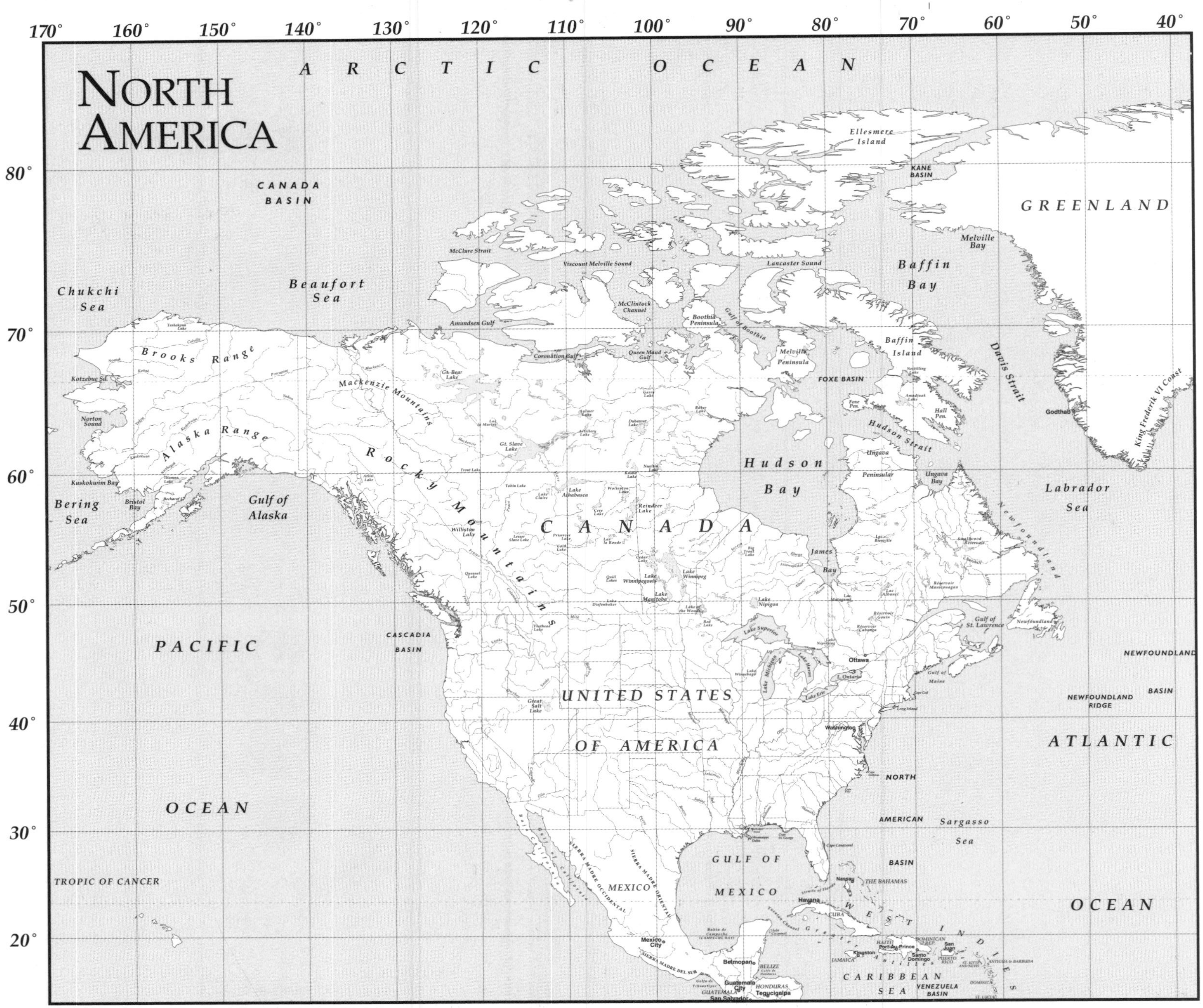
NORTH AMERICA
ARCTIC OCEAN
CANADA BASIN
Beaufort Sea
Chukchi Sea
Bering Sea
Gulf of Alaska
PACIFIC OCEAN
CASCADIA BASIN
TROPIC OF CANCER
Brooks Range
Alaska Range
Mackenzie Mountains
Rocky Mountains
Kotzebue Sd.
Norton Sound
Kuskokwim Bay
Bristol Bay
McClure Strait
Viscount Melville Sound
McClintock Channel
Amundsen Gulf
Coronation Gulf
Queen Maud Gulf
Boothia Peninsula
Gulf of Boothia
Lancaster Sound
Ellesmere Island
KANE BASIN
GREENLAND
Melville Bay
Baffin Bay
Baffin Island
Melville Peninsula
FOXE BASIN
Davis Strait
Godthab
King Frederik VI Coast
Hudson Strait
Hall Pen.
Ungava Peninsular
Ungava Bay
Hudson Bay
James Bay
Labrador Sea
Newfoundland
Gulf of St. Lawrence
CANADA
Gt. Bear Lake
Gt. Slave Lake
Lake Athabasca
Reindeer Lake
Lake Winnipeg
Lake Winnipegosis
Lake Manitoba
Lake Nipigon
Lake Superior
Lake Michigan
Lake Huron
Lake Erie
L. Ontario
Great Salt Lake
Ottawa
Washington
UNITED STATES OF AMERICA
MEXICO
SIERRA MADRE OCCIDENTAL
SIERRA MADRE ORIENTAL
SIERRA MADRE DEL SUR
Mexico City
GULF OF MEXICO
Havana
CUBA
Nassau
THE BAHAMAS
JAMAICA
Kingston
HAITI
Port-au-Prince
Santo Domingo
PUERTO RICO
San Juan
WEST INDIES
CARIBBEAN SEA
VENEZUELA BASIN
BELIZE
Belmopan
GUATEMALA
Guatemala City
HONDURAS
Tegucigalpa
San Salvador
NORTH AMERICAN BASIN
Sargasso Sea
NEWFOUNDLAND BASIN
NEWFOUNDLAND RIDGE
ATLANTIC OCEAN
170° 160° 150° 140° 130° 120° 110° 100° 90° 80° 70° 60° 50° 40°
80° 70° 60° 50° 40° 30° 20°

WEBSTER'S
NEW CENTURY
DICTIONARY

Other reference works from Random House Value Publishing:

WEBSTER'S COMPACT DICTIONARY

WEBSTER'S COMPACT THESAURUS

WEBSTER'S CONCISE ENCYCLOPEDIA

WEBSTER'S TREASURY OF RELEVANT QUOTATIONS

WEBSTER'S SYNONYMS, ANTONYMS AND HOMONYMS

WEBSTER'S CROSSWORD PUZZLE DICTIONARY

WEBSTER'S NEW CENTURY DICTIONARY

Gramercy Books
New York

This 2001 edition is published by Gramercy Books™, an imprint of
Random House Value Publishing, Inc., 280 Park Avenue, New York, NY 10017,
by arrangement with Geddes & Grosset, Scotland, UK.

Gramercy Books™ and design are trademarks of Random House Value Publishing, Inc.

Printed and bound in Great Britain.

Random House
New York . Toronto . London . Sydney . Auckland
http://www.randomhouse.com/

A CIP catalog record for this title is available from the Library of Congress.

WEBSTER'S NEW CENTURY DICTIONARY
ISBN: 0-517-21881-X

9 8 7 6 5 4 3 2 1

Contents

TABLE OF CONTENTS

List of Abbreviations

The following abbreviations are used throughout the dictionary.

abbr	abbreviation	*med*	medicine
adj	adjective	*meteorol*	meteorology
adv	adverb	*mil*	military
alg	algebra	*mus*	music
anat	anatomy	*myth*	mythology
approx	approximately	*n*	noun
arch	archaic	*naut*	nautical
archit	architecture	*neut*	neuter
astrol	astrology	*news*	news media
astron	astronomy	*NT*	New Testament
astrophys	astrophysics	*nf*	noun feminine
Austral	Australia, Australasia	*npl*	noun plural
aux	auxiliary	*n sing*	noun singular
b.	born	*obs*	obsolete
bank	banking	*org chem*	organic chemistry
biol	biology	*orig*	original, originally, origin
biochem	biochemistry	*OT*	Old Testament
bot	botany	*p*	participle
Brit	Britain, British	*pers*	person, personal
c.	circa, about	*pharm*	pharmaceutical
cap	capital	*philos*	philosophy
cent	century	*photog*	photography
chem	chemical, chemistry	*phys*	physics
colloq	colloquial	*pl*	plural
com	commercial	*poet*	poetical
compar	comparative	*poss*	possessive
comput	computing	*pp*	past participle
conj	conjunction	*prep*	preposition
d.	died	*pres t*	present tense
demons	demonstrative	*print*	printing
dent	dentistry	*pron*	pronoun
derog	derogatory, derogatorily	*pr p*	present participle
dimin	diminutive	*psychol*	psychology
eccles	ecclesiastical	*pt*	past tense
econ	economics	*RC*	Roman Catholic
e.g.	exempli gratia, for example	*reflex*	reflexive
elec	electricity	*Scot*	Scotland
esp	especially	*sing*	singular
etc	etcetera, and others	*sl*	slang
fig	figuratively	*stock exch*	stock exchange
geneal	genealogy	*superl*	superlative
geog	geography	*theat*	theater
geol	geology	*transp*	transport
geom	geometry	*TV*	television
gram	grammar	*typog*	typography
her	heraldry	*UK*	United Kingdom
hist	history	*US*	United States
i.e.	id est, that is	*USA*	United States of America
imper	imperative	*usu*	usually
incl	including	*vb*	verb
inf	informal	*vb aux*	auxiliary verb
ins	insurance	*vi*	intransitive verb
interj	interjection	*vt*	transitive verb
math	mathematics	*vti*	transitive or intransitive verb
meas	measurement	*vulg*	vulgar, vulgarly
mech	mechanics	*zool*	zoology

American English

Pronunciation and Development

American English pronunciation

The lists below show the pronunciation of vowel and consonant sounds using familiar words.

There are many different accents of American English. Differences in accents are most noticeable in the vowel sounds. There is no "right" or "wrong" accent.

Vowel sounds

a	bay	bat
e	bee	bet
i	bite	bit
o	boat	pot
u	huge	but, putt
u		put
y	try	hymn

Consonant sounds

b	baby
c	cap
ch	chin
d	do
f	face
g	go
h	hat
j	job
k	kid
l	lie
m	me
n	no
ng	sing
p	pat
r	red
s	so
sh	show
t	tie
th	thin
th	then
v	very
w	we
y	yes
z	zone

The development of American English

American English developed originally from an early dialect of English that was brought to England by Germanic tribes called Jutes, Angles, and Saxons. This early dialect is now known as Anglo-Saxon or Old English. Many of our most common words come from Anglo-Saxon, for example *house, good* and *big* are all Anglo-Saxon words.

Later, Scandinavian words such as *call* and *gate,* and Latin words including *candle* and *school* were added to the language. The most important influence, though, was from France after the Norman Invasion of England in 1066.

French affected the pronunciation and spelling of existing words and contributed thousands of new words such as *government, battle, chair,* and *music.*

These foreign borrowings explain why there are so many synonyms in modern English. For example, *ask* is originally English, *question* is French, and *interrogate* is Latin. *Rise* is the old English word, *mount* is the French synonym, and *ascend* is Latin. The Latin words tend to sound the most formal or bookish of the three.

Pronunciation and spelling

Over the centuries, the pronunciation of many words changed. This is one of the reasons that the way words look, or the way they are spelled, does not always match the way they sound. When the printing press was invented in 1476, spelling began to be standardized but pronunciation continued to change.

Silent letters such as the "k" in *knife* and the "gh" in *night* were pronounced in Shakespeare's time. We have retained the spelling, but not the pronunciation.

The early colonists

American English began to develop with the arrival of British colonists in the 17th century. Many of the things the colonists saw around them, such as plants and animals, were new so they borrowed Native American words such as *racoon* and *moose* to describe them. American English also adopted words from Dutch, French, German and Spanish. Settlers also made up new words.

The groups of people in the early settlements, one in New England and the other in Virginia, were from different linguistic backgrounds. The New England colonists came mainly from the Eastern part of England; the Virginian colonists were primarily from the southwest. Each group had its own distinct accent. One feature that is noticeably different is the pronunciation of "r" after vowels. The Virginian settlers pronounced this "r", the New England settlers did not. Modern-day New Englanders still tend not to pronounce "r" after a vowel.

A new identity

After the American Revolution and the spirit of independence, there was a wish to distance the United States from Britain. The culture, customs, laws, and politics of the United States were different from England and different words were used to describe them. Noah Webster saw a need for a distinctively American dictionary that reflected these differences.

At first, Webster was against such radical simplification and opposed change. He later sided with Franklin but eventually took a more moderate stand and endorsed changes such as *centre* to *center* and the omission of "u" from *colour* to *color* .

Webster's first dictionary was published in 1806 but it wasn't until 1828, when he was seventy years old, that his famous *An American Dictionary of the English Language* finally appeared. It had many new words including thousands of technical and scientific words, and included senses of words that had changed through use in the American context.

New words, new uses for old words

American English keeps on changing and growing. New words are constantly being added, particularly scientific and technical words. Computer related terms such as *input*, *output*, *interface*, and *software* abound. Business, politics, art, and popular culture also contribute new words and uses.

People also invent, change, and adapt words. We make up new words or use old words in new ways. Take the word *mouse* for example. It has been in the language since the early days—but it now has an entirely new meaning in addition to the original one. Similarly, *icon*, *virus*, *surf*, and *crash* have totally new meanings. Imagine what Noah Webster would make of them.

Modern communications, especially the Internet, mean that these new words and new uses spread very quickly. Someone coins a phrase in California and soon we hear it in Miami. In addition to spreading new words, the Internet itself is a huge source of new words. We talk about *websites*, *emails*, and *e-businesses*. These words would have been unknown to most people twenty years ago.

Email itself has given us a new style of writing and a whole range of new abbreviations. Email shorthand for phrases such as TIA (thanks in advance), BTW (by the way), and IMHO (in my humble opinion) is very common. Text messaging has taken these abbreviations further. Some parents and teachers are worried that, as their children spend more and more time writing text messages, they will not learn or will forget how to spell words correctly. It is interesting to wonder how Ben Franklin would react to GR8 2 C U (Great to see you). Presumably it would be too radical, even for him.

A multicultural language

We have continued to borrow words from other languages. The multicultural society of the United States is reflected in its rich and varied vocabulary. We have eaten at Scandinavian "smorgasboards" and run in "marathons" for many years, but we are constantly adding to our collection with borrowings like *sushi*.

As long as people need words, they will keep inventing and borrowing. Just as we need special training to read the English of 400 years ago, people 400 years from now will need training in order to be able to read this.

A

a, A the first letter of the English language; the first vowel of the English language.

a *adj, determiner* the indefinite article; one; any; per.

a *symbol* acceleration; area.

A *symbol* (*chem*) argon (element); (*temperature*) absolute; (*mus*) the sixth note of the scale of C, the note to which instruments of an orchestra are usu tuned; (*astrophys*) a Fraunhofer line caused by terrestrial oxygen.

Å *symbol* (*phys*) = Ångstrom unit.

a *abbr* = acre; (*Latin*) *ad*, "at," or "to"; (*Latin*) *anno*, "in the year"; (*com*) (*Latin*) *annus*, "year"; (*Latin*) *ante*, "before"; anterior; (*Latin*) *atto*, "110–18."

a. *abbr* = (*com*) about; acre, or acres; acting; active; adjective; after; afternoon; alto; amateur; ampere; (*chem*) ana-; (*Latin*) *anno*, "in the year"; (*Latin*) *annus*, "year"; anode; anonymous; answer; (*Latin*) *ante*, "before"; (*com*) approved; (*Latin*) *aqua*, "water"; (*metric system*) are; area; argent; artillery; assists; at.

A *abbr* = absolute, as in temperature; (*Latin*) *absolvo*, "I absolve"; academy; academician; America; American; ampere(s); April; area; associate; alcohol.

A1, A-1, *or* **A-one** *adj* (*inf*) first-class; in perfect condition; physically fit; excellent.

AA *abbr* = Alcoholics Anonymous; Architectural Association; Associate of Arts; Automobile Association; anti-aircraft.

AAA *abbr* = American Academy of Achievement; American Academy of Art; American Automobile Association; Automobile Association of America.

AAA. *abbr* = (*chem*) amalgama.

AAIB *abbr* = Aircraft Accident Investigation Board.

Aalto *n* **Hugo Alvar Henrik** (1898–1976) Finnish architect who influenced 20th-century architecture away from the strong geometric shapes of constructivism. His notable works include Finlandia Concert Hall, Helsinki, and Massachusetts Institute of Technology student hostel.

A & I *abbr* = accident and indemnity.

A & R *abbr* = Artist and Repertoire.

aaO *abbr* (*German*) = *am angeführten Orte*, "at the place quoted."

aar *abbr* = average annual rainfall; against all risks.

aardvark *n* a nocturnal African mammal with a long snout that feeds on termites.

aardwolf *n* (*pl* **aardwolves**) the earth wolf, a South African carnivore like a hyena.

AARG *abbr* = Aerial Archeology Research Group.

AARM *abbr* = Association of Aquatic and Recreation Management.

Aarnio *n* **Eero** (1932–) Finnish interior and industrial designer, best known for his chair designs.

Aaron *n* (*Bible, OT*) the first high priest and head of the Levites, said to be a great grandson of Levi the son of Jacob; Moses' elder brother.—*See also* **Levites.**

Aaronic *adj* pertaining to Aaron; relating to the Israelite high priesthood; (*Mormon Church*) pertaining to the second order of the Mormon priesthood.

AAUW *abbr* = American Association of University Women.

ab *prep* (*Latin*) meaning "from", as in *ab initio.*

Ab *symbol* (*chem*) alabamine (element).

ab *abbr* (*chem*) = the pure albite molecule, $Na_2O.Al_2O_3.6SiO_2.$

AB *abbr* = Advisory Board; able-bodied seaman; (*Latin*) *Artium Baccalaureus*, "Bachelor of Arts."

ab- *prefix* away, from, apart.

abaca *n* Manila hemp.

aback *adv* **taken aback** startled.

abactinal *adj* (*zool*) (of organisms) situated away from the mouth. *Also* **aboral.**—**abactinally** *adv.*

abacus *n* (*pl* **abaci, abacuses**) a frame with sliding beads for doing arithmetic; (*archit*) a flat stone slab forming the uppermost part of a capital.

ABACUS *abbr* = Association of Bibliographic Agencies of Britain, Australia, Canada and the United States.

Abaddon *n* a destroying angel, the devil; hell.

abaft *adv, prep* (*naut*) behind.

abalone *n* an edible mollusc having an ear-shaped shell lined with mother-of-pearl.

abandon *vt* to leave behind; to desert; to yield completely to an emotion or urge. * *n* freedom from inhibitions.—**abandonment** *n.*

abandoned *adj* (*behavior*) showing abandon, unrestrained.—**abandonedly** *adv.*

Abaris *n* (*Greek myth*) a priest of Apollo to whom the god gave a golden arrow on which to ride through the air, making him invisible (the dart of Abaris).

ABAS *abbr* = Amateur Basketball Association of Scotland; Association of Business Administration Studies.

abase *vt* to degrade, humiliate.—**abasement** *n.*

abash *vt* to cause a feeling of shame, embarrassment or confusion.—**abashment** *n.*

abashed *adj* ashamed, embarrassed.

abate *vti* to make or become less; (*law*) to end.—**abatement** *n.*

abatis *n* (*pl* **abatis, abatises**) a defense work of fallen trees with the branches towards the enemy.

abattoir *n* a slaughterhouse.

abb. *abbr* = abbess; abbey; abbot.

Abba *n* Aramaic word for father used by Jesus when he prayed in the Garden of Gethsemane.—*See also* **Gethsemane.**

ABBA *abbr* = Amateur Basketball Association.

abbacy *n* (*pl* **abbacies**) the office or rights of an abbot.

Abbado *n* **Claudio** (1933–) Italian conductor; principal conductor of the London Symphony Orchestra in 1979 and of the Berlin Philharmonic Orchestra in 1989. His specialty is 19th and 20th century music.

abbandono *adv* (*mus*) (*Italian*) "passionately."

abbatial *adj* of an abbey or abbot.

abbé *n* a French ecclesiastic.

abbess *n* the woman who heads a convent of nuns.

Abbevillian *adj* (*archeo*) relating to a lower Paleolithic culture and handaxe industry whose name is derived from the type site at Abbeville, France.

Abbey *n* **Edwin Austen** (1852–1911) American illustrator and painter of historical scenes. One of his best-known paintings is the portrait of *Richard, Duke of Gloucester, and Lady Anne.*

abbey *n* a building occupied by monks or nuns; a church built as part of such a building; the community of monks or nuns.

Abbey Theatre *n* Irish theater founded in Dublin in 1904 by W B Yeats and Lady Gregory.

Abbot *n* 1. **Bud [William]** (1898–1974) American comedian; comedy partner of Lou Costello (1908–50). 2. **George Francis** (1887–1995) American playwright, actor director, and producer whose work includes *The Fall Guy* (1925); winner of a Pulitzer prize for drama in 1960. 3. **Jacob** (1803–79) American clergyman and founder of the Mount Vernon School for Girls in Boston. 4. **Robert Sengstacke** (1868–1940) American founder and editor of the *Chicago Defender.*

abbot *n* the head of an abbey of monks.

abbr. *or* **abbrev.** *abbr* = abbreviated; abbreviation.

abbreviate *vt* to make shorter, esp to shorten (a word) by omitting letters.

abbreviation *n* the process of abbreviating; a shortened form of a word.

ABC[1] *n* the alphabet; the basic facts of a subject.

ABC[2] *abbr* = American Broadcasting Corporation; Associated British Cinemas; automatic binary computer; Australian Broadcasting Corporation.

Abdera *n* an ancient Greek city on the Thracian coast; the birthplace of the philosophers Democritus and Protagoras.

Abderus *n* (*Greek myth*) a friend of Heracles, eaten by the horses of Diomedes, king of Thrace.

abdicate *vti* to renounce an official position or responsibility, etc.—**abdication** *n.*

ABDO *abbr* = Association of British Dispensing Opticians.

abdomen *n* the region of the body below the chest containing the digestive organs; the belly; (*insects, etc*) the section of the body behind the thorax.—**abdominal** *adj.*—**abdominally** *adv.*

ABDP *abbr* = Association of British Directory Publishers.

abducent *adj* (*anat*) (a limb, etc) drawn from its natural position.

abduct *vt* to carry off (a person) by force; (*anat*) to draw (a limb, etc) from its natural position.—**abduction** *n.*—**abductor** *n.*

ABE *abbr* = Association of British Editors; Association of Building Engineers; Association of Business Executives.

abeam *adv* (*naut*) at right angles to a ship's length, abreast.

abecedarian *adj* of the ABC, elementary; arranged alphabetically. * *n* one learning the ABC, a beginner, a learner.

Abéché *n* a city in Chad.

abed *adv* in bed.

Abednego *n* (*Bible*) one of Daniel's companions cast into the fiery furnace. *See also* **Daniel.**

Abel *n* (*Bible*) second son of Adam and Eve; a shepherd killed by his brother, Cain. *See also* **Cain.**

Abel *n* **Carl Friedrich** (1723–87) German composer and noted player of the viola da gamba. He wrote pieces specifically for the viola da gamba in addition to other types of chamber music, as well as symphonies.

Abelard *n* **Peter** (1079–1142) French theologian and philosopher whose love affair with his pupil, Héloïse, resulted in his castration.

Abell Catalog *n* a catalog of clusters of galaxies.

abelmosk *n* an Asian herb of the mallow family yielding musk.

Abelson *n* **Philip Hauge** (1913–) American physical chemist who played a role in the development of the atomic bomb.

Abendlied *n* (*mus*) (*German*) an "evening song," often of religious significance.

Abendmusik *n* (*mus*) (*German*) an "evening performance of music," particularly performances of mainly religious music given at the Protestant church of Lübeck in Germany between 1673 and 1810.

ABEng *abbr* (*Brit*) = Associate Member of the Association of Building Engineers.

Aberdeen *n* important Scottish city in the United Kingdom of Great Britain and Northern Ireland (UK).

Abernathy *n* **Ralph David** (1926–90) American civil rights leader; president of the SCLC 1968–77.

aberrant *adj* deviating from that regarded as normal or right.—**aberrance, aberrancy** *n*.

aberration *n* a deviation from the normal; a mental or moral lapse; (*astron*) the apparent displacement of a star from its true position caused by the finite velocity of light; (*optics, phys*) a form of image imperfection caused by light rays focusing at slightly different positions in an optical system.

ABES *abbr* = Association for Broadcast Engineering Standards.

ABET *abbr* = Advisory Board on Educational Technology.

abet *vt* (**abetted, abetting**) to encourage or assist, esp to do wrong.—**abetment** *n*.—**abetter,** (*esp law*) **abettor** *n*.

abeyance *n* (*usu preceded by* in) (*law, etc*) suspended temporarily.

ABFM *abbr* = American Board of (Commissioners for) Foreign Missions.

abhor *vt* (**abhorred, abhorring**) to detest, despise.

abhorrence *n* detestation.

abhorrent *adj* detestable.

Abiathar *n* (*Bible*) priest and companion of David in his outlaw days. *See also* **David.**

abide *vt* (**abiding, abode** *or* **abided**) to endure; to put up with.

abiding *adj* permanent.—**abidingly** *adv*.

Abidjan *n* a city on the Côte D'Ivoire.

abigail *n* a lady's maid.

Abilene *n* a district of Lebanon. *See also* **Lysanias.**

ability *n* (*pl* **abilities**) the state of being able; power to do; talent; skill.

Abimelech *n* (*Bible*) king of Gerar who made covenant with Abraham at Beersheba. *See also* **Gerar.**

ab init. *abbr* (*Latin*) = *ab initio*.

ab initio *adv* (*Latin*) "from the beginning."

abiogenesis *n* spontaneous generation.—**abiogenetic** *adj*.

abject *adj* wretched; dejected.—**abjection** *n*.—**abjectly** *adv*.

abjure *vt* to renounce.—**abjuration** *n*.—**abjurer** *n*.

abl. *abbr* = ablative.

ablactation *n* the act of weaning a child from the breast.

ablate *vti* (**ablating, ablated**) (*med*) to remove surgically any part of the body; (*astrophysics*) to melt or vaporize when entering the earth's atmosphere; (*geol*) to erode, to waste or wear away; (*geol*) to remove a surface snow or ice by melting or evaporation.—**ablation** *n*.

ablative *adj* (*gram*) expressing source, instrumentality, etc; (*astrophysics*) ablating. * *n* one of the cases of Latin nouns, expressing chiefly separation and instrumentality and sometimes place.

ablative absolute *n* a particular construction in Latin of a noun and a participle in the ablative case, agreeing in gender and number, and forming a clause by themselves, but unconnected grammatically with the rest of the sentence.

ablaut *n* (*linguistics*) a vowel permutation, the change of a root vowel in the derivation of a word, as *do, did,* or *sing, sang, sung, song*.

ablaze *adj* burning, on fire.

able *adj* having the competence or means (to do); talented; skilled.—**ably** *adv*.

-able *adj suffix* capable of, as in *suitable*.

able-bodied *adj* fit, strong.

able-bodied seaman *n* a trained seaman in the (merchant) navy.—*also* **able seaman.**

abloom *adv* in bloom, blooming.

ablution *n* (*usu pl*) a washing or cleansing of the body by water; the ritual cleansing of vessels or hands.—**ablutionary** *adj*.

ably *adv* in an able manner.

ABM *abbr* = Association of Board Makers; Association of Breastfeeding Mothers; Association of British Maltsters; Association of British Music; Association of Button Merchants; anti-ballistic missile.

ABMC *abbr* = American Battle Monuments Commission

ABMEWS *abbr* = anti-ballistic missile early warning system.

ABMU *abbr* = American Baptist Missionary Union.

ABNA *abbr* = Anorexia Bulimia Nervosa Association.

abnegate *vt* to deny oneself (a right, etc); to renounce.—**abnegation** *n*.

Abner *n* (*Bible*) commander of Saul's army; plotted with David but killed by Joad who feared his influence. *See also* **David, Joab.**

abnormal *adj* unusual, not average or typical; irregular. —**abnormally** *adv*.

abnormality *n* (*pl* **abnormalities**) deformity; irregularity; difference or departure from a regular type or rule.

ABO *abbr* = Association of British Orchestras; antigen-based blood group-classification.—*see* **blood grouping.**

aboard *adv* on or in an aircraft, ship, train, etc.—*also prep*.

abode[1] *n* a home, residence.

abode[2] *see* **abide.**

abolish *vt* to bring to an end, do away with.—**abolisher** *n*.—**abolishment** *n*.

abolition *n* the act of abolishing; (*with cap*) in UK, the ending of the slave trade (1807) or slavery (1833), in US, the emancipation of the slaves (1863).

abolitionist *n* one who is in favor of the repeal or abolition of some existing law or custom; (*often with cap*) one in favor of Abolition.

abomasum *n* (*pl* **abomasa**) the fourth stomach of a ruminant animal.—**abomasal** *adj*.

A-bomb *abbr* = atomic bomb.

abominable *adj* despicable, detestable; (*inf*) very unpleasant.—**abominably** *adv*.

abominable snowman *n* a huge creature of legend resembling a man or an animal, said to be found in the Himalayas.—*also* **yeti.**

abominate *vt* to abhor; to regard with feelings of disgust or hatred.—**abominator** *n*.

abomination *n* detestation; a loathsome person or thing; something which causes disgust or loathing.

aboriginal *adj* existing in a place from the earliest times; of aborigines. * *n* another term for **aborigine**; the species of animals or plants presumed to have originated within a given area.

aborigine *n* any of the first known inhabitants of a region; (*with cap*) one of the original inhabitants of Australia before the arrival of European settlers.

abort *vti* to undergo or cause an abortion; to terminate or cause to terminate prematurely; (*comput*) to cancel or terminate a process or procedure while it is in progress. * *n* the premature termination of a rocket flight, etc.

abortifacient *n* a drug used to bring about an induced abortion.

abortion *n* the removal of an embryo, or fetus, from the uterus, either by natural expulsion or by human intervention.

abortionist *n* a person who performs abortions, esp illegally.

abortive *adj* failing in intended purpose; fruitless; causing abortion.—**abortively** *adv*.

aboulia *see* **abulia.**

abound *vi* to be in abundance; to have in great quantities.

about *prep* on all sides of; near to; with; on the point of; concerning. * *adv* all around; near; to face the opposite direction.

about-turn, about-face *n* a complete reversal in direction or opinion, etc. * *vi* to make an about-turn.

above *prep* over, on top of; better or more than; beyond the reach of; too complex to understand. * *adv* in or to a higher place; in addition; (*text*) mentioned earlier.

aboveboard *adj, adv* without trickery; in open sight.

aboveground *adj* situated on or above the ground.

above-the-line *adj* (*com*) referring to those entries that appear above a horizontal line in a profit and loss account, which divides the entries that establish the profit or loss that has been achieved from the entries that indicate how the profit is distributed; (*media*) referring to expenditure on mass media promotion or advertising. *See* **below-the-line.**

Abp. or **abp.** *abbr* = Archbishop; archbishop.

ABP *abbr* = arterial blood pressure.

abr. *abbr* = abridged; abridger; abridgement.

abracadabra *n* a cabalistic word used as a charm, a spell; gibberish.

abradant *adj* having the property of rubbing away. * *n* a substance employed for abrading or scouring.

abrade *vti* to wear or rub away; to remove as by friction or abrasion; to corrode, as by acids.—**abrader** *n*.

Abraham *n* (*Bible*) called and trusted by God, and considered the father of the Jews; Jesus' family tree is traced to Abraham. *See also* **Patriarch.**

Abramovitz *n* **Gerald** (1928–) 1. South African-born architect, whose cantilevered desk lamp won the 1966 Design Center Award. 2. **Max** (1908–) American architect. His notable works include Krannert Center, University of Illinois.

abranchiate, abranchial *adj* (*zool*) devoid of gills. * *n* an animal without gills.

abrasion *n* the act or process of rubbing away by friction, etc; a scraped area; (*geol*) the effect of the wearing away of rock by fragments of other rock carried by moving ice, water or wind; (*med*) a superficial injury caused by the mechanical rubbing off of the skin surface.—*also* **graze.**

abrasive *adj* causing abrasion; harsh, irritating. * *n* a substance or tool used for grinding or polishing, etc.—**abrasively** *adv*.

ABRC *abbr* = Advisory Board for Research Councils; Association of British Research Councils; Advisory Board for Redundant Churches.

abreact *vt* (*psychoanal*) to remove (a complex) by acting it out or talking it out.—**abreaction** *n*.—**abreactive** *adj*.

abreast *adv* side by side and facing the same way; informed (of); aware.

ABRFM *abbr* = Association of British Roofing Felt Manufacturers.

abridge *vt* to shorten by using fewer words but keeping the substance.

abridgment, abridgement *n* the state of being contracted or curtailed; a shortened version of a text; an epitome.

ABRO *abbr* = Animal Breeding Research Organization; Army Base Repair Organization.

abroach *adj, adv* letting out; broached, pierced so as to let the liquor run.

abroad *adv* in or to a foreign country; over a wide area; out in the open; in circulation, current.

abrogate *vt* to repeal, cancel.—**abrogator** *n*.

abrogation *n* the act of abrogating; the repeal or annulling of a law.

abrupt *adj* sudden; unexpected; curt.—**abruptly** *adv*.—**abruptness** *n*.

abruptio placentae *n* bleeding from the placenta.

abruption *n* a separation with violence; a sudden or abrupt termination.

abs. *abbr* = absolute (temperature); absolutely; abstract.

ABS *abbr* = American Bible Society; (*German*) *antiblockiersystem* (car brake; "anti-lock system").

ABSA *abbr* = Association for Business Sponsorship of the Arts.

Absalom *n* (*Bible*) third and favorite son of David; led a revolt against his father; killed by Joab, to David's grief. *See also* **Ahithophel, David, Joab**.

abscess *n* a collection of pus at a localized site resulting from an infection; an inflamed area of the body containing pus.

abscissa *n* (*pl* **abscissas, abscissae**) (*geom*) one of the two coordinates fixing the position of a point; the x-co-ordinate, the distance of a point from the y-axis.

abscission *n* the act of severance; (*bot*) the shedding of parts; breaking off in a sentence, leaving the rest implied; (*med*) the surgical removal of tissue by cutting.

abscond *vi* to hide, run away, esp to avoid punishment for a wrongdoing.

abseil *vi* to descend a rock face by means of a double rope attached to a higher point.—**abseiling** *n*.

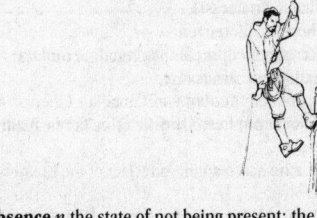

absence *n* the state of not being present; the time of this; a lack; inattention.

absent *adj* not present; not existing; inattentive. * *vt* to keep (oneself) away.—**absently** *adv*.

absentee *n* a person who is absent, as from work or school.

absenteeism *n* persistent absence from work, school, etc.

absently *adv* in an abstracted manner.

absent-minded *adj* inattentive; forgetful.

ABSFAM *abbr* = Association of British Solid Fuel Appliance Manufacturers.

ABSFCE *abbr* = Association of British Salted Fish Curers and Exporters.

ABSI *abbr* = Association of the Boot and Shoe Industry.

absinthe, absinth *n* a potent, green, brandy-based liqueur flavored with wormwood.

absit omen (*Latin*) may the foreboding caused by some unlucky word or event not come to pass.

ABSM (TTD) *abbr* = Diploma of the Birmingham School of Music.

ABSO *abbr* = Association of British Security Officers.

absolute *adj* unrestricted, unconditional; complete; positive; perfect, pure; not relative; (*monarch, ruler, etc*) authoritarian, despotic; (*inf*) utter, out-and-out.

absolute cost advantage *n* (*com*) an advantage enjoyed by a country that enables it to produce certain goods more cheaply than others.

absolute dating *n* or **chronometric dating** *n* fixing the date of an artifact using any of a number of scientific instrumental methods.

absolute humidity *n* the amount of water vapor in the air, expressed in grams per cubic centimeter.

absolutely *adv* completely; unconditionally; (*inf*) I completely agree, certainly.

absolute magnitude *n* the apparent magnitude a star would have if seen from a standard distance of ten parsecs.

absolute music *or* **abstract music** *n* (*mus*) instrumental music that exists purely as music and does not attempt to relate to a story or image. It is the opposite of program music.

absolute pitch *or* **perfect pitch** *n* (*mus*) the sense by which some people can exactly identify, or sing without an accompanying instrument, any note they hear.

absolute temperature *n* a temperature measured on the Kelvin scale with respect to absolute zero.

absolute zero *n* the lowest temperature theoretically attainable, at which point the particles that make up any body of matter would have their lowest possible energy.—0K = -273.15°C (-459.67°F).

absolution *n* forgiveness; remission of sin or its penalty.

absolutism *n* the state of being absolute; the principle or system of absolute government.—**absolutist** *n, adj*.

absolve *vt* to clear from guilt or blame; to give religious absolution to; to free from a duty, obligation, etc.

absolver *n* one who absolves, or pronounces absolution.

absorb *vt* to take in; to soak up; to incorporate; to pay for (costs, etc); to take in (a shock) without recoil; to occupy one's attention or interest completely.—**absorber** *n*.—**absorptive** *adj*.

absorbable *adj* capable of being absorbed.—**absorbability** *n*.

absorbefacient *adj* inducing or causing absorption. * *n* something that causes absorption.

absorbent *adj* capable of absorbing moisture, etc.—**absorbency** *n*.

absorbent cotton *n* raw cotton that has been bleached and sterilized for use as a dressing, etc.—*also* **cotton wool**.

absorbing *adj* engrossing.—**absorbingly** *adv*.

absorption *n* the process or act of absorbing; the state of being absorbed; entire preoccupation of the mind; (*com*) a procedure in which the overheads of a firm are assigned to production by means of absorption costs; (*phys*) decrease in the intensity of radiation by interaction with matter.—**absorptive** *adj*.

absorption coefficient *n* the ratio (reduction in intensity) for radiation passing through unit thickness of material.

absorption costing *n* a system of product costing that assigns overhead costs in a firm to production by employing a process known as absorption.

absorption lines *npl* dark lines in the spectrum produced by the absorption of cool vapors through which the light has passed.

absorption nebula *n* a nebula shown by its absorption of radiation from other sources rather than its own emissions.

absorption rate *n* (*com*) a rate established for the charging of overheads to products.

absorption spectrum *n* a system of absorption lines or bands seen in a bright continuous spectrum from a wideband source on passing through relatively cool matter.

absorptivity *n* the power of absorption; (*phys*) the rate of absorption of radiation by a material.

ABSSG *abbr* = Associate of the British Society of Scientific Glassblowers.

abstain *vi* to keep oneself from some indulgence, esp from drinking alcohol; to refrain from using one's vote.

abstainer *n* one who abstains, esp from intoxicants.

abstemious *adj* sparing in consuming food or alcohol.—**abstemiously** *adv*.—**abstemiousness** *n*.

abstention *n* the act of holding off or abstaining; the withholding of a vote.—**abstentious** *adj*.—**abstentionist** *n*.

abstergent *adj* possessing cleansing or purging properties. * *n* that which cleanses or purges; a detergent.

abstinence *n* an abstaining or refraining, esp from food or alcohol.

abstinent *adj* refraining from over-indulgence, esp with regard to food and drink. * *n* an abstainer.—**abstinently** *adv*.

abstr. *abbr* = abstract; abstracted.

abstract *adj* having no material existence; theoretical; (*art*) non-representational. * *n* (*writing, speech*) a summary or condensed version. * *vt* to remove or extract; to separate; to summarize.

abstract art *n* art that intentionally avoids representation of the observed world.

abstracted *adj* not paying attention.—**abstractedly** *adv*.—**abstractedness** *n*.

abstract expressionism *n* art that is based on freedom of expression, spontaneity, and random composition and is characterized by loose, unrestrained brushwork and often indistinct forms, usu on large canvases.

abstraction *n* preoccupation, inattention; an abstract concept.—**abstractive** *adj*.

abstractionism *n* the theory and art of the abstract, esp non-representational painting.—**abstractionist** *adj, n*.

abstract music *see* absolute music.

abstract noun *n* the name of a state or quality considered apart from the object to which it belongs.

abstract of judgment *n* (*law*) a public notice that a judgment against a person or company has been rendered in a court of law and that this judgment may be enforced against real property.

abstruse *adj* obscure; hidden; difficult to comprehend; profound.—**abstrusely** *adv*.—**abstruseness** *n*.

absurd *adj* against reason or common sense; ridiculous.—**absurdly** *adv*. *See also* **theater of the absurd**.

absurdity *n* (*pl* **absurdities**) the state of being absurd; that which is absurd.

Absyrtus *n* (*Greek myth*) a son of Aeëtes, king of Colchis, and brother of Medea.—*also* **Apsyrtus**.

abt. *abbr* = about.

ABT *abbr* = American Board of Trade; Australian Broadcasting Tribunal.

ABTM *abbr* = American Board of Tropical Medicine; Association of British Transport Museums.

Abu Ghurob *n* (*Egypt*) site in the Saqqara area of Egypt, on the west bank of the Nile, south of Cairo, Egypt, of the sun temple of the Pharaoh Neuserre (Fifth Dynasty) and the best guide to the appearance of the now vanished sun temple of Heliopolis.

Abuja *n* capital city of Nigeria.

abulia *n* (*psychol*) loss of willpower.—*also* **aboulia**.—**abulic** *adj*.

abundance *n* a plentiful supply; a considerable amount; (*astron*) the ratio of the number of atoms or ions of an element to the number of atoms or ions of hydrogen in the same volume.

abundant *adj* plentiful; rich (in).—**abundantly** *adv*.

abuse *vt* to make wrong use of; to mistreat; to insult, attack verbally. * *n* misuse; mistreatment; insulting language; immoderate or illegal use of drugs or other stimulants.—**abuser** *n*.

Abu Simbel *n* the site near the River Nile of two temples that were carved from the rock face by Pharaoh Rameses II, *c*. 1250 BC.

abusive *adj* insulting.—**abusively** *adv*.—**abusiveness** *n*.

abut *vi* (**abutting, abutted**) to adjoin, border or lean (on, against).

abutment *or* **abuttal** *n* that which borders upon something else; (*archit*) the solid structure that supports the extremity of a bridge, arch, or vault.

abutter *n* (*law*) the owner of an adjoining property.

Abu Zabi (Abu Dhabi) *n* capital city of the United Arab Emirates (UAE).

abuzz *adv* filled with buzzing sounds; active, alive.

ABVT *abbr* = American Board on Veterinary Toxicology.

ABYC *abbr* = American Boat and Yacht Council.

Abydos *n* (*Egypt*) site in Upper Egypt, to the west of the Nile, about 100 miles (160 kilometers) northwest of Thebes, the location of tombs from the earliest dynasties onwards.

abysm *n* (*arch*) an abyss, a gulf.

abysmal *adj* extremely bad, deplorable.—**abysmally** *adv*.

abyss *n* a bottomless depth; anything too deep to measure; hell.

abyssal *adj* pertaining to oceanic depths.* *n* the bottom zone of the ocean, below 9842 feet (3000 meters), where light does not penetrate and temperatures are below 4°C (39°F).

Abyssinia *n* previous name of the African country of Ethiopia.

ABZ *abbr* = Association of British Zoologists.

Ac *symbol* (*chem*) actinium (element).

ac¹ *abbr* (*chem*) = alicyclic; acetate; acetyl.

ac² *abbr* (*med*) = *ante cibum*, Latin "before food."

ac. *abbr* = acre, or acres; money of account.

AC *abbr* (*elec*) = Air Command Air Corps; Alpine Club; Alpine Convention; (*elec*) alternating current; Ambulance Corps; Analytical Chemist; Appeal Court; Army Corps; Arts Council; Assistant Commissioner; Athletic Club; alternating current (used in physics); (*French*) *appellation contrôlée*, "regulated naming," used in the origin of wines; aircraftman; (*Latin*) *ante Christum*, "before Christ."

A/C, a/c *abbr* = account; account current.

ac- *prefix* the form of *ad-* before *c, k, g*.

ACA *abbr* = Acoustic Corporation of America; Afro-Caribbean Association; Agricultural Council of America; Aircrewmen Association; American Cartographic Association; Asian Christian Association; Association of Canadian Archivists; Australian Coal Association.

ACAA *abbr* = Asian Christian Art Association.

ACAAI *abbr* = Air Cargo Agents Association of India.

ACAC *abbr* = American Christian Action Council; Arab Civil Aviation Authority; Australian Chemicals Advisory Committee.

Acacetus *n* one who does nothing badly, a name given to Hermes because of his eloquence.

ACACHE *abbr* = Association of Career Advisers in Colleges of Higher Education.

acacia *n* a genus of shrubby or arboreous leguminous plants of warmer regions with white or yellow flowers, several species of which yield gum.

acad. *abbr* = academy; academic.

academe *n* the world of higher education; the academic environment.

academia *n* the academic world, academe.

academic *adj* pertaining to a school, college or university; scholarly; purely theoretical in nature. * *n* a member of a college or university; a scholarly person.

academic freedom *n* the liberty to teach, discuss and pursue knowledge without interference or censorship.

academically *adv* theoretically, unpractically.

academician *n* a member of an Academy.

Académie Française a literary academy founded by Cardinal Richelieu in 1635 to supervise the purity of the French language.

academy *n* (*pl* **academies**) a school for specialized training; (*Scot*) a secondary school; (*with cap*) a society of scholars, writers, scientists, etc.

Academy Award *n* a golden statuette, "Oscar," awarded yearly by the Academy of Motion Picture Arts and Sciences for excellence in various categories of film-making.

academy of art *n* institution of professional artists or scholars. The National Academy of Design was founded in the USA in 1924 by a breakaway group of young members from the American Academy of Fine Arts, founded in 1802.

Acadian *adj* of Acadia, a region of Canada, Nova-Scotian.

ACADS *abbr* = Association for Computer Aided Design.

ACAE *abbr* = Australian Commission on Advanced Education.

ACAF *abbr* = Aero-Club Air France.

ACAHA *abbr* = Association of Chief Administrators of Health Authorities.

ACAI *abbr* = Accademia Archeologica Italiana.

ACAIP *abbr* = Advisory Committee on Animal Import Priorities.

ACAN *abbr* = Action Committee Against Narcotics.

acanthine *adj* pertaining to or resembling the plant acanthus. * *n* ornamentation in the shape of the acanthus leaf.

acanthus *n* (*pl* **acanthuses, acanthi**) a genus of herbaceous plants with sharp-toothed leaves; (*archit*) ornamentation adopted in the capitals of the Corinthian and Composite orders, and resembling the foliage of the acanthus.

ACANZ *abbr* = Agricultural Council of Australia and New Zealand.

ACAO *abbr* = Association of Chief Ambulance Officers.

a cappella *or* **alla capella** *adj* (*mus*) (*Italian*) literally "in the chapel style"; it is a term that has come to mean unaccompanied choral singing.

ACAQ *abbr* = Advisory Committee on Air Quality.

ACARD *abbr* = Advisory Council for Applied Research and Development.

acarid *n* a tick or mite of the *Acarina* order of insects, etc, in which the divisions of head, thorax and abdomen are not apparent.—*also adj*.

ACARMA *abbr* = Agricultural Chemical and Animal Remedies Manufacturing Association of New Zealand.

Acarnania *n* ancient name for the most westerly portion of northern Greece.—**Acarnanian** *adj*.

acarpellous, acarpelous *adj* (*bot*) without carpels.

acarpous *adj* (*bot*) not producing fruit; sterile or barren.

ACAS *abbr* = Advisory, Conciliation and Arbitration Service; Association of Concerned African Scholars.

ACASS *abbr* = Association of Chartered Accountant Students Societies.

Acastus *n* (*Greek myth*) a son of Pelias, king of Iolcus, and one of the Argonauts.

ACAT *abbr* = Action de Chrétiens pour l'Abolition de Torture; African Cooperative Action Trust.

acatalectic *adj* (*verse*) with a complete number of syllables, not catalectic.—*also n*.

ACATCM *abbr* = All-China Association of Traditional Chinese Medicine.

ACATS *abbr* = Association of Civil Aviation Technical Staffs.

acaudal, acaudate *adj* (*zool*) without a tail.

acaulescent *adj* (*bot*) stemless or with a very short stem.—**acaulescence** *n*.

ACAV *abbr* = Agence Centrafrique de Voyage; American Committee on Arthropod-borne Viruses.

ACAVA *abbr* = Association for Cultural Advancement through Visual Art.

ACAVC *abbr* = Advisory Committee on Agricultural and Veterinary Chemicals.

ACB *abbr* = Agricultural Cooperatives Bank of Iran; American Council of the Blind; Arab Central Bank; Associación Costarricense de Bibliotecarios; Association Canadienne des Bibliothèques.

ACBA *abbr* = Aggregate Concrete Block Association.

ACBB *abbr* = American Council for Better Broadcasts.

ACBC *abbr* = Australian Catholic Bishops' Conference.

acc. *abbr* = acceptance; accepted; accompanied; accompaniment; accordant; according; according (to); account; accountant; accusative.

ACC *abbr* = Aboriginal Coordinating Council; Academy of Canadian Cinema; Air Combat Command; American Catholic Committee; Army Catering Corps; Australian Chamber of Commerce.

ACCA *abbr* = American Cotton Cooperative Association; Associate of the Chartered Association of Certified Accountants.

ACCAD *abbr* = Advisory Committee for the World Climate Applications and Data Programs.

Accadian *see* **Akkadian**.

ACCART *abbr* = Australian Council for Care of Animals in Research and Teaching.

ACCBD *abbr* = Advisory Committee on Conservation of Biological Diversity.

ACCC *abbr* = Advisory Committee to the Canada Center for Inland Waters; American Council of Christian Churches; Association of Classic Car Clubs.

ACCDU *abbr* = African Caribbean Community Development Unit.

ACCE *abbr* = Association of Christian Centers in Europe (Germany); Association of County Chief Executives.

accede *vi* to take office; to agree or assent to (a suggestion).

accel. *abbr* (*mus*) (*Italian*) = *accelerando*, "more quickly."

accelerando *adv, adj* (*mus*) (*Italian*) "quickening," with gradual increase of speed. * *n* (*pl* **accelerandos**) a piece of music played in this way; a gradual speeding up of pace.

accelerate *vti* to move faster; to happen or cause to happen more quickly; to increase the velocity of (a vehicle, etc).—**accelerative, acceleratory** *adj*.

accelerated depreciation *n* a rate of depreciation that is faster than the rate that is usu allowed for in considering the useful life of an asset.

acceleration *n* (*phys*) an increase in the speed at which an object is traveling.

acceleration of gravity *n* the gravitational acceleration of a mass allowed to drop freely near the surface of the Earth.

accelerator *n* a device for increasing speed; a throttle; (*phys*) an apparatus that imparts high velocities to elementary particles.

accelerator board *n* (*comput*) an adapter for the computer containing a more advanced microprocessor than the one already in the computer.

accent *n* emphasis on a syllable or word; a mark used to indicate this; any way of speaking characteristic of a region, class, or an individual; the emphasis placed on something; rhythmic stress in music or verse; (*mus*) the emphasis given to specific notes to indicate the rhythm of a piece of music. * *vt* to express the accent, or denote the vocal division of a word by stress or modulation of the voice; to pronounce; to mark or accent a word in writing by use of a sign; to dwell upon or emphasize, as a passage of music.

accentuate *vt* to emphasize.

accentuation *n* the act of accentuating by stress or accent; speaking or writing with emphasis or distinction.

accept *vt* to receive, esp willingly; to approve; to agree to; to believe in; to agree to pay.

acceptable *adj* satisfactory; welcome; tolerable.—**acceptability** *n*.—**acceptably** *adv*.

acceptance *n* the act of accepting; the act of being accepted or received with approbation; agreement; the subscription to a bill of exchange; the bill accepted or the sum contained in it; (*com*) the signature on a bill of exchange that shows that the person on whom the bill is drawn accepts its conditions; a bill of exchange that has been duly accepted in this way; an agreement to accept the terms of an offer.

acceptance sampling *n* a quality-control process in which a sample is taken from a batch of raw materials, work in progress or finished products and deemed to be representative of the quality of the whole.

acceptation *n* the act of accepting or state of being accepted or acceptable; the meaning or sense of a word or statement in which it is to be understood.

accepter, acceptor *n* one who accepts; the person who accepts a bill of exchange.

accepting house *n* a financial institution that specializes in accepting, or guaranteeing to honor, bills of exchange.

acceptor *n* the person who signs the face of a bill of exchange and thereby accepts liability for it.

access *n* approach, or means of approach; the right to enter, use, etc. * *vt* (*comput*) to retrieve (information) from a storage device; to gain access to.

access code *n* (*comput*) the means of gaining entry into a computer or system by use of a password or specific identification number.

access provider *n* (*comput*) a company that provides connections to the Internet.

accessible *adj* able to be reached; open (to).—**accessibility** *n*.—**accessibly** *adv*.

accession *n* the act of reaching or assuming a rank or position.—**accessional** *adj*.

accessorize *vt* to decorate or to provide with accessories.

accessory *adj* additional; extra. * *n* (*pl* **accessories**) a supplementary part or item, esp of clothing; a person who aids another in a crime.—**accessorial** *adj*.

ACCET *abbr* = Asian Center for Comparative Education.

ACCI *abbr* = Association of Chambers of Commerce of Ireland; Australian Chamber of Commerce and Industry.

acciaccatura *n* (*pl* **acciaccaturas, acciaccature**) (*mus*) (*Italian*) a half-note or grace note (ornamental or auxiliary note), normally the semitone below the principal note, played just before or at the same time as the principal note and immediately released while the latter is held.

accidence *n* (*gram*) the part of grammar that deals with the inflections of words, which are accidents, not essentials; a book containing the rudiments of grammar; the rudiments themselves.

accident *n* an unexpected event; a mishap or misfortune, esp one resulting in death or injury; chance.

accidental *adj* occurring or done by accident; non-essential; (*mus*) a note in a piece of music that departs by one or two semitones from the key signature. It is indicated by a sharp, flat or natural sign before it.—**accidentally** *adv*.

accident-prone *adj* having a tendency to suffer accident or injury.

accidie *n* sloth, torpor, apathy.

accipiter *n* a generic name for birds of prey, as the common hawk.

accipitrine *adj* hawk-like, rapacious.

acclaim *vt* to praise publicly (the merits of a person or thing); to welcome enthusiastically. * *vi* to shout approval. * *n* a shout of welcome or approval.

acclamation *n* a shout of applause or other demonstration of hearty approval, loud united assent; an outburst of joy or praise; the adoption of a resolution *viva voce*; a mode of papal election.—**acclamatory** *adj*.

acclimatize *vt* to adapt to a new climate or environment * *vi* to become acclimatized.—**acclimatization** *n*.

acclivity *n* (*pl* **acclivities**) an ascent or upward slope of the earth; the talus of a rampart.—**acclivitous** *adj*.

ACCM *abbr* = Advisory Council for the Church's ministry.

ACCME *abbr* = Accreditation Council for Continuing Medical Education.

ACCO *abbr* = Association of Child Care Officers; Australian Council of Consumer Organizations.

accolade *n* praise; approval; an award; a ceremonial touch on the shoulder with a sword to confer knighthood.

accommodate *vt* to provide lodging for; to oblige, supply; to adapt, harmonize.

accommodating *adj* obliging, willing to help.—**accommodatingly** *adv*.

accommodation *n* lodgings; the process of adapting; willingness to help.

accommodation bill *n* a bill of exchange that is signed by the person who is acting as guarantor, such a person being known as the accommodation party.

accommodation ladder *n* a ladder or stairway suspended at the gangway of a ship.

accommodative *adj* disposed or tending to accommodate.

accomp. *abbr* = accompaniment.

accompaniment *n* something that accompanies; (*mus*) an instrumental part, provided by an orchestra, organ or, most usu, a piano, supporting a solo instrument, a voice, or a choir.

accompanist, accompanyist *n* one who plays a musical accompaniment.

accompany *vt* (**accompanying, accompanied**) (*person*) to go with; (*something*) to supplement.

accomplice *n* a partner, esp in committing a crime.

accomplish *vt* to succeed in carrying out; to fulfill.

accomplished *adj* done; completed; skilled, expert; polished.

accomplishment *n* a skill or talent; the act of accomplishing; something accomplished.

accord *vi* to agree; to harmonize (with). * *vt* to grant. * *n* consent; harmony.

accordance *n* agreement; conformity.

accordant *adj* corresponding; of the same mind.

accordant drainage *n* a drainage pattern related to the structure of the underlying rocks where the main stream flows in the same direction as the dip of the rock.

accordant junctions *n* tributaries that join a stream or river at the same elevation as that of the larger watercourse.

accordant summits *n* hills or mountain tops at approximately the same height above sea level.

according *prep* as stated by or in; (*with* **to**) in conformity with; (*with* **as**) depending on whether. * *adj* agreeing, harmonious.

accordingly *adv* consequently; therefore; suitably.

accordion *n* a portable keyboard instrument with manually operated folding bellows that force air through metal reeds.—**accordionist** *n*.

accost *vt* to approach and speak to, often to accuse of crime or to solicit sexually.

account *n* a description; an explanatory statement; a business record or statement; a credit arrangement with a bank, department store, etc; importance, consequence. * *vt* to think of as; consider. * *vi* to give a financial reckoning (to); (*with* **for**) to give reasons (for); (*with* **for**) to kill, dispose of.

accountable *adj* liable; responsible; explainable.—**accountability** *n*.—**accountably** *adv*.

accountancy *n* the profession or practice of an accountant.

accountant *n* one whose profession is auditing business accounts.

account book *n* a book for the entering of accounts, or in which particulars of sales, purchases, etc, are kept.

account executive *n* an agency executive who manages the accounts of one or more clients.

accounting *n* the process of recording a company's financial transactions by means of recognized book-keeping records.

account payable *n* (*pl* **accounts payable**) the balance due to a creditor.

accounting period *n* the period over which a company prepares its accounts or financial records.

account receivable *n* (*pl* **accounts receivable**) the balance due from a debtor.

accounts *npl* the financial statements of a company prepared from a system of recorded financial transactions. They consist at least of a profit and loss account and the balance sheet of the company.

accouter, accoutre *vt* to dress; to equip; to array in military dress; to furnish with accoutrements.—**accouterment, accoutrement** *n*.

accouterments, accoutrements *npl* equipage; dress; military equipment.

Accra *n* capital city of Ghana.

accredit *vt* to give credit or authority to; to have confidence in; to authorize; to stamp with authority; to believe and accept as true.—**accreditation** *n*.

accredited *adj* authorized officially; accepted as valid; certified as being of a prescribed quality.

accrescent *adj* (*bot*) increasing; growing.

accrete *vi* to adhere, to grow together; to be added. * *vt* to cause to grow or unite. * *adj* (*bot*) grown into one.

accretion *n* an increase by natural growth; the addition of external parts; the growing together of parts or members naturally separate; capture of matter by a celestial object, largely by gravitation; the growth of land by the offshore depositions of a sediment. —**accretive, accretionary** *adj*.

accrual *n* an expense that is outstanding at the end of an accounting period and requires to be included in the accounts for the period.

accrual accounting *n* an accounting procedure in which all the costs and revenue occurring in the course of a company's transactions are counted in the company's accounts on the date on which the costs are incurred or the revenues earned.

accrue *vi* (**accruing, accrued**) to come as a natural increase or addition; (money, etc) to accumulate or be added periodically.—**accrual, accrument** *n*.

acct. *abbr* = account.

ACCT *abbr* = Association of Cinematograph, Television and Allied Technicians.

ACCTVS *abbr* = Association of Closed Circuit Television Surveyors.

acculturation *n* the process whereby one society takes up a characteristic, feature or attribute of another society.

accumbent *adj* (*bot*) reclining or recumbent; (*hist*) of the Roman style of reclining on a couch at meals.—**accumbency** *n*.

accumulate *vti* to collect together in increasing quantities, to amass.

accumulated profits *npl* the amount of profit in a company's accounting period that can be carried forward to the next accounting period after dividends and taxes are paid.

accumulating shares *npl* ordinary shares that are issued to shareholders in a company instead of a dividend.

accumulation *n* the act of accumulating or amassing; the addition of interest to principal; the mass accumulated.

accumulation zone *n* the part of a slope that gains material, leading to a progressive raising of the ground surface.

accumulative *adj* cumulative; acquisitive.

accumulator *n* a rechargeable battery; (*borseracing*) a bet that accumulates in value over successive races; (*comput*) a storage register.

accuracy *n* (*pl* **accuracies**) the quality of being accurate; exactness or correctness.

accurate *adj* conforming with the truth or an accepted standard; done with care, exact.—**accurately** *adv*.

accursed, accurst *adj* under or subject to a curse; ill-fated, doomed to destruction; detestable; execrable.

accusation *n* the act of accusing or being accused; an allegation; the charge of guilt brought against a person.

accusative *n* (*gram*) the case expressing the direct object of a word.

accusatorial, accusatory *adj* accusing, or containing an accusation; (*law*) in which prosecutor and judge are not the same (opposite to inquisitorial).

accuse *vt* to charge with a crime, fault, etc; to blame.—**accuser** *n*.—**accusingly** *adv*.

accused *n* (*law*) (*with* **the**) the defendant in court facing a criminal charge.

accuser *n* one who accuses; one who formally charges an offence against another.

accustom *vt* to make used (to) by habit, use, or custom.

accustomed *adj* usual, customary; used to.

ACD *abbr* = Advisory Committee on National Health Service Drugs; Association for Curriculum Development.

ACDA *abbr* = United States Arms Control and Disarmament Agency

AC/DC *abbr* = alternating current/direct current.

ACDP *abbr* = Advisory Committee on Dangerous Pathogens.

ACDS *abbr* = Advisory Committee on Dangerous Substances; Anglo-Continental Dental Society.

ace *n* the one spot in dice, playing cards, dominoes, etc; a point won by a single stroke, as in tennis; an expert. * *adj* (*inf*) excellent.

ACE *abbr* = Access Committee for England; Advisory Center for Education; Age Concern England; Agricultural Communicators in Education; (*med*) alcohol, chloroform, and ether (mixture); Alliance for everage Cartons and the Environment; American College of Ecology; Association for Coal in Europe; Association for Cultural Exchange; Association for the Conservation of Energy; Association of Children's Entertainers; Association of Circulation Executives; Association of Comics Enthusiasts; Association of Conference Executives; Association of Consulting Engineers; Association of Cost Engineers; Athens Center of Ekistiks; Australian Christian Endeavor Union.

ACEA *abbr* = Associate of the Association of Cost and Executive Accountants.

-acea *n suffix* forming the plural names for orders of animals, e.g., Crustacea, Crustaceae.

-aceae *n suffix* forming plural names for families of plants, e.g., Rosaceae.

acedia *n* an abnormal condition of the mind, characterized by lassitude, listlessness, and general indifference.

ACEG *abbr* = Afghan Carpet Exporters' Guild.

ACEI *abbr* = Association of Consulting Engineers of Ireland.

acellular *adj* (*biol*) without any cells; not made up of cells.

Ac-Em *abbr* (*chem*) = actinon, *or* actinon emanation.

acentric *adj* away from the center; having no center.

ACENVO *abbr* = Association of Chief Executives of National Voluntary Organizations.

ACEO *abbr* = Association of Chief Education Officers.

acephalous *adj* headless; without a leader; an ovary of a plant that has its style springing from the base instead of the apex.

ACER *abbr* = Advisory Committee on Environmental Resources; Afro-Caribbean Education Resource Center; Australian Council for Educational Research.

acerbic *adj* bitter and harsh to the taste; astringent.

Acerbis *n* influential Italian furniture manufacturer founded in 1870 by a cabinet maker of that surname.

acerbity *n* (*pl* **acerbities**) sharpness of speech or manner; (of taste) bitterness.

acerose *adj* (*bot*) like a needle, very narrow, rigid, and tapering to a point.

ACERT *abbr* = Advisory Committee for the Education of Romany and other Travelers.

ACertCM *abbr* = The Archbishop of Canterbury's Certificate in Church Music.

acervate *adj* growing in closely compacted clusters.

ACES *abbr* = American Catholic Esperanto Society; Applied Computational Electromagnetics Society; Arab Center for Energy Studies.

Acestes *n* a Sicilian who, according to Virgil's *Aeneid*, in a trial of skill discharged his arrow with such force that it caught fire (the arrow of Acestes).

ACESW *abbr* = Association of Chief Education Social Workers.

ACET *abbr* = AIDS Care Education and Training; Association of Consultants in Education and Training.

acet-, aceto- *prefix* vinegar.

acetabulum *n* (*pl* **acetabula, acetabulums**) the cavity of the hip bone into which the femur fits; one of the cup-like suckers on the arms of the cuttlefish; the posterior sucker of the leech; the saucer-shaped fructification of certain lichens; the receptacle of various fungi; a cup to hold vinegar.

acetabulum *see* **hip joint**.

acetanilide, acetanilid *n* a pungent white powder, formed by the action of acetyl choride on aniline, used in medicine as an antipyretic.

acetate *n* a salt or ester of acetic acid; a fabric made from cellulose acetate.

acetic *adj* of acetic acid or vinegar.

acetic acid *n* a clear liquid with a strong acid taste and sharp smell, present in a dilute form in vinegar.

acetify *vt* (**acetifying, acetifed**) to turn into vinegar.—**acetification** *n*.—**acetifier** *n*.

acetometer *n* an instrument for gauging the strength or purity of vinegar or acetic acid.

acetone *n* a clear flammable liquid used as a solvent.

acetonuria *see* **ketonuria**.

acetous, acetose *adj* of the nature of vinegar; sour; causing acetification.

acetylcholine *n* an important organic chemical substance involved in the transmission of electrical impulses along nerves.

acetylene *n* a gas that burns with a hot flame, used for welding, etc.

acetylsalicylic acid *n* the chemical name for aspirin.

ACF *abbr* = Active Citizen Force (South Africa); Administration for Children and Families; Agricultural Co-operative Federation; Anarchist Communist Federation; Army Cadet Force; Association of Charitable Foundations; Australian Cotton Foundation; Automobile Club de France.

ACFA *abbr* = Air Charter Forwarders Association; American Council for Free Asia; Army Cadet Force Association; Association of Cystic Fibrosis Adults.

ACFAI *abbr* = All-China Federation of Automobile Industry.

ACFHE *abbr* = Association of Colleges for Further and Higher Education.

ACFI *abbr* = Associate of the Clothing and Footwear Institute.

ACFM *abbr* = Advisory Committee on Fisheries Management; Association of Cereal Food Manufacturers.

ACFSS *abbr* = Aged Christian Friend Society of Scotland.

ACG *abbr* = Anti-Counterfeiting Group; Arts Center Group; automatic control gear.

ACGA *abbr* = American Cricket Growers' Association.

ACGB *abbr* = Aircraft Corporation of Great Britain; Arts Council of Great Britain.

ACGF *abbr* = Australian Citrus Growers Foundation.

ACGI *abbr* = Associate of the City and Guilds of London Institute (at City and Guilds College, Imperial College, London).

ACGM *abbr* = Advisory Committee on Genetic Manipulation.

ACGME *abbr* = Accreditation Council for Graduate Medical Education.

ACh *abbr* = acetylcholine.

ACH *abbr* = Association for Comparative Hematology; Association of Clinical Hypnotherapists; Association of Community Homes; Association of Contemporary Historians.

Achaea *see* **Achaia**.

Achaeans, Achaians *npl* one of the four races into which the ancient Greeks were divided, used by Homer to refer to the Greeks in general.

Achaemenid *n* the generic term for descendants of Achaemenes who formed the Persian royal family. These include Cyrus II, Darius I and Xerxes.

Achaeus *n* (*Greek myth*) son of Xuthus and Creusa, and the brother of Ion and grandson of Hellen.

Achaia *n* (*Bible*) ancient name for part of Greece which included Corinth.—**Achaian, Achaean** *adj*.

achalasia *n* a failure to relax the muscle fibers surrounding the opening of the esophagus.

Achan *n* (*Bible*) man of Judah stoned to death for looting after the fall of Jericho.

ACHAS *abbr* = Acoustical Commission of the Hungarian Academy of Sciences.

Achates *n* a faithful friend, from Aeneas's friend in Virgil's *Aeneid*.

ACHCEW *abbr* = Association of Community Health Councils for England and Wales.

ache *n* a dull, continuous pain. * *vi* to suffer a dull, continuous mental or physical pain; (*inf*) to yearn.—**achy** *adj*.

ACHE *abbr* = Action on Child Exploitation.

Achelous *n* the largest river in Greece, which in Greek mythology was worshiped as a god.

Achernar *or* **Alpha Eridani** *n* a star of the first magnitude, the leading star in the southern constellation Eridanus.

Acheron *n* the ancient name of several rivers in Greece and Italy, all of which were connected by legend with the underworld.

Acherusia *n* (*Greek myth*) a cavern said to lead down to the underworld, through which Heracles dragged Cerberus to earth.

Acheson *n* **Dean** [**Gooderham**] (1893–1971) American lawyer and statesman who played an important role in developing the Marshall Plan and the establishment of NATO.

Acheulian *adj* (*archeo*) relating to a late, lower Paleolithic culture and handaxe industry which is seen as a development of the Abbevilian.

achieve *vt* to perform successfully, accomplish; to gain, win. —**achievable** *adj*.—**achiever** *n*.

achievement *n* a thing achieved, esp by great effort, courage, determination, etc; accomplishment; (*ber*) an escutcheon in memory of a distinguished feat.

Achilles *n* a Greek legendary hero, the chief character in Homer's *Iliad*, son of Peleus and Thetis, by whom he was dipped in the River Styx. He was killed in battle at Troy by an arrow which struck his vulnerable heel.

Achilles' heel *n* a person's vulnerable or weak point.

Achilles' tendon *n* a tendon attaching the heel to the calf muscles.

achlamydeous *adj* having neither calyx nor corolla.

achondrite *n* a stony meteorite lacking chondrules, similar to igneous rock of low silica content on Earth.

achondroplasia *n* the commonest cause of dwarfism, in which the long bones of the limbs are abnormally short.

ACHP *abbr* = Advisory Council on Historic Preservation

ACHRO *abbr* = Asian Coalition of Human Rights Organizations.

achromatic *adj* colorless; transmitting light without decomposing it.—**achromatically** *adv*.—**achromaticity, achromatism** *n*.

achromatic lens *n* a lens combination designed to overcome chromatic aberration over a particular wavelength range.

achromatize *vt* to deprive of the power of transmitting color; to render achromatic.—**achromatization** *n*.

ACHSTS *abbr* = African Council for the Training and Promotion of Health Sciences Teachers and Specialists.

ACHSWW *abbr* = American Committee on the History of the Second World War.

ACIA *abbr* = Associate of the Corporation of Insurance Brokers.

ACIArb *abbr* = Associate of the Chartered Institute of Arbitrators.

ACIB *abbr* = Associate of the Chartered Institute of Bankers.

ACIBS *abbr* = Associate of the Chartered Institute of Bankers in Scotland.

ACIBSE *abbr* = Associate of the Chartered Institution of Building Services Engineers.

acicula *n* (*pl* **aciculae**) a spine or prickle.

acicular *adj* needle-shaped.

aciculate, aciculated *adj* in the shape of a needle; acicular.

acid *adj* sharp or sour to the taste. * *n* (*chem*) a substance that releases hydrogen ions during a chemical reaction, one that with certain other substances forms salts; a sour substance; (*sl*) LSD.—**acidly** *adv*.

acid-head *n* (*sl*) a frequent consumer of LSD.

acid house *n* a party where people take drugs and dance to House music; the style of popular music played.

acidic *adj* containing a large proportion of the acid element; opposed to basic.

acidifier *n* a substance having the property of imparting an acid quality.

acidify *vti* (**acidifying, acidified**) to make or become acid.—**acidification** *n*.

acidimeter *n* an instrument for measuring the strength of acids.—**acidimetric** *adj*.—**acidimetrically** *adv*.—**acidimetry** *n*.

acidity *n* (*pl* **acidities**) the quality or condition of being acid.

acidosis *n* a condition in which the acidity of the blood and body fluids rise to an abnormally high level. —**acidotic** *adj*.

acid rain *n* rain made acidic by air pollution from power stations, etc.

acid rock *n* a type of rock music characterized by lyrics and sound supposedly inspired by drug-induced experiences.

acid soil *n* a soil with a pH of less than 7.

acid test *n* a crucial or conclusive test.

acidulate *vt* to render slightly acid. —**acidulation** *n*.

acidulous, acidulent *adj* somewhat acid; tart; peevish.

acierate *vt* (**acierating, acierated**) to change into steel.—**acieration** *n*.

ACIF *abbr* = African Caribbean Institute of Jamaica; Agricultural Construction Industry Association.

ACIG *abbr* = Animal Cruelty Investigation Group.

ACII *abbr* = Associate of the Chartered Insurance Institute.

ACILA *abbr* = Associate of the Chartered Institute of Loss Adjusters.

acinaciform *adj* (*bot*) resembling a scimitar in shape, as an acinaciform leaf or pod.

acini *npl* milk-producing glands found in the female breast.

aciniform *adj* grape-like; clustered like grapes; acinous.

acinous *adj* consisting of acini.—*Also* **acinose**.

ACIOB *abbr* = Associate of the Chartered Institute of Building.

-acious *adj suffix* forming adjectives meaning full of, inclined to, as mendacious.

Acis *n* (*Greek myth*) a beautiful shepherd of Sicily, loved by Galatea and crushed to death by his rival, the Cyclops Polyphemus.

ACIS *abbr* = African Church Information Service; American Committee for Irish Studies; American Council for International Studies; Associate of the Institute of Chartered Secretaries; Association of Contemporary Iberian Studies.

-acity *n suffix* forming corresponding nouns of quality, as mendacity.

ACIUCN *abbr* = Australian Committee for the International Union for the Conservation of Nature and Natural Resources.

ACJA *abbr* = American Criminal Justice Association.

ack. or **ackgt.** *abbr* (*bank*) = acknowledgment.

ack-ack *n* (*mil*) (*sl*) an anti-aircraft gun; anti-aircraft fire.

Ackermann *n* **Rudolf** (1764–1834) German-born coach designer who designed Admiral Nelson's funeral carriage in 1806.

Acking *n* **Carl-Axel** (1910–) Swedish architect, influential in furniture and interior design.

acknowledge *vt* to admit that something is true and valid; to show that one has noticed or recognized.

acknowledgment, acknowledgement *n* the act of acknowledging; the admission or recognition of a truth; confession; the expression of appreciation of a favor or benefit conferred; a printed recognition by an author of others' works used or referred to; a receipt.

aclinic line *n* the imaginary point near the equator where the magnetic needle has no dip, the magnetic equator.

ACLM *abbr* = American College of Legal Medicine; Antigua Caribbean Liberation Movement; Association of Contact Lens Manufacturers.

ACLS *abbr* = American Council of Learned Societies; Automatic Carrier Landing System.

ACM *abbr* = Air Chief Marshal; American council on Marijuana and other Psychoactive Drugs; Arab Common Market; Association for College Management; Association of Clinical Microbiologists; Australian Chamber of Manufacturers.

ACMA *abbr* = Agricultural Co-operative Managers Association; Aluminum Coin Manufacturers' Association; American Cutlery Manufacturers Association; Associate of the Institute of Cost and Management Accountants.

ACMC *abbr* = Advanced Composites Manufacturing Center; American Common Market Club; Association of Canadian Medical Colleges.

ACMD *abbr* = Advisory Council on the Misuse of Drugs.

acme *n* the peak or highest point; the height of perfection.

ACME *abbr* = Advisory Council on Medical Establishments (Scotland); Association of Cotton Merchants in Europe.

Acmeist group *n* a school of Russian poetry that emerged in the early 20th century.

ACML *abbr* = Anti-Common Market League; Arab Center for Medical Literature (Kuwait); Association of Canadian Map Libraries.

ACN *abbr* = Aid to the Church in Need; Action Christian National Party (Namibia); *ante Christum natum*, Latin "before the birth of Christ".

acne *n* a disorder of the skin in adolescents (because of hormonal influence), characterized by the presence of pustules and blackheads.

ACO *abbr* = African Curriculum Organization; American College of Orgonomy; Association of Charity Officers; Association of Conservation Officers.

ACOLF *abbr* = Advisory Committee on Live Fish.

acolyte *n* an assistant or follower, esp of a priest.

aconite, aconitum *n* the plant wolf's-bane or monk's-hood; the drug prepared from the plant.—**aconitic** *adj*.

ACOP *abbr* = Advisory Committee on Pilotage; Association of Chief Officers of Police; Association of Chief Officers of Probation.

ACOPS *abbr* = Advisory Committee on Oil Pollution of the Sea; Advisory Committee on Protection of the Sea.

ACORBAT *abbr* = Association for Co-operation in Banana Research in the Caribbean and Tropical America.

ACORD *abbr* = Advisory Council on Research and Development For Fuel and Power; Asian Center for Organization, Research and Development; Euro Action-Agency for Cooperation and Research and Development.

acorn *n* the nut of the oak tree.

ACORN *abbr* (*comput*) = automatic checkout and recording network.

ACOST *abbr* = Advisory Committee on Science and Technology.

ACOSVO *abbr* = Association of Chief Officers of Scottish Voluntary Organizations.

acotyledon *n* (*bot*) a plant with seeds (spores) that have no cotyledons (seed lobes).—**acotyledonous** *adj*.

acoustic, acoustical *adj* of the sense of hearing or sound; of acoustics; (*mus*) not amplified, e.g., a guitar.—**acoustically** *adv*.

acoustic coupler *n* (*comput*) a cradle that holds a telephone handset and allows modems to communicate through the telephone.

acoustic guitar *see* guitar.

acoustician *n* one skilled in acoustics.

acoustics *npl* (*room, concert hall, etc*) properties governing how clearly sounds can be heard in it; (*phys*) a branch of physics that is concerned with sound.

acoustic wave *n* a wave motion in which compressions and rarefactions of the material through which the wave travels occur in the direction of travel; a sound wave.

ACP *abbr* = American College of Prosthodontics; Associate of the College of Preceptors; Association of Canadian Publishers; Association of Child Psychotherapists; Association of Circus Proprietors of Great Britain; Association of Clinical Pathologists; Association of Computer Professionals; Australian College of Pediatrics.

ACPA *abbr* = American Capon Producers Association; American Cleft Palate Association; Association of Christians in Planning and Architecture.

ACPM *abbr* = Advisory Committee on Program Management; Associate of the Confederation of Professional Management; Association of Corrugated Paper Makers.

ACPO *abbr* = Association of Chief Police Officers.

ACPP *abbr* = Association for Child Psychology and Psychiatry.

ACPSM *abbr* = Association of Chartered Physiotherapists in Sports Medicine; Australasian College of Physical Scientists in Medicine.

acpt. *abbr* (*bank*) = acceptance.

ACQS Association of Consultant Quantity Surveyors.

acquaint *vt* to make (oneself) familiar (with); to inform; (*with* **with**) to introduce (to).

acquaintance *n* a person whom one knows only slightly.

acquainted *adj* having personal knowledge; (*with* **of, with**) familiar, known.

acquiesce *vi* (*with* **in**) to comply with readily, or put up no opposition to.

acquiescence *n* compliance; assent.—**acquiescent** *adj*.

acquire *vt* to gain by one's own efforts; to obtain.—**acquirable** *adj*.

acquired *adj* (*med*) a term used to describe a condition or malady that is not congenital but arises after birth.

acquired immune deficiency syndrome *see* **AIDS**.

acquired taste *n* something that may at first seem unpleasant but for which one later develops a liking.

acquirement *n* the act of acquiring; that which is acquired; mental attainment.

acquisition *n* the act of gaining, acquiring; someone or something that is acquired, often of special worth or talent.

acquisitive *adj* eager or greedy for possessions.—**acquisitively** *adv.*—**acquisitiveness** *n*.

acquit *vt* (**acquitting, acquitted**) to free from an obligation; to behave or conduct (oneself); to declare innocent.

acquittal *n* the act of releasing or acquitting, the state of being acquitted; a judicial discharge from accusation; the performance (of duty).

acquittance *n* a discharge or release from debt or other liability; a receipt barring a further demand.

ACQWeb *abbr* = Office of the Under Secretary of Defense for Acquisition and Technology

ACR *abbr* = Association for Consumer Research; Association of Clinic Research; Association of Countryside Rangers; Australian Catholic Relief.

ACRA *abbr* = Aluminum Can Recycling Association; Aontacht Cumann Riartha Aitreabhthoiri; Association of College Registrars and Administrators; Association of Company Registrations Agents; Australian Cultivar Registration Authority.

acre *n* a measure of area equal to 4840 square yards.

ACRE *abbr* = Action with Communities in Rural England; Association for Consumer Research; Association of Community Councils in Rural England.

acreage *n* area measured in acres.

acrid *adj* sharp and bitter of taste or smell; caustic, critical in attitude or speech.—**acridity** *n*.—**acridly** *adv*.

acrimony *n* (*pl* **acrimonies**) bitterness of manner or language.—**acrimonious** *adj.*—**acrimoniously** *adv*.

Acrisius *n* (*Greek myth*) son of Abas and twin brother of Proetus, with whom he is said to have quarreled even in the womb, and father of Danaè.

acro- *prefix* topmost, extreme.

acrobat *n* a skillful performer of spectacular gymnastic feats.—**acrobatic** *adj.*—**acrobatically** *adv*.

acrobatics *npl* acrobatic feats.

acrocarpous *adj* (*bot*) having (like the mosses) the fruit at the end of the primary axis.

acrogen *n* (*bot*) a nonflowering plant increasing by growth from the top, as ferns and mosses.—**acrogenic, acrogenous** *adj*.

acrolith *n* a sculptured figure, with head and extremities of stone and the rest of wood.

acromegaly *n* an abnormal growth of bones and tissues in the hands, head, feet and chest. —**acromegalic** *adj*.

acronycal, acronical *adj* (*astron*) (*stars*) rising at sunset and setting at sunrise.

acronym *n* a word formed from the initial letters of other words (as *laser*).

acrophobia *n* dread of heights.—**acrophobe** *n*.—**acrophobic** *adj, n*.

acropolis *n* the citadel or chief place of an ancient Greek city, usu on an eminence commanding the town.

acrospire *n* (*bot*) the sprout of a seed.

across *prep* from one side to the other of; on or at an angle; on the other side of. * *adv* crosswise; from one side to the other.

across-the-board *adj* (*wage increase, cut, etc*) applying equally to all; (*horseracing*) winning a bet if the horse comes first, second or third.

acrostic *n* a poem or word puzzle in which the initial letters of each line spell a complete word, etc.—**acrostically** *adv*.

acroter *n* (*pl* **acroteria**) (*archit*) a plinth for a statue placed on the apex and lower ends of pediments.

ACRR *abbr* = Advisory Council on Race Relations.

Acrux *or* **Alpha Crucis** *n* (*astron*) a binary star of the first magnitude, the brightest in the constellation Southern Cross.

acrylic *adj* of or derived from acrylic acid. * *n* an acrylic fiber or resin.

acrylic paint *n* a versatile synthetic paint that is quick-drying and can be used in thick, heavy layers or thin washes on almost any surface.

acrylic resin *n* a thermoplastic formed by polymerization of amides or esters.

ACS *abbr* = Additional Curates Society; Age Concern Scotland; American Camellia Society; Armstrong Clan Society; Association of Certified Secretaries of South Africa; Association of Commonwealth Students; Association of Consulting Scientists; Association of Cricket Statisticians; Australian Customs Service.

ACS *abbr* = Additional Curates Society; American Chemical Society; American College of Surgeons; American Colonization Society.

ACSA *abbr* = Associate of the Institute of Chartered Secretaries and Administrators.

ACSHEE *abbr* = Advisory Committee on the Safety of Household Electrical Equipment.

ACSI *abbr* = Association of Christian Schools International.

ACSIL *abbr* = Admiralty Center for Scientific Information and Liaison.

ACSIR *abbr* = Advisory Council for Scientific and Industrial Research.

ACSO *abbr* = Association of County Supplies Officers.

A/cs Pay. *abbr* = accounts payable.

A/cs Rec. *abbr* = accounts receivable.

act *vi* to perform or behave in a certain manner; to perform a specific function; to have an effect; to perform on the stage; (*with* **up**) (*inf*) to misbehave; to malfunction. * *vt* to portray by actions, esp on the stage; to pretend, simulate; to

take the part of, as a character in a play. * *n* something done, a deed; an exploit; a law; a main division of a play or opera; the short repertoire of a comic, etc; something done merely for effect or show.

act. *abbr* = active.

ACT *abbr* = Action by Christians Against Torture; Agricultural Central Trading; Aid for Children with Tracheostomies; Arts Counseling Trust; Asian Confederation of Teachers; Association of Career Teachers; Association of Christian Teachers; Associate in Corporate Treasury Management; Association of Cycle Traders; Association of Cytogenetic Technologists; Australian Capital Territory; Northern Ireland Advisory Committee on Travelers; advance corporation tax.

act of God *n* a direct and unforeseeable act of nature that could not reasonably have been guarded against.

ACTA *abbr* = Animal Consultants and Trainers' Association; Association of Cardiothoracic Anesthetists; Association of Chart and Technical Analysts; Australian City Transit Authority.

ACTAC *abbr* = Association of Community Technical Aid Centers.

Actaeon *n* (*Greek myth*) son of Autonoè, a great hunter who was turned into a stag by Artemis for looking on her when she was bathing and torn to pieces by his own dogs.

ACTAF *abbr* = Association of Community Trusts and Foundations.

Actg. *abbr* = acting.

ACTH *abbr* = Association for Cushing's Treatment and Help; adrenocorticotropic hormone (medical).

ACTHCM *abbr* = Associate Member of the Confederation of Tourism, Hotel and Catering Management.

acting *n* the art of an actor. * *adj* holding an office or position temporarily.

actinia *n* (*pl* **actiniae, actinias**) any of a genus of sea anemones that resemble flowers when the tentacles of the mouth are spread out.

actinide *n* (*chem*) a group of elements in the periodic table from actinium to lawrencium.

actiniform, actinoid *adj* having the form of rays; star-shaped.

actinism *n* the property of light by which chemical changes are caused, as in photography.—**actinic** *adj.*—**actinically** *adv*.

actinium *n* a radioactive element occurring as a decay product of uranium.

actinozoan *see* **anthozoan**.

action[1] *n* the process of doing something; an operation; a movement of the body; gesture; a land or sea battle; a lawsuit; the unfolding of events in a play, novel, etc; (*inf*) (*with* **the**) the center of (social) activity.

action[2] *n* (*mus*) the mechanism of a keyboard instrument that links the keyboard to the strings or, in the case of an organ, to the pipes and stops; the gap between the strings and fingerboard of a stringed instrument as dictated by the height of the bridge.

ACTION *abbr* = Active Citizens To Improve Our Neighborhood.

action painting *n* a form of abstract expressionism in which the paint is applied to the canvas in the course of a series of actions or movements by the artist. Jackson Pollock was a prominent exponent of action painting.

action potential *n* a biochemical change produced in a nerve by a stimulus such as pain.

actionable *adj* providing grounds for legal action.—**actionably** *adv*.

activate *vt* to make active; to set in motion; to make radioactive.—**activation** *n*.—**activator** *n*.

activated carbon *n* a highly absorbent carbon often used in deodorization.

activation energy *n* (*chem*) the energy required to start a chemical reaction between compounds.

active *adj* lively, physically mobile; engaged in practical activities; energetic, busy; (of a volcano) liable to erupt; capable of producing an effect; radioactive; (*mil*) in full-time service. * *n* (*gram*) the verb form having as its subject the doer of the action.—**actively** *adv.*—**activeness** *n*.

active cell *n* (*comput*) the cell in a spreadsheet in which the cursor is currently positioned, allowing a number or formula to be entered.

active glacier *n* a glacier that is receiving new ice above the snow line but is losing ice by ablation below the snow line.

active matrix display *n* (*comput*) a liquid crystal display (LCD) in which each of the display's electrodes is under the control of its own transistor.

active region *n* (*astron*) gas clouds where star formation occurs; a galactic nucleus with a black hole causing copious energy output; an area on the Sun giving rise to a flare.

active remote-sensing system *n* a remote sensing system having its own source of electromagnetic radiation sensors.

active service, active duty *n* full-time service in a military force, esp during a war.

active window *n* (*comput*) the current window, where multiple windows are open, indicated by a colored bar at the top of the window.

Active X *n* (*comput*) a programming language created by Microsoft™ that enables programmers to write small applications programs called applets which extend the capability of a browser.

activist *n* an advocate of direct or militant action, esp in politics.—**activism** *n*.

activity *n* (*pl* **activities**) the state of being active; energetic, lively action; specific occupations.

activity-based costing *npl* a system of product costing that considers the total cost to the business of making a product.

ACTO *abbr* = Association of Chief Technical Officers.

Acton *n* Sir **Harold** [Marino Mitchell] (1904–94) English poet, historian, and writer whose two volumes of memoirs shed light on the literary world of John Betjeman and Evelyn Waugh.

actor *n* a person who acts in a play, film, etc.—**actress** *nf*.

ACTR *abbr* = American Council of Teachers of Russian.

ACTRAM *abbr* = Advisory Committee on the Safe Transport of Radioactive Materials.

ACTS *abbr* = Action of Churches Together in Scotland; African Center for Technology Studies; Australian Catholic Truth Society.

Acts of the Apostles *n* (*Bible*) *NT* book probably written by Luke in the second half of the first century AD; generally recognized as the first history of the Christian Church. *See also* **Luke**.

ACTSS *abbr* = Association of Clerical, Technical and Supervisory Staffs.

ACTT *abbr* = Association of Cinematograph Television and Allied Technicians.

act tune *n* (*mus*) an instrumental piece of music that is played between the acts of a play while the curtain is down. Also **curtain music**. *See* **entr'acte**; **intermezzo**.

actual *adj* real; existing in fact or reality.

actuality *n* (*pl* **actualities**) the state of being real or actual; that which is in full existence; reality.

actualize *vt* to realize in action; to describe realistically; to make actual.—**actualization** *n*.

actually *adv* as an existing fact, really; strange though it seems.

actuals *npl* commodities that can be bought and used rather than goods that are traded on the basis of a futures contract.

actuary *n* (*pl* **actuaries**) a person who calculates insurance risks, premiums, etc; a trained statistician.—**actuarial** *adj*.

actuate *vt* to move or incite to action; to put in motion; to impel, influence.—**actuation** *n*.—**actuator** *n*.

ACu *abbr* = alto-cumulus.

ACU *abbr* = American Congregational Union; Association of Commonwealth Universities.

acuity *n* sharpness of thought or vision.

aculeate *adj* pointed; (*zool*) equipped with a sting; (*bot*) having aculei or sharp prickles.

aculeus *n* (*pl* **aculei**) a prickle.

acumen *n* sharpness of mind, perception.

acuminate *adj* ending in a sharp point. * *vt* (**acuminating, acuminated**) to sharpen.—**acumination** *n*.

acupuncture *n* a method of Chinese traditional healing involving the insertion of fine needles at various points beneath the skin, sometimes being employed as an alternative to anesthesia.—**acupuncturist** *n*.

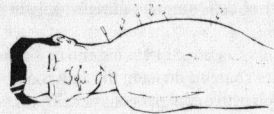

acute *adj* perceptive; sharp-witted; (*hearing*) sensitive; (*pain*) severe; very serious; (*geom*) angle between 0° and 90°; (*med*) a term used to describe a disease or condition that is short-lived and starts rapidly with severe symptoms.—**acutely** *adv*.—**acuteness** *n*.

acute accent *n* a mark (´) over a vowel in certain languages to indicate emphasis or special quality.

ACV *abbr* = actual cash value; air cushion vehicle.

ACW *abbr* = Aircraftwoman; alternating continuous waves.

ACWW *abbr* = Associated Countrywomen of the World.

ACY *abbr* = average crop yield.

-acy *n suffix* forming nouns of state or quality, e.g., piracy.

ACYC *abbr* = Association of Combined Youth Clubs.

ACYF *abbr* = Administration for Children, Youth, and Families

ACYW *abbr* = Associate of the Community and Youth Work Association.

a.d. *abbr* = after date; (*Latin*) *ante diem* , "before the day."

ad *prep* to, as in *ad absurdum*.

Ad *symbol* (*chem*) Aldebaranium (element).

ad *abbr* = accumulated dose (radiation); (*Latin*) *ante diem*, "before the day."

ad. *abbr* = (*Latin*) *addatur*, "let there be added"; adverb; advertisement.

AD *abbr* = (*Latin*)*anno domini*, "in the year of Our Lord"; in dates of the Christian era, indicating the number of years since the birth of Christ; average deviation; Alzheimer's disease; air defense; active duty.

ad- *prefix* to, as in *adhere*.

Ada *n* (*comput*) a high-level structured programming language designed around 1980 for US Government operations.

ADA *abbr* = Action for Dysphasic Adults; Aluminum Development Association; American Dental Association; Americans with Disabilities Act of 1990; Anti-Dumping Authority; Antiquities Dealers' Association; Association of Drainage Authorities; Australian Dental Association.

ad absurdum (*Latin*) "to absurdity."

adactylous *adj* without toes or fingers.

adage *n* a proverb, old saying.

adagietto *adj, adv* (*mus*) (*Italian*) "slow" but not as slow as adagio. * *n* a short composition in an adagio tempo.

adagio *adj, adv* (*mus*) (*Italian*) literally "at ease," i.e., at a slow tempo, slowly, gracefully. * *n* (*pl* **adagios**) a slow movement.

adagissimo *adj, adv* (*mus*) (*Italian*) "very slow."

Adalbert *n* **Saint** (956–997) born in Bohemia; became bishop of Prague when he was only 27. He was martyred in 997. His feast day is 23 April.

Adam *n* (*Bible*) first man in the story of the Creation in the book of Genesis; used in the Bible to refer to mankind in general. *See also* **Eve**.

Adam *n* 1. **Robert** (1728–92) Scottish architect son of leading architect William Adam, famous for his individualistic interpretations of Palladian and Renaissance styles in domestic architecture. His notable works include Culzean Castle, Ayrshire, Scotland; Harewood House near Leeds, England; Keddleston House in Derbyshire, England. 2. **James** (1730–94), brother of Robert, worked with him as a draftsman and also designed buildings of his own.

adamant *adj* inflexible, unyielding. * *n* adamantine, an extremely hard substance.

adamantine *adj* made of adamantine; impenetrable, very hard. * *n* an extremely hard substance; the diamond (—*also* **adamant**).

Adamite *n* a child of Adam; a member of a sect who went naked; a nudist.—**Adamitic** *adj*.

Adamnan *n* **Saint** (*c.* 625–704) Irish abbot, born in Ulster, in the part that is now Donegal. He joined the Columban brotherhood of Iona when he was 28, becoming abbot in 679. Best known for his *Life of St Columba*. His feast day is 23 September.

Adams *n* 1. **Ansel [Easton]** (1902–84) American photographer mainly of landscapes of the southwest USA of the 1930s. 2. **Brian Guy** (1959–) Canadian rock musician. 3. **Gerry [Gerald]** (1948–) Northern Ireland politician and president of Sinn Féin. 4. **Henry Brooks** (1838–1918) American historian whose nine-volume *History of the United States* is a landmark in American historical writing. 5. **John** (1735–1826) American Federalist statesman and second US president (1797–1801) who helped draft the Declaration of Independence (1776). 6. **John Collidge** (1947–) American composer whose works include the opera *Nixon in China* (1987). 7. **John Quincy Adams** (1767–1848) sixth US president (1825–29). 8. **Richard George** (1920–) English novelist; author of *Watership Down* (1972). 9. **Samuel** (1722–1803) American Revolutionary leader; a signatory of the Declaration of Independence.

Adam's apple *n* a projection of the thyroid cartilage of the larynx, which is visible beneath the skin of the throat.

Adam's needle *n* a popular name of the yucca.

Adana *n* a city in Turkey.

adapt *vti* to make or become fit; to adjust to a new purpose or circumstances.—**adaptability** *n*.—**adaptable** *adj*.—**adapter** *n*.

ADAPT *abbr* = Access for Disabled People in Arts Premises Today.

adaptation *n* the process or condition of being adapted; something produced by modification; a version of a literary composition rewritten for a different medium; (*biol*) the change that occurs in an organism in response to its environment.

adapter *n* a device that allows an item of equipment to be put to new use; a device for connecting parts of differing size and shape; an electrical plug using one socket for different appliances.—*also* **adaptor.**

adapter card *n* (*comput*) a card with electronic components that plugs into the computer's main circuit board and provides enhanced capabilities.

adaptive radiation *n* (*biol*) a response to adaptation in which a species of animal evolves into numerous descendent species.

ADAR *abbr* = Art and Design Admissions Registry.

ADAS *abbr* = Agricultural Development and Advisory Service.

adaxial *adj* towards the axis.

ADb or **ADB** *abbr* (*comput*) = Apple (*trademark*) desktop bus.

ADB *abbr* = Asian Development Bank.

ADC *abbr* = Aboriginal Development Commission; Aide-de-Camp; Alternative Defense Commission; Association of District Councils; analogue-to-digital converter.

ADCJ *abbr* = Association of District Council Treasurers.

ADCM *abbr* = Archbishop of Canterbury's Diploma in Church Music.

ADCO *abbr* = Andean Development Company.

add *vt* to combine (two or more things together); to combine numbers or amounts in a total; to remark or write further. * *vi* to perform or come together by addition.

add. *abbr* = (*Latin*) *addatur*, "let there be added"; additional; additions.

ADD *abbr* = Administration on Developmental Disabilities.

ADD *abbr* = Action on Disability and Development; Action on Drinking and Driving.

Ad Dammam *n* a city in Saudi Arabia.

Addams n **Charles Samuel** (1912–88) American cartoonist. Born in New Jersey, he worked for *New Yorker* magazine from 1935 and became particularly well known for his humorously macabre style.

addax n (*pl* **addaxes, addax**) a large North African antelope with twisted horns.

added sixth n (*mus*) a frequently used chord created by adding the sixth note from the root to a major or minor triad.

added value n (*econ*) the net increase in the value of goods measured as the difference between the total revenue of the goods less the cost of the raw materials used in the process of production.

addendum n (*pl* **addenda**) a thing to be added; supplementary text appended to a book, etc.

adder n the venomous viper.

adder's-tongue n a kind of fern whose spike resembles the tongue of a snake.

addict n a person who is dependent upon a drug. * vt to devote or give oneself up to; to practice sedulously (usu pejorative).—**addiction** n.—**addictive** adj.

addiction n a broadly used term that describes a state of physical and psychological dependence on a substance or drug.

Addis Ababa (Adis Abeba) n capital city of Ethiopia.

Addison n **Joseph** (1672–1719) English essayist and poet and cofounder of *The Spectator* newspaper with Richard Steele in 1711.

Addison's disease n a disease caused by the failure of the adrenal glands to secrete adrenocortical hormones because the adrenal cortex has been damaged, possibly as a result of disturbances in the immune system.

addition n the act or result of adding; something to be added; an extra part.

additional adj added, extra; supplementary.—**additionally** adv.

additional accompaniments n (*mus*) new or revised parts for extra instruments written by later composers.

additive adj produced by addition. * n a substance added (to food, etc) to improve texture, flavor, etc.

addle vb (**addling, addled**) vt to make corrupt, putrid or confused. * vi to become addled. * adj rotten.

addle-headed, addle-pated adj stupid, weak-brained; muddled.

addorsed adj (*archit*) of two similar or identical ornamental figures placed exactly back to back.

address vt to write directions for delivery on (a letter, etc); to speak or write directly to; to direct one's skills or attention (to); (*golf*) to adjust one's stance and aim before hitting the ball; * n a place where a person or business resides, the details of this on a letter for delivery; a speech, esp a formal one; (*comput*) a specific memory location where information is stored.—**addressable** adj.

address book n (*comput*) a facility within the program for e-mail which enables the user to record e-mail addresses and access them easily when sending a new message.

address bus n (*comput*) an electronic channel linking the microprocessor to the RAM along which the addresses of memory locations are transmitted.

addressee n a person or company to whom a letter is addressed.

Addressograph n (*trademark*) an addressing machine.

adduce vt to offer as an example or evidence.

adducent adj bringing forward or together.

adducible, adduceable adj capable of being adduced.

adduct vt to pull towards; (*of muscles*) to draw to a common center.—**adduction** n.—**adductive** adj.

adductor muscle n a muscle that draws certain parts to a common center.

Adelaide n a city in Australia.

Adelaide of Burgundy n Saint (*c.* 931–999) widow of Lothair, king of Italy; married the emperor Otto the Great; crowned empress by Pope John XII in 962; founded a convent in Alsace, where she died. Her feast day is 16 December.

ademption n (*law*) the revocation of a grant; the lapse of a legacy.

Aden (Adan) n Commercial capital of Yemen.

aden-, adeno- *prefix* gland.

Adena n (*archeo*) a North American Woodland culture based in the Ohio valley and commencing *c* 1250 BC.

Adenauer n **Konrad** (1876–1967) German statesman; chancellor of West Germany (1949–63).

adenitis n inflammation of one or more glands or lymph nodes.

adenoid n (*usu pl*) a clump of lymphoid tissue situated at the back of the nose (the nasopharynx).

adenoidectomy n the removal, by surgery, of the adenoids.

adenoma n (*pl* **adenomas, adenomata**) a gland-like benign tumor.

adenosine triphosphate *see* ATP.

adept adj highly proficient. * n a highly skilled person.—**adeptly** adv.—**adeptness** n.

adequacy n adequateness; sufficiency for a particular purpose.

adequate adj sufficient for requirements; barely acceptable.—**adequately** adv.—**adequateness** n.

à deux (*French*) for two; intimate.

à deux cordes (*French*) *see* **a due corde**.

adf abbr = automatic direction finder.

ADF abbr = African Development Foundation

ad fin abbr = (*Latin*) *ad finem*, "near the end".

ad gr. gust abbr = (*Latin*) *ad gratum gustum*, "to an agreeable taste".

ADH abbr = antidiuretic hormone (medical).

Adhara or **Epsilon Canis Majoris** n a star in the constellation of the Plough.

ADHD abbr = attention deficit hyperactivity disorder.

adhere vi to stick, as by gluing or suction; to give allegiance or support (to); to follow.

adherence n the act or state of adhering; unwavering attachment.

adherent adj sticking, attached. * n a supporter of a political party, idea, etc.

adhesion n the action or condition of adhering; the attachment of normally separate tissues in the body.

adhesive adj sticky; causing adherence. * n a substance used to stick, such as glue, paste, etc.—**adhesiveness** n.

ad hoc adj for a particular purpose.

ADHOC abbr = Association of Departmental Heads of Catering.

ad hominem (*Latin*) "to the man", personal.

ADI abbr = Approved Driving Instructor; acceptable daily intake.

adiabatic adj (*physics*) not gaining or losing heat.—**adiabatically** adv.

adiabatic change n (*phys*) a change that occurs with no alteration in the heat content of the system.

adiabatic temperature change n a temperature change that involves no heat transfer but is due to a change in pressure.

adiaphorous adj (*theol*) tolerant in non-essential points of religion; morally indifferent; (*med*) neither helping nor harming.

adieu n (*pl* **adieux, adieus**) farewell, goodbye; good wishes at parting.

ad imt. abbr = (*Latin*) *ad initium*, "at the beginning."

ad inf. abbr = (*Latin*) *ad infinitum*, "to infinity."

ad infinitum adv without end, forever.

ad init. abbr = (*Latin*) *ad initium*, "near the beginning."

ad int. abbr = (*Latin*) *ad interim*, "for the moment."

adios interj (*Spanish*) goodbye; farewell.

adipocere n a fatty substance resulting from decomposition of animal bodies in moist places.—**adipocerous** adj.

adipose adj of, like or containing animal fat; fatty.—**adiposity** n.

adipose tissue n a type of loose, fibrous, connective tissue containing a mass of fat cells.

adit n (*archit*) an entrance or passage; an entrance to a mine more or less horizontal.

adj. abbr = adjective; adjourned; adjunct; (*bank*) adjustment.

Adj. or Adjt. abbr = Adjutant.

Adj. Gen. abbr = Adjutant General.

adjacent adj nearby; adjoining, contiguous.—**adjacency** n.

adjective n a word used to add a characteristic to a noun or pronoun.—**adjectival** adj.—**adjectivally** adv.

adjoin vt to unite or join. * vi to lie next to.

adjoining adj beside, in contact with.

adjourn vt to suspend (a meeting) temporarily. * vi (*inf*) to retire (to another room, etc).

adjournment n the act of adjourning; the postponement of a meeting.

adjudge vt (**adjudging, adjudged**) to decide or award judicially; to sentence; to determine in a controversy, to adjudicate.—**adjudgment, adjudgement** n.

adjudicate vt (*law*) to hear and decide (a case). * vi to serve as a judge (in or on).—**adjudicator** n.

adjudication n the act of determining judicially; a judicial sentence; a court's decision.

adjunct n something joined or added but inessential.—**adjunctive** adj.

adjuration n the solemn charging on oath; the oath used.

adjure vt to command on oath under pain of a penalty; to charge solemnly, request earnestly.

adjust vt to arrange in a more proper or satisfactory manner; to regulate or modify by minor changes; to decide the amount to be paid in settling (an insurance claim). * vi to adapt oneself.—**adjustable** adj.—**adjuster** n.

adjustment n the act of adjusting; arrangement.

adjutancy n (*pl* **adjutancies**) the office of an adjutant.

adjutant n a military staff officer who assists the commanding officer.

adjutant general n (*pl* **adjutants general**) the chief staff officer of an army, through whom all orders, etc, are received and issued by the general commanding.

adjuvant adj assisting, helpful. * n a helper, an auxiliary.

ADL abbr = activities of daily living (medical).

Adler n 1. **Alfred** (1870–1937) Austrian psychiatrist and associate of Freud. 2. **Larry [Lawrence Cecil]** (1914–) American musician and harmonica player.

ad-lib vti (**ad-libbing, ad-libbed**) (*speech, etc*) to improvise. * n an ad-libbed remark. * adv spontaneously, freely.—**ad-libber** n.

ad lib. abbr = *ad libitum*, "as you like."

ad libitum n (*mus*) (*Latin*) literally, "at pleasure," usu abbreviated to ad lib. In music, the term is used to indicate that, when playing a piece, a performer can (*a*) alter the tempo or rhythm of the music, (*b*) choose an alternative passage by the composer, (*c*) improvise a cadenza, and (*d*) include or omit a passage if he so chooses.

ad loc. abbr = (*Latin*) *ad locum*, "at the place cited."

adm. abbr = administrative; administrator.

Adm. abbr = Admiral; Admiralty.

Adm. Co. abbr = admiralty court.

Adm'l, Adml abbr = Admiral.

ADMA abbr = American Drug Manufacturers Association; Association of Dance and Mime Artists.

adman n (*pl* **admen**) (*inf*) a person who works in the advertising business.

admass n the public targeted by or influenced by advertising.

admeasure vt (**admeasuring, admeasured**) to measure dimensions; to apportion.

admeasurement n a measurement by a rule; adjustment of proportions; dimensions.

Admetus n (*Greek myth*) king of Pherae in Thessaly, and husband of Alcestis, who gave proof of her love by consenting to die in order to prolong her husband's life.

ADMG abbr = Association of Deer Management Groups.

admin n (*inf*) administration.

administer vt to manage, direct; to give out as a punishment; to dispense (medicine, punishment, etc); to tender (an oath, etc).

administered price n a price for a product that is established and controlled by an individual supplier, a group of suppliers or the government rather than being the result of market forces.

administrate vti to manage or control the affairs of a business, institution, etc.

administration n management; the people who administer an organization; the government; (*with cap*) the executive officials of a government, their policies, and term of office.

administrative adj of management; executive.—**administratively** adv.

administrator n a person who manages or supervises; (*law*) one appointed to settle an estate.

admirable adj deserving of admiration or approval.—**admirably** adv.

admiral n the commanding officer of a fleet; a naval officer of the highest rank.

admiralty n (*pl* **admiralties**) the department of a government having authority over naval affairs; the building in which naval affairs are transacted; the office of an admiral.

admiration n a feeling of pleasurable and often surprised respect or approval; an admired person or thing.

admire vt to regard with honor, approval and pleasure; to express admiration for.—**admirer** n.—**admiring** adj.—**admiringly** adv.

admissible adj that may be admitted or allowed.—**admissibility, admissibleness** n.

admission n an entrance fee; a conceding, confessing, etc; a thing conceded, confessed, etc.—**admissive** adj.

admit vb (**admitting, admitted**) vt to allow to enter or join; to concede or acknowledge as true. * vi to give access; (*with of*) to allow or permit.

admittance n the act of admitting; the right to enter.

admittedly adv acknowledged as fact, willingly conceded.

admix vt to mix with something else; to add as an extra ingredient.

admixture n a mixture, a compound of substances mixed together.

admonish vt to remind or advise earnestly; to reprove gently.

admonition n a friendly reproof or warning.—**admonitory** adj.

admr., adms., admstr. abbr = administrator.

adnate adj (*bot*) with organic cohesion of unlike parts.

ad nauseam adv to a sickening degree.

Adnet n **Jacques** (1900–84) French architect, who created modern furniture designs and accessories in metal and glass.

ado n fuss, excitement, esp over trivial matters.

ado. abbr = adagio.

ADO abbr = Army Digitization Office, Association of Dispensing Opticians

adobe n a brick made of sun-dried clay; clay for making adobe bricks; a building using such bricks.

Adobe Type Manager or **ATM** n, trademark (*comput*) a program that smoothes out the edges of type for presentation on the screen.

adolescence n the period of life between puberty and maturity; youth.

adolescent adj pertaining to the stage between childhood and maturity; (*inf*) immature. * n an adolescent person.

Adonijah n (*Bible*) fourth son of David; plotted to succeed David but Bathsheba interceded on Solomon's behalf and he was put to death. *See also* **Bathsheba, David, Joab.**

Adonis n (*astron*) a small asteroid; (*Greek myth*) a great favorite of Aphrodite, who was killed by a wild boar, and the goddess made the anemone flower grow from his blood. He represents the reproductive principle, nature's decay in winter and its revival in spring.

adopt vt to take legally into one's family and raise as one's child; to select and pursue, e.g. a course of action; to take as one's own.—**adoption** n.

adoptive adj made or related by adoption.

adorable adj worthy of being adored; extremely charming.—**adorably** adv.

adoration n worship, homage; profound regard.

adoratrice of Amun n (*Egypt*) Egyptian female chief priestess instead, divine worshippers, of Amun-Ra.

adore vt to worship; to love deeply.—**adoringly** adv.

adorn vt to decorate; to make more pleasant or attractive.—**adornment** n.

Adorno n **Theodor [Wiesengrund]** (1903–69) German philosopher, sociologist and music critic. His theorizing on the oppressive nature of all philosophical inquiry is regarded as a significant influence on the 1960s radical movement.

ADP abbr = Anguilla Democratic Party; Association for Dental Prosthesis; Association of Database Producers; Association of Disabled Professionals; Australian Democrats Party; (*med*) adenosine diphosphate; automatic data processing.

ADPCM abbr = (*comput*) adaptive differential pulse code modulation.

ADRA abbr = Adventist Development and Relief Agency International; Animal Diseases Research Association; Association for the Study of Reptiles and Amphibia.

Adrastea n a small rocky satellite of Jupiter.

Adrastus n (*Greek myth*) a king of Argos, who led the expedition of the Seven against Thebes to restore his exiled son-in-law Polynices to his native city.

ad rem adj, adv to the point or purpose.

adrenal adj of or near the kidney.

adrenal gland n important endocrine organ producing hormones that regulate various body functions.—*also* **suprarenal gland.**

adrenaline n a hormone produced by the adrenal glands, which, when released, prepares the body for "fright, flight or fight."—*also* **epinephrine.**

adrenocorticotrophic hormone (ACTH) n substance produced and stored by the anterior pituitary gland that regulates the release of corticosteroid hormones from the adrenal glands.

adret n the sunny side of a hill or valley.

Adrian of Canterbury n **Saint** (*d.* 710) born in Africa; abbot of Nerida; instructed by the pope to travel to England where he was installed in the abbey that became **St Augustine**'s; influential teacher and esteemed scholar of Greek and Latin. His feast day is 9 January.

adrift adj, adv afloat without mooring, drifting; loose; purposeless.

adroit adj skillful and clever, sharp-witted.—**adroitly** adv.—**adroitness** n.

ads. abbr = advertisements; (*Latin*) ad sectam , "at the suit."

ADSA abbr = Art Deco Societies of America; Automated Door Suppliers' Association.

adscititious adj taken in addition; added from without; additional, supplementary.

ADSCLAT abbr = Associations of Distributors to the Self-Service and Coin-Operated Laundry and Allied Trades.

ADSL abbr = (comp) asynchronous digital subscriber loop.

adsorb vti to accumulate on a surface, to collect by adsorption.—**adsorbable** adj.

adsorbent n (*med*) substance that is capable of absorbing gas, liquid, etc.

adsorption n the action of a solid in condensing and holding a gas upon it.

ADsPH abbr = Association of Directors of Public Health.

ADT abbr = American District Telegraph; Addictive Diseases Trust.

ADTA abbr = American Dance Therapy Association.

ADTS abbr = automatic data and telecommunications service.

a due corde adj (*mus*) (*Italian*) "on two strings"; when applied to music for stringed instruments, the term means that a piece should be played on two strings, not just on one.

adulate vt to flatter excessively or basely.—**adulator** n.—**adulatory** adj.

adulation n excessive flattery.—**adulatory** adj.

Adullam n (*Bible*) cave in the hills where David hid as a fugitive from Saul; he became leader of a group of rebels. *See also* **David.**

adult adj fully grown; mature; suitable only for adults, as in pornography, etc. * n a mature person, etc.—**adulthood** n.

adulterant adj adulterating. * n the person or thing that adulterates.

adulterate vt to make impure or inferior, etc by adding an improper substance.—**adulteration** n.—**adulterator** n.

adulterer n a person who commits adultery.—**adulteress** nf.

adulterine adj resulting from adulterous intercourse; fake, spurious; illegal.

adulterous adj guilty of adultery.

adultery n (*pl* **adulteries**) sexual intercourse between a married person and someone other than their legal partner.

adult respiratory distress syndrome n a condition of severe respiratory failure brought about by a number of different disorders to the lungs, by infection or by an adverse reaction following surgery or transfusion. It is often fatal.

adumbral adj overshadowing; shady.

adumbrate vt to foreshadow; to overshadow; to give a faint semblance of.—**adumbration** n.—**adumbrative** adj.

adv. abbr = (*Latin*) ad valorem "according to value"; (*Latin*) adversus, "against"; advent; adverb; adverbial; adverbially; adversus; advertisement; advice; advocate; (*banking*) advise.

Adv. abbr = advertising.

ad val. abbr = (*Latin*) ad valorem, "according to value."

ad valorem adj (*com*) referring to a tax that is calculated as a percentage of the total invoice value or price of goods rather than on the number of items involved.

advance vt to bring or move forward; to promote; to raise the rate of; (*money*) to lend. * vi to go forward; to make progress; to rise in rank, price, etc. * n progress; improvement; a rise in value; payment beforehand; (*pl*) friendly approaches, esp to please. * adj in front; beforehand.

advanced adj in front; old; superior in development or progress.

advancement n promotion to a higher rank; progress in development.

advantage n superiority of position or condition; a gain or benefit; (*tennis*) the first point won after deuce. * vt to produce a benefit or favor to.

advantageous adj producing advantage, beneficial.—**advantageously** adv.

advection n the horizontal transfer of heat in gases and liquids.

advent n an arrival or coming; (*with cap*) (*Christianity*) the coming of Christ; the four-week period before Christmas.

Advent Sunday *n* the Sunday nearest (before or after) to St Andrew's Day (30 November).

Adventist *n* a person who believes in Christ's second coming to set up a kingdom on earth.—**Adventism** *n*.

adventitious *adj* happening by chance; casual; fortuitous; accidental; produced out of normal and regular order; growing in an abnormal position.—**adventitiously** *adv*.—**adventitiousness** *n*.

adventure *n* a strange or exciting undertaking; an unusual, stirring, often romantic, experience.

adventure playground *n* a children's playground equipped with materials and objects for building, climbing, hiding in, etc.

adventurer *n* a person who seeks adventure; someone who seeks money or power by unscrupulous means.—**adventuress** *nf*.

adventuresome *adj* daring; venturesome.

adventurism *n* reckless political or financial activities.

adventurous *adj* inclined to incur risk; full of risk; rash; enterprising; daring.—**adventurously** *adv*.

adverb *n* a word that modifies a verb, adjective, another adverb, phrase, clause or sentence and indicates how, why, where, etc.—**adverbial** *adj*.—**adverbially** *adv*.

adversary *n* (*pl* **adversaries**) an enemy or opponent.

adversative *adj* (*words*) denoting opposition or contrariety; expressing opposition.

adverse *adj* hostile; contrary or opposite; unfavorable.—**adversely** *adv*.

adversity *n* (*pl* **adversities**) trouble, misery, misfortune.

advert *vt* to refer (to); to turn attention (to). * *n* (*inf*) an advertisement.

advertence, advertency *n* attention; heedfulness.—**advertent** *adj*.

advertently *adv* in an intentional manner.

advertise *vt* to call public attention to, esp in order to sell something, by buying space or time in the media, etc. * *vi* to call public attention to things for sale; to ask (for) by public notice.—**advertiser, advertizer** *n*.

advertisement *n* advertising; a public notice, usu paid for by the provider of a good or service.

advertising *n* the promotion of goods or services by public notices; advertisements; the business of producing adverts.

advertising objective *n* a specific target aimed at by advertising, such as increasing the consumer's awareness of a product or brand or improving a company's market share of sales of a product.

Adv. Gen. *abbr* = Advocate General.

advice *n* recommendation with regard to a course of action; formal notice or communication.

advice note *n* a note that is sent to a customer by a supplier to advise him or her that an order for goods has been fulfilled.

advisable *adj* prudent, expedient.—**advisability** *n*.

advise *vt* to give advice to; to caution; to recommend; to inform. * *vi* to give advice.—**adviser, advisor** *n*.

advised *adj* acting with caution; deliberate; judicious.—**advisedly** *adv*.

advisory *adj* having or exercising the power to advise; containing or giving advice.

advocaat *n* a sweet egg-based liqueur.

advocacy *n* (*pl* **advocacies**) the function of an advocate; a pleading in support (of).

advocate *n* a person who argues or defends the cause of another, esp in a court of law; a supporter. * *vt* to plead in favor of, to recommend.

advs. *abbr* = adversus.

advt. *abbr* = advertisement.

advtg. *abbr* = advertising.

ADW *abbr* = Air Defense Warning.

ADX *abbr* = automatic data exchange; automatic digital exchange.

adynamia *n* want of vital power, prostration, weakness.—**adynamic** *adj*.

adytum *n* (*archit*) an inner room or sanctuary in a Greek temple.

adz, adze *n* a type of ax with a blade at right angles to the handle for cutting and shaping wood.

AE *abbr* = account executive; age exemption; Agricultural Engineer; atomic energy.

AE and P *abbr* = Ambassador Extraordinary and Plenipotentiary.

ae., aet., aetat. *abbr* (*Latin*) = *aetatis* "of age," "at the age of."

AEA *abbr* = American Electrolysis Association; Anglican Evangelical Association; (*Eire*) Association of Established Agents; Association of European Airlines; Atomic Energy Authority.

Aeacus *n* (*Greek myth*) king of the island of Aegina, after his death a judge of the ghosts in Hades.

AEB *abbr* = American Egg Board; Associated Examining Board; (*Japan*) Atomic Energy Bureau.

aec *abbr* = at earliest convenience.

AECB *abbr* = Association for Environment Conscious Building; Association for the Export of Canadian Books.

AECI *abbr* = Associate Member of the Institute of Employment Consultants; Association of Electrical Contractors of Ireland; Association of European Cooperative Insurers.

Aed *n* (*d.* 878) king of Scots. Reigned in 878.

Aeda *n* (*Irish Celtic myth*) Aeda was a dwarf at the court of Fergus mac Leda. He was taken by the fili, Eisirt, to the court of Iubdan, the king of the diminutive Faylinn, to prove that there was a race of supposed giants elsewhere.

Aed Abrat *n* (*Irish Celtic myth*) Aed Abrat was the father of Fand and Li Ban.

Aed Find *n* (*d. c.*778) king of Scots. Reigned from 768 to 778.

Aed Finnliath *n* (*d. c.*879) High king of Ireland. Reigned from 862 to 868.

aedile *n* a Roman magistrate who exercised supervision over the temples, public and private buildings, the markets, public games, sanitation, etc, hence a municipal officer.—*also* **edile**.

AEE *abbr* = Association for Experiential Education; Atomic Energy Establishment.

Aeëtes *n* (*Greek myth*) king of Colchis at the time when the golden fleece was brought there, father of Medea.

AEEU *abbr* = (*Brit*) Amalgamated Engineering and Electrical Union.

AEF *abbr* = Airfields Environment Federation; Allied Expeditionary Force; Amalgamated Union of Engineering and Foundry; American Euthanasia Foundation Workers; American Expeditionary Force.

Aegaeon *see* **Briareus**.

Aegean Sea *n* the part of the Mediterranean which adjoins the eastern shores of Greece and the western coast of Turkey.

Aegeus *n* (*Greek myth*) king of Athens and father of Theseus, who, mistakenly thinking his son was dead, threw himself into the sea, named the Aegean Sea.

Aegidius *see* **Giles**.

Aegina *n* a Greek island in the Gulf of Aegina, south of Athens.

aegis *n* protection, sponsorship; (*Greek myth*) shielding or protecting power from the shield of Zeus or from a metal cuirass or breastplate, in which was set the head of the Gorgon Medusa, and which protected the goddess Athena.—*also* **egis**.

AEGIS *abbr* = Aid for the Elderly in Government Institutions; Australian Electronic Government Information Service.

Aegisthus *n* (*Greek myth*) the lover of Clytemnestra, with whom he killed her husband Agamemnon, king of Mycenae.

Aegyptus *n* (*Greek myth*) the conqueror of the country of Melampodes, which he called Aegypt after his own name. All his 50 sons except one were killed by their brides, the daughters of his brother Danaus.

Aeken *n* **Jerom van** *see* **Bosch, Hieronymus**.

Aelfheah *see* **Alphege**.

Aelfric *n* (*c.*955–*c.*1020) English monk and author of lives of the saints.

Aelfwald *n* (*d.* 749) king of East Anglia. Reigned from 713 to 749. An under-king of Mercia under the powerful Ethelbald from 740.

AELTC *abbr* = All England Lawn Tennis Club.

Aelle *n* 1. (*d.* 588) king of Deira (roughly modern Humberside, England. Reigned from *c.*560–588). A son of Ida. 2. (*d.* 867) king of Northumbria (reigned from 866–867). 3. (*d. c.*514) king of Sussex. Came to be regarded as *Bretwalda*, or overlord among the Anglo-Saxon kings of southern England.

AEMSM *abbr* = Association of European Metal Sink Manufacturers.

AEMT *abbr* = Association of Electrical Machinery Trades; Association of Emergency Medical Technicians.

AEMTM *abbr* = Association of European Machine Tool Merchants.

AENA *abbr* = All England Netball Association.

Aeneas *n* the hero of Virgil's *Aeneid*, a Trojan, who deserted Dido, queen of Carthage, and after many adventures by land and sea reached Italy.

Aeneid *see* **Virgil**.

AENOC *abbr* = Association of European National Olympic Committees.

Aeolian *adj* pertaining to Aeolis in Asia Minor or to the Aeolic race; (*Greek myth*) of Aeolus, the Greek god of winds; pertaining to the wind.

Aeolian harp *n* (*mus*) a stringed instrument, the wires of which are set in motion and sounded by the wind.

Aeolian Islands *npl* a group of volcanic islands in the Tyrrhenian Sea, one of which is an active volcano and was considered the home of Vulcan in Roman mythology.

Aeolian mode *n* (*mus*) a mode that, on the piano, uses the white notes from A to A.

Aeolians *npl* one of the four races into which the ancient Greeks were divided, originally inhabiting the district of Aeolis, in Thessaly, from which they spread over other parts of Greece.

Aeolic *n* the Aeolic dialect of ancient Greece.

aeolina *n* a type of harmonica.

aeoline *n* a soft organ stop that imitates the sound of the Aeolian harp.

Aeolus *n* (*Greek myth*) the god of the winds, which he kept confined in a cave in the Aeolian Islands, releasing them when he wished or when he was commanded by the superior gods.

AEOM *abbr* = Association of European Open Air Museums.

aeon *n* a period of immense duration; an age.—*also* **eon**.

aeonian *adj* everlasting.—*also* **eonian**.

AEP *abbr* = Association of Educational Psychologists; Association of Embroiderers and Pleaters.

AEPA *abbr* = All-Ethiopia Peasants Association.

aerate *vt* to supply (blood) with oxygen by respiration; to supply or impregnate with air; to combine or charge a liquid with gas.—**aeration** *n*.

aerated concrete *n* a modern building material made of fine sand, chemical components and fuel ash.

A

aerator *n* an apparatus for making aerated waters.

AERE *abbr* = Atomic Energy Research Establishment.

aerial *adj* belonging to or existing in the air; of aircraft or flying. * *n* a radio or TV antenna.

aerialist *n* a trapeze or high-wire artist.

aerial reconnaissance *n* the survey of a site using an aircraft, usu involving the taking of aerial photographs.

aerie *see* **eyrie**.

aeriform *adj* having the form of air; gaseous; like air; unsubstantial.

aerify *vt* (**aerifying, aerified**) to combine with air.—**aerification** *n*.

aero- *prefix* aviation; air vessel

aerobatics *npl* stunts performed while flying an aircraft.

aerobe, aerobium *n* (*pl* **aerobes, aerobia**) a microbe that cannot live without air.

aerobic *adj* (*exercise*) that conditions the heart and lungs by increasing the efficient intake of oxygen by the body. * *n* (*pl* **aerobics**) aerobic exercises.

aerobic respiration *n* (*biol*) a set of reactions that occur in plant and animals cells in which food molecules are broken down to form energy.

aerodrome *n* (*Brit*) an airfield.

aerodynamics *npl* the study of the forces exerted by air or other gases in motion, esp around solid bodies such as aircraft.—**aerodynamic** *adj*.—**aerodynamically** *adv*.

aerofoil *n* (*Brit*) *see* **airfoil**.

aerogram, aerogramme *n* a radio telegraphic message.

aerolite *n* a stone falling from the air, a meteorite.

aerology *n* the science that deals with the air and the atmosphere.—**aerologic, aerological** *adj*.—**aerologist** *n*.

aerometer *n* an instrument for weighing the air.—**aerometric** *adj*.

aerometry *n* the branch of physics concerned with air, pneumatics.

aeronaut *n* an aviator; the pilot or navigator of an aircraft.

aeronautical, aeronautic *adj* of or pertaining to aeronautics or an aeronaut.—**aeronautically** *adv*.

aeronautics *n* the science dealing with the operation of aircraft; the art or science of flight.

aeronomy *n* the study of the physics and chemistry of Earth's upper atmosphere.

aerophone *n* (*mus*) any instrument in which movement of air causes sound; for example, organ, oboe, trumpet, flute, etc.

aeroplane *n* (*Brit*) *see* **airplane**.

aerosol *n* a suspension of fine solid or liquid particles in gas, esp as held in a container under pressure, with a device for releasing it in a fine spray.

aerospace *n* the earth's atmosphere and the space beyond. * *adj* technology for flight in aerospace.

Aero Sq., Aer. Sq. *abbr* = Aero Squadron.

aerostat *n* a balloon; a balloonist.

aerostatics *n* (*used as sing*) the science that studies the equilibrium of bodies sustained in air; the science of air navigation.—**aerostatic, aerostatical** *adj*.

aerostation *n* ballooning.

aeruginous *adj* of or like verdigris or copper rust.

aery *see* **eyrie**.

AES *abbr* = American Electrochemical Society.

Aesc *n* (*d.* 512) king of Kent (488–512). Son of Hengest and nephew of Horsa, the first Jutish kings of Kent, England.

Aescwine *n* 1. king of Essex, England (*c.*527–*c.*587). 2. king of Wessex, England (674–676). The son of Cenfus and a descendant of King Coel.

AESC *abbr* = American Engineering Standards Committee.

Aeschylus *n* (524–456 BC) Greek dramatist whose plays include the *Oresteia* trilogy.

Aesculapian *adj* of or pertaining to Aesculapius, the god of medicine, or to medicine.

Aesculapius, Asclepius *n* (*Greek myth*) the god of medicine, also adopted by the Romans, worshiped in particular at Epidaurus. His symbol is a staff entwined with a snake.

Aeson *n* (*Greek myth*) father of Jason. Usurped by his half-brother, Pelias, he sent Jason to Chiron the Centaur for protection.

Aesop *n* (*c.*620–564 BC) supposed Greek author of fables in which human characteristics are satirized in the form of dialogs between animals.

aesthete *n* a person who has a high degree of sensitivity toward the beautiful, esp in the arts.—*also* **esthete**.

aesthetic *adj* pertaining to a sense of beauty or aesthetics.—*also* **esthetic**.

aesthetical *adj* of or pertaining to aesthetics.—*also* **esthetical**.

aesthetically *adv* according to aesthetics and its principles.—*also* **esthetically**.

aesthetician *n* a person familiar with the concept of aestheticism.—*also* **esthetician**.

aestheticism *n* the application and acceptance of aesthetic standards.—*also* **estheticism**.

Aesthetic Movement *n* an English cultural movement that developed in the late 19th century, characterized by an affected and mannered approach to life and the arts.

aesthetics *npl* (*perceived as singular*) the study of the qualities perceived in the arts.—*also* **esthetics**.

aestival *see* **estival**.

aestivation *see* **estivation**.

aet *abbr* = after extra time.

aet., aetat. *abbr* = (*Latin*) *aetatis*, "of his/her age."

Aether *n* (*Greek myth*) the personification of the clear upper air breathed by the Olympians.

Aethra *n* (*Greek myth*) the mother of Theseus. She was carried off to Lacedaemon and became a slave of Helen, with whom she was taken to Troy, where she was freed at the request of Agamemnon.

aetiology, aetiological, aetiologist *see* **etiology**.

Aetolia *n* in ancient Greece, a western division of northern Greece, and one of the original independent states of Greece.—**Aetolian** *adj*.

AEU *abbr* = Amalgamated Engineering Union.

AEW *abbr* = airborne early warning.

AEWHA *abbr* = All England Women's Hockey Association.

AEWLA *abbr* = All England Women's Lacrosse Association.

a.f. *abbr* = audio frequency.

a/f, A/F *abbr* = as found.

Af. *abbr* = Africa; African.

AF *abbr* = Associate Fellow; Admiral of the Fleet; Air Force; Anglo-French.

af- *prefix* the form of *ad-* before *f*.

AFA *abbr* = African Farmers Association; (*med*) atrial fibrillation.

Afagddu *n* (*Welsh Celtic myth*) the son of Cerridwen. He was so ugly that his mother sought to give him intellectual skills to compensate for his unattractive appearance.

AFAM *abbr* = Ancient Free and Accepted Masons.

afar *adv* at, to, or from a great distance.

AFAS *abbr* = Associate of the Faculty of Architects and Surveyors.

AFASIC *abbr* = Association for All Speech-Impaired Children.

AFB *abbr* = Action for Bosnia; Airforce Base; American Foundation of the Blind.

AFBA *abbr* = Associate of the Faculty of Business Administrators.

AFBC *abbr* = Association of Football Badge Collectors.

AFBD *abbr* = Association of Futures Brokers and Dealers.

AFBPSS *abbr* = Associate Fellowship of the British Psychological Society.

AFBS *abbr* = American and Foreign Bible Society.

afc *abbr* = automatic flight control; automatic frequency control.

AFC *abbr* = Air Force Cross; Association Football Club; Association of Fish Canners; Australian Forestry Council; Authors For Choice.

AFCA *abbr* = Associate of the Association of Financial Controllers and Administrators.

afce *abbr* = automatic flight control equipment.

AFCI *abbr* = Associate of the Faculty of Commerce and Industry Ltd.

afco *abbr* = automatic fuel cut-off.

afcs *abbr* = automatic flight control system.

AFCS *abbr* = Associate of the Faculty of Secretaries.

AFDB *abbr* = African Development Bank

AFDC *abbr* = Aid to Families with Dependent Children

AFEI *abbr* = Americans for Energy Independence; Arab Federation of Engineering Industries; Association of Finnish Electric Industries; (*Eire*) Association of Freelance Editors and Indexers.

AFEMS *abbr* = European Association of Sporting Ammunition Manufacturers.

AFETUK *abbr* = Anne Frank Educational Trust.

aff. *abbr* = affectionate; affirmative(ly); affirming.

affable *adj* friendly; approachable.—**affability** *n*.—**affably** *adv*.

affair *n* a thing done or to be done; (*pl*) public or private business; (*inf*) an event; a temporary romantic or sexual relationship.

affaire (de coeur) *n* a love affair.

affannato*n* (*mus*) (*Italian*) "distressingly."

affannosamente*n* (*mus*) (*Italian*) "restlessness."

affannoso *n* (*mus*) (*Italian*) "sadly."

AFFD *abbr* = Association of Fashion Fabric Distributors.

affect[1] *vt* to have an effect on; to produce a change in; to act in a way that alters or affects the feelings of.

affect[2] *vt* to pretend or feign (an emotion); to incline to or show a preference for.

affect[3] *n* an emotion, feeling or desire associated with a certain stimulus.

affectation *n* a striving after or an attempt to assume what is not natural or real; pretence.

affected *adj* (*manner, etc*) assumed artificially.—**affectedly** *adv*.—**affectedness** *n*.

affecting *adj* having power to excite the emotions; moving; pathetic.—**affectingly** *adv*.

affection *n* tender feeling; liking.—**affectional** *adj*.

affectionate *adj* showing affection, loving.—**affectionately** *adv*.

affective *adj* arousing the emotions, emotional.—**affectivity, affectiveness** *n*.

Affektenlehre *n* (*mus*) (*German*) a musical theory formulated in Germany during the 18th century, which held that music should be judged by the way in which it arouses certain emotions, such as sorrow, happiness, etc.

afferent *n* (*med*) a term meaning "inwards to an organ," esp the brain or spinal cord. * *adj* conveying inwards or to a part. *Compare* **efferent**.

affettuoso *adj, adv* (*mus*) (*Italian*) literally "tender" or "affectionate," i.e., an indication that a piece of music should be played with tender feeling.

AFFHC *abbr* = Australian Freedom from Hunger Campaign.

affiance *vt* to promise in marriage, betroth. * *n* faith, trust; a marriage contract.

affiche *n* a paper affixed to a wall, a poster.

affidavit *n* (*law*) a sworn written statement.

affiliate *vt* to connect as a subordinate member or branch; to associate (oneself with). * *vi* to join. * *n* an affiliated person, club, etc.—**affiliation** *n*.

affinity *n* (*pl* **affinities**) attraction, liking; a close relationship, esp by marriage; similarity, likeness; (*chem*) a tendency in certain substances to combine.

affinity card *n* a loyalty card issued by a retailer whereby discounts or rewards can be collected and redeemed.

AffIP *abbr* = Affiliate of the Institute of Plumbing.

affirm *vt* to assert confidently or positively; to confirm or ratify; (*law*) to make an affirmation.

affirmation *n* affirming; an assertion; a solemn declaration made by those declining to swear an oath, e.g., on religious grounds.

affirmative *adj* confirming; indicating agreement. * *n* a positive word or statement, e.g., *yes*.—**affirmatively** *adv*.

affirmative action *n* specific attempts to employ, or to improve educational opportunities for, members of minority groups and women.

AffIRTE *abbr* = Affiliate of the Institute of Road Traffic Engineers.

AffIWHTE *abbr* = Affiliate of the Institution of Works and Highways Technician Engineers.

affix *vt* to fasten; to add, esp in writing; to attach.

afflatus *n* a breath or blast of wind; poetic or divine inspiration; creative power.

afflict *vt* to cause persistent pain or suffering to; to trouble greatly.—**afflictive** *adj*.

affliction *n* persistent pain, suffering; a cause of this.

affluence *n* an abundant supply, as of thoughts, words, riches; wealth.

affluent *adj* rich, well provided for.—**affluently** *adv*.

affluenza *n* a psychological disease resulting from an excess of affluence.

afflux *n* a flowing towards; an increase; an influx.

afford *vt* to be in a position to do or bear without much inconvenience; to have enough time, money, or resources for; to supply, produce.

afforest *vt* to plant trees to cover with forest.—**afforestation** *n*.

affranchise *vt* to free from an obligation or slavery; to enfranchise.—**affranchisement** *n*.

affray *n* a noisy fight.

affreightment *n* the hire of a ship for the transportation of goods or freight.

affright *vt* (*arch*) to frighten, to terrify; to alarm; to confuse.

affront *vi* to insult or offend openly or deliberately. * *n* such an insult or offence.

affronted *adj* (*archit*) of two similar or identical ornamental figures, placed so that they exactly face one another.

afft. *abbr* (*law*) = affidavit.

affusion *n* the act of pouring upon, esp in baptism.

afghan *n* a knitted or crocheted wool cover or blanket.

Afghan *adj* pertaining to Afghanistan. * *n* a native of Afghanistan.—*also* **Afghani**.

afghani *n* the standard monetary unit of Afghanistan, made up of 100 puls.

Afghanistan *n* a landlocked republic in southern Asia.

AFHQ *abbr* = Allied Forces Headquarters.

AFI *abbr* = Acupuncture Foundation of Ireland; Aid for India; Arthritis Foundation of Ireland; Association for Futures Investment; Association of Finnish Industries.

AFIA *abbr* = Apparel and Fashion Industry Association of Great Britain.

aficionado *n* (*pl* **aficionados**) a devotee of a particular sport, activity, etc.

afield *adv* far away from home; to or at a distance; astray.

AFIMA *abbr* = Associate Fellow of the Institute of Mathematics and its Applications.

afire *adj*, *adv* on fire.

AFIS *abbr* = American Forces Information Service

aflame *adj*, *adv* flaming, ablaze, in a glow.

afloat *adj*, *adv* floating; at sea, on board a ship; debt-free; flooded.

AFM *abbr* = Air Force Medal; audio-frequency modulation.

afoot *adj*, *adv* on foot; astir; on the move; in operation.

afore *adv*, *prep* in front, before; previously.

aforementioned *adj* mentioned previously.

aforesaid *adj* referred to previously.

aforethought *adj* premeditated.

afoul *adv* **to fall** or **run afoul of** to be in conflict or collision with.

AFP *abbr* (*med*) = alpha fetoprotein.

AFPRB *abbr* = Army Forces Pay Review Board.

AFPVA *abbr* = Advertising Film and Videotape Producers Association.

Afr. *abbr* = Africa; African.

AFRAeS *abbr* = Associate Fellow of the Royal Aeronautical Society.

afraid *adj* full of fear or apprehension; regretful.

AFRC *abbr* = Air Force Reserve Command.

afreet *n* (*Arabian myth*) an evil demon.

afresh *adv* anew, starting again.

AFrI *abbr* = Action From Ireland.

Africa *n* the second largest of the continents, bounded by the Mediterranean in the north, the Atlantic in the west and the Red Sea, Gulf of Aden, and Indian Ocean in the east.

African *adj* pertaining to Africa. * *n* a native of Africa.

African art *n* a term generally used to describe African tribal art in the countries south of the Sahara Desert. Examples of typical art forms include richly carved wooden masks and figures.

African trypanosomiasis *see* **sleeping sickness**.

African violet *n* any of various African plants popular as houseplants, with purple, pink or white flowers and velvet-textured leaves.

Afrikaans *n* a language derived from Dutch used in South Africa.

Afrikander, Africander *n* (any of) a breed of southern African beef cattle.

Afrikaner *n* a South African native white, esp of Dutch descent.

Afrit *n* (*Egypt*) a desert spirit embodied in the whirlwind summoned up by Seth.

AFRL *abbr* = Air Force Research Laboratory

Afro *n* (*pl* **Afros**) a bushy hairstyle.

Afro- *prefix* Africa or African.

Afro-American *n* a Black American. * *adj* of or relating to Black Americans, or their culture, history, etc.

afrormosia *n* a hard wood similar to teak, used in furniture.

AFROTC *abbr* = Air Force Reserve Officer Training Corps

AFRTS *abbr* = Armed Forces Radio and Television Service

AFS *abbr* = American Fern Society; Associate of the Faculty of Architects and Surveyors; Association for Stammerers; Association of Football Statisticians; Australian Fishing Service; Auxiliary Fire Service.

AFSC *abbr* = Armed Forces Staff College (replaced by JFSC)

AFSOC *abbr* = Air Force Special Operations Command

AFSPC *abbr* = Air Force Space Command

aft *adv* at, near, or towards the stern of a ship or rear of an aircraft.

aft. *abbr* = afternoon.

AFT *abbr* = Association for Family Therapy.

AFTA *abbr* = Atlantic Free Trade Area.

AFTCom *abbr* = Associate of the Faculty of Teachers in Commerce.

after *prep* behind in place or order; following in time, later than; in pursuit of; in imitation of; in view of, in spite of; according to; about, concerning; subsequently. * *adv* later; behind. * *conj* at a time later than. * *adj* later, subsequent; nearer the stern of a ship or aircraft.

after all *adv* nevertheless; when everything is considered.

afterbirth *n* the placenta expelled from the womb after giving birth.

afterburner *n* a device in a jet engine used to provide extra thrust by igniting additional fuel.

aftercare *n* care following hospital treatment, etc.

afterdamp *n* the carbonic acid found in coal mines after an explosion of fire damp; choke damp.

aftereffect *n* an effect that occurs some time after its cause.

afterglow *n* the glow in the sky after sunset.

after-hours *adj* after regular business hours; (*bar*, *etc*) open past the established or legal closing time. * *n* an after-hours club; a speakeasy.

afterimage *n* the image that remains momentarily after the eye has been withdrawn from a bright object.

afterlife *n* life after death.

aftermath *n* the result, esp an unpleasant one.

aftermost *adj* hindmost; farthest aft, nearest to the stern.

afternoon *n* the time between noon and sunset or evening.

afternote *n* (*mus*) the second or unaccented note, which takes its time from the first or accented note.

afterpain *n* (*usu pl*) pains following a birth, caused by uterine contractions that help to restore the uterus to its normal size.

aftershave *n* lotion for use after shaving.

aftershock *n* a tremor or a relatively small earthquake occurring after the initial earthquake.

aftertaste *n* the taste that remains after eating or drinking.

after-tax *n* the value of a product or the amount of money remaining following the payment of taxes, esp. income tax.

afterthought *n* a thought or reflection occurring later.

afterwards, afterward *adv* at a later time.

afterwit *n* wisdom that comes too late.

afterworld *n* a world or place existing after death.

AF of L *abbr* = American Federation of Labor.

a fortiori adj, adv (*Latin*) with stronger reason, more conclusively.

AFTO *abbr* = Association of Flight Training Officers.

AFV *abbr* = armored fighting vehicle.

Ag *symbol* (*chem*) silver (element).

Ag. *abbr* = August.

AG *abbr* = Accountant General; Adjutant General; Agent General; (*German*) *Aktiengesellschaft*, "limited company"; Attorney General.

ag- *prefix* the form of *ad-* before *g*.

aga *n* in Turkey, a commander or chief officer; a title of respect.—*also* **agha**.

AGA *abbr* = American Gas Association; Arab Geologists' Association; Architectural Granite Association; Asparagus Growers' Association; (*med*) appropriate for gestational age.

Agabus *n* (*Bible*) prophet from Jerusalem who foretold a great famine over all the world; this led to relief collections for Christians in Judea.

Agadez *n* a city in Niger.

Agag *n* (*Bible*) king of the Amalekites; killed by Saul.

again *adv* once more; besides; on the other hand.

against *prep* in opposition to; unfavorable to; in contrast to; in preparation for; in contact with; as a charge on.

agalloch *n* a fragrant resinous heartwood.—*also* **eaglewood**.

agama *n* a short-tongued lizard found in India and Africa.

Agamemnon *n* (*Greek myth*) son of Atreus, king of Mycenae and Argos, and commander of the allied Greeks at the siege of Troy. Returning home after the fall of Troy, he was assassinated by his wife, Clytemnestra, and her lover, Aegisthus. He was the father of Orestes, Iphigeneia, and Electra.

agami *n* a South American bird allied to the cranes; a trumpeter bird.

agamic *adj* (*biol*) produced without sexual action, asexual.—**agamically** *adj*.

agamogenesis *n* (*biol*) asexual reproduction.—**agamogenetic** *adj*.—**agamogenetically** *adv*.

Agana *n* capital city of Guam.

Aganippe *n* (*Greek myth*) nymph of a fountain on Mount Helicon, sacred to the Muses, which had the property of giving poetic inspiration to those who drank from it.

agapanthus *n* an ornamental plant with bright blue flowers.

agape *adj* open-mouthed.

Agape *n* the love feast of the early Christians at communion time.

agar *n* a preparation of seaweed used for jelly, glue and bacteria culture.

agaric *n* a mushroom or other fungus of the genus *Agaricus*.

Agassi *n* **Andre** (1970–) American tennis player.

agate *n* stone with striped or clouded coloring used as a gemstone.

Agatha *n* **Saint** (*d*. 251) born in Sicily; patron saint of bell-founders. Her feast day is 5 February.

Agave *n* a daughter of Cadmus, king of Thebes, and sister of Semele, who was driven mad by the gods and tore her son, Pentheus, to pieces.

agave *n* a genus of plants of which the chief species is the century plant.

agb, a.g.b. *abbr* = any good brand.

AGBI *abbr* = Artists' General Benevolent Institution.

AGBM *abbr* = Association of Grey Board Makers.

AGC *abbr* = Agricultural Genetics Company.

AGCA *abbr* = automatic ground-controlled approach.

AGCD *abbr* = Association of Green Crop Driers.

AGCL *abbr* = automatic ground-controlled landing.

AGCS *abbr* = Association of Golf Club Secretaries.

agcy. *abbr* = agency.

AGD *abbr* = Adjutant General's Department.

age *n* the period of time during which someone or something has lived or existed; a stage of life; later years of life; a historical period; a division of geological time; (*inf: often pl*) a long time. * *vti* (**ageing** *or* **aging, aged**) to grow or make old, ripe, mature, etc.

AGE *abbr* = automatic guidance electronics.

age analysis *n* (*com*) a summary analysis of how long debts on a company's books have been outstanding.

aged *adj* very old; of a specified age. * *n* (*with* **the**) the elderly.

ageism *n* discrimination on grounds of age.—*also* **agism**.—**ageist, agist** *adj*.

ageless *adj* timeless; appearing never to grow old.

age-long *see* **age-old**.

agency *n* (*pl* **agencies**) action; power; means; a firm, etc empowered to act for another; an administrative government division.

agenda, agendum *n* (*pl* **agendas, agendums**) a list of items or matters of business that have been tabled for discussion at a business meeting.

agenesis *n* imperfect development of the body.—**agenetic** *adj*.

Agenor *n* (*Greek myth*) king of Phoenicia and father of Europa and five sons. When Europa was carried off by Zeus, Agenor sent his sons in search of her and told them not to return without her. As Europa was not to be found, none of them returned, and all settled in foreign countries.

agent *n* a person appointed by someone, called the principal, to act on his or her behalf in some capacity; a person or thing that acts or has an influence; a substance or organism that is active; a government representative; a spy.

Agent Orange *n* an extremely toxic and powerful herbicide employed as a defoliant, esp during the Vietnam War.

agent provocateur *n* (*pl* **agents provocateurs**) a person hired to tempt or provoke suspected persons into illegal acts so as to incriminate themselves.

age-old *adj* ancient.—*also* **age-long**.

Agfa *trademark, abbr* (*German*) = *Aktiengesellschaft für Anilinfabrikation*, Dye-Manufacture Company.

agger *n* (*archeo*) a low bank or causeway upon which most Roman roads were constructed.

agglomerate *vti* to gather into a heap; to accumulate; to collect into a mass. * *n* a heap or mass; a rock of volcanic origin made up of fine fragments cemented together in a fine matrix.—**agglomeration** *n*.—**agglomerative** *adj*.

agglutinate *vti* to stick or fuse together; to form words into compounds. * *adj* glued together.—**agglutination** *n*.—**agglutinative** *adj*.

aggradation *n* the building up of the surface of land by water-borne or wind-borne material.

aggrandize *vt* to increase the power, rank, wealth, or reputation of.—**aggrandizement** *n*.

aggravate *vt* to make worse; (*inf*) to annoy, irritate.—**aggravation** *n*.

aggravated *adj* (*law*) denoting a grave form of a specified offence.

aggravating *adj* making worse or more heinous; (*inf*) annoying, irritating.

aggregate *adj* formed of parts combined into a mass or whole; taking all units as a whole. * *n* a collection or sum of individual parts; sand, stones, etc mixed with cement to form concrete. * *vt* to collect or form into a mass or whole; to amount to (a total).—**aggregation** *n*.

aggression *n* an unprovoked attack; a hostile action or behavior.

aggressive *adj* boldly hostile; quarrelsome; self-assertive, enterprising.—**aggressively** *adv*.—**aggressiveness** *n*.

aggressor *n* a person or country that attacks first.

aggrieve *vt* to pain; to injure; to have a grievance; to bear heavily upon; to oppress.—**aggrieved** *adj*.—**aggrievedly** *adv*.

aggro *n* (*sl*) aggression.

agha *see* **aga**.

aghast *adj* utterly horrified.

AGHS *abbr* = Australian Garden History Society.

Aghulhas current *n* a warm ocean current off the coast of southeast Africa.

AGHW *abbr* = Association of Gardening and Hardware Wholesalers.

AGI *abbr* = Associate of the Greek Institute.

agiatamente *adj, adv* (*mus*) (*Italian*) literally "comfortably," i.e., an indication that a piece should be played with a certain amount of liberty.

agile *adj* quick and nimble in movement; mentally acute.—**agility** *n*.

agio *n* (*pl* **agios**) the premium on changing paper money into cash or for exchanging one currency for another.—**agiotage** *n*.

Agip *abbr* = *Agenzia Generale Italia Petroli*, Italian General Petrol Agency.

agism *see* **ageism**.

agitate *vt* to shake, move; to disturb or excite the emotions of. * *vi* to stir up public interest for a cause, etc.—**agitation** *n*.—**agitator** *n*.

agitato *adj, adv* (*mus*) in a hurried or agitated manner.

agitator *n* one who starts or keeps up a political or other agitation; an implement for stirring.

AGK *abbr* = Astronomische Gesellschaft Katalog, a compilation of the positions of all stars brighter than ninth magnitude.

AGL *abbr* = above ground level.

Aglaia, Aglaea *n* (*Greek myth*) wife of Hephaestus and one of the three Graces, the other two being Euphrosyne and Thalia.

aglet *n* a tag (of a shoelace, etc); a spangle, a metallic ornament; a catkin.—*also* **aiglet**.

AGLMH *abbr* = Association for Great Lakes Maritime History.

aglow *adj* radiant with warmth or excitement.

AGLOW *abbr* (*Brit*) = Association of Greater London Older Women.

AGM *abbr* = air-to-ground missile; annual general meeting.

agnail *n* a sore under or near the nail, a hangnail.

agnate *adj* related by the father's side or with the same male ancestor. * *n* a relative by the father's side.—**agnatic** *adj*.

Agnew *n* **Spiro [Theodore]** (1918–96) American Republican politician, vice-president (1969–73) in Nixon's administration. Resigned following revelations of political corruption and was sentenced to three years' probation.

Agnes *n* **Saint** (*d*. 303) born in Rome; died aged 13, having suffered under the persecution of the Christians ordered by the Roman emperor Diocletian. Her feast day is 21 January.

agnomen *n* (*pl* **agnomina**) the fourth name of a person in ancient Rome; an additional name or epithet, as *Milton, the poet*.—**agnominal** *adj*.

agnostic *n* one who believes that knowledge of God is impossible. * *adj* pertaining to the agnostics or their teachings; expressing ignorance.—**agnostically** *adv*.—**agnosticism** *n*.

Agnus Dei (*Latin*) *n* a figure of a lamb bearing a banner or cross, symbolic of Christ and associated emblematically with St John the Baptist; the lamb and flag; a medal of wax or precious metal stamped with the figure of the Agnus Dei and blessed by the pope for distribution on Low Sunday; (*mus*) "O Lamb of God"; the concluding part of the Latin Mass. Numerous musical settings have been written for the Agnus Dei.

ago *adv* in the past. * *adj* gone by; past.

AGO *abbr* = Adjutant General's Office; Association of Gypsy and Romany Organizations.

AGOD *abbr* = International Association on the Genesis of Ore Deposits.

agog *adj, adv* in agitation or expectation; eager, on the lookout.

agogic *n* (*mus*) a note that is made to stand out by being lingered on rather than by being played more loudly.

agonic *adj* making no angle.

agonic line *n* a line drawn on a map joining the north and south magnetic poles.

agonistic *adj* of athletic contests; athletic; polemic; melodramatic; strained; unnatural.

agonize *vti* to suffer or cause to suffer agony; to strive.—**agonizingly** *adv*.

agony *n* (*pl* **agonies**) extreme mental or physical suffering.

agony aunt *n* a person who replies to readers' problem letters in an agony column.

agony column *n* the column of a newspaper devoted to advertisements relating to lost relatives, etc; a column in a magazine containing readers' letters with helpful replies to problems.

AGOR *abbr* = Advisory Group on Ocean Research.

agoraphobia *n* abnormal fear of public places or open spaces.—**agoraphobic** *adj, n*.

agorot *see* **shequel**.

agouti *n* (*pl* **agoutis, agouties**) a rodent similar to the guinea pig found in the West Indies and South America.

agr. *abbr* = agricultural; agriculture.

AGR *abbr* = advanced gas-cooled reactor.

AGRA *abbr* = Association of Genealogists and Record Agents.

agraphia *n* the inability to write due to mental illness.

agrarian *adj* of or relating to fields, or their cultivation; of or relating to farmers or agricultural life. * *n* an advocate of redistribution of property in land.

agrarianism *n* the principle of a uniform division of land; agitation with respect to land tenure.

agree *vi* (**agreeing, agreed**) to be of similar opinion; to consent or assent (to); to come to an understanding about; to be consistent; to suit a person's digestion; (*gram*) to be consistent in gender, number, case, or person. * *vt* to concede, grant; to bring into harmony; to reach terms on.

agreeable *adj* likeable, pleasing; willing to agree.—**agreeableness** *n*.—**agreeably** *adv*.

agreed bid *n* (*com*) a takeover bid that has the backing of the majority of the shareholders of the target company.

agreement *n* harmony in thought or opinion, correspondence; (*law*) a legal document which is a settlement on a set of facts between two or more parties.

agrestic *adj* rustic; uncouth.

agric. *abbr* = agricultural; agriculture; agriculturist.

AGRICOLA *abbr* = Agricultural OnLine Access

agriculture *n* the science or practice of producing crops and raising livestock; farming.—**agricultural** *adj.*—**agriculturally** *adv.*—**agriculturist, agriculturalist** *n*.

agrimony *n* (*pl* **agrimonies**) a yellow-flowered plant.

Agrippa, Herod *n* (*Bible*) grandson of Herod the Great; a persecutor of the early Church. *See also* **Herod**.

agronomics *n* (*used as sing*) the part of economics concerned with the management and distribution of farming lands.—**agronomic, agronomical** *adj*.

agronomy *n* the science of land cultivation and management, husbandry.—**agronomist** *n*.

agrost. *abbr* = agrostology.

agrostology *n* the branch of botany that treats of the grasses.

aground *adj, adv* on or onto the shore.

AGS *abbr* = (*China*) Aero-Geophysical Survey; Alpine Garden Society; American Goat Society; Association for Gravestone Studies; Association of Geotechnical Specialists.

AGSM *abbr* = Associate of the Guildhall School of Music and Drama.

agst *abbr* = against.

Agt, agt *abbr* = against; agent; agreement.

AGT *abbr* = advanced gas turbine.

AGTO *abbr* = Association of Group Tour Operators.

aguardiente *n* an inferior Spanish brandy.

ague *n* malaria, an intermittent fever; the cold fit of the intermittent fever.—**aguish** *adj*.

agw *abbr* = actual gross weight.

AGW Association of Garden Wholesalers; Association of Golf Writers.

ah *interj* an exclamation of sudden emotion.

ah, a.h. *abbr* = ampere-hour; ampere-hours.

AH *abbr* (*Latin*) = *anno Hegira*, "in the year of the Hegir," used in dates of the Muslim era.

aha *interj* an exclamation of satisfaction, triumph or mockery.

Aha *n* (*Egypt*) the first known king of a unified Egypt, from around 3150 BC. His reign marks the beginning of the dynasties. He is also known as Meni and Narmer..

AHA *abbr* = American Hominological Association; Arab Historians Association; Area Health Authority; Association of Housing Aid.

Ahab *n* (*Bible*) king of Israel 869–850 BC and a renowned warrier, particularly against the threat of Assyria; he married Jezebel, who encouraged the worship of Baal.

Ahaz *n* (*Bible*) king of Judah *c*.735–715 BC.

Ahaziah *n* (*Bible*) grandson of Ahab and king of Judah *c*.842 BC; killed by Jehu. *See also* **Ahab, Jehu**.

AHC *abbr* = Army Hospital Corps.

AHCIMA *abbr* = Associate of the Hotel, Catering and Institutional Management Association.

AHCPR *abbr* = Agency for Health Care Policy and Research

ahead *adj, adv* in or to the front; forward; onward; in advance; winning or profiting.

ahem *interj* an exclamation to call attention.

AHFS *abbr* = Associate of the Council of Health Fitness and Sports Therapists.

Ahithophel *n* (*Bible*) counselor of David who hanged himself after supporting Absalom's rebellion. *See also* **Absalom, David**.

ahl *abbr* (*Latin*) = *ad hunc locum*, "at this place."

Ahmadabad *n* a city in India.

AHMS *abbr* = American Home Missionary Society.

Ahmosis *n* (*Egypt*) Egyptian first king of the New Kingdom and Eighteenth Dynasty, coming to power around 1550 BC.

Ahnighito meteorite *n* a meteorite found by the explorer Peary in 1897 at Cape York in West Greenland.

ahoy *interj* a term used in hailing a vessel.

AHPCRC *abbr* = Army High Performance Computing Research Center

AHPP *abbr* = Association of Humanistic Psychology Practitioners.

AHPWJC *abbr* = Association of High Pressure Water Jetting Contractors.

AHQ *abbr* = Allied Headquarters; Army Headquarters.

ahr *abbr* = acceptable hazard rate.

AHRC *abbr* = Alister Hardy Research Center.

Ahrensburgian *adj* (*archeo*) relating to a culture found in northern Germany and the Low Countries that dates back to about the 9th century BC.

AHRQ *abbr* = Agency for Healthcare Research and Quality

AHS *abbr* = American Harp Society; Antiquarian Horological Society; Association for Humanist Sociology; Australian Herpetological Society; (*Latin*) *anno humanae salutis*, "in the year of human salvation."

AHSS *abbr* = Architectural Heritage Society for Scotland.

AHUA *abbr* = Association of Heads of University Administrations.

ahv *abbr* (*Latin*) = *ad hanc vocem*, "at this word."

AHWA *abbr* = Association of Hospital and Welfare Administrators.

ai *n* (*pl* **ais**) a South American three-toed sloth.

Ai *n* (*Bible*) town in Canaan destroyed by Joshua.

a.i. *abbr* (*Latin*) = *ad interim*, "in the meantime."

AI *abbr* = artificial insemination; American Institute; (*comput*) artificial intelligence; Amnesty International.

AIA *abbr* = Abrasives Industries Association; Academy of Irish Art; Acupuncture International Association; Allergy-Induced Autism Support and Self-Help Group; American Institute of Architects; Anglo-Indian Association; Artists International Association; Asbestos International Association; Associate of the Institute of Actuaries; Association of Automobile and Allied High Duty Ironfounders.

AIAB *abbr* = Associate of the International Association of Bookkeepers.

AIAT *abbr* = Associate of the Institute of Asphalt Technology.

AIB *abbr* = African Immigrants Bureau; Allied Irish Banks; American Institute of Baking; Associate of the Institute of Bankers; Association of Independent Businesses; Association of Insurance Brokers.

AIBA *abbr* = Associate of the Institution of Business Agents.

AIBCM *abbr* = Associate of the Institute of British Carriage and Automobile Manufacturers; Association of Industrialized Building Component Manufacturers.

AIC *abbr* = Agricultural Improvement Council; American Institute of Chemists; Appraisal Institute of Canada; Asbestos Information Center; Association Internationale de Cybernétique; Association of Independent Cinemas; Association of Indian Communists.

AICE *abbr* = American Institute of Chemical Engineers.

Aichleach *n* (*Irish Celtic myth*) according to one story Fionn mac Cumhaill was murdered by Aichleach during a rebellion of the Fianna.

AICR *abbr* = Association for International Cancer Research.

AICS *abbr* = Associate of the Institute of Chartered Shipbrokers.

aid *vti* to help, give assistance to. * *n* anything that helps; a specific means of assistance, e.g., money, equipment; a helper.

AID *abbr* = acute infectious disease; Agency for International Development; Alternative for India Development; Army Intelligence Department; artificial insemination (by) donor.

Aidan, Saint *n* (*d.* 651) Irish Scot and a monk of Iona; founded the Northumbrian church. Many miracles were attributed to Aidan. When he died, his body was taken to Lindisfarne and buried there. His feast day is 31 August.

aide *n* an aide-de-camp; assistant.

aide-de-camp *n* (*pl* **aides-de-camp**) a military officer serving as an assistant to a senior officer.

aide-mémoire *n* (*pl* **aides-mémoire**) a summarized document; a memorandum, etc, as an aid to the memory.

Aiden (Mac Gabrain) (*d.* 606) king of Scots. Reigned from *c*.575 to 606. Ordained at Dunadd by St Columba.

Aido *n* **Yusuke** (1931–) Japanese designer of popular, industrially-produced pottery.

AIDPM *abbr* = Associate of the Institute of Data Processing Management.

AIDS, Aids *abbr* = Acquired Immune Deficiency Syndrome, in which the body loses its immunity to infection, caused by the human immunodeficiency virus known as HIV.

AIDS-related complex *n* a condition in which mild symptoms of AIDS (e.g., fever, weight loss) precede development of the full-blown disease.

AIDTA *abbr* = Associate of the International Dance Teachers' Association.

AIEE *abbr* = American Institute of Electrical Engineers.

AIEM *abbr* = Associate of the Institute of Executives and Managers.

AIEP *abbr* = Association of Independent Electricity Producers.

AIExpE *abbr* = Associate of the Institute of Explosives Engineers.

AIF *abbr* = Australian Imperial Force.

AIFA *abbr* = Associate of the Institute of Field Archeologists.

AIFF *abbr* = Associate of the Institute of Freight Forwarders.

AIGD *abbr* = Associate of the Institute of Grocery Distribution.

aiglet *see* **aglet**.

aigrette, aigret *n* a small white heron; a plume arranged in imitation of the feathers of the heron, worn on helmets and as a hat decoration.

aiguille *n* a sharp peak of rock.

aiguillette *n* an ornamental tag or lace worn on uniforms and liveries.

AIH *abbr* = American Institute of Homeopathy; Association of Independent Hospitals; Australian Institute of Horticulture; artificial insemination by husband.

AIIB *abbr* = Allied Irish Investment Bank.

AIIM *abbr* = Associate of the Institution of Industrial Managers; Association for Information and Image Management; Association of Independent Investment Managers; Association of International Industrial Irradiation.

AIIMR *abbr* = Associate of the Institute of Investment Management and Research.

AIIRSM *abbr* = Associate of the International Institute of Risk and Safety Management.

Aiken *n* **Conrad Potter** (1889–1973) American poet, novelist, short-story writer, and critic. Collections of his poems include *Earth Triumphant*.

aikido *n* a 20th-century Japanese martial art.

ail *vt* to give or cause pain. * *vi* to feel pain; to be afflicted with pain.

AIL *abbr* = Associate of the Institute of Linguists.

AILAM *abbr* = Associate of the Institute of Leisure and Amenity Management.

Ailas *abbr* = automatic instrument landing approach system.

aileron *n* a hinged section on the wing of an aircraft used for lateral control.

Ailill (*Irish Celtic myth*) Ailill was the husband of Medb, queen of Connacht, she sought to acquire Donn Cuailgne, the great brown bull of Ulster.

ailing *adj* unwell.

Aillaud *n* **Émile** (b. 1902) French architect. His notable works include Les Courtillières housing estate, near Paris.

ailment *n* a slight illness.

ailurophobia *n* cat fear; a morbid dread of cats and a consciousness of their presence even when they are not in sight.—**ailurophobe** *n*.

aim *vti* to point or direct towards a target so as to hit; to direct (one's efforts); to intend. * *n* the act of aiming; purpose, intention.

AIM *abbr* = Action in International Medicine; alternative investment market; American Indian Movement; Associazione Italiana di Metallurgia; Atlantic International Marketing Committee; Australasian Institute of Metals.

AIM & ME, AIME *abbr* = American Institute of Mining and Metallurgical Engineers.

AIMBM *abbr* = Associate of the Institute of Maintenance and Building Management.

AIMechE *abbr* = Associate of the Institution of Mechanical Engineers.

AIMgt *abbr* = Associate of the Institute of Management.

AIMinE *abbr* = Associate of the Institute of Mining Engineers.

AIMIT *abbr* = Associate of the Institute of Musical Instrument Technology.

aimless *adj* without purpose or object.—**aimlessly** *adv*.—**aimlessness** *n*.

AIMLS *abbr* = Associate of the Institute of Medical Laboratory Sciences.

AIMM *abbr* = Associate of the Institute of Massage and Movement.

AInstAM *abbr* = Associate Member of the Institute of Administrative Management.

AInstBA *abbr* = Associate of the Institute of Business Administration.

AInstBB *abbr* = Associate of the Institute of British Bakers.

AInstBCA *abbr* = Associate of the Institute of Burial and Cremation Administration.

AInstMC *abbr* = Associate of the International Management Center.

AInstP *abbr* = Associate of the Institute of Physics.

AInstPM *abbr* = Associate of the Institute of Professional Managers.

AInstSMM *abbr* = Associate of the Institute of Sales and Marketing Management.

AInstTA *abbr* = Associate of the Institute of Transport Administration.

ain't = am not, is not, are not, has not, have not.

A. Inv. *abbr* = (*Latin*), *Anno Inventionis*, "in the Year of Invention."

AIOC *abbr* = Associate of the Institute of Carpenters.

AIOFMS *abbr* = Associate of the Institute of Financial and Management Studies.

AIP *abbr* = Associate of the Institute of Plumbing; American Independent Party; Association of Independent Producers; Australian Institute of Packaging.

AIPM *abbr* = Associate of the Institute of Personnel Management.

AIQS *abbr* = Associate of the Institute of Quantity Surveyors.

air *n* the mixture of invisible gases surrounding the earth; the earth's atmosphere; empty, open space; a light breeze; aircraft, aviation; outward appearance, demeanor; a pervading influence; (*mus*) a simple melody or song; (*mus*) a melodious Baroque composition; (*pl*) an affected manner. * *vt* to expose to the air for drying, etc; to expose to public notice; (*clothes*) to place in a warm place to finish drying.

AIR *abbr* = All-India Radio; Alliance of Independent Retailers; American Institutes for Research in the Behavioral Sciences; Australian Institute of Radiography.

airbag *n* a safety device in a motor vehicle that automatically inflates to protect the occupants in the event of an accident.

air base *n* a base for military aircraft.

air bath *n* a lengthened exposure of the body to the action of the air and sun; an arrangement for drying articles by exposing them to air of any regulated temperature.

air bed *n* an inflatable mattress usu of plastic or rubber.

airborne *adj* carried by or through the air; aloft or flying.

air box *n* a tube for conveying fresh air to a mine; a flue supplying air to a furnace; a chamber behind the fire box of a furnace to assist combustion by supply of air.

air brake *n* a brake operated by compressed air.

air brick *n* a brick with holes in the sides through which air for ventilation can pass.

airbrush, air brush *n* a brush, powered by compressed air, that is used to spray paint. It produces a fine mist of color, giving delicate tonal gradations and a smooth finish. Its principal use is in the fields of advertising and graphic design.—*also vti*.

airbus *n* a jet aircraft designed for short-distance intercity flights.

air conditioning *n* regulation of air humidity and temperature in buildings, etc.

air-cooled *adj* cooled by having air passed over, into, or through.

air corridor *n* any air route established through international agreement.

air course *n* a ventilating passage in a mine.

air cover *n* protection for ground forces given by fighter aircraft; the aircraft giving this protection.

aircraft carrier *n* a warship with a large flat deck, for the carrying, taking off and landing of aircraft.

aircraft *n* (*pl* **aircraft**) any machine for traveling through air.

aircrew *n* the crew of an aircraft.

air cushion *n* an inflatable cushion usu of plastic or rubber.

air drop *n* a dropping by parachute of troops and supplies.

Airedale *n* a large rough-coated terrier.

air embolism *n* a bubble of air in a blood vessel that interferes with the outward flow of blood from the heart.

airfare *n* the amount paid for travel by airplane.

airfield *n* a field where aircraft can take off and land.

air flow, airflow *n* the air currents that result from the movement of an object.

airfoil *n* a wing, the lifting surface of an airplane.

air force *n* the aviation branch of a country's armed forces.

air frost *n* air with a temperature at or below 0°C (32°F).

air gas *n* an illuminating gas made from air charged with the vapor of petroleum, naphtha, etc.

airglow *n* a faint luminescence of Earth's upper atmosphere emitted from the whole sky at all times.

airgun *n* a gun that fires pellets by compressed air.

airhead *n* (*sl*) a stupid person.

air hostess *n* a stewardess on a passenger aircraft.

airing *n* exposure to the open air for drying or freshening; exercise in the open air; exposure to public view.

airless *adj* stuffy; sultry.—**airlessness** *n*.

air letter *n* a sheet of light writing paper that is folded and sealed for sending by airmail.

airlift *n, vt* the transport of cargo, troops, passengers, etc by air, esp in an emergency.

airline *n* a system or company for transportation by aircraft; a beeline.

airliner *n* a large passenger airplane.

airlock *n* a blockage in a pipe caused by an air bubble; an airtight compartment giving access to a pressurized chamber.

airmail *n* mail transported by aircraft.

airman *n* (*pl* **airmen**) a male civilian or military pilot, etc.—**airwoman** *nf* (*pl* **airwomen**).

air mass *n* an area of the atmosphere that, horizontally, has more or less uniform temperature and humidity and extends for hundreds of miles.

air miles *n* an incentive scheme where points or credits are earned by the user taking part by making appropriate transactions.

airmiss *n* the near collision of aircraft in flight.

air passage, airway *n* (*usu pl*) all the openings and passages through which air enters and is taken into the lungs.

air photography, aerial photography *see* **aerial reconnaissance**.

air piracy *n* the hijacking of an airplane during its travel.—**air pirate** *n*.

airplane *n* a power-driven aircraft.

air plant *n* a plant that derives its nourishment from the air, an epiphyte.

airplay *n* the playing of a recording over radio or TV.

air pocket *n* a patch of rarefied air causing aircraft to drop abruptly.

airport *n* a place where aircraft can land and take off, with facilities for repair, etc.

air pump *n* a machine for exhausting the air from a receiver; the pump used to exhaust the water and gases from the condenser of a steam engine.

air raid *n* an attack by military aircraft on a surface target.

air rifle *n* a low-powered rifle employing compressed air to fire small pellets.

airs *npl* affected behavior for the purpose of impressing others.

air-sea rescue *n* a rescue at sea, accomplished by aircraft.

airship *n* a self-propelled steerable aircraft that is lighter than air.

airsick *adj* nauseated due to the motion of an aircraft.

airspace *n* the space above a nation over which it maintains jurisdiction.

airspeed *n* the speed of an aircraft relative to the outside air.

airstream or **air stream** *n* a current of air passing over some surface, blowing from an identifiable source..

airstrip *n* an area of land cleared for aircraft to land on; a runway.

AIRTE *abbr* = Associate of the Institute of Road Transport Engineers.

airtight *adj* too tight for air or gas to enter or escape; (*alibi, etc*) invulnerable.

airtime *n* (*radio, TV*) the time allotted to a programme, item, commercial, etc; the time at which the broadcast begins.

air-to-air *adj* (*weaponry, communications, etc*) activated between aircraft in flight.

air-traffic control *n* a system used to direct air traffic by radio contact.—**air-traffic controller** *n*.

air valve *n* a valve regulating the supply of air to a boiler or pipe.

air vesicle *n* a dilatation of the trachea of certain insects enabling them to ascend or descend by its inflation or expiration; a vesicle filled with air in certain fish, connected with the swim bladder.

airwaves *npl* (*inf*) radio waves, the medium used to transmit radio and TV signals.

airway *n* an aircraft route; a ventilation passage, as in a mine; a passage for air into the lungs; (*med*) a device to maintain the airway of an unconscious person.

airworthy *adj* safe to fly.—**airworthiness** *n*.

airy *adj* (**airier, airiest**) open to the air; breezy; light as air; graceful; lighthearted; flippant.—**airily** *adv*.—**airiness** *n*.

Airy disk *n* the central spot in the diffraction pattern produced from a point source of light by a circular aperture, named after Sir George Airy.

AIS *abbr* = Androgen Insensitivity Support Group; Association for Information Systems; Association for Integrative Studies; Australian Institute of Sport; (*Algeria*) Islamic Salvation Army.

AISA *abbr* = Associate of the Incorporated Secretaries Association.

aisle *n* (*archit*) a corridor or wing of a building; a division at the side of a church, running along the length of the building and divided off by a colonnade of pillars; a passageway, as between rows of seats.

AISOB *abbr* = Associate of the Incorporated Society of Organ Builders.

AISTD *abbr* = Associate of the Imperial Society of Teachers of Dancing.

AISTDDip *abbr* = Associate Diploma of the Imperial Society of Teachers of Dancing.

AIStructE Associate of the Institution of Structural Engineers.

ait *n* a small island in a river or lake.—*also* **eyot**.

AIT *abbr* = Association of Inspectors of Taxes; Association of Insurance Teachers.

AITC *abbr* = American Institute for Timber Construction; Association of Investment Trust Companies; Australian Industry and Technology Commission.

aitch *n* the letter H.

aitchbone *n* the rump bone; the cut of meat lying over it.

Aitchison *n* George (1825–1910) British architect trained at the Royal Academy Schools and University College, London.

AITO *abbr* = Association of Independent Tour Operators.

AITSA *abbr* = Associate of the Institute of Trading Standards Administration.

AIWEM *abbr* = Associate of the Institution of Water and Environmental Management.

AIWSc *abbr* = Associate Member of the Institute of Wood Science.

AIX *abbr* (*comput*) = Advanced Interactive eXecutive. A variant of the UNIX operating system developed by IBM primarily for their workstations.

AJA *abbr* = Amateur Judo Association of Great Britain; (*Brit*) Anglo-Jewish Association; Australian Journalists Association.

AJAG Assistant Judge Advocate General.

ajar *adv* partly open, as a door.

Ajax *n* (*Greek myth*) son of Telamon, a Greek hero and king of Salamis, who sailed with 12 ships to join the fight against Troy. When the armor of Achilles was awarded to Odysseus, he became insane and killed himself.

AJR *abbr* = Association of Jewish Refugees in Great Britain.

AJSM *abbr* = Association of Jute Spinners and Manufacturers.

AK *abbr* = Alaska.

aka, a.k.a, AKA *abbr* = also known as.

AKC *abbr* (*Brit*) = Associateship of King's College, University of London.

akh *n* (*Egypt*) one of the five elements forming the human being seen as an aspect of the sun, the link between the human and the luminous life force. It left the body at death to join the circumpolar stars. In hieroglyphics it is denoted by the crested ibis.

Akhenaten *n* 1. *or* **Amenophis IV** (ruled 1352–1338 son of Amenophis III of Egypt, after a period of co-regency with his father, he assumed sole reign, with Nefertiti as his queen. 2. **Akhenaten, Ikhnaton** the name taken by the heretic pharaoh of Egypt, Amenhotep IV, who reigned for 17 years until 1352 BC.

Akhetaten *see* **Amarna**.

Akhmatova *n* Anna [Anna Andreyevna Gorenko] (1889–1966) Russian poet associated with the Acmeist group whose poem on the suffering of the Russian people under Stalin's rule, *Requiem*, was first published in Munich in 1963.

Akihito *see* **Hirohito**.

akimbo *adv* having the hands on the hips and the elbows bent outwards.

akin *adj* related; essentially similar, compatible.

Akkadian, Accadian *n* an ancient Babylonian language preserved in cuneiform inscriptions. * *adj* of Akkad or Accad, the Babylonian city.

A.kr. *abbr* = Austrian krone.

Akureyri *n* a city in Iceland.

Al *symbol* (*chem*) = aluminum (element).

al. *abbr* (*Latin*) = *alii*, "others."

AL *abbr* = Alabama; Arab League.

al- *prefix* the form of *ad-* before *l*.

-al *adj suffix* of, of the nature of, as in *mortal, colossal*. * *n suffix* esp of verbal action, as in *approval*.

à la *prep* in the style of.

Ala. *abbr* = Alabama.

ALA *abbr* = Agricultural Law Association; American Landrace Association; American League of Automobilists; American Library Association; (*Brit*) Association of London Authorities Automobile Legal Association.

Alabama (AL) *n* a state of the United States of America (USA) of which the capital is Montgomery.

"Alabama" *n* the official song of the American State, Alabama.

alabaster *n* (*art*) a fine-grained type of gypsum that can be translucent, white, or streaked with color. It is soft and easy to carve and is, therefore, a popular medium for windows, decorative artifacts, and statues.—**alabastrine** *adj*.

ALAC *abbr* = Artificial Limb and Appliance Center.

à la carte *adj* (*menu*) with dishes listed and priced as separate items.

alack *interj* an exclamation of blame, sorrow, or surprise.

alacrity *n* promptness, eager readiness.—**alacritous** *adj*.

AlAgrE *abbr* = Associate of the Institution of Agricultural Engineers.

Alajuela *n* a city in Costa Rica.

ALAM *abbr* = Association of Licensed Automobile Manufacturers.

alameda *n* a public promenade planted with trees.

alamode *n* a thin, light, glossy black silk.

à la mode *adv* in the fashion. * *adj* fashionable.

alar *adj* of wings; winged; wing-like; wing-shaped.—*also* **alary**.

ALAR *abbr* = Association of Light Alloy Refiners.

alarm *n* a signal warning of danger; an automatic device to arouse from sleep or to attract attention; the fear arising from the apprehension of danger. * *vt* to give warning of danger; to fill with apprehension or fear.

alarm clock *n* a clock with an apparatus that can be set to ring loudly at a particular time.

alarming *adj* frightening, disconcerting.—**alarmingly** *adv*.

alarmist *n* one who keeps prophesying danger, a panic-monger.—**alarmism** *n*.

alarum *n* (*arch*) an alarm.

alary *see* **alar**.

alas *n* (*geog*) a large, steep-sided, flat-bottomed depression occurring in a permafrost area. * *interj* expressive of misery, unhappiness, grief, etc.

Alas. *abbr* = Alaska.

Alaska (AK) *n* a state of the United States of America (USA) of which the capital is Juneau.

"Alaska's Flag" *n* the official song of the American State, Alaska.

Alaska time *n* the time in the tenth time zone west of Greenwich that includes most of Alaska.

alate *adj* having wings or wing-like side appendages.

Alavoine Interieurs *n* French interior decoration company, influential from the 1920s to the 1970s.

ALAWP *abbr* = all letters answered with photograph.

alb *n* a white priestly vestment reaching to the feet, worn at the celebration of the Eucharist in the RC Church and in some Anglican churches.

Alb. *abbr* = Albanian; Albany.

Alba *abbr* = Alberta (Canada).

albacore *n* a large species of mackerel or tunny found in the Atlantic and Pacific Oceans.

Alba Longa *n* a city of Latium in ancient Italy, built by Ascanius, the son of Aeneas, 300 years before the foundation of Rome, at one time the most powerful city of Latium. It ultimately fell under the dominion of Rome.

Alban *n* Saint (*d. c.* 304) the first English martyr, said to have been martyred during the persecution of Diocletian around 304–305. His feast day is 20 June.

Alban. *abbr* = Albanian.

Albania *n* a small mountainous republic in the Balkan region of southeastern Europe.

Albany *n* the capital city of the state of the USA, New York.

Al-Basrah *n* a city in Iraq.

albata *n* an alloy imitating silver; German silver.

albatross *n* any of various large web-footed seabirds; a heavy burden, as of debt, guilt, etc; (*golf*) a score of three under par.

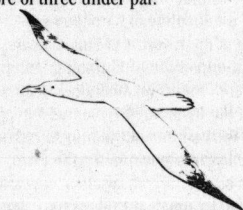

albedo *n* the reflective power of a non-luminous celestial body.

Albee *n* Edward [Franklin] (1928–) American dramatist whose plays include *Who's Afraid of Virginia Woolf?* (1962).

albeit *conj* although, even though, notwithstanding.

Albéniz *n* Isaac (1860–1909) Spanish pianist and composer who was a child prodigy and went on to write operas, orchestral pieces and songs. He is best known for his piano suite *Iberia*.

Alberic *n* Saint (also known as Aubrey) (*d.* 1109) one of the founders of the mother house of the Cistercian order, the basis of one of the most influential religious orders. His feast day is 26 January.

Albers *n* Josef (1888–1976) German-born American painter and designer, closely connected with the **Bauhaus**. His series of paintings entitled *Homage to the Square* explore color relationships through various compositions of flat squares set one inside the other.

Albert *n* Calvin (1918–) American sculptor in the school of abstract expressionism. Much of his work involved special metal welding techniques and he undertook commissions for decorative sculptures in churches and synagogues.

Albert Hall *see* **Royal Albert Hall**.

Albert *n* Prince (1819–61) husband of Queen Victoria.

Albert the Great *n* Saint (1206–80) born in Swabia in southern Germany, a prolific writer, sometimes called the "Universal Teacher"; patron saint of students of natural sciences. His feast day is 15 November.

Alberti bass *n* (*mus*) a simple accompaniment to a melody consisting of "broken" or spread chords arranged in a rhythmic pattern; so called because Domenico Alberti used it in his keyboard sonatas.

Alberti *n* Domenico (1710–40) an Italian singer, composer and harpsichordist who wrote many unremarkable works and is largely remembered for his use of "broken" chords in his pieces for harpsichord.

Alberti n **Leon Battista** (1404–72) Italian writer, architect, sculptor, and painter. A prominent Renaissance figure, his wide-ranging interests and talents including music and athletics are representative of the "universal man" ideal of his humanist views. His notable works include Palazzo Rucellai, Florence and churches at Mantua.

Albertus n **Gundorph** (1887–1970) Danish silversmith and brother-in-law of Georg Jensen.

albescent adj shading into white; whitish; becoming white.—**albescence** n.

Albini n **Franco** (1905–1977) Italian architect. His notable works include Municipal office, Genoa.

albinism n an inherited disorder in which there is a lack of pigmentation (melanin) in the skin, hair and eyes.

albino n (pl **albinos**) a person lacking normal coloration, so that they have white skin and pink eyes; an animal or plant with abnormal pigmentation.

Albinoni n **Tomaso** (1671–1750) a prolific Italian composer, he was among the earliest to write concertos for solo violin. He wrote more than 40 operas. Bach composed fugues on themes by Albinoni.

Albinson n **Don** (1915–) American furniture designer who became head designer at **Knoll**.

Albion n (arch) Britain.

ALBM abbr = air-launched ballistic missile.

alborada n (mus) (Spanish) literally "morning song"; a form of popular Spanish music for bagpipes and side drum.

Ålborg n a city in Denmark.

album n a book with blank pages for the insertion of photographs, autographs, etc; a long-playing record, cassette, or CD.

Albumblatt n (mus) (German) literally "album leaf"; a popular title given by 19th-century composers to short, instrumental compositions often for the piano and of a personal nature.

albumen n the white of an egg.

albumenize vt to coat (paper) with an albuminous solution.

albumin n a water-soluble protein that coagulates when heated and is found in plasma, egg white, etc.

albuminoid adj like albumen. * n any of a class of simple proteins like keratin or gelatin.

albuminous adj like, or containing, albumin.

albuminuria n the presence of albumin in the kidneys and the urine.

alburnum n the white and softer part of wood between the bark and the heartwood; sapwood.

alc. abbr = alcohol.

alcahest see **alkahest**.

Alcaic n, adj a kind of lyric verse form consisting of four lines of four feet devised by the 7th-century BC Greek poet Alcaeus.

alcaide n the commander of a castle in Spain; the warder of a Spanish jail.

alcalde, alcade n a magistrate or mayor in Spain or Portugal.

Alcathous n (Greek myth) king of Megara, who won the kingdom when Megareus offered his daughter and his kingdom to whoever should kill the Cythaeronian lion.

alcazar n a Spanish or Moorish palace or castle.

Alcestis n (Greek myth) wife of Admetus, king of Thessaly. Her husband was ill, and, according to an oracle, would die unless someone made a vow to die in his place. This was done by Alcestis, and Admetus recovered. After her death Heracles brought her back from the underworld.

alchemist n one who studies or practices alchemy.

alchemize vt to transmute.

alchemy n (pl **alchemies**) chemistry as practiced during medieval times, with the aim of transmuting base metals into gold.—**alchemic, alchemical** adj.—**alchemist** n.

Alchred king of Northumbria. Reigned from 765 to 774.

Alcinous n (Greek myth) king of the Phaeacians, who entertained on his island the Argonauts on their return from Colchis, and with the help of his queen, Arete, protected Medea from the pursuing Colchians. Odysseus was shipwrecked on the island of Alcinous, and this episode is related in detail in Homer's Odyssey.

ALCM abbr = (Brit) Associate of the London College of Music; air-launched cruise missile.

Alcmaeon n (Greek myth) a son of Amphiaraus and Eriphyle. After the fall of Thebes he killed his mother, in fulfillment of the command of his father, for which he was made insane by the Furies.

Alcmene, Alcmena n (Greek myth) the wife of Amphitryon and the mother of Heracles by Zeus and of Iphicles by Amphitryon. Hera, jealous of Alcmene, delayed the birth of Heracles for seven days so that Eurystheus might be born first and thus be entitled to greater rights.

alcohol n a liquid, generated by distillation and fermentation, that forms the intoxicating agent in wine, beer and spirits; a liquid containing alcohol; a chemical compound of this nature; (chem) an organic compound with an oxygen/hydrogen group, (hydroxyl), attached to the molecule.

alcoholic adj of or containing alcohol; caused by alcohol. * n a person suffering from alcoholism.

alcoholism n a disease caused by excessive consumption of alcohol.

alcoholize, (Brit) **alcoholise** vt to subject to the influence of alcohol; to rectify (spirits of wine).—**alcoholization,** (Brit) **alcoholisation** n.

alcoholometer n an instrument for determining the strength of spirits.

Alcor or **80 Ursae Majoris** n (astron) a faint star of magnitude four in the constellation of the Great Bear.

Alcoran n the Koran, the Muslim bible.

Alcott n **Louisa M[ay]** (1832–88) American novelist and social reformer, remembered for her children's novels, e.g., Little Women, Good Wives.

alcove n a small, vaulted recess separated from the main part of the room by an entrance or partition; a recess in a garden often containing a seat.

Ald. or **Aldm.** abbr = Alderman.

Aldebaran or **Alpha Tauri** (astron) a star of the first magnitude, one of the 15 brightest stars.

aldehyde n (chem) an organic compound made up of carbon, hydrogen and oxygen; a volatile fluid with a suffocating smell, obtained from alcohol.

al dente adj (of pasta, etc) cooked but still firm to the teeth.

alder n a genus of plants growing in moist land and related to the birch.

alderman n (pl **aldermen**) in US, a member of certain municipal councils; (formerly) in England and Wales, a senior councilor.—**aldermanic** adj.

Aldhelm n **Saint** [also known as Ealdhelm] (c. 640–709) born in Wessex, England; abbot of Malmesbury around 673 and bishop of Sherborne in 705; wrote Latin treatises, letters and verses; buried at Malmesbury abbey. His feast day is 25 May.

Aldington n **Richard** (1892–1962) English poet and dramatist whose best-known novel Death of a Hero is a semi-autobiographical account of his experiences in World War I.

Aldrich n 1. **Henry** (1648–1710) English architect. His notable works include All Saints', Oxford. 2. **Thomas Bailey** (1836–1907) American poet, novelist, and editor of Atlantic Monthly (1881–90).

Aldrin, Edwin "Buzz" see **Armstrong, Neil**.

ALDU abbr = Association of Lawyers for the Defense of the Unborn.

Aldwulf n 1. king of East Anglia, England (663–713); son of Ethelhere and a Northumbrian princess, Hereswith of Deira. 2. **king** of Sussex, England (c.765); known to have made a land grant to the Church.

ale n beer.

ALEA abbr = Air Line Employees Association International; American Law and Economics Association.

aleatory adj depending on dice or chance.

aleatory music n (mus) music which contains unpredictable or chance elements so that no two performances of a piece are ever similar. It is a form explored since 1945 by composers such as Cage in his Music of Changes, and Stockhausen and Morton Feldman.

Alecheim n **Sholom**, real name **Solomon J Rabinowitz** (1859–1916) American Jewish writer, born in Russia. His work Tevye the Milkman was made into the musical Fiddler on the Roof.

Alecto n (Greek myth) one of the three Furies, the others being Megaera and Tisiphone.

alee adj, adv (naut) on the lee, to leeward.

alegar n vinegar made from ale.

alehouse n a place where ale is sold.

Aleijadinho n **Antonio F L** (b. 1738) Brazilian architect. His notable works include São Francisco, Ouro Preto.

alembic n an apparatus formerly used in distilling.

Alençon n a fine lace made at Alençon in France.

alert adj watchful; active, brisk. * n a danger signal. * vt to warn of impending danger, put in a state of readiness.—**alertly** adv.—**alertness** n.

alert box n (comput) an on-screen warning that an error has occurred or the command chosen may result in lost work.

Alessi n **Galeazzo** (1512–72) Italian architect. His notable works include Palazzo Marino.

A-level abbr (Brit) = Advanced Level.

Alexander I (the Fierce) n (1077–1124) king of Scots. Reigned from 1107 to 1124. The fifth son of Malcolm III (Canmore), the first king of all Scotland, and Margaret of England.

Alexander II n (1198–1249) king of Scots. Reigned from 1214 to 1249. The son of William I, "the Lion," and Ermengarde de Beaumont.

Alexander III n (1241–1286) king of Scots. Reigned from 1249 to 1286. The only son of Alexander II and Marie de Coucy, he succeeded his father when still only eight years of age.

Alexander VI, Pope see **Borgia, Rodrigo**.

Alexander n **Christopher** (1936–) English architect. His notable works include Mexican housing at Mexicali.

Alexander Nevsky n **Saint** (1219–63) stood out against a papal attempt to reunite the Greek and Roman churches; canonized in 1547. Peter the Great honored his memory by founding the knightly order of Alexander Nevsky. His feast day is 23 November.

Alexander Technique n a technique developed by Australian actor Frederick Matthias Alexander (d. 1955) to improve the posture.

Alexander the Great n (356–323 BC) Macedonian king who conquered Greece, Egypt, and the Persian Empire and founded the city of Alexandria.

Alexandra, Feodorovna see **Nicholas II**.

Alexandra, Queen see **Edward VII**.

Alexandria (El Iskandarîya) n a city in Egypt; (Egypt) the capital of Ptolemaic Egypt and the first really large city of Egypt. It was named in honor of Alexander the Great, who founded it.

alexandrine n a heroic verse of six iambic feet, or 12 syllables.—also adj.

alexia n the inability to read, due to mental illness.

alexin *n* a disease-resisting protein in blood serum.

Alexis *n* **Saint** (*c.* 4AD) known as the "Man of God"; the patron saint of a society of nurses known as the Alexian Brothers. His feast day is 17 July.

Alf *abbr* = automatic letter facer (mail sorting machine).

ALF *abbr* (*Brit*) = Animal Liberation Front.

alfalfa *n* a deep-rooted leguminous plant grown widely for hay and forage.—*also* **lucerne.**

Alfieri *n* 1. **Benedetto** (*b.* 1699) Italian architect. His notable works include Carignano Parish Church. 2. **Count Vittorio** (1749–1803) Italian poet and tragedian whose works display enthusiasm for Italian nationalism and reform.

Alfred the Great (849–899) king of Wessex, England. Reigned from 871 to 899. Alfred was born at Wantage in Berkshire, his father being Ethelwulf, son of Egbert, king of the West Saxons.

alfresco *adj* taking place outside in the open.—*also adv.*

Alfvén's theory *n* a theory of frozen-in-flux, in which a plasma can be considered trapped by magnetic field lines, developed by the Swedish astrophysicist Hannes Alfvén, Nobel Prizewinner in 1970.

alg. *abbr* = algebra.

Alg. *abbr* = Algiers.

ALG *abbr* (*Brit*) = Association for London Government.

alga *n* (*pl* **algae**) any of a group of chiefly aquatic lower plants without root, stem or leaves, classified according to color.—**algal** *adj.*

Algardi *n* **Alessandro** (1598–1654) Italian baroque sculptor. His major works include the tomb of Leo XI (*c.*1645) Rome, the sculptured group, *The Decapitation of St Paul*, in Bologna.

algarroba, algaroba *n* the carob tree and bean; St John's bread.

algebra *n* the branch of mathematics dealing with the properties and relations of numbers; the generalization and extension of arithmetic.—**algebraic, algebraical** *adj.*—**algebraist** *n.*

Alger *n* **Horatio** (1834–99) American author of adventure stories, e.g., *Ragged Dick.*

Algeria *n* a large country in northern Africa with a Mediterranean Sea coastline in the north. The Democratic and Popular Republic of Algeria is the second largest country in Africa.

Algerian *adj* pertaining to Algeria or Algiers. * *n* a native of Algeria or Algiers.

Algerine *adj* Algerian.

-algia *n suffix* pain.—**algic** *adj.*

algicide *n* a chemical used to eliminate algae.

algid *adj* cold, chilly.

Algiers (**Alger**) *n* capital city of Algeria.

ALGOL *n* (*comput*) a high-level programming language used for solving general problems in science and mathematics.

Algol[1] *or* **Beta Persei** *n* (*astron*) the second brightest star in the constellation Perseus.

Algol[2] *abbr* (*comput*) = Algebraically Oriented Language.

algology *n* the study of algae.—**algologist** *n.*

Algonquian *n* a family of North American Indian languages; the language spoken by Algonquins.

Algonquin *n* a member of a North American Indian people of Canada; the language of this people.

Algonquin Park *n* a National Park in southeast Ontario containing more than 1200 lakes.

algor *n* the rigor or chill on the onset of fever.

algorism *n* the arabic (decimal) numeration; arithmetic.—**algorismic** *adj.*

algorithm *n* (*comput*) a set of straightforward logical mathematical steps that provide a solution to a problem.—**algorithmic** *adj.*—**algorithmically** *adv.*

Algren *n* **Nelson** (1909–81) American novelist, two of whose novels, *The Man with the Golden Arm* and *Somebody in Boots*, are classic portrayals of urban underclass life.

Al Hudaydah *n* a city in Yemen.

Ali *n* **Muhammad** [Cassius Clay] (1942–) American boxer and world heavyweight champion (1964–67, 1974–78, 1978). Regarded as one of the greatest boxers of all time.

ALI *abbr* = (*Sweden*) Alfa-Laval International; American Law Institute; American Library Institute; Associate of the Landscape Institute.

alias *adv* otherwise called. * *n* (*pl* **aliases**) an assumed name; (*comput*) a small file that directs the computer to the original file and can be used as if it were the original.

aliasing *n* (*comput*) *see* **jaggies.**

alibi *n* (*pl* **alibis**) (*law*) the plea that a person charged with a crime was elsewhere when it was committed; (*inf*) any excuse.

alien *adj* foreign; strange; distasteful to, counter to. * *n* a person from another country, place, etc; a person of foreign birth who has not been naturalized; a being from outer space.

alienable *adj* (*law*) (*property*) able to be transferred.—**alienability** *n.*

alienage *n* the state or legal status of an alien.

alienate *vt* to render hostile or unfriendly; to make less affectionate or interested.

alienation *n* estrangement; transference; diversion to another purpose; mental derangement.

alienation effect *n* an effect that is supposed to occur upon an audience when the audience is reminded by action, dialog or song that it is, in fact, an audience watching a play, and not, for example, waiting for a bus.

alienee *n* (*law*) one to whom property is transferred.

alienism *n* the study and treatment of mental alienation.—**alienist** *n.*

alienor *n* (*law*) one who transfers property to another.

aliform *adj* wing-shaped.

alight[1] *vi* (**alighting, alighted** *or* **alit**) to come down, as from a bus; to land after a flight.

alight[2] *adj* on fire; lively.

align *vt* to place in a straight line, to bring into agreement, etc. * *vi* to line up.

alignment *n* the act of laying out or adjusting by a line; the ground plan of a railway or road.

alike *adj* like one another. * *adv* equally; similarly.

aliment *n* food; the necessaries of life generally; an allowance for support by decree of court. * *vt* to make provision for the maintenance of; to make provision for the support of parents or children respectively.—**alimental** *adj* .

alimentary *adj* pertaining to nourishment, food.

alimentary canal *n* the tube extending within the body from the mouth to the anus through which food passes and is absorbed.

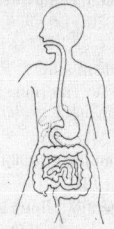

alimentation[1] *n* the act of giving nourishment; the function of the alimentary canal.—**alimentative** *adj.*

alimentation[2] *n* the snow and ice, together with any re-frozen meltwater, that accumulates on a glacier.

alimony *n* (*pl* **alimonies**) an allowance for support made by one spouse to the other, esp a man to his wife or former wife, pending or after a legal separation or divorce.

aliped *adj* having wing-like limbs, as the bat.

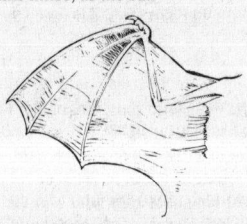

aliphatic *adj* (*chem*) containing carbon atoms in open chains (organic compound); pertaining to fat.

aliquant *adj*, *n* (*math*) being a part of a number that does not divide it without a remainder, as eight is the aliquant part of 25.

aliquot *adj*, *n* (*math*) being a part of a number of quantity that will divide it without a remainder, as eight is the aliquot part of 24.—*also n.*

alive *adj* having life; active, alert; in existence, operation, etc.

alizarin *n* a red coloring matter found in madder but now produced from anthracene.

alkahest *n* the supposed universal solvent of the alchemists.—*also* **alcahest.**

alkali *n* (*pl* **alkalis, alkalies**) (*chem*) any salt or mixture that neutralizes acids and with a pH value greater than 7.—**alkaline** *adj.*

alkalify *vt* (**alkalifying, alkalified**) (*chem*) to form or convert into alkali. * *vi* to become an alkali.

alkalimeter *n* (*chem*) an instrument used to determine the relative strength of alkalis.

alkalimetry *n* (*chem*) the process of determining the strength of an alkaline mixture or liquid.—**alkalimetric** *adj.*

alkaline *adj* (*chem*) pertaining to, or having the properties of, an alkali.—**alkalinity** *n.*

alkaline soil *n* a soil having a pH greater than 7 usu indicating a high concentration of carbonates, mainly of sodium or calcium.

alkalize, (*Brit*) **alkalise** *vt* (*chem*) to convert into an alkali or render alkaline.—**alkalizable**, (*Brit*) **alkalisable** *adj.*—*also* **alkalinize, alkalinise.**

alkaloid *n* (*chem*) an organic substance found in plants that protects them from being eaten; a body or substance containing alkaline properties. * *adj* resembling an alkali in its properties.

alkalosis *n* an abnormal rise in the alkalinity (a decrease in pH) of the blood and body fluids because of a failure of the mechanisms that regulate the balance in the body.

Alkan *n* **Charles Henri Valentin** [the pseudonym of **Morhange** *n* **Charles Henri Valentin**] (1813–88) French composer and pianist who was a close friend of Liszt and Chopin. One of the foremost piano teachers of his day, he wrote many piano pieces of great complexity, often using ideas ahead of the time.

alkanal *see* **aldehyde.**

alkane *n* (*chem*) a saturated compound containing hydrogen and carbon with single bonds between each carbon atom.

alkanet *n* a rich red dye; the plant the root of which yields it.

alkene n (*chem*) an unsaturated compound containing hydrogen and carbon with double bonds between the carbon atoms.

Al Khaburah n a city in the Sultanate of Oman.

alkyne n (*chem*) an unsaturated compound containing hydrogen and carbon with triple bonds between the carbon atoms.

all *adj* the whole amount or number of; every one of. * *adv* wholly; supremely; completely; entirely. * n the whole number, quantity; everyone; everything.

ALL *abbr* = acute lymphoblastic leukemia.

all along *adv* throughout.

alla breve *adj, adv* (*mus*) (*Italian*) an instruction that indicates a piece of music should be performed twice as fast as the notation would suggest, with one double whole note (breve) to a measure. * n 2/2 time.

Allah n the Muslim name of God.

all-American *adj* composed entirely of parts from the US; typical of American values; (*sport*) indicating excellence in American collegiate sports events. * n one who is considered the best; one who represents American ideals.

allargando *adj, adv* (*mus*) (*Italian*) literally "getting broader," i.e., an indication that a piece should be played grandly whilst at the same time getting slower.

all-around *see* all-round.

alla tedesca *adj, adv* (*mus*) (*Italian*) an abbreviation of *alla danza tedesca*, meaning "in the style of a German dance."

allantoid *adj* of or pertaining to the allantois; (*bot*) sausage-shaped. * n the allantois.—**allantoidal** *adj*.

allantois n (*pl* allantoides) a membranous appendage of most vertebrate embryos.

alla turca *adj, adv* (*mus*) (*Italian*) "in the Turkish style."

alla zingarese *adj, adv* (*mus*) (*Italian*) "in the style of gypsy music."

alla zoppa *adj, adv* (*mus*) (*Italian*) "in a limping way," i.e., in a syncopated rhythm. *See* syncopation.

allay *vt* to lighten, alleviate; to pacify or make calm.

all but *adv* almost.

all clear n a signal indicating that a danger has passed or that it is safe to proceed.

allegation n the act of alleging; assertion; declaration; that which is asserted or alleged; that which is offered as a plea, an excuse, or justification; the statement as yet unproved of a party to a suit.

allege *vt* to assert or declare, esp without proof; to offer as an excuse.

allegedly *adv* asserted without proof.

allegiance n the obligation of being loyal to one's country, etc; devotion, as to a cause.

allegorical, allegoric *adj* pertaining to, consisting of, or in the nature of allegory; figurative.—**allegorically** *adv*.

allegorize, (*Brit*) **allergorise** *vt* to put in the form of an allegory.—**allegorization,** (*Brit*) **allegorisation** n.

allegory n (*pl* allegories) a fable, story, poem, etc in which the events depicted symbolize an underlying moral or spiritual quality or represent a hidden meaning beneath the literal one expressed.—**allegorist** n.

allegretto *adj, adv* (*mus*) (*Italian*) a term indicating light and moderately quick movement, but not as fast as allegro. * n (*pl* allegrettos) a piece of music played in this way.

allegro *adj, adv* (*mus*) (*Italian*) literally "lively", i.e., in a quick tempo. The term is often used as the title of a bright composition or movement. * n (*pl* allegros) a piece of music played in this way.

allele n (*genetics*) either of a pair of contrasting characteristics one or the other of which is found unmixed in descendants of a cross between parental forms respectively possessing them.—*also* **allelomorph.**—**allelic** *adj*.—**allelism** n.

alleluia *see* hallelujah.

allemande n (*mus*) (*French*) an abbreviation of *danse allemande* or "German dance," of which there are two forms: a) a moderately slow dance used by 17th- and 18th-century composers as the first movement of a suite of four contrasting dances, b) a brisk dance, in three-quarter time, of the 18th and 19th centuries, similar to the waltz.

all-embracing *adj* including everything; complete.

Allen n 1. **Davis** (1916–) American interior designer, influenced by Hugo **Aalto.** 2. **Woody [Allen Stewart Konigsberg]** (1935–) American actor, writer and film director whose films include *Annie Hall* (1977) which won three academy awards.

Allende n 1. **Isabel** (1942–) Chilean novelist and goddaughter of Salvador Allende. Her novels include *The House of the Spirits* (1985). 2. **[Gossens] Salvador** (1908–73) Chilean politician and Marxist president from 1970. He was killed in a coup that brought Pinochet to power.

Allende meteorite n a meteorite found in Mexico weighing about two tons and consisting of carbonaceous chondrites.

allentando *adj, adv* (*mus*) (*Italian*) "slowing down," i.e., a term used to indicate that the tempo of a piece of music should be slowed down.

allergen n any substance, usu a protein, that causes a hypersensitive (allergic) reaction in a person who is exposed to the allergen.

allergenic *adj* causing an allergic reaction.

allergist n a physician whose specialty is treating allergies.

allergy n (*pl* allergies) an abnormal reaction of the body to substances (certain foods, pollen, etc) normally harmless; antipathy.—**allergic** *adj*.

allerion n (*her*) an eagle displayed without feet or beak.

alleviate *vt* to lessen or relieve (pain, worry, etc).—**alleviation** n.—**alleviator** n.

alleviative *adj* tending to alleviate. * n that which alleviates.

alley n a narrow street between or behind buildings; a bowling lane.

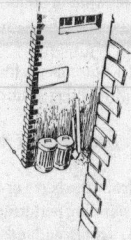

all fours *adv* on hands and knees.

"All Hail to Massachusetts" *phr* the song of the American State, Massachusetts.

All-hallowe'en n Hallowe'en.

All-hallows *npl* All Saints' Day, celebrated on 1 November, in honor of all the saints.

alliaceous *adj* of the nature or property of garlic or the onion.

alliance n a union by marriage or treaty for a common purpose; an agreement for this; the countries, groups, etc in such an association.

allied *see* ally.

Allies *npl* in World War I, all the nations allied against the Central Powers of Europe; in World War II, the nations allied against the Axis powers.

alligator n a large reptile similar to the crocodile but having a short, blunt snout.

alligator pear n the avocado.

all in *adj* (*price, etc*) all-inclusive.

all-in *adj* (*inf*) exhausted.

all in all *adj* taking everything into consideration.

all-inclusive *adj* including everything.

alliteration n the repetition of the same sound at the beginning of two or more words in a phrase, etc.—**alliterative** *adj*.

allo *abbr* (*mus*) (*Italian*) = *allegro*, "lively."

allocate *vt* to distribute or apportion in shares; to set apart for a specific purpose.

allocation n the act of allotting, allocating, or assigning; an allotment or assignment; an allowance made on an account; (*com*) in a company, the breakdown of costs and revenues between different departments or products; (*com*) the assigning of materials that are held in stock to fulfil product orders.

allocution n a formal address, esp as one delivered by the Pope to his clergy or to the Church generally.

allodial *adj* freehold; not feudal. * n land thus held.

allodium, allod n (*pl* allodia, allods) freehold estate; land that is the absolute property of the owner.

allogamy n (*biol*) cross-fertilization.—**allogamous** *adj*.

allograph n a signature by one person on behalf of another, opposite of autograph.—**allographic** *adj*.

allomorphism n (*chem*) the property in certain substances of assuming a different form while remaining the same in constitution.

all one *adj, n* in effect the same.

all' ongarese *adj, adv* (*mus*) (*Italian*) "in the style of Hungarian (gypsy) music."

allopath, allopathist n (*med*) one who favors or practices allopathy.

allopathy n (*med*) the orthodox medical practice of treating disease by inducing an action opposite to the disease it is sought to cure, opposite of homeopathy.—**allopathic** *adj*.—**allopathically** *adv*.

all or nothing *adj* accepting or risking everything or nothing.

allot *vt* (allotting, allotted) to distribute, allocate.

allotment n allotting; a share allotted; a small area of land rented for cultivation.

allotropy, allotropism n (*chem*) the capability shown by certain chemical elements to assume different forms, each characterized by peculiar qualities, as the occurrence of carbon in the form of the diamond, charcoal and plumbago respectively.—**allotropic** *adj*.—**allotropically** *adv*.

all'ott. *abbr* (*mus*) (*Italian*) = *all' ottava*, "at the octave."

allotted shares *npl* (*com*) shares, previously unissued, that are allocated to intending shareholders who have made application to the company for shares.

allottee n one to whom an allotment or share is granted or assigned; a plot-holder.

all out *adv* with maximum capacity.

all-out *adj* using maximum effort.

all-over *adj* covering the whole surface.

allow *vt* to permit; to acknowledge, admit as true; (*money*) to give, grant as an allowance at regular intervals; to estimate as an addition or deduction. * *vi* to admit the possibility (of).

allowable *adj* permissible.—**allowably** *adv*.

allowance[1] n an amount or sum allowed or given at regular times; a discount; a portion of income not subject to income tax; permission; admission, concession.

allowance[2] n (*com*) a tax-free amount of money that is allowed to be deducted before tax is calculated; money that is paid by an employer to an employee for expenses incurred in the course of his or her work for the company; an agreed time added to the basic time that a worker should take to perform a task; the additional raw materials or component parts that are added to the basic materials allowed for the completion of a particular product; a price reduction or rebate that is given to a customer for some reason, such as an exceptionally large order.

alloy n a solid substance comprising a mixture of two or more metals; something that degrades the substance to which it is added. * *vt* to make into an alloy; to degrade or spoil by mixing with an inferior substance.

all-purpose *adj* suitable for many uses.

all right *adv* good enough, acceptable; without doubt. * *adj* satisfactory; safe, well; agreeable. * *interj* (used to express consent).—*also* **alright**.

all-round *adj* efficient in all respects, esp sport.

All Saints' Day *n* (*Christian Church*) 1 November, a festival in honor of all the saints.

all-singing, all-dancing *adj phr* having every feature and possibility; all encompassing.

All Souls' Day *n* (*RC Church*) the day, celebrated 2 November, in honor of the departed.

allspice *n* an aromatic spice made from the berry of a West Indian tree.

all-star *adj* made up entirely of outstanding performers.

Allston *n* **Washington** (1779–1843) American landscape painter and leading figure in the beginnings of romanticism in the US. His work was large in scale and concentrated on the monumental, mysterious, and dramatic elements of nature and religious subjects. *See also* **Hudson River School**.

all that *adv* to an extent.

all the same *adv* regardless; of little or no importance.

all there *adj* (*sl*) not mentally wanting.

all-time *adj* unsurpassed until now.

all told *adv* with all counted; all in all.

allude *vi* to refer indirectly to.

allure *vt* to entice, charm. * *n* fascination; charm.—**allurement** *n*.

alluring *adj* attractive.

allusion *n* alluding; an implied or indirect reference.—**allusive** *adj*.

allusive *adj* having reference to something not definitely expressed.—**allusively** *adv*.—**allusiveness** *n*.

alluvion *n* the wash of the sea or river against a shore; land added to a shore or riverbank by the action of the water; an overflow.

alluvium *n* (*pl* **alluviums, alluvia**) the deposits, e.g., earth, sand, gravel, etc, produced as a result of the action of streams or rivers.—**alluvial** *adj*.

ally *vti* (**allying, allied**) to join or unite for a specific purpose; to relate by similarity of structure, etc. * *n* (*pl* **allies**) a country or person joined with another for a common purpose.

Almagest *n* an astronomical and mathematical encyclopedia completed in about 140 AD by Ptolemy of Alexandria; (*without cap*) other similar treatises.

alma mater *n* one's school, college, or university.

almanac *n* an annual publication featuring a collection of data, astronomical, meteorological, etc, such as positions and brightness of celestial objects for the year ahead, and a calendar for the coming year; a compendium of useful and interesting facts.

almanack *n* (*arch*) an almanac.

almandine *n* a violet-red variety of garnet, tinged sometimes with blue or yellow.

Alma-Tadema *n* **Sir Lawrence** (1836–1912) Dutch-born painter and furniture designer, who moved to England in 1870; elected to the Royal Academy.

Almaty *n* a city in Kazakhstan.

Al Mawsil *n* a city in Iraq.

Almeria *n* a southeast coastal area of Spain which has agricultural communities of early Neolithic age (*c*.5500–4300 BC).

almighty *adj* all-powerful. * *n* (*with cap*) God, the all-powerful.—**almightily** *adv*.—**almightiness** *n*.

almond *n* the edible kernel of the fruit of a tree of the rose family; the tree bearing this fruit. * *adj* (*eyes, etc*) oval and pointed at one or both ends.

almoner *n* (*arch*) one who dispenses or distributes alms or charity; an alms purse; a pouch or purse which in early times was suspended from the girdle.

almost *adv* all but, very nearly but not quite all.

Almquist *n* **Osvald** (1884–1950) Swedish architect. His notable works include hydro-electric power plants.

alms *npl* money or other gifts given to the poor in the name of God.

almshouse *n* a house endowed by private or public charity and appropriated to the use of the poor.

aloe *n* (*pl* **aloes**) a succulent plant with tall spikes of flowers.

aloes *n* (*used as sing*) the bitter juice of the aloe plant used in medicine.

aloft *adv* in the air, flying; high up.

aloha *interj* (*Hawaii*) used as a greeting or a farewell.

alone *adj* isolated; without anyone or anything else; unassisted; unique. * *adv* exclusively.

along *adv* onward, forward; over the length of; in company and together with; in addition. * *prep* in the direction of the length of; in accordance with.

alongside *prep* close beside. * *adv* at the side.

aloof *adv* at a distance; apart. * *adj* cool and reserved.—**aloofness** *n*.

Alope *n* (*Greek myth*) a daughter of Cercyon, king of Eleusis, who abandoned her baby son, Hippothoon. The child survived, suckled by mares, and was found by shepherds, but when Cercyon recognized the baby's clothes, he killed Alope.

alopecia *n* baldness; loss of hair through skin disease.

aloud *adv* with a normal voice; loudly; spoken.

alow *adv* (*naut*) to or in a lower part; below.

Aloysius *n* **Saint** (1568–91) born Luigi Gonzaga near Brescia in Italy; canonized in 1726; joined the Society of Jesus (the Jesuits) in 1585; devoted himself to caring for the sick and died of plague. His feast day is 21 June.

alp *n* a mountain peak, a shoulder of land in mountainous terrain standing above a glaciated trough and stretching up to the summer snow line.

ALP *abbr* = automated language processing.

ALPA *abbr* = Airline Pilots' Association.

alpaca *n* a Peruvian llama with long fine wool; a fabric made of this wool.

alpenglow *n* a peculiar purple glow on the snow on the Alps seen just before sunrise and after sunset.

alpenhorn *n* a long and nearly straight horn used by the mountaineers of the Alps.

alpenstock *n* a stout staff with an iron spike, used by mountain climbers.

Alpha *n* first letter in the Greek alphabet; used with Omega to express the greatness of God. *See also* **Omega**; (*astron*) the name given to the brightest star in a constellation.

alphabet *n* a set of letters, signs or symbols used in writing a language and communication.

alphabetical, alphabetic *adj* pertaining to an alphabet; in the order of the alphabet.—**alphabetically** *adv*.

alphabetize *vt* to arrange in alphabetical order.—**alphabetization** *n*.

Alpha Centauri *n* (*astron*) brightest of three stars in the constellation Centaurus.

alpha fetoprotein *n* (*biol*) a type of protein formed in the liver and gut of the fetus, detectable in the amniotic fluid and maternal blood.

alphanumeric *adj* (*comput*) using numerals to nine and the alphabet.

alphanumeric character *n* (*comput*) any keyboard character, such as A to Z in either uppercase or lowercase, numbers one to ten and punctuation marks.

alpha particle *n* (*phys*) a helium nucleus with a short straight range from the source of emission, one of the earliest particles recognized in radioactivity.

alpha ray *n* (*phys*) radiation of alpha particles.

Alphard *or* **Alpha Hydrae** *n* (*astron*) the brightest star, second magnitude, of the constellation Hydra.

alpha wave *n* brain waves, with a frequency of ten per second, that occur when the person is awake. *See* **electroencephalogram**.

Alphege *n* **Saint,** also known as **Aelfheah** (954–1012) bishop of Winchester in 984; archbishop of Canterbury in 1005; taken prisoner by marauding Danes in 1011 and was put to death with an axe. His feast day is 19 April.

Alphekka *or* **Alpha Corona Borealis** *n* (*astron*) the brightest star, second magnitude but variable, of the northern constellation Corona Borealis.

Alpheratz *or* **Alpha Andromedae** *n* (*astron*) the brightest star, second magnitude, of the constellation Andromeda.

Alpheus, Alpheius *n* the largest river of the Peloponnese, now Rufia; (*Greek myth*) a river-god, the son of Oceanus and Tethys.

Alphorn *n* (*mus*) (*German*) a primitive type of wooden horn which has no valves and was traditionally played by Swiss herdsmen to call in their cattle in the evening.

Alpin *n* (*d. c*.840) king of Scots. Reigned from *c*.837 to *c*.840. This semi-legendary king ruled Dalriada for only a short period before being killed by an unknown assailant. The 34th king of Dalriada, thought to be the son of **Eochaid** "the Venomous," and the father **of Kenneth mac-Alpin** and **Donald I**.

alpine *adj* (*with cap*) of the Alps; of high mountains. * *n* a mountain plant, esp a small herb.

alpinist *n* a mountaineer who climbs in the Alps or in areas of similar mountains.—**alpinism** *n*.

Alps *npl* a high mountain range in south central Europe; (*astron*) mountains on the Moon: the lunar Alps.

Alpurcoms *abbr* = all-purpose communications system.

ALRA *abbr* = Abortion Law Reform Association; Adult Literacy Resource Agency.

already *adv* by or before the time specified; before the time expected.

Alric *n* king of Kent, England (reigned 747–762). Succeeded his brother Eadbert I as joint ruler with his other brother, Ethelbert II.

alright *adv* a frequent spelling of all right.

ALS Academy of Leisure Sciences; Alliance of Literary Societies; Associate of the Linnean Society; approach lighting system.

Alsatian *n* a German shepherd; a native of Alsace.

al seg. *abbr* = al segno.

al segno *adv* (*mus*) (*Italian*) literally, "to the sign" (i.e., to a standard symbol used in musical notation). The term is used in two ways: it can instruct the player either to go *back* to the sign and start again, or to *continue* until the sign is reached.

ALSEP *abbr* = Apollo Lunar Surface Experiments Package *n* a self-contained package of experimental apparatus left on the Moon by the Apollo astronauts.

also *adv* in addition, besides.

also-ran *n* a defeated contestant in a race, an election, etc.

alt *abbr* (*mus*) (*Latin*) = *in alto,* "high." It is used for the notes in the octave rising from G above the treble clef; the notes in the octave above that are said to be *in altissimo.*

alt. *abbr* = alternate; alternating; alternations; altitude; alto.

Alta *abbr* = Alberta.

Altaic *adj* pertaining to the Altaic mountain regions, partly bounding Russia and China. * *n* the language of the region.

Altair *or* **Alpha Aquilae** *n* (*astron*) the brightest star, first magnitude, of the constellation Aquila.

Altamira *n* a the site in northern Spain of prehistoric rock paintings dating from about 13000 BC from the Magdalenian culture, the first ever to be discovered, in 1879.

altar *n* a raised structure, often of stone or marble, on which offerings were placed and sacrifices offered to God, allowing the smoke and smell to rise heavenwards; in Christian churches, a communion table.

altarage *n* the offerings placed upon the altar to be devoted to the church, or appropriated by the priest as stipend.

altar boy *n* in RC Church and Anglican Church, a boy who assists a priest in the course of a religious service.

altar cloth *n* a general term for the coverings of the altar.

altar ledge *n* a step or ledge behind the altar of a church, slightly raised above it for holding lights, flowers, and other symbolical ornaments; a retable.

altarpiece *n* a decorated wall, screen, or sectional painting set behind the altar of a Christian church, a feature of church decor dating from the 11th century.

altarscreen *n* a screen or partition separating the altar from the choir; a reredos.

altar slab *n* the top of an altar; the consecrated part of an altar (the mensa).

altarwise *adv* placed in the usual position of an altar, with the ends towards the north and south, and the front to the west.

Altay *n* a city in Mongolia.

altazimuth *n* (*astron*) an instrument for determining the altitudes and azimuths of the stars and planets.

altazimuth mounting *n* (*astron*) a form of two-axis telescope mounting where rotation about the altitude axis, which is a horizontal axle, lets the telescope sweep out in a vertical semicircular arc over the observer's head.

altazimuth system *n* (*astron*) a system of coordinates to locate the position of a celestial object on the celestial sphere.

alt. dieb. *abbr* (*Latin*) = *alternis diebus,* "every other day."

Altdorfer *n* **Albrecht** (1480–1538) German painter and printmaker. His themes were mainly religious, but his outstanding contribution to art is in the development of landscape painting as a genre in its own right.

alter *vti* to make or become different in a small way; to change.—**alterable** *adj.*—**alterability** *n.*

alter ego *n* one's other self; a constant companion.

alteration *n* the act of altering or changing; the change or modification effected.

alterative *adj* producing change; having the power to alter. * *n* a medicine that restores the healthy functions of the body.

altercate *vi* to contend in words; to wrangle; to dispute with anger or heat.

altercation *n* an angry or heated quarrel.

alternant *adj* alternating; composed of alternate layers.

alternate angles *npl* the internal angles made by two lines with a third on opposite sides of it.

alternate *vt* to do or use by turns. * *vi* to act, happen, etc by turns; to take turns regularly; *adj* occurring or following in turns.—**alternately** *adv.*

alternating current *n* an electric current that reverses the direction of its flow regularly.

alternation *n* the act of alternating, or state of being alternate; reciprocal succession; antiphonal singing or reading.

alternative *adj* presenting a choice between two things. * *n* either of two possibilities.—**alternatively** *adv.*

alternative comedy *n* a form of comedy that avoids conventional humor (e.g., racist and sexist jokes), characterized by aggressively delivered and blackly humorous stand-up routines that usu challenge political and social orthodoxy.

alternative medicine *n* forms of healing other than Western-orientated medical practice, including acupuncture, homeopathy, osteopathy, naturopathy, faith healing and herbal remedies.—*also* **complementary medicine**

alternator *n* an electric generator that produces alternating current.

althaea, althea *n* a genus of plants including the marshmallow and the hollyhock.

Althaea *n* (*Greek myth*) the mother of Meleager, whose death she caused to avenge her brothers, killed by Meleager in a quarrel. She then took her own life in remorse.

alt. hor. *abbr* (*Latin*) = *alternis horis,* "every other hour."

althorn *n* a musical instrument of the saxhorn class, frequently used in military bands.

although *conj* though; in spite of that.

altimeter *n* an instrument for indicating height above sea level.

altimetry *n* any measurement of the height of an object above some reference level; the art of measuring altitudes by the use of the altimeter.—**altimetrical** *adj.*

altissimo *adj* (*mus*) of the part or notes situated above F in alt.

altitude *n* (*geom*) the distance from the corner of a figure to the opposite side; (*astron*) the angle measured from the horizon upwards to a planetary object; height, esp above sea level.—**altitudinal** *adj.*

altitude sickness *n* a condition occurring at high altitudes with symptoms such as nausea, fatigue and breathlessness that are attributable to oxygen deficiency.

Altman *n* **Robert** (1925–) American film director whose films include *M*A*S*H* (1970).

alt. noct. *abbr* (*Latin*) = *alternis noctibus,* "every other

alto[1] *n* (*pl* **altos**) the range of the highest male voice; a singer with this range; a contralto. * *adj* high.

alto[2] *n* clouds between 9840 and 19,684 feet (3000 and 6000 meters) high, as in *altocumulus.*

alto clef *n* the C clef placed on the third line of the staff.

altocumulus *n* a roll of cloud in small segments, occurring at medium altitude.

altogether *adv* in all; on the whole; completely.

alto-relievo, alto-rilievo *n* (*pl* **alto-relievos, alto-rilievos**) high relief; figures or other objects that stand out boldly from the background, and having more than half their thickness projecting.

altostratus *n* a layer of cloud with a uniform appearance, occurring at medium altitude.

altruism *n* unselfish concern for or dedication to the interests or welfare of others.—**altruist** *n.*—**altruistic** *adj.*—**altruistically** *adv.*

ALU *abbr* = Aboriginal Liaison Unit; Aluminum Can Recycling Association; (*comput*) arithmetic logic unit.

aludel *n* one of the pear-shaped glass or earthenware pots, open at both ends, used in sublimation.

alum *n* a double sulphate formed of aluminum and some other element, usu an alkali metal.

alum. *abbr* = aluminum.

alum root *n* a popular name given to certain astringent roots of saxifrages.

alum schist *n* a thin-bedded fissile rock from which alum is procured.

alumina *n* the single oxide of aluminum, the most abundant of the earth's minerals; a notable constituent of common clay, alumina is largely used in dyeing and calico printing as a mordant.

aluminiferous *adj* containing or yielding alum, alumina, or aluminum.

aluminous *adj* of, containing or resembling alum or alumina.

aluminum *n* a light metal that is easily shaped and drawn out into wire and that is also a good conductor of electricity.

aluminum foil *n* thin sheets of aluminum wrap used to protect food.

alumna *n* (*pl* **alumnae**) a female graduate or pupil of a university or college.

alumnus *n* (*pl* **alumni**) a former pupil or student.—**alumna** *nf* (*pl* **alumnae**).

alunite *n* subsulphate of alumina and potash.

alure *n* (*archit*) a walkway esp that behind the parapet of a fortified castle wall, or around a church roof.

alveolar *adj* of tooth sockets.

alveolate *adj* with deep pits or cells resembling the honeycomb.—**alveolation** *n.*

alveolus *n* (*pl* **alveoli**) a small pit, cell, cavity, or socket; the socket in which a tooth is fixed; the cell of a honeycomb; (*med*) a small sac or cavity that in numbers forms the alveolar sacs at the end of the bronchioles in the lungs.

alvine *adj* pertaining or belonging to the intestines or belly.

always *adv* at all times; in all cases; repeatedly; forever.

Alzheimer's disease *n* a degenerative disease of the cerebral cortex for which there is no cure. Symptoms include progressive loss of memory and speech and paralysis.

am *see* **be.**

Am *symbol* (*chem*) americium (element).

am *abbr* (*Latin*) = *ante meridiem,* "before noon."

aM *abbr* (*German*) = *am Main,* "on the Main," for places near this river.

Am. *abbr* = America, American; ammeter; amplitude modulation, a radio band; (*mil*) ammunition (party).

AM *abbr* = Academy of Management; Action Monégasque; Air Marshal; Albert Medal; (*Latin*) *anno mundi,* "in the year of the world"; (*Latin*) *Artium Magister,* "Master of Arts"; Associate Member; (*phys*) amplitude modulation (when radio waves are altered to transmit broadcasting signals).

AMA *abbr* = American Medical Association; American Missionary Association.

Amadeo *n* **Giovanni A** (1447–1522) Italian architect. His notable works include the façade of the Cortosa outside Pavia.

amadou *n* a styptic and a tinder prepared by steeping the solid portions of a fungus affecting trees in a solution of saltpeter; German tinder.

amah *n* an East Indian nurse or female servant.

Amalekites *n* (*Bible*) nomadic tribe which plundered the Israelites during the Exodus.

amalgam *n* an alloy of mercury and another metal; a mixture.

amalgamate *vt* to combine, unite.

amalgamation *n* the act or process of compounding mercury with another metal; the separation of precious metals from the mother rock by means of quicksilver; the blending or mixing of different elements or things; (*com*) the union or consolidation of two or more companies or businesses into one concern, a merger.

Amalthea *n* (*astron*) a satellite of Jupiter discovered in 1892.

amanuensis *n* (*pl* **amanuenses**) one who is employed to write at the dictation or direction of another; a secretary.

amaranth *n* an imaginary flower said by poets to be unfading; a plant of the genus *Amarantus*; a color mixture in which magenta is the chief ingredient; red coloring added to some foods.

amaranthine *adj* pertaining to the amaranth; never-fading, like amaranth; purplish.

amaretto *n* an Italian almond-flavored liqueur.

Amarna (Tel-el-Amarna) *n* (*Egypt*) this site in Middle Egypt, downstream from Thebes, was chosen by the Eighteenth-Dynasty Pharaoh Akhenaten as his new capital when, in a move unprecedented in Egypt's long history, he abandoned Thebes.

Amarna Period *n* (*Egypt*) a period of the New Kingdom, 1348–1336 BC, corresponding to the reign of Akhenaten, which was centered at his capital on the site of el-Amarna. The Amarna Period saw distinctive changes in the arts of sculpture and painting.

amaryllis *n* a genus of bulbous flowering plants to which the belladonna lily and narcissus belong.

amass *vt* to bring together in a large quantity; to accumulate.—**amasser** *n*.—**amassment** *n*.

amateur *n* one who engages in a particular activity as a hobby, and not as a profession. * *adj* of or done by amateurs.—**amateurism** *n*.

amateurish *adj* lacking expertise.—**amateurishly** *adv*.—**amateurishness** *n*.

Amati *n* (*mus*) the name of a famous family of violin-makers who worked in Cremona, Italy, in the 16th and 17th centuries. The most famous member of the family was **Nicolo Amati** (1596–1684), who taught Antonio Stradivari and Andrea Guarneri.

amatol *n* a high explosive.

amatory, amatorial *adj* relating to or expressive of love.

amaurosis *n* loss or decay of sight due to partial, periodic, or complete paralysis of the optic nerve.—**amaurotic** *adj*.

amaze *vt* to fill with wonder, astonish.—**amazing** *adj*.—**amazingly** *adv*.

amazement *n* the state of being amazed; astonishment; perplexity arising from sudden surprise.

amazon ant *n* a species of ant found in Europe and America, which seizes the neuters of other species in the pupa stage and brings them up with their own larvae.

Amazon *n* (*Greek myth*) a race of women warriors who permitted no men to live among them. They fought under the command of a queen, and were said to burn off the right breast in order to use the bow; a tall strong athletic woman.—**Amazonian** *adj*.

amazon stone *n* a beautiful green feldspar found near the Amazon.

amazonite *n* the amazon stone gemstone.

amb., Amb. *abbr* = ambassador.

Amb. *abbr* (*mil*) = ambulance (party).

AMBA *abbr* = Associate Member of the British Arts.

ambary, ambari *n* (*pl* **ambaries, ambaris**) a plant of Asia that produces a jute-like fiber; the fiber.

ambassador *n* the highest-ranking diplomatic representative from one country to another; an authorized messenger.—**ambassadorial** *adj*.—**ambassadress** *nf*.

ambassador extraordinary *n* an ambassador sent on a special mission.

ambassador plenipotentiary *n* an ambassador sent with full powers to make a treaty.

ambassador-at-large *n* (*pl* **ambassadors-at-large**) a high-ranked minister not associated with a particular government or monarch.

AMBBA *abbr* = Associated Master Barbers and Beauticians of America.

Amb. Co. *abbr* = Ambulance Company.

AMBCS *abbr* = Associate Member of the British Computer Society.

amber *n* a hard yellowish fossil resin of pine trees, used for jewelry and ornaments, etc; the color of amber.

ambergris *n* a waxy substance found in tropical seas, which is secreted by sperm whales and is used in perfumery as a fixative.

amberoid, amberoid *n* pressed amber; synthetic amber.

amber tree *n* the common name for various species of African evergreen shrubs with fragrant leaves.

ambidextrous *adj* able to use the left and the right hand equally well.—**ambidexterity** *n*.

ambience, ambiance *n* surrounding influence, atmosphere.

ambient *adj* surrounding.

ambiguity *n* (*pl* **ambiguities**) double or dubious significance; vagueness.

ambiguous *adj* capable of two or more interpretations; indistinct, vague.—**ambiguously** *adv*.—**ambiguousness** *n*.

AMBII *abbr* = Associate Member of the British Institute of Innkeeping.

ambit *n* a circuit or compass; the line or sum of the lines by which a figure is bounded; the perimeter; sphere of action.

ambition *n* desire for power, wealth and success; an object of ambition.

ambitious *adj* having or governed by ambition; resulting from or showing ambition; requiring considerable effort or ability.—**ambitiously** *adv*.

ambivalent *adj* having mixed feelings toward the same object.—**ambivalence** *n*.

amble *vi* to walk in a leisurely way. * *n* an easy pace.—**ambler** *n*.

amblyopia *n* dimness of vision; amaurosis.—**amblyopic** *adj*.

ambo *n* (*pl* **ambos, ambones**) a pulpit; a reading desk.

amboyna, amboina *n* a beautifully mottled and curled variegated wood used in cabinet work.

Ambracia *n* in ancient Greece, a gulf, town and river in northwest Greece, modern Arta.

Ambrose *n* **Saint** (340–397) born at Trèves; bishop of Milan; patron saint of Milan. His feast day is 7 December.

ambrosia *n* (*class myth*) the food of the gods; anything exquisitely pleasing to taste or smell; a genus of weeds allied to wormwood.—**ambrosial, ambrosian** *adj*.

Ambrosian chants *n* (*mus*) a collection of chants or plainsong, used in Milan Cathedral, which are named after St Ambrose, Bishop of Milan.

ambrotype *n* (*photog*) a process by which the light parts of a photograph are produced in silver, the dark parts showing as a background through the clear glass.

ambry *n* (*pl* **ambries**) a recess in a church wall for sacred vessels; a repository for arms; a cupboard for money tools, etc.

ambsace *n* two ones, the lowest throw at dice; bad luck.

ambulacrum *n* (*pl* **ambulacra**) a perforation in the shell of echinoderms through which the tube feet are protruded.—**ambulacral** *adj*.

ambulance *n* a special vehicle for transporting the sick or injured.

ambulance chaser *n* one who attempts to profit from disaster.

ambulant *adj* (of a patient) able to walk, not bed-ridden; moving from place to place.

ambulate *vi* to walk about; to move about; to wander.—**ambulation** *n*.

ambulatory *adj* of or pertaining to walking; movable; temporary; capable of walking. * *n* (*pl* **ambulatories**) (*archit*) a place for walking in; a roofed passage for walking in, generally within a church.

ambuscade *n* (*milit*) a strategic disposition of troops in ambush.

ambush *n* the concealment of soldiers, etc to make a surprise attack; the bushes or other cover in which they are hidden. * *vti* to lie in wait; to attack from an ambush.

ambush marketing *n* the practice of taking advantage of another's official event to advertise one's own products.—*also* **ambushing**.

AMC *abbr* = American Mining Congress; Australian Maritime College.

AMCS *abbr* = Airborne Missile Control System.

am. cur. *abbr* (*Latin*) = *amicus curiae*, "friend of the court."

AMD *abbr* = Army Medical Department.

AMDG *abbr* (*Latin*) = *ad majorem Dei gloriam*, "to the greater glory of God."

ameba *n* (*pl* **amebae, amebas**) a microscopic invertebrate found in fresh water, damp soil and the digestive tracts of animals that consists of a gelatinous mass which constantly alters its state.—*also* (*Brit*) **amoeba**.—**amebic, amoebic** *adj*.

amebiasis *n* an intestinal infection caused by amebae.

amebic dysentery *n* a disease caused by *Entamoeba histolytica*, which is spread via infected food or water and occurs mainly in the tropics and subtropics.

ameer *see* **amir**.

ameliorate *vti* to make or become better.—**ameliorative** *adj*.—**ameliorator** *n*.

amelioration *n* the making or growing better; improvement.

Amen[1] *interj* Hebrew word used as a religious response meaning "So be it"; spoken at the end of prayers, blessings.

Amen[2], **Amon** *n* the main god of the city of Thebes, on the east bank of the Nile in Upper Egypt.

amenable *adj* easily influenced or led, tractable; answerable to legal authority.—**amenability** *n*.—**amenably** *adv*.

amend *vt* to remove errors, esp in a text; to modify, improve; to alter in minor details.—**amendable** *adj*.—**amender** *n*.

amendatory *adj* tending to amend; corrective.

amende honorable *n* (*pl* **amendes honorables**) a public apology and reparation; a punishment formerly inflicted in France on traitors and the sacrilegious.

amendment *n* the act of amending, correction; an alteration to a document, etc; (*law*) a filed document changing the intent of a previously filed document or modifying certain aspects within it.

amends *npl* (*used as sing*) compensation or recompense for some loss, harm, etc.

Amenhotep *n* the dynastic name of four pharaohs from the New Kingdom, in the 18th dynasty.

amenity *n* (*pl* **amenities**) pleasantness, as regards situation, convenience, or service.

Amenophis I *n* Egyptian king of the Eighteenth Dynasty (ruled 1526–1506 BC), son of Ahmosis, who benefited from Ahmosis's conquests.

Amenophis II *n* Egyptian king of the Eighteenth Dynasty (ruled 1425–1401 BC). The successor to the great Tuthmosis III, he is remembered for his great physical strength and for a degree of cruelty unusual in Egyptian monarchs.

Amenophis III *n* Egyptian king of the Eighteenth Dynasty (ruled 1390–1352 BC). His principal wife, Tiy, mother of his successor, Akhenaten, was an Egyptian commoner whose father was Master of the Stud Farms. She was elevated to a special status as Great Royal Wife.

Amenophis IV *see* **Akhenaten**.

amenorrhea *n* abnormal absence of menstruation.

ament, amentum *n* (*pl* **aments, amenta**) a catkin, as of the willow.

amentia *n* want of reason; mental deficiency.

Amer. *abbr* = America; American.

Amerasian *n* a person of mixed American and Asian lineage.—*also adj.*

amerce *vt* to punish by an arbitrary fine.—**amerceable** *adj.*—**amercement** *n*.

Amerenglish *n* the English language as spoken in the United States.

"America the Beautiful" *phr* the poem which has become the national song of the USA; poem written in 1893 by Katharine Lee Bates (1859–1929). More than 60 tunes have been written for the poem, but those by Will C Macfarlane (1870–1945) and S A Ward are the most famous.

American *adj* belonging to or characteristic of America. * *n* an inhabitant of the US.

Americana *n* artifacts associated with American tradition, history or geography; a collection of these objects.

American Designers' Gallery *n* founded in 1928 in New York, this was one of the first attempts to accord design its rightful status as a creative art.

American eagle *n* the bald eagle.

American in Paris *n* **An** a descriptive piece for orchestra by Gershwin (1928) in which, amongst other unusual instruments, four taxi horns are played.

American Indian *n* any member of the original native peoples of North America, Central America or South America, excluding the Inuit.

American National Standards Institute *n* a non-governmental organization founded in 1981 to approve the specification of computer data processing standards and define high-level programming languages.

Americanism *n* a form of expression peculiar to the US; a custom peculiar to the US; attachment to the US.

Americanize *vt* to render American; to assimilate to the political and social institutions of the US.—**Americanization** *n*.

American organ *n* (*mus*) a reed organ, similar to a harmonium except that air is sucked through the reeds instead of being blown through them. *Also* **cabinet organ.**

American Samoa *n* an "unincorporated" territory of the USA lying close to Western Samoa in the Pacific Ocean and comprising five main volcanic islands and two coral atolls.

American Sign Language *n* a sign language for the deaf that uses hand gestures to convey meaning.—*also* **Ameslan.**

American Society of Interior Designers *n* American professional association founded in 1975.

American Standard Code for Information Interchange *see* **ASCII.**

America's Cup *n* an international yachting race; the winning trophy of this race.

americium *n* a white radioactive metallic element derived from plutonium.

Amerindian, Amerind *n* an American Indian.—**Amerindic** *adj*.

AMES *abbr* = Ames Laboratory

Ameslan *see* **American Sign Language.**

ametabolic *adj* (*certain insects*) not undergoing metamorphosis.

amethyst *n* a gemstone consisting of bluish-violet quartz; the color of an amethyst.—**amethystine** *adj*.

AMF *abbr* = Allied Mobile Force (NATO).

Amhairghin *or* **Amairgen** (*Irish Celtic myth*) Irish warrior and a fili. He is said to have been a son of Mil and to have been part of the expedition of the Sons of Mil Espaine that invaded Ireland.

AM Herculis stars *npl* (*astron*) stars showing regular change in both brightness and polarization of light, sometimes called polars.

AMI *abbr* = Association of Meat Inspectors; acute myocardial infarction.

AMIA *abbr* = Affiliated Member of the Association of International Accountants.

amiable *adj* friendly in manner, congenial.—**amiability** *n*.—**amiably** *adv*.

AMIAEA *see* AMInstAEA.

AMIAgrE *abbr* = Associate Member of the Institution of Agricultural Engineers.

amianthus *n* earth or mountain flax, a fibrous variety of asbestos.—**amianthine, amianthoid, amianthoidal** *adj*.

AMIAP *abbr* = Associate of the Institution of Analysts and Programmers.

AMIAT *abbr* = Associate Member of the Institute of Asphalt Technology.

AMIBC *abbr* = Associate Member of the Institute of Building Control.

AMIBCM *abbr* = Associate Member of the Institute of British Carriage and Automobile Manufacturers.

AMIBCO *abbr* = Associate Member of the Institution of Building Control Officers.

amicable *adj* friendly; peaceable.—**amicability, amicableness** *n*.—**amicably** *adv*.

amice *n* a square of white linen formerly worn on the head but now worn about the neck and shoulders by celebrant priests while saying Mass; a pilgrim's cloak.

AMICE *abbr* = Associate Member of the Institution of Civil Engineers.

AMICorrST *abbr* = Associate Member of the Institution of Corrosion Science and Technology.

amicus curiae *n* (*pl* **amici curiae**) (*law*) a friend of the court; a disinterested adviser.

amid, amidst *prep* in or to the middle of; during.

amide *n* any of several compounds produced by the replacement of a hydrogen atom of ammonia by an acid radical or metal atom.

amidships *adv* (*naut*) in the middle of a ship.

AMIEE *abbr* = Associate Member of the Institution of Electrical Engineers.

AMIEIE *abbr* = Associate Member of the Institution of Electrical and Electronics Incorporated Engineers.

AMIEx *abbr* = Associate Member of the Institute of Export.

AMIGasE *abbr* = Associate Member of the Institution of Gas Engineers.

amigo *n* (*pl* **amigos**) (*Spanish*) a friend.

AMIHIE *abbr* = Associate Member of the Institute of Highway Incorporated Engineers.

AMIHT *abbr* = Associate Member of the Institution of Highways and Transportation.

AMIIEXE *abbr* = Associate Member of the Institution of Incorporated Executive Engineers.

AMIISE *abbr* = Associate Member of the International Institute of Social Economics.

AMIM *abbr* = Associate Member of the Institute of Materials.

AMIManf *abbr* = Associate Member of the Institute of Manufacturing.

AMIMarE *abbr* = Associate Member of the Institute of Marine Engineers.

AMIMatM *abbr* = Associate Member of the Institute of Materials Management.

AMIMechE *abbr* = Associate Member of the Institution of Mechanical Engineers.

AMIMechIE *abbr* = Associate Member of the Institution of Mechanical Incorporated Engineers.

AMIMI *abbr* = Associate Member of the Institute of the Motor Industry.

AMIMinE *abbr* = Associate Member of the Institute of Mining Engineers.

AMIMS *abbr* = Associate Member of the Institute of Management Specialists.

Amin [Dada] *n* Idi (1925–) Ugandan dictator (1971–79).

amine *n* (*chem*) any of several organic compounds formed by replacing hydrogen atoms of ammonia by one or more univalent hydrocarbon radicals; naturally occurring compound in the body derived from amino acids.

amino acid *n* (*chem*) any of the 20 standard organic compounds from which all the protein components of the body are built up.

amino-acid racemization *n* a method, based on changes in amino acids, for dating animal or human bone up to 100,000 years old.

AMInstAEA *abbr* = Associate Member of the Institute of Automotive Engineers Assessors.

AMInstBE *abbr* = Associate Member of the Institute of British Engineers.

AMInstE *abbr* = Associate Member of the Institute of Energy.

AmInstEE *abbr* = American Institute of Electrical Engineers.

AMInstME, AMInstME(Dip) *abbr* = Associate Member of the International Institute of Management Executives.

AMInstTA *abbr* = Associate Member of the Institute of Transport Administration.

AMIPA *abbr* = Associate Member of the Institute of Practitioners in Advertising.

AMIPC *abbr* = Associate Member of the Institute of Production Control.

AMIPlantE *abbr* = Associate Member of the Institution of Plant Engineers.

AMIPM *abbr* = Associate Member of the Institute of Personnel Management.

AMIPR *abbr* = Associate Member of the Institute of Public Relations.

AMIQ *abbr* = Associate Member of the Institute of Quarrying.

AMIQA *abbr* = Associate Member of the Institute of Quality Assurance.

amir *n* (*formerly*) the Muslim ruler of Afghanistan.—*also* **ameer.**

AMIRSO *abbr* = Associate Member of the Institute of Road Safety Officers.

AMIRT *abbr* = Associate Member of the Institute of Reprographic Technology.

AMIRTE *abbr* = Associate Member of the Institute of Road Transport Engineers.

Amis *n* 1. Sir **Kingsley** (1922–95) English novelist and poet whose novels include *Lucky Jim* and *The Old Devils*. 2. his son **Martin** (1949–) English novelist whose works include The *Rachel Papers*.

AMISM *abbr* = Associate Member of the Institute of Supervisory Management.

amiss *adj* wrong, improper. * *adv* in an incorrect manner.

AMIStructE *abbr* = Associate Member of the Institution of Structural Engineers.

AMITD *abbr* = Associate Member of the Institute of Training and Development.

amity *n* (*pl* **amities**) friendship.

AMIWPC *abbr* = Associate Member of the Institute of Water Pollution Control.

AML *abbr* = acute myelogenous leukemia.

AMM *abbr* (*mil*) = anti-missile missile.

amm. *abbr* = amalgama.

Amman *n* capital city of the Hashemite Kingdom of Jordan.

Ammanati *n* **Bartolomeo** (1511–92) Italian sculptor and architect. His architectural works include the Ponte Santa Trinità and the court of the Pitti Palace, both in Florence.

Ammenemes I *n* Egyptian Middle Kingdom pharaoh of the Twelfth Dynasty (ruled 1991–1962 BC) who was assassinated as the result of a conspiracy that began in the women's quarters.

ammeter *n* an instrument for measuring electric current in amperes.

AMMI *abbr* = Affiliate of the Institute of the Motor Industry.

ammo *n* (*sl*) ammunition.

ammonal *n* a highly explosive compound.

ammonia *n* a colorless gas with an irritating smell, used as a cleaning agent; a pungent colorless gas composed of nitrogen and hydrogen.

ammoniac[1] *n* a gum resin.—*also* **gum ammoniac.**

ammoniac², ammoniacal *adj* of, pertaining to, like or containing ammonia.

ammonite *n* a fossil shell, twisted like a ram's horn; snakestone.—**ammonitic** *adj*.

Ammonites *n* (*Bible*) semitic people said to be descended from Lot; notorious for their cruelty; repeatedly clashed with the Israelites and defeated by Saul at Jabesh-Gilead. *See also* **Jabesh-Gilead**, **Saul**.

ammonium *n* the hypothetical base of ammonia.

ammunition *n* bullets, shells, rockets, etc; any means of attack or defense; facts and reasoning used to prove a point in an argument.

amnesia *n* a partial or total loss of memory.—**amnesiac, amnesic** *n, adj*.

amnesty *n* (*pl* **amnesties**) a general pardon, esp of political prisoners; a pardon granted for a limited time. * *vt* (**amnestying, amnestied**) to pardon (an offence).

AMNI *abbr* = Associate Member of the Nautical Institute.

amniocentesis *n* (*med*) the extraction by hollow needle of a sample of amniotic fluid from the womb to test for fetal abnormalities.

amniography a special X-ray performed late in pregnancy.

amnion *n* (*pl* **amnions, amnia**) the thin innermost membrane surrounding the fetus in the womb of mammals, birds, and reptiles.—**amniotic** *adj*.

amnioscopy *n* the procedure by which an endoscope is inserted through the mother's abdominal wall, either by means of an incision or through her cervix, in order to view the fetus.

amniotic cavity *n* the cavity filled with fluid, that is enclosed by the amnion and surrounds the fetus.

amniotic fluid *n* the liquid in the amniotic cavity. Amniotic fluid is released when the membranes rupture during labor.

amniotic sac *n* a membrane that forms around a fertilized egg and surrounds the developing fetus.

amniotomy *n* the artificial rupture of membranes (ARM) which is carried out in order to induce the onset of labor.

amoeba *see* **ameba**

amoebean *adj* (*verse form*) alternately answering.

amoebiasis *see* **amebiasis**.

amoebic *see* **amebic**.

amoebic dysentery *see* **amebic dysentery**.

amok *adj, adv* **run amok** to run about armed, in a state of frenzy, attacking all that come in the way; indiscriminate slaughter; headstrong violence.—*also* **amuck**.

Amon *n* (*Bible*) son of Manasseh and king of Judah *c*.642–640 BC; assassinated by his servants. *See also* **Manasseh**.

among, amongst *prep* in the number of, surrounded by; in the group or class of; within a group, between; by the joint efforts of.

amontillado *n* (*pl* **amontillados**) a dry kind of light-colored sherry.

Amor *n* (*Roman myth*) a name for Cupid, the god of love, equivalent to the Greek Eros; (*astron*) an asteroid of diameter about 0.6 miles, which was discovered in 1932.

amoral *adj* neither moral nor immoral; without moral sense.—**amorality** *n*.—**amorally** *adv*.

amoretto, amorino *n* (*pl* **amoretti, amorini**) a small plump naked boy used in painting and sculpture to represent a cupid or children.—*also* **putto** (*pl* **putti**).

amorist *n* an amateur in love, a philanderer.

Amorites *n* (*Bible*) semitic tribes who invaded the fertile crescent *c*. 2000 BC, regarded as enemies of the Israelites. *See also* **Canaan**.

amoroso *adj, adv* (*mus*) (*Italian*) literally "lovingly," indicating that a piece should be played in a tender, amatory style.

amorous *adj* displaying or feeling love or desire.—**amorously** *adv*.—**amorousness** *n*.

amor patriae *n* love of one's country.

amorphous *adj* (*chem*) non-crystalline; lacking a specific shape, shapeless; unrecognizable, indefinable.—**amorphism** *n*.

amortization *n* (*com*) the repayment of debt by a borrower in a series of installments; the system of regarding as an expense the annual amount that is considered to waste away from a fixed asset, such as a lease; the act of alienating lands to a corporation in mortmain.—**amortizement** *n*.

amortize *vt* to put money aside at intervals for gradual payment of (a debt, etc).—**amortization** *n*.

Amos, the Book of *n* (*Bible*, *OT*) one of the twelve minor prophets; the Book is concerned with social justice, hypocrisy and visions of doom.

amount *vi* to be equivalent (to) in total, quantity or significance. * *n* the total sum; the whole value or effect; a quantity.

amour *n* a love affair; an intrigue.

amour propre *n* self-love, vanity; self-respect.

amp *abbr* = (*phys*) ampere, a unit of electric current; (*inf*) an amplifier.

amp.-hr. *abbr* = ampere-hour.

AMP *abbr* (*med*) = adenosine monophosphate.

AMPA *abbr* = Associate Member of the Master Photographers Association.

AMPDE *abbr* = Associated Master Plumbers & Domestic Engineers.

ampelopsis *n* kinds of vine creeper, incl the Virginia creeper.

amperage *n* the strength of an electric current measured in amperes.

ampere *n* the standard SI unit by which an electric current is measured.

ampersand *n* the sign (&) meaning "and."

amphetamine *n* an addictive drug chemically similar to adrenaline used esp as a stimulant and to suppress appetite.

amphi- *prefix* of both kinds; on both sides; around.

Amphiaraus *n* (*Greek myth*) a seer and one of the Seven against Thebes, who was persuaded by his wife to join the expedition although he foresaw its outcome.

While being pursued by the enemy, he was swallowed up by the earth, and Zeus made him immortal.

amphibian *n* an animal living on land but breeding in water; an aircraft that can take off and land on water or land; a vehicle that can travel on land and through water.

amphibious *adj* living on both land and in water; (*mil*) involving both sea and land forces.

amphibole *n* a rock-forming mineral occurring in many different rock types.

amphibology, amphiboly *n* (*pl* **amphibologies, amphibolies**) an ambiguous phrase, as a sentence that may be construed in two distinct ways, as "The duke yet lives that Henry shall depose"; a quibble.

amphibrach *n* (*verse*) a foot of three syllables, the middle long, the first and last short.—**amphibrachic** *adj*.

amphimacer *n* (*verse*) a foot of three syllables, the middle short, the first and last long.

amphimixis *n* (*pl* **amphimixes**) a mingling of male and female gametes in sexual reproduction.

Amphion *n* (*Greek myth*) a son of Zeus and Antiope, who had miraculous skill in music, and with his twin brother, Zethus, was said to have used music to build the walls of Thebes.

amphioxus *n* (*pl* **amphioxi, amphioxuses**) the name of the lancelet, a fish with a body tapering at both ends, the lowest in organization of the vertebrates.

amphipod *n* any of the *Amphipoda* order of crustaceans having feet for both walking and swimming, including the sandhoppers and sand fleas.

amphiprostyle *adj* (*archit*) with a portico at both ends. * *n* a building of this kind, esp a temple.—**amphiprostylar** *adj*.

amphisbaena *n* (*pl* **amphisbaenae, amphisbaenas**) a fabled serpent with a head at each end; a kind of lizard or worm.—**amphisbaenic** *adj*.

amphitheater *n* (*archit*) a Roman theater, usu circular or oval, with an arena encircled by rising tiers of seats.

Amphitrite *n* (*Greek myth*) the wife of Poseidon, represented with a trident in her hand; the personification of the sea.

Amphitryon *n* (*Greek myth*) king of Thebes and husband of Alcmene. During his absence from home in order to punish the murderers of his wife's brothers, Alcmene was seduced by Zeus in the disguise of Amphitryon, who himself returned home the next day.

amphora *n* (*pl* **amphorae, amphoras**) a large vessel used for storage that had two handles, a bulbous and sometimes elongate body and narrow neck. They were commonly used by the Romans.

amphoteric *adj* (*chem*) capable of reacting as either an acid or a base.

ampicillin *n* a type of semi-synthetic penicillin used to treat various infections.

ample *adj* large in size, scope, etc; plentiful.—**amply** *adv*.

amplification *n* the act of amplifying or expanding; enlargement.

amplifier *n* a device that increases electric voltage, current, or power, or the loudness of sound; (*mus*) any device, particularly an electric one, which renders a sound louder.

amplify *vt* (**amplifying, amplified**) to expand more fully, add details to; (*electrical signals, etc*) to strengthen.

amplitude *n* largeness of extent, scope; abundance; the maximum value of any regularly varying quantity during one period; (*phys*) the intensity of a sound wave, the maximum deviation of an oscillation from the mean or zero.

amplitude modulation *n* (the transmitting of information by) the modulation of the amplitude of a radio carrier wave in accordance with the amplitude of the signal carried.

ampolloso *adj, adv* (*mus*) (*Italian*) "inflated style."

ampoule, ampul, ampule *n* a small plastic or glass bubble that is sterile and sealed, usu containing one dose of a drug to be administered by injection.

ampoulé *adj, adv* (*mus*) (*French*) "bombastic."

AMPRI *abbr* = Association Member of the Plastics and Rubber Institute.

AMProfBTM *abbr* = Associate Member of Professional Business and Technical Management.

AMPS Association of Management and Professional Staffs; Association of Motorists Protection Service; automated message-processing system.

ampulla *n* (*pl* **ampullae**) an ancient vessel which contained unguents for the bath; a drinking vessel; a vessel for consecrated oil or chrism used in church rites and at the coronation of sovereigns.—**ampullar, ampullary** *adj*.

amputate *vt* to cut off, esp by surgery.

amputation *n* the surgical removal of any body part, but generally referring to a limb.

amputee *n* one who has undergone an amputation.

AMPW *abbr* = Association of Makers of Printings and Writings.

AMR *abbr* = Associate of the Association of Health Care Information and Medical Record Officers; Association of Minor Railway Companies; automatic message routing.

AMRA *abbr* = Ancient Mediterranean Research Association; Automotive Manufacturers Racing Association.

AMRAAM *abbr* (*mil*) = advanced medium-range air-to-air missile.

Amratian *adj* relating to a culture from Egypt dated at 4500–4000 BC.

AMRSH Associate Member of the Royal Society of Health.

AMS *abbr* = Agricultural Manpower Association; Agricultural Marketing Service; American Magnolia Society; Ancient Monuments Society; Army Medical Service; Army Medical Staff; Associate of the Institute of Management Services Association of Metal Sprayers; Association of Missionary Societies; Assurance Medical Society; Australian Musicology Society.

AMS(Aff) *abbr* = Affiliate, Association of Medical Secretaries, Practice Administrators and Receptionists.

AMSE *abbr* = Associate Member of the Society of Engineers (Incorporated).

AMSL *abbr* = above mean sea level.

AmSocCE *abbr* = American Society of Civil Engineers.

AmSocME *abbr* = American Society of Mechanical Engineers.

Amst. *abbr* = Amsterdam.

Amsterdam *n* capital city of the Netherlands.

amt. *abbr* = amount.

AMTDA *abbr* = American Machine Tool Distributors Association.

AMTE *abbr* = Admiralty Marine Technology Establishment.

AMTRA *abbr* = Animal Medicine Training Regulatory Authority.

Amtrak *abbr* = National Railroad Passenger Corporation

AMTRI *abbr* = Advanced Manufacturing Technology Research Association.

amu *abbr* = atomic mass unit.

AMU *abbr* = American Malacological Union; Associated Metalworkers Union; Association of Master Upholsterers; Association of Minicomputer Users.

amuck *see* **amok.**

Amudian *adj* relating to an industry from Syria, Palestine and the Levant based upon blades and burins.

amulet *n* something worn as a charm against evil.

Amulius *n* (*Roman myth*) a king of Alba Longa, who drove his brother from power and killed his nephews, and when his niece gave birth to twin sons, Romulus and Remus, had them put in a basket on the Tiber so that they would die. However, they survived and later killed Amulius before restoring their grandfather Numitor to the throne.

Amundsen *n* **Roald** (1872–1928) Norwegian explorer and navigator, leader of the first expedition to reach the South Pole in 1911.

amuse *vt* to entertain or divert in a pleasant manner; to cause to laugh or smile.—**amusing** *adj.*

amusement arcade *n* an indoor or roofed area with mechanical games for entertainment.

amusement *n* that which amuses; the state of being amused; an entertainment; a pastime.

amusement park *n* an outdoor area with fairground entertainments.

AMusLCM *abbr* (*Brit*) = Associate in Music of the London College of Music.

AMusTCL *abbr* (*Brit*) = Associate in Music of Trinity College of Music, London.

Amun or **Amen** *n* (*Egypt*) Egyptian God with a ram's head, symbolizing fertility, identified by the Egyptians with the national deity **Amun-Ra.**

Amun-Ra or **Amen-Ra** *n* (*Egypt*) the Egyptian sun god; the principal deity of Theban hegemony.

AMWES *abbr* = Associate Member of the Women's Engineering Society.

Amyclae *n* a town of ancient Greece, the chief seat of the Achaeans in Laconia, a short distance from Sparta, by which it was conquered about 800 BC.

Amyclas *n* (*Greek myth*) a son of Lacedaemon and Sparta, king of Laconia and the founder of Amyclae.

amygdalate *adj* of or belonging to the almond.

amygdalin *n* a white crystalline substance obtained from the kernels of almonds.

amygdaloid *adj* almond shaped. * *n* an igneous rock containing almond-shaped nodules of some mineral.

amyl *n* (*formerly*) the alcohol radical of many chemical compounds.

amylaceous *adj* of starch, starchy.

amylase *n* a digestive enzyme that breaks down starch and glycogen.

amylene *n* a hydrocarbon obtained by the removal of water from amyl alcohol.

amyl nitrite *n* a drug inhaled to relieve spasms.

amyloid *n* a starchy food.

amylopsin *n* (*chem*) a pancreatic ferment converting starch into sugar.

an *adj* the indefinite article ("a"), used before words beginning with the sound of a vowel except "u."

An *symbol* (*chem*) actinon (element).

an *abbr* = above named; anno; anonymous; the pure anorthite molecule CaO.Al2O3.2SiO2.

an. *abbr* (*Latin*) = *anno*, "in the year."

a.n. *abbr* (*shipping*) = arrival notice.

a/n *abbr* = advice note.

AN *abbr* = Anglo-Norman.

an- *prefix* the form of *ad-* before *n*.

-an, -ain, -ane *adj suffix* of, of the nature of, as in *suburban, certain, humane.*

ana. *abbr* = anastomosing.

ANA *abbr* = Administration for Native Americans; American Naprapathic Association; Anguilla National Alliance; Associate National Academician; Article Number Association; Association of Nordic Aeroclubs; Association of Nurse Administrators; Australian National Airways.

ana- *prefix* up, anew, again.

-ana, -iana *n suffix* sayings of, publications about, as *Shakespeariana*, etc.

Anabaptist *n* one who believes in the rebaptizing of adults on their profession of faith; one who holds the invalidity of infant baptism; (*pl*) the sect of Baptists.—**Anabaptism** *n*.

anabas *n* a genus of Indian fishes allied to the perch, remarkable for their power of living a long time out of water and of travelling on land.

anabasis *n* (*pl* **anabases**) (*Greek*) the name given to Xenophon's account of the expedition of Cyrus the Younger (401 BC); an inland military expedition; (*mus*) a succession of ascending tones.

anabatic *adj* (*of wind*) caused by upward current of air.

anabatic wind *n* an upslope wind formed when air on the sides of a valley is heated more quickly than air above the valley floor.

anabiosis *n* a coming to life again, resuscitation.

anableps *n* (*pl* **anableps**) a genus of the perch family found in Guiana, remarkable for the structure of its eye.

anabolic steroid *n* a synthetic male sex hormone used to enhance tissue growth by promoting the build-up of protein, e.g., to enhance muscle bulk. *See* **steroid.**

anabolism *n* constructive metabolism, in which simple molecules synthesize into more complex ones.—**anabolic.**

anabranch *n* a stream that leaves a river and rejoins it lower down.

anachronism *n* a person, custom, or idea regarded as out of date or out of its period.—**anachronistic** *adj.*—**anachronistically** *adv.*

anacoluthia *n* want of grammatical sequence, esp in a sentence.—**anacoluthic** *adj*.

anacoluthon *n* (*pl* **anacolutha**) a sentence in which one part belongs to a different construction from the other.

anaconda *n* a large South American semiaquatic snake that kills its prey by constriction.

Anacreon *n* (*c.* 5 BC) Greek lyric poet noted for his poems on love and wine.

Anacreontic *adj* after the manner of Anacreon, the Greek poet (*c.* 5 BC); amatory, erotic. * *n* a poem in praise of love and wine.

anacrusis *n* (*pl* **anacruses**) (*Greek*) *anakrousis*, (*linguistics*) an unstressed syllable at the beginning of a verse; (*mus*) literally "a prelude," an unstressed note or grouping of notes at the beginning of a musical phrase.—**anacrustic** *adj*.

anadiplosis *n* (*rhetoric*) the repetition of the last word of a line or clause at the beginning of the next.

anadromous *adj* (*fish*) ascending from the sea to freshwater rivers to deposit spawn, as the salmon, etc.

Anadyomene *n* a name given to Aphrodite when she was represented as rising from the sea.

anaemia *see* **anemia.**

anaemic *see* **anemic.**

anaerobe, anaerobium *n* (*pl* **anaerobes, anaerobia**) a microbe that can live without air.

anaerobic respiration *n* (*biol*) a form of respiration in which biochemical reactions occur without oxygen being present.

anaerobiosis *n* life devoid of oxygen.—**anaerobic** *adj*.—**anaerobically** *adv*.

anaesthesia *see* **anesthesia.**

anaesthesiology *see* **anesthesiology.**

anaesthetic *see* **anesthetic.**

anaesthetist *see* **anesthetist.**

anaesthetize *see* **anesthetize.**

ana-front *n* a front where warm air rides over colder air.

anaglyph[1] *n* an ornament or work of art carved in low relief, as distinguished from intaglio.—**anaglyphic, anaglyphical, anaglyptic, anaglyptical** *adj*.

anaglyph[2] *n* a method of obtaining a three-dimensional image of topography by viewing two adjoining aerial photographs that have been printed by using special lenses.

anagnorisis *n* (*pl* **anagnorises**) the denouement in a drama.

anagoge, anagogy *n* an allegorical or mystical interpretation, a hidden sense.—**anagogic, anagogical** *adj*.—**anagogically** *adv*.

anagram *n* a word or sentence formed by rearranging another word or sentence.—**anagrammatic, anagrammatical** *adj*.—**anagrammatically** *adv*.

anagrammatize *vt* to make into an anagram. * *vi* to construct anagrams.—**anagrammatism** *n*.—**anagrammatist** *n*.

Anakim *n* (*Bible*) legendary race of giants.

anal *adj* of or situated near the anus.

anal. *abbr* = analogous; analogy; analysis; analytic; analytical; analyze; analyzer.

analects, anelecta *npl* literary passages or extracts selected from published works by different authors.—**analectic** *adj*.

analeptic *adj* restorative. * *n* a restorative drug.

analgesia *n* a state of reduced reaction to pain, but without loss of consciousness.

analgesic *adj* relieving pain. * *n* a drug or substance that relieves pain, varying in potency from mild, such as paracetamol and aspirin, to very strong, e.g., pethidine and morphine.

analog *n* (*Brit* **analogue**) a word or thing analogous to something else. * *adj* varying continuously to reflect actual changes. A thermometer is an analog measurement device, as the temperature varies so does the height of the mercury.

analog computer *n* a computer whose numerical data types are represented by changes in physical magnitudes of electrical signals.

analog data *n* information represented or collected in continuous form.

analogism *n* a reasoning from the cause to the effect; study and examination of matters and things by reference to their analogies.—**analogist** *n*.

analogize *vt* to reason or expound by reference to analogy, to draw comparisons. * *vi* to treat or investigate by use of analogy.

analogous *adj* corresponding in certain respects (to).—**analogously** *adv*.

analogue *see* **analog.**

analogy *n* (*pl* **analogies**) a similarity or correspondence in certain respects between two things.—**analogical, analogic** *adj*.

analysand *n* anyone undergoing psychoanalysis.

analyse *see* **analyze.**

analysis *n* (*pl* **analyses**) the process of analyzing; a statement of the results of this; psychoanalysis.

analyst *n* a person who analyzes; a psychoanalyst.

analyt. *abbr* = analytical.

analytic, analytical *adj* pertaining to analysis.—**analytically** *adv*.

analyzable *adj* capable of being resolved by, or that may be subjected to, analysis.

analyze *vt* to separate (something) into its constituent parts to investigate its structure and function, etc; to examine in detail; to psychoanalyze.—*also* (*Brit*) **analyse**.

anamnesis *n* (*pl* **anamneses**) recollection; a patient's case history.—**anamnestic** *adj*.—**anamnestically** *adv*.

anamorphosis *n* (*pl* **anamorphoses**) the irregular and distorted representation of an object as viewed directly, but which is corrected and reduced to its proper proportion when regarded from a different point of view, or reflected by a curved mirror; the abnormal or monstrous development of a portion of a plant or flower; a gradual progression from one type to another.

ananas *n* a genus of tropical plants to which the pineapple belongs.

anandrous *adj* without stamens.

Ananias *n* (*Bible*) disciple in Damascus who sought out Saul and helped restore his sight. *See also* **Paul**.

ananthous *adj* without flowers.

anapaest, anapest *n* (*verse*) a foot comprising two short syllables and one long syllable.—**anapaestic, anapestic** *adj*.

Anaphe *n* a small mountainous island in the south of the Greek Archipelago, east of Thera.

anaphora *n* (*rhetoric*) the repetition at the beginning of the succeeding clauses of sentences of the word or words used in beginning the first; that part of the Eucharistic service which starts with the Sursum Corda; the oblique ascension of a star.—**anaphoric** *adj*.—**anaphorically** *adv*.

anaphrodisia *n* impotence of the sexual organs; absence of venereal desire.

anaphrodisiac *adj* tending to diminish sexual desire. * *n* a remedy that produces such an effect.

anaphylaxis *n* a response exhibited by a hypersensitive individual resulting from the release of histamine in body tissues. Death may follow if the individual is not soon treated with adrenaline by injection.—**anaphylactic** *adj*.—**anaphylactically** *adv*.

anaplasia *n* the condition typical in malignant tumors in which cells and tissues become less distinctive and revert to a more primitive form.

anaplasty *n* the repairing of wounds by the transplantation of adjacent healthy tissue, plastic surgery.—**anaplastic** *adj*.

Anarawd *n* king of Gwynedd, Wales. Reigned from 878 to 916. The son of **Rhodi Mawr**.

anarchism *n* lawlessness; confusion; anarchy; the doctrines of the anarchists.

anarchist *n* a person who believes that all government is unnecessary and should be abolished.—**anarchistic** *adj*.

anarchy *n* the absence of government; political confusion; disorder, lawlessness.—**anarchic, anarchical** *adj*.

anarthria *n* the loss of the ability to speak. **and/or** *conj* indicating that either *and* or *or* may be used.

anarthrous *adj* without the article; destitute of joints; without articulated limbs.

anasarca *n* (*med*) dropsy.—**anasarcous** *adj*.

Anasazi *n* a North American culture that can be traced from the 6th and 7th centuries AD. The people cultivated crops and built large villages, *see* **pueblo**.

anastigmat *n* a lens corrected of astigmatism.—**anastigmatic** *adj*.

anastomosis *n* (*pl* **anastomoses**) the area of communication between the end branches of adjacent blood vessels; (*med*) the artificial joining together of two or more tubes that are normally separate, e.g., between parts of the intestine or blood vessels; a cross-connection of arteries, rivers, etc.—**anastomotic** *adj*.

anastrophe *n* (*rhetoric*) an inversion of the sequence of words in a sentence, as "echoed the hills," for "the hills echoed."

anat. *abbr* = anatomical; anatomist; anatomy.

anathema *n* (*pl* **anathemas**) anything greatly detested; an ecclesiastical curse or denunciation accompanied by excommunication.

anathematize *vt* to pronounce a decree of excommunication against. * *vi* to curse.—**anathematization** *n*.

Anathoth *n* (*Bible*) home of the prophet Jeremiah, near Jerusalem.

anatomist *n* one possessing a knowledge of anatomy by dissection.

anatomize *vt* to dissect; to study the structure of; to analyze.—**anatomization** *n*.

anatomy *n* (*pl* **anatomies**) the science of the physical structure of plants and animals; the structure of an organism.—**anatomical** *adj*.—**anatomically** *adv*.

anbury *n* (*pl* **anburies**) a soft wart or tumor on horses and cattle; a disease in turnips.

anc. *abbr* = ancient; anciently.

ANC *abbr* = African National Congress; (*Latin*) *Ante Nativitatem Christi*, "before the birth of Christ."

-ance *n suffix* denoting quality or action, as in *arrogance, penance*.

ancestor *n* one from whom a person is descended, a forefather; an early animal or plant from which existing types are descended; something regarded as a forerunner.—**ancestress** *nf*.

ancestral *adj* belonging to, or connected with, one's ancestors; derived from one's progenitors; lineal.

ancestry *n* (*pl* **ancestries**) ancestors collectively; lineage.

Anchises *n* (*Greek myth*) the father by Aphrodite of the Trojan hero Aeneas, who carried him off on his shoulders at the burning of Troy and made him the companion of his voyage to Italy, described by Virgil in his *Aeneid*.

anchor *n* a heavy metal implement that lodges at the bottom of the sea or a river to hold a ship in position; something that gives support or stability. * *vt* to fix by an anchor; to secure firmly.

anchorage *n* a safe anchoring place for ships; the charge for anchoring.

anchorite *n* one who voluntarily secludes him or herself from society and lives a solitary life devoted to religious or philosophic meditation.—**anchoress** *nf*.

anchorman *n* (*pl* **anchormen**) (*sport*) the last man in a team to compete and whose contribution is vital; the main presenter of a television show.

anchor stock *n* the crossbar at the top of the shank, at right angles to the arms.

anchor watch *n* the watch on board ship when at anchor; the seamen on this watch.

anchovy *n* (*pl* **anchovies, anchovy**) a small Mediterranean fish resembling a herring with a very salty taste.

anchovy pear *n* a West Indian fruit like the mango, used as a pickle.

anchylose *see* **ankylose**.

anchylosis *see* **ankylosis**.

ancien régime *n* (*pl* **anciens régimes**) the old order, esp that ruling France before the Revolution.

ancient *adj* very old; dating from the distant past; of the period and civilizations predating the fall of the Roman Empire; old-fashioned. * *n* a person who lived in the ancient period; (*pl*) the members of the classical civilizations of antiquity, esp of Greece and Rome.

Ancient of Days *n* (*Bible*) God, as described in the Book of Daniel.

Ancients, The *npl* a group of romantic artists working in England between 1824 and the early 1830s. Their work was mainly pastoral in theme, much inspired by Blake's illustrations of Virgil.

ancillary *adj* subordinate (to); auxiliary; supplementary. * *n* (*pl* **ancillaries**) a subordinate or auxiliary person or thing.

ancipital, ancipitous *adj* (*biol*) two-edged and sharp.

ancon, ancone *n* (*pl* **ancones**) (*archit*) a bracket or projection for the support of a cornice; the elbow.—**anconal, anconeal** *adj*.

ancora *adv* (*mus*) (*Italian*) literally "again," "yet," or "still," as in *ancora forte* meaning "still loud," and *ancora più forte* meaning "yet louder."

Ancus Marcius *n* according to Roman legend, the fourth king of Rome, who succeeded Tullus Hostilius in 638 and died in 614 BC.

and *conj* in addition to; together with; plus; increasingly; as a consequence, afterwards; expressing contrast.

AND *see* **formula**; **logical operator**.

and. *abbr* (*Italian*) = *andante*, "flowing" (term used to indicate speed in music).

andalusite *n* a silicate of alumina.

andante *adj, adv* (*mus*) (*Italian*) moderately slow, naturally and easily. Literally "going" or "moving," usu indicates a moderate tempo. *Più andante* means "moving more" or slightly faster. * *n* a movement written and to be played in andante time.

andantino *adj, adv* (*mus*) (*Italian*) "less slow" (i.e., slightly faster) than andante. * *n* (*pl* **andantinos**) a movement slower than an andante.

Andersen *n* 1. **Carl David** *see* **Hess, Victor Francis**. 2. **Hans Christian** (1805–75) Danish writer remembered for his fairy tales, e.g., *The Ugly Duckling*. 3. **Ib Joust** (1884–1943) Danish painter and sculptor who became a designer of pewter. 4. **Sherwood** (1876–1941) American novelist and short-story writer whose *Winesburg, Ohio* focuses on the tragedies of small-town life.

andesite *n* a silicate of alumina, soda, and lime.

andiron *npl* metal standards used for open fires to support the logs; fire dogs.

Ando *n* **Tadao** (*b.* 1941) Japanese architect. His notable works include domestic house design.

Andorra *n* a tiny republic situated high in the eastern Pyrenees between France and Spain.

Andorra la Vella *n* capital city of Andorra.

Andre *n* **Carl** (1935–) American sculptor whose minimalist style emphasizes the real in art as opposed to the metaphoric.

Andrea del Castagno *n* (*c.*1421–57) Florentine artist. One of the leading painters of his generation.

Andrea del Sarto *n* (1486–1530) Florentine painter. A major figure of the High Renaissance, his work was among the greatest examples of contemporary classical art.

Andretti *n* **Mario Gabriele** (1940–) American racing driver; world champion (1978).

Andrew *n* **Prince** *see* **Elizabeth II**.

Andrew *n* **Saint** (first century) the first apostle to be called by Jesus; brother of Peter; patron saint of Scotland, Greece and Russia; according to tradition, he was the first to preach the gospel in Russia. His feast day is 30 November.

Andrewes *n* **Lancelot** (1555–1626) English theologian and bishop, and one of the translators of the Authorized Version of the Bible.

Andrews *n* 1. **Ernest Clayton** (1870–1948) Australian geologist who specialized in physiography; president of the Australasian Association for the advancement of Science. 2. **Frank M[axwell]** (1884–1943) American air force commander who succeeded Eisenhower as commander of US forces in Europe during World War II. 3. **John** (1933–), Australian architect. His notable works include Canadian National Tower, Toronto. 4. **Julie**, originally **Julia Elizabeth Wells** (1935–), English singer and actress most famous for her appearances in musicals; won an Academy Award for her performance in *Mary Poppins* (1964).

Androco n (fl. AD 20) high king of the British tribes. Son of Caswallon, he ruled the Catuvellauni tribe based around Hertfordshire.

androgen n one of a group of hormones that is responsible for the development of the sex organs and also the secondary sexual characteristics in the male.

androgenous adj (biol) having only male offspring.

androgynous adj combining both sexes or bearing both male and female organs; hermaphroditical.—**androgyne** n.—**androgyny** n.

android n (science fiction) a robot in human form.—also adj.

Andromache n (Greek myth) wife of Hector, whose son was hurled from the wall of Troy when the city was captured, while she herself was taken by the Greek Neoptolemus.

Andromeda n (Greek myth) daughter of the Ethiopian king Cepheus, who was chained to a rock to appease Poseidon after he sent a sea monster to punish her people. She was rescued by Perseus and after death was changed into a constellation;

ndromeda n (astron) a northern sky constellation, one hour right ascension, 40° N declination.

Andromeda galaxy n (astron) a spiral galaxy found in the constellation Andromeda, referred to as NGC24 or M31, visible to the unaided eye.

Andropov n Yuri [Vladimirovich] (1914–84) Soviet statesman and former head of the KGB and president of the USSR (1983–84).

androsphinx n (pl androsphinxes, androsphinges) a sphinx with the body of a lion and the head of a man.

anecdotal adj relating to anecdotes; (evidence, etc) obtained from experience, not scientific.

anecdote n a short entertaining account about an amusing or interesting event.

anemia n a decrease in the ability of the blood to carry oxygen because of a reduction in the number of red blood cells or in the amount of hemoglobin that they contain, resulting in paleness, weakness, etc. also—(Brit) **anaemia.**

anemic adj relating to or suffering from anemia. also—(Brit) **anaemic.**

anemograph n an instrument for registering the force or direction of the wind.

anemography n the scientific description of winds, and the measurement and registration of their force and direction.—**anemographic** adj.—**anemographically** adv.

anemology n the science and literature of the winds.

anemometer n a device that measures the force or speed of the wind.

anemone n a plant of the buttercup family.

anemophilus adj (bot) fertilized by pollen carried by the wind, wind-pollinated.—**anemophily** n.

anemoscope n an apparatus for exhibiting the direction of the wind.

anencephaly n a failure in the development of a fetus, sometimes associated with spina bifida, resulting in the absence of the cerebral hemispheres of the brain and some skull bones.—**anencephalic** adj.

anent prep, adv (Scot) with regard or respect to; concerning.

aneroid adj having no liquid, as quicksilver. * n a barometer shaped like a watch, the action depending on the varying pressure of the atmosphere on the top of an elastic metal box.

aneroid barometer n a barometer that measures air pressure by its effect on the flexible lid of a box containing a partial vacuum.

anesthesia n a loss of sensation or feeling in the whole or part of the body so that surgery can be performed without pain.—also (Brit) **anaesthesia.**

anesthesiology n the study and application of anesthetics.—also (Brit) **anaesthesiology.**—**anesthesiologist, anesthesiologist** n.

anesthetic n a drug, gas, etc used to produce anesthesia, as before surgery. * adj of or producing anesthesia.—also (Brit) **anaesthetic.**

anesthetist n a doctor who is medically specialized in the administration of anesthetics.—also (Brit) **anaesthetist**

anesthetize vt to administer an anesthetic.—also (Brit) **anaesthetize.**—**anesthetization, anaesthetization** n.

anestrus n (biol) the period of sexual inactivity in mammals between periods of estrus.—also (Brit) **anoestrus.**—**anestrous, anoestrous** adj.

aneuploidy n (med) a condition in which an abnormal number of chromosomes are present in the cells of an affected individual.

aneurysm, aneurism n (med) a balloon-like swelling in the wall of an artery that occurs when it becomes weakened or damaged in some way.

anew adv afresh; again, once more; in a new way or form.

Anfang n (mus) (German) "the beginning"; Anfangs means "from the beginning."

Anfo abbr = ammonium nitrate and fuel oil.

anfractuous adj winding, intricate.—**anfractuosity** n (pl anfractuosities).

ang. abbr = (chem) angular.

ANG abbr = Air National Guard

angary n a belligerent's right to seize and use neutral property, for which it pays indemnity.

angel n messenger from God, usu beneficial, or heavenly being; also 'guardian angel'; a very beautiful or kind person; in art frequently shown in gleaming white, with wings, and sheathed in an other-worldly radiance; (inf) one who gives financial backing to an enterprise.

angel cake n a small round cake with a round fruit on the top.

Angeleno n (pl Angelenos) (inf) an inhabitant of the city of Los Angeles.

angelfish n (pl angelfish, angelfishes) a species of shark with large pectoral fins, which give to it a winged appearance.

angelic, angelical adj belonging to or resembling an angel in nature or function.—**angelically** adv.

angelica n the candied stalks of a fragrant plant used esp in cake decoration.

Angelico n Fra (1400–1455) Dominican monk and Florentine painter of the early Renaissance. His major work is the series of about 50 in his monastery of San Marco, now a museum housing a large collection of his art.

Angelou n Maya [Marguerite Johnson] (1928–) American dramatist, poet, and short-story writer, and author of the autobiographical I Know Why the Caged Bird Sings.

angel shark n a species of shark with large pectoral fins that give it a winged appearance.

Angelus n (RC) a devotional exercise commemorating the Incarnation, during which the Ave Maria is twice repeated, morning, noon, and night; the bell that is rung to announce the time of such devotions.

anger n strong displeasure, often because of opposition, a hurt, etc. * vti to make or become angry.

angina n sharp stabbing pains in the chest, usu caused by angina pectoris.

angina pectoris n a heart disease causing a spasmodic gripping pain in the chest.

angiocardiography n an X-ray examination of the activity of the heart, involving the injecting of a radio-opaque substance.

angiography n an examination of blood vessels using X-rays, made possible by first injecting a radio-opaque substance.

angiology n (anat) the branch of anatomy that deals with the blood vessels and lymphatics.

angioma n (pl angiomas, angiomata) a tumor caused by the enlargement of a blood vessel; a clump of distended blood vessels pushing onto the surface of the brain that may cause epilepsy.—**angiomatous** adj.

angioplasty n a surgical method used to widen or reopen a narrowed or blocked blood vessel or heart valve.

angiosperm n (bot) a plant having its seeds protected by a covering.—**angiospermous** adj.

angitis n a condition in which there is inflammation of the walls of small blood vessels, usu in patches.—also **vasculitis**

Angkor n the capital of the Kampuchian Khmer empire, established in the 9th century AD.

anglaise n (mus) (French) short for danse anglaise or "English dance," i.e., a lively dance in quick time, such as a hornpipe.

angle[1] n a corner; the point from which two lines or planes extend or diverge; a specific viewpoint; an individual method or approach (e.g., to a problem). * vt to bend at an angle; to move or place at an angle; to present information, news, etc from a particular point of view.

angle[2] vi to fish with a hook and line; to use hints or artifice to get something.

angle bracket n either of the punctuation marks < >.

angle of declination n the angle between true north and the direction of the magnetic meridian.

angle of inclination n the angle between two planes.

angler n one who fishes with rod and line; the name of a fish with filamentary appendage that attracts smaller fish on which it feeds.

Angles n a Germanic people that in archeological terms have been subsumed by the Anglo-Saxons.

Anglican adj belonging to or of the Church of England and other churches in communion with it. * n a member of the Anglican Church; a ritualist.

Anglican chant n (mus) a characteristically English way of setting to music prose, psalms and canticles, in which the number of syllables per line can vary. In many respects, it is a simple form of Gregorian chant.

Anglicanism n the principles and ritual of the Anglican Church.

Anglicism n a form of speech, an English idiom; a principle or mannerism peculiar to England.

anglicize vt to make or to render into English; to accord with English manners and customs.—**anglicization** n.

angling n the art or act of fishing with rod and line.

Anglo- prefix English, British.

Anglo-American adj pertaining to England and the United States conjointly, as to commerce or population. * n an American citizen of English descent.

Anglo-Australian Observatory n an observatory, jointly funded by Britain and Australia, situated on a mountain top at Siding Spring, north of Canberra.

Anglo-Australian Telescope n a telescope 3.9 meters (approx. 13 feet) in diameter, in operation since 1975 with particularly well-formed optical and guidance systems.

Anglo-Catholic adj Catholic according to the teachings and ritual of the English Church; in the strictest Catholic sense; high church. * n a member of the English Church, popularly a ritualist or high churchman, who repudiates the term "Protestant."

Anglo-Catholicism *n* the principles and ritual of the Anglican Church interpreted in their strictest Catholic sense.

Anglo-French *adj* English and French. * *n* the old French language introduced into England by the Normans.

Anglo-Indian *adj* pertaining to England and India conjointly. * *n* one of English descent born or residing in India.

Anglo-Irish *adj* pertaining to England and Ireland, or to the English settled in Ireland and their descendants; having the father or mother of English or Irish race. * *npl* English born or resident in Ireland.

Anglomania *n* a predilection carried to excess for everything that is English, in the sense of being peculiar to England.

Anglo-Norman *adj* common to England and Normandy. * *n* one of the Norman settlers in England after the Conquest (AD 1066).

Anglophile *n* a person who loves England or anything English.—*also* **Anglophil**.

Anglophobe *n* one who hates or fears England and the English.

Anglophobia *n* an intense aversion or fear of everything English.—**Anglophobe** *n*.

Anglophone, anglophone *adj* of, pertaining to, or being an English-speaking person or population.

Anglo-Saxon *adj* pertaining to the Saxon settlers in England prior to the Conquest, or to their language. * *n* one of the Saxon settlers in England as distinguished from those on the Continent; Old English, the language of the settlers; (*pl*) the English race; a Germanic people, comprising the Angles and Saxons, who settled in England in the 5th century AD.

Anglo-Saxon art *n* a term for works of art produced in England between the 5th century AD and 1066. The major source of surviving artifacts is the 7th-century excavation site at Sutton Hoo, and much of the Anglo-Saxon jewelry collection at the British Museum comes from there.

Angola, People's Republic of *n* a country situated on the Atlantic coast of southern Africa.

angora *n* a long-haired variety of cat, rabbit or goat; fabric made from the hair of angora goats or rabbits.

angostura bark *n* a bitter aromatic bark used for medicinal purposes.

angostura bitters *npl* a bitter flavoring made from the bark of a South American tree.

angry *adj* (**angrier, angriest**) full of anger; inflamed.—**angrily** *adv*.

angry young men *n* a group of English writers of the mid–1950s with leftist sympathies and a hatred of provincialism and intellectual pretentiousness, including Kingsley Amis and John Osborne.

angst *n* a feeling of anxiety, fear or remorse.

angström *n* (*phys*) the unit of measurement, one hundred millionth of a centimeter, formerly used for optical wavelengths, now largely displaced by the vanometer.

Anguilla *n* a British overseas territory, formerly part of St Kitts and Nevis.

anguilliform *adj* shaped like an eel or a serpent.

anguine *adj* snakelike.

anguish *n* agonizing physical or mental distress.

angular *adj* having one or more angles; forming an angle; measured by an angle; stiff and clumsy in manner, thin and bony.

angularity *n* (*pl* **angularities**) the quality of being angular in any sense.

angular measure *n* (*astron*) a mathematical measurement of astronomical distances.

angular momentum *n* (*phys*) a vector property characteristic of the rotatory motion of a body around an axis: the product of the angular velocity and moment of inertia.

angular velocity *n* (*phys*) the rate of rotation of a body measured in radians/second.

angulate *adj* constructed of angles; having the form of an angle.

angulation *n* the exact measurement of angles; an angular shape.

anhydride *n* (*chem*) an oxygen compound formed by substituting an acid radicle for the whole of the hydrogen in one or two molecules of water.

anhydrite *n* anhydrous sulphate of lime.

anhydrous *adj* without water, applied to minerals in which the water of crystallization is not present.

ani *n* (*pl* **anis**) a tropical American bird of the cuckoo family.

Ani *n* (*Egypt*) Egyptian author of the *Maxims of Ani*, a widely copied text of the New Kingdom period, drawing on earlier models, intended to lead the reader towards the harmonious life so much appreciated by the Egyptians.

ANIC *abbr* = Australian National Insect Collection.

aniconic *adj* (*idols*) not of human or animal form.

anil *n* the indigo plant; a dye yielded by it.

anile *adj* resembling an old woman; aged.—**anility** *n*.

aniline *n* a base used in the formation of many rich dyes obtained from coal tar but more extensively from benzole. * *adj* of or pertaining to aniline.

anim. *abbr* (*mus*) (*Italian*) = *animato*, "animated."

anima *n* (*mus*) (*Italian*) literally "soul" or "spirit," as in *con anima*, which means that a piece should be played "with soul" or "with emotion."

animadversion *n* the act of observing; capacity for perception; censure; criticism; stricture.

animadvert *vi* to give the mind to; to pass comment or stricture upon, to criticize.

animal *n* any living organism except a plant or bacterium, typically able to move about; a lower animal as distinguished from man, esp mammals; a brutish or bestial person. * *adj* of or like an animal; bestial; sensual.

animal companion *n* an animal such as a cat or dog kept as a pet.

animalcule, animalculum *n* (*pl* **animalcules, animalcula**) one of a class of minute or microscopic organisms abounding in water and infusions.—**animalcular** *adj*.

animal cult *n* the worship of animals like bulls, rams, crocodiles, ibex and falcons who were all identified with gods, often, as with bulls and rams, with more than one deity. Animal cults existed in cultures such as Indian and Egyptian.

animal husbandry *n* a branch of agriculture concerned with the care and breeding of domestic animals.

animalism *n* the state of being animal, or actuated by animal instincts or appetites; the theory that regards humankind as merely animal; sensuality.—**animalist** *n*.—**animalistic** *adj*.

animality *n* the state or quality of being an animal, or possessing animal characteristics, animal nature.

animalize *vt* to make animal; to impart animal life, form, and attributes; to sensualize or bestialize; to convert into animal substance by assimilation.—**animalization** *n*.

animal kingdom *n* beings endowed with animal life and regarded collectively, one of the three great divisions of nature.

animal liberation *n* freeing animals from captivity and exploitation (e.g., in laboratories) by humans, action esp associated with organizations such as the Animal Liberation Front.

animal magnetism *n* another name for mesmerism; attractiveness, esp to the opposite sex.

animal rights *n* a movement that seeks to extend certain rights, such as freedom from captivity and exploitation by humans, to animals.

animal spirits *npl* vivacity; liveliness of disposition.

animal starch *see* **glycogen**.

animal worship *n* the worship of animals as symbols of deities, as among the ancient Egyptians, Hindus, etc.

animate *vt* to give life to; to liven up; to inspire, encourage. * *adj* alive; lively.

animated *adj* lively, full of spirit.

animated cartoon *n* a film made by photographing a series of drawings, giving the illusion of movement.

animation *n* (*comput*) a fast display of a sequence of images, like a cartoon; the skill of making animated films; liveliness; movement;

animato *adj, adv* (*mus*) (*Italian*) "animated," with vigor.

animator, animater *n* an artist who draws and produces animated cartoons.

animé *n* an amber-colored resin, resembling copal, obtained from a tropical American tree and used in varnish.

animism *n* in primitive religion, the belief that natural effects are due to spirits and that inanimate objects have spirits; the belief in a human apparitional soul, having the form and appearance of the body, existing after death as semi-human.—**animist** *n*.—**animistic** *adj*.

animo *n* (*mus*) (*Italian*) literally "spirit," so *con animo* indicates that a piece should be performed "with spirit."

animosity *n* (*pl* **animosities**) strong dislike; hostility.

animoso *n* (*mus*) (*Italian*) "spirited."

animus *n* an actuating spirit; a bitter or hostile feeling (against); hostility.

ANIN *abbr* = Associated Northern Ireland Newspapers.

anion *n* (*chem*) a negatively charged ion; the element in a body decomposed by voltaic action, which is evolved at the positive pole or anode.—**anionic** *adj*.

anise *n* the common name for a plant (indigenous in Egypt) yielding the seeds used in aniseed.

aniseed *n* the seed of the anise plant, used as a flavoring.

anisette *n* a liqueur prepared from aniseed.

Ankara *n* capital city of Turkey.

ankh *n* an Egyptian cross with a loop or handle at the top, the symbol of life.—*also* **crux ansata**.

ankle *n* the joint between the foot and leg, the part of the leg between the foot and calf.

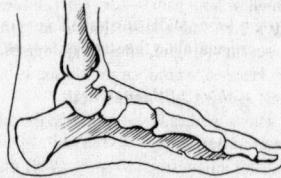

anklebone *n* the talus.

anklet *n* an ornamental chain worn round the ankle.

ankylose *vt* to consolidate or join by bony growth; to stiffen as a joint. * *vi* to grow together; to become stiff.—*also* **anchylose**.

ankylosing spondylitis *n* a rheumatic disease of the spinal column and sacroiliac joints (i.e., those of the sacrum and ilium), causing pain and stiffness in the hip and shoulder. It may result in the spine becoming rigid. *See* **kyphosis**.

ankylosis *n* (*zool*) the joining or consolidation of parts formerly or normally separate or movable by means of bony growth; (*med*) the stiffening of a joint by fibrous bands or union of bones.—*also* **anchylosis**.—**ankylotic, anchylotic**.

ANL *abbr* = Anti-Nazi League; Argonne National Laboratory; Australian National Line.

ann. *abbr* = (*Latin*) *annales*, "annals"; (*Latin*) *anni*, "years"; (*Latin*) *anno*, "in the year"; annual; annuities; annuity.

ANN *abbr* = Anti-Nuclear Network; Asian-Pacific News Network.

anna *n* an Indian coin, one sixteenth of a rupee.

Anna *n* 1. (*Bible*) (first century) an old widow and prophetess who visited the Temple daily and witnessed the dedication of the infant Jesus. 2. (*d.* 654) king of East Anglia, Britain (*c.*633–654). A devout Christian son of Ine. He was killed in battle fighting Penda of Mercia.

Annaba *n* a city in Algeria.

annals *npl* a written account of events year by year; historical records; periodical reports or records of a society.—**annalist** *n*.—**annalistic** *adj*.

Annapolis *n* the capital city of Maryland, a state of the USA.

Annas *n* (*Bible*) former high priest of the Temple, and father-in-law of Caiaphas. *See also* **Caiaphas**.

annates *npl* (*RC*) the sum paid to the pope by an abbot or bishop on his appointment to a benefice or see and consisting of the first year's revenue of the living, now chiefly supplied by Peter's Pence.

Anne *n* (1665–1714) Queen of England and later Great Britain and Ireland. Reigned from 1702 to 1714. The second daughter of James II, then Duke of York, and Anne Hyde, daughter of the Earl of Clarendon.

Anne, Princess *see* **Elizabeth II**.

Anne *n* **Saint** (first century BC) mother of the Virgin **Mary**; first mentioned in Christian literature in the fourth century AD. Many miracles were attributed to St Anne in the Middle Ages. Her feast day is 26 July.

Anne of Cleves *n* (1515–57) German princess, queen consort of England, 4th wife of Henry VIII. The marriage was annulled after six months.

anneal *vt* to fix by heat; to temper and render malleable; to bake or fuse.—**annealer** *n*.

annealing *n* a process whereby metal or glass is heated to a specific temperature before controlled cooling.

annelid *n* any of a class of invertebrates which includes the worms, whose bodies are composed of numerous segments or ring-like divisions.—**annelidan** *adj*.

annex *n* an extension to a main building; something added, a supplement. * *vt* to attach, esp to something larger; to incorporate into a state the territory of (another state).

annexation *n* the act of annexing; that which is annexed.—**annexational** *adj*.—**annexationism** *n*.—**annexationist** *n*.

Annigoni *n* **Pietro** (1910–88) Italian painter whose realistic and dramatic works reflect the Renaissance techniques that he adopted. He is best known for his portraits, including those of President John Kennedy (1955) and Queen Elizabeth II (1970).

annihilate *vt* to destroy completely; (*inf*) to defeat convincingly, as in an argument.—**annihilable** *adj*.—**annihilative** *adj*.—**annihilator** *n*.

annihilation *n* the act of annihilating; nonexistence.

anniversary *n* (*pl* **anniversaries**) the yearly return of the date of some event; a celebration of this.—*also adj*.

anno Domini *adv* (*abbr* AD) "in the year of our Lord," dating from the birth of Christ. * *n* (*inf*) advancing age.

annot. *abbr* = annotator.

annotate *vti* to provide with explanatory notes.—**annotative** *adj*.—**annotator** *n*.

annotation *n* the act of noting or commenting upon; a note, remark, or criticism made in a book.

announce *vt* to bring to public attention; to give news of the arrival of; to be an announcer for. * *vi* to serve as an announcer.

announcement *n* the act of announcing; that which is announced; a proclamation.

announcer *n* a person who reads the news, etc on the radio or TV.

annoy *vt* to vex, tease, irritate, as by a repeated action.—**annoyingly** *adv*.

annoyance *n* the act of annoying or causing vexation; the state of being annoyed; the thing or act that annoys.

annual *adj* of or measured by a year; yearly; coming every year; living only one year or season. * *n* a plant that lives only one year; a periodical published once a year.—**annually** *adv*.

annual accounts *npl* (*com*) the financial statements of a company or organization that are published annually.

annual general meeting *n* (*abbr* AGM) an annual meeting of the shareholders of a company that must be called to allow the shareholders an opportunity to discuss the annual accounts.

annual percentage rate *n* (*abbr* APR) (*bank*) an interest rate expressed as the rate for the year.

annual ring *n* a concentric layer of wood produced by woody plants throughout a season of growth.

annuitant *n* one who is in receipt of, or is entitled to receive, an annuity.

annuity *n* a contract between an individual and an insurance company in which the individual pays a premium to the company and the company in return pays him or her an agreed sum of money at regular, periodic intervals for the rest of his or her life or for an agreed, specified length of time; the payment made on the basis of such a contract.

annul *vt* (**annulling, annulled**) to do away with; to deprive of legal force, nullify.

annular *adj* ring-like; in the form of a ring or annulus. * *n* (*astron*) the ring of light surrounding the moon's body in an annular eclipse of the sun; (*archit*) a ring-shaped vault or passageway.

annulate *adj* ringed; having ring-like bands or circles.

annulation *n* a ring-like formation.

annulet *n* a small ring; (*archit*) a small fillet encircling a column.

annulment *n* the act of reducing to nothing; abolition; invalidation.

annulose *adj* composed of a succession of rings; segmented.

annulus *n* (*pl* **annuli, annuluses**) a ringlike part, structure, figure or marking.

annunciate *vt* to make known officially or publicly; to announce, proclaim.—**annunciation** *n*.—**annunciative, annunciatory** *adj*.

Annunciation *n* (*Bible*) the intimation of the Incarnation made by the angel Gabriel to the Virgin Mary (Luke 1:28–33); the Church festival (Lady Day, 25 Mar) commemorating this.

annunciator *n* a signaling apparatus; an indicator connected with bells and telephones, to show where attendance is required.

Annw *n* (*Welsh Celtic myth*) Annw was the Otherworld realm ruled over by Arawn.

anode *n* (*elect*) the positive electrode by which electrons enter an electric circuit.

anodize *vt* to electrolytically subject (a metal) to a protective oxide coat.

anodizing *n* the process of depositing a coat of oxide on the surface of a metal (often aluminum) in electrolysis.

anodyne *n* (*med*) a drug that relieves pain; anything that relieves pain or soothes.

anoint *vt* to pour oil on the head or body, usu in a sacred ceremony.—**anointment** *n*.

anole *n* any of various tropical New World lizards.

anomalistic month *n* (*astron*) the interval of 27.555 days between two successive passages of the Moon in its orbit round the Earth through perigee.

anomalistic year *n* (*astron*) the interval of 365.26 mean solar days between two successive passages of the Sun in its apparent motion through perigee.

anomalous *adj* deviating from the common order, abnormal.

anomaly[1] *n* (*pl* **anomalies**) abnormality; anything inconsistent or odd.—**annomalistic** *adj*.—**anomalistically** *adv*.

anomaly[2] *n* (*astron*) one of three angles used in describing the orbit of a body in an ellipse.

anon *adv* soon; at another time; * *abbr* (*arch*) = anonymous.

anonym *n* an unnamed person; an assumed name.

anonymous *adj* having or providing no name; written or provided by an unnamed person; lacking individuality.—**anonymity** *n*.—**anonymously** *adv*.

anonymous FTP site or **directory** *n* (*comput*) holds files that anyone can download. *See* **FTP**.

anopheles *n* (*pl* **anopheles**) any of a genus of mosquitos, which transmits the microbe of malaria.

anorak *n* (*Brit*) a parka, waterproof jacket with a hood; (*sl Brit*) an unfashionable and obsessive person.

anorexia *n* loss of appetite.—**anorexic** *adj*.

anorexia nervosa *n* the psychological condition causing fear of becoming overweight and reluctance to eat even to the point of starvation and death.

anosmia *n* the inability to smell.—**anosmatic, anosmic** *adj*.

another *adj, pron* a different or distinct (thing or person); an additional one of the same kind; some other.

Anouilh *n* **Jean** (1910–87) French dramatist whose plays include *The Waltz of the Toreadors* and *Beckett*.

anovulatory bleeding *n* bleeding from the vagina without ovulation.

anoxia *n* a condition in which the body tissues do not receive sufficient oxygen.—**anoxic** *adj*.

ANS *abbr* = American Name Society; Army Nursing Service; Australian Numismatic Society; autonomic nervous system.

ans. *abbr* = answer; answered.

ansa lunata *n* a type of handle on a cup or bowl. The top is similar to a capital T but the arms are curved as in a crescent.

ansate *adj* with a handle, as a vase.

Anschluss *n* the union of Nazi Germany with Austria in 1938; the annexation of one territory by another for the benefit of the more powerful.

Anselm *n* **Saint** (1033–1109) Italian Benedictine monk; born at Aosta; wrote a treatise on the Incarnation, *Cur Deus Homo*. Buried in Canterbury, England. His feast day is April 21.

anserine, anserous *adj* of, relating to or resembling a goose; stupid as a goose.

ANSI *see* **American National Standards Institute**.

ANSM *abbr* = Former award of Associate of the Northern School of Music.— *see* **GNSM**.

answer *n* a spoken or written reply or response; the solution to a problem; a reaction, response; (*mus*) the second entry of the main subject (theme) of a fugue which is played a fifth higher or lower than the first entry. In a *real answer,* the subject and answer are identical; in a *tonal answer,* the intervals in the answer are changed. * *vt* to speak or write in reply; to satisfy or correspond to (e.g., a specific need); to justify, offer a refutation of. * *vi* to reply; to act in response (to); to be responsible (for); to conform (to).

answerable *adj* capable of being refuted; (*with* **for** *or* **to**) responsible, accountable.—**answerability** *n*.—**answerableness** *n*.

answering machine *n* an apparatus that records incoming telephone calls.

ant *n* any of a family of small, generally wingless insects of many species, all of which form and live in highly organized groups.

ant. *abbr* = antiquarian; antiquities; antonym.

-ant *adj suffix* as in *repentant*. * *n suffix* denoting agent, as in *celebrant*.

anta *n* (*pl* **antae**) (*archit*) a square pilaster at either corner of a building, or at either side of a door.

antacid *n* a substance that counters excessive acidity.

Antaeus *n* (*Greek myth*) the giant son of Poseidon and Ge, who was invincible so long as he was in contact with the earth. Heracles grasped him in his arms and stifled him suspended in the air, thus preventing him from touching the earth.

antagonism *n* antipathy, hostility; an opposing force, principle, etc.

antagonist *n* an adversary; an opponent.

antagonistic *adj* acting in opposition; opposed.—**antagonistically** *adv*.

antagonistic action *n* (*med*) an action in which systems or processes act against each other so that the activity of one reduces that of the other.

antagonize *vt* to arouse opposition in.—**antagonization** *n*.

antalkali *n* (*pl* **antalkalis, antalkalies**) a substance that counteracts the presence of alkali in the system; an acid.—**antalkaline** *adj, n*.

Antananarivo *n* capital city of Madagascar.

Antarctic *adj* of the South Pole or its surroundings. * *n* the regions south of the Antarctic circle, 66.6°S; the Antarctic Ocean.

Antarctica *n* the land mass within the Antarctic circle.

Antarctic convergence *n* the zone around Antarctica where cold, heavy seas sink below warmer waters to the north.

Antares *or* **Alpha Scorpii** *n* (*astron*) a variable binary star of the first magnitude, the brightest in the constellation Scorpius.

ant bear *n* the aardvark.

ant bird *n* one of an extensive group of South American birds.

ant cow *n* an aphid or similar insect collected by ants for the sweet secretion in its body.

ante *n* a player's stake in poker; (*inf*) money contributed as a share in a joint project.

ante- *prefix* in front of; earlier than.

anteater *n* an ant-eating animal, as the pangolin.

ante-bellum *adj* of the period prior to a war.

antecede *n* to precede or go before in time or space.

antecedence *n* precedence; going before; priority.

antecedent *adj* prior in time, previous. * *n* a preceding event or happening; (*pl*) ancestry; (*pl*) the previous events of a person's life.

antechamber *n* an anteroom.

antechurch *n* (*archit*) an extension or outer part of the west end of a church or chapel.

antecourt *n* (*archit*) an outer court before the main court of a great mansion.

antedate *vt* to carry back to an earlier period; to anticipate. * *n* a date esp on a document earlier than the date on which it was drawn up.

antediluvian *adj* of or pertaining to the world before the Flood; belonging to very ancient times; antiquated, primitive. * *n* one who lived before the Flood; an old-fashioned person.

antefix *n* (*pl* **antefixes** *or* **antefixa**) (*archit*) decorative ornamental tile concealing the edges of roof tiles, situated above the eaves.

antelope *n* (*pl* **antelopes, antelope**) any of the family of fast-running and graceful deer-like animals of Africa and Asia.

antemeridian *adj* before noon.

ante meridiem *n* the period between midnight and noon. * *abbr* a.m.

antenatal *see* **pre-natal**.

antenna *n* (*pl* **antennae**) either of a pair of feelers on the head of an insect, crab, etc; a metal device for transmitting and receiving radio waves.

antennule *n* a little antenna.

Antenor *n* (*Greek myth*) a Trojan hero who advised Helen to return to Menelaus.

antependium *n* (*pl* **antependia**) a covering for the front of an altar.

antepenult *n* the last but two, usu of syllables.

antepenultimate *adj* pertaining to the last but two. * *n* that which is last but two, antepenult.

Antequera *n* a town in Southern Spain famous for three chambered tombs from the Copper Age.

anterior *adj* a term meaning situated towards the front, the opposite of posterior; earlier; previous.

anteroom *n* (*archit*) a small room forming an outer chamber to a more important room within a mansion.

Anteros *n* (*Greek myth*) the god of mutual love; the enemy of love, the god of antipathy.

Antheil *n* **George** (1900–59) American composer and pianist of Polish descent who gained notoriety by incorporating the sounds of motor horns, door bells and airplane engines in some of his compositions, most notably his *Ballet mécanique*, first performed in Paris in 1926.

anthelion *n* (*pl* **anthelia**) (*astron*) a luminous halo, opposite the sun, formed around the shadow of the head of the observer, as projected on a cloud or fog bank.

anthem *n* (*mus*) a religious choral song; a song of praise or devotion, as to a nation; the Anglican equivalent to the Roman Catholic motet.

anther *n* the part of a flower's stamen containing pollen.—**antheral** *adj*.

anthill *n* a mound thrown up by ants or termites in digging their nests.

anthologize *vt* to compile or include in an anthology.

anthology *n* (*pl* **anthologies**) a collection of poetry or prose.—**anthological** *adj*.—**anthologist** *n*.

Anthony *n* **Susan Bromwell** (1820–1906) American women's suffrage leader and anti-slavery campaigner; also founder of the National American Woman Suffrage Association (1869) and the International Woman Suffrage Alliance (1904).

anthozoan *n* any of a class of radiated soft marine zoophytes, which includes the sea anemones, corals, etc.—*also* **actinozoan**.

anthracene *n* a complex hydrocarbon obtained from coal tar, the source of a red dye.

anthracite *n* a hard coal that gives off a lot of heat and little smoke.—**anthracitic** *adj*.

anthrax *n* (*pl* **anthraces**) a contagious bacterial disease of cattle and sheep, etc that can be transmitted to people.

anthrop. *or* **anthropol.** *abbr* = anthropological; anthropology.

anthropic principle *n* (*astron*) the idea that for the universe to take the form it has and provide a home for intelligent life to evolve, there is very little latitude possible in the values of many fundamental constants.

anthropo- *prefix* man.

anthropocentric *adj* centering in man.—**anthropocentrism** *n*.

anthropoid *adj* resembling man. * *n* one of the higher apes resembling man.—**anthropoidal** *adj*.

anthropology *n* the scientific study of human beings, their origins, distribution, physical attributes and culture.—**anthropological** *adj*.—**anthropologist** *n*.

anthropometry *n* the measurement of the human body; the branch of anthropology relating to such measurement of persons at various ages and in different tribes, races, occupations, etc.—**anthropometric, anthropometrical** *adj*.—**anthropometrist** *n*.

anthropomorphism *n* the ascription of human behavior to other animals or to things.—**anthropomorphic** *adj*.—**anthropomorphist** *n*.

anthropomorphize *vt* to invest with human qualities.

anthropomorphous *adj* in the form of a human being.

anthropophagi *npl* (*sing* **anthropophagus**) cannibals, men-eaters.

Anti *n* Egyptian falcon-god, associated with war, worshipped in Upper Egypt, with his cult center at Deir-el-Gebrawi.

anti- *prefix* opposed to; against.

anti-aircraft *adj* for use against aircraft.

anti-aliasing *n* (*comput*) the process whereby the jagged appearance of a sloping line in a bit-mapped image is made smooth. *See* **dither** and **jaggies**.

antiar *n* the upas tree of Java; a poison obtained from one species of it.

antiballistic missile *n* a defensive missile used to destroy a ballistic missile in flight.

antibiotic *n* (*med*) a substance, derived from a microorganism, that kills or inhibits the multiplication of other microorganisms, usu bacteria.

antibody *n* (*pl* **antibodies**) a protein produced by an organism in response to the action of a foreign body, such as the toxin of a parasite, that neutralizes its effects.

antic *n* a ludicrous action intended to amuse.

Antichrist *n* (*Bible*) an opponent of Christ, esp the great personal opponent expected to appear before the end of the world (1 John 2:22).

Antichristian *n* one who is an opponent of the Christian religion. * *adj* pertaining to Antichrist; opposed to the Christian religion.

anticipant *adj* operating beforehand. * *n* one who looks forward.

anticipate *vt* to give prior thought and attention to; to use, spend, act on in advance; to foresee and take action to thwart another; to expect. * *vi* to speak, act, before the appropriate time.

anticipation *n* the act of taking beforehand; expectation; hope; preconception; (*mus*) the sounding of a note (or notes) of a chord before the rest of the chord is played.

anticlastic *adj* (*archit*) of a surface that curves in opposite ways (convex and concave) and in different directions through any given point.

anticlerical *adj* opposed to the power of the clergy or church, esp in secular affairs. * *n* a person opposed to the power of the church.—**anticlericalism** *n*.

anticlimax *n* a sudden drop from the important to the trivial; an ending to a story or series of events that disappoints one's expectations.—**anticlimactic** *adj*.—**anticlimactically** *adv*.

anticlinal *adj* (*strata*) inclining or folding with the convex side upwards; inclined in opposite directions.

anticlockwise *see* **counterclockwise**.

anticoagulant *n* a drug that delays or tends to prevent blood clotting.

anticonvulsant *n* a drug that decreases or suppresses convulsions, used to reduce the severity of epileptic fits.

anticyclone *n* a body of air rotating about an area of high atmospheric pressure.—**anticyclonic** *adj*.

antidepressant *n* a drug that is administered in order to alleviate depression and its accompanying symptoms.

antidiuretic hormone *see* **vasopressin**.

antidote *n* a substance that counteracts the effect of a particular poison.

antiemetic *n* a drug taken to prevent vomiting, such as is used for travel sickness.

antifebrile *adj* capable of allaying fever. * *n* a medicine for allaying fever.

antifreeze *n* a substance used, as in a car radiator, to prevent freezing up.

antifungal *adj* fungicidal.

antigen *n* a substance introduced into the blood to stimulate production of antibodies; any substance that the body sees as being foreign.—**antigenic** *adj*.—**antigenically** *adv*.

Antigone *n* (*Greek myth*) the daughter of Oedipus and Jocasta, famous for her devotion to her brother Polynices, for burying whom against the decree of King Creon she was killed.

antigravity *n* the effect of decreasing or canceling a gravitational field.

Antigua and Barbuda *n* a tiny state comprising three islands – Antigua, Barbuda and Redonda, an uninhabited rocky islet, located on the eastern side of the Leeward Islands. Formerly under British rule, they became independent in 1981.

antihero *n* (*pl* **antiheroes**) a leading character in a book, film, etc who lacks the conventional heroic attributes.

antihistamine *n* (*med*) any of a group of drugs that inhibit the action of histamines, used in treating allergic conditions.

anti-inflammatory *adj* (*med*) describes anything that reduces inflammation such as antihistamines and non-steroidal anti-inflammatory drugs.

Antilochus *n* (*Greek myth*) a son of Nestor, distinguished among the younger heroes who took part in the Trojan War by beauty, bravery, and speed in running.

anti-lock *adj* denoting a system of braking in a motor vehicle that allows sudden braking without lacking of the wheels.

antilog *n* an antilogarithm.

antilogarithm *n* a number which a logarithm represents.—**antilogarithmic** *adj*.

antilogy *n* (*pl* **antilogies**) a contradiction.

antimacassar *n* an ornamental covering for chairbacks, etc, to prevent their being soiled (formerly by macassar oil, once used as a pomade).

antimasque *n* a droll or grotesque interlude between parts of a more serious nature in a masque.

antimatter *n* a form of matter in which electrical charge or other property of each fundamental particle is the reverse of the property of usual matter in our universe.

antimere *n* (*biol*) one of two or more corresponding parts or organs on opposite sides of animals.—**antimeric** *adj*.—**antimerism** *n*.

antimeridian *n* any meridian that is 180° of longitude from any other meridian.

antimetabolite *n* (*med*) one of a group of drugs, used particularly in the treatment of certain cancers, that mimic substances (metabolites) present in the cells.

antimonic, antimonous *adj* relating to, composed of, or obtained from antimony.

antimony *n* (*pl* **antimonies**) a brittle metallic element used in making alloys.—**antimonial** *adj, n*.

antinomy *n* (*pl* **antinomies**) (*law*) contradiction in law or authorities or conclusions; the opposition of one law or part of a law to another.—**antinomic** *adj*.—**antinomically** *adv*.

antinovel *n* a novel in which traditional or conventional novelistic elements are rejected.

Antioch *n* Pisidian Antioch, a town in the Roman province of Galatia visited by Paul and Barnabas on their first journey.

Antioch *n* third city of the Roman Empire and capital of the province of Syria; one of the first great centers of the Christian Church. *See also* **Syria**.

Antiope *n* (*Greek myth*) the mother of the twins, Amphion and Zethus, by Zeus, who, afraid of her father's anger, fled from Thebes and went to Sicyon, where she married King Epopeus.

antioxidant *n* a compound that inhibits oxidation.

antiparallel *adj* running parallel, but in an opposite direction. * *n* one of two or more lines making equal angles with two other lines, but in contrary order.

antiparticle *n* an elementary particle with the same mass as its corresponding particle but having an equal and opposite electric charge, resulting in mutual destruction when brought into contact.

Antipas, Herod *n* ruled from 4 BC to 39 AD. *See also* **Herod**.

antipathetic, antipathetical *adj* possessing or causing a natural antipathy or aversion (to).—**antipathetically** *adv*.

antipathy *n* (*pl* **antipathies**) a fixed dislike; aversion; an object of this.

antiperiodic *adj* (*med*) preventive of a return in periodic or intermittent disease. * *n* a medicine for periodic diseases.

antipersonnel *adj* (*mil*) (of a weapon) used to destroy people rather than objects.

antiperspirant *n* a substance used to stem excessive perspiration.

antiphlogistic *adj* (*med*) efficacious in counteracting fever or inflammation. * *n* any remedy that checks inflammatory symptoms.

antiphon *n* a verse or sentence sung by one choir in response to another, as in Roman Catholic church services; an anthem.

antiphonal *adj* characterized by responsive singing; sung alternately. * *n* a collection of antiphons.—**antiphonally** *adv*.

antiphonary *n* (*pl* **antiphonaries**) a book of responses used in church services; an antiphonal. * *adj* antiphonal or responsive.

antiphony *n* (*pl* **antiphonies**) the alternate or responsive rendering of psalms or chants by a dual choir; a musical setting of sacred verses arranged for alternate singing.

antiphrasis *n* (*rhetoric*) the use of words in a sense opposite to the true one.

antipodes *npl* the regions on the earth's surface opposite each other; (*with cap preceded by* **the**) Australia and New Zealand.—**antipodean** *adj*.

antipope *n* one who usurps or is elected to the papal office in opposition to a pope canonically elected; a rival pope.

antipyretic *adj* (*med*) preventive of, or remedial to fever. * *n* a fever-allaying drug.—**antipyresis** *n*.

antipyrine *n* (*med*) a drug obtained from coal tar and used to relieve neuralgia, etc, and to reduce heat in fevers.

antiq. *abbr* = antiquarian; antiquities.

antiquarian *adj* connected with the study of antiquities. * *n* an antiquary.

antiquary *n* (*pl* **antiquaries**) a person who studies or collects antiquities.

antiquated *adj* old-fashioned; obsolete.

antique *adj* from the distant past; old-fashioned. * *n* a relic of the distant past; a piece of furniture, pottery, etc dating from an earlier historical period and sought after by collectors.

antiquity *n* (*pl* **antiquities**) the far distant past, esp before the Middle Ages; (*pl*) relics dating from the far distant past.

antirrhinum *n* snapdragon.

antisabbatarian *adj* opposed to the observance of the Sabbath.—*also n*.

antiscorbutic *n* a remedy against scurvy.—*also adj*.

anti-Semite *n* one who is hostile toward or discriminates against Jews as a religious or racial group.—**anti-Semitic** *adj*.—**anti-Semitism** *n*.

antiseptic *n* a substance that destroys or prevents the growth of disease-producing microorganisms. * *adj* destroying harmful organisms; very clean; (*inf*) unexciting.—**antiseptically** *adv*.

antiserum *n* (*pl* **antiserums, antisera**) (*med*) a serum injected against a particular disease or toxin that contains a high concentration of antibodies against a particular antigen.

antisocial *adj* avoiding the company of other people, unsocial; contrary to the interests of society in general.

antispasmodic *adj* counteractive to or curative of spasms. * *n* a medicine having such an effect.

antistatic *adj* counteracting the effects of static electricity.

antistrophe *n* a stanza or movement of a Greek chorus alternating with the strophe, sung in moving to the right.—**antistrophic** *adj*.

antithesis *n* (*pl* **antitheses**) a contrast or opposition, as of ideas; the exact opposite.—**antithetical, antithetic** *adj*.

antitoxin *n* a substance that acts against a specific toxin in the body; a serum containing an antitoxin, injected into a person to prevent disease.—**antitoxic** *adj*.

antitrade *n* a tropical wind blowing steadily in an opposite direction to the trade wind.

antitrust *adj* (*law*) restricting or opposing the activities of cartels and monopolies.

antitussive *adj* (*med*) able to relieve coughing.

antitype *n* that which a type or symbol stands for; that which preceded the type and of which the type is the representation.

antivenin *n* (*med*) an antidote to snake poison.

anti-virus program *n* (*comput*) a program that checks for the existence of a virus and informs the user if there is one present on the computer's secondary storage.

antivivisectionist *n* a person who opposes scientific experimentation on live animals.

antler *n* the branched horn of a deer or related animal.—**antlered** *adj*.

antler sleeve *n* a piece of antler from a deer used in an axe. It had a stone axe head inserted at one end and the other end attached to a wooden handle.

antlion *n* a neuropterous insect whose larva constructs a pitfall for ants and other insects.

Antoine *n* **Jacques-Denis** (*b*. 1733) French architect. His notable works include the Mint, Paris.

Antonelli *n* **Alessandro** (1798–1888) Italian architect. His notable works include Novara Cathedral.

Antonello da Messina *n* (*c*.1430–79) Sicilian painter, whose work helped to popularize oil painting in Italy. A good example of this combination is his *Crucifixion* in London's National Gallery.

Antonine Wall *n* a defensive structure constructed in 143 AD which stretched about 40 miles from the Firth of Forth to the Firth of Clyde in Scotland.

Antonini *n* **Carlo** publisher of the *Manual of Various Ornament* from 1777.

Antonioni, Michelangelo (1912–) Italian film director. His films include *L'Avventura* and *Blow-Up*.

antonomasia *n* (*rhetoric*) the use of an attribute or epithet, or style of dignity or office, in place of the proper noun, e.g., "the Stagirite" for Aristotle, or the reverse, of a proper noun for a common noun, e.g., "some mute inglorious Milton".—**antonomastic** *adj*.—**antonomastically** *adv*.

Antony *n* **Mark [Marcus Antonius]** (*c*. 83–30 BC) Roman soldier who fought with Julius Caesar in the Gallic wars. He deserted his wife for the Egyptian queen, Cleopatra.

Antony of Padua *n* **Saint** (1195–1231) born at Lisbon in Portugal; canonized by Pope Gregory IX in 1232; patron saint of the lower orders of animals. He was first an Augustinian monk, but later became one of the order of the Franciscans' foremost propagators. His feast day is 13 June.

Antony the Great n **Saint** (251–356) Egyptian hermit said to be the founder of the concept of the monastic community as a way of life. His feast day is 17 January.

antonym n a word that has the opposite meaning to another.

antrum n (pl **antra**) (anat) a cavity, esp in the upper jawbone.

Antwerp n a city in Belgium.

Anzti n ancient Egyptian Delta god whose cult center was at Busiris. Uniquely among nome deities, he was represented in human form, bearing the crook of a shepherd and the whip of a cowherd.

Anubis n a god of ancient Egypt that guarded tombs and the underworld. It had the head of a jackal.

anuresis n (med) the inability to urinate.

anuria n (med) a failure of the kidneys to produce urine.

anurous adj (zool) tailless.

anus n the excretory opening of the alimentary canal.

anvil n the heavy iron block on which metal objects are shaped with a hammer; (mus) a percussion instrument consisting of steel bars that are struck with a wooden or metal mallet.

anxiety n (pl **anxieties**) the condition of being anxious; eagerness, concern; a cause of worry.

anxious adj worried; uneasy; eagerly wishing; causing anxiety.—**anxiously** adv.—**anxiousness** n.

any adj one out of many, some; every.

anybody pron any person; an important person.

anyhow adv in any way whatever; in any case.

any more, anymore adv now; nowadays.

anyone pron any person; anybody.

anything pron any object, event, fact, etc. * n a thing, no matter what kind.

anyway adv in any manner; at any rate; haphazardly.

anywhere adv in, at, or to any place.

ANZA abbr = Association of New Zealand Advertisers.

Anzac or **ANZAC** abbr = Australian and New Zealand Army Corps. * n a member of this corps.—also adj.

ANZUS abbr = Australia, New Zealand, United States Security Treaty.

a/o, AO abbr = account of.

aO abbr (German) = an der Oder, "on the Oder," for places in Germany near this river.

AO abbr = Aide Olympique; Association of Optometrists; Army Order.

AOA abbr = Administration on Aging; Ambulance Officers' Association; American Ontoanalytic Association; Association of Official Architects.

AOB abbr = Association of Ballrooms; Association Ornithologique de Belgique; any other business.

Aobh n (Irish Celtic myth) the daughter of Bodb Dearg and the wife of Lir. She bore him four children. On her death, Lir married her sister, **Aoife**[1].

AOC abbr = Air Officer Commanding; (French) appellation d'origine contrôlée, "regulated naming," used in the origin of wines; Army Ordnance Corps; (EU) Associated Overseas Countries; Association of Old Crows.

AOCB abbr = any other competent business.

AOCI abbr = Airport Operators Council International.

AOC-in-C abbr = Air Officer Commander-in-Chief.

AOCP abbr = Associated Owners of City Properties.

AOD abbr = Ancient Order of Druids; Army Ordnance Department.

AOD abbr = Army Ordnance Department.

AOF abbr = Ancient Order of Foresters; Australian Orchid Foundation.

Aoife n (Irish Celtic myth) 1. the sister of Aobh and the second wife of Lir. She was so jealous of Lir's four she turned them into swans for 900 years. 2. or **Aife** the great rival of Scathach who taught Cuchulainn war skills. While studying with Scathach, Cuchulainn defeated Aoife in battle. Later he had an affair with her, the result of the union being a son, Connlai.

A-OK, A-Okay adj working perfectly; excellent.

AOL abbr (trademark) = America On-line.

AONB abbr = Area of Outstanding Natural Beauty.

AOPA abbr = Aircraft Owners and Pilots Association.

aor. abbr = aorist.

aorist n (gram) an indeterminate past tense of the verb expressing completed action. * adj indefinite; pertaining to the aorist tense.—**aoristic** adj.—**aoristically** adv.

aorta n (pl **aortas, aortae**) (anat) the main artery that carries blood from the heart to be distributed through the body.—**aortic, aortal** adj.

aortic stenosis n a narrowing of the opening of the aortic valve, resulting in the obstruction of blood flow from the left ventricle to the aorta.

AOSE abbr = American Order of Stationary Engineers.

AOSS abbr (Latin) = Americanae Orientalis Societatis Socius, "Fellow of the American Oriental Society."

AOU abbr = American Ornithologists' Union.

aoudad n a wild sheep-like animal of North Africa, somewhat resembling the chamois.

ap abbr = additional premium; (med) (Latin) ante prandium, "before meals."

ap. abbr (Latin) = apud, "in the works of."

a.p. abbr = assessment paid; author's proof.

A/P abbr = authority to pay.

Ap. abbr = April.

AP abbr = (mil) airplane; Associated Press; anti-personnel; armor-piercing.

ap- prefix the form of ad- before p.

APA abbr = Airhawk Pilots Association; Aluminum Prefabs Association; American Philological Association; American Protective Association; Army Parachute Association; Association for the Prevention of Addiction; Association of Pediatric Anesthetists; Association of Piping Adjudicators; Association of Preventive Medicine; Association of Professional Astrologers; Association of Public Analysts; Association of Publishing Agencies; Australian Physiotherapy Association.

apace adv at a swift pace.

apache n a Parisian street ruffian, a hooligan.

Apache n (pl **Apaches, Apache**) a tribe of North American Indians.

APACS abbr = Association for Payment Clearing Services.

apagoge n (logic) the establishing of a proposition by demonstrating the untenability of its opposite.—**apagogic, apagogical** adj.—**apagogically** adv.

apanage see **appanage**.

apart adv at a distance, separately, aside; into two or more pieces.

apartheid n a policy of racial segregation implemented in South Africa.

apartment n a room or set of rooms in a building.

apathetic adj devoid of or insensible to feeling or emotion.—**apathetically** adv.

apathy n lack of feeling; lack of concern, indifference.—**apathetic** adj.—**apathetically** adv.

apatite n a crystalline phosphate of lime.

APC abbr = (mil) armored personnel carrier; Army Pay Corps; (med) aspirin, phenacetin and caffeine; automatic public convenience; automatic phase control.

APCC abbr = Animal Population Control Clinic.

APD abbr = Airport Passenger Duty.

APD abbr = Army Pay Department.

ape n a chimpanzee, gorilla, orangutan, or gibbon; any monkey; a mimic. * vt to imitate.

apeak adv (naut) nearly vertical in position.

APEC abbr = (Canada) Atlantic Provinces Economic Council; Asia Pacific Economic Cooperation.

Apelles n Greek painter from the 4th century BC and court painter to Philip of Macedon and Alexander the Great.

apeman n (pl **apemen**) an extinct creature supposedly intermediate in development between apes and man.

Apennine adj relating to a Bronze Age culture from the Italian mountains of the same name.

Apennines n (astron) mountains on the Moon.

aperçu n a first view; a rapid survey; a brief outline.

aperient adj gently laxative; opening the bowels. * n a mild laxative medicine.

aperiodic adj without periodicity.—**aperiodically** adv.—**aperiodicity** n.

aperitif, apéritif n an alcoholic drink taken before a meal as an appetizer.

aperto vt (mus) (Italian) "use damper pedal."

aperture n an opening; a hole; a slit; in optical instruments, the (diameter of the) opening allowing or controlling the amount of light or radiation to enter.

aperture synthesis n a technique used chiefly in radio astronomy to obtain the higher resolving power of a large aperture by using small antennae separated by large distances.

apery n (pl **aperies**) mimicry.

apetalous adj without petals or corolla.—**apetaly** n.

apex n (pl **apexes, apices**) the highest point, the tip; the culminating point; the vertex of a triangle; the point on the celestial sphere towards which the Sun, and thus the Solar System, is moving.

Apex abbr (Brit) = Apex Trust for the Advancement of the Employment Prospects of Ex-Offenders; advance purchase excursion (travel tickets).

apex stone n (archit) uppermost stone in a gable end.—also **saddle stone**

apgar score n a method of assessing the health of an infant immediately after birth, carried out at one minute and five minutes after delivery.

APH abbr (med) = antepartum hemorrhage.

aphaeresis see **apheresis**.

aphagia n the inability to swallow.

aphasia n loss of the power of speech or the appropriate use of words due to disease or injury of the brain.—**aphasic** adj.

aphelion n (pl **aphelia**) that point in the orbit of a planet or a comet which is farthest from the sun.

apheliotropic adj (bot) turning from the sun.

apheresis n (pl **aphereses**) (linguistics) the removal of a letter or syllable from the beginning of a word.—also **aphaeresis**.

aphesis n (linguistics) the gradual loss of an unaccented vowel at the beginning of a word, as in "squire" for "esquire".—**aphetic** adj.—**aphetically** adv.

aphid n any of various small insects, such as the greenfly, that suck the juice of plants.

aphis n (pl **aphides**) an aphid.

APHIS abbr = Animal and Plant Health Inspection Service

aphonia, aphony n dumbness; (med) loss of the voice caused by disease or by damage to the larynx, mouth or nerves controlling throat muscles, or may be the result of hysteria.—**aphonic** adj.

aphorism n a brief, wise saying; an adage.—**aphoristic** adj.

aphotic zone n a zone deeper than 635 feet (300 meters) in lakes and oceans where light does not penetrate and photosynthesis, the process whereby plants turn the Sun's energy into food, is impossible.

aphrodisiac adj arousing sexually. * n a food, drug, etc that excites sexual desire.

Aphrodite *n* (*Greek myth*) the goddess of erotic love and marriage, counterpart of the Roman Venus. She was said to have arisen from the sea foam surrounding the severed genitals of Uranus.

aphtha *n* (*pl* **aphthae**) the small round white ulcers infesting the interior of the mouth; thrush.

aphyllous *adj* (*bot*) without leaves.—**aphylly** *n*.

API *abbr* = American Petroleum Institute.

Apia *n* capital city of Western Samoa.

a piacere *adj, adv* (*mus*) (*Italian*) "at pleasure," meaning that the performer of a piece of music is permitted to take a certain amount of liberty, particularly with tempo, while playing it.

apian *adj* of, pertaining to, or like bees.

apiarian *adj* of or relating to beekeeping.

apiarist *n* a beekeeper.

apiary *n* (*pl* **apiaries**) a place with hives where bees are kept.

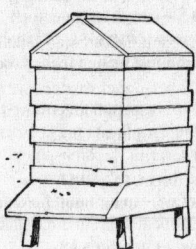

apical *adj* of, pertaining to, belonging to, or at the apex.—**apically** *adv*.

apices *see* **apex**.

apiculate *adj* terminated abruptly by a point, as leaves.

apiculture *n* beekeeping.—**apicultural** *adj*.—**apiculturist** *n*.

apiece *adv* to, by, or for each one.

Apiru *n* tribe or tribes of displaced persons who lived in Egypt during the later New Kingdom, identified by some writers as the exiled Hebrews.

Apis *n* ancient Egyptian bull-headed god, worshipped in Memphis at the Serapeum.

apish *adj* like an ape in manners; foolish; imitative.—**apishness** *n*.

apivorous *adj* feeding on bees.

Apl. *abbr* = April.

APL *abbr* (*comput*) = A Program Language. A high-level programming language designed for handling engineering and mathematical functions and as a notation for communication between mathematicians.

aplacental *adj* without a placenta.

aplanatic *adj* (*phys*) free from, or correcting, spherical or chromatic aberration.—**aplanatically** *adv*.

aplasia *n* a complete or partial failure in the correct development of an organ or tissue.

aplastic *adj* without plasticity; not easily molded.

aplenty *adj* existing in abundance.

aplomb *n* poise; self-possession.

apnea *n* a temporary halt in breathing, common in newborn infants, which may result from a number of different causes.—**apnoeic** *adj*.

apo. *abbr* = apogee.

apo- *prefix* off, from, away; un-; quite.

Apoc. *abbr* = Apocalypse; Apocrypha; Apocryphal.

apocalypse *n* a cataclysmic event, the end of the world; revelation, esp that of St John.

Apocalypse *n* the last book of the New Testament; the revelation of St John.—**apocalyptic** *adj*.—**apocalyptically** *adv*.

apocarpous *adj* (*bot*) having the carpels of the ovary separate or distinct.

apochromat *n* a highly achromatic lens.—**apochromatic** *adj*.

apocopate *vt* to cut off or drop the last letter or syllable of a word.—**apocopation** *n*.

apocope *n* (*linguistics*) the cutting off or deletion of the last letter or syllable of a word.

Apocr. *abbr* = Apocrypha.

apocrine *adj* pertaining to sweat glands that occur in hairy parts of the body.

Apocrypha *npl* (*used as sing*) books of the Old Testament, e.g., Ecclesiasticus, accepted as an authentic part of the Holy Scriptures by the RC Church but not by Protestants; name given to the 14 books not included in the Authorized Version of the Bible because they were "not of divine inspiration."

apocryphal *adj* doubtful; untrue; invented.—**apocryphally** *adv*.

Apocryphal *adj* of the Apocrypha.

apodal *adj* without feet.

apodictic, apodeictic *adj* clearly established, unquestionably true.—**apodictically, apodeictically** *adv*.

apodosis *n* (*pl* **apodoses**) (*gram*) the latter portion, or consequent clause, of a conditional sentence.

apogamy *n* the absence of sexual reproduction; asexual reproduction.—**apogamic** *adj*.—**apogamous** *adj*.

apogee *n* (*astron*) the point at which a satellite orbiting the Earth is at its greatest distance from the Earth.

apolitical *adj* uninterested or uninvolved in politics.

Apollinaire *n* Guillaume (1880–1918) French art critic and writer of great influence, he originated the term surrealism in 1917 in a preface to his play *The Breasts of Tiresias*.

Apollo *n* (*Greek myth*) son of Zeus and Leto. He was skilled in the use of the bow, and his killing of the serpent Python five days after his birth was the first of his many exploits. He was originally the sun-god, but he came to be regarded as the god of song and prophecy, the god that heals suffering and disease, the institutor and guardian of civil and political order, and the founder of cities; (*astron*) an irregularly shaped asteroid with a mean diameter of 0.87 miles, found in 1932; (*astron*) the American Moon-landing project.

Apollodorus *n* 1. a Greek writer who flourished about 140 BC, author of the *Bibliotheca*, a concise account of the mythology of Greece down to the heroic age; 2. an Athenian painter from the 5th century BC. According to Pliny, he was the first artist to depict light and shadow in the modeling of his figures, an important development in art history.

Apollonius of Rhodes *n* a Greek rhetorician and poet, who flourished about 230 BC, author of the *Argonautica*, an epic poem telling the story of the Argonauts' expedition.—*also* **Apollonius Rhodius**.

Apollos *n* (*Bible*) a Jew who spoke in Ephesus of repentance and baptism; later instructed by Aquila and Priscilla; his presence prompted Paul's call for unity in the Christian church. *See also* **Aquila**.

apologetic *adj* expressing an apology; contrite; presented in defense.—**apologetically** *adv*.

apologetics *n* (*used as sing*) the defense and vindication of the principles and laws of Christian belief.

apologia *n* a written defense of one's principles or conduct.

apologist *n* a person who makes an apology; a defender of a cause.

apologize *vi* to make an apology.

apologue *n* a moral fable; a fiction or allegory embodying a moral application, as *Aesop's Fables*.

apology *n* (*pl* **apologies**) an expression of regret for wrongdoing; a defense or justification of one's beliefs, etc; (*with* **for**) a poor substitute.

Apophis *n* Egyptian god who personified the negative force of darkness against the light of Ra, attacking the sun-god's sky-ship during the darkness of night but always repulsed by dawn. Certain Hyksos kings also bore the name.

apophthegm *n* a pithy saying embodying a wholesome truth or precept, a maxim.—*also* **apothegm**.

apophyge *n* (*archit*) the slight concave curve at the end of a column where it joins the astragal at the top and the fillet above the base at the bottom.

apoplectic *adj* of, causing, or exhibiting symptoms of apoplexy; (*inf*) furious.

apoplexy *n* a sudden loss of consciousness and subsequent partial paralysis, usu caused by a broken or blocked artery in the brain.

aport *adv* (*naut*) on or towards the port or left side of a ship.

aposematic *adj* (*coloration*) conspicuous and so serving to warn.

aposiopesis *n* (*pl* **aposiopeses**) (*rhetoric*) a sudden breaking off in speech for effect, e.g., "Bertrand is—what I dare not name."—**aposiopetic** *adj*.

apostasy *n* (*pl* **apostasies**) abandonment of one's religion, principles or political party.

apostate *n* a person who commits apostasy.

apostatize *vi* to abandon one's faith, church or party; to change one's religion for another.

a posteriori *adj* (*logic*) inductively, from effect to cause, founded on observation of facts, effects or consequences.

apostil *n* a marginal note.

apostle *n* one who is sent as a messenger; the first or principal supporter of a new belief or cause.

Apostle *n* one of the 12 disciples of Christ, chosen to be witnesses of his life and work, and some later followers such as Paul.

apostle spoon *n* a spoon having a figure of one of the Apostles at the top of the handle.

Apostles' Creed *n* the shortest of the three creeds, so named as containing a summary of apostolic doctrine.

apostolate *n* the dignity or office of an apostle, now restricted to that of the pope.

apostolic *adj* of or relating to the Apostles or their teachings; of or relating to the pope as successor to the Apostle St Peter.

Apostolic Church, Apostolic See *n* the Christian church as founded and governed by the Apostles on their doctrine and order. The name originally applied to the Churches of Rome, Antioch, Ephesus, Alexandria and Jerusalem.

Apostolic succession *n* the regular and uninterrupted transmission of ministerial authority by bishops from the Apostles.

apostrophe[1] *n* a mark (') showing the omission of letters or figures, also a sign of the possessive case or the plural of letters and figures; a breaking off in speech to appeal to someone dead or absent.—**apostrophic** *adj*.

apostrophe[2] *n* (*rhetoric*) a digression made in a speech or address, esp one directed at a person.

apostrophize *vt* to address by apostrophe; to omit a letter or letters; to mark an omission by the sign ('). * *vi* to make an apostrophe or short digressive address in speaking.

apothecaries' weight *n* a system of weights used for dispensing drugs, comprising the pound (12 oz), the ounce (8 drachms), the drachm (3 scruples), the scruple (20 grains), and the grain.

apothecary *n* (*pl* **apothecaries**) (*arch*) one who prepares and dispenses medicines and drugs, a pharmacist.

apothecium *n* (*pl* **apothecia**) the shield-like receptacle of lichens.—**apothecial** *adj*.

apothegm *see* **apophthegm**.

apotheosis *n* (*pl* **apotheoses**) deification; glorification of a person or thing; the supreme or ideal example.

apotheosize *vt* to exalt to the rank of a god; to deify.

app. *abbr* = apparent; apparently; appended; appendix; appointed; apprentice.

App. *abbr* = Apostles; Appellate.

APPA *abbr* = Aluminum Powder and Paste Association; Aluminum Primary Producers' Association; Antigua Planned Parenthood Association.

appall, appal *vt* (*or* **appalls, appals, appalling, appalled**) to fill with terror or dismay.

appalling *adj* shocking, horrifying.—**appallingly** *adv*.

appanage *n* provision for the younger sons of kings, etc; a perquisite; a dependency; an attribute.—*also* **apanage**.

appar. *abbr* = apparent; apparently.

apparatus *n* (*pl* **apparatus, apparatuses**) the equipment used for a specific task; any complex machine, device, or system.

apparel *n* clothing, dress. * *vt* (**apparelling, apparelled** *or* **appareling, appareled**) to dress; to clothe.

apparent *adj* a descriptive word given to a measurement where full allowance has not been made for all factors capable of influencing the observation; easily seen, evident; seeming, but not real.—**apparently** *adv*.

apparent luminosity *n* (*astron*) the luminosity of a celestial object as it appears from Earth, with no allowance made for reduction in brightness by distance or by light absorption in the interstellar medium.

apparent magnitude *n* (*astron*) the magnitude of a star as it appears from Earth with no allowance made for reductions in brightness by distance or by light absorption in the interstellar medium.

apparent motion *n* (*astron*) the motion that many celestial objects appear to have against the background of the fixed stars when viewed from Earth.

apparent time *n* local time, established from the time when the Sun is at its highest.

apparition *n* an appearance or manifestation, esp something unexpected or unusual; a ghost.

appassionato, appassionata *adj, adv* (*mus*) (*Italian*) "impassioned," hence the title *Sonata appassionata* which was given to Beethoven's Piano Sonata in F Minor (Opus 57).

appeal *vi* (*law*) to take a case to a higher court; to make an earnest request; to refer to a witness or superior authority for vindication, confirmation, etc; to arouse pleasure or sympathy. * *n* (*law*) the referral of a lawsuit to a higher court for rehearing; an earnest call for help; attraction, the power of arousing sympathy; a request for public donations to a charitable cause.—**appealable** *adj*.—**appealer** *n*.—**appealing** *adj*.

appear *vi* to become or be visible; to arrive, come in person; to be published; to present oneself formally (before a court, etc); to seem, give an impression of being.

appearance *n* the act or occasion of appearing; that which appears; external aspect of a thing or person; outward show, semblance.

appease *vt* to pacify; to allay; to conciliate by making concessions.—**appeasement** *n*.

appellant *n* (*law*) a person who makes an appeal to a higher court.

appellate *adj* pertaining to appeals; dealing with appeals. * *n* the person appealed against or called upon to appear.

appellation *n* the name, title or designation by which a person or thing is called or known; the act of appealing.

appellative *n* (*gram*) a common, as distinguished from a proper, name; the designation of a class. * *adj* serving to distinguish, as a name or denomination of a group or class; common, as a noun.

appellee *n* the person appealed against; (*law*) the defendant in an appeal.

appenato *adj, adv* (*mus*) (*Italian*) "with suffering or grief."

append *vt* to attach; to add, esp to the end as a supplement, etc.

appendage *n* something appended; an external organ or part, as a tail.

appendant *adj* attached or annexed; attached in a subordinate capacity to another. * *n* that which is appended or added.

appendectomy, appendicectomy *n* (*pl* **appendicectomies, appendectomies**) *n* (*med*) surgical operation to remove the vermiform appendix that grows from the intestine.

appendicitis *n* (*med*) inflammation of the appendix that grows from the intestine.

appendicle *n* a small appendage.

appendix *n* (*pl* **appendixes, appendices**) a section of supplementary information at the back of a book, etc; (*med*) a blind-ended tube about four inches long that projects from the caecum of the large intestine. *See* **appendicitis**.

apperception *n* (*psychol*) perception with consciousness of self.—**apperceptive** *adj*.

appertain *vi* to belong or pertain to, as by relation or custom.

appetence, appetency *n* (*pl* **appetences, appetencies**) desire, craving; affinity.

appetite *n* sensation of bodily desire, esp for food; (*with* **for**) a strong desire or liking, a craving.

appetizer *n* a food or drink that stimulates the appetite; something that whets one's interest.

appetizing *adj* stimulating the appetite.—**appetizingly** *adv*.

Apphia *n* (*Bible*) a Christian woman of Colossae, probably wife of Philemon. *See also* **Philemon**.

applaud *vt* to show approval, esp by clapping the hands; to praise.

applause *n* approval expressed by clapping; acclamation.

apple *n* a round, firm, fleshy, edible fruit.

apple brandy *n* a liqueur distilled from cider.

applecart *n* **upset the applecart** to spoil one's plans.

Apple Computer, Inc. *trademark* (*comput*) one of the largest and most innovative manufacturers of personal computers (brand name Macintosh) in the world.

Apple desktop bus *trademark* (*comput*) a standard interface for Apple computers that allows connection of input devices such as keyboards, mice, graphics tablets and trackballs to all Macintosh computers.

applejack *n* apple brandy.

apple-pie bed *n* a bed made with the sheets folded so that one's legs cannot get down.

apple-pie order *n* perfect order.

apple sauce *n* a sauce of stewed apples usu served with pork; (*sl*) nonsense, flattery.

AppleShare *trademark* (*comput*) a network operating system that converts an Apple Macintosh computer into a file server for a network.

applet *n* (*comput*) a minor "cross-platform" application or program that runs within an application program commonly written using Java language and can be found on the Internet.

AppleTalk *trademark* (*comput*) a program that connects computers and other hardware such as printers together in a local area network.

Appleton layer *n* the upper layer of the ionosphere, which is approximately 990 feet (300 kilometers) above the Earth's surface.

appliance *n* a device or machine, esp for household use.

applicable *adj* that may be applied; appropriate, relevant (to).—**applicability** *n*.

applicant *n* a person who applies, esp for a job.

application for listing *n* the process by which a company makes an application to a stock exchange so that its securities can be traded on it.

application *n* the act of applying; the use to which something is put; a petition, request; concentration, diligent effort; relevance or practical value; (*law*) an instrument applying for the achievement of some goal.

application program *n* (*comput*) a computer program that performs specific tasks such as letter writing, statistical analysis, design, etc.

applicative *adj* capable of being applied.

applicator *n* a device for applying something.

applicatory *adj* fit to be applied.

applied *adj* practical.

applied arts *npl* art that serves a useful purpose or that ornaments functional objects; often a synonym for design. Subjects included under this term are architecture, interior design, ceramics, furniture, graphics, etc.

appliqué *n* ornamental fabricwork applied to another fabric. * *vt* (**appliquéing, appliquéed**) to decorate with appliqué.

apply *vb* (**applying, applied**) *vt* to bring to bear; to put to practical use; to spread, lay on; to devote (oneself) with close attention. * *vi* to make a formal, esp written, request; to be relevant.

appoggiando *adj, adv* (*mus*) (*Italian*) "leaning"; when applied to musical notes, this implies that they should pass very smoothly from one to the next.

appoggiatura *n* (*pl* **appoggiaturas, appoggiature**) (*mus*) (*Italian*) a grace note, a "leaning" note, immediately preceding a principal note with which it is connected, and taking its time from the latter.

appoint *vt* to fix or decide officially; to select for a job; to prescribe.

appointed *adj* equipped; furnished.

appointee *n* a person appointed.

appointment *n* an appointing; a job or position for which someone has been selected; an arrangement to meet; (*law*) an instrument appointing an individual or a company to perform some task in behalf of another person or company.

apport *n* (*spiritualism*) the act of conjuring up or moving an object; an object so produced or moved.

apportion *vt* to divide into shares; allot.—**apportionable** *adj*.—**apportioner** *n*.—**apportionment** *n*.

appose *vt* to apply; to place opposite or in juxtaposition.

apposite *adj* esp pertinent, appropriate.—**appositely** *adv*.

apposition *n* the act of adding; addition by application, or placing together; (*gram*) the placing of a second noun in the same case in juxtaposition to the first, which it characterizes or explains, as *St Mark, the Evangelist*.—**appositional** *adj*.

appraisal, appraisement *n* the act of appraising or valuing, esp the putting of a price upon with a view to sale; a valuation.

appraise *vt* to estimate the value or quality of.—**appraiser** *n*.

appreciable *adj* capable of being perceived or measured; fairly large.—**appreciably** *adv*.

appreciate *vt* to value highly; to recognize gratefully; to understand, be aware of; to increase the value of. * *vi* to rise in value.

appreciation *n* gratitude, approval; sensitivity to aesthetic values; an assessment or critical evaluation of a person or thing; a favorable review; (*finance*) an increase in value of an asset usu as a result of inflation; an increase in the value of one foreign currency against another or others in a floating exchange system.—**appreciative** *adj*.

apprehend *vt* to arrest, capture; to understand, to perceive.

apprehension *n* anxiety; the act of arresting; understanding; an idea.

apprehensive *adj* uneasy; anxious.—**apprehensively** *adv*.

apprentice *n* one being taught a trade or craft; a novice. * *vt* to take on as an apprentice.—**apprenticeship** *n*.

apprise, apprize *vt* to give notice to; to inform.

approach *vi* to draw nearer. * *vt* to make a proposal to; to set about dealing with; to come near to. * *n* the act of approaching; a means of entering or leaving; a move to establish relations; the final descent of an aircraft.

approachable *adj* within approaching distance; easy to approach; inviting friendship.—**approachability** *n*.—**approachably** *adv*.

approbation *n* formal approval; sanction.

appropriate *adj* fitting, suitable. * *vt* to take for one's own use, esp illegally; (*money, etc*) to set aside for a specific purpose.—**appropriately** *adv*.—**appropriateness** *n*.

appropriation *n* (*com*) an allocation of the net profits of a company in its accounts; the allocation of payments to one particular debt of several debts owed by the same debtor; the act of setting apart or reserving for one's own use; a sum of money set aside for a particular purpose.

approval *n* the act of approving; favorable opinion; official permission.

approve *vt* to express a good opinion of; to authorize. * *vi* (*with* of) to consider to be favorable or satisfactory.

approved deferred share trust *n* a trust fund set up by a company that purchases shares in the company for the benefit of its employees.

approx. *abbr* = approximate; approximately.

approximate *adj* almost exact or correct. * *vt* to come near to; to be almost the same as. * *vi* to come close.—**approximately** *adv*.

approximation *n* a close estimate; a near likeness.

appulse *n* a coming towards; (*astron*) the near approach of a planet to a conjunction with the sun or any fixed star.—**appulsive** *adj*.

appurtenance *n* that which belongs or relates to something else; an adjunct or appendage; that which belongs it, is accessory to; an estate or property.—**appurtenant** *adj, n*.

Apr. *abbr* = April.

APR *abbr* (*bank*) = annual percentage rate.

APRC *abbr* (*Latin*) = *anno post Romam conditam*, "in the year from the founding of Rome."

après-midi d'un faune, Prélude à l' (**Prelude to the Afternoon of a Faun**) *n* (*mus*) an orchestral tone poem by Debussy, written in 1892–94 and first performed in Paris in 1894.

après-ski *n* social activity after skiing.—*also adj*.

apricot *n* a small, oval, orange-pink fruit resembling the plum and peach.

April Fool *n* the victim of a trick played on 1 April, **April Fool's Day**.

April *n* the fourth month of the year, having 30 days.

a priori (*Latin*) deductively, from cause to effect.

apron *n* a garment worn to protect clothing; anything resembling the shape of an apron used for protection; (*archit*) a raised panel, sometimes ornamental, directly below a window sill; the paved surface on an airfield where aircraft are parked, etc.

apropos *adv* at the right time; opportunely; appropriately. * *adj* appropriate. * *prep* (*with* of) regarding, in reference to.

APS *abbr* = American Peace Society; American Philatelic Society; American Philosophical Society; American Physical Society.

apse *n* (*archit*) a domed or vaulted recess, esp in a church.

apse line *n* (*astron*) a line drawn between the foci of an elliptical orbit and extended to cut the orbit (giving the major axis) at two points called the apses where the orbiting body is closest to the massive body to which it is attracted.

apsis *n* (*pl* **apsides**) (*astron*) one of two points in the orbit of a planet situated at the furthest or the least distance from the central body or sun; the imaginary line connecting these points.—**apsidal** *adj*.

apt *adj* ready or likely (to); suitable, relevant; able to learn easily.—**aptness** *n*.

Apt. *abbr* = apartment.

APT *abbr* = advanced passenger train; automatic picture transmission; (*comput*) a computer programming language.

apteral *adj* (*archit*) without side columns.

apterous *adj* without wings.

apterygial *adj* lacking wings or fins.

apteryx *n* the kiwi, a New Zealand bird with rudimentary wings and no tail.

aptitude *n* suitability; natural talent, esp for learning.

aptitude test *n* a standardized test used to measure a person's ability to develop skills or acquire knowledge.

Apts. *abbr* = apartments.

Apuleius *n* (2nd century AD) North African Latin author of a satirical romance, *The Golden Ass*.

Apulia *n* a region in the southeast of Italy on the Adriatic. In Greek mythology, it was settled by Diomedes, who founded its principal cities.—**Apulian** *adj*.

APWR *abbr* = advanced pressurized water reactor.

APWU *abbr* = Amalgamated Postal Workers' Union.

apx. *abbr* = appendix.

apyretic *adj* without fever, or with intermission of fever.

aq *abbr* = aqua.

AQ *abbr* = achievement quotient.

Aqaba *n* a city in the Hashemite Kingdom of Jordan.

AQPS *abbr* (*French*) = *autre que pur sang*, "other than pure blood" (term used in horse breeding).

aqua *n* (*pl* **aquae, aquas**) water as used in pharmacy.

aquaculture *n* the cultivation and breeding of fish and other marine organisms.—*also* **aquiculture**.—**aquacultural** *adj*.—**aquaculturist** *n*.

aqualung *n* portable diving gear comprising air cylinders connected to a face mask.

aquamarine *n* a variety of bluish-green beryl used as a gemstone; its color.

aquaplane *n* a plank towed at high speed. * *vi* to ride on one.

aquarelle *n* the French term for watercolor painting, where a water-based paint is applied to dampened paper in thin glazes that are gradually built up into areas of varying tone.—**aquarellist** *n*.

aqua fortis *n* impure nitric acid.

aqua regia *n* a mixture of nitric and hydrochloric acids, capable of dissolving gold.

Aquarids *n* meteor showers to be seen in late April–early May, associated with Halley's comet and having a radiant in the constellation Aquarius.

aquarist *n* an individual who keeps an aquarium.

aquarium *n* (*pl* **aquariums, aquaria**) a tank, pond, etc for keeping aquatic animals or plants; a building where collections of aquatic animals are exhibited.

Aquarius *n* (*astron*) a zodiacal constellation between Capricorn and Pisces at 23 hours right ascension, 10° south declination, with brightest stars of third magnitude; (*astrol*) the eleventh sign of the zodiac, the water-carrier, operative 20 January–18 February.—**Aquarian** *adj, n*.

aquatic *adj* of or taking place in water; living or growing in water.

aquatics *npl* water sports.

aquatint *n* an etching technique where a resin-coated metal plate is placed in a bath of acid that bites into the resin, producing a pitted surface; a style of etching resembling a watercolor drawing in Indian ink or in sepia; an engraving produced by this process. * *vt* to etch or engrave in aquatint.

aqua vitae *n* (*Latin*) "water of life," unrectified alcohol; archaic name for brandy and other ardent spirits.

aqueduct *n* a large pipe or conduit for carrying water; an elevated structure supporting this.

aqueous *adj* of, like, or formed by water.

aqueous humor *n* a limpid fluid of the eye, filling the space between the crystalline lens and the cornea. *See* **glaucoma**.

aquiculture *n* hydroponics; another name for aquaculture.—**aquicultural** *adj*.—**aquiculturist** *n*.

aquifer *n* a layer of rock, sand or gravel that is porous and therefore allows the passage and collection of water.

Aquila[1] *n* (*astron*) an equatorial constellation in a populous region of the Milky Way Galaxy;

Aquila[2] *n* (*Bible*) a Jew who, with his wife Priscilla, befriended Paul and became early Christian teachers. *See also* **Apollos**, **Priscilla**.

aquilegia *n* columbine.

aquiline *adj* of or like an eagle; (*nose*) hooked, like an eagle's beak.

Aquinas *n* **Saint Thomas** (1226–74) Italian theologian, scholar and Dominican friar; the patron saint of all universities, colleges and schools. His *Summa Theologica*, which was to contain the whole of the Christian religion from the existence of God to the precepts of morality, with every conceivable objection stated and answered was never finished. His feast day is 28 January.

Aquino *n* **[Maria] Corazon** (1933–) Filipino politician and president of the Philippines (1986–92).

Ar *symbol* (*chem*) argon (element).

aR *abbr* (*German*) = *am Rhein*, "on the Rhine," used for places near the river.

a/r, A/R *abbr* (*marine insurance*) = all risks.

Ar. *abbr* = Arabic; Aramaic.

AR *abbr* = Amateur Riders' Association of Great Britain; Anti-Racist Alliance; Arkansas; Australian Robot Association; (*Latin*) *anno regni*, "in the year of the reign of"; autonomous republic; (*med*) assisted respiration.

ar- *prefix* the form of *ad-* before *r*.

-ar *adj suffix* of, belonging to, as in *angular, popular*.

ARA *abbr* = American Railway Association; American Relief Administration.

ARAA *abbr* = Associate of the Royal Academy of Arts.

Arab *n* a native of Arabia; one of the Arabic races spread over the African and Syrian deserts. * *adj* pertaining to Arabia or the Arabs.

Arab. *abbr* = Arabic.

Araba, Sea of *n* alternative name for the Dead Sea. *See also* **Dead Sea**.

Arabeske (*German*) *see* **arabesque**.

arabesque *n* a decorative design incorporating organic motifs, such as leaves and flowers, in an intricate pattern, deriving from Moresque patterns of the 16th century; a posture in which a dancer (in ballet) balances on one leg with one arm extending forwards and the other arm and leg extending backwards; (*mus*) a lyrical piece of music that employs an exaggerated and elaborate style, as used by Schumann and Debussy. * *adj* (*mus*) a florid treatment of thematic music.

Arabia *n* large desert peninsula lying between Egypt and Mesopotamia (Iraq), bounded by the Red Sea, the Indian Ocean and the Persian Gulf.

Arabia Ceramics *n* a company founded in 1873 which later helped establish Modern Scandinavian design.

Arabian *adj* of Arabia, Arab. * *n* an Arab.

Arabian camel *n* a camel with a single hump.

Arabian Nights' Entertainments, The *n* a compilation of stories, probably originating in Persia, that were translated into Arabic in the mid–9th century AD and have become classics of Arab and world literature. Also called **The Thousand and One Nights**.

Arabic *n* the Arabian language. * *adj* of or pertaining to the Arabic language and the countries in which it is spoken.

Arabic numeral *n* one of the numbers 0, 1, 2, 3, 4, 5, etc.

arable *adj* suitable for ploughing or planting crops.—*also n*.

arable land *n* land that is suitable for growing crops.

Arachne *n* (*Greek myth*) a virgin from Lydia who was changed into a spider by Athena after challenging the goddess to a weaving contest.

arachnid *n* any of a class of animals including spiders, scorpions, mites and ticks.—**arachnidan** *adj, n.*

arachnoid *adj* pertaining to spiders; resembling the web of a spider. * *n* (*anat*) the enveloping membrane of the brain and spinal cord, between the dura mater and the pia mater.

arachnoid mater *n* (*anat*) the enveloping membrane of the brain and spinal cord, between the dura mater and the pia mater.

arachnoids *n* (*astron*) spider-shaped patterns of cracks of volcanic origin on Venus.

Arad *n* a city in Romania.

Arafat *n* **Yasser** (1929–) Palestinian leader. He signed the Israeli-Palestinian Peace Accord in 1993 with Israeli prime minister Yitzhak Rabin.

Aragon *n* **Louis** (1897–1982) French poet, novelist, and essayist, and one of the founders of Dadaism and surrealism.

aragonite *n* a variety of carbonate of lime.

arak *see* **arrack**.

Aram. *abbr* = Aramaic.

Aramaic *n* the language of Palestine at the time of Christ.

araneid *n* a member of the *Arachnida* order, the spider family.

Ararat *n* range of mountains where Noah's ark came to rest when the waters of the flood receded.

ARAS *abbr* (*Brit*) = Association of the Royal Astronomical Society.

araucaria *n* one of a genus of coniferous trees, found principally in South America and Australia, which includes the monkey puzzle.

Arawn *n* (*Welsh Celtic myth*) king of Annw, the Welsh Otherworld. He is best known in legend for his association with Pwyll, lord of Dyfed.

ARBA *abbr* = Army Review Boards Agency

arbalest *n* a crossbow with a drawing mechanism.

Arbeth *n* (*Welsh Celtic myth*) Arbeth was the chief court of Pwyll.

arbiter *n* a person having absolute power of decision or absolute control.

arbitrage *n* (*com*) the buying and selling of commodities, financial securities or foreign currencies between two or more markets.—*also* **index arbitrage**.

arbitrament *n* an arbiter's judgment; an authoritative decision.

arbitrary not bound by rules; despotic, absolute; capricious, unreasonable.—**arbitrarily** *adv*.—**arbitrariness** *n*.

arbitrate *vi* to act as an arbitrator. * *vt* to submit to an arbiter; to act as an arbiter upon.

arbitration *n* a procedure for settling an industrial dispute in which a third party is called in to settle the dispute.

arbitrator *n* a person chosen to settle a dispute between contending parties.

arbor[1] *n* a place shaded by trees, foliage, etc; a bower.—*also* **arbour**.

arbor[2] *n* the main support of a machine; an axis, a spindle.

arboraceous *adj* pertaining to, or of the nature of, a tree or trees; living on or among trees.

Arbor Day *n* a day legally set apart in certain states of the US for planting trees.

arboreal *adj* of or living in trees.

arboreous *adj* wooded.

arborescent *adj* growing or formed like a tree.—**arborescence** *n*.

arboretum *n* (*pl* **arboreta**, **arboretums**) a botanical tree garden where rare trees are cultivated and exhibited.

arboriculture *n* the cultivation of trees and shrubs, forestry.

arborist *n* one who specializes in growing trees.

arborization *n* a tree-like appearance.

arbor vitae *n* an evergreen tree extensively cultivated in gardens, etc.

arbour *see* **arbor**.

Arbus *n* **André** (1903–69) French decorator who produced elegant furniture for *Epoque*, his Paris store.

arbutus *n* (*pl* **arbutuses**) one of a genus of tree-like evergreen shrubs to which the strawberry tree belongs.

arc *n* a portion of the circumference of a circle or other curve; a luminous discharge of electricity across a gap between two electrodes or terminals. * *vi* to form an electric arc.

ARC *abbr* = AIDS-related condition; American (National) Red Cross; Appalachian Regional Commission.

ARCA *abbr* (*Brit*) = Associate of the Royal College of Art.

arcade *n* (*archit*) a series of arches supported by columns, which may be a decorative feature against a wall (a blind arcade); a covered area containing stores, usu featuring a high, vaulted roof.

Arcadia *n* the central and most mountainous portion of the Peloponnese in Greece, which in ancient times was famous for its pastoral character. It became the archetypal setting for rural bliss and innocence in the arts. In Greek mythology the lyre was invented there by Hermes, and the syrinx, the musical instrument of the shepherds, was the invention of Pan.

Arcadian *adj* of or pertaining to Arcadia, a department of Greece, or its inhabitants; rurally simple. * *n* an inhabitant of Arcadia.

Arcady *n* (*poet*) ideal countryside.

arcane *adj* secret or esoteric.

arcanum *n* (*pl* **arcana**) a secret, a mystery; a valuable elixir.

Arcas *n* (*Greek myth*) the ancestor and eponymous hero of the Arcadians, from whom Arcadia and its inhabitants derived their name.

arch[1] *n* a curved structure spanning an opening; (*archit*) a curved opening constructed without the use of a lintel; an opening on the sea coast where two caves, originally on opposite sides of a headland, have been eroded until they meet; (*med*) a part or structure of the body that is curved, e.g., the vault formed by the tarsus and metatarsal bones of the foot. * *vti* to span or cover with an arch; to curve, bend into an arch.

arch[2] *adj* (*criminal, etc*) principal, expert; clever, sly; mischievous.—**archly** *adv*.—**archness** *n*.

arch. *abbr* = archaic; archaism; archery; archipelago; architect; architectural; architecture.

Arch. *abbr* = Archbishop.

Archaean *see* **Archean**.

archaeology *see* **archeology**.

archaeopteryx *n* oldest fossil bird.

archaic *adj* belonging to ancient times; (*language*) no longer in common use.

archaic period *n* (*archeo*) a term describing the early stages of certain civilizations.

archaism *n* an archaic word or phrase.—**archaistic** *adj*.

archaize *vti* to affect the archaic; to make archaic.—**archaizer** *n*.

archangel *n* a principal angel.—**archangelic** *adj*.

archbishop *n* a bishop of the highest rank.

archbishopric *n* the jurisdiction, office or see of an archbishop.

Archd. *abbr* = Archdeacon.

archdeacon *n* a clergyman ranking next under a bishop.

archdeaconry *n* (*pl* **archdeaconries**) the office, rank, jurisdiction, or residence of an archdeaon.

archdiocese *n* the diocese of an archbishop.—**archdiocesan** *adj*.

archducal *adj* of or pertaining to an archduchess, an archduchy or an archduke.

archduchess *n* a daughter of the emperor of Austria; the wife or widow of an archduke.

archduchy *n* (*pl* **archduchies**) the territory or rank of an archduke or an archduchess.

archduke *n* a prince of the imperial house of Austria.

Archean *adj* of the earliest geological period or strata.—*also* **Archaean**.

archegonium *n* (*pl* **archegonia**) (*bot*) the pistillidium or female organ of the higher cryptogams (ferns, etc).

Archelaus, Herod *n* (*Bible*) son of Herod the Great and notorious for his cruelty. *See also* **Herod**.

archenemy *n* (*pl* **archenemies**) a principal enemy; Satan.

archeol. *abbr* = archeology.

archeology *n* the study of past human societies through their extant remains.—*also* **archaeology**.—**archeological, archaeological** *adj*.—**archeologist, archaeologist** *n*.

archeomagnetism *or* **paleomagnetism** *n* the magnetism of a past time that has been preserved in an artifact.

archer *n* a person who shoots with a bow and arrow.

Archer *n* **Thomas** born 1668, English architect. His notable works include St John Church, Smith Square, London.

archerfish *n* (*pl* **archerfish**, **archerfishes**) a scaly-finned fish of the Java seas, which catches insects by darting drops of water upon them.

archery *n* the art or sport of shooting arrows from a bow.

archet *n* (*mus*) (*French*) a bow, such as is used to play a stringed instrument.

archetype *n* (*psychol*) an image or symbol drawn from the collective unconscious; the original pattern or model; a prototype.—**archetypal, archetypical** *adj*.

archfiend *n* a chief fiend; Satan.

archi *npl* (*mus*) (*Italian*) "bows." * *adj* a term that refers to all stringed instruments played with a bow.

archidiaconal *adj* of or pertaining to an archdeacon or to his office.

archidiaconate *n* the office of an archdeacon.

archiepiscopal *adj* of or pertaining to an archbishop or to his office.

archiepiscopate, archiepiscopacy *n* the rule or dignity of an archbishop.

archil *see* orchil.

archimagus, archimage *n* the high priest of the Persian magi or fire-worshippers; a chief magician.

archimandrite *n* (*Greek Orthodox Church*) the abbot of a monastery, or an abbot-general having the charge and superintendence of several monasteries.

Archimedean screw *n* an instrument for raising water, consisting of a flexible tube wound spirally around or within a cylinder in the form of a screw. When placed in an inclined position, with the lower end immersed in water, by the revolution of the screw the water is raised to the upper end.

Archimedes' principle *n* (*phys*) a law that when a body is immersed in a liquid, the weight it appears to have lost equals the weight of the displaced liquid.

archipelago *n* (*pl* **archipelagoes, archipelagos**) a sea filled with small islands; a group of small islands.—**archipelagic, archipelagian** *adj*.

Archipenko *n* Alexander (1887–1946) Ukrainian-born American sculptor whose influence on 20th-century European and American sculpture has been considerable.

Archit. *abbr* = architecture.

architect *n* a person who designs buildings and supervises their erection; someone who plans something.

architectonic *adj* pertaining to design or construction; skilled in architecture; expert in constructing; of the systematizing of knowledge.—**architectonically** *adv*.

architectonics *n* (*used as sing*) the science of architecture; structure.

architecture *n* the art, profession, or science of designing and constructing buildings; the style of a building or buildings; the design and organization of a computer's parts.—**architectural** *adj*.—**architecturally** *adv*.

architrave *n* an epistyle, the lowest division of an entablature, the part resting immediately on a column; the parts round a door or window.

archival standards *npl* the standards set by the US Bureau of Standards used to assure permanence of microfilm.

archive *n* (*comput*) a store of files kept as a backup in case the original files are corrupted or damaged. Often stored in a compressed format (*see* compress).

archives *npl* the location in which public records are kept; the public records themselves.—**archival** *adj*.

archivist *n* a keeper of public records.

archivolt *n* the undercurve of an arch or the molding on it.

archpriest *n* a chief priest; a rural dean.

Archt. *abbr* = architect.

archway *n* an arched or vaulted passage, esp that leading into a castle.

ARCIC *abbr* = Anglican-Roman Catholic International Commission.

arc light *n* light produced by a current of electricity passing between two carbon points placed a short distance from each other.

ARCM *abbr* (*Brit*) = Associate of the Royal College of Music.

ARCnet *abbr* = attached resource computer network.

arco *n* (*mus*) (*Italian*) the singular of archi. * *vt* instruction to play with the bow after playing pizzicato.

ARCO *abbr* (*Brit*) = Associate of the Royal College of Organists.

ARCO(CHM) *abbr* (*Brit*) = Associate of the Royal College of Organists (Choir-training Diploma).

ARCS *abbr* (*Brit*) = Associateship of the Royal College of Science, Imperial College, University of London.

Arctic *n* regions north of the Arctic circle, 66.6°N. * *adj* pertaining to these regions; (*inf*) very cold, icy.

Arctic Circle *n* an imaginary circle around the arctic regions parallel to the equator.

arctic fox *n* a small species of fox, whose fine fur is used for muffs, trimmings, etc.

Arctic front *n* a front lying between 50°N and 60°N where cold Arctic air meets slightly warmer polar air.

Arctic Ocean *n* the ocean that washes the northern coasts of Europe, Asia and North America.

Arctic smoke *n* fog formed in high latitudes when cold air condenses as it passes over a warmer water surface.

Arcturus *or* **Alpha Boötis** *n* (*astron*) a star of the first magnitude in the constellation Boötes.

arcuate *adj* bent or curved in the form of a bow.

arcuation *n* the act of bending; the state of being bent or curved; a method of propagating trees by bending branches to the ground and covering portions of them with earth.

ARCUK *abbr* = Architects' Registration Council of the United Kingdom.

ARCVS *abbr* (*Brit*) = Associate of the Royal College of Veterinary Surgeons.

arc welding *n* welding using an electric arc.

ARD *abbr* = acute respiratory disease.

Ardea *n* an ancient city of Latium, situated on a small river near the sea, south of Rome.

Arden *n* John (1930–) English dramatist whose early plays, e.g., *Serjeant Musgrave's Dance* (1959), attacked the evils of social corruption and violence.

ardent *adj* passionate; zealous.—**ardency** *n*.—**ardently** *adv*.

ardent spirits *npl* alcoholic beverages, as brandy, whisky, etc.

ardor, ardour *n* warmth of feeling; extreme intensity.

ARDS *abbr* = acute respiratory distress syndrome.

arduous *adj* difficult, laborious; steep, difficult to climb. —**arduously** *adv*.—**arduousness** *n*.

ARE *abbr* = Admiralty Research Establishment.

are[1] *see* be.

are[2] *n* a metric unit of measure equal to 100 square meters.

area *n* an expanse of land; a total outside surface, measured in square units; a specific part of a house, district, etc; scope or extent.

Area Code, area code *n* a number that identifies telephone service areas.

areca *n* a genus of lofty palms, including the tree from which the betelnut and the astringent juice Catechu are obtained.

Arecibo Observatory *n* an observatory in Puerto Rico, south of Arecibo town, with the world's most powerful single-dish radio telescope.

ARELS-FELCO *abbr* = Association for Recognized English Language Teaching Establishments in Britain.

aren't = are not.

arena *n* a shallow, usu circular, basin surrounded by higher land; an area within a sports stadium, etc where events take place; a place or sphere of contest or activity; (*archit*) the central circular space of an amphitheater.

arenaceous *adj* sandy; abounding in, or having the properties of, sand.

Arend-Roland comet *n* a comet whose nucleus reached first magnitude in 1957.

Arendt *n* Hannah (1906–75) German-born American philosopher. Her best-known work is *The Origins of Totalitarianism* (1951).

Arensky *n* Anton Stepanovich (1861–1906) a Russian composer, born in Novgorod, who studied under Rimsky-Korsakov at the St Petersburg Conservatory. His best-known works are his piano pieces, esp his Piano Trio in D Minor (Opus 32).

areography *n* the geography of Mars.

areola (*pl* **areolae, areolas**) *n* a very small area; an interstice in tissue; the brown-colored, pigmented ring around the nipple of the breast.—**areolar, areolate** *adj*.—**areolation** *n*.

Areopagus *n* (*Bible*) hill in Athens where Paul preached the God of heaven and earth to the council of Greek philosophers; the oldest of the ancient Athenian courts of justice, named from its place of meeting, on the Hill of Ares.

Arequipa *n* a city in Peru.

Ares *n* (*Greek myth*) the god of war whose Roman counterpart is Mars. He was a lover of Aphrodite, by whom he had several children.

arête *n* (*geog*) a sharp, rugged ridge on a mountain between two cirques.

Arethusa *n* (*Greek myth*) a nymph changed by Artemis into a fountain in order to free her from the pursuit of the river-god Alpheus.

aretic *n* an area that does not have flowing streams. An example is hot deserts, where any precipitation either soaks into the ground or evaporates.

Aretinian Syllables *npl* (*mus*) ut, re, mi, fa, sol, la, by which Guido Aretinus or d'Arezzo, a 10th-century French Benedictine monk and teacher of music designated the hexachord tones.

Aretino *n* Pietro (1492–1556) Italian poet and dramatist whose name became a byword for witty licentiousness.

ARF *abbr* = acute renal failure; acute respiratory failure.

arg. *abbr* = (*Latin*) argentum, "silver"; arguendo; argent; argentum.

Arg. Rep. *abbr* = Argentine Republic.

argali *n* (*pl* **argalis, argali**) a large wild Asiatic sheep, remarkable for its huge curved horns.

argent *n* (*her*) silver, represented in a drawing or engraving of a coat of arms by a plain white surface, symbolic of purity, beauty, etc. * *adj* made of or resembling silver; silvery white; bright like silver.

argentiferous *adj* producing or containing silver.

Argentina *n* the world's eighth largest country, which stretches from the Tropic of Capricorn to Cape Horn on the southern tip of the South American continent.

argentine *adj* pertaining to or resembling silver; silvery. * *n* a silvery-white slaty variety of calcite; white metal coated with silver, imitation silver.

argil *n* clay, esp potter's clay or earth.

argillaceous *adj* of or containing clay, clayey.

argilliferous *adj* producing or containing clay.

argillite *n* clay-slate.—**argillitic** *adj*.

arginine *n* an essential amino acid.

Argives *n* the inhabitants of Argos in ancient Greece; in Homer, a generic name for all the Greeks.

argle-bargle *see* argy-bargy.

Argo *n* (*Greek myth*) the ship of the Argonauts.

argol *n* a deposit of crude tartar on the sides of wine vessels; crude tartar from which cream of tartar is prepared.

Argolis *n* the territory surrounding the ancient Greek town of Argos, near Mycenae.

argon *n* an inert gas used in lamps and fluorescent tubes and as a shield in arc welding.

Argonaut *n* a mollusk; a prospector in the California gold rush (1849).

Argonauts *npl* (*Greek myth*) 50 Greek heroes who performed a dangerous voyage to Colchis, a country at the eastern extremity of the Black Sea, in the ship *Argo* under the command of Jason. Their quest was to fetch the golden fleece, guarded by a fire-breathing dragon.

Argo Navis *n* an anciently recognized constellation now split into three.

Argos *n* a town of Greece, in the north-east of the Peloponnese.

argosy *n* (*pl* **argosies**) a large, richly laden merchant ship.

argot *n* the special vocabulary of any set of persons, as of lawyers, criminals, etc.—**argotic** *adj*.

arguable *adj* debatable; able to be asserted; plausible.—**arguably** *adv*.

argue *vt* (**arguing, argued**) to try to prove by reasoning; to debate, dispute; to persuade (into, out of). * *vi* to offer reasons for or against something; to disagree, exchange angry words.—**arguer** *n*.

argufy *vi* (**argufying, argufied**) (*sl*) to argue tediously, to wrangle.

argument *n* a disagreement; a debate, discussion; a reason offered in debate; an abstract, summary.

argumentation *n* systematic reasoning; argument, discussion.

argumentative *adj* prone to arguing.—**argumentatively** *adv*.—**argumentativeness** *n*.

Argus *n* (*Greek myth*) a giant with a hundred eyes.

argus-eyed *adj* extremely watchful, from Argus, a monster in Greek mythology said to have a hundred eyes, which after his death were put in the tail of the peacock.

argy-bargy *n* (*pl* **argy-bargies**) a tedious discussion. * *vi* to argue at length.

argyle, argyll *n* a varicolored, diamond-shaped pattern; a sock knit in this pattern.

Århus *n* a city in Denmark.

ARI acute respiratory infection.

aria *n* (*mus*) (*Italian*) a song or air. Originally the term was used for any song for one or more voices but it has come to be used exclusively for a long, solo song as found in oratorio and opera.

ARIA *abbr* = Accounting Researchers International Association; automated radio-immuno-assay.

Arica *n* a city in Chile.

Ariadne *n* (*Greek myth*) a daughter of Minos, king of Crete, who gave Theseus a ball of thread to conduct him out of the labyrinth after his defeat of the Minotaur. Theseus promised to marry her but abandoned her on the island of Naxos, where she was found by Dionysus, who married her.

Arian *adj* pertaining to the doctrines of the Arian sect, which held that Christ is not divine. * *n* a follower of Arianism.

Arianism *n* the doctrine of Arius.

Ariane *n* the European Space Agency rocket-launching vehicle.

ARIBA *abbr* = Associate of the Royal Institute of British Architects.

ARIC *abbr* (*Brit*) = Associateship of the Royal Institute of Chemistry.

ARICS *abbr* (*Brit*) = Professional Associate of the Royal Institution of Chartered Surveyors.

arid *adj* very dry, parched; uninteresting; dull.—**aridity** *n*.—**aridly** *adv*.

arid area *n* one with less than 10 inches (250 millimeters) of precipitation annually, which is insufficient to support vegetation

arid zone *n* where the potential for evaporation exceeds precipitation.

ariel *n* a gazelle.

Ariel *n* one of the five major satellites of Uranus, discovered in 1851; the first international co-operative Earth satellite, launched in 1962.

Aries *n* (*astron*) a zodiacal constellation lying between Pisces and Taurus at three hours right ascension and 20° north declination; (*astrol*) the first sign of the zodiac, the Ram, operative 21 March–21 April.—**Arian** *adj, n*.

arietta *n* a short aria, song or air.

aright *adv* correctly.

aril *n* (*bot*) an accessory covering or appendage of certain seeds.

Arima *n* town in Trinidad and Tobago.

Arimathea *n* (*Bible*) town in Judaea, the home of Joseph, who buried the body of Jesus in his own tomb. *See also* **Joseph**.

Arion *n* an ancient Greek poet and musician, born on the island of Lesbos, flourished about 625 BC. To escape from some murderous sailors, he threw himself into the sea, where a dolphin carried him to land.

arioso *adj, adv* (*mus*) (*Italian*) "like an aria," in a smooth melodious style. * *n* a melodious and song-like recitative; a short air in an opera or oratorio; an instrumental piece that follows the style of a vocal arioso.

Ariosto *n* **Ludovico** (1474–1533) Italian poet best known for his epic verse romance Orlando Furioso (1532).

ARIPHH *abbr* (*Brit*) = Associate of the Royal Institute of Public Health and Hygiene.

arise *vi* (**arising, arose**, *pp* **arisen**) to get up, as from bed; to rise, ascend; to come into being, to result (from).

arista *n* (*pl* **aristae**) the awn or beard of grasses; a bristle.

Aristarchus *n* (*Bible*) a faithful companion and fellow-prisoner of Paul.

aristate *adj* bearded; having a beard or bristle, as certain grasses.

Aristeas *n* (*Greek myth*) a personage who lived over many centuries, disappearing and reappearing by turns.

aristocracy *n* (*pl* **aristocracies**) (a country with) a government dominated by a privileged minority class; the privileged class in a society, the nobility; those people considered the best in their particular sphere.

aristocrat *n* a member of the aristocracy; a supporter of aristocratic government; a person with the manners or taste of a privileged class.

aristocratic *adj* relating to or characteristic of the aristocracy; elegant, stylish in dress and manners.—**aristocratically** *adv*.

Aristophanes *n* (*c*.448–380 BC) Greek comic dramatist whose works include *Lysistrata*.

Aristotelian *adj* pertaining to, or characteristic of, Aristotle (384—322 BC) or his philosophy.

Aristotle *n* (384–322 BC) Greek philosopher whose writings greatly influenced intellectual inquiry until the Renaissance.

arith. *abbr* = arithmetic; arithmetical.

arithmetic *n* (*math*) computation (addition, subtraction, etc) using real numbers; calculation.—**arithmetic, arithmetical** *adj*.—**arithmetically** *adv*.

arithmetic operator *n* (*comput*) a symbol that indicates which arithmetical operation to perform, e.g., adding (+), subtracting (-), multiplying (*) or dividing (/).

arithmetic series *n* (*math*) the sum of the terms in a sequence of quantities.

arithmetician *n* one skilled in the science of numbers.

Arius *n* (c 250–336) Greek Christian theologian who was considered heretical in his belief that Christ was not of one substance with the Father; originator of the doctrine of Arianism.

Ariz. *abbr* = Arizona.

Arizona (AZ) *n* a state of the United States of America (USA) of which the capital is Phoenix.

"Arizona" *n* the official song of the American State, Arizona.

Arizona meteorite crater *n* a 164 yards deep circular depression of diameter 0.75 miles in the Arizona desert formed 40,000 years ago by the impact of a metallic meteorite.

ark *n* (*Bible*) the boat in which Noah and his family and two of every kind of creature survived the Flood; a place of safety; a box or chest; an enclosure in a synagogue for the scrolls of the Torah.

Ark. *abbr* = Arkansas.

Arkansas (AR) *n* a state of the United States of America (USA) of which the capital is Little Rock.

"Arkansas" *n* the official song of the American State, Arkansas.

Ark of the Covenant *n* (*Bible*) the chest containing the two stone tablets inscribed with the Ten Commandments.

ARL *abbr* = Army Research Laboratory

Arlen *n* **Harold** (1905–86) American composer whose songs include "Stormy Weather."

ARLL *abbr* (*comput*) = advanced run-length limited.

arm. *abbr* = armature.

Arm. *abbr* = Armenian; Armoric.

Ar.M. *abbr* (*Latin*) = *Architecturae Magister*, "Master of Architecture."

ARM *abbr* = artificial rupture of the membranes; anti-radar missile.

arm[1] *n* the upper limb from the shoulder to the wrist; something shaped like an arm, as a support on a chair; a sleeve; power, authority; an administrative division of a large organization.

arm[2] *n* (*usu pl*) (*mil*) a weapon; a branch of the military service; (*pl*) heraldic bearings. * *vt* to provide with weapons, etc; to provide with something that protects or strengthens, etc; to set a fuse ready to explode. * *vi* to prepare for war or any struggle.

armada *n* a fleet of warships or aircraft.

armadillo *n* (*pl* **armadillos**) a small animal from South America with a body covering of small bony plates.

Armageddon *n* (*Bible*) hill of Megiddo; in the Book of Revelations referred to as the location of the final battle between good and evil. *See also* **Megiddo**.

Armagnac *n* a brandy of superior quality made in southwestern France.

armament *n* (*often pl*) all the military forces and equipment of a nation; all the military equipment of a warship, etc; the process of arming or being armed for war.

Armant *n* important Egyptian Pre-dynastic Period site, cult center of the god Montu, in the heart of Theban territory.

armature *n* (*elect*) a piece of iron connecting the poles of a magnet or electromagnet to preserve and increase the magnetic force; the revolving part of a dynamo; arms, armor, that which serves as a means of defense; iron bars or framework used to strengthen a building; a framework supporting clay, etc, in sculpture or modeling.

armband *n* a strip of cloth worn around the arm, usu symbolically.

armchair *n* a chair with side rests for the arms. * *adj* lacking practical experience.

armed forces *npl* the military forces of a nation.—*also* **armed services**.

Armenia *n* the smallest republic of the former USSR and part of the former kingdom of Armenia which was divided between Turkey, Iran and the former USSR. It declared independence from the USSR in 1991.

armful *n* as much as the arms can hold.

armhole *n* an opening for the arm in an item of clothing.

armiger *n* one entitled to use heraldic bearings, an esquire.—**armigerous** *adj*.

armillary *adj* of or resembling a bracelet; consisting of circles or rings.

armillary sphere *n* a skeleton celestial globe showing the relative positions of the stars, etc.

Arminianism *n* a Christian Protestant doctrine that denies Calvin's doctrine of predestination.—**Arminian** *adj, n*.

armistice *n* a truce, preliminary to a peace treaty.

armlet *n* an ornamental or protective band worn around the arm; a badge worn on the arm; a small arm of the sea.

armoire *n* a clothes cabinet.

armor, armour *n* any defensive or protective covering.

Armor. *abbr* = Armoric.

armored, armoured *adj* covered or protected with armor; equipped with tanks and armor vehicles.

armored car *n* a military vehicle often with a mounted machine gun; an armored truck used to transport money or valuables.

armorer, armourer *n* the custodian of the arms of a battleship, etc; (formerly) a maker of arms or armor; one who had charge of the armor of another.

armor plate, armor plate *n* a plate of iron or steel affixed to a ship or tank as part of a casing for protection against shellfire.

armorial *adj* pertaining to armor or the arms or escutcheon of a family. * *n* a book or dictionary of heraldic devices and the names of persons entitled to use them.

armory, armoury *n* (*pl* **armories, armouries**) an arsenal; a place where armor or ammunition is stored.

Armory Show *n* the international exhibition of modern art held at the 69th Regimental Armory in New York in 1913, one of the most influential exhibitions ever shown in the US. It served the function of restoring the life and vitality of contemporary art and critical debate in the US.

armpit *n* the hollow underneath the arm at the shoulder.

ARMS *abbr* = Action for Research into Multiple Sclerosis.

arms *see* arm².

arms race *n* a continuous build-up of weapons and forces by two or more competing nations.

Armstrong *n* 1. **[Daniel] Louis "Satchmo"** (meaning "satchel mouth.") (1900–71) Popular Black American jazz trumpeter, singer, and band born in New Orleans who remains one of the greatest figures in jazz history. 2. **John** (1893–1973) British painter and designer who designed stage sets, murals and posters. 3. **Neil [Alden]** (1930–) American astronaut; commander of Apollo 11 moon landing and first man to walk on the moon, followed by the lunar module pilot **Edwin "Buzz" Aldrin** (1930–). The other member of the mission was the orbiting module pilot **Michael Collins** (1930–).

army *n* (*pl* **armies**) a large organized body of soldiers for waging war, esp on land; any large number of persons, animals, etc.

army ant *n* any of various chiefly tropical New World ants that form large colonies that move from place to place.

army worm *n* the larva of a moth that devastates grain and other crops, esp destructive in North America; the larva of a European small two-winged fly.

Arne *n* 1. **Michael** (1740–86) an English singer and composer who was the illegitimate son of Thomas Arne. His best works were for the stage and he worked with the great impresario, David Garrick. 2. **Thomas Augustine** (1710–78) a prolific English composer of operas, oratorios and instrumental pieces. His operas include *Artaxerxes* and *Thomas and Sally*, but his best-known work is his masque *Alfred*, which contains the song "Rule, Britannia!"

ARNet *abbr* = Acquisition Reform Network

arnica *n* a genus of perennial herbs, esp mountain tobacco, whose roots and flowers are used to make a tincture for treating bruises.

Arnold *n* 1. **Malcolm** (1921–) an English composer, trumpeter and conductor. He is best known for his score for the film *The Bridge on the River Kwai* (1957). 2. **Matthew** (1822–88) English poet and critic, and an important commentator on Victorian society whose works include the poem "Dover Beach." 3. **Thomas** (1795–1842), father of Matthew Arnold and English educational reformer.

Arnolfo di Cambio (1245–1302?) Italian sculptor and architect, who was one of the most important Italian architects in the Gothic style.

aroma *n* a pleasant smell; a fragrance.

aromatherapy *n* the massage of fragrant oils into the skin to relieve tension and promote wellbeing.

aromatic *adj* giving out an aroma; fragrant, spicy; odoriferous. * *n* a plant, herb or drug yielding a fragrant smell.—**aromatically** *adv*.

aromatize *vt* to render fragrant, to perfume, to scent.—**aromatization** *n*.

arose *see* arise.

around *prep* on all sides of; on the border of; in various places in or on; approximately, about. * *adv* in a circle; in every direction; in circumference; to the opposite direction.

arousal *n* the act of awakening or stimulating; the state of being awakened or stimulated.

arouse *vt* to wake from sleep; to stir, as to action; to evoke.

Arp *n* **Jean, Hans** (1887–1966) French abstract sculptor of great merit; a founder of the Dada group. He worked on the development of collage together with the Swiss painter, Sophie Taeuber, who later became his wife.

arp. *abbr* (*Italian*) = arpeggio, "harped" (i.e., notes in music played as a broken chord).

ARP *abbr* = air raid precautions.

ARPA *abbr* = Advanced Research Projects Agency

Arpanet *abbr* = Advanced Research Projects Agency Network (early Internet).

arpeggiare *vt* (*mus*) (*Italian*) literally "to play the harp," i.e., to play chords "spread out" as they are on the harp.

arpeggio *n* (*pl* **arpeggios**) (*mus*) (*Italian*) "harp-wise," the playing of notes of a chord in rapid succession, instead of simultaneously; a passage or chord so played.

arpeggione *n* (*mus*) an obsolete instrument invented in 1823, which is a cross between a violoncello (cello) and a guitar.

arpent *n* an old French unit of land measurement nearly equal to an acre.

ARPS *abbr* (*Brit*) = Associate of the Royal Photographic Society.

arquebus *n* an old-fashioned handgun fired from a forked rest.—*also* **harquebus**.

arr. *abbr* = arranged; arrangements; arrival, or arrivals; arrive, or arrives; arrived.

ARR *abbr* = Association for Radiation Research; (*Latin*) *anno regni reginae*, "in the year of the queen's reign"; (*Latin*) *anno regni regis*, "in the year of the king's reign."

ARRA *abbr* = Amateur Radio Retailers Association.

arrack *n* an alcoholic spirit distilled in some Asian countries from rice, molasses, the juice of the date palm, etc.—*also* **arak**.

arraign *vt* to put on trial; to indict, accuse; to censure publicly; to impeach.—**arraigner** *n*.—**arraignment** *n*.

arrange *vt* to put in a sequence or row; to settle, make preparations for; (*mus*) to prepare a composition for different instruments other than those intended.* *vi* to come to an agreement; to make plans.—**arranger** *n*.

arrangement *n* the act of putting in proper form or order; that which is ordered or disposed; the method or style of disposition; a preparatory measure; preparation; settlement; classification; adjustment; adaptation; (*mus*) an adaptation of a piece of music for a medium different from that for which it was originally composed; (*pl*) plans.

arrant *adj* notorious; unmitigated; downright, thorough; shameless.

arras *n* a tapestry; hangings made of a rich figured fabric.

Arras *adj* relating to a culture of the 5th to 1st century BC that seems to have originated in eastern France and the Rhineland.

Arrau *n* **Claudio** (1903–91) an influential Chilean pianist who opened his own piano school in Santiago, Chile, and taught in Berlin from 1925–40. He was recognized as one of the greatest interpreters of works by Beethoven.

array *n* an orderly grouping, esp of troops; an impressive display; fine clothes; (*comput*) an ordered data structure that allows information to be easily indexed; (*astron*) a regularly spaced group of antennae for radio astronomy * *vt* to set in order, to arrange; to dress, decorate.—**arrayal** *n*.

arrears *npl* overdue debts; work, etc still to be completed.

arrest *vt* to stop; to capture, apprehend esp by legal authority; to check the development of a disease; to catch and hold the attention of. * *n* a stoppage; seizure by legal authority.

arrestee *n* one who has been arrested.

arrester *n* one who or that which stops or seizes, or causes to be detained.

arresting *adj* striking or attracting to the mind or eye; impressive.—**arrestingly** *adv*.

arrhythmia *n* any irregularity in the rhythm or force of the heartbeat.—**arrhythmic** *adj*.

ARRI *abbr* = Aboriginal Rural Resource Initiative.

arrière-pensée *n* (*pl* **arrière-pensées**) a mental reservation.

arris *n* (*archit*) a sharp edge produced when two curved or flat surfaces meet as in a V-shaped gutter; the ridge formed at the junction of two surfaces, as on the center line of a sword.

arrival *n* arriving; a person or thing that has arrived.

arrive *vi* to reach any destination; to come; (*with* **at**) to reach agreement, a decision; to achieve success, celebrity.

arriviste *n* an ambitious person, a self-seeker.

arrogance *n* an exaggerated assumption of importance.

arrogant *adj* overbearing; aggressively self-important.—**arrogantly** *adv*.

arrogate *vt* to assume or lay claim to unduly or presumptuously.—**arrogation** *n*.—**arrogative** *adj*.—**arrogator** *n*.

arrondissement *n* a subdivision of a French department; a municipal subdivision of Paris, etc.

arrow *n* a straight, pointed weapon, made to be shot from a bow; a sign used to indicate direction or location.

ARROW *abbr* = Active Resistance to the Roots of War; Asian-Pacific Research Center for Women.

arrowhead *n* the head or barb of an arrow; an aquatic plant so named from the shape of its leaves.

arrowroot *n* a starch obtained from the rootstocks of several species of West Indian plants.

arrowwood *n* a wood once used for arrows by American Indians.

arroyo *n* a watercourse or rivulet; the dry bed of a small stream.

ARRRI *abbr* = Alligator Rivers Region Research Institute.

ars. *abbr* = arsenal.

ARS *abbr* = Agricultural Research Service

ars antiqua *n* (*mus*) (*Latin*) the "old art," i.e., music of the 12th and 13th centuries as opposed to *ars nova*, the new style of music that evolved in the 14th century.

ars nova (*Latin*) *see* **ars antiqua**.

ARSA *abbr* (*Brit*) = Associate of the Royal Society of Arts.

ARSCM *abbr* (*Brit*) = Associate Member of the Royal School of Church Music.

arse *n* (*vulg*) the buttocks.

arsenal *n* a workshop or store for weapons and ammunition.

arsenate *n* a salt formed by combination of arsenic acid with any base.

arsenic *n* a soft grey metallic element, highly poisonous.

arsenical *adj* pertaining to or containing arsenic.

arsenious, arsenous *adj* pertaining to or containing arsenic.

arsenite *n* a salt of arsenious acid.

arsis *n* (*poet*) the part of a metrical foot where the accent is placed.

arson *n* the crime of using fire to destroy property deliberately.—**arsonist** *n*.

ARSR *abbr* = air route surveillance radar.

art[1] *n* human creativity; skill acquired by study and experience; any craft and its principles; the making of things that have form and beauty; any branch of this, as painting, sculpture, etc; drawings, paintings, statues, etc; (*pl*) the creative and nonscientific branches of knowledge, esp as studied academically.

art[2] (*arch*) the second person singular indicative mood and present tense of the verb to be.

art. *abbr* = article; artificial; artillery; artist.

Artaud *n* Antonin (1896–1948) French actor and director whose essays on the theater, *The Theater and Its Double*, have had a lasting effect on Western drama, particularly theater of cruelty.

art autre, art informel *n* a name coined by art critic Michel Tapie in *Un Art Autre* (1952); he used it to describe non-geometric abstract expressionism.

Artaxerxes *n* king of Persia (*Bible*) 464–424 BC; he gave permission for Nehhemiah to rebuild the walls of Jerusalem. *See also* **Nehemiah**.

art brut *n* the work of anyone not linked to the art world either as professional or amateur, for example psychiatric patients or prisoners, etc. The term can also include graffiti and the work of young children. It refers to any work uninfluenced by the art world and its fashions. *See also* **Dubuffet**.

ARTC *abbr* = air route traffic control.

Art Déco *n* the decorative art of the 1920s and 1930s in Europe and North America, originally called Jazz Modern. It was classical in style, with slender, symmetrical, geometric, or rectilinear forms. Major influences were Art Nouveau architecture and ideas from the arts and crafts movement and the Bauhaus.

artefact *see* **artifact**.

artel *n* a workers' guild in the former USSR.

Artemis *n* (*Greek myth*) goddess of hunting and the moon, daughter of Zeus and Leto and twin sister of Apollo, identified with the Roman Diana.

artemisia *n* a large genus of plants to which the common wormwood belongs, yielding a volatile oil (the chief ingredient of absinthe).

arterial *adj* pertaining to an artery or the arteries; contained in an artery; (of blood) oxygenated, of a lighter red color than venous blood; (of road) major, with many branches.

arterial blood *n* blood carried from the heart by arteries

arterialize *vt* to convert as venous blood into arterial blood by exposure to oxygen in the lungs.—**arterialization** *n*.

arteriectomy *n* the surgical removal of a part or the whole of an artery.

arteriogram *n* the recording of an arterial pulse on an oscilloscope screen or paper strip, which appears in wave form.

arteriography *n* the X-ray examination of an artery.

arteriole *n* a small branch of an artery leading to a capillary.

arterioplasty *n* surgery to reconstruct an artery.

arteriosclerosis *n* (*med*) hardening of the walls of the arteries due to the action of fatty deposits, which impairs blood circulation.—**arteriosclerotic** *adj*.

arteritis *n* inflammation of an artery.

artery *n* (*pl* **arteries**) a tubular vessel that conveys blood from the heart; any main channel of transport or communication.

artesian basin *n* an area where water seeps into and saturates permeable rocks so that the water is under pressure.

artesian well *n* a well in which water rises to the surface by internal pressure.

art form *n* any activity considered as an artistic expression.

artful *adj* skillful at attaining one's ends; clever, crafty.—**artfully** *adv*.—**artfulness** *n*.

Artgal *n* (*d*. 871) king of Strathclyde. His kingdom was subject to raids from Norse invaders and in 870 they sacked Dumbarton.

arthritis *n* inflammation of the joints or spine, the symptoms of which are pain and swelling, restriction of movement, redness and warmth of the skin.—**arthritic** *adj*.

arthropathy *n* any joint disorder or disease.

arthroplasty *n* an operation to repair a diseased joint by constructing a new one, often involving the insertion of artificial materials.

arthropod *n* a member of the largest group of invertebrate animals with jointed legs, such as the butterfly, spider, crab, centipede.

Arthur (*c*. 500) British tribal king; a legendary Celtic warrior-king of post-Roman Britain who may have organized resistance against the Saxon invaders.

Arthur *n* Chester Alan (1830–86) 21st president of the US. He served as Republican vice-president (1880) and president (1881–85).

Arthurian legend *n* any of the tales of brave knights and holy quests associated with the court of King Arthur that became popular throughout Europe in the early Middle Ages.

artichoke *n* a thistle-like plant with a scaly flower head, parts of which are eaten as a vegetable.

article *n* a separate item or clause in a written document; an individual item on a particular subject in a newspaper, magazine, etc; a particular or separate item; (*gram*) a word placed before a noun to identify it as definite or indefinite.

articled *adj* apprenticed to, as an articled clerk to a solicitor.

articles of association *npl* the legal constitution of a company.

articular *adj* of a joint or structural components in a joint.

articulate *adj* capable of distinct, intelligible speech, or expressing one's thoughts clearly; jointed. * *vti* to speak or express clearly; to unite or become united (as) by a joint.—**articulatedly** *adv*.—**articulateness** *n*.

articulated truck, articulated lorry *n* a large vehicle composed of a tractor and one or more trailers connected by flexible joints for greater maneuverability.— *also* **trailer truck**.

articulation *n* the act of jointing; the act of speaking distinctly; a distinct utterance; the state of being articulated; a joint or juncture between bones; the point of separation of organs or parts of a plant; a node or joint of the stem, or the space between two nodes.—**articulatory** *adj*.

articulator *n* one who pronounces distinctly; any organ of the mouth, etc, that moves to produce speech sounds.

artifact *n* a product of human craftsmanship, esp a simple tool or ornament.— *also* **artefact**.

artifice *n* a clever contrivance or stratagem; a trick, trickery.

artificer *n* a skilled or artistic worker; a maker or constructor; an inventor.

artificial *adj* lacking natural qualities; man-made.—**artificiality** *n*.— **artificially** *adv*.

artificial insemination *n* injection of semen into the womb by artificial means so that conception takes place without sexual intercourse.

artificial intelligence *n* (*comput*) the ability of an artificial mechanism to exhibit intelligent behavior by modifying its actions through reasoning and learning from experience; the research discipline in which artificial mechanisms that exhibit intelligence are developed and studied.

artificial respiration *n* an emergency procedure carried out when normal respiration has ceased.

artillery *n* (*pl* **artilleries**) large, heavy guns; the branch of the army that uses these.

artisan *n* a skilled workman.

artist *n* one who practices fine art, esp painting; one who does anything very well.— **artistic** *adj*.

artiste *n* a professional, usu musical or theatrical, entertainer.

artistic *adj* pertaining to art or to artists; characterized by aesthetic feeling or conformity to the principles of a school of art or design.—**artistically** *adv*.

artistry *n* artistic quality, ability, work, etc.

artless *adj* simple, natural; without art or skill.—**artlessly** *adv*.—**artlessness** *n*.

Art Nouveau *n* A style of art and decoration that developed in the late 19th century, characterized by flowing curves and designs in imitation of nature. Its principal exponents were the Scottish architect Charles Rennie Mackintosh and the American designer Louis Comfort Tiffany (1848–1933).

arts. *abbr* = articles.

Arts and Crafts Movement *n* an English movement in the decorative arts towards the end of the 19th century. The motive was to re-establish the value of handcrafted objects at a time of increasing mass production and industrialization. The most active and important leader of the movement was William Morris.

artwork *n* work in the graphic or plastic arts; (*media*) the decorative and graphic portions of a publication, as opposed to the text.

arty *adj* (**artier, artiest**) (*inf*) having a pretentious or affected interest in art.

Arty. *abbr* = Artillery.

arty-crafty, artsy-craftsy *adj* (*inf*) relating to arts and crafts, esp when affecting a simple, traditional style.

ARU *abbr* = American Railway Union.

Aruba *n* one of the islands in the Netherlands Antilles in the Caribbean Sea. It has been a self-governing Dutch territory since 1986.

arum *n* a genus of plants with small flowers within a hood-shaped leaf.

Arundel *n* Thomas Howard 2nd Earl of (1586–1646) English patron of the arts, collector, and antiquarian, and also a prominent figure at the court of Charles I. His impressive art collection was broken up after his death, although the bulk of his classical sculpture is in the Ashmolean Museum in Oxford.

arundinaceous *adj* pertaining to or resembling a reed or cane.

ARV *abbr* = Aids-associated retrovirus; American Standard Revised Version.

-ary *adj suffix*, *n suffix* connected with, as *dictionary*.

Aryan *n* a member of the Indo-European race; according to Nazi belief, a Caucasian, esp of the Nordic type, with no Jewish blood. * *adj* pertaining to the Aryans, or to their language.

as[1] *adv* equally; for instance; when related in a certain way. * *conj* in the same way that; while; when; because. * *prep* in the role or function of.

as[2] *n* (*pl* **asses**) a Roman weight equivalent to the libra or pound; a Roman copper coin.

As *symbol* (*chem*) arsenic (element).

as *abbr* (*org chem*) = asymmetric.

a.s. *abbr* = assistant secretary; at sight.

As. *abbr* = Asia; Asian; Asiatic.

AS *abbr* = Academy of Science; Act or Acts, of Sederunt; Aetherius Society; Air Service; Aristotelian Society; Association of Secretaries; Association of Stammerers;

Association of Surgeons of Great Britain and Ireland; Assistant Secretary; Avicultural Society; air speed; (*mus*) (*Italian*) *al segno*, "to the sign"; (*Latin*) *anno salutis*, " in the year of salvation."

A/S *abbr* = (*Danish*)*Aktieselskab*, "joint-stock company"; (*Norwegian*)*Aksjeselskap*, "limited company"; account sales; after sight.

Asa *n* (*Bible*) king of Judah who defeated a huge Ethiopian invading army.

ASA *abbr* = Advertising Standards Authority; American Statistical Association; Acoustical Society of America; Atomic Scientists Association; Australian Society of Archivists; Austrian Space Agency; (*chem*) acetylsalicylic acid (aspirin).

asafetida, asafoetida *n* a foul-smelling gum resin obtained from the roots of several large umbelliferous plants and used in medicine.

asap *abbr* = as soon as possible.

ASAT *abbr* = anti-satellite.

asb. *abbr* = asbestos.

ASB *abbr* (*med*) = anencephaly and spina bifida.

asbestos, asbestus *n* a fine fibrous mineral used for making incombustible and chemical-resistant materials.

asbestosis *n* (*med*) a disease of the lungs caused by the inhalation of asbestos fibers.

ASBM *abbr* = air-to-surface ballistic missile.

ASBTH *abbr* = Associate of the Society of Health and Beauty Therapists.

ASC *abbr* = Army Service Corps.

ASCA *abbr* = Airline Sports and Cultural Association; Arab Society of Certified Accountants; (*Taiwan*) Asian Crystallographic Association; Associate of the Institute of Company Accountants.

Ascanius *n* (*Greek myth*) the son of Aeneas, who accompanied his father on his journey from Troy to Italy.—*also* **Iulus**.

ASCC *abbr* = Association of Scottish Chambers of Commerce; Australian Society of Cosmetic Chemists.

ASCE *abbr* = American Society of Civil Engineers.

a.s.e., ase *abbr* = air standard efficiency.

ascend *vti* to go up; to succeed to (a throne).

ascendancy, ascendency *n* governing or dominating influence; power; sway.

ascendant, ascendent *adj* rising upwards; dominant.

ascender *n* one who ascends; the top part of letters such as b, d, h.

ascending order *n* (*comput*) a method of sorting data in a list so that the data is arranged from 1 to 10 or A to Z. Descending order reverses the sort order.

ascension *n* the act of ascending or rising.—**ascensional** *adj*.

Ascension *n* (*Bible*) the ascent of Christ to heaven is celebrated in the Christian Church on the Thursday ten days before Whitsunday.

Ascension Day *n* a movable feast commemorating the Ascension, celebrated on the Thursday next but one before Whit Sunday.—*also* **Holy Thursday**.

ascent *n* an ascending; an upward slope; the means of, the way of ascending.

ascertain *vt* to acquire definite knowledge of, to discover positively.—**ascertainable** *adj*.

ascetic *adj* self-denying, austere. * *n* a person who practices rigorous self-denial as a religious discipline; any severely abstemious person.—**ascetically** *adv*.—**asceticism** *n*.

Ascham *n* **Roger** (*c*.1515–68) English educationalist and classics tutor to Queen Elizabeth I whose book on education, *The Scholemaster*, is a landmark in humanist educational theory.

ascidian *n* a type of mollusk with a leathery tunic resembling a double-necked bottle, a sea squirt.—*also adj*.

ascidium *n* (*pl* **ascidia**) (*bot*) a pitcher-shaped or flask-shaped organ peculiar to certain plants, as the pitcher plants.

ASCII *abbr* (*comput*) = American Standard Code for Information Interchange. A standard set of codes that defines the way information is transferred from one computer to another. It represents binary code by alphanumeric codes.

ASCII file *n* (*comput*) a file composed entirely of ASCII characters. A txt file is often the same as an ASCII file.

ascites *n* (*pl* **ascites**) an abnormal accumulation of fluid in the abdominal cavity.—**ascitic** *adj*.

Asclepius *see* **Aesculapius**.

ascomycete *n* one of a family of the fungi, including most of the lichens, which form free spores within elongated spore cases.—**ascomyetous** *adj*.

ascorbic acid *n* vitamin C, found esp in citrus fruit and fresh green vegetables.

ascot *n* a kind of scarf or necktie.

ascribe *vt* to attribute, impute or refer; to assign.—**ascribable** *adj*.—**ascription, adscription** *n*.

ASCT *abbr* = Associate of the Society of Cardiological Technicians.

ascus *n* (*pl* **asci**) the spore case of lichens and fungi.

ASD *abbr* = atrial septal defect.

Asda *trademark* = Associated Dairies.

ASDC *abbr* = Associate of the Society of Dyers and Colorists.

ASDIC *abbr* = Anti-Submarine Detection Investigation Committee (a name for sonar equipment; an apparatus for locating submarines; an echo sounder).

ASDSFB *abbr* = Association of Scottish District Salmon Fishery Boards.

ASE *abbr* = American Society of Enologists; Association for Science Education; Associate of the Society of Engineering; Association for Science Engineering; (*Brit*) Astronomical Society of Edinburgh; Athens Stock Exchange; Australian Society of Endodontology.

asea *adv* at sea; toward or on the sea.

aseismic plates *n* any of the Earth's crustal plates where there are few earthquakes.

Asenath *n* (*Bible*) daughter of a priest of Egypt and mother of Ephraim, the second son of Joseph. *See also* **Ephraim**, **Joseph**.

asepsis *n* an absence of disease or putrefaction; a surgical method aiming at this.—**asceptic** *adj*.

asexual *adj* lacking sex or sexual organs; (*reproduction*) produced without the union of male and female germ cells.—**asexuality** *n*.—**asexually** *adv*.

ash[1] *n* a tree with silver-grey bark; the wood of this tree.

ash[2] *n* powdery residue of anything burnt; fine, volcanic lava.

Ash. *abbr* (*mil*) = airship.

ASH *abbr* = Action on Smoking and Health; Association Suisse des Horticulteurs.

ashamed *adj* feeling shame or guilt.—**ashamedly** *adv*.

A-shares *npl* (*com*) ordinary shares in a company that usu do not confer voting rights on their owners.

Ashbee *n* **Charles Robert** (1863–1942) British architect and designer who was a leading force in the **Arts and Crafts Movement**.

Ashbery *n* **John** (1927–) American poet and critic whose poetry, e.g., *The Double Dream of Spring*, is renowned for its vivid imagery.

ash can *n* a container for household refuse, a garbage can.

Ashcan School *n* a group of American painters of urban realism between 1908 and 1918. Their joint aim was to declare themselves primarily American painters, and they painted what they saw as American life, generally rejecting subject matter of academic approval.

Ashcroft *n* **Dame Peggy** (1907–91) English actress. She won an Oscar for her role in *A Passage to India* (1984).

Ashe *n* **Arthur** (1943–93) American tennis player and the first black tennis player to win the major titles.

ashen *adj* like ashes, esp in color; pale.

ashen light *n* (*astron*) a faint illumination sometimes seen in the unlit side of Venus.

Asherah *n* (*Bible*) alternative name to Astoroth.

Ashkenazi *n* (*pl* **Ashkenazim**) a Jew from Germany or eastern Europe.

Ashkhabad (Ashgabat) *n* capital city of Turkmenistan.

ashlar *n* (*archit*) blocks of building stone with square edges and even faces; masonry of this.

ashlaring *n* a wall faced with ashlar; a low wall of a garret, built close to where the rafters reach the floor.

Ashley *n* **Laura** (1926–88) British fashion and fabric designer who revived the English country cottage design in the early 1950s.

ashore *adv* to or on the shore; to or on land.—*also adj*.

ashram *n* a Hindu religious retreat.

Ashtaroth *n* (*Bible*) female counterpart in Canaanite fertility cults to Baal, the male lord or master. *See also* **Baal**.

Ashton *n* **Sir Frederick [William Mallandaine]** (1906–88) British choreographer and co-founder of the Royal Ballet.

Ashtoreth *n* (*Bible*) alternative name to Astoroth.

ashtray *n* a small receptacle for tobacco ash and cigarette stubs.

Ash Wednesday *n* the first day of Lent; a special day set apart for fasting.

ashy *adj* (**ashier, ashiest**) of ashes; ash-colored, pale.

ASI *abbr* = Adam Smith Institute; Ambulance Service Institute; Anti-Slavery International; ; Astronomy Society of India; Aviation Society of Ireland; air speed indicator.

ASIAD *abbr* = Associate of the Society of Industrial Artists and Designers.

Asian *adj* of or relating to the continent of Asia, its inhabitants or languages.—*also n* .

Asiatic cholera *n* a virulent form of cholera.

ASIC *abbr* = application specific integrated circuit.

aside *adv* on or to the side; in reserve; away from; notwithstanding. * *n* words uttered and intended as inaudible, esp as spoken by an actor to the audience and supposedly unheard by the other actors on the stage.

ASIF *abbr* = Amateur Swimming International Federation.

Asimov *n* **Isaac** (1920–92) Russian-born American science fiction author, whose many novels and short stories, e.g., *I Robot*, have been very influential.

asinine *adj* silly, stupid.—**asininity** *n*.

ask *vt* to put a question to, inquire of; to make a request of or for; to invite; to demand, expect. * *vi* to inquire about.—**asker** *n*.

askance, askant *adv* with a sideways glance; with distrust.

askew *adv* to one side; awry.—*also adj*.

askos *n* a vessel with one handle towards the rear and an opening with a neck.

ASL *abbr* = above sea level.

aslant *adv* not at right angles; obliquely. * *prep* slantingly across, athwart.

ASLDC *abbr* (*Brit*) = Association of Social and Liberal Democrat Councillors.

asleep *adj* sleeping; inactive; numb. * *adv* into a sleeping condition.

ASLEF *abbr* = Associated Society of Locomotive Engineers and Firemen.

ASLIB *abbr* = Association for Information Management (formerly Association of Special Libraries and Information Bureaux).

ASLO *abbr* = Associated Scottish Life Officers; Australian Scientific Liaison Office.

asm. *abbr* = assembly.

ASM *abbr* = air-to-surface missile; assistant stage manager.

ASMA *abbr* = Associate of the Society of Sales Management Administrators Ltd.

ASME *abbr* = American Society of Mechanical Engineers.

ASN *abbr* = Army service number.

ASNNA *abbr* = Associate of the Society of Nursery Nursing Administrators.

asocial *adj* not capable of or avoiding social contact; antisocial.

Asopus *n* the name of several rivers in ancient Greece; Greek river-god, the father of Aegina.

asp *n* a small poisonous snake.

ASP *abbr* = American Society of Papyrologists; Association of Service Providers; Australian Society of Prosthodontists.

asparagus *n* a plant cultivated for its edible young shoots.

aspartame *n* an artificial sweetener derived from an amino acid.

ASPCA *abbr* = American Society for Prevention of Cruelty to Animals.

aspect *n* the look of a person or thing to the eye; a particular feature of a problem, situation, etc; the direction something faces; view; the direction a slope faces; (*astrol*) the position of the planets with respect to one another, regarded as having an influence on human affairs.

aspen *n* a species of poplar with leaves that tremble in the slightest breeze. * *adj* (*arch*) quivering.

aspergillus *n* (*pl* **aspergilli**) a genus of microscopic fungi, to which several of the moulds belong.

asperity *n* (*pl* **asperities**) hardship, severity; sharpness of temper.

asperse *vt* to slander; (*rare*) to besprinkle, to bespatter.—**asperser** *n*.—**aspersive** *adj*.

aspersions *npl* slander; an attack on a person's reputation.

aspersorium *n* (*pl* **aspersoria, aspersoriums**) a vessel containing holy water for sprinkling; a brush or metallic instrument used for sprinkling the water.

asphalt *n* a hard, black bituminous substance, used for paving roads, etc. * *vt* to surface with asphalt.—**asphaltic** *adj*.

asphalt *n* a naturally occurring tar, usu thick and viscous.

asphodel *n* a favorite plant among the ancient Greeks, who planted it round their tombs and associated it with Persephone, the dead, and the underworld; one of several plants of the lily family; (*poet*) the daffodil; (*poet*) an immortal, unfading flower that bloomed in the meadows of Elysium (possibly the narcissus).

asphyxia *n* the state of suffocation during which breathing eventually stops and oxygen fails to reach tissues and organs.

asphyxiate *vt* to suffocate.—**asphyxiation** *n*.—**asphyxiator** *n*.

aspic *n* a savory jelly used to coat fish, game, etc.

aspidistra *n* an Asian plant with broad leaves, grown as a house plant.

aspirant *n* someone who aspires to something.

aspirate *n* the sound of *h*. * *vt* to pronounce with an *h*; to suck out using an aspirator.

aspiration *n* strong desire; ambition; the act of aspirating; the act of breathing; the withdrawal of air or fluid from a body cavity. (*med*) the process of removing fluid or gases from cavities in the body by means of suction.—**aspiratory** *adj*.

aspirator *n* a device used to suck (air, fluid, etc) from a (body) cavity.

aspire *vi* to desire eagerly; to aim at high things.—**aspirer** *n*.—**aspiring** *adj*.

aspirin *n* (*pl* **aspirin, aspirins**) acetylsalicylic acid used to relieve mild pain, e.g., headache, and also helpful in the prevention of coronary thrombosis.

Asplund *n* **Gunnar E.** (1885–1940) Swedish architect. His notable works include extension to Göteborg Town Hall.

ASPS *abbr* = Association of Scottish Police Superintendents.

asquint *adv, adj* with a squint, to or out of the corner of the eye; obliquely.

Asquith *n* **Herbert Henry [1st Earl of Oxford and Asquith]** (1852–1928) British statesman; Liberal prime minister (1908–16).

ASR *abbr* = airport surveillance radar; answer, send and receive; air-sea rescue; automatic send and receive.

ASRA *abbr* = Association for the Study of Reptilia and Amphibia.

A/SRS *abbr* = air-sea rescue service.

ass *n* a donkey; a silly, stupid person; (*sl*) the arse, the buttocks.

ass. *abbr* = assistant; association.

Ass. *abbr* = Associated; Associate; Association.

ASS *abbr* = Anti-Slavery Society.

assagai *see* **assegai**.

assai *adv* (*mus*) (*Italian*) very, more, extremely, as in *allegro assai*, "very fast."

assail *vt* to attack violently either physically or verbally.—**assailable** *adj*.—**assailer** *n*.—**assailment** *n*.

assailant *n* an attacker.

assassin *n* a murderer, esp one hired to kill a leading political figure, etc.

assassinate *vt* to kill a political figure, etc; to harm (a person's reputation, etc).—**assassination** *n*.

assault *n* a violent attack; (*law*) an unlawful threat or attempt to harm another physically. * *vti* to make an assault (on); to rape.—**assaulter** *n*.

assault course *n* an obstacle course used for military training .

assay *n* (*chem*) the chemical analysis of a mixture to determine the amount of a particular constituent; the analysis of the quantity of metal in an ore or alloy, esp the standard purity of gold or silver; a test. * *vt* (**assaying, assayed**) to subject to analysis; to determine the quantity or proportion of one or more of the constituents of a metal.—**assayable** *adj*.—**assayer** *n*.

ASSC *abbr* = Air Service Signal Corps.

assd. *abbr* = assigned.

assegai, assagai *n* (*pl* **assegais, assagais**) (*S Africa*) a light hardwood javelin or spear for casting or stabbing.

assemblage *n* a gathering of persons or things; (*art*) a form of collage.

assemble *vti* to bring together; to collect; to fit together the parts of; (*comput*) to translate using an assembler.

assembler *n* (*comput*) a program that converts low-level mnemonic symbols into machine code.

assembly *n* (*pl* **assemblies**) assembling or being assembled; a gathering of persons, esp for a particular purpose; the fitting together of parts to make a whole machine, etc.

assembly language *n* (*comput*) a low-level programming language that is based on instructions that relate directly to the processing chip. (*See also* **high-level programming language**.)

assembly line *n* a series of machines, equipment and workers through which a product passes in successive stages to be assembled.

assemblyman *n* (*pl* **assemblymen**) a member of a legislative assembly.—**assemblywoman** *nf* (*pl* **assemblywomen**).

assent *vi* to express agreement to something. * *n* consent or agreement.—**assentor, assenter** *n*.

assentation *n* compliance with the opinion of another, in flattery or obsequiousness.

assert *vt* to declare, affirm as true; to maintain or enforce (e.g., rights).—**assertible** *adj*.

assertion *n* asserting; a statement that something is a fact, usu without evidence.

assertive *adj* self-assured, positive, confident; dogmatic.—**assertively** *adv*.—**assertiveness** *n*.

assess *vt* to establish the amount of, as a tax; to impose a tax or fine; to value, for the purpose of taxation; to estimate the worth, importance, etc of.—**assessable** *adj*.

assessment *n* the act of assessing or determining an amount to be paid; an official valuation of property, or income, for the purpose of taxation; the specific sum levied as tax, or assessed for damages.

assessor *n* a person appointed to assess property or persons for taxation; an expert appointed to assist a judge or magistrate as an adviser on special points of law.—**assessorial** *adj*.

asset *n* an article or property that is owned by a company or individual and has a monetary value; a desirable thing; (*pl*) all the property, accounts receivable, etc of a person or business; (*pl*) (*law*) property usable to pay debts.

asset value per share *n* (*com*) the total value of the assets of a company minus its liabilities divided by the number of ordinary shares.

asset-stripping *n* the acquisition of a company with a view to selling its assets for financial profit rather than with a view to running it as a going concern.—**asset-stripper** *n*.

asseverate *vt* to declare solemnly; to affirm or aver positively.—**asseveration** *n*.

assez *adj, adv* (*mus*) (*French*) "moderately," as in *assez vite*, "moderately quick."

ASSGB *abbr* = Association of Ski Schools in Great Britain.

asshole *n* (*sl*) a stupid person; (*vulg*) the anus.

assibilate *vt* (*phonetics*) to pronounce with a hissing sound; to alter to a sibilant.—**assibilation** *n*.

assiduity *n* (*pl* **assiduities**) close application, steady attention; diligence; (*usu pl*) constant attentions.

assiduous *adj* persistent or persevering; diligent.—**assiduously** *adv*.—**assiduousness** *n*.

assign *vt* to allot; to appoint to a post or duty; to ascribe; (*law*) to transfer (a right, property, etc).—**assignable** *adj*.—**assigner** *n*.

assignat *n* a money or currency bond secured on state lands, issued by the French Revolutionary Government (1789–96).

assignation *n* the act of assigning; a meeting, esp one made secretly by lovers.

assignee *n* (*law*) one to whom an assignment of anything is made, either in trust or for his or her own use and enjoyment.

assignment *n* the act of assigning; something assigned to a person, such as a share, task, etc; (*law*) the transfer of an interest in a bond, mortgage, lease or other instrument by writing.

assignor *n* (*law*) one who assigns or transfers an interest.

assigt. *abbr* = assignment.

assimilate *vt* to absorb; to digest; to take in and understand fully; to be ascribed; to be like.—**assimilable** *adj*.—**assimilation** *n*.

assimilative, assimilatory *adj* having the power of assimilating, or causing assimilation, tending to produce assimilation.

assist *vti* to support or aid.—**assister** *n*.

assistance *n* help; furtherance; aid; succor; support.

assistant *n* one who or that which assists; a helper; an auxiliary; a subordinate; (*comput*) a series of steps in an application program that assists the user to create a particular document style. * *adj* helping; lending aid; auxiliary.

assisted conception *n* conception of a fetus by in vitro fertilization.

assize *n* (*pl* **assizes**) (*law*) a court or session of justice for the trial by jury of civil or criminal cases; (*usu pl*) (*formerly*) the sessions held periodically in each county of England by judges of the Supreme Court; (*usu pl*) the time or place of holding the assize.

assn. *abbr* = association.

assoc. *abbr* = associate; associated; association.

associable *adj* capable of being joined or associated; liable to be affected by sympathy with kindred parts or organs.

associate *vt* to join as a friend, business partner or supporter; to bring together; to unite; to connect in the mind. * *vi* to combine or unite with others; to come together as friends, business partners or supporters. * *adj* allied or connected; having secondary status or privileges. * *n* a companion, business partner, supporter, etc; something closely connected with another; a person admitted to an association as a subordinate member.

associated company *n* a company in which another company has a significant interest but not a majority interest.

association *n* an organization of people joined together for a common aim; the act of associating or being associated; a connection in the mind, memory, etc; (*archeo*) a number of objects which are found together at an archeological site; (*astron*) a loose form of star cluster.

association football *n* football played with a round ball that is not handled, soccer.

associationism *n* (*psychol*) the mental connection existing between an object and the ideas related to it.

associative *adj* tending to or characterized by association; (*math*) having elements whose result is the same despite the grouping.

assonance *n* a correspondence in sound between words or syllables.—**assonant** *adj*, *n*.—**assonantal** *adj*.

assort *vt* to arrange in groups according to kind. * *vi* to agree in kind.—**assortative, assortive** *adj*.—**assorter** *n*.

assorted *adj* distributed according to sorts; miscellaneous.

assortment *n* a collection of people or things of different sorts.

asst *abbr* = assistant.

ass't. *abbr* = assessment.

ASSU *abbr* = American Sunday School Union.

assuage *vt* to soften the intensity of; to soothe.—**assuager** *n*.—**assuagement** *n*.—**assuasive** *adj*.

assume *vt* to take on, to undertake; to usurp; to take as certain or true; to pretend to possess.—**assumable** *adj*.—**assumer** *n*.

assumed name *n* (*law*) a legal document establishing the fact that an individual or corporation are planning to do business in the county under the assumed name declared on the document.

assuming *adj* presumptuous.

assumption *n* something taken for granted; the taking on of a position, esp of power; (*with cap*) the ascent of the Virgin Mary into heaven; (*RC Church*) the Christian feast in remembrance of this, celebrated 15 August.—**assumptive** *adj*.

Assur or **Ashur** *n* (*archeo*) the name of the principal city of Assyria and also the Assyrians' sun god.

assurance *n* a promise, guarantee; a form of life insurance; a feeling of certainty, self-confidence.

Assurbanipal *n* Egyptian king of the Assyrians (ruled Egypt 669–640 BC), son of Esarhaddon, who had conquered Lower Egypt.

assure *vt* to make safe or certain; to give confidence to; to state positively; to guarantee, ensure.—**assurable** *adj*.—**assurer** *n*.

assured *adj* certain; convinced; self-confident.—**assuredness** *n*.

assuredly *adv* certainly.

assurgent *adj* ascending, rising; (*bot*) rising in a curve.

Assyr. *abbr* = Assyrian.

Assyria *n* great empire on the river Tigris in Mesopotamia; it destroyed the kingdom of Israel but failed to capture Jerusalem, capital of Judah; the empire was overrun on 612 BC by the Medes and Chaldeans of Babylon.

Assyrian *adj* pertaining to Assyria, an ancient kingdom of Mesopotamia, or to its inhabitants or language. * *n* the language spoken in Assyria; an inhabitant of Assyria.

Assyrians *npl* one of the major peoples in the Near East in ancient times, with their capital at Nineveh.

Assyriology *n* the science or study of the extinct language and the antiquities of Assyria.—**Assyriologist** *n*.

AST *abbr* = Association of Stress Therapists; Association of Swimming Therapy; Astronomical Society of Tasmania; Atlantic Salmon Trust; Atlantic Standard Time; advanced supersonic transport; automatic station tuning.

ASTA *abbr* = American Seed Trade Association; Association of Shippers to Africa; Association of Short-Circuit Testing Authorities; Associate of the Swimming Teachers' Association; Auckland Science Teachers Association.

Astaire *n* **Fred [Frederick Austerlitz]** (1899–1987) American dancer, singer, and actor and partner of **Ginger Rogers** in song-and-dance films, e.g., *Top Hat* (1935).

Astana *n* capital city of Kazakhstan.

astatic *adj* having a tendency not to stand still; unstable.—**astatically** *adv*.—**astaticism** *n*.

astatine *n* a radioactive element.

aster *n* a kind of plant with round composite flowers; a Michaelmas daisy.

-aster *n* *suffix* petty imitation, as in *poetaster*.

asteriated *adj* (*crystal, etc*) radiated; having the form of a star.

asterisk *n* a sign (*) used in writing or printing to mark omission of words, a footnote or other reference, etc. * *vt* to mark with an asterisk.

asterism *n* (*astron*) a chance grouping of stars forming a distinctive pattern, usu forming part of a constellation; three asterisks placed in the form of a triangle to direct attention to a particular passage; the star-like appearance in certain crystals.

astern *adv* behind a ship or aircraft; at or towards the rear of a ship, etc; backward.

asternal *adj* (*anat*) (of ribs) not joined to the sternum or breastbone.

asteroid *n* (*astron*) a rocky or metallic body that orbits the sun between the orbits of Mars and Jupiter.

asthenia *n* debility, weakness.—**asthenic** *adj*.

asthenopia *n* eyestrain.—**asthenopic** *adj*.

asthenosphere *n* the higher layer of the upper mantle of the Earth.

asthma *n* a chronic respiratory condition causing difficulty with breathing.—**asthmatic** *adj*.—**asthmatically** *adv*.

asthmatic *adj* of or suffering from or good for asthma. * *n* an asthmatic person.—**asthmatically** *adv*.

astigmatism *n* a defect in vision caused by abnormal curvature of the cornea that results in sight being blurred and distorted.—**astigmatic** *adj*.—**astigmatically** *adv*.

astir *adv* moving or bustling about; out of bed.

ASTM *abbr* = American Society for Testing Materials.

astomatous *adj* (*biol*) lacking a mouth; without breathing pores.

astonish *vt* to fill with sudden or great surprise.—**astonishing** *adj*.—**astonishment** *n*.

Astor *n* 1. **John Jacob** (1763–1849) German-born American fur trader and financier. He donated the Astor Public Library (now the New York Public Library) to New York city. 2. **Nancy Witcher [Langhorne] [Viscountess Astor]** (1879–1964) American-born British Conservative politician. The first woman to be elected to the British parliament.

Astori *n* **Antonia** (1940–) Italian designer who founded **Drade** with her brother, Enrico.

astound *vt* to astonish greatly.—**astounding** *adj*.—**astoundingly** *adv*.

astr. *abbr* = astronomer; astronomical; astronomy.

ASTRA *abbr* = Association in Scotland to Research into Astronautics.

astraddle *adv* astride, straddling.

Astraea, Astraia *n* (*Greek myth*) the daughter of Zeus and Themis and the goddess of justice; goddess of the constellation Virgo; (*astron*) an asteroid discovered in 1845.

astragal *n* (*archit*) a small molding or bead of semicircular form; a ring of molding round the top or bottom of a column.

astragalus *n* (*pl* **astragali**) the ball of the ankle joint.

astrakhan *n* the dark curly fleece of lambs from Astrakhan in Russia; a cloth with a curled pile made from or imitating this.

astral *adj* of or from the stars.

astraphobia *n* the fear of thunder and lightning.— **astraphobic** *adj*.

astray *adv* off the right path; into error.

astride *adv* with a leg on either side. * *prep* extending across.

astringent *adj* that contracts body tissues; stopping blood flow, styptic; harsh; biting. * *n* an astringent substance.—**astringency** *n*.

astro- *prefix* (*astron*) of a star or stars.

astrobleme *n* an ancient, crater-like feature on the Earth's surface, thought to have been caused by collision with an extraterrestrial body.

astrodome *n* a large sports stadium covered with a domed translucent roof.

astrograph *n* a telescope designed for accurate photography of the sky in which the relative positions of stars can be measured to a high degree of precision.

astrol. *abbr* = astrologer; astrological; astrology.

astrolabe *n* an early instrument for reckoning time and for other observational purposes.

astrology *n* the study of planetary positions and motions to determine their supposed influence on human affairs.—**astrologer, astrologist** *n*.—**astrological** *adj*.—**astrologically** *adv*.

astrometry *n* accurate measurement of the positions of stars and other objects on the celestial sphere using two coordinates, declination and right ascension; the art by which the apparent relative magnitude of the stars is determined.—**astrometric, astrometrical** *adj*.

astron. *abbr* = astronomer, astronomical; astronomy.

astronaut *n* one trained to make flights in outer space.

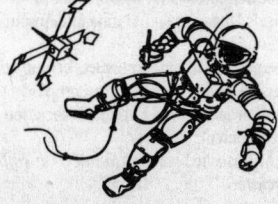

astronautics *npl* (*used as sing*) the scientific study of space flight and technology.

Astronomer Royal *n* (*Brit*) an honorary title given to an eminent British astronomer.

astronomical, astronomic *adj* enormously large; of or relating to astronomy.—**astronomically** *adv*.

astronomical clock *n* a clock that keeps sidereal time.

astronomical unit the mean distance of the Earth from the Sun, approx. 93 million miles, which forms the basis of astronomical distance measurements.

astronomical year *n* a year the length of which is determined by astronomical observations.

astronomy *n* the science of all celestial objects and of anything in the universe beyond our own Earth.—**astronomer** *n*.

astrophotography *n* photography of the heavenly bodies.—**astrophotographic** *adj*.

astrophys. *abbr* = astrophysics; astrophysical.

astrophysics *n* (*used as sing*) the branch of astronomy that deals with the physical and chemical constitution of the stars.—**astrophysical** *adj*.—**astrophysicist** *n*.

AstroTurf *n* (*trademark*) an artificial grasslike surface.

astute *adj* clever, perceptive; crafty, shrewd.—**astutely** *adv*.—**astuteness** *n*.

astylar *n* (*archit*) a classical façade without pilasters or columns.

Asunción *n* capital city of Paraguay.

asunder *adv* apart in direction or position; into pieces.

ASW *abbr* = anti-submarine warfare.

Aswan *n* Egyptian settlement on the Nile, now site of the High Dam. The Aswan quarries were the source of a prized red granite.

asylum *n* a place of safety, a refuge; (*formerly*) an institution for the blind, the mentally ill, etc.

asym., asymm. *abbr* = asymmetric; asymmetrical.

asymmetric, asymmetrical *adj* lacking symmetry.—**asymmetrically** *adv*.

asymmetry *n* a lack of symmetry or proportion between the parts of a thing.

asymptote *n* (*geom*) the line that continually approaches nearer to a given curve without ever meeting it.—**asymptotic, asymptotical** *adj*.

asynchronous *adj* not occurring at the same time.— **asynchronism** *n*.

asynchronous communication *n* (*comput*) a commonly used mode of transmitting data over telephone lines, where characters are sent or received one at a time.

asyndeton *n* (*pl* **asyndetons, asyndeta**) (*gram*) a figure of speech in which conjunctions are omitted, as "I came, I saw, I conquered"; such a figure.

Asyut *n* settlement in Middle Egypt, with large stone quarries nearby. A temple site and nome capital, whose local deity, the jackal-headed Wepwawet, became one of the guardians of the Osirian Underworld.

at[1] *prep* on; in; near; by; used to indicate location or position.

at[2] (@) *symbol* (*comput*) at; the part of an e-mail/Internet address that separates a user name from a domain name.

At *symbol* (*chem*) astatine (element).

at. *abbr* = atmospheres; atomic; attorney.

a.t. *abbr* = ampere turn, turns; arch treasurer; assay ton.

AT *abbr* = alternative technology; anti-tank; appropriate technology; automatic transmission.

A/T *abbr* = American terms (*grain trade*).

at- *prefix* the form of *ad-* before *t*.

ATA *abbr* = Africa Travel Association; Air Transport Auxiliary; American Trucking Association; Angling Trade Association; Animal Technicians Association; Atlantic Treaty Association.

Atalanta, Atalante *n* (*Greek myth*) a hunting heroine of Arcadia, who was to be married only to a man who could outrun her in a race, the consequence of failure being death. Melanion threw behind him three golden apples as he ran, and Atalanta stopped to pick them up.

AT & T *abbr* = American Telephone and Telegraph Company.

ataraxia, ataraxy *n* impassivity; peace of mind.

Atatürk *n* **Kemal [Mustafa Kemal Atatürk]** (1881–1938) Turkish general and statesman, regarded as the creator of the modern Turkish state.

atavism *n* the appearance in plants or animals of characteristics typical in more remote ancestors; reversion to a more primitive type.—**atavistic** *adj*.—**atavistically** *adv*.

ataxia *n* a loss of coordination in the limbs as a result of a disorder of the central nervous system.—**ataxic, atactic** *adj*.

ATB *abbr* = Agricultural Training Board; advanced technology bomber.

Atbara *n* a tributary of the Nile, rising in Ethiopia and joining the main stream at Atbara, north of Khartoum.

ATC *abbr* = Air Traffic Control; Air Training Corps; Art Teacher's Certificate; automated train control.

ATCC *abbr* = air traffic control center.

ATCL *abbr* (*Brit*) = Associate Diploma in Speech and Drama, Trinity College, London; Associate of Trinity College, London.

ATCRBS *abbr* = air traffic control radar beacon system.

ATD *abbr* = Art Teacher's Diploma; actual time of departure.

ate *see* **eat**.

Ate *n* (*Greek myth*) the goddess of hate, injustice, crime, and retribution.

ATE *abbr* = Automatic Telephone and Electric Company; Association of Tanzania Employers; Association of Teachers of English; Association of Therapeutic Education; automatic test equipment.

-ate *adj suffix* having or furnished with, as *foliate*. * *n suffix* forming the equivalent of *pp*, as in *associate*.

atelier *n* (*French*) a workshop; the studio of a painter or sculptor.

a tem. *abbr* (*mus*) = a tempo.

a tempo *adj, adv* (*mus*) (*Italian*) "in time"; a term that indicates that a piece should revert to its normal tempo after a change of speed.

a tempo giusto *n* (*mus*) (*Italian*) a direction to a performer to sing or play in strict time.

a tempo primo *see* **a tempo**.

atemporal *adj* timeless.

Aten *or* **Aton** *n* (*Egypt*) the name of the one god; the disc of the sun, its brilliantly visible aspect, as distinct from its mystical, creative aspects, which are linked with Amun, the "hidden god." Aten, on the other hand, was there for all to see and was established by the heretic pharaoh Akhenaten, who ruled until 1352 BC, as a universal god.

ATF *abbr* = Bureau of Alcohol, Tobacco and Firearms

ATG *abbr* = Appropriate Technology Group; Association of Teachers of Geology.

Athaliah *n* (*Bible*) 1. the daughter of Ahab and Jezebel. 2. married King Jehoram of Judah. 3 she followed the example of her mother by encouraging the worship of Baal, and tried to destroy the royal line of David. *See also* **Ahab**, **Baal**, **Jezebel**.

Athamas *n* (*Greek myth*) son of Aeolus, brother of Sisyphus and king of Orchomenus in Boeotia.

Athanasian Creed *n* one of the three creeds thus named as containing an exposition of the doctrines of the Trinity and incarnation of Christ, which Athanasius, bishop of Alexandria (*c*.296–373), defended.

Athanasius *n* **Saint** (296–373) born in Alexandria in Egypt; bishop of Alexandria; writer of two treatises, *Against the Gentiles* and *On the Incarnation*. His life was constantly in danger because he championed Christian orthodoxy over Arianism. His feast day is 2 May.

atheism *n* belief in the nonexistence of God.—**atheist** *n*.—**atheistic, atheistical** *adj*.

atheling *n* an Anglo-Saxon title of honor conferred on royal children and young nobles.

Athelstan *see* **Ethelstan**.

athematic music *n* (*mus*) music that does not have any themes or tunes as such; it is concerned with exploring the unconventional possibilities of sounds.

Athena, Athene *n* a Greek goddess, identified by the Romans with Minerva, the representative of the intellectual powers, born fully grown and in complete armor from the head of Zeus. She was the special patroness of the state of Athens.—*also* **Pallas Athene**.

athenaeum *n* a public institution, club or building devoted to the purposes or study of literature, science and art; a literary club.—*also* **atheneum**.

Athenaeum *n* the temple of Athena in ancient Athens, where scholars met.—*also* **Atheneum**.

Athenian *adj* pertaining to Athens, the capital of Greece. * *n* a native or citizen of Athens.

Athens (Athínai) *n* capital city of Greece; in ancient times the capital of Attica and center of Greek culture. A site that has been occupied for about 4000 years, from the Late Neolithic period. The end of Athens' power came in the mid-4th century BC with war against Sparta and the rise of Macedon.—**Athenian** *adj*.

athermanous *adj* resisting the passage of heat; nonconducting.—**athermany** *n*.

atheroma *n* a degenerative condition of the arteries.

atherosclerosis *n* (*pl* **atheroscleroses**) a degenerative disease of the arteries characterized by deposition of fatty material on the inner arterial walls.—**atherosclerotic** *adj*.

athirst *adj* thirsty; eager (for).

athl. *abbr* = athletics.

athlete *n* a person trained in games or exercises requiring skill, speed, strength, stamina, etc.

athlete's foot *n* a fungal infection of the skin, particularly between the toes and often caused by ringworm.

athletic *adj* of athletes or athletics; active, vigorous.—**athletically** *adv*.—**athleticism** *n*.

athletics *n* (*used as sing or pl*) running, jumping, throwing sports, games, etc.

athletic supporter *n* a jockstrap.

athwart *prep* across, from side to side. * *adv* crosswise; obliquely; across the course or direction of a ship; adversely (to).

ATIG *abbr* = Alternative Technology Information Group.

atilt *adv* in the position or with the action of a person making a thrust; tilted.

-ation *n suffix* denoting action or its result, as in *flirtation, vacation*.

Atl. *abbr* = Atlantic.

ATL *abbr* = Association of Teachers and Lecturers.

Atlanta *n* the capital city of Georgia, a state of the USA.

atlantes *see* **atlas**.

Atlantic *adj* of, near or relating to the Atlantic Ocean.

Atlantic-type coast *n* where the ridges and valleys determined by the underlying geology run transversely to the coast.

Atlantis *n* (*Greek myth*) a large island which, according to Plato, existed in the Atlantic beyond the Pillars of Hercules (Straits of Gibraltar), was the home of a great nation, and was finally swallowed up by the sea in an earthquake nine thousand years before his time.

atlas[1] *n* a book containing maps, charts and tables; (*pl* **atlantes**)

atlas² (*archit*) a figure or half-figure of a man, used in place of a column or pilaster to support an entablature.—*also* **telamon**.

atlas³ *n* (*med*) the first cervical vertebra of the spinal column.

Atlas¹ *n* (*astron*) a small satellite of Saturn; catalog recording positions of stars; (*Greek myth*) leader of the Titans, who attempted to storm the heavens, and was punished by having to hold up the vault of heaven on his head and hands at the western extremity of the earth, on the mountains in the northwest of Africa still called by his name.

Atlas² *abbr* = automated telephone line address system; automatic tabulating, listing and sorting package.

Atlas rockets *n* rockets used as launch vehicles for space research.

ATLB *abbr* = Air Transport Licensing Boards.

atm. *abbr* = atmosphere, *or* atmospheres; atmospheric.

ATM¹ *abbr*, *trademark* (*comput*) = **Adobe Type Manager**.

ATM² *abbr* = anti-tank missile; Automated/Automatic Teller Machine.

atmo- *prefix* vapor, air, atmosphere.

atmometer *n* an instrument for measuring the rate and amount of evaporation from a moist surface.—**atmometry** *n*.

atmosphere *n* the gaseous mixture that surrounds the earth or the other stars and planets; a unit of pressure equal to the pressure of the atmosphere at sea level; any dominant or surrounding influence; special mood or aura.—**atmospheric, atmospherical** *adj*.

atmospheric pressure *n* the pressure exerted by the atmosphere, 1.01325 x 105 Newtons at sea level.

atmospheric window *n* a region in the electromagnetic spectrum to which Earth's atmosphere is transparent.

atmospherics *npl* interference in radio reception, etc caused by atmospheric disturbances.

atm. press. *abbr* = atmospheric pressure.

at. no. *abbr* = atomic number.

atoll *n* a circular or horseshoe-shaped coral reef surrounding a lagoon, particularly common in the Pacific Ocean.

atom *n* (*chem*) the smallest particle that makes up all matter and still retains the chemical properties of the element.

ATOM *abbr* = Against Tests on Muroroa.

atom bomb *see* **nuclear fission**.

atomic *adj* pertaining to or consisting of atoms; extremely minute.—**atomically** *adv*.

atomic absorption spectrometry (AAS) *n* an analytical technique used to determine the chemical elements in a sample.

atomic age *n* the current era.

atomic bomb *n* a bomb whose explosive power derives from the atomic energy released during nuclear fission or fusion.—*also* **A-bomb**.

atomic clock *n* a device for measuring time where the mechanically oscillating mass of an ordinary timepiece is replaced by a much more constant atomic vibration.

atomic energy *n* the energy derived from nuclear fission.

atomicity *n* the number of atoms in a molecule of an element; equivalence; the combining capacity of an element, valency.

atomic number *n* (*chem*) the number of protons in the nucleus of an atom.

atomic theory *n* the theory that elemental bodies consist of ultimate atoms of definite weight, and that atoms of different elements unite chemically with each other in fixed proportions.

atomic weight *n* the weight of the atom of any element as compared with another taken as a standard, usu hydrogen, taken as 1.

atomism *n* the doctrine of atoms, atomic theory.—**atomist** *n*.—**atomistic, atomistical** *adj*.

atomize *vt* to reduce to a fine spray or minute particles.—**atomization** *n*.—(*Brit*) **atomise**.

atomizer *n* a device for atomizing liquids, usu perfumes or cleaning agents.

atom smasher *n* an atomic accelerator.

atonal *adj* (*mus*) avoiding traditional tonality; not written in any established key, particularly associated with the works of Schoenberg.—**atonality** *n*.—**atonally** *adv*.

atone *vi* to give satisfaction or make amends (for).—**atonable, atoneable** *adj*.—**atoner** *n*.

atonement *n* satisfaction, reparation; (*Christianity: with cap*) the reconciliation of humankind with God through Christ's self-sacrifice.

Atonement, Day of *n* (*Bible*) the day on which the high priest entered the innermost shrine of the Temple to make offerings for the priests and for the whole people. *See also* **high priest**.

atonic *adj* unaccented (word, etc); lacking tone, or vital energy. * *n* an unaccented word or syllable; a medicine to allay excitement.—**atonicity** *n*.

atony *n* lack of tone; debility; weakness of any organ.

atop *adv* on or at the top.

ATP *abbr* = adenosine triphosphate, an important molecule found in the mitochondrion, that is synthesized or broken down to produce energy to drive metabolic processes; Association for Teaching Psychology; Association of Tennis Professionals ; Automatic Train Protection; (*med*) adenosine triphosphate; advanced turboprop.

ATPL *abbr* = Airline Transport Pilot's License.

ATR *abbr* = advanced test reactor.

Atreus *n* (*Greek myth*) king of Mycenae and father of Agamemnon and Menelaus, who killed the sons of Thyestes and served their flesh in a banquet to their father.

atrial *adj* the term used to describe anything relating to the atrium of the heart.

atrip *adv* (*naut*) (anchor) just clear of the ground.

atrium *n* (*pl* **atria**) (*anat*) a minor chamber of the heart, considered to be a reservoir as blood passes from it into the ventricle; (*archit*) an open, inner courtyard in a Roman building; an entrance court, usu rectangular and flanked by columns; an entrance hall that rises up several storeys, often with a glass roof.

atrocious *adj* extremely brutal or wicked; (*inf*) very bad, of poor quality.—**atrociously** *adv*.

atrocity *n* (*pl* **atrocities**) a cruel act; something ruthless, wicked, repellent.

atrophy *n* (*pl* **atrophies**) a wasting away or failure to grow of a bodily organ. * *vti* (**atrophying, atrophied**) to cause or undergo atrophy.

atropine, atropin *n* a crystalline alkaloid of a very poisonous nature extracted from the deadly nightshade (belladonna), having the singular property of producing dilatation of the pupil of the eye.

a.t.s., ats *abbr* (*law*) = at the suit of.

ATS *abbr* = American Temperance Society; American Thyroid Society; American Tolkien Society; American Tract Society; Army Transport Service; (*comput*) administrative terminal system; (*med*) anti-tetanus serum.

ATSDR *abbr* = Agency for Toxic Substances and Disease Registry

ATSP *abbr* = Association of Teachers of Spanish and Portuguese.

ATSS *abbr* = Association for Teaching of the Social Sciences.

att. *abbr* = attorney.

ATT *abbr* = Association of Taxation Technicians.

attacca *n* (*mus*) a direction to a performer at the end of a movement to follow on with the next without pause. * *vt* "attack," start the next movement without a pause.

attach *vt* to fix or fasten to something; to appoint to a specific group; to ascribe, attribute. * *vi* to become attached; to adhere.—**attachable** *adj*.—**attacher** *n*.

attaché *n* a technical expert on a diplomatic staff.

attaché case *n* a flat case for carrying documents, etc.

attached *adj* fixed; feeling affection for.

attachment *n* a fastening; affection, devotion; something attached; a device or part fixed to a machine, implement, etc; the act of attaching or being attached; (*comput*) a file sent with an e-mail which may be an EPS, TIF or similar format or it may be a spreadsheet, word processing, or desk-top publishing file (which are all binary files).

attack *vt* to set upon violently; to assault in speech or writing; to invade, as of a disease. * *vi* to make an assault. * *n* an assault; a fit of illness; severe criticism; an enthusiastic beginning of a performance, task, undertaking, etc.—**attacker** *n*.

attain *vt* to succeed in getting or arriving at; to achieve. * *vi* to come to or arrive at by growth or effort.—**attainable** *adj*.—**attainability** *n*.

attainder *n* loss of estate and civil rights following conviction for high treason.

attainment *n* something attained; an accomplishment.

attaint *vt* to subject to attainder; to infect; to stain, to disgrace.

attar *n* a fragrant essential oil extracted from rose petals and used in making perfume.

ATTC *abbr* = Association of Travel Trades Clubs.

attempt *vt* to try to accomplish, get, etc. * *n* an endeavor or effort to accomplish; an attack, assault.—**attemptable** *adj*.—**attempter** *n*.

Attenborough *n* 1. **Sir David [Frederick]** (1926–) English naturalist and broadcaster. 2. **Sir Richard [Samuel]** (1923–) English film director, producer, and actor; brother of Sir David Attenborough.

attend *vt* to take care of; to go with, accompany; to be present at. * *vi* to apply oneself (to); to deal with, give attention to.—**attender** *n*.

attendance *n* attending; the number of people present; the number of times a person attends.

attendant *n* a person who serves or accompanies another; someone employed to assist or guide. * *adj* accompanying, following as a result; being in attendance.

attention *n* the application of the mind to a particular purpose, aim, etc; awareness, notice; care, consideration; (*usu. pl*) an act of civility or courtesy; (*usu. pl*) indications of admiration or love; (*mil*) a soldier's formal erect posture.

attention deficit disorder *n phr* any of a wide range of behavioral problems, i.e., learning difficulties, hyperactivity etc. esp. in children.

attentive *adj* observant, diligent; courteous.—**attentively** *adv*.—**attentiveness** *n*.

attenuate *vt* to make thin; to weaken; to reduce the force or severity of. * *vi* to become thin; to weaken.—**attenuation** *n*.

attest *vt* to state as true; to certify, as by oath; to give proof of. * *vi* to testify, bear witness (to).—**attestable** *adj*.—**attestation** *n*.—**attester, attestor** *n*.

attestation *n* the act of attesting; testimony or evidence given on oath or by official declaration; swearing in.

Att. Gen. *abbr* = Attorney General.

attic *n* the room or space just under the roof; a garret.

Attic *adj* pertaining to Attica in Greece; classical; elegant. * *n* a dialect of ancient Athens.

Attica *n* in ancient times one of the independent states of ancient Greece, the capital of which was Athens.

atticism *n* an elegant expression; (*with cap*) a peculiarity of style or idiom characterizing the Attic rendering of the Greek language.

Attic order *n* a square column of any of the five Greek orders of architecture.

Attic salt, Attic wit *n* delicate wit.

attire *vt* to clothe; to dress up. * *n* dress, clothing.

ATTITB *abbr* = Air Transport and Travel Industry Training Board.

attitude *n* posture, position of the body; a manner of thought or feeling; behavior; the position of an aircraft or spacecraft in relation to certain reference points.—**attitudinal** *adj*.

attitudinize *vi* to assume affected postures, to pose for effect.—**attitudinizer** *n*.

Attlee *n* **Clement [Richard] [1st Earl Attlee]** (1883–1967) British statesman; Labour prime minister (1945–51).

attorn *vti* to transfer; to make legal acknowledgment of a new landlord.—**attornment** *n*.

attorney *n* (*pl* **attorneys**) one legally authorized to act for another; a lawyer.

attorney at law *n* a lawyer.

attorney general *n* (*pl* **attorneys general, attorneys generals**) the chief law officer of a state or nation acting as its legal representative and advising the chief executive on legal matters.

attract *vt* to pull towards oneself; to get the admiration, attention, etc of. * *vi* to be attractive.—**attractable** *adj*.—**attractor** *n*.

attraction *n* the act of attraction; the power of attracting, esp charm; (*phys*) the mutual action by which bodies tend to be drawn together.

attractive *adj* pleasing in appearance, etc; arousing interest; able to draw or pull.—**attractively** *adv*.—**attractiveness** *n*.

attrib. *abbr* = attribute; attributive; attributively.

attribute *n* a quality, a characteristic of; (*archeo*) a basic characteristic or aspect of an artifact. Attributes include color, shape and raw material.—*vt* to regard as belonging to; to ascribe, impute (to).—**attributable** *adj*.

attribution *n* the act of attributing, esp a work of art, etc to a particular creator; a designation; a function.—**attributional** *adj*.

attributive *adj* expressing an attribute; (*gram*) qualifying. * *n* a word joined to and describing a noun; an adjective or adjective phrase.—**attributively** *adv*.

attrition *n* a grinding down by or as by friction; a relentless wearing down and weakening; natural wastage or reduction of a workforce by not employing replacements for those who resign or leave.—**attritional** *adj*.—**attritive** *adj*.

attritional age profile *n* (*archeo*) where the teeth (or bones) from a site are of more young and old animals than expected, suggesting that these animals were hunted.

attune *vt* to bring (a person or thing) into harmony with; to adapt.

Attwood *n* **Thomas** (1765–1838) an English composer who was organist at St Paul's Cathedral, London. He was a pupil of Mozart in Vienna and became a close friend to Mendelssohn. He wrote anthems for the coronations of George IV and William IV.

atty *abbr* = attorney.

Atty Gen. *abbr* = Attorney General.

Atum *n* (*Egypt*) the local god of the Delta city of Heliopolis, represented in human form and originally seen as creator of the world. The priests of Heliopolis then joined his cult with that of **Ra**, the universal sun-god, with the name of **Atum-Ra**.

ATV *abbr* = Associated Television; all-terrain vehicle.

at. vol. *abbr* = atomic volume.

atwitter *adj* of or being in a state of nervous excitement.

Atwood *n* **Margaret Eleanor** (1939–) Canadian poet and novelist whose novel *Surfacing*, established her as one of Canada's important modern writers.

at. wt. *abbr* = atomic weight.

atypical *adj* not according to type; without definite typical character.—**atypically** *adv*.

Atys, Attis *n* (*Classical myth*) the shepherd lover of Cybele, who, having broken the vow of chastity which had made her, castrated himself.

Au *symbol* (*chem*) gold (element).

au *abbr* = astronomical unit.

AU *abbr* = Angstrom unit; (*Afghanistan*) Artists' Union.

AUA *abbr* = American Unitarian Association.

aubade *n* (*mus*) (*French*) "morning music," as opposed to a serenade, or evening music.

Auber *n* **Daniel François Esprit** (1782–1871) a French composer who wrote some 45 operas, including *La Muette de Portici* (1828) and *Fra Diavolo* (1830). In 1842 he followed Cherubini as director of the Paris Conservatoire.

auberge *n* an inn.

aubergine *see* **eggplant**.

Aubrey *n* **John** (1626–97) English antiquary and biographer noted for his *Lives of Eminent Men*.

Aubrey, Saint *see* **Alberic**.

aubrietia, aubretia *n* a small purple-flowered perennial plant.

AUBTW *abbr* = Amalgamated Union of Building Trade Workers.

auburn *adj* reddish brown.

AUC *abbr* = Air Transport Users Committee; American University in Cairo; Association of Underwater Contractors; (*Latin*) *ab urbe condita*, "from the building of the city"; (*Latin*) *anno urbis conditae*, "in the year from the building of the city".

AUCET *abbr* = Association of University Chemical Education Tutors.

Auckland *n* a city in New Zealand.

AUCL *abbr* = Association of University and College Lecturers.

au contraire *adv* on the contrary.

au courant *adj* well-informed, esp in current affairs.

auction *n* a public sale of items to the highest bidder. * *vt* to sell by or at an auction.

auction bridge *n* a form of bridge in which the players contract to take a certain number of tricks, with extra tricks counting towards game.

auctioneer *n* one who conducts an auction.

aud. *abbr* = auditor.

Aud.-Gen. *abbr* = Auditor-General.

audacious *adj* daring, adventurous; bold; rash; insolent.—**audaciously** *adv*.—**audaciousness** *n*.

audacity *n* (*pl* **audacities**) boldness; daring; spirit; presumptuousness; impudence; effrontery.

Auden *n* **W[ystan] H[ugh]** (1907–73) English-born American poet and librettist who became the leading voice of a new generation of young poets, the "Auden generation."

audible *adj* heard or able to be heard.—**audibility** *n*.—**audibly** *adv*.

audience *n* a gathering of listeners or spectators; the people addressed by a book, play, film, etc; a formal interview or meeting, esp one in which one's views are heard.

audile *adj* received through hearing.

audio *n* sound; the reproduction, transmission or reception of sound.

audio frequency *n* a frequency audible to the human ear.

audiometer *n* an instrument for gauging the power of hearing.—**audiometric** *adj*.—**audiometrically** *adv*.—**audiometry** *n*.

audiotape *n* a sound tape recording; a cassette tape.

audiotypist *n* a typist who works from a recording.

audiovisual *adj* using both sound and vision, as in teaching aids.

audit *n* an independent examination of a company's financial statements by a qualified auditor. * *vt* to make such an inspection.

audition *n* a trial to test a performer. * *vti* to test or be tested by audition.

auditor *n* a professional accountant who is trained to conduct an independent assessment of the accuracy and fairness of a company's financial statements, called an audit.—**auditorial** *adj*.

auditorium *n* (*pl* **auditoriums, auditoria**) the part of a building allotted to the audience; a building or hall for speeches, concerts, etc.

auditory *adj* of or relating to the sense of hearing.

Audrey, Saint *see* **Etheldreda**.

Audsley *n* **George Ashdown** (1838–1925) British architect who incorporated decorative work into his buildings, largely influenced by Christopher **Dresser**.

Audubon *n* **John James** (1784–1851) American naturalist and artist. His passion for ornithology resulted in the magnificent plates for his famous *Birds of America*. which is among the most valuable and beautiful of illustrated books.

Auerbach *n* **Frank** (1931–) German-born British painter. Figures and portraits predominate in his work, executed either in chalk and charcoal or a heavy impasto of oil paint.

AUEW *abbr* = Amalgamated Union of Engineering Workers.

AUEW-TASS *abbr* = Amalgamated Union of Engineering Workers, Technical, Administrative and Supervisory Section.

au fait *adj* (*French*) fully informed about; competent.

au fond *adv* (*French*) fundamentally.

auf Wiedersehen *interj, n* (*German*) till we meet again.

aug. *abbr* = augmentative; augmented.

Aug. *abbr* = August.

Augean stables *npl* (*Greek myth*) the stables, not cleaned for 30 years, in which Augeas kept 3,000 oxen, which Heracles cleaned in one day by turning the course of the River Alpheus through them.

Augeas, Augeias *n* (*Greek myth*) king of the Epeans in Elis, killed by Heracles after refusing to pay him the promised wage for cleaning his stables.

auger *n* (*archeo*) a large drill bit (similar to a corkscrew) with a handle which is turned into the ground to obtain a small sample of soil.

aught *n* anything; any part. * *adv* (*arch*) in any degree, in any way; at all.—*also* **ought**.

augite *n* a variety of pyroxene of a black or dark green color.—**augitic** *adj*.

augment *vti* to increase.—**augmentable** *adj*.—**augmenter, augmentor** *n*.

augmentation *n* enlargement, addition, increase; (*mus*) the increase in time value of the notes of a theme; (*her*) an additional charge to a coat of arms bestowed as a mark of honor.

augmentative *adj* having the quality or power of augmenting; (*gram*) increasing in force the idea of a word. * *n* a word or affix that expresses with greater force the idea conveyed by the term from which it is derived, opposite of diminutive.

augmented interval *n* (*mus*) the interval formed by increasing any perfect or major interval by a semitone.

augmented sixth *n* (*mus*) a chord based on the flattened submediant that contains the augmented sixth interval.

augmented triad *n* (*mus*) a triad of which the fifth is augmented.

au gratin *adj* topped with breadcrumbs or breadcrumbs and cheese, and cooked until crisp.

augur *vti* to prophesy; to be an omen (of).—**augural** *adj*.

augury *n* (*pl* **auguries**) the art or practice of foretelling events by reference to natural signs or omens; an omen; prediction; presage.

august *adj* imposing; majestic.

August *n* the eighth month of the year, having 31 days.

Augusta *n* the capital city of Maine, a state of the USA.

Augustan *adj* of or pertaining to Augustus Caesar, emperor of Rome, or his reign, during which Roman literature gained its highest point; of or pertaining to the period of the highest stage of literary excellence in other countries.

Augustine of Canterbury *n* **Saint**, also known as **Austine** (*d*. 604) Roman monk sent by Pope Gregory the Great to convert the British (597) and to establish the authority of Rome over the English church (601). He was the first archbishop of Canterbury (601–604). His feast day is 27 May.

Augustine of Hippo *n* **Saint** (354–430)) Latin Church Father, born in Numidia (present-day Algeria) in North Africa; perhaps the greatest of the Latin fathers and an influence in both Catholic and Protestant theology; the son of St Monica. He wrote many theological works, including *Confessions* and *De Civitate Dei*. His feast day is 28 August.

Augustus *n* [**Gaius Octavianus**] (63 BC–AD 14) Augustus Caesar, the official title of Octavian the first emperor of Rome in 31 BC after defeating Mark Antony; ruled 27 BC–AD 14.

au jus *adj* (*French*) served in its natural juices or with gravy.

auk *n* a northern sea bird with short wings used as paddles.

au lait *adj* (*French*) with milk.

auld lang syne *n* (*Scot*) days of old; long ago.

AUM *abbr* = air-to-underwater missile.

a una corda *adv* (*mus*) (*Italian*) "on one string" (*compare* **a due corde**). In the context of a piano, it means left-hand pedal, i.e., reducing the volume.

au naturel *adj*, *adv* in the natural state; cooked plainly; raw; nude.

aunt *n* a father's or mother's sister; an uncle's wife.

auntie, aunty *n* (*pl* **aunties**) (*inf*) aunt.

au pair *n* a person, esp a girl, from abroad who performs domestic chores, child-minding, etc in return for board and lodging.

aur. *abbr* = aurum.

aura *n* (*pl* **auras, aurae**) a particular quality or atmosphere surrounding a person or thing.

aural[1] *adj* of the ear or the sense of hearing.—**aurally** *adv*.

aural[2] *adj* of the air or an aura.

aureate *adj* golden; gilded; golden yellow.

Aurelius *n* **Marcus** (121–80) Roman emperor and philosopher.

aureole *n* (*astron*) a ring sometimes seen around the sun or moon; (*art*) a halo, radiance, or luminous cloud encircling the figures of Christ, the virgin and the saints in sacred pictures; anything resembling an aureole.

au revoir *n* (*French*) goodbye for the present.

Auric *n* **Georges** (1899–1983) a French composer and the youngest member of *Les Six*. His compositions include operas, piano and chamber pieces, as well as music for films (particularly those of René Clair [1898–1981] and Jean Cocteau [1899–1963]) and ballets, the most notable of which is *Les Matelots*.

auric *adj* of or pertaining to gold.

auricle *n* (*anat*) the external part of the ear flap, the pinna; an ear-shaped appendage of the atrium of the heart.

auricula *n* (*pl* **auriculas, auriculae**) a species of primrose with leaves the shape of a bear's ear.

auricular *adj* of or received by the ear; shaped like an ear; spoken privately; relating to the auricles of the heart.

auriculate *adj* ear-shaped; having ears or ear-like appendages.

auriferous *adj* gold-bearing; yielding or containing gold.

Auriga *n* a northern sky constellation.

aurochs *n* (*pl* **aurochs**) an extinct wild ox of North Africa, Europe and Asia.

aurora *n* (*pl* **auroras, aurorae**) either of the luminous bands seen in the night sky in the polar regions caused by the ionization of atmospheric molecules by solar and cosmic radiation.—*also* **northern lights**.

Aurora *n* (*Roman myth*) the goddess of the dawn, the equivalent of the Greek Eos.

aurora australis *n* the aurora seen at the South Pole.

aurora borealis *n* the aurora seen at the North Pole.

aurous *adj* of or bearing gold.

AURPO *abbr* = Association of University Radiation Protection Officers.

Aus. *abbr* = Austria; Austrian.

auscultate *vt* to examine by auscultation.—**auscultator** *n*.—**auscultatory** *adj*.

auscultation *n* a listening to the sounds of the heart, lungs, etc in the chest for medical diagnosis.

auspex *n* (*pl* **auspices**) one who divined by observation of birds in ancient Rome.

auspice *n* (*pl* **auspices**) an omen; (*pl*) sponsorship; patronage.

auspicious *adj* showing promise, favorable.—**auspiciously** *adv*.

Aussie *n* (*sl*) an Australian.

Aust. *abbr* = Austria; Austrian.

Austen *n* **Jane** (1775–1817) English novelist whose novels, e.g., *Pride and Prejudice*, *Emma* and *Persuasion*, are set within the middle-class society in which she lived and display masterly dialog, a finely tuned sense of satire, and moral judgment.

austere *adj* stern, forbidding in attitude or appearance; abstemious; severely simple, plain.—**austerely** *adv*.—**austereness** *n*.

austerity *n* (*pl* **austerities**) being austere; economic privation.

Austin[1] *n* 1. **Alfred** (1835–1913) minor English poet who became poet laureate in succession to Tennyson in 1896. 2. **John Langshaw** (1911–60) English philosopher; he stressed the need for simplicity and use of ordinary language in philosophical speculation, as seen in his posthumously published lectures, *Sense and Sensibilia* and *How to do Things with Words* (both 1962).

Austin[2] *n* the capital city of Texas a, state of the USA.

Austine *see* **Augustine of Canterbury.**

austral *adj* southern.

Austral. *abbr* = Australia; Australian; Australasia; Australasian.

Australasian *adj* of or pertaining to Australasia (Australia, New Zealand and adjacent islands). * *n* a native or inhabitant of Australasia.

Australia *n* the world's smallest continental landmass, situated in the southern hemisphere.

Australia Day *n* in Australia, 26 January, or the first Monday following this date, a national holiday to commemorate the landing of the British (1788).

Australian *adj* of or pertaining to Australia. * *n* a native or inhabitant of Australia.

Australian Dollar *n* currency of Australia, Kiribati, and Nauru.

Australoid *adj* of the variety of human population that includes the Australian aborigines. * *n* an Australoid person.

Australopithecus *n* the generic name of the earliest hominids, i.e. related to man. These appeared in Africa probably around four million years ago.

Austria *n* is a landlocked country in central Europe which is surrounded by seven nations: Italy, Germany, Switzerland, the Czech Republic, the Slovak Republic, Hungary and Slovenia.

aut. *abbr* = automatic.

AUT *abbr* = Association of University Teachers.

autarchy *n* (*pl* **autarchies**) absolute or autocratic rule or sovereignty; a country governed in such a way; autarky.—**autarchic, autarchical** *adj*.

autarky *n* (*pl* **autarkies**) self-sufficiency, esp in the economic sphere; the policy of encouraging economic self-sufficiency.—**autarkic, autarkical** *adj*.

auth. *abbr* = authentic; author; authoress; authorized.

Auth. Ver. *abbr* = Authorized Version.

authentic *adj* genuine, conforming to truth or reality; trustworthy, reliable.—**authentically** *adv*.—**authenticity** *n*.

authenticate *vt* to demonstrate the authenticity of; to make valid; to verify.—**authentication** *n*.—**authenticator** *n*.

author *n* a person who brings something into existence; the writer of a book, article, etc. * *vt* to be the author of.—**authoress** *nf*.—**authorial** *adj*.

authoring *n* the term used for the creation or compilation of documents or layouts in the field of electronic publishing.

authoritarian *adj* favoring strict obedience; dictatorial. * *n* a person advocating authoritarian principles.—**authoritarianism** *n*.

authoritative *adj* commanding or possessing authority; accepted as true; official.—**authoritatively** *adv*.

authority *n* (*pl* **authorities**) the power or right to command; (*pl*) officials with this power; influence resulting from knowledge, prestige, etc; a person, writing, etc cited to support an opinion; an expert.

authorize *vt* to give authority to, to empower; to give official approval to, sanction.—**authorization** *n*.

authorized share capital *n* the maximum amount of share capital that may be issued by a company as set out in the company's articles of association.

Authorized Version *n* a translation of the Bible published in 1611, the powerful and poetic language of which made it very influential on writers in English from the early 17th century on. Also called **King James Bible** or **King James Version**.

authorship *n* the writing profession; origin (of book).

autism *n* a mental state, usu of children, marked by disregard of external reality—**autistic** *adj*.

AUTM *abbr* = Association of Unit Trust Managers; Association of Used Tire Manufacturers.

auto *n* (*pl* **autos**) (*inf*) an automobile.

auto. *abbr* = automatic; automotive.

auto- *prefix* self; by oneself or itself.

autoantibody *n* an antibody produced by the body against one of its own tissues.

autobahn *n* a German, Austrian or Swiss freeway.

autobiography *n* (*pl* **autobiographies**) the biography of a person written by himself or herself.—**autobiographer** *n*.—**autobiographical** *adj*.

Auto CAD *n* (*comput*) a widely used but very expensive CAD program.

autocephalous *adj* having its own head; independent.

autochondriac *n* a person who is preoccupied with his or her automobile.

autochthon *n* (*pl* **autochthons, autochthones**) an earliest known inhabitant, an aboriginal.

autochthonous, autochthonal *adj* pertaining to primitive inhabitants; indigenous, native to the soil.—**autochthonism, autochthony** *n*.

autoclave *n* a strong container used for chemical reactions at high temperatures and pressures; a device for sterilizing implements using steam at high pressure.

autocracy *n* (*pl* **autocracies**) government by one person with absolute power.

autocrat *n* an absolute ruler; any domineering person.—**autocratic** *adj*.—**autocratically** *adv*.

autocross *n* cross-country motor racing.

Autocue *n* (*trademark*) a prompting device used in TV, etc, which provides speakers with a script that remains invisible to the audience.—*also* **Teleprompter**.

auto-da-fé *n* (*pl* **autos-da-fé**) a public judgment by the Spanish Inquisition upon prisoners tried for heresy and other offences against the religious or civil law; the subsequent execution of such sentences by burning.

auto dial *n* (*comput*) a communications programs feature, in which the program automatically dials the appropriate phone number and makes a connection with the answering computer.

auto dial/auto answer modem *n* (*comput*) a modem that is able to generate tones to dial the receiving computer and also to answer the telephone and establish a link when a call is received.

autodidact *n* an individual who is self-taught.

autoerotism, autoeroticism *n* self-produced sexual emotion.—**autoerotic** *adj*.

autogamy *n* self-fertilization.—**autogamous** *adj*.

autogenesis, autogeny *n* spontaneous generation.—**autogenetic** *adj*.

autogenous *adj* self-generated; produced independently.

autograft *n* a graft of skin or tissue taken from one part of a person's body and transferred to another region.

autograph *n*

autograph *n* a person's signature; (*art*) a term used to denote a painting by one artist only, and not assisted by pupils or assistants. * *vt* to write one's signature in or on.—**autographic** *adj*.—**autographically** *adv*.

autography *n* one's own handwriting; a lithographic process by which copies of writings or drawings are reproduced in facsimile.

autogyro, autogiro *n* (*pl* **autogyros, autogiros**) an aircraft like a helicopter but with unpowered rotor blades.

autoharp *n* (*mus*) a type of zither in which chords are produced by pressing down keys that dampen some of the strings but let others vibrate freely. The instrument was invented in the late-19th century and was popular with American folk musicians.

autohypnosis *n* self-hypnosis.

autoimmune *adj* of, relating to, or caused by the action of antibodies or lymphocytes against the body's own tissues.

autoimmune disease *n* one of a number of conditions resulting from the production of antibodies by the body that attack its own tissues.

autoimmunity *n* a failure of the immune system in which the body develops antibodies that attack components or substances belonging to itself.

autolysis *n* the destruction of cells of a body by the action of its own serum.—**autolytic** *adj*.

automaker *n* a manufacturer of automobiles.

automat *n* a restaurant equipped with slot machines for dispensing food and drink; a vending machine.

automate *vt* to control by automation; to convert to automatic operation.

automated telling machine *n* a device that provides cash and other banking services automatically when activated by a plastic card issued to customers; a cash dispenser.—*also* **autoteller**.

automatic *adj* involuntary or reflexive; self-regulating; acting by itself. * *n* an automatic pistol or rifle.—**automatically** *adv*.

automatic pilot *n* a device that can maintain an aircraft or ship on a previously set course.—*also* **autopilot**.

automatic transmission *n* a system in a motor vehicle for changing gears automatically.

automation *n* the use of automatic methods, machinery, etc in industry.

automatism *n* automatic action; involuntary action; mechanical routine; the doctrine that assigns all animal functions to the active operation of physical laws.—**automatist** *n*.

automaton *n* (*pl* **automatons, automata**) any automatic device, esp a robot; a human being who acts like a robot.

automatous *adj* spontaneous; of the nature of an automaton.

automobile *n* a usu four-wheeled vehicle powered by an internal combustion engine.—*also* **motor car**.

automotive *adj* relating to motor vehicles.

autonomic nervous system *n* the part of the nervous system that controls body functions that are not under conscious control, e.g., the heartbeat.

autonomy *n* (*pl* **autonomies**) freedom of self-determination; independence, self-government.—**autonomous** *adj*.

autopilot *n* automatic pilot.

autoplasty *n* the process of repairing lesions by application of tissue removed from another part of the same body.—**autoplastic** *adj*.

autopsy *n* (*pl* **autopsies**) a post-mortem examination to determine the cause of death.

autoresponder *n* (*comput*) a means whereby a message can automatically be sent to the e-mail address of anyone sending a simple e-mail message.

autoroute *n* a French freeway.

autosome *n* any chromosome other than a sex chromosome.

autostrada *n* an Italian freeway.

auto save *n* (*comput*) a utility that regularly saves the work being done on a computer onto the hard disk.

autosuggestion *n* (*psychol*) self-applied suggestion.—**autosuggestive** *adj*.

autoteller *see* **automated telling machine**.

autotoxin *n* a poisonous substance produced by changes within an organism.—**autotoxic** *adj*.

autotransplant *see* **transplantation**.

autotroph *n* an organism, such as a green plant, that is able to manufacture its own food.—**autotrophic** *adj*.

autumn, fall *n* the season between summer and winter.

autumnal *adj* belonging or peculiar to autumn or fall; produced or gathered in autumn; pertaining to the period of life when middle age is past. * *n* a plant that flowers in autumn.

aux. or auxil. *abbr* = auxiliary.

auxiliary *adj* providing help, subsidiary; supplementary. * *n* (*pl* **auxiliaries**) a helper; (*gram*) a verb that helps form tenses, moods, voices, etc of other verbs, as *have, be, may, shall,* etc.

auxiliary storage *n* (*comput*) a term for **secondary storage**.

av, a.v. *abbr* (*Latin*) = *annos vixit,* "lived (so many) years."

av. *abbr* = avenue; average; avoirdupois.

a/v or A/V or AV *abbr* (*Latin*) = *ad valorem,* "according to value" (a tax system).

Av., av. *abbr* = avenue.

AV *abbr* = Artillery Volunteers; (*Bible*) Authorized Version; alternative vote; (*med*) arteriovenous; (*med*) atrioventricular; (*med*) auriculoventricular; audiovisual.

AVA *abbr* = Academy of Visual Arts; American Ventilation Association; Association of Veterinary Anesthetists; (*Belgium*) Atlantic Visitors Association; Audio Visual Association.

avadavat *n* a small Asian finch-like bird, kept as a caged bird for its song.

avail *vti* to be of use or advantage to. * *n* benefit, use or help.

available *adj* ready for use; obtainable, accessible.—**availability** *n*.—**availably** *adv*.

avalanche *n* a mass of snow, ice, and rock tumbling down a mountainside; a sudden overwhelming accumulation or influx.

avalanche wind *n* the blast of air that moves before an avalanche, that can be very destructive, causing buildings to explode before the avalanche actually reaches them.

AVAMA *abbr* = Audio Visual Aids and Allied Manufacturers Association.

avant-garde *n* (*French*) literally "vanguard," those ideas and practices regarded as in advance of those generally accepted. * *adj* pertaining to such ideas and practices and their creators.—**avant-gardism** *n*.

avarice *n* greed for wealth.—**avaricious** *adj*.—**avariciously** *adv*.

Avaris *n* (*Egypt*) site in the eastern Delta, close to Piramesse, where the Hyksos kings established their first base before establishing themselves at Memphis.

AVASS *abbr* = Association of Voluntary Aided Secondary Schools.

avast *interj* (*naut*) stop! cease! hold!

avatar *n* (*Hinduism*) the descent to earth of a deity in an incarnate form; manifestation or embodiment; transference of personality.

AVB *abbr* = atrioventricular block.

AVC *abbr* = additional voluntary contribution; automatic volume control.

AVCA *abbr* = Agriculture and Veterinary Chemicals Association.

AVCI *abbr* = Association of Vocational Colleges International.

AVCPT *abbr* = Association of Veterinary Clinical Pharmacology and Therapeutics.

AVCU *abbr* = Agriculture and Veterinary Chemicals Unit.

AVD *abbr* = Army Veterinary Department.

avdp. *abbr* = avoirdupois.

ave *interj* hail; farewell. * *n* an Ave Maria; a salutation.

Ave, ave *abbr* = avenue.

Avebury *n* (*archeo*) an important archeological site west of Marlborough in England. It features a large stone circle measuring 1200 feet in diameter.

Ave Maria *n* (*Latin*) "Hail Mary," a prayer to the Virgin Mary used in the RC Church. It has been set to music by numerous composers including Schubert, and Liszt, and Gounod in particular.

aven *n* a vertical opening into a limestone cave.

avenge *vt* to get revenge for.—**avenger** *n*.

avens *n* (*pl* **avens**) the popular name of plants to which the herb bennet belongs.

aventurine *n* a brown, gold-spangled kind of Venetian glass; a variety of micaceous quartz or feldspar.

avenue *n* a street, drive, etc, esp when broad; means of access; the way to an objective.

aver *vt* (**averring, averred**) to state as true; to assert.—**averment** *n*.

average *n* the result of dividing the sum of two or more quantities by the number of quantities; the usual kind, amount, quality, etc. * *vt* to calculate the average of; to achieve an average number of.

average cost *n* the unit cost of a product estimated by dividing the total output cost by the total number of units produced.

average stock *n* a method of accounting for stock movements that assumes that goods are taken out of stock at the average cost of the goods in stock.

Averroës [Ibn Rushd] (1126–88) Arab philosopher, judge, scholar and court physician in Morocco. His works, notably his *Commentaries* on Aristotle, were profoundly influential on European scholarship.

averse *adj* unwilling; opposed (to).

aversion *n* antipathy; hatred; something arousing hatred or repugnance.

avert *vt* to turn away or aside from; to prevent, avoid.—**avertible, avertable** *adj*.

Avery *n* 1. **Milton** (1893–1965) American self-taught painter. His best-known paintings include *Mother and Child* (1944) and *Swimmers and Sunbathers* (1945). 2. **Tex [Frederick Bean]** (1908–80) American cartoonist; creator of cartoon characters Daffy Duck and Bugs Bunny.

avg. *abbr* = average.

AVI *abbr* = Automatic Vehicle Identification.

avian *adj* of or pertaining to birds.

aviary *n* (*pl* **aviaries**) a building or large cage for keeping birds.

aviate *vi* to pilot or travel in an aircraft.

aviation *n* the art or science of flying aircraft.

aviator *n* a pilot, esp in the early history of flying.

aviatrix *n* (*pl* **aviatrixes**) a female pilot.

aviculture *n* the breeding and rearing of birds.—**aviculturist** *n*.

avid *adj* eager, greedy.—**avidly** *adv*.

avidity *n* greediness; eagerness; strong appetite.

avifauna *n* (*pl* **avifaunae**) the birds of a region regarded collectively.—**avifaunal** *adj*.

avionics *n* (*used as sing*) the application of electronics in aviation.—**avionic** *adj*.

Avison *n* **Charles** (1709–70) an English organist and composer, and the author of the controversial treatise *An Essay on Musical Expression*, which was first published in 1752.

AVLP *abbr* = Association of Valuers of Licensed Property.

AVM *abbr* = Air Vice-Marshal; automatic vending machine.

avo *n* the monetary unit of Macao, equal to one hundredth of a pataca.

avocado *n* (*pl* **avocados**) a thick-skinned, pear-shaped fruit with yellow buttery flesh.

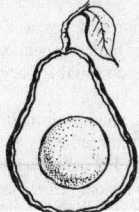

avocation *n* a hobby; a job or vocation.

avocet *n* one of several species of wading birds, characterized by very long legs and an extremely slender curved bill.

avoid *vt* to keep clear of, shun; to refrain from.—**avoider** *n*.

avoidable *adj* able to be avoided.

avoidance *n* the act of annulling or making void; the act of shunning; the state of being vacant.

avoir. *abbr* = avoirdupois.

avoirdupois *n* the system of weights based on the pound of 16 ounces; (*inf*) excess weight.

avow *vt* to declare confidently; to acknowledge.—**avowed** *adj*.—**avowedly** *adv*.—**avower** *n*.

avowal *n* an open declaration; a frank acknowledgment; a confession.

AVPC *abbr* = Association of Vice-Principals of Colleges.

AVR *abbr* = Army Volunteer Reserve.

AVRC *abbr* = Applied Vision Research Center.

AVRDC *abbr* = Asian Vegetable Research and Development Center.

AVRO *abbr* = Animal Virus Research Organization; Association of Vehicle Recovery Operators.

AVS *abbr* = American Vacuum Society; Anti-Vivisection Society.

AVS *abbr* = Army Veterinary Service.

AVTRW *abbr* = Association of Veterinary Teachers and Research Workers.

avulsion *n* a separation by violence; the sudden removal of land, without change of ownership, caused by a flood, etc.

avuncular *adj* like an uncle.

a/w *abbr* = actual weight; artwork.

A/W *abbr* = all water.

AWACS *abbr* = Airborne Warning and Control System (surveillance system used in 1991 Gulf War).

await *vti* to wait for; to be in store for.

awake *vb* (**awaking, awoke** *or* **awaked,** *pp* **awoken** *or* **awaked**) *vi* to wake; to become aware. * *vt* to rouse from sleep; to rouse from inaction. * *adj* roused from sleep, not asleep; active; aware.

awaken *vti* to awake.

awakening *n* the act of rousing from sleep; a revival of religion, or activity of a particular religious sect. * *adj* rousing; exciting; alarming.

award *vt* to give, as by a legal decision; to give (a prize, etc); to grant. * *n* (*law*) a decision, as by a judge; (*law*) a legal document which lists an award granted to a party by a court of law or a governing body; a prize.

aware *adj* realizing, having knowledge; conscious; fully conversant with and sympathetic towards (*ecologically aware*).—**awareness** *n*.

awash *adj* filled or overflowing with water.

away *adv* from a place; in another place or direction; off, aside; far. * *adj* absent; at a distance.

AWB *abbr* = Agricultural Wages Board; Asian Wetland Bureau; Australian Wool Board.

AWC *abbr* = Assembly of Welsh Counties; Association for Women in Computing; Australian Wool Corporation.

AWCF *abbr* = Associate of the Worshipful Company of Farriers.

AWCH *abbr* (*Eire*) = Association for the Welfare of Children in Hospital.

AWCVIE *abbr* = Ancient and Worshipful Company of Village Idiots.

AWD *abbr* = Association of Welding Distributors.

awe *n* a mixed feeling of fear, wonder and dread. * *vt* to fill with awe.

AWE *abbr* = Afghan Wool Enterprises.

aweather *adv* (*naut*) on the weather side, or towards the wind. * *n* opposed to the alee.

AWEBB *abbr* = Association of Wholesale Electrical Bulk Buyers.

aweigh *adj, adv* (*naut*) (*anchor*) atrip, just drawn out of the ground and hanging perpendicularly.

awe-inspiring *adj* worthy of respect or admiration; spellbinding.

AWeldI *abbr* = Associate of the Welding Institute.

AWES *abbr* = Association of West Europe Shipbuilders.

awesome *adj* inspiring awe; (*inf*) marvelous, terrific.

awestricken, awestruck *adj* struck with awe.

AWF *abbr* = Animal Welfare Foundation.

awful *adj* very bad; unpleasant. * *adv* (*inf*) very.—**awfulness** *n*.

awfulize *vt* to envisage a situation as being worse than it is.—*also* **catastrophize**.

awfully *adv* in an awful manner; excessively; (*inf*) very.

AWG *abbr* = American wire gauge; Art Workers Guild.

awhile *adv* for a short time.

AWID *abbr* = Association of Women Industrial Designers.

AWISE *abbr* = Association for Women in Science and Engineering.

awkward *adj* lacking dexterity, clumsy; graceless; embarrassing; embarrassed; inconvenient; deliberately obstructive or difficult to deal with.—**awkwardly** *adv*.—**awkwardness** *n*.

awl *n* a small pointed tool for boring or piercing, used by shoemakers, etc.

a.w.l. *abbr* = absent with leave.

AWLA *abbr* = Association of Welsh Local Authorities.

AWLREM *abbr* = Association of Webbing Load Restraint Equipment Manufacturers.

AWMC *abbr* = Association of Wardens of Mountain Centers.

awn *n* the beard or bristle-like appendage of the outer glume of wheat, barley, and numerous grasses.

awning *n* a structure, as of canvas, extended above or in front of a window, door, etc to provide shelter against the sun or rain.

awoke *see* **awake**.

AWOL *abbr* = absent without official leave.

AWPR *abbr* = Association of Women in Public Relations.

AWRE *abbr* = Atomic Weapons Research Establishment.

awry *adv* twisted to one side. * *adj* contrary to expectations, wrong.

AWS *abbr* = Agricultural Wholesale Society; Association of Women Solicitors.

AWT *abbr* = Animal Welfare Trust.

AWTA *abbr* = Australian Wool Testing Authority.

awu *abbr* = atomic weight unit.

ax, axe *n* (*pl* **axes**) a tool with a long handle and bladed head for chopping wood, etc. * *vt* to trim, split, etc with an ax.

ax. *abbr* = axiom.

axe *n* a flat, heavy cutting tool of metal or stone with the cutting edge parallel to the handle.

axial *adj* of, forming or round an axis.—**axially** *adv*.

axil *n* (*bot*) the angle formed by the upper side of an organ or branch with the stem or trunk to which it is attached.

axile *adj* (*bot*) of, lying or situated in, or attached to, an axis.

axilla *n* (*pl* **axillae, axillas**) the armpit, or cavity in the junction of the arm and shoulder; the axil of a leaf.

axillary *adj* of or pertaining to the armpit; (*bot*) pertaining to, springing from, or situated in, the axil. * *n* (*pl* **axillaries**) a feather from the axilla of a bird.

axiom *n* a widely held or accepted truth or principle.

axiomatic *adj* pertaining to, or of the nature of, an axiom.—**axiomatically** *adv*.

axis[1] *n* a straight line, usu imaginary, indicating a direction of particular symmetry or importance; the Earth's axis is the line joining the north and south poles, around which the Earth rotates every 24 hours; (*with cap*) a partnership, alliance, esp of Germany and Italy, 1936 to the end of World War II.—**axial** *adj*.

axis[2] *n* (*pl* **axises**) a small deer of India and Asia with slender antlers.

axle *n* a rod on or with which a wheel turns; a bar connecting two opposite wheels, as of a car.

axletree *n* a bar connecting the opposite wheels of a carriage, on the rounded ends of which the wheels revolve.

A

axolotl *n* a Mexican amphibian like the salamander, having gills.

axon *n* a long threadlike extension of a nerve cell that conducts nerve impulses from the cell.

AXrEM *abbr* = Association of X-ray Equipment Manufacturers.

ay, aye[1] *adv* (*arch*) for ever, always; continually.

ay, aye[2] *adv, interj* yes; even so; indeed. * *n* (*pl* **ayes**) an affirmative answer or vote in a parliamentary division; the members so voting.

ayah *n* a native Indian nurse or lady's maid.

ayatollah *n* a Shiite Muslim leader; a title of respect.

Ayckbourn *n* **Alan** (1939–) English dramatist noted for his satirical comedies including *The Norman Conquests* (1974).

aye-aye *n* a small nocturnal quadruped, native to Madagascar and allied to the lemurs.

Ayer *n* **Sir A[lfred] J[ules]** (1910–89) English philosopher whose work is based on logical positivism and the rejection of metaphysics. His work, *Language, Truth and Logic*, has been highly influential on British philosophy.

AYF *abbr* = Asian Yachting Federation.

AYM *abbr* = Ancient York Mason; Ancient York Masonry.

Aymonino *n* **Carlo** (1926–) Italian architect. His notable works include city center design Turin, Florence.

Ayres *n* **Gillian** (1930–) British painter much influenced in her early work by American abstract expressionism, particularly the work of Jackson Pollock.

AYRO *abbr* = Action on Youth Rights and Opportunities.

AYRS *abbr* = Amateur Yacht Research Society.

AYSA *abbr* = American Yarn Spinners Association.

Ayub Khan, Mohammed (1907–74) Pakistani field marshal and statesman, president of Pakistan (1958–69). His suspension of civil liberties and increasingly dictatorial style of leadership led to his fall in 1969.

az *abbr* = azimuth; azure.

AZ *abbr* = Arizona.

azalea *n* a flowering shrub-like plant.

azan *n* the call to public prayers in Islamic countries.

Azariah *see* **Uzziah**.

azedarach *n* an Asian tree, the bark or root of which was formerly used as a drug.

Azerbaijan *n* a republic of the former USSR on the southwest coast of the Caspian Sea, which declared itself independent in 1991.

AZF *abbr* = American Zionist Federation.

Azikiwe, [Benjamin] Nnamdi (1904–96) Nigerian statesman, first president of Nigeria (1963–66).

Azilian *adj* of a Mesolithic geological stage characterized by bone harpoon heads and painted stone pebbles.

azimuth *n* (*astron*) a vertical arc from the zenith to the horizon; the angular distance of this from the meridian.—**azimuthal** *adj*.

azoic *adj* without life; (*geol*) without fossils, older than the lowermost series of rocks containing traces of organic life.

azonal *n* a young soil developing on a bare rock surface, e.g., sand dunes and alluviums.

azote *n* an old name for nitrogen.

AZRC *abbr* (*Australia*) = Arid Zone Research Centre.

AZT *abbr* = azidothymidine, a drug that has been effective in alleviating symptoms in some AIDS sufferers.

Aztec *adj* pertaining to the Aztec race that ruled Mexico before the Spanish conquest. * *n* a member of the Aztec race.

azure *adj* sky-blue.

azurite *n* blue carbonate of copper; blue malachite or chessylite; lazulite.

azygous *adj* (*anat*) single, as a muscle or vein; not one of a pair.

B

b, B *n* the second letter of the English alphabet.

B[1] *symbol* (*mus*) the seventh note of the scale of C major.

B[2] *symbol* (*chem*) boron (element).

b *abbr* = billion; born; bowled; breadth; (*cricket*) bye.

B *abbr* = (*mus*) bass; Bachelor (as in B.Mus., Bachelor of Music); Baron; Bible; Britain; British.

B/- *abbr* = bag; bale.

B2 *n* French design partnership, founded by Bruno Berrione and Bruno Lefebre in 1980.

ba *n* an Egyptian term approximating to "soul," one of the five elements constituting the human being.

ba. *abbr* = bachelor.

Ba *symbol* (*chem*) barium (element).

BA *abbr* (*Latin*) = *Baccalaureus Agriculturae*, "Bachelor of Agriculture"; (*Latin*) *Baccalaureus Artium*, "Bachelor of Arts" (a degree in education; British Academy; British Airways; Buenos Aires.

baa *n* the bleat of a sheep. * *vi* to bleat as a sheep.

BAA *abbr* = Biodynamic Agricultural Association; British Acupuncture Association; British Archaeological Association; British Airports Authority.

BAAB *abbr* = British Amateur Athletic Board.

BAAC *abbr* = British Association of Aviation Consultants.

BAACI *abbr* = British Association of Allergy and Clinical Immunology.

Baade *n* **Wilhelm Heinrich Walter** (1893–1960) German-born American astronomer.

Baader Andreas *see* **Meinhoff, Ulrike.**

BAAG *abbr* = British Aerospace Aircraft Group.

Baal *n* (*Bible*) a general term in the *OT* for fertility gods for bountiful harvests and plentiful offspring; worship of Baal gods was strongly opposed by *OT* prophets and writers. *See also* **Ahaziah, Carmel, Jezebel, Jehu.**

BAAL *abbr* = British Association of Applied Linguistics.

BAAP *abbr* = British Association of Academic phonetians; British Association of Audiological Physicians.

BAAPS *abbr* = British Association of Aesthetic Plastic Surgeons.

BAAR *abbr* = British Acupuncture Association and Register.

BAARC *abbr* = British Association of Automation and Robotics in Construction.

BAAS *abbr* = British Academy for the Advancement of Science.

BAB *abbr* = British Aerospace Board.

baba *n* a small sponge cake soaked in (usu rum) flavored syrup.

Babbage *n* **Charles** (1792–1871) English mathematician. His primitive "calculating machines" were the precursors of the modern computer.

Babbitt *n* **Milton [Byron]** (1916–) American modernist composer and mathematician. His compositions include several orchestral and choral pieces as well as *Composition for Synthesizer* and *Vision and Prayer.*

Babbitt metal *n* an anti-friction alloy of copper, tin and zinc, used in crank and axle bearings, etc.

Babbittry *n* (*derog*) businessman's or middle-class person's standards or blinkered outlook.—**Babbitt** *n.*

babble *vi* to make sounds like a baby; to talk incoherently, endlessly or senselessly; to give away secrets; to murmur, as a brook. * *n* incoherent talk; chatter; a murmuring sound.—**babbler** *n.*

babe *n* a baby; a naive person; (*sl*) a girl or young woman.

Babel *n* (*Bible*) Hebrew for Babylon; the tower in Shinar (Genesis 11); a lofty structure; a confused and meaningless sound of voices; a scene of confusion and noise. *See also* **Babylon.**

Babel *n* **Isaac** (1894–?1941) Russian writer whose works include *Red Cavalry* and who is assumed to have died in a Soviet labor camp.

BABIE *abbr* = British Association for Betterment of Infertility and Education.

babies'-breath *see* **baby's-breath.**

Babinski reflex *n* a reflex action response of the foot. When the sole is stroked, the big toe turns up and the others fan out. This is normal for infants up to two years but abnormal thereafter.

babirusa, babiruossa, babirussa *n* the wild hog of Eastern Asia.

baboon *n* a large, short-tailed monkey.

Babs *abbr* = blind approach beacon system.

BABS *abbr* = British Aluminium Building Service; British Association for Brazing and Soldering; British Association of Barbershop Singers.

BABT *abbr* = British Approval Board for Telecommunications.

BABTAC *abbr* = British Association of Beauty Therapy and Cosmetology.

babul *n* the rind of the East Indian acacia.

Baburen Dirck van *see* **Utrecht School.**

babushka *n* a woman's headscarf; in Russia, an old woman.

baby *n* (*pl* **babies**) a newborn child or infant; a very young animal; (*sl*) a girl or young woman; a personal project. * *vt* (**babying, babied**) to pamper.—**babyish** *adj.*

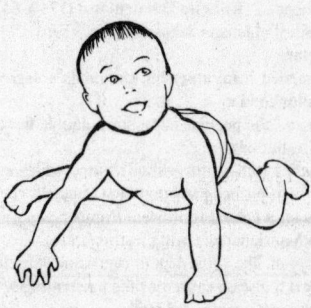

baby boom *n* a sharp rise in the birth rate.

baby-boomer *n* a person born in the period immediately after World War II when the birthrate increased sharply (*baby boom*).

baby break *n* a period, often five years, when a parent raises children before returning to work.

baby burst *n* a sudden fall in birth rate.

baby carriage *n* a small four-wheeled carriage, usu with a folding top for pushing a baby around in.

baby grand *n* (*mus*) the smallest size of grand piano.

Babylon *n* (*Bible*) the original Hebrew homeland; excavations have shown the high artistic level which existed there; it was from Babylon that Nebuchadrezzar destroyed Jerusalem and took the Jewish people into exile; a city in Iraq, on the River Euphrates. It became important when Hammurabi adopted it as his capital at the end of the 18th century BC.

Babylonian *adj* of or pertaining to the ancient kingdom of Babylonia; magnificent; luxurious. * *n* an inhabitant of Babylonia; its language.

baby's-breath *n* any of several plants with small, pleasantly scented flowers.—*also* **babies'-breath.**

baby-sit *vti* (**baby-sitting, baby-sat**) to look after a baby or child while the parents are out.—**baby-sitter** *n.*

baby snatcher *n* (*inf*) one who marries or has a liaison with a much younger person; a person who steals a baby.

baby tooth *n* a milk tooth.

baby wipe *n* a disposable paper towel, ready moistened.

BAc *abbr* = Bachelor of Acupuncture.

BAC *abbr* = British Aerospace Campaign; British Aircraft Corporation; British Atlantic Committee; Burma Airways Corporation; blood alcohol concentration.

BACA *abbr* = Baltic Air Charter Association; British Advisory Committee for Aeronautics.

Bacall *n* **Lauren**, originally **Betty Joan Perske** (1924–) American actress, best known for her acting partnership with her husband **Humphrey Bogart**. Notable films include *The Big Sleep*, *Key Largo*, *and How to Marry a Millionaire.*

BACAN *abbr* = British Association for the Control of Aircraft Noise.

baccalaureate *n* the university degree awarded to a Bachelor of Arts etc; a commencement address.

baccarat *n* a card game where players bet against the banker.

baccate *adj* having many berries; berry-shaped.

bacchanal *n* a priest of Bacchus, the god of wine; a drunken reveler; a drunken feast.—**bacchanalian** *adj.*

bacchanalia *npl* ancient Athenian feasts in honor of Bacchus or Dionysus, characterized by licentiousness and revelry; generally refers to drunken revels.—*also* **dionysia.**

bacchant *n* (*pl* **bacchants, bacchantes**) a priest or votary of Bacchus; a drunkard; a person taking part in revels in honor of Bacchus.—**bacchante** *nf* (*pl* **bacchantes**).

Bacchic *adj* pertaining to Bacchus or the feasts in his honor; riotous, or mad with drink.

Bacchus *n* the Roman name, and one of the Greek names, for Dionysus, the god of wine.

BACCHUS *abbr* = British Aircraft Corporation Commercial Habitat under the Sea.

bacciferous *adj* bearing or producing berries.

bacciform *adj* berry-shaped.

baccivorous *adj* eating or subsisting on berries.

BAce *abbr* = Bachelor of Accountancy.

BACE *abbr* = British Association of Corrosion Engineers.

Bach *n* 1. **Carl Philipp Emanuel** (1714–88) German composer and harpsichordist who was the second son and pupil of Johann Sebastian Bach. 2. **Johann (John) Christian** (1735–82) German composer and the eleventh and youngest son of Johann Sebastian Bach by his second wife. 3. **Johann Christoph** (1642–1703) German organist and composer who was the cousin of Johann Sebastian Bach's father. He composed several choral and instrumental pieces of which *Ich lasse dich nicht* is the best known. 4. **Johann Christoph Friedrich** (1732–95) German composer who was the eldest surviving son of Johann Sebastian Bach's marriage to his second wife. 5. **Johann Michael** (1648–94) German organist and composer who was the son of Johann Sebastian Bach's great-uncle and the father of the great composer's first wife, Maria Barbara. 6. **Johann Sebastian** (1685–1750) German composer who was one of the most influential in history. His works include choral masterpieces such as the *St Matthew Passion*, and works for harpsichord, clavichord and the organ. 7. **Wilhelm Friedemann** (1710–84) German composer and organist; the eldest of Johann Sebastian Bach's sons.

bach. *abbr* = bachelor.

bachelor *n* an unmarried man; a person who holds a degree from a college or university.—**bachelorhood** *n*.

bachelor's buttons *npl* the popular name for a double-flowered buttercup with blossoms resembling buttons.

Bach trumpet *n* (*mus*) a 19th-century valved trumpet which was designed to make it easier to play the high-pitched parts that were originally composed by Bach and his contemporaries for a natural (unvalved) trumpet.

BACI *abbr* = British Association of Caving Instructors.

bacillary, bacillar *adj* of, like, caused by, or consisting of bacilli; rod-shaped.

bacillary dysentery *n* a disease caused by the bacterium *Shigella* and spread by contact with a carrier or contaminated food.

bacilliform *adj* rod-shaped, like a bacillus.

bacillus *n* (*pl* **bacilli**) any of a genus of rod-shaped bacteria; (*loosely*) bacteria in general.

Bacillus Calmette-Guérin vaccine *see* **BCG vaccine**.

back[1] *n* the rear surface of the human body from neck to hip; the corresponding part in animals; a part that supports or fits or makes firm the back of anything; the part farthest from the front; (*sport*) a player or position behind the front line. * *adj* at the rear; (*streets, etc*) remote or inferior; (*pay, etc*) of or for the past; backward. * *adv* at or towards the rear; to or towards a former condition, time, etc; in return or requital; in reserve or concealment. * *vti* to move or go backwards; to support; to bet on; to provide or be a back for; to supply a musical backing for a singer; (*with* **down**) to withdraw from a position or claim; (*with* **off**) to move back (or away, etc); (*with* **out**) to withdraw from an enterprise; to evade keeping a promise, etc; (*with* **up**) to support; to move backwards; to accumulate because of restricted movement; (*comput*) to make a copy (of a data file, etc) for safekeeping.

back[2] *n* a large shallow cistern or vat used by brewers, etc, for liquids.

backache *n* an ache or pain in the back.

backbencher *n* in UK, Australia, etc, a member of parliament who does not hold office.

backbite *vt* (**backbiting, backbit**, *pp* **backbitten** *or* **backbit**) to talk spitefully or ill of behind a person's back.—**backbiter** *n*.—**backbiting** *n*.

backboard *n* a board at the back of a cart; a board worn at the back to support the back; a thin wooden backing used for picture frames, mirrors, etc.

backbone *n* the spinal column; main support; strength, courage; (*comput*) the main "trunk route" of the pathways that carry traffic, i.e., information, on the net. Smaller networks are connected to it. *See* **spinal column**.

backbreaking *adj* arduous; physically exhausting.

backchat *n* (*inf*) cheeky repartee.

backcomb *vt* to comb hair towards the roots to give body.

backcross *vt* to mate (a first-generation hybrid) with a parent.

backdate *vt* to declare valid from some previous date.

backdoor *adj* indirect, concealed, devious.

backdown *n* the act of backing down; the withdrawal of a claim, etc.

backdrop *n* a curtain, often scenic, at the back of a stage; background.

back end *n* (*dial*) autumn.

backer *n* a patron; one who bets on a contestant.

backfire *vi* (*cars*) to ignite prematurely causing a loud bang from the exhaust; to have the opposite effect from that intended, usu with unfortunate consequences.—*also n*.

backgammon *n* a board game played by two people with pieces moved according to throws of the dice.

background *n* the distant part of a scene or picture; an inconspicuous position; social class, education, experience; circumstances leading up to an event; "interference," which affects the reading of a signal that is being measured.

background level *n* the naturally occurring level of radiation activity; levels of pollution.

background task *n* (*comput*) a lower priority procedure where more than one task is being carried out simultaneously.

backhand *n* (*tennis, etc*) a stroke played with the hand turned outwards.

backhanded *adj* (*compliment*) indirect, ambiguous.— **backhandedly** *adv*.

backhander *n* a backhanded stroke; (*inf*) a backhanded remark; (*sl*) a bribe.

backing[1] *n* a change of direction of wind, anticlockwise in the northern hemisphere and clockwise in the southern hemisphere.

backing[2] *n* support; supporters; a lining to support or strengthen the back of something; musical accompaniment to a (esp pop) singer.

backlash *n* a violent and adverse reaction; a recoil in machinery.

backlist *n* books published in past years that are still in print.

backlit screen *n* (*comput*) an LCD display mostly used in notebook or laptop computers. The text is contrasted against the background.

backlog *n* an accumulation of work, etc still to be done.

back number *n* a former issue (of a magazine, etc); an out-of-date person.

backpack *n* a rucksack; an equipment pack carried on the back of an astronaut, etc. * *vi* to travel, hike, etc wearing a backpack.

back pay *n* an increase in wages or salary paid retrospectively.

back-pedal *vi* (**back-pedaling, back-pedaled** *or* **back-pedalling, back-pedalled**) to work the pedals of a bicycle backwards; to modify or withdraw one's original argument or action.

backroom *adj* of or pertaining to a place in which some type of confidential information is being decided upon or work carried out and from which indirect influence is often exercised.

back-seat driver *n* a passenger in a car who irritates the driver with persistent unwanted advice.

backshore *n* the part of a beach between high water during normal spring tides and the foot of the cliff.

backside *n* (*inf*) buttocks.

backslide *vi* (**backsliding, backslid**, *pp* **backslid** *or* **backslidden**) to return to one's (bad) old ways.—**backslider** *n*.

back slope *n* the slope of a cuesta, which is more gentle and follows the dip of the strata.

backspace *n* (*comput*) a keyboard key that moves the cursor to the left, deleting any previously typed characters. * *vi* to move a typewriter carriage or cursor of a word processor back one space.

backspin *n* (*sport*) a backward spin in a ball to slow it down.

backstage *adv* behind the stage of a theater in areas hidden from the audience; (*inf*) away from public view.—*also adj*.

backstairs *npl* stairs in the back part of a house; stairs for private use. * *adj* indirect; underhand; secret; intriguing.

backstay *n* (*naut*) a long rope extending from the masthead to the side of a ship, supporting the mast.

backstitch *n* an overlapping stitch. * *vt* to sew with this stitch.

backstop *n* (*sport*) a fence used to keep a ball within a playing area.

backstreet *n* a side or small street. * *adj* operating or performing secretly or illegally.

backstretch *n* a straight part of a racecourse, esp farthest from the finish.

backstroke *n* (*swimming*) a stroke using backward circular sweeps of the arms whilst lying face upwards.

Backstrom *n* 1. **Monica** (1939–) Swedish glassware designer who designed for **Boda**. 2. **Olaf** (1922–) Swedish engineer who turned to designing kitchen tools.

backsword *n* a sword with one sharp edge, a broadsword; a stick with a basket handle used in the game of singlestick.

backtalk *n* an insolent or impudent retort.

back-to-back *adj* facing in opposite directions, often with the backs touching.

back-to-back loan *n* a loan arrangement in which money is lent by a company in one country to a company in another, usu in a different currency.

backtrack *vi* to return along the same path; to reverse or recant one's opinion, action, etc.

backup *n* an alternate or auxiliary; support, reinforcement; (*comput*) a copy of a program or data file that is kept for archive purposes usu on a removable floppy or hard disk.

backup utility *n* (*comput*) a program that automatically makes a copy of the main storage disk of a computer.

back wall *n* the steep rock wall at the back of a glacially eroded hollow or cirque.

backward *adj* turned toward the rear or opposite way; shy; slow or retarded. * *adv* backwards.—**backwardness** *n*.

backwardation *n* the difference between the spot price of a commodity and the forward price.

backward compatible *n* (*comput*) an application program that works not only with the most recent version of an operating system but also with previous versions.

backwards *adv* towards the back; with the back foremost; in a way opposite the usual; into a less good or favorable state or condition; into the past.

backwash *n* the return flow of water to the sea after a wave has broken; water receding from the action of an oar, propeller, etc; the consequences of an event.

backwater *n* a pool of still water fed by a river; a remote, backward place.

backwoods *npl* uncleared forest land; an isolated, thinly populated area.— **backwoodsman** *n* (*pl* **backwoodsmen**).

backyard *n* a yard at the back of a house.

baclava *see* **baklava**.

BACM *abbr* = British Association of Colliery Management.

BACMA *abbr* = British Artists Colour Manufacturers Association.

BACO *abbr* = British Aluminium Company.

bacon *n* salted and smoked meat from the back or sides of a pig; **to bring home the bacon** to succeed; to help materially; **to save one's bacon** to have a narrow escape.

Bacon *n* 1. **Francis** (1561–1626) English philosopher and statesman whose writings on philosophy and the need for rational scientific method are landmarks in the history of human thought. 2. **Francis** (1909–92) Irish painter noted for his richly colored distorted figures. 3. **Roger** (*c.*1214–92) English monk and philosopher noted for his wide learning and anti-scholastic speculation.

Baconian theory *n* a theory developed in the late 19th century that Shakespeare's plays were written by Francis Bacon, the philosopher.

BACSA *abbr* = British Association for Cemeteries in South Asia.

Bact. *abbr* = bacteriology.

BACT *abbr* = British Association of Canoe Trades; British Association of Conference Towns; British Association of Creative Therapists.

bacteria *npl* (*sing* **bacterium**) (*biol*) single-celled organisms that underpin all life-sustaining processes, identified by shape.—**bacterial** *adj*.

bactericide *n* (*biol*) a substance that destroys bacteria.—**bactericidal** *adj*.

bacteriology *n* (*biol*) the scientific study of bacteria.—**bacteriological** *adj*.—**bacteriologist** *n*.

bacteriolysis *n* (*biol*) destruction of bacteria by a serum.—**bacteriolytic** *adj*.

bacteriophage, phage (*biol*) *n* a virus that attacks bacteria by replicating the host, which is ultimately destroyed as new phages are released.

bacterium *see* **bacteria**

Bactrian camel *n* a camel with two humps.

bad[1] *adj* (**worse, worst**) not good; not as it should be; inadequate or unfit; rotten or spoiled; incorrect or faulty; wicked; immoral; mischievous; harmful; ill; sorry, distressed.—**badness** *n*.

bad[2] *see* **bid**.

BAD *abbr* = British Association of Dermatologists.

BADA *abbr* = British Antique Dealers' Association; British Audio Dealers Association.

Badb *n* (*Irish Celtic myth*) Irish war-goddess said to have been able to select those who would die in battle.

bad blood *n* enmity, hostility.

bad debt *n* an amount of money owed that is considered unlikely ever to be repaid.

badderlocks *n* a large dark-green edible seaweed.

baddie, baddy *n* (*pl* **baddies**) (*inf*) a villain.

bade *see* **bid**.

bad faith *n* dishonesty. * *adv* **in bad faith** dishonestly.

badge *n* an emblem, symbol or distinguishing mark.

badger *n* a hibernating, burrowing black and white mammal related to the weasel. * *vt* to pester or annoy persistently.

bad hair day *n phr* term used to describe a day when nothing seems to go as planned.

badinage *n* light or playful raillery or banter; (*mus*) (*French*) literally "frolic"; a term for fast, frivolous music.

badlands *n* country that is difficult to travel across because of frequent deep ravines and gullies and steep, sharp ridges, usu created by fluvial erosion in a semi-arid area.

badly *adv* (**worse, worst**) poorly; inadequately; unsuccessfully; severely; (*inf*) very much.

BAdmin *abbr* = Bachelor of Administration.

badminton *n* a court game for two or four players played with light rackets and a shuttlecock volleyed over a net.

badmouth *vt* (*sl*) to speak ill of; to slander.

BADS *abbr* = British Association for Day Surgery.

bad sector *n* (*comput*) a part of a disk that cannot be used to record data generated in manufacturing, caused by damage in handling the disk, or by dust.

BAe *abbr* = British Aerospace.

BAE *abbr* = British Academy of Experts; British Association of Electrolysists.

BAEA *abbr* = British Actors' Equity Association.

BAEC *abbr* = Bangladesh Atomic Energy Commission.

BA(Econ) *abbr* = Bachelor of Arts in Economics and Social Studies.

BA(Ed) *abbr* = Bachelor of Arts (Education).

Baez *n* **Joan** (1941–) American folksinger, renowned for her protest songs on civil rights and the Vietnam war in the 1960s.

BAF *abbr* = British Abrasive Federation; British Aerophilatelic Federation; British Allergy Foundation; British Athletics Federation.

baffle *vt* to bewilder or perplex; to frustrate; to make ineffectual. * *n* a plate or device used to restrict the flow of sound, light or fluid.—**bafflement** *n*.—**baffling** *adj*.

BAFM *abbr* = British Association of Forensic Medicine; British Association of Friends of Museums.

BAFMA *abbr* = British and Foreign Maritime Agencies.

BAFO *abbr* = British Army Forces Overseas.

BAFTA *abbr* = British Academy of Film and Television Arts.

bag *n* a usu flexible container of paper, plastic, etc that can be closed at the top; a satchel, suitcase, etc; a handbag; a purse; game taken in hunting; a bag-like shape or part; (*derog*) an old, unpleasant or ugly woman; (*inf: in pl*) plenty (of). * *vti* (**bagging, bagged**) to place in a bag; to kill in hunting; (*inf*) to get; to make a claim on; to hang loosely.

BAGA *abbr* = British Amateur Gymnastics Association.

bagasse *n* sugar-cane refuse after crushing, used as a fuel.

bagatelle *n* (*French*) something of little value; a piece of light music usu for piano; a board game in which balls struck with a cue or by a spring are aimed at holes or pinned spaces.

BAGB *abbr* = Baltic Association of Great Britain.

Bagehot *n* **Walter** (1826–77) English social scientist and literary critic whose works include *The English Constitution* (1867) and *Literary Studies* (1879–95).

bagel *n* a ring-shaped bread roll, hard and glazed on the outside, soft in the center.

bagful *n* (*pl* **bagfuls**) as much as will fill one bag.

baggage *n* suitcases; luggage; **bag and baggage** with one's entire possessions; entirely.

bagging *n* the act of putting into bags; a coarse cloth or other material used for bags; filtration through canvas bags.

baggy *adj* (**baggier, baggiest**) hanging loosely in folds.—**baggily** *adv*.—**bagginess** *n*.

bag lady *n* (*pl* **bag ladies**) a homeless woman who wanders the streets carrying her possessions in shopping bags or carrier bags.

bagman *n* (*pl* **bagmen**) (*formerly*) a traveling salesman who carried his wares in saddlebags; a person who collects or distributes illegally obtained money for another.

bagnio *n* (*pl* **bagnios**) a brothel; a bath house; an oriental prison.

bag of bones *n* a very thin individual or animal.

bagpipe *n* (*often pl*) (*mus*) a musical instrument consisting of an air-filled bag fitted with pipes.

BAgr *abbr* = Bachelor of Agriculture.

BAgric *abbr* = Bachelor of Agriculture.

BAgrSc *abbr* = Bachelor of Agricultural Science.

baguette *n* (*French*) a type of bread loaf that is long and thin; (*archit*) a small molding with a semicircular profile; a frame with small bead molding.

bah *interj* used to express impatience or contempt.

Bahamas *n* a constitutional monarchy comprising an archipelago of 700 islands located in the Atlantic Ocean off the southeast coast of Florida.

BAHO *abbr* = British Association of Helicopter Operators.

BAHOH *abbr* = British Association of the Hard of Hearing.

Bähr *n* **Georg** (*b*. 1666), German architect. His notable works include Frauenkirche, Dresden (destroyed in World War II).

Bahrain *n* a small, oil-rich Emirate; a hereditary monarchy; comprises 33 low-lying islands situated between the Qatar Peninsula and the mainland of Saudi Arabia.

baht *n* the monetary unit of Thailand, made up of 100 satang.

BAHVS *abbr* = British Association of Homoeopathic Veterinary Surgeons.

BAIE *abbr* = British Association of Industrial Errors.

bail[1] *n* money lodged as security that a prisoner, if released, will return to court to stand trial; such a release; the person pledging such money. * *vt* to free a person by providing bail; (*with* **out**) to help out of financial or other difficulty; (*government, bank, etc*) to assist a floundering business.—**bailable** *adj*.

bail[2] *vti* (*usu with* **out**) to scoop out (water) from (a boat).

bail[3] *n* (*cricket*) either of two wooden crosspieces that rest on the three stumps; a bar separating horses in an open stable; a metal bar that holds the paper against the roller of a typewriter.

bailee *n* (*law*) the person to whom goods are delivered in trust.

bailey *or* **ward** *n* (*archit*) the outer wall of a castle; a castle yard.

Bailey *n* **David** (1938–) British photographer who came to prominence in the 1960s.

Bailey bridge *n* a prefabricated bridge of steel easily and quickly assembled for temporary use.

bailie *n* (*Scot*) a municipal officer corresponding to an alderman.

bailiff *n* a sheriff's officer who serves writs and summonses; a minor official in some US courts, usu a messenger or usher. In UK, the agent of a landlord or landowner.

bailiwick *n* the district within which a bailiff has jurisdiction; a person's special sphere of knowledge or activity or jurisdiction.

Baillie Scott *n* **Mackay Hugh** (1865–1945) British-born architect, who collaborated with Archibald **Knox**.

bailment *n* (*law*) a delivery of goods in trust to another; the action of becoming surety for one in custody.

bailor *n* (*law*) one who delivers goods in trust.

bail-out *n* assistance by a bank, government, etc, to help (a company) in financial trouble.

bailsman *n* (*pl* **bailsmen**) one who gives bail for another.

Baily's beads *n* an arc of bright spots round the edge of the Moon seen during a total eclipse of the Sun.

Bainbridge *n* **Beryl** (1934–) English novelist whose works include *Another Part of the Wood* and *Young Adolf*.

bain-marie *n* (*pl* **bains-marie**) a vessel that holds hot water for cooking or warming food.

BAIR *abbr* = British Airports Information Retrieval.

Baird *n* 1. **John Logie** (1888–1946) Scottish engineer who invented a mechanically scanned system of television in 1926. 2. **Spencer Fullerton** (1823–87) American ornithologist and natural history writer; author of *Catalogue of North American Birds* (1858).

bairn *n* (*Scot*) a child.

BAIS *abbr* = British Association for Irish Studies.

bait *n* food attached to a hook to entice fish or make them bite; any lure or enticement. * *vt* to put food on a hook to lure; to set dogs upon (a badger, etc); to persecute, worry or tease, esp by verbal attacks; to lure, to tempt; to entice.

baiza *n* the monetary unit of Oman, equal to one hundredth of a rial.

baize *n* a coarse, green woolen fabric used to cover snooker tables.

BAJ *abbr* = Bachelor of Arts, Journalism; British Association of Journalists.

bake *n* (*pottery*) to dry and harden by heating in the sun or by fire; (*food*) to cook by dry heat in an oven. * *vi* to do a baker's work; to dry and harden in heat; (*inf*) to be very hot. * *n* all the food baked at one time or baking; a party or picnic featuring one baked item, e.g., a *clambake*.

baked beans *npl* cooked haricot beans canned in tomato sauce.

bakehouse *n* a bakery.

Bakelite *n* (*trademark*) a hard synthetic resin used for dishes, etc.

baker *n* a person who bakes and sells bread, cakes, etc.

Baker *n* 1. **Chet [Chesney Henry]** (1929–88) American jazz trumpet player noted for his "cool" style. 2. **Dame Janet** (1933–) an English mezzo-soprano (formerly a contralto) of international repute. She was appointed a DBE in 1976. 3. **Sir Herbert** (*b.* 1862), English architect. His notable works include Bank of England and Church House, Westminster; government buildings in Pretoria.

baker's dozen *n* thirteen.

bakery *n* (*pl* **bakeries**) a room or building for baking; a shop that sells bread, cakes, etc; baked goods.

baking powder *n* a leavening agent containing sodium bicarbonate and an acid-forming substance.

baking soda *n* sodium bicarbonate.

baklava *n* a cake made with thin, flaky pastry, honey and nuts.—*also* **baclava.**

baksheesh *n* a present of money as a bribe or tip to expedite service.

Bakst *n* **Léon** (1866–1924) Russian designer and painter. He designed spectacular ballet sets for the theaters, including the Russian Ballet. He also had his own school where Marc Chagall and the dancer, Nijinsky, were among his pupils.

bal. *abbr* = balance; balancing.

BAL *abbr* = basic assembly language (computing); blood alcohol level.

Balaam *n* (*Bible*) soothsayer summoned by the king of Moab to curse the invading Israelites; later Balaam's ass saw the angel of the Lord standing in the way, and it reproached Balaam when he struck it.

balaclava (helmet) *n* a woolen hood that covers the ears and neck.

Balakirev *n* **Mily Alexeyevich** (1837–1910) Russian composer, famed for his leadership of a group known as The Five, or "The Mighty Handful." His works include two symphonies, two symphonic poems (*Russia* and *Tamara*), an overture (*King Lear*), a piano sonata, and songs.

balalaika *n* (*mus*) (*Russian*) a folk instrument of the guitar family, with a triangular body.

BA(Lan) *abbr* = Bachelor of Languages.

balance *n* a device for weighing, consisting of two dishes or pans hanging from a pivoted horizontal beam; equilibrium; mental stability; the power to influence or control; a remainder.—**in the balance** a state of uncertainty.—**on balance** having considered all aspects or factors. * *vt* to weigh; to compare; to equalize the debit and credit sides of an account. * *vi* to be equal in power or weight, etc; to have the debits and credits equal.—**balanceable** *adj*.—**balancer** *n*.

balance of payments *n* (*finance*) a record of a country's trading deals and financial transactions with other countries in the world.

balance of power *n* the distribution of power between nations.

balance of trade *n* (*finance*) the record of a country's trading deals with other countries in the world. It is a component part of the balance of payments.

balancer *n* one who or that which keeps anything in equilibrium; an acrobat.

balance sheet *n* an accounting statement of the assets and liabilities of a company issued on the last day of an accounting period or trading period.

balance wheel *n* a wheel that regulates the speed of a clock or watch.

balas *n* a variety of spinel ruby of a pale rose-red color.

balata *n* dried gum from a South American tree, used as a substitute for guttapercha.

BA(Law) *abbr* = Bachelor of Arts in Law.

balboa *see* **centesimo**.

Balch *n* **Emily Greene** (1867–1961) American pacifist. She helped found the Women's League of Freedom (1919) and won the Nobel peace prize in 1946.

balcony *n* (*pl* **balconies**) a projecting platform from an upper storey enclosed by a railing; an upper floor of seats in a theater, etc, often projecting over the main floor.—**balconied** *adj*.

bald *adj* lacking a natural or usual covering, as of hair, vegetation, or nap; (*tire*) having little or no tread; (*truth*) plain or blunt; bare, unadorned.—**baldly** *adv*.—**baldness** *n*.

BALD *abbr* = British Association of Laser Dentistry.

baldachine, baldacchino or **baldaquin** *n* (*archit*) a canopy above an altar, throne or doorway which is suspended from the ceiling or projects from a wall. —*see* **ciborium**.

bald eagle *n* a large North American eagle with a dark body and wings, a yellow bill and a white head and tail.

balderdash *n* nonsense.

balding *adj* becoming bald.

baldness *n* the gradual depletion of hair on the head, which is, to a great extent, hereditary.—*also* **alopecia**

baldric *n* a broad belt, often richly ornamented, worn round the waist, or over one shoulder and across the breast.

Baldung Grien *n* **Hans** (1484–1545) German engraver and painter thought to have worked in Dürer's workshop and certainly influenced by him, as in *The Knight, Death and the Maiden* (1505).

Baldwin *n* 1. **Billy** (1903–84) American interior designer of the 1930s. 2. **James** (1924–87) American novelist and essayist, whose works, e.g., *Go Tell it on the Mountain* and *The Fire Next T ime*, depict the problems of Black and homosexual identity. 3. **Stanley [1st Earl Baldwin of Bewdley]** (1867–1947) British statesman and Conservative prime minister (1923–24, 1924–29, 1935–37).

bale[1] *n* a large bundle of goods, as raw cotton, compressed and bound. * *vt* (*bay etc*) to make into bales. * *vi* (*with* **out**) to parachute from an aircraft, usu in an emergency.

bale[2] *n* a great evil; woe.

baleen *n* whalebone.

baleful *adj* evil; harmful; deadly; ominous.—**balefully** *adv*.—**balefulness** *n*.

Balfe *n* **Michael William** (1808–70) Irish composer, baritone singer and violinist, noted for his roles as a singer as Figaro in *The Barber of Seville* and Papageno in *The Magic Flute*. He wrote 29 operas, of which *The Bohemian Girl* (1843) is the best known.

BALH *abbr* = British Association for Local History.

balk *vt* to obstruct or foil. * *vi* to stop and refuse to move and act.—*also* **baulk.**

ball[1] *n* a spherical or nearly spherical body or mass; a round object for use in tennis, soccer, etc; a throw or pitch of a ball; a missile for a cannon, rifle, etc; any rounded part or protuberance of the body; (*pl: sl*) testicles; nonsense. * *interj* (*pl*) (*sl*) nonsense! * *vti* to form into a ball; (*vulg sl*) to have sexual intercourse with.

ball[2] *n* a formal social dance; (*inf*) a good time.—**ballroom** *n*.—**ballroom dancing** *n*.

ballabile *adj*, *adv* (*mus*) (*Italian*) "in a dancing style."

ballad *n* a narrative song or poem; a slow, sentimental, esp pop, song.—**balladeer** *n*.—**balladry** *n*.

ballade (*French*) a type of medieval French poetry, often set to music by troubadours; a 19th-century term, coined by Chopin, for a long, romantic instrumental piece. Chopin wrote four outstanding ballades.

balladmonger *n* a dealer in ballads; an inferior poet, a poetaster.

ballad opera *n* (*mus*) a popular opera composed of dialog and songs with tunes borrowed from folk music, popular songs, and sometimes opera. They first appeared in the 18th century in England, probably the best-known being *The Beggar's Opera*.

ball and socket joint *n* joint permitting all-round movement, e.g., the hip.

Ballantine *n* **James** (1808–77) Scottish house painter involved in a revival of the art of stained glass.

ballast *n* heavy material carried in a ship or vehicle to stabilize it when it is not carrying cargo; crushed rock or gravel, etc used in railway tracks.

ball bearing *n* a device for lessening friction by having a rotating part resting on small steel balls; one of these balls.

ball boy *n* (*tennis*) a boy who retrieves balls that go out of play.—**ball girl** *nf*.

ballcock *n* a device that uses a floating ball to regulate the flow of water in a cistern, tank, etc.

ballerina *n* a female ballet dancer.

ballet *n* (*mus*) a theatrical representation of a story, set to music and performed by dancers; the troupe of dancers.

balletomane *n* an enthusiastic lover of ballet.—**balletomania** *n*.

ballflower *n* (*archit*) ornamentation in the form of a ball cupped by the three petals of a globular-shaped flower.

ball game *n* any of various games played with a ball.

Ballin *n* **Mogens** (1871–1914) Danish metalworker, based in Copenhagen.

Balliol *n* 1. **Edward** (1287–1364) king of Scots (1332–1341). The son of John Balliol. 2. **John** (1249–1313) king of Scots (1292–1296). The son of Devorguilla Balliol, John married the daughter of the Earl of Surrey. His claim to the throne in 1291 was contested by a dozen rivals (known as the Competitors), including Robert Bruce of Annandale, the grandfather of **Robert I**.

ballistic *adj* relating to the flight of projectiles.

ballistic missile *n* a missile whose trajectory is initially guided then ballistic.

ballistics *n* (*used as sing*) the scientific study of projectiles and firearms.

Ball *n* **Lucille Desirée** (1910–1989) American actress and television comedienne; star of *I Love Lucy* (1951–55).

Ballo in Maschera, Un *see* **Masked Ball, A**.

ballonet *n* a small balloon; a subdivision of a balloon's or an airship's gasbag for controlling descent.

balloon *n* a large airtight envelope that rises up when filled with hot air or light gases, often fitted with a basket or gondola for carrying passengers; a small inflatable rubber pouch used as a toy or for decoration; a balloon-shaped line enclosing speech or thoughts in a strip cartoon. * *vti* to inflate; to swell, expand; to travel in a balloon.—**balloonist** *n*.

ballooning *n* the art or practice of managing balloons or making balloon ascents.

balloon jib, balloon sail *n* (*naut*) a light triangular sail used by yachts in a slight breeze.

balloon mortgage *n* a mortgage in which at the end of the mortgage agreement period there is still some of the original capital and some interest still outstanding.

ballot *n* a paper used in voting; the process of voting; the number of votes cast; the candidates offering themselves for election. * *vi* (**balloting, balloted**) to vote.— **balloter** *n*.

ballot box n a secure container for ballot papers.

ballottement n a technique in which a floating structure in the body, e.g., a fetus, moves when it is gently pushed, and then rebounds.

ballpark n a stadium, arena or park in which ball games are played; (*inf*) a situation.

ballplayer n one who plays in a ball game, esp a baseball game.

ballpoint pen n a pen with a tiny ball, which rotates against an inking cartridge, as its writing tip.

ballroom dancing n formal, social dancing with traditional steps.

ball valve n a valve that is opened or shut by the rising or falling of a ball.

ballyhoo n vulgar, noisy publicity or advertisement.

ballyrag (**ballyragging, ballyragged**) vt to hustle, to jeer at. * vi to indulge in horseplay.—*also* **bullyrag**.

balm n a fragrant ointment used in healing and soothing; anything comforting and soothing.

balm of Gilead n any of various fragrant resins, as that of the evergreen terebinth tree of Arabia or the balsam fir; a North American poplar with broad heart-shaped leaves.

balmoral n a laced boot; a Scottish bonnet of wool; a petticoat.

balmy adj (**balmier, balmiest**) having a pleasant fragrance; soothing; (*weather*) mild, warm.

balneology n the science of therapeutic baths and their effect.—**balneological** adj.—**balneologist** n.

baloney n (*inf*) foolish talk; nonsense.—*also* **boloney**.

Balor of the Evil Eye n (*Irish Celtic myth*) king of the Fomorii. A giant with one eye.

BALPA abbr = British Air Line Pilots' Association.

BALPPA abbr = British Association of Leisure Parks, Piers and Attractions.

balsa n lightweight wood from a tropical American tree.

balsam n a fragrant, resinous substance; the tree yielding it.—**balsamic** adj.

balsam fir n a North American evergreen pine with flat needles and yielding balsam.

balsamiferous adj producing or yielding balsam.

Balt. abbr = Baltimore.

BALT abbr = British Association for Language Teaching.

Baltard n **Victor** (b.1805) French architect. His notable works include Les Halles, Paris.

Baltimore n a port in N Maryland, USA.

Baltimore oriole n an American bird nearly related to the starlings with bright orange and black plumage.

baluster n (*archit*) any of the small posts of a railing, as on a staircase.—**balustered** adj.

balustrade n an ornamental row of balusters joined by a rail.

Balzac n **Honoré de** (1799–1850) French novelist whose works include *The Human Comedy*, a series of over 90 separate works.

BAM abbr = Brothers to All Men International.

bambino n (*pl* **bambinos, bambini**) a child or baby; (*RC Church*) a figure of the infant Christ wrapped in swaddling clothes, exhibited in churches from Christmas to Epiphany.

bamboo n (*pl* **bamboos**) any of various, often tropical, woody grasses, used for furniture.

bamboo shoots npl the edible shoots of certain bamboos.

bamboozle vt (*inf*) to deceive; to mystify.—**bamboozlement** n.—**bamboozler** n.

BAMW abbr = British Association of Meat Wholesalers.

ban[1] n a condemnation, an official prohibition. * vt (**banning, banned**) to prohibit, esp officially; to forbid.

ban[2] n (*feudal*) a public proclamation or summons to arms.

BAN abbr = British Association of Neurologists.

banal adj trite, commonplace.—**banally** adj.

banality n (*pl* **banalities**) anything trite or trivial; a commonplace remark, etc.

banana n a herbaceous plant bearing its fruit in compact, hanging bunches.

banana republic n (*derog*) a small country, esp in Central America, that is dominated by foreign interests.

bananas adj (*sl*) insane; wild.

banana skin n (*inf*) an unforeseen occurrence that causes embarrassment.

banana split n ice cream served on a lengthwise sliced banana and topped with syrup, nuts, cream, etc.

banausic adj merely mechanical; mean, illiberal.

BANC abbr = British Association of Nature Conservationists; British Association of National Coaches.

banco n the bet in certain gambling games for the entire amount the banker offers to accept.

band[1] n a strip of material used for binding; a stripe; (*radio*) a range of wavelengths.

band[2] n a group of people with a common purpose; a group of musicians playing together, an orchestra; (*archeo*) a group of Paleolithic hunter-gatherer people consisting of 100 or fewer individuals. * vti to associate together for a particular purpose.

Banda n **Hastings [Kamuzu]** (1905–97) First president of Nyasaland from 1963 and president of Malawi (formerly Nyasaland) from 1966.

bandage n a material pad or strip wrapped around a part of the body to hold a dressing in place, immobilize a limb or maintain pressure on a compress. * vt to bind a wound.

Band-Aid n (*trademark*) a small adhesive bandage.

bandanna, bandana n a large colored handkerchief.

B & B or **b. and b.** abbr = bed and breakfast.

bandbox n a light box of pasteboard, etc, for holding collars or hats.

bandeau n (*pl* **bandeaux**) a band for the hair; a fitting band inside a hat.

banderilla n a barbed dart, used by a banderillero in bullfights to exasperate the bull.

banderole, banderol n a long narrow flag with a cleft end; a streamer; a small flag carried at the head of a lance or mast; a scroll or band with an inscription.—*also* **bannerol**.

B & FBS abbr = British and Foreign Bible Society.

bandicoot n a large rat, native to India and Sri Lanka, very destructive to rice fields and gardens; the name given to rat-like marsupials of several species found in Australia and Tasmania.

bandit n (*pl* **bandits, banditti**) a robber.—**banditry** n.

bandmaster n the conductor of a musical, esp brass, band

bandolier, bandoleer n a belt worn over the chest with pockets for holding ammunition.

bandore, bandora n an ancient stringed instrument resembling a zither.—*also* **pandora, pandore**.

band saw n a motorized, toothed steel belt used for sawing.

bandsman n (*pl* **bandsmen**) a player in a musical, esp brass, band.

band spectrum n a absorption or emission spectrum where the principal features are broad bands of darkness or brightness usu with one sharp edge.

bandstand n a platform for a musical band.

b & w abbr = black and white.

bandwagon n a wagon for carrying a band in a parade; a movement, idea, etc that is (thought to be) heading for success.

bandwidth n the range of frequencies within a given waveband for radio or other types of transmission.

bandy[1] vt (**bandying, bandied**) to pass to and fro; (*often with* **about**) (*rumors, etc*) to spread freely; to exchange words, esp angrily.

bandy[2] adj (**bandier, bandiest**) having legs curved outwards at the knee.

bandy-legged adj bandy.

bane n a person causing distress or misery; something bringing destruction or death; a poison.—**baneful** adj.

baneberry n (*pl* **baneberries**) a plant of the buttercup family bearing white or red poisonous berries; its berry.—*also* **herb Christopher, cohosh**.

banette n a clip for holding the hair in place.

bang[1] n a hard blow; a sudden loud sound. * vt to hit or knock with a loud noise; (*door*) to slam. * vi to make a loud noise; to hit noisily or sharply. * adv with a bang, abruptly; successfully; (*inf*) precisely.

bang[2] n hair cut straight across the forehead to form a fringe; false hair so worn. * vt to cut the hair across the forehead to form a fringe.

bang[3] see **bhang**.

Bang & Olufsen n Danish electronics manufacturers founded in 1925.

banger n an exploding firework; (*sl*) a sausage.

Bangladesh n the People's Republic of Bangladesh, formerly the Eastern Province of Pakistan, is the world's eighth most populated country, situated in southeast Asia.

bangle n a bracelet worn on the arm or ankle.

banian see **banyan**.

banish vt to exile from a place; to drive away; to get rid of.—**banishment** n.

banister n the railing or supporting balusters in a staircase.—*also* **bannister**.

banjo n (*pl* **banjos, banjoes**) (*mus*) a guitar-like, stringed instrument (banjos can have between four and nine strings) of African American origin, comprising a shallow metal (sometimes wood) drum with parchment stretched over the top while the bottom is (usually) left open.—**banjoist** n.

bank[1] n a mound or pile; the sloping side of a river; elevated ground in a lake or the sea; a row or series of objects, as of dials, switches. * vti to form into a mound; to cover (a fire) with fuel so that it burns more slowly; (*aircraft*) to curve or tilt sideways.

bank[2] n an institution that offers various financial services, such as the safekeeping, lending and exchanging of money; the money held by the banker or dealer in a card game; any supply or store for the future, such as a *blood bank*. * vti (*checks, cash, etc*) to deposit in a bank; to work as a banker.

bank. abbr = banking.

bank account n money deposited in a bank and credited to the depositor.

bank bill n a bill of exchange that is issued or guaranteed (accepted) by a bank.

bankbook n a book in which a record is kept of deposits and withdrawals of money into a personal account.

bank charge n the amount that a bank charges a customer for a specific transaction.

bank deposit n an amount of money that a customer places in a bank account.

bank discount n a deduction made according to the current rate of interest.

bank draft n a check that is drawn by a bank on itself or on one of its agents.

banker n a person who runs a bank; the keeper of the bank at a gaming table.

banker's acceptance n a form of promissory note that promises to pay a certain sum of money and has been accepted by a bank.

banker's bill see **bank draft**.

banker's card see **check card**.

banker's reference n a report on someone's creditworthiness that is supplied by a bank to a third party.

Bankhead n **Tallulah** (1903–80) American actress whose films include *Lifeboat* (1944).

bank holiday n a weekday when banks are officially closed; (*Brit*) a legal holiday.

banking n the activity or occupation of running a bank. * adj of or concerning a bank.

bank loan *n* a specified sum of money that has been lent to an individual or company (the borrower) by a bank, usu for a fixed period of time and usu at a specified rate of interest.

bank rate *n* the rate at which the central bank lends to other banks.

bank reconciliation statement *n* a statement showing how the bank balance of a company can be reconciled with the bank statement.

bankroll *n* money in one's possession. * *vt* (*sl*) to finance.

bankrupt *n* a person, etc legally declared unable to pay his debts; one who becomes insolvent. * *adj* judged to be insolvent; financially ruined; devoid of resources, ideas, etc. * *vt* to make bankrupt.—**bankruptcy** *n*.

bankruptcy *n* the state of individuals who are unable to pay their debts.

bank shot *n* (basketball) a shot made by rebounding the ball off the backboard into the basket.

bank statement *n* a statement issued regularly by a bank or other institution that records the financial transactions of an individual or company.

Banks *n* **Sir Joseph** (1743–1820) English botanist and explorer who accompanied Cook on his 1768–71 voyage round the world.

banksia *n* (*bot*) any of an Australian genus of flowering shrubs with evergreen leaves.

banner *n* a flag or ensign; a headline running across a newspaper page; a strip of cloth bearing a slogan or emblem carried between poles in a parade.

banner ad *n* (*comput*) a banner advertisement which appears on a website.

banneret *n* (*hist*) an order of knighthood conferred on the field of battle for distinguished service or a deed of valor; the person on whom the degree was conferred and who ranked between a baron and a knight.

bannerette *n* a little banner or flag.

bannerol *see* **banderole**.

Bannister *n* **Sir Roger** (1929–) British athlete. He was the first man to run a mile in less than four minutes (May 1954).

bannister *see* **banister**.

bannock *n* a thick flat cake made of oatmeal or barley and baked on a griddle.

banns *npl* public declaration of intention, esp in church, to marry.

BANPR *abbr* = British Association of Nursery and Pram Retailers.

banquet *n* a feast; an elaborate and sometimes formal dinner in honor of a person or occasion. * *vt* (**banqueting, banqueted**) to hold a banquet.—**banqueter** *n*.

banquette *n* a cushioned bench; a step along the inside of a parapet on which soldiers stood to fire upon the enemy; the footway of a bridge when raised above the carriageway.

BANS *abbr* = British Association of Numismatic Societies.

banshee *n* (*folklore*) a female fairy whose wail portends a death in the family.—*see* **Bean Sidhe**.

bantam *n* a dwarf breed of domestic fowl; a small, aggressive person; (*boxing*) a bantamweight.

bantamweight *n* a boxing weight (112–118 lbs; 51–53.5 kg) between featherweight and flyweight.

banter *vt* to tease good-humoredly.—**banterer** *n*.

Banting *n* **Sir Frederick [Grant]** (1891–1941) Canadian physician whose research with American physiologist Charles Herbert Best (1899–1978) isolated insulin in a form suitable for treating diabetes.

Bantock *n* **Granville** (1868–1946) influential English composer. His works, which included symphonic poems, operas and choral pieces, followed the romantic tradition. Perhaps his best known work is his tone poem *Fifine at the Fair*. He was knighted in 1930.

Bantu *n* (*pl* **Bantu, Bantus**) one of a group of Southern African peoples or their language.

banyan *n* an Indian fig tree with vast, rooting branches.—*also* **banian.**

banzai *interj* a Japanese greeting or salute; a shout used in Japanese combat during attack.

banzai attack *n* a desperate suicidal attack practiced by Japanese troops in World War II.

BAO *abbr* = Bachelor of Obstetrics; Bankruptcy Annulment Order.

baobab *n* an African tree with an enormously thick trunk.

BAOR *abbr* = British Army of the Rhine.

BAOT *abbr* = British Association of Occupational Therapists.

bap *n* a large soft bread roll.

bap. *abbr* = baptized.

Bap. *abbr* = Baptist.

BAPA *abbr* = British Amateur Press Association.

BAPC *abbr* = British Aircraft Preservation Council; British Association of Paperback Collectors; British Association of Print and Copyshops.

BAPE *abbr* = Barbados Association of Professional Engineers.

BAPH *abbr* = British Association of Paper Historians.

BAppArts *abbr* = Bachelor in Applied Arts.

BAppSc *abbr* = Bachelor in Applied Science.

BAPS *abbr* = British Association of Paediatric Surgeons; British Association of Plastic Surgeons.

bapt. *abbr* = baptized.

Bapt. *abbr* = Baptist; Baptiste.

baptism *n* the sprinkling of water on the forehead, or complete immersion in water, as a rite of admitting a person to a Christian church; any initiating experience.—**baptismal** *adj*.—**baptismally** *adv*.

Baptist *n* a member of a Protestant Christian denomination holding that the true church is of believers only, who are all equal, that the only authority is the Bible, and that adult baptism by immersion is necessary.

baptistry, baptistery *n* (*pl* **baptistries, baptisteries**) the part of a church where baptism takes place.

baptize *vt* to christen, to name.—**baptizer** *n*.

BAPTO *abbr* = British Association of Pool Table Operators.

bar[1] *n* a straight length of wood or metal; a counter where alcoholic drinks or other refreshments are served; a place with such a counter; an oblong piece, as of soap; anything that obstructs or hinders; a band or strip; a strip or bank of sand or mud near and in line with the shore or across a river or harbor; (*mil*) a badge signifying a second award; (*with cap*) barristers or lawyers collectively; the legal profession; (*mus*) a vertical line dividing a staff into measures; (*mus*) a measure. * *vt* (**barring, barred**) to secure or fasten as with a bar; to exclude or prevent; to oppose. * *prep* except for.

bar[2] *n* a unit of atmospheric pressure.

bar[3] *see* **barre**.

bar. *abbr* = barleycorn; barometer; barometric; barrel; barrister.

Bar. *abbr* = Baruch.

BAR *abbr* = British Association of Removers.

Barabbas *n* (*Bible*) a condemned criminal who was pardoned by Pilate at Jesus' trial. When Pilate offered to release Jesus, Jewish leaders incited the crowd to ask for Barabbas to be released instead.

Barak *n* (*Bible*) defeated Sisera in a battle at the river Kishon. *See also* **Deborah**.

barathea *n* a type of fine woolen material.

barb *n* the sharp backward point of a fish-hook, etc; one of the sharp parts combined to form barbed wire; a pointed or critical remark; a beard-like growth. * *vt* to provide with a barb.—**barbed** *adj*.

Barb. *abbr* = Barbados.

BARB *abbr* = British Association Representing Breeders; Broadcasters' Audience Research Board.

Barbados *n* the most easterly island of the West Indies. Barbados is a constitutional monarchy.

barbarian *n* an uncivilized, primitive person; a cruel vicious person.—*also adj*.

barbaric *adj* of or suitable for barbarians.—**barbarically** *adv*.

barbarism *n* a barbarous act; the state of being a barbarian; an expression or word that is tasteless or not standard; an object or act that offends.

barbarity *n* (*pl* **barbarities**) savage cruelty; a vicious act.

barbarize *vti* to make or become barbarous.

barbarous *adj* uncivilized, cruel, coarse.—**barbarously** *adv*.

Barbary ape *n* a tailless macaque monkey of North Africa and Gibraltar.

barbate *adj* tufted, bearded.

Barbe *n* **Pierre** (1900–95) French architect and designer specializing in furniture.

barbecue *n* a metal frame for grilling food over an open fire; an open-air party where barbecued food is served. * *vt* (**barbecuing, barbecued**) to cook on a barbecue.

barbed drainage *n* a pattern of drainage in which tributaries meet the main river at an obtuse angle as though they are trying to flow upstream.

barbed wire *n* wire with barbs at close intervals.—*also* **barbwire**.

barbel *n* a freshwater fish with beard-like filaments at its mouth; such a filament.—**barbelled** *adj*.

barbell *n* a metal rod with weights at each end, used in weightlifting.

barber *n* a person who cuts hair and shaves beards.

Barber *n* **Samuel** (1910–81) American composer and singer whose works include two operas (*Vanessa* and *Antony and Cleopatra*), ballets, symphonies, concertos, choral works and piano compositions. His best-known work is *Adagio for Strings* (1936), which is taken from a string quartet.

barberry *n* (*pl* **barberries**) a thorny shrub with yellow flowers; its red berry.

barbershop *n* the business premises of a barber.

barbershop quartet *n* a quartet of amateur male singers who perform close-harmony arrangements. The tradition originated in barber shops in New York in the late 19th century.

barbet *n* a tropical bird with tufts of feathers at the base of the bill.

barbette *n* a raised platform for guns to fire over a parapet; a type of armored turret in a warship.

barbican *n* a defensive tower over the gate or drawbridge of a castle or fortification.

Barbiere di Siviglia, Il *see* **Barber of Seville** *n* **The**.

Barbirolli *n* **Sir John (Giovanni Battista)** (1899–1970) English conductor, of Italian origin, knighted in 1949; conducted the British National Opera Company, the Scottish Orchestra, and the New York Philharmonic Orchestra; conductor of the Hallé Orchestra (1943); conductor of the Houston Symphony Orchestra (1961–67).

barbitone, barbital *n* a habit-forming, toxic, hypnotic and sedative drug.

barbiturate *n* a drug that has anesthetic, hypnotic or sedative effects.

Barbizon School *n* a group of French landscape painters in the 1840s who based their art on direct study from nature. Their advanced ideas represented a move away from academic conventions, and their interest in daylight effects and their bold use of color helped prepare the way for impressionism.

barbotine *adj* a type of decoration applied to pots consisting of a pattern made in thick slip.

barbule *n* a minute barb; a filament fringing the barb of a feather.

barbwire *see* **barbed wire**.

barcarole, barcarolle *n* a Venetian gondolier's song; an instrumental piece resembling this.

BArch *abbr* = Bachelor of Architecture.

bar chart *or* **bar graph** *n* a diagram that indicates statistical data, such as sales figures, by means of bars or rectangles of varying heights.

BArchE *abbr* = Bachelor of Architectural Engineering.

bar code *n* (*comput*) a series of printed vertical bars of differing widths that represent numbers to identify items, usu for stock control and sales pricing.

bard *n* (*mus*) a Celtic minstrel, part of whose job it was to compose songs for his master.

BARD *abbr* = Bangladesh Academy for Rural Development; British Association of Rally Doctors; British Association of Record Dealers.

Bardeen *n* **John** (1908–91) American physicist and electrical engineer. He won two Nobel prizes, one (1956) for research leading to invention of the transistor, another (1972) for research into superconductivity.

Bardot *n* **Brigitte** (1934–) French actress and leading "sex symbol" of the 1950s.

bare *adj* without covering; unclothed; naked; simple, unadorned; mere; without furnishings. * *vt* to uncover; to reveal.—**bareness** *n*.

bareback *adj* on a horse with no saddle.—*also adv*.

barefaced *adj* with the face shaven or uncovered; shameless.—**barefacedly** *adv*.

barefoot, barefooted *adj* with the feet bare.—*also adv*.

barefoot doctor *n* a medical worker in rural areas of developing countries.

barège, barege *n* a thin gauze-like fabric, usu of silk and worsted.

barehanded *adj* without using weapons.

barely *adv* openly; merely; scarcely.

Barenboim *n* **Daniel** (1942–) Argentine-born Israeli pianist and conductor famed for his interpretation of late-19th and early-20th-century music.

barfly *n* (*pl* **barflies**) (*sl*) one who often frequents bars.

bargain *n* an agreement laying down the conditions of a transaction; something sold at a price favorable to the buyer; **into the bargain** as well; in addition. * *vt* to make a bargain, to haggle; (*with* **for**) to expect or hope for.

bargaining chip *n* something offered in negotiations by one side in an attempt to get concessions from the other side.

barge *n* a flat-bottomed vessel, used to transport freight along rivers and canals; a large boat for excursions or pleasure trips. * *vi* to lurch clumsily; (*with* **in**) to interrupt (a conversation) rudely; (*with* **into**) to enter abruptly.

bargeboard *n* (*archit*) a projecting board, often decorated, placed on the verge of gables to hide the ends of the horizontal roof timbers.—*also* **vergeboard**

barge couple *n* one of two beams bounding a gable, mortised and tenoned together and used for strengthening a building.

barge course *n* the tiling that projects beyond the principal rafters in a building; a wall coping constructed of bricks set on edge.

bargee *n* the owner of or one employed on a barge; a bargeman.

bar graph *see* **bar chart**.

barilla *n* an alkali made from kinds of marine plant or seaweed.

barit. *abbr* = baritone.

barite *see* **barytes**.

baritone *n* (*mus*) a male voice, midway between bass and tenor with a range of approximately two octaves; a singer with such a voice; a brass instrument of the saxhorn family.

barium *n* (*chem*) a white metallic element.

barium sulphate *n* a white insoluble fine heavy powder which is opaque to X-rays, swallowed by a patient before X-ray of the alimentary canal.

Bar-Jesus *see* **Elymas**.

bark[1] *n* the harsh or abrupt cry of a dog, wolf, etc; a similar sound, such as one made by a person. * *vi* to make a loud cry like a dog; to speak or shout sharply or angrily.

bark[2] *n* the outside covering of a tree trunk. * *vt* to remove the bark from; to scrape; to skin (the knees, etc).

bark[3] *see* **barque**.

barkentine *see* **barquentine**.

barker *n* one who or that which barks; a person who shouts his wares, etc, usu at a fairground.

Barker *n* 1. **Arizona Donnie Clark ("Ma")** (1872–1935) American gangster, head of the "Bloody Barkers," a family of violent criminals including her husband, and sons **Herman** (1894–1927), **Lloyd** (1896–1949), **Arthur** ["Doc"] (1899–1935) and **Fred** (1902–1939). 2. **George** [**Granville**] (1913–91) English poet, noted for his highly dramatic, often surreal verse, e.g., *Eros in Dogma*.

barking *n* the process of stripping bark from trees; the process of tanning leather or dyeing with bark.

BARLA *abbr* = British Amateur Rugby League Association.

Barlach *n* **Ernst** (1870–1938) German expressionist sculptor. Notable among his works is the war memorial at Gustrow Cathedral.

barley *n* a grain used in making beer and whisky, and for food.

barleycorn *n* a grain of barley; (*formerly*) a measure of length, one-third of an inch (0.85 cm).

barley sugar *n* a transparent amber-colored sweet.

barm *n* the froth on fermenting liquor used as leaven in breadmaking, yeast.

BARMA *abbr* = Boiler and Radiator Manufacturers Association.

barmaid *n* a female serving alcohol in a bar.

barman *n* (*pl* **barmen**) a man serving alcohol in a bar.

Barmecide, Barmedcidal *adj* like the Barmecide's feast in *The Arabian Nights*; imaginarily satisfying; unreal, illusory.

bar mitzvah *n* (*Judaism*) the ceremony marking the thirteenth birthday of a boy, who then assumes full religious obligations; the boy himself.

barn *n* a farm building used for storing grain, hay, etc, and sheltering animals.

Barnabas *n* (*Bible*) Jewish Christian named Joseph, nicknamed Barnabas, who sold a field and gave the proceeds to help the needy.

Barnack *n* **Oscar** (1879–1936) German industrial designer, who created the revolutionary Leica 35mm camera.

barnacle *n* a marine crustacean that attaches itself to rocks and ship bottoms.

barnacle goose *n* a wild European gray-winged goose that breeds in the Arctic.

Barnard *n* 1. **Christian** [**Neethling**] (1922–) South African surgeon. He performed the world's first heart transplant in 1967. 2. **George Grey** (1863–1938) American sculptor. He studied in Chicago and Paris and was inspired by a line from Victor Hugo to produce his best-known work, *The Nature of Man*.

Barnard's star *n* a dim 10th magnitude star, about 2 parsec from the Solar System.

barn owl *n* any of a genus of owl with brownish plumage above and white plumage below.

barnstorm *vi* to tour (rural areas) as an actor, or making speeches in a political campaign, or demonstrating flying stunts.—**barnstormer** *n*.

Barnum *n* **Phineas Taylor** (1810–1991) American showman, famous for his touring circus "The Greatest Show on Earth."

barnyard *n* the area around a barn.

barogram *n* the record traced by a barograph.

barograph *n* a self-recording aneroid barometer.—**barographic** *adj*.

barometer *n* an instrument for measuring atmospheric pressure and imminent changes in the weather; anything that marks change.—**barometric** *adj*.—**barometrically** *adv*.

baron *n* a member of a rank of nobility, the lowest in the British peerage; a powerful businessman.—**baroness** *nf*.

baronage *n* the whole body of barons; the dignity or rank of a baron.

baronet *n* the lowest hereditary title of honor in Britain.

baronetage *n* the collective body of baronets; the dignity or rank of a baronet.

baronetcy *n* (*pl* **baronetcies**) the dignity or rank of a baronet.

baronial *adj* pertaining to or suitable for a baron.

barony *n* (*pl* **baronies**) the rank or lands of a baron; (*Scot*) a large manor; (*Ireland*) a division of a county.

baroque *n* (*French*) literally "grotesque," (*archit*) a style of architecture, mainly associated with the 17th and early 18th century, with its origins in Italy, and characterized by exuberant decoration; (*mus*) the lush style of music typical of the 17th and early-18th centuries, also applied to other arts. * *adj* extravagantly ornamented.

baroscope *n* an instrument for indicating variations in the pressure of the atmosphere without actual measurement of its weight.—**baroscopic** *adj*.

barouche *n* a 19th-century roomy four-wheeled carriage for four with a folding top.

barque *n* (*poet*) a ship; a three-masted vessel with the foremast and main mast square-rigged and the mizzen fore-and-aft.—*also* **bark**.

barquentine, barquantine *n* (*naut*) a three-masted vessel with the foremast square-rigged and the main mast and mizzenmast fore-and-aft or schooner-rigged.—*also* **barkentine**.

barr. *abbr* = barrister.

Barraband *n* **Jacques** (*c*.1767–1809) professor of Floral Design at the Lyon Ecole des Beaux Arts from 1807.

barrack *vti* to shout or protest at.—**barracker** *n*.

barracks *n* (*used as sing*) a building for housing soldiers.

barracuda *n* (*pl* **barracuda, barracudas**) a fierce fish with edible flesh.

Barragán *n* **Luis** (1902–88) Mexican architect. His notable works include Mexico city suburbs.

barrage *n* a man-made dam across a river; heavy artillery fire; (*of protests, questions, etc*) continuous and heavy delivery.

barrage balloon *n* a large balloon anchored to the ground and trailing cables or nets, used as a defense against low-flying enemy aircraft.

barranca, barranco *n* (*pl* **barrancas, barrancos**) a deep mountain gully or ravine.

Barraqué *n* **Jean** (1928–73) French experimental composer who explored the possibilities of voice and percussion instruments, as in his piece entitled *Le Temps Restitué*.

barratry *n* the defrauding or injury of a ship's owner, freighter or insurer by the master or crew; the practice of inciting and encouraging lawsuits or litigation.—**barrator** *n*.—**barratrous** *adj*.

Barrau *n* **Gerard** (1945–) French industrial designer specializing in store layouts.

barre *n* a horizontal rail used for ballet practice.

barred *see* **bar**[1].

barred owl *n* a North American owl with bars of darker feathers on the breast.

barrel *n* a cylindrical container, usu wooden, with bulging sides held together with hoops; the amount held by a barrel; a tubular structure, as in a gun. * *vt* (**barreling, barreled** *or* **barrelling, barrelled**) to put into barrels.

barrel-chested *adj* having a large, outward-curving chest.

barrel organ *n* (*mus*) a mechanical piano or organ played by a revolving cylinder with pins that operate the keys or valves to produce sound.

barrel roll *n* an aircraft maneuver consisting of a complete rotation.

barrel vault *n* (*archit*) the simple tunnel-shaped vault, used by the Romans and later in Romanesque architecture.

B

barren *adj* infertile; incapable of producing offspring; unable to bear crops; unprofitable; (*with* **of**) lacking in.

barrette *n* a small clasp used to hold hair in place.

barricade *n* a barrier or blockade used in defense to block a street; an obstruction. * *vt* to block with a barricade.

Barrie *n* Sir J[ames] M[atthew] (1860–1937) Scottish dramatist and novelist, remembered principally for *Peter Pan* (1904).

barrier *n* anything that bars passage, prevents access, controls crowds, etc, such as a fence; obstruction; hindrance.

barrier beach *n* an elongated sand or shingle bank that is not submerged at high tide.

barrier lake *n* any lake formed by a naturally occurring barrier that interrupts the normal flow of a river.

barrier reef *n* a reef of coral parallel to the shore but some distance from it.

barring *prep* excepting; leaving out of account.

barrister *n* a qualified lawyer who has been called to the bar in England.

Barron *n* Phyllis (1890–1964) British textile designer.

barrow[1] *n* a wheelbarrow or hand-cart used for carrying loads.

barrow[2] *n* (*archeo*) a long or round earth mound constructed over burial places in Britain from the early Neolithic period onwards.

Barry *n* 1. James (1741–1806) Irish painter patronized and financed in his early career by the writer Edmund Burke. His most famous and ambitious work is *The Progress of Human Culture* (1777–83), which he painted gratis for the Society of Arts. 2. Sir Charles (1795–1860), English architect. His notable works include Houses of Parliament.

Barrymore *n* John (1882–1942) American stage and film actor, known as "The Great Profile."

Barsac *n* a French white wine.

bar sinister *n* (*her*) in error for **bend sinister**, the badge of illegitimacy.

Bart *abbr* = Baronet.

barter *vt* to trade commodities or services without exchanging money. * *vi* to haggle or bargain. * *n* trade by the exchanging of commodities.—**barterer** *n*.

Barth *n* Karl (1886–1968) Swiss Protestant theologian and courageous opponent of Nazism.

Barthes *n* Roland (1915–80) French critic and writer who applied structuralism to literature.

Bartholdi *n* Frédéric Auguste (1834–1904) French sculptor, famous for his monumental sculptures, the most notable of which is *Liberty Enlightening the World*, the "Statue of Liberty" in New York Bay.

Bartholomew *n* (*Bible*) one of the twelve apostles; also referred to as Nathanael.

Bartimaeus *n* (*Bible*) blind beggar outside Jericho; he called Jesus the Son of David, and his sight was restored.

bartizan *n* (*archit*) an overhanging turret at the top of a tower or wall.

Bartók *n* Béla (1881–1945) Hungarian composer and pianist. Bartók's principal works include: Duke Bluebeard's Castle (opera); *The Miraculous Mandarin* (ballet); *Cantata profana* (a choral piece); and six influential string quartets.

Bartolommeo *n* Fra (*c.*1472–1571) Florentine painter of the High Renaissance. Famous among his works are *The Vision of St Bernard, The Marriage of St Catherine* and the *Salvador Mundi*.

bartonellosis *see* **sandfly fever**.

Baruch *n* (*Bible*) Jeremiah's companion who wrote down his message and read it to the people of Jerusalem; it was later burnt by the King.

barycentre *n* the common center of mass round which the stars in a binary star system rotate.

baryon *n* an elementary particle (nucleon or hyperon) with a mass greater than or equal to that of the proton.

barytes *n* a white crystalline mineral of great weight, consisting mainly of barium sulfate.—*also* **barite, heavy spar**.

baryton *n* (*mus*) (*German*) an 18th-century German stringed instrument, played with a bow.

BAS *abbr* = Bachelor of Applied Science; Bachelor of Agricultural Science; Brewers' Association of Scotland; British Alpine Society; British Ambulance Society; British Antarctic Survey; British Association of Stammerers; Bulgarian Academy of Sciences; Bureau of Analysed Samples.

BASA *abbr* = Bahamas Association of Shipping Agents; British Adhesives and Sealants Association; British Air Survey Association; British Amputee and Les Autres Sports Association; British Architectural Students' Association; British Association of Seed Analysts; British Australian Studies Association; British Automatic Sprinkler Association.

basal *adj* pertaining to, at or forming the base; fundamental. * *n* a basal part.—**basally** *adv*.

basal ganglion (*pl* **basal ganglia**) *n* gray matter at the base of the cerebrum that is involved in the subconscious control of voluntary movement.

basal metabolism *n* (*biol*) the minimum amount of energy required to maintain life in an organism.

basalt *n* (*geol*) a dark, fine-grained igneous rock containing feldspar, pyroxene and possibly olivine, occurring as lavas and associated with volcanic activity. — **basaltic** *adj*.

BASc *abbr* = Bachelor of Agricultural Science; Bachelor of Applied Science.

bascule *n* a mechanical arrangement on the seesaw principle by which the lowering of one end raises the other; a kind of drawbridge so operated.

base *n* the bottom part of anything; the support or foundation; the fundamental principle; the center of operations (e.g., military); (*baseball*) one of the four corners of the diamond; (*archit*) the part beneath the shaft of a column and the pedestal; (*chem*) any substance that dissociates in water to produce hydroxide ions; (*math*) a base is the number raised to a certain power, which will produced a fixed number. * *adj* low in morality or honor; worthless; menial.—**basely** *adv*.—**baseness** *n*. * *vt* to use as a basis; to found (on); (*with* **at, in**) to place, to station.—**basal** *adj*.

baseball *n* the US national game, involving two teams that score runs by hitting a ball and running round four bases arranged in a diamond shape on the playing area.

baseboard *n* a molding used to conceal the joint between a wall and a floor.

baseborn *adj* (*arch*) of low or mean birth; illegitimate; mean.

base hit *n* (*baseball*) a hit enabling the batter to reach base safely, without a force play or error being made.

baseless *adj* without a base; unfounded.

baseline *n* a line on the ground that is surveyed extremely accurately and from which other readings are taken during a survey; the line at each end of a games court marking the limit of play; (*baseball*) the line between any two consecutive bases.

BASELT *abbr* = British Association for State English Language Teaching.

baseman *n* (*pl* **basemen**) (*baseball*) a fielder placed at the first, second, and third bases respectively.

basement *n* the part of a building that is partly or wholly below ground level.

base metal *n* any metal other than the precious metals.

base rate *n* the interest rate used as a basis by banks when setting the interest rates that they charge their customers.

base stock *n* a volume of stock held by a company that is assumed to be at a constant level, stock levels not being allowed to fall below this level.

bash *vt* (*inf*) to hit hard; to dent by striking. * *n* (*inf*) a heavy blow; (*inf*) a try or attempt; (*sl*) a party.

Bashan *n* (*Bible*) district by the River Jordan famous in *OT* times for its agriculture. *See also* **Og**.

bashful *adj* easily embarrassed, shy.—**bashfully** *adv*.—**bashfulness** *n*.

bashibazouk *n* a volunteer or irregular in the Turkish army.

Basho *n* [Matsuo] (1644–94) Japanese poet who devised the haiku.

basic *adj* fundamental; simple. * *n* (*often pl*) a basic principle, factor, etc; the rudiments.—**basically** *adv*.

BASIC *abbr* (*comput*) = Beginner's All-purpose Symbolic Instruction Code. A popular, flexible and relatively easy computer programming language, developed in the USA in 1964; British American Security Information Centre.

basicity *n* the state of being a base; (*chem*) the power of an acid to unite with one or more atoms of a base.

basic rocks *n* (*geol*) quartz-free igneous rocks that have a low silica content but a high proportion of magnesium iron and calcium; e.g., basalt and gabbro.

BASICS *abbr* = British Association for Immediate Care Schemes.

basic slag *n* the phosphates of lime and oxidized impurities left as a brittle powder in steelmaking and used as a fertilizer.

basic training *n* the initial period of training for a new recruit.

basidium *n* (*pl* **basidia**) the cell to which the spores of certain fungi are attached.—**basidial** *adj*.

Basie *n* "Count" (William) (1904–84) African American jazz pianist, band leader and composer. On "discovering" jazz he formed his own band in 1935, famous for its driving rhythms as well as its virtuoso soloists.

basify *vt* (**basifying, basified**) to convert into a base, make basic.

basil *n* a plant with aromatic leaves used for seasoning food.

Basil *n* Saint, also called Basil the Great (329–379) born at Caesarea, the capital of Cappadocia, an ancient region of east Asia Minor; bishop of Caesarea (370). One of the first to adopt the community system for monks and a devoted opponent of Arianism. His feast day (with **Gregory Nazianzens**) is 2 January.

basilar, basilary *adj* (*anat*) pertaining to or situated at the base, esp of the skull.

basilica *n* a church with a broad nave, side aisles, and an apse; (*RC Church*) a church with special ceremonial rites; an important Roman public building, used as a center of commerce and hall of justice.—**basilican** *adj*.

basilisk *n* a fabulous creature dealing death by its gaze, sometimes identified with the cockatrice; a lizard with an inflatable crest. * *adj* pertaining to the basilisk; penetrating or malignant.

basin *n* a wide shallow container for liquid; its contents; (*geol*) a depression in the land surface; a huge depression occupied by sea water, e.g., an ocean basin; the catchment area of a river system; a geological feature, such as a large depression filling with sediment or a sinking caused by solution and removal of mineral deposits; (*astron*) a surface feature of planets and moons; a shallow, circular depression.

basinet *n* a light steel helmet of medieval times, often with a visor.

basis *n* (*pl* **bases**) a base or foundation; a principal constituent; a fundamental principle or theory.

bask *vi* to lie in sunshine or warmth; to enjoy someone's approval.

basket *n* a container made of interwoven cane, wood strips, etc; the hoop through which basketball players throw the ball to score.

basketball *n* a game in which two teams compete to score by throwing the ball through an elevated net basket or hoop; this ball.

basket case *n* one who is completely worn-out, incapacitated or inoperative; an amputee with all four limbs removed.

basket hilt *n* the hilt of a sword shaped like a basket.

basket of currencies *n* a group of selected currencies that is used to set a value on some other currency.

basketry *n* woven, interlocking strips of vegetable fibers fashioned to form a container.

basking shark *n* a large shark of northern seas, which is harmless and has the habit of basking at the surface in the sun.

Baskin *n* **Leonard** (1929–) American sculptor, graphic arts teacher and founder of the Gehenna Press.

BASMA *abbr* = Boot and Shoe Manufacturers Association and Leather Trades Protection Society; British Adhesives & Sealants Manufacturers' Association.

basque *n* a woman's jacket with a short skirt.

Basque *n* one of a people inhabiting the western Pyrenees; their language.

BASRA *abbr* = British Amateur Scientific Research Association.

bas-relief *n* a low relief; a form of relief in which the figures stand out very slightly from the ground.—*also* **basso-rilievo**.

bass[1] *n* (*mus*) the range of the lowest male voice; a singer or instrument with this range. * *adj* of, for or in the range of a bass.

bass[2] *n* (*pl* **bass**) any of numerous freshwater food and game fishes.

BASS *abbr* = Belgian Archives for the Social Sciences; British Association of Ship Suppliers; British Association of Sports Sciences.

bassa *adj, adv* (*mus*) (*Italian*) "low."

BASSA *abbr* = British Airline Stewards and Stewardesses Association.

bass-bar *n* (*mus*) a strip of wood glued as reinforcement under the bridge inside the belly of instruments of the violin family.

bass clarinet *n* (*mus*) a single-reed instrument built an octave lower than the clarinet, with a crook and upturned bell.

bass clef *n* (*mus*) the character C placed at the beginning of the bass staff.

bass dance, base dance *n* (*mus*) a slow dance resembling the minuet.

bass drum *n* (*mus*) a large percussion instrument consisting of a cylindrical wooden hoop which is usu covered on both sides with vellum.

basse danse *n* (*mus*) (*French*) literally "low dance," i.e., a dance in which the feet are kept low to the ground.

basset[1], **basset hound** *n* a smooth-haired hound with short legs.

basset[2] *vi* (**basseting, basseted**) (*geol*) to crop out at the surface. * *n* an outcrop.

basset horn *n* (*mus*) an alto clarinet.

bass flute *n* (*mus*) an alto flute with a pitch a fourth lower than a "concert" or normal flute.

bassinet *n* a wickerwork or wooden cradle with a hood; a pram.

bassist *n* a player of the double bass.

basso *n* (*pl* **bassos, bassi**) one who sings bass.

basso continuo *see* **figured bass**.

bassoon *n* an orchestral, deep-toned woodwind instrument.—**bassoonist** *n*.

basso ostinato *n* (*mus*) (*Italian*) "obstinate bass," a ground bass, i.e., a bass figure that is repeated many times throughout a composition (or part of a composition) while the upper parts vary.

basso profundo *n* (*pl* **basso profundos**) the lowest bass voice; a singer with such a voice.

basso-rilievo *n* (*pl* **basso-rilievos**) a bas-relief.

bass viol *n* a large stringed instrument of the violin class for playing bass, the violoncello.

bast *n* the tough inner fibrous bark of various trees, esp of the lime; rope or matting made from this bark.

basta *interj* enough!

bastard *n* a person born of unmarried parents; (*offensive*) an unpleasant person; (*inf*) a person (*lucky bastard*); (*inf*) a difficult task, situation, etc. * *adj* illegitimate (by birth); false; not genuine.—**bastardy** *n*.

bastardize *vt* to declare illegitimate; to falsify or corrupt.—**bastardization** *n*.

baste[1] *vt* to drip fat over (roasting meat, etc).

baste[2] *vt* to sew with long loose stitches as a temporary seam.

Bastet *n* (*Egypt*) a cat-headed goddess, guardian of the Delta area, with her center of cult at Bubastis.

Bastide *n* **Thomas** (1954–) French glass designer, who became Head of Design at Baccarat in 1983.

bastille, bastile *n* a prison; a fortress.

bastinado *n* (*pl* **bastinadoes**) a caning of the soles of the feet as a form of torture. * *vt*. (**bastinadoing, bastinadoed**) to torture in this way.

bastion *n* (*archit*) a projection built out from the angle of a fortified building allowing the occupants to defend the ground in front of the ramparts; one who strongly upholds or supports a principle, etc; any strong defense;—**bastioned** *adj*.

bastle *n* (*archit*) a type of farmhouse, dating from 1650–1750, built in the Scottish borders, housing farm animals at ground level and the family above.

basuco *n* the dregs of cocaine after refining, which are packaged and sold in Colombia.

BASW *abbr* = British Association of Social Workers.

bat[1] *n* a wooden club used in cricket, baseball, etc; a batsman; a paddle used in table tennis. * *vt* (**batting, batted**) to hit as with a bat. * *vi* to take one's turn at bat.

bat[2] *n* a nocturnal, mouse-like flying mammal with forelimbs modified to form wings.

bat[3] *vt* (**batting, batted**) (*one's eyelids*) to wink or flutter.

bat. or batt. *abbr* = battalion; battery.

BAT[1] *n* (*comput*) the common extension used at the end of a batch file name.

BAT[2] *abbr* = British-American Tobacco Company.

BATA *abbr* = Bakery Allied Traders Association; British Air Transport Association.

batch *n* the quantity of bread, etc produced at one time; one set, group, etc; an amount of work for processing by a computer in a single run.

batch costing *n* (*business*) a form of product costing in which unit costs are given on the basis of a batch produced.

batch file *n* (*comput*) a file containing DOS commands that is accessed by typing the file name at the DOS prompt.

batch processing *n* (*comput*) a type of computer operation that processes a series or batch of commands at one time without user intervention.

batch production *n* (*business*) a form of manufacturing production in which a number of identical products or components are passed through the various production processes as a batch.

batch size *n* (*business*) the number of items that make up a batch in batch production.

bate *vt* to lessen or reduce; to deduct.

bateau *n* (*pl* **bateaux**) a light boat used esp on Canadian rivers.

Bates *n* **H[erbert] E[rnest]** (1905–74) English novelist and short-story writer whose works include *The Darling Buds of May* (1958).

bath *n* water for washing the body; a bathing; a bathtub; (*pl*) a building with baths for public use; a municipal swimming pool.

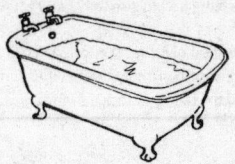

BATHC *abbr* = British Amateur Treasure Hunting Clubs.

bath chair *n* a wheeled chair for invalids.

bathe *vt* to dampen with any liquid. * *vi* to take a bath; to go swimming; to become immersed.—**bather** *n*.

bathhouse *n* a public building with baths; a building in which bathers can change clothes.

bathing suit *n* a garment that is worn for swimming, a swimsuit.

bathmat *n* a washable mat placed in front of a bathtub.

bathometer *n* an apparatus for measuring depths.

bathos *n* anticlimax; descent from the elevated to the ordinary in speech or writing.

bathrobe *n* a loose-fitting garment of absorbent fabric for use after bathing or as a dressing gown.

bathroom *n* a room with a bath or shower and usu a lavatory and washbasin.—*also* **lavatory**.

Bathsheba *n* (*Bible*) wife of Uriah the Hittite whom David married after Uriah was killed in battle; she bore David a son, Solomon, and interceded on his behalf as David was dying. *See also* **David**, **Nathan**, **Solomon**, **Uriah**.

Bath stone *n* (*archit*) a creamy-fawn colored building stone quarried near Bath in England.

bathtub *n* a usu fixed tub for bathing.

bathymetry *n* the art or science of sounding or of measuring sea depths.—**bathymetric** *adj*.—**bathymetrically** *adv*.

bathyscaphe *n* a submersible vessel for deep-sea observation and exploration.

bathysphere *n* a hollow steel sphere for descending to great depths in the sea.

batik *n* a method of printing colored designs on fabric; fabric produced by this method.

batiste *n* a kind of cambric; a fabric like cambric.

batman *n* (*pl* **batmen**) (*mil*) in UK, an officer's servant.

bat mitzvah, bat mizvah *n* a female bar mitzvah; a bar mitzvah ceremony for a girl.

batn. *abbr* = battalion.

baton *n* a staff serving as a symbol of office; (*mus*) the stick used by a conductor to give his commands to performers; a hollow cylinder carried by each member of a relay team in succession; a policeman's truncheon.

Baton *n* (*Greek myth*) the charioteer of Amphiaraus who with him was swallowed up by the earth after the battle of Seven against Thebes.

batrachian *n* one of the amphibians, which includes frogs and toads. * *adj* of or pertaining to frogs or toads.

BATS *abbr* = British Association of Tennis Supporters; British Association of Trauma in Sport; Brotherhood of Asian Trade Unionists; Building and Allied Trades Union (Eire).

batsman *n* (*pl* **batsmen**) (*cricket, baseball*) the player whose turn it is to bat.

battalion *n* an army unit consisting of three or more companies; a large group.

batten[1] *n* a strip of wood or metal; a strip of wood put over a seam between boards; (*archit*) a long, thin piece of rectangular-shaped timber supporting roof tiles, or lath and plaster. * *vt* to fasten or supply with battens.

batten[2] *vt* to make fat by rich living; to fertilize or enrich. * *vi* to grow or become fat; to thrive at the expense of others.

batter[1] *vt* to beat with repeated blows; to wear out with heavy use; to criticize strongly and at length. * *vi* to strike heavily and repeatedly. —**batterer** *n*.

batter[2] *n* a mixture of flour, egg, and milk or water used in cooking.

batter[3] *n* (*archit*) a sloping wall or face that is wider at the bottom and narrower at the top.

batterie *n* (*mus*) (*French*) a 17th- and 18th-century term for arpeggio; the percussion section of an orchestra. *Also* **battery**.

battering ram *n* (*hist*) a military machine for breaching the walls of besieged places, consisting of a large beam with an iron head resembling the head of a ram.

Battersby *n* **George Martin** (1914–1982) British illustrator and a recognized expert on Art Nouveau.

battery *n* (*pl* **batteries**) a set of heavy guns; a small unit of artillery; an electric cell that supplies current; an unlawful beating; an arrangement of hens' cages designed to increase egg laying.

battle *n* a combat or fight between two opposing individuals or armies; a contest; any struggle towards a goal. * *vti* to fight; to struggle.—**battler** *n*.

battle-axe, battle-ax *n* (*pl* **battle-axes**) an old-fashioned two-headed axe; (*inf*) a domineering woman.

battle cruiser *n* a heavy-gunned ship with higher speed and lighter armor than a battleship.

battle cry *n* a war cry; a slogan used to rally supporters of a political campaign, etc.

battledore *n* a wooden bat used in washing, baking, etc; a bat used in **battledore and shuttlecock**.

battlefield *n* the land on which a battle is fought.

battlement *n* (*archit*) a parapet with embrasures, originally for defensive purposes.

battle royal *n* (*pl* **battles royal**) a fight with many combatants; a general engagement; a melee.

battleship *n* a large, heavily armored warship.

battue *n* (*hunting*) the driving up of game by beaters towards the guns; wholesale slaughter.

battue ice *n* large ice floes that obstruct the St Lawrence estuary in winter.

Battus *n* legendary founder of the Greek colony of Cyrene in Libya, about 650 BC. There were eight rulers of the family founded by him, bearing alternately the names Battus and Arcesilaus.

battuta *see* **al battuta**.

batty[1] *adj* (**battier, battiest**) (*inf*) crazy; eccentric.—**battiness** *n*.

batty[2] *abbr* = battery.

BAU *abbr* = Bangladesh Agricultural University; British Association Unit; business as usual.

bauble *n* a showy toy; a shining ball hung on a Christmas tree as a decoration; a worthless trifle or ornament.

Baucis and Philemon *n* (*Greek myth*) an elderly peasant couple who entertained Zeus and Hermes after the two gods were refused hospitality by everyone else in the region. They were saved when everyone else was drowned in a flood.

baud *n* (*comput*) a unit used in measuring the speed of electronic data transmissions.

Baudelaire *n* **Charles** (1821–67) French symbolist poet. Works include *Les fleurs du Mal*.

Bauernleyer *n* (*mus*) (*German*) hurdy-gurdy.

Bauhaus *n* German school of architecture and applied arts founded by the architect Walter Gropius (1883–1969) at Weimar in 1919. A number of Bauhaus masters emigrated to the US, where their ideas continued to be influential.

baulk[1] *n* (*archeo*) an area of undisturbed earth left between excavation trenches so that the stratigraphy can be sampled.

baulk[2] *see* **balk**.

Baumann *n* **Hans Theo** (1924–) Swiss ceramic artist.

Baumgarten *n* **CF** (*fl*. late 18th century) composer of operas and pantomimes, including *Robin Hood* (1786) and *Blue Beard* (1792), while leader of the English Opera at Covent Garden, London (1780–1794).

bauxite *n* the primary ore source for aluminum, formed by the weathering of aluminum-bearing rocks in tropical conditions.

Bav. *abbr* = Bavarian.

BAW *abbr* = Basketball Association of Wales.

Bawa *n* **Geoffrey** born 1919, Sri Lankan architect. His notable works include University of Ruhuna, Matara.

BAWA *abbr* = British Amateur Wrestling Association.

bawd *n* a woman who runs a brothel; a prostitute.

Bawden *n* **Edward** (1903–1995) British painter who designed many seminal advertising campaigns.

bawdy *adj* (**bawdier, bawdiest**) humorously indecent; obscene, lewd.—**bawdily** *adv*.—**bawdiness** *n*.

bawdyhouse *n* a brothel.

bawl *vti* to shout; to weep loudly. * *n* a loud shout; a noisy weeping.—**bawler** *n*.—**bawling** *n*.

Bax *n* **Sir Arnold Edward Trevor** (1883–1953) English composer and pianist, influenced by Irish folklore and by the poetry of W B Yeats (1865–1939). Notable for his symphonic poems (e.g., *The Garden of Fand, Overture to a Picaresque Comedy* and *Tintagel*). He was knighted in 1937, and was appointed Master of the King's Musick in 1942.

bay[1] *n* a deep howl or growl; (at) **bay**, forced to turn and face attackers; * *vi* to howl (at) in deep prolonged tones; * *vt* to utter in a loud prolonged tone; to drive or hold at bay, at a distance.

bay[2] *n* (*archit*) a principal vertical division of the interior or exterior of a building.

bay[3] *n* (*geol*) an open, curving recess in the coastline of a sea or lake.

bay[4] *n* (*bot*) a Mediterranean laurel.

bay[5] *n* a light, reddish brown color; an animal of this color, esp a horse

bayberry *n* (*pl* **bayberries**) any of various shrubs, esp the wax myrtle of North America; the gray waxy berry of the wax myrtle; a West Indian tree with fragrant leaves used in bay rum.

Bayer *n* **Herbert** (1900–1985) Austrian born designer, trained at the **Bauhaus**.

bay leaf *n* the leaf of the laurel dried and used as a flavoring for food.

bay leaf garland *n* (*archit*) a small molding, cylindrical in shape and ornamented to look like a string of beads.

bayonet *n* a blade for stabbing attached to the muzzle of a rifle. * *vt* (**bayoneting, bayoneted** *or* **bayonetting, bayonetted**) to kill or stab with a bayonet.

bayou *n* in the southern US, the marshy inlet or outlet of a lake or river.

bay rum *n* a perfumed cosmetic obtained from the leaves of the bayberry.

bay window *n* (*archit*) a window which projects out from the wall forming a recess within a room.

bazaar *n* a marketplace; a street full of small shops; a benefit sale for a church, etc.

Bazhenov *n* **Vasily** (1738–99) Russian architect. His notable works include Yushkov House, Moscow.

bazooka *n* a portable anti-tank weapon that fires rockets from a long tube.

BB[1] *n* a standard size of lead shot.

BB[2] *abbr* = double black (pencils).

BBA *abbr* = Bachelor of Business Administration.

BBAC *abbr* = British Balloon and Airship Club.

BBB *abbr* = Bulletin Board Service (internet); triple black (pencils).

BBBC *abbr* = British Boxing Board of Control.

BBC *abbr* = British Broadcasting Corporation.

BBCS *abbr* = British Butterfly Conservation Society.

BBEM *abbr* = bed, breakfast and evening meal.

BBF *abbr* = Brother's Brother Foundation.

BBFC *abbr* = British Board of Film Classification; British Board of Film Censors.

BB gun *n* a small air rifle or pistol that uses BB shot as ammunition.

BBIP *abbr* = British Books in Print.

BBKA *abbr* = British Beekeepers Association.

bbl. *abbr* = barrel; barrels.

BBL *abbr* = British Bridge League.

bbls. *abbr* = barrels.

BBO *abbr* = British Ballet Organisation.

BBQC *abbr* = British Board of Quality Control.

BBS *abbr* = Bachelor of Business Science; Bachelor of Business Studies; Barbados Broadcasting Society; Brittle Bone Society; Burma Broadcasting Service.

bc *abbr* = *basso continuo*, Italian "continuous bass."

BC *abbr* = before Christ (for dates in Christian calendar); (*Latin*) *Baccalaureus Chirurgiae*, "Bachelor of Surgery"; Bachelor of Chemistry; Bachelor of Commerce; British Columbia; British Council.

B/C *abbr* = bill for collection.

BCA *abbr* = Bomber Command Association; Business Council of Australia.

BCAB *abbr* = British Computer Association for the Blind.

BCAC *abbr* = British Conference on Automation and Computation.

BCAP *abbr* = British Code of Advertising Practice.

BCAR *abbr* = British Council for Aid to Refugees; British Civil Airworthiness Requirements.

BCBC *abbr* = British Cattle Breeders Club; British Citizens Band Council.

BCC *abbr* = British Copyright Council; Burundi Coffee Company; basal-cell carcinoma.

BCCA *abbr* = Beer Can Collectors of America.

BCCF *abbr* = British Calcium Carbonates Federation; British Cast Concrete Federation.

BCCG *abbr* = British Chamber of Commerce in Germany.

BCD *abbr* (*comput*) = binary coded decimal notation.

BCDP *abbr* = balloon catheter dilatation of the prostate.

BCE *abbr* = Bachelor of Chemical Engineering; Bachelor of Civil Engineering.

BCE *abbr* = Bachelor of Chemical Engineering; Bachelor of Civil Engineering; before Christian era.

B-cell *n* a type of lymphocyte.

BCF *abbr* = British Chess Federation.

BCFS *abbr* = British Columbia Forestry Society.

BCG *abbr* = bacillus of Calmette and Guérin.—*see* **BCG vaccine**.

BCGTMA *abbr* = British Ceramic Gift and Tableware Manufacturers Association.

BCG vaccine, Bacillus Calmette-Guérin vaccine *n* a vaccine named after the two French bacteriologists who first introduced it in France in 1908 and used as a vaccine against tuberculosis

BCh *abbr* = *Baccalaureus Chirurgiae*, Latin "Bachelor of Surgery."

BChD *abbr* = *Baccalaureus Chirurgiae Dentalis*, Latin "Bachelor of Dental Surgery."

BChE *or* **BChemEng** *abbr* = Bachelor of Chemical Engineering.

BChir *abbr* = *Baccalaureus Chirurgiae*, Latin "Bachelor of Surgery."

BCIS *abbr* = Building Cost Information Service.

BCL *abbr* = Bachelor of Civil Law; Bachelor of Canon Law.

BCLA *abbr* = British Contact Lens Association.

BCLDI *abbr* = British Clayware Land Drain Industry.

BCMA *abbr* = Breast Care and Mastectomy Association; British Complementary Medicine Association.

BCO *abbr* = British College of Optometrists.

BCOG *abbr* = British College of Obstetricians and Gynaecologists.

BCom *abbr* = Bachelor of Commerce.

BCombStuds *abbr* = Bachelor of Combined Studies.

BComm *abbr* = Bachelor of Commerce.

BCommunications *abbr* = Bachelor of Communications.

BComSc *abbr* = Bachelor of Commercial Science.

BCP *abbr* = Book of Common Prayer.

BCPL *abbr* = Basic Computer Programming Language.

BCRC *abbr* = British Columbia Research Council.

BCRU *abbr* = British Committee on Radiological Units.

BCRUM *abbr* = British Committee on Radiation Units and Measurements.

BCS *abbr* = Bachelor of Combined Studies; Bachelor of Chemical Science; Bachelor of Commercial Science.

BCT *abbr* = Building Conservation Trust.

BCTA *abbr* = British Canadian Trade Association.

bd *abbr* = (*Latin*) *bis die*, "twice a day"; band; board; bond; bound; bundle.

Bd. *abbr* = Band (G., volume).

Bd. or **B/d** *abbr* = brought down (*bookkeeping*).

BD *abbr* = Bachelor of Divinity; bills discounted.

B/D *abbr* = bank draft.

BDA *abbr* = British Deaf Association; British Dental Association; British Diabetic Association; British Dyslexia Association.

BDAMA *abbr* = British Distributors of Animal Medicines Association.

BDBJ *abbr* = Board of Deputies of British Jews.

BDC *abbr* = Book Development Council.

Bde. *abbr* = Brigade.

bdellium *n* a fragrant gum used medicinally and as a perfume; the African and Asian tree yielding it.

BDentSc *abbr* = Bachelor of Dental Science.

BDF *abbr* = Ballroom Dancers Federation; Barbados Defense Force; British Digestive Foundation.

BDFA *abbr* = British Dairy Farmers' Association.

bd. ft. *abbr* = board foot.

BDH *abbr* = British Drug Houses Limited.

BDI *abbr* = British Dyslexia Institute.

BDL *abbr* = below detectable limits.

BDM *abbr* = branch delegates' meeting.

bds. *abbr* = (bound in) boards; bundles.

BDS *abbr* = Bachelor of Dental Surgery.

BDSc *abbr* = Bachelor of Dental Science.

BDU *abbr* = Bomb Disposal Unit.

be *vi* (*pres t* **am, are, is,** *pt* **was, were,** *pp* **been**) to exist; to live; to take place.

Be *symbol* (*chem*) beryllium (element).

Bé. *abbr* = Baumé.

BE *abbr* = Bachelor of Economics; Bachelor of Education; Bachelor of Elocution; Bachelor of Engineering; Bank of England; Board of Education.

B/E or **b.e.** *abbr* = bill of exchange.

be- *prefix* all over, thoroughly, as in *bespatter*; to make, as in *bedim*; to call, as in *bedevil*; to form a transitive verb from an intransitive, as *bewail*.

BEA *abbr* = British Epilepsy Association; British Esperanto Association.

BEAB *abbr* = British Electrotechnical Approvals Board.

beach *n* a flat, sandy shore of the sea. * *vi* to bring (a boat) up on the beach from the sea.

beach ball *n* a large round inflatable ball esp for games on the beach or in the water.

beachboy *n* a male attendant or instructor at the beach.

beach budget *n* the balance between the material lost on beaches by erosion or backwash and the deposits carried in from other areas, by rivers, longshore drift, or swash.

beach buggy *n* a car designed to be driven in sand.

beachcomber *n* a person who hangs about the shore on the lookout for wreckage or plunder; a long curling wave rolling in from the ocean.—**beachcombing** *n*.

beachhead *n* an area of seashore captured from the enemy by an advance force in preparation for a full-scale landing of troops and equipment.

beach music *n* a style of pop music originating on the coast of South Carolina, based on soul music and rhythm and blues.

beacon *n* a light, esp on a high place, tower, etc, for warning or guiding. * *vi* to guide, to act as a beacon.

BEACON *abbr* = British Electronic Auction Comparing Network.

bead *n* a small ball pierced for stringing; (*pl*) a string of beads; (*pl*) a rosary; a bubble or droplet of liquid; the sight of a rifle.—**beaded** *adj*.

BEADA *abbr* = British Export Accessory and Design Association.

beading *n* molding or edging in the form of a series of beads; a wooden strip, rounded on one side, used for trimming.—*also* **beadwork**.

beadle *n* an officer of a parish or church; a mace-bearer; (*formerly*) an officer in a law court.

Beadle *n* George Wells *see* **Tatum, Edward Lawrie.**

beady *adj* (**beadier, beadiest**) (eyes) small, round and bright, sometimes calculating or unfriendly.—**beadily** *adv*.—**beadiness** *n*.

BEAG *abbr* = British Egg Art Guild.

beagle *n* a small hound with short legs and drooping ears.

beak *n* a bird's bill; any projecting part; the nose.—**beaked** *adj*.

beaker *n* a large drinking cup, or the amount it holds; a cylindrical vessel with a pouring lip used by chemists and pharmacists; (*archeo*) a pottery drinking cup without a handle, mainly associated with a group formerly named the Beaker Culture or People.

beakhead *n* (*archit*) a decorative motif consisting of carved human, animal or bird heads with a beak.

Bealdred *n* king of Kent, England (807–825). Ruled as an under-king of Mercia under the control of Cuthred's brother, King Coenwulf. He was driven out in 825 by Egbert of Wessex.

beam *n* a long straight piece of timber or metal; (*archit*) a horizontal, transverse timber in the roof of a building. the crossbar of a balance; a ship's breadth at its widest point; a slender shaft of light, etc; a radiant look, smile, etc; a steady radio or radar signal for guiding aircraft or ships. * *vt* (*light, etc*) to send out; to smile with great pleasure.

BEAMA *abbr* = British Electrical and Allied Manufacturers' Association.

beam width *n* the distance or area between the edge rays of a beam of radiation.

beamy *adj* (**beamier, beamiest**) emitting rays of light; resembling a beam in size and weight; (*ship*) broad; (*inf*) having broad hips.

bean *n* a plant bearing kidney-shaped seeds; a seed or pod of such a plant; any bean-like seed.

bean bag *n* a small cloth bag filled with dried beans and used in games; a larger cloth bag filled with plastic granules and used for sitting on.

bean curd *n* soft cheese made from soya milk.—*also* **tofu.**

beanfeast *n* (*inf*) an annual dinner given by an employer for his employees; (*inf*) any festive meal.

beanie *n* a small cap without a brim.

Beann Ghulban *n* (*Irish Celtic myth*) a monstrous boar without ears or a tail that originally had been born as a human child to the wife of Donn.

Bean Sidhe *n* (*Irish Celtic myth*) a female fairy or spirit that became attached to a particular family. Known in English as **banshee.**

bean sprout *n* the shoot of the mung bean used in Chinese cooking.

bear[1] (**bearing, bore,** *pp* **borne**) *vt* to carry; to endure; to support, to sustain; to conduct (oneself); to produce or bring forth; (*with* **out**) to show to be true, confirm. * *vi* to be productive; (*with* **down**) to press or weigh down; to overwhelm; (*with* **on** or **upon**) to have reference to, be relevant to; (*with* **out**) to confirm the truth of; (*with* **up**) to endure with courage; (*with* **with**) to listen to patiently.

bear[2] *n* (*pl* **bears, bear**) a large mammal with coarse black, brown or white fur, short legs, strong claws and feeding mainly on fruit and insects; a gruff or ill-mannered person; a teddy bear; a speculator who sells stock in anticipation of a fall in price so that he may buy them back at a lower price.

bearable *adj* endurable.—**bearably** *adv*.

bear baiting *n* the former sport of setting dogs to attack captive bears.

beard *n* hair covering a man's chin; similar bristles on an animal or plant. * *vt* to defy, oppose openly.—**bearded** *adj*.

Bearden *n* Romare (1914–88) American painter from Charlotte, North Carolina. His work was concerned with the life experience of African Americans.

beardless *adj* without a beard; youthful.

Beardsley *n* Aubrey Vincent (1872–98) English illustrator in the Art Nouveau style and a prominent figure of aestheticism in the 1890s.

bearer *n* a person who bears or presents; a person who carries something (a coffin, etc); (*finance*) a person who presents for payment a check or bill of exchange, the check or bill being marked "pay bearer."

bearer security *n* a form of financial security for which possession of the relevant security certificate is proof of ownership.

bear garden *n* (*formerly*) a place where bears were kept for sport; any scene or place of tumult or disorder.

bear hug *n* (*wrestling*) a hold in which the opponent's arms and chest are pinned in a tight embrace; any tight embrace.

bearing *n* demeanor; conduct; a compass direction; the horizontal angle between a baseline and the point being surveyed; (*with* **on, upon**) relevance; a machine part on which another part slides, revolves, etc; (*usu pl*) one's position, orientation.

bearing rein *n* a short fixed rein for holding up the head of a horse.—*also* **checkrein.**

bearish *adj* resembling a bear in qualities; rude, surly.—**bearishly** *adv*.—**bearishness** *n*.

bear market *n* a situation on the stock exchange or currency market in which there is persistent selling and limited buying, thereby causing prices to fall.

bear's breech *n* one of two tall plants of the acanthus genus with purple-tinged white flowers.

bear's ear *see* **auricula.**

bearskin *n* the skin of a bear used as a garment, rug, etc; a tall furry cap worn by a guardsman in the British army.

beast *n* a large, wild, four-footed animal; a brutal, vicious person; (*inf*) something difficult, an annoyance.

beastings *see* **beestings.**

beastly *adj* (**beastlier, beastliest**) (*inf*) disagreeable. * *adv* (*inf*) very (e.g., beastly cold).

beast of burden *n* an animal used to transport loads.

beat *vb* (**beating, beaten,** *pp* **beat**) *vt* to strike, dash or pound repeatedly; to flog; to overcome or counteract; to win against, to arrive first; to find too difficult for; (*mus*) to mark (time) with a baton, etc; (*eggs, etc*) to mix by stirring vigorously; (*esp wings*) to move up and down; (*a path, way, etc*) to form by repeated trampling; (*sl*) to baffle; (*with* **up**) (*inf*) to cause grievous bodily harm to by severe and repeated blows and kicks. * *vi* to hit, pound, etc repeatedly; to throb; (*naut*) to sail against the wind. * *n* a recurrent stroke, pulsation, as in a heartbeat or clock ticking; (*mus*) a unit of rhythmic measure in music; a form of 20th-century popular music with a steady and powerful rhythm; the area patrolled by a police officer.—**beatable** *adj*.

beaten *adj* defeated; (*metal*) shaped or formed by pounding; (*a path*) formed by constant trampling.

beater *n* an implement for beating, such as an attachment for an electric food mixer; one who rouses game birds from cover.

Beat Generation *n* a term invented by Jack Kerouac to describe a group of young liberal Americans who expressed disillusionment with Western values in the 1950s.

beatific *adj* showing great happiness; making blessed.—**beatifically** *adv*.

beatify *vt* (**beatifying, beatified**) (*RC Church*) to declare that one who has died is among the blessed in heaven; to make blissfully happy.—**beatification** *n*.

beating *n* the act of striking or thrashing; throbbing or pulsation; a defeat.

beatitude *n* blessedness; heavenly happiness; (*with cap*) (*Bible*) one of Christ's eight sayings in the Sermon on the Mount (Matthew 5).

beatitudes *n* special blessings particularly in the Books of the Psalms and Proverbs.

beatnik *n* a member of the Beat Generation in the 1950s, esp one who showed disregard for conventional norms.

Beaton *n* **Cecil** (1904–80) British dilettante designer and celebrity/fashion photographer who won Oscars for his designs on *My Fair Lady* (1965).

Beatty *n* **Warren** (1937–) American actor, director, and producer. His films include *Bonnie and Clyde* (1967).

beau *n* (*pl* **beaus, beaux**) a woman's suitor or sweetheart.

Beaufort scale *n* an international system of indicating wind strength, from 0 (calm) to 12 (hurricane), developed in 1805 by Admiral Sir Francis Beaufort.

beau geste *n* (*pl* **beaux gestes**) a fine gesture; a gesture that appears noble but is meaningless.

beau ideal *n* (*pl* **beaux ideals**) ideal excellence, a standard of perfection.

beaujolais *n* (*often with cap*) a popular fruity red or white wine from Burgundy in France.

beau monde *n* the fashionable world.

Beaumont *n* **Sir Francis** (1584–1616) English dramatist who collaborated with John Fletcher on tragicomedies such as *The Maid's Tragedy*.

beaut *adj* (*sl*) good. * *n* (*sl*) beauty.

beauteous *adj* (*poet*) beautiful.

beautician *n* one who works in a beauty salon offering cosmetic treatments.

beautiful *adj* having beauty; very enjoyable.—**beautifully** *adv*.

Beautiful Gate *n* (*Bible*) a gate of the Temple in Jerusalem in *NT* times.

beautify *vti* (**beautifying, beautified**) to make or become beautiful.—**beautification** *n*.

beauty *n* (*pl* **beauties**) the combination of qualities in a person or object that cause delight or pleasure; a very attractive woman or girl; good looks; a very fine specimen.

beauty parlor, beauty salon, beauty shop *n* an establishment that offers cosmetic beauty treatments.

beauty queen *n* the winner of a beauty contest.

beauty sleep *n* sleep taken before midnight, supposed to be more restorative than that taken later.

beauty spot *n* a scenic location; a small birthmark or artificial patch on the cheek, regarded as a mark of beauty.

Beauvoir *n* **Simone de** (1908–86) French novelist and essayist whose essay *The Second Sex* is a cornerstone of the feminist movement.

beaver[1] *n* a large semi-aquatic dam-building rodent; its fur; a hat made from beaver fur. * *vi* (*often with* **away**) to work hard (at).

beaver[2] *n* the lower or movable part of a helmet's face guard.

Beaverbrook *n* **Max [William Maxwell Aitken, 1st Baron Beaverbrook]** (1879–1964) Canadian-born British newspaper proprietor and Conservative politician.

Bebo *n* (*Irish Celtic myth*) the wife of Iubdan and so the queen of Faylinn. She went with her husband to Ulster to visit what to the diminutive people of Faylinn was a race of giants. They were held captive there.

bebop *n* (*mus*) a jazz development of the 1940s in which complex rhythms and harmonic sequences were carried out against rapidly played melodic improvisation. It is particularly associated with Charlie Parker.

Bebung *n* (*mus*) (*German*) literally "trembling," i.e., a vibrato effect caused by shaking a finger holding down a key. * *adj* pertaining to a clavichord.

BEc *abbr* = Bachelor of Economics.

BEC *abbr* = Bermuda Employer's Council; British Evangelical Council; Building Employers' Confederation.

becalm *vt* to make calm; to make (a ship) motionless from lack of wind.—**becalmed** *adj*.

became *see* **become**.

because *conj* since; for the reason that.

because of *prep* by reason of.

BECC *abbr* = British Empire Cancer Campaign.

beccafico *n* (*pl* **beccaficos**) a small bird of the warbler family, eaten as a delicacy in Italy.

béchamel sauce *n* a thick, rich white sauce.

bêche-de-mer *n* (*pl* **bêches-de-mer**) the trepang, a sea slug dried and eaten as a food in China; a form of pidgin English used in the islands of the Pacific.—*also* **beach-la-mar**.

Bechet *n* **Sidney** (1897–1959) American jazz saxophonist and clarinettist.

Bechstein *n* **Friedrich Wilhelm Karl** (1826–1900) German piano manufacturer who, after working in Germany, France and England, established his own company in Berlin in 1856 and produced his first piano in 1859.

beck[1] *n* a wave or nod with the finger or head.

beck[2] *n* a brook, a mountain stream.

becket *n* (*naut*) a rope loop, a hook, or a bracket for securing sails, tackle, etc.

Becket *n* **Thomas à, Saint** (1118–70) English saint. He became Archbishop of Canterbury in 1162 and was murdered by King Henry II's knights. He was canonized in 1173.

Beckett *n* **Samuel** (1906–89) Irish dramatist and novelist whose work is noted for its brilliant dialogues or monologues of despair. His best-known play is *Waiting for Godot*. He was awarded the Nobel prize for literature in 1969.

Becklin–Neugebauer object *n* a powerful source of infrared radiation in the Orion nebula.

Beckmann *n* **Max** (1884–1950) one of Germany's most important expressionist painters.

beckon *vti* to summon by a gesture.—**beckoner** *n*.—**beckoning** *adj*.

becloud *vt* to obscure by clouds, to dim.

become *vb* (**becoming, became,** *pp* **become**) *vi* to come or grow to be. * *vt* to be suitable for.

becoming *adj* appropriate; seemly; suitable to the wearer.—**becomingly** *adv*.

BEcon *abbr* = Bachelor of Economics.

becquerel *n* (*physics*) a unit of radioactivity in the SI scheme.

Becquerel *n* 1. **Alexandre Edmond** (1820–91) French physicist, son and assistant of Antoine Cesar. 2. **Antoine Cesar** (1788–1878) French physicist The first to use electrolysis as a means of isolating metals from their ores. 3. **Antoine Henri** (1852–1908) French physicist. Son of Alexandre Edmond). He discovered the rays (becquerel rays) emitted from the uranium salts in pitchblende. Shared the 1903 Nobel prize with the **Curies**.—*see* **Curie, Marie**.

Becrux or **Beta Crucis** *n* a star of the first magnitude, the second brightest in the constellation of the Southern Cross.

BECTA *abbr* = British Engineers' Cutting Tools Association.

BECTO *abbr* = British Electric Cable Testing Organisation.

BECTU *abbr* = Broadcasting, Entertainment, Cinematograph and Theatre Union.

bed *n* a piece of furniture for sleeping on; the mattress and covers for this; a plot of soil where plants are raised; the bottom of a river, lake, etc; (*geol*) a layer of rock within a sedimentary rock sequence that differs in composition, texture or structure from other layers; any flat surface used as a foundation; a stratum. * *vt* (**bedding, bedded**) to put to bed; to embed; to plant in a bed of earth; to arrange in layers.

BEd *abbr* = Bachelor of Education.

bed and breakfast *n* (*Brit, business*) a process on the stock exchange in which a shareholder sells shares at the end of a trading day and buys them back when trading opens the next morning; overnight accommodation and breakfast the following morning, as offered in hotels and guesthouses, etc.—**bed-and-breakfast** *adj*.—**b and b** *abbr*.

bedaub *vt* to smear all over.

bedazzle *vt* to dazzle so completely as to blind or confuse.

bedbug *n* a bloodsucking wingless insect that infests dirty bedding.

bedchamber *n* a bedroom.

bedclothes *npl* sheets, blankets, etc for a bed.

bedding *n* bedclothes; litter (straw, etc) for animals; a bottom layer, foundation.

bedding plane *n* (*geol*) the surface that separates each bed in a sequence of sedimentary rocks.

bedding plant *n* a young plant suitable for a garden bed.

Bede *n* **Saint**, known as the "**Venerable Bede**" (*c*. 673–735) English monk, scholar, historian and theologian. The most important of his more than forty works is an *Ecclesiastical History of the English People*. Bede has been called the "father of English history." His feast day is 25 May.

bedeck *vt* to cover with finery, to adorn.

bedevil *vt* (**bedeviling, bedeviled** or **bedevilling, bedevilled**) to plague or bewilder.—**bedevilment** *n*.

bedew *vt* to moisten, to sprinkle.

bedfellow *n* a sharer of a bed; an associate, ally, etc, esp a temporary one.

Bedford *n* **David** (1937–) a prolific English composer who was, for a time, a member of the pop group The Whole World. His best-known work is *Star's End* (1974), a composition for electric instruments as well as orchestra.

bedim *vt* (**bedimming, bedimmed**) to make dim.

bedizen *vt* to adorn or dress gaudily.—**bedizenment** *n*.

bedlam *n* (*arch*) a madhouse; uproar.

Bedouin *n* (*pl* **Bedouins, Bedouin**) an Arab desert nomad; a gypsy.

bedpan *n* a vessel used as a lavatory by a bedridden person; a warming pan.

bedplate *n* the base plate or frame or platform on which a machine is fixed.

bedpost *n* any of the four vertical posts at the corners of some types of beds.

bedraggle *vt* to make untidy or dirty by dragging in the wet or dirt.—**bedraggled** *adj*.

bedridden *adj* confined to bed through illness.

bedrock *n* solid rock underlying soil, etc; the base or bottom; fundamentals.

bedroom *n* a room for sleeping in. * *adj* suggestive of sexual relations; (*area, suburb, etc*) inhabited by commuters.

bedside *n* the space beside a bed. * *adj* situated or conducted at the bedside; suitable for someone bedridden.

bedside manner *n* the attitude and conduct of a physician in a patient's presence.

bedsitter, bedsit, bedsitting room *n* a single room with sleeping and cooking facilities.

bed sores *npl* sore and ulcerated skin caused by constant pressure when lying in bed.—*also* **pressure sores; decubitus ulcers.**

bedspread *n* a covering for a bed, usu decorative.

bedspring *n* the network of springs that supports the mattress of a bed; a box spring.

bedstead *n* a frame for the spring and mattress of a bed.

bedstraw *n* a plant of the madder family used formerly as straw for stuffing beds.

bedwetting *n* urinating in bed.—**bedwetter** *n*.

bee[1] *n* a social, stinging four-winged insect that is often kept in hives to make honey; any of numerous insects that also feed on pollen and nectar and are related to wasps; (*Egypt*) the ancient emblem of Lower Egypt (the Delta town of Buto).

bee[2] *n* a social meeting for work on behalf of a neighbor or a charitable object.

bee[3] *n* (*naut*) strips of wood bolted each side of a bowsprit, through which the fore topmast stays are reeved.

BEE *abbr* = Bachelor of Electrical Engineering.

beebread *n* a brown bitter substance consisting of the pollen of flowers collected and stored by bees as food for larvae.

beech *n* a tree with smooth silvery-gray bark; its wood.

Beecham *n* **Sir Thomas** (1879–1961) English conductor who founded the London Philharmonic Orchestra in 1932 and the Royal Philharmonic Orchestra in 1946; noted for his interpretations of Berlioz and Delius. He was knighted in 1914 and succeeded to his father's baronetcy in 1916.

beechmast *n* beechnuts collectively.

beechnut *n* the triangular nut of the beech, which yields an oil.

bee-eater *n* any of the numerous species of bee-eating birds.

beef *n* (*pl* **beefs**) the meat of a full-grown cow, steer, etc; (*inf*) muscular strength; (*inf*) a complaint, grudge; (*pl* **beeves**) cows, ox, steers, etc bred for their meat. * *vt* (*with* **up**) to add weight, strength or power to.

beefburger *n* a flat grilled or fried cake of minced beef.

beefcake *n* (*sl*) muscular men displayed provocatively, esp in photographs.

beef cattle *npl* cattle that are raised for their meat.

beefeater *n* an eater of beef; (*inf*) in UK, a yeoman of the royal guard, attending the sovereign on state occasions.

beef tea *n* stewed beef juice.

beefy *adj* (**beefier, beefiest**) brawny, muscular.

beehive *n* a container for keeping honeybees; a scene of crowded activity.

beehive construction *n* (*archit*) an ancient type of one-roomed dwelling house built in a beehive shape.

beekeeper *n* one who keeps bees for producing honey.—**beekeeping** *n*.

beeline *n* the straight course pursued by a bee returning laden to the hive; a direct line or course.

Beelzebub *n* (*Bible*) a fallen angel, lord of the flies, next in power to Satan; in *NT* times the name came to signify the prince of devils. *See also* **Devil**, **Satan**.

bee moth *n* a moth that lays its eggs in beehives, and whose larvae feed upon the wax.

been *see* **be**.

Beene *n* **Geoffrey** (1927–) American fashion designer.

beep *n* the brief, high-pitched sound of a horn or electronic signal. * *vti* to make or cause to make this sound.

beeper *n* an electronic pager; one who or that which beeps.

beer *n* an alcoholic drink made from malt, sugar, hops and water fermented with yeast.

Beer *n* **Michael** (*d*. 1666) German architect. His notable works include Benedictine Abbey Church, Weingarten.

beer belly *n* a person's fat stomach, usu resulting from drinking beer or other alcoholic beverages.

Beerbohm *n* **Sir [Henry] Max[imilian]** (1872–1956) English parodist, caricaturist, and essayist.

Beersheba *n* (*Bible*) ancient Biblical town in the south of Palestine; an important oasis.

beery *adj* (**beerier, beeriest**) smelling or tasting of beer.

beestings *npl* the first milk given by a cow after calving.—*also* **biestings, beastings**.

beeswax *n* wax secreted by bees, refined and used for polishing.

beeswing *n* a gauze-like crust that occurs in port and some other wines, indicative of age.

beet *n* a red, edible root used as a vegetable, in salads, etc; a source of sugar.

Beethoven *n* **Ludwig van** (1770–1827) German composer and pianist of Flemish descent, of immense influence. His principal compositions include: nine symphonies; *Fidelio* (opera); *The Creatures of Prometheus* (ballet); *Christus am Olberg* (oratorio); five piano concertos; the violin concerto; two Masses; numerous pieces of chamber music; thirty-two piano sonatas; ten violin sonatas; five cello sonatas; a horn sonata; and several songs.

beetle[1] *n* any of an order of insects having hard wing covers.

beetle[2] *n* a heavy wooden mallet for driving wedges, etc; a club for beating linen, etc, in washing. * *vt* to use a beetle on; to beat with a heavy wooden mallet.

beetle[3] *vi* to be prominent; to jut out, overhang, as a cliff.—**beetling** *adj*.

beetroot *n* (*pl* **beetroot**) the fleshy root of beet used as a vegetable, in salads, etc.—*also* **red beet**.

beeves *see* **beef**.

beezer *n* (*sl*) a fellow; (*sl*) a nose.

bef. *abbr* = before.

BEF *abbr* = British Employers Federation; British Equestrian Federation; British Expeditionary Force.

BEFA *abbr* = British Emigrant Families Association.

befall *vti* (**befalling, befell**, *pp* **befallen**) to happen or occur to.

befit *vt* (**befitting, befitted**) to be suitable or appropriate for; to be right for.—**befittingly** *adv*.

befog *vt* (**befogging, befogged**) to involve in a fog, to confuse.

befool *vt* to make a fool of.

before *prep* ahead of; in front of; in the presence of; preceding in space or time; in preference to; rather than. * *adv* beforehand; previously; until now. * *conj* earlier than the time that; rather than.

beforehand *adv* ahead of time; in anticipation.

befoul *vt* to make foul, to soil.—**befouler** *n*.—**befoulment** *n*.

befriend *vt* to be a friend to, to favor.

befuddle *vt* to confuse, stupefy, often with drink.

beg *vti* (**begging, begged**) to ask for money or food; to ask earnestly; to implore.

began *see* **begin**.

beget *vt* (**begetting, begot** *or* **begat**, *pp* **begotten** *or* **begot**) to become the father of; to cause.—**begetter** *n*.

beggar *n* a person who begs or who lives by begging; a pauper; (*inf*) a person. * *vt* to reduce to poverty; (*description*) to render inadequate.

beggarly *adj* like, or in the condition of, a beggar; poor; mean, contemptible.—**beggarliness** *n*.

Beggar's Opera, The a ballad opera by John Gay first performed in London in 1728; essentially a play interspersed with songs to tunes of the day, which satirizes contemporary politics and Italian operatic conventions. The musical arrangement was by Johann Christoph Pepusch.

beggary *n* the state of a beggar; extreme poverty; beggars collectively.

begin *vti* (**beginning, began**, *pp* **begun**) to start doing, acting, etc; to originate.

Begin *n* **Menachem** (1913–92) Polish-born Israeli statesman; commander of the Irgun militant Zionist group (1943–48) and prime minister of Israel (1977–84). He shared the Nobel peace prize with Sadat in 1978.

beginner *n* one who has just started to learn or do something; a novice.

beginning *n* source or origin; commencement.

begird *vt* (**begirding, begirded** *or* **begirt**) to gird round, to encompass, surround.

begone *interj* go away! be off!

begonia *n* a tropical plant cultivated for its showy petalless flowers and ornamental lopsided leaves.

begorra *interj* by God.

begot, begotten *see* **beget**.

begrime *vt* to make grimy, to soil deeply.

begrudge *vt* to grudge; to envy.—**begrudgingly** *adv*.

beguile *vt* (**beguiling, beguiled**) to cheat or deceive; to charm; to fascinate.—**beguilement** *n*.—**beguiler** *n*.—**beguilingly** *adv*.

beguine *n* a West Indian dance in bolero rhythm; the music for this.

begum *n* a Muslim queen or lady of high rank.

begun *see* **begin**.

behalf *n* in *or* on behalf of in the interest of; for.

Behan *n* **Brendan** (1923–64) Irish dramatist, noted for his plays based on his experiences as a youthful member of the Irish Republican Army, e.g., *The Hostage*.

behave *vti* to act in a specified way; to conduct (oneself) properly.

behavior, behaviour *n* way of behaving; conduct or action.—**behavioral, behavioural** *adj*.

behaviorism, behaviourism *n* the doctrine that human action is governed by external stimuli.—**behaviorist, behaviourist** *adj, n*.—**behavioristic, behaviouristic** *adj*.

behead *vt* to cut the head off.

beheld *see* **behold**.

behemoth *n* (*Bible*) an enormous animal described in Job, possibly the hippopotamus.

behest *n* a command; a precept.

behind *prep* at the rear of; concealed by; later than; supporting. * *adv* in the rear; slow; late.

behindhand *adj, adv* late, in arrears.

Behistun Rock *n* (*or* **Bisutun**) a monument carved in a rock face in Iran to celebrate a Persian victory over the Achaemenid empire.

Behn *n* **Aphra** (1640–89) English dramatist and novelist whose most famous play, *Oroonoko*, attacks the horrors of slavery.

behold (**beholding, beheld**) *vt* to look at; to observe. * *vi* to see.—**beholder** *n*.

beholden *adj* indebted to; bound under an obligation.

behoof *n* advantage; interest; profit; use; behalf.

behoove, behove *vt* to be necessary or fit for, to be incumbent.

Behrens *n* **Peter** (1868–1940) German designer who worked on factory buildings and electrical goods.

BEIC *abbr* = British Egg Industry Council.

Beiderbecke *n* [Leon] **Bix** (1903–31) American jazz cornet player, pianist, and composer.

beige *n* a very light brown.

being *n* life; existence; a person or thing that exists; nature or substance.

bejewel *vt* (**bejeweling, bejeweled** *or* **bejewelling, bejewelled**) to ornament or furnish with jewels.

Békésy *n* Georg von (1899–1972) Hungarian-born American physiologist and winner of the 1961 Nobel prize for physiology or medicine for his discoveries on the mechanics of hearing.

bel *n* a unit equal to 10 decibels, used in the measurement of the intensity of sound, named after its inventor, Alexander Graham Bell (1847–1922). *See also* decibel.

Bel. *abbr* = Belgian; Belgic; Belgium.

belabor, belabour *vt* to beat soundly, to thump; to criticize severely.

Bélanger *n* François-Joseph (*b.* 1744) French architect. His notable works include Bagatelle, Bois de Boulogne, Paris.

Belarus, Belorussia, Byelorussia *n* a republic of the former USSR, which declared itself independent in 1991. It borders Poland to the west, Ukraine to the south, Latvia and Lithuania to the north, and the Russian Federation to the east.

belated *adj* coming late.—**belatedly** *adv*.

belay *vti* (**belaying, belayed**) to secure (a rope) by winding it round a spike, piton; to secure by a rope.

bel canto *adj, adv* (*mus*) (*Italian*) literally "beautiful singing," a style of singing characterized by elaborate technique, associated with 18th-century Italian opera.

belch *vti* to expel gas from the stomach by the mouth; to eject violently from inside.— *also n*.

beldam, beldame *n* an old woman, esp an ugly or loathsome one.

beleaguer *vt* to besiege, to blockade; to harass.

belemnite *n* a pointed fossil internal bone or shell of an extinct family of cuttlefish.

Belenus *or* **Belenos** *or* **Bel** (*Gaulish Celtic myth*) a god who was associated with light, the word *bel* meaning "bright." He was also associated with the sun and with healing and later became linked with the classical god Apollo.

bel esprit *n* (*pl* **beaux esprits**) a person of wit or genius.

belfry *n* (*archit*) a movable tower used by those laying siege; a watch tower or bell tower; the upper chamber in a church tower where the bells are housed.

Belg. *abbr* = Belgian; Belgic; Belgium.

Belgae *n* a group of tribal peoples whose origins date back to the 5th century. They gradually spread northwards, incorporating other Celtic cultures.

Belgian *adj* of or pertaining to Belgium or its inhabitants. * *n* a native or inhabitant of Belgium.

Belgium *n* a highly industrialized, relatively small country in northwest Europe with a short coastline on the North Sea. Belgium is a constitutional monarchy.

Beli *n* 1. (*d.* 722) king of Strathclyde, Scotland. He successfully defended his kingdom from attacks by Oengus, king of the Picts. 2. (*Welsh Celtic myth*) the father of Lludd and Llefelys. He is also said to have been the husband of Don.

Belial *n* a demon or devil; a fallen angel.

belie *vt* (**belying, belied**) to show to be a lie; to misrepresent; to fail to live up to (a hope, promise).—**belier** *n*.

belief *n* a principle or idea considered to be true; religious faith.

believe *vt* to accept as true; to think; to be convinced of. * *vi* to have religious faith.—**believable** *adj*.—**believer** *n*.

believing *adj* trustful.

Belinda *n* a satellite of Uranus.

belittle *vt* (*a person*) to make feel small; to disparage.—**belittlement** *n*.—**belittler** *n*.—**belittlingly** *adv*.

Belize *n* a small Central American country on the southeast of the Yucatan Peninsula in the Caribbean Sea.

bell[1] *n* a hollow metal object which rings when struck; anything bell-shaped; the sound made by a bell.

bell[2] *n* the cry of a stag in rut. * *vi* to make this cry.

Bell *n* 1. **Alexander Graham** (1847–1922) Scottish inventor and scientist who patented the telephone in 1876. 2. **Vanessa** (1879–1961) British painter and leading figure of the Bloomsbury group (her sister was the novelist Virginia Woolf).

belladonna *n* the deadly nightshade plant, whose flowers, leaves and stalk are poisonous.

Bellamy *n* **Edward** (1850–98) American novelist whose best-known work, *Looking Backward, 2000–1887*, describes a future America in which capitalism has disappeared.

Bellany *n* **John** (1942–) Scottish painter who was a prominent figure in the Renaissance movement in Scottish art in the 1960s.

bellbird *n* an American bird whose note resembles a bell; an Australian bird with a similar call.

bell buoy *n* a buoy with a warning bell activated by wave movement.

belle *n* a pretty woman or girl.

Bellerophon *n* (*Greek myth*) a hero who, riding the winged horse Pegasus, overpowered the monster Chimera.

belles-lettres *n* (*used as sing*) artistic literature, including poetry, essays, etc.—**belletrist** *n*.—**belletristic** *adj*.

bellfounder *n* a person who casts bells.—**bellfoundry** *n*.

bellhop, bellboy *n* one who carries luggage, runs errands, etc in a hotel or club.

bellicose *adj* war-like; ready to fight.—**bellicosity** *n*.

belligerent *adj* at war; of war; war-like; ready to fight or quarrel.—**belligerence** *n*.—**belligerently** *adv*.

Bellini *n* 1. **Giovanni** (1430–1516) Venetian painter and an important member of a family of artists. A common theme is the Madonna and Child, of which the *Barberini Madonna* is a notable example. 2. **Vincenzo** (1801–35) Italian composer who studied in Naples under the composer Nicola Zingarelli. He is famed for his operas which include *Il Pirata, La Sonnambula*, the fine, lyrical *Norma*, and *I Puritani*.

bell jar *n* a protective glass cover in the shape of a bell.

bell metal *n* an alloy of copper and tin, used for the manufacture of bells.

bellman *n* (*pl* **bellmen**) one who uses a bell for public announcement, a town crier.

Belloc *n* **Hilaire** (1870–1953) French-born English poet, essayist, historian, and Liberal member of the British parliament. He was noted for his verse for children and collaborated with Chesterton.

Bellona *n* (*Roman myth*) the goddess of war and companion of Mars.

bellow *vi* to roar; to make an outcry. * *vt* to utter loudly. * *n* the roar of a bull; any deep roar.

Bellow *n* **Saul** (1915–) Canadian-born American novelist and winner of the 1976 Nobel prize for literature. His novels include *More Die of Heartbreak* (1987).

bellows *n* (*used as pl or sing*) a device for creating and directing a stream of air by compression of its collapsible sides.

Bellows *n* **George Wesley** (1882–1925) American social realist painter whose painting is characterized by a bold, direct style. He was a progressive and outgoing artist and one of the organizers of the Armory Show.

bellpull *n* a rope or handle for a bell.

bell punch *n* a punch with a signal bell used for punching tickets and checking the number of fares issued.

bellpush *n* a button that operates a bell.

bells *n* (*mus*) (*orchestral*) cylindrical metal tubes (*tubular bells*) of different lengths which are suspended from a frame and struck with a wooden mallet.

bells and whistles *n* (*comput*) the advanced features that an application program contains.

Bell's palsy *n* a paralysis of the facial muscles on either or both sides of the face, caused by infection or inflammation.

bell tower *n* (*archit*) a tower, either attached to, or separate from a church in which the bells are hung.

bellwether *n* the leading sheep of a flock with a bell round its neck.

belly *n* (*pl* **bellies**) the lower part of the body between the chest and the thighs; the abdomen; the stomach; the underside of an animal's body; the deep interior, as of a ship; (*mus*) the upper part of the body or soundbox of a stringed instrument. * *vti* (**bellying, bellied**) to swell out; to bulge.

bellyache *n* (*inf*) a pain in the stomach. * *vi* (*sl*) to complain constantly.

bellyband *n* a band that encircles the belly of a horse, a saddle girth.

bellybutton *n* (*inf*) the navel.

belly dance *n* a solo dance performed by a woman with sinuous, provocative movements of the belly and hips.—**belly dancer** *n*.

belly-flop *vt* (**belly-flopping, belly-flopped**) to dive in such a way that the body lands almost flat against the water.—**belly flop** *n*.

bellyful *n* (*sl*) as much as one can tolerate of something.

belong *vi* to have a proper place; to be related (to); (*with* **to**) to be a member; to be owned; (*inf*) to fit in socially.

belongings *npl* personal effects, possessions.

beloved *adj* dearly loved. * *n* one who is dearly loved.

below *prep* lower than; unworthy of. * *adv* in or to a lower place; south of; beneath; later (in a book, etc).

below-the-line[1] *adj* referring to entries that occur below the horizontal line in a company's profit and loss account. *See* above-the-line.

below-the-line[2] *adj* referring to expenditure on advertising that does not involve payments of commission or fees to an advertising agency. *See* above-the-line.

Belshazzar *n* (*Bible*) king of Babylon, who gave a feast during which a hand wrote on the wall; it was interpreted by Daniel to predict the kingdom's downfall. *See also* **Daniel**.

belt *n* a band of leather, etc worn around the waist; any similar encircling thing; a belt as an award for skill, e.g., in boxing, judo; a continuous moving strap passing over pulleys and so driving machinery; a distinctive region or strip; (*sl*) a hard blow. * *vt* to surround, attach with a belt; to thrash with a belt; (*sl*) to deliver a hard blow; (sl) to hurry; (with out) (sl) to sing or play loudly; (with up) to fasten with a belt. * vi (with up) (inf) to wear a seat belt; (sl:often imper) to be quiet.

Beltane or **Beltaine** or **Beltene** n one of the four great annual Celtic festivals; formerly observed on 1 May in Scotland, and in Ireland on June 21 by the kindling of huge bonfires. It was named after Belenus.

Belt of Orion n a distinctive feature of three visible stars across the middle of the constellation Orion.

beluga n a large sturgeon; its caviar; a white whale.

belvedere n (archit) an elevated turret on the top of a house constructed for obtaining a view. See also gazebo.

Belyayev n **Mitrofan** (1836–1904) Russian music publisher who was an enthusiastic sponsor of the "New" composers. Borodin, Rimsky-Korsakov and many others used to congregate at his house regularly on Fridays and collectively wrote Les Vendredis (Fridays) in his honor.

BEM abbr = British Empire Medal.

bema n (archit) in ancient Greece an elevated platform from which an orator addressed an audience; a raised pulpit in a place of worship; a speaker's platform.

bemire vt to soil with mire; to be stuck in mud.

bemoan vti to lament.

bemuse vt to muddle; to preoccupy.—**bemused** adj.—**bemusement** n.

ben n the Scottish Gaelic term for a mountain or peak.

ben, bene adj, adv (mus) (Italian) "well," as in ben marcato meaning "well marked."

BEN abbr = Black Empire Network.

Ben Bella n [Mohammed] Ahmed (1916–) Algerian statesman. He became prime minister in 1962 and was deposed in 1965.

Ben-ben n (Egypt) a truncated obelisk set on a podium in the temple of the sun-god at Heliopolis, a fetish object representing the sun as creator and also set up in other sun temples.

bench n a long hard seat for two or more persons; a long table for working at; the place where judges sit in a court of law; the status of a judge; judges collectively; (sport) the place where reserves, etc, sit during play.

bencher n one who sits on a bench; in UK, a senior member of an Inn of Court, one of the governing body, usu a judge.

bench mark n a surveyor's mark for making measurements; something that serves as a standard; (comput) a measurement standard used to compare the performance of different computers and equipment.

benchmarking n the process undergone by a company of trying to establish the best production and marketing practices.

bench warrant n a warrant issued by a court or judge for someone's arrest.

bend (bending, bent) vt to form a curve; to make crooked; to turn, esp from a straight line; to adapt to one's purpose, distort. * vi to turn, esp from a straight line; to yield from pressure to form a curve; (with over or down) to curve the body; to give in. * n a curve, turn; a bent part; (pl: used as sing or pl) decompression sickness in divers.—**bendable** adj.

bender n one who or that which bends; (sl) a bout of drinking.

Bendigeid Vran or **Bendigeidfran** n known as **Bran the Blessed**, (Welsh Celtic myth) the son of Llyr, the brother of Branwen and Manawydan, and the half-brother of Efnisien and Nisien. He is best known for the expedition that he led to Ireland to rescue his sister Branwen from her husband, the Irish king, Matholwch.

B endorphin n a painkiller released by the pituitary in response to pain and stress.

bends n a condition caused by the formation of nitrogen bubbles in the blood, that may affect workers operating at depth underwater if they surface too rapidly.— also **compressed air illness; caisson disease.**

bend sinister n (her) a bar or band drawn from the upper corner of the shield at the left (sinister) to the opposite base at the right (dexter), a sign of illegitimacy.

beneath prep underneath; below; unworthy. * adv in a lower place; underneath.—also adj.

benedicite n a blessing, a grace; (with cap) canticle known as The Song of the Three Holy Children, used during Lent as an alternative to the Te Deum in the Anglican Service of Morning Prayer.

benedict n a newly married man, esp if previously a confirmed bachelor.

Benedict n 1. Saint (480–543) Italian monk; aged fourteen, he renounced the world and went to live as a hermit in the mountains. Founded the order of Benedictines at Monte Cassino (540), which set the pattern for western monasticism for the next six hundred years. His feast day is 11 July. 2. **Sir Julius** (1804–85) an English composer and conductor who wrote many operas and oratorios but is best remembered for his opera The Lily of Killarney (1862). He was knighted in 1871.

Benedictine adj of or relating to the order of St Benedict. * n a monk of the Benedictine order; a kind of liqueur made from herbs and spices.

benediction n a blessing; an invocation of a blessing, esp at the end of a church service.—**benedictory** adj.

Benedict's test n a test for glucose and reducing sugars.

Benedictus n (mus) (Latin) the second part of the sanctus of a Roman Catholic Mass; the canticle "Benedictus Dominus Israel" or "Blessed be the Lord God of Israel"; the Song of Zacharias (Luke 1) used as a canticle after the second lesson at morning prayer when the Jubilate is not sung.

Benedictus n **Edouard** (1878–1930) French designer of textiles.

benefaction n the act of doing good; the money or help given.

benefactor n a patron.—**benefactress** nf.

benefice n a church office yielding an income to a clergyman.

beneficence n active kindness, the act of doing good; a benefaction.

beneficent adj generous; conferring blessings.—**beneficence** n.—**beneficently** adv.

beneficial adj advantageous.—**beneficially** adv.

beneficiary n (pl beneficiaries) a person who receives or will receive benefit, as from a will, etc.

benefit n advantage; anything contributing to improvement; (often pl) allowances paid by a government, insurance company, etc; a public performance, bazaar, etc, the proceeds of which are to help some person or cause. vt (**benefiting, benefited**) to help. * vi to receive advantage.

benefit of clergy n a sanctioning by the church; (hist) exemption from trial by a secular court.

benefit society, benefit association n an association for mutual insurance against sickness, etc.

benefits in kind npl benefits other than actual cash that a person obtains from his or her employment.

Benelux abbr = Belgium, Netherlands, Luxembourg (Benelux Economic Union).

Benét n **Stephen Vincent** (1898–1943) American poet whose works include John Brown's Body and whose poem "American Names" contains his most famous line, "Bury my heart at Wounded Knee."

benevolence n inclination to do good; kindness; generosity; (formerly) a royal tax levied under the guise of a gratuity to the sovereign.—**benevolent** adj.—**benevolently** adv.

BEng abbr = Bachelor of Engineering.

BEng and Man abbr = Bachelor of Mechanical Engineering, Manufacture and Management.

BEngA abbr = Bachelor of Agricultural Engineering.

Bengali n a native or inhabitant of the Bengal province of India; the language spoken in Bengal. * adj of or pertaining to Bengal, its inhabitants or language.

Bengal light n a firework used also for signals, giving a steady bright blue light.

Benguela current n n a cold ocean current flowing northwards off the west coast of South Africa.

Ben-Gurion n **David [David Gruen]** (1886–1973) Polish-born Israeli statesman. He was the first prime minister of Israel (1948–53) and prime minister again (1955–63).

benighted adj overtaken by night; in moral darkness or ignorance.

benign adj favorable; kindly; gentle or mild; (med) not malignant.—**benignly** adv.

benignant adj kind; benign.—**benignancy** n.

benignity n (pl benignities) kindliness.

Beni-Hasan n (Egypt) capital of the Oryx nome in Upper Egypt, with large limestone deposits and tombs of governors.

Benin n a republic on the southern coast of west Africa.

Benioff zone n the earthquake zone where one continental plate is pushed under another when they meet.

benison n (arch) a benediction or blessing.

Benjamin n 1. (Bible) youngest son of Jacob, whose descendants are the tribe of Benjamin, said to be brave warriors; they include Saul, first king, and Paul the apostle. 2. **Arthur** (1893–1960) Australian composer and pianist renowned for his humorous but accomplished style. His principal operas include The Devil Take Her (1931) and Prima Donna (1931). His popular Jamaican Rumba for two pianos (1938) is still widely played.

Benn n **Tony [Anthony Neil Wedgwood Benn, formerly Viscount Stansgate]** (1925–) English left t-wing Labour politician; retired 2001.

benne n the sesame, an Asian annual cultivated for its seeds, which yield oil.

Bennett n 1. [Enoch] Arnold (1867–1931) English novelist, dramatist, and essayist whose novels include the Clayhanger series. 2. **James Gordon** (1795–1872) American journalist and founder of the New York Herald (1835). 3. **James Gordon** (1841–1918) journalist son of James Gordon Bennett. 4. **Richard Rodney** (1936–) English composer and pianist, best known for the popular tunes from his film scores, such as Far from the Madding Crowd (1967) and Murder on the Orient Express (1974). 5. **Bennett** n **Sir William Sterndale** (1816–75) English composer and pianist who was a friend of Mendelssohn and Schumann and founded the Bach Society in 1849. His works include a symphony, four piano concertos, and songs. He was knighted in 1871.

benny n (pl bennies) (sl) a tablet of amphetamine.

Benny n **Jack [Benjamin Kubelsky]** (1894–1974) American comedian and film actor.

BENS abbr = British Electroless Nickel Society.

bent¹ see bend.

bent² n aptitude; inclination of the mind. * adj curved or crooked; (with on) strongly determined; (sl) dishonest; sexually deviant.

bent³ n a kind of coarse stiff grass; a withered grass stalk; a heath.

Bentham n **Jeremy** (1748–1832) English philosopher.

benthic n, adj (biol) a plant or animal living on the bottom of a lake or sea.

benthos n (biol) the flora and fauna at the bottom of the sea; the sea bottom itself.—**benthic, benthonic** adj.

Bentley n 1. **Edmund Clerihew** (1875–1956) English civil servant, noted for his classic detective novel Trent's Last Case and for the invention of the verse form called the clerihew. 2. **John F.** born 1839, English architect. His notable works include Westminster Cathedral, London.

Benton n **Thomas Hart** (1889–1975) American painter. Famous among his works are his mural commissions on American Life and a series of paintings, Art of the West.

Bentsen n **Lloyd Millard Jnr** (1921–) American politician; secretary of the treasury under Clinton (1992–94).

bentwood *adj* (*furniture*) made of wood that is bent and shaped by heat.

benumb *vt* to make numb.—**benumbed** *adj*.

benzene *n* (*chem*) an organic chemical compound, which is a hydrocarbon containing carbon and hydrogen, used as a solvent, in the manufacture of plastics, and as motor fuel.

benzhexol *n* a drug prescribed in the treatment of Parkinson's disease.—*also* **benzhexol hydrochloride; trihexyphenidyl hydrochloride**

benzine, benzol *n* a volatile mixture of lighter hydrocarbons from petroleum, used as a solvent and as motor fuel.

benzocaine *n* a local anesthetic for relief of painful skin conditions, including those within the mouth.

benzodiazepines *npl* a group of drugs that act as tranquilizers, hypnotics, and anticonvulsants, depending on the duration of action.

benzoic acid *n* an antiseptic used to preserve certain pharmaceutical preparations and foodstuffs.

benzoin *n* a resin of the benjamin tree of Sumatra. Used chiefly in cosmetics, perfumes, incense and in the preparation of compounds such as friar's balsam, that are inhaled in the treatment of colds, bronchitis, etc.—**benzoic** *adj*.

benzothiadiazine *n* a diuretic compound, taken orally, that lowers the blood pressure and relieves edema in heart failure.

benzoyl peroxide *n* a bactericidal agent used as a bleach in the food industry and also as a treatment for acne.

Beonna *n* king of East Anglia (reigned *c.*760). Known to have issued a coinage during his reign.

Beonred *n* king of Mercia. Reigned in 757. The successor to the throne of King Ethelbald of Mercia.

Beorhtwulf *n* (*d.* 853) king of Mercia (840–853).

Beornwulf *n* (*d.* 827) king of Mercia (823–827).

Beortric *n* (*d.* 802) king of Wessex (757–802). He married Eadburga of Mercia, a daughter of Offa, and was succeeded by Egbert.

BEP *abbr* = Bureau of Engraving and Printing

BEPA *abbr* = British Edible Pulses Association; British Egg Products Association; British European Potato Association.

bequeath *vt* (*property, etc*) to leave by will; to pass on to posterity.—**bequeathal** *n*.—**bequeather** *n*.

bequest *n* act of bequeathing; something that is bequeathed, a legacy.

Ber. *abbr* = Berlin.

BER *abbr* = Board for Engineers' Registration.

Berain *n* **Jean** (1640–1711) French engraver and designer.

berate *vt* to scold severely.

berberine *n* an alkaloid used in dyeing and medicine, and obtained as a bitter yellow substance from the barberry and other plants.

berceuse *n* (*mus*) (*French*) (*pl* **berceuses**) a cradle song; a tender or soothing musical composition.

bereave *vt* to deprive (of) a loved one through death.—**bereaved** *adj*.—**bereavement** *n*.

bereft *adj* deprived; bereaved.

Berenson *n* **Bernard** (1865–1959) Lithuanian-born American art critic who was highly influential in the early development of art history.

beret *n* a flat, round, brimless, soft cap.

berg *n* the German word for mountain; a colloquial word for an iceberg.

Berg *n* 1. **Alban** *n* (*mus*) (1885–1935) Austrian composer and exponent of atonal composition and the twelve-note system. He established his reputation with his first opera, *Wozzeck*, in 1921. His second opera, *Lulu*, was unfinished when he died, and a version of it was not performed until 1979. 2. **Berg G A** (1884–1957) Swedish furniture designer who was an influential **modernist** in Sweden.

bergamot *n* a variety of lemon, the rind of which yields a valuable oil used in perfumery; the oil of the bergamot; a variety of pear; a variety of mint; a coarse kind of tapestry.

Berger *n* **Thomas** (1924–) American novelist, best known for his novels contrasting the American dream with the actual way of life, e.g., *Reinhart in Love* (1962), and his novel of the American West *Little Big Man*.

Bergman *n* 1. **Ingmar** (1918–) Swedish film and stage director. His film *Fanny and Alexander* (1982) won an Oscar for Best Foreign Language Film. 2. **Ingrid** (1915–82) Swedish film actress whose films include *Casablanca* (1942).

bergomask *see* **bergamasca**.

bergschrund *n* a crevasse between a glacier and the side of its valley.

Bergson *n* **Henri Louis** (1859–1941) French philosopher and winner of 1927 Nobel prize for literature.

berg wind *n* a hot, dry wind that blows down from the high interior of South Africa towards the east coast, causing oppressive conditions.

Berhtun *n* (*d.* 686) king of Sussex, England (reigned in 686). Ruling for less than a year, he was killed during an invasion of Kent.

Beria *n* **Lavrenti Pavlovich** (1899–1953) Georgian-born Soviet politician. He was head of the secret police (1938–53) under Stalin.

beri-beri *n* (*med*) a serious disease of the nervous system caused by a lack or deficiency of vitamin B1 (thiamine).

Berin, Saint *see* Birinus.

Berio *n* **Luciano** (1925–) Italian composer and conductor of avant-garde technique. The piece *Circles* in 1960, has text by e e cummings and the female singer is given

a certain amount of freedom with regard to which notes she sings. His experiments with electronic music have produced *Mutations*, *Theme*, and *Chantas parallèles*.

Berkeley *n* 1. **Busby** [**William Busby Enos**] (1895–1976) American film director noted for his dance choreography. 2. **Berkeley** *n* **Sir Lennox Randal Francis** (1903–89) English composer who was influenced by Stravinsky and is best known for his symphonies and operas, e.g., *Ruth*, *Nelson*, *A Dinner Engagement*, and *The Castaway*.

berkelium *n* a radioactive metallic element derived from americium.

Berkowitz *n* **David** (1953–) American murderer who called himself "Son of Sam." He killed six people in New York (1976–77) before capture.

Berlage *n* **Hendrik Petrus** (1856–1934) Dutch architect and designer who introduced the work of Frank Lloyd Wright to Europe. His notable works include Amsterdam Exchange.

berlin *n* a fine dyed knitting wool; an 18th-century four-wheeled carriage with a hood behind.

Berlin *n* 1. **Irving** (originally **Israel Baline**) (1888–1989) American composer of Russian origin. Among his best known songs are *Alexander's Ragtime Band, White Christmas* and *God Bless America*. His musicals, include *Top Hat, Annie Get Your Gun*, and *Call Me Madam*. 2. **Sir Isaiah** (1909–97) Latvian-born British philosopher and historian.

Berlioz *n* **(Louis) Hector** (1803–69) French composer, conductor, and critic. His principal compositions include: *Benvenuto Cellini* (opera); *The Trojans* (opera); *Béatrice et Bénédict* (opera); Symphonie Fantastique; *Harold in Italy* (viola and orchestra); *Romeo et Juliette* (dramatic symphony); and *Les Nuits d'été* (song cycle).

berm, berme *n* (*archeo*) an area of level ground that separates, for example, an earth mound of a barrow or fortification from its surrounding ditch or trench; a high ridge of shingle on a beach marking the limit of swash; a narrow shelf along a slope; a shoulder of a road.

Bermuda *n* a British overseas territory comprising a group of 150 small islands in the western Atlantic Ocean.

Bermuda grass *n* a valuable variety of pasture grass.

Bermuda-rigged *adj* (*naut*) rigged with a high tapering mainsail.

Bermuda shorts *npl* close-fitting knee-length shorts.

Bernadette *n* **Saint**, born Bernadette Soubirous (1844–79) daughter of a miller at Lourdes in southern France. Her visions of the Virgin Mary, who told her that a spring lay below the ground, led to the establishment of a shrine at Lourdes. Canonized in 1933. Her feast day is 16 April.

Bernadotte *n* **Count Sigvard** (1907–1995) Son of King Gustavus VI of Sweden and silversmith.

Bernard *n* **Oliver Percy** (1881–1939) British architect who started out as a stage set designer.

Bernard of Clairvaux *n* **Saint** (1091–1153) French abbot and theologian; born at Fontaines near Dijon; founded a strict branch of the order of the Cistercians. His feast day is 20 August.

Bernardaud *n* **Porcelaines** French ceramics company founded in 1863.

Berners *n* **Lord** (**Gerald Hugh Tyrwhitt-Wilson**) (1883–1950) English composer, diplomat, author and painter, mainly remembered for his ballets, e.g., *The Triumph of Neptune* and *A Wedding Bouquet*. He also wrote scores for the films *Champagne Charlie* and *Nicholas Nickleby*.

Bernini *n* **Giovanni Lorenzo** (1598–1680) Italian baroque sculptor, also painter, architect, designer, and playwright. His notable works include Palazzo Odescalchi, the colonnade at St Peters, Rome.

Bernoulli *n* (*comput*) a type of disk drive, usu holding over 20 megabytes of data, that uses removable cartridges.

Bernstein *n* **Leonard** (1918–90) American conductor, composer, pianist and musical director of the New York Philharmonic (1958-70); wrote the musicals *West Side Story* and *On the Town*. He also wrote three symphonies, an opera, *Trouble in Tahiti*, an operetta, *Candide*, and music for the film *On the Waterfront* (1954).

berry *n* (*pl* **berries**) any small, juicy, stoneless fruit (eg blackberry, holly berry). * *vti* (**berrying, berried**) to bear, produce or gather berries.

Berryman *n* **John** (1914–72) American poet whose verse is intensely personal, self-critical and highly proficient and includes *The Dispossessed*.

BERSA *abbr* = British Elastic Rope Sports Association.

berserk *adj* frenzied; destructively violent.—*also adv*.

berth *n* a place in a dock for a ship at mooring; a built-in bed, as in a ship or train; (*inf*) a job. * *vt* to put into or furnish with a berth; to moor a ship. * *vi* to occupy a berth.

bertha *n* a wide lace collar.

Berthelemy *n* **Jean Simon** (1743–1811) French painter who won the Prix de Rome in 1767.

Bertillon system *n* a method of identifying criminals by body measurements.

Bertolucci *n* **Bernardo** (1940–) Italian film director; films include *The Last Emperor*.

Bertotti-Scamozzi *n* **Ottavio** born 1719, Italian architect. His notable works include Palazzo Franceschini, Vicenza.

Berwald *n* **Franz Adolf** (1796–1868) a distinguished Swedish composer and violinist whose work included four symphonies, concertos, symphonic poems, and several operas, e.g., *A Rustic Betrothal in Sweden*.

beryl *n* a mineral found in some igneous and metamorphic rocks, regarded as a precious stone (usu green).

beryllium *n* a hard lightweight silvery-white metallic element used in making alloys.

Bes *n* a demi-god dating from New Kingdom times in Ancient Egypt. He is depicted as an animal-like dwarf.

BES *abbr* = Bachelor of Engineering Science; Business Expansion Scheme.

beseech *vt* (**beseeching, beseeched** *or* **besought**) to implore, to entreat; to beg earnestly for.

beset *vt* (**besetting, beset**) to surround or hem in; to attack from all sides; to harass.

besetting *adj* constantly harassing.

BESI *abbr* = bus electronic scanning indicator.

beside *prep* at, by the side of, next to; in comparison with; in addition to; aside from; **beside oneself** extremely agitated.

besides *prep* other than; in addition; over and above. * *adv* in addition; also; except for that mentioned; moreover.

besiege *vt* to hem in with armed forces; to close in on; to overwhelm, harass, etc.

besmear *vt* to smear with sticky stuff; to soil.

besmirch *vt* to sully; to make dirty, to soil.

besom *n* a broom made of twigs; (*Scot*) a naughty or silly woman.

besotted *adj* muddled with drunkenness or infatuation; dull, stupid.—**besottedly** *adv*.

besought *see* **beseech.**

bespangle *vt* to adorn with spangles; to dot or sprinkle with something that glitters.

bespatter *vt* to soil by spattering; to spot with mud; to asperse with calumny.

bespeak *vt* (**bespeaking, bespoke**, *pp* **bespoken** *or* **bespoke**) to speak for beforehand; to order or arrange in advance; to be evidence of; to indicate, as by signs or marks.

bespectacled *adj* wearing eyeglasses.

bespoke *adj* (*clothes*) custom-made; (*tailor*) making such clothes.

besprent *adj* (*poet*) sprinkled; scattered.

besprinkle *vt* to sprinkle over (with).

BESS *abbr* = Bank of England Statistical Summary.

best *adj* (*superl of* **good**) most excellent; most suitable, desirable, etc; largest; above all others. * *n* one's utmost effort; the highest state of excellence. * *adv* (*superl of* **well**) in or to the highest degree. * *vt* to defeat, outdo.

Best *n* 1. **Charles Herbert** *see* **Banting, Sir Frederick.** 2. **George** (1946–) Northern Irish former British soccer player.

BEST *abbr* = Biomonitoring of Environmental Status and Trends

bestial *adj* brutal; savage.—**bestially** *adv*.

bestiality *n* (*pl* **bestialities**) brutal or brutish behavior; a brutal or savage action or practice; sexual intercourse by a person with an animal.

bestialize *vt* to make like a beast; to degrade to the level of a brute.

bestiary *n* (*pl* **bestiaries**) a medieval treatise on beasts.

bestir *vt* (**bestirring, bestirred**) to put into brisk or vigorous action; to rouse, exert (oneself).

best man *n* the principal attendant of the bridegroom at a wedding.

bestow *vt* to present as a gift or honor.—**bestowal** *n*.—**bestower** *n*.

bestrew *vt* (**bestrewing, bestrewed**, *pp* **bestrewed** *or* **bestrewn**) to strew or scatter over; to lie scattered over.

bestride *vt* (**bestriding, bestrode**, *pp* **bestridden**) to stand, sit on or mount with the legs astride.

best seller *n* a book or other commodity that sells in vast numbers; the author of such a book.—**best-selling** *adj*.

bet *n* a wager or stake; the thing or sum staked; a person or thing likely to bring about a desired result; (*inf*) belief, opinion. * *vti* (**betting, bet** *or* **betted**) to declare as in a bet; to stake (money, etc) in a bet (with someone).

bet. *abbr* = between.

beta *n* the second letter of the Greek alphabet; (*chem*) the second of two or more isomerous modifications of the same compound; (*biol*) the second subspecies or permanent variety of a species.

Beta *n* (*astron*) the name used to distinguish the second brightest star in a constellation.

beta blocker *n* a drug that subdues cardiac activity, used in the treatment of high blood pressure.

Beta Centauri *n* a bright giant star of first magnitude, the second brightest star in the constellation Centaurus, also known as Agena or Hadar.

Beta Cephei Star *n* a variable star, named after the first studied of the class, Beta Cephei, the second brightest star in the constellation Cepheus.

beta decay *n* one form of natural radioactivity where an unstable nucleus spontaneously emits a beta particle, a high-speed electron, converting a neutron to a proton and forming a new element one place higher in the periodic table.

betake *vt* (**betaking, betook**, *pp* **betaken**) to have recourse (to), to resort; to take oneself (to), to go.

Beta Lyrae *n* a star of third magnitude, the second brightest in the constellation Lyra.

Beta Lyrae stars *n* a class of eclipsing binary star where, in addition to brightness variation produced by eclipses, there are variations in the light output of the individual stars.

beta particle *n* an electron or positron ejected from the nucleus of an atom during radioactive disintegration.

beta ray *n* a stream of penetrating rays emitted by radioactive substances.

beta testing *n* (*comput*) the final stage of testing of a computer program before it is released for general sale.

beta wave *n* an electrical rhythm of the brain associated with normal waking consciousness.

betel *n* an Asian pepper, the leaves of which are mixed with betel nuts and chewed as a stimulant or narcotic.

betel nut *n* the seed of the betel palm.

betel palm *n* a palm tree of tropical Asia with feathery leaves and scarlet or orange fruit.

Betelgeuse *or* **Alpha Orion** *n* a star of first magnitude, the brightest star in the constellation Orion.

bête noir *n* (*pl* **bêtes noires**) (*French*) pet hate.

Bethany *n* (*Bible*) village on the slope of the Mount of Olives near Jerusalem.

bethel *n* a hallowed spot; a seamen's church; in UK, a nonconformist chapel.

Bethel *n* (*Bible*) a well-known holy place in *OT* times.

be there for *v phr* to be ready and available to perform a supportive role for another, at times of grief, stress etc.

Bethesda *n* (*Bible*) "house of mercy," located outside Jerusalem, where sick persons attended; Jesus healed a man who had been there for thirty-eight years.

Bethlehem *n* (*Bible*) town about five miles south of Jerusalem, famous as the birthplace of David and of Jesus.

Bethphage *n* (*Bible*) village on the slope of the Mount of Olives from which Jesus' disciples fetched an ass for his entry into Jerusalem.

Bethsaida *n* (*Bible*) town on the shore of the Sea of Galilee, the home of Peter, Andrew and Philip; the name means "house of fishers."

Bethune *n* **Mary McLeod** (1875–1955) American educator. She founded the Bethune-Cookman College and was founder and president of the National Council of Negro Women (1935–49).

betide *vt* to happen to, to befall. * *vi* to come to pass.

betimes *adv* (*arch*) in good time; before it is too late; early; soon.

bêtise *n* folly; an ill-chosen remark.

Betjeman *n* **Sir John** (1906–84) English poet and essayist, appointed British poet laureate in 1972.

betoken *vt* to signify, to indicate by signs; to augur, to foreshadow.

béton brut *n* (*archit*) concrete which is left in its natural unfinished state once the formwork has been removed.

betony *n* (*pl* **betonies**) a purple-flowered woodland plant formerly used in medicine and as a dye.

betook *see* **betake.**

betray *vt* to aid an enemy; to expose treacherously; to be a traitor to; to reveal unknowingly.—**betrayal** *n*.—**betrayer** *n*.

betroth *vt* to promise in marriage.

betrothal *n* the state of being engaged to marry; a mutual promise for future marriage made between a man and a woman.

betrothed *adj* affianced, engaged to be married. * *n* a fiancé or fiancée.

better[1] *adj* (*compar of* **good**) more excellent; more suitable; improved in health; larger. * *adv* (*compar of* **well**) in a more excellent manner; in a higher degree; more. * *n* a person superior in position, etc; a more excellent thing, condition, etc. * *vt* to outdo; to surpass.

better[2] *n* someone who bets.

betterment *n* an improvement.

between *prep* the space, time, etc separating (two things); (*bond, etc*) connecting from one or the other.

betweentimes, betweenwhiles *adv* at or during intervals.

betwixt *prep* between; in the space that separates.

betyl *n* (*archeo*) a stone of religious significance, usu standing and worked so that it is shaped like a cone.

Beuys *n* **Joseph** (1921–86) German sculptor and important influence on 1970s avante-garde artists. He was a pioneer of "actions" or "happenings" as in *Coyote* (1974), in which he spent a week in New York having a conversation with a coyote.

BeV *abbr* = billion electron-volts.

Bevan *n* **Aneurin** (1897–1960) Welsh statesman. As Labour minister of health under Clement Attlee, he oversaw the formation of the welfare state in Britain.

bevel *n* an angle other than a right angle; the inclination that one surface makes with another when not at right angles; a tool for setting of angles. * *vb* (**beveling, bevelled** *or* **bevelling, bevelled**) *vt* to cut on the slant. * *vi* to slant or incline.

bevel gear *n* a gear in which the axis or shaft of the driving wheel forms an angle with the shaft of the wheel driven.

beverage *n* a drink, esp one other than water.

Beveridge *n* **William Henry [1st Baron Beveridge]** (1879–1963) Indian-born English economist. His *Report on Social Insurance and Allied Services* (1942) became the basis for the British welfare state.

Bevin *n* **Ernest** (1881–1951) English trade unionist and statesman; co-founder of the Transport and General Workers Union (1922) and Labour foreign secretary (1945–51).

bevy *n* (*pl* **bevies**) a flock of quails; a large group (esp of girls).

bewail *vt* to mourn or weep aloud for, to lament. * *vi* to express grief.—**bewailer** *n*.—**bewailing** *n*.

beware *vti* to be wary or careful (of).

Bewick *n* **Thomas** (1753–1828) British wood-engraver from Newcastle upon Tyne, he became famous for his illustrations of *A General History of Quadrupeds* (1790) and *A History of British Birds* I (1797–1804).

bewilder *vt* to perplex; to confuse hopelessly.—**bewilderingly** *adv*.—**bewilderment** *n*.

bewitch *vt* to cast a spell over; to fascinate or enchant.

bewitching *adj* fascinating, enchanting, captivating, alluring.—**bewitchingly** *adv*.

bey *n* a Turkish title of respect; a title similar to Mr; (*formerly*) a governor of a province or district in the Turkish dominions.

Beyer *n* **Johann Christian Wilhelm** (1725–1806) German-born sculptor, painter and architect.

beyond *prep* further on than; past; later than; outside the reach of (*beyond help*). * *adv* further away. * *n* (*with* **the**) life after death.

bezant *n* a gold coin of Byzantium or Constantinople, issued in the Middle Ages and current in Europe until the fall of the Eastern Empire, 1472; (*her*) a small circle of gold representing the coin.

bezel *n* the sloping edge of a chisel; the rim that holds a gem in its setting; the groove in which the glass of a watch is fitted.

Bezier curve *n* (*comput*) a style of curve that depends on vector forces of power and angle to determine its shape.

bezique *n* a game of cards for two, three, and four persons using two decks of cards with sixes and cards below omitted.

bezoar *n* a calcareous concretion found in the intestines of certain animals.

bf *or* **b.f.** *abbr* = bold-faced (type).

b.f. *abbr* = *bona fide*, *Latin* "genuine," "genuinely."

BF *abbr* = Bachelor of Finance; Bachelor of Forestry.

B/F *abbr* = brought forward (*bookkeeping*).

BFA *abbr* = Bachelor of Fine Arts.

BFBS *abbr* = British Forces Broadcasting Service.

BFF *abbr* = Born Free Foundation.

BFFS *abbr* = British Federation of Film Societies.

BFI *abbr* = British Film Institute.

BFMP *abbr* = British Federation of Master Printers.

BFN *abbr* = British Forces' Network (radio).

BFO *abbr* = beat frequency oscillator.

BFor *abbr* = Bachelor of Forestry.

BForSc *abbr* = Bachelor of Forestry Science.

BFP *abbr* = Bureau of Freelance Photographers.

BFPO *abbr* = British Forces Post Office.

BFSS *abbr* = British Field Sports Society.

bg. *abbr* = bag.

BG *abbr* = Brigadier General; blood group.

BGA *abbr* = Behavior Genetics Association.

bg. adj. *abbr* = brigade adjutant.

bg. c. *abbr* = brigade commander.

BGH *abbr* = bovine growth hormone.

bgs. *abbr* = bags.

BGS *abbr* = Brigadier, General Staff; British Geological Survey.

bg.sf.p.o. *abbr* = brigade staff petty officer.

b/h *abbr* = bill of health.

Bh *abbr* = bohrium (chemical element).

BH *abbr* = Bachelor of Humanics.

BHA *abbr* = Black History for Action; British Homoeopathic Association; British Humanist Association; British Hypnotherapy Association.

bhang *n* the dried leaves of Indian hemp, chewed or smoked as an intoxicant or narcotic, hashish.—*also* **bang**.

BHB *abbr* = British Hockey Board.

BHC *abbr* = British High Commissioner.

BHE *abbr* = Bachelor of Home Economics.

BHF *abbr* = British Heart Foundation.

BHI *abbr* = British Horological Institute.

BHL *abbr* = biological half-life.

BHort *abbr* = Bachelor of Horticulture.

BHortSc *abbr* = Bachelor of Horticultural Science.

BHP *or* **b.h.p.** *abbr* (*mech*) = brake horsepower.

BHQ *abbr* = Brigade Headquarters.

BHS *abbr* = British Home Stores; British Hypertension Society.

BHSI *abbr* = British Horse Society's Instructor's Certificate.

BHTA *abbr* = British Herb Trade Association.

Bhuilg *n* (*Irish Celtic mythology*) Irish god after whom **Fir Bholg** was named.

Bhutan *n* a constitutional monarchy surrounded by India to the south and China to the north.

Bhutto *n* 1. **Benazir** (1953–) daughter of Zulfikar Bhutto; prime minister of Pakistan (1988–90, 1993–97). 2. **Zulfikar Ali** (1928–79) Pakistani statesman; the first civilian president of Pakistan (1971–73), then prime minister (1973–77).

Bi *symbol* (*chem*) bismuth.

BI *abbr* = Agricultural Society of Iceland; Befrienders International.

bi- *prefix* having two; doubly; happening twice during; every two; using two or both; joining or involving two; having twice the amount of acid or base.

Bia *n* (*Greek myth*) the personification of might and force, in some legends male, in others female.

BIA *abbr* = Bureau of Indian Affairs.

Bianca *n* a small satellite of Uranus.

biannual *adj* occurring twice a year.—**biannually** *adv*.

bias *n* a slanting or diagonal line, cut or sewn across the grain in cloth; a weight inside a bowl in a game of bowls slanting its course when rolled; partiality; prejudice. * *vt* (**biasing, biased** *or* **biassing, biassed**) to prejudice.

Bias *n* (*Greek myth*) brother of Melampus, who helped him win Pero as his wife, by bringing her father Neleus the oxen of Iphicles.

biathlon *n* (*sport*) an athletic event combining cross-country skiing and rifle shooting.

biauriculate, biauricular *adj* having two auricles, as the heart of the higher vertebrates; (*bot*) having two ear-like projections at the base, as a leaf.

biaxial *adj* having two (optic) axes.—**biaxially** *adv*.

bib[1] *n* a cloth or plastic cover tied around a baby or child to prevent food spillage on clothes; the upper part of dungarees or an apron.

bib[2] *vi* (**bibbing, bibbed**) (*arch*) to drink, to tipple.

bib[3] *n* a kind of fish, whiting pout.

Bib. *abbr* = Bible; Biblical.

BIBBA *abbr* = British Isles Bee Breeders' Association.

bibcock *n* a tap with the nozzle bent downward.

bibelot *n* a trinket, a knickknack.

Bibl. *or* **bibl.** *abbr* = biblical; bibliographical; bibliotheca (*Latin*, library).

Bible *n* the sacred book of the Christian Church; the Old and New Testaments; (*without cap*) an authoritative book on a particular subject.

Bible Belt *n* sections of the US where Protestant fundamentalism prevails.

Bible thumper *n* (*inf*) a religious fanatic.

biblical *adj* of or referring to the Bible.—**biblically** *adv*.

Biblicist *n* a biblical scholar; a fundamentalist.—**Biblicism** *n*.

biblio- *prefix* book or books.

bibliog. *abbr* = bibliography.

bibliography *n* (*pl* **bibliographies**) a list of writings on a given subject or by a given author; the study of the history of books and book production. —**bibliographer** *n*.—**bibliographic** *adj*.—**bibliographical** *adj*.

bibliolatry *n* book worship; excessive reverence for the letter of the Bible.—**bibliolater** *n*.—**bibliolatrous** *adj*.

bibliomania *n* a mania for acquiring rare and curious books.—**bibliomaniac** *adj, n* .

bibliophile, bibliophil *n* a book lover.—**bibliophilistic** *adj*.—**bibliophism** *n*.

bibliopole, bibliopolist *n* a bookseller, esp one who deals in rare works.—**bibliopolic** *adj*.—**bibliopoly** *n*.

bibliotheca *n* (*pl* **bibliothecas, bibliothecae**) a library; a list of books.

BIBRA *abbr* = British Industrial Biological Research Association.

bibulous *adj* readily absorbing or imbibing fluids; spongy; addicted to drink.—**bibulously** *adv*.—**bibulousness** *n*.

BIC *abbr* = Business Information Center

bicameral *adj* (*legislature*) having two chambers.

bicarb. *abbr* = sodium bicarbonate.

bicarbonate *n* (*chem*) an acid salt of carbonic acid in which one hydrogen atom is replaced by a metal; sodium bicarbonate.

BICC *abbr* = British Insulated Callender's Cables Limited.

bicentenary *adj* occurring every two hundred years. * *n* (*pl* **bicentenaries**) a two hundredth anniversary or its celebration.

bicentennial *adj* lasting or occurring every two hundred years.

bicephalous, bicephalic *adj* (*biol*) two-headed.

biceps *n* (*pl* **biceps, bicepses**) a muscle with two points of origin, esp the large muscles of the upper arm (biceps brachii) and the back of the thigh (biceps femoris).

bichloride *n* (*chem*) a compound of two or more atoms of chlorine combined with a base; dichloride.

bicipital *adj* (*anat*) having two heads, as a biceps muscle; dividing into two parts at either extremity.

bicker *vi* to squabble, quarrel.—*also* *n*.—**bickerer** *n*.

bicoastal *adj* pertaining to both the west and east coasts of the United States.

biconcave *adj* hollow on both sides.—**biconcavity** *n*.

biconvex *adj* rounded on both sides.

bicorn, bicornuate *adj* having two horns.

bicuspid *adj* having two points or prominences (—*also* **bicuspidate**). * *n* one of the two double-pointed teeth forming the first pair of molars on either side of the jaw, above and below.

bicuspid valve *see* **mitral valve**.

bicycle *n* a vehicle consisting of a metal frame on two wheels, driven by pedals and having handlebars and a seat. * *vti* to ride or travel on a bicycle.—**bicyclist, bicycler** *n*.

bid[1] *n* an offer of an amount one will pay or accept; (*cards*) a statement of the number of tricks that a player intends to win. * *vi* (**bidding, bid**) to make a bid.—**bidder** *n*.

bid[2] *vt* (**bidding, bade** *or* **bid**, *pp* **bidden** *or* **bid**) to command or ask; to summon; (*farewell, etc*) to express.

bid *abbr* = *bis in die*, *Latin* "twice daily."

BID *abbr* = Bachelor of Industrial Design.

biddable *adj* docile, obedient; worth bidding on.—**biddability** *n*.—**biddably** *adv*.

bidding *n* an order; command; an invitation; the act of offering a price at auction.

biddy[1] *n* (*pl* **biddies**) (*inf*) a woman, esp an old or meddlesome one.

biddy² *n* (*pl* **biddies**) (*dial*) a fowl or chicken.

bide (**biding, bided** *or* **bode**) *vi* to wait; to dwell. * *vt* to endure, suffer; to wait for.

bidentate *adj* having two teeth, or two tooth-like processes.

bidet *n* a low, bowl-shaped bathroom fixture with running water for bathing the crotch and anus.

bidirectional *adj* (*comput*) describes a device that can do two opposite things, e.g., printer ports capable of sending and receiving data.

bid price *n* the price at which a dealer in a financial security, foreign currency or commodity is prepared to buy.

BIE *abbr* = Bachelor of Industrial Engineering.

Biedermeier *n* a style in art and architecture in Austria and Germany between 1815 and 1848. Architecture associated with the style is solid and utilitarian, paintings are meticulous and devoid of imagination; term first coined in 1890s to refer to the simple design style of the 1820s and 1830s in a derogatory way.

biennial *adj* lasting two years; occurring every two years. * *n* a plant that lasts for two years.—**biennially** *adv*.

bier *n* a portable framework on which a coffin is put.

Bierce *n* **Ambrose** (1842–1914?) American journalist and short-story writer whose best-known work is *The Devil's Dictionary*.

Bierstadt *n* **Albert** (1830–1902) German-born American landscape painter. He is famous for his dramatic depictions of the Rocky Mountains countryside, as in *Thunderstorm on the Rocky Mountains* (1859).

biestings *see* **beestings**.

BIET *abbr* = British Institute of Engineering Technology.

bifacial *adj* having two faces or fronts; (*leaves*) having upper and lower surfaces that are dissimilar; having opposite surfaces alike.

bifarious *adj* (*bot*) two-fold; two-rowed; pointing in two ways.

BIFD *abbr* = British Institute of Funeral Directors.

biff *n* (*sl*) a blow. * *vt* to hit, strike.

BIFF *abbr* = British Industrial Fasteners Federation.

bifid *adj* divided by a deep cleft, partially divided into two.—**bifidity** *n*.—**bifidly** *adv*.

bifilar *adj* two-threaded; fitted with two threads.—**bifilarly** *adv*.

bifocal *adj* (*spectacles*) having two different focuses.

bifocals *npl* spectacles with bifocal lenses for near and distant vision.

bifoliate *adj* (*bot*) having two leaves.

BIFU *abbr* = Banking, Insurance and Finance Union.

bifurcate *vti* to divide into two branches.—**bifurcation** *n*.

bifurcation *n* (*medical*) the branching of the trachea where it forms two bronchi.

big *adj* (**bigger, biggest**) large; of great size; important; influential; grown-up; pregnant; generous; boastful.—**bigness** *n*.

bigamist *n* a person guilty of bigamy.

bigamy *n* (*pl* **bigamies**) the act of marrying a second time when one is already legally married.—**bigamous** *adj*.—**bigamously** *adv*.

Big Apple *n* a nickname for New York City.

big band *n* (*mus*) a large band, most commonly associated with the swing era. Such bands were famed for the strong dance rhythms they produced.

Big Bang *n* (*Brit, finance*) the informal name given to the occurrence of major changes on the London Stock Exchange which were introduced on 27 October 1986.

big bang theory *n* (*astron*) the theory that the universe originated in a cataclysmic explosion and is still expanding.

Big Ben *n* a clock tower in the Houses of Parliament in London, England; the big bell in this tower that tolls the hour.

Big Blue *n* (*comput*) the colloquial name given to IBM, one of the largest computer companies in the world.

big brother *n* an older brother; a person who fills that protective role; (*with caps*) a ruthless and sinister dictator, corporation, etc that wields absolute power.

big business *n* large corporations and enterprises collectively, esp when regarded as exploitative.

big cat *see* **cat**.

big deal *n* an important achievement. * *interj* (*sl*) an expression of scorn or contempt.

big dipper *n* a roller coaster; (*with caps*) the seven main stars in the constellation Ursa Major.

big dry *n* a period of drought longer than normal.

bigeminal *adj* twinned; occurring in pairs.— **bigeminy** *n*.

bigfoot *n* a big, hairy man-like creature supposed to exist in northwestern US and western Canada.—*also* **Sasquatch**.

big game *n* large animals or fish hunted for sport; an important, usu risky objective.

biggin¹ *n* a close-fitting child's hood or cap.

biggin² *n* a small building; a cottage.

big gun *n* a **bigwig**.

bighead *n* (*inf*) a boastful or conceited person.—**bigheaded** *adj*.

big-hearted *adj* benevolent.

bighorn *n* (*pl* **bighorns, bighorn**) the wild sheep of the Rocky Mountains.

big house *n* (*sl*) a penitentiary.

bight *n* a loop or bend of a rope, in distinction from the ends; a bend in a coastline forming an open bay; a small bay between two headlands.

big league *n* (*baseball*) a major league; big time.—**big-league** *adj*.

bigmouth *n* (*inf*) a loud-mouthed, bragging or indiscreet person.

big name *n* a famous person, esp in entertainment.

bigot *n* an intolerant person who blindly supports a particular political view or religion.—**bigoted** *adj*.

bigotry *n* (*pl* **bigotries**) the state or condition of a narrow-minded, intolerant person; blind and obstinate attachment to a particular creed, party or opinion; intolerance; fanaticism.

big screen *n* (*inf*) the cinema (industry).

big shot *n* (*inf*) an important person.

big stick *n* the threat of force.

big time *n* the top level in any profession.

big top *n* a large circus tent.

biguanide *n* a substance, taken orally, that reduces blood sugar level and is used in the treatment of diabetes mellitus.

bigwig *n* (*inf*) an important person.

BIHA *abbr* = British Ice Hockey Association.

BII *abbr* = British Institute of Innkeeping.

BIIBA *abbr* = British Insurance and Investment Brokers' Association.

bijou *n* (*pl* **bijoux**) a jewel; any small and elegantly finished article. * *adj* (*often derog*) small and elegant.

bijouterie *n* bijoux collectively, jewelery.

BIJS *abbr* = British Institute of Jazz Studies.

bijugate, bijugous *adj* (*bot*) having two pairs of leaflets; having two heads in profile, one of which overlaps the other.

bike *n* (*inf*) a bicycle; a motorcycle.

bikini *n* (*pl* **bikinis**) a scanty two-piece swimsuit for women.

Biko *n* **Steve** (1947–77) South African Black radical leader. He helped found the Black People's Convention against apartheid and died in police custody.

bilabiate *adj* (*bot*) having two lips, as a flower.

bilateral *adj* having two sides; affecting two parties reciprocally.—**bilaterally** *adv*.

bilberry *n* (*pl* **bilberries**) an edible dark-blue berry.

bilbo *n* (*pl* **bilboes**) a rapier or sword; (*pl*) a long bar of iron with sliding shackles for the feet and a lock at the end, formerly used as fetters.

Bildungsroman *n* (*German* for "education novel") a novel that describes the growth of a character from youthful naivety to a well-rounded maturity.

bile *n* a viscous alkaline solution produced by the liver and stored in the gall bladder which aids in fat digestion and absorption of nutrients.

bile duct *n* a duct that carries bile from the liver.

bilge *n* the lowest part of a ship's hull; filth that collects there.

bilge keel *n* a piece of timber secured edgeways under the bottom of a vessel to prevent heavy rolling.

bilge water *n* foul water in a ship's bilge.

bilharzia *n* a tropical disease caused by a parasitic worm.

bilharziasis *see* **schistosomiasis**.

biliary *adj* of or pertaining to the bile; conveying bile.

bilingual *adj* written in two languages; able to speak two languages.—**bilingualism** *n*.—**bilingually** *adv*.

bilious *adj* suffering from or caused by disorder of the bile; peevish.—**biliously** *adv*.—**biliousness** *n*.

bilirubin *n* one of the two important orange or yellow bile pigments, formed primarily from the breakdown of hemoglobin from red blood cells

biliverdin *n* a green pigment in the bile, the oxidized form of bilirubin.

bilk *vt* to deceive or defraud, as by evading a payment; to leave in the lurch; (*cribbage*) to spoil the score of an opponent. * *n* a swindler; the act of spoiling the score of an opponent at cribbage.—**bilker** *n*.

bill¹ *n* a bird's beak; a beak-like headland.

bill² *n* a statement for goods supplied or services rendered, the money due for this; a list, as a menu or theater programme; a poster or handbill; a draft of a proposed law, to be discussed by a legislature; a bill of exchange; a piece of paper money; (*law*) a written declaration of charges and complaints filed. * *vt* to make out a bill of (items); to present a statement of charges to; to advertise by bills.

billabong *n* (*Aus*) Aboriginal term to describe a pond or a stagnant pool connected to a river.

billboard *n* a large panel designed to carry outdoor advertising; a hoarding.

bill broker *n* a broker who buys bills of exchange from traders and sells them to banks or discount houses, or, alternatively, holds them until the date of their maturity.

billet¹ *n* a written order to provide lodging for military personnel; the lodging; a position or job. * *vt* (**billeting, billeted**) to assign to lodging by billet.

billet² *n* a small stick or log of wood, as for fuel; (*archit*) a molding ornament, resembling a billet of wood.

billet-doux *n* (*pl* **billets-doux**) a love letter.

bill fold *n* a notecase or wallet.

billhook *n* a small curved cutting tool with a hooked point.

billiards *n* a game in which hard balls are driven by a cue on a felt-covered table with raised, cushioned edges.

billing *n* the order in which actors' names are listed.

Billings *n* **William** (1746–1800) American who worked as a tanner and composed hymns, anthems and songs in his spare time; considered to be the first "all-American" composer of any worth. His *New England Psalm-Singer* was published in 1770.

billingsgate *n* coarse or profane language; virulent abuse.

billion *n* (*pl* **billions, billion**) a thousand millions, the numeral 1 followed by 9 zeros; in UK, a million million, a trillion.—**billionaire** *n*.—**billionth** *adj, n*.

Bill *n* **Max** (1908–1995) Swiss designer, painter and architect.

bill of exchange *n* a written order instructing one person to pay a certain sum of money to a named person on demand or at a specified time in the future.

bill of fare *n* a menu.

bill of health *n* a ship's certificate of health; a report on a situation or condition, usu favorable.

bill of lading *n* a receipt issued to a shipper by a carrier, listing the goods received for shipment.

bill of rights *n* a charter or summary of basic human rights.

bill of sale *n* a written statement transferring ownership by sale.

billon *n* an alloy of gold and silver, with a large proportion of copper or other base metal, used in coinage of low value.

billow *n* a large wave; any large swelling mass or surge, as of smoke. * *vi* to surge or swell in a billow.—**billowy** *adj*.

billposter *n* a person who pastes up bills.

bill rate *n* the rate at which bills of exchange are discounted by banks etc.

billsticker *n* a billposter.

billy, billycan *n* (*pl* **billies, billycans**) (*Austral*) a can used as a kettle by campers.

billy boots *npl* (*inf*) rain boots.

billy club *n* a small wooden club, usu a policeman's club.

billy-goat *n* a male goat.

bilobate, bilobed *adj* divided into two lobes or segments, with two lobes.

bilocular, biloculate *adj* divided into, or containing, two cells.

biltong *n* (*S Africa*) strips of meat, salted and dried in the sun.

BIM *abbr* = British Institute of Management; British Insulin Manufacturers.

bimanous *adj* (*zool*) having two hands.

BIMAS *abbr* = BioInformatics Molecular Analysis Section

bimbo *n* (*pl* **bimbos, bimboes**) (*sl*) an attractive, but brainless, young woman, often one who has an affair with a prominent person.

bimetallic *adj* of or containing two metals; of or based on bimetallism.

bimetallism *n* a monetary system using both gold and silver as a standard currency at a fixed relative value.—**bimetallist** *n*.

bimonthly *adj* every two months; loosely twice a month.

bin *n* a box or enclosed space for storing grain, coal, etc; a dustbin. * *vt* (**binning, binned**) to put or store in a bin; (*inf*) to discard, throw away.

binary *adj* made up of two parts; double; denoting or of a number system in which the base is two, each number being expressed by using only two digits, specifically 0 and 1. * *n* (*comput*) the language of all computers in which all numbers, letters and special characters are represented by 0 and 1. It is called base two notation. (*See* **binary numbers**.)

binary digit *n* (*comput*) *see* **bit**.

binary file (*see also* **attachment**) *n* (*comput*) a file where all the available bits (eight) of information in the byte are used. ASCII text differs in that it requires only seven bits and this simpler form is the basis for simple text files.

binary form *n* (*mus*) a structure, common in baroque music, consisting of two related sections which were repeated. Sonata form evolved from it.

binary numbers *npl* (*comput*) the use of a base notation of two compared with a base notation of 10 in normal decimal numbers. In base two, there are only two states, 0 or 1 ("on" or "off").

binary star *n* a double star or sun whose members revolve round their common center of gravity.

binary system *n* (*math*) a type of code in arithmetic that uses a combination of the two digits 0 and 1, expressed to the base 2.

binate *adj* (*bot*) occurring or growing in pairs.—**binately** *adv*.

binaural *adj* of or used with both ears; (*sound*) transmitted from two sources.—**binaurally** *adv*.

bind (**binding, bound**) *vt* to tie together, as with rope; to hold or restrain; to encircle with a belt, etc; to fasten together the pages of (a book) and protect with a cover; to obligate by duty, love, etc; (*with* **over**) to compel, as by oath or legal restraint; (*often with* **up**) to bandage. * *vi* to become tight or stiff; to stick together; to be obligatory; (*sl*) to complain. * *n* anything that binds; (*inf*) a difficult situation.

binder *n* a folder for keeping loose papers together; a bookbinder; something used to bind; a sheaf-binding machine.

bindery *n* (*pl* **binderies**) a bookbinder's workshop.

Bindesboll *n* **Thorvald** (1846–1908) the most prolific of the Danish Art Nouveau designers.

binding *n* the covering of a book holding the pages together.

bindweed *n* a common name for twining plants belonging to the genus Convolvulus.

bine *n* the slender stem of a twining plant, esp hop; one of these plants.

Bing and Grøndahl Porcelaenfabrik *n* Danish ceramics manufacturer founded in 1853.

Bing *n* **Samuel** (1838–1905) German collector, whose store, L'Art Nouveau, gave its name to that artistic movement.

binge *n* (*inf*) a heavy drinking session; immoderate indulgence in anything.

Bingham *n* **George Caleb** (1811–79) American painter from Missouri. His precisely composed genre paintings of river life have a fresh and pleasing quality of zest and color, as in *Fur Traders Descending the Missouri* (1845).

bingo *n* a game of chance in which players cover numbers on their cards according to the number called aloud. * *interj*, *n* a cry of delight, surprise or success.

binnacle *n* a turret-shaped box containing a ship's compass.

binocular *adj* for or using both eyes.

binoculars *npl* a viewing device for use with both eyes, consisting of two small telescope lenses joined together.

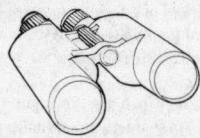

binomial *n* (*math*) an expression or quantity consisting of two terms connected by the sign plus (+) or minus (–). * *adj* consisting of two terms; pertaining to binomials; (*biol*) using two names, esp of classification by genus and species.—**binomially** *adv*.

binomial theorem *n* the general algebraic formula, discovered by Newton, by which any power of a binomial quantity may be found with performing the progressive multiplication.

binturong *n* a prehensile-tailed civet of India.

binucleate, binucleated, binuclear *adj* having two nuclei.

bio- *prefix* life.

bioassay *vb* the determination of a drug's activity by comparing its effects on a living organism with that of a reference sample of known strength.

biochemistry *n* the study of the chemistry of biological processes and substances in living organisms.—**biochemical** *adj*.—**biochemist** *n*.

biocide *n* a toxic chemical substance capable of killing living organisms.

bioclimatology *n* the study of climate and its effect on living things, esp in relation to their health.

biodegradable *adj* readily decomposed by bacterial action.

bioengineering *n* the application of engineering principles in the biological and medical sciences.—**bioengineer** *n*.

biofeedback *n* the practice of monitoring and recording involuntary mental and physiological processes (e.g., brainwaves) in order to attempt to bring them under conscious control.

biog. *abbr* = biographer; biographical; biography.

biogenesis *n* the theory that only living matter can produce living matter; the science of life development.—**biogenetic** *adj*.—**biogenetically** *adv*.

biogeosphere *n* the upper crust and surface of the Earth, that contains organic life.

biography *n* (*pl* **biographies**) an account of a person's life written by another; biographical writings in general.—**biographer** *n*.—**biographical** *adj*.

biol. *abbr* = biological; biologist; biology.

biological clock *n* the intrinsic biological mechanism responsible for time-dependent aspects of certain behaviors in living organisms.

biological warfare *n* warfare with biological weapons, e.g., disease-producing microorganisms or organic biocides.

biology *n* the study of living organisms.—**biological** *adj*.—**biologically** *adv*.—**biologist** *n*.

bioluminescence *n* (*biol*) the emission of visible light by living organisms, e.g., fireflies.

biomass *n* the total mass of all the living organisms in a given area that can be supported at each level in the food chain, expressed as mass per unit area.

biometry, biometrics *n* (*used as sing*) the statistics of biology or probable duration of life.—**biometric, biometrical** *adj*.—**biometrically** *adv*.—**biometrician** *n*.

bionics *n* the study of electronically operated mechanical systems that function like living organisms.—**bionic** *adj*.

bionomics *n* (*used as sing*) ecology.—**bionomic, bionomical** *adj*.—**bionomist** *n*.

biophysics *n* the application of physics to biology.—**biophysical** *adj*.—**biophysicist** *n*.

bioplasm *n* living germinal matter, living protoplasm.—**bioplasmic** *adj*.

biopsy *n* (*pl* **biopsies**) the removal of parts of living tissue for medical diagnosis.

biorhythm *n* a cyclical pattern in physiological activity said to determine a person's intellectual, emotional and physical moods and behavior.—**biorhythmic** *adj*.

BIOS *abbr* (*comput*) = Basic Input Output System. A code that resides on a ROM chip and controls basic hardware operations such as the processor's interaction with disk drives, displays, and keyboard.

biosphere *n* the part of the Earth's surface that is inhabited or could be inhabited by any living organism.

biosynthesis *n* (*pl* **biosyntheses**) (*biol*) the formation of chemical compounds by living organisms.—**biosynthetic** *adj*.—**biosynthetically** *adv*.

biota *n* all the plants and animals of a given area.

biotechnology *n* the commercial and industrial application of biological processes, such as the use of microorganisms to dye cloth.

biotic *adj* relating to life or living things.

biotin *n* a B-complex vitamin that is synthesized by bacteria in the intestine.

biparous *adj* producing two at once in time or place; (*zool*) producing two at a birth; (*bot*) having two branches.

bipartisan *adj* of, representing or supported by two political parties.—**bipartisanship** *n*.

bipartite *adj* having two parts; involving two.—**bipartition** *n*.

biped *n* an animal having two feet.—*also adj*.—**bipedal** *adj*.

bipinnate *adj* (*bot*) having lobes that are lobed themselves.—**bipinnately** *adv*.

biplane *n* an airplane with two sets of wings.

bipod *n* a stand with two legs for supporting a weapon, etc.

bipolar *adj* having two poles or opposite extremities; of or affecting both the earth's poles; having or expressing two directly opposite ideas or qualities.—**bipolarity** *n*.

biquadratic *adj* (*math*) pertaining to the fourth power. * *n* the fourth power, arising from the multiplication of a square number or quantity by itself.

BIR *abbr* = British Institute of Radiology.

BIRC *abbr* = British Industry Roads Campaign.

birch *n* a tree with a smooth white bark and hard wood; a bundle of birch twigs used for thrashing. * *vt* to flog.—**birchen** *adj*.

bird *n* any class of warm-blooded, egg-laying vertebrates with a feathered body, scaly legs, and forelimbs modified to form wings; (*sl*) a woman; (*sl*) time in prison; **for the birds** useless, worthless, unimportant; **get** *or* **give the bird** (*inf*) to boo an entertainer off the stage.

birdbath *n* a water-filled basin in a park or garden in which birds may bathe.

birdbrain *n* (*inf*) a stupid or frivolous person.—**bird-brained** *adj*.

birdcage *n* an enclosure for birds.

birdcall *n* a bird's cry or song, birdsong.

bird dog *n* a dog used to hunt birds.

birdhouse *n* a small box used as a refuge for birds; an aviary.

birdie *n* (*inf*) a small bird; (*golf*) a score of one stroke under par for a hole.

birdlime *n* a viscous substance used for snaring small birds; a thing that snares. * *vt* to smear or trap with birdlime.

bird of passage *n* a migratory bird; a transient person.

bird of prey *n* a meat-eating bird (as a hawk, owl, falcon, etc) that hunts other animals for food.

bird's beak molding *n* (*archit*) a type of molding used in ancient Greece which resembles a bird's beak.

birdseed *n* a mixture of seeds for feeding wild or caged birds.

Birdseye *n* **Clarence** (1886–1956) American businessman, inventor, and food processing pioneer. He was president of Birdseye Frosted Foods (1930–34) and Birdseye Electric Company (1935–38).

bird's-eye *adj* seen from above; dappled to resemble the eye of a bird. * *n* any of several plants with flowers resembling a bird's eye.

birds of a feather *npl* people with similar tastes.

birdsong *n* a bird's cry or song, birdcall.

bird watcher *n* one who makes a study of birds in the wild.—**bird watching** *n*.

BIRE *abbr* = British Institute of Radio Engineers.

bireme *n* an ancient galley with two tiers of oars.

biretta *n* a square cap with three corners worn by Roman Catholic clergy.

Birinus *n* **Saint**, also known as Berin or Birin (*d.* 649) Italian bishop, probably born in Lombardy. In 633, sailed from Genoa to preach the Gospel in the parts of Britain it had not yet reached. His feast day is 3 December.

Biro *n* (*trademark*) (*pl* **Biros**) a ball-point pen.

Biro *n* **Laszlo** (1889–1965) Hungarian painter, sculptor and inventor, who developed the first Biro pen.

birr[1] *vi* to make a whirring sound, like that of a spinning wheel. * *n* a whirring sound.

birr[2] *n* the standard monetary unit of Ethiopia and Eritrea, made up of 100 cents.

BIRS *abbr* = British Institute of Recorded Sound.

birth *n* the act of being born; childbirth; the origin of something; lineage, ancestry.

birth canal *n* the passage traveled by the fetus during birth, out of the uterus and through the vagina.

birth certificate *n* an official record of a person's parentage, place and date of birth.

birth control *n* the use of contraceptive drugs or devices to limit reproduction.

birthday *n* the day of birth; the anniversary of the day of birth.

birthday suit *n* (*inf*) a state of nakedness.

birthmark *or* **nevus** *n* an agglomeration of dilated blood vessels that creates a malformation of the skin which can now be treated by laser. *See also* **mole**.

birthplace *n* the place where one is born.

birth rate *n* the number of births per thousand of population per year.

birthright *n* privileges or property that a person is believed entitled to by birth.

birthstone *n* a gem symbolizing the month of one's birth.

Birtwistle *n* **Sir Harrison** (1934–) English composer of operas and symphonies who experimented with electronic music; noted for *The Triumph of Time* (for orchestra), and the operas *Punch and Judy, Gawain, Yan Tan Tethera,* and *The Mask of Orpheus.* He was knighted in 1991.

bis *adj, adv* twice; (*mus*) (*French*) "twice," "again."

bis. *abbr* = bissextile.

BIS *abbr* = Bank for International Settlements; Bird Information Service; British Ichthyological Society; British Interplanetary Society; Bureau of Indian Standards.

biscuit *n* (Brit) a cookie * *adj* pale brown in color.

bise *n* a piercing dry northeast wind prevalent in Switzerland.

bisect *vt* to split into two equal parts; (*geom*) to divide into two equal parts.—**bisection** *n*.

bisector *n* a line bisecting.

bisexual *adj* sexually attracted to both sexes; having the characteristics of both sexes. * *n* a person sexually attracted to both sexes.—**bisexualism, bisexuality** *n*.

BISF *abbr* = British Iron and Steel Federation.

bishop *n* a high-ranking clergyman governing a diocese or church district; a chessman that can move in a diagonal direction.

Bishop *n* 1. **Sir Henry Rowley** (1786–1855) English composer and conductor; the first British musician to be knighted (1842); adapted a number operas for the English stage. Much of his own work is forgotten, save his song *Home, Sweet Home,* a version of which appears in Donizetti's opera *Anna Bolena* (1830). 2. **Isabel** (1902–88) American painter from Ohio, who was prominent during the 1930s as a painter of social realism.

bishopric *n* the office, dignity or jurisdiction of a bishop; a diocese.

Bismarck *n* **Prince Otto von** (1815–98) German statesman. He was prime minister of Prussia (1862–90) and first chancellor of a united Germany.

bismuth *n* one of the elements, a light reddish-colored metal of brittle texture.—**bismuthal, bismuthic** *adj*.

bison *n* (*pl* **bison**) a wild ox of Europe and America.—*also* **buffalo**.

BISP *abbr* = British Institute of Sewage Purification.

BISPA *abbr* = British Independent Steel Producers' Association.

bisque[1] *n* a thick cream soup made from shellfish.

bisque[2] *n* an unglazed white porcelain, used for statuettes, etc, biscuit porcelain.

bisque[3] *n* (*croquet, tennis, golf*) a stroke allowed to an inferior player or side.

bissextile *n* a leap year. * *adj* pertaining to a leap year.

bister *n* a warm brown pigment made from wood soot. * *adj* of this color.—*also* **bistre**.

bistort *n* a herb with twisted roots, snakeweed.

bistoury *n* (*pl* **bistouries**) a surgeon's knife, a scalpel.

bistre, bister *n* (*art*) a warm brown pigment prepared from the soot of wood, esp of the beech.

bistro *n* (*pl* **bistros**) a small restaurant.

bisulcate *adj* having two furrows or grooves; cloven-footed.

bisulfate, bisulphate *n* a salt of sulfuric acid in which half of its hydrogen is replaced by a positive element.

bisulfite, bisulphite *n* a salt of sulfurous acid, half the hydrogen of which is replaced by the base.

BISYNC *abbr* = binary synchronous communications.

bit[1] *n* a small amount or piece; in US, a small coin worth one eighth of a dollar; a small part in a play, film, etc, a bit part.—**a bit** slightly, rather.

bit[2] *n* a metal mouthpiece in a bridle used for controlling a horse; a cutting or boring attachment for use in a brace, drill, etc. * *vt* (**bitting, bitted**) to put a bridle upon; to put the bit in the mouth of.

bit[3] *abbr* (*comput*) = Binary digIT. The smallest unit of information in a digital computer. It has a value of 0 or 1 that represents yes/no and either/or choices. A collection of eight bits is called a byte.

bit[4] *see* **bite**.

bitch *n* a female dog or wolf; (*sl*) a spiteful woman; (*inf*) an unpleasant or difficult situation. * *vi* (*inf*) to grumble; to act spitefully; (*with* **up**) to make a mess of, to ruin.

bite (**biting, bit,** *pp* **bitten**) *vt* to grip or tear with the teeth; to sting or puncture, as an insect; to cause to smart; to take the bait. * *vi* to press or snap the teeth (into, at, etc); (*with* **back**) to stop oneself from saying something offensive, embarrassing, etc. * *n* the act of biting with the teeth; a sting or puncture by an insect.

Bith *n* (*Irish Celtic myth*) Bith was a son of Noah and the father of Cesair. With Fintan and Ladra, he was one of the three men who took part in her invasion of Ireland.

Bithynia *n* an ancient territory in the northwest of Asia Minor, on the Black Sea and Sea of Marmara, at one time an independent kingdom, afterwards a Roman province.—**Bithynian** *adj*.

biting *adj* severe; critical, sarcastic.—**bitingly** *adv*.—**bitingness** *n*.

bitmap *n* (*comput*) a method of storing graphics information in memory in which a bit is devoted to each pixel (picture element) on screen.

bitonality *n* (*mus*) the use of two keys simultaneously.

bit part *n* a small acting role in a play, film, etc.

bits per second *n* (*comput*) a measure of speed of data transmission, esp in connection with the performance of modems. * *abbr* **bps**.

bitt *n* (*usu pl*) (*naut*) a post of wood or iron to which cables are made fast. * *vt* to put round the bitts.

bitter *adj* having an acrid or sharp taste; sorrowful; harsh; resentful; cynical; (*weather*) extremely cold.—**bitterly** *adj*.—**bitterness** *n*.

bitter end *n* final extremity.

bittern[1] *n* a wading bird of the heron family, with a booming cry.

bittern[2] *n* the liquid that remains after cystallization of common salt from sea water or the brine of salt springs.

bitters *npl* liquor in which herbs or roots are steeped.

bittersweet *n* the woody nightshade, the roots and leaves of which when chewed produce first a bitter then a sweet taste; a variety of apple. * *adj* simultaneously sweet and bitter; pleasantly sad.

bitty *adj* (**bittier, bittiest**) small, tiny; made up of scraps of something.

bitumen *n* any of several substances obtained as residue in the distillation of coal tar, petroleum, etc, or occurring naturally as asphalt.—**bituminous** *adj*.

bituminize *vt* to make into or mix with bitumen.—**bituminization** *n*.

bivalent *adj* (*chem*) having a valency of two; (*genetics*) having two homologous chromosomes; (*logic*) having two truth values. * *n* an element, one of the atoms of which can replace two atoms of hydrogen; (*genetics*) a pair of homologous chromosomes.—**bivalency** *n*.

bivalve *n* any mollusk having two valves or shells hinged together, as a clam.—**bivalvular** *adj*.

bivouac *n* a temporary camp, esp one without tents or other cover. * *vi* (**bivouacking, bivouacked**) to spend the night in a bivouac.

biweekly *adj* every two weeks; twice a week. * *n* (*pl* **biweeklies**) a periodical published every two weeks.

BIWS *abbr* = Bureau of International Whaling Statistics.

bizarre *adj* odd, unusual.

Bizet *n* **Georges** (originally **Alexandre César Léopold Bizet**) (1838–75) French composer who is best known for his operas, e.g., *The Pearl Fishers, Ivan the Terrible, Carmen*, and *The Fair Maid of Perth*.

BJ *abbr* = Bachelor of Journalism.

BJA *abbr* = Bureau of Justice Assistance

Bjorn *n* **Acton** (1910–92) founder of Denmark's first industrial design practice in 1949.

BJS *abbr* = Bureau of Justice Statistics

BJuris *abbr* = Bachelor of Jurisprudence.

Bk *symbol* (*chem*) berkelium (element).

bk. *abbr* = bank; block; book.

bkg. *abbr* = banking.

bkpt *abbr* = bankrupt.

bks. *abbr* = banks; books.

BKS *abbr* = barracks.

bkt *abbr* = basket; bracket.

bl *abbr* = bill of lading.

bl. *abbr* = bale; barrel; black.

Bl. *abbr* = The Blessed.

BL, B.L. *abbr* = Bachelor of Laws; Bachelor of Letters; Bachelor of Literature; (*mil*) breech-loading; British Library; Broad Left.

B/L *abbr* = bill of lading.

BLA *abbr* = Bachelor of Liberal Arts; British Legal Association.

blab *vti* (**blabbing, blabbed**) to reveal (a secret); to gossip. * *n* a gossip.—**blabber** *n*.

blabbermouth *n* (*sl*) one who talks indiscreetly and at length.

black *adj* of the darkest color, like coal or soot; having dark-colored skin and hair; without light; dirty; evil, wicked; sad, dismal; sullen; angry; (*coffee, etc*) without cream or milk. * *n* black color; (*often with cap*) a Negro, Australian Aborigine; black clothes, esp when worn in mourning; (*chess, checkers*) black pieces.—**in the black** without debts, in credit. * *vt* to make black; to blacken; (*shoes*) to polish with blacking; to boycott; (*with out*) (*lights*) to extinguish, obliterate; (*broadcast*) to prevent transmission. * *vi* (*with out*) to lose consciousness or vision.—**blackly** *adv*.—**blackness** *n*.

black-and-blue *adj* livid with bruises.

black-and-white *adj* (*film, photography, drawing*) in black and white, not color; (*ideas, etc*) highly simplistic.

black art *n* black magic, witchcraft.

blackball *vt* to ostracize.

black belt *n* a black belt awarded to an expert of the highest skill in judo or karate; a person who holds a black belt.

blackberry *n* (*pl* **blackberries**) a woody bush with thorny stems and berry-like fruit; its black or purple edible fruit (—*also* **bramble**). * *vt* to gather blackberries.

blackbird *n* any of various birds, the male of which is almost all black.

blackboard *n* a black or dark green board written on with chalk.

black body radiation *n* electromagnetic radiation that perfectly absorbs and emits all wavelengths of the electromagnetic spectrum.

black book *n* a record of offenders; **in someone's black books** in disfavor; **little black book** (*sl*) an address book with names and telephone numbers of women.

black box *n* a flight recorder on an aircraft.

black bread *n* rye bread.

black bryony *n* a European climbing plant with small green flowers and poisonous red berries.

blackcap *n* the popular name of several black-crested birds.

blackcock *n* the male of the European black grouse or black game.

black comedy *n* a comedy with a tragic theme.

blackcurrant *n* a Eurasian shrub that produces small edible berries.

Black Death *n* the name given to the bubonic plague that ravaged Europe and Asia in the 14th century.

black dwarf *n* the final stage in stellar evolution, often a white dwarf star that has exhausted all its nuclear fuel.

black economy *n* a form of economic activity that is undisclosed, unrecorded and thus not liable for taxation.

blacken *vt* to make black; to defame.

black eye *n* (*inf*) discoloration around the eye caused by a blow; (*sl*) shame.

blackfish *n* (*pl* **blackfish, blackfishes**) a female salmon immediately after spawning; a common name for several species of British and American fish.

black flag *n* the flag of a pirate with a skull and crossbones emblazoned upon it.

blackfly *n* (*pl* **blackflies**) any of various dark insects, esp a North American fly that sucks the blood of mammals.

black frost *n* a severe frost without a rime that damages vegetation.

black gold *n* crude oil.

blackguard *n* a villain, scoundrel.—**blackguardism** *n*.—**blackguardly** *adj*.

Black Hawk *n* (1767–1838) Native American leader; chief of the Sauk people in Illinois. He led his people in the Black Hawk War (1832) against federal troops and was defeated at Bad Axe River.

blackhead *n* a small spot or pimple clogging a pore in the skin.

black-hearted *adj* evil or wicked.

black hole *n* (*astron*) a region in space from which no material or light escapes due to its enormous gravitational force; hypothetical, invisible region in space.

black humor *n* a humor of the morbid and the absurd.

black ice *n* a thin transparent coating of ice on roads or other surfaces.

blacking *n* black shoe polish.

blackish *adj* rather black.—**blackishly** *adv*.—**blackishness** *n*.

blackjack[1] *n* a gambling game with cards in which players try to obtain points better than the banker's but not more than 21.—*also* **pontoon, twenty-one, vingt-et-un**.

blackjack[2] *n* a large leather vessel or drinking cup; a short leather club with a flexible handle. * *vt* to hit with a blackjack.

blackjack oak *n* a dark shrubby oak of North America.

black knight *n* (*business*) an individual or company that makes an unwelcome or hostile takeover bid for a company. *See* white knight.

black lead *n* plumbago, graphite.

blackleg *n* a person who takes a striker's place, a scab; a person who endeavors to obtain money by cheating at races or cards, a rook; a disease affecting sheep and cattle. * *vti* (**blacklegging, blacklegged**) to act or injure, as a blackleg.

black letter *n* the old English or Gothic type used in early manuscripts and the first printed books. * *adj* written or printed in black letter.

blacklist *n* a list of those censored, refused employment, regarded as suspicious politically or generally not to be trusted. * *vt* to put on such a list.

black lung *n* a disease of chronic inflammation of the lung, often suffered by coal miners.

black magic *n* sorcery, witchcraft.

blackmail *vt* to extort money by threatening to disclose discreditable facts. * *n* the crime of blackmailing.—**blackmailer** *n*.

Black Maria *n* a prison van, a patrol wagon.

black market *n* the illegal buying and selling of goods, esp banned goods, e.g., drugs, or when rationing is in force.—**black marketeer, black marketer** *n*.

black mass *n* a travesty of the Mass used by Satanists.

Black *n* **Misha** (1910–77) British industrial and exhibit designer who founded the first multi-skilled design group in Britain with Milner **Gray**.

Blackmore *n* **R[ichard] D[oddridge]** (1825–1900) English poet and novelist whose classic novel *Lorna Doone* is a tale of love, outlawry and feuding set in 17th-century Exmoor.

blackout *n* the darkness when all lights are switched off; temporary loss of consciousness or electricity; a breakdown of communications between a spacecraft and ground control; a closing down of radio or TV broadcasting due to strike action or government ban.

black power *n* a movement of black people whose goal is political, social and economic equality with whites.

black pudding *n* a dark (blood) sausage with a large proportion of blood.

Black Rod *n* in UK, the usher belonging to the Order of the Garter and the House of Lords, so called from the black rod of the office.

Black Sea *n* a sea situated between Europe and Asia and connected with the Mediterranean by the Bosphorus, Sea of Marmara, and Hellespont.

black sheep *n* a person regarded as disreputable or a disgrace by their family.

Blackshirt *n* a fascist, esp a member of Mussolini's Italian Fascist party.

blacksmith *n* a metal worker, esp one who shoes horses.

black spot *n* an area where traffic accidents frequently happen; a difficult or dangerous place; a disease affecting leaves, esp of roses.

blackstrap (molasses) *n* a very dark and thick molasses.

black tea *n* a dark tea, the leaf of which is completely fermented or oxidized before drying.

blackthorn *n* the sloe; a walking stick cut from the stem of the sloe.

black tie *n* semi-formal evening wear.

blackwater fever *n* a severe and sometimes fatal form of malaria.

black widow *n* a poisonous spider found in America, the female of which devours its mate.

bladder *n* a sac of fibrous and muscular tissue that contains secretions and can increase and decrease in capacity, esp one that holds urine flowing from the kidneys; any inflatable bag. *See also* **gall bladder**.

bladderwort *n* any of a genus of water plants, some of which trap insects.

bladderwrack *n* a type of seaweed with trailing fronds containing small air bladders.

blade *n* the cutting edge of a tool or knife; the broad, flat surface of a leaf; a straight, narrow leaf of grass; the flat part of an oar or paddle; the runner of an ice skate; (*archeo*) a long, narrow flake of flint or chert that was struck from a larger worked core of rock.—**bladed** *adj*.

blah[1] *n* (*sl*) nonsense, exaggeration; a blunder.

blah[2] *adj* (*sl*) boring; mediocre.

Blaich *n* Robert (1931–) influential American industrial designer.

blain *n* an inflamed sore, a blister.

Blair *n* Tony [Anthony] (1953–) English Labour statesman who became British prime minister in 1997 after leading the Labour Party to its first election victory since 1974.

BLAISE *abbr* = British Library Automated Information Service.

Blake *n* William (1757–1827) English poet and artist in the Romantic tradition who published his own poems with handwritten text and drawings. The great feature of his work is the power of his visionary imagination. His notable works include *Songs of Innocence*, *Songs of Experience*, *The Marriage of Heaven and Hell*, and *Jerusalem*.

Blakelock *n* Ralph Albert (1847–1919) American self-taught painter. Representative works include *Indian Encampment and Pipe Dance* (1872) and *Moonlight Sonata* (1892).

blame *vt* to hold responsible for; to accuse. * *n* responsibility for an error; reproof.—**blamable, blameable** *adj*.

blameful *adj* meriting blame; guilty.—**blamefully** *adv*.—**blamefulness** *n*.

blameless *adj* innocent; free from blame.—**blamelessly** *adv*.—**blamelessness** *n*.

blameworthy *adj* deserving blame.—**blameworthiness** *n*.

blanch *vt* to whiten or bleach; to make pale; (*vegetables, almonds, etc*) to scald. * *vi* to turn pale.

blanche *n* (*mus*) (*French*) literally "white"; the French word for a minim.

blancmange *n* a dessert made from gelatinous or starchy ingredients (as cornflour) and milk.

bland *adj* mild; gentle; insipid.—**blandly** *adv*.—**blandness** *n*.

blandish *vti* to flatter in order to coax; to cajole.

blandishment *n* (*usu pl*) a winning expression or action, an artful caress, cajolery.

blank[1] *adj* (*paper*) bearing no writing or marks; vacant; (*mind*) empty of thought; (*look*) without expression; (*denial, refusal*) utter, complete; (*check*) signed but with no amount written in. * *n* an empty space, esp one to be filled out on a printed form; an empty place or time.—**blankly** *adv*.—**blankness** *n*.

blank[2] *n* a powder-filled cartridge without a bullet.

blank check, blank cheque *n* a signed check with the amount left blank to be filled by the payee; complete freedom of action.

blanket *n* a large, soft piece of cloth used for warmth, esp as a bed cover; (*of snow, smoke*) a cover or layer. * *adj* applying to a wide variety of cases or situations. * *vt* to cover.

blanket bog *n* a continuous covering of peat bog formed where there is high rainfall and acid soil.

blank verse unrhymed verse in iambic pentameters, i.e., a line of verse with five short-long "feet" that reached its highest peak in Shakespeare's great plays.

blare *vti* to sound harshly or loudly. * *n* a loud, harsh sound.

blarney *n* wheedling talk, flattery. * *vt* (**blarneying, blarneyed**) to influence or talk over by soft wheedling speeches; to humbug with flattery.

Blarney Stone *n* a stone in the wall of Blarney Castle, Cork, on kissing which a person is said to become an adept in flattery.

blasé *adj* bored, indifferent; sated with pleasure.

Blasius *n* Saint, also called **Blaise** (*d.* 316) Armenian physician and bishop of Sebaste. Persecuted for his beliefs, he had the flesh torn from his back with metal hooks. Finally, along with his two children, he was beheaded. His feast day is 3 February.

blaspheme *vt* to speak irreverently of (God, a divine being or sacred things). * *vi* to utter blasphemy.—**blasphemer** *n*.

blasphemous *adj* impious, grossly insulting (to God, etc).

blasphemy *n* (*pl* **blasphemies**) impious speaking; speaking irreverently of God, a divine being or sacred things.

blast *n* a sharp gust of air; the sound of a horn; an explosion; an outburst of criticism. * *vt* to wither; to blow up, explode; to criticize sharply. * *vi* to make a loud, harsh sound; to set off explosives, etc; (*with* **off**) to be launched.

blasted *adj* withered; (*inf*) damned.

blastema *n* (*pl* **blastemas, blastemata**) (*biol*) the point of growth of an organ as yet unformed, from which it is developed.—**blastemal, blastemic, blastematic** *adj*.

blast furnace *n* a smelting furnace using compressed air.

blasto- *prefix* bud; germination.

blastoderm *n* a layer of embryonic cells in an egg from which an organism is formed.—**blastodermic** *adj*.

blastoff *n* the launch of a space vehicle or rocket; the time when this takes place.

blastogenesis *n* reproduction by budding.—**blastogenic, blastogenetic** *adj*.

blatant *adj* noisy; glaringly conspicuous.—**blatancy** *n*.—**blatantly** *adv*.

blather *see* **blether**.

blatherskite *n* a blethering or blustering person.

BLAVA *abbr* = British Laboratory Animals Veterinary Association.

blaze[1] *n* an intensive fire; a bright light; splendor; an outburst (of emotion). * *vi* to burn brightly; to shine with a brilliant light; to be excited, as with anger.

blaze[2] *n* a white mark on the face of a horse or other quadruped; a white mark cut on a tree to serve as a guide. * *vt* to mark, as trees, by removing a portion of the bark; to indicate, as a path or boundary, by blazing trees; **blaze a trail** to act as a pioneer.

blaze[3] *vt* to proclaim, to publish widely.

blazer *n* a lightweight jacket, often in a bright color representing membership of a sports club, school, etc.

blazon *vt* to proclaim publicly; to adorn; to describe (heraldic or armorial bearings) in technical terms. * *n* the terminology of coats of arms.—**blazoner** *n*.—**blazonment** *n*.

blazonry *n* (*pl* **blazonries**) a heraldic device; the art of describing and explaining coats of arms; decoration, as with heraldic devices; a bright display.

BLBEG *abbr* = British Lawn Bowls Export Group.

BLBSD *abbr* = British Library, Bibliographic Services Division.

BLD *abbr* = Bachelor of Landscape Design.

bldg. or **blg.** *abbr* = building.

bldr. *abbr* = builder.

BLDSC *abbr* = British Library Document Supply Centre.

BLE *abbr* = Bachelor of Land Economy.

bleach *vti* to make or become white or colorless. * *n* a substance for bleaching.—**bleachable** *adj*.—**bleacher** *n*.

bleachers *npl* the unroofed seats at a baseball field or sports ground.

bleaching powder *n* a white powder, chloride of lime, used for bleaching.

bleak[1] *adj* cold; exposed; bare; harsh; gloomy; not hopeful.—**bleakly** *adv*.—**bleakness** *n*.

bleak[2] *n* (*pl* **bleak, bleaks**) a small European river fish with brilliant silvery scales.

blear *adj* (*eyes*) sore or dim with inflammation. * *vt* to make (eyes) sore or watery; to dim or blur.

bleary *adj* (**blearier, bleariest**) (*eyesight*) dim with water or tears; obscure, indistinct.—**blearily** *adv*.—**bleariness** *n*.

bleary-eyed *adj* with eyes dulled by tears or tiredness; dull.

bleat *vi* to cry as a sheep, goat or calf; to complain. * *n* a bleating cry or sound.—**bleater** *n*.—**bleatingly** *adv*.

bleb *n* a small blister; a bubble in water or glass.

Bleddyn *n* (*Welsh Celtic myth*) Bleddyn was the son of the brothers Gwydion fab Don and Gilfaethway and the brother of Hydwyn and Hwychdwn. Born in the shape of a wolf

bleed *vb* (**bleeding, bled**) *vi* to lose blood; to ooze sap, color or dye; to die for a country or an ideal; to sympathize (often ironically). * *vt* to remove blood or sap from; (*inf*) to extort money or goods from.

bleeder *n* one who bleeds, esp blood from another; (*inf*) a person with hemophilia; (*sl*) an annoying person.

bleeding-heart *n* a pink-flowered plant; an excessively sympathetic person.

bleep *vi* to emit a high-pitched sound or signal (e.g., a car alarm). * *n* a small portable electronic radio receiver that emits a bleep to convey a message.—*also* **bleeper**.

blemish *n* a flaw or defect, as a spot. * *vt* to mar; to spoil.

Blemmyes *n* (*Egypt*) a southern desert people, a source of troops for Old Kingdom rulers.

blench *vi* to flinch; to blanch.

blend *vt* (*varieties of tea, etc*) to mix or mingle; to mix so that the components cannot be distinguished. * *vi* to mix, merge; to shade gradually into each other, as colors; to harmonize. * *n* a mixture.

blende *n* any of various minerals composed mainly of metallic sulfides; a yellow to brownish-black zinc ore, sphalerite.

blended whiskey *n* a whiskey made from a blend of straight whiskeys, or whiskeys and neutral spirits.

blender *n* something or someone that blends; an electrical device for preparing food.—*also* **liquidizer**.

blenny *n* (*pl* **blennies, blenny**) a small elongated spiny-finned sea fish.

blepharitis *n* inflammation of the eyelids.—**blepharitic** *adj*.

Blériot *n* Louis (1872–1936) French aviator and aeronautical engineer who made the first flight across the English Channel in one of his monoplanes in 1909.

blesbok *n* (*pl* **blesboks, blesbok**) a South African white-faced antelope.

BLESMA *abbr* = British Limbless Ex-Servicemen's Association.

bless *vt* (**blessing, blessed** *or* **blest**) to consecrate; to praise; to call upon God's protection; to grant happiness; to make the sign of the cross over.

blessed *adj* holy, sacred; fortunate; blissful; beatified.—**blessedly** *adv*.—**blessedness** *n*.

blessing *n* a prayer or wish for success or happiness; a cause of happiness; good wishes or approval; a grace said before or after eating.

blest *see* **bless**.

blet *n* a decayed spot in fruit.

blether *vi* (*inf*) to talk foolishly. * *n* (*inf*) foolish talk; one who talks it.—*also* **blather**.

blew *see* **blow²**.

BLHSS *abbr* = British Library, Humanities and Social Sciences.

BLI *abbr* = Bachelor of Literary Interpretation.

BLib *abbr* = Bachelor of Librarianship.

BLibSc *abbr* = Bachelor of Library Science.

blight *n* any insect, disease, etc that destroys plants; anything that prevents growth or destroys; someone or something that spoils. * *vt* to destroy; to frustrate.

blimp *n* a small, nonrigid airship; any airship; a soundproof cover for a camera.

blind *adj* sightless; unable to discern or understand; not directed by reason; (*exit*) hidden, concealed; closed at one end. * *n* something that deceives; a shade for a window; (*sl*) a drinking bout. * *vti* to make sightless, to deprive of insight; to dazzle (with facts, a bright light, etc); to deceive.—**blindly** *adv*.—**blindness** *n*.

blind alley *n* a street closed at one end; an occupation or inquiry that leads to nothing.

blind date *n* a date between two individuals who have never met before; either individual on a blind date.

blinder *n* a horse's blinkers.

blindfish *n* (*pl* **blindfish, blindfishes**) a diminutive fish of a pale color and with rudimentary eyes, which inhabits underground waters.

blindfold *n* a cloth or bandage used to cover the eyes. * *adj* having the eyes covered, so as not to see; reckless. * *vt* to cover the eyes with a strip of cloth, etc; to hamper sight or understanding; to mislead.

blind man's buff *n* a game in which a blindfold person tries to catch and identify others.

blindness *n* the inability to see.

blind spot *n* a point on the retina of the eye that is insensitive to light; a place where vision is obscured; a subject on which someone is ignorant.

blindstory, blindstorey *n* (*pl* **blindstories, blindstoreys**) (*archit*) the storey below the clerestory, admitting no light.

blind tracery *n* (*archit*) the tracery work on wood panels or walls, characteristic of Gothic architecture.

blind valley *n* a steep-sided valley with a cliff across the lower end.

blind window *n* (*archit*) a false window where there is no opening.

blindworm *n* the slowworm, a small, slender limbless lizard with very small eyes.

BLing *abbr* = Bachelor of Linguistics.

blini, blinis *npl* (*sing* **blin**) buckwheat pancakes.

blink *vi* to open and close the eyes rapidly; (*light*) to flash on and off; (*with* at) to ignore. * *vt* (*with* at) to be amazed or surprised. * *n* a glance, a glimpse; a momentary flash.

blinker *n* one who blinks; that which obscures the sight or mental perception; (*pl*) a screen for a horse's eye, to prevent it from seeing sideways; (*sl*) the eyes.

blip *n* a trace on a radar screen; a recurring sound; a temporary setback. * *vi* (**blipping, blipped**) to make a blip.

bliss *n* supreme happiness; spiritual joy.—**blissful** *adj*.—**blissfully** *adv*.

Bliss *n* **Sir Arthur** (1891–1975) English composer noted for *The Olympians* (opera), *Checkmate* and *Miracle of the Gorbals* (ballets), as well as *Rout* (a piece for soprano and ten instruments). He also wrote music for films, including H G Wells's *Things to Come* and *Men of Two Worlds*.

blister *n* a raised patch on the skin, containing water, as caused by burning or rubbing; a raised bubble on any other surface. * *vti* to cause or form blisters; to lash with words.

blistering *adj* (*criticism*) scornful, cruel.

BLit(t) *abbr* = Baccalaureus Lit(t)erarum (*Latin*, Bachelor of Literature, *or of* Letters).

blithe *adj* happy, cheerful, gay.—**blithely** *adv*.—**blitheness** *n*.

blithering *adj* (*inf*) stupid, idiotic.

blithesome *adj* blithe, merry.—**blithesomely** *adv*.—**blithesomeness** *n*.

blitz *n* heavy aerial bombing; any sudden destructive attack; a determined effort. * *vt* to subject to a blitz.

blitzkrieg *n* warfare in which blitz is employed; any swift combined action.

blizzard *n* a severe storm of wind and snow, which may lead to a white-out.

blk. *abbr* = black; block.

BLL *abbr* = Baccalaureus Legum (*Latin*, Bachelor of Laws).

BLLD *abbr* = British Library, Lending Division.

BLM *abbr* = Bureau of Land Management

BLNL *abbr* = British Library Newspaper Library.

bloat *vti* to swell as with water or air; to puff up, as with pride; to cure or dry (fish) in smoke.—**bloated** *adj*.

bloater *n* a herring or mackerel smoked and partially dried, but not split open.

blob *n* a drop of liquid; a round spot (of color, etc).

bloc *n* a group of parties, nations, etc united to achieve a common purpose.

Bloch *n* **Ernest** (1880–1959) American composer, born in Geneva, Switzerland. His music is noted for being Jewish in character, e.g., *Hakdesh*, and his *Israel Symphony*, *American Symphony*, and *Schelomo*. He also wrote music for piano, strings, a violin concerto, and an opera, *Macbeth*.

block *n* a solid piece of stone or wood, etc; a piece of wood used as a base (for chopping, etc); a group or row of buildings; a number of things as a unit; the main body of an internal combustion engine; a building divided into offices; an obstruction; a child's building brick; (*sl*) the head. * *vt* to impede or obstruct; to shape; (*often with* out) to sketch roughly. * *vi* to obstruct an opponent in sports.—**blocker** *n*. * *n, vt* (*comput*) a selection of information that can be dealt with by one series of commands.

blockade *n* (*mil*) the obstruction of an enemy seaport by warships; any strategic barrier. * *vt* to obstruct in this way.—**blockader** *n*.

blockage *n* an obstruction.

blockbuster *n* (*sl*) a very heavy bomb of great penetrative power; a conspicuously powerful or effective person or thing; one who engages in blockbusting.

blockbusting *n* the practice of persuading house owners to sell their houses quickly by convincing them that property values will drop.

block chords *n* (*mus*) a harmonic procedure in which the notes of chords are moved simultaneously in "blocks."

blocked account *n* a bank account from which money may not be withdrawn, even when this is not overdrawn.

blocked currency *n* a currency that, because of strict exchange controls, cannot be removed from a country and is not freely convertible into other currencies.

blockhead *n* a dolt, a stupid person.

blockhouse *n* a small fort, usu of timber; a log house; a concrete fortification with loopholes for observation or firing from.

blocking course *n* (*archit*) a plain course of stone or brick above a classical cornice on the top of a building; a projecting course at the base of a building.

block letter *n* a handwritten capital letter similar to a printed letter.

block vote *n* at a conference, a total vote represented by one delegate.

Blodeuwedd *n* (*Welsh Celtic myth*) a beautiful maiden whose name translates as "flower face." She was created out of oak, broom and meadowsweet by Gwydion and Math to be the bride of Lleu Llaw Gyffes.

bloke *n* (*Brit, inf*) a man.

Blomdahl *n* **Karl-Birger** (1916–68) Swedish composer who wrote three symphonies and the opera, *Aniara* (1959), which is set on a spaceship and contains electronic effects.

blond, blonde *adj* having light-colored hair and skin; light-colored. * *n* a blond person.—**blondness, blondeness** *n*.

blonde lace *n* a silk lace.

blood *n* a suspension of red blood cells (or corpuscles) called erythrocytes, white blood cells (leucocytes), and platelets (small disc-shaped cells involved in blood clotting) in a liquid medium, blood plasma. It circulates around the body in arteries and veins and transports many substances, including oxygen; the sap of a plant; the essence of life; kinship; descent; hatred; anger; bloodshed; guilt of murder.

blood-and-thunder *adj* melodramatic. * *n* a sensational story or play.

blood bank *n* a place where blood is taken from blood donors and stored.

blood bath *n* a massacre.

blood brother *n* one of two men or boys pledged to treat the other as a brother, as confirmed by the ceremonial mingling of blood.

blood cell *n* a red or white cell present in the blood.

blood clot *n* a hard mass of blood platelets formed after tissue damage, trapped red blood cells, and fibrin.

blood clotting *n* a process that stops blood from leaking out of an area of injured tissue.

blood count, complete blood count (CBC) *n* the determination of the numbers of red and white corpuscles in a sample of blood.

bloodcurdling *adj* exciting terror, horrifying, chilling.

blood donor *n* a person who donates his or her blood for transfusion.

blooded *adj* having a specific kind of blood (*hot-blooded*); of fine breed; initiated.

blood feud *n* a long-lasting dispute, usu between or within families.

blood group *n* the classification of four main groups of human blood based on the compatibility of antigens on the surface of the red blood cells (corpuscles). This gives rise to four groups: group O; group A; group B; both A and B (hence blood group AB). —*also* **blood type**.

blood grouping *n* a method for classifying blood types by checking which particular antigens are present on the surface of red blood cells.

blood heat *n* the normal heat of the human blood in health (37˚C, 98.4˚F).

bloodhound *n* a large breed of hound used for tracking; a detective.

bloodless *adj* without blood or slaughter; unfeeling.—**bloodlessly** *adv*.—**bloodlessness** *n*.

bloodletting *n* phlebotomy; bloodshed, e.g., a massacre.

blood line *n* a pedigree; a line of descent of a family group through the generations.

blood money *n* money obtained at the cost of another's life; the reward paid for the discovery or capture of a murderer; compensation paid to the next of kin of a person slain by another.

blood plasma *n* blood from which all the blood cells have been removed.

blood poisoning *n* septicemia.

blood pressure *n* the pressure of the blood on the heart and blood vessels in the system of circulation.

blood pudding *n* blood sausage.

blood-red *adj* red as blood.

blood relation, blood relative *n* a person related by descent, not marriage.

blood sausage *n* a dark sausage with a large proportion of blood.

blood serum *n* plasma from which one of the proteins, called fibrinogen, has been removed.

bloodshed *n* killing.

bloodshot *adj* (*eye*) suffused with blood, red and inflamed.

blood sport *n* any sport in which an animal is hunted and killed.

bloodstain *n* a stain made by blood.

bloodstained *adj* stained with blood; responsible for killing.

bloodstock *n* thoroughbred horses collectively.

bloodstone *n* a dark green quartz flecked with red jasper; heliotrope.

bloodstream *n* the flow of blood through the blood vessels in the human body.

bloodsucker *n* an animal that sucks blood, a leech; a person who sponges or preys on another, an extortionist.—**bloodsucking** *adj, n.*

blood sugar *n* glucose concentration in the blood. *See also* **hypoglycemia; hyperglycemia**.

blood test *n* an examination of a blood specimen to ascertain blood group, alcohol intake, etc.

bloodthirsty *adj* (**bloodthirstier, bloodthirstiest**) eager for blood, cruel, warlike.—**bloodthirstiness** *n.*

blood transfusion *n* the replacement of blood lost because of injury, surgery, etc. Blood from donors is matched to the recipient for blood group and hemoglobin.

blood type *see* **blood group**.

blood vessel *n* the veins and arteries and their smaller branchings (venules and arterioles) through which blood is carried to and from the heart.

bloody *adj* (**bloodier, bloodiest**) stained with or covered in blood; bloodthirsty; cruel, murderous; (*sl*) as an intensifier (*a bloody good hiding*). * *vt* (**bloodying, bloodied**) to cover with blood.—**bloodily** *adv.*—**bloodiness** *n.*

Bloody Mary *n* (*pl* **Bloody Marys**) a drink made with vodka and tomato juice.

bloody-minded *adj* (*inf*) deliberately obstructive.—**bloody-mindedness** *n.*

bloom¹ *n* a flower or blossom; the period of being in flower; a period of most health, vigor, etc; a youthful, healthy glow; the powdery coating on some fruit and leaves. * *vi* to blossom; to be in one's prime; to glow with health etc.

bloom² *n* a rough mass of incandescent iron for hammering or rolling into bars. * *vt* to make (iron) into bloom.

bloomer¹ *n* a plant that flowers.

bloomer² *n* (*Brit, inf*) a stupid mistake;

bloomer³ *n* (*Brit*) a medium-sized loaf with a glazed surface.

bloomers *npl* (*inf*) women's long loose underpants.

blooming *adj* blossoming, flowering; flourishing; (*sl*) confounded, bloody.—**bloomingly** *adv.*

Bloomsbury Group *n* a group of writers and artists, of whom the most important was Virginia Woolf who lived and worked in the Bloomsbury area of London in the early 20th century.

blooper *n* (*inf*) a blunder; (*baseball*) a ball that falls just beyond the infield for a hit.

blossom *n* a flower, esp one that produces edible fruit; a state or time of flowering. * *vi* to flower; to begin to develop.—**blossomy** *adj.*

blot *n* a spot or stain, esp of ink; something that diminishes or spoils the beauty of; a blemish in reputation. * *vt* (**blotting, blotted**) to spot or stain; to obscure; to disgrace; to absorb with blotting paper.

blotch *n* a spot or discoloration on the skin; any large blot or stain. * *vt* to cover with blotches.—**blotched** *adj.*—**blotchily** *adv.*—**blotchy** *adj.*

blotter *n* a piece of blotting paper.

blotting paper *n* absorbent paper used to dry freshly written ink.

blotto *adj* (*sl*) very drunk.

blouse *n* a shirt-like garment worn by women.

blow¹ *n* a hard hit, as with the fist; a sudden attack; a sudden misfortune; a setback.

blow² *vb* (**blowing, blew**, *pp* **blown**) *vi* to cause a current of air; to be moved or carried (by air, the wind, etc); (*mus*) to make a sound by forcing in air with the mouth; (*often with* **out**) to burst suddenly; to breathe hard; (*with* **out**) to become extinguished by a gust of air; (*gas or oil well*) to erupt out of control; (*with* **over**) to pass without consequence. * *vt* to move along with a current of air; to make a sound by blowing; to inflate with air; (*a fuse, etc*) to melt; (*inf*) to spend (money) freely; (*sl*) to leave; (*sl*) to divulge a secret; (*sl*) to bungle; (*often with* **up**) to burst by an explosion; (*with* **out**) to extinguish by a gust; (*storm*) to dissipate (itself) by blowing; (*with* **over**) to pass over or pass by; (*with* **up**) to enlarge a photograph; (*with* **up**) (*inf*) to lose one's temper.

blow³ *vi* (**blowing, blew**, *pp* **blown**) to blossom, to flower. * *n* a mass of blossom; the state or condition of flowering.

blow-by-blow *adj* told or shown in great detail.

blow-dry *vi* (**blow-drying, blow-dried**) to style recently washed hair with a hand-held drier.

blower *n* one who blows; a braggart; a device for producing a stream of gas or air.

blowfly *n* (*pl* **blowflies**) a fly that lays its eggs in rotting meat.

blowhole *n* a nostril of a whale; a vent for the escape of gas, air, etc; a hole in ice used for breathing by whales, seals, etc; a hole of gas in metal capturing during the solidifying process.

blow job *n* (*sl*) fellatio.

Blow *n* **John** (1649–1708) English composer and organist at Westminster Abbey and at the chapel royal, where he was also appointed composer. He wrote numerous anthems and songs, and the masque, *Venus and Adonis*.

blowlamp, blowtorch *n* a gas-powered torch that produces a hot flame for welding, etc.

blown *adj* swollen or bloated.

blowout¹ *n* (*inf*) a festive social event; a bursting of a container (as a tire) by pressure on a weak spot; an uncontrolled eruption of a gas or oil well.

blowout² *n* (*geog*) a deflation hollow in sand dunes that lacks vegetation cover, caused by wind erosion.

blowpipe *n* a tube through which a current of air or gas is driven upon a flame to concentrate its heat on a substance, e.g., glass, to fuse it; a long tube of cane or reed used to discharge arrows by the force of the breath.

blowup *n* an explosion; an enlarged photograph; (*sl*) an angry outburst.

blowy *adj* (**blowier, blowiest**) breezy, windy.

blowzy, blowsy *adj* (**blowzier, blowziest** *or* **blowsier, blowsiest**) (*esp a woman*) fat and ruddy, slatternly.—**blowzily, blowsily** *adv.*—**blowziness, blowziness** *n.*

BLR *abbr* = breech-loading rifle; breech-loading rifled (gun).

BLRD *abbr* = British Library, Reference Division.

bls. *abbr* = bales; barrels.

BLS *abbr* = Bachelor of Library Studies; Bachelor of Library Science; Bureau of Labor Statistics.

blubber¹ *vi* to weep loudly.

blubber² *n* whale fat; excessive fat on the body.

bludgeon *n* a short, heavy stick used for striking. * *vti* to strike with a bludgeon; to bully or coerce.

blue *adj* (**bluer, bluest**) of the color of the clear sky; depressed; (*film*) indecent, obscene. * *n* the color of the spectrum lying between green and violet; (*with* **the**) the sky, the sea; (*pl: with* **the**) (*inf*) a depressed feeling; (*pl: with* **the**) a style of vocal and instrumental jazz. * *vt* (**blueing** *or* **bluing, blued**) to make or dye blue; to dip in blue liquid; (*sl*) to squander.

blue baby *n* the condition in a newborn infant causing a blueness of the skin. Deoxygenated blood does not go through the lungs to be oxygenated but is pumped around the body because of a congenital malformation of the heart.

blue-band *n* a band of bluer ice in a glacier, caused by being bubble-free and denser than the surrounding ice.

bluebell *n* any of several plants with a one-sided cluster of blue bell-shaped flowers.

blueberry *n* (*pl* **blueberries**) the edible blue or blackish berry of any of several plants of the heath family; a shrub, e.g., the huckleberry, producing these berries.

bluebird *n* any of various small songbirds prevalent in North America.

blue blood *n* royal or aristocratic descent.

bluebonnet *n* a Scottish cap of blue cloth; a name given to the Scottish troops before the Union, 1707; a Scotsman.

blue book *n* a governmental official report, etc, bound in blue paper covers; a directory of socially prominent persons; a booklet in which students answer examination questions.

bluebottle *n* a large fly; (*inf*) a policeman.

blue cheese *n* cheese with veins of blue mold.

blue chip *adj* (*stocks, shares*) providing a reliable return.

blue-chip company *n* a company with considerable assets and a well-established reputation.

blue-collar worker *n* a manual worker, so called because of the blue overalls worn by manual workers in factories, etc. *See* white-collar worker.

blue devils *npl* low spirits; mental depression; delirium tremens.

bluegrass *n* any of several rich pasture grasses with bluish green blades, esp in Kentucky; (*mus*) a type of folk music originally from Kentucky, USA. *See* Country and Western.

blue gum *n* a lofty eucalyptus tree of Australia, valuable for its timber and essential oil.

blueing *n* the process of imparting a blue tint; the indigo, etc, used by washerwomen.—*also* **bluing**.

bluejacket *n* a seaman in the US or UK navy.

blue jay, bluejay *n* a North American jay with a blue crested head.

blue jeans *npl* blue denim pants.

blue mold *n* a minute fungus that attacks bread and other foodstuffs.

Blue Nile n (*Egypt*) the right-hand branch (looking north) of the Nile, which rises in the mountains of Ethiopia and joins the White Nile at Khartoum.

bluenose n a puritanical person; a prude; a Nova Scotian.

blue note n (*mus*) a note in jazz, usu the third or seventh, played slightly flat.

blue peter n a small blue flag with a white square in the center, hoisted when a ship is about to sail.

blueprint n a blue photographic print of plans; a detailed scheme, template of work to be done; basis or prototype for future development.

blue ribbon n in UK, the broad ribbon of a dark blue color worn by members of the Order of the Garter; a prized distinction; a mark of success; a thin blue strip worn as a badge of teetotalism.

blue rinse n a rinse giving a blue tint to gray hair. * *adj* (*inf*) describing mature, assured, social women and their background.

blues npl (*used as sing or pl*) depression, melancholy; (*mus*) a 20th-century Black American song or lamentation following a simple form of twelve bars to each verse. Blues music formed the basis for jazz; musicians favored such instruments as the guitar and harmonica.

bluestocking n a woman of literary tastes or occupation; a member of small, mostly female groups in English 18th-century social life who held informal discussion groups on literary and scholarly matters.

bluestone n a gray sandstone used for building, etc; copper sulfate in crystalline form.

blue whale n a rorqual, the largest mammal known.

bluey n (*Austral*) a bushman's bundle.

bluff[1] *adj* rough in manner; abrupt, outspoken; * n a broad, steep bank or cliff.—**bluffness** n.

bluff[2] *vti* to mislead or frighten by a false, bold front.* n deliberate deception.—**bluffer** n.

bluing *see* blueing.

Blum n **Léon** (1872–1950) French statesman; the first socialist and Jewish prime minister of France (1936–37, 1938, 1946–47).

Blumberg n **Baruch Samuel** (1925–) American biochemist and winner of the 1976 Nobel prize for physiology or medicine. He introduced a vaccine for hepatitis B (1969).

Blume n **Peter** (1906–92) Russian-born American painter. His work is concerned with the communication of ideas through storytelling. His most famous work is *The Eternal City* (1934–7), a satirical attack on the Fascist movement.

blunder *vi* to make a foolish mistake; to move about clumsily. * n a foolish mistake.—**blunderer** n.—**blundering** *adj*.—**blunderingly** *adv*.

blunderbuss n (*hist*) a short gun or firearm with a wide bore, firing many balls; a clumsy person.

blunge *vt* (*pottery*) to mix clay with water.

blunt *adj* not having a sharp edge or point; rude, outspoken, unsubtle. * *vti* to make or become dull.—**bluntly** *adv*.—**bluntness** n.

Blunt n 1. **Anthony [Frederick]** (1907–83) English art historian who was disgraced in 1979 following the revelation that he had been a Soviet spy. 2. **Wilfrid Scawen** (1840–1922) English poet and traveler whose verse collections, e.g., *In Vinculus*, reflect his two main interests, women and politics.

blur n a stain, smear; an ill-defined impression. * *vti* (**blurring, blurred**) to smear; to make or become indistinct in shape, etc; to dim.—**blurred** *adj*.—**blurredly** *adv*.—**blurry** *adj*.

blurb n a promotional description, as on a book cover; an exaggerated advertisement.

blurt *vt* (*with* out) to utter impulsively.

blush n a red flush of the face caused by embarrassment or guilt; any rosy color. * *vi* (*with* for, at) to show embarrassment, modesty, joy, etc involuntarily, by blushing; to become rosy.

blusher n a cosmetic that gives color to the cheeks.

blush wine n rosé wine, a blend of red and white wines.

bluster *vi* to make a noise like the wind; to bully. * n a blast, as of the wind; bullying or boastful talk, often to hide shame or embarrassment.—**blusterer** n.—**blustery** *adj*.—**blusteringly, blusterously** *adv*.

Blvd, blvd. *abbr* = Boulevard.

Blyton n **Enid [Mary]** (1897–1968) English children's writer; creator of Noddy and Big Ears and *The Famous Five* books

memory"; British Museum; bench mark.

BM *abbr* = Baccalaureus Medicinae (*Latin*, Bachelor of Medicine); Baccalaureus Musicae (*Latin*, Bachelor of Music); Beata Maria (*Latin*, the blessed Mary); bishop and martyr; British Museum; bench mark.

BM, BCh *abbr* = conjoint degree of Bachelor of Medicine, Bachelor of Surgery.

BM, BS *abbr* = conjoint degree of Bachelor of Medicine, Bachelor of Surgery.

BMA *abbr* = Baby Milk Action; Blanket Manufacturers' Association; British Medical Association; British Midland Airways.

BMAA *abbr* = British Marine Aquarists Association; British Microlight Aircraft Association.

BMath *abbr* = Bachelor of Mathematics.

BMC *abbr* = British Medical Council.

BMDO *abbr* = Ballistic Missile Defense Organization

BME *abbr* = Bachelor of Mechanical Engineering.

BMechE *abbr* = Bachelor of Mechanical Engineering.

BmedBiol *abbr* = Bachelor of Medical Biology.

BMedSci *abbr* = Bachelor of Medical Science.

BmedSci(Speech) *abbr* = Bachelor of Medical Sciences (Speech).

BMEP *abbr* = brake mean effective pressure.

BMet *abbr* = Bachelor of Metallurgy.

BMetE *abbr* = Bachelor of Metallurgical Engineering.

BMEWS *abbr* = ballistic missile early warning system.

BMI *abbr* = ballistic missile interceptor.

BMJ *abbr* = *British Medical Journal*.

BML *abbr* = British Museum Library.

BMLBS *abbr* = British Matchbox Label and Booklet Society.

B-movie n (*cinema*) a film made as a supporting feature, esp in the 1940s and 1950s.

bmp *abbr* = brake mean power.

BMR *abbr* = basal metabolic rate.

BMRB *abbr* = British Market Research Bureau.

BMS *abbr* = Baptist Missionary Society.

BMSc *abbr* = Bachelor of Medical Science.

BMTA *abbr* = British Motor Trade Association.

BMus *abbr* = Bachelor of Music.

BMV *abbr* (*Latin*) = *Beata Maria Virgo* "Blessed Mary the Virgin."

BMW *abbr* (*German*) = *Bayerische Motoren Werke*, "Bavarian Motor Works."

BMWS *abbr* = ballistic missile weapon system.

BMX *abbr* = bicycle motocross.

bn *abbr* = battalion; billion.

BN *abbr* = Bachelor of Nursing; bank note.

BNA *abbr* = Bureau of National Affairs.

BNB *abbr* = Barbados National Bank; British National Bibliography.

BNC *abbr* = British National Corpus.

BNCAR *abbr* = British National Committee for Antarctic Research.

BNCC *abbr* = British National Committee for Chemistry.

BNCOLD *abbr* = British National Committee on Large Dams.

BNCSR *abbr* = British National Committee on Space Research.

BNEC *abbr* = British Nuclear Energy Council; British National Export Council.

BNF *abbr* = British Nutrition Foundation; Backus-Naur Form (computing).

BNFL *abbr* = British Nuclear Fuels plc.

BNHQ *abbr* = battalion headquarters.

BN Nursing *abbr* = Bachelor of Nursing, Nursing Studies.

BNOC *abbr* = British National Opera Company; British National Oil Corporation.

BNP *abbr* = British National Party.

BNS *abbr* = British Neuropathological Society; British Numismatic Society.

BNSc *abbr* = Bachelor of Nursing Science.

BNTVA *abbr* = British Nuclear Test Veterans' Association.

BNurs *abbr* = Bachelor of Nursing.

b/o *abbr* = brought over. (*Bookkeeping*)

BO *abbr* = (*inf*) body odor; bowels opened; box office; broker's order; buyer's option; Bachelor of Oratory; Board of Ordnance.

BOA *abbr* = British Octopus Association; British Olympic Association; British Oncological Association; British Optical Association; British Orthopaedic Association.

boa n any of various large South American snakes that crush their prey; a long fluffy scarf of feathers.

BOAC *abbr* = Bank of the Arab Coast (Dubai); British Overseas Airways Corporation.

boa constrictor n the largest boa, remarkable for its length and power of destroying its prey by constriction.

Boadicea *see* **Boudicca**.

Boanerges n (*Bible*) name given by Jesus to the brothers James and John; it means sons of thunder. See also **James**, **John**.

Boann n (*Irish Celtic myth*) the mother of Oenghus by the Daghda. At that time she was the wife of Elcmar, and the Daghda had tricked him into going away while he had sexual relations with his wife.

boar n a male pig, a wild hog.

board n meals, esp when provided regularly for pay; a long, flat piece of sawed wood, etc; a flat piece of wood, etc for some special purpose; pasteboard; a council; a group of people who supervise a company; the side of a ship (*overboard*). * *vt* to provide with meals and lodging at fixed terms; to come onto the deck of (a ship); to get on (a train, bus, etc). * *vi* to provide with meals, or room and meals, regularly for pay; (*with* up) to cover with boards; **to take on board** to appoint to a position; to adopt new ideas.

boarder n one who is provided with board.

board game n a game as chess, checkers, etc, played by moving pieces on a marked board.

boarding n light timber collectively; a covering of planks; the act of supplying, or state of being supplied with, food and lodging for a stipulated sum; the act of entering a ship or aircraft.

boarding house n a house for boarders.

boarding school n a school where the students are boarded.

board of directors n a group of directors responsible for running a company.

board of trade n a chamber of commerce; a commodities exchange; (*with caps*) in UK, a government department concerned with commerce and industry.

boardroom n a room where meetings of a company's board are held.

board rule n a figured scale for finding the number of square feet in a board without calculation.

boardsailing n the sport of skimming along the surface of the water standing on a surfboard fitted with a sail.—*also* **windsurfing**.

boardwalk *n* a footway of boards, esp by the sea.

boarish *adj* coarse; brutal; cruel.

boart *see* **bort**.

boast[1] *vi* to brag. * *vt* to speak proudly of; to possess with pride. * *n* boastful talk.—**boaster** *n*.—**boastingly** *adv*.

boast[2] *vt* to dress stone with a broad chisel and mallet; to dress a block in outline for a statue, etc, prior to more detailed or delicate work.

boastful *adj* given to boasting.—**boastfully** *adv*.—**boastfulness** *n*.

boat *n* a small, open, waterborne craft; (*inf*) a ship. * *vi* to travel in a boat, esp for pleasure.

boatbill(ed heron) *n* a South American wading bird with a boat-shaped bill.

boat burial *n* (*archeo*) a form of burial used in northern Europe, particularly by the Vikings.

boater *n* a stiff flat straw hat.

boathook *n* a hooked pole for drawing a boat to land, fending off, etc.

boathouse *n* a shed for boats.

boating *n* rowing, sailing, etc, for pleasure.

boatload *n* the load that can be carried by a boat; the passengers or freight carried by a boat.

boatman *n* (*pl* **boatmen**) a person who works on, deals in, or operates boats.

boat people *npl* refugees fleeing by boat.

boat pit *n* (*Egypt*) stone-lined pits, often found close to Old Kingdom pyramids. Boat pits provide the dead king with a sky vessel in which to accompany the sun-god.

boatswain *n* a ship's officer in charge of hull maintenance and related work.—*also* **bosun**.

boat train *n* a train for steamer or ferry passengers.

Boaz *n* (*Bible*) wealthy farmer who befriended and later married Ruth. *See also* **Ruth**.

bob *vb* (**bobbing, bobbed**) *vi* to move abruptly up and down, often in water; to nod the head; to curtsey. * *vt* (*hair*) to cut short. * *n* a jerking motion up and down; the weight on a pendulum, plumb line, etc; a woman's or girl's short haircut.

bobbery *n* (*pl* **bobberies**) a rumpus, a row, a noisy disturbance; a pack of hunting dogs.

bobbin *n* a reel or spool on which yarn or thread is wound.

bobbinet *n* a machine-made cotton netting or lace in imitation of pillow lace.

bobble *n* a small wooly ball used for ornament or trimming; a bobbing movement; (*inf*) a mistake; a fumble. * *vti* to bob up and down; to make a mistake; to fumble with (a ball).

bobby *n* (*pl* **bobbies**) (*Brit*) a policeman.

bobby pin *n* a clip for holding hair in position; a hairgrip.

bobcat *n* (*pl* **bobcats, bobcat**) a medium-sized feline of eastern North America with a black-spotted reddish-brown coat and a short tail.

Boberg *n* **Ferdinand** (1860–1946) Swedish architect and designer famous for his furniture designs for the Swedish Royal Family.

BOBMA *abbr* = British Oat and Barley Millers Association; British Oil-Burners Manufacturers Association.

bobolink *n* an American migratory songbird.—*also* **reedbird, ricebird**.

BOBS *abbr* = Board of Banking Supervision.

bobsled, bobsleigh *n* a long racing sled. * *vi* (**bobsledding, bobsledded**) to ride or race on a bobsled.

bobstay *n* (*naut*) a rope holding the bowsprit down to the stem.

bobtail *n* a short tail or a tail cut short; an animal with a docked tail; the rabble (*rag-tag and bobtail*). * *adj* with a docked tail.—**bobtailed** *adj*.

BOC *abbr* = British Orchid Council; British Ornithologists' Club; British Oxygen Corporation.

bocage *n* a landscape comprising small fields and low hedges, typical of Brittany and Normandy.

Boccaccio *n* [**Giovanni**] (1313–75) Italian poet and author noted particularly for his collection of 100 short tales, the *Decameron*.

bocca chiusa *n* (*mus*) (*Italian*) literally "closed mouth," i.e., humming.

Boccherini *n* **Luigi** (1743–1805) prolific Italian composer and acclaimed cellist, who died in poverty in Madrid. His work includes a total of 125 string quintets, 102 string quartets, cantatas, oratorios, 29 symphonies, and the opera, *Clementina*.

Boccioni *n* **Umberto** (1882–1916) Italian futurist painter and sculptor. One of his early and most important paintings is *The City Rises* (1910).

Boche *n* (*pl* **Boche**) (*sl*) a German, esp a soldier.

bock *n* a variety of lager beer of double strength; a glass of beer.

Böcklin *n* **Arnold** (1827–1901) Swiss painter whose work is characterized by his use of mythological creatures to create a symbolic imagery relating to primeval human fears and emotions.

BOCM *abbr* = British Oil and Cake Mills Limited.

BOD *abbr* = biological oxygen demand.

Boda (Kosta Boda) *n* Swedish glass manufacturer founded in 1864. Produced a much-copied glass with a bubble entrapped in the stem in 1938.

Bodb Dearg *n* (*Irish Celtic myth*) said to have been the son of the Daghda and to have succeeded him as father of the gods.

bode *vt* to be an omen of.

bodega *n* a wine vault, cellar or shop where wine is sold from the cask; a store specializing in Hispanic groceries.

bodice *n* the upper part of a woman's dress.

bodiless *adj* without a body, incorporeal.—**bodilessness** *n*.

bodily *adj* physical; relating to the body. * *adv* in the flesh; as a whole; altogether.

bodkin *n* a large blunt needle, a tool for piercing holes; a pin for fastening hair; a small dagger.

Bodley *n* **George F** (1827–1907), Scottish architect. His notable works include Queen's College Chapel, Cambridge.

body *n* (*pl* **bodies**) the whole physical substance of a person, animal, or plant; the trunk of a person or animal; a corpse; the principal part of anything; a distinct mass; substance or consistency, as of liquid; a richness of flavor; a person; a distinct group of people. * *vt* (**bodying, bodied**) to give shape to.

BODY *abbr* = British Organ Donor Society.

body bag *n* a large plastic sack, usu zipped, to carry a corpse from the scene of a disaster.

body check *n* (*ice hockey*) the obstruction of an opponent using the body. * *vti* to block with a body check.

bodybuilding *n* strengthening and enlarging the muscles through exercise and diet for competitive display.— **bodybuilder** *n*.

body double *n* a substitute or stand-in for an actor, often a stuntman used in situations during the recording of film sequences where particular skills or risks are involved.

bodyguard *n* a person or persons assigned to guard someone.

body image *n* a person's concept of their identity, shape, etc.

body language *n* gestures, unconscious bodily movements, etc, that function as a means of communication.

body paint *see* **gouache**.

body piercing *n* the piercing of body parts as a form of decoration, in order to attach rings, pins or studs.

body politic *n* the collective body of people living under an organized political government.

body shop *n* a garage that specializes in car body repair work.

body-snatcher *n* (*formerly*) one who stole corpses from graves for dissection by anatomists.

body stocking *n* a woman's tight-fitting garment that covers the torso and sometimes the legs.

body warmer *n* a sleeveless, quilted outer garment.

bodywork *n* the outer shell of a motor vehicle.

BoE *abbr* = Bank of England.

Boehm *n* **Michael** (1944–) German ceramic and glassware designer who joined **Rosenthal** in 1966.

Boehm system *n* (*mus*) an improved system of keys and levers for the flute, named after its German inventor, Theobald Boehm (1794–1881). The system is also applied to other instruments, e.g., the clarinet.

Boeotia *n* one of the independent states of ancient Greece, of which Thebes was the chief city.

Boeotian *adj* pertaining to Boeotia in central Greece, noted for its moist and heavy atmosphere; dull, stupid. * *n* an inhabitant of Boeotia; a dull, stupid person.

Boer *n* a Dutch-descended South African.—*also adj*.

BOF *abbr* = British Organic Farmers; British Orienteering Federation; British Othello Federation; British Overseas Fairs Limited.

boffin *n* (*inf*) a military research scientist.

boffo *adj* (*sl*) wonderful, amazing.

Boffrand *n* **Gabriel G** (born 1667) French architect. His notable works include Château de Saint Ouen.

Bofill *n* **Ricardo** (1939–) Spanish architect. His notable works include housing complexes.

bog *n* an area of waterlogged, spongy ground, made up primarily of decaying vegetation, esp rough grass, rushes and sphagnum moss. * (**bogging, bogged**) *vt* to sink or submerge in a bog or quagmire. * *vi* to sink or stick in a bog.—**boggy** *adj*

Bogarde *n* **Sir Dirk [Derek Jules Gaspard Ulric Niven van den Bogaerde]** (1920–99) English actor and author whose films include *Death in Venice* (1970).

Bogart *n* **Humphrey [De Forest]** (1899–1957) American actor who formed a famous screen partnership with his (fourth) wife **Lauren Bacall**. Notable films include *The Maltese Falcon*, *Casablanca* and *The Big Sleep*.

bogey[1] *n* (*pl* **bogeys**) (*golf*) one stroke more than par on a hole.

bogey[2] *n* (*pl* **bogeys**) a goblin; a cause of worry.—*also* **bogy** (*pl* **bogies**).

bogeyman *n* (*pl* **bogeymen**) an imaginary monster commonly used to frighten children.

boggle *vi* to be surprised; to hesitate (at). * *vt* to confuse (the imagination, mind, etc).

Boghaz Köy (Hattusas) *n* a village in central Turkey which is the site of the ancient capital of the Hittite empire.

bogie *n* an assembly of four or six wheels on a rail carriage.

bogle *n* a goblin, a specter; a scarecrow.

Bogler *n* **Theodor** (1897–1968) German ceramic designer who studied at the **Bauhaus**.

bogus *adj* counterfeit, spurious.

bogy *see* **bogey**[2].

Boh. *abbr* = Bohemia; Bohemian.

bohea *n* a black China tea of the lowest quality.

Bohem. *abbr* = Bohemian.

Bohemian *adj* of or pertaining to Bohemia in Czechoslovakia; unconventional. * *n* an inhabitant of Bohemia; a person who disregards social conventions or evinces a wild or roving disposition; a gipsy.

Bohemianism *n* the life or habits of a person, usu artistic or literary, who by natural inclination leads a free and easy unconventional existence.

Böhm *n* 1. **Dominikus** (*b.* 1880) German architect. His notable works include St Engelbert Church, Cologne-Riehl. 2. **Gottfried** (1920–) German architect. His notable works include Town Hall, Bensberg. 3. **Karl** (1894–1981) Austrian conductor esp associated with the works of Mozart and Richard Strauss; conductor of the Munich Opera in the 1920s and director of the Vienna State Opera, 1943–45. 4. **Niels [Henrik David]** (1885–1962) Danish physicist; winner of 1922 Nobel prize for physics. He was the first to apply the quantum theory to explain the stability of the nuclear model of the atom.

Boiceau *n* **Ernest** (1881–1950) Swiss designer best known for tapestries and embroidery.

boil[1] *vi* to change rapidly from a liquid to a vapor by heating; to bubble when boiling; to cook in boiling liquid; to be aroused with anger; (*with* **down**) to reduce by boiling; to condense; (*with* **over**) to overflow when boiling; to burst out in anger. * *vt* to heat to boiling point; to cook in boiling water.—**boilable** *adj*.

boil[2] *n* a skin infection in a hair follicle or gland that produces inflammation and pus.—*also* **furuncle.**

Boileau *n* **Louis-Auguste** (1812–96) French architect. His notable works include St Eugène, Paris.

boiler *n* a container in which to boil things; a storage tank in which water is heated and steam generated; a device for providing central heating and hot water.

boilermaker *n* a boiler repairman or maker.

boilerplate *n* (*comput*) a standard passage of text used in memos, reports or letters. (Compare with **template.**)

boilersuit *n* coveralls.

boiling point *n* the temperature at which a substance changes from the liquid state to the gaseous state; the point at which a person loses his temper; the point of crisis.

Boissevain *n* **Antoinette** (1898–1973) Dutch painter and lighting designer who managed London-based Merchant Adventurers from 1924.

boisterous *adj* wild, noisy; stormy; loud and exuberant.—**boisterously** *adv*.

Boito *n* **Arrigo** (1842–1918) an Italian composer and librettist who wrote the libretti for Verdi's *Otello* and *Falstaff.* He also wrote an opera, *Mefistofele*, and another, *Nerone*, unfinished at his death, was performed in 1924 to little acclaim.

Bojeson *n* **Kay** (1886–1958) Danish silversmith and ceramicist who pioneered Danish Modern style.

Bok globules *n* relatively small (10[3] to 10[5] astronomical units) dark nebulae in the Milky Way Galaxy, lying in regions where there is not much other gas.

Bol. *abbr* = Bolivia.

BOL *abbr* = Bachelor of Oriental Languages.

bola, bolas *n* a South American hunting implement consisting of two or more balls of iron or stone attached to the ends of a leather cord, used to entangle the legs of an animal.

bold *adj* daring or courageous; fearless; impudent; striking to the eye; (*print*) set in boldface type.—**boldly** *adv*.—**boldness** *n*.

boldface type *n* type characters with thickened, heavy strokes.

bold-faced *adj* brazen; impudent; set or printed in boldface type.

bole[1] *n* the trunk or stem of a tree.

bole[2] *n* friable clay or clayey shale, usu colored by oxide of iron.

bolection molding *n* (*archit*) a projecting molding concealing the join between two surfaces at different levels.

bolero *n* (*pl* **boleros**) (*mus*) (*Spanish*) a lively Spanish dance; the music accompanying such a dance; a short jacket-shaped bodice.

boletus *n* (*pl* **boletuses, boleti**) any of a large genus of thick-stemmed fungi containing edible or poisonous species.

bolide *n* a large meteor that explodes on coming into contact with air, a fire ball.

bolivar *n* the standard monetary unit of Venezuela, made up of 100 centimos.

Bolivar *n* **Simon** (1783–1830) Venezuelan-born revolutionary who overthrew Spanish rule in Venezuela, Ecuador, Colombia, and Peru. Upper Peru was renamed Bolivia in his honor.

Bolivia *n* a republic in South America surrounded by land on all sides.

boliviano *n* the standard monetary unit of Bolivia, made up of 100 centavos.

boll *n* the pod of a plant, esp of cotton or flax.

Böll *n* **Heinrich** (1917–85) German novelist, short-story writer, and critic. His masterpiece is the novel *The Lost Honor of Katharina Blum* (1975).

bollard *n* a strong post on a wharf around which mooring lines are secured; one of a line of posts closing off a street to traffic; an illuminated marker on a traffic island.

bollocks *npl* (*chiefly Brit taboo sl*) testicles. * *interj* used to express utter disbelief, ridicule, etc.

boll weevil *n* an American weevil that infests cotton bolls.

Bologna *n* **Giovanni, Giambologna** (1529–1608) Flemish-born Italian sculptor in the mannerist tradition, best known for his popular *Flying Mercury* and *The Rape of the Sabines* (1583), both in Florence.

Bologna *n* Italian city; the seat of the first Italian school of music.

bologna *n* smoked sausage meat made of pork, veal, etc, and seasonings, sold ready for eating cold.

bolometer *n* an instrument for measuring radiation.—**bolometric** *adj*.—**bolometrically** *adv*.

boloney *see* **baloney.**

bolo tie *n* a cord with an ornamental adjustable fastening, worn as a necktie.

Bolshevik *n* (*pl* **Bolsheviks, Bolsheviki**) a Russian communist; a revolutionary; an opponent of an existing social order.

Bolshevism *n* the doctrines and practices of the Bolsheviks; the communist form of government adopted in Russia in March 1917.—**Bolshevist** *adj, n*.

bolshie, bolshy *adj* (*sl*) left-wing; rebellious. * *n* (*pl* **bolshies**) (*often with cap*) a Bolshevik; a revolutionary.

bolster *n* a long narrow pillow; any bolster-like object or support. * *vt* (*often with* **up**) to support or strengthen.—**bolsterer** *n*.—**bolsteringly** *adv*.

bolt[1] *n* a bar used to lock a door, etc; an arrow for a crossbow; a flash of lightning; a threaded metal rod used with a nut to hold parts together; a roll (of cloth, paper, etc); a sudden dash. * *vt* to lock with a bolt; to eat hastily; to say suddenly; to blurt (out); to abandon (a party, group, etc). * *vi* (*horse*) to rush away suddenly * *adv* erectly upright.—**bolter** *n*.

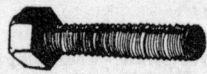

bolt[2] *vt* to sift or separate coarser from finer particles; to examine with care, to investigate; to separate.—*also* **boult.**—**bolter** *n*.

Bolt *n* **Robert [Oxton]** (1924–95) English dramatist, the best known of whose plays is the historical drama *A Man for all Seasons*.

bolthole *n* an escape route; a safe and secret hiding place; a person's private refuge.

BOLTOP *abbr* = better on lips than on paper.

boltrope *n* (*naut*) a rope to which the edges of sails are sewn.

Boltzmann equation *n* an equation linking the absolute or Kelvin temperature to the average kinetic energy of a particle.

bolus *n* a chewed lump of food ready for swallowing; (*medical*) a large pill; a method of drug delivery in which a small quantity of a drug is injected directly into an organ where a maximum concentration is required; anything disagreeable, which must be accepted.

bomb *n* a projectile containing explosives, incendiary material, or chemicals used for destruction; (*with* **the**) the hydrogen or atomic bomb; (*comput*) an unexpected termination of an application, similar to a crash, often caused by a software conflict; (*sl*) a lot of money. * *vt* to attack with bombs. * *vi* to fail, to flop.

bombard *vt* to attack with bombs or artillery; to attack verbally.—**bombardment** *n*.

bombardier *n* the crew member who releases the bombs in a bomber; in Britain and Canada, a noncommissioned artillery officer.

bombardier beetle *n* any of various coleopterous insects that, when irritated, expel a fluid from the abdomen with a slight report.

bombast *n* pretentious or boastful language.—**bombastic** *adj*.—**bombastically** *adv*.

bombazine *n* a twilled fabric of which the warp is silk and the weft worsted.

bombe *n* a frozen dessert molded into a round shape.

bomber *n* a person who bombs; an airplane that carries bombs.

Bomberg *n* **David** (1890–1957) English painter. He is now considered one of the pioneers of British expressionism.

bomber jacket *n* a waist-length bloused jacket with a zip.

bombshell *n* a shocking surprise.

bomb shelter *n* a shelter, esp underground, affording protection from bombs.

bombsight *n* a manual or electronic device for aiming bombs.

bomb site *n* an area devastated by bombing; a vacant area cleared after a bombing raid.

bombycid *n* any of a family of moths, including the silkworm moth.

BON *abbr* = British Organization of Non-Parents.

Bona Dea *n* (*Roman myth*) a goddess, whose name means "good goddess," worshipped from earliest times exclusively by women.—*also* **Fauna.**

bona fide *adj* in good faith; genuine or real.

bona fides *n* good faith; honorable dealing.

bonanza *n* a rich vein of ore; any source of wealth; unexpected good fortune or luck.

Bonatz *n* **Paul** born 1877, German architect. His notable works include Stuttgart railroad station.

Bonaventure *n* **Saint**, also called **Bonaventura**, real name **John of Fidenza** (1221–74) Italian (Tuscan) Franciscan monk; bishop of Albano and cardinal in 1273. He was canonized in 1482. His feast day is 15 July.

bonbon *n* a small piece of candy, a sweet.

bond *n* anything that binds, fastens, or unites; (*chem*) the force that holds atoms together to form a molecule; (*pl*) shackles; an obligation imposed by a contract, promise, etc; the status of goods in a warehouse until taxes are paid; (*finance*) a financial security that is issued by a borrower to a lender. Bonds usu issued for a set number of years and usu fixed-interest. Once issued, bonds can be bought and sold on the stock market; surety against theft, absconding, etc. * *vt* to join, bind, or otherwise unite; to provide a bond for; to place or hold (goods) in bond; to put together bricks or stones so that they overlap to give strength. * *vi* to hold together by means of a bond.—**bondable** *adj*.—**bonder** *n*.

bondage *n* slavery, captivity.

bond dissociation energy *n* (*chem*) the amount of energy needed to break a particular bond holding two atoms together.

bonded goods *npl* goods on which customs duty or excise duty has not yet been paid, although the goods are liable for duty.

Bond n **Edward** (1934–) English dramatist, notable for the extreme violence of his early work, e.g., *Saved*.

bonded warehouse n a warehouse for the storing of goods that are liable for duty but on which customs duty or excise duty has not yet been paid. *See* bonded goods.

bondholder n one who holds a government or corporation bond.

bonding n the process by which people form a relationship with one another, esp parent and child.

bond paper n a durable paper, originally made for bonds.

bondstone n a long stone running through a wall and so binding it.

Bon Jovi n **John [John Francis Bongiovi]** (1962–) American rock singer and lead singer of Bon Jovi.

bon mot n (*pl* bons mots) a witty saying, a fitting remark.

bon ton n the style of persons in high life; good breeding; fashionable society; height of fashion.

bon vivant n (*pl* bons vivants) a gourmet.

bon voyage n, *interj* an expression used to wish travelers a pleasant trip.

bone n (*anat*) a hard material that forms the skeleton of most vertebrate animals; any constituent part of the skeleton; (*pl*) the skeleton; the essentials or basics of anything. * *vti* to remove the bones from, as meat; (*with* up) (*inf*) to study hard.—**boneless** *adj*.

bone ash n the residue from bones burned in an open furnace, used as a fertilizer and in china manufacture.

bone black n a black pigment made partly from charcoal obtained by roasting animal bones.

bone china n china made from clay mixed with bone ash.

bone-dry *adj* completely dry.

bonehead n (*sl*) a fool.

bone marrow n a soft tissue found in the spaces of bones.

bone meal n fertilizer or feed made of crushed or ground bone.

bone of contention n a source of strife.

bones n (*mus*) a pair of small sticks (originally bones) that are held in the hands and clicked together rhythmically.

bonesetter n one who treats fractures or dislocated limbs without medical qualification to do so.

boneyard n (*inf*) a cemetery.

Bonfils n **Robert** (1886–1971) French painter and designer who created bookbindings and ceramics for Sèvres.

bonfire n an outdoor fire.

bongo[1] n (*pl* bongos) (*mus*) either of a pair of small drums of different pitch struck with the fingers.

bongo[2] n (*pl* bongo, bongos) a large striped African antelope.

bongos n (*mus*) pairs of small, upright Cuban drums that are often found in dance bands. They are played with the hands.

Bonhoeffer n **Dietrich** (1906–45) German Lutheran pastor, theologian, and writer who was active in the anti-Nazi resistance during World War II and was hanged by the Gestapo.

bonhomie n good-heartedness; a frank good-natured manner.—**bonhomous** *adj*.

Boniface n **Saint** (*c.* 680–755) English monk; traveled as a missionary to Frisia (corresponds to modern Holland). Many were converted and baptized. In 755 an armed crowd attacked Boniface and his companions and killed them. His feast day is 5 June.

Bonington n **Richard Parkes** (1802–28) English painter. He was a first-class watercolorist, noted for the lightness and fluidity of his style.

bonito n (*pl* bonitos, bonito) one of several species of warm-sea game fishes allied to the tuna.

bonk *vt* (*inf*) to hit; (*inf*) to have sexual intercourse with.—**bonking** n.

bonkers *adj* (*sl*) crazy.

Bonnard n **Pierre** (1867–1947) French impressionist painter; a member of the Nabis group in Paris and a founder member of the Salon d'Automne.

bonne n a French nursemaid.

Bonner Durchmusterung *or* **the Bonn Survey** n a star catalog listing the position and magnitude of 324,188 northern stars.

bonnet n a hat with a chin ribbon, worn by women and children; (*Brit*) a case or covering, usu of sheet metal, placed over a motor.—*also* hood.

bonnet tile n (*archit*) a curved tile with a rounded top which joins with the plain tiles along the hip of the roof.

bonny, bonnie *adj* (bonnier, bonniest) healthy, attractive looking.

Bonomi n **Joseph** (1739–1806) Italian architect. His notable works include St James Church, Great Packington, Warwickshire.

bonsai n (*pl* bonsai) a miniature tree or shrub that has been dwarfed by selective pruning; the art of cultivating bonsai.

bonspiel n (*Scot*) a curling match between players of different clubs.

bontebok n (*pl* bonteboks, bontebok) a pied antelope of South Africa.

bonus n (*pl* bonuses) an amount paid over the sum due as interest, dividend, or wages.

bonus dividend n a dividend that is issued to shareholders of a company in addition to those that are expected.

bonus payment *see* bonus.

bonus shares *npl* additional shares that are issued to existing shareholders in a company without any further payment being made by them.

Bonvallet n **Lucien** (1861–1919) French designer and master of copperware.

bony *adj* (bonier, boniest) of or resembling bones; having large or prominent bones; full of bones.

bonze n a Buddhist monk.

boo *interj* an expression of disapproval. * n (*pl* boos) hooting. * *vi* (booing, booed) to low like an ox; to groan. * *vt* to hoot at.

boob n a stupid awkward person; a blunder; (*sl*) a female breast.

BOOBA *abbr* = British Olive Oil Buyers' Association.

boo-boo n (*pl* boo-boos) (*inf*) a small error, a mistake.

boob tube n (*sl*) a television set; a strapless, tight-fitting sleeveless woman's top; a strapless brassiere.

booby n (*pl* boobies) a foolish person; the loser in a game.

booby prize n a prize of little value for the lowest score.

booby trap n a trap for playing a practical joke on someone; a camouflaged explosive device triggered by an unsuspecting victim.

boodle n money paid for votes or undue political influence; graft; lot, caboodle.

boogeyman, boogieman *see* bogeyman.

boogie *vi* (boogieing, boogied) to dance to pop music or jazz. * n (*mus*) fast, rhythmic music for dancing.

boogie-woogie n (*mus*) a jazz and blues style of piano playing in which the left hand plays a persistent bass rhythm while the right hand plays a melody.

boohoo *vi* (boohooing, boohooed) to weep noisily or to pretend to do so. * n (*pl* boohoos) the sound of noisy weeping.

book n a bound set of printed or blank pages; a literary composition of fact or fiction; the script or libretto of a play or musical; (*pl*) written records of transactions or accounts; a book or record of bets. * *vt* to make a reservation in advance; to note a person's name and address for an alleged offence. * *vi* to make a reservation.

bookbindery n a place where books are bound.

bookbinding n the art or process of putting covers on books.—**bookbinder** n.

bookcase n a piece of furniture with shelves for books.

book club n an organization that sells books to its members at cheaper prices, usu by mail order.

book end *npl* a prop at the end of a row of books to keep them upright.

Booker prize n a prize that is awarded annually for a work of fiction by a British, British Commonwealth, or Irish writer.

bookie n (*inf*) a bookmaker.

bookish *adj* fond of reading.—**bookishness** n.

book-keeping n the systematic recording of business accounts. *See* accounting.—**bookkeeper** n.

book learning n theoretical, not practical, knowledge.—**book-learned** *adj*.

booklet n a small book, usu with a paper cover; a pamphlet.

bookmaker n a person who takes bets on horse races, etc and pays out winnings; a manufacturer or publisher of books.

bookman n (*pl* bookmen) a literary man, a scholar; one who works in publishing.

bookmark[1], **bookmarker** n a thing to mark a place in a book.

bookmark[2] n (*comput*) a link which can mark an internet site then at a later date the site can be reaccessed. The term has been adopted from Netscape Navigator™. In Microsoft Explorer™ it is called Favorites.

Book of Caverns n (*Egypt*) a set of religious illustrations and texts found on the walls of royal tombs of the New Kingdom period showing the progress of Ra through the six caverns of the underworld.

Book of Common Prayer n the once-official book of services for the Church of England, first published in 1549.

Book of the Dead n (*Egypt*) religious writings which were placed within the coffins of important Egyptians in New Kingdom times.

bookplate n a label in a book with the owner's name on it.

bookseller n a person who sells books.

bookstall n a stall for the sale of books, magazines, etc.

bookstand n a support for holding a book open for the reader; a bookstall.

bookstore n a store where books are sold.

book value n the value of an asset as it is stated in the account books of a company.

bookworm n an insect that feeds on books; a person who reads a lot.

Boolean algebra n (*math*) a system of symbolic logic used in the manipulation of sets and other mathematical entities, and in computing science.

boom[1] n a spar on which a sail is stretched; a barrier across a harbor; a long pole carrying a microphone.

boom[2] *vi* to make a deep, hollow sound. * n a resonant sound, as of the sea.

boom[3] *vi* to flourish or prosper suddenly. * n (*econ*) a period of vigorous economic activity.

boomer n the male of the great kangaroo; one who starts or promotes a boom; (*sl*) a migratory worker.

boomerang n a curved stick that, when thrown, returns to the thrower; an action that unexpectedly rebounds and harms the agent.—*also vi*.

boom town n a town that suddenly grows and increases in economic prosperity.

boon[1] n something useful or helpful; a blessing; a favor.

boon[2] adj bountiful; convivial, jolly; specially friendly (*boon companion*).

boondocks npl (*sl*) a wild, inhospitable area; a dull, provincial region.—**boondock** adj.

boondoggle vi to waste time or money on pointless work.—*also* n.

boonies npl (*sl*) boondocks.

boor n an ill-mannered or coarse person.—**boorish** adj.—**boorishly** adv.—**boorishness** n.

boost vt (*sales, etc*) to increase; to encourage, to improve; to push; to help by advertising or promoting. * n a push.

booster n a thing or person that increases the effectiveness of another mechanism; the first stage of a rocket, which usu breaks away after launching; a substance that increases the effectiveness of medication.

booster cable n a jumper cable.

boosterism n the practice of boosting an image or product commercially.

booster shot, booster injection n a supplementary dose of medicine, esp a vaccine.

boot[1] n a strong covering for the foot and lower part of the leg; (*sl: with* **the**) dismissal from employment; (Brit) the rear compartment of a car used for holding luggage, etc (—*also* **trunk**). * vt to kick; to get rid of by force; (*comput*) to bring a program from a disc into the memory.

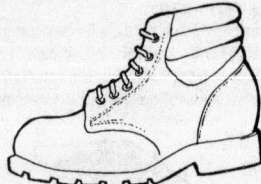

boot[2] n (*arch*) advantage, use; **to boot** as well. * vi (*arch*) to avail.

bootblack n one who shines shoes.

boot camp n (*sl*) in US, a Navy or Marine Corp camp for basic training.

Boote n **T and R** British ceramics manufacturer, which patented a new method of tile production in 1863.

booted adj wearing boots.

bootee n a knitted or soft shoe for a baby.

Boötes n (*Greek myth*) the son of Demeter who invented the plow and cultivated the soil.—*also* **Philomelus**; a constellation beside Ursa Major.

booth n a stall for selling goods; a small enclosure for voting; a public telephone enclosure; (*Bible*) temporary dwelling made of woven branches.

Booth n 1. **Charles** (1844–93) British stained-glass designer who designed windows for the Jefferson Market Courthouse. 2. **John Wilkes** (1839–65) American assassin of Abraham Lincoln. 3. **William** (1829–1912) English religious leader and founder of the Salvation Army in 1878.

bootjack n an appliance for drawing off boots.

bootleg vt (**bootlegging, bootlegged**) to smuggle illicit alcohol; to deal in illegally made records and tapes of live music, etc.—**bootlegger** n.

bootless adj useless, unavailing.—**bootlessly** adv.—**bootlessness** n.

bootlicker n a person who ingratiates himself or herself to gain favor, a toady.

boots n (*pl* **boots**) in UK, the servant in a hotel who cleans the boots of the guests.

boots and saddles n a cavalry signal to mount.

bootstrapping n (*comput*) a program routine designed to make a computer ready for use.

booty n (*pl* **booties**) spoils obtained as plunder.

booze vi (*inf*) to drink alcohol excessively. * n alcohol.—**boozer** n.

boozy adj (**boozier, booziest**) (*sl*) addicted to drink; drunk.—**boozily** adv.

bop n (*mus*) short for **bebop**, a style of 1940s jazz music.

BOP abbr = Federal Bureau of Prisons

BOPA abbr = British Outdoor Professionals Association.

BOptom abbr = Bachelor of Optometry.

bor. abbr = boron.

BOR abbr = Bureau of Reclamation

bora n a fierce dry northeast wind that blows from the Balkan mountains to the Adriatic Sea.

boracic adj of or yielding boron.—*also* **boric**.

boracic acid n a white solid acid used in manufacturing and as a mild antiseptic.

borage n a blue-flowered herb used in salads, etc.

borax n a mineral composed of the sodium salt compounded of boracic acid chiefly from the dried beds of certain lakes, used in the manufacture of glass, enamel, antiseptics, soaps, etc; (*sl*) shoddy merchandise.

Bordeaux n any of several red, white or rosé wines from around Bordeaux in France.

bordello n (*pl* **bordellos**) a brothel.

border n the edge, rim, or margin; a dividing line between two countries; a narrow strip along an edge. * vi (*with* **on, upon**) to be adjacent; to approach, to verge on. * vt to form a border.

Border ballad n a form of ballad describing the violent world of the English/Scottish Borders from the late Middle Ages to the 17th century.

bordereau n (*pl* **bordereaux**) a memorandum of contents, a docket.

borderer n a dweller on a frontier.

borderland n land forming a border or frontier; an uncertain or debatable district; an intermediate state.

borderline n a boundary. * adj on a boundary; doubtful, indefinite.

Bordone n Paris (1500–71) Italian painter. He worked and studied in Venice from 1510 and was a pupil of Titian.

Borduas n Paul Emile (1905–60) Canadian painter; notable works include *Sous le Vent de l'Ile* (1947), *Floraison Massive* (1951), *Pulsation* (1955) and *The Seagull* (1957).

bordure n (*her*) a border round a shield.

bore[1] vt to drill so as to form a hole; * n a hole made by drilling; the diameter of a gun barrel.

bore[2] vt to weary, by being dull or uninteresting; * n a dull or uninteresting person.

bore[2] *see* **bear**[1].

bore[3] n a tidal wave that breaks in the estuaries of some rivers and, impeded by a narrowing channel, rises in a ridge and courses along with great force and noise.

boreal adj of or pertaining to the north, or to the north wind; situated on the northern side; of a northern character.

Boreal adj relating to a climatic zone typified by short summers and long winters that are cold and snowy; adj denoting an early post-glacial era within Europe that has been dated at 7500–5500 BC and was drier than the present climate.

boreal forest n the coniferous forest of the temperate latitudes of the northern hemisphere.

Boreas n (*myth*) the north wind as personified by the Greeks and Romans.

boredom n tedium.

borehole n a hole drilled during prospecting for coal, oil or natural gas to enable samples to be taken.

borer n (*archeo*) a flint tool, mainly from the Lower Paleolithic period, which was used for a variety of different purposes.

Borg n Bjorn (1956–) Swedish tennis player; five times Wimbledon champion (1976–80).

Borges n Jorge Luis (1899–1986) Argentinian poet, critic and short-story writer whose fiction, e.g., *Labyrinths*, is noted for its use of fantastic themes to make philosophical points.

Borgia n Cesare (1476–1507) Italian soldier and politician, the son of Rodrigo Borgia (1431–1503). He became a cardinal in 1493 and with his sister Lucrezia (1480–1519) acquired a reputation for conspiracy.

Borglum n Gutzon (1867–1941) American sculptor; famous for the portraits, at Mount Rushmore in South Dakota, of Presidents Washington, Jefferson, Lincoln, and Theodore Roosevelt. This massive feat of engineering began in 1930 and was not finished until after the artist's death.

boric acid *see* **boracic acid**.

boric *see* **boracic**.

boring adj dull, tedious; making holes.

born pp of **bear**[1]. * adj by birth, natural.

born-again adj having undergone a revival of personal faith or conviction.

borne *see* **bear**[1].

bornite n a valuable ore of copper.

Borodin n Aleksandr Porfiryevich (1833–87) Russian composer and scientist. A member of "The Five." Noted for *In the Steppes of Central Asia* (tone poem), and *Prince Igor* (an opera completed after his death by Rimsky-Korsakov and Glazunov).

boron n a nonmetallic element found in borax.

borough n a self-governing, incorporated town; an administrative area of a city, as in New York or London.

borough English n (*formerly*) a custom existing in some parts of England by which an estate descended to the youngest son instead of the eldest, or, if there were no son, to the youngest brother.

Borrelli n Corrado (1947–) Italian industrial and graphic designer working in Milan.

Borromini n Francesco (1599–1667) Italian architect. His notable works include S. Carlo alle Quattro Fontane.

borrow vt to obtain (an item) with the intention of returning it; (*an idea*) to adopt as one's own; (*loan, money*) to obtain from a financial institution at definite rates of interest.—**borrower** n.

Borrow n George (1803–81) English novelist and travel writer whose best-known works are semi-autobiographical novels of gypsy life, e.g., *Lavengro*, and his travel book, *The Bible in Spain*.

Borsani n Osvaldo (1911–1995) Italian furniture designer who founded his company, Tecno, in 1954.

Borsato n Giuseppe (1770–1849) Venetian painter who achieved fame by designing for Napoleon I and his circle.

borscht, borsch n a type of soup (*orig* from Russia) made with beetroot.

borstal system n (*often cap*) (*Brit*) (*formerly*) a reformatory system by which the sentence depended on the prisoner's conduct; now called a youth custody center.

bort, bortz n an imperfect or inferior diamond used for polishing other stones; a fragment of diamond made in the cutting.—*also* **boart**.

borzoi n (*pl* **borzois**) a tall hound with a long, silky coat and a long head, a Russian wolfhound.

BOS abbr = British Origami Society; British Orthoptic Society.

BOSCA abbr = British Oil Spill Control Association.

boscage, boskage n ground covered with trees and shrubs; woods; thickets; a wooded landscape.

Bosch n Hieronymus [Jerome van Aeken, Aken] (*c*.1450–1516) Dutch painter, known for his allegorical paintings. His best-known and most intriguing works are bizarre and confusing, as in *The Garden of Earthly Delights*.

Bose *n* **Subhas Chandra** (1897–1945) Indian nationalist leader; president of the Indian National Congress (1938–39). In collaboration with the Japanese in World War II, he organized the Indian National Army to combat British rule.

bosh *n* (*inf*) nonsense.—*also interj*.

bosing *n* (*archeo*) (*or* **bowsing**) a method for detecting buried structures. The ground is struck with a heavy object and the sound emitted changes over the buried feature.

bosk *n* a small wood, a thicket.

bosky *adj* (**boskier, boskiest**) wooded, bushy.—**boskiness** *n*.

Bosnia-Herzegovina *n* a Republic, more commonly known as Bosnia, which declared its independence from the former Yugoslavia in 1992.

bosom *n* the breast of a human being, esp a woman; the part of a dress that covers it; the seat of the emotions. * *adj* (*friend*) very dear, intimate.

boson *n* a subatomic particle whose spin is an integral number.

Bosporus, Bosphorus *n* the strait joining the Black Sea with the Sea of Marmara, also known as the Strait of Constantinople.

boss[1] *n* (*archit*) a projecting, rounded, ornamental knob used on ceilings or vaults where stone ribs or wooden beams converged. * *vt* to ornament with studs or knobs.

boss[2] *n* (*geol*) a roughly circular, steep-sided outcrop of intrusive igneous rock that is usu a few square miles in area.

boss[3] *n* (*inf*) the manager or foreman; a powerful local politician. * *vt* to domineer; to be in control.

bossa nova *n* a dance from Brazil similar to the samba; the music for this.

Bossanyi *n* **Elvin** (1891–1975) Hungarian stained-glass designer whose work includes glass for the Senate House of London University (1934).

Boss General Catalog *n* a star catalog started by the American astronomer Lewis Boss in 1895, planned to give the positions and motions of stars in the northern hemisphere as seen from Albany and in the southern hemisphere from Argentina.

bossy *adj* (**bossier, bossiest**) (*inf*) domineering, fond of giving orders.—**bossily** *adv*.—**bossiness** *n*.

Boston ivy *n* a woody vine of the grape family with three-lobed leaves.

Boston lettuce *n* a type of lettuce with soft leaves and a small loose head.

bosun *see* **boatswain**.

Boswell *n* **James** (1740–95) Scottish lawyer and writer remembered for his *Life of Samuel Johnson*, one of the great biographies.

bot *n* the larva of the botfly, which infests horses, cattle, sheep, etc; (*pl*) the disease that it causes.—*also* **bott**.

bot. *abbr* = botanical; botanist; botany; bottle.

BoT, BOT *abbr* = Board of Trade.

botanical, botanic *adj* pertaining to plants and botany.—**botanically** *adv*.

botanical garden *n* a place where indigenous and exotic plants are grown for scientific study and for show.

botanize *vi* to study plants, esp on a field trip.—**botanizer** *n*.

botany *n* (*pl* **botanies**) the study of plants.—**botanist** *n*.

BOTB *abbr* = British Overseas Trade Board.

botch *n* a poorly done piece of work. * *vt* to mend or patch clumsily; to put together without sufficient care.—**botcher** *n*.

botchy *adj* (**botchier, botchiest**) clumsily made or done; marked with botches.—**botchily** *adv*.—**botchiness** *n*.

botfly *n* (*pl* **botflies**) any of many winged insects with larvae parasitic on humans and livestock.

both *adj, pron* the two together; the one and the other. * *conj* together equally.—*also adv* .

Botha *n* **1. Louis** (1862–1919) South African general and statesman, the first prime minister of South Africa (1910–19). **2. P[ieter] W[illem]** (1916–) South African politician. As prime minister (1978–84) and then president (1984–89), he introduced limited reforms of apartheid.

Botham *n* **Ian** (1955–) English cricket captain (1980–81).

bother *vt* to perplex or annoy; to take the time or trouble. * *n* worry; trouble; someone who causes problems, etc.

botheration *n* bother.—*also interj*.

bothersome *adj* causing bother.

bothy *n* (*pl* **bothies**) (*Scot*) a small cottage or hut, esp a hut or barrack serving as farm servants' quarters; a shelter for climbers on mountains.

bo tree *n* the peepul, the sacred tree of the Buddhists.

botryoidal *adj* resembling a bunch of grapes.—**botryoidally** *adv*.

Botswana *n* a landlocked republic in southern Africa which straddles the Tropic of Capricorn.

bott *see* **bot**.

Botta *n* **Mario** (1943–), Swiss architect. His notable works include Casa Rotondo, Stabio.

Botticelli *n* **Sandro** (1445–1510) Florentine painter *The Madonna of the Magnificat* (1480s), his best-known altarpiece, is one of several Virgin and Child paintings.

bottle[1] *n* a glass or plastic container for holding liquids; its contents; (*sl*) courage, nerve. * *vt* to put in bottles; to confine as if in a bottle.

bottle[2] *n* (*dial*) a quantity of hay or grass bundled up.

bottle-feed *vt* (**bottle-feeding, bottle-fed**) to feed (a baby) from a bottle rather than from the breast.

bottle green *adj* dark green.

bottleneck *n* a narrow stretch of a road where traffic is held up; a congestion in any stage of a process.

bottlenose *n* a dolphin with a sharp protruding beak; a moderately large toothed whale with a prominent beak.

bottom *n* the lowest or deepest part of anything; the base or foundation; the lowest position (e.g., in a class); the buttocks; (*naut*) the part of a ship's hull below water; the seabed. * *vt* to be based or founded on; to bring to the bottom, to get to the bottom of. * *vi* to become based; to reach the bottom; (*with* **out**) to flatten off after dropping sharply.

bottomlands *npl* rich flat low-lying land along watercourses in the western states of the US.

bottomless *adj* very deep; without limit.

bottom line *n* the crux; the final result; (accounts) a term used in accounting to denote the net profit from a business after all costs have been paid.—**bottom-line** *adj*.

bottomry *n* (*pl* **bottomries**) the borrowing of money by the owner on the security of his or her ship. * *vt* to pledge (a ship) thus.

botulism *n* (*med*) the very dangerous type of food poisoning caused by a bacterium, *Clostridium botulinum*.

bouche fermée (*French*) *see* **bocca chiusa**.

Boucher *n* **1. François** (1703–70) French rococo painter whose work was elegant and frivolous. Notable among his works are *The Triumph of Venus* (1740), *The Reclining Girl* (1751) and *The Rising* and *The Setting of the Sun* (1753). **2. Guy** (1935–1992) French designer and engineer who designed drinking glasses for **Daum**.

bouclé, boucle *n* a type of looped yarn or fabric.

Boudicca *or* **Boadicea** *n* (*d.* 62 AD) warrior queen of the Iceni tribe. Wife of Prasutagus, a client of Rome, whose lands in Norfolk and Suffolk were taken by the Romans after his death. Boudicca raised a campaign against the Romans and met with some success until she was eventually defeated in battle. She is said to have taken poison after the defeat.

Boudin *n* **Eugene** (1824–98) French painter who had a strong influence on the impressionists.

boudoir *n* a woman's bedroom.

bouffant *adj* puffed out; (*of hair*) backcombed.

bouffe *see* **opéra bouffe**.

bougainvillea, bougainvillaea *n* a tropical plant with large rosy or purple bracts.

bough *n* a branch of a tree.

bought *see* **buy**.

bought deal *n* a method of raising capital used by a company in which market makers or banks are invited to bid for new shares, these are sold to the highest bidder who then sells them on the stock market with a view to making a profit.

Boughton *n* **Rutland** (1878–1960) an English composer of operas, the most famous of which were based on Arthurian legends, e.g., *The Immortal Hour*, immediately popular and performed first at Glastonbury in 1914, and *The Birth of Arthur*.

bougie *n* a wax candle; (*med*) a slender flexible tube for inserting into the gullet, etc; a catheter.

bouillabaisse *n* a French fish stew.

bouillon *n* a clear seasoned stock or broth.

boul. *abbr* = boulevard.

Boulanger *n* (**Juliette**) **Nadia** (1887–1979) French composer and conductor but who is mainly remembered for being an outstanding teacher of composition. Among her pupils were Berkeley, Copland and Piston.

boulder *n* a large stone or mass of rock rounded by the action of erosion.

boulder clay *n* a deposit of rocks embedded in clay left by a glacier that has since melted.

boule[1] *n* an imitation gemstone.

boule[2] *n* in ancient Athens, a higher popular assembly; (*with cap*) the lower house of the modern Greek legislative assembly.

boule[3] *see* **boulle**.

boules *n* (*used as sing*) a French game similar to bowls played with small, hard balls.

Boulestin *n* **X Marcel** (*fl.* 1906–1930) French interior designer who started the fashion for "java paper" lampshades.

boulevard *n* a broad, often tree-lined road.

boulevardier *n* a frequenter of a boulevard, esp a Parisian; a man about town.

bouleversement *n* an overturning, overthrow.

Boulez *n* **Pierre** (1925–) French avant-garde composer, conductor and pianist. His most noted works include *Le Marteau sans maître* (for voice and chamber orchestra), and *Pli selon pli* (for soprano and orchestra).

boulle *n* decorative inlaying for cabinetwork, consisting of brass or other metal, tortoiseshell, etc, worked into scrolls or other patterns; the articles so ornamented.—*also* **boule, buhl**.

Boullée *n* **Étienne-Louis** (1728–99) French architect. His notable works include Hôtel Alexandre, Paris.

boult *see* **bolt**[2].

Boult *n* **Sir Adrian Cedric** (1889–1983) English conductor notable for conducting the first performance of Holst's suite *The Planets* in 1918; conductor of the BBC Symphony Orchestra (1930–49) and was knighted in 1937.

bounce *vi* to rebound; to jump up suddenly; (*sl: check*) to be returned because of lack of funds; (*with* **back**) to recover easily, e.g., from misfortune or ill health. * *vt* to cause a ball to bounce; (*sl*) to put (a person) out by force; (*sl*) to fire from a job. * *n* a leap or springiness; capacity for bouncing; sprightliness; boastfulness, arrogance.

bounced e-mail *n* (*comput*) an e-mail message that could not be delivered and which is returned to the sender.

bouncer *n* (*sl*) a man hired to remove disorderly people from nightclubs, etc.

bouncing *adj* big, healthy, etc.

bouncy *adj* able to spring or bound; elastic; vigorous, lively.—**bouncily** *adv*.—**bounciness** *n*.

bound[1] *see* **bind.**

bound[2] *n* (*usu pl*) the limit or boundary. * *vt* to limit, confine or surround; to name the boundaries of.

bound[3] *n* a jump or leap. * *vi* to jump or leap.

bound[4] *adj* (*with* **for**) intending to go to, on the way to.

boundary *n* (*pl* **boundaries**) the border of an area; the limit; (*cricket*) the limit line of a field; a stroke that goes beyond the boundary line.

boundary current *n* the current flowing at depth in the ocean where there is a marked difference in temperature and salinity between the current and the rest of the sea.

bounden *adj* (*duty*) obligatory.

bounden duty *n* a moral obligation.

bounder *n* one who or that which bounds; (*inf*) an insolent, ill-bred man, who makes himself disagreeable to those whom he meets.

boundless *adj* unlimited, vast.—**boundlessly** *adv*.—**boundlessness** *n*.

bounteous *adj* giving freely, bountiful, generous; plentiful.—**bounteously** *adv*.—**bounteousness** *n*.

bountiful *adj* generous in giving.—**bountifully** *adv*.—**bountifulness** *n*.

bounty *n* (*pl* **bounties**) generosity in giving; the gifts given; a reward or premium.

bounty hunter *n* one who hunts predatory animals for the reward offered; one who tracks down outlaws and captures them when a reward is offered.

bouquet *n* a bunch of flowers; the perfume given off by wine.

bouquet garni *n* (*pl* **bouquets garnis**) herbs tied in a small bundle used for flavoring stews, soups, sauces, etc.

bourbon *n* a whiskey distilled in the US from corn mash.

Bourdelle *n* **Emile Antoine** (1861–1929) French sculptor; notable among his works are the several versions of *Beethoven, Tragic Mask* and the statue *Meracles Archer* (1910).

bourdon *n* the bass drone of the bagpipe; a bass stop of an organ.

bourgeois *n* (*pl* **bourgeois**) a member of the bourgeoisie or middle class; a conventional and unimaginative individual. * *adj* smug, respectable, conventional; mediocre.

bourgeoisie *n* the class between the lower and upper classes, mostly composed of professional and business people.—*also* **middle class**.

bourn, bourne[1] *n* a small stream; a temporary stream, after heavy rainfall, in chalk country.

bourn, bourne[2] *n* (*arch*) a boundary; a destination, goal; a realm.

bourne, bourrée *n* (*mus*) (*French*) a lively French dance dating from the 17th century.

bourrée *n* (*mus*) a composition of a lively character, similar to the gavotte; the music for this.

bourse *n* a stock exchange for the transaction of business; (*with cap*) the stock exchange of Paris.

bouse *vi* (*naut*) to pull or haul hard.—*also* **bowse.**

boustrophedon *n* an ancient mode of writing lines alternately from left to right and from right to left.—**boustrophedonic** *adj*.

bout *n* a spell, a turn, a period spent in some activity; a contest or struggle, esp boxing or wrestling; a time of illness.

boutique *n* a small shop, usu selling fashionable clothing and accessories.

boutonniere, boutonnière *n* a buttonhole; a spray of flowers worn in it.

Bouts *n* **Dierick** (*c*.1415–1475) Dutch painter whose style is distinctive in its use of perspective, controlled composition, richness of color, and lyrical treatment of landscape.

bouzouki *n* (*mus*) a Greek stringed instrument with a long, fretted neck. Its six strings are plucked, often to provide an emotionally charged accompaniment to songs. The sound of the bouzouki reached a worldwide audience with the film music of the Greek composer Mikis Theodorakis.

bovine *adj* relating to cattle; dull; sluggish. * *n* an ox, cow etc.

bovine spongiform encephalopathy (**BSE**) *n* a disease of cattle that proves fatal and is similar to scrapie in sheep and Creutzfeldt-Jakob disease in humans. Commonly known as mad cow disease.

bow[1] *vi* to bend the knee or to lean the head (and chest) forward as a form of greeting or respect or shame; (*with* **before**) to accept, to submit; (*with* **out**) to withdraw or retire gracefully. * *vt* to bend downwards; to weigh down; to usher in or out with a bow. * *n* a lowering of the head (and chest) in greeting.

bow[2] *n* (*mil*) a weapon for shooting arrows; (*mus*) an implement for playing the strings of a violin; a decorative knot of ribbon, etc. * *vti* to bend, curve.

bow[3] *n* (*naut*) the forward part of a ship.

bow compass *n* (*geom*) a compass with jointed legs.

Bowdler *n* **Dr Thomas** (1754–1825) Scottish physician and editor who published an edition of Shakespeare suitable for family reading, i.e., with all indecency and blasphemy removed, thus adding the word "bowdlerize" to the English language.

bowdlerize *vt* to expurgate, to remove indelicate words from.—**bowdlerism** *n*.—**bowdlerization** *n*.

bowed harp *n* (*mus*) a primitive violin, dating back to at least the 12th century. It was held on the knee and played vertically.

bowel *n* the intestine; (*pl*) entrails; (*pl*) the deep and remote part of anything.

bowel movement *n* the process of discharging waste matter from the bowels, defecation; matter so discharged, feces.

Bowen *n* **Elizabeth** (1899–1973) Anglo-Irish novelist and short-story writer whose works, e.g., *The Death of the Heart*, have been highly praised.

bower[1] *n* an arbor, a shady recess; (*poet*) dwelling.

bower[2] *n* (*naut*) an anchor carried at the bow of a ship.

bower[3] *n* (*cards*) one of the two highest cards in some card games, or the second and third highest (when the joker is used).

bowerbird *n* one of various Australian birds belonging to the starling family.

Bowe *n* **Riddick** (1967–) American heavyweight boxer, nicknamed "Big Daddy," winner of WBO heavyweight title (1995).

bow hand *n* (*mus*) usu the right hand.

bowhead *n* an Arctic whale with a large mouth; Greenland whale.

bowie knife *n* a long hunting knife, a sheath knife.

bowing *n* (*mus*) the technique of using a bow to play an instrument; the particular style of execution. *See also* **legno**.

bowl[1] *n* a roll or throw of a ball, as in bowling; a wooden ball having a bias used in bowling; (*pl*) a game played on a smooth lawn with bowls. * *vti* to play the game of bowls; to move smoothly (along) like a bowl; to throw or roll a ball; (*cricket*) to send a ball to a batsman; to dismiss (a batsman) by hitting the wicket with a bowled ball; (*with* **over**) to knock over; (*inf*) to astonish.

bowl[2] *n* a deep, rounded dish; the rounded end of a pipe; a sports stadium.

bow legs *n* (*usu pl*) a deformity in which the legs curve outwards, producing a gap between the knees when standing.—*also* **genu varum**.—**bow-legged** *adj*.

bowler[1] *n* a person who plays bowls; (*cricket*) the player who delivers the ball.

bowler[2] *n* a stiff felt hat.—*also* **derby**.

Bowles *n* **Paul** (1910–1999) American novelist, short-story writer, who is best-known for his novel *The Sheltering Sky*, and musical compositions include piano pieces, three operas and "Blue Mountain Ballads."

bowline *n* (*naut*) a knot used in making a fixed end loop; (*naut*) a rope from the weather side of a square sail to the bow to keep the ship near the wind.

bowling *n* a game in which a heavy wooden ball is bowled along a bowling alley at ten wooden skittles; the game of bowls.

bowling alley *n* a long narrow wooden lane, usu one of several in a building designed for them.

bowling green *n* a smooth lawn for bowls.

bowman[1] *n* (*pl* **bowmen**) (*mil*) an archer.

bowman[2] *n* (*pl* **bowmen**) (*naut*) the oarsman nearest the bow.

bowsaw *n* a saw with a blade under tension for cutting curves.

bowse *see* **bouse**.

bowsprit *n* (naut) a large boom or spar running out from the stem of a (sailing) ship to carry its sails forward.

bowstring *n* the string of a bow.

bow tie *n* a necktie tied in the shape of a bow.

bow window *n* a curved bay window.

bow-wow *n* a dog's bark; a child's name for a dog. * *vi* to bark like a dog.

bowyer *n* a maker or seller of archery bows.

box[1] *n* a container or receptacle for holding anything; (*theater*) a compartment with seats; (*archit*) a small country home or minor residence, e.g., a shooting box; (*inf*) a television set. * *vt* to put into a box; to enclose; (*with* **in**) to restrict.

box[2] *vt* to hit using the hands or fists. * *vi* to fight with the fists. * *n* a blow on the head or ear with the fist.

box[3] *n* an evergreen shrub or small tree yielding a hard close-grained wood; the wood. * *adj* of box or boxwood.

boxcar *n* an enclosed freight car.

boxer *n* a person who engages in boxing; a breed of dog with smooth hair and a stumpy tail.

boxer shorts *npl* loose underpants that resemble the pants worn by boxers.

box-frame *n* (*archit*) a concrete structure designed like a series of boxes one on top of the other where the cross walls carry the loads.

box girder *n* a girder constructed from rectangular metal plates.

boxing *n* the skill or sport of fighting with the fists.

Boxing Day the weekday following December 25, Christmas, when traditionally presents are given to tradesmen, employees, etc.

boxing glove *n* a padded mitten used to protect the hand in boxing.

box lunch *n* the ingredients for lunch for one person contained in a box, esp when professionally catered.

box office *n* a theater ticket office; the popularity of a play, film, actor.—**box-office** *adj*.

box pleat *n* a double pleat in cloth made by two facing folds.

box score *n* a record of a (baseball) game presented in boxlike form in order to summarize the performance of the contestants statistically.

box seat *n* a seat in a box in a theater.

box spring *n* a bedspring consisting of spiral springs enclosed in a cloth-covered frame.

boxwood *n* the hard wood of the box tree; the tree itself.

boxy *adj* resembling a box.

boy *n* a male child; a son; a lad; a youth. * *interj* an exclamation of surprise or joy.

boyar *n* (*formerly*) a Russian landed proprietor of an old aristocratic order abolished by Peter I.

Boyce *n* William (1711–79) an English composer and organist whose works include twenty symphonies and numerous pieces of church and chamber music. Most famous for writing "Heart of Oak," in *Harlequin's Invasion*, a pantomime by David Garrick (1717–79) first performed in 1759.

boycott *vt* to refuse to deal with or trade with in order to punish or coerce.—*also n.*

Boyd *n* William [Andrew Murray] (1953–) Ghanaian-born Scottish novelist whose novels include *The New Confessions* and *Brazzaville Beach*.

boyfriend *n* a male friend with whom a person is romantically or sexually involved.

boyhood *n* the time, or state, of being a boy.

boyish *adj* like a boy; puerile; with the appeal of a boy.—**boyishly** *adv*.—**boyishness** *n*.

Boyle's law *n* (*chem*) a law that at a constant temperature the volume of a gas lessens in proportion to an increase in the pressure of the gas.

Boy Scout *n* a scout; (*without cap*) (*inf*) a man with a strong sense of duty.

boysenberry *n* (*pl* **boysenberries**) (the fruit of) a hybrid shrub developed by crossing the loganberry and various blackberries and raspberries.

bp *abbr* = boiling point; blood pressure; birthplace.

bp. *abbr* = birthplace; bishop.

BP *abbr* = *Baccalaureus Pharmaciae* (*Latin*, Bachelor of Pharmacy); *Baccalareus Philosophiae* (*Latin*, Bachelor of Philosophy); British Petroleum; British Pharmacopoeia; before present (with **B/P**); bills payable.

BP, B/P *abbr* = blood pressure.

BPA *abbr* = Bonneville Power Administration.

BPAS *abbr* = British Pregnancy Advisory Service.

BPCRA *abbr* = British Professional Cycle Racing Association.

BPd or **BPe** *abbr* = *Baccalaureus Pedagogiae* (*Latin*, Bachelor of Pedagogy).

BPE *abbr* = Bachelor of Physical Education.

BPF *abbr* = Buddhist Peace Fellowship.

BPGA *abbr* = British Potplant Growers' Association.

BPGMA *abbr* = British Pressure Gauge Manufacturers Association.

BPGS *abbr* = British Pelargonium and Geranium Society.

BPh *abbr* = Bachelor of Philosophy.

BPH *abbr* = benign prostatic hypertrophy.

BPharm *abbr* = Bachelor of Pharmacy.

BPHC *abbr* = Bureau of Primary Health Care

BPhil *abbr* = *Baccalaureus Philosophiae* (*Latin*, Bachelor of Philosophy).

BPhil(Ed) *abbr* = Bachelor of Philosophy (Education).

BPHS *abbr* = British Percheron Horse Society; British Polled Hereford Society.

bpi *abbr* = bytes per inch; bits per inch.

BPIF *abbr* = British Printing Industries Federation.

bpl. *abbr* = birthplace.

BPL *abbr* = Bachelor of Planning.

BPO *abbr* = Berlin Philharmonic Orchestra.

bps *abbr* = (*comput*) bit per second; bytes per second.

BPsych *abbr* = Bachelor of Psychology.

BPy *abbr* = Bachelor of Pedagogy.

Bq (*symbol*) bequerel.

bque. *abbr* = barque.

br. *abbr* = branch; brig; bronze; brother.

Br *symbol* (*chem*) bromine (element);

Br *abbr* = British; brother.

BR *abbr* = British Rail.

B/R. *abbr* = Bill of Rights.

BRA *abbr* = Bee Research Association; Brain Research Association.

bra *n* a brassiere.

Brabançonne, La *n* the Belgian national anthem, written in 1830.

brace *n* (*archit*) a secondary length of straight or curved timber fixed diagonally to strengthen a structure; (*mus*) the vertical line, usu with a bracket, which joins two staves of music to indicate that they are played together; a prop; a support to stiffen a framework; a hand tool for drilling; (*pl* **brace**) a pair, esp of game; (*pl*) straps for holding up trousers; a dental appliance for straightening the teeth. * *vt* to steady.

brace and bit *n* a revolving tool for boring.

bracelet *n* an ornamental chain or band for the wrist; (*pl: sl*) handcuffs.

bracer[1] *n* something that braces; a pick-me-up.

bracer[2] *n* a wrist guard in archery.

bracero *n* a Mexican laborer admitted to the US, esp for seasonal contract work in agriculture.

brachial *adj* a term used to describe the upper arm.

brachiate *adj* having arms; (*bot*) having branches in pairs, nearly horizontal and each pair at right angles to the next.—**brachiation**.

brachiopod *n* an animal like a mollusk with two spirally coiled armlike appendages, one on each side of the mouth.

brachy- *prefix* short.

brachycephalic, brachycephalous *adj* (*anat*) having the skull short in proportion to its breadth, short-headed.—**brachycephaly** *n*.

brachylogy *n* (*pl* **brachylogies**) conciseness; a condensed expression.—**brachylogous** *adj*.

brachypterous *adj* (*insects*) short-winged.

brachyuran *adj* of or belonging to a group of ten-footed crustaceans, including the crabs, marked by an undeveloped abdomen (—*also* **brachyurous**) * *n* a member of this group.

bracing *adj* refreshing, invigorating.—**bracingly** *adv*.

bracken *n* a large, coarse fern; a wide area of these growing on hills or moorland.

bracket *n* (*archit*) a projection from a wall, used to support the weight of another structure such as a shelf; a projecting metal support for a shelf; a group or category of people classified according to income; (*pl*) a pair of characters (), [], {}, used in printing or writing as parentheses. * *vt* to support with brackets; to enclose by brackets; (*people*) to group together.

brackish *adj* a term for slightly salty water, intermediate between sea and fresh water, containing between 15 and 30 parts of salt per 1000 parts of water. * *adj* somewhat salty; nauseating.—**brackishness** *n*.

bract *n* a modified leaf growing from a flower stem or enveloping a head of flowers.—**bracteal** *adj*.

bracteate *adj* (*plant*) furnished with bracts. * *n* a plate or dish made of a thin beaten precious metal and decorated.

brad *n* a slender flat nail with a projection on one side.

bradawl *n* a small boring tool for making holes for brads.

Bradbury *n* 1. Malcolm [Stanley] (1932–2000) English novelist and critic whose best-known novel is *The History Man* and whose critical works include *The Novel Today*. 2. Ray (1920–) American science fiction novelist and short-story writer whose works include *Fahrenheit 451* and *The Martian Chronicles*.

Bradlee *n* 1. Benjamin Crowninshield (1921–) American journalist. He was the editor of *The Washington Post* when the Watergate scandal was exposed. 2. Will (1868–1962) American graphic designer and typographer, influenced by Aubrey Beardsley.

Bradman *n* [Sir] Don[ald George] (1908–2001) Australian cricketer; Australian captain (1936–48).

brady- *prefix* slow.

bradycardia *n* slowness of the heartbeat and pulse to below 60 per minute.

bradykinesia *n* the condition in which there is abnormally slow movement of the body and limbs and slowness of speech, as may be caused by Parkinsonism.

bradykinin *n* a polypeptide derived from plasma proteins that causes smooth muscle to contract.

brae *n* (*Scot*) a hillside; sloping ground.

brag *vti* (**bragging, bragged**) to boast. * *n* a boast or boastful talk.—**bragger** *n*.

Bragg *n* Melvyn (1939–) English novelist and arts broadcaster.

braggadocio *n* (*pl* **braggadocios**) bragging talk, empty boasting; a boaster, braggart.

braggart *n* a loud arrogant boaster.

Brahma[1] *n* (*Hinduism*) a supreme god; divine essence.

Brahma[2] *n* a useful variety of large domestic fowl with feathered legs.

Brahman[1] *n* (*pl* **Brahmans**) (*Hinduism*) a member of the highest caste, formerly consisting only of priests; Brahma.—**Brahmanic, Brahmanical** *adj*.

Brahman[2] *n* (*pl* **Brahmans, Brahman**) a breed of Indian cattle with a large hump used in crossbreeding beef cattle.

Brahmani *n* (*pl* **Brahmanis**) a female Brahman.

Brahmanism *n* the religion or doctrines of the Brahmans.—**Brahmanist** *n*.

Brahmin *n* a Brahman; a member of an upper-class New England family.

Brahms *n* Johannes (1833–97) German classical composer, one of the most influential of the 19th century. His works include the choral *German Requiem* (1869), symphonies, and chamber music.

braid *vt* to interweave three or more strands (of hair, straw, etc); to make by such interweaving. * *n* a narrow band made by such interweaving for decorating clothing; a plait.—**braider** *n*.

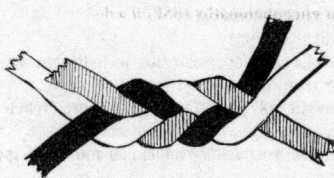

braided channel *n* a river channel that has deposited bars and islands. Braiding occurs where it becomes shallow.

brail *n* (*naut*) one of certain ropes used to gather up the foot and leeches of a sail prior to furling. * *vt* (*usu with* **up**) to haul in by the brails.

Braille *n* printing for the blind, using a system of raised dots that can be understood by touch.—*also adj*.

brain *n* nervous tissue contained in the skull of vertebrates that controls the nervous system; intellectual ability; (*inf*) a person of great intelligence; (*often pl*) the chief planner of an organization or enterprise. * *vt* to shatter the skull of; (*sl*) to hit on the head.

brainchild *n* (*pl* **brainchildren**) the result of creative thought; a clever and original idea or plan.

brain death *n* the irreversible cessation of brain activity, but not of the heartbeat, widely accepted as a criterion of death. *See* **brain-stem death**.

Brain n **Dennis** (1921–57) English horn player who became the outstanding exponent of this instrument in his day. Britten wrote *Serenade* (for tenor, horn and strings) especially for him.

brain disease n impairment of a facility, e.g., a loss of sensation or an alteration in behavior. *See also* **aphasia; concussion; epilepsy; hydrocephalus; meningitis.**

brain drain n the loss of highly skilled scientists, technicians, academics, etc through emigration.

brainless adj (*inf*) stupid.—**brainlessness** n.

brainpan n the cranium.

brain-stem death, brain death n a complete and continuous absence of the vital reflexes controlled by centers in the brain stem (breathing, pupillary responses, etc).

brainstorm n a violent mental disturbance; a brain wave.

brainstorming n the unrestrained offering of ideas by all members of a group to seek solutions to problems.

brainteaser n a mathematical puzzle; a difficult problem.

brainwash vt to change a person's ideas or beliefs by physical or mental conditioning, usu over a long period.—**brainwasher** n.—**brainwashing** n.

brain wave n an electrical impulse in the brain; (*inf*) a bright idea.

brainy adj (**brainier, brainiest**) (*inf*) having a good mind; intelligent.— **braininess** n.

braise vt (*meat, vegetables, etc*) to sauté lightly and cook slowly in liquid with the lid on.

brake[1] n a device for slowing or stopping the motion of a wheel by friction. * vt to retard or stop by a brake. * vi to apply the brake on a vehicle; to become checked by a brake.

brake[2] n bracken.

brake[3] n a place overgrown with brushwood, etc; a thicket.

brake drum n a heavy metal cylinder attached to the hub of a wheel, to which pressure is applied to slow down rotation of the wheel.

brake horsepower n the rate of work of an engine measured in terms of its resistance to a brake.

brakeman n (*pl* **brakemen**) a person in charge of a brake; a guard on a train; the person at the back of a bobsled team.

brake shoe n that part of a brake which presses against the wheel.

Bramante n **Donate** (1444–1514) Italian architect and painter. He was a leading and influential architect of the High Renaissance. His notable works include St Peter's Basilica, Rome; parts of the Vatican palace; Church of Santa Maria delle Grazie, Milan.

bramble n a prickly shrub or vine, esp of blackberries and raspberries.— **brambly** adj.

brambling n a migratory European finch with bright plumage.

bran n the husks of grain separated by sieving from the flour; a food containing these.

Bran n (*Irish Celtic myth*) **1.** the son of Febal; lured away to the Otherworld by the vision of a beautiful woman. **2.** one of the sons of Tuireann, who was born to her when she had been turned into a wolfhound by the mistress of her husband, Illan. Bran and his brother, Sgeolan, were born as wolfhounds and became the hounds of **Fionn mac Cumhaill**.

Branagh n **Kenneth** (1961–) Irish-born British actor and director.

branch n an offshoot extending from the trunk or bough of a tree or from the parent stem of a shrub; a separately located subsidiary or office of an enterprise or business; a part of something larger, e.g., a road or railroad; (*comput*) a section of a program that causes the program to divert to a subroutine when certain criteria are met and return to the main trunk on completion; a section of a directory. * vi to possess branches; to divide into branches; to come out (from a main part) as a branch; (*with* out) to extend or enlarge one's interests, activities, etc.

branchia n (*pl* **branchiae**) a respiratory organ of fishes and some amphibians, a gill.—**branchial** adj.

branchiate adj having permanent gills.

branchio- prefix gills.

branchiopod n one of a group of crustaceans, including the water flea, the gills of which are situated on the feet.

Brancusi n **Constantin** (1876–1957) Romanian-born French sculptor. The essential simplicity of his style, his excellent craftsmanship, and sensitivity to materials made him one of the most influential and well-respected sculptors of the 20th century.

brand n an identifying mark on cattle, imprinted with hot iron; a burning piece of wood; a mark of disgrace; (*business*) a particular product that is produced or distributed by a company, distinguished from products offered by competing companies by a name, symbol or design. * vt to burn a mark with a hot iron; to fix in the memory; to denounce.

brand extension n (*business*) the use of an existing successful brand name to launch a new or modified product.

brand image n (*business*) the perception of brand that manufacturers and distributors try to create in consumers by advertising, sales promotion, etc, in order to persuade them to buy it and to keep buying it.

branding iron n a metal rod with an iron at one end that is heated and used for branding cattle.

brandish vt (*a weapon, etc*) to wave or flourish in a threatening manner.— **brandisher** n.

brandling n a small brownish-red earthworm used as bait by freshwater anglers.

brand loyalty n (*business*) the tendency shown by consumers to buy a particular brand and to keep on buying it.

brand mark n (*business*) the symbol, distinctive lettering or design that is used to indicate a particular brand of product.

brand name n (*business*) the name that is used to identify a particular product, manufacturer or distributor.—**brand-name** adj.

brand-new adj entirely new and unused.

Brando n **Marlon** (1924–) American film and stage actor. Notable films *include A Streetcar Named Desire*, *On the Waterfront*, and *The Godfather*.

Brandt n 1. **Edgar** (1880–1960) French designer, the leading exponent of decorative ironwork of his day. 2. **Marianne** (1893–1983) German designer who became head of the **Bauhaus** metal workshops in 1928. 3. **Brandt Willy [Herbert Ernst Karl Frahm]** (1913–92) German statesman; chancellor of West Germany (1969–74); winner of the Nobel peace prize (1971).

Brandubh n (*Irish Celtic myth*) king of Leinster; abducted Dubh Lacha and was tricked into marrying a hag by Mongan.

brand value n (*business*) the value that is attached to a brand name.

brandy n (*pl* **brandies**) an alcoholic liquor made from distilled wine or fermented fruit juice.

Brangwyn n **Sir Frank** (1867–1956) Belgian-born Welsh artist who designed tapestries for William Morris. He is best known for his large colorful murals.

branle n (*mus*) (*French*) a French folk dance from the 15th century, which had a swaying movement.

Brans-Dicke theory n the theory that the constant of universal gravitation occurring in Newton's Law of gravitation is not constant.

brant n the brent goose, the smallest species of the wild goose.

Bran the Blessed n (*Welsh Celtic myth*) a name popularly given to Bendigeid Vran.

Branwen n (*Welsh Celtic myth*) Branwen was the sister of Bendigeid Vran and wife of Matholwch.

Braque n **Georges** (1882–1963) French painter and, along with Picasso, one of the founders of cubism. Typical of his work are his series paintings of *Still Lifes* (1920s), *Atelier* (1948–50) and *Oiseaux* (1958).

Braquernond n **Joseph Auguste** (1833–1914) French artist and designer who sparked the French and British enthusiasm for Japanese design.

brash[1] adj bold; loud-mouthed; reckless.—**brashly** adv.—**brashness** n.

brash[2] n (*geol*) broken, loose and angular fragments of rock underlying alluvial deposits; small broken pieces of ice; hedge clippings.

brash[3] n acid eructation, a fit of sickness; a rash; a burst of rain.

Brasiae n in ancient Greece, a town on the coast of northern Laconia where according to myth the infant Dionysus was washed up, after having been locked in a chest with his mother Semele and cast into the sea.

brasilin see **brazilin**.

brass n an alloy of copper and zinc; (*inf*) impudence; nerve; cheek; money; (*often pl*) the brass instruments of an orchestra or band; (*sl*) officers or officials of high rank.

brassard, brassart n armor for the upper arm; an armlet for the upper arm.

brass band n (*mus*) a type of band, particularly associated with the north of England, which consists of brass instruments and drums only.

brasserie n a bar and restaurant.

brassica n any of a group of plants that includes cabbages, turnips and mustards.— **brassicaceous** adj.

brassie n (*golf*) a wooden club *orig* with a brass sole, now No.2 wood.

brassiere n a woman's undergarment for protecting and supporting the breasts, a bra.

brass instruments n (*mus*) a family of wind instruments which are made of metal but not always brass. Brass instruments include the trombone, cornet, bugle, trumpet, French horn, tuba, and euphonium.

brass knuckles npl a metal bar with holes for the fingers worn over the knuckles for fighting.

brass tacks npl (*inf*) basic facts.

brassy adj (**brassier, brassiest**) like brass; brazen, cheeky.—**brassily** adv.— **brassiness** n.

brat n an ill-mannered, annoying child.

Brateau n **Jules-Paul** (1844–1923) French metalworker and jewelry designer who helped to revive interest in pewter.

bratpack n a group of precociously young actors, writers, etc.

Brattain, Walter see **Shockley, William Bradford**.

brattice n (*mining*) a wooden partition or separating wall in a level or shaft to form an air passage. * vt to divide by a brattice.

brattishing n (*archit*) a carved ornamental cresting on the top of a parapet, cornice or screen.

bratwurst n a type of seasoned German sausage made from pork.

Braun n German domestic appliance maker, founded by Max Braun in 1921, which made design-led products.

bravado n (*pl* **bravadoes, bravados**) pretended confidence; swaggering.

brave adj showing courage; not timid or cowardly; fearless; handsome; of excellent appearance. * vt to confront boldly; to defy. * n a North American Indian warrior.— **bravely** adv.

bravery n (*pl* **braveries**) the quality of being brave; courage, fearlessness; finery, magnificence.

bravo interj well done! * n (*pl* **bravoes, bravos**) a cry or shout of "bravo!"

bravura n, adj bold daring; dash; (*mus*) (*Italian*) literally "bravery," as in a "bravura passage"; a passage that demands a virtuoso display by the performer.

brawl *n* a loud quarrel; a noisy fight. * *vi* to quarrel loudly.—**brawler** *n*.

brawn *n* strong, well-developed muscles; physical strength; pickled pork.

brawny *adj* (**brawnier, brawniest**) muscular, tough.—**brawnily** *adv*.—**brawniness** *n*.

bray[1] *n* the sound of a donkey; any harsh sound. * *vi* (**braying, brayed**) to make similar sounds.—**brayer** *n*.

bray[2] *vt* (**braying, brayed**) to pound or beat fine or small.

brayer *n* (*print*) a hand roller used to rub down and temper ink.

Braz. *abbr* = Brazil; Brazilian.

braze[1] *vt* to solder with an alloy of brass and zinc.—**brazer** *n*.

braze[2] *vt* to cover or ornament with brass; to color like brass.

brazen *adj* made of brass; shameless. * *vt* (*usu with* **out**) to face a situation boldly and shamelessly.—**brazenness** *n*.

brazenfaced, brazen-faced *adj* marked by bold disrespect.

brazier[1] *n* a metal container for hot coals.

brazier[2] *n* a worker in brass.

brazil *n* brazilwood; a dye of various tints of esp red and orange obtained from brazilin.

Brazil *n* a huge South American federal republic bounded to the north, south and east by the Atlantic Ocean.

brazilin *n* the coloring substance extracted from brazilwood.—*also* **brasilin.**

brazil nut *n* a large three-cornered nut, the seed of a tall tree of Brazil.

brazilwood *n* a very heavy wood of a red color from various species of Central and South American trees.

BRC *abbr* = British Refugee Council.

BRCS *abbr* = British Red Cross Society.

BRD *abbr* = Biological Resource Division.

BRDB *abbr* = British Rubber Development Board.

BRDC *abbr* = British Research and Development Corporation.

BRE *abbr* = Bachelor of Religious Education; Building Research Establishment.

BREA *abbr* = Bahamas Real Estate Association.

breach *n* a break or rupture; violation of a contract, promise, etc; a break in friendship. * *vt* to make an opening in.

breach of contract *n* a failure of one of the parties involved in a contract to carry out the obligations imposed by the contract.

breach of promise *n* the breaking of a promise to marry.

breach of the peace *n* a public disturbance.

bread *n* a dough, made from flour, yeast and milk, that is baked; nourishment; (*sl*) money; **bread and butter** (*inf*) one's livelihood. * *vt* to coat meat, fish, etc with breadcrumbs before cooking.

bread-and-butter *adj* (*job*) providing a basic income; (*issues, etc*) fundamental, basic; (*letter*) thanking for hospitality.

breadbasket *n* a basket for holding bread; (*sl*) the stomach; a source of food.

breadboard *n* a wooden board for cutting bread on; board used for constructing experimental electric circuits.

breaded *adj* coated with breadcrumbs.

breadfruit *n* (*pl* **breadfruits, breadfruit**) the fruit of a tree growing in the Pacific islands, which, when roasted, is eaten as bread.

breadline *n* a line-up for free food from a charity or government; **on the breadline** poverty-stricken, only just able to subsist.

breadth *n* measurement from side to side, width; extent; liberality (e.g., of interests).

breadthways, breadthwise *adv* from side to side.

breadwinner *n* the principal wage-earner of a family.

break *vt* (**breaking, broke**, *pp* **broken**) to smash or shatter; to tame; (*rules*) to violate; to discontinue; to cause to give up a habit; (*fall*) to lessen the severity of; to ruin financially; (*news*) to impart; to decipher or solve; (*with* **down**) to crush or destroy; to analyse; (*with* **in**) to intervene; to train. * *vi* to fall apart; (*voice*) to assume a lower tone at puberty; to cut off relations with; to suffer a collapse, as of spirit; (*news*) to become public in a sudden and sensational way; (*with* **down**) to fail completely; to succumb emotionally; (*with* **even**) to suffer neither profit nor loss (after taking certain action); (*with* **in**) to force a way in; (*with* **out**) to appear, begin; to erupt; to throw off restraint, escape; (*with* **up**) to disperse; to separate; to collapse. * *n* a breaking; an interruption; a gap; a sudden change, as in weather; a rest or a short holiday; an escape; (*snooker, billiards*) a continuous run of points; (*sl*) a fortunate opportunity; (*mus*) in jazz, a short, improvised, solo passage; the point in a vocal or instrumental range where the register changes.

breakable *adj* able to be broken. * *n* a fragile object.

breakage *n* the action of breaking; something broken.

breakaway *n* secession, disassociation.

break dancing *n* dancing that involves acrobatic movements.

breakdown *n* a mechanical failure; failure of health; nervous collapse; an analysis.

breakdown truck *n* a tow truck.

breaker[1] *n* a very steep wave that breaks with a pronounced swash onto the shoreline. *Plunging breakers*, which curl over and break with a crash, are destructive. *Spilling breakers*, which break gradually over some distance, and *surging breakers*, which surge up the beach, are constructive and deposit material on the beach.

breaker[2] *n* (*naut*) a small cask for holding water.

breakeven *n* the point at which costs are covered but no profit is made.

breakeven point *n* (*business*) the level of production, sales, etc, at which a company makes neither a profit nor loss.

breakfast *n* the first meal of the morning; the food consumed. * *vi* to have breakfast.

break-in *n* the unlawful entering of premises, esp by thieves.

breaking bulk *n* (*business*) the practice of buying large quantities (bulk-buying) of goods and then selling on smaller quantities of these to consumers.

breakneck *adj* dangerously steep or fast.

break of day *n* dawn.

break-out *n* an escape, esp from prison.

breakthrough *n* the action of breaking through an obstruction; an important advance or discovery.

break-up *n* separation; collapse; dispersal.

break-up value *n* (*business*) the value of an asset of a company as estimated if it was sold off separately as opposed to being sold as part of the sale of a company as a going concern.

breakwater *n* a barrier that protects a harbor or area of coast against the force of the waves.

bream[1] *n* (*pl* **bream**) a freshwater fish.

bream[2] *vt* (*naut*) to clear (a ship's bottom) of shells, seaweed, etc, by heating and scraping.

Bream *n* **Julian** (1933–) English guitar and lute player who has done much to revive interest in classical guitar music.

Breasal *n* (*Irish Celtic myth*) king of Hy-Breasal.

breast *n* the chest; one of the two mammary glands that produce milk; the seat of the emotions. * *vt* to oppose, confront; to arrive at the top of; to confess (*make a clean breast of*).

breastbone *n* (*anat*) the flat narrow bone in the center of the chest that connects the ribs, the sternum.

breast cancer *n* a carcinoma or sarcoma, which is the commonest cancer in women.

breast cysts *n* cysts in the breasts caused by blocked milk ducts.

breast-feed *vt* (**breast-feeding, breast-fed**) to allow a baby to suck milk from the breast.

breastplate *n* armor covering the front of the body; a part of the vestment of a Jewish high priest.

breast screening *n* procedure adopted to detect breast cancer as early as possible.

breaststroke *n* a swimming stroke in which both arms are brought out sideways from the chest.

breastwork *n* a hastily constructed work thrown up breast-high for defense; the parapet of a building.

breath *n* the inhalation and exhalation of air in breathing; the air taken into the lungs; life; a slight breeze; (*scandal*) a hint.

Breathalyzer, Breathalyser *n* (*trademark*) a device for measuring the amount of alcohol in a person's breath.

breathe *vi* to inhale and exhale, to respire air; to take a rest or pause; to exist or live; to speak or sing softly; to whisper. * *vt* to emit or exhale; to whisper or speak softly.

breather *n* a pause during exercise to recover one's breath.

breathing *n* respiration; air in gentle motion; a gentle influence; a pause; (*phonetics*) an accent (‘) whether an initial vowel is aspirated or not.

breathing space *n* a pause in which to recover, get organized or get going.

breathless *adj* out of breath; panting; gasping; unable to breathe easily because of emotion.—**breathlessly** *adv*.—**breathlessness** *n*.

breathlessness *n* excessive and/or labored breathing to gain more air as a result of depleted blood oxygen.

breathtaking *adj* very exciting.

breathy *adj* (**breathier, breathiest**) (*voice*) not clear sounding.—**breathily** *adv*.—**breathiness** *n*.

B

B.Rec. or **b. rec.** *abbr* = bills receivable.

breccia *n* (*geol*) a sedimentary rock comprising coarse angular rock fragments indicating deposition very close to the source area.—**brecciated** *adj*.

Brecht *n* Bertolt (1898–1956) German dramatist, poet, and advocate of the alienation effect whose works include *The Threepenny Opera* (for which Kurt Weill wrote the music) and the play *Mother Courage*.

breckland *n* heathland.

bred *see* **breed**.

Bred *n* (*d.* 842) king of Picts. Reigned in 842. He ascended the throne on the death of his father, Uurad, but his reign did not last the year as he was deposed by his brother, Kineth.

bree *n* (*Scot*) broth; juice or liquor in which something has been steeped or boiled.

breech *n* the back part of a gun barrel.

breech delivery, breech birth *n* the birth of a baby buttocks or feet first.

breeches *npl* pants extending just below the knee.

breeches buoy *n* a lifebuoy on a hawser to take people off a wreck.

breeching *n* the harness that passes round a horse's hindquarters; a strong rope to check the recoil of a gun.

breechloader *n* a gun loaded at the breach.—**breechloading** *adj*.

breech presentation *n* the position of a baby in the uterus whereby it would be delivered buttocks first instead of the usual head-first delivery.

breed *vb* (**breeding, bred**) *vt* to engender; to bring forth; (*dogs*) to raise; to give rise to. * *vi* to produce young; to be generated. * *n* offspring; lineage or race; species (of animal).—**breeder** *n*.

breeder reactor *n* a nuclear reactor that produces more fissile material than it consumes.

breeding *n* the bearing of offspring; one's education and training; refined behavior.

breeze[1] *n* a light gentle wind; something easy to do. * *vi* (*inf*) to move quickly or casually.

breeze[2] *n* sifted ashes and cinders used in burning bricks; house sweepings; refuse.

breeze block *n* a lightweight building brick composed mainly of the ashes of coal and coke.

breezy *adj* (**breezier, breeziest**) windy; nonchalant; light-hearted, cheerful.—**breezily** *adv*.—**breeziness** *n*.

breit *adj, adv* (*mus*) (*German*) "broadly" or "grandly"; a term used to describe the manner in which a piece should be played.

BREL *abbr* = British Rail Engineering Limited.

bremsstrahlung *n* electromagnetic radiation emitted or absorbed when a free electron is decelerated or accelerated by the electric field of a nucleus without being captured by it.

Brendan the Navigator *n* Saint (484–577) Irish monk, traveled in a coracle in search of "the mysterious land far from human ken"; thought to have reached Scotland or even Iceland; founded a monastery at what is now Clonfert in County Galway. His feast day is 16 May.

Brendel *n* Alfred (1931–) Austrian pianist who lives in London and who has acquired an international reputation as a soloist. He is also highly respected as a musicologist, and his master-classes are immensely popular.

brent (goose) *n* the smallest species of the wild goose.—*also* **brant**.

Brenton *n* Howard (1942–) English dramatist whose plays include *The Romans in Britain* and (in collaboration with David Hare) *Pravda*.

br'er *n* (*dial*) brother

Bres *n* (*Irish Celtic myth*) took over from Nuada when he lost an arm in battle and had to abdicate as king of the Tuatha De Danann; was a bad and tyrannical ruler.

bressumer *n* (*archit*) the main horizontal beam in a timber-framed construction supporting a wall or projecting gable.

brethren *see* **brother**.

Breton *adj* of or relating to Brittany, its people or language. * *n* an inhabitant of Brittany; the Celtic language of Brittany.

Breton *n* André (1896–1966) French poet and author of the first *Surrealist Manifesto* in 1924.

Breuer *n* Marcel Lajos (1902–81) Hungarian-born designer who produced the *Wassily* chair in 1925.

Breughel *see* **Brueghel**.

Breuhaus de Groot *n* Fritz-August (1883–1960) German architect and designer who worked on the interior design of the first Zeppelin.

brev. *abbr* = brevet; brevetted.

breve[1] *n* a mark (˘) used to indicate a short vowel.

breve[2] *n* (*mus*) the longest note now used, equal to two whole notes (two semibreves or four minims). It is only occasionally used.—*also* **double whole note**.

Brever *n* Marcel (*b.* 1902) Hungarian architect. His notable works include Whitney Museum, New York.

brevet *n* (*mil*) a commission to an officer in the army conferring a higher rank but without increase of pay; a warrant; a license. * *adj* conferred by brevet; nominal, honorary. * *vt* (**brevetting, brevetted** *or* **breveting, breveted**) to confer brevet rank on.—**brevetcy** *n*.

brevi- *prefix* short.

breviary *n* (*pl* **breviaries**) (*RC Church*) a book containing the daily offices and prayers.

brevirostrate *adj* (*birds*) short-billed.

brevity *n* (*pl* **brevities**) briefness; conciseness.

brew *vt* to make (beer, ale, etc) from malt and hops by boiling and fermenting; to infuse (tea, etc); to plot, scheme. * *vi* to be in the process of being brewed; to be about to happen. * *n* a brewed drink.

brewage *n* something made by brewing; the brewing process.

brewer *n* a person who brews, usu beer.

brewery *n* (*pl* **breweries**) a place where beer, etc is brewed.

Brezhnev *n* Leonid Ilyich (1906–82) Soviet statesman who became general secretary of the Communist Party (1977–82) and Soviet president (1977–82).

BRF *abbr* = Bible Reading Fellowship; British Road Federation.

brg. *abbr* = bearing.

br.g. *abbr* = brown gelding.

br.h. *abbr* = brown horse.

Brian *n* William Havergal (1876–1972) English composer of 32 symphonies, which sometimes demanded outrageously large orchestras, the opera *The Tigers*, and *By the Waters of Babylon* for chorus and orchestra.

Brian Boru *n* (*c.*941–1014) high king of Ireland (1002–1014). The king of Munster from 976.

briar *see* **brier**.

Briareus *n* (*Greek myth*) a giant with a hundred arms and fifty heads, who aided Zeus in the great war waged with the Titans and was rewarded with Cympola, daughter of Zeus.—*also* **Aegaeon**.

bribe *n* money or gifts offered illegally to gain favor or influence; the gift to achieve this. * *vt* to offer or give a bribe to.—**bribable** *adj*.—**briber** *n*.

bribery *n* (*pl* **briberies**) the giving or taking of bribes.

bric-a-brac *n* curios, ornamental or rare odds and ends.

Brice *n* Saint, also known as **Britius** (*d.* 443) French monk brought up by St Martin in his monastery nears Tours; bishop of Tours. His feast day is 13 November.

brick *n* a rectangular block of mud or clay, dried in the sun or fired in a kiln for use in building; a similar shaped block of other material. * *vt* to lay or wall up with brick.

brickbat *n* a piece of brick, esp one used as a weapon; an unfavorable remark.

bricklayer *n* a person who lays bricks.

brick red *n* a grayish red color.—**brick-red** *adj*.

brickwork *n* a structure formed of bricks.

Bricriu *n* (*Irish Celtic myth*) an Ulster champion who was famous for his malice and love of mischief.

bridal *adj* relating to a bride or a wedding.

bridal wreath *n* a shrub of the rose family with sprays of small, white double flowers.

bride *n* a woman about to be married or recently married.

Bride, Saint *see* Bridget.

bridegroom *n* a man about to be married or recently married.

Bridei I *n* (*d.* 586) king of Picts (556–586). His royal court at Inverness was visited by St Columba but he did not convert to Christianity.

Bridei II *n* (*d.* 641) king of Picts (635–641). A brother of Garnard.

Bridei III *n* (*d.* 692) king of Picts (671–692).

Bridei IV *n* (*d.* 706) king of Picts (696–706). The son of Drest's sister.

Bridei V *n* (*d.* 763) king of Picts (761–763). The brother of Oengus.

bridesmaid *n* a young girl or woman attending the bride during a wedding.

bridge[1] *n* a structure built to convey people or traffic over a river, road, railway line, etc; the platform on a ship where the captain gives directions; the hard ridge of bone in the nose; (*mus*) a piece of wood that stands on the belly of stringed instruments and supports the strings; a passage in a composition that links two important themes together.; a mounting for false teeth.* *vt* to be or act as a bridge; to be a connecting link between.—**bridgeable** *adj*.

bridge[2] *n* a card game for two teams of two players based on whist.

Bridge *n* Frank (1879–1941) English composer, viola player, conductor and teacher. He wrote numerous works of all kinds, e.g., four string quartets, songs, and *A Prayer*, for chorus and orchestra.

bridgeboard *n* a notched board into which the ends of the steps of wooden stairs are fastened.

bridgehead *n* a defensive work covering the end of a bridge nearest the enemy; a foothold in enemy territory.

Bridges *n* Robert (1844–1930) English poet, appointed poet laureate in 1913.

Bridget *n* Saint, also known as **Bridgit**, **Brigit Brigid** and **Bride** (453–523) Irish abbess; patron saint of Ireland. Her feast day is 1 February; (*Irish Celtic myth*) a pagan goddess who was both a single goddess and a triple goddess.

bridgework *n* a false tooth or teeth secured to the natural teeth.

bridging *n* a piece of wood between two beams to keep them apart.

bridging loan *n* (*finance*) a form of short-term loan taken out by a borrower to bridge the gap between the purchase of one asset and the sale of another.

bridle *n* the headgear of a horse, controlling its movements; a restraint or check; (*naut*) a mooring cable. * *vt* to put a bridle on (a horse); to restrain or check. * *vi* to draw one's head back as an expression of anger, scorn, etc.—**bridler** *n*.

bridle path *n* a trail suitable for horse riding.

bridoon *n* the light snaffle and rein of a military bridle.

Brie *n* creamy white soft cheese.

brief *n* a summary of a client's case for the instruction of a barrister in a trial at law; an outline of an argument, esp that setting out the main contentions; (*pl*) men's or women's close-fitting underpants. * *vt* to provide with a precise summary of the facts. * *adj* short, concise.—**briefly** *adv*.—**briefness** *n*.

briefcase *n* a flat case for carrying documents, etc.

brier *n* a plant with a thorny or prickly woody stem; a mass of these; a tobacco pipe made from the root of the brier.—*also* **briar**.—**briery, briary** *adj*.

brig[1] *n* a hard, rocky, coastal headland.

brig[2] *n* a two-masted square-rigged vessel; a naval prison, esp on a ship.

Brig. *abbr* = Brigade; Brigadier.

Brig. Gen. *abbr* = Brigadier General.

brigade *n* an army unit, smaller than a division, commanded by a brigadier; a group of people organized to perform a particular function.

brigadier *n* an officer commanding a brigade and ranking next below a major general.

brigand *n* a bandit, usu one of a roving gang.

brigantine *n* a small two-masted vessel, square-rigged on the foremast only and with raking masts.

bright *adj* clear, shining; brilliant in color or sound; favorable or hopeful; intelligent, illustrious. * *adv* brightly.—**brightly** *adv*.—**brightness** *n*.

brighten *vti* to make or become brighter.—**brightener** *n*.

brightness *n* the subjective visual sensation related to intensity of light.

brightness temperature *n* the temperature of a black body which emits radiation of the observed intensity at a given wavelength.

Bright's disease *n* a kidney disease characterized by the presence of albumin in the urine.

Brigid, Saint *see* Bridget.

brill *n* (*pl* **brill, brills**) a European flatfish resembling the turbot.

brill. *abbr* = **brillante**, Italian "brilliant" (music).

brilliance *n* intense radiance, luster, splendor.

brilliancy *n* the quality of being brilliant; shining quality, lustrousness, shining brightness.

brilliant *adj* sparkling, bright; splendid; very intelligent.—**brilliantly** *adv*.

brilliantine *n* a cosmetic oil giving a gloss to the hair; a shiny fabric of cotton and mohair.

brim *n* the rim of a hollow vessel; the outer edge of a hat. * *vti* (**brimming, brimmed**) to fill or be filled to the brim; (*with* **over**) to overflow.

brimful *adj* completely full; overflowing.

brimstone *n* sulfur; a yellow butterfly.

brindisi *n* (*mus*) (*Italian*) literally "a toast," a drinking song in an opera during which toasts are often given.

brindled *adj* streaked brown or gray, or with flecks of a darker color.

brine *n* salt water; the sea.

bring *vt* (**bringing, brought**) to fetch, carry or convey "here" or to the place where the speaker will be; to cause to happen (e.g., rain, relief), to result in; to lead to an action or belief; to sell for; (*with* **about**) to induce, to effect; (*with* **down**) to cause to fall by or as if by shooting; (*with* **forth**) to give birth to; (*with* **forward**) to present something for consideration; to transfer a total figure from the bottom of a page to the top of the next page; (*with* **in**) to yield a profit or return; to return a verdict in court; to introduce (a legislative bill); to earn (an income); (*with* **off**) to achieve a success, often against odds; accomplish; (*with* **out**) to cause to appear; to produce (a play) or publish (a book); to demonstrate clearly, expose to view; to help someone with encouragement; (*with* **over**) to convince a person to change their loyalties; (*with* **round**) to convince a person to change their opinion; to get someone to agree or give support; to restore a person to consciousness, revive; (*with* **up**) to educate, rear a child; to raise (a matter) for discussion; to vomit.—**bringer** *n*.

brink *n* the verge of a steep place; the edge of the sea; the point of onset; the threshold of danger.

brinkmanship, brinksmanship *n* the pursuing of a policy, esp in international relations, that brings serious risk of danger in order to gain advantage.

briny *adj* (**brinier, briniest**) salty. * *n* the sea.—**brininess** *n*.

brio *n* vivacity. * *adj, adv* (*mus*) (*Italian*) "vigor," so "con brio" means "with vigor."

brioche *n* a small, slightly sweet, bread roll.

briony *see* **bryony**.

briquette, briquet *n* a compacted brick usu of fine compressed material, esp charcoal.

brisé *adj, adv* (*mus*) (*French*) literally "broken"; a term which indicates that a chord should be played in arpeggio fashion, or that music for stringed instruments should be played with short movements of the bow.

Briseïs *n* (*Greek myth*) the concubine of Achilles at Troy, whom Agamemnon took, thereby starting a quarrel which led to Achilles refusing to fight for the Greeks.

brisk *adj* alert; quick; vigorous; sharp in tone.—**briskly** *adv*.—**briskness** *n*.

brisket *n* meat from the breast of an animal.

brisling *n* a small fish like a sardine.

bristle *n* a short, coarse hair. * *vi* to stand up, as bristles; to have the bristles standing up; to show anger or indignation; to be thickly covered (with).

bristly *adj* (**bristlier, bristliest**) covered with bristles; rough.—**bristliness** *n*.

Bristol board *n* a thick smooth white pasteboard.

brit *n* the young of the herring and sprat; small animals upon which whales feed.

Brit *n* (*inf*) a British person.

Brit. *abbr* = Britain; British.

Britannia *n* Britain or its former empire personified.

Britannia metal *n* a white metal alloy of tin, copper, antimony and bismuth, resembling pewter.

Britannic *adj* of Britain; British.

Briticism *n* a word, phrase, etc, peculiar to or characteristic of British English.

British *adj* of or pertaining to Great Britain or its inhabitants; pertaining to the ancient Britons. * *n* the people of Britain; the language of the ancient Britons.

Britisher *n* a British subject.

Britishism *n* a Briticism.

Britius *n* Saint *see* Brice.

Britomartis *n* (*Greek myth*) a Cretan goddess and the daughter of Zeus, associated with hunting and fishermen.

Briton *n* a native of Great Britain, esp before the Anglo-Saxon conquest.

Britten *n* (**Edward**) **Benjamin** (1913–76) English composer, conductor and pianist. Britten's major works include the operas *Peter Grimes*, *The Rape of Lucretia*, *Albert Herring*, *Billy Budd*, *The Turn of the Screw*, *A Midsummer Night's Dream*, and *Death in Venice*. He is considered to be one of the most influential of all 20th-century composers.

brittle *adj* easily cracked or broken; fragile; sharp-tempered.—**brittleness** *n*.

brittle bone disease *see* **osteogenesis imperfecta**.

britzka, britzska *n* an open carriage with a hooded top and space for reclining.

brl. *abbr* = barrel.

brls. *abbr* = barrels.

br.m. *abbr* = brown mare.

BRM *abbr* = British Racing Motors.

BRMA *abbr* = Board of Registration of Medical Auxiliaries; Boiler and Radiator Manufacturers Association; British Reinforcement Manufacturers Association; British Rubber Manufacturers' Association.

BRNC *abbr* = Britannia Royal Naval College.

bro *n* (*inf*) mate, buddy.

bro. *abbr* = brother.

BROA *abbr* = British Rig Owners' Association.

broach *n* a spit for roasting meat; a tapered bit for shaping or enlarging a hole in metal; a device for broaching; a hole made by broaching; a brooch. * *vt* (*a topic*) to introduce for discussion; to pierce (a container) and draw out liquid.

broad *adj* of large extent from side to side; wide; spacious; giving an overall view or idea; (*humor*) coarse; strongly marked in dialect or pronunciation. * *n* (*sl*) a woman.—**broadly** *adv*.—**broadness** *n*.

broad arrow *n* an arrow with a broad barbed head; a UK government mark to distinguish its property.

broad band *adj* (*comput*) an analog communications method using high bandwidth, operating at high speeds and over long distances.

broad bean *n* a plant widely grown for its large flat edible seed.

broadcast *n* a program on radio or television. * *vti* (**broadcasting, broadcast**) to transmit on radio or television; to make known widely; to scatter seed.—**broadcaster** *n*.

broadcloth *n* a fine woolen cloth with a smooth finished surface.

Broad Church *n* a section or party intermediate between the High and the Low Church of England; any group that opposes rigid dogma.—**Broad-Church** *adj*.

broaden *vti* to grow or make broad; to widen.

broad gauge *n* a railroad gauge wider than standard gauge.—**broad-gauge, broad-gauged** *adj*.

broadloom *adj* (*carpets*) woven on a wide loom.

broad-minded *adj* tolerant; liberal in outlook.—**broad-mindedly** *adv*.—**broad-mindedness** *n*.

broads *n* a series of shallow, reed-fringed lakes linked by a slow flowing river.

broad seal *n* the official seal of a nation.

broadsheet *n* a large paper printed on one side only; a large format newspaper, approx 15 by 24 inches (38 by 61cms).

broadside *n* the entire side of a ship above the waterline; a simultaneous volley from one side of a warship; a sheet printed on one side containing information of a popular nature or an attack on some public person; any verbal or written attack.

broadside ballad *n* a form of ballad, popular until the late 19th century, that described battles, executions, etc.

broad-spectrum *adj* efficacious against a wide range (of diseases, microorganisms).

broadsword *n* (*mil*) a cutting sword with a broad straight blade.

Brobdingnagian *adj* resembling one of the giant inhabitants of the land of Brobdingnag in Swift's *Gulliver's Travels*; gigantic.

brocade *n* a heavy fabric woven with raised patterns, *orig* in gold and silver. * *vt* to work with a raised pattern.

brocatelle, brocatel *n* a figured brocade of silky texture; a variegated marble from Italy and Spain.

broccoli *n* (*pl* broccoli) a kind of cauliflower with loose heads of tiny green buds.

broch *n* (*Scot*) a dry-built circular tower of the Iron Age, common as a dwelling in prehistoric northern Scotland.

brochette *n* (food cooked on) a skewer or small spit.

brochure *n* an advertising booklet.

brock *n* (*dial*) a badger.

Brodrick *n* **Cuthbert** (1822–1905) English architect. His notable works include Hull and Leeds Town Halls.

Brodsky *n* **Joseph** (1940–1996) Russian poet who settled in the USA, becoming an American citizen in 1977. He was awarded the Nobel prize for literature in 1987.

brogan *n* a sturdy ankle-high work shoe.

brogue *n* a sturdy shoe; a dialectical accent, esp Irish.

broil[1] *vti* to cook by exposure to direct heat; to grill.

broil[2] *n* a noisy quarrel, a tumult. * *vi* to be heated with passion.

broiler *n* a pan, grill, etc for broiling; a bird fit for broiling.

broke *pt* of **break**. * *adj* (*inf*) hard up, having no money.

broken *pp* of **break**. * *adj* splintered, fractured; violated; ruined; tamed; disconnected, interrupted; overwhelmed by sorrow or ill fortune; (*speech*) imperfect.—**brokenly** *adv*.—**brokenness** *n*.

broken-down *adj* extremely infirm; worn out.

brokenhearted *adj* grief-stricken; very sad.

broken link *n* (*comput*) the link is the means whereby surfing on the Internet becomes practicable.The very fluid nature of the Internet means it is often the case that a link becomes inoperable, i.e., broken, resulting in an error message. *See* **link**.

broken octaves *n* (*mus*) a term used to describe a passage of notes that are played alternately an octave apart; they frequently occur in piano music.

broken-winded *adj* (*horse*) having the heaves.

broker *n* (*finance*) an agent who negotiates contracts of purchase and sale (as of commodities or securities); a power broker; a stockbroker; (*or* **dealer**) a member of the Stock Exchange.

brokerage *n* (*finance*) a broker's business; the fee charged by a broker.

bromate *n* a salt of bromic acid.

brome (**grass**) *n* any of a genus of oat-like grasses with drooping clusters of spikelets.

bromic acid *n* a compound of bromine and oxygen.

bromide *n* a compound of bromine; a sedative; (*sl*) a bore; a trite remark.

bromine *n* an evil-smelling nonmetallic element related to chlorine and iodine.—**bromic** *adj*.

Bromios *n* (*Greek myth*) a name given to Dionysus, meaning "thunderer."

bronchi (*sing* **bronchus**) *npl* (*anat*) two air passages supported by rings of cartilage branching off from the trachea. *See* **bronchus**.

bronchia *npl* (*sing* **bronchium**) (*anat*) the bronchial tubes.

bronchial *adj* (*anat*) of or pertaining to the bronchial tubes.

bronchial tube *n* (*anat*) either of the two main branches of the windpipe.

bronchioles *n pl* (*anat*) very fine tubes occurring as branches of the bronchi.

bronchitis *n* inflammation of the bronchi, which occurs in two forms, acute and chronic. Bacteria or viruses cause the acute form, while chronic bronchitis is identified by an excessive production of mucus and may be the result of recurrence of the acute form. —**bronchitic** *adj*.

bronchodilator *n* a drug used to relax the smooth muscle of the bronchioles, thus increasing the air supply to the lungs.

bronchopneumonia *n* diffuse inflammation of the lungs and bronchi. *See* **pneumonia**.

bronchus *n* (*pl* **bronchi**) one of two tubes which divide off from the windpipe or trachea.

bronco *n* (*pl* **broncos**) a wild or half-tamed horse of North America.

broncobuster *n* a cowboy who breaks in broncos.—**broncobusting** *n*.

Brongniart *n* **Alexandre-Theodore** (1739–1813) French architect who designed many buildings in Paris.

Brontë *n* 1. **Anne** (1820–49) English novelist and author of *Agnes Grey* and *The Tenant of Wildfell Hall* under the pen name Acton Bell; her sister 2. **Charlotte** (1816–55), English novelist and author of *Jane Eyre*, *Villette* and *The Professor* under the pen name Currer Bell, and her sister, 3. **Emily** (1818–48) English novelist and poet and author of *Wuthering Heights* under the pen name Ellis Bell.

brontosaur, brontosaurus *n* (*pl* **brontosauruses**) a large plant-eating dinosaur.—**brontosaurian** *adj*.

Bronx cheer *n* (*inf*) a rude sound made with the lips; a raspberry.

bronze *n* a copper and tin alloy, sometimes other elements, that takes a good polish and is harder and more fusible than copper. It has been used as a medium for sculpture since ancient times; any object cast in bronze; a reddish-brown color. * *adj* made of, or like, or of the color of bronze; (*skin*) tanned.—**bronzy** *adj*.

Bronze Age *n* (*archeo*) stage between the Stone and Iron Ages, beginning in the Middle East around 4500 BC, which began with the discovery of the production of bronze.

brooch *n* a small ornament with an attached pin to fasten it to a garment.

brood *vi* to incubate or hatch (eggs); to ponder over or worry about. * *n* a group having a common nature or origin, esp the children in a family; the number produced in one hatch.

broody *adj* (**broodier, broodiest**) contemplative, moody; (*inf*) wanting to have a baby.—**broodily** *adv*.—**broodiness** *n*.

brook[1] *n* a freshwater stream.

brook[2] *vt* to tolerate.—**brookable** *adj*.

Brook *n* **Edward William** (1919–) American Republican politician; the first African American to serve on the Senate (1967–79) since Reconstruction.

Brooke *n* 1. **Peter [Stephen Paul]** (1925–) English stage and experimental film director based in Paris. 2. **Rupert** (1887–1915) English poet, whose patriotic poems on the outbreak of World War I, *1914 and Other Poems*, were very popular during the war.

brooklet *n* a small brook.

Brookner *n* **Anita** (1938–) English novelist and art historian whose novels include *Hotel du Lac* and *Latecomers* and whose works on art include *Jacques-Louis David*.

Brooks *n* 1. **Gwendolyn** (1917–2000) American poet; the first African American to be awarded the Pulitzer Prize. 2. **James** (*b.* 1825) English architect. His notable works include Holy Saviour Church, Hoxton. 3. **James** (1906–92) American painter. His work in the 1930s with the Federal Arts Project was a colorful, monumental realism that developed into abstract expressionism during the 1940s. He turned to action painting in the 1950s. 3. **Mel [Melvin Kaminsky]** (1926–) American comedian, film writer, and director whose best films include *Blazing Saddles* and *Young Frankenstein*.

broom[1] *n* a bundle of fibers or twigs attached to a long handle for sweeping.

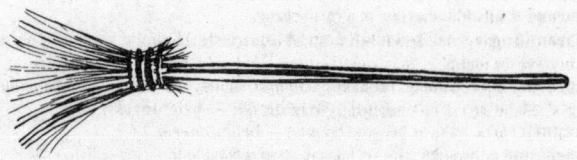

broom[2] *n* a shrub bearing large yellow flowers.

broomstick *n* the handle of a broom.

bros. *abbr* = brothers.

Bros *abbr* = Brothers.

brose *n* (*Scot*) a kind of porridge made by pouring boiling water or milk or meat liquor on oatmeal.

broth *n* a thin or thick soup made by boiling meat, etc in water.

brothel *n* a house where prostitutes work.

brother *n* a male sibling; a friend who is like a brother; a fellow member of a group, profession or association; a lay member of a men's religious order; (*pl* **brethren**) used chiefly in formal address or in referring to the members of a society or sect.

brotherhood *n* the state or quality of being a brother, brotherliness; a fraternity, an association.

brother-in-law *n* (*pl* **brothers-in-law**) the brother of a husband or wife; the husband of a sister.

Brother Jonathan *n* (*hist*) a humorous personification of the US.

brotherly *adj* like a brother; kind; affectionate.—**brotherliness** *n*.

brougham *n* a light closed four-wheeled carriage for one or two horses.

brought *see* **bring**.

brouhaha *n* a fuss; uproar.

Brouwer *n* **Adriaen** (*c.*1605–38) Flemish painter who provides an important link between the Flemish and Dutch traditions.

brow *n* the forehead; the eyebrows; the top of a cliff; the jutting top of a hill.

browbeat *vt* (**browbeating, browbeat**, *pp* **browbeaten**) to intimidate with threats, to bully.

brown *adj* having the color of chocolate, a mixture of red, black and yellow; tanned. * *n* a brown color. * *vti* to make or become brown, esp by cooking.—**brownish** *adj*.—**brownness** *n*.

Brown *n* 1. **Eleanor McMillen** (1890–1991) American interior designer whose clients included the Winthrops and the Rockefellers. 2. **F. Gregory** (1887–1948) British commercial artist and designer. 3. **Ford Madox** (1821–93) English painter. Born in France, Brown became a founder member of **Morris** and Co in 1861. His best-known picture is *The Last of England* (1855), and he also designed glass and furniture for the William Morris Company. 4. **James** (1926–) American singer and songwriter, noted for his soul sound. His songs include "Get Up Offa That Thing" (1976). 5. **John** (1800–59) American anti-slavery campaigner. His attempts to start a slave insurrection in Virginia resulted in defeat and his execution for treason. 6. **Lancelot "Capability"** (1716–83) English architect. His notable works include Claremount House, the gardens of Harewood and Blenheim Houses.

brown-bag *vti* (**brown-bagging, brown-bagged**) to take (lunch) to school or work, esp in a brown paper bag; to take (wine, etc) into a place that does not provide liquor.— **brown bagging** *n*.

brown bear *n* a large wild bear of a brownish color that lives in forests in temperate areas of Asia, North America and Europe; a brown variety of the American black bear.

brown bread *n* bread made from wholemeal flour.

brown coal *n* lignite.

Browne *n* **Sir Thomas** (1605–82) English physician and author whose two most famous works are *Religio Medici* and *Hydriotaphia or Urn Burial*.

brown earth *n* free-draining soils rich in humus where the vegetation is, or was, deciduous forest.

browned-off *adj* (*sl*) fed up, depressed.

brown goods *npl* goods such as television sets, hi-fi equipment, etc, so called because they are often brown in color.

Brownian motion (or **movement**) *n* (*physics*) a random movement of minute particles in gases and liquids.

brownie *n* a square of flat, rich chocolate cake; a friendly helpful elf; (*with cap*) a member of the junior branch of the Girl Scout or Guide movement.

Brownie point *n* a credit gained by having scored some success.

Browning *n* an automatic or semi-automatic gas-operated rifle; an automatic machine gun.

Browning *n* 1. **Elizabeth Barrett** (1806–81) English poet whose works include *Sonnets from the Portuguese* and *Aurora Leigh*; her husband 2. **Robert** (1812–89), English poet who became one of England's great poets and whose masterpiece is *The Ring and the Book* and whose "A Child's Story, The Pied Piper of Hamelin" is perennially popular.

brown-nose *vt* (*sl*) to seek approval or favor by fawning behavior.—**brownnose, brown-noser** *n*.

brownout *n* a diminution of electric light caused by a shortage of, or to conserve, electric power.

brown rice *n* unpolished rice.

brownshirt *n* (*often cap*) a member of the Nazi Party; a storm trooper.

brown star *n* a possible celestial object intermediate between a planet and a star.

brownstone *n* a kind of sandstone; a house built of this.

brown study *n* a reverie.

brown sugar *n* sugar that is unrefined or partially refined.

browse *vti* to nibble, to graze; to examine (a book) at one's leisure or casually.

browser *n* someone that browses; (*comput*) an Internet software program that enables the web to be searched, or "surfed."

BRPF *abbr* = Bertrand Russell Peace Foundation.

brt. *abbr* = brought.

Brubeck *n* **Dave** (1920–) American jazz composer and pianist, esp known for adapting classical music for jazz. He formed the "Dave Brubeck Quartet" in 1951.

Bruce *n* 1. **Edward** (1276–1318) high king of Ireland (1315–1318). 2. **Lenny** (1925–66) controversial American comedian. 3. **Sir William** (1630–1710) Scottish architect. His notable works include Hopetoun House.

brucellosis *n* an infectious disease of livestock, esp cattle, caused by a species of bacillus, *Brucella*, which can be passed to human beings.

Bruch *n* **Max** (1838–1920) German composer of Jewish origin. Among the posts he held was that of conductor of the Liverpool Philharmonic Society. Perhaps the best known of his works are his 1st Violin Concerto and his setting of *Kol Nidrei* for cello and orchestra.

Brücke *n* **Die** an association of German artists founded in 1905 in Dresden by Kirchner and others.

Bruckner *n* **Anton** (1824–96) Austrian composer noted for his ten symphonies as well as his choral and chamber music.

Brude *n* (*d.* 845) king of Picts (843–845).

Bruegel, Brueghel *n* 1. **Pieter the Elder** (*c*.1525–69) Flemish painter and draftsman and father of Pieter Brueghel the Younger and Jan Brueghel. A prominent figure in Flemish art in the mid-16th century, he remains one of the world's most admired and outstanding painters. 2. **Jan** (1568–1625) Flemish painter; also called "Velvet" Brueghel, son of Pieter Bruegel the Elder. He painted mainly landscapes and still lifes, particularly flowers, which were richly colored and detailed. 3. **Pieter the Younger** (1564–1638) Flemish painter, also called "Hell" Brueghel, son of Pieter Bruegel the Elder. He had a penchant for scenes of fire and brimstone, as in *The Burning of Troy*.

bruin *n* the brown bear personified.

bruise *vt* to injure and discolor (body tissue, surface of fruit) without breaking the skin; to break down (as leaves and berries) by pounding; to inflict psychological pain on. * *vi* to inflict a bruise; to undergo bruising. * *n* an injury of, and leakage of blood into, the subcutaneous tissue but without an open wound; a similar injury to plant tissue; an injury, to the feelings.

bruiser *n* a tough, pugnacious man; a boxer.

bruit *n* a report; a rumor; fame. * *vt* to report; to noise abroad.

brumal *adj* of or like winter, wintry.

brume *n* fog, mist; a thick vapor.—**brumous** *adj*.

brummagen *adj* showy but worthless. * *n* a cheap and showy thing, esp imitation jewelry.

brunch *n* breakfast and lunch combined.

Brunei *n* a sultanate located on the northwest coast of the island of Borneo in southeast Asia.

Brunel *n* 1. **Isambard Kingdom** (1806–59) English engineer; son of Sir Marc Isambard. He designed many bridges, tunnels, railway lines, etc in Britain. 2. **Sir Marc Isambard** (1769–1849) a French engineer who designed a tunnel under the Thames in London.

Brunelleschi *n* **Filippo** (1377–1446) Italian sculptor and architect; a major project was building the dome of Florence Cathedral.

brunette, brunet *adj* having dark brown or black hair, often with dark eyes. * *n* a brunette person; (*mus*) (*French*) a folk love-song popular in the 17th and 18th centuries.

Bruno *n* **Saint** (*c.* 1040–1101) French monk; founded the order of the Carthusians; canonized in 1628. His feast day is 6 October.

brunt *n* the main force or shock of a blow; the hardest part.

brush[1] *n* a device made of bristles set in a handle, used for grooming the hair, painting or sweeping; a short unfriendly meeting or exchange of words; a fox's bushy tail; a light stroke or graze, made in passing. * *vt* to groom or sweep with a brush; to remove with a brush; (*with aside*) to ignore, to regard as little account; (*with up*) to refresh one's memory of or skill in a subject; to wash and tidy oneself. * *vi* to touch lightly or graze; (*with up*) to smarten one's appearance.—**brusher** *n*.

brush[2] *n* brushwood.

brush fire *n* a fire in brushwood; a local war that could spread if not controlled.

brush-off *n* a curt dismissal.

brush-up *n* a smartening of one's appearance; refreshment of memory or skill.

brushwood *n* rough, close bushes; a thicket, a coppice; small wood or twigs suitable for the fire.

brushwork *n* (*art*) the "handwriting" of a painter, i.e., the distinctive way in which he or she applies paint; a particular or characteristic style of painting.

brusque *adj* blunt and curt in manner.—**brusquely** *adv*.—**brusqueness** *n*.

Brussels carpet *n* a strong kind of woolen carpet.

Brussels lace *n* a fine, expensive lace with a floral pattern made *orig* in Brussels.

Brussels sprout *n* a plant of the cabbage family with a small edible green head.

brut *adj* (*wines*) dry, unsweetened.

brutal *adj* inhuman; savage, violent; severe.—**brutally** *adv*.

brutality *n* (*pl* **brutalities**) the quality of being brutal; pitiless cruelty; a brutal act.

brutalize *vt* to treat brutally; to degrade.—**brutalization** *n*.

brute *n* any animal except man; a brutal person; (*inf*) an unpleasant or difficult person or thing. * *adj* (*force*) sheer, physical.

brutish *adj* brutal; stupid; savage, violent; coarse.—**brutishly** *adv*.—**brutishness** *n*.

Brutus *n* (*Romano-British Celtic myth*) said to have been the founder of the British people. The great-grandson of the Trojan Aeneas.

bryol. *abbr* = bryology.

bryology *n* the scientific study of mosses.—**bryological** *adj*.—**bryologist** *n*.

bryony *n* (*pl* **bryonies**) any of several climbing plants of Europe and North Africa; black bryony; white bryony.—*also* **briony**.

bryophyte *n* any plant of the division that includes mosses and liverworts.

bryozoan *n* any small animal belonging to the class Polyzoa, forming moss-like colonies by budding.

b.s. *abbr* = balance sheet.

B/s *abbr* = bags; bales.

BS *abbr* = Bachelor of Science; Bachelor of Surgery; Blessed Sacrament; Bookplate Society; British Shipbuilders; British Standard.

B/S *abbr* = bill of sale.

BSA *abbr* = Bachelor of Agricultural Science; Bachelor of Science in Agriculture; Botanical Society of America; Boy Scouts of America; Byzantine Studies Association; body surface area.

BSAA *abbr* = British School of Archaeology at Athens.

BSAC *abbr* = British Screen Advisory Council.

BSAgr, BS(Agr) *abbr* = Bachelor of Science in Agriculture.

BSAP *abbr* = British Society of Animal Production.

BSArch *abbr* = Bachelor of Science in Architecture.

BSAVA *abbr* = British Small Animal Veterinary Association.

BSBA *abbr* = Bachelor of Science in Business Administration.

BSBSW *abbr* = Boilermakers, Shipwrights, Blacksmiths and Structural Workers.

BSBus *abbr* = Bachelor of Science in Business.

bsc *abbr* = binary synchronous communications.

BSc *abbr* = *Baccalaureus Scientiae* (*Latin*, Bachelor of Science).

BSC *abbr* = Bachelor of Christian Science; Bachelor of Science in Commerce; British Safety Council; British Steel Corporation; Broadcasting Standards Council.

BScAg or **BScAgr** *abbr* = Bachelor of Science in Agriculture.

BScAgr *abbr* = Bachelor of Science in Agriculture.

BSc(Architecture) *abbr* = Bachelor of Science (Architecture).

BSCC *abbr* = British Society for Clinical Cytology.

BScChemE *abbr* = Bachelor of Science in Chemical Engineering.

BScD *abbr* = Bachelor of Dental Science.

BSCD *abbr* = British Ski Club for the Disabled.

BSCDA *abbr* = British Stock Car Drivers Association.

BSc(DentSci) *abbr* = Bachelor of Science in Dental Science.

BSCE *abbr* = Bachelor of Science in Civil Engineering; Bird Strike Committee Europe.

BSc(Econ) *abbr* = Bachelor of Science in Economics.

BScEng *abbr* = Bachelor of Science in Engineering.

BS(CerE) *abbr* = Bachelor of Science in Ceramic Engineering.

BScF or **BScFor** *abbr* = Bachelor of Science in Forestry.

B

BScMed *abbr* = Bachelor of Medical Science.

BSc(MedSci) *abbr* = Bachelor of Science (Medical Sciences).

BSCP *abbr* = British Standard Code of Practice.

BScSoc *abbr* = Bachelor of Social Sciences.

BSc(Social Science) *abbr* = Bachelor of Science (Social Science).

BScTech *abbr* = Bachelor of Technical Science.

BSD *abbr* = Bachelor of Didactic Science; British Society of Dowsers; bound stock date.

BSE *abbr* = Bachelor of Science in Education; bovine spongiform encephalopathy.

BSEd *abbr* = Bachelor of Science in Education.

BSF *abbr* = Bachelor of Science in Forestry; British Screen Finance.

BSFA *abbr* = British Science Fiction Association; British Steel Founders Association.

BSG *abbr* = British Standard Gauge.

bsh. *abbr* = bushel.

BSH *abbr* = British Society for Haematology; British Society of Hypnotherapists.

BSHA *abbr* = Bachelor of Science in Hospital Administration; British Skater Hockey Association.

BSI *abbr* = Bloody Sunday Initiative; British Society for Immunology; British Standards Institution; Building Societies' Institute.

BSIDA *abbr* = British Starch Importer & Dealers Association.

BSIE Bachelor of Science in Industrial Engineering.

BS in Econ. *abbr* = Bachelor of Science in Economics.

BSJA British Show Jumping Association.

bskt. *abbr* = basket.

Bs/L. *abbr* = bills of lading.

BSL *abbr* = Botanical Society of London; British Sign Language.

BSM *abbr* = Battalion Sergeant Major.

BSM *abbr* = British School of Motoring; British Society of Mycopathology.

BSMA *abbr* = British Secondary Metals Association; British Skate Makers Association; British Strapping Merchants Association.

BSMALTPS *abbr* = Boot and Shoe Manufacturers' Association and Leather Trades' Protection Society.

BSME or BS(MinE) *abbr* = Bachelor of Science in Mining Engineering.

BSMGP *abbr* = British Society of Master Glass Painters.

BSMMA *abbr* = British Sugar Machinery Manufacturers Association.

BSN *abbr* = Bachelor of Science in Nursing.

BSocSc *abbr* = Bachelor of Social Science.

BSOUP *abbr* = British Society of Underwater Photographers.

BSP *abbr* = Bachelor of Science in Pharmacy.

BSPA *abbr* = British Sports Photographers Association.

BSPGR *abbr* = British Society for Plant Growth Regulation.

BSPP *abbr* = British Society of Plant Pathology.

BSpPS *abbr* = British Spotted Pony Society.

BSR *abbr* = Board for Social Responsibility (Church of England).

BSRA *abbr* = British Sound Recording Association.

BSS *abbr* = Bachelor of Social Science; British Standards Specification.

BSSAA *abbr* = British Snoring and Sleep Apnoea Association.

BSSC *abbr* = Bachelor of Social Science; British Shooting Sports Council.

BSSEA *abbr* = British Special Ships Equipment Association.

BSSG *abbr* = British Society of Scientific Glassblowers.

BST *abbr* = British Standard Time; British Summer Time; bovine somatotrophin.

bt. *abbr* = bought.

Bt. *abbr* = Baronet.

BT *abbr* = *Baccalaureus Theologiae* (*Latin*, Bachelor of Theology); Board of Trade; Book Trust; British Telecom.

BTA *abbr* = British Tourist Authority; British Travel Association; Bulgarian Telegraph Agency.

bt. c. *abbr* = battalion commander.

BTC *abbr* = Bachelor of Textile Chemistry.

BTCV *abbr* = British Trust for Conservation Volunteers.

BTE *abbr* = Bachelor of Textile Engineering.

BTFHA *abbr* = British Touch for Health Association.

BTG *abbr* = British Technology Group; British Toymakers' Guild.

BTh *abbr* = Bachelor of Theology.

BThU *abbr* = British Thermal Unit.

BTIA *abbr* = British Tape Industry Association; British Turf Irrigation Association.

BTO *abbr* = British Trust for Ornithology.

BTP *abbr* = Bachelor of Town and Country Planning.

Btry *abbr* = Battery.

BTS *abbr* = Blood Transfusion Service; Burma Translation Society.

BTTMC *abbr* = British Truck Trailer Manufacturers Association.

Btu *abbr* = British thermal unit.

BTU *abbr* = Board of Trade unit.

bu *abbr* = base unit.

bu. *abbr* = bureau; bushel; bushels.

BU *abbr* = Baptist Union of Great Britain and Ireland.

Buatta *n* Mario (1936–) American interior designer, dubbed "the prince of chintz."

BUAV *abbr* = British Union for the Abolition of Vivisection.

bub *n* (*inf*) a boy; brother.

Bubastis *n* (*Egypt*) a religious site in the Nile Delta, nome capital and seat of the cult of the cat-goddess Bastet.

bubble *n* a film of liquid forming a ball around air or gas; a tiny ball of gas or air in a liquid or solid; a transparent dome; a scheme that collapses. * *vi* to boil; to rise in bubbles; to make a gurgling sound.

bubble and squeak *n* meat and vegetables fried together.

bubble bath *n* perfumed crystals or liquid added to a bath to soften the water and produce foam; a bath to which this has been added.

bubble gum *n* chewing gum that can be blown into large bubbles.

bubblejet *n* (*comput*) *see* **inkjet**.

bubbly *adj* (**bubblier, bubbliest**) having bubbles, effervescent; cheerful, high-spirited. * *n* (*inf*) champagne.

Buber *n* Martin (1878–1965) Austrian-born Jewish theologian and existentialist philosopher.

bubo *n* (*pl* **buboes**) an inflamed swelling in the groin or armpit.—**bubonic** *adj*.

bubonic plague *n* a disease which is transmitted to humans from infected rats by the rat flea.

bubonocele *n* a rupture or hernia in the groin.

BUC *abbr* = Bangor University College.

buccal *adj* a term used generally to pertain to the mouth, specifically the inside of the cheek or the gum next to the cheek.

buccaneer *n* a sea robber, a pirate. * *vi* to be a pirate.

buccinator *n* a flat muscle of the cheek, also called the trumpeter's muscle from its use in blowing wind instruments.

Buchan *n* John [1st Baron Tweedsmuir] (1875–1940) Scottish novelist, statesman, and historian; governor-general of Canada from 1935–40. He is now remembered chiefly for his adventure novels, e.g., *The Thirty-nine Steps*.

Buchanan *n* James (1791–1868) American statesman and 15th president of the US (1856–61).

Buchman *n* Frank [Nathan Daniel] (1878–1961) American evangelist who founded the Oxford Group and the Moral Rearmament.

Buchmanism *see* **Oxford Group**.

buck *n* the male of animals such as the deer, hare, rabbit, antelope; (*inf*) a dashing young man; (*sl*) a dollar. * *vti* (*horse*) to rear upwards quickly; (*inf*) to resist; (*with* **up**) (*inf*) to make or become cheerful; to hurry up.

buck. *abbr* = buckram. *Bookbinding*.

Buck *n* Pearl S[ydenstricker] (1892–1973) American novelist whose most famous work, *The Good Earth*, is based on her experiences as a missionary. She was awarded the Nobel prize for literature in 1938.

buckaroo *n* (*pl* **buckaroos**) a cowboy.

buckbean *n* a water plant with pinkish flowers.

buckboard *n* a light four-wheeled carriage with a flexible board bearing the seats.

bucket *n* a container with a handle for carrying liquid or substances in small pieces; (*comput*) a direct-access storage area from which data can be retrieved; (*inf*) a wastepaper bin. * *vt* to drive fast or recklessly; to pour with rain.

bucket brigade *n* a group of people cooperating in a line to extinguish a fire by passing buckets of water.

bucket seat *n* a single, contoured seat with an adjustable back as in a car, etc.

bucket shop *n* (*sl*) a dishonest brokerage firm; a business that sells cheap airline tickets.

buckeye *n* a North American tree with white or reddish flowers growing in clusters, the American horse chestnut; its nut; a native of Ohio.

buck fever *n* a novice hunter's nervous excitement when first sighting game.

buckjumper *n* a vicious untrained horse that endeavors to throw its rider by arching its back and drawing its feet together.

buckle *n* a fastening or clasp for a strap or band; a bend or bulge. * *vti* to fasten with a buckle; to bend under pressure, etc; (*with* **down**) (*inf*) to apply oneself diligently.

buckler *n* a small shield; protection. * *vt* to defend.

bucko *n* (*pl* **buckoes**) (*naut: sl*) a swaggering bully; (*Irish*) a young man.

buckpasser *n* (*inf*) one who regularly shifts the blame or responsibility to someone else.

buckram *n* a coarse linen or cotton cloth stiffened with dressing. * *adj* made of, or resembling, buckram; stiff, precise. * *vt* (**buckraming, buckramed**) to stiffen with or bind in buckram.

bucksaw *n* a saw whose blade is set in a frame tensioned across the back and operated by both hands.

buckshee *n* (*sl*) an extra allowance, a windfall. * *adj, adv* free, for nothing.

buckshot *n* shot of a large size for shooting game.

buckskin *n* a soft leather of deerskin, etc; (*pl*) breeches or shoes made of this; (*hist*) a native American. * *adj* made of buckskin.

buckthorn *n* any of several shrubs or trees with small greenish flowers, black berries and thorny branches.

bucktooth *n* (*pl* **buckteeth**) a projecting front tooth.

buckwheat *n* a plant cultivated for its triangular seeds, which are ground into meal and used as a cereal.

bucolic *adj* pastoral; rustic. * *n* a pastoral poem; a rustic.—**bucolically** *adv*.

BUCOP *abbr* = British Union Catalogue of Periodicals.

bud¹ *n* an embryo shoot, flower, or flower cluster of a plant; an early stage of development. * *vi* (**budding, budded**) to produce buds; to begin to develop.

bud² *n* (*inf*) buddy.

Buddha *n* one who has arrived at the state of perfect enlightenment; an image of Siddharta Gautama, founder of Buddhism.

Buddhism *n* a system of ethics and philosophy based on teachings of Buddha.

Buddhist *n* a follower of Buddhism.

budding *n* being in an early stage of development; promising or showing promise.

buddle *n* an inclined trough in which ore is separated from earth by the action of running water. * *vt* to wash ore in a buddle.

buddleia *n* a shrub with lilac or yellow flowers.

buddy *n* (*pl* **buddies**) (*inf*) a friend; a term of informal address; one who helps and supports another, esp an AIDS sufferer. * *vi* (**buddying, buddied**) to help as a buddy.

buddy system *n* an arrangement by which two people are paired, usu for mutual safety or comfort.

budge[1] *vti* to shift or move.

budge[2] *n* lambskin dressed with the wool outwards.

budgerigar *n* a small Australian parrot bred as a cage bird in many varieties of different colors.

budget *n* (*finance*) an estimate of income and expenditure within specified limits of a country, a business, etc; the total amount of money for a given purpose; a stock or supply; **on a budget** restricting one's expenditure. * *vi* (**budgeting, budgeted**) to make a budget; * *vt* to put on a budget; to plan; (*with* **for**) to allow for or save money for a purpose or aim.—**budgetary** *adj*.

budgie *n* (*inf*) a budgerigar.

BUF *abbr* = British Union of Fascists.

buff *n* a heavy, soft, brownish-yellow leather; a dull brownish yellow; (*inf*) a devotee, fan; (*inf*) a person's bare skin. * *adj* made of buff; of a buff color. * *vt* to clean or shine, *orig* with leather or a leather-covered wheel.

buffa *see* **opéra bouffe**.

buffalo *n* (*pl* **buffalo, buffaloes** *or* **buffalos**) a wild ox; a bison.

buffer[1] *n* anything that lessens shock, as of collision; something that serves as a protective barrier; (*chem*) a chemical substance that is able to keep the pH of a solution at the same level when other substances are added; (*comput*) an electronic memory storage device that is used for temporary storage of data passing in or out of the computer, e.g., from a computer to a printer.

buffer[2] *n* (*sl*) a good-tempered somewhat foolish person; an elderly man.

buffer state *n* a neutral country between two powerful and usu warlike neighbors.

buffer zone, buffer state *n* an area intended to separate; a neutral area.

buffet[1] *n* a blow with the hand or fist. * *vt* (**buffeting, buffeted**) to hit with the hand or fist; to batter (as of the wind). * *vi* to make one's way esp under difficult conditions.—**buffeter** *n*.

buffet[2] *n* a counter where refreshments are served; a meal at which guests serve themselves food.

Buffet *n* **Bernard** (1928–) French painter whose distinctive linear style was popular and much admired by younger contemporary artists.

buffet car *n* a railroad coach where light refreshments are served.

buffeting *n* repeated battering.

buffing wheel *n* a leather or cloth-covered wheel for polishing metal.

buffo *n* (*pl* **buffi, buffos**) a comic actor, esp in an opera. * *adj* comic; burlesque.

buffoon *n* a clown, a jester; a silly person.

buffoonery *n* ridiculous behavior.

BUFORA *abbr* = British Unidentified Flying Object Research Association.

bug *n* an insect with sucking mouth parts; any insect; (*inf*) a germ or virus; (*sl*) a defect, as in a machine; (*comput*) a mistake – a hardware or software error; (*sl*) a hidden microphone; an obsession, an enthusiasm. a continuing source of irritation. * *vt* (**bugging, bugged**) (*sl*) to plant a hidden microphone; (*sl*) to annoy, anger, etc.

bugaboo *n* (*pl* **bugaboos**) a bugbear.

Bugatti *n* **Carlo** (1855–1940) Italian designer and furniture maker best known for his futuristic-style furniture. His son, **Ettore** (1881–1947) achieved lasting fame as an auto designer.

bugbear *n* an object that causes great fear and anxiety.

bugger *n* a sodomite; (*sl*) a contemptible or annoying person or thing. * *vt* to practice buggery with; (*sl*) to ruin; to exhaust; (*with* **off**) to leave. * *interj* an exclamation of annoyance.

buggery *n* anal sexual intercourse.

buggy *n* (*pl* **buggies**) a light four-wheeled, one-horse carriage with one seat; a small stroller for a baby; a small vehicle.

bughouse *n* (*sl*) a mental home. * *adj* crazy.

bugle[1] *n* (*mus*) a valveless brass instrument with a conical tube and a cup-shaped mouthpiece which was widely used for giving military signals. *vti* to signal by blowing a bugle.—**bugler** *n*.

bugle[2] *n* an elongated glass bead, usu black.

bugle[3] *n* bugleweed.

bugleweed *n* a plant of Europe and Asia with spikes or clusters of small blue or white flowers.

bugloss *n* any of various plants with hairy leaves and stems.

buhl *see* **boulle**.

BUI *abbr* = Badminton Union of Ireland.

build *vt* (**building, built**) to make or construct, to establish, base; (*with* **up**) to create or develop gradually. * *vi* to put up buildings; (*with* **up**) to grow or intensify; (*health, reputation*) to develop. * *n* the way a thing is built or shaped; the shape of a person; the physical appearance or weight or size of a person.—**builder** *n*.

building *adj* the skill or occupation of constructing houses, boats, etc; something built with walls and a roof.

building and loan association *see* **savings and loan association**.

building block *n* a block of material used for construction, e.g., a brick or block of precast concrete.

building society *n* (*Brit, finance*) in the UK, a financial institution that accepts deposits from savers and makes long-term loans for house purchase secured by mortgage.

built-in *adj* incorporated as an integral part of a main structure; inherent.

built-up *adj* made higher, stronger, etc with added parts; having many buildings on it, e.g., *built-up area*.

BUJ *abbr* = *Baccalaureus Utriusque Juris*, *Latin* "Bachelor of Both Laws" (civil and canon).

bul. *abbr* = bulletin.

bulb *n* the underground bud of plants such as the onion and daffodil; a glass bulb in an electric light; a rounded shape.—**bulbous** *adj*.

bulbiferous *adj* (*plants*) producing bulbs.

bulbil *n* (*bot*) a small bulb formed at the side of an old one; a small solid or scaly bud, which detaches itself from the stem, becoming an independent plant.

bulb of percussion *n* (*archeo*) a small, rounded protuberance on the upper surface of a blade or flake formed when this was struck from the flint or stone core.

bulbul *n* an Eastern songbird; (*poet*) the Persian nightingale.

Bulfinch *n* **Charles** (1763–1844) American architect. His notable works include Boston State House.

Bulg. *abbr* = Bulgaria; Bulgarian.

Bulgakov *n* **Mikhail** (1891–1940) Russian novelist and dramatist whose masterpiece is the novel *The Master and Margarita*, a grimly comic fantasy.

Bulgari *n* **Sotirio** (1857–1932) Greek jeweler who started out selling from a stall in Rome.

Bulgaria *n* a southeast European republic located on the east of the Balkan Peninsula with a coast on the Black Sea to the east.

bulge *n* a swelling; a rounded projected part; a significant rise in numbers (of population). * *vti* to swell or bend outward.—**bulgy** *adj*.

bulgur *n* parched cracked wheat.

bulimia *n* insatiable hunger, voracity.

bulimia nervosa *n* an illness characterized by bouts of compulsive eating followed by misuse of laxatives or self-induced vomiting to avoid weight gain.

bulk *n* magnitude; great mass; volume; the main part; **in bulk** in large quantities. * *adj* total, aggregate; (*goods*) not packaged.

bulk buying *n* the large-scale buying of one commodity usu at a cost reduction; the purchase by one country of the total output of a product of another country.

bulk carrier *n* a ship carrying as cargo one unpackaged commodity.

bulkhead *n* a wall-like partition in the interior of a ship, aircraft or vehicle.

bulky *adj* (**bulkier, bulkiest**) large and unwieldy.—**bulkily** *adv*.—**bulkiness** *adj*.

bull[1] *n* an adult male bovine animal; a male whale or elephant; (*finance*) a speculator who buys in anticipation of reselling at a profit; the bull's-eye; (*sl*) nonsense; bullshit. * *adj* male; rising in price.

bull[2] *n* an official edict issued by the pope, with the papal seal on it.

bull[3] *n* a ludicrous inconsistency in language.—*also* **Irish bull**.

Bull *n* 1. **John** (1563–1628) English organist and composer whose best-known works are keyboard and church music. 2. **Ole Børneman** (1810–80) Norwegian violinist and composer.

bull. *abbr* = bulletin.

bulla *n* (*pl* **bullae**) a lead seal on a papal document; a blister.—**bullous** *adj*.

bullace *n* a wild European species of plum cultivated as the damson.

bullate *adj* blistered; puffy.

bulldog *n* a variety of dog of strong muscular build, remarkable for its courage and ferocity, formerly used for baiting bulls; a short-barrelled pistol with a large caliber. * *adj* characterized by the courage of a bulldog; tenacious.

bulldog clip *n* a spring clip with a powerful grip.

bulldoze *vt* to demolish with a bulldozer; (*inf*) to force.

bulldozer a tractor with caterpillar tracks, having a large, broad, blunt metal blade for moving earth and rocks; one who bulldozes; (*inf*) an overbearing or bullying person.

bullet *n* a small metal missile fired from a gun or rifle.

bulletin *n* an announcement; a short statement of news or of a patient's progress.

bulletin board *n* a board on which notices are posted; (*comput*) an information or services exchange accessed through a modem and telephone lines, set up by like-minded groups.

bulletproof *adj* providing protection against bullets.

bullfight *n* a combat between armed men and a bull or bulls.

bullfighting *n* the sport of goading and then killing bulls, popular in Spain, etc.—**bullfighter** *n*.

bullfinch *n* a common brightly colored European songbird.

bullfrog *n* a large North American frog found in marshy places, remarkable for its loud bellowing croak.

bullheaded *adj* stubborn; stupid.—**bullheadedly** *adv*.—**bullheadedness** *n*.

bullhorn *n* a portable electronic voice amplifier.

bullion *n* gold or silver in the form of bars or ingots before coinage.

bullish *adj* of or resembling a bull; (*stock, shares, etc*) rising or expected to rise; optimistic, hopeful.—**bullishly** *adv*.—**bullishness** *n*.

bull market *n* (*finance*) a situation on the stock exchange or currency market in which there is persistent buying and limited selling, thereby causing prices to rise.

bull-necked *adj* having a short thick neck.

bullock *n* a gelded bull; steer.

bullpen *n* a pen for bulls; a temporary detention room in a jail; (*baseball*) a practice area for relief pitchers.

bullring *n* an arena for bullfighting.

bullroarer *see* **thunder stick**.

bull's-eye *n* (*darts, archery*) the center of a target; something resembling this; a direct hit; a large round peppermint boiled sweet.

bullshit *n* (*vulg sl*) nonsense; exaggeration, pretentious talk. * *vti* (**bullshitting, bullshitted**) (*vulg sl*) to claim knowledge that is lacking; to talk boastfully.—**bullshitter** *n*.

bullsnake *n* a large, nonpoisonous North American snake.

bull terrier *n* a dog bred by a cross between the bulldog and the terrier.

bullwhip *n* a whip with a long lash for driving cattle. * *vt* (**bullwhipping, bullwhipped**) to whip with this.

bully *n* (*pl* **bullies**) a person, adult or child, who hurts or intimidates others weaker than himself or herself. * *vt* (**bullying, bullied**) to intimidate, oppress or hurt. * *vi* (*with* **off**) (*hockey*) to cross sticks in a bully-off to start a match. * *adj* (*inf*) very good, as in *bully for you*.

bully beef *n* canned corned beef.

bully boy *n* a hoodlum, a ruffian, usu one hired to beat up someone.

bullyrag *see* **ballyrag**.

Bülow *n* **Hans Guido von** (1830–94) German pianist, conductor and composer best remembered as a conductor who was greatly influenced by Wagner.

bulrush *n* a tall marsh plant.

bulwark *n* a defensive wall or rampart; (*naut*) a fence-like structure projecting above the deck of a ship; an object or person acting as a means of defence.

bum *n* (*inf*) a tramp; an idle person; (*inf*) a devotee, as of skiing or tennis; (*sl*) buttocks or anus. * *adj* broken; useless. * *vti* (**bumming, bummed**) to beg, to sponge; to live as a vagabond; (*with* **around**) to be idle, to loaf about.

bumble *vi* to do or say something clumsily or in a confused way; to stumble.—**bumbler** *n*.

bumblebee *n* a large, furry bee.

bumboat *n* a boat used for conveying provisions, fruit, etc, for sale to vessels lying off shore.

Bumbry *n* **Grace** (1937–) American soprano (formerly mezzo-soprano) who made her début in Aida in 1960. In 1961 she appeared at Bayreuth, the first black singer to do so.

bummer *n* a worthless person who sponges on others; a low politician; an unpleasant experience, esp due to drug taking.

bump *vi* to knock with a jolt, or the noise of it; a lump produced by a blow. * *vt* to hurt by striking or knocking; (*inf*) (*with* **into**) to collide with; (*inf*) to meet by chance; (*with* **off**) (*sl*) to kill, murder; (*with* **up**) (*inf*) to increase prices, size or bulk; (*sl*) to decline a pre-booked passenger their seat on a flight, due to overbooking. * *n* a jolt; a knock; the noise made by a bump or a collision; a swelling or lump; one of the bulges on the head supposedly indicating a special faculty.

bumper *n* (Brit) a shock-absorbing bar fixed to the front and rear of a motor vehicle (also **fender**); a brimming glass for a toast. * *adj* exceptionally large.

bumper car *n* a small electrically powered vehicle driven in a special rink at an amusement arcade to bump into other cars.—*also* **dodgem**.

bumper sticker *n* an adhesive label with a printed slogan, joke, etc, for fixing to an automobile bumper.

bumpkin *n* an awkward or simple country person.

bumptious *adj* offensively conceited or self-assertive.—**bumptiously** *adv*.—**bumptiousness** *n*.

bumpy *adj* (**bumpier, bumpiest**) having many bumps; rough; jolting, jerky.—**bumpily** *adv*.—**bumpiness** *n*.

bum steer *n* (*sl*) false or deceptive information or advice.

bun *n* a roll made of bread dough and currants, spices and sugar; a bun-shaped coil of hair at the nape of the neck.

BUN *abbr* = Biomass Users' Network.

bunch *n* a cluster; a number of things growing or fastened together; (*inf*) a group of people. * *vi* to group together; * *vt* to make into a bunch.—**bunchy** *adj*.—**bunchiness** *n*.

Bunche *n* **Ralph Johnson** (1904–71) American diplomat and UN official who won the Nobel peace prize in 1950, for his attempt at reconciling Israel and the Arab states (1948–49).

bunco *n* (*pl* **buncos**) (*sl*) a swindle.

buncombe *see* **bunkum**.

bund[1], **Bund** *n* (*pl* **bunds, Bünde**) a league, a confederacy.

bund[2] *n* an embankment to protect land against inundation.

bundle *n* a number of things fastened together; a fastened package; (*sl*) a large sum of money. * *vt* to put together in bundles; to push hurriedly into.—**bundler** *n*.

bundled software *n* (*comput*) software that is provided with a computer as part of the overall purchase price.

Bundy *n* **Ted [Theodore Robert]** (1946–89) American lawyer and serial killer. He carried out some 40 rapes and murders from 1974 until he was brought to trial in 1979. He was executed in 1989.

bung *n* a cork or rubber stopper. * *vt* to close up with or as with a bung; (*sl*) to throw, toss.

bungalow *n* a single story dwelling house.

bungee jumping *n* the practice of stepping into space from a high platform of some kind, where the participant is attached by the ankles, by an elasticated rope and harness.

bungle *n* a mistake or blunder; something carried out clumsily. * *vt* to spoil something through incompetence or clumsiness.—**bungler** *n*.—**bungling** *adj, n* .

bunion *n* a swollen joint between the toe and the first metatarsal bone caused by tight-fitting footwear.

bunk[1] *n* a narrow, shelf-like bed; a bunk bed.

bunk[2] *n* (*sl*) a hurried departure.

bunk[3] *n* (*sl*) bunkum, buncombe.

bunk bed *n* one of two or three single beds arranged one above the other in a compact unit.

bunker *n* a large storage container, esp for coal; a sand pit forming an obstacle on a golf course; an underground shelter.

bunkhouse *n* a dormitory for farm workers, ranch hands, etc.

bunkmate *n* one who sleeps in an adjacent bunk in a bunkhouse.

bunkum *n* idle or showy speech; nonsense.—*also* **buncombe**.

bunny *n* (*pl* **bunnies**) a pet name for a rabbit; a nightclub waitress dressed to resemble a rabbit.

Bunsen burner *n* (*chem*) a burner that mixes gas and air to produce a smokeless flame of great heat, used in science laboratories.

bunt[1] *vti* (*animal*) to butt; (*baseball*) to tap (the ball) within the infield. * *n* this stroke.

bunt[2] *n* a species of fungus that produces the smut disease in wheat.

bunt[3] *n* the bulge of a sail, net, etc.

bunting[1] *n* a cotton fabric used for making flags; a line of pennants and decorative flags.

bunting[2] *n* a bird allied to the finches and sparrows.

buntline *n* (*naut*) one of the ropes attached to the foot rope of a square sail to draw the sail up to the yard.

Buñuel *n* **Luis** (1900–83) Spanish-born film director and master of surrealist cinema.

Bunyan *n* **John** (1628–88) English author and writer of the *Pilgrim's Progress* (1678–84), perhaps the greatest allegory in the English language.

buoy *n* a bright, anchored, marine float used for mooring and for making obstacles. * *vt* to keep afloat; (*usu with* **up**) to hearten or raise the spirits of; to mark with buoys.

buoyancy *n* ability to float or rise; cheerfulness; resilience.

buoyant *adj* able to float; light, elastic; not easily depressed, cheerful.—**buoyantly** *adv*.

BUP *abbr* = British United Press.

BUPA *abbr* = British United Provident Association.

bur *n* a prickly seed-case of a plant; a person hard to shake off; a rough edge left after drilling or cutting; a burr. * *vt* (**burring, burred**) to pick burs off.

bur. *abbr* = bureau.

burble *vi* to make a gurgling sound; to speak incoherently, esp from excitement.—**burbler** *n*.

burbot *n* (*pl* **burbot, burbots**) a freshwater fish like the eel.

Burchfield *n* **Charles** (1893–1967) American painter from Ohio, who studied at Cleveland Museum School of Art.

Burckhardt *n* **Ernst F** (1900–1958) Swiss architect and set designer whose buildings include the Zurick Volkstheater (1950).

burden[1] *n* a load; something worrisome that is difficult to bear; responsibility. * *vt* to weigh down, to oppress.

burden[2] *n* the chorus or refrain of a song; a topic dwelt on in speech or writing.

burden of proof *n* the responsibility of proving what is asserted.

burdensome *adj* onerous; oppressive; heavy.—**burdensomely** *adv*.

burdock *n* a large wayside weed with prickly flowers and rough broad leaves.

bureau *n* (*pl* **bureaus, bureaux**) a writing desk; a chest of drawers; a branch of a newspaper, magazine or wire service in an important news center; a government department.

bureaucracy *n* (*pl* **bureaucracies**) a system of government where the administration is organized in a hierarchy; the government collectively; excessive paperwork and red tape.

bureaucrat *n* an official in a bureaucracy, esp one who adheres inflexibly to this system.—**bureaucratic** *adj*.—**bureaucratically** *adv*.

burette, buret *n* (*chem*) a narrow, graduated glass tube, usu with a tap, for measuring the volume of liquids.

burg *n* a town; (*formerly*) a fortified town.

burgee *n* a swallow-tailed flag or pennant flown on the mast of a yacht to show membership of a club or of a merchant vessel to show ownership.

burgeon *vt* to start to increase rapidly; (*plant*) to bloom copiously.

burger *n* (*inf*) hamburger.

Burges *n* **William** (1827–81), English architect involved in the Gothic revival movement. His notable works include Cork Cathedral.

burgess *n* in UK, a citizen or freeman of a borough; (*formerly*) a member of parliament for a borough or university; in US, a representative sent by a town to the colonial legislative body of Virginia or Maryland.

Burgess *n* **[Wilson] [John] Anthony** (1917–93) English novelist, musician, and critic whose huge output included several important novels, e.g., the nightmarish fantasy *A Clockwork Orange*. 2. **Guy** (1911–63) English diplomat and spy. Recruited by Soviet Intelligence in the 1930s, he worked for MI5 and served at the British Embassy in Washington DC. He fled to the USSR with fellow agent Donald Maclean (1913–83) in 1951.

burgh *n* (*Scot*) a borough.—**burghal** *adj*.

burgher *n* a citizen or freeman of a burgh or borough; a prosperous person of the middle classes.

burglar *n* a person who trespasses in a building with the intention of committing a crime, such as theft.

burglary *n* (*pl* **burglaries**) the act or crime of breaking into a house or any building with intent to commit a felony, esp theft.

burgle, burglarize *vti* to commit burglary (in or on).

burgomaster *n* the chief magistrate of a municipal town in Holland, Belgium or Germany.

burgonet *n* a kind of steel cap or helmet of the 16th century.

Burgred *n* king of Mercia (853–874).

Burgundy *n* (*pl* **Burgundies**) a dryish wine, red or white, made in the Burgundy region of eastern France; a similar wine produced elsewhere; a dark purplish red color.

burial *n* the laying of a body or ashes of burnt remains in the ground or a cave or structure created by man.

burial ground *n* a graveyard.

burin *n* a chisel used for engraving metal, wood or marble; (*archeo*) a stone or flint tool fashioned from a blade, usu with a narrow, sharp tip made by striking off a flake from either side; (*art*) an instrument for engraving on copper, steel, and so on, made of tempered steel (*also* **graver**).

burke *vt* to murder by suffocation; to dispose of quietly; to hush up.

Burke *n* **Edmund** (1729–97) Anglo-Irish statesman and philosopher who defended constitutionalism, attacked government abuses and its policy towards the American colonies and whose most important works are *A Philosophical Inquiry into the Origin of our Ideas of the Sublime and Beautiful* and *Reflections on the Revolution in France*.

Burkina Faso *n* a landlocked country in west Africa. The People's Democratic Republic of Burkina Faso was formerly called Upper Volta.

burl *n* a small knot or lump in thread or cloth; a knot in wood; a wood veneer with knots in it. * *vt* to pick knots, etc, from, as in finishing cloth.

burl. *abbr* = burlesque.

burla *n* **burlesca** (*Italian*) a short and jolly piece of music.

burlap *n* a coarse fabric made of jute, hemp, etc, used for bagging or in upholstery.

burlesque *n* a caricature; a literary or dramatic satire. * *vti* (**burlesquing, burlesqued**) to make fun of, to caricature. * *adj* of or like burlesque; mockingly imitative.

Burlington *n* **Richard B.** (1695–1753) English architect. His notable works include Assembly Rooms, York.

burly *adj* (**burlier, burliest**) heavily built; sturdy.—**burliness** *n*.

burn[1] *vt* (**burning, burned** *or* **burnt**) to destroy by fire; to injure by heat. * *vi* to be on fire; to feel hot; to feel passion; (*inf*) to suffer from sunburn; (*with* **off**) to clear ground by burning all vegetation; to get rid of (surplus gas, energy) by burning or using up; (*with* **out**) (*fire*) to go out; (*person*) to lose efficiency through exhaustion, excess or overwork. * *n* a scorch mark; injury caused by dry heat, flame, electric current or by chemicals. In superficial burns the skin regrows, while in deep burns grafting may be necessary.

burn[2] *n* (*Scot*) a small stream, a brook.

Burne-Jones *n* **Sir Edward Coley** (1833–1898) British painter, designer, and illustrator. Much of his work dwelt on escapist themes of myth and legend, imbued with a dreamlike, unreal quality of his own imagination.

burner *n* the part of a lamp or stove that produces a flame.

burnet *n* a brown-flowered plant of the rose family.

Burnet, Sir Frank Macfarlane *see* **Medawar, Sir Peter Brian.**

Burney *n* 1. **Dr Charles** (1726–1814) English composer and author of *General History of Music*. 2. His daughter, **Fanny** [Frances, Madame D'Arbley] (1752–1840) English novelist whose works include *Evelina*.

Burnham *n* **Daniel H** (1846–1912) American architect. His notable works include Monadnock building, Chicago.

burn-in *n* (*comput*) a period of time during which computer components are tested.

burning *adj* intense, passionate; urgent.—**burningly** *adj*.

burning glass *n* a double convex lens used to focus the sun's rays on combustible substances to ignite them.

burnish[1] *n* a polish applied as a finish to the surface of a metal or pottery vessel or artifact; luster; polish. *vt* to make shiny by rubbing; to polish. —**burnishable** *adj*.—**burnisher** *n*.

burnish[2] **burnous, burnoose** *n* a long, hooded cloak worn by Arabs.

Burns *n* **Robert** (1759–96) Scottish poet renowned as both a lyric poet and a satirist.

burnt *see* **burn**.

burnt offering *n* something offered and burnt upon an altar as a sacrifice or an atonement for sin; it was believed that the smoke and smell ascending to heaven from an animal sacrifice would propitiate the gods and bring favor. *See also* **sacrifice**.

burnt sienna *n* an orange-reddish pigment used in painting.

burp *vi* to belch. * *vt* to pat a baby on the back to cause it to belch. * *n* a belch.

burp gun *n* (*sl*) a submachine gun or automatic pistol.

burr[1] *see* **bur**.

burr[2] *n* a whirring sound; a gruff pronunciation of the letter *r*. * *vti* to pronounce with a burr.

burrito *n* a tortilla baked with a savory filling.

burro *n* (*pl* **burros**) a donkey.

Burroughs *n* **William S[eward]** (1914–97) American novelist who became one of the leading figures of the beat generation and whose works include *The Naked Lunch*.

burrow *n* an underground hide or tunnel dug by a rabbit, badger or fox, etc for shelter. * *vi* to dig a burrow; to live in a burrow; to hide (oneself); to grope into the depths of one's pockets.—**burrower** *n*.

burry *adj* (**burrier, burriest**) full of burs; rough; prickly.

bursa *n* (*pl* **bursae, bursas**) (*anat*) a fibrous sac or sac-like cavity, esp between joints, full of a fluid that lessens friction.—**bursal** *adj*.

bursar *n* a treasurer; a person in charge of the finances of a college or university; a student holding a bursary.—**bursarial** *adj*.

bursary *n* (*pl* **bursaries**) a scholarship awarded to a student.—**bursarial** *adj*.

bursitis *see* **housemaid's knee.**

burst *vt* (**bursting, burst**) to break open; to cause to explode. * *vi* to emerge suddenly; to explode; to break into pieces; to give vent to. * *n* an explosion; a burst; a volley of shots; a sudden increase of activity; a spurt.—**burster** *n*.

burton *n* (*naut*) a tackle formed of two or more blocks or pulleys; **go for a burton** to die; to be no longer useful.

Burton *n* 1. **Decimus** (1800–81), English architect. His notable works include Colosseum, Regent's Park. 2. **Richard [Richard Jenkins]** (1925–84) Welsh actor; screen partner of Elizabeth Taylor, to whom he was married twice (1964–70, 1975–76).

Burundi *n* a small, densely populated republic in central east Africa.

bury *vt* (**burying, buried**) (*bone, corpse*) to place in the ground; to inter; to conceal, to cover; to blot out of the mind; **bury the hatchet** to make peace; to be reconciled.

bus *n* (*pl* **buses, busses**) a motor coach for public transport; (*comput*) a channel through which data passes. * *vti* (**busing, bused** *or* **bussing, bussed**) to transport or travel by bus; to take by bus children from one area to another, esp to balance racial numbers.

bus. *abbr* = bushels; business.

bus boy *n* a waiter's assistant who cleans tables, brings water, etc.—**bus girl** *nf*.

busby *n* (*pl* **busbies**) a tall, fur hat, esp one worn by a guardsman.

Busby *n* **Sir Matt[hew]** (1909–94) Scottish footballer and manager of the British football club Manchester United (1946–69).

BUSF *abbr* = British Universities Sports Federation.

bush[1] *n* a low shrub with many branches; a cluster of shrubs forming a hedge; woodland; (*with* **the**) uncultivated land, esp in Africa, Australia, New Zealand, Canada; a thick growth, e.g., of hair; a fox's tail or brush.

bush[2] *n* a metal lining of a hole in which an axle turns to reduce wear by friction (— *also* **bushing**). * *vt* to furnish with a bush.

Bush *n* 1. **George [Herbert Walker]** (1924–) American Republican politician and 41st president of the US. He was vice-president under Reagan (1980–88) and president from 1988–1992. He led the UN coalition in the Gulf War (1991). 2. **George W** (1946–) American Republican statesman and 43rd president of the US; son of George Bush. Defeated Al Gore to become president in 2001, succeeding Clinton.

bush. *abbr* = bushel.

bushbaby *n* (*pl* **bushbabies**) a small tree-dwelling nocturnal lemur from Africa.

bushed *adj* (*inf*) tired, exhausted; (*Austral*) lost in the bush.

bushel[1] *n* a dry measure containing eight gallons (UK) or 64 pints (US); a vessel of such a capacity; a large quantity.

bushel[2] *vt* (**busheling, busheled** *or* **bushelling, bushelled**) to patch or repair, esp clothes.—**busheler, busheller** *n*.

bushfire *n* a fire, often widespread, in bush or scrubland.

bushing *see* **bush**[2].

bushman *n* (*pl* **bushmen**) a woodsman; (*Austral*) a settler in the bush or newly opened country; (*with cap*) one of a tribe of South African aboriginals near the Cape of Good Hope.

bushmaster *n* a large deadly South American snake with brown and gray markings.

bush pilot *n* one who pilots small aircraft in country areas, esp in Africa.

bushranger *n* a frontiersman; (*Austral: formerly*) a criminal who escaped and lived a lawless life in the bush.

bush telegraph *n* a means of communicating news by drumbeat across a large area; (*inf*) a means of spreading gossip.

bush veld *n* a mix of open grassland and trees in varying proportions in Africa. It is a type of savanna vegetation.

bushwhack *vi* to work one's way through the bush; to ambush.

bushwhacker *n* a backwoodsman; a guerrilla fighter; an implement for cutting brushwood.

bushy *adj* (**bushier, bushiest**) covered with bushes; (*hair*) thick.—**bushiness** *n*.

business *n* trade or commerce; occupation or profession; a firm; a factory; one's concern or responsibility; a matter; the agenda of a business meeting.

business card *n* a small card printed with the name, address and telephone number of a company and with the name of its employee, used for information or as an introduction.

business cycle *n* the process by which business and economic activity tends to fluctuate up and down in a relatively regular pattern.

businesslike *adj* efficient, methodical, practical.

businessman *n* (**businessmen**) a person who works for an industrial or commercial company, esp as an executive.—**businesswoman** *nf* (*pl* **businesswomen**).

business plan *n* a detailed statement of the aims and plans of a business over a stated period.

busing *see* **bussing**.

Busiris *n* (*Greek mythology*) a mythical Egyptian king, a son of Poseidon, who, during a severe drought sacrificed strangers to Zeus, and was defeated and killed by Heracles; (*Egypt*) a religious site and nome capital in the Delta, a focus of the cult of Osiris.

busker *n* a street entertainer.—**busking** *n*.

buskin *n* a half boot or high shoe; a high boot once worn by tragic actors to increase their height; a tragic drama.

busman's holiday *n* a holiday spent doing what one usually does at work.

Busoni *n* **Ferruccio Benvenuto** (1866–1924) Italian composer, pianist, theorist and teacher, remembered mainly for his operas, e.g., *Die Brautwahl, Arlecchino*, and *Doktor Faust*.

Busquet *n* **Edouard Wilfred** (*fl.*1920s) French lighting designer who patented the first anglepoise lamp.

buss *n* a smacking kiss. * *vt* to kiss.

bussing *n* the transport of children to a school in another district to achieve racially balanced classes.—*also* **busing**.

bus stop *n* a place on a bus route, usu indicated by a sign, where passengers board or alight.

bust¹ *n* the chest or breast of a human being, esp a woman; a sculpture of the head and chest.

bust² *vti* (**busting, busted** *or* **bust**) (*inf*) to burst or break; to make or become bankrupt or demoted; to hit; to arrest. * *n* (*inf*) a failure; financial collapse; a punch; a spree; an arrest.

BUSTA *abbr* = British Universities Student Travel Association.

bustard *n* any of a genus of large swift-running birds of Europe and Africa.

buster *n* a person or thing that busts; something very large; a frolic; a violent wind; (*with cap*) (*inf*) boy, man, a form of address.

bustle¹ *vi* to move or act noisily, energetically or fussily. * *n* noisy activity, stir, commotion.—**bustler** *n*.—**bustling** *adj*.

bustle² *n* a pad placed beneath the skirt of a dress to cause it to puff up at the back.

bust-up *n* (*inf*) a fight or quarrel; a noisy brawl; the permanent ending of a relationship.

busy *adj* (**busier, busiest**) occupied; active; crowded; full; industrious; (*painting*) having too much detail; (*room, telephone*) engaged, in use. * *vt* (**busying, busied**) to occupy; to make or keep busy (esp oneself).—**busily** *adv*.—**busyness** *n*.

busybody *n* (*pl* **busybodies**) a meddlesome person.

busywork *n* an activity whose main purpose is to occupy time.

but *prep* save; except. * *conj* in contrast; on the contrary, other than. * *adv* only; merely; just. * *n* an objection.

butane *n* (*chem*) a chemical substance that is easily changed from a gas to a liquid, allowing it to be stored and used as a fuel.

butch *adj* (*sl*) tough; aggressively male; (*often of a woman*) male-looking.

butcher *n* a person who slaughters meat; a retailer of meat; a ruthless murderer. * *vt* to slaughter; to murder ruthlessly; to make a mess of or spoil.

butcherbird *n* any of a genus of shrikes that suspend their slaughtered prey from thorns.

butcher's-broom *n* a low-growing evergreen shrub with rigid branched stems and spiny leaves.

butchery *n* (*pl* **butcheries**) the preparation of meat for sale; slaughter.

BUTEC *abbr* = British Underwear Testing Evaluation Centre.

Buthelezi *n* **Chief Gatsha** (1928–) South African Zulu chief and politician; a founder of the Inkatha Freedom Party.

butler *n* a manservant, usu the head servant of a household, etc.

Butler *n* 1. **Reg** (1913–81) British sculptor. He began making sculptures, as an assistant to Henry Moore, from 1947. He rose to fame in 1953 after winning a competition for a monument to the *Unknown Political Prisoner*. 2. **Samuel** (1613–80) English poet and author of a satire on Puritan intolerance, *Hudibras*, which achieved instant success in Restoration England. 3. **Samuel** (1835–1902) English novelist whose best novel is *Erewhon* and whose best-known book is *The Way of All Flesh*.

Buto *n* (*Egypt*) a snake-goddess of Lower Egypt, to whom the cobra was sacred.

butt¹ *vti* to strike or toss with the head or horns, as a bull, etc; (*with* **in**) to interfere, to enter into unasked. * *n* a push with the head or horns.—**butter** *n*.

butt² *n* a large cask for wine or beer.

butt³ *n* a mound of earth behind targets; a person who is the target of ridicule or jokes; (*pl*) the target range.

butt⁴ *n* the thick or blunt end; the stump; (*sl*) a cigarette; (*sl*) the buttocks. * *vti* to join end to end.

butte *n* (*geol*) a steep-sided, flat-topped hill of layered strata found in dry or semi-arid areas.

butte *n* an abrupt isolated hill or ridge.

butter *n* a solidified fat made from cream by churning. * *vt* to spread butter on; (*with* **up**) (*inf*) to flatter.

butterball *n* a small piece of butter shaped into a ball; a variety of North American duck; (*inf*) a fat person.

butter bean *n* a variety of lima bean cultivated for its large, flat, pale, edible, seeds.

buttercup *n* any of various plants with yellow, glossy, cup-shaped flowers.

butterfat *n* the fatty content of milk from which butter is made.

Butterfield *n* **William** (1814–1900) British Gothic Revival architect famous for his patterned brickwork. His notable works include All Saints Church, London; Keble College, Oxford.

butterfingers *n* (*used as sing*) a person who lets (a ball, etc) slip through his or her fingers.—**butterfingered** *adj*.

butterfly *n* (*pl* **butterflies**) an insect with a slender body and four usu brightly colored wings; a swimming stroke.

butterfly diagram *n* a diagram showing the variation of solar latitude with time for the first appearance of sunspots through the 11 year sunspot cycle.

buttermilk *n* the sour liquid that remains after separation from the cream in buttermaking.

butternut *n* a North American tree of the walnut family; its large oily nut; its hard wood; the color of the butternut, a brownish gray, the color of the Confederate uniform in the American Civil War; one who wore the uniform of the Confederate army.

butterscotch *n* a sauce made of melted butter and brown sugar; a kind of hard toffee made from this; its flavor; a brownish-yellow color.

butterwort *n* a violet-flowered bog plant with leaves that secrete a viscid fluid to entrap small insects.

buttery¹ *adj* like or tasting of butter; insincere.

buttery² *n* (*pl* **butteries**) a storeroom for wine or food.

buttock *n* either half of the human rump.

button *n* a disc or knob of metal, plastic, etc used as a fastening; a badge; a small button-like sweet; an electric bell push; a knob at the point of a fencing foil; (*comput*) a graphic that represents a particular command, selected when the mouse clicks on it. * *vti* to fasten with a button or buttons.

button-down *adj* (*shirt collar*) with the pointed ends secured by buttons; (*person*) conventional, unimaginative.

buttonhole *n* the slit through which a button is passed; a single flower in the buttonhole. * *vt* to make buttonholes; to sew with a special buttonhole stitch; (*person*) to keep in conversation.

buttonhook *n* a tool for fastening buttons on shoes or gloves.

buttress *n* a rugged, rocky ridge or face that projects from the side of a mountain; (*archit*) a projecting mass of brickwork or masonry built out from a wall as a support, usu to counteract the weight and lateral thrust of the roof. * *vt* to support or prop.

butut *see* **dalasi**.

butyraceous *adj* like butter in consistency, appearance or properties.

butyrate *n* a salt of butyric acid.

butyric acid *n* a colorless liquid obtained from butter, also present in cod-liver oil and sweat glands.

buxom *adj* plump and healthy; (*woman*) big-bosomed.—**buxomness** *n*.

Buxtehude *n* **Diderik** *or* **Dietrich** (*c.*1637–1707) Danish composer and noted organist, much admired by Bach. His compositions include works for organ, church cantatas, and sonatas for orchestra.

buy *vt* (**buying, bought**) to purchase (for money); to bribe or corrupt; to acquire in exchange for something; (*inf*) to believe; (*with* **off**) to pay (someone) to ensure that some undesired action is not taken; (*with* **out**) to purchase a controlling interest in or share of; to secure the release of (e.g., a person from the army) by payment; (*with* **up**) to purchase the total supply of something; to acquire a controlling interest in. * *n* a purchase.

buyer *n* a person who buys; a customer; an employee who buys on behalf of his or her employer, esp a company or store.

buyer's market *n* a market in which, because the supply exceeds the demand, the buyers control the price.

buy-out *see* **management buy-out**.

Buys Ballot's Law *n* in the northern hemisphere, winds blow anticlockwise round a depression and clockwise round an anticyclone; the converse is true in the southern hemisphere.

buzz *vi* to hum like an insect; to gossip; to hover (about). * *vt* spread gossip secretly; (*inf*) to telephone. * *vi* (*with* **off**) to go away. * *n* the humming of bees or flies; a rumor; (*sl*) a telephone call; (*sl*) a thrill, a kick.

buzzard *n* a large bird of prey of the hawk family.

buzzer *n* a device producing a buzzing sound.

buzz saw *n* a circular saw.

buzzword *n* (*inf*) a vogue or jargon word; a word or phrase that was once a technical or specialist term and which has suddenly become popular, often used mainly for effect.—*also* **fuzzword**.

b.v. *abbr* = *bene vale* (*Latin*, farewell).

B/v *abbr* = book value.

BV *abbr* = (*Latin*) *Beata Virgo*, "Blessed Virgin"; (*Dutch*) *Besloten Vennootschap*, "Company Limited"; (*Latin*) *bene vale*, "farewell"; blood vessel; blood volume.

BVA *abbr* = Board of Veterans Appeals

BVetMed *abbr* = Bachelor of Veterinary Medicine.

BVetSc *abbr* = Bachelor of Veterinary Science.

BVM *abbr* = (*Latin*) *Beata Virgo Maria*, "Blessed Virgin Mary"; Bachelor of Veterinary Medicine.

BVMS, BVM&S *abbr* = Bachelor of Veterinary Medicine and Surgery.

BVS *abbr* = Bachelor of Veterinary Surgery.

BVSc *abbr* = Bachelor of Veterinary Science.

bvt. *abbr* = brevet; brevetted.

BW *abbr* = British Waterways; biological warfare; body weight; body water.

BWA *abbr* = Baptist World Alliance; Black Watch Association.

BWAHDA *abbr* = British Warm Air Hand Drier Association.

bwana *n* (*E Africa*) an employer, a boss; (*with cap*) a form of address.

BWR *abbr* = boiling-water reactor.

BWV *abbr* = (*German*) *Bach Werke Verzeichnis*, "catalogue of Bach's works."

bx. *abbr* = box.

Bx. *abbr* = Brix (scale).

BXA *abbr* = Bureau of Export Administration

bxs. *abbr* = boxes.

by *prep* beside; next to; via; through the means of; not later than. * *adv* near to; past; in reserve, aside.

by-, bye- *prefix* subordinate, side, secret.

by and by *adv* presently, before long; later; eventually; in the future.—**by-and-by** *n*.

by and large *adv* on the whole.

Byatt *n* A[ntonia] S[usan] (1936–) English novelist and critic whose novels include *The Game* and *Possession*.

BYBA *abbr* = British Youth Band Association.

Byblis *n* (*Greek myth*) twin sister of Caunus, who hanged herself for love of her brother.

by-blow *n* a side blow; a bastard.

Byblus, Byblos *n* an ancient maritime city of Phoenicia, north of Beirut, on the Syrian coast, famous as the birthplace and center of worship of Adonis or Tammuze, now Jebail.

by. c. *abbr* = battery commander.

BYC *abbr* = British Youth Council.

bye *n* something subordinate or incidental; an odd man in a knockout competition; (*cricket*) a run scored without the ball being hit by the batsman; (*golf*) holes left after a match is decided; (*lacrosse*) a goal; (*sport*) the position of one who draws no opponent for a round in a tournament and so advances to the next round.

bye *interj* goodbye.

bye-bye[1] *interj* (*inf*) goodbye.

bye-bye[2] *n* (*inf*) sleep; bed.

by-election, bye-election *n* an election held other than at a general election.

bygone *adj* past. * *n* (*pl*) past offences or quarrels.

bylaw, bye-law *n* a rule or law made by a local authority or a company.

by-line *n* a line under a newspaper article naming its author.

BYNA *abbr* = British Young Naturalists Association.

BYO *abbr* = bring your own.

bypass *n* a main road built to avoid a town; a channel redirecting the flow of something around a blockage; (*med*) an operation to redirect the flow of blood into the heart. * *vt* (**bypassing, bypassed**) to go around; to avoid, to act by ignoring the usual channels.

bypath *n* a secluded path.

BYPC *abbr* = Beijing Youth Politics College.

byplay *n* action or dumb show aside from the main action.

byproduct, by-product *n* something useful produced in the process of making something else.

Byrd *n* **William** (1543–1623) English composer. His compositions include Masses, anthems, and other church music.

byre *n* a shed for cows.

byroad *n* an unfrequented or side road.

Byron *n* **Lord George Gordon** (1788–1824) English poet whose best-known works include *Don Juan* (1819–21) and *Childe Harold's Pilgrimage*, a work that introduced the Byronic hero.

Byronic hero a lonely, handsome, melancholy, flawed man, fatally attractive to women, as created by Lord Byron.

byssus *n* (*pl* **byssuses, byssi**) (*biol*) a tuft of long soft silky filaments by which certain mollusks attach themselves to rocks; a fine linen used by the ancient Egyptians for wrapping mummies.

bystander *n* a chance onlooker.

byte *n* (*comput*) a sequence of 8 or 16 bits representing one character or a unit of memory

by the by, by the bye *adv* incidentally.

by the way *adv* incidentally.

byway *n* a side road; a specialist or abstruse interest or area of study.

byword *n* a well-known saying; a perfect example; an object of derision.

Byzantine *adj* of or pertaining to Byzantium, the ancient capital of the Eastern Roman Empire; (*archit*) in the style of the Eastern Empire. * *n* an inhabitant of Byzantium.

Byzantine architecture *n* (*archit*) a style of architecture associated with the Byzantine Empire, mainly to be seen in churches and monastic buildings and characterized by domed roofs, rounded arches, flat ornamentation and extensive use of mosaics.

Byzantine music *n* (*mus*) music of the Christian Church of the Eastern Roman Empire which was established in AD 330 and lasted until 1435.

Bz *abbr* (*chem*) = benzene (organic chemical compound); benzoyl

BZS *abbr* = Britain-Zimbabwe Society.

B

C

c, C *n* the third letter of the English alphabet.

C *or* **C language** *n* (*comput*) a versatile medium-level computer language developed in 1972.

C¹ *symbol* (*chem*) carbon (*element*).

C² *symbol* (*mus*) the key-note or tonic of the scale of C major.

°C *symbol* degrees Celsius.

© *symbol* copyright.

c *abbr* = capacity; (*Latin*) *caput*, "chapter"; carat; century; centi- (hundredth); cubic; (*phys*) specific heat.

c. *abbr* = candle; canine (teeth); (*elec*) capacity; caput; carat; carton; case; cathode; cent; centavo; center; centime, *or* centimes; centigrade; centimeter; century; cervical; chairman; chancellor; chancery; chapter; chief; child; church; circa; circiter; (*Latin*) *circum*, "about"; (*meteor*) cirrus; (*Italian*) *col, colla* "with the"; colt; companion; (*Italian*) *con* "with"; conductor; confessor; (*Latin*) *congius*, "gallon"; congress; conservative; (*maths*) constant; consul; copy; copper; copyright; corps; cost; coupon; court; (*volumetry*) cubic; currency; current; cuspid; cutter; codex; hundredweight; (*phys*) specific heat capacity.

c. *abbr* (*Latin*) = *circa*, "about" (used with dates that are not certain).

C *abbr* = 100 (Roman numeral); Canon; Captain; Catholic; Celsius *or* centigrade; century; Chancellor; (*phys, chem*) chemical constant; (*phys, chem*) concentration; Congress; Conservative; Constable; contralto; Corps; Council; County; (*phys, chem*) Curie's constant; (*phys, chem*) molecular heat; (*astrophysics*) a Fraunhofer line characteristic of hydrogen coulomb; (*math*) third known quantity.

C. *abbr* = Cape; Catholic; Celsius *or* centigrade; Celtic; (*Latin*) Gaius.

C4 *abbr* (*Brit*) = Channel Four (commercial television channel).

C18 *abbr* = Combat 18.

Ca *symbol* (*chem*) calcium (element).

ca *abbr* = (*Latin*) *circa*, "about"; (*mus*) (*Italian*) *coll' arco*, "with the bow," as opposed to pizzicato.

ca. *abbr* = (*Law*) case, cases; cathode; centare; (*Latin*) *circa*, "about."

c.a. *abbr* = chartered accountant; chief accountant; church association; commercial agent; consular agent; controller of accounts; court of appeal.

c/a *abbr* = capital account; credit account; current account.

CA *abbr* = California; Central America; Champagne Association; Chartered Accountant; Church Army; Classical Association; Coast Artillery; Confederate Army.

C/A *abbr* = capital account; close annealed; commercial agent; credit account; current account.

CAA *abbr* = Chinese Aeromedical Association; Christian Adventure Association; Cigar Association of America; Cinema Advertising Association; Civil Aviation Authority.

CAADRP *abbr* = civil aircraft airworthiness data recording program.

CAAIS *abbr* = computer-assisted action information system.

CAAT *abbr* = Campaign Against Arms Trade.

cab *n* a taxicab; the place where the driver sits in a truck, crane, etc.

CAB *abbr* = Citizens' Advice Bureau; Condensation Advisory Bureau; Corrosion Advice Bureau.

cabal *n* a conspiracy, a secret plot; a small group of people united in perpetrating this; a clique. * *vi* (**caballing, caballed**) to form a cabal, to plot.

cabala, cabbala *n* a mystic interpretation of Scripture by Jewish rabbis; occult lore.—*also* **kabala, kabbala.**—**cabalism, cabbalism** *n*.—**cabalist, cabbalist** *n*.—**cabalistic, cabbalistic** *adj*.

cabaletta *n* (*mus*) (*Italian*) a simple aria with an insistent rhythm, or an emphatically rhythmical ending to an aria or duet.

Caballé *n* **Monserrat** (1933–) Spanish soprano whose dramatic singing has, since her début at Basle in 1956, been heard in all the great opera houses of the world.

caballero *n* (*pl* **caballeros**) a Spanish knight or gentleman; a horseman; a Spanish dance.

cabana *n* a small hut or shelter used as a dressing room on a beach.

cabaret *n* entertainment given in a restaurant or nightclub.

CABAS *abbr* = City and Borough Architects Society.

cabbage *n* a garden plant with thick leaves formed usu into a compact head, used as a vegetable.

cabbage rose *n* a large full rose.

cabby, cabbie *n* (*pl* **cabbies**) (*inf*) a person who drives a taxi.

CABE *abbr* = Companion of the Association of Business Executives.

Cabell *n* **James Branch** (1879–1958) American novelist whose mock-courtly novels set in an imaginary medieval French kingdom had a huge following in the 1920s.

caber *n* a rough pole, usu cut from a tree, tossed as a trial of strength at Highland games.

CABFAA *abbr* = Coach and Bus First Aid Association.

CABG *abbr* = coronary artery bypass graft.

cabin *n* a small house, a hut; a room in a ship; the area where passengers sit in an aircraft.

cabin boy *n* a boy servant on a ship.

cabin cruiser *n* a powerful motorboat with living accommodation.

cabinet *n* a case or cupboard with drawers or shelves; a case containing a TV, radio, etc; (*often with cap*) a body of official advisers to a government; the senior ministers of a government.

cabinetmaker *n* a person who makes fine furniture.

cabinet organ *see* **American organ**.

cable *n* a strong thick rope often of wire strands; an anchor chain; an insulated cord that carries electric current; a cablegram; a bundle of insulated wires for carrying cablegrams, TV signals, etc; (*naut*) a cable length. * *vti* to send a message by cablegram.

cable car *n* a car drawn by a moving cable, as up a steep incline.

cablecast *n* a cable television broadcast.

cablegram *n* a message transmitted by telephone line, submarine cable, or satellite; a cable.

cable-laid *adj* (*rope*) composed of three triple strands.

cable length *n* (*naut*) (*UK*) a unit of length, about 100 fathoms, 608 feet or one tenth of a nautical mile; (*US*) 120 fathoms, 720 feet.

cable molding *n* (*archit*) a type of Romanesque molding resembling a twisted rope.

cable stitch *n* a pattern of knitting stitches resembling a cable.

cable television *n* TV transmission to subscribers by cable.

cabman *n* (*pl* **cabmen**) the driver of a taxi.

cabochon *n* a precious stone polished but not faceted.

caboodle *n* (*sl*) a lot, a set (*the whole caboodle*).

caboose *n* the guard's car at the rear of a freight train; a kitchen on a ship's deck.

cabriolet *n* a covered carriage with two or four wheels drawn by one horse; a car body with a folding hood and fixed sides.

CABS *abbr* = Conservation Association of Botanical Societies; coronary artery bypass surgery.

Ca/c *abbr* = current account.

CAC *abbr* = Campaign Against Censorship; Central Advisory Committee; Central Arbitration Committee; Coast Artillery Corps; Colonial Advisory Council.

CACA *abbr* = Canadian Agricultural Chemicals Association.

CACAC *abbr* = Civil Aircraft Control Advisory Committee.

cacao *n* a tropical tree; its seed, from which cocoa and chocolate are obtained.

CACC *abbr* = Civil Aviation Communications Center.

caccia *n* (*mus*) (*Italian*) literally a "hunt," as in *corno da caccia,* hunting horn. It can also mean a 14th-century hunting poem about country life set to music.

Caccini *n* **Giulio** (*c*.1550–1618) Italian singer and composer who was a member of the Florentine group, the Camerata, which helped to establish opera. He wrote many songs and the early opera *L'Euridice.*

CACE *abbr* = Central Advisory Council for Education.

cachalot *n* the sperm whale.

cache *n* a secret hiding place; a store of weapons or treasure; a store of food left for use by travellers, etc; (*comput*) part of a computer's random access memory (*see* **RAM**), used as a temporary storage for frequently used data for faster access. * *vt* to place in a cache.

cachepot *n* an ornamental pot to hold a flowerpot.

cachet *n* a mark of authenticity; any distinguishing mark; prestige.

cachexia, cachexy *n* (*med*) a bad state of general health, weakness.—**cachectic** *adj*.

cachinnate *vi* to laugh loudly and unrestrainedly.—**cachinnation** *n*.

cachou¹ *see* **catechu**.

cachou² *n* a lozenge for sweetening the breath.

cachucha *n* (*mus*) a Spanish solo dance in 3/4 time, resembling the bolero; the music for it.

cacique *n* a West Indian or American Indian chief; a political boss.

cackle *n* the clucking sound of a hen; shrill or silly talk or laughter. * *vi* to utter with a cackle.

CACLB *abbr* = Churches' Advisory Committee on Local Broadcasting.

caco- *prefix* bad.

cacodemon, cacodaemon *n* an evil spirit.

cacodyl *n* an evil-smelling compound of arsenic and methyl.

cacoethes *n* a bad habit or propensity of the body or mind; an uncontrollable urge.—**cacoethic** *adj*.

cacography *n* bad handwriting or spelling, the opposite of calligraphy and orthography.—**cacographic** *adj*.

cacophonous *adj* harsh, ill-sounding, discordant.

cacophony *n* (*pl* **cacophonies**) an ugly sound, a discord.

CACTM *abbr* = Central Advisory Council for the Ministry.

cactus *n* (*pl* **cactuses, cacti**) a plant with a thick fleshy stem that stores water and is often studded with prickles.

cad *n* (*inf*) a man who behaves in an ungentlemanly or dishonorable way.—**caddish** *adj*—**caddishly** *adv*.—**caddishness** *n*.

cad. *abbr* (*mus*) (*Italian*) = cadenza, "final flourish."

CAD *abbr* = compact audio disc; (*comput*) computer-aided design; (*comput*) computer-aided drafting.

CADA *abbr* = Campaign Against Drug Addiction.

cadastre, cadaster *n* a register of the real estate of a district or county as a basis for taxation.—**cadastral** *adj*.

cadaver *n* a dead body.—**cadaveric** *adj*.

cadaverous *adj* gaunt, haggard; pallid, livid.—**cadaverousness** *n*.

Cadbury *n* **George** (1839–1922) English businessman, social reformer and philanthropist. With his brother Michael Cadbury (1835–99) he established the model village of Bournville, near Birmingham, England.

CADCAM *abbr* (*comput*) = computer-aided design and manufacture.

CADD *abbr* (*comput*) = computer-aided drafting and design.

caddie, caddy *n* (*pl* **caddies**) a person who carries a golfer's clubs.—*vi* (**caddying, caddied**) to perform as a caddie.

caddis *n* the larva of the mayfly used as bait.

caddy *n* (*pl* **caddies**) a small box or tin for storing tea.

cade *n* a lamb, etc, bred by hand.

CADE *abbr* = Coalition Against Dangerous Exports; (*comput*) computer-aided design evaluation.

Cadell *n* **Francis Campbell Boileau** (1883–1937) Scottish painter, influenced by Cézanne and by post-impressionist art. *Interior – The Orange Blind* (*c*.1928) is typical of his non-landscape works.

cadence *n* a falling of the voice; the intonation of the voice; rhythm; measured movements as in marching.

cadent *adj* rhythmic; falling.

cadenza *n* (*mus*) (*Italian*) an ornamental flourish at the close of a movement; an elaborate ending to an operatic aria.

cadet *n* a student at an armed forces academy, police college, etc; a school pupil in a school army training corps.

cadge *vti* to beg or obtain by begging.—**cadger** *n*.

cadi *n* a minor Mohammedan judge.

CADMAT *abbr* (*comput*) = computer-aided design, manufacture and testing.

cadmium *n* a whitish metallic element.

cadmium cell *n* a photocell sensitive to ultraviolet light.

Cadmus *n* (*Greek myth*) the founder of the city of Thebes, who killed the dragon and sowed its teeth in the ground. From these sprang up armed men who killed each other until only five were left.

CADPOS *abbr* = Communications and Data Processing Operations System.

cadre *n* a permanent nucleus or framework of a political or military unit.

caduceus *n* (*pl* **caducei**) the winged wand of Hermes (Mercury) entwined with two serpents, the emblem of the medical profession; an ancient herald's wand.

caducity *n* the quality or condition of being caducous; senility.

caducous *adj* (*biol*) (*parts of a plant*) falling off quickly or before maturity; fleeting; perishable.

CADV *abbr* = Campaign Against Domestic Violence.

CADW *abbr* (*Brit*) = Welsh Historic Monuments.

Cadwalla *n* (*c*.658–689) king of Wessex, Britain (685–688).

Cadwallon *n* (*d*. 633) king of Gwynedd, Wales (*c*.625–633).

CAE *abbr* (*comput*) = computer-aided engineering.

caecum *see* **cecum.**

Caelani *n* **Michelangelo** (1803–83) Italian patron, painter and jewelry designer.

Caer *n* (*Irish Celtic myth*) the daughter of Ethal Anubal. Oenghus had a dream about a beautiful maiden and fell in love with her. He was able to identify the girl as Caer.

CAES *abbr* = compressed air energy storage.

Caesar *n* **[Gaius] Julius** (100–44 BC) Roman soldier and historian. He formed the First Triumvirate with Marcus Licinius Crassus (*c*.114–53 BC) and Pompey [Gnaeus Pompeius Magnus] (106–48 BC) in 60 BC. He became dictator in 49 BC.

Caesar *n* the title of Roman emperors, esp Julius Caesar (*c*. 100–44 BC); (*without cap*) any ruler.

Caesarea *n* Roman town and military headquarters on the coast of Palestine.

Caesarea Philippi *n* town in Palestine near the source of the river Jordan.

Caesarean *adj* pertaining to Caesar or the Caesars; (*med*) sometimes l.c., usu spelled **cesarean**—*also* **Caesarian, Cesarean, Cesarian.**

caesarean section *or* **Caesarean section** *see* **cesarean section.**

caesium *see* **cesium.**

caesura *n* (*pl* **caesuras, caesurae**) a natural pause in the rhythm of a verse line.—**caesural** *adj*.

caf *abbr* = cost and freight.

CAF (*also* **c.a.f.**) *abbr* = cost and freight; cost, assurance, and freight.

CAFE *abbr* = Council of American Forensic Entomologists.

cafe, café *n* a diner, a small restaurant, a coffee bar, a nightclub, etc.

café au lait *n* coffee with milk; a light brown color.

café noir *n* coffee without milk.

cafeteria *n* a self-service restaurant.

cafetière *n* (*French*) a usu glass coffee pot with a plunger to press down coffee grounds.

caffeine *n* (*chem*) a chemical substance found in tea leaves and coffee beans that acts as a weak stimulant on the central nervous system.—**caffeinic** *adj*.

cafm *abbr* = commercial air freight movement.

CAFOD *abbr* = Catholic Fund for Overseas Development.

caftan *n* a long-sleeved, full-length, voluminous garment originating in the Middle East.—*also* **kaftan.**

CAFU *abbr* = Civil Aviation Flying Unit.

cage *n* a box or enclosure with bars for confining an animal, bird, prisoner, etc; a car for raising or lowering miners. * *vt* to shut in a cage, to confine.

Cage *n* **1. John** (1912–92) American composer and pianist famous for his experimental works. His works include *Music of Changes*, *4' 33"* (4 minutes 33 seconds of silence), *Radio Music* (for one to eight radios), and *Imaginary Landscape* (for twelve radios with two players at each radio). **2. Nicolas [Nicholas Coppola]** (1964–) American actor whose movies include *Leaving Las Vegas* (1995), which earned him an academy award.

CAGE *abbr* = Commercial and Government Entity

cagey, cagy *adj* (**cagier, cagiest**) (*inf*) wary, secretive, not frank.—**cagily** *adv*.—**caginess** *n*.

Cagney *n* **James** (1899–1986) American movie actor famed for gangster roles, e.g. in *Angels with Dirty Faces* (1938).

Cagnola *n* **Marchese L.** (1762–1833) Italian architect, whose notable works include Arco della Pace, Milan.

cahier *n* sheets of paper put loosely together, a notebook.

cahoots *npl* partnership; **in cahoots** in league or partnership.

CAI *abbr* = (*comput*) Computer-Assisted Instruction; Container Aid International (Belgium).

CAIAD *abbr* = Campaign Against Immigration Act Detentions.

Caiaphas *n* (*Bible*) high priest of the Temple who succeeded his father-in-law Annas and presided at the trial of Jesus.

CAIB *abbr* = Certified Associate of the Institute of Bankers.

CAIC *abbr* = Chinese Academy of International Culture.

Cailleres *n* **Jean Pierre** (1941–) French architect and designer who designed the first dishes for microwaves.

CAILS *abbr* = Chinese Association of Indian Literature Studies.

caiman *n* (*pl* **caimans**) an alligator of South and Central America.—*also* **cayman.**

Cain *n* (*Bible*) the elder son of Adam and Eve who killed his brother Abel, was cursed by God and became a wanderer of the earth.

Cain *n* **James M[allahan]** (1892–1977). American novelist noted for his thrillers, e.g. *The Postman Always Rings Twice* (1934).

caique, caïque *n* a skiff or light rowing boat used on the Bosphorus in Turkey.

Cairbre *n* (*Irish Celtic myth*) the son of Cormac mac Airt and a king of Ireland.

cairn *n* a stone mound placed as a monument or marker.

cairngorm *n* (a gemstone of) a yellow or brown variety of quartz or rock crystal.

Cairo (**El Qâhira**) *n* capital city of Egypt.

caisson *n* a watertight chamber used for carrying out underwater repairs or construction work; an apparatus for floating or lifting a vessel.

caisson disease *see* **bends.**

caitiff *n* (*arch*) a coward; a rascal. * *adj* (*arch*) base, despicable, cowardly.

cajole *vti* to persuade or soothe by flattery or deceit.—**cajoler** *n*.—**cajolingly** *adv*.

cajolery, cajolement *n* (*pl* **cajoleries, cajolements**) the action or practice of cajoling; persuasion by false arts.

Cajun, Cajan *n* an inhabitant of Louisiana descended from 18th-century French-Canadian immigrants; the dialect spoken by Cajuns.

cake *n* a mixture of flour, eggs, sugar, etc baked in small, flat shapes or a loaf; a small block of compacted or congealed matter. * *vti* to encrust; to form into a cake or hard mass.

cakewalk *n* an elaborate step dance; a task accomplished without difficulty.

cal *abbr* = calendar; caliber; calorie.

cal. *abbr* = (*mus*) (*Italian*) *calando*, "decreasing"; calendar; calends; caliber; calomel; small calorie or calories.

Cal *abbr* = California; Calorie; (*computing*) computer-aided learning.

Cal. *abbr* = California; large calorie or calories.

CAL *abbr* = (*comput*) Conversational Algebraic Language.

Calabar bean *n* a West African plant; its poisonous bean.

calabash *n* the fruit of the calabash tree of tropical America, used when dried as a vessel for liquids, etc.

calaboose *n* (*inf*) a jail.

calamanco *n* (*pl* **calamancoes, calamancos**) a glossy woolen fabric, brocaded or checkered.

calamander *n* a fine variety of Indian ebony of a very hard texture.

calamari *n* squid eaten as a food.

calamary *n* (*pl* **calamaries**) squid.

calamine *n* a zinc oxide powder used in skin lotions, etc for its soothing effect.

calamint *n* an aromatic herb of the mint family.

calamite *n* a fossil plant resembling a horsetail.

calamitous *adj* producing or resulting from calamity; disastrous.—**calamitously** *adv*.—**calamitousness** *n*.

calamity *n* (*pl* **calamities**) a disastrous event, a great misfortune; adversity.

Calamity Jane *n* [**Martha Jane Burke**] (1852–1903) American frontierswoman, and one-time associate of Wild Bill Hickok [James Butler Hickok] (1837–76).

calamus *n* (*pl* **calami**) any of a genus of palms producing the rattan canes; the sweet flag.

calando *adv* (*mus*) (*Italian*) gradually slower and softer.

calash *n* a light carriage with low wheels and a folding removable top; (*Canada*) a two-wheeled single-seater carriage; a hood formerly worn by women.—*also* **caleche**.

Calatin *n* (*Irish Celtic myth*) Calatin and his twenty-seven sons were killed by Cuchulainn. His wife bore him six monstrous children posthumously.

calcaneus (*pl* **calcanei**) *n* bone which forms the heel.

calcar *n* (*pl* **calcaria**) a tube or spur at the base of a petal or sepal; a furnace used in glass-making.

calcareous *adj* of the nature of, or containing, lime.—**calcareousness** *n*.

calceiform, calceolate *adj* (*bot*) slipper-shaped.

calceolaria *n* any of a genus of South American ornamental plants with slipper-shaped flowers.

Calchas *n* (*Greek myth*) a seer with the Greek forces during the Trojan War, who foretold the length of the siege and predicted that Troy could not be won without the help of Achilles.

calcic *adj* of or containing calcium.

calciferol *n* a form of vitamin D that is manufactured in the skin in the presence of sunlight or derived from certain foods (liver and fish oils).

calciferous *adj* containing or yielding carbonate of lime.

calcification the deposition of calcium salts, which is normal in the formation of bone but may occur at other sites in the body.

calcify *vt* (**calcifying, calcified**) to convert into lime. * *vi* to harden by conversion into lime.

calcimine *n* a white or tinted wash for walls or ceilings.—*also* **kalsomine**.

calcination *n* the act or process of reducing to powder by heat.

calcine *vt* to reduce a substance to chalky powder by the action of heat; to burn to ashes. * *vi* to undergo calcination.

calcite *n* crystallized carbonate of lime.—**calcitic** *adj*.

calcitonin *n* a hormone produced by the thyroid gland that regulates levels of calcium in the blood.

calcium *n* (*chem*) the chemical element prevalent in bones and teeth.

calcium carbide *n* (*chem*) a fusion of coal or coke with lime in an electrical furnace, which, with water, produces acetylene gas.

calcium carbonate *n* (*chem*) a common chemical compound found in limestone, chalk, marble, bones, and shells.

calcium-channel blocker *n* a drug that inhibits the movement of calcium ions into smooth muscle and cardiac muscle cells.*æalso* **calcium antagonist**.

calcium chloride *n* (*chem*) a drying agent.

calcium hypochlorite *n* (*chem*) a white powder used as a bleaching agent, bactericide or fungicide.

calcium phosphate *n* (*chem*) a white crystalline substance used in baking powder.

calcsinter *n* (*chem*) a crystalline deposit from lime springs.

calcspar *n* (*chem*) calcite, a crystalline carbonate of lime.

calculate *vti* to reckon or compute by mathematics; to suppose or believe; to plan.—**calculable** *adj*.

calculated *adj* adapted or suited (to); deliberate, cold-blooded, premeditated.—**calculatedly** *adv*.

calculated field *n* (*comput*) in a database management program a field that contains the result of a formula.

calculating *adj* shrewd, scheming.—**calculatingly** *adv*.

calculation *n* the act of calculating; the result obtained from this; an estimate.—**calculational** *adj*.

calculator *n* a device, esp a small, electronic, hand-held one, for doing mathematical calculations rapidly; one who calculates.

calculous *adj* stony; gritty.

calculus *n* (*pl* **calculi, calculuses**) an abnormal, stony mass in the body; (*math*) a mode of calculation using symbols.

Calcutta *n* a city in India.

Calder *n* **Alexander** (1898–1976) American sculptor famous for his moving sculptures or "mobiles"; non-moving ones he called "stabiles".

caldera *n* a large depression at the center of a volcano with a diameter many times that of the original vent.

caldron *n* a large kettle or boiling pot; a state of violent agitation.—*also* **cauldron**.

Caldwell *n* **Erskine** (1903–87) American novelist whose works, e.g. *Tobacco Road*, are concerned with the lives of poor Whites in the southern states.

caleche *see* **calash**.

Caledonian *adj* pertaining to Caledonia, the ancient name of Scotland; Scottish. *n* a native of Scotland.

Caledonian orogeny *n* a period of mountain-building that occurred during the late Silurian/early Devonian periods, roughly 430–360 million years ago.

calefacient *adj* producing or exciting heat. * *n* a heat-producing substance.—**calefaction** *n*.

calendar *n* a system of determining the length and divisions of a year; a chart or table of months, days and seasons; a list of particular, scheduled events.

calendar month *n* a solar month reckoned according to the calendar, as distinguished from the lunar month.

calender[1] *n* a press with rollers for finishing the surface of cloth, paper, etc. * *vt* to press in a calender.—**calenderer** *n*.

calender[2] *n* a mendicant dervish.

calends *npl* in the Roman calendar, the first day of each month.—*also* **kalends**.

calendula *n* any of a genus of plants, including the marigold, from which a medical tincture is obtained.

calenture *n* a tropical fever with delirium.

CALF *abbr* = Campaign Against Leather and Fur.

calf[1] *n* (*pl* **calves**) the young of a cow, seal, elephant, whale, etc; the leather skin of a calf; a piece of floating sea ice that has broken away from a larger piece of sea ice or from land ice; a small island beside a larger one, as in the Calf of Man beside the Isle of Man.

calf[2] *n* (*pl* **calves**) the fleshy back part of the leg below the knee.

calf love *n* puppy love; an immature infatuation.

calfskin *n* the skin of a calf made into leather.

Calgary *n* a city in Canada.

Cali *n* a city in Colombia.

Caliari *n* Paolo *see* **Veronese, Paolo**.

caliber, calibre *n* the internal diameter of a gun barrel or tube; capacity, standing, moral weight.

calibrate *vt* to measure the caliber of a gun; to adjust or mark units of measurement on a measuring scale or gauge.—**calibration** *n*.—**calibrator** *n*.

calico *n* (*pl* **calicoes, calicos**) a kind of cotton cloth. * *adj* made of this.

caliduct *n* (*archit*) a pipe for carrying hot air, steam or water as part of a heating system.

calif *see* **caliph**.

Calif. *abbr* = California.

califate *see* **caliphate**.

California (CA) *n* a state of the United States of America (USA) of which the capital is Sacramento.

California Current *n* a cold ocean current flowing southwards along the west coast of the USA.

californium *n* an artificial radioactive metallic element.

Caligula *n* [**Gaius Caesar Augustus Germanicus**] (AD 12–41) Roman emperor (AD 37–41), assassinated and succeeded by his uncle, Claudius.

calipash *n* the part of a turtle belonging to the upper shell, enclosing a dull greenish gelatinous edible substance.

calipee *n* the part of a turtle belonging to the lower shell, enclosing a light yellow gelatinous edible substance.

caliper *n* a metal framework for supporting a crippled or weak leg; paper thickness measured in microns; (*pl*) a two-legged measuring instrument. * *vt* to measure with or use calipers.—*also* **calliper**.

caliph *n* the former title assumed by the successors of Mohammed as rulers; title of a Turkish sultan.—*also* **calif**.

caliphate *n* the office, dignity or government of a caliph.—*also* **califate**.

calisthenics *npl* light gymnastic exercises.—*also* **callisthenics**.—**calisthenic, callisthenic** *adj*.

calix *n* (*pl* **calices**) a chalice; a cup-like cavity or organ.

calk[1] *see* **caulk**.

calk[2] *n* the part of a horseshoe that projects downwards to prevent slipping; a semicircular piece of iron nailed to the heel of a boot.

call *vi* to shout or cry out; to pay a short visit; to telephone; to guess the result of a coin toss; (*with* **in**) to pay a brief or informal visit; (*with* **on**) to pay a visit; to ask, to appeal to. * *vt* to summon; to name; to describe as specified; to awaken; to give orders for; to stop a baseball game due to bad weather or darkness; (*poker*) to equal an opponent's bet; (*with* **down**) to invoke; (*with* **in**) to summon for advice or help; to bring out of circulation; to demand payment of (a loan); (*with* **off**) to cancel; (*an animal*) to call away in order to stop, divert; (*with* **out**) to cry aloud; to order (workers) to come out on strike; to challenge to a duel; to summon (troops) to action; (*with* **up**) to telephone; to summon to military action, as in time of war; to recall. * *n* a summons; the note of a bird; a vocation, esp religious; occasion; a need; a demand; a short visit; the use of a telephone; a cry, a shout; the decision of an umpire or referee.—**on call** available for duty.

Callao *n* a city in Peru.

call box *n* a telephone booth; a roadside box containing a telephone for making emergency calls.

call girl *n* (*inf*) a prostitute who makes appointments by telephone.

call letters *npl* letters used to identify a radio or TV station.

call loan *n* a loan subject to recall without notice.

call option *n* an agreement to buy a stock or a commodity for a fixed price within a specified time period; (a demand for payment of) the unpaid portion of the price of a share.

call report *n* a report that is completed at regular intervals by a sales representative indicating the number of sales calls made and the results of these, such as the number of sales concluded.

call sign *n* a signal identifying a particular radio transmitter.

calla (lily) *n* an ornamental plant of the arum family with a large white spathe that enfolds a yellow spadix.

callable bonds *npl* fixed-rate bonds the issuer of which has the right to redeem or call the bond at par during the bonds' lifetime.

Callaghan *n* [Leonard] James [Baron Callaghan of Cardiff] (1912–) British Labour statesman; prime minister (1976–79).

callant, callan *n* (*Scot*) a lad, a youth.

Callas *n* Maria (originally **Maria Kalogeropoulou**) (1923–77) soprano of Greek origins, born in the USA; the most celebrated singer of her day.

callboy *n* a prompter's attendant who tells actors when to go on.

caller[1] *n* one who calls, esp by telephone; one who pays a brief visit.

caller[2] *adj* (*food*) (*Scot*) cool, fresh; in season; (*fish*) recently caught.

calligraphy *n* handwriting; beautiful writing.—**calligrapher, calligraphist** *n*.—**calligraphic** *adj*.—**calligraphically** *adv*.

calling *n* the act of summoning; a summons or invitation; a vocation, trade or profession; the state of being divinely called.

calling card *n* a social or business card with one's name, address and phone number.

calliope *n* a steam organ; (*with cap*) (*Greek myth*) the muse of epic poetry.

calliper *see* caliper.

callisthenics *see* calisthenics.

Callisto *n* (*Greek myth*) a huntress and companion of Artemis, who was loved by Zeus and was changed by him into a bear. She was killed by Artemis during a hunt and was placed among the stars as Arctos; (*astron*) a Galilean satellite of Jupiter, observed in 1610, probably a mixture of rock and ice.

callosity *n* (*pl* callosities) the state or quality of being hardened; a callus.

Callot *n* Jacques (1592–1635) French engraver whose macabre cartouches were the inspiration for designs by many goldsmiths.

callous *adj* (*skin*) hardened; (*person*) unfeeling.—**calloused** *adj*—**callously** *adv*.—**callousness** *n*.

callow *adj* inexperienced, undeveloped.—**callowness** *n*.

Calloway *n* Cab[ell] (1907–94) American bandleader and jazz singer.

call-up *n* a summons to military service.

callus *n* (*pl* calluses) a hardened, thickened place on the skin; material that forms around the end of a broken bone containing bone-forming cells, cartilage, and connective tissue.

calm *adj* windless; still, unruffled; quiet, peaceful. * *n* the state of being calm; stillness; tranquility. * *vti* to become or make calm.—**calmly** *adv*.—**calmness** *n*.

calmative *adj* (*med*) sedating. * *n* a sedative.

calo. *abbr* (*mus*) (*Italian*) = *calando*, "decreasing."

calomel *n* a preparation of mercury used as a purgative.

caloric *adj* of or pertaining to heat or calories.—**calorically** *adv*.

calorie *n* a unit of heat; a measure of food energy.—*also* **calory**.

Calorie *n* a unit of heat equalling 1,000 calories.

calorific *adj* heat-producing; (*inf*) causing fat.—**calorifically** *adv*.

calorimeter *n* an instrument for measuring quantities of heat.—**calorimetric, calorimetrical** *adj*.—**calorimetry** *n*.

Caloris basin *n* the largest feature on Mercury, an impact crater 808 miles in diameter.

calory *see* calorie.

calotte *n* a small plain skullcap of satin, etc, worn by priests.

calotype *n* a photographic process in which the image is received on paper prepared with iodide of silver.

caloyer *n* a Greek monk of the order of St Basil.

calpac, calpack *n* a tall brimless sheepskin cap worn by Turks and Armenians.—*also* **kalpak**.

CALPOM *abbr* = Committee for the Liberation of Prisoners of Opinion in Morocco.

caltrop, caltrap, calthrop *n* any of various plants with prickly fruit; an iron instrument with four spikes, placed in ditches, etc, to hinder the advance of troops.

calumet *n* the tobacco pipe of the North American Indians, smoked as a symbol of peace or to ratify treaties.

calumniate *vt* to accuse falsely and maliciously. * *vi* to utter calumnies.—**calumniation** *n*.—**calumniator** *n*.

calumny *n* (*pl* calumnies) a slander; a lie, a false accusation.—**calumnious** *adj*.—**calumniously** *adv*.

calvados *n* apple brandy distilled in Normandy in France.

calvary *n* (*pl* calvaries) a place or representation of the crucifixion of Christ; an experience of intense mental suffering; (*with cap*) the place where Christ was crucified.

calve *vti* to give birth to a calf; (*glacier, iceberg*) to break up and release ice.

calves *see* calf.

Calvin *n* John (1509–64) French religious reformer. His *Institutes of the Christian Religion* is the founding text of Calvinism.

Calvin cycle *n* (*chem*) a series of chemical reactions that take place in some plant cells during the last stage of photosynthesis.

Calvinism *n* the doctrines of John Calvin, esp those relating to predestination and election.—**Calvinist** *n*.—**Calvinistic** *adj*.

Calvino *n* Italo (1923–89) Cuban-born Italian novelist whose style varies from a grueling realism, e.g. *The Path of the Nest of Spiders*, to later complex explorations of fantasy and myth, e.g. *Invisible Cities*.

calvities *n* (*med*) baldness.

calx *n* (*pl* calxes, calces) the powder left when a metal or mineral has been subjected to great heat.

calycine, calycinal *adj* having a calyx; of or on the calyx.

calycle, calyculus *n* (*pl* calycles, calyculi) a whorl of small bracts forming a secondary calyx below the true one.

Calydon *n* the ancient capital city of Aetolia in northern Greece, ruled by Oeneus and famous in Greek mythology for the Calydonian Boar.

Calydonian Boar *n* (*Greek myth*) a boar sent by Artemis to ravage Calydon, finally killed by Meleager.

calypso *n* (*pl* calypsos) a West Indian folk song that comments on current events or personalities.

Calypso *n* (*Greek myth*) a nymph, a daughter of Atlas, who inhabited the island of Ogygia, where Odysseus was shipwrecked, and detained him there seven years; (*astron*) a satellite of Saturn.

calyptra *n* (*bot*) the hood-like covering of the spore case of mosses.—**calyptrate** *adj*.

calyx *n* (*pl* calyxes, calyces) the outer series of leaves that form the cup from which the petals of a flower spring.

Calzabigi *n* Raniera da (1714–95) Italian writer and librettist of the operas of Gluck.

cam *n* a device to change rotary to reciprocating motion.

CAM *abbr* = Campaign Against Militarism; Chinese Association of Musicians; Commonwealth Association of Musicians; (*comput*) computer-aided manufacture.

Camaguey *n* a city in Cuba.

camaraderie *n* friendship, comradeship.

camarilla *n* a political clique, a cabal.

camber *n* a slight upward curve in the surface of a road, etc; (*archit*) a horizontal roof timber with ends lower than the center, giving a shallow convex curve * *vti* to curve upwards slightly.—**cambered** *adj*.

cambiata *abbr* (*mus*) (*Italian*) = *nota cambiata*, "changing note."

cambist *n* an expert in exchanges; a dealer in bills of exchange.

cambium *n* (*pl* cambiums, cambia) the formative layer of cellular tissue that lies between the young wood and the bark of exogenous trees.—**cambial** *adj*.

Cambodia *n* a southeast Asian state, bounded by Thailand, Laos and Vietnam with its southern coast lying on the Gulf of Thailand, formerly called Kampuchea.

Cambrian *adj* of Wales; (*geol*) of the earliest Paleozoic period, before the Silurian. * *n* the strata underlying the Silurian rocks, now classed with them.

cambric *n* a fine white linen or cotton cloth.

Cambridge *n* major English city in United Kingdom of Great Britain and Northern Ireland (UK).

Cambridge Platonist *n* any of a group of 17th-century English clergymen in Cambridge whose writings and teachings were much influenced by humanist thinkers such as Erasmus and by the tolerant, learned writings of the Anglican divine Hooker.

camcorder *n* a portable video recorder with built-in sound recording facilities.

CAMDA *abbr* = Car and Motorcycle Drivers Association.

came *see* come.

camel *n* a large four-footed, long-necked animal with a humped back; a fawny-beige color.—*also adj*.

cameleer *n* a camel driver.

camellia *n* an oriental evergreen shrub with showy blooms.—*also* **japonica**.

camelopard *n* the giraffe.

Camelot *n* (*legend*) the site of King Arthur's Court; any time or place of unusual beauty, peace and enlightenment.

camel's hair, camelhair *n* the hair of a camel; cloth from this; its fawn-tan color; the hair from a squirrel's tail used as a paintbrush.—**camel's-hair, camelhair** *adj*.

Camembert *n* a soft white cheese originating in Normandy.

cameo *n* (*pl* cameos) an onyx or other gem carved in relief, often showing a head in profile; an outstanding bit role, esp in a motion picture; a short piece of fine writing.

camera *n* the apparatus used for taking still photographs or television or motion pictures; a judge's private chamber; **in camera** in private, esp of a legal hearing excluding the public; **off camera** outside the area being filmed; **on camera** being filmed, before the camera.

camera lucida *n* an optical device for projecting images onto a flat surface.

cameraman *n* (*pl* cameramen) a movie or television camera operator.

camera obscura *n* a darkened chamber or box in which, by means of lenses, external objects are exhibited on paper, glass, etc.

camera-ready *adj* (*printing*) ready for photographic platemaking.

camera-shy *adj* unwilling to, or against, being filmed or photographed.

Cameron *n* Charles (c.1743–1812) London-born Scottish architect who worked for Catherine the Great.

Cameroon *n* a triangular-shaped republic in west central Africa.

camion *n* a heavy truck, a wagon.

camise *n* a light loose robe, a chemise.

camisole *n* a woman or girl's loose sleeveless underbodice.

camlet *n* a kind of light cloth.

camomile *see* chamomile.

Camorra n a secret terrorist organization in southern Italy; a lawless clique.

camouflage n a method (esp using coloring) of disguise or concealment used to deceive an enemy; a means of putting people off the scent. * vt to conceal by camouflage.

camp[1] n the ground on which tents or temporary accommodation is erected; the occupants of this, such as vacationers or troops; the supporters of a particular cause. * vi to lodge in a camp; to pitch tents.—**camping** n.

camp[2] adj (sl) theatrical, exaggerated; effeminate; homosexual. * vi (with **up**) to make or give an exaggerated display of camp characteristics.

campaign n a series of military operations; a series of operations with a particular objective, such as election of a candidate or promotion of a product; organized course of action. * vi to take part in or conduct a campaign.—**campaigner** n.

campanelli (Italian) see **glockenspiel**.

campanile n (archit) a bell tower detached from the body of a church.

campanology n the art of bell ringing.—**campanologist** n.

campanula n a plant with bell-shaped flowers.

campanulate adj (flower) bell-shaped.

Campbell n 1. **Sir Malcolm** (1885–1948) English racing driver who set a land speed record of 246 mph in 1931. 2. **Donald [Malcolm]** (1921–67) son of Sir Malcolm Campbell. He held the water speed record, 276 mph, before his death on Lake Coniston. 3. **Roy** (1923–57) South African poet whose works include the allegorical The Flaming Terrapin, bitingly satirical verse, and some fine lyric poetry.

Campbell-Bannerman n **Sir Henry** (1836–1908) British statesman and Liberal prime minister (1905–08).

Campbell-Stokes recorder see **sunshine recorder**.

Campen n **Jacob van** (1595–1657) Dutch architect. His notable works include Town Hall (Royal Palace), Amsterdam.

camper n one who lives in a tent; a person on a camping vacation; a vehicle equipped with all domestic facilities.

campfire n an outdoor fire at a camp; a social gathering around such a fire.

camp follower n a civilian, esp a prostitute, who provides unofficial services to military personnel; a person who is sympathetic to the aims of a particular group but is not a member.

camphene n rectified oil of turpentine.

camphor n a solid white transparent essential oil with a pungent taste and smell used to repel insects, as a stimulant in medicine, etc.—**camphoric** adj.

camphorate vt to saturate or treat with camphor.

camphor tree n a species of laurel that yields camphor.

Campin n **Robert** (c.1378–1444) Flemish painter, also known as the Master of Flemalle, whose development of perspective and chiaroscuro techniques had a considerable influence on the beginnings of the Netherlandish School.

campion n any of various wild plants of the pink family, the commonest having red or white flowers.

Campion (Campian) n **Thomas** (1567–1620) English poet, songwriter, physician, and lawyer, who published several books of lute songs and many masques for performance at court.

camp meeting n an outdoor religious meeting.

camp-robber see **Canada jay**.

campsite n a camping ground, often with facilities for vacationers.

campstool n a folding stool or seat.

campus n (pl **campuses**) the grounds, and sometimes buildings, of a college or university.

campus novel a novel with a university setting, usu satirical.

CAMRA abbr = Campaign for Real Ale.

camshaft n the rotating shaft to which cams are fitted to lift valves in engines.

Camus n **Albert** (1913–60) Algerian-born French existentialist novelist, essayist, and dramatist; winner of the Nobel prize for literature (1957). His novels include The Outsider.

can[1] vt (pt **could**) to be able to; to have the right to; to be allowed to.

can[2] n a container, usu metal, with a separate cover in which gasoline, film, etc is stored; a tin in which meat, fruit, drinks, etc are hermetically sealed; the contents of a can; (sl) jail; (sl) a lavatory; **in the can** (movie) shot and edited and ready for showing; (inf) accomplished, agreed, tied up. * vti (**canning, canned**) to preserve (foods) in a can.—**canner** n.

can. abbr = cancellation; canon; canto; cantoris.

Can abbr = Canada; Canadian.

CAN abbr = Climate Action Network; Committee on Aircraft Noise.

Cana n (Bible) village in Galilee where Jesus performed two miracles.

CANA abbr = Center for Advice on Natural Alternatives; Clergy Against Nuclear Arms.

Canaan n (Bible) OT name for the promised land, or a land flowing with milk and honey, which lay between the River Jordan and the Mediterranean; later it came to be known as Palestine.

Canaanites npl a group of Semitic-speaking peoples who occupied the eastern Mediterranean region during the middle and later Bronze Age (c. 2000–1200 BC).

Canada n the second largest country in the world, lying to the north of the USA. Canada is a federal parliamentary state.æ **Canadian** adj, n.

Canada balsam n a resin obtained from a species of fir.

Canada Day n a national Canadian holiday, July 1, commemorating its dominion status (established 1867).

Canada goose n a large gray goose with a black head and neck and a white throat patch.

Canada jay n a crestless jay.—also **camp-robber, whiskey-jack**.

Canadian Dollar n currency of Canada.

canaille n a rabble, the lowest orders.

canal n an artificial waterway cut across land; a duct in the body; an underground cave passage that is filled with water; a long narrow arm of water connecting two larger seas. * vt (**canaling, canaled** or **canalling, canalled**) to provide with canals.

Canaletto n **Giovanni Antonio Canal** (1697–1768) Venetian painter whose work includes many views of Venice.

canalize, canalise vt to provide with a canal or channel. * vi to flow in or into a channel; to establish new channels or outlets.—**canalization, canalisation** n.

canapé n a small piece of pastry, bread or toast with a savory spread or topping.

canard n a false report, an absurd story, a baseless rumor.

Canaries Current a cold current that flows southwards past the Canary Islands and the north coast of Africa.

canary n (pl **canaries**) a small finch, usu greenish to yellow in color, kept as a songbird.

canasta n a card game played with two packs of cards, for two to six players.

Canberra n capital city of Australia.

cancan n an energetic dance performed by women, involving high kicks and the lifting of frothy petticoats.

cancel vt (**canceling, canceled** or **cancelling, cancelled**) to cross out; to obliterate; to annul, suppress; (reservation, etc) to call off; to countermand; vti (comput) to undo a command; (with **out**) to make up for.—**canceler, canceller** n.

cancel n (mus) a note which is neither sharpened nor flattened.—also **natural**.

cancelation, cancellation n the act of canceling; annulment; something that has been canceled; the mark made by canceling.

cancelli n (archit) a grille in early Christian churches dividing the choir from the main part of the building.

cancellous, cancellate, cancellated adj (med) marked with cross lines or ridges.

cancer n the abnormal and uncontrollable growth of the cells of living organisms, esp a malignant tumour; an undesirable or dangerous expansion of something.—**cancerous** adj.

Cancer n (astron) the Crab, a northern constellation; (astrol) the 4th sign of the zodiac, operative 21 June–21 July.—**Cancerian** adj.

Cancer, Tropic of n the imaginary line round the Earth at latitude $23° 32´$N, where the Sun's rays are vertical at noon on 21 June.

CANCIRCO abbr = Cancer International Research Co-operative.

cancrizans n (mus) literally "crab-like," a type of music that makes sense if it is played backwards; retrograde motion.

cancroid adj resembling a cancer; like a crab.

CAND abbr = Campaign Against Nuclear Dumping.

c & b abbr = caught and bowled by (cricket).

c & d, C and D or **c. and d.** abbr = collection and delivery.

C & E abbr = Customs and Excise.

candela n a unit of luminous intensity.

Candela n **Felix** (1910–97) Spanish architect. His notable works include Church of Our Lady of Miracles, Mexico City.

candelabrum n (pl **candelabra**) a branched and ornamented candlestick or lampstand.

candescent adj glowing; white-hot.—**candescence** n.

c & f abbr = cost and freight.

c & i abbr = cost and insurance.

candid adj frank, outspoken; unprejudiced; (photograph) informal.—**candidly** adv.—**candidness** n.

candidate n a person who has nomination for an office or qualification for membership or award; a student taking an examination.—**candidacy** n.—**candidature** n.

candid camera n a small camera for photographing people unexpectedly or unknowingly.

candidiasis see **thrush**.

candied adj preserved in or encrusted with sugar.

c & lc abbr (printing) = capital and lower case.

candle n a stick of wax with a wick that burns to give light. * vt to check the freshness of eggs by examining in front of a light.

candlelight n the light produced by a candle or candles.

Candlemas (Day) n the Feast of the Purification of the Virgin Mary (2 February).

candlepower n a unit of measurement of the intensity of a light source, measured in candelas.

candlestick n a holder for one or more candles.

candlewick n a cotton fabric with raised pattern of tufted yarn.—also adj.

candor, candour n sincerity, openness, frankness.

c & p abbr = carriage and packing.

C & PC abbr = Corrosion & Protection Center.

c & r abbr = convalescence and rehabilitation.

c & sc abbr (printing) = capital and small capitals.

C & W abbr (mus) = country and western.

candy n (pl **candies**) a solid confection of sugar or syrup with flavoring, fruit, nuts, etc, a sweet. * vt (**candying, candied**) to preserve by coating with candy; to encrust with crystals. * vi to become candied.

candyfloss n a confection of spun sugar.—also **cotton candy**.

candy-striped adj (cloth) with narrow stripes of color on a white background.

candytuft n a plant with pink, white or purple tufted flowers.

cane *n* the slender, jointed stem of certain plants, as bamboo; a plant with such a stem, as sugar cane; (*usu with* **the**) a stick of this used for corporal punishment; strips of this used in furniture making, etc, or for supporting plants; a walking stick. * *vt* to thrash with a cane; to weave cane into; (*inf*) to beat, e.g. in a game.

CANE *abbr* = Consumers Against Nuclear Energy.

canebrake *n* a thicket of canes.

canella *n* an aromatic and tonic bark of a West Indian tree.

canescent *adj* (*biol*) growing white, hoary.

cane sugar *n* sugar made from sugar cane.

Canes Venatici *n* (*astron*) a constellation of the northern sky.

Canetti *n* **Elias** (1905–94) Bulgarian-born German writer whose two best-known works are the novel *Auto da Fé* and the grim sociological study of mass behavior, *Crowds and Power*, awarded the Nobel prize for literature in 1981.

cangue *n* (*formerly*) a square wooden collar worn as a punishment by criminals in China.

canine *adj* of or like a dog; of the family of animals that includes wolves, dogs and foxes; pertaining to a canine tooth. * *n* a dog or other member of the same family of animals; in humans, a pointed tooth next to the incisors.

Canis Major *or* **The Greater Dog** *n* (*astron*) a constellation of the southern sky.

Canis Minor *or* **The Lesser Dog** *n* (*astron*) a constellation of the northern sky.

canister *n* a small box or container usu of metal for storing tea, flour, etc; a tube containing tear gas which explodes and releases its contents on impact.

canker *n* an erosive or spreading sore; a foot disease in horses; an ear disease in cats and dogs; a fungal disease of trees; a corrupting influence.—**cankerous** *adj*.

cankerworm *n* a caterpillar destructive to trees or plants.

canna *n* a showy American tropical plant.

Cannabich *n* **Christian** (1731–98) German violinist, composer and conductor, whose conducting was particularly admired by Mozart.

cannabin *n* a narcotic resin extracted from hemp.

cannabis *n* a narcotic drug obtained from the hemp plant; the hemp plant.—*also* **hashish, marijuana**.—**cannabic** *adj*.

canned *adj* stored in sealed tins; recorded for reproduction; (*sl*) drunk.

canned hunt *n* (*sl*) an organized big-game hunt carried out within an area from which the quarry cannot escape.

cannel (coal) *n* a hard bituminous coal burning with a clear bright flame.

cannelloni *npl* stuffed pasta tubes.

cannelure *n* a groove or fluting.

cannery *n* (*pl* **canneries**) a building, etc, where foods are canned.

cannibal *n* a person who eats human flesh; an animal that feeds on its own species. * *adj* relating to or indulging in this practice.—**cannibalism** *n*.—**cannibalistic** *adj*.

cannibalize *vti* to strip (old equipment) of parts for use in other units.—**cannibalization** *n*.

cannikin *n* a small can.

cannon *n* (*pl* **cannon**) a large mounted piece of artillery; an automatic gun on an aircraft; (*pl* **cannons**) (*billiards*) a carom. * *vi* to collide with great force (with **into**); to rebound; (*billiards*) to make a carom.

cannonade *n* a heavy, continuous artillery attack. * *vti* to attack with cannon.

cannonball *n* the heavy, round shot fired from a cannon; (*tennis*) a low, fast service stroke. * *vi* to move along at great speed.

cannoneer *n* an artilleryman.

cannon fodder *n* soldiers regarded as expendable in war.

cannonry *n* (*pl* **cannonries**) artillery.

cannot = can not.

cannula *n* (*pl* **cannulas, cannulae**) (*med*) a small tube for inspecting or withdrawing fluids.

canny *adj* (**cannier, canniest**) knowing, shrewd; cautious, careful; thrifty.—**cannily** *adv*.—**canniness** *n*.

Cano *n* (*d. c.*688) semi-legendaryson of a Scottish king; exiled to Ireland.

canoe *n* a narrow, light boat propelled by paddles.—*also vi* (**canoeing, canoed**).—**canoeist** *n*.

canola oil *n* an edible oil made from rape seed.

canon *n* a decree of the Church; a general rule or standard, criterion; a list of the books of the Bible accepted as genuine; the works of any author recognized as genuine; a list of canonized saints; a member of a cathedral chapter; a part of the mass containing words of consecration; (*mus*) a round.

canoness *nf* (*RC Church*) one of a number of women living under canon law but not compelled to take religious vows.

canonical *adj* pertaining to a rule or canon; according to or established by ecclesiastical laws; belonging to the canon of scripture. * *n* (*pl*) the official dress of the clergy.—**canonically** *adv*.

canonical hour *n* (*RC Church*) one of the hours appointed by ecclesiastical law for daily prayer: matins with lauds, prime, sext, nones, vespers, and compline.

canonist *n* an expert in canon law.—**canonistic** *adj*.

canonize *vt* (*RC Church*) to declare officially (a person) a saint.—**canonization** *n*.

canon law *n* rules or laws relating to faith, morals, and discipline that regulate church government, as laid down by popes and councils.

canonry *n* (*pl* **canonries**) the office of a cathedral canon.

canoodle *vti* (*sl*) to cuddle, to fondle.

canopic jar *n* a jar made out of stone, alabaster, pottery, or wood which was used to hold one of the preserved organs of a mummified cadaver in Ancient Egypt.

Canopus *or* **Alpha Carinae** *n* a star of first magnitude, the brightest star in the constellation Carina.

canopy *n* (*pl* **canopies**) a tent-like covering over a bed, throne, etc; any roof-like structure or projection; the transparent cover of an airplane's cockpit; the tops of trees in a forest; the sky regarded as a covering. * *vt* (**canopying, canopied**) to cover with or as with a canopy.

Canova *n* **Antonio** (1757–1822) Italian sculptor. One of the major neoclassical sculptors of the 18th century.

cans *npl* (*sl*) headphones.

CANSAD *abbr* = Caribbean Network of Cooperation in Small Animal Development (Chile).

CANSG *abbr* = Civil Aviation Navigational Services Group.

CANSTAT *abbr* = Canadian Society of Teachers of the Alexander Technique.

cant[1] *n* insincere or hypocritical speech; language specific to a group (e.g. thieves, lawyers); cliched talk, meaningless jargon. * *vi* to talk in or use cant.

cant[2] *n* an inclination or tilt; a slanting surface, bevel. * *vti* to slant, to tilt; to overturn by a sudden movement.

can't = can not.

cantab. *abbr* = cantabile.

Cantab. *abbr* (*Latin*) = *Cantabrigiensis*, "of Cambridge."

cantabile *adj, adv* (*mus*) (*Italian*) literally "song-like," to be performed flowingly or melodiously. *n* an instrumental piece played in a singing style.

Cantabrigian *n* a student or graduate of Cambridge University, England; an inhabitant of Cambridge.—*also adj*.

cantaloupe, cantaloup *n* a variety of melon with orange flesh.

cantankerous *adj* ill-natured, bad-tempered, quarrelsome.—**cantankerously** *adv*.—**cantankerousness** *n*.

cantata *n* (*mus*) a composition for voices of a story or religious text.

cantatrice *nf* a female singer, esp one who sings in operas.

canteen *n* a restaurant attached to factory, school, etc, catering for large numbers of people; a flask for carrying water; (a box containing) a set of silverware.

Cantelli *n* **Guido** (1920–56) Italian conductor of international renown. He died in an air crash at the age of 36.

canter *n* a horse's three-beat gait resembling a slow, smooth gallop.—*also vti*.

Canterbury bell *n* a large variety of campanula with handsome bell-shaped blossoms.

cantharides *npl* (*sing* **cantharis**) (*med*) a diuretic preparation made from dried Spanish flies, formerly considered an aphrodisiac.—*also* **Spanish fly**.

cant hook *n* a wooden pole with a sharp iron grip at one end, used to roll a log.—*also* **peavy**.

canthus *n* (*pl* **canthi**) the angle made by the meeting of the eyelids.

canticle *n* a song taken from the Bible (e.g. the Magnificat).

cantilever bridge *n* a bridge supported by cantilevers springing from piers.

cantilever *n* a projecting beam that supports a balcony, etc.

cantina *n* a bar or saloon in the southwestern USA.

cantino *n* (*mus*) (*Italian*) a violin's E string.

cantle *n* a corner; a piece; the rising rear part of a saddle.

canto *n* (*pl* **cantos**) a division of a long poem; (*mus*) (*Italian*) the upper voice part in concerted music, which carries the melody.

canton *n* a political and administrative division of Switzerland.—**cantonal** *adj*.

Cantonese *n* (*pl* **Cantonese**) a Chinese language deriving from Canton; an inhabitant or native of Canton.—*also adj*.

cantonment *n* a part of a town or village allotted to a body of troops; in India, a permanent military station.

cantor *n* a singer of liturgical solos in a synagogue; the leader of singing in a church choir; the principal of a college of church music; the head of a musical institution.

cantorial *adj* of or pertaining to a precentor's or the north side of the choir of a church.

cantrip *n* a prank, a piece of mischief; a magic spell.

Cantuar. *abbr* (*Latin*) = *Cantuariensis*, "of Canterbury."

cantus firmus *n* (*mus*) (*Latin*) "fixed song," i.e. a melody in polyphonic music, often taken from plainsong, with long notes against which counterpoint tunes are sung.æ*also* **cantus mensurabilis**.

Canuck *n* (*inf*) a Canadian.—*also adj*.

Canute (*c.*994–1035) king of England, Denmark and Norway. Reigned (England) from 1014–1035. The son of Sweyn Forkbeard.

canvas *n* a strong coarse cloth of hemp or flax, used for tents, sails, etc, and for painting on; a ship's sails collectively; a tent or tents; an oil painting on canvas.

canvasback *n* (*pl* **canvasbacks, canvasback**) a North American duck esteemed for the delicacy of its flesh.

canvass *vti* to go through (places) or among (people) asking for votes, opinions, orders, etc.—*also n*.—**canvasser** *n*.

canyon *n* a long, narrow valley between high cliffs.

canzone, canzona, canzon *n* (*pl* **canzoni, canzone**) (*mus*) a song or air resembling the madrigal; an instrumental piece in the style of a madrigal.

canzonet, canzonette *n* (*mus*) a short light song.

CAO *abbr* = Chief Administrative Officer.

caoutchouc *n* rubber.—*also adj*.

cap *n* any close-fitting headgear, visored or brimless; the special headgear of a profession, club, etc; the top of a mushroom or toadstool; a cap-like thing, as an artificial covering for a tooth; a top, a cover; a percussion cap in a toy gun; a type of contraceptive device; (*sport*) the headgear presented to a player chosen for a team. * *vt* (**capping, capped**) to put a cap on; to cover (the end of); to award a degree at a university; to seal (an oil or gas well); to equal, outdo or top; to limit the level of a tax increase, etc; (*sport*) to choose a player for a team.

cap. *abbr* = (*Latin*) *capiat*, "let him take"; capital; capitalize; captain; (*Latin*) *caput*, "chapter."

CAP *abbr* = Campaign Against Pornography; Canadian Association of Palynologists; Church Action on Poverty; Code of Advertising Practice; (*Europe*) Common Agricultural Policy; Commonwealth Association of Museums; Community Action Projects; computer-aided production.

Capa *n* **Robert [André Friedmann]** (1913–54) Hungarian photographer whose war photography is renowned.

capability *n* (*pl* **capabilities**) the quality of being capable; an undeveloped faculty.

capable *adj* able or skilled to do; competent, efficient; susceptible (of); adapted to.—**capably** *adv*.

capacious *adj* able to hold a great deal; roomy.—**capaciousness** *n*.

capacitance *n* (a measure of) the ability of a system to store an electric charge.

capacitate *vt* to make capable; to enable; to qualify.—**capacitation** *n*.

capacitor *n* (*elect*) a device for storing electric charge.

capacity *n* (*pl* **capacities**) the power of holding or grasping; cubic content; mental ability or power; character; the position held; legal competence; the greatest possible output or content; (*comput*) the amount of information that can be held in a storage device.

Capaneus *n* (*Greek myth*) one of the Seven against Thebes, killed by a thunderbolt from Zeus.

cap-a-pie *adv* from head to foot.

caparison *n* an ornamental covering for a horse; rich clothing. * *vt* to cover (a horse) with rich clothing; to adorn with rich dress.

CAPD *abbr* = continuous ambulatory peritoneal dialysis.

cape[1] *n* a headland or promontory running into the sea.

cape[2] *n* a sleeveless garment fastened at the neck and hanging over the shoulders and back.

CAPE *abbr* = Children's Alliance for Protection of the Environment; Council for American Private Education.

Cape Town *n* legislative capital city of South Africa.

Cape Verde *n* a republic situated in the Atlantic Ocean comprising ten islands and five islets.

Cape Verde Escudo *n* currency of Cape Verde.

Capek *n* **Karel** (1890–1938) Czech novelist and dramatist whose best-known play is *R.U.R.*, which introduced the word "robot" into the English language, and who co-wrote (with his brother Josef) *The Insect Play*, a prophetic satire on totalitarianism.

capelin, caplin *n* a small sea fish of the smelt family, largely used as bait for cod.

Capella *n* a star of first magnitude, the brightest star in the constellation Auriga.*æalso* **Alpha Aurigae**.

caper[1] *vi* to skip about playfully, to frolic. * *n* a playful leap or skip; (*sl*) an escapade; (*sl*) a criminal activity.

caper[2] *n* a low, prickly Mediterranean shrub; its pickled flower buds, used in cooking (e.g. caper sauce).

capercaillie, capercailzie *n* the largest Old World grouse.

Capernaum *n* (*Bible*) prosperous city on the shore of the Sea of Galilee where Jesus made his home and the center of much of his healing and teaching.

Capetian *adj* of or pertaining to the dynasty founded by Hugh Capet, who ascended the French throne in 987.

capful *n* the amount a cap will hold.

cap gun *n* a toy gun that fires caps by means of a cocked hammer.—*also* **cap pistol**.

Caphtor *n* (*Bible*) OT name for Crete.

capias *n* (*law*) a writ for arrest.

capillarity *n* (*pl* **capillarities**) the power possessed by porous bodies of drawing up a fluid; surface tension.

capiliary *adj* of or as fine as a hair; (*tube, pipe*) of a hair-like caliber; (*anat*) of the capillaries. * *n* (*pl* **capillaries**) one of the very fine blood vessels connecting arteries and veins.

capillary action *n* an activity related to surface tension that results in liquid rising or falling in a narrow tube.

capital[1] *adj* of or pertaining to the head; (*offense*) punishable by death; serious; chief, principal; leading, first-class; of, or being the seat of government; of capital or wealth; relating to a large letter, upper case; (*inf*) excellent. * *n* a city that is the seat of government of a country; a large letter; accumulated wealth used to produce more; stock or money for carrying on a business; a city, town, etc pre-eminent in some special activity.—**capitally** *adv*.

capital[2] *n* (*archit*) the head or top part of a column or pillar.

capital account *n* a business account stating the owner's or shareholder's interest in the assets.

capital assets *npl* physical property; shares.

capital budgeting *n* the process of planning future expenditure in a firm.

capital expenditure *n* money spent to acquire or improve buildings and equipment.

capital gain *n* the profit made on the sale of an asset.

capital goods *npl* goods (e.g. machinery) used to produce other goods.

capitalism *n* the system of individual ownership of wealth; the dominance of such a system.

capitalist *n* a person who has money invested in business for profit; a supporter of capitalism. * *adj* of or favoring capitalism.—**capitalistic** *adj*.

capitalize *vti* (*with on*) to use (something) to one's advantage; to convert into money or capital; to provide with capital; to write in or print in capital letters.—**capitalization** *n*.

capital levy *n* tax based on capital (to be distinguished from tax on income).

capital loss *n* the deficit that occurs when a capital asset realizes a price that is lower than the original cost of the asset.

capitally *adv* in a capital manner; excellently.

capital punishment *n* the death penalty for a crime.

capital reserves *npl* profits that are not distributed to shareholders as dividends.

capital stock *n* the total stock authorized or issued by a corporation; the book value of the outstanding shares of a corporation.

capital structure *n* the composition of the capital of a company or organization indicating the portion of capital that is made up of shares and the portion that is made up of loan capital; the balance between the assets and liabilities of a company.

capital turnover *n* the ratio of sales to the capital employed in a company.

capitate *adj* (*bot*) shaped like a head; head-like.

capitation *n* a direct, uniform tax imposed on each person, a tax per head.

CAPITB *abbr* = Clothing and Allied Products Industry Training Board.

Capitol *n* (*with* **the**) the building where the US Congress meets; the temple of Jupiter on the Capitoline in Rome.

capitular *adj* of or pertaining to a chapter. * *n* a member of a cathedral chapter.

capitulary *n* (*pl* **capitularies**) a statute passed in a chapter, as of knights or canons; (*pl*) the body of statutes of a chapter or of an ecclesiastical council.

capitulate *vi* to surrender on terms; to give in.—**capitulation** *n*.—**capitulator** *n*.—**capitulatory** *adj*.

capo *n* (*pl* **capos**) a device attached across the fingerboard of a guitar to raise the pitch of the strings.

capon *n* a castrated cockerel fattened for eating.

Capone *n* **Al[phonse]** (1899–1947) Italian-born American gangster nicknamed "Scarface."

caponize *vt* to make a cock a capon by castration.

caporal *n* a French tobacco.

capotasto *n* (*mus*) (*Italian*) the "head of the fingerboard," i.e., the raised part or "nut" at the top of the fingerboard of a stringed instrument that defines the lengths of the strings.

capote *n* a long coarse cloak; a long mantle for women.

Capote *n* **Truman** (1924–84) American novelist and socialite whose works include *Breakfast at Tiffany's* (1958), and *In Cold Blood* (1966).

capped mortgage *n* a mortgage in which the variable interest rate that is paid by the borrower cannot rise above a specified level, although it can be reduced if interest rates in general fall.

cappella, **a** *see* **a cappella**.

cappuccino *n* (*pl* **cappuccinos**) frothy, milky coffee usu served sprinkled with chocolate powder.

Capra *n* **Frank** (1897–1991) Italian-born American movie director whose movies include *It's a Wonderful Life* (1946).

capreolate *adj* (*bot*) furnished with tendrils.

Capriati *n* **Jennifer** (1976–) American tennis player.

capriccio *n* (*pl* **capriccios, capricci**) (*mus*) (*Italian*) a light musical composition in a fantastic, whimsical style.

capriccioso *adv* (*mus*) (*Italian*) in a free, fantastic style.

caprice *n* a passing fancy; an impulsive change in behavior, opinion, etc; a whim.

capricious *adj* unstable, inconstant; unreliable.—**capriciously** *adv*.—**capriciousness** *n*.

Capricorn *n* (*astron*) the Goat, a southern constellation; (*astrol*) the tenth sign of the zodiac, operative 21 December–19 January.—**Capricornean** *adj*.

Capricorn, Tropic of *n* the imaginary line round the Earth at latitude 23° 32´S, where the Sun's rays are vertical at noon on 21 December.

caprification *n* a process of accelerating the ripening of the fig by puncturing it.

caprine *adj* of, pertaining to, or like a goat.

capriole *n* a leap of a horse made without advancing; a caper. * *vi* to execute a capriole, to kick up the heels.

cap rock *n* an impervious rock containing oil or gas overlying a source rock containing hydrocarbons, e.g. limestone, shale, evaporite, and clay-rich sandstone.

caps. *abbr* = capitals, i.e., capital letters.

CAPS *abbr* = Captive Animals' Protection Society.

capsaicin *n* an alkaloid extracted from several species of capsicum.

Capsian *adj* relating to a Mesolithic culture originally centered on Gafa in southern Tunisia and Tehassa in eastern Algeria.

capsicum *n* a tropical plant with bell-shaped fruits containing hot or mild seeds; the fruit of this plant used as a vegetable.—*also* **red** *or* **green pepper**.

capsize *vti* to upset or overturn.

capstan *n* an upright drum around which cables are wound to haul them in; the spindle in a tape recorder that winds the tape past the head.

capstone *n* a flat slab of stone forming part of the roof of a cist or Megalithic chamber tomb.

capsulate, capsulated *adj* furnished with or enclosed in a capsule.—**capsulation** *n*.

capsule *n* a small gelatin case enclosing a drug to be swallowed; a metal or plastic container; (*bot*) a seed case; (*medical*) a sheath of connective tissue or membrane surrounding an organ; the orbiting and recoverable part of a spacecraft.—**capsular** *adj*.

capsulize *vt* to present (information) in a concise or condensed form.—**capsulization** *n*.

Capt. *abbr* = Captain.

CAPT *abbr* = Child Accident Prevention Trust.

captain *n* a chief, leader; the master of a ship; the pilot of an aircraft; a rank of army, naval, and marine officer; the leader of a team, as in sports; a leading employer in industry; a police officer responsible for a precinct. * *vt* to be captain of.—**captaincy** *n*.

captaincy, captainship *n* (*pl* **captaincies, captainships**) the rank, post, or commission of a captain.

caption *n* a heading in a newspaper, to a chapter, etc; a legend or title describing an illustration; a subtitle. * *vti* to provide with a caption.

captious *adj* ready to find fault or take offense; carping, quibbling.—**captiously** *adv*.

captivate *vt* to fascinate; to charm.—**captivating** *adj*.—**captivation** *n*.—**captivator** *n*.

captive *n* one kept confined; a prisoner; a person obsessed by an emotion. * *adj* taken or kept prisoner; unable to avoid being addressed (*a captive audience*); unable to refuse (a product) through a lack of choice (*a captive market*); captivated.

captive market *n* a group of people who are in such a position for some reason or other that they are obliged to buy a particular product or products.

captive product *n* a product that has to be purchased on a continuing basis because it has to be used with another main product, for example razor blades for a razor.

captive product pricing *n* the pricing of a captive product.

captivity *n* (*pl* **captivities**) the state of being a captive; a period of imprisonment.

captor *n* a person or animal who takes a prisoner.

capture *vt* to take prisoner; (*fortress, etc*) to seize; to catch; to gain or obtain by skill, attraction, etc, to win. * *n* the act of taking a prisoner or seizing by force; anything or anyone so taken.

capuche *n* a monk's hood or cowl; the hood of a cloak.

capuchin *n* a monkey with hair resembling a cowl; a pigeon with cowl-like feathers; a woman's cloak and hood; (*with cap*) a Franciscan monk of the mendicant order.

capybara *n* a large South American rodent that lives mostly in water.

car *n* a self-propelled motor vehicle, an automobile, a motorcar; the passenger compartment of a train, airship, elevator, etc; a train carriage.

car. *abbr* = carat; carpentry.

CAR *abbr* = compounded annual rate.

CARA *abbr* = combat air rescue aircraft.

carabineer, carabinier *see* **carbineer**.

carabiner *n* (*climbing*) a type of shackle with a snap link, used to secure a rope.

caracal *n* a kind of lynx; its fur.

Caracas *n* capital city of Venezuela.

Caractacus, *or* **Caratacus,** *or* **Caradoc** *n* (*d*. 54) British chieftan of a Celtic tribe called the Catuvellauni. He led a campaign against the Roman invaders but he was handed over to his Roman enemies by Cartimandua, the queen of the Brigantes.

caracole, caracol *vi* (*horse*) to make a half turn to the right or left. * *n* a half turn, right or left; a spiral staircase.

Caradawc *n* (*Welsh Celtic myth*) a son of Bendigeid Vran. When his father set out for Ireland to challenge Matholwch for his treatment of Branwen, he left Caradawc with six companions in charge of his kingdom.

Caradoc *n* (*d. c.*54) king of the Catuvellauni tribe of Britain. A son of Cunobelinus.

CARAF *abbr* = Christians Against Racism and Fascism.

carafe *n* an open-topped bottle for serving water or wine at table.

carageen *see* **carrageen**.

caramel *n* burnt sugar, used in cooking to color or flavor; a type of sweet tasting of this.

caramelize *vti* to turn or be turned into caramel.

carapace *n* the upper shell of the tortoise, turtle, crab, etc.

carat *n* a measure of weight for precious stones; a measure of the purity of gold.—*also* **karat**.

Caravaggio *n* **Michelangelo Amerighi da** (1573–1610) Italian painter from Milan, who worked in Rome from 1592. His paintings from the last four years of his life include the famous *Beheading of John the Baptist*.

caravan *n* (*esp Brit*) a trailer; a band of merchants traveling together for safety. * *vi* (**caravanning, caravanned**) to travel with a caravan, esp on vacation.

caravanserai, caravansary *n* (*pl* **caravanserais, caravansaries**) in the East, a large inn surrounding a spacious courtyard, where caravans rest at night.

caravel, caravelle *n* an ancient small light fast Spanish ship with broad bows, a narrow high poop, four masts and lateen sails.—*also* **carvel**.

caraway *n* a biennial plant with pungent aromatic seeds used as a flavoring.

carbide *n* (*chem*) a compound of carbon with another element, esp calcium carbide.

carbine *n* a light, semiautomatic or automatic rifle.

carbineer *n* a mounted soldier armed with a carbine.—*also* **carabineer, carabinier**.

carbo-, carb- *prefix* carbon.

carbohydrate *n* a compound of carbon, hydrogen, and oxygen, esp in sugars and starches as components of food. * *npl* starchy foods.

carbolic acid *n* phenol.

carbolize *vt* to sterilize with carbolic acid.

carbon *n* (*chem*) a nonmetallic element, a constituent of all organic matter; a duplicate made with carbon paper.

carbon-12 *n* an isotope of carbon, used as the standard for atomic weight.

carbon-14 *n* a radioisotope used in medicine as a tracer and in carbon dating.

carbonado *n* (*pl* **carbonadoes, carbonados**) a piece of meat cut crossways for grilling.

carbonaceous *adj* pertaining to, composed of or resembling carbon.

carbonaceous chondrite *n* a stony meteorite containing granules known as chondrules.

carbonaceous rock *n* a sedimentary rock containing carbon derived from plant material.

carbonate *n* (*chem*) a salt of carbonic acid. * *vt* to treat with carbon dioxide, as in making soft, fizzy drinks.—**carbonated** *adj*.

carbon copy *n* a copy of typed or written material made by using carbon paper; (*inf*) an exact copy of something or someone.

carbon cycle *n* the circulation of carbon compounds in the natural world by various metabolic processes of many organisms; (*astron*) the principal nuclear fusion reaction responsible for the energy of many main sequence stars (*æalso* **carbon-nitrogen cycle, Bethe cycle**).

carbon dating *n* a scientific method of dating material by measuring the amount of carbon-14 it contains.

carbon dioxide *n* (*chem*) a colorless gas occurring in the atmosphere which solidifies at -78.5ºC.

carbonic *adj* (*chem*) of or obtained from carbon.

carbonic acid *n* (*chem*) a weakly acidic solution of carbon dioxide in water.

carboniferous *adj* coal-bearing, yielding carbon; (*with cap*) of or relating to strata of the Paleozoic Age from which coal is derived.

carbonize *vt* to convert into carbon or a carbon residue.—**carbonization** *n*.

carbon monoxide *n* (*chem*) a colorless gas, odorless and highly poisonous, formed during the incomplete burning of coke and similar fuels.

carbon paper *n* a sheet of paper covered with a dark pigment inserted between sheets of paper for making copies of writing or typing.

Carborundum *n* (*trademark*) a compound of carbon and silicon used for polishing and grinding.

carboxylic acid *n* (*chem*) an organic acid containing one or more carboxyl groups.

carboy *n* a, usu cushioned, container of glass, plastic or metal for the safe transportation of liquids.

carbuncle *n* a red, knob-shaped gemstone, esp a garnet; a large inflamed boil; a pimple.—**carbuncular** *adj*.

carburet *vt* (**carbureting, carbureted**) to combine with carbon.

carburetor *n* a device in an internal-combustion engine for making an explosive mixture of air and fuel vapor.

carburize *vt* to combine with carbon.—**carburization** n.

carcajou *n* a wolverine.

carcanet *n* (*arch*) a collar of jewels.

carcass *n* the dead body of an animal; a framework, skeleton, or shell; (*derog*) the body of a living person.

Carchemish *n* an important archeological site situated beside the River Euphrates on the Turkish/Syrian border.

carcinogen *n* (*med*) a substance that produces cancer.—**carcinogenic** *adj*.

carcinoma *n* (*pl* **carcinomas, carcinomata**) a tumor caused by a cancer.

card[1] *n* a small piece of cardboard; a piece of this with a figure or picture for playing games or fortune-telling; a piece of this filed in a card index; a membership card; a piece of card with a person or firm's name, address or with an invitation, greeting, message, etc; (*comput*) a circuit board made up of plastic backing with circuits etched onto the plastic; (*inf*) an entertaining or eccentric person; a small piece of plastic identifying a person for banking purposes, e.g. a check card, credit card; (*pl*) card games; (*pl*) card playing; (*pl*) employees' insurance and tax documents held by the employer.

card[2] *n* a toothed instrument for combing cotton, wool, or flax fibers off. * *vt* (*wool, etc*) to comb.

Card. *abbr* (*RC Church*) = Cardinal.

CARD *abbr* = compact automatic retrieval device; Campaign Against Racial Discrimination.

cardamom, cardamum, cardanon *n* a tropical Asian plant the seed pods of which are used as a spice.

cardboard *n* thick stiff paper, often with a clay coating, for boxes, cartons, etc. * *adj* made of this; lacking substance; makeshift.

card-carrying *adj* being an official member of a political party, organization, etc.

card catalog *n* a catalog, each item of which is entered on a separate card.æ*also* **card file**.

Carder *n* **Frederick C** (1863–1963) British glassware designer who founded the **Steuben** Glassworks with Thomas Hawkes, and is regarded as the father of modern glass-making.

Cardew *n* **Michael** (1901–83) British ceramicist, a pupil of Bernard **Leach**, who revived the art of British slip-ware.

cardi- *prefix* heart.

cardia *n* (*med*) the opening of the esophagus into the stomach.

cardiac *adj* relating to the heart. * *n* a person suffering a disorder of the heart; a drug to stimulate the heart.

cardiac arrest *n* heart failure.

cardiac cycle *n* the sequence of events that produces a heartbeat.

cardiac massage *n* a means of restoring the heartbeat if this has suddenly ceased.

cardiac muscle *n* specialized muscle unique to the heart, consisting of branching, elongated fibers possessing the ability to contract and relax continuously.

cardiac pacemaker *see* **pacemaker**.

cardialgia *n* (*med*) heartburn.—**cardialgic** *adj*.

Cardiff *n* major Welsh city in United Kingdom of Great Britain and Northern Ireland (UK).

cardigan *n* a knitted sweater fastening up the front.

cardinal[1] *adj* of chief importance, fundamental; of a bright red. * *n* an official appointed by the Pope to his councils; bright red.—**cardinally** *adv*.

cardinal[2] *n* a North American bird with bright red plumage.

cardinalate, cardinalship *n* the office, rank, or dignity of a cardinal; the body of cardinals.

cardinal numbers *npl* numbers that express how many (1, 2, 3, 4 etc).

cardinal points *npl* the four chief points of the compass: north, south, east, west.

cardinal virtues *npl* justice, prudence, temperance, and fortitude.

cardio- *prefix* heart.

cardiogram *n* an electrocardiogram.

cardiograph *n* a device for recording heart movements; an electrocardiograph.

cardiology *n* the branch of medicine concerned with the heart and its diseases.—**cardiological** *adj*.—**cardiologist** *n*.

cardiomyopathy *n* a disease or disorder of the cardiac muscle.

cardiopulmonary *adj* of or concerned with or affecting the heart and lungs.

cardiopulmonary bypass *n* (*med*) an artificial mechanism (heart-lung machine) for maintaining the body's circulation while the heart is intentionally stopped in order to carry out cardiac surgery.

cardiovascular *adj* of or pertaining to the heart and the blood vessels.

cardiovascular system *n* (*anat*) the organization of the heart, arteries, and veins of the human body.

carditis *n* inflammation of the muscular tissue of the heart.

cardoon *n* a plant related to and resembling the artichoke and used as a vegetable in Spain and France.

cards *see* **card**[1].

cardsharp(er) *n* a person who cheats at cards.

care *n* anxiety; concern; serious attention, heed; consideration; charge, protection; the cause or object of concern or anxiety. * *vt* to feel concern; to agree, like, or be willing (to do something); **care of** at the address of, c/o; **in, into care** (*person*) taken charge of by a local authority by court order. * *vi* (*usu with* **for** *or* **about**) to feel affection or regard; to have a desire (for); to provide for, have in one's charge.

CARE *abbr* = Christian Action for Research and Education; Community Action in the Rural Environment; Cottage and Rural Enterprises Limited.

careen *vt* to bring (a ship) over on one side for calking, cleansing, or repairing. * *vi* to incline to one side, as a ship under press of sail.

career *n* progress through life; a profession, occupation, esp with prospects for promotion. * *vi* to rush rapidly or wildly.

career break *n* an interruption to the career of an individual, usu for the purpose of taking care of children.

careerist *n* a person who is ambitious to advance in a chosen profession.

career woman *n* a woman primarily interested in her job and in furthering her career.

carefree *adj* without cares, lively, light-hearted.

careful *adj* painstaking; cautious; thoughtful.—**carefully** *adv*.—**carefulness** *n*.

careless *adj* not careful; unconcerned, insensitive; carefree.—**carelessly** *adv*.—**carelessness** *n*.

Carême *n* **Marie Antoine** (1714–1833) famous French cook who built elaborate table decorations out of powdered sugar.

carer *n* one who takes on (professionally) the care of a dependent person.

ca. resp. *abbr* (*Latin*) = *capias ad respondendum*.

caress *n* any act or expression of affection; an embrace. * *vt* to touch or stroke lovingly.—**caresser** *n*.—**caressingly** *adv*.

caret *n* a mark (∧) showing where something omitted in text is to be inserted.

caretaker *n* a person put in charge of a place or thing; (*government*) one temporarily in control.

Carew *n* **Thomas** (c.1595–1640) English Cavalier poet.

careworn *adj* showing signs of stress, worry.

carfare *n* fare charged to a passenger.

cargo *n* (*pl* **cargoes, cargos**) the load carried by a ship, truck, aircraft, etc; freight.

Caria *n* an ancient country in the southwest corner of Asia Minor.æ**Carian** *adj*.

Carib *n* (*pl* **Caribs, Carib**) a member of an Indian people of the Lesser Antilles and neighbouring parts of the South American coast, or of their descendants; their language * *adj* of or pertaining to the Carib people or language.

Caribbean *adj* of or pertaining to the Caribbean Sea and its islands. * *n* the Caribbean Sea.

caribou *n* (*pl* **caribou, caribous**) a large North American reindeer.

caricature *n* a likeness made ludicrous by exaggeration or distortion of characteristic features. * *vt* to make a caricature of, to parody.—**caricaturist** *n*.

caries *n* (*pl* **caries**) decay of bones or teeth.

carillon *n* a chime of bells diatonically tuned and played by hand or machinery; a simple air adapted for playing on a set of bells; an organ stop which produces a bell-like sound.

carina *n* (*pl* **carinae, carinas**) a keel; the two lower petals of a papilionaceous flower (as the furze) partially joined; the keel of the breastbone of birds.

Carina *n* (*astron*) a southern sky constellation.

carinate, carinated *adj* shaped like a keel.

caring *adj* compassionate; of or dealing with people's welfare, usu professionally.

carioca *n* a ballroom dance; (*with cap*) a native of Rio de Janeiro.

carious *adj* affected with caries; decayed.

Carissimi *n* **Giacomo** (1605–74) an Italian composer, particularly of church music, noted for his oratorios, e.g., *Jephte* and *Jonas Baltazar*.

CARJ *abbr* = Catholic Association for Racial Justice.

carjacking *n* the violent hijacking and theft of an automobile, possibly involving the abduction or kidnaping of the driver or passenger.

carling *n* a ship's timber running fore and aft from one transverse deck beam to another, serving as a foundation for the planks of the deck.

Carliol. *abbr* (*Latin*) = *Carliolensis*, "of Carlisle."

carload *n* the amount an automobile will carry.

Carlovingian *see* **Carolingian**.

Carlyle *n* **Thomas** (1795–1881) Scottish historian and essayist whose works include *Sartor Resartus* and *Past and Present*.

carmagnole *n* a popular song and dance of the time of the French Revolution; a costume adapted by the revolutionists; a bombastic report from the French armies during the Revolution.

carman *n* (*pl* **carmen**) a streetcar driver.

Carme *n* (*astron*) a small satellite of Jupiter.

Carmel *n* (*Bible*) range of hills stretching from Samaria to Mount Carmel on the coast of Palestine, scene of the conflict between Elijah and the priests of Baal.

Carmelite *n* a member of a mendicant order founded on Mount Carmel in the 12th century, a white friar; a variety of pear; a kind of fine woolen cloth. * *adj* of or belonging to the order of Carmelites.

carminative *n* a medicine that expels wind and relieves colic and flatulence. * *adj* expelling wind.

carmine *n* a rich crimson pigment; the essential coloring principle of cochineal.

Carnac *n* a site in Brittany, France where there are over 3000 aligned menhirs, along with long cairn burial mounds dating from the Neolithic to the beginning of Bronze Age period.

carnage *n* great slaughter.

carnal *adj* of the flesh; sexual; sensual; worldly.—**carnality** *n*.—**carnally** *adv*.

carnal knowledge *n* sexual intercourse.

Carnap *n* **Rudolf** (1891–1970) German-born American philosopher regarded as a leading logical positivist.

Carnarvon *n* **Lord** (1866–1923) British aristocrat and passionate amateur Egyptologist, who sponsored the excavations of Howard Carter at Thebes, which led to the discovery of the tomb of Tutankhamun.

carnation *n* a garden flower, the clove pink.

carnauba *n* (a palm tree that provides) a type of natural wax used as a polish.

Carné *n* **Marcel** (1909–) French movie director.

Carnegie *n* 1. **Andrew** (1835–1919) Scottish-born American industrialist and philanthropist. 2. **Hattie** (1886–1956) she opened her first store, Carnegie-Ladies' Hatters, in 1909, which she expanded into a chain by 1929.

Carnegie Hall *n* concert hall in New York endowed by the Scottish-born philanthropist and millionaire, Andrew Carnegie (1835–1919).

carnelian *see* **cornelian**.

carnet *n* a customs permit or license, esp for a vehicle; a book of tickets, etc.

carnival *n* public festivities and revelry; a traveling fair with sideshows, etc.

carnivore *n* (*zool*) any animal that eats the flesh of other animals.

carnivorous *adj* (*animals*) feeding on flesh; (*plants*) able to trap and digest insects.

Caro *n* **Sir Anthony** (1924–) British sculptor, whose early work is simplistic in form with an emphasis on surface texture while later sculptures are prefabricated pieces of metal bolted or welded together and then painted, as in *Midday* (1960).

carob *n* an edible, sugary pod of a Mediterranean tree.

carol *n* a joyful song or hymn; a Christmas hymn. * *vi* (**caroling, caroled** *or* **carolling, carolled**) to sing carols; to sing with happiness.

Carolina *n* former British colony (est. 1663) on the east coast of the USA, split into the states of North and South Carolina in 1729.

"Carolina" *n* the song of the American State, South Carolina.

Caroline, Carolean *adj* belonging to the period of Charles I or Charles II.

Carolingian *adj* of or pertaining to the medieval Frankish dynasty that once ruled France. * *n* a member of this dynasty.—*also* **Carlovingian**.

Carolinian *adj* of or pertaining to either North or South Carolina.

carom *n* (*billiards*) a shot in which the cue ball hits two others successively. * *vi* to make a carom.—*also* **cannon**.

carotenoid *n* (*chem*) an orange, red or yellow pigment found in carrots and tomatoes.

carotid (**artery**) *n* (*anat*) one of the two principal arteries, one on either side of the neck, which convey blood from the aorta to the head.—**carotidal** *adj*.

carotid body *n* (*anat*) a small area of specialized reddish-colored tissue situated on either side of the neck where the common carotid artery branches to form the internal and external carotids.

carousal *n* a feast or festival; a noisy drinking bout or revel.

carouse *vi* to drink and have fun.—**carousal** *n*.—**carouser** *n*.

carousel *n* a merry-go-round; a revolving circular platform, as in an airport luggage conveyor.

carp[1] *vi* to find fault, esp continually.

carp[2] *n* (*pl* **carp, carps**) a brown and yellow freshwater fish.

carp. *abbr* = carpentry.

Carpaccio *n* **Vittore** (*c*.1450–1525) Venetian painter; a notable favorite is *Two Courtesans*, a fragment of a larger painting, which was much copied.

carpal *adj* pertaining to the carpus or wrist.

car park *n* a parking lot.

carpe diem (*Latin*) seize the day; take advantage of a present opportunity.

Carpeaux *n* **Jean-Baptiste** (1827–75) French sculptor and painter. His work was expressive and emotional and represented a move away from neoclassical trends.

carpel *n* (*bot*) a simple pistil, or one of the parts of a compound pistil or ovary of a flower.—**carpellary** *adj*.

carpellate *adj* having a carpel.

carpenter *n* a person skilled in woodwork, esp in house building.—**carpentry** *n*.

Carpenter *n* **John Alden** (1876-1951) American businessman and noted composer whose works include *Krazy Kat*, a jazz pantomime, ballets, e.g. *The Birthday of the Infanta* (1918) and *Skyscrapers* (1926), and two symphonies.

carpenter bee *n* a bee that makes nests in wood.

carpentry *n* the art of cutting, framing, and joining timber; work done by a carpenter.

carpet *n* a woven fabric for covering floors; any thick covering. * *vt* to cover with carpet; (*inf*) to issue a reprimand, to have on the carpet to rebuke.

carpetbag *n* a carrying bag formerly made of carpeting.

carpetbagger *n* a Northerner who went south after the American Civil War, seeking political or financial advantage; an outsider, esp a nonresident who meddles in politics.

carpeting *n* cloth for carpets; carpets in general.

carpet snake *n* a harmless Australian snake with a patterned back.

carpet sweeper *n* a mechanical device for removing dirt, etc, from a carpet.

carphone *n* a cellular telephone fitted in and operated from a car.

carpology *n* the branch of botany that treats of the structure of fruits in general.—**carpological** *adj*.—**carpologist** *n*.

car pool *n* an agreement by which several commuters take turns in driving each other to work; a group of commuters entering into such an agreement.

carpophore *n* (*bot*) a slender prolongation of the axis that bears the carpels.

carport *n* an open-sided shelter for an automobile extending from the side of a house.

carpus *n* (*pl* **carpi**) (*anat*) the bones between the forearm and the hand, forming the wrist in man and the corresponding bones in other animals.

Carr *n* 1. **Alwyn C. E.** (1872–1940) British silversmith, who worked with Omar Ramsden at their company, St Dunstan's. 2. **John** (*b*. 1723) English architect, whose notable works include The Crescent, Buxton.

Carrà *n* **Carlo** (1881–1966) Italian painter. In 1915, he and de Chirico founded metaphysical painting.

Carracci *n* **Annibale** (1560–1609) Bolognese painter, famous as the father of modern caricature, rated alongside Caravaggio in greatness and achievement.

carrack *n* a large round-built vessel formerly used by the Portuguese and Spaniards in the East Indian and American trade.

carrageen, carragheen *n* a seaweed very common on the rocks of the Irish coast that, when dried and bleached, is known as Irish moss and is used for blancmanges, soup, etc.—*also* **carageen**.

carrel *n* a small study room or cubicle, esp in a library; a small niche in the cloister of a monastery where a monk would sit and meditate or work.

Carreras *n* **José [Maria]** (1946–) Spanish lyric tenor regarded as one of the finest tenors of the late 20th century.

carriage *n* the act of carrying, transport; the cost of this; deportment, bearing; behavior; a rail coach or compartment; a wheeled coach drawn by horses; a frame with wheels to carry a gun; the moving part of a typewriter.

carriage cost *n* the cost of delivering goods.

carriage dog *n* the spotted Dalmatian.

carriage forward *n* the cost of delivery to be met by the purchaser.

carriage free *or* **carriage paid** *n* the cost of delivery to be met by the seller.

carrick bend *n* (*naut*) a particular kind of knot for splicing two hawsers together.

carrick bitt *n* (*naut*) one of the bitts supporting the windlass.

carrier *n* one who carries or transports goods, esp for rental; a device for carrying; a person or animal transmitting an infectious disease without being affected by it; an aircraft carrier; a plastic or paper bag with handles for holding things; a portable seat for a baby, a carrycot.

Carrier-Belleuse *n* **Albert-Ernest** (1824–87) French ceramicist and modeler.

carrier pigeon *n* a homing pigeon used to carry messages.

carrier wave *n* an electromagnetic wave that can be modulated in frequency, amplitude, etc, to transmit (radio, TV, etc) signals.

carrion *n* the dead putrefying flesh of an animal.

carrion crow *n* the common crow of Europe.

Carroll *n* **Lewis [Charles Lutwidge Dodgson]** (1832–98) English author, clergyman, and mathematician best known for *Alice's Adventures in Wonderland*.

carronade *n* a short cannon of large bore for close range, formerly used in the navy.

carron oil *n* a mixture of linseed oil and lime water used as a liniment for burns.

carrot *n* a plant grown for its edible, fleshy orange root; an inducement, often illusory.

carrot-and-stick *adj* combining threat and reward to produce a desired response.

carroty *adj* orange-red in color.

carry *vt* (**carrying, carried**) to convey or transport; to support or bear; to involve, have as a result; to hold (oneself); to extend or prolong; to gain by force; to win over; to stock; to be pregnant; (*with* **away**) to delight; to arouse to extreme enthusiasm; to remove violently; (*with* **forward**) (*book-keeping*) to transfer (a total) to the next column, page, etc; (*with* **off**) to cause to die; to remove by force, capture; (*situation*) to handle successfully; (*with* **out**) to perform (a task, etc); to accomplish; (*with* **over**) to carry forward; (*with* **through**) to complete. * *vi* (*with* **away**) to be filled with joy or emotion; (*with* **on**) to persevere; to conduct a business, etc; (*inf*) to have an affair; (*inf*) to cause a fuss; (*with* **through**) to enable to survive; to persist.

carryall *n* an overnight or holdall bag.

carrycot *n* a baby carrier, a portable cot.

carrying charges *npl* interest charged on an unpaid balance.

carry-out *n* food or drink sold by a restaurant but consumed elsewhere.—*also adj*.

carry-over *n* something reserved for future use; a sum transferred to a new column.

Carshemish *n* (*Bible*) early civilization in Mesopotamia.

carsick *adj* ill or queasy from the motion of a moving vehicle.—**carsickness** *n*.

Carson *n* **Johnny [John William]** (1925–) American television presenter; presenter of *The Tonight Show* (1962–92).

Carson City *n* the capital city of Nevada, a state of the USA.

cart *n* a two-wheeled vehicle drawn by horses; any small vehicle for carrying loads. * *vt* to carry in a cart; (*inf*) to transport with effort.

CART *abbr* = Community Alliance for Responsible Transport; collision avoidance radar trainer.

cartage *n* conveyance in a cart; the charge made for this.

Cartagena *n* a city in Colombia.

carte blanche *n* (*pl* **cartes blanches**) full authority to act as one thinks best.

cartel *n* an illegal association of business firms to coordinate production, prices, etc to avoid competition and maximize profits; a union of political parties to achieve common aims.

Carter *n* 1. **Elliot** (1908–) American composer of ballets, chamber music, symphonies, and a piano concerto. He held many teaching posts at prestigious American colleges, and his works include *Variations for Orchestra, Symphony of Three Orchestras*, and *Penthode*. 2. **Jimmy [James Earl Carter]** (1924–) American Democratic statesman and 39th president of the US (1977–81). He defeated Gerald Ford in the 1976 presidential campaign. 3. **John** (1748–1817) British architect and antiquarian, trained as a marble carver and mason. 4. **Howard** (1874–1939) British Egyptologist, who discovered the tomb of Tutankhamun, with its treasures still intact, in 1922. He also found the tombs of Hatshepsut and Tuthmosis IV.

Cartesian *adj* pertaining to the French philosopher and mathematician René Descartes (1596–1650) or his philosophical or mathematical works. * *n* a follower of Descartes or his philosophy.

Carthage *n* a Phoenician city on the north coast of Africa, the capital of one of the great empires of the ancient world, situated on a peninsula in the region now known as Tunis. The Carthaginians had conflicts with Greece and later with Rome.—**Carthaginian** *adj*.

cart-horse *n* a large, sturdy horse suitable for pulling heavy loads.

Carthusian *n* one of an order of monks founded (1086) by St Bruno in the Grande Chartreuse, France.

Cartier French court jewelers, who in 1917 created the *Tank* watch and became known for their Art Deco mantel clock.

Cartier-Bresson *n* **Henri** (1908–) French photographer and movie director.

cartilage *n* tough, elastic tissue attached to the bones of animals; gristle.—**cartilaginous** *adj*.

Cartimandua (*fl*.70) queen of the Brigantes tribe of Britain. A leader of one of the largest British tribes which had York as its center.

cartload *n* the amount a cart will hold.

cartogram *n* a map showing statistical information in diagrammatic form.

cartography *n* the drawing and publishing of maps.—**cartographer** *n*.—**cartographic, cartographical** *adj*.

carton *n* a cardboard box or container.

cartoon *n* a humorous picture dealing with current events; a comic strip; an animated cartoon; a full-size preparatory sketch for reproduction on a fresco, etc.—**cartoonist** *n*.

cartouche, cartouch *n* a cartridge; a canvas cartridge case; an ornament in the form of an unrolled scroll; on Egyptian monuments, etc, an oval figure containing the name or title of a sovereign or deity.

cartridge *n* the case that contains the explosive charge and bullet in a gun or rifle; a sealed case of film for a camera; (*comput*) a removable unit used as a secondary or backup storage, or, in a printer, containing ink; the device containing the stylus on the end of the pick-up arm of a record player.

cartridge belt *n* a belt with loops for holding spare cartridges.

cartridge clip *n* a detachable container for cartridges in an automatic firearm.

cartridge paper *n* a thick paper originally manufactured for soldiers' cartridges but now extensively used in art.

cartulary *n* (*pl* **cartularies**) a collection or register of charters.—*also* **chartulary**.

cartwheel *n* an acrobatic handspring in which the body revolves with the weight on each hand in turn and the legs spread like the spokes of a wheel.

Cartwheel Galaxy *n* (*astron*) a galaxy, A0035, of unusual shape with a central hub of older, mainly red stars surrounded by a vast ring of spectacular brilliant blue and white stars.

cartwright *n* a person who makes carts.

caruncle *n* a small fleshy excrescence on a bird's head, as the comb or wattle of a fowl; an appendage surrounding the hilum of a seed.—**caruncular, carunculate** *adj*.

Caruso *n* **Enrico** (1873–1921) Italian tenor, regarded as the most outstanding operatic tenor of all time. The first tenor to make recordings.

carve *vt* to shape by cutting; to adorn with designs; to cut up (meat, etc); (*with* **up**) to cut into pieces or shares; (*sl*) to share out illegal proceeds; to slash someone with a knife or razor.

carvel *see* **caravel**.

carvel-built *adj* (*vessel*) with the outer boards or plates meeting flush, not overlapping.

Carver *n* **Raymond** (1939–88) American poet and short-story writer whose collections of stories include *What We Talk About When We Talk about Love*. His poetry includes *Where Water Comes Together With Other Water*.

carving *n* a figure or design carved from wood, stone, etc; the act of carving.

Carwardine *n* **George** (1887–1948) British automobile engineer and lighting designer who produced the first commercially successful anglepoise lamp in 1934.

caryatid *n* (*pl* **caryatids, caryatides**) (*archit*) a figure of a woman in long robes supporting an entablature.—**caryatic, caryatidic, caryatidal, caryatidean** *adj*.

caryophyllaceous *adj* (*flowers*) belonging to the pink family.

caryopsis *n* (*pl* **caryopses, caryopsides**) a small dry fruit with the thin pericarp adherent to the seed, as in wheat, etc.

CAS *abbr* = Canadian Astronomical Society; Caribbean Air Services; Catgut Acoustical Society; Center for Agricultural Strategy; Certification of Accountancy Studies; Chief of Air Staff; Church Adoption Society; Collision Avoidance System; Committee on Atlantic Studies; Contemporary Art Society.

ca. sa. *abbr* (*Latin*) = *capias ad satisfaciendum*.

casaba *n* a variety of winter melon with a yellow rind and sweet flesh.—*also* **cassaba**.

Casablanca (Dar el Beida) *n* a city in Morocco.

Casali *n* **Giovanni Battista** (1715–92) Italian composer of church music and the operas *Campasbe* (1740) and *Antigone* (1752). He was chapelmaster at St John's Lateran, Rome, from 1759, until his death.

Casals *n* **Pablo** (1876–1973) Catalan cellist, conductor, and composer whose worldwide performances did much to raise the status of the cello as a solo instrument. His compositions include the oratorio *El pessebre* (*The Manger*).

Casanova *n* a man of amorous reputation.

cascade *n* a small, steep waterfall; a shower, as of sparks, etc. * *vti* to fall in a cascade.

cascading windows *npl* (*comput*) several open windows displayed so that the title bar of each window is visible.

cascara *n* Californian bark used as an aperient; a bark canoe.

cascarilla *n* the bark of a West Indian shrub, possessing aromatic and bitter properties; the shrub itself, from which is obtained a white bitter crystalline substance, cascarillin.

CASD *abbr* = Campaign Against Sea Dumping.

case[1] *n* a covering; a suitcase; its contents; the binding covering a book.

case[2] *n* an instance; a state of affairs; a condition, circumstance; a lawsuit; an argument for one side; (*sl*) a character; a person of a specific type; (*med*) a patient under treatment; (*gram*) the relationship between nouns, pronouns and adjectives in a sentence; **in case** in order to prevent, lest.

CASE *abbr* = Caithness and Sutherland Enterprise; Campaign Against the Sale of Estates; Campaign for the Advancement of State Education; Committee on the Atlantic Salmon Emergency; computer-aided software engineering; computer-aided systems engineering.

case-harden *vt* to make the surface (of iron or steel) harder than the interior.

case-hardened *adj* with a hard surface; made callous.

case history *n* a record of a person's medical background, etc.

casein *n* a protein in the curd matter of milk.

case knife *n* a sheath knife.

case law *n* law as settled by precedent.

Casella *n* **Alfredo** (1883–1947) Italian composer, conductor, teacher, pianist, and author. His works include operas, e.g., the one-act operas, *Il Deserto Tentato* and *La Favola d'Orfeo*, and the full-length opera *La Donna serpente* and the ballet *La Giara*.

casemate *n* a bomb-proof vault or battery in a fortification; an armored enclosure for a gun in a warship; a hollow molding.

casement *n* a window or its frame with a side hinge for opening; a wide, concave, hollow molding found in window and door jambs.

Casement *n* **Sir Roger [David]** (1864–1916) British consular official and Irish nationalist, hanged for treason.

caseous *adj* like cheese, cheesy.

casern, caserne *n* a lodging or barrack for soldiers in a garrison town.

case sensitive *adj* (*comput*) the ability of a program to differentiate between uppercase and lowercase characters.

case study *n* an analysis arrived at from studying more than one case history.

casework *n* social work based on the close monitoring of individuals or families.—**caseworker** *n*.

cash[1] *n* money in coins or bills; immediate payment, as opposed to that by check or on credit. * *vt* to give or get cash for; (*with* **in**) to exchange something for money; (*inf*) to gain an advantage or seize an opportunity to profit from; (*sl*) to die. * *vi* (*with* **in**) to exploit for profit; to take advantage of.—**cashable** *adj*.

cash[2] *n* (*pl* **cash**) the name of various Eastern coins of low value.

cash. *abbr* = cashier, a teller.

Cash *n* **Johnny** (1932–) American country and western singer and songwriter whose songs include "I Walk the Line."

cash and carry *n*, *adj* (a policy of) selling for cash without delivery of goods.

cash-book *n* a book in which a register is kept of money received or paid out.

cash box *n* a box with compartments and a lid used to keep money.

cash cow *n* a business that requires little investment in time, effort, or money, and that produces a regular profit.

cash crop *n* a crop grown for market not for consumption.

cash discount *n* a reduction in the money owed by a customer to a supplier of goods and services in return for prompt payment or in return for payment in cash.

cash dividend *n* a dividend that is paid in cash rather than in shares.

cashew *n* the small, edible nut of a tropical tree.

cash flow *n* money which is paid into and out of a business during its operations.

cashier[1] *n* a teller, a person in charge of the paying and receiving of money in a bank, store, etc.

cashier[2] *vt* to dismiss (an officer) from military service; to discharge.

cashier's check *n* a check signed by a bank officer, which is drawn on the bank's own funds.

cashmere *n* a fine wool from Kashmir goats; a material made from this.

cash on delivery *n* an arrangement by which goods that have been ordered are paid for at the time of delivery.

cash register *n* an automatic or electronic machine that shows and records the amount placed in it.

casimere *see* **cassimere**.

casing *n* any protective or outer covering; the material for this.

casino *n* (*pl* **casinos**) a room or building where gambling takes place.

cask *n* a barrel of any size, esp one for liquids; its contents.

casket *n* a small box or chest for jewels, etc; a coffin.

casque *n* (*poet*) a helmet.

CASS *abbr* = Certificate of Applied Social Studies.

cassaba *see* **casaba**.

Cassady *n* **Neal** (1926–68) American novelist and a leading member of the Beat Generation.

Cassandra *n* (*Greek myth*) a daughter of Priam and Hecuba, who was given the power by Apollo to foretell the future, but whose prophecies would never be believed; a name often used of one who takes pessimistic views of the political or social future.

Cassat *n* **Mary** (1845–1926) American painter, who lived and worked mainly in Paris. Notable works include *Lady at the Tea Table* (1885) and *Gathering Fruit* (1892).

cassation *n* (*mus*) an 18th-century term for instrumental music devised for open-air performance, similar to the serenade.

cassava *n* a plant of tropical America and Africa cultivated for its tuberous roots, which yield a nutritious starch from which cassava bread and tapioca are made.

Cassegrain telescope *n* a form of reflecting telescope.

Casse-Noisette *see* **Nutcracker, The**.

casserole *n* a covered dish for cooking and serving; the food so cooked and served. * *vt* to cook in a casserole.

cassette *n* a case containing magnetic tape or film for loading into a tape recorder or camera.

cassia *n* one of several tropical leguminous plants, the leaves of several species of which constitute the drug senna.

Cassibile *n* a cemetery site in Sicily near Syracuse consisting of around two thousand tombs excavated in the rocks of the steep hillside.

cassimere *n* a thin twilled woolen cloth used for men's garments.—*also* **casimere**.

Cassini's division *n* (*astron*) a dark gap between the two principal bands of Saturn's rings.

Cassiopeia *n* (*astron*) a conspicuous constellation in the northern hemisphere, situated next to Cepheus and often called the Lady in her Chair.

cassis *n* a blackcurrant bush; a cordial or liqueur flavored with blackcurrants.

cassiterite *n* a native tin dioxide; the principal ore of tin.

cassock *n* a long close-fitting black garment worn by certain clergy and by choristers.

cassowary *n* (*pl* **cassowaries**) a large running bird resembling the ostrich, inhabiting Australia and New Guinea.

cast *vt* (**casting, cast**) to throw or fling; to throw off or shed; to record; to direct; to shape in a mold; to calculate; to select actors, etc for a play; to throw a fishing line into the water. * *vi* to throw, hurl; (*with* **off**) to untie a ship from its moorings; (*knitting*) to loop off stitches from a needle without letting them unravel; (*with* **on**) to loop the first row of stitches onto a needle. * *n* act of casting; a throw; a plaster form for immobilizing an injured limb; a mold for casting; type or quantity; a tinge of color; the actors assigned roles in a play; the set of actors; a slight squint in the eye.

Castalia *n* a fountain on the slope of Parnassus, above Delphi, sacred to Apollo and the Muses. Its waters were supposed to give poetic inspiration to those who drank from it.

castanets *npl* hollow shell-shaped pieces of wood held between the fingers and rattled together, esp to accompany Spanish dancing.

castaway *adj* shipwrecked; discarded. * *n* a shipwrecked person.

cast down *adj* depressed.

caste *n* any of the Hindu hereditary social classes; an exclusive social group.

castellan *n* the governor of a castle.

castellated *adj* having turrets and battlements, as a castle.

caster *see* **castor**.

castigate *vt* to chastise; to punish; to correct.—**castigation** *n*.

casting *n* the art of working metals by pouring them while in a fluid condition into molds in which they solidify and harden into the form of the mold that they fill.

casting vote *n* the deciding vote used by the chairperson of a meeting when the votes on each side are equal.

cast iron *n* an iron-carbon alloy melted and run into molds.

cast-iron *adj* made of cast iron; untiring; rigid, unadaptable.

castle *n* a fortified building; a chess piece (—*also* **rook**). * *vi* (*chess*) to make a simultaneous and strategic move of the rook and king. * *vt* to move (the king) by castling.

Castle *n* **Richard** (1690–1751) German architect whose notable works include Leinster House, Dublin.

cast-off *adj* laid aside or rejected.—**castoff** *n*.

castoff *n* a rejected item; a rough estimate of the number of pages of a finished book, etc.

castor *n* a small container with a perforated top for sprinkling salt, sugar, etc; a small swiveled wheel on a table leg, etc.—*also* **caster**.

Castor¹ *n* a Roman site near Peterborough in England.

Castor² *n* the brightest star in the constellation Gemini.æ*also* **Alpha Geminorum**.

Castor and Pollux *n* (*Greek myth*) twin divinities, sons of Zeus. Castor was mortal, but Pollux was immortal. Zeus placed the brothers among the stars as Gemini.—*also* **Dioscuri**.

castor oil *n* a vegetable oil used as a cathartic and lubricant.

castrate *vt* to remove the testicles of, to geld.—**castration** *n*.—**castrator** *n*.

castrato *n* (*pl* **castrati, castratos**) (*mus*) (*Italian*) a male castrated in childhood to prevent a change of voice at the age of puberty; an artificial male soprano.

Castries *n* capital city of St Lucia.

Castro [Ruz] *n* **Fidel** (1927–) Cuban statesman, prime minister (1959–76) and Communist president (1976–).

castrum *n* (*archit*) a Roman army camp based on a rectangular plan with an outer defensive rampart and wall.

cast stone *n* (*archit*) a type of building material made from an aggregate of various types of natural stone.

casual *adj* accidental, chance; unplanned; occasional; careless, offhand; unmethodical; informal. * *n* someone who works occasionally; (*pl*) informal or leisure clothing, shoes.—**casually** *adv*.—**casualness** *n*.

casualty *n* (*pl* **casualties**) a person injured or killed in a war or in an accident; something damaged or destroyed.

casuarina *n* a tree of Australia and southeast Asia having jointed branches.

casuist *n* one who studies or resolves cases of conscience; one skilled in casuistry.—**casuistic, casuistical** *adj*.—**casuistically** *adv*.

casuistry *n* (*pl* **casuistries**) the study or application of rules of right and wrong; sophistical or equivocal reasoning, esp on moral matters.

casus belli *n* (*pl* **casus belli**) an act or occurrence justifying war.

Caswallon *n* (d. c.60) high king of the British tribes. Leader of the Catuvellauni.

cat *n* a small, domesticated feline mammal kept as a pet; a wild animal related to this; lions, tigers, etc (—*also* **big cat**); (*inf*) a spiteful woman; (*sl*) a man.

cat. *abbr* = catalog; cataplasm; catechism.

Cat. *abbr* = Catalan.

CAT¹ *abbr* = Center for Alternative Technology; Certificate for Accounting Technicians; College of Advanced Technology; computer-aided typesetting.

CAT² (*acronym*) computerized axial tomography (—*also* **computer-aided** or **computer-assisted tomography**); the production of detailed three-dimensional images from scans of cross-sections of internal organs (**CAT scans**) using a computer-controlled X-ray machine (**CAT scanner**).

cata- *prefix* down; wrongly; thoroughly.

catabolism *n* (*chem*) a downward series of changes by which complex bodies are broken down into simpler forms.—**catabolic** *adj*.—**catabolically** *adv*.

catabolize *vti* to subject to or undergo catabolism.

catachresis *n* (*pl* **catachreses**) misapplication of words; formation of words on a false analogy.—**catachrestic** *adj*.—**catachrestically** *adv*.

cataclysm *n* a violent disturbance or disaster.—**cataclysmic** *adj*.

cataclysmic variable *n* (*astron*) a star which suddenly changes its brightness by several magnitudes due to nuclear fusion reactions taking place on the surface of the receiving star.

catacomb *n* (*usu pl*) an underground burial place.

catadromous *adj* going down to the sea to spawn.

catafalque *n* a temporary structure erected, usu in a church, to support the coffin on the occasion of a lying in state.

catal. *abbr* = catalog.

Catalan *adj* of or pertaining to Catalonia, a province of Spain, or to its inhabitants or language. * *n* an inhabitant of Catalonia; the language of Catalonia.

catalectic *adj* (*poetry*) lacking a syllable in the last foot.

catalepsy *n* (*pl* **catalepsies**) a state of temporary rigidity and unconsciousness.—**cataleptic** *adj*.

Çatal Hüyük (Çatalhöyük) *n* one of the oldest known settlements, in southern central Turkey, the earliest levels of which date back to c.7000 BC.

catalog, catalogue *n* a list of books, names, etc in systematic order; (*astron*) a collection of data about celestial objects: stars, nebulae, galaxies, etc. * *vti* to list, to make a catalog of.—**cataloger, cataloguer** *n*.

catalog store *n* a retail outlet in which there are very few goods on display, the majority being sold through the medium of a catalog in which the goods are displayed.

catalogue raisonné *n* (*French*) a catalog of books, paintings, etc, classed according to their subjects.

catalpa *n* an American tree with trumpet-shaped flowers.

catalysis *n* (*pl* **catalyses**) (*chem*) the acceleration or retardation of a chemical reaction by the action of a catalyst. —**catalytic** *adj*.

catalyst *n* a substance which accelerates or retards a chemical reaction without itself undergoing any permanent chemical change; a person or thing which produces change.

catalytic converter *n* a filter device in vehicles to reduce pollution from exhaust produced by combustion, e.g., carbon monoxide, nitrogen oxide, etc.

catalyze *vt* (*chem*) to accelerate or retard (a chemical reaction) by catalysis.—**catalyzer** *n*.

catamaran *n* a (sailing) boat with twin hulls; a raft of logs.

catamenia *n* menstruation.—**catamenial** *adj*.

catamite *n* a boy kept by a sodomite.

catamount, catamountain *n* the wild cat; the puma, cougar, or mountain lion.

cataplasm *n* a poultice.

cataplexy *n* (*pl* **cataplexies**) a sudden shock to the nerves causing paralysis.

catapult *n* a slingshot; a device for launching aircraft from the deck of an aircraft carrier. * *vt* to shoot forwards as from a catapult.

cataract *n* a waterfall, esp a large sheet one; a disease of the eye causing dimming of the lens and loss of vision.

catarrh *n* inflammation of a mucous membrane, esp in the nose and throat, causing a flow of mucus.—**catarrhal** *adj*.

catarrhine *adj* of or pertaining to a group of monkeys and apes of the Old World, which have the nostrils close together and pointing downwards.

catastrophe *n* a great disaster.—**catastrophic** *adj*.—**catastrophically** *adv*.

catastrophic age profile *n* (*archeo*) where the teeth (or bones) of animals from a site reflect the normal distribution of a wild group and may indicate that the animals were slaughtered.

catastrophize *vt* to envisage a situation as being worse than it is.—*also* **awfulize**.

catatonia *n* a form of schizophrenia in which a trance-like state is punctuated by periods of hyperactivity.—**catatonic** *adj*.

Catawba *n* (*pl* **Catawba, Catawbas**) a member of a North American Indian people formerly of North and South Carolina; a light red variety of American grape; a light wine made from this grape.

catbird *n* a gray or black North American perching bird; an American barer bird; an Australian bowerbird.

catboat *n* a small boat with one sail on a single mast near the bows.

cat burglar *n* a burglar who enters by climbing.

catcall *n* a shrill whistle or cry used to express disapproval. * *vt* to express disapproval by a catcall.

catch *vt* (**catching, caught**) to take hold of, to grasp; to capture; to ensnare or trap; to be on time for; to detect; to apprehend; to become infected with (a disease); to attract (the eye); (*inf*) to see, hear, etc; to grasp (a meaning); (*with* **out**) (*inf*) to detect (a person) in a mistake. * *vi* to become entangled; to begin to burn; (*with* **on**) (*inf*) to become popular; to understand; (*with* **up**) to reach or come level with (e.g., a person ahead); to make up for lost time, deal with a backlog. * *n* the act of catching; the amount or number caught; a device for fastening; someone worth catching; a hidden difficulty; (*mus*) a round for three or more voices.

catch-22 *n* a predicament from which a victim is powerless to escape due to conditions beyond his or her control.

catch-all *adj, n* (something) intended to cover all eventualities.

catcher *n* (*baseball*) the player who stands behind the batter to catch the ball.

catching *adj* infectious; attractive.

catchment *n* the collecting or the drainage of water.

catchment area *n* the area from which a body of water is fed, eg a river or reservoir; a geographic area served by a particular institution.

catchpenny *n* (*pl* **catchpennies**) an article of little value got up attractively to effect a quick sale.

catch phrase *n* a well-known phrase or slogan, esp one associated with a particular group or person.

catchpole *n* (*Brit*) a sheriff's officer; a constable in medieval England.

catchup *see* **ketchup**.

catchweight *n* a weight left to the choice of an owner of a horse. * *adv* without being handicapped.

catchword *n* a guide word; a word or expression, briefly popular, representative of a person or point of view; a cue in the theater.

catchy *adj* (**catchier, catchiest**) easily remembered, as a tune.—**catchiness** *n*.

CATE *abbr* = Committee for the Accreditation of Teacher Education.

catechetical, catechetic *adj* instructing orally; proceeding by question and answer; of catechism.—**catechetically** *adv*.

catechin *n* a tannic acid extracted from catechu.

catechism *n* a simple summary of the principles of religion in question and answer form, used for instruction; continuous questioning.—**catechismal** *adj*.

catechize *vt* to instruct by question and answer.—**catechization** *n*.—**catechist, catechizer** *n*.

catechu *n* a brown astringent substance obtained from tropical plants and used in the arts and as a medicine.—*also* **cachou, cutch**.

catechumen *n* one who is under religious instruction prior to receiving baptism; a beginner in the first principles of knowledge.

categorical *adj* unconditional, absolute; positive, explicit.—**categorically** *adv*.

categorical imperative *n* (*philos*) the absolute and unconditional command of moral law.

categorize *vt* to place in a category.—**categorization** *n*.

category *n* (*pl* **categories**) a class or division of things.

catena *n* (*pl* **catenae, catenas**) a series of notions; things connected with each other like the links of a chain; a systematic arrangement of selections from authors to illustrate a doctrine.

catenary *n* (*pl* **catenaries**) a curve formed by a hanging chain. * *adj* of or resembling a chain (—*also* **catenarian**).

catenate *vt* (*biol*) to link together.—**catenation** *n*.

catenulate *adj* (*bot*) consisting of little links.

cater *vi* (*with* **for** or **to**) to provide with what is needed or desired, esp food and service, as for parties.—**caterer** *n*.

cateran *n* a kern; a Highland or Irish irregular soldier; a Highland freebooter.

caterpillar *n* the worm-like larvae of a butterfly or moth; the ribbed band in place of wheels on a heavy vehicle; a vehicle (e.g., tank, tractor) equipped with such tracks.

caterwaul *vi* to make a howling noise like a cat. * *n* such a cry.

catfish *n* (*pl* **catfish, catfishes**) a large, usu freshwater, fish with whisker-like feelers around the mouth.

catgut *n* a strong cord made from animal intestines, used for the strings of musical instruments, sports rackets, and surgical ligatures.

cath. *abbr* = cathedral.

Cath. *abbr* = Catholic.

Cathal O'Connor *n* (*d*. 1224) king of Connaught (1202–24). The last provincial monarch in Ireland.

catharsis *n* (*pl* **catharses**) emotional relief given by art, esp tragedy; (*med*) purgation; (*psychoanal*) relief obtained by the uncovering of buried repressions, etc.

cathartic *adj* bringing about catharsis; purgative. * *n* a purgative medicine.—**cathartically** *adv*.

Cathbad or **Cathbhadh** *n* (*Irish Celtic myth*) a druid at the court of Conchobar mac Nessa. He is said to have been the father of Deichtire and so the grandfather of Cuchulainn.

cathead *n* a beam projecting from a ship's bows to which the anchor is secured.

cathedra *n* (*pl* **cathedrae**) a bishop's throne in the cathedral of his diocese; an official or professional chair.

cathedral *n* the chief church of a diocese. * *adj* having or belonging to a cathedral.

Cather *n* **Willa Sibert** (1876–1947) American novelist, whose novels of immigrant life on the Great Plains, e.g., *O Pioneers!* and *My Antonia*, were based on her childhood experiences in Nebraska and have been widely acclaimed for their realism.

Catherine II *n* [**the Great**] (1729–96) Russian empress (1762–96). She expanded the Russian Empire by conquest.

Catherine of Alexandria *n* **Saint** (4th century) Christian martyr who was tortured on a spiked wheel and beheaded. Her feast day is 25 November.

Catherine of Siena *n* **Saint** (1348–80) Italian mystic who, aged six, had a vision of Christ. Patron saint of the order of the Dominicans. Her feast day is 29 April.

Catherine wheel *n* a rotating firework.—*also* **pinwheel**.

catheter *n* a flexible tube inserted into the bladder for drawing off urine.

catheterize *vt* to insert a catheter into.—**catheterization** *n*.

cathode *n* (*elect*) the negative terminal; the electrode by which current leaves.—**cathodal** *adj*.—**cathodic, cathodical** *adj*.

cathode rays *npl* a stream of electrons emitted by a cathode in a vacuum tube.

cathode-ray tube *n* a vacuum tube in which electron beams are directed onto a fluorescent screen to produce luminous images, as used in television sets.

catholic *adj* universal, all-embracing; broad-minded, liberal; general, not exclusive.

Catholic *n* a member of the Roman Catholic Church. * *adj* relating to the Roman Catholic Church; embracing the whole body of Christians.—**Catholicism** *n*.

Catholic Epistles *npl* the Epistles of the Apostles addressed to believers generally, ie James 1 and 2, Peter 1, 2, and 3, John, and Jude.

Catholicism *n* the belief of, or adherence to, the Catholic or faith, esp to that of the Roman Catholic Church.

catholicity *n* the quality of being catholic; universality, comprehensiveness; accordance with Catholic, esp Roman Catholic, church doctrine.

catholicize *vt* to convert to the Roman Catholic Church.—**catholicization** *n*.

catholicon *n* a universal remedy, a panacea.

cathouse *n* a brothel.

cation *n* a positively charged ion.—**cationic** *adj*.

cation-ratio dating *n* a method of dating rock art from archeological sites in arid regions. It is based on comparison between changes in different chemicals.

catkin *n* a hanging spike of small flowers, e.g., on birch, willow, and hazel trees.

cat-like *adj* like a cat; stealthy, noiseless.

Catlin *n* **George** (1796–1824) American painter, a self-taught artist, who painted portraits including over 500 of American Indians, among whom he lived from 1830–36.

catmint, catnip *n* a strongly-scented plant attractive to cats.

catnap *n* a short, light or intermittent sleep, a snooze, a doze.—*also vi* (**catnapping, catnapped**).

cat-o'-nine-tails *n* (*pl* **cat-o'-nine-tails**) a whip with nine lashes of knotted cord, formerly used as a punishment in the army and navy.

catoptric, catoptrical *adj* of or pertaining to mirrors or reflected light.

Cat scan, Cat scanner *see* **CAT**².

cat's cradle *n* a game of making designs with string looped over the fingers.

cat's-eye *n* a hard semi-transparent variety of quartz.

cat's-paw *n* a person used as a tool by another, a dupe; (*naut*) a light breeze that slightly ripples the surface of the water.

catsup *see* **ketchup**.

cattery *n* (*pl* **catteries**) a place for boarding or breeding cats.

cattle *npl* domesticated bovine mammals such as bulls and cows.

cattle-grid *n* a metal grid over a ditch allowing the passage of people and vehicles, but not cattle, sheep, etc.

cattleman *n* (*pl* **cattlemen**) one who tends or drives cattle; a breeder of cattle.

cattle prod *n* an electrified prod for driving cattle.

catty¹ *adj* (**cattier, cattiest**) (*inf*) spiteful, mean.—**cattily** *adv*.—**cattiness** *n*.

catty² *n* (*pl* **catties**) an East Indian weight equal to one and a third pounds; a name applied to a Chinese kin or pound; a Siamese coin.

CATU *abbr* = Ceramic and Allied Trades Union.

CATV *abbr* = cable television; community antenna television.

catwalk *n* a narrow, raised pathway on a stage, bridge, etc; fashion modeling (*with* **the**).

Caucasian *adj* of the light-skinned racial group of humankind; of or relating to the Caucasus Mountains. * *n* a Caucasian person.—**Caucasoid** *adj*.

Caucasus *n* a mountain range in the southwest USSR (*with* **the**).—*also* **Caucasus Mountains**.

caucus *n* (*pl* **caucuses**) a private meeting of leaders of a political party or faction, usu to plan strategy.

caudal *adj* of or pertaining to a tail.—**caudally** *adv*.

caudate, caudated *adj* having a tail; having a tail-like appendage.

caudex *n* (*pl* **caudices, caudexes**) the main trunk or axis of a plant.

caudle *n* a warm drink made of wine or ale, spiced or sugared, and mixed with bread, eggs, etc.

caught *see* **catch**.

caul *n* the membrane covering a fetus; part of this covering the head of some infants at birth.

cauldron *see* **caldron**.

caulescent *adj* having a true stem or stalk.

caulicle *n* a small or rudimentary stem.

cauliflower *n* a kind of cabbage with an edible white flower-head used as a vegetable.

cauliflower ear *n* a thickening condition of the ear, common to boxers, caused by repeated blows.

cauline *adj* of, on or belonging to a stem.

caulk *vt* to make (a boat) watertight by stopping up the seams with pitch.—*also* **calk**.—**caulker, calker** *n*.

Caunus *see* **Byblis**.

caus. *abbr* = causation; causative.

causal *adj* forming or being a cause; involving, expressing or implying a cause.—**causally** *adv*.

causality *n* (*pl* **causalities**) the relationship between cause and effect.

causation *n* causality; the act of causing something to happen.—**causational** *adj*.

causative *adj* that causes; effective as a cause; expressing causation.

cause *n* that which produces an effect; reason, motive, purpose, justification; a principle for which people strive; a lawsuit. * *vt* to bring about, to effect; to make (to do something).—**causer** *n*.

cause célèbre *n* (*pl* **causes célèbres**) (*French*) a famous lawsuit, trial or celebrated issue.

causeless *adj* without cause; groundless.

causerie *n* a discursive conversational article; an informal chat.

causeway *n* a raised road across wet ground or water.

causewayed camp *n* (*archeo*) a circular monument consisting of one to four rings of ditches and earth banks with solid causeways in several places.*æalso* **enclosure**.

caustic *adj* burning tissue, etc, by chemical action; corrosive; sarcastic, cutting. * *n* a caustic substance.—**caustically** *adv*.—**causticness, causticity** *n*.

caustic potash *n* potassium hydroxide, a white substance acting as a powerful bleach, much used in medicine and manufacturing.

caustic soda *n* sodium hydroxide, a white solid substance, largely used in soapmaking.

cauterize *vt* to burn with a caustic substance or a hot iron so as to destroy dead tissue, stop bleeding, etc; to deaden.—**cauterization** *n*.

cautery *n* (*pl* **cauteries**) a burning or searing; an instrument or drug used for such a purpose.

caution *n* care for safety, prudence; a warning, esp a formal one, to a suspect or accused person. * *vt* to warn (against); to admonish.

cautionary *adj* of a warning nature.

cautious *adj* careful, circumspect.—**cautiously** *adv*.—**cautiousness** *n*.

cav. *abbr* = cavalier; cavalry.

c.a.v. *abbr* (*Latin*) = *curia advisari vult*, "the court wishes to consider" (used in law to indicate that a court will consider a case privately before giving judgment).

cavalcade *n* a procession of riders on horseback; a dramatic sequence or procession.

cavalier *adj* free and easy, careless; offhand, brusque. * *n* a horseman; a lady's escort; (*with cap*) a royalist in the English Civil War.—**cavalierly** *adv*.

Cavalieri *n* **Emilio de'** (*c*.1550-1602) Italian amateur composer who wrote four music dramas which heralded the way for the oratorio form. His best-known work is the morality play *La Rappresentazione de Anima e di Corpo*.

Cavalier poet any of a loose grouping of lyric poets associated with the court or cause of Charles I during his clashes with the English Parliament and the ensuing Civil War.

Cavalli *n* **Pietro Francesco** (originally **Pier Caletti-Bruni**) (1602-76) Italian composer who wrote more than forty operas as well as church music. His operas, include *L'Ormindo*, *La Callisto*, and *Egisto*.

cavalry *n* (*pl* **cavalries**) combat troops originally mounted on horseback.

cavatina *n* (*pl* **cavatine**) (*mus*) (*Italian*) a short simple melody.

cave *n* a hollow place inside the earth open to the surface. * *vti* (*with* in) to collapse or make collapse; (*inf*) to yield, submit.—**cave-in** *n*.

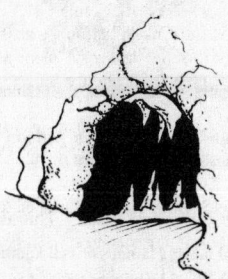

cave painting *n* prehistoric painting on cave walls.

caveat *n* (*law*) a process to suspend proceedings; a warning.

caveat emptor (*Latin*) let the buyer beware.

cavefish *n* (*pl* **cavefish, cavefishes**) a fish belonging to the family Amblyopsidae, species of which inhabit cave streams of the US.

Cavell *n* **Edith [Louisa]** (1865-1915) English nurse who worked in Brussels during the German occupation and was executed by the German authorities.

caveman *n* (*pl* **cavemen**) a prehistoric cave dweller; (*inf*) a person who acts in a primitive or crude manner.

Cavendish *n* **Michael** (*c*.1565-1628) English composer of songs for lutes and of madrigals. He also composed "Ayres for four Voyces," 1599; and, with nine other composers, *The Whole Booke of Psalmes*, published in 1592.

cavern *n* a large cave.—**cavernous** *adj*.

cavernous sinus *n* (*anat*) one of a pair of cavities located on either side of the sphenoid bone behind the eye sockets at the base of the skull.

cavetto *n* (*pl* **cavetti**) (*archit*) a round concave molding.

caviar, caviare *n* salted roe of the sturgeon or other large fish.

CAVIAR *abbr* = Cinema and Video Industry Audience Research.

cavil *vi* (**caviling, caviled** *or* **cavilling, cavilled**) to make trifling objections, to find fault. * *n* a trifling objection.—**caviler** *n*.

caving *n* the sport of exploring caves.—**caver** *n*.

cavity *n* (*pl* **cavities**) a hole; a hollow place, esp in a tooth.

cavort *vi* to frolic, prance.

cavy *n* (*pl* **cavies**) one of several kinds of small rodent including the guinea pig.

caw *n* the cry of the crow, rook, or raven. * *vi* to utter this cry.

CAW *abbr* = Campaign Against the Witchhunt; Co-ordinating Animal Welfare.

CAWTU *abbr* = Church Action With The Unemployed.

Caxton *n* **William** (*c*.1422-91) English printer, translator, and author of *Recuyell of the Historyes of Troye*, printed at Bruges in 1475, the first book to be printed in English. Soon afterwards, he began printing books at Westminster in London.

cay *n* a small low island.—*also* **key**.

CAYA *abbr* = Catholic Association of Young Adults.

cayenne, cayenne pepper *n* a hot red pepper made from capsicum.

Cayenne *n* capital city of French Guiana or Guyane.

cayman *see* **caiman**.

Cayman Islands *n* a British overseas territory comprising three low-lying islands situated in the Caribbean Sea some 240 kilometers or 149 miles south of Cuba.

Cayman Islands Dollar *n* currency of Cayman Islands.

Cayuse *n* (*pl* **Cayuse, Cayuses**) a member of an American Indian tribe of Oregon and Washington; their language; (*without cap*) (*pl* **cayuses**) a range pony of the western USA.

CAZS *abbr* = Center for Arid Zone Studies.

Cb *symbol* (*chem*) columbinium (element).

cb *abbr* = circuit breaker.

c.b. *abbr* = cashbook; cavalry brigade; center of buoyancy; confined to barracks.

c/b *abbr* (*cricket*) = caught and bowled.

CB *abbr* = Cape Breton; (*Latin*) *Chirurgiae Baccalaureus*, "Bachelor of Surgery"; (*radio*) citizens' band; (*mus*) (*Italian*) *contrabasso*, "double bass."

C/B *abbr* = cashbook.

CBA *abbr* = Citizens Band Association; Council for British Archaeology; (*Brit*) Criminal Bar Association.

CBC *abbr* = Canadian Broadcasting Corporation; complete blood count; Cyprus Broadcasting Corporation.

cbd *abbr* = cash before delivery.

CBD *abbr* = Commerce Business Daily

CBE *abbr* = Commander of the Order of the British Empire.

CBF *abbr* = cerebral blood flow.

cbi *abbr* = computer-based information.

CBI *abbr* = Confederation of British Industry; Cooperative Business International.

CBIAC *abbr* = Chemical and Biological Defense Information Analysis Center

CBiol *abbr* = Chartered Biologist.

CBIS *abbr* = computer-based information system.

c. bl. *abbr* = carte blanche.

CBMIS *abbr* = computer-based management information system.

CBO *abbr* = Congressional Budget Office

C-bomb *abbr* = cobalt bomb.

CBR *abbr* = complete bed rest.

CBRD *abbr* = cattle birth record document.

CBRW *abbr* = chemical, biological, and radiological warfare; chemical, biological, and radiological weapons.

CBT *abbr* = computer-based training.

CBW *abbr* = chemical and biological warfare.

cc *abbr* = carbon copy; chapters; courtesy copy; cubic centimeter(s).

c.c. *abbr* = carbon copy; cashier's check; chief clerk; circuit court; city council; civil court; (*Brit*) clerk of the (privy) council; common councilman; company commander; (*French*) *compte courant*, "current account"; consular clerk; contra credit; cricket club; (*Brit*) crown cases; (*Brit*) crown clerk; curate in charge.

CC *abbr* = Cape Colony; Central Committee; Chamber of Commerce; Charity Commission; Chief Clerk; City Council; Code Civil; Countryside Commission; County Council; County Councilor.

CCA *abbr* = Canadian Center for Architecture; Caribbean Conservation Association.

CCAT *abbr* = Central Council for the Amateur Theater.

CCBN *abbr* = Central Council for British Naturism.

CCBW *abbr* = Committee on Chemical and Biological Warfare.

CCC *abbr* = Caribbean Council of Churches; Catholic Communications Center; Central Criminal Court.

CCCBR *abbr* = Central Council of Church Bell Ringers.

CCCM *abbr* = Central Committee for Community Medicine.

CCCO *abbr* = Committee on Climatic Changes and the Ocean.

CCCR *abbr* = Coordinating Committee for Cancer Research.

CCD *abbr* = cattle control document; charge coupled device.

CCE *abbr* = Counsel and Care for the Elderly.

CCF *abbr* = Combined Cadet Force; Congress for Cultural Freedom; congestive cardiac failure.

CCFA *abbr* = Combed Cadet Force Association.

CCHE *abbr* = Central Council for Health Education.

CChem *abbr* = Chartered Chemist.

CCHF *abbr* = Children's Country Holidays Fund.

CCHMS *abbr* = Central Committee for Hospital Medical Services.

CCIA *abbr* = Commission of the Churches on International Affairs.

CCIS *abbr* = command control information system.

CCIVS *abbr* = Coordinating Committee for International Voluntary Service.

CCJ *abbr* = Council for Christians and Jews.

CCLGF *abbr* = Consultative Committee on Local Government Finance.

CCM *abbr* = (*Brit*) Cornish Chamber of Mines.

CCMP *abbr* = Coordinating Committee for the Moon and Planets.

CCNR *abbr* = Consultative Committee on Nuclear Research.

ccol *abbr* = Chartered Colorist.

CCP *abbr* = Code of Civil Procedure.

CCPR *abbr* = Central Council for Physical Recreation.

CCR *abbr* = Commission on Civil Rights

CCrP *abbr* = Code of Criminal Procedure.

CCS *abbr* = Center for Cognitive Science; Corporation of Secretaries.

CCSC *abbr* = Commercial Computer Security Center.

CCSEM *abbr* = computer-controlled scanning electron microscope.

CCSS *abbr* = (*Brit*) Cambridge Center for Sixth Form Studies.

CCSU *abbr* = Council of Civil Service Unions.

CCT *abbr* (*Brit*) = Chamber of Coal Traders; Cockburn Conservation Trust.

CCTA *abbr* = Central Computer and Telecommunications Agency.

CCTV *abbr* = closed circuit television.

CCU *abbr* = coronary care unit.

CCW *abbr* = Caribbean Church Woman; International Committee on Chemical Warfare.

CCWA *abbr* = Conservation Council of Western Australia.

CCWC *abbr* = Campaign for Cold Weather Credits.

CCWM *abbr* = Congregational Council for World Mission.

Cd *symbol* (*chem*) cadmium (element).

cd *abbr* = candela.

c.d. *abbr* = cash discount; (*mus*) (*Italian*) *colla destra*, "with the right hand"; (*Latin*) *cum dividendo*, "with dividend."

c/d *abbr* = carried down.

CD *abbr* = certificate of deposit; (*Poland*) Christian Democracy; Civil Defense; compact disc; condemned; contagious disease; (*French*) *corps diplomatique*.

C/D *abbr* = certificate of deposit.

CDA *abbr* = Chinese Dancers' Association; Commonwealth Dental Association.

CDAA *abbr* = Churches Drought Action in Africa.

CDC *abbr* = Centers for Disease Control; Commonwealth Development Corporation; Control Data Corporation.

CDEE *abbr* = Chemical Defense Experimental Establishment.

CDEU *abbr* = Christian Democratic European Union.

CDEV *abbr* (*comput*) = control panel device.

CDH *abbr* = congenital disease of the heart.

CDI *abbr* (*comput*) = Compact Disc Interactive.

CDipAF *abbr* = Certified Diploma in Accounting and Finance.

CDL *abbr* = central door locking.

CDMF *abbr* = Community Dance and Mime Foundation.

cDNA *abbr* = complementary DNA.

CDP *abbr* = Community Drug Project.

CD ROM *abbr* (*comput*) = Compact Disk Read Only Memory. A data-storage system invented by Phillips in 1983, capable of holding in excess of 600 megabytes of data.

cds. *abbr* = cards.

CDSC *abbr* = Communicable Disease Surveillance Center.

CDSE *abbr* = computer-driven simulation environment.

CDSO *abbr* = Companion of the Distinguished Service Order.

CDT *abbr* = Central Daylight Time.

CDTV *abbr* = compact disk television.

CDU *abbr* = (*Germany*) Christian Democratic Union.

CDV *abbr* = canine distemper virus; CD-video; Civil Defense Volunteers.

Ce *symbol* (*chem*) cerium (element).

ce *abbr* (*Latin*) = *caveat emptor*, "let the buyer beware."

CE *abbr* = Chancellor of the Exchequer; Chemical Engineer; Chief Engineer; Christian Endeavor; Church of England (*also* **C of E**); civil engineer; Common Entrance; (*French*) *Communauté Européenne*, "European Community," an EU safety approval mark; Common Era; Council of Europe.

CEA *abbr* = Cinematograph Exhibitors Association of Great Britain; Council for Educational Advance; Council of Economic Advisers.

cease *vti* to stop, to come to an end; to discontinue.

ceasefire *n* a period of truce in a war, uprising, etc.

ceaseless *adj* without ceasing; incessant.—**ceaselessly** *adv*.

Ceausescu *n* **Nicolae** (1918–89) Romanian dictator, secretary general of the Romanian Communist Party from 1969 and president of Romania from 1974. He was overthrown in 1989 and executed.

Ceawlin *n* (*d. c.*593) king of Wessex, Britain (577–591).

CEBAR *abbr* = Chemical, Biological, and Radiological Warfare.

cebell *n* (*mus*) a 17th-century English dance similar to the gavotte.

CEBIS *abbr* (*Brit*) = Centre for Environment and Business in Scotland.

Cebu *n* a city in Philippines.

CEC *abbr* = Catholic Education Council; Central Ethical Committee; chief executive officer; Clarence Environment Center; Commonwealth Engineers Council; Council for Exceptional Children.

Cecil *n* **William [1st Baron Burghley]** (1520–98) English statesman.

Cecilia *n* **Saint** the patron saint of music who was martyred in the 2nd or 3rd century. Her feast day is 22 November.

Cecrops *n* (*Greek myth*) the founder of Athens and the first king of Attica, sometimes represented as half man and half dragon.

CECS *abbr* = Church of England Children's Society.

cecum *n* (*pl* **ceca**) (*anat*) the pouch at the beginning of the large intestine containing the vermiform appendix.—*also* **caecum**.—**cecal** *adj*.

CEDA *abbr* = Canadian Electrical Distributors Association; Catering Equipment Distributors Association; Chinese Exploration and Design Association; (*Eire*) Consumer Electronics Distributors' Association.

cedar *n* a large coniferous evergreen tree; its wood.—**cedarwood** *n*.

Cedd *n* **Saint** (*d.* 664) English monk who converted the East Saxons to Christianity, brother of St Chad. His feast day is 7 January.

cede *vt* to yield to another, give up, esp by treaty; to assign or transfer the title of.—**ceder** *n*.

cedi *see* **pesewa**.

Cedi *n* currency of Ghana.

cedilla *n* a character written under a c in certain languages, "ç," to indicate that it is pronounced as an "s" not "k."

CEDO *abbr* = Center for Education Development Overseas.

CEDR *abbr* = Center for Dispute Resolution.

CEEC *abbr* = Council for European Economic Co-operation.

CEF *abbr* = Canadian Expeditionary Force(s); College Employers Forum; Construction Employers' Federation.

CEG *abbr* = Computer Education Group.

CEGB *abbr* = Central Electricity Generating Board.

CEI *abbr* = Center for Environmental Information; Committee for Environmental Information; Conference of the Electronics Industry.

ceil *vt* to overlay or cover the inner surface of a roof; to furnish with a ceiling.

ceilidh *n* (*mus*) (*Gaelic*) a gathering at which songs, folk music, and dances are performed esp in Scotland and Ireland.

ceiling *n* the inner roof of a room; the lining of this; any upper limit; the highest altitude a particular aircraft can fly.

CEIM *abbr* = Conservative Evangelicals in Methodism.

cel. *abbr* = celebrated.

Cel., Cels. *abbr* = Celsius.

celadon *n* a soft pale sea-green color; porcelain or fine earthenware of such a color. * *adj* having the color of celadon.

celandine *n* one of several kinds of wild plant with star-shaped yellow flowers.

celebrant *n* one who celebrates, esp the principal officiating priest in offering mass or celebrating the Eucharist.

celebrate *vt* to make famous; to praise, extol; to perform with proper rites; to mark with ceremony; to keep (festival).—**celebrant** *n*.

celebrated *adj* famous.

celebration *n* the act of celebrating; an observance or ceremony to celebrate anything.

celebrity *n* (*pl* **celebrities**) fame; a famous or well-known person.

celeriac *n* a variety of celery with a turnip-like root.

celerity *n* quickness, dispatch.

celery *n* (*pl* **celeries**) a vegetable with long juicy edible stalks.

celesta, celeste *n* a kind of glockenspiel with a keyboard.

celestial *adj* in or of the sky; heavenly; divine.—**celestially** *adv*.

celestial body *n* (*astron*) a star or planet.

celestial equator *n* (*astron*) the circle created by the meeting of a projection into space of the plane of the Earth's equator.

celestial mechanics *n* (*astron*) the study of the motion, etc, of celestial bodies, usu under gravitation.

celestial poles *npl* (*astron*) the points at which imaginary northerly and southerly extensions of the Earth's axis meet the celestial sphere.

celestial sphere *n* (*astron*) an imaginary sphere which places an observer at its center and all the stars on the inner surface of the sphere.

Celestine V *n* **Saint, Peter di Morrone** (1215–96) Italian monk, elected pope in 1294. He resigned his office and was imprisoned by his successor, Boniface VIII. He was canonized in 1313. His feast day until 1969 was 19 May.

celestite *n* native strontium sulphate.

celiac *adj* of or pertaining to the abdomen. * *n* a person with celiac disease.—*also* **coeliac**.

celiac disease *n* a chronic digestive disease of young children, causing malnutrition and diarrhea.—*also* **gluten enteropathy**

celibacy *n* (*pl* **celibacies**) the unmarried state; complete sexual abstinence.

celibate *n* a person who remains unmarried, esp one who has taken religious vows; a person who abstains from sexual intercourse.—*also adj.*

cell *n* a small room for one in a prison or monastery; a small cavity as in a honeycomb; a device that converts chemical energy into electricity; a microscopic unit of living matter; a small group of people bound by common aims within an organization or political party; (*comput*) an element or block of a spreadsheet into which data, numbers or formulae are placed.—**cellular** *adj.*

cella *n* (*archit*) the main area of a classical temple containing the statue of the deity.

cellar *n* a basement; a stock of wines.

cellarage *n* cellars collectively; the space occupied by cellars; a charge for storage in cellars.

cellarer *n* an official in a monastery who superintends the cellar and distribution of provisions; an official of the chapter who has charge of the temporals.

cellarete, cellaret *n* a case for holding bottles of wine or liquor.

cell division *n* mitosis, the process by which cells divide and multiply.

Cellini *n* **Benvenuto** (1500–71) Italian goldsmith who designed in Mannerist style.

cellnet *n* a portable radio telephone used in cellular radio.

cello *n* (*pl* **cellos**) the violoncello, a large four-stringed bass instrument of the violin family, held between the knees.—**cellist** *n.*

cellophane *n* a thin transparent paper made from cellulose, used for wrapping.

Cellphone *n* (*trademark*) a cellular telephone, a portable mobile telephone operated by cellular radio.

cellular *adj* of, resembling, or containing cells; (*textiles*) of an open texture.

cellular phone *n* a portable mobile telephone operated by microwave radio.

cellular radio *n* a computer-controlled radio communications system for Cellphones, etc, using a network of transmitters serving small zones called cells, as users move between cells the transmitters/receivers are transferred automatically.

cellular telephone *or* **cellphone** *n* a mobile telephone operated by cellular radio.

cellule *n* a small cell or cavity.

cellulite *n* a form of fat on the hips, thighs, and buttocks that causes puckering of the skin surface.

celluloid *n* a type of plastic made from cellulose nitrate and camphor; a plastic coating on film; cinema film.

cellulose *n* a starch-like carbohydrate forming the cell walls of plants, used in making paper, textiles, film, etc.

cellulose acetate *n* a compound used in the manufacture of artificial textiles, film, and varnishes.

CELS *abbr* = Center for European Legal Studies; Coalition for Education in the Life Sciences.

Celsius *adj* pertaining to a thermometer scale with a freezing point of 0 degrees and a boiling point of 100 degrees.

celt *n* a prehistoric edged instrument or weapon of stone or bronze, resembling a chisel or blade of an ax, found in ancient tumuli.

Celt *n* a member of an ancient people who inhabited pre-Roman Britain, Gaul and Spain.

Celtic *adj* of or relating to the Celts; the language of the Celts, including Scots or Irish Gaelic, Manx, Welsh, Cornish, and Breton. Celtic languages formed a group that was a branch of the Indo-European family of languages. They are sometimes divided into Continental Celtic and Insular Celtic.

Celtic art *or* **La Tène art** *n* an art form first developed and used by high-ranking Celts around the River Rhine in Germany.

Celticist, Celtist *n* a student of Celtic antiquities, languages, etc.

Celts *n* a group of people whose origins can be traced to the region around the Rhine in Germany. They were also known as the Galatians and Gauls.

cembalo *n* (*mus*) (*Italian*) a dulcimer; an abbreviation of *clavicembalo*, which is the Italian for harpsichord.

cement *n* a powdered substance of lime and clay, mixed with water, etc, to make mortar or concrete, which hardens upon drying; any hard-drying substance. * *vt* to bind or glue together with or as if with cement; to cover with cement.—**cementer** *n.*

cementation *n* the act of cementing; a process for converting iron into steel, glass into porcelain, etc.

cementum *n* a thin hard substance resembling bone that covers the root of a tooth.

CEMEP *abbr* = European Committee of Manufacturers of Electrical Machines and Power Electronics.

cemetery *n* (*pl* **cemeteries**) a place for the burial of the dead.

CEMS *abbr* = Church of England Men's Society.

CEMYC *abbr* = Council of Europe Minority Youth Committees.

cen. *abbr* = central; century.

Cenfus *n* king of Wessex, Britain (reigned in 674). A grandson of Ceolwulf.

CEng *abbr* = Chartered Engineer.

CEngFIProdE *abbr* = Fellow of the Institution of Production Engineers.

CEngMIProdE *abbr* = Member of the Institution of Production Engineers.

CENMAC *abbr* = Center for Micro-Assisted Communication.

cenobite *n* one of a religious order living in a convent or in community.—*also* **coenobite**.

cenotaph *n* a monument to a person who is buried elsewhere.—**cenotaphic** *adj.*

Cenozoic *adj* of the third geological period, Tertiary.

Cenred *n* king of Mercia, Britain (716–718) succeeded the murdered King Osred.

cense *vt* to perfume with incense.

censer *n* a covered cup-shaped vessel pierced with holes in which incense is burned.

censor *n* an official with the power to examine literature, movies, mail, etc, and remove or prohibit anything considered obscene, objectionable, etc. * *vt* to act as a censor.—**censorable** *adj.*—**censorial** *adj.*—**censorship** *n.*

censorious *adj* expressing censure; fault-finding.—**censoriously** *adv.*—**censoriousness** *n.*

censure *n* an expression of disapproval or blame. * *vt* to condemn as wrong; to reprimand.—**censurable** *adj.*

census *n* (*pl* **censuses**) an official count of the population, including details of age, sex, occupation, etc; any official count.

cent *n* a hundredth of a dollar; (*inf*) a negligible amount of money.

cent. *abbr* = centigrade; centime; centimeter; centimeters; central; (*Latin*) *centum*, "a hundred"; century.

CENTA *abbr* = Combined Edible Nut Trade Association.

centaur *n* a fabulous monster, half man, half horse; an expert horseman.

Centaurus *n* (*astron*) a southern sky constellation.

Centaurus A *n* (*astron*) an elliptical galaxy in the constellation Centaurus.

centaury *n* (*pl* **centauries**) a medicinal herb.

centavo *n* (*pl* **centavos**) the hundredth part of a dollar or peso in use in the South American republics.

centenarian *n* one who is one hundred years old or more.—*also adj.*

centenary *n* (*pl* **centenaries**) a hundredth anniversary or its celebration. * *adj* of a hundred years.

centennial *adj* happening every hundred years. * *n* a centenary.

center *n* the approximate middle point or part of anything, a pivot; interior; point of concentration; a place where a particular activity goes on; source; political moderation; (*sport*) a player at the center of the field, etc, a center-forward. * *adj* of or at the center. * *vt* (**centering, centered**) to place in the center; to concentrate; to be fixed; (*football, hockey*) to kick or hit the ball into the center of the pitch.—*also* **center**.

center bit *n* a carpenter's tool turning upon a center, for boring holes.

center of gravity *n* that point of a body through which the resultant of all the forces acting upon it in consequence of the earth's attraction will pass.

center of mass *n* a point, not necessarily in a body, where the whole mass of the body or bodies appears to act.

centerboard *n* a keel so constructed that it may be raised within the hull of a vessel or lowered, extensively used by racing craft; a yacht with this.—*also* **centerboard**.

centerfold *n* a color illustration spread across the two facing pages in the middle of a newspaper or magazine.

centerpiece *n* a central ornament or decoration.

centesimal *adj* counting or counted by hundredths. * *n* a hundredth part.

centesimo *n* a monetary unit of Italy and San Marino, equal to one hundredth of a lira; a monetary unit of Panama, equal to one hundredth of a balboa; a monetary unit of Uruguay, equal to one hundredth of a peso.

centi- *prefix* one hundredth.

centiare, centare *n* a square meter, equal to the hundredth part of an are.

centig. *abbr* = centigrade.

centigrade *adj* Celsius.

centigram, centigramme *n* one hundredth of a gram.

centiliter, centilitre *n* one hundredth of a liter.

centime *n* a small french coin, the hundredth part of a franc.

centimeter, centimetre *n* one hundredth of a meter.

centimeter-gram-second *n* a unit system in which the centimeter, the gram, and the mean solar second are taken respectively as the units of length, mass, and time (usu abbreviated **cgs units**).

centimo *n* a monetary unit of Cost Rica and various other countries.

centipede *n* a crawling creature with a long body divided into numerous segments each with a pair of legs.

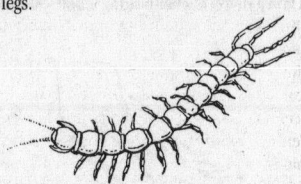

centner *n* a weight divisible first into a hundred parts and then into smaller parts; in many European countries the commercial name for a hundredweight.

cento *n* (*pl* **centos**) a literary or musical composition formed by selections from various authors or composers and arranged in a new order.

CENTO *abbr* = Central Treaty Organization.

central *adj* in, at, from, or forming the center; main; principal; important.—**centrally** *adv*.—**centrality** *n*.

Central African Republic *n* a landlocked republic in central Africa bordered by Chad in the north, Cameroon in the west, Sudan in the east, and the Congo and the Democratic Republic of Congo in the south.

central bank *n* a national bank that handles government transactions as opposed to private business.

central heating *n* a system of heating by pipes from a central boiler or other heat source.

Central Intelligence Agency *n* a US government agency that coordinates intelligence gathering.

centralism *n* the policy or process of bringing under central control.—**centralist** *adj, n*.

centralize *vt* to draw to the center; to place under the control of a central authority, esp government.—**centralization** *n*.

central nervous system *n* (*biol*) in vertebrates, the brain and spinal cord which coordinates an animal's activity.

central processing unit *n* (*comput*) the core of a computer system, which contains the integrated circuits needed to interpret and execute instructions and perform the basic computer functions.

Central Standard Time *n* the sixth time zone west of Greenwich that covers much of the central US, six hours behind GMT.

centric, centrical *adj* placed in the center; central.—**centricity** *n*.

centrifugal *adj* moving away from the center of rotation.—**centrifugally** *adv*.

centrifugal force *n* (*physics*) a force that acts in direct and equal opposition to a body that is spinning fast around a central point.

centrifuge *n* a device used to separate milk, blood, etc, by rotating at very high speed.—**centrifugation** *n*.

centripetal *adj* tending to move towards the center.—**centripetally** *adv*.

centripetal drainage system *n* a pattern of streams arranged radially and draining inwards towards a single river or lake.

centripetal force *n* (*physics*) a force that pulls a spinning body in towards the center.

centrist *n* a person of moderate political opinions, etc.—**centrism** *n*.

centrobaric *adj* relating to the center of gravity or to the method of its determination.

centroid *n* the center of mass or gravity of a body.

centuple *adj* multiplied by a hundred.

centurion *n* an officer commanding a hundred Roman soldiers.

century *n* (*pl* **centuries**) a period of a hundred years; a set of a hundred; (*cricket*) 100 runs made by a batsman in a single innings; a company of a Roman legion.

century plant *n* a name of the American aloe, from the supposition that it flowered once only in a hundred years.

Centwine *n* king of Wessex, Britain (676–685) brother of Cenwahl.

Cenwahl *n* king of Wessex, Britain (643–672). The son of Cyneglis.

CEO *abbr* = Center for Earth Observation; Chief Executive Officer.

Ceol *n* king of Wessex, Britain (591–597). Came to the throne after the abdication of Ceawlin.

Ceolred *n* king of Mercia, Britain (709–716). The son of Ethelred.

Ceolwulf *n* (*d*. 760) king of Northumbria, Britain (729–737). A brother of Cenred.

Ceolwulf I *n* king of Mercia, Britain (821–823). Succeeded his brother, Coenwulf, but reigned for only two years before being deposed by Beornwulf.

Ceolwulf II *n* king of Mercia, Britain (874–c.880). The last Mercian king was chosen by the Danish overlords to rule the subordinate western half of the kingdom. He was deposed.

Ceolwulf *n* king of Wessex, Britain (597–611). He succeeded his brother, Ceol.

Ceorl *n* king of Mercia, Britain (c.606–626). Related to Pybba, his daughter married the dominant king of Northumbria, Edwin.

CEOS *abbr* = Child Exploitation and Obscenity Section.

cep *n* an edible woodland fungus with a shiny brown cap and a white underside.

cephalalgia *n* a headache.

cephalic *adj* of the head.

Cephalic index *n* an index obtained by taking measurements of the length and breadth of the human skull.

cephalization *n* the tendency in animal development to localize important parts or organs in or near the head.

Cephalonia, Kephallenia *n* a mountainous island of Greece, the largest of the Ionian Islands.—**Cephalonian, Kephallenian** *adj*.

cephalopod *n* a marine mollusc, such as an octopus, characterized by a well-developed head and eyes and a ring of sucker-bearing tentacles.—**cephalopodan** *n, adj*.

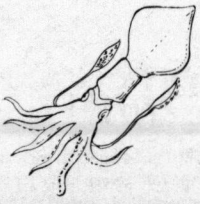

cephalosporin *n* one of a group of semi-synthetic antibiotics effective against a broad spectrum of micro-organisms and derived from a mold called *Cephalosporium*.

cephalothorax *n* (*pl* **cephalothoraxes, cephalothoraces**) the anterior part of the body in the higher crustaceans, spiders, etc.

Cephalus *n* (*Greek myth*) ruler of Phocis, and husband of Procris, whom he accidentally killed with a hunting spear.

Cephas *n* (*Bible*) Aramaic name of Peter, meaning rock or stone.

Cepheid variable *n* (*astron*) one of a class of regular variable stars, typically brighter stars that can be seen over great distances.

Cepheus *n* (*Greek myth*) a king of Ethiopia, husband of Cassiopeia and father of Andromeda; (*astron*) a north sky constellation close to the pole.

Cephissus *n* the name of two rivers in ancient Greece, one in Attica, the other in Boeotia.

CEPO *abbr* = County Emergency Planning Officers Society.

CEPR *abbr* = Center for Economic Policy Research.

CEPS *abbr* = Center for Earth and Planetary Studies

CEQ *abbr* = Council on Environmental Quality

ceraceous *adj* resembling wax.

ceram. *abbr* = ceramics.

ceramic *adj* of earthenware, porcelain, or brick. * *n* something made of ceramic.

ceramics *n* (*sing*) work executed wholly or partly in clay and baked; the art of pottery.—**ceramist, ceramicist** *n*.

cerastes *n* (*pl* **cerastes**) the horned viper.

cerate *n* a thick ointment of wax, etc.

ceratodus *n* (*pl* **ceratoduses**) a genus of Australian fishes containing the barramunda, or native salmon.

Cerberus *n* (*Greek myth*) the dog-monster that guarded Hades, variously described as having a hundred, fifty, or three heads. He was subdued by Heracles, who, in the last test of his strength, snatched Cerberus from the halls of Hades.

CERC *abbr* = Chemical Energy Research Center; Civil Engineering Research Council.

CERCI *abbr* = Center for Educational Resources in the Construction Industry.

CERCLIS *abbr* = Comprehensive Environmental Response, Compensation, and Liability Information System

Cerdic *n* king of Wessex, Britain (519–534). Recorded as the first king of the West Saxons.

cere[1] *n* a wax-like membrane at the base of the bill of many birds, as the parrot.

cere[2] *vt* to cover or close with cerecloth.

cereal *n* a grass grown for its edible grain, e.g., wheat, rice; the grain of such grasses; a breakfast food made from such grains. * *adj* of corn or edible grain.

cerebellum *n* (*pl* **cerebellums, cerebella**) a part of the brain below and behind the cerebrum which coordinates voluntary movements.—**cerebellar** *adj*.

cerebral *adj* of or relating to the cerebrum; intellectual.—**cerebrally** *adv*.

cerebral cortex *n* the outer layer of the cerebral hemispheres active in the higher nervous functions.

cerebral hemisphere *n* one of the two lateral halves of the cerebrum.

cerebral palsy *n* a disability caused by brain damage before, during, or immediately after birth resulting in poor muscle co-ordination.

cerebrate *vi* to use the brain; to think.

cerebration *n* the conscious or unconscious action of the brain; thought or thinking.

cerebrospinal *adj* of the brain and spinal cord.

cerebrospinal fluid *n* a clear, colorless fluid with a similar composition to lymph which fills the ventricles and cavities in the central nervous system and bathes all the surfaces of the brain and spinal cord.

cerebrovascular accident *see* **stroke**.

cerebrum *n* (*pl* **cerebrums, cerebra**) the front part of the brain of vertebrates; the dominant part of the brain in man, associated with intellectual function; the brain as a whole.

cerecloth *n* a cloth saturated with wax or some gummy substance, used for wrapping embalmed bodies in.

cerement *n* a grave cloth or shroud; (*pl*) grave clothes.

ceremonial *adj* of or with ceremony; formal. * *n* a set of rules for ceremonies.—**ceremonially** *adv*.

ceremonialism *n* adherence to, or fondness for, ceremonial observance; ritualism.—**ceremonialist** *n*.

ceremonious *adj* observant of ceremony; marked by formality; overpolite.—**ceremoniously** *adv*.

ceremony *n* (*pl* **ceremonies**) a sacred rite; formal observance or procedure; behaviour that follows rigid etiquette.

Cerenkov radiation *n* electromagnetic radiation emitted when highly energetic particles traveling close to the velocity of light enter a medium in which they are moving faster than the velocity of light in that medium.

Ceres *n* (*Roman myth*) a goddess corresponding to the Greek Demeter, the goddess of the earth, responsible for its fertility; (*astron*) an asteroid 621 miles in diameter, the first to be found.

CERES Center for the Education of Racial Equality in Scotland; Consumers for Ethics in Research Group.

cerise *n* a light and clear red.—*also adj*.

cerium *n* a gray metallic element used in various metallurgical and nuclear applications.

CERN *abbr* (*French*) = *Conseil Européen pour la Recherche Nucléaire*, European Organization for Nuclear Research.

Cernunnos *n* (*Celtic myth*) lord of the animals. His name means "the horned one". He is usu depicted as wearing horns or antlers, sometimes decorated with a torc, and often has both human and animal ears.

cero- *prefix* wax.

Cerri *n* **Pierluigi** (1939–) Italian architect, industrial, graphic and exhibition designer who designed the 1976 Venice Biennale.

Cerridwen *or* **Carridwen** *n* (*Welsh Celtic myth*) the mother of a very ugly son, Afagddu, and a very beautiful daughter, Crearwy. Said to have been the keeper of the cauldron in the Otherworld. She was associated with the sow, a symbol of fecundity.

cert *n* (*sl*) certainty.

cert. *abbr* = certificate; certified; certify.

CERT *abbr* = Charities Effectiveness Review Trust.

certain *adj* sure, positive; unerring, reliable; sure to happen, inevitable; definite, fixed; some; one; unnamed, unspecified.

certainly *adv* without doubt; yes.

certainty *n* (*pl* **certainties**) something undoubted, inevitable; the condition of being certain.

CertBDS *abbr* (*Brit*) = Special Category Membership of the British Display Society Ltd.

CertBibKnowl *abbr* = Certificate of Bible Knowledge.

CertDesRCA *abbr* (*Brit*) = Certificate of Designer of the Royal College of Art.

CertEd *abbr* = Certificate in Education.

CertHSAP *abbr* = Certificate in Health Services Administration Practice.

CertHSM *abbr* = Certificate in Health Services Management.

certif. *abbr* = certificate; certificated.

certifiable *adj* able to be certified; (*sl*) fit to be declared insane.—**certifiably** *adv*.

certificate *n* a document formally attesting a fact; a testimonial of qualifications or character.—**certificated** *adj*.

certificate of origin *n* a document that states the country from which a consignment of goods has originated in international trading.

certified check *n* a check guaranteed by a bank.

certified mail *n* first-class mail for which the addressee must sign.

certified public accountant *n* an accountant who has qualified by passing official examinations; a chartered accountant.

certified stock *n* stocks of a commodity that have been passed as acceptable in fulfilment of contracts on a futures market.

certify *vt* (**certifying, certified**) to declare in writing or attest formally; to endorse with authority.—**certification** *n*.

certiorari *n* (*law*) a writ issuing from a superior court calling for the records of an inferior court, or to remove a case from a court below.

certitude *n* freedom from doubt.

CertOccHyg *abbr* = Certificate of Operational Competence in Comprehensive Occupational Hygiene.

cerulean *adj* deep blue.

cerumen *n* wax of the ear.—**ceruminous** *adj*.

ceruse *n* white lead used as a pigment and from which a cosmetic is prepared.

Cervantes [Saavedra] *n* **Miguel de** (1547–1616) Spanish novelist, dramatist, and poet whose satirical masterpiece is *Don Quixote de la Mancha*. He wrote other fine works, notably the short stories in *Exemplary Tales*.

cervical *adj* of the neck of the uterus.

cervical cancer *n* cancer of the neck or cervix of the uterus.

cervical smear *n* (*med*) a sample of cells taken from the cervix for detection of cancer; the taking of the sample.

cervine *adj* of or pertaining to the deer family; of a tawny or fawn color.

cervix *n* (*pl* **cervixes, cervices**) a neck-like structure, esp *cervix uteri* or neck of the uterus.

CES *abbr* = Center for Environmental Studies; Charities Evaluation Studies; Christian Evidence Society.

CESA *abbr* = Catholic Ex-Servicemen's Association; Cultural Exchange Society of America.

Cesair *n* (*Irish Celtic myth*) the granddaughter of Noah and daughter of Bith, who led the first invaders to Ireland before the Flood, a group consisting of fifty women and three men, Bith, Ladra and Fintan. Cesair became the wife of Fintan. Her journey features in the *Leabhar Gabhala Eireann*.

Cesarean section, Caesarean section *n* the delivery of a child from the uterus by a surgical operation involving incision into the abdomen and uterus.—*also* l.c.

CESC *abbr* = Conference on European Security and Co-operation.

CESDA *abbr* = Confederation of European Soft Drinks Associations.

cesium *n* a rare silvery alkaline metal.—*also* **caesium.**

CESPA *abbr* = Campaign for Equal State Pension Ages.

cespitose *adj* (*bot*) growing in tufts.

cess[1] *vt* to impose a tax; to assess. * *n* a rate or tax, esp the land tax.

cess[2] *n* (*Irish*) luck or fortune.

CESSAC *abbr* = Church of England Soldiers', Sailors', and Airmen's Clubs.

cessation *n* a stoppage; a pause.

cession *n* a giving up, a surrender; something ceded.

cessionary *n* (*pl* **cessionaries**) (*law*) a giving or yielding up.

cesspit, cesspool *n* a covered cistern for collecting liquid waste or sewage; (*fig*) a place of sin and depravity.

Cesti *n* **Antonio** (1623-69) Italian opera composer. His works helped to develop the operatic form, e.g., *Orontea*.

cestoid *adj* of or pertaining to the Cestoda, an order of parasitic flat worms to which the tapeworms belong. * *n* a flat intestinal worm.

Cestr. *abbr* (*Latin*) = *Cestrensis*, "of Chester."

Cet *n* (*Irish Celtic myth*) a warrior of Connacht who, with his brother Anluan, was invited by Medb to take part in the quest for the Donn Cuailgne.

CET *abbr* = Central European Time; European Ceramic Tile Manufacturers Federation.

CETA *abbr* = Conference of Engineering Trades Associations.

cetacean *n* a member of an order of aquatic, usu marine, mammals that includes whales, dolphins and porpoises. * *adj* belonging to this order (—*also* **cetaceous**).

CETEC *abbr* = Topographic Engineering Center

ceteris paribus (*Latin*) other things being equal.

CETHV *abbr* = Certificate of Education in Training as Health Visitor.

Ceto *n* (*Greek myth*) a sea monster, the daughter of Ge and Pontus and mother of the Gorgons.

cetology *n* the study of cetaceous creatures.— **cetological** *adj*.—**cetologist** *n*.

cet. par. *abbr* (*Latin*) = *ceteris paribus*, "other things being equal."

Cetus *n* (*astron*) an equatorial constellation.

Cézanne *n* **Paul** (1839–1906) French painter, whose notable works are *Mont Ste Victoire* and *L'Estaque*; his work had a huge influence on cubism and 20th-century art generally.

Cf *symbol* (*chem*) californium (element).

cf. *abbr* = (*binding*) calf; (*Latin*) *confer*, "compare."

c.f., CF *abbr* = (*mus*) (*Latin*) *cantus firmus*, "fixed song"; cost and freight.

c/f *abbr* (*book-keeping*) = carried forward.

CF, C.F. *abbr* = Chaplain to the Forces; Compassionate Friends; cystic fibrosis.

CFA *abbr* = Commonwealth Forestry Association; Council for Acupuncture.

CFA Franc *n* currency of Benin, Burkina Faso, Cameroon, Central African Republic, Chad, Côte D'Ivoire, Equatorial Guinea, Eritrea, Gabon, Mali, Niger, Senegal, the Congo, and Togo.

CFAL *abbr* = current food additives legislation.

CF and I, c. f. and i. *abbr* = cost, freight, and insurance.

CFB *abbr* = Council of the Corporation of Foreign Bondholders.

CFC *abbr* = Caribbean Food Corporation; chlorofluorocarbon.

CFDA *abbr* = Catalog of Federal Domestic Assistance

CFE *abbr* = College of Further Education.

CFFA *abbr* = Commonwealth Families and Friendship Association.

CFGB *abbr* = Canadian Foodgrains Bank.

CFHS *abbr* = Catholic Family History Society.

cfi, c.f.i. *abbr* = cost, freight, and insurance.

CFI *abbr* = Campaign for Freedom of Information; Campaign for Industry; Clothing and Footwear Institute; Confederation of Finishing Industries; cost, freight, and insurance; Council of the Forest Industries of British Columbia.

CFIC *abbr* = Canned Food Information Center.

CFL *abbr* = Creation for Liberation.

CFLP *abbr* = Central Fire Liaison Panel.

c.f.m. *abbr* = cubic feet per minute.

CFM *abbr* = Center for Facilities Management; Center for Franchise Marketing.

CFMA *abbr* = Chair Frame Manufacturers Association.

CFMEU *abbr* = Construction, Forestry, Mining, and Energy Union.

CfN *abbr* = Council for Nature.

CFO *abbr* = Chief Fire Officer.

CFOA *abbr* = Chief Fire Officers' Association.

CFOCFA *abbr* = Commission For Our Common Future.

CFP *abbr* = Common Fisheries Policy.

CFR *abbr* = Code of Federal Regulations; commercial fast reactor

c.f.s. *abbr* = cubic feet per second.

CFS *abbr* = Canadian Forestry Service; Chinese Foot Society.

CFSA *abbr* = Charge Families' Support Association.

CFSAN *abbr* = National Center for Food Safety and Applied Nutrition

CFSL *abbr* = Central Forensic Science Laboratory.

CFT *abbr* = Campaign Free Tibet; Cystic Fibrosis Trust.

CFTA *abbr* = Celtic Film and Television Association.

CFTC *abbr* = Commodity Futures Trading Commission

CFTF *abbr* = (*French*) *Centre Technique Forestier Tropical*.

CFW *abbr* = Care For the Wild; Concern for Family and Womanhood.

CFWI *abbr* (*Brit*) = County Federation of Women's Institutes.

cg. *abbr* = centigram; centigrams.

c.g. *abbr* = captain of the guard; center of gravity; centigram; commanding general; commissary general; consul general.

CG *abbr* = Captain of the Guard; coast guard; (*Brit*) Coldstream Guards; Commanding General; Common Ground; consul general; (*Brit*) Covent Garden.

CGA *abbr* = Cyprus Geographical Association.

CGAT *abbr* = City Gallery Arts Trust.

CGB *abbr* = Commonwealth Geographic Bureau.

CGC *abbr* = Commonwealth Games Council.

CGDEM *abbr* = Council of Gas Detection Equipment Manufacturers.

CGE *abbr* = Conservative Group for Europe.

CGF *abbr* = Commonwealth Games Federation.

cgh *abbr* = computer-generated hologram.

CGH *abbr* = Cape of Good Hope.

CGI *abbr* = Catholic Guides of Ireland; (*Brit*) City and Guilds of London Institute.

CGIT *abbr* = Canadian Girls in Training.

CGLI *abbr* (*Brit*) = City and Guilds of London Institute.

cgm. *abbr* = centigram.

CGM *abbr* = Computer Graphics Metafile; Conspicuous Gallantry Medal.

CGMA *abbr* = Casein Glue Manufacturers Association.

CGP *abbr* (*Brit*) = College of General Practitioners.

CGRA *abbr* = Canadian Good Roads Association; China and Glass Retailers Association.

c.g.s., cgs, CGS *abbr* (*system*) = centimeter-gram-second.

CGS *abbr* = Carolina Geological Society; Chief of General Staff; Commissary General of Subsistence; Cottage Garden Society.

c.g.s.e. *or* **cgse.** *abbr* (*system*) = centimeter-gram-second-electrostatic.

c.g.s.m. *or* **cgsm.** *abbr* (*system*) = centimeter-gram-second-electromagnetic.

CGT *abbr* = capital gains tax.

ch. *abbr* = chain; chaldron; chancery; chapter; (*chess*) check; chief; child; children; (*Latin*) *chirurgiae*, "of surgery"; choir; church.

c.h. *abbr* = courthouse; customhouse.

Ch. *abbr* = Chaplain; Chief; China; Chinese; Church.

CH *abbr* = clearinghouse; (*Brit*) Companion of Honour.

CHA *abbr* = Canadian Historical Association; Caribbean Hotel Association; (*Eire*) Catholic Headmasters' Association; Commercial Horticultural Association; Community Hospitals Association; Countrywide Holidays Association.

chablis *n* (*often with cap*) a dry white wine from Chablis, France.

Chabrier *n* **Alexis Emmanuel** (1841–94) French, self-taught composer, a devotee of Wagner. His most famous piece is his lively orchestral rhapsody, *España*.

cha-cha(-cha) *n* a ballroom dance orig from Latin America; the music for this.

chacma *n* a South African baboon.

chaconne *n* an old Spanish dance; the music for such a dance.

chad *n* (*comput*) the little scraps of paper or cardboard left by the punching of holes in computer cards or paper tape.

Chad *n* a landlocked republic in the center of northern Africa.

Chad *n* **Saint** (*d.* 672) English monk, who succeeded his brother St Cedd as abbot of Lastingham, and became bishop of York. His feast day is 2 March.

chador *n* a long black garment worn by Muslim women, covering the head, body and part of the face.

Chadwick *n* 1. **Lynn** (1914–) British sculptor who experimented with "balancing sculptures" and mobiles in welded iron, inspired by animal and insect forms. 2. **Sir James** (1891–1974) English physicist, who discovered the neutron in 1932 and won the Nobel prize for physics in 1935.

chafe *vti* to restore warmth by rubbing; to make or become sore by rubbing; to irritate; to feel irritation, to fret.

chafer *n* any of various large beetles.

chaff[1] *n* husks of grain separated from the seed by threshing or winnowing; cut hay or straw; worthless stuff.

chaff[2] *vt* to banter; to make a game of. * *vi* to use bantering language. * *n* good-natured teasing, banter.

chaffer *vi* to bargain, haggle. * *n* the act of bargaining.

chaffinch *n* a European songbird.

chaffy *adj* resembling, or full of, chaff; anything light or worthless.

chafing dish *n* a vessel for heating or cooking food on a table; a small portable grate for coals.

Chagall *n* **Marc** (1887–1985) Russian-born French painter. His style suggests the influences of cubism and orphism, but his unique, juxtaposed imagery is drawn from his own childhood memories.

Chagas' disease *n* a form of sleeping sickness that is found in South and Central America.

chagrin *n* annoyance; vexation; disappointment.

CHAH *abbr* = Committee of Heads of Australian Herbaria.

Chaikovsky *see* **Tchaikovsky**.

chain *n* a series of connected links or rings; a continuous series; a series of related events; a bond; a group of stores, hotels, etc, owned by the same company; a unit of length equal to 66 feet; a range of mountains; a group of islands; (*pl*) anything that restricts or binds; fetters. * *vt* to fasten with a chain or chains.

Chain *n* **Sir Ernst Boris** (1906–79) German-born British biochemist. He prepared penicillin for clinical use and shared the 1945 Nobel prize for physiology or medicine with Florey and Alexander Fleming.

chain gang *n* a group of prisoners chained together.

chain letter *n* a letter requesting the recipient to send out copies to a specified number of people.

chain mail *n* flexible armor formed of metal links interwoven.

chain reaction *n* a process in which a chemical, atomic, or other reaction stimulates further reactions, e.g., combustion or nuclear fission; a series of events, each of which stimulates the next.

chain saw *n* a power-driven saw with teeth linked as in a chain.

chain-smoke *vti* to smoke (cigarettes) one after the other.—**chain-smoker** *n*.

chain stitch *n* an embroidery stitch that resembles the links of a chain.

chain store *n* one of a series of retail stores owned by one company.

chair *n* a separate seat for one, with a back and legs; a seat of authority; a chairperson; a professorship; the electric chair. * *vt* to preside as chairman of.

chair lift *n* a series of seats suspended from a cable for carrying tourists or skiers uphill.

chairman *n* (*pl* **chairmen**) a person who presides at a meeting; the president of a board or committee.—**chairwoman** *nf* (*pl* **chairwomen**).—*also* **chairperson**.

chairman's report *n* a report that gives a summary of the year's activities of a company and a short survey of the likely activities of the coming year.

chair rail *n* (*archit*) a wooden molding running around the walls of a room at chair back height.

CHAIS *abbr* = Consumer Hazards Analysis Information Service.

chaise *n* a light two-wheeled carriage; any carriage.

chaise longue *n* (*pl* **chaise longues, chaises longues**) a couch-like chair with a long seat.

chal. *abbr* = chaldron.

Chal. *or* **Chald.** *abbr* = Chaldaic; Chaldaism; Chaldean.

chalcedony *n* (*pl* **chalcedonies**) a form of quartz used as a gemstone.

chalco- *prefix* copper.

Chalcolithic *adj* (*archeo*) relating to a time when stone and copper implements were used together.

chalcopyrite *n* a copper ore.

Chaldea *n* ancient land identified with Babylon.

Chaldean, Chaldaean *adj* pertaining to Chaldea, or ancient Babylon, or its language. * *n* the language of ancient Babylon.

chalet *n* a Swiss hut; any similar building used in a holiday camp, as a ski lodge, etc.

Chalgrin *n* **Jean** (1739–1811) French architect, whose notable works include the Arc de Triomphe, Paris.

Chaliapin *n* **Fedor Ivanovich** (1873–1933) Russian bass singer. Between 1921 and 1925 he was a member of the Metropolitan Opera New York. Of his many outstanding roles, he is best remembered for his Boris Gudunov.

chalice *n* a large cup with a base; a communion cup.

chalk *n* calcium carbonate, a soft white limestone; such a stone or a substitute used for drawing or writing. * *vt* to write, mark or draw with chalk; (*with* **up**) (*inf*) to score, get, achieve; to charge or credit.

chalkboard *n* black or green slate used for writing on with chalk.

chalky *adj* (**chalkier, chalkiest**) containing or resembling chalk.—**chalkiness** *n*.

challenge *vt* to summon to a fight or contest; to call in question; to object to; to hail and interrogate; to demand proof of identity. * *n* the act of challenging; a summons to a contest; a calling in question; a problem that stimulates effort.—**challenger** *n*.—**challenging** *adj*.

challis *n* a light all-wool fabric.

Chalon *n* **Louis** (1866–1916) French painter and designer whose most popular bronze items had a *femme-fleur* theme.

chalumeau *n* (*mus*) (*French*) a generic term for a type of reed-pipe; the lower register of the clarinet.

chalybeate *adj* (*water*) impregnated with iron. * *n* spring water containing a high concentration of dissolved compounds of iron, reputed to be of therapeutic value.

chamber *n* a room, esp a bedroom; a deliberative body or a division of a legislature; a room where such a body meets; a compartment; a cavity in the body of an organism; part of a gun cylinder holding the cartridge; (*pl*) a judge's office.

chambered nautilus *n* a mollusk with a partitioned shell.

chamberlain *n* an official in charge of the household of a monarch or nobleman; a steward, treasurer, or factor of a municipal corporation.

Chamberlain *n* **[Arthur] Neville** (1869–1940) British statesman and Conservative prime minister (1937–40).

chambermaid *n* a woman employed to clean bedrooms in a hotel, etc.

chamber music *n* music for performance by a small group, as a string quartet.

chamber of commerce *n* (*often cap*) an organization of representatives from local businesses formed to promote and protect their interests.

chamber orchestra *n* a small orchestra, sometimes solely of stringed instruments, for performing chamber music.

chamber pot *n* a vessel for urine.

Chambers *n* **Sir William** (1723–96) Swedish architect whose notable works include Somerset House, London.

chamber tomb *n* (*archeo*) a tomb, of various types, constructed from stone.

chameleon *n* a lizard capable of changing color to match its surroundings; a person of variable moods or behavior; an adaptable person.—**chameleonic** *adj*.

chamfer *n* a flat surface made in wood or metal by paring off an angle, a bevel. * *vt* to groove, channel or flute.—**chamferer** *n*.

Chaminade *n* **Cécile** (1857–1944) French pianist and composer who is best known for her songs and piano pieces.

chamois *n* (*pl* **chamois**) a small antelope found in Europe and Asia; a piece of chamois leather.

chamois leather, chammy (leather) *n* a soft, pliable leather formerly made from chamois skin, and now obtained from sheep, goats, and deer; a piece of this for polishing.—*also* **shammy (leather)**.

chamomile *n* an aromatic plant with daisy-like flowers used medicinally for its soothing property and as a hair lightener, and in making camomile tea.—*also* **camomile**.

champ[1] *vti* to munch noisily, chomp; **champ at the bit** to be impatient.

champ[2] *n* (*inf*) a champion.

champagne *n* a sparkling white wine; a pale straw color.

champaign *n* flat open country, a level expanse. * *adj* level, open.

Champaigne *n* **Philippe de** (1602–74) Flemish-born French painter. He was a successful portrait painter and also worked on frescoes at the Sorbonne and decoration for the Palais Royale in Paris.

champerty *n* (*pl* **champerties**) (*law*) the maintenance of a party in a suit on condition that, if successful, the property is shared; the offense of aiding another's lawsuit in order to share in gains from it.—**champertous** *adj*.

champêtre *adj* (*mus*) (*French*) "rural" or "rustic."

champignon *n* an edible mushroom that grows in circular clusters.

champion *n* a person who fights for another; one who upholds a cause; a competitor successful against all others. * *adj* first-class; (*inf*) excellent. * *vt* to defend; to uphold the cause of.

Champion *n* **Georges** (1889–1940) French decorator and furniture designer who used severe geometric shapes and contrasting colors.

championship *n* the act of championing; the process of determining a champion; a contest held to find a champion.

champlevé *n* enamel bearing indentations filled with color.—*also adj*.

Champollion *n* **Jean-François** (1790–1832) French Egyptologist, who first analyzed the hieroglyphic script of ancient Egypt. His further work was published as *Monuments d'Egypte et Nubie*, and *Grammaire Egyptien*.

CHAMPVA *abbr* = Civilian Health and Medical Program of the Veterans Administration.

Chan *n* **Kwok Hoi** (1939–87) Chinese architect and interior designer who collaborated on the design of some interiors for the liner, *Queen Elizabeth II*.

Chanaux *n* **Adolphe** (1887–1965) French designer and interior decorator who in 1941 became artistic advisor to the House of Guerlain in Paris.

Chanc. *abbr* = Chancellor; Chancery.

chance *n* a course of events; fortune; an accident, an unexpected event; opportunity; possibility; probability; risk. * *vti* to risk; to happen; to come upon unexpectedly. * *adj* accidental, not planned.

chancel *n* the part of a church around the altar, for the clergy and the choir.

chancellery, chancellory *n* (*pl* **chancelleries, chancellories**) a chancellor's department or office; an office attached to an embassy.

chancellor *n* a high government official, as, in certain countries, a prime minister; in some universities, the president or other executive officer.—**chancellorship** *n*.

chance-medley *n* (*law*) justifiable homicide in self-defense; inadvertency.

chancery *n* (*pl* **chanceries**) a court of equity; in England a division of the High Court of Justice; the office for public records.

chancre *n* a syphilitic ulcer.—**chancrous** *adj*.

chancy *adj* (**chancier, chanciest**) (*inf*) risky, uncertain.—**chancily** *adv*.

chandelier *n* an ornamental hanging frame with branches for holding lights.

chandler *n* a dealer or merchant, esp in candles, oil, soap, etc.

Chandler *n* **Raymond Thornton** (1888–1959) American novelist whose detective novels, e.g. *Farewell, My Lovely*, have been widely praised for their sharp, wise-cracking dialog.

Chandler wobble *n* a periodic movement of the Earth's rotation axis which causes latitude to vary with a period of about 14 months.

chandlery *n* (*pl* **chandleries**) a chandler's store or stock.

Chandrasekkar limit *n* (*astron*) the maximum mass of a white dwarf star, about 1.44 times the Sun's mass.

Chanel *n* **Coco** [**Gabrielle Bonheur Chanel**] (1883–1971) French couturière and perfumer.

change *vt* to make different, to alter; to transform; to exchange; to put fresh clothes on. * *vi* to become different, to undergo alteration; to put on fresh clothes; to continue one's journey by leaving one station, etc, or mode of transport and going to and using another. * *n* alteration, modification; substitution; variety; a fresh set, esp clothes; money in small units; the balance of money returned when given in a larger denomination as payment.—**changer** *n*.

changeable *adj* able to be changed; altering rapidly between different conditions; inconstant.—**changeability** *n*.—**changeably** *adv*.

changeful *adj* often changing.

changeless *adj* constant, immutable.—**changelessly** *adv*.—**changelessness** *n*.

changeling *n* a child secretly left in place of another.

change of life *n* the menopause.

changeover *n* a complete change of system, method, state, attitude, etc.

change-ringing *n* (*mus*) an English method of ringing a peal of church bells.

Chang-hua *n* a city in Taiwan.

changing note *or* **cambiatta** *n* (*mus*) a dissonant passing note which is a third away from the preceding note, before being resolved.

channel[1] *n* the bed or the deeper part of a river, harbor, etc; a body of water joining two larger ones; a navigable passage; a means of passing or conveying or communicating; a band of radio frequencies reserved for a particular purpose, e.g., television station; a path for an electrical signal; a groove or line along which liquids, etc, may flow. * *vt* (**channeling, channeled** *or* **channelling, channelled**) to form a channel in; to groove; to direct.

channel[2] *n* a projection from a ship's side to spread the shrouds and keep them clear of the bulwarks.

channeled decoration *n* (*archeo*) wide incised lines applied to various items.

chanson *n* (*pl* **chansons**) a song.

chant *vti* to sing; to recite in a singing manner; to sing or shout (a slogan) rhythmically. * *n* sacred music to which prose is sung; sing-song intonation; a monotonous song; a rhythmic slogan, esp as sung or shouted by sports fans, etc.

chanter *n* a person who chants; the tenor or treble pipe of a bagpipe on which the melody is played.

chanterelle[1] *n* (*mus*) the highest string on a bowed, stringed instrument e.g., the E string on a violin.

chanterelle[2] *n* an edible yellow mushroom.

chanteuse *n* a woman who sings in a nightclub.

chantey, chanty *n* (*pl* **chanteys, chanties**) a shanty.

chanticleer *n* a rooster.

chantry *n* (*pl* **chantries**) a chapel endowed for the saying or singing mass daily for the soul of the founder; such an endowment.

chaology *n* the study of chaos theory.—**chaologist** *n*.

chaos *n* utter confusion, muddle; (*astron*) a complex, interrelated, moving, or dynamic system where known physical laws govern the behavior but where the complexity is such that a slight alteration in some part of the system has consequences which seem quite unpredictable; (*myth*) in old theories of the earth, the void out of which arose all things or in which they existed in a confused, unformed shape before they were separated into kinds.

chaos theory *n* (*physics*) the theory that the behavior of dynamic systems is haphazard rather than mathematical.

chaotic *adj* completely without order or arrangement.—**chaotically** *adv*.

chap[1] *vti* (**chapping, chapped**) (*skin*) to make or become split or rough in cold weather. * *n* a chapped place in the skin.

chap[2] *n* (*inf*) a man.

chap[3] *n* (*usu pl*) one of the jaws or its fleshy covering; the mouth of a channel.

chap. *abbr* = chaplain; chapter.

chaparejos *npl* a cowboy's leather leg coverings.—*also* **chaps**.

chaparral *n* a poor grassland with short, dense bushes.

chapatti, chapati *n* (*pl* **chapattis, chapatis**) in Indian cookery, flat unleavened bread.

chapbook *n* a small book of ballads, romances, etc, formerly hawked by a chapman.

chape *n* the metal tip of a scabbard; the part attaching a scabbard to a belt.

chapeau *n* (*pl* **chapeaux, chapeaus**) a hat or head covering.

chapel *n* a building for Christian worship, not as large as a church; an association or trade union of printers in a printing office.

Chapel Royal *n* (*Brit*) the body of musicians and clergymen who serve a British monarch in his or her court.

chaperon, chaperone *n* a woman who accompanies a girl at social occasions for propriety. * *vt* to attend as a chaperon.—**chaperonage** *n*.

chapfallen *adj* with the jaw hanging down, dejected, dispirited.—*also* **chopfallen**.

chapiter *n* (*archit*) the upper part or capital of a column.

chaplain *n* a clergyman serving in a religious capacity with the armed forces, or in a prison, hospital, etc.—**chaplaincy** *n*.

chaplet *n* a wreath or garland encircling the head; a rosary; a round molding carved into beads, olives, etc.—**chapleted** *adj*.

Chaplin *n* **Sir Charlie** [**Spencer**] (1889–1977) English comedian and movie director whose gentleman-hobo character featured in many comic silent movies.

chapman *n* (*pl* **chapmen**) formerly a merchant or trader; a hawker.

Chapman *n* **John** (1774–1845) American pioneer known as "Johnny Appleseed." He is reputed to have gone in advance of the line of frontier settlers, planting apple orchards.

chaps *npl* chaparejos.

CHAPS *abbr* = Clearing House Automated Payment System.

chapter *n* a main division of a book; the body or meeting of canons of a cathedral or members of a monastic order; a sequence of events; an organized branch of a society or association.

chapterhouse *n* a room for the meetings of a cathedral chapter.

char[1] *vt* (**charring, charred**) to burn to charcoal or carbon. * *vti* to scorch.

char[2] *n* (*pl* **char, chars**) a red-bellied fish allied to the salmon.—*also* **charr**.

char[3] *n* a charwoman. * *vti* (**charring, charred**) to work as a charwoman.

Char. *abbr* = Charter.

CHAR *abbr* = Campaign for Homeless People (formerly Campaign for Homeless and Rootless).

charabanc, char-a-banc *n* (*Brit*) a bus used for tours by groups of tourists.

character *n* the combination of qualities that distinguishes an individual person, group or thing; moral strength; reputation; disposition; a person of marked individuality; an eccentric; (*comput*) a single letter, number, space, or symbol that can be made to appear on screen by using the keyboard; (*inf*) a person; a person in a play or novel; a guise, role; a letter or mark in writing, printing, etc.

character assassination *n* slander.

characterful *adj* full of character, unusual.

characteristic *adj* marking or constituting the particular nature (of a person or thing). * *n* a characteristic or distinguishing feature.—**characteristically** *adv*.

characterization studies *n* (*archeo*) the use of various analytical techniques to identify the characteristic properties of the material from which artifacts are made.

characterize *vt* to describe in terms of particular qualities; to designate; to be characteristic of, mark.—**characterization** *n*.

characterless *adj* ordinary, undistinguished.

character piece *n* (*mus*) a term used by composers for a short instrumental piece, such as may attempt to describe a specific mood. Examples are Schumann's *Fantasiestücke*, *Nachtstücke*, and *Albumblätter*.

character set *n* (*comput*) the full set of numbers, punctuation marks, alphabetic characters, and symbols that a particular computer system uses and that a printer is capable of producing.

character sketch *n* a summary of a person's distinguishing features or qualities.

characters per inch, cpi *n* (*comput*) the number of characters that occupy one inch of text when printed.

characters per second, cps *n* (*comput*) a measurement of the speed at which a printer can produce type.

charade *n* a travesty; an absurd pretense; (*usu pl*) a game of guessing a word from the acted representation of its syllables and the whole.

Charalambides Divanis *n* **Sonia** (1948–) Greek furniture designer who combined architecture and computer science to research design methods.

charcoal *n* the black carbon matter obtained by partially burning wood and used as fuel, as a filter or for drawing.

chard *n* a type of beet with edible leaves and stalks.

Chardin *n* **Jean-Baptiste Simeon** (1699–1779) French painter. His small-scale genre paintings and still lifes were realistically direct and natural, as in *Rayfish, Cat and Kitchen Utensils* (1728).

Chardzhou *n* a city in Turkmenistan.

charge *vt* to ask as the price; to record as a debt; to load, to fill, saturate; to lay a task or trust on; to burden; to accuse; to attack at a run; to build up an electric charge (in). * *n* a price charged for goods or service; a build-up of electricity; the amount which a receptacle can hold at one time; the explosive required to fire a weapon; trust, custody; a thing or person entrusted; a task, duty; accusation; an attack.

chargeable *adj* liable to be charged.—**chargeability** *n*.

charge account *n* an account with a store, etc, to which the cost of goods are charged for later payment.

charge card *n* a type of credit card issued by a chain store or other organization.

charge-coupled device *n* a light-sensitive semiconductor chip which is divided into a regular array of small areas called pixels.

chargé d'affaires *n* (*pl* **chargés d'affaires**) an ambassador's deputy; a minor diplomat.

charge-hand *n* a sub-foreman of a work crew.

charger *n* a cavalry horse; a device for charging a battery.

charily *adv* reluctantly; cautiously.

chariness *n* a being chary.

chariot *n* a two-wheeled vehicle driven by two or more horses in ancient warfare, races, etc.—**charioteer** *n*.

charisma, charism *n* (*pl* **charismata, charisms**) personal quality enabling a person to influence or inspire others; a God-given power or gift.—**charismatic** *adj*.

charitable *adj* of or for charity; generous to the needy, benevolent; lenient in judging others, kindly.—**charitableness** *n*.—**charitably** *adv*.

charitable trust *n* a trust that is set up for some charitable purpose.

Charites *npl* (*Greek myth*) the Graces.

charity *n* (*pl* **charities**) leniency or tolerance towards others; generosity in giving to the needy; a benevolent fund or institution.

charivari *n* a mock serenade of discordant music; hurly-burly.—*also* **shivaree**.

charlatan *n* a person who pretends to be what he or she is not; one who professes knowledge dishonestly, esp of medicine.—**charlatanism, charlatanry** *n*.

Charlemagne *n* (*c*.742–814) king of the Franks and Holy Roman emperor.

Charleroi *n* a city in Belgium.

Charles I *n* (1600–1649) king of Great Britain and Ireland (1625–49). The son of James I (James VI of Scotland) and Anne, daughter of King Ferdinand II of Denmark. The only saint canonized by the English church since the Reformation. His feast day is 30 January.

Charles II *n* (1630–1685) king of Great Britain and Ireland (1660–85). The eldest surviving son of Charles I and Henrietta Maria of France and the brother of James, Duke of York, later James VII.

Charles *n* **Ray** [Ray Charles Robinson] (1930–) American singer, pianist, and songwriter.

Charles, Prince *n* [Charles Philip Arthur George, Prince of Wales] (1948–) heir apparent to Elizabeth II of the United Kingdom.

Charles Borromeo *n* **Saint** (1538–84) Italian doctor, archbishop of Milan (1560), who founded the Helvetic College at Milan (1570). His feast day is 4 November.

Charleston *n* (*also without cap*) a lively dance with sidekicks from the knee.

Charlestown[1] *n* a city in St Kitts and Nevis.

Charlestown[2] *n* the capital city of West Virginia, a state of the USA.

charley horse *n* (*sl*) a muscle cramp.

charlock *n* wild mustard.

charlotte *n* a pudding of stewed fruit covered with breadcrumbs.

Charlotte Amalie *n* capital city of the US Virgin Islands.

charlotte russe *n* whipped cream custard enclosed in a sponge cake.

Charlton *n* 1. **Bobby** [Robert Charlton] (1937–) English footballer, capped over 100 times for England. 2. **Jack** [John] (1935–) brother of Bobby Charlton; led the Irish team to the World Cup finals in 1990 and 1994.

charm *n* an alluring quality, fascination; a magic verse or formula; something thought to possess occult power; an object bringing luck; a trinket on a bracelet. * *vt* to delight, captivate; to influence as by magic.—**charmer** *n*.

charmed *adj* having charm; protected as if by a charm.

charmed circle *n* an exclusive group.

charming *adj* delightful, attractive.—**charmingly** *adv*.

charnel house *n* a vault containing cadavers or bones.

Charon *n* (*Greek myth*) the old man who transported the dead over the rivers of the underworld in his ferry; (*astron*) the only satellite of Pluto so far discovered (1978).

Charpentier *n* 1. **Alexandre** (1856–1909) French sculptor, medalist and designer, who was regarded as one of the best representatives of the Art Nouveau style. 2. **Gustave** (1860–1956) French composer whose works include instrumental pieces and songs. His most memorable piece is the opera *Louise*. 3. **Marc-Antoine** (1634–1704) French composer of stage and church music but whose most impressive works were the operas, *Les Amours d'Acis et de Galatée* and *Médée*.

charpoy *n* a light portable Indian bedstead.

charqui *n* beef cut into strips and sun-dried.

charr *see* **char**[2].

chart *n* a map, esp for use in navigation; an information sheet with tables, graphs, etc; a weather map; a table, graph, etc; (*pl with* **the**) a list of the most popular music recordings. * *vt* to make a chart of; to plan (a course of action).

Chart. *abbr* (*pharm*) = chartula.

charter *n* a document granting rights, privileges, ownership of land, etc; the rental of transportation. * *vt* to grant by charter; to rent.

charter member *n* an original or founding member of a group.

chartered accountant *n* an accountant who has qualified by passing the official examinations; a certified public accountant.

chartism *n* the use of charts, diagrams, and graphs to monitor price movements of shares, foreign currencies, etc, with a view to trying to forecast future price movements.

Chartism *n* a democratic reforming movement in England for the extension of political power to the working class, embodied in the People's Charter of 1838.—**Chartist** *adj, n* .

Chartreuse *n* (*trademark*) a yellowish green liqueur; (*without cap*) its color.

chartulary *see* **cartulary**.

charwoman *n* (*pl* **charwomen**) a woman employed to clean a house.

chary *adj* (**charier, chariest**) cautious; sparing; (*with* **of**) unwilling to risk.

Charybdis *n* an eddy or whirlpool in the Strait of Messina, notorious in ancient times and dangerous to navigators because in attempting to escape it they ran the risk of being wrecked upon Scylla, a rock opposite to it.

CHAS *abbr* = Catholic Housing Aid Society; (*Brit*) Children's Hospice Association Scotland.

chase[1] *vt* to pursue; to run after; to drive (away); to hunt; (*inf: usu with* **up**) to pursue in a determined manner. * *n* pursuit; a hunt; a quarry hunted; a steeplechase.

chase[2] *n* a frame for securing a page of type; a groove; (*archit*) a narrow channel dug into a floor or wall to house pipes, cables, etc; that part of a cannon in front of the trunnions.

chase[3] *vt* to work or emboss precious metals; to cut a screw.

Chase *n* **William Merritt** (1849–1916) American artist and teacher who influenced a whole generation of artists and designers at the New York School of Fine and Applied Art, which he founded.

chaser *n* a horse used in steeplechasing; a person that chases; (*inf*) a drink taken after another, as in beer after a whiskey.

chasm *n* a deep cleft, an abyss, a gaping hole; a wide difference in opinions, etc.—**chasmal, chasmic** *adj*.

chassé *n* a rapid gliding step in dancing. * *vi* to perform a chassé.

chasseur *n* a French light-armed foot or cavalry soldier; a domestic dressed in military or hunting costume.

Chassey *adj* (*archeo*) relating to a Neolithic culture, first identified in the Midi region of France, dating from *c*.4300 BC.

chassis *n* (*pl* **chassis**) the frame, wheels, engine of an automobile, airplane, or other vehicle.

chaste *adj* pure, abstaining from unlawful sexual intercourse; virgin; modest; restrained, unadorned.—**chastely** *adv*.—**chasteness** *n*.

chasten *vt* to correct by suffering, discipline; to restrain.—**chastener** *n*.

chastise *vt* to punish; to beat; to scold.—**chastisement** *n*.

chastity *n* sexual abstinence; virginity; purity.

chastity *n* sexual abstinence; virginity; purity.

chastity belt *n* a garment designed to prevent women from having sexual intercourse.

chasuble *n* a rich sleeveless vestment worn over the alb by a priest celebrating mass.

chat *vti* (**chatting, chatted**) to talk in an easy or familiar way; (*with* **up**) (*inf*) to talk in a flirtatious way with another person. * *n* informal conversation.

chateau, château *n* (*pl* **chateaus, châteaux**) a castle or large country estate in France.

chatelaine *n* the lady of a country house; a bunch of chains to which are attached keys, etc, worn at the waist by ladies.

chat forum *n* (*comput*) a conference area dedicated to a particular subject provided by an on-line service provider, which allows two or more users to type messages and converse in real time.

Chatham, William Pitt, 1st Earl of *see* **Pitt, William**.

chatoyant *adj* changing in color or luster.—**chatoyancy** *n*.

chat show *n* a television or radio program with informal interviews and conversation.

chattel *n* (*usu pl*) goods, possessions; (*law*) personal property except freehold.

chatter *vi* to talk aimlessly and rapidly; (*animal, etc*) to utter rapid cries; (*teeth*) to rattle together due to cold or fear. * *n* idle rapid talk; the sound of chattering.—**chatterer** *n*.

chatterbox *n* an incessant talker.

Chatterton *n* **Thomas** (1752–70) English poet whose pseudo-medieval poems were published posthumously following his suicide.

chatty *adj* (**chattier, chattiest**) talkative, full of gossip.—**chattily** *adv*.—**chattiness** *n*.

Chaucer *n* **Geoffrey** (*c*.1340–70) English poet whose masterpiece is *The Canterbury Tales* (*c*.1387).

Chauchet-Guillere *n* **Charlotte** (1878–1964) French artistic director of the Primavera workshop of the Au Printemps department store, Paris.

chauffeur *n* a person who drives an automobile for someone else. * *vt* to drive as a chauffeur.—**chauffeuse** *nf*.

Chausson *n* **Ernest** (1855–99) French composer of romantic operas and orchestral pieces, including *Le Roi Arthur* (opera) and his *Poème* for violin and orchestra.

chauvinism *n* aggressive patriotism; excessive devotion to a belief, cause, etc, esp a man's belief in the superiority of men over women.—**chauvinist** *n*.—**chauvinistic** *adj*.

Chávez (y Ramirez) *n* **Carlos** (1899–1945) Mexican composer and conductor whose work was much influenced by Indian folk music and folklore, e.g. *Sinfonía India* and *Xochipilli-Macuilxochitl* (ballet).

chaw *vt* (*dial*) to chew, to munch, esp tobacco. * *n* a plug of tobacco.

ChB *abbr* (*Latin*) = *Chirurgiae Baccalaureus*, "Bachelor of Surgery."

CHB *abbr* = complete heart block.

CHCF *abbr* = Catholic Handicapped Children's Fellowship.

ChClk *abbr* = chief clerk.

chd. *abbr* = chaldron.

ChD *abbr* = (*Latin*) *Chirurgiae Doctor*, "Doctor of Surgery"; Doctor of Chemistry.

CHD *abbr* = Center for Human Development; coronary heart disease.

CHDL *abbr* = computer hardware description language.

ChE *abbr* = Chemical Engineer.

CHE *abbr* = Campaign for Homosexual Equality.

cheap *adj* low-priced, inexpensive; good value; of little worth, inferior; vulgar.—**cheaply** *adv*.—**cheapness** *n*.

cheapen *vti* to make or become cheap; to lower the value, worth or reputation of.

cheap-jack *n* (*inf*) a person who sells cheap or worthless goods. * *adj* worthless, inferior.

cheap shot *n* an unjust action or statement made against a vulnerable target.

cheapskate *n* (*inf*) a mean or dishonorable person.

cheat *vti* to defraud, to swindle; to deceive; to play unfairly. * *n* a fraud, deception; a person who cheats.—**cheater** *n*.

Chebar *n* (*Bible*) river or canal of Babylon beside which the exiles of Judah settled after the fall of Jerusalem.

check *vti* to bring or come to a stand; to restrain or impede; to admonish, reprove; to test the accuracy of, verify; (*with* **in**) to sign or register arrival at a hotel, work, an airport, etc; (*with* **out**) to settle the bill and leave a hotel; to investigate. * *n* repulse; stoppage; a pattern of squares; a control to test accuracy; a tick against listed items; a bill in a restaurant; (*chess*) a threatening of the king; a money order to a bank (—*also* **cheque**).

checkbook *n* a book containing blank checks to be drawn on a bank.

check box *n* (*comput*) a small box that is used to toggle between different options in a dialog box.

check digit *n* (*comput*) a digit added to data digits to test accuracy and check for corruption.

checked *adj* having a square pattern; restrained; held up or stopped.

checker[1] *n* a pattern of squares (—*also* **checker**); a flat counter used in the game of checkers (—*also* **draughtsman**); (*pl*) a game for two players who each move twelve round flat pieces over a checkerboard (—*also* **draughts**).

checker[2] *n* a teller in a supermarket.

checkerboard *n* a draughtboard.

checkered *adj* marked with a variegated pattern; having a career marked by fluctuating fortunes.—*also* **chequered**.

check-in *n* the act, time or place of checking in at a hotel or an airport.

checking account *n* a bank account, usu with no interest, from which money is withdrawn by checks or cash cards; a current account.

check list *n* a list of items, used for reference or verification.

checkmate *n* (*chess*) the winning position when the king is threatened and unable to move; utter defeat. * *vt* (*chess*) to place in checkmate; to defeat, foil.

check-off *n* the authorized collection of trades union dues.

checkout *n* a place where traffic may be halted for inspection; the place in a store where goods are paid for.

checkpoint *n* a place where visitors' passports or other official documents may be examined.

checkrein *see* **bearing rein**.

checkroom *n* a temporary repository for luggage, coats, etc.

check sum *n* (*comput*) an error detection technique commonly used in data communications.

checkup *n* a thorough examination; a medical examination, usu repeated at intervals.

Cheddar *n* a type of hard, white or yellow cheese originally made in Cheddar, England.

cheek *n* the side of the face below the eye; (*sl*) buttock; impudence.

cheekbone *n* the zygomatic bone.

cheek piece *n* a bar made out of metal or bone that was fastened to a horse's bit and to which the reins were attached; a protective leather or metal flap on a helmet which covered the wearer's cheek.

cheeky *adj* (**cheekier, cheekiest**) disrespectful, impudent.—**cheekily** *adv*.—**cheekiness** *n*.

cheep *n* the frail squeak of a young bird. * *vi* to make such a sound.

cheer *n* a shout of applause or welcome; a frame of mind, spirits; happiness. * *vt* to gladden; to encourage; to applaud.

cheerful *adj* in good spirits; happy.—**cheerfully** *adv*.—**cheerfulness** *n*.

cheerleader *n* a person who leads organized cheering, esp at a sports event.

cheerless *adj* dismal, depressing.

cheers *interj* (*inf*) an expression used in offering a toast, as a form of farewell or thanks.

cheery *adj* (**cheerier, cheeriest**) lively, genial, merry.—**cheerily** *adv*.—**cheeriness** *n*.

cheese *n* the curds of milk pressed into a firm or hard mass; a boss or important person (*big cheese*).

cheeseburger *n* a hamburger with melted cheese on top.

cheesecake *n* a cake made with cottage or cream cheese; (*sl*) attractive women or men displayed as sex objects in photographs, etc.

cheesecloth *n* a thin cotton fabric.

cheesed-off *adj* (*sl*) angry.

cheeseparing *adj* niggardly, mean.

cheesy *adj* (**cheesier, cheesiest**) like cheese.—**cheesiness** *n*.

cheetah *n* a large spotted cat, similar to a leopard.

Cheever *n* **John** (1912–82) American short-story writer and novelist whose short-story collections include *The Enormous Radio and Other Stories* and whose four novels include *The Wapshot Chronicle* and *Falconer*. *The Stories of John Cheever* won the Pulitzer prize in 1979.

chef *n* a professional cook.

chef-d'oeuvre *n* (*pl* **chefs-d'oeuvre**) (*French*) a masterpiece.

cheiro-, chiro- *prefix* hand.

Chekhov *n* **Anton Pavlovich** (1860–1904) Russian dramatist and short-story writer whose great plays, e.g. *Uncle Vanya*, *Three Sisters*, and *The Cherry Orchard*, deal with the lives and problems of the Russian middle classes. His short stories include "My Life" and "The Lady with the Little Dog."

CHEL *abbr* = Cambridge History of English Literature.

chela *n* (*pl* **chelae**) a claw-like pincer of the crab, etc.—**cheliferous** *adj*.

chelation *n* (*chem*) a reaction between a metal ion and an organic molecule that ties up the metal into a closed stable ring structure.

cheloid *see* **keloid**.

chelonian *n* any of the order of reptiles, including turtles and tortoises.—*also adj*.

chem. *abbr* = chemical; chemist; chemistry.

CHEMA *abbr* = Container Handling Equipment Manufacturers' Association.

ChemE *abbr* = Chemical Engineer.

chemical *n* a substance used in, or arising from, a chemical process. * *adj* of, used in, or produced by chemistry.—**chemically** *adv*.

chemical engineering *n* the branch of engineering dealing with the design, construction, and manufacture of plant used in industrial chemical processes.

chemical reaction *n* an interaction between substances that changes their chemical structure or energy content.

chemical warfare *n* warfare in which poison gases and other chemicals are used.

chemin de fer *n* a gambling game, a kind of baccarat.

chemise *n* a woman's undergarment; a loose-fitting dress.

chemisette *n* a short bodice worn over the breast; lace, etc, filling the neck opening of a dress.

chemist *n* a pharmacy; a manufacturer of medicinal drugs; a person skilled in chemistry.

chemistry *n* (*pl* **chemistries**) the science of the properties of substances and their combinations and reactions; chemical structure.

chemoreceptor *n* an organ, such as a taste bud, that responds to chemical stimulus.

chemotherapy *n* the treatment of disease, esp cancer, by drugs and other chemical agents.

Cheney *n* **Richard B** (1941–) American Democrat statesman; secretary of defense (1989–93); vice-president in 2001.

Chengdu *n* a city in China.

chenille *n* silk or worsted cord.

Cheops *or* **Khufu** *n* Egyptian pharaoh of the Fourth Dynasty (between 2625 and 2510 BC) for whom the Great Pyramid at Giza was constructed.

Chephren *or* **Khephren** *n* Egyptian pharaoh of the Fourth dynasty (between 2625 and 2510 BC) whose pyramid is found close to that of Cheops, at Giza.

cheque *see* **check**.

chequebook *see* **checkbook**.

chequer *see* **checker**.

chequered *see* **checkered.**

chequer work *n* (*archit*) a decorative pavement or wall using alternate squares of different materials to produce a checker board pattern.

Cherenkov *n* **Pavel Alekseievich** (1904–90) Soviet physicist who discovered Cherenkhov radiation; winner of the 1958 Nobel prize for physics.

Cheret *n* **Joseph** (1834–94) French sculptor and ceramicist who in 1887 succeeded his father-in-law, Carrier-Belleuse, as artistic director of the modeling studio at Sèvres.

cherish *vt* to tend lovingly, foster; to keep in mind as a hope, ambition, etc.—**cherisher** *n*.

Chermayeff *n* **Serge Ivan** (1900–1995) Russian architect and designer who pioneered the design of tubular steel furniture.

cheroot *n* a cigar cut square at each end.

cherry *n* (*pl* **cherries**) a small red, pitted fruit; the tree bearing it; a bright red color.

cherry picker *n* a crane, usu on a truck, with a long elbow-jointed arm carrying a platform that can be raised and lowered.

chersonese *n* (*poet*) a peninsula.

chert *n* an impure flint-like quartz or hornstone, used for the construction of tools and implements.—**cherty** *adj*.

cherub *n* (*pl* **cherubim**) an angel of the second order; a winged child or child's head; (*pl* **cherubs**) an angelic, sweet child.—**cherubic** *adj*.

Cherubini *n* **[Maria] Luigi [Carlo Zenobia Salvatore]** (1760–1842) Italian composer who wrote operas, e.g., *Médée*, *Les Deux Journées*, *Faniska* and *Ali Babar*, and other works.

chervil *n* an aromatic herb used for flavoring.

Cheshire cheese *n* a mildflavored cheese, originally made in Cheshire, England.

chess[1] *n* a game played by two people with 32 pieces on a chessboard.

chess[2] *n* one of the flooring planks of a pontoon bridge.

Chessa *n* **Paolo Antonio** (1922–) Italian architect-turned-furniture designer best known for his *Butterfly* chair.

chessboard *n* a board checkered with 64 squares in two alternate colors, used for playing chess or draughts.

chessman *n* (*pl* **chessmen**) any of the 16 pieces used by each player in chess.

chest *n* a large strong box; the part of the body enclosed by the ribs, the thorax.

chesterfield *n* a large, stuffed couch with straight ends; a man's overcoat.

Chesterton *n* **G[ilbert] K[eith]** (1874–1936) English essayist, novelist, critic, and poet who also wrote detective stories, e.g. *The Innocence of Father Brown*, and collaborated with Hilaire Belloc.

chestnut *n* a tree or shrub of the beech family; the edible nut of a chestnut; the wood of the chestnut; a horse with chestnut coloring; (*inf*) an old joke. * *adj* of the color of a chestnut, a deep reddish brown.

chest of drawers *n* a piece of furniture containing several drawers.

chest voice *n* (*mus*) the lower register of voice, so called because notes seem to emanate from the chest.

chesty *adj* (**chestier, chestiest**) (*inf*) prone to chest infections; having a large chest or bosom.—**chestily** *adv*.—**chestiness** *n*.

Cheti *n* **Fede** (1905–78) Italian textile designer, backed by Gio Ponti, noted for her large motifs and printed and painted chintzes.

chetrum *n* a monetary unit of Bhutan, equal to one hundredth of a ngultrum.

Chevakinsky *n* **Savva** (*b.* 1713) Russian architect, whose notable works include St Nicholas Cathedral, Leningrad.

Cheval *n* **Ferdinand** (1836–1924) French self-taught architect, who built his *Palais ideal*, designated an historic monument in 1969.

cheval-de-frise *n* (*pl* **chevaux-de-frise**) (*French*) a fence constructed of a bar armed with long spikes.

chevalet *n* (*mus*) (*French*) the bridge of a stringed instrument.

cheval glass *n* a full-length mirror which can swivel in its frame.

chevalier *n* a knight; a horseman; a member or knight of an honorable order; the lowest title or rank of the old French nobility; a gallant.

Chevalier *n* **Georges** (1894–1987) French designer who was connected with Baccarat for most of his working life.

chevet *n* an apse; a group of apses.

cheviot *n* a rough cloth made from the wool of sheep bred on the Cheviot Hills along the border between England and Scotland.

chevron *n* the V-shaped bar on the sleeve of a uniform, showing rank; (*archit*) a type of Romanesque molding in a zig-zag pattern.

chevrotain *n* a small musk deer.

chew *vt* to grind between the teeth, to masticate; (*with* **over**) to ponder, think over; (*with* **up**) to spoil by chewing; **to chew the rag** *or* **the fat** (*sl*) to chat. * *n* the act of chewing; something to chew, as a sweet or tobacco.—**chewable** *adj*.—**chewer** *n*.

chewed-up *adj* (*sl*) made nervous or worried.

chewing gum *n* a flavored gum made from chicle, for chewing.

chewy *adj* (**chewier, chewiest**) needing to be chewed.

Cheyenne *n* the capital city of Wyoming, a state of the USA.

chez *prep* (*French*) at the home of.

CHF *abbr* = congestive heart failure.

ch.g. *abbr* (*horse*) = chestnut gelding.

chg. *abbr* = charge.

chgd. *abbr* = charged.

chgs. *abbr* = charges.

chi *n* the 22nd letter of the Greek alphabet.

CHIA *abbr* = Canadian Hovercraft Industries Association; Craft and Hobby Industry Association.

Chiang Ch'ing, Jiang Qing *n* (1913–91) Chinese Communist politician and actress who married Mao Tse-tung in 1939 and was one of the "Gang of Four." She was the main force behind the Cultural Revolution purges.

Chiang Kai-shek, Jiang Jie Shi *n* (1887–1975) Chinese general and statesman; president of China (1928–38, 1943–49). He lost the civil war to Mao Tse-tung and established the nationalist republic of China in Formosa, of which he was president (1950–57).

Chiang Mai *n* a city in Thailand.

Chianti *n* a dry red or white wine from Italy.

chiaro, chiara *adj* (*mus*) (*Italian*) "clear," "distinct."

chiaroscuro *n* (*pl* **chiaroscuros**) the effects of light and shade; the treatment of this in painting, drawing, or engraving; the use of contrast and relief in literature. * *adj* pertaining to such treatment.—**chiaroscurism** *n*.—**chiaroscurist** *n*.

chiasma, chiasm *n* (*pl* **chiasmas, chiasmata, chiasms**) the central body of nervous matter formed by the junction and the crossing of the fibers of the optic nerves.—**chiasmal** *adj*.—**chiasmic** *adj*.

chiasmus *n* (*pl* **chiasmi**) a figure of speech by which the order of words in the first of two parallel clauses is reversed in the second, e.g., "to stop too fearful and too faint to go."—**chiastic** *adj*.

Chiaveri *n* **Gaetano** (1689–1770) Italian architect. His notable works include Hofkirche, Dresden.

chibouk, chibouque *n* a long Turkish tobacco pipe.

chic *n* elegance, style. * *adj* stylish.

Chicago *n* a city in the United States of America (USA).

chicane *n* a hand at bridge without trumps; a barrier or obstacle on a motor-racing course; chicanery.

chicanery *n* (*pl* **chicaneries**) underhand dealing, trickery; verbal subterfuge.

Chicano *n* (*pl* **Chicanos**) a Mexican-American.—*also adj.*

chick *n* a young bird; (*sl*) a young attractive woman or girl.

chickadee *n* the American blackcap titmouse.

chickaree *n* the American red squirrel.

chicken *n* a young, domestic fowl; its flesh. * *adj* cowardly, timorous. * *vi* (*with* **out**) (*inf*) to suffer a failure of nerve or courage.

chicken feed *n* poultry food; (*inf*) a trifling amount of money.

chicken-hearted, chicken-livered *adj* cowardly.

chickenpox *n* a contagious viral disease that causes a rash of red spots on the skin.

chicken wire *n* light wire netting with a hexagonal mesh.

chickpea *n* (the seed eaten as a vegetable of) an Asian leguminous plant.

chickweed *n* a small white-flowered plant of the pink family.

Chiclayo *n* a city in Peru.

chicle *n* the milky gum of a tropical American tree used to make chewing gum.

chicory *n* (*pl* **chicories**) endive, a salad plant; its dried, ground, roasted root used to flavor coffee or as a coffee substitute.

chide *vt* (**chiding, chided** *or* **chid**; *pp* **chided, chid** *or* **chidden**) to rebuke, scold.—**chider** *n*.—**chidingly** *adv*.

chief *adj* principal, most important. * *n* a leader; the head of a tribe or clan.

chief executive (officer), CE, CEO *n* the person in a company or organization who has overall responsibility for the management of a firm.

chief justice *n* the presiding judge of a court; (*with caps*) the presiding judge of the US Supreme Court.

Chief of Staff *n* the senior military officer of an army, navy or airforce; the head of any staff.

chief petty officer *n* the highest ranking non-commissioned officer in the navy or coast guard.

chiefly *adv* especially; mainly; for the most part.

chieftain *n* the head of a Scottish clan; a chief.

chiffchaff *n* a European warbler.

chiffon *n* a thin gauzy material. * *adj* made of chiffon; (*pie filling, etc*) having a light fluffy texture.

chiffonier, chiffonnier *n* a high chest of drawers; a wide, low cupboard.

chignon *n* a mass of hair worn in a roll at the back of the head, a bun.

chigoe *n* a species of West Indian and South American flea that burrows beneath the skin of the feet, causing irritation and ulcers.—also **jigger**.

Chihuahua *n* a tiny dog with erect ears, originally from Mexico.

chilblain *n* an inflamed swelling on the hands, toes, etc, due to cold.

child *n* (*pl* **children**) a young human being; a son or daughter; offspring; an innocent or immature person.

child abuse *n* physical, mental or sexual maltreatment of a child by parents or any other adult.

childbearing *n* pregnancy and childbirth.—also *adj*.

childbirth *n* the process of giving birth to children.

child care *n* care by an authority of homeless children or those from a disturbed home background.

childe *n* (*arch*) a term formerly applied to the scions of knightly houses before their admission into knighthood; a youth of noble birth.

childhood *n* the period between birth and puberty in humans.

childish *adj* of, like or suited to a child; foolish.—**childishly.**—**childishness** *n*.

child labor *n* illegal employment of children below a certain age.

childless *adj* having no children.

child-like *adj* like a child; innocent, simple, candid.

child's play *n* an easy task.

child-proof *adj* made safe against tampering by children.

children *see* **child**.

Chile *n* a republic in South America.

Chilean Peso n currency of Chile.

chili *n* (*pl* **chilies**) the hot-tasting pod of some of the capsicums, dried and used as flavoring.

chiliad *n* a thousand; a thousand years.—**chiliadal, chiliadic** *adj*.

chiliasm *n* the doctrine of the millennium.—**chiliast** *n*.—**chiliastic** *adj*.

chili con carne *n* a spicy stew of ground beef, beans, onions, and tomatoes flavored with chilli powder or chillies.

chill *n* a sensation of coldness; an illness caused by exposure to cold and marked by shivering; anything that dampens or depresses. * *adj* shivering with cold; feeling cold; unemotional, formal. * *vti* to make or become cold; to harden by cooling; to depress.

chillum *n* the bowl of a hookah; a hookah; smoking.

chilly *adj* (**chillier, chilliest**) cold; unfriendly.—**chilliness** *n*.

chilopod *n* any of an order of the class Myriopoda, containing the centipedes.

Chi-lung n a city in Taiwan.

chime[1] *n* the harmonious sound of a bell; accord; harmony; (*pl*) a set of bells or metal tubes, etc, tuned in a scale; their ringing. * *vi* to ring (a bell); (*with* **in**) (*inf*) to join in in agreement; to interrupt a conversation; (*with* **with**) to agree. * *vt* to indicate the hour by chiming, as a clock.

chime[2], **chimb** *n* the rim formed by the ends of the staves of a cask.

chimera, chimaera *n* (*Greek myth*) a fire-breathing monster with the head of a lion, the body of a goat, and the tail of a dragon; a fantastic hybrid; an impossible fancy.

chimere *n* a loose silk robe worn by an Anglican bishop, either sleeveless or with lawn sleeves.

chimerical, chimeric *adj* merely imaginary; fantastic, visionary; unreal.—**chimerically** *adv*.

chimney *n* (*pl* **chimneys**) a passage for smoke, hot air, or fumes, a funnel; a chimney stack; the vent of a volcano; a vertical crevice in rock large enough to enter and climb.

chimneypiece *n* a mantelpiece.

chimneypot *n* a pipe extending a chimney at the top.

chimney stack *n* the chimney above roof level.

chimney sweep *n* a person who removes soot from chimneys.

chimney swift *n* a North American bird that often nests in chimneys.

chimp *n* (*inf*) chimpanzee.

chimpanzee *n* an African anthropoid ape.

chin *n* the part of the face below the mouth.

Chin. *abbr* = China; Chinese.

china *n* fine porcelain; articles made from this.

China *or* **The People's Republic of China** *n* the third largest country in the world, dominating the region of East Asia.

china clay *n* kaolin, a clay formed from the alteration of granite rocks due to weathering.

Chinatown *n* the Chinese quarter of any city.

chinch *n* a tropical American insect destructive to corn crops; a bedbug.

chinchilla *n* a small South American rodent with soft gray fur; a breed of domestic cat; a breed of rabbit.

chine *n* the backbone or spine of an animal; a piece of the backbone of an animal with adjacent parts cut for cooking; a ridge; a rocky ravine or large fissure in a cliff.

Chinese *adj* of or pertaining to China. * *n* (*pl* **Chinese**) an inhabitant of China.

Chinese checkers *n* a board game played with marbles.

Chinese gooseberry *see* **kiwi fruit**.

Chinese lantern *n* a collapsible paper lantern.

Chinese puzzle *n* an intricate puzzle based on fitting boxes within boxes; any very difficult puzzle or complex problem.

Chinese restaurant syndrome *n* an ailment characterized by chest pain, dizziness, flushing, allegedly caused by consuming in quantity monosodium glutamate found in Chinese food.

Chinese wall *n* the segregation of the various sections of a financial institution or business so as to prevent information spreading from one section to another with a view to protecting the interests of the clients.

Chinese white *n* a white pigment; white zinc oxide.

chink[1] *n* a narrow opening; a crack or slit.

chink[2] *n* the sound of coins clinking together.

Chinnereth *n* (*Bible*) OT name for the Sea of Galilee. *See also* **Sea of Galilee**.

chino *n* (*pl* **chinos**) a strong, hardwearing twilled cotton; (*pl*) pants made of this fabric.

chinoiserie *n* (an object or objects in) a style of decoration copying Chinese motifs.

chinook *n* a warm dry southwesterly wind of the eastern slopes of the Rocky Mountains; a warm moist wind blowing onto the northwest coast of America.

Chinook *n* a jargon of native and foreign words used on the northwest Pacific coast by Indians and whites.

chinook salmon *n* a northern Pacific salmon; the king or tyee salmon.

chinquapin *n* the dwarf chestnut of the US; its nut.

chintz *n* a glazed cotton cloth printed with colored designs.

chintzy *adj* (**chintzier, chintziest**) of or describing furniture, decor, etc, covered in chintz; cheap; tasteless in a flowery way.

chinwag *vi* (**chinwagging, chinwagged**) (*sl*) to talk, to gossip. * *n* (*sl*) a chatty conversation, a gossip.

Chios *n* an island belonging to Greece, in the Aegean Sea, which claimed to be the birthplace of Homer.—**Chian** *adj*.

chip *vt* (**chipping, chipped**) to knock small pieces off; to shape or make by chipping. * *n* a small piece cut or broken off; a mark left by chipping; a thin strip of fried potato, french fry; a counter used in games; (*comput*) a tiny piece of semiconducting material, such as silicon, printed with a microcircuit and used as part of an integrated circuit.

chipboard *n* a thin stiff material made from compressed wood shavings and other waste pieces combined with resin.

chipmunk *n* a small, striped, squirrel-like animal of North America.

Chippendale *adj* of the light style of furniture introduced in the middle of the 18th century by the furniture maker and designer, Thomas Chippendale (1718–79).

Chippendale *n* **Thomas** (1718–79) British furniture designer whose book, *The Gentleman and Cabinet-maker's Director, is* one of the most important pattern books of the century.

chipper *adj* active; lively, cheerful.

CHIPS *abbr* = Christian International Peace Service; Clearing House Inter-Bank Payments System.

chip shot *n* a short, lofted approach shot in golf.

ChirDoct *abbr* (*Latin*) = *Chirurgiae Doctor*, "Doctor of Surgery."

Chirico *n* **Giorgio de** (1888–1978) Greek-born Italian painter.

chiro-, cheiro- *prefix* hand.

chirography *n* the art of writing, calligraphy; judgment of character by the handwriting.—**chirographer** *n*.—**chirographic, chirographical** *adj*.

chiromancy *n* palmistry.—**chiromancer** *n*.

Chiron, Cheiron *n* (*Greek myth*) the most famous of the Centaurs, famous for his wisdom and skill in healing, hunting, music, and prophecy.

Chiron *n* (*astron*) an asteroid discovered in 1977, with an eccentric orbit that takes it out well beyond Saturn.

chiropody *n* the care and treatment of the feet.—**chiropodist** *n*.

chiropractic *n* the manipulation of joints, esp of the spine, to alleviate nerve pressure as a method of curing disease.—**chiropractor** *n*.

chirp *n* the sharp, shrill note of some birds or a grasshopper. * *vi* to make this sound.—**chirper** *n*.

chirpy *adj* (**chirpier, chirpiest**) lively, cheerful.—**chirpily** *adv*.—**chirpiness** *n*.

chirr *n* the shrill rasping sound of a grasshopper. * *vi* to make this sound.—*also* **churr**.

C

chirrup *vi* (*birds*) to twitter; to make a clicking sound to a horse. * *n* chirruping sound.—**chirruper** *n*.—**chirrupy** *adj*.

chisel *n* a tool with a square cutting end. * *vt* (**chiseling, chiseled** or **chiselling, chiselled**) to cut or carve with a chisel; (*sl*) to defraud.—**chiseler** *n*.

Chisinau *n* capital city of Moldova (Moldavia).

chi-squared test *n* (*statistics*) a test used to determine how well data obtained from an experiment fits in with the data expected to occur by chance.

chit[1] *n* a voucher or a sum owed for drink, food, etc; a note; a requisition.

chit[2] *n* a child; (*derog*) an impudent girl.

CHIT *abbr* = Child Head Injury Trust.

chitarrone *n* (*mus*) (*Italian*) a large lute.

chitchat *n* gossip, trivial talk.

chitin *n* the white horny substance that forms the outer covering of many invertebrate animals.—**chitinoid** *adj*.—**chitinous** *adj*.

chiton *n* in ancient Greece, a knee-length tunic; a full-length woman's dress; a genus of mollusks.

chitterlings, chitlins, chitlings *npl* the small edible entrails of pigs.

Chittim *n* (*Bible*) OT name for Cyprus.

chivalrous *adj* relating to chivalry; war-like; high-spirited; brave, gallant; generous to the weak.—**chivalrously** *adv*.

chivalry *n* (*pl* **chivalries**) the medieval system of knighthood; knightly qualities, bravery, courtesy, respect for women.—**chivalric** *adj*.—**chivalrous** *adj*.—**chivalrously** *adv*.

chive, chives *n* a plant whose onion-flavored leaves are used in cooking and salads.

CHIVE *abbr* = Council for Hearing-Impaired Visits and Exchanges.

chivvy, chivy *vt* (**chivvying, chivvied** or **chivying, chivied**) to annoy, harass, nag.

ChJ *abbr* = Chief Justice.

chlamydia *n* (*pl* **chlamydiae**) a sexually transmitted disease.—**chlamydial** *adj*.

chlor-, chloro- *prefix* green.

chloral (hydrate) *n* a bitter white crystalline compound used as a sedative or anesthetic.

chlorate *n* a salt of chloric acid.

chlorhexidine *n* an antiseptic substance that is used in preparations to cleanse the skin or in lozenges for mild infections of the mouth and throat.—*also* **hibitane**.

chloric *adj* pertaining to or containing chlorine.

chloric acid *n* an acid containing hydrogen, oxygen, and chlorine.

chloride *n* any compound containing chlorine.—**chloridic** *adj*.

chloride of lime *n* a compound of chlorine with lime used in bleaching.

chlorinate *vt* to treat or combine with chlorine; to disinfect with chlorine.—**chlorination** *n*.

chlorine *n* a nonmetallic element, a yellowish-green poisonous gas used in bleaches, disinfectants, and in industry.

chloro-, chlor- *prefix* green.

chlorofluorocarbon, CFC *n* any of various compounds containing carbon, chlorine, fluorine, and hydrogen, used in refrigerants, aerosol propellants, etc, and thought to be harmful to the earth's atmosphere.

chloroform *n* a colorless volatile liquid formerly used as an anesthetic.

chlorophyl, chlorophyll *n* the green photosynthetic coloring matter in plants.

chloroplast *n* (*bot*) an organelle found within the cells of green plants and algae, where photosynthesis takes place.

chlorosis *n* a disease affecting young women, characterized by anemia.—**chlorotic** *adj*.

CHLW *abbr* = commercial high-level waste.

chm. *abbr* = chairman; checkmate.

ch. m. *abbr* (*horse*) = chestnut mare.

ChM *abbr* (*Latin*) = *Chirurgiae Magister*, "Master of Surgery."

CHM *abbr* = Choir-Training Diploma of the Royal College of Organists.

CHME *abbr* = Conference on Hospitality Management Education.

chmn. *abbr* = chairman.

chn. *abbr* = (*measure*) chain; chairman.

CHO *abbr* = Confederation of Healing Organizations.

chock *n* a block of wood or other material used as a wedge. * *vt* to secure with a chock.

chock-a-block *adj* completely full.—*also* **chock-full**.

chocolate *n* a powder or edible solid made of the roasted, pounded cacao bean; a drink made by dissolving this powder in boiling water or milk; a sweet with a center and chocolate coating. * *adj* flavored or coated with chocolate; dark reddish brown.—**chocolaty** *adj*.

chocolate-box *adj* sweetly pretty; oversentimental.

CHOGM *abbr* = Commonwealth Heads of Government Meeting.

choice *n* act of choosing; the power to choose; selection; alternative; a thing chosen; preference; the best part. * *adj* of picked quality, specially good.—**choicely** *adv*.—**choiceness** *n*.

choir *n* an organized group of singers, esp of a church; the part of a church before the altar used by them.

choirbook *n* (*mus*) a large medieval volume that usu included both words and music and was designed to be read by various members of a choir.

choirboy *n* one of the young trebles in a choir.

choirmaster *n* one who trains and conducts the singers in a choir.

choir organ *n* (*mus*) the section of an organ that is played from the lowest manual and is soft enough to accompany a church choir

choke *vti* to stop the breath of, stifle; to throttle; to suffocate; to block (up); to check, esp emotion, to choke back or up. * *n* a fit of choking; a choking sound; a valve that controls the flow of air in a carburetor.

chokebore *n* a shotgun with a bore narrowing towards the muzzle.

chokedamp *n* carbonic acid gas generated in mines.

choker *n* a necklace worn tight round the neck; a high collar.

choking *n* a violent coughing and interference in breathing caused by an obstruction in the airway in the region of the larynx.

choler *n* bile; irascibility, anger.

cholera *n* a severe, infectious intestinal disease.

choleric *adj* irascible; tending to anger; angry.

cholesterol, cholesterin *n* a substance found in animal tissues, blood and animal fats, thought to be a cause of hardening of the arteries.

choluria *n* bile in the urine, which occurs when there is an elevated level of bile in the blood.

chomp *vt* to chew noisily and with relish, champ.

Chomsky *n* Noam [Avram] (1928–) American linguist, philosopher, and political activist. A notable opponent of the Vietnam war.

chon *n* a monetary unit of North Korea and South Korea, equal to one hundredth of a won.

chondr-, chondri-, chondro- *prefix* cartilage.

chondrify *vti* (**chondrifying, chondrified**) to change into cartilage.—**chondrification** *n*.

chondrite *n* a stony meteorite, containing granules known as chondrules.

chondrule *n* small nodule-like grain formed from solidified drops of once molten rock.

Chongjin *n* a city in the Democratic People's Republic of Korea.

choose *vt* (**choosing, chose**, *pp* **chosen**) to select (one thing) rather than another. * *vi* to decide, to think fit.—**chooser** *n*.

chooser *n* (*comput*) a utility program for the Apple Macintosh that controls the selection of printers, fax cards, and file servers.

choosy *adj* (**choosier, choosiest**) (*inf*) cautious; fussy, particular.—**choosily** *adv*.—**choosiness** *n*.

chop[1] *vt* (**chopping, chopped**) to cut by striking; to cut into pieces. * *n* a cut of meat and bone from the rib, loin, or shoulder; a downward blow or motion; **get the chop** (*sl*) to be dismissed from one's employment; to be killed.

chop[2] *n* a mark or brand denoting quality.

chopfallen *see* **chapfallen**.

Chopin *n* Frédéric [François] (1810–49) Polish pianist and composer. His works include mazurkas, piano concertos, and preludes.

chopper *n* a tool for chopping; a cleaver; a small hand ax; (*sl*) a helicopter.

chopping tool *n* (*archeo*) a stone tool with a cutting edge made by chipping flakes from two adjacent faces. *See also* **pebble tool**.

choppy *adj* (**choppier, choppiest**) (*sea*) running in rough, irregular waves; jerky.—**choppily** *adv*.—**choppiness** *n*.

chops *npl* the jaws or cheeks.

chopsticks *n* a pair of wooden or plastic sticks used in Asian countries to eat with.

chop suey *n* a Chinese-American dish consisting of stir-fried vegetables and meat or seafood served with rice.

choral[1] *adj* relating to, sung by, or written for, a choir or chorus.—**chorally** *adv*.

chorale, choral[2] *n* a slow hymn or psalm sung to a traditional or composed melody, esp by a choir.

choral symphony *n* (*mus*) a symphony in which a chorus is used at some point or a symphony written entirely for voices.

chorale cantata *n* (*mus*) a cantata that was written to be performed in a (Lutheran) church.

Chorazim *n* (*Bible*) town on the shore of the Sea of Galilee.

chord[1] *n* (*mus*) three or more notes played simultaneously.—**chordal** *adj*.

chord[2] *n* a straight line joining the ends of an arc; a feeling of sympathy, recognition or remembering (**strike a chord**).

chordophone *n* (*mus*) any instrument in which stretched strings are vibrated to produce sound, e.g., a violin.

chore *n* a piece of housework; a regular or tedious task.

chorea *n* a neurological disorder characterized by jerky involuntary movements, esp of the arms, legs and face.—**choreal, choreic** *adj*.

choreograph *vt* to devise the steps for a ballet, dance, etc.

choreography *n* the art of devising ballets or dances.—**choreographer** *n*.—**choreographic** *adj*.—**choreographically** *adv*.

choric *adj* of or for a Greek chorus.

chorine *n* a chorus girl.

chorion *n* the exterior membrane of a seed or fetus.—**chorionic, chorial** *adj*.

chorionic gonadotrophic hormone, human chorionic gonadotrophin (HCG) *n* a hormone, the basis of most pregnancy tests and produced during pregnancy, large amounts of which are present in the urine of a pregnant woman.

chorister *n* a member of a choir.

chorizo *n* (*pl* **chorizos**) a spicy pork sausage.

chorography *n* the geographical description of a region.—**chorographer** *n*.—**chorographic, chorographical** *adj*.

choroid *n* the vascular membrane of the retina.

choroid plexus *n* an extensive network of blood vessels present in the ventricles of the brain and responsible for the production of the cerebrospinal fluid.

choroids *n* the blood supply for the outer half of the retina of the eye.

chorology *n* the study of the geographical distribution of plants and animals.

chortle *vi* to chuckle exultantly.—*also n*.

chorus *n* (*pl* **choruses**) a group of singers and dancers in the background to a play, musical, etc; a group of singers, a choir; music sung by a chorus; a refrain; an utterance by many at once. * *vt* (**chorusing, chorused**) to sing, speak or shout in chorus.

chorus girl *n* one who sings and dances in the chorus of a musical.—**chorus boy** *nm*.

chose, chosen *see* **choose**.

Chou dynasty *n* the Chinese dynasty that conquered and replaced that of Shang in 1027 BC. In 256 BC it was annihilated by the Ch'in.

Chou En-lai *or* **Zhou En Lai** (1898–1976) Chinese Communist statesman; prime minister (1949–76) of the People's Republic of China.

chough *n* a red-legged crow.

Choukoutien *n* (*archeo*) a village near Peking in China where the remains of 45 extinct humans, named *Homo erectus*, were discovered.

Choula *n* one of the most important ancient cities of Mexico, which first developed between 800 and 300 BC.

chow *n* a breed of thick-coated dog, originally from China (—*also* **chow chow**); (*sl*) food.

chow-chow *n* a relish of chopped pickles in a mustard sauce.

chowder *n* a thick clam and potato soup.

chow mein *n* a Chinese-American dish of fried, crispy noodles with meat and vegetables.

Choybalsan *n* a city in Mongolia.

CHP *abbr* = Certificate in Hypnosis and Psychology; combined heat and power.

CHPA *abbr* = Combined Heat and Power Association.

Chq. *or* **chq.** *abbr* = cheque.

CHQ *abbr* = Corps Headquarters.

chr. *abbr* = chrestomathy.

Chr. *abbr* = Christ; Christian.

chrestomathy *n* (*pl* **chrestomathies**) a collection of extracts for learning a foreign language; a phrasebook; an anthology.

CHRI *abbr* = Commonwealth Human Rights Initiative.

chrism *n* consecrated oil.—**chrismal** *adj*.

chrisom *n* an infant's baptismal robe.

Christ *n* Jesus of Nazareth, regarded by Christians as the Messiah.

Christchurch *n* a city in New Zealand.

christen *vt* to enter the Christian Church by baptism; to give a name to; (*inf*) to use for the first time.—**christener** *n*.—**christening** *n*.

Christendom *n* all Christians, or Christian countries regarded as a whole.

Christian *n* a person who believes in Christianity. * *adj* relating to, believing in, or based on the doctrines of Christianity; kind, gentle, humane.

Christian Era *n* the present era reckoned from the birth of Christ.

Christianity *n* the religion based on the teachings of Christ.

Christianize *vt* to convert to Christianity.—**Christianization** *n*.—**Christianizer** *n*.

Christianly *adj* like or befitting a Christian.

Christian name *n* a name given when one is christened; (*loosely*) any forename.

Christian Science *n* a system of religion founded by Mary Baker Eddy, 1866, in which sin and disease are regarded as mental errors to be overcome by faith.—**Christian Scientist** *n*.

Christie *n* [Dame] Agatha [Clarissa Mary] (1890–1976) English detective story writer.

Christlike *adj* resembling Christ.

Christmas *n* (*pl* **Christmases**) an annual festival (25 December) in memory of the birth of Christ.

Christmas card *n* a greeting card, usu decorative, sent at Christmas.

Christmas Eve *n* the day and esp the night before Christmas Day.

Christmas rose *n* the black hellebore.

Christmas stocking *n* a stocking hung by a child on Christmas Eve for Santa Claus to fill with presents.

Christmastide *n* Christmas Eve (24 December) to Epiphany (6 January).

Christmas tree *n* an evergreen tree decorated at Christmas; an imitation tree.

Christo *n* Javacheff (1935–) Bulgarian-born American sculptor, who experimented with assemblage and "packaging."

Christology *n* the branch of theology that studies Christ's nature.—**Christological** *adj*.—**Christologist** *n*.

Christopher *n* **Saint** (third century?) Christain martyr; patron saint of travelers. He carried a child across a river, his burden suddenly became almost too heavy for him and its voice revealed that he was in fact carrying Christ. His feast day is 25 July.

christy *n* (*pl* **christies**) a ski turn used to change direction or stop.

chrom-, chromo- *prefix* color.

chromate *n* a salt or ester of chromic acid.

chromatic *adj* of or in color; (*mus*) using tones outside the key in which the passage is written.—**chromatically** *adv*.—**chromaticism** *n*.

chromatic aberration *n* an image imperfection occurring in optical instruments using lenses.

chromatics *n* (*sing*) the science of color.

chromatic scale *n* a twelve-note musical scale that proceeds by semitones.

chromatin *n* a protoplasmic substance in a cell nucleus forming chromosomes.—**chromatinic** *adj*.

chromatography *n* the separation of the components of a substance by passing it over or through a substance that absorbs selectively.—**chromatograph** *n*.—**chromatographer** *n*.—**chromatographic** *adj*.—**chromatographically** *adv*.

-chrome *adj suffix* colored. * *n suffix* color, pigment.

chrome *n* chromium; a chromium pigment; something plated with an alloy of chromium.

chrome green *n* a green pigment made from a compound of chromium.

chrome red *n* a red pigment made from a compound of chromium.

chrome yellow *n* a yellow pigment made from a compound of chromium.

chromic *adj* of chromium.

chromium *n* a hard metallic element used in making steel alloys and electroplating to give a tough surface.

chromo-, chrom- *prefix* color.

chromogen *n* the coloring matter of plants.—**chromogenic** *adj*.

chromolithography *n* the art of printing in colors from stone.—**chromolithograph** *n*.—**chromolithographer** *n*.—**chromolithographic** *adj*.

chromosome *n* (*biol*) any of the microscopic rod-shaped bodies bearing genes.

chromosphere *n* the rose-colored outer gaseous envelope of the sun above the photosphere.—**chromospheric** *adj*.

chron. *or* **chronol.** *abbr* = chronological; chronology.

Chron. *abbr* (*Bible*) = Chronicles.

chron-, chrono- *prefix* time.

chronic *adj* (*disease*) long-lasting; regular; habitual;.—**chronically** *adv*.—**chronicity** *n*.

chronicle *n* a record of events in chronological order; an account; a history. * *vt* to record in a chronicle.—**chronicler** *n*.

Chronicles, 1 and 2 *n* (*Bible*) OT books forming part of a larger work, which contain genealogical tables and historical events, esp building the Temple.

chronogram *n* an inscription which includes in it the date of some event.—**chronogrammatic, chronogrammatical** *adj*.

chronograph *n* an instrument for recording minute intervals of time; a stopwatch.—**chronographer** *n*.—**chronographic** *adj*.

chronological, chronologic *adj* arranged in order of occurrence.—**chronologically** *adv*.

chronology *n* (*pl* **chronologies**) the determination of the order of events, e.g., in history; the arrangement of events in order of occurrence; a table of events listed in order of occurrence.—**chronologist** *n*.

chronometer *n* a very accurate instrument for measuring time exactly.

chronometry *n* the scientific measurement of time.—**chronometric, chronometrical** *adj*.—**chronometrically** *adv*.

chronoscope *n* an instrument for measuring by electricity the velocity of a projectile.—**chronoscopic** *adj*.

chrys-, chryso- *prefix* gold.

chrysalis *n* (*pl* **chrysalises, chrysalides**) the pupa of a moth or butterfly, enclosed in a cocoon.

chrysanthemum *n* a plant with a brightly colored flower head.

chryselephantine *adj* composed (or overlaid) partly with gold and partly with ivory.

chrysoberyl *n* a yellowish-green gem.

chrysolite *n* a green-colored and sometimes transparent gem.—**chrysolitic** *adj*.

chrysoprase *n* a variety of chalcedony of an apple-green color.

chs. *abbr* = chapters.

CHS *abbr* = Clarinet Heritage Society; Clydesdale Horse Society.

CHSA *abbr* = Chest Heart and Stroke Association.

cht. *abbr* = chest.

CHT *abbr* = Church Housing Trust.

chthonian, chthonic *adj* (*Greek gods*) of the underworld, as opposed to Olympian.

chub *n* (*pl* **chub, chubs**) a small freshwater fish of the carp family.

chubby *adj* (**chubbier, chubbiest**) plump.—**chubbiness** *n*.

chuck¹ *vt* to throw, to toss; (*inf*) to stop, to give up. * *n* (*usu with* **the**) a giving up; dismissal.

chuck² *n* a device on a lathe, etc, that holds the work or drill; a cut of beef from the neck to the ribs.

chuck³ *vt* to make a noise like a hen calling to her chickens. * *n* a hen's call.

chuck⁴ *n* (*dial*) darling.

chuckle *vt* to laugh softly; to gloat. * *n* a quiet laugh.—**chuckler** *n*.

chuck wagon *n* a wagon with food and cooking equipment, used as a portable kitchen on cattle drives.

chuff¹ *n* a surly fellow, a boor.

chuff² *vi* to make a puffing sound, as a steam engine. * *n* such a sound.

chug *n* the explosive sound of an automobile exhaust, etc. * *vi* (**chugging, chugged**) to make such a sound.

chukka[1] *n* an ankle-length boot.

chukker, chukka[2] *n* each period of play in a game of polo.

CHULS *abbr* = Committee of Heads of University Law Schools.

chum *n* (*inf*) a close friend, esp of the same sex. * *vi* (**chumming, chummed**) to be friendly (with); to room together.

chummy *adj* (**chummier, chummiest**) friendly, close to.—**chummily** *adv*.—**chumminess** *n*.

chump *n* (*inf*) a stupid person; a fool.

chunk *n* a short, thick piece or lump, as wood, bread, etc.—**chunky** *adj*.

chunky *adj* (**chunkier, chunkiest**) short and thick; (*clothing*) of heavy material.—**chunkily** *adv*.—**chunkiness** *n*.

Chunnel *n* (*inf*) the Channel Tunnel linking England and France.

church *n* a building for public worship, esp Christian worship; the clerical profession; a religious service; (*with cap*) all Christians; (*with* the) a particular Christian denomination.

Church *n* Frederick Edwin (1826–1900) American painter, who painted huge epic works based on sketches of South American scenery, e.g. *The Heart of the Andes* (1859).

churchgoer *n* one who goes to church regularly.—**churchgoing** *adj, n*.

Churchill *n* Sir Winston [Leonard Spencer] (1874–1965) British Conservative statesman and writer; prime minister (1940–45). He served under both Liberal and Conservative governments.

churchman *n* (*pl* **churchmen**) a member of the Church; a clergyman.—**churchwoman** *n* (*pl* **churchwomen**).

churchwarden *n* in the Anglican church, an elected lay representative who administers the secular matters of a parish church.

churchyard *n* the yard around a church often used as a burial ground.

churl *n* formerly one of the lowest orders of freemen; a peasant; a surly ill-bred person.

churlish *adj* surly, ill-mannered.—**churlishly** *adv*.—**churlishness** *n*.

churn *n* a large metal container for milk; a device that can be vigorously turned to make milk or cream into butter. * *vt* to agitate in a churn; to make (butter) this way; to stir violently; (*with* **out**) (*inf*) to produce quickly or one after the other or without much effort.

churr *see* **chirr**.

Churriguera *n* José Benito (1665–1725) Spanish sculptor and architect and prominent member of a family of artists famous for their ornate designs for church sculptures and altarpieces.

chute *n* an inclined trough or a passage for sending down water, logs, rubbish, etc; a fall of water, a rapid; an inclined slide for children; a slide into a swimming pool.

chutney *n* a relish of fruits, spices, and herbs.

chutzpah, chutzpa *n* shameless audacity, presumption, or gall.

chyle *n* a milk-like fluid separated from digested matter in the stomach, absorbed by the lacteal vessels and assimiliated into the blood.—**chylaceous, chylous** *adj*.

chyme *n* the pulpy mass of digested food prior to the separation of the chyle.

Ci *symbol* curie.

c.i. *abbr* = cast iron; (*roofing*) corrugated iron.

Ci. *abbr* = cirrus.

CI *or* **c.i.** *abbr* = cost and insurance.

CI *abbr* = Channel Islands; Chief Inspector; Combustion Institute; Commonwealth Institute.

C/I *abbr* = certificate of insurance.

CI and F *or* **c. i. and f.** *abbr* = cost, insurance, and freight.

CIA *abbr* = Cancer Information Association; Central Intelligence Agency; Chemical Industries Association; Cigar Institute of America; Credit Insurance Association.

CIAC *abbr* = Ceramics Industry Advisory Committee; Construction Industry Advisory Council.

ciaccona *see* **chaconne**.

Cian *n* (*Irish Celtic myth*) the son of Dian Cecht, the god of medicine.

ciao *interj* (*Italian*) used to express greeting or farewell.

CIAO *abbr* = Critical Infrastructure Assurance Office

CIArb *abbr* = Chartered Institute of Arbitrators.

CIB *abbr* = Campaign for an Independent Britain; Chartered Institute of Bankers; Corporation of Insurance Brokers; corporate and institutional banking.

Cibber *n* Colley (1671–1757) English actor and dramatist who became poet laureate in England in 1730.

Cibic *n* Aldo (1955–) Italian architect who specialized in store design, watches, and furniture for the Memphis group.

ciborium *n* (*pl* **ciboria**) a covered chalice for holding the sacrament; a canopy over an altar.

CIBS *abbr* = Chartered Institute of Building Societies.

CIC *abbr* = Capital Issues Committee; Caribbean Investment Corporation; Cinema International Corporation; Commander-in-Chief; Consumer Information Center; Construction Industry Council; Council for International Contact.

C-I-C *or* **CIC** *abbr* = Commander-in-Chief.

cicada, cicala *n* (*pl* **cicadas, cicadae** *or* **cicalas, cicale**) a large fly-like insect with transparent wings, the male producing a loud chirp or drone.

cicatrix *n* (*pl* **cicatrices**) the scar remaining after a wound has healed; a scarlike mark.—**cicatricial** *adj*.—**cicatricose** *adj*.

cicatrize *vt* to heal a wound by inducing the skin to form a cicatrix; to mark with scars.—**cicatrization** *n*.—**cicatrizer** *n*.

CICB *abbr* = Criminal Injuries Compensation Board.

CICCA *abbr* = Committee for International Cooperation between Cotton Associations.

cicely *n* (*pl* **cicelies**) a species of umbelliferous plants allied to chervil.

cicerone *n* (*pl* **cicerones, ciceroni**) a guide who explains the antiquities and chief features of a place.

Cicestr. *abbr* (*Latin*) = *Cicestrensis*, "of Chichester."

CICF *abbr* (*Eire*) = Cork International Choral Festival.

CICRA *abbr* = Crohn's in Childhood Research Association.

CiCu *abbr* = cirro-cumulus.

CID *abbr* = Criminal Investigation Department; Council of Industrial Design; U.S. Army Criminal Investigation Command.

-cide *n suffix* killing, or killer of, as in *regicide*.

cider *n* fermented apple juice as an alcoholic drink; unfermented apple juice.

CIDIE *abbr* = Committee of International Development Institutions on the Environment.

CIDST *abbr* = Committee for Scientific and Technical Information and Documentation.

CIE *abbr* = Center for International Economics; Choice in Education; Companion of the Order of the Indian Empire; (*Gaelic*) *Córas Iompair Éireann*, "Transport Organization of Ireland."

CIEC *abbr* = Chemical Industry Education Center.

CIEE *abbr* = Companion of the Institution of Electrical Engineers.

CIEL *abbr* = Center for International Environmental Law.

CIEx *abbr* = Companion of the Institute of Export.

cif *abbr* = charged in full; cost, insurance, and freight.

CIF *abbr* (*Eire*) = Construction Industry Federation.

CIF *or* **c.i.f.** *abbr* = cost, insurance, and freight.

CIFA *abbr* = Corporation of Insurance and Financial Advisers.

CIF and C *or* **c. i. f. and c.** *abbr* = cost, insurance, freight, and charges.

CIF and E *or* **c. i. f. and e.** *abbr* = cost, insurance, freight, and exchange.

CIF and I *or* **c. i. f. and i.** *abbr* = cost, insurance, freight, and interest.

cifc *abbr* = cost, insurance, freight, and commission.

CIFC *abbr* = Council for the Investigation of Fertility Control.

CIFC and I *or* **c.i.f.c. and i.** *abbr* = cost, insurance, freight, collection, and interest.

cifci *abbr* = cost, insurance, freight, commission, and interest.

cife *abbr* = cost, insurance, freight, and exchange.

CIFE *abbr* = Colleges and Institutes of Further Education; Conference for Independent Further Education.

CIFER *abbr* = Colorado Institute for Fuels and High Altitude Engine Research.

cifi *abbr* = cost, insurance, freight, and interest.

CIFOR *abbr* = Center for International Forestry Research.

CIG *abbr* = Cataloguing and Indexing Group; Conference Interpreters' Group; Conservative Integration Group.

cigar *n* a compact roll of tobacco leaf for smoking.

cigarette *n* shredded tobacco rolled in fine paper for smoking.

CIGAS *abbr* = Cambridge Intercollegiate Graduate Application Scheme.

CIGS *abbr* = Chief of the Imperial General Staff.

Cigfa *n* (*Welsh Celtic myth*) the wife of Pryderi. She and Pryderi had various adventures along with Manawydan and Rhiannon.

CIH *abbr* = Commonwealth Institute of Helminthology.

CIHE *abbr* = Council for Industry and Higher Education.

CII *abbr* = Chartered Insurance Institute.

CIIA *abbr* = Council of Independent Inspecting Authorities.

CIID *abbr* = Communications and Information Industries Division.

CIIG *abbr* = Construction Industry Information Group.

CIIR *abbr* = Catholic Institute for International Relations.

CIJ *abbr* = Chartered Institute of Journalists.

CIL *abbr* = Center for Independent Living; Commissioners of Irish Lights.

Cilèa *n* Francesco (1866-1950) Italian composer, teacher and administrator, best known for his successful operas, including and *L'Arlesiana* (*The Woman of Arles*), and *Adriana Lecouvreur*. The leading tenor parts in both operas were created by Caruso in 1897 and 1902.

cilia *npl* (*sing* **cilium**) the hair of the eyelids; long, minute, hair-like appendages on the margins of vegetable bodies; the minute vibrating filaments lining or covering certain organs.—**ciliated** *adj*.

ciliary body *n* part of the eye which secretes the aqueous humor.

cilice *n* haircloth.

Cilicia *n* coastal plain of Asia Minor, the chief city being Tarsus; (*Bible*) a Roman province in NT times.

CILT *abbr* = (*Brit*) Campaign to Improve London's Transport; (*Brit*) Centre for Independent Transport Research in London; Center for Information on Language Teaching.

Cilydd *n* (*Welsh Celtic myth*) Cilydd was the husband of Goleud-dydd and father of Culhwch.

CIM *abbr* = Chartered Institute of Marketing; Commission for Industry and Manpower; Cooperative Investigation in the Mediterranean.

CIMA *abbr* = Chartered Institute of Management Accountants.

Cimarosa *n* Domenico (1749-1801) Italian composer, whose most successful opera was *Il Matrimonio segreto* (*The Secret Marriage*). He also wrote Masses and oratorios.

CIMB *abbr* = Construction Industry Manpower Board.

cimbal, cimbalom *see* **dulcimer**.

CIMCLG *abbr* = Construction Industry Metric Change Liaison Group.

CIME *abbr* = Council of Industry for Management Education.

CIMgt *abbr* = Companion of the Institute of Management.

CIMGTechE *abbr* = Companion of the Institution of Mechanical and General Technician Engineers.

CIMM *abbr* = Canadian Institute of Mining and Metallurgy.

Cimmerian *adj* intensely dark; gloomy; pertaining to the Cimmerii, a legendary people mentioned by Homer as living in perpetual darkness.

Cimmerians *npl* a nomadic tribe who inhabited the steppes of Russia in the 8th century BC.

CIMO *abbr* = Confederation of Importers and Marketing Organizations in Europe of Fresh Fruit and Vegetables.

CIMP *abbr* = Committee on Igneous and Metamorphic Petrogenesis.

CIMS *abbr* = Center for Innovation Management Studies.

Cin. *abbr* = Cincinnati.

C in C, C-in-C *abbr* = Commander in Chief.

cinch *n* (*sl*) a firm hold, an easy job; a saddle band or girth.

cinchona *n* a South American tree that yields quinine and other drugs.

cinchonism *n* a medical condition characterized by buzzing in the ears, deafness, etc, caused by the excessive use of quinine.

cincture *n* a belt or girdle worn round the waist; a raised or carved ring at the bottom and top of a pillar.

cinder *n* a tiny piece of partly burned wood, etc; (*pl*) ashes from wood or coal.— **cindery** *adj*.

cinder block *n* a lightweight building brick composed mainly of the ashes of coal and coke, bonded with cement.—*also* **breeze block, clinker block**.

cinder cone *n* a cone surrounding a volcanic vent composed of small fragments of glassy, solidified lava.

cine- *prefix* motion picture or cinema, as in *cinecamera*, *cinefilm*.

cineast, cineaste *n* a movie enthusiast.

cinema *n* a place where motion pictures are shown; film as an industry or art form.— **cinematic** *adj*.—**cinematically** *adv*.

cinéma vérité *n* cinema photography of real-life scenes and situations, etc, to create realism.

cinematography *n* the art or science of motion-picture photography.—**cinematographic** *adj*.—**cinematographer** *n*.

cineraria *n* a genus of garden plants of the aster family with bright flowers.

cinerarium *n* (*pl* **cineraria**) a place for keeping a person's ashes after cremation.

cinerary *adj* of, pertaining to, or containing, ashes.

cinerary urn *n* an urn containing cremated ashes that was then buried.

cinereous *adj* ash-gray.

cingulum *n* (*pl* **cingula**) belt.

Cinioch *n* (*d.* 631) king of Picts, Britain. Son of Gartnart's sister, the dates of his reign are not known.

Ciniod *n* king of Picts, Britain. (763–775). Son of Oengus's sister.

cinnabar *n* red sulphide of mercury. * *adj* vermilion.

cinnamon *n* a tree of the laurel family; its aromatic edible bark; a spice made from this; a yellowish-brown color. * *adj* yellowish brown.—**cinnamonic, cinamic** *adj*.

cinnamon stone *n* a variety of the garnet.

cinque *n* a five at dice or cards.

cinquecento *n* the 16th century and Italian fine art of that period. * *adj* designed or executed in such Italian style.

cinquefoil *n* a plant with leaves divided into five lobes; (*archit*) ornamentation resembling five leaves.

CIO *abbr* = Church Information Office.

CIOB *abbr* = Chartered Institute of Building.

CIoH *abbr* = Chartered Institute of Housing.

CIP *abbr* = Canadian Industrial Preparedness Association; Caribbean Institute of Perinatology; Center for International Policy; Common Industrial Policy; Council of Iron Producers.

CIPA *abbr* = Chartered Institute of Patent Agents.

CIPFA *abbr* = Chartered Institute of Public Finance and Accountancy.

cipher *n* the numeral 0, zero; any single Arabic numeral; a thing or person of no importance, a nonentity; a method of secret writing. * *vt* to convert (a message) into cipher.—*also* **cypher**.

CIPRIS *abbr* = Coordinated Interagency Partnership Regulating International Students

CIPS *abbr* = Chartered Institute of Purchasing and Supply; Choice in Personal Safety; Commonwealth International Philatelic Society.

cir. *abbr* = (*Latin*) *circa, circiter, circum*, "about"; circular.

CIR *abbr* = Commission for Industrial Relations.

CIRA *abbr* = Cast Iron Research Association; Confederation of Industrial Research Associations.

cir.bkr. *abbr* = circuit breaker.

circ. *abbr* (*Latin*) = *circa, circiter, circum*, "about."

CIRC *abbr* = Center for International Research Cooperation.

circa *prep* about.

circadian *adj* of or pertaining to biological processes that occur in 24-hour cycles.

Circe *n* (*Greek myth*) a sorceress who changed people into the shapes of wolves and lions. Odysseus stayed with her for a year during his voyage home from Troy.

circinate *adj* (*leaf*) rolled up with the tip inwards.

circle *n* a perfectly round plane figure; the line enclosing it; anything (built) in the form of a circle; the curved seating area above the stalls in a theater; a group, set or class (of people); extent, scope, as of influence. * *vti* to encompass; to move in a circle; to revolve (round); to draw a circle round.— **circler** *n*.

CIRCLE *abbr* = Cultural and Information Research Centers in Europe.

circlet *n* a small circle; a circular band or hoop.

circuit *n* a distance round; a route or course; an area so enclosed; the path of an electric current; a visit to a particular area by a judge to hold courts; the area itself; a chain or association, e.g., of cinemas controlled by one management; sporting events attended regularly by the same competitors and at the same venues; a motor-racing track.—**circuital** *adj*.

circuit board *n* (*comput*) a plastic board onto which circuits are etched and to which components such as chips and other electronics are connected.

circuit breaker *n* a switch that interrupts an electric circuit under certain abnormal conditions.

circuit of capital *n* the process whereby the capitalist invests money to pay for the production of goods, paying wages to the workforce, who in turn buy goods, while the profit on sales provides further capital for investment.

circuitous *adj* roundabout, indirect.—**circuitously** *adv*.

circuitry *n* (*pl* **circuitries**) the plan of an electric circuit; the components of a circuit.

circular *adj* shaped like a circle, round; (*argument*) using as evidence the conclusion which it is seeking to prove; moving round a circle. * *n* an advertisement, etc addressed to a number of people.—**circularity, circularness** *n*.

circular breathing *n* (*mus*) the technique of sustaining a note when playing a wind instrument by breathing in through the nose while sounding the note.

circular reference *n* (*comput*) a situation occurring in a spreadsheet that is the result of a cell containing a formula that depends on the result of the formula.

circular saw *n* a power-driven saw with a circular blade.

circularize *vt* to make circular; to send circulars to; to canvass.—**circularization** *n*.—**circularizer** *n*.

circulate *vti* to pass from hand to hand or place to place; to spread or be spread about; to move round, finishing at the starting point.—**circulative** *adj*.—**circulator** *n*.—**circulatory** *adj*.

circulating capital *n* working capital.

circulating decimal *n* the recurring decimal.

circulating library *n* a lending library.

circulation *n* the act of circulating; a movement to and fro; the regular cycle of blood flow in the body; the number of copies sold of a newspaper, etc; currency.

circum- *prefix* round, about.

circumambient *adj* enclosing, or being surrounded, on all sides.—**cicumambience, cicumabiency** *n*.

circumcise *vt* to cut off the foreskin of (a male) or the clitoris of (a female), esp as a religious rite.

circumcision *n* the act of circumcising; spiritual purification.

circumference *n* the line bounding a circle, a ball, etc; the length of this line.— **circumferential** *adj*.

circumference of Earth *n* the equatorial circumference is 24,902 miles (40,076 kilometers). The circumference around the poles is 24,860 miles (40,008 kilometers).

circumflex *n* an accent (^) placed over a vowel to indicate contraction, length, etc.— **circumflexion** *n*.

circumfuse *vt* to pour or spread around; to bathe (with).—**circumfusion** *n*.

circumlocution *n* the use of more words than are necessary; a roundabout or evasive expression.—**circumlocutory** *adj*.

circumnavigate *vt* to sail or fly completely round (the world).—**circumnavigable** *adj*.—**circumnavigation** *n*.—**circumnavigator** *n*.

circumnutate *vi* (*bot*) to turn successively to all points of the compass.— **circumnutation** *n*.

circumpolar *adj* near the north or south pole; (*astron*) (stars that appear) always above the horizon.

circumscribe *vt* to draw a line around; to enclose; to limit or restrict.— **circumscription** *n*.

circumspect *adj* prudent, cautious; careful; discreet.—**circumspection** *n*.— **circumspective** *adj*.

circumstance *n* an occurrence, an incident; a detail; ceremony; (*pl*) a state of affairs; condition in life.

circumstantial *adj* detailed; incidental; (*law*) strongly inferred from direct evidence.— **circumstantially** *adv*.

circumstantiality *n* (*pl* **circumstantialities**) the state of being circumstantial; fullness of detail.

circumstantiate *vt* to describe or verify in detail.—**circumstantiation** *n*.

circumvallate *vt* to surround with a rampart.—**circumvallation** *n*.

circumvent *vt* to evade, bypass; to outwit.—**circumventer, circumventor** *n*.—**circumvention** *n*.

circumvolution *n* the act of rolling round; the state of being rolled round; a coil.—**circumvolutory** *adj*.

circus *n* (*pl* **circuses**) a large arena for the exhibition of games, feats of horsemanship, etc; a carnival, a traveling show of acrobats, clowns, etc; a company of people traveling round giving displays; houses built in a circle; an open space in a town where streets meet; (*archit*) in ancient Rome an open-air stadium surrounded by tiers of seats; (*inf*) noise, disturbance; loud, extravagant behavior.

CIRDAP *abbr* = Center for Integrated Rural Development for Asia and the Pacific.

cire perdue *or* **lost wax process** *n* a method of casting awkwardly shaped metal objects, particularly figurines or statuettes, in bronze or gold.

CIRET *abbr* = Center for International Research on Economic Tendency.

cirque *n* a natural amphitheater or ring formed by the erosion effect of a glacier.

cirrhosis *n* a hardened condition of the tissues of an organ, esp the liver.—**cirrhosed** *adj*.—**cirrhotic** *adj*.

cirriped, cirripede *adj* having feet resembling cirri; pertaining to the Cirripedia, a subclass of parasitic crustaceans, as the barnacles and acorn shells.

cirrocumulus *n* (*pl* **cirrocumuli**) a cloud broken up into small fleecy masses.

cirrostratus *n* (*pl* **cirrostrati**) a horizontal or slightly inclined light fleecy cloud.

cirrouse, cirrous *adj* terminating in a curl, tuft, or tendril.

cirrus *n* (*pl* **cirri**) thin, wispy clouds.

CIRSE *abbr* = Cardiovascular and Interventional Radiological Society of Europe.

CIRSSE *abbr* = Center for Intelligent Robotic System for Space Exploration.

CIS *abbr* = Center for Institutional Studies; Center for International Security; China Instrument Society; Commonwealth of Independent States (a federation of former Soviet republics, such as Russia, Ukraine, who wish to retain voluntary links with one another).

cis- *prefix* on this side of.

CISA *abbr* = Coach Industry Suppliers' Association.

cisalpine *adj* this side of the Alps with regard to Rome, south of the Alps.

CISC *abbr* = Citizens' Study Income Center; complex instruction-set computer.

cisco *n* (*pl* **ciscoes, ciscos**) the Canadian lake herring.

CISCO *abbr* = Civil Service Catering Organization.

CISE *abbr* = Council of the Institution of Structural Engineers.

cismontane *adj* on this (northern) side of the Alps.

CISOB *abbr* = Counsellor of the Incorporated Society of Organ Builders.

CISS *abbr* = Center for International Sports Studies.

Cissa *n* king of Sussex, Britain (*c*.514). Participated in the siege of Pevensey in 491, the *Anglo–Saxon Chronicle* does not mention the South Saxons again until 661.

CiSt *abbr* = cirro-stratus.

cist *n* a prehistoric stone tomb consisting of two rows of stone and covered with a flat stone slab; a box or chest.

Cistercian *n* one of a Benedictine order of monks, founded 1098 at Citeaux, France. * *adj* pertaining to the Cistercians.

cistern *n* a tank or reservoir for storing water, esp in a toilet.

CISV *abbr* = Children's International Summer Villages.

CISWO *abbr* = Coal Industry Social Welfare Organisations.

cit. *abbr* = citation; cited; citizen.

CIT *abbr* = Center for Information Technology; Coda International Training.

citadel *n* a fortress in or near a city.

citation *n* a quotation; a source or authority cited; a commendation, esp for bravery; (*law*) a summons to appear.

CITB *abbr* = Carpet Industry Training Board; Construction Industry Training Board.

cite *vt* to summon officially to appear in court; to quote; to give as an example or authority.—**citable, citeable** *adj*.

CITES *abbr* = Campaign Against International Trade in Endangered Species; Convention on International Trade in Endangered Species of Wild Fauna and Flora.

CITG *abbr* = Coal Industry Tripartite Group.

CITHA *abbr* = Confederation of International Trading Houses Association.

Cithaeron *n* a mountain of ancient Greece, modern Elatea. On its northern slope stood the city of Plataea.

cithara *n* an ancient lyre.—*also* **kithara**.

citify *vt* (**citifying, citified**) to assume city ways, habits, dress.

citizen *n* a member of a city, state or nation.—**citizenship** *n*.

citizenry *n* (*pl* **citizenries**) citizens collectively.

citizen's arrest *n* an arrest made by a citizen on his or her own authority.

citizen's band *n* a shortwave band reserved for private radio communication.

cito disp. *abbr* (*Latin*) = *cito dispensetur*, "let there quickly be dispensed."

citole *n* (*mus*) a medieval instrument and ancestor of the cittern.

citrate *n* a salt or ester of citric acid.

citric *adj* of or obtained from citrus fruits or citric acid.

citric acid *n* a sour acid found in fruits and used as a flavoring.

citric acid cycle *n* (*biochemistry*) a complicated series of biochemical reactions controlled by enzymes.

citrine *adj* lemon-colored.

citron *n* a large fruit-like a lemon; the tree bearing it; a yellow-green color.

citronella *n* a fragrant Asian grass which yields an aromatic oil used in soap, perfumes, and in insect repellents.

citrus *n* (*pl* **citruses**) a genus of trees including the lemon, orange, etc; the fruit of these trees. * *adj* of or relating to citrus trees or shrubs or their fruit.

cittern *n* a medieval stringed instrument.

city *n* (*pl* **cities**) an important or cathedral town; a town created a city by charter; the people of a city; business circles, esp financial services.—*also adj*.

City *n* (*Brit*) the part of London in which are situated the head offices of many financial institutions.

city editor *n* the editor in charge of local news.

city fathers *npl* the people who take part in running a city.

city hall *n* the townhall; the government of a city or its officers; (*inf*) bureaucracy.

City of Refuge *n* (*Bible*) place of sanctuary provided by OT law for people who had committed murder unintentionally.

city slicker *n* (*inf*) one who adopts city ways; a suave, unreliable person.

city-state *n* (*hist*) a sovereign state comprising a city and its surrounding territory.

CIU *abbr* = Workingmen's Club and Institute Union.

Ciudad del Este *n* a city in Paraguay.

CIUL *abbr* = Council for International Urban Liaison.

civ. *abbr* = civil; civilian.

civet *n* a cat-like animal of central Africa and South Asia; the pungent substance secreted by this animal used in perfumery.

civic *adj* of a city, citizen or citizenship. * *npl* the principles of good citizenship; the study of citizenship.—**civically** *adv*.

civil *adj* of citizens or the state; not military or ecclesiastical; polite, obliging; (*law*) relating to crimes other than criminal ones or to private rights.—**civilly** *adv*.

civil ceremony *n* a legal marriage performed by a civic official, not involving a church.

civil defense *n* the organization of civilians against enemy attack.

civil disobedience *n* refusal to pay taxes, etc, as part of a political campaign; nonviolent protest to achieve an end.

civil engineer *n* an engineer who designs and constructs roads, bridges, etc.

civilian *n* a person who is not a member of the armed forces.

civility *n* (*pl* **civilities**) good manners, politeness.

civilization *n* the state of being civilized; the process of civilizing; an advanced stage of social culture; moral and cultural refinement.

civilize *vt* to bring out from barbarism; to educate in arts and refinements.—**civilizer** *n*.

civilized *adj* no longer in a savage or uncultured state.

civil law *n* law pertaining to private rights.

civil liberties *npl* the right of free speech, association, etc, subject to the law.

civil rights *npl* the personal rights of a citizen.

civil service *n* those employed in the service of a state apart from the military.—**civil servant** *n*.

civil war *n* a war between citizens of the same state or country.

civil year *n* the calendar year as used in ordinary life, consisting of 365 days in ordinary years and 366 in leap years.

civvy *adj* (*sl*) civilian. * *n* (*pl* **civvies**) (*sl*) civilian clothes.

CIWF *abbr* = Compassion in World Farming.

CIYC *abbr* = Church of Ireland Youth Council.

cj. *abbr* = conjectural.

CJ *abbr* = Chief Judge; Chief Justice.

CJA & HSA *abbr* = Council of Justice to Animals and Humane Slaughter Association.

CJCan *abbr* = Corpus Juris Canonici.

CJCC *abbr* = Commonwealth Joint Communications Committee.

CJCiv *abbr* = Corpus Juris Civilis.

CJD *see* **Creutzfeld-Jakob disease**.

CJEC *abbr* = Court of Justice of the European Communities.

ck. *abbr* = cask; check.

cks. *abbr* = casks; checks.

Cl *symbol* (*chem*) chlorine (element).

cl *abbr* = centiliter(s).

cl. *abbr* = centiliter; claim; class; clause; clearance; clergyman; clerk; cloth.

c.l. *abbr* = carload; carload lots; civil law; common law.

CL *abbr* = Celtic League; Communist League.

C/L *abbr* = cash letter.

CLA *abbr* = Canadian Lung Association; Cantonese Language Association; Commonwealth Lawyers Association; Computer Law Association; Copyright Licensing Agency; Country Landowners' Association.

CLABE *abbr* = Center for Language & Business in Europe.

clack *vt* to make a sudden, sharp sound; to chatter rapidly and continuously. * *n* a sudden, sharp sound as of wood striking wood.

clad[1] *see* **clothe**.

clad[2] *vt* (**cladding, clad**) to bond one material to another for protection (*iron cladding*).—**cladding** *n*.

CL(ADO) *abbr* = Diploma in Contact Lens Fitting of the Association of Dispensing Opticians.

CIAgrE *abbr* = Companion of the Institution of Agricultural Engineers.

claim *vt* to demand as a right; to call for; to require; to profess (to have); to assert; to declare to be true. * *n* the act of claiming; a title, right to something; a thing claimed, esp a piece of land for mining.—**claimable** *adj*.—**claimer** *n*.

claimant *n* a person who makes a claim.

Clairborne *n* **Liz** (1929–) American fashion designer.

clairvoyance *n* the power of seeing things not present to the senses, second sight.

clairvoyant *n* a person with the gift of clairvoyance. * *adj* possessing clairvoyance; having remarkable insight.

clam *n* an edible marine bivalve mollusk. * *vt* (**clamming, clammed**) to gather clams. * *vi* (*with* **up**) (*inf*) to remain silent, refuse to talk.

clamant *adj* insistent, crying; clamorous.

clambake *n* clams baked with seaweed; a picnic at which baked clams form the chief dish.

clamber *vi* to climb with difficulty, using the hands as well as the feet. * *n* a climb performed in this way.—**clamberer** *n*.

clammy *adj* (**clammier, clammiest**) damp and sticky.—**clammily** *adv*.—**clamminess** *n*.

clamor, clamour *n* a loud confused noise; an uproar; an insistent demand. * *vi* to demand loudly; to make an uproar.—**clamorous** *adj*.

clamp *n* a device for gripping objects tightly together. * *vt* to grip with a clamp; to attach firmly. * *vi* (*with* **down**) to put a stop to forcefully. * *vt* to attach a wheelclamp to a wheel to immobilize an illegally parked car.

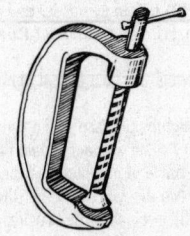

clan *n* a group of people with a common ancestor, under a single chief; people with the same last name; a party or clique.

CL & CGB *abbr* = Church Lads' and Church Girls' Brigade.

clandestine *adj* done secretly; surreptitious; sly.—**clandestinely** *adv*.

clang *n* a loud metallic sound. * *vti* to make or cause to make a clang.

clangor, clangour *n* a sharp clang; repeated clanging.—**clangorous, clangourous** *adj*.—**clangorously, clangourously** *adv*.

clank *n* a short, harsh metallic sound. * *vt* to make or cause to make a clank.

clannish *adj* closely united and excluding others.—**clannishly** *adv*.

clansman *n* (*pl* **clansmen**) a member of a clan.—**clanswoman** *nf* (*pl* **clanswomen**).

clap[1] *vti* (**clapping, clapped**) to strike (the hands) together sharply; to applaud in this way; to slap; to flap (wings) loudly; to put or place suddenly or vigorously. * *n* the sound of hands clapping; a sudden sharp noise; a sudden sharp slap.

clap[2] *n* (*vulg*) venereal disease, gonorrhea.

CLAPA *abbr* = Cleft Lip and Palate Association.

clapboard *n* a narrow, thin board used for building by overlapping each piece.

clapper *n* the tongue of a bell; (*pl*) (*mus*) virtually any kind of percussion instrument comprising two similar pieces that can be struck together, e.g. bones, spoons, sticks.

clapperboard *n* a pair of boards clapped together to aid in synchronization of sound in film making.

Clapton *n* **Eric** (1945–) English guitarist; he played with the Yardbirds (1963–65) and Cream (1966–68).

claptrap *n* flashy display, empty words.

claque *n* an organized body of people paid to applaud or express disapproval at theaters; interested admirers.

clar. *abbr* = clarinet.

CLARA *abbr* = Center for the Law of Rural Areas.

Clare[1] *n* a county of the Republic of Ireland

Clare *n* **John** (1793–1864) English poet whose popularity derived from his poems on rural life, in volumes such as *The Shepherd's Calendar*. From 1837 he spent most of his life in insane asylums, where he wrote many original and beautiful poems.

Clare of Assisi *n* **Saint** (*c*. 1194–1253) Italian nun, founder of the Franciscan order of the Poor Clares. Her feast day is 11 August.

clarence *n* a closed four-wheeled carriage with a curved front.

claret *n* a dry red wine of Bordeaux in France; its purple-red color.

claret cup *n* a summer drink composed of iced claret, lemon, brandy, etc.

clarify *vti* (**clarifying, clarified**) to make or become clear or intelligible; to free or become free from impurities.—**clarification** *n*.—**clarifier** *n*.

clarinet *n* an orchestral woodwind instrument.—**clarinetist** *n*.

clarion *n* a shrill trumpet formerly used in war; a rousing sound. * *adj* ringing.

clarity *n* clearness.

Clark *n* 1. **Jim** [James Clark] (1936–68) Scottish racing driver and world champion (1963, 1965). 2. **William** (1770–1838) American explorer and frontiersman who led and expedition to the Pacific Northwest with Meriwether Lewis.

Clarke *n* 1. **Jeremiah** (*c*.1673-1707) English composer and organist at St Paul's Cathedral in London. He is best remembered for "The Prince of Denmark's March," otherwise known as the "Trumpet Voluntary" (formerly attributed to Purcell). 2. **Martha** (1944–) American dancer and choreographer.

clarkia *n* a bright-flowered garden plant.

CLARNICO *abbr* = Clark, Nichols and Coombes Limited (confectioners).

clàrsach *n* (*mus*) (*Gaelic*) a small harp of the Scottish Highlands and Ireland.

clary *n* (*pl* **claries**) meadow and wild sage.

clash *n* a loud noise of striking weapons, cymbals, etc; a contradiction, disagreement; a collision. * *vti* to make or cause to make a clash by striking together; to conflict; to collide; to be at variance (with); (*colors*) to be unsuitable or not pleasing when put together.—**clasher** *n*.

Clashing Rocks *npl* (*myth*) two rocks on either side of the northern entrance of the Bosporus, also known as the Symplegades. They were said to clash together when the wind blew strongly.

clasp *n* a hold, an embrace; a catch or buckle. * *vt* to grasp firmly, to embrace; to fasten with a clasp.—**clasper** *n*.

clasp knife *n* a knife with a blade or blades that shut into the handle.

class *n* a division, a group; a kind; a set of students who are taught together; a grade of merit or quality; standing in society, rank; (*inf*) high quality, excellence; style. * *vt* to put into a class.

class. *abbr* = classic; classical; classification.

CLASS *abbr* = Concrete Lintel Association.

class action *n* a legal action taken on behalf of all who share the grievance of the claimants.

class-conscious *adj* aware of and taking part in the conflict between laboring and other classes.—**class-consciousness** *n*.

classic *adj* of the highest class or rank, esp in literature; of the best Greek and Roman writers; of music conforming to certain standards of form, complexity, etc; traditional; authoritative. * *n* a work of literature, art, cinema, etc, of the highest excellence; a definitive work of art.

classical *adj* influenced by, of or relating to ancient Roman and Greek art, literature and culture; traditional; serious; refined; (*mus*) (music) adhering to basic conventions and forms that are more concerned with carefully controled expression rather than unrestrained emotion.—**classicality** *n*.—**classically** *adv*.

classical architecture *n* the style of building of the ancient Greek and Roman civilization, simple in form and variety, but with infinite attention paid to line and proportion.

classical order *n* (*archit*) the system of orders invented by the ancient Greeks, Doric, Ionic, and Corinthian, each consisting of a vertical column usu resting on a base, with a shaft, capital, and entablature.

classicism, classicalism *n* the use of ancient Roman and Greek style.

classicist, classicalist *n* a scholar of the classics.—**classicistic** *adj*.

classics *n* (*with* **the**) the study of ancient Greek and Roman literature; any literature considered to be a model of its type.

classification *n* the organization of knowledge into categories; a category or a division of a category into which knowledge or information has been put.—**classificational** *adj*.—**classificatory** *adj*.

classified *adj* arranged by a system of classification; (*information*) secret and restricted to a select few; (*advertisements*) grouped according to type.

classify *vt* (**classifying, classified**) to arrange in classes, to categorize; to restrict for security reasons.—**classifiable** *adj*.—**classifier** *n*.

classless *adj* not divided into classes; not belonging to a particular class.—**classlessness** *n*.

classmate *n* a member of the same class in a school, college, etc.

classroom *n* a room where pupils or students are taught.

class struggle *n* conflict between the interests of different social classes.

classy *adj* (**classier, classiest**) (*sl*) stylish; elegant.—**classily** *adv*.—**classiness** *n*.

clastic *adj* (*geol*) composed of fragments.

clatter *n* a rattling noise; noisy talk. * *vti* to make or cause a clatter.—**clattery** *adj*.

Claude Lorraine, Claude Gellée *n* (1600–82) French painter who had a great influence on 17th- and 18th-century landscape painters. Notable works include *Landscape at Sunset* (1639) and *The Expulsion of Hagar* (1668).

Claudius *n* (10 BC–AD 54) Roman emperor who extended the Roman empire and initiated the conquest of Britain.

clause *n* a single article or stipulation in a treaty, law, contract, etc; (*gram*) a short sentence; a division of a sentence.—**clausal** *adj*.

claustral *adj* of or pertaining to a cloister, cloistral.

claustrophobia *n* a morbid fear of confined spaces.—**claustrophobe** *n*.—**claustrophobic** *adj*.—**claustrophobically** *adv*.

CLAVA *abbr* = County Land Agents' and Valuers Association.

clavate, claviform *adj* club-shaped.

clavecin *see* **harpsichord**.

claves *n* (*mus*) short sticks that are held in the hand and clicked together to emphasize a beat or rhythm.

clavicembalo *see* **harpsichord**.

clavichord *n* a medieval keyboard instrument, the predecessor of the piano.—**clavichordist** *n*.

clavicle *n* one of the two bones that connect the shoulder blades with the breast bone, the collarbone.—**clavicular** *adj*.

clavier *n* a musical instrument with a keyboard; the keyboard.

claw *n* the sharp hooked nail of an animal or bird; the pointed end or pincer of a crab, etc; a claw-like thing. * *vti* to seize or tear with claws or nails; to clutch or scratch (at); (*with* **back**) to recover (something) with difficulty; to get back money by taxing; to take back part of what was handed out, esp by taxation.—**clawer** *n*.

CLAW *abbr* (*Brit*) = Consortium of Local Authorities in Wales.

clawback *n* money that a government retrieves from people who have been given some form of welfare, the money being "clawed back" in the form of taxes.

claw hammer *n* a hammer with a claw for drawing out nails.

CLAWS *abbr* = Community Land and Workspace Services Limited.

clay *n* a sticky ductile earthy material composed of clay minerals that are hydrous aluminum silicates.—**clayey** *adj*.

clay court *n* a tennis court with a clay surface.

claymore *n* a large two-edged sword formerly used in Scotland.

clay pigeon *n* a brittle clay disk or other object propelled into the air as a shooting target; someone in a vulnerable position.

CLB *abbr* = Church Lads' Brigade; Communist League of Britain.

CLC *abbr* = Central Land Council; Children's Legal Center; Commonwealth Liaison Committee.

CLCB *abbr* (*Brit*) = Committee of the London Clearing Banks.

cld. *abbr* = cleared; colored.

c.l.d. *abbr* = cost laid down.

CLD *abbr* = Christian Literature Development; chronic liver disease; Doctor of Civil Law.

CLE *abbr* = Center for Languages in Education; Committee of Liberal Exiles; Council of Legal Education.

CLEA *abbr* = Commonwealth Legal Education Association; Council of Local Education Authorities.

clean *adj* free from dirt or impurities; unsoiled; morally or ceremonially pure; complete, decisive; free of errors; free of suggestive language; not carrying firearms or drugs. * *adv* entirely; outright; neatly. * *vti* to remove dirt from; (*with* **out**) to remove dirt out of; (*sl*) to take away everything from someone, esp money; (*with* **up**) to leave clean; (*sl*) to get rid of corrupt people, a system, etc; to gain a large profit.—**cleanable** *adj*.—**cleanness** *n*.

clean-cut *adj* sharply defined, clear-cut; well-shaped.

cleaner *n* a substance or device used for cleaning; a person employed to clean; (*pl*) a dry cleaner.

clean-limbed *adj* having well-proportioned or shapely limbs.

cleanly *adj* (**cleanlier, cleanliest**) clean in habits or person; pure; neat. * *adv* in a clean manner.—**cleanliness** *n*.

clean price *n* the price of a gilt-edged security excluding the interest that has accrued since payment of the previous dividend.

cleanse *vt* to make clean or pure.—**cleansable** *adj*.

cleanser *n* something that cleanses, esp a detergent, face cream, etc.

clean-up *n* a thorough cleansing; the set of routine tasks performed at the end of a project.

clear *adj* bright, not dim; transparent; without blemish; easily seen or heard; unimpeded, open; free from clouds; quit (of); plain, distinct, obvious; keen, discerning; positive, sure; without debt. * *adv* plainly; completely; apart from. * *vti* to make or become clear; to rid (of), remove; to free from suspicion, vindicate; to disentangle; to pass by or over without touching; to make as a profit; (*comput*) to remove a part of a document; (*with* **off**) (*inf*) to depart; (*with* **up**) to explain; to tidy up; (*weather*) to become fair.—**clearness** *n*.

CLEAR *abbr* = Campaign for Lead-Free Air; Center for Lake Erie Area Research.

clearance *n* the act of clearing; permission, authority to proceed; the space between two objects in motion.

clear-cut *adj* having a sharp, clearly defined outline, as if chiseled; straightforward and open; of a method of logging in which all trees of a certain species are felled.

clear-eyed *adj* mentally acute; perceptive; keen-sighted.

clear felling *n* the cutting down of all trees on a site, leaving the soil unprotected against erosion.

clear-headed *adj* showing sense, alertness, judgment.—**clear-headedly** *adv*.—**clear-headedness** *n*.

clearing *n* a tract of land cleared of trees, etc, for cultivation.

clearing bank *n* a bank that uses a clearing house to exchange checks and credits with other banks.

clearing house *n* an office where checks are sorted and exchanged by the clearing banks; centralized system for settling indebtedness between the financial institutions that are members; a central agency for the collection, classification and distribution of information.

clearly *adv* in a clear manner; evidently.

clear-sighted *adj* discerning, objective.

clearstory *see* **clerestory**.

cleat *n* a wedge; a strip of wood nailed crossways to a footing, etc; a projection for making ropes fast to; a grip or spur on a shoe or boot to prevent slipping, or to aid in climbing.

cleavage *n* the way a thing splits; divergence; the hollow between the breasts; (*biochemistry*) the tendency of minerals and rocks to shear and split along particular planes.

cleave[1] *vti* (**cleaving, cleft, cleaved** or **clove,** *pp* **cleft, cleaved** or **cloven**) to divide by a blow; split; to sever.—**cleavable** *adj*.

cleave[2] *vi* (**cleaved, clave**) to be faithful to; to stick.

cleaver *n* a butcher's heavy chopper; (*archeo*) a special type of stone tool made from a flake or core.

cleavers *n* goose-grass.

cleek *n* an iron-headed golf club with a narrow straight face; (*Scot*) a large hook or crook.

Cleese *n* **John [Marwood]** (1939–) English comedy actor and writer; one of the main talents in *Monty Python's Flying Circus* (1969–74).

clef *n* a sign on a music stave that indicates the pitch of the notes.

cleft *n* a fissure or crack.

cleft palate *n* a congenital fissure of the hard palate in the roof of the mouth.

cleistogamy *n* (*bot*) self-fertilization without opening of the flower.—**cleistogamous, cleistogamic** *adj*.

Cleland *n* **John** (1709–89) English writer and novelist, notable for his novel *Memoirs of a Woman of Pleasure*, now known universally as *Fanny Hill*.

clematis *n* a climbing plant with large colorful flowers.

Clemenceau *n* **Georges [Eugène Benjamin]** (1841–1929) French left-wing statesman and prime minister (1906–19, 1917–20).

clemency *n* (*pl* **clemencies**) mercy, leniency; mildness, esp of weather.

clement *adj* merciful, gentle; (*weather*) mild.

Clement I *n* **Saint** (*d. c.*100) third bishop of Rome after the Apostles, and became pope (88?–97? AD). His feast day is 23 November.

Clementi *n* **Muzio** (1752–1832) Italian composer and pianist. He wrote many symphonies, some 60 piano sonatas, and *Gradus ad Parnassum*, 100 studies for the piano.

clementine *n* a citrus fruit thought to be a hybrid between a tangerine and a small sweet orange.

clench *vt* (*teeth, fist*) to close tightly; to grasp. * *n* a firm grip.

Clendenning *n* **Max** (1924–) British architect noted for his distinctive interiors using minimal furniture, often made of plywood, and the use of white.

Cleopas *n* (*Bible*) one of the two disciples who met the risen Jesus on the road to Emmaus on the first day of the week after the Crucifixion.

Cleopatra *n* (69–30 BC) Greek queen of Egypt; the last independent ruler of ancient Egypt (ruled 51–30 BC).—*see also* **Antony, Mark**.

CLEPR *abbr* = Council on Legal education for Professional Responsibility.

clerestory *n* (*pl* **clerestories**) the upper story, with windows, of the nave of a church.—*also* **clearstory**.—**clerestoried, clearstoried** *adj*.

Clerget *n* **Charles Ernest** (*b.* 1812) French designer of porcelain for the Sèvres factory and tapestry for the Gobelins factory.

clergy *n* (*pl* **clergies**) pastors of the Christian church collectively.

clergyman *n* (*pl* **clergymen**) a member of the clergy.

cleric *n* a member of the clergy.

clerical *adj* of or relating to the clergy or a clergyman; of or relating to a clerk or a clerk's work.—**clerically** *adv*.

clerical collar *n* a narrow stiff white collar buttoned at the back and worn by the clergy.—*also* **dog collar**.

clericalism *n* clerical influence, esp of an undue kind.

clerihew *n* a short nonsensical or satirical poem, usu in four lines of varying length, e.g., Sir Christopher Wren / Said, "I'm going to dine with some men. / If anyone calls, / Say I'm designing St Paul's."

clerk *n* an office worker who types, keeps files, etc; a layman with minor duties in a church; a public official who keeps the records of a court, town, etc.—**clerkdom** *n*.—**clerkship** *n*.

clerkly *adj* (**clerklier, clerkliest**) pertaining to a clerk, or to penmanship. * *adv* in a scholarly manner.

CLES *abbr* = Center for Local Economic Strategies.

Cleveland *n* **[Stephen] Grover** (1837–1908) American Democrat statesman and 22nd and 24th president of the US (1885–89, 1893–97).

clever *adj* able; intelligent; ingenious; skilful, adroit.—**cleverly** *adv*.—**cleverness** *n*.

clew *n* a ball of thread; the corner of a sail to which a sheet is attached. * *vt* to truss up (sails) to the yard of a ship.

CLIC *abbr* = Cancer and Leukaemia in Childhood Trust.

cliché *n* a hackneyed phrase; something that has become commonplace.—**cliché'd, clichéd** *adj*.

click *n* a slight, sharp sound. * *vi* to make such a sound; (*comput*) (*usu with* **on**) to press and release the mouse button; (*inf*) to establish immediate friendly relations with; to succeed; (*inf*) to become plain or evident; to fall into place.—**clicker** *n*.

client *n* a person who employs another professionally; a customer; (*comput*) a personal computer or workstation in a local area network that is used to request information from a network's file server.—**cliental** *adj*.

client document *n* (*comput*) a document that is connected to another document (primary) in another computer on a network. When the primary document is updated the client document is updated immediately.

clientele *n* clients, customers.

cliff *n* a high steep rock face.

Cliff *n* **Clarice** (1899–1972) British ceramicist and painter who produced brilliantly-colored, geometric patterns, best-known being her *Bizarre* pattern.

cliffhanger *n* the perilous situation at the climax of each episode of a serialized film or book; any dramatic or suspenseful situation.—**cliffhanging** *adj*.

climacteric *n* a critical period, a turning point, esp in the life of an individual; the male menopause. * *adj* forming a crisis (—*also* **climacterical**).

climate *n* the weather characteristics of an area; the prevailing attitude, feeling, atmosphere.—**climatic, climatical, climatal** *adj*.

climatology *n* the science of climates.—**climatologic, climatological** *adj*.—**climatologist** *n*.

climax *n* the highest point; a culmination; sexual orgasm; the highlight or most interesting part of a story, drama or music. * *vti* to reach, or bring to a climax.—**climactic, climactical** *adj*.

climb *vti* to mount with an effort; to ascend; to rise; (*plants*) to grow upwards by clinging onto walls, fences, or other plants; (*with* **down**) to descend from a higher level; to retreat from a position previously held, e.g., in a debate or argument; to yield. * *n* an ascent.

climber *n* a mountaineer or rock climber; a climbing plant; a socially ambitious person.

clime *n* (*poet*) a country, region, or tract.

CLIMEX *abbr* = Information Exchange System on Country Activities on Climate Change.

clin. *abbr* = clinical.

clinch *vt* (*argument, etc*) to confirm or drive home. * *vi* (*boxing*) to grip the opponent with the arms to hinder his punching. * *n* the act of clinching; (*inf*) an embrace.

clincher *n* a decisive point in an argument.

Cline *n* **Patsy** [**Virginia Petterson**] (1932–63) American country and western singer.

cling *vi* (**clinging, clung**) to adhere, to be attached (to); to keep hold by embracing or entwining.—**clinger** *n*.

clinging vine *n* (*sl*) a person who is unnaturally dependent on his or her spouse.

clingstone *n* a fruit, e.g. the peach, with pulp adhering to the stone.—*also adj*.

clinic *n* a place where outpatients are given medical care or advice; a place where medical specialists practice as a group; a private or specialized hospital; the teaching of medicine by treating patients in the presence of students.

clinical *adj* of or relating to a clinic; based on medical observation; plain; simple; detached, cool, objective.—**clinically** *adv*.

clink[1] *n* a slight metallic ringing sound. * *vti* to make or cause to make such a sound.

clink[2] *n* (*sl*) prison.

clinker *n* very hard-burnt brick; a mass of partly vitrified brick; slag; a fine specimen.

clinker block *see* **cinder block**.

clinker-built *adj* (*boat*) built so that the planks overlap each other like clapboard.

clinkstone *n* an igneous rock that emits a clinking sound when struck.

clinometer *n* an instrument for measuring the angles of slopes or the dip of rock strata; a kind of plumb level.—**clinometric, clinometrical** *adj*.—**clinometry** *n*.

clinquant *adj* glittering. * *n* tinsel.

Clinton *n* **Bill** [**William Jefferson Davis**] (1946–) American politician and 42nd president of the US (1992–2001).

Clio, Cleio *n* (*Greek myth*) one of the nine Muses, dedicated to history and epic poetry.

clip[1] *vt* (**clipping, clipped**) to cut or trim with scissors or shears; to punch a small hole in, esp a ticket; (*words*) to shorten or slur; (*inf*) to hit sharply. * *n* the piece clipped off; a yield of wool from sheep; an extract from a movie; (*inf*) a smart blow; speed.

clip[2] *vt* (**clipping, clipped**) to hold firmly; to secure with a clip. * *n* any device that grips, clasps or hooks; a magazine for a gun; a piece of jewelry held in place by a clip.

clip art *n* (*comput*) a collection of ready-drawn pieces of art that are available to copy and paste into any document.

clipboard *n* (*comput*) a temporary storage area containing the results of a cut and paste or copy and paste command.

clipboard *n* a writing board with a spring clip for holding paper.

clip joint *n* (*sl*) a place, such as nightclub or restaurant, that overcharges or defrauds its customers.

clipper *n* a fast sailing ship.

clippers *n* a hand tool, sometimes electric, for cutting hair; nail clippers.

clipping *n* an item cut from a publication, movie, etc, a cutting.

clique *n* a small exclusive group, a set.—**cliquey, cliquish** *adj*.

CLISG *abbr* = Commonwealth Land Information Support Group.

CLit *abbr* = Companion of Literature.

clitoridectomy *n* (*pl* **clitoridectomies**) the excision of the clitoris.

clitoris *n* a small sensitive erectile organ of the vulva.—**clitoral** *adj*.

Clive *n* 1. **Kitty** *see* **Garrick, David**. 2. **Sir Robert** [**1st Baron Clive of Plassey**] (1725–74) English general and administrator in India; governor of Bengal (1764–67).

clk. *abbr* = clerk; clock.

CLL *abbr* = chronic lymphocytic leukaemia.

CLLR *abbr* = Computing in Literary and Linguistic Research.

CLMC *abbr* (*N. Ireland*) = Combined Loyalist Military Command.

ClntMC *abbr* = Companion of the International Management Center.

CLOA *abbr* = Chief Leisure Officers Association.

cloaca *n* (*pl* **cloacae**) a sewer; the cavity receiving the alimentary canal and urinary duct in birds, reptiles, many fishes, and the lower mammals.—**cloacal** *adj*.

cloak *n* a loose sleeveless outer garment; a covering; something that conceals, a pretext. * *vt* to cover as with a cloak; to conceal.

cloak-and-dagger *adj* involving intrigue or espionage; undercover.

cloakroom *n* a room where overcoats, luggage, etc, may be left.

clobber *vt* (*sl*) to hit hard and repeatedly; to defeat; to criticize severely.

cloche *n* a bell-shaped glass or plastic cover for food or outdoor plants; a woman's bell-shaped hat.

clock[1] *n* a device for measuring time; any timing device with a dial and displayed figures; a dandelion head after flowering. * *vt* to time (a race, etc) using a stopwatch or other device; (*inf*) to register a certain speed; (*sl*) to hit; (*with* **off, out**) to stop work, esp by registering the time of one's departure on a card; (*with* **on, in**) to start work, esp by registering the time of one's arrival on a card.

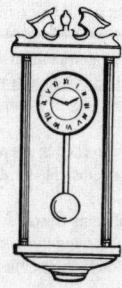

clock[2] *n* a woven or embroidered ornament on a sock or stocking.

clock radio *n* a radio with a timer that functions as an alarm clock.

clock speed *n* (*comput*) the speed of a microprocessor usu described in megahertz (one million cycles per second). The system clock emits a stream of electrical pulses or clicks that synchronize all the processor's activities.

clock-watcher *n* (*sl*) a person who constantly watches the time while working.

clockwise *adv* moving in the direction of a clock's hands.—*also adj*.

clockwork *n* the mechanism of a clock or any similar mechanism with springs and gears. * *adj* mechanically regular.

clod *n* a lump of earth or clay; a stupid person.

cloddish *adj* stupid; phlegmatic.

clodhopper *n* (*inf*) a clumsy person; (*usu pl*) a large heavy shoe.

clog *n* a wooden-soled shoe. * *vt* (**clogging, clogged**) to cause a blockage in; to impede, obstruct.

cloggy *adj* (**cloggier, cloggiest**) lumpy, clogging; adhesive, sticky.—**clogginess** *n*.

cloisonné *n* enamel decoration with the colors of the pattern set in spaces partitioned off by wires. * *adj* inlaid with partitions; decorated in outline with bands of metal.

cloister *n* a roofed pillared walk, usu with one side open, in a convent, college, etc; a religious retreat. * *vt* to confine or keep apart as if in a convent.

cloistered *adj* solitary, secluded.

cloister vault *see* **domical vault**.

cloistral *adj* pertaining to or confined in a cloister; secluded; claustral.

clone *n* a group of organisms or cells derived asexually from a single ancestor; an individual grown from a single cell of its parent and genetically identical to it; (*comput*) the original name given to computers that succeeded in replicating the features of an IBM personal computer; (*inf*) a person or thing that resembles another. * *vt* to propagate a clone from; to make a copy of.—**clonal** *adj*.

cloning *n* (*biol*) an artificial process used in the breeding of plants.

clonus *n* (*pl* **clonuses**) (*med*) a series of convulsive spasms.—**clonic** *adj*.—**clonicity** *n*.

close[1] *adj* near; reticent, secret; nearly alike; nearly even or equal; dense, compact; cut short; sultry, airless; narrow; careful; restricted. * *adv* closely; near by. * *n* a courtyard; the entrance to a courtyard; the precincts of a cathedral.—**closely** *adv*.—**closeness** *n*.

close[2] *vt* to make closed; to stop up (an opening); to draw together; to conclude; to shut; (*with* **down**) to wind up, eg a business. * *vi* to come together; to complete; to finish. * *vti* (*comput*) to command to finish working with a computer file. * *n* a completion, end.

Close *n* 1. **Chuck** (1940–) American painter and pioneer of "superrealism" as a reaction against the strong emotions of abstract expressionism. 2. **Glenn** (1947–) American movie actress whose movies include *Dangerous Liaisons* (1988).

close call *n* a close shave, a narrow escape.

close company *n* a company of which the share capital is held or controlled by five or fewer people or by people who are all directors of the company.

close corporation, closed corporation *n* a corporation in which vacancies are filled up by its members.

closed *adj* shut up; with no opening; restricted; not open to question or debate; not open to the public, exclusive.

closed book *n* something too difficult to understand; something put aside for ever.

closed-captioned *adj* (*TV broadcast*) with captions that appear only on sets equipped with special receivers.

closed circuit *n* the transmission of TV signals by cable to receivers connected in a particular circuit.

closed shop *n* a firm employing only members of a trade union.

close-fisted *adj* mean with money.

close harmony *n* (*mus*) harmony in which the notes of the chords are close together.

close-hauled *adj* with sails trimmed to keep as near to the wind as possible.

close-knit *adj* having strong social or cultural ties.

close-mouthed *adj* taciturn.

close price *n* the price of a share or commodity when the difference between the bid price and the offer price is very small.

close season, closed season *n* certain months in the year in which it is illegal to kill certain game, protected wild birds, fish, etc.

close shave, close thing *n* a close call, a narrow escape.

closet *n* a small room or a cupboard for clothes, supplies, etc; a small private room. * *vt* to enclose in a private room for a confidential talk.

close-up *n* a movie or television shot taken from very close range; a close examination.

closing balance *n* the balance, whether debit or credit, on a ledger at the end of a company's accounting period, that will be carried forward to the next accounting period.

closing prices *npl* buying and selling prices that are recorded at the close of a day's trading on the stock market or on a commodity market.

closing stock *n* the stock that remains in a company at the end of an accounting period.

clostridium *n* one of a group of bacteria that are present in the intestines of humans and animals. Some species are responsible for diseases such as botulism, tetanus, and gas gangrene.

closure *n* closing; the condition of being closed; something that closes; (*parliament, etc*) a decision to end further debate and move to an immediate vote.

clot *n* a thickened mass, esp of blood; (*sl*) an idiot.* *vti* (**clotting, clotted**) to form into clots, to curdle, coagulate.

cloth *n* (*pl* **cloths**) woven, knitted or pressed fabric from which garments, etc, are made; a piece of this; a tablecloth; clerical dress; (*with* **the**) the clergy.

cloth binding *n* a book binding of linen over cardboard.

clothe *vt* (**clothing, clothed** *or* **clad**) to cover with garments; to dress; to surround, endow (with).

clothes *npl* garments, apparel.

clotheshorse *n* a wooden or metal frame for drying linen, etc; a dressy person.

clothesline *n* a rope on which washing is hung to dry.

clothespin *n* a plastic, wooden, or metal clip for attaching washing to a line.

clothier *n* one who manufactures or sells cloth and clothes.

clothing *n* clothes.

Clotho *n* (*Greek myth*) one of the three Fates, whose duty it was to put the wool for the thread of life round the spindle.

cloud *n* a visible mass of water vapor floating in the sky; a mass of smoke, etc; a threatening thing, a gloomy look; a multitude; **on cloud nine** (*inf*) blissfully happy; **under a cloud** suspected of wrongdoing, disgraced. * *vt* to darken or obscure; to confuse; to depress.—**cloudless** *adj*.

cloudberry *n* (*pl* **cloudberries**) a species of wild dwarf raspberry.

cloudburst *n* a sudden rainstorm.

cloud chamber *n* (*physics*) a chamber filled with vapor used for detecting the tracks of high-energy particles.—*also* **Wilson cloud chamber**.

cloud-cuckoo-land *n* a realm of fantasy, imagination and impossible dreams.

cloudlet *n* a small cloud.

cloudy *adj* (**cloudier, cloudiest**) of or full of clouds; not clear; gloomy.—**cloudily** *adv*.—**cloudiness** *n*.

Clouet *n* François (*c*.1510–72) French painter, whose excellence as a portraitist can be seen in his collection of drawings in the Musée Condé at Chantillyson.

Clough *n* Arthur Hugh (1819–61) English poet, whose *Amours de Voyage* explores the uneasy intellectual attitudes of his age. "Say not the struggle nought availeth" is his most famous title, if not poem.

clout *n* a blow; (*sl*) power, influence.

clove[1] *see* **cleave**.

clove[2] *n* a segment of a bulb, as garlic.

clove[3] *n* the dried flower bud of a tropical tree, used as a spice.

clove hitch *n* a knot used to secure a rope around a spar or pole.

clove pink *n* the carnation.

cloven *adj* divided; split.—*see also* **cleave**.

cloven hoof *n* the split hoof of oxen, sheep, etc; the mark of the Devil; an evil influence.

clover *n* a low-growing plant with three leaves used as fodder; a trefoil; **in clover** (*inf*) luxury.

cloverleaf *n* connecting roads built in the shape of a clover leaf.

Clovis point *n* (*archeo*) a form of projectile point discovered at sites in North America, and dating from at least 10,000 BC.

clown *n* a person who entertains with jokes, antics, etc, esp in a carnival; a clumsy or boorish person. * *vi* to act the clown, behave comically or clumsily.—**clownish** *adj*.

cloy *vt* to sicken with too much sweetness or pleasure.—**cloyingly** *adv*.

CLP *abbr* (*Brit*) = Constituency Labour Party.

CLPA *abbr* = Common Law Procedure Acts.

CLR *abbr* = computer language recorder.

CLS *abbr* = Certificate in Library Science.

CLSB *abbr* (*Brit*) = Committee of London and Scottish Bankers.

CLSP *abbr* = Community Landcare Support Program.

CLSS *abbr* (*Eire*) = Coast Life Saving Service.

CLT *abbr* = Campaign for Local Television; Co-operative League of Thailand; computer language translator.

CLU *abbr* = Chartered Life Underwriter.

club *n* a heavy stick used as a weapon; a stick with a head for playing golf, etc; an association of people for athletic, social, or common purposes; its premises; a suit of playing cards with black clover-like markings. * *vt* (**clubbing, clubbed**) to beat with or use as a club. * *vi* to form into a club for a common purpose.

clubbable, clubable *adj* suitable for a club, sociable.

clubfoot *n* a congenital malformation of the foot.

clubhaul *vt* (*naut*) to tack by dropping the lee anchor as soon as the wind is out of the sails, bringing the ship's head to the wind.

clubhouse *n* premises used by a club.

club moss *n* the lycopodium.

club sandwich *n* a three-layered sandwich.

cluck *n* the call of a hen. * *vi* to make such a noise.

clue *n* a guide to the solution of a mystery or problem. * *vt* (**cluing, clued**) (*with* **in, up**) to provide with helpful information.

clueless *adj* (*inf*) stupid, incompetent.

clumber *n* a breed of spaniel, a field spaniel.

clump *n* a cluster of trees; a cluster of bacteria; a lump; (*of hair*) a handful; the sound of heavy footsteps.

clumsy *adj* (**clumsier, clumsiest**) unwieldy; awkward; lacking tact, skill or grace.—**clumsily** *adv*.—**clumsiness** *n*.

clung *see* **cling**.

clunk *n* a dull metallic sound. * *vi* to make this sound.

clupeid *n* one of the genus of fishes to which the herring belongs.—*also adj*.

cluster *n* a bunch, esp of things growing or tied together; a swarm; a group. * *vti* to form or arrange in a cluster.—**clustery** *adj*.

cluster analysis *n* (*archeo*) a statistical technique in which groups of objects at different sites are analyzed according to similarity.

cluster bomb *n* a bomb containing small fragmentation bombs that are dispersed on impact.

clutch[1] *vt* to seize, to grasp tightly; to snatch at. * *n* a tight grip; a device for throwing parts of a machine into or out of action; the pedal operating this device; (*pl*) power.

clutch[2] *n* a nest of eggs; a brood of chicks.

clutter *n* a disordered mess; confusion. * *vti* to litter; to put into disorder.

Clydesdale *n* a heavy breed of carthorse.

clypeal, clypeate *adj* shield-shaped.

clypeus *n* (*pl* **clypei**) a shield-like part of an insect's head.

clyster *n* a liquid injected into the lower intestines by a syringe, an enema.

Clytemnestra *n* (*Greek myth*) the wife of Agamemnon. During the absence of her husband in the Trojan War, she became the mistress of Aegisthus and with him murdered Agamemnon on his return from Troy.

Cm *symbol* (*chem*) curium (element).

cm *abbr* = centimeter; centimeters.

c.m. *abbr* = (*Latin*) *causa mortis*, "by reason of death"; church missionary; corresponding member; courtmartial; (*pharm*) (*Latin*) *cras mane*, "tomorrow morning."

CM *abbr* = Certificated Master; Certificated Mistress; (*Latin*) *Chirurgiae Magister*, "Master of Surgery"; common meter; Corresponding Member.

CMA Cable Makers' Association; Carrot Marketing Association; Case Makers' Association; Castor Manufacturers' Association; (*Brit*) Catering Managers Association of Great Britain; Center for Management Agriculture; Certificate in Management Accountancy; Chinese Medical Association; Church Music Association; Communication Managers Association; Country Music Association.

CMAC *abbr* = Catholic Marriage Advisory Council.

CMB *abbr* = Christian Mission to Buddhists.

CMBHI *abbr* (*Brit*) = Craft Member of the British Horological Institute.

CMC *abbr* = Catholic Media Council; Congregation of Mother of Carmel; Culture Ministers Council; Curriculum Ministers Council.

CMD *abbr* = common meter double.

CMDA *abbr* (*Brit*) = Cornish Mining Development Association.

CMDC *abbr* = Central Milk Distributive Committee.

cmdg. *abbr* = commanding.

CMF *abbr* = Cast Metal Federation; Coal Merchants' Federation.

CMG *abbr* = Companion of the Order of St Michael and St George.

CMHERA *abbr* = Community and Mental Handicap Educational and Research Association.

CMHS *abbr* = Center for Mental Health Services

CMI *abbr* = Canadian Mediterranean Institute; Carmelites of Mary Immaculate; computer-managed instruction; Cordage Manufacturers' Institute.

CMIBCM *abbr* (*Brit*) = Commercial Membership of the Institution of British Carriage and Automobile Manufacturers.

CMIM *abbr* = Center for Measurement & Information Medicine.

CMIWHTE *abbr* = Companion Member of the Institution of Works and Highways Technician Engineers.

CMIWSc *abbr* = Member of the Institute of Wood Science.

cml. *abbr* = commercial.

CML *abbr* = Central Music Library; chronic myeloid leukaemia; computer-managed learning; Council of Mortgage Lenders.

CMO *abbr* = Chief Medical Officer.

CMOS *abbr* (*comput*) = complementary metal oxide semiconductor.

CMP *abbr* = Center for Multiprocessors; Christian Movement for Peace; (*Brit*) Commissioner of the Metropolitan Police.

CMPA *abbr* = Chinchilla Pelt Marketing Association.

CmpnlAP *abbr* = Companion of the Institution of Analysts and Programmers.

CMR *abbr* = Center for Materials Research; cerebral metabolic rate.

CMRC *abbr* = Colonial Medical Research Committee.

CMRS *abbr* = Conference of Major Religious Superiors.

CMRSHR *abbr* = Chinese Medical Research Society of Health Recovery.

c.m.s. *abbr* (*pharm*) (*Latin*) = *cras mane sumendus*, "to be taken tomorrow morning."

CMS *abbr* = Catholic Missionary Society; Center for Mediterranean Studies; Certificate in Management Studies; Church Missionary Society; Church Monuments Society; Clay Minerals Society; (*Latin*) (*pharm*) *cras mane sumendus*, "to be taken tomorrow morning"; Cricket Memorabilia Society;

CMT *abbr* = Common Market Travel Association.

CMU *abbr* (*Eire*) = Communication Managers Union.

CMV *abbr* = cytomegalovirus.

CMW *abbr* (*Brit*) = Council of Museums in Wales.

c.n. *abbr* (*pharm*) (*Latin*) = *cras nocte*, "tomorrow night".

CN *abbr* (*French*) = Code Napoléon.

C/N *abbr* = carbon/nitrogen; (*bank*) circular note; (*com*) credit note.

CNAA *abbr* = Council for National Academic Awards.

CNAR *abbr* = compound net annual rate.

CNAUK *abbr* (*Brit*) = Chemical Notation Association UK.

CNC *abbr* (*N. Ireland*) = Committee for Nature Conservancy; computer numeric control.

CNCC *abbr* = Council for Nature Conservation and the Countryside; Czech National Committee for Chemistry.

CND *abbr* = Campaign for Nuclear Disarmament.

CNDA *abbr* = Cherished Numbers Dealers Association.

CNF *abbr* = Commonwealth Nurses' Federation.

CNG *abbr* = compressed natural gas.

CNHC *abbr* = Churches National Housing Coalition.

CNHS *abbr* = Cherokee National Historical Society.

CNIDR *abbr* = Center for Networked Information

CNIPA *abbr* = Committee of National Institutes of Patent Agents.

CNN *abbr* = Cable News Network; Certified Nursery Nurse.

CNO *abbr* = Chief of Naval Operations; Council of National Organisations.

CNOOC *abbr* = China National Offshore Oil Corporation.

CNP *abbr* = (*Brit*) Cornish National Party; Council for National Parks; Croatian National Party.

CNPP *abbr* = Center for Nutrition Policy and Promotion

CNR *abbr* = Canadian National Railways.

c.n.s. *abbr* (*pharm*) (*Latin*) = *cras nocte sumendus*, "to be taken tomorrow night."

CNS *abbr* = Center for Neuroscience; central nervous system; Chief of Naval Staff; Chinese Nutrition Society; Cognitive Neuroscience Society; (*pharm*) (*Latin*) *cras nocte sumendus*, "to be taken tomorrow night."

CNSA *abbr* (*Gaelic*) = *Combhairle Nan Sgoiltean Araich*, Pre-School Council.

CNSF *abbr* = Cornell National Supercomputer Facility.

CNSLD *abbr* = chronic non-specific lung disease.

CNT *abbr* = Commission for the New Towns.

CNTMA *abbr* = Chinese National Traditional Medical Association.

Co *symbol* (*chem*) cobalt (element).

co. *abbr* = colon.

c.o. *abbr* (*French*) = *compte ouvert*, "open account."

c/o *abbr* = care of; (*book-keeping*) carried over.

Co. *or* **co.** *abbr* = Company; County.

CO *abbr* = Colorado; Commanding Officer; Commissioner for Oaths; Commonwealth Office; Criminal Office; Crown Office; conscientious objector.

C/O *abbr* (*banking*) = cash order.

co- *prefix* together with, jointly.

COA *abbr* = Cathedral Organists' Association; China Orchid Association.

coach *n* a long-distance bus; a train carriage; a large, covered four-wheeled horse-drawn carriage; a sports instructor; a tutor in a specialized subject. * *vti* to teach or train.

coach dog *n* a Dalmatian dog.

coachman *n* (*pl* **coachmen**) the driver of a horse carriage.

coachwood *n* a close-grained Australian wood.

coaction *n* compulsion; an acting together.—**coactive** *adj*.—**coactivity** *n*.

coad. *abbr* = coadjutor.

Coade stone *n* (*archit*) a type of artificial stone fired in a kiln and used for ornament and sculpture.

coadjutor *n* a helper; an assistant to a bishop.—**coadjutrix** *nf*.

coadunate *adj* (*bot*) united, growing together.—**coadunation** *n*.—**coadunative** *adj*.

coagulant *n* a substance that causes coagulation.

coagulate *vti* to change from a liquid to partially solid state, to clot, curdle.—**coagulation** *n*.—**coagulative** *adj*.—**coagulator** *n*.

coagulation factors *n* substances present in plasma that are involved in the process of blood coagulation.

coagulum *n* (*pl* **coagula**) a clot (of blood); a curdled mass.

coal *n* a black mineral used for fuel; a piece of this; an ember.

coalesce *vi* to come together and form one, to merge.—**coalescence** *n*.—**coalescent** *adj*.

coalfield *n* a region yielding coal.

coalfish *n* (*pl* **coalfish**, **coalfishes**) the pollock.

coal gas *n* gas obtained from coal and formerly used for lighting and heating.

coalition *n* a temporary union of parties or states.—**coalitional** *adj*.—**coalitionist**, **coalitioner** *n*.

Coal Measure *n* that part of the Carboniferous series in which coal is found.

coal oil *n* petroleum; kerosene.

coal tar *n* a thick opaque liquid distilled from bituminous coal and from which many rich dye colors are obtained.

coaming *n* the raised wood or iron border round the outside of a ship's hatch.

co-anchor *n* a person who anchors a news broadcast with another.—*also vt*.

coaptation *n* the adjustment or adaptation of parts to one another.

coarctation *n* a narrowing, esp of the aorta.

coarse *adj* rough; large in texture; rude, crude; inferior.—**coarsely** *adv*.—**coarseness** *n*.

coarse fish *n* those freshwater fish that are neither salmon or trout.

coarse-grained *adj* having a coarse grain; ill-tempered; gross.

coarsen *vti* to make or become coarse.

coast *n* an area of land bordering the sea; the seashore. * *vi* to sail along a coast; to travel down a slope without power; to proceed with ease.—**coastal** *adj*.

coaster *n* a ship engaged in coastal trade; a tray for a decanter; a small mat for drinks; a roller coaster.

coastguard *n* an organization which monitors the coastline and provides help for ships in difficulties, prevents smuggling, etc.

coastline *n* the outline of the shore.

coat *n* a sleeved outer garment; the natural covering of an animal; a layer. * *vt* to cover with a layer or coating.

coat hanger *n* a piece of wood, wire, or plastic curved to fit the shoulders for hanging a garment from a hook.

coat of arms *n* the heraldic bearings of a family, city, institution, etc.

coat of mail *n* chain mail.

Coates *n* 1. **Eric** (1886-1957) an English composer and viola player whose orchestral works, e.g., *Countryside*, *The Three Bears* and the *London Suite*, are light but well crafted. He wrote more than 100 songs and marches, such as *The Knightsbridge March* and the march for the movie *The Dam Busters* (1955). 2. **Wells** (*b.* 1895) English architect, whose notable works include Palace Gate flats, London.

coati, coatimundi *n* a raccoon-like South American animal.

coating *n* a surface coat or layer; material for coats.

co-author *n* a joint author.

coax *vt* to persuade gently; to obtain by coaxing; to make something work by patient effort.—**coaxer** *n*.—**coaxingly** *adv*.

coaxial *adj* having a common axis.

coaxial cable *n* a transmission cable having a double conductor separated by insulating material, as for a television.

cob[1] *n* a sturdy riding horse; a corn cob; a round lump of coal; a male swan.

cob[2] *n* a composition of clay and straw used for building.

cobalamin *see* **hydroxocobalamin**.

cobalt *n* a metallic element; a deep blue pigment made from it.

cobalt-60 *n* a radioisotope used in radiotherapy.

cobalt-blue *n* a greenish-blue pigment derived from cobalt.

cobalt bomb *n* a radioisotope (cobalt-60) used in radiotherapy; a nuclear weapon made from a hydrogen bomb encased in cobalt.

Cobán *n* a city in Guatemala.

COBBA *abbr* = Council of Brass Bands Association.

cobber *n* (*Austral*) (*sl*) a chum, a pal.

Cobbett *n* **William** (1763–1835) English essayist and political reformer whose best-known work is *Rural Rides*.

cobble[1] *n* a cobblestone, a rounded stone used for paving. * *vt* to pave with cobblestones.

cobble[2] *vt* to repair, to make (shoes); to put together roughly or hastily.

cobbler[1] *n* a person who mends shoes; a clumsy workman.

cobbler[2] *n* an iced drink of wine or spirits, fruit and sugar; fruit covered with a rich crust as a pudding.

COBCOE *abbr* (*Brit*) = Council of British Chambers of Commerce in Continental Europe.

Cobden-Sanderson *n* **Thomas James** (1840–1922) British bookbinder and printer, credited with coining the name of the Arts and Crafts Movement.

cobelligerent *n* a power cooperating with another in carrying on a war.

COBI *abbr* = Council on Biological Information.

cobnut *n* a large hazelnut.

Cobol *n* (*comput*) a high-level programing language for general business use (Common Business Orientated Language).

cobra *n* a venomous hooded snake of Africa and India.

Cobthach Coel *n* (*Irish Celtic myth*) drove Labhraidh Loingsech into exile and was the cause of him losing his voice.

cobweb *n* a spider's web; a flimsy thing; an entanglement.—**cobwebbed** *adj*.—**cobwebby** *adj*.

coca *n* either of two South American shrubs; their leaves, chewed as a stimulant.

Coca-Cola *n* (*trademark*) a brown-colored carbonated soft drink flavored with coca leaves, etc.

cocaine, cocain *n* an intoxicating addictive drug obtained from coca leaves, used in anesthesia.

cocainism *n* a morbid state resulting from excess of cocaine.

cocainize *vt* to subject to, or render insensible by, cocaine; to treat with cocaine.—**cocainization** *n*.

COCAST *abbr* = Council for Overseas Colleges of Arts Science and Technology.

cocci *see* **coccus**.

coccidiosis *n* a disease of animals resulting from a parasitic infection of the intestines.

coccus *n* (*pl* **cocci**) a spherical bacterium; one of the separable carpels of a dry fruit.—**coccal, coccoid** *adj*.

coccyx *n* (*pl* **coccyges**) a small triangular bone at the base of the spine.—**coccygeal** *adj*.

COCF *abbr* = Council for Our Common Future.

coch., cochl. *abbr* (*pharm*) (*Latin*) = *cochleare*, "spoonful."

Cochabamba *n* a city in Bolivia.

cochineal *n* a scarlet dye obtained from dried insects.

Cochise *n* an offshoot of the desert culture in southeast Arizona and southwest New Mexico dating from before 7000 BC.

cochlea *n* (*pl* **cochleae**) the spiral-shaped cavity of the inner ear.

cochleate, cochleated *adj* shell-shaped, screw-like.

cock[1] *n* the adult male of the domestic fowl; the male of other birds; a faucet or valve; the hammer of a gun; a cocked position; (*vulg*) the penis. * *vt* to set erect, to stick up; to set at an angle; to bring the hammer (of a gun) to firing position; (*with* **up**) to make a complete mess of.—**cockup** *n*.

cock[2] *n* a small pile of hay.

cockade *n* a rosette worn on the hat as a badge.

cock-a-hoop *adj* elated, exultant.

Cockaigne *n* an imaginary land of plenty (—*also* **Cockayne**); (*mus*) a concert overture by Elgar subtitled "In London Town."

cock-a-leekie *n* soup made of chicken boiled with leeks, etc.

cockalorum *n* a young cock; a perky or self-important person.

cock-and-bull story *n* an incredible story.

cockatoo *n* (*pl* **cockatoos**) a large crested parrot.

cockatrice *n* a fabulous serpent possessing the power of killing by a glance of its eye, a basilisk.

Cockayne *see* **Cockaigne**.

cockchafer *n* a large winged beetle.

Cockcroft *n* **Sir John Douglas** (1897–1967) English nuclear physicist. With Sir Ernest [Thomas Sinton] Walton (1903–95), he produced the first laboratory splitting of an atomic nucleus and won the 1951 Nobel prize for physics.

cockcrow *n* the time of dawn, early morning.

cocked hat *n* a hat with turned-up brims pointed in front and behind; **to knock into a cocked hat** to beat easily.

cockerel *n* a young cock, rooster.

Cockerell *n* 1. **Charles R** (1788–1863) English architect, whose notable works include Cambridge University Library. 2. **Sir Christopher Sydney** (1910–99) English engineer and inventor of the hovercraft. 3. **Samuel P** (1754–1827) English architect, whose notable works include Sezincote House.

cocker spaniel *n* a small breed of spaniel.

cockeyed *adj* (*inf*) having a squint; slanting; daft, absurd.

cockfight *n* an organized fight between gamecocks.

cockhorse *n* a rocking horse.

cockle[1] *n* an edible shellfish with a rounded shell.

cockle[2] *vti* to curl up, to pucker. * *n* a wrinkle, a bulge.

cockle[3] *n* a purple-flowered weed, the plant corncockle or darnel.

cockleshell *n* the shell of a cockle; a frail boat.

cockloft *n* a small upper loft; a garret.

cockney *n* (*pl* **cockneys**) a person born in the East End of London; the dialect of this area.

cock of the walk *n* an arrogant or domineering person.

cockpit *n* the compartment of a small aircraft for the pilot and crew, the flight deck; an arena for cock fighting; the driver's seat in a racing car.

cockroach *n* a nocturnal beetle-like insect.

cockscomb *n* a cock's crest; a jester's cap resembling a cock's comb; a decorative plant with red or yellow flowers; a vain young fop.—*also* **coxcomb**.

cockshy *n* (*pl* **cockshies**) a thing set up to be thrown at; a throw at a cockshy.

cocksure *adj* quite certain; over-confident.

cocktail *n* an alcoholic drink containing a mixture of spirits or other liqueurs; an appetizer, usu containing shellfish, served as the first course of a meal.

cocktail party *n* a party, usu in the early evening, at which cocktails are served.

cocky *adj* (**cockier, cockiest**) cheeky; conceited; arrogant.—**cockily** *adv*.—**cockiness** *n*.

coco *n* (*pl* **cocos**) the coconut palm.

cocoa *n* a powder of ground cacao seeds; a drink made from this.

cocoa bean *n* the seed of the cacao plant.

cocoa butter *n* a waxy substance derived from cocoa beans and used in perfumery, confectionery, etc.

coconut *n* the fruit of the coconut palm.

coconut matting *n* rough matting made from the fibrous outer husks of coconuts.

coconut palm *n* a tall palm tree that is grown widely in the tropics for its fruit, the coconut.

coconut shy *n* a fairground stall where coconuts are set up as targets.

cocoon *n* a silky case spun by some insect larvae for protection in the chrysalis stage; a cozy covering. * *vt* to wrap in or as in a cocoon; to protect oneself by cutting oneself off from one's surroundings.

COCOS *abbr* = Co-ordinating Committee for Manufacturers of Static Converters in the Common Market Countries.

cocotte[1] *n* a small fireproof dish for cooking and individual serving of food.

cocotte[2] *n* a promiscuous woman.

COCRIL *abbr* = Council of City Research and Information Libraries.

COCSU *abbr* = Council of Civil Service Unions.

Cocteau *n* **Jean** (1889–1963) French movie director, novelist, dramatist, poet, and critic whose movies include *Orphee* and *La belle et la bête*.

Cocytus *n* a river of ancient Greece, in Greek mythology supposed to be connected with the underworld.

cod *n* (*pl* **cod, cods**) a large edible fish of the North Atlantic.

cod. *abbr* = codex, codicil.

COD *or* **c.o.d.** *abbr* = cash on delivery; collect on delivery.

Cod. Civ. *abbr* = Code Civil.

coda *n* (*mus*) a passage at the end of a composition or section to give a greater sense of finality; a supplementary section at the end of a novel.

CODA *abbr* = Community Data.

Codasyl *abbr* = Conference on Data Systems Languages.

codd. *abbr* = codices.

coddle *vt* to treat as an invalid, to pamper; to cook (eggs) in lightly boiling water.—**coddler** *n*.

code *n* a system of letters, numbers or symbols used to transmit secret messages, or to simplify communication; a systematic body of laws; a set of rules or conventions; (*comput*) a set of program instructions. * *vt* to put into code.

Code N. *abbr* (*French*) = Code Napoléon.

codeine *n* an analgesic substance.

code of conduct *or* **code of practice** *n* a set of guidelines indicating what is regarded as acceptable behavior and ethical standards relating to a particular profession or organization.

codetta *n* (*mus*) (*Italian*) a "little tail," i.e., a shorter version of a coda.

codeword, codename *n* a word used in planning and when referring to a secret operation.

codex *n* (*pl* **codices**) a volume of ancient manuscripts.

codger *n* (*sl*) a buffer, an old man.

codicil *n* an addition to a will modifying, adjusting, or supplementing its contents.—**codicillary** *adj*.

codify *vt* (**codifying, codified**) to collect or arrange (laws, rules, regulations, etc) into a system.—**codifier** *n*.—**codification** *n*.

CODIR *abbr* = Campaign for the Defense of Iranian People's Rights.

codlin *n* a kind of stewing apple.

codling *n* a young cod.

cod-liver oil *n* oil derived from the livers of cod and related fish which is rich in vitamins A and D.

Codman Jr. *n* **Ogden** (1863–1951) American interior designer and architect who wrote the influential book *The Decoration of Houses* (1897) with novelist, Edith Wharton.

CODOT *abbr* = Classification of Occupations and Directory of Occupational Titles.

codpiece *n* a baggy appendage once worn in front of men's breeches.

Codrus *n* (*Greek myth*) the last king of Athens.

codswallop *n* (*sl*) nonsense.

Codussi *n* **Mauro** (*b.* 1440) Italian architect, whose notable works include numerous palaces.

Cody *n* **William F[rederick]** (1846–1917) American showman who toured under the name of "Buffalo Bill" with his Wild West Show.

COE *abbr* = Chamber Orchestra of Europe.

co-ed *adj* (*inf*) coeducational. * *n* (*inf*) a girl attending a coeducational school or college.

COED *abbr* = computer-operated electronic display.

coeducation *n* the teaching of students of both sexes in the same institution.—**coeducational** *adj*.—**coeducationally** *adv*.

coeff. *abbr* = coefficient.

coefficient *n* (*math*) a numerical or constant factor in an algebraic term.

Coel *n* (Old Coel the Splendid) (*fl.*420) British tribal king. The "Old King Cole" of nursery-rhyme fame was overlord of several British tribes and ruled much of lowland Scotland.

coelacanth *n* a type of primitive fish that is extinct except for one species.

coelenterate *n* any of a group of aquatic creatures with a bulbous or tube-shaped body and a mouth surrounded by tentacles, such as sea anemones, jellyfish and corals.—*also adj*.

coeliac *see* **celiac**.

coelostat *n* a flat mirror on a mechanically driven mounting which is arranged to direct the light from any selected area of sky constantly onto some observing instrument.

coenobite *see* **cenobite**.

Coenred *n* king of Mercia, Britain (704–709). The eldest son of Wulfhere.

Coenwulf *n* king of Mercia, Britain (796–821). A descendant of Penda's youngest brother.

coequal *adj* having complete equality.—**coequality** *n*.—**coequally** *adv*.

coerce *vt* to compel; to force by threats.—**coercible** *adj*.—**coercion** *n*.

coercion *n* the act of coercing; forcible compulsion; government by force.—**coercionary** *adj*.—**coercionist** *n*.

coercive *adj* having the power to force; compelling.—**coerciveness** *n*.

coessential *adj* of the same substance.—**coessentiality, coessentialness** *n*.

coeternal *adj* equally eternal.—**coeternally** *adv*.

coeval *adj* contemporaneous. * *n* a person of the same age, a contemporary.—**coevality** *n*.—**coevally** *adv*.

coexist *vi* to exist together at the same time; to live in peace together.—**coexistence** *n*.—**coexistent** *adj*.

coextensive *adj* extending over the same space or time; equally extensive.

COF *abbr* = Community Organising Foundation.

C of A *abbr* = Certificate of Airworthiness.

COFA *abbr* = Commonwealth and Overseas Families Association.

C of C *abbr* = Chamber of Commerce.

C of E *abbr* = Church of England; Council of Europe.

coffee *n* a drink made from the seeds of the coffee tree; the seeds, or the shrub; a light-brown color.

coffee bean *n* the seed of the coffee plant.

coffee house, coffee bar, coffee shop *n* a refreshment house where coffee is served.

coffee mill *n* a machine for grinding coffee beans.

coffeepot *n* a pot for making coffee in.

coffee table *n* a low table for holding drinks, books, etc.

coffee table book *n* a large book for display, not reading.

coffer *n* a strong chest for holding money or valuables.

COFFER *abbr* = Coalition for Fair Electricity Regulation.

cofferdam *n* a watertight structure enclosing a submerged area which can be pumped dry to allow construction or essential repair work.

coffering *n* (*archit*) a type of ceiling decoration consisting of geometric sunken panels.

coffin *n* a casket for a dead body to be buried or cremated in.

coffin bone *n* a bone inside a horse's hoof.

coffin texts *npl* (*Egypt*) funerary inscriptions made on sarcophagi to ensure that the spirit of the deceased passed successfully through to the afterworld.

coffle *n* a gang of slaves, animals, etc, chained together.

C of GH *abbr* = Cape of Good Hope.

C of I *abbr* = Church of Ireland.

COFO *abbr* = Committee on Forestry.

C of S *abbr* = Chief of Staff; Church of Scotland.

cog[1] *n* a tooth-like projection on the rim of a wheel.

cog[2] *vti* (**cogging, cogged**) to load dice in order to cheat. * *n* a trick.

cog. *abbr* = cognate.

COG *abbr* = Consultant Orthodontists' Group.

COGB *abbr* = Certified Official Government Business.

COGDEM *abbr* = Council of Gas Detection Equipment Manufacturers.

COGENE *abbr* = Committee on Genetic Experimentation.

cogent *adj* persuasive, convincing.—**cogently** *adv*.—**cogency** *n*.

COGEODATA *abbr* = Committee on Storage, Automatic Processing, and Retrieval of Geological Data.

Cogidummus *n* (*fl.*75) king of the Regni tribe, Britain. A client king of the Romans.

cogitate *vi* to think deeply, to ponder.—**cogitation** *n*.—**cogitator** *n*.

COGMA *abbr* = Concrete Garage Manufacturers' Association.

cognac *n* a superior grape brandy distilled in France.

cognate *adj* having a common source or origin; kindred, related.—**cognation** *n*.

cognition *n* the mental act of perceiving; knowledge.—**cognitive** *adj*.

cognizable *adj* knowable; (*law*) within the cognizance of a court.

cognizance *n* judicial knowledge or notice; extent of knowledge; awareness, perception; (*her*) a distinctive crest or badge.

cognizant *adj* aware, informed (of).

cognize *vt* to have cognition of.

cognomen *n* (*pl* cognomens, cognomina) a last name; a nickname.

cognoscente *n* (*pl* cognoscenti) (*usu pl*) a connoisseur.

cogwheel *n* a wheel with a toothed rim for gearing.

cohabit *vi* to live together as husband or wife.—**cohabitant, cohabiter** *n*.—**cohabitation** *n*.

cohere *vi* to stick together; to remain united; to be consistent.

coherent *adj* cohering; capable of intelligible speech; consistent.—**coherently** *adv*.—**coherence** *n*.

cohesion *n* the act of cohering or sticking together; the force that causes this; interdependence; (*biol*) the attraction between molecules in a liquid that allows thin films and drops to form.—**cohesive** *adj*.

cohort *n* a tenth part of a Roman legion; any group of persons banded together; a follower, a comrade.

coho salmon *n* a salmon native to the Pacific Northwest.

COHSE *abbr* (*Brit*) = Confederation of Health Service Employees.

COI *abbr* = Central Office of Information.

COID *abbr* = Council of Industrial Design; Council on International Development.

COIE *abbr* = Committee on Invisible Exports.

coif *n* a close-fitting cap.

COIF *abbr* = Control of Intensive Farming.

coiffeur *n* a hairdresser.—**coiffeuse** *nf*.

coiffure *n* a hairstyle.

coil[1] *vti* to wind in rings or folds; to twist into a circular or spiral shape. * *n* a coiled length of rope; a single ring of this; (*elect*) a spiral wire for the passage of current; an intrauterine contraceptive device.—**coiler** *n*.

coil[2] *n* (*arch*) tumult, disturbance.

Coimbra *n* a city in Portugal.

coin *n* a piece of legally stamped metal used as money. * *vt* to invent (a word, phrase); to make into money, to mint; to make a lot of money quickly.

coinage *n* the act of coining; the issue of coins, currency; a coined word.

coincide *vi* to occupy the same portion of space; to happen at the same time; to agree exactly, to correspond.

coincidence *n* the act of coinciding; the occurrence of an event at the same time as another without apparent connection.

coincident *adj* coinciding.

coincidental *adj* happening by coincidence.—**coincidentally** *adv*.

coin-op *n* a self-service laundromat, etc, where the machines are operated by coins.

Cointreau (*trademark*) *n* a clear liqueur with orange flavoring.

coir *n* the prepared fiber of the husks of coconuts.

coitus, coition *n* sexual intercourse.—**coital** *adj*.

coitus interruptus *n* the interruption of coitus by withdrawal of the penis before ejaculation.

coke[1] *n* coal from which gas has been expelled. * *vt* to convert (coal) into coke.

coke[2] *n* (*sl*) cocaine.

Coke *n* (*trademark*) short for Coca-Cola.

col *n* a pass between mountain peaks; an atmospheric depression between two anticyclones.

col, coll', colla, colle (*Italian*) "with the," as in *col basso* meaning "with bass," *colle voce*, "with voice."

col. *abbr* = (*pharm*) (*Latin*) *cola*, "strain"; (*pharm*) coliander; collect; collected; collections; collector; college; collegiate; colonel; colony; color; colored; column.

Col. *abbr* = Colonel; Colorado; Colossians; Columbia.

COL *abbr* = computer-orientated language, cost of living.

col- *prefix* the form of *com-* before *l*.

cola[1] *see* **colon**[1].

cola[2] *n* a carbonated drink flavored with extracts from the kola nut and coca leaves.—*also* **kola**.

COLA *abbr* = Camping and Outdoor Leisure Association.

colander *n* a bowl with holes in the bottom for straining cooked vegetables, pasta, etc.

Colani *n* **Luigi** (1928–) German designer of speedboats, fashion, furniture, and ceramics, best-known for his teapot for Rosenthal.

cola nut *see* **kola nut**.

colcannon *n* an Irish dish of boiled cabbage and potatoes mashed together and seasoned with salt, pepper, etc.

colchicum *n* meadow saffron; a narcotic made from its seeds.

Colchis *n* the ancient name of a region at the eastern extremity of the Black Sea, famous in Greek mythology as the destination of the Argonauts, and the native country of Medea.

colcothar *n* red peroxide of iron used as a pigment.

cold *adj* lacking heat or warmth; lacking emotion, passion or courage; unfriendly; dead; (*scent*) faint; (*sl*) unconscious. * *adv* (*inf*) without prior knowledge or preparation; completely. * *n* absence of heat; the sensation caused by this; cold weather; a virus infection of the respiratory tract (—*also* **common cold**).—**coldish** *adj*.—**coldly** *adv*.—**coldness** *n*.

COLD *abbr* = chronic obstructive lung disease.

cold-blooded *adj* having a body temperature that varies with the surrounding air or water, as reptiles and fish; without feeling; callous; ruthless; in cold blood.—**cold-bloodedness** *n*.

cold boot *see* **bootstrapping**.

cold calling *n* a method of selling by which approaches are made by representatives, often by means of door-to-door calls, to people who have not previously shown any interest in the product or service.

cold chisel *n* a tempered chisel for cutting cold iron.

cold comfort *n* that which gives little cheer or consolation.

cold cream *n* a creamy preparation for cleansing and softening the skin.

cold desert[1] *n* polar regions where plant life is hindered by low temperatures and lack of free moisture.

cold desert[2] *n* the enclosed basins of central Asia where mean temperature is less than 42°F (6°C) for at least one month and there is little rainfall.

cold feet *n* (*inf*) fear.

cold frame *n* an unheated plant frame with a glass top for protecting seedlings, etc.

cold front *n* (*meteorol*) the forward edge of a cold air mass approaching a warmer mass.

cold-hearted *adj* unfeeling; stern.—**cold-heartedly** *adv*.—**cold-heartedness** *n*.

cold link *see* **link**.

cold-shoulder *vt* (*inf*) to treat with indifference or hostility.—**cold shoulder** *n*.

cold sore *n* one or more blisters appearing near the mouth, caused by the virus herpes simplex.

cold storage *n* storage in refrigerated areas; (*with* **in**) (*inf*) abeyance, being set aside for future use.

cold sweat *n* a cooling and moistening of the skin usu associated with fear or shock.

cold turkey *n* (*sl*) sudden withdrawal of narcotic drugs from an addict as a cure; the symptoms (e.g., nausea, vomiting, cramps) resulting from this withdrawal.

cold war *n* enmity between two nations characterized by military tension and political hostility.

cold water desert *n* an arid but often foggy desert where the climate is affected by a cold ocean current, e.g. western California.

cole *n* cabbage plants in general.

Cole *n* 1. **Eric Kirkham** (1901–65) British electronics industrialist who founded Ecko Radio, the earliest in wooden casings copying conventional furniture. 2. **Sir Henry** (1808–82) publisher of the first Christmas card, and founder of what later became the Victoria and Albert Museum in London. 3. **Nat "King" [Nathaniel Adams]** (1919–65) American singer and pianist whose songs include "Unforgettable." 4. **Thomas** (1801–48) English-born American painter; a pioneer of American landscape painting.

colectomy *n* (*pl* **colectomies**) surgical removal of all or part of the colon.

Colefax *n* **Sybil** (*c*.1875–1950) British designer who established salons at Onslow Square and Argyll House, London.

coleopteran *n* (*pl* **coleopterans, coleoptera**) any of the beetles, an order of insects having the outer pair of wings formed into hard sheaths for the inner pair.—**coleopterous** *adj*.

Coleridge *n* **Samuel Taylor** (1772–1834) English poet and critic, who with Wordsworth published *Lyrical Ballads* in 1798. Coleridge's main contribution to the book was "The Rime of the Ancient Mariner."

Coleridge-Taylor *n* **Samuel** (1875-1912) English composer, whose mother was English and father was from Sierra Leone. He wrote famous settings for poems by Henry Longfellow (1807–82), e.g., *Hiawatha's Wedding Feast* and *The Death of Minnehaha*, and also composed orchestral, stage and chamber music.

coleslaw *n* raw shredded cabbage, carrots, onions in a dressing, used as a salad.

Colette *n* **[Sidonie Gabrielle]** (1873–1954) French novelist whose works include *Chéri* and *Gigi*.

coleus *n* (*pl* **coleuses**) a plant cultivated for its variegated foliage.

colic *n* acute spasmodic pain in the abdomen.—**colicky** *adj*.

coliform bacteria *npl* a group of bacteria found in human and animal intestines, some of which cause disease.

COLING *abbr* = International Conference on Computational Linguistics.

coliseum *n* a large building, such as a stadium, used for sports events and other public entertainments; (*with cap*) the Colosseum.

colitis *n* inflammation of the colon.—**colitic** *adj*.

coll. *abbr* = colleague; collect; collection; collections; collective; collector; college; collegiate; colloquial; colloquially.

collab. *abbr* (*music*) = collaboration; collaborator.

collaborate *vi* to work jointly or together, esp on a literary project; to side with the invaders of one's country.—**collaboration** *n*.—**collaborator** *n*.—**collaborative** *adj*.

collage *n* a piece of art created by sticking pieces of paper, fabric, wood, etc, on to a flat surface.

collagen *n* a protein present in connective tissue and bones which yields gelatin when boiled.

collapse *vi* to fall down; to come to ruin, to fail; to break down physically or mentally. * *n* the act of collapsing; a breakdown, prostration.

collapsible, collapsable *adj* designed to fold compactly.—**collapsibility** *n*.

collar *n* the band of a garment round the neck; a decoration round the neck, a choker; a band of leather or chain put round an animal's neck. * *vt* to put a collar on; (*inf*) to seize; to arrest.

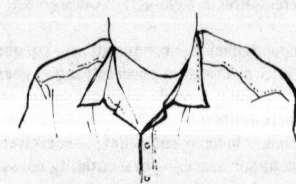

collarbone *n* one of the two bones that connect the shoulder blades with the breast bone, the clavicle.

collard *n* a variety of kale with edible leaves.

collat. *abbr* = collateral; collaterally.

collate *vt* to examine and compare (manuscripts, etc); to put (pages) together in sequence; (*bishop*) to appoint to a benefice.—**collation** *n*.—**collator** *n*.

collateral *n* security pledged for the repayment of a loan. * *adj* side by side; accompanying but secondary; descended from the same ancestor but not directly.—**collaterally** *adv*.

collation *n* the act of collating, a comparison; a light meal; the presentation to a benefice by a bishop, who is the patron.

colleague *n* an associate in the same profession or office; a fellow worker.

collect[1] *vti* to bring together, gather or assemble; to regain command of (oneself); to concentrate (thoughts, etc); to ask for or receive money or payment. * *adj* (*telephone call*) paid for by the person called.

collect[2] *n* a short comprehensive prayer for a particular occasion.

collectanea *npl* passages selected from various authors; a miscellany.

collected *adj* self-possessed, cool.—**collectedly** *adv*.

collectible, collectable *adj* (*antiques, etc*) of interest to a collector. * *n* an object worth collecting.

collection *n* act of collecting; an accumulation; money collected at a meeting, etc; a group of things collected for beauty, interest, rarity or value; the periodic showing of a designer's fashions; a regular gathering of mail from a mailbox.

collective *adj* viewed as a whole, taken as one; combined, common; (*gram*) used in the singular to express a multitude. * *n* a collective enterprise, as a farm.—**collectively** *adv*.

collective bargaining *n* negotiations on working conditions between representatives of employees and management.

collective farm *n* a farm or number of smallholdings run on a cooperative basis, usu under state supervision.

collective noun *n* a singular noun covering a number of person or things (e.g. *family*, *flock*).

collective unconscious *n* (in Jungian psychology) a sort of reservoir in the unconscious mind that is filled with memories and instincts common to all human beings and that is accessed by means of archetypes.

collectivism *n* the political or economic theory of collective ownership of the means of production and distribution by the state or people.—**collectivist** *n*.—**collectivistic** *adj*.

collectivize *vt* to bring into public ownership in accordance with the principle of collectivism.—**collectivization** *n*.

collector *n* a person who collects things, eg stamps, butterflies, as a hobby or so as to inspect them, as tickets.

colleen *n* (*Irish*) a girl.

college *n* an institution of higher learning; a school offering specialized knowledge; the buildings housing a college; an organized body of professionals.

collegian *n* a student or recent graduate of a college.

collegiate, collegial *adj* of or belonging to a college; containing, connected with or having the status of a college.

col legno *see* **legno**.

collet *n* the part of a ring in which the stone is set.

collide *vi* to come into violent contact (with); to dash together; to conflict; to disagree.

collie *n* a breed of dog with a pointed muzzle and long hair, used as a sheepdog.

collier *n* a coal miner.

colliery *n* (*pl* **collieries**) a coal mine.

colligate *vt* to bind together; to bring (isolated facts) under a general principle.—**colligation** *n*.—**colligative** *adj*.

colligative property *n* (*chem*) a property of a solution that depends entirely upon the concentration of the dissolved particles rather than their nature.

collimate *vt* to bring into the same line; to make parallel.—**collimation** *n*.

collimator *n* an apparatus for forming light into a parallel beam, used in spectrometry.

collinear *adj* in the same straight line.—**collinearity** *n*.

Collins *n* 1. **Michael** (1890–1922) Irish Republican politician and Sinn Féin leader. He negotiated the 1922 peace treaty with Britain leading to the establishment of the Irish Free State. 2. **Michael** (1930–) American astronaut, who took part in the Apollo 11 mission to the Moon in 1969. 3. **[William] Wilkie** (1824–89) English novelist, noted particularly for his detective novel *The Moonstone*.

collision *n* state of colliding together; a violent impact of moving bodies, a crash; a clash of interests, etc; (*physics*) an interaction or meeting between particles in which momentum is maintained.

collision course *n* one that, if continued on, will end in disaster.

collision margin *n* the boundary of two continental plates.

collocate *vt* to place together; to arrange.

collocation *n* a placing in a particular order; an arrangement, relative situation.

collodion *n* a preparation of soluble pyroxylin with ether, used in photography.

colloid *adj* like glue or jelly; (*chem*) of a gummy noncrystalline kind. * *n* a viscid inorganic transparent substance.—**colloidal** *adj*.—**colloidality** *n*.

collop *n* a slice of meat.

colloq. *abbr* = colloquial; colloquialism; colloquially.

colloquial *adj* used in familiar but not formal talk, not literary.—**colloquially** *adv*.

colloquialism *n* a colloquial word or phrase.

colloquium *n* (*pl* **colloquiums, colloquia**) a conference, seminar.

colloquy *n* (*pl* **colloquies**) a conversation; a written dialog.

coll' ott. *abbr* (*mus*) (*Italian*) = coll' ottava, "in octaves."

collotype *n* a gelatine photographic plate used for printing from in ink.—**collotypic** *adj*.

collr. *abbr* = collector.

collude *vi* to act together; to conspire, esp to defraud.

collusion *n* the act of colluding; an agreement to commit fraud or deception.—**collusive** *adj*.

collyrium *n* (*pl* **collyria, collyriums**) an eye salve.

collywobbles *npl* (*sl*) abdominal pain or discomfort; nervousness.

Colman of Lindisfarne *n* **Saint** (*d*. 676) Irish monk at Iona, Scotland. His feast day is 18 February (and 8 August in Ireland).

Colo. *abbr* = Colorado.

colobus *n* any of a genus of long-tailed African monkeys with shortened or absent thumbs.

colocynth *n* a kind of cucumber; the pulp it yields dried and powdered and used as a purgative.

cologne *n* eau-de-Cologne, a scented liquid.

Cologne (Köln) *n* a city in Germany.

Colombia *n* a republic situated in the north of South America.

Colombian Pesov *n* currency of Colombia.

Colombo *n* capital city of Sri Lanka.

colon[1] *n* (*pl* **colons, cola**) the part of the large intestine from the cecum to the rectum.—**colonic** *adj*.

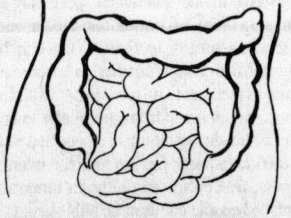

colon[2] *n* (*pl* **colons**) a punctuation mark (:) between the semicolon and the full stop, usu written before an explanation or a list.

colon[3] *n* the standard monetary unit of Costa Rica, equal to 100 centimos; the standard monetary unit of El Salvador, made up of 100 centavos.

Colon *n* currency of Costa Rica.

Colón[1] *n* currency of El Salvador.

Colón[2] *n* a city in Panama.

colonel *n* a commissioned officer junior to a brigadier but senior to a lieutenant colonel.—**colonelcy, colonelship** *n*.

colonial *adj* of or pertaining to a colony or colonies; (*with cap*) pertaining to the thirteen British colonies that became the US. * *n* a person who takes part in founding a colony, a settler.—**colonially** *adv*.

colonialism *n* the policy of acquiring and governing colonies.—**colonialist** *adj, n*.

colonist *n* a person who settles in a colony.

colonize *vt* to establish a colony in; to settle in a colony.—**colonization** *n*.—**colonizer** *n*.

Colonna *n* **Edward** (1862–1948) (*b*. Edouard Klonne) German-born designer, who worked for Bing's L'Art Nouveau store.

colonnade *n* a range of columns placed at regular intervals; a similar row, as of trees.

colony *n* (*pl* **colonies**) an area of land acquired and settled by a distant state and subject to its control; a community of settlers; a group of people of the same nationality or interests living in a particular area; (*biol*) a collection of organisms in close association.

colophon *n* a publisher's imprint or decorative device on a book; (*formerly*) an inscription at the end of a book giving the printer's or writer's name.

color *n* the eye's perception of wavelengths of light with different colors corresponding to different wavelengths; the attribute of objects to appear different according to their differing ability to absorb, emit, or reflect light of different wavelengths; color of the face or skin; pigment; dye; paint; (*literature*) use of imagery, vividness; (*mus*) depth of sound; (*pl*) a flag; a symbol of a club, team, etc. * *vt* to give color to, paint; to misrepresent; to influence. * *vi* to emit color; (*face*) to redden in anger or embarrassment; to blush; to change color, to ripen.

colorable *adj* capable of being colored; specious, plausible.

Colorado (CO) *n* a state of the United States of America (USA) of which the capital is Denver.

Colorado beetle *n* a yellowish beetle with ten longitudinal black stripes on its back, destructive to potatoes.

colorant *n* a coloring matter.

coloration *n* coloring.

coloratura, colorature *adj* (*mus*) (*Italian*) highly ornamented or florid. * *n* a vocal passage sung in this way.

color bar *n* discrimination based on race, esp by White races against other races.

color-blind *adj* unable to distinguish colors, esp red and green.—**color blindness** *n*.

color code *n* a system of identifying by colors, e.g., of electrical wires.

colored *adj* possessing color; biased, not objective; of a darker skinned race. * *n* a person of a darker skinned race.

colorfast *adj* of a material made with non-running or non-fading colors after washing.—*also* **colorfast**.

color field painting *n* a movement begun by abstract expressionists whose paintings were large areas of pure, flat color, the mood and atmosphere being created by the shape of the canvas and by sheer scale.

color filter *n* (*photog*) a thin plate or layer for adjusting depth and brightness of required colors.

colorful *adj* full of color; vivid.—**colorfully** *adv*.

color graphics adapter *n* (*comput*) a VDU display standard offering resolutions of 640 x 200 pixels in monochrome and 320 x 200 in four colors.

color guard *n* a ceremonial escort for the flag of a miliary unit or a nation.

colorific *adj* producing color.

colorimeter *n* an instrument for measuring the intensity of color, strength of dyes, etc.—**colorimetric, colorimetrical** *adj*.—**colorimetry** *n*.

color index *n* (*astron*) a simplified method of classifying stars by using colored light filters to find the most significant features of their spectra.

coloring *n* appearance in term of color; disposition or use of color; a substance for giving color.

colorist *n* an artist whose works are characterized by beauty of color.—**coloristic** *adj*.

colorize *vt* to add color to a black-and-white film using a Colorizer device.

colorless *adj* lacking color; dull, uninteresting, characterless.—**colorlessly** *adv*.—**colorlessness** *n*.

color monitor *n* (*comput*) a VDU that displays multicolor images as opposed to a monochrome screen.

color separation *n* (*comput*) (an image) separated into its component colors, Cyan (blue), magenta (red), yellow, and black, by scanning.

color temperature *n* the temperature of a usually inaccessible incandescent body determined by comparing its emission spectrum with that of a black body whose temperature can be adjusted until the two match.

Coloss. *abbr* (*Bible*) = Colossians.

Colossae *n* (*Bible*) a city of Phrygia in Asia Minor mentioned by Paul at the beginning of his Letter to the Colossians.

colossal *adj* gigantic, immense; (*inf*) amazing, wonderful.—**colossally** *adv*.

Colosseum *n* a large amphitheater in Rome built in the 1st century.

Colossians, Letter of Paul to the *n* (*Bible*) NT book.

Colossi of Memnon *npl* (*Egypt*) two colossal statues carved in the reign of Amenophis III (Eighteenth Dynasty) as guardian figures to his mortuary temple at Malkata on the west bank of the Nile, at Thebes.

colossus *n* (*pl* **colossi, colossuses**) a gigantic statue; something immense.

colostomy *n* (*pl* **colostomies**) a surgical opening into the bowl forming an artificial anus.

colostrum *n* the first milk secreted after parturition; biestings.—**colostral** *adj*.

colotomy *n* (*pl* **colotomies**) an incision in the colon.

colour *see* **color**.

colourable *see* **colorable**.

coloured *see* **colored**.

colourfast *see* **colorfast**.

colourful *see* **colorful**.

colouring *see* **coloring**.

colourist *see* **colorist**.

colourize *see* **colorize**.

colourless *see* **colorless**.

colporteur *n* a person who hawks books, esp bibles.

COLS *abbr* = communications for online systems.

colt *n* a young male horse; a young, inexperienced person; an inexperienced player of a sport.

Colt *n* **Samuel** (1814–62) American inventor who patented a revolver, which was named after him.

coltish *adj* like a colt; frisky; inexperienced.

Coltrane *n* **John [William]** (1926–67) American jazz saxophonist.

coltsfoot *n* (*pl* **coltsfoots**) a yellow-flowered weed.

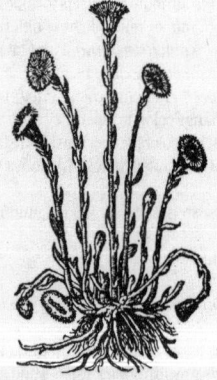

colubrine *adj* of, like or pertaining to snakes.

Columba *n* **Saint** (521–97) Irish missionary who founded a monastic settlement on the island of Iona, and established Christianity in Scotland. His feast day is 9 June.

Columban *n* **Saint** (543–615) Irish missionary sent to Europe, who in 612 founded the monastery of Bobbio in the Apennines. His feast days are 21 and 23 November.

columbarium *n* (*pl* **columbaria**) a dovecote; a place with niches for cinerary urns.

Columbia *n* the capital city of South Carolina, a state of the USA.

Columbian *adj* pertaining to the US.

columbine[1] *adj* pertaining to or like a dove or pigeon.

columbine[2] *n* a garden plant, aquilegia.

Columbine *n* a female character or dancer in a pantomime, sweetheart of Harlequin.

columbium *n* a metallic element now called niobium.

Columbus *n* the capital city of Ohio, a state of the USA.

Columbus *n* **Christopher** (1451–1506) Italian navigator who discovered the New World in 1492.

Columbus Day *n* a legal holiday in most US states, 12 October, commemorating Columbus' landing in the Americas, 1492.

columella *n* (*pl* **columellae**) (*biol*) a central axis or column.—**columellar** *adj*.

columination *n* (*archit*) a building in which columns are used.

column *n* a round pillar for supporting or decorating a building; something shaped like this; a vertical division of a page; a narrow-fronted deep formation of troops; a long line of people; a feature article appearing regularly in a newspaper, etc; (*comput*) a vertical block of word-processor text or spreadsheet cells.—**columnar** *adj*.—**columned, columnated** *adj*.

column inch *n* a unit of advertising space in a magazine or newspaper, measuring one column wide by one inch deep.

columnist *n* a journalist who contributes a regular newspaper or magazine column.

colza *n* rape seed.

colza oil *n* an oil made from rape seed.

com. *abbr* = comedy; comic; comma; commander; commentary; commerce; commercial; commission; commissioned; commissioner; committee; commodore; common; commoner; commonly; commune; communicate; communicated; communication; community.

Com. *abbr* = Commander; Commission; Committee; Commodore; Communist.

COM *abbr* = Committee on Mutagenicity of Chemicals in Food, Consumer Products and the Environment; computer output on microfilm.

coma[1] *n* (*pl* **comas**) deep prolonged unconsciousness.

coma[2] *n* (*pl* **comae**) (*astron*) the nebulous hair-like envelope around the nucleus of a comet; (*astron*) a temporary atmosphere; (*bot*) the silky hairs at the end of a seed; the branches forming the leafy head of a tree; (*optics*) a form of aberration in optical instruments in which a point image is distorted into a pear-shaped patch when it is not on the axis of the instrument.—**comal** *adj*.

COMA *abbr* = Coke Oven Managers Association; Committee on Medical Aspects of Food Policy.

COMAL *abbr* = Common Algorithmic Language.

COMARE *abbr* = Committee on Medical Aspects of Radiation in the Environment.

COMATAS *abbr* = Committee for Monitoring Agreements on Tobacco Advertising and Sponsorship.

comate *adj* (*bot*) hairy.

comatose *adj* in a coma; lethargic, sleepy.

comb *n* a toothed instrument for separating hair, wool, etc; a part of a machine like this; the crest of a cock; a honeycomb. * *vt* to arrange (hair) or dress (wool) with a comb; to seek for thoroughly.

combat *vti* to strive against, oppose; to do battle. * *n* a contest; a fight; struggle.—**combatable** *adj*.—**combater** *n*.

COMBAT *abbr* = Association to Combat Huntington's Chorea.

combatant *adj* fighting. * *n* a person engaged in a fight or contest.

combat fatigue *n* a nervous disorder caused by the stress of battle.

combative *adj* aggressive, keen to fight.

combe *or* **coombe** *n* a dry valley in the chalky areas of southern England that ends in a steep-sided hollow.

combed ornament *n* a pattern of parallel lines on pottery produced by passing the teeth of a special comb over the surface of the soft clay.

comber *n* a wool-combing machine; a long curling wave, a breaker.

combination *n* the act of combining; a union of separate parts; persons allied for a purpose; a sequence of numbers which opens a combination lock; a motorcycle and sidecar.

combination lock *n* a lock which can only be opened by moving a set of dials to show a specific sequence of numbers.

combinations *npl* an all-in-one undergarment also covering the arms and legs.

combination tone *n* (*mus*) a faint (third) note that is heard when two notes are sounded simultaneously.*æalso* **resultant tone**.

combine *vti* to join together; to unite intimately; to possess together; to cooperate; (*chem*) to form a compound with. * *n* an association formed for commercial or political purposes; a machine for harvesting and threshing grain.—**combinable** *adj*.—**combiner** *n*.

combo *n* (*pl* **combos**) a small jazz band; (*inf*) any small group.

combust *vt* to burn.

combustible *adj* capable of burning; easily set alight; excitable. * *n* a combustible thing.—**combustibility, combustibleness** *n*.

combustion *n* the process of burning; the process in which substances react with oxygen in air to produce heat.

combustion chamber *n* the space in the cylinder of an engine in which the gas compressed by the piston is exploded.

COMCIAM *abbr* = Climate Impacts Assessment and Management Program for Commonwealth Countries.

COMDA *abbr* = Canadian Office Machine Dealers Association.

COMDEX *n* (*comput*) the largest computer show in the world, which takes place in the USA twice per year.

comdg. *abbr* = commanding.

comdr. *abbr* = commander.

comdt. *abbr* = commandant.

come *vi* (**coming, came**, *pp* **come**) to approach; to arrive; to reach; to happen (to); to originate; to turn out (to be); to occur in a certain order; to be derived or descended; to be caused; to result; to be available; (*sl*) to experience a sexual orgasm; (*with* **about**) to happen; (*naut*) to change to a new tack; (*with* **across**) to meet with unexpectedly; to communicate the intended information or impression; to provide what is expected; (*sl*) to pay up; (*with* **along**) to make progress; (*with* **at**) to find out; to attack; (*with* **away**) to get detached; to leave with; (*with* **between**) to cause the estrangement of (two people); (*with* **by**) to obtain, esp by chance; to pass; (*with* **down**) to descend; to fall; to suffer an illness; to leave university; (*with* **down on**) to reprimand; (*with* **forward**) to offer oneself for some duty, volunteer; (*with* **from**) (*inf*) to have an awareness of the circumstances causing one's attitudes or actions; to understand what someone means; (*with* **in**) to enter, arrive; (*race*) to finish in a certain position; to perform a certain function; to become popular or fashionable; (*money*) to be received as income; to turn out to be; (*with* **into**) to enter; to receive as an inheritance; (*with* **of**) to result from; (*with* **off**) to become detached; to fall from; to emerge from or finish something in a specified way; to succeed; to be reduced in price, etc; (*inf*) to happen; (*inf*) to have the intended effect; (*with* **on**) to advance, make progress; (*electricity, etc*) to begin functioning; to enter on to the stage or set; (*with* **out**) to become public or be published; to go on strike; to declare oneself in public; to present oneself openly as homosexual; to transpire; to make one's debut; (*with* **over**) to change sides; to communicate effectively; to make an impression; (*inf*) to become affected with a certain feeling; (*with* **round, around**) to recover one's normal state; to look in as a visitor; to regain consciousness; to change one's opinion, accede to something; (*with* **to**) to regain consciousness, revive; (*total*) to amount to; (*with* **through**) to overcome; to survive; (*with* **under**) to be subjected to; to be classed among; (*with* **up**) to approach; to grow; to come to a higher place or rank; (*sun*) to rise; to occur; to arise for discussion, etc; (*with* **upon**) to discover or meet unexpectedly; (*with* **up with**) to pass; to put forward for discussion.

comeback *n* (*inf*) a return to a career or to popularity; (*inf*) a witty answer.

comedian *n* an actor of comic parts; an entertainer who tells jokes; a person who behaves in a humorous manner.

comedienne *nf* a female comedian.

comedown *n* a downfall; a disappointment.

comedy *n* (*pl* **comedies**) an amusing play or movie; drama consisting of amusing plays; an amusing occurrence; humor.—**comedic** *adj*.

comedy of errors *n* an undertaking beset from the beginning with a multitude of errors.

comedy of manners a form of comedy that features intrigues, invariably involving sex and/or money, among an upper region of society.

comehither *adj* (*sl*) flirtatious; charmingly seductive.

comely *adj* (**comelier, comeliest**) pleasing to the eye, good-looking.—**comeliness** *n*.

come-on *n* (*inf*) an enticement, lure.

comer *n* (*inf*) a person or thing showing promise of success.

comestible *n* (*usu pl*) anything to eat.

comet *n* a celestial body that travels in an irregular orbit round the sun, with a visible nucleus and a luminous tail.—**cometary, cometic** *adj*.

comeuppance *n* (*inf*) a deserved retribution.

COMEX *abbr* = Commonwealth Expedition; (*New York*) Commodity Exchange.

comfit *n* a candy; a sugared almond.

comfort station *n* (*inf*) a public lavatory.

comfort *vti* to bring consolation to; to soothe; to cheer. * *n* consolation; relief; bodily ease; (*pl*) things between necessities and luxuries.—**comforting** *adj*.

comfortable *adj* promoting comfort; at ease; adequate; (*inf*) financially well off.—**comfortably** *adv*.

comforter *n* one who comforts; a woolen scarf; a baby's dummy teat; a quilted bedcover.

comfrey *n* a tall bell-flowered hairy plant.

comfy *adj* (**comfier, comfiest**) (*inf*) comfortable.

comic *adj* of comedy; causing amusement. * *n* a comedian; an entertaining person; a paper or book with strip cartoons.

comical *adj* funny, laughable; droll, ludicrous.—**comically** *adv*.

comic book *n* a book or magazine containing stories told in strip cartoons.

comic opera *n* a musical play with a comic theme.

comic relief *n* a humorous scene or character in a tragedy that alleviates tension.

comic strip *n* a series of drawings that depict a story in stages.

Com-in-Chf *abbr* = Commander in Chief.

coming *adj* approaching next; of future importance or promise.

comitia *n* (*pl* **comitia**) one of the three Roman public assemblies for passing laws, declaring war, etc.

comity *n* (*pl* **comities**) civility, politness; acts of international courtesy.

comm. *abbr* = commander; commentary; commerce; commission; committee; commonwealth.

comma *n* a punctuation mark (,) that indicates a slight pause or break in a sentence or separates items in a list.

comma delimited file *n* (*comput*) a method of saving a file in which each data field is separated by a comma.

command *vti* to order; to bid; to control; to have at disposal; to evoke, compel; to possess knowledge or understanding of; to look down over; to be in authority (over), to govern. * *n* an order; control; knowledge; disposal; position of authority; something or someone commanded; an instruction to a computer.

commandant *n* an officer in command of troops or a military establishment, esp a fortress.

command button *n* (*comput*) a button appearing in dialog boxes that initiates a command, e.g., cancel.

command.com *n* (*comput*) a command file that is required for DOS to run.

commandeer *vt* to seize for military purposes; to appropriate for one's own use.

commander *n* a person who commands, a leader; a naval officer ranking next below a captain.—**commandership** *n*.

commander in chief *n* the commander of a state's entire forces.

commanding *adj* in command; dominating; impressive.

command key *n* (*comput*) on a Macintosh keyboard a special key that is used in conjunction with other keys to provide shortcuts for commands.

command line *n* (*comput*) a line of instructions or commands input to the computer through a keyboard.

commandment *n* a command; a divine law, esp one of the Ten Commandments in the Bible.

Commandments *npl* (*Bible*) the Ten Commandments, forming part of the code of law which the OT traces back to Moses.

command module *n* the operational part of a spacecraft.

commando *n* (*pl* **commandos, commandoes**) a member of an elite military force trained to raid enemy territory.

command performance *n* a theatrical performance requested by a head of state.

command post *n* a military field headquarters.

commedia dell'arte *n* a theatrical comedy characterized by an improvised plot and stock characters.

comme il faut (*French*) as it should be; correct; well bred.

commemorate *vt* to keep in the memory by ceremony or writing; to be a memorial of.—**commemoration** *n*.—**commemorative, commemoratory** *adj*.—**commemorator** *n*.

commence *vti* to begin.

commencement *n* a start; a ceremony of conferring degrees; the day of this.

commend *vt* to speak favorably of, to praise; to recommend; to entrust.—**commendable** *adj*.—**commendably** *adv*.—**commendatory** *adj*.

commendation *n* the act of commending, praise; an award.

commensal *adj* (*biol*) living together, but not at the expense of another; (*person, organization*) living and feeding with another. * *n* one of two commensal plants or animals; a dinner companion.—**commensalism, commensality** *n*.

commensurable *adj* measurable by the same standard; divisible without a remainder by the same quantity; proportionate (to).—**commensurability** *n*.

commensurate *adj* having the same extent or measure; proportionate.—**commensuration** *n*.

comment *n* a remark, observation, criticism; an explanatory note; talk, gossip. * *vi* to make a comment (upon); to annotate.—**commenter** *n*.

commentary *n* (*pl* **commentaries**) a series of explanatory notes or remarks; a verbal description on TV or radio of an event as it happens, esp sport (—*also* **running commentary**).—**commentarial** *adj*.

commentate *vt* to act as a commentator.

commentator *n* one who reports and analyzes events, trends, etc, as on television.

commerce *n* trade in goods and services on a large scale between nations or individuals.

commercial *adj* of or engaged in commerce; sponsored by an advertiser; intended to make a profit. * *n* a broadcast advertisement.—**commerciality** *n*.—**commercially** *adv*.

commercial art *n* art designed for use in all aspects of advertising and packaging.—**commercial artist** *n*.

commercial bank *n* a bank that provides a wide range of financial services to businesses and to the general public.

commercial bill *n* a bill of exchange other than a Treasury bill.

commercialism *n* commercial methods or principle.—**commercialist** *n*.—**commercialistic** *adj*.

commercialize *vt* to put on a business basis; to exploit for profit.—**commercialization** *n*.

commercial traveler *n* a sales representative or traveling salesman.

COMMET *abbr* = Council of Mechanical and Metal Trade Association.

commie *n* (*pl* **commies**) (*derog*) a communist.

commination *n* a threatening of divine punishment and vengeance, denunciation, cursing.—**comminatory** *adj*.

commingle *vti* to mix together, to mingle.

comminute *vt* to reduce to minute particles or powder.—**comminution** *n*.

comminuted fracture *n* a serious injury to a bone in which more than one break occurs accompanied by splintering and damage to the surrounding tissues.

commiserate *vti* to sympathize (with); to feel pity for.—**commiseration** *n*.—**commiserator** *n*.

commissar *n* (*formerly*) a head of a government department in the USSR.

commissariat *n* a supply of provisions; the department in charge of this, as for an army.

commissary *n* (*pl* **commissaries**) a store, as in an army camp, where food and supplies are sold; a restaurant in a movie studio, factory, etc.—**commissarial** *adj*.

commission *n* authority to act; a document bestowing this; appointment as a military officer of the rank of lieutenant or above; a body of people appointed (by government) for specified duties; a task or duty or business committed to someone; a special order for something, esp a picture or other art object; a percentage on sales paid to a salesman or agent; brokerage. * *vt* to empower or appoint by commission; to employ the service of; to authorize.—**commissional, commissionary** *adj*.

commissioner *n* a person empowered by a commission; various types of civil servant; a member of a commission.

commissionnaire *n* a uniformed doorman; a security guard.

commissr. *abbr* = commissioner.

commissure *n* (*anat*) a line of junction, a seam; the point of union between two bodies.—**commissural** *adj*.

commit *vti* (**committing, committed**) to entrust; to consign (to prison); to do, to perpetrate a crime, etc; to pledge, to involve.—**committer** *n*.

commitment *n* the act of committing; an engagement that restricts freedom; an obligation; an order for imprisonment or confinement in a mental institution (—*also* **committal**).

committed *adj* dedicated; pledged by a commitment.

committed costs *npl* costs, such as rent, that a company or organization have a long-term commitment to pay.

committee *n* a body of people appointed from a larger body to consider or manage some matter.

Commius *n* (*fl*. 50) king of the Atrebates tribe, Britain. Leader of the tribe which settled in what are now Hampshire and Sussex after fleeing Gaul.

commn. *abbr* = commission.

commod. *abbr* = commodity.

commode *n* a chamber pot enclosed in a stool; a chest of drawers.

commodious *adj* roomy; (*arch*) useful.

commodity *n* (*pl* **commodities**) an article of trade; a useful thing; (*pl*) goods.

commodity broker *n* a broker who deals in commodities, esp one who trades on behalf of others in the commodity market.

commodity market *n* a market for the trading of commodities, the main markets being in London and New York.

commodore *n* a naval officer ranking below a rear admiral and above a captain; the senior commander of a fleet; the president of a yacht club.

common *adj* belonging equally to more than one; public; usual, ordinary; widespread; familiar; frequent; easily obtained, not rare; low, vulgar; (*noun*) applying to any of a class. * *n* a tract of open public land; (*pl*) the common people; (*Brit*) the House of Commons.—**commonality** *n*.—**commonly** *adv*.—**commonness** *n*.

common carrier *n* a carrier prepared to transport any passengers or goods by land, water, or air.

common chord *n* (*mus*) a note accompanied by its third and fifth.

common denominator *n* a common multiple of the denominators of two or more fractions; a characteristic in common.

common land *n* land that is owned privately by an individual or organization but the legal rights of which are held by others.

common law *n* the body of law developed in England based on custom and judicial precedents, as distinct from statute law. * *adj* denoting a marriage recognized in law not by an official ceremony, but after a man and woman have cohabited for a number of years.

common logarithm *see* **logarithm**.

common market *n* a grouping of nations formed to facilitate trade by removing tariff barriers; (*with caps*) the European Economic Community.

common measure *n* a number that will divide two or more numbers without a remainder.

common sense *n* ordinary, practical good sense.—**common-sense** *adj*.

common stock *n* ordinary capital shares; equity stock.

common time *n* (*mus*) two or four beats in a bar.

commonage *n* the right of pasturing on common land.

commonalty, commonality *n* (*pl* **commonalties, commonalities**) the common people.

commoner *n* an ordinary person, not a member of the nobility.

commonplace *adj* ordinary, unremarkable. * *n* a platitude; an ordinary thing.

commonplace book *n* a diary containing literary excerpts and comment.

Commons *n* (*with* **the**) the House of Commons, the lower House of the British Parliament.

commonweal *n* the public good.

commonwealth *n* a political community; a sovereign state, republic; a federation of states; (*with cap*) an association of sovereign states and dependencies ruled or formerly ruled by Britain.

commotion *n* a violent disturbance; agitation; upheaval.—**commotional** *adj*.

communal *adj* of a commune or community; shared in common.—**communality** *n*.—**communally** *adv*.

communalism *n* a political system based on local self-government.—**communalist** *n*.—**communalistic** *adj*.

communalize *vt* to make over to a community.—**communalization** *n*.

communard *n* one who advocates government by communes.

commune[1] *n* a group of people living together and sharing possessions; the smallest administrative division in several European countries.

commune[2] *vi* to converse intimately; to communicate spiritually.

communicable *adj* able to be communicated; (*disease*) easily passed on.—**communicability, communicableness** *n*.

communicant *n* a person who receives Holy Communion.

communicate *vti* to impart, to share; to succeed in conveying information; to pass on; to transmit, esp a disease; to be connected.—**communicator** *n*.—**communicatory** *adj*.

communication *n* the act of communicating; information; a connecting passage or channel; (*pl*) connections of transport; (*pl*) means of imparting information, as in newspapers, radio, television.

communications port *n* (*comput*) a port at the rear of a computer into which a serial device such as a printer or a modem can be plugged.

communications program *n* (*comput*) a program that allows a computer to connect with another computer through a modem.

communications protocol *n* (*comput*) a list of standards that control the transfer of information or exchange of data between computers connected via the telephone network.

communications satellite *n* an artificial satellite orbiting the earth used to relay telephone, radio and TV signals.

communications settings *n* (*comput*) the set of standards used by the main computer in an on-line network.

communicative *adj* inclined to talk and give information.

communion *n* common possession, sharing; fellowship; an emotional bond with; union in a religious body; (*with cap*) Holy Communion, the Christian sacrament of the Eucharist when bread and wine are consecrated and consumed.—**communional** *adj*.

communiqué *n* an official communication, esp to the press or public.

communism *n* a social system under which private property is abolished and the means of production are owned by the people; (*with cap*) a political movement seeking the overthrow of capitalism based on the writings of Karl Marx; the system as instituted in the former USSR and elsewhere.—**communistic** *adj*.

communist *n* a supporter of communism; (*with cap*) a member of a Communist party.

community *n* (*pl* **communities**) an organized political or social body; a body of people in the same locality; the general public, society; any group having work, interests, etc in common; joint ownership; common character; a group of plants and animals of a region, dependent on each other for life and survival; (*comput*) the population of an on-line information service or bulletin board expressing itself in conferences, discussion boards, and electronic mail.

community center *n* a place providing social and recreational facilities for a local community.

commutation *n* the right to receive an instant sum in cash in return for accepting smaller annual payments at some point in the future.

commutative *n* relating to or involving substitution; (*math*) having a result that is independent of the order in which the elements are combined; (*addition, etc*) showing this property.

commutator *n* a device for reversing the direction of electric current.

commute *vti* to travel a distance daily from home to work; to exchange (for); to change (to); to reduce (a punishment) to one less severe.—**commutable** *adj*.—**commutation** *n*.

commuter *n* a person who commutes to and from work.

comodo *n* (*mus*) (*Italian*) "convenient," as in *tempo comodo,* "at a convenient speed."

com. off. *abbr* = commissioned officer.

Comorian Franc *n* currency of Comoros.

Comoros *n* a federal Islamic republic, comprising three volcanic islands in the Indian Ocean situated between mainland Africa and Madagascar.

comose *adj* hairy; tufted.

comp. *abbr* = companion; comparative; compare; comparison; compensating; compilation; compiled; compiler; composer; composition; compositor; (*Latin*) *compositus*, "compound"; compound; (*pharm*) compounded; comprising.

Compa *abbr* = Company.

COMPAC *abbr* = Commonwealth Trans-Pacific Telephone Cable.

compact[1] *n* an agreement; a contract, a treaty.

compact[2] *adj* closely packed; condensed; terse; firm; taking up space neatly. * *vt* to press or pack closely; to compose (of). * *n* a small cosmetic case, usu containing face powder and a mirror.—**compacter** *n*.—**compactly** *adv*.—**compactness** *n*.

compact disc *n* a small mirrored disc containing music (or audio-visual material) encoded digitally in metallic pits which are read optically by a laser beam.

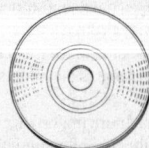

compactor *n* a device for compressing garbage into disposable bundles.

compact video disc *n* a laser disc, similar to an audio compact disc, which plays sound and pictures.

companion[1] *n* an associate in an activity; a partner; a friend; one of a pair of matched things; (*Brit*) a low-ranking member of an order of knighthood.—**companionship** *n*.

companion[2] *n* a wooden shelter over a companionway.

companionable *adj* friendly, sociable.—**companionability** *n*.—**companionably** *adv*.

Companion IEE *abbr* = Companion of the Institution of Electrical Engineers.

Companion IGasE *abbr* = Companion of the Institution of Gas Engineers.

companionway *n* a ladder or staircase on a ship.

company *n* (*pl* **companies**) any assembly of people; an association of people for carrying on a business, etc; a society; a military unit; the crew of a ship; companionship, fellowship; a guest, visitor(s).

company registrar *n* the officer of a company whose duty it is to maintain an up-to-date company share register, to issue new share certificates, and cancel old share certificates as shares are bought and sold.

company secretary *n* the officer of a company whose duties include the preparation of the agenda for directors' meetings, the submission of annual returns, and the keeping of minutes at meetings.

Compaq™ *n* (*comput*) a major manufacturer of IBM™-compatible computers.

compar. *abbr* = comparative; comparison.

comparable *adj* able or suitable to be compared (*with* **with**); similar.—**comparably** *adv*.—**comparability** *n*.

comparative *adj* estimated by comparison; relative, not absolute; (*gram*) expressing more.—**comparatively** *adv*.

comparator *n* any device for comparing one item with another, or with a standard.

compare *vt* to make one thing the measure of another; to observe similarity between, to liken; to bear comparison; (*gram*) to give comparative and superlative forms of (an adjective). * *vi* to make comparisons; to be equal or alike.—**comparer** *n*.

comparison *n* the act of comparing; an illustration; a likeness; (*gram*) the use of *more* or *er* with an adjective.

compartment *n* a space partitioned off; a division of a train carriage; a separate section or category.—**compartmental** *adj*.—**compartmented** *adj*.

compartmentalize *vt* to divide into categories, esp excessively.—**compartmentalization** *n*.

compass *n* a circuit, circumference; an extent, area; the range of a voice; an instrument with a magnetic needle indicating north, south, east, west; (*often pl*) a two-legged instrument for drawing circles, etc.—**compassable** *adj*.

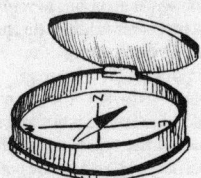

compassion *n* sorrow for another's sufferings; pity.

compassionate *adj* showing compassion; merciful.—**compassionately** *adv*.

compass points *n* north, south, east, west, etc.

compatible *adj* agreeing or fitting in (with); of like mind; consistent; (*body organ*) able to be transplanted successfully; (*comput*) (hardware or software) able to accept and process data prepared by another machine.—**compatibly** *adv*.—**compatibility** *n*.

compatriot *n* a fellow countryman.—*also adj*.—**compatriotic** *adj*.

compeer *n* an equal; a companion.

compel *vt* (**compelling, compelled**) to force, constrain; to oblige; to obtain by force.—**compeller** *n*.

compelling *adj* evoking powerful feelings, eg interest, admiration.

compendious *adj* containing much in a small space, succinct.

compendium *n* (*pl* **compendiums, compendia**) an abridgement; a summary; a collection; an assortment of things in one box.

compensate *vti* to counterbalance; to make up for; to recompense.—**compensator** *n*.—**compensatory, compensative** *adj*.

compensation *n* the act of compensating; a sum given to compensate, esp for loss or injury; an exaggerated display of ability in one area as a cover-up for a lack in another.

Comper *n* **John N** (1864–1960) English architect, whose notable works include St Mary's Church, Wellingborough.

compere *n* a master of ceremonies.

COMPETA *abbr* = Computer and Peripherals Equipment Trade Association.

compete *vi* to strive; to contend; to take part in a competition, esp sporting.

competence *n* the quality of being capable; sufficiency; capacity; an adequate income to live on.

competency *n* (*pl* **competencies**) competence; (*law*) the capacity to testify in court.

competent *adj* fit, capable; adequate; with enough skill for; legally qualified.—**competently** *adv*.

competition *n* act of competing; rivalry; a contest in skill or knowledge; a match.

competitive *adj* of, or involving, competition; of sufficient value in terms of price or quality to ensure success against rivals.—**competitively** *adv*.—**competitiveness** *n*.

competitor *n* a person who competes; an opponent; a rival.

competitor analysis *n* the process of studying and assessing the production and marketing methods adopted by a company's key competitors.

compile *vt* to collect or make up from various sources; to amass; to gather data, etc for a book; (*comput*) to translate high-level program instructions into machine code using a compiler.—**compilation** *n*.

compiled map *n* a map produced by using information from an existing map and not from an original survey.

compiler *n* a person who compiles a book, etc; (*comput*) a program that translates high-level program instructions into machine code.

COMPIP *abbr* = Companion of the Institute of Plumbing.

complacency, complacence *n* (*pl* **complacencies, complacences**) self-satisfaction; gratification.

complacent *adj* self-satisfied.—**complacently** *adv*.—**complacency, complacence** *n*.

complain *vi* to find fault, to grumble; to be ill; (*poet*) to express grief, to make a mourning sound.—**complainer** *n*.

complainant *n* (*law*) a plaintiff.

complaint *n* a statement of some grievance; a cause of distress or dissatisfaction; an illness.

complaisant *adj* disposed to please, obliging; compliant.—**complaisance** *n*.

complement *n* something making up a whole; a full allowance (of equipment or number); the entire crew of a ship, including officers. * *vt* to make complete.

complementary *adj* completing; together forming a balanced whole.

complementary angles *npl* (*math*) two angles totaling 90°.

complementary color *n* one of a pair of colors that make white or gray when mixed in the correct proportion.

complementary medicine *see* **alternative medicine**.

complete *adj* entire; free from deficiency; finished; thorough. * *vt* to make complete; to finish.—**completeness** *n*.—**completer** *n*.—**completive** *adj*.

completely *adv* entirely, utterly.

completion *n* the act of completing; accomplishment; fulfillment.

complex *adj* having more than one part; intricate, not simple; difficult. * *n* a complex whole; a collection of interconnected parts, buildings, or units; a group of mostly unconscious impulses, etc, strongly influencing behaviour; (*inf*) an undue preoccupation; a phobia.—**complexity** *n* (*pl* **complexities**).

complex fraction *n* (*math*) a fraction with fractions for the numerator or denominator or both.

complexion *n* a color, texture, and look of the skin; aspect, character.

complexity *n* (*pl* **complexities**) the state of being complex, complexness.

complex number *n* (*math*) a number having both real and imaginary parts.

complex sentence *n* a sentence with one principal clause and one or more subordinate clauses.

compliance, compliancy *n* the act of complying with another's wishes; acquiescence.

compliant *adj* yielding, submissive.—**compliantly** *adv*.

complicate *vt* to make intricate or involved; to mix up.

complicated *adj* intricately involved; difficult to understand.

complication *n* a complex or intricate situation; a circumstance that makes (a situation) more complex; (*med*) a condition or disease following an original illness.

complicity *n* (*pl* **complicites**) partnership in wrongdoing.

compliment *n* a polite expression of praise, a flattering tribute; (*pl*) a formal greeting or expression of regard. * *vt* to pay a compliment to, to flatter; to congratulate (on).

complimentary *adj* conveying or expressing a compliment; given free of charge.

complin, compline *n* (*RC Church*) the last service of the day following vespers.

comply *vi* (**complying, complied**) to act in accordance (with); to yield, to agree.—**complier** *n*.

compo *n* (*pl* **compos**) a mixture of plaster, stucco, etc; (*sl*) compensation.

component *adj* going to the making of a whole, constituent. * *n* a component part.—**componential** *adj*.

comport *vti* to conduct (oneself); to be compatible, to accord (with).—**comportment** *n*.

compose *vt* to make up, to form; to construct in one's mind, to write; to arrange, to put in order; to settle, to adjust; to tranquilize; (*print*) to set up type * *vi* to create musical works, etc.

composed *adj* calm, self-controlled.—**composedly** *adv*.

composer *n* a person who composes, esp music.

composite *adj* made up of distinct parts or elements; (*archit*) blending Ionic and Corinthian orders; (*bot*) having many flowers in the guise of one, as the daisy. * *n* a composite thing or flower.

composite construction *n* (*archit*) a building component made of two or more types of material.

composite map *n* a compiled map that uses information from several other maps and displayed to enable comparisons to be made between sets of data.

composite number *n* an integer divisible by itself and at least one other number.

composition *n* the act or process of composing; a work of literature or music, a painting; a short written essay; the general make-up of something; a chemical compound.—**compositional** *adj*.

compositor *n* a person who puts together, or sets up, type for printing.

compos mentis *adj* (*Latin*) of sound mind, sane.

compost *n* a mixture of decomposed organic matter for fertilizing soil.

composure *n* the state of being composed, calmness.

compote *n* fruit preserved in syrup.

compound[1] *n* a substance or thing made up of a number of parts or ingredients, a mixture; a compound word made up of two or more words; (*chem*) two or more elements combined in a substance in definite proportions, in the form of molecules held together by chemical bonds. * *vt* to combine (parts, elements, ingredients) into a whole, to mix; to intensify by adding new elements; to settle (debt) by partial payment. * *vi* to become joined in a compound; to come to terms of agreement. * *adj* compounded or made up of several parts; not simple.—**compounder** *n*.

compound[2] *n* an enclosure in which a building stands.

compound annual return *n* the total return that is available from an investment in which the interest is employed to increase the investment.

compound eye *n* the eye in insects consisting of numerous separate visual units.

compound fracture *n* a fracture in which the shattered bone protrudes through the skin.

compound interest *n* interest paid on the principal sum of capital and the interest that it has accrued.

compound interval *n* (*mus*) an interval which is greater than an octave.

compound number *n* a quantity expressed in different units of measure, such as pounds and ounces.

compound sentence *n* a sentence with more than one principal clause.

compound time *n* (*mus*) musical time in which each beat in a bar is divisible by three, e.g., 6/8, 9/8, and 12/8 time.

comprador *n* a native agent for a foreign company in China or Japan.

comprehend *vt* to grasp with the mind, to understand; to include, to embrace.—**comprehendible** *adj*.—**comprehension** *n*.

comprehensible *adj* capable of being understood.—**comprehensibly** *adv*.—**comprehensibility** *n*.

comprehensive *adj* wide in scope or content, including a great deal; (*automobile insurance policy*) covering most risks including third party, fire, theft. * *n* a comprehensive school.—**comprehensively** *adv*.—**comprehensiveness** *n*.

compress *vt* to press or squeeze together; to bring into a smaller bulk; to condense; (*comput*) to reduce the space taken up by files in order to reduce the disk space that is used to store the compressed files. * *n* a soft pad for compressing an artery, etc; a

C

wet or dry bandage or pad for relieving inflammation or discomfort.—**compressed** *adj*.—**compressible** *adj*.—**compressive** *adj*.

compressed air *n* air under greater than atmospheric pressure, used as a portable oxygen supply or to power a mechanical device.

compression *n* the act of compressing; the increase in pressure in an engine to compress the gases so that they explode.—**compressional** *adj*.

compressor *n* a machine for compressing air or other gases.

comprise *vt* to consist of, to include.—**comprisable** *adj*.—**comprisal** *n*.

compromise *n* a settlement of a dispute by mutual concession; a middle course or view between two opposed ones. * *vti* to adjust by compromise; to lay open to suspicion, disrepute, etc.—**compromiser** *n*.

compromised *adj* (*reputation*) open to disrepute, tarnished.

COMPSAC *abbr* = Computer Software and Applications Conference.

Compton *n* **Arthur Holly** (1892–1962) American physicist and prominent researcher into radiation and nuclear energy. He discovered the Compton effect, and was the winner of the 1927 Nobel prize for physics. 2. **Denis [Charles Scott]** (1918–) English cricketer.

Compton-Burnett *n* [**Dame**] **Ivy** (1884–1969) English novelist whose novels, e.g. *Brothers and Sisters*, are composed almost entirely of dialog and are mainly concerned with the traumas and hypocrisies of upper-middle-class family life.

Compton scattering *n* (*physics*) the effect of an interaction of X-rays with electrons.

comptroller *n* the form of controller used in some titles.

compulsion *n* the act of compelling; something that compels; an irresistible urge.

compulsive *adj* compelling; acting as if compelled.—**compulsively** *adv*.

compulsory *adj* enforced, obligatory, required by law, etc; involving compulsion; essential.—**compulsorily** *adv*.

compulsory purchase *n* the compulsory acquisition of land or property by the state, usu because the land is necessary for some public use, such as the building of a new road.

compunction *n* pricking of the conscience; remorse; scruple.—**compunctious** *adj*.

Compuserve *n*, *trademark* (*comput*) an on-line information service provider that provides a wide variety of services such as electronic mail, news services, information, etc, plus access to the internet.

computation *n* the act or process of computing; a reckoning, an estimate.—**computational** *adj*.

compute *vt* to determine mathematically; to calculate by means of a computer. * *vi* to reckon; to use a computer.—**computability** *n*.—**computable** *adj*.—**computation** *n*.

computed axial tomography *or* **CAT** *or* **CT scanner images** *n* examination of the internal structures of a human body by means of a CAT scanner, which produces cross-sectional images.

computer *n* an electronic device that processes data in accordance with programed instructions.

computer game *n* a game on cassette or disk to play on a home computer by means of operating the keys according to the images appearing on the screen.

computer-generated music music that is created by feeding a formula or program into a computer, which then translates the program into sounds.

computer graphics *n* the production and manipulation of pictorial images on a computer screen.

computerize *vt* to equip with computers; to control or perform (a process) using computers; to store or process data using a computer.—**computerization** *n*.

computerized axial tomography *see* **CAT**[2].

computer language *n* a code used to provide instructions and data to a computer.

computer literate *adj* capable of or proficient in using computers.

computer virus *n* a program introduced into a computer system with the intention of sabotaging or destroying data.

compy. *abbr* = company.

Comr. *abbr* = Commissioner.

comrade *n* a companion; a fellow member of a Communist party.—**comradely** *adv*.—**comradeship** *n*.

comsat *n* communications satellite.

COMSAT *abbr* = communications satellite.

ComSec *abbr* = Commonwealth Secretariat.

COMSER *abbr* = (UN) Commission on Marine Science and Engineering Research.

Com. Ver. *abbr* (*Bible*) = Common Version.

con[1] *vt* (**conning, conned**) (*inf*) to swindle, trick. * *n* (*inf*) a confidence trick.

con[2] *n* against, as in **pro and con**.

con[3] *prep* with.

con[4] *vt* (**conning, conned**) (*ship*) to direct the course of.

con[5] *vt* (**conning, conned**) to study; to learn by heart.

con[6] *n* (*sl*) a convict.

con. *abbr* = concerto; conclusion; conformist; (*Latin*) *conjunx*, "wife"; connection; consol; consolidated; consul; (*Latin*) *contra*, "against"; conundrum; conversation.

con- *prefix* com-.

Conaire Mor *n* (*Irish Celtic myth*) according to some sources, the son of Eochaidh Airemh and his own daughter—*see* **Midhir**. He ignored warnings not to go to Da Derga's Hostel and he met his death there.

Conakry *n* capital city of Guinea.

Conall *n* king of Picts, Britain (787–789). The son of Alpin II's sister, he succeeded Talorgen but was deposed within two years by Constantine.

Conall Cernach *or* **Cearnach** *n* also known as **Conall of the Victories** (*Irish Celtic myth*) one of the three warriors who vied for the honor of carving the roast meat at the feast of Bricriu.

con amore *adj*, *adv* (*mus*) with love.

conation *n* (*psychol*) the faculty of voluntary agency, including volition and desire.

conative *adj* (*verb*) expressing endeavor or effort; pertaining to the faculty of conation.

CONBA *abbr* (*Brit*) = Council of National Beekeeping Associations of the United Kingdom.

con brio *adj*, *adv* (*mus*) with spirit.

conc. *abbr* = concentrate; concentrated; concentration; concerning; (*Latin* (*eccles*) (*Latin*) *concilium*, "council."

concatenate *vt* to link together. * *adj* linked.

concatenation *n* a string of connected ideas or events; (*comput*) the adding of two or more fields or pieces of text together to form one item.

concave *adj* curving inwards, hollow. * *n* a concave line or surface.—**concavity** *n* (*pl* **concavities**).

concavo-concave *adj* hollow on both surfaces, as a lens.

concavo-convex *adj* concave on one side, convex on the other.

CONCAWE *abbr* = Oil Companies European Organisation for Environmental and Health Protection.

concd. *abbr* = concentrated.

conceal *vt* to hide, to keep from sight; to keep secret.—**concealment** *n*.

concede *vt* to grant; to admit to be true, to allow; to agree to be certain in outcome.—**conceder** *n*.

conceit *n* an over-high opinion of oneself; vanity; a far-fetched comparison, a quaint fancy.

conceited *adj* full of conceit, vain.—**conceitedly** *adv*.

conceivable *adj* capable of being imagined or believed; possible.—**conceivably** *adv*.

conceive *vti* to become pregnant (with); to form in the mind; to think out, to imagine; to understand; to express.

concenter *vti* to bring or come to a common center.—*also* **concenter**.

concentrate *vt* to bring or converge together to one point; to direct to a single object or purpose; to collect one's thoughts or efforts; (*chem*) to increase the strength of by diminishing bulk, to condense. * *n* a concentrated product, esp a food reduced in bulk by eliminating fluid; a foodstuff relatively high in nutrients.—**concentrator** *n*.

concentration *n* the act or process of concentrating; the direction of attention to a single object; a drawing together of forces; the simultaneous firing of many weapons; (*chem*) the quantity of a substance dissolved in a fixed amount of liquid to form a solution.æ**concentrative** *adj*.

concentration camp *n* a camp where persons (as prisoners of war, political prisoners, and refugees) are detained or confined.

concentre *see* **concenter**.

concentric, concentrical *adj* having a common center.—**concentrically** *adv*.—**concentricity** *n*.

concept *n* a general idea, esp an abstract one.

conceptacle *n* (*bot*) that which holds anything; a follicle.

conception *n* the act of conceiving; the fertilizing of an ovum by a sperm; a thing conceived; an idea, a notion.—**conceptional** *adj*.

Concepcion *n* a city in Chile.

Concepción *n* a city in Paraguay.

concept testing *n* the trying out of a new product or an existing product that has been modified in some way on a sample of likely consumers with a view to assessing consumer reaction to the product.

conceptual *adj* of mental conception or concepts.

conceptual art *n* art meant to convey an idea or concept by non-traditional means.

conceptualism *n* (*philos*) the theory that universal truths exist in the mind apart from any concrete embodiment.—**conceptualist** *n*.—**conceptualistic** *adj*.

conceptualize *vt* to form a concept of in the mind based on evidence, experience, etc.—**conceptualization** *n*.

concern *vt* to relate or apply to; to fill with anxiety; to interest (oneself) in; to take part, to be mixed up (in). * *n* a thing that concerns one; anxiety, misgiving; interest in or regard for a person or thing; a business or firm.

concerned *adj* troubled, worried; interested.—**concernedly** *adv*.

concerning *prep* about; regarding.

concert *n* a musical entertainment; harmony; agreement or union; **in concert** working together; (*musicians*) playing together.

concerted *adj* planned or arranged by mutual agreement; combined; (*mus*) arranged in separate parts for musicians or singers.

concert grand *n* (*mus*) a large grand piano that is used in concert halls.

concertina *n* a hexagonal musical instrument, similar to an accordion, which produces sound by squeezing bellows which pass air over metal reeds.

concertino *n* (*pl* **concertini**) a short concerto.

concertmaster *n* (*mus*) the first violinist, or leader of an orchestra.

concerto *n* (*pl* **concertos, concerti**) a musical composition for a solo instrument and orchestra; a work for several contrasted instruments; an orchestral work in several movements, containing passages for groups of solo instruments (**concerto grosso**).

concert overture *n* (*mus*) an orchestral piece of one movement, similar to an opera overture, but written solely for performance in a concert hall.

concert-party agreement *n* an agreement between shareholders of a company who are apparently unconnected to act together as a unit to try to influence the management of a company or to influence the share price.

concert pitch *n* a pitch slightly above normal; (*mus*) the internationally agreed pitch, according to which A above middle C (in the middle of the treble clef) is fixed at 440 hertz (cycles per second); a state of exceptional efficiency.

Concertstück, Konzertstück *n* (*mus*) (*German*) a short concerto.

concession *n* the act of conceding; something conceded; a grant of rights, land, etc by a government, corporation, or individual; the sole right to sell a product within an area; a reduction in price (of admission, travel, etc) for certain people.—**concessionary** *adj*.—**concessible** *adj*.

concessionaire, concessioner *n* a person holding a concession.

concessive *adj* of or expressing concession.

conch *n* (*pl* **conchs, conches**) a tropical marine spiral shell, sometimes used as a trumpet.

conch. *abbr* = conchology.

concha *n* (*pl* **conchae**) the external ear or its cavity; (*archit*) the dome of a semicircular apse.—**conchal** *adj*.

conchiferous *adj* producing shells.

Conchobar mac Nessa *n* (*Irish Celtic myth*) king of Ulster.

conchology *n* the branch of zoology that studies mollusks and their shells.—**conchological** *adj*.—**conchologist** *n*.

concierge *n* a resident doorkeeper or janitor, esp in France.

conciliar *adj* of or pertaining to ecclesiastical councils.

conciliate *vt* to win over from hostility; to make friendly; to appease; to reconcile.—**conciliation** *n*.—**conciliator** *n*.—**conciliatory** *adj*.

conciliation *n* a form of intervention in industrial disputes in which a third party tries to assist the two parties involved in the dispute to resolve their differences and reach an agreement that is satisfactory to both of them.

concinnity *n* (*pl* **concinnities**) neatness, elegance, esp in speech or writing.—**concinnous** *adj*.

concise *adj* brief, condensed, terse.—**concisely** *adv*.—**conciseness** *n*.

concision *n* conciseness; (*arch*) mutilation.

concitato *adj* (*mus*) (*Italian*) "agitated."

conclave *n* a private or secret meeting; a meeting of cardinals in seclusion to choose a pope; the meeting place.—**conclavist** *n*.

conclude *vti* to bring or come to an end, to finish; to effect, to settle; to infer; to resolve.

conclusion *n* concluding; the end or close; an inference; a final opinion; (*logic*) a proposition deduced from premises.

conclusive *adj* decisive; convincing, removing all doubt.—**conclusively** *adv*.

concn. *abbr* = concentration.

concoct *vt* to make by combining ingredients; to devise, to plan; to invent (a story).—**concocter, concoctor** *n*.—**concoctive** *adj*.

concoction *n* the act of concocting; something concocted; a mixture; a lie.

concomitance *n* the state of being concomitant; coexistence.

concomitant *n* an accompanying thing or circumstance.—*also adj*.

concord *n* agreement, harmony; a treaty; grammatical agreement; (*mus*) a combination of sounds (such as a chord) that are satisfactory and sound agreeable, the opposite of dissonance.—**concordant** *adj*.

Concord *n* the capital city of New Hampshire, a state of the USA.

concordance *n* agreement; an alphabetical index of words in a book or in the works of an author with their contexts.

concordance file *n* (*comput*) a file that contains a list of words that are to appear in an index.

concordant *adj* agreeing, harmonious.

concordant coast *n* a coast that lies parallel to the topography of the area and itself is determined by the underlying geology.

concordat *n* a compact or agreement, esp between church and state.

concourse *n* a crowd; a gathering of people or things, e.g. events; an open space or hall where crowds gather, e.g. a railroad or airport terminal.

con. cr. *abbr* = contra credit.

concrescence *n* (*biol*) a growing together, coalescence.—**concrescent** *adj*.

concrete *adj* having a material existence; (*gram*) denoting a thing, not a quality, not abstract; actual, specific (*a concrete example*); made of concrete. * *n* anything concrete; a mixture of sand, cement, etc, with water, used in building. * *vti* to form into a mass, to solidify; to build or cover with concrete.

concrete art *n* a term used to describe severely geometrical abstract art.

concretion *n* a solidified mass; a stone-like mass found in some parts of the body, calculus.—**concretionary** *adj*.

concretions, calculi (*sing* **calculus**) *npl* hard, stony masses of various sizes formed within the body.

concrete music *see* **musique concrète**.

concubinage *n* the act of living with a woman without being legally married.

concubine *n* a secondary wife (in polygamous societies); (*formerly*) a mistress of a king or nobleman.—**concubinage** *n*.

concupiscence *n* sexual desire, lust.—**concupiscent** *adj*.

concur *vi* (**concurring, concurred**) to happen together, to coincide; to cooperate; to be of the same opinion, to agree.—**concurrence** *n*.

concurrence *n* the act of concurring; agreement; consent.

concurrent *adj* existing, acting or occurring at the same time; coinciding.—**concurrently** *adv*.

concuss *vt* to shake violently, to agitate; to cause concussion of the brain to.

concussion *n* the violent shock of an impact or explosion; loss of consciousness caused by a violent blow to the head.—**concussive** *adj*.

cond. *abbr* = (*mus*) conducted; conductivity; conductor.

condemn *vt* to express strong disapproval of; to find guilty; to blame or censure; to declare unfit for use; to force into unwillingly.—**condemnable** *adj*.—**condemnation** *n*.—**condemnatory** *adj*.—**condemner** *n*.

condensation *n* (*meteorol, chem*) the process by which a substance changes from gas to liquid.

condense *vt* to reduce to a smaller compass, to compress; to change from a gas into a liquid; to concentrate; to express in fewer words. * *vi* to become condensed.—**condensable, condensible** *adj*.—**condenser** *n*.—**condensation** *n*.

condensed milk *n* milk that has been sweetened and reduced by evaporation.

condensed type *n* (*comput*) a type style that reduces the width of characters so that more characters are printed per inch of space.

condenser *n* an apparatus for reducing gases or vapor to a liquid or solid form; a device for storing electricity; a lens for concentrating light.

condescend *vi* to waive one's superiority; to deign, to stoop; to act patronizingly.—**condescension** *n*.

condescending *adj* kindly in a lordly fashion to inferiors; patronizing.

condescension *n* a condescending act or manner.

condign *adj* deserved, merited; suitable.

condiment *n* a seasoning or relish.

condition *n* the state or nature of things; anything required for the performance, completion or existence of something else; physical state of health; an abnormality, illness; a prerequisite; (*pl*) attendant circumstances. * *vt* to be essential to the happening or existence of; to stipulate; to agree upon; to make fit; to make accustomed (to); to bring about a required effect by subjecting to certain stimuli.

conditional *adj* depending on conditions; not absolute; (*gram*) expressing condition. * *n* a conditional clause or conjunction.—**conditionality** *n*.—**conditionally** *adv*.

conditional sale agreement *n* a form of contract of sale by which the price of the goods purchased is payable by installments and the seller remains the owner of the goods until they are paid in full, although the goods are in the possession of the purchaser.

conditional statement *n* (*comput*) a statement used in programing to determine the next operation.

conditioner *n* a person or thing that conditions; a creamy substance for bringing the hair into a glossy condition.

conditioning *n* a bringing into a required state or state of fitness for an objective.

condo *n* (*pl* **condos, condoes**) (*inf*) a condominium.

condole *vt* (**with** with) to express sympathy for another.—**condolatory** *adj*.—**condoler** *n*.

condolence, condolement *n* sympathy.

con dolore *adv* (*mus*) mournfully.

condom *n* a sheath for the penis, used as a contraceptive and to prevent infection.

condominium *n* (*pl* **condominiums**) a block of apartments, each apartment being individually owned; joint rule; a country ruled by more than one other country.

condominium declaration *n* (*law*) an instrument which creates a condominium: describes the condominium and gives a declaration of the covenants and conditions of its use.

condone *vt* to overlook, to treat as nonexistent; to pardon an offense.—**condonation** *n*.—**condoner** *n*.

condor *n* a large South American vulture.

condottiere *n* (*pl* **condottieri**) a military adventurer, a captain of mercenaries.

conduce *vi* to tend to bring about, to contribute (to).—**conducer** *n*.

conducive *adj* leading to or helping to cause or produce a result.

conduct *vti* to lead; to guide; to convey; to direct (an orchestra); to carry on or manage (a business); to transmit (electricity, heat); to behave (oneself). * *n* management, direction; behavior.—**conductible** *adj*.—**conductibility** *n*.

conductance *n* the ability of a specified system to conduct electricity.

conducting *n* (*mus*) the art of directing and controlling an orchestra or choir (or operatic performance) by means of gestures.

conduction *n* the conducting or transmission of heat or electricity through a medium; the transmission of nerve impulses.

conductive *adj* having the power to transmit heat or electricity.—**conductivity** *n* (*pl* **conductivities**).

conductivity *n* (*elect*) the reciprocal or opposite of resistance in an electric circuit.

conductor *n* a person who conducts an orchestra; one in charge of passengers on a train, or who collects fares on a bus; a substance that conducts heat or electricity.—**conductress** *nf*.

conduit *n* a channel or pipe that carries water, etc.

conduplicate *adj* (*bot*) folded lengthwise along the middle.—**conduplication** *n*.

condyle *n* (*anat*) the rounded head at the end of a bone fitting into another bone.—**condylar** *adj*.

condyloid *adj* shaped like, resembling, or connected with a condyle.

cone *n* a solid pointed figure with a circular or elliptical base; any cone-shaped object (*an ice-cream cone*); a warning bollard on roads, etc; the scaly fruit of the pine, fir, etc; type of photoreceptor (light-sensitive cell) found in the retina of the eye, which detects color.

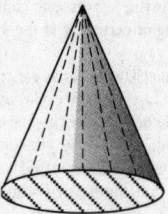

con esp., con espr. *abbr* (*mus*) (*Italian*) = *con expressione*, "with expression."

coney *see* cony.

conf. *abbr* = (*pharm*) (*Latin*) *confectio*, "confection"; (*Latin*) *confer*, "compare"; conference; confessor.

confab *n* (*inf*) an informal talk, chat.

confabulate *vi* to talk familiarly together.—**confabulation** *n*.—**confabulator** *n*.—**confabulatory** *adj*.

confect *vt* to put together, to make; to make into a confection.

confection *n* candy, ice cream, preserves, etc; anything overfussy, fanciful or ornate.

confectionary *n* (*pl* **confectionaries**) a place where confectionery is made or sold. * *adj* of or pertaining to confectionery.

confectioner *n* a person who makes or sells confectionery.

confectionery *n* (*pl* **confectioneries**) candies.

Confed. *abbr* = Confederate.

confederacy *n* (*pl* **confederacies**) a union of states, an alliance; a combination of persons for illegal purposes; (*with cap*) the Confederate States of America.

confederate *adj* banded together by treaty, united in confederation. * *vti* to bring or come into alliance or confederacy. * *n* a member of a confederacy; a partner in design, an accomplice; an ally.

Confederate States *npl* in US history, the eleven Southern States that seceded from the Union in 1861, leading to the Civil War in which they were defeated in 1865.

confederation *n* the act or state of confederating; an alliance of individuals, organizations, states, or cantons (as in Switzerland).—**confederationism** *n*.—**confederationist** *n*.

confer *vt* (**conferring, conferred**) to grant or bestow; to compare views or take counsel; to consult.—**conferment, conferral** *n*.—**conferrable** *adj*.—**conferrer** *n*.

conferee, conferree *n* one on whom something is conferred; a member of a conference.

conference *n* a meeting for discussion or consultation.—**conferential** *adj*.

conferva *n* (*pl* **confervae, confervas**) a genus containing green freshwater algae.—**conferval** *adj*.—**confervoid** *adj*.

confess *vt* to acknowledge or admit; to disclose (sins) to a confessor; (*priest*) to hear confession of. * *vi* to make or hear a confession.

confessedly *adv* avowedly.

confession *n* admission or acknowledgement of a fault or sin, esp to a confessor; a thing confessed; a statement of one's religious beliefs, creed.—**confessionary** *adj*.

confessional *n* an enclosure in a church where a priest hears confessions.

confessor *n* a priest who hears confessions and grants absolution; one who confesses.

confetti *npl* small bits of colored paper thrown at weddings.

confidant *n* a person trusted with one's secrets.—**confidante** *nf*.

confide *vti* to put confidence (in); to entrust; to impart a confidence or secret.—**confider** *n*.

confidence *n* firm trust, faith; belief in one's own abilities; boldness; something revealed confidentially.

confidence man *n* a con man, a swindler.

confidence trick *n* the persuading of a victim to hand over valuables as proof of confidence.

confident *adj* full of confidence; positive, assured.—**confidently** *adv*.

confidential *adj* spoken or written in confidence, secret; entrusted with secrets.—**confidentiality, confidentialness** *n*.—**confidentially** *adv*.

confiding *adj* unsuspicious.—**confidingly** *adv*.

config.sys *n* (*comput*) a DOS file that contains commands that set up the computer's operating system.

configuration[1] *n* arrangement of parts; external shape, general outline; aspect; (*astrol*) the relative position of the planets; the make-up of a computer system.—**configurational, configurative** *adj*.

configuration[2] *n* (*comput*) the machines that are interconnected and programed to operate as a computer system, usu a central processing unit with keyboard, VDU, printer and a disk drive; the setting up of a computer system or program to ensure that it matches the needs of the user.

confine *vt* to restrict, to keep within limits; to keep shut up, as in prison, a sickbed, etc; to imprison. * *n* (*pl*) borderland, edge, limit.—**confinable, confineable** *adj*.

confined *adj* narrow, enclosed, of limited space.

confinement *n* a being confined; the period of childbirth.

confirm *vt* to make stronger; to establish firmly; to make valid, to ratify; to corroborate; to administer rite of confirmation to.

confirmation *n* the act of confirming; convincing proof; the rite by which people are admitted to full communion in Christian churches.

confirmatory, confirmative *adj* giving extra proof; corroborative.

confirmed *adj* habitual; settled in belief, mode of life, etc; having undergone the rite of confirmation.

confiscate *vt* to appropriate to the state as a penalty; to seize by authority.—**confiscable** *adj*.—**confiscation** *n*.—**confiscator** *n*.—**confiscatory** *adj*.

conflagration *n* a massively destructive fire.—**conflagrative** *adj*.

conflation *n* a fusing together; a combining of two variant readings of a text into one.—**conflate** *vt*.

conflict *n* a fight; a contest; strife, quarrel; emotional disturbance. * *vi* to be at variance; to clash (with); to struggle.—**confliction** *n*.—**conflictive, conflictory** *adj*.

conflicting *adj* contradictory.

confluence, conflux *n* the point where two rivers meet; a coming together.

confluent *adj* flowing or running together. * *n* a tributary river or stream.

confocal *adj* having a common focus.

conform *vi* to comply, to be obedient (to); to act in accordance with. * *vt* to adapt; to make like.—**conformer** *n*.

conformable *adj* compliant; corresponding, adapted (to); in parallel order.—**conformability, conformableness** *n*.—**conformably** *adv*.

conformation *n* arrangement of parts, structure; adaptation.

conformist *n* one who conforms to established rules, standards, etc; compliance with the rites and doctrines of an established church.—**conformism** *n*.

conformity, conformance *n* (*pl* **conformities, conformances**) correspondence; agreement; conventional behavior; compliance.

confound *vt* to mix up, to obscure; to perplex, to astound; to overthrow; to mistake one thing for another.—**confounder** *n*.

confounded *adj* astonished; confused; annoying; (*inf*) damned.—**confoundedly** *adv*.

confraternity *n* (*pl* **confraternities**) a brotherhood or society of men associated for a common purpose.—**confraternal** *adj*.

confrère *n* an associate, a colleague.

confront *vt* to stand in front of, to face; to bring face to face (with); to encounter; to oppose.—**confronter** *n*.

confrontation *n* the coming face to face with; hostility without actual warfare, esp between nations.

Confucian *adj* pertaining to Confucius, the Chinese philosopher. * *n* a follower of the teachings of Confucius.

confuse *vt* to throw into disorder; to mix up; to mistake one thing for another; to perplex, to disconcert; to embarrass; to make unclear.—**confusable** *adj*.—**confusing** *adj*.—**confusingly** *adv*.

confused *adj* perplexed; disordered; mentally unbalanced.—**confusedly** *adv*.

confusion *n* the act or state of being confused; disorder; embarrassment, discomfiture; lack of clarity.

confute *vt* (*argument, etc*) to prove wrong; to convict of error; to overcome in argument.—**confutation** *n*.—**confutative** *adj*.—**confuter** *n*.

cong. *abbr* = (*pharm*) (*Latin*) *congius*, "gallon"; congregation.

Cong. *abbr* = Congregational; Congregationalist; Congregationist; Congress; Congressional.

conga *n* a Cuban dance in which the dancers move along in a long line; music for this; a tall, narrow drum which is played with the hands. * *vi* (**congaing, congaed**) to do this dance.

conga drum *n* a tall narrow drum beaten with the hands.

con game *n* a swindle in which someone is defrauded after his or her confidence has been gained.

congé *n* dismissal; (*arch*) a formal bow, esp at parting.

congeal *vti* to change from a liquid to a solid by cooling, to jell.—**congealment** *n*.

congelation *n* the act of congealing; a congealed state or substance.

congener *n* a person or thing of the same kind as another.

congeneric *adj* of the same genus or origin.

congenial *adj* of a similar disposition or with similar tastes, kindred; suited, agreeable (to).—**congenially** *adv*.—**congeniality, congenialness** *n*.

congenital *adj* existing or dating since birth, as in certain defects.—**congenitally** *adv*.

congenital hyperthyroidism *see* cretinism.

conger eel *n* a large marine eel.

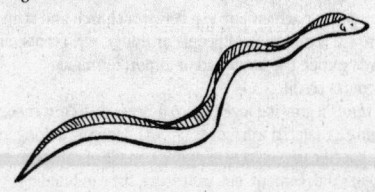

congeries *n* (*used as sing or pl*) a gathered mass, a heap; a conglomeration.

congest *vt* to overcrowd. * *vi* (*med*) to affect with congestion.—**congested** *adj*.—**congestible** *adj*.

congestion *n* an overcrowding; (*med*) an excessive accumulation of blood in any organ; an accumulation of traffic causing obstruction.—**congestive** *adj*.

Congl. *abbr* = Congregational.

conglobate *vti* to form into a mass.—**conglobation** *n*.

conglomerate *adj* stuck together in a mass. * *vt* to gather into a ball. * *n* a coarse-grained rock of embedded pebbles; a large corporation consisting of companies with varied and often unrelated interests.—**conglomeratic, conglomeritic** *adj*.

conglomeration *n* the act of conglomerating; a mass stuck together; a miscellaneous collection.

conglutinate *vt* to glue together. * *adj* glued together; united by an adhesive substance.—**conglutination** *n*.—**conglutinative** *adj*.

Congo, the Democratic Republic of *n* a country formerly known as Zaire, situated in west central Africa.

Congolese Franc *n* currency of the Democratic Republic of the Congo (DRC).

congou *n* a kind of black Chinese tea.

congratulate *vt* to express sympathetic pleasure at success or good fortune of, to compliment; to feel satisfied or pleased with oneself.—**congratulation** *n*.—**congratulator** *n*.—**congratulatory** *adj*.

congratulations *npl* an expression of joy or pleasure.

congregate *vti* to flock together, to assemble; to gather into a crowd or mass.—**congregator** *n*.

congregation *n* a gathering, an assembly; a body of people assembled for worship.

congregational *adj* of a congregation; (*with cap*) of or pertaining to Congregationalism.

Congregationalism *n* a form of church government in which each congregation has management of its own affairs.—**Congregationalist** *adj*, *n*.

congress *n* an association or society; an assembly or conference, esp for discussion and action on some question; (*with cap*) the legislature of the US, comprising the Senate and the House of Representatives.

congressional *adj* of, or relating to, a congress.—**congressionalist** *n*.

Congressman *n* (*pl* **Congressmen**) a member of Congress.—**Congresswoman** *nf* (*pl* **Congresswomen**).

Congreve *n* William (1670–1729) English dramatist whose comedies, e.g. *The Way of the World*, are notable for their witty dialog and sharp observation of social behavior in Restoration England.

congruent *adj* in agreement; harmonious; (*geom*) having identical shape and size so that all parts correspond.—**congruence, congruency** *n*.

congruous *adj* accordant; fit.—**congruity** *n*.

CONGU *abbr* = Council of National Golf Unions.

CONIAC *abbr* = Construction Industry Advisory Committee.

conic, conical *adj* of a cone; cone-shaped.

conics *n* (*used as sing*) the branch of geometry that deals with conic sections.

conic section *n* a curve formed from a cone—an ellipse, a parabola, or a hyperbola.

conidium (*pl* **conidia**) a reproductive cell formed of certain fungi.—**conidial** adj.

conifer *n* any evergreen trees and shrubs with true cones (as pines) and others (as yews).—**coniferous** *adj*.

coniferous *adj* bearing fruit cones.

coniferous forest *n* a forest of needle-leaved trees that are usu evergreen and shallow-rooted and bear cones.

conine, conin *n* a very poisonous alkaloid existing in the hemlock.

conium *n* a genus of biennial poisonous plants including the hemlock.

conj. *abbr* = conjunction; conjunctive; conjugation.

conjectural *adj* depending on conjecture, doubtful.—**conjecturally** *adv*.

conjecture *n* a guess, guesswork. * *vt* to make a conjecture, to guess, surmise.—**conjecturer** *n*.—**conjecturable** *adj*.—**conjectural** *adj*.

conjoin *vt* to join together; to connect or associate. * *vi* to be joined.—**conjoinedly** *adv*.—**conjoiner** *n*.

conjoined twins *see* **Siamese twins**.

conjoint *adj* united, combined; cooperating.—**conjointly** *adv*.

conjugal *adj* of or relating to marriage.—**conjugality** *n*.—**conjugally** *adv*.

conjugate *vt* to give the parts of (a verb); to unite.—**conjugable** *adj*.—**conjugation** *n*.—**conjugator** *n*.—**conjugative** *adj*.

conjugation *n* the act of conjugating; a group of verbs with the same inflections; the union of cells in reproduction.—**conjugational** *adj*.

conjunct[1] *adj* joined together; associated.

conjunct[2] *n* (*mus*) a succession of notes of different pitch.

conjunction *n* (*gram*) a word connecting words, clauses or sentences; a union; a simultaneous occurrence of events; (*astron*) the apparent proximity of two or more planets.—**conjunctional** *adj*.

conjunctiva *n* (*pl* **conjunctivas, conjunctivae**) the mucous membrane that lines the inner surface of the eyelids and the exposed area of the eyeball.—**conjunctival** *adj*.

conjunctive *adj* serving to unite; closely connected; (*gram*) of or pertaining to conjunctions. * *n* a conjunction.—**conjunctively** *adv*.

conjunctivitis *n* inflammation of the conjunctiva.

conjuncture *n* a combination of many circumstances or causes; a critical time.—**conjunctural** *adj*.

conjuration *n* the act of conjuring or invoking; an incantation; an enchantment; a solemn entreaty.

conjure *vti* to practice magical tricks; to call up (spirits) by invocation.

conjurer, conjuror *n* one who conjures or is skilled in sleight of hand.

conk *n* (*sl*) the nose or head. * *n* a blow to the nose or head. * *vt* to hit, esp on the head. * *vi* (*with out*) (*sl*) (*machine*) to break down entirely; to collapse suddenly from exhaustion.

conker *n* (*inf*) the horse chestnut; (*pl*) a children's game using conkers on a string.

con man *n* (*inf*) a swindler, one who defrauds by means of a confidence trick.

con moto *adj* (*mus*) (*Italian*) spirited.

Conn. *abbr* = Connecticut.

Connacht *n* (*Irish Celtic myth*) one of the five provinces into which the Fir Bholg divided Ireland. Traditionally it was the great rival and enemy of Ulster.

connate *adj* inborn, congenital; (*leaves*) united at the base.

connatural *adj* congenital; having the same nature.

connect *vti* to fasten together, to join; to relate together, to link up; (*trains, buses, etc*) to be timed to arrive as another leaves so that passengers can continue their journey; to establish a link by telephone; (*sl*) to punch or kick; to uncover (a source of drugs).—**connectible, connectable** *adj*.—**connector, connecter** *n*.

Connecticut (**CT**) *n* a state of the United States of America (USA) of which the capital is Hartford.

connection *n* the act of connecting; the state of being connected; a thing that connects; a relationship, bond; a train, bus, etc, timed to connect with another; an opportunity to transfer between trains, buses, etc; context; a link between components in an electric circuit; a relative; (*sl*) a supply or the supplier of illicit drugs; (*pl*) clients, customers.—**connectional** *adj*.

connective *adj* serving to connect.—**connectively** *adv*.

connective tissue *n* (*biol*) supporting or packing tissue within the body that holds or separates other tissues and organs.

connectivity *n* (*comput*) the ability of computers of different kinds to communicate.

connect time *n* (*comput*) the former basis of charging customers for time using computer online systems.

Connery *n* Sir Sean [Thomas] (1930–) Scottish movie actor who achieved fame as Ian Fleming's character James Bond, Oscar winner for his role in *The Untouchables* (1987).

conning tower *n* the armored pilot house of a submarine.

conniption *n* (*sl*) a fit of hysteria or rage.

connivance *n* the act of conniving; pretense of ignorance; passive cooperation in a crime or fault; collusion.

connive *vi* to permit tacitly; to wink (at); to plot.—**conniver** *n*.

connivent *adj* converging.

Connlai *or* **Conall** *n* (*Irish Celtic myth*) who was the child of Cuchulainn by Aoife[2]. Defeated and killed by Conall Cernach.

connoisseur *n* a trained discriminating judge, esp of the fine arts.

Connolly *n* Cyril [Vernon] (1903–74) English critic who edited the literary magazine *Horizon* whose works include a novel, *The Rock Pool*, collections of essays, and his best-known work, *The Unquiet Grave*, reflections on Western culture.

Connors *n* Jimmy (1952–) American tennis player. He won the US Open championships five times and Wimbledon twice.

connotation *n* a consequential meaning, an implication—**connotative, connotive** *adj*.

connote *vt* to imply; to indicate; to mean.

connubial *adv* of or relating to marriage.—**connubiality** *n*.—**connubially** *adv*.

conoid *n* (*geom*) a solid formed by revolution of a conic section about its axis. * *adj* somewhat conical (—*also* **conoidal**).

conquer *vt* to gain victory (over), to defeat; to acquire by conquest; to overcome, to master. * *vi* to be victor.—**conqueror** *n*.

conquest *n* conquering; the winning of a person's affection; a person or thing conquered.

Conquest *n* [George] Robert (1917–) English poet, historian, and critic whose works include *Poems* and, with Kingsley Amis, a comedy of sexual intrigue, the novel *The Egyptologists*.

conquistador *n* (*pl* **conquistadors, conquistadores**) a member of the Spanish forces that conquered Mexico and Peru in the 16th century.

Conrad *n* Joseph (1857–1924) Polish-born English master mariner and novelist whose third language was English and whose works include the novel *The Outcast of the Islands* and the novella *Heart of Darkness*.

Conrail *abbr* = Consolidated Rail Corporation

Conran *n* Sir Terence Orby (1931–) British designer and entrepreneur who opened his first Habitat stores in 1964.

cons. *abbr* = consecrated; consigned; consignment; consolidated; consonant; constable; constitution; constitutional; construction; consul; consulting.

consanguineous, consanguine *adj* related by blood or birth.—**consanguinity** *n*.

conscience *n* the knowledge of right and wrong that affects action and behavior; the sense of guilt or virtue induced by actions, behavior, etc; an inmost thought; conscientiousness.

conscience clause *n* a clause in an act giving relief to persons having religious scruples to some requirement in it.

conscience investment *n* the investment in companies whose activities do not offend the investor's moral principles.—*also* **ethical investment**.

conscience money *n* money paid, usu anonymously, to atone for some dishonest act or illegal monetary gain.

conscience-stricken *adj* feeling extreme guilt or remorse.

conscientious *adj* following the dictates of the conscience; scrupulous; careful, thorough.—**conscientiously** *adv*.—**conscientiousness** *n*.

conscientious objector *n* a person who refuses to serve in the military forces on moral or religious grounds.

conscionable *adj* governed by conscience, just.—**conscionably** *adv*.

conscious *adj* aware (of); awake to one's surroundings; (*action*) realized by the person who does it, deliberate.—**consciously** *adv*.

consciousness *n* the state of being conscious; perception; the whole body of a person's thoughts and feelings.

conscript *adj* enrolled into service by compulsion; drafted. * *n* a conscripted person (as a military recruit). * *vt* to enlist compulsorily.

conscription *n* compulsory military or naval service; the persons enrolled.—**conscriptional** *adj*.

consecrate *vt* to set apart as sacred, to sanctify; to devote (to).—**consecration** *n*.—**consecrator** *n*.—**consecratory, consecrative** *adj*.

consecration *n* the act of consecrating; a setting apart or devoting to a sacred use or office; (*with cap*) (*RC Church*) the part of Mass when the bread and wine are blessed.

con. sect. *abbr* = conic section *or* sections.

consecution *n* a following on; a logical sequence.

consecutive *adj* following in regular order without a break; successive; (*gram*) expressing consequence.—**consecutively** *adv*.

consensual *adj* caused by sympathetic action.

consensus *n* an opinion held by all or most; general agreement, esp in opinion.

consent *vi* to agree (to); to comply; to acquiesce * *n* agreement, permission; concurrence.—**consenter** *n*.

consequence *n* a result, an outcome; importance; (*pl*) an unpleasant result of an action; a game in which each player writes part of a story without knowing what has gone before.

consequent *adj* occurring as a result.

consequential *adj* pompous, self-important; resultant.—**consequentiality, consequentialness** *n*.—**consequentially** *adv*.

consequently *adv* as a result, therefore.

CONSER *abbr* = Cooperative Online Serials

conservancy *n* (*pl* **conservancies**) (*UK*) an authority controlling a river or port; conservation.

conservation *n* the act of conserving; preservation of the environment and natural resources.—**conservational** *adj*.—**conservationist** *n*.

conservationist *n* one who advocates or practices the protection of natural resources and wildlife.

conservation of energy *n* the fact that the amount of energy in a closed system remains the same although its form changes.

conservatism *n* opposition to change; a political ideology favoring preservation and defense of tradition.

conservative *adj* traditional, conventional; cautious; moderate. * *n* a conservative person; (*with cap*) a member of the Conservative Party in Britain and other countries.—**conservatively** *adv*.

conservatoire *n* an institution for instruction in music.

conservator *n* a custodian, a keeper; a preserver; a member of a conservancy.

conservatory *n* (*pl* **conservatories**) a greenhouse attached to a house; a conservatoire.

conserve *vt* to keep from loss or injury; to preserve (a foodstuff) with sugar. * *n* a type of jam using whole fruit.—**conservable** *adj*.—**conserver** *n*.

consider *vti* to reflect (upon), to contemplate; to examine, to weigh the merits of; to take into account; to regard as; to be of the opinion; to act with respect; to allow for.—**considerer** *n*.

considerable *adj* a fairly large amount; worthy of respect.—**considerably** *adv*.

considerate *adj* careful of the feelings of others.—**considerately** *adv*.

consideration *n* the act of considering; deliberation; a point of importance; an inducement; thoughtfulness; deference; a payment.

considered *adj* well thought out.

considering *prep* in view of. * *adv* all in all. * *conj* seeing that.

consign *vt* to hand over, to commit; to send goods addressed (to).—**consignable** *adj*.—**consignation** *n*.

consignee *n* the person to whom goods are consigned.

consignment *n* consigning; goods, etc consigned; (*business*) an arrangement between an exporter and an importer by which the exporter receives payment for goods only when they have been transported and sold by the importer.

consignor *n* the person by whom goods are consigned.

consist *vi* to be made up (of); to be comprised (of).

consistency *n* (*pl* **consistencies**) degree of density, esp of thick liquids; the state of being consistent.

consistent *adj* compatible, not contradictory; uniform in thought or action.—**consistently** *adv*.

consistory *n* a solemn assembly or the place where it meets; the ecclesiastical court of the pope and cardinals, of an Anglican bishop, or of Presbyterian presbyters.—**consistorial, consistorian** *adj*.

consol. *abbr* = consolidated.

consolation *n* someone or something that offers comfort in distress.—**consolatory** *adj*.

consolation prize *n* a prize for the runner up or loser in a competition.

console[1] *vt* to bring consolation to, to cheer in distress.—**consolable** *adj*.—**consoler** *n*.

console[2] *n* a desk containing the controls of an electronic system; (*comput*) the terminal that is used to control the computer system; the part of an organ containing the pedals, stops, etc; an ornamental bracket supporting a shelf or table.

consolidate *vti* to solidify; to establish firmly, to strengthen; to combine into a single whole.—**consolidator** *n*.

consolidation *n* the act of consolidating; solidification.

consols *npl* (*Brit*) government securities consolidated into a single stock.

consommé *n* a clear soup made from meat stock.

consonance, consonancy *n* (*pl* **consonance, consonancies**) agreement of sounds; harmony; concord.

consonant *n* a letter of the alphabet that is not a vowel; the sound representing such a letter. * *adj* consistent, in keeping (with).—**consonantal** *adj*.

consort[1] *n* a husband or wife, esp of a reigning queen or king; a ship sailing with another. * *vti* to associate, to keep company with (often dubious companions).—**consorter** *n*.

consort[2] *n* (*arch*) an ensemble of musical instruments, e.g., a consort of viols.

consortium *n* (*pl* **consortia**) an international banking or financial combination.—**consortial** *adj*.

cons. sp. *abbr* = constant speed.

conspectus *n* a general sketch or digest of some subject, a synopsis.

conspicuous *adj* easily seen, prominent; outstanding, eminent.—**conspicuousness** *n*.—**conspicuously** *adv*.

conspiracy *n* (*pl* **conspiracies**) a secret plan for an illegal act; the act of conspiring.

conspirator *n* one who conspires.—**conspiratorial, conspiratory** *adj*.—**conspiratorially** *adv*.

conspire *vti* to combine secretly for an evil purpose; to plot, to devise.

con spirito *adj, adv* (*mus*) (*Italian*) with spirit.

const. *abbr* = constant; constitution.

constable *n* (*UK*) a policeman or policewoman of the lowest rank; a governor of a royal castle.

Constable *n* John (1776–1837) English painter regarded as an oustanding landscape painter.

constabulary *n* (*pl* **constabularies**) (*UK*) a police force.—*also adj*.

constancy *n* being constant; steadfastness; fidelity.

constant *adj* fixed; unchangeable; unchanging; faithful; firm and steadfast; continual. * *n* (*math, physics*) a quantity that does not vary; (*comput*) a fixed value used in a spreadsheet.

Constanta *n* a city in Romania.

Constantine[1] *n* a city in Algeria.

Constantine[2] *n* (*d.* 820) king of Picts (789–820). The first Constantine to rule in Scotland was the son of Alpin II's sister.

Constantine I 1. *n* (*d.* 878) king of Scots (862–877) the son of Kenneth Mac-Alpin, he succeeded Kenneth's brother, Donald, to the throne and bore the title of Constantine I. **2.** (*c.*274–337) Roman emperor who became the first Christian emperor in 312 and moved the capital to Byzantium (renamed Constantinople) in 330.

Constantine II *n* (*d.* 952) king of Scots (900–942).

Constantine III *n* (*d.* 997) king of Scots (995–997). The grandson of Constantine II and son of Cuilean.

constantly *adv* continually, continuously, often.

constellate *vti* to form into a constellation.

constellation *n* a group of fixed stars; an assembly of the famous.—**constellatory** *adj*.

consternate *vt* to dismay.

consternation *n* surprise and alarm; shock; dismay.

constipate *vt* to cause constipation in.—**constipated** *adj*.

constipation *n* infrequent and difficult movement of the bowels.

constituency *n* (*pl* **constituencies**) a body of electors; the voters in a particular district or area.

constituent *adj* forming part of a whole, component; having the power to revise the constitution. * *n* a component part; a member of an elective body; a voter in a district.

constitute *vt* to set up by authority, to establish; to frame, to form; to appoint; to compose, to make up.—**constituter, constitutor** *n*.

constitution *n* fundamental physical condition; disposition; temperament; structure, composition; the system of basic laws and principles of a government, society, etc; a document stating these specifically.

constitutional *adj* of or pertaining to a constitution; authorized or limited by a constitution, legal; inherent, natural. * *n* a walk for the sake of one's health.—**constitutionally** *adv*.—**constitutionality** *n*.

constitutionalism *n* constitutional government; adherence to constitutional principles.—**constitutionalist** *n*.

constitutive *adj* having the power to enact, constituent; elemental; essential; productive.

constr. *abbr* = construction; construed.

constrain *vt* to compel, to force; to hinder by force; to confine, to imprison.—**constrainer** *n*.

constrained *adj* enforced; embarrassed, inhibited; showing constraint.

constraint *n* compulsion; forcible confinement; repression of feeling; embarrassment; a condition that restricts freedom.

constrict *vt* to draw together, to squeeze, to compress.

constricted *adj* narrowed, cramped.

constriction *n* compression; tightness.—**constrictive** *adj*.

constrictor *n* a constrictive muscle; a snake that crushes its prey.

construct *vt* to make, to build, to fit together; to compose. * *n* a structure; an interpretation; an arrangement, esp of words in a sentence.—**constructible** *adj*.—**constructor, constructer** *n*.

construction *n* a constructing; anything constructed; a structure, building; interpretation, meaning; (*gram*) two or more words grouped together to form a phrase, clause, or sentence.—**constructional** *adj*.

constructive *adj* helping to improve, promoting development.—**constructively** *adv*.

constructive dismissal *n* a situation in a workplace in which an employer or a member of the management team behaves towards an employee in such a way that the employee claims that he or she had no choice but to resign.

constructivism *n* nonrepresentational art, esp sculpture based on movement and using machine-made materials.

constructivist theater *n* a form of theater in which stage sets use technological artefacts derived from industrial processes to emphasize the kinetic, active nature of the stage developed from futurism.

construe *vti* (**construing, construed**) to translate word for word; to analyze grammatically; to take in a particular sense, to interpret.—**construer** *n*.

consubstantiation *n* the doctrine that the body and blood of Christ are in a mysterious manner substantially present in the Eucharistic elements after Consecration.

consuetude *n* an established custom.—**consuetudinary** *adj*.

consul *n* a government official appointed to live in a foreign city to attend to the interests of his country's citizens and business there.—**consular** *adj*.

consulate *n* the official residence of a consul; the office of a Roman consul.

consult *vti* to seek advice from, esp a doctor or lawyer; to seek information from, e.g., a work of reference; to deliberate, to confer.—**consulter, consultor** *n*.

consultant *n* a specialist who gives professional or technical advice; a senior physician or surgeon in a hospital; a person who consults another.—**consultancy** *n* (*pl* **consultancies**).

consultation *n* the act of consulting; a conference, esp with a professional adviser.—**consultative, consultatory, consultive** *adj*.

consultative, consultatory *adj* advisory; deliberative.

consumable *adj* able to be consumed. * *n* (*usu pl*) something bought to be used.

consume *vti* to destroy; to use up; to eat or drink up; to waste away; to utilize economic goods.

consumer *n* a person who uses goods and services, the end user.

consumer durables *npl* goods, such as television sets, automobiles, etc, that have a useful life that extends over a relatively long period of time, unlike consumer non-durables.

consumer goods *npl* commodities for domestic consumption which are not used for the production of other goods and services.

consumer non-durables *npl* goods, such as food, that are purchased by members of the public and are used either immediately or within a relatively short time, unlike consumer durables.

consumer price index *n* an index of the prices of the food, clothing, and housing necessary for life.

consumer research *n* research that indicates consumer needs and preferences.

consumerism *n* protection of the interests of consumers; encouragement to buy consumer goods.

consummate¹ *vt* to bring to perfection, to be the crown of; (*marriage*) to complete by sexual intercourse.—**consummation** *n*.—**consummative, consummatory** *adj*.—**consummator** *n*.

consummate² *adj* complete, perfect, highly skilled.

consumption *n* the act of consuming; the state of being consumed or used up; (*econ*) expenditure on goods and services by consumers; tuberculosis.

consumptive *adj* tending to consume; affected with consumption. * *n* a person with tuberculosis.

cont. *abbr* = containing; contents; continent; continue; continued; contra; contract.

Cont. *abbr* = Continental.

cont. bon. mor *abbr* (*Latin*) = *contra bonos mores*, "contrary to good manners."

cont. rem. *abbr* (*Latin*) = *continuantur remedia*, "let the remedies be continued."

contact *n* touch, touching; connection; an acquaintance, esp one willing to provide help or introductions in business, etc; a connection allowing the passage of electricity; (*med*) a person who has been in contact with a contagious disease.* *vti* to establish contact with.—**contactual** *adj*.

contact lens *n* a thin correctional lens placed over the cornea of the eye.

contact print *n* a photographic print made by exposing a negative in direct contact with a photosensitive surface.

contagion *n* the communicating of a disease by contact; a disease spread in this way; a corrupting influence.

contagious *adj* (*disease*) spread by contact; capable of spreading disease by contact; (*influence*) catching, infectious.—**contagiousness** *n*.

contain *vt* to hold, to enclose; to comprise, to include; to hold back or restrain within fixed limits.

container *n* a receptacle, etc, designed to contain goods or substances; a standardized receptacle used to transport commodities.

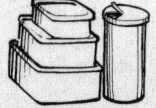

container ship *n* a ship built specifically to transport containerized cargo.

containerize *vt* to put or convey (cargo) in large standardized containers.

containment *n* the prevention of the expansion of a hostile power; the prevention of the release of dangerous quantities of radioactive material from a nuclear reactor.

containment building *n* a building enclosing a nuclear reactor to limit the spread of radiation, esp in the event of an accident.

contaminate *vt* to render impure by touch or mixing, to pollute, esp by radioactive contact.—**contaminant** *n*.—**contaminator** *n*.

contamination *n* the act of contaminating; the state of being contaminated; a thing that contaminates.

contd. *abbr* = continued.

conte *n* a short story.

contemn *vt* to despise; to disregard scornfully.—**contemner, contemnor** *n*.—**contemnible** *adj*.

contemp. *abbr* = contemporary.

contemplate *vti* to look at steadily; to reflect upon, to meditate; to have in view, to intend.—**contemplator** *n*.

contemplation *n* the act of contemplating; pious meditation; intention.

contemplative *adj* thoughtful, meditative, of or given to contemplation; dedicated to religious contemplation.—**contemplatively** *adv*.—**contemplativeness** *n*.

contemporaneous *adj* existing or occurring at the same time; of the same period.—**contemporaneously** *adv*.—**contemporaneity** *n*.

contemporary *adj* living or happening at the same time; of about the same age; present day; of or following present-day trends in style, art, fashion, etc. * *n* (*pl* **contemporaries**) a person living at the same time; a person of the same age.—**contemporarily** *adv*.

contempt *n* the feeling one has towards someone or something considered low, worthless etc; the condition of being despised; disregard.

contemptible *adj* deserving contempt.—**contemptibly** *adv*.—**contemptibility** *n*.

contemptuous *adj* showing or feeling contempt; disdainful.—**contemptuously** *adv*.—**contemptuousness** *n*.

contend *vti* to take part in a contest, to strive (for); to quarrel; to maintain (that), to assert or argue strongly for.—**contender** *n*.

content¹ *n* (*usu pl*) what is in a container; (*usu pl*) what is in a book; substance or meaning.

content² *adj* satisfied (with), not desiring more; willing (to); happy; pleased. * *n* quiet satisfaction. * *vt* to make content; to satisfy.—**contentment** *n*.

contented *adj* content; gratified, satisfied.—**contentedly** *adv*.

contention *n* contending, struggling, arguing; a point in dispute; an assertion in an argument.—**contentional** *adj*.

contentious *adj* tending to argue; likely to cause dispute, controversial.—**contentiously** *adv*.

content provider *n* (*comput*) a company that provides material for preservation on another company's website or online service.

conterminous *adj* having a common boundary (with), contiguous.—*also* **coterminous**.

Contes d'Hoffmann *see* **Tales of Hoffmann**.

contest *vti* to call in question, to dispute; to fight to gain, to compete for; to strive. * *n* a struggle, an encounter; a competition; a debate; a dispute.—**contestable** *adj*.—**contestation** *n*.—**contester** *n*.

contestant *n* a competitor in a contest; a person who contests.

context *n* the parts of a written work or speech that precede and follow a word or passage, contributing to its full meaning; associated surroundings, setting.—**contextual** *adj*.—**contextually** *adv*.

context sensitive help *n* (*comput*) an information system in application programs that automatically finds the relevant pages to assist with a command or operation.

contextualize *vt* to place in or treat as part of a context.

contexture *n* a structure; a fabric; a style of composition.—**contextural** *adj*.

contg. *abbr* = containing.

contiguous *adj* touching, adjoining; near; adjacent.—**contiguity** *n*.

contiguous zone *n* a zone beyond the territorial seas over which a nation claims exclusive rights.

contin. *abbr* = continued; continuer; (*Latin*) *continuetur*, "let it be continues."

continent¹ *n* one of the six or seven main divisions of the earth's land; (*with cap*) the mainland of Europe, excluding the British Isles; a large extent of land.

continent² *adj* able to control urination and defecation; practicing self-restraint; chaste.—**continence, continency** *n*.

continental *adj* of a continent; (*with cap*) of or relating to Europe, excluding the British Isles; (*Brit*) of or relating to the former thirteen British colonies later forming the USA. * *n* an inhabitant of the Continent.—**continentalism** *n*.—**continentalist** *n*.—**continentally** *adv*.

continental air mass *n* a usu dry air mass originating over a continental interior where high atmospheric pressure occurs, forming in low or high latitudes.

continental breakfast *n* a light morning meal of coffee and rolls.

continental Celtic *n* a branch of the Indo-European family of languages now extinct; spoken from about 500 BC to AD 500 from the Black Sea to Iberia.

continental climate *n* the type of climate found in the interiors of large land masses in mid-latitudes, with low rainfall, cold winters and hot summers.

continental crust *n* the Earth's crust, which lies beneath the continents and continental shelves.

continental divide *n* high ground on either side of which the rivers of a continent flow in opposite directions.

continental drift *n* (geol) the (theoretical) gradual process of separation of the continents from their original solid land mass.

continental shelf *n* the sea bed, under relatively shallow seas, bordering a continent.

continental slope *n* the slope between the edge of the continental shelf and the deep sea floor.

contingency *n* (*pl* **contingencies**) a possibility of a future event or condition; something dependent on a future event.

contingency plan *n* a plan formulated by a company that can be put into practice in the event of some circumstance occurring.

contingent *adj* possible, that may happen; chance; dependent (on); incidental (to). * *n* a possibility; a quota of troops.—**contingently** *adv*.

contingent liability *n* a liability that may occur if a certain circumstance occurs.

continual *adj* frequently repeated, going on all the time.—**continuality** *n*.—**continually** *adv*.

continuance *n* uninterrupted succession; duration.

continuant *n* a consonant whose sound can be prolonged, as *f*, *v*.

continuation *n* a continuing; prolongation; resumption; a thing that continues something else, a sequel, a further installment.

continue *vt* to go on (with); to prolong; to extend; to resume, to carry further. * *vi* to remain, to stay; to last; to preserve.—**continuable** *adj*.—**continuer** *n*.—**continuingly** *adv*.

continuity *n* (*pl* **continuities**) continuousness; uninterrupted succession; the complete script or scenario in a movie or broadcast.

continuo *abbr* (*mus*) (Italian) = *basso continuo*, in 17th century Baroque music the bass line on which a keyboard player could effect a harmonic accompaniment. *See also* **figured bass**.

continuous *adj* continuing; occurring without interruption.—**continuously** *adv*.—**continuousness** *n*.

continuous processing *n* (*manufacture*) a process in which extremely high volumes of a product are produced continuously on plant specifically designed for the purpose.

continuous spectrum *n* a spectrum formed by the complete and unbroken range of electromagnetic waves.

continuum *n* (*pl* **continua, continuums**) a continuous and homogeneous whole.

contort *vti* to twist out of a normal shape, to pull awry.—**contorted** *adj*.—**contortion** *n*.—**contortional** *adj*.

contortionist *n* a person who can twist his or her body into unusual postures, esp as entertainment.—**contortionistic** *adj*.

contour *n* the outline of a figure, land, etc; the line representing this outline; a contour line. * *adj* made according to a shape or form (*contour chair*).

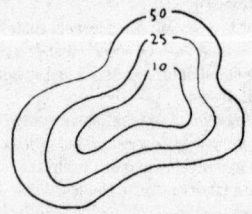

contour fort *n* (*archeo*) a hill fort in which the defensive earthworks follow the line of a contour round the hill.

contour line *n* a line on a map that passes through all points at the same altitude.

contour ploughing *n* a method of ploughing parallel to the contours to prevent erosion.

contr. *abbr* = contract; contracted; contraction; contractions; contralto; contrary; control; controller.

contra *n* a thing that may be argued against.

contra- *prefix* against.

contraband *n* smuggled goods; smuggling. * *adj* illegal to import or export.—**contrabandist** *n*.

contraband of war *n* certain commodities used in warfare; the traffic in them with belligerent states; goods supplied to one belligerent and seizable by another.

contrabass *n* an instrument sounding an octave lower than another instrument of the same class; the largest instrument of the violin class, the double bass.—**contrabassist** *n*.

contrabassoon *n* the largest instrument of the oboe class.—**contrabassoonist** *n*.

contraception *n* the deliberate prevention of conception, birth control.

contraceptive *n* a contraceptive drug or device.—*also adj*.

contract *vt* to draw closer together; to confine; to undertake by contract; (*debt*) to incur; (*disease*) to become infected by; (*word*) to shorten by omitting letters. * *vi* to shrink; to become smaller or narrower; to make a contract; (*with* out) to decide not to take part in or join, eg a pension scheme. * *n* a bargain; an agreement to supply goods or perform work at a stated price; a written agreement enforceable by law.—**contractibility** *n*.—**contractible** *adj*.

contract bridge *n* a form of bridge in which the players contract to take a certain number of tricks.

contractile *adj* able or causing to grow smaller.—**contractility** *n*.

contraction *n* the act of contracting; the state of being contracted; a contracted word; a labor pain in childbirth.—**contractional** *adj*.—**contractive** *adj*.

contract note *n* a document that is sent out by a broker to a client as proof that securities or commodities have been bought or sold according to the client's instructions.

contract of employment *n* an agreement by which an employee undertakes to work for an employer for a certain remuneration and which sets out the terms and conditions of employment.

contractor *n* a person who makes a business contract, esp a builder; something that draws together, e.g. a muscle.

contractual *adj* of a contract.—**contractually** *adv*.

contradance *see* **contredanse**.

contradict *vti* to assert the contrary or opposite of; to deny; to be at variance (with); to lack consistency.—**contradictable** *adj*.—**contradicter, contradictor** *n*.

contradiction *n* the act of contradicting; a denial.—**contradictory** *adj*.

contradistinction *n* a distinction by opposite qualities.—**contradistinctive** *adj*.

contradistinguish *vt* to mark the difference between two things by contrasting their opposite qualities.

contrail *n* a line of vapor formed in the wake of an aircraft or rocket.

contraindicate *vt* (*med*) to indicate the inadvisability of (a particular treatment, drug, etc).—**contraindication** *n*.—**contraindicative** *adj*.

contralto *n* (*pl* **contraltos**) a singing voice having a range between tenor and mezzo-soprano; a person having this voice.

contraposition *n* opposition, antithesis.

contraption *n* (*inf*) a device, a gadget.

contrapuntal *adj* of or according to counterpoint.—**contrapuntally** *adv*.

contrapuntist *n* one skilled in the rules of counterpoint.

contrariety *n* (*pl* **contrarieties**) opposition; inconsistency, discrepancy.

contrariwise *adv* on the other hand; conversely.

contrary *adj* opposed; opposite in nature; wayward, perverse. * *n* (*pl* **contraries**) the opposite. * *adv* in opposition to; in conflict with.—**contrarily** *adv*.—**contrariness** *n*.

contrary motion *see* **inversion**.

contrast *vi* to show marked differences. * *vt* to compare so as to point out the differences. * *n* the exhibition of differences; difference of qualities shown by comparison; the degree of difference between colors or tones when put together.

contratenor *n* (*mus*) (in the 14th and 15th centuries) a voice with approximately the same range as a tenor.

contravene *vt* to infringe (a law), to transgress; to conflict with, to contradict.—**contravener** *n*.—**contravention** *n*.

contredanse *n* a dance in which the partners are arranged in opposite lines; the music for this.—*also* **contradance**.

contretemps *n* (*pl* **contretemps**) a confusing, embarrassing or awkward occurrence.

contrib. *abbr* = contributor.

contribute *vti* to give to a common stock or fund; to write (an article) for a magazine or newspaper; to furnish ideas, etc.—**contributive** *adj*.

contribution *n* the act of contributing; something contributed; a literary article; a payment into a collection.

contributor *n* a person who contributes, esp the writer of an article for a newspaper, etc; a factor, a contributory cause.—**contributorial** *adj*.

contributory *adj* giving, donating; partly responsible, sharing in.

con trick *n* (*inf*) confidence trick.

contrite *adj* deeply repentant, feeling guilt.—**contritely** *adv*.—**contrition** *n*.

contrivance *n* something contrived, esp a mechanical device, invention; inventive ability; an artificial construct; a stratagem.

contrive *vt* to plan ingeniously; to devise, to design; to manage; to achieve, esp by some ploy or trick; to scheme.—**contriver** *n*.

contrived *adj* skillful but overdone; (*writing*) not spontaneous or natural or flowing.

control *n* restraint; command, authority; a check; a means of controlling; a standard of comparison for checking an experiment; (*business*) the direction of the financial and operational policies of a company, making sure that these are efficient and effective and taking corrective action where necessary; (*pl*) mechanical parts by which an automobile, airplane, etc, is operated. * *vt* (**controlling, controlled**) to check; to restrain; to regulate; to govern; (*experiment*) to verify by comparison.

control panel *n* (*comput*) a utility program designed to allow the user to alter the look and feel of the computer environment.

control point *or* **control station** *n* a point on the ground whose exact position and elevation has been determined with great accuracy used as a reference point when carrying out survey work.

control tower *n* a tower at an airport from which flight directions are given.

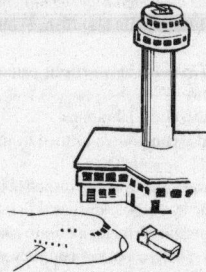

controllable *adj* able to be controlled.—**controllably** *adv*.

controlled drug *n* a drug that is subject to restrictions.

controller *n* a person who controls, esp one in charge of expenditure or finances.

controlling interest *n* a financial interest in a company that gives the person holding the investment control of the company.

controversial *adj* causing controversy, open to argument.—**controversialism** *n*.—**controversialist** *n*.—**controversially** *adv*.

controversy *n* (*pl* **controversies**) a discussion of contrary opinions; dispute, argument.

controvert *vt* to contend against; to refute; to disprove.—**controverter** *n*.—**controvertible** *adj*.

contumacious *adj* resisting authority, insubordinate; obstinate.

contumacy *n* (*pl* **contumacies**) stubborn resistance to authority, esp contempt of court.—**contumacious** *adj*.

contumelious *adj* haughtily contemptuous or offensive; supercilious.

contumely *n* (*pl* **contumelies**) haughty and contemptuous rudeness; scornful and insolent abuse; reproach, disgrace.

contuse *vt* to wound or bruise without breaking the skin.—**contusive** *adj*.

contusion *n* a wound that does not break the skin, a bruise.—**contusioned** *adj*.

conundrum *n* a riddle involving a pun; a puzzling question.

conurbation *n* a vast urban area around and including a large city.

conv. *abbr* = convent; convention; conversation; converter.

convalesce *vi* to recover health and strength after an illness; to get better.—**convalescence** *n*.

convalescence *n* the gradual recovery of a person's health and strength after a disease or operation.

convalescent *adj* recovering health; aiding the recovery of full health. * *n* a patient recovering after an illness.

convection *n* the transmission of heat through a liquid by currents; the process whereby warmer air rises while cooler air drops.—**convectional** *adj*.—**convective** *adj*.

convection current *n* any current of warm fluid, gas or liquid that rises and is replaced by colder fluid.

convection rain *n* rain which occurs when moist air is warmed and rises, then cools and if its temperature falls below dew point, clouds form and heavy rain falls (associated with equatorial climates and the cold fronts of polar air masses).

convection zone *n* a region where heat energy is principally carried by convection currents, i.e. by movement of a fluid from regions at a higher temperature to regions at a lower one.

convector *n* a heater that circulates warm air.

convene *vti* to call together for a meeting.—**convenable** *adj*.—**convener** *n*.

convenience food *n* food that is easily and quickly prepared.

convenience *n* what suits one; a useful appliance.

convenient *adj* handy; suitable; causing little or no trouble.—**conveniently** *adv*.

convent *n* a house of a religious order, esp an establishment of nuns.

conventicle *n* a meeting house; a secret meeting; an assembly for worship, usu by a schism; (*formerly*) a prohibited meeting of Nonconformists or Covenanters.

convention *n* a political or ecclesiastical assembly or meeting; an agreement between nations, a treaty; established usage, social custom.

conventional *adj* of or based on convention or social custom; not spontaneous; lacking imagination or originality; following accepted rules; (*weapons*) non-nuclear.—**conventionality** *n* (*pl* **conventionalities**).—**conventionally** *adj*.

conventionalism *n* that which is received as established by usage, etc; adherence to established usage.—**conventionalist** *n*.

conventionalize *vt* to make conventional.—**conventionalization** *n*.

conventional wisdom *n* a body of established and generally accepted opinion.

conventual *adj* belonging to a convent. * *n* a member or inmate of a convent.

converge *vti* to come or bring together.—**convergence, convergency** *n*.—**convergent** *adj*.

conversable *adj* disposed to converse, sociable.

conversant *adj* well acquainted; proficient; familiar (with).—**conversance, conversancy** *n*.

conversation *n* informal talk or exchange of ideas, opinions, etc between people.—**conversational** *adj*.—**conversationally** *adv*.

conversationalist, conversationist *n* a person who is good at conversation.

conversation piece *n* originally an 18th-century picture showing a group in an outdoor or indoor setting; something unusual or novel that provokes conversation; a play that focuses interest on dialog as much as on action.

conversazione *n* (*pl* **conversazioni, conversaziones**) a meeting for conversation, esp on literary or scientific topics.

converse¹ *vi* to engage in conversation (with). * *n* familiar talk, conversation.—**converser** *n*.

converse² *adj* opposite, contrary. * *n* something that is opposite or contrary.—**conversely** *adv*.

conversion *n* change from one state, or from one religion, to another; something converted from one use to another; an alteration to a building undergoing a change in function; (*rugby*) a score after a try by kicking the ball over the crossbar.—**conversional, conversionary** *adj*.

conversion cost *n* the costs involved in a production process in which raw material is converted into finished product.

convert *vt* to change from one thing, condition or religion to another; to alter; to apply to a different use; (*rugby*) to make a conversion after a try. * *n* a converted person, esp one who has changed religion.

converter reactor *n* a nuclear reactor that changes fertile material to fissile material.

converter, convertor *n* one who converts; an iron retort used for converting pig iron into steel in the Bessemer process; a kind of electrical induction coil.

convertibility *n* (*finance*) the extent to which a financial security, such as a foreign currency, can be freely exchanged for another.

convertible *adj* able to be converted. * *n* an automobile with a folding or detachable roof.—**convertibility** *n*.

convertible currency *n* (*finance*) a currency that can be freely converted into the currency of another country.

convex *adj* curving outward like the surface of a sphere.—**convexly** *adv*.—**convexity** *n*.

convexo-concave *adj* convex on one side, concave on the other.

convexo-convex *adj* curving outwards on both sides, as a lens.

convey *vt* to transport; to conduct, to transmit; to make known, to communicate; (*law*) to make over (property).—**conveyable** *adj*.—**conveyor, conveyer** *n*.

conveyance *n* the act of conveying; a means of transporting, a vehicle; (*law*) the act of transferring property.—**conveyancer** *n*.

conveyancing *n* the business of drawing up deeds, leases, etc, and investigating titles to property.

conveyor belt *n* a continuous moving belt or linked plates for moving objects in a factory.

convict *vt* to prove or pronounce guilty. * *n* a convicted person serving a prison sentence.

conviction *n* act of convicting; a settled opinion; a firm belief.

convince *vt* to persuade by argument or evidence; to satisfy by proof.—**convincer** *n*.—**convincible** *adj*.

convincing *adj* compelling belief.—**convincingly** *adv*.

convivial *adj* sociable, jovial.—**conviviality** *n*.—**convivially** *adv*.

convocation *n* the act of convoking an assembly, esp of bishops, clergy or heads of a university; an assembly of clergy.—**convocational** *adj*.—**convocator** *n*.

convoke to call or summon together; to convene.—**convoker** *n*.

convolute *vt* to form into a rolled or coiled shape. * *adj* (*bot*) rolled upon itself; coiled.

convoluted *adj* twisted; coiled; complicated, difficult to understand.

convolution *n* a rolling together, a coiling; a fold, a twist; a complicated or confused matter.

convolve *vt* to roll together.

convolvulus *n* (*pl* **convolvuluses, convolvuli**) a twining plant with bell-shaped flowers.

convoy *n* a group of ships or vehicles traveling together for protection. * *vt* to travel thus.

convulse *vt* to agitate violently; to shake with irregular spasms. * *vi* (*inf*) to cause to shake with uncontrollable laughter.—**convulsive** *adj*.—**convulsively** *adv*.

convulsion *n* a violent involuntary contraction of a muscle or muscles; an agitation, tumult; (*pl*) a violent fit of laughter.

cony, coney *n* (*pl* **conies, coneys**) rabbit, or the skin or fur of a rabbit used in making clothes.

coo *n* the note of the pigeon; a soft murmuring sound. * *vt* (**cooing, cooed**) to utter the cry of a dove or pigeon; to speak softly; to act or murmur in a loving manner.

cook *vt* to prepare (food) by heat; (*inf*) to fake (accounts, etc); to subject to great heat. * *vi* to be a cook; to undergo cooking; (*with* up) to plot; to make up a story. * *n* a person who cooks; one whose job is to cook.—**cookable** *adj*.

Cook *n* (Captain) James (1728–79) English explorer who claimed the east coast of Australia for Britain and discovered New Caledonia.

cookbook, cookery book *n* a book of recipes and other information for preparing food.

cook-chill *n* (*catering*) a method in which meals are pre-cooked, chilled rapidly, and then reheated as required.

cooker *n* an electric or gas appliance for cooking.

cookery *n* the art or practice of cooking.

cookhouse *n* a kitchen, esp outdoors.

cookie¹, cooky *n* (*pl* **cookies**) a small flat sweet cake; (*sl*) a person.

cookie² *n* (*comput*) a small file created by a Web server which is transmitted to, and stored on, the hard disk of the computer making the connection. It matches the data and "recognises" the individual browser. The cookie records what was looked at and the site last visited.

cookout *n* a meal cooked and eaten outdoors, a barbecue.

cool *adj* moderately cold; calm; indifferent; unenthusiastic; cheeky. * *vti* to make or become cool. * *n* coolness; composure.—**coolly** *adv.*—**coolness** *n*.

coolabah, coolibah *n* an Australian eucalyptus tree.

coolant *n* a fluid or other substance for cooling machinery.

cooler *n* that which cools; a vessel for cooling liquids, etc; a drink of spirits; (*sl*) prison.

Cooley's anemia *see* **thalassemia**.

cool-headed *adj* not easily excited.

Coolidge *n* 1. **(John) Calvin** (1872–1933) American Republican politician and 30th president of the US (1923–39). He succeeded Warren Harding. 2. **Susan [Sarah Chauncey Woolsey]** (1835-1905) American children's writer best-known for the *Katy* books, e.g. *What Katy Did* (1872).

coolie, cooly *n* (*pl* **coolies**) an Indian or Chinese hired laborer.

cooling tower *n* a tall hollow construction used in some industries, in which water is cooled and reused.

coombe *see* **combe**.

coon *n* a raccoon; (*derog*) a black person.

cooncan *n* a card game for two.

co-op *n* a cooperative.

co-op. *abbr* = co-operative.

coop *n* a small pen for poultry. * *vt* to confine as in a coop.

cooper *n* one who makes and repairs barrels, etc.

Cooper *n* 1. **Gary [Frank James Cooper]** (1901–61) American movie actor whose movies include *High Noon*. 2. **James Fenimore** (1789–1851) American novelist whose adventure novels include *The Last of the Mohicans*. 3. **Samuel** (1609–72) English painter of miniature portraits. 4. **Susie [Susan Vera]** (1902–1996) British ceramicist who became the first woman to have her name stamped on wares.

cooperage *n* the business or workshop of a cooper; the price for a cooper's work.

cooperate *vi* to work together, to act jointly.—**cooperation** *n*.—**cooperator** *n*.

cooperative *adj* willing to cooperate; helpful. * *n* an organization or enterprise owned by, and operated for the benefit of, those using its services.—**cooperatively** *adv*.

co-ops. *abbr* = co-operatives.

co-opt *vt* to elect or choose as a member by the agreement of the existing members; to appropriate; to take over by assimilation.—**co-optation, co-option** *n*.—**co-optative, co-optive** *adj*.

coordinate *vt* to integrate (different elements, etc) into an efficient relationship; to adjust to; to function harmoniously. * *n* an equal person or thing; any of a series of numbers that, in a given frame of reference, locate a point in space; (*pl*) separate items of clothing intended to be worn together. * *adj* equal in degree or status.—**coordinately** *adv*.—**coordinator** *n*.

coordinate system *n* a system of numbers, essentially representing lengths, indicating the position of a required point relative to the origin or starting point.

coordination *n* the act of coordinating; the state of being coordinated; balanced and harmonious movement of the body.

coot *n* a European water-bird with dark plumage and a white spot on the forehead; a silly person.

cootie *n* (*sl*) a louse.

cop[1] *vt* (**copping, copped**) (*sl*) to arrest, catch. * *vi* (*with* **out**) (*sl*) to fail to perform, to renege. * *n* (*sl*) capture; a policeman.

cop[2] *n* a conical ball of thread on a spindle.

cop. *abbr* = copper; copyrighted.

Cop. *abbr* = Copernican; Coptic.

COP *abbr* = Coastal Ocean Program

copacetic *adj* (*sl*) in order; first-rate.

copaiba *n* an aromatic resinous balsam from various South American and West Indian trees.

copal *n* a gum resin used in varnishes.

coparcenary *n* joint heirship.

coparcener *n* a coheir.

copartner *n* a joint partner.—**copartnership** *n*.

COPD *abbr* = chronic obstructive pulmonary disease.

cope[1] *vi* to deal successfully with; to contend on even terms (with).

cope[2] *n* a large semicircular ecclesiastical vestment worn by bishops and priests over the surplice; a canopy, esp of heaven.

COPEC *abbr* = Conference of Politics, Economics and Christianity.

Copeland *n* (*comput*) the code name for a version of the Macintosh operating system.

Copenhagen (København) *n* capital city of Denmark.

Coper *n* **Hans** (1921–1981) German-born ceramicist who settled in Britain in 1939.

Coperario *n* **John** (*c*.1575–1626) English composer and noted player of the lute and viola da gamba.

Copernican *adj* of or relating to Copernicus and his teaching that the earth and planets revolve around the sun (**Copernican system**).

Copernicus *n* **Nicolas** (1473–1543) Polish astronomer. His great work *De Revolutionibus* (1543) sets out his theory that the planets orbit the sun.

copestone *n* the top stone of a structure; a crowning touch.

copier *n* a copying machine, a photocopier.

copilot *n* a second pilot in an aircraft.

coping *n* the top masonry of a wall.

coping saw *n* a saw with a U-shaped frame and narrow blade used for cutting outlines in wood.

copious *adj* plentiful, abundant.—**copiously** *adv*.—**copiousness** *n*.

Copland *n* **Aaron** (1900–90) American composer, conductor, pianist, and teacher. His best-known works include the ballets *Billy the Kid*, *Appalachian Spring*, *Rodeo*, and *Fanfare for the Common Man*. He also wrote symphonies, a piano concerto, and chamber music.

Copley *n* **John Singleton** (1738–1815) American painter and one of the greatest portraitists of the 18th century.

COPOL *abbr* = Council of Polytechnic Librarians.

copolymer *n* (*chem*) a polymer compound, formed by the polymerization of two or more monomers.

cop-out *n* (*sl*) an evasion; a means of avoiding responsibility.

Coppélia *n* a ballet with music by Delibes which was first performed in 1870.

copper[1] *n* a reddish ductile metallic element; a bronze coin. * *adj* made of, or of the color of, copper. * *vt* to cover with copper.—**coppery** *adj*.

copper[2] *n* (*sl*) a police officer.

Copper Age *n* a period, often not apparent, between the Stone Age and the Bronze Age.

copper-bottomed *adj* to be trusted; financially sound.

copperhead *n* a South American snake.

copperplate *n* a polished plate of copper for engraving or printing; a print from this; copybook writing.

coppersmith *n* a worker in copper.

Coppola *n* **Francis Ford** (1939–) American movie director and screenwriter. His movies include *Apocalypse Now* (1979).

COPPSSO *abbr* = Conference of Professional and Public Service Organizations.

copra *n* the dried kernel of the coconut after the oil has been removed.

COPRA *abbr* = Conference of Private Residents Associations.

copro- *prefix* dung.

coprocessor *n* (*comput*) a secondary or support chip that is used alongside the main chip to provide added power for specific operations e.g. graphics display.

coprolite *n* fossil dung.—**coprolitic** *adj*.

coprophagous *adj* feeding on dung, as certain beetles.—**coprophagy** *n*.

coprophilia *n* an abnormal interest in feces; love of obscenity.

coprophilous *adj* growing in dung.

COPS *abbr* = Office of Community Oriented Policing Services

copse *n* a thicket of small trees and shrubs.

Copt *n* a native Egyptian Christian.

Copt. *abbr* = Coptic.

copter *n* a helicopter.

Coptic *adj* pertaining to the Copts, their church or their language. * *n* the language spoken by Copts.

copula *n* (*pl* **copulas, copulae**) a link, a connecting part; (*gram*) a word that joins the subject and predicate in a sentence or proposition.—**copular** *adj*.

copulate *vi* to have sexual intercourse.—**copulation** *n*.—**copulatory** *adj*.

copulative *adj* joining, uniting; (*gram*) serving as a copula; uniting ideas as well as words. * *n* a copulative conjunction.

COPUOS *abbr* = UN Committee on the Peaceful Uses of Outer Space.

COPUS *abbr* = Committee on the Public Understanding of Science.

copy *n* (*pl* **copies**) a reproduction; a transcript; a single specimen of a book; a model to be copied; a manuscript for printing; newspaper text; text for an advertisement; subject matter for a writer. * *vt* (**copying, copied**) to make a copy of, to reproduce; to take as a model, to imitate; (*comput*) to create a duplicate of a file, graphic or program without changing the original version.

copybook *n* a book of handwriting exercises.

copy-edit *vt* to correct and prepare text for printing.

copyhold *n* (*English law*) a tenure of estate by copy of the court roll or custom of the manor.

copyholder *n* a tenant by copyhold; (*print*) a reader's assistant.

copyist *n* one who copies.

copy protection *n* (*comput*) a method of preventing, or at least reducing, the user's ability to copy a program illegally.

copyright *n* the exclusive legal right to the publication and sale of a literary, dramatic, musical, or artistic work in any form. * *adj* protected by copyright.

copywriter *n* a writer of advertising or publicity copy.—**copywriting** *n*.

coq. *abbr* (*pharm*) (*Latin*) = *coque*, "boil."

coq au vin *n* a dish of chicken cooked in wine.

coquet *vi* (**coquetting, coquetted**) to flirt with; to seek to attract attention or admiration; to trifle.

coquetry *n* (*pl* **coquetries**) the act of coquetting; flirtatious behavior.

coquette *n* a woman who trifles with men's affections.—**coquettish** *adj*.

coquito *n* (*pl* **coquitos**) a tall Chilean palm producing edible nuts and palm honey.

cor *see* **horn**.

cor. *abbr* = corner; cornet; coroner; corpus; corrected; correction; corrective; correlative; correspondence; correspondent; corresponding; corrupted; corruption.

Cor. *abbr* (*Bible*) = Corinthians.

COR *abbr* = The Club of Rome.

CORA *abbr* = Chemical and Oil Recycling Association.

CORAA *abbr* = Council of Regional Arts Associations.

coracle *n* a boat with a wicker frame covered with leather.

coracoid *n* a hook-like process of the scapula or bladebone.

coral *n* the hard skeleton secreted by certain marine polyps. * *adj* made of coral, esp jewelry; of the color of coral, deepish pink.

CORAL *abbr* = Common Real-Time Application Language.

coralline, coralloid *adj* consisting of, or like, coral; of a color like coral. * *n* a coral-like seaweed or animal.

coral reef *n* a formation or bank of coral.

coral snake *n* a venomous American snake with black, red, and yellow markings.

coral tree *n* an American tree with blood-red flowers.

coranach *n* (*mus*) (*Gaelic*) a lament sung at Scottish funerals.

Coranaid *npl* (*Welsh Celtic myth*) a group of small people who could overhear everything, no matter how low it was whispered. They were one of three plagues that disturbed the reign of Lludd.

co-range line *n* a line drawn on a map joining either climatic stations showing the same temperature range between January and July or points with an equal tidal range.

cor anglais *n* (*mus*) an alto oboe pitched a fifth below the standard oboe.

coranto *see* **courante**.

CORAS *abbr* = Center for Operational Research & Applied Statistics.

CORAT *abbr* = Christian Organizations Research and Advisory Trust.

Coray *n* **Hans** (1906–1991) Swiss designer who promoted the use of aluminum in furniture design.

corban *n* an offering to God in fulfilment of a vow.

corbeil *n* (*archit*) a sculptured basket of flowers, fruit, etc.

corbel *n* a stone or wood projection from a wall to support something. * *vt* (**corbeling, corbeled** *or* **corbelling, corbelled**) to furnish with or support by corbel.

corbelling *n* (*archeo*) the method of roofing a chamber (often a tomb) by successively overlapping the courses of stone.

corbicula *n* (*pl* **corbiculae**) the receptacle for pollen in the honey bee.

CORCA *abbr* = Committee of Registered Clubs Associations.

cord *n* a thick string or thin rope; something that binds; a slender electric cable; a ribbed fabric, esp corduroy; (*pl*) corduroy pants any part of the body resembling string or rope (*spinal cord*).

corda *n* (*mus*) (*Italian*) "string," as in "piano string". The term *una corda* means "one string," an indication to use the "soft" pedal on the piano.

CORDA *abbr* = Coronary Artery Disease Research Association.

cordage *n* a quantity of cords or ropes; ropes and rigging collectively.

cordate *adj* heart-shaped.

Cordelia *n* (*astron*) a small satellite of Uranus.

cordial *adj* hearty, warm; friendly; affectionate. * *n* a fruit-flavored drink.—**cordially** *adv*.—**cordialness** *n*.

cordiality *n* (*pl* **cordialities**) sincere sympathethic geniality; sincerity; heartiness.

cordiform *adj* heart-shaped.

cordillera *n* a continuous ridge or chain of mountains, esp of the Andes mountains.

cordite *n* an explosive used in bullets and shells.

cordless *adj* (*electrical device*) operated by a battery.

cordoba *n* the standard monetary unit of Nicaragua, equal to 100 centavos.

Cordoba *n* a city in Argentina.

Córdoba Oro *n* currency of Nicaragua.

cordon *n* a chain of police or soldiers preventing access to an area; a piece of ornamental cord or ribbon given as an award; (*archeo*) a decorative strip of clay, often with some form of indented pattern, pressed onto the surface of a vessel before it was fired; (*archit*) a circular stone molding below the parapet of the retaining wall of a fort. * *vt* (*with* **off**) (*area*) to prevent access to.

cordon bleu *n* the highest distinction in any profession; a first-class cook.—*also adj*.

cordon sanitaire *n* a barrier around an infected area; a buffer zone.

cord ornament *n* (*archeo*) a form of decoration applied to pottery by pressing a twisted "rope" of clay into the surface before firing.

cordovan *n* a Spanish leather made of goatskin or split horsehide, tanned and dressed.—*also* **cordwain**.

cords *npl* (*inf*) corduroy pants.

corduroy *n* a strong cotton fabric with a velvety ribbed surface; (*pl*) pants of this.

corduroy road *n* a roadway formed of logs laid crosswise across swampy ground, etc.

cordwain *see* **cordovan**.

cordwainer *n* (*arch*) a worker in leather; a shoemaker.

core *n* the innermost part, the heart; the inner part of an apple, etc containing seeds; the region of a nuclear reactor containing the fissile material; (*comput*) a form of magnetic memory used to store one bit of information; (*archeo*) a piece of rock, usu flint, from which flakes or blades were chipped off to produce stone tools; (*astron*) the innermost, usu spherical, heart of any celestial object. * *vt* to remove the core from.—**corer** *n*.

COREE *abbr* = Conference on Organic Environmental Economics.

Corelli *n* **Arcangelo** (1653–1713) an Italian violinist and composer who spent much of his early life in France and Germany as a virtuoso performer. His most important pieces include sonatas (e.g., twelve *Sonate a tre*) and twelve *Sonate da camera a tre*.

coreopsis *n* a kind of plant with rayed flowers and seeds with two small horns at the end.

core sampling *n* (*geol*) a method of withdrawing samples of soil, peat, rock, or ice from the area under examination.

corespondent *n* (*law*) a person named as having committed adultery with the husband or wife from whom a divorce is sought.—**corespondency** *n*.

corgi *n* (*pl* **corgis**) a Welsh breed of dog with short legs and a sturdy body.

CORGI *abbr* = Confederation for Registration of Gas Installers.

coriaceous *adj* of leather; leathery.

coriander *n* a plant with aromatic seeds used for flavoring food.

Corinth *n* in ancient Greece an important city-state on the isthmus of the same name which joins the Peloponnese to northern Greece.—**Corinthian** *adj*.

Corinthian *adj* of or pertaining to Corinth, a Greek city noted for its luxury and licentiousness; luxurious; conducted by amateurs; (*archit*) denoting the Corinthian order. * *n* a man about town; a gentleman yachtsman or sportsman.

Corinthian order *n* the lightest and most ornate of the classic orders of architecture, with a bell-shaped capital and ornamented with acanthus leaves.

Corinthians, the First and Second Letter of Paul to the *n* (*Bible*) NT book revealing Paul's concern for the development of the Church there.

Coriolis force *n* (*physics*) a theoretical force used when calculating the movement of particles in relation to a spinning or rotating body.

corium *n* (*pl* **coria**) the innermost layer of skin of the cuticle.

cork *n* the outer bark of the cork oak used esp for stoppers and insulation; a stopper for a bottle, esp made of cork. * *adj* made of cork. * *vt* to stop up with a cork; to give a taste of cork to (wine).

Cork *n* a city in the Republic of Ireland.

corkage *n* a charge made by a restaurant for serving wine, esp when brought in by the customer from outside.

corked *adj* (*wine*) contaminated by a decayed cork.

corker *n* (*sl*) something conclusive or superlatively good; a flagrant lie.

corkscrew *n* a tool for drawing corks from wine bottles. * *adj* spiral-shaped, resembling a corkscrew.

corky *adj* made of, or like, cork.

corm *n* the bulb-like underground stem of the crocus, etc; a solid bulb.—**cormous** *adj*.

Cormac mac-Art *or* **Cormac mac Airt** *n* (*d. c*.360) high king of Ireland. A semi-legendary warrior king who reigned from Tara. Said to have been the father of Cairbre and Grainne.

Corman *n* **Roger** (1926–) American movie director and producer.

cormel *n* a new corm developing from a mature one.

Cor. Mem. *abbr* = Corresponding Member.

cormorant *n* a large voracious sea bird with dark plumage and webbed feet.

corn[1] *n* a grain or seed of a cereal plant; plants that yield grain; maize; (*sl*) something corny.

corn[2] *n* a small hard painful growth on the foot.

corn[3] *vt* to preserve or cure, as with salt.

cornbread *n* a sweet loaf bread made of cornmeal.

corn circle *see* **crop circle**.

corncob *n* the central part of an ear of maize to which the corn kernels are attached; a corncob pipe.

corncockle *n* a plant with purplish flowers that grows among corn.

corncrake *n* a bird with a harsh cry, the landrail.

corncrib *n* a storehouse for corn.

cornea *n* (*pl* **corneas, corneae**) the transparent membrane in front of the eyeball.—**corneal** *adj*.

corneal graft *n* a surgical procedure to replace a damaged or diseased cornea with one from a donor.—*also* **keratoplasty**.

corn(ed) beef *n* cooked salted beef.

Corneille *n* **Pierre** (1606–84) French dramatist whose best-known plays are the tragedies *Le Cid*, *Horace*, *Cinna*, and *Polyeucte* and who is regarded as the main founder of French neoclassical tragedy.

cornel *n* the cornelian cherry or dogwood, yielding an acrid edible red berry.

cornelian *n* a dull-red semi-transparent form of chalcedony.—*also* **carnelian**.

Cornelius *n* (*Bible*) Roman centurion sympathetic to the Jewish faith and customs, who was baptized together with his household.

Cornelius *n* 1. **Peter** (1824–74) a German composer and writer who was a friend of Wagner and Liszt. His works include the operas *The Barber of Baghdad* and *The Cid*. 2. **Peter von** (1783–1867) German painter who revived German interest in monumental fresco painting, a notable example of which is the *Last Judgement* in the Ludwigskirche in Munich.

Cornell *n* 1. **Ezra** (1807–74) American industrialist and philanthropist. He founded the Western Union Telegraph company (1855) and Cornell University with Andrew Dickson White (1832–1918). 2. **Cornell** *n* **Joseph** (1903–73) American self-taught sculptor and pioneer of assemblage techniques. His style is constructivist in approach with surrealist overtones.

corneous *adj* horny.

corner *n* the point where sides or streets meet; an angle; a secret or confined place; a difficult or dangerous situation; (*football*, *hockey*) a free kick from the corner of the pitch; a monopoly over the supply of a good or service giving control over the market price; one of the opposite angles in a boxing ring. * *vt* to force into a corner; to monopolize supplies of (a commodity). * *vi* to turn round a corner; to meet at a corner or angle.

cornerstone *n* the principal stone, esp one at the corner of a foundation; an indispensable part; the most important thing or person.

cornet *n* a tapering valved brass musical instrument; a cone-shaped wafer for ice cream.

cornetist, cornettist *n* a performer on the cornet.

cornett *n* an obsolete wind instrument dating from the Middle Ages. It comprised a tube of wood, pierced with seven holes which were covered by the fingers and with a cup-shaped mouthpiece.

cornfield *n* a field planted with corn or other cereal plants.

cornflakes *npl* a breakfast cereal made from split and toasted maize.

cornflower *n* a blue-flowered wild plant growing in cornfields.

corn husk *n* the leafy husk surrounding an ear of corn.

cornice *n* a plaster molding round a ceiling or on the outside of a building.

corniche *n* a coastal road, esp one along a cliff offering spectacular views.

corniculate *adj* horned; spurred.

Corn Laws *npl* British laws (1436–1834) for regulating the import and export of corn, repealed 1846–9.

cornmeal *n* meal ground from corn.

corn pone *n* a type of Indian cornbread made with milk and eggs.

cornstalk *n* a stem of corn; (*sl*) a youth or girl of Australian birth.

cornstarch *n* a type of corn or maize flour used for thickening sauces.—*also* **cornflour.**

cornucopia *n* a horn-shaped container overflowing with fruits, flowers, etc; great abundance, an inexhaustible store.

cornute, cornuted *adj* (*biol*) horned; horn-like.

corny *adj* (**cornier, corniest**) (*inf*) hackneyed; banal; trite; overly sentimental.—**cornily** *adv*.—**corniness** *n*.

corol. or **coroll.** *abbr* = corollary.

corolla *n* the inner envelope of a flower composed of two or more petals.

corollary *n* (*pl* **corollaries**) an additional inference from a proposition already proved; a result.

corona *n* (*pl* **coronas, coronae**) a top; a crown; a luminous halo or envelope round the sun or moon; the flat projecting part of a cornice.

coronal *adj* pertaining to the corona. * *n* a crown or garland.

coronary *adj* pertaining to the arteries supplying blood to the heart. * *n* (*pl* **coronaries**) a coronary artery; coronary thrombosis.

coronary arteries *npl* the arteries that supply blood to the heart and arise from the aorta.

coronary artery disease *n* any abnormal condition that affects the arteries of the heart. Angina is a common symptom of such diseases.

coronary bypass graft *n* a surgical operation that is carried out when one or more of the coronary arteries have become narrowed by disease and by which a section of vein from a leg is grafted in to bypass the obstruction.

coronary thrombosis *n* blockage of one of the coronary arteries by a blood clot.

coronation *n* the act or ceremony of crowning a sovereign.

coroner *n* a public official who inquires into the causes of sudden or accidental deaths.—**coronership** *n*.

coronet *n* a small crown; an ornamental headdress.

Coronis *n* (*Greek myth*) the mother of Aesculapius by Apollo.

Corot *n* Jean-Baptiste Camille (1796–1875) French painter who greatly influenced landscape painting in the late 19th century.

corp. *abbr* = corporal; corporation.

Corp. Jur. Civ. *abbr* = Corpus Juris Civilis.

corpn. *abbr* = corporation.

corpora *see* **corpus.**

corporal[1] *n* a noncommissioned officer below the rank of sergeant.—**corporalship** *n*.

corporal[2] *adj* of or relating to the body; physical, not spiritual.—**corporality** *n*.—**corporally** *adv*.

corporal[3] *n* a communion cloth.

corporate *adj* legally united into a body; of or having a corporation; united.—**corporately** *adv*.

corporate governance *n* the manner in which a company is managed and the nature and effectiveness of management responsibility.

corporate restructuring *n* a change in a company's internal system of organization; a change in a company's business strategy.

corporation *n* a group of people authorized by law to act as one individual; a city or town council.—**corporative** *n*.

corporation tax *n* a tax that is levied on the total profits of a company in each accounting period.

corporator *n* a member of a corporation.

corporeal *adj* having a body or substance, material.—**corporeality, corporealness** *n*.—**corporeally** *adv*.

corposant *n* a flame-like electric discharge from a ship's mast and rigging in thundery weather, St Elmo's fire.

corps *n* (*pl* **corps**) an organized subdivision of the military establishment; a group or organization with a special function (*medical corps*).

corps de ballet *n* all the dancers in a ballet company.

corps diplomatique *n* all the ambassadors at a particular capital, the diplomatic corps.

corpse *n* a cadaver, a dead body. * *vi* (*theat sl*) to laugh or create laughter mischievously on stage.

corpulent *adj* fleshy, fat.—**corpulence, corpulency** *n*.

corpus *n* (*pl* **corpora**) a body or collection, esp of written works; the chief part of an organ.

Corpus Christi *n* (*RC Church*) a festival in honor of the Eucharist, held on the Thursday after Trinity Sunday.

corpuscle *n* a red or white blood cell.—**corpuscular** *adj*.

corpus delicti *n* (*law*) the essence of a crime charged.

Corpus Jur. Can. *abbr* = Corpus Juris Canonici.

corpus luteum *n* (*anat*) the tissue that forms within the ovary after the structure that contains the egg ruptures and releases an ovum at the time of ovulation.

corr. *abbr* = corrected; correspond; correspondence; correspondent; corresponding; corrupt; corrupted; corruption.

corral *n* a pen for livestock; an enclosure with wagons; a strong stockade. * *vt* (**corralling, corralled**) to form a corral; to put or keep in a corral.

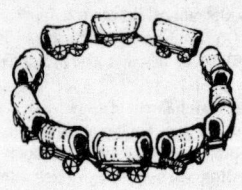

Corrca *n* Charles M. (*b.* 1930) Indian architect, whose notable works include Parliament Buildings, Bhopal.

correct *vt* to set right, to remove errors from; to reprove, to punish; to counteract, to neutralize; to adjust. * *adj* free from error; right, true, accurate; conforming to a fixed standard; proper.—**correctable, correctible** *adj*.—**correctly** *adv*.—**correctness** *n*.—**corrector** *n*.

correction *n* the act of correcting; punishment.—**correctional** *adj*.

correctitude *n* correctness, esp of conduct.

corrective *adj* serving to correct or counteract. * *n* that which corrects.—**correctively** *adv*.

Correggio *n* Antonio Allegri da (*d.* 1534) Italian painter from Parma, a leading figure of the High Renaissance.

correlate *vti* to have or to bring into mutual relation; to correspond to one another. * *n* either of two things so related that one implies the other.—**correlation** *n*.—**correlative** *adj*.

correlation *n* reciprocal relation; similarity or parallelism of relation or law; the interdependence of functions, organs, natural forces, or phenomena.—**correlational** *adj*.

correlative *adj* having or expressing reciprocal or mutual relation. * *n* the antecedent to a pronoun.—**correlativeness, correlativity** *n*.

corresp. *abbr* = correspondence; corresponding.

correspond *vi* to answer, to agree; to be similar (to); to tally; to communicate by letter.

correspondence *n* communication by writing letters; the letters themselves; agreement.

correspondence school *n* an institution offering tuition (**correspondence courses**) by mail.

correspondent *n* a person who writes letters; a journalist who gathers news for newspapers, radio, or television from a foreign country. * *adj* similar, analogous.

correspondent bank *n* a bank in a foreign country that provides banking services to the customers of a bank in another country, there usu being a reciprocal agreement between the two banks.

Corr. Fell. *abbr* = Corresponding Fellow.

corridor *n* a long passage into which compartments in a train or rooms in a building open; a strip of land giving a country without a coastline access to the sea.

corrie *n* (*Scot*) a round hollow on a hillside.

corrigendum *n* (*pl* **corrigenda**) an error in a book, etc, for which a correction slip is printed.

corrigible *adj* capable of being amended, correct, or reformed.—**corrigibility** *n*.

Corr. Mem. *abbr* = Corresponding Member.

corroborant *adj* corroborating. * *n* a corroborating fact.

corroborate *vt* to confirm; to make more certain; to verify.—**corroboration** *n*.—**corroborative** *adj*.—**corroborator** *n*.

corroboree *n* an Australian festivity and dance.

corrode *vti* to eat into or wear away gradually, to rust; to disintegrate.—**corrodant, corrodent** *n*.—**corroder** *n*.—**corrodible** *adj*.—**corrosion** *n*.

corrosion *n* the act of corroding; a corroded condition.

corrosive *adj* causing corrosion. * *n* a corrosive substance, as acid.—**corrosively** *adv*.—**corrosiveness** *n*.

corrosive sublimate *n* a poisonous compound of mercury.

corrugate *vt* to form into parallel ridges and grooves.—**corrugated** *adj*.—**corrugation** *n*.

corrugated iron *n* sheet iron pressed in alternate parallel ridges and grooves and galvanized.

corrugated paper *n* paper used for packaging with one surface in parallel ridges.

corrupt *adj* dishonest; taking bribes; depraved; rotten, putrid. * *vti* to make or become corrupt; to infect; to taint.—**corrupter, corruptor** *n*.—**corruptive** *adj*.—**corruptly** *adv*.—**corruptness** *n*.

corrupted file *n* (*comput*) a file or part of a file that has become unreadable.
corruptible *adj* open to corruption.—**corruptibility** *n*.
corruption *n* the act of corrupting; the state of being corrupted; physical dissolution.—**corruptionist** *n*.
corsage *n* a small bunch of flowers for pinning to a dress; the part of a woman's dress covering the bust.
corsair *n* a pirate; a pirate ship.
corse *n* (*poet*) a cadaver.
Cor. Sec. *abbr* = Corresponding Secretary.
corselet, corslet *n* light body armor, esp for the breast.
corset *n* a close-fitting undergarment, worn to support the torso.

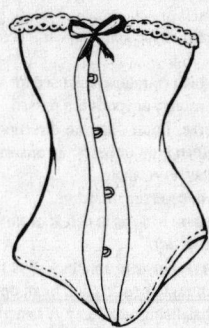

corsetière *n* a woman who makes and fits corsets.—**corsetier** *nm*.
cort. *abbr* = cortex.
CORT *abbr* = Council of Regional Theaters; Council of Repertory Theaters.
cortege, cortège *n* a train of attendants; a retinue; a funeral procession.
Cortes *n* the national and legislative assembly of Spain and (formerly) Portugal.
cortex *n* (*pl* **cortices**) an outer layer of tissue of any organ, e.g., the outer gray matter of the brain; the outer tissue of a plant stem; bark of a tree.—**cortical** *adj*.
corticate, corticated *adj* covered with bark or a bark-like substance.—**cortication** *n*.
corticosteroid *n* any steroid hormone manufactured by the adrenal cortex.
cortisone *n* a hormone produced by the adrenal glands, the synthetic version of which is used to treat arthritis, allergies, and skin disorders, etc.
corundum *n* a hard mineral of many colors used as an abrasive and as gemstones.
coruscate *vi* to sparkle, to flash.—**coruscation** *n*.
corvée *n* the exacting of unpaid labor in the feudal system.
corves *see* **corf**.
corvette *n* a fast escort warship.
corvine *adj* of or pertaining to a crow or raven.
Corvus *n* a southern sky constellation.
Corybants *npl* (*Greek myth*) male attendants of the goddess Cybele.
corymb *n* an inflorescence with the flowers all nearly at the same level and the lower stalks are the longest.—**corymbose, corybous** *adj*.
coryphaeus *n* (*pl* **coryphaei**) the leader of the chorus in ancient Greek drama.
coryphée *n* a ballet dancer.
coryza *n* a severe cold in the head with inflammation of the mucous membrane of the nose.
Cos, Kos *n* an island in the Aegean Sea.—**Coan, Koan** *adj*.
cos *abbr* (*math*) = cosine.
cos. *abbr* = companies; counties.
c.o.s. *or* **cos** *abbr* = cash on shipment.
CoS *abbr* = Chief of Staff.
COS *abbr* = Canadian Otolaryngological Society; Central Orchid Society; Charity Organization Society; (*mil*) Chief of Section; Cinema Organ Society.
co. sa. *abbr* (*mus*) (*Italian*) = *come sopra*, "as above."
COSAWR *abbr* = Committee on South African War Resistance.
Cosby *n* **Bill [William Henry]** (1937–) American comedian and actor; star of several television shows, including *The Cosby Show* (1984–92).
COSCO *abbr* = China Ocean Shipping Company.
cosec *abbr* (*geom*) = cosecant.
cosecant *n* (*geom*) the secant of the complement of the given angle or arc of 90 .
cosech *abbr* (*geom*) = hyperbolic cosecant.
coseismal, coseismic *adj* showing simultaneous shocks of an earthquake.
COSFPS *abbr* = Commons, Open Spaces, and Footpaths Preservation Society.
Cosgrave *n* **W[illiam] T[homas]** (1880–1965) Irish nationalist politician; first president of the Irish Free State (1922–32).
cosh *vt* (*sl*) to bludgeon.
cosh *abbr* (*geom*) = hyperbolic cosine.
cosher *vt* to pamper, to coddle.
COSHH *abbr* = Control of Substances Hazardous to Health.
cosignatory *n* a person signing along with another.
cosine *n* a trigonometrical function of an angle that in a right-angled triangle is equal to the ratio of the length of the adjacent side to the hypotenuse.
COSLA *abbr* = Convention of Scottish Local Authorities.
cosmetic *n* a preparation for improving the beauty, esp of the face. * *adj* beautifying or correcting faults in the appearance.—**cosmetically** *adv*.

cosmetic surgery *n* surgery carried out to improve the appearance.
cosmic, cosmical *adj* of or pertaining to the universe and the laws that govern it; vast in extent, intensity, or comprehensiveness.—**cosmically** *adv*.
cosmic rays *npl* (*astron*) rays of radiation coming from various sources in space such as the sun and solar wind.
cosmo- *prefix* universe.
cosmogony *n* (*pl* **cosmogonies**) the origin of the universe; a theory or treatise on this.—**cosmogonal** *adj*.—**cosmogonic, cosmogonical** *adj*.—**cosmogonist** *n*.
cosmography *n* the description and mapping of the universe or the earth as a whole.—**cosmographer, cosmographist** *n*.—**cosmographic, cosmographical** *adj*.
cosmology *n* the science of the nature, origins, and development of the universe.—**cosmological, cosmologic** *adj*.—**cosmologist** *n*.
cosmonaut *n* a Russian astronaut.
cosmopolitan *adj* of all parts of the world; free from national prejudice; at home in any part of the world. * *n* a well-traveled person; a person without national prejudices.—**cosmopolitanism** *n*.
cosmopolite *n* a citizen of the world, a person without patriotism; an animal or plant found worldwide.—**cosmopolitism** *n*.
cosmos *n* the universe as an ordered whole; any orderly system.
COSPOIR *abbr* (*Eire*) = National Sports Council.
coss. *abbr* (*Latin*) = *consules*, "consuls."
Cossack *n* a member of a Russian people skilled as horsemen. * *adj* pertaining to Cossacks.
COSSEC *abbr* (*Brit*) = Cambridge, Oxford, and Southern School Examinations Council.
cosset *vt* to make a pet of; to pamper.
cost *vt* (**costing, cost**) to involve the payment, loss, or sacrifice of; to have as a price; to estimate and fix the price of. * *n* a price; an expense; expenditure of time, labor, etc; a loss, a penalty; (*pl*) the expenses of a lawsuit.
costa[1] *n* (*pl* **costae**) a rib.—**costal** *adj*.
costa[2] *n* (*Spanish*) coastline.
COSTA *abbr* = Council of Subject Teaching Associations.
Costa *n* **Lucio** (*b.* 1902) Brazilian architect, designer of plans for Brasilia.
costal cartilage *n* (*anat*) a type of cartilage connecting a rib to the sternum (breastbone).
co-star *n* an actor or actress sharing top billing in a movie, play, etc.
costard *n* a large kind of English apple; (*arch*) a head.
Costa Rica *n* a small republic bounded by Nicaragua to the north, Panama to the south, the Pacific Ocean to the south and west, and the Caribbean Sea to the east.
costate *adj* ribbed.
cost-effective *adj* giving a satisfactory return for the amount spent on outlay.
costive *adj* constipated.
costly *adj* (**costlier, costliest**) expensive; involving great sacrifice.—**costliness** *n*.
costmary *n* (*pl* **costmaries**) a perennial plant with fragrant leaves, formerly used for flavoring ale.
cost of capital *n* the cost to a company of the capital that is used to finance its business activities.
cost-of-living index *n* consumer price index.
cost-plus *adj* (*price*) based on the cost of production plus an agreed percentage of profit.
costume *n* a style of dress, esp belonging to a particular period, fashion, etc; clothes of an unusual or historical nature, as worn by actors in a play, etc; fancy dress.
costume drama *n* a dramatization in which the actors wear period costumes.
costumer, costumier *n* a dealer in fancy dress for the theater, etc.
costume jewelry *n* imitation gems or cheap jewelry worn for decorative effect.
cosy *see* **cozy**.
cot[1] *n* a child's box-like bed; a narrow collapsible bed.

cot[2] *abbr* = cotangent.
COT *abbr* = Committee on Toxicity of Chemicals in Food, Consumer Products, and the Environment.
cotangent *n* a trigonometrical function of an angle that in a right-angled triangle is equal to the ratio of the length of the adjacent side to the opposite side.
cot death *see* **crib death**.
cote *n* a shed or shelter for animals or birds, esp doves.
côte *n* (*French*) coast; steep slope.
Côte d'Ivoire *n* a former French colony in west Africa.
cotenant *n* a joint tenant.—**cotenancy** *n*.
coterie *n* a small circle of people with common interests; a social clique.
coterminous *see* **conterminous**.
coth *abbr* = hyperbolic cotangent.
cotidal *adj* (*chart lines*) joining those places where high tide occurs at the same time.

C

cotillion *n* a brisk, lively dance for eight or more people; music for such a dance; a formal ball.

Cotman *n* **John Sell** (1782–1842) English draftsman and painter, who is best known for his sepia and watercolor landscapes, such as *Greta Bridge* (1805).

cotoneaster *n* an ornamental shrub of the rose family with red or orange berries.

Cotonou *n* a city in Benin.

COTS *abbr* = Childlessness Overcome Through Surrogacy.

cotta *n* (*pl* **cottae, cottas**) a short surplice.

cottage *n* a small house, esp in the country.

cottage cheese *n* a soft cheese made from loose milk curds.

cottage industry *n* manufacture carried out in the home, e.g. weaving, basketry.

cottage piano *n* a small upright piano.

cottager *n* a person who lives or vacations in a cottage.

cotter¹, cottar *n* a farm laborer who has the use of a cottage for which he works in lieu of rent.

cotter² *n* a bolt, wedge, etc, used to secure parts of machinery to prevent movement.

cotter pin *n* a split pin that secures (a cotter, etc) by spreading the ends after insertion.

Cottier *n* **Daniel** (1838–91) British stained-glass designer and decorator who designed for the Green Memorial Alcove in the New York Society Library.

cotton *n* soft white fiber of the cotton plant; fabric or thread made of this; thread. * *adj* made of cotton. * *vi* (*with* **on**) (*inf*) to realize the meaning of, to understand; to take a liking to.—**cottony** *adj*.

cotton batting *n* cotton fiber used as stuffing or padding.

cotton gin *n* a machine for separating the seeds and hulls from cotton fibers.

cotton grass *n* a plant with long silky hairs.

cottontail *n* an American rabbit.

cottonwood *n* a poplar of the eastern and central US with a tuft of cottony hairs on the seed; its soft wood.

cotton wool *n* raw cotton that has been bleached and sterilized for use as a dressing, etc; absorbent cotton; a state of being protected.

cotyledon *n* a seed lobe or rudimentary leaf or leaves of an embryo; kinds of plant, chiefly evergreens.—**cotyledonal** *adj*.—**cotyledonary** *adj*.—**cotyledonous, cotyledonoid** *adj*.

cotyloid, cotyloidal *adj* cup-shaped.

couch *n* a piece of furniture, with a back and armrests, for seating several persons; a bed, esp as used by psychiatrists for patients. * *vt* to express in words in a particular way; to lie down; to deposit in a bed or layer; (*arch*) to crouch ready for springing; to depress or remove (a cataract in the eye).—**coucher** *n*.

couchant *adj* (*her*) lying down with the head up.

couch grass *n* a kind of coarse grass that spreads rapidly.

couching *n* the operation of removing a cataract from the eye by depressing or removing the crystalline lens; a style of embroidery.

couch potato *n* (*sl*) a person who would rather watch television in leisure time than participate in sports, etc.

cougar *n* a puma.

cough *vi* to expel air from the lungs with a sudden effort and noise; (*with* **up**) (*inf*) to hand over or tell unwillingly. * *n* the act of coughing; a disease causing a cough.

cough drop *n* a lozenge that when sucked relieves a cough.

cough syrup *n* a medicinal liquid to relieve coughing.

could *see* **can¹**.

couldn't = could not.

coulee *n* a dry ravine with sloping sides; a flow of lava; a gorge gouged out by the sudden, violent release of water from a dammed lake; a tongue of fine debris formed by periglacial processes.

coulisse *n* a piece of grooved wood in which anything slides; one of the side scenes of a stage; (*pl*) the space between the side scenes.

couloir *n* a steeply ascending gorge in a mountainside.

coulomb *n* an SI unit of electric charge; the quantity of electricity conveyed by a current of one ampere in one second.

coulter *n* a vertical blade at the front of a ploughshare.—*also* **colter**.

couma *see* **dram**.

coumarin *n* an aromatic crystalline substance obtained from the tonka bean and used in perfumes and medicines.—**coumaric** *adj*.

council *n* an elected or appointed legislative or advisory body; a central body uniting a group of organizations; an executive body whose members are equal in power and authority.—**councilor, councillor** *n*.—**councilorship, councillorship** *n*.

councilman *n* (*pl* **councilmen**) a member of a council, a councilor.

councilor, councillor *n* a member of a council.—**councilorship, councillorship** *n*.

counsel *n* advice; consultation, deliberate purpose or design; a person who gives counsel, a lawyer or a group of lawyers; a consultant. * *vt* (**counseling** *or* **counselling**, **counseled** *or* **counselled**) to advise; to recommend. * *vi* to give or take advice.

counseling, counselling *n* professional guidance for an individual or a couple from a qualified person.

counselor, counsellor *n* one who gives advice, esp legal advice, an adviser.

count¹ *n* a European noble.

count² *vt* to number, to add up; to reckon; to consider to be; to call aloud (beats or time units); to include or exclude by counting; (*with* **against**) to have an adverse effect. * *vi* to name numbers or add up items in order; to mark time; to be of importance or value; to rely (upon); (*with* **on**) to rely on: (*with* **out**) (*inf*) to exclude, leave out; to pronounce after a count a floored boxer to be the loser. * *n* an act of numbering or reckoning; the total counted; a separate and distinct charge in an indictment; rhythm.

countdown *n* the descending count backwards to zero, e.g. to the moment a rocket lifts off.

countenance *n* the whole form of the face; appearance; support. * *vt* to favor, give approval to.

counter¹ *n* one who or that which counts; a disk used for scoring, a token; a table in a bank or store across which money or goods are passed.

counter² *adv* contrary; adverse; in an opposite direction; in the wrong way. * *adj* opposed; opposite. * *n* a return blow or parry; an answering move. * *vti* to oppose; to retort; to give a return blow; to retaliate.

counter- *prefix* rival; opposed; reversed; matched.

counteract *vt* to act in opposition to so as to defeat or hinder; to neutralize.—**counteraction** *n*.—**counteractive** *adj*.

counterattack *n* an attack in response to an attack. * *vt* to make a counterattack.

counterattraction *n* a rival attraction; attraction in an opposite direction.

counterbalance *n* a weight balancing another. * *vt* to act as a counterbalance; to act against with equal power.

counterchange *vti* to interchange; to checker.

countercharge *n* an opposing charge, esp by an accused person against his or her accuser. * *vt* to charge in opposition to another.

countercheck *n* a check on a check; an opposing check; (*arch*) a retort.

counterclaim *n* an opposing claim, esp by a defendant in a lawsuit.—**counterclaimant** *n*.

counterclockwise *adj* moving in a direction contrary to the hands of a clock as viewed from the front.—*also adv*.—*also* **anticlockwise**.

counterculture *n* a culture (of youth) alienated by traditional social values and norms.

counterespionage *n* spying on or exposing enemy spies.

counterfeit *vt* to imitate; to forge; to feign, simulate. * *adj* made in imitation, forged; feigned, sham. * *n* an imitation, a forgery.—**counterfeiter** *n*.

counterfoil *n* a detachable section of a check or ticket, kept as a receipt or record; a stub.

counterinsurgency *n* measures taken by a state against rebels or terrorists.

counterintelligence *n* activities intended to frustrate enemy espionage and intelligence-gathering operations.

counterirritant *n* an application or action irritating the body surface to relieve internal inflammation.—**counterirritation** *n*.

countermand *vt* to revoke or annul, as an order or command; to cancel the orders of another. * *n* a command canceling another.

countermarch *vti* to march in the reverse direction. * *n* such a march.

countermeasure *n* an action taken to neutralize or retaliate against some threat or danger, etc.

countermine *n* a mine made to intercept that of an enemy. * *vi* to make a countermine; to counterplot.

counteroffensive *n* a counterattack, esp by defenders of a position.

counterpane *n* a bedspread.

counterpart *n* a thing exactly like another, a duplicate; a corresponding or complementary part or thing.

counterplot *n* a plot to defeat another plot. * *vi* (**counterplotting, counterplotted**) to plot in retaliation.

counterpoint *n* (*mus*) a melody added as an accompaniment to another. * *vt* to set in contrast.

counterpoise *n* a weight, force, or influence that balances another; equilibrium. * *vt* to counterbalance.

counterproductive *adj* producing a contrary effect on productivity or usefulness; hindering the desired end.

Counter-Reformation *n* the reforming movement in the Roman Catholic Church following the Protestant Reformation.

counter-revolution *n* a revolution undoing the work of a previous one.—**counter-revolutionary** *adj, n*.

countersign *vt* to authenticate a document by an additional signature. * *n* an additional signature to a document to attest it; a word to be given in answer to a sentry's challenge; an additional mark.—**countersignature** *n*.

countersink *vt* (**countersinking, countersunk**) to enlarge the upper part of a hole so that the screw head will sit flush with, or below, the surface; to drive (a screw) into such a hole. * *n* a tool for countersinking.

counterspy *n* (*pl* **counterspies**) a spy working to oppose enemy spying.

counter-subject *n* (*mus*) a melody, found in a fugue, that is contrapuntal to the main theme (subject), i.e. after singing the subject, a voice carries on to sing the countersubject while the answer is sung.

countertenor *n* a high tenor voice with an alto range; a person who sings countertenor.

counterterrorism *n* terrorist act(s) perpetrated in revenge for former terrorist act(s).

countertrading *n* (in international trading) the practice of paying for goods by means other than cash, usu by the direct or indirect exchange of goods.

countervail *vt* to counterbalance, compensate for.

countervailing duty *n* import duty that is levied on certain goods as an extra tax, usu in an effort to prevent the dumping of goods.

counterweight *n* a counterbalancing weight or power.

countess *nf* a woman with the rank of count or earl; the wife or widow of a count.

counting house *n* a book-keeping office or department.

countless *adj* innumerable.

countrified, countryfied *adj* in the manner of the country; rural.

country *n* (*pl* **countries**) a region or district; the territory of a nation; a state; the land of one's birth or residence; rural parts; country-and-western. * *adj* rural.

country-and-western *n* a style of white folk music of the southeastern US.—*also* **country music**.

country bumpkin *n* a simple country dweller; a hayseed.

country club *n* a social and sporting facility in a rural setting.

country code *see* **domain name**

country cousin *n* a country dweller unfamiliar with urban life.

country dance *n* a dance with the couples face to face in two lines.

country house *n* a gentleman's country residence.

countryman *n* (*pl* **countrymen**) a person who lives in the country; a person from the same country as another.—**countrywoman** *nf* (*pl* **countrywomen**).

countryside *n* a rural district.

county *n* (*pl* **counties**) an administrative subdivision of a state; (*UK*) an administrative subdivision for local government.—*also adj*.

county palatine *n* a county having royal powers in the administration of justice.

county town, county seat *n* the capital of a county.

coup *n* a sudden telling blow; a masterstroke; a coup d'état.

coup de grâce *n* (*pl* **coups de grâce**) a finishing or fatal blow.

coup d'état *n* (*pl* **coups d'état**) a sudden and unexpected bold stroke of policy; the sudden overthrow of a government.

coup de théâtre *n* (*pl* **coups de théâtre**) a sudden dramatic or sensational action.

coupé *n* a closed, four-seater, two-door automobile with a sloping back.

Couperin *n* François ["le Grand"] (1668–1733) a French composer and organist who wrote music for the harpsichord. His book *L'Art de toucher le clavecin*, published in 1716, gave instructions on how to play his harpsichord pieces and had an influence on Bach.

couple *n* two of the same kind connected together; a pair; a husband and wife; a pair of equal and parallel forces. * *vt* to link or join together. * *vi* to copulate.

couplet[1] *n* two consecutive lines of verse that rhyme with each other.

couplet[2] *n* (*mus*) the same as duplet; a two-note slur; a song in which the same music is repeated for every stanza.

coupling *n* a device for joining parts of a machine or two train carriages.

coupon *n* a detachable certificate on a bond, presented for payment of interest; a certificate entitling one to a discount, gift, etc; (*finance*) the rate of interest that is paid on a fixed-interest security.

courage *n* bravery; fortitude; spirit.—**courageous** *adj*.—**courageously** *adv*.—**courageousness** *n*.

courante *n* (*mus*) (*French*) *danse courante*, "running dance," a lively Baroque dance in triple time.

Courbet *n* Gustave (1819–77) French painter regarded as the founder of realism.

courgette *n* a zucchini.

courier *n* a messenger, esp diplomatic; a tourist guide; a carrier of illegal goods between countries.

course *n* a race; a path or track; a career; a direction or line of motion; a regular sequence; the portion of a meal served at one time; conduct; behavior; the direction a ship is steered; a continuous level range of brick or masonry of the same height; the chase of a hare by greyhounds; a length of time; an area set aside for a sport or a race; a series of studies; any of the studies. * *vt* to hunt. * *vi* to move swiftly along an indicated path; to chase with greyhounds.

courser *n* one who courses; a dog trained for coursing; (*poet*) a swift and spirited horse.

coursing *n* the sport of pursuing game with hunting dogs. **court** *n* an uncovered space surrounded by buildings or walls; a short street; a playing space, as for tennis, etc; a royal palace; the retinue of a sovereign; (*law*) a hall of justice; the judges, etc engaged there; address; civility; flattery. * *vt* to seek the friendship of; to woo; to flatter; to solicit. * *vi* to carry on a courtship.

court *n* an uncovered space surrounded by buildings or walls; a short street; a playing space, as for tennis, etc; a royal palace; the retinue of a sovereign; (*law*) a hall of justice; the judges, etc engaged there; address; civility; flattery. * *vt* to seek the friendship of; to woo; to flatter; to solicit; to risk. * *vi* to carry on a courtship.

Court cairn *n* (*archeo*) a type of Megalithic chamber tomb found in Northern Ireland and southwest Scotland. *Also* **Clyde-Carlingford tomb**.

courteous *adj* polite; obliging.—**courteously** *adv*.—**courteousness** *n*.

courtesan *n* (*formerly*) a prostitute, or mistress of a courtier.

courtesy *n* (*pl* **courtesies**) politeness and kindness; civility; a courteous manner or action.

courthouse *n* a public building that houses law courts.

courtier *n* one in attendance at a royal court.

courtly *adj* (**courtlier, courtliest**) well-mannered; polite; of a court.—**courtliness** *n*.

court martial *n* (*pl* **courts martial, court martials**) a court of justice composed of naval or military officers for the trial of disciplinary offenses.

court-martial *vt* (**court-martialing, court-martialed** *or* **court-martialling, court-martialled**) to try by court martial.

court plaster *n* a superior kind of sticking plaster, originally used by ladies at court for ornamental patches on the face.

courtship *n* the act of wooing.

courtyard *n* an enclosed space adjoining or in a large building.

couscous *n* a North African dish of cracked wheat steamed and served with a meat and vegetable stew.

cousin *n* the son or daughter of an uncle or aunt.—**cousinly** *adj*.—**cousinship** *n*

Cousteau *n* Jacques [Yves] (1910–97) French oceanographer and inventor of the aqualung (1943).

couture *n* the design and manufacture of expensive fashion clothes.

couturier *n* a designer of expensive fashion clothes.—**couturière** *nf*.

couvade *n* a primitive custom by which when a child is born the father takes to his bed, where he receives the attentions usu given to the mother.

covalent bond *n* (*chem*) the joining of two atoms due to the equal sharing of their electrons.

Covarrubias *n* Alonso de (*b*. 1488) Spanish architect, whose notable works include Chapel of the New Kings, Toledo Cathedral.

cove *n* a small sheltered bay or inlet in a body of water; a curved molding at the juncture of a wall and ceiling (—*also* **coving**).

coven *n* an assembly of witches.

covenant *n* a written agreement; a solemn agreement of fellowship and faith between members of a church; an agreement to pay annually a sum to a charity. * *vt* to promise by a covenant. * *vi* to enter into a formal agreement.—**covenantal** *adj*.—**covenanted** *adj*.

covenantee *n* one in whose favor a covenant is made.

covenantor *n* one who enters into a covenant.

cover *vt* to overspread the top of anything with something else; to hide; to save from punishment; to shelter; to clothe; to understudy; to insure against damage, loss, etc; to report for a newspaper; to include; to make a journey over; (*male animal*) to copulate. * *vi* to spread over, as a liquid does; to provide an excuse or alibi (for); to work, e.g., as a salesman, in a certain area; to have within firing range. * *n* that which is laid on something else; a bedcover; a shelter; a covert; an understudy; something used to hide one's real actions, etc; insurance against loss or damage; a place laid at a table for a meal.—**coverer** *n*.

coverage *n* the amount, extent, etc covered by something; the amount of reporting of an event for newspaper, television, etc.

coverall *n* (*usu pl*) a one-piece garment that completely covers and protects one's clothing.

cover charge *n* a charge made by a restaurant over and above the cost of the food and service.

cover crop *n* a temporary crop planted to prevent soil erosion.

covered wagon *n* a horse-drawn wagon with a canvas top used by American pioneers for traveling.

cover girl *n* an attractive girl whose picture is used on magazine covers.

covering *n* that which covers or protects; dress.

covering letter *n* a letter containing an explanation of an accompanying item.

coverlet *n* a bedspread.

covers *abbr* (*math*) = coversed sine.

coversine *n* (*math*) the versed sine of the complement of an angle or arc.

covert *adj* covered; secret, concealed. * *n* a place that protects or shelters; a thicket; shelter for game.—**covertly** *adv*.

coverture *n* a cover; shelter; (*law*) the status of a married woman.

cover-up *n* something used to hide one's real activities, etc; a concerted effort to keep an act or situation from being made public.

covet *vt* to desire earnestly; to lust after; to long to possess (what belongs to another).—**coveter** *n*.—**covetous** *adj*.—**covetousness** *n*.

covetous *adj* avaricious, grasping, acquisitive.—**covetousness** *n*.

covey *n* a hatch or brood of birds, esp partridges.

coving *n* a curved molding at the juncture of a wall and ceiling.—*also* **cove**.

cow[1] *n* the mature female of domestic cattle; the mature female of various other animals, as the whale, elephant, etc; (*sl*) a disagreeable woman.

cow[2] *vt* to take the spirit out of, to intimidate.

coward *n* a person lacking courage; one who is afraid.

Coward *n* Sir Noel [Pierce] (1899–1973) English dramatist, actor, and songwriter, best known for his witty "sophisticated" comedies of life on the fringes of English upper-middle-class society, e.g. *Private Lives* and *Blithe Spirit*.

cowardice *n* lack of courage.

cowardly *adj* of, or like, a coward.—**cowardliness** *n*.

cowbane *n* water hemlock.

cow bell *n* a square cow bell with the clapper taken out and played with a drumstick, used as a percussion instrument in an orchestra.

cowbird *n* an American blackbird so called from its accompanying cattle.

cowboy *n* a person who tends cattle or horses (—*also* **cowhand**); (*inf*) one who is engaged in dubious business activities.

cowcatcher *n* a wedge-shaped iron frame on the front of a locomotive to push aside obstacles.

Cowell *n* Henry Dixon (1897–1965) American composer, pianist, teacher, and writer who developed a technique of playing what he called "tone clusters" on the piano, which involved hitting the keyboard with a fist or elbow. Notable works are *The Building of Banba* and *Atlantis*, and *O'Higgins of Chile*.

cower *vi* to crouch or sink down through fear, etc; to tremble.

cowfish *n* (*pl* **cowfish, cowfishes**) a name given to various fishes and other marine animals, as the dolphin.

cowgirl *n* a woman who works as a cowhand.

cowherd *n* a person employed to tend cattle.

cowhide *n* the tanned and dressed skins of cows; a stout flexible whip made of rawhide.

cowl *n* a hood; the hooded habit of a monk; the draped neckline of a woman's dress or sweater; a metal revolving hood for a chimney which improves ventilation.

Cowley *n* Abraham (1618–67) English poet whose most important works are *The Mistress*, a collection of metaphysical love poems, "Davideis," a Scriptural epic in rhymed couplets, and several odes, e.g. *Ode, upon the Blessed Restoration*.

cowlick *n* a tuft of hair turned up or brushed over the forehead.

cowling *n* the metal covering of an airplane engine.

coworker *n* a fellow worker.

cow pat *n* a piece of cow dung.

Cowper *n* William (1731–1800) English poet who is now regarded as an important transitional figure between the 18th century and the romantic era.

cow pony *n* a mustang used by cowboys.

cowpox *n* a disease of cows that produces vesicles from which the vaccine for inoculation against smallpox is obtained.

cowpuncher, cowpoke *n* a cowboy.

cowry, cowrie *n* (*pl* **cowries**) a marine mollusk with a glossy, brightly speckled shell.

cowslip *n* a common wild plant with small fragrant yellow flowers.

cow town *n* a small town in cattle-raising country.

cox *n* a coxswain. * *vt* to act as a coxswain.

coxa *n* (*pl* **coxae**) the hip joint.—**coxal** *adj*.

coxalgia *n* a pain in, or disease of, the hip joint.—**coxalgic** *adj*.

coxcomb *n* a cockscomb; a vain conceited person, a fop.

coxcombry *n* (*pl* **coxcombries**) affected airs, foppishness.

coxswain *n* a person who steers a boat, esp a lifeboat or racing boat.—*also* **cockswain**.

coy *adj* playfully or provocatively demure; bashful.—**coyly** *adv*.—**coyness** *n*.

Coy. *or* **coy.** *abbr* = company.

coyote *n* (*pl* **coyotes, coyote**) a small prairie wolf of North America.

COYPSS *abbr* = Coalition on Young People and Social Security.

coypu *n* (*pl* **coypus, coypu**) an aquatic beaver-like animal, originally from South America.

coz *n* (*arch*) cousin.

COZAC *abbr* = Conservation Zone Advisory Committee.

cozen *vt* to cheat, to beguile; to act deceitfully.—**cozenage** *n*.—**cozener** *n*.

cozy *adj* (**cozier, coziest**) warm and comfortable; snug; friendly for an ulterior motive. * *n* a cover to keep a thing warm.—*also* **cosy**.—**cozily** *adv*.—**coziness** *n*.

Cozzens *n* James Gould (1903–1978) American novelist who won the Pulitzer prize for *Guard of Honour* (1948).

cp *abbr* = candlepower; carriage paid; chemically pure.

cp. *abbr* (*Latin*) = *compara*, "compare."

c.p. *abbr* = center of pressure; chemically pure; civil power; clerk of the peace; code of procedure; common pleas; court of probate.

c/p *abbr* (*grain trade*) = custom of port.

Cp *abbr* = cassiopeium; molecular heat at constant pressure.

CP *abbr* = Cape Province; center of pressure; cerebral palsy; Chief Patriarch; Common Prayer; Communist Party; (*Latin*) *Congregatio Passionis*, "Congregation of the Passion" (RC monastic order); Court of Probate; (*Brit*) Royal College of Preceptors.

C/P *abbr* = charter party.

CP Catalog *n* the *True Visual Magnitude Photographic Star Atlas* (1850.0) by Christos Papadopoulos.

CPA *abbr* = Canadian Postmasters Association; Carpet Planners Association; Center for Policy on Ageing; Certified Public Accountant; Chartered Patent Agent; Chartered Public Accountant; Chick Producers Association; China Photographers' Association; Chipboard Promotion Association; City Property Association; Cocoa Producers Alli-

ance; Commonwealth Parliamentary Association; Concrete Pipe Association; Construction Plant-hire Association; Contractors Plant Association; Craftsmen Potters Association; Credit Protection Association; critical path analysis.

CPAC *abbr* = Consumer Protection Advisory Committee; Corrosion Prevention Advisory Center.

CPAG *abbr* = Child Poverty Action Group.

CPB *abbr* = cardiopulmonary bypass; Communist Party of Britain.

CPBF *abbr* = Campaign for Press and Broadcasting Freedom.

CPBS *abbr* (*Eire*) = Connemara Pony Breeders' Society.

CPC *abbr* = Campaign Against Pornography and Censorship; Caring Professions Concern; Center for Peaceful Change; Certificate of Professional Competence; (*Brit*) Clerk of the Privy Council; Coffee Promotion Council; Commonwealth Palaeontological Collection; Conservative Political Center.

CPCG *abbr* = Children's Panel Chairmen's Group.

cpd. *abbr* = compound.

CPDA *abbr* = Clay Pipe Development Association.

CPEA *abbr* = Confederation of Professional and Executive Associations; Cyprus Professional Engineers' Association.

CPFS *abbr* = Council for the Promotion of Field Studies.

CPG *abbr* = Coronary Prevention Group.

CPGB *abbr* = Communist Party of Great Britain.

CPH *abbr* = Certificate in Public Health.

cpi *abbr* (*comput*) = characters per inch.

CPI *abbr* = consumer price index.

CPIC *abbr* = Canadian Police Information Center; Comprehensive Pig Information Center.

CPIM *abbr* = Certificate in Production and Inventory Management.

CPISRA *abbr* = Cerebral Palsy International Sports and Recreation Association.

CPJ *abbr* = Committee to Protect Journalists.

Cpl *abbr* = Corporal.

CPL *abbr* = Cats' Protection League; commercial pilot's license.

cpm *abbr* = characters per minute; cycles per minute.

CPM *abbr* = common particular meter.

CP/M *abbr* (*comput*) = Control Program for Microcomputers; Control Program Monitor.

CPMS *abbr* = Defense Civilian Personnel Management Service

CPNA *abbr* = Community Psychiatric Nurses' Association.

CPO *abbr* = Chief Petty Officer; Crime Prevention Officer; compulsory purchase order.

CPPA *abbr* = Canadian Pulp and Paper Association; Coal Preparation Plant Association.

CPR *abbr* = cardiopulmonary resuscitation.

CPRE *abbr* = Council for the Protection of Rural England.

cps *abbr* (*comput*) = characters per second.

cps. *abbr* = coupons.

CPS *abbr* = Carnivorous Plant Society; Center for Public Services; Certificate in Pastoral Studies and Applied Theology; Citizens Protection Society; Communist Party of Scotland; Crown Prosecution Service; (*Latin*) *Custos Privati Sigilli*, "Keeper of the Privy Seal."

CPSA *abbr* = Civil and Public Services.

CPSC *abbr* = Consumer Product Safety Commission

CPSR *abbr* = Computer Professionals for Social Responsibility.

CPsychol *abbr* (*Brit*) = Chartered Member of the British Psychological Society.

cpt. *abbr* = counterpoint.

CPT *abbr* (*Brit*) = Confederation of British Road Passenger Transport.

CPTB *abbr* = Clay Products Technical Bureau.

CPU *abbr* (*comput*) = central processing unit.

CPVE *abbr* = Certificate of Pre-Vocational Education.

CQM *abbr* = Chief Quartermaster; Company Quartermaster.

CQMS *abbr* = Company QuarterMaster-Sergeant.

CQSW *abbr* = Certificate of Qualification in Social Work.

Cr *symbol* (*chem*) chromium (element).

cr. *abbr* = center; created; credit; creditor; creek; (*mus*) (*Italian*) *crescendo*, "increasing"; crown.

c.r. *abbr* = carrier's risk; center of resistance; class rate; company rate; company's risk.

CR *abbr* = Chief Ranger (*foresters*); (*Latin*) *Civis Romanus*, "Roman citizen."

CRA *abbr* = Commercial Rabbit Association; Community Radio Association; Computing Research Association; Concrete Repair Association; (*Eire*) County Registrars' Association; Crime Reporters' Association.

crab *n* any of numerous chiefly marine broadly built crustaceans. * *vi* (**crabbing, crabbed**) to fish for crabs; to complain. *vt* to spoil.

CRAB *abbr* = Center for Research in Aquatic Biology.

crab-apple *n* a wild apple.

Crabbe *n* **George** (1754–1832) English poet whose works present a bitter and true picture of rural poverty in England. The "Peter Grimes" section of his poem *The Borough* inspired Benjamin Britten's great opera of the same name.

crabbed *adj* bad-tempered, morose; (*writing*) cramped; hard to decipher.

crabby *adj* bad-tempered.—**crabbily** *adv*.—**crabbiness** *n*.

crab grass *n* a coarse grass with creeping stems that root freely.

crab louse *n* a species of body louse.

Crab Nebula *or* **M1 and NGC1952** *n* (*astron*) a nebula in the constellation Taurus, thought to be the remnant of a supernova explosion of AD 1054.

crabs (*pl*) infestation by body lice.

crabstick *n* a cudgel; a surly person.

CRAC *abbr* = Careers Research and Advisory Center.

crack *vt* to burst, break or sever; to utter a sharp, abrupt cry; to injure; to damage mentally; to open a bottle; (*sl*) to make (a joke); (*inf*) to break open (a safe); to decipher (a code). * *vi* to make a sharp explosive sound; (*inf*) to lose control under pressure; to shift erratically in vocal tone; (*with* **up**) (*inf*) to be unable to cope; (*sl*) to take the drug crack. * *n* a chink or fissure; a narrow fracture; a sharp sound; a sharp resonant blow; an altered tone of voice; a chat, gossip; a wisecrack; (*inf*) an attempt; an expert; (*sl*) the drug cocaine packaged in the form of pellets.

crackbrained *adj* crazy.

crackdown *n* repressive action to quell disorder, etc.

cracked *adj* split, broken; blemished; insane; legally imperfect.

cracker *n* a firework that explodes with a loud crack; a paper tube that when pulled explodes harmlessly and releases a paper hat and plastic toy; a thin, crisp biscuit; (*sl*) a person or thing of great ability or excellence.

crackerbarrel *adj* (*inf*) homespun, as the informal chat of people who regularly assemble at a general store.

crackerjack *n* (*sl*) a fine specimen.

crackers *adj* (*sl*) crazy.

crackhead *n* (*sl*) a person who is addicted to the drug crack.

crack house *n* (*sl*) a place where the drug crack is made available by dealers.

cracking *adj* (*inf*) fast-moving; excellent. * *n* the act of hacking into computer games; (*chem*) an industrial process in which large complicated molecules are broken down into smaller ones. **to get cracking** to start to do something with vim and vigor.

crackle *vi* to make a slight, sharp explosive noise. * *vt* to cover with a delicate network of minute cracks. * *n* a noise of frequent and slight cracks and reports; a surface glaze on glass or porcelain.—**crackly** *adj*.

crackling *n* (*usu pl*) the browned crisp rind of roast pork.

cracknel *n* a thick puffy dry fancy biscuit.

crackpot *n* (*inf*) an eccentric, a crazy person. * *adj* (*inf*) crazy, unpractical.

cracksman *n* (*pl* **cracksmen**) a burglar.

-cracy *n suffix* government by, as in *democracy*.

CRAD *abbr* = Committee for Research into Apparatus for the Disabled.

cradle *n* a baby's crib or a small bed, often on rockers; infancy; birthplace or origin; a case for a broken limb; a framework of timbers, esp for supporting a boat; the rest for a telephone handset. * *vt* to rock or place in a cradle; to nurse or train in infancy.

cradle cap *n* a form of seborrhea or dermatitis of the scalp which affects young babies.

cradlesnatcher *n* (*inf*) one who takes a much younger spouse or lover, a babysnatcher.

cradlesong *n* a lullaby.

cradling *n* the open timbers or ribs of a vaulted ceiling.

CRAE *abbr* = Committee for the Reform of Animal Experimentation.

craft *n* manual skill; a skilled trade; the members of a skilled trade; cunning; (*pl* **craft**) a boat, ship, or aircraft.

Craftiny *n* (*Irish Celtic myth*) the harpist whose magic harp revived the powers of speech of Labhraidh Loingsech.

craftsman *n* (*pl* **craftsmen**) a person skilled in a particular craft.—**craftsmanship** *n*.—**craftswoman** *nf* (*pl* **craftswomen**).

crafty *adj* (**craftier, craftiest**) cunning, wily.—**craftily** *adv*.—**craftiness** *n*.

crag *n* a rough steep rock or cliff.

CRAG *abbr* = Cellular Radio Advisory Group.

craggy, cragged *adj* (**craggier, craggiest**) full of crags; rugged.—**cragginess** *n*.

Craiova *n* a city in Romania.

crake *n* the corncrake.

cram *vt* (**cramming crammed**) to pack tightly, to stuff; to fill to overflowing; (*inf*) to prepare quickly for an examination. * *vi* to eat greedily.

Cram *n* **Ralph A** (1863–1942) American architect, whose notable works include Cathedral of St John the Divine, New York.

crambo *n* (*pl* **cramboes**) a game in which rhymes have to be found for a given word.

Cramer *n* **Johann Baptist** (1771–1858) German-born composer and pianist most noted for his piano pieces and his book of *Studies*, which he wrote to pass on his skills and which is still used by young pianists today.

cramp *n* a spasmodic muscular contraction of the limbs; (*pl*) abdominal spasms and pain; a clamp. * *vt* to affect with muscular spasms; to confine narrowly; to hamper; to secure with a cramp. * *vi* to suffer from cramps.

cramped *adj* restricted, narrow; (*handwriting*) small and irregular.

crampon, crampoon *n* a metal frame with spikes attached to boots for walking or climbing on ice.

CRAMRA *abbr* = Convention on the Regulation of Antarctic Mineral Resource Activities.

Cranach *n* 1. **Lucas** (1472–1553) German painter who painted a number of portraits of Martin Luther. 2. **Wilhelm Lucas von** (1861–1918) German painter, jeweler, and decorator who designed French and Belgian style Art Nouveau jewelry.

cranberry *n* (*pl* **cranberries**) a small red sour berry; the shrub it grows on.

crane *n* a large wading bird with very long legs and neck, and a long straight bill; a machine for raising, shifting, and lowering heavy weights. * *vti* to stretch out (the neck).

Crane *n* 1. **[Harold] Hart** (1899–1932) American poet who published only two volumes of verse, *White Buildings* and *The Bridge*. 2. **Stephen [Townley]** (1871–1900) American journalist, poet, and novelist whose greatest work is *The Red Badge of Courage*, a study of the shattering impact of the Civil War upon a young soldier. 3. **Walter** (1845–1915) British illustrator and designer who became an important propagandist for the **Arts and Crafts Movement**.

crane fly *n* the daddy-longlegs.

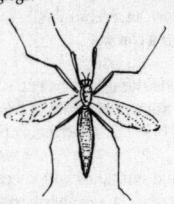

cranesbill *n* a kind of wild geranium.

cranial nerves *npl* 12 pairs of nerves that arise directly from the brain, each with dorsal and ventral branches known as roots. Each root remains separate and is assigned a Roman numeral as well as a name.

craniol. *abbr* = craniology.

craniology *n* the scientific study of skulls and their characteristics.—**craniological** *adj*.—**craniologist** *n*.

craniom. *abbr* = craniometry.

craniometer *n* an instrument for measuring the skull.

craniometry *n* the measurement and study of skulls.—**craniometric, craniometrical** *adj*.

craniotomy *n* (*pl* **craniotomies**) the operation of crushing the head of a dead fetus for facilitating delivery; the operation of opening the skull for neurosurgery.

cranium *n* (*pl* **craniums, crania**) the skull, esp the part enclosing the brain.—**cranial** *adj*.

crank *n* a right-angled arm attached to a shaft for turning it; (*inf*) an eccentric person, usu one with strange or unorthodox opinions; an irritable or rude person. * *vt* to provide with a crank; to turn or wind; (*with* **up**) (*engine*) to start with a crank handle; (*inf*) to speed up; (*sl*) to inject a narcotic drug.

crankcase *n* the housing for a crankshaft in an internal combustion engine, etc.

crankpin *n* a cylindrical pin parallel with the shaft axis of a crank upon which the connecting rod acts to turn the crank.

crankshaft *n* a shaft with one or more cranks for transmitting motion.

cranky *adj* (**crankier, crankiest**) (*inf*) eccentric; shaky; cross.—**crankily** *adv*.—**crankiness** *n*.

Cranmer *n* **Thomas** (1489–1556) English prelate. As newly appointed Archbishop of Canterbury, he pronounced the annulment of the marriage of Henry VIII to Catherine of Aragon in 1533.

crannog *n* a lake dwelling built on an artificial island.

cranny *n* (*pl* **crannies**) a fissure, crack, crevice.

crap *n* (*sl*) nonsense; (*vulg*) feces. * *vi* (**crapping, crapped**) (*vulg*) to defecate.—**crappy** *adj*.

crape *n* crepe; a black gauze-like crimped silk material used for mourning.

craps *n* (*sing or pl*) a gambling game played with two dice.

crapshooter *n* a player of craps.

crapulence *n* sickness from drinking to excess.—**crapulent, crapulous** *adj*.

craquelure *n* a network of tiny cracks found on old paintings caused by cracking of the varnish.

crash *n* a loud, sudden confused noise; a violent fall or impact; a sudden failure, as of a business or a computer; a collapse, as of the financial market. * *adj* done with great speed, suddenness, or effort. * *vti* to clash together with violence; to make a loud clattering noise; (*aircraft*) to land with a crash; to involve an automobile in a collision with one or more other vehicles or with a hard object; to collapse, to ruin; (*inf*) to intrude into (a party); (*with* **out**) *vi* (*sl*) to fall asleep; to pass out; to stay the night somewhere other than home.

Crashaw *n* **Richard** (1613–49) English poet whose often highly florid and elaborate imagery was inspired by his reading of Spanish mystical writers. His main work is *Steps to the Temple*.

crash dive *n* an emergency dive by a submarine.

crash helmet *n* a cushioned helmet worn by airmen, motorcyclists, etc for protection.

crash-land *vti* (*aircraft*) to make an emergency landing without lowering the undercarriage, or to be landed in this way.—**crash-landing** *n*.

crass *adj* gross; dense; very stupid.—**crassly** *adv*.—**crassness, crassitude** *n*.

-crat *n suffix* a supporter or member of a particular form of government or class.

cratch *n* a rack for fodder.

crate *n* an open box of wooden slats, for shipping; (*sl*) an old vehicle or aircraft. * *vt* to pack in a crate.

crater *n* the mouth of a volcano; a cavity caused by the landing of a meteorite, the explosion of a bomb, shell, etc; an ancient Greek goblet.—**craterous** *adj*.

Crater *n* (*astron*) a southern sky constellation, whose brightest stars are fourth magnitude.

Cratos *n* (*Greek myth*) the personification of strength, a son of Uranus and Ge.

cravat *n* a neckcloth.

crave *vt* to have a strong desire (for); to ask humbly, to beg.—**craving** *n*.

craven *adj* spiritless, cowardly. * *n* a coward.

craw *n* a bird's crop.

crawfish *n* (*pl* **crawfish**) a crayfish; the spiny lobster.

Crawford *n* 1. **Joan [Lucille Le Sueur]** (1908–77) American movie actress whose movies include *Mildred Pierce* (1945). 2. **Thomas** (1814–57) American sculptor in the neoclassical tradition.

crawl *vi* to move along the ground on hands and knees; to move slowly and with difficulty; to creep; (*inf*) to seek favor by servile behavior; to swarm (with). * *n* the act of crawling; a slow motion; a racing stroke in swimming.—**crawler** *n*.

crawl space *n* space that gives access to plumbing or wiring in a building, as under a floor or roof.

crayfish *n* (*pl* **crayfish**) any of numerous freshwater crustaceans; the spiny lobster.

crayon *n* a stick or pencil of colored chalk mixed with oil or wax used for drawing; a drawing done with crayons. * *vt* to draw with a crayon.—**crayonist** *n*.

craze *n* a passing infatuation; excessive enthusiasm; a crack in pottery glaze. * *vt* to produce cracks; to render insane.—**crazed** *adj*.

crazy *adj* (**crazier, craziest**) (*inf*) insane; foolish; ridiculous; unsound; madly in love with; (*paving*) composed of irregular pieces.—**crazily** *adv*.—**craziness** *n*.

crazy quilt *n* a quilt made of patchwork pieces of cloth; a haphazard or disorderly thing.—**crazy-quilt** *adj*.

CRC *abbr* = camera-ready copy; Cancer Research Campaign; Chemical Rubber Company; Civil Rights Center; Clinical Research Center; Confederation of Roofing Contractors; Cotton Research Corporation;.

CRCC *abbr* = Canadian Red Cross Committee.

CRCP *abbr* (*Brit*) = Certificant of the Royal College of Physicians.

CRCS *abbr* (*Brit*) = Certificant of the Royal College of Surgeons.

CRD *abbr* = chronic respiratory disease.

CRE *abbr* = Campaign for Real Education; Coal Research Establishment; Commission for Racial Equality; Conference of the Regions of Europe; cumulative radiation effect.

creak *vi* to make a shrill grating sound. * *n* such a sound.

creaky *adj* (**creakier, creakiest**) apt to creak.—**creakiness** *n*.

cream *n* the rich, fatty part of milk; the choicest part of anything; a yellowish white color; a type of face or skin preparation; any preparation of the consistency of cream (e.g. *shoe cream*). * *vt* to add or apply cream to; to beat into a soft, smooth consistency; to skim cream from; to remove the best part of. * *vi* to form cream or scum; to break into a creamy froth.

cream cheese *n* soft cheese made from soured milk or cream.

creamer *n* a machine or dish for separating cream from milk; a pitcher for cream or milk; a powder used as a substitute for cream in drinks.

creamery *n* (*pl* **creameries**) a place where dairy products are made or sold.

cream of tartar *n* purified tartar or argol, potassium bitartrate.

creamy *adj* (**creamier, creamiest**) like cream.—**creaminess** *n*.

crease *n* a line made by folding; a wrinkle; (*cricket*) a line made by a batsman or bowler marking the limits of their position. * *vti* to make or form creases; to become creased; (*sl*) to find something very funny.

create *vt* to cause to come into existence; to form out of nothing. * *vi* to make something new, to originate; (*sl*) to make a fuss.

creatine, creatin *n* a white crystalline substance in muscular tissue.

creation *n* the act of creating; the thing created; the whole world or universe; a production of the human mind; (*with cap*) the universe as created by God.—**creational** *adj*.

creationism *n* the belief in special creation, not evolution; the belief that God creates a soul for every human being at birth.—**creationist** *adj, n*.

creative *adj* of creation; having the power to create; imaginative, original, constructive.—**creatively** *adv*.—**creativeness** *n*.—**creativity** *n*.

creative accounting *n* a method of accounting that seeks to use all means possible that are not actually illegal to present the financial position of a company in as favorable a light as possible.

creator *n* one who creates, esp God.

creature *n* a living being; a created thing; one dependent on the influence of another.—**creatural, creaturely** *adj*.

crèche *n* a day nursery for very young children.

credence *n* belief or trust, esp in the reports or testimony of another.

credentials *npl* documents proving the identity, honesty, or authority of a person.

credibility gap *n* a gap between what is claimed in official statements and the true facts of a situation.

credible *adj* believable; trustworthy.—**credibility, credibleness** *n*.—**credibly** *adv*.

credit *n* belief; trust; honor; good reputation; approval; trust in a person's ability to pay; time allowed for payment; a sum at a person's disposal in a bank; the entry in an account of a sum received; the side of the account on which this is entered; (*educ*) a distinction awarded for good marks in an examination; (*pl*) a list of those responsible for a movie, television program, etc. * *vt* to believe; to trust; to have confidence in; to attribute to; to enter on the credit side of an account.

creditable *adj* worthy of praise.—**creditableness, creditability** *n*.—**creditably** *adv*.

credit card *n* a card issued by a bank, department store, etc authorizing the purchase of goods and services on credit.

credit control *n* a system operated by a company to make sure that customers pay outstanding debts within a reasonable period of time.

credit note *n* a document given to a customer by a supplier giving the customer credit for any goods that have been returned by the customer and for which the supplier has already received payment.

creditor *n* a person to whom money is owed.

credit rating *n* an appraisal of a person's or a business's creditworthiness.

credits *npl* a list of those involved in the production of a movie or television show.

creditworthy *adj* worthy of being given credit as judged by the capacity to earn, repay debts promptly, etc.—**creditworthiness** *n*.

credo[1] *n* (*pl* **credos**) a creed.

credo[2] *n* (*Latin*) "I believe," the first word in the Roman Catholic Creed.

credulous *adj* over-ready to believe; easily imposed on.—**credulously** *adv*.—**credulity** *n*.

creed *n* a system of religious belief or faith; a summary of Christian doctrine; any set of principles or beliefs.—**creedal, credal** *adj*.

creek *n* a natural stream of water smaller than a river; a tidal channel in a coastal marsh or between sandbanks.

creel *n* a wicker fishing basket; a wickerwork cage.

creep *vi* (**creeping, crept**) to move slowly along the ground, as a worm or reptile; (*plant*) to grow along the ground or up a wall; to move stealthily or slowly; to fawn; to cringe; (*flesh*) to feel as if things were creeping over it. * *n* (*geog*) the slow gravitational movement of soil, scree or glacial ice down a slope; (*inf*) a dislikable or servile person; (*pl: inf*) shrinking horror.

creeper *n* a creeping or climbing plant.

creepy *adj* (**creepier, creepiest**) making one's flesh crawl; causing fear or disgust.—**creepily** *adv*.—**creepiness** *n*.

creepy-crawly *n* (*pl* **creepy-crawlies**) (*inf*) a small crawling insect.

CREG *abbr* = Center for Research and Education on Gender.

cremate *vt* to burn (a cadaver) to ashes.—**cremation** *n*.—**cremationism** *n*.—**cremationist** *n*.

crematorium *n* (*pl* **crematoriums, crematoria**) a place where bodies are cremated.

crematory *adj* pertaining to cremation. * *n* (*pl* **crematories**) a place for burning the dead, a crematorium.

crème, creme *n* cream.

crème de la crème *n* the cream of the cream, the very best.

crème de menthe *n* a green-colored peppermint liqueur.

crenate, crenated *adj* (*leaves*) scalloped.—**crenation, crenature** *n*.

crenelated, crenellated *adj* having battlements.—**crenelation, crenellation** *n*.

crenulate, crenulated *adj* (*leaves*) finely notched, indented.—**crenulation** *n*.

Creoda *n* (d. 593) king of Mercia, Britain (c.585–593). The first named king of the Mercians, he is thought to have been the son of Icel, the first continental Angle king to settle in Britain.

creole *n* a language combining two or more original languages, one of which is European.

Creole *n* a descendant of European settlers in the West Indies or South America; a white descendant of French settlers in the southern US; a person of mixed European and Negro ancestry; the language of any of these groups.

Creon *n* (*Greek myth*) the brother of Jocasta and successor to Oedipus as king of Thebes.

creosol *n* an oily liquid resembling phenol, a constituent of creosote.

creosote *n* an oily substance derived from tar used as a wood preservative. * *vt* to treat with creosote.—**creosotic** *adj*.

crepe, crêpe *n* a thin, crinkled cloth of silk, rayon, wool, etc (—*also* **crape**) ; thin paper like crepe; a thin pancake.

crepe de Chine *n* a silk crepe.

crepe paper, crêpe paper *n* a thin soft colored paper that resembles crepe.

crepe ring *n* (*astron*) one of the rings of Saturn, discovered by Dawes in 1850.

crepe rubber *n* a type of ribbed rubber used for the soles of shoes.

crêpe suzette *n* (*pl* **crêpes suzettes**) a thin orange-flavored pancake with a hot liqueur sauce.

crepitate *vi* to make a slight, sharp crackling noise.—**crepitation** *n*.

crepitus *n* (*medical*) a grating sound, heard when the ends of fractured bones rub together, from arthritic joints and from a roughening of the inner surface of the kneecap.

crept *see* **creep**.

crepuscular *adj* pertaining to or resembling twilight; active at twilight, as certain animals.

cres. or cresc. *abbr* (*mus*) (*Italian*) = *crescendo*, "increasing."

CRES *abbr* = Chinese Rare Earth Society.

crescendo *adv* (*mus*) gradually increasing in loudness or intensity; moving to a climax. * *n* (*pl* **crescendos, crescendi**) a crescendo passage or effect.

crescent *n* the figure of the moon in its first or last quarter; a narrow, tapering curve; a curving street. * *adj* crescent-shaped; (*arch*) increasing.—**crescentic** *adj*.

cresol *n* a phenol obtained from coal and wood tar.

cress *n* any of various plants with pungent leaves, used in salads.

cresset *n* a light set on a beacon; an open frame of iron containing fire, used as a torch.

Cressida *n* (*astron*) a small satellite of Uranus.

crest *n* a plume of feathers on the head of a bird; the ridge of a wave; the summit of a hill; a distinctive device above the shield on a coat of arms. * *vti* to mount to the top of; to take the form of a crest; to provide or adorn with a crest, to crown.— **crested** *adj*.

CReSTeD *abbr* = Council for the Registration of Schools Teaching Dyslexic Pupils.

crestfallen *adj* dejected.

cresting *n* an ornamental finish, esp along a rooftop; ornamentation on top of furniture, a mirror, etc.

Creston *n* **Paul** [originally **Joseph Guttoveggio**] (1906–85) American self-taught composer of Italian origin. His works include five symphonies, choral pieces and concertos.

Creswellian *adj* (*archeo*) relating to a Paleolithic culture, the type site of which is Creswell Crags in Derbyshire, England.

cretaceous *adj* composed of or like chalk; chalky.

Cretaceous *n* a geological group between the Jurassic and Tertiary formations. * *adj* of the last Mesozoic era.

Cretan *adj* of or pertaining to Crete or its inhabitants.

Crete *n* a large mountainous island in the Mediterranean, famous for its Minoan civilization.—**Cretan** *adj*.

cretin *n* a person suffering from mental and physical retardation due to a congenital thyroid disorder; (*inf*) an idiot.—**cretinism** *n* (*also* **congenital hyperthyroidism**).—**cretinoid, cretinous** *adj*.

cretonne *n* an unglazed cotton fabric printed with colored patterns on one side.

Creusa *n* (*Greek myth*) a daughter of Priam and Hecuba, and the wife of Aeneas.

Creutzfeldt-Jakob disease (CJD) *n* a fatal disease of the brain, thought to be caused by a slow virus connected with similar diseases in animals such as bovine spongiform encephalopathy (BSE) in cattle and scrapie in sheep, which may be transmittable to humans and has already caused many deaths.—*also* **spongiform encephalopathy**.

crevasse *n* a deep cleft in a glacier; a deep crack.

crevice *n* a crack, a fissure.

crew *n* the people operating a ship or aircraft; a group of people working together. * *vi* to act as a member of the crew of a ship, etc.

crewcut *n* a very short hairstyle for men.

crewel *n* a fine twisted or worsted yarn used in embroidery.—**crewelist** *n*.

crew neck *n* a plain closely-fitting neckline in sweaters.

CRFA *abbr* = Canadian Restaurant and Foodservers Association.

CRI *abbr* = Center for the Study of Regulated Industries; Children's Relief International.

crib *n* a rack for fodder, a manger; a child's cot with high sides; a model of the manger scene representing the birth of Jesus; (*inf*) something copied from someone else; (*inf*) a literal translation of foreign texts used (usu illicitly) by students in examinations, etc. * *vti* (**cribbing, cribbed**) (*inf*) to copy illegally, plagiarize.

cribbage *n* a card game for two to four players.

crib death *n* the sudden death of a baby during sleep from an unexplained cause.— *also* **cot death**.

cribellum *n* (*pl* **cribella**) a spinning organ in front of the spinnerets of certain spiders.

cribriform *adj* with small holes like a sieve.

CRIC *abbr* = Commercial Radio International Committee.

crick *n* a painful stiffness of the muscles of the neck. * *vt* to produce a crick in.

Crick *n* **Francis** [**Harry Compton**] (1916–) English molecular biologist who discovered the structure of DNA with James Dewey Watson. He won the 1962 Nobel prize for physiology or medicine.

cricket[1] *n* a leaping grasshopper-like insect.

cricket[2] *n* a game played with wickets, bats, and a ball, by eleven players on each side.—**cricketer** *n*.

CRICT *abbr* = Center for Research into Innovation and Culture Technology.

cried *see* **cry**.

crier *n* one who cries; an officer who makes public proclamations.

crim. *abbr* = criminal.

crim. con. *abbr* = criminal conversation.

crime *n* a violation of the law; an offense against morality or the public welfare; wrongdoing; (*inf*) a shame, disappointment.

CRIMES *abbr* = Child Rape and Incest Merit Effective Sentencing.

criminal *adj* of the nature of, or guilty of, a crime. * *n* a person who has committed a crime.—**criminality** *adv*.—**criminally** *adv*.

criminal conversation *n* (*formerly*) a legal action for damages for illegal sexual intercourse; adultery.

criminology *n* the scientific study of crime.—**criminological, criminologic** *adj*.— **criminologist** *n*.

crimp[1] *vt* to press into small folds; to frill; to corrugate; (*hair*) to curl.—**crimper** *n*.

crimp[2] *n* a person luring or pressganging sailors aboard a vessel. * *vt* to decoy thus.

crimson *n* a deep-red color inclining to purple. * *adj* crimson-colored. * *vti* to dye with crimson; to blush.

cringe *vi* to shrink in fear or embarrassment; to cower; to behave with servility; to fawn.

cringle *n* a loop of rope containing a metal ring for another rope to pass through.

crinite *adj* hairy.

crinkle *vt* to wrinkle; to corrugate; to crimp; to rustle. * *vi* to curl; to be corrugated or crimped. * *n* a wrinkle.—**crinkly** *adj*.

crinoid *adj* lily-shaped. * *n* a stone lily, a kind of sea urchin.

crinoline *n* a hooped skirt made to project all round; a stiff fabric for stiffening a garment.

crinum *n* any of several handsome tropical plants.

Criosphinx *n* (*Egypt*) a ram-headed Sphinx.

Crippen *n* **Hawley Harvey** (1862–1910) American doctor who poisoned his wife in London in 1910.

cripple *vt* to deprive of the use of a limb; to disable. * *n* a lame or otherwise disabled person. * *adj* lame.

crippling *adj* harmful; unbearable.

Cripps *n* **Sir** [**Richard**] **Stafford** (1889–1952) British Labour statesman.

CRIS *abbr* = command retrieval information system.

CRISA *abbr* = Car Radio Industry Specialists' Association.

crisis *n* (*pl* **crises**) a turning point; a critical point in a disease; an emergency; a time of serious difficulties or danger.

crisp *adj* dry and brittle; bracing; brisk; sharp and incisive; decided; very clean and tidy. * *n* a potato chip. * *vt* to make crisp.—**crisply** *adv*.—**crispness** *n*.

crispate, crispated *adj* curled; (*bot*) with a wavy margin.—**crispation** *n*.

Crispin and Crispinian *n* Saints (*d.* 285) Italian brothers beheaded for their Christianity, patron saints of shoemakers. Their feast day is 25 October.

crispy *adj* (**crispier, crispiest**) crisp.—**crispily** *adv*.—**crispiness** *n*.

crisscross *vti* to intersect; to mark with cross lines. * *n* an intersecting; a mark of a cross; a game of noughts and crosses. * *adj* crossing; in cross lines. * *adv* crosswise.

cristate, cristated *adj* crested; tufted.

Cristofori *n* **Bartolomeo** (1655–1731) Italian instrument maker who first devised the hammer mechanism for the piano.

crit. *abbr* = critical; criticism; criticized.

criterion *n* (*pl* **criteria**) a standard, law, or rule by which a correct judgment can be made.

critic *n* a person skilled in judging the merits of literary or artistic works; one who passes judgment; a fault-finder.

critical *adj* skilled in criticism; censorious; relating to the turning point of a disease; crucial.—**critically** *adv*.

criticism *n* being critical; an adverse comment; a review or analysis of a book, play, work of art, etc by a critic.

criticize *vt* to pass judgment on; to find fault with; to examine critically.—**criticizer** *n*.

critique *n* a critical article or review.

critter *n* (*dial*) a creature.

CRJ *abbr* = Commission for Racial Justice.

CRL *abbr* = Certified Record Librarian; Certified Reference Librarian.

CRLS *abbr* = Coastguard Radio Liaison Station.

CRM *abbr* = counter-radar missile.

CRMF *abbr* = Cancer Relief Macmillan Fund.

CRMP *abbr* = Corps of Royal Military Police.

CRM Soc *abbr* = Charles Rennie Mackintosh Society.

CRN *abbr* = Co-op Reform Network; Countryside Recreation Network.

CRNA *abbr* = Campaign for the Restoration of the National Anthem and Flag.

CRNCM *abbr* (*Brit*) = Companionship of the Royal Northern College of Music.

CRO *abbr* = cathode-ray oscillograph (or oscilloscope); Citizens' Rights Office; Companies Registration Office; Criminal Records Office.

croak *n* a deep hoarse discordant cry. * *vti* to utter a croak; (*inf*) to die, to kill.— **croakily** *adv*.—**croakiness** *n*.—**croaky** *adj*.

Croatia *n* a republic of former Yugoslavia, which made a unilateral declaration of independence on 25 June 1991.

Croatian, Croat *adj* of or pertaining to Croatia, its people or language. * *n* an inhabitant of Croatia; the language of Croatia, a dialect of Serbo-Croatian.

croche *n* (*mus*) (*French*) an eighth note (quaver).

crochet *n* a kind of knitting done with a hooked needle. * *vti* (**crocheting, crocheted**) to do this; to make crochet articles.—**crocheter** *n*.

crocidolite *n* blue asbestos.

crock[1] *n* an earthenware pot.

crock[2] *n* a broken-down horse; (*sl*) a worn-out or unfit person. * *vti* to become or make unfit.

crock³ n soot on a kettle, etc. * vt to blacken with soot.

crocked adj (sl) drunk.

crockery n china dishes, earthenware vessels, etc.

crocket n a small curved ornament on the angles of spires, canopies, etc.

Crockett n Davy [David] (1786–1836) American frontiersman.

crocodile n a large amphibious reptile, similar to an alligator; its skin, used to make handbags, shoes, etc; a line of schoolchildren walking in pairs.

crocodile clip n a clasp with serrated interlocking edges for electrical connections

crocodile tears npl insincere grief.

crocodilian adj pertaining to crocodiles. * n any of the order of reptiles that includes alligators and crocodiles.

crocus n (pl **crocuses**) a bulbous plant with yellow, purple, or white flowers.

croft n a small plot of land with a rented farmhouse, esp in Scotland.—**crofter** n.

Croft n **William** (1678-1727) English composer who was for a time organist at Westminster Abbey. He is best known for his odes and anthems, esp the hymn tune "St Anne" to which is sung "O God our Help in Ages Past."

Crohn's disease n chronic inflammation of the bowel, esp the ileum.

croissant n (French) "crescent"; a rich, buttery crescent-shaped, bread roll originating from France.

Cro-Magnon n a natural rock hollow in cliffs in the Dordogne region of France, in which the first human (*Homo sapiens*) remains were discovered in 1868.

Cro-Magnon man n a race of man living in late Palaeolithic times.

cromlech n a prehistoric monument of rough stones in a circle and usu surrounding a lofty pillar of stone.

Cromwell n 1. **Oliver** (1599–1658) English soldier and statesman. Following the Civil War, he was nominated "Lord Protector" of the Commonwealth in 1653. He was succeeded as Protector (1658–59) by his son, Richard Cromwell (1626–72). 2. **Thomas** (c.1485–1540) English statesman and Henry VIII's chief adviser. He fostered the passing of Reformation legislation, establishing the king as head of the Church in England.

crone n a withered old woman.

Cronin n **A(rchibald) J(oseph)** (1896–1981) Scottish novelist, dramatist, and physician.

Cronkite n **Walter Leland Jnr** (1916–) American journalist and broadcaster. He distinguished himself covering events of World War II and later as a reporter for CBS.

Cronos, Cronus, Kronos n (*Greek myth*) a son of Uranus and Ge (Heaven and Earth) and youngest of the Titans, identifed with the Roman Saturn. He was the ruler of the world after Uranus was deposed.

crony n (pl **cronies**) an intimate friend.

crook n a shepherd's hooked staff; a bend, a curve; (*mus*) a detachable section of tubing that was inserted into a brass or woodwind instrument between the mouthpiece and the body of the instrument to give it a different key; a swindler, a dishonest person. * adj (sl) unwell. * vti to bend or to be bent into the shape of a hook.

crooked adj bent, twisted; dishonest.—**crookedly** adv.—**crookedness** n.

croon vi to hum in a low gentle voice. * vt to sing songs in a soft gentle manner.—**crooner** n.

crooning n (*mus*) a soft, sentimental style of singing, often to dance music. Bing Crosby was a noted "crooner."

crop n a year's or a season's produce of any cultivated plant; harvest; any collection of things appearing at the same time; a pouch in a bird's gullet; a hunting whip; hair cut close or short. * vti (**cropping, cropped**) to clip short; to bite off or eat down (grass); (*land*) to yield; to sow, to plant; (*geol*) to come to the surface; to sprout; (*with* **up**) (*inf*) to occur or appear by chance or unexpectedly.

crop circle n a circular patch of corn in a cornfield that has been flattened by an as yet unexplained whirling movement.

crop-dusting n the aerial spraying of crops.

crop-eared adj with clipped ears; short-haired.

cropper n a thing that crops; a cloth-facing machine; a pouter pigeon; (*sl*) a heavy fall.

cropping n (*comput*) a feature of graphics programs that enables users to trim an image.

crop rotation n the renewal of soil by the successive planting of different crops.

croquet n a game played with mallets, balls and hoops. * vt (**croqueting, croqueted**) to drive away an opponent's ball by striking one's own placed in contact with it.

croquette n a ball of ground meat, fish, or potato seasoned and fried brown.

crore n unit of currency in India, Pakistan, and Bangladesh, equal to 100 lakhs.

Crosby n **Bing [Harry Lillis Crosby]** (1904–77) American singer and actor who co-starred with Bob Hope in the *Road to . . .* series.

crosier n the pastoral staff of a bishop.—*also* **crozier**.

cross n a figure formed by two intersecting lines; a wooden structure, consisting of two beams placed across each other, used in ancient times for crucifixion; the emblem of the Christian faith; a symbol or mark (X); a focal point in a town; a burden, or affliction; a device resembling a cross; a cross-shaped medal; a hybrid. * vti to pass across; to intersect; to meet and pass; to place crosswise; to mark with a cross; to make the sign of the cross over; to thwart, to oppose; to modify (a breed) by intermixture (with). * adj transverse; reaching from side to side; intersecting; out of temper, peevish.—**crosser** n.—**crossly** adv.—**crossness** n.

cross. abbr = crossing.

Cross n **Joan** (1900–) English soprano, who was one of the greatest of the 20th century. She was particularly associated with the works of Britten.

crossbar n a horizontal bar, as that across goal posts or a bicycle frame.

crossbill n a bird whose mandibles cross when the bill is closed.

crossbow n a bow set crosswise on the stock from which bolts are shot along a groove.

crossbreed vt (**crossbreeding, crossbred**) to breed animals by mating different varieties. * n an animal produced in this way.

crosscheck vt to verify by checking different opinions or sources.

cross-country adj across fields; denoting cross-country racing or skiing.—also n.

cross-cultural adj of or involving two or more cultures.—**cross-culturally** adv.

crosscurrent n a current that flows across another in water or air; ideas running counter to those generally held.

crosscut vti (**crosscutting, crosscut**) to cut transversely across; (*film*) to cut between alternate shots. * adj made or used for cutting transversely; cut on the bias. * n a crosswise cut; a short cut; (*film*) an alternation between shots; (*mining*) a level intersecting a vein.

cross-domed church n (*archit*) an early Christian or Byzantine church in the form of a cross with a central domed roof.

crosse n a long-handled racket in which the ball is caught and carried in lacrosse.

Crosse n **Gordon** (1937–) English composer whose works include pieces for children, e.g., *Ahmet the Woodseller*, and four operas, including *Purgatory* and *Potter Thompson*.

cross-examine vt to question closely; (*law*) to question (a witness) who has already been questioned by counsel on the other side.—**cross-examiner** n.—**cross-examination** n.

cross-eyed adj squinting.—**cross-eye** n.

cross-fertilization n fertilization of the ovules of a flower by the pollen of another.

cross-fertilize vt to fertilize (a plant) with pollen from another.

crossfire n converging gunfire from two or more positions; animated debate or argument.

cross-grained adj contrary or awkward; with an irregular grain or fiber.

crosshatch vt to shade with crossed lines.

crossing n an intersection of roads or railroad lines; a place for crossing a street; the crossbreeding of animals and plants.

cross-in-square n (*archit*) the most common plan for a Byzantine church, having a large square central bay with a domed roof resting on four piers.

cross-legged adj seated with one leg crossed over the other.

crosspatch n (*inf*) a bad-tempered person.

crosspiece n a transverse piece.

cross-platform n (*comput*) the use of software and files on computer with a different hardware system.

cross-purpose n a contrary purpose; **be at cross-purposes** to talk without either party realizing that the other is talking about a different thing.

cross-question vt to question to elicit details or test the accuracy of an account already given.—**cross-questioning** n.

cross-refer vt to mark (text, a book, etc) in such a way as to direct the reader to another page, etc with more information.

cross-reference n a note directing the reader to a different section of a book or document.

cross rhythms n (*mus*) rhythms that appear to have conflicting patterns and are performed at the same time as one another.

crossroad n a road crossing another; (*pl*) a four way, where two roads cross; (*fig*) the time when a decisive action has to be made.

cross section n a cutting at right angles to length; the surface then shown; a random selection of the public.—**cross-sectional** adj.

cross-stitch n a stitch formed of two stitches of the same length, one crossing the other.

crosstalk n interference in lines of communication, esp telephone lines; a quick-witted flow of conversation; repartee.

crosstie n a railroad tie.

crosstree n (*naut*) one of several pieces of timber across the head of a lower mast to support the mast above.

crosswalk n a street crossing for pedestrians.

crosswind n a side or unfavorable wind.

crosswise, crossways adv in the manner of a cross.

crossword (puzzle) n a puzzle in which interlocking words to be inserted vertically and horizontally in a squared diagram are indicated by clues.

crotch n the region of the body where the legs fork, the genital area; any forked region.

crotchet n (*mus*) a quarter note, a note equal to the duration of a half-minim.—*also* **quarter note**.

crotchety adj peevish, ill-tempered.—**crotchetiness** n.

Crotti n **Jean** (1878–1958) Swiss painter and stained glass craftsman who was active in the Dada movement.

crouch vi to squat or lie close to the ground; to cringe, to fawn.

croup¹ n inflammation of the windpipe causing coughing and breathing problems, esp in children.—**croupous, croupy** adj.

croup², **croupe** n the rump or buttocks of certain animals; the place behind the saddle of a horse.

croupier n a person who presides at a gaming table and collects or pays out the money won or lost.

crouton n a small piece of fried or toasted bread sprinkled onto soups.

crow n any of various usu large, glossy, black birds; a cawing cry, the shrill sound of a cock. * vi (**crowing**, **crowed** or **crew**) to make a sound like a cock; to boast in triumph; to utter a cry of pleasure.—**crower** n.

crowbar n an iron bar for use as a lever.

crowd n a number of people or things collected closely together; a dense multitude, a throng; (inf) a set; a clique. * vti to press closely together; to fill to excess; to push, to thrust; to importune.—**crowded** adj.

crowfoot n (pl **crowfoots**) any of several kinds of buttercup with yellow or white flowers and leaves like a crow's foot.

crown n a wreath worn on the head; the head covering of a monarch; regal power; the sovereign; the top of the head; the top of a tree; a summit; a reward; the part of a tooth above the gum; (archit) the area of the upper surface of a vault, where the ribs intersect. * vt to invest with a crown; to adorn or dignify; to complete; to reward; to put an artificial crown on a tooth; (sl) to strike on the head.

crown colony n a British colony subject to the control of the home government.

crown glass n a fine, thick kind of glass.

crown land n (UK) land or real property belonging to the sovereign.

crown prince n the heir apparent to a throne.

crown princess nf the heiress apparent to a throne; the wife of a crown prince.

crown saw n a kind of circular saw.

crownwork n the covering or replacement of the crown of a tooth; the making of crowns; a fortified outwork.

crow's-foot n (pl **crow's-feet**) a wrinkle at the corner of the eye; an arrangement of cords to suspend an awning; a decorative embroidery stitch.

crow's-nest n a lookout or watchtower on the main topmast of a sailing vessel.

crozier see **crosier**.

CRP abbr = Community Rights Project.

CRPB abbr (Scot) = Clyde River Purification Board.

crs. abbr = creditors; credits.

CRS abbr = (Eire) Centre for Retail Studies; Cereals Research Station; Christian Rescue Service; Conflict Research Society.

CRSA abbr = Cold Rolled Sections Association.

CRSOA abbr = County Road Safety Officers Association.

CRT abbr = cathode-ray tube; Ship Owners' Refrigerated Cargo Research Association.

CRTC abbr = Clay Roofing Tile Council.

cruces see **crux**.

crucial adj decisive; severe; critical.—**crucially** adv.

cruciate adj (bot) cross-shaped.

crucible n a heat-resistant container for melting ores, etc.

crucifer n any of many plants with four petals arranged like a cross, as the mustard, etc; the bearer of a large cross in a religious procession.

crucifier n one who crucifies.

crucifix n a cross with the sculptured figure of Christ.

crucifixion n a form of execution by being nailed or bound to a cross by the hands and feet; (with cap) the death of Christ in this manner.

cruciform adj cross-shaped.

cruciform village n a village that has formed at the intersection of two different routes.

crucify vt (**crucifying**, **crucified**) to put to death on a cross; to cause extreme pain to; to defeat utterly in an argument; to ridicule mercilessly.

cruck construction n (archit) a Saxon building using crucks, curved timbers extending from ground level to meet at an apex above, as the framework for walls and roof.

crud n (sl) a deposit of encrusted filth; nuclear waste; a contemptible person.

crude adj in a natural state; unripe; raw; immature; harsh in color; unfinished, rough; lacking polish; blunt; vulgar. * n petroleum.—**crudely** adv.—**crudeness** n.

crude oil n unrefined petroleum.

crudités npl coarsely chopped raw vegetables eaten with a dip.

crudity n (pl **crudities**) crudeness; a crude act or expression.

cruel adj (**crueler**, **cruelest**) disposed to give pain to others; merciless; hard-hearted; fierce; painful; unrelenting.—**cruelly** adv.—**cruelty** n.

cruelty n (pl **cruelties**) inhumanity; savageness; a cruel act.

cruet n a small glass bottle for vinegar and oil, used at the table; a set of containers holding salt, pepper, vinegar.

cruise vi to sail to and fro; to wander about; to move at the most efficient speed for sustained travel. * vt to cruise over or about. * n a voyage from place to place for military purposes or in a liner for pleasure.

Cruise n Tom [Tom Cruise Mapother IV] (1962–) American movie actor who won an academy award for best actor for Born on the 4th of July (1989).

cruise missile n a subsonic low-flying guided missile.

cruiser n fast warship smaller than a battleship; a pleasure yacht or motorboat.

crumb n a fragment of bread; the soft part of bread; a little piece of anything; (sl) a despicable person. * vi to cover food with breadcrumbs before cooking.

crumble vt to break into crumbs; to cause to fall into pieces. * vi to disappear gradually, to disintegrate.—**crumbly** adj.

crumby adj (**crumbier**, **crumbiest**) in crumbs; soft.—**crumbiness** n.

crumhorn see **Krumhorn**.

crummy adj (**crummier**, **crummiest**) (sl) dirty, squalid, worthless; slightly ill.—**crumminess** n.

crump n a bursting shell; the crunching or exploding sound of this. * vi to explode. * vt to shell; to hit (a ball) hard.

crumpet n a soft cake with holes on one side, often eaten toasted; (sl) a sexually attractive woman.

crumple vti to twist or crush into wrinkles; to crease; to collapse. * n a wrinkle or crease made by crumpling.—**crumply** adj.

crunch vti to crush with the teeth; to tread underfoot with force and noise; to make a sound like this; to chew audibly. * n the sound or act of crunching; (with the) (inf) the crucial moment, the time of vital decision.

crunchy adj (**crunchier**, **crunchiest**) crisp; able to be crunched.—**crunchily** adv.—**crunchiness** n.

crupper n a looped leather band attached to the back of a saddle and passing under the horse's tail; the hindquarters of a horse.

crural adj of the leg or thigh; leg-shaped.

crus n (pl **crura**) the leg proper; a part resembling a leg.

crusade n a medieval Christian military expedition to recover the Holy Land; a vigorous concerted action for the defense of a cause or the advancement of an idea. * vi to engage in a crusade.—**crusader** n.

cruse n a small earthenware pot or dish for holding liquids.

crush vt to press between two opposite bodies; to squeeze; to break by pressure; to bruise; to ruin; to quell, to defeat; to mortify. * vi to be pressed out of shape or into a smaller compass. * n a violent compression or collision; a dense crowd; (inf) a large party; a drink made from crushed fruit; (sl) an infatuation.—**crushable** adj.—**crusher** n.

crust n any hard external coating or rind; the exterior solid part of the earth's surface; a shell or hard covering; (sl) a means of livelihood. * vti to cover or become covered with a crust.—**crusty** adj (**crustier**, **crustiest**).—**crustily** adv.—**crustiness** n.

crustacean n any aquatic animal with a hard shell, including crabs, lobsters, shrimps, and barnacles .—also adj.—**crustaceous** adj.

crutch n a staff with a crosswise head to support the weight of a lame person; something that supports; a prop; the crotch.

crux n (pl **cruxes**, **cruces**) a difficult problem; the essential or deciding point.

Crux n (astron) a southern sky constellation, the smallest of all constellations.

Cruzeiro n currency of Brazil.

cry vi (**crying**, **cried**) to call aloud; to proclaim; to exclaim vehemently; to implore; to shed tears; (with off) (inf) to cancel (an agreement, arrangement, etc); to renege; (with out) to shout due to fear or pain. * vt to utter loudly and publicly; (with out for) to be in dire need of. * n (pl **cries**) an inarticulate sound; an exclamation of wonder or triumph; an outcry; clamor; an urgent appeal; a spell of weeping; a battle cry; a catchword; the particular sound made by an animal or bird.

crybaby n (pl **crybabies**) a child who weeps easily; a person who cries or complains often.

cryo- prefix frost; freezing.

cryoextraction n the extraction of juice from grapes that have been frozen before pressing to obtain a higher level of sugar and fruitier taste.

cryogen n a substance for producing freezing temperatures.

cryogenics n (sing) the science of very low temperatures and their effects.

cryolite n a mineral from which aluminum is produced.

cryometer n an instrument for measuring very low temperatures.—**cryometry** n.

cryonic suspension n the process of freezing a cadaver in the hope that it may be restored to life in the future.

cryonics n (sing) the use of extreme cold to preserve living tissue (e.g. organs) for future use.

cryosurgery n surgery involving freezing to destroy or remove diseased tissue.

crypt n an underground chamber or vault, esp under a church, used as a chapel or for burial.

crypt-, **crypto-** prefix hidden.

cryptesthesia, **cryptaesthesia** n clairvoyance; extrasensory perception.

cryptic, **cryptical** adj hidden, secret; mysterious.

cryptogam n a plant without stamens or pistil, a non-flowering plant, as mosses, ferns, etc.—**cryptogamic**, **cryptogamous** adj.

cryptogram n a coded message, cipher.

cryptograph n a piece of writing in cipher.

cryptography n the art of code writing and breaking; (comput) the process of converting data into a secret code by using an encryption algorithm.—**cryptographer** n.—**cryptographic** adj.

cryptozoology *n* the study of creatures whose existence has yet to be proved, e.g. the yeti, the Loch Ness monster.

cryst. *abbr* = crystalline; crystallized; crystallography.

crystal *n* a solid piece, e.g. of quartz, geometrically shaped owing to regular arrangement of its atoms; very clear, brilliant glass; articles of such glass, as goblets; (*sl*) the drug methamphetamine packaged and sold as a stimulant in powdered form (— *also* **crystal meth**). * *adj* made of crystal.—**crystalline** *adj*.

crystal. *abbr* = crystallography.

crystal gazing *n* fortune telling by peering into a ball of crystal.

crystalline *adj* pertaining to or having the form of a crystal; clear; transparent.— **crystallinity** *n*.

crystalline lens *n* a transparent biconvex solid body enclosed in a capsule between the vitreous and acqueous humors of the eye.

crystallize *vti* to form crystals; to give definite form; to express clearly the theme and content of an argument, proposition, etc.—**crystallization** n.

crystallography *n* the science of the forms and structure of crystals.—**crystallographer** *n*.—**crystallographic** *adj*.

crystalloid *adj* resembling a crystal; of a crystalline structure, opposite to colloid. * *n* a crystalloid substance; one of certain bodies that in solution diffuse readily through animal membranes.

Cs *symbol* (*chem*) cesium (element).

cs *abbr* (*mus*) (*Italian*) = *come sopra*, "as above."

c.s. *abbr* = capital stock; cast steel; chemical society; civil service; clerk of session; clerk to the signet; court of sessions.

cs. *abbr* = cases; commanders; (*Latin*) *communis*, "common."

c/s *abbr* = cycles per second.

Cs *abbr* = (*meteorol*) cirrostratus.

CS *abbr* = cesarean section; Cafe Society; Chemical Society; Chocolate Society; Christian Science; Christian Scientist; Civil Service; Cliometric Society; Coleopterists Society; Concrete Society; Confederate States; Conservation Society; Court of Session; Cultural Survival; Cyclamen Society.

C/s *abbr* = cases.

CSA *abbr* = (*Scot*) Campaign for a Scottish Assembly; Channel Swimming Association; Child Support Agency; Choir Schools' Association; (*Eire*) Civil Service Alliance; Confederate States Army; Confederate States of America; (*Scot*) Council for Scottish Archaeology; Creative Services Association.

CSAB *abbr* = Civil Service Appeal Board.

CSAC *abbr* = Catholic Scout Advisory Council.

CSAP *abbr* = Center for Substance Abuse Prevention

csárdás *see* **czárdás**.

CSAT *abbr* = Center for Substance Abuse Treatment

CSB *abbr* = Bachelor of Christian Science; Central Statistical Board; Chemical Safety and Hazard Investigation Board; Congregation of Saint Basil.

CSBF *abbr* = Civil Service Benevolent Fund.

CSBTA *abbr* = (*Eire*) Civil Service Blind Telephonists' Association.

csc *abbr* (*math*) = cosecant.

CSC *abbr* = Catholic Students Council; Christian Service Center; Civil Service Commission; Conspicuous Service Cross; Construction Safety Campaign; Cuba Solidarity Campaign.

CSCAW *abbr* = Catholic Study Circle for Animal Welfare.

CSCB *abbr* (*Scot*) = Committee of Scottish Clearing Bankers.

CSCFE *abbr* = Civil Service Council for Further Education.

CSD *abbr* = Center for Sustainable Development; Chartered Society of Designers; Civil Service Department; Commonwealth Society for the Deaf; Doctor of Christian Science.

CSE *abbr* = Campaign for State Education; Center for Software Engineering; Certificate of Secondary Education; Office of Child Support Enforcement.

CSES *abbr* = Chinese Solar Energy Society.

CSEU *abbr* = Confederation of Shipbuilding and Engineering Unions.

CSF *abbr* = cerebrospinal fluid; Coil Spring Federation.

CSG *abbr* = Catholic Stage Guild; Chinese Society of Geriatrics.

CS gas *n* an irritant gas used in quelling riots and disturbances.

CSGB *abbr* (*Brit*) = Cartophilic Society of Great Britain.

CSI *abbr* = Center for the Study of Intelligence; Chartered Surveyors Institution; (*Eire*) Coeliac Society of Ireland; Construction Surveyors Institute.

CSII *abbr* = Center for the Study of Industrial Innovation.

CSIP *abbr* = Committee for the Scientific Investigation of the Paranormal.

CSIR *abbr* = Council for Industrial and Scientific Research.

CSIRO *abbr* = Commonwealth Scientific and Industrial Research Organization.

csk. *abbr* = cask.

CSL *abbr* = computer simulation language.

CSM *abbr* = (*Brit*) Cambridge Society of Musicians; Christian Socialist Movement; Commission for Synoptic Meteorology; Committee on the Safety of Medicines; Company Sergeant-Major.

CSMA *abbr* = carrier-sensed multiple access.

CSN *abbr* = Confederate States Navy.

CSO *abbr* = Central Selling Organisation (of Diamond Producers); Central Statistical Office; (*Scot*) Chief Scientist Office; Chief Signal Officer; Chief Staff Officer; Committee of Senior Officials; community service order.

Cs. o. S. *abbr* (*mil*) = Chiefs of Section.

CSP *abbr* = Chartered Society of Physiotherapists; Council for Scientific Policy.

CSPA *abbr* = Congress of Catholic Secondary School Parents Associations.

CSPEC *abbr* = Confederation of the Socialist Parties of the European Community.

CSR *abbr* = Center for Scientific Review

CSRA *abbr* = Committee of Secretaries of Research Associations; Copper Smelters and Refiners Association.

CSREES *abbr* = Cooperative State Research, Education, and Extension Service

CSRF *abbr* = Civil Service Retirement Fellowship.

CSS *abbr* = Certificate in Social Service; Clan Stewart Society; computer systems simulator.

CSSA *abbr* = Cactus and Succulent Society of America; Computer Society of South Africa.

CSSC *abbr* = Civil Service Sports Council.

CSSR *abbr* (*Latin*) = *Congregatio Sanctissimi Redemptoris*, "Congregation of the Most Holy Redeemer."

CST *abbr* = Central Standard Time; College of Science and Technology; College of Speech Therapists; convulsive shock therapy.

CSTA *abbr* = Canadian Society of Technical Agriculturists; (*N. Ireland*) Catholic Secondary Teachers Association.

Cstat *abbr* = Chartered Statistician.

CSU *abbr* = catheter specimen of urine; Civil Service Union.

CSV *abbr* = Community Service Volunteers.

CSW *abbr* (*Scot*) = Central Scotland Woodlands.

CSWG *abbr* (*Scot*) = Church of Scotland Women's Guild.

CSYS *abbr* (*Scot*) = Certificate of Sixth Year Studies.

Ct *symbol* (*chem*) celtium (element).

ct *abbr* = carat; cent; court.

ct. *abbr* = cent; (*Latin*) *centum* "a hundred"; court.

c.t. *abbr* = certified teacher; commercial traveler.

CT *abbr* = Cambodia Trust; Civic Trust; College of Technology; cerebral thrombosis; cerebral tumour; computer-aided axial tomography; Connecticut; coronary thrombosis.

C/T *abbr* = cable transfer; (*grain trade*) Californian terms.

c.t.a. *abbr* (*Latin*) = *cum testamento annexo*.

CTA *abbr* = Cable Television Association.

CTB *abbr* = Chief of Tariff Bureau; comprehensive test ban.

CTBT *abbr* = comprehensive test ban treaty.

CTC *abbr* = carbon tetrachloride; Central Training Council; Citizens' Training Camps *or* Corps; City Technical College; Clothing Technology Center; Coach Tourism Council; Cyclists' Touring Club.

CTCC *abbr* = Central Transport Consultative Committee.

CTD *abbr* = classified telephone directory.

CTEB *abbr* = Council of Technical Examining Bodies.

ctenidium *n* (*pl* **ctenidia**) one of the respiratory organs of mollusks.

ctenoid *adj* having a comb-like margin.

ctf. *abbr* = certificate.

CTF *abbr* = Catholic Teachers' Federation; (*UK*) Children's Tropical Forests.

CTFMA *abbr* = Copper Tube Fittings Manufacturers Association.

CTGA *abbr* = Ceylon Tea Growers Association.

ctge. *abbr* = cartage.

CTGWE *abbr* = Christmas Tree Growers of Western Europe.

CTHCM *abbr* = Confederation of Tourism, Hotel and Catering Management.

CTMB *abbr* = Canal Transport Marketing Board.

CTMO *abbr* = Community Trade Marks Office.

ctn *abbr* (*math*) = cotangent.

cto. *abbr* = concerto.

CTOL *abbr* = conventional take-off and landing.

C to S *or* **c. to s.** *abbr* = carting to shipside.

CTPA *abbr* = Cosmetic Toiletry and Perfumery Association.

ctr. *abbr* = center.

cts. *abbr* = centimes; cents; certificates.

CTS *abbr* = Incorporated Catholic Truth Society.

CT scanner *see* **CAT**[2].

CTT *abbr* = capital transfer tax.

CTTH *abbr* = Cathedrals Through Touch and Hearing.

CTU *abbr* = Conservative Trade Unionists.

CTVM *abbr* = Center for Tropical Veterinary Medicine.

Cu *symbol* (*chem*) copper (element).

cu. *abbr* = cubic; (*meteorol*) cumulus.

Cu. *abbr* = (*meteorol*) cumulus.

CU *abbr* = Cambridge University; Casualties Union; Church Union; Commercial Union; Customs Union.

CUA *abbr* = common user access; Conference of University Administrators.

CUAG *abbr* = Computer Users Association Group.

CUAP *abbr* = College and University Affiliations Program

cub *n* a young carnivorous mammal; a young, inexperienced person; (*with cap*) a Cub Scout. * *vi* (**cubbing, cubbed**) to bring forth cubs.

cub. *abbr* = cubic.

Cuba *n* the largest and most westerly of the Greater Antilles group of islands in the West Indies. Cuba is a socialist republic.

cubage, cubature *n* the act of determining the contents of a solid; the contents so measured.

Cuban Peso *n* currency of Cuba.

cubbyhole *n* a small or snug place; a pigeonhole.

cube *n* a solid body with six equal square sides or faces; a cube-shaped block; the product of a number multiplied by itself twice. * *vt* to raise (number) to the third power, or cube; to cut into cube-shaped pieces.

cubeb *n* a species of pepper of Asia; its small spicy berry dried and used as a stimulant.

cube root *n* the number that gives the stated number when cubed.

cubic *adj* having the form or properties of a cube; three-dimensional.

cubical *adj* of or pertaining to volume; cube-shaped.

cubicle *n* a small separate sleeping compartment in a dormitory, etc.

cubiculum *n* (*pl* **cubicula**) a burial chamber in a catacomb.

cubism *n* a style of painting in which objects are depicted as fragmented and reorganized geometrical forms.—**cubist** *n*.—**cubistic** *adj*.—**cubistically** *adv*.

cubit *n* an ancient measure of about 18 inches (46 centimeters); the forearm from the elbow to the wrist.

cubital *adj* of the forearm.

Cubitt *n* Thomas (1788-1855) English architect, whose notable works include Gordon and Eaton Squares, London.

cuboid *adj* like a cube. * *n* a regular solid contained by parallelograms.

Cub Scout *n* a junior branch of the Scout Association.

CUC *abbr* = Coal Utilization Council.

Cuchulainn *n* (*Irish Celtic myth*) the epitome of the Irish warrior hero; said to be the son of Deichtire and Lugh, although some say that Conchobar mac Nessa was his father.

cuckold *n* a man whose wife has committed adultery.—**cuckoldry** *n*.

cuckoo *n* a bird with a dark plumage, a curved bill, and a characteristic call that lays its eggs in the nests of other birds; (*mus*) a short pipe with a single finger hole, which gives two notes that imitate the sound of the bird. * *adj* (*inf*) crazy, silly.

cuckoo clock *n* a clock that strikes the hours with a cuckoo call.

cuckoopint *n* a European plant with large leaves, purple flowers, and bearing red berries.

cuckoo spit *n* a white froth exuded by froghopper larvae on the leaves of plants.

cu. cm. *abbr* = cubic centimeter.

cucullate, cucullated *adj* hooded; hood-shaped.

cucumber *n* a long juicy fruit used in salads and as a pickle; the creeping plant that bears it.

cucurbit *n* any of an order of succulent, climbing, tendril-bearing plants with a fleshy fruit, including cucumbers, pumpkins, melons, etc.

cud *n* the food that a ruminating animal brings back into the mouth to chew again; **chew the cud** to consider and mull over.

cudbear *n* a purple dye made from lichens.

cuddle *vt* to embrace or hug closely. * *vt* to nestle together. * *n* a close embrace.

cuddlesome *adj* tempting to cuddle.

cuddly *adj* (**cuddlier, cuddliest**) given to cuddling; tempting to cuddle.

cuddy *n* (**cuddies**) (*naut*) the cabin of a half-decked boat; a small cabin, a galley.

cudgel *n* a short thick stick for beating. * *vt* (**cudgeling, cudgeled** *or* **cudgelling, cudgelled**) to beat with a cudgel.—**cudgeler, cudgeller** *n*.

cudweed *n* a plant with a fine down, belonging to the aster family.

CUE *abbr* = Committee for University English.

cue[1] *n* the last word of a speech in a play, serving as a signal for the next actor to enter or begin to speak; any signal to do something; a hint. * *vt* (**cueing** *or* **cuing, cued**) to give a cue to.

cue[2] *n* a tapering rod used in snooker, billiards, and pool to strike the cue ball.

cue ball *n* (*snooker, etc*) the ball that a player strikes in order to hit other balls.

Cuenca *n* a city in Ecuador.

CUEP *abbr* = Central Unit on Environmental Pollution.

cuesta *n* (*geog*) an asymmetrical ridge with a long, gentle slope on one side and a short, steep slope or escarpment on the other, produced when the slopes erode at different rates.

CUEW *abbr* (*Brit*) = Congregational Union of England and Wales.

cuff[1] *n* a blow with the fist or the open hand. * *vt* to strike such a blow.

cuff[2] *n* the end of a sleeve; a covering round the wrist; the turn-up on pants.

cufflink *n* a decorative clip for fastening the edges of a shirt cuff.

CUG *abbr* = closed user group.

Cui *n* César Antonovich (1835–1918) Russian military engineer who rose to the rank of general, composer, critic, and member of "The Five." He wrote fifteen operas, including *The Captive of the Caucasus, William Ratcliffe, The Saracen* and *Mam'zelle Fifi*, but is best remembered for his witty writings.

Cuilean *n* (*d*. 971) king of Scots (966–971). He was killed in battle fighting the Britons of Strathclyde.

cu. in. *abbr* = cubic inch.

cuirass *n* defensive armor for the breast and back, a breastplate.

cuirassier *n* a cavalry soldier armed with a cuirass.

cuisine *n* a style of cooking or preparing food; the food prepared.

cuisse *n* defensive armor for the thighs.

cuj. *abbr* (*Latin*) = *cujus* "of which."

CUKT *abbr* = Carnegie United Kingdom Trust.

CUL *abbr* = Cambridge University Library.

culch *n* materials forming a spawning bed for oysters; oyster spawn.

cul-de-sac *n* (*pl* **culs-de-sac, cul-de-sacs**) a street blocked off at one end; a blind alley; a position, job leading nowhere.

-cule *n suffix* forming diminutives, as *animalcule*.

Culhwch *n* (*Welsh Celtic myth*) legendary Welsh warrior. The son of Cilydd and Goleuddydd.

culinary *adj* of or relating to cooking.

cull *vt* to select; to pick out, gather. * *n* the selection of certain animals with the intention of killing them.—**culler** *n*.

cullet *n* broken or refuse glass for recycling.

culm[1] *n* the stem of grasses.

culm[2] *n* inferior anthracite coal.

culminate *vti* to reach the highest point of altitude, rank, power, etc; (*astron*) to reach the meridian; to bring to a head or the highest point.—**culminant** *adj*.—**culmination** *n*.

culmination *n* (*astron*) the highest or lowest altitude, above or below the horizon, attained by a celestial object as it crosses the observer's meridian.

culottes *npl* a women's flared pants that resemble a skirt.

culpable *adj* deserving censure; criminal; blameworthy.—**culpably** *adv*.—**culpability** *n*.

culprit *n* a person accused, or found guilty, of an offense.

cult *n* a system of worship; devoted attachment to a person, principle, etc; a religion regarded as unorthodox or spurious; its body of adherents; a current fashion.—**cultic** *adj*.—**cultism** *n*.—**cultist** *n*.

cultivate *vt* to till and plant; to improve by care, labor, or study; to seek the society of; to civilize or refine.—**cultivated** *adj*.

cultivation *n* the act of cultivating; the state of being cultivated; tillage; culture.

cultivator *n* a machine for breaking up soil for cultivation; someone who cultivates.

cultrate, cultrated *adj* (*bot*) shaped like a pruning knife; pointed and sharp-edged.

cultural *adj* pertaining to culture.—**culturally** *adv*.

culture *n* appreciation and understanding of the arts; the skills, arts, etc of a given people in a given period; the entire range of customs, beliefs, social forms, and material traits of a religious, social, or racial group; the scientific cultivation of plants to improve them and find new species; improvement of the mind, manner, etc; a growth of bacteria, etc in a prepared substance.* *vt* to cultivate bacteria for study or use.

cultured *adj* educated to appreciate the arts; having good taste; artificially grown, as cultured pearls.

cultured pearl *n* a pearl induced to grow artificially by the injection of a foreign body into the closed shell.

culture shock *n* loss of bearings and distress caused by an uprooting from a familiar environment or culture.

culverin *n* a 16th-century long cannon with serpent-shaped handles.

culvert *n* a drain or conduit under a road.

cum *prep* (*Latin*) with.

CUM *abbr* = Cambridge University Mission.

cumarin *see* **coumarin**.

cumber *vt* to hamper, to burden. * *n* a hindrance.

cumbersome *adj* inconveniently heavy or large, unwieldy.

cum div. *or* **cum d.** *abbr* (*Latin*) = *cum dividendo* "with dividend."

Cumhaill *see* **Fionn mac Cumhaill**.

cumin, cummin *n* a plant cultivated for its seeds which are used as a spice.

cum int. *abbr* = "with interest."

cummerbund *n* a sash worn as a waistband, esp with a man's tuxedo.

cummings *n* e[dward] e[stlin] (1894–1962) American poet, novelist, and artist. His novel, *The Enormous Room*, won him international recognition and his experimental free verse and distinctive use of typography were of great influence.

cum. pref. *abbr* = cumulative preference.

cumshaw *n* in China, a present or bonus.

cumulate *vt* to accumulate; to combine into one; to build up by adding new material.—**cumulation** *n*.

cumulative *adj* augmenting or giving force; growing by successive additions; gathering strength as it grows.—**cumulatively** *adv*.

cumulative preference share *n* a type of preference share that allows the owner to receive any dividends that were not paid in previous years.

cumulative voting *n* a system of voting in which each voter has as many votes as there are candidates, and may give all to one candidate.

cumulonimbus *n* (*pl* **cumulonimbi, cumulonimbuses**) (*meteorol*) large bulging clouds with a dark base that reach great heights.

cumulus *n* (*pl* **cumuli**) (*meteorol*) a well-defined cloud form having a flat base and rounded outlines.

CUNA *abbr* = Credit Union National Association.

CuNb *abbr* (*meteorol*) = cumulonimbus.

cuneate *adj* wedge-shaped.

Cunedda *n* (*fl*.390) Welsh tribal king. A chieftain settled by the Romans in north Wales where he defended the country against attacks from Ireland. Kings of Gwynedd claim descent from him.

cuneiform *adj* wedge-shaped (—*also* **cuneal**). * *n* the wedge-shaped characters of ancient Assyrian and Persian writing.

C

cunnilingus *n* sexual stimulation of the female genitals by the tongue.

cunning *adj* ingenious; sly; designing; subtle. * *n* slyness, craftiness.

Cunninghame Graham *n* **Robert Bontine** (1852–1936) Scottish travel and short-story writer, essayist, and politician whose books include *Mogreb-el-Acksa*, a description of exploration in Morocco.

Cunobelinus *n* (*fl*.43) high king of the British tribes. The Shakespearean Cymbeline.

cunt *n* (*vulg*) the female genitals, the vagina; (*derog, offensive*) a woman; (*offensive*) an obnoxious person.

CUNY *abbr* = City University of New York.

cup *n* a small, bowl-shaped container for liquids, usu with a handle; the amount held in a cup; a drink made from a mixture of drinks with one main ingredient (e.g. *claret cup*); one of two shaped supporting parts of a brassiere; an ornamental cup used as a trophy. * *vt* (**cupping, cupped**) to take or put as in a cup; to curve (the hands) into the shape of a cup.

CUP *abbr* = Cambridge University Press.

cupbearer *n* one who serves wine at a banquet, esp an officer of a royal household.

cupboard *n* a closet or cabinet with shelves for cups, plates, utensils, food etc.

cupel *n* a small flat vessel used to assay precious metals. * *vt* (**cupeling, cupeled** *or* **cupelling, cupelled**) to refine precious metals from lead in a cupel.

cupful *n* (*pl* **cupfuls**) as much as a cup will contain.

Cupid *n* (*Roman myth*) the god of love, also known as Amor, corresponding to the Greek Eros. He is represented as a winged boy, naked, armed with a bow and a quiver full of arrows.

cupidity *n* greed of gain; covetousness.

cup mark *n* (*archeo*) a decoration carved into stone, consisting of a cup-shaped hollow that may be ringed with a series of circles.*ææalso* **cup and ring mark**.

cupola *n* a dome, esp of a pointed or bulbous shape; a furnace for melting metals.—**cupolated** *adj*.

cupreous *adj* of or like copper; coppery.

cupric, cuprous *adj* containing copper.

cupriferous *adj* yielding copper.

cuprite *n* red oxide of copper.

cupule *n* (*biol*) a cup-shaped part, as of the acorn.

cur *n* a mongrel dog; a despicable person.

cur. *abbr* = currency.

cur., curr. *or* **curt.** *abbr* = current (of the present month).

curable *adj* able to be cured, remediable.—**curability** *n*.—**curably** *adv*.

curaçao *n* an orange-flavored liqueur.

curacy *n* (*pl* **curacies**) the office or district of a curate.

curare, curari *n* a substance extracted from vines and used by South American Indians to poison arrows.

curarine *n* an alkaloid extract of curare used as a muscle relaxant.

curarize *vt* to poison with curare.—**curarization** *n*.

curassow *n* a large turkey-like bird of South America.

curate *n* an assistant of a vicar or rector.

curative *adj* tending to cure. * *n* a curative agent or drug.

curator *n* a superintendent of a museum, art gallery, etc.—**curatorial** *adj*.

curb *vt* to restrain; to check; to keep in subjection. * *n* that which checks, restrains, or subdues; a line of raised stone forming the edge of a sidewalk (—*also* **kerb**).

CURB *abbr* = Campaign on the Use and Restriction of Barbiturates.

curbing *n* curbstones collectively; material for curbstones.—*also* **kerbing**.

curb roof *n* a roof with a double slope, the lower being steeper.

curbstone *n* the stone edge of a path.—*also* **kerbstone**.

curcuma *n* one of several kinds of plant including turmeric.

curd *n* the coagulated part of soured milk, used to make cheese.—**curdy** *adj*.—**curdiness** *n*.

curdle *vti* to turn into curds; to coagulate; (*with* **the blood**) to cause terror.—**curdler** *n*.

cure *n* the act or art of healing; a remedy; restoration to health. * *vt* to heal; to rid of; to preserve meat or fish by drying, salting, etc.

curé *n* a French parish priest.

Curetes *npl* (*Greek myth*) the attendants of Rhea, who saved the infant Zeus from his father Cronos, and then became a bodyguard to the god.

curettage *n* surgical scraping to remove growths or dead tissue, etc.

curette, curet *n* a surgical instrument for scraping a body cavity. **vt* (**curetting, curetted**) to scrape with this.

curfew *n* a signal, as a bell, at a fixed evening hour as a sign that everyone must be indoors; the signal or hour.

curia *n* (*pl* **curiae**) the papal court; a senate house of ancient Rome; one of the divisions of the Roman people; a medieval court of justice.

curie *n* a unit of radioactivity.

Curie *n* **Marie** (1867–1934) Polish-born French chemist. She won the 1903 Nobel prize for physics for work on radioactivity with her husband Pierre Curie (1859–1906) and physicist Antoine Henri Becquerel (1852–1908). She also won the 1911 Nobel prize for chemistry for the discovery of radium and polonium.

curio *n* (*pl* **curios**) an item valued as rare or unusual.

curiosa *npl* curiosities; books on exotic subjects, esp erotica.

curiosity *n* (*pl* **curiosities**) the quality of being curious; inquisitiveness; a strange, rare or interesting object.

curious *adj* anxious to know; prying, inquisitive; strange, remarkable, odd.—**curiously** *adv*.—**curiousness** *n*.

Curitiba *n* a city in Brazil.

curium *n* an artificially made radioactive metallic element derived from plutonium.

curl *vti* to form into a curved shape, to coil; to twist into ringlets; to proceed in a curve, to bend; to play at curling; (*with* **up**) to rest with the body in a curved shape and the legs drawn up; to relax in a comfortable place; (*inf*) to give up; to be embarrassed and sickened by. * *n* a ringlet of hair; a spiral form, a twist; a bend or undulation.

CURL *abbr* = Consortium of University Research Libraries.

curler *n* a small pin or roller used for curling the hair; a person who plays curling.

curlew *n* a bird with a long curved bill and long legs.

curlicue *n* an exaggerated ornamental curl.

curling *n* a Scottish game in which two teams slide large smooth stones on ice into a target circle.

curling iron, curling tong *n* a heated, rod-shaped implement for forming curls by winding a lock around the rod.

curling stone *n* a heavy round flat stone with a handle used in curling.

curling tongs *n* a pair of tongs heated to curl hair.

curly *adj* (**curlier, curliest**) full of curls.—**curliness** *n*.

curmudgeon *n* an ill-natured churlish person; a miser.—**curmudgeonly** *adj*.

Cu Roi mac Dairi *n* (*Irish Celtic myth*) king of Munster and a sorcerer; involved in several legends relating to Cuchulainn.

currant *n* a small variety of dried grape; a shrub that yields a red or black fruit.

currency *n* (*pl* **currencies**) the time during which a thing is current; the state of being in use; the money current in a country.

currency bar *n* (*archeo*) a narrow piece of iron, 15 to 36 inches in length, used as a form of currency in parts of the British Isles before the introduction of coins.

current *adj* generally accepted; happening now; presently in circulation. * *n* a body of water or air in motion, a flow; the transmission of electricity through a conductor; a general tendency.

current account *n* a checking account; a bank account, usu with no interest, from which money is withdrawn by checks or cash cards.

current affairs, current events *npl* topical news, esp in politics and international affairs.

current assets *npl* (*business*) assets, such as stock-in-trade, cash, and money owed by debtors, that are used up or turned over fairly soon in the course of the business and production activities of a business.

current liabilities *npl* (*business*) all the liabilities of a company, such as payments due to trade creditors, that are payable at some date in the relatively near future.

currently *adv* at the present time.

current ratio *n* (*business*) the ratio of the current assets of a business to the current liabilities, used as a test of a company's liquidity.

curricle *n* a two-wheeled open carriage drawn by two horses abreast.

curriculum *n* (*pl* **curricula, curriculums**) a prescribed course of study.—**curricular** *adj*.

curriculum vitae *n* (*pl* **curricula vitae**) a résumé of one's career.

currier *n* a leather dresser.—**curriery** *n*.

currish *adj* snappy; quarrelsome; rude.

curry[1] *n* (*pl* **curries**) a spicy dish with a hot sauce; curry seasoning. * *vt* (*pl* **currying, curried**) to flavor with curry.

curry[2] *vt* (**currying, curried**) to rub down and groom (a horse); to dress leather after tanning; to beat; (*with* **favor**) to use flattery to ingratiate.

Curry *n* **John Steuart** (1897–1946) American regionalist painter, who painted scenes of American life in the midwest. Typical of his work is *Baptism in Kansas* (1928).

currycomb *n* a metal comb for grooming horses.

curse *n* a calling down of destruction or evil; a profane oath; a swear word; a violent exclamation of anger; a scourge. * *vti* to invoke a curse on; to swear, to blaspheme; to afflict, to torment.

cursed *adj* damnable.

cursive *adj* running; flowing. * *n* a script with the letters joined, as in handwriting.

cursor *n* a flashing indicator on a computer screen indicating position; the transparent slide on a slide rule.

cursorial *adj* (*bird*) with limbs adapted for running or walking.

cursory *adj* hasty, passing; superficial, careless.—**cursorily** *adv*.

curt *adj* short; abrupt; concise; rudely brief.—**curtly** *adv*.—**curtness** *n*.

curtail *vt* to cut short; to reduce; to deprive of part (of).—**curtailment** *n*.

curtain *n* a cloth hung as a screen at a window, etc; the movable screen separating the stage from the auditorium; (*pl: sl*) the end, death. * *vt* to enclose in, or as with, curtains.

curtain call *n* (*theat*) a call from the audience for performers to appear at the end to receive applause.

curtain lecture *n* a private reprimand from a wife to her husband.

curtain music *see* **act tune**.

curtain-raiser *n* a short play preceding the main one; an introductory item.

curtain wall *n* (*archit*) in a medieval castle, the outer wall fortified by towers; a type of non-load-bearing wall erected to protect a building from the weather.

curtall *n* (*mus*) a small bassoon of the 16th and 17th centuries.

curtilage *n* (*law*) a yard, garden, or enclosure of a house, included in the same fence.

Curtis *n* **Tony [Bernard Schwartz]** (1925–) American actor whose movies include *Some Like it Hot* (1959).

curtsy, curtsey *n* (*pl* **curtsies, curtseys**) a formal gesture of greeting or respect, involving bending the knees, made by women. * *vi* (**curtsying, curtsied** *or* **curtseying, curtseyed**) to make a curtsy.

curvaceous *adj* (*inf*) having an attractive body with shapely curves.

curvature *n* a bending; a curved form.

curve *n* a bending without angles; a bent form or thing; (*geom*) a line of which no part is straight. * *vti* to form into a curve, to bend.—**curvy** *adj* (**curvier, curviest**).

curve ball *n* (*baseball*) a pitch thrown so that it swerves from its expected course; an unexpected thing or event.

curvet *n* a particular leap of a horse; a frisk or bound. *vi* (**curveting, curveted** *or* **curvetting, curvetted**) to leap as a horse; to frisk or bound.

curvilinear, curvilineal *adj* consisting of or bounded by curved lines.—**curvilinearity** *n*.

cusec *n* a unit of flow of one cubic foot of water per second.

Cush *n* (*Bible*) Hebrew name for Ethiopia.

Cushing's syndrome *n* a metabolic disorder that results from excessive amounts of corticosteroids in the body because of an inability to regulate cortisol or adrenocorticotropic hormone (ACTH).

cushion *n* a case stuffed with soft material for resting on; the elastic border around a snooker table; the air mass supporting a hovercraft. * *vt* to furnish with cushions; to protect by padding; to give protection against difficulties, etc; to soften the effect of.—**cushiony** *adj*.

cushy *adj* (**cushier, cushiest**) (*inf*) easy, comfortable.

cusp *n* an apex or point; the point at each end of a crescent moon; (*astrol*) the transitional point of a house; (*archit*) the pointed intersection between two arcs; a cone-shaped point on a tooth; a fold or flap of a heart valve.

cuspid *n* a canine tooth.

cuspidate, cuspidal *adj* of, like or having a cusp; (*leaves, etc*) ending in a point.

cuspidor *n* a spittoon.

cuss *n* (*sl*) an annoying person; a curse. * *vt* (*sl*) to curse.

cussed *adj* (*sl*) cursed; stubborn, perverse.

cussedness *n* (*sl*) contrariness.

custard *n* a sauce mixture of milk, eggs and sugar.

custard apple *n* a West Indian tree; its dark fruit with a soft edible pulp.

Custer *n* **George Armstrong** (1839–76) American soldier; commander of the American cavalry, famous for the Battle of the Little Big Horn and "Custer's last stand" (1876), in which he and hundreds of his troops were killed by Native American warriors.

custodian *n* one who has the care of anything; a keeper; a caretaker.

custody *n* (*pl* **custodies**) guardianship; imprisonment; security.—**custodial** *adj*.

custom *n* a regular practice; usage; traditions of a people or a society; frequent repetition of the same act; business patronage; (*pl*) duties on imports.

customary *adj* habitual; conventional; common.—**customarily** *adv*.

custom-built *adj* made to a customer's specifications.

customer *n* a person who buys from a store or business, esp regularly; (*inf*) a person.

custom house *n* an office or building where duties are paid on exported or imported goods and vessels are entered and cleared.

customization *n* the adaptation or development of goods or services to accord with the special requirements of a specific customer.

customs duty *n* a form of tax that is levied by the government on foreign products that are imported into the country.

custom software *n* (*comput*) a computer program that is written specifically for a client to match the systems that the client operates in his or her business.

cut *vt* (**cutting, cut**) to cleave or separate with a sharp instrument; to make an incision; to wound with a sharp instrument; to divide; to trim; to intersect; to abridge; to diminish; to pass deliberately without recognition; to wound the feelings deeply; to reduce or curtail; to grow a new tooth through the gum; to divide (a pack of cards) at random; to switch off (a light, an engine); (*inf*) to stay away from class, school, etc; (*with* **back**) to prune vegetation; to economize; (*with* **down**) to fell a tree; to reduce expenditure, consumption, etc; to make a smaller garment from an old one; to kill; (*with* **off**) to take away by cutting or slicing; to stop abruptly, esp a telephone conversation; to sever relations; to be so placed as to foil something, e.g. an escape; (*with* **out**) to delete; to cut into shapes; (*inf*) to force out a rival; to give up an indulgence or habit; (*with* **up**) to cut into pieces; to wound with a knife; (*inf*) to affect deeply. * *vi* to make an incision; to perform the work of an edged instrument; to grow through the gums; (*cinema*) to change to another scene, to stop photographing; (*with* **in**) to butt in; to interpose oneself; to interrupt with comments; to drive between two vehicles, leaving insufficient space; (*with* **out**) (*engine*) to stop working. * *n* an incision or wound made by a sharp instrument; a gash; a sharp stroke; a sarcastic remark; a passage or channel cut out; a slice; a block on which an engraving is cut; the fashion or shape of a garment; the deliberate ignoring of an acquaintance; the division of a pack of cards; a diminution in price below another merchant; (*sl*) a share, as of profits. * *adj* divided or separated; gashed; having the surface ornamented or fashioned; not wrought or hand-made; reduced in price.

CUT *abbr* = Chartered Union of Taxpayers.

cutaneous *adj* pertaining to the skin.

cutaway *n* a drawing (of a machine) with part of the exterior covering cut away to show the internal mechanism; (*film*) a scene shot separately from but relevant to the main action.

cutback *n* a reduction, esp in expenditure; a flashback.

cutch *see* **catechu**.

cute *adj* (*inf*) acute, shrewd; pretty or attractive, esp in a dainty way.—**cutely** *adv*.—**cuteness** *n*.

cut glass *n* flint glass cut into facets or figures.

Cuthbert *n* **Saint** (*d.* 687) Scottish monk who saw, in a vision, the soul of St Aidan transported to heaven, bishop of Lindisfarne. His feast day is 20 March.

Cuthred *n* (*d.* 756) king of Wessex, Britain (740–756). He defeated Ethelbald of Mercia at Burford, Oxfordshire in 752.

cuticle *n* the skin at the base of the fingernail or toe nail; epidermis.—**cuticular** *adj*.

cutie *n* (*sl*) a bright smart girl.

cutis *n* (*pl* **cutes, cutises**) the vascular layer of the skin, below the epidermis.

cutlass *n* a sailor's short heavy sword.

cutler *n* a maker of or dealer in knives.

cutlery *n* silverware, knives, forks, etc for eating and serving food.

cutlet *n* a neck chop of lamb, etc; a small slice cut off from the ribs or leg; ground meat in the form of a cutlet.

cutoff *n* a short or straight road; a new shorter channel cut by a river across a bend; a device for stopping steam from entering a cylinder.

cutout *n* a switch to cut off an electric light from a circuit.

cutpurse *n* a pickpocket.

cutter *n* someone or something that cuts; a small, swift sailing vessel; a light boat carried by larger ships.

cutthroat *n* a murderer. * *adj* merciless; (*razor*) having a long blade in a handle.

cutting *n* a piece cut off or from; an incision; a newspaper clipping; a slip from a plant for propagation; a passage or channel cut out; the process of editing a film or recording; a recording. * *adj* (*wind*) sharp, biting; (*remarks*) hurtful.

cuttlebone *n* the internal bone of the cuttlefish, used for polishing, etc.

cuttlefish *n* (*pl* **cuttlefish, cuttlefishes**) any of a family of 10-armed squidlike marine mollusks with a calcified internal shell.

cutwater *n* the fore part of a ship's prow.

cutwork *n* appliqué work.

Cuvillies *n* **Jean François Vinzent Joseph** (1695–1768) French-born architect who designed several rococo buildings.

Cuyp *n* **Aelbert** (1620–91) Dutch landscape painter whose work was inspired by the river landscapes of northern Europe, of the Maas (Meuse), and the Rhine, his favorite subjects being fields of cows.

Cuypers *n* **Petrus J.H.** (1827–1921) Dutch architect, whose notable works include Central Station, Amsterdam.

Cuzco *n* a city in Peru.

cv *abbr* (*pharm*) (*Latin*) = *cras vespere*, "tomorrow evening."

Cv *abbr* = molecular heat at constant volume.

CV *abbr* = calorific value; cardiovascular; cerebrovascular; (*Bible*) Common Version; curriculum vitae (a resumé) .

CVA *abbr* = cerebrovascular accident (stroke).

CVD *abbr* = cerebrovascular disease.

CVI *abbr* = common variable immunodeficiency.

CVO *abbr* = Center for Voluntary Organisation; Chief Veterinary Officer.

CVRTC *abbr* = Commercial Vehicle and Road Transport Club.

CVS *abbr* = cardiovascular system; chorionic villus sampling.

CVT *abbr* = Camphill Village Trust Limited.

CVWS *abbr* = combat vehicle weapons system.

CVWW *abbr* = Council of Voluntary Welfare Work.

CW *abbr* = chemical warfare; chemical weapons; child welfare; (*radio*) continuous wave.

CWA *abbr* = Crime Writers' Association.

CWBW *abbr* = chemical and biological warfare.

CWC *abbr* = Catering Wages Commission.

CWCC *abbr* = Children's World Community Chest.

CWCT *abbr* = Countrywide Workshops Charitable Trust.

CWD *abbr* = Caribbean Women for Democracy; civilian war dead; (*Brit*) Council of Welsh Districts.

CWF *abbr* = Commonwealth Weightlifting Federation; Conservative Way Forward.

CWG *abbr* = Cooperative Women's Guild.

CWGC *abbr* = Commonwealth War Graves Commission.

CWI *abbr* = Clean World International.

CWL *abbr* = Catholic Women's League; Children with Leukaemia Charitable Trust.

CWM *abbr* = Council for World Mission.

CWME *abbr* = Commission on World Mission and Evangelism.

cwo *abbr* = cash with order.

CWO *abbr* = Chief Warrant Officer.

CWP *abbr* = Coordinating Working Party on Atlantic Fishery Statistics.

CWR *abbr* = continuous welded rail; Crusade for World Revival.

CWS *abbr* = Co-operative Wholesale Society.

cwt. *abbr* = hundredweight.

CWU *abbr* (*Eire*) = Communication Workers' Union.

CWVA *abbr* = Commonwealth Veterinary Association.

CWVYS *abbr* (*Brit*) = Council for Wales Voluntary Youth Services.

CXR *abbr* = chest X-ray.

CXT *abbr* = Common External Tariff.

cy. *abbr* = capacity; currency; cycles.

Cy *abbr* = cyanogen.

cyan *n* a blue color, one of the primary colors.

cyanamide, cyanamid *n* a chemical compound of calcium carbide and nitrogen, used as a fertilizer.

cyanate *n* a compound of cyanic acid with a base.

cyanic acid *n* a strong acid composed of cyanogen and oxygen.

cyanide *n* a poison, salts of hydrocyanic acid.

cyanide process *n* the process of obtaining gold and silver from ores by treating them with sodium cyanide.

cyanogen *n* a colorless poisonous gas burning with a purple flame and with the odor of peach blossom.

cyanosis *n* a condition of the body in which its surface becomes blue due to insufficient aeration of the blood.—**cyanotic** *adj*.

cyanotype *n* a photographic process in which the picture is taken in Prussian blue; a blueprint.

Cybele *n* (*myth*) originally a goddess of the Phrygians, the Great Mother Deity, and the symbol of the moon. The Greeks identified her with an ancient earth goddess.

cyber café *n* (*comput*) a diner where customers can browse the Internet, play computer games, or look at CDS.

cybernetics *n* (*sing*) the study of communication and control functions in living organisms, and in mechanical and electronic systems.—**cybernetic** *adj*.

cyberphobia *n* a morbid fear or intense dislike of computers.—**cyberphobic** *adj*.

cyberspace *n* all of the data stored on a large computer or network through which a virtual reality user can move.

cyc. *abbr* = cycling; cyclopedia; cyclopedic.

Cyclades *npl* the principal group of islands in the Greek Archipelago. The largest islands of the group are Andros, Paros, Mykonos, Naxos, Melos, and Thera (or Santorini).—*also* **Kyklades.**—**Cycladic, Kykladic** *adj*.

cyclamen *n* a plant of the primrose family, with pink, purple, or white flowers.

cycle *n* a recurring series of events or phenomena; the period of this; a body of epics or romances with a common theme; a group of songs; a bicycle, motorcycle, or tricycle. * *vi* to go in cycles; to ride a bicycle or tricycle.

cyclic, cyclical *adj* moving or recurring in cycles.—**cyclically** *adv*.

cyclist *n* a person who rides a bicycle.

cyclo. *abbr* = cyclopedia; cyclopedic.

cyclogenesis *n* the formation of cyclones.

cycloid *n* a curve traced by a point on a circle as it rolls along a straight line.—**cycloidal** *adj*.

cyclometer *n* an instrument for registering the revolutions of a wheel.—**cyclometry** *n*.

cyclone *n* a violent circular storm; an atmospheric movement in which the wind blows spirally round towards a center of low barometric pressure.—**cyclonic** *adj*.

Cyclopean *adj* pertaining to the Cyclops, the legendary one-eyed giant; one-eyed; huge and rough; vast, massive; (*archit*) built of huge stones without mortar.

cyclopedia, cyclopaedia *n* an encyclopedia.—**cyclopedic, cyclopaedic** *adj*.

Cyclops *n* (*pl* **Cyclops, Cyclopes**) (*Greek myth*) member of a race of one-eyed giants.

cyclorama *n* a series of moving pictures extended circularly so as to appear in natural perspective to the viewer standing in the center.—**cycloramic** *adj*.

cyclothem *n* (*geol*) a feature of some sedimentary rocks in which a set of deposits is repeated in a cycle or sequence.

cyclotron *n* an apparatus for accelerating charged particles in a magnetic field.

cygnet *n* a young swan.

Cygnus *n* (*astron*) a northern sky constellation.

Cygnus X1 *n* (*astron*) a binary star system identified by its X-ray emission, possibly a supergiant and a black hole in orbit round each other.

Cygnus A *n* (*astron*) the first radio galaxy to be found in constellation Cygnus, and one of the brightest radio sources in the sky.

Cygnus Loop *or* **Veil Nebula** *n* the remnants of the outer layers of a star that exploded as a supernova.

cyl. *abbr* = cylinder; cylindrical.

CYL *abbr* = Communist Youth League.

cylinder *n* a hollow figure or object with parallel sides and circular ends; an object shaped like a cylinder; any machine part of this shape; the piston chamber in an engine.—**cylindrical** *adj*.—**cylindrically** *adv*.

cylindroid *adj* like a cylinder. * *n* a solid body resembling a cylinder but with the ends elliptical.

Cyllene *n* a mountain of ancient Arcadia in southern Greece, in myth the birthplace of Hermes, modern Ziria.

CYM *abbr* = Center for Young Musicians; Commonwealth Youth Movement.

cyma *n* (*pl* **cymae, cymas**) (*archit*) ogee molding of a cornice.

cymatogeny *n* th warping of the Earth's crust on a massive scale, resulting in domes and basins.

cymbal *n* (*mus*) one of a pair of two brass plates struck together to produce a ringing or clashing sound.—**cymbalist** *n*.

cymbalo *see* **dulcimer.**

cyme *n* a flower cluster in which the main stem ends in a flower, while from each side of the main stem secondary stems branch off to end in a flower, and tertiary stems from those, etc.—**cymose** *adj*.

Cymric *adj* pertaining to the Cymry, or the Welsh. * *n* the Welsh language.

CYMS *abbr* = Catholic Young Men's Society.

Cyneglis *n* (*d.* 643) king of Wessex, Britain (611–643). He failed in a plot to murder Edwin of Northumbria in 626.

Cynewulf *n* (*d.* 786) king of Wessex, Britain (757–786). A client of Offa of Mercia.

cynic *n* a morose, surly, or sarcastic person; a skeptic about people, motives and actions; one of a sect of ancient Greek philosophers.—**cynicism** *n*.

cynical *adj* skeptical of or sneering at goodness; shameless in admitting unworthy motives.—**cynically** *adv*.

cynosure *n* a center of attraction or admiration.

Cynric *n* king of Wessex, Britain (534–560). He extended his kingdom by fighting the Britons at Salisbury in 552 and at Badbury, near Swindon in 556. He was succeeded by his son, Ceawlin.

Cynthia, Cynthius *n* (*Greek myth*) names respectively of Artemis and Apollo.

cypher *see* **cipher.**

cypress *n* an evergreen tree with hard wood.

Cyprian *adj* of Cyprus; of Aphrodite, the Greek goddess of love; wanton, lascivious. * *n* a native of Cyprus; a prostitute.

Cyprian *n* Saint (*d.* 258) martyred bishop of Carthage. His feast day is 16 September.

cyprinid *n* any of a family of freshwater fishes, including the carp.

cyprinoid *adj* of or resembling a cyprinid; carp-like.

Cypriot *adj* pertaining to Cyprus, or to its inhabitants. * *n* a native of Cyprus.

Cyprus *n* an island republic which lies in the eastern Mediterranean about 85 kilometers or 53 miles south of Turkey.

Cyprus pound *n* currency of Cyprus.

Cyrano de Bergerac *n* Savinien (1619–55) French soldier, poet, and dramatist famous for having an enormous nose and for reputedly fighting around a thousand duels, inspiring Rostand's eponymous play.

Cyrene[1] *n* (*Greek myth*) a nymph who was loved by Apollo. He carried her to Libya, where Cyrene derived its name from her.

Cyrene[2] *n* in ancient times a Greek city in north Africa.

Cyril *n* Saint (827–69) Greek missionary monk and inventor of the Cyrillic alphabet, brother of Saint Methodius (826–885). They became known as the Apostles of the Slavs. Their feast day is 14 February (11 May in the Greek Church).

Cyrillic *adj* of or pertaining to St Cyril, or to the Slavonic alphabet. * *n* the alphabet of the Slavonic languages.

Cyril of Alexandria *n* Saint (376–444) patriarch of Alexandria in 412. His feast day is 27 June.

Cyril of Jerusalem *n* Saint (315–86) Bishop of Jerusalem from 350 until his death, persecuted by Arians who denied Christ's divinity. His feast day is March 18.

Cyrus *n* **the Great** founder of the Persian empire and ruler from 548–529 BC, who allowed exiled Jews to return to Jerusalem and rebuild the Temple.

CYS *abbr* = Catholic Youth Services; Center for Youth Studies.

CYSA *abbr* = Community Youth Services Association.

cyst *n* a closed sac developing abnormally in the structure of plants or animals.—**cystic** *adj*.

cystic fibrosis *n* a congenital disorder in young children characterized by chronic respiratory and digestive problems.

cystitis *n* inflammation of the urinary bladder.

cystocele *n* a hernia caused by protrusion of the bladder.

cystoid *adj* cyst-like. * *n* a growth resembling a cyst.

cystolith *n* a stone in the bladder.

cystoscope *n* an instrument for examining the urinary bladder.—**cystoscopic** *adj*.—**cystoscopy** *n*.

cystotomy *n* (*pl* **cystotomies**) the opening of the human bladder for the removal of a stone, etc.

cyt-, cyto- *prefix* cell.

Cythera *n* a Greek island in the Mediterranean, in Greek mythology, the home of the goddess Aphrodite.—*also* **Kithera.**

cytogenesis, cytogeny *n* cell formation in plants and animals.

cytogenetics *n* the scientific study of the structure and behavior of chromosomes.

cytology *n* the scientific study of cells; cell structure.—**cytological** *adj*.—**cytologist** *n*.

cytoplasm *n* the substance of a cell as opposed to its nucleus.—**cytoplasmic** *adj*.

cytoscreening *n* the examination of smear tests for indications of cervical cancer.

cytotoxic *adj* of a substance that damages or destroys cells.

CYWU *abbr* = Community Youth Workers' Union.

CZ *abbr* (*Panama*) = Canal Zone.

czar *see* **tsar.**

czardas *n* a Hungarian national dance with varying tempos; the music for it.

czarevitch *see* **tsarevitch.**

czarina, czaritsa *see* **tsarina, tsaritsa.**

Czech *n* a native, or the language, of the Czech Republic.

Czech Republic *n* a landlocked country at the heart of central Europe, which was constituted on January 1 1993 with the dissolution of the 74-year-old federal republic of Czechoslovakia.

Czerny *n* Karl (1791–1857) Austrian-born composer and piano teacher who was taught by Beethoven and in turn taught Liszt. He published many influential books on piano playing.

Cz. kr. *abbr* = Czechoslovakian kronen.

D

d, D the fourth letter of the English alphabet.

D¹ *n* (*mus*) the second note of the scale of C major.

D² (*symbol*) (*chem*) deuterium; the Roman numeral for 500; the second note of the C major scale.

d. *abbr* = (*mech*) angular deformation; (*Latin*) *da*, "give"; dam (in pedigrees); date; daughter; day; dead; (*elec*) deci- (tenth); deciduous; (*Latin*) *decretum*, "decree"; degree; (*Latin*) *dele*, "delete"; democrat; democratic; (*Latin*) *denarii*, "pennies"; (*Latin*) *denarius*, "penny" (*UK currency before 1971*); (*phys*) density; depth; deputy; deserter; (*chem*) dextro-; diameter; (*chem*) didymium; died; (*alg*) differentiation; dime; dinar; diopter(s); (*bank*) director; dividend; dollar; (*theat*) door; dorsal; dose; duke.

D *abbr* = December; (*math*) degree of curve; (*army*) Department (*math*) derivation; (*Latin*) *Deus*, "God"; (*cards*) diamonds; (*chem*) didymium; one of two Fraunhofer lines caused by sodium; dinar(s); Director; doctor; dominant; (*Latin*) *Dominus*, "Lord"; dong; Duchess; Duke.

3-D *abbr* = three-dimensional.

da. *abbr* = daughter; day(s).

d/a *abbr* = days after acceptance.

Da. *abbr* = Danish.

DA *abbr* Department of the Army; (*bank*) deposit account; developmental age; direct-action; Diploma in Anesthetics; Diploma of Art; District Attorney; (*com*) documents against *or* for *or* on acceptance; dopamine.

D/A *abbr* = digital-to-analog; (*chartering*) discharge afloat.

DAAG *abbr* = Deputy Assistant Adjutant-General.

dab¹ *vt* (**dabbing, dabbed**) to touch lightly with something moist or soft. * *n* a quick light tap; a small lump of anything moist or soft.—**dabber** *n*.

dab² *n* a species of European flounder.

dab³ *n* (*inf*) a dab hand.

dabble *vi* to move hands, feet, etc gently in water or another liquid; (*usu with* **at, in, with**) to do anything in a superficial or dilettante way. * *vt* to splash.—**dabbler** *n*.

dabchick *n* a water bird, the little grebe.

dab hand *n* (*inf*) an adept person, an expert.

DAC *abbr* = digital-to-analog converter.

da capo *adj, adv* (*mus*) from the beginning. * *abbr* DC.

dace *n* (*pl* **dace**) a small freshwater fish of the carp family.

dacha *n* in Russia, a house in the country used as a holiday and summer residence.

dachshund *n* a breed of short-legged, long-bodied hound.

dacoit *n* one of a group of robbers in India and Burma, who plunder in bands.— *also* **dakoit**.

DACOR *abbr* = data correction.

DACS *abbr* = Design and Artists Copyright Society Limited.

dactyl *n* a poetic foot of three syllables, one long and two short.—**dactylic** *adj, n*.

dactylogram *n* a fingerprint.

dactylography *n* the science of fingerprints.—**dactylographer** *n*.— **dactylographic** *adj*.

dactylology *n* the art of communicating ideas with the fingers; sign language.

Dactyls *npl* (*Greek myth*) beings whose name means literally "fingers," credited with the discovery of iron and the art of smelting.

dad *n* (*inf*) father.

Dada *n* a school of art and literature that aims at suppressing all relations between thought and expression.—**Dadaism** *n*.— **Dadaist** *n*.—**Dadaistic** *adj*.

Daddi *n* **Bernardo** (1290–1349) Florentine painter, whose popularity and influence continued into the late 14th century.

daddy *n* (*pl* **daddies**) (*inf*) father.

daddy longlegs *n* (*inf*) any of various spiders or insects with long, slender legs, esp a crane fly.

Da Derga's Hostel *n* (*Irish Celtic myth*) a place owned by a Leinster chief where travelers were always welcome; the place to which Conaire Mor insisted on travelling, having broken a geis or bond by so doing.

dado *n* (*pl* **dadoes**) the lower part of a room wall when separately paneled or decorated; (*archit*) the part of the pedestal in a classical column above the base; a rectangular groove in wood into which a board may be fitted; such a fitting.

dado rail *see* **chair rail**

Daedalus *n* (*Greek myth*) an architect and sculptor, who built on Crete the famous labyrinth to confine the Minotaur. He invented wings for himself and his son Icarus with which to fly across the sea.

DAES *abbr* = Diploma in Advanced Educational Studies.

DAF *abbr* (*Dutch*) = *Doorn Automobielfabriek* "Doorn Car Factory".

daff *vi* (*Scot*) to sport, to play.

daffodil *n* a yellow spring flower, a narcissus; its pale yellow color.

DAFS *abbr* (*Brit*) = Department of Agriculture and Fisheries for Scotland.

daft *adj* (*Brit inf*) silly, weak-minded; giddy; mad.—**daftly** *adv*.—**daftness** *n*.

Dafydd ap Llywelyn (*d.* 1246) king of Gwynedd, Wales (1240–1246). The second son and successor of Llywelyn ap Iorwerth.

Dafydd ap Opwain (*d.* 1194) king of Gwynedd, Wales (1170–1194). He married Henry II's illegitimate half-sister, Emma.

DAG *abbr* = Debendox Action Group; Deputy Adjutant-General; Divorce Action Group (Republic of Ireland).

dagger *n* a short weapon for stabbing; a reference mark used in printing (†). — *also* **obelisk**.

Daghda *or* **Dagda, The** *n* (*Irish Celtic myth*) meaning "the good god" and which has various variants, was a father-god and the chief of the Tuatha De Danann. He was the son of Eladu.

DAGMAR *abbr* = defined advertising goals for measured advertising results.

dago *n* (*pl* **dagos, dagoes**) (*offensive*) a foreigner, esp from Spain or Portugal.

DAgr *abbr* = Doctor of Agriculture.

DAgrSc *abbr* = Doctor of Agricultural Science.

daguerreotype *n* an early photographic process using a copper plate; a picture taken by this process.—**daguerreotypy** *n*.

DAH *abbr* = disordered action of the heart.

Dahl *n* **Roald** (1916–90) English author (of Norwegian parentage), whose children's stories include *Charlie and the Chocolate Factory*. His stories for adults include the collection *Kiss, Kiss*.

dahlia *n* a half-hardy tuberous perennial of the aster family grown for its colorful blooms.

Dahmer *n* **Jeffrey Lionel** (1960–94) American serial killer who murdered some 17 young men, some of whom he cannibalized, between 1974 and 1991. He was killed by fellow prisoners in 1994.

Dahshur *n* (*Egypt*) an important funerary site in the Memphis area, on the west bank of the Nile, just south of Saqqara.

DAI *abbr* = death from accidental injuries.

daily *adj, adv* (happening) every day; constant(ly), progressive(ly). * *n* (*pl* **dailies**) a newspaper published every weekday; (*inf*) a charwoman.

daimon, daemon *n* (*myth*) a kind of spirit usu associated with a particular place or object, such as a tree, stream, mountain, etc.

dainty *adj* (**daintier, daintiest**) delicate; choice; nice, fastidious. * *n* (*pl* **dainties**) a tidbit, a delicacy.—**daintily** *adv*.—**daintiness** *n*.

daiquiri *n* (*pl* **daiquiris**) a cocktail of rum, sugar and lime juice.

Dair *n* **Thomas** (1954–) American industrial designer.

Daire *n* (*Irish Celtic myth*) a son of Fionn mac Cumhaill. Legend has it that he was swallowed by a monster but succeeded in hacking his way out of the creature's stomach.

dairy *n* (*pl* **dairies**) a building or room where milk is stored and dairy products made; a shop selling these; a company supplying them.

dairy cattle *npl* cows reared for milk production.

dairying *n* the business or occupation of a dairy farmer.

dairyman *n* (*pl* **dairymen**) a man who works in a dairy or deals in dairy products.

dairy products *npl* milk and products made from it, e.g., butter, cheese, yogurt.

dais *n* a low platform at one end of a hall or room.

daisy *n* (*pl* **daisies**) any of various plants with a yellow center and white petals.

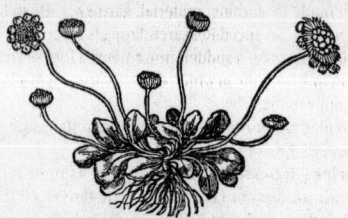

daisywheel *n* (*comput*) a flat, wheel-shaped, printing device with characters at the ends of spokes; the print wheel for a daisywheel printer.

Dakar *n* capital city of Senegal.

dal *n* a split-grain pulse commonly used in Indian cooking.—*also* **dhal**.

dal. *abbr* = dekaliter.

Daladier *n* **Edouard** (1884–1970) French socialist statesman; prime minister (1933, 1934, 1938–40) and signatory of the Munich Pact of 1938.

Dalai Lama *n* [**Tenzin Gyatso**] (1935–) Tibetan spiritual and temporal leader; winner of the 1989 Nobel Peace Prize. He became 14th Dalai Lama in 1940, but fled Tibet in 1959 following the Chinese invasion.

Dalap-Uliga-Darrit (on Majuro Atoll) *n* capital city of the Marshall Islands.

dalasi *n* the standard monetary unit of The Gambia, made up of 100 bututs.

dale *n* a valley.

Dale *n* **Sir Henry Hallett** (1875–1968) English physiologist. He and Otto Lowei (1873–1961) won the 1936 Nobel Prize for Physiology or Medicine for their work on nerve-impulse transmission.

Dali *n* **Salvador** (1904–89) Spanish surrealist painter.

Dall. *abbr* = Dallas's Reports, US Supreme Court.

Dallas *n* a city in the United States of America (USA).

Dallapiccola *n* **Luigi** (1904–75) Italian pianist and composer whose work includes anti-fascist songs, e.g., *Canti di Prigionia* ("Songs of Captivity") and several operas, including *Il Prigioniero* (*The Prisoner*) and *Ulisse* (*Ulysses*), and two ballets.

dalliance *n* idle or frivolous time-wasting; trifling; flirtation.

dally *vi* (**dallying, dallied**) to lose time by idleness or trifling; to play or trifle (with); to flirt.—**dallier** *n*.

dallymoney *n* (*sl*) alimony paid by one partner in a former sexual relationship to the other.

Dalmatian *n* a large short-haired dog with black spot-like markings on a white body.

Dalmatian-type coast *n* an example of Pacific or concordant coast.

dalmatic *n* a loose vestment with open sides worn esp by a bishop.

Daloa *n* a city in Côte D'Ivoire.

DALPA *abbr* = Danish Airline Pilots' Association.

Dalpayrat *n* **Pierre-Arden** (1844–1910) French porcelain painter and ceramicist, who specialized in stoneware.

Dálriada *n* a Scottish kingdom established in the 5th century, when the Scots crossed from Ireland.

dal s. *abbr* (*Italian*) = *dal segno*, "from the sign".

dal segno *n* (*mus*) from the sign, i.e., go back to the point in the music marked by the relevant symbol and repeat the music which follows it. * *abbr* dal s., DS.

Dalton *n* **William Bower** (1868–1965) British watercolorist and potter, who published three influential books on pottery design.

dam[1] *n* an artificial embankment to retain water; water so contained. * *vt* (**damming, dammed**) to retain (water) with such a barrier; to stem, obstruct, restrict.

dam[2] *n* the mother of a four-footed animal.

damage *n* injury, harm; loss; (*inf*) price, cost; (*pl*) (*law*) payment in compensation for loss or injury. * *vt* to do harm to, to injure.—**damageable** *adj*.—**damager** *n*. —**damaging** *adj*.

damar *see* **dammar**.

Damascus (Dimashq) *n* capital city of Syrian Arab Republic; probably the oldest inhabited city in the world; (*Bible*) Saul was converted on the road to Damascus. *See also* **Syria**.

damask *n* a reversible, figured, woven fabric, esp linen or silk. * *adj* made of this; having a pinkish color like a damask rose.

damask rose *n* a rose with grayish-pink blooms and a sweet fragrance used in perfume making.

Damasus I *n* **Saint** (*c*. 306–84) born in Rome of Spanish descent; pope (366). Zealous opponent of the Arians. His feast day is 11 December.

dambo *n* a shallow depression at the head of a drainage system but one that has no identifiable drainage streams.

dame *n* the comic, female role in a pantomime, usu played by a man; (*sl*) a woman; (*with cap*) the title of a woman who has been awarded an order of chivalry equivalent to the title of a knight; the wife of a knight or baronet.

dammar, damar *n* a resin used for varnish.

damn *vt* to condemn, censure; to ruin; to curse; to consign to eternal punishment. * *vti* to prove guilty. * *interj* (*sl*) expressing irritation or annoyance. * *n* (*sl*) something having no value. * *adj, adv* damned.

damnable *adj* deserving damnation; despicable; hateful; offensive; wicked; (*inf*) annoying.—**damnably** *adv*.

damnation *n* the state of being condemned to hell; the act of damning. * *interj* expressing annoyance, irritation, etc.

damnatory *adj* assigning to, or containing a threat of, damnation.

damned *adj* (*inf*) damnable. **adv* extremely.

damnify *vt* (**damnifying, damnified**) (*law*) to cause loss or damage to.

damp *n* humidity, moisture; in mines, poisonous or foul gas. * *adj* slightly wet, moist. * *vt* to moisten; (*with* **down**) to stifle, reduce; (*mus*) to stop the vibrations of (an instrument) by touching it, or part of it, e.g., the strings of a harp or the skin of a drum.—**damply** *adv*.—**dampness** *n*.

dampen *vti* to make or become damp. * *vt* to stifle.—**dampener** *n*.

damper *n* a depressive influence; a metal plate in a flue for controlling combustion; (*mus*) a device for stopping vibration in stringed instruments; (*Austral*) unleavened bread.

Dämpfer *see* **mute**.

Damrosch *n* **Walter Johannes** (1862–1950) American composer and conductor of German birth. His best-known works include *Cyrano de Bergerac*, *The Scarlet Letter*, and *The Man without a Country*. His brother, **Frank Heino Damrosch** (1859–1937), and his father, **Leopold Damrosch** (1832–85), were also notable conductors and musicians.

damsel *n* (*formerly*) a girl.

damselfly *n* (*pl* **damselflies**) an insect resembling the dragonfly but having wings that fold when at rest.

damson *n* a small, dark purple variety of plum; the color of this; the tree on which this fruit grows.

Dan[1] *n* the most northerly town in Palestine.

Dan[2] *n* (*Bible*) one of the twelve tribes of Israel

Dan. *abbr* = Danish.

DAN *abbr* = Direct Action Network.

Dana *see* **Danu**.

Danaè *n* (*Greek myth*) daughter of the king of Argos, who was shut up by her father in a tower, as there was a prophecy that her son would kill him. Zeus descended to her in a shower of gold and she bore him a son, Perseus.

Danaïdes *npl* (*Greek myth*) the fifty daughters of Danaus, who, all except one, murdered their husbands on their wedding night.

Dà Nang *n* a city in Vietnam.

Danaus *n* (*Greek myth*) king of Argos, who gave each of his daughters a dagger and urged them to murder their bridegrooms in revenge for the treatment he had received from Aegyptus.

dance *vti* to move rhythmically, esp to music; to skip or leap lightly; to execute (steps); to cause to dance or to move up and down. * *n* a piece of dancing; a dance performance of an artistic nature; a party with music for dancing; music for accompanying dancing.—**dancer** *n*.—**dancing** *adj, n*.

Dance *n* **George** (*b*. 1741) English architect. His notable works include Mansion House, London.

D & B *abbr* = Dun and Bradstreet (financial reports).

D and C *n* (*med*) dilatation (of the cervix) and curettage (of the womb).

d & d *abbr* = drunk and disorderly.

dandelion *n* a common wild plant with ragged leaves, a yellow flower and a fluffy seed head.

dander[1] *n* scurf from various animals, e.g., cats and dogs, that may be allergenic; temper; fighting spirit.

dander[2] *vi* (*Scot*) to saunter. * *n* a sauntering stroll.

D & HAA *abbr* (*Brit*) = Dock and Harbour Authorities' Association.

Dandie Dinmont *n* a breed of terrier.

dandify *vt* (**dandifying, dandified**) to give the character or style of a dandy to; to make trim or smart like a dandy.—**dandification** *n*.

dandle *vt* to play with (a baby) on the knee, to fondle.—**dandler** *n*.

d & p *abbr* = developing and printing.

dandruff *n* scales of skin on the scalp, under the hair, scurf.—**dandruffy** *adj*.

d & s *abbr* (*bank*) = demand and supply.

D & V *abbr* = diarrhea and vomiting.

dandy *n* (*pl* **dandies**) a man who likes to dress too fashionably. * *adj* (**dandier, dandiest**) (*inf*) excellent, fine.—**dandyish** *adj*.—**dandyism** *n*.

dandy-brush *n* a stiff brush for grooming horses.

Dane *n* a native or citizen of Denmark.

Danegeld *n* an annual tax imposed in England in the reign of Ethelred II to maintain forces against the Danes.

Danelaw, Danelagh *n* the code of laws established by the Danes on their settlement in England; that part of the country where these laws were in force.

dang *adj, adv, interj, n* a euphemistic form of **damn**.

danger *n* exposure to injury or risk; a source of harm or risk.

dangerous *adj* involving danger; unsafe; perilous.—**dangerously** *adv*.—**dangerousness** *n*.

dangle *vi* to hang and swing loosely. * *vt* to carry something so that it hangs loosely; to display temptingly.—**dangler** *n*.

Dani (*Irish Celtic history*) one of the last Celtic kings to rule at Tara before the arrival of St Patrick.

Daniel *n* (*Bible*) the principal character of the book of the same name; the real author lived in the 2nd century BC at a time when the Jews were being persecuted. *See also* **Balshazzar**.

Daniel, the Book of *n* (*Bible*) a fictional work of the Old Testament, which describes Daniel surviving ordeals such as the fiery furnace and the den of lions, as well as a number of visions.

Danish *adj* of the people or language of Denmark. * *n* the language of Denmark.

Danish krone *n* currency of Denmark, the Faeroe Islands, and Greenland.

Danish pastry *n* a sweet pastry topped with fruity icing and nuts.

dank *adj* disagreeably damp.—**dankly** *adv*.—**dankness** *n*.

D'Annunzio *n* Gabriele (1863–1938) Italian poet, novelist, dramatist, and political adventurer.

danseur *n* a professional dancer, a ballet dancer.—**danseuse** *nf*.

Dante *n* [Alighieri] (1265–1321) Italian poet, expelled from Florence in 1309. His best known work is *The Divine Comedy*.

Danton *n* Georges Jacques (1759–94) French revolutionary. As minister of justice, he voted for the death of King Louis XVI.

Danu *or* **Dana** *n* (*Irish Celtic myth*) Danu was a mother-goddess and the mother of the Tuatha De Danann.

Danube School *see* **Altdorfer, Albrecht**.

Danubian *adj* relating to an early farming culture in central and eastern Europe, which first started *c*. 5300 BC.

dap *vi* (**dapping, dapped**) to drop bait gently into water * *vt* to dip lightly; to bounce (a ball) * *n* a bounce.

dap *abbr* = documents against payment.

DAP *abbr* = distributed array processor.

daphne *n* a genus of small evergreen shrubs with fragrant flowers, allied to the laurel.

Daphne *n* (*Greek myth*) a nymph who was changed into a laurel tree while fleeing from the advances of the god Apollo.

dapper *adj* nimble; neat in appearance, spruce.

dapple *vti* to mark with or show patches of a different color; to variegate. * *adj* marked in such a way. * *n* something so marked.

dapple-gray *adj* mottled with darker gray. * *n* a horse of this color.

DAppSc *abbr* = Doctor of Applied Science.

DAR *abbr* = Daughters of the American Revolution.

Dar'a *n* a city in the Syrian Arab Republic.

DArch *abbr* = Diploma in Architecture; Doctor of Architecture.

Dardania *n* the area around or including the ancient city of Troy.

Dardanian, Dardan *adj* pertaining to Dardania, an ancient city of Troy, in Asia Minor, or its people. * *n* a Trojan.

Dardanus *n* (*Greek myth*) the ruler of Dardania and the Dardanians, who are identified with the Trojans.

dare *vti* to be bold enough; to venture, to risk; to defy, to challenge. * *n* a challenge.—**darer** *n*.

daredevil *n* a rash, reckless person. * *adj* daring, bold; courageous.—**daredevilry, daredeviltry** *n*.

Dar es Salaam *n* town in Tanzania.

Dargomizhsky *n* Alexander Sergeievich (1813–69) Russian composer, whose works include the operas *The Russalka* and *The Stone*.

daring *adj* fearless; courageous; unconventional. * *n* adventurous courage.—**daringly** *adv*.

Darius I, also known as **Darius the Great** *n* (*c*. 522–486 BC), king of the Persians and suzerain of Egypt (548–486 BC).

Darius II *n* king of the Persians (424–405 BC).

dark *adj* having little or no light; of a shade of color closer to black than white; (*person*) having dark brown or black skin or hair; gloomy; (*inf*) secret, unknown; mysterious. * *n* a dark state or color; ignorance; secrecy.—**darkly** *adv*.—**darkness** *n*.

darken *vti* to make or become dark or darker.—**darkener** *n*.

dark horse *n* a competitor about whom little is known; a person of reserved character; a surprise political candidate.

darkish *adj* quite dark.

dark matter *n* material that may exist in the universe but be "invisible," in the sense that not only does it not shine with its own light nor reflect light, but it reacts so rarely or weakly with the visible matter that it is difficult to detect.

dark nebulae *npl* (*astron*) clouds of thick gas and dust common throughout the Milky Way and other galaxies.

darkroom *n* a room for processing photographs in darkness or safe light.

darksome *adj* gloomy.

darling *n* a dearly loved person; a favorite. * *adj* lovable; much admired.

darn[1] *vt* to mend a hole in fabric or a garment with stitches. * *n* an area that has been darned.—**darner** *n*.

darn[2] *interj* a form of **damn** as a mild oath.—*also adj*.

darnel *n* a kind of rye grass.

darning *n* a patch made by darning; material, garments, etc to be darned.

DARPA *abbr* = Defense Advanced Research Projects Agency

dart *n* a small pointed missile; a sudden movement; a fold sewn into a garment for shaping it; (*pl*) an indoor game in which darts are thrown at a target. * *vti* to move rapidly; to send out rapidly.

dartboard *n* a circular cork or wooden target used in the game of darts.

darter *n* one of several kinds of bird or fish.

Darwin *n* 1. **Charles [Robert]** (1809–82) English naturalist; grandson of physician and poet Erasmus Darwin (1731–1802). He developed the theory of evolution by natural selection. 2. **Robin** (1910–74) British design educator.

Darwinian *adj* pertaining to Charles Darwin, the naturalist, or Darwinism. * *n* an evolutionist.

Darwinism *n* the theory of natural selection advocated by Charles Darwin.—**Darwinist** *n*.

das *abbr* = delivered alongside ship.

DAS *abbr* = data acquisition system.

DASA *abbr* = Domestic Appliance Service Association.

DASD *abbr* = direct-access storage device.

dash *vti* to fling violently; to rush quickly; (*hopes*) to shatter; (*one's spirits, etc*) to depress, confound; to write quickly. * *n* a short race; a rush; a small amount of something added to food; a tinge; a punctuation mark (—); a dashboard; vigor, verve; display.

dashboard *n* an instrument panel in a car.

dasher *n* one who or that which dashes; a dashing person; the part of a churn that agitates cream.

dashing *adj* debonair; spirited, stylish, dapper.—**dashingly** *adv*.

DASS *abbr* = Depressives Associated.

dastard *n* a malicious coward.

dastardly *adj* mean, cowardly; base.—**dastardliness** *n*.

dasyure *n* a small carnivorous Australian marsupial.

dat. *abbr* = dative.

DAT *abbr* = dementia of the Alzheimer type; digital audio tape.

data *npl* (*sing* **datum**) (*often used as sing*) facts, statistics, or information, either historical or derived by calculation or experimentation.

data bank, database *n* a large store of information for analysis, esp one held in a computer.

database management system *n* (*comput*) a software system for managing the storage, access, updating and maintenance of a database. *abbr* DBMS.

data bits *npl* (*comput*) the elements of a character sent during asynchronous communications that contain the actual data.

data bus *see* **bus**.

data capture *n* the process of translating information into computer-readable form.

Datacom *abbr* = data communications.

data file *n* a computer file containing data as opposed to an application or program.

Datanet *abbr* = data network.

data processing *n* the preparing and storing, handling or processing of data through a computer.

data protection *n* protection relating to personal information about individuals that is stored on computer systems.

Datastor *abbr* = data storage.

data warehouse *n* a system that collects data from a wide range of sources, and is processed as a management tool regarding trends, marketing etc.

DATCO *abbr* = Disability Appeal Tribunal Central Office.

date[1] *n* a day or time of occurrence; a statement of this in a letter, etc; a period to which something belongs; a duration; an appointment, esp with a member of the opposite sex. * *vt* to affix a date to; to note the date of; to reckon the time of; (*inf*) to make a date with; (*inf*) to see frequently a member of the opposite sex. * *vi* to reckon from a point in time; to show signs of belonging to a certain period.—**datable, dateable** *adj*.—**dater** *n*.

date[2] *n* the sweet fruit of the date palm; a palm tree of tropical regions.

DATEC *abbr* = Art and Design Committee of the Technician Education Council.

dated *adj* old-fashioned; out of style; bearing a date.—**datedness** *n*.

Datel *abbr* = Data and telecommunications.

dateless *adj* without a date; timeless; classic.

dateline *n* a line on a newspaper story giving the date and place of writing. * *vt* to provide with a dateline.

date line *n* the line running north to south along the 180-degree meridian, east of which is one day earlier than west of it.—*also* **International Date Line**.

dating *n* (*archeo*) the technique whereby a particular event, artifact, etc is given an age, enabling archeologists to place it in a sequence of events.

dative *adj* (*gram*) denoting an indirect object. * *n* the dative case.—**datival** *adj*.—**datively** *adv*.

Datran *abbr* = data transmission.

Datrec *abbr* = data recording.

datum *n* (*pl* **data**) a single unit of information; a thing given or taken for granted; something known or assumed as fact and made the basis of reasoning or calculation; an assumption or premise from which inferences are drawn; (*pl* **datums**) (*geol*) a level, line or point used as a reference in surveying.

datum level *or* **datum line** *n* the zero level or line from which all land altitudes and water depths are calculated, usu taken as sea level or a mean based on tide levels.

datura *n* any of several kinds of strongly scented narcotic plant.

DAU *abbr* = Defense Acquisition University

dau. *abbr* = daughter.

daub *vt* to smear or overlay (with clay, etc); to paint incompetently. * *n* a smear; a poor painting; (*archeo*) clay that is spread onto a framework or structure such as intertwined twigs (wattle) to provide building material. —**dauber** *n*.

Daubigny *n* **Charles François** (1817–79) French painter; a pioneer of *plein air* landscape painting.

Daugavpils *n* a city in Latvia.

daughter *n* a female child or descendant; a female member of a family, race, etc; a woman in relation to her native country or place; (*phys*) a nucleus, particle, etc produced from another by radioactive decay; (*biol*) a cell produced by the division of another.

daughter board *n* (*comput*) a printed circuit board that plugs into the main board, or motherboard, in a computer to add processing power or other facilities.

daughter-in-law *n* (*pl* **daughters-in-law**) the wife of one's son.

daughterly *adj* of or befitting a daughter.—**daughterliness** *n*.

Daum *n* **Auguste** (1853–1909), **Antonin** (1864–1930) and **Paul** (*d.* 1943) famous French glassware designers and manufacturers.

Daumier *n* **Honoré** (1808–79) French satirical cartoonist, painter, and sculptor.

daunt *vt* to intimidate; to discourage.—**daunter** *n*.—**dauntingly** *adv*.

dauntless *adj* incapable of being discouraged; intrepid, fearless.—**dauntlessly** *adv*.—**dauntlessness** *n*.

dauphin *n* the title of the eldest son of the king of France, 1349–1830.

dauphine, dauphiness *n* the wife of the dauphin.

Davao *n* a city in Philippines.

davenport *n* a large sofa, often able to be converted into a bed; a small ornamental writing desk.

David[1] *n* 1. (*Bible*) second king of the Hebrews (*c*.1000–962 BC). 2. **Jacques Louis** (1748–1825) French painter; leading artist of the French Revolution. 3. **Saint** also known as Dewi (*d. c*. 601) Welsh bishop; patron saint of Wales. His feast day is 1 March.

David[2] *n* a city in Panama.

David I ("the Saint") *n* (*c*.1081–1153) king of Scots (1124–1153). The sixth son of Malcolm III Canmore's second marriage to Margaret, sister of Edgar the Aetheling.

David II (1324–1371) king of Scots. Reigned with interruptions from 1329–1371. Born at Dunfermline, the son of Robert I (the Bruce) by his second wife, Elizabeth de Burgh.

Davie *n* **Alan** (1920–) Scottish painter. His style of mystical expressionism is vigorous and dynamic.

Davies *n* 1. **Arthur Bowen** (1862–1928) American artist. He helped organize the Armory Show. He later worked on the establishment of the Museum of Modern Art in New York. 2. Sir **Henry Walford** (1869–1941) Welsh composer and organist, best known and remembered for his music for festivals. 3. Sir **John** (1569–1626) English poet and statesman, who developed acrostics. 4. Sir **Peter Maxwell** (1934–) English composer and one of the Manchester School. As well as writing operas, notably *Taverner*, and orchestral pieces, he has also composed movie music, e.g., for Ken Russell's *The Devils* (1971). 5. **Robertson** (1913–95) Canadian novelist, playwright, literary critic, and essayist, who gained acclaim for the scale and quiet humor of his work, e.g., *The Cornish Trilogy*. 6. **W[illiam] H[enry]** (1871–1940) Welsh poet, who emigrated to the USA but after losing a leg in an accident returned to England where he survived as a tramp, scraping together enough money to publish a volume of poems, *The Soul's Destroyer*. His best-known prose work is *The Autobiography of a Super-Tramp*.

Davis *n* 1. **Alexander J.** (1903–) American architect. His notable works include United States Custom House, New York. 2. **Bette [Ruth Elizabeth Davis]** (1908–89) American actress, whose movies include *All About Eve*. 3. **Carl** (1937–) American composer, whose scores for movies and television include *The Naked Civil Servant* and *The World at War*. In 1981 he wrote the music for the movie *The French Lieutenant's Woman*. 4. Sir **Colin [Rex]** (1927–) English conductor esp associated with the works of Mozart, Stravinsky, Berlioz and Tippett. 5. **Jefferson** (1808–89) American statesman; president of the Confederate states during the period of the Civil War (1861–65). 6. **Miles** (1926–91) American jazz trumpeter and band leader and one of the most influential of all contemporary jazz. He made numerous recordings, which include *Sketches of Spain* and *Miles Ahead*. 7. **Owen William** (1838–1913) British architect noted for his fabric and wallpaper designs. 8. **Stuart** (1894–1964) American painter. His mature work is bright and decorative, as in *Oah! In Sao Pao* (1951).

Davisson, Clinton Joseph *see* **Thomson, Sir George Paget.**

davit *n* a small crane with tackle for raising or lowering a lifeboat, etc over a ship's side.

DAvMed *abbr* = Diploma in Aviation Medicine.

Davy *n* **Sir Humphry** (1778–1829) English chemist who discovered many new metals, and invented the "Davy lamp" in 1815.

Davy Jones *n* the spirit of the sea.

Davy Jones's locker *n* the seabed, the deep, esp as the grave of those who die at sea.

daw *n* a bird of the crow family; a jackdaw.

DAW *abbr* (*Brit*) = Drama Association of Wales.

dawdle *vi* to move slowly and waste time, to loiter.—**dawdler** *n*.

Dawes *n* **Charles G[ates]** (1865–1951) American banker; devised the Dawes Plan of 1924; was US Vice-President (1925–29); winner of the 1925 Nobel Peace Prize.

Dawes limit *n* an expression for the resolution obtained by a telescope used visually, established by W R Dawes.

dawn *vi* (*day*) to begin to grow light; to begin to appear. * *n* daybreak; a first sign.

dawn raid *n* an attempt made, often as part of a takeover bid, to buy a substantial shareholding in the company that is the target of the takeover bid as soon as the Stock Exchange opens so as to take the directors of the target company by surprise.

Dawson *n* **Nelson Ethelrad** (1889–1942) British architect who in 1901 founded the Artificers' Guild with his wife, Edith.

day *n* the time when the sun is above the horizon; the 24 hours from midnight to midnight; daylight; the time for one revolution of the earth about its axis; a particular period of success or influence; (*usu pl*) a period, an epoch.

Day *n* 1. **Doris [Doris Kappelhoff]** (1924–) American movie actress and singer. 2. **Lewis Foreman** (1845–1910) British designer of stained glass in the Arts and Crafts tradition. 3. **Lucienne** (1917–) British textile designer, whose Calyx pattern is an archetypal image for the 1950s. 4. **Robin** (1915–) British furniture designer.

Dayan *n* **Moshe** (1915–81) Israeli general and statesman. He played a leading role in the Israel-Egypt peace treaty of 1979.

daybook *n* a diary; an account book for recording the day's transactions.

daybreak *n* the first appearance of daylight, dawn.

day care *n* care provided in the daytime for the children of working parents or for elderly people.—**day-care** *adj*.

daydream *n* a reverie. * *vi* to have one's mind on other things; to fantasize.—**daydreamer** *n*.

Day-Lewis *n* **Cecil** (1904–72) Irish-born British poet; poet laureate in 1968.

daylight *n* the light of the sun; dawn; publicity; a visible gap; the dawning of sudden realization or understanding.

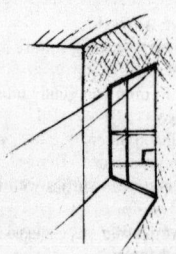

days *adv* during the day regularly.

days of grace *npl* the extra time that is granted for payment of an insurance premium or bill of exchange after the due date.

daytime *n* the time of daylight.

day-to-day *adj* daily; routine.

daze *vt* to stun, to bewilder. * *n* confusion, bewilderment.—**dazedly** *adv*.—**dazedness** *n*.

dazzle *vt* to confuse the sight of or be partially blinded by strong light; to overwhelm with brilliance. * *n* the act of dazzling; a thing that dazzles; an overpoweringly strong light; bewilderment.—**dazzlement** *n*.—**dazzler** *n*.—**dazzlingly** *adv*.

Db *symbol* (*chem*) dubnium (element).

db *abbr* = daybook; double bass; double bed; doubly biased.

dB *abbr* = decibel(s).

DB *abbr* = database; delayed broadcast; Domesday Book.

dba *abbr* = doing business as/at.

DBA *abbr* = dihydro-dimethyl-benzopyranbutyric acid (for sickle-cell anemia).

DBB *abbr* = dinner, bed, and breakfast.

DBE *abbr* (*Brit*) = Dame (Commander, Order) of the British Empire.

d.b.h. *abbr* = diameter at breast height; diameter breast high.

D. Bib. or **D. Bible** *abbr* (*Bible*) = Douay Bible.

dbk. *abbr* = drawback.

dbl. *abbr* = double.

DBM *abbr* = Diploma in Business Management.

DBMC *abbr* = Danish Bacon and Meat Council.

DBMS *abbr* (*comput*) = database management system.

DBO *abbr* = Diploma of the British Orthoptic Society.

DBS *abbr* = direct broadcasting by satellite; direct broadcast by satellite; Donkey Breed Society.

DBW *abbr* = desirable body weight.

DC = (*Italian*) *da capo*, "from the beginning"; death certificate; (*cataloging*) decimal system; depth charge; (*Brit*) Detective Constable; Diplomatic Corps; (*elec*) direct current; District of Columbia.

DCAA *abbr* = Defense Contract Audit Agency

DCAe *abbr* = Diploma of the College of Aeronautics.

DCAS *abbr* = Divorce Conciliation and Advisory Service.

DCC *abbr* = digital compact cassette.

DCDH *abbr* = Diploma in Child Dental Health.

DCDSTF *abbr* = Digital Cartographic Data Standards Task Force.

DCE *abbr* = data communications equipment; Doctor of Civil Engineering.

DCF *abbr* = discounted cash flow.

DCG *abbr* = Diploma in Careers Guidance.

DCh *abbr* = *Doctor Chirurgiae*, "Doctor of Surgery."

DCH *abbr* = Diploma in Child Health.

DChD *abbr* (*Latin*) = *Doctor Chirurgiae Dentalis*, "Doctor of Dental Surgery."

DChE *abbr* = Doctor of Chemical Engineering.

DCHT *abbr* = Diploma in Community Health in Tropical Countries.

DCI *abbr* = Detective Chief Inspector.

DCL *abbr* (*Brit*) = Doctor of Civil Law.

DCLF *abbr* = Diploma in Contact Lens Fitting.

DCLP *abbr* = Diploma in Contact Lens Practice.

DCM *abbr* (*Brit*) = Distinguished Conduct Medal.

DCMA *abbr* = Defense Contract Management Agency

DCMG *abbr* (*Brit*) = Dame Commander of the Order of St Michael and St George.

DCnL *abbr* = Doctor of Canon Law.

D C of S *abbr* = Deputy Chief of Staff.

DComL *abbr* = Doctor of Commercial Law.

DCompL *abbr* = Doctor of Comparative Law.

DCP *abbr* = Diploma in Clinical Pathology.

DCR *abbr* = Diploma of the College of Radiographers.

DCS *abbr* = Doctor of Christian Science; Doctor of Commercial Science.

DCT *abbr* = Doctor of Christian Theology.

DCVO *abbr* (*Brit*) = Dame Commander of the Royal Victorian Order.

dd *abbr* = day's date; delayed delivery; delivered to docks; direct debit; double deck.

dd., d/d *abbr* = delivered.

D.d. *abbr* (*Latin*) = *Deo dedit*, "he gave to God."

DD *abbr* = dangerous drug; (*Latin*) *dedicavit*, "he dedicated it"; (*Latin*) *Divinitatis Doctor*, "Doctor of Divinity"; (*Latin*) *dono dedit*, "he gave as a gift"; double density (of computer disk).

D/D, D/d *abbr* = days after date; days after delivery; days' *or* day's date; demand draft.

DD214 *n* (*law*) a military discharge.

DDA *abbr* = Dangerous Drugs Act; Disabled Drivers' Association.

D-day *n* the date (June 6, 1944) of the Allied cross-channel invasion of France during World War II; any date set aside for an important event.

ddc *abbr* = direct digital control.

DDC *abbr* = Defense Distribution Center; Dewey Decimal Classification.

DDD *abbr* (*Latin*) = *dat, dicat, dedicat*, "gives, devotes and dedicates"; *dono, dedit, dedicavit*, "gave and dedicated as a gift."

DDE *abbr* = direct data entry.

DDH *abbr* = Diploma in Dental Health.

d. d. in d. *abbr* (*Latin*) = *de die in diem*, "from day to day".

ddl *abbr* = data definition language; digital data link.

DDMC *abbr* = Disabled Drivers' Motor Club.

DDOrthRCPS Glas *abbr* (*Brit*) = Diploma in Dental Orthopaedics of the Royal College of Physicians and Surgeons of Glasgow.

ddp *abbr* = distributed data processing.

DDPHRCSEng *abbr* (*Brit*) = Diploma in Dental Public Health, Royal College of Surgeons of England.

DDRB *abbr* = Doctors' and Dentists' Review Body.

DDS *abbr* = Dewey Decimal System; digital data storage; Doctor of Dental Surgery.

dd/s *abbr* = (*grain trade*) delivered sound.

DDSc *abbr* = Doctor of Dental Science.

DDT *abbr* = dichlorodiphenyltrichloroethane, a chemical used as an insecticide.

de *prep* from; concerning; of.

DE *abbr* = (*Irish Gaelic*) *Dáil Éireann*, "Assembly of Representatives", the lower house of Irish parliament; Department of Employment; Doctor of Entomology.

de- *prefix* down; off; completely.

DEA *abbr* = Dance Educators of America; Drug Enforcement Administration.

Dea. *abbr* = Deacon.

de-accessioning *n* the disposal, usu by selling, of an artifact or painting in a public collection.

deacon *n* (*Anglican & RC Churches*) an ordained member of the clergy ranking below a priest; (*Presbyterian Church*) a lay church officer who assists the minister.—**deaconship** *n*.

deaconess *n* a churchwoman appointed to do work in a parish; a member of an institution or order trained to carry on regular charitable work; in a convent, the nun who attends to the altar.

deactivate *vt* (*bomb*) to make inactive or harmless.—**deactivation** *n*.—**deactivator** *n*.

dead *adj* without life; inanimate, inert; no longer used; lacking vegetation; emotionally or spiritually insensitive; without motion; (*fire, etc*) extinguished; (*limb, etc*) numb; (*color, sound etc*) dull; (*ball*) out of play; complete, exact; unerring. * *adv* in a dead manner; completely; utterly. * *n* a dead person; the quietest time.—**deadness** *n*.

deadbeat *n* (*inf*) a lazy or socially inept person; a vagrant.

dead cave *n* a cave that was made by the sea but is now above sea level because the sea level has fallen or the land has been raised.

dead cliff *n* a cliff that was eroded by the sea but is now above sea level.

dead duck *n* (*sl*) a person or thing destined to fail.

deaden *vt* to render numb or insensible; to deprive of vitality; to muffle.—**deadener** *n*.—**deadeningly** *adv*.

dead end *n* a cul-de-sac; a hopeless situation.

dead-end *adj* (*job*) holding no chance of advancement; (*kid*) having no hope of success in the future.

deadening *n* material for soundproofing a room.

deadeye *n* an expert marksman; (*naut*) a round, laterally flattened, wooden block pierced with three holes through which the lanyards are passed, used for extending the shrouds.

deadfall *n* a trap with a falling weight, which can kill or disable; a tangled mass of fallen trees.

deadhead *n* a person who has a free pass on trains or to places of amusement, etc; a transport vehicle traveling empty. * *vt* to remove dead flower heads from (a plant); to provide free admission to. * *vi* to travel or gain admission without payment; to drive an empty transport vehicle.

dead heat *n* a race in which two or more finish equal, a tie.

dead letter *n* a law or rule that is no longer enforced; a letter that cannot be delivered and is returned to the sender.

deadlight *n* (*naut*) a storm shutter for a cabin window; a skylight not made to open.

deadline *n* the time by which something must be done.

deadlock *n* a clash of interests making progress impossible; a standstill.—*also vt*.

deadly *adj* (**deadlier, deadliest**) fatal; implacable; (*inf*) tedious. * *adv* deathlike; intensely.—**deadliness** *n*.

deadly nightshade *n* a poisonous plant with purple flowers and black berries.—*also* **belladonna**.

deadpan *adj* (*inf*) deliberately expressionless or emotionless.—*also adv*.

dead reckoning *n* the taking of a ship's position by log and compass, not astronomical observations.

Dead Sea *n* a lake between Israel and Jordan. The lowest stretch of water in the world, it has no outlet, and there are no fish because it is so salty. *See also* **Sodom, Gomorrah**.

Dead Sea Scrolls *npl* the oldest known Hebrew books, written about 2000 years ago. They were first discovered in the late 1940s in Qumran, Palestine.

dead set *adv* with determination.

dead space *n* the volume of air in each breath taken into the lungs that does not contribute directly to the respiratory process.

dead weight *n* a very heavy load; an oppressive burden.

dead wood *n* (*inf*) a useless person or thing.

deaf *adj* unable to hear; hearing badly; not wishing to hear.—**deafly** *adv*.—**deafness** *n*.

deafen *vt* to deprive of hearing.—**deafeningly** *adv*.

deaf-mute *n* a person who is unable to hear or speak.

deal[1] *vt* (**dealing, dealt**) (*a blow*) to deliver, inflict; (*cards, etc*) to distribute; (*with* **with**) to do business with; (*problem, task*) to solve. * *vi* to do business (with); to trade (in). * *n* a portion, quantity; (*inf*) a large amount; a dealing of cards; a business transaction.

deal[2] *n* fir or pine wood.—*also adj*.

dealer *n* a trader of any kind; a person who deals for himself or herself as a principal on the Stock Exchange rather than as an agent or broker.

dealer *n* a trader; a person who deals cards; (*sl*) a seller of illegal drugs.

Dealgnaid *n* (*Irish Celtic myth*) the wife of Partholan. She is said to have accompanied him to Ireland. She was the mother of Rury.

dealings *npl* personal or business transactions.

dealt *see* **deal**[1].

dean *n* the head of a cathedral chapter; a college fellow in charge of discipline; the head of a university or college faculty.—**deanship** *n*.

Dean *n* 1. **Christopher** *see* **Torvill, Jayne**. 2. **Jay Hannah** (1911–74) American baseball player, who played with the St Louis Cardinals (1932–37) and the Chicago Cubs (1938–41). 3. **James [Byron]** (1931–55) American movie actor and a cult figure for his roles in *East of Eden* and *Rebel Without a Cause*.

deanery *n* (*pl* **deaneries**) the office or residence of a dean.

dear *adj* loved, precious; charming; expensive; a form of address in letters. * *n* a person who is loved. * *adv* at a high price.—**dearness** *n*.

dearie, deary *n* (*pl* **dearies**) (*inf*) a darling, a dear.

dearly *adv* with great affection; at a high price or rate.

dearth *n* scarcity, lack.

death *n* the end of life, dying; the state of being dead; the destruction of something.

deathbed *n* the bed in which a person dies or is about to die.

deathblow *n* a blow causing death.

death duty *n* (*Brit*) death tax.

deathless *adj* immortal.—**deathlessly** *adv*.—**deathlessness** *n*.

deathly *adj* like death, pale, still; deadly. * *adv* in a manner causing or tending to death; to a degree resembling death; (*inf*) extremely (*deathly quiet*).—**deathliness** *n*.

death mask *n* a plaster cast of a face taken immediately after death.

death rate *n* the yearly proportion of deaths to population.—*also* **mortality rate**.

death rattle *n* a deep gurgling noise sometimes made by a dying person.

death row *n* the section of a prison housing inmates sentenced to death.

death's head *n* a skull or representation of a skull, emblematic of death.

death's-head moth *n* a large moth with skull-like markings.

deathtrap *n* an unsafe place, thing, or structure.

death warrant *n* official authorization for the execution of a person condemned to death; anything that guarantees the destruction of hope or expectation.

deathwatch *n* a vigil beside a dying person; a guard over a criminal prior to execution.

deathwatch beetle *n* a small beetle that makes a ticking sound, superstitiously supposed to forebode death.

death wish *n* a usually unconscious wish for one's own death or that of another.

deb *n* (*inf*) a debutante.

deb., deben. *abbr* = debenture.

debacle *n* a sudden disastrous break-up or collapse; a break-up of river ice.

debar *vt* (**debarring, debarred**) to exclude, to bar.—**debarment** *n*.

debark *vti* to land from a ship, to disembark.—**debarkation** *n*.

debase *vt* to lower in character or value; (*coinage*) to degrade.—**debasement** *n*.—**debaser** *n*.

debatable *adj* open to question, disputed.—**debatably** *adv*.

debate *n* a formal argument; a discussion, esp in parliament. * *vt* to consider, contest. * *vi* to discuss thoroughly; to join in debate.—**debater** *n*.

debauch *vti* to corrupt, to dissipate; to lead astray, to seduce.—**debaucher** *n*.

debauchee *n* a dissolute person, a libertine.

debauchery *n* (*pl* **debaucheries**) depraved over-indulgence; corruption; profligacy.

deben *n* (*Egypt, arch*) a standard weight, equivalent to about 3¼ ounces (91 grams), used for expressing values in trade.

debenture *n* a bond with guaranteed interest and forming a first charge on assets; a certificate acknowledging a debt; a certificate entitling a refund of customs duty.

debilitate *vt* to weaken, to enervate.—**debilitation** *n*.—**debilitative** *adj*.

debility *n* (*pl* **debilities**) weakness, infirmity.

debit *n* an entry on the left-hand or debtor side of a double-entry company accounts. *See* **double-entry book-keeping**.

debit *n* the entry of a sum owed, opposite to the credit; the left side of a ledger used for this. * *vt* to charge to the debit side of a ledger.

debit note *n* a document that is sent by a company to an organization or individual indicating the cost of products or services supplied and as yet not paid for.

de Boer *n* Antoinette (1939–) German textile designer, who succeeded Margret Hildebrand as artistic director of the Stuttgarter Gardinenfabrik.

debonair *adj* having a carefree manner; courteous, gracious, charming.—**debonairly** *adv*.

Deborah *n* (*Bible*) Israelite prophetess who summoned Barak to attack Sisera, who was defeated at the river Kishon; regarded as a "mother of Israel." *See also* **Barak**, **Kishon**, **Sisera**.

debouch *vi* to march or to flow out from a narrow space to open ground.—**debouchment** *n*.

Debrecen *n* a city in Hungary.

debrief *vt* (*diplomat, etc*) to make a report following a mission; to obtain such information.—**debriefing** *n*.

debris *n* broken and scattered remains, wreckage; (*geol*) material, such as scree, gravel, sand or clay, formed by the breaking up of rocks, that has been moved by ice or water from its original site to another location.

debt *n* a sum owed; a state of owing; an obligation.

debt collection agency *n* an organization that is responsible for the collection of the outstanding debts of its clients.

debtor *n* a person, company, etc who owes money to another.

debug *vt* (**debugging, debugged**) (*inf*) (*room, etc*) to clear of hidden microphones; (*machine, program, plan, etc*) to locate and remove errors from; to remove insects from.

debunk *vt* (*inf*) (*claim, theory*) to expose as false.—**debunker** *n*.

Debussy *n* [Achille] Claude (1862–1918) French composer, regarded as the founder of impressionism in music. His works include the opera *Pelléas et Mélisande*.

debut *n* a first appearance as a public performer or in society. * *vi* to make one's debut; (*mus*) (*French*) "beginning," i.e., a first appearance.

debutant *n* one making a debut, esp a sportsman.

debutante *n* a young woman making her first appearance in upper-class society; a young woman regarded as wealthy, aristocratic and indolent.

DEC *abbr* = Disasters Emergency Committee.

dec. *abbr* = deceased; decimeter; declaration; declension; declination; decorative; decrease; (*Italian*) *decrescendo*, "becoming softer".

Dec. *abbr* = December.

DeCA *abbr* = Defense Commissary Agency

decade *n* a period of ten years; a group of ten.—**decadal** *adj*.

decadence, decadency *n* a state of deterioration in standards, esp of morality.

decadent *adj* deteriorating; self-indulgent.—**decadently** *adv*.

decaffeinated *adj* (*coffee, tea, carbonated drinks, etc*) with caffeine reduced or removed.

decagon *n* a ten-sided plane figure.—**decagonal** *adj*.

decahedron *n* a solid with ten faces.—**decahedral** *adj*.

decalcify *vt* (**decalcifying, decalcified**) to deprive (bone, etc) of its lime.

decaliter *n* a unit of ten liters.

Decalog *n* the Ten Commandments.

decameter *n* a unit of ten meters.

decamp *vi* to leave suddenly or secretly.—**decampment** *n*.

decanal *adj* of a dean or a dean's office; of the south side of the choir of a church, etc.

decant *vt* (*wine, etc*) to pour from one vessel to another, leaving sediment behind.—**decantation** *n*.

decanter *n* an ornamental bottle (usu glass) for holding wines, etc.

decapitate *vt* to behead.—**decapitation** *n*.—**decapitator** *n*.

decapod *adj* having ten feet or ten arms. * *n* a ten-footed crustacean, or ten-armed cephalopod.—**decapodal, decapodan, decapodous** *adj*.

Decapolis *n* a group of ten cities. *See also* **Gadara**.

decarbonate *vt* to remove carbon dioxide or carbonic acid from.—**decarbonation** *n*.

decarbonize *vt* take carbon or carbon deposit from.—**decarbonization** *n*.

decare *n* a measure of 1000 square meters.

de Castelbajac *n* Jean-Charles (1949–) French fashion designer, born in Casablanca.

decasyllable *n* a ten-syllabled line or word.—**decasyllabic** *adj, n*.

decathlon *n* a track-and-field contest consisting of ten events.—**decathlete** *n*.

decay *vti* to rot, to decompose; to deteriorate, to wither. * *n* the act or state of decaying; a decline, collapse; (*phys*) the decrease in amplitude or intensity with time.

decd. *abbr* = deceased.

decease *n* death. * *vi* to die.

deceased *adj* dead. * *n* the dead person.

deceit *n* the act of deceiving; cunning; treachery; fraud.

deceitful *adj* treacherous; insincere; misleading.—**deceitfully** *adv*.—**deceitfulness** *n*.

deceive *vt* to cheat; to mislead; to delude; to impose upon.—**deceivable** *adj*.—**deceiver** *n*.—**deceivingly** *adv*.

decelerate *vt, vi* to reduce speed.—**deceleration** *n*.—**decelerator** *n*.

deceleration parameter *n* (*astron*) a parameter, or number, describing the rate at which the expansion of the universe is slowing down because of the gravitational attractions within it.

December *n* the 12th and last month of the year, with 31 days.

Decembrist *n* one of the conspirators who took part in the insurrection against Tsar Nicholas I of Russia, on his accession, December 1825.

decency *n* being decent; conforming to accepted standards of proper behavior.

decennial *adj* lasting for, or occurring, every ten years.—**decennially** *adv*.

decennium *n* (*pl* **decenniums, decennia**) a ten-year period, a decade.

decent *adj* respectable, proper; moderate; not obscene; (*inf*) quite good; (*inf*) kind, generous.—**decently** *adv*.

decentralize *vt* (*government, organization*) to divide among local centers.—**decentralist** *adj, n*.—**decentralization** *n*.

deception *n* the act of deceiving or the state of being deceived; illusion; fraud.

deceptive *adj* apt to mislead; ambiguous; unreliable.—**deceptively** *adv*.—**deceptiveness** *n*.

deci- *prefix* one tenth.

decibel *n* a unit for measuring sound level.

decide *vti* to determine, to settle; to give a judgment on; to resolve.—**decidable** *adj*.

decided *adj* unhesitating; clearly marked.

decidedly *adv* definitely, certainly.

decider *n* a deciding round, a final heat.

deciduas *n* the soft epithelial tissue that forms a lining to the uterus during pregnancy and is shed in birthing.

deciduous *adj* (*trees, shrubs*) shedding all leaves annually, at the end of the growing season.—**deciduousness** *n*.

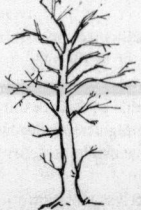

deciliter *n* a unit equal to one tenth of a liter.

decillion *n* in the US, the 11th power of a thousand, a unit followed by 33 zeros; in the UK, the tenth power of a million, a unit followed by 60 zeros.—**decillionth** *adj*.

decimal *adj* of tenths, of numbers written to the base ten. * *n* a tenth part; a decimal fraction.—**decimally** *adv*.

decimal classification *see* **Dewey Decimal System**.

decimal currency *n* currency in which units are divisible by ten.

decimal fraction *n* a fraction whose denominator is ten or a power of ten, indicated by figures after a decimal point.

decimalize *vt* to express as a decimal or to convert to a decimal system.—**decimalization** *n*.

decimal numbers *npl* (*math*) a structured system of numbers based on ten

decimal point *n* a dot written before the numerator in a decimal fraction (e.g., $0.5 = \frac{1}{2}$).

decimal system *n* a system of weights and measures in which units are related in multiples or submultiples of ten.

decimate *vt* to kill every tenth person; to reduce by one tenth; to kill a great number.—**decimation** *n*.—**decimator** *n*.

decimeter *n* a measure of length, one tenth of a meter.

decipher *vt* to decode; to make out (indistinct writing, meaning, etc).—**decipherable** *adj*.—**decipherer** *n*.—**decipherment** *n*.

decision *n* a settlement; a ruling; a judgment; determination, firmness; (*boxing*) a win on points.—**decisional** *adj*.

decisive *adj* determining the issue, positive; conclusive, final.—**decisively** *adv*.—**decisiveness** *n*.

deciso *adj, adv* (*mus*) with decision.

deck *n* the floor on a ship, aircraft, bus or bridge; a pack of playing cards; the turntable of a phonograph; the playing mechanism of a tape recorder; (*sl*) the ground, the floor. * *vt* to cover; to adorn.

deck chair *n* a folding chair made of canvas suspended in a frame.

deck hand *n* sailor who performs manual tasks.

deckle *n* a gauge on a paper-making machine for determining the width.

deckle edge *n* a ragged edge, as on handmade paper.—**deckle-edged** *adj*.

decl. *abbr* = declension; declensional.

declaim *vti* to state dramatically; to recite.—**declaimer** *n*.

declamation *n* the art of declaiming according to rhetorical rules; impassioned oratory; distinct and correct enunciation of words in vocal music.

declamatory *adj* pertaining to, or characterized by, declamation; noisy in style; appealing to the passions.—**declamatorily** *adv*.

declaration *n* the act of declaring or proclaiming; that which is declared; an assertion; publication; a statement reduced to writing; (*law*) a legal document declaring a fact or set of facts.

declarative *adj* making a declaration.—**declaratively** *adv*.

declaratory *adj* declarative; explanatory, affirmative.—**declaratorily** *adv*.

declare *vt* to affirm, to proclaim; to admit possession of (dutiable goods). * *vi* (*law*) to make a statement; (*with* **against, for**) to announce one's support.—**declarable** *adj*.

déclassé *adj* fallen in the social scale.

declassify *vt* (**declassifying, declassified**) to remove (a document, etc) from the list of official secrets.—**declassification** *n*.

declension *n* (*gram*) variation in the form of a noun and its modifiers to show case and number; a complete set of such variations of a noun, etc.—**declensional** *adj*.

declination *n* a downward bend; (*astron*) the angular distance of a star and the celestial equator; (*compass*) the angle between true north and the magnetic north..—**declinational** *adj*.

declination axis *n* an axle permitting an instrument such as a telescope to be moved up and down to different angles of declination.

declination circle *n* a circle graduated in degrees and subdivisions allowing an instrument such as a telescope to be set to any required angle of declination.

decline *vi* to refuse; to move down; to deteriorate, fall away; to fail; to diminish; to draw to an end; to deviate. * *vt* to reject, to refuse; (*gram*) to give the cases of a declension. * *n* a diminution; a downward slope; a gradual loss of physical and mental faculties.—**declinable** *adj*.—**decliner** *n*.

declining region *n* a region suffering the economic problems associated with factory closure, unemployment, old-fashioned working methods, etc.

declivity *n* (*pl* **declivities**) a downward slope.—**declivitous** *adj*.

decoct *vt* to boil something to extract its essence.

decoct. *abbr* (*Latin*) = *decoctum*, "a decoction".

decoction *n* an extract obtained by boiling or digesting in hot water; the act of decocting.

decode *vt* to translate (a code) into plain language.

decoder *n* one who decodes; (*comput*) a device for converting data from one form to another, e.g., binary to decimal.

decollate *vt* to separate (collated papers); (*arch*) to behead

decollation *n* the act of decollating; (*art*) a representation of a beheading, esp of St John the Baptist.

decollator *n* (*comput*) a machine that separates the sheets of a multipart form or continuous paper, i.e., it separates the top sheet from the second sheet.

décolletage *n* a low-cut dress or neckline.

décolleté *adj* having a low neckline.

decolonize *vt* to allow a colony to become independent.

decolorize *vt* to remove color from, to bleach.—**decoloration** *n*.—**decolorization** *n*.

decompose *vti* to separate or break up into constituent parts, esp as part of a chemical process; to resolve into its elements. * *vi* to decay.—**decomposable** *adj*.

decomposer *n* (*biol*) any organism that breaks down dead organic material, which may be remains of plants or animals or waste.

decomposition *n* (*chem, biol*) the breakdown of a substance from a more complicated form into a simpler one.

decompress *vt* to decrease the pressure on, esp gradually; to return (a diver, etc) to a condition of normal atmospheric pressure.—**decompression** *n*.—**decompressive** *adj*.—**decompressor** *n*.

decompression chamber *n* a chamber in which air pressure can be controlled to allow divers, astronauts, etc, to return to normal pressure without developing decompression sickness.

decompression sickness *n* a condition affecting divers, astronauts, etc, resulting from too rapid a return from high pressure to atmosphere and characterized by cramps and paralysis.

DEcon *abbr* = Doctor of Economics.

decongestant *n* a medical preparation that relieves congestion, e.g., catarrh.

DEconSc *abbr* = Doctor of Economic Science.

deconsecrate *vt* to transfer (a church) from ecclesiastical use.—**deconsecration** *n*.

deconstruction *n* in literary criticism a concept developed by Jacques Derrida for the process of examining the elements (signs) of language in isolation from other elements, thus exposing the contradictions inherent within language.—*also* **poststructuralism**.

decontaminate *vt* to free from (radioactive, etc) contamination.—**decontamination** *n*.—**decontaminator** *n*.

decontrol *vt* (**decontrolling, decontrolled**) to release from control, esp government control.

décor, decor *n* general decorative effect, e.g., of a room; scenery and stage design.

decorate *vt* to ornament; to paint or wallpaper; to honor with a badge or medal.

decoration *n* decorating; an ornament; a badge or an honor.

decorative *adj* ornamental, pretty to look at.—**decoratively** *adv*.—**decorativeness** *n*.

decorator *n* a person who decorates, esp houses.

decorous *adj* proper, decent; showing propriety and dignity.—**decorously** *adv*.—**decorousness** *n*.

decorticate *vt* to remove the bark, rind, or husk from; to remove the cortex of an organ by surgery. * *vi* to peel or come off, as bark, skin.—**decortication** *n*.—**decorticator** *n*.

decorum *n* what is correct in outward appearance, propriety of conduct, decency.

decoupage *n* the art or skill of decorating with shapes cut from paper, card, etc; something produced in this way.

decoupling era *n* an early period in the development of Big Bang theory when matter and radiation became distinct.

decoy *vt* to lure into a trap. * *n* anything intended to lure into a snare.—**decoyer** *n*.

decrease *vti* to make or become less. * *n* a decreasing; the amount of diminution.—**decreasingly** *adv*.

decree *n* an order, edict or law; a judicial decision; (*law*) a legal document declaring a fact or set of facts. * *vt* (**decreeing, decreed**) to decide by sentence in law; to appoint.—**decreeable** *adj*.—**decreer** *n*.

decrement *n* a decrease; the amount of this; (*math*) a negative increment of a variable.—**decremental** *adj*.

decrepit *adj* worn out by the infirmities of old age; in the last stage of decay.—**decrepitly** *adv*.

decrepitate *vti* to heat (a salt or mineral) until it crackles; to crackle under extreme heat.—**decrepitation** *n*.

decrepitude *n* the state or condition of being decrepit; feebleness and decay, esp that due to old age.

decres. or decresc. *abbr* (*Italian*) = *decrescendo*, "decreasing".

decrescendo *n* (*pl* **decrescendos**) (*mus*) a sign (>) that the volume of sound is to be gradually reduced; a gradual decrease in force of tone or a passage where this occurs. * *adj* gradually diminishing in loudness.—*also* **diminuendo**.

decrescent *adj* growing less; (*moon*) waning.—**decrescence** *n*.

decretal *n* (*RC Church*) a papal decree; a book of edicts. * *adj* of a decree or decretal.

decry *vt* (**decrying, decried**) to disparage, to censure as worthless.—**decrial** *n*.—**decrier** *n*.

decryption *n* (*comput*) the process of decoding or deciphering data from an encrypted form so that the data can be read and used. *See* **encryption**.

dectet *n* a group of eight musicians or voices.

decubitus ulcer *see* **bed sore**.

decumanus maximus *n* (*archeo*) the main street in a Roman camp or town. It commonly runs from gates in opposite walls.

decumbent *adj* lying down, prostrate, reclining; (*bot*) resting on the ground, trailing.—**decumbence, decumbency** *n*.

decuple *adj* tenfold * *n* a number repeated ten times * *vt* to increase tenfold.

decurion *n* a Roman officer commanding ten men.

decurrent *adj* (*plant*) running or extending downward.

DECUS *abbr* = Digital Equipment Computer Users.

decussate *vti* to intersect in the form of an X * *adj* X-shaped; (*leaves*) in pairs, at right angles to those above and below.—**decussation** *n*.

DED *abbr* = Department of Economic Development (N. Ireland).

DEd *abbr* = Doctor of Education.

dedicate *vt* to consecrate to some sacred purpose; to devote wholly or chiefly; to inscribe to someone.—**dedicatee** *n*.—**dedicator** *n*.—**dedicatory, dedicative** *adj*.

dedicated *adj* devoted to a particular cause, profession, etc; single-minded; assigned to a particular function.

dedicated line *n* (*comput*) a communications cable line that is dedicated exclusively to a particular communication function.

dedication *n* the act of dedicating; a dedicatory inscription in a book, etc; devotion to a cause, ideal, etc; a legal document that dedicates something to the public or to an individual, e.g., allowing public access to something.

deduce *vt* to derive (knowledge, a conclusion) from reasoning; to infer.—**deducible** *adj*.

deduct *vt* to take from; to subtract.

deductible *adj* capable of being deducted; allowable as a deduction against income tax.—**deductibility** *n*.

deduction *n* deducting; the amount deducted; deducing; a conclusion that something is true because it necessarily follows from a set of general premises known to be valid.—**deductive** *adj*.—**deductively** *adv*.

deductions at source *npl* a form of tax collection in which a person who is paying money to another for work carried out deducts income tax from the money paid before giving the money to the employee.

deed *n* an act; an exploit; a legal document recording a transaction.

deed of covenant *n* a legal document that authorizes regular amounts of money to be transferred from an individual to another individual or organization, e.g., a registered charity.

deed of trust *n* a legal document by which the legal title to a property is placed in a trustee to secure the repayment of a sum of money owed to a person other than the trustee.—*also* **mortgage**.

deem *vti* to judge; to think, to believe.

deep *adj* extending or placed far down or far from the outside; fully involved; engrossed; profound, intense; heartfelt; penetrating; difficult to understand; secret; cunning; sunk low; low in pitch; (*color*) of high saturation and low brilliance. * *adv* in a deep manner; far in, into. * *n* that which is deep; the sea.—**deeply** *adv*.—**deepness** *n*.

DEEP *abbr* = Directly Elected European Parliament.

deepen *vt* to make deeper in any sense; to increase. * *vi* to become deeper.—**deepener** *n*.

deep-freeze *vt* (**deep-freezing, deep-froze** or **deep-freezed**, *pp* **deep-frozen, deep-freezed**) to freeze (food) so that it keeps for a long period of time; to store in a freezer. * *n* a freezer.

deep-fry *vt* (**deep-frying, deep-fried**) to fry (food) in deep fat in order to cook or brown it without turning.—**deep-fryer** *n*.

deep-laid *adj* (*plans, etc*) secret and elaborate.

deep-rooted *adj* (*feelings, opinions, etc*) firmly established; ingrained.

deep-seated *adj* having its seat far beneath the surface; deep-rooted.

deep-six *vt* (*sl*) to destroy (papers, etc); to dispose of.

Deep South *n* the southeastern states of the USA.

deep space *n* the region of outer space beyond our solar system.

Deep Space Network *n* a spacecraft communications network established by the American NASA organization.

deer *n* (*pl* **deer, deers**) a four-footed animal with antlers, esp on the males, including stag, reindeer, etc.

deerfly *n* (*pl* **deerflies**) a bloodsucking fly similar to a horsefly.

deerhound *n* a large rough-haired greyhound.—*also* **Scottish deerhound**.

deerstalker *n* a person who hunts deer; a soft hat peaked at the front and back.

de-escalate *vti* to reduce the intensity of.—**de-escalation** *n*.

def. *abbr* = defendant; deferred; defined; definite; definition.

deface *vt* to disfigure; to obliterate.—**defaceable** *adj*.—**defacement** *n*.—**defacer** *n*.

de facto *adv* in fact; in reality.—*also adj*.

defalcate *vi* to embezzle money held in trust.—**defalcation** *n*.—**defalcator** *n*.

de Falla *see* **Falla**.

defamation *n* the act of injuring someone's good name or reputation without justification, either orally or in writing; the condition of being defamed.

defamatory *adj* containing that which is injurious to the character or reputation of someone.—**defamatorily** *adv*.

defame *vt* to destroy the good reputation of; to speak evil of.—**defamer** *n*.

default *n* neglect to do what duty or law requires; failure to fulfill a financial obligation; (*comput*) a basic setting or instruction to which a program reverts. * *vi* to fail in one's duty (as honoring a financial obligation, appearing in court).

defaulter *n* one who defaults; one who fails to appear in court when required, or to make a proper account of money or property entrusted to his or her charge; on the Stock Exchange, one who fails to meet his or her engagements.

Defcon *abbr* = defense readiness condition.

defeasance *n* (*law*) annulment; a condition annexed to a deed, which being performed renders the deed void.

defeasible *adj* able to be annulled.—**defeasibility** *n*.

defeat *vt* to frustrate; to win a victory over; to baffle. * *n* a frustration of plans; overthrow, as of an army in battle; loss of a game, race, etc.—**defeater** *n*.

defeatism *n* disposition to accept defeat.—**defeatist** *n*, *adj*.

defecate *vi* to empty the bowels. * *vt* (*chem*) to free from impurities, to refine.—**defecation** *n*.—**defecator** *n*.

defect *n* a deficiency; a blemish, fault. * *vi* to desert one's country or a cause, transferring one's allegiance to another.—**defector** *n*.

defection *n* desertion of duty or allegiance.

defective *adj* having a defect; faulty; incomplete. * *n* a person defective in physical or mental powers.—**defectively** *adv*.—**defectiveness** *n*.

defend *vt* to guard or protect; to maintain against attack; (*law*) to resist, as a claim; (*law*) to contest (a suit); (*sport*) to protect (one's goal); (*sport*) to defend (one's title). * *vi* (*sport*) to compete to retain one's title.—**defendable** *adj*.—**defender** *n*.

defendant *n* a person accused or sued in a lawsuit.

defenestration *n* the act of throwing (a person) out of a window.

defense *n* resistance or protection against attack; a means of resisting an attack; protection; vindication; (*law*) a defendant's plea; the defending party in legal proceedings; (*sport*) defending (the goal, etc) against the attacks of the opposing side; the defending players in a team.—**defenseless** *adj*.—**defenselessness** *n*.

defensible *adj* able to be defended or justified.—**defensibly** *adv*.—**defensibility** *n*.

defensive *adj* serving to defend; in a state or posture of defense.—**defensively** *adv*.—**defensiveness** *n*.

defer[1] *vt* (**deferring, deferred**) to put off to another time; to delay.—**deferrable, deferable** *adj*.—**deferrer** *n*.

defer[2] *vi* (**deferring, deferred**) to yield to another person's wishes, judgment or authority.

deference *n* a deferring or yielding in judgment or opinion; polite respect.

deferent *adj* deferential (*anat*) conveying (a fluid, etc) away.

deferential *adj* expressing deference or respect.—**deferentially** *adv*.

deferment *n* a delay; postponement.

deferral *n* a deferment.

deferred *adj* postponed; (*stock, shares*) having the dividend payable after other shares.

deferred annuity *n* a form of annuity in which payments do not begin right away but begin either at a specified date in the future or when the policyholder reaches a specified age.

de Feure *n* George (1868–1928) Dutch decorative artist, who designed for Maison Fleury before joining Bing's store in Paris.

defiance *n* the act of defying; willful disobedience; a challenge.

defiant *adj* characterized by defiance; challenging.—**defiantly** *adv*.

defibrillation *n* the application of electricity to the heart to stop fillibration and restore normal contractions.

deficiency *n* (*pl* **deficiencies**) being deficient; lack, shortage; deficit.

deficiency disease *n* a disease that is caused by a lack of vitamins or other essential dietary items, e.g., beriberi, pellagra, or scurvy.

deficient *adj* insufficient, lacking.—**deficiently** *adv*.

deficit *n* the amount by which an amount falls short of what is required; excess of expenditure over income, or liabilities over assets.

deficit spending *n* government expenditure in excess of revenues, which is financed by borrowing, resulting in a budget deficit.

defilade *vt* to raise (a rampart) to protect defensive lines from guns placed in a high position. * *n* protection provided in this way.

defile[1] *vt* to pollute or corrupt.—**defilement** *n*.—**defiler** *n*.

defile[2] *n* a long, narrow pass or way, through which troops can pass only in single file. * *vt* to march in single file.

define *vt* to fix the bounds or limits of; to mark the limits or outline of clearly; to describe accurately; to fix the meaning of.—**definable** *adj*.—**definer** *n*.

definite *adj* defined; having distinct limits; fixed; exact; clear.—**definiteness** *n*.

definitely *adv* certainly; distinctly. * *interj* used to agree emphatically.

definition *n* a description of a thing by its properties; an explanation of the exact meaning of a word, term, or phrase; sharpness of outline.—**definitional** *adj*.

definitive *adj* defining or limiting; decisive, final.—**definitively** *adv*.—**definitiveness** *n*.

definitude *n* the quality of being definite; definiteness, precision.

deflagrate *vt* to set fire to * *vi* to cause to burn with sudden and sparkling combustion.—**deflagration** *n*.

deflate *vt* to release gas or air from; to reduce in size or importance; to reduce the money supply, restrict credit, etc to reduce inflation in the economy.—**deflator** *n*.

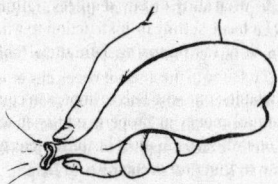

deflation *n* deflating; a reduction in the supply of money, causing a fall in prices.—**deflationary** *adj.*—**deflationist** *adj*, *n*.

deflation hollow *n* a large basin formed by the action of the wind in removing loose clay, silt or sand from the surface of the ground.

deflect *vti* to turn or cause to turn aside from a line or proper course.—**deflective** *adj.*—**deflector** *n*.

deflection *n* the action of deflecting or the state of being deflected from a straight line or regular path; deviation; the turning of a magnetic needle away from its zero; the amount of this.

defloration *n* a deflowering.

deflower *vt* to deprive of virginity; to corrupt the beauty or innocence of.—**deflowerer** *n*.

Defoe *n* Daniel (1660–1731) English novelist and pamphleteer whose works include *Robinson Crusoe* (1719).

defoliant *n* a chemical that kills foliage.

defoliate *vt* to strip (a plant or tree) of its leaves.—**defoliation** *n*.—**defoliator** *n*.

deforce *vt* (*law*) to keep (property) out of the legal owner's possession by force; (*Scots Law*) to resist (an officer of law in execution of his or her duty).—**deforcement** *n*.

deforest *vt* to clear of trees.—**deforestation** *n*.—**deforester** *n*.

deform *vt* to spoil the natural form of; to put out of shape.

deformation *n* the act of deforming; a change for the worse; a perverted form of word; (*geol*) a process that rocks may undergo over a long period of time during which they are changed from their original state.

deformed *adj* misshapen; warped.

deformity *n* (*pl* **deformities**) the condition of being deformed; a deformed part of the body; a defect.

defraud *vt* to remove (money, rights, etc) from a person by cheating or deceiving.—**defrauder** *n*.

defray *vt* to provide money to pay (expenses, etc).—**defrayable** *adj.*—**defrayal** *n*.—**defrayer** *n*.

defrock *vt* to expel from the priesthood, to unfrock.

defrost *vt* to unfreeze; to free from frost or ice.* *vi* to become unfrozen.

defroster *n* a device, e.g., in a freezer, that accelerates de-icing.

deft *adj* skillful, adept; nimble.—**deftly** *adv.*—**deftness** *n*.

deft. *abbr* = defendant.

defunct *adj* no longer being in existence or functioning or in use.—**defunctive** *adj*.

defuse *vt* to disarm (a bomb or mine) by removing its fuse; to decrease tension in (a situation).

defy *vt* (**defying**, **defied**) to resist openly and without fear; to challenge (a person) to attempt something considered dangerous or impossible; to resist attempts at, to elude.—**defier** *n*.

deg. *abbr* = degree(s).

dégagé *adj* unconstrained, at ease.

Degas *n* [Hilaire Germain] Edgar (1834–1917) French impressionist painter and sculptor.

de Gaulle *n* Charles [André Joseph Marie] (1890–1970) French general, statesman, and first president (1958–69) of the Fifth Republic; president of the provisional government in 1945–46.

degauss *vt* to neutralize or remove a magnetic field.—**degausser** *n*.

degearing *n* the process by which some of the loan stock of a company is replaced by ordinary share capital.

degeneracy *n* (*pl* **degeneracies**) the condition or quality of being degenerate; an instance of degeneracy; something that is degenerate.

degenerate *adj* having declined in physical or moral qualities; sexually deviant. * *vi* to become or grow worse.—*n* a degenerate person.—**degenerately** *adv*.

degenerate star *n* a star in which the matter of the core is so compacted and crushed that it does not behave in an ordinary way.

degeneration *n* the act, state, or process of growing worse; degeneracy; decline; the morbid impairment of any structural tissue or organ.

degenerative *adj* of the nature of, or tending to, degenerate.—**degeneratively** *adv*.

deglutinate *vt* to extract gluten from; to unglue.—**deglutination** *n*.

deglutition *n* the power to swallow, a swallowing.

degradable *adj* capable of being broken down by biological or chemical action.

degradation *n* a degrading or being degraded in quality, rank or status; a degraded state; (*geol*) a lowering of land by erosion; (*RC Church*) the unfrocking of a priest.

degrade *vt* to reduce in rank or status; to disgrace; to decompose; to be lowered by erosion.—**degrader** *n*.

degrading *adj* humiliating; (*geol*) eroding.—**degradingly** *adv*.

degrease *vt* to remove the grease from.

degree *n* a step in an ascending or descending series; a stage in intensity; the relative quantity in intensity; a unit of measurement in a scale; an academic title awarded as of right or as an honor; (*alg*) an equation defined by the sum of its exponents; (*geom*) the 360th part of the circumference of a circle; (*mus*) a step of the diatonic scale; (*gram*) one of three grades in the comparison of adjectives or adverbs; (*law*) the classification of a crime.

degression *n* a going down; a decrease, esp in taxation rate.—**degressive** *adj*.

dehisce *vi* (*fruits, seed pods, etc*) to burst open.

dehiscent *adj* (*fruits*) opening to release seeds.—**dehiscence** *n*.

dehorn *vt* to cut back, or deprive of, horns. —**dehorner** *n*.

dehumanize *vt* to remove human qualities from; to deprive of personality or emotion, to render mechanical.—**dehumanization** *n*.

dehumidify *vt* (**dehumidifying, dehumidified**) to remove moisture from (air).

dehydrate *vt* to remove water from. * *vi* to lose water, esp from the bodily tissues.—**dehydrator** *n*.

dehydration *n* the removal of water; (*med*) the loss of water from the body through diuresis, sweating, etc.; (*chem*) the removal of a water molecule from a compound or a more complex molecule by the action of heat.

dehypnotize *vt* to rouse from a hypnotic state.

Deïaneira *n* (*Greek myth*) the wife of Heracles, who killed herself after she accidentally killed him with a poisoned potion that she believed to be a harmless love potion.

de-ice *vt* to prevent the formation of ice on or remove ice from (a surface).—**de-icer** *n*.

Deichtire *or* **Deichtine** *n* (*Irish Celtic myth*) the daughter of the druid Cathbad and the mother of Cuchulainn, perhaps by the god Lugh.

deicide *n* the killing of a god; the killer of a god.—**deicidal** *adj*.

deictic *adj* (*gram*) demonstrative; (*logic*) proving directly.—**deictically** *adv*.

deific *adj* making, or tending to make, divine.

deify *vt* (**deifying, deified**) to make into a god; to worship as a god, glorify.—**deification** *n*.—**deifier** *n*.

deign *vi* to condescend; to think it worthy to do something.

deil *n* (*Scot*) the devil.

Deimos *n* the outermost of two satellites of Mars, first located in 1877.

Deïphobus *n* (*Greek myth*) husband of Helen, after the death of Paris.

Deïphontes *n* (*Greek myth*) a leader of the Heraclids, who became king of Argos.

Deir el Bahri *n* (*Egypt*) the site of the Eighteenth-Dynasty tomb of Queen Hatshepsut, and the pyramid and temple of Mentuhotpe, in the hills of the west bank of the Nile, opposite Thebes.

Deir el Medina *n* (*Egypt*) dating from the Ramessid period, this is the site of a well-preserved workmen's village for 120 artisans and their families. In the Eleventh Dynasty it was a cemetery area, an extension of Deir el Bahri.

Deirdre *or* **Derdriu** *n* (*Irish Celtic myth*) the druid Cathbad forecast that she would become the fairest woman in all of Ireland but that she would bring death and destruction to the country.

deism *n* belief in the existence of God, but not religious revelation.—**deist** *n*.—**deistic, deistical** *adj*.

deity *n* (*pl* **deities**) a god or goddess; the rank or essence of a god; (*with cap and the*) God.

déjà vu *n* the illusion that you have already experienced the present situation.

deject *vt* to have a depressing effect on.

dejecta *npl* excrement, droppings.

dejected *adj* morose, depressed.—**dejectedly** *adv.*—**dejectedness** *n*.

dejection *n* depression; lowness of spirits.

de jure *adv* according to the law, by right.

Dekker *n* Thomas (*c*.1570–*c*.1632) English dramatist and pamphleteer, who collaborated with Middleton on the tragedy *The Honest Whore*.

de Klerk *n* F[rederik] W[illem] (1936–) South African statesman, who succeeded P W Botha as president (1989). He was defeated in South Africa's first free elections in 1994 by Nelson Mandela.

de Kooning *n* Willem (1904–97) Dutch-born American painter important in the abstract expressionist movement.

del. *abbr* = delegate; delete; (*Latin*) *delineavit*, "drew it"; deliver.

Del. *abbr* = Delaware.

Delacroix *n* Eugène (1798–1863) French painter, whose work influenced artists of the Barbizon School.

delaine *n* a light fabric of wool and cotton.

de la Mare *n* Walter [John] (1873–1956) English poet and novelist.

de Lanux *n* Eyre "Lise" (1894–1995) American designer who designed Cubist-style furniture in Paris in the 1920s.

delate *vt* (*formerly*) to inform against (a person); to report (an offense).—**delation** *n*.—**delator** *n*.

Delaunay *n* Robert (1885–1941) French painter and founder of "orphism."

Delaware (DE) *n* a state of the United States of America (USA) of which the capital is Dover.

delay *vt* to postpone; to detain, obstruct. * *vi* to linger. * *n* a delaying or being delayed; the time period during which something is delayed.—**delayer** *n*.

deld. *abbr* = delivered.

dele *vt* (**deleing, deled**) (*print*) to take out (a letter, etc) in proofreading. * *n* a mark that a letter, etc is to be deleted.

delectable *adj* delightful, delicious.—**delectability** *n*.—**delectably** *adv*.

delectation *n* delight, enjoyment.

delegate *vt* to appoint as a representative; to give powers or responsibilities to (an agent or assembly). * *n* a deputy or an elected representative.—**delegable** *adj*.

delegation *n* the act of delegating; a group of people empowered to represent others.

delete *vt* to strike out (something written or printed); to erase.

deleterious *adj* harmful or destructive.

deletion *n* the act of deleting; a word, passage, etc deleted from a text; the absence of a normal part of a chromosome.

delft, delftware *n* a type of blue-glazed earthenware, originally from Delft in Holland.

Delhi *n* a city in India.

deli *n* (*pl* **delis**) (*inf*) a delicatessen.

Delia *n* (*Greek myth*) a name sometimes applied to Artemis, from the island of Delos, her birthplace.

deliberate *vt* to consider carefully. * *vi* to discuss or debate thoroughly; to consider. * *adj* well thought out; intentional; cautious.—**deliberately** *adv*.—**deliberateness** *n*.—**deliberator** *n*.

deliberation *n* careful consideration; thorough discussion; caution.

deliberative *adj* of or appointed for deliberation; resulting of deliberation.—**deliberatively** *adv*.

Delibes *n* [Clément Philibert]- Léo (1836–91) French composer of opera and organ pieces, who was also a teacher. His best-known works include the ballet *Coppélia* and the opera *Lakmé*.

delicacy *n* (*pl* **delicacies**) delicateness; the state of requiring tact or careful handling; subtle discrimination; a luxurious food.

delicatamente *adv* (*mus*) "delicately."

delicate *adj* fine in texture; fragile, not robust; requiring tactful handling; subtle, not obvious; discriminating; of exquisite workmanship; requiring skill in techniques.—**delicately** *adv*.—**delicateness** *n*.

delicatessen *n* a store selling prepared foods, esp imported delicacies.

delicato *adj* (*mus*) "delicate."

delicious *adj* having a pleasurable effect on the senses, esp taste; delightful.—**deliciously** *adv*.—**deliciousness** *n*.

delict *n* a legal offense.

delight *vt* to please greatly. * *vi* to have or take great pleasure (in). * *n* great pleasure; something that causes this.—**delighter** *n*.

delighted *adj* very pleased; filled with delight.—**delightedly** *adv*.—**delightedness** *n*.

delightful *adj* giving great pleasure.—**delightfully** *adv*.—**delightfulness** *n*.

Delilah *n* (*Bible*) the Philistine woman who enticed Samson to reveal the secret of his great strength and then betrayed him to the Philistines. *See also* **Samson**.

delimit, delimitate *vt* to fix or mark the boundaries of.—**delimitation** *n*.—**delimitative** *adj*.

delimiter *n* (*comput*) a character that is used to show the end of a command or the end of a field of data in a data record, e.g., a comma or a tab.

delineate *vt* to describe in great detail; to represent by drawing.—**delineation** *n*.—**delineative** *adj*.

delineator *n* one who delineates; an adjustable tailor's pattern.

delinquency *n* (*pl* **delinquencies**) neglect of or failure in duty; a misdeed; a fault; antisocial or illegal behavior, esp by young people.—*also* **juvenile delinquency**.

delinquent *adj* negligent; guilty of an offense. * *n* a person guilty of a misdeed, esp a young person who breaks the law.

deliquesce *vi* to melt and become liquid by absorbing moisture from the atmosphere.—**deliquescence** *n*.—**deliquescent** *adj*.

delirious *adj* mentally confused, light-headed; wildly excited.—**deliriously** *adv*.—**deliriousness** *n*.

delirium *n* (*pl* **deliriums, deliria**) a state of mental disorder, esp caused by a feverish illness; wild enthusiasm.

delirium tremens *n* a disorder of the brain, causing delusions and violent trembling, as the result of excessive drinking.

Delius *n* Frederick (1862–1934) English composer, born of German parents, whose works include *A Village Romeo and Juliet* and large orchestral pieces.

deliver *vt* to transport (goods, letters, etc) to a destination; to distribute regularly; to liberate, to rescue; to give birth to; to assist at a birth; to launch (a blow); (*baseball*) to pitch; to utter (speech).—**deliverable** *adj*.—**deliverer** *n*.

deliverance *n* the act of rescuing or liberating.

delivery *n* (*pl* **deliveries**) the act of delivering; anything delivered or communicated; the manner of delivering (a speech, etc); the manner of bowling in cricket, etc; the act of giving birth.

delivery note *n* a document, usu in duplicate, that is sent by a supplier to a customer when goods are delivered.

dell *n* a small hollow, usu with trees.

Dello Joio *n* Norman (1913–) American composer, pianist and organist. He has written operas, including *The Ruby* and *The Trial at Rouen*, as well as organ, choral, and piano music.

Del Mar *n* Norman (1919–) English conductor, particularly associated with 20th-century music. He is a guest conductor with many international orchestras.

Del Marie *n* Felix (1889–1952) French painter and designer, who espoused Italian futurism.

delocalize *vt* to deprive of local character; to remove from a locality.—**delocalization** *n*.

Delos *n* the central and smallest island of the Cyclades, in the Aegean Sea. In Greek mythology, it was a floating island, but was fixed to the bottom of the sea by Zeus in order to provide a safe place for the birth of Apollo and Artemis.—**Delian** *adj*.

delouse *vt* to rid the lice from.

Delphi *n* a Greek town, in ancient times the seat of the famous oracle of Apollo.

Delphic, Delphian *adj* relating to the ancient Greek city or its famous oracle, which imparted enigmatic prophecies; obscure or ambiguous in meaning.

delphinium *n* a garden plant with spikes of, usu blue, flowers.

Delphinius *n* (*Greek myth*) a name applied to Apollo, possibly because he assumed the shape of a dolphin to lead Cretan colonists to Delphi.

Delphinus *n* (*Greek myth*) the Dolphin, a small constellation which is identified with the dolphin that saved the life of Arion.

Delphyne *n* a mythical Greek monster who was half serpent and half woman.

delt. *abbr* (*Latin*) = *delineavit*, "he drew."

delta *n* the fourth letter of the Greek alphabet; an alluvial deposit at the mouth of a river.—**deltaic** *adj*.

Delta *n* the great fan-shaped area of marshland, over 100 miles (161 kilometers) long, north of Memphis, Egypt.

delta wave *n* one of the four types of brain waves and the slowest of the four. Delta waves are associated with deep sleep.

delta wing *n* a triangular-shaped aircraft wing.

deltoid *adj* of the shape of the letter delta; triangular * *n* (*anat*) a muscle that lifts the upper arm.

delude *vt* to mislead, to deceive.—**deluder** *n*.

deluge *n* a flood; anything happening in a heavy rush. * *vt* to inundate.

delusion *n* a false belief; a persistent false belief that is a symptom of mental illness.—**delusional** *adj*.

delusive *adj* deluding or tending to delude; deceptive; false.—**delusively** *adv*.

delusory *adj* delusive.

deluxe *adj* luxurious, of superior quality.

delve *vti* to search deeply; to dig.—**delver** *n*.

Dem. *abbr* = Democrat; Democratic.

De Maestra *n* Georges (*fl.*1940s–50s) Swiss inventor of the tape fastener known as Velcro.

demagnetize *vt* to remove the magnetic properties of.—**demagnetization** *n*.—**demagnetizer** *n*.

demagogic, demagogical *adj* of, pertaining to, or characteristic of a demagogue.—**demagogically** *adv*.

demagogue *n* a political orator who derives power from appealing to popular prejudices.

demagoguery *n* demagogy; the rhetoric of a demagogue.

demagogy *n* the principles or practice of a demagogue; rule by a demagogue.

demand *vt* to ask for in an authoritative manner. * *n* a request or claim made with authority for what is due; an urgent claim; desire for goods and services shown by consumers.—**demandable** *adj*.—**demander** *n*.

demandant *n* a plaintiff.

demand curve *n* a line on a chart indicating the relationship between the price of a product and the quantity of a product demanded.

demanding *adj* constantly making demands; requiring great skill, concentration or effort.—**demandingly** *adv*.

demand note *n* a note that is payable on demand.

demand-pull inflation *n* a rise in prices caused by an excess of demand over supply.

demantoid *n* an emerald-green garnet used as a gem.

demarcate *vt* to delimit; to define or mark the bounds of.—**demarcator** *n*.

demarcation *n* the act of marking off a boundary or setting a limit to; a limit; the strict separation of the type of work done by members of different trade unions.

demarcation dispute *n* an industrial dispute based on the allocation of tasks in a workplace.

démarche *n* a diplomatic announcement of policy or plan.

demark *vt* to demarcate.

Demas *n* (*Bible*) a fellow worker of Paul's who proved unreliable and left him.

dematerialize *vti* to deprive of or give up material form.—**dematerialization** *n*.

Dembowska *n* a small asteroid.

deme *n* a territorial subdivision or township of ancient Greece; (*biol*) a group within a species with similar cell structure, etc.

demean *vt* to lower in dignity.—**demeaning** *adj*.

demeanor *n* behavior; bearing.

dement *vt* to make insane, drive mad.

demented *adj* crazy, insane.—**dementedly** *adv*.

dementia *n* the failure or loss of mental powers.

demerge *vt* to separate (a previously merged business corporation) into several companies.

demerger *n* the break-up of one company into two or more separate companies.

demerit *n* a fault, a defect; a mark recording poor work by a student, etc.

demersal *adj* (*zool*) found in deep water or on the sea bottom.

demesne *n* (*law*) one's own land; (*hist*) a landed estate attached to a manor; a domain.

Demeter *n* (*Greek myth*) one of the twelve principal deities, the great mother-goddess, goddess of corn and of the earth and its fertility, known as Ceres to the Romans.—*also* **Deo**.

Demetrius *n* (*Bible*) silversmith in Ephesus who stirred up his fellow craftsmen against Paul because his preaching threatened their livelihood.

demi- *prefix* half.

demigod *n* a being that is part mortal, part god; a god-like individual.—**demigoddess** *nf*.

demijohn *n* a large bottle, often in a wicker case.

demilitarize *vt* to remove armed forces, weapons systems, etc from.—**demilitarization** *n*.

demilitarized zone *n* an area required by treaty to have no military installations or forces in it.

de Mille *n* **Agnes George** (1905–93) American choreographer, who choreographed many major musicals, e.g., *Paint Your Wagon* (1951).

de Mille *n* **Cecil B[lount]** (1881–1959) American movie producer and director, whose movies include *The Ten Commandments* (1923).

demimondaine *n* a member of the demimonde, a courtesan.

demimonde *n* a class of women not recognized by society, esp in 19th-century France, because of promiscuity; any socially disreputable group.

demise *n* (*formal*) death; termination, end. * *vt* to give or grant by will. * *vi* to pass by bequest or inheritance.—**demisable** *adj*.

demisemiquaver *n* (*mus*) a note with a time value of half a semiquaver.—*also* **thirty-second note**.

demitasse *n* a small cup (of black coffee).

demiurge *n* in Platonic philosophy, the creator of the world; in Gnostic philosophy, an agent of the Supreme Being in the creation of man and the material universe; in ancient Greece, the chief magistrate of some states.—**demiurgic** *adj*.

demo *n* (*pl* demos) (*inf*) a demonstration; (*comput*) a program that is partially restricted but still shows a potential user the main features of the program.

demob *vt* (**demobbing, demobbed**) (*inf*) to demobilize. * *n* (*inf*) demobilization.

demobilize *vt* to discharge from the armed forces.—**demobilization** *n*.

democracy *n* (*pl* democracies) a form of government by the people through elected representatives; a country governed by its people; political, social or legal equality.

democrat *n* a person who believes in or promotes democracy; (*with cap*) a member of the Democratic Party.

democratic *adj* of, relating to, or supporting the principles of democracy; favoring or upholding equal rights; (*with cap*) of or pertaining to the Democratic Party.—**democratically** *adv*.

democratize *vt* to make democratic. * *vi* to become democratic.—**democratization** *n*.

démodé *adj* out of fashion.

demodulate *vt* to extract a modulating radio, video, etc wave or signal from (a modulated carrier wave).—**demodulator** *n*.

demodulation *see* **modem**.

demographic segmentation *n* the division of a market into socio-economic groups according to such demographic variables as age, sex, occupation, education, income, etc.

demography *n* the study of population statistics concerning birth, marriage, death and disease.—**demographer, demographist** *n*.—**demographic** *adj*.—**demographically** *adv*.

demoiselle *n* a damsel; a small crane of North Africa, southeast Europe and central Asia.

demolish *vt* to pull down or knock down (a building); to defeat (an argument); (*inf*) to eat up.—**demolisher** *n*.—**demolishment** *n*.

demolition *n* a demolishing or being demolished, esp by explosives.—**demolitionist** *adj, n*.

demon *n* an evil spirit; a cruel person; someone who is very skilled, energetic, hard-working, etc.—**demonic** *adj*.—**demonically** *adv*.

demon. *abbr* = demonstrative.

demonetize *vt* to withdraw (coin) from circulation; to abandon (gold, etc) as a currency.—**demonetization** *n*.

demoniac, demoniacal *adj* of or like a demon; possessed by evil; frenzied, energetic. * *n* a person possessed by a demon.—**demoniacally** *adv*.

demonism *n* belief in demons; the nature of a demon.—**demonist** *n*.

demonize *vt* to make into or represent as a demon.

demonolater *n* a demon worshiper.—**demonolatry** *n*.

demonology *n* the study of demons and superstitions about them.—**demonologist** *n*.

demonstrable *adj* able to be demonstrated or proved.—**demonstrability** *n*.—**demonstrably** *adv*.

demonstrate *vt* to indicate or represent clearly; to provide certain evidence of, prove; to show how (a machine, etc) works. * *vi* to show one's support for a cause, etc by public parades and protests; to act as a demonstrator of machinery, etc.—**demonstrational** *adj*.

demonstration *n* proof by evidence; a display or exhibition; a display of feeling; a public manifestation of opinion, as by a mass meeting, march, etc; a display of armed force.

demonstrative *adj* displaying one's feelings openly and unreservedly; indicative; conclusive; (*gram*) describing an adjective or pronoun indicating the person or thing referred to.—**demonstratively** *adv*.—**demonstrativeness** *n*.

demonstrator *n* a person who shows consumer goods to the public; one who or that which shows how a machine, etc works; a person who takes part in a public protest.

Demophon, Demophoön *n* (*Greek myth*) a hero who fought in the Trojan War.

demoralize *vt* to lower the morale of, discourage.—**demoralization** *n*.—**demoralizer** *n*.

De Morgan *n* **William** (1839–1917) British painter, ceramicist, and tilemaker.

demos *n* in ancient Greece, the common people of a state; the population personified.

demo tape *n* a tape recording of a song, singer, band, etc, used to demonstrate quality or performance.

demote *vt* to reduce in rank or position.—**demotion** *n*.

demotic *adj* pertaining to the people; in the simplified style of ancient Egyptian writing.

Dempsey *n* **Jack [William Harrison Dempsey]** (1895–1983) American boxer.

DemU *abbr* = Democratic Unionist.

demulcent *adj* softening; soothing. * *n* a medicine that allays irritation.

demur *vi* (**demurring, demurred**) to raise objections.—**demurral** *n*.

demure *adj* modest, reserved; affectedly quiet and proper; coy.—**demurely** *adv*.—**demureness** *n*.

demurrage *n* a charge for keeping a ship, truck, etc beyond the time agreed for unloading.

demurrer *n* (*law*) a plea that an opponent's facts are irrelevant; exception taken.

Demuth *n* **Charles** (1883–1935) American painter and leading precisionist artist. He was also a proficient illustrator and his best-known work, based on a poem by William Carlos Williams, is *I Saw the Figure Five in Gold* (1928).

demy *n* (*pl* demies) a size of paper for printing (22$\frac{1}{2}$ x 17$\frac{1}{2}$ ins) or writing (20 x 15$\frac{1}{2}$ ins).

demyelination *n* the process whereby the myelin sheath surrounding a nerve fiber is destroyed, resulting in impaired nerve function.

demystify *vt* (**demystifying, demystified**) to remove the mystery from; to clarify.—**demystification** *n*.

demythologize *vt* to eliminate mythological or mystical elements from (a text, esp the Bible); to restate or recast (a text, etc) in rational terms.

den *n* a cave or lair of a wild beast; a place where people gather for illegal activities; a room in a house for relaxation or study.

Den *n* (*Egypt*) Egyptian king of the First Dynasty (ruled 3050–2995 BC).

Den. *abbr* = Denmark.

denarius *n* (*pl* denarii) in ancient Rome, a silver coin; a gold coin worth 25 silver denarii.

denary *adj* of ten; decimal.

denationalize *vt* to transfer (industry, etc) from state control to private ownership.—**denationalization** *n*.

denaturalize *vt* to make unnatural; to deprive of acquired citizenship.—**denaturalization** *n*.

denature *vt* to modify the nature of; to change the properties of (a protein) by the action of an acid or heat; to render (alcohol) unfit for consumption.—**denaturant** *n*.—**denaturation** *n*.

Dendera *n* (*Egypt*) the site in Upper Egypt, close to Edfu, of a major temple of the goddess Hathor.

dendriform *adj* branching, like a tree.

dendrite *n* a stone or mineral with tree-like markings; a fine branch of one of the nerve cells that conduct impulses.—**dendritic** *adj*.

dendrochronology *n* the dating of past events by studying the annual growth rings in trees.—**dendrochronological** *adj*.

dendroid *adj* resembling a tree in appearance.

dendrology *n* the scientific study of trees.—**dendrologic, dendrological** *adj*.—**dendrologist** *n*.

dene *n* a low sandy tract near sea, a dune.

Dene *n* (*pl* **Dene, Denes**) a member of a people inhabiting the Northwest Territories of Canada.

Deneb *or* **Alpha Cygni** *n* the brightest star in the constellation Cygnus.

denegation *n* a denial.

DEng *abbr* = Doctor of Engineering.

dengue *n* a tropical disease transmitted by the mosquito, causing fever and pain in the joints.

Deng Xiaoping *or* **Teng Hsiao-p'ing** *n* (1904–97) Chinese Communist statesman. Denounced in the Cultural Revolution, he re-emerged as a powerful figure in the 1970s.

DENI *abbr* (*Brit*) = Department of Education for Northern Ireland.

deniable *adj* able to be denied; questionable.—**deniably** *adv*.

denial *n* the act of denying; a refusal of a request, etc; a refusal or reluctance to admit the truth of something.

denier[1] *n* a unit of weight used to measure the fineness of silk, nylon, or rayon fiber, esp as used in women's panty hose, etc.

denier[2] *n* one who denies.

denigrate *vt* to disparage the character of; to belittle.—**denigration** *n*.—**denigrator** *n*.

denim *n* a hard-wearing cotton cloth, esp used for jeans; (*pl*) denim trousers or jeans.

De Niro *n* **Robert** (1943–) American actor, whose movies include *The Godfather Part II* (1974), for which he won an Academy Award.

Denis[1] *n* Saint, also known as **Denys** or **Dionysius of Paris** (*d.* 273) patron saint of France, sent by Clement to preach the Gospel in Gaul (modern France). He was put to death at Montmartre in Paris. His feast day is October 9.

Denis[2] *n* **Maurice** (1870–1943) French decorator, who was one of the founders of the Nabis group in the late 1880s.

denizen *n* an inhabitant or resident; an animal or plant established in a region where it is not native.

Denmark *n* a constitutional monarchy in northern Europe.

den mother *n* a woman who leads a Scout troop; a person regarded as leader or nurturer of a group.

denominate *vt* to give a name to; to designate.

denomination *n* a name or title; a religious group comprising many local churches, larger than a sect; one of a series of related units, esp monetary.

denominational *adj* of, belonging to, or controlled by a religious denomination.—**denominationally** *adv*.

denominationalism *n* denominational spirit, policy, or principles; adherence to these.—**denominationalist**.

denominative *adj* giving a name; (*gram*) formed from a substantive or adjectival stem; connotative. * *n* a verb formed from a substantive or adjectival stem.

denominator *n* (*math*) the number below the line in a vulgar fraction.

denotation *n* the action of denoting; expression by marks, signs, or symbols; a sign, indication; a mark by which a thing is made known; a designation, meaning.

denotative *adj* having the power to denote or point out; significant.—**denotatively** *adv*.

denote *vt* to indicate, be the sign of; to mean.—**denotement** *n*.

denouement, dénouement *n* the resolution of a plot or story; the solution, the outcome.

denounce *vt* to condemn or censure publicly; to inform against; to declare formally the ending of (treaties, etc).—**denouncement** *n*.—**denouncer** *n*.

dense *adj* difficult to see through; massed closely together; dull-witted, stupid.—**densely** *adv*.—**denseness** *n*.

density *n* (*pl* **densities**) the degree of denseness or concentration; stupidity; the ratio of mass to volume; (*comput*) a measure of the amount of information, in bits, that can be stored on a magnetic medium such as a floppy disk.

density wave *or* **shock wave** *n* a sharp change in pressure, and thus density, in a narrow region in a gas caused by an explosion or other disturbance.

dent *n* a depression made by pressure or a blow. * *vti* to make a dent in or become dented.

dent. *abbr* = dental; dentist; dentistry.

dental *adj* of or for the teeth.—**dentally** *adv*.

dental floss *n* waxed thread for cleaning between the teeth.

dental hygienist *n* a professionally trained and qualified person who checks and cleans teeth.—*also* **hygienist**.

dentate *adj* toothed, notched.

denticle *n* a small tooth or tooth-like projection.

denticulate *adj* (*leaf*) having small teeth.

dentiform *adj* tooth-shaped.

dentifrice *n* toothpowder or toothpaste.

dentil *n* (*arch*) a small, square, projecting block on a molding.

dentin, dentine *n* the hard, bone-like substance forming the main part of teeth.

dentist *n* a person qualified to treat tooth decay, gum disease, etc.

dentistry *n* the area of medicine dealing with the care of teeth and the treatment of diseases of the teeth and gums; the practice of this as a profession.

dentition *n* the process or period of cutting the teeth; the arrangement of the teeth.

dentoid *adj* tooth-shaped.

denture *n* (*usu pl*) a set of artificial teeth.

denude *vt* to make naked; to deprive, strip.—**denuder** *n*.

denudation *n* (*geog*) the stripping bare of a land surface by the forces of climate and weather.

denunciate *vt* (*rare*) to denounce.—**denunciator** *n*.

denunciation *n* the act of denouncing; a threat.—**denunciator** *n*.—**denunciatory** *adj*.

Denver *n* the capital city of Colorado, a state of the USA.

deny *vt* (**denying, denied**) to declare to be untrue; to repudiate; to refuse to acknowledge; to refuse to assent to a request, etc.

Deoca *n* (*Irish Celtic myth*) fiancée of Lairgnen. She begged him to bring her the singing swans who were actually the children of Lir.

deodand *n* (*law, hist*) a chattel that, having caused death, was forfeited to the crown.

deodar *n* a tall Himalayan cedar tree yielding a valuable timber.

deodorant *n* a substance that removes or masks unpleasant odors.

deodorize *vt* to remove the odor or smell from.—**deodorization** *n*.—**deodorizer** *n*.

deoxidize *vt* to deprive of oxygen.

deoxyribonucleic acid *see* DNA.

dep. *abbr* = department; departs; (*naut*) departure; deponent; deposed; deputy.

Dep. *abbr* = (*bank*) deposit; (*mil*) depot.

Depardieu *n* **Gérard** (1948–) French actor, whose movies include *Green Card* (1990).

depart *vi* to go away, leave; to deviate (from).

departed *adj* (*time, etc*) long past; (*person*) recently dead.

department *n* a unit of specialized functions into which an organization or business is divided; a province; a realm of activity.

departmental *adj* of, having, or organized into departments.—**departmentally** *adv*.

departmentalism *n* departmental structure, esp a bureaucratic one.

departmentalize *vt* to split into departments; to subdivide.—**departmentalization** *n*.

department store *n* a large store divided into various departments selling different types of goods.

departure *n* a departing; a deviating from normal practice; a new venture, course of action, etc.

DEPCA *abbr* = International Study Group for the Detection and Prevention of Cancer.

depend *vi* to be determined by or connected with anything; to rely (on), put trust (in); to be reliant on for support, esp financially.

dependable *adj* able to be relied on.—**dependably** *adv*.—**dependability** *n*.

dependant[1], dependent *n* a person who is dependant on another, esp financially.

dependant[2], dependent *adj* relying on another person, thing, etc for support, money, etc; contingent; subordinate.

dependence, dependance *n* the state of being dependent; reliance, trust; a physical or mental reliance on a drug, person, etc.

dependency *n* (*pl* **dependencies**) dependence; a territory controlled by another country.

dependent variable *n* in a mathematical expression, the quantity with a value that depends on the other independent variables.

depersonalize *vt* to eliminate the individual character from (a person, organization, etc); to make impersonal.—**depersonalization** *n*.

depict *vt* to represent pictorially; to describe.—**depicter, depictor** *n*.—**depiction** *n*.

depilate *vt* to remove hair from.—**depilation** *n*.—**depilator** *n*.

depilatory *n* (*pl* **depilatories**) a substance for removing superfluous hair. * *adj* removing hair.

deplane *vti* to alight or unload from an aircraft.

deplete *vt* to use up a large quantity of.—**depletion** *n*.—**depletive** *adj*.

deplorable *adj* shocking; extremely bad.—**deplorably** *adv*.

deplore *vt* to regret deeply; to complain of; to deprecate.—**deplorer** *n*.—**deploringly** *adv*.

deploy *vt* to distribute and position strategically (military forces). * *vi* to adopt strategic positions within an area.—**deployment** *n*.

deplume *vt* to strip of feathers, to pluck; to strip of position, honor, etc.—**deplumation** *n*.

depolarize *vt* to deprive of or counteract the polarity of.—**depolarization** *n*.

depone *vti* (*Scot*) to testify upon oath, depose.

deponent *adj* (*gram*) (*verb*) passive in form but active in meaning. * *n* (*gram*) a deponent verb; (*law*) one who makes a deposition.

depopulate *vt* to reduce the population of.—**depopulation** *n*.—**depopulator** *n*.

deport *vt* to expel (an undesirable person) from a country; to behave in a certain manner.—**deportable** *adj*.

deportation *n* forcible removal from a country, esp of an undesirable person.

deportee *n* a deported person.

deportment *n* manners; bearing; behavior.

depose *vt* to remove from power; to testify, esp in court.—**deposable** *adj*.—**deposer** *n*.

deposit *vt* to place or lay down; to pay (money) into a bank or other institution for safekeeping, to earn interest, etc; to pay as a first installment; to let fall, leave. * *n* something deposited for safekeeping; money put in a bank; money given in part payment or security; material left in a layer, e.g., sediment.

deposit account *n* a bank account from which money cannot be withdrawn by check and which usu attracts a higher rate of interest than a checking account.

depositary *n* (*pl* **depositaries**) the person to whom something is entrusted; a depository.

deposition *n* the act of depositing or deposing; a being removed from office or power; a sworn testimony, esp in writing; (*geol*) the laying down of sediments (clay, mud, silt, sand, etc., and also mineral veins in rocks).

depositor *n* a person who deposits money in a bank, etc.

depository *n* (*pl* **depositories**) a place where anything is deposited; a depositary.

depot *n* a warehouse, storehouse; a place for storing military supplies; a military training center; a bus or railway station.

depot preparation *n* a drug, usu hormonal, that is injected deeply and intramuscularly and allows the slow release of the drug over days, weeks or months.

depr. *abbr* = depreciation.

deprave *vt* to pervert; to corrupt morally.—**depravation** *n*.—**depraver** *n*.

depraved *adj* morally debased; corrupt; made bad or worse.—**depravedly** *adv*.

depravity *n* (*pl* **depravities**) moral corruption; extreme wickedness.

deprecate *vt* to criticize, esp mildly or politely; to belittle.—**deprecation** *n*.—**deprecative** *adj*.—**deprecator** *n*.

deprecatory *adj* apologetic; disapproving, belittling.

depreciate *vti* to make or become lower in value.—**depreciator** *n*.—**depreciatory**, **depreciative** *adj*.

depreciation *n* a fall in value, esp of an asset through wear and tear; an allowance for this deducted from gross profit; the reduction in value of the currency of one country against another; disparagement.

depredate *vt* to pillage; to rob; to lay waste; to prey upon.—**depredator** *n*.

depredation *n* plundering; pillage.

DePree *n* **Dirk Jan** (1891–1990) American furniture manufacturer who, with Robert Propst, produced the open-plan Action Office.

depress *vt* to push down; to sadden, dispirit; to lessen the activity of.—**depressing** *adj*.—**depressingly** *adv*.

depressant *adj* causing depression. * *n* a substance that reduces the activity of the nervous system; a drug that acts as a depressant.

depressed *adj* cast down in spirits; lowered in position; flattened from above, or vertically.

depression *n* excessive gloom and despondency; an abnormal state of physiological inactivity; a phase of the business cycle characterized by stagnation, widespread unemployment, etc; a falling in or sinking; a lowering of atmospheric pressure, often signaling rain.

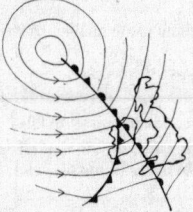

depressive *adj* depressing; tending to suffer from mental depression.—**depressively** *adv*.

depressor *n* one who or that which depresses; a muscle that draws down an organ or part.

deprive *vt* to take a thing away from; to prevent from using or enjoying.—**deprivation** *n*.

deprived *adj* lacking the essentials of life, such as adequate food, shelter, education, etc.

dept. *abbr* = department; deponent; deputy.

depth *n* deepness; the distance downward or inward; the intensity of emotion or feeling; the profundity of thought; intensity of color; the mid point of the night or winter; the lowness of sound or pitch; the quality of being deep.

depth charge *n* a bomb designed to explode under water, used against submarines.

depth perception *n* the ability to judge the distance of and between objects.

depurate *vti* to free or become free from impurities.—**depuration** *n*.—**depurative** *adj*.—**depurator** *n*.

deputation *n* a person or group appointed to represent others.

depute *vt* to appoint as one's representative; to delegate.

deputize *vi* to act as deputy.—**deputization** *n*.

deputy *n* (*pl* **deputies**) a delegate, representative, or substitute.

De Quincey *n* **Thomas** (1785–1859) English essayist and critic, whose best-known work is *Confessions of an English Opium Eater*.

der. or **deriv.** *abbr* = derivation; derivative; derive; derived.

deracinate *vt* to tear up by the roots.—**deracination** *n*.

derail *vti* to cause (a train) to leave the rails.—**derailment** *n*.

derailleur *n* a system of gearing on a bicycle.

Derain *n* **André** (1880–1945) French painter; founded Fauvism along with Matisse. He was one of the first to be influenced by African tribal art, creating granite masks, and block-like figure sculptures.

Derain *n* **André** (1880–1954) French painter; a leading Fauvist, influenced by Picasso and Braque.

derange *vt* to throw into confusion; to disturb; to make insane.—**deranged** *adj*.—**derangement** *n*.

Derbe *n* town in Asia Minor visited by St Paul.

derby *n* (*pl* **derbies**) a felt hat with a crown.

Derdriu *see* Deirdre.

DERE *abbr* (*Brit*) = Dounreay Experimental Reactor Establishment.

deregulate *vt* to remove (e.g., government) regulations or controls from (an industry, etc).—**deregulation** *n*.

derelict *adj* abandoned, deserted and left to decay; negligent. * *n* a person abandoned by society; a wrecked ship or vehicle.

dereliction *n* neglect (of duty); abandonment.

deride *vt* to scorn, mock.

de rigueur *adj* required by fashion or etiquette.

derisible *adj* open to derision.

derision *n* ridicule.

derisive *adj* full of derision; mocking, scornful.—**derisively** *adv*.—**derisiveness** *n*.

derisory *adj* showing or deserving of derision.

derivation *n* the tracing of a word to its root; origin; descent.—**derivational** *adj*.

derivative *adj* derived from something else; not original. * *n* something that is derived; a word formed by derivation; (*math*) the rate of change of one quantity with respect to another.—**derivatively** *adv*.

derive *vt* to take or receive from a source; to infer, deduce (from). * *vi* to issue as a derivative (from).—**derivable** *adj*.—**deriver** *n*.

dermal *adj* of the skin; consisting of skin.

dermatitis *n* inflammation of the skin.

dermatol. *abbr* = dermatological; dermatologicy.

dermatology *n* the science of the skin and its diseases.—**dermatologic, dermatological** *adj*.—**dermatologist** *n*.

dermic *adj* dermal.

dermis *n* the fine skin below the epidermis containing blood vessels.

derogate *vti* to detract (from); to lose face; to degenerate; to take a part (from).—**derogation** *n*.

derogatory *adj* disparaging; deliberately offensive.—**derogatorily** *adv*.

derrick *n* any crane-like apparatus; a tower over an oil well, etc, holding the drilling machinery.

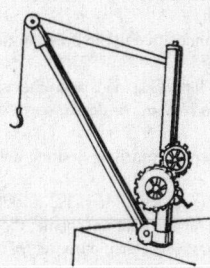

Derrida *n* **Jacques** (1930–) French philosopher, who developed the theory of deconstruction in literary criticism.

derring-do *n* bravery, reckless valor.

derringer *n* a pocket pistol with a short barrel of very large caliber.

DERV *abbr* = diesel-engined road vehicle.

dervish *n* a member of a Muslim religious order vowing chastity and poverty, noted for frenzied, whirling dancing.

DES *abbr* = data encryption standard; Department of Education and Science.

DESA *abbr* = Department of Economic and Social Affairs

Desai *n* **Morarji [Ranchhodji]** (1896–1995) Indian statesman and prime minister (1977–79). He founded the Janata Party in opposition to Indira Gandhi's Congress Party.

desalinate *vt* to remove the salt from (seawater, etc).—**desalination** *n*.—**desalinator** *n*.

Desalvo *n* **Albert** (1931–73) American sex offender, who was arrested for sexual assaults on women in 1964. He confessed to being the Boston Strangler but was not tried for murder. Sentenced to life for the sex attacks, he was killed in prison in 1973.

desc. *abbr* = descendant.

DESC *abbr* = Defense Energy Support Center

descant *n* a musical accompaniment sung or played in counterpoint to the main melody; (*mus*) a general term for all forms of polyphony used from the 12th century.—*also vi*.

Descartes *n* **René** (1596–1650) French philosopher and mathematician, famous for the dictum "I think, therefore I am."

descend *vi* to come or climb down; to pass from a higher to a lower place or condition; (*with* **on, upon**) to make a sudden attack upon or visit unexpectedly; to sink in morals or dignity; to be derived. * *vt* to go, pass, or extend down.

descendant *n* a person who is descended from an ancestor; something derived from an earlier form.

descendent *adj* descending; sinking.

descendible *adj* (*law*) that may be inherited; transmissible.

descending order *see* **ascending order**.

descent *n* a descending; a downward motion or step; a way down; a slope; a raid or invasion; lineage, ancestry.

describe *vt* to give a verbal account of; to trace out.—**describable** *adj*.—**describer** *n*.

description *n* a verbal or pictorial account; a sort, a kind.

descriptive *adj* tending to or serving to describe.—**descriptively** *adv*.—**descriptiveness** *n*.

descry *vt* (**descrying, descried**) to catch sight of.

Desdemona *n* small satellite of Uranus.

desecrate *vt* to violate (a sacred place) by destructive or blasphemous behavior.—**desecration** *n*.—**desecrator, desecrater** *n*.

desegregate *vt* to abolish racial or sexual segregation in.—**desegregation** *n*.

desensitization *n* (*med*) the technique whereby an individual builds up resistance to an allergen by taking gradually increasing doses of the substance over a period of time; (*med*) the treatment of phobias by which a patient is gradually faced with the thing that is feared and concurrently learns to relax and reduce anxiety.

desensitize *vt* to remove or reduce the sensitivity of (e.g., photographic film, an allergic person).

desert[1] *n* (*often pl*) a deserved reward or punishment.

desert[2] *vti* to leave or abandon, with no intention of returning; to abscond from the armed forces without permission.—**deserter** *n*.—**desertion** *n*.

desert[3] *n* a dry, barren region, able to support little or no life; a place lacking in some essential quality.

desert culture *n* a way of life associated with arid and semi-arid conditions in the American West after the Pleistocene epoch.

desertification *n* the transformation of fertile land into arid waste or desert through soil erosion, over-cultivation, etc.

desert pavement *n* a wide area of wind-polished, rounded stones in a desert, formed when the sand has been blown away, protecting the underlying ground from further erosion.

deserve *vt* to merit or be suitable for (some reward, punishment, etc).

deserved *adj* justly earned, merited.—**deservedly** *adv*.—**deservedness** *n*.

deserving *adj* worthy of support, esp financially.

deshabille *see* **dishabille**.

De Sica *n* **Vittorio** (1902–74) Italian movie director and actor.

desiccant *adj* desiccating; serving to dry. * *n* (*chem*) a substance that absorbs water, used as a drying agent.

desiccate *vti* to dry or become dried up; to preserve (food) by drying.—**desiccation** *n*.—**desiccative** *adj*.

desiccator *n* an apparatus for drying foods and other substances.

desiderate *vt* to feel the lack of, to desire earnestly.—**desideration** *n*.—**desiderative** *adj*.

desideratum *n* (*pl* **desiderata**) anything desired; a want or desire generally felt and recognized.

design *vt* to plan; to create; to devise; to make working drawings for; to intend. * *n* a working drawing; a mental plan or scheme; the particular form or disposition of something; a decorative pattern; purpose; (*pl*) dishonest intent.

designate *vt* to indicate or specify; to name; to appoint to or nominate for a position or office. * *adj* (*after noun*) appointed to office but not yet installed.—**designator** *n*.

designated hitter *n* (*baseball*) a player nominated at the start of the game to bat in place of the pitcher, with the pitcher remaining on the field. *abbr* DH.

designation *n* the act of designating; nomination; a distinguishing name or title.

designedly *adv* intentionally.

designer *n* a person who designs things; a person who is renowned for creating high-class fashion clothes. * *adj* (*inf*) trendy, of the latest, esp expensive, fashion.

designer drug *n* a synthetic narcotic or hallucinogenic substance which mimics the chemical structure and effects of banned drugs but is not yet covered by anti-drug laws.

designing *adj* crafty, scheming. * *n* the art or practice of making designs.

desirable *adj* arousing (sexual) desire; advisable or beneficial; worth doing.—**desirability** *n*.—**desirably** *adv*.

desire *vt* to long or wish for; to request, ask for. * *n* a longing for something regarded as pleasurable or satisfying; a request; something desired; sexual craving.

desirous *adj* desiring; craving.

desist *vi* to stop doing something.—**desistance** *n*.

desk *n* a piece of furniture with a writing surface and usu drawers; a counter behind which a cashier, etc sits; the section of a newspaper responsible for a particular topic.

desk accessory *n* (*comput*) a small utility program that can help in a computer user's productivity, e.g., on-screen calculators.

desktop *n* (*comput*) in a graphical user interface, the computer representation of a physical desk top onto which files and folders can be placed.

desktop publishing *n* the use of a microcomputer with sophisticated page-layout programs and a laser printer to produce professional-looking printed matter. *abbr* DTP.

desman *n* (*pl* **desmans**) a small amphibious animal similar to a mole.

desmoid *adj* having the characteristics of, or resembling, a ligament; (*tumor*) fibrous.

Des Moines *n* the capital city of Iowa, a state of the USA.

desolate *adj* solitary, lonely; devoid of inhabitants; laid waste; forlorn, disconsolate; overwhelmed with grief. * *vt* to devastate or lay waste; to make barren or unfit for habitation; to leave alone, forsake, abandon; to overwhelm with grief.—**desolately** *adv*.—**desolateness** *n*.—**desolator, desolater** *n*.

desolated *adj* wretched, lonely, miserable.

desolation *n* destruction, ruin; a barren state; loneliness; wretchedness.

desp. *abbr* = despatch.

despair *vi* to have no hope. * *n* utter loss of hope; something that causes despair.

despatch *see* **dispatch**.

despatcher *see* **dispatcher**.

desperado *n* (*pl* **desperadoes, desperados**) a violent criminal.

desperate *adj* (almost) hopeless; reckless through lack of hope; urgently requiring (money, etc); (*remedy*) extreme, dangerous.—**desperately** *adv*.—**desperateness** *n*.

desperation *n* loss of hope; recklessness from despair.

despicable *adj* contemptible, worthless.—**despicableness** *n*.—**despicably** *adv*.

Despina *n* a satellite of Neptune.

despise *vt* to regard with contempt or scorn; to consider as worthless, inferior.

despite *prep* in spite of.

despoil *vt* to plunder, rob.—**despoiler** *n*.—**despoilment** *n*.

Despoina *n* (*Greek myth*) the daughter of Demeter and Poseidon.

despoliation *n* despoilment; pillage.

despond *vi* to lose hope, to be dejected. * *n* despondency.

despondency, despondence *n* a being despondent; depression or dejection of spirits through loss of resolution or hope.

despondent *adj* dejected, depressed.—**despondently** *adv*.

despot *n* a ruler possessing absolute power; a tyrant.

despotic, despotical *adj* of, pertaining to, or of the nature of a despot or of despotism; arbitrary, tyrannical.—**despotically** *adv*.

despotism *n* absolute power, tyranny; a state governed by a despot.

Despres *n* **Jean** (1889–1980) French airplane pilot who turned to silver- and goldsmithing.

desquamate *vti* to peel or scale off.—**desquamation** *n*.

dessert *n* the sweet course at the end of a meal.

dessertspoon *n* a spoon in between a teaspoon and a tablespoon in size, used for eating desserts.

De Stijl *n* a Dutch art and design movement founded in 1917, which was strongly influenced by cubism.

destination *n* the place to which a person or thing is going.

destine *vt* to set aside for some specific purpose; to predetermine; to intend.

destiny *n* (*pl* **destinies**) the power supposedly determining the course of events; the future to which any person or thing is destined; a predetermined course of events.

destitute *adj* (*with* **of**) lacking some quality; lacking the basic necessities of life, very poor.

destitution *n* extreme poverty.

destn. *abbr* = destination.

destroy *vt* to demolish, ruin, put an end to; to kill.

destroyer *n* one who or that which destroys; a fast small warship.

destruct *vt* to destroy deliberately (a missile, etc). * *n* the act of destructing (a missile, etc).

destructible *adj* subject to destruction; able to be destroyed.—**destructibility** *n*.

destruction *n* the act or process of destroying or being destroyed; ruin.

destructionist *n* an anarchist.

destructive *adj* causing destruction; (*with* **of, to**) ruinous; (*criticism*) intended to discredit, negative.—**destructively** *adv*.—**destructivity** *n*.

destructor *n* a furnace for burning up rubbish, etc; an explosive device for blowing up a malfunctioning rocket, etc.

desuetude *n* disuse, discontinuance.

desultory *adj* going aimlessly from one activity or subject to another, not methodical.—**desultorily** *adv*.—**desultoriness** *n*.

det. *abbr* = (*mil*) detachment; (*Latin*) *detur*, "let it be given."

DET *abbr* = diethyltriptamine (a drug).

detach *vt* to release; to separate from a larger group; (*mil*) to send off on special assignment.

detachable *adj* able to be detached.—**detachability** *n*.—**detachably** *adv*.

detached *adj* separate; free from bias or emotion; (*house*) not joined to another; aloof.

detached retina *n* the condition in which the retina of the eye becomes detached from the choroid (a layer of the eyeball with blood vessels and pigment that absorbs excess light, preventing blurred vision).

detachment *n* indifference; freedom from emotional involvement or bias; the act of detaching; a thing detached; a body of troops detached from the main body and sent on special service.

detail *vt* to describe fully; (*mil*) to set apart for a particular duty. * *n* an item; a particular or minute account; (*art*) treatment of smaller parts; a reproduction of a smaller part of a picture, statue, etc; a small detachment for special service.

detailed *adj* giving full details; thorough.

detain *vt* to place in custody or confinement; to delay.—**detainment** *n*.

detainee *n* a person who is held in custody.

detainer *n* the (wrongful) detaining of person or goods; a writ for holding on another charge a person already arrested.

detect *vt* to discover the existence or presence of; to notice.

detectable *adj* able to be detected.—**detectability** *n*.

detection *n* a discovery or being discovered; the job or process of detecting.

detective *n* a police officer or other person employed to find evidence of crimes.

detector *n* a device for detecting the presence of something.

detent *n* a catch for locking machinery or regulating the striking of a clock.

détente, detente *n* relaxation of tension between countries.

detention *n* the act of detaining or withholding; a being detained; confinement; the act of being kept in school after hours as a punishment.

deter *vt* (**deterring, deterred**) to discourage or prevent from acting.—**determent** *n*.

deterge *vt* to cleanse (a wound, etc).

detergent *n* a cleaning agent, esp one made from a chemical compound rather than fats, as soap. * *adj* having cleaning power.

deteriorate *vt* to make or become worse.—**deterioration** *n*.—**deteriorative** *adj*.

determinable *adj* capable of being definitely ascertained; defined with clearness; terminable.—**determinability** *n*.—**determinably** *adv*.

determinant *adj* determining. * *n* something that determines, a decisive factor; (*math*) an algebraic term expressing the sum of certain products arranged in a square or matrix.

determinate *adj* definitely bounded in time, space, position, etc; fixed; clearly defined; distinct; resolute, decisive; (*bot*) having the terminal flower bud opening first, followed by those on lateral branches.—**determinately** *adv*.—**determinateness** *n*.

determination *n* the act or process of making a decision; a decision resolving a dispute; firm intention; resoluteness.

determinative *adj* determining, limiting, or defining; tending to define the genus or species * *n* that which serves to determine the quality or character of something else; a demonstrative pronoun; an ideograph.—**determinatively** *adv*.

determine *vt* to fix or settle officially; to find out; to regulate; to impel. * *vi* to come to a decision.

determined *adj* full of determination, resolute.—**determinedly** *adv*.—**determinedness** *n*.

determiner *n* one who or that which determines; (*gram*) a word that limits the meaning of a noun, esp an article or possessive pronoun.

determinism *n* the theory that all events, including human actions, are determined by preceding causes, thereby precluding free will.—**determinist** *n*.—**deterministic** *adj*.—**deterministically** *adv*.

deterrent *n* something that deters; a nuclear weapon that deters attack through fear of retaliation. * *adj* deterring.—**deterrence** *n*.

detest *vt* to dislike intensely.—**detester** *n*.

detestable *adj* intensely disliked, abhorrent.—**detestably** *adv*.

detestation *n* extreme dislike; a detestable person or thing.

dethrone *vt* to remove from a throne, depose.—**dethronement** *n*.—**dethroner** *n*.

detinue *n* (*law*) a writ for recovery of property wrongfully detained.

detonate *vti* to explode or cause to explode rapidly and violently.

detonation *n* a sudden explosion with a loud report.

detonator *n* a device that sets off an explosion.

detour *n* a deviation from an intended course, esp one serving as an alternative to a more direct route. * *vti* to make or send by a detour.

detoxification center *n* an institution that treats alcoholism or drug addiction.

detoxify *vt* (**detoxifying, detoxified**) to extract poison or toxins from.—**detoxification** *n*.

detract *vt* to take away. * *vi* to take away (from).—**detractor** *n*.

detraction *n* defamation; slander; depreciation.—**detractive** *adj*.—**detractively** *adv*.

detrain *vt, vi* to set down or alight from a train.—**detrainment** *n*.

detriment *n* (a cause of) damage or injury.

detrimental *adj* harmful.—**detrimentally** *adv*.

detrital mineral *n* a mineral derived from a parent rock by the mechanical breakdown of the rock by weathering and erosion.

detrition *n* a wearing down by rubbing or friction.

detritus *n* debris; loose matter, esp formed by rubbing away or erosion of a larger mass, e.g. a rock.—**detrital** *adj*.

Detroit *n* major city in the United States of America (USA).

de trop *adj* too much; out of place; (*person*) not wanted.

detumescence *n* the diminution of a swelling, esp of an erect penis.—**detumescent** *adj*.

Deucalion *n* (*Greek myth*) the king of Phthia. When Zeus sent a flood to destroy humans, Deucalion built a ship in which he and his wife Pyrrha were saved from the flood. When they reached Mount Parnassus, the oracle told them to throw the bones of their mother behind them. They threw stones, which became men and women.

deuce[1] *n* a playing card or dice with two spots; (*tennis*) the score of forty all.

deuce[2] *interj* (*inf*) an exclamation of surprise or annoyance.

deuced *adj* (*inf*) confounded.

deus ex machina *n* divine intervention; an artificial solution of difficulties, esp in a play.

Deut. *abbr* = Deuteronomy.

Deutsche Mark *n* currency of Germany.

deuteragonist *n* (*Greek drama*) the second principal actor.

deuterium *n* heavy hydrogen, used as a moderator in nuclear reactors to slow the rate of fission.

deuter(o)- *prefix* second.

deuterocanonical *adj* of or belonging to a second canon or to the Apocrypha.

deuterogamy *n* a second marriage.

deuteron *n* the nucleus of a heavy hydrogen atom.

Deuteronomy *n* (*Bible*) an Ool Testament book, the name of which means the second law; it is a key book of the Old Testament, setting out the highest ideals of the Jewish faith.

deutoplasm *n* the albuminous part of the yolk that provides food for the embryo in an egg.—**deutoplasmic** *adj*.

Deutschland über Alles *n* (*German*, "Germany above Everything") the German national anthem, written just before the revolution of 1848 and sung to a tune by Haydn. *See* **Emperor's Hymn**.

Deutschmark *n* the monetary unit of Germany.

deutzia *n* a small shrub of the saxifrage family with clusters of white flowers.

deux temps *n* (*mus*) 2/2 time. A *valse à deux temps* is a waltz which has only two dance steps to every three beats of the bar.

deva *n* (*Hinduism*) a god.

De Valera *n* **Eamon** (1882–1975) American-born Irish statesman, prime minister (1932–48, 1951–54, 1957–59), and president (1959–73).

devaluate *vt* to devalue.

devalue *vt* (**devaluing, devalued**) to reduce the exchange value of (a currency).—**devaluation** *n*.

devastate *vt* to lay waste; to destroy; to overwhelm.—**devastatingly** *adv*.—**devastation** *n*.—**devastator** *n*.

develop *vt* to evolve; to bring to maturity; to show the symptoms of (e.g., a habit or a disease); to treat (a photographic film or plate) to reveal an image; to improve the value of. * *vi* to grow (into); to become apparent.

developer *n* a person who develops; a person or organization that develops property; a reagent for developing photographs.

developing country *n* a poor country that is attempting to improve its social conditions and encourage industrial growth.

development *n* the process of growing or developing; a new situation that emerges; a piece of land or property that has been developed; the expansion or changing in some way of parts of a theme of music that have already been heard; the use of resources to improve the standard of living.—**developmental** *adj*.

development costs *npl* costs incurred by a company in making improvements to a product or process marketed by it.

Deverel-Rimbury *adj* relating to a local culture in southern England dating from the 15th to 12th centuries BC.

deviant *adj* deviating from an accepted norm. * *n* a person whose behavior deviates from the accepted standards of society.—**deviance, deviancy** *n*.

deviate *vi* to diverge from a course, topic, principle, etc.—**deviator** *n*.

deviation *n* a deviating from normal behavior, official ideology, etc; deflection of a compass needle by magnetic disturbance; (*statistics*) difference from a mean.

device *n* a machine, implement, etc for a particular purpose; an invention; a scheme or plot.

device driver *n* (*comput*) in DOS, a utility program that extends the capabilities of the operating system to allow hardware devices such as a mouse, CD-ROM drive, printer, or hard disk to work with the computer.

devil *n* (*with cap*) in Christian and Jewish theology, the supreme spirit of evil, Satan; any evil spirit; an extremely wicked person; (*inf*) a reckless, high-spirited person; (*inf*) someone or something difficult to deal with; (*inf*) a person. * *vt* to cook (food) with a hot seasoning. * *vi* to act as a drudge to someone; to do research for an author or barrister.

devilfish *n* (**devilfish, devilfishes**) the manta, a very large ray; a large species of octopus.

devilish *adj* fiendish; mischievous. * *adv* (*inf*) very.—**devilishly** *adv*.—**devilishness** *n*.

devil-may-care *adj* audacious, contemptuous of authority.

devilment *n* mischievous behavior.

devilry *n* (*pl* **devilries**) wickedness; malicious mischief.

devil's advocate *n* a person who advocates an opposing cause, esp for the sake of argument.

Devine *n* **George** [**Alexander Cassady**] (1910–65) English stage director and administrator.

devious *adj* indirect; not straightforward; underhand, deceitful.—**deviously** *adv*.—**deviousness** *n*.

devisable *adj* capable of being imagined; (*law*) (*real estate*) capable of being bequeathed.—**devisability** *n*.

devise *vt* to invent or contrive; to plan; (*law*) to leave (real estate) by will. * *n* (*law*) a bequest (of real estate); property so bequeathed.—**deviser** *n*.

devisee *n* (*law*) a person to whom real estate has been bequeathed.

devisor *n* (*law*) a person who bequeaths, esp real estate.

devitalize *vt* to deprive of vitality or vigor.—**devitalization** *n*.

DeVito *n* **Danny** (1944–) American movie actor, best known for his comic roles, whose movies include *Batman Returns* (1992).

devitrify *vt* (**devitrifying, devitrified**) to deprive of glassy quality; to make opaque.—**devitrification** *n*.

devoid *adj* (*with* **of**) lacking; free from.

devoirs *npl* civilities; one's best.

devolution *n* a transfer of authority, esp from a central government to regional governments; a passing on from one person to another.

devolve *vti* to hand on or be handed on to a successor or deputy.—**devolvement** *n*.

Devorgilla *or* **Derbhorgill** *n* (*Irish Celtic myth*) rescued from the Fomorii by Cuchulainn. She and her handmaidens changed themselves into swans so that they could follow Cuchulainn.

devote *vt* to give or use for a particular activity or purpose.

devoted *adj* zealous; loyal; loving.—**devotedly** *adv*.—**devotedness** *n*.

devotee *n* (*with* **of, to**) a person who is enthusiastically or fanatically devoted to something; a religious zealot.

devotion *n* given to religious worship; piety; strong affection or attachment (to); ardor; (*pl*) prayers.

devotional *adj* of devotions; devout. * *n* a brief religious service.

devour *vt* to eat up greedily; to consume; to absorb eagerly by the senses or mind.

devout *adj* very religious, pious; sincere, dedicated.—**devoutly** *adv*.—**devoutness** *n*.

De Vries *n* 1. **Hugo [Marie]** (1848–1935) Dutch botanist and geneticist, who developed the theory of evolution through the mutation of genes. 2. **Peter** (1910–93) American novelist, whose works include *The Tunnel of Love* (1954).

dew *n* air moisture, deposited on a cool surface, esp at night.

DEW *abbr* = distant early warning.

dewberry *n* (*pl* **dewberries**) a kind of trailing blackberry plant; its dark blue fruit.

dewclaw *n* a rudimentary toe above a dog's paw or above the hoof of a deer, etc.

dewdrop *n* a drop of dew.

Dewey Decimal System *n* a method of classifying library books into ten main subject areas.—*also* **decimal classification**.

dewlap *n* a flap of skin hanging under the throat of some animals, e.g., cows; loose skin on the throat of an elderly person.

DEW line *n* a distant early warning line, any of a series of early-warning radar stations situated across the top of North America.

De Wolfe *n* **Elsie** (1865–1950) American actress, who became America's first professional interior designer.

dew point *n* the air temperature at which dew forms.

dew worm *n* a large earthworm that surfaces at nightfall.

dewy *adj* (**dewier, dewiest**) wet with dew.—**dewily** *adv*.—**dewiness** *n*.

dewy-eyed *adj* sentimental, naive.

dexter *adj* right; (*her*) to the viewer's left and the wearer's right.

dexterity *n* manual skill, adroitness.

dexterous *adj* possessing manual skill; quick, mentally or physically; adroit; clever.—**dexterously** *adv*.—**dexterousness** *n*.

dextral *adj* on the right-hand side; right-handed; (*shell*) with whorls going to the right.—**dextrality** *n*.—**dextrally** *adv*.

dextrin, dextrine *n* a white gummy substance found in plant sap, etc, and used as gum and a thickening agent.

dextrorotation *n* right-handed or clockwise rotation.—**dextrorotary, dextrorotatory** *adj*.

dextrorse *adj* (*bot*) twining spirally from left to right.—**dextrorsely** *adv*.

dextrose *n* a form of glucose found in fruit, honey and animal tissues.

dextrous *adj* dexterous.

DF *abbr* = Dean of the Faculty; (*Latin*) *Defensor Fidei*, "Defender of the Faith"; direction-finding; (*Spanish*) *Districto Federal*, "Federal District."

D/F *abbr* (*radio*) = direction-finding.

d.-f. *abbr* = double-fronted.

DFC *abbr* = Distinguished Flying Cross.

DFD *abbr* = data function diagram; Dogs for Disabled.

DfEE *abbr* (*Brit*) = Department for Education and Employment.

DFLP *abbr* = Democratic Front for the Liberation of Palestine.

DFM *abbr* = Diploma in Forensic Medicine.

dft *abbr* = defendant; draft.

dg *abbr* = decigram.

DG *abbr* = (*Latin*) *Dei gratia*, "by the grace of God"; (*Latin*) *Deo gratias*, "thanks to God"; Director General.

DGM *abbr* = Diploma in General Medicine.

DGO *abbr* = Diploma in Gynecology and Obstetrics.

DGS *abbr* = Diploma in General Surgery; Diploma in Graduate Studies.

DH *abbr* (*Brit*) = Department of Health; (*baseball*) designated hitter.

DHA *abbr* (*Brit*) = District Health Authority.

dhak *n* an Indian tree with brilliant red flowers.

Dhaka *n* capital city of Bangladesh.

dhal *see* **dal**.

dharma *n* (*Hinduism, Buddhism*) the law requiring virtue and righteousness; its practice in daily life.

DHC *abbr* = Domestic Heating Council.

DHDS *abbr* = Dolmetsch Historical Dance Society.

DHE *abbr* (*Brit*) = Diploma in Horticulture, Royal Botanic Gardens, Edinburgh.

DHF *abbr* = Dag Hammarskjold Foundation.

DHI *abbr* = David Hume Institute.

DHL *abbr* = Doctor of Hebrew Literature.

DHM *abbr* = Daughters of the Heart of Mary.

DHMSA *abbr* (*Brit*) = Diploma in the History of Medicine, Society of Apothecaries of London.

dhobi *n* (*pl* **dhobis**) in India, a laundryman.

dhole *n* (*pl* **dholes, dhole**) an Asian wild dog that hunts in packs.

dhoti *n* (*pl* **dhotis**) a loincloth worn by men in India.

dhow *n* an Arab coastal vessel with a triangular sail.

DHP *abbr* = Diploma in Hypnosis and Psychotherapy.

DHQ *abbr* = District Headquarters; Divisional Headquarters.

DHS *abbr* = Design History Society; Domestic Heating Society.

dhw *abbr* = domestic hot water.

DHy *abbr* = Doctor of Hygiene.

di. *abbr* = diameter.

Di *abbr* (*chem*) = didymium.

DI *abbr* = Defence Intelligence; Detective Inspector; diabetes insipidus.

di- *prefix* two; twice; double.

dia. *abbr* = diameter.

DIA Defence Industry Association; Defense Intelligence Agency.

diabase *n* dolerite, a dark-colored igneous rock.

Diabelli *n* **Anton** (1781–1858) Austrian composer and founder of a firm of music publishers, best known for inviting a number of composers to write variations on a waltz tune of his own.

diabetes *n* a medical disorder marked by the persistent and excessive discharge of urine.

diabetes insipidus *n* a rare condition that is completely different from diabetes mellitus and is characterized by excessive thirst and polyuria.

diabetes mellitus *n* a breakdown in the body's ability to absorb carbohydrates caused by a deficiency of insulin, which results in abnormally high levels of sugar in the blood and urine.

diabetic *adj* of or suffering from diabetes. * *n* a person with diabetes.

diablerie *n* a devil's work, sorcery; devil lore; mischief.

diabolic *adj* devilish; cruel, wicked.—**diabolically** *adv*.—**diabolicalness** *n*.

diabolical *adj* diabolic; (*inf*) extremely bad or annoying.

diabolism *n* devil worship; witchcraft.—**diabolist** *n*.

diabolize *vt* to make into or represent as a devil.

diaconal *adj* of or pertaining to a deacon.

diaconate *n* the office or dignity of a deacon; deacons collectively.

diacritic *adj* diacritical. * *n* a diacritical mark.

diacritical *adj* distinguishing, distinctive, esp of accents, etc attached to letters to indicate pronunciation.—**diacritically** *adv*.

diacritical mark *n* a mark, such as an accent, used above or below a letter to indicate differences in sound.

diactinic *adj* transparent to actinic rays.—**diactinism** *n*.

diadelphous *adj* (*flowers*) with stamens in two bundles.

diadem *n* a crown or jeweled headband worn by royalty.

diag. *or* **diagr.** *abbr* = diagram.

diagenesis *n* (*geol*) the changes that occur in a sediment after deposition.

Diaghilev *n* **Sergei [Pavlovich]** (1872–1929) Russian ballet impresario. He founded the Ballet Russe de Diaghilev in 1911.

diagnose *vt* to ascertain by diagnosis.—**diagnosable** *adj*.

diagnosis *n* (*pl* **diagnoses**) the identification of a disease from its symptoms; the analysis of the nature or cause of a problem.—**diagnostician** *n*.

diagnostic *adj* of or aiding diagnosis; characteristic * *n* a symptom distinguishing a disease; a characteristic; (*pl: used as sing*) the art of diagnosing.—**diagnostically** *adv*.

diagnostic program *n* (*comput*) a utility program designed to test computer hardware and operating systems for errors.

diagonal *adj* slanting from one corner to an opposite corner of a polygon. * *n* a straight line connecting opposite corners.—**diagonally** *adv*.

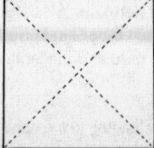

diagram 187 dicta

diagram *n* a figure or plan drawn in outline to illustrate the form or workings of something. * *vt* (**diagramming, diagrammed**) to demonstrate in diagram form.

diagrammatic, diagrammatical *adj* having the form or nature of a diagram; of or pertaining to diagrams.—**diagrammatically** *adv*.

diagraph *n* an instrument for enlarging maps, etc mechanically.

dial *n* the face of a watch or clock; a graduated disk with a pointer used in various instruments; the control on a radio or television set indicating wavelength or station; the numbered disk on a telephone used to enter digits to connect calls; an instrument for telling the time by the sun's shadow. * *vt* (**dialing, dialed**) to measure or indicate by a dial; to make a telephone connection by using a dial or numbered keypad.

dial. *abbr* = dialect; dialectal; dialectic; dialectical.

dialect *n* the form of language spoken in a particular region or social class.—**dialectal** *adj*.—**dialectally** *adv*.

dialectic *n* the pursuit of truths in philosophy through logical debate.—**dialectical** *adj*.—**dialectically** *adv*.

dialectology *n* the study of dialects.—**dialectological** *adj*.—**dialectologist** *n*.

dialog *n* a conversation, esp in a play or novel; an exchange of opinions, negotiation.

dialog box *n* (*comput*) a window used to convey information or request information from the user about the operations of a program.

dial tone *n* a sound heard over the telephone indicating that the line is clear.

dial-up *n* (*comput*) the process of locating and retrieving information over telephone lines.

dialysis *n* (*pl* **dialyses**) the removal of impurities from the blood by filtering it through a membrane; (*chem*) a method for separating small molecules from larger ones in a solution.—**dialytic** *adj*.—**dialytically** *adv*.

dialyze *vt* to separate crystalline from colloid parts of a mixture by filtration.—**dialyzation** *n*.

dialyzer *n* a machine for dialyzing, esp one that acts as a kidney.

diam. *abbr* = diameter.

diamagnetic *adj* cross-magnetic, tending to point east and west.—**diamagnetically** *adv*.

diamagnetism *n* the property of certain bodies when under the influence of magnetism and freely suspended of taking a position at right angles to the magnetic meridian.

diamanté *adj* glittering with rhinestones, sequins or imitation jewels. * *n* a material ornamented in this way.

diameter *n* a straight line bisecting a circle; the length of this line.

diametric, diametrical *adj* of or along a diameter; completely opposed.—**diametrically** *adv*.

diamond *n* a valuable gem, a crystallized form of pure carbon; (*baseball*) the playing field, esp the infield; a suit of playing cards denoted by a red lozenge. * *adj* composed of, or set with diamonds; shaped like a diamond; denoting the 60th (or 75th) anniversary of an event.

Diamond *n* **David Leo** (1915–) American composer, whose work, *Rounds,* for string orchestra, is probably his best-known piece.

diamondback *n* a large rattlesnake with diamond-shaped markings.

diamond-ring effect *n* (*astron*) an optical effect seen in the last stages of a total eclipse of the sun.

diamorphine hydrochloride *see* **heroin**.

Diana *n* 1. (*Roman myth*) the goddess of hunting. See also **Ephesus**. 2. Diana, Princess of Wales, original name Lady Diana Francis Spencer (1961–97). Married Charles, Prince of Wales in 1981; divorced 1996. Killed in a car crash in Paris while being pursued by members of the press.

Dian Cecht *n* (*Irish Celtic myth*) the god of healing, often depicted as a giant leech.

DIANE *abbr* = Direct Information Access Network for Europe.

dianthus *n* (*pl* **dianthuses**) any of a large genus of ornamental plants, including carnations and pinks.

diapason *n* the entire compass of a voice or instrument; a recognized musical standard of pitch; the foundation stops of an organ; a tuning fork.

diapason normal *n* (*mus*) concert pitch.

diaper *n* a square of absorbent material arranged between a baby's legs and fastened at its waist to absorb excrement.

diaper work *n* (*archit*) a decoration, all over a surface, consisting of flowers in a geometric outline.

diaphanous *adj* (*fabric*) delicate, transparent.—**diaphanously** *adv*.—**diaphanousness** *n*.

diaphoretic *adj* causing profuse perspiration. * *n* a diaphoretic drug.

diaphragm *n* the midriff, a muscular structure separating the chest from the abdomen; any thin dividing membrane; a device for regulating the aperture of a camera lens; a contraceptive cap covering the cervix; a thin vibrating disk used in a telephone receiver, microphone, etc.—**diaphragmatic** *adj*.—**diaphragmatically** *adv*.

diaphragm arch *n* (*archit*) a transverse arch that forms a line separating vaulting bays.

diaphysis *n* (*pl* **diaphyses**) the central part or shaft of a long bone.

diarchy *n* (*pl* **diarchies**) government by two independent authorities.—*also* **dyarchy**.

diarist *n* one who keeps a diary; the author of a diary.

Diarmaid ua Duibhne *n* (*Irish Celtic myth*), the son of Donn, received the "love spot," on his forehead to make any woman who saw it instantly fall in love with him.

diarrhea, (*Brit*) **diarrhoea** *n* excessive looseness of the bowels.—**diarrheal, diarrheic,** (*Brit*) **diarrhoeal, diarrhoeic** *adj*.

diary *n* (*pl* **diaries**) a daily record of personal thoughts, events, or business appointments; a book for keeping a daily record.

Diaspora *n* the dispersion of the Jews after the Babylonian captivity; the Jewish communities outside Israel; (*without cap*) the dispersion of any peoples outside their native area.

diastase *n* any enzyme that converts starch into sugar.—**diastatic, diastasic** *adj*.

diastasis *n* the separation of a growing bone from the shaft.

diastole *n* the dilation of the chambers of the heart during which they fill with blood.—**diastolic** *adj*.

diatessaron *n* the combination of the four Gospels into a single narrative.

diathermancy *n* the property of transmitting radiant heat.—**diathermanous** *adj*.

diathermic *adj* having diathermancy; allowing heat rays to pass freely.

diathermy *n* the use of electric current to warm or destroy body tissues as part of medical treatment.

diathesis *n* (*pl* **diatheses**) a constitutional tendency, esp to disease; a predisposing factor.

diatom *n* a microscopic alga found in fresh and seawater and in soil.—**diatomaceous** *adj*.

diatomite *n* soft earth formed from the shells of diatoms and used as a filter, etc.

diatonic *adj* (*mus*) using only the major and minor scales, as opposed to the chromatic scale.—**diatonically** *adv*.—**diatonicism** *n*.

diatribe *n* a lengthy and abusive verbal attack.

diazepam *see* **tranquilizer**.

dib *vti* (**dibbing, dibbed**) to dibble; (*fishing*) to drop bait gently into water; to dip lightly.

dibasic *adj* containing two atoms of hydrogen replaceable by a basic radical.—**dibasicity** *n*.

dibber *n* a dibble.

dibble *n* a pointed tool used to make holes in the ground for seedlings. * *vt* to make a hole in the ground with a dibber.

Dibdin *n* **Charles** *n* (1745–1814) English composer, who wrote successful short operas, *The Padlock,* and numerous songs, one of the best known being "Tom Bowling."

dibs *npl* (*sl*) money, esp in small amounts; a claim; a right (to something).

DIC *abbr* = Diamond Information Center; Diploma of Membership of Imperial College of Science and Technology.

dicast *n* in ancient Athens, a juryman.

dice *n* (*the pl of* **die**[2] *but used as sing*) a small cube with numbered sides used in games of chance. * *vti* to gamble using dice; to cut (food) into small cubes.

DICE *abbr* = Dairy and Ice Cream Equipment Association; Durrell Institute of Conservation and Ecology.

dicentra *n* a member of a genus of perennial plants with heart-shaped flowers.

dicephalous *adj* two-headed.

dicey *adj* (**dicier, diciest**) (*inf*) risky.

DIChem *abbr* = Diploma in Industrial Chemistry.

dichloride *see* **bichloride**.

dichogamous, dichogamic *adj* (*bot*) with stamens and pistils maturing at different times, preventing self-fertilization.—**dichogamy** *n*.

dichotomy *n* (*pl* **dichotomies**) a division into two parts.—**dichotomous, dichotomic** *adj*.

dichroic, dichroitic *adj* (*crystal*) showing two colors; dichromatic.

dichroism *n* the property by which a crystallized body exhibits different colors according to the direction of light transmitted through it.

dichromatic *adj* two-colored (—*also* **dichroic**); being able to see only two of the three primary colors, color-blind; (*biol*) having one of two varieties of seasonal coloration.—**dichromatism** *n*.

dichromic *adj* seeing only two of the three primary colors, dichromatic.

dick *n* (*sl*) a detective; (*sl*) a person; (*vulg*) a penis.

dickens *interj* (*inf*) the Devil.

Dickens *n* **Charles [John Huffam]** (1812–70) English novelist, whose novels include *David Copperfield*.

dicker *vi* to barter or trade on a small scale; to haggle. * *n* a barter; a deal; haggling.

Dickinson *n* **Emily** (1830–86) American poet, who was a virtual recluse from her late twenties onward, only seven of her c.2000 highly original poems being printed in her lifetime.

dicky, dickey[1] *n* (*pl* **dickies, dickeys**) a false shirt-front; a seat at the back of a sports car.

dicky, dickey[2] *adj* (**dickier, dickiest**) (*sl*) shaky, unsound.

dicrotic *adj* having a double or secondary pulse beat.—**dicrotism** *n*.

dict. *abbr* = dictator; dictionary.

dicta *see* **dictum**.

Dictaphone *n* (*trademark*) a machine that records dictation and later reproduces it for typing.

dictate *vt* to say or read for another person to write or for a machine to record; to pronounce, order with authority. * *vi* to give dictation; to give orders (to). * *n* an order, rule, or command; (*usu pl*) an impulse, ruling principle.

dictation *n* the act of dictating words to be written down by another; the thing dictated; an authoritative utterance.

dictator *n* a ruler with absolute authority, usu acquired by force.

dictatorial *adj* like a dictator; tyrannical; domineering.—**dictatorially** *adv*.

dictatorship *n* the office or government of a dictator; a country governed by a dictator; absolute power.

Dicte *n* (*Greek myth*) a mountain in Crete where the infant Zeus was sheltered.

diction *n* a way of speaking, enunciation; a person's choice of words.

dictionary *n* (*pl* **dictionaries**) a reference book containing the words of a language or branch of knowledge alphabetically arranged, with their meanings, pronunciation, origin, etc.

Dictograph *n* (*trademark*) a sound-recording instrument used for recording or monitoring telephone conversations.

dictum *n* (*pl* **dictums, dicta**) an authoritative pronouncement.

Dictys *n* (*Greek myth*) a fisherman who became king of Seriphos.

did *see* **do**.

Didache *n* the title of a 2nd-century AD treatise on Christian doctrine and order, discovered 1883.

didactic *adj* intended to teach; instructive; in a lecturing manner.—**didactically** *adv*.—**didacticism** *n*.

didactics *n* (*used as sing*) the art of teaching.

diddle *vt* (*sl*) to cheat.—**diddler** *n*.

Diderot *n* **Denis** (1713–84) French philosopher and co-editor of the great *Encyclopédie*.

didgeridoo, didjeridoo *n* (*mus*) a tubular-shaped Australian Aboriginal wind instrument producing a deep vibratory tone.

didn't = did not.

Dido *n* (*Greek myth*) the founder and queen of Carthage. According to Virgil's *Aeneid*, she killed herself because she was deserted by Aeneas.—*also* **Elissa**.

didymium *n* a mixture of rare earths, formerly thought to be an element, used for coloring glass.

didymous *adj* (*biol*) growing in pairs; paired or double.

Didymus *n* (*Bible*) Greek for "twin"; applied to Thomas, one of the twelve disciples.

die[1] *vi* (**dying, died**) to cease existence; to become dead; to stop functioning; to fade; to become weak or faint; to stop; (*sl*) to receive a poor response (from an audience); (*with* **down**) to abate; (*with* **out**) to become extinct; (*with* **for**) to feel a deep longing; (*often with* **of**) (*inf*) to be overcome. * *vt* to experience (a particular form of death).

die[2] *n* a dice.

die[3] *n* (*pl* **dies**) an engraved stamp for pressing coins; a casting mold; a tool used in cutting the threads of screws or bolts, etc.

DIE *abbr* = Diploma in Industrial Engineering.

dieb. alt. *abbr* (*Latin*) = *diebus alternis*, "every other day."

die-cast *vt* (**die-casting, die-cast**) to shape (molten metal or plastic) under pressure in a mold.

diecious *see* **dioecious**.

diehard *n* a person who prolongs futile resistance, usu an extreme conservative.

dielectric *adj* nonconducting * *n* any medium, as glass, that transmits electric force by induction.

Dientzenhofer *n* 1. **Georg** (*b.* 1643) German architect, whose notable works include the Church at Kappel. 2. **Johann** (*b.* 1663) German architect, whose notable works include the Abbey at Banz. 3. **Kilian I.** (*b.* 1689) German architect, whose notable works include the Thomas Kirche in Prague.

dieresis *n* (*pl* **diereses**) a sign (¨) placed over the second of two separate vowels to show that each has a separate sound in pronunciation, as *Zoë*; a division in a line of verse.—**dieretic** *adj*.

dièse *adj* (*mus*) sharp.

diesel *n* a vehicle driven by a diesel engine.

diesel engine *n* an internal-combustion engine in which ignition is produced by the heat of highly compressed air alone.

diesel oil *n* a form of petroleum for diesel engines, ignited by the heat of compression.

diesis *n* (*pl* **dieses**) the double dagger used in printing (‡); (*mus*) the difference between a greater and lesser semitone.

diet[1] *n* food selected to adjust weight, to control illness, etc; the food and drink usu consumed by a person or animal. * *vt* to put on a diet. * *vi* to eat according to a special diet.—**dieter** *n*.

diet[2] *n* a legislative assembly in some countries.

dietary *adj* pertaining to a diet.

dietetic, dietetical *adj* regulating food or diet.—**dietetically** *adv*.

dietetics *n* (*used as sing*) the scientific study of diet and nutrition.

dietician, dietitian *n* a person trained to plan meals in hospitals, schools, etc.

Dietrich *n* **Marlene [Maria Magdelene von Losch]** (1902–92) German-born American movie actress and singer.

dif. *abbr* = differ; difference.

diff. *abbr* = difference; different; differs.

differ *vi* to be unlike, distinct (from); to disagree.

Differdange *n* a city in the Grand Duchy of Luxembourg.

difference *n* the act or state of being unlike; disparity; a distinguishing feature; the amount or manner of being different; the result of the subtraction of one quantity from another; a disagreement or argument.

different *adj* distinct, separate; unlike, not the same; unusual.—**differently** *adv*.

differentia *n* (*pl* **differentiae**) (*logic*) what distinguishes a thing from others, esp one subclass from another of the same class.

differential *adj* of or showing a difference; (*math*) relating to increments in given functions. * *n* something that marks the difference between comparable things; the difference in wage rates for different types of labor, esp within an industry.—**differentially** *adv*.

differential calculus *n* the branch of calculus dealing with the rate of change of given functions with respect to their variables.

differential gear *n* a type of gear that allows powered wheels in a motor vehicle to turn at different speeds (e.g., when cornering).

differentiate *vt* to make different; to become specialized; to note differences; (*math*) to calculate the derivative of.

differentiated marketing *n* product differentiation.

differentiation *n* the act of differentiating; (*biol*) specialization; (*math*) the calculation of a differential; (*geol*) the process by which several types of rock are produced from one "parent" magma.

difficult *adj* hard to understand; hard to make, do, or carry out; not easy to please.

difficulty *n* (*pl* **difficulties**) the state of being difficult; a problem, etc that is hard to deal with; an obstacle; a troublesome situation; a disagreement.

diffidence *n* lack of confidence in one's own ability; shyness, modesty.

diffident *adj* shy, lacking self-confidence, not assertive.—**diffidently** *adv*.

diffract *vti* to cause, or cause to undergo, diffraction.—**diffractive** *adj*.

diffraction *n* the breaking up of a ray of light into colored bands of the spectrum, or into a series of light and dark bands.

diffraction grating *n* a useful instrument which consists of thousands of closely spaced lines ruled on glass, each line acting as a slit to incoming light, thus producing a diffraction pattern.

diffuse *vt* to spread widely in all directions. * *vti* (*gases, fluids, small particles*) to intermingle. * *adj* spread widely, not concentrated; wordy, not concise.—**diffusely** *adv*.

diffusion *n* the act of diffusing; a spreading abroad; the passing by osmosis through animal membranes; (*chem*) the natural process by which molecules will disperse evenly throughout a particular substance; (*archeo*) the means whereby a particular trait of culture, e.g., trade, war or imitation, is spread from its source.

diffusive *adj* extending; spreading widely.—**diffusively** *adv*.—**diffusiveness** *n*.

diffusivity *n* (*chem*) the rate at which heat diffuses through a material.

dig *vti* (**digging, dug**) to use a tool or hands, claws, etc in making (a hole) in the ground; to unearth by digging; to excavate; to investigate; to thrust (into); to nudge; (*sl*) to understand, approve. * *n* (*sl*) a thrust; an archeological excavation; a cutting remark.

dig. *abbr* = digest.

DIG *abbr* = Disablement Income Group; Drinks Industry Group (Republic of Ireland).

digamist *n* one who marries for a second time.—**digamous** *adj*.—**digamy** *n*.

digamma *n* a letter of the ancient Greek alphabet, in sound approaching that of V or W.

digastric *adj* (*muscle*) with two swollen ends. * *n* a neck muscle that helps lower the jaw.

digenesis *n* (*biol*) an alternating process of reproduction, sexual in one generation, asexual in the following.—**digenetic** *adj*.

digest[1] *vt* to convert (food) into assimilable form; to reduce (facts, laws, etc) to convenient form by classifying or summarizing; to form a clear view of (a situation) by reflection. * *vi* to become digested.

digest[2] *n* an abridgment of any written matter; a periodical synopsis of published or broadcast material.

digester *n* one who makes a digest; a thing that digests; an apparatus for extracting the essence of a substance by heat.

digestible *adj* capable of being digested.—**digestibility** *n*. **digestibly** *adv*.

digestion *n* the act or process of digesting.—**digestional** *adj*.

digestive *adj* pertaining to, performing, or aiding, digestion. * *n* a thing that aids digestion; (*Brit*) a sweet wholewheat biscuit.

digestive gland *n* (*anat*) a gland that secretes digestive enzymes.

digestive system *n* (*anat*) the connected organs that enable food to be digested.

digger *n* an implement or machine for digging; (*inf*) an Australian or New Zealander (used as a form of address).

digispeak *n* (*comput*) the use of acronyms in on-line communication in which frequently used terms or phrases are abbreviated into their initial letters commonly with numbers.

digit *n* any of the basic counting units of a number system, including zero; a human finger or toe.

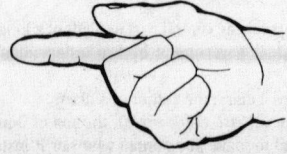

digital *adj* of, having or using digits; using numbers rather than a dial to display measurements; of or pertaining to a digital computer or digital recording. * *n* (*mus*) one of the keys on the keyboard of a piano or organ.—**digitally** *adv*.

digital audio tape *n* a magnetic tape capable of being used in digital recording, giving high-quality audio reproduction.

digital clock *n* a clock that displays the time in figures.

digital computer *n* a computer that processes information in the form of characters and digits in electronic binary code.

digitalin *n* a poison extracted from foxglove leaves.

digitalis *n* a drug derived from foxglove leaves, used as a heart stimulant.

digital money *n* (*comput*) money in electronic form to make purchases via the Internet.

digital recording *n* the conversion of sound into discrete electronic pulses (representing binary digits) for recording.

digital signature *n* (*comput*) an electronic version of a signature, which is encrypted and sent with a message, guaranteeing that the recipient gets a document that has not been opened by an unauthorized person.

digital video disk *or* **digital versatile disk** *n* (*comput*) a storage/reply medium commonly used for audio video usage. *abbr* **DVD**.

digital watch *n* a watch that displays the time in figures.

digitate, digitated *adj* having separate fingers or toes.—**digitation** *n*.

digitigrade *adj* (*cats, dogs, etc*) walking on the toes. * *n* an animal that walks in this way.

digitize *vt* to translate (data or images) into digital form for input into a computer.—**digitization** *n*.

diglot *adj* bilingual. * *n* a book with the text in two languages.

dignified *adj* possessing dignity; noble; serious.—**dignifiedly** *adv*.

dignify *vt* (**dignifying, dignified**) to confer dignity on; to exalt; to add the appearance of distinction to.

dignitary *n* (*pl* **dignitaries**) a person in a high position or rank.

dignity *n* (*pl* **dignities**) noble, serious, formal in manner and appearance; sense of self-respect, worthiness; a high rank, e.g., in the government.

digraph *n* a combination of two sounds or characters to represent one simple sound, as *ph* in *phone*.—**digraphic** *adj*.—**digraphically** *adv*.

digress *vi* to stray from the main subject in speaking or writing.—**digression** *n*.

digressive *adj* tending to digress; deviating from the subject.—**digressively** *adv*.—**digressiveness** *n*.

DIGS *abbr* (*Brit*) = Disablement Income Group Scotland.

DIH *abbr* = Diploma in Industrial Health.

dihedral *adj* (*angle*) having two intersecting plane faces or sides. * *n* a dihedral angle; the angle between aircraft wings for improving stability.

dik-dik *n* a small East African antelope.

dike[1] *n* an embankment to prevent flooding or form a barrier to the sea; a ditch; a causeway.—*also* **dyke**.

dike[2] *see* **dyke**[2].

dil. *abbr* = dilute.

dilapidate *vt* to bring into partial ruin by neglect or misuse.

dilapidated *adj* in a state of disrepair; shabby.

dilapidation *n* a state of damage or disrepair.

dilatation *n* a dilating, esp as part of a medical procedure; an abnormal enlargement of an organ, etc.—**dilatational** *adj*.

dilatation and curettage *n* a surgical procedure for opening the cervix and scraping the uterus. * *abbr* **D and C.**

dilate *vti* to make wider or larger; to increase the width of; to expand, amplify, enlarge; to extend in time, protract, prolong, lengthen. * *vi* to become wider or larger; to spread out, widen, enlarge, expand; to discourse or write at large; to enlarge.—**dilatable** *adj*.—**dilatability** *n*.

dilation *n* the action or process of dilating; something dilated.

dilator *n* that which dilates; a surgical instrument for opening or expanding an orifice; a muscle that dilates the parts on which it acts.

dilatory *adj* tardy; causing or meant to cause delay.—**dilatorily** *adv*.—**dilatoriness** *n*.

dildo *n* (*pl* **dildos**) an artificial penis used for sexual stimulation.

dilemma *n* a situation in which each of two alternative courses is undesirable; any difficult problem or choice.—**dilemmatic** *adj*.

dilettante *n* (*pl* **dilettantes, dilettanti**) a person who dabbles in a subject for amusement only.

diligence[1] *n* careful attention; assiduity; industry.

diligence[2] *n* (*formerly*) a French stagecoach.

diligent *adj* industrious; done with proper care and effort.—**diligently** *adv*.

dill *n* a yellow-flowered herb whose leaves and seeds are used for flavoring and in medicines.

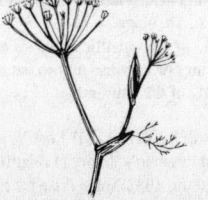

dillydally *vi* (**dillydallying, dillydallied**) (*inf*) to dawdle, loiter.

dilute *vt* to thin down, esp by mixing with water; to weaken the strength of. * *adj* diluted.—**diluter, dilutor** *n*.—**diluteness** *n*.

dilution *n* the act of diluting; a weak liquid.

dilution of equity *n* (*com*) a decrease in earnings from shares and a reduction in control experienced by existing shareholders in a company when new shares are issued to attract new shareholders.

diluvial, diluvian *adj* pertaining to, produced by, or resulting from, a deluge or flood, esp the Flood of the Bible.

diluvium *n* (*pl* **diluviums, diluvia**) (*formerly*) geological deposits caused by water action, drift.

dim *adj* (**dimmer, dimmest**) faintly lit; not seen, heard, understood, etc clearly; gloomy; unfavorable; (*inf*) stupid. * *vti* (**dimming, dimmed**) to make or cause to become dark.—**dimly** *adv*.—**dimness** *n*.

dim. *abbr* = dimension; (*Italian*) *diminuendo*, "becoming softer."

DIM *abbr* = Diploma in Industrial Management.

DiMaggio *n* Joe [Joseph Paul] (1914–99) American baseball player; member of the New York Yankees (1936–51); nicknamed "Joltin' Joe" and "The Yankee Clipper."

dime *n* a US or Canadian coin worth ten cents.

dimension *n* any linear measurement of width, length, or thickness; extent; size.

dimensional *adj* of or pertaining to dimension or magnitude; (*geom*) of or pertaining to (a specified number of) dimensions.—**dimensionality** *n*.—**dimensionally** *adv*.

dimerous *adj* (*flowers*) having two members in each whorl; (*insects*) having a foot composed of two parts.

dimeter *n* (a line of) verse of two measures, a measure being one or two feet, according to the meter.

dimin. *abbr* = diminutive; (*Italian*) *diminuendo*, "becoming softer."

diminish *vti* to make or become smaller in size, amount, or importance.—**diminishable** *adj*.—**diminishment** *n*.

diminished interval *n* (*mus*) a perfect or major interval reduced by one half step (semitone) by flattening the upper note or sharpening the lower one.

diminished seventh chord *n* (*mus*) a chord which covers a minor seventh diminished by one half step (semitone).

diminished triad *n* (*mus*) a minor triad in which the fifth is flattened (diminished), e.g., in the key of C major, c-e-g flat.

diminution *n* act or process of being made smaller; (*mus*) the shortening of note time values, so that a melody is played more quickly, usu at double speed.

diminutive *adj* very small. * *n* a word formed by a suffix to mean small (e.g., *duckling*) or to convey affection (e.g., *Freddie*).

dimity *n* (*pl* **dimities**) a light, strong, striped or figured, cotton cloth used for curtains, etc.

DIMM *abbr* (*comput*) = Double In-line Memory Module, a small circuit board containing RAM chips that increase the amount of memory available to a computer. *See also* **SIMM**.

dimmer *n* a switch for reducing the brightness of an electric light.

dimorphism *n* the quality of assuming, crystallizing or existing in two forms.—**dimorphic, dimorphous** *adj*.

dimple *n* a small hollow, usu on the cheek or chin. * *vti* to make or become dimpled; to reveal dimples.—**dimply** *adj*.

DIMS *abbr* = data and information management system.

dimwit *n* (*inf*) an idiotic person, a fool.—**dimwitted** *adj*.—**dimwittedly** *adv*.—**dimwittedness** *n*.

din *n* a loud persistent noise. * *vt* (**dinning, dinned**) to make a din; (*with* **into**) to instill by continual repetition.

dinar *n* the monetary unit of Albania, Algeria, Bahrain, Bosnia-Herzegovina, Iraq, Jordan, Kuwait and Yemen, Tunisia, Libya, Serbia, the Former Yugoslav Republic of Macedonia (FYROM) and Yugoslavia.

d'Indy *see* **Indy, Vincent d'**.

dine *vi* to eat dinner. * *vt* to entertain to dinner.

Dine *n* Jim [James] (1935–) American artist, noted particularly for collage work.

diner *n* a person who dines; a dining car on a train; a small, cheap eating place.

Dinesen *n* Isak [Baroness Karen Blixen] (1885–1962) Danish short-story writer whose autobiographical account of life on a Kenyan coffee farm, *Out of Africa*, was filmed in 1985.

dinette *n* a small area in a house for eating in.

DINFOS *abbr* = Defense Information School

ding *vi* to sound, as a bell, with a continuous monotonous tone. * *vt* to impress by noisy repetition. * *n* the ringing sound of a bell.

DIng *abbr* (*Latin*) = Doctor Ingeniariae, "Doctor of Engineering."

ding-dong *n* the sound of a metallic body produced by blows, as a bell; (*inf*) a violent argument. * *adj* characterized by a rapid succession of blows; (*insults, etc*) vigorously maintained. * *vi* to ring as or like a bell. * *vt* to assail with constant repetition; to repeat with mechanical regularity.

dinghy *n* (*pl* **dinghies**) a small open boat propelled by oars or sails; a small inflatable boat.

dingle *n* a small wooded hollow.

dingo *n* (*pl* **dingoes**) an Australian wild dog.

dingy *adj* (**dingier, dingiest**) dirty-looking, shabby.—**dingily** *adv*.—**dinginess** *n*.

Dinh Van *n* **Jean** (1927–) French jewelry designer noted for his simple, innovative shapes.

dining car *n* a restaurant car on a train.

dining room *n* a room used for eating meals.

dinkum *adj* (*Austral*) genuine, honest.

dinky *adj* (**dinkier, dinkiest**) (*inf*) small; of no consequence, unimportant; (*Scot*) neat and attractive, smart.

DINKY *abbr* = dual income, no kids yet.

dinner *n* the principal meal of the day; a formal meal in honor of a person or occasion.

dinner jacket *n* a tuxedo.

dinosaur *n* any of an order of extinct reptiles, typically enormous in size; (*inf*) a person or thing regarded as outdated.

dinothere *n* a huge, extinct animal like an elephant.

dint *n* (*arch*) a mark left by a blow, a dent; **by dint of** by force of. * *vt* make a dint in.

dioc. *abbr* = diocesan; diocese.

diocesan *adj* of or pertaining to a diocese; the bishop of a diocese.

diocese *n* the district over which a bishop has authority.

diode *n* a semiconductor device for converting alternating to direct current; a basic thermionic valve with two electrodes.

dioecious, diecious *adj* (*bot, zool*) having male and female organs respectively in separate individuals.

diogenite *n* a stony meteorite lacking in chondrules.

Diomedes *n* 1. (*Greek myth*) the king of the Bistones in Thrace, who fed his horses on the human flesh of strangers who entered his territories. 2. (*Greek myth*) one of the heroes at the siege of Troy.—*also* **Diomede**.

Dione[1] *n* (*Greek myth*) a female Titan, a daughter of Oceanus and Tethys.

Dione[2] *n* a satellite of Saturn, discovered in 1684.

dionysia *see* **bacchanalia**.

Dionysus *n* the Greek god of wine, also called Bacchus by the Greeks and the Romans.

Dionysius of Paris *see* Denis.

dioptase *n* a vitreous emerald-green ore of copper.

diopter *n* a unit for measuring the refractive power of a lens.

dioptric, dioptrical *adj* assisting vision by means of the refraction of light in viewing distant objects.

dioptrics *n* (*used as sing*) the area of optics dealing with the refraction of light.

Dior *n* **Christian** (1905–57) French couturier, who created the "New Look" of the late 1940s.

diorama *n* a miniature three-dimensional scene, esp in a museum; any small-scale model with figures; a device for producing changing effects using special lighting on a translucent picture.—**dioramic** *adj*.

diorite *n* a granite-like rock consisting of feldspar and hornblende.

Dioscuri *see* **Castor and Pollux**.

dioxide *n* an oxide with two molecules of oxygen to one molecule of the other constituents.

dip *vt* (**dipping, dipped**) to put (something) under the surface (e.g., of a liquid) and lift quickly out again; to immerse (e.g., a sheep in an antiseptic solution). * *vi* to go into water and come out quickly; to suddenly drop down or sink out of sight; to read superficially; to slope downward. * *n* a dipping of any kind; a sudden drop; a mixture in which to dip something; (*geol*) the angle of inclination of a plane, measured from the horizontal and perpendicular to the strike, esp a rock outcrop in which the orientation of the bedding or cleavage is measured.

dip., Dip. *abbr* = diploma.

DipAD *abbr* = Diploma in Art and Design.

DipAE *abbr* = Diploma in Adult Education.

DipAgr *abbr* = Diploma in Agriculture.

DipAgrComm *abbr* = Diploma in Agricultural Communication.

DipALing *abbr* = Diploma in Applied Linguistics.

DipAppSc *abbr* = Diploma in Applied Science.

DipArch *abbr* = Diploma in Architecture.

DipBA *abbr* = Diploma in Business Administration.

DipCD *abbr* = Diploma in Community Development.

DipCE *abbr* = Diploma in Civil Engineering.

DipChemEng *abbr* = Diploma in Chemical Engineering.

DipClinPath *abbr* = Diploma in Clinical Pathology.

DipCom *abbr* = Diploma in Commerce.

DipCOT *abbr* = Diploma of the College of Occupational Therapists.

DipCT *abbr* = Diploma in Corporate Treasury Management.

DipDS *abbr* = Diploma in Dental Surgery.

DipEd *abbr* = Diploma in Education.

DipEF *abbr* = Diploma in Executive Finance.

DipEH *abbr* = Diploma in Environmental Health.

DipEMA *abbr* = Diploma in Executive and Management Accountancy.

DipEng *abbr* = Diploma in Engineering.

DipEngLit *abbr* = Diploma in English Literature.

DipESL *abbr* = Diploma in English as a Second Language.

DipFD *abbr* = Diploma in Funeral Directing, National Association of Funeral Directors.

DipFS *abbr* = Financial Studies Diploma.

DipHE *abbr* = Diploma of Higher Education.

diphtheria *n* an acute infectious disease causing inflammation of the throat and breathing difficulties.—**diphtherial** *adj*.

diphtheritic, diphtheric *adj* of or like diphtheria; affected by diphtheria.

diphthong *n* the union of two vowel sounds pronounced in one syllable; a ligature.—**diphthongal** *adj*.

diphyllous *adj* (*bot*) having two leaves.

DipISW *abbr* = Diploma of the Institute of Social Welfare.

dipl. *abbr* = diplomatic; diplomatist.

DipLE *abbr* = Diploma in Land Economy.

diplegia *n* (*med*) paralysis on both sides of the body.

diploblastic *adj* (*zool*) with two germ layers.

diplodocus *n* (*pl* **diplodocuses**) an extinct reptile with a very long tail and neck and a small head.

diploe *n* the soft spongy tissue between the two layers of the skull.—**diploic** *adj*.

diploid *adj* (*biol*) (*cell*) having two of each chromosome in its nucleus.

diploma *n* (*pl* **diplomas**) a certificate given by a college or university to its graduating students; the course of study leading to a diploma; (*pl often* **diplomata**) an official document, a charter.

diplomacy *n* (*pl* **diplomacies**) the management of relations between nations; skill in handling affairs without arousing hostility.

diplomat *n* a person employed or skilled in diplomacy.

diplomatic, diplomatical *adj* of diplomacy; employing tact and conciliation; tactful.—**diplomatically** *adv*.

diplomatic corps *n* all the ambassadors at a particular capital, the corps diplomatique.

diplomatic immunity *n* the exemption from local laws and taxes accorded to foreign diplomats in the country where they are stationed.

diplomatist *n* a diplomat.

diplopia *n* (*med*) double vision caused by dysfunction in the muscles that move the eyeballs so that rays of light fall in different places on the two retinae.

DipLSc *abbr* = Diploma in Library Science.

DipMechE *abbr* = Diploma in Mechanical Engineering.

DipMetEng *abbr* = Diploma in Meteorological Engineering.

DipN *abbr* = Diploma in Nursing.

dipole *n* two equal and opposite electric charges or magnetic poles a small distance apart; a molecule in which the centers of negative and positive charge do not coincide; a directional aerial consisting of two metal rods.—**dipolar** *adj*.

dipper *n* a ladle; any of various diving birds.

DipPharmMed *abbr* = Diploma in Pharmaceutical Medicine.

DipPhil *abbr* = Diploma in Philosophy.

dippy *adj* (**dippier, dippiest**) (*sl*) eccentric; crazy.

dipso *n* (*pl* **dipsos**) (*inf*) a dipsomaniac.

DipSoc *abbr* = Diploma in Sociology.

dipsomania *n* a compulsive craving for alcohol.

dipsomaniac *n* a person with an uncontrollable craving for alcohol. * *adj* of or having dipsomania.—**dipsomaniacal** *adj*.

dipstick *n* a rod with graduated markings to measure fluid level.

DipSW *abbr* = Diploma in Social Work.

dip switch *n* (*comput*) a Dual In-line Package switch, one of a collection of small "on" and "off" switches used to select options on a circuit board without having to modify the hardware.

DipTEFL *abbr* = Diploma in Teaching English as a Foreign Language.

dipteral *adj* (*archit*) having a double row of columns, as a temple, etc. * *n* (*archit*) a peristyle with a double colonnade.

dipteran *n* any of a large order of insects including flies, mosquitoes, midges, having one pair of true wings and piercing or sucking mouthparts.

dipterous *adj* (*insects*) two-winged; (*seeds*) with appendages resembling wings.

DipTESOL *abbr* = Diploma in Teaching of English to Speakers of Other Languages.

DipTh *abbr* = Diploma in Theology.

DipTHP *abbr* = Diploma in Therapeutic Hypnosis and Psychotherapy.

diptych *n* a pair of paintings or carvings on two panels hinged together.

DipUniv *abbr* = Diploma of the University.

dir. *abbr* = director.

Dirac *n* **Paul Adrien Maurice** (1902–84) English physicist, who devised a mathematical formulation of Einstein's theory of relativity and predicted the existence of antimatter. He shared the 1933 Nobel Prize for Physics with Schrödinger.

Dirae *npl* (*Roman myth*) one of the names by which the Furies were known.

Dirce *n* (*Greek myth*) daughter of Helios, who was killed by a bull, and in the spot where she died Dionysus made a spring appear.

dire *adj* dreadful; ominous; desperately urgent.—**direly** *adv*.—**direness** *n*.

direct *adj* straight; in an unbroken line, with nothing in between; frank; truthful. * *vt* to manage, to control; to tell or show the way; to point to, aim at; to address (a letter or parcel); to carry out the organizing and supervision of; to train and lead performances; to command. * *vi* to determine a course; to act as a director. * (*mus*) a sign placed at the end of a line or page of old music that indicates the pitch of the following note or notes.—**directness** *n*.

direct costs *or* **prime costs** *npl* costs incurred by a company that can be directly traced to the production of a particular product or service.

direct current *n* an electric current that flows in one direction only.

direct debit *n* an order given to a bank by an account holder to pay regular amounts from his or her account to an organization or individual.

direction *n* management, control; order, command; a knowing or telling what to do, where to go, etc; any way in which one may face or point; (*pl*) instructions.

directional *adj* relating to direction in space; (*antenna*) transmitting in one direction only. **directionality** *n*.—**directionally** *adv*.

direction finder *n* a device used to locate the direction of incoming radio signals, used in navigation.

directive *adj* directing; authoritatively guiding or ruling. * *n* an order, instruction.

direct labor *n* workers in a company who are directly concerned with the production of a product or service.

directly *adv* in a direct manner; immediately; in a short while.

direct-mail selling *n* a form of direct marketing in which sales and advertising literature is sent directly to a series of selected potential customers.

direct marketing *n* a method of marketing in which the seller deals directly with the consumers rather than through a retailer.

direct materials *npl* materials that are directly incorporated in a particular product made by a company and so their cost is included in direct costs.

Directoire *adj* of or imitating the low-necked high-waisted dress or curving oriental furniture of the Directoire period in France (1795–99).

director *n* person who directs, esp the production of a show for stage or screen; one of the persons directing the affairs of a company or an institution.—**directorial** *adj*.— **directorship** *n*.

directorate *n* a board of directors; the position of a director.

directory *n* (*pl* **directories**) an alphabetical or classified list, as of telephone numbers, members of an organization, charities, etc.; (*comput*) the table of contents of a computer file system that allows convenient access to specific files.

direct tax *n* a tax paid by the actual person or organization on which it is levied.— **direct taxation** *n*.

Dire Dawa *n* a city in Ethiopia.

direful *adj* dreadful, dire.—**direfully** *adv*.

dirge *n* a song or hymn played or sung at a funeral; a slow, mournful piece of music.

dirham *n* a monetary unit of Morocco, the United Arab Emirates, Qatar, and Libya.

dirigible *adj* able to be steered. * *n* an airship.

dirk *n* a small dagger, esp as part of Scottish Highland dress.

dirndl *n* a woman's full skirt with a tight waistband.

dirt *n* filth; loose earth; obscenity; scandal. * *adj* made of dirt.

dirt-cheap *adj* (*inf*) very cheap.

dirty *adj* (**dirtier, dirtiest**) filthy; unclean; dishonest; mean; (*weather*) stormy; obscene. * *vti* (**dirtying, dirtied**) to make or become dirty.—**dirtily** *adv*.—**dirtiness** *n*.

dirty work *n* illegal or unpleasant activity, esp in behalf of another.

Dis *n* (*Roman myth*) a contraction of Dives, a name sometimes given to Pluto, god of the underworld.

dis. *abbr* = discipline; discount; distance; distant; distribute.

DIS *abbr* = Development Information System (UN); Diploma in Industrial Studies.

dis- *prefix* not, the reverse of; away from, apart; to deprive of.

DISA *abbr* = Defense Information Systems Agency

disability *n* (*pl* **disabilities**) a lack of physical, mental or social fitness; a physical or mental handicap.

disable *vt* to make useless; to cripple; (*law*) to disqualify.—**disablement** *n*.

disabled *adj* having a physical or mental handicap.

disabuse *vt* to free from a mistaken impression.

disaccord *vi* to disagree, be at variance. * *n* disagreement, incongruity.

disadvantage *n* an unfavorable condition or situation; loss, damage. * *vt* to put at a disadvantage.

disadvantaged *adj* deprived or discriminated against in social and economic terms.

disadvantageous *adj* causing disadvantage; unfavorable.—**disadvantageously** *adv*.

disaffected *adj* discontented, no longer loyal.—**disaffectedly** *adv*.— **disaffection** *n*.

disaffirm *vt* (*law*) to set aside, to reverse.—**disaffirmation** *n*.

disafforest *vt* to change from the legal state of forest to that of ordinary land; to remove forest from.—**disafforestation** *n*.

disagree *vi* (**disagreeing, disagreed**) to differ in opinion; to quarrel; (*with* **with**) to have a bad effect (on).—**disagreement** *n*.

disagreeable *adj* nasty, bad-tempered.—**disagreeableness** *n*.— **disagreeably** *adv*.

disagreement *n* refusal to agree; a difference; a quarrel or dispute.

disallow *vt* to refuse to allow or to accept the truth or value of.—**disallowance** *n*.

disannul *vt* (**disannulling, disannulled**) to annul completely; to make void.

disappear *vi* to pass from sight completely; to fade into nothing.— **disappearance** *n*.

disappoint *vt* to fail to fulfill the hopes of (a person).—**disappointed** *adj*.—**disappointing** *adj*.—**disappointingly** *adv*.

disappointment *n* the frustration of one's hopes; annoyance due to failure; a person or thing that disappoints.

disapprobation *n* disapproval, condemnation.

disapproval *n* the action or fact of disapproving; condemnation of what is wrong.

disapprove *vti* to express or have an unfavorable opinion (of).— **disapprovingly** *adv*.

disarm *vt* to deprive of weapons or means of defense; to defuse (a bomb); to conciliate. * *vi* to abolish or reduce national armaments.

disarmament *n* the reduction or abolition of a country's armed forces and weaponry.

disarming *adj* allaying opposition, conciliating; ingratiating, endearing.— **disarmingly** *adv*.

disarrange *vt* to make untidy; to disorganize.—**disarrangement** *n*.

disarray *n* disorder, confusion; undress. * *vt* to put into disorder.

disarticulate *vt* to separate, to take to pieces.—**disarticulation** *n*.— **disarticulator** *n*.

disaster *n* a devastating and sudden misfortune; utter failure.—**disastrous** *adj*.— **disastrously** *adv*.

disavow *vt* to deny, disclaim; to repudiate.—**disavowal** *n*.—**disavower** *n*.

disband *vt* to disperse; to break up and separate.—**disbandment** *n*.

disbar *vt* (**disbarring, disbarred**) to deprive (a barrister) of the right to practice.—**disbarment** *n*.

disbelief *n* a disbelieving; mental rejection of a statement or assertion; positive unbelief.

disbelieve *vt* to believe to be a lie. * *vi* to have no faith (in).—**disbeliever** *n*.

disburden *vt* to throw off a burden; to relieve of anything annoying or oppressive * *vi* to ease one's mind.—**disburdenment** *n*.

disburse *vt* to pay out.—**disburser** *n*.

disbursement *n* a paying out (of money); expenditure.

disc *see* **disk**.

disc. *abbr* = discount; discovered; discoverer.

discalced *adj* (*friars, etc*) barefoot, wearing sandals.

discard *vti* to cast off, get rid of; (*cards*) to throw away (a card) from one's hand. * *n* something discarded; (*cards*) a discarded card.

disc brake, disk brake *n* a brake in which two flat disks press against a central plate on the wheel hub.

discern *vt* to perceive; to see clearly.—**discernible** *adj*.—**discernibly** *adv*.

discerning *adj* discriminating; perceptive.—**discerningly** *adv*.—**discernment** *n*.

disch. *abbr* = discharged.

dis. ch. *abbr* (*chess*) = discovered check.

discharge *vt* to unload; to send out, emit; to release, acquit; to dismiss from employment; to shoot (a gun); to fulfill (e.g., duties). * *vi* to unload; (*gun*) to be fired; (*fluid*) to pour out. * *n* the act or process of discharging; something that is discharged; an authorization for release, acquittal, dismissal, etc.

disciple *n* a person who believes in and helps to spread another's teachings, a follower; (*with cap*) one of the twelve apostles of Christ.—**discipleship** *n*.

disciplinarian *n* a person who insists on strict discipline.

disciplinary *adj* of or for discipline.

discipline *n* a field of learning; training and conditioning to produce obedience and self-control; punishment; the maintenance of order and obedience as a result of punishment; a system of rules of behavior. * *vt* to punish to enforce discipline; to train by instruction; to bring under control.—**disciplinable** *adj*.— **disciplinal** *adj*.

disc jockey *n* (*inf*) a person who announces records on a program of broadcast music, or in night clubs or discos.

disclaim *vt* to deny connection with; to renounce all legal claim to.

disclaimer *n* a denial of legal responsibility; a written statement embodying this.

disclose *vt* to bring into the open, reveal.

disclosure *n* the act of revealing anything secret; discovery; an uncovering.

disco *n* (*pl* **discos**) (*inf*) an occasion when people gather to dance to recorded pop music; a night club or party, etc where this takes place; equipment for playing such music.

discography *n* (*pl* **discographies**) a classified list or survey of phonograph records or CDs.—**discographer** *n*.

discoid *adj* round and flat like a disk.—*also* **discoidal**. * *n* anything with the shape of a disk.

discolor *vti* to ruin the color of; to fade or stain.—**discoloration** *n*.

discombobulate *vt* to disconcert, upset, confuse.—**discombobulation** *n*.

discomfit *vt* to defeat; to rout; to frustrate; to thwart; to disconcert.

discomfiture *n* defeat; disappointment; confusion.

discomfort *n* uneasiness; something causing this. * *vt* to make uncomfortable; to make apprehensive or uneasy.

discommode *vt* to put to inconvenience.

discompose *vt* to disturb the calmness of; to ruffle.—**discomposure** *n*.

disconcert *vt* to confuse; to upset; to embarrass.—**disconcerting** *adj*.—**disconcertingly** *adv*.

disconnect *vt* to separate or break the connection of.—**disconnection** *n*.

disconnected *adj* not connected, detached; disjointed; incoherent.—**disconnectedly** *adv*.—**disconnectedness** *n*.

disconsolate *adj* miserable; dejected.—**disconsolately** *adv*.—**disconsolation** *n*.

discontent *n* lack of contentment, dissatisfaction (—*also* **discontentment**). * *adj* not content; dissatisfied; discontented. * *vt* to deprive of contentment; to dissatisfy.

discontented *adj* feeling discontent; unhappy, unsatisfied.—**discontentedly** *adv*.

discontinuance *n* a discontinuing or breaking off; interruption; (*law*) the termination of a suit by the plaintiff.

discontinuation *n* a discontinuing; discontinuance; a breach or interruption of continuity.

discontinue *vti* to stop or come to a stop; to give up, esp the production of something; (*law*) to terminate (a suit).

discontinuity *n* (*pl* **discontinuities**) a being discontinuous; lack or failure of continuity or sequence; a break or gap in a structure; (*geol*) a point at which the character of the earth alters abruptly; (*math*) a function that is discontinuous.

discontinuous *adj* not continuous, incoherent, intermittent; (*math*) of a function that varies discontinuously and whose differential coefficient may therefore become infinite.—**discontinuously** *adv*.

discord *n* lack of agreement, strife; (*mus*) a lack of harmony; harsh, clashing sounds.

discordant *adj* at variance; inharmonious; jarring; incongruous.—**discordance, discordancy** *n*.—**discordantly** *adv*.

discordant coast *see* **Atlantic-type coast**.

discordant drainage *see* **accordant drainage**.

discordant junction *n* a junction where a tributary falls steeply just before it joins a river.

discotheque, discothèque *n* a disco.

discount *n* a reduction in the amount or cost; the percentage charged for doing this; (*com*) the amount by which the market price of a financial security is below its par value; (*com*) a deduction from a bill of exchange when it is purchased before its maturity date. * *vt* to deduct from the amount or cost; to allow for exaggeration; to disregard; to make less effective by anticipation. * *vi* to make and give discounts.—**discountable** *adj*.—**discounter** *n*.

discount house *n* (*com*) a financial institution that specializes in the buying and selling of bills of exchange.

discount rate *n* (*com*) the interest rate at which future cash inflows and cash outflows associated with a particular investment projected are discounted in order to allow for the timing of these cash flows.

discount store *n* (*com*) a retail store, usu a self-service store, that routinely sells a range of standard products at discounted prices.

discountenance *vt* to refuse moral support to; to discourage, frown upon.

discourage *vt* to deprive of the will or courage (to do something); to try to prevent; to hinder.—**discouragingly** *adv*.

discouragement *n* the action or fact of discouraging; the state or feeling of being discouraged; something that discourages; a disheartening or deterring influence.

discourse *n* a formal speech or writing; conversation. * *vi* to talk or write about.

discourteous *adj* lacking in courtesy, rude.—**discourteously** *adv*.—**discourteousness** *n*.

discourtesy *n* (*pl* **discourtesies**) lack of courtesy or consideration; rudeness; an inconsiderate or rude act.

discover *vt* to see, find or learn of for the first time.—**discoverable** *adj*.—**discoverer** *n*.

discovert *adj* (*law*) (*single woman, divorcée, widow*) without a husband.—**discoverture** *n*.

discovery *n* (*pl* **discoveries**) the act of discovering or state of being discovered; something discovered; (*law*) a process obliging on the parties to an action to disclose relevant facts or documents.

discredit *n* damage to a reputation; doubt; disgrace; lack of credibility. * *vt* to damage the reputation of; to cast doubt on the authority or credibility of.

discreditable *adj* bringing discredit or disgrace.—**discreditably** *adv*.

discreet *adj* wisely cautious, prudent; unobtrusive.—**discreetly** *adv*.—**discreetness** *n*.

discrepancy *n* (*pl* **discrepancies**) difference; a disagreement, as between figures in a total.

discrepant *adj* inconsistent; not tallying.—**discrepantly** *adv*.

discrete *adj* individually distinct; discontinuous.—**discretely** *adv*.—**discreteness** *n*.

discretion *n* the freedom to judge or to choose; prudence; wise judgment; skill.

discretionary *adj* left to or done at one's own discretion.

discriminate *vi* to be discerning in matters of taste or judgment; to make a distinction; to treat differently, esp unfavorably due to prejudice.

discriminating *adj* judicious; discerning; discriminatory.—**discriminatingly** *adv*.

discrimination *n* prejudicial treatment of a person, minority group, etc based on sex, religion, race, etc; penetration, discernment.

discriminative *adj* serving to discriminate or distinguish; discerning; discriminatory.—**discriminatively** *adv*.

discriminator *n* one who or that which discriminates; (*electronics*) a circuit that converts a property of a signal into an amplitude variation.

discriminatory *adj* discriminating; showing prejudice or favoritism; biased.—**discriminatorily** *adv*.

dist. *abbr* = discount.

discursive *adj* wandering from one subject to another; digressive.—**discursively** *adv*.—**discursiveness** *n*.

discus *n* (*pl* **discuses, disci**) a heavy disk with a thickened middle, thrown by athletes.

discuss *vt* to talk over; to investigate by reasoning or argument.—**discussible, discussable** *adj*.

discussion *n* an argument; a debate; the airing of a question.

disdain *vt* to scorn, treat with contempt. * *n* scorn; a feeling of contemptuous superiority.

disdainful *adj* showing or feeling disdain; contemptuous; haughty.—**disdainfully** *adv*.—**disdainfulness** *n*.

disease *n* an unhealthy condition in an organism caused by infection, poisoning, etc; sickness; a harmful condition or situation.—**diseased** *adj*.

disembark *vti* to land from a ship, debark.—**disembarkation** *n*.

disembarrass *vt* to free from embarrassment; to relieve (of); to disentangle.—**disembarrassment** *n*.

disembody *vt* (**disembodying, disembodied**) to free (a soul, spirit, etc) from the body.—**disembodiment** *n*.

disembogue *vti* (**disemboguing, disembogued**) (*river etc*) to discharge, pour forth (its water).

disembowel *vt* (**disemboweling, disemboweled**) to remove the entrails of; to remove the substance of.—**disembowelment** *n*.

disenchant *vt* to disillusion.—**disenchantment** *n*.

disencumber *vt* to free from burden or hindrance.

disendow *vt* to deprive (a church) of endowments.—**disendowment** *n*.

disenfranchise *see* **disfranchise**.

disengage *vt* to separate or free from engagement or obligation; to detach, release.—**disengaged** *adj*.—**disengagement** *n*.

disentail *vt* to release from entail.—*also n*.

disentangle *vt* to untangle; to free from complications.—**disentanglement** *n*.

disenthrall *vt* to free from bondage, to emancipate.

disentomb *vt* to remove from a tomb.

disestablish *vt* to displace from a settled position; to sever (a church) from connection with the state.—**disestablishment** *n*.

disesteem *vt* to regard with disfavor, dislike. * *n* lack of favor or regard.

diseur *n* a reciter of monologs for entertainment.—**diseuse** *nf*.

disfavor *n* dislike; disapproval. * *vt* to treat with disfavor.

disfeature *vt* to disfigure.

disfigure *vt* to spoil the beauty or appearance of.—**disfigurer** *n*.

disfigurement, disfiguration *n* the act of disfiguring; a disfigured state; a thing that disfigures; a blemish, a defect.

disfranchise *vt* to deprive of the right to vote.—*also* **disenfranchise**.—**disfranchisement, disenfranchisement** *n*.

disgorge *vt* to emit violently from the throat, to vomit; to empty; to surrender (e.g., stolen property).—**disgorgement** *n*.

disgrace *n* a loss of trust, favor, or honor; something that disgraces. * *vt* to bring disgrace or shame upon.—**disgracer** *n*.

disgraceful *adj* causing or deserving disgrace, shameful.—**disgracefully** *adv*.—**disgracefulness** *n*.

disgruntled *adj* dissatisfied, resentful.—**disgruntlement** *n*.

disguise *vt* to hide what one is by appearing as something else; to hide what (something) really is. * *n* the use of a changed appearance to conceal identity; a false appearance.—**disguisedly** *adv*.—**disguiser** *n*.

disgust *n* sickening dislike; repugnance; aversion. * *vt* to cause disgust in.—**disgustedly** *adv*.

dish *n* any of various shallow concave vessels to serve food in; the amount of food served in a dish; the food served; a shallow concave object, as a dish antenna; (*inf*) an attractive person. * *vt* (*with* **out**) (*inf*) to distribute freely; (*with* **up**) to serve food at mealtimes; (*inf*) to present (e.g., facts).

dishabille *n* a partly clad state, undress.—*also* **deshabille**.

dish antenna *n* a microwave antenna used in radar, telescopes, telecommunications, etc having a concave reflector.

disharmonize *vt* to put out of harmony; to set at variance.

disharmony *n* (*pl* **disharmonies**) a lack of harmony between sounds; discord; a discordant situation, etc.—**disharmonious** *adj*.

dishcloth *n* a cloth for washing dishes.

dishearten *vt* to discourage.—**dishearteningly** *adv*.—**disheartenment** *n*.

disheveled *adj* rumpled, untidy.—**dishevelment** *n*.

dishonest *adj* not honest.—**dishonestly** *adv*.—**dishonesty** *n*.

dishonor *n* loss of honor; disgrace, shame. * *vt* to bring shame on, disgrace; to refuse to pay (e.g., a check).

dishonorable *adj* lacking honor, disgraceful.—**dishonorably** *adv*.

dishtowel *n* a towel for drying dishes.

dishwasher *n* an appliance for washing dishes; a person employed to wash dishes.

dishwater *n* water used for washing dishes; something that looks like or tastes like this.

dishy *adj* (**dishier, dishiest**) (*inf*) physically attractive, good-looking.

disillusion *vt* to free from mistaken ideals or illusions. * *n* the state of being disillusioned.—**disillusionment** *n*.

disincentive *n* a discouragement to action or effort.

disinclination *n* reluctance, unwillingness.

disinclined *adj* unwilling.

disinfect *vt* to destroy germs in.

disinfectant *n* any chemical agent that inhibits the growth of or destroys germs.

disinfection *n* the process of killing pathogenic organisms (not spores) to prevent the spread of infection.

disinformation *n* false information given out by intelligence agencies to mislead foreign spies.

disingenuous *adj* insincere, not candid or straightforward.—**disingenuously** *adv*.—**disingenuousness** *n*.

disinherit *vt* to deprive of the right to an inheritance.—**disinheritance** *n*.

disintegrate *vti* to break or cause to break into separate pieces.—**disintegrator** *n*.

disintegration *n* (*chem*) the process by which one or more particles is given off from the nucleus of an atom.

disinter *vt* (**disinterring, disinterred**) to take out of a grave; to bring out from obscurity, to unearth.—**disinterment** *n*.

disinterest *n* lack of partiality or bias. * *vt* to cease to concern (oneself).

disinterested *adj* impartial; objective.—**disinterestedly** *adv*.—**disinterestedness** *n*.

disjoin *vt* to separate. * *vi* to become detached.

disjoint *vt* to dislocate; to take to pieces. * *adj* (*math*) having no elements in common; (*obs*) disjointed.

disjointed *adj* incoherent, muddled, esp of speech or writing.—**disjointedly** *adv*.—**disjointedness** *n*.

disjunction *n* severance, disconnection (—*also* **disjuncture**); (*logic*) a compound proposition presenting alternative terms only one of which is true.

disjunctive *adj* disjoining; alternative; (*gram*) marking an adverse or oppositional sense; syntactically independent; (*logic*) presenting alternative terms.—**disjunctively** *adv*.

disk, disc *n* any flat, thin circular body; something resembling this, e.g., the sun; a cylindrical pad of cartilage between the vertebrae; a phonograph record; (*comput*) a storage device in a computer, either floppy or hard.

disk brake *see* **disc brake**.

disk cache *see* **cache**.

disk drive *n* (*comput*) a mechanism that allows a computer to read data from, and write data to, a disk.

diskette *n* (*comput*) a floppy disk.

dislike *vt* to consider unpleasant. * *n* aversion, distaste.—**dislikable** *adj*.

dislocate *vt* to put (a joint) out of place, displace; to upset the working of.

dislocation *n* the act of dislocating; an injury to a joint in which bones are displaced from their normal, respective positions; an imperfection in a crystalline structure; (*geol*) a displacement of stratified rocks, a fault.

dislodge *vt* to force or move out of a hiding place, established position, etc.—**dislodgment** *n*.

disloyal *adj* unfaithful; false to allegiance, disaffected.—**disloyally** *adv*.

disloyalty *n* (*pl* **disloyalties**) the state of being unfaithful; a disloyal act.

DISMAC *abbr* = digital scene-matching area correlation sensors.

dismal *adj* gloomy, miserable, sad; (*inf*) feeble, worthless.—**dismally** *adv*.

dismantle *vt* to pull down; to take apart.—**dismantlement** *n*.

dismast *vt* to deprive (a ship) of a mast or masts.

dismay *n* apprehension, discouragement. * *vt* to fill with dismay.

dismember *vt* to cut or tear off the limbs from; to cut or divide into pieces.—**dismemberment** *n*.

dismiss *vt* to send away; to remove from an office or employment; to stop thinking about; (*law*) to reject a further hearing in court; (*cricket*) to bowl (a batsman or side) out.—**dismissible** *adj*.

dismissal *n* the act of dismissing; a removal from office, etc.

dismissive *adj* rejecting; offhand.—**dismissively** *adv*.

dismount *vti* to alight from (a horse or bicycle); to remove from a mount or setting.

Disney *n* **Walt[er Elias]** (1901–66) American cartoonist and movie producer, the creator of Mickey Mouse, Donald Duck, etc.

disobedience *n* the withholding of obedience; a refusal to obey; violation of a command by omitting to conform to it, or of a prohibition by acting in defiance of it; an instance of this.

disobedient *adj* failing or refusing to obey.—**disobediently** *adv*.

disobey *vt* (**disobeying, disobeyed**) to refuse to follow the orders of.

disoblige *vt* to ignore the wishes of; to inconvenience.—**disobligingly** *adv*.

disorder *n* lack of order; untidiness; a riot; an illness or interruption of the normal functioning of the body or mind. * *vt* to throw into confusion; to upset.

disorderly *adj* untidy; unruly, riotous.—**disorderliness** *n*.

disorganize *vt* to confuse or disrupt an orderly arrangement.—**disorganization** *n*.

disorient, disorientate *vt* to cause the loss of sense of time, place or identity; to confuse.—**disorientation** *n*.

disown *vt* to refuse to acknowledge as one's own.

disp. *abbr* = dispensatory.

disparage *vt* to belittle.—**disparagingly** *adv*.—**disparagement** *n*.

disparate *adj* unequal, completely different.—**disparately** *adv*.—**disparateness** *n*.

disparity *n* (*pl* **disparities**) essential difference; inequality.

dispassionate *adj* unemotional; impartial.—**dispassionately** *adv*.—**dispassionateness** *n*.

dispatch, despatch *vt* to send off somewhere; to perform speedily; to kill. * *n* a sending off (of a letter, a messenger etc); promptness; haste; a written message, esp of news.

dispatcher, despatcher *n* one who dispatches; a person who schedules taxis, trains, airplanes, buses, etc; a person who directs the destination of police cars.

dispel *vt* (**dispelling, dispelled**) to drive away and scatter.

dispensable *adj* able to be done without; unimportant.—**dispensability** *n*.

dispensary *n* (*pl* **dispensaries**) a place in a hospital, a drugstore, etc where medicines are made up and dispensed; a place where medical treatment is available.

dispensation *n* the act of distributing or dealing out; exemption from a rule, penalty, etc.

dispense *vt* to deal out, distribute; to prepare and distribute (medicines); to administer.

dispenser *n* a person who dispenses medicines; a machine, etc, that dispenses measured quantities or units of something.

dispermous *adj* (*bot*) two-seeded.

dispersal *n* the act of dispersing; dispersion.

disperse *vt* to scatter in different directions; to cause to evaporate; to spread (knowledge); to separate (light, etc) into different wavelengths. * *vi* to separate, become dispersed.—**dispersedly** *adv*.

dispersion *n* a dispersing, or state of being dispersed; (*phys*) the separation of light into colors by diffraction or refraction; (*statistics*) the scattering of data about a mean. *See also* **diaspora**.

dispersion measure *n* (*phys*) a determination of how well a given prism or grating separates the wavelengths in, e.g., a spectrometer.

dispersive *adj* tending to disperse; producing dispersion.—**dispersively** *adv*.

dispirit *vt* to depress the spirits of; to dishearten; to render cheerless.

dispirited *adj* depressed, discouraged.—**dispiritedly** *adv*.

displace *vt* to take the place of, oust; to remove from a position of authority.

displaced person *n* a person who has become a refugee from his or her own country, e.g., due to war or famine.

displacement *n* the act of displacing; substitution; apparent change of position; the weight of water displaced by a solid body immersed in it; the distance moved by a particle or body in a given direction; a vector quantity.

display *vt* to show, expose to view; to exhibit ostentatiously. * *n* a displaying; an eye-catching arrangement, exhibition; a computer monitor for presenting visual information.

displease *vt* to cause offense or annoyance to.

displeasure *n* a feeling of being displeased; dissatisfaction.

disport *vt* to amuse or divert (oneself) * *vi* to display gaily.

disposable *adj* designed to be discarded after use; available for use. * *n* something disposable, e.g., a baby's diaper.

disposable income *n* the income that a person has available to spend after the usual deductions, such as income tax, social-security contributions and pension contributions, have been removed from his or her salary or wage.

disposal *n* a disposing of something; order, arrangement.

dispose *vt* to place in order, arrange; to influence. * *vi* to deal with or settle; to give, sell or transfer to another; to throw away.

disposed *adj* inclined (toward something).

disposition *n* a natural way of behaving toward others; tendency; arrangement.—**dispositional** *adj*.

dispossess *vt* to deprive, rid (of); to eject.—**dispossession** *n*.—**dispossessor** *n*.

dispraise *vt* to disparage; to censure. * *n* depreciation; a reproach.—**dispraisingly** *adv*.

disproof *n* a disproving or refuting; evidence that refutes.

disproportion *n* a lack of symmetry, a being out of proportion. * *vt* to render or make out of due proportion.—**disproportional** *adj*.—**disproportionally** *adv*.

disproportionate *adj* out of proportion.—**disproportionately** *adv*.

disprove *vt* to prove (a claim, etc) to be incorrect.—**disprovable** *adj*.

disputable *adj* likely to cause dispute, arguable.—**disputability** *n*.—**disputably** *adv*.

disputant *n* a person involved in a dispute.

disputation *n* an argument; an exercise in debate.

disputatious *adj* fond of argument, contentious.—**disputatiously** *adv*.—**disputatiousness** *n*.

dispute *vt* to make the subject of an argument or debate; to query the validity of. * *vi* to argue. * *n* an argument; a quarrel.

disqualify *vt* (**disqualifying, disqualified**) to make ineligible because of a violation of rules; to make unfit or unsuitable, disable.—**disqualifier** *n*.—**disqualification** *n*.

disquiet *vt* to trouble, disturb; to make uneasy or restless. * *n* disturbance; uneasiness, anxiety, worry; restlessness. * *adj* restless; uneasy; disturbed.—**disquieting** *adj*.

disquietude *n* restlessness; disturbance; a feeling, occasion, or cause of disquiet.

disquisition *n* a careful examination of a subject.

Disraeli *n* **Benjamin [1st Earl of Beaconsfield]** (1804–81) British statesman and novelist, Conservative prime minister (1868, 1874–80).

disregard *vt* to pay no attention to; to consider as of little or no importance. * *n* lack of attention, neglect.

disrelish *vt* to dislike.—*also n*.

disrepair *n* a worn-out condition through neglect of repair.

disreputable *adj* of bad reputation; not respectable; discreditable.—**disreputably** *adv*.

disrepute *n* disgrace, discredit.

disrespect *n* lack of respect, rudeness.—**disrespectful** *adj*.—**disrespectfully** *adv*.

disrobe *vti* to undress; to uncover.

disrupt *vti* to break up; to create disorder or confusion; to interrupt.—**disruption** *n*.

disruptive *adj* causing disruption.—**disruptively** *adv*.

diss. *abbr* = dissertation.

dissatisfaction *n* disapproval; discontent; something that dissatisfies.

dissatisfactory *adj* unsatisfactory.

dissatisfy *vt* (**dissatisfying, dissatisfied**) to fail to please, make discontented.

dissect *vt* to cut apart (a plant, an animal, etc) for scientific examination; to analyze and interpret in fine detail.—**dissection** *n*.—**dissector** *n*.

disseise, disseize *vt* to deprive of possession; to dispossess unlawfully.—**disseisor, disseizor** *n*.

disseisin, disseizin *n* the act of unlawfully dispossessing a person or an estate.

dissemble *vti* to pretend or to conceal (e.g., true feelings) by pretense.—**dissemblance** *n*.—**dissembler** *n*.

disseminate *vt* to spread or scatter (ideas, information, etc) widely.—**dissemination** *n*.—**disseminator** *n*.

dissension *n* disagreement, esp when resulting in conflict.

dissent *vi* to hold a different opinion; to withhold assent. * *n* a difference of opinion.—**dissenter** *n*.

dissentient *adj* disagreeing with the majority. * *n* a person who dissents.

dissepiment *n* (*biol*) a calcareous or membranous partition, a septum.

dissertate *vi* to hold forth, discourse.—**dissertator** *n*.

dissertation *n* a written thesis, esp as required for a university degree, etc.

disservice *n* an ill turn, a harmful action.

dissever *vti* to cut apart, to disunite.—**disseverance, disseverment** *n*.

dissident *adj* disagreeing. * *n* a person who disagrees strongly with government policies, esp one who suffers harassment or imprisonment as a result.—**dissidence** *n*.

dissimilar *adj* unlike, different.—**dissimilarly** *adv*.

dissimilarity *n* (*pl* **dissimilarities**) lack of similarity; a difference, distinction.

dissimulate *vt* to dissemble.—**dissimulation** *n*.—**dissimulator** *n*.

dissipate *vt* to scatter, dispel; to waste, squander (money, etc). * *vi* to separate and vanish.—**dissipater, dissipator** *n*.

dissipated *adj* dissolute, indulging in excessive pleasure; scattered, wasted.—**dissipatedly** *adv*.—**dissipatedness** *n*.

dissipation *n* dispersion; wastefulness; frivolous or dissolute living.

dissociate *vti* to separate or cause to separate the association of (people, things, etc) in consciousness; to repudiate a connection with.

dissociation *n* a dissociating or being dissociated; (*chem*) decomposition of a molecule into single atoms, etc; (*psychol*) the separation of an attitude, belief, etc, from the rest of the personality.

dissoluble *adj* soluble.—**dissolubility** *n*.

dissolute *adj* lacking moral discipline, debauched.—**dissolutely** *adv*.—**dissoluteness** *n*.

dissolution *n* separation into component parts; the dissolving of a meeting or assembly (e.g., parliament); the termination of a business or personal relationship; death; the process of dissolving; (*chem*) the dissolving of a substance in a liquid to form a solution in which all the material is evenly distributed.

dissolve *vt* to cause to pass into solution; to disperse (a legislative assembly); to melt; to break up (a partnership or marriage) legally, annul. * *vi* to become liquid; to fade away; to be overcome by emotion.—**dissolvable** *adj*.—**dissolver** *n*.

dissolvent *adj* able to dissolve. * *n* a substance that dissolves.

dissonance *n* a harsh or inharmonious sound; discord; lack of agreement; (*mus*) an incomplete or unfulfilled chord requiring resolution into harmony.

dissonant *adj* inharmonious; discordant; disagreeing; (*mus*) producing dissonance.—**dissonantly** *adv*.

dissuade *vt* to prevent or discourage by persuasion.—**dissuasion** *n*.—**dissuasive** *adj*.

dissyllable *see* **disyllable**.

dissymmetry *n* (*pl* **dissymmetries**) an absence or lack of symmetry; symmetry in opposite directions, like right and left hands.—**dissymmetrical, dissymmetric** *adj*.

dist. *abbr* = discount; distance; distant; distinguish; distinguished; district.

distaff *n* the stick on which wool for flax is wound for spinning; (*arch*) a woman or women.

distaff line *n* the female line of a family.

distal *adj* (*anat*) (of a muscle, bone, limb, etc) relatively distant from the center of the body or point of attachment.—**distally** *adv*.

distance *n* the amount of space between two points or things; a distant place or point; remoteness, coldness of manner; *n* (*phys*) the measurement of how far an object has traveled along a particular path; (*math*) the length of a line needed to join particular points. * *vt* to place at a distance, physically or emotionally; to outdistance in a race, etc.

distant *adj* separated by a specific distance; far off in space, time, place, relation, etc; not friendly, aloof.—**distantly** *adv*.

distaste *n* aversion; dislike.

distasteful *adj* unpleasant, offensive.—**distastefully** *adv*.—**distastefulness** *n*.

Dist. Atty. *abbr* = District Attorney.

distemper *n* an infectious and often fatal disease of dogs and other animals; a type of paint made by mixing color with egg or glue instead of oil; a painting made with this.

distend *vti* to swell or cause to swell, esp from internal pressure.

distensible *adj* able to be distended.

distension, distention *n* a distending or being distended; a swelling.

distich *n* (*pl* **distichs**) (*poetry*) a couplet.

distichous *adj* (*bot*) arranged in two rows on opposite sides of an axis.—**distichously** *adv*.

distill *vti* to treat by, or cause to undergo, distillation; to purify; to extract the essence of; to let or cause to fall in drops.

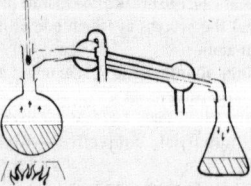

distillate *n* a product of distillation.

distillation *n* the conversion of a liquid into vapor by heat and then cooling the vapor so it condenses again, separating out the liquid's constituents or purifying it in the process; a distillate.—**distillatory** *adj*.

distiller *n* an individual or organization that distills, e.g., a brewery.

distillery *n* (*pl* **distilleries**) a place where distilling, esp of alcoholic spirits, is carried on.

distinct *adj* different, separate (from); easy to perceive by the mind or senses.—**distinctly** *adv*.—**distinctness** *n*.

distinction *n* discrimination, separation; a difference seen or made; a distinguishing mark or characteristic; excellence, superiority; a mark of honor.

distinctive *adj* clearly marking a person or thing as different from another; characteristic.—**distinctively** *adv*.—**distinctiveness** *n*.

distingué *adj* of superior manner, distinguished, striking.

distinguish *vt* to see or recognize as different; to mark as different, characterize; to see or hear clearly; to confer distinction on; to make eminent or known. * *vi* to perceive a difference.—**distinguishable** *adj*.

distinguished *adj* eminent, famous; dignified in appearance or manners.

Distinguished Flying Cross *n* a US military decoration for gallantry or heroism in flying operations.

distort *vt* to pull or twist out of shape; to alter the true meaning of, misrepresent.

distortion *n* a distorting or being distorted; a distorted feature; (*optics*) a faulty image; (*electronics*) an unwanted change in a signal, etc.—**distortional** *adj*.

distr. *abbr* = distributed; distribution; distribution.

distract *vt* to draw (e.g., the mind or attention) to something else; to confuse.—**distractingly** *adv*.

distracted *adj* bewildered, confused.—**distractedly** *adv*.

distraction *n* something that distracts the attention; an amusement; perplexity; extreme agitation.—**distractive** *adj*.—**distractively** *adv*.

distrain *vt* to seize and hold (goods or chattels) as security for payment of a debt.—**distrainer, distrainor** *n*.—**distrainment** *n*.

distrainee *n* a person who is distrained upon.

distraint *n* the act of distraining for debt; seizure.

distrait *adj* absent-minded, preoccupied.

distraught *adj* extremely distressed.

distress *n* physical or emotional suffering, as from pain, illness, lack of money, etc; a state of danger, desperation. * *vt* to cause distress to.—**distressingly** *adv*.

distressful *adj* suffering or causing distress.—**distressfully** *adv*.—**distressfulness** *n*.

distributary *n* (*pl* **distributaries**) a river branch that does not return to the main stream.

distribute *vt* to divide and share out; to spread, disperse throughout an area.—**distributable** *adj*.

distribution *n* a distributing or a being distributed; allotment; a thing distributed; diffusion; the geographical range or occurrence of an organism; classification; (*archeo*) a visual representation of an archeological feature or trait, which can cover a site, region, or country; (*law*) the apportioning of an estate among the heirs; (*com*) the marketing of goods to customers, their handling and transport; (*statistics*) the way numbers denoting characteristics in a statistical population are distributed.—**distributional** *adj*.

distribution channel *n* the network used in the distribution of a product from the manufacture to the customer.

distributor *n* an agent who sells goods, esp wholesale; a device for distributing current to the spark plugs in an engine.

district *n* a territorial division defined for administrative purposes; a region or area with a distinguishing character.

district attorney *n* a lawyer who is the State's prosecutor in a judicial district.

District of Columbia (DC) *n* a federal area whose boundary is that of Washington, the capital.

distrust *n* suspicion, lack of trust. * *vt* to withhold trust or confidence from; to suspect.—**distrustful** *adj*.—**distrustfully** *adv*.—**distrustfulness** *n*.

disturb *vt* to interrupt; to cause to move from the normal position or arrangement; to destroy the quiet or composure of.

disturbance *n* a disturbing or being disturbed; an interruption; an outbreak of disorder and confusion.

disturbed *adj* showing symptoms of emotional illness.

disulfate *n* a sulfate containing one atom of hydrogen, replaceable by a basic element.

disulfide *n* a sulfide in which two atoms of sulfur are contained.

disunite *vt* to divide, disrupt. * *vi* to separate.

disuse *n* the state of being neglected or unused.—**disused** *adj*.

disyllable *or* **dissyllable** *n* a word of two syllables.—**disyllabic** *or* **dissyllabic** *adj*.

DITB *abbr* = Distributive Industry Training Board.

ditch *n* any long, narrow trench dug in the ground. * *vt* to make a ditch in; (*sl*) to drive (a car) into a ditch; (*sl*) to make a forced landing of (an aircraft); (*sl*) to get rid of.

dither *vi* to hesitate, vacillate. * *vt* (*comput*) to combine small dots of different colors or shades to produce the effect of a new color or shade. * *n* a state of confusion; uncertainty.—**ditherer** *n*.

dithyramb *n* a hymn sung in honor of Dionysus, the Greek god of wine; an impassioned speech or writing.—**dithyrambic** *adj*, *n*.—**dithyrambically** *adv*.

dittany *n* (*pl* **dittanies**) an aromatic pink-flowered plant of the mint family, formerly considered to have magical properties.

ditto *n* (*pl* **dittos**) the same again, as above—used in written lists and tables to avoid repetition. * *vt* (**dittoing, dittoed**) to repeat.

ditto marks *npl* two small marks (") placed under an item repeated.

ditty *n* (*pl* **ditties**) a simple song.

diuresis *n* (*med*) an increase in urine production as a result of disease, drugs, hormone imbalance, or increased fluid intake.

diuretic *n* (*med*) a substance or drug that acts to increase the discharge of urine.—also *adj*.

diurnal *adj* occurring daily; of the daytime; having a daily cycle.—**diurnally** *adv*.

diurnal motion *n* movement taking place in the course of a day.

diurnal parallax *n* the apparent shift in position of a celestial object due to the rotation of the Earth.

diurnal range *n* a measure of the difference between maximum and minimum temperatures recorded in one 24-hour period.

div. *abbr* = divergence; diversion; divide; divided; dividend; divine; divisi; division; divisor; divorced.

Div. *abbr* = Divinity.

diva *n* (*pl* **divas, dive**) an accomplished female opera singer; a prima donna.

divalent *adj* (*chem*) having a valence of two.

divan *n* a long couch without back or sides; a bed of similar design.

dive *vi* (**diving, dove, dived**) to plunge headfirst into water; (*aircraft*) to descend or fall steeply; (*diver, submarine*) to submerge; to plunge (e.g., the hand) suddenly into anything; to dash headlong, lunge. * *n* a headlong plunge; a submerging of a submarine, etc; a sharp descent; a steep decline; (*sl*) a disreputable public place.

dive bomber *n* an aircraft designed to release its bombs during a steep dive for superior accuracy.—**dive-bomb** *vt*.

diver *n* a person who dives; a person who works or explores under water from a diving bell or in a diving suit; any of various aquatic birds.

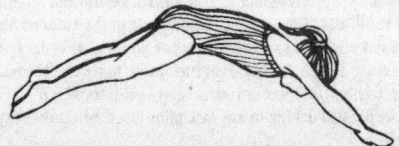

diverge *vi* to branch off in different directions from a common point; to differ in character, form, etc; to deviate from a path or course.—**divergence** *n*.—**divergent** *adj*.

divergent junction *or* **constructive boundary** *n* (*geol*) a boundary between two of the Earth's crustal plates that are moving apart because new material is being made.

divers *adj* (*arch*) various; sundry.

diverse *adj* different; assorted, various.—**diversely** *adv*.—**diverseness** *n*.

diversify *vt* (**diversifying, diversified**) to vary; to invest in a broad range of securities to lessen risk of loss. * *vi* to engage in a variety of commercial operations to reduce risk.—**diversification** *n*.

diversion *n* turning aside from a course; a recreation, amusement; a drawing of attention away from the principal activity; a detour when a road is temporarily closed to traffic.—**diversionary** *adj*.

diversity *n* (*pl* **diversities**) the condition or quality of being diverse; unlikeness; a difference, distinction; variety.

divert *vt* to turn aside from one course onto another; to entertain, amuse.

diverticulitis *n* inflammation of a diverticulum.

diverticulosis *n* the condition in which there are diverticula in the large intestine, occurring primarily in the lower colon.

diverticulum *n* (*pl* **diverticula**) a pocket or side branch off a passage or cavity in the body, esp the intestine.

divertimento *n* (*pl* **divertimenti, divertimentos**) a light, pleasant vocal or instrumental composition.

divertissement *n* an amusement; a recreation, a light entertainment, a ballet, etc, as an interlude between the acts of a play; an entr'acte; a short ballet incorporated into an opera or play; (*mus*) a short piece that includes well-known tunes taken from another source; (*mus*) a divertimento.

divest *vt* to strip of clothing, equipment, etc; to deprive of rights, property, power, etc.—**divestiture** *n*.

divestment *n* the selling off or closure by a firm of part of its operation.

divide *vt* to break up into parts; to distribute, share out; to sort into categories; to cause to separate from something else; to separate into opposing sides; (*parliament*) to vote or cause to vote by division; (*math*) to ascertain how many times one quantity contains another. * *vi* to become separated; to diverge; to vote by separating into two sides. * *n* a watershed; a split.—**dividable** *adj*.

divided highway *n* a road with traffic traveling in opposite directions separated by a central reservation.

dividend *n* a number that is to be divided; the money earned by a company and divided among the shareholders; a bonus derived from some action.

dividend warrant *n* the check that is issued to a shareholder in payment of a dividend.

divider *n* something that divides; a screen, furniture or plants, etc used to divide up a room; (*pl*) measuring-compasses.

divi-divi *n* (*pl* **divi-divis**) a South American tropical plant; its astringent husks used for dyeing and tanning.

divination *n* the art of foretelling the future or discovering hidden knowledge by supernatural means; intuitive perception.—**divinatory** *adj*.

divine *adj* of, from, or like God or a god; (*inf*) excellent. * *n* a clergyman; a theologian. * *vt* to foretell the future by supernatural means; to discover intuitively; to dowse. * *vi* to practice divination.—**divinely** *adv*.—**diviner** *n*.

diving bell *n* an open-bottomed chamber for working under water, supplied with compressed air.

diving board *n* a platform or springboard for diving from.

diving suit *n* a watertight suit with a helmet and air supply, used by divers.

divining rod *n* a forked twig used for dowsing.

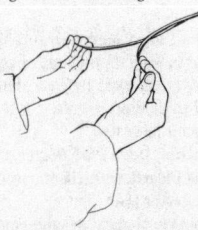

divinity *n* (*pl* **divinities**) any god; theology; the quality of being God or a god.

divisi *or* **divisé** *adj* (*mus*) divided: used to indicate that, where a part is written in double notes, performers should not attempt to play all the notes but should divide themselves into groups to play them.

divisible *adj* able to be divided.—**divisibility** *n*.

division *n* a dividing or being divided; a partition, a barrier; a portion or section; a military unit; separation; (*parliament*) a separation into two opposing sides to vote; a disagreement; (*math*) the process of dividing one number by another; (*mus*) a 17th-century type of variation in which the long notes of a melody were split up into shorter ones; (*mus*) long vocal runs used by composers such as Bach and Handel.—**divisional** *adj*.

divisionalization *n* the breaking-up of an organization into separate divisions, based on differences of product or services, geographical location, etc.

divisive *adj* creating disagreement or disunity.—**divisively** *adv*.—**divisiveness** *n*.

divisor *n* a number that is to be divided into another number (the dividend).

divorce *n* the legal dissolution of marriage; separation. * *vti* to terminate a marriage by divorce; to separate.

divorcé, divorcee *n* a divorced person.—**divorcée** *nf*.

divorcement *n* the act or process of divorcing.

divot *n* a lump of turf dug from the ground while making a golf swing, etc.

divulge *vt* to tell or reveal.—**divulgence** *n*.

divvy *n* (*pl* **divvies**) a portion. * *vt* (**divvying, divvied**) (*usu with* **up**) to share out.

Dix *n* **Otto** (1891–1969) German painter in the social-realist tradition of the *neue Sachlichkeit*. His work is meticulously detailed and realistic, his criticism of society undiluted, as in *The City* triptych (1927–28).

Dixie *n* the southern States of the US.

Dixieland *n* Dixie; a New Orleans jazz style.

DIY *abbr* = do-it-yourself.

dizzy *adj* (**dizzier, dizziest**) confused; causing giddiness or confusion; (*sl*) silly; foolish. * *vt* (**dizzying, dizzied**) to make dizzy; to confuse.—**dizzily** *adv*.—**dizziness** *n*.

DJ *abbr* = dinner jacket; disc jockey; District Judge; (*Latin*) *Doctor Juris*, "Doctor of Law."

Djadjat *n* (*Egypt*) a local council of elders and notables, advisers to the provincial governor as part of the legal system.

DJAG *abbr* = Deputy Judge Advocate General.

DJF *abbr* = Disc Jockeys' Federation.

DJI *abbr* = Dow Jones Index.

Djibouti[1] *n* a republic situated in northeast Africa.

Djibouti[2] *n* the capital city of Djibouti.

Djibouti Franc *n* currency of Djibouti.

DJS *abbr* = Doctor of Juridical Science.

dk. *abbr* = dark; deck; dock; duck (fabric).

dl *abbr* = deciliter.

dl *or* **d-l** *or* **d + l** *abbr* (*chem*) = dextro-levo.

DL *abbr* = Deputy Lieutenant.

D/L *abbr* = demand loan.

DLA *abbr* = Decorative Lighting Association; Defense Logistics Agency; Dental Laboratories Association.

DLAPS *abbr* = Defense Logistics Agency Publishing System

DLC *abbr* = Distance Learning Center.

DLCC *abbr* = Disabled Living Centers Council.

DLCO-EA *abbr* = Desert Locust Control Organization for Eastern Africa.

DLF *abbr* = Disabled Living Foundation.

DLIS *abbr* = Defense Logistics Information Service

DLIS *abbr* = Desert Locust Information Service.

DLit *or* **DLitt** *abbr* (*Latin*) = *Doctor Litterarum*, "Doctor of Letters" or "Doctor of Literature."

DLO *abbr* = dead letter office; Diploma of Laryngology and Otology.

DLP *abbr* = Diploma in Legal Practice.

DLPA *abbr* = Dry Lining and Partition Association.

DLR *abbr* = Docklands Light Railway.

DLRI *abbr* = Dalian Diesel Locomotive Research Institute.

dls *abbr* = debt liquidation schedule.

dls. *abbr* = dollars.

DLS *abbr* = Doctor of Library Science.

DLSA *abbr* = Defense Legal Services Agency.

DLSc *abbr* = Doctor of Library Science.

DLSC *abbr* = Defense Logistics Support Command.

DLSRT *abbr* = Dunkirk Little Ships Restoration Trust.

dm *abbr* = decimeter.

dm. *abbr* = decameter; decimeter.

DM *abbr* = Daughters of Our Lady of Mercy; Deputy Master; Deutschmark; Doctor of Medicine; Doctor of Music; diabetes mellitus; diastolic murmur.

DMA *abbr* = Dance Masters of America; Defense Manufacturers' Association; Defense Mapping Agency; direct memory access.

dmc *abbr* = direct manufacturing costs.

DMD *abbr* = (*Latin*) *Dentariae Medicinae Doctor*, "Doctor of Dental Medicine"; Doctor of Mathematics and Didactics; Duchenne muscular dystrophy.

DMDC *abbr* = Defense Manpower Data Center.

DMedRehab *abbr* = Diploma in Medical Rehabilitation.

DMet *abbr* = Doctor of Metallurgy.

DMF *abbr* = decayed, missing and filled (teeth); Disabled Motorists' Federation.

DMJ *abbr* = Daughters of Mary and Joseph.

DMJ(Clin) *or* **DMJ(Path)** *abbr* (*Brit*) = Diploma in Medical Jurisprudence (Clinical or Pathological), Society of Apothecaries of London.

DML *abbr* = data manipulation language.

DMO *abbr* = District Medical Officer.

DMRD *abbr* = Diploma in Medical Radio-Diagnosis.

DMRT *abbr* = Diploma in Radiotherapy.

DMS *abbr* = database management system; Defense Mapping School; Diploma in Management Studies; Doctor of Medical Sciences.

DMSA *abbr* = Domestic Manufacturing Stationers' Association.

DMT *abbr* = dimethyltriptamine.

DMU *abbr* = Diploma in Medical Ultrasound; (*Brit*) directly managed unit (hospital in National Health Service).

DMus *abbr* = Doctor of Music.

DMusCantuar *abbr* = the Archbishop of Canterbury's Doctorate in Music.

DMZ *abbr* = demilitarized zone.

DN *abbr* = debit note; Diploma in Nursing; (*Latin*) *Dominus Noster*, "Our Lord."

DNA *abbr* = deoxyribonucleic acid, the main component of chromosomes that stores genetic information; District Nursing Association.

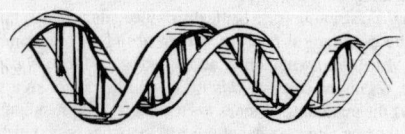

DNB *abbr* = Dictionary of National Biography.

DNC *abbr* = distributed numerical control.

Dnepropetrovsk *n* a city in Ukraine.

DNF *abbr* = did not finish.

DNFSB *abbr* = Defense Nuclear Facilities Safety Board.

DNH *abbr* = Department of National Heritage.

DNJC *abbr* = (*Latin*) *Dominus Noster Jesus Christus*, "Our Lord Jesus Christ."

DNPP *abbr* = (*Latin*) *Dominus Noster Papa Pontifex*, "Our Lord the Pope."

DNR *abbr* = do not resuscitate.

DNS *abbr* = Department of National Savings; Domain Name System (of the Internet).

DNSC *abbr* = Defense National Stockpile Center.

DNT *abbr* = dinitrotoluene.

do[1] *vt* (*pres t* **does, doing, did**, *pp* **done**) to perform; to work; to end, to complete; to make; to provide; to arrange, to tidy; to perform; to cover (a distance); to visit; (*sl*) to serve (time in prison); (*sl*) to cheat or rob; (*sl*) to assault; (*with* **in**) (*inf*) to kill; to tire out. * *vi* to act or behave; to be satisfactory; to manage. * *n* (*pl* **dos, do's**) (*inf*) a party; (*inf*) a hoax. *Do* has special uses where it has no definite meaning, as in asking questions (*Do you like milk?*), emphasizing a verb (*I do want to go*), and standing for a verb already used (*My dog goes where I do*).

do[2] *n* (*mus*) the spoken name for the first note of a major scale in tonic sol-fa.

do. *abbr* (*Italian*) = *ditto*, "the same."

DO *abbr* = deferred ordinary (shares); Diploma in Ophthalmology; Diploma in Osteopathy; District Office; District Officer; Doctor of Oratory; Doctor of Osteopathy.

D/O *or* **d.o.** *abbr* = delivery order.

DOA *abbr* = date of availability; dead on arrival.

DOAE *abbr* = Defense Operational Analysis Establishment.

dob *abbr* = date of birth.

Doberman (pinscher) *n* a breed of dog with a smooth, glossy, black-and-tan coat and docked tail.

DOBETA *abbr* = Domestic Oil Burning Equipment Testing Association.

dobra *n* the standard monetary unit of São Tomé e Principe.

Dobson *n* 1. **Frank** (1888–1963) British painter and sculptor, active in many of the artists' groups of the early 1920s. 2. **John** (1787–1865) English architect, whose notable works include Central Railway Station, Newcastle.

DObstRCOG *abbr* (*Brit*) = Diploma in Obstetrics of the Royal College of Gynaecologists and Obstetricians.

Dobzhansky *n* **Theodosius** (1900–75) Russian-born American geneticist.

doc *n* (*inf*) doctor.

doc. *abbr* = document.

DOC *abbr* = Department of Commerce; District Officer Commanding.

docent *n* a person licensed to teach in a university, but of lower grade and authority than a professor.

docile *adj* easily led; submissive.—**docilely** *adv*.—**docility** *n*.

dock[1] *vt* to cut short (an animal's tail); to deduct a portion of (someone's wages, etc).

dock[2] *n* a wharf; an artificial enclosed area of water for ships to be loaded, repaired, etc; (*pl*) a dockyard. * *vt* to come or bring into dock; to join (spacecraft) together in space.

dock[3] *n* an enclosed area in a court of law reserved for the accused.

dockage *n* the provision of accommodation for the docking of vessels; money paid for the use of a dock.

docker *n* a laborer who works at the docks.—*also* **longshoreman**.

docket *n* a label or document recording the contents of a package, delivery instructions, payment advice, or details of payment of customs duties; a list of lawsuits to be tried by a court. * *vt* to put a docket on (goods); to enter (a lawsuit) on a docket.

docking station *n* (*comput*) a hardware device into which a notebook computer can be connected to provide added facilities, e.g., disk drive, CD-ROM, etc.

dockyard *n* an area with docks and facilities for repairing and refitting ships.

Docomomo *abbr* = International Working Party for the Documentation and Conservation of Buildings, Sites and Neighborhoods of the Modern Movement.

doctor *n* a person qualified to treat diseases or physical disorders; the holder of the highest academic degree. * *vt* to treat medically; to patch up (machinery, etc); to tamper with, falsify; (*inf*) to castrate or spay.—**doctoral** *adj*.

doctorate *n* the highest degree in any discipline given by a university, conferring the title of doctor.

doctrinaire *adj* obsessed by theory rather than by experience. * *n* a person so obsessed.—**doctrinairism** *n*.

doctrine *n* a principle of belief.—**doctrinal** *adj*.—**doctrinally** *adv*.

document *n* a paper containing information or proof of anything; (*comput*) a piece of work created in a word-processing or database management program, or a spreadsheet. * *vt* to provide or prove with documents.—**documental** *adj*.

documentary *adj* consisting of documents; presenting a factual account of an event or activity. * *n* (*pl* **documentaries**) a non-fiction film.

documentation *n* (*comput*) books or disks that provide information and instruction in the use of a piece of hardware or software.

document reader *n* (*comput*) a hardware device that scans printed text, converting the text into digital signals. *See also* **scanner**.

dod *abbr* = date of death.

DOD *abbr* = Department of Defense.

dodder *vt* to tremble or shake through old age or weakness; to walk slowly and shakily.—**dodderer** *n*.—**doddery** *adj*.

DODDS *abbr* = Department of Defense Dependents' Schools.

dodecagon *n* a geometric figure with twelve angles and sides.

dodecahedron *n* a solid figure with twelve faces.—**dodecahedral** *adj*.

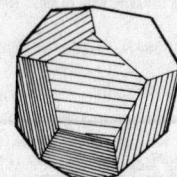

dodecaphonic *adj* (*mus*) relating to dodecaphony, the 12-note system of composition.

dodge *vi* to move quickly in an irregular course. * *vt* to evade (a duty) by cunning; to avoid by a sudden movement or shift of position; to trick. * *n* a sudden movement; (*inf*) a clever trick.—**dodger** *n*.

dodgem *see* **bumper car**.

dodgy *adj* (**dodgier, dodgiest**) (*inf*) cunning; risky.

DoDISS *abbr* = DoD Index of Specifications and Standards.

dodo *n* (*pl* **dodos, dodoes**) a large, clumsy bird, now extinct.

Dodoma *n* capital city of Tanzania.

Dodona *n* the site of an important oracle of ancient Greece, where the oracle of Zeus was given by the rustling of leaves on an oak tree.

doe *n* (*pl* **does, doe**) a female deer, rabbit, or hare.

DoE *abbr* = Department of the Environment.

DOE *abbr* = Department of Energy.

D.Oec. *abbr* (*Latin*) = *Doctor Oeconomiae*, "Doctor of Economics."

Doenitz *see* **Dönitz**.

doer *n* a person who acts, as opposed to thinking or talking; an active, energetic person.

does *see* **do**.

Doesburg *n* **Theo van** (1883–1931) Dutch painter; founder member of the De Stijl group. Examples of his work include *The Cow* (1916–17) and *Counter-composition in Dissonances no. XVI* (1925).

doeskin *n* the skin of a doe; a fine woolen cloth with a smooth finish.

doesn't = does not.

doff *vt* to take off (esp one's hat) in greeting or as a sign of respect.

D of L *abbr* = Duchy of Lancaster.

dog *n* a canine mammal of numerous breeds, commonly kept as a domestic pet; the male of the wolf or fox; a despicable person; a device for gripping things. * *vt* (**dogging, dogged**) to pursue relentlessly.—**dog-like** *adj*.

DOG *abbr* = Directory of Opportunities for Graduates.

dogcart *n* a light, two-wheeled carriage with cross seats back to back.

dog collar *n* a collar for a dog; (*inf*) a clerical collar.

dog days *npl* the warmest days of the year.

doge *n* (*formerly*) the chief magistrate in republican Venice and Genoa.

dog-eared *adj* worn, shabby; (*book*) having the corners of the pages turned down.—**dog-ear** *vt*.

dogfight *n* (*loosely*) a fiercely disputed contest; combat between two fighter planes, esp at close quarters.

dogfish *n* (*pl* **dogfish, dogfishes**) any of various small shark-like fish.

dogged *adj* tenacious.—**doggedly** *adv*.—**doggedness** *n*.

doggerel *n* trivial or worthless verse.

doggish *adj* like a dog, surly; (*sl*) showily stylish.—**doggishly** *adv*.—**doggishness** *n*.

doggo *adv* (*sl*) silent and still; **lie doggo** to lie low, stay hidden.

doggone *interj* (*sl*) darn, damn. * *adj* (*sl*) cursed, confounded. * *vt* (*sl*) to damn.

doggy *adj* (**doggier, doggiest**) of or like a dog; fond of dogs; (*sl*) showily stylish. * *n* (*pl* **doggies**) a pet name for a dog; a little dog.—*also* **doggie**.

doghouse *n* a dog kennel; **in the doghouse** (*inf*) in disgrace.

dogleg *n* something having a sharp angle or a sharp bend, as a road or fairway on a golf course. * *adj* crooked like a dog's hind leg.—*also* **doglegged**.

dogma *n* (*pl* **dogmas, dogmata**) a belief taught or held as true, esp by a church; a doctrine; a belief.

dogmatic, dogmatical *adj* pertaining to a dogma; forcibly asserted as if true; overbearing.—**dogmatically** *adv*.

dogmatics *n* (*used as sing*) the study of religious dogmas; doctrinal theology.

dogmatize *vt* to assert in a dogmatic manner.—**dogmatism** *n*.—**dogmatist** *n*.

do-gooder *n* a well-meaning person, esp if naive or ineffectual.—**do-gooding** *n*.

dog paddle *n* an elementary form of swimming in which the arms and legs paddle rapidly in the water.—**dog-paddle** *vi*.

dog rose *n* a prickly wild rose.

dog's age *n* (*inf*) a long time.

dogsbody *n* (*pl* **dogsbodies**) (*inf*) a drudge.

Dog star *n* the star Alpha Canis Majoris or Sirius.

dogtooth *n* (*pl* **dogteeth**) a canine tooth; (*archit*) a small conical ornament resembling a petal in Early English architecture.

dogtrot *n* a gentle trot; a covered passageway.

Dog Waltz *see* **Minute Waltz**.

dogwatch *n* (*naut*) one of two watches on board ship of two hours each, between 4 and 8 pm.

dogwood *n* any of several shrubs with clusters of small flowers.

DoH *abbr* (*Brit*) = Department of Health.

Doha (Ad Dawhah) *n* capital city of Qatar.

Dohnányi *n* **Ernö** *or* **Ernst von** (1877–1960) Hungarian composer and pianist; best known for his *Variations on a Nursery Theme* (for piano and orchestra).

Dohner *n* **Donald R.** (1907–44) American industrial designer, who was an influential teacher at the Carnegie Institute of Technology.

DoI *abbr* = Department of Industry.

DOI *abbr* = Department of the Interior; died of injuries.

doily *or* **doyley** *n* (*pl* **doilies** *or* **doyleys**) a small ornamented mat, laid under food on dishes, e.g., cakes.

doing *n* an action or its result; (*pl*) things done; actions.

doit *n* a small old Dutch copper coin; a thing of little value.

do-it-yourself *n* domestic repairs, woodwork, etc undertaken as a hobby or to save money.—*also adj*.—**do-it-yourselfer** *n*.

DOJ *abbr* = Department of Justice.

dol. *abbr* = (*Italian*) *dolce*, "sweet"; dollar(s).

DOL *abbr* = Department of Labor; Doctor of Oriental Languages.

dolabriform, dolabrirate *adj* (*bot*) hatchet-shaped.

Dolby *n* (*trademark*) an electronic noise-reduction system used in sound-recording and playback systems.

dolce *adj* soft. * *adv* (*mus*) gently.

dolciss. *abbr* (*Italian*) = *dolcissimo*, "very sweet."

dolcissimo *adj* (*mus*) "very sweet."

doldrums *npl* inactivity; depression; boredom; the regions of the ocean about the Equator where there is little wind.

dole *n* (*inf*) money received from the state while unemployed; a small portion. * *vt* to give (out) in small portions.

doleful *adj* sad, gloomy.—**dolefully** *adv*.—**dolefulness** *n*.

dolente *adj* (*mus*) "sorrowful."

dolerite *n* a dark-colored, basic, igneous rock composed of augite, feldspar and iron; basaltic greenstone.

dolichocephalic *adj* with a skull long in proportion to its breadth, long-headed.—**dolichocephaly** *n*.

Dolius *n* (*Greek myth*) an elderly slave of Penelope, wife of Odysseus.

doll *n* a toy in the form of a human figure; a ventriloquist's dummy; (*sl*) a woman.

dollar *n* the unit of money in the US, Canada, Australia, and many other countries.

Dollfus *n* **Engelbert** (1892–1934) Austrian statesman, who became leader of the Christian Socialist Party and was elected chancellor (1932–34).

dollop *n* (*inf*) a soft mass or lump; a portion, serving.

dolls. *or* **dols.** *abbr* = dollars.

dolly *n* (*pl* **dollies**) (*inf*) a child's word for a doll; a wheeled platform for a camera. * *vi* (**dollying, dollied**) to maneuver a camera dolly.

dolman *n* (*pl* **dolmans**) a loose robe; a short cloak.

dolman sleeve *n* a full, wide sleeve narrowing to a wristband.

dolmen *n* a prehistoric structure of two or more erect stones supporting a horizontal slab.

dolomite *n* a white mineral obtained from sedimentary rock; a sedimentary rock similar to limestone.—**dolomitic** *adj*.

Dolon *n* (*Greek myth*) a Trojan herald in the Trojan War.

dolor *n* grief, sorrow, distress.

doloroso *adv* (*mus*) sadly.

dolorous *adj* mournful, doleful.—**dolorously** *adv*.—**dolorousness** *n*.

dolphin *n* a marine mammal with a beak-like snout, larger than a porpoise but smaller than a whale.

dolphinarium *n* (*pl* **dolphinariums, dolphinaria**) a large pool or aquarium for keeping and displaying dolphins.

dolt *n* a dull or stupid person.—**doltish** *adj*.—**doltishly** *adv*.—**doltishness** *n*.

Dom *n* (*RC Church*) the title of certain dignitaries; a former Portuguese title of rank, as Don.

dom *abbr* = date of marriage.

dom. *abbr* = domestic; dominion.

Dom. *abbr* = Dominicus; Dominus.

DOM *abbr* = (*Latin*) *Deo optimo maximo*, "to God, the best and greatest"; (*Latin*) *Dominus omnium magister*, "God the master of all."

domain *n* an area under the control of a ruler or government; a field of thought, activity, etc.

domain name *n* (*comput*) the name referring to an Internet site, service, or computer and in the main representing a business or an organization.

domain name system *n* (*comput*) the means whereby the name of a website is converted into an Internet protocol number to enable a connection to be made to the appropriate site. * *abbr* DNS.

domain type *n* (*comput*) a part of an e-mail address that indicates what sort of organization is involved, e.g., "com" designates a company, "org" designates a non-profit organization.

Dom. Can. *abbr* = Dominion of Canada.

dome *n* a large, rounded roof; something high and rounded.—*also vt*.

dome *n* a rounded roof, convex in shape, which covers part or all of a building.

dom. econ. *abbr* = domestic economy.

domed *adj* having, or shaped like, a dome.

Domenichino *n* (1581–1641) Italian painter; from 1610, Rome's leading painter. He painted the *Life of St Cecilia* fresco (1611–14) in the Church of San Luigi dei Francesca, which is classical in style, and the baroque *Four Evangelists* (1624–8) in the Church of San Andrea della Valle.

Domenico Veneziano *n* (*c.*1400–61) Italian painter. His best-known surviving work is the *St Lucy* altarpiece (*c.*1445), with its strong perspectives and fully rounded figures.

domesday *n* the day of God's Last Judgment of mankind.—*also* **doomsday**.

Domesday Book *n* the record of William I's survey of England in 1086.

domestic *adj* belonging to the home or family; not foreign; (*animals*) tame. * *n* a servant in the home.—**domestically** *adv*.

domesticate *vt* to tame; to make home-loving and fond of household duties.—**domestication** *n*.

domesticity *n* home life; being domestic.

domestic science *n* the study of household skills; home economics.

domical vault *n* (*archit*) a vault shaped like a low dome on a square or polygonal base.—*also* **cloister vault.**

domicile *n* a house; a person's place of residence. * *vt* to establish, to settle permanently.—**domiciliary** *adj*.

domiciliate *vt* to domicile.—**domiciliation** *n*.

dominance *n* (*genetics*) the situation in which one particular allele or gene for a certain characteristic is dominant over another.

dominant *adj* commanding, prevailing over others; overlooking from a superior height. * *n* (*mus*) the fifth note of a diatonic scale; (*mus*) the reciting note of Gregorian chants.—**dominantly** *adv*.

dominate *vt* to control or rule by strength; to hold a commanding position over; to overlook from a superior height.—**domination** *n*.—**dominator** *n*.

domineer *vti* to act in an arrogant or tyrannical manner.—**domineeringly** *adv*.

Domingo *n* Placido (1941–) Spanish tenor, regarded as one of the finest modern operatic tenors.

Dominic *n* St (*c.* 1170–1221) Spanish monk; founded the Dominican Order of monks; canonized 1234.

Dominica *n* the most northerly of the Windward Islands in the West Indies.

dominical *adj* pertaining to Christ as Lord, or to Sunday.

Dominican Peso *n* currency of the Dominican Republic.

Dominican Republic *n* the eastern portion of the island of Hispaniola in the West Indies.

dominie *n* (*Scot*) a schoolteacher; (*inf*) a clergyman.

dominion *n* a territory with one ruler or government; the power to rule; authority.

Dominique *n* French interior design company, founded in 1922 by André Domin and Marcel Genevrière in Paris.

domino *n* (*pl* **dominoes, dominos**) a flat oblong tile marked with up to 12 dots; (*pl*) a popular game usu using a set of 28 dominoes; a loose cloak, usu worn with an eye mask, at masquerades.

Domino *n* Fats [Antoine] (1928–) American rhythm-and-blues and jazz pianist and singer whose songs include "Blueberry Hill."

DOMMDA *abbr* = Drawing Office Material Manufacturers' and Dealers' Association.

DOMO *abbr* = Dispensing Opticians' Manufacturing Organization.

DOMS *abbr* = Diploma in Ophthalmic Medicine and Surgery.

DOMSAT *abbr* = domestic communications satellite.

don[1] *vt* (**donning, donned**) to put on; to invest with; to assume.

don[2] *n* a head, fellow, or tutor at Oxford or Cambridge Universities; (*loosely*) any university teacher; a Mafia leader.

Don[1] *n* a Spanish title for a gentleman or nobleman.—**Doña** *nf*.

Don[2] *n* (*Welsh Celtic myth*) the Welsh equivalent of the Irish Danu; said to have been the daughter of Mathonwy and the wife of Beli. Her children include Gwydion, Gilfaethwy and Aranrhod.

Donald I (*d.* 862) king of Scots (858–862). The son of Alpin and brother of Kenneth I.

Donald II (*d.* 900) king of Scots (889–900). The son of Constantine I, he was the first king of both the Scots and Picts to be referred to as *ri alban* or king of Alba.

Donald III Bane (1031–1097) king of Scots (1093–1097). The sobriquet 'Bane' means 'fair'. He retreated to the Hebrides on the death of his father, Duncan I, at the hands of his rival, Macbeth.

Donald Breac (*d.* 642) king of Scots (*c.*635–642). The tenth king of Dalriada.

Donald Brothers *npl* Scottish fabric manufacturers, who employed notable designers of the 1930s.

donate *vt* to give as a gift or donation, esp to a charity.

Donatello *n* [Donato di Niccolò di Betto Bardi] (*c.*1386–1466) Florentine sculptor of the Renaissance, whose most notable work is the bronze statue of *David* (1430s).

donation *n* a donating; a contribution or gift, esp to a charity.

donative *n* a gift; largess, a donation. * *adj* given by donation.

Donati's Comet *n* a comet discovered in 1858 with a coma that produced a fountain effect.

done[1] *see* **do**.

done[2] *adj* completed; cooked sufficiently; socially acceptable; (*with* **for**) (*sl*) doomed; dead; exhausted; discarded.

donee *n* a person to whom a gift is made.

Donetsk *n* a city in Ukraine.

dong *see* **hao, trinh, xu**.

donga *n* in South Africa, a steep-sided gully produced by soil erosion, often the result of floods; in Australia, a circular depression left when the roof of a cave has collapsed.

Dongen *n* Kees van (1877–1968) Dutch painter, who from 1910 painted mainly nudes and society portraits, e.g., *Women on the Balcony* (1910).

Dönitz, Doenitz *n* Karl (1891–1980) German admiral and commander of the German navy (1943–45), who became head of the Nazi state following Hitler's suicide and surrendered to the Allies. He was tried for war crimes.

Donizetti *n* Gaetano (1797–1848) Italian composer of 75 operas, some serious, others comic; includes *Don Pasquale, Lucia di Lammermoor, Lucrezia Borgia*, and *La Favorita*.

donjon *n* the central tower of a castle, a keep.

donkey *n* (*pl* **donkeys**) a small animal resembling a horse.

donkey engine *n* a portable auxiliary engine.

donkey jacket *n* a thick waterproof jacket, esp worn by laborers.

donkey's years *npl* (*inf*) a very long time.

donkey-work *n* the groundwork; drudgery.

Donleavy *n* J[ames] P[atrick] (1926–) American-born Irish novelist whose works include *The Ginger Man*.

Donn (*Irish Celtic myth*) **1.** the god of death. **2.** one of the Sons of Mil Espaine. In terms of the invasion of Ireland by the Sons of Mil Espaine, he is better known as **Eber Donn**. **3** the name of the father of Diarmaid ua Duibhne.

Donna *n* a term of respect to a woman in Italy.

Donn Cuailgne *n* (*Irish Celtic myth*) the great brown bull of Ulster. Medb tried to get hold of it and caused a war between Ulster and Connacht. It was killed and torn to pieces Finnbhenach, the white-horned bull of Connacht,

Donne *n* John (1573–1631) English metaphysical poet and divine.

donnish *adj* (*inf*) resembling a university don.—**donnishly** *adv*.—**donnishness** *n*.

donor *n* a person who donates something; a person who gives his or her blood, organs, etc for medical use.

donor insemination *see* **artificial insemination**.

don't = do not.

donut *see* **doughnut.**

doodad *n* (*inf*) a small item whose name is lost or forgotten.

doodle *vi* to scribble aimlessly. * *vt* to draw (something) absent-mindedly. * *n* a meaningless drawing or scribble.—**doodler** *n*.

doom[1] *n* a grim destiny; ruin. * *vt* condemn to failure, destruction, etc.

doom[2] *see* **doum**.

doomsday *see* **domesday**.

door *n* a movable barrier to close an opening in a wall; a doorway; a means of entry or approach.

doorjamb *n* one of the two vertical sides of a door frame; a doorpost.

doorkeeper *n* a person guarding a door.

doorman *n* (*pl* **doormen**) a uniformed attendant stationed at the entrance to large hotels, offices, etc.

doormat *n* a mat placed at the entrance to a doorway for wiping one's feet; (*inf*) a submissive or easily bullied person.

doornail *n* (*formerly*) a large nail with which doors were studded; **dead as a door-nail** most certainly dead.

doorplate *n* a plate with the name of the occupant of a building.

doorpost *n* the straight vertical side-post of a door, jamb.

doorstop *n* a device for preventing a door from moving or fixed to the bottom of a door to prevent it hitting a wall when opening, etc.

doorway *n* an opening in a wall, etc filled by a door.

dopa *n* an amino acid compound that is a precursor of dopamine and noradrenaline.

dopamine *n* a catecholamine derived from dopa and an intermediate in the synthesis of noradrenaline found mainly in the basal ganglia of the brain. A deficiency is typical in Parkinsonism.

dope *n* a thick pasty substance used for lubrication; (*inf*) any illegal drug, esp cannabis; (*sl*) a stupid person; (*sl*) information. * *vt* to treat with dope. * *vi* to take addictive drugs.

dopey, dopy *adj* (**dopier, dopiest**) (*sl*) stupid; (*inf*) half asleep.—**dopiness** *n*.

doppelgänger, doppelganger *n* a ghostly double of a living person.

doppio *adj, adv* (*mus*) double, as in *doppio movimento*, meaning "twice as fast."

Doppler effect *n* (*phys*) a change in the apparent frequency of a wave experienced if the source of the wave is moving.

DOpt *abbr* = Diploma in Ophthalmic Optics.

DORA *abbr* (*Brit*) = Defence of the Realm Act.

Dorcas *n* (*Bible*) a female disciple widely known for her acts of charity. After she died, the Christians sent for Peter who prayed and raised her to life.

Doré *n* **Gustave** (1832–83) French sculptor, painter, and illustrator.

Dorian *adj* of or relating to an early Greek race that overthrew the Mycenean civilization. * *n* a member of that race.

Dorian mode *n* (*mus*) a term applied to the ascending scale that is played on the white keys of a piano beginning at D.

Doric *adj* of the Dorians or their dialect; of or belonging to the oldest and simplest style of Greek architecture. * *n* the dialect of the Dorians; any broad dialect.

Doris *n* in ancient times, a small, mountainous region of northern Greece, at one time the home of the Dorians.

dormant *adj* sleeping; quiet, as if asleep; inactive.—**dormancy** *n*.

dormer *n* an upright window that projects from a sloping roof.

dormitory *n* (*pl* **dormitories**) a large room with many beds, as in a boarding school.

dormitory town *n* a town the majority of whose residents work elsewhere.

dormouse *n* (*pl* **dormice**) a small mouse-like creature that hibernates in winter.

Dorn *n* **Marion Victoria** (1899–1964) American-born fabric designer, who was the best-known carpet designer in the UK by the 1930s.

Dorner *n* **Marie-Christine** (1960–) French furniture designer, born in Strasbourg and trained in Paris.

Dornoni *n* a city in Comoros.

dorp *n* (*South African*) a small town.

DORRA *abbr* = DLA Office of Operations Research and Resource Analysis

dorsal *adj* of, on, or near the back; (*med*) relating to the posterior part of an organ.—**dorsally** *adv*.

dorsiventral *adj* (*leaves*) having a differentiated back and front.

DOrth *abbr* = Diploma in Orthoptics.

DOrthRCSEdin *abbr* (*Brit*) = Diploma in Orthodontics, Royal College of Surgeons of Edinburgh.

DOrthRCSEng *abbr* (*Brit*) = Diplomate in Orthodontics, Royal College of Surgeons of England.

Dortmund *n* a city in Germany.

Dorus *n* (*Greek myth*) the ancestor of the Dorians.

dory[1] *n* (*pl* **dories**) a light, flat-bottomed boat with a sharp bow and high sides.

dory[2] *n* (*pl* **dories**) an edible, yellow seafish.—*also* **John Dory**.

DOS *abbr* = Department of State; (*comput*) Disk Operating System; Doctor of Optical Science.

dosage *n* the administration of a medicine in doses; the size of a dose; the operation of dosing.

dose *n* the amount of medicine, radiation, etc administered at one time; a part of an experience; (*sl*) a sexually transmitted disease. * *vt* to administer a dose of medicine to.

Dos Passos *n* **John** (1896–1970) American novelist, whose masterpiece is his great trilogy of American life, *U.S.A.*

doss *vi* (*Brit*) to sleep, esp in a dosshouse.

dossal, dossel *n* a hanging of silk or damask at the back and sides of an altar.

dosseret *n* (*archit*) a four-faced impost block placed on top of an abacus before the arch above.

dosshouse *n* (*Brit*) a cheap lodging house.

Dossi *n* **Dosso** (c. 1490–1542) Italian painter. His best-known work, *Circe*, which is in Rome, is a landscape peopled by magnificently dressed inhabitants.

dossier *n* a collection of documents about a subject or person, a file.

Dostoyevsky *n* **Fyodor Mikhailovich** (1821–81) Russian novelist, whose novels include *Crime and Punishment*.

dot *n* a small, round speck, a point; the short signal in Morse code. * *vt* (**dotting, dotted**) to mark with a dot; to scatter about.—**dotter** *n*.

DoT *abbr* (*Brit*) = Department of Tourism; Department of Transport.

DOT *abbr* = Department of Trade; Department of Transportation

dotage *n* weakness and infirmity caused by old age.

dotard *n* a person in his or her dotage.

dote *vi* (*with* **on** *or* **upon**) to show excessive affection.—**doter** *n*.

dot matrix printer *n* (*comput*) a printer in which each printed character is formed by pins selected from a rectangular array.

dot pitch *n* (*comput*) a measure of the resolution of computer screens or printers. The smaller the dot pitch the sharper the image that is displayed.

dots per inch *npl* (*comput*) a measure of the resolution of a screen or printer. The more dots per inch that the computer can display or print the higher the resolution. * *abbr* dpi.

dotted *see* **dot**.

dotterel, dottrel *n* a small plover of Europe and Asia, now rare; a similar Australian bird.

dottle *n* a remnant of tobacco left in a smoked pipe.

dotty *adj* (**dottier, dottiest**) (*inf*) eccentric, slightly mad.—**dottily** *adv*.—**dottiness** *n*.

Dou *n* **Gerrit** (1613–75) Dutch painter who studied with Rembrandt, on some of whose works he may have collaborated, e.g., *The Blind Tobit and his Wife Anne* (c. 1630).

Douala *n* a city in Cameroon.

double *adj* twice as large, as strong, etc; designed or intended for two; made of two similar parts; having two meanings, characters, etc; (*flower*) having more than one circle of petals; (*mus*) pertaining to certain instruments that are built an octave lower than normal; denoting a type of variation found in 17th-century French instrumental music in which melody notes are embellished with ornamentation. * *adv* twice; in twos. * *n* a number or amount that is twice as much; a person or thing identical to another; a person closely resembling an actor and who takes his or her place to perform stunts, etc in a movie; (*pl*) a game between two pairs of players. * *vti* to make or become twice as much or as many; to fold, to bend; to bend sharply backward; to sail around; to have an additional purpose.—**doubly** *adv*.

double agent *n* a spy secretly acting for two governments at the same time.

double ax *n* (*archeo*) an ax with a double cutting edge and a shaft hole through the center of the ax head.

double-barreled *adj* (*gun*) having two barrels; (*surname*) having two parts; (*question*) serving a double purpose.

double bass *n* the largest instrument of the violin family.—**double bassist** *n*.

double boiler *n* two pots fitting into each other so that the contents of the upper are cooked while boiling in the lower.

double-breasted *adj* (*suit*) having one half of the front overlapping the other.

double-click *vti* (*comput*) to click (the mouse button) twice in quick succession to select and open a program or file.

double counterpoint *n* (*mus*) counterpoint in which the two parts can change places, i.e., the higher can become the lower and vice versa.

double cream *n* cream with a high fat content.

double-cross *vt* to betray (an associate), cheat. * **double cross** *n*.—**double-crosser** *n*.

double-dealing *n* treachery, deceit.—**double-dealer** *n*.

double decomposition *n* (*chem*) a chemical reaction between two substances that results in their breakdown and two new substances being formed from the parts.

double-density disk *n* (*comput*) a floppy disk that can store approximately 720 kilobytes of data.

double-edged *adj* acting in two ways; (*remarks*) having two possible meanings (e.g., well-meaning or malicious).

double entendre *n* a word or phrase with two meanings, one of which is usu indecent.

double entry *n* (*bookkeeping*) a system where each transaction is entered as a debit in one account and a credit in another.—**double-entry** *adj*.

double-faced *adj* having two faces; hypocritical.

double fugue *n* (*mus*) a fugue with two subjects. In one type of double fugue both subjects are introduced at the start; in another type the second subject appears after the first and the two are eventually combined.

double glazing *n* windows with two layers of glass with an air space between designed to provide thermal and sound insulation.

double-jointed *adj* having joints that allow the limbs, figures, etc an unusual degree of flexibility.

double-park *vt* to park alongside a car which is already parked beside the curb.

double-quick *adj, adv* very quick. * *vti* to march quickly.

double-sided disk *n* (*comput*) a floppy disk with both surfaces available for storage of data.

double standard *n* a principle that is applied more strictly to one person or group than to another.

doublet *n* (*formerly*) a man's close-fitting jacket; one of a pair of similar things.

double taxation *n* taxation on income and profit in more than one country, the country in which they are earned and the country to which the income and profit is remitted.

doublethink *n* a belief in two conflicting ideas, principles, etc.

doubleton *n* two cards only of a suit (in a player's hand).

double whole note *n* (*mus*) the longest note.—*also* **breve**.

doubloon *n* an old Spanish gold coin.

doubt *vi* to be uncertain or undecided. * *vt* to hold in doubt; to distrust; to be suspicious of. * *n* uncertainty; (*often pl*) lack of confidence in something, distrust.—**doubter** *n*.

doubtful *adj* feeling doubt; uncertain; suspicious.—**doubtfully** *adv*.—**doubtfulness** *adv*.

doubtful debts *npl* money that is owed to a company but that it is unlikely ever to receive.

doubtless *adv* no doubt; probably. * *adj* assured; certain.—**doubtlessly** *adv*.—**doubtlessness** *n*.

douce *adj* (*Scot*) sober; sedate; prudent; modest.

Doucet *n* **Jacques** (1853–1929) French couturier and patron of the arts, who encouraged Paul Poiret.

douceur *n* a gift for services rendered, or to secure a favor; a bribe.

douche *n* a jet of water directed on or into a part of the body; a device for applying this. * *vt* to cleanse or treat with a douche.

dough *n* a mixture of flour and water, milk, etc used to make bread, pastry, or cake; (*inf*) money.

doughboy *n* a boiled dumpling; (*sl*) a soldier.

doughnut *n* a small, fried, usu ring-shaped, cake.—*also* **donut**.

doughty *adj* (**doughtier, doughtiest**) valiant; strong.—**doughtily** *adv*.—**doughtiness** *n*.

doughy *adj* (**doughier, doughiest**) soft, like dough.—**doughiness** *n*.

Douglas *n* 1. **Kirk** (1916–) American movie actor, whose movies include *Spartacus* (1960). 2. **Michael** (1944–) American movie actor and son of Kirk Douglas, whose movies include *Wall Street* (1987), which earned him An academy Award.

Douglas *n* **Lord Alfred** (1870–1945) English poet, whose homosexual relationship with Oscar Wilde led to the latter's imprisonment.

Douglas-Home *n* **Sir Alec [Baron Home of the Hirsel]** (1903–95) Scottish Conservative politician who succeeded Harold Macmillan as British prime minister.

doum, doom *n* an Egyptian palm tree.

dour *adj* stern; sullen; grim.—**dourly** *adv*.—**dourness** *n*.

douse *vt* to plunge into or soak with water; to put out, extinguish.

DOV *abbr* = double oil of vitriol, sulfuric acid.

dove[1] *see* **dive**.

dove[2] *n* a small bird of the pigeon family; (*politics, diplomacy*) an advocate of peace or a peaceful policy.

Dove *n* **Arthur Garfield** (1880–1946) American painter. The development of his style is comparable with the abstract art of his contemporary, Kandinsky.

dovecote, dovecot *n* a shelter and breeding place for domesticated pigeons.

Dover *n* the capital city of Delaware, a state of the USA.

dovetail *n* a wedge-shaped joint used in woodwork. * *vt* to fit or combine together.

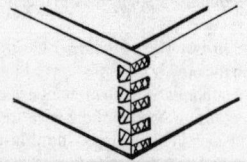

DOW *abbr* = died of wounds.

dowager *n* a widow possessing property or title from her husband; (*inf*) a dignified elderly woman.

dowdy *adj* (**dowdier, dowdiest**) poorly dressed, not stylish.—**dowdily** *adv*.—**dowdiness** *n*.

dowel *n* a headless wooden or metal pin used for fastening wood or stone. * *vt* (**doweling, doweled**) to fasten with dowels.

dower *n* a widow's share of her husband's estate.

Dow Jones Industrial Average *n* an index of share prices that is issued by Dow Jones & Co, an American firm that supplies financial information, and is used on the New York Stock Exchange.

Dowland *n* 1. **John** (1563–1626) English composer and lute player, who is now considered to be a great and innovative composer of songs. 2. **Robert Dowland** (*c*.1585–1641) noted English lutenist and composer and son of John Dowland.

down[1] *n* soft, fluffy feathers or fine hairs.

down[2] *adv* toward or in a lower physical position; to a lying or sitting position; toward or to the ground, floor, or bottom; to a source or hiding place; to or in a lower status or in a worse condition; from an earlier time; in cash; to or in a state of less activity. * *adj* occupying a low position, esp lying on the ground; depressed, dejected. * *prep* in a descending direction in, on, along, or through. * *n* a low period (as in activity, emotional life, or fortunes); (*inf*) a dislike or prejudice. * *vti* to go or cause to go or come down; to defeat; to swallow.

down[3] *n* (*usu pl*) (*Brit*) a tract of bare hilly land used for pasturing sheep; banks or rounded hillocks of sand.

downbeat *n* (*mus*) the first beat in the bar, the downward gesture of a conductor's baton. * *adj* (*inf*) dismal; relaxed.

downcast *adj* dejected; (*eyes*) directed downward.

downer *n* (*sl*) a depressant drug, esp a barbiturate; a depressing experience or situation.

downfall *n* a sudden fall (from power, etc); a sudden or heavy fall of rain or snow.

downgrade *n* a descending slope. * *vt* to reduce or lower in rank or position; to disparage.

download *vti* (*comput*) to copy (a file) from an on-line information service or from another computer to your computer. *See also* **upload**.

down payment *n* a deposit.

downpour *n* a heavy fall of rain.

downright *adj* frank; absolute. * *adv* thoroughly.

downscale, down-market *adj* (*goods, services*) of inferior quality.

downside *n* the less appealing or advantageous aspect of something.

downsize *vt* to produce a smaller version of (e.g., a car); to reduce the numbers in (a workforce) by means of redundancy.

Down's syndrome *n* a chromosomal abnormality resulting in a flat face, slanting eyes and mental retardation.

downstage *adv* to the front of the stage.

downstairs *adv* to or on a lower floor. * *adj* on the first floor or a lower floor. * *n* (*used as sing or pl*) the lower part of a house, the first floor.

downtime *n* the period of time during which a computer or piece of machinery is not operational.

down-to-earth *adj* practical, sensible.

downtown *n* the main business district of a town or city.—*also adj*.

downtrodden *adj* oppressed, trampled underfoot.

downturn *n* a decline in (economic) activity or prosperity.

down under *n* (*inf*) Australia or New Zealand.

downward *adj* moving from a higher to a lower level, position, or condition. * *adv* toward a lower place, position, etc; from an earlier time to a later.

downwind *adv* in the direction the wind is blowing.—*also adj*.

downy *adj* (**downier, downiest**) like, covered with, or made of, down.

dowry *n* (*pl* **dowries**) the money or possessions that a woman brings to her husband at marriage.

dowse *vi* to search for water, treasure, etc with a divining rod.—**dowser** *n*.

doxology *n* (*pl* **doxologies**) a hymn of praise to God.

doxy *n* (*pl* **doxies**) (*arch*) a sweetheart, a prostitute.

doyen *n* a senior member of a group; an expert in a field; the oldest example of a category.—**doyenne** *nf*.

Doyle *n* **Sir Arthur Conan** (1859–1930) Scottish writer and physician; creator of Sherlock Holmes.

doyley *see* **doily**.

D'Oyly Carte *n* **Richard** (1844–1901) English impresario, who brought together Gilbert and Sullivan and founded the D'Oyly Carte Opera Company to perform their operas, for which he built the Savoy Theatre in London.

doz. *abbr* = dozen(s).

doze *vi* to sleep lightly. * *n* a light sleep, a nap.—**dozer** *n*.

dozen *n* a group of twelve.—**dozenth** *adj*.

dozy *adj* (**dozier, doziest**) drowsy; (*inf*) stupid.—**dozily** *adv*.—**doziness** *n*.

dp *abbr* = damp-proof; dual-purpose.

d.p. *abbr* = (*com*) documents for payment; double pole; (*elec*) potential difference.

DP *abbr* = data processing; Democratic Party; Diploma in Psychotherapy; displaced person; Doctor of Philosophy.

D/P *abbr* = (*com*) documents against payment.

DPA *abbr* = (*Brit*) Dartmoor Preservation Association; Data Protection Agency; Diary Publishers' Association; Diploma in Public Administration; Directory Publishers' Association; Duck Producers' Association.

DPAA *abbr* (*Brit*) = Draught Proofing Advisory Association.

DPAG *abbr* = Dangerous Pathogens Advisory Group.

DPAS *abbr* = Discharged Prisoners' Aid Society.

DPath *abbr* = Diploma in Pathology.

DpBact *abbr* = Diploma in Bacteriology.

dpc *abbr* = damp-proof course.

DPC *abbr* = Defence Planning Committee (NATO).

DPCM *abbr* = differential pulse-code modulation.

DPD *abbr* = Diploma in Public Dentistry.

DPE *abbr* = Diploma in Physical Education.

DPh *abbr* (*Latin*) = *Doctor Philosophiae*, "Doctor of Philosophy."

DPH *abbr* = Diploma in Public Health; Doctor of Public Health; Doctor of Public Hygiene.

DPhil *abbr* = Doctor of Philosophy.

DPHRCSEng (*Brit*) *abbr* = Diploma in Dental Public Health, Royal College of Surgeons of England.

dpi *abbr* (*comput*) = dots per inch.

DPI *abbr* = Department of Public Information (UN).

DPL *abbr* Denied Persons List

DPM *abbr* = (*Brit*) Deputy Prime Minister; Diploma in Psychological Medicine.

DPMI *abbr* = DOS/Protected Mode Interface.

DPMO *abbr* = Defense Prisoner of War/Missing Personnel Office.

d.p.o. *abbr* = distributing post office.

DPP *abbr* (*Brit*) = Director of Public Prosecutions.

DPR *abbr* = Data Protection Register.

DPRTF *abbr* = Drought Policy Review Task Force.

DPS *abbr* = (*Brit*) Dales Pony Society; Diploma in Pastoral Studies and Applied Theology; Diploma in Professional Studies; Disabled Photographers' Society.

DPSE *abbr* = Diploma in Professional Studies in Education.

DPSPA *abbr* = Display Producers' and Screen Printers' Association.

DPSSC *abbr* = Drugs and Poisons Schedule Standing Committee.

dpt. *abbr* = department; deponent.

DPT *abbr* = diphtheria, pertussis, tetanus (vaccine).

DPTAC *abbr* = Disabled Persons' Transport Advisory Committee.

DPTRI *abbr* = Drilling and Production Technology Research Institute.

dpu *abbr* = data processing unit.

DQMG *abbr* = Deputy Quartermaster General.

dr *abbr* = debit; debtor; drachma; dram(s); drawer; drawing paper.

d.r. *abbr* = dead reckoning; deposit receipt; differential rate; district registry; dock receipt; drill regulations.

Dr *abbr* = Doctor; driver; drummer.

DR *abbr* = Daughters of the Revolution.

D/R *abbr* = deposit receipt.

DRA *abbr* = Danish Robot Association; Defense Research Agency.

drab *adj* (**drabber, drabbest**) dull, uninteresting; of a dull brown color. * *n* a dull yellow-brown color; cloth of this color.—**drably** *adv*.—**drabness** *n*.

drabble *vt* to make wet or dirty by dragging through mud or water.

Drabble *n* **Margaret** (1939–) English novelist whose works, e.g., *The Millstone* and *The Middle Ground*, frequently feature the dilemmas and life crises of intelligent, married career women. She edited the fifth edition of *The Oxford Companion to English Literature*.

DrAc *abbr* = Doctor of Acupuncture.

dracena *n* any of a genus of tropical liliaceous palm-like plants.

drachm *n* in the UK, a unit of capacity (¹/8th fluid ounce); in the US, a dram; a drachma.

drachma *n* (*pl* **drachmas, drachmae**) the monetary unit of Greece.

Draco *n* a northern sky constellation, near Polaris, the Pole Star.

draconian *adj* (*laws, etc*) very cruel, severe; (*with cap*) of the 7th-century Athenian statesman Draco or his extremely harsh laws.

draft *n* a rough plan, preliminary sketch; an order for the payment of money by a bank; a smaller group selected from a larger for a specific task; conscription; a current of air, esp in an enclosed space; the pulling of a load using an animal, etc; something drawn; a dose of medicine or liquid; an act of swallowing; the depth of water required to float a ship; beer, wine, etc stored in bulk in casks. * *vt* to draw a rough sketch or outline of; to select for a special purpose; to conscript,

draft board *n* an official body of civilians that selects men for compulsory military service in the US.

draftee *n* a conscript.

draft mode *n* (*comput*) the quickest, low-resolution output from a dot matrix or inkjet printer.

draftsman *n* a person who makes detailed drawings or plans.—**draftsmanship** *n*.

drafty *adj* letting in or exposed to drafts of air.— **draftiness** *n*.

drag *vt* (**dragging, dragged**) to pull along by force; to draw slowly and heavily; (*comput*) to hold down the mouse button and move the mouse pointer across the screen, thus selecting (an area of text or cells, or a group of document icons in a desktop window); to search in (water) with a dragnet or hook. * *vi* to trail on the ground; to move slowly and heavily; (*sl*) to draw on a cigarette. * *n* something used for dragging, a dragnet, a heavy harrow; something that retards progress; a braking device; (*sl*) something boring or tedious; (*sl*) women's clothes worn by a man; (*sl*) a draw at a cigarette.

drag and drop *vt* (*comput*) to select (text or files) with the drag command and drop them somewhere else.

dragée *n* a coated nut or ball of sugar; a silver coated ball used as a cake decoration; a pill coated with sugar.

draggle *vt* to wet or soil by dragging in the mud or along the ground * *vi* to become dirty or wet by dragging.

dragnet *n* a net for scouring a riverbed, pond, etc to search for anything; a coordinated hunt for an escaped criminal, etc.

dragon *n* a mythical winged reptile; an authoritarian or grim person, esp a woman.

dragonfly *n* (*pl* **dragonflies**) an insect with a long, slender abdomen, large eyes and iridescent wings.

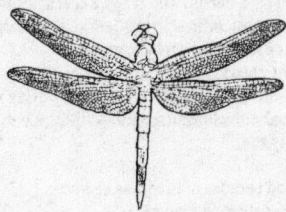

dragoon *n* a soldier on horseback, a cavalryman. * *vt* to force into submission by bullying commands.

drail *n* a weighted fishhook for dragging through water.

drain *vt* to draw off (liquid) gradually; to make dry by removing liquid gradually; to exhaust physically or mentally; to drink the entire contents of (a glass). * *vi* to flow away gradually; to become dry as liquid trickles away. * *n* a sewer, pipe, etc by which water is drained away; something that causes exhaustion or depletion.—**drainer** *n*.

drainage *n* a draining; a system of drains; something drained off; the movement of water over the land and through it in subterranean waterways that results in its eventual discharge into the sea.

draining board, drainboard *n* a sloping, usu grooved, surface beside a sink for draining washed dishes.

drainpipe *n* a pipe that carries waste liquid, sewage, etc out of a building.

drake *n* a male duck.

Drake *n* **Sir Francis** (*c*.1540–1596) English navigator and pirate, who circumnavigated the world (1577–80) and was prominent in the victory over the Spanish Armada (1588).

dram[1] *n* a small drink of spirits; a small amount; a unit of capacity (¹/8th fluid ounce); a unit of weight (avoirdupois 27.243 grains or 0.00265 ounce/apothecaries' weight 3 scruples or 60 grains).

Dram[2] *n* the standard monetary unit of Armenia.

DRAM *abbr* (*comput*) = dynamic random access memory.

drama *n* a play for the stage, radio, or television; dramatic literature as a genre; a dramatic situation or a set of events.

dramatic *adj* of or resembling drama; exciting, vivid.—**dramatically** *adv*.

dramatics *n* (*used as sing or pl*) the producing or performing of plays; (*used as sing*) exaggerated behavior, histrionics.

dramatis personae *n* the characters in a play.

dramatist *n* a person who writes plays.

dramatization *n* the action or process of dramatizing; an event or novel, etc, adapted to the form of a play.

dramatize *vt* to write or adapt in the form of a play; to express in an exaggerated or dramatic form.—**dramatizer** *n*.

dramaturge, dramaturg *n* a playwright; a literary adviser; an expert in dramaturgy.

dramaturgy *n* the art of dramatic composition; representation and stage effect.—**dramaturgic, dramaturgical** *adj*.

dram. pers. *abbr* (*Latin*) = *dramatis personae*, "characters present in the drama."

drank *see* **drink**.

dr. ap. *abbr* = apothecaries' dram.

drape *vt* to cover or hang with cloth; to arrange in loose folds; to place loosely or untidily. * *n* a hanging cloth or curtain; (*pl*) curtains.

draper *n* a seller of cloth.

Draper *n* **Dorothy** (1889–1969) American interior designer, who influenced much 1940s and 1950s furniture in the US.

Draper classification *n* a system of classifying stars by their spectrum, based on the Henry Draper catalog of stars.

drapery *n* (*pl* **draperies**) fabrics or curtains, esp as arranged in loose folds; the trade of a draper.

drastic *adj* acting with force and violence.—**drastically** *adv*.

drat *interj* (*sl*) a euphemism for "damn."

dratted *adj* (*sl*) confounded; annoying.

draughtboard *n* (*Brit*) a checkerboard.

draughtsman *n* (*pl* **draughtsmen**) (*Brit*) a checker.

Dravidian *adj* pertaining to an ancient race and their languages, spoken in southern India and Sri Lanka. * *n* a member of this race; a family of languages spoken by the Dravidians.

draw *vti* (**drawing, drew**, *pp* **drawn**) to haul, drag; to cause to go in a certain direction; to pull out; to attract; to delineate, sketch; to receive as a salary; to bend (a bow) by pulling back the string; to leave (a contest) undecided; to write up or draft (a will); to produce or allow (a current of air); to get information from; (*ship*) to require (a certain depth) to float; (*with* **on**) to approach; to use (a resource); to withdraw (money) from an account, etc; to put on (clothes); (*with* **out**) to extract; to prolong, extend; to cause (someone) to speak freely; (*with* **up**) to bring or come to a standstill; to draft (a document); to straighten oneself; to form soldiers into an array. * *n* the act of drawing; (*inf*) an event that attracts customers, people; the drawing of lots; a drawn game.

DRAW *abbr* = direct read after write.

drawback *n* a hindrance, handicap.

drawbridge *n* a bridge (e.g., over a moat) designed to be drawn up.

drawee *n* one on whom an order, a bill of exchange, or a draft is drawn.

drawer *n* a person who draws; a person who draws a check; a sliding box-like compartment (e.g., in a table, chest, or desk); (*pl*) knickers, underpants.

drawing *n* a figure, plan, or sketch drawn by using lines.

drawing pin *n* (*Brit*) a thumbtack.

drawing room *n* a room where visitors are entertained, a living room.

drawl *vt* to speak slowly and with elongated vowel sounds. * *n* drawling speech.—**drawler** *n*.—**drawlingly** *adv*.

drawn[1] *see* **draw**.

drawn[2] *adj* looking strained because of tiredness or worry.

draw program *see* **object-oriented program**.

drawstring *n* a string or tape threaded through fabric which when pulled gathers it up or closes an opening.

dray *n* a low, stoutly built cart used for heavy loads.

Drayton *n* **Michael** (1563–1631) English dramatist and poet, remembered for the sonnet beginning "Since there's no hope, come let us kiss and part," and "Agincourt," whose first line is "Faire stood the wind for France."

DRC *abbr* = Dictionary Research Center.

drch. *abbr* = drachma.

DRCOG (*Brit*) *abbr* = Diploma of the Royal College of Obstetricians and Gynaecologists.

DRCPath (*Brit*) *abbr* = Diploma of the Royal College of Pathologists.

DRD *abbr* = Diploma in Restorative Dentistry.

DRDW *abbr* = direct read during write.

DRE *abbr* = Diploma in Remedial Electrolysis.

dread *n* great fear or apprehension. * *vt* to fear greatly.

dreadful *adj* full of dread; causing dread; extreme (*dreadful tiredness*); (*sl*) bad, disagreeable.—**dreadfully** *adv*—**dreadfulness** *n*.

dreadlocks *npl* hair worn in long, matted strands, esp by male Rastafarians.

dreadnought *n* a battleship with main armament entirely of big guns; a heavy cloth; an overcoat of this cloth.

dream *n* a stream of thoughts and images experienced during sleep; a day-dreaming state, a reverie; an ambition; an ideal. * *vi* (**dreaming, dreamt** *or* **dreamed**) to have a dream during sleep; to fantasize. * *vt* to dream of; to imagine as a reality; (*with* **up**) to devise, invent.—**dreamer** *n*.

dreamy *adj* (**dreamier, dreamiest**) given to dreaming, unpractical; (*inf*) attractive, wonderful.—**dreamily** *adv*.—**dreaminess** *n*.

dreary *adj* (**drearier, dreariest**) dull; cheerless.—**drearily** *adv*.—**dreariness** *n*.

dredge[1] *n* a device for scooping up material from the bottom of a river, harbor, etc. * *vt* to widen, deepen, or clean with a dredge; to scoop up with a dredge; (*with* **up**) (*inf*) to discover, reveal, esp through effort.

dredge[2] *vt* to coat (food) by sprinkling.

dredger[1] *n* a vessel fitted with dredging equipment.

dredger[2] *n* a container with a perforated lid for sprinkling.

dreggy *adj* (**dreggier, dreggiest**) full of dregs; like dregs.

dregs *npl* solid impurities that settle on the bottom of a liquid; residue; (*inf*) a worthless person or thing.

Dreier *n* **Hans** (1885–1966) German movie designer, who was head of design at Paramount Stufios from 1928 to 1951.

Dreiser *n* **Theodore** (1871–1945) American naturalistic novelist, whose works include *Sister Carrie* and *An American Tragedy*, as well as non-fiction documentary works such as *America is Worth Saving*.

drench *vt* to soak, saturate.

Dr. Eng. *abbr* = Doctor of Engineering.

dress *n* clothing; a one-piece garment worn by women and girls comprising a top and skirt; a style or manner of clothing. * *vt* to put on or provide with clothing; to decorate; (*wound*) to wash and bandage; (*animal*) to groom; to arrange (the hair); to prepare (food, e.g., poultry or fish) for eating by cleaning, gutting, etc; (*with* **up**) to attire in best clothes; to improve the appearance of. * *vi* to put on clothes; to put on formal wear for an occasion; (*with* **up**) to put on fancy dress, etc.

dressage *n* the training of a horse in deportment and obedience.

dress circle *n* the first tier of seats in a theater above the stalls.

dresser *n* a person who assists an actor to dress; a type of kitchen sideboard.

Dresser *n* **Christopher** (1834–1904) British botanist and designer, born in Glasgow and trained in London.

dressing *n* a sauce or stuffing for food; manure spread over the soil; dress or clothes; the bandage, ointment, etc applied to a wound.

dressing-down *n* a severe scolding.

dressing gown *n* a loose garment worn when one is partially clothed, a bath robe.

dressings *npl* (*archit*) stones worked to provide a smooth or molded finished face and used around a window as a feature.

dressmaker *n* a person who makes clothes.—**dressmaking** *n*.

dress rehearsal *n* rehearsal in full costume.

dressy *adj* (**dressier, dressiest**) stylish; elaborate; showy.—**dressily** *adv*.—**dressiness** *n*.

Drest I king of Picts, Scotland (663–671). The brother of Gartnait, succeeded by Bridei III who crushed Egfrith's army at Nechtansmere in 685.

Drest II (*d.* 729) king of Picts, Scotland (724–729). The son of Nechton's sister.

Drest III (*d.* 780) king of Picts, Scotland (reigned in 780). The son of Alpin II's sister.

Drest IV (*d.* 837) king of Picts, Scotland (834–837). He was the son of Uen.

drew *see* **draw**.

Dreyfus *n* **Alfred** (1859–1935) French army officer, who was imprisoned in 1894 on Devil's Island on a false charge of espionage.

Dreyfuss *n* **Henry** (1903–72) American stage designer, who designed Bell Telephones, Hoover products, and passenger cars for the New York Central Railroad.

Dr. Hy. *abbr* = Doctor of Hygiene.

DRI *abbr* = Diploma in Radionuclide Imaging.

Driade *n* Italian furniture manufacturer, set up in 1968 by Enrico Astori, his sister Antonia Astori, and his wife Adelaide.

dribble *vi* to flow in a thin stream or small drips; to let saliva trickle from the mouth. * *vt* (*soccer, basketball, hockey*) to move (the ball) along little by little with the foot, hand, stick, etc. * *n* the act of dribbling; a thin stream of liquid.—**dribbler** *n*.

driblet *n* a small amount; a drop, trickle.

dried *see* **dry**.

drier *see* **dry, dryer**.

drift *n* a heap of snow, sand, etc deposited by the wind; natural course, tendency; the general meaning or intention (of what is said); the extent of deviation (of an aircraft, etc) from a course; an aimless course; the action or motion of drifting. * *vt* to cause to drift. * *vi* to be driven or carried along by water or air currents; to move along aimlessly; to be piled into heaps by the wind.

driftage *n* matter that drifts ashore; deviation from a course caused by air or sea currents.

drifter *n* a person who wanders aimlessly.

driftwood *n* wood cast ashore by tides.

drill[1] *n* an implement with a pointed end that bores holes; the training of soldiers, etc; repetitive exercises or training as a teaching method; (*inf*) correct procedure or routine. * *vt* to make a hole with a drill; to instruct by drilling.

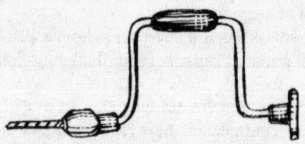

drill[2] *n* a machine for planting seeds in rows; a furrow in which seeds are planted; a row of seeds planted in this way.—*also vt*.

drilling platform *n* the fixed or mobile structure supporting the equipment and accommodation facilities, etc for drilling an offshore oil well.

drilling rig *n* the machinery required to drill an oil well.

drily *see* **dry**.

drink *vt* (**drinking, drank,** *pp* **drunk**) to swallow (a liquid); to take in, absorb; to join in a toast. * *vi* to consume alcoholic liquor, esp to excess. * *n* liquid to be drunk; alcoholic liquor; (*sl*) the sea.—**drinker** *n*.

drip *vti* (**dripping, dripped**) to fall or let fall in drops. * *n* a liquid that falls in drops; the sound of falling drops; (*med*) a device for administering a fluid slowly and continuously into a vein; (*archit*) a projection, often in the form of a molding or tablet, above doorways, windows, etc to direct rainwater away from the wall below; (*inf*) a weak or ineffectual person.—**dripper** *n*.

drip-dry *adj* (*clothing*) drying easily and needing relatively little ironing.—*also vti*.

dripping *n* fat that drips from meat during roasting.

drive *vt* (**driving, drove,** *pp* **driven**) to urge, push, or force onward; to direct the movement or course of; to convey in a vehicle; to carry through strongly; to impress forcefully; to propel (a ball) with a hard blow. * *vi* to be forced along; to be conveyed in a vehicle; to work, to strive (at). * *n* a trip in a vehicle; a stroke to drive a ball (in golf, etc); a driveway; a military attack; an intensive campaign; dynamic ability; the transmission of power to machinery.

drive-in *n* a cinema, restaurant, etc, where customers are served in their cars.—*also adj*.

drivel *n* nonsense. * *vi* (**driveling, driveled**) to talk nonsense.—**driveler** *n*.

driven *see* **drive**.

driver *n* one who or that which drives; a chauffeur; (*golf*) a wooden club used from the tee; (*comput*) a file containing information which allows a program to control and operate a peripheral device, e.g., a printer, scanner, or monitor.

driveway *n* a road for vehicles, often on private property.

drizzle *n* fine light rain.—*also vi*.—**drizzly** *adj*.

Dr. Jur. (*Latin*) *abbr* = *Doctor juris*, "Doctor of Law."

Dr. Med. *abbr* (*Latin*) = *Doctor medicae*, "Doctor of Medicine."

DRMS *abbr* = Defense Re-utilization and Marketing Service.

drogue *n* a sea anchor; a small parachute that slows down or stabilizes something, e.g., a jet aircraft; a funnel-shaped device that enables an airplane to be refueled from a tanker plane while in flight; a buoy at the end of a harpoon line; a windsock.

droit *n* equity; a right of ownership, esp in land; custom; duty.

droll *adj* oddly amusing; whimsical.—**drollness** *n*.—**drolly** *adv*.

drollery *n* (*pl* **drolleries**) the quality of being droll; buffoonery; a droll act.

dromedary *n* (*pl* **dromedaries**) a one-humped camel.

dromos *n* a long entrance passage, resembling a corridor, leading to a tholos or chamber tomb.

drone *n* a male honey bee; a lazy person; a deep humming sound; a monotonous speaker or speech; (*mus*) a pipe that sounds a continuous note of fixed pitch as a permanent bass, used in bagpipes; a similar effect produced by stringed instruments fitted with "drone strings"; an aircraft piloted by remote control. * *vi* to make a monotonous, humming sound; to speak in a monotonous manner.

drool *vi* to slaver, dribble; to show excessive enthusiasm for.

droop *vi* to bend or hang down; to become weak or faint. * *n* the act or an instance of drooping.

droopy *adj* (**droopier, droopiest**) drooping; tending to droop; (*sl*) tired, depressed.—**droopily** *adv*.—**droopiness** *n*.

drop *n* a small amount of liquid in a roundish shape; something shaped like this, e.g., a sweet; a tiny quantity; a sudden fall; the distance down; (*pl*) liquid medicine, etc dispensed in small drops. * *vi* (**dropping, dropped**) to fall in drops; to fall suddenly; to go lower, to sink; to come (in); (*with* **in**) to visit (with) informally; (*with* **out**) to abandon or reject (a course, society, etc). * *vt* to let fall, cause to fall; to lower or cause to descend; to set down from a vehicle; to mention casually; to cause (the voice) to be less loud; to give up (an idea).—**dropper** *n*.

drop-dead *adv* (*sl*) referring to a very attractive person (*drop-dead gorgeous*).

drop-down menu *n* (*comput*) a list of command options that appears only when the main command is selected.

drop kick *n* a kick made by dropping the ball onto the ground and kicking as it bounces.—**drop-kick** *vt*.

droplet *n* a tiny drop (of liquid).

dropout *n* a student who abandons a course of study; a person who rejects normal society.

droppings *npl* animal dung.

dropsy *n* an unnatural accumulation of serious fluid in any cavity of the body or its tissues.—**dropsical** *adj*.

droshky *or* **drosky** *n* (*pl* **droshkies** *or* **droskies**) a light four-wheeled open Russian carriage.

drosophila *n* a fruit fly of that is used a great deal in genetic research because it breeds easily and quickly.

dross *n* a surface scum on molten metal; rubbish, waste matter.

drought *n* a long period of dry weather.—**droughty** *adj*.

drove[1] *see* **drive**.

drove[2] *n* a group of animals driven in a herd or flock, etc; a large moving crowd of people.

drover *n* a person whose occupation is to drive cattle.

drove road *n* a broad track, used by herders to walk their animals to markets in towns or cities, before other means of transport were available.

drown *vti* to die or kill by suffocation in water or other liquid. * *vt* to flood; to drench; to become deeply immersed in some activity; to blot out (a sound) with a louder noise; to remove (sorrow) with drink.

drowned valley *n* a river valley that has been submerged as a result of a rise in sea level, often caused by postglacial melting.

drowned valleys *n* (*geol*) a river valley that has been flooded due to a rise in sea level.

drowse *vi* to be nearly asleep.

drowsy *adj* (**drowsier, drowsiest**) sleepy; soporific; lethargic; inactive.—**drowsily** *adv*.—**drowsiness** *n*.

Dr. P.H. *abbr* = Doctor of Public Health; Doctor of Public Hygiene.

Dr. Phil. *abbr* (*Latin*) = *Doctor Philosophiae*, "Doctor of Philosophy."

DR(RCA) *abbr* (*Brit*) = Doctor of the Royal College of Art.

DRSAM *abbr* (*Latin*) = Diploma of the Royal Scottish Academy of Music and Drama.

DRT *abbr* = Disability Research Team.

drub *vt* (**drubbing, drubbed**) to thrash; to defeat convincingly.

drudge *vi* to do boring or very menial work. * *n* a person who drudges, esp a servant.—**drudger** *n*.—**drudgingly** *adv*.

drudgery *n* (*pl* **drudgeries**) dull, boring work.

drug *n* any substance used in medicine; a narcotic. * *vt* (**drugging, drugged**) to administer drugs to; to stupefy.

drug binding *n* the attaching of a drug to a protein, fat, or component of tissues.

drug clearance *n* the volume of blood that in one minute is completely cleared of a drug.

drugget *n* a coarse woolen or cotton fabric; a rug made of this.

druggist *n* a pharmacist.

drug interaction *n* interaction between some or all simultaneous medications.

drug metabolism *n* the process by which a drug is altered by the body into a metabolite (i.e., necessary for metabolic action).

drugstore *n* a retail store selling medicines and miscellaneous articles, such as cosmetics, film, etc.

druid *n* (*often with cap*) a priest of the ancient inhabitants (probably Celtic) of Britain, Gaul, and Germany; a member of a modern society reviving druidism.—**druidic, druidical** *adj*.

druidism *n* the beliefs, manners, rites, and customs of the druids.

drum *n* a round percussion instrument, played by striking a membrane stretched across a hollow, cylindrical frame; the sound of a drum; anything shaped like a drum, e.g., a container for liquids. * *vi* (**drumming, drummed**) to play a drum; to beat or tap rhythmically. * *vt* (*with* **in**) to instill (knowledge) into a person by constant repetition; (*with* **up**) to summon as by drum; to create (business, etc) by concerted effort; to originate.

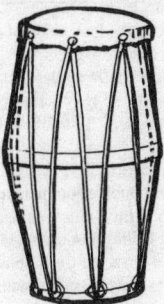

drum brake *n* a brake on a wheel that operates by rubbing two shoes against the inside wall of a brake drum.

drumhead *n* the membrane stretched across the end of a drum.

drum kit *n* a set of drums and cymbals that are arranged in such a way that they can all be played by one person sitting on a stool.

drumlin *n* an oval accumulation of boulder clay deposited by glaciation that forms a small hill.

drummer *n* a person who plays a drum; (*inf*) a traveling salesman.

drum scanner *see* **scanner**.

drumstick *n* a stick for beating a drum; the lower part of a cooked leg of poultry.

drunk[1] *see* **drink**.

drunk[2] *adj* intoxicated with alcohol. * *n* a drunk person.

drunkard *n* an habitual drunk.

drunken *adj* intoxicated; caused by excessive drinking.—**drunkenly** *adv*.—**drunkenness** *n*.

drupe *n* a fleshy fruit with a stone, e.g., a plum.—**drupaceous** *adj*.

drupelet *n* a small drupe in a compound fruit, e.g. a raspberry.

druse *n* a crust of crystals; a rock cavity lined with this.

Druse, Druze *n* a member of a fanatical politico-religious sect in Syria and Lebanon.

Drust (*d.* 848) king of Picts, Scotland (845–848). One of the sons of Uurad.

dry *adj* (**drier, driest**) free from water or liquid; thirsty; marked by a matter-of-fact, ironic, or terse manner of expression; uninteresting, wearisome; (*bread*) eaten without butter, etc; (*wine*) not sweet; not selling alcohol. * *vti* (**drying, dried**) to make or become dry; (*with* **out**) to be treated for alcoholism or drug addiction.—**drily, dryly** *adv*.—**dryness** *n*.

dryad *n* (*pl* **dryads, dryades**) (*Greek myth*) a wood nymph.

dry-clean *vt* to clean with solvents as opposed to water.—**dry-cleaner** *n*.—**dry-cleaning** *n*.

Dryden *n* John (1631–1700) English poet, dramatist, and critic, whose works include *All for Love*.

dry dock *n* a dock that can be drained of water to make ship repairs easier.

dryer *n* a device for drying, as a tumble-drier; a clothes horse.—*also* **drier**.

dry ice *n* solid carbon dioxide.

dry rot *n* decay of timber caused by a fungus; any form of moral decay or corruption.

dry run *n* (*inf*) a rehearsal.

dry-salt *vt* to cure (meat, etc) by salting and drying.

drysalter *n* (*formerly*) a dealer in dyes, oils, etc.—**drysaltery** *n*.

dry valley *n* (*geol*) a valley once carved out by a river but now dry.

d.s. *abbr* = (*com*) days after sight; document signed.

Ds *symbol* (*chem*) = dysprosium (element).

DS *abbr* = (*Italian*) *dal segno*, "from the sign"; debenture stock; Detective Sergeant; disseminated sclerosis; Doctor of Science; Doctor of Surgery; Down's syndrome.

d/s *abbr* = (*com*) days after sight; (*com*) days' *or* day's sight.

D/S *abbr* = dextrose saline.

DSA *abbr* = Direct Selling Association; Door and Shutter Association; Down's Syndrome Association; Drilling and Sawing Association; Driving Standards Agency.

DSAC *abbr* = Defense Scientific Advisory Council.

DSBA *abbr* (*Brit*) = Sheep Breeders' Association.

DSc *abbr* (*Latin*) = *Doctor Scientiae*, "Doctor of Science."

DSC *abbr* = Dangerous Sports Club; Desert Society of China; Distinguished Service Cross; Doctor of Christian Science.

DScEcon *abbr* = Doctor in the Faculty of Economics and Social Studies.

DSc(Econ) *abbr* = Doctor of Science (Economics) *or* in Economics.

DSc(Eng) *abbr* = Doctor of Science (Engineering).

DSc(Social Sciences) *abbr* = Doctor of Science in the Social Sciences.

DScTech *abbr* = Doctor of Technical Science.

dsDNA *abbr* = double-stranded deoxyribonucleic acid.

DSM *abbr* = deputy stage manager; Distinguished Service Medal.

DSMA *abbr* = Door and Shutter Manufacturers' Association.

DSMP *abbr* = Daughters of St Mary of Providence.

DSO *abbr* = Distinguished Service Order; District Staff Officer.

DSocSc *abbr* = Doctor of Social Science.

dsp *abbr* = (*Latin*) *decessit sine prole*, "died without issue"; digital signal processing.

DSP *abbr* = Democratic Socialist Party.

DSPCA *abbr* = Dublin Society for the Prevention of Cruelty to Animals.

d.s.q. *abbr* (*mil*) = discharged to sick quarters.

DSS *abbr* = Defense Security Service; (*Brit*) Department of Social Security; (*Latin*) *Doctor Sacrae Scripturae*, "Doctor of Holy Scripture."

DSSA *abbr* = Dental System Suppliers' Association; Direct Sales and Service Association.

DSSc *abbr* = Doctor of Social Science.

DST *abbr* = Daylight Saving Time; Double Summer Time; Doctor of Sacred Theology.

DSTA *abbr* = Diploma Member of the Swimming Teachers' Association.

DSWA *abbr* (*Brit*) = Dry Stone Walling Association of Great Britain.

d.t. *abbr* = (*elec*) double-throw (switch); (*mil*) double time.

DT *abbr* = Daily Telegraph; data transmission; Doctor of Theology.

DTA *abbr* = Development Trusts Association.

DTAG *abbr* = Development Training Advisory Group.

dtba *abbr* = date to be advised.

DTC *abbr* = Department of Technical Co-operation.

DTCD *abbr* = Diploma in Tuberculosis and Chest Diseases.

DTCH *abbr* = Diploma in Tropical Child Health.

d.t.d. *abbr* (*Latin*) = *detur talis dosis*, "let such a dose be given."

DTD *abbr* = document type definition.

DTE *abbr* = data terminal equipment.

DTech *abbr* = Doctor of Technology.

DTF *abbr* = Dairy Trade Federation; Domestic Textiles Federation.

DTh *abbr* (*Latin*) = *Doctor Theologiae*, "Doctor of Theology."

DTI *abbr* (*Brit*) = Department of Trade and Industry.

DTIC *abbr* = Defense Technical Information Center.

DTM *abbr* = Diploma in Tropical Medicine; Doctor of Tropical Medicine.

DTM&H *abbr* = Diploma in Tropical Medicine and Hygiene.

DTp *abbr* = Department of Transport.

DTP *abbr* = desktop publishing.

DTR *abbr* = double taxation relief.

DTRA *abbr* = Defense Threat Reduction Agency

DTRP *abbr* = Diploma in Town and Regional Planning.

DTs *abbr* = delerium tremens.

DTTAC *abbr* = Distributive Trades Technology Advisory Center.

Du. *abbr* = Dutch.

DU *abbr* = died unmarried; duodenal ulcer.

dual *adj* double; consisting of two.

dual carriageway *see* **divided highway**.

dual economy *n* a system found in many developing countries where a relatively advanced economy exists alongside a traditional economy but the two rarely come into contact.

dualism *n* a twofold division; (*philos*) the doctrine that the universe is based on two principles, e.g., good and evil, mind and matter.—**dualist** *n*.—**dualistic** *adj*.—**dualistically** *adv*.

duality *n* (*pl* **dualities**) the condition or quality of being two or in two parts, dualism; dichotomy.

dub[1] *vt* (**dubbing, dubbed**) to confer knighthood on; to nickname.

dub[2] *vt* (**dubbing, dubbed**) to replace the soundtrack of (a movie), e.g., with one in a different language; to add sound effects or music to (a movie, broadcast, etc); to transfer (a recording) to a new tape.

dub. *abbr* = (*Latin*) *dubitans*, "doubting"; (*Latin*) *dubitatur* "it is doubted"; dubious.

Dubai (Dubayy) *n* a city in the United Arab Emirates (UAE).

dubbin *or* **dubbing** *n* a grease for softening and waterproofing leather.

Dubcek *n* **Alexander** (1921–92) Czech statesman; first secretary of the Communist Party (1968–69); appointed chairman of the federal assembly (1989) following Czechoslovakian independence.

Dubh (*d.* 966) king of Scots (962–966). The son of Malcolm I, he was killed in battle.

Dubhe *n* Alpha Ursae Majoris, one of the pointer stars.

dubiety *n* (*pl* **dubieties**) doubtfulness, uncertainty; a matter of doubt.

dubious *adj* (*with* **about, of**) doubtful; uncertain as to the result; untrustworthy.—**dubiously** *adv*.—**dubiousness** *n*.

Dublin *n* capital city of the Republic of Ireland.

Dubois *n* **Ferard** (*b.* 1859) Belgian sculptor and metalworker, whose most famous piece is the five-branched candelabrum in the Horta Museum, Brussels.

Dubreuil *n* **Andre** (1951–) French interior and furniture designer.

Dubuffet *n* **Jean** (1901–85) French painter, whoe ideas about pure, untrained art influenced trends in modern abstract and surrealist art.

Duc *n* **Christian** (1949–) Vietnamese designer, who set up a gallery in Paris in 1977.

ducal *adj* of or pertaining to a duke, a dukedom or a duchy.—**ducally** *adv*.

ducat *n* a gold or silver coin formerly in use in Europe; (*pl*) (*sl*) money.

Duccio di Buonisegna *n* (1278–1318) Italian painter, little of whose work is clearly documented apart from his masterpiece, the *Maestà* (1311) for the Siena Cathedral altarpiece.

duce *n* a chief, a leader; (*with cap*) the title used by the Italian Fascist dictator, Benito Mussolini (1922–43).

Du Cerceau *n* **Jacques Androuet** (*c.* 1515–*c.* 85) important pattern designer, whose ideas were disseminated across Europe.

Duchamp *n* **Marcel** (1887–1968) French-born American painter and sculptor, who was a pioneer of Dadaism.

Duchamp-Villon *n* **Raymond** (1876–1918) French sculptor. The brother of Marcel Duchamp, he was an important member of the Section d'Or group. His most famous masterpiece is *The Horse* (1912–14).

duchess *n* the wife or widow of a duke; a woman having the same rank as a duke in her own right.

duchy *n* (*pl* **duchies**) the territory of a duke, a dukedom.

duck[1] *vt* to dip briefly in water; to lower the head suddenly, esp to avoid some object; to avoid, dodge. * *vi* to dip or dive; to move the head or body suddenly; to evade a duty, etc. * *n* a ducking movement.

duck[2] *n* (*pl* **ducks, duck**) a water bird related to geese and swans; the female of this bird; its flesh used as food.

duck[3] *n* a plain cotton cloth; (*pl*) trousers or light clothes made from this and worn in hot climates.

duckbill, duck-billed platypus *n* an Australian egg-laying furred mammal with webbed feet and a broad bill.—*also* **platypus**.

duckboard *n* a path of wooden slats laid over muddy or wet ground.

duckling *n* a young duck.

duckweed *n* a common floating freshwater plant.

ducky, duckie *adj* (**duckier, duckiest**) (*Brit inf*) fine; satisfactory; cute. * *n* (*pl* **duckies**) (*Brit inf*) a term of endearment, darling.

duct *n* a channel or pipe for fluids, electric cable, etc; a tube in the body for fluids to pass through.

ductile *adj* malleable; yielding.

ductility *n* (*chem*) the property of metals that allows them to be drawn out into a wire.

ductless gland *n* a gland that releases its secretion directly into the blood for transport around the body, e.g., the pituitary or thyroid.

ductus arteriosus *n* a duct that takes fetal blood from the pulmonary artery to the aorta, so bypassing the lungs. The duct stops functioning soon after birth.

dud *adj* (*sl*) worthless. * *n* (*sl*) anything worthless; an ineffectual person.

dude *n* a dandy; a city person on holiday in a ranch.

dudeen *n* a short clay tobacco pipe.

Dudelange *n* a city in the Grand Duchy of Luxembourg.

dudgeon *n* resentment, indignation; (*arch*) the hilt of a dagger.

Dudok *n* **Willem M.** (1884–1974) Dutch architect, whose notable works include Hilversum Town Hall.

due *adj* owed as a debt; immediately payable; fitting, appropriate; appointed or expected to do or arrive. * *adv* directly, exactly. * *n* something due or owed; (*pl*) fees.

due corde *n* (*mus*) two strings: a term used in violin music indicating that a passage that could theoretically be played on one string should nevertheless be played on two to produce the desired effect.

due date *n* the date on which a debt of some kind is due to be settled.

duel *n* combat with weapons between two persons over a matter of honor, etc; conflict of any kind between two people, sides, ideas, etc. * *vi* (**dueling, dueled**) to fight in a duel.—**duelist** *n*.

duello *n* (*pl* **duellos**) the duelists' code.

duenna *n* an older woman acting as a chaperone of young women in Spanish or Portuguese families.

due process *n* proceedings (esp a legal process) in accordance with established principles and practice.

duet *n* a musical composition for two performers.—**duettist** *n*.

Dufay *n* **Guillaume** (*c.* 1400–74) Flemish composer, who in 1940 founded the most important of his time. Although he wrote some secular songs, he is best known for his church music and masses, e.g., *L'Homme armé*, based on a secular folk song.

Dufet *n* **Michel** (1888–1985) French interior designer, who designed the first cubist wallpapers in 1924.

duffel, duffle *n* a coarse, heavy, woolen cloth.

duffel bag, duffle bag *n* a large, cylindrical drawstring bag for personal belongings.

duffel coat, duffle coat *n* a heavy, hooded overcoat, fastened with toggles.

duffer *n* an incompetent person, esp an elderly one.

Dufrène *n* **Maurice** (1876–1955) French designer, who in 1940 founded the Société des Artistes Décorateurs, as a reaction to the excesses of Art Nouveau.

Dufy *n* **Raoul** (1877–1953) French painter, associated with the Fauve school of artists, but active as a designer of letterheads and fabrics.

dug *see* **dig**.

dugong *n* an aquatic, herbivorous mammal resembling the seal and walrus; the sea cow.

dugout *n* a boat made from the hollowed out tree trunk; a rough underground shelter.

duiker *n* (*pl* **duikers, duiker**) a small South African antelope.

Dukas *n* **Paul** (1865–1935) French composer and critic. His output was comparatively small but includes some of the most important works of the early 20th century, such as the scherzo for orchestra *The Sorcerer's Apprentice*, the opera *Ariadne and Bluebeard*, and the ballet *La Péri*.

duke *n* the highest order of British nobility; the title of a ruler of a European duchy.

dukedom *n* a duchy; the rank, position or title of a duke.

Dulac *n* **Edmund** (1881–1953) French illustrator, who produced wax caricatures of celebrities, chocolate wrappers, and stamps.

dulcet *adj* sweet-sounding, melodious.—**dulcetly** *adv*.

dulcimer *n* a musical instrument with wire strings that are struck with a hammer; a folk-music instrument with usu three strings that are played by plucking.—*also* **dulcimore**.

dulcimer *n* (*mus*) an ancient instrument consisting of a shallow box over which strings are stretched. The instrument is placed on the knees and the strings struck with small hammers.—*also* **cymbalo**.

dulcitone *n* (*mus*) a keyboard instrument containing tuning forks that are struck with hammers, as in a piano.

dulia *n* the veneration paid to saints and angels as the servants of God.

dull *adj* not sharp or pointed; not bright or clear; stupid; boring; not active. * *vti* to make or become dull.—**dully** *adv*.—**dullness** *n*.

dullard *n* a slow-witted person.

Dulles *n* 1. **Allan Welsh** (1893–1969) American intelligence officer, who became head of the CIA (1953–63). 2. **John Foster** (1888–1959) American Republican statesman and lawyer, secretary of state (1953–59) under Eisenhower. He developed the foreign policy of "brinkmanship" in the Cold War.

Dulles dullness *see* **resonance**.

dulse *n* a red, edible seaweed found on rocks.

duly *adv* properly; suitably.

Dumas *n* 1. **Alexandre [Dumas père]** (1802–70) French novelist and dramatist, author of *The Three Musketeers*. 2. **Alexandre Dumas [Dumas fils]** (1824–95) French novelist and dramatist and son of Dumas père. 2. **René** (1937–) Greek architect and interior designer, who became designer of leather goods for Hèrmes in 1962.

Du Maurier *n* Dame **Daphne** (1907–89) English novelist and short-story writer, whose works include *Rebecca* (1938).

dumb *adj* not able to speak; silent; (*inf*) stupid.—**dumbly** *adv*.—**dumbness** *n*.

dumbbell *n* one of a pair of heavy weights used for muscular exercise; (*sl*) a fool.

dumbfound, dumfound *vti* to astonish, surprise.

dumbstruck *adj* rendered silent with astonishment.

dumb terminal *n* (*comput*) a computer terminal that lacks its own central processing unit and disk drives.

dumbwaiter *n* a stand with revolving shelves for holding food; a revolving tray for holding food; a small elevator for carrying food, etc, between floors.

dumdum *n* (*sl*) a stupid person; a dummy.

dumdum (bullet) *n* a soft-nosed, expanding bullet.

Dumée *n* **Guillaume** (*fl.* 1601–1626) French decorative painter, who was curator of the royal paintings at Saint-Germain.

dumka *n* (*mus*) a Slavonic folk ballad or lament, which may have a fast middle section.

dummy *n* (*pl* **dummies**) a figure of a person used to display clothes; (*Brit sl*) a soother or pacifier for a baby; a stupid person; an imitation; (*bridge*) the exposed cards of the dealer's partner.

Dumoulin *n* **Georges** (1882–1959) French ceramic and glass designer, who worked at Manufacture de Sèvres for nine years.

dump *vt* to drop or put down carelessly in a heap; to deposit as rubbish; to abandon or get rid of; (*comput*) to transfer (data) to another storage medium; to sell goods abroad at a price lower than the market price abroad; (*football*) to throw a pass to either end of the offensive line; (*with* on) (*sl*) to censure strongly the words or actions of others. * *n* a place for refuse; a temporary store; (*comput*) the process of transferring the contents of memory in one storage device to another storage device or item of hardware; (*inf*) a dirty, dilapidated place; (*pl*) (*inf*) despondency, low spirits.—**dumper** *n*.

dumping *n* the process of selling goods on the export market at a price well below that charged on the domestic market.

dumpling *n* a rounded piece of dough cooked by boiling or steaming; a short, fat person.

dumpster *n* a large garbage can.

dumpy *adj* (**dumpier, dumpiest**) short and thick.—**dumpily** *adv*.—**dumpiness** *n*.

dun[1] *adj* (**dunner, dunnest**) grayish-brown.—**dunness** *n*.

dun[2] *vt* (**dunning, dunned**) to press persistently for payment of a debt.

dun[3] *n* (*archeo*) an ancient fortification; a natural feature that resembles an ancient dun.

Dunaway *n* [**Dorothy**] **Faye** (1941–) American actress whose movies include *Mommie Dearest* (1981).

Dunbar *n* **William** (*c.*1465–*c.*1530) Scottish poet and divine, noted mainly for his very fine poem "Lament for the Makaris" (*makar* is the Scots word for "poet").

Duncan I (1010–1040) king of Scots (1034–1040). The son of Crinan, Abbot of Dunkeld, and Bethoc, daughter of Malcolm II, Duncan succeeded his grandfather and founded the Dunkeld dynasty.

Duncan II (1060–94) king of Scots (reigned in 1094). The eldest son of Malcolm III from his first marriage.

Duncan *n* **Isadora** (1878–1927) American dancer and choreographer who played an important role in the development of modern dance.

dunce *n* a person who is stupid or slow to learn.

Dundee *n* major Scottish city in the United Kingdom of Great Britain and Northern Ireland (UK).

dunderhead *n* a stupid person, a dunce.—**dunderheaded** *adj*.

dune *n* a hill of sand piled up by the wind.

Dunedin *n* a city in New Zealand.

Dunelm. *abbr* (*Latin*) = *Dunelmensis*, "of Durham."

dung *n* excrement; manure; filth. * *vt* to spread with manure.—**dungy** *adj*.

dungaree *n* a coarse cotton cloth; (*pl*) overalls or trousers made from this.

dungeon *n* an underground cell for prisoners.

dunghill *n* a heap of dung.

DUniv *abbr* = Doctor of the University.

dunk *vti* to dip (cake, etc) into liquid, e.g., coffee.

dunlin *n* a small red-backed sandpiper of northern regions.

dunnage *n* loose wood, etc, used to pack cargo or keep it out of bilge water in a ship's hold; baggage.

dunnite *n* a powerful explosive used esp in shells.

Dunsany *n* **Edward** *n* **18th Baron** (1878–1957) Anglo-Irish novelist, dramatist, and short-story writer, whose works include the fantasy stories in *The Book of Wonder*.

Dunstable *n* **John** (*c.*1385–1453) English musician, astrologer, and mathematician, of whose early life very little is known. However, he is considered one of the most important composers of the 15th century and was probably one of the first to write instrumental accompaniments to church music.

Dunstan *n* **Saint** (*c.* 924–88) English priest and the archbishop of Canterbury (959–988). He encouraged education and revived monasticism in England. His feast day is May 19.

duo *n* (*pl* **duos, dui**) a pair of performers; (*inf*) two persons connected in some way.

duodecimal *adj* of twelve; proceeding by twelves. * *n* a twelfth; a system of computing by twelves.

duodecimo *n* (*pl* **duodecimos**) a book of sheets folded into 12 leaves; this book size.—*also* **twelvemo**.

duodenal ulcer *n* the commonest type of peptic ulcer. Duodenal ulcers may occur after the age of 20 and are more common in men.

duodenary *adj* duodecimal.

duodenum *n* (*pl* **duodena, duodenums**) the first part of the small intestine.—**duodenal** *adj*.

Duoduo *n* [Li Shizheng] (1951–) Chinese poet. He is a strong admirer of Western poets yet works very much as a traditional Chinese poet. He has lived in exile since the Tiananmen Square Massacre of 1989.

duolog *n* a play with two actors; a conversation between two people.

dup *vt* (**dupping, dupped**) (*arch*) to open.

dup. *abbr* = duplicate.

DUP *abbr* = Democratic Unionist Party.

Dupas *n* **Jean** (1882–1964) French artist, whose decorations of the Church of Saint-Esprit, in Paris, brought him fame.

du Pasquier *n* **Nathalie** (1957–) French textile designer, who designs fashion fabrics for Pink Dragon, Esprit, and Missoni.

dupe *n* a person who is cheated. * *vt* to deceive; to trick.—**dupable** *adj*.—**duper** *n*.—**dupery** *n*.

duple *adj* double; (*mus*) of two beats to the bar.

duplet *n* (*mus*) a group of two notes of equal value that are played in the time normally taken by three.

duple time *n* (*mus*) a form of musical time in which the number of beats in a bar is a multiple of two, e.g., 2/4 (two quarter notes) and 6/8 (six eighth notes in two groups of three).

duplex *adj* having two parts, double. * *n* an apartment on two floors. *See also* **full duplex**.—**duplexity** *n*.

duplicate *adj* in pairs, double; identical; copied exactly from an original. * *n* one of a pair of identical things; a copy. * *vt* to make double; to make an exact copy of; to repeat.—**duplicable** *adj*.

duplication *n* the act of duplicating; a copy; multiplication by two.—**duplicative** *adj*.

duplicator *n* a machine for making copies, esp of a document.

duplicity *n* (*pl* **duplicities**) treachery; deception.—**duplicitous** *adj*.

du Pré *n* **Jacqueline** (1945–87) English cellist of worldwide repute, whose career ended in 1973, after she developed multiple sclerosis.

dur *adj* (*mus*) major (*major key*).

durable *adj* enduring, resisting wear, etc.—**durability** *n*.—**durably** *adv*.

Duralumin *n* (*Trademark*) a strong alloy of aluminum with copper, magnesium, manganese and silicon.

dura mater *n* the tough outer membrane that envelops the brain and spinal cord.

duramen *n* the inner heartwood of a tree.

durance *n* imprisonment.

Durand *n* **Asher Brown** (1796–1886) American painter. His early portrait and landscape prints established his reputation in this field. Notable works include *Kindred Spirits* (1849).

duration *n* the time in which an event continues.

Durban *n* a city in South Africa.

durbar *n* (*formerly*) a state levee or reception in India or Africa.

Dürer *n* **Albrecht** (1471–1528) German engraver and painter; a leading figure of the Northern Renaissance.

duress *n* compulsion by use of force or threat; unlawful constraint; imprisonment.

durian, durion *n* an oval fruit with a foul smell and a pleasant taste; the Asian tree that bears it.

during *prep* throughout the duration of; at a point in the course of.

durmast *n* a dark European oak yielding a tough wood.

Durrell *n* **Lawrence [George]** (1912–90) English poet, novelist, and travel writer.

Durrès n a city in Albania.

Du Ry *n* **Paul** (*b.* 1640) French architect, whose notable works include various buildings in Kassel.

Dushanbe *n* capital city of Tajikistan.

dusk *n* (the darker part of) twilight.

dusky *adj* (**duskier, duskiest**) having a dark color.—**duskily** *adv*.—**duskiness** *n*.

Dussek *n* **Jan Ladislav** (originally **Dusik**) (1760–1812) Czech pianist and composer, who earned a reputation as a virtuoso performer in his own lifetime. His works include 28 piano sonatas and 15 piano concertos, as well as many sonatas for violin and flute.

Düsseldorf *n* a city in Germany.

dust *n* fine particles of solid matter. * *vt* to free from dust; to sprinkle with flour, sugar, etc.

dustbin *n* (*Brit*) a garbage can or trash can.

dust bowl *n* a drought area subject to dust storms.

dust cover *n* a dust jacket.

dust devil *n* a small, short-lived whirlwind that picks up loose soil or sand and sweeps it around a central vortex, caused when land in dry areas gets very hot and convection currents form.

duster *n* (*Brit*) a cloth for dusting; a device for dusting; a duster coat; a light housecoat.

duster (coat), dustcoat *n* a woman's coat for keeping off dust, worn esp formerly for traveling in an open car.

dust jacket *n* a paper cover for a book.

dustman *n* (*pl* **dustmen**) a garbageman.

dust storm *n* a storm in dry or semi-arid areas where great quantities of dust are whipped up by the wind, causing serious loss of visibility.

dust tail *n* part of the tail of a comet consisting of dust grains liberated from the nucleus as it evaporates in the sun's radiation.

dust wrapper *n* a dust jacket.

dusty *adj* (**dustier, dustiest**) covered with dust.—**dustily** *adv*.—**dustiness** *n*.

Dutch *adj* of the people or language of Holland. * *n* the language of Holland.

Dutch courage *n* courage obtained from drinking alcohol; alcoholic drink.

Dutch elm disease *n* a fungal disease that withers the foliage of elm trees and eventually kills them.

Dutch oven *n* a metal box for cooking before an open fire.

Dutch treat *n* a meal, etc, where each pays for himself or herself.

Dutch uncle *n* a person with stern kindness.

duteous *adj* (*poet*) dutiful.—**duteously** *adv*.—**duteousness** *n*.

dutiable *adj* (*goods, etc*) subject to duty.—**dutiability** *n*.

dutiful *adj* performing one's duty; obedient.—**dutifully** *adv*.—**dutifulness** *n*.

duty *n* (*pl* **duties**) an obligation that must be performed for moral or legal reasons; respect for one's elders or superiors; actions and responsibilities arising from one's business, occupation, etc; a tax on goods or imports, etc.

duty-free *adj* free from tax or duty.

duumvir *n* (*pl* **duumvirs, duumviri**) in ancient Rome, either of two officers of high rank acting together in one capacity or public function; either member of a duumvirate.

duumvirate *n* a governing body of two; two such people.

duvet *n* a thick, soft quilt used instead of bedclothes.—*also* **continental quilt**.

DV *abbr* (*Bible*) = Douay Version.

DV *abbr* (*Latin*) = *Deo volente*, "God willing"; defective vision; Douay version (of the Bible); double vision.

DVA *abbr* (*Brit*) = Dunkirk Veterans' Association.

DVD *abbr* digital versatile disk; digital video disk.

DVE *abbr* = Diploma in Vocational Education.

DVetMed *abbr* = Doctor of Veterinary Medicine.

DVH *abbr* = Diploma in Veterinary Hygiene.

DVI *abbr* (*comput*) = digital video imaging; digital video interface.

DVLA *abbr* (*Brit*) = Driver and Vehicle Licensing Agency.

DVM *abbr* = Doctor of Veterinary Medicine.

DVM&S, DVMS *abbr* = Doctor of Veterinary Medicine and Surgery.

Dvorak *n* **Antonin** (1841–1904) Czech composer, whose most famous work is *Symphony No. 9 from the New World*.

Dvorak keyboard *n* (*comput*) a keyboard that is an alternative to the QWERTY keyboard.

d.v.p. *abbr* = (*Latin*) *decessit vita patris*, "he died in his father's lifetime."

DVS *abbr* = Doctor of Veterinary Science; Doctor of Veterinary Surgery.

DVSc *abbr* = Doctor of Veterinary Science.

DVSC *abbr* = Doctor of Veterinary Science; Doctor of Veterinary Surgery.

d.w. *abbr* = dead weight.

DW *abbr* = Daughters of Wisdom.

D/W *abbr* = dock warrant.

DWA *abbr* = Drystone Walling Association; driving without awareness.

dwarf *n* (*pl* **dwarfs, dwarves**) a person, animal, or plant of abnormally small size. * *vt* to stunt; to cause to appear small.

dwarf galaxy *n* a smaller galaxy, usu elliptical, that contains perhaps one or two million times the mass of the sun in a diameter of about 2000 parsec.

dwarfish *adj* like a dwarf; very small.—**dwarfishness** *n*.

dwarfism *n* an abnormal underdevelopment of the body manifested by small stature.

dwarf nova *n* a variable star thought to be a very close binary star, where matter is being transferred from one component to the other. —*also* **cataclysmic variable**.

dwarf star *n* a star of ordinary or low luminosity and relatively small mass and size.

DWAS *abbr* = Doctor Who Appreciation Society.

dwc *abbr* = deadweight capacity.

dweeb *n* (*inf*) a bore or a person considered unfashionable, a dull person.—**dweeby, dweebish** *adj*.

dwell *vi* (**dwelling, dwelt** *or* **dwelled**) to live (in a place); (*with* **on**) to focus the attention on; to think, talk, or write at length about.—**dweller** *n*.

dwelling *n* the house, etc where one lives, habitation.

dwindle *vi* to shrink, diminish; to become feeble.

Dworkin *n* **Andrea** (1946–) American feminist writer.

dwt *abbr* = deadweight tonnage; pennyweight.

DX *abbr* = (*radio*) distance.

DXR *abbr* = deep X-ray.

DXRT *abbr* = deep X-ray therapy.

Dy *symbol* (*chem*) dysprosium (element).

D/y *abbr* = delivery.

dyad *n* a pair; (*chem*) a bivalent atom, element, or radical.—**dyadic** *adj*.

dyarchy *see* **diarchy**.

Dyce *n* **William** (1806–64) Scottish painter and educationalist, who was heavily involved in the fresco revival of the 1940s.

Dyck *n* **Sir Anthony van** (1599–1641) Flemish painter, who developed his own unique and influential style of portraiture, investing his sitters with extraordinary character and refinement of detail.

dye *vt* (**dyeing, dyed**) to give a new color to. * *n* a coloring substance, esp in solution; a color or tint produced by dyeing.—**dyer** *n*.

dyed-in-the-wool *adj* uncompromising in attitude or opinion.

dyeing *n* the process or work of giving color to fabrics using dyes.

dyestuff *n* material yielding a dye.

Dyfed *n* a former county and an ancient realm in Wales.

Dyfnwal 1. (*d.* 934) king of Strathclyde, Scotland (*c.*920–934). He recognized Edward the Elder as overlord in 925. 2. (*d.* 975) king of Strathclyde, Scotland (934–*c.*973). He killed the king of Scots, Cuilean, in battle in 971 and died whilst on a pilgrimage to Rome.

dying¹ *see* **die¹**.

dying² *adj* passing away from life; decaying physically; drawing to a close; expiring. * *n* death.

dyke *n* (*geol*) an intrusion if igneous rock forced up from the hot molten material beneath the Earth's crust and which has become solid.

dyke *or* **dike¹** *n* igneous intrusion that occurs as a sheet-like body with near-parallel sides; normally discordant, cutting across the host rock.

dyke *or* **dike**² *n* an artificial embankment to prevent flooding.

dyke *or* **dike**³ *n* an artificial drainage ditch.

dyke¹ *see* **dike**¹.

dyke² *n* (*derog*) a lesbian.—*also* **dike**.

Dylan *n* **Bob** [Robert Allen Zimmerman] (1941–) American folk-rock singer and songwriter; the most prominent "protest" folksinger of the 1960s.

Dylan Eil Ton *n* (*Welsh Celtic myth*) the first of the two sons to be born to Aranrhod when she was taking the virginity test for the post of foot-holder to Math.

dyn. *or* **dynam.** *abbr* = dynamics.

dynamic *adj* relating to force that produces motion; (*person*) forceful, energetic.—**dynamically** *adv*.

dynamic accents *npl* (*mus*) accents which correspond to the regular rhythm of a piece of music, as indicated by the time signature.

dynamical *adj* relating to any quantity involving motion.

dynamical parallax *n* (*astron*) a method of estimating the parallax, and hence distance, of a binary star system.

dynamic data exchange *n* (*comput*) an interprocess channel through which correctly prepared programs can exchange data and control other programs.

dynamic equilibrium *n* (*phys*) a state of balance despite the physical changes taking place.

dynamic link *n* (*comput*) a method of linking data shared by two separate programs, required in multi-user networks.

dynamics *n* (*used as sing*) the branch of physics that deals with forces and their effect on the motion of bodies.

dynamism *n* dynamic influence or power; (*philos*) the theory that the universe is constituted of forces.—**dynamist** *n*.—**dynamistic** *adj*.

dynamite *n* a powerful explosive; a potentially dangerous situation; (*inf*) an energetic person or thing. * *vt* to blow up with dynamite.—**dynamiter** *n*.

dynamo *n* (*pl* **dynamos**) a device that generates electric current.

dynamoelectric, dynamoelectrical *adj* of or denoting the production of electricity from mechanical energy or of mechanical energy from electricity.

dynamometer *n* an instrument for measuring energy expended.

dynast *n* a ruler, usu a hereditary one.

dynasty *n* (*pl* **dynasties**) a line of hereditary rulers or leaders of any powerful family or similar group.—**dynastic** *adj*.—**dynastically** *adv*.

dyne *n* a unit of force, causing in one gram an acceleration per second of one centimeter per second; the unit of force in the cgs system.

dys- *prefix* bad, unfavorable.

dysarthria *n* poorly articulated speech that sounds weak or slurred because of impairment in the control of the muscles that affect speech.

dysentery *n* painful inflammation of the large intestine with associated diarrhea.—**dysenteric** *adj*.

dysergy *n* (*com*) the possibility that the merger of two companies will produce a combined operation of less productivity and efficiency, the opposite of synergy.

dysfunction *n* a failure in normal functioning.—**dysfunctional** *adj*.

dysgenic *adj* having a bad effect on the hereditary qualities of a race.

dysgenics *n* (*used as sing*) the study of the causes of reduction in quality of a race.

dyslexia *n* impaired ability in reading or spelling.—**dyslexic** *adj*, *n*.

dysmenorrhea *n* painful menstruation.—**dysmenorrheal** *adj*.

Dyson *n* Sir **George** *n* (1883–1964) English composer and teacher, whose works include one symphony and several cantatas, such as *The Canterbury Pilgrims*.

dyspepsia *n* indigestion, esp chronic.

dyspeptic *adj* of or afflicted with indigestion. * *n* a dyspeptic sufferer.

dysphagia *n* difficulty in swallowing.—**dysphagic** *adj*.

dysphasia *n* a deficiency in the use or understanding of language.—**dysphasic** *adj*.

dysphoria *n* morbid restlessness, the fidgets.—**dysphoric** *adj*.

dyspnea *n* shortness of breath, difficulty in breathing.—**dyspneal** *or* **dyspneic** *adj*.

dysprosium *n* a soft metallic element used in lasers and magnetic alloys. *symbol* Dy.

dyss *n* (*pl* **dysser**) (*archeo*) a type of megalithic cist from the late Danish Early Neolithic period.

dystrophy *n* any of various hereditary disorders causing progressive weakening of the muscles (*muscular dystrophy*).—**dystrophic** *adj*.

dysuria *n* difficulty in passing urine.—**dysuric** *adj*.

dz. *abbr* = dozen.

DZ *abbr* = Doctor of Zoology.

D

E

e, E the fifth letter of the English alphabet.

e *symbol* (*phys*) (the numerical value of the) electric charge of an electron or proton.

E *symbol* (*mus*) the third note (mediant) of the scale of C major.

e *abbr* = early; Earth; English; coefficient of impact or of restitution of elasticity; electromotive force; emmetropia; engineer; engineering; (*theat*) entrance; (*phys*) erg, the centimeter-gram-second unit of work or energy; (*mech*) longitudinal strain per unit length.

E *abbr* = East; Ecstasy (slang term for the drug); (*math*) eccentricity of a curve; English; earth (on electrical circuits); (*phys*) energy; elasticity (Young's modulus of); European (concerning weights which comply with EU regulations).

E- *prefix* used to indicate a standard system (for packaging, weight, content, etc) within the European Community.

ea. *abbr* = each.

EA *abbr* = East Anglia; educational age; Evangelical Alliance; enemy aircraft.

EAA *abbr* = Electrical Appliance Association; Entertainments Agents Association; European Aluminium Association; European Athletic Association.

EAACI *abbr* = European Academy of Allergology and Clinical Immunology.

EAAE *abbr* = European Association of Agricultural Economists.

EAAS *abbr* = East Anglian Aviation Society.

EAC *abbr* = Elderly Accommodation Counsel; Engineering Applications Center; Evangelical Association of the Caribbean.

EACC *abbr* = Edinburgh Airport Consultative Committee.

EACE *abbr* = European Association for Cognitive Ergonomics.

each *adj* every one of two or more.

Eachtach *n* (*Irish Celtic myth*) the daughter of Grainne and Diarmaid ua Duibhne. She attacked Fionn mac Cumhaill so severely that it took him four years to recover from his wounds.

EACN *abbr* = European Air Chemistry Network.

EACRO *abbr* = European Association of Contract Research Association.

EADA *abbr* = Eastern Dredging Association.

Eadbert *n* (*d.* 768) king of Northumbria, Britain (737–758). Came to the throne after the abdication of his cousin Ceolwulf.

Eadbert I *n* (*d.* 748) king of Kent, Britain (725–748). Joint ruler of the kingdom with his brother, Ethelbert II.

Eadbert II Praen *n* (*d. c.*810) king of Kent, Britain (796–798).

Eadric *n* (*d.* 688) king of Kent (*c.*685–687). Joint ruler with the East Saxon, Suabhard, under the overlordship of the South Saxons.

Eadwig *see* **Edwy.**

EAECMI *abbr* = Export Association of the Electric Cable Making Industry.

EAEE *abbr* = European Association of Earthquake Engineering.

EAES *abbr* = European Atomic Energy Society.

EAFA *abbr* = European Aluminium Foil Association.

EAG *abbr* = Environmental Assessment Group; European Atherosclerosis Group.

EAGB *abbr* = Executives Association of Great Britain; Eyecare Association of Great Britain.

eager *adj* enthusiastically desirous (of); keen (for); marked by impatient desire or interest.—**eagerly** *adv*.—**eagerness** *n*.

eager beaver *n* (*inf*) an exceptionally diligent person.

eagle *n* a bird of prey with keen eyes and powerful wings; (*golf*) a score of two strokes under par; (*Bible*) in the gospels a symbol of inspiration, hence its frequent use as a lectern in churches.

EAGLE *abbr* = European Association for Grey Literature Exploitation.

eagle-eyed *adj* having very sharp eyesight.

eagle owl *n* a type of large owl, also known as the great horned owl.

eaglet *n* a young eagle.

EAGO *abbr* = European Association of Gynaecologists and Obstetricians.

eagre *n* a bore or sudden tidal flood in an estuary.

EAHF *abbr* = eczema, asthma, hay fever.

EAHP *abbr* = European Association for Humanistic Psychology; European Association of Hospital Pharmacists.

EAHTMA *abbr* = Engineers and Allied Hand Tool Makers Association.

EAIA *abbr* = Early American Industries Association.

Eakins *n* **Thomas** (1844–1916) American painter of strongly realistic works, as in *The Gross Clinic* (1875), although his portraits show a more dramatic interest in the use of tonal contrasts; e.g. *Max Schmitt in a Single Scull* (1871).

Ealdhelm, Saint *see* **Aldhelm.**

Eames *n* 1. **Charles** (1907–78) American architect and one of the most influential furniture designers of the century. 2. **Ray** (1912–88) his wife, she edited *Arts and Architecture* and, from the late 1940s, worked on designs with her husband.

EAN *abbr* = European Academic Network; European Article Number (computer coding on retail items); effective atomic number.

e & e *abbr* = each and every.

E & OE *abbr* = errors and omissions excepted, which is often printed on invoice forms to protect the interests of the sender of the invoice in case an error has been introduced in the recipient's favor.

Eanfrith *n* king of Bernicia, Britain (633–634). The son of Ethelfrith, he married a Pictish princess, and their son, Talorcen, became a king of the Picts. He was killed by the Welsh king, Cadwallon.

EANI *abbr* = Energy Action Northern Ireland.

Eanna *n* (*Irish Celtic myth*) the father of Sgathach.

Eanred *n* (*d.* 850) king of Northumbria (809–841). A son of Eardwulf, he did homage to Egbert of Wessex in 827.

EAON *abbr* = except as otherwise noted.

EAP *abbr* = Environment Action Plans.

EAPA *abbr* = English Apples and Pears Association; European Asphalt Pavement Association.

EAPAC *abbr* = Eggs Authority Producer Advisory Committee.

ear *n* the sense organ used for detection of sound and maintenance of balance; the part of a cereal plant, e.g. corn, maize, that contains the seeds.

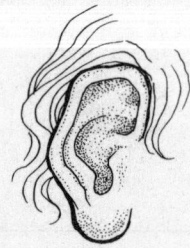

EAR *abbr* = Export Administration Regulations.

earache *n* pain in the ear that may be caused directly by inflammation of the middle ear but is often referred pain from other conditions, e.g. infections of the nose or larynx or tooth decay.

Eardley *n* **Joan** (1921–63) English-born Scottish painter. Her best-known works are landscapes and seascapes around the northeast coast of Scotland.

eardrum *n* the membrane within the ear that vibrates in response to sound waves.

Eardwulf *n* 1. (*d.* 762) king of Kent (747–762). The son of Eardbert, he was a joint ruler of the kingdom with Ethelbert II. 2. king of Northumbria (796–809). He deposed Osbald and was succeeded by his son, Enred.

eared *adj* having ears.

Earhart *n* **Amelia** (1898–1937) American aviator and the first woman to fly solo across the Atlantic (1932).

earing *n* (*naut*) a rope attaching the upper corner of a sail to a yard or stanchion.

earl *n* a member of the British nobility ranking between a marquis and a viscount.—**countess** *nf*.

Earl *n* **Ralph** (1751–1801) American painter. The bulk of his works are portraits of members of wealthy Connecticut families, e.g. *Oliver Ellsworth and his Wife* (1782).

earldom *n* the position or estate of an earl.

early *adj* (**earlier, earliest**) before the expected or normal time; of or occurring in the first part of a period or series; of or occurring in the distant past or near future.—*also adv*.—**earliness** *n*.

early adopter *n* one of a group of consumers who begin to use a new product very soon after it has been put on the market.

earmark *vt* to set aside for a specific use; to put an identification mark on. * *n* a distinguishing mark.

earmuff *n* one of a pair of joined cloth or fur pads for keeping the ears warm.

earn *vt* to gain (money, etc) by work or service; to acquire; to deserve; to earn interest (on money invested, etc).

EARN *abbr* = European Academic and Research Network.

earned income *n* income that is earned from employment or self-employment.

earnest *adj* sincere in attitude or intention.—**earnestly** *adv*.—**earnestness** *n*.

earnings *npl* wages or profits; something earned.

earnings per share *npl* the net profit after tax that is attributable to each ordinary share in a company.

earnings yield *n* the net profit after tax per ordinary share (earnings per share) for a specified accounting period expressed as a percentage of the current market price per share.

earn-out agreement *n* an agreement to buy a company, under which the buyer agrees to pay a lump sum at the time of purchase but agrees to a contingency agreement by which a larger amount will be paid if certain criteria are met during a specified number of years after purchase.

EAROM *abbr* = electrically alterable read-only memory.

Earp *n* **Wyatt [Berry Stapp]** (1848–1929) American gunfighter famous for his part in the gunbattle at the OK Coral in Tombstone, Arizona in 1881.

earphone *n* a device held to or worn over the ear, through which sound is transmitted; a headphone.

earpiece *n* a telephone earphone.

earplug *n* a piece of wadding or wax inserted in the ear to prevent noise or water penetration.

earring *n* an ornament worn on the ear lobe.

earshot *n* hearing distance.

ear-splitting *adj* very loud.

earth building *n* (*archit*) a crude method of construction using adobe, cob (clay soil with straw or roots) or pisé (dry loam with or without cement) with thick walls providing good insulation.

Earth *n* the third planet in the solar system with its orbit between Venus and Mars; the world that we inhabit; solid ground, as opposed to sea; soil; the burrow of a badger, fox, etc; a connection between an electric device or circuit with the earth; (*inf*) a large amount of money. * *vt* to cover with or bury in the earth; to connect an electrical circuit or device to earth.

earthborn *adj* mortal.

earthbound *adj* confined to the earth; heading towards the earth.

earthen *adj* composed of earth; made of baked clay.

earthenware *n* pottery, etc made from baked clay.

earthly *adj* (**earthlier, earthliest**) of the earth; material, worldly.—**earthliness** *n*.

earthquake *n* the often violent movement of the earth along a fault or fault zone due to tectonic upheaval.

earth science *n* any of the sciences (e.g., geology) concerned with the nature and composition of the earth.

earth station *n* a dish-shaped amplifier, antenna, receiver, or transmitter used to communicate directly with orbiting satellites.

Earth's magnetic field *see* **geomagnetism**.

earth tremor *n* a small earthquake that is unlikely to cause any damage.

earthwards, earthward *adv* towards the earth.

earthwork *n* an excavation of earth; a fortification.

earthworm *n* any of various common worms that live in the soil.

earthy *adj* (**earthier, earthiest**) of or resembling earth; crude.—**earthiness** *n*.

earwax *n* cerumen, the brown wax found in the ear.

earwig *n* a small insect with a pincer-like appendage at the end of its body.

EAS *abbr* = Energy Action Scotland; Epilepsy Association of Scotland; European Aquaculture Society; equivalent air speed; electronic article surveillance.

ease *n* freedom from pain, discomfort, or disturbance; rest from effort or work; effortlessness; lack of inhibition or restraint, naturalness. * *vt* to relieve from pain, trouble, or anxiety; to relax, make less tight, release; to move carefully and gradually. * *vi* (*often with* **off**) to become less active, intense, or severe.

easeful *adj* restful.

easel *n* a supporting frame, esp one used by artists to support their canvases while painting.

easement *n* (*law*) a legal document which conveys the right of real estate from one party to another usually for the building or maintaining of roads, sewage lines, electrical lines, or other public or private utilities; relief; something that gives ease or relief.

easily *adv* with ease; by far; probably.

east *n* the direction of the sunrise; the compass point opposite west; (*with cap* *preceded by* **the**); the area of the world east of Europe. * *adj, adv* in, towards or from the east.

East Caribbean Dollar *n* currency of Dominica, Grenada, Montserrat, St Kitts and Nevis, St Vincent and the Grenadines, and St Lucia.

Easter *n* the Christian festival observed on a Sunday in March or April in commemoration of the resurrection of Christ.

Easter Island *n* one of the most remote islands on earth, situated in the Pacific Ocean, and famous for its many enormous stone statues.

easterly *adj* situated towards or belonging to the east, coming from the east. * *n* (*pl* **easterlies**) a wind from the east.

eastern *adj* of or in the east.

eastern hemisphere *n* the eastern half of the globe beyond the Atlantic Ocean, encompassing Europe, Asia, and Africa.

Eastern Standard Time *n* the fifth time zone west of Greenwich (five hours behind GMT) that includes the eastern US.

easterner *n* someone from the east.

easternmost *adj* farthest to the east.

easting *n* the distance traveled by a vessel eastwards from a given meridian; the first part of a grid reference, representing distance measured eastwards from the reference line of the grid.

Eastlake *n* **Charles Locke** (1836–1906) British architect whose 1868 *Hints on Household Taste in Furniture, Upholstery, and Other Details* was a popular and significant guide.

Eastman *n* **George** (1854–1932) American inventor and philanthropist who invented the Kodak roll-film camera, and developed color photography.

eastward *adj* towards the east.—**eastwards** *adv*.

easy *adj* (**easier, easiest**) free from pain, trouble, anxiety; not difficult or requiring much effort; (*manner*) relaxed; lenient; compliant; unhurried; (*inf*) open to all alternatives. * *adv* with ease.—**easiness** *n*.

easy chair *n* a comfortable chair.

easygoing *adj* placid, tolerant, relaxed.

eat *vt* (**eating, ate,** *pp* **eaten**) to take into the mouth, chew, and swallow as food; to have a meal; to consume, to destroy bit by bit; (*also with* **into**) to corrode; (*inf*) to bother, cause anxiety to; (*with* **up**) to consume completely; (*inf*) to listen or absorb avidly; (*inf*) to preoccupy. * *vi* (*with* **out**) to eat away from home, esp in a restaurant. * *n* (*pl: inf*) food.—**eater** *n*.

EAT *abbr* = Employment Appeals Tribunal (Eire); Environmental Awareness Trust.

EATA *abbr* = East Asia Travel Association.

eatable *adj* suitable for eating; fit to be eaten. * *n* (*pl*) food.

EATB *abbr* = East Anglia Tourist Board.

eating disorder *n* a psychological disorder identified by unusual or abnormal eating patterns.—*See* **anorexia; bulimia nervosa**.

eau de Cologne *n* (*pl* **eaux de Cologne**) a perfume originally from Cologne.

eau de vie *n* brandy.

EAVA *abbr* = Ethnographic Audio Visual Archive.

eave *n* (*pl* **eaves**) the underneath part or overhanging edge of a sloping roof that overhangs a wall.

eavesdrop *vi* (**eavesdropping, eavesdropped**) to listen secretly to a private conversation.—**eavesdropper** *n*.

EAW *abbr* = Electrical Association for Women.

EAX *abbr* = electronic automatic exchange.

e.b. *abbr* = eastbound.

EB *abbr* = Encyclopaedia Britannica; Epstein-Barr (virus); epidermolysis bullosa (skin disease).

EBA *abbr* = Electric Boat Association; English Basketball Association; English Bowling Association; European Boardsailing Association.

EBAA *abbr* = Eye Bank Association of America.

ebb *n* the flow of the tide out to sea; a decline. * *vi* (*tide water*) to flow back; to become lower, to decline.

EBBS *abbr* = European Brain and Behaviour Society.

EBC *abbr* = English Bowls Council; European Brewery Convention.

EBCIDIC *abbr* = extended binary coded decimal interchange code (computing).

EBEA *abbr* = Economics and Business Education Association; Electronic and Business Equipment Association.

Ebedmelech *n* (*Bible*) the eunuch in Jerusalem who rescued the prophet Jeremiah.

Eber *or* **Eber Donn** *n* (*Irish Celtic myth*) one of the leaders of the expedition undertaken by the Sons of Mil Espaine to Ireland.

Eber Finn *n* (*Irish Celtic myth*) one of the leaders of the expedition made by the sons of Mil Espaine to Ireland. He was the brother of Eber Donn.

Eberhart *n* **Richard Ghormley** (1904–) American poet in the romantic tradition.

Eberson *n* **John** American designer of fantastic cinema interiors, including the Majestic Theater, Houston, Texas, in 1923.

EBF *abbr* = English Bowling Federation; European Baptist Federation.

E b N *abbr* = east by north.

EBOA *abbr* = Export Buying Offices Association.

ebon *n* (*poet*) ebony.

ebonite *n* a hard black rubber substance.

ebonize *vt* to make black by staining like ebony.

ebony *n* (*pl* **ebonies**) a hard heavy wood. * *adj* black as ebony.

Ebor. *abbr* (*Latin*) = *Eboracensis*, "of York"; *Eboracum*, "York."

ebracteate *adj* without bracts.

EBRD *abbr* = European Bank for Reconstruction and Development.

EbS *abbr* = east by south.

EBS *abbr* = Emergency Bed Service; European Book Society; European Business School; emergency broadcast system.

EBSA *abbr* = Estuarine and Brackish-Water Sciences Association.

EBSC *abbr* = Equine Behavior Study Circle; European Bird Strike Committee.

EBU *abbr* = English Bridge Union; European Badminton Union; European Boxing Union; European Broadcasting Union.

ebullient *adj* exuberant, enthusiastic; boiling.—**ebullience, ebulliency** *n*.—**ebulliently** *adv*.

ebullition *n* boiling; an outburst (of passion, feeling, etc).

EBV *abbr* = Epstein-Barr Virus.

e.c. *abbr* (*Latin*) = *exempli causa*, "for example."

EC *abbr* = East Central; Engineering Corps; Engineering Council; Episcopal Church; Established Church; European Community; European Council of Ministers; expansive system (of cataloguing).

ECA *abbr* = Bureau of Educational and Cultural Affairs; Economic Commission for Africa; Educational Centers Association; Electrical Contractors Association; Employment Conditions Abroad; English Clergy Association; English Curling Association; Environmental Contaminants Authority; European Cockpit Association; European Commission on Agriculture.

ECAB *abbr* = Employees' Compensation Appeals Board

ECAMA *abbr* = European Citric Acid Manufacturers' Association.

ECAT *abbr* = emission computerized axial tomography.

ECATRA *abbr* = European Car and Truck Rental Association.

ECAZA *abbr* = European Community Association of Zoos and Aquaria.

ECBC *abbr* = European Carbon Black Centre.

ECBO *abbr* = European Community Baroque Orchestra; European Conference of British Bus and Coach Operators.

ECC *abbr* = Electricity Consumers Council; English Ceramic Circle; European Crystallographic Committee.

ECCA *abbr* = European Coil Coating Association.

ECCC *abbr* = English Country Cheese Council.

eccentric *adj* deviating from a usual or accepted pattern; unconventional in manner or appearance, odd; (*circles*) not concentric; off center; not precisely circular. * *n* an eccentric person.—**eccentrically** *adv*.

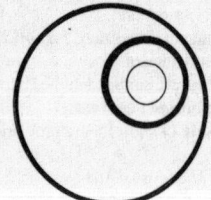

eccentricity *n* (*pl* **eccentricities**) strangeness of behavior; an eccentric or unusual habit.

eccl., eccles. *abbr* = ecclesiastical; ecclesiology.

Ecclesiastes *n* (*Bible*) OT book, the title of which means the preacher.

ecclesiastic *n* a member of the clergy.

ecclesiastical *adj* of or relating to the Christian Church or clergy.—**ecclesiastically** *adv*.

ecclesiasticism *n* excessive attachment to the forms, usages, organization, and privileges of the Christian Church.

ecclesiology *n* the study of the Christian Church and its development; the study of church architecture and decoration.—**ecclesiological** *adj*.—**ecclesiologist** *n*.

Ecclus. *abbr* = Ecclesiasticus.

ECCM *abbr* = electronic counter-countermeasures.

ECCO *abbr* = European Culture Collections' Organization.

ECCP *abbr* = European Committee on Crime Problems.

ECCU *abbr* = English Cross-Country Union.

ECDU *abbr* = European Christian Democratic Union.

ecdysis (*pl* **ecdyses**) *n* sloughing of skin, molting.

ECE *abbr* = Economic Commission for Europe.

ECF *abbr* = East China Fair; Eastern Counties Farmers; European Caravan Federation; European Coffee Federation; European Commission on Forestry and Forest Products; European Cyclists Federation.

ECG *abbr* = Ecosystem Conservation Group; Export Credit Guarantee; electrocardiogram.

ECGD *abbr* = Export Credits Guarantee Department.

echelon *n* a stepped formation of troops, ships, or aircraft; a level (of authority) in a hierarchy.

Echemus *n* (*Greek myth*) a king of Arcadia.

Echetus *n* (*Greek myth*) a king of Epirus who was noted for his terrible cruelty.

ECHG *abbr* = English Churches Housing Group; Equipment for Charity Hospitals Overseas.

Echid *n* (*Irish Celtic myth*) the grandfather of Concho-bar mac Nessa.

echidna *n* (*pl* **echidnas, echidnae**) an Australian nocturnal, toothless, spiny, egg-laying animal.

Echidna *n* (*Greek myth*) a monster, half girl and half serpent, who lived in a cave and ate passers-by.

echinococcosis *n* the condition created when cysts from the larval stages of a tapeworm create malignant tumors in the brain, lungs, or liver.

echinoderm *n* one of a class of animals which includes starfish and sea urchins.

echinus *n* (*pl* **echini**) a sea urchin.

Echion *n* (*Greek myth*) one of the Sparti, the five survivors of the group of armed men that rose up from the teeth of the dragon at Thebes sown by Cadmus.

echo *n* (*pl* **echoes**) a repetition of sound caused by the reflection of sound waves; imitation; the reflection of a radar signal by an object. * *vb* (**echoing, echoed**) *vi* to resound; to produce an echo. * *vt* to repeat; to imitate; to send back (a sound) by an echo. *vi* (*comput*) to show on screen the commands being executed by a computer as they are being performed

Echo *n* (*Greek myth*) a mountain nymph, whom the goddess Hera punished by depriving her of speech, unless first spoken to. She fell in love with Narcissus, who did not return her affection, and faded away until nothing was left but her voice.

echocardiography *n* the use of ultrasound to study the heart and its movements.

echography *n* the use of sound waves (ultrasound) to create an image of the deeper structures of the body.—*see also* **ultrasonography**.

echoic *adj* like an echo; imitative.

echolocation *n* finding unseen objects by means of reflected sound waves.

echo sounder *n* an instrument for determining the depth beneath a ship using sound waves.—**echo sounding** *n*.

echovirus *n* a virus that can cause symptoms of the common cold, mild meningitis, and intestinal and respiratory infections.

ECHR *abbr* = European Court of Human Rights; European Commission on Human Rights.

echtrai or **eachtra** *n* (*Irish Celtic myth*) a class of adventure legends usually relating to a mortal's journey to the Otherworld.

ECIMOT *abbr* = European Central Inland Movements of Transport.

ECJ *abbr* = European Court of Justice.

Eckmann *n* **Otto** (1865–1902) German designer and painter who was one of the main proponents of Jugendstil.

ecl., eclec. *abbr* = eclectic.

éclair *n* a small oblong shell of choux pastry covered with chocolate and filled with cream.

eclampsia *n* convulsions that occur during pregnancy, usu at the later stages or during delivery.

éclat *n* success; applause; striking effect; social distinction.

eclectic *adj* selecting from or using various styles, ideas, methods, etc; composed of elements from a variety of sources. * *n* a person who adopts an eclectic method.—**eclectically** *adv*.—**eclecticism** *n*.

eclipse *n* (*astron*) the total or partial disappearance of one astronomical body by passing into the shadow of another; a decline into obscurity, as from overshadowing by others. * *vt* to cause an eclipse of; to overshadow, darken; to surpass.—**eclipser** *n*.

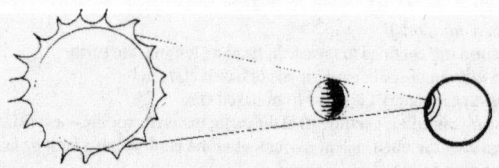

ecliptic *n* the apparent path of the sun's motion relative to the stars.—**ecliptically** *adv*.

eclogue *n* a short, esp pastoral poem.

ECMA *abbr* = European Collectors and Modellers Association; European Computer Manufacturers Association.

ECMWF *abbr* = European Centre for Medium-Range Weather Forecasting.

ECNC *abbr* = Economic Committee of the Nordic Council; European Centre for Nature Conservation.

Eco *n* **Umberto** (1932–) Italian critic and novelist who made his mark as the writer of *A Theory of Semiotics*, and whose best-known novel is *The Name of the Rose*.

ECO *abbr* = English Chamber Orchestra; English Channel Organization; Irish Environmental Conservation Organization for Youth; Malta Ecological Society.

eco- *prefix* ecology; ecological.

ECoG *abbr* = electrocorticogram.

ecol. *abbr* = ecological; ecology.

E. coli *abbr* (*Latin*) = *Escherichia coli*, a type of bacteria.

ecology *n* (the study of) the relationships between living things and their environments.—**ecological** *adj*.—**ecologist** *n*.

ECOM *abbr* = electronic computer-originated mail.

e-commerce or **electronic commerce** *n* (*comput*) the undertaking of business transactions online.

econ. *abbr* = economic; economics; economy.

econometrics *n* the employment of statistical techniques in the analysis of economic data.

economic *adj* pertaining to economics or the economy; (*business, etc*) capable of producing a profit.

economical *adj* thrifty.—**economically** *adv*.

economic growth *n* an increase in the output of a country's economy in terms of goods and services.

economics *n* (*sing*) the social science concerned with the production, consumption, and distribution of goods and services; (*pl*) financial aspects.

economic sanctions *npl* restriction on imports or exports imposed on a country by another country or group of countries in order to cause damage to its economic interests and so bring pressure on it to bring about political or social change.

economic value *n* the present value of expected future cash flows.

economies of scale *npl* reductions in the average cost of production, and thus in unit costs, when production output has been increased.

economist *n* an expert in economics.

economize *vt* to spend money carefully; to save; to use prudently.—**economization** *n*.

economy *n* (*pl* **economies**) careful use of money and resources to minimize waste; an instance of this; the management of the finances and resources, etc of a business, industry, or organization; the economic system of a country.

ECOSOC *abbr* = Economic and Social Council

ecosphere *n* the parts of the universe where life can exist.

écossaise *n* (*mus*) (*French*) abbreviation of *danse écossaise*, i.e. "Scottish dance," although in fact the term has little to do with Scottish dancing and merely refers to a quick dance in 2/4 time.

ecosystem *n* an ecological community that includes all organisms that occur naturally within a specific area.

Ecovast *abbr* = European Council for the Village and Small Town.

ECP *abbr* = English Collective of Prostitutes; European Confederation for Plant Protection Research.

ECPS *abbr* = European Centre for Population Studies.

ECR *abbr* = electronic cash register.

ecru *n* beige.

ECS *abbr* = European Communications Satellite.

ECSA *abbr* = Estuarine and Coastal Studies Association; European Chips and Snacks Association.

ECSC *abbr* = Energy Conservation and Solar Center; European Coal and Steel Community.

ECST *abbr* = European Convention on the Suppression of Terrorism.

ecstasy *n* (*pl* **ecstasies**) intense joy; (*sl: often with cap*) the synthetic amphetamine-based drug MDMA, which reduces social and sexual inhibitions.—**ecstatic** *adj*.—**ecstatically** *adv*.

ECT *abbr* = electroconvulsive therapy.

ECTA *abbr* = Electrical Contractors' Trading Association.

ECTF *abbr* = Edinburgh Centre for Tropical Forests.

ECTG *abbr* = European Channel Tunnel Group.

ECTMAC *abbr* = East Coast Trawl Management Advisory Committee.

ecto-, ect- *prefix* outside.

ectoderm *n* the outer layer of an embryo or skin.

ectomorph *n* a person with a lightly built physique.—**ectomorphic** *adj*.—**ectomorphy** *n*.

-ectomy *n suffix* denoting surgical removal of a part.

ectopic *adj* a term used to refer to something that is not in its usual place or occurring at its usual time, e.g. an ectopic pregnancy is one in which the fertilized egg implants outside the uterus.

ectoplasm *n* the outer layer of the cytoplasm of a cell; a substance supposedly exuded from the body of spiritualist mediums during trances.—**ectoplasmic** *adj*.

ECTU *abbr* = European Confederation of Trade Unions.

ectype *n* a reproduction or imitation of an original design.

ECU *abbr* = English Church Union; European Chiropractors Union; European Customs Union; European currency unit.

Ecuador *n* an Andean country situated in the northwest of the South American continent.

ecumenical *adj* of the whole Christian Church; seeking Christian unity worldwide.—**ecumenicalism, ecumenicism** *n*.—**ecumenically** *adv*.

ECW *abbr* = Emergency Conservation Work.

ECWS *abbr* = English Civil War Society.

ECY *abbr* = European Conservation Year.

ECYO *abbr* = European Community Youth Orchestra.

eczema *n* an inflammation of the skin that causes itching, a red rash, and often small blisters that weep and become encrusted. It is often the case that eczema, hay fever, and asthma are found in the family history.—**eczematous** *adj*.

ed. *abbr* = edited; edition; editor

e.d. *abbr* = *ex dividend*; (*mil*) extra duty.

ED *abbr* = Doctor of Engineering; Eastern Department.

EDA *abbr* = Eating Disorders Association; Ecological Design Association; Economic Development Administration; English Draughts Association; European Dyslexia Association.

Edain *see* Etain.

edacious *adj* gluttonous, greedy.—**edacity** *n*.

Edam *n* a mild-flavored round Dutch cheese, usu with a red waxy rind.

EDANA *abbr* = European Disposables and Nonwovens Association.

EdB *abbr* = Bachelor of Education.

Edbald *n* (*d.* 640) king of Kent (616–640). On succeeding his father, Ethelbert, he promptly renounced Christianity, which had been introduced to the kingdom by St Augustine in his father's reign.

EDBS *abbr* = expert database system.

EDC *abbr* = Early Dance Circle; Education Development Center; European Defence Community; ethylene dichloride; (*med*) expected date of confinement .

EdD *abbr* = Doctor of Education.

EDD *abbr* = (*med*) expected date of delivery; English Dialect Dictionary.

Eddington *n* **Sir Arthur Stanley** (1882–1944) English astronomer and physicist who published several popular and highly readable books explaining such topics as Einstein's theory of relativity, e.g. *Mathematical Theory of Relativity* (1923) and *The Expanding Universe* (1933).

eddy *n* a roughly circular movement within a body of air or water that can be much stronger than the smooth current in which they form. * *vi* (**eddying, eddied**) to move round and round.

Eddy *n* **Mary Baker** (1821–1910) American religious leader who devised a system of faith healing called "Christian Science," and founded the Church of Christ, Scientist, in Boston (1879).

edelweiss *n* a small white-flowered alpine herb.

edema *n* an accumulation of fluid in the body, possibly beneath the skin or in cavities or organs.—*also* **oedema**.—**edematous** *adj*.

Eden *n* (*Bible*) the garden where Adam and Eve lived in the creation story in Genesis.

Eden *n* **Sir [Robert] Anthony [1st Earl of Avon]** (1897–1977) British Conservative prime minister (1955–57).

edentate *adj* (*zool*) toothless.

EDF *abbr* = European Development Fund.

Edgar *n* **David** (1948–) English dramatist whose two most important works are *Destiny* and his adaptation of Dickens's *The Life and Adventures of Nicholas Nickleby*.

EDGAR *abbr* = Electronic Data Gathering, Analysis, and Retrieval

edge *n* the border, brink, verge, margin; the sharp cutting side of a blade; sharpness, keenness; force, effectiveness. * *vt* to supply an edge or border to; to move gradually.—**edger** *n*.

edgeways, edgewise *adv* with the edge forwards; sideways.

Edgeworth *n* **Maria** (1768–1849) Irish novelist whose many works include a treatise on education, children's stories, romantic novels, and historical novels, e.g. *Castle Rackrent*.

Edfu *n* (*Egypt*) an ancient site in Upper Egypt, south of Thebes, on the western bank of the Nile.

Edgar *n* **1.** (1074–1107) king of Scots (1097–1107). The fourth son of Malcolm III's second marriage. He died unmarried, and the kingdom passed to his brother Alexander I. **2.** (943–975) king of England (957–975). The second son of Edmund I and Elgifu, he replaced Edwy as ruler of Northumbria and Mercia. His legitimate sons were Edward (the Marytr), Edmund (the Aetheling) and Ethelred II (the Unready).

edging *n* any border for decoration or strengthening.

edgy *adj* (**edgier, edgiest**) irritable.—**edgily** *adv*.—**edginess** *n*.

edible *adj* fit or safe to eat.—**edibility, edibleness** *n*.

edict *n* a decree; a proclamation.—**edictal** *adj*.

edicule *n* (*archit*) in classical architecture, a shrine or small room.

edifice *n* a substantial building; any large or complex organization or institution.—**edificial** *adj*.

edify *vt* (**edifying, edified**) to improve the moral character or mind of (a person).—**edification** *n*.—**edifier** *n*.—**edifyingly** *adv*.

edile *n* a magistrate of ancient Rome.

Edinburgh *n* major Scottish city in United Kingdom of Great Britain and Northern Ireland (UK).

Edinburgh Tapestry Company textile firm established by the 4th Marquess of Bute in 1912.

Edinburgh Weavers *npl* fabric and carpet manufacturers established in Edinburgh in 1929 with a reputation for the innovative use of modern avant-garde designs.

Edis *n* **Robert William** (1839–1927) British architect who promoted the red-brick Queen Anne style for buildings.

Edison *n* **Thomas Alva** (1847–1931) American physicist and inventor who invented, amongst other things, the gramophone (1877) and the incandescent light bulb (1877).

edit *vt* to prepare (text) for publication by checking facts, grammar, style, etc; to be in charge of a publication; (*cinema*) to prepare a final version of a film by selection and arrangement of photographed sequences; (*comput*) to change or alter text, graphics, or values that appear in a file.

edit. *abbr* = edited; edition.

editio princeps (*pl* **editiones principes**) *n* the first printed edition of a book.

edition *n* a whole number of copies of a book, etc printed at a time; the form of a particular publication.

editor *n* a person in charge of a newspaper or other publication; a person who edits written material for publication; one who prepares the final version of a film; a person in overall charge of the form and content of a radio or television show.—**editorship** *n*.

editorial *adj* of or produced by an editor.* *n* an article expressing the opinions of the editor or publishers of a newspaper or magazine.—**editorialist** *n*.—**editorially** *adv*.

EDLS *abbr* = European Divine Life Society.

EdM *abbr* = Master of Education.

Edmund *n* **Saint** (841–70) said to have been a Saxon prince. His feast day is November 20.

Edmund I *n* (921–946) king of England (939–946). The eldest son of Edward the Elder and Edgifu, he succeeded his half-brother Ethelstan as king. He married twice and had two sons who became kings: Edgar and Edwy.

Edmund II Ironside *n* (993–1016) king of England. Reigned for seven months in 1016. The eldest surviving son of Ethelred II and Elfled.

Edmund Rich *n* Saint [**Edmund of Abingdon**] (*c*.1170–1240) English priest who led a life of extreme mortification; wrote the treatise *Speculum Ecclesiae*; archbishop of Canterbury (1233); canonized in 1247. His feast day is November 16.

edoc *abbr* = effective date of change.

Edom *n* (*Bible*) the land of Edom, meaning red, which lay between the Dead Sea and the Red Sea.—*also* **Idumea**.

Edonians *npl* a tribe of Thracia in ancient Greece.—*also* **Edoni**.

EDP *abbr* = electronic data processing.

Edred *n* (923–955) king of England (946–955). The youngest son of Edward the Elder and Edgifu, succeeded to the throne on the murder of his brother, Edmund I, in 946.

eds. *abbr* = editors.

EDS *abbr* = English Dialect Society.

Edsat *abbr* = educational television satellite.

educ. *abbr* = educated; education; educational.

educable, educatable *adj* able to be educated.

educate *vt* to train the mind, to teach; to provide schooling for.—**educator** *n*.

education *n* the process of learning and training; instruction as imparted in schools, colleges, and universities; a course or type of instruction; the theory and practice of teaching.—**educational** *adj*.—**educationally** *adv*.

educationalist, educationist *n* an expert in education.

educative *adj* educating.

educe *vt* to elicit (information, etc); to infer.—**educible** *adj*.

edulcorate *vt* to free from acids and other impurities by washing.—**edulcoration** *n*.

edutainment *n* (*comput*) computer software that educates the user while being entertaining.

Edward *n* (1964–) English prince; the third son of Queen Elizabeth II of England. *See* **Elizabeth II**.

Edward I *n* (Hammer of the Scots) (1239–1307) king of England, Wales, Scotland and Ireland (1272–1307). The eldest surviving son of Henry III and Eleanor of Provence.

Edward II *n* (1284–1327) king of England and Wales (1307–1327). The only surviving son of Edward I and Eleanor of Castile.

Edward III *n* (1312–1377) king of England and Wales (1327–1377). The eldest son of Edward II and Isabella of France.

Edward IV *n* (1442–1483) king of England and Wales (1461–1483). The son of Richard Plantagenet, Duke of York, and grandson of Edmund, Earl of Cambridge and Duke of York, fourth son of Edward III, he became the first Yorkist king after ousting Henry VI in the dynastic civil wars, later called the Wars of the Roses.

Edward V *n* (1470–1483) king of England and Wales. Reigned for 77 days in 1483. The eldest son of Edward IV and Elizabeth Woodville, he became Prince of Wales in 1471 and was in his thirteenth year when he succeeded his father.

Edward VI *n* (1537–1553) king of England and Ireland (1547–1553). The only son of Henry VIII by Jane Seymour.

Edward VII *n* (1841–1910) king of the United Kingdom of Great Britain and Ireland and British Dominions overseas; Emperor of India (1901–1910). The eldest son of Queen Victoria and Prince Albert of Saxe-Coburg-Gotha.

Edward VIII *see* **Windsor, Duke of**.

Edward the Confessor *n* [Saint] (*c*.1004–66) English saint and king; saint; son of Ethelred II the Unready. He succeeded to the throne in 1042 and founded Westminster Abbey. His feast day is October 13.

Edward the Elder *n* (870–924) king of Wessex (899–924). The son of Alfred the Great. His sons Elfward, Ethelstan, Edmund I and Edred, all became kings.

Edward the Martyr *n* (St Edward) (963–978) king of England (975–978). The only son of Edgar and Ethelfled. When he went to visit his stepbrother Ethelred at Corfe, he was stabbed in the back. His feast day is March 18

Edwards *n* 1. **Edward B** (1873–1948) American graphic designer and illustrator, became director of the American Institute of Graphic Art. 2. **Jonathan** (1703–58) American divine whose writings, e.g. *The Freedom of the Will*, had a strong influence on many 18th and 19th-century writers.

Edwin *n* (*d*. 633) king of Northumberland, Britain (616–633). The city of Edinburgh in Scotland derives its name from being Edwin's northern outpost.

Edwy *or* **Eadwig** *n* (940–959) king of England (955–959). The eldest son of Edmund I and Elfgifu.

EE *abbr* = Early English; Electrical Engineer; ells English; English Estates; errors excepted.

EEA *abbr* = Employment Equality Agency (Eire); European Energy Association; European Evangelical Alliance.

EE & MP *abbr* = Envoy Extraordinary and Minister Plenipotentiary.

EEBB *abbr* = East Europe Boxing Bureau.

EEC *abbr* = European Economic Community (now European Union).

EED *abbr* = electro-explosive device.

EEF *abbr* = Engineering Employers' Federation.

EEG *abbr* = Essence Export Group; electroencephalogram; electroencephalograph.

EEIBA *abbr* = Electrical and Electronics Industries Benevolent Association.

eel *n* a snake-like fish.

eelpout *n* a type of freshwater fish, found in Europe, North America, and Asia.—*also* **burbot**.

e'en *n* (*poet*) evening.

EENT *abbr* = eye, ear, nose, and throat.

EEO *abbr* = Energy Efficiency Office.

EEOC *abbr* = Equal Employment Opportunities Commission.

EEPROM *abbr* = electrically erasable programmable memory (computing).

e'er *adv* (*poet*) ever.

eerie *adj* (**eerier, eeriest**) causing fear; weird.—**eerily** *adv*.—**eeriness** *n*.

EEROM *abbr* = electrically erasable read-only memory.

EES *abbr* = European Exchange System.

EET *abbr* = Eastern European Time.

Eètion *n* (*Greek myth*) an ally of the Trojans. He and his seven sons were killed by Achilles in one day.

EETPU *abbr* = Electrical, Electronic, Telecommunications, and Plumbing Union.

EETS *abbr* = Early English Text Society.

EEZ *abbr* = exclusive economic zone.

EF! *abbr* = Earth First!

EFA *abbr* = Electrical Floorwarming Association; Eton Fives Association; European Free Alliance; European Fighter Aircraft; essential fatty acids.

EFAA *abbr* = English Field Archery Association.

EFDSS *abbr* = English Folk Dance and Song Society.

EFEC *abbr* = European Fashion Export Council.

efface *vt* to rub out, obliterate; to make (oneself) humble or inconspicuous.—**effaceable** *adj*.—**effacement** *n*.—**effacer** *n*.

effect *n* the result of a cause or action by some agent; the power to produce some result; the fundamental meaning; an impression on the senses; an operative condition; (*pl*) personal belongings; (*pl: theater, cinema*) sounds, lighting, etc to accompany a production. * *vt* to bring about, accomplish.—**effecter** *n*.—**effectible** *adj*.

effective *adj* producing a specified effect; forceful, striking in impression; actual, real; operative.—**effectively** *adv*.—**effectiveness** *n*.

effective tax rate *n* the average tax rate that is applicable in a given situation.

effector *n* a motor or sensory nerve ending that terminates in a muscle, gland, or organ and stimulates contraction or secretion.

effectual *adj* able to produce the desired effect.—**effectuality, effectualness** *n*.—**effectually** *adv*.

effectuate *vt* to make happen.—**effectuation** *n*.

effeminate *adj* (*man*) displaying what are regarded as feminine qualities.—**effeminacy, effeminateness** *n*.

effendi (*pl* **effendis**) *n* a Turkish title of respect, equivalent to sir or Mr.

efferent *n* (*med*) a term meaning "outwards from an organ, etc," especially the brain or spinal cord, e.g. an efferent nerve. *Compare* **afferent**.

effervesce *vt* (*liquid*) to froth and hiss as bubbles of gas escape; to be exhilarated.—**effervescence** *n*.—**effervescent** *adj*.—**effervescible** *adj*.

effete *adj* decadent, weak.—**effeteness** *n*.

efficacious *adj* achieving the desired result.—**efficacy, efficaciousness** *n*.

efficient *adj* achieving results without waste of time or effort; competent.—**efficiently** *adv*.—**efficiency** *n* (*pl* **efficiencies**).

effigy *n* (*pl* **effigies**) a sculpture or portrait; a crude figure of a person, esp for exposure to public contempt and ridicule.

effloresce *vi* to blossom; (*chem*) to turn to powder when exposed to air, to crystallize; to become encrusted with crystals as a result of loss of water.—**efflorescence** *n*.—**efflorescent** *adj*.

effluence, efflux *n* something that flows out.

effluent the flow of sewage, fertilizers in solution, liquid industrial waste, or other liquid pollution into streams, rivers, lakes, or the sea.

effluent stream *n* a small distributary that should not be confused with effluent as in pollution.

effluvium *n* (*pl* **effluvia, effluviums**) an offensive vapor or smell.—**effluvial** *adj*.

Effner *n* Joseph (*b*.1687) German architect. His notable works include the Gallery of Ancestors in Münich.

effort *n* exertion; an attempt, try; a product of great exertion.—**effortful** *adj*.

effortless *adj* done with little effort, or seemingly so.—**effortlessly** *adv*.—**effortlessness** *n*.

effrontery *n* (*pl* **effronteries**) impudent boldness, insolence.

EFFTA *abbr* = European Fishing Tackle Trade Association.

effulgent *adj* radiant, brilliant.—**effulgence** *n*.

effuse *vt* (*liquid, words*) to flow or pour out.

effusion *n* a pouring out; an unrestrained outpouring, as of emotion; something poured out.

effusive *adj* gushing, emotionally unrestrained; demonstrative.—**effusiveness** *n*.

EFG *abbr* = Economic Forestry Group.

EFGA *abbr* = English Farmers and Growers Association.

EFH *abbr* = Elizabeth Fitzroy Homes.

EFI *abbr* = Electronic Forum for Industry; Equestrian Federation of Ireland.

EFL *abbr* = English as a foreign language.

Efnisien *n* (*Welsh Celtic myth*) the brother of Nisien and the half-brother of Bendigeid Vran, Branwen and the rest of the children of Llyr. He was known as a mischief-maker, and his brother Nisien was known as a peacemaker.

eft *n* a newt.

EFT *abbr* = electronic funds transfer.

EFTA *abbr* = European Free Trade Association.

EFTPOS *abbr* = electronic funds transfer at point of sales (the transfer of monies by electronic means from one bank account to another).

EFTS *abbr* = electronic funds transfer system.

EFTU *abbr* = Engineering and Fastener Trade Union.

EFU *abbr* = European Football Union.

e.g. *abbr* (*Latin*) = *exempli gratia*, "for example."

Eg. *abbr* = Egypt; Egyptian; Egyptology

EG *abbr* = Engineers' Guild.

EGA *abbr* (*comput*) = Enhanced Graphic Adapter. A color bit-mapped VDU display adapter for IBM-compatible personal computers. *See* **bitmap**.

egad *interj* (*arch*) an exclamation of surprise, pleasure, or admiration.

egalitarian *adj* upholding the principle of equal rights for all.—*also n.*—**egalitarianism** *n*.

Egbert *n* (Egbert III of Kent) (775–839) king of Wessex, England (802–839).

Egbert I *n* **1.** (*d.* 873) king of Bernicia, Britain. Installed as ruler of this kingdom in Northumbria by the Vikings in 867. **2.** king of Kent, Britain (664–673). He extended his kingdom to include Surrey.

Egbert II *n* **1.** (*d.* 878) king of Bernicia, Britain (876–878). The last of the Viking-installed rulers. **2.** king of Kent, Britain (765–780). Failed to win independence from the Mercian overlords at the Battle of Otford in 766.

Egeria *n* (*Roman myth*) a nymph who was made a goddess; said to have been the source of the laws of the Romans.

egest *vt* to excrete.—**egestion** *n*.

egesta *npl* excrement.

Egfrith *n* **1.** (*d.* 685) king of Northumbria, Britain (670–685). The son of Oswy and Eanfled of Deira. **2.** (*d.* 796) king of Mercia, Britain (787–796). The son of the powerful Offa, he survived his father by only 141 days, having ruled jointly with him since 787.

egg[1] *n* the oval hard-shelled reproductive cell laid by birds, reptiles, and fish; the egg of the domestic poultry used as food; ovum.—**eggy** *adj*.

egg[2] *vt* (*with* **on**) to incite (someone to do something).

egg and dart *n* (*archit*) an ovolo molding that is decorated with half egg shapes and arrow heads, alternating along the molding.

egger *n* a type of large moth.

egghead *n* (*inf*) an intellectual.

eggnog *n* a drink made from egg, beaten up with hot milk, sugar, and brandy.

eggplant *n* a plant producing a smooth, dark-purple fruit; this fruit is used as a vegetable. *See* **aubergine**.

eggshell *n* the hard outer covering of an egg. * *adj* fragile; (*paint*) having a slight sheen.

EGI *abbr* = Edward Grey Institute (of Field Ornithology).

Egk *n* **Werner** (1901–83) a German composer and conductor who was influenced by Stravinsky. His important works include the operas *Peer Gynt*, *Irish Legend*, and *The Government Inspector*. He also wrote ballet and choral music.

eglantine *n* the sweetbrier; the wild rose.

EGM *abbr* = extraordinary general meeting.

ego *n* (*pl* **egos**) the self; self-image, conceit.

egocentric *adj* self-centered.—**egocentricity** *n*.

egoism *n* self-concern; self-centeredness.—**egoist** *n*.—**egoistic, egoistical** *adj*.—**egoistically** *adv*.

egotism *n* excessive reference to oneself; conceit.—**egotist** *n*.—**egotistic, egotistical** *adj*.—**egotistically** *adv*.

ego trip *n* (*inf*) an activity undertaken to boost one's own self-esteem or importance in the eyes of others.—**ego-trip** *vi*.

egregious *adj* outstandingly bad.—**egregiousness** *n*.

egress *n* the way out, exit.

egression *n* the act of going out or emerging; egress.

egret *n* a type of heron.

Egric *n* (*d.* 637) king of East Anglia, England (634–637).

EGS *abbr* = English Goethe Society.

EGSF *abbr* = Equine Grass Sickness Fund.

EGU *abbr* = English Golf Union.

Egypt *n* desert country watered by the River Nile in North Africa.—**Egyptian** *adj*.

Egypt. *abbr* = Egyptian.

Egyptian Pound *n* currency of Egypt.

Egyptology *n* the scholarly study of ancient Egypt in all its aspects.—**Egyptologist** *n*.

eh *interj* an exclamation of inquiry or surprise.

EHA *abbr* = Economic History Association; European Helicopter Association.

EHB *abbr* = European Homograft Bank.

EHF *abbr* = European Hockey Federation; extremely high frequency.

EHIA *abbr* = European Herbal Infusions Association.

EHO *abbr* = Environmental Health Officer.

e.h.p. *abbr* = effective horsepower; electric horsepower.

EHPS *abbr* = Endurance Horse and Pony Society of Great Britain.

Ehrenburg *n* **Ilya Grigoryevich** (1891–1969) Russian war correspondent and novelist whose greatest novel is *The Thaw*, the first major work published in the USSR to address the horrors of the Stalin era.

Ehrlich 1. *n* **Franz** (1907–83) German designer, trained at the Bauhaus, who worked for Walter Gropius in Berlin. **2. Paul** (1854–1915) German bacteriologist who developed a cure for syphilis (1910). He was the winner of the 1908 Nobel prize for physiology or medicine.

EHS *abbr* = Ecclesiastical History Society.

EHT *abbr* = extra high tension.

EIA *abbr* = Energy Information Administration; environmental impact assessment.

EIB *abbr* = European Investment Bank.

EIBA *abbr* = English Indoor Bowling Association.

EICA *abbr* = East India Cotton Association.

Eichler *n* **Fritz** (1911–91) German teacher and designer, who established Braun's distinctive stark forms.

Eichmann *n* **[Karl] Adolf** (1906–62) Austrian Nazi leader and war criminal who oversaw the deportation of Jews to death camps. He was executed for his war crimes.

eider *n* a large marine duck, the down of which has commercial value as a filling for quilts etc.

eiderdown *n* the down of the eider duck used for stuffing quilts, etc; a thick quilt with a soft filling.

eidolon *n* (*pl* **eidolons, eidola**) *n* an apparition or phantom.

Eiffel *n* **Gustave** (1832-1923) French engineer. His notable works include the Eiffel Tower, Paris.

EIG *abbr* = Ethical Investors' Group.

eight *n, adj* one more than seven; (the crew of) an eight-oared rowing boat. * *symbol* 8, VIII, viii.

Eight *n* **The** a group of American painters who for the most part were realist painters. They campaigned vigorously on the development of progressive art away from the strictures of academic tradition.

eighteen *n, adj* one more than seventeen. * *symbol* 18, XVIII, xviii.—**eighteenth** *adj*.

eighteenmo *n* (*pl* **eighteenmos**) a book whose sheets are folded into eighteen leaves.

eightfold *adj, adv* consisting of eight units; being eight times as great or many.

eighth *adj, n* one after seventh; one of eight equal parts.

eighth-note *n* (*mus*) a note which is half the length of a quarter note (crotchet) and an eighth of a whole note (semibreve). Known in British notation as a **quaver**.

eighty *n* (*pl* **eighties**) eight times ten; (*pl*) the numbers from 80 to 89. * *symbol* 80, LXXX, lxxx.—**eightieth** *adj, n*.

Eigtued *n* **Nils** (*b.* 1701) Danish architect. His notable works include Amalienborg, Copenhagen.

Eijkman *n* **Christiaan** (1858–1930) Dutch physician who discovered the cause of beriberi. She shared the 1929 Nobel prize for physiology or medicine with Sir Frederick Hopkins.

Eileithyia *n* (*Greek myth*) the goddess of childbirth.

Eilshemius *n* **Louis Michel** (1864–1941) American painter. His earliest works were impressionist-style landscapes, but he later developed a more primitivist approach, e.g. *New York at Night* (1917).

Einarsdottir *n* **Sigrun** (1951–) Icelandic glassware designer who set up the first hot-glass workshop in Iceland.

Einarsson *n* **Gudmundur** (1895–1963) Icelandic ceramicist, who set up the first ceramic workshop in Iceland in 1927.

E-in-C *abbr* = Engineer-in-Chief.

Eindhoven *n* a city in the Netherlands.

Einem *n* **Gomried von** (1918–) Austrian composer who was born in Switzerland. He is most noted for his operas *Danton's Death* and *The Old Lady's Visit*, performed at Glyndebourne in 1973, and the ballet *Princess Turandot*. He has also written orchestral and choral pieces.

Einstein *n* **Albert** (1879–1955) German-born physicist and mathematician who formulated the special theory of relativity (1906) and general theory of relativity (1916), and researched quantum theory. He was the winner of the 1921 Nobel prize for physics.

einsteinium *n* an artificial radioactive element.

Einstein's law *or* **Einstein's equation** *n* the mass-energy equation, $E = mc2$, devised by the physicist Albert Einstein.

Eire *n* the name given to the Republic of Ireland today. The name derives from the goddess Eriu.

EIS *abbr* = Environmental Information Services; Epidemic Intelligence Service.

Eisen *n* **Charles** (1720–78) French artist and book illustrator, much admired by Voltaire.

Eisenhower *n* **Dwight D[avid]** (1890–1969) American general and Republican statesman, known as "Ike." He became supreme commander of the Allied Forces in 1943 and was the 34th president of the US (1953–60).

Eisenstein *n* **Sergei Mikhailovich** (1898–1948) Soviet film director whose films include *Battleship Potemkin* (1925).

Eisirt *n* (*Irish Celtic myth*) the bard at the court of Iubdan, king of the Faylinn, a diminutive people.

eisteddfod *n* (*pl* **eisteddfods, eisteddfodau**) a Welsh competitive festival of the arts, esp singing.—**eisteddodic** *adj*.

Eitelberger-Edelberg *n* **Rudolf von** (1817–85) Austrian teacher whose articles led to the foundation of the Austrian Museum for Art and Industry.

either *adj, n* the one or the other of two; each of two. * *conj* correlative to *or*.

ejaculate *vti* to emit a fluid (as semen); to exclaim.—**ejaculation** *n*.—**ejaculator** *n*.—**ejaculatory** *adj*.

EJCS *abbr* = English Jersey Cattle Society.

eject *vt* to turn out, to expel by force. * *vi* to escape from an aircraft or spacecraft using an ejector seat.—**ejection** *n*.—**ejector** *n*.

ejecta *npl* matter discharged by an erupting volcano.

ejector seat *n* an escape seat, esp in combat aircraft, that can be ejected with its occupant in an emergency by means of explosive bolts.

EJMA *abbr* = English Joinery Manufacturers' Association.

e-journal *n* (*comput*) an online publication which can be accessed on the Web, commonly used in the academic world.

ejusd. *abbr* (*Latin*) = *ejusdem*, "of the same."

Ekco Radio *see* **Cole, Eric Kirkham**.

eke *vt* (*with* **out**) to supplement; to use (a supply) frugally; to make (a living) with difficulty.

Ekman effect *or* **Ekman spiral** *n* the combined effect of wind and the rotation of the Earth on the oceans.

el *n* (*inf*) elevated railroad, a rail transport system running on pillars or trestles above the streets, as in Chicago.—*also* **L.**

el. *abbr* = elevation.

elaborate *adj* highly detailed; planned with care and exactness. * *vt* to work out or explain in detail. —**elaborateness** *n*.—**elaboration** *n*.—**elaborative** *adj*.—**elaborator** *n*.

Eladu *n* (*Irish Celtic myth*) the father of the Daghda.

Elam *n* a wide valley in southwest Iran, the empire of the Elamites whose main settlement was at Susa.

élan *n* verve, spirit.

eland *n* an African antelope with spirally twisted horns.

elapse *vi* (*time*) to pass by.

elasmobranch *n* (*pl* **elasmobranchs**) a member of a class of fish that includes sharks and skates.

elastic *adj* returning to the original size and shape if stretched or squeezed; springy; adaptable. * *n* fabric, tape, etc incorporating elastic thread.—**elastically** *adv*.—**elasticity** *n*.

elasticated *adj* made elastic by the use of elastic thread.

elasticity *n* a property of any material that will stretch when forces are applied to it and recover when the forces are relaxed.

elastin *see* **fibrous tissue**.

elastomer *n* a synthetic material with the capacity to return to its original state after being extended.

elate *vt* to fill with happiness or pride.—**elated** *adj*.—**elatedness** *n*.—**elation** *n*.

Elath *n* town at the head of the Gulf of Aqaba; present-day name is Elat.

Elatha *n* (*Irish Celtic myth*) a Fomorii leader who had an affair with Eri, one of the Tuatha De Danann women. She gave birth to Bres as a result of this affair.

Elba *n* an island off the west coast of Italy, known in classical times as Aethalia or Ilva.

elbow *n* the joint between the forearm and upper arm; the part of a piece of clothing covering this; any sharp turn or bend, as in a pipe. * *vt* to shove away rudely with the elbow; to jostle.

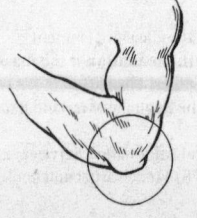

elbow grease *n* (*inf*) effort, hard work.

elbowroom *n* space to move, scope.

ELBS *abbr* = English Language Book Society.

Elcmar *n* (*Irish Celtic myth*) the foster-father of Oenghus, a god of love.

elder[1] *n* a tree or shrub with flat clusters of white or pink flowers.

elder[2] *n* an older person; an office bearer in certain churches.—**eldership** *n*.

elderberry *n* (*pl* **elderberries**) (the fruit of) an elder.

elderly *adj* quite old.—**elderliness** *n*.

eldest *n* oldest, first born.

ELDO *abbr* = European Launcher Development Organization.

El Dorado, eldorado *n* an imaginary land of vast wealth.

Eldoret *n* a town in Kenya.

eldritch, eldrich *adj* (*Scot*) weird; hideous.

elec. *abbr* = electric; electrical; electricity; electuary.

elecampane *n* a plant of the aster family, from the roots of which a tonic medicine is made.

elect *vti* to choose by voting; to make a selection (of); to make a decision on. * *adj* chosen for an office but not installed.

elect. *abbr* = electric; electrical; electrician; electricity.

election *n* the public choice of a person for office, esp a politician.

election campaign contribution and expenditure report *n* (*law*) a report filed by an individual declaring the itemized contributions he has received for the purpose of running for a county elected position.

electioneer *vi* to work on behalf of a candidate for election.—**electioneering** *n*.

elective *adj* pertaining to, dependant on, or exerting the power of, choice.—**electivity, electiveness** *n*.

elector *n* a person who has a vote at an election.—**electorship** *n*.

electoral *adj* of elections or electors.

electorate *n* the whole body of qualified electors.

Electra *n* (*Greek myth*) a daughter of Agamemnon and Clytemnestra. After the murder of her father by her mother and her mother's lover, Aegisthus, she helped her brother Orestes with Pylades to kill Clytemnestra and Aegisthus.

electric *adj* of, producing or worked by electricity; exciting, thrilling. * *npl* electric fittings.

electrical *adj* of or relating to electricity.—**electrically** *adv*.

electric blanket *n* a blanket containing an internal element that can be heated to warm a bed.

electric chair *n* a chair used in executing condemned criminals by electrocution.

electric current *n* (*elect*) a flow of electric charge through a conductor.

electric eel *n* an eel-like fish capable of giving an electric shock.

electric eye *n* a photoelectric cell.

electric guitar *n* a guitar that is electronically amplified.

electrician *n* a person who installs and repairs electrical devices.

electricity *n* a form of energy comprising certain charged particles, such as electrons and protons; an electric current.

electrify *vt* (**electrifying, electrified**) to charge with electricity; to modify or equip for the use of electric power; to astonish or excite.—**electrifiable** *adj*.—**electrification** *n*.—**electrifier** *n*.

electro-, electr- *prefix* of or by electricity.

electrocardiogram *n* a record of the changes in the heart's electrical potential made on an instrument called an electrocardiograph.

electrocardiograph *or* **ECG** *n* equipment used to record the current and voltage associated with contractions of the heart.—**electrocardiographic, electrocardiographical** *adj*.—**electrocardiography** *n*.

electrocautery *n* cautery, using an electrically heated wire or needle.

electrochem. *abbr* = electrochemistry; electrochemical.

electrochemistry *n* the area of chemistry dealing with chemical changes caused by electricity.—**electrochemical** *adj*.—**electrochemist** *n*.

electroconvulsive therapy *or* **ECT** *n* a somewhat drastic treatment for severe depression and sometimes schizophrenia where an electric current is passed through the brain.

electrocute *vt* to kill or execute by electricity.—**electrocution** *n*.

electrode *n* a conductor that enables an electric current to be passed into or out of a liquid, a gas, or a vacuum.

electrodynamics *n* (*sing*) the area of physics dealing with electric currents.—**electrodynamic, electrodynamical** *adj*.

electroencephalogram *or* **EEG** *n* a record of the brain's electrical activity or brain waves, measured on an electroencephalograph.

electroencephalograph *n* a device for recording the electrical activity of the brain.—**electroencephalographic** *adj*.—**electroencephalographically** *adv*.—**electroencephalography** *n*.

electrokinetics *n* (*sing*) the area of physics dealing with electricity in motion.—**electrokinetic** *adj*.

Electrolux *n* Swedish domestic appliance manufacturer, founded as AB Lux, in 1901.

electrolysis *n* (*chem*) chemical decomposition achieved by passing an electric current through a substance in solution or molten form; a chemical process which is sometimes used to clean metal; the passage of an electric current through an electrolyte to effect chemical change.

electrolyte *n* a compound that dissolves in water to produce a solution, containing ions, that is able to conduct an electrical charge.

electrolyze *vt* to cause to undergo electrolysis.—**electrolyzation** *n*.—**electrolyzer** *n*.

electromagnet *n* a metal core rendered magnetic by the passage of an electric current through a surrounding coil.

electromagnetic *adj* pertaining to or produced by electromagnetism.—**electromagnetically** *adv*.

electromagnetic waves *n* the effects of oscillating electric and magnetic fields that are capable of traveling across space.

electromagnetism *n* magnetism produced by an electric current; the area of science dealing with the relations between electricity and magnetism.

electrometallurgy *n* metallurgy using a slow electric current to precipitate certain metals from their solutions, or to separate metals from their ores.—**electrometallurgical** *adj*.—**electrometallurgist** *n*.

electrometer *n* an instrument for measuring electricity.—**electrometric, electrometrical** *adj*.—**electrometry** *n*.

electromotive *adj* producing an electric current.

electromotive force *n* a source of energy producing an electric current; the amount of energy drawn from such a source per unit current of electricity passing through it, measured in volts.

electron *n* an indivisible particle that is negatively charged and free to orbit the positively charged nucleus of every atom.

electron microscope *n* a microscope that uses a beam of electrons rather than a beam of light striking an object.

electronegative *adj* with a negative electrical charge.

electronic *adj* of or worked by streams of electrons flowing through semiconductor devices, vacuum, or gas; of or concerned with electrons or electronics.—**electronically** *adv*.

electronic data interchange *n* an electronic data-transmission system that enables firms to exchange business documents.

electronic funds transfer at point of sale *n* when a purchase is made the automatic debiting of a customer's bank account or credit-card account using a computer link between the check-out till and the bank or credit-card company.

electronic instruments *npl* (*mus*) a generic term for instruments that convert electrical energy into sound, such as the synthesizer.

electronic mail *see* **E-mail**.

electronic marketplace *n* (*comput*) the business of employing the Internet to buy and sell goods

electronic point of sale *n* an electronic system of recording purchases in retail outlets.

electronic publishing *n* the use of the Internet and other electronic means to publish and distribute work.

electronics *n* (*sing*) the study, development, and application of electronic devices; (*pl*) electronic circuits.

electronic shopping *n* a form of electronic direct marketing by which consumers can make purchases from a computerized list on a screen by means of a cable or telephone link to the seller.

electron pair *n* two electrons, one each from the outer shells of two atoms, which are shared by the adjacent nuclei to form a bond.

electron probe microanalysis *n* (*archeo*) a technique for analyzing the composition of the various layers of a metal or pottery objects, using a scanning electron microscope.

electronvolt *n* a unit of energy equivalent to the energy gained by an electron that has been accelerated through a potential difference of one volt.

electrophoresis *n* (*physics*, *chem*) a method for separating the molecules within a solution using an electric field.

electrophorus *n* (*pl* **electrophori**) an instrument for generating static electricity by induction.

electrophys. *abbr* = electrophysical; electrophysics.

electroplate *vt* to plate or cover with metal (e.g., silver) by electrolysis. * *n* electro-plated objects.—**electroplater** *n*.

electropositive *adj* with a positive electrical charge.

electroscope *n* an instrument for showing the presence or quality of electricity.—**electroscopic** *adj*.

electrostatics *n* (*elect*) the part of the science of electricity dealing with the phenomena associated with electrical charges at rest.

electrotherapeutics *n* (*sing*) the area of medicine dealing with the use of electrotherapy.

electrotherapy *n* the treatment of disease using electricity.—**electrotherapist** *n*.

electrotype *n* (*print*) a facsimile made by covering a mold or plate of the original with a coating of copper or nickel. * *vt* to make a copy in this way.—**electrotyper** *n*.

electrum *n* (*archeo*) an alloy of silver and gold that was used mainly for the decoration of valuable items.

Electryon *n* (*Greek myth*) son of Perseus and Andromeda who inherited the throne of Mycenae from his father.

electuary *n* (*pl* **electuaries**) a medicinal drug mixed with honey or syrup.

eleemosynary *adj* dependent on charity; (*money*) given as charity.

elegant *adj* graceful; refined; dignified and tasteful in manner and appearance.—**elegance, elegancy** *n*.—**elegantly** *adv*.

elegiac *adj* characteristic of elegy; mournful.

elegize *vt* to write an elegy about.—**elegist** *n*.

elegy *n* (*pl* **elegies**) a slow mournful song or poem.

elem. *abbr* = elementary; elements.

element *n* a constituent part; any of the 105 known substances composed of atoms with the same number of protons in their nuclei; a favorable environment for a plant or animal; a wire that produces heat in an electric cooker, kettle, etc; any of the four substances (earth, air, fire, water) that in ancient and medieval thought were believed to constitute the universe; (*pl*) atmospheric conditions (wind, rain, etc); (*pl*) the basic principles, rudiments.

elemental *adj* of elements or primitive natural forces.—**elementally** *adv*.

elementary *adj* concerned with the basic principles of a subject.—**elementariness** *n*.

elementary particle *n* any of the subatomic particles, such as electrons, protons, and neutrons, not made up of other particles.

elemi *n* (*pl* **elemis**) a resin used in medicines and varnishes.

Elen *n* (*Welsh Celtic myth*) the daughter of Eudaf, from whom the kings of Cornwall are supposed to be descended.

elenchus *n* (*pl* **elenchi**) (*logic*) refutation of an argument.—**elenctic** *adj*.

elephant *n* (*pl* **elephants, elephant**) a large heavy mammal with a long trunk, thick skin, and ivory tusks.—**elephantoid** *adj*.

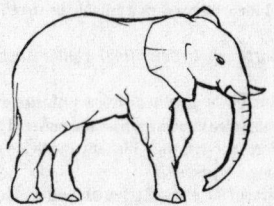

elephantiasis *n* a dramatic and debilitating enlargement of skin and underlying connective tissue caused by parasitic worms (filariae), which are carried to humans by mosquitoes.—**elephantiasic** *adj*.

elephantine *adj* of or like elephants; very big or clumsy.

Eleusinian Mysteries *npl* the sacred rites observed in ancient Greece at the annual festival of Demeter or Ceres, so named from their original site in Eleusis near Athens.

Eleusis *n* a town of ancient Attica in Greece, famous as the chief site of the worship of Demeter or Ceres.—**Eleusinian** *adj*.

elev. *abbr* = elevation.

elevate *vt* to lift up; to raise in rank; to improve in intellectual or moral stature.

elevated *adj* raised; (*fig*) inflated; (*inf*) tipsy.

elevation *n* a raised place; the height above the earth's surface or above sea level; the angle which a gun is aimed above the horizon; a drawing that shows the front, rear, or side view of something.

elevator *n* a cage or platform for moving something from one level to another; a moveable surface on the tailplane of an aircraft to produce motion up and down; a lift; a building for storing grain.

eleven *adj, n* one more than ten; (*soccer, etc*) a team of eleven players. * *symbol* 11, XI, xi.—**eleventh** *adj, n*.

elf *n* (*pl* **elves**) a mischievous fairy.—**elfin** *adj*.—**elfish, elvish** *adj*.

ELF *abbr* = Earth Liberation Front; Elimination of Leukemia Fund; Environmental Law Foundation; extra/extremely low frequency.

ELFA *abbr* = Educational Film Library Association; Electric Light Fittings Association.

Elffin *n* (*Welsh Celtic myth*) the boy who found the leather bag containing Taliesin in his father's fish weir, where Cerridwen had thrown it.

elflock *n* an intricately twisted lock of hair.

Elfward *n* (*d.* 924) king of Wessex, Britain (reigned in 924). An illegitimate son of Edward the Elder, his reign lasted only a few months. His half-brother Ethelstan succeeded him.

Elfwold *n* (*d.* 788) king of Northumbria (779–788). The grandson of king Eadbert, he deposed Ethelred to take the throne.

Elgar *n* **Sir Edward William** (1857–1934) English composer well known for "Land of Hope and Glory," the popular name for the first of the set of five Pomp and Circumstance Marches.

Elgin Marbles *n* part of the Parthenon Frieze which was removed by Lord Elgin at the beginning of the 19th century and sold to the British Museum.

El Greco *n* [**Domenikos Theotocopolous**] (1541–1614) Cretan-born Spanish painter, sculptor, and architect. In the main, he painted religious subjects, including many portrayals of St Francis. His style was emotional and spiritually evocative.

Elhanan *n* (*Bible*) an alternative source suggests that Elhanan, not David, slew Goliath. *See also* **David; Goliath**.

E

Elhred *n* king of Northumbria (765–774). He was succeeded by Ethelred, the son of Ethelwald.

Eli *n* (*Bible*) a priest at the shrine at Shiloh where the Ark was kept; Hannah brough her young son Samuel to Eli "to serve the Lord". *See also* **Hannah**.

Elias *n* Greek form of Elijah; the form used in the Gospels.

elicit *vt* to draw out (information, etc).—**elicitable** *adj*.—**elicitation** *n*.—**elicitor** *n*.

elide *vt* (*linguistics*) to cut off a syllable or vowel.

Elien. *abbr* (*Latin*) = *Eliensis*, "of Ely" (bishop's see).

eligible *adj* suitable to be chosen, legally qualified; desirable, esp as a marriage partner.—**eligibility** *n*.—**eligibly** *adv*.

Elijah *n* (*Bible*) stormy prophet of Israel in the 9th century BC; he challenged the priests of Baal on Mt Carmel, and the house of Ahab for propagating the heathen gods of Baal and seizing the vineyard of Naboth. *See also* **Ahab; Baal; Naboth**.

eliminate *vt* to expel, get rid of; to eradicate completely; (*sl*) to kill; to exclude (e.g., a competitor) from a competition, usu by defeat.—**eliminable** *adj*.—**elimination** *n*.—**eliminative, eliminatory** *adj*.—**eliminator** *n*.

Elint *abbr* = electronic intelligence.

Eliot *n* 1. George [Mary Ann Evans] (1819–80) English novelist whose works, e.g. *The Mill on the Floss* and *Middlemarch*, deal with the problems of ethical choice in the rapidly changing rural environment of 19th-century England. 2. T[homas] S[tearns] (1888–1965) American-born British poet and critic whose early volumes of poetry, notably *Prufrock and Other Observations* and *The Waste Land*, are concerned with the disarray of the post-World War I era.

Elis *n* a maritime state of ancient Greece in the west of the Peloponnese, where Olympia, site of the Olympic Games, was situated.—**Elian** *adj*.

Elisha *n* (*Bible*) farmer's son who was Elijah's successor in 9th-century Israel after the latter had been taken up to heaven in a whirlwind; a helper of ordinary people and counselor of kings.

elision *n* (*linguistics*) the cutting off of a syllable or vowel.

Elissa *see* **Dido**.

elite, élite *n* a superior group; (*typewriting*) a letter size having twelve characters to the inch.

elitism *n* leadership or rule by an elite; advocacy of such a system.—**elitist** *n*.

elixir *n* (*alchemy*) a substance thought to have the power of transmuting base metals into gold, or of conferring everlasting life; any medicine claimed as a cure-all; a sweet syrup containing a medicine.

Elizabeth *n* (*Bible*) wife of the priest Zechariah and mother of John the Baptist.

Elizabeth I (1533–1603) queen of England. The daughter of Henry VIII and Anne Boleyn, she was crowned Queen in 1558. She established the Church of England over the years 1559–63.

Elizabeth II *n* (1926–) queen of the United Kingdom of Great Britain and Northern Ireland and other realms and territories from 1952; daughter of George VI; married Prince Philip in 1947; has four children: Prince Charles (1948–), Princess Anne (1950–), Prince Andrew (1960–) and Prince Edward (1964–).

Elizabethan *adj* pertaining to Queen Elizabeth I of England and her reign (1558–1603); pertaining to Queen Elizabeth II of Great Britain and her reign (1952–). * *n* a person alive in the reign of Elizabeth I.

Elizabethan architecture *n* the style of design and construction practiced during the reign of Queen Elizabeth I of England (1558–1603), characterized by features of the Renaissance and Flemish architecture.

Elizabeth of Hungary *n* Saint (1205–29) Hungarian princess and saint who devoted her life to acts of charity. Her feast day is November 17.

elk *n* (*pl* **elks, elk**) the largest existing deer of Europe and Asia.

ell *n* an old measure of length used for cloth, based on the length of a man's arm, approximately equal to 45 inches (1.15 meters).

Ellington *n* Edward Kennedy "Duke" (1899–1974) American jazz composer, pianist, and band leader; among his compositions are *Mood Indigo*, *Take the "A"-Train*, *Concerto for Cootie* and *Creole Rhapsody*.

ellipse *n* (*geom*) a closed plane figure formed by the plane section of a right-angled cone; a flattened circle.

ellipsis *n* (*pl* **ellipses**) the omission of words needed to complete the grammatical construction of a sentence; the mark (...) used to indicate such omission.

ellipsoid *n* (*geom*) an elliptical spheroid; an oval.—**ellipsoidal** *adj*.

elliptic, elliptical *adj* of or like an ellipse; having a part understood.—**elliptically** *adv*.

ellipticity *n* (*geom*) the extent of deviation of an oval from a circle or sphere.

Ellis *n* Alice Thomas [Anna Haycraft] (1932–) Anglo-Welsh novelist, regarded by many critics as one of the wittiest modern British writers. Her novels include *The Sin Eater*. 2. Eileen (1933–) British textile designer who in 1960 formed the Orbit Design Group. 3. Harvey (1852–1904) American architect who was active as

a painter in Rochester, New York. 4. [Henry] Havelock (1859–1939) English physician and sexologist. His seven-volume *Studies on the Psychology of Sex* (1897–1928, revised edition 1936) were very influential in bringing the discussion of sexual matters into the realm of open debate. 5. Peter (*b*.1804) English architect. His notable works include the Oriel Chambers in Liverpool.

Ellison *n* Ralph (1914–94) American writer whose Kafkaesque and partly autobiographical novel *Invisible Man* describes the alienated life of a young African-American man in New York.

elm *n* a tall deciduous shade tree with spreading branches and broad top; its hard heavy wood.

ELMA *abbr* = Electric Lamp Manufacturers' Association; European Association for Length Measuring Instruments and Machines.

Elmslie *n* George Grant (1871–1952) Scottish architect who moved to America in 1885.

El Niño *n* a south-flowing current along the west coast of South America from Colombia to Ecuador that has far reaching and often extreme consequences on world weather conditions.

ELO *abbr* = European Leisure Organization.

elocution *n* skill in public speaking.—**elocutionary** *adj*.—**elocutionist** *n*.

elongate *vti* to make or become longer.—**elongation** *n*.

elope *vi* to run away secretly with a lover, esp to get married.—**elopement** *n*.—**eloper** *n*.

eloquence *n* skill in the use of words; speaking with fluency, power, or persuasiveness.

eloquent *adj* (*speaking, writing, etc*) fluent and powerful.

Eloth *n* (*Bible*) alternative spelling of Elath.

El Salvador *n* a republic in Central America.

else *adv* besides; otherwise.

elsewhere *adv* in another place.

Elsheimer *n* Adam (1578–1610) German painter and etcher. Notable works include *Rest on the Flight into Egypt* (1609).

ELSS *abbr* = emergency life support system.

ELT *abbr* = English Language Teaching.

Elton *n* Charles Sutherland (1900–) English ecologist. His field studies of animal communities in their environments raised awareness of the ability of animals to adapt to changing habitats, and popularized such terms as "ecological niche."

ELU *abbr* = English Lacrosse Union.

elucidate *vt* to make clear, to explain.—**elucidation** *n*.—**elucidative, elucidatory** *adj*.—**elucidator** *n*.

elude *vt* to avoid stealthily; to escape the understanding or memory of a person.—**eluder** *n*.—**elusion** *n*.

elusive *adj* escaping; baffling; solitary, difficult to contact.—**elusiveness** *n*.

ELV *abbr* = expendable launch vehicle.

elver *n* a young eel.

elves, elvish *see* **elf**.

ELWW *abbr* = European Laboratory Without Walls.

Elymas *n* (*Bible*) a magician and false prophet who called himself Bar-Jesus (the Son of Jesus).

Elysian *adj* of or resembling Elysium; paradisiacal, blissful.

Elysium *n* in Greek and Roman mythology, the regions inhabited by the blessed after death.

elytron, elytrum *n* (*pl* **elytra**) one of the hard wing cases of a beetle.—**elytroid, elytrous** *adj*.

em *n* (*print*) a measure of width, equal to one sixth of an inch (approx 4 mm).

Em, Em. *abbr* (*chem*) = emanation.

EM *abbr* = electromagnetic; electromotive; electron microscope; evening meal.

EMA *abbr* = European Monetary Agreement; European Motorcycle Association; Excavator Makers Association; Executives and Managers Association of Great Britain and Ireland.

EMAC *abbr* = Extra-Mural Activity Association.

emaciate *vti* to make or become very thin and weak.—**emaciated** *adj*.

emaciation *n* particularly severe leanness caused by lack of nourishment or disease.

E-mail, e-mail *or* **email** *n* a form of electronic communication by which computer-originated messages can be sent by means of a telecommunication network and a modem. Each e-mail user has an e-mail address; the commonly-used abbreviation for electronic mail. * *vt* to send a piece of electronic mail; to contact a person by this method.

emanate *vi* to issue from a source.—**emanative** *adj*.—**emanator** *n*.—**emanatory** *adj*.

emanation *n* something coming from or caused by something else.—**emanational** *adj*.

emancipate *vt* to liberate, esp from bondage or slavery.—**emancipative** *adj*.—**emancipator** *n*.—**emancipatory** *adj*.

emancipation *n* the act of freeing; freedom, liberation.—**emancipationist** *n*.

emarginate, emarginated *adj* (*leaf*) notched at the edges or tip.—**emargination** *n*.

emasculate *vt* to castrate; to deprive of vigor, strength, etc.—**emasculation** *n*.—**emasculative, emasculatory** *adj*.—**emasculator** *n*.

emb. *abbr* = embargo.

embalm *vt* to preserve (a dead body) with drugs, chemicals, etc.—**embalmer** *n*.—**embalmment** *n*.

embank *vt* to enclose or protect with an embankment.

embankment *n* an earth or stone mound made to hold back water or to carry a roadway.

embargo *n* (*pl* **embargoes**) an order of a government forbidding ships to enter or leave its ports; any ban or restriction on commerce by law; a prohibition, ban. * *vt* (**embargoing, embargoed**) to lay an embargo on; to requisition.

embark *vti* to put or go on board a ship or aircraft to begin a journey; to make a start in any activity or enterprise.—**embarkation** *n*.—**embarkment** *n*.

embarrass *vt* to make (a person) feel confused, uncomfortable, or disconcerted.—**embarrassing** *adj*.—**embarrassment** *n*.

embassy *n* (*pl* **embassies**) a person or group sent to a foreign government as ambassadors; the official residence of an ambassador.

embattle *vt* to arrange troops for battle; to prepare for battle.—**embattled** *adj*.

embay *vt* to bring or drive a ship into a bay.

embed *vt* (**embedding, embedded**) to fix firmly in surrounding matter.—**embedment** *n*.

embellish *vt* to decorate, to adorn.—**embellisher** *n*.—**embellishment** *n*.

ember *n* a piece of glowing coal or wood in a fire; (*pl*) the smoldering remains of a fire.

embezzle *vt* to steal (money, securities, etc entrusted to one's care).—**embezzlement** *n*.—**embezzler** *n*.

embitter *vt* to cause to feel bitter.—**embitterment** *n*.

emblazon *vt* to make bright with color; to ornament with heraldic devices.—**emblazonment** *n*.

emblazonry *n* heraldic decoration, blazonry.

emblem *n* a symbol; a figure adopted and used as an identifying mark.

emblematic, emblematical *adj* of emblems; symbolic.—**emblematically** *adv*.

emblements *npl* (*law*) the annual crops produced by the labor of the cultivator; the profit from these crops.

embody *vt* (**embodying, embodied**) to express in definite form; to incorporate or include in a single book, law, system, etc.—**embodiment** *n*.

embolden *vt* to inspire with courage; to make bold.

embolectomy *n* the surgical, and often emergency, removal of an embolus or clot to clear an arterial obstruction.

embolism *n* the obstruction of a blood vessel by a blood clot, air bubble, etc.—**embolismic** *adj*.

embolus (*pl* **emboli**) *n* material carried by the blood which then lodges elsewhere in the body.

embonpoint *n* plumpness.

emboss *vt* to ornament with a raised design.—**embosser** *n*.—**embossment** *n*.

embouchure *n* the mouth of a river; (*mus*) the mouthpiece of a brass or wind instrument; the correct positioning of the mouth when playing a wind instrument.

embowel *vt* (**emboweling, emboweled** *or* **embowelling, embowelled**) (*arch*) to remove the intestines from, disembowel; to embed, to bury.

embrace *vt* to take and hold tightly in the arms as a sign of affection; to accept eagerly (e.g., an opportunity); to adopt (e.g., a religious faith); to include. * *n* the act of embracing, a hug.—**embraceable** *adj*.—**embracement** *n*.

embracer *n* one who embraces; (*law*) one who attempts to influence a jury corruptly.

embracery *n* (*law*) the act of attempting to corrupt or influence a jury.

embranchment *n* the act of branching out.

embrasure *n* (*archit*) an opening in a wall, for a window or door, in which the sides are slanted from within; an opening in a parapet (also known as crenel) which is slanted on the inside.

embrocate *vt* to rub a diseased or injured part of the body with a lotion.

embrocation *n* a liniment for applying to or rubbing an injured part of the body.

embroider *vt* to ornament with decorative stitches; to embellish (e.g., a story).—**embroiderer** *n*.

embroidery *n* (*pl* **embroideries**) decorative needlework; elaboration or exaggeration (of a story, etc).

embroil *vt* to involve (a person) in a conflict, argument, or problem.—**embroiler** *n*.—**embroilment** *n*.

embryo *n* (*pl* **embryos**) an animal during the period of its growth from a fertilized egg up to the third month; a human product of conception up to about the second month of growth; a thing in a rudimentary state.—**embryoid** *adj*.

embryology *n* the study of the embryo, its growth, and development from fertilization to birth.—**embryological, embryologic** *adj*.—**embryologist** *n*.

embryonic, embryonal *adj* immature, existing at an early stage.—**embryonically** *adv*.

embryo transfer *n* the fertilization of an ovum by sperm and its development into an early embryo, outside the mother, and its subsequent implantation in the mother's uterus. *See also* **in vitro fertilization**.

EMC *abbr* = Early Music Center; European Muscle Club.

emcee *n* (*inf*) a master of ceremonies, a compere. * *vi* (**emceeing, emceed**) (*inf*) to act as master of ceremonies, to compere.

e.m.d.p. *abbr* = electromotive difference of potential.

emend *vt* to correct mistakes in written material.—**emendable** *adj*.—**emendation** *n*.

emerald *n* a rich green gemstone; its color.

Emer *n* (*Irish Celtic myth*) the daughter of Forgall and the wife of Cuchulainn.

emerge *vi* to appear up out of, to come into view; to be revealed as the result of investigation.—**emergence** *n*.—**emergent** *adj*.

emergency *n* (*pl* **emergencies**) an unforeseen situation demanding immediate action; a serious medical condition requiring instant treatment.

emergent shoreline *n* any shoreline that is currently either raised above high water mark or is inland from the present coastline, as a result of uplift of the land or fall in sea level.

emergicenter *n* walk-in facility for minor ailments and injuries often located in shopping malls or along highways.

emeritus *adj* retired but still holding one's title or rank.—*also n*.

emersed *adj* (*bot*) rising out of water.

emersion *n* the act of emerging.

Emerson *n* **Ralph Waldo** (1803–82) American philosopher, essayist, and poet, and an exponent of transcendentalism. His ideas are contained in his early work *Nature* and *Essays, First and Second Series*.

emery *n* a hard granular mineral used for grinding and polishing; a hard abrasive powder.

emery board *n* a nailfile made from cardboard covered with powdered emery.

emery paper *n* a stiff paper covered with powdered emery.

emesis *n* the medical term for vomiting.

emetic *n* a substance that causes vomiting such as mustard in water, copper sulfate, alum, or a lot of salty water

emf *abbr* = electromotive force (term used in physics).

EMF *abbr* = European Monetary Fund.

EMFEC *abbr* = East Midland Further Education Council.

Emhain Macha *n* (*Irish Celtic myth*) the seat of the kings of Ulster, which was the centre of the Red Branch. It is supposed to have been established by Macha, hence its name. It was the court of Conchobar mac Nessa.

emi *abbr* = electromagnetic interference.

EMI *abbr* = Electrical and Musical Industries.

emigrant *n* a person who emigrates.

emigrate *vi* to leave one's country for residence in another.—**emigration** *n*.

émigré *n* an emigrant, usually someone forced to emigrate.

eminence, eminency *n* (*pl* **eminences, eminencies**) high rank or position; a person of high rank or attainments; (*with cap*) the title for a cardinal of the RC Church; a raised piece of ground, a high place.

eminent *adj* famous; conspicuous; distinguished.—**eminently** *adv*.

eminent domain *n* the right of the state to confiscate private property for public use.

emir *n* a ruler in parts of Africa and Asia.

emirate *n* the territory governed by an emir.

emissary *n* (*pl* **emissaries**) a person sent on a mission on behalf of another, esp a government.

emit *vt* (**emitting, emitted**) to send out (light, heat, etc); to put into circulation; to express, to utter.—**emission** *n*.—**emissive** *adj*.—**emitter** *n*.

EML *abbr* = Environmental Measurement Laboratory

EMLC *abbr* = Ethnic Minorities Law Center.

Emmanuel *n* (*Bible*) means "God with us"; Isaiah foretold "A young woman shall conceive and bear a son and shall call his name Emmanuel."

Emmaus *n* (*Bible*) village where two disciples met Jesus after he had risen from the dead.

Emmenthal(er), Emmental *n* a hard Swiss cheese with lots of holes.

emmer wheat *n* a primitive form of wheat, derived from wild emmer grass, cultivated in the Middle East at an early period.

emmet *n* (*dial*) an ant.

emollient *n* a substance that softens or soothes the skin, whether in the form of a powder, oil, or preparation.

emoluments *npl* the total amount of financial benefit from an employment or office, including salary, fee or wage, expenses, and perquisites.

emote *vi* to display emotion theatrically.

emoticon *or* **smiley** an icon representing emotion (hence the name) made up of standard keyboard characters. A few examples are: :)—smiling face, :-)—smile, :-D—big smile

emotion *n* a strong feeling of any kind.

emotional *adj* of emotion; inclined to express excessive emotion.—**emotionality** *n*.—**emotionally** *adv*.—**emotionalism** *n*.

emotive *adj* characterized by or arousing emotion.—**emotiveness, emotivity** *n*.

EMP *abbr* = European Member of Parliament; electromagnetic pulse.

EMPA *abbr* = European Marine Pilots Association.

empanel *vt* (**empaneling, empaneled** *or* **empanelling, empanelled**) (*law*) to enroll (for a jury); to enter on a jury list.—*also* **impanel**.

empathize *vi* to treat with or feel empathy.

empathy *n* the capacity for participating in and understanding the feelings or ideas of another.—**empathic, empathetic** *adj*.

emperor *n* the sovereign ruler over an empire.—**emperorship** *n*.

emperor penguin *n* an Antarctic penguin, the largest species known.

empery *n* (*pl* **emperies**) (*arch*) power, dominion.

emphasis *n* (*pl* **emphases**) particular stress or prominence given to something; force or vigor of expression; clarity of form or outline.

emphasize *vt* to place stress on.

E

emphatic *adj* spoken, done, or marked with emphasis; forceful, decisive.—**emphatically** *adv*.—**emphaticalness** *n*.

emphysema *n* in the main, an abnormal condition of the lungs in which the walls of the alveoli are over-inflated and distended and changes in their structure occur.—**emphysematous** *adj*.

empire *n* a large state or group of states under a single sovereign, usu an emperor; nations governed by a single sovereign state; a large and complex business organization.

empiric *adj* empirical. * *n* an empirical worker; a quack.

empirical *adj* based on observation, experiment, or experience only, not theoretical.—**empirically** *adv*.—**empiricalness** *n*.

empirical formula *n* (*chem*) a chemical formula of a compound that shows the simplest ratio of atoms present in the compound.

empiricism *n* (*philos*) the theory that experience is the only source of knowledge; the use of empirical methods.—**empiricist** *n*.

emplacement *n* a position prepared for a gun or artillery.

emplane *vti* to put on board a plane; to board a plane.

employ *vt* to give work and pay to; to make use of.—**employable** *adj*.

employee *n* a person who is hired by another person for wages.

employee participation *n* the participation by the workforce in the decision-making processes.

employer *n* a person, business, etc that employs people.

employers' liability insurance *n* a form of insurance, compulsory by law, that covers an employer's legal liability to pay compensation to employees in the event of injury or death at work.

employment *n* an employing; a being employed; occupation or profession.

employment agency *n* an agency that maintains a list of employment vacancies as provided by prospective employers and a list of people seeking work and acts as an agent between the two.

empoison *vt* to taint, corrupt.

emporium *n* (*pl* **emporiums, emporia**) a large shop carrying many different items.

empower *vt* to give official authority to.

empowerment *n* the allotting of increased responsibility and a degree of control to employees.

empress *n* the female ruler of an empire; the wife or widow of an emperor.

Empson *n* Sir **William** (1906–84) English poet and critic whose *Seven Types of Ambiguity* is a modern classic of literary criticism.

empty *adj* (**emptier, emptiest**) containing nothing; not occupied; lacking reality, substance, or value; hungry. * *vb* (**emptying, emptied**) *vt* to make empty; to transfer or discharge (the contents of something) by emptying. * *vi* to become empty; to discharge contents. * *n* (*pl* **empties**) empty containers or bottles.—**emptily** *adv*.—**emptiness** *n*.

empty-handed *adj* with nothing in one's hands; without gain.

empty-headed *adj* scatterbrained.

empyema *n* (*pl* **empyemata**) a collection of pus, esp in the chest.—**empyemic** *adj*.

empyrean *n* (*arch*) the highest heaven. * *adj* pertaining to the highest heaven; celestial.

EMR *abbr* = electronic magnetic resonance.

EMS *abbr* = European Monetary System; Emergency Medical Service; expanded memory specification.

emu *n* a fast-running Australian bird, related to the ostrich.

emu, e.m.u., EMU *abbr* = electromagnetic units.

EMU *abbr* = European Monetary Union; economic and monetary union; electromagnetic unit.

emulate *vt* (*comput*) to duplicate the function of a program, operating system, or hardware device in another computer system; to try to equal or do better than; to imitate; to rival or compete.

emulous *adj* wanting to excel; competitive.

emulsify *vti* (**emulsifying, emulsified**) to make or become an emulsion.—**emulsification** *n*.—**emusifier** *n*.

emulsion *n* a mixture of mutually insoluble liquids in which one is dispersed in droplets throughout the other; a light-sensitive substance on photographic paper or film.—**emulsive** *adj*.

emunctory *n* (*pl* **emunctories**) (*anat*) an excretory

en *n* (*print*) a measure of width, equal to half an em.

EN *abbr* = English Nature; Enrolled Nurse.

ENA *abbr* = English Newspaper Association; European Needlemakers Association.

enable *vt* to give the authority or means to do something; to make easy or possible.—**enabler** *n*.

enact *vt* to make into law; to act (a play, etc).—**enactive** *adj*.—**enactment** *n*.—**enactor** *n*.—**enactory** *adj*.

enamel *n* a glass-like substance used to coat the surface of metal or pottery; the hard outer layer of a tooth; a usu glossy paint that forms a hard coat. * *vt* (**enameling, enameled** *or* **enamelling, enamelled**) to cover or decorate with enamel.—**enameler, enameller, enamelist, enamellist** *n*.—**enamelware** *n*.

enamor, enamour *vt* to inspire with love.—**enamored, enamoured** *adj*.

enarthrosis *n* (*pl* **enarthroses**) (*anat*) a ball-and-socket joint.

ENB *abbr* = English National Board.

en bloc *adv* in a mass.

enc. *abbr* = encyclopedia.

ENC *abbr* = Eisenhower National Clearinghouse.

encage *vt* to shut up in or as in a cage.

encamp *vt* to place or stay in a camp.—**encampment** *n*.

encapsulate *vt* to enclose or be enclosed in, as a capsule; to summarize.—**encapsulation** *n*.

Encarnación *n* a city in Paraguay.

encase *vt* to enclose (as if) in a case.—**encasement** *n*.

encaustic *adj* (*ceramics*) with colors burned in. * *n* the art of painting in melted wax; a piece of work done by this method; a manner of painting murals with a medium composed principally of wax dissolved by heat, practiced in ancient times.

enceinte *adj* pregnant.

Enceladus *n* (*Greek myth*) one of the hundred armed giants who made war upon the gods. He was killed by Zeus, by a flash of lightning, and buried under Mount Etna.

encephalic *adj* of the brain.

encephalitis *n* inflammation of the brain.—**encephalitic** *adj*.

encephalogram *n* an electroencephalogram.—**encephalograph** *n*.

encephalography any technique that is used to record brain structure or activity.

encephaloid *n* the term given to a form of cancer that superficially resembles brain tissue.

encephalomyelitis *n* inflammation of the brain and spinal cord, typified by headaches, fever, stiff neck, and back pain, with vomiting.

encephalopathy *n* any disease affecting the brain or an abnormal condition of the brain's structure and function.

enchain *vt* to hold fast with, or as with, a chain.—**enchainment** *n*.

enchant *vt* to bewitch, to delight.—**enchanter** *n*.—**enchantment** *n*.—**enchantress** *nf*.

enchase *vt* to engrave, to emboss.

encircle *vt* to surround; to move or pass completely round.—**encirclement** *n*.

enclasp *vt* to clasp.

enclave *n* a small area within a country that is administered by another country.

enclitic *adj* (*linguistics*) attached to the preceding word and treated as a suffix, e.g. "thee" in "prithee". * *n* an enclitic word.—**enclitically** *adv*.

enclose *vt* to shut up or in; to put in a wrapper or parcel, usu together with a letter.—**enclosable** *adj*.—**encloser** *n*.

enclosure *n* an enclosing; an enclosed area; something enclosed with a letter, in a parcel, etc.

encode *vt* to put (a message, etc) into code.— **encoder** *n*.

encomiast *n* a composer of an encomium.—**encomiastic** *adj*.

encomium *n* (*pl* **encomiums, encomia**) a usu formal expression of high praise in speech or writing.

encompass *vt* to encircle or enclose; to include.—**encompassment** *n*.

encore *adv* (*mus*) (*French*) literally "again"; the call from an English audience (the French equivalent is in fact *bis*) for more music. **n* the performance of additional at the end of a concert.—*also vt*.

encounter *vt* to meet, esp unexpectedly; to fight, engage in battle with; to be faced with (problems, etc). * *n* a meeting; a conflict, battle.

encourage *vt* to inspire with confidence or hope; to urge, incite; to promote the development of.—**encouragement** *n*.—**encourager** *n*.—**encouragingly** *adv*.

encroach *vi* to infringe another's territory, rights, etc; to advance beyond an established limit.—**encroacher** *n*.—**encroachingly** *adv*.—**encroachment** *n*.

encrust *vt* to cover with a hard crust; to form a crust on the surface of; to decorate a surface with jewels.—**encrustation** *n*.

encryption *n* (*comput*) encoding data so that unauthorized users cannot read or otherwise use the data.

encumber *vt* to weigh down; to hinder the function or activity of.—**encumberingly** *adv*.

encumbrance *n* something that is a hindrance or burden.

encumbrancer *n* a person who has a legal claim on an estate.

encyclical *adj* circulated widely (—*also* **encyclic**). * *n* a letter addressed by the pope to all Roman Catholic bishops.

encyclopedia *n* a book or series of books containing information on all branches of knowledge, or treating comprehensively a particular branch of knowledge, usu in alphabetical order.

encyclopedic, *adj* comprehensive.—**encyclopedically,** *adv*.

encyclopedist *n* a compiler of an encyclopedia.

encyst *vti* (*biol*) to enclose, or become enclosed in, a cyst or vesicle.—**encystment** *n*.

end *n* fragment; death or destruction; the manner or cause of this; (*football*) the player or position at the end of a line; the last part; the place where a thing stops; purpose; result, outcome; (*football*) the player or position at the end of a line. * *vt* to bring to an end; to destroy. * *vi* to come to an end; to result (in). * *adj* final; ultimate

end. *abbr* = endorsement.

end-, endo- *prefix* within.

endanger *vt* to put in danger.—**endangerment** *n*.

endear *vt* to make loved or more loved.—**endearing** *adj*.—**endearingly** *adv*.

endearment *n* something that endears; a word or words of affection.

endeavor *vi* to try or attempt (to). * *n* an attempt.

endemic *adj* (*disease*) locally prevalent; (*plant*) peculiar to a locality. * *n* an endemic disease; an endemic plant.—**endemicity** *n*.—**endemically** *adv*.

endgame *n* the final stages of a game, esp chess, when only a few pieces remain on the board; any final stage.

ending *n* reaching or coming to an end; the final part.

endive *n* an annual or biennial herb widely cultivated as a salad plant; a variety of chicory used in salads.

endless *adj* unending; uninterrupted; extremely numerous.—**endlessly** *adv*.—**endlessness** *n*.

endocarditis *n* inflammation of the endocardium, heart valves, and muscle, caused by a bacterium, virus, or rheumatic fever.—**endocarditic** *adj*.

endocardium *n* a fine membrane lining the heart, which forms a continuous membrane with the lining of veins and arteries.

endocarp *n* the inner coat or shell of a fruit.—**endocarpal, endocarpic** *adj*.

endocrine *adj* secreting internally, specifically producing secretions that are distributed in the body by the bloodstream (—*also* **endocrinal**). * *n* an endocrine gland.

endocrine glands *n* ductless glands that produce hormones for secretion directly into the bloodstream (or lymph).

endocrine system *n* (*physiology*) the network of glands that release hormones directly into the bloodstream.

endocrinology *n* the study of the endocrine glands, the hormones secreted by them and the treatment of any problems.—**endocrinologic, endocrinological** *adj*.—**endocrinologist** *n*.

endoderm *n* the inner layer of embryonic cells in an egg from which an organism is formed.—*also* **entoblast, entoderm**.—**endodermal, endodermic, entodermal, entodermic** *adj*.

endogamy *n* the practice of marrying only within the same tribe.—**endogamous** *adj*.

endogenous *adj* what is within the body, whether growing within, originating from within or the result of internal causes.—**endogeny** *n*.

endometriosis *n* the occurrence of endometrium in other parts of the body, e.g. within the muscle of the uterus, in the ovary, Fallopian tubes, peritoneum, and possibly the bowel.

endometritis *n* inflammation of the endometrium .

endometrium *n* the mucous membrane lining of the womb.

endomorph *n* a mineral enclosed within another mineral; a person with a heavily built physique.—**endomorphic** *adj*.—**endomorphy** *n*.

endomorphism *n* (*geol*) metamorphosis of molten rock within older rock.

endoparasite *n* an internal parasite.—**endoparasitic** *adj*.

endoplasm *n* (*biol*) the inner layer of protoplasm.

endorphin *n* one of a group of peptides that occur in the brain and have pain-relieving qualities similar to morphine.

endorse *vt* to write one's name, comment, etc on the back of to approve; to recommend (a product, service, etc) publicly, often for payment; to record an offence on a driving license; to support.—**endorsable** *adj*.—**endorsee** *n*.—**endorsement** *n*.—**endorser** *n*.

endorsement *n* the act or instance of endorsing; something used to endorse, such as a signature; support; a supplementary provision altering the terms of an insurance policy; an advertisement recommending a product, etc.

endoscope *n* the general term for an instrument used to inspect the interior of a body cavity or organ.—**endoscopic** *adj*.—**endoscopist** *n*.—**endoscopy** *n*.

endosmosis *n* (*biol*) osmosis inwards through the porous membrane of a cell, etc, by a surrounding liquid.

endosperm *n* the albumen of a seed.—**endospermic** *adj*.

endothelium *n* (*pl* **endothelia**) (*anat*) a tissue which lines blood vessels.

endothermic reaction *n* (*chem*) a chemical reaction in which heat energy is absorbed.

endow *vt* to give money or property to provide an income for; to provide with a special power or attribute.—**endower** *n*.

endowment assurance *n* a life assurance scheme by which a specified amount of money is paid out either on the death of the person whose life is assured or at an agreed date, whichever of these occurs first

endpaper *n* either of two folded sheets of paper pasted against the inside covers of a book and attached to the first and last pages.

end pin *see* **tail pin**.

end product *n* the final result of a manufacturing or other process.

endue *vt* (**enduing, endued**) to provide with a quality or power.—*also* **indue**.

endurance *n* the ability to withstand pain, hardship, strain, etc.

endure *vt* to undergo, tolerate (hardship, etc) esp with patience. * *vi* to continue in existence, to last out.—**endurable** *adj*.—**endurability** *n*.—**endurably** *adv*.

enduring *adj* lasting, permanent.—**enduringly** *adv*.

endways *adv* on end, with the end foremost.

Endymion *n* (*Greek myth*) a hunter, a shepherd, or a king of Elis, who received eternal sleep as a punishment; a personification of the sun, or of the plunge of the setting sun into the sea.

ENE *abbr* = east-northeast.

enema *n* (*pl* **enemas, enemata**) the procedure of putting fluid into the rectum for purposes of cleansing or therapy.

enemy *n* (*pl* **enemies**) a person who hates or dislikes, and wishes to harm another; a military opponent; something harmful or deadly.

energetic *adj* lively, active; done with energy.—**energetically** *adv*.

energetics *n* (*sing*) the science of energy.

energize *vt* to fill with energy; to invigorate; to apply an electric current to.—**energizer** *n*.

energy *n* (*pl* **energies**) capacity of acting or being active; vigor, power; (*physics*) capacity to do work.

enervate *vt* to lessen the strength or vigor of; to enfeeble in mind and body.—**enervation** *n*.—**enervative** *adj*.—**enervator** *n*.

Enescu *n* George (1881–1955) Romanian composer of symphonies, rhapsodies, and chamber music. He also wrote an opera, *Oedipe*.

enface *vt* to write or stamp on the face of a document.

enfant terrible *n* (*pl* **enfants terribles**) (*French*) a person who makes awkward remarks.

enfeeble *vt* to make feeble.—**enfeeblement** *n*.—**enfeebler** *n*.

enfeoff *vt* (*law*) to give a freehold property to; to convey.—**enfeoffment** *n*.

enfilade *n* gunfire directed (at troops, etc) in a line from end to end; (*archit*) the architectural feature in which a series of internal doors to rooms are aligned so that a long view is obtained when all the doors are open; long rows of trees planted so as to create a long view.—*also vt*.

enfold *vt* to wrap up; to hug in the arms.—**enfolder** *n*.—**enfoldment** *n*.

enforce *vt* to compel obedience by threat; to execute with vigor.—**enforceable** *adj*.—**enforcement** *n*.—**enforcer** *n*.

enfranchise *vt* to admit to citizenship; to grant the vote to.—**enfranchisement** *n*.—**enfranchiser** *n*.

Enfrith *n* (*d.* 633) king of Bernicia, Britain (reigned in 633). The eldest son of Ethelfrith. Killed after reigning for less than a year by the Welsh king, Cadwallon.

eng. *abbr* = engine; engineer; engineering; engraved; engraver; engraving.

EN(G) *abbr* = Enrolled Nurse (General).

ENG *abbr* = electronic news gathering.

Eng. *abbr* = England; English.

engage *vt* to pledge as security; to promise to marry; to keep busy; to hire; to attract and hold, esp attention or sympathy; to cause to participate; to bring or enter into conflict; to begin or take part in a venture; to connect or interlock, to mesh.—**engager** *n*.

engaged *adj* entered into a promise to marry; reserved, occupied, or busy.

engagement *n* the act or state of being engaged; a pledge; an appointment agreed with another person; employment; a battle; (*med*) the stage in a pregnancy when the presenting part of the fetus, which is usually the head, descends into the pelvis of the mother.

engaging *adj* pleasing, attractive.—**engagingly** *adv*.—**engagingness** *n*.

EngD *abbr* = Doctor of Engineering.

Engel *n* Carl L (*b*.1778) German architect. His notable works include Helsinki Cathedral.

Engels *n* Friedrich (1820–95) German socialist and political philosopher who lived in England from 1849 and collaborated with Karl Marx on *The Communist Manifesto* and edited volumes of *Das Kapital*.

engender *vt* to bring into existence.—**engenderment** *n*.

engine *n* a machine by which physical power is applied to produce a physical effect; a locomotive; (*formerly*) a mechanical device, such as a large catapult, used in war.

engineer *n* a person trained in engineering; a person who operates an engine, etc; a member of a military group devoted to engineering work; a designer or builder of engines. * *vt* to contrive, plan, esp deviously.

engineering *n* the art or practice of constructing and using machinery; the art and science by which natural forces and materials are utilized in structures or machines.

English *adj* of, relating to or characteristic of England, the English people, or the English language. * *n* the language of the English people, the US, and many areas formerly under British control; English language and literature as a subject of study.

English horn *n* a large alto oboe.

engorge *vt* to congest with blood; to consume (food) greedily.—**engorgement** *n*.

engr. *abbr* = engineer; engraved; engraver; engraving.

engrained *see* **ingrained**.

engrave *vt* to produce by cutting or carving a surface; to cut to produce a representation that may be printed from; to lodge deeply (in the mind, etc).—**engraver** *n*.

engraving *n* a technique of cutting an image into a metal or wood plate using special tools; a print produced in this way.

engross *vt* to occupy (the attention) fully; to copy in large handwriting; to prepare the final text of.—**engrossing** *adj*.—**engrossment** *n*.

engrossed *adj* having one's attention entirely occupied.

engrossing *adj* holding one's attention completely.—**engrossingly** *adv*.

EngTech *abbr* = Engineering Technician.

engulf *vt* to flow over and enclose; to overwhelm.—**engulfment** *n*.

enhance *vt* to increase in value, importance, attractiveness, etc; to heighten.—**enhancement** *n*.—**enhancer** *n*.

enharmonic intervals *n* (*mus*) intervals that are so small that they do not exist on keyboard instruments; an example is the interval from A sharp to B flat.

E

enigma *n* someone or something that is puzzling or mysterious.—**enigmatic, enigmatical** *adj*.—**enigmatically** *adv*.

Enigma Variations *n* [**Variations on an Original Theme**] a work for orchestra by Elgar first performed in 1899.

enjoin *vt* to command, order someone with authority; to forbid, to prohibit.—**enjoiner** *n*.—**enjoinment** *n*.

enjoy *vt* to get pleasure from, take joy in; to use or have the advantage of; to experience.—**enjoyment** *n*.

enjoyable *adj* giving enjoyment.—**enjoyably** *adv*.

enkephalin *n* a peptide that acts as a neurotransmitter.

enkindle *vt* to set on fire; (*fig*) to inflame.

enl. *abbr* = enlarged; enlisted.

enlace *vt* to entwine; to enfold.—**enlacement** *n*.

enlarge *vti* to make or grow larger; to reproduce (a photograph) in a larger form; to speak or write at length (on).

enlargement *n* an act, instance, or state of enlarging; a photograph, etc that has been enlarged.

enlarger *n* a device for making photographic enlargements.

enlighten *vt* to instruct; to inform.—**enlightening** *adj*.—**enlightenment** *n*.

enlightened *adj* well-informed, tolerant, unprejudiced.

enlist *vt* to engage for service in the armed forces; to secure the aid or support of. * *vi* to register oneself for the armed services.—**enlistee** *n*.—**enlistment** *n*.

enliven *vt* to make more lively or cheerful.—**enlivening** *adj*.—**enlivenment** *n*.

EN(M) *abbr* = Enrolled Nurse (Mental).

en masse *adv* all together; in a large group.

enmesh *vt* to catch in a net; to entangle.—*also* **inmesh, immesh**.

EN(MH) *abbr* = Enrolled Nurse (Mental Handicap).

enmity *n* (*pl* **enmities**) hostility, esp mutual hatred.

ennage *n* (*print*) the number of ens in a text.

ennea- *prefix* nine.

ennead *n* a set of nine; (*Egypt*) a group of nine deities comprising Ra-Atum, Shu, Tefnut, Geb, Nut, Osiris, Isis, Nephthys and Seth.—**enneadic** *adj*.

enneagon *n* a plane figure with nine sides and nine angles.

ennoble *vt* to make noble, dignify; to raise (a person) to a rank of nobility.—**ennoblement** *n*.—**ennobler** *n*.

ennui *n* boredom, apathy.

ENO *abbr* = English National Opera.

enology *n* the science of wines.—*also* **oenology**.—**enological, oenological** *adj*.—**enologist, oenologist** *n*.

enormity *n* (*pl* **enormities**) great wickedness; a serious crime; huge size, magnitude.

enormous *adj* extremely large.—**enormously** *adv*.

enough *adj* adequate, sufficient. * *adv* so as to be sufficient; very; quite. * *n* a sufficiency. * *interj* stop!

enounce *vt* to proclaim, to enunciate.

en passant *adv* in passing.

enquire, enquirer *see* **inquire**.

enquiry *see* **inquiry**.

enrage *vt* to fill with anger.—**enraged** *adj*.—**enragement** *n*.

enrapture *vt* to fill with pleasure or delight.

Enred *n* (*d. c.*841) king of Northumbria (809–*c.*841). A son of Eardwulf.

enrich *vt* to make rich or richer; to ornament; to improve in quality by adding to.—**enricher** *n*.—**enrichment** *n*.

Enrich *abbr* = European Network for Research in Global Change.

enroll, enrol *vti* (**enrolls** *or* **enrols, enrolling, enrolled**) to enter or register on a roll or list; to become a member of a society, club, etc; to admit as a member.—**enrollee** *n*.—**enroller** *n*.—**enrollment, enrolment** *n*.

en route *adv* along or on the way.

Ens. *abbr* = Ensign.

ENS *abbr* = European Nuclear Society.

ENSA *abbr* = Entertainments National Services Association.

ensanguine *vt* to smear or cover with blood.

ensconce *vt* to establish in a safe, secure, or comfortable place.

ensemble *n* something regarded as a whole; the general effect; the performance of the full number of musicians, dancers, etc; a group of players or singers; a movement in opera for several singers; a complete harmonious costume.

enshrine *vt* to enclose (as if) in a shrine; to cherish as sacred.—*also* **inshrine**.—**enshrinement** *n*.

enshroud *vt* to cover with, or as with, a shroud.

ensiform *adj* sword-shaped.

ensign *n* a flag; the lowest commissioned officer in the US Navy.

ensilage *n* storage in a pit or silo; silage.

ensile *vt* to store in a silo.—**ensilability** *n*.

enslave *vt* to make into a slave; to subjugate.—**enslavement** *n*.—**enslaver** *n*.

ensnare *vt* to trap in, or as in, a snare.—**ensnarement** *n*.

Ensor *n* **James** (1860–1949) Belgian painter. He is considered as a forerunner of expressionism and surrealism.

ensue *vi* (**ensuing, ensued**) to occur as a consequence or in time.—**ensuing** *adj*.

en suite *adv, adj* in a single unit.

ensure *vt* to make certain, sure, or safe.—**ensurer** *n*.

enswathe *vt* to wrap, swathe.

ent. *abbr* = entomology.

ENT *abbr* = ear, nose, and throat (mainly hospital departments or specialist clinics).

entablature *n* (*archit*) the part of the structure, or order, which lies upon the columns, consisting of the lower architrave, followed by the frieze and the uppermost cornice.

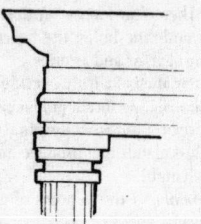

entablement *n* a platform for a statue, above the dado and base.

entail *vt* to involve, necessitate as a result; to restrict the inheritance of property to a designated line of heirs. * *n* the act of entailing or the estate entailed.—**entailer** *n*.—**entailment** *n*.

entangle *vt* to tangle, complicate; to involve in a tangle or complications.—**entanglement** *n*.—**entangler** *n*.

entd. *abbr* = entered.

Entebbe *n* a city in Uganda.

entelechy *n* (*pl* **entelechies**) (*philos*) actuality.

entente (cordiale) *n* a friendly understanding or relationship between two or more countries.

enter *vi* to go or come in or into; to come on stage; to begin, start; (*with* **for**) to register as an entrant. * *vt* to come or go into; to pierce, penetrate; (*an organization*) to join; to insert; (*proposal, etc*) to submit; to record (an item) in a diary, etc.—**enterable** *adj*.—**enterer** *n*.

enteral, enteric *adj* a term meaning relating to the intestine.

enteral feeding *n* the procedure of feeding through a tube via the nose to the stomach.

enteric, enteral *adj* intestinal.

enteric fever *see* **typhoid fever; paratyphoid fever**.

enteritis *n* inflammation of the intestine, usually caused by a viral or bacterial infection, resulting in diarrhea.

enterotomy *n* (*pl* **enterotomies**) dissection of, or an incision into, the bowels.

enterovirus *n* a virus that enters the body via the gut, where it multiplies and from where it attacks the central nervous system, e.g. poliomyelitis.

enterprise *n* a difficult or challenging undertaking; a business project; readiness to engage in new ventures.—**enterpriser** *n*.

enterprise zone *n* an area in economic decline that is chosen for development.

enterprising *adj* adventurous, energetic, and progressive.—**enterprisingly** *adv*.

entertain *vt* to show hospitality to; to amuse, please (a person or audience); to have in mind; to consider.

entertainer *n* a person who entertains in public, esp professionally.

entertaining *adj* amusing; diverting.—**entertainingly** *adv*.

entertainment *n* entertaining; amusement; an act or show intended to amuse and interest an audience, etc.

enthrall, enthral *vt* (**enthralls** *or* **enthrals, enthralling, enthralled**) to captivate.—**enthrallment, enthralment** *n*.

enthrone *vt* to install ceremonially, as a monarch or bishop.—**enthronement** *n*.

enthuse *vti* to fill with or express enthusiasm.

enthusiasm *n* intense interest or liking; something that arouses keen interest.

enthusiast *n* a person filled with enthusiasm for something.

enthusiastic *adj* filled with enthusiasm.—**enthusiastically** *adv*.

enthymeme *n* (*logic*) a syllogism in which one premise is suppressed.

entice *vt* to attract by offering some pleasure or reward.—**enticement** *n*.—**enticer** *n*.—**enticing** *adj*.

entire *adj* whole; complete.—**entireness** *n*.

entirely *adv* fully; completely.

entirety *n* (*pl* **entireties**) completeness; the total.

entitle *vt* to give a title to; to give a right (to).—**entitlement** *n*.

entity *n* (*pl* **entities**) existence, being; something that has a separate existence.

entoblast, entoderm *see* **endoderm**.

entom. *abbr* = entomological, entomology.

entomb *vt* to place in, or as in, a tomb.—**entombment** *n*.

entomic *adj* of insects.

entomo-, entom- *prefix* insect.

entomology *n* the branch of zoology that deals with insects.—**entomological, entomologic** *adj.*—**entomologist** *n.*

entomophagous *adj* insect-eating.

entomophilous *adj* fertilized by insects.

entopic *adj* (*anat*) in a normal position.

entourage *n* a retinue, group of attendants.

entozoan *n* (*pl* **entozoa**) a parasite which lives inside an animal.

entozoic *adj* living within an animal.

entr'acte *n* a light entertainment, a ballet, etc, as an interlude between the acts of a play or opera. *See also* act tune, interlude, intermezzo.

entrails *npl* the insides of the body, the intestines.

entrain *vti* to put or get onto a train.

entrance[1] *n* the act of entering; the power or authority to enter; a means of entering; an admission fee.

entrance[2] *vt* to put into a trance; to fill with great delight.—**entrancement** *n.*—**entrancing** *adj.*

entrance grave *or* **undifferentiated passage grave** *n* (*archeo*) a form of chamber tomb in which there is no clear entry passage leading into the burial chamber.

entrant *n* a person who enters (e.g., a competition, profession).

entrap *vt* (**entrapping, entrapped**) to catch, as if in a trap; to lure into a compromising or incriminatory situation.—**entrapment** *n.*—**entrapper** *n.*

entreat *vt* to request earnestly; to implore, beg.—**entreaty** *n* (*pl* **entreaties**).

entrecôte *n* a boned cut of beef from between the ribs.

entrée, entree *n* a dish served before the main meal; in US, the principal dish of a meal; the right or power of admission.

entremets *n* (*pl* **entremets**) a dessert.

entrench *vt* to dig a trench as a defensive perimeter; to establish (oneself) in a strong defensive position.—**entrencher** *n.*—**entrenchment** *n.*

entrepôt *n* a point of entry where goods are imported without attracting duty before being sent on to another country.

entrepôt trade *n* a form of international trading in which goods are temporarily imported into a country and then re-exported.

entrepreneur *n* a person who invests in a new business and bears the risk associated with that investment.—**entrepreneurial** *adj.*—**entrepreneurship** *n.*

entresol *n* a floor between the ground and first floor, a mezzanine.

entropy *n* (*pl* **entropies**) a measure of the unavailable energy in a closed thermodynamic system; disorder, disorganization; (*physics*) a measure of the randomness or disorder of a system.

entrust *vt* (*usu with* **with**) to confer as a responsibility, duty, etc; (*usu with* **to**) to place something in another's care.—**entrustment** *n.*

entry *n* (*pl* **entries**) the act of entering; a place of entrance; an item recorded in a diary, journal, etc; a person or thing taking part in a contest.

entwine *vt* to twine together or around. —**entwinement** *n.*

enucleate *vt* to remove the nucleus from.

Enugu *n* a city in Nigeria.

E number *n* a series of numbers with the prefix E used to identify food additives within the European Union.

enumerate *vt* to count; to list.—**enumeration** *n.*—**enumerator** *n.*

enunciate *vt* to state definitely; to pronounce clearly.—**enunciation** *n.*—**enunciator** *n.*—**enunciative** *adj.*

enure *see* **inure**.

enuresis *n* urinary incontinence; bedwetting.—**enuretic** *adj.*

envelop *vt* to enclose completely (as if) with a covering.—**envelopment** *n.*

envelope *n* something used to wrap or cover, esp a gummed paper container for a letter; the bag containing the gas in a balloon or airship.

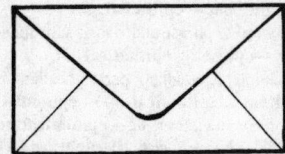

envemon *vt* to put poison into; (*fig*) to embitter.

Env. Ext. *abbr* = Envoy Extraordinary.

enviable *adj* causing envy; fortunate.—**enviably** *adv.*

envious *adj* filled with envy.—**enviously** *adv.*

environ *vt* to surround or enclose.

environment *n* external conditions and surroundings, esp those that affect the quality of life of plants, animals, and human beings; (*comput*) the style or setting in which the user enters commands into or performs tasks with the computer—**environmental** *adj.*—**environmentally** *adv.*

environmentalist *n* a person who is concerned with improving the quality of the environment.—**environmentalism** *n.*

environs *npl* the surrounding area or outskirts of a district or town.

envisage *vt* to have a mental picture of.—**envisagement** *n.*

envoy *n* a diplomatic agent; a representative.

envy *n* (*pl* **envies**) resentment or discontent at another's achievements, possessions, etc; an object of envy. * *vt* (**envying, envied**) to feel envy of.—**envier** *n.*

ENWRAC *abbr* = European Network for Women's Right to Abortion and Contraception.

enwrap *vt* to wrap up.

enzootic *adj* (*disease*) affecting animals in a particular district.

enzyme *n* any protein molecule that acts as a natural catalyst and is found in the bodies of all bacteria, plants, and animals.

eo *abbr* (*Latin*) = *ex officio*, "by right of office."

EO *abbr* = Education Officer; Education Otherwise; Equal Opportunities; Executive Officer; Executive Order.

EOA *abbr* = examination, opinion, and advice.

EOC *abbr* = Equal Opportunities Commission.

Eocha *n* (*d.* 889) king of Scots (878–889). The son of Run, king of Strathclyde, and grandson of Kenneth mac-Alpin. He ruled jointly with his cousin, Giric I, the son of Donald I, before being deposed.

Eochaid I (the Yellow-Haired) *n* (*d. c.*629) king of Scots. The son and successor of Aiden.

Eochaid II *n* (*d. c.*679) king of Scots. Also known as "Eochaid the Crook-Nose."

Eochaid III *n* (*d. c.*733) king of Scots. The last to rule in Irish Dalriada.

Eochaid IV *n* (the Venomous) (*d. c.*737) king of Scots. Reigned between 733 and 737. His son, Alpin, was the father of Kenneth mac-Alpin who became the first king of the Dalriadan Scots and the Picts.

Eochaidh Airemh *n* (*Irish Celtic myth*) Eochaidh Airemh married the reincarnation of Etain and then refused to return her to Midhir, her husband, in her original form.

EODC *abbr* = Earth Observation Data Center.

e.o.h.p. *abbr* = except as otherwise herein provided.

eoliths *n* (*archeo*) chipped stones found in geological deposits dating either from before the last Ice Age (Pleistocene) or to the beginning of that period.

e.o.m. *abbr* = end of the month (payments).

eon *n* (*geol*) the largest geological unit of time.

eonism *n* (*psychiatry*) a tendency in a male to adopt female clothing and mannerisms, transvestitism.

Eormenric *n* (*d. c.*560) king of Kent (*c.*540–560). A son of Aesc.

Eorpwold *n* (*d.* 627) king of East Anglia (*c.*617–627). A son of Redwald, he was converted to Christianity by Edwin of Northumbria.

EORTC *abbr* = European Organization for Research into the Treatment of Cancer.

Eos *n* (*Greek myth*) the goddess of the dawn.

EOSC *abbr* = Employments Occupational Standards Council.

eosin, eosine *n* a pink coal tar dye.—**eosinic** *adj.*

EOUSA *abbr* = Executive Office for United States Attorneys

ep *abbr* (*French*) = *en passant*, "while passing" (chess).

ep. *abbr* = epistle.

e.p. *abbr* = electric primer; electrically polarized.

Ep. *abbr* (*Latin*) = *Episcopus*, "bishop."

EP *abbr* = European Parliament; electroplate; extended play (record).

EPA *abbr* = Emergency Powers Act; Employment Protection Act; English Pool Association; Environmental Protection Agency; European Productivity Agency.

epact *n* (*astron*) the difference between the solar and the lunar month, about eleven days in the year.

EPACT *abbr* = European Promotion Association for Composite Tanks and Tubulars.

Epaphras *n* (*Bible*) companion and beloved fellow-servant of Paul.

Epaphroditus *n* (*Bible*) a native of Philippi who brought gifts to Paul when he was imprisoned in Rome.

Epaphus *n* (*Greek myth*) a son of Zeus and Io, who was born on the River Nile after the long wanderings of his mother. He later became king of Egypt and built the city of Memphis in Egypt. He had one daughter, Libya, from whom the African country received its name.

eparch *n* (*Greek Orthodox Church*) a metropolitan or other bishop; a governor of an eparchy.

eparchy, eparchate *n* (*pl* **eparchies, eparchates**) a Greek province; the diocese of an eparch.—**eparchial** *adj.*

epaulet, epaulette *n* a piece of ornamental fabric or metal worn on the shoulder, esp on a uniform.

EPC *abbr* = Educational Publishers Council; Emergency Preparedness Canada; European Pancreatic Club; Export Publicity Council.

EPCC *abbr* = Edinburgh Parallel Computing Centre.

EPCIA *abbr* = Expanded Polystyrene Cavity Insulation.

EPDA *abbr* = Emergency Powers Defence Act.

épée *n* a sword used in fencing.—**épéeist** *n.*

epenthesis *n* (*pl* **epentheses**) *n* (*linguistics*) the insertion of a letter or syllable in the middle of a word.

epergne *n* a branched centerpiece or ornamental stand for a dinner table.

epexegesis *n* (*pl* **epexegeses**) (*linguistics*) the use of additional words to clarify a meaning.—**epexegetic, epexegetical** *adj.*

EPG *abbr* = Eminent Persons' Group.

ephah *n* (*Bible*) Hebrew dry measure of quantity; approximately a basketful.

ephebe *n* a young citizen (aged 18 to 20) of ancient Greece.

ephedrine *n* an alkaloid used to treat asthma and hay fever.

ephemeral *adj* existing only for a very short time. * *n* an ephemeral thing or organism.—**ephemerality, ephemeralness** *n.*

ephemeris *n* (*astron*) a published table providing the projected position and movements of planets and comets.

Ephes. *abbr* (*Bible*) = Ephesians.

Ephesians *n* **Letter of Paul to the** *n* (*Bible*) NT book, one of four "letters from prison" although some scholars do not believe it was written by Paul.

Ephesus *n* seaport in Asia Minor at the mouth of the Meander and Hermus rivers in western Turkey and capital of the Roman province of Asia.

ephod *n* (*Bible*) piece of linen shaped like an apron once worn by a Jewish high priest.

ephor *n* (*pl* **ephors, ephori**) a magistrate in ancient Greece.

Ephraim *n* (*Bible*) one of the tribes of Israel, based in hilly country in central Canaan; together with other northern tribes they established the kingdom of Israel, though it was still often called Ephraim.

Ephraim *n* (*Bible*) second son of Joseph and Asenath, daughter of an Egyptian priest. *See also* **Asenath; Joseph.**

EPI *abbr* = European Peace Initiative.

epi-, ep- *prefix* upon, at, in addition.

epiblast *n* the outer layer of the embryonic cells in an egg from which an organism is formed.—**epiblastic** *adj*.

epic *n* a long poem narrating the deeds of a hero; any literary work, film, etc in the same style. * *adj* relating to or resembling an epic.

Epic *abbr* = European Philosophical Inquiry Centre.

epicarp *n* the outer skin of a fruit.

epicene *adj* having characteristics of both sexes; lacking characteristics of either sex, sexless.

epicenter *n* the point or line on the Earth's surface that is directly above the focus of an earthquake.—**epicentral** *adj*.

epicure *n* a person who has cultivated a refined taste in food, wine, literature, etc.— **epicurism, epicureanism** *n*.

epicurean *adj* given to sensuous enjoyment.

Epicurus *n* (341–271 BC) Greek philosopher and founder of the Epicurean school of philosophy.

epicycle *n* (*geom*) a small circle, the center of which is situated on the circumference of a larger circle.—**epicyclical** *adj*.

epicycloid *n* (*geom*) a curve described by a point in the circumference of one circle which rolls round the circumference of another circle.

Epidaurus *n* a town of ancient Greece in the Peloponnese, famous for its temple of Aesculapius.

epidemic *n* a disease that affects a large proportion of the population at the same time. —**epidemical** *adj*.

epidemiology *n* the area of medicine dealing with epidemic diseases.— **epidemiological** *adj*.—**epidemiologist** *n*.

epidermis *n* the outer layer of the skin, which comprises four layers and overlies the dermis.—**epidermal, epidermic, epidermoid** *adj*

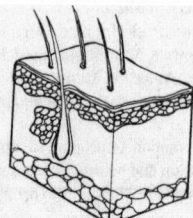

epidiascope *n* a projector for magnifying opaque as well as transparent pictures.

epidural *or* **extradural** *adj* outside the *dura mater* enveloping the spinal chord.

epidural anesthesia *n* anesthesia in the region of the pelvis, abdomen, or genitals produced by local anesthetic injected into the epidural space of the spinal column.

epidural space *n* the space between the vertebral canal and the *dura mater* of the spinal cord.

epigastrium *n* (*pl* **epigastria**) the upper part of the abdomen.

epigenesis *n* the theory that an organism is created by the division or segmentation of a fertilized egg cell; a form of geological metamorphism of rock brought about by outside forces; the depositing of ore in already formed rock.—**epigenesist, epigenist** *n*.—**epigenetic** *adj*.—**epigentically** *adv*.

epiglottis *n* a thin piece of cartilage situated at the base of the tongue, enclosed in mucous membrane that covers the larynx.—**epiglottal, epiglottic** *adj*.

epiglottitis *n* inflammation of the mucous membrane of the epiglottis.

Epigoni *npl* (*Greek myth*) the sons of the Seven against Thebes, who ten years later conducted a war against Thebes to avenge their fathers. They were Alcmaeon, Aegialeus, Diomedes, Promachus, Sthenelus, Thersander, and Eurylus.

epigram *n* a short witty poem or saying.—**epigrammatic** *adj*.— **epigrammatically** *adv*.

epigrammatize *vti* to compose an epigram (about).—**epigrammatist** *n*.

epigraph *n* a quotation at the beginning of a book or chapter; an inscription on a building or monument.—**epigraphic, epigraphical** *adj*.

epigraphy *n* the study of inscriptions.—**epigraphist, epigrapher** *n*.

epilepsy *n* a disorder of the nervous system marked typically by convulsive attacks and loss of consciousness caused by damaged tissue in the brain .

epileptic *adj* of or affected with epilepsy. * *n* a person affected with epilepsy.— **epileptically** *adv*.

epilogue *n* the concluding section of a book or other literary work; a short speech addressed by an actor to the audience at the end of a play.—**epilogist** *n*.

Epimetheus *n* (*Greek myth*) the brother of Prometheus and Atlas, and husband of Pandora.

epinaos *n* (*archit*) the open space beneath the rear portico roof behind the naos, in a Greek temple.

Épinay *n* [**Louise Florence Pétronille] Madame d'** (1726–83) French writer who became acquainted with Rousseau and gave him a cottage where he lived for some time. Her *Conversations d'Émilie* is a companion volume to Rousseau's *Émile*.

epinephrine *see* **adrenaline**.

Epiph. *abbr* = Epiphany.

epiphany *n* (*pl* **epiphanies**) a moment of sudden revelation or insight; (*with cap*) a festival of the Christian Church in commemoration of the coming of the Magi to Christ.

epiphenomenon *n* (*pl* **epiphenomena**) a by-product; (*med*) an attendant symptom.

epiphysis (*pl* **epiphyses**) *n* the softer end of a long bone that is separated from the shaft by a plate of cartilage.

epiphyte *n* (*bot*) a plant which grows on another plant but is not fed by it.— **epiphytic** *adj*.

Epirus *or* **Epeirus** *n* the ancient name of a part of northern Greece.

Epis., Episc. *abbr* = Episcopal.

episcopacy *n* (*pl* **episcopacies**) the system of church government by bishops.

Episcopal *adj* of bishops; governed by bishops.—**Episcopally** *adv*.

Episcopal Church *n* a church outside England in communion with the Anglican Church; the Protestant Episcopal Church.

Episcopalian *adj* of or pertaining to the Episcopal Church; (*without cap*) pertaining to episcopacy. * *n* a member of the Episcopal Church or the Protestant Episcopal Church; (*without cap*) a supporter of episcopacy.— **Episcopalianism** *n*.

episcopate *n* the office of a bishop.

episiotomy *n* (*med*) the process of making an incision in the perineum to enlarge a woman's vaginal opening to facilitate delivery of a child.

episode *n* a piece of action in a dramatic or literary work; an incident in a sequence of events; (*mus*) in a fugue, a passage that connects entries of the subject; in a rondo, a contrasting section that separates entries of the principal theme.

episodic, episodical *adj* happening at irregular intervals; digressive.— **episodically** *adv*.

epispastic *adj* producing a blister.

epistaxis *n* (*med*) nosebleed.

epistemology *n* the science of the processes and grounds of knowledge.

epistle *n* (*formal*) a letter.

Epistle *n* (*Bible*) a letter written by one of Christ's Apostles to various churches and individuals.

epistler *n* someone who reads the Epistle in the communion service; one who writes an epistle.

epistolary *adj* pertaining to, contained in, or conducted by letters.

epistolary novel a novel in the form of a series of letters written to and from the main characters, sometimes presented by the author in the anonymous role of "editor." The form flourished in the 18th century.

epistrophe *n* (*rhetoric*) the practice of ending several successive clauses or sentences with the same word.

epistyle *n* an architrave.

epit. *abbr* = epitaph; epitome.

epitaph *n* an inscription in memory of a dead person, usu on a tombstone.— **epitaphic** *adj*.—**epitaphist** *n*.

epithalamium *n* (*pl* **epithalamia**) a nuptial song or poem.—**epithalamic** *adj*.

epithelioma *n* (*med*) an epithelial tumor, used formerly to describe any carcinoma. — **epitheliomatous** *adj*.

epithelium (*pl* **epithelia**) *n* tissue made up of cells packed closely together and bound by connective material that covers the outer surface of the body and lines vessels and organs in the body.—**epithelial** *adj*.

epithet *n* a descriptive word or phrase added to or substituted for a person's name, e.g. Vlad the Impaler.—**epithetic, epithetical** *adj*.

epitome *n* a typical example; a paradigm; personification; a condensed account of a written work.—**epitomic, epitomical** *adj*.—**epitomist** *n*.

epitomize *vt* to be or make an epitome of.—**epitomization** *n*.—**epitomizer** *n*.

EPNS *abbr* = English Place Name Society; electroplated nickel silver.

EPO *abbr* = Earthnet Program Office.

epoch *n* a date in time used as a point of reference; an age in history associated with certain characteristics; a unit of geological time subsidiary to the period, and forming several ages.—**epochal** *adj*.

EPOCH *abbr* = End Physical Punishment of Children.

epode *n* a kind of lyric poem; the last part of a lyric ode.

Epona *n* (*Gaulish Celtic myth*) a horse-goddess; also thought to have been associated with death.

eponym *n* a person after whom something is named; a name so derive;. a mythical person created to account for the name of a tribe or people. —**eponymous, eponymic** *adj*.—**eponymy** *n*.

epopee *n* an epic poem; epic poetry.

Epopeus *n* (*Greek myth*) a son of Poseidon who became king of Sicyon.

epos *n* early unwritten epic poetry; an epic poem; the subject of an epic poem.

EPOS *abbr* = electronic point of sale.

epoxy *adj* (*chem*) of or containing an oxygen atom and two other groups, usually carbon, which are themselves linked with other groups.

epoxy resin *n* a strong synthetic resin containing epoxy groups, used in laminates and adhesives.

epp. *abbr* = epistles.

EPP *abbr* = European People's Party.

EPPAPA *abbr* = European Pure Phosphoric Acid Producers' Association.

Eppilus *n* (*c.*AD 15) king of the Atrebates tribe. One of the three sons of Commius who divided his kingdom and used the Roman title *Rex* meaning "king."

EPROM *abbr* (*comput*) = Erasable Programmable Read Only Memory. A memory chip that can be programmed, erased, and reprogrammed.

EPS *abbr* = Experimental Psychology Society.

EPSF *abbr* = European Paintball Sports Federation.

EPSG *abbr* = Epiphytic Plant Study Group; European Pineal Study Group; European Production Study Group.

EPS graphic *abbr* (*comput*) = Encapsulated PostScript graphic. An object-oriented graphics file format developed by Apple.

epsilon *n* the fifth letter of the Greek alphabet.

Epstein *n* Sir Jacob (1880–1959) American-born British sculptor in the romantic tradition. Notable works include *Christ* (1919), *Genesis* (1931), and *Adam* (1939).

Epstein-Barr virus *n* a virus, similar to herpes, that causes infectious mononucleosis (glandular fever) and is implicated in hepatitis.

EPT *abbr* = Environmental Protection Technology; Exploring Parenthood Trust.

EPTA *abbr* = Electrophysiological Technologists Association; European Paltrusion Technology Association; European Piano Teachers Association; European Power Tool Association.

EPU *abbr* = European Payments Union; European Picture Union.

eq *abbr* = equal; equalizer; equalizing; equation; equivalent.

EQ *abbr* (*psychol*) = educational quotient.

EQA *abbr* = European Quality Alliance.

equable *adj* level, uniform; (*climate*) free from extremes of hot and cold; even-tempered.—**equability, equableness** *n*.—**equably** *adv*.

equable climate *n* a climate with little variation throughout the year.

equal *adj* the same in amount, size, number, or value; impartial, regarding or affecting all objects in the same way; capable of meeting a task or situation. * *n* a person that is equal. * *vt* (**equaling, equaled** *or* **equalling, equalled**) to be equal to, esp to be identical in value; to make or do something equal to.—**equally** *adv*.

equality *n* (*pl* **equalities**) being equal.

equalize *vti* to make or become equal; (*games*) to even the score.—**equalization** *n*.—**equalizer** *n*.

equal pay *n* the right of men and women to be paid the same rate of pay for performing the same job or work of equal value.

equal temperament *n* (*mus*) a convenient, but technically incorrect, way of tuning a keyboard in which all half tones, or half steps (semitones), are considered equal, e.g. F sharp and G flat are taken to be identical notes when theoretically they are not. Such a system makes complex modulations practicable.

equanimity *n* (*pl* **equanimities**) evenness of temper; composure.—**equanimous** *adj*.

equate *vt* to make, treat, or regard as comparable. * *vi* to correspond as equal.

equation *n* an act of equaling; the state of being equal; a usu formal statement of equivalence (as in logical and mathematical expressions) with the relations denoted by the sign =; an expression representing a chemical reaction by means of chemical symbols.—**equational** *adj*.

equator *n* the imaginary great circle round the Earth at latitude 0°. It is 24,902 miles (40,076 kilometers) long.—**equatorial** *adj*.

equatorial *adj* (*astron*) of a telescope, positioned so that when it is set on a star, that body will be kept in the field of view.

equatorial climate *n* the type of climate occurring on low ground near the equator, with high temperatures and humidity, and little seasonal change.

equatorial currents *n* surface currents in the oceans near the Equator that flow at about 2 knots.

Equatorial Guinea *n* a republic situated on the coast of west Africa.

equatorial trough *see* doldrums.

equerry *n* (*pl* **equerries**) an officer in the British royal household.

equestrian *adj* pertaining to horses and riding; on horseback. * *n* a skilled rider.—**equestrienne** *nf*.—**equestrianism** *n*.

equi- *prefix* equal.

equiangular *adj* having equal angles.

equidistant *adj* at equal distances.—**equidistance** *n*.

equilateral *adj* having all sides equal.

equilibrate *vti* to balance.—**equilibration** *n*.—**equilibrator** *n*.

equilibrist *n* a tightrope walker; an acrobat.—**equilibristic** *adj*.

equilibrium *n* (*pl* **equilibriums, equilibria**) a state of balance of weight, power, force, etc; (*chem*) a condition in which the proportion of the chemicals reacting together and the products being formed is constant.

equine *adj* of or resembling a horse.

equinox *n* the two times of the year when night and day are equal in length (around 21 March and 23 September); the point of intersection between the Sun's apparent path in the sky, relative to the stars and the celestial Equator.—**equinoctial** *adj*.

equip *vt* (**equipping, equipped**) to provide with all the necessary tools or supplies.—**equipper** *n*.

equipage *n* a carriage with horses and liveried attendants.

equipment *n* the tools, supplies, and other items needed for a particular task, expedition, etc.

equipoise *n* balance, equilibrium.

equipollent *adj* equal in power.—**equipollence** *n*.

equiponderant *vti* to make or be equal in weight.—**equiponderant** *adj*.

equisetum *n* (*pl* **equisetums, equiseta**) a plant of the group that includes horsetails.

equitable *adj* just and fair; (*law*) pertaining to equity as opposed to common or statute law.—**equitableness** *n*.—**equitably** *adv*.

equitation *n* horsemanship.

equity *n* (*pl* **equities**) fairness; (*law*) a legal system based on natural justice developed into a body of rules supplementing the common law; (*pl*) ordinary shares in a company; the net assets of a company after all debts and liabilities have been paid; the ordinary share capital of a company; the amount of money that is returned to a borrower in a mortgage or other loan agreement after the asset involved has been sold and the full repayment of the sum lent; the value of an asset after the deduction of any liabilities outstanding on it.

equiv. *abbr* = equivalent.

equivalence, equivalency *n* (*pl* **equivalences, equivalencies**) equality of value or power; (*chem*) the property of having equal valency.

equivalent *adj* equal in amount, force, meaning, etc; virtually identical, esp in effect or function. * *n* an equivalent thing.

equivocal *adj* ambiguous; uncertain; questionable; arousing suspicion.—**equivocality, equivocacy** *n*.—**equivocally** *adv*.

equivocate *vi* to use ambiguous language, esp in order to confuse or deceive.—**equivocation** *n*.—**equivocator** *n*.—**equivocatory** *adj*.

equivoque, equivoke *n* a pun; an ambiguous expression.

Er *symbol* (*chem.*) erbium.

ER *abbr* (*Latin*) = *Elizabeth Regina*, "Queen Elizabeth."

era *n* an historical period typified by some special feature; a chronological order or system of notation reckoned from a given date as a basis; (*geol*) a unit of geological time which comprises several periods.

ERA *abbr* = Education Reform Act; Emergency Relief Administration; Eritrean Relief Association; European Renal Association; European Rifle Association (Luxembourg).

ERAD *abbr* = Eradication of Animal Diseases Board (Eire).

eradiate *vti* to emit rays, to radiate.—**eradiation** *n*.

eradicate *vt* to obliterate.—**eradicable** *adj*.—**eradication** *n*.—**eradicator** *n*.

erasable storage *n* (*comput*) a read/write secondary storage device in which data can be written and erased repeatedly.

erase *vt* to rub out, obliterate; to remove a recording from magnetic tape; to remove data from a computer memory or storage medium.—**erasable** *adj*.—**erasion** *n*.

eraser *n* a piece of rubber, etc for rubbing out marks or writing.

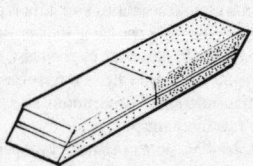

Erasmus *n* **Desiderius** (1467–1536) Dutch scholar, one of the greatest of the Renaissance and Reformation period. A humanist rather than a reformer or theologian, he took no direct part in the Reformation but waged war on ignorance and superstition.

ERASMUS *abbr* = European Community Action Scheme for the Mobility of University Students.

erasure *n* an erasing; something rubbed out.

Erato *n* (*Greek myth*) one of the nine Muses, who presided over lyric and esp love poetry.

erbium *n* a soft metallic element of the rare earth group.

ERBM *abbr* = extended-range ballistic missile.

Erc *n* (*Irish Celtic myth*) is said to have killed Cuchulainn. He joined forces with Medb and the monstrous children of Calatin and marched in battle against Cuchulainn.

ERC *abbr* = Earth Resources Center.

Erconbert *n* (*d.* 664) king of Kent, Britain (*c.*660–664). He married Sexburga, one of King Anna of East Anglia's four daughters.

Erdmannsdorff *n* **Friedrich Wilhelm** (1736–1800) German painter and architect, who was sponsored by Duke Friedrich-Franz of Anhalt-Dessau. His notable works include Wörlitz Palace.

ere *prep, conj* (*poet*) before.

Erebus *n* (*Greek myth*) the son of Chaos (darkness) and father of Aether and Hemera (day); a name for the underworld.

Erechtheus *n* (*Greek myth*) a hero of Attica, and king of Athens, in whose honor the Erechtheum Temple was built on the Acropolis.—*also* **Erichthonius**.

erect *adj* upright; not leaning or lying down; (*sexual organs*) rigid and swollen with blood from sexual stimulation. * *vt* to construct, set up.—**erectable** *adj*.—**erecter, erector** *n*.—**erectness** *n*.

erectile *adj* (*penis, clitoris, etc*) able to become enlarged and rigid through sexual stimulation.—**erectility** *n*.

erection *n* construction; something erected, as a building; (*biol*) the condition in which erectile tissue in the penis (and to some degree in the clitoris) is engorged with blood, making it swell and become hard.

erector *n* a person who, or a thing that, erects; a muscle that erects.

eremite *n* a hermit.—**eremitic, eremitical** *adj*.—**eremitism** *n*.

Eremon *n* (*Irish Celtic myth*) the first king to rule over all Ireland; one of the Sons of Mil Espaine who invaded Ireland.

ERES *abbr* = European Rare Earth and Actinide Society.

erethism *n* (*med*) an abnormal degree of excitement in an organ or tissue of the body.

ERF *abbr* = European Rotorcraft Forum.

erg *n* the unit for measuring work or energy.

ergo *adv* therefore.

ergometer *n* an instrument for measuring work performed or force produced.

ergonomics *n* (*sing*) the study of the interaction between people and their working environment with the aim of improving efficiency and providing safe, comfortable working conditions.—**ergonomic** *adj*.—**ergonomically** *adv*.—**ergonomist** *n*.

ergot *n* a disease of rye and other cereals caused by a fungus; this fungus; a medicine derived from an ergot fungus.

ergotism *n* (*med*) a toxic condition in humans caused by ergot fungus or chronic excessive use of an ergot drug.

Eric *n* (*d.* 918) king of East Anglia, England (900–902). He succeeded his father, Guthrum, and was killed fighting Edward the Elder's army. He was the last Dane to rule the kingdom of East Anglia.

ERIC *abbr* = Educational Resources Information Center.

Erica *n* a genus of flowering plants, including the heaths and some heathers.

ericaceous *adj* of the heath family.

Erickson *n* **Arthur C** (1924–) Canadian architect. His notable works include the Government offices, Vancouver.

Eridanus *n* the name of various rivers in ancient Greece and Europe, including the River Po.

Erik Bloodaxe *n* (*d.* 954) king of York, England (947–954). After being deposed as King of Norway in 934 he fled to England and seized Northumbria from Edred in 947. He was killed along with his brother and a son in an ambush at Stainmore by Edred's army.

Erikson *n* **Erik Homburger** (1902–94) American psychoanalyst and author of several works, including *Childhood and Society* (1950).

Erinyes *see* **Furies**.

Eris *n* (*Greek myth*) the goddess of discord, who, not being invited to the marriage of Peleus, took revenge by means of the golden apple of discord.

eristic, eristical *adj* (*logic*) seeking to win an argument rather than find the truth.

Eritrea *n* an autonomous province in Ethiopia, which gained independence in May 1993.

Eriu *n* (*Irish Celtic myth*) the goddess who gave her name to Ireland. Amhairghin promised that the country would be named Eire. Eriu is one of the three aspects of the sovereignty of Ireland, the other two being Fotla or Fodla and Banbha or Banb.

Erlanger *n* **Joseph** (1874–1965) American physiologist. He shared the 1944 Nobel prize for physiology or medicine with Herbert Spencer Gasser for their work on nerve fibers and the transmission of nerve impulses.

ERM *abbr* = exchange rate mechanism.

ERMA *abbr* = Ernest Read Music Association; European Resin Manufacturers' Association.

ERMCO *abbr* = European Ready Mixed Concrete Organization.

ermine *n* (*pl* **ermines, ermine**) the weasel in its winter coat; the white fur of the winter coat; a rank or office whose official robe is edged with ermine.

erne, ern *n* the sea eagle.

ERNIE *abbr* = Electronic Random Number Indicator Equipment. A computer used to draw random winning numbers of British premium bonds.

Ernst *n* **Max** (1891–1976) German painter and sculptor. Self-taught, he founded the Dada movement in 1914 with Jean Arp. He was also a founder member of surrealism with Breton in 1922 and moved to the US in 1941.

ERO *abbr* = Ethiopian Relief Organization.

erode *vt* to eat or wear away gradually.

erogenous *adj* sexually arousing; sensitive to sexual stimulation.

EROM *abbr* = erasable read-only memory.

Eros *n* (*Greek myth*) the god of love, whom the Romans called Cupid.

erosion *n* the act of eroding; gradual destruction or eating away; an eroded part; (*geol*) the breakdown and transport of material by water, ice, and wind and the continued wearing down of the land surface.

erotic, erotical *adj* of sexual love; sexually stimulating.—**erotically** *adv*.

erotica *n* sexually explicit literature or art.

eroticism, erotism *n* erotic nature; sexually arousing themes in literature and art; sexual desire.

erotomania *n* excessive sexual desire.—**erotomaniac** *n*.

err *vi* to be or do wrong.

ERR *abbr* = Earth Resources Research.

ERRA *abbr* = European Recovery and Recycling Association (Belgium).

errand *n* a short journey to perform some task, usu on behalf of another; the purpose of this journey.

errant *adj* going astray, esp doing wrong; moving aimlessly.

errantry *n* (*pl* **errantries**) the state or conduct of a knight errant.

erratic *adj* capricious; irregular; eccentric, odd.—**erratically** *adv*.

erratum *n* (*pl* **errata**) a written or printed error; a page bearing a list of corrigenda (—*also* **corrigendum**).

Errazuriz *n* **Eugenie** (1861–1954) Chilean society hostess, whose Paris salon influenced the styles of painters, including Pablo Picasso.

erron. *abbr* = erroneous; erroneously.

erroneous *adj* incorrect; mistaken.—**erroneously** *adv*.

error *n* a mistake, an inaccuracy; a mistaken belief or action; (*statistics*) the difference between an approximation of a value and the actual value, usu expressed as a percentage.

error message *n* (*comput*) a message displayed on-screen that indicates that the computer has detected an error or malfunction.

errors and omissions excepted *see* **E & OE**.

ERS *abbr* = Economic Research Service; Electoral Reform Society; Electric Railway Society; European Respiratory Society.

ersatz *adj* made in imitation; synthetic.

Erse *n* Scottish Gaelic; Irish Gaelic.—*also adj*.

Erskine *n* **Ralph** (1914 -) English architect. His notable works include Byker housing in Newcastle.

erstwhile *adv* formerly. * *adj* former.

Erté *n* [**Romain de Tirtoff**] (1892–1990) Russian designer, illustrator, and costume designer who became one of the most notable exponents of Art Deco style and worked on Hollywood sets.

Ertebølle or **Kitchen Midden Culture** *adj* (*archeo*) relating to a Mesolithic culture defined by kitchen midden sites in the west Baltic region.

ERU *abbr* = English Rugby Union.

eructation *n* the act of belching.

erudite *adj* scholarly, having great knowledge.—**eruditely** *adv*.—**erudition** *n*.

erupt *vi* to burst forth; to break out into a rash; (*volcano*) to explode, ejecting ash and lava into the air.—**eruptible** *adj*.

eruption *n* the ejection of lava from a volcano; an outbreak; pimples; (*med*) an outbreak or rash on the skin, usually in the form of a red and raised area, possibly with fluid-containing blisters or scales/crusts.—**eruptional** *adj*.—**eruptive** *adj*.

eryngo, eringo *n* (*pl* **eryngoes, eryngos, eringoes, eringos**) one of a genus of plants including the sea holly.

erysipelas *n* an infectious disease, caused by *Streptococcus pyogenes*. It produces an inflammation of the skin with associated redness.

erythema *n* an inflammation or redness of the skin in which the tissues are congested with blood..—**erythematic, erythematous, erythemic** *adj*.

erythroblast *n* a cell occurring in the red bone marrow that develops into a red blood cell (erythrocyte).

erythrocyte *n* the red blood cell that is made in the bone marrow and occurs as a red disc, concave on both sides, full of hemoglobin.

erythroderma *see* **dermatitis**.

erythromycin *n* an antibiotic used for bacterial and mycoplasmic infections, similar to penicillin in its activity, that can be taken for infections that penicillin cannot treat.

Eryx *n* an ancient city and a mountain in the west of Sicily; modern San Giuliano.

ESAA *abbr* = English Schools Athletic Association.

ESAG *abbr* = Escalator Safety Action Group.

Esaias *n* (*Bible*) Greek form of Isaiah, used in the NT.

Esarhaddon *n* (*Egypt*) king of Assyria and conqueror of Egypt in 671 BC,

Esau *n* (*Bible*) a skilled hunter and the favorite son of Isaac; older twin brother of Jacob who tricked him out of their father's blessing and had to flee to escape Esau's anger. *See also* **birthright; Jacob**.

ESB *abbr* = English-speaking Board; European Settlement Board; electrical stimulation of the brain.

esc. *abbr* = escadrille.

ESC *abbr* = English Ski Council; Entomological Society of Canada; Ethiopia Solidarity Campaign; European Shippers' Council; Executive Secretaries Club.

ESCA *abbr* = East of Scotland College of Agriculture; English Schools Cricket Association; European Speech Communication Association; electronic spectroscopy for chemical analysis.

escalade *n* the act of scaling the walls of a fortified place by ladders.

escalate *vi* to increase rapidly in magnitude or intensity.—**escalation** *n*.

escalation clause *n* a clause in a contract that gives authorization to a contractor to increase the contracted price under certain specified conditions.

escalator *n* a motorized set of stairs arranged to ascend or descend continuously.

escallop *n* a scallop.

escalope *n* a thin cut of meat, esp veal.

escapade *n* a wild or mischievous adventure.

escape *vt* to free oneself from confinement, etc; to avoid, remain unnoticed; to be forgotten. * *vi* to achieve freedom; (*gas, liquid*) to leak. * *n* an act or instance of escaping; a means of escape; a leakage of liquid or gas; a temporary respite from reality.—**escapable** *adj.*—**escaper** *n*.

escape clause *n* a clause in a contract that allows for the release of one party from all or part of the obligations imposed by the contract under certain specified conditions.

escapee *n* a person who has escaped, esp a prisoner.

escape key (esc) *n* (*comput*) a nonprinting character or keyboard control key that causes an interruption in the normal program sequence.

escapement *n* a device in a watch or clock by which the motions of the pendulum or balance are regulated; (*mus*) the mechanism in a piano which releases the hammer, allowing a string to vibrate freely after it has been struck.

escape velocity *n* (*astron*) the velocity required of an object, e.g. a rocket or space probe, to escape from the gravitational pull of a larger body, e.g. a planet.

escapism *n* the tendency to avoid or retreat from reality into fantasy.—**escapist** *n, adj.*

escapologist *n* a performer who escapes from handcuffs, locked boxes, etc.—**escapology** *n*.

escargot *n* a snail prepared as food.

Esarhaddon *n* (*Egypt*) king of Assyria and conqueror of Egypt in 671 BC,

escarp *n* a steep bank in front of a rampart.

escarpment or **scarp** *n* (*geog*)a cliff or steep slope at the edge of a flat or gently sloping area, generated by a combination of original geology and the attitude of the rocks, and subsequent erosion.

ESCB *abbr* = European System of Central Banks.

eschar *n* a scab or slough formed after living tissue has been destroyed by a burn, cautery, or gangrene.

eschatology *n* (*pl* **eschatologies**) the study of death, judgment, heaven, and hell, and how humanity relates to them.

escheat *n* (*law*) (*formerly*) the lapsing of property to the state in the absence of an heir or by forfeiture; property that passes to the state in this way. * *vt* to confiscate property by escheat. * *vi* to revert to the state by escheat.

Escher *n* **Mauritz Corneille** (1898–1970) Dutch graphic artist famous for his popular optical-illusion drawings, such as *Endless Staircase*.

Escherichia *n* a group of rod-shaped bacteria, *E. coli*, normally found in the intestines and common in water, milk, etc.

eschew *vt* to avoid as habit, esp on moral grounds.—**eschewal** *n*.—**eschewer** *n*.

Esch-sur-Algette *n* a city in the Grand Duchy of Luxembourg.

Escoffier *n* **Georges Auguste** (1846–1935) French chef, who is regarded as one of the greatest chefs of all time. He invented peach melba in honor of Dame Nellie Melba.

escort *n* a person, group, ship, aircraft, etc accompanying a person or thing to give protection, guidance, or as a matter of courtesy; a person who accompanies another on a social occasion. * *vt* to attend as escort.

escritoire *n* a writing desk.

escrow *n* (*law*)a deed that has been signed and sealed but will be delivered on the condition that it will not become operative until the occurrence of some stated

escudo *n* the standard monetary unit of Portugal, Madeira, and Cape Verde, being made up of 100 centavos.

esculent *adj* edible.

escutcheon *n* a shield bearing a coat of arms.

Esd. *abbr* = Esdras.

ESD *abbr* = European Society of Dacryology.

Esdraelon *n* (*Bible*) Greek form of Jezreel.

e.s.e., ESE *abbr* = east-southeast.

ESE *abbr* = Engineering Associate of the Society of Engineers (Incorporated).

ESF *abbr* = European Script Fund; European Social Fund; European Surfing Federation.

ESFA *abbr* = English Schools Football Association.

Esfahan *n* a city in Islamic Republic of Iran.

ESG *abbr* = Euphorbia Study Group; European Seal Group.

ESGA *abbr* = English Schools Gymnastics Association.

ESH *abbr* = European Society of Hypnosis.

ESI *abbr* = Ecological Studies Institute; electricity supply industry.

Esias *n* (*Irish Celtic myth*) Esias was a wizard who lived in Gorias. He is said to have presented the invincible spear to Lugh and to have been one of the wizards who taught magical arts to the Tuatha De Danann.

esker *n* (*geol*) a steep-sided ridge made of sands and gravels, the remains of a stream that ran beneath or within a glacier.

Eskimo *see* **Inuit.**

ESL *abbr* = English as a second language.

ESMG *abbr* = Electric Steel Makers' Guild.

ESN *abbr* = educationally subnormal.

ESOP *abbr* = employee share ownership plan.

esophagitis *n* (*med*) inflammation of the esophagus. *See also* **heartburn.**

esophagoscope *n* an instrument for inspecting the esophagus. It has a light source and can be used to open the tube if narrowed, remove material for biopsy or clear an obstruction.

esophagus *n* (*anat*) the first part of the alimentary canal, lying between the pharynx and stomach.

ESOT *abbr* = European Society for Organ Transplantation.

esoteric *adj* intended for or understood by a select few; secret; private.—**esoterically** *adv.*—**esotericism** *n*.

esp. *abbr* = especially; espressivo.

ESP *abbr* = extrasensory perception; English for special purposes.

espadrille *n* a flat shoe usu having a fabric upper and rope soles.

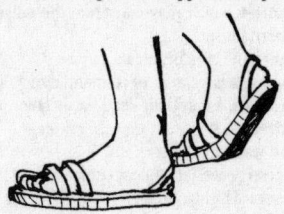

espalier *n* a plant (as a fruit tree) trained to grow flat against a support; the trellis on which such plants are trained.

esparto *n* (*pl* **espartos**) either of two Spanish and Algerian grasses used esp in paper-making.

especial *adj* notably special, unusual; particular to one person or thing.—**especially** *adv*.

Esperanto *n* an artificial international language.

espionage *n* spying or the use of spies to obtain information.

esplanade *n* a level open space for walking or driving, esp along a shore.

espouse *vt* to adopt or support a cause.—**espousal** *n*.—**espouser** *n*.

espressivo *n* (*mus*) (*Italian*) expressively.

espresso *n* (*pl* **espressos**) coffee brewed by forcing steam through finely ground darkly roasted coffee beans; an apparatus for making espresso.

ESPRIT *abbr* = European Strategic Programme of Research into Information Technology.

esprit de corps *n* a sense of loyalty and attachment to a group to which one belongs; wit; liveliness.

espy *vt* (**espying, espied**) to catch sight of.—**espial** *n*.—**espier** *n*.

Esq. *abbr* = esquire.

ESQA *abbr* = English Slate Quarries Association.

esquire *n* (usu *Brit*) a general courtesy title used instead of Mr in addressing letters.

esquisse *n* (*mus*) (*French*) literally a "sketch," a title sometimes given to short instrumental pieces.

ESRA *abbr* = European Safety and Reliability Association; European Synthetic Rubber Association.

ESRC *abbr* = Economic and Social Research Council.

ESRO *abbr* = European Space Research Organization.

ESRS *abbr* = European Sleep Research Society.

ess. *abbr* = essences.

ESS *abbr* = evolutionarily stable strategy.

essay *n* a short prose work usu dealing with a subject from a limited or personal point of view; an attempt. * *vt* (**essaying, essayed**) to try, to attempt.

essayist *n* an essay writer.

Essen *n* a city in Germany.

essence *n* that which makes a thing what it is; a substance distilled or extracted from another substance and having the special qualities of the original substance; a perfume.

essential *adj* of or containing the essence of something; indispensable, of the greatest importance. * *n* (*often pl*) indispensable elements or qualities.—**essentiality, essentialness** *n*.—**essentially** *adv*.

essential amino acid *n* (*biol*) any of eight amino acids that are required for normal health and growth, and must be supplied by diet as they are manufactured in the body in insufficient quantities if at all.

essential fatty acid *n* (*biol*) three polyunsaturated acids which cannot be produced in the body – arachidonic, linoleic, and linolenic.

essential hypertension *n* (*med*) high blood pressure with no identifiable cause. *See also* **hypertension**.

essential oil *n* any of various plant oils used in perfumery.

Esslinger *n* **Hartmut** (1945–) German designer of radios for Wega (now Sony), porcelain, and lighting.

Esso *abbr* = Standard Oil (from the initials SO).

est. *abbr* = established; estimated.

EST *abbr* = electric shock treatment.—also **ECT.**

estab. *abbr* = established.

establish *vt* to set up (e.g., a business) permanently; to settle (a person) in a place or position; to get generally accepted; to place beyond dispute, prove as a fact.—**establisher** *n*.

established *adj* of church or religion, officially recognized as the national church or religion of a country.

establishment *n* the act of establishing; a commercial organization or other large institution; the staff and resources of an organization; a household; (*with cap*) those people in institutions such as the government, civil service and commerce who use their power to preserve the social, economic, and political status quo.

establishmentarian *adj, n* of an established church; supporting the established church system. * *n* a person who advocates official recognition of a church or religion.—**establishmentarianism** *n*.

Etain *or* **Edain** *n* (*Irish Celtic myth*) the daughter of Ailill. Midhir fell in love with her and his first wife, Fuamnach turned her into various shapes in order to destroy the marriage.

estaminet *n* a café.

estampie *n* (*mus*) (*French*) a form of dance accompanied by song, dating from the 13th and 14th centuries, which may constitute the oldest type of instrumental composition in Western music.

estancia *n* a cattle ranch in Latin America.

estate *n* landed property; a large area of residential or industrial development; a person's total possessions, esp at their death; a social or political class.

estate agent *see* **realtor**.

estate car *see* **station wagon**.

ESTEC *abbr* = European Space Technology Centre.

esteem *vt* to value or regard highly; to consider or think. * *n* high regard, a favorable opinion.

ester *n* (*chem*) an organic hydrocarbon compound formed from organic acids.

Estes *n* **Richard** (1936–) American painter. His work depicts American streets in a "superrealist" style.

Esther *n* (*Bible*) Jewish heroine purported to have saved her people from destruction

Esther *n* **the Book of** (*Bible*) OT book of historical fiction, which describes anti-Semitism in ancient Persia.

esthete, esthetics *see* **aesthete, aesthetics**.

estheticism *see* **aestheticism**.

estimable *adj* worthy of esteem; calculable.

estimate *vt* to judge the value, amount, significance of; to calculate approximately. * *n* an approximate calculation; a judgment or opinion; a preliminary calculation of the cost of a particular job.—**estimative** *adj*.

estimation *n* estimating; an opinion, judgment; esteem.

estimator *n* someone or something that estimates.

estinto *n* (*mus*) (*Latin*) literally "extinct," i.e. as soft as possible.

estival *adj* of or occurring in summer.

estivation *n* (*bot*) the arrangement of petals in a flower bud; (zool) the spending of the dry season in a dormant state.

ESTOC *abbr* = European Smokeless Tobacco Council.

Estonia *n* a low-lying republic in northeastern Europe.

estop *vt* (**estopping, estopped**) (*law*) to prohibit by estoppel.

estoppel *n* (*law*) a legal impediment arising as a result of one's previous action.

ESTRA *abbr* = English Speaking Tape Respondents Association.

estradiol *n* (*biol*) the major female sex hormone. It is produced by the ovary and is responsible for development of the breasts, sexual characteristics, and premenstrual uterine changes.

estrange *vt* to alienate the affections or confidence of.—**estranged** *adj*.—**estrangement** *n*.

estrogen *n* (*biol*) one of a group of steroid hormones secreted mainly by the ovaries and, to a lesser extent, by the adrenal cortex and placenta. The testicles also produce small amounts.

estrus, estrum *n* violent desire, frenzy; the period of ovulation of mammals, when they are said to be on heat.

estuarine *adj* pertaining to, or formed in, an estuary.

estuary *n* a partially enclosed stretch of water that is subjected to marine tides and fresh water draining from land, is usually created as a drowned valley, as a result of a post-glacial rise in sea level.

esu *abbr* = electrostatic unit.

esurient *adj* voracious, greedy.—**esurience** *n*.

ESV *abbr* = earth satellite vehicle; emergency shut-down valve.

ESVA *abbr* = English Schools Volleyball Association.

ET *abbr* = English Translation; extra-terrestrial; embryo transfer.

eta[1] *n* the seventh letter of the Greek alphabet.

eta[2]**, ETA** *abbr* = estimated time of arrival.

étagère *n* an ornamental stand.

et al. *abbr* (*Latin*) = *et alii*, "and others," used in bibliography.

étang *n* a small brackish lake among coastal sand dunes or beach ridges.

ETB *abbr* = English Tourist Board.

etc *abbr* (*Latin*) = *et cetera, etcetera*, "and the rest."

etceteras *npl* the usual extra things or persons.

etch *vti* to make lines on (metal, glass) usu by the action of acid; to produce (as a design) by etching; to delineate clearly.—**etcher** *n*.

Etchells *n* **Frederick** (1886–1973) British painter and architect.

etching *n* a technique of making an engraving in a metal plate, using acid to bite out the image rather than tools; a print produced in this way.

ETD *abbr* = estimated time of departure.

Eteocles *n* (*Greek myth*) son of Oedipus and brother of Polynices and Antigone. Eteocles usurped the throne to the exclusion of his brother, an act which led to an expedition by Polynices and six others against Thebes, a war known as the Seven against Thebes. The two brothers killed each other.

eternal *adj* continuing forever without beginning or end, everlasting; unchangeable; (*inf*) seemingly endless.—**eternality, eternalness** *n*.—**eternally** *adv*.

eternalize *vt* to make eternal.—**eternalization** *n*.

eternity *n* (*pl* **eternities**) infinite time; the timelessness thought to constitute life after death; (*inf*) a very long time.

etesian *adj* (*winds*) blowing from the northwest in the Mediterranean for about forty days each summer.

ETF *abbr* = electronic transfer of funds.

Eth. *abbr* = Ethiopia; Ethiopic.

Ethal Anubal *n* (*Irish Celtic myth*) a prince of Connacht and the father of Caer.

ethane *n* (*chem*) a colorless gaseous hydrocarbon found in natural gas and used esp as fuel.

ethanol *n* (*chem*) an alcohol that has a functional hydroxyl group in place of one hydrogen atom in the structure of ethane.

Ethelbald *n* **1.** (834–860) king of Wessex, Britain (858–860). He ascended the throne on the death of his father Ethelwulf. He married his stepmother Judith. **2.** (*d.* 757) king of Mercia (716–757).

Ethelbert *n* 1. (836–865) king of Wessex, Britain (857–865). The third son of Ethelwulf. 2. (St Ethelbert) (*d.* 792) king of East Anglia, Britain. Reigned in 792. He was executed by his father-in-law, King Offa of Mercia, and is the patron saint of Hereford Cathedral.

Ethelbert I *n* (*d.* 616) king of Kent, Britain (560–616). Ruler of all England south of the Humber, he married Bertha, daughter of the Frankish King Charibert, *c.* 589.

Ethelbert II *n* (*d.* 762) king of Kent, Britain (725–762). The son of Wihtred and Cynegyth, he reigned jointly to 748 with his brother, Eadbert, and then with his half-brothers, Alric and Eardwulf.

Etheldreda *n* **Saint [Audrey]** (*d.* 679) East Anglian princess and saint; founded a monastery for men and women. Her feast day is June 23.

Ethelfrith *n* (*d.* 617) king of Northumbria, Britain (604–617). The third of Ida's six sons.

Ethelheard *n* (*d.* 740) king of Wessex, Britain (726–*c*.740). Succeeded Ine as king in 726.

Ethelhere *n* (*d.* 654) king of East Anglia, Britain (reigned in 654). A younger brother of Anna, he reigned for only a few months before being killed in the Battle of Winwaed.

Ethelred (II) *n* **the Unready** (968–1016) king of England (978–1016). The son of Edgar and Emma of Norway, he succeeded his brother, Edward the Martyr, and, for his lack of vigour and capacity, earned the name of 'the Unready'.

Ethelred I *n* (*d.* 796) king of Northumbria, Britain (774–796). The son of Ethelwold Moll.

Ethelred I *n* (St Elthelred) (840–871) king of Wessex, Britain (865–871). The son of Ethelwulf, he succeeded his brother, Ethelbert. Ethelred's devout Christianity was recognised in his popular title of St Ethelred.

Ethelred II *n* king of Northumbria, Britain (841–850). The son of Eanred.

Ethelred *n* king of Mercia, Britain (675–704). A brother of Wulfhere, he abdicated to become a monk.

Ethelric *n* king of Bernicia, Britain (568–572). A son of the Saxon king Ida, Ethelric ruled Bernicia, which, with Deira, ruled by his brother Aelle, later formed the kingdom of Northumbria. Bernicia supplied most of the kings in the merged kingdom.

Ethelstan *or* **Athelstan** *n* (895–939) king of England (924–939). The eldest son of Edward the Elder and Egwina. The first Saxon king with effective control of all England (with the exception of Cumbria).

Ethelwalh *n* king of Sussex, Britain. Reigned before 685. He received the Isle of Wight from Wulferhere of Mercia in 661 and in turn gave Wilfred the bishopric of Selsey.

Ethelweard *n* king of Mercia, Britain (*c*.837–850).

Ethelwold *n* (Moll) king of Northumbria, Britain (759–765).

Ethelwold *n* king of Mercia, Britain (654–663). The youngest brother of Anna.

Ethelwulf *n* (800–858) king of Wessex, Britain (839–858). He succeeded his father, Egbert. Alfred the Great was the youngest of his five children.

ethene *see* **ethylene**.

ether *n* (*chem*) a light flammable liquid used as an anesthetic or solvent; the upper regions of space, the invisible elastic substance formerly believed to be distributed evenly through all space.—**etheric** *adj*.

ethereal *adj* delicate; spiritual; celestial.—**ethereality, etherealness** *n*.—**ethereally** *adv*.

etherealize *vt* to make ethereal; to regard as ethereal.—**etherealization** *n*.

Etherege, Etheredge *n* **Sir George** (*c*.1635–92) English dramatist, whose play *The Comical Revenge* established the main pattern of Restoration comedy.

etherize *vt* (*patient*) to anesthetize, using ether.—**etherization** *n*.

Ethernet *n* (*trademark*) (*comput*) a local area network hardware standard capable of linking up to 1,024 computers in a network. Ethernet can transfer up to 10 megabits per second.

EtherTalk *n* (*trademark*) (*comput*) an implementation of the Ethernet local area network developed by Apple (*trademark*) and the 3com (*trademark*) corporation, designed to work with the Appleshare network system.

ethic *n* a moral principle or set of principles. * *adj* ethical.

ethical *adj* of or pertaining to ethics; conforming to the principles of proper conduct, as established by society, a profession, etc; (*med*) legally available only on prescription.—**ethically** *adv*.—**ethicalness, ethicality** *n*.

ethical investment *n* an investment made in a company that is not engaged in business activity that the investor considers as unethical or is engaged in a business activity that the investor considers to be of a particularly ethical nature, such as something that will be of help in improving or preserving the environment. *See also* **conscience investment**.

ethics *n* (*sing*) the philosophical analysis of human morality and conduct; system of conduct or behavior, moral principles.—**ethicist** *n*.

Ethiopia *n* a landlocked, east African republic formerly known as Abyssinia.

Ethiopian *adj* of or pertaining to Ethiopia, its languages or people.—*also n*.

Ethiopian Birr *n* currency of Ethiopia.

Ethlinn *or* **Eithne** *or* **Ethne** *n* (*Irish Celtic myth*) the daughter of Balor. Because of a prophecy that he would be killed by his grandson, Balor had her confined in a tower, probably the Glass Tower.

ethmoid *adj* (anat) denoting a light, spongy bone that forms the roof of the nose (—*also* **ethmoidal**). * *n* the ethmoid bone.

ethnic, ethnical *adj* of races or large groups of people classed according to common traits and customs.—**ethnically** *adv*.

ethnic cleansing *n* the planned expulsion, extermination or removal of people from a religious or ethnic minority within an area, region, or country.

ethnic group *n* a group of people with their own distinctive culture and customs, living within a larger, different society and subject to the laws of that larger society.

ethno- *prefix* indicating race; people; culture.

ethnocentrism *n* belief in the superiority of the national, racial, social, or cultural group to which one belongs.—**ethnocentric** *adj*.— **ethnocentrically** *adv*.— **ethnocentricity** *n*.

ethnog. *abbr* = ethnographical; ethnography.

ethnography *n* the area of anthropology dealing with the scientific description of human races.—**ethnographer** *n*. **ethnographic, ethnographical** *adj*.

ethnol. *abbr* = ethnological; ethnology.

ethnology *n* the scientific study of the origins and culture, etc, of different races and peoples.—**ethnologic, ethnological** *adj*.—**ethnologist** *n*.

ethology *n* the scientific study of animal behavior.—**ethologic, ethological** *adj*.—**ethologist** *n*.

ethos *n* the distinguishing character, sentiment, moral nature, or guiding beliefs of a person, group, or institution.

ethyl *n* the radical from which common alcohol and ether are derived.

ethylene glycol *n* (*chem*) a colorless liquid used in antifreeze and as coolants for engines.

ethylene *n* a colorless sweet-smelling gaseous hydrocarbon obtained from petroleum and used to manufacture chemicals including polythene. *See also* **ethene**.

ethyne *n* (*chem*) a highly flammable gas that, when burned with oxygen, will produce the high-temperature flame characteristic of the oxyacetylene torch.

etiolate *vti* (*green plants*) to bleach by depriving of light; to make or become pale and sickly.—**etiolation** *n*.

etiology *n* the scientific study of the causes of disease.

etiquette *n* the form of conduct or behavior prescribed by custom or authority to be observed in social, official or professional life.

Etna *n* a volcanic mountain in Sicily. In mythology, a giant was said to have been buried under the mountain by Zeus.—*also* **Aetna**.

ETRA *abbr* = European Textile Rental Association.

Etruria *n* ancient name of region of Italy corresponding partly with modern Tuscany.—**Etruscan, Etrurian** *adj*.

Etruscans *n* a group of people who developed a highly advanced civilization and culture of great influence in Tuscany, Italy.

ETSA *abbr* = English Table Soccer Association.

et seq. *abbr* (*Latin*) = *et sequens*, "and the following."

ETSMA *abbr* = European Tyre Stud Manufacturers Association.

ETTA *abbr* = English Table Tennis Association.

ETTU *abbr* = European Table Tennis Union.

Etty *n* **William** (1787–1849) American-born English painter; notable mainly for his nude female paintings, which, despite having attracted criticism for weakness in draftsmanship, display a fine sense of sensual form, texture, and color.

ETU *abbr* = Electrical Trades Union.

ETUC *abbr* = European Trade Union Confederation.

étude *n* (*mus*) (*French*) a "study" or piece of music evolved from a single phrase or idea. Studies are also written purely as exercises to improve technique or fingering.

étui *n* (*pl* **étuis**) a pocket case for sewing implements and other small articles.

etym., etymol. *abbr* = etymological; etymology.

etymology *n* (*pl* **etymologies**) the study of the source and meaning of words; an account of the source and history of a word.—**etymological, etymologic** *adj*.—**etymologist** *n*.

etymon *n* (*pl* **etymons, etyma**) the root of a word, or its original meaning.

Eu *symbol* (*chem*) europium (element).

EU *abbr* = European Union; Evangelical Union.

ÉUA *abbr* (*French*) = États-Unis Amérique (USA).

Euboea *n* a Greek island, the second largest island of the Aegean Sea.— **Euboean** *adj*.

eucalyptol *n* a liquid contained in eucalyptus oil.

eucalyptus, eucalypt *n* (*pl* **eucalyptuses, eucalypti** *or* **eucalypts**) any of a genus of mostly Australian evergreen trees cultivated for their resin, oil, and wood; a type of oil obtained from its leaves.

Eucharist *n* the Christian sacrament of communion in which bread and wine are consecrated; the consecrated elements in communion.—**Eucharistic, Eucharistical** *adj*. *See* **Lord's Supper**.

euchre *n* a card game for two, three or four players.

Euclidean *adj* pertaining to or accordant with the geometrical principles of Euclid, the Greek mathematician (*fl* 3rd century BC).

eudemonism, eudaemonism *n* the ethical doctrine that regards happiness as the chief end in moral conduct.

eudiometer *n* an instrument for measuring the amount of oxygen in the air.

eugenics *n* the study of how the inherited characteristics of the human population can be improved by genetics or selective/controlled breeding.

euhemerism *n* the theory that the classical deities are deified heroes and that the myths connected with them are based on real history.—**euhemerist** *n*.— **euhemeristic** *adj*.—**euhemeristically** *adv*.

eukaryote *n* (*biol*) any member of a class of living organisms (except viruses) that has in each of its cells a nucleus within a membrane.

eulogize *vt* to extol in speech or writing.—**eulogist, eulogizer** *n*.— **eulogistic, eulogistical** *adj*.—**eulogistically** *adv*.

eulogy *n* (*pl* **eulogies**) a speech or piece of writing in praise or celebration of someone or something.

Eumenides *see* **Furies**.

Eunice *n* (*Bible*) a Jewish-Christian and the mother of Timothy whom Paul met.

eunuch *n* a castrated man.

euonymus *n* a genus of small trees, containing the spindle tree.

euphemism *n* a mild or inoffensive word substituted for a more unpleasant or offensive term; the use of such inoffensive words.—**euphemistic** *adj*.— **euphemistically** *adv*.

euphonic, euphonical *adj* sounding pleasant to the ear.—**euphonically** *adv*.

euphonium *n* (*mus*) a large brass instrument, a tenor tuba, which is mainly used in brass and military bands.

euphony *n* (*pl* **euphonies**) a pleasing sound, esp words.—**euphonious** *adj*.

Euphorbia *n* a member of the large genus of plants of the spurge family.

euphoria *n* a feeling of elation.—**euphoric** *adj*.—**euphorically** *adv*.

euphotic zone *n* the upper layers of the sea or lakes where light can penetrate and where life is possible since photosynthesis can take place.

Euphrates *n* largest river of western Asia, along whose banks grew some of the greatest civilizations of the ancient world such as Babylon, Carchemish, Ur, and Mari; (*Bible*) known in the OT as "the river".

Euphrosyne *n* (*Greek myth*) one of the Graces.

euphuism *n* an affected style of prose using elaborate antithesis, alliteration, and conceits; the pedantic or affected use of words or language.—**euphuist** *n*.— **euphuistic, euphuistical** *adj*.

euploid *n* a term used to describe a chromosome number that is an exact multiple of the normal (haploid) number.

Eur. *abbr* = Europe; European.

EURABIA *abbr* = European Coordinating Committee of Friendship Societies with the Arab World.

Eurasian *adj* of Europe and Asia (Eurasia) taken as one continent; of mixed European and Asian descent.—*also n*.

EURATOM *abbr* = European Atomic Energy Community.

eureka *interj* used to express triumph on a discovery.

Eureka Company *n* the American manufacturer, founded in Detroit in 1909, now located in Bloomington, Illinois.

eurhythmics *n* (*mus*) a system of teaching musical rhythm by graceful physical movements. It was invented in 1905 by Émile Jaques-Dalcroze, whose training institute was founded in Dresden in 1910 .

EURING *abbr* = European Union for Bird Ringing.

Euripides *n* (480–406 BC) Greek dramatist, 19 of whose plays are extant, the most notable being *Alcestis, Medea, Orestes*, and *The Trojan Women*.

Euro *n* the currency unit used in the European Monetary Union.

Euro- *prefix* Europe; European.

EuroACE *abbr* = European Association for the Conservation of Energy.

Eurocrat *n* a member of the administration of the European Community.

eurocurrency *n* a currency held in a European country other than its country of origin. For example, dollars that are deposited in a European bank are known as eurodollars.

Europa *n* (*Greek myth*) the daughter of a king, who was abducted by Zeus in the form of a bull to the island of Crete, where she bore him three sons; in ancient geography the known world around the Mediterranean, named after the mythical Europa.

Europe *n* a continent extending from Asia in the east to the Atlantic Ocean in the west.

European *adj* relating to or native to Europe. * *n* a native or inhabitant of Europe; a person of European descent.

European Commission *n* the body that administers the work of the European Union.

European Community *n* an association of 12 European countries, formerly the European Economic Community, with common social, monetary, and political objectives. * *abbr* **EC**.

European Currency Unit *n* a currency medium and unit of account that was established in 1979 to act as the accounting unit and reserve asset of the European Monetary System. * *abbr* **ECU**. *See* European Monetary Union.

European Economic Community *n* the former European Common Market set up by six western European countries in 1957 which broadened into the European Community and then the European Union in 1993. * *abbr* **EEC**.

European Free Trade Association *n* a trade association established in 1960 between Austria, Denmark, Norway, Portugal, Sweden, Switzerland, and the UK. Finland, Iceland, and Liechtenstein joined later. In 1973, the UK and Denmark left to join the European Community and Portugal joined them in 1986.

European Monetary System *n* a system established in 1979 to coordinate and stabilize the exchange rates of the member countries of the European Community. * *abbr* **EMS**.

European Monetary Union *n* a system by which the members of the European Union will have a single European currency, the Euro, and a European central bank. * *abbr* **EMU**.

European Union *n* an association of European countries formed in 1993 to extend the European Community with the aim of providing close economic, social, and political links among its 15 members.

europium *n* a soft metallic element of the rare earth group.

EURORAD *abbr* = European Association of Manufacturers of Radiators.

EUROSAG *abbr* = European Salaried Architects Group.

Eurosswyd *n* (*Welsh Celtic myth*) Eurosswyd was the father of Efnisien and Nisien by Penardun.

Eurotas *n* (*Greek myth*) a hero who created the river to carry the waters in the plain of Lacedaemon to the sea; the river was named after him.

Eurydice *n* (*Greek myth*) the wife of Orpheus.

Eurystheus *n* (*Greek myth*) a king of Mycenae and persecutor of Heracles, for whom he set a series of difficult tasks.

Eurytion *n* (*Greek myth*) king of Phthia, who was accidentally killed by his son-in-law Peleus.

Eusden *n* **Laurence** (1688–1730) English poet who succeeded as poet laureate in England in 1718, more for political reasons than for poetic ones.

Eustachian tube *n* one of two tubes that connect the middle ear to the pharynx named after the 16th-century Italian anatomist Eustachio.

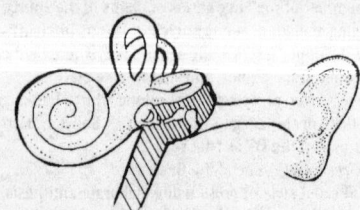

eustasy *n* a worldwide change of sea level that may be the result of climatic change causing either the growth or melting of ice sheets; a change in the shape of ocean basins.

Euterpe *n* (*Greek myth*) one of the Muses, who presided over lyric poetry and invented the flute.

euthanasia *n* the intentional hastening of the death of someone who is suffering from a disease that is painful, incurable, and inevitably fatal.

eutrophication *n* the enrichment of a lake or river by pollution nutrients that use up all the oxygen from the water.

Eutychus *n* (*Bible*) the young man from Troas who was restored to life by Paul.

EUVEPRO *abbr* = European Vegetable Protein Federation.

Euxine Sea *n* the ancient name for the Black Sea.

EV *abbr* = electronvolt (electronic volt, electron-volt); English Version (of Bible).

EVA *abbr* = extravehicular activity (astronautics).

evacuate *vti* to move (people, etc) from an area of danger to one of safety; to leave or make empty; to discharge wastes from the body.—**evacuation** *n*.—**evacuative** *adj*.—**evacuator** *n*.

evacuee *n* an evacuated person.

evade *vt* to manage to avoid, esp by dexterity or slyness.—**evadable** *adj*.—**evader** *n*.

evaluate *vt* to determine the value of; to assess.—**evaluation** *n*.—**evaluator** *n*.

Evander *n* (*Greek myth*) a hero who founded a town on the banks of the Tiber in Italy.

evanescent *adj* fading away, vanishing; ephemeral.—**evanescence** *n*.

evang. *abbr* = evangelical; evangelist.

evangel *n* the Christian gospel.

evangelical *adj* of or agreeing with Christian teachings, esp as presented in the four Gospels; pertaining to various Christian sects that believe in salvation through personal conversion and faith in Christ.—**evangelicalism** *n*.

evangelism *n* preaching the Christian gospel; missionary zeal.

evangelist *n* a person who preaches the gospel; one of the writers of the four Gospels.—**evangelistic** *adj*.—**evangelistically** *adv*.

evangelize *vt* to preach or spread the gospel; to seek converts to a particular cause.—**evangelization** *n*.—**evangelizer** *n*.

Evans *n* 1. **Dame Edith [Mary Booth]** (1888–1976) English actress. 2. **Sir Arthur [John]** (1851–1941) English archaeologist. His excavations of the palace of Knossos in Crete led to the rediscovery of Minoan civilization. 3. **Sir Geraint** (1922–92) Welsh baritone and opera producer particularly famous for his roles in Mozart operas.

Evanson *n* **James** (1946–) American lighting designer who specialized in large lighting constructions that emulated city skylines.

evaporate *vti* to change into a vapor; to remove water from; to give off moisture; to vanish; to disappear.—**evaporable** *adj*.—**evaporative** *adj*.—**evaporator** *n*.

evaporated milk *n* tinned unsweetened milk thickened by evaporation.

evaporation *n* (*chem*) the process by which a substance changes from a liquid to a vapor (gas).

evaporite *n* (*geol*) sedimentary rocks formed by precipitation from solution during evaporation of lagoons, salt pans, and salt lakes

evasion *n* the act of evading; a means of evading, esp an equivocal reply or excuse.—**evasive** *adj*.—**evasively** *adv*.—**evasiveness** *n*.

eve *n* the evening or the whole day, before a festival; the period immediately before an event; (*formerly*) evening.

Eve *n* (*Bible*) the first woman, wife of Adam and "mother of all living," beguiled by the serpent, she persuaded Adam to eat the forbidden fruit and God drove them from the garden of Eden; mother of Cain and Able. *See also* **Adam**.

evection *n* (*astron*) a periodical irregularity of the moon's motion.

Evelyn *n* **John** (1620–76) English author and diarist whose diary, first published in full in 1955, is full of valuable details of domestic and social life in 17th-century England.

even *adj* level, flat; smooth; regular, equal; balanced; exact; divisible by two. * *vti* to make or become even; (*with* up) to balance (debts, etc). * *adv* exactly; precisely; fully; quite; at the very time; used as an intensive to emphasize the identity of something (*be looked content, even happy*), to indicate something unexpected (*she refused even to look at him*), or to stress the comparative degree (*she did even better*).—**evenly** *adv*.—**evenness** *n*.

even-handed *adj* impartial, fair.—**even-handedness** *n*.

evening *n* the latter part of the day and early part of the night.

evening primrose *n* a plant with yellow flowers that open in the evening.

evening star *n* Venus (or Mercury), seen in the western sky around sunset.

evens *npl* (*bet*) winning the same as the stake if successful; offered at such odds, as a horse. *See also* **even money**.

evensong *n* vespers; evening prayers. *See also* **Nunc Dimittis**.

event *n* something that happens; a social occasion; contingency; a contest in a sports Programme.

event-driven program *n* (*comput*) a program that is constructed to react to the computer user who initiates events by clicking a mouse rather than a command-driven program, which requires specific commands to be typed into the computer to obtain results.

even-tempered *adj* calm

eventful *adj* full of incidents; momentous

event horizon *n* (*astron*) the boundary of a black hole, which is thought to be spherical.

eventide *n* (*formerly*) evening.

eventual *adj* happening at some future unspecified time; ultimate.—**eventually** *adv*.

eventuality *n* (*pl* eventualities) a possible occurrence.

eventuate *vi* to result.—**eventuation** *n*.

ever *adv* always, at all times; at any time; in any case.

everglade *n* marshy ground with tall, coarse grass and occasional trees usually flooded during the summer rainy season; e.g. Florida Everglades.

Evergood *n* **Philip** (1901–75) American painter. His preferred subject matter was social-realist issues, e.g. *Lily and the Sparrows*.

evergreen *adj* (*plants, trees*) having foliage that remains green all year.—*also n*.

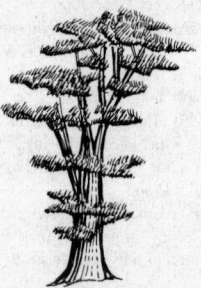

everlasting *adj* enduring forever; (*plants*) having flowers that may be dried without loss of form or color.—**everlastingly** *adv*.

evermore *adv* forever.

evert *vt* to turn inside out.—**eversible** *adj*.—**eversion** *n*.

Evert *n* **Chris[tine]** **Marie** (1952–) American tennis player; winner of 18 singles grand slam titles.

every *adj* being one of the total.

everybody, everyone *pron* every person.

everyday *adj* happening daily; commonplace; worn or used on ordinary days.

everything *pron* all things, all; something of the utmost importance.

everywhere *adv* in every place.

evg. *abbr* = evening.

evict *vt* to expel from land or from a building by legal process; to expel.—**eviction** *n*.—**evictor** *n*.

evidence *n* an outward sign; proof, testimony, esp matter submitted in court to determine the truth of alleged facts. * *vt* to demonstrate clearly; to give proof or evidence for.

evident *adj* easy to see or understand.—**evidently** *adv*.

evidential *adj* relating to, providing, or based on evidence.—**evidentially** *adv*.

evil *adj* wicked; causing or threatening distress or harm. * *n* a sin; a source of harm or distress.—**evilly** *adv*.—**evilness** *n*.

evildoer *n* a wicked person.—**evildoing** *n*.

evil eye *n* a stare superstitiously believed to inflict harm; the power to cause harm in this manner.

evince *vt* to indicate that one has (e.g., a quality); to demonstrate.—**evincible** *adj*.—**evincive** *adj*.

eviscerate *vt* to take out the intestines of, disembowel.—**evisceration** *n*.—**eviscerator** *n*.

evocative *adj* serving to evoke.—**evocatively** *n*.

evoke *vt* to call forth or up.—**evocable** *adj*.—**evocation** *n*.—**evoker** *n*.

evolution *n* a process of change in a particular direction; the process by which something attains its distinctive characteristics; a theory that existing types of plants and animals have developed from earlier forms.—**evolutionary, evolutional** *adj*.

evolutionist *adj* pertaining to evolution. * *n* someone who believes in the theory of evolution.

evolve *vi* to develop by or as if by evolution.—**evolvable** *adj*.—**evolvement** *n*.

EW *abbr* = early warning; electronic warfare.

ewe *n* a female sheep.

ewer *n* a large pitcher or jug with a wide spout.

EWF *abbr* = European Wax Federation; European Weightlifting Federation.

EWIA *abbr* = External Wall Insulation Association.

Ewing's sarcoma *n* a malignant bone cancer that develops from the marrow in the pelvis or long bones, named after the American pathologist James Ewing.

ex[1] *n* (*inf*) a former husband, wife, etc.

ex[2] *prep* out of, from.

ex. *abbr* = examined; example; exception; exchange; excursion; executed; executive.

Ex. *abbr* = Exodus.

ex- *prefix* out, forth; quite, entirely; formerly.

exacerbate *vt* to make more violent, bitter, or severe.—**exacerbatingly** *adv*.—**exacerbation** *n*.

exact *adj* without error, absolutely accurate; detailed. * *vt* to compel by force, to extort; to require.—**exactable** *adj*.—**exactness** *n*.—**exactor, exacter** *n*.

exacting *adj* greatly demanding; requiring close attention and precision.—**exactingness** *n*.

exaction *n* the extortion of money, etc; an outrageous demand; something exacted.

exactitude *n* (the state of) being exact.

exactly *adv* in an exact manner; precisely. * *interj* quite so!

exaggerate *vt* to enlarge (a statement, etc) beyond what is really so or believable.—**exaggeration** *n*.—**exaggerative** *adj*.—**exaggerator** *n*.

exalt *vt* to raise up, esp in rank, power, or dignity.—**exalted** *adj*.—**exalter** *n*.

exaltation *n* elevation; rapture; a flock of larks.

exam. *abbr* = examination; examining.

examination *n* an examining, close scrutiny; a set of written or oral questions designed as a test of knowledge; the formal questioning of a witness on oath.—**examinational** *adj*.

examine *vt* to look at closely and carefully, to investigate; to test, esp by questioning.—**examinable** *adj*.—**examiner** *n*.

examinee *n* a person who is being tested in an examination.

example *n* a representative sample; a model to be followed or avoided; a problem to be solved in order to show the application of some rule; a warning to others.

exanimate *adj* dead, defunct, lifeless.—**exanimation** *n*.

ex. aq. *abbr* (*Latin*) = ex aqua, "from water."

exarch *n* a bishop of the Eastern Orthodox Church; the governor of a province under the Byzantine Empire.

exarchate, exarchy *n* the area of jurisdiction of an exarch.

exasperate *vt* to annoy intensely.—**exasperatedly** *adv*.—**exasperating** *adj*.—**exasperation** *n*.

Ex.B.L. *abbr* = exchange bill of lading.

exc. *abbr* = excellency; excellent; except; excepted; exception; exchange.

Excalibur *n* in legend, King Arthur's sword.

ex cathedra *adj* with authority.

excavate *vt* to form a hole or tunnel by digging; to unearth; to expose to view (historical remains, etc) by digging away a covering.—**excavation** *n*.—**excavator** *n*.

exceed *vt* to be greater than or superior to; to go beyond the limit of.—**exceedable** *adj*.—**exceeder** *n*.

exceedingly *adv* very, extremely.

excel *vb* (**excelling, excelled**) *vt* to outdo, to be superior to. * *vi* (*with* **in, at**) to do better than others.

excellence *n* that in which one excels; superior merit or quality; (*with cap*) a title of honor given to certain high officials (—*also* **Excellency**).

excellent *adj* very good, outstanding.—**excellently** *adv*.

excelsior *interj* higher. * *n* soft wood shavings for stuffing.

except *vt* to exclude, to take or leave out. * *prep* not including; other than.—**exceptable** *adj*.

excepting *prep* except, not including.

exception *n* the act of excepting; something excepted; an objection.

exceptionable *adj* open to objection.—**exceptionably** *adv*.

exceptional *adj* unusual, forming an exception; superior.—**exceptionally** *adv*.

exceptional items *see* extraordinary items.

excerpt *n* an extract from a book, film, etc. * *vt* to select or quote (a passage from a book).—**exerptible** *adj*.—**excerption** *n*.

excess *n* the exceeding of proper established limits; the amount by which one thing or quantity exceeds another; (*pl*) overindulgence in eating or drinking; unacceptable conduct.

excess capacity *n same as* overcapacity.

excessive *adj* greater than what is acceptable, too much.—**excessively** *adv*.—**excessiveness** *n*.

exch. *abbr* = exchange; exchequer.

exchange *vt* to give and take (one thing in return for another); to give to and receive from another person. * *n* the exchanging of one thing for another; the thing exchanged; the conversion of money in one currency into a sum of equivalent value in another currency; the system of settling commercial debts between foreign governments, e.g. by bills of exchange; a place where things and services are exchanged, esp a marketplace for securities; a center or device in which telephone lines are interconnected.—**exchangeable** *adj*.—**exchangeability** *n*.—**exchanger** *n*.

exchange rate *n* the rate at which one foreign currency may be exchanged for another.

exchange rate mechanism *n* a system under which participating countries of the European Union undertake to commit themselves to maintain the values of their currencies within agreed limits. * *abbr* **ERM**.

exchequer *n* (*with cap*) the British governmental department in charge of finances; (*inf*) personal finances.

excise[1] *n* a tax on the manufacture, sale, or use of certain articles within a country.—**excisable** *adj*.

excise[2] *vt* to remove by cutting out.—**excision** *n*.

excise duty *n* an indirect tax that is imposed by the government on certain products, such as alcoholic drinks and tobacco products.

exciseman *n* (*pl* **excisemen**) (*formerly*) an officer employed to collect and enforce excise.

excision *n* (*med*) the cutting out or removal of, for example, a gland or tumor from the body.

excitable *adj* easily excited.—**excitability, excitableness** *n*.

excitant *n* a stimulant. * *adj* stimulating.

excitation *n* the act of exciting; the state of excitement.—**excitative, excitatory** *adj*.

excite *vt* to arouse the feelings of, esp to generate feelings of pleasurable anticipation; to cause to experience strong emotion; to stir up, agitate; to rouse to activity; to stimulate a physiological response, e.g. in a bodily organ.

excited *adj* experiencing or expressing excitement.—**excitedly** *adv*.—**excitedness** *n*.

excitement *n* a feeling of strong, esp pleasurable, emotion; something that excites.

exciting *adj* causing excitement; stimulating.—**excitingly** *adv*.

excl., exclam. *abbr* = exclamation.

exclaim *vti* to shout out or utter suddenly and with strong emotion.—**exclaimer** *n*.

exclamation *n* a sudden crying out; a word or utterance exclaimed.—**exclamational** *adj*.

exclamation point, exclamation mark *n* the punctuation mark (!) placed after an exclamation.

exclamatory *adj* of or expressing exclamation.—**exclamatorily** *adv*.

exclave *n* a small part of a country lying within the territory of another country.

exclude *vt* to shut out, to keep out; to reject or omit; to eject.—**excluder** *n*.—**exclusion** *n*.

exclusive *adj* excluding all else; reserved for particular persons; snobbishly aloof; fashionable, high-class, expensive; unobtainable or unpublished elsewhere; sole, undivided.—**exclusively** *adv*.—**exclusiveness** *n*.—**exclusivity** *n*.

exclusive distribution *n* a distribution system in which a distributor carries the goods of only one manufacturer, or in which only one retailer or wholesaler is allowed to sell a manufacturer's goods in a particular area.

EXCO *abbr* = Express Coach Operators' Association (Eire).

excogitate *vt* to devise, to invent; to discover by thinking.—**excogitation** *n*.—**excogitative** *adj*.

Ex. Com. *abbr* = Executive Committee.

excommunicate *vt* to bar from association with a church; to exclude from fellowship.—**excommunication** *n*.—**excommunicative** *adj*.—**excommunicator** *n*.

excoriate *vt* to strip of the skin; to flay.

excoriation *n* (*med*) injury of the surface of the skin (or other part of the body) caused by the abrasion or scratching of the area.

ex. cp., x/cp. *abbr* = ex coupon.

excrement *n* waste matter discharged from the bowels.—**excremental, excrementitious** *adj*.

excrescence *n* an outgrowth, esp abnormal, from a plant or animal; a disfigurement.

excrescent *adj* pertaining to excrescence; superfluous.

excreta *npl* waste matter discharged from the body, feces, urine.

excrete *vt* to eliminate or discharge wastes from the body.—**excreter** *n*.—**excretion** *n*.—**excretive, excretory** *adj*.

excretion *n* (*biol*) the removal of all waste material from the body, including urine and feces, the loss of water and salts through sweat glands, and the elimination of carbon dioxide and water vapor from the lungs.

excruciate *vt* to inflict severe pain upon; to torture.—**excruciation** *n*.

excruciating *adj* intensely painful or distressful; (*inf*) very bad.—**excruciatingly** *adv*.

exculpate *vt* to free (a person) from alleged fault or guilt.—**exculpable** *adj*.—**exculpation** *n*.

exculpatory *adj* tending or serving to exculpate.

excurrent *adj* (*bot*) (*leaf*) having a midrib running beyond the edge; (*tree*) having a projecting stem; (*zool*) having a duct, etc, whose contents flow out.

excursion *n* a pleasure trip; a short journey.

excursionist *n* someone going on an excursion.

excursive *adj* digressing, rambling.—**excursively** *adv*.

excursus *n* (*pl* **excursuses, excursus**) a dissertation added as a supplement to a work, giving additional information on certain points; a digression from the main subject of a work.

excusable *adj* able to be excused.—**excusably** *adv*.

excuse *vt* to pardon; to forgive; to give a reason or apology for; to be a reason or explanation of; to let off. * *n* an apology, a plea in extenuation.

exd. *abbr* = examined.

ex d., ex div. *abbr* = ex dividend

ex-directory *adj* (*telephone number*) not listed in the telephone directory by request.

exec. *abbr* = executive; executor.

execrable *adj* appalling.—**execrableness** *n*.

execrate *vt* to denounce as evil; to abhor.—**execration** *n*.—**execrative, execratory** *adj*.

executant *n* a person who executes or performs, esp an artist, musician, etc.

execute *vt* to carry out, put into effect; to perform; to produce (e.g., a work of art); to make legally valid; to put to death by law; (*comput*) to carry out the individual steps called for by the program in a computer.—**executable** *adj*.—**executer** *n*.

execution *n* the act or process of executing; the carrying out or suffering of a death sentence; the style or technique of performing, e.g. music.

executioner *n* a person who executes a death sentence upon a condemned prisoner.

executive *n* a person or group concerned with administration or management of a business or organization; the branch of government with the power to put laws, etc into effect. * *adj* having the power to execute decisions, laws, decrees, etc.

executive director *n* a director of a company who is also an employee, usually a full-time employee, of that company.

executor *n* a person who is named in a will to carry out the task of gathering in any assets relating to the estate of the deceased, discharging any liabilities and distributing any remaining assets to the beneficiaries named in the will.—**executorial** *adj*.—**executorship** *n*.

executory *adj* (*law*) pertaining to the execution of laws; to be carried out at a future date.

executrix *n* (*pl* **executrices, executrixes**) a female executor.

execx. *abbr* = executrix.

exegesis *n* (*pl* **exegeses**) an explanation or interpretation of a text or passage, esp of the Bible.

exegetic, exegetical *adj* expository; interpretative.

exegetics *n* (*sing*) the study of exegesis.

exemplar *n* a model; a typical instance or example.

exemplary *adj* deserving imitation; serving as a warning.—**exemplarily** *adv*.—**exemplariness** *n*.

exemplify *vt* (**exemplifying, exemplified**) to illustrate by example; to be an instance or example of.—**exemplification** *n*.—**exemplifier** *n*.

exempt *adj* not liable, free from the obligations required of others. * *vt* to grant immunity (from).—**exemptible** *adj*.—**exemption** *n*.

exercise *n* the use or application of a power or right; regular physical or mental exertion for health, amusement or acquisition of some skill; something performed to develop or test a specific ability or skill; (*often pl*) maneuvers carried out for military training and discipline. * *vt* to use, exert, employ; to engage in regular physical activity to strengthen the body, etc; to train (troops) by means of drills and maneuvers; to engage the attention of; to perplex.—**exercisable** *adj*.

exergue *n* the space below the principal design on a coin or medal for the insertion of a date, etc.—**exergual** *adj*.

exert *vt* to bring (e.g., strength, influence) into use.

exertion *n* an exerting; a strenuous effort.—**exertive** *adj*.

exeunt (*Latin*) "they go off", a stage direction.

ex factory *see* **ex works.**

exfoliate *vi* to flake off; (*tree*) to shed bark. —**exfoliation** *n*.

exfoliation *n* the process whereby rocks are gradually worn away by the flaking off of layers or shells.

ex. gr. *abbr* (*Latin*) = "ex gratia."

ex gratia *adj* given as a favor or where no legal obligation exists.

exhalant *adj* exhaling. * *n* a duct, organ, etc used for exhaling.

exhalation *see* **respiration.**

exhale *vt* to breathe out.—**exhalation** *n*.

exhaust *vt* to use up completely; to make empty; to use up, tire out; (*subject*) to deal with or develop completely. * *n* the escape of waste gas or steam from an engine; the device through which these escape.—**exhausted** *adj*.—**exhauster** *n*.—**exhaustible** *adj*.—**exhausting** *adj*.

exhaustion *n* the act of exhausting or being exhausted; extreme weariness.

exhaustive *adj* comprehensive, thorough.—**exhaustively** *adv*.

exhib. *abbr* (*Latin*) (*pharm*) = *exhibeatur*, " let it be administered."

exhibit *vt* to display, esp in public; to present to a court in legal form. * *n* an act or instance of exhibiting, something exhibited; something produced and identified in court for use as evidence.—**exhibitor** *n*.—**exhibitory** *adj*.

exhibition *n* a showing, a display; a public show; an allowance made to a student.

exhibitioner *n* a student who holds an exhibition.

exhibitionism *n* an excessive tendency to show off one's abilities; a compulsion to expose oneself indecently in public.—**exhibitionist** *n*. —**exhibitionistic** *adj*.

exhilarant *adj* exhilarating. * *n* something that exhilarates.

exhilarate *vt* to make very happy; to invigorate.—**exhilarating** *adj*.—**exhilaration** *n*.—**exhilarator** *n*.

exhort *vt* to urge or advise strongly.—**exhortation** *n*.—**exhortative, exhortatory** *adj*.—**exhorter** *n*.

exhume *vt* to dig up (a dead person) for detailed examination.—**exhumation** *n*.—**exhumer** *n*.

exigency, exigence *n* (*pl* **exigencies, exigences**) a pressing need; emergency.

exigent *adj* urgent; exacting.—**exigently** *adv*.

exigible *adj* (*debt etc*) liable to be exacted.

exiguous *adj* very small in amount, meager.—**exiguity, exiguousness** *n*.

exile *n* prolonged absence from one's own country, either through choice or as a punishment; an exiled person. * *vt* to banish, to expel from one's native land.—**exilic, exilian** *adj*.

Exile *n* (*Bible*) the period spent by the Jews in captivity in Babylon following the destruction of Jerusalem in 587 BC by Nebuchadrezzar; they preserved their Jewish identity and faith, and were able to return after Cyrus had overrun Babylon. *See also* **Babylon; Cyrus.**

Ex-Im Bank *abbr* = Export-Import Bank of the United States

ex int. *abbr* = ex interest.

Exion-Geber *n* (*Bible*) alternative name for Elath.

exist *vi* to have being; to just manage a living; to occur in a specific place under specific conditions.

existence *n* the state or fact of existing; continuance of life; lifestyle; everything that exists.

existent *adj* real, actual; existing; current.

existential *adj* of or pertaining to existence; existentialist.

existentialism *n* a philosophical position based on a perception of life in which man is an actor forced to make choices in an essentially meaningless universe that functions as a colossal and cruel theater of the absurd. .—**existentialist** *n*, *adj*.

exit *n* a way out of an enclosed space; death; a departure from a stage. * *vi* to leave, withdraw; to go offstage.

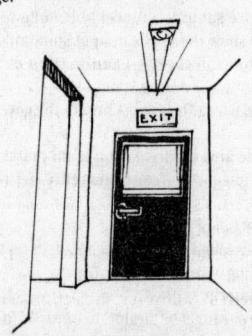

exit value *n* the market price of an asset at the date of a balance sheet less the selling price, making it the net realizable value.

ex lib. *abbr* (*Latin*) = *ex libris*, ""from the library of."

ex libris *n* (*pl* **ex libris**) a book plate.

exmr. *abbr* = examiner.

exocrine *adj* secreting though a duct; of or relating to exocrine glands or their secretions.

exocrine gland *n* (*biol*) a gland that discharges its secretions through a duct, e.g. salivary glands and sweat glands. *Compare* **endocrine gland**. *See also* **perspiration**.

Exod. *abbr* = Exodus.

exoderm *see* **ectoderm**.

exodus *n* the departure of many people; (*Bible*) the second book of the Old Testament.

Exodus *n* the departure of the Israelites from Egypt led by Moses.

ex officio *adv, adj* by virtue of an official position.

exogamy *n* the practice of marrying only outside one's own tribe.—**exogamous** *adj*.

exogenous *adj* (*med*) a term used to describe something originating outside the body, including an outside organ of the body.—**exogenously** *adv*.

exonerate *vt* to absolve from blame; to relieve from a responsibility, obligation.—**exoneration** *n*.—**exonerative** *adj*.—**exonerator** *n*.

exophthalmos, exophthalmus *n* protrusion of the eyeball.—**exophthalmic** *adj*.

exorbitant *adj* (*prices, demands, etc*) unreasonable, excessive.—**exorbitance** *n*.

exorcise, exorcize *vt* to expel an evil spirit (from a person or place) by ritual and prayer.—**exorciser, exorcizer** *n*.—**exorcism** *n*.—**exorcist** *n*.

exordium *n* (*pl* **exordiums, exordia**) the opening part of a speech or composition.—**exordial** *adj*.

exoteric *adj* accessible to ordinary people; external.—**exoterically** *adv*.—**exotericism** *n*.

exothermic reaction *n* (*chem*) a chemical reaction in which heat energy is released to the surrounding environment.

exotic *adj* foreign; strange; excitingly different or unusual.—**exotically** *adv*.—**exoticism** *n*.—**exoticness** *n*.

exotica *npl* exotic items, esp as a collection.

exp. *abbr* = (*law*) (*Latin*) *ex parte* ; expenses; exponential; export; exportation; exported; express.

expand *vt* to increase in size, bulk, extent, importance; to describe in fuller detail. * *vi* to become larger; to become more genial and responsive.—**expandable, expandible** *adj*.—**expander** *n*.

expanse *n* a wide area of land, etc; the extent of a spread-out area.

expansible *adj* capable of expansion, or of being expanded.—**expansibility** *n*.

expansile *adj* capable of expansion, or of causing expansion.

expansion *n* the act of expanding or being expanded; something expanded; the amount by which something expands; the fuller development of a theme, etc.—**expansionary** *adj*.

expansion bus *see* **bus**.

expansion card *n* (*comput*) a printed circuit board that is fitted into the main computer board and enhances the power of the computer, providing facilities such as modems, etc.

expansion slot *n* (*comput*) a port in the main computer system that allows the fitting of an expansion card.

expansive *adj* able to or having the capacity to expand or cause expansion; comprehensive; (*person*) genial, communicative.—**expansively** *adv*.—**expansiveness** *n*.

ex parte *adj* (*law*) (*Latin*) legal terminology for "in the interests of one party."

expatiate *vi* to speak or write at length; to enlarge.—**expatiation** *n*.—**expatiator** *n*.

expatriate *adj* living in another country; self-exiled or banished. * *n* an expatriate person. * *vti* to exile (oneself) or banish (another person).—**expatriation** *n*.

expect *vt* to anticipate; to regard as likely to arrive or happen; to consider necessary, reasonable or due; to think, suppose.

expectant *adj* expecting, hopeful; filled with anticipation; pregnant.—**expectantly** *adv*.—**expectancy, expectance** *n*.

expectation *n* the act or state of expecting; something that is expected to happen; (*pl*) prospects for the future, esp of inheritance.—**expectative** *adj*.

expectorant *n* one of a group of drugs that are taken to help in the removal of secretions from the lungs, bronchi, and trachea.

expectorate *vti* to bring up (mucus) from the respiratory tract by coughing; to spit.—**expectoration** *n*.—**expectorator** *n*.

expediency, expedience *n* (*pl* **expediencies, expediences**) fitness, suitability; an inclination towards expedient methods.—**expediential** *adj*.

expedient *adj* suitable or desirable under the circumstances. * *n* a means to an end; a means devised or used for want of something better.—**expediently** *adv*.

expedite *vt* to carry out promptly; to facilitate.—**expediter, expeditor** *n*.

expedition *n* a journey to achieve some purpose, as exploration, etc; the party making this journey; speedy efficiency, promptness.

expeditionary *adj* of or constituting an expedition.

expeditious *adj* speedy; efficient.—**expeditiously** *adv*.

expel *vt* (**expelling, expelled**) to drive out, to eject; to banish.—**expellable** *adj*.—**expellee** *n*.—**expeller** *n*.

expend *vt* to spend (money, time, energy, etc); to use up, consume.—**expender** *n*.

expendable *adj* able to be consumed, not worth keeping; available for sacrifice to achieve some objective.—**expendability** *n*.

expenditure *n* the act or process of expending money, etc; the amount expended.

expenditure tax *n* a tax on the expenditure of individuals.

expense *n* a payment of money for something, expenditure; a sum spent for goods or services in a company that is normally set against profit in the profit and loss account; money spent by an employee in the course of his or her work for a company and subject to refund by the company.

expense account *n* an account of expenses to be reimbursed to an employee.

expensive *adj* causing or involving great expense; costly.—**expensively** *adv*.—**expensiveness** *n*.

experience *n* observation or practice resulting in or tending towards knowledge; knowledge gained by seeing and doing; a state of being affected from without (as by events); an affecting event. * *vt* to have experience of.

experienced *adj* wise or skilled through experience.

experiential *adj* of or based on experience.

experiment *n* any test or trial to find out something; a controlled procedure carried out to discover, test, or demonstrate something. * *vi* to carry out experiments.—**experimentation** *n*.—**experimenter** *n*.

experimental *adj* of, derived from, or proceeding by experiment; empirical; provisional.—**experimentalism** *n*.—**experimentally** *adv*.

experimental psychology *n* a branch of psychology using laboratory experiments to study topics such as learning.

expert *adj* thoroughly skilled; knowledgeable through training and experience. * *n* a person with special skills or training in any art or science.—**expertly** *adv*.—**expertness** *n*.

expertise *n* expert knowledge or skill.

expert system *n* (*comput*) a program that uses the accumulated expertise in a specific area of many people in order to assist non-experts who wish to solve problems.

expiate *vt* to pay the penalty for; to make amends for.—**expiation** *n*.—**expiator** *n*.—**expiatory** *adj*.

expiration *see* **respiration**.

expire *vti* to come to an end; to lapse or become void; to breathe out; to die.—**expiration** *n*.—**expirer** *n*.

expired costs *npl* costs the advantages of which are used up during a current accounting period and which thus do not get carried over to the next accounting period in the form of closing stock or a prepayment.

expiry *n* (*pl* **expiries**) the ending of a period of validity, e.g. of a passport.

explain *vt* to make plain or clear; to give a reason for, account for.—**explainable** *adj*.—**explainer** *n*.

explanation *n* an act or process of explaining; something that explains, esp a statement.

explanatory, explanative *adj* serving as an explanation.—**explanatorily** *adv*.

expletive *n* a violent exclamation or swearword.

explicable *adj* able to be explained.

explicate *vt* to analyze the implications of; to explain in great detail.—**explication** *n*.—**explicative, explicatory** *adj*.—**explicator** *n*.

explicit *adj* clearly stated, not merely implied; outspoken, frank; graphically detailed.—**explicitly** *adv*.—**explicitness** *n*.

explode *vti* to burst or cause to blow up with a loud noise, as in the detonation of a bomb; (*emotions*) to burst out; (*population*) to increase rapidly; to expose (a theory, etc) as false.—**exploder** *n*.

exploit *n* a bold achievement. * *vt* to utilize, develop (raw materials, etc); to take unfair advantage of, esp for financial gain.—**exploitable** *adj*.—**exploitation** *n*.—**exploitative** *adj*.

exploratory, explorative *adj* for the purpose of exploring or investigating.

explore *vti* to examine or inquire into; to travel through (a country) for the purpose of (geographical) discovery; to examine minutely.—**exploration** *n*.—**explorer** *n*.

Explorer *n* (*trademark*) (*comput*) the file manager utility that comes with Windows (*trademark*) software and which shows the directories/folders, files, and other information about a computer's disks.

explosion *n* an act or instance of exploding; a sudden loud noise caused by this; an outburst of emotion; a rapid increase or expansion.

explosive *adj* liable to or able to explode; liable or threatening to burst out with violence and noise. * *n* an explosive substance.—**explosively** *adv*.

exponent *n* a person who explains or interprets something; a person who champions, advocates, or exemplifies; (*math*) a symbol, usually a number, that appears as a superscript to the right of a mathematical expression and indicates the power to which an expression is raised.

exponential *adj* of, relating to or having an exponent; (*math*) having a variable in an exponent; able to be expressed by an exponential function. * *n* an exponential function.—**exponentially** *adv*.

exponential function *n* a mathematical function in which the constant quantity of the expression is raised to the power of a variable quantity, i.e. the exponent.

export *vt* to send out (goods) of one country for sale in another; (*comput*) to create a data file in one program that can be transferred to another computer and be read by another program. * *n* the act of exporting; the article exported.—**exportable** *adj*.—**exportation** *n*.—**exporter** *n*.

exports *npl* goods or services that are sold to buyers in foreign countries.

exposé *n* a revelation of crime, dishonesty, etc.

expose *vt* to deprive of protection or shelter; to subject to an influence (as light, weather); to display, reveal; to uncover or disclose.—**exposable** *adj*.—**exposal** *n*.—**exposer** *n*.

exposed *adj* open to view; not shielded or protected.—**exposedness** *n*.

exposition *n* a public show or exhibition; a detailed explanation; a speech or writing explaining a process, thing, or idea; (*mus*) in the sonata form, the first section of a piece in which the main themes are introduced before they are developed;.—**expositional** *adj*.

expositive, expository *adj* of, pertaining to or conveying exposition; explanatory.—**expositively, expositorily** *adv*.

ex post facto *adj* (*law*) (*Latin*) legal terminology for "enacted retrospectively." * *adv* after the fact.

expostulate *vi* to argue with, esp to dissuade.—**expostulation** *n*.—**expostulator** *n*.—**expostulatory, expostulative** *adj*.

exposure *n* an exposing or state of being exposed; time during which light reaches and acts on a photographic film, paper or plate; publicity.

expound *vt* to explain or set forth in detail.—**expounder** *n*.

express *vt* to represent in words; to make known one's thoughts, feelings, etc; to represent by signs, symbols, etc; to squeeze out. * *adj* firmly stated, explicit; (*train, bus, etc*) traveling at high speed with few or no stops. * *adv* at high speed, by express service. * *n* an express train, coach, etc; a system or company for sending freight, etc at rates higher than standard.—**expresser** *n*.—**expressible** *adj*.

expression *n* an act of expressing, esp by words; a word or phrase; a look; intonation; a manner of showing feeling in communicating or performing (e.g., music); (*math*) a collection of symbols serving to express something.—**expressional** *adj*.—**expressionless** *adj*.

expressionism *n* a style of art, literature, music, etc that seeks to depict the subjective emotions aroused in the artist by objects and events, not objective reality.—**expressionist** *n*.—**expressionistic** *adj*. See also **abstract expressionism**.

expressive *adj* serving to express; full of expression.—**expressively** *adv*.—**expressiveness** *n*.

expressly *adv* explicitly; for a specific purpose.

expressway *n* a high-speed divided highway with partially or totally controlled access..

expropriate *vt* to remove (property) from its owner, to dispossess.—**expropriable** *adj*.—**expropriation** *n*.—**expropriator** *n*.

EXPS *abbr* = Exmoor Pony Society.

expulsion *n* the act of expelling or being expelled.—**expulsive** *adj*.

expunge *vt* to obliterate, to erase.—**expunction** *n*.—**expunger** *n*.

expurgate *vt* to cut from a book, play, etc any parts supposed to be offensive or erroneous.—**expurgation** *n*.—**expurgator** *n*.—**expurgatory, expurgatorial** *adj*.

exquisite *adj* very beautiful, refined; sensitive, showing discrimination; acutely felt, as pain or pleasure.—**exquisitely** *adv*.

exr. *abbr* = executor; ex rights.

exrx. *abbr* = executrix.

exsanguinate *vt* to drain of blood.—**exsanguination** *n*.

exsanguine *adj* bloodless.

exscind *vt* to cut off; to cut out, excise.

exsert *vt* to thrust outwards.—**exsertile** *adj*.—**exsertion** *n*.

exsiccate *vt* to dry up.—**exsiccation** *n*.

ext. *abbr* = extension; externally; extinct; extra; extract.

extant *adj* still existing.

extemporaneous, extemporary *adj* spoken, acted, etc without preparation.—**extemporaneously, extemporarily** *adv*.

extempore *adv, adj* without preparation, impromptu.

extemporize *vi* to do something extemporaneously.—**extemporization** *n*. See also **improvisation**.

extend *vt* to stretch or spread out; to stretch fully; to prolong in time; to cause to reach in distance, etc; to enlarge, increase the scope of; to hold out (e.g., the hand); to accord, grant; to give, offer, (e.g., sympathy). * *vi* to prolong in distance or time; to reach in scope.

extended family *n* a family with three or more generations of blood relations living as a unit.

extended memory specification *see* **XMS**.

extendible, extendable *adj* able to be extended.—**extendibility, extendability** *n*.

extensible, extensile *adj* extendible.—**extensibility, extensibleness** *n*.

extension *n* the act of extending or state of being extended; extent, scope; an added part, e.g. to a building; an extra period; a Programme of extramural teaching provided by a college, etc; an additional telephone connected to the principal line; (*comput*) a set of three characters after the file name that helps in recognizing the file type; (*law*) an instrument which, for example, grants an extension to a previously filed instrument.

extensive *adj* large; having a wide scope or extent.—**extensively** *adv*.—**extensiveness** *n*.

extensometer *n* a type of micrometer for measuring the expansion of a body.

extensor *n* (*med*) a muscle that extends or stretches to cause an arm, leg, etc, to move.—*also* **antagonist**. *Compare* **flexor**.

extent *n* the distance over which a thing is extended; the range or scope of something; the limit to which something extends.

extenuate *vt* to make (guilt, a fault, or offence) seem less.—**extenuating** *adj*.—**extenuator** *n*.—**extenuatory** *adj*.

extenuation *n* an extenuating or being extenuated, partial justification; something that extenuates, an excuse.

exterior *adj* of, on, or coming from the outside; external; (*paint, etc*) suitable for use on the outside. * *n* the external part or surface; outward manner or appearance.

exteriorize *vt* to externalize; (*med*) to move (an organ, etc) out of the body, usu to facilitate surgery.

exterminate *vt* to destroy completely.—**exterminable** *adj*.—**extermination** *n*.—**exterminatory** *adj*.

exterminator *n* one who or that which exterminates; a person who is employed to destroy pests, etc.

extern, externe *n* a non-resident doctor.

external *adj* outwardly perceivable; of, relating to, or located on the outside or outer part. * *n* an external feature.—**externally** *adv*.

external audit *n* an audit of a company carried out by an auditor who is not part of the organization but is an independent auditor who works outside the firm.

external growth *n* a form of business growth in which expansion comes not from internal, organic growth but from external business activities such as mergers or takeovers.

externality *n* (*pl* **externalities**) a being external or externalized; something external; (*philos*) a being external to the perceiving mind.

externalize *vt* to make external; to attribute an external existence to; to express (feelings, etc) esp in words; (*psychol*) to project (opinions, feelings) onto others or one's surroundings.—**externalization** *n*.

exterritorial *adj* extraterritorial.—**exterritoriality** *n*.

extinct *adj* (*animals*) not alive, no longer existing; (*fire*) not burning, out; (*volcano*) no longer active.—**extinction** *n*.

extine *n* (*bot*) the outer coat of the pollen grain.

extinguish *vt* to put out (a fire, light, etc); to bring to an end.—**extinguishable** *adj*.—**extinguishment** *n*.

extinguisher *n* a device for putting out a fire.

extirpate *vt* to destroy totally, as by uprooting.—**extirpation** *n*.—**extirpative** *adj*.—**extirpator** *n*.

extoll, extol *vt* (**extolls** *or* **extols, extolling, extolled**) to praise highly.—**extoller** *n*.—**extollment, extolment** *n*.

extort *vt* to obtain (money, promises, etc) by force or improper pressure.—**extorter** *n*.—**extortive** *adj*.

extortion *n* the act or practice of extorting; the criminal instance of this; oppressive or unjust exaction.—**extortionary** *adj*.—**extortioner, extortionist** *n*.

extortionate *adj* exorbitant; excessively high in price.—**extortionately** *adv*.

extra *adj* additional. * *adv* unusually; in addition. * *n* something extra or additional, esp a charge; a special edition of a newspaper; a person who plays a non-speaking role in a film.

extra- *prefix* outside, beyond.

extract *vt* to take or pull out by force; to withdraw by chemical or physical means; to abstract, excerpt. * *n* the essence of a substance obtained by extraction; a passage taken from a book, play, film, etc.—**extractable, extractible** *adj*.—**extractability, extractibility** *n*.

extraction *n* the act of extracting; lineage; something extracted.

extractive *adj* tending or serving to extract.

extractor *n* one who extracts; a thing that extracts, esp a device for removing teeth or delivering a baby; a device for extracting stale air or fumes from a room (—*also* **extractor fan**).

extracurricular *adj* not part of the regular school timetable; beyond one's normal duties or activities.

extradite *vt* to surrender (an alleged criminal) to the country where the offence was committed.—**extraditable** *adj*.—**extradition** *n*.

extrados *n* (*pl* **extrados** *or* **extradoses**) (*archit*) the outer curve of an arch on top of the voussoirs.

extragalactic *adj* outside the Galaxy.

extrajudicial *adj* out of the ordinary course of legal proceedings.

extramarital *adj* occurring outside marriage, esp sexual relationships.

extramundane *adj* beyond the material world.

extramural *adj* (*course, studies*) outside the usual courses run by a university, etc; outside a city's walls or boundaries.—**extramurally** *adv*.

extraneous *adj* coming from outside; not essential.—**extraneously** *adv*.

extraordinary *adj* not usual or regular; remarkable, exceptional.—**extraordinarily** *adv*.—**extraordinariness** *n*.

extraordinary general meeting *n* any general meeting of a company or association other than the annual general meeting.

extraordinary items *npl* costs or income that do not stem from the normal, routine activities of the company and that affect a company's profit and loss account.

extrapolate *vti* to predict the unknown value of a measurement or function using known values.—**extrapolation** *n*.—**extrapolator** *n*.

extrasensory perception *n* the claimed ability to obtain information by means of other than the ordinary physical senses.

extrasystole *or* **ectopic beat** *n* a heartbeat that is outside the normal rhythm of the heart and is the result of an impulse generated outside the sinoatrial node. It may go unnoticed or it may seem that the heart has missed a beat.

extraterritorial *adj* outside territorial boundaries; (*embassy etc*) outside the jurisdiction of the country in which it is.—*also* **exterritorial**.

extraterritoriality *n* exemption granted to foreign diplomats from the legal jurisdiction of the country to which they are posted; a country's jurisdiction over its nationals abroad.

extravagant *adj* lavish in spending; (*prices*) excessively high; wasteful; (*behavior, praise, etc*) lacking in restraint, flamboyant, profuse.—**extravagantly** *adv*.—**extravagance** *n*.

extravaganza *n* an elaborate musical production; a spectacular show, play, film, etc.

extravagate *vi* (*arch*) to wander; to be extravagant.—**extravagation** *n*.

extravasate *vt* (*anat*) to force blood, etc out of its proper vessel; to exude. * *vi* to flow out.—**extravasation** *n*.

extraversion *see* **extroversion**.

extravert *see* **extrovert**.

extreme *adj* of the highest degree or intensity; excessive, immoderate, unwarranted; very severe, stringent; outermost. * *n* the highest or furthest limit or degree; (*often pl*) either of the two points marking the ends of a scale or range.—**extremely** *adv*.—**extremeness** *n*.

extremist *n* a person of extreme views, esp political.—**extremism** *n*.

extremity *n* (*pl* **extremities**) the utmost point or degree; the most remote part; the utmost violence, vigor, or necessity; the end; (*pl*) the hands or feet.

extricable *adj* able to be extricated.

extricate *vt* to release from difficulties; to disentangle.—**extrication** *n*.

extrinsic *adj* external; not inherent or essential.—**extrinsically** *adv*.

extrorse *adj* (*bot*) turned outwards.

extroversion *n* the state of having thoughts and activities directed towards things other than oneself.—*also* **extraversion**.

extrovert *n* a person more interested in the external world than his own thoughts and feelings.—*also* **extravert**.—**extroverted, extraverted** *adj*.

extrude *vt* to force or push out; to mould (metal or plastic) by forcing through a shaped die.—**extrusion** *n*.—**extrusive** *adj*.

extrusive rocks *n* (*geol*) a general term to encompass rocks of volcanic origin that are discharged onto the Earth's surface, e.g. lava flows.

exuberant *adj* lively, effusive, high-spirited; profuse.—**exuberance** *n*.—**exuberantly** *adv*.

exuberate *vi* to be exuberant; (*arch*) to abound.

exudate *n* exuded matter, e.g. sweat.

exudation *n* an exuding or being exuded; exuded matter, e.g. sweat.—**exudative** *adj*.

exude *vt* to cause or allow to ooze through pores or incisions, as sweat, pus; to display (confidence, emotion) freely.

exult *vi* to rejoice greatly.—**exultation** *n*.

exultant *adj* exulting, joyful; triumphant.—**exultantly** *adv*.

exuviae *npl* the cast-off skins, shells, etc, of animals.—**exuvial** *adj*.

exuviate *vt* (*skin*) to shed, slough.—**exuviation** *n*.

ex warehouse *n* a term indicating delivery terms for goods in which the purchaser pays for the delivery of the goods but the seller pays the loading charges for road or rail transport.

ex works, ex factory *n* a term indicating delivery terms for goods in which the purchaser has to pay for transporting them from the factory.

exx. *abbr* = executrix.

eyas *n* a nesting hawk.

EYC *abbr* = European Young Conservatives.

Eyck *n* **Jan van** (*d*. 1441) Dutch painter. He was a master in the medium of oil painting. His representation of light and detail remains unsurpassed.

eye *n* the complicated organ of sight; the iris; the faculty of seeing; the external part of the eye; something resembling an eye, as the hole in a needle, the leaf-bud on a potato; the calm area at the center of a hurricane. * *vt* (**eyeing** *or* **eying, eyed**) to look at; to observe closely.

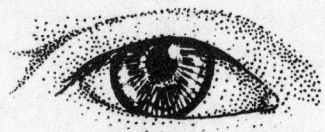

EYE *abbr* = European Youth Exchange.

eyeball *n* the ball of the eye. * *vt* (*sl*) to stare at.

eyebright *n* a plant with small white and purplish flowers, formerly used as a lotion to treat disorders of the eye.

eyebrow *n* the hairy ridge above the eye.

eye-catching *adj* attractive or striking in appearance.—**eye-catcher** *n*.

eyeful *adj* (*inf*) a close look, gaze; an attractive vision, esp a woman.

eyeglass *n* a lens for correcting defective vision, a monocle.

eyeglasses *npl* spectacles.

eyelash *n* the fringe of fine hairs along the edge of each eyelid.

eyeless *adj* without eyes; blind.

eyelet *n* a small hole for a rope or cord to pass through, as in sails, garments, etc.

eyelid *n* the lid of skin and muscle that moves to cover the eye.

eye-liner *n* a cosmetic used to apply a line round the eye.

Eye of Horus *n* (*Egypt*) the eye painted on the prow of Egyptian ships and much used as a protective amulet; in his epic battle with Seth, Horus lost an eye, which was later reassembled by Thoth.

eye-opener *n* something that comes as a shock or surprise.

eyephone *n* a device in the style of a headset which provides the user with stereoscopic images and stereo sound used in virtual reality simulation.

eyepiece *n* the lens or lenses at the end nearest the eye of an optical instrument, e.g. a telescope.

eyeprint *n* the pattern of veins in the retina, which is unique to an individual and used as a means of identification.

eye-shadow *n* a colored powder applied to accentuate or decorate the eyelids.

eyeshot *n* seeing distance.

eyesight *n* the faculty of seeing.

eyesore *n* anything offensive to the sight.

eyespot *n* a rudimentary visual organ; (*on butterflies, etc*) a marking resembling an eye.

eyestrain *n* tiredness or soreness of the eyes.

eyetooth *n* (*pl* **eyeteeth**) a canine tooth in the upper jaw.

eyewash *n* (*inf*) nonsense, drivel.

eye-witness *n* a person who sees an event, such as an accident or a crime, and can describe what happened.

eyot *see* **ait**.

eyrie *n* the nest of an eagle or other bird of prey; any high inaccessible place or position.

eyrir *n* a monetary unit of Iceland, equal to one hundredth of a krona.

Eysenck *n* **Hans [Jürgen]** (1916–97) German-born British psychologist.

Ezek. *abbr* = Ezekiel.

Ezekiel *n* prophet of the sixth century BC in Judah and a priest of the Temple, who was carried into Exile.

Ezekiel *n* **the Book of** (*Bible*) OT book which proclaims Ezekiel's "word from the Lord" that Jerusalem shall be restored.

Ezra *n* (*Bible*) priest who was in Exile in Babylonia in the reign of Artaxerxes, king of Persia; on his return, he established the ritual worship in the Temple.

Ezra *n* **the Book of** (*Bible*) OT book linked with Nehemiah and with Chronicles; tells of Jews returning to Jerusalem after being released by Cyrus; it lays down strict regulations including the requirement for wives to be Jewish.

E

F

f, F *n* the sixth letter of the English alphabet.

F *symbol* (*chem*) fluorine (element).

f *abbr* = (*phys, chem*) fugacity (of gases); fathom; feet; female; filly; fine; formula; frequency; furlong.

f *abbr* (*mus*) = *forte* (loud).

f. *abbr* = (*Latin*) *fac*, "make"; farad; father; fathom; (*eccl*) feast; feet; feminine; (*Latin*) *fiat*, "let it be done"; fine; form; (*theat*) flat; florin, florins; flower; fluid (ounce); folio, folios; following; foot; formula, formulas; forte; franc, francs; furlong.

F *abbr* = (*phys*) free energy; (*astrophys*) a Fraunhofer line caused by hydrogen; (*math*) function; (*mus*) the fourth note of the scale of C major; Fahrenheit; Father; February; Fellow; Finance; France; French; Friday; fathom; farad.

F. *abbr* (*Rom calendar*) = (*dies*) *fastus*.

fa *n* (*mus*) the fourth note in the sol-fa musical notation.—*also* **fah**.

f.a. *abbr* = football association; freight agent; freight association; freight auditor.

FA *abbr* = Family Allowance; Football Association; field artillery.

f.a.a, FAA *abbr* = free of all average.

FAA *abbr* = Federal Aviation Administrations; Film Artistes Association.

FAAAS *abbr* = Fellow of the American Association for the Advancement of Science; Fellow of the American Academy of Arts and Sciences.

FAACE *abbr* = Fight Against Animal Cruelty in Europe.

FAB *abbr* = Farm Apprenticeship Board (Eire); Feline Advisory Board; Feminist Audio Books; Flour Advisory Board.

FABAC *abbr* = Fellow of the Association of Business and Administrative Computing.

fabaceous *adj* (*bot*) bean-like.

FABE *abbr* = Fellow of the Association of Business Executives.

Fabergé *n* **Peter Carl** (1846–1920) Russian goldsmith and jeweler, born in St Petersburg.

Fabian *adj* pertaining to the tactics of the Roman general, Fabius Maximus; cautiously persistent; watchful. * *n* a member of the Fabian Society.

Fabian *n* **Saint** (*d.* 250) bishop of Rome; pope for sixteen years. His feast day is January 20.

Fabiansen *n* **Ib** (1927–) Danish architect who designed Illum's Bolighus store.

Fabian Society *n* a society seeking socialism by moral persuasion.

fable *n* a story, often with animal characters, intended to convey a moral; a lie, fabrication; a story involving mythical, legendary, or supernatural characters or events.

fabled *adj* related in fables; fictitious.

fabric *n* cloth made by knitting, weaving, etc; framework, structure.

fabricate *vt* to construct, manufacture; to concoct, e.g. a lie; to forge.—**fabrication** *n*.—**fabricator** *n*.

Fabricius *n* **Preben** (1931–) Danish designer who, in 1952, designed seating for the United Nations Building in New York.

Fabritius *n* **Carel** (1622–54) Dutch painter. His subject matter included portrait, genre, and still life as well as animal paintings.

Fabry–Perot interferometer *n* a very high resolution device for examining the fine structure of spectral lines, often used along with a spectrometer.

fabulist *n* a writer of fables; a liar.

fabulous *adj* told in fables; incredible, astonishing; (*inf*) very good.—**fabulously** *adv*.

faburden *n* (*mus*) literally "false bass" or "drone," the lowest of three voices in the English 15th-century improvised harmonization of plainsong melody.

fac. *abbr* = facsimile.

FAC *abbr* = Feminists Against Censorship; Food Aid Convention.

FACA *abbr* = Federal Alcohol Control Administration.

façade, facade *n* an outward appearance, esp concealing something hidden; (*archit*) the main front or face of a building.

FACD *abbr* = Fellow of the American College of Dentists.

face *n* the front part of the head containing the eyes, nose, mouth, chin, etc; facial expression; the front or outer surface of anything; external show or appearance; dignity, self respect; impudence, effrontery; a coal face. * *vt* to be confronted by (a problem, etc); to deal with (an opponent, problem, etc) resolutely; to be opposite to; to turn (a playing card) face upwards; to cover with a new surface. * *vi* to turn the face in a certain direction; to be situated in or have a specific direction.

face card *n* the king, queen, or jack in a pack of cards.

faceless *adj* lacking a face; anonymous.

face-lift *n* plastic surgery to smooth and firm the face; an improvement or renovation, esp to the outside of a building.

facer *n* someone who, or something which, faces; (*inf*) an unexpected setback.

face-saving *adj* allowing the preservation of dignity and prevention of humiliation.

facet *n* a small plane surface (as on a cut gem); an aspect of character, a problem, issue, etc.

facetiae *npl* witty sayings; books characterized by coarse wit.

face-time *n* (*sl*) a spell of duty, esp by US Secret Service agents guarding the President or others.

facetious *adj* joking, esp in an inappropriate manner.—**facetiously** *adv*.—**facetiousness** *n*.

face value *n* the value indicated on the face of (e.g. a coin or share certificate); apparent worth or significance.

Fachtna *n* (*Irish Celtic myth*) king of Ulster and the husband or lover of Nessa.

facia *see* **fascia**.

facial *adj* of or pertaining to the face. * *n* a beauty treatment for the face.—**facially** *adv*.

facial nerve *n* a cranial nerve that has a number of branches and supplies the muscles that control facial expression.

facial paralysis *n* paralysis of the facial nerve, which leads to a loss of function in the muscles of the face, producing a lack of expression in the affected side.

facies *n* (*pl* **facies**) the general appearance of a person or a group of plants, animals, or rocks; the face.

facile *adj* easy to do; superficial.

facilitate *vt* to make easier; to help forward.—**facilitator** *n*.—**facilitation** *n*.

facility *n* (**facilities**) the quality of being easily done; aptitude, dexterity; something, e.g. a service or equipment that makes it easy to do something.

facing *n* a lining at the edge of a garment; a covering on a surface for decoration or protection; (*archit*) the surface applied to the exterior of a building to finish it off.

FACP *abbr* = Fellow of the American College of Physicians.

FACS *abbr* = Fellow of the American College of Surgeons.

facsimile *n* an exact copy of a book, document, etc; a method of transmitting printed matter (text and graphics) through the telephone system.—*also* **fax**.

fact *n* a thing known to have happened or to exist; reality; a piece of verifiable information; (*law*) an event, occurrence, etc as distinguished from its legal consequences.

FACT *abbr* = Federation Against Copyright Theft; Food Additives Campaign Team.

faction[1] *n* a small group of people in an organization working together in a common cause against the main body; dissension within a group or organization.—**factional** *adj*.—**factionally** *adv*.—**factious** *adj*.

faction[2] *n* a book, film, etc based on facts but presented as a blend of fact and fiction.

factitious *adj* contrived, artificial.—**factitiously** *adv*.

factitive *adj* (*gram*) causative.

factor *n* any circumstance that contributes towards a result; (*math*) any of two or more numbers that, when multiplied together, form a product; a person who acts for another.

factor VIII *or* **antihemophilic factor** *n* one of the coagulation factors normally present in the blood. If the factor is deficient in males, it results in hemophilia.

factorage *n* a factor's commission.

factorial *n* (*math*) an integer multiplied by all lower integers, e.g. $4 \times 3 \times 2 \times 1$.

factoring *n* the purchasing of the trade debts of a company in order to provide it with enough finance with which to operate (working capital).

factorize *vt* to reduce to factors.—**factorization** *n*.

factors of production *n* factors that are required to produce goods, usually classed as capital, labor, and land.

factory *n* (*pl* **factories**) a building or buildings where things are manufactured.

factory farm *n* a farm which rears livestock intensively using modern manufacturing processes.—**factory farming** *n*.

factory ship *n* a ship that processes the catch of a fishing fleet.

factotum *n* a person employed to do all kinds of work.

facts of life *npl* knowledge of human sexual reproduction.

factual *adj* based on, or containing, facts; actual.—**factually** *adv*.

facula *n* (*pl* **faculae**) a bright spot or streak on the surface of the sun.

facultative *adj* enabling; optional; contingent.

faculty *n* (*pl* **faculties**) any natural power of a living organism; special aptitude; a teaching department of a college or university, or the staff of such a department.

fad *n* a personal habit or idiosyncrasy; a craze.—**faddish, faddy** *adj*.—**faddism** *n*.—**faddist** *n*.

fade *vi* to lose vigor or brightness of color gradually; to vanish gradually. * *vt* to cause (an image or a sound) to increase or decrease in brightness or intensity gradually.—*also n*.

fadeless *adj* unfading.

fading *n* decay; loss of color; (*radio*) a deterioration in quality of reception.

fado *n* (*mus*) (*Portuguese*) a type of melancholy song with a guitar accompaniment.

FADO *abbr* = Fellow of the Association of Dispensing Opticians.

faeces *see* **feces**.

faerie, faery *n* (*pl* **faeries**) (*arch*) a fairy; the fairy world; enchantment. * *adj* of or like a fairy; enchanted.

Faeroe Islands *n* a self-governing region of Denmark since 1948, comprising a group of 18 basaltic islands and situated in the North Atlantic, approximately halfway between the Shetland Islands and Iceland.

Faeroese *n* (*pl* **Faeroese**) an inhabitant of the Faeroes in the North Atlantic; the language of the Faeroes.—*also adj*.—*also* **Faroese**.

FAFPIC *abbr* = Forestry and Forest Products Industry Council.

FAFS *abbr* = Farm and Food Society.

fag *vti* (**fagging, fagged**) to become or cause to be tired by hard work. * *n* (*formerly*) a British public schoolboy who performs chores for senior pupils; (*inf*) drudgery; (*sl*) a homosexual; (*sl*) a cigarette.

FAG *abbr* = Friedreich's Ataxia Group.

fag end *n* the useless remains of anything; (*sl*) a cigarette-end.

faggot[1] *see* **fagot**.

faggot[2] *n* (*sl*) a male homosexual.

fagot *n* a bundle of sticks for fuel; (*sl*) a nasty old woman.

fagoting, faggoting *n* a method of decorating textile fabrics.

FAGS *abbr* = Fellow of the American Geographical Society.

fah *see* **fa**.

Fah. *abbr* = Fahrenheit.

Fahrenheit *n* (*chem*) a temperature scale with a freezing point of 32° and boiling point at 212°. * *adj* of or using the Fahrenheit temperature scale

FAIA *abbr* = Fellow of the American Institute of Architects; Fellow of the Association of International Accountants.

FAIE *abbr* = Fellow of the British Association of Industrial Editors.

faïence, faience *or* **Egyptian faience** *n* a glaze made from a mixture of clay and quartz sand that, when fired at a high temperature, produces a blue-green colored glassy surface; a type of decorated earthenware.

fail *vi* to weaken, to fade or die away; to stop operating; to fall short; to be insufficient; to be negligent in duty, expectation, etc; (*exam, etc*) to be unsuccessful; to become bankrupt. * *vt* to disappoint the expectations or hopes of; to be unsuccessful in an exam, etc; to leave, to abandon; to grade (a candidate) as not passing a test, etc. * *n* failure in an examination.

failing *n* a fault, weakness. * *prep* in default or absence of.

faille *n* a soft silk, used for dresses and hat trimmings.

fail-safe *adj* designed to operate safely even if a fault develops; foolproof.

failure *n* failing, non-performance, lack of success; the ceasing of normal operation of something; a deficiency; bankruptcy; an unsuccessful person or thing.

failure costs *npl* the cost to a manufacturer of goods that are defective.

fain *adv* (*arch*) willingly; gladly. * *adj* willing; glad.

fainéant, faineant *adj* indolent.

faint *adj* dim, indistinct; weak, feeble; timid; on the verge of losing consciousness. * *vi* to lose consciousness temporarily from a decrease in the supply of blood to the brain, as from shock. * *n* an act or condition of fainting.—**faintly** *adv*.—**faintness** *n*.

faint-hearted *adj* lacking courage and resolution.

fainting *n* a temporary and brief loss of consciousness caused by a sudden drop in the blood supply to the brain.—*also* **syncope**

fair[1] *adj* pleasing to the eye; clean, unblemished; (*hair*) light-colored; (*weather*) clear and sunny; (*handwriting*) easy to read; just and honest; according to the rules; moderately large; average. * *adv* in a fair manner; squarely.—**fairness** *n*.

fair[2] *n* a gathering for the sale of goods, esp for charity; a competitive exhibition of farm, household, or manufactured goods; a fun-fair.

Fairbanks *n* 1. **Douglas [Douglas Elton Ullman]** (1883–1939) American film actor and producer. 2. **Douglas** (1909–2000) son of Douglas Fairbanks and also an actor.

fair game *n* a legitimate target for attack or ridicule.

fairground *n* an open area where fairs are held.

fairing *n* a structure attached to the exterior of an aircraft, ship, motor vehicle, etc to reduce drag.

fairly *adv* in a fair manner; justly; moderately.

fair play *n* justice, honesty; impartiality.

fairway *n* a navigable channel; the mowed part of a golf course between the tee and the green.

fair-weather *adj* (*friend*) unreliable in troubled times.

fairy *n* (*pl* **fairies**) an imaginary supernatural being, *usu* in human form; (*sl*) a male homosexual.

fairyland *n* the country of fairies; a beautiful, enchanting place.

Fairy Queen, The *n* an operatic masque with music by Purcell, based on Shakespeare's *Midsummer Night's Dream*, first performed in 1692.

fairy ring *n* a dark or bare ring in grass caused by fungi.

fairy story *or* **fairy tale** *n* a story about fairies; an incredible story; a fabrication.

Faisalabad *n* a city in the Islamic Republic of Pakistan.

fait accompli *n* (*pl* **faits accomplis**) something already done; an irreversible act.

faith *n* trust or confidence in a person or thing; a strong conviction, esp a belief in a religion; any system of religious belief; fidelity to one's promises, sincerity.

Faith *n* Saint (*d. c.* 304) French virgin saint who was martyred at Agen during the persecution of Diocletian. Her feast day is October 6.

faithful *adj* loyal; true; true to the original, accurate.—**faithfully** *adv*.—**faithfulness** *n*.

faithless *adj* treacherous, disloyal; untrustworthy.—**faithlessly** *adv*.—**faithlessness** *n*.

Faiyum *n* (*Egypt*) a fertile area to the west of the Nile Valley, south of the Delta, which was empty marshland during the Old Kingdom but was drained and exploited in the Middle Kingdom.

fake *vt* to make (an object) appear more real or valuable in order to deceive; to pretend, simulate. * *n* a faked article, a forgery; an impostor. * *adj* counterfeit, not genuine.—**faker** *n*.

fakir *n* a Muslim or Hindu religious mendicant or ascetic.

Falangist *n* a supporter of the Spanish Falange, a fascist party founded in 1933.

falbala *n* a flounce on a dress.

falcate, falciform *adj* sickle-shaped.

falchion *n* a broad, curved sword.

falcon *n* a type of hawk trained for use in falconry.

falconer *n* a person who hunts with, or who breeds and trains hawks for hunting.—**falconry** *n*.

falconet *n* a small falcon.

falderal *n* a trifling ornament.

faldstool *n* an armless chair, used by a bishop.

Falias *n* (*Irish Celtic myth*) one of the four great deities of the Tuatha De Danann before they went to Ireland. It was the home of Morfessa.

Falkland Islands *n* a British crown colony situated in the South Atlantic about 650 kilometers or 410 miles east of southern Argentina.

Falkland Islands Pound *n* currency of Falkland Islands.

fall *vi* (**falling, fell**, *pp* **fallen**) to descend by force of gravity; to come as if by falling; to collapse; to drop to the ground; to become lower, weaker, less; to lose power, status, etc; to lose office; to slope in a downward direction; to be wounded or killed in battle; to pass into a certain state; to become pregnant; to take place, happen; to be directed by chance; to come by inheritance; (*with* **about**) to laugh uncontrollably; (*with* **back**) to retreat; (*with* **behind**) to fail to keep up with; to become in arrears with; (*with* **for**) to fall in love with; to be fooled by (a lie, trick, etc); (*with* **out**) to quarrel; to leave one's place in a military formation; (*with* **through**) to fail to happen. * *n* act or instance of falling; something which falls; the amount by which something falls; a decline in status, position; overthrow; a downward slope; a decrease in size, quantity, value; autumn; (*wrestling*) a scoring move by pinning both shoulders of an opponent to the floor at once.

Falla *n* **Manuel de** (1876–1946) Spanish composer and pianist. Compositions include *El amor brujo* (Love the Magician), *Noches en los jardines de Espana* (Nights in the Gardens of Spain), and *Fantasia betica*.

fallacious *adj* misleading.—**fallaciously** *adv*.—**fallaciousness** *n*.

fallacy *n* (*pl* **fallacies**) a false idea; a mistake in reasoning.

fallal *n* a piece of finery, an ornament.

fallen *adj* sunk to a lower state or condition; overthrown.

fall guy *n* (*inf*) a person who is easily cheated; a scapegoat.

fallible *adj* liable to make mistakes.—**fallibly** *adv*.— **fallibility** *n*.

fall-off analysis *n* (*archeo*) a study of the way in which particular items that have been traded become less common with increasing distance from their source.

Fallopian tube *n* either of the two tubes through which the egg cells pass from the ovary to the uterus.

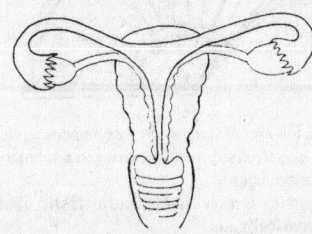

fall-out *n* a deposit of radioactive dust from a nuclear explosion; a by-product.

fallow¹ *adj* of land, ploughed and left unplanted for a season or more.

fallow² *adj* yellowish-brown.

fallow deer *n* a small European deer with a brownish-yellow coat which becomes spotted with white in summer.

false *adj* wrong, incorrect; deceitful; artificial; disloyal, treacherous; misleading, fallacious.—**falsely** *adv.*—**falseness** *n*.

false alarm *n* an alarm that proves needless; an occasion when a forecast danger does not occur.

false ceiling *n* a second ceiling constructed below the level of the original one, to reduce the height of a room.

false color *n* a term used in remote sensing when, using infrared photography, images of objects can be obtained from the infrared radiation that they emit by using special dyes on films.

false entrance *n* (*archeo*) a blind entrance to a barrow constructed in the expected place when the real entrance was elsewhere.

falsehood *n* a being untrue; the act of deceiving; a lie.

false origin *n* a point from which a grid is imposed on a map, chosen to prevent negative coordinates from appearing.

false pretenses *npl* (usu *with* **under**) a deception to acquire or influence dishonestly.

false relation *or* **cross relation** *n* (*mus*) in harmony, the occurrence of a note bearing an accidental, which is immediately followed, in another part, by the same note which does not bear an accidental, or vice versa.

false relief *n* two rows of triangular shapes pressed or cut out from the surface, giving the surrounding pattern the appearance of standing out above the surface.

false rib *see* **rib**.

falsetto *n* (*pl* **falsettos**) (*mus*) (*Italian*) an adult male voice, used in the register above its normal range. It has often been used, to comic effect, in operas.

falsies *npl* (*inf*) foam, cloth, or rubber pads worn under clothing to exaggerate the size of the breasts.

falsify *vt* (**falsifying, falsified**) to misrepresent; to alter (a document, etc) fraudulently; to prove false.—**falsification** *n*.

falsity *n* (*pl* **falsities**) the quality of being false; an error, a lie.

falter *vi* to move or walk unsteadily, to stumble; to hesitate or stammer in speech; to be weak or unsure, to waver.—**falteringly** *adv*.

fam. *abbr* = familiar; family.

FAM *abbr* = Federal Air Mail; Free and Accepted Masons.

Famagusta *n* a city in Cyprus.

fame *n* the state of being well known; good reputation.—**famed** *adj*.

FAMEM *abbr* = Federation of Associations of Mine Equipment Manufacturers.

familiar *adj* well-acquainted; friendly; common; well-known; too informal, presumptuous. * *n* a spirit or demon supposed to aid a witch, etc; an intimate.—**familiarly** *adv.*—**familiarity** *n*.

familiarize *vt* to make well known or acquainted; to make (something) well known.—**familiarization** *n*.

family *n* (*pl* **families**) parents and their children; a person's children; a set of relatives; the descendants of a common ancestor; any group of persons or things related in some way; a group of related plants or animals; a unit of a crime syndicate (as the Mafia).

family brand *n* a group of brand names for the products of a company in which the names contain the same word.

family circle *n* close relatives.

family name *n* a surname.

family planning *n* birth control.

family tree *n* a genealogical diagram.

famine *n* an acute scarcity of food in a particular area; an extreme scarcity of anything.

famish *vti* to make or be very hungry.

famous *adj* renowned; (*inf*) excellent.—**famously** *adv*.

FAMS *abbr* = Fellow of the Association of Medical Secretaries, Practice Administrators and Receptionists.

famulus *n* (*pl* **famuli**) a magician's assistant.

FAMW *abbr* = Federation of African Media Women.

fan¹ *n* a handheld or mechanical device used to set up a current of air. * *vt* (**fanning, fanned**) to cool, as with a fan; to ventilate; to stir up, to excite; to spread out like a fan.

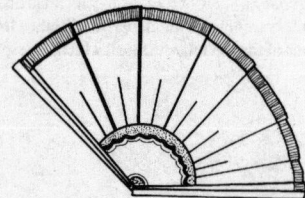

fan² *n* an enthusiastic follower of some sport, hobby, person, etc.

fan³ *n* (*geog*) an area of detrital sediment occurring in a submarine environment at the base of cliffs or mountains.

fanatic *n* a person who is excessively enthusiastic about something.—**fanatical** *adj.*—**fanatically** *adv*.

fanaticism *n* excessive enthusiasm.

fanaticize *vti* to make or become fanatical.

fan belt *n* the belt that drives the cooling fan in a car engine.

fancied *adj* imaginary.

fancier *n* a person with a special interest in something, esp plant or animal breeding.

fanciful *adj* not factual, imaginary; indulging in fancy; elaborate or intricate in design.—**fancifully** *adv*.

Fanciulla del West, La *see* **Girl of the Golden West, The**.

fan club *n* an organized group of followers of a celebrity.

fancy *n* (*pl* **fancies**) imagination; a mental image; a whim; fondness. * *adj* (**fancier, fanciest**) not based on fact, imaginary; elegant or ornamental. * *vt* (**fancying, fancied**) to imagine; to have a fancy or liking for; (*inf*) to be sexually attracted to.

fancy dress *n* a costume worn at masquerades or parties, usu representing an animal, historical character, etc.

fancy-free *adj* uncommitted, carefree.

fancy man *n* (*sl*) a woman's lover; a pimp.

fancy woman *n* (*sl*) a mistress, prostitute.

fancywork *n* ornamental needlework.

Fand *n* (*Irish Celtic myth*) a daughter of Aed Abrat and sister of Li Ban. She was the wife of Manannan mac Lir.

f & a *abbr* = fore and aft.

fandango *n* (*pl* **fandangos**)(*mus*) a lively Spanish dance, thought to be South American in origin, in triple time, usually accompanied by guitar and castanets; music for this dance, tomfoolery.

f & f *abbr* = fixtures and fittings.

F & M *abbr* = foot and mouth.

F & T *abbr* = fire and theft.

fanfare *n* (*mus*) a flourish of trumpets or other instruments (e.g., the organ) that imitate the sound of trumpets.

fang *n* a long sharp tooth, as in a canine; the long hollow tooth through which venomous snakes inject poison.

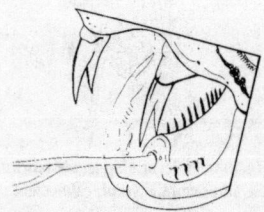

fanlight *n* (*archit*) a window above a doorway, semicircular in shape with glazing bars radiating out from the center resembling a fan; any window above a door.

Fannie Mae *abbr* = Federal National Mortgage Association.

fanny *n* (*pl* **fannies**) (*sl*) the part of the body that we sit on; buttocks; bottom.

fantail *n* a pigeon with a tail that opens out like a fan.

fantan *n* a Chinese gambling game in which players make guesses about hidden counters.

fantasia *n* (*mus*) (*Italian*) a piece in which the composer follows his imagination in free association rather than composing within a particular conventional form; an improvised musical or prose composition.

Fantasie (*German*) *or* **fantaisie** (*French*) *n* a fantasia.

fantasize *vt* to imagine in an extravagant way. * *vi* to daydream.

fantast *n* a visionary or dreamer.

fantastic *adj* unrealistic, fanciful; unbelievable; imaginative; (*inf*) wonderful.—**fantastically** *adv*.

Fantastici *n* **Agostino** 19th-century Italian architect who designed elegant furniture in the neo-classical style.

fantasy *n* (*pl* **fantasies**) imagination; a product of the imagination, esp an extravagant or bizarre notion or creation; an imaginative poem, play, or novel.

Fantin-Latour *n* **Henri** (1836–1904) French painter and lithographer. He is best known for his paintings of flowers and his group portraits, such as *Homage to Delacroix* (1864).

fan vault *n* (*archit*) a vault with paneling in the shape of a fan, having curving ribs of equal length arising from a single point at the top of the wall.

FANY *abbr* = First Aid Nursing Yeomanry.

fanzine *n* a magazine produced by and for the fans of a celebrity, football club, etc.

fao *abbr* = for the attention of.

FAO *abbr* = Food and Agricultural Organization.

FAPA *abbr* = Federation of Asian Pharmaceutical Associations.

FAPRS *abbr* = Federal Assistance Programs Retrieval System (replaced by CFDA).

FAPS *abbr* = Fellow of the American Physical Society.

f.a.q. *abbr* = fair average quality; free at quay.

FAQ *abbr* = fair average quality; free at quay; (*comput*) frequently asked question.

far *adj* (**farther, farthest** *or* **further, furthest**) remote in space or time; long; of political views, etc extreme * *adv* very distant in space, time, or degree; to or from a distance in time or position, very much.—**farness** *n*.

far. *abbr* = farad; farriery; farthing.

FAR *abbr* = Federal Acquisition Regulation.

farad *n* (*elect*) a unit of electrical capacitance.

faraday *n* (*chem*) a quantity of charge carried by one mole of electrons.

Faraday *n* **Michael** (1791–1867) English chemist and physicist.

faradic *adj* pertaining to the phenomenon of induced electricity, or to faradization.

faradize *vt* to treat by use of a faradic current.—**faradization** *n*.—**faradizer** *n*

farandole *n* a lively dance, originating in Provence.

faraway *adj* distant, remote; dreamy.

farce *n* a style of light comedy; a drama using such comedy; a ludicrous situation.—**farcical** *adj*.—**farcically** *adv*.

farceur, farceuse *n* a writer of or actor in a farce; a wit.

farcy *n* (*pl* **farcies**) a disease of horses, closely allied to glanders.

fardel *n* (*arch*) a bundle or burden.

fare *n* money paid for transportation; a passenger in public transport; food. * *vi* to be in a specified condition.

Far East *n* the countries of East and Southeast Asia including China, Japan, North and South Korea, Indochina, Eastern Siberia, and adjacent islands.

farewell *interj* goodbye.—*also n*.

far-fetched *adj* unlikely.

far-flung *adj* spread over a wide area; remote.

farina *n* flour or meal obtained by grinding the seeds of cereals and leguminous plants; starch.

farinaceous *adj* consisting of, or made from, farina; mealy.

farinose *adj* producing farina; resembling farina.

farm *n* an area of land (with buildings) on which crops and animals are raised. * *vt* to grow crops or breed livestock; to cultivate, as land; to breed fish commercially; (*with* **out**) to put out (work, etc) to be done by others, to subcontract.

farmer *n* a person who manages or operates a farm.

Farmer Mac *abbr* = Federal Agricultural Mortgage Corporation

farmer's lung *n* an allergic condition caused by sensitivity to inhaled dust and the fungal spores that are found in moldy hay or straw.

farm-hand *n* a worker on a farm.

farmhouse *n* a house on a farm.

farming *adj* pertaining to, or engaged in, agriculture. * *n* the business or practice of agriculture.

farmstead *n* a farm with the buildings belonging to it.

farmyard *n* a yard close to or surrounded by farm buildings.

faro *n* a gambling card game.

Faro *n* a city in Portugal.

farouche *adj* sullen; unsociable.

Farouk, King *see* **Nasser, Gamal Abdel.**

far-out *adj* (*sl*) weird, bizarre; fantastic, wonderful. * *interj* used to express delight.

Farquhar *n* **George** (1678–1707) Irish dramatist whose plays, e.g. *The Recruiting Officer* and *The Beaux Strategem*, are the best of the late Restoration comedies.

farrago *n* (*pl* **farragoes**) a confused collection.—**farraginous** *adj*.

far-reaching *adj* having serious or widespread consequences.

Farrell *n* 1. **J[ames] G[ordon]** (1935–79) English novelist whose novels explore the end of the British Empire, e.g. *Troubles*, *The Siege of Krishnapur*, and *The Singapore Grip*. 2. **J[ames] T[homas]** (1904–79) American novelist whose work is mainly set in the Irish slums of Chicago and whose best-known work is the *Studs Lonigan* trilogy.

farrier *n* a person who shoes horses.

farrow *n* a litter of pigs. * *vti* to give birth to (pigs).

far-seeing *adj* having foresight.

fart *vi* (*vulg*) to expel wind from the anus.—*also n*.

farther *adj* at or to a greater distance. * *adv* to a greater degree.

farthest *adj* at or to the greatest distance. * *adv* to the greatest degree.

farthing *n* a former British monetary unit.

farthingale *n* a hooped support worn beneath a skirt to expand it at the hip line.

f.a.s. *abbr* = free alongside ship.

FAS *abbr* = Federation of Astronomical Societies; Fellow of the Anthropological Society; Fellow of the Antiquarian Society; Fellow of the Society of Arts; Funding Agency for Schools; Foreign Agricultural Service; free alongside ship; fetal alcohol syndrome.

FASA *abbr* = Fellow of the Acoustical Society of America.

FASAB *abbr* = Federal Accounting Standards Advisory Board.

fasc. *abbr* = fasciculus.

fasces *npl* a bundle of rods with an ax used in ancient Rome as a symbol of authority.

fascia[1] *n* (*pl* **fasciae**) (*archit*) a long flat surface between moldings.

fascia[2] *n* (*pl* **fasciae**) (*anat*) fibrous tissue enclosing muscles and muscle groups.

fascia[3] *n* (*pl* **fasciae**) the instrument panel of a motor vehicle, the dashboard; the flat surface above a shop front, with the owner's name, etc.—*also* **facia**.

fascicle *n* one part of a book published by installments (—*also* **fascicule**); a small collection, group, or bundle; (*bot*) a cluster of leaves, roots, etc.

fascicular, fasciculate *adj* (*bot*) arranged in fascicles.

fascicule *n* a fascicle.

fasciculus *n* (*pl* **fasciculi**) (*anat*) a bundle of nerve fibers; a fascicle.

fascinate *vt* to hold the attention of, to attract irresistibly.—**fascination** *n*.

fascinating *adj* having great interest or charm.

fascine *n* a long bundle of sticks bound together, used for fortifying ditches, building earthworks, etc.

fascioliasis *n* a disease of the liver and bile ducts caused by the organism *Fasciola hepatica* or liver fluke.

Fascism *n* a system of government characterized by dictatorship, belligerent nationalism, racism, and militarism.—**Fascist** *n*, *adj*.

fash *vti* (*Scot*) to bother, worry. * *n* worry; trouble.

fashion *n* the current style of dress, conduct, speech, etc; the manner or form of appearance or action. * *vt* to make in a particular form; to suit or adapt.—**fashioner** *n*.

fashionable *adj* conforming to the current fashion; attracting or frequented by people of fashion.—**fashionably** *adv*.

FASI *abbr* = Fellow of the Architects and Surveyors Institute.

FASS *abbr* = Federation of Associations of Specialists and Sub-contractors.

Fassbinder, Rainer Werner (1946–82) German film director whose films show the underside of the German "economic miracle" but his analysis of oppression is by no means simplistic.

Fassett *n* **Kaffe** (1937–) American designer noted for his bold use of color in knitting patterns, fabric, and interiors.

FASST *abbr* = Farming for Agriculturally Sustainable Systems in Tasmania; Friends of Aerospace Supporting Science and Technology.

fast[1] *adj* swift, quick; (*clock*) ahead of time; firmly attached, fixed; (*color, dye*) non-fading; wild, promiscuous. * *adv* firmly, thoroughly, rapidly, quickly.

fast[2] *vi* to go without all or certain foods. * *n* a period of fasting.

FAST *abbr* = Federation Against Software Theft.

fastback *n* a car with a roof that slopes to the back.

fast breeder reactor *n* a nuclear reactor that produces more fissile material than it uses.

fast buck *n* (*inf*) money acquired quickly and easily, and possibly by dishonest means.

fasten *vti* to secure firmly; to attach; to fix or direct (the eyes, attention) steadily.

fastener, fastening *n* a clip, catch, etc for fastening.

fast food *n* food, such as hamburgers, kebabs, pizzas, etc prepared and served quickly.

fast-forward *vt* to move (video or music tape, etc) on at high speed.

fast ice *n* a large area of sea ice joined to ice on the land that breaks up to form ice floes and pack ice.

fastidious *adj* hard to please; daintily refined; over-sensitive.—**fastidiously** *adv*.—**fastidiousness** *n*.

fastigiate *adj* (*biol*) narrowing at the apex.

fastness *n* swiftness; colorfast quality; a stronghold.

fast one *n* (*inf*) a deceptive or dishonest trick.

fast-talk *vt* to persuade by fluent or deceptive talk.—**fast talker** *n*.

fast track *n* a hectic and competitive lifestyle or career. * *vt* to speed up a process.—**fast-track** *adj*.

fat *adj* (**fatter, fattest**) plump; thick; fertile; profitable. * *n* an oily or greasy material found in animal tissue and plant seeds; the richest or best part of anything; a superfluous part.—**fatness** *n*. *See also* **adipose tissue.**

FAT *see* **file allocation table.**

fatal *adj* causing death; disastrous (to); fateful.—**fatally** *adv*.

fatalism *n* belief that all events are predetermined by fate and therefore inevitable; acceptance of this doctrine.—**fatalist** *n*.—**fatalistic** *adj*.

fatality *n* (*pl* **fatalities**) a death caused by a disaster or accident; a person killed in such a way; a fatal power or influence.

fat cat *n* (*sl*) a rich person.

fate *n* the ultimate power that predetermines events, destiny; the ultimate end, outcome; misfortune, doom, death.

fated *adj* doomed; destined by fate.

fateful *adj* having important, usu unpleasant, consequences.—**fatefully** *adv*.

Fates *npl* (*myth*) in Greek and Roman mythology, the sisters who were engaged in spinning the thread of human life. Clotho put the wool for the thread of life round the spindle, Lachesis spun it,, and Atropos cut it when the time had come.

fath. *abbr* = fathom.

fathead *n* (*inf*) an idiot.

father *n* a male parent; an ancestor; a founder or originator; (*with cap*) God; a title of respect applied to monks, priests, etc. * *vt* to be the father of; to found, originate.—**fatherhood** *n*.

father-in-law *n* (*pl* **fathers-in-law**) the father of one's husband or wife.

fatherland *n* one's native country.

fatherless *adj* without a living father.

fatherly *adj* pertaining to a father; kind, affectionate, as a father. * *adv* like a father.

fathogram *n* a chart of the sea floor obtained by taking echo soundings.

fathom *n* a measurement of sea depth. 1 fathom = 6 feet (1.829 meters), 100 fathoms = 1 cable, and 1000 fathoms = 1 nautical mile. * *vt* to measure the depth of; to understand.

Fathy *n* **Hassan** (1900–) Egyptian architect. His notable works include village of New Gournia, Luxor.

fatidic, fatidical *adj* having the gift of prophecy.

fatigue *n* tiredness from physical or mental effort; the tendency of a material to break under repeated stress; any of the menial or manual tasks performed by military personnel; (*pl*) the clothing worn on fatigue or in the field. * *vti* (**fatiguing, fatigued**) to make or become tired.

fatling *n* a young animal fattened for slaughter.

fats *npl* (*chem*) a group of organic compounds that occur widely in plants and animals and serve as long-term energy stores.

fatten *vt* to make fat or fleshy; to make abundant.—**fattening** *adj*.

fat transfer *n* a cosmetic surgery procedure to take fat from parts of the body, e.g. hips, and insert it in the face to reduce wrinkling.

fatty *adj* (**fattier, fattiest**) resembling or containing fat. * *n* (*pl* **fatties**) (*inf*) a fat person.

F

fatty acids *npl* (*chem*) a class of organic compounds containing a long hydrophobic hydrocarbon chain and a terminal carboxylic acid group which is extremely hydrophilic.

fatuous *adj* foolish, idiotic.—**fatuously** *adv*.—**fatuousness** *n*.—**fatuity** *n*.

fatwa, fatwah *n* a decision by a mufti or Muslim judge.

faubourg *n* a suburb, esp of Paris in France.

faucal *adj* deeply guttural; (*anat*) of the fauces.

fauces *n* (*pl* **fauces**) (*anat*) the upper part of the throat.

faucet *n* a fixture for draining off liquid (as from a pipe or cask); a device controlling the flow of liquid through a pipe or from a container (—*also* **tap**).

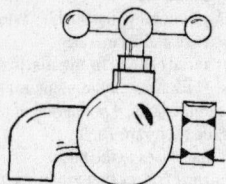

faugh *interj* an expression of disgust or abhorrence.

Faulkner *n* 1. **Kate** (*d.* 1898) British decorator who painted tiles for her brother's company, Morris, Marshall, Faulkner & Co. 2. **William [Harrison]** (1897–1962) American novelist; winner of the 1949 Nobel prize for literature. His best-known work is *The Sound and the Fury*.

fault[1] *n* a failing, defect; a minor offence; (*tennis, etc*) an incorrect serve or other error. * *vt* to find fault with, blame. * *vi* to commit a fault.

fault[2] *n* (*geol*) a flat plane caused by the brittle deformation of rocks that are displaced on one side of the fault plane relative to the other.

fault *see* **folds and faults**.

fault breccia *n* (*geol*) a zone composed of broken, angular, and crushed rock fragments generated by movement along a fault.

fault-finding *adj* censorious, critical.—**fault-finder** *n*.

faultless *adj* without fault; perfect; blameless.—**faultlessly** *adv*.—**faultlessness** *n*.

faulty *adj* (**faultier, faultiest**) imperfect; defective; wrong.—**faultily** *adv*.—**faultiness** *n*.

Faun *n* (*Roman myth*) a rural deity or demi-god, with the tail, ears, and horns of a goat, similar to a Satyr.

fauna *n* (*pl* **faunas, faunae**) the animals of a region, period, or specific environment.

Fauna *n* (*Roman myth*) the female complement of Faunus, also called Bona Dea.

FAUNA *abbr* = Friends of Animals Under Abuse.

Faunus *n* (*Roman myth*) an ancient king who instructed his subjects in agriculture and the management of flocks and was afterwards worshiped as the god of fields and shepherds.

Fauré *n* **Gabriel Urbain** (1845–1924) French composer, organist, and teacher. His Requiem Mass has become one of his best-known compositions.

Faustulus *n* (*Roman myth*) the shepherd who found the abandoned twins Romulus and Remus.

faute de mieux (*French*) in the absence of anything better.

fauteuil *n* (*French*) an armchair; a stall in a theater.

Fauves, Fauvists *n* a group of French painters including Matisse, Derain, Vlaminck, and others, who painted in a particularly vivid and colorful style.

fauxbourdon *n* (*mus*) (*French*) a 15th-century continental technique of improvising a bass part for a plainsong melody.

faux pas *n* (*pl* **faux pas**) (*French*) an embarrassing social blunder.

favela *n* a South American term for a shanty town outside a city.

faveolate *adj* honeycombed.

favism *n* (*med*) an inherited disorder that takes the form of severe hemolytic anemia (destruction of red blood cells), brought on by eating broad beans.

favonian *adj* of or pertaining to the west wind; (*poet*) favorable.

favor, favour *n* goodwill; approval; a kind or helpful act; partiality; a small gift given out at a party; (*usu pl*) a privilege granted or conceded, esp sexual. * *vt* to regard or treat with favor; to show support for; to oblige (with); to afford advantage to, facilitate.

favorable, favourable *adj* expressing approval; pleasing; propitious; conducive (to).—**favorably, favourably** *adv*.

favorite, favourite *n* a favored person or thing; a competitor expected to win. * *adj* most preferred.

favoritism, favouritism *n* the showing of unfair favor.

Favorites *n* (*comput*) the Microsoft Internet Explorer™ equivalent to Bookmarks in Netscape Navigator™. It enables the user to build up a list of frequently visited sites.

Favre-Pinsard *n* **Gisèle** (*fl.*1930s–40s) French ceramicist who co-founded Les Quatre Potiers.

FAW *abbr* = Federation of Army Wives.

FAWC *abbr* = Farm Animal Welfare Council.

Fawcett *n* **Dame Millicent [Millicent Garrett]** (1847–1929) English feminist. She became first president of the National Union of Women Suffrage Societies (1897–1919), and opposed the more militant tactics of Pankhurst.

fawn[1] *n* a young deer; a yellowish-brown color. * *adj* fawn-colored.

fawn[2] *vi* (*dogs, etc*) to crouch, etc in a show of affection; to flatter in an obsequious manner.—**fawner** *n*.—**fawning** *n*.

fax *n* a document sent by facsimile transmission; a device for sending faxes. * *vt* to send (a document) by facsimile transmission.

fay *n* a fairy.

Faylinn *n* (*Irish Celtic myth*) Faylinn was the kingdom of diminutive people who were ruled over by Iubdan.

Fayum, Faiyum, Fayoum *n* a large natural basin near the west bank of the River Nile about 50 miles south of Cairo.

faze *vt* (*inf*) to disturb; to discompose, to disconcert; to daunt.

Fazioli *n* **Domenico** (1937–) Italian architect and furniture designer.

fb *abbr* = full back; freight bill.

f.b. *abbr* = freight bill.

FB *abbr* = Faculty of Building; Federation of Bakers; Fenian Brotherhood; Free Baptist; fire brigade.

FBA *abbr* = Farm Buildings Association; Federation of Bloodstock Agents; Federation of British Astrologers; Fellow of the British Academy; Freshwater Biological Association; Fur Breeders Association.

FBAA *abbr* = Fellow of the British Association of Accountants and Auditors.

FBAE *abbr* = Fellow of the British Academy of Experts.

FBDO *abbr* = Fellow of the Association of British Dispensing Opticians.

FBEI *abbr* = Fellow of the Institution of Body Engineers.

FBEng *abbr* = Fellow of the Association of Building Engineers.

FBI *abbr* = Federal Bureau of Investigation; Federation of British Industries.

FBIBA *abbr* = Fellow of the British Insurance Brokers' Association.

FBID *abbr* = Fellow of the British Institute of Interior Design.

FBIM *abbr* = Fellow of the British Institute of Management.

FBIPP *abbr* = Fellow of the British Institute of Professional Photography.

FBIS *abbr* = Foreign Broadcast Information Service.

FBIST *abbr* = Fellow of the British Institute of Surgical Technologists.

FBM *abbr* = fleet ballistic missile.

FBMA *abbr* = Finnish Boat and Motor Association.

FBOA *abbr* = Fellow of the British Optical Association.

FBPS *abbr* = Fellow of the British Psychological Society.

FBR *abbr* = fast-breeder reactor.

FBS *abbr* = Fellow of the Botanical Society.

FBT *abbr* = Fellow of the Association of Beauty Teachers.

FBTO *abbr* = Federation of British Trawler Officers.

FBW *abbr* = fly by wire.

fc. *abbr* = franc.

FC *abbr* = Fighter Command; Football Club; Forestry Commission; Free Church.

FCA *abbr* = Fellow of the (Institute of) Chartered Accountants; Fishing Clubs of Australia.

F C and S, f. c. and s. *abbr* (*transp*) = free of capture and seizure.

fcap. *abbr* = foolscap.

FCBSI *abbr* = Fellow of the Chartered Building Societies Institute.

FCC *abbr* = Federal Communications Commission; First Class Certificate.

FCCA *abbr* = Fellow of the Chartered Association of Certified Accountants.

FCDRC *abbr* = Family & Community Dispute Research Center.

FCEA *abbr* = Fellow of the Association of Cost and Executive Accountants.

FCES *abbr* = Fellow of the Faculty of Executive Secretaries.

FCF *abbr* = Fellow of the Faculty of Community Finance.

FCFC *abbr* = Free Church Federal Council.

FCFI *abbr* = Fellow of the Clothing and Footwear Institute.

FCGI *abbr* = Fellow of the City and Guilds of London Institute.

FCH *abbr* = Flower Council of Holland.

FCI *abbr* = Foreign and Commonwealth Institute.

FCIA *abbr* = Fellow of the Corporation of Insurance Agents.

FCIB *abbr* = Fellow of the Chartered Institute of Bankers.

FCIBSE *abbr* = Fellow of the Chartered Institution of Building Services Engineers.

FCIC *abbr* = Federal Consumer Information Center; Federal Crop Insurance Corporation.

FCII *abbr* = Fellow of the Chartered Insurance Institute.

FCILA *abbr* = Fellow of the Chartered Institute of Loss Adjusters.

FCIM *abbr* = Fellow of the Chartered Institute of Marketing.

FCIMA *abbr* = Fellow of the Chartered Institute of Management Accountants.

FCIOB *abbr* = Fellow of the Chartered Institute of Building.

FCIPS *abbr* = Fellow of the Chartered Institute of Purchasing and Supply.

FCIS *abbr* = Fellow of the Institute of Chartered Secretaries and Administrators.

FCIT *abbr* = Fellow of the Chartered Institute of Transport.

FCJ *abbr* = Faithful Companions of Jesus.

FCM *abbr* = Friends of Cathedral Music.

FCMA *abbr* = Fellow of the Institute of Cost and Management Accountants.

fco. *abbr* = franco.

FCO *abbr* = Foreign and Commonwealth Office.

FCollP *abbr* = Ordinary Fellow of the College of Preceptors.

FCOphth *abbr* = Fellow of the College of Ophthalmology.

F corona *n* the outermost region of the Sun's corona.

fcp. *abbr* = foolscap.

FCP *abbr* = Fellow of the College of Preceptors.

FCPM *abbr* = Fellow of the Confederation of Professional Management.

FCPWA *abbr* = Fellow of the Faculty of Community, Personal and Welfare Accounting.

FCPWG *abbr* = Federal Credit Policy Working Group.

FCS *abbr* = Fellow of the Chemical Society.

f.c.s., FCS *abbr* (*transp*) = free of capture and seizure.

fcs. *abbr* = francs.

FCSA *abbr* = Fellow of the Institute of Chartered Secretaries and Administrators.

FCSD *abbr* = Fellow of the Chartered Society of Designers.

FCSP *abbr* = Fellow of the Chartered Society of Physiotherapy.

FCST *abbr* = Fellow of the College of Speech Therapists.

FCT *abbr* = Fellow of the Association of Corporate Treasurers.

fd *abbr* = flight deck; focal distance; free delivery; free dispatch.

FD *abbr* = Financial Director; (*Latin*) *Fidei Defensor*, *Fidei Defensatrix*, "Defender of the Faith."

FDA *abbr* = Food and Drugs Administration.

FDC *abbr* = (philately) first-day cover; (*French*) *fleur de coin*, "excellent impression" (referring to coins in mint condition).

FDF *abbr* = Food and Drink Federation.

FDFU *abbr* = Federation of Documentary Film Units.

FDIC *abbr* = Federal Deposit Insurance Corporation

FDPA *abbr* = Furniture Design Protection Association.

FDR *abbr* = Franklin Delano Roosevelt (president); (*German*)*Freie Demokratische Republik*, "Free Democratic Republic" (formerly West Germany).

FDS *abbr* = Fellow in Dental Surgery.

FDTF *abbr* = Food, Drink and Tobacco Federation (Eire).

Fe *symbol* (*chem*) iron (element).

f.e. *abbr* = for example.

Fe. *abbr* = February.

FE *abbr* = further education.

fealty *n* (*pl* **fealties**) (*feudal society*) the loyalty due from a vassal to his feudal lord.

fear *n* an unpleasant emotion excited by danger, pain, etc; a cause of fear; anxiety; deep reverence. * *vt* to feel fear, be afraid of; to be apprehensive, anxious; to be sorry. * *vi* to be afraid or apprehensive.—**fearless** *adj*.—**fearlessly** *adv*.—**fearlessness** *n*.

Fear *n* **Jeffrey** (1945–) Canadian designer of contract furniture.

fearful *adj* causing intense fear; timorous; apprehensive (of); (*inf*) very great, very bad.—**fearfully** *adv*.

fearless *adj* brave, intrepid.—**fearlessly** *adv*.—**fearlessness** *n*.

fearnought, fearnaught *n* a strong woolen cloth.

fearsome *adj* causing fear, frightful.

feasible *adj* able to be done or implemented, possible.—**feasibly** *adv*.—**feasibility** *n*.

feast *n* an elaborate meal prepared for some special occasion; something that gives abundant pleasure; a periodic religious celebration. * *vi* to have or take part in a feast. * *vt* to entertain with a feast.—**feaster** *n*.

feasts *see* **Passover, Penticost, Tabernacles**.

feat *n* an action of remarkable strength, skill, or courage.

feather *n* any of the light outgrowths that form the covering of a bird, consisting of a hollow central shaft with a vane of fine barbs on each side; a plume; something resembling a feather; the water thrown up by the turn of the blade of an oar. * *vt* to ornament with feathers; to turn (an oar or propeller blade) so that the edge is foremost.—**feathering** *n*.—**feathery** *adj*.

feather bed *n* a mattress stuffed with feathers.

featherbedding *n* the practice of overmanning or limiting production to ensure maximum employment

featherbrain *or* **featherhead** *n* (*inf*) a silly, forgetful person.

featherbrained *adj* frivolous, giddy.

featheredge *n* a thin piece of board with one wedge-shaped side.

featherstitch *n* a zigzag stitch with a featherlike appearance.

featherweight *n* a lightweight thing or person; an insignificant thing or person; a boxer weighing from 118–126 lbs (53.5–57 kg); a wrestler weighing from 127–137 lbs (58–62 kg).

feathery *adj* like or covered with feathers.—**featheriness** *n*.

feature *n* any of the parts of the face; a characteristic trait of something; a special attraction or distinctive quality of something; a prominent newspaper article, etc. * *vti* to make or be a feature of (something).

featureless *adj* lacking prominent or distinctive features.

Feb. *abbr* = February.

FEB *abbr* = Federal Executive Board.

febrifuge *n* a drug that reduces fever.—**febrifugal** *adj*.

febrile *adj* having a fever; feverish.

February *n* (*pl* **Februaries**) the second month of the year, having 28 days (or 29 days in leap years).

FEC *abbr* = Federal Election Commission; Fair Employment Commission (N. Ireland); Fluid Engineering Center; Free Europe Committee.

fec. *abbr* (*Latin*) = *fecit*, "he made" or "she made."

feces, faeces *npl* stools; excrement; the end waste products of digestion, which are formed in the colon and discharged via the anus.—**fecal, faecal** *adj*.

FECI *abbr* = Fellow of the Institute of Employment Consultants.

feckless *adj* incompetent, untrustworthy.—**fecklessly** *adv*.—**fecklessness** *n*.

feculent *adj* muddy, turbid; full of dregs or sediment.—**feculence** *n*.

fecund *adj* fertile, prolific.—**fecundity** *n*.

fecundate *vt* to impregnate.—**fecundation** *n*.

fed *see* **feed**.

Fed. *abbr* = Federal.

Fed. Rep. *abbr* = Federal Reporter.

FEDA *abbr* = Further Education Development Association.

fedayee *n* (*pl* **fedayeen**) an Arab commando or guerrilla.

FEDC *abbr* = Federation of Engineering Design Consultants.

federal *adj* designating or of a union of states, etc, in which each member surrenders some of its power to a central authority; of a central government of this type.—**federalism** *n*.—**federalist** *n*.—**federally** *adv*.

Federal Arts Project *n* a series of American government aid schemes to assist artists during the years of the Depression (1933–43).

Federal Reserve Bank *n* one of the twelve banks that form the Federal Reserve System in the USA.

Federal Reserve System *n* the organization consisting of twelve banks situated in various cities in the USA which acts as the central bank of the USA.

federal tax lien *n* (*law*) the right of the Internal Revenue Service (IRS) to make a claim to or sell any property the tax payer owns if the tax payer did not pay any or all of his federal income tax.

federalism *n* a two-tier system of government designed to allow regions to have some control over their own affairs.

federalize *vt* to unite (states, etc) in a federal union; to put under federal authority.—**federalization** *n*.

federate *vti* to unite in a federation. * *adj* united in a league; on a federal basis.—**federative**.*adj*.

federation *n* a union of states, groups, etc, in which each subordinates its power to a central authority; a federated organization.

federmesser *n* (*archeo*) small blades produced by Upper Paleolithic peoples in the northern Europe during the latter part of the last Ice Age (Pleistocene).

FEDIX *abbr* = Federal Information Exchange Inc.

fedora *n* a soft felt hat with a curled brim and a crown creased lengthways.

FEDRIP *abbr* = Federal Research in Progress Database.

fee *n* the price paid for the advice or service of a professional; a charge for some privilege, as membership of a club; (*law*) an inheritance in land.

feeble *adj* weak, ineffective.—**feebly** *adv*.—**feebleness** *n*.

feeble-minded *adj* mentally defective; of low intelligence.

feed *vb* (**feeding, fed**) *vt* to give food to; to give as food to; to supply with necessary material; (*comput*) to supply paper to a printer; to gratify. * *vi* to consume food. * *n* food for animals; material fed into a machine; the part of a machine supplying this material.

feedback *n* a return to the input of part of the output of a system; information about a product, service, etc returned to the supplier for purposes of evaluation.

feedback mechanism *n* (*biol*) a control mechanism that uses the products of a process to regulate that same process by activating or repressing it.

feedbag *n* a bag containing fodder hung from a horse's muzzle for feeding; **to put on the feedbag** (*sl*) to eat.

feeder *n* a person or thing that feeds; a baby's feeding-bottle; a device for supplying material to a machine; a subsidiary road, railway, etc acting as a link with the central transport network.

feel *vb* (**feeling, felt**) *vt* to perceive or explore by the touch; to find one's way by cautious trial; to be conscious of, experience; to have a vague or instinctual impression of; to believe, consider. * *vi* to be able to experience the sensation of touch; to be affected by; to convey a certain sensation when touched. * *n* the sense of touch; feeling; a quality as revealed by touch.

feeler *n* a tactile organ (as a tentacle or antenna) of an animal; a tentative approach or suggestion to test another person's reactions.

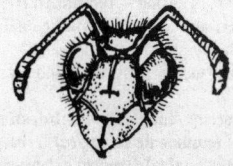

feel-good *adj* that which generates the feeling of well-being; feel-good factor.

feeling *n* the sense of touch; mental or physical awareness; a physical or mental impression; a state of mind; sympathy; emotional sensitivity; a belief or opinion arising from emotion; (*pl*) emotions, sensibilities.

FEEM *abbr* = Federation of European Explosive Manufacturers.

fee simple *n* (*pl* **fees simple**) (*law*) an inheritable estate without restrictions as to the category of heir.

feet *see* **foot**.

FEFG *abbr* = Far East Fracture Group.

Fehling's test *n* a test, now replaced by more modern methods, for detecting the presence of sugar in the urine.

feign *vt* to invent; to pretend.

Feininger *n* **Lyonel** (1871–1956) American painter. He was in Europe from 1887 until 1937, and from 1919 until 1933 he taught at the Bauhaus. His work incorporates cubist and futurist features.

feint *n* a pretended attack, intended to take the opponent off his guard, as in boxing.— *also vi.*

FEIS *abbr* = Fellow of the Educational Institute of Scotland.

feisty *adj* (**feistier, feistiest**) (*sl*) exuberant; frisky; touchy; aggressive.

FELASA *abbr* = Federation of European Laboratory Animal Science Associations.

Feldman *n* **Morton** (1926–87) American composer who experimented with alternative forms of music and music notation. His most noted pieces include *Projections* (chamber music) and *Vertical Thoughts* (keyboard pieces).

feldspar *n* (*geol*) any member of the group of hard rock-forming minerals.—*also* **felspar**.—**feldspathic, felspathic** *adj*.

Felicitas, Saint *see* Perpetua.

felicitate *vt* to congratulate.—**felicitation** *n*.

felicitous *adj* (*words, etc*) apt, well-chosen; agreeable in manner; happy.— **felicitously** *adv*.

felicity *n* (*pl* **felicities**) happiness; apt and pleasing style in writing, speech, etc.

feline *adj* of cats; cat-like.—**felinity** *n*.

Felix *n* (*Bible*) Roman governor of Judea before whom Paul appeared for trial .

fell[1] *n* an open mountainside of moors and rough grazing.

fell[2] *see* **fall**.

fell[3] *vt* to cut, beat, or knock down; to kill, to sew (a seam) by folding one raw edge under the other.

fell[4] *n* a skin, hide, pelt.

fell[5] *adj* (*poet*) cruel, fierce, bloody, deadly.

fellah *n* (*pl* **fellahs, fellahin, fellaheen**) an Arab peasant.

fellatio *n* sexual stimulation of the penis with the mouth.

Fellini *n* **Federico** (1920–93) Italian film director whose best known film is *La Dolce Vita* (1960).

felloe, felly *n* (*pl* **felloes, fellies**) one of the curved pieces of wood which form the outer section of a wheel; the outer section of a wheel, the circumference.

fellow *n* an associate; a comrade; an equal in power, rank, or position; the other of a pair, a mate; a member of the governing body in some colleges and universities; a member of a learned society; (*inf*) a man or boy. * *adj* belonging to the same group or class.

fellow feeling *n* mutual sympathy or understanding; an experience held in common.

fellowship *n* companionship; a mutual sharing; a group of people with the same interests; the position held by a college fellow.

fellow traveler *n* a traveling companion; a non-Communist who openly or secretly supports the Communist Party.

felo de se *n* (*pl* **felones de se, felos de se**) the act of suicide; a person who commits suicide.

felon *n* a person guilty of a felony.

felonious *adj* done with the intention of committing a crime; criminal; malignant.— **feloniously** *adv*.—**feloniousness** *n*.

felony *n* (*pl* **felonies**) (*formerly*) a grave crime.

Fels *n* **Jerry** (1917–1996) American costume jeweler.

felspar *see* **feldspar**.

felt[1] *see* **feel**.

felt[2] *n* a fabric made from woolen fibers, often mixed with fur or hair, pressed together. * *vti* to make into or become like felt.

felting *n* the material from which felt is made; the process of manufacturing felt.

felucca *n* a small boat with oars and lateen sails, used in the Mediterranean.

fem. *abbr* = feminine.

FEMA *abbr* = Federal Emergency Management Agency

female *adj* of the sex that produces young; of a woman or women; (*pipe, plug, etc*) designed with a hollow part for receiving an inserted piece. * *n* a female animal or plant.

female impersonator *n* a male stage performer who acts and dresses like a woman.

FEMC *abbr* = Federation of Earth Moving Contractors.

feminine *adj* of, resembling or appropriate to women; (*gram*) of that gender to which words denoting females belong.—**femininity** *n*.

feminine cadence *n* (*mus*) an ending in which the final chord occurs on a weak beat of the bar and not the more usual strong beat.

feminism *n* the movement to win political, economic, and social equality for women.—**feminist** *adj, n*.

feminize *vti* to make or become feminine.—**feminization** *n*.

femme de chambre *n* (*pl* **femmes de chambre**) (*French*) a chambermaid.

femme fatale *n* (*pl* **femmes fatales**) (*French*) a dangerously seductive woman.

femoral *adj* the term used to describe the femur or that area of the thigh, e.g. femoral artery, vein, nerve, and canal.

femur *n* (*pl* **femurs, femora**) the thigh bone, which is the long bone extending from the hip to the knee and is the strongest bone in the body.

fen *n* an area of low-lying marshy or flooded land.

fen *see* **yuan**.

fence *n* a barrier put round land to mark a boundary, or prevent animals, etc from escaping; a receiver of stolen goods. * *vt* to surround with a fence; to keep (out) as by a fence. * *vi* to practice fencing; to make evasive answers; to act as a fence for stolen goods.—**fencer** *n*.

fencing *n* fences; material for making fences; the art of fighting with foils or other types of sword.

fend *vi* (*with* **for**) to provide a livelihood for.

fender *n* anything that protects or fends off something else, as old tires along the side of a vessel, or the part of a car body over the wheel.

fenestrated, fenestrate *adj* having windows.

fenestration *n* (*archit*) the design and arrangement of windows in a building.

feng shui *n* a form of geomancy with it base in Chinese mythology concerning the placement positioning of buildings and household items and their relationship to their surroundings as they affect people.

fennec *n* a type of small fox, found in Africa.

fennel *n* a European herb of the carrot family grown for its foliage and aromatic seeds; a herb grown for its edible bulbous stem tasting of aniseed.

fennelflower *n* one of a variety of Mediterranean plants, with white, blue, or yellow flowers.—*also* **love-in-a-mist**.

Fennemore *n* **Thomas Acland** (1922–55) British pottery, wallpaper and textile designer.

fenny *adj* marshy.

fenugreek *n* a Mediterranean plant with white flowers and pungent seeds.

feoff *see* **fief**.

FEPOWA *abbr* = Far East Prisoners of War Association.

FERA *abbr* = Federal Emergency Relief Administration.

feral, ferine *adj* wild, untamed; like a wild beast.

Ferber *n* **Edna** (1885–1968) American writer and winner of the Pulitzer prize for *So Big* (1924).

FERC *abbr* = Federal Energy Regulatory Commission.

fer-de-lance *n* a yellowish, highly poisonous snake of tropical America.

Ferdia *n* (*Irish Celtic myth*) the foster brother and friend of Cuchulainn. Legend has it that he was goaded into single combat with Cuchulainn. Ferdia was killed by Cuchulainn, who was grief-stricken.

Ferdinand V *n* [Ferdinand the Catholic] (1452–1516) Ferdinand became the first king of a united Spain. He brought the Inquisition into Spain in 1478, and financed Columbus's voyage to the New World.

feretory *n* (*pl* **feretories**) a shrine for the relics of a saint; a chapel for keeping this.

Fergus mac Leda *n* (*Irish Celtic myth*) king of Ulster at the time that Iubdan and his wife went from Faylinn to visit Ulster to see for themselves what was to them a race of giants.

Fergus mac Roth *n* (*Irish Celtic myth*) king of Ulster. He was in love with Nessa, and gave up his throne for a year to her son, Conchobar mac Nessa.

Fergus Mor *n* (*d.* 501) king of Scots. The son of Erc, he was the ruler of the kingdom of Dalriada in Argyll. All kings of Dalriada for the following 343 years claimed descent from either Fergus or Loarn, another son of Erc.

Ferguson *n* **Howard** (1908–99) Northern Irish composer and teacher. His works include the ballet, *Chauntecleer, Diversions on Ulster Airs* for orchestra, as well as chamber and piano music.

Fergusson *n* **John Duncan** (1874–1961) Scottish painter; one of the Scottish colorists.

ferial *adj* (*RC Church*) describes an ordinary day, not a festival or a fast day.

Ferlinghetti *n* **Lawrence** (1919–) American poet and publisher whose bookshop in San Francisco was a breeding ground for Beat Generation writers.

Fermat *n* **Pierre de** (1601–65) French mathematician; the founder of number theory. He initiated, with Pascal, the study of probability theory.

fermata *see* **pause**.

ferment *n* an agent causing fermentation, as yeast; excitement, agitation. * *vti* to (cause to) undergo fermentation; to (cause to) be excited or agitated.— **fermentable** *adj*.—**fermenter** *n*.

fermentation *n* the breakdown of complex molecules in organic components caused by the influence of yeast or other substances.

fermentative *adj* of or pertaining to fermentation; capable of or causing fermentation.

Fermi *n* Enrico (1901–54) Italian-born American physicist; winner of the Nobel prize for physics (1938) for his work in nuclear science. He built the first nuclear reactor at Chicago (1942).

Fermilab *abbr* = Fermi National Accelerator Laboratory

fermion *n* a type of subatomic particle.

fermium *n* an artificially-produced radioactive metallic element.

fern *n* any of a large class of nonflowering plants having roots, stems, and fronds, and reproducing by spores.—**ferny** *adj*.

fernery *n* (*pl* **ferneries**) a place for growing ferns.

ferny *adj* (**fernier, ferniest**) full of ferns; of or characteristic of ferns.

ferocious *adj* savage, fierce.—**ferociously** *adv*.—**ferocity, ferociousness** *n*.

Ferrabosco *n* Alfonso (1543–88) Italian composer who wrote madrigals, motets, and pieces for lute.

ferrate *n* a salt of ferric acid.

ferret *n* a variety of the polecat, used in unearthing rabbits. * *vt* to drive out of a hiding-place; (*with* **out**) to reveal by persistent investigation. * *vi* to hunt with ferrets.—**ferreter** *n*.—**ferrety** *adj*.

Ferrex *n* (*Brit Celtic myth*) a son of Gorboduc and Judon and the brother of Porrex.

ferriage *n* the act of conveying by ferry; the fare paid for this.

ferric *adj* of or containing iron.

Ferrier *n* Kathleen (1912–53) English contralto. The part of Lucretia in Britten's opera *Rape of Lucretia* was written for her (Glyndebourne, 1946).

ferriferous *adj* yielding iron.

Ferris wheel *n* a large upright revolving wheel with suspended seats, popular in amusement parks.

ferroconcrete *n* reinforced concrete.

ferrocyanic acid *n* an acid formed by the union of iron and cyanogen.

ferromagnetism *n* magnetism possessed by iron and some other metals, which is retained even after the removal of the magnetizing field.—**ferromagnetic** *adj*.

ferromanganese *n* an alloy of iron and manganese.

ferrotype *n* a photograph taken on a sensitized iron plate.

ferrous *adj* containing iron.

ferruginous *adj* containing or impregnated with iron; rust-colored, reddish brown.

ferrule *n* a metal ring or cap on a cane, umbrella, etc.—*also* **ferule**.

ferry *vt* (**ferrying, ferried**) to convey (passengers, etc) over a stretch of water; to transport from one place to another, esp along a regular route. * *n* (*pl* **ferries**) a boat used for ferrying; a ferrying service; the location of a ferry.—**ferryman** *n* (*pl* **ferrymen**).

fertile *adj* able to bear offspring; (*land*) easily supporting plants and vegetation; (*animals*) capable of breeding; (*eggs*) able to grow and develop; prolific; (*mind, brain*) inventive.—**fertility, fertileness** *n*.

fertility *n* the state or quality of being fertile.

fertility drug *n* any of various compounds used to stimulate ovulation in (otherwise infertile) women.

fertility rate *n* the number of live births in a given population during a given period.

fertilization *n* the fusion of sperm and ovum to form a zygote, which then undergoes cell division to become an embryo.

fertilize *vt* to make (soil) fertile by adding nutrients; to impregnate; to pollinate.

fertilizer *n* natural organic or artificial substance used to enrich the soil and improve crops and their yield.

ferula *n* (*pl* **ferulas, ferulae**) a genus of plants of the parsley family, from one of which asafetida is produced.

ferule *see* **ferrule**.

fervency *n* earnestness; ardor.

fervent, fervid *adj* passionate; zealous.—**fervently, fervidly** *adv*.—**fervency** *n*.

fervor, fervour *n* intensity of feeling; zeal; warmth.

Fès *n* a city in Morocco.

FES *abbr* = foil, épée, and saber (fencing).

fescue *n* a kind of grass, often grown for pasture and fodder.

fesse *n* (*her*) a broad horizontal band across the middle of a shield.

festal *adj* of a feast or holiday; festive.—**festally** *adv*.

fester *vti* to become or cause to become infected; to suppurate; to rankle.

festival *n* a time of celebration; performances of music, plays, etc given periodically.

festive *adj* merry, joyous.—**festively** *adv*.—**festiveness** *n*.

festivity *n* (*pl* **festivities**) a festive celebration.

festoon *n* a decorative garland of flowers, etc hung between two points. * *vt* to adorn as with festoons.—**festoonery** *n*.

Festus *n* (*Bible*) Roman governor of Judea who succeeded Felix.

FET *abbr* = Future of Europe Trust; field-effect transistor.

feta *n* a type of white goat's milk cheese, esp popular in Greece.

FETA *abbr* = Federation of Environmental Trade Associations; Fire Extinguishing Trades Association.

fetal *adj* pertaining to the fetus.—*also* **foetal**.

FETC *abbr* = Federal Energy Technology Center.

fetch[1] *vt* to go for and bring back; to cause to come; (*goods*) to sell for (a certain price); (*inf*) to deal (a blow, slap, etc); (*with* **up**) to come to stand, arrive at; **fetch and carry** to run errands for another.—**fetcher** *n*.

fetch[2] *n* an apparition of a living person, a wraith; a person's double.

fetching *adj* attractive.—**fetchingly** *adv*.

fête, fete *n* a festival; a usu outdoor sale, bazaar, or entertainment in aid of charity. * *vt* to honor or entertain (as if) with a fête.

fetial *n* (*pl* **fetiales**) a priestly herald in ancient Rome who performed rites accompanying a declaration of war or peace.

feticide *n* the destruction of a fetus in the womb.—*also* **foeticide**.

fetid *adj* stinking.—*also* **foetid**.

fetish, fetich *n* an object believed by primitive peoples to have magical properties; any object or activity regarded with excessive devotion.

fetishism, fetichism *n* the transfer of sexual desire to an inanimate object, or to some part of the body other than the sexual organs; worship of, or belief in, fetishes—**fetishist, fetichist** *n*.

fetlock, fetterlock *n* the joint on a horse's leg behind and above the hoof.

fetter *n* (*usu pl*) a shackle for the feet; anything that restrains. * *vt* to put into fetters; to impede, restrain.—**fetterer** *n*.

fettle *n* good condition or repair.

fettucine, fettuccine, fettucini *n* a kind of pasta cut in strips.

fetus *n* (*pl* **fetuses**) the unborn young of an animal, esp in its later stages; in humans, the offspring in the womb after the eighth week of development until birth.—*also* **foetus** (*pl* **foetuses**).—**fetal, foetal** *adj*.

FEU *abbr* = Further Education Unit.

Feuchère *n* Leon (1804–57) French architect hailed as the greatest decorator of his day.

Feuchtwanger *n* Lion (1884–1958) German novelist who fled to the USA in 1940 and whose best-known work is the historical novel *Jew Süss*.

feud *n* a state of hostilities, esp between individuals, families, or clans; a dispute.—*also vi*.

feud. *abbr* = feudal.

feudal *adj* pertaining to feudalism; (*inf*) old-fashioned, redundant.

feudalism *n* the economic and social system in medieval Europe, in which land, worked by serfs, was held by vassals in exchange for military and other services to overlords.—**feudalist** *n*.—**feudalistic** *adj*.

feudality *n* (*pl* **feudalities**) the state of being feudal; a feudal estate.

feudalize *vt* to make feudal.—**feudalization** *n*.

feudatory *adj* pertaining to, or held by, feudal tenure.

feudist *n* someone taking part in a feud or argument.

feuilleton *n* in France, etc, the section of a newspaper containing reviews, fiction, etc; an article in this; serialization in a newspaper.—**feuilletonist** *n*—**feuilletonistic** *adj*

fever *n* an abnormally increased body temperature; any disease marked by a high fever; a state of restless excitement.—**fevered** *adj*.

feverfew *n* a perennial European herb, formerly used to reduce fevers.

feverish, feverous *adj* having a fever; indicating a fever; restlessly excited.—**feverishly** *adv*.—**feverishness** *n*.

few *adj, n* a small number, not many.—**fewness** *n*.

FEW *abbr* = Freemen of England and Wales.

fey *adj* strange and unusual.—**feyness** *n*.

Feydeau *n* Georges (1862–1921) French dramatist known for his farces, e.g. *A Flea in Her Ear*.

Feynman *n* Richard (1918–88) American physicist who shared the 1965 Nobel prize for physics for his work in quantum electrodynamics.

fez *n* (*pl* **fezzes**) a red brimless high cap, usu with black tassel, worn esp by men in eastern Mediterranean countries.

ff *abbr* = (*Latin*) *fecerunt*, "they made it"; fixed focus; fully fashioned; fully furnished and fitted.

ff *abbr* (*mus*) (*Italian*) = *fortissimo* "very loud."

ff. *abbr* = (*Latin*) *fecerunt*, "they made it"; folios; following (pages); *fortissimo*.

f.f. *abbr* (*photog*) = fixed focus.

FF *abbr* = Feminist Forum; (*Gaelic*) *Fianna Fáil* "Warriors of Ireland," an Irish political party.

f.f.a. *abbr* = foreign freight agent.

f.f.a., FFA *abbr* = free foreign agency; free from alongside (ship); free from average.

FFA *abbr* = Future Farmers of America; South Pacific Forum Fisheries Agency.

FFB *abbr* = Federal Financing Bank; Fellow of the Faculty of Building.

FFBA *abbr* = Fellow of the Faculty of Business Administrators.

FFCA *abbr* = Federal Farm Credit Administration.

FFCI *abbr* = Fellow of the Faculty of Commerce and Industry Ltd.

FFCS *abbr* = Fellow of the Faculty of Secretaries.

FFDO *abbr* = Fellow of the Faculty of Dispensing Opticians.

fff *abbr* (*music*) (*Italian*) = *fortississimo*, "as loud as possible."

FFF *abbr* = Fish Friers' Federation.

FFHC *abbr* = Freedom from Hunger Campaign.

FFHom *abbr* = Fellow of the Faculty of Homeopathy.

FFHS *abbr* = Federation of Family History Societies.

FFI *abbr* = Fellow of the Institute of Journalists.

FFMA *abbr* = Flavor and Fragrance Manufacturers' Association (Japan).

FFMC *abbr* = Federal Financial Managers Council; Federal Farm Mortgage Corporation.

FFP *abbr* = Forests for the People (Sri Lanka); Fund for Peace.

FFPHM *abbr* = Fellow of the Faculty of Public Health Medicine.

FFPHMIrel *abbr* = Fellow of the Faculty of Public Health Medicine, Royal College of Physicians of Ireland.

FFPS *abbr* = Fauna and Flora Preservation Society; Fellow of the Faculty of Physicians and Surgeons.

FFR *abbr* = Fellow of the Faculty of Radiologists.

FFRC *abbr* = Food Freezer Refrigeration Council.

FFRRCSIrel *abbr* = Fellow of the Faculty of Radiologists, Royal College of Surgeons in Ireland.

FFS *abbr* = Fellow of the Faculty of Architects and Surveyors; Farm & Food Society.

FFTA *abbr* = Finnish Foreign Trade Association.

FFTCom *abbr* = Fellow of the Faculty of Teachers in Commerce.

FFVIB *abbr* = Fresh Fruit and Vegetable Information Bureau.

FFVMA *abbr* = Fire Fighting Vehicle Manufacturers Association.

FFV(s) *abbr* = First Families of Virginia.

f.g. *abbr* = field gun; fine grain; friction glaze; fully good.

FG *abbr* = Federal Government.

f.g.a., FGA *abbr* = foreign general average; (*marine ins*) free of general average.

FGA *abbr* = Fellow of the Gemmological Association.

FGCM *abbr* = Field General Court Martial.

f.g.f. *abbr* = fully good, fair.

FGS *abbr* = Fellow of the Geological Society.

FGSA *abbr* = Fellow of the Geological Society of America.

FGSM *abbr* = Fellow of the Guildhall School of Music and Drama.

f.h. *abbr* = (*pharm*) (*Latin*) *fiat haustus*, "let a draft be made"; (*naut*) forehatch.

f/h *abbr* = freehold; fly half; foghorn.

FH *abbr* = fire hydrant.

FH *see* **growth hormone**.

FHA *abbr* = Future Homemakers of America; Federal Housing Administration.

FHC *abbr* = Food Hygiene Center.

FHF *abbr* = Federation of Hardware Factors.

FHFB *abbr* = Federal Housing Finance Board.

FHG *abbr* = Fellow of the Institute of Heraldic and Genealogical Studies.

FHH *abbr* = fetal heart heard.

FHLB *abbr* = Federal Home Loan Bank (Board).

FHNH *abbr* = fetal heart not heard.

f. hosp. *abbr* = field hospital.

fhp *abbr* = friction horsepower.

FHR *abbr* = foetal heart rate; Federal House of Representatives.

FHS *abbr* = Fellow of the Heraldry Society.

FHSM *abbr* = Fellow of the Institute of Health Services Management.

FHWA *abbr* = Federal Highway Administration.

f.i. *abbr* = for instance.

FI *abbr* = Falkland Islands; Fiji Islands; Faeroe Islands.

FI Inst. *abbr* = Fellow of the Imperial Institute.

fi. fa. *abbr* (*legal*) (*Latin*) = *fieri facias*, "see that it is done."

f.i.a., FIA *abbr* (*ins*) = full interest admitted.

FIA *abbr* = Federal Insurance Administration; Fellow of the Institute of Actuaries; Fitness Industry Association; Friends of Israel Association; Fruit Importers Association.

FIAB *abbr* = Fellow of the International Association of Book-keepers.

Fiachna mac Retach *n* (*Irish Celtic myth*) sought the help of Laoghaire mac Crimthann to retrieve his wife and daughter, who had been abducted by Goll of Magh Mell.

Fiachtra *n* (*Irish Celtic myth*) a daughter of Aobh and Lir. She was one of the four children of Lir who were turned into swans by their stepmother, Aoife.

fiacre *n* a type of horse-drawn carriage.

FIAEA *abbr* = Fellow of the Institute of Automotive Engineer Assessors.

FIAgrE *abbr* = Fellow of the Institution of Agricultural Engineers.

Fianarantsoa *n* a city in Madagascar.

fiancé *n* a person engaged to be married.—**fiancée** *nf*.

Fianna *n* (*Irish Celtic myth*) a group of warriors who formed a military elite who guarded the high king of Ireland. At one point they were led by Fionn mac Cumhaill.

FIAP *abbr* = Fellow of the Institution of Analysts and Programmers.

fiard *see* **fjard**.

fiasco *n* (*pl* **fiascos, fiascoes**) a complete and humiliating failure.

fiat *n* an order by authority; a decree.

FIAT *abbr* = (*Italian*) *Fabbrica Italiana Automobili Torino*, "Italian Motor Works, Turin"; Fellow of the Institute of Animal Technicians; Fellow of the Institute of Asphalt Technology; Forest Industries Association of Tasmania.

fiat money *n* money that has been declared by a government to be legal tender, although it has no intrinsic value and is not backed by government reserves.

fib *n* a lie about something unimportant. * *vi* (**fibbing, fibbed**) to tell a gib.—**fibber** *n*.

FIB *abbr* = Fellow of the Institute of British Foundrymen; Fellow of the Institute of Bankers.

FIBA *abbr* = Fellow of the Institution of Business Agents.

FIBC *abbr* = Fellow of the Institute of Building Control.

FIBCM *abbr* = Fellow of the Institute of British Carriage and Automobile Manufacturers.

FIBCO *abbr* = Fellow of the Institution of Building Control Officers.

fiber, fibre *n* a natural or synthetic thread, e.g. from cotton or nylon, which is spun into yarn; a material composed of such yarn; texture; strength of character; a fibrous substance, roughage.—**fibered, fibred** *adj*.

fiberglass, fibreglass *n* glass in fibrous form, often bonded with plastic, used in making various products.

fiber optics, fibre optics *n* (*sing*) the transmission of information in the form of light signals along thin transparent fibers of glass.—**fiber-optic, fibre-optic** *adj*.

fiberoptic endoscopy *n* a method of viewing hollow internal structures, such as the digestive tract and tracheo-bronchial tree, using fiberoptics.

FIBiol *abbr* = Fellow of the Institute of Biology.

FIBP *abbr* = Fellow of the Institute of British Photographers.

fibril, fibrilla *n* (*pl* **fibrils, fibrillae**) a small fiber.—**fibrilar, fibrillar, fibrillose** *adj*.

fibrillation *n* the rapid and irregular twitching of muscle fibers, esp in the heart.

fibrin *n* the end product of the process of blood coagulation, comprising threads of insoluble protein.

fibrinogen *n* a protein in the blood, which causes it to form clots, due to action by the enzyme thrombin.

fibrinous *adj* composed of, or resembling, fibrin.

fibrocystic disease of the pancreas *see* **cystic fibrosis**.

fibroid *adj* (*anat*) containing or resembling fiber. * *n* a benign tumor in the uterus composed of fibrous and muscular tissue and varying in size from fractions of an inch to a mass weighing several pounds..

fibroin *n* a protein that is the main constituent of silk and cobwebs.

fibroma *n* (*pl* **fibromata, fibromas**) a benign fibrous tumor.

fibrosarcoma *n* a malignant tumor of connective tissue, found in the limbs, esp the legs.

fibrosis *n* the abnormal growth of fibrous tissue in an organ or part of the body usually as a result of injury or inflammation. *See also* **cystic fibrosis**

fibrositis *n* inflammation of fibrous connective tissue, muscles, and muscle sheaths, esp in the back, legs, and arms, causing pain and stiffness.

fibrous *adj* composed of fibers.—**fibrousness** *n*.

fibrous tissue *n* a tissue type that occurs abundantly throughout the body. *See* **white fibrous tissue; yellow fibrous tissue.**

fibula[1] *n* (*pl* **fibulae, fibulas**) the outer of the two bones of the lower leg.—**fibular** *adj*.

fibula[2] *n* (*pl* **fibulae, fibulas**) (*archeo*) a decorative metal brooch, usually fashioned in bronze, with a "safety-pin" fastening, designed to secure draped clothing

FIC *abbr* = Federal Information Center.

FICA *abbr* = Forest Industries Campaign Association; Formula 1 Constructors Association.

FICE *abbr* = Fellow of the Institution of Civil Engineers.

fiche *n* (*pl* **fiche**) a microfiche.

FIChemE *abbr* = Fellow of the Institution of Chemical Engineers.

FIChor *abbr* = Fellow of the Benesh Institute of Choreology.

fichu *n* a woman's light three-cornered scarf worn over the neck and shoulders.

fickle *adj* inconstant; capricious.—**fickleness** *n*.

FICM *abbr* = Fellow of the Institute of Credit Management.

FICO *abbr* = Fellow of the Institute of Careers Officers.

FICorr *abbr* = Fellow of the Institute of Corrosion.

FICS *abbr* = Fellow of the Institute of Chartered Shipbrokers.

FICSA *abbr* = Federation of International Civil Servants' Associations.

fict. *abbr* = fiction; (*Latin*) *fictilis*, "made of clay, earthen."

fictile *adj* molded from clay; able to be molded from clay.

fiction *n* an invented story; any literary work with imaginary characters and events, as a novel, play, etc; such works collectively.—**fictional** *adj*.—**fictionally** *adv*.

fictitious *adj* imaginary, not real; feigned.—**fictitiously** *adv*.

fictive *adj* pertaining to fiction; creating or created by the imagination.—**fictively** *adv*.

FICW *abbr* = Fellow of the Institute of Clerks of Works of Great Britain Incorporated.

fid *n* (*naut*) an iron or wooden bar used to support a topmast; a pin used to open the strands of a rope.

fid. *abbr* = fidelity; fiduciary.

FID *abbr* = Falkland Island Dependencies; Field Intelligence Department; Fellow of the Institute of Directors.

FIDA *abbr* = Falkland Islands Development Agency; Federation of Industrial Development Association.

FIDASE *abbr* = Falkland Islands and Dependencies Aerial Survey Expedition.

fidchell *n* (*Irish Celtic myth*) a game like chess, in legends often used as a method of settling disputes. The Welsh equivalent of the game was gwyddbwyll.

Fid. Def. *abbr* (*Latin*) = *Fidei Defensor, Fidei Defensatrix*, "Defender of the Faith."

fiddle *n* (*mus*) a generic term for a range of primitive stringed instruments played with a bow, as used in parts of Asia, Africa and Eastern Europe; (*inf*) a colloquial term for a violin, especially in folk music; (*sl*) a swindle. * *vt* (*inf*) to play on a violin; (*sl*) to swindle; to falsify. * *vi* to handle restlessly, to fidget.—**fiddler** *n*.

fiddle-de-dee *interj* an expression of incredulity or impatience.

fiddle-faddle *n* nonsense; trifles. * *vi* to fuss over unimportant matters.

fiddlehead *n* an ornament at the prow of a ship.

fiddler *n* one who fiddles; (*inf*) a violinist.

fiddlestick *n* a bow for playing the violin.

fiddlesticks *interj* nonsense!

fiddling *adj* trifling, petty.

fidelity *n* (*pl* **fidelities**) faithfulness, loyalty; truthfulness; accuracy in reproducing sound.

fidelity bonus *n* a business reward accorded to loyal customers by a supplier.

fidget *vi* to (cause to) move restlessly. * *n* nervous restlessness; a fussy person.—**fidgetingly** *adv*.—**fidgety** *adj*.

FIDO *abbr* = Film Industry Defense Organization; Forklift Independent Distributors Organization; Frizzier Island Defenders Organization.

FIDTA *abbr* = Fellow of the International Dance Teachers' Association.

fiducial *adj* (*physics*) taken as a standard of reference; based on trust or faith.—**fiducially** *adv*.

fiduciary *adj* of, held or given in trust; (*paper currency*) depending on public confidence for value. * *n* a trustee.

fie *interj* for shame; an expression of disgust or dismay.

FIED *abbr* = Fellow of the Institution of Engineering Designers.

FIEE *abbr* = Fellow of the Institution of Electrical Engineers.

fief *n* (*feudalism*) heritable land held by a vassal; an area in which one has control or influence.—*also* **feoff**.

FIEIE *abbr* = Fellow of the Institution of Electrical and Electronics Incorporated Engineers.

field¹ *n* an area of land cleared of trees and buildings, used for pasture or crops; an area rich in a natural product, e.g. gold, coal; a battlefield; a sports ground; an area affected by electrical, magnetic, or gravitational influence, etc; the area visible through an optical lens; a division of activity, knowledge, etc; all competitors in a contest; (*comput*) a section of a record in a database. * *vt* (*cricket, baseball, etc*) to catch or stop and return the ball as a fielder; to put, e.g. a team, into the field to play; (*inf*) to handle, e.g. questions, successfully. *See also* **electric field**; **magnetic field**.

field² *see* **fjeld**.

Field *n* 1. **Eugene** (1850–95) American journalist and poet who is famous for his nursery rhymes, e.g. "Wynken, Blynken and Nod." 2. **John** (1782–1837) Irish composer and pianist.

FIELD *abbr* = Foundation for International Environmental Law and Development.

field curvature *n* a lens aberration or optical defect in which, over the field of view, only the central region is in sharp focus, the outer sections being brought to a focus in a slightly different plane.

field day *n* a day of sports and athletic competition; (*inf*) any day of unusual happenings or success.

fielder *n* (*cricket, baseball, etc*) a person who is not in the batting side, a person who fields.—*also* **fieldsman** (*pl* **fieldsmen**).

field event *n* (*usu pl*) an athletic competition involving jumping or throwing, as opposed to running.

fieldfare *n* a European thrush, which migrates to Britain for winter.

field glasses *npl* small, portable binoculars for use outdoors.

field hockey *n* an outdoor game played by two teams of 11 players with a ball and clubs curved at one end —*also* **hockey**.

Fielding *n* **Henry** (1707–54) English novelist and dramatist whose greatest work is *Tom Jones* (1749).

fieldmouse *n* a small, nocturnal mouse that lives in woods and fields.

field of view¹ *n* (*astron*) the area in an optical telescope on the celestial sphere, or any large body, which is in view at any one time through the eyepiece.

field of view² *n* a remote sensing term for the angle through which an instrument can sense electromagnetic radiation.

Fields *n* 1. **Dame Gracie [Grace Stansfield]** (1898–1979) English singer and comedienne whose 1930s films, e.g. *Sally in Our Alley* (1931) and *Sing As We Go* (1934), were very popular in England. 2. **W C [William Claude Dukenfield]** (1880–1946) American comedian.

fieldstone *n* stone as found in a field and used unaltered in building.

field systems *or* **Celtic fields** *npl* (*archeo*) patchworks of small squares of land dating mainly from the late Bronze Age.

field test *n* a practical trial in a natural environment, as opposed to a laboratory.

field trip *n* a visit, as by students, to observe and experience something first-hand.

fieldwork *n* research done outside the laboratory or place of work by scientists, archaeologists, social workers, etc.—**fieldworker** *n*.

FIEM *abbr* = Fellow of the Institute of Executives and Managers.

fiend *n* an evil spirit; an inhumanly wicked person; (*inf*) an avid fan.—**fiendish** *adj*.—**fiendishly** *adv*.

fierce *adj* ferociously hostile; angry, violent; intense; strong, extreme.—**fiercely** *adv*.—**fierceness** *n*.

fiery *adj* (**fierier, fieriest**) like or consisting of fire; the color of fire; intensely hot; spicy; passionate, ardent; impetuous; irascible.—**fierily** *adv*.—**fieriness** *n*.

fiesta *n* a religious celebration, a festival, esp in Spain and Latin America.

FIEx *abbr* = Fellow of the Institute of Export.

FIExpE *abbr* = Fellow of the Institute of Explosives Engineers.

FiF *abbr* = Forward in Faith.

FIFA *abbr* (*French*) = *Fédération Internationale de Football Association*, "International Association Football Federation."

fife *n* a type of small flute with a shrill sound used esp in military music to accompany drums.—**fifer** *n*.

fife rail *n* (*naut*) a rail round the mast holding belaying pins.

FIFF *abbr* = Fellow of the Institute of Freight Forwarders.

FIFireE *abbr* = Fellow of the Institution of Fire Engineers.

FIFO *abbr* = first-in-first-out.

FIFST *abbr* = Fellow of the Institute of Food Science and Technology.

fifteen *adj, n* one more than fourteen; the first point scored by a side in a game of tennis; a rugby football team. * *symbol* 15, XV, xv.—**fifteenth** *adj, n*.

fifth¹ *adj, n* last of five; (being) one of five equal parts; a gear in a motor vehicle used when driving at speed.—**fifthly** *adv*.

fifth² *n* (*mus*) an interval of five notes (the first and last notes are counted) or seven semitones (half steps), e.g. from C to G.

fifth column *n* a subversive organization within a country, which is ready to give help to an enemy.—**fifth columnist** *n*.

fifth generation computer *n* (*comput*) the next stage of computer development, which will incorporate technologies such as parallel processing, speech recognition, integrated communications, etc.

fifty *adj, n* (*pl* **fifties**) five times ten. * *symbols* 50, L, l.—**fiftieth** *adj*.

fifty-fifty *adj, adv* (*inf*) evenly, equally; (*chance*) the equal possibility of winning or losing.

fig *n* a tree yielding a soft, pear-shaped fruit; a thing of little or no importance.

fig. *abbr* = figurative; figuratively; figure; figures.

FIGA *abbr* = Fretted Instrument Guild of America.

FIGasE *abbr* = Fellow of the Institution of Gas Engineers.

FIGD *abbr* = Fellow of the Institute of Grocery Distribution.

FIGeol *abbr* = Fellow of the Institution of Geologists.

fight *vb* (**fighting, fought**) *vi* to engage in battle in war or in single combat; to strive, struggle (for). * *vt* to engage in or carry on a conflict with; to achieve (one's way) by fighting; to strive to overcome; (*with* **off**) to repel; to ward off or repress through effort. * *n* fighting; a struggle or conflict of any kind; a boxing match.—**fighting** *n*.

fighter *n* a person who fights; a person who does not yield easily; an aircraft designed to destroy enemy aircraft.

fighting chance *n* a small chance of success given supreme effort.

Figini *n* **Luigi** (1903–84) Italian architect. His notable works include Olivetti Headquarters, Iurea.

figment *n* something imagined or invented.

Figueroa *n* **Leonardo de** (1650–) Spanish architect. His notable works include Salvador Church, Seville.

figurant *n* a ballet dancer who performs as one of a group.—**figurante** *nf*.

figuration *n* the giving of form; representation; a figure, a shape; (*mus*) the use of florid counterpoint.

figurative *adj* metaphorical, not literal; using or full of figures of speech; emblematic; pictorial.—**figuratively** *adv*.

figurative art *n* art that recognizably represents figures, objects, or animals from real life, as opposed to abstract art.—*also* **representational art**.

figure *n* a character representing a number; a number; value or price; bodily shape or form; a graphic representation of a thing, person, or animal; a design; a geometrical form; a statue; appearance; (*mus*) a short musical phrase that is repeated in the course of a composition; a personage; (*dancing, skating*) a set of steps or movements; (*pl*) arithmetic. * *vt* to represent in a diagram or outline; to imagine; (*inf*) to consider; (*inf*) to believe; (*with* **out**) (*inf*) to solve. * *vi* to take a part (in), be conspicuous (in); to calculate.—**figurer** *n*.

figured *adj* depicted as a figure; adorned with figures.

figured bass *n* (*mus*) the bass part of a composition which has numerical figures written below the notes to indicate how the harmony above should be.

figure eight, figure of eight *n* something shaped like the numeral eight; a type of knot; an embroidery stitch; a dance pattern in ice skating.

figurehead *n* a carved figure on the bow of a ship; a nominal head or leader.

figure of speech *n* an expression not intended to be taken literally, as a metaphor or simile.

figure skating *n* ice skating in which prescribed figures are outlined.

figurine *n* a statuette in the shape of a human, animal, or mythical creature, usually having some religious significance.

FIH *abbr* = Fellow of the Institute of Housing.

FIHEC *abbr* = Fellow of the Institute of Home Economics.

FIHIE *abbr* = Fellow of the Institute of Highway Incorporated Engineers.

FIHT *abbr* = Fellow of the Institution of Highways and Transportation.

FIIM *abbr* = Fellow of the Institution of Industrial Managers.

FIIMR *abbr* = Fellow of the Institute of Investment Management and Research.

FIInfSc *abbr* = Fellow of the Institute of Information Scientists.

FIIRSM *abbr* = Fellow of the International Institute of Risk and Safety Management.

FIISE *abbr* = Fellow of the International Institute of Social Economics.

FIISec *abbr* = Fellow of the Institute of Industrial Security.

Fiji *n* a republic of more than 800 islands comprising a part of Melanesia in the Western Pacific.

F

Fijian Dollar *n* currency of Fiji.

FIL *abbr* = Fellow of the Institute of Linguists.

filagree *see* **filigree**.

FILAM *abbr* = Fellow of the Institute of Leisure and Amenity Management.

filament *n* a slender thread or strand; a fiber; the fine wire in an electric light bulb that is made incandescent by current; (*bot*) the anther-bearing stalk of a stamen; (*astron*) a fine thread-like feature seen on the Sun's surface, particularly in the penumbra of a sunspot associated with a gas flow.—**filamentary, filamentous** *adj*.

filar *adj* of or pertaining to thread; (*microscope, etc*) having fine threads in the eyepiece for measuring tiny distances.

filariasis *n* a tropical and subtropical disease caused by nematode worms in the lymphatic system and carried to humans by mosquitoes, causing swelling (elephantiasis).

filar micrometer *n* a set of very fine crosswires which can be moved by a sensitive micrometer screw gauge.

filature *n* the reeling of silk from cocoons; a place where this is done.

filbert *n* the edible nut of the cultivated hazel.

filch *vt* to steal (something of little value); to pilfer.—**filcher** *n*.

file[1] a container for keeping papers, etc, in order; an orderly arrangement of papers; a line of persons or things; (*comput*) a collection of related data under a specific name. * *vt* to dispatch or register; to put on public record. * *vi* to move in a line; to apply.—**filer** *n*.

file[2] *n* a tool, usu steel, with a rough surface for smoothing or grinding. * *vt* to cut or smooth with, or as with, a file; to polish, improve.—**filer** *n*.

file allocation table *n* (*comput*) a table held on a computer disk that keeps a record of the location on a disk of all the files. * *abbr* FAT.

file association *n* (*comput*) a link between a document file and the program that created it so that when a document file is selected by double clicking it opens the program and hence the file.

file attribute *n* (*comput*) information held in a file directory that contains details about the file and how the computer can access it.

file compression *n* (*comput*) the process of condensing a file so that it takes up around half the normal space on a disk.

file compression utility *n* (*comput*) a program that is designed to compress files. *See also* **file compression**.

file conversion *n* (*comput*) the conversion of a computer file in one format so that it is readable and usable in the accepting application, and also that as much of the original formatting as possible is retained.

file conversion utility *n* (*comput*) a program that is designed to convert files created in one program for use by another program.

file extension *see* **extension; file name**

filefish *n* (*pl* **filefish, filefishes**) a tropical fish, of the family of triggerfish, with a narrow body and rough skin.

file format *n* (*comput*) the method that an operating system or program uses to store data on a disk. *See also* **file conversion utility**.

file manager *n* (*comput*) a utility program that allows the user to copy, delete, add, or move files around without reverting to the DOS commands, and to create directories.

file name *n* (*comput*) a name given to a file by the computer user so that the operating system recognizes the file. Every name must include a file extension, which identifies the file with the software with which it was produced.

file recovery *n* (*comput*) the process of retrieving or restoring a file that has been previously erased.

file server *n* (*comput*) a high-powered PC in a network that provides access to other computers in the network. *See also* **server**.

filester *see* **fillister**.

filet *n* a net with a square mesh.

file transfer protocol *see* FTP

fili *n* (*pl* **filidh**) (*Irish Celtic*) a learned bard or poet, often one who was attached to a royal court.

filial *adj* of, or expected from, a son or daughter.—**filially** *adv*.—**filialness** *n*.

filiation *n* the relation of child to father; lineage, line of descent; the formation of branches of a society, etc; a branch so formed.

filibeg *n* a kilt.—*also* **philabeg**.

filibuster *n* a member of a legislature who obstructs a bill by making long speeches. * *vti* to obstruct (a bill) by such methods.—**filibusterer** *n*.

filiform *adj* threadlike.

filigree *n* a kind of lace-like ornamental work in precious metal. * *vt* (**filigreeing, filigreed**) to decorate with filigree.—*also* **filagree**.

filing *n* a particle rubbed off with a file.

Filipino *n* (*pl* **Filipinos**) a native or inhabitant of the Philippines.—*also adj*.

fill[1] *n* (*comput*) an operation that is used in a spreadsheet program to enter values in a range of cells.

fill[2] *vt* to put as much as possible into; to occupy wholly; to put a person into (a position or job, etc); to supply the things called for (in an order, etc); to close or plug (holes, etc); (*with* in) to complete (a form, design, etc) by writing or drawing; (*inf*) to provide with the latest news or facts; (with **out**) to make fuller or heavier; to fill in (a form, etc). * *vi* to become full; (with **in**) to act as a substitute for; (with **out**) to become fuller or heavier. * *n* enough to make full or to satisfy; anything that fills.

filler[1] *n* a monetary unit of Hungary, equal to one hundredth of a forint.

filler[2] *n* one who or that which fills; a substance used to plug a hole or increase the bulk of something.

fillet *n* a thin boneless strip of meat or fish; a ribbon, etc worn as a headband; (*archit*) a narrow band used between moldings. * *vt* to bone and slice (fish or meat).

filling *n* a substance used to fill a tooth cavity; (*geog*) the movement of air into a lower pressure area so that the depression dies away; the contents of a sandwich, pie, etc. * *adj* (*meal, etc*) substantial.

filling station *n* a place where fuel is sold to motorists, a service station.

fillip *n* a blow with the nail of the finger; a stimulus.

fillister, filister *n* a plane used to cut grooves, rabbets, etc.—*also* **filester**.

Fillmore *n* Millard (1800–74) 13th president of the US (1848–52).

filly *n* (*pl* **fillies**) a young female horse, usu less than four years.

film *n* a fine, thin skin, coating, etc; a flexible cellulose material covered with a light-sensitive substance used in photography; a haze or blur; a motion picture. * *vti* to cover or be covered as with a film; to photograph or make a film (of).—**filmic** *adj*.

film card *see* **microfiche**.

film star *n* a leading cinema actor or actress.

filmy *adj* (**filmier, filmiest**) gauzy, transparent; blurred, hazy.—**filmily** *adv*.—**filminess** *n*.

FILO *abbr* = first-in-last-out.

filose *adj* threadlike.

fils *n* a monetary unit of Bahrain, Iraq, Jordan, and Kuwait, equal to one thousandth of a dinar; a monetary unit of the United Arab Emirates, equal to one hundredth of a dirham; a monetary unit of Yemen, equal to one hundredth of a riyal and one thousandth of a dinar.

filter *n* a device or substance straining out solid particles, impurities, etc, from a liquid or gas; a device for removing or minimizing electrical oscillations, or sound or light waves of certain frequencies; (*optics*) a device which allows a limited range of the electromagnetic spectrum to pass through; a traffic signal at certain road junctions that allows vehicles to turn left or right while the main lights are red. * *vti* to pass through or as through a filter; (*comput*) to select certain files from a database by setting up a set of criteria; to remove with a filter.—**filterable, filtrable** *adj*.

filter paper *n* (*chem*) a pure cellulose paper used in the laboratory for the separation of solids from liquids by filtration.

filter tip *n* the porous tip of a cigarette designed to reduce the intake of tar during smoking.—**filter-tipped** *adj*.

filth *n* dirt; obscenity.

filthy *adj* (**filthier, filthiest**) dirty, disgusting; obscene; (*inf*) extremely unpleasant.—**filthily** *adv*.—**filthiness** *n*.

filtrate *vt* to filter. * *n* a liquid that has been filtered; (*chem*) the liquid remaining after filtration, having been separated from a solid/liquid mixture.—**filtration** *n*.

filtration *n* (*chem*) separation of a solid from a liquid by passing the mixture through a suitable separation medium.

FIM *abbr* = Fellow of the Institute of Materials.

FIMA *abbr* = Fellow of the Institute of Mathematics and its Applications.

FIManf *abbr* = Fellow of the Institute of Manufacturing.

FIMatM *abbr* = Fellow of the Institute of Materials Management.

FIMBM *abbr* = Fellow of the Institute of Maintenance and Building Management.

fimbria *see* **fallopian tubes**.

fimbriate, fimbriated *adj* (*bot*) fringed.

FIMC *abbr* = Fellow of the Institute of Management Consultants.

FIMechE *abbr* = Fellow of the Institution of Mechanical Engineers.

FIMechIE *abbr* = Fellow of the Institution of Mechanical Incorporated Engineers.

FIMgt *abbr* = Fellow of the Institute of Management.

FIMI *abbr* = Fellow of the Institute of the Motor Industry.

FIMinE *abbr* = Fellow of the Institution of Mining Engineers.

FIMIT *abbr* = Fellow of the Institute of Musical Instrument Technology.

FIMLS *abbr* = Fellow of the Institute of Medical Laboratory Sciences.

FIMS *abbr* = Fellow of the Institute of Management Specialists.

FIMunE *abbr* = Fellow of the Institution of Municipal Engineers.

fin *n* an organ by which a fish, etc, steers itself and swims; a rubber flipper used for underwater swimming; any fin-shaped object used as a stabilizer, as on an aircraft or rocket. * *vb* (**finning, finned**) *vi* (*fish, whale. etc*) to agitate the fins. * *vt* to furnish with fins.

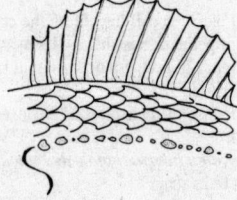

fin. *abbr* (*Latin*) = ad finem, "at" or "towards the end."

Fin. *abbr* = Finland; Finnish.

FIN *abbr* = Food Irradiation Network.

finable, fineable *adj* liable to a fine.

finagle *vt* (*inf*) to obtain or achieve through cunning or deceit; to use trickery or deceit on someone.

final *adj* of or coming at the end; conclusive. * *n* (*often pl*) the last of a series of contests; a final examination.—**finally** *adv*.

final accounts *npl* a company's financial accounts prepared at the end of its financial year, which must be audited.

finale *n* the concluding part of any public performance; the last section in a musical composition.

finalist *n* a contestant in a final.

finality *n* (*pl* **finalities**) the state or quality of being final; completeness, conclusiveness.

finalize *vt* to make complete, to bring to an end.—**finalization** *n*.

finally *adv* at last; lastly; completely.

finance *n* the management of money; (*pl*) money resources. * *vt* to supply or raise money for.

finance house *n* a financial institution that specializes in the supply of installment credit to borrowers and is often owned by a commercial bank.

financial *adj* of finance.—**financially** *adv*.

financial security *n* a means of borrowing money and raising new capital issued by companies and financial organizations.

financial statement *n* (*law*) a statement of assets entailing a legal right to sell personal property or claim the assets of a debtor.

Financial Times Share Index *n* a number of share indexes that are published by the *Financial Times* newspaper in the UK as a guide to share prices generally on the London Stock Exchange.

financial year *n* a year concerned in some way with a company's finances, such as a period of a year for which budgets are prepared.

financier *n* a person skilled in finance.

finback *n* a whale with a prominent dorsal fin; the rorqual.

FINCEN *abbr* = Financial Crimes Enforcement Network.

finch *n* any of numerous songbirds of the *Fringillidae* family.

find *vb* (**finding, found**) *vt* to discover by chance; to come upon by searching; to perceive; to recover (something lost); to reach, attain; to decide and declare to be; (*with* out) to discover; to solve; to detect in an offence. * *vi* to reach a decision (as by a jury). * *n* a discovery, something found.—**findable** *adj*.

Findabair or **Findabar** or **Findbhair** *n* (*Irish Celtic myth*) the daughter of Medb and Ailill. She fell in love with Fraoch.

finder[1] *n* one who or that which finds; a discoverer; a device for sighting the field of view of a camera, telescope, etc.

finder[2] *n* (*comput*) a utility program that manages memory and files in conjunction with the Macintosh operating system.

fin de siècle *adj* of or typical of the end of a century, esp the 19th century. * *n* the end of a century.

finding *n* a discovery; the conclusion reached by a judicial enquiry.

fine[1] *adj* very good; with no impurities, refined; (*weather*) clear and bright; not heavy or coarse; very thin or small; sharp; subtle; elegant. * *adv* in a fine manner; (*inf*) very well.—**finely** *adv*.—**fineness** *n*.

fine[2] *n* a sum of money imposed as a punishment. * *vt* to punish by a fine.—**finable, fineable** *adj*.

fine arts *npl* painting, sculpture, engraving, etc, valued for their esthetic qualities. *See also* **applied arts**.

fine-draw *vt* (**fine-drawing, fine-drew,** *pp* **fine-drawn**) to sew up (a darn) so neatly that the join cannot be noticed; to draw out (wire) to an extreme fineness.—**fine-drawn** *adj*.

Finegas *n* (*Irish Celtic myth*) a druid to whom Fionn mac Cumhaill was sent to learn poetry and knowledge.

finely *adv* in a fine manner; discriminatingly; subtly; in tiny pieces.

fineness *n* the state or quality of being fine; the quantity of pure metal contained in an alloy.

finery *n* (*pl* **fineries**) elaborate clothes, jewelry, etc.

finespun *adj* delicate, fine; over-subtle.

finesse *n* delicacy or subtlety of performance; skillfulness, diplomacy in handling a situation; (*bridge*) an attempt to take a trick with a card lower than a higher card held by an opponent. * *vt* to achieve by finesse; to play (a card) as a finesse.

fine-tooth(ed) comb *n* a comb with closely set fine teeth for trapping nits, etc.

fine-tune *vt* to make fine adjustments to something in order to improve its effectiveness.

finger *n* one of the digits of the hand, usu excluding the thumb; anything shaped like a finger; (*inf*) the breadth of a finger. * *vt* to touch with fingers; (*mus*) to use the fingers in a certain way when playing; to mark this way on music; (*sl*) to inform against.—**fingerer** *n*.

fingerboard *n* the part of a violin, guitar, etc, against which the strings are pressed by the fingers.

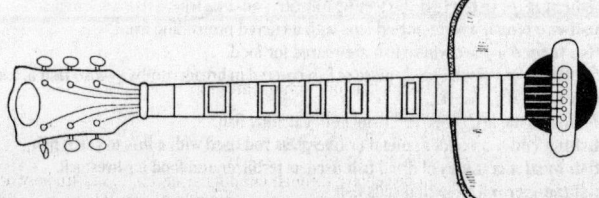

finger bowl *n* a small bowl containing water for rinsing the fingers at the table.

fingered *adj* marked by handling; having a finger or fingers; (*mus*) marked to show how the fingers are used.

fingering[1] *n* the manner of using the fingers in playing a musical instrument; the indication of this in a musical score.

fingering[2] *n* a fine knitting yarn.

fingerling *n* a young fish, esp a trout.

fingernail *n* the nail on a finger.

finger painting *n* the technique of painting using the fingers and hands.

fingerpost *n* a direction post in the shape of a pointing finger.

fingerprint *n* the impression of the ridges on a fingertip, esp as used for purposes of identification. —*also vt*.

fingerstall *n* a protective covering for a finger.

finial *n* (*archit*) a pointed ornament at the top of a spire, gable, etc.—**finialed** *adj*.

Finias *n* (*Irish Celtic myth*) one of the four great cities of the Tuatha De Danann before they went to Ireland. It was the home of Uscias.

finical *adj* fastidious, over-particular, fussy; affectedly fine.—**finicality** *n*.—**finically** *adv*.

finicky, finicking *adj* too particular, fussy.

fining *n* the act or process of clarifying or refining; a liquid used to clarify wine, beer, etc.

finis *n* the end, used at the conclusion of books, films, etc.

finish *vt* to bring to an end, to come to the end of; to consume entirely; to perfect; to give a desired surface effect to. * *vi* to come to an end. * *n* the last part, the end; anything used to finish a surface; the finished effect; means or manner of completing or perfecting; polished manners, speech, etc.—**finisher** *n*.

finished *adj* completed, ended; perfect; consummate; provided with a particular surface treatment, polished; destroyed, ruined.

finishing school *n* a private school for girls which teaches social etiquette.

finite *adj* having definable limits; (*verb form*) having a distinct grammatical person and number.—**finitely** *adv* —**finiteness** *n*.

fink *n* (*sl*) a nasty person; an informer; a strikebreaker, blackleg. * *vi* (*sl*) to inform on.

Finland *n* a north European republic sharing borders with Sweden in the northwest, Norway in the north and the Russian Federation in the east.

Finn *n* a native of Finland.

Finn. *abbr* = Finnish.

finnan haddock, Finnan haddie *n* a kind of smoked haddock, named after *Findon*, a Scottish fishing village.

Finnbhenach *n* (*Irish Celtic myth*) the white-horned bull of Connacht. Owned by Medb, but it transferred itself into the ownership of Medb's husband, Ailill. Medb acquired the Donn Cuailgne, she took it back to her camp where it had a terrible fight with Finnbhenach who was reduced to pieces.

finned *adj* having a fin or fins.

Finney *n* Albert (1936–) English actor and film star. His portrayal of the rebellious young working-class hero of the film *Saturday Night and Sunday Morning* (1960) had a strong impact on British cinema.

Finnish *adj* of or relating to Finland or its language. * *n* the language of Finland.

FINNPAP *abbr* = Finnish Paper Mills' Association.

finny *adj* (**finnier, finniest**) pertaining to, or abounding in, fish; having a fin or fins.

fino *n* (*mus*) (*Italian*) as far as, so *fino al segno* means "as far as the sign."

fino[2] *n* (*pl* **finos**) a dry sherry.

Fin. Sec. *abbr* = Financial Secretary.

Fintan *n* (*Irish Celtic myth*) Fintan was the husband of Cesair, the granddaughter of Noah, who led the first invaders to Ireland before the Flood.

FIntMC *abbr* = Fellow of the International Management Center.

Finzi *n* Gerald (1901–56) English composer who is best known for his musical settings of poems by Thomas Hardy.

fio *abbr* = for information only.

FIOC *abbr* = Fellow of the Institute of Carpenters.

FIOFMS *abbr* = Fellow of the Institute of Financial and Management Studies.

Fionn mac Cumhaill *n* (*Irish Celtic myth*) Irish hero and warrior; sometimes anglicized as **Finn mac Cool**; the son of Cumhaill, who fell in love with Muirne, the daughter of a druid.

FIOP *abbr* = Fellow of the Institute of Plumbing; Fellow of the Institute of Printing.

fiord *see* **fjord**.

fioritura *n* (*mus*) (*Italian*) literally a "flowering," i.e. an embellishment.

fipple flute *see* **flageolet; recorder**.

fir *n* a kind of evergreen, cone-bearing tree; its timber.

fir. *abbr* = firkin.

FIR *abbr* = Fellow of the Institute of Population Registration; fuel indicator reading.

FIRA *abbr* = Furniture Industry Research Association.

Firbank *n* [Arthur Annesley] Ronald (1886–1926) English novelist whose weirdly exotic works, e.g. *Valmouth*, bear the stamp of the esthetic movement.

Fir Bholg or **Firbolg** *n* (*Irish Celtic myth*) the leaders of the invasion of Ireland after the Nemedians. They are said to have divided Ireland into five provinces. The Tuatha De Danann ended the Fir Bholg's rule of Ireland when they defeated them at the first Battle of Magh Tuiredh.

fire *n* the flame, heat, and light of combustion; something burning; burning fuel in a grate to heat a room; an electric or gas fire; a destructive burning; a strong feeling; a discharge of firearms. * *vti* to ignite; to supply with fuel; to bake (bricks, etc) in a kiln; to excite or become excited; to shoot (a gun, etc); to hurl or direct with force; to dismiss from a position.—**fireable** *adj*.—**firer** *n*.

fire alarm *n* a device that uses a bell, hooter, etc to warn of a fire.

fire and brimstone *interj* hell, damn, an exclamation of extreme annoyance.

firearm *n* a handgun.

fireball *n* a ball of fire; a meteor; the hot gas cloud created by a nuclear explosion.

firebox *n* the furnace in a steam locomotive.

firebrand *n* a piece of burning wood; a person who starts trouble.

firebreak *n* a strip of land cleared of vegetation to halt the spread of a fire.

firebrick *n* a brick made of fireclay to withstand the action of fire.

fire brigade *n* an organized body specially trained and equipped for fighting fires.

firebug *n* (*inf*) an arsonist.

fireclay *n* a fire-resisting clay.

firecracker *n* a small explosive firework.

firedamp *n* a combustible mine gas, chiefly methane.

firedog *n* a metal standard used for open fires to support the logs; andirons.

fire drill *n* a rehearsal of evacuation procedure in case of fire.

fire-eater *n* a performer who pretends to eat fire; a quarrelsome person.—**fire-eating** *adj, n*.

fire engine *n* a vehicle equipped for fire-fighting.

fire escape *n* a means of exit from a building, esp a stairway, for use in case of fire.

fire extinguisher *n* a container with a spray nozzle, holding water or chemicals for putting out a fire

firefighter *n* a person who fights fires, esp a member of a fire department; fireman.

firefly *n* (*pl* **fireflies**) a winged nocturnal beetle whose abdomen glows with a soft intermittent light.

fireguard *n* a protective grating placed in front of a fire.

fire insurance *n* insurance against loss by fire.

fire irons *npl* tools for tending a domestic fire, esp a poker, tongs, and shovel.

firelighter *n* a prepared block of ignitable material used for lighting a fire.

firelock *n* a flintlock.

fireman *n* (*pl* **firemen**) a member of a fire brigade; firefighter; a person employed to tend furnaces.

fireplace *n* a place for a fire, esp a recess in a wall; the area surrounding this.

fireplug *n* a connection in a water main for a hose; a hydrant.

fire power *n* the amount of fire that a military unit can deliver on a target.

fireproof *adj* not easily destroyed by fire. * *vt* to make fireproof.

fire raiser *n* an arsonist.—**fire raising** *n*.

fire resistance *n* the degree to which a component of a building can resist the passing of a fire to another part, or can continue to support its load or perform its function.

fire sale *n* a sale of fire-damaged goods.

firescreen *n* a movable ornamental screen for keeping the heat of a fire off the face; a screen for decorating an empty fireplace.

fireship *n* a ship filled with explosives to set an enemy's ships on fire.

fireside *n* the area in a room nearest the fireplace; home.

fire station *n* a building where firemen and fire-fighting equipment are based.—*also* **firehouse, station house**.

firestorm *n* a blaze producing intense heat that generates high winds, usu as a result of bombing.

firetrap *n* a building easily set on fire or hard to get out of if on fire.

firewarden *n* an officer responsible for protecting forests against fire.

firewater *n* (*inf*) strong alcoholic drink.

firewood *n* wood for fuel.

firework *n* a device packed with explosive and combustible material used to produce noisy and colorful displays; (*pl*) such a display; (*pl*) a fit of temper, an outburst of emotions.

firing[1] *n* (*mus*) ringing all the bells in a tower together as an expression of joy, and of mourning, when muffled.

firing[2] *n* baking in intense heat, esp of clay; fuel; the act of discharging a firearm; the act of adding fuel to a fire.

firing line *n* the front line of a military position; the forefront of any activity.

firing squad *n* a detachment with the task of firing a salute at a military funeral or carrying out an execution.

firkin *n* a small wooden barrel containing butter, etc; (*Brit*) a measure of one quarter of a barrel (41 liters/9 gallons).

firm[1] *adj* securely fixed; solid, compact; steady; resolute; definite. * *vti* to make or become firm.—**firmly** *adv*.—**firmness** *n*.

firm[2] *n* a business partnership; a commercial company.

firmament *n* the sky, viewed poetically as a solid arch or vault.—**firmamental** *adj*.

firmware *n* (*comput*) the part of the system software that is stored permanently in the computer's read only memory. *See* **ROM**. Firmware cannot be altered or modified.

firn *n* (*geog*) a compacted snow that forms an intermediate between snow and glacial ice and has survived the melting of a summer.

FIRSE *abbr* = Fellow of the Institute of Railway Signal Engineers.

FIRSO *abbr* = Fellow of the Institute of Road Safety Officers.

first *adj* before all others in a series; 1st; earliest; foremost, as in rank, quality, etc. * *adv* before anyone or anything else; for the first time; sooner. * *n* any person or thing that is first; the beginning; the winning place, as in a race; low gear; the highest award in a university degree.

first aid *n* emergency treatment for an injury, etc, before regular medical aid is available.

first-born *n* the eldest child in a family. * *adj* eldest.

first-class *adj* of the highest quality, as in accommodation, travel. * *n* the best accommodation on a plane, train, etc; the highest class in an examination, etc.

first-degree burn *n* (*med*) a mild burn causing a painful reddening of the skin but no blistering or charring.

first fruits *npl* fruit which is the first to ripen; the earliest returns or results from an enterprise.

first-generation *adj* denoting a native-born citizen of a country whose parents were foreign; denoting a foreign-born, naturalized citizen or inhabitant of a country.

firsthand *adj* obtained directly from a source.

first-in-first-out *n* a system of valuing units of raw material, components, or finished products issued from stock that is based on the principle of using the earliest unit value as a means of pricing the issues until all the stock at that price has been used up. * *abbr* **FIFO**.

First Lady *n* the wife of the US president.

firstling *n* the first offspring.

firstly *adv* in the first place.

first mate *n* an officer next in rank to the captain on a merchant ship.

first night *n* the opening performance of a play.

first person *n* (*gram*) pronouns and verbs referring to the person speaking.

first quarter *n* a particular phase of the Moon when it is seen as exactly half illuminated, the limit to the illuminated area appearing as a straight line.

first-rate *adj, adv* of the best quality; (*inf*) excellent.

first strike *n* a pre-emptive nuclear missile attack designed to cripple an enemy's capacity for effective retaliation.

FIRTE *abbr* = Fellow of the Institute of Road Transport Engineers.

firth *n* a Scottish term for a narrow arm of the sea, esp a river mouth.—*also* **frith**.

fis *abbr* = flight information service.

FIS *abbr* = Fellow of the Institute of Statisticians; Family Income Supplement; Federation of Irish Societies.

FISA *abbr* = Federation of Insurance Staffs Associations; Fellow of the Incorporated Secretaries Association.

FISC *abbr* = Foundation for International Scientific Coordination; Fund for International Student Cooperation.

fiscal *adj* of or relating to public revenue; financial. * *n* a prosecuting official in some countries.

fiscal year *n* the government's accounting year, which is used for assessing personal income tax.

FISCC *abbr* = Fruit Industry Sugar Concession Committee (Australia).

Fischer *n* 1. **Bobby [Robert James Fischer]** (1943–) American chess player and the first US player to win the world championship (1972). 2. **Johann M** (1692–) German architect. His notable works include Benedictine Abbey Church, Ottobeuren. 3. **Uwe** (1958–) German designer who set up the Gimbande Studio in Frankfurt.

Fischer-Dieskau *n* Dietrich (1925–) German baritone and conductor who is especially admired for his huge repertoire.

Fischer von Erlach *n* Johann B (1656–) Austrian architect. His notable works include Karlskirche, Vienna.

fish[1] *n* (*pl* **fish, fishes**) any of a large group of cold-blooded animals living in water, having backbones, gills for breathing and fins; the flesh of fish used as food. * *vi* to catch or try to catch fish; (*with* **for**) to try to obtain by roundabout methods. * *vt* (*often with* **out**) to grope for, find, and bring to view.—**fishable** *adj*.

fish[2] *n* a rigid strip of wood or metal used to strengthen a mast, joint, etc. * *vt* to strengthen or join with a fish.

fishbone chart *n* a chart that shows the various constituent operations that are used in the manufacture of products.

Fishbourne *n* a Roman palace built in 70 AD near Chichester in England.

fisher *n* a person who fishes; (*zool*) another name for the pekan, a marten found in North America.

Fisher *n* Alexander (1864–1936) British silversmith whose most notable works include plaques showing Wagnerian scenes.

fisherman *n* (*pl* **fishermen**) a person who fishes for sport or for a living; a ship used in fishing.

fisherman's knot *n* an overhand knot used for securing two lines of equal thickness.

fishery *n* (*pl* **fisheries**) the fishing industry; an area where fish are caught.

fish-eye lens *n* a wide-angled lens with a curved protruding front.

fish farm *n* a place where fish are reared for food.

fishfinger *n* a small oblong piece of fish covered in breadcrumbs.—*also* **fish stick**.

fish hawk *n* an osprey.

fishing *n* the art, sport, or business of catching fish.

fishing rod *n* a wooden, metal or fiberglass rod used with a line to catch fish.

fish meal *n* granules of dried fish used as fertilizer and food for livestock.

fishmonger *n* a shop that sells fish.

fishnet *n* a coarse open-mesh fabric.—*also adj*.

fishplate *n* an iron plate, one of a pair used to join railway rails.

fishpond *n* a pond in which fish are kept.

fish stick *see* **fishfinger**.

fishwife *n* (*pl* **fishwives**) a woman who guts or sells fish; a coarse, scolding woman.

fishy *adj* (**fishier, fishiest**) like a fish in odor, taste, etc; (*inf*) creating doubt or suspicion.—**fishily** *adv*.—**fishiness** *n*.

FISOB *abbr* = Fellow of the Incorporated Society of Organ Builders.

fissile *adj* capable of undergoing nuclear fission; easily split.—**fissility** *n*.

fission *n* a split or cleavage; the reproductive division of biological cells; the splitting of the atomic nucleus resulting in the release of energy, nuclear fission.—**fissionable** *adj*.

fission track dating *n* a method of dating based on the fission of a naturally occurring isotope of uranium (^{238}U).

fissiparous *adj* multiplying or propagating by fission.

fissiped, fissipedal *adj* (*zool*) having the toes separated, e.g. dogs, cats, etc.

fissirostral *adj* (*birds*) with a deeply cleft beak, e.g. swallows.

fissure *n* a narrow opening or cleft; abnormal break in the skin or mucous membrane, e.g. an anal fissure. * *vti* to split.

fist *n* the hand when tightly closed or clenched.

FIST *abbr* = Fellow of the Institute of Science Technology.

FISTD *abbr* = Fellow of the Imperial Society of Teachers of Dancing.

fistic *adj* (*joc*) of or pertaining to boxing.

fisticuffs *npl* a fight with the fists.

FIStructE *abbr* = Fellow of the Institution of Structural Engineers.

fistula *n* (*pl* **fistulas, fistulae**) an abnormal passage, as from an abscess to the skin.

fistulous *adj* resembling a fistula; hollow, like a pipe.

fit[1] *adj* (**fitter, fittest**) suited to some purpose, function, etc; proper, right; healthy; (*sl*) inclined, ready. * *n* the manner of fitting. * *vb* (**fitting, fitted**) *vt* to be suitable to; to be the proper size, shape, etc, for; to adjust so as to fit; (*with* **out**) to equip, to outfit. * *vi* to be suitable or proper; to have the proper size or shape.—**fittable** *adj*.—**fitly** *adv*.—**fitness** *n*.

fit[2] *n* any sudden, uncontrollable attack, as of coughing; an outburst, as of anger; a short period of impulsive activity; a seizure involving convulsions or loss of consciousness. *See also* **convulsions**.

f.i.t., FIT *abbr* = free in truck; free of income tax.

FIT *abbr* = Federation of International Traders.

FITC *abbr* = Foundry Industry Training Committee.

fitch *n* the polecat; the hair of a polecat; a brush made of this.

FITD *abbr* = Fellow of the Institute of Training and Development.

fitful *adj* marked by intermittent activity; spasmodic.—**fitfully** *adv*.—**fitfulness** *n*.

fitment *n* a piece of equipment, esp fixed furniture.

FITSA *abbr* = Fellow of the Institute of Trading Standards Administration.

fitter *n* a person who specializes in fitting clothes; a person skilled in the assembly and operation of a particular piece of machinery.

fitting *adj* appropriate; suitable, right. * *n* an act of one that fits, esp a trying on of altered clothes; a small often standardized electrical part.—**fittingly** *adv*.—**fittingness** *n*.

Fitzgerald *n* 1. **Edward** (1809–83) English poet whose best-known work is his very free translation of *The Rubaiyat of Omar Khayyám*. 2. **Ella** (1918–96) American jazz singer. 3. **F[rancis] Scott [Key]** (1896–1940) American novelist and short-story writer whose works, e.g. *The Great Gatsby* and *Tender is the Night*, are moralistic fables of extravagance and glamour. 4. **Penelope** (1916–2000) English novelist whose novels include *Human Voices*.

five *adj, n* one more than four. * *symbol* 5, V, v.

Five, The *n* (*mus*) the name given to a group of nationalistic 19th-century Russian composers who were known in Russia as *Moguchaya Kuchka* (The Mighty Handful). The five were Rimsky-Korsakov, Balakirev, Borodin, Cui, and Mussorgsky.

five-and-ten *or* **five-and-dime store** *n* a store that sells a range of inexpensive household items, orig for either 5 or 10 cents.

five-finger exercise *n* a piano exercise for five fingers.

fivefold *adj, adv* having five units or members; being five times as great or as many.

fivepins *n sing* a bowling game using five pins.

fiver *n* (*inf*) in US, a $5 bill, in UK, a £5 note.

fives *n* (*sing*) a ball game similar to squash, played in a walled court.

FIWEM *abbr* = Fellow of the Institution of Water and Environmental Management.

fix *vt* to fasten firmly; to set firmly in the mind; to direct (one's eyes) steadily at something; to make rigid; to make permanent; to establish (a date, etc) definitely; to set in order; to repair; to prepare (food or meals); (*inf*) to influence the result or action of (a race, jury, etc) by bribery; (*inf*) to punish. * *vi* to become fixed; (*inf*) to prepare or intend. * *n* the position of a ship, etc, determined from the bearings of two known positions; (*inf*) a predicament; (*inf*) a situation that has been fixed; (*inf*) something whose supply becomes continually necessary or greatly desired, as a drug, entertainment, activity, etc.—**fixable** *adj*.

fixated *adj* having a fixation.

fixation *n* a fixing; (*psychol*) an unhealthy obsession, esp one leading to arrested emotional development.

fixative *n* a substance used to fix things in position; a substance that prevents (colors, perfumes, etc) fading or evaporating.

fixed *adj* firm; not moving; lasting; intent.—**fixedly** *adv*.—**fixedness** *n*.

fixed asset *or* **capital asset** *n* a permanent asset, such as buildings, land, plant, and machinery, that is used long-term in the trade or business of a company rather than for resale.

fixed disk *see* **hard disk**.

fixed exchange rate *n* an exchange rate between one currency and another that is fixed by government.

fixed idea *n* an obsession with a single thing, person, etc.

fixed overheads *npl* indirect costs, the level of which does not vary with the level of production output or sales.

fixed star *n* a star at such a great distance from the Earth that it appears to be fixed in position throughout the year.

fixer *n* a chemical that fixes photographs, making the image permanent; (*sl*) a person who fixes something, esp by illegal means.

fixings *npl* trimmings.

fixity *n* (*pl* **fixities**) the state of being fixed; stability; permanence.

fixture *n* what is fixed to anything, as to land or to a house; a fixed article of furniture; a firmly established person or thing; a fixed or appointed time or event.

fizz *vi* to make a hissing or sputtering sound. * *n* this sound; any effervescent drink.—**fizzy** *adj*.—**fizziness** *n*.

fizzle *vi* to make a weak fizzing sound; (*with* **out**) (*inf*) to end feebly, die out, esp after a promising start.

fjard *or* **fiard** *n* a sea inlet between low banks occurring on a drowned coastline found on the southern coast of Sweden.

FJC *abbr* = Federal Judicial Center.

fjeld *n* in Scandinavia, a high, barren plateau.—*also* **field**.

FJI *abbr* = Fellow of the Institute of Journalists.

fjord *n* a long, narrow inlet of the sea between high cliffs, esp in Norway.—*also* **fiord**.

FKC *abbr* = Fellow of King's College, London.

Fl *symbol* (*chem*) fluorine.

fl *abbr* (*Latin*) = *falsa lectio*, "a false reading."

fl. *abbr* = (*Latin*) *flores*, "flowers"; florin, florins (former unit of currency); (*Latin*) *floruit*, "he flourished"; floor; flower; fluid; flute.

Fl. *abbr* = Florida.

FL *abbr* = Flight/Flag Lieutenant.

Fla. *abbr* = Florida.

FLA *abbr* = Film Laboratory Association; Free Lebanese Army.

flab *n* (*inf*) fat.

flabbergast *vt* (*inf*) to astonish, startle.

flabby *adj* (**flabbier, flabbiest**) fat and soft; weak and ineffective.—**flabbily** *adv*.—**flabbiness** *n*.

flabellate, flabelliform *adj* (*bot*) fan-shaped.

flabellum *n* (*pl* **flabella**) (*RC*) a large fan.

FLAC *abbr* = Free Legal Advice Centres (Eire).

flaccid *adj* not firm or stiff; limp, weak.—**flaccidity** *n*.

flack *see* **flak**.

flacon *n* a small bottle or flask.

flag[1] *vi* (**flagging, flagged**) to grow limp; to become weak, listless.

flag[2] *n* a piece of cloth, usu with a design, used to show nationality, party, a particular branch of the armed forces, etc, or as a signal. * *vt* (**flagging, flagged**) to decorate with flags; to signal to (as if) with a flag; (*usu with* **down**) to signal to stop.

flag[3] *n* a hard, flat stone used for paving, a flagstone. * *vt* (**flagging, flagged**) to pave with flagstones.

flag[4] *n* a plant with a sword-shaped leaf, the iris; a long thin plant blade.

flag day *n* a day on which charitable donations are solicited in exchange for small flags.

Flag Day *n* 14 June, the anniversary of the adoption of the stars and stripes, 1777.

flagellant *n* a person who scourges himself or herself or others as a sign of religious penance or for sexual gratification.—**flagellantism** *n*.

flagellate *vt* to scourge, to whip.—**flagellation** *n*.—**flagellator** *n*..

flagelliform *adj* long, tapering and flexible; shaped like the thong of a whip.

flagellum *n* (*pl* **flagella, flagellums**) (*biol, zool*) a whiplike appendage; (*bot*) a runner.

flageolet[1] *n* (*mus*) a small, end-blown flute with six holes, four in front and two at the back, popular in the 17th century.

flageolet[2] *n* a type of edible bean.

flagging *n* a pavement of flagstones.

flagitious *adj* atrocious, abominably wicked.—**flagitiously** *adv*.—**flagitiousness** *n*.

flag of convenience *n* a flag of a country flown by a ship registered there by the owners to benefit from less rigorous taxes or safety regulations.

F

flagon *n* a pottery or metal container for liquids with a handle and spout and often a lid.

flagrant *adj* conspicuous, notorious.—**flagrancy, flagrance** *n*.—**flagrantly** *adv*.

flagrante delicto *adv* in the very act, red-handed.

flagrante delicto *see* **in flagrante delicto**.

flagship *n* the ship that carries the admiral and his flag; the most important vessel of a shipping line; the chief or leading item of a group or collection.

Flagstad *n* **Kirsten** (1895–1962) Norwegian soprano who is noted for her performances in Wagner's operas.

flagstaff *or* **flagpole** *n* a pole on which a flag is displayed.

flagstone *n* hard, evenly stratified rock easily split into slabs for paving.

flag-waver *n* an excessively patriotic person, a jingoist.

Flaherty *n* **Robert [Joseph]** (1884–1951) American documentary film director whose films include *Nanook of the North*.

flail *n* a tool for threshing by hand. * *vt* to beat with a flail. * *vi* (*usu with* **about**) to wave (the arms, etc) wildly.

flair *n* natural ability, aptitude; discernment; (*inf*) stylishness, sophistication.

flak *n* shells fired by anti-aircraft guns; criticism, opposition.—*also* **flack**.

flake *n* a small piece of snow; a small, thin layer chipped from a larger mass of something; (*archeo*) a stone tool, usually made of flint, produced by striking off a fragment from a larger core. * *vt* to form into flakes. * *vi* (*with* **out**) (*inf*) to collapse or fall asleep from exhaustion.—**flaker** *n*.

flaky *adj* (**flakier, flakiest**) of or resembling flakes; liable to flake; (*sl*) nervous; (*sl*) odd, eccentric.—**flakily** *adv*.—**flakiness** *n*.

flam *vt* (**flamming, flammed**) (*dial*) to deceive.

flambé, flambée *adj* (*food*) covered with flaming brandy or other spirit.—*also vt*.

flambeau *n* (*pl* **flambeaux, flambeaus**) a lighted, flaming torch; a large ornamental candlestick.

flamboyant *adj* brilliantly colored; ornate; strikingly elaborate; dashing, exuberant.—**flamboyance, flamboyancy** *n*.—**flamboyantly** *adv*.

flame *n* the burning gas of a fire, appearing as a tongue of light; the state of burning with a blaze; a thing like a flame; an intense emotion; (*inf*) a sweetheart. * *vi* to burst into flame; to become bright red with emotion.

flamen *n* (*pl* **flamens, flamines**) in ancient Rome, a priest devoted to the service of a special deity.

flamenco *n* (*pl* **flamencos**) (*mus*) a generic term for a type of Spanish song from Andalusia, usually sad and often accompanied by guitar and dancing. Flamenco guitar playing relies heavily on the strumming of powerful, dynamic rhythms.

FLAMES *abbr* = Fabrication Labor and Material Estimating Service.

flame test *n* (*chem*) a simple test used for the detection of metals, which is useful for distinguishing between different metals.

flame-thrower *n* a weapon that shoots a jet of flaming liquid.

flaming *adj* emitting flames; very hot; gaudy; exaggerated; intense.—**flamingly** *adv*.

flamingo *n* (*pl* **flamingos, flamingoes**) any of several wading birds with rosy-pink plumage and long legs and neck.

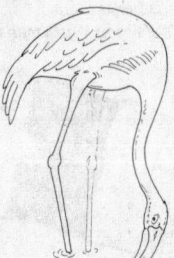

flammable *adj* easily set on fire.—**flammability** *n*.

flamy *adj* (**flamier, flamiest**) resembling flame; flame-colored.

flan *n* an open case of pastry or sponge cake with a sweet or savory filling.

flânerie *n* idleness.

flâneur an idle person, a lounger.

flange *n* a raised edge, as on a wheel rim to keep it on a rail; a projecting rib. * *vt* to provide with a flange.—**flanged** *adj*.

flank *n* the fleshy part of the side from the ribs to the hip; the side of anything; the right or left side of a formation of troops. * *vt* to attack the flank of; to skirt the side of; to be situated at the side of.

flanker *n* (*mil*) a soldier or fortification used to protect a flank.

flannel *n* a soft light cotton or woolen cloth; a small cloth for washing the face and hands; (*sl*) nonsense, equivocation; (*pl*) trousers of such cloth. * *vt* (**flanneling, flanneled** *or* **flannelling, flannelled**) to wash with a flannel; (*inf*) to flatter.—**flannelly** *adj*.

flannelette *n* a soft cotton fabric.

flap[1] *n* (*med*) a section of tissue, usually skin, that is excised from the underlying tissues except for one thin strip that is left for blood and nervous supply. *See* **skin grafting**.

flap[2] *vi* (**flapping, flapped**) to move up and down, as wings; to sway loosely and noisily, as curtains in the wind, etc; to move or hang like a flap; (*inf*) to get into a panic or fluster. * *n* the motion or noise of a flap; anything broad and flexible, either hinged or hanging loose; a light blow with a flat object; (*inf*) agitation, panic.

flapdoodle *n* (*inf*) nonsense.

flapjack *n* a kind of pancake; a cake made with oats and syrup.

flapper *n* someone who, or something which, flaps; (*inf*) a fashionable young woman of the 1920s.

flare *vi* to burn with a sudden, bright, unsteady flame; to burst into emotion, esp anger; to widen out gradually. * *n* an unsteady flame; a sudden flash; a bright light used as a signal or illumination; a widened part or shape; (*astron*) a sudden outburst of radiation from a star, or more particularly from the lower atmosphere of the Sun.

flare star *n* an explosive variable star which in a few seconds may increase its brightness by several magnitudes, returning to its former state in a few tens of minutes.

flare-up *n* a sudden burst of fire; (*inf*) a sudden burst of emotion.

flash *n* a sudden, brief light; a brief moment; a sudden brief display; (*TV, radio*) a sudden brief news item about an important event; (*photog*) a device for producing a brief intense light; a sudden onrush of water; **flash in the pan** a misfire; a showy start not followed up. * *vi* to send out a sudden, brief light; to sparkle; to come or pass suddenly; (*sl*) to expose the genitals indecently. * *vt* to cause to flash; to send (news, etc) swiftly; (*inf*) to show off. * *adj* (*inf*) flashy.—**flasher** *n*.

flashback *n* an interruption in the continuity of a story, etc, by telling or showing an earlier episode.

flashboard *n* a board placed on a dam to increase its height and hence the depth of the water contained.

flashbulb *n* a small bulb giving an intense light used in photography.

flash flood *n* a sudden brief flood caused by a heavy rainfall.

flash gun *n* (*photog*) a device for holding and operating a flashbulb.

flashing *n* a piece of lead or other metal, used to keep a roof watertight.

flashlight *n* an electric torch; a flash of electric light used to take photographs in dark conditions.

flash memory *n* (*comput*) a type of memory device that can be programmed, erased and reprogrammed.

flashpoint *n* the lowest temperature at which vapor, as from oil, will ignite with a flash; the point where a situation will erupt into violence.

flash spectrum *n* a line spectrum of the limb of the Sun taken just before or just after totality in an eclipse of the sun.

flashy *adj* (**flashier, flashiest**) pretentious; showy, gaudy.—**flashily** *adv*.—**flashiness** *n*.

flask *n* a slim-necked bottle; a vacuum flask.

flasket *n* a small flask; a long, shallow basket.

flat *adj* (**flatter, flattest**) having a smooth level surface; lying spread out; broad, even, and thin; not fluctuating; (*tyre*) deflated; dull, tedious; (*drink*) not fizzy; (*battery*) drained of electric current. * *adv* in a flat manner or position; exactly; (*mus*) below true pitch. * *n* anything flat, esp a surface, part, or expanse; (*Brit*) a flat tire; a set of rooms on one floor of a building (—*also* **apartment**).—**flatly** *adv*.—**flatness** *n*.

flatbed scanner *n* (*comput*) a hardware device that is used to transfer text and graphics from paper into a digitized format that can then be edited in a computer program. *See also* **optical character recognition**.

flatcar *n* an open, sideless rail truck.

flat file database *n* (*comput*) a database management program that can access only one record or file at a time.

flatfish *n* (*pl* **flatfish, flatfishes**) any of an order of marine fishes that as adults have both eyes on one side.

flatfoot *n* a condition in which the arch of the instep is flattened; (*pl* **flatfeet, flatfoots**) (*sl*) a policeman.

flat-footed *adj* having flatfoot; (*inf*) awkward; (*inf*) unprepared; (*inf*) determined, blunt.—**flat-footedly** *adv*.—**flat-footedness** *n*.

flatiron *n* an iron used for clothes, linen, etc, heated by being placed upon a hot stove, etc.

flat spin *n* a spin or maneuver in which an aircraft is more horizontal than vertical; (*inf*) a confused or agitated state.

flatten *vti* to make or become flat.—**flattener** *n*.

flatter *vt* to praise excessively or insincerely, esp out of self-interest or to win favor; to display to advantage; to represent as more attractive, etc than reality; to gratify the vanity of; to encourage falsely.—**flatterer** *n*.—**flattering** *adj*.—**flatteringly** *adv*.

flattery *n* (*pl* **flatteries**) compliments; insincere praise.

flattie *n* (*inf*) a woman's shoe with a flat heel.

flatting *n* (*metallurgy*) the process of rolling metal into flat sheets.

flatulence, flatulency *n* (*med*) a build-up of gas in the stomach or bowels that is released through the mouth or anus; windiness; verbosity; pomposity.

flatulent *adj* causing or affected with intestinal gas; pretentious, vain.—**flatulently** *adv*.

flatways, flatwise *adv* flat side downwards.

flatworm *n* any of various parasitic worms having a flattened body.

Flaubert *n* **Gustave** (1821–80) French novelist whose best-known work is *Madame Bovary* (1857).

flaunt *vi* to move or behave ostentatiously; (*flag*) to wave in the wind. * *vt* to display.—**flaunter** *n*.—**flauntingly** *adv*.

flaunty *adj* (**flauntier, flauntiest**) inclined to flaunting.

flautist *n* a flute player.—*also* **flutist**.

flavescent *adj* turning yellow; yellowish.

flavin, flavine *n* a yellow dye and antiseptic.

flavor, flavour *n* the taste of something in the mouth; a characteristic quality. * *vt* to give flavor to.—**flavorer, flavourer** *n*.—**flavorsome, flavoursome**.*adj*.

flavoring, flavouring *n* any substance used to give flavor to food.

flavorous *adj* tasty.

flaw¹ *n* a defect; a crack. * *vti* to make or become flawed.

flaw² *n* a gust of wind, a squall.

flawless *adj* perfect.—**flawlessly** *adv*.—**flawlessness** *n*.

flax *n* a blue-flowered plant cultivated for its fiber and seed; the fiber of this plant.

flaxen, flaxy *adj* made of flax; pale yellow.

Flaxman *n* **John** (1755–1826) British sculptor and designer whose masterpiece in silver design was the Shield of Achilles.

flaxseed *n* the seed of the flax plant, from which linseed oil is obtained.

flay *vt* to strip off the skin; to berate, criticize severely.—**flayer** *n*.

FLBA *abbr* = Family Law Bar Association.

FLC *abbr* = Federal Laboratory Consortium.

FLCM *abbr* = Fellow of the London College of Music.

FLCSP(Phys) *abbr* = Fellow of the London and Counties Society of Physiologists.

FLD *abbr* = Friends of the Lake District.

flea *n* a small wingless jumping bloodsucking insect.

fleabane *n* a plant of the aster family.

fleabite *n* the bite of a flea; a minor inconvenience.

fleabitten *adj* marked with fleabites; (*inf*) shabby, wretched; (*horses*) flecked with red spots on a light ground.

flea collar *n* a collar for animals which is impregnated with an insecticide to kill fleas.

fleam *n* a lancet used for bleeding cattle.

flea market *n* an open-air street market, usu selling second-hand articles.

fleapit *n* (*inf*) a shabby cinema or theatre.

flèche *n* (*archit*) a slender spire, esp at the intersection of the nave and transept.—*also* **spirelet**.

Flecheux *n* **Luc** (1966–) French designer of furniture and tableware.

fleck *n* a spot or speckle of color; a tiny particle. * *vt* to mark with flecks.

flection *see* **flexion**.

fled *see* **flee**.

Fledermaus *n* **Die** [The Bat] an operetta by Johann Strauss the Younger to a libretto by C.Haffner and R Genée first performed in 1874.

fledge *vt* (*birds*) to rear until ready to fly; to cover or provide with feathers, esp an arrow.

fledgling, fledgeling *n* a young bird just fledged; an inexperienced person, a trainee.

flee *vti* (**fleeing, fled**) to run away from danger, etc; to pass away quickly, to disappear.—**fleer** *n*.

fleece *n* the woolen coat of sheep or similar animal. * *vt* to remove wool from; to defraud.

fleecy *adj* (**fleecier, fleeciest**) like a fleece, woolly.—**fleecily** *adv*.—**fleeciness** *n*.

fleer *n* a derisive look, sneer. * *vti* to sneer (at), to mock.

fleet¹ *n* a number of warships under one command; (*often with cap*) a country's navy; any group of cars, ships, buses, etc, under one control.

fleet² *adj* swift moving; nimble.—**fleetly** *adv*.—**fleetness** *n*.

fleeting *adj* brief, transient.—**fleetingly** *adv*.

Fleischer *n* **Max** (1883–1972) American cartoonist best known as the creator of Popeye and Betty Boop.

Flemalle, Master of *see* **Campin, Robert**.

Fleming *n* a native or inhabitant of Flanders.

Fleming *n* 1. **Sir Alexander** (1881–1955) Scottish bacteriologist who discovered the antibacterial qualities of the enzyme lysozome, "penicillin." He shared the 1945 Nobel prize for physiology or medicine with Chain and Florey. 2. **Erik** (1894–1954) a Swedish baron who founded the Atelier Borgila, which became one of Sweden's leading modern silver workshops. 3. **Ian** [Lancaster] (1908–64) English novelist whose James Bond novels, e.g. *Goldfinger* (1959), have all been produced as films.

Flemish *adj* of the people of Flanders, or their language.

flense, flench *vt* (*whale, seal*) to strip blubber from.

flesh *n* the soft substance of the body, esp the muscular tissue; the pulpy part of fruits and vegetables; meat; the body as distinct from the soul; all mankind; a yellowish-pink color. * *vt* (*usu with* out) to give substance to.

flesh and blood *n* the body; humankind; human nature; one's own family; relatives. * *adj* real as opposed to imaginary.

fleshings *npl* flesh-colored tights.

fleshly *adj* (**fleshlier, fleshliest**) having to do with the body and its desires, material, sensual.—**fleshliness** *n*.

flesh wound *n* a superficial wound.

fleshy *adj* (**fleshier, fleshiest**) of or resembling flesh; plump; succulent; sensual.—**fleshiness** *n*.

FLETC *abbr* = Federal Law Enforcement Training Center.

Fletcher *n* **John** (1579–1625) English dramatist who frequently collaborated with other dramatists, most notably Sir Francis Beaumont and Shakespeare.

fleur-de-lis, fleur-de-lys *or* **flower-de-luce** *n* (*pl* **fleurs-de-lis, fleurs-de-lys, flowers-de-luce**) a heraldic lily, the emblem of France.

Fleuron *n* **The** (1923–30) a magazine concerned with all aspects of typography.

fleury *adj* (*her*) decorated with a fleur-de-lis.—*also* **flory**.

flew *see* **fly**.

flews *npl* the pendulous lips of a bloodhound, etc.

flex *vti* to bend (a limb or joint, etc); to contract (a muscle). * *n* an insulated cable used to connect electric appliances to the mains.—*also* **cord**.

flex. *abbr* = flexible.

flexible *adj* easily bent, pliable; adaptable, versatile; docile.—**flexibility** *n*.—**flexibly** *adv*.

flexible budget *n* a firm's budget which is designed to alter in line with the level of business activity that is actually achieved.

flexile *adj* supple; docile; flexible.—**flexility** *n*.

flexion *n* the act or process of bending; a curve; (*gram*) an inflection.—*also* **flection**.

flexitime, flextime *n* the staggering of working hours to enable each employee to work the full quota of time but at periods most convenient for the individual.

flexor *or* **agonist** *n* a muscle that acts to bend a joint or limb. *See* **voluntary muscle**.

flexuous, flexose *adj* winding, sinuous; unsteady.—**flexuosity** *n*.

flexure *n* the act of bending; the state of being bent; (*math*) the curving of a line or surface.—**flexural** *adj*.

FLI *abbr* = Fellow of the Landscape Institute.

flibbertigibbet *n* an impish, flighty, or gossipy person.

flick *n* a light stroke or blow; (*inf*) a cinema film. * *vt* to strike or propel with a flick; a flicking movement.

flicker *vi* to burn unsteadily, as a flame; to move quickly to and fro. * *n* a flickering moment of light or flame; a flickering movement; (*comput*) a distortion that occurs on a VDU, caused by a low rate of refreshment of the screen.—**flickeringly** *adv*.—**flickery** *adj*.

flick knife *n* a knife with a retractable blade released by pressing a button.

Fliegende Hollander, Der *see* **Flying Dutchman, The**.

flier *see* **flyer**.

flies *see* **fly**.

flight¹ *n* the act, manner, or power of flying; distance flown; a group of creatures or things flying together; an aircraft scheduled to fly a certain trip; a trip by aircraft; a set of stairs, as between landings; a mental act of soaring beyond the ordinary; a set of feathers on a dart or arrow.

flight² *n* an act or instance of fleeing.

flight attendant *n* a steward or stewardess on an aircraft.

flight-deck *n* the cockpit of an aircraft.

flightless *adj* (*birds, insects*) incapable of flying.

flight path *n* the course through the air of an aircraft, spacecraft, or projectile.

flight recorder *n* a device that records information about the flight performance of an aircraft.

flighty *adj* (**flightier, flightiest**) irresponsible, capricious, frivolous.—**flightily** *adv*.—**flightiness** *n*.

flimflam *vt* (**flimflamming, flimflammed**) to deceive. * *n* nonsense; a trick.

flimsy *adj* (**flimsier, flimsiest**) weak, insubstantial; light and thin; (*excuse etc*) unconvincing. * *n* (*pl* **flimsies**) thin paper; copy written on this.—**flimsily** *adv*.—**flimsiness** *n*.

flinch *vi* to draw back, as from pain or fear; to wince.—**flincher** *n*.—**flinchingly** *adv*.

flinders *npl* fragments.

fling *vb* (**flinging, flung**) *vt* to cast, throw aside, esp with force; to put or send suddenly or without warning. * *vi* to kick out violently; to move or rush quickly or impetuously. * *n* the act of flinging; a lively dance; a period of pleasurable indulgence.—**flinger** *n*.

flint *n* a very hard and brittle rock that produces sparks when struck with steel, as well as fragments with sharp points and cutting edges; an alloy used for producing a spark in lighters.

flint glass *n* a lustrous kind of glass; lead glass.

flintlock *n* a type of old-fashioned gun fired by sparks from a flint.

flinty *adj* (**flintier, flintiest**) like flint, hard; cruel.—**flintily** *adv*.—**flintiness** *n*.

flip¹ *n* a drink made from any alcoholic beverage sweetened and mixed with beaten egg.

flip² *vb* (**flipping, flipped**) *vt* to toss with a quick jerk, to flick; to snap (a coin) in the air with the thumb; to turn or turn over. * *vi* to move jerkily; (*inf*) to burst into anger.

F

flip-flop *n* a backward handspring; an electronic circuit that can assume either of two states when activated; a rubber-soled sandal with a strap that fits between the toes —*also* **thong**.

flippant *adj* impertinent; frivolous.—**flippancy** *n*.—**flippantly** *adv*.

flipper *n* a limb adapted for swimming; a flat rubber shoe expanded into a paddle, used in underwater swimming.

flip side *n* the reverse side of a gramophone record; the less attractive or well-known aspect of a person or thing.

flirt *vi* to make insincere amorous approaches; to trifle or toy, e.g. with an idea. * *n* a person who toys amorously with the opposite sex.—**flirtation** *n*.—**flirter** *n*.—**flirtingly** *adv*.

flirtatious *adj* fond of flirting, coquettish.—**flirtatiously** *adv*.

flit *vi* (**flitting, flitted**) to move lightly and rapidly; to vacate (a premises) stealthily. * the act of flitting, a removal.

flitch *n* a side of bacon, salted and cured; a plank cut from a tree.

Flitcroft *n* **Henry** (1687–1769) English architect. His notable works include Chatham House and Woburn Abbey.

flitter *vi* to flit about; to flicker, flutter.

flivver *n* (*sl*) an old or cheap car.

float *vi* to rest on the surface of or be suspended in a liquid; to move lightly; to wander aimlessly. * *vt* to cause to float; to put into circulation; to start up a business, esp by offering shares for sale. * *n* anything that floats; a cork or other device used on a fishing line to signal that the bait has been taken; a low flat vehicle decorated for exhibit in a parade; a small sum of money available for cash expenditures.—**floatable** *adj*.

floatage *see* **flotage**.

floatation *see* **flotation**.

floater *n* something that floats; a person lacking strong political convictions; (*inf*) a blunder.

floating *adj* swimming, or buoyed up, on the surface of a liquid; (*anat*) displaced; (*vote, etc*) not settled; (*capital*) in circulation, available for use.

floating exchange rate *n* an exchange rate between currencies that is not fixed but that is allowed to float or vary according to market forces.

floating point calculation *n* (*comput*) calculation where the decimal point in a number is not fixed but floats, allowing a high level of accuracy.

floating ribs *npl* (*anat*) the last two pairs of ribs, which are unattached and end freely in the muscle of the thoracic wall. *See* **ribs**.

floccose *adj* tufted.

floccule *n* a mass of fleecy material; a small tuft or flake.

flocculent *adj* woolly or flaky.—**flocculence, flocculency** *n*.

flocculus *n* (*pl* **flocculi**) a tufted mass; (*astron*) a mass of gas appearing as a mark on the sun (—*also* **plage**.

floccus *n* (*pl* **flocci**) down, such as that found on young birds; a tuft of hair.

flock[1] *n* a group of certain animals as birds, sheep, etc, living and feeding together; a group of people or things. * *vi* to assemble or travel in a flock or crowd.

flock[2] *n* a tuft of wool or cotton fiber; woolen or cotton waste used for stuffing furniture.—**flocky** *adj*.

floe *n* a sheet of floating ice.

flog *vt* (**flogging, flogged**) to beat harshly with a rod, stick, or whip; (*sl*) to sell.—**flogger** *n*.—**flogging** *n*.

flong *n* (*printing*) paper used for stereotyping.

flood *n* an overflowing of water on an area normally dry; the rising of the tide; a great outpouring, as of words. * *vt* to cover or fill, as with a flood; to put too much water, fuel, etc on or in. * *vi* to gush out in a flood; to become flooded.—**floodable** *adj*.—**flooder** *n*.

floodgate *n* a gate for controlling the flow of water, a sluice.

floodlight *n* a strong beam of light used to illuminate a stage, sports field, stadium, building exterior, etc. * *vt* (**floodlighting, floodlit**) to illuminate with floodlights.

flood plain *n* the flat land surrounding a river which is subject to periodic flooding.

Flood *n* **The** (*Bible*) because of man's wickedness God sent a Flood to destroy man and every living creature; he told Noah to build an ark to preserve himself, his family, and two of every animal, bird and creeping thing. *See also* **ark; Noah**.

flood tide *n* the incoming current of sea after low water. *See* **ebb tide**.

floor *n* the inside bottom surface of a room, flooring; the bottom surface of anything, as the ocean; a story in a building; the area in a legislative assembly where the members sit and debate; the lower limit, the base. * *vt* to provide with a floor; to knock down (a person) in a fight; (*inf*) to defeat; (*inf*) to shock, to confuse.

floorage *n* the area of a floor.

floorboard *n* one of the boards making up a floor.

floor finish *n* material laid to form a finished surface on the sub-floor.

flooring *n* material for making or covering a floor; a floor.

floor plan *n* a scale drawing of the layout of a floor of a building.

floor show *n* entertainment with singers and dancers, etc, in a nightclub.

floozy, floozie, floosie *n* (*pl* **floozies, floosies**) (*sl*) a disreputable woman.

flop *vi* (**flopping, flopped**) to sway or bounce loosely; to move in a heavy, clumsy, or relaxed manner; (*inf*) to fail. * *n* a flopping movement; a collapse; (*inf*) a complete failure.

floppy *adj* (**floppier, floppiest**) limp, hanging loosely. * *n* (*pl* **floppies**) a floppy disk.—**floppily** *adv*.—**floppiness** *n*.

floppy disk *n* (*comput*) a removable medium of data storage, made of magnetic-coated plastic, and usu protected by a rigid plastic cover.

floptical disk *n* (*comput*) a floppy disk that, because of its construction, allows the disk drive's read/write heads to align very accurately with the disk, allowing a far greater amount of information to be stored on a disk.

Flor. *abbr* = Florida.

flora *n* (*pl* **floras, florae**) the plants of a region or a period.

Flora *n* (*Roman myth*) the goddess of flowers and spring, and of youthful vitality.

Flora group *n* (*astron*) a family of asteroids which have more or less identical orbits, about 2.2 astronomical units radius.

floral *adj* pertaining to flowers.—**florally** *adv*.

Florence (Firenze) *n* a city in Italy.

Florentine *n* a native or inhabitant of Florence.—*also adj*.

florescence *n* the process, state, or time of flowering.

floret *n* one of the small flowers forming the head of a plant.

Florey *n* **Howard Walter [Baron Florey of Adelaide]** (1898–1968) Australian pathologist who shared the 1945 Nobel prize for physiology or medicine with Sir Alexander Fleming and Chain for their work on penicillin.

floriated, floreated *adj* ornamented with floral decorations; flowery.

floribunda *n* any of several varieties of hybrid roses with large clusters of flowers.

floriculture *n* the cultivation of flowers.—**floricultural** *adj*.—**floriculturist** *n*.

florid *adj* flowery; elaborate; (*complexion*) ruddy.—**floridity** *n*.—**floridly** *adv*.

Florida (FL) *n* a state of the United States of America (USA) of which the capital is Tallahassee.

Florida current *n* an important warm ocean current of the north Atlantic that flows rapidly from the Caribbean through the Florida Straits to the Atlantic where it forms the southern part of the Gulf Stream.

Florin *n* currency of Aruba.

Florio *n* **John** (*c*.1553–1625) English author who compiled an Italian-English dictionary, *A World of Words*.

Floris *n* **Cornelis** (1514–75) Dutch architect whose notable works include Antwerp Town Hall.

florist *n* a person who sells or grows flowers and ornamental plants.

flory *see* **fleury**.

floss *n* a mass of short silky fibers, as from the rough outside of the silkworm's cocoon; fine silk used in embroidery; dental floss.

flossy *adj* (**flossier, flossiest**) like floss, silky, downy; (*sl*) flashy.

flotage *n* flotation; a craft afloat; flotsam.—*also* **floatage**.

flotation[1] *n* the act or process of floating.—*also* **floatation**.

flotation[2] *n* the process by which a new company is launched as a public limited company for the first time and offers shares for sale to the public.

flotilla *n* a small fleet of ships.

Flotow *n* **Friedrich von** (1812–83) German composer, popular in his own lifetime, who is best known for his operas such as *Alessandro Stradella* and *Marta* (Martha).

flotsam *n* wreckage or debris found floating in the sea.

flounce[1] *vi* to move in an emphatic or impatient manner.* *n* the act of flouncing, a plunge.

flounce[2] *n* a frill of material sewn to the skirt of a dress. * *vt* to add flounces to.

flouncing *n* a material used for making flounces.

flounder[1] *vi* to move awkwardly and with difficulty; to be clumsy in thinking or speaking.

flounder[2] *n* (*pl* **flounder, flounders**) a small flatfish used as food.

flour *n* the finely ground powder of wheat or other grain. * *vt* to sprinkle with flour.—**floury** *adj*.

flourish *vi* (*plants*) to grow luxuriantly; to thrive, prosper; to live and work at a specified time. * *vt* to brandish dramatically. * *n* embellishment; a curve made by a bold stroke of the pen; a sweeping gesture; a musical fanfare.—**flourisher** *n*.

flout *vt* to treat with contempt, to disobey openly. * *n* an insult.—**flouter** *n*.—**floutingly** *adv*.

flow *vi* (*liquids*) to move (as if) in a stream; (*tide*) to rise; to glide smoothly; (*conversation, etc*) to continue effortlessly; (*comput*) when data is imported into a page layout document and the imported text runs into the available columns and around any graphic images; to be characterized by smooth and easy movement; to hang free or loosely; to be plentiful. * *n* a flowing; the rate of flow; anything that flows; the rising of the tide.

flow chart *n* a diagram representing the sequence of and relationships between different steps or procedures in a complex process, e.g. manufacturing.

flower *n* the seed-producing structure of a flowering plant, blossom; a plant cultivated for its blossoms; the best or finest part. * *vt* to cause to bear flowers. * *vi* to produce blossoms; to reach the best stage.

floweret *n* a little flower.

flowerpot *n* a pot used to contain a growing plant.

flowery *adj* full of or decorated with flowers; (*language*) full of elaborate expressions.—**floweriness** *n*.

flown *see* fly.

fl. oz. *abbr* = fluid ounce.

fl. pl. *abbr* (*Latin*) = *flore pleno*, "in full bloom."

flr. *abbr* = florin.

FLRA *abbr* = Federal Labor Relations Authority.

FLS *abbr* = Fellow of the Linnean Society; Folklore Society.

FLSPT *abbr* = Fellowship of the London School of Polymer Technology.

flt. *abbr* (*mil*) = flight.

flu *n* (*inf*) influenza.

fluctuate *vi* (*prices, etc*) to be continually varying in an irregular way.—**fluctuation** *n*.

flue[1] *n* a shaft for the passage of smoke, hot air, etc, as in a chimney.

flue[2] *n* soft downy matter; fluff.

flue[3] *n* a type of fishing net.

fluent *adj* able to write and speak a foreign language with ease; articulating, speaking, and writing easily and smoothly; graceful.—**fluency** *n*.—**fluently** *adv*.

flue pipes *n* (*mus*) all organ pipes that have narrow openings or flues, into which air passes.

fluff *n* soft, light down; a loose, soft mass, as of hair; (*inf*) a mistake, bungle. * *vt* to pat or shake until fluffy; (*inf*) to forget, to bungle.

fluffy *adj* (**fluffier, fluffiest**) like fluff; soft and downy; feathery.—**fluffily** *adv*.—**fluffiness** *n*.

Flügelhorn *n* (*mus*) (*German*) a soprano brass instrument invented by Adolphe Sax which is similar to a bugle in shape, but with three pistons.

fluid *n* a substance able to flow freely, as a liquid or gas does. * *adj* able to flow freely; able to change rapidly or easily.—**fluidal** *adj*.—**fluidity** *n*.—**fluidly** *adv*.

fluidics *n* the investigation and application of flowing liquid or gas in tubes to simulate the flow of electrons in conductors.—**fluidic** *adj*.

fluid ounce *n* a unit of capacity equal to one sixteenth of a pint; a UK unit of capacity equal to one twentieth of an imperial pint.

fluke[1] *n* a flatfish; a flattened parasitic worm.

fluke[2] *n* the part of an anchor that fastens in the sea bed, river bottom, etc; the barbed end of a harpoon; one of the lobes of a whale's tail.

fluke[3] *n* a stroke of luck. * *vti* to make or score by a fluke.

fluky, flukey *adj* (**flukier, flukiest**) obtained by luck; uncertain.—**flukiness** *n*.

flume *n* a channel for water; a ravine with a stream; a chute with a flow of water into a swimming pool. * *vt* to transport or divert by a flume.

flummery *n* (*pl* **flummeries**) (*inf*) an empty compliment; a pudding, a kind of custard or blancmange.

flummox *vt* (*inf*) to bewilder, perplex.

flung *see* fling.

flunk *vti* (*sl*) to fail, as in school work; to shirk.

flunky, flunkey *n* (*pl* **flunkies, flunkeys**) a servile person, toady; a person who does menial work; a liveried servant.

fluor *see* fluorspar.

fluoresce *vi* to display fluorescence.

fluorescence *n* the property of producing light when acted upon by radiant energy; light so produced.—**fluorescent** *adj*.

fluorescent lamp *n* a glass tube coated with a fluorescent substance that emits light when acted upon by ultraviolet radiation.

fluoridate *vt* to add fluoride to drinking water to reduce tooth decay.—**fluoridation** *n*.

fluoride *n* any of various compounds of fluorine.

fluorinate *vt* to treat or mix with fluorine.—**fluorination** *n*.

fluorine, fluorin *n* a chemical element, a pale greenish-yellow corrosive gas.

fluorine test *n* (*archeo*) comparing the relative ages of bones or teeth based on the amount of calcium phosphate replaced by the fluorine in groundwater.

fluoro-, fluor- *prefix* fluorine; fluorescence.

fluorocarbon *n* an organic compound in which fluorine replaces some or all of the hydrogen atoms in the hydrocarbon. *See also* **CFC**.

fluoroscope *n* an instrument with a fluorescent screen, used for studying X-ray images.—**fluoroscopy** *n*.

fluorspar *n* a transparent or semi-transparent material, composed of calcium fluoride.—*also* **fluor**.

flurry *n* (*pl* **flurries**) a sudden gust of wind, rain, or snow; a sudden commotion. * *vti* (**flurrying, flurried**) to (cause to) become flustered.

flush[1] *n* a rapid flow, as of water; sudden, vigorous growth; a sudden excitement; a blush; a sudden feeling of heat, as in a fever. * *vi* to flow rapidly; to blush or glow; to be washed out by a sudden flow of water. * *vt* to wash out with a sudden flow of water; to cause to blush; to excite. * *adj* level or in one plane with another surface; (*inf*) abundant, well-supplied, esp with money.—**flusher** *n*.

flush[2] *vt* to make game birds fly away suddenly.—**flusher** *n*.

flush[3] *n* (*poker, etc*) a hand of cards all of the same suit.

flush[4] *adj* (*archit*) of a flat surface which is level with any adjacent surface.

flush bead molding *n* (*archit*) a rounded convex molding sunk in so that its outer surface is level with the surface of the adjacent wall or door.

fluster *vti* to make or become confused. * *n* agitation or confusion.

flute[1] *n* a tall, slender wineglass used esp for champagne.

flute[2] *n* an orchestral woodwind instrument in the form of a straight pipe (with finger holes and keys) held horizontally and played through a hole located near one end; a decorative groove. * *vi* to play or make sounds like a flute; to cut grooves in.—**fluty** *adj*.

fluter *n* a person who makes flutes; a tool used in making flutes; a flute player.

fluting *n* decorative channels or grooves in pillars, etc; pleats like this in a skirt, etc.

flutist, flautist *n* a flute player.

flutter[1] *vi* (*birds*) to flap the wings; to wave about rapidly; (*heart*) to beat irregularly or spasmodically. * *vt* to cause to flutter. * *n* rapid, irregular motion; nervous excitement; commotion, confusion; (*inf*) a small bet.—**flutterer** *n*.—**fluttery** *adj*.

flutter[2] *n* (*med*) an abnormal disturbance of heartbeat rhythm that may affect the atria or ventricles but is less severe than fibrillation.

fluty *adj* (**flutier, flutiest**) soft and clear like the sound of a flute.—**flutily** *adv*.—**flutiness** *n*.

fluvial, fluviatile *adj* of or found in streams and rivers.

fluviatile deposits *npl* (*geol*) sediments deposited by a river, often comprising sands and gravels.

flux[1] *n* a continual flowing or changing; a substance used to help metals fuse together, as in soldering.

flux[2] *n* (*med*) an excessive and abnormal flow from any of the natural openings of the body, e.g. alvine flux, which is diarrhea.

fluxion *n* a flowing; an excessive flow; (*math*) differential calculus.—**fluxional, fluxionary** *adj*.

fly[1] *n* (*pl* **flies**) a two-winged insect; a natural or imitation fly attached to a fish-hook as bait.

fly[2] *vb* (**flying, flew,** *pp* **flown**) *vi* to move through the air, esp on wings; to travel in an aircraft; to control an aircraft; to take flight, flee; to pass quickly; (*inf*) to depart quickly. * *vt* to cause to fly, as a kite; to escape, flee from; to transport by aircraft. * *n* a flap that conceals buttons, a zip, etc on trousers; material forming the outer roof of a tent; a device for regulating machinery, a flywheel.—**flyable** *adj*.

fly[3] *adj* (*inf*) sly, astute.

fly agaric *n* a poisonous woodland fungus characterized by a bright red cap flecked with white.

Flyaway *adj* (*hair etc*) loose; (*person*) flighty.

flyblow *n* the egg or larva of a fly. * *vt* (**flyblowing, flyblew,** *pp* **flyblown**) to contaminate (meat, etc) by laying eggs (esp of a blowfly) in it.

flyby *n* (*pl* **flybys**) a flight past a target, esp by a spacecraft past a celestial body to collect scientific data.

fly-by-night *adj* (*inf*) unreliable, untrustworthy; transitory. * *n* an untrustworthy person, esp one who evades responsibilities or debts by flight.

flycatcher *n* a bird that catches insects on the wing.

flyer *n* something that flies or moves very fast; a pilot.—*also* **flier**.

fly fishing *n* fishing using artificial flies as lures.—**fly-fish** *vi*.

flying *adj* capable of flight; fleeing; fast-moving. * *n* the act of flying an aircraft, etc.

flying boat *n* a sea plane in which the boat forms the fuselage and float.

flying buttress *n* a buttress connected to a wall by an arch, serving to resist outward pressure.

flying colors *npl* great success; triumph.

flying doctor *n* a doctor who visits patients (e.g. in isolated communities) by aircraft.

flying fish *n* any of numerous fishes of warm seas with winglike fins used in gliding through the air.

flying fox *n* a large fruit bat of Africa and Asia.

flying saucer *n* an unidentified flying disc-shaped object, purportedly from outer space.

flying squad *n* a small detachment of police officers mobilized for swift action.

F

flying squirrel *n* a nocturnal squirrel with folds of skin joining its legs, enabling it to glide.

flying start *n* a start in a race when the competitor is already moving when passing the starting line; a promising start in anything.

flyleaf *n* (*pl* **flyleaves**) the blank leaf at the beginning or end of a book.

Flynn *n* **Errol [Leslie Thomas Flynn]** (1909–59) Australian-born American film actor.

flyover *n* (*Brit*) a bridge that carries a road or railway over another; a fly-past.

flypaper *n* paper with a sticky poisonous coating that is hung up to trap and kill flies.

fly-past *n* a processional flight of aircraft.

fly swatter *n* a flat square of wire or plastic mesh fixed to a handle, used for killing flies.

flytrap *n* any of various insect-eating plants; a device for catching flies.

flyweight *n* a boxer weighing not more than 112 pounds (51 kg).

flywheel *n* a heavy wheel which stores energy by inertia, used to regulate machinery.

Fm *symbol* (*chem*) fermium.

fm, f.m. *abbr* (*pharm*) = *fiat mistura*, "let a mixture be made."

fm. *abbr* = fathom; from.

FM *abbr* = Field Marshal; Foreign Mission or Missions; (*Latin*) *Fraternitas Medicorum*, Fraternity of Physicians; frequency modulation.

FMA *abbr* = Family Mediators Association; Fan Manufacturers' Association; Fellow of the Museums Association; Fertilizer Manufacturers' Association; Football Membership Authority.

FMB *abbr* = Federation of Master Builders.

FMC *abbr* = Finnish Management Council; Federal Maritime Commission.

FMCS *abbr* = Federal Mediation and Conciliation Service.

FMCSA *abbr* = Federal Motor Carrier Safety Administration.

f.m.d. *abbr* = foot and mouth disease.

FMD *abbr* = foot and mouth disease.

FMDIYR *abbr* = Federation of Multiple DIY Retailers.

FMDM *abbr* = Franciscan Missionaries of the Divine Motherhood.

FMDV *abbr* = foot and mouth disease virus.

FME *abbr* = Foundation for Management Education.

FMF *abbr* = Food Manufacturers Federation; foetal movements felt.

FMG *abbr* = Food Machinery Group.

FMLA *abbr* = Family and Medical Leave Act.

FMO *abbr* = Fleet/Flight Medical Officer.

FMPA *abbr* = Fellow of the Master Photographers Association.

FMR *abbr* = Fellow of the Association of Health Care Information and Medical Records Officers; field maintenance request.

FMS *abbr* = Fellow of the Institute of Management Services; Fellow of the Medical Society; Financial Management Service; flight management system.

FMSE *abbr* = Federation of Medium and Small Employers.

FMSHRC *abbr* = Federal Mine Safety and Health Review Commission.

FMSPA *abbr* = Fish and Meat Spreadable Products Association.

FMT *abbr* = Federation of Merchant Tailors.

FMTA *abbr* = Farm Machinery and Tractor Trade Association of New South Wales.

FNCP *abbr* = Fellow of the National Council of Psychotherapists.

FNCS *abbr* = Food, Nutrition, and Consumer Services.

FNI *abbr* = Fellow of the Nautical Institute.

FNIMH *abbr* = Fellow of the National Institute of Medical Herbalists.

FNMA *abbr* = Federal National Mortgage Association.

FNO *abbr* = Fleet Navigation Officer.

FNS *abbr* = Food and Nutrition Service.

FNSSA *abbr* = Field Naturalists Society of South Australia.

f-number *n* (*photog*) a number used to calculate the ratio of light passing through a lens.

fo. *abbr* = folio.

f.o. *abbr* = field officer; field orders; (*music*) full organ.

F/o. *abbr* = for orders.

FO *abbr* = Faculty of Ophthalmologists; Field Officer; Flag Officer; Flying Officer; Foreign Office (*Brit*).

Fo *n* **Dario** (1926–) Italian dramatist and director whose satirical farces target social issues such as police corruption and the oppression of women. He was awarded the Nobel prize for literature in 1997.

FOAA *abbr* = Flying Optometrists Association of America.

FOAL *abbr* = Friends of Animals League.

foal *n* the young of the horse or a related animal. * *vti* to give birth to a foal.

foam *n* froth or fine bubbles on the surface of liquid; something like foam, as frothy saliva; a rigid or springy cellular mass made from liquid rubber, plastic, etc. * *vi* to cause or emit foam.

foamy *adj* (**foamier, foamiest**) of, like, or covered with foam.—**foamily** *adv*.—**foaminess** *n*.

FOAS *abbr* = Friends of Afghanistan Society.

fob[1] *n* the chain or ribbon for attaching a watch to a waistcoat; any object attached to a watch chain; a small pocket in a waistcoat for a watch.

fob[2] *vt* (**fobbing, fobbed**) (*with* **off**) to cheat; to put off; to palm off (upon).

fob, f.o.b. *abbr* = free on board.

FOB *abbr* = Friends of Blue; free on board.

FOBS *abbr* = fractional-orbit bombardment system.

foc *abbr* = free of charge.

FOC *abbr* = Father of the Chapel (union official).

focal *adj* of or pertaining to a focus.—**focally** *adv*.

focalize *vti* to (cause to) focus.—**focalization** *n*.

focal length *n* the distance between the focal point and optical center of a lens or mirror.

focal point *n* the point on the axis of a lens or mirror at which rays meet after reflection or refraction.

Foch *n* **Ferdinand** (1851–1929) French general and marshal of France (1918). He led the Allies to victory following the arrival of US troops in July 1918.

fo'c's'le, fo'c'sle *see* **forecastle.**

focus[1] *n* (*pl* **focuses, foci**) a point where rays of light, heat, etc, meet after being bent by a lens, curved mirror, etc; correct adjustment of the eye or lens to form a clear image; a center of activity or interest. * *vt* (**focusing, focused** *or* **focussing, focussed**) to adjust the focus of; to bring into focus; to concentrate.—**focusable** *adj*.—**focuser** *n*.

focus[2] *n* the point of origin of an earthquake.

focus group *n* a group of people who are appointed to carry out a detailed discussion and to give views on a particular topic or concept.

fodder *n* dried food for cattle, horses, etc.

foe *n* an enemy, an adversary.

FOE *abbr* = Friends of the Earth.

foederati *n* tribes outside the boundaries of the Roman Empire but who had a relationship with Rome established by treaty.

foehn *see* **föhn.**

foeman *n* (*arch*) an adversary in war.

foetal *see* **fetal.**

foeticide *see* **feticide.**

foetid *see* **fetid.**

foetus *see* **fetus.**

FOFA *abbr* = follow-on forces' attack.

fog[1] *n* (a state of poor visibility caused by) a large mass of water vapor condensed to fine particles just above the earth's surface; a state of mental confusion; (*photog*) cloudiness on a developed photograph. * *vti* (**fogging, fogged**) to make or become foggy.

fog[2] *n* a second growth of grass in autumn; winter pasture; (*Scot*) moss.

fogbound *n* unable to function due to fog.

fogey, fogy *n* (*pl* **fogeys, fogies**) a person of old-fashioned or eccentric habits.—**fogeyish, fogyish** *adj*.

foggy *adj* (**foggier, foggiest**) thick with fog; mentally confused; indistinct, opaque.—**foggily** *adv*.—**fogginess** *n*.

foghorn *n* a horn (in a ship, etc) sounded in a fog as a warning.

fogy *see* **fogey.**

FOH *abbr* (*theat*) = front of house.

föhn *n* a warm, dry, Alpine wind.—*also* **foehn.**

FOI *abbr* = Freedom of Information.

FOIA *abbr* = Freedom of Information Act.

foible *n* a slight weakness or failing; an idiosyncrasy; the weakest part of the blade of a sword.

FOIC *abbr* = Flag Officer in Charge.

foil[1] *vt* to defeat; to frustrate; to trample a trail to spoil scent. * *n* (*arch*) the trail of hunted game.—**foilable** *adj*.

foil[2] *n* a very thin sheet of metal; a backing for a mirror or gem; anything that sets off or enhances another by contrast; (*archit*) a small arc or space in the tracery of a window. * *vt* to cover, back, or adorn with foil; to set off.

foil[3] *n* a long, thin blunted sword used for fencing.

foison *n* (*arch*) an abundance.

foist *vt* (*with* **in** *or* **into**) to introduce stealthily or without permission; (*with* **off** *or* **on**) to pass off as genuine.

Fokine *n* **Michel** (1880–1942) Russian-born American ballet dancer and choreographer.

Fokker *n* **Anthony [Anthony Herman Gerard]** (1890–1939) Dutch aeronautical engineer, founder of the Fokker aircraft factory in Germany, which built planes for the German airforce in World War II.

fol. *abbr* = folio; following.

folacin *see* **folic acid.**

-fold *suffix* times repeated, e.g. *tenfold*.

fold[1] *vt* to cover by bending or doubling over so that one part covers another; to wrap up, envelop; to interlace (one's arms); to clasp (one's hands); to embrace; to incorporate (an ingredient) into a food mixture by gentle overturnings. * *vi* to become folded; to fail completely; to collapse, esp to go out of business. * *n* something folded, as a piece of cloth; a crease or hollow made by folding.—**foldable** *adj*.

fold[2] *n* a pen for sheep; a group of people or institutions having a common belief, activity, etc. * *vt* to pen in a fold.

fold[3] *n* (*geol*) a curve or bend in a flat bed of rock due to the application of immense forces over a long period of time.

foldaway *adj* (*bed, etc*) collapsible.

folder[1] *n* a folded cover or large envelope for holding loose papers.

folder[2] *n* (*comput*) in graphical user interface systems, the directory in which files are located or stored.

folderol *see* **falderal**.

folding *n* the act or process of folding. * *adj* which folds or can be folded.

folia *n* (*mus*) (*Portuguese*) literally "the folly," a wild and noisy Portuguese dance.

foliaceous *adj* resembling or having leaves; (*rock*) having thin layers.

foliage *n* leaves, as of a plant or tree.

foliar *adj* of or pertaining to leaves.

foliate *adj* resembling or having leaves. * *vti* to beat (metal) into foil; to divide into thin layers; to produce leaves; (*archit*) to decorate with foils; to number the leaves of (a book).

foliation *n* (*bot*) the act of producing leaves or the state of having leaves; the act or process of beating a metal into thin plates.

folic acid *n* (*biol*) a compound that forms part of the vitamin B complex, found in green vegetables, whole wheat products, peas, and beans.—*also* **folacin**.

folio *n* (*pl* **folios**) a large sheet of paper folded once to make two leaves of a book; a book of sheets in this size, the largest commonly used; the number of a page in a book. * *vt* (**folioing, folioed**) to number the pages of.

foliose *adj* (*bot*) having many leaves; of or resembling leaves.

folk *n* (*pl* **folk, folks**) a people of a country or tribe; people in general, esp those of a particular area; relatives; folk music. * *adj* of or originating among the ordinary people.—**folkish** *adj*.

folk dance *n* (*mus*) any dance, performed by ordinary people, in a pre-industrial society, that has evolved over the years and gained a traditional form.

folk etymology *n* the perversion of a word in an attempt to explain it, as "sparrow grass" for "asparagus."

folklore *n* the traditional beliefs, customs, legends, etc, of a people; the study of these.—**folkloric, folkloristic** *adj*.—**folklorist** *n*.

folk medicine *n* traditional medicine as practiced nonprofessionally, esp the use of herbal remedies.

folk music *n* traditional music.

folk song *n* (*mus*) properly, any song that has been preserved by oral tradition.

folksy *adj* (**folksier, folksiest**) (*inf*) simple, plain; friendly.—**folksiness** *n*.

folktale *n* an anonymous, timeless, and placeless tale circulated orally among a people.

foll. *abbr* = following.

follicle *n* any small sac, cavity, or gland, e.g. hair follicles.—**follicular, folliculate, folliculated** *adj*.

follicle-stimulating hormone *n* a hormone produced by males and females that controls, directly or indirectly, growth of the ova and sperm. * *abbr* FSH. *See* **gonadotrophines**.

Follot *n* **Paul** (1877–1941) French decorative artist whose early work has much in common with the Pre-Raphaelites.

follow *vt* to go or come after; to pursue; to go along (a path, road, etc); to copy; to obey; to adopt, as an opinion; to watch fixedly; to focus the mind on; to understand the meaning of; to monitor the progress of; to come or occur after in time; to result from; (*with* **through**) to pursue (an aim) to a conclusion; (*with* **up**) to pursue a question, inquiry, etc, that has been started. * *vi* to go or come after another; to result; (*with* **on**) (*cricket*) to take a second innings immediately after a first; (*with* **suit**) to play a card of the same suit; to do the same thing; (*with* **through**) (*sport*) to continue a stroke or motion of a bat, club, etc after the ball has been struck; (*with* **up**) to pursue steadily; to supplement.—**followable** *adj*.

follower *n* a disciple or adherent; a person who imitates another.

following *n* a body of adherents or believers. * *adj* next after; now to be stated.

follow-on *n* (*cricket*) an immediate return to bat by a side which has scored a certain number of runs fewer than its opponents in the first innings.

follow-through *n* (*golf, tennis, etc*) the continuation of a swing after hitting the ball.

follow-up *n* the continuing after a beginning; a steady pursuit.

folly[1] *n* (*pl* **follies**) a lack of sense; a foolish act or idea.

folly[2] *n* (*archit*) an extravagant useless construction usually in the form of Gothic ruins, a tower, or fanciful structure of some kind.

Fomalhaut *or* **Alpha Piscis Austrini** *n* (*astron*) a first magnitude hot dwarf star.

Fomboni *n* a city in Comoros.

FOMC *abbr* = Federal Open Market Committee.

foment *vt* to stir up (trouble); to bathe with warm water or lotions.—**fomenter** *n*.

fomentation *n* the act of fomenting; instigation; the application of a warm lotion to ease pain or swelling. *See also* **poultice**.

Fomorii *or* **Fomhoire** *or* **Fomoire** *or* **Fomorians** *n* (*Irish Celtic myth*) a race of demonic beings, many of whom were half-human, half-monster, translated both as "sea giants" and as "under-demons."

fond *adj* loving, affectionate; doting, indulgent; (*arch*) overcredulous, simple; (*with* **of**) having a liking for.—**fondly** *adv*.— **fondness** *n*.

Fonda *n* 1. **Henry** (1905–82) American film actor. 2. **Jane** (1937–) daughter of Henry Fonda and an actress. She was an outspoken critic of the Vietnam war.

fondant *n* a soft sugar mixture for sweets and icings; a sweet made from this.

fondle *vt* to caress.—**fondler** *n*.—**fondlingly** *adv*.

fondue *n* melted cheese used as a dip with small pieces of bread.

font[1] *n* a receptacle for baptismal water; a receptacle for holy water.—**fontal** *adj*.

font[2] *see* **fount**[1].

font[3] *n* a complete set of letters, numbers, special characters, and punctuation marks of a particular size and for one identifiable typeface whether roman or bold (the weight), italic or upright (the posture).

Fontaine *n* **Pierre** (1762–1853) French architect. His notable works include the restoration of the Palais Royal, Paris.

Fontana *n* 1. **Carlo** (1638–1714) Italian draftsman who became architect of St Peter's, in Rome, in 1697. 2. **Domenico** (1543–1607) Italian architect. His notable works include the Vatican Library.

fontanameter *n* a device for measuring the pressure within the skull of a fetus in the womb.

fontanel, fontanelle *n* an opening in the skull of newborn and young infants in whom the bone is not wholly formed and the sutures are incompletely fused.

Fontenay *n* **Eugene** (1823–87) French goldsmith, best-known for his delicate decorations inspired by ancient Etruscan styles.

Fonteyn *n* **Dame Margot [Margaret Hookham]** (1919–91) English prima ballerina. She partnered Rudolf Nureyev at the age of 43.

font family *n* (*comput*) a set of fonts sharing the same typeface but differing in the size and the boldness of the type.

food *n* any substance, esp a solid, taken in by a plant or animal to enable it to live and grow; anything that nourishes.

food chain *n* (*ecology*) a series of organisms in a community, each of which is dependent on the next for food.

foodie *n* (*pl* **foodies**) (*inf*) a person who takes great delight in cooking and eating.

food poisoning *n* an acute illness caused by harmful bacteria or toxins in food.

food processor *n* an electric appliance used to perform various functions when preparing food, as chopping, mixing, and grating.

foodstuff *n* a substance used as food.

food vessel *n* (*archeo*) a container of variable form found in a particular type of early Bronze Age burial in Ireland and northerly parts of the British Isles.

fool *n* a person lacking wisdom or common sense; (*Middle Ages*) a jester; a dupe; a cold dessert made from whipped cream mixed with fruit purée. * *vt* to deceive, make a fool of. * *vi* to act jokingly; to spend time idly; to tease or meddle with.

foolery *n* (*pl* **fooleries**) foolish behavior, buffoonery.

foolhardy *adj* (**foolhardier, foolhardiest**) foolishly bold; rash.—**foolhardiness** *n*.

foolish *adj* unwise; ridiculous; ill-judged.—**foolishly** *adv*.—**foolishness** *n*.

foolproof *adj* proof against failure; easy to understand; easy to use.

foolscap *n* a large size of writing paper.

fool's errand *n* a pointless undertaking.

fools' gold *n* any of various minerals, such as pyrites, that can be mistaken for gold.

fool's paradise *n* illusory happiness.

foot *n* (*pl* **feet**) the end part of the leg, on which one stands; anything a resembling foot, as the lower part of a chair, table, etc; the lower part or edge of something, bottom; a measure of length equal to 12 inches (30.48 cm); the part of a garment that covers the foot; an attachment on a sewing machine that grips the fabric; a group of syllables serving as a unit of meter in verse. * *vi* to dance. * *vt* to walk, dance over or on; to pay the entire cost of (a bill).

Foot *n* **Michael [Mackintosh]** (1913–) British Labour politician and leader of the Labour Party (1980–83).

footage *n* measurement in feet, esp film exposed.

foot-and-mouth disease *n* a contagious disease of cattle.

foot soldier *n* a soldier who fights on foot; an infantryman.

football *n* in US and Canada, a game played by two teams of eleven players using an oval leather ball which may be handled; rugby football; soccer.—**footballer** *n*.

footboard *n* a treadle on a machine; a step on a carriage.

footbridge *n* a narrow bridge for pedestrians.

Foote *n* **Samuel** (1720–77) English actor and dramatist whose plays and performances frequently satirized his contemporaries.

footer[1] *n* (*sl*) football.

footer[2] *n* (*comput*) text positioned at the foot of a page by a word processing program.

footfall *n* the sound of a footstep.

foot-fault *n* (*tennis*) overstepping the base line when serving. * *vi* to commit a foot-fault.

footgear *n* shoes and socks, etc.

foothill *n* a hill at the foot of higher hills.

foothold *n* a ledge, etc for placing the foot when climbing, etc; a place from which further progress may be made.

footie *see* **footy**.

footing *n* the basis upon which something rests; status; relationship; a foothold; (*archit*) a projecting course at the base of a wall.

footle *vi* to potter.

footlights *npl* a row of lights in front of a stage floor.

footling *adj* trifling.

footloose *adj* free, untrammeled.

footman *n* (*pl* **footmen**) a liveried servant or attendant.

footmark *n* a footprint.

footnote *n* a note or comment at the foot of a page.

footpad *n* (*arch*) a highwayman on foot.

footpath *n* a narrow path for pedestrians.

foot-pound *n* a unit of energy, equal to the work required to raise a one pound weight through one foot; equivalent to 0.042 joule.

footprint[1] *n* the impression left by a foot.

footprint[2] *n* (*comput*) a physical measure of the amount of desk space that a computer and its peripheral devices take up when sitting on the user's desk.

foot-rot *n* an inflammation of the feet of sheep and cattle; a plant disease affecting stalks and trunks; (*sl*) athlete's foot.

foots *npl* the sediment of oil or sugar.

footsie *n* (*inf*) amorous touching together of feet; (*inf*) clandestine dealings.

footslog *vt* (**footslogging, footslogged**) (*inf*) to march.

footsore *adj* having painful feet from excessive walking.

footstalk *n* (*bot*) the supporting stem of a plant or flower; (*zool*) the attachment of a barnacle.

footstall *n* a woman's stirrup (used on a sidesaddle)

footstep *n* a step forward in walking; the sound of this; a footmark; a single step on a stair, etc; (*pl*) another's example.

footstool *n* a stool for the feet of a seated person.

footwear *n* shoes and socks, etc.

footwork *n* skillful use of the feet in boxing, football, dancing, etc.

footy *n* (*sl*) football.—*also* **footie**.

foozle *n* (*golf*) a bungled shot. * *vi* to bungle (a shot).

fop *n* someone obsessed with fashion and appearance.

FOP *abbr* = forward observation post.

foppery *n* (*pl* **fopperies**) the appearance, manner, or dress of a fop.

foppish *adj* affected in dress and manners.—**foppishly** *adv*.—**foppishness** *n*.

for *prep* because of, as a result of; as the price of, or recompense of; in order to be, to serve as; appropriate to, or adapted to; in quest of; in the direction of; on behalf of; in place of; in favor of; with respect to; notwithstanding, in spite of; to the extent of; throughout the space of; during. * *conj* because.

for. *abbr* = foreign; forestry.

f.o.r., FOR *abbr* = free on rail.

FoR *abbr* = Fellowship of Reconciliation.

for- *prefix* expressing prohibition or neglect; bad effect; intensity.

forage *n* food for domestic animals, esp when taken by browsing or grazing; a search for provisions. * *vi* to search for food.—**forager** *n*.

Forain *n* Jean Louis (1852–1931) French painter and caricaturist. His work reveals the cartoonist's economical sense of line and gesture.

foramen *n* (*pl* **foramina, foramens**) a short passage or opening, esp in a bone.

foraminifer *n* a member of a group of protozoa having a shell with very minute apertures, through which parts of its body pass.

forasmuch as *conj* seeing that, since.

foray *n* a sudden raid. * *vti* to plunder.—**forayer** *n*.

forbad, forbade *see* **forbid.**

Forbay *n* (*Irish Celtic myth*) the son of Conchobar mac Nessa. He is said to have killed Medb with a slingshot as she bathed in a lake on the island where she lived after the death of her husband, Ailill.

forbear *vb* (**forbearing, forbore,** *pp* **forborne**) *vi* to endure, to avoid. * *vt* to hold oneself back from.—**forbearer** *n*.—**forbearingly** *adv*.

forbearance *n* patience; self-control.

Forbicini *n* Fulvio (1952–) Italian industrial designer who started out with Roche Bobois, before opening his own studio.

forbid *vt* (**forbidding, forbad** *or* **forbade,** *pp* **forbidden** *or* **forbid**) to command (a person) not to do something; to render impossible, prevent.—**forbiddance** *n*.—**forbidder** *n*.

forbidden line *n* an emission line formed by an electron making a drop from a higher energy level to a lower one, changing quantum numbers in a way which cannot normally happen.

forbidding *adj* unfriendly, solemn, strict.—**forbiddingly** *adv*.

forbore, forborne *see* **forbear.**

Forbush effect *n* an occasional decrease in the intensity of cosmic rays at times when solar flares are prominent, possibly associated with the coincident magnetic fields.

FORC *abbr* = Financial Options Research Center.

force *n* strength, power, effort; (*physics*) (the intensity of) an influence that causes movement of a body or other effects; a body of soldiers, police, etc prepared for action; effectiveness; violence, compulsion; legal or logical validity. * *vt* to compel or oblige by physical effort, superior strength, etc; to achieve by force; to press or drive against resistance; to produce with effort; to break open, penetrate; to impose, inflict; to cause (plants, animals) to grow at a greater rate than normal.—**forceable** *adj*.—**forcer** *n*.

forced *adj* compulsory; strained.—**forcedly** *adv*.—**forcedness** *n*.

forced march *n* a long and arduous march, esp by soldiers.

force-feed *vt* (**force-feeding, force-fed**) to compel a person to swallow food.

forceful *adj* powerful, effective.—**forcefully** *adv*.—**forcefulness** *n*.

force majeure *n* compelling force, unavoidable circumstances.

forcemeat *n* finely chopped meat, seasoned and used as a stuffing.

force of habit *n* action performed routinely or unconsciously through custom or frequent repetition.

forceps *n* (*pl* **forceps, forcipes**) an instrument for grasping and holding firmly, or exerting traction upon objects, esp by jewelers and surgeons.

force pump *n* a pump that forces water beyond the range of atmospheric pressure.

forcible *adj* powerful; done by force.—**forcibleness** *n*.—**forcibly** *adv*.

ford *n* a shallow crossing place in a river, stream, etc. * *vt* to wade across.—**fordable** *adj*.

Ford *n* 1. **Ford** Madox (1873–1939) English novelist, editor, and critic whose most important works are the novel *The Good Soldier* and the tetralogy *Parade's End*. 2. **Gerald R[udolph]** (1913–) American Republican statesman and 38th president of the US (1974–77). 3. **Harrison** (1942–) American film actor whose films include the *Indiana Jones* series, e.g. *Indiana Jones and the Last Crusade* (1989). 4. **Henry** (1863–1947) American car designer and manufacturer. The production of his Model T Ford, introduced in 1908, became a role model for industry. 5. **John** (1585–*c*.1639) English dramatist, notable for such revenge tragedies as "*'Tis Pity She's a Whore* and *The Broken Heart*. 6. **John [Sean Aloysius O'Fearna]** (1895–1973) American film director whose films include *Stagecoach* (1939).

FORDS *abbr* = Floating Ocean Research and Development Station.

fore *adj* in front. * *n* the front. * *adv* in, at or towards the front. * *interj* (*golf*) a warning cry to anybody who may be hit by the ball.

fore- *prefix* in front; beforehand.

fore-and-aft *adj* (*naut*) (situated) at both bow and stern.

forearm[1] *n* the arm between the elbow and the wrist.

forearm[2] *vt* to arm in advance.

forebear *n* (*usu pl*) an ancestor.

forebode *vt* to be a sign or warning (of trouble, etc) in advance; to have a premonition of (an event).—**foreboder** *n*.

foreboding *n* a feeling that evil is going to happen, a presentiment.

forebrain *n* the part of the brain that consists of the thalamus and hypothalamus.

forecast *vt* (**forecasting, forecast** *or* **forecasted**) to predict (an event, the weather, etc) through rational analysis; to serve as a forecast of. * *n* a prediction, esp of weather; foresight.—**forecaster** *n*.

forecastle *n* the forward part of a ship containing the crew's quarters.—*also* **fo'c's'le, fo'c'sl**.

foreclose *vt* to remove the right of redeeming (a mortgage); to bar, exclude; to hinder.—**foreclosable** *adj*.—**foreclosure** *n*.

forecourt *n* an enclosed space in front of a building, as in a filling station.

foredeep *see* **deep**.

fore-dune *n* on a beach, the dune or line of dunes nearest the sea.

forefather *n* (*usu pl*) an ancestor.

forefinger *n* the finger next to the thumb.

forefoot *n* (*pl* **forefeet**) a front foot of an animal; (*naut*) the foremost piece of the keel.

forefront *n* the very front, vanguard.

Forgall *n* (*Irish Celtic myth*) the father of Emer, who married Cuchulainn.

foregather *see* **forgather**.

forego[1] *see* **forgo**.

forego[2] *vt* (**foregoing, forewent,** *pp* **foregone**) to precede.—**foregoer** *n*.

foregoing *adj* going before, preceding.

foregone conclusion *n* an inevitable result, easily predictable.

foreground *n* the part of a picture or view nearest the spectator's vision.

foreground task *n* (*comput*) the priority job that the computer is undertaking. *See also* **background task**.

forehand *n* (*tennis, etc*) a stroke made with the hand facing forwards; the part of a horse in front of the rider. * *adj* (*tennis stroke*) made with the palm leading.

forehanded *adj* thrifty; well-off.—**forehandedness** *n*.

forehead *n* the part of the face above the eyes.

foreign *adj* of, in, or belonging to another country; involving other countries; alien in character; introduced from outside.

foreign correspondent *n* a journalist employed to send news from a foreign country.

foreigner *n* a person from another country; a stranger.

foreign exchange *n* the currency of other countries; commercial dealings in foreign currencies.

foreign exchange market *n* an international market in which foreign currencies are bought and sold.

foreign investment *n* investment in a country's domestic economy by foreign companies or individuals.

foreignism *n*.a foreign mannerism, custom, or saying, or an imitation of any of these.

foreign minister *n* the government minister responsible for dealings with other countries.

foreign office *n* the government department which handles foreign affairs.—*also* **state department**.

foreign policy *n* the political policies of a state with regard to other states in the international community.

forejudge *vti* to judge before hearing evidence.

foreknow *vt* (**foreknowing, foreknew,** *pl* **foreknown**) to know beforehand.— **foreknowledge** *n*.

foreland *n* a promontory, a headland.

foreleg *n* a front leg of an animal.

forelock *n* the lock of hair growing above the forehead.

foreman *n* (*pl* **foremen**) a person who supervises workers in a factory, etc; the spokesperson of a jury.—**forewoman** *nf* (*pl* **forewomen**).

foremast *n* the mast nearest the bow of a sailing vessel.

foremost *adj* first in importance; most advanced in rank or position. * *adv* in the first place.

forenoon *n* time before midday; morning.

forensic *adj* of, belonging to or used in courts of law.—**forensicality** *n*.—**forensically** *adv*.

forensic medicine *n* the application of medical expertise to legal and criminal investigations.

foreordain *vt* to arrange in advance; to predestine.—**foreordainment, foreordination** *n*.

forepeak *n* (*naut*) the end of a ship's hold in the angle of the bow.

foreplay *n* mutual sexual stimulation before intercourse.

forerun *vt* (**forerunning, foreran,** *pp* **forerun**) to precede, to foreshadow.

forerunner *n* a person or thing that comes in advance of another; a portent.

foresail *n* (*naut*) the largest sail on the foremast of a sailing vessel.

foresee *vt* (**foreseeing, foresaw,** *pp* **foreseen**) to be aware of beforehand.— **foreseeable** *adj*.—**foreseer** *n*.

foreshadow *vt* to represent or indicate beforehand.—**foreshadower** *n*.

foresheet *n* a rope for controlling a foresail; (*pl*) the inner part of a boat's bows.

foreshock *n* an earth tremor that occurs shortly before an earthquake.

foreshore *n* a strip of land next to the shore; the shore between the high and low water marks.

foreshorten *vt* in drawing, etc, to shorten some lines of (an object) to give the illusion of proper relative size.

foresight *n* foreseeing; the power to foresee; prudent provision for the future.— **foresighted** *adj*.—**foresightedness** *n*.

foreskin *n* the loose skin that covers the end of the penis.

forest *n* a thick growth of trees, etc covering a large tract of land; something resembling a forest. * *vt* to plant with trees; to make into forest.—**forestal, forestial** *adj*.

FOREST *abbr* = Freedom Organization for the Right to Enjoy Smoking Tobacco.

forestall *vt* to prevent by taking action beforehand; to anticipate.—**forestaller** *n*.— **forestalment, forestallment** *n*.

forestation *n* the planting of trees over a large area.

forestay *n* (*naut*) a strong rope reaching from the top of the foremast to the bow of a vessel.

forester *n* a person trained in forestry.

forestry *n* the science of planting and cultivating forests.

foretaste *n* partial experience in advance; anticipation. * *vt* to taste before possession; to have a foretaste of.

foretell *vt* (**foretelling, foretold**) to forecast, to predict.—**foreteller** *n*.

forethought *n* thought for the future; provident care.—**forethoughtful** *adj*.

foretime *n* the past, old times.

foretoken *vt* to portend, foreshadow. * *n* an omen.

foretop *n* (*naut*) a platform at the head of the foremast.

fore-topgallant mast *n* the mast above the fore-topmast, carrying the fore-topgallant sail.

fore-topmast *n* (*naut*) the mast immediately above the foremast, carrying the fore-topsail.

for ever, forever *adv* for all future time; continually.

for evermore, forevermore *adv* for ever.

forewarn *vt* to warn beforehand.—**forewarner** *n*.—**forewarningly** *adv*.

forewent *see* **forego**.

forewind *n* (*naut*) a favorable wind.

forewoman *n* (*pl* **forewomen**) a person who supervises workers in a factory, etc; the spokesperson of a jury.

foreword *n* an introduction to a book to explain its purpose, often by someone other than the author.

forfeit *n* something confiscated or given up as a penalty for a fault; (*pl*) a game in which a player redeems a forfeit by performing a ludicrous task. * *vt* to lose or be penalized by forfeiture.—**forfeiter** *n*.—**forfeiture** *n*.

forfend *vt* to protect; (*arch*) to avert, ward off.

forficate *adj* (*zool*) scissor-shaped, forked.

forg. *abbr* = forgery.

Forgall *n* (*Irish Celtic myth*) the father of Emer, who married Cuchulainn.

forgather *vi* to assemble, meet.—*also* **foregather**.

forgave *see* **forgive**.

forge[1] *n* (a workshop with) a furnace in which metals are heated and shaped. * *vt* to shape (metal) by heating and hammering; to counterfeit, e.g. a signature. * *vi* to commit forgery.—**forgeable** *adj*.—**forger** *n*.

forge[2] *vt* to move steadily forward with effort.

forgery *n* (*pl* **forgeries**) fraudulently copying; a forged copy; a spurious thing.

forget *vti* (**forgetting, forgot,** *pp* **forgotten**) to be unable to remember; to overlook or neglect; **forget oneself** to lose self-control; to act unbecomingly.—**forgettable** *adj*.—**forgetter** *n*.

forgetful *adj* apt to forget, inattentive.—**forgetfully** *adv*.—**forgetfulness** *n*.

forget-me-not *n* a plant with bright-blue or white flowers.

forgive *vt* (**forgiving, forgave,** *pp* **forgiven**) to cease to feel resentment against (a person); to pardon. * *vi* to be merciful or forgiving.—**forgivable** *adj*.— **forgiveness** *n*.—**forgiver** *n*.

forgiving *adj* willing to forgive; merciful, kind.—**forgivingly** *adv*.

forgo *vt* (**forgoing, forwent,** *pp* **forgone**) to give up, abstain from.—*also* **forego**.— **forgoer** *n*.

forgot, forgotten *see* **forget**.

forint *n* the standard monetary unit of Hungary, made up of 100 filler.

fork *n* a small, usu metal, instrument with two or more thin prongs set in a handle, used in eating and cooking; a pronged agricultural or gardening tool for digging, etc; anything that divides into prongs or branches; one of the branches into which a road or river divides; the point of separation. * *vi* to divide into branches; to follow a branch of a fork in a road, etc. * *vt* to form as a fork; to dig, lift, etc with a fork; (*with* **out**) (*sl*) to pay or hand over (money, goods, etc).

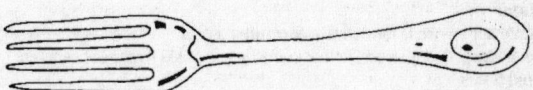

forked *adj* shaped like a fork; branching, opening into two or more parts; zigzag, e.g. lightning.

fork-lift truck *n* a vehicle with power-operated prongs for raising and lowering loads.

forlana *n* (*mus*) (*Italian*) an Italian dance from northern Italy that is especially associated with Venetian gondoliers.

forlorn *adj* alone; wretched.—**forlornly** *adv*.

forlorn hope *n* a faint hope; a desperate enterprise.

form[1] *n* general structure; the figure of a person or animal; a mold; a particular mode, kind, type, etc; arrangement; a way of doing something requiring skill; a conventional procedure; a printed document with blanks to be filled in; a class in school; condition of mind or body; a chart giving information about racehorses; changed appearance of a word to show inflection; (*sl*) a criminal record. * *vt* to shape; to train; to develop (habits); to constitute. * *vi* to be formed.— **formable** *adj*.

form[2] *see* **forme**.

formal *adj* in conformity with established rules or habits; regular; relating to the outward appearance only; ceremonial; punctilious; stiff.—**formally** *adv*.

formaldehyde *n* a colorless pungent gas used in solution as a disinfectant and preservative.

formalin *n* an aqueous solution of formaldehyde used as an antiseptic or preservative.—*also* **formol**.

formalism *n* strict observance of outward form or conventional usage.— **formalist** *n*.—**formalistic** *adj*.

formality *n* (*pl* **formalities**) strict observance of established rules or customs; an act or procedure required by law or convention.

formalize *vt* to make formal; to clothe with legal formality.—**formalization** *n*.

Forman *n* Milos (1932–) Czech film director, resident in the US since 1968. His American films include the very successful black comedy *One Flew Over the Cuckoo's Nest* (1975) and *Amadeus* (1988), the latter being mostly filmed in Prague.

format[1] *n* the size, form, shape in which books, etc, are issued; the general style or presentation of something, e.g. a television show. * *vt* (**formatting, formatted**) to arrange in a particular form, esp for a computer.

format[2] *n* (*comput*) the preparation of a hard disk or floppy disk for use by laying down clearly defined recording areas; the overall arrangement of labels and values in the separate cells of a spreadsheet, database management, or word processing program.

formate *n* a salt of formic acid..

formation *n* form of making or producing; that which is formed; structure; regular array or prearranged order; (*geol*) a group of strata with common characteristics.— **formational** *adj*.

F

formative *adj* pertaining to formation and development; shaping; (*gram*) used in forming words.—**formatively** *adv*.—**formativeness** *n*.

formatting *n* (*comput*) the process of instruction that produces the desired format of text in a document for on-screen display or printing.

forme *n* a frame with type assembled in it for printing.—*also* **form**.

former *adj* of or occurring in a previous time; the first mentioned (of two).—**formerly** *adv*.

formeret *n* (*archit*) a non-structural rib in a vault bay constructed along the side wall in order to complete a design.—*also* **wall rib**.

formerly *adv* previously; heretofore.

formic acid *n* a colorless pungent liquid found esp in ants and many plants.

formic *adj* of or pertaining to ants or formic acid.

Formica *n* (*trademark*) a heat-resistant laminated sheeting.

formicary, formicarium *n* (*pl* **formicaries, formicaria**) an anthill.

formication *n* an irritation of the skin, resembling the sensation made by insects crawling over it.

formidable *adj* causing fear or awe; difficult to defeat or overcome; difficult to handle.—**formidability** *n*.—**formidably** *adv*.

formless *adj* without distinct form, shapeless.—**formlessness** *n*.

form-line *n* a line drawn on a map to give an impression of the terrain. There is not sufficient information to draw an accurate contour line, probably because the area has not been surveyed.

formol *see* **formalin**.

formula *n* (*pl* **formulas, formulae**) a set of symbols expressing the composition of a substance; a general expression in algebraic form for solving a problem; a prescribed form; a formal statement of doctrines; a list of ingredients, as for a prescription or recipe; a fixed method according to which something is to be done; a prescribed recipe for baby food.—**formulaic** *adj*.

formularize *vt* to formulate.—**formularization** *n*.—**formularizer** *n*.

formulary *n* (*pl* **formularies**) a book of prescribed forms or of prayers, ritual, etc; (*med*) a book giving details of the formulas and preparation of pharmaceutical products. * *adj* of formulas or ritual.

formulate *vt* to express in a formula; to devise.—**formulation** *n*.—**formulator** *n*.

formulism *n* adherence to formulas.—**formulist** *adj, n*.

formwork *n* (*archit*) any structure that contains and holds fresh, wet concrete in place until it sets.

Fornasetti *n* **Piero** (1913–88) Italian artist taken up by Gio Ponti.

Fornax *n* (*astron*) a southern sky constellation, with no stars brighter than the fourth magnitude.

fornicate[1] *vi* to have sexual intercourse without being married.—**fornication** *n*.—**fornicator** *n*.

fornicate[2], **fornicated** *adj* (*archit*) vaulted, arched.

fornix *n* (*pl* **fornices**) (*anat*) an arch-shaped part.

forsake *vt* (**forsaking, forsook**, *pp* **forsaken**) to desert; to give up, renounce.—**forsaker** *n*.

Forseth *n* **Einar** (1892–1988) Swedish-born church decorator who later specialized in stained glass and mosaics.

forsooth *adv* (*arch*) in truth.

Forster *n* **E[dward] M[ontagu]** (1879–1970) English novelist and critic whose novels, e.g. *Howards End*, are mainly concerned with moral and ethical choices, and whose best-known work is *A Passage to India*.

forswear *vb* (**forswearing, forswore**, *pp* **foresworn**) *vt* to reject, renounce; to deny; to perjure (oneself).

Forsyth *n* **Gordon Mitchell** (1879–1953) Scottish ceramicist who specialized in lustreware. His *Twentieth Century Ceramics* was published in 1936.

forsythia *n* a widely cultivated, yellow-flowered shrub.

fort *n* a fortified place for military defense.

fort. *abbr* = fortification; fortified.

Fort-de-France *n* capital city of Martinique.

forte[1] *n* something at which a person excels.

forte[2] *adv* (*mus*) loudly.

forte-piano *adj, adv* (*music*) loud then soft.

fortepiano *n* (*mus*) (*Italian*) an early word for pianoforte. Not to be confused with *forte-piano* (loud then soft).

forth *adv* forwards; onwards; out; into view; **and so forth** and the like.

forthcoming *adj* about to appear; readily available; responsive.—**forthcomingness** *n*.

forthright *adv* frank, direct, outspoken; decisive.—**forthrightly** *adv*.—**forthrightness** *n*.

forthwith *adv* immediately, without delay.

fortification *n* the act or process of fortifying; a wall, barricade, etc built to defend a position.

fortify *vt* (**fortifying, fortified**) to strengthen physically, emotionally, etc; to strengthen against attack, as with forts; to support; (*wine, etc*) to add alcohol to; (*milk*) to add vitamins to.—**fortifiable** *adj*.—**fortifier** *n*.

fortissimo *adv* (*mus*) very loud. * *n* (*pl* **fortissimos, fortissimi**) (*mus*) a passage played very loudly.

fortitude *n* courage in adversity; patient endurance, firmness.—**fortitudinous** *adj*.

fortnight *n* (*Brit*) a period of two weeks or fourteen consecutive days.

fortnightly *adj, adv* (*Brit*) once a fortnight.

Fortran *n* (*comput*) a high-level programming language used for scientific and mathematical problem-solving.

FORTRAN *abbr* (*comput*) = formula translation.

fortress *n* a strong fort or fortified town.

fortuitous *adj* happening by chance.—**fortuitously** *adv*.—**fortuitousness** *n*.

fortuity *n* (*pl* **fortuities**) fortuitousness; accident, chance.

Fortuna *n* (*Roman myth*) the goddess of chance or success, corresponding to the Greek Tyche.

fortunate *adj* having or occurring by good luck.—**fortunately** *adv*.

fortune hunter *n* someone who seeks to become rich, esp by marrying for money.

fortune *n* the supposed arbitrary power that determines events; luck; destiny; prosperity, success; vast wealth.

fortune-teller *n* a person who claims to foretell a person's future.—**fortune-telling** *n*.

Fortuny y Madrazo *n* **Mariano** (1871–1949) Spanish designer most famous for his silk fabric designs.

forty *n* (*pl* **forties**) four times ten. * *symbol* 40, XL, xl.—*also adj*.—**fortieth** *adj*.

forty-five *n* a gramophone record played at 45 revolutions per minute.

Forty-Five, the *n* the Jacobite Rebellion of 1745.

forty-niner *n* a pioneer who went to California in 1849 to look for gold.

forty winks *n* (*sing or pl*) a nap.

forum *n* (*pl* **forums, fora**) an assembly or meeting to discuss topics of public concern; a medium for public debate, as a magazine; the marketplace and center of public affairs in ancient Rome.

forward *adj* at, toward, or of the front; advanced; onward; prompt; bold; presumptuous; of or for the future. * *vt* to promote; to send on. * *n* (*sport*) an attacking player in various games. * *adv* toward the front; ahead.—**forwardness** *n*.

FORWARD *abbr* = Foundation for Women's Health Research and Development.

forward exchange contract *n* a contract to purchase foreign exchange at a specified date in the future at an agreed exchange rate.

forwardly *adv* pertly; promptly; forwards.

forward market *see* **futures market**.

forwards *adv* towards the front, in an onward direction

forwent *see* **forgo**.

forz. *abbr* (*mus*) (*Italian*) = forzando.

forza *n* (*mus*) (*Italian*) force, so *con forza* means "with force."

forzando *adv* (*music*) with sudden emphasis.

forzato *adj* (*mus*) (*Italian*) forced.

fos *abbr* = free on ship; free on station.

Fosbury *n* **Dick [Richard]** (1947–) American athlete who won Olympic Gold in the high jump in 1968, using the technique now known as the "Fosbury Flop."

Fosdic *abbr* = film optical sensing device (computing).

FOSFA *abbr* = Federation of Oils, Seeds, and Fats Associations.

Foss *n* **Lukas [Fuchs]** (1922–) composer of German parentage. He settled in the United States in 1937 and wrote operas, symphonies, piano concertos and an oratorio.

fossa *n* (*pl* **fossae**) (*anat*) a groove, pit, or cavity.

fosse, foss *n* a ditch or moat, esp in a fortification.

fossick *vt* to search for by picking over, to rummage.—**fossicker** *n*.

fossil *n* the petrified remains of an animal or vegetable preserved in rock; (*inf*) a thing or person regarded as outmoded or redundant. * *adj* of or like a fossil; dug from the earth.

fossil fuels *n* natural gas, petroleum (oil), and coal, which are the major fuel sources today, formed from the bodies of aquatic organisms that were buried and compressed on the bottoms of seas and swamps millions of years ago.

fossiliferous *adj* containing fossils.

fossilization *n* (*geol*) the formation of a fossil.

fossilize *vti* to change or become changed into a fossil.

fossorial *adj* (*zool*) used for digging.

foster *vt* to encourage; to bring up (a child that is not one's own). * *adj* affording, giving, sharing, or receiving parental care although not related.—**fosterer** *n*.

Foster *n* 1. **Jodie [Alicia Christian Foster]** (1962–) American film actress and winner of several academy awards, e.g. for *Taxi Driver* (1976). 2. **Norman** (1935–) British architect, who pioneered high-tech design. 3. **Stephen Collins** (1826–64) American composer of popular songs, including "My old Kentucky Home" and "Beautiful Dreamer."

fosterage *n* the act of fostering.

foster child *n* a child raised by a person other than its parent.

fosterling *n* a foster child.

fot *abbr* = free of tax.

f.o.t., FOT *abbr* = free on truck.

Foucault's pendulum *n* a pendulum consisting of a very heavy bob suspended from a very long wire and set in motion in a particular plane; the pendulum remains in this plane, in space, whilst the Earth rotates beneath it.

foudroyant *adj* sudden and overwhelming; dazzling, like lightning.

fought *see* **fight**.

foul *adj* stinking, loathsome; extremely dirty; indecent; wicked; (*language*) obscene; (*weather*) stormy; (*sports*) against the rules. * *adv* unfairly. * *vt* to make filthy; to dishonor; to obstruct; to entangle (a rope, etc); to make a foul against, as in a game; (*with* **up**) to contaminate; to ruin, bungle; to cause to become blocked or entangled. * *vi* to be or become fouled; (*with* **up**) to become blocked or entangled. * *n* (*sports*) a hit, blow, move, etc that is foul.—**foully** *adv*.—**foulness** *n*.

foul play *n* fouls in sport; violent crime, murder.

foulard *n* a light silk or silk-cotton fabric; a scarf made of this fabric.

foul-mouthed *adj* using abusive or obscene language.

found¹ *see* **find**.

found² *vt* to bring into being; to establish (as an institution) often with provision for future maintenance.

found³ *vt* to melt and pour (metal) into a mould to produce castings.

foundation *n* an endowment for an institution; such an institution; the base of a house, wall, etc; a first layer of cosmetic applied to the skin; an underlying principle, etc; a supporting undergarment, as a corset.—**foundational** *adj*.—**foundationary** *adj*.

foundation stone *n* a stone laid at a special ceremony to mark the foundation of a new building.

founder¹ *n* one who founds an institution, a benefactor.

founder² *n* a person who casts metal.

founder³ *vi* (*ship*) to fill with water and sink; to collapse; to fail.

foundling *n* a deserted child whose parents are unknown.

found object *or* **objet trouvé** *n* a form of art that began with Dada and continued with surrealism, where an object, either natural or manufactured, is displayed as a piece of art in its own right.

foundry *n* (*pl* **foundries**) a workshop or factory where metal castings are produced.

fount¹ *n* a set of printing type or characters of one style and size.—*also* **font**.

fount² *n* a source.

fountain *n* a natural spring of water; a source; an artificial jet or flow of water; the basin where this flows; a reservoir, as for ink. * *vti* to (cause to) flow or spurt like a fountain.

fountainhead *n* a spring from which a stream flows; a first source.

fountain pen *n* a pen with an internal reservoir or cartridge of ink which supplies the nib.

Fouquet *n* **Jean** (*c*.1420–81) French painter. His work is dominated by his excellent draftsmanship, bringing a grace and purity to miniatures and larger works alike.

four *n* one more than three; the fourth in a series or set; something having four units as members (as a four-cylinder engine); a four-oared boat or its crew. * *symbol* 4, IV, iv.—*also adj*.

Four *n* **The** *see* **MacNair, J Herbert**.

fourchette *n* (*anat*) a fold of skin situated at the rear of the vulva.

four-dimensional *adj* consisting of the four dimensions of length, breadth, depth, and time.

four flush *n* a poker hand with four cards of one suit.

four-flusher *n* a bluffer.

fourfold *adj* having four units or members; being four times as great or as many.—*also adv*.

fourhanded *adj* for four players; (*mus*) for two players.

four-in-hand *n* a narrow necktie with a flat slipknot and long dangling ends; a vehicle with four horses driven by a single person.

four-letter word *n* any of various words regarded as offensive or obscene typically containing four letters.

four-poster *n* a bed with four posts and a canopy.

fourscore *n* eighty.

Four Seasons *n* **The** [*Le quattro stagioni*] a set of four beautifully evocative and perennially popular violin concertos by Vivaldi, depicting the seasons' changes of aspect and mood.

foursome *n* a group or set of four; (*golf*) a game between two pairs in which each pair has one ball.

Foursquare *adj* square; firm. * *adv* squarely; firmly.

four-stroke *adj* (*internal-combustion engine*) having a piston that operates a cycle of four strokes for every explosion.

fourteen *n*, *adj* four and ten. * *symbol* 14, XIV, xiv.—**fourteenth** *adj*.

fourth¹ *adj* next after third. * *n* one of four equal parts of something.—**fourthly** *adv*.

fourth² *n* (*mus*) an interval of four notes (including the first and last) or five semitones (half step), e.g. C to F.

fourth dimension *n* time as added to the three spatial dimensions (length, breadth, depth).

fourth estate *n* journalists or the press in general.

fourth generation computer *n* (*comput*) the current generation of computers that use chips.

Fourth of July *n* Independence Day of U.S.A.

fovea (*pl* **foveae**) *n* (*med*) any small depression, often referring to the one that occurs in the retina of the eye.

f.o.w., FOW *abbr* = first open water (*chartering*).

fowl *n* any of the domestic birds used as food, as the chicken, duck, etc; the flesh of these birds. * *vi* to hunt or snare wildfowl.—**fowler** *n*.—**fowling** *n*.

Fowler *n* 1. **H[enry] W[atson]** (1858–1933) English lexicographer. The second of his two books on English usage, *A Dictionary of English Usage* (1926), was for many years the standard work on the subject. 2. **John** (1933–) British interior designer who became a major decorator for high society together with Sybil Colefax.

Fowles *n* **John [Robert]** (1926–) English novelist whose works include *The Collector*, *The Magus*, and *The French Lieutenant's Woman*.

FOWP *abbr* = Fertilizers from Organic Wastes Program.

fox *n* (*pl* **foxes**, **fox**) any of various small, alert wild mammals of the dog family; the fur of the fox; a sly, crafty person. * *vt* to deceive by cunning. * *vi* (*inf*) to bemuse, puzzle.

Fox *n* 1. **Charles James** (1749–1806) English Whig statesman and a vigorous opponent of the slave trade. 2. **George** (1624–91) English religious leader who founded the Society of Friends ("Quakers") in 1647.

Fox *abbr* = Futures and Options Exchange.

foxglove *n* a tall plant with spikes of purple or white flowers.

foxhole *n* a pit dug in the ground as a protection against enemy fire.

foxhound *n* any of various large swift powerful hounds of great endurance used in hunting foxes.

foxtail *n* a type of grass found in Europe, Asia, and South America.

fox-terrier *n* any of a breed of small lively terriers formerly used to dig out foxes.

foxtrot *n* a dance for couples in 4/4 time. * *vi* (**foxtrotting, foxtrotted**) to dance the foxtrot.

foxy *adj* (**foxier, foxiest**) reddish-brown; crafty; resembling a fox; physically attractive.—**foxily** *adv*.—**foxiness** *n*.

foyer *n* an anteroom; an entrance hallway, as in a hotel or theatre.

Foyt *n* **A[nthony] J[oseph] Jnr** (1935–) American racing driver; four times winner of the Indianapolis 500, and winner of the Le Mans 24-hour race (1967).

fp *abbr* = (*mus*) (*Italian*) *forte piano*, "loud and then immediately soft"; (*Latin*) *fiat pilula*, "let a pill be made"; (*Latin*) *fiat potio*, "let a drink be made"; fine paper; fixed price; footpath; freezing point; frontispiece; fully paid.

fp *abbr* (*mus*) (*Italian*) = *forte piano* , "loud and then soft."

f.p. *abbr* = fine paper; freezing point; fully paid; freezing point; foot-pound.

FP *abbr* = fireplug; former pupil; foot-pound.

FPA *abbr* = Family Planning Association; Film Production Association of Great Britain; Fire Protection Association; Flexible Packaging Association; Flowers and Plants Association; Free Pacific Association.

f.p.a., FPA *abbr* = free of particular average.

f.p.a.a.c., FPAAC *abbr* = free of particular average, American conditions.

FPAS *abbr* = Frank Patterson Appreciation Society.

fpb *abbr* = fast patrol boat.

FPB *abbr* = Forum of Private Business.

FPC *abbr* = Family Practitioner Committee; Flowers Publicity Council.

FPCS *abbr* = Farm Planning Computer Service.

FPD *abbr* = Forum of People with Disabilities (Eire).

FPDS *abbr* = Federal Procurement Data System.

FPFC *abbr* = Fair Play For Children.

FPIA *abbr* = Family Planning International Assistance.

f. pil. *abbr* (*Latin*) (*pharm*) = *fiat pilula*, "let a pill be made."

fpm, f.p.m. *abbr* = feet per minute.

FPMI *abbr* = Forest Pest Management Institute (Canada).

FPO *abbr* = field post office.

FPPTE *abbr* = Federation of Public Passenger Transport Employers.

FPRC *abbr* = Flying Personnel Research Committee.

FPRI *abbr* = Fellow of the Plastics and Rubber Institute.

FProfBTM *abbr* = Fellow of Professional Business and Technical Management.

fps *abbr* = feet per second; foot-pound-second; frames per second (photography).

f.p.s., fps *abbr* = feet per second; foot-pound-second.

FPS *abbr* = Federation of Petroleum Suppliers; Federation of Piling Specialists; Fell Pony Society; Free Painters and Sculptors; Fellow of the Philological Society; Fellow of the Philosophical Society; foot-pound-second.

FPSC *abbr* = Family Policy Studies Center.

FPTP *abbr* = first past the post (voting system).

Fr *symbol* (*chem*) francium (element).

fr *abbr* = franc.

fr. *abbr* = fragment; franc; from.

f.r. *abbr* (*Latin*) = *folio recto*, "right-hand page."

Fr. *abbr* (*Latin*) = *frater*, "brother"; (*eccl*) Father; France; French; Friar; Friday; Frau.

FR *abbr* = Federal Register.

Fra *n* (*title*) a friar.

FRA *abbr* = Federal Railroad Administration; Federal Re-employment Administration.

fracas *n* (*pl* **fracas, fracases**) uproar; a noisy quarrel.

fractals *npl* (*comput*) groups of shapes that are alike but not identical, such as leaves or snowflakes.

fraction *n* a small part, amount, etc; (*math*) a quantity less than a whole, expressed as a decimal or with a numerator and denominator.—**fractionary** *adj*.—**fractionally** *adv*.

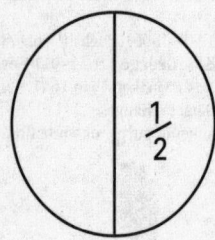

fractional *adj* of or pertaining to fractions; inconsiderable, very small.

fractional distillation *or* **fractionation** *n* (*chem*) the process used for separating a mixture of liquids into component parts by distillation.

fractionate *vt* to separate (elements of a mixture) by distillation.—**fractionation** *n*.

fractionize *vt* to divide into fractions.—**fractionization** *n*.

fractious *adj* quarrelsome; peevish.—**fractiously** *adv*.—**fractiousness** *n*.

fracture *n* any break in a bone, which may be complete or incomplete. In a simple fracture, the skin remains more or less intact, but in a compound fracture there is an open wound connecting the bone with the surface.

fracture *n* the breaking of any hard material, esp a bone. *See also* **comminuted fracture**. * *vti* to break; to cause or suffer a fracture.—**fracturable** *adj*.—**fractural** *adj*.

FRAD *abbr* = Fellow of the Royal Academy of Dancing.

FRAeS *abbr* = Fellow of the Royal Aeronautical Society.

fragile *adj* easily broken; frail; delicate.—**fragilely** *adv*.—**fragility, fragileness** *n*.

fragment *n* a piece broken off or detached; an incomplete portion. * *vti* to break or cause to break into fragments.—**fragmentation** *n*.

fragmentary *adj* consisting of fragments; incomplete.—**fragmentarily** *adv*.—**fragmentariness** *n*.

fragmentation *n* (*comput*) the storage of files on a disk that uses non-contiguous sectors to store the file. Disks can be defragmented using a utility program.

Fragonard *n* Jean-Honoré (1732–1806) French painter. One of the great exponents of rococo, he is best known for his small, picturesquely pretty canvases, such as *The Swing* (1766).

fragrance, fragrancy *n* (*pl* **fragrances, fragrancies**) a pleasant scent, a perfume.

fragrant *adj* sweet-scented.—**fragrantly** *adv*.

FRAI *abbr* = Fellow of the Royal Anthropological Institute.

frail[1] *adj* physically or morally weak; fragile.—**fraily** *adv*.—**frailness** *n*.

frail[2] *n* a rush basket; the quantity of fruit held in a frail.

frailty *n* (*pl* **frailties**) physical or moral weakness; infirmity; a failing.

fraise *n* a palisade of pointed sticks, used in a rampart; a type of neck ruff; a tool used to enlarge a drill hole.

FRAM *abbr* = Fellow of the Royal Academy of Music.

frambesia, framboesia *n* an infectious tropical disease, causing red skin eruptions and joint pain.—*also* **yaws**.

frame *vt* to form according to a pattern; to construct; to put into words; to enclose (a picture) in a border; (*sl*) to falsify evidence against (an innocent person). * *n* something composed of parts fitted together and united; the physical make-up of an animal, esp a human body; the framework of a house; the structural case enclosing a window, door, etc; an ornamental border, as around a picture; (*snooker*) a triangular mould for setting up balls before play; (*snooker*) a single game.—**framable, frameable** *adj*.—**framer** *n*.

Frame *n* Janet (1924–) New Zealand novelist and short-story writer whose work includes ten highly regarded novels.

FRAME *abbr* = Fund for the Replacement of Animals in Medical Experiments.

frame construction *n* (*archit*) a building supported by a frame rather than weight-bearing walls, as in timber framing and steel-frame construction.

frame of reference *n* an arbitrary system of axes for describing the position or motion of something or from which physical laws are derived; a set or system (as of facts and ideas) serving to orient; a viewpoint, a theory.

frame-up *n* (*sl*) a conspiracy to have someone falsely accused of a crime.

framework *n* a structural frame; a basic structure (as of ideas); frame of reference.

Frampton *n* George (1860–1928) British sculptor whose most famous sculpture is *Peter Pan* in Kensington Gardens, London.

franc *n* the standard monetary unit of Andorra, Belgium, Benin, Burkina-Faso, Burundi, Cameroon, the Central African Republic, Chad, Comoros, Congo, Côte d'Ivoire, Djibouti, Equitorial Guinea, France, French Guiána or Guyane, French Polynesia, Gabon, Guadelope; Guinea, Liechtenstein, Luxembourg, Madagascar, Mali, New Caledonia or Nouvelle Calédonie, Niger, Monaco, Réunion Rwanda, Senegal, Switzerland, Tahiti, and Togo the Wallis and Futuna Islands, made up of 100 centimes.

Françaix *n* Jean (1912–) French composer of operas, ballets, and orchestral works, e.g. *Les Demoiselles de la nuit* (ballet), and *La Maine de Gloire*, an opera in four acts.

France *n* a republic in Western Europe with coastlines on the English Channel, Mediterranean Sea, and Atlantic Ocean.

France *n* Anatole [Jacques Anatole Thibault] (1844–1924) French novelist who specialized in social and political satire, his best-known work being *Penguin Island*. He was awarded the Nobel prize for literature in 1921.

Francesca *n* Piero della (*c*.1416–92) Italian early Renaissance painter. From *c*.1460 he was at the court of Federico da Montefeltro of Urbino, and during this time he painted some of his finest masterpieces.

franchise *n* the right to vote in public elections; authorization to sell the goods of a manufacturer in a particular area. * *vt* to grant a franchise.—**franchisement** *n*.

Francis I *see* **Maria Theresa**.

Francis II *see* **Mary, Queen of Scots**.

Francis *n* Sam (1923–94) American painter; influenced by Japanese art and American abstract expressionists, such as Jackson Pollock, e.g. *Big Red* (1953).

Franciscan *n* a member of the Order of Friars Minor founded by St Francis of Assisi in 1209.

Francis de Sales *n* Saint (1567–1622) French priest; bishop of Geneva (1602); ruled his diocese with gentleness and gave away his private fortune. He wrote *An Introduction to the Devout Life* (1608) and *Treatise on the Love of God* (1616). His feast day is January 29.

Francis of Assisi *n* Saint [Giovanni Bernardone] (1181–1226) Italian monk born at Assisi; founder of the order of the Franciscans; led a life of prayer, hard work, and poverty; had a remarkable affinity with wild animals. Italian monk. He was canonized in 1228. His feast day is October 4 .

Francistown *n* a city in Botswana.

Francis Xavier *n* Saint (1506–52) Spanish missionary; a founding member of the Society of Jesus (the Jesuits); known as "the Apostle of the Indies." He regarded baptism as the most important part of a missionary's work. His feast day is December 3.

francium *n* a radioactive metallic element.

Franck *n* 1. César Auguste (1822-90) Belgian composer and organist, whose compositions include oratorios, operas, and his *Variations symphoniques* (for piano and orchestra) for which he is probably most famed. 2. James (1882–1964) German-born American physicist. He shared the 1925 Nobel prize for physics for work on the quantum theory with the German physicist Gustav Ludwig Hertz.

Franc Malgache *n* currency of Madagascar.

Franco *n* Francisco (1892–1975) Spanish general and dictator who ruled Spain from 1939. He led the right-wing rebellion during the Spanish Civil War (1936–39) and became leader of the Fascist Falange Party in 1937.

Franco- *prefix* France; French.

francolin *n* a kind of partridge, found in Africa and Asia.

Francophile *n* a lover of France or its customs, etc.

francophone *n* a French-speaking person. * *adj* speaking French as a native language.

frangible *adj* fragile, easily broken.—**frangibility** *n*.

frangipane *n* a paste or cake made with almonds and cream.

frangipani *n* (*pl* **frangipanis, frangipani**) a tropical American shrub, the flowers of which are used to make a perfume.

frank *adj* free and direct in expressing oneself; honest, open. * *vt* to mark letters, etc with a mark denoting free postage. * *n* a mark indicating free postage.—**frankly** *adv*.—**frankness** *n*.

Frank *n* a member of a West Germanic people who conquered Gaul in the 4th century AD.—**Frankish** *adj*.

Frank *n* 1. Anne (1929–45) German-born Dutch Jewish girl whose journal documents Jewish suffering under Nazi rule during World War II. 2. Jean-Michel (1895–1941) French interior decorator who introduced the use of white-leaded wood in the 1920s.

Frankenstein *n* a person who creates something that brings about his ruin.

Frankenthaler *n* Helen (1928–) American painter whose work forms a significant link between abstract expressionism and color field painting.

Frankfort *n* the capital city of Kentucky, a state of the USA.

Frankfurt *n* a city in Germany.

frankfurter *n* a type of smoked sausage.

frankincense *n* a fragrant gum resin.

Frankl *n* 1. Paul Theodore (1887–1958) Austrian designer who was the main force behind the formation of the American Designers' Gallery and the American Union of Decorative Artists and Designers. 2. Peter (1935–) Hungarian-born pianist who has been a British citizen since 1967. He is a renowned concert hall soloist.

franklin *n* a middle-class landowner in England in the 14th and 15th century.

Franklin *n* 1. **Aretha** (1942–) American soul singer regarded as "The Queen of Soul." 2. **Benjamin** (1706–90) American author, statesman, and scientist who helped draft the American Declaration of Independence, and was active in American politics. 3. **Rosalind Elsie** (1920–58) British chemist whose research into DNA contributed to the discovery of its structure by James Watson and Francis Crick.

frantic *adj* violently agitated; furious, wild.—**frantically, franticly** *adv*.

Franz *n* **Robert** (1815–92) German composer, admired by both Schumann and Liszt, who wrote more than 250 songs.

Fraoch *n* (*Irish Celtic myth*) a very handsome man who fell in love with Findabair, the daughter of Medb and Ailill. She returned his love, but her parents were reluctant for her to marry him and tried to kill him.

frap *vt* (**frapping, frapped**) (*naut*) to bind tightly.

frappé *adj* iced; chilled.

FRAS *abbr* = Fellow of the Royal Astronomical Society; Fellow of the Royal Asiatic Society.

Fraser *n* 1. **Claud Lovat** (1890–1921) British textile and theatre designer and illustrator whose designs for *The Beggar's Opera* were a sensation. 2. **[John] Malcolm** (1930–) Australian Liberal statesman. He was installed as caretaker prime minister (1975–83) and won the ensuing 1975 election by a large majority.

frater[1] *n* a friar.

frater[2] *n* (*arch*) a refectory.

fraternal *adj* of or belonging to a brother or fraternity; friendly, brotherly.—**fraternalism** *n*.—**fraternally** *adv*.

fraternal twins *n* (*biol*) twins that are not identical and that develop when two ova are fertilized at the same time.

fraternity *n* (*pl* **fraternities**) brotherly feeling; a society of people with common interests.

fraternize *vt* to associate in a friendly manner.—**fraternization** *n*.

fratricide *n* the murder of a brother; a person guilty of this.—**fratricidal** *adj*.

Frattini *n* **Gianfranco** (1926–) Italian architect who also designed many items of furniture.

Frau *n* (*pl* **Frauen, Fraus**) (a title of) a married German woman.

Frau *n* **Renzo** (1880–) Italian designer who designed the famous *Poltrona* armchair.

fraud *n* deliberate deceit; the acquiring of a financial advantage by means of deliberate deception or false representation; an act of deception; (*inf*) a deceitful person; an impostor.

fraudulent *adj* deceiving or intending to deceive; obtained by deceit.—**fraudulence, fraudulency** *n*.—**fraudulently** *adv*.

fraught *adj* filled or loaded (with); (*inf*) anxious; difficult.

Fräulein *n* (*pl* **Fräulein, Fräuleins**) (a title of) an unmarried German woman.

Fraunhofer lines *n* (*astron*) dark lines crossing the continuous spectrum of the Sun caused by a relatively cooler layer, the reversing layer, above the photosphere where atoms absorb light from the continuous spectrum.

fraxinella *n* a white-flowered Eurasian plant.

fray[1] *n* a fight, a brawl.

fray[2] *vti* (*fabric, etc*) to (cause to) wear away into threads, esp at the edge of; (*nerves, temper*) to make or become irritated or strained.

Frayn *n* **Michael** (1933–) English dramatist and novelist, noted for his dry, sardonic humor.

Frazer *n* **Sir James George** (1854–1941) Scottish scholar and anthropologist whose study of religious customs and myth, *The Golden Bough*, was a major influence on 20th-century writers.

Frazier *n* **Joe** (1944–) American boxer; world heavyweight champion (1968–73); the first man to beat Muhammad Ali in a professional match.

frazil *n* the ice that forms in a stream.

frazzle *vt* to exhaust; to fray, tatter. * *n* (*inf*) a state of exhaustion.

FRB *abbr* = Federal Reserve Bank; Federal Reserve Board.

FRC *abbr* = Federal Radio Commission.

FRCA *abbr* = Fellow of the Royal College of Anaesthetists; Fellow of the Royal College of Art.

FRCGP *abbr* = Fellow of the Royal College of General Practitioners.

FRCM *abbr* = Fellow of the Royal College of Music.

FRCO *abbr* = Fellow of the Royal College of Organists.

FRCO(CHM) *abbr* = Fellow of the Royal College of Organists (Choir-training Diploma).

FRCOG *abbr* = Fellow of the Royal College of Obstetricians and Gynaecologists.

FRCP *abbr* = Fellow of the Royal College of Physicians.

FRCPath *abbr* = Fellow of the Royal College of Pathologists.

FRCPEdin *abbr* = Fellow of the Royal College of Physicians of Edinburgh.

FRCPS *abbr* = Fellow of the Royal College of Physicians and Surgeons.

FRCPsych *abbr* = Fellow of the Royal College of Psychiatrists.

FRCR *abbr* = Fellow of the Royal College of Radiologists.

FRCS *abbr* = Fellow of the Royal College of Surgeons.

FrCu *abbr* = fracto-cumulus.

FRCVS *abbr* = Fellow of the Royal College of Veterinary Surgeons.

freak[1] *n* an unusual happening; any abnormal animal, person, or plant; (*inf*) a person who dresses or acts in a notably unconventional manner; an ardent enthusiast. * *vi* (*with* out) (*inf*) to hallucinate under the influence of drugs; to experience intense emotional excitement.—**freakish** *adj*.

freak[2] *vt* to variegate; to spot or streak.

freakish *adj* very unusual; changing suddenly.—**freakishly** *adv*.—**freakishness** *n*.

freckle *n* a small, brownish spot on the skin. * *vti* to make or become spotted with freckles.—**freckled, freckly** *adj*.

FREconS *abbr* = Fellow of the Royal Economic Society.

FRED *abbr* = Fast Reactor Experiment, Dounreay.

Frederick II [**Frederick the Great**] (1712–86) Prussian king. A sickly child, he became King of Prussia in 1740. He expanded Prussian territory and fought the Seven Years War (1756–63) with great military skill.

free *adj* (**freer, freest**) not under the control or power of another; having social and political liberty; independent; able to move in any direction; not burdened by obligations; not confined to the usual rules; not exact; generous; frank; with no cost or charge; exempt from taxes, duties, etc; clear of obstruction; not fastened. * *adv* without cost; in a free manner. * *vt* (**freeing, freed**) to set free; to clear of obstruction, etc.—**freely** *adv*.

free association *n* a method in psychoanalysis of probing a patient's unconscious by eliciting immediate verbal responses to a series of keywords.

freebie *n* (*sl*) something provided free of charge.

freeboard *n* the part of the side of a ship between the upper side of the deck and the water-line.

freebooter *n* a pirate; a plunderer.

freeborn *adj* born of free parents, as opposed to in slavery.

free capital *n* the shares in a public company that are available to members of the general public; capital in the form of cash.

freedman *n* (*pl* **freedmen**) an emancipated slave.

freedom *n* being free; exemption from obligation; unrestricted use; a right or privilege.

freedom fighter *n* a person violently resisting an oppressive political regime.

freedom of the seas *n* the right of a merchant vessel to sail in any waters except territorial waters during a time of peace or war.

free energy or **Gibb's free energy** *n* (*chem*) a thermodynamic quantity that gives a direct measure of spontaneity of reaction in a reversible process.

free enterprise *n* the freedom of business from government intervention or control.

free enterprise economy or **private enterprise economy** *n* an economic system in which private individuals and companies, as opposed to the state, control the means of production with the minimum of state interference.

free fall *n* the descent of a body under the force of gravity alone, as a parachutist before the parachute opens.

free fight *n* an indiscriminate contest, a mêlée.

free-floating *adj* uncommitted, esp politically.

free-for-all *n* (*inf*) a disorganized fight or brawl involving as many participants as are willing.

free form database *n* (*comput*) a form of database that has no preset structure of information on each record.

free hand *n* freedom to act as desired.

freehand *adj* (*drawing, etc*) drawn by the hand without the aid of instruments.

freehanded *adj* generous; liberal.—**freehandedly** *adv*.—**freehandedness** *n*.

freehold *n* tenure without rent; absolute ownership; an estate so held.—**freeholder** *n*.

freehold property *n* property that is legally held outright by a person or company.

free house *n* (*Brit*) a public house which is allowed to sell drinks from more than one brewer.

free kick *n* (*soccer, rugby*) a place kick awarded because of a foul or infringement by an opponent.

freelance *n* a person who pursues a profession without long-term commitment to any employer (—*also* **freelancer**). * *vt* to work as a freelance.

free-living *n* (*organisms*) not parasitic.—**free-liver** *n*.

freeload *vi* to impose upon another's hospitality.—**freeloader** *n*.

free love *n* sexual intercourse without the restraints of marriage.

freeman *n* (*pl* **freemen**) someone who is not a slave; someone with civic rights.

free market *n* a market governed by supply and demand and with no government interference.

freemartin *n* a sexually imperfect and sterile cow calf, born as the twin of a bull calf.

Freemason *n* a member of the secretive fraternity (Free and Accepted Masons) dedicated to mutual aid.

freemasonry *n* mutual help between persons of similar interests.

free on board *adj* a term used to denote the basis on which an export contract has been made. By a free-on-board arrangement, the seller pays the cost of transporting the goods to the port of shipment. Thereafter the transport costs are the responsibility of the purchaser.

free port *n* a port where goods are received and shipped free of customs duty.

Freeport *n* a city in Bahamas.

free-range *adj* (*hens*) allowed to roam freely, not confined in a battery; (*eggs*) produced by hens raised in this way.

free reed *n* (*mus*) a type of reed found in such instruments as the accordion and harmonica.

freesheet *n* a newspaper distributed free of charge.

freesia *n* a sweet-scented African plant of the iris family.

freespoken *adj* outspoken, blunt.—**freespokenness** *n*.

freestanding *adj* (*furniture*) standing on its own; not attached.

F

freestone *n* a type of limestone or sandstone that is suitable for working.

freestyle *n* a swimming competition in which the competitor chooses the stroke.

freethinker *n* a person who rejects authority in religion, etc; a skeptic.

free trade *n* the export and import of goods and services from one country to another without the imposition of restrictions such as tariffs or quotas.—**free-trader** *n*.

Freetown *n* capital city of Sierra Leone.

free verse *or* **vers libre** *n* any form of verse, rhymed or unrhymed, without traditional metrical or stanzaic form, usually characterized by the use of rhythmic "natural speech" cadences and dependent on alliteration and the subtle placing of syllabic stresses.

freeware *n* (*comput*) copyrighted programs that are provided by the author free of charge.

freeway *n* an expressway with controlled access, a fast road, a toll-free highway.

freewheel *n* a device for temporarily disconnecting and setting free the back wheel of a bicycle from the driving gear. * *vi* to ride a bicycle with the gear disconnected; to drive a car with the gear in neutral.—**freewheeler** *n*.

freewheeling *adj* unrestrained; carefree.

free will *n* voluntary choice or decision; freedom of human beings to make choices that are not determined by prior causes or by divine intervention.

freeze *vb* (**freezing, froze,** *pp* **frozen**) *vi* to be formed into, or become covered by ice; to become very cold; to be damaged or killed by cold; to become motionless; to be made speechless by strong emotion; to become formal and unfriendly. * *vt* to harden into ice; to convert from a liquid to a solid with cold; to make extremely cold; to act towards in a stiff and formal way; to act on usu destructively by frost; to anesthetize by cold; to fix (prices, etc) at a given level by authority; to make (funds, etc) unavailable to the owners by authority.—**freezable** *adj*.

freeze-dry *vt* (**freeze-drying, freeze-dried**) to preserve (food) by rapid freezing and then drying in a vacuum.

freeze-drying *n* a process used when dehydrating heat-sensitive substances so that they may be preserved without being damaged during the process.

freeze-frame *n* a frame of a motion picture or television film that is repeated to give the illusion of a static picture.

freezer *n* a compartment or container that freezes and preserves food for long periods.

freezing *adj* very cold.

freezing point *n* the temperature at which a liquid solidifies.

Frege *n* [**Friedrich Ludwig**] **Gottlob** (1848–1925) German mathematician and philosopher.

FREGG *abbr* = Free Range Egg Association.

freight *n* the transport of goods by water, land, or air; the cost for this; the goods transported. * *vt* to load with freight; to send by freight.

freightage *n* the conveyance of cargo; the cargo conveyed; a charge made for transporting cargo.

freight car *n* a rail truck for carrying freight.

freighter *n* one who freights; a ship or aircraft carrying freight.

freight train *n* railroad train for transporting goods.

Fremiet *n* **Emmanuel** (1824–1910) French sculptor who brought his sculpting talents to lighting design.

French *adj* of France, its people, culture, etc. * *n* the language of France.

French *n* **Daniel Chester** (1850–1931) American sculptor, best known for his civic commissions. These include the seated figure of *Abraham Lincoln* (1922) in Washington DC.

French bread *n* bread in a long, slender loaf.

French chalk *n* a soapstone used as a dry lubricant and to mark cloth, etc.

French cuff *n* a double cuff formed by turning back a wide soft cuff and fastened by cuff links.

French doors *see* **French windows**.

French dressing *n* a salad dressing made from vinegar, oil, and seasonings.

French fries, french fries *npl* thin strips of potato fried in oil, etc, chips.

French Guiana *or* **Guyane** *n* an overseas department of France bounded to the south and east by Brazil and to the west by Suriname.

French horn *n* an orchestral brass instrument with a narrow conical tube wound twice in a circle, a funnel shaped mouthpiece, and a flaring bell.

Frenchify *vti* (**Frenchifies, Frenchifying, Frenchified**) (*inf*) to make or become French.

French kiss *n* an open-mouthed kiss involving tongue contact.

French leave *n* leave taken without permission; a hasty or secret departure.

French letter *n* a condom.

French polish *n* a shellac varnish for furniture.

French Polynesia *n* an island territory comprising 5 separate archipelagos in the southeast Pacific Ocean.

French roof *n* a mansard roof.

French sixth *see* **augmented sixth**.

French toast *n* toast with one side buttered and the other toasted; bread soaked in milk and batter and fried lightly.

French windows *npl* a pair of casement windows extending to the floor that are placed in an outside wall and open on to a patio, garden, etc.—*also* **French doors**.

frenetic *adj* frantic, frenzied.—**frenetically** *adv*.

frenulum lingae *see* **tongue**.

frenzy *n* (*pl* **frenzies**) wild excitement; violent mental derangement. * *vt* (**frenzying, frenzied**) to infuriate, to madden.—**frenzied** *adj*.—**frenziedly** *adv*.

freq. *abbr* = frequent; frequentative; frequently.

freq. m. *abbr* = frequency meter.

frequency modulation *n* the transmission of signals by radio waves whose frequency varies according to the amplitude of the signal.

frequency[1] *n* (*pl* **frequencies**) repeated occurrence; the number of occurrences, cycles, etc in a given period.

frequency[2] *n* (*comput*) a measure of the speed at which a computer processor operates, measured in megahertz.

frequent *adj* coming or happening often. * *vi* to visit often; to resort to.—**frequenter** *n*.—**frequently** *adv*.

frequentative *adj* (*gram*) expressing repetition and intensity (of a verb). * *n* a frequentative verb.

fresco *n* (*pl* **frescos, frescoes**) a picture painted on walls covered with damp freshly laid plaster. * *vt* (**frescoing, frescoed**) to paint in fresco.

Frescobaldi *n* **Girolamo** (1583–1643) Italian composer who was one of the outstanding organists of his era. For much of his life, he was organist at St Peter's in Rome.

fresh *adj* recently made, grown, etc; not salted, pickled, etc; not spoiled; lively, not tired; not worn, soiled, faded, etc; new, recent; inexperienced; cool and refreshing; (*wind*) brisk; (*water*) not salt; (*inf*) presumptuous, impertinent. * *adv* newly.—**freshly** *adv*.—**freshness** *n*.

freshen *vi* to make or become fresh.—**freshener** *n*.

fresher *n* (*pl* **freshers**) a freshman.

freshet *n* a flood caused by melting snow or heavy rain; a stream of fresh water.

freshman *n* (*pl* **freshmen**) a first year student at university, college, or high school.

freshwater *adj* of a river; not sea-going.

fret[1] *vti* (**fretting, fretted**) to make or become worried or anxious; to wear away or roughen by rubbing.

fret[2] *n* a running design of interlacing small bars. * *vt* (**fretting, fretted**) to furnish with frets.

fret[3] *n* any of a series of metal ridges along the finger-board of a guitar, banjo, etc used as a guide for depressing the strings.

fretful *adj* troubled; peevish; irritable; impatient.—**fretfully** *adv*.—**fretfulness** *n*.

fretsaw *n* a narrow saw held under tension in a frame used for cutting intricate designs in wood or metal.

fretwork *n* decorative carving consisting of frets.

Freud *n* 1. **Sigmund** (1856–1939) Austrian psychiatrist who founded psychoanalysis. 2. **Anna** (1895–1982) daughter of Sigmund Freud; she pioneered child psychology in the UK. 3. **Lucien** (1922–) German-born British painter; the grandson of Sigmund Freud; renowned for his nudes and portraits.

Freudian *adj* of or pertaining to the psychoanalytic theories of Sigmund Freud. * *n* a psychoanalyst who follows the theories of Freud.—**Freudianism** *n*.

Freudian slip *n* a slip of the tongue said to betray an unconscious feeling.

Frey *n* **Patrick** (1947–) French fabric designer.

Freyssinet *n* **Eugène** (1879–1962) French architect. His notable works include St Michael Bridge, Toulouse.

FRG *abbr* = Federal Republic of Germany.

FRGS *abbr* = Fellow of the Royal Geographical Society.

frgt. *abbr* = freight.

FRHB *abbr* = Federation of Registered House Builders.

FRHistS *abbr* = Fellow of the Royal Historical Society.

FRHS *abbr* = Fellow of the Royal Horticultural Society.

Fri. *abbr* = Friday.

FRI *abbr* = Federation of Reclamation Industries; Flowers Research Institute (China).

friable *adj* easily crumbled.—**friability** *n*.

friar *n* a member of certain Roman Catholic religious orders.

friarbird *n* an Australasian songbird with a tongue specially adapted to extract nectar.

friar's balsam *n* a compound containing benzoin, which is mixed with hot water and the resulting vapor inhaled to relieve colds, etc.

friary *n* (*pl* **friaries**) a monastery of friars.

FRIBA *abbr* = Fellow of the Royal Institute of British Architects.

fribble *vt* to fritter away. * *vi* to trifle.—**fribbler** *n*.

fricandeau, fricando *n* (*pl* **fricandeaus, fricandeaux, fricandoes**) a dish made from spiced, stewed veal.

fricassee *n* a dish made of stewed poultry, rabbit, etc in a white sauce. * *vt* (**fricasseing, fricasseed**) to cook in this way.

fricative *n* (*phonetics*) a sound, e.g. "f," produced by the friction of breath in a narrow opening. * *adj* pertaining to a fricative.

FRICS *abbr* = Fellow of the Royal Institution of Chartered Surveyors.

friction *n* a rubbing of one object against another; conflict between differing opinions, ideas, etc; the resistance to motion of things that touch.—**frictional** *adj*.

frictional unemployment *n* the degree of unemployment that is considered to be consistent with the efficient running of an economy.

friction clutch *n* a clutch that transmits motion by friction.

friction layer *n* (*astron*) the layer in the atmosphere in which the effects of surface friction are registered.

Friday *n* the sixth day of the week.

Frideswide *n* **Saint** (*d. c.*730) English nun who founded a convent; daughter of Mercian prince. Devoted herself to working with the poor, sick and wretched. Her feast day is October 19.

fridge *n* (*inf*) a refrigerator.

fried *see* **fry**[1].

Friedman *n* **Milton** (1912–) American economist and winner of the 1976 Nobel prize for economics.

Friedreich's ataxia *n* an inherited disorder that is caused by degeneration of nerve cells in the brain and spinal cord. *See also* **ataxia**.

Friedrich *n* **Caspar David** (1774–1840) German romantic painter. His works have a melancholy atmosphere peculiar to the Northern European temperament.

friend *n* a person whom one knows well and is fond of; an ally, supporter, or sympathizer. * *vt* (*arch*) to befriend.—**friendless** *adj.*—**friendship** *n*.

friendly *adj* (**friendlier, friendliest**) like a friend; kindly; favorable. * *n* a sporting game played for fun, not in competition.—**friendlily** *adv.*—**friendliness** *n*.

friendly society *n* an association for mutual insurance against sickness, etc.

friendship *n* the state of being friends; intimacy united with affection or esteem; mutual attachment; goodwill.

frier *see* **fry**[1].

frieze[1] *n* a decorative band along the top of the wall of a room; (*archit*) the part of an entablature between the architrave and cornice, often filled with sculpture.

frieze[2] *n* a coarse woolen cloth with a rough shaggy nap on one side.

frigate *n* a warship smaller than a destroyer used for escort, anti-submarine, and patrol duties.

frigate bird *n* a swift-flying tropical sea bird.

fright *n* sudden fear; a shock; (*inf*) something unsightly or ridiculous in appearance.

frighten *vt* to terrify, to scare; to force by frightening.—**frightener** *n*.—**frighteningly** *adv*.

frightful *adj* terrible, shocking; (*inf*) extreme, very bad.—**frightfully** *adv.*—**frightfulness** *n*.

frigid *adj* extremely cold; not warm or friendly; unresponsive sexually.—**frigidity** *n*.—**frigidly** *adv*.

Frigid Zone *n* either of the areas within the Arctic or Antarctic circles.

frigorific *adj* (*arch*) causing cold.

frijol *n* (*pl* **frijoles**) a type of bean, widely cultivated for eating in Mexico.

frill *n* a piece of pleated or gathered fabric used for edging; something superfluous, an affectation. * *vt* to decorate with a frill or frills.—**frilled** *adj.*—**frilly** *adj*.

FRIN *abbr* = Fellow of the Royal Institution of Navigation.

FRINA *abbr* = Fellow of the Royal Institution of Naval Architects.

fringe *n* a decorative border of hanging threads; hair hanging over the forehead; an outer edge; a marginal or minor part. * *vt* to be or make a fringe for. * *adj* at the outer edge; additional; minor; unconventional.

fringe benefit *n* any benefit given to an employee by his or her employer in addition to salary or wages; benefits given by a company to its shareholders in addition to their dividends.

FRIPHH *abbr* = Fellow of the Royal Institute of Public Health and Hygiene.

frippery *n* (*pl* **fripperies**) cheap, gaudy clothes or ornaments; trivia.

Frisbee *n* (*trademark*) a plastic disc that is spun through the air for recreation or sport.

Frisch *n* 1. **Karl von** (1886–1982) Austrian zoologist and ethologist who discovered that bees communicate information on food sources and direction by "dancing." He shared the 1973 Nobel prize for physiology or medicine with Lorenz and Niko Tinbergen. 2. **Otto Robert** (1904–79) Austrian-born British nuclear physicist. He and his aunt, Lise Meitner, discovered nuclear fission, and their work led to the invention of the atom bomb.

Frisch, Ragnar *see* **Tinbergen, Jan**.

frisette *n* a curly fringe, esp of false hair.—*also* **frizette**.

Frisians *n* a Germanic race of people who occupied the coastal plains of north Germany and Holland.

frisk *vi* to leap playfully. * *vt* (*inf*) to search (a person) by feeling for concealed weapons, etc. * *n* a gambol, dance, or frolic.—**frisker** *n*.

frisky *adj* (**friskier, friskiest**) lively, playful.—**friskily** *adv.*—**friskiness** *n*.

frisson *n* an emotional thrill, a shiver of excitement.

frit fly *n* a small fly destructive to grain.

frit, fritt *n* the mixture of sand and fluxes from which glass is made. * *vt* (**fritting, fritted**) to make into frit.

frith *see* **firth**.

fritillary *n* (*pl* **fritillaries**) a flowering plant of the lily kind, the petals of which are variegated with purple, dice-shaped marks; a butterfly with brownish wings spotted with black or silver.

fritt *see* **frit**.

fritter[1] *n* a slice of fruit or meat fried in batter.

fritter[2] *vt* (*with* **away**) to waste; to break into tiny pieces.—**fritterer** *n*.

frivol *vb* (**frivolling, frivolled** *or* **frivoling, frivoled**) *vi* to behave in a frivolous way; to trifle. * *vt* to squander.

frivolity *n* (*pl* **frivolities**) a trifling act, thought, or action.

frivolous *adj* irresponsible; trifling; silly.—**frivolously** *adv.*—**frivolousness** *n*.

frizette *n see* **frisette**.

frizz *vti* (*hair*) to (cause to) form into small tight curls. * *n* hair that is frizzed.—**frizzer** *n*.

frizzle[1] *vt* to frizz. * *n* a small tight curl.—**frizzler** *n*.

frizzle[2] *vti* to sizzle, as in frying; to scorch by frying.

frizzy, frizzly *adj* (**frizzier, frizziest** *or* **frizzlier, frizzliest**) (*hair*) in tight wiry curls.—**frizziness, frizzliness** *n*.

frl. *abbr* = fractional.

Frl. *abbr* = Fräulein.

FRLSU *abbr* = Forum for Research into the Languages of Scotland and Ulster.

frm. *abbr* = from.

FRMedSoc *abbr* = Fellow of the Royal Medical Society.

FRMetS *abbr* = Fellow of the Royal Meteorological Society.

FRMS *abbr* = Fellow of the Royal Microscopical Society.

FRN *abbr* = Furniture Recycling Network.

FrNb *abbr* = fracto-nimbus.

FRNCM *abbr* = Fellow of the Royal Northern College of Music.

FRNS *abbr* = Fellow of the Royal Numismatic Society.

fro *adv* away from; backward; **to and fro** back and forward.

FRO *abbr* = Fire Research Organization.

frock *n* a dress; a smock; a loose wide-sleeved gown worn by a monk. * *vt* to put on a frock; to invest with the office of priest.

frock coat *n* a double-breasted skirted coat for men.

frog[1] *n* a small tailless web-footed jumping amphibian; (*offensive*) a French person.

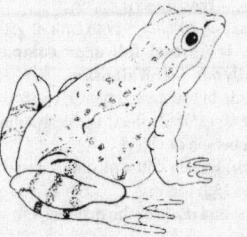

frog[2] *n* a decorative loop used to fasten clothing; an attachment on a belt for carrying a sword.—**frogged** *adj*.

frog[3] *n* a section of rail where two lines cross.

frog[4] *n* a tender horny substance growing in the middle of the sole of a horse's foot.

frogfish *n* (*pl* **frogfish, frogfishes**) a variety of angler fish.

froggy *adj* (**froggier, froggiest**) resembling or containing a frog or frogs.

froghopper *n* a small jumping insect whose larvae secrete a spittle-like protective covering.

frogman *n* (*pl* **frogmen**) a person who wears a rubber suit, flippers, oxygen supply, etc, and is trained in working underwater.

frogmarch *vt* to carry an unwilling person by the legs and arms face down; to move (a person) by force.—*also* **n**.

frolic *n* a lively party or game; merriment, fun. * *vi* (**frolicking, frolicked**) to play happily.—**frolicker** *n*.

frolicsome, frolicky *adj* fond of frolicking; playful.

from *prep* beginning at, starting with; out of; originating with; out of the possibility or use of.

fromage frais *n* a smooth white curd cheese eaten plain or with added fruit as a dessert.

Froment-Meurice *n* **François-Désiré** (1802–55) influential French goldsmith who was dubbed the "19th-Century Cellini."

fromenty *see* **frumenty**.

Fromm *n* **Erich** (1900–80) German-born American psychoanalyst and social philosopher. His work is based on the principle that social and economic factors determine human behavior.

frond *n* a large leaf with many divisions, esp of a palm or fern.

frondescence *n* (*bot*) the act of producing leaves; foliage.—**frondescent** *adj*.

frons *n* (*pl* **frontes**) a plate found on the head of an insect.

front *n* outward behavior; (*inf*) an appearance of social standing; etc; the part facing forward; the first part; a forward or leading position; the promenade of a seaside resort; the advanced battle area in warfare; a person or group used to hide another's activity; an advancing mass of cold or warm air. * *adj* at, to, in, on, or of the front. * *vti* to face; to stand or be situated opposite to or over against; to serve as a front (for); to have the front turned in a particular direction.

frontage *n* the front part of a building or plot of land; the width or extent of the front of a shop, building, piece of land, etc.

frontal *adj* of or belonging to the front; of or pertaining to the forehead. * *n* a decorative covering for the front of an altar; a small pediment over a window or door.—**frontally** *adv*.

frontal lobe *n* the anterior part of each cerebral hemisphere of the cerebrum of the brain.

front bench *n* in the British House of Commons, either of the two rows of benches occupied by the leading figures (**front benchers**) in the Government or Opposition.

front door *n* a main entrance to a building.

frontier *n* the border between two countries; the limit of existing knowledge of a subject.

F

frontiersman *n* (*pl* **frontiersmen**) a person who lives or works on the frontier.

frontispiece *n* an illustration opposite the title page of a book; (*archit*) the main face of a building.

frontlet *n* a band worn on the forehead; an animal's forehead.

frontline *adj* designed for or intended for use in the military front line; conspicuous; (*country*) close to the front line or enemy territory.

front line *n* the leading military units in a battle; the forefront.

front man[1] *n* (*mus*) the person who stands at the front of the stage during a performance of jazz and who is therefore the focus of the audience's attention.

front man[2] *n* a person serving as a front or cover.

frontrunner *n* the favorite to win a race, election, etc.

frontwards, frontward *adj, adv* towards the front.

Fronzini *n* **A G** (1923–96) Italian architect and editor of *Casabella*.

frost *n* temperature at or below freezing point; a coating of powdery ice particles; coldness of manner. * *vt* to cover (as if) with frost or frosting; to give a frost-like opaque surface to (glass).

Frost *n* **Robert Lee** (1874–1963) American poet whose work is concerned mainly with the people and landscape of New England.

frostbite *n* damage to the skin and underlying tissues caused by extreme cold and especially affecting the "extremities," i.e. the fingers, toes, nose, and cheeks.

frostbite *n* injury to a part of the body by exposure to cold.—**frostbitten** *adj*.

frost heave *n* a bulge in the ground or pavement caused by the freezing of moist earth.

frosting *n* icing for a cake.

frosty *adj* (**frostier, frostiest**) cold with frost; cold or reserved in manner, chilly, distant.—**frostily** *adv*.—**frostiness** *n*.

froth *n* foam; foaming saliva; frivolity. * *vi* to emit or gather foam.

frothy *adj* (**frothier, frothiest**) full of or composed of froth; frivolous; insubstantial.—**frothily** *adv*.—**frothiness** *n*.

frottage *n* (a design made by) rubbing a pencil, crayon, etc, over an object placed under paper to create a textured effect; the derivation of sexual pleasure from rubbing, e.g. against a person or object.

frottola *n* (*mus*) (*Italian*) literally "little mixture," a type of Italian polyphonic song that was popular in the 15th century.

froufrou *n* the rustling sound made by the material, esp silk, of a dress etc, when in motion.

froward *adj* (*arch*) obstinate; wayward.

frown *vi* to contract the brow as in anger or thought; (*with* **upon**) to regard with displeasure or disapproval. * *n* a wrinkled brow; a stern look.—**frowner** *n*.—**frowningly** *adv*.

frowst *n* (*inf*) a close, stuffy atmosphere.

frowsty *adj* stuffy; musty.

frowzy, frowsy *adj* (**frowzier, frowziest** *or* **frowsier, frowsiest**) dirty and untidy; unkempt.

froze *see* **freeze**.

frozen[1] *see* **freeze**.

frozen[2] *adj* formed into or covered by ice; damaged or killed by cold; (*food, etc*) preserved by freezing; motionless; made speechless by strong emotion; formal and unfriendly; extremely cold; (prices, wages, etc) fixed at a given level; (funds, etc) unrealizable.

frozen assets *npl* assets that cannot be either used or realized.

frozen shoulder *n* painful stiffness of the shoulder joint, which limits movement.

FRPharms *abbr* = Fellow of the Royal Pharmaceutical Society of Great Britain.

FRPS *abbr* = Fellow of the Royal Photographic Society.

frs. *abbr* = francs.

FRS *abbr* = Federal Reserve System; Federal Relay Service; Fellow of the Royal Society.

FRSA *abbr* = Fellow of the Royal Society of Arts.

FRSC *abbr* = Fellow of the Royal Society of Chemistry; Fellow of the Royal Society, Canada.

FRSCM *abbr* = Fellow of the Royal School of Church Music.

FRSE *abbr* = Fellow of the Royal Society of Edinburgh.

FRSH *abbr* = Fellow of the Royal Society of Health.

FRSL *abbr* = Ffestiniog Railway Society.

FRSM *abbr* = Fellow of the Royal Society of Medicine.

FrSt *abbr* = fracto-stratus.

frt. *abbr* = freight.

FRTIB *abbr* = Federal Retirement Thrift Investment Board.

FRTPI *abbr* = Fellow of the Royal Town Planning Institute.

FRTRA *abbr* = Federation of Radio and Television Retailers Association.

FRU *abbr* = Free Representation Unit.

fructiferous *adj* (*plant etc*) bearing fruit.

fructify *vb* (**fructifies, fructifying, fructified**) *vt* to make fruitful, fertilize. * *vi* to bear fruit; to become fruitful.—**fructification** *n*.

fructose *n* a type of sugar found in ripe fruit and honey.

fructuous *adj* fruitful.

frugal *adj* economical, thrifty; inexpensive, meager.—**frugality** *n*.—**frugally** *adv*.

frugivorous *adj* fruit-eating.

fruit machine *n* a coin-operated gambling machine, using symbols of fruit to indicate a winning combination.

fruit *n* the seed-bearing part of any plant; the fleshy part of this used as food; the result or product of any action. * *vti* to bear or cause to bear fruit.

fruit salad *n* a dish of various fruits sliced and mixed.

fruitage *n* the process of bearing fruit; a collective term for all fruits.

fruiter *n* a fruit grower; a fruit tree.

fruiterer *n* a dealer in fruit.

fruitful *adj* producing lots of fruit; productive.—**fruitfully** *adv*.—**fruitfulness** *n*.

fruition *n* a coming to fulfillment, realization.

fruitless *adj* unproductive; pointless; useless.—**fruitlessly** *adv*.—**fruitlessness** *n*.

fruity *adj* (**fruitier, fruitiest**) like, or tasting like, fruit; (*inf*) (*voice*) mellow; (*inf*) salacious.—**fruitiness** *n*.

frumenty *n* a sort of porridge, made from hulled wheat and boiled milk.—*also* **fromenty, furmenty**.

frump *n* a drab and dowdy woman.—**frumpish, frumpy** *adj*.

frust. *abbr* (*Latin*) = *frustillatim*, "in small portions" or "pieces."

frustrate *vt* to prevent from achieving a goal or gratifying a desire; to discourage, irritate, tire; to disappoint.—**frustrater** *n*.—**frustratingly** *adv*.—**frustration** *n*.

frustule *n* the shell of a diatom.

frustum *n* (*pl* **frustums, frusta**) (*geom*) the part of a cone, pyramid, etc, left after the top is cut off.

frutescent *adj* pertaining to, having the form of, or resembling a shrub.

fruticose *adj* resembling a shrub.

FRVA *abbr* = Fellow of the Rating and Valuation Association.

Fry *n* 1. **C[harles] B[urgess]** (1872–1956) English all-round sportsman who represented England in athletics, cricket, and soccer. 2. **Christopher [Harris]** (1907–) English dramatist whose verse dramas such as *A Phoenix too Frequent* and *The Lady's Not for Burning* were popular with both critics and the public. 3. **Edwin M** (1899–1987) English architect. His notable works include Impington Village College. 4. **Elizabeth** (1780–1845) English prison reformer, Quaker, and preacher. 5. **Roger** (1866–1934) British writer and artist; curator of paintings at the Metropolitan Museum of Art, New York (1906–10).

fry[1] *vti* (**frying, fried**) to cook over direct heat in hot fat. * *n* (*pl* **fries**) a dish of things fried.

fry[2] *n* (*pl* **fries**) recently hatched fishes; the young of a frog, etc.

fryer *n* a person who fries; a pan, etc, for frying in; a piece of meat for frying.—*also* **frier**.

fs. *abbr* = facsimile.

f.s. *abbr* = (*French*) *faire suivre* , " to be forwarded"; foot-second.

FS *abbr* = Forest Service; Fabian Society; Faraday Society; Fertilizer Society; Flight Sergeant; Fountain Society; Friendly Society; Free State; Field Service; Fleet Surgeon; .feasibility study.

FSA *abbr* = Fellow of the Society of Antiquaries; Fellow of the Society of Arts; Farm Service Agency.

FSAA *abbr* = Fellow of the Society of Incorporated Accountants and Auditors.

FSAO *abbr* = Fellow of the Scottish Association of Opticians.

FSAPP *abbr* = Fellow of the Society of Advanced Psychotherapy Practitioners.

FSAW *abbr* = Federation of South African Women.

FSBP *abbr* = Fellow of the Society of Business Practitioners.

FSBTH *abbr* = Fellow of the Society of Health and Beauty Therapists.

FSC *abbr* = Field Studies Council; Fiji Sugar Corporation; Forest School Camps; Forestry Stewardship Council.

FSCA *abbr* = Fellow of the Institute of Company Accountants.

FSCT *abbr* = Fellow of the Society of Cardiological Technicians.

FSDC *abbr* = Fellow of the Society of Dyers and Colourists.

FSE *abbr* = Fellow of the Society of Engineers (Inc).

FSElec *abbr* = Fellow of the Society of Electroscience.

FSG *abbr* = Factoring Services Group; Fellow of the Society of Genealogists; Fortress Study Group.

FSGT *abbr* = Fellow of the Society of Glass Technology.

FSH[1] *abbr* = follicle-stimulating hormone.

FSH[2] *see* **gonadotrophins**.

FSIAD *abbr* = Fellow of the Society of Industrial Artists and Designers.

FSID *abbr* = Foundation for the Study of Infant Deaths.

FSIS *abbr* = Food Safety and Inspection Service

FSK *abbr* = Frequency Shift Keying (computing).

FSL *abbr* = First Sea Lord; Folger Shakespeare Library.

FSMA *abbr* = Fellow of the Society of Sales Management Administrators Ltd.

FSMF *abbr* = Furniture Spring Makers Federation.

FSMGB *abbr* = Federation of Small Mines of Great Britain.

FSNNA *abbr* = Fellow of the Society of Nursery Nursing Administrators.

FSPG *abbr* = Fire Service Preservation Group.

FSPS *abbr* = Federation of Sailing and Powerboat Schools.

FSPYOA *abbr* = Farm Shop and Pick Your Own Association.

FSR *abbr* = Field Service Regulations.

FSRC *abbr* = Federal Surplus Relief Corporation.

FSS *abbr* = Federal Supply Service; Fellow of the Finnish Sauna Society; Fellow of the Royal Statistical Society.

FSSCH *abbr* = Fellow of the School of Surgical Chiropody.

FSSU *abbr* = Federated Superannuation Scheme for Universities.

f-stop *n* any of the standard settings of the aperture in a camera lens.

FSVA *abbr* = Fellow of the Incorporated Society of Valuers and Auctioneers.

ft *abbr* = (*Latin*) (*pharm*) *fiat*, "let there be made'; feet/foot (imperial measure of distance equal to 30.48 cm); fort.

ft. *abbr* = faint; feet; (*Latin*) (*pharm*) *fiat*, "let there be made'; flat; foot; fort; fortification; fortified.

FT *abbr* = *Financial Times*; full term (pregnancy).

FTA *abbr* = Federal Transit Administration; Fair Trials Abroad; Flotation Tank Association; Freight Transport Association; Free Trade Area.

FTA Index *abbr* = *Financial Times* Actuaries Share Index.

FTAM *abbr* = file transfer, access, and management.

FTASI *abbr* = *Financial Times* Actuaries All-Share Index.

FTAT *abbr* = Fair Trials Abroad Trust; Furniture, Timber and Allied Trades Union.

FTB *abbr* = first-time buyer.

FTBD *abbr* = full-term, born dead.

FTC *abbr* = Federal Trade Commission; Feed the Children; Forestry Training Council.

FTCD *abbr* = Fellow of Trinity College, London.

FTCL *abbr* = Fellow of the Trinity College of Music, London.

FTF *abbr* = Fibre Trade Federation.

fth., fthm. *abbr* = fathom.

FTI *abbr* = Fellow of the Textile Institute.

FT Index *abbr* = *Financial Times* Ordinary Share Index.

FT-IR *abbr* = Fourier-transform infra-red.

FTIT *abbr* = Fellow of the Institute of Taxation.

FTND *abbr* = full-term, normal delivery.

FT-NMR *abbr* = Fourier-transform nuclear magnetic resonance.

FT Ord. *abbr* = *Financial Times* Industrial Ordinary Share Index.

FTP *abbrev* (*comput*) = File transfer protocol, a standard that controls asynchronous communications by telephone to ensure error-free transmission of files.

FTS *abbr* = Federal Technology Service.

FTSC *abbr* = Fellow in the Technology of Surface Coatings.

FT-SE 100 *abbr* = *Financial Times* Stock Exchange 100-Share Index.

FTSKO *abbr* = Federation of Textile Societies and Kindred Organizations.

FTT *abbr* = failure to thrive.

FTWN *abbr* = Farmers' Third World Network.

FTZ *abbr* = Free Trade Zone.

Fuamnach *n* (*Irish Celtic myth*) the first wife of Midhir. She was so jealous when Midhir fell in love with Etain and took her for his wife that she turned the beautiful young woman into a series of shapes, starting with a pool of water.

Fuchs *n* 1. **Klaus [Emil Julius]** (1911–88) German-born British physicist who worked on British atom-bomb research from 1941 and was jailed in 1950 for passing details to the Soviet Union. 2. **Sir Vivian** (1908–99) English explorer and scientist who led the first overland crossing of Antarctica.

fuchsia *n* any of a genus of decorative shrubs with purplish-red flowers.

fuchsine, fuchsin *n* a crystalline substance, made into a dark red dye.

fuck *vti* (*vulg*) to have sexual intercourse with. * *n* (*vulg*) an act of sexual intercourse. * *interj* (*vulg*) expressing anger, frustration, etc.

fucus *n* (*pl* **fuci, fucuses**) a kind of large brown flat seaweed.—**fucoid, fucoidal** *adj*.

fuddle *vt* to make drunk; to make confused.

fuddy-duddy *n* (*pl* **fuddy-duddies**) a person with old-fashioned or staid views.

fudge[1] *n* a soft sweet made of butter, milk, sugar, flavoring, etc; (*print*) a piece of late matter inserted in the stop-press column of a newspaper; a made-up story. * *vi* to refuse to commit oneself; to cheat; to contrive by imperfect or improvised means. * *vt* to fake; to fail to come to grips with; to make or do anything in a bungling, careless manner.

fudge[2] *n* nonsense. * *interj* expressing annoyance or disbelief.

fuehrer *see* **führer**.

fuel *n* material burned to supply heat and power, or as a source of nuclear energy; anything that serves to intensify strong feelings. * *vti* (**fueling, fueled** *or* **fuelling, fuelled**) to supply with or obtain fuel.—**fueler, fueller** *n*.

fuel oil *n* liquid fuel used as a substitute for coal in furnaces and engines.

fug *n* (*inf*) a hot, stale atmosphere.

Fuga *n* **Ferdinando** (1699–1781) Italian architect. His notable works include the Palazzo Corsini in Rome.

fugacious *adj* fleeting; elusive; volatile; (*bot*) (*petals, etc*) falling off very early.—**fugaciously** *adv*.—**fugaciousness** *n*.

fugacity *n* fugaciousness; the property of a gas to escape or expand.

Fugard *n* **Athol** (1932–) South African dramatist whose plays, e.g. *The Blood Knot*, explore the tragedy of racial tension caused by apartheid in South Africa.

fugitive *n* a person who flees from danger, pursuit, or duty. * *adj* fleeing, as from danger or justice; fleeting, transient; not permanent.—**fugitively** *adv*.

fugleman *n* (*pl* **fuglemen**) (*formerly*) a soldier who stands in front of others to demonstrate drill; a ringleader.

fugue *n* a polyphonic musical composition with its theme taken up successively by different voices.—**fugal** *adj*.—**fugally** *adv*.

fuguist *n* a composer of fugues.

führer *n* (*German*) a leader, esp a dictator.

Führer *n* **Der** the title of Adolf Hitler (1889-1945), leader of the German Nazi party.

Fujie *n* **Kazuko** (1947–) Japanese designer who founded the Field Shop Office in 1977.

-ful *adj suffix* full of, e.g. *doleful*. * *n suffix* the amount needed to fill, e.g. *cupful*.

fulcrum *n* (*pl* **fulcrums, fulcra**) the fixed point on which a lever turns; a critical factor determining an outcome.

fulfill, fulfil *vt* (**fulfills** *or* **fulfils, fulfilling, fulfilled**) to carry out (a promise, etc); to achieve the completion of; to satisfy; to bring to an end, complete.—**fulfiller** *n*.—**fulfillment, fulfilment** *n*.

fulgent *adj* (*poet*) shining, radiant.—**fulgency** *n*.—**fulgently** *adv*.

fulgurate *vi* to flash (like lightning).—**fulgurant** *adj*.

fulgurite *n* rock or sand that has been vitrified by lightning.

fuliginous *adj* sooty, smoky.—**fuliginously** *adv*.

full[1] *adj* having or holding all that can be contained; having eaten all one wants; having a great number (of); complete; having reached to greatest size, extent, etc. * *n* the greatest amount, extent etc. * *adv* completely, directly, exactly.

full[2] *vt* to clean and thicken (cloth) by beating.

fullback *n* (*football, rugby, hockey, etc*) one of the defensive players at the back; the position held by this player.

full backup utility *n* (*comput*) a utility program that creates a full backup of the files on a disk.

full-blooded *adj* vigorous, hearty.—**full-bloodedly** *adv*.

full-blown *adj* in full bloom; matured, fully developed.

full-bodied *adj* (*flavor*) characterized by richness and fullness.

full close *see* **cadence**.

full dress *n* dress worn for formal or ceremonial occasions.—**full-dress** *adj*.

full duplex *n* (*comput*) a protocol for asynchronous communications, which allows the sending and receiving of signals at the same time.

fuller[1] *n* someone who fulls cloth.

fuller[2] *n* a tool used for grooving and shaping iron; a groove made by this.

Fuller *n* **[Richard] Buckminster** (1895–1983) American architect and engineer who invented the "geodesic dome."

fuller's earth *n* a type of clay used for fulling cloth.

full face *adj, adv* seen from in front.

full-frontal *adj* (*inf*) of a nude person or photograph, with the genitals clearly visible; unrestrained.—**full frontal** *n*.

full house *n* (*poker*) a hand with three cards of the same value and a pair (—*also* **full hand**); (*theater, etc*) a performance for which all seats are sold; (*bingo*) a complete set of winning numbers.

full moon *n* a particular phase of the Moon when it is seen as exactly fully illuminated; the period of this.

full nelson *n* (*wrestling*) a hold in which both hands reach under an opponent's arms from behind, and then are clasped against the back of the opponent's neck.

fullness *n* the state of being full; **fullness of time** the proper or destined time.—*also* **fulness**.

full organ *n* (*mus*) a term used in organ music to indicate that all the loud stops are to be used together.

full-scale *adj* actual size.

full-stop *or* **period** *n* the punctuation mark (.) used at the end of a sentence, and after abbreviations, etc.

full tilt *adv* at maximum speed.

full time *n* the finish of a match.

full-time *adj* working or lasting the whole time.—**full-timer** *n*.

fully *adv* thoroughly, completely; at least.

fully-fledged *adj* (*bird*) mature; having full status.—*also* **full-fledged**.

fulmar *n* an Arctic sea bird.

fulminant *adj* fulminating; sudden; (*pain*) sharp, piercing.

fulminate *vi* to issue protests with violence or threats; to inveigh (against). * *vt* to utter or exclaim, as a denunciation. *n* an explosive compound of fulminic acid. —**fulmination** *n*. —**fulminator** *n*. —**fulminatory** *adj*.

fulminic acid *n* an unstable acid composed of cyanogen and oxygen.

fulness *see* **fullness**.

FULS *abbr* = Federation of Ulster Local Studies.

fulsome *adj* excessively praising, obsequious.—**fulsomely** *adv*.—**fulsomeness** *n*.

Fulton *n* **Robert** (1765–1815) American engineer who designed the river steamboat *Clermont* (1807).

fulvous *adj* tawny.

fumarole *n* a vent in a volcanically active area from which high-temperature gases are emitted

fumatorium *n* (*pl* **fumatoriums, fumatoria**) an airtight room where insects, plants, etc, are fumigated.

fumble *vi* to grope about. * *vt* to handle clumsily; to say or act awkwardly; to fail to catch (a ball) cleanly. * *n* an awkward attempt.—**fumbler** *n*.—**fumblingly** *adv*.

fume *n* (*usu pl*) smoke, gas, or vapor, esp if offensive or suffocating. * *vi* to give off fumes; to express anger. * *vt* to subject to fumes.—**fumer** *n*.—**fumingly** *adv*.

Fumiani *n* **Giovanni Antonio** (1643–1710) Venetian-born painter, famed for his decoration of the church of St Pantaleone.

fumigate *vt* to disinfect or exterminate (pests, etc) using fumes.—**fumigation** *n*.—**fumigator** *n*.

fumitory *n* (*pl* **fumitories**) a plant, found mainly in Europe, the leaves of which were formerly used as a treatment for skin diseases.

fun *n* (what provides) amusement and enjoyment. * *vi* (**funning, funned**) to joke.

Funafuti *n* capital city of Tuvalu.

Funakoshi *n* **Saburo** (1931–) Japanese glassware designer.

funambulist *n* a tightrope walker.

function[1] *n* the activity characteristic of a person or thing; the specific purpose of a certain person or thing; an official ceremony or social entertainment; (*math*) a quantity whose value depends on the varying value of another. * *vi* to perform a function; to act, operate.

function² *n* (*comput*) any single operation of a computer or word processor, e.g. editing; within programs such as spreadsheets, a procedure that will perform a particular sequence of operations to produce a result.

function key *n* (*comput*) a special purpose key on the keyboard of a word processor or computer system that enables the user to perform a particular task or execute a command.

functional *adj* of a function or functions; practical, not ornamental; (*disease*) affecting the functions only, not organic.—**functionally** *adv*.

functional budget *n* a budget that has relevance to a particular function of a firm, such as production, marketing, etc.

functional group *n* (*chem*) an arrangement of atoms joined to a carbon skeleton, which gives an organic compound its particular chemical properties.

functionalism[1] *n* the theory and practice of design for practical application.—**functionalist** *adj*, *n*.

functionalism[2] *n* an architectural theory developed from the idiom that form should reflect function. It evolved into a style in the 1920s, but more effectively formed the basis for modernism.

functionary *n* (*pl* **functionaries**) a person in an official capacity.

fund *n* a supply that can be drawn upon; a sum of money set aside for a purpose; (*pl*) ready money. * *vt* to provide funds for; to convert (a debt) into stock; to place in a fund.

fundament *n* foundation, basis; (*euphemism*) the buttocks; the anus.

fundamental *adj* basic; essential. * *n* that which serves as a groundwork; an essential.—**fundamentality, fundamentalness** *n*.—**fundamentally** *adv*.

fundamentalism *n* belief in the literal truth of the Bible, Koran etc.—**fundamentalist** *adj*, *n*.—**fundamentalistic** *adj*.

fundamental particle *see* **elementary particle**.

fundus[1] *n* (*pl* **fundi**) (*anat*) the base or deepest part of an organ.

fundus[2] *n* (*pl* **fundi**) (*anat*) a point in the retina of the eye opposite the pupil.

funeral *n* the ceremony associated with the burial or cremation of the dead; a procession accompanying a coffin to a burial.

funeral director *n* a person who manages funerals.

funereal *adj* suiting a funeral, dismal, mournful.—**funereally** *adv*.

fungal *adj* of or pertaining to a fungus; caused by a fungus.

fungal disease *n* disease or infection caused by a fungus.

fungible *adj* (*law*) replaceable by another, similar specimen. * *n* a fungible thing, e.g. a coin.

fungibles[1] *npl* interchangeable securities, goods, etc, that allow for the replacement of one by another without any loss of value occurring.

fungibles[2] *npl* perishable goods.

fungicide *n* a substance that destroys fungi.—**fungicidal** *adj*.

fungiform *adj* resembling a mushroom

fungoid *adj* resembling a fungus.

fungous *adj* of, pertaining to or like fungi; fungal; developing suddenly.

fungus *n* (*pl* **fungi, funguses**) any of a major group of lower plants, as mildews, mushrooms, yeasts, etc, that lack chlorophyll and reproduce by spores.—**fungic** *adj*.

funicular *adj* of rope or its tension. * *n* a cable railway ascending a mountain.

funiculus *n* (*pl* **funiculi**) (*anat*) a small cord, ligature, or fiber.

funk[1] *n* (*inf*) panic, fear; a coward. * *vti* (*inf*) to show fear; to shirk.—**funker** *n*.

funk[2] *n* (*mus*) a form of heavily syncopated, rhythmic African-American dance music, originating in the United States.

funky[1] *adj* (**funkier, funkiest**) panicky; fearful.

funky[2] *adj* (**funkier, funkiest**) (*inf*) (*mus*) soulful, bluesy; fashionable.—**funkiness** *n*.

funnel *n* an implement, usually a cone with a wide top and tapering to a narrow tube, for pouring fluids, powders, into bottles, etc; a metal chimney for the escape of smoke, steam, etc. * *vti* (**funneling, funneled** *or* **funnelling, funnelled**) to pour or cause to pour through a funnel.

funny *adj* (**funnier, funniest**) causing laughter; puzzling, odd; (*inf*) unwell, queasy. * *n* (*pl* **funnies**) a joke; (*pl*) comic strips, esp in a newspaper.—**funnily** *adv*.—**funniness** *n*.

funny bone *n* the part of the elbow where a sensitive nerve rests close to the bone, producing a tingling sensation if struck.

FUO *abbr* = fever of uncertain origin.

fuoco *n* (*mus*) (*Italian*) literally "fire," so *con fuoco* means "with fire."

fur *n* the short, soft, fine hair on the bodies of certain animals; their skins with the fur attached; a garment made of fur; a fabric made in imitation of fur; a fur-like coating, as on the tongue. * *vti* (**furring, furred**) to cover or become covered with fur.

fur. *abbr* = furlong; further.

furbelow *n* a flounce or other trimming on clothing.

furbish *vt* to polish, to burnish; to renovate.—**furbisher** *n*.

FURC *abbr* = Foundation for Underdeveloped Regions in China.

furcate *vi* to fork, divide. * *adj* forked, branching.—**furcation** *n*.

furfur *n* (*pl* **furfures**) scurf, dandruff.

furfuraceous *adj* resembling bran; resembling dandruff.

Furies *npl* (*Roman myth*) three winged virgins who live in the depths of Tartarus and punished crimes, called Erinyes or Eumenides in Greek mythology.

furioso *adv* (*mus*) wildly.

furious *adj* full of anger; intense; violent, impetuous.—**furiously** *adv*.—**furiousness** *n*.

furl *vt* to roll up (a sail, flag, etc) tightly and make secure; to fold up, close.—**furlable** *adj*.—**furler** *n*.

furlong *n* 220 yards, one-eighth of a mile (201 meters).

furlough *n* leave of absence from duty, esp for military personnel. * *vt* to grant a furlough to.

furmenty *see* **frumenty**.

furnace *n* an enclosed chamber in which heat is produced to burn refuse, smelt ore, etc.

Furness *n* Frank (1839–1912) American architect who designed buildings in an aggressive Gothic style.

furnish *vt* to provide (a room, etc) with furniture; to equip with what is necessary; to supply.—**furnisher** *n*.

furnishings *npl* furniture, carpets, etc.

furniture *n* the things in a room, etc that equip it for living, as chairs, beds, etc; equipment.

furore, furor *n* fury, indignation; widespread enthusiasm.

furrier *n* a dealer in furs.

furriery *n* (*pl* **furrieries**) the fur trade; a collective name for furs.

furrow *n* the groove in the earth made by a plough; a groove or track resembling this; a wrinkle. * *vti* to make furrows in; to wrinkle.—**furrower** *n*.—**furrowy** *adj*.

furry *adj* (**furrier, furriest**) like, made of, or covered with, fur.—**furrily** *adv*.—**furriness** *n*.

further *adv* at or to a greater distance or degree; in addition. * *adj* more distant, remote; additional. * *vt* to help forward, promote.—**furtherer** *n*.

furtherance *n* a helping forward.

furthermore *adv* moreover, besides.

furthermost *adj* most remote.

furthest *adj* at or to the greatest distance.

furtive *adj* stealthy; sly.—**furtively** *adv*.—**furtiveness** *n*.

furuncle *n* (*med*) a boil.—**furuncular** *adj*. *See* **boil**.

fury *n* (*pl* **furies**) intense rage; a frenzy; a violently angry person.

furze *n* gorse.

fus. *abbr* = fusiliers.

fuscous *adj* dark-colored, esp brownish-black.

fuse *n* (*elect*) a device for maintaining the current in a circuit by preventing it from rising too high if a fault should occur.—*also* **fuze**.

fusee *n* a large-headed match; a conical spindle in a clock, around which the chain is wound.—*also* **fuzee**.

fusel oil *n* a poisonous liquid mixture of various alcohols, formed as a byproduct of distillation.

fuselage *n* the body of an aircraft.

Fuseli *n* Henry (1741–1825) Swiss painter. His paintings are mannered and romantic with a strange sense of the grotesque and macabre, which was later to appeal to surrealist artists.

fusible *adj* able to be fused; (*metal, alloy*) having a melting point below 148.9° C (300° F) and used in fuses, etc.—**fusibility** *n*.—**fusibly** *adv*.

fusiform *adj* spindle-shaped.

fusil *n* a light flintlock musket.

fusilier, fusileer *n* (*formerly*) a British soldier armed with a flintlock musket; a soldier in certain infantry regiments.

fusillade *n* a firing of shots in continuous or rapid succession; an outburst, as of criticism. * *vt* to attack or shoot down by fusillade.

fusion[1] *n* the act of melting, blending, or fusing; a product of fusion; union, partnership.

fusion[2] *n* (*physics*) a nuclear reaction in which unstable nuclei combine to create larger, more stable nuclei with the release of vast amounts of energy.

fuss *n* excited activity, bustle; a nervous state; (*inf*) a quarrel; (*inf*) a showy display of approval. * *vi* to worry over trifles; to whine, as a baby.—**fusser** *n*.

fussy *adj* (**fussier, fussiest**) worrying over details; hard to please; fastidious; overelaborate.—**fussily** *adv*.—**fussiness** *n*.

fustian *n* a kind of coarse twilled cotton cloth, e.g. corduroy; ranting language, bombast. * *adj* made of fustian; turgid.

fustic *n* a large tropical American tree; its wood; the yellow obtained from it.

fusty *adj* (**fustier, fustiest**) smelling of mold or damp; outmoded in ideas or opinions.—**fustily** *adv*.—**fustiness** *n*.

fut. *abbr* = future.

futhark, futharc, futhork, futhorc *n* a phonetic alphabet made up of runes.

futile *adj* useless; ineffective.—**futilely** *adv*.—**futility** *n*.

futtock *n* (*naut*) one of those timbers raised over the keel which form the breadth of the ship.

futon *n* a light cotton mattress.

future *adj* that is to be; of or referring to time yet to come. * *n* the time to come; future events; likelihood of eventual success; (*gram*) the future tense; (*pl*) commodities purchased at a prescribed price for delivery at some future date.

futures contract *n* an agreement to buy or sell a specified quantity of a fixed security, currency, or commodity at a specified price at a specified date in the future.

futures market *or* **forward market** *n* a market that deals in futures contracts.

futurism *n* a movement of writers and artists, originating in early 20th-century Italy, that extolled the virtues of the new, dynamic machine age but which was a spent force by the 1930s.—**futurist** *adj, n*.

futuristic *adj* forward-looking in design, appearance, intention, etc.—**futuristically** *adv*.

futurity *n* (*pl* **futurities**) time or events yet to come.

futurology *n* the forecasting of future trends in human affairs.—**futurologist** *n*.

Fux *n* **Johann Joseph** (1663–1741) Austrian composer, organist, and theorist who specialized in church music.

fuze *vti* to join or become joined by melting; to (cause to) melt by the application of heat; to equip a plug, circuit, etc with a fuse; to (cause to) fail by blowing a fuse. * *n* a tube or wick filled with combustible material for setting off an explosive charge; a piece of thin wire that melts and breaks when an electric current exceeds a certain level.—*also* **fuse; fuzee**. *See* **fusee**.

fuzz *n* fine light particles of fiber (as of down or fluff); a blurred effect; fluff; (*sl*) police. * *vi* to fly off in minute particles; to become blurred.

fuzzword *see* **buzzword**.

fuzzy *adj* (**fuzzier, fuzziest**) like fuzz; fluffy; blurred.—**fuzzily** *adv*.—**fuzziness** *n*.

fuzzy logic *n* (*comput*) a description of the development away from strict logical arguments to take account of human or non-logical behavior.

f.v. *abbr* (*Latin*) = *folio verso*, "on the back of the page" or the left-hand page.

FVPC *abbr* = Federation of Visual Planning Consultants.

FVPG *abbr* = Film and Video Press Group.

FWAG *abbr* = Farming and Wildlife Advisory Group.

FWB *abbr* = Free-will Baptists.

fwd. *abbr* = four-wheel drive; front-wheel drive.

FWeldI *abbr* = Fellow of the Welding Institute.

fwh *abbr* = flexible working hours.

FWN *abbr* = Farmers' World Network.

FWS *abbr* = Fish and Wildlife Service.

fwt *abbr* = fair wear and tear.

FWT *abbr* = Farming and Wildlife Trust.

FWVFA *abbr* = Federation of World Volunteer Firefighters Associations.

FWWCP *abbr* = Federation of Worker Writers and Community Publishers.

Fx *abbr* = fracture.

FX *abbr* = foreign exchange.

FX *abbr* = sound effects; special effects.

-fy *vb suffix* to make, e.g. *solidify*.

fya *abbr* = first-year allowance.

FYC *abbr* = Family and Youth Concern.

FYD *abbr* = Fellowship of the Youth Development Association.

FYDA *abbr* = Associate Fellowship of the Youth Development Association.

FYF *abbr* = Find Your Feet.

fyi *abbr* = for your information.

fz *abbr* (*mus*) (*Italian*) = *forzando*, "to be strongly accentuated."

FZS *abbr* = Fellow of the Zoological Society.

FZY *abbr* = Federation of Zionist Youth.

G

g, G *n* the seventh letter of the English alphabet.

G *symbol* (*mus*) the 5th note of the scale of C; gravitational constant; (*phys*) conductance; giga; (*sl*) grand ($1000 or £1000); Great; Gulf.

g *abbr* = gallons(s); gram(s); gravity; acceleration due to gravity.

g. *abbr* = (*elect*)conductance ; gauge; gelding; gender; general (staff); genitive; gingival; gold; grain; grand; green; guide; gulf.

G. *abbr* = German; Germany; specific gravity; a Fraunhofer line caused by iron.

G3 *abbr* = Group of Three (most powerful Western economies).

G5 *abbr* = Group of Five (nations taking part in exchange-rate stabilization).

G7 *abbr* = Group of Seven (the leading industrialized nations).

G10 *abbr* = Group of Ten (the nations that are lending money to the IMF).

G24 *abbr* = Group of Twenty-Four (the industrialized nations).

G77 *abbr* = Group of Seventy-Seven (developing nations).

g.a., G/A *abbr* (*marine ins*) = general average.

g/a *abbr* = ground to air.

Ga *symbol* (*chem*) gallium (element).

Ga. *abbr* = Gallic; Georgia.

GA *abbr* = Galvanizers Association; Gamblers Anonymous; Gemmological Association of Great Britain; General Agent; General Assembly, Georgia; Giftware Association; Green Alliance; Greening Australia; gestational age.

GAA *abbr* = Gaelic Athletic Association; Greenhouse Action Australia.

gab *vi* (**gabbing, gabbed**) (*inf*) to talk in a rapid or thoughtless manner, chatter. * *n* (*inf*) idle talk.—**gabber** *n*.

Gabaline *n* (*Irish Celtic myth*) an ancient blind seer whom Medb consulted.

gabardine *n* a firm cloth of wool, rayon, or cotton; gaberdine.

gabble *vti* to talk or utter rapidly or incoherently; to utter inarticulate or animal sounds.—**gabbler** *n*.

gabbro *n* (*pl* **gabbros**) a dark igneous rock like granite.—**gabbroic** *adj*.

gabby *adj* (**gabbier, gabbiest**) (*inf*) talkative.

gabelle *n* (*formerly*) a tax on salt in France.

gaberdine *n* (*formerly*) a long, loose upper garment worn by pilgrims, Jews etc; a raincoat.

Gabhra or **Gowra** *n* (*Irish Celtic myth*) the Battle of Gabhra, known also as Gowra, was the last great battle in which the Fianna took part. It led to the loss of their supremacy in Ireland and to the death of most of them.

gabion *n* (*formerly*) a large cylindrical basket filled with earth or stones, used in military defense; a similar metal container used in engineering and underwater construction.

gable *n* the triangular upper part of a wall enclosed by the sloping ends of a pitched roof.—**gabled** *adj*.

Gable *n* [William] **Clark** (1901–60) American film actor.

gablet *n* a small ornamental gable used for the summit of niches etc.

Gabo Naum *n* (1890–1979) Russian-born sculptor; one of the first to experiment with kinetic art; important commissions include sculptures for the Baltimore Museum of Art (1951).

Gabon *n* a small republic in west central Africa.

Gabor *n* **Dennis** (1900–79) British engineer and winner of 1971 Nobel prize for physics for his invention (1947) of the hologram.

Gaborone *n* capital city of Botswana.

Gabriel *n* archangel, the traditional messenger of God. *See also* **angel**.

Gabriel *n* 1. **Ange-Jacques** (1698–1782) French architect. His notable works include Petit Trianon, Versailles. 2. **René** (1890–1950) French decorator who designed wallpaper, fabric, rugs, and limited-edition furniture.

Gabrieli *n* 1. **Andrea** (*c*.1517–86) Italian organist and composer of madrigals, motets, masses, and instrumental pieces. 2. **Giovanni** (*c*.1557–1612) the nephew of Andrea Gabriele, and also a noted composer, organist, and teacher. He was one of the greatest Venetian composers of motets.

gad *vi* (**gadding, gadded**) (*usu with* **about**) to wander restlessly or idly in search of pleasure.—**gadder** *n*.

gadabout *n* (*inf*) a person that wanders restlessly in search of pleasure or amusement.

Gadara *n* (*Bible*) one of the towns of the Decapolis near the Sea of Galilee. *See also* **Decapolis**.

Gaddafi, Qaddafi *n* Moammar al (1942–) Libyan statesman and militar y dictator who took power in a coup in 1969 and became president in 1977.

Gade *n* Niels Wilhelm (1817–90) a Danish violinist and composer whose output was influenced by Mendelssohn and Schumann. His principal works include eight symphonies, six overtures, and several cantatas, e.g. *The Crusaders*.

gadfly *n* (*pl* **gadflies**) any of various flies that bite or annoy livestock; an irritating person.

gadget *n* a small, often ingenious, mechanical, or electronic tool or device.—**gadgety** *adj*.

gadgetry *n* gadgets; the use of gadgets.

gadoid *adj, n* (a fish) of the cod family.

gadolinite *n* a silicate of yttrium.

gadolinium *n* a magnetic metallic element of the rare earth group.—**gadolinic** *adj*.

gadroon *n* an ornamental edge of inverted fluting; a decorative border, esp on silver.

gadwall *n* (*pl* **gadwalls, gadwall**) a large freshwater duck, prized as game.

Gaea *see* **Ge**.

Gae-Bholg *n* (*Irish Celtic myth*) a famous spear belonging to Cuchulainn.

Gael *n* a person who speaks Gaelic, esp a Scottish Highlander or Irishman.

Gael. *abbr* = Gaelic.

Gaelic *n* the Celtic language of Ireland, the Scottish Highlands, and the Isle of Man.—*also adj*.

gaff *n* a pole with a sharp hook for landing large fish; (*naut*) a high boom or yard for hoisting a sail aft of a mast; (*sl*) one's home. * *vt* to land (a fish) with a gaff.

gaffe *n* a social blunder.

gaffer *n* an old man, often a countryman; an overseer or foreman; the senior electrician of a film crew.

gaff-topsail *n* (*naut*) a light sail set above a gaff.

GAFTA *abbr* = Grain and Free Trade Association.

gag *n* something put over or into the mouth to prevent talking; any restraint of free speech; a joke. * *vb* (**gagging, gagged**) *vt* to cause to retch; to keep from speaking, as by stopping the mouth of. * *vi* to retch; to tell jokes.

gaga *adj* (*inf*) senile; slightly crazy.

Gagarin *n* Yuri [Alekseevich] (1934–68) Soviet cosmonaut who became the first man in space in 1961, when his *Vostok I* satellite circled the earth.

gage *see* **gauge**.

gaggle *n* a flock of geese when not in flight; (*inf*) a disorderly collection of people.

Gagnère *n* Olivier (1952–) a designer with the Memphis Group in Milan, before setting up his own consultancy.

gahnite *n* a greenish and dark-brown mineral.

GAI *abbr* = General Assembly of International Sports Federations; Guild of Architectural Ironmongers.

Gaible *n* (*Irish Celtic myth*) the son of Nuada. He stole a bundle of twigs that Ainge had gathered to build a tub for herself. Gaible threw the twigs awayand a wood sprang up where the twigs fell.

Gai Dearg *n* (*Irish Celtic myth*) the name Gai Dearg was given to the magical red-handled spear owned by Diarmaid.

gaiety *n* (*pl* **gaieties**) happiness, liveliness; colorful appearance.

gaige *n* the Chinese word for "radical reform" or peristroika.

Gaillard *n* Eugène (1862–1933) French jewelry designer, associated with Bing's Paris store.

Gailioin or **Galioin** *n* (*Irish Celtic myth*) the Gailioin was one of the three companies that made up the descendants of Nemedh, who came from Greece and invaded Ireland. *See also* **Laighin**.

gaily *adv* in a cheerful manner; with bright colors.

gain *vt* to obtain, earn, esp by effort; to win in a contest; to attract; to get as an addition (esp profit or advantage); to make an increase in; to reach. * *vi* to make progress; to increase in weight. * *n* an increase esp in profit or advantage; an acquisition.

gainful *adj* profitable.—**gainfully** *adv*.—**gainfulness** *n*.

gainsay *vt* (**gainsaying**, **gainsaid**) (*formal*) to dispute; to deny.—**gainsayer** *n*.

Gainsborough *n* **Thomas** (1727–88) English portrait painter whose keen interest in landscape painting pervades most of his work, his sitters often being portrayed in an outdoor setting, e.g. *Mr and Mrs Andrews* (1748).

gainsharing *n* a system of paying workers by which a proportion of pay is linked to gains in the level of productivity or to a reduction in the level of costs.

gait *n* a manner of walking or running; the sequence of footsteps made by a moving horse.

gaiter *n* a cloth or leather covering for the lower leg.

Gaitskell *n* **Hugh [Todd Naylor]** (1906–63) British Labour politician; Labour Party leader (1955–63).

gal¹ *n* (*sl*) a girl.

gal², **gall.** *abbr* = gallon.

gala *n* a celebration, festival.

galactic *adj* of a galaxy; huge.

galactic center *n* (*astron*) the center of the Milky Way Galaxy.

galactic coordinates *n* (*astron*) coordinates using angular measure to specify the position of any object or point in the Milky Way Galaxy.

galactic halo *n* (*astron*) a collection of stars, gas, and dust, nearly spherical in shape, which has the same center as the galaxy.

galactic noise *n* (*astron*) background noise from galactic sources.

galactic nucleus *n* (*astron*) the assembly of stars at the center of a galaxy and similar spirals.

galactic plane *n* (*astron*) the plane which passes through the center of the Milky Way.

galactic rotation *n* (*astron*) the rotation of the galaxy, and all its gas, stars, and dust, which increases towards its center.

galactorrhea *n* the flow of milk from the breast, not associated with childbirth or nursing.

galago *n* (*pl* **galagos**) an African genus of lemurs; a bushbaby.

Galahad *n* (*Welsh Celtic myth*) originally **Gwalchafed**, which translates as the "falcon of summer." In the medieval Arthurian legend, Galahad went in quest of the Holy Grail.

Galan Mai *n* (*Welsh Celtic culture*) the Welsh equivalent of Beltane. Galan Mai was held on May 1.

galant *n* (*mus*) (*French*) literally "polite"; a term applied to certain graceful styles of court music, especially of the 18th century.

galanterie *n* (*mus*) an 18th-century German term for a keyboard piece in the galant style.

galantine *n* a dish composed of chicken, veal, or other white meat, boned, seasoned, tied up, boiled, shaped, and served cold in its own jelly.

galatea *n* a cotton fabric, often with blue and white stripes.

Galatea *n* 1. (*Greek myth*) a nymph who rejected the advances of the Cyclops Polyphemus in favor of the shepherd Acis. 2. (*Roman myth*) the name of a statue brought to life by Venus in answer to the prayer of the sculptor Pygmalion.

Galati *n* a city in Romania.

Galatians *n sing* (*Bible*, *NT*) the epistles of St Paul addressed to the Galatians.

galavant *see* **gallivant**.

galaxy *n* (*pl* **galaxies**) any of the systems of stars in the universe; any splendid assemblage; (*with cap*) the galaxy containing the Earth's solar system; the Milky Way.

galbanum *n* an odorous and bitter gum resin used in medicine.

Galbraith *n* **John Kenneth** (1908–) Canadian-born American economist and diplomat; American ambassador to India (1961–63). His written works include *The Affluent Society*.

gale *n* (*meteorol*) a strong wind, specifically one with an average speed of 42 mph (67.6 kph) and gusts in excess of 50 mph (80.5 kph); an outburst.

galea *n* (*pl* **galeae**) (*bot*, *zool*) a helmet-like structure.—**galeate**, **galeated** *adj*.

galena *n* (*chem*) a sulfide of lead.

Galenic *adj* of Galen (*c*.AD130–200), the Greek physician and philosopher, or his works.

GALHA *abbr* = Gay and Lesbian Humanist Association.

Galian *n* (*Irish Celtic myth*) the ancient name for Leinster. *See* **Laighin**.

Galilean¹ *adj* of Galilee or its inhabitants * *n* a native of Galilee; (*often pl*) a Christian; (*with the*) Jesus Christ.

Galilean² *adj* of or pertaining to Galileo (1564–1642), the Italian astronomer and mathematician.

Galilean satellites *n* (*astron*) the four satellites of Jupiter first observed by Galileo in 1610: Io, Europa, Ganymede, and Callisto.

Galilean telescope *n* (*astron*) a refracting telescope (i.e., one using lenses only) invented by Galileo Galilei. *See* **Galilei** *n* **Galileo**.

galilee *n* (*archit*) a small chapel or porch at the western entrance to a church.

Galilee *n* a northern region of Israel, frequently overrun by invading armies from the north; (*Bible*) the location of the early ministry of Christ.

Galilee Sea of [**Lake Tiberius**] freshwater lake in northeast Israel fed by the River Jordan; it lies some 700 feet below sea level.

Galilei *n* **Alessandro M G** (*b*.1691) Italian architect. His notable works include the Corsini Chapel, Rome.

Galileo, Galilei *n* (1564–1642) Italian astronomer, mathematician, and natural philosopher. He demonstrated the isochronism of the pendulum, and showed that falling bodies of differing weight descend at the same rate.

galingale, galangal *n* a kind of sedge; the aromatic root of an Asian plant.

galiot, galliot *n* a heavily built two-masted Dutch trading vessel; (*formerly*) a small light galley used in the Mediterranean.

galipot *n* a white resinous juice that exudes from pine trees.

galivant *see* **gallivant**.

gall¹ *n* bile; bitter feeling; (*inf*) impudence.

gall² *n* a diseased growth on plant tissue produced by fungi, insect parasites, or bacteria.

gall³ *n* a skin sore caused by rubbing. * *vt* to chafe or hurt by rubbing; to irritate.

gallant *adj* dignified, stately; brave; noble; (*man*) polite and chivalrous to women.—**gallantly** *adv*.—**gallantness** *n*. —**gallantry** *n* (*pl* **gallantries**).

gallantry *n* (*pl* **gallantries**) (an act of) bravery, dashing courage; courtliness, a polite act.

gall bladder *n* a membranous sac attached to the liver in which bile is stored.

Gallé *n* **Émile** (1864–1904) influential French glassware designer who founded the Alliance Provinciale des Industries d'Art.

galleass *n* a large low-built three-masted vessel propelled by sails and oars, and carrying twenty or more guns.

galleon *n* a large sailing ship of the 15th–18th centuries.

gallery *n* (*pl* **galleries**) a covered passage for walking; a long narrow outside balcony; a balcony running along the inside wall of a building; (the occupants of) an upper area of seating in a theater; a long narrow room used for a special purpose, e.g. shooting practice; a room or building designed for the exhibition of works of art; the spectators at a golf tournament, tennis match, etc.—**galleried** *adj*.

gallery forest *n* a strip of forest along river banks in an otherwise treeless landscape.

gallery grave *n* (*archeo*) a type of chamber tomb in which there is no distinct entrance way and the burial chambers are adjacent to one another beneath a long mound.

galleting *n* (*archit*) the primarily decorative technique of pushing pebbles or chips of stone into mortar which is still soft.

galley *n* a long, usu low, ship of ancient or medieval times, propelled by oars; the kitchen of a ship, aircraft; (*print*) a shallow tray for holding type; proofs printed from such type (—*also* **galley proof**).

galliard *n* (*mus*) (*French*) a lively dance in triple time.

gallic *adj* of or made of gallnuts; (*chem*) of or containing gallium in the trivalent state.

Gallic *adj* of or pertaining to France; of ancient Gaul or its people.

Gallican *adj* of the Roman Catholic Church in France.

Gallicanism *n* the doctrine of the national party in the French Roman Catholic Church, tending to restrict papal control, opposed to Ultramontanism.

Gallice *adv* in French.

Gallicism *n* a French expression or idiom.

Gallicize, Gallicise *vt* to make French in manners, idiom etc.

galligaskins *n pl* trousers, leggings worn in the 16th and 17th centuries.

gallimaufry *n* (*pl* **gallimaufries**) a medley, a hotch-potch.

gallinaceous *adj* of or relating to a group of heavy-bodied largely land-loving birds including pheasants and domestic fowl.

galling *adj* irritating, exasperating.

gallipot *n* a small glazed pot, esp for medicine.

gallium *n* a metallic element that is liquid at room temperature and is used in thermometers, semiconductor devices, etc.

gallivant *vi* (*inf*) to go about in search of amusement.—*also* **galivant, galavant**.

galliwasp *n* a West Indian lizard.

gallnut *n* a round excrescence produced on the oak by the puncturing of the leaf buds by an insect, the gall beetle.

gallon *n* a unit of liquid measure comprising 4 quarts or 3.78 liters (in UK, 4.54 liters); (*pl*) (*inf*) a large amount.

galloon *n* a narrow braid or trimming of silk, gold lace, embroidery etc.

gallop *n* the fastest gait of a horse, etc; a succession of leaping strides; a fast pace. * *vti* to go or cause to go at a gallop; to move swiftly.—**galloper** *n*.

gallowglass *n* a heavily armed footsoldier; a chief's retainer in Ireland in the 13th–16th centuries.

gallows *n* (*pl* **gallowses, gallows**) a wooden frame used for hanging criminals.

gallstone *n* a small solid mass in the gall bladder.

Gallup *n* **George Horace** (1901–84) American statistician who developed the "Gallup poll."

Gallup poll *n* a sampling of public opinion, esp to help forecast an election.

galoot *n* (*sl*) a clumsy or foolish person.

galop *n* (*mus*) a dance.

galore *adv* in great quantity; in plentiful supply.

galosh *n* a waterproof overshoe.

gals. *abbr* = gallons.

Galsworthy *n* **John** (1867–1933) English novelist and dramatist; winner of the 1932 Nobel prize for literature. His novels include the *Forsythe Saga* series.

Galt *n* **John** (1789–1839) Scottish novelist who described his novels, e.g. *Annals of the Parish*, as "theoretical histories" of the changing social patterns of Scottish country life.

Galton *n* **Sir Francis** (1822–1911) English scientist and explorer who made significant contributions to meteorology, and developed the science of fingerprinting.

galumph *vi* (*inf*) to prance triumphantly or clumsily.

galv. *abbr* = galvanic; galvanism; galvanized.

G

galvanic *adj* producing electricity by chemical action; stimulating (people) into action.—**galvanically** *adv*.

galvanic cell *n* (*chem*) an electrochemical cell that generates energy.

galvanism *n* (*arch*) electricity produced by the chemical action of certain bodies or an acid on a metal; the medical use of this.

galvanize *vt* to apply an electric current to; to startle; to excite; to plate (metal) with zinc.—**galvanization** *n*. —**galvanizer** *n*.

galvanizing *n* (*chem*) the industrial process by which one type of metal is coated with a thin layer of another, more reactive metal.

galvanometer *n* an instrument for detecting or measuring small electric currents.—**galvanometric, galvanometrical** *adj*.—**galvanometry** *n*.

galvanoscope *n* an instrument for measuring the direction and presence of electricity by movements of a magnetic needle.

Galway *n* a city in the Republic of Ireland.

Galway *n* James (1939–) Northern Irish flautist and composer who has done much to popularize the flute.

gam[1] *n* a school of whales; a visit by one captain of a whaler to another; * *vb* (**gams, gammed, gamming**) *vt* to call upon the captain of a whaler. * *vi* (*whales*) to gather together in schools .

gam[2] *n* (*sl*) a well-shaped leg.

gam. *abbr* = gamut.

Gama *n* Vasco da (*c*.1469–1525) Portuguese navigator who discovered the route to India round the Cape of Good Hope (1497–99). He became Portuguese viceroy in India in 1524.

Gamaliel *n* (*Bible*) liberal Pharisee who was a member of the Council of the Jews; he spoke for tolerance and caution during the trial of Peter.

gambado (*pl* **gambados, gambadoes**) *n* a kind of leather legging used by horsemen; a flourish or curvet.

Gambia *n* a republic which is the smallest country in Africa.

gambier, gambir *n* a vegetable extract used medicinally as an astringent, and also for tanning and dyeing.

gambit *n* (*chess*) an opening in which a piece is sacrificed to gain an advantage; any action to gain an advantage.

gamble *vi* to play games of chance for money; to take a risk for some advantage. * *vt* to risk in gambling, to bet. * *n* a risky venture; a bet.—**gambler** *n*. —**gambling** *n*.

gamboge *n* a yellow gum resin from SE Asia, used as a pigment and as a purgative (—*also* **cambogia**); a bright yellow color.

gambol *vi* (**gamboling, gamboled** *or* **gambolling, gambolled**) to jump and skip about in play; to frisk. * *n* a caper, a playful leap.

gambrel *n* the hock of a horse; a bent stick of wood or metal resembling a horse's leg, used by butchers; a gambrel roof.

gambrel roof *n* (*archit*) a curved roof with a small gable at each end; a roof with a double slope on each side so that each side is shaped like a horse's leg.

game[1] *n* any form of play, amusement; activity or sport involving competition; a scheme, a plan; wild birds or animals hunted for sport or food, the flesh of such animals. * *vi* to play for a stake. * *adj* (*inf*) brave, resolute; (*inf*) willing.—**gamely** *adv*.—**gameness** *n*.

game[2] *adj* (*limbs*) injured, crippled, lame.

gamecock *n* (*formerly*) a cock bred and trained for fighting.

gamekeeper *n* a person who breeds and takes care of game birds and animals, as on an estate.—**gamekeeping** *n*.

gamelan *adj* (*mus*) pertaining to a type of traditional orchestra found principally in Indonesia and South-East Asia with an array of gongs, drums, and chimes. * *n* the music produced by such an orchestra.

game point *n* (*tennis*) the situation when the next point scored wins the game for one side or player.

Games *n* Abram (1914–) British graphic artist and industrial designer , best known for his posters for the War Office.

gamesmanship *n* (*inf*) the art of winning games by questionable acts just short of cheating.

gamesome *adj* sportive.

gamester *n* a gambler.

gamete *n* (*biol*) a reproductive cell that unites with another to form the cell that develops into a new individual.—**gametal, gametic** *adj*.

gamic *adj* (*zool*) having a sexual character.

gamin *n* a mischievous urchin.

gamine *n* a boyish girl or woman with impish appeal.

gaming *n* the act of playing games for stakes; gambling. —*also adj*.

gamma[1] *n* the third letter of the Greek alphabet.

Gamma[2] *n* (*astron*) the name for the third brightest star in a constellation.

gamma globulin, immune gamma globulin *n* a concentrated form of the antibody part of human blood. *See also* **globulin**.

gamma radiation, gamma rays *n* (*physics*) short-wave electromagnetic radiation from a radioactive substance.

gamma-ray astronomy *n* the study of gamma rays produced by natural processes anywhere in the universe.

gamma-ray bursts *n* rapid fluctuations in the output of gamma rays from a source.

gammer *n* (*rare*) an old woman.

gammon *n* cured or smoked ham; meat from the hindquarters of a side of bacon.

gamogenesis *n* (*bot*) sexual reproduction.

gamopetalous *adj* with petals united at the base.

gamophyllous *adj* (*flowers*) with leaves cohering at the edges.

gamosepalous *adj* (*flowers*) with sepals united at the edges to form a calyx.

gamut *n* a complete range or series; (*mus*) the whole range of notes of a voice or instrument.

gamy, gamey *adj* (**gamier, gamiest**) having the strong smell or flavor of cooked game; (*inf*) spirited, lively.—**gaminess** *n*.

-gamy *n suffix* marriage; sexual union.

GAN *abbr* = Green Academic Network.

G & AE *abbr* = general and administrative expenses.

gander *n* an adult goose; (*inf*) a quick look.

Gandhi *n* 1. **Indira** (1917–84) Indian stateswoman and prime minister; daughter of Nehru; prime minister (1966–77) and from 1980 until her assassination in 1984. Her son Rajiv (1944–91) became prime minister in 1984, and was killed in a suicide bomb attack. 2. **Mahatma [Mohandas Karamchand Gandhi]** (1869–1948) Indian nationalist statesman and spiritual leader whose non-violent campaign against British rule in India impressed world public opinion.

G & O *abbr* = gas and oxygen.

Gandon *n* James (1743–1823) Irish architect. His notable works include the Four Courts, Dublin.

G & SS *abbr* = Gilbert & Sullivan Society.

g and t *abbr* = gin and tonic.

gandy dancer *n* a laborer on a railroad; a seasonal laborer.

gang *n* a group of persons, esp laborers, working together; a group of persons acting or associating together, esp for illegal purposes. * *vti* to form into or act as a gang.—**ganged** *adj*.

gang hook *n* several fishhooks joined together at the shanks.

gangland *n* the criminal fraternity.

gangling, gangly *adj* tall, thin, and awkward in appearance and movement.

ganglion *n* (*pl* **ganglia, ganglions**) (*med*) a mass of nerve cells from which nerve impulses are transmitted.—**ganglionic** *adj*. *See* **basal ganglion**.

gangplank *n* a moveable ramp by which to board or leave a ship.

gangrene *n* death of body tissue when the blood supply is obstructed.—**gangrenous** *adj*. *See also* **gas gangrene**.

gangsta *n* a variant of rap music with its source the US West Coast with lyrics focused on gang culture; a performer of this style of music; *adj* **gangsta** belonging to gangsta music.

gangster *n* a member of a criminal gang.

gangue, gang *n* the earth or matrix in which ore is found

gangway *n* a passageway, esp an opening in a ship's side for loading, etc; a gangplank.

ganister, gannister *n* a kind of silicious clay rock or hard sandstone; a refractory material used for lining furnaces.

ganja *n* marijuana.

gannet *n* any of various large voracious fish-eating sea birds.

ganoid *adj* (*fish*) having enameled bony scales, like the sturgeon. * *n* a ganoid fish.

gantlet *see* **gauntlet**.

gantline *n* a rope used in a block on a ship for hoisting.

gantry *n* (*pl* **gantries**) a metal framework, often on wheels, for a traveling crane; a wheeled framework with a crane, platforms, etc for servicing a rocket to be launched.

Ganymede[1] *n* a satellite of Jupiter discovered by Galileo in 1610.

Ganymede[2], **Ganymedes** *n* (*Greek myth*) an exceptionally beautiful youth who was carried off by an eagle to Olympus, where he served as cup-bearer to the gods.

Gao *n* town in Mali.

GAO *abbr* = General Accounting Office

gaol, gaolbird, gaoler *see* **jail, jailbird, jailer**.

gap *n* a break or opening in something, as a wall or fence; an interruption in continuity, an interval; a mountain pass; a divergence, disparity. * *vt* (**gapping, gapped**) to make a gap in.—**gappy** *adj*.

GAP *abbr* = Girls Alone Project; great American public; gross agricultural product.

gap analysis *n* a technique used in marketing that aims to establish the extent to which customers are satisfied by the products or services provided by a company.

gape *vi* to open the mouth wide; to stare in astonishment, esp with the mouth open; to open widely. * *n* the act of gaping; a wide opening.—**gaping** *adj*.—**gapingly** *adv*.

gaper *n* a person who gapes; one of various types of shellfish that have a space between the valves.

gap year *n* a break of one year between school and college or university planned for the student to access work or experience seen as valuable in terms of personal development.

gar *n* (*pl* **gar, gars**) a garfish.

garage *n* an enclosed shelter for motor vehicles; a place where motor vehicles are repaired and serviced, and fuel sold. * *vt* to put or keep in a garage.

garage sale *n* a sale of unwanted household goods, held in a garage or other part of the house.

garb *n* clothing, style of dress. * *vt* to clothe.

garbage *n* food waste; unwanted or useless material; rubbish; (*comput*) useless data.

garbageman *n* (*pl* **garbagemen**) a person employed to remove garbage.

Garbe *n* **Richard** (*d*.1957) British sculptor who designed for Doulton of Burslem.

garble *vt* to distort (a message, story, etc) so as to mislead.—**garbler** *n*.

Garbo *n* **Greta [Greta Louisa Gustafson]** (1905–90) Swedish-born American film actress whose films include *Queen Christina*.

garboard (strake) *n* (*naut*) the plank or plate on a ship's bottom next to the keel.

garbology *n* the study of the disposal of waste material.—**garbologist** *n*.

garçon *n* a waiter.

Gardella *n* **Ignazio** (1905–95) Italian architect of notable classical façades and designer of furniture.

garden *n* an area of ground for growing herbs, fruits, flowers, or vegetables; a yard; a fertile, well-cultivated region; a public park or recreation area, usu laid-out with plants and trees. * *vi* to make, or work in, a garden.—**gardener** *n*. — **gardening** *n*.

gardenia *n* a tree or shrub with beautiful fragrant white or yellow flowers.

garderobe *n* a wardrobe in medieval houses for storing clothes or items of value; medieval term for a lavatory.

Gardner *n* 1. **Erle Stanley** (1889–1970) American writer who is famous as the creator of Perry Mason, lawyer and investigator. 2. **James** (1907–95) British jewelry designer for Cartier from 1924 to 1931.

garfish *n* (*pl* **garfish, garfishes**) a long, slender freshwater fish with a spearlike snout and a thick-scaled body.

garg. *abbr* (*Latin*) = *gargarisma*, "a gargle."

gargantuan *adj* colossal, prodigious.

garget *n* a disease in cattle.

gargle *vti* to rinse the throat by breathing air from the lungs through liquid held in the mouth. * *n* a liquid for this purpose; the sound made by gargling.—**gargler** *n*.

gargoyle *n* a grotesquely carved face or figure, usu acting as a spout to drain water from a gutter; a person with an ugly face.—**gargoyled** *adj*.

garibaldi *n* a type of loose blouse, orig red.

Garibaldi *n* **Giuseppe** (1807–82) Italian patriot. Exiled in 1834, he returned to Italy in 1848, and defended Rome against the French. He took Naples and Sicily in 1860 for the newly united Italy.

garish *adj* crudely bright, gaudy.—**garishly** *adv*.—**garishness** *n*.

garland *n* a wreath of flowers or leaves worn or hung as decoration. * *vt* to decorate with a garland.

Garland *n* **Judy [Frances Gumm]** (1922–69) American film actress, singer, and star of *The Wizard of Oz*, *Easter Parade*, and *A Star is Born*.

garlic *n* a bulbous herb cultivated for its compound bulbs used in cookery; its bulb.—**garlicky** *adj*.

garment *n* an item of clothing.

Garnard *n* (*d*. 635) king of Picts (631–635). The son of Cinoich's sister.

garner *vt* to gather, store.

garnet *n* a semiprecious stone, red, yellow or green in color.

garnish *vt* to decorate; to decorate (food) with something that adds color or flavor. * *n* something used to garnish food.—**garnisher** *n*. —**garniture** *n*.

garnishee *vt* (**garnisheeing, garnisheed**) (*law*) to warn by garnishment. * *n* (*law*) the person into whose hands the property of another is attached pending the satisfaction of the claims of a third party.

garnishment *n* embellishment; (*law*) notice to holder of another's attached property not to give it to him but to account for it in court; a summons; (*arch*) notice to third party to appear in suit.

garniture *n* embellishment, trimmings (esp on a dish of food).

garpike *n* the garfish.

Garrard *n* British goldsmiths and jewelers who in 1843 became the crown jewelers.

garret *n* an attic.

Garrick *n* **David** (1717–79) English actor and dramatist who dominated the English theater of his time.

garrison *n* troops stationed at a fort; a fortified place with troops. * *vt* to station (troops) in (a fortified place) for its defense.

Garrison *n* **William Lloyd** (1805–79) American anti-slavery campaigner and founder of the American Anti-Slavery Society (1833).

garrotte, garrote, garotte *n* a method of execution by strangling with an iron collar; the iron collar used. * *vt* to execute by garrotte; to half-throttle and rob.—**garrotter, garroter, garotter** *n*.

garrulous *adj* excessively talkative.—**garrulously** *adv*.—**garrulousness, garrulity** *n*.

garter *n* an elasticized band used to support a stocking or sock.

garter belt *n* a strap or belt with fasteners for supporting undergarments.

garter snake *n* any of various non-venomous American snakes marked with longitudinal stripes.

garth *n* a courtyard surrounded by a cloister; (*arch*) a yard, garden, or paddock.

Gartnait *n* (*d*. 663) king of Picts (657–663). The son of Talorcen's sister.

Gartnart *n* (*d*. 597) king of Picts (reigned *c*.586–597). The son of Bridei I's sister.

Gärtner *n* **Friedrich von** (*b*.1792) German architect. His notable works include the State Library, Münich.

gas *n* (*pl* **gases, gasses**) (*chem*) an air-like substance with the capacity to expand indefinitely and not liquefy or solidify at ordinary temperatures; any mixture of flammable gases used for lighting or heating; any gas used as an anesthetic; any poisonous substance dispersed in the air, as in war; (*inf*) empty talk; gasoline. * *vt* (**gases** *or* **gasses, gassing, gassed**) to poison or disable with gas; (*inf*) to talk idly and at length.

GAS *abbr* = Glasgow Archeological Society.

gasbag *n* (*inf*) an idle talker.

gas chamber *n* an airtight room where animals or people are killed by poisonous gas.

gas cloud *n* an isolated accumulation of gas, often with dust mixed through.

GASCO *abbr* = General Aviation Safety Committee.

gasconade *n* (*rare*) boastful or blustering talk. * *vi* to bluster, to boast.

gaseous *adj* having the form of or being gas; of or being related to gases; lacking substance or solidity.—**gaseousness** *n*.

gaseous exchange *n* the exchange of respiratory gases (oxygen and carbon dioxide) by diffusion across the walls of the alveoli in the lungs.

gas gangrene *n* a form of gangrene that occurs when wounds are infected with soil bacteria of the genus *Clostridium*.

gash *n* a long, deep, open cut. * *vt* to cut deep.

gasholder *n* a circular hollow tank, open at the bottom and closed at the top, for storing gas prior to distribution.

GASI *abbr* = Graduate Member of the Ambulance Service Institute.

gasify *vti* (**gasifying, gasified**) to turn into gas.—**gasification** *n*.

Gaskell *n* **Mrs Elizabeth [Elizabeth Cleghorn Stevenson]** (1810–65) English novelist whose most popular novel is *Cranford*.

gasket *n* a piece or ring of rubber, metal, etc, sandwiched between metal surfaces to act as a seal.

Gaskin *n* **Arthur Joseph** (1862–1928) British painter, silversmith, and jeweler who, together with his wife, designed the *Cymric* range of jewelry for Liberty.

gas laws *n* (*chem*) the rules that relate to the pressure, temperature, and volume of an ideal gas, allowing useful information about a gas to be gained by calculation instead of by experimentation.

gaslight *n* a type of lamp using a jet of gas to provide illumination.

gasman *n* (*pl* **gasmen**) an employee of a gas company who reads meters, etc.

gas mask *n* a respirator worn over the face, which protects against poisonous gases.

gasolier, gaselier *n* a branched hanging support for gas lights.

gasoline, gasolene *n* a liquid fuel or solvent distilled from petroleum.—*also* **petrol**.—**gasolinic** *adj*.

gasometer *n* an instrument for measuring gas; a gasholder.

gasometry *n* the science or process of measuring gas.

gasp *vi* to draw in the breath suddenly and audibly, as from shock; to struggle to catch the breath. * *vt* to utter breathlessly. * *n* the act of gasping.—**gaspingly** *adv*.

GASP *abbr* = Group Against Smog Pollution.

gassy *adj* (**gassier, gassiest**) impregnated with or like a gas; given to pretentious talk; inflated.

gastr-, gastro- *prefix* stomach.

gastralgia *n* (*med*) a term meaning pain in the stomach.

gastrectomy *n* (*med*) the surgical removal of part of the stomach.

gastric *adj* of, in, or near the stomach.

gastric glands *n* glands that are situated in the mucous membrane of the stomach and secrete gastric juice.

gastric juice *n* digestive fluid secreted by glands in the stomach lining.

gastric ulcer *n* an ulcer of the lining of the stomach.

gastrin *n* a hormone that stimulates excess production of acidic gastric juice.

gastritis *n* inflammation of the stomach.—**gastric** *adj*.

G

gastroenteric *adj* of or pertaining to the stomach or intestinal tract.

gastroenteritis *n* inflammation of the mucous membrane of the stomach and intestines.—**gastroenteritic** *adj*.

gastroenterology *n* the study of diseases that affect the gastrointestinal tract, including the pancreas, gall bladder, and bile duct in addition to the stomach and intestines.

gastroenterostomy *n* an operation making an opening in the stomach and the nearby small intestine and joining the two together, undertaken to reroute food from the stomach to enable an obstruction to be relieved.

gastrointestinal *adj* of or pertaining to the stomach or intestines.

gastrointestinal tract *see* **alimentary canal**.

gastrology, gastroenterology *n* the study of diseases of the stomach and intestinal tract.

gastronome, gastronomer, gastronomist *n* a connoisseur of food.

gastronomic, gastronomical *adj*.—**gastronomically** *adj*.

gastronomy *n* the art and science of good eating.—**gastropod** *n* any of a large class of mollusks (as snails) with a flattened foot for moving and usu with stalk-like sense organs.—**gastropodan** *adj, n*. —**gastropodous** *adj*.

gastroscope *n* (*med*) a flexible instrument, comprising fiber optics or a miniature video camera, that permits internal visual examination of the stomach.

gastrostomy *n* (*med*) the creation, usually by surgery, of an opening into the stomach from the outside to permit food to be given.

gastrula *n* (*pl* **gastrulas, gastrulae**) the fertilized ovum at a certain period in its development.

gasworks *n sing* a place where gas is manufactured.

GAT *abbr* = Greenwich apparent time.

GATB *abbr* = General Aptitude Test Battery.

GATCO *abbr* = Guild of Air Traffic Control Officers.

gate *n* a movable structure controlling passage through an opening in a fence or wall; a gateway; a movable barrier; a structure controlling the flow of water, as in a canal; a device (as in a computer) that outputs a signal when specified input conditions are met; the total amount or number of paid admissions to a football match, etc. * *vt* to supply with a gate; to keep within the gates (of a university) as a punishment.

gâteau, gateau *n* (*pl* **gâteaux, gateaux**) a large cream cake.

gate-crasher *n* a person who attends a party, etc without being invited.—**gatecrash** *vi*.

gatefold *n* an oversize page in a book or magazine that is folded in.

gatehouse *n* a house built over or beside a gate.

gatekeeper *n* a person who controls entrance to a gate.

gate-leg(ged) table *n* a table with drop leaves supported by movable legs.

gatepost *n* a post on which a gate is hung or to which it is attached when closed.

gateway *n* an opening for a gate; a means of entrance or exit.

Gath *n* (*Bible*) the home of Goliath; Gath was one of five Philistine cities on the coast of Palestine. *See also* **Goliath**.

gather *vt* to bring together in one place or group; to get gradually; to collect (as taxes); to harvest; to draw (parts) together; to pucker fabric by pulling a thread or stitching; to understand, infer. * *vi* to come together in a body; to cluster around a focus of attention; (*sore*) to swell and fill with pus.—**gatherable** *adj*.—**gatherer** *n*.

gathering *n* the act of gathering or assembling together; an assembly; folds made in a garment by gathering.

Gatling *n* **Richard Jordan** (1818–1903) American inventor famous for the invention of the "Gatling gun" (1862).

Gatling gun *n* a machine gun with clustered barrels, which are discharged in succession by turning a handle.

GATT *abbr* = General Agreement on Tariffs and Trade.

gauche *adj* socially inept; graceless, tactless.—**gauchely** *adv*.—**gaucheness** *n*.

gaucherie *n* awkwardness, tactlessness; a tactless or awkward act.

gaucho *n* (*pl* **gauchos**) a cowboy of the pampas of South America.

gaud *n* a piece of finery, a trinket or ornament.

gaudery *n* (*pl* **gauderies**) cheap, showy finery.

Gaudí *n* **Antoni** (1852–1926) Spanish architect whose most famous building is the unfinished Sagrada Familia Church in Barcelona.

gaudy *adj* (**gaudier, gaudiest**) excessively ornamented; tastelessly bright.—**gaudily** *adv*.—**gaudiness** *n*.

GAUFCC *abbr* = General Assembly of Unitarian and Free Christian Churches.

gauffer *see* **goffer**.

gauge *n* measurement according to some standard or system; any device for measuring; the distance between rails of a railway; the size of the bore of a shotgun; the thickness of sheet metal, wire, etc. * *vt* to measure the size, amount, etc of.—*also* **gage**.—**gaugeable, gagable** *adj*.—**gauger, gager** *n*.

Gauguin *n* 1. **Jean** (1881–1961) French ceramicist whose most important work was done for Bing and Grøndahl, Denmark. 2. **Paul** (1848–1903) French painter and one of the greatest exponents of post-impressionism.

Gaul *n* an ancient region of Western Europe corresponding roughly to modern France, Switzerland and Belgium; a native of Gaul.

Gaullism *n* the policies pertaining to General de Gaulle, first president of the Fifth Republic in France (1959–69); the political movement based on de Gaulle's policies and principles.—**Gaullist** *n, adj*.

gaunt *adj* excessively thin as from hunger or age; looking grim or forbidding.—**gauntness** *n*.

gauntlet[1] *n* a knight's armored glove; a long glove, often with a flaring cuff.—*also* **gantlet** *n*.

gauntlet[2] *n* (*formerly*) a type of military punishment in which a victim was forced to run between two lines of men who struck him as he passed.

gaur *n* a large fierce, dark-colored ox found in Southeast Asia and India.

gauss *n* (*pl* **gauss, gausses**) the unit of measurement for magnetic flux density.

gauze *n* any very thin, loosely woven fabric, as of cotton or silk; a firm woven material of metal or plastic filaments; a surgical dressing.

gauzy *adj* (**gauzier, gauziest**) like gauze, thin, transparent.—**gauzily** *adv*.—**gauziness** *n*.

GAV *abbr* = gross annual value.

GAVA *abbr* = Guild of Aviation Artists.

gavage *n* (*med*) forced feeding by stomach tube or naso-gastric tube.

Gavaskar *n* **Sunil Manohar** (1949–) Indian cricketer . He was captain of India (1978–83, 1984–85). He was dubbed the "Little Master" for his skill (and stature) and scored 34 test centuries.

gave *see* **give**.

gavel *n* a hammer used by a chairman, auctioneer, judge, etc to command proceedings.

gavial *n* an Indian crocodile with a long narrow snout.

Gavin *n* **Bernard** (1940–) F rench interior designer who created several furniture ranges.

gavotte *n* (*mus*) a lively dance of French peasant origin.

GAW *abbr* = Gay Authors Workshop; Global Atmosphere Watch.

gawk *vi* to stare at stupidly.

gawky *adj* (**gawkier, gawkiest**) clumsy, awkward, ungainly.—**gawkily** *adv*.—**gawkiness** *n*.

gay *adj* joyous and lively; colorful; homosexual. * *n* a homosexual.—**gayness** *n*.

Gay *n* **John** (1685–1732) English dramatist and poet whose masterpiece is *The Beggars' Opera* (1728), on which Brecht based his *Threepenny Opera*.

Gaye *n* **Marvin** (1939–84) American soul singer. One of his most famous songs is "*I heard it through the grapevine*" (1968).

gaz. *abbr* = gazette; gazetteer.

Gaza *n* (*Bible*) one of the five Philistine cities on the coast of Palestine.

Gaza City *n* capital city of West Bank and Gaza Strip.

gaze *vi* to look steadily. * *n* a steady look.—**gazer** *n*.

gazebo *n* (*pl* **gazebos, gazeboes**) a summerhouse or belvedere, elevated to command a wide view.

gazelle *n* (*pl* **gazelles, gazelle**) any of numerous small swift Asian or African antelopes.

gazette *n* a newspaper, now mainly in newspaper titles; an official publication listing government appointments, legal notices, etc.

gazetteer *n* an index of geographical place names.

gazpacho *n* a Spanish soup of tomatoes and other vegetables, served cold.

Gazza Ladra, La *see* **Thieving Magpie, The**.

gb *abbr* = gall bladder.

GB *abbr* = Girls' Brigade; Gas Board; Great Britain; Guidebook; gunboat.

GBA *abbr* = Governing Bodies Association; Alderney.

GB and I *abbr* = Great Britain and Ireland.

GBC *abbr* = Gibraltar Broadcasting Corporation.

gbe *abbr* = gilt-beveled edge.

GBE *abbr* = Knight/Dame Grand Cross/Orderof the British Empire.

GBG *abbr* = Guernsey.

GBH *abbr* = grievous bodily harm.

GBJ *abbr* = Jersey.

GBM *abbr* = Isle of Man.

GBMPC *abbr* = Great Britain Map Postcard Club.

GBNE *abbr* = Guild of British Newspaper Editors.

gbo *abbr* = goods in bad order.

GBP *abbr* = Gay Bereavement Project.

GBRMPA *abbr* = Great Barrier Reef Marine Park Authority.

GBSM *abbr* = Graduate of the Birmingham School of Music.

GBZ *abbr* = Gibraltar.

gc *abbr* = going concern; gigacycle; good condition.

GC *abbr* = Gas Council; General Circular; George Cross; Grand Chancellor; Grand Conductor; Grand Cross; Golf Club; gas chromatography.

GCA *abbr* = Garden Center Association; General Claim Agent; Global Commission on AIDS; Grains Council of Australia; ground controlled approach (aircraft landing system).

g-cal. *abbr* = gram calorie; gram calories.

GCB *abbr* = Dame/Knight Grand Cross of the Order of the Bath; Greyhound Consultative Council; Guernsey Cattle Breeders' Association.

GCBS *abbr* = General Council of British Shipping.

GCC *abbr* = Gas Consumers' Council; Game Conservancy Council; Gulf Co-operation Council.

GCCA *abbr* = Greeting Card and Calendar Association.

GCCF *abbr* = Governing Council of the Cat Fancy.

GCD *abbr* = greatest common divisor.

GCE *abbr* (*Brit*) = General Certificate of Education, an examination formerly taken at Ordinary and Advanced levels ("O" and "A" levels) but replaced by the GCSE.

GCF *abbr* = greatest common factor.

GCFR *abbr* = gas-cooled fast reactor.

GCH *abbr* = Knight Grand Cross of Hanover; gas central heating.

GCHQ *abbr* = Government Communications Headquarters.

GCI *abbr* = ground-controlled interception.

GCIC *abbr* = Gifted Children's Information Center.

GCL *abbr* = ground-controlled landing.

GCLH *abbr* = Grand Cross of the Legion of Honor.

g.c.m., GCM *abbr* = general court martial; greatest common measure.

GCMG *abbr* = Dame/Knight Grand Cross of the Order of St Michael and St George.

GCMS *abbr* = gas-chromatography mass spectroscopy.

GCR *abbr* = gas-cooled reactor; ground controlled radar.

GCRN *abbr* = General Council and Register of Naturopaths.

GCRO *abbr* = General Council and Register of Osteopaths.

GCSE *abbr* (*Brit*) = General Certificate of Secondary Education, an examination in the UK for 16-year-old children.

GCVO *abbr* = Dame/Knight Grand Cross of the Royal Victorian Order.

GCWT *abbr* = Golf Course Wildlife Trust.

Gd *symbol* (*chem*) gadolinium.

gd. *abbr* (*mil*) = guard.

g.d. *abbr* = good delivery; gravimetric density.

GD *abbr* = Grand Duchess; Grand Duke; Grand Duchy.

Gdansk *n* a city in Poland.

GDBA *abbr* = Guide Dogs for the Blind Association.

GDC *abbr* = General Dental Council.

GDP *abbr* = Gross Domestic Product.

GDPA *abbr* = General Dental Practitioners' Association.

GDR *abbr* = German Democratic Republic (the former East Germany).

gds. *abbr* = goods.

gdt *abbr* = graphic display terminal.

gdu *abbr* = graphic display unit.

Ge *n* (*Greek myth*) the earth or the earth goddess.—*also* **Gaea**.

Ge *symbol* (*chem*) germanium.

ge *abbr* = gilt edges.

GE *abbr* = gastroenterology.

gear *n* clothing; equipment, esp for some task or activity; a toothed wheel designed to mesh with another; (*often pl*) a system of such gears meshed together to transmit motion; a specific adjustment of such a system; a part of a mechanism with a specific function. * *vt* to connect by or furnish with gears; to adapt (one thing) to conform with another.

gearbox *n* a metal case enclosing a system of gears.

gearing *n* a particular arrangement of gears; (*econ*) the ratio of a company's capital supplied by long-term funds having a fixed interest charge to its share capital.

gearshift *n* a lever used to engage or change gear, esp in a motor vehicle.

gearwheel *n* a cogwheel.

Geb *n* (*Egypt*) the Egyptian earth-god in the Heliopolitan cosmology, from whose union with the sky-goddess, Nut, came the four children Isis, Osiris, Seth and Nephthys.

GEBCO *abbr* = General Bathymetric Chart of the Oceans.

Gebel Barkal *n* (*Egypt*) temple site in Nubia, Egypt, close to Napata. The temple had been dedicated to Amun by Tuthmosis III.

GEC *abbr* = General Electric Company.

Gecchelin *n* **Bruno** (1939–) Italian architect who designed the F iat Panda auto, and glassware for Venini.

gecko *n* (*pl* **geckos, geckoes**) a small lizard of warm regions that feeds on insects.

GED *abbr* = general educational development.

gedämpft *adj* (*mus*) (*German*) "muted."

Geddes *n* **Norman Bel** (1893–1958) American industrial and theatrical designer responsible for over 200 theatrical productions.

gee[1] *vi* (**geeing geed**) (*often with* **up**) to make a horse go faster. * *interj* a mild oath.

gee[2] *interj* (*sl*) an exclamation of surprise.

gee[3] *n* (*inf*) gravitational acceleration; (*sl*) a thousand of something, a grand.

geis *n* (*Irish Celtic myth*) a bond that people were placed under. If someone placed under such a bond broke it, he or she would either die or face extreme dishonor.

geek *n* (*comput*) a synonym for nerd.

geese *see* **goose**.

geest *n* a heathland landscape on glacial sand and gravel, common in northern Germany.

geezer *n* (*sl*) an old man.

GEF *abbr* = Global Environment Facility.

Gehry *n* **Frank O.** (1930–) Canadian architect who created innovative furniture from inexpensive industrial materials.

Geige *n* (*mus*) (*German*) "fiddle" or "violin."

Geiger counter *n* an electronic device for detecting and measuring radioactive emissions.

Geiger tube *or* **Geiger-Müller tube** *n* (*physics*) an instrument that can detect and measure radiation.

geisha *n* (*pl* **geisha, geishas**) a Japanese girl trained as an entertainer to serve as a hired companion to men.

gel *n* (*chem*) a jelly-like substance, as that applied to style and sculpt hair before drying it. * *vti* (**gelling, gelled**) to become or cause to become a gel.—*also* **jell**.

gelatin, gelatine *n* a tasteless, odorless substance extracted by boiling bones, hoofs, etc and used in food, photographic film, medicines, etc.

gelatinize *vt* to make or become gelatinous; to coat with gelatin.— **gelatinization** *n*. —**gelatinizer** *n*.

gelatinous *adj* of or like gelatin; jelly-like in consistency.

gelation *n* solidification (of liquids) by cold.

geld *vt* (**gelding, gelded, *or* gelt**) to castrate, esp a horse.

gelding *n* a castrated horse.

gelid *adj* intensely cold; icy.—**gelidity** *n*.

gelignite *n* an explosive consisting of nitroglycerin absorbed in a base of wood pulp mixed with sodium or potassium nitrate.

Gell-Mann *n* **Murray** (1929–) American physicist who introduced the quark hypothesis into physics and won the 1969 Nobel prize for physics.

gem *n* a precious stone, esp when cut and polished for use as a jewel; a person, or thing regarded as extremely valuable or beloved. * *vt* (**gemming, gemmed**) to decorate or set with gems.

Gemcos *abbr* = Generalized Message Control System.

geminate, geminated *adj* growing or occurring in pairs.

gemination *n* duplication; (*rhetoric*) the repetition of a word, etc, for effect.

Gemini[1] *n* (*astrol*) the third sign of the zodiac, represented by the twins Castor and Pollux, operative May 21–June 20.

Gemini[2] (*astron*) zodiacal constellation, between Cancer and Taurus.

Gemini[3] *n* (*astronautics*) any one of a series of manned US spacecraft launched between the Mercury and Apollo space missions.

Geminiani *n* **Francesco** (*c*.1679–1762) an Italian violinist who wrote a ballet, *La Foresta Incantana*, and several impressive sonatas, trios, and concertos. His book *The Art of Playing on the Violin*, was the first of its kind.

gemma *n* (*pl* **gemmae**) a growth on an animal or plant budding off as a separate individual.

gemmate *vi* to have buds; to propagate by gemmae.—**gemmation** *n*. — **gemmiparous** *adj*.

gemmule *n* a small bud or gemma; an ovule; a cell produced by certain moulds.

gemot, gemote *n* an assembly or local court in pre-Norman England.

GEMS *abbr* = Global Environment Monitoring System.

gemsbok *n* (*pl* **gemsbok, gemsboks**) a large, straight-horned South African antelope with a broad black stripe along its length.

gemshorn *or* **chamois horn** *n* (*mus*) an early type of recorder made from the horn of an animal; an organ stop with a light tone.

gemstone *n* a mineral or substance used as a gem.

gen. *abbr* = gender; genera; general; generally; generic; generator; genitive; genus.

Gen. *abbr* = (*army*) General; Genesis; Geneva; Genevan.

gendarme *n* an armed policeman in France and Belgium.

gendarmerie, gendarmery *n* a force of gendarmes.

gender *n* the classification by which words are grouped as feminine, masculine, or neuter; the sex of a person.

gene *n* (*biol*) any of the complex chemical units in the chromosomes by which hereditary characteristics are transmitted. *See also* **sex-linked disorder**.

geneal. *abbr* = genealogy.

genealogy *n* (*pl* **genealogies**) a recorded history of one's ancestry; the study of family descent; lineage.—**genealogical** *adj*.—**genealogist** *n*.

gene cloning *n* a method of genetic engineering in which certain genes are extracted from host DNA and introduced into the cell of another host.

genera *see* **genus**.

generable *adj* capable of being generated.

general *adj* not local, special, or specialized; of or for a whole genus, relating to or covering all instances or individuals of a class or group; widespread, common to many; not specific or precise; holding superior rank, chief. * *n* something that involves or is applicable to the whole; a commissioned officer above a lieutenant general; a leader, commander; the title of the head of some religious orders.— **generalness** *n*.

general anesthetic *n* an anesthetic effecting the whole body and producing unconsciousness.

general delivery *n* the department of a post office that will hold mail until it is called for.—*also* **poste restante**.

general election *n* a national election to choose representatives in every constituency.

generalissimo *n* (*pl* **generalissimos**) a military commander of combined air, naval, and ground forces.

generalist *n* a person skilled in a variety of different fields.—**generalism** *n*.

generality *n* (*pl* **generalities**) the quality or state of being general; a vague or inadequate statement.

generalization *n* general inference; induction; a general notion formed by attributing the characteristic(s) of a particular part or member (of a class, community etc) to the whole.

generalize *vti* to form general conclusions from specific instances; to talk (about something) in general terms.—**generalization** *n*. —**generalizer** *n*.

generally *adv* widely; popularly; usually; not specifically.

Generalpause *n* (*mus*) (*German*) a rest of one or more bars for all the members of an orchestra. * *abbr* G.P.

general practitioner *n* a non-specialist doctor who treats all types of illnesses in the community.

general price level *n* an index that gives an indication of the purchasing power of money.

general-purpose *adj* having all kinds of uses.

generalship *n* the office of general; military skill; management skill.

general staff *n* officers who advise and assist a military commander.

general strike *n* a strike of all workers in a city, region, or country.

generate *vt* to bring into existence; to produce.

generation *n* the act or process of generating; a single succession in natural descent; people of the same period; production, as of electric current.

generation gap *n* the difference in attitudes and understanding between one generation and another.

generative *adj* pertaining to generation; having the power to generate.

generator *n* one who or that which generates; a machine that changes mechanical energy to electrical energy. *See also* **dynamo**.

generic *adj* of a whole class, kind, or group.—**generically** *adv*.

generic name *n* the general name used to identify a product or class of products, as opposed to the supplier's tradename or brand name that is used to identify a product. Thus vacuum cleaner is a generic name while Hoover is a tradename.

generosity *n* (*pl* **generosities**) the quality of being generous; liberality; munificence; a generous act.

generous *adj* magnanimous; of a noble nature; willing to give or share; large, ample.—**generously** *adv*.—**generousness** *n*.

genesis *n* (*pl* **geneses**) the beginning, origin; (*with cap*) the first book of the Old Testament.

genet *n* an animal of southern Europe, western Asia and Africa, related to the civet and valued for its fur; any fur made in imitation of genet.

Genet *n* Jean (1910–86) French dramatist and novelist.

genetic, genetical *adj* of or relating to the origin, development, or causes of something; of or relating to genes or genetics.—**genetically** *adv*.

genetic adaptation *see* **adaptation**.

genetic code *n* the order of genetic information in a cell, which determines hereditary characteristics.

genetic counseling *n* the provision of advice to families about the nature and likelihood of inherited disorders and the options available in terms of prevention and management.

genetic engineering *n* (*biol*) the modification of genetic information in the cell of a plant or animal to improve yield, performance, etc. —*also* **recombinant DNA technology**.

genetic fingerprinting *n* the analysis of bodily tissue or fluids to identify the unique genetic character of an individual, as used in criminal investigations, the determination of paternity, etc.

genetics *n sing* the branch of biology dealing with heredity and variation in plants and animals.—**geneticist** *n*.

genetic screening *n* the procedure whereby individuals are tested to determine whether their gene make-up suggests they carry a particular disease or condition. *See also* **sex-linked disorder**.

Geneva (**Genève**) *n* a city in Switzerland.

Geneviere, Marcel *see* **Dominique**.

Genghis Khan *n* [Temujin] (*c*.1162–1227) Mongol leader who united the Mongol tribes and conquered China, establishing an empire from the Black Sea to the Pacific.

Gen. Hosp. *abbr* (*mil*) = General Hospital.

genial[1] *adj* kindly, sympathetic, and cheerful in manner; mild, pleasantly warm.—**geniality, genialness** *n*. —**genially** *adv*.

genial[2] *adj* of the chin.

geniculate, geniculated *adj* having knee-like joints; bent at a sharp angle.

genie *n* (*pl* **genies, genii**) (*fairy tales*) a spirit with supernatural powers which can fulfil your wishes.—*also* **jinni**.

genit. *abbr* = genitive.

genital *adj* of reproduction or the sexual organs.

genital herpes *n* a sexually transmitted disease that produces painful blisters on and around the genitals.

genitals, genitalia *npl* the (external) sexual organs.—**genitalic** *adj*.

genitive *adj* (*gram*) of or belonging to the case of nouns, pronouns, and adjectives expressing ownership or relation. * *n* the genitive case.—**genitival** *adj*.

genito-urinary medicine *n* the subdiscipline concerned with all aspects of sexually transmitted diseases.

genito-urinary tract *n* (*biol*) the genital and urinary organs and associated structures: kidneys, ureter, bladder, urethra, and genitalia.

genius *n* (*pl* **geniuses**) a person possessing extraordinary intellectual power; (*with* **for**) natural ability, strong inclination.

genl. *abbr* = general.

Gennesaret *n* (*Bible*) fertile place west of the Sea of Galilee.

Genoa (**Genova**) *n* a city in Italy.

genocide *n* the systematic killing of a whole race of people.—**genocidal** *adj*.

genome *n* (*biol*) the total genetic information stored in the chromosomes of an organism.

genotype *n* (*biol*) the particular combination of the genes in an individual's genetic make-up.

genre *n* (*art*) a distinctive type or category, esp of literary composition; a style of painting in which everyday objects are treated realistically.

genre painting *n* a painting that has as its subject a scene from everyday life, as opposed to a historical event or mythological scene, etc.

gens *n* (*pl* **gentes**) in ancient Rome, a clan or house; one of a number of related families claiming a common ancestor or having a name or religious rites etc in common.

Gensoli *n* Maurice (1892–) Algerian ceramicist who became head of decorating at Sèvres.

gent *n* (*inf*) a gentleman.

gent., Gent. *abbr* = gentleman; gentlemen.

genteel *adj* polite or well-bred; affectedly refined.—**genteelly** *adv*.—**genteelness** *n*.

gentes *see* **gens**.

gentian *n* an alpine plant, usu with blue flowers.

gentian violet *n* a crystalline substance used as an antiseptic.

gentile *n* a person who is not a Jew.—*also adj*.

Gentile *n* 1. **Giovanni** (1875–1944) Italian philosopher and politician. He became a long-term supporter of Mussolini and a Fascist minister and was assassinated by partisans. 2. **Thomas** (1936–) American jewelry designer whose pieces have been exhibited in many of the world's leading museums.

Gentile da Fabriano *n* (*c*.1370–1427) Italian painter in the International Gothic tradition. Little of his work has survived, but he is thought to have established his reputation with frescos, since lost, for the Doge's Palace in Venice.

Gentileschi *n* 1. **Orazio** (1563–1639) Italian painter, his earliest work was mannerist in style but the major influence on his art was his friend and older contemporary Carvaggio. 2. **Artemisia** (1593–*c*.1652) daughter of Orazio, she was a powerful exponent of the Caravaggesque style and was responsible for its predominance in Naples, where she settled in 1630.

gentility *n* (*pl* **gentilities**) refinement, good manners.

gentle *adj* belonging to a family of high social station; refined, courteous; generous; kind; kindly; patient; not harsh or rough.—**gentleness** *n*. —**gently** *adv*.

gentleman *n* (*pl* **gentlemen**) a man of good family and social standing; a courteous, gracious, and honorable man; a polite term of address.—**gentlemanly** *adj*.

Gentleman *n* David (1930–) British painter whose best-known work is a series of murals painted for the London Underground in the 1980s.

gentleman-at-arms *n* (*pl* **gentlemen-at-arms**) one of the bodyguard of the UK sovereign on state occasions.

gentleman-farmer *n* (*pl* **gentlemen-farmers**) a person who farms for pleasure and does not depend on it for a living.

gentleman's agreement, gentlemen's agreement *n* an agreement in which the parties are bound by honor but not by law.

gentlewoman *n* (*pl* **gentlewomen**) a woman of noble or gentle birth; a lady.

gentrify *vt* (**gentrifying, gentrified**) to convert a working-class house or district to more expensive middle-class tastes.—**gentrification** *n*.

gentry *n* people of high social standing; (*formerly*) landed proprietors not belonging to the nobility.

genuflect *vi* to act in a servile way; to bend the knee in worship or respect.—**genuflection** *n*. —**genuflector** *n*.

genuine *adj* not fake or artificial, real; sincere.—**genuinely** *adv*.—**genuineness** *n*.

genus *n* (*pl* **genera**) (*biol*) a taxonomic division of plants and animals below a family and above a species; a class of objects divided into several subordinate species.

genu varum *see* **bow legs**.

geo *n* a narrow inlet in a sea cliff, worn by marine erosion along a weak line in the rock.

Geo. *abbr* = Georgia.

GEO *abbr* = geostationary earth orbit.

geo- *prefix* earth.

geocentric *adj* (*astron*) viewed as from the center of the earth; having the earth as a center.—**geocentrically** *adv*.

geochemistry *n* (*geol*) a part of geology that deals with the chemical make-up of the Earth.

geochronology *n* (*geol*) the study of time on a geologic scale through the use of absolute and relative age-dating methods.

geocorona *n* the outermost part of Earth's atmosphere, extending out to about 15 Earth radii.

geod *abbr* = geodesic; geodesy; geodetic.

geode *n* (*geol*) a cavity lined with crystals, usu within a rock.

geodemographic segmentation *n* a form of market segmentation in which consumers are divided and categorized according to demographic variables such as income, age, marital status, etc.

geodesic *adj* (*geom*) (*path*) geodetic (—*also* **geodesical**). * *n* (*math*) the shortest distance between two points on a curved surface, determined by triangulation.

geodesic dome *n* (*archit*) a lightweight domed structure made of interlocking polygons.

geodesy *n* (*math*) the mathematical determination of the exact positions of geographical points and the shape and size of the earth.—**geodesic** *adj*.—**geodic** *adj*.

geodetic, geodetical *adj* of, pertaining to, determined by, or carried out by geodesy.

Geoffrey of Monmouth *n* (*c*.1100 – *c*.1155) a Welsh cleric of Breton origin; writer of the medieval Arthurian saga *Historia Regum Britanniae*, "History of the Kings of Britain."

geog. *abbr* = geographer; geographic; geographical; geography.

geographic information system *n* a computer-based mapping system that enables archeologists to create a representation of an ancient landscape.

geographics *n* a computer printout perspective model of the terrain produced from grid-based map data.

geography *n* (*pl* **geographies**) the science of the physical nature of the earth, such as land and sea masses, climate, vegetation, etc, and their interaction with the human population; the physical features of a region.—**geographer** *n*. —**geographical, geographic** *adj*.—**geographically** *adv*.

geol. *abbr* = geologic; geological; geologist; geology.

geological timescale *n* a division of time since the formation of the Earth (4,600 million years ago) into units, during which rock sequences were deposited, deformed and eroded, and life of diverse types emerged, flourished and, often, ceased.

geologize *vti* to study geology or the geology of.

geology *n* the science relating to the history and structure of the earth's crust, its rocks and fossils.—**geological, geologic** *adj*.—**geologically** *adv*.—**geologist, geologer** *n*.

geom. *abbr* = geometer; geometric; geometrical; geometry.

geomagnetic field *n* the magnetic field of the Earth, almost certainly caused by motion in the fluid core.

geomagnetic reversal *n* (*archeo*) a total reversal of the magnetic field of the Earth. Evidence for reversals is preserved in rocks and can be useful for dating sites.

geomagnetic storm *n* a disturbance of the interaction of the Earth's magnetic field in the magnetosphere with incoming charged particles, often a result of a solar flare.

geomagnetism *n* the study of the Earth's magnetic field.

geomancy *n* divination by figures or lines.—**geomancer** *n*. —**geomantic** *adj*.

geometer, geometrician *n* one who studies or is skilled in geometry.

geometric, geometrical *adj* pertaining to, or done by, geometry; (*design, etc*) consisting of simple geometric shapes.—**geometrically** *adv*.

geometric progression *n* a sequence in which the terms differ by a constant ratio (e.g., 1, 2, 4, 8, 16...).

geometrize *vti* to work or make by geometrical methods; to study geometry.

geometry *n* (*math*) the branch of mathematics dealing with the properties, measurement, and relationships of points, lines, planes, and solids.—**geometric, geometrical** *adj*.—**geometrically** *adv*.

geomorphology *n* the study of the Earth's surface.

GEON *abbr* = gyro-erected optical navigation.

geophagy, geophagia, geophagism *n* the practice of eating certain kinds of clay, earth, or chalk.—**geophagist** *n*. —**geophagous** *adj*.

geophysics *n sing* (*physics*) the physics of the earth.— **geophysical**.—*adj*.—**geophysicist** *n*.

geopolitics *n sing* the study of the relationship between the geographical situation of a nation and its politics; the study of the effect of a nation's geography on its politics, esp in relation to that nation's relationship with other nations.

geoponic *adj* agricultural.

geoponics *n sing* the scientific study of agriculture.

Georef. *abbr* = World Geographic Reference System.

George *n* **Saint** (*d*. 303) Palestinian-born soldier and Christian martyr; patron saint of England, the Italian city of Genoa, and of soldiers and sailors. His feast day is April 23.

George I *n* (1660–1727) king of Great Britain and Ireland. The elector of Hanover since 1698, he became the first Hanoverian British king in 1714. Unable to speak English and with a marked preference for living in Hanover, he was not the most popular of British monarchs.

George II *n* (1683–1760) king of Great Britain and Ireland (1727–60). He was the last British monarch to fight in battle, at Denigen in 1743. The Jacobite rebellion of 1745 was efficiently crushed by his second son, William, Duke of Cumberland (1721–65), effectively ending any challenge to Hanoverian rule.

George III *n* (1738–1820) king of Great Britain and Ireland (1760–1820). Regarded as the least unattractive of the Hanoverian kings, he had much better relations with his subjects than his predecessors. American independence was established during his reign in 1783. He became insane in 1811, after which his son George became Regent.

George IV (1762–1830) king of Great Britain and Ireland (1820–30). In the Hanoverian manner, he detested his father, and became Prince Regent in 1811

when his father went insane. He acquired a public reputation for being dissolute but he was also a noted patron of the arts.

George V (1865–1936) king of Great Britain and Northern Ireland and emperor of India (1910–36). He was the second son of Edward VII, and changed the surname of the Royal Family from Saxe-Coburg to Windsor in 1917. He was a very popular monarch.

George VI (1895–1952) king of Great Britain and Northern Ireland (1936–1952) and emperor of India (1936–1947). He was the second son of George V, and succeeded to the throne following the abdication of his elder brother, the Duke of Windsor. He was succeeded by his eldest daughter, Elizabeth II.

georgette *n* a thin silk fabric.

George Town *n* 1. capital city of Cayman Islands. 2. a city in Malaysia.

Georgetown *n* capital city of Guyana.

Georgia *n* 1. (**GA**) a state of the United States of America (USA) of which the capital is Atlanta. 2. a republic in the southwest of the former USSR which gained full independence from Russia in 1991.

Georgian *adj* of the times or reigns of the four Georges (1714–1830) or of George V (1910–36) who ruled Britain; pertaining to Georgia in the US; pertaining to Georgia in the Caucasus. * *n* a person from Georgia; a person who lived in Georgian times; one who lives as if he or she belonged to Georgian times.

Georgian architecture *n* (*archit*) architecture of the period 1714 to 1830, when four King Georges reigned in Great Britain and Ireland, characterized by classical design and elaborate interiors.

"Georgia on my mind" *nphr* the official song of the American State, Georgia.

georgic, georgical *adj* of or pertaining to husbandry; rural. * *n* a poem on agriculture; (*with cap: pl*) a poem on agriculture by Virgil.

GEOS *abbr* = geodetic orbiting satellite.

geostationary satellite *n* a satellite used for communication, weather forecasting and remote sensing that appears stationary to observers on the Earth because its velocity in orbit matches that of the Earth.

Geosynchronous orbit *or* **geostationary orbit** *n* an orbit with a period of exactly one day in which a satellite rotates with the Earth, appearing to be stationary vertically above one point on the surface.

geothermal, geothermic *adj* of, relating to, or using the heat of the earth's interior.

geotropism *n* (*bot*) a tendency in the roots of certain plants to turn in the direction of the earth.—**geotropic** *adj*.—**geotropically** *adv*.

GEP *abbr* = Grasslands Ecology Program.

Ger., Germ. *abbr* = German; Germany.

geranium *n* a garden plant with red, pink, or white flowers.

Gerar *n* (*Bible*) kingdom on the southern coast of Palestine. *See also* **Abimilech**.

gerbil, gerbille *n* a type of burrowing desert rodent of Asia and Africa.—*also* **jerbil**.

Gerbil *abbr* (*Brit*) = Great Education Reform Bill (1988).

Gere *n* **Richard** (1949–) American film actor whose films include *An Officer and a Gentleman* (1982).

gerent *n* (*rare*) a ruler, a manager.

gerfalcon *see* **gyrfalcon**.

Gergenses *n* (*Bible*) not identified – probably Gadara. *See also* **Gadara**.

geriatric *adj* relating to geriatrics or old people; (*inf*) old, decrepit. * an aged person.

geriatrics *n sing* a branch of medicine dealing with the diseases and care of old people.—**geriatrician, geriatrist** *n*.

Géricault *n* **Théodore** (1791–1824) French painter who is seen as the originator of romanticism in painting.

germ *n* a simple form of living matter capable of growth and development into an organism; any microscopic, disease-causing organism; an origin or foundation capable of growing and developing.

german *adj* of the same stock or parentage; germane.

German *adj* of or relating to Germany, its people or their language. * *n* a native of Germany.

German *n* 1. **Saint [Germanus]** (*c*.378–448) one of the six governors of Gaul; ordained priest against his will, and became bishop. From then on, he devoted himself to the work of Christ. His feast day is July 31. 2. **Sir Edward [Edward German Jones]** (1862–1936) Welsh composer who is best known for the incidental music he wrote for Shakespeare's plays, e.g. *Henry VIII*.

germander *n* a plant of the mint family.

germane *adj* relevant.—**germanely** *adv*.—**germaneness** *n*.

Germanez *n* **Christian** (1940–) French designer of office furniture and the *Half and Half* seat produced by Airborne in 1966.

Germanic *adj* of Germans or Germany, or of a German-speaking nation. * *n* the family of languages derived from Indo-European that comprises the English, Dutch, German, Scandinavian, and Gothic languages.

Germanism *n* a German idiom, custom, or characteristic.

germanium *n* a rare metallic element used in transistors.

Germanize *vti* to make or become German in language, custom, manners etc.—**Germanization** *n*.

German measles *n* (*sing*) a mild contagious disease similar to measles.—*also* **rubella**.

Germanophile *n* a lover of Germany or its customs, etc.

Germanophobe *n* a person who has an irrational fear of Germany.—**Germanophobia** *n*.

G

German shepherd *n* any of a breed of large smooth-haired dogs often used by the police and for guarding property.—*also* **Alsatian**.

German silver *n* an alloy of nickel, copper, and zinc.—*also* **nickel silver**.

German sixth *see* **augmented sixth**.

Germanus, Saint *see* **German**.

Germany *n* a large country in northern central Europe that comprises the former East and West German Republics, reunified in 1990.

germ cell *n* a reproductive cell.

germicide *n* a substance used to destroy germs.—**germicidal** *adj*.

germinal *adj* incipient; of or pertaining to a germ or germs or seed buds; in the French revolutionary calendar, the seventh month (March 22–April 20).

germinate *vti* to start developing; to sprout, as from a seed.—**germinable**, **germinative** *adj*.—**germination** *n*. —**germinator** *n*.

germs *n* microorganisms. The term is used particularly for microorganisms that are pathogenic.

germ warfare *n* the use of disease-causing bacteria against enemy forces.

gerontocracy *n* (*pl* **gerontocracies**) government by old men.—**gerontocratic** *adj*.

gerontology *n* the study of aging and its effects and problems.—**gerontological** *adj*.—**gerontologist** *n*.

gerrymander *vt* to rearrange the boundaries of (voting districts) to favor a particular party or candidate.

Gershwin *n* George (1898–1937) American composer and pianist who wrote songs for many musical shows, often with his lyricist brother, Ira. His most famous pieces include *Rhapsody in Blue* and the opera *Porgy and Bess*.

Gertrude *n* **Saint** (*d*.664) born into a Frankish noble family; Charlemagne's great-aunt and abbess of Nivelles. She built churches and hospitals, and was later believed to protect departed spirits. Her feast day is March 17. She is also a patron saint of travelers. *See also* **Christopher, Saint**.

gerund *n* the participle of a verb used as a noun.—**gerundial** *adj*.

gerundive *adj* of or like a gerund. * *n* a passive verbal adjective.

Geryon, Geryones *n* (*Greek myth*) a king who had three heads or the body of three men from the waist down, the son of the Gorgon Medusa.

Gerza *n* (*Egypt*) site in Upper Egypt, important in Pre-dynastic times; has given its name to a phase of Pre-dynastic culture, also known as Naqada, after another Upper Egypt site.—**Gerzean** *adj*.—*also* **Gerzean Period** *n*.

Gerzean *adj* (*archeo*) relating to an ancient Egyptian pre-dynastic culture dating from *c*.4,000 BC, named after the site at El Gerza.

GES *abbr* = Global Epidemiological Surveillance and Health Situation.

Gesamtkunstwerk *n* A concept founded in Germany in the early 19th century, defining a bringing together of all the arts and epitomized by the operas of Richard Wagner.

GESM *abbr* = Group for Educational Services in Museums.

gesso *n* (*pl* **gessoes**) a prepared ground of plaster for painting on; plaster of Paris.

gest, geste *n* an adventure, exploit; a tale of adventure, esp in verse.

gestalt *n* (*pl* **gestalts, gestalten**) an integral pattern or system of phenomena forming a functional unit in which the whole is more than the sum of its parts.

Gestapo *n* the secret police of Nazi Germany.

gestate *vt* to carry (young) in the womb during pregnancy; to develop (a plan, etc) gradually in the mind.—**gestational, gestative** *adj*.—**gestatory** *adj*.

gestation *n* the act or period of carrying young in the womb; pregnancy. *See also* **pregnancy**.

gestation period *n* (*biol*) the period from conception to birth in mammals.

gesticulate *vi* to make expressive gestures, esp when speaking.—**gesticulation** *n*. —**gesticulative** *adj*.—**gesticulator** *n*.

gesture *n* movement of part of the body to express or emphasize ideas, emotions, etc. * *vi* to make a gesture.—**gestural** *adj*.—**gesturer** *n*.

Gesualdo *n* Carlo (*c*.1560–1613) Italian composer and lutist; Prince of Venosa. He wrote outstanding madrigals and motets which were far in advance of their time.

get *vb* (**getting, got,** *pp* **got, gotten**) *vt* to obtain, gain, win; to receive; to acquire; to go and bring; to catch; to persuade; to cause to be; to prepare; (*inf*) (*with vb aux* **have** *or* **has**) to be obliged to; to possess; (*inf*) to strike, kill, baffle; defeat, etc; (*inf*) to understand; (*with* **across**) to cause to be understood; (*with* **in**) to bring in; (*crops, etc*) to gather; to insert; (*with* **off**) to acquit, to secure favorable treatment of; (*letters*) to post; (*with* **out**) to cause to leave or escape; to cause to become known or published; (*with* **out of**) to avoid doing; (*with* **over**) to communicate effectively. * *vi* to come; to go; to arrive; to come to be; to manage or contrive; (*with* **about, around**) to be up and on one's feet, esp after being unwell; to be socially active; (*news, gossip*) to become circulated; (*with*) **across**) to be understood; (*with* **at**) to reach; (*inf*) to mean, imply; to irritate, pester relentlessly; (*inf*) to criticize; (*inf*) to corrupt, bribe, influence illegally; (*with* **away**) to escape; (*with* **by**) (*inf*) to manage, to survive; (*with* **in**) (*vehicle, etc*) to enter; to arrive; (*university, college, etc*) to be offered a place; (*with* **off**) to come off, down, or out of; to be acquitted; to escape the consequences of; to begin, depart; (*with* **on**) to go on or into; to put on; to proceed; to grow older; to become late; to manage; to succeed; (*with* **on with**) to establish a friendly relationship; (*with* **out**) to go out or away; to leave or escape; to take out; to become known or published; (*with* **over**) to overcome; to recover from; to forget; (*with* **round, around**) to evade, circumvent; to coax, cajole; (*with* **through**) to use up, spend, consume; to finish; to manage to survive; (*examination, test*) to succeed or pass; to contact by telephone; (*with* **up**) to rise to one's feet; to get out of bed; (*inf*) to organize; (*inf*) to dress in a certain style; (*inf*) to be involved in (mischief, etc).—**getable, gettable** *adj*.

GET *abbr* = gastric emptying time.

get-at-able *adj* accessible.

getaway *n* the act of escaping; a start in a race, etc.

Gethsemane *n* (*Bible*) place at the foot of the Mount of Olives where Jesus went with his disciples to pray on the night of his betrayal and arrest.

getter *n* one who gets or acquires.

get-together *n* (*inf*) an informal social gathering or meeting.

Getty *n* **J[ean] Paul** (1892–1976) American industrialist and art collector. He made his money in oil and was a billionaire by the late 1960s. The J Paul Getty Museum in Malibu, California, houses his art collection.

get-up *n* (*inf*) dress, costume.

get-up-and-go *n* (*inf*) energy, enthusiasm.

geum *n* a genus of the rose family, with yellow, orange, red, or white flowers.

GeV *abbr* = giga-electronvolt.

GEW *abbr* = gram equivalent weight.

gewgaw *n* a showy ornament; a trinket.

geyser *n* (*geog*) a natural spring from which columns of boiling water and steam gush into the air at intervals; a water heater.

gf *abbr* = glass fiber; girlfriend.

GF *abbr* = General Foods; growth factor.

GFA *abbr* = general freight agent.

GFCH *abbr* = gas-fired central heating.

GFG *abbr* = Good Food Guide.

GFOF *abbr* = Geared Futures and Options Funds.

GFR *abbr* = German Federal Republic.

GFS *abbr* = Girls' Friendly Society.

GFSA *abbr* = Gold Fields of South Africa.

gg *abbr* = gas generator; gamma globulin.

GG *abbr* = Girl Guides; Grenadier Guards; Governor General.

GGA *abbr* = Good Gardeners Association; Guernsey Growers Association.

GGE *abbr* = Guild of Glass Engravers.

GGGS *abbr* = Golden Guernsey Goat Society.

g.gr. *abbr* = great gross.

GGSM *abbr* = Graduate of Guildhall School of Music.

GH *abbr* = General Hospital; Guild of Hairdressers; growth hormone.

Ghana *n* a republic located on the southern coast of west Africa between Côte d'Ivoire and Togo.

gharry, gharri *n* (*pl* **gharries**) a cart or carriage in India that is available for hire.

ghastly *adj* (**ghastlier, ghastliest**) terrifying, horrible; (*inf*) intensely disagreeable; pale, unwell looking.—**ghastliness** *n*.

ghat, ghaut *n* in India, a mountain pass or a chain of mountains; a landing-place with steps; a flight of steps to a river or a temple.

ghazi *n* (*pl* **ghazies**) a Muslim slayer of infidels; a Turkish title bestowed on distinguished commanders; a warrior champion.

ghee *n* clarified butter.

Ghent *n* a city in Belgium.

gherkin *n* a small cucumber used for pickling.

ghetto *n* (*pl* **ghettos, ghettoes**) a section of a city in which members of a minority group live, esp because of social, legal, or economic pressure.

ghetto blaster *n* (*inf*) a large portable stereo cassette player and radio with built-in speakers.

GHI *abbr* = Good Housekeeping Institute.

Ghiberti *n* **Lorenzo** (1378–1455) Florentine sculptor. He was an outstanding and highly talented figure of the late Gothic and early Renaissance periods.

ghillie *n* (*pl* **ghillies**) a gillie.

Ghirlandaio *n* **Domenico** (1449–94) Florentine painter, who produced frescos and altarpieces for a number of churches in Florence, e.g. *The Life of St John the Baptist* (1845–90) in the Church of Santa Maria Novella.

GHMS *abbr* = Graduate in Homeopathic Medicine and Surgery.

ghost *n* the supposed disembodied spirit of a dead person, appearing as a shadowy apparition; a faint trace or suggestion; a false image in a photographic negative. * *vt* to ghostwrite.

Ghost *abbr* = global horizontal sounding technique.

ghostly *adj* (**ghostlier, ghostliest**) of or like a ghost.—**ghostliness** *n*.

ghost town *n* a town abandoned by most or all of its inhabitants.

Ghost Trio *see* **Geistertrio**.

ghost wall *n* (*archeo*) a trench left by removal of foundations so the stones or bricks can be used to make new buildings.

ghostwrite *vt* (**ghostwriting, ghostwrote,** *pp* **ghostwritten**) to write books, speeches, articles, etc for another who professes to be the author.—**ghostwriter** *n*.

ghoul *n* (*Muslim folklore*) an evil spirit that robs graves and feeds on the dead; a person with macabre tastes or interests.—**ghoulish** *adj*.—**ghoulishly** *adv*.

GHQ *abbr* (*mil*) = General Headquarters.

GHRF *abbr* = growth hormone releasing factor.

GHS *abbr* = Garden History Society; Girls' High School.

Ghz *abbr* = gigahertz.

gi *abbr* = galvanized iron.

gi. *abbr* = gill; gills.

GI *abbr* = Gideons International; Government Issue (slang for ordinary servicemen); gastrointestinal.

Giacometti *n* **Alberto** (1910–66) and **Diego** (1902–85) Swiss artists and designers who worked in Paris.

Giambologna *see* **Bologna, Giovanni**.

giant *n* a huge legendary being of great strength; a person or thing of great size, strength, intellect, etc. * *adj* incredibly large.—**giantess** *nf*.

giantism *n* the condition or quality of being a giant; gigantism.

giant panda *n* a large black and white bear-like herbivore.—*also* **panda**.

giant planets *n* Jupiter, Saturn, Neptune, and Uranus, which have much greater masses and diameters than the other planets in the Solar System.

giant star *n* (*astron*) a star in a spectral class that is brighter than the main stars in the class. *See* **spectral types**.

giaour *n* (*derog*) a Muslim term for an unbeliever, esp a Christian.

Giap *n* **Vo Nguyen** (1912–) Vietnamese general who commanded the North Vietnamese army against the US during the Vietnam War.

Gib. *abbr* = Gibraltar.

GIB *abbr* = Gibraltar Information Bureau.

gibber *vi* to utter meaningless or inarticulate sounds.

Gibberd *n* **Sir Frederick** (1908–) English architect. His notable works include buildings in Harlow New Town.

gibberellin *see* **hormone**.

gibberish *n* unintelligible talk, nonsense.

gibbet *n* a gallows; a structure from which bodies of executed criminals were hung and exposed to public scorn.

gibbon *n* a small tailless ape of Southeast Asia and the East Indies.

Gibbon *n* 1. **Edward** (1737–94) English historian, author of *History of the Decline and Fall of the Roman Empire* (1776–88). 2. **Lewis Grassic [James Leslie Mitchell]** (1901–35) Scottish novelist whose masterpiece is his trilogy *A Scots Quair*.

Gibbons *n* 1. **Cedric** (1893–1960) Irish-born American movie-set designer who introduced early three-dimensional sets. 2. **Orlando** (1583–1625) English composer and organist who wrote motets, madrigals, and stately anthems, e.g. *This is the Record of John*. His son, Christopher, was also an organist and composer of note.

gibbous *adj* protuberant; humped; irregularly rounded; (*moon*) between full and half.

Gibbs *n* 1. **Cecil Armstrong** (1889–1960) English composer who is best known for his songs. He also composed an opera as well as a choral symphony, *Odysseus*. 2. **James** (1682–1754) Scottish architect. His notable works include St Martin-in-the-Fields, London.

Gibb's free energy *see* **free energy**.

Gibbs surround *n* (*archit*) the extremity of a window or doorway which contains blocks of stone set around the frame.

GIBCM *abbr* = Graduate of the Institute of British Carriage and Automobile Manufacturers.

gibe *n* a taunt, sneer. * *vti* to jeer, scoff (at).—*also* **jibe**.—**giber, jiber** *n*. — **gibingly, jibingly** *adv*.

GIBiol *abbr* = Graduate of the Institute of Biology.

giblets *npl* the edible internal organs of a bird.

Gibraltar *n* 1. a self-governing British colony comprising a limestone promontory situated at the end of a peninsula that forms the southernmost tip of Spain. 2. capital city of Gibraltar.

Gibraltar Pound *n* currency of Gibraltar.

Gibson *n* **Mel** (1956–) American-born Australian film actor and academy award winner for best director and best actor for *Braveheart* (1995).

gid *n* a disease in sheep, marked by staggering.

giddy *adj* (**giddier, giddiest**) frivolous, flighty; having a feeling of whirling around as if about to lose balance and fall; causing giddiness. * *vti* (**giddying, giddied**) to make giddy, to become giddy.—**giddily** *adv*.—**giddiness** *n*. *See also* **vertigo**.

Gide *n* **André** (1860–1951) French novelist whose novels, e.g. *Fruits of the Earth*, are usually studies of sexual and social self-deception. He was awarded the Nobel prize for literature in 1947.

Gideon *n* (*Bible*) a hero of the Book of Judges, also known as Jerubbaal, who led his people against the Midianites who had invaded Canaan from Arabia and, like locusts, were eating their crops.

gie *vt* (*Scot*) to give.

GIE *abbr* = Graduate of the Institute of Engineers.

Gielgud *n* **Sir [Arthur] John** (1904–2000) English stage and film actor and producer; a leading Shakespearean actor.

Gierek *n* **Edward** (1913–) Polish Communist statesman who became leader of the Polish United Workers Party in 1971. He presided over increasing industrial unrest and the rise of Solidarity and was forced to resign in 1980. *See* **Walesa, Lech**.

GIF *abbr* = (*comput*) Graphics Interchange Format; Garden Industry Federation; growth-hormone inhibiting factor.

gift *n* something given; the act of giving; a natural ability. * *vt* to present with or as a gift.—**giftedness** *n*.

GIFT *abbr* = gamete intra-Fallopian transfer, a technique that helps infertile couples to have children.

gifted *adj* having great natural ability.

gift of tongues *n* unintelligible speech uttered while in a state of religious ecstasy—*also* **glossolalia**.

gifts inter vivos *npl* gifts that are made during the giver's lifetime as opposed to being bequeathed under the terms of the will of a deceased person.

gig[1] *n* a light two-wheeled horse-drawn carriage; a long, light boat.

gig[2] *n* (*inf*) a single booking for a jazz or pop band, etc; a single night's performance. * *vi* (**gigging, gigged**) to perform a gig.

gig[3] *n* an arrangement of hooks on a line used to snag fish; a fish spear. * *vti* (**gigging, gigged**) to catch or spear with a gig.

giga *see* **gigue**.

giga- *prefix* (*comput*) a prefix meaning one billion, and abbreviated to g.

gigabyte *n* (*comput*) one billion bytes or 1,000 megabytes, although, strictly speaking, a gigabyte is 1,073,741,824 bytes.

gigantesque *adj* as if by or for a giant.

gigantic *adj* exceedingly large.—**gigantically** *adv*.—**giganticness** *n*.

gigantism *n* abnormal enlargement of the body due to hormonal imbalance (—*also* **giantism**); the condition or quality of being gigantic.

giggle *vi* to laugh in a nervous or silly manner. * *n* a laugh in this manner; (*inf*) a prank, a joke.—**giggler** *n*. —**giggly** *adj*.

Gignoux *n* **Michèle** (1944–) French "pop romantic" artist who designed the 1967 Cube photo frame.

GIGO *abbr* (*comput*) = Garbage In, Garbage Out. Where poor or distorted results from a program are caused by incorrect input, so the quality of the output is only as good as the quality of the input.

gigolo *n* (*pl* **gigolos**) a man paid to be a woman's escort.

gigot *n* a leg of mutton.

gigue *n* (*mus*) (*French*) a lively tune; a dance similar to a jig.

Gihon *n* (*Bible*) a spring in the Kidron valley. *See also* **Siloam**.

Gilbert *n* 1. **Alfred** (1854–1934) British sculptor whose most famous work is Eros, in Piccadilly Circus, London. 2. **Cass** (1859–1934), American architect. His notable works include the Woolworth Building, New York. 3. **Sir W[illiam] S[chwenck]** (1836–1911) English dramatist and librettist whose collaboration with Arthur Sullivan resulted in the "Savoy operas," e.g., *The Pirates of Penzance* and *The Gondoliers*, of which there are 13 in all. He was also a fine parodist and wrote much excellent light verse.

Gilboa *n* Mt one of a range of mountains in the north of Palestine; (*Bible*) Saul and his sons were killed there in a battle with the Philistines. *See also* **Saul**.

gild[1] *see* **guild**.

gild[2] *vt* (**gilding, gilded**, *or* **gilt**) to coat with gold leaf; to give a deceptively attractive appearance to.—**gilder** *n*

Gildas *n* British monk; possibly the writer of the part history, part mythology of the Celts *De Excidio Et Con-questu Britanniae*, "On the Ruin and Conquest of Britain," written sometime between *c*.516 and 547 AD.

gilder *see* **guilder**.

gilding *n* the art or process of overlaying or covering with gold leaf; gold leaf applied to a surface; a superficial covering.

Gilead *n* (*Bible*) grandson of Manaseh; ancestor of the Coileadites; (*geog*) mountainous area east of the River Jordan famous for its sheep and the balm or resin from the trees which grew there.

Giles *n* Saint [Aegidius] a 7th century Greek hermit in France; the patron saint of cripples and beggars. His feast day is September 1.

Gilfaethwy *n* (*Welsh Celtic myth*) the son of Don. He fell in love with Goewin.

Gilgal *n* (*Bible*) "circle of stones"; the name is used for several ancient places in the OT.

gill[1] *n* an organ, esp in fish, for breathing in water.

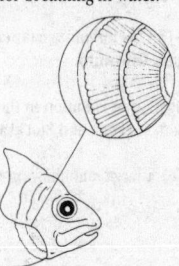

gill[2] *n* in US a liquid measure equal to 4 fluid ounces (0.25 pint) or 23.6 millimeters; in UK, 5 fluid ounces (0.25 pint) or 28.4 millimeters.

Gill *n* 1. **[Arthur] Eric [Rowton]** (1882–1940) English typographer, writer, sculptor, and engraver. His type designs include Perpetua and Gill Sans-serif, his sculpture the *Prospero and Ariel* sculpture for Broadcasting House, and his books *Art* and *Autobiography*. 2. **Irving John** (1870–1936) American architect. His notable works include Laughlin House, Los Angeles.

Gillespie *n* **Dizzy [John Birks Gillespie]** (1917–93) American virtuoso jazz trumpeter and bandleader.

gillie, gilly n (pl **gillies**) (Scot) a Highland attendant, esp one who accompanies a shooting or fishing party.—also **ghillie**.

gills npl the wattle below the beak of a bird, as in certain domestic fowl; one of the radiating plates under the cap of a mushroom; a person's cheeks or jowls.

gillyflower n one of various scented plants of the mustard family, e.g. wallflower, stock, etc.

GILS abbr = Government Information Locator Service.

gilt[1] see **gild**.

gilt[2] n gilding; a substance used for this.

gilt-edged adj (securities) considered a secure investment.

gilt-edged security n a fixed interest security or stock issued by the UK government as a means of borrowing money.

gimbal n (usu pl) one of two rings moving within each other at right angles, used to suspend a ship's compass, etc.

gimcrack adj showy, cheap, and useless.

GIMechE abbr = Graduate of the Institution of Mechanical Engineers.

GIMI abbr = Graduate of the Institute of the Motor Industry.

gimlet n a small tool with a screw point for boring holes.

gimmick n a trick or device for attracting notice, advertising, or promoting a person, product, or service.—**gimmickry** n. —**gimmicky** adj.

gimp n an interlaced silk twist or trimming interwoven with wire or cord, used for furniture, dresses etc.—also **guimpe**.

Gimson n **Ernest** (1864–1919) British architect who turned to chair-making.

gin[1] n an alcoholic spirit distilled from grain and flavored with juniper berries.

gin[2] n a trap for catching small animals; a type of crane; a machine for separating the seeds from raw cotton. * vt (**ginning, ginned**) to trap with a gin; to separate seeds from cotton.

Ginastera n **Alberto** (1916–) Ar gentinean composer particularly well known for his operas, Don Rodrigo, Bomarzo, and Beatrix.

ginger n a tropical plant with fleshy roots used as a flavoring; the spice prepared by drying and grinding; (inf) vigor; a reddish-brown.—**gingery** adj.

ginger ale, ginger beer n a carbonated soft drink flavored with ginger.

gingerbread n a cake flavored with ginger.

gingerly adv with care or caution. * adj cautious.—**gingerliness** n.

ginger snap n a ginger-flavored biscuit.

gingham n a cotton fabric with stripes or checks.

gingival adj of the gums.

gingivitis n inflammation of the gums.

ginglymus n (pl **ginglymi**) (anat) a joint like a hinge.

gink n (sl) a boy or man, esp an eccentric one.

ginkgo n (pl **ginkgoes**) a Japanese tree with handsome fan-shaped foliage; the maidenhair tree.

Ginnie Mae abbr = Government National Mortgage Association.

Gino abbr = graphical input/output.

Ginsberg n **Allen** (1926–97) American poet regarded as the leading poet of the beat generation.

ginseng n a plant found in China and North America; its root, said to have an invigorating effect on the mind and body.

GInstP abbr = Graduate of the Institute of Physics.

GInstT abbr = Graduate of the Institute of Transport.

GIntMC abbr = Graduate of the International Management Center.

GINucE abbr = Graduate of the Institution of Nuclear Engineers.

giocoso adj (mus) (Italian) "merry."

gioioso adj (mus) (Italian) "joyful."

Giona mac Lugha n (Irish Celtic myth) the son of the warrior daughter of Fionn mac Cumhaill, who became a leader of the Fianna.

Giordano n **Umberto** (1867–1948) an Italian composer of operas, e.g. Mala vita, Andrea Chenier and Fedora.

Giorgione n [**Giorgio da Castelfranco**] (c.1477–1510) Venetian painter. Little of his work has survived, although he was one of the most influential painters of his time.

Giotto di Bondone n (1267–1337) Florentine painter and architect.

Giovanni Bologna see **Bologna, Giovanni.**

gip see **gyp.**

GIPME abbr = Global Investigation of Pollution in the Marine Environment.

GIPSA abbr = Grain Inspection, Packers, and Stockyards Administration.

Gipsy see **Gypsy.**

giraffe n (pl **giraffes, giraffe**) a large cud-chewing mammal of Africa, with very long legs and neck.

girandole, girandola n a branched chandelier; a revolving firework or water jet; a pendant or earring with small stones around a larger one; one of several mines connected in a group.

Girard n **Alexander Hayden** (1907–93) American architect who designed the interiors of the 1943 Ford and 1946 Lincoln autos.

girasol, girosol, girasole n a variety of opal; the fire opal.

gird vt (**girding, girded,** or **girt**) to encircle or fasten with a belt; to surround; to prepare (oneself) for action.

girder n a large steel beam for supporting joists, the framework of a building, etc.

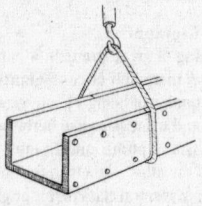

girdle n a belt for the waist.

Giric I n (d. 889) king of Scots (878–889). The cousin of Aed, whom he is thought to have murdered to take the throne. He ruled jointly with Eocha.

Giric II n (d. 1005) king of Scots (997–1005). The son of Kenneth III with whom he shared the throne.

girl n a female child; a young woman; (inf) a woman of any age.—**girlhood** n. —**girlish** adj.

girlfriend n a female friend, esp with whom one is romantically involved.

Girl Guide n a member of the Girl Guides, a scouting organization founded in Britain in 1910.

girlie n a little girl; a young woman; (inf) a woman.

girlie magazine n a magazine that contains photographs of nude or semi-nude females.

girlish adj of or like a girl.—**girlishly** adv.—**girlishness** n.

Girl of the Golden West n **The** (La Fanciulla del West) an opera by Puccini to a libretto by G. Civinini and C. Zangarini.

Girl Scout n a member of the Girl Scouts, a youth organization founded in the US in 1912.

giro (pl **giros**) a credit-transfer system between financial organizations; a payment so made.

Girondist n a member of the Gironde, the moderate Republican party during the Revolution in France (1791–93).

girt[1] see **gird**.

girt[2] adj (naut) moored so taut by two cables as not to swing to the wind or tide.

girth n the thickness round something; a band put around the belly of a horse, etc to hold a saddle or pack.

GIS abbr = Geographic Information Systems.

Giscard d'Estaing n **Valéry** (1926–) F rench statesman. He was minister of finance under de Gaulle (1962–66) and Pompidou (1969–74) and became president (1974–81) following the latter's death.

Gispen n **Willem H.** (1890–1981) Dutch metalworker who also made wooden furniture and lighting.

GISS abbr = Goddard Institute for Space Studies.

Gissing n **George** (1857–1903) English novelist whose novels, e.g. New Grub Street, are unrelentingly grim works designed to expose the horrors of social injustice.

gist n the principal point or essence of anything.

GITB abbr = Gas Industry Training Board.

gîte n self-catering holiday accommodation in France.

GITS abbr = Government Information Technology Services.

Giugiaro n **Giorgio** (1938–) Italian auto designer who, together with Aldo Mantovani, was responsible for over 40 autos, including the 1983 Fiat Uno.

giusto adj (mus) (Italian) "exact," as in tempo giusto, which can mean either "strict time" or "appropriate speed."

give vb (**giving, gave,** pp **given**) vt to hand over as a present; to deliver; to hand over in or for payment; to pass (regards etc) along; to act as host or sponsor of; to supply; to yield; (advice) to offer; (punishment, etc) to inflict; to sacrifice; to perform; (with **away**) to make a gift of; to give (the bride) to the bridegroom; to sell cheaply; to reveal, betray; (with **in**) to deliver, hand in (a document, etc); (with **off**) to emit (fumes, etc); (with **out**) to discharge; to make public, to announce; to emit; to distribute; (with **over**) to devote time to a specific activity; to cease (an activity); to transfer to another; to set aside for a particular purpose; (with **up**) to hand over; to stop, renounce; to cease; to resign (a position); to stop trying; to despair of; to surrender; to devote oneself completely (to). * vi to bend, move, etc from force or pressure; (inf) to be happening; (with **in**) to concede, admit defeat; (with **out**) to become used up or exhausted; to fail; (with **over**) (inf) to stop (an activity). * n capacity or tendency to yield to force or strain; the quality or state of being springy; (with **in**) to submit; (with **out**) to become worn out; (with **up**) to accept defeat or failure to do something, to surrender.—**givable, giveable** adj.

give-and-take n mutual concessions; free-flowing exchange of ideas and conversation.

giveaway n (inf) an unintentional revelation; a free gift to encourage sales; a freesheet.

"Give Me Louisiana" *n* the song of the American state, Louisiana.

given[1] *see* **give**.

given[2] *adj* accustomed (to) by habit, etc; specified; assumed; granted.

given name *n* a first name.

giver *n* a person who gives.

GIX *abbr* = Government Information Xchange (replaced by First Gov).

Giza (El Gîza) *n* a city in Egypt; the site of a pyramid complex set on a plateau a few miles southwest of modern Cairo. Includes the Great Pyramid, the Great Sphinx and many other monuments in a vast funerary.

gizzard *n* the second stomach of a bird, used for grinding food.

gj *abbr* = gigajoule.

gk *abbr* = goalkeeper.

GKA *abbr* = Garter King of Arms.

GKN *abbr* = Guest, Keen and Nettlefold.

Gl *symbol* (*chem*) glucinum or glucinium.

gl. *abbr* = gill; gloss; (*Latin*) *gloria*, "glory."

g/l *abbr* = grams per liter.

Gl. *abbr* (*Latin*) = *Gloria Patri*, "Glory be to the Father."

GL *abbr* = ground level; (*French*) *grande luxe*, "great luxury."

GLAAS *abbr* (*Brit*) = Greater London Association of Alcohol Services.

glabella *n* (*pl* **glabellae**) the smooth projection above the bridge of the nose.—**glabellar** *adj*.

glabrous *adj* without hair, smooth-skinned.

glacé *adj* candied, covered in icing, as fruit. * *vt* (**glacéing, glacéed**) to cover with icing; to candy.

glacial *adj* extremely cold; of or relating to glaciers or a glacial epoch.—**glacially** *adv*.

glacial action *n* (*geol*) all processes that are related to the action of a glacier.

glacial deposits *n* (*geol*) the deposits formed by actions of glaciers.

glacial erosion *n* (*geol*) the removal and wearing down of rock by glaciers and associated streams.

glacial lake *n* (*geol*) a small lake dammed by ice between the edge of a glacier and the side of its valley or moraine.

glacial outburst *n* (*geol*) the sudden release of water from a glacial lake.

glaciate *vti* to subject to glacial action; to cover or become covered with glaciers.—**glaciation** *n*.

glaciated valley *n* (*geol*) a U-shaped valley with steep sides and a wide floor gouged out by glacial erosion.

glaciation *n* (*geol*) an ice age, with all its effects, processes and products.

glacier *n* (*geol*) a large mass of snow and ice moving slowly down a mountain.

glacis *n* (*pl* **glacis**) a sloping bank of earth in front of a fortification for its defense; a slope (on a tank) to throw off hostile shot.

Glackens *n* **William James** (1870–1938) American painter. He was a member of the New York realists and The Eight and was involved in organizing the Armory Show, in which he exhibited.

glad *adj* (**gladder, gladdest**) happy; causing joy; very willing; bright.—**gladly** *adv*.—**gladness** *n*.

gladden *vti* to make or become glad.—**gladdener** *n*.

glade *n* an open space in a wood or forest.

glad hand *n* a warm greeting; a fulsome welcome prompted by ulterior motives.—**glad-hand** *vti*.

gladiate *adj* sword-shaped.

gladiator *n* (*ancient Rome*) a person trained to fight with men or beasts in a public arena.—**gladiatorial** *adj*.

gladiolus *n* (*pl* **gladiolus, gladioli**) any of a genus of the iris family with sword-like leaves and tall spikes of funnel-shaped flowers.

gladsome *adj* joyous.

Gladstone *n* **William Ewart** (1809–98) British statesman who became leader of the Liberals in 1867, and prime minister (1868–74, 1880–85, 1886, 1892–94).

glair *n* white of egg; size made from this; a sticky substance; any sticky or glairy matter * *vt* to smear with glair.—**glaireous** *adj*.

glairy *adj* (**glairier, glairiest**) like or smeared with glair.—**glairiness** *n*.

glam *abbr* = greying, leisured, affluent, married.

glamor, glamour *n* charm, allure; attractiveness, beauty.—**glamorous, glamourous** *adj*.—**glamorousness, glamourousness** *n*.

glamorize, glamourize *vt* to make glamorous.—**glamorization, glamourization** *n*.—**glamorizer, glamourizer** *n*.

glance *vi* to strike obliquely and go off at an angle; to flash; to look quickly. * *n* a glancing off; a flash; a quick look.—**glancingly** *adv*.

gland *n* an organ that separates substances from the blood and synthesizes them for further use in, or for elimination from, the body.

glanders *n* (*sing or pl*) a contagious bacterial disease esp of horses, often fatal.—**glandered** *adj*.—**glanderous** *adj*.

glandular *adj* of, having or resembling glands; (*plants*) covered with hairs tipped with glands.

glandular fever *n* an infectious viral disease caused by the Epstein-Barr virus producing a sore throat and swelling in neck lymph nodes (also those in the armpits and groin).—*also* **infectious mononucleosis**.

glans *n* the head of the penis, which is normally covered by the foreskin.

glare *n* a harsh uncomfortably bright light, esp painfully bright sunlight; an angry or fierce stare; (*comput*) the reflection of light from the computer screen. * *vi* to shine with a steady, dazzling light; to stare fiercely.

glaring *adj* dazzling; obvious, conspicuous.—**glaringly** *adv*.—**glaringness** *n*.

Glaser *n* **Milton** (1929–) America president of P ush Pin Studios in New York from 1954 to 1974 and designer of Bob Dylan posters.

Glas Ghaibhnenn *n* (*Irish Celtic myth*) a magic cow that was stolen by Balor. He took it to Tory Island, but Cian went in pursuit and rescued the cow.

Glasgow *n* major Scottish city in United Kingdom of Great Britain and Northern Ireland (UK).

Glasgow *n* **Ellen** (1873–1945) American novelist whose novels, usually set in her native Virginia, are closely observed dramas of social and political tension.

Glasgow Boys *n* a group of painters centered in Glasgow in the 1880s and 90s who established an outpost of the European vogue for naturalism and romantic lyricism in landscape painting.

Glasgow School *n* a group of architect-designers, including Charles Rennie Mackintosh, Frances and Margaret MacDonald and George MacNair who developed a conservative version of Art Nouveau.

Glashow, Sheldon *see* **Weinberg, Steven.**

glasnost *n* the Russian word for "openness," now applied to the policy, initiated by President Gorbachev of the former USSR, of greater frankness and openness in Soviet affairs.—**glasnostian** *adj*.

Glaspell *n* **Susan** (1882–1948) American novelist and winner of the Pulitzer prize for *Alison's House* (1930).

glass *n* a hard brittle substance, usu transparent; glassware; a glass article, as a drinking vessel; (*pl*) spectacles or binoculars; the amount held by a drinking glass. * *adj* of or made of glass. * *vt* to equip, enclose, or cover with glass.

Glass *n* **Philip** (1937–) American composer whose work includes pieces for voice and a broad variety of instruments, as well as the opera *Einstein on the Beach.*

glass-blowing *n* the art, skill or process of blowing air into molten glass and shaping it.—**glass-blower** *n*.

glass ceiling *n* the name given to the invisible barrier, usually created by discrimination, that prevents women from reaching posts in senior management in companies.

glass cutter *n* a tool for cutting glass; a person who cuts glass or etches on glass.

glass eye *n* an artificial eye made of glass.

glass harmonica *n* (*mus*) at its simplest, a set of goblets which are played by rubbing a moistened finger around the rims.

glass jaw *n* vulnerability (esp in boxers) to a knockout punch.

Glass Tower or **Glass Castle** *n* (*Irish Celtic myth*) the Fomorii are said to have built a glass tower or castle. Balor is said to have imprisoned his daughter in the Glass Tower.

glassware *n* objects made of glass, esp drinking vessels.

glasswort *n* a fleshy plant of marshy areas, from which soda was formerly obtained for use in making glass.

glassy *adj* (**glassier, glassiest**) resembling glass; smooth; expressionless, lifeless.—**glassily** *adv*.—**glassiness** *n*.

Glastonbury *n* (*archeo*) a very important Iron Age site in Somerset, England. It was a lake settlement and lasted from *c*. 300 BC until the Roman invasion.

Glastonbury Tor *n* the hill at Glastonbury in the Vale of Avalon in Somerset, England, known as Glastonbury Tor, was said to have been a kind of gate between the mortal world and the Otherworld. Its Celtic name was Ynys Wittrin, "island of glass."

Glauce *n* (*Greek myth*) the daughter of Creon, king of Corinth, who was killed by a poisonous robe given to her by Jason's wife Medea, to prevent her marrying Jason.

glaucoma *n* a disease of the eye caused by pressure.—**glaucomatous** *adj*.

glaucous *adj* sea-green; covered with bloom of a bluish-white color, green with a bluish-grey tinge.

Glaucus *n* (*Greek myth*) a son of Minos and Pasiphaè, who as a child drowned in a large jar of honey, and was revived by a seer.

glaze *vt* to provide (windows etc) with glass; to give a hard glossy finish to (pottery, etc); to cover (foods, etc) with a glossy surface. * *vi* to become glassy or glossy. * *n* a glassy finish or coating.—**glazer** *n*.

glazier *n* a person who fits glass in windows.—**glaziery** *n*.

glazing *n* a glaze; the operation of setting glass or applying a glaze; windowpanes; glass; semi-transparent colors passed thinly over other colors to tone down their effect.

Glazunov *n* **Alexander Konstantinovich** (1865–1936) a Russian composer who wrote eight symphonies and seven quartets, and whose other works include the ballet *Raymonda.*

GLB *abbr* = Girls' Life Brigade.

GLC *abbr* (*Brit*) Greater London Council; gas-liquid chromatography.

GLCM *abbr* = (*Brit*) Graduate Diploma of the London College of Music; ground-launched cruise missile.

gld. *abbr* = guilder.

G

gleam *n* a subdued or moderate beam of light; a brief show of some quality or emotion, esp hope. * *vi* to emit or reflect a beam of light.—**gleamingly** *adv*.

glean *vti* to collect (grain left by reapers); to gather (facts, etc) gradually.—**gleanable** *adj*.—**gleaner** *n*.

gleaning *n* the act of collecting after reapers; (*often pl*) that which is collected laboriously from various sources.

glee *n* joy and gaiety; delight; (*mus*) a song in parts for three or more male voices.—**gleeful** *adj*.—**gleefully** *adv*.—**gleefulness** *n*.

glee club *n* a chorus organized for singing choral music; originated in meetings held at the house of Robert Smith, London, England in 1783, at which songs were sung after dinner; was organized at the Newcastle Coffee House, 1787, and gave entertainments in which the best English musicians participated until its dissolution in 1857.

gleeful *adj* merry, joyous; triumphant.—**gleefully** *adv*.—**gleefulness** *n*.

gleet *n* a thin mucous discharge, esp from the urethra, resulting from gonorrheal disease.

glen *n* a narrow valley.

glengarry *n* (*pl* **glengarries**) (*often cap*) a boat-shaped cap originating in Scotland.

Glenn *n* **John Herschel** (1921–) American astronaut and the first American to orbit the earth (1962).

gley soil *n* a mottled, blue-grey clay soil formed when the soil becomes waterlogged, and iron is changed to its ferrous form, giving the characteristic blue-grey color.

glia, neuroglia, glial cells *npl* connective tissue in the central nervous system composed of a variety of cells.

GLIAS *abbr* (*Brit*) = Greater London Industrial Archeological Society.

glib *adj* (**glibber, glibbest**) speaking or spoken smoothly, to the point of insincerity; lacking depth and substance.—**glibly** *adv*.—**glibness** *n*.

glide *vti* to move smoothly and effortlessly; to descend in an aircraft or glider with little or no engine power. * *n* a gliding movement.—**glidingly** *adv*.

glider *n* an engineless aircraft carried along by air currents.

gliding *n* the sport of flying gliders.

Glière *n* **Reinhold Moritzovich** (1875–1956) Russian composer of Belgian descent. His most important works include the opera *Shah Senem* and the ballet *Red Poppy*.

Glifieu *n* (*Irish Celtic myth*) one of the seven survivors of the expedition that was mounted by Bendigeid Vran, or Bran the Blessed, to go to Ireland and retrieve Branwen, who was being ill-treated by her husband, Matholwch.

glim *n* (*sl*) a light, a candle.

glimmer *vi* to give a faint, flickering light; to appear faintly. * *n* a faint gleam; a glimpse, an inkling.

glimmering *n* a faint gleam; a glimpse, an inkling.

glimpse *n* a brief, momentary view. * *vt* to catch a glimpse of.—**glimpser** *n*.

Glinka *n* **Mikhail Ivanovich** (1804–57) Russian composer, influenced by folk-music. His best known works are his operas *A Life for the Tsar* (*Ivan Sussanin*) and *Russlan and Ludmilla*.

glint *n* a brief flash of light; a brief indication. * *vti* to (cause to) gleam brightly.

glioma *n* (*pl* **gliomata, gliomas**) a tumor of rapid growth on the brain, spinal cord, or auditory nerve.

glissade *vi* to slide down a snow-covered slope without the aid of skis. * *n* a sliding ballet step.—**glissader** *n*.

glissando *n* (*pl* **glissandi, glissandos**) (*mus*) (*Italian*) a run by sliding the fingers over the keys of a piano; a quick slur on a violin.

glisten *vi* to shine, as light reflected from a wet surface.—**glisteningly** *adv*.

glister *vi* (*poet*) to sparkle, to glitter.—*also n*.

glitch *n* a malfunction in a, usu electronic, system.

glitter *vi* to sparkle; (*usu with* **with**) to be brilliantly attractive. * *n* a sparkle; showiness, glamor; tiny pieces of sparkling material used for decoration.—**glittering** *adj*.—**glittery** *adj*.

glitz *n* (*sl*) gaudiness; ostentatious glamor.—**glitzy** *adj* (**glitzier, glitziest**)

gloaming *n* twilight.

gloat *vi* to gaze or contemplate with wicked or malicious satisfaction.—**gloater** *n*.—**gloatingly** *adv*.

global[1] *adj* worldwide; comprehensive.—**globally** *adv*.

global[2] *n* (*comput*) a style or format that is applied throughout a document or program.

globalization *or* **internationalization** *n* the investment in financial markets on an international basis.

global warming *n* the process caused by a blanket of "greenhouse gases" building up around the earth trapping heat from the sun. Carbon dioxide, released by burning fossil fuels is one of the main causes.—*see* **greenhouse effect**.

globate, globated *adj* globe-shaped.

globe *n* anything spherical or almost spherical; the earth, or a model of the earth.

Globecom *abbr* = Global Communications System.

globeflower *n* a plant with round yellow flowers.

globetrotter *n* a person who travels widely.—**globetrotting** *n*, *adj*.

globin *n* a constituent of red blood corpuscles.

globoid *adj* nearly globular. * *n* a globoid figure.

globose, globous *adj* globe-like, spherical.

globosity, globoseness *n*

globular *adj* spherical.

globular cluster *n* (*astron*) a spherical arrangement of stars, closely packed together, and containing up to many millions of stars.

globule *n* a small spherical particle; a drop, pellet; a blood corpuscle; (*astron*) a nebula made up of opaque dust and gas, an early stage of star formation.

globulin *n* an albuminous protein forming one of the constituents of blood, muscle, and the cellular tissue of plants.

glockenspiel *n* (*mus*) (*German*) an orchestral percussion instrument with tuned metal bars, played with hammers.

glomerate *adj* gathered into a roundish head or mass; compactly clustered.

glomerule *n* a clustered flowerhead.

glomerulus *n* a knot of capillaries within the kidney.

gloom *n* near darkness; deep sadness. * *vti* to look sullen or dejected; to make or become cloudy or murky.

gloomy *adj* (**gloomier, gloomiest**) almost dark, obscure; depressed, dejected.—**gloomily** *adv*.—**gloominess** *n*.

gloria *n* a halo or aureole; a light fabric of silk, etc; (*with cap*) a prayer of praise, esp the *Gloria in excelsis* and *Gloria patri*; a musical setting of these.

glorify *vt* (**glorifying, glorified**) to worship; to praise, to honor; to cause to appear more worthy, important, or splendid than in reality.—**glorifiable** *adj*.—**glorification** *n*. —**glorifier** *n*.

glorious *adj* having or deserving glory; conferring glory or renown; beautiful; delightful.—**gloriously** *adv*.—**gloriousness** *n*.

glory *n* (*pl* **glories**) great honor or fame, or its source; adoration; great splendor or beauty; heavenly bliss. * *vi* (**glorying, gloried**) (*with in*) to exult, rejoice proudly.

gloss[1] *n* the luster of a polished surface; a superficially attractive appearance. * *vt* to give a shiny surface to; (*with over*) to hide (an error, etc) or make seem right or inconsequential.—**glosser** *n*.

gloss[2] *n* an explanation of an unusual word (in the margin or between the lines of a text); a misleading explanation; a glossary. * *vt* to provide with glosses; to give a misleading sense of.—**glosser** *n*.

gloss. *abbr* = glossary.

glossa *n* (*pl* **glossae, glossas**) the tongue, esp of insects.—**glossal** *adj*.

glossary[1] *n* (*pl* **glossaries**) a list of specialized or technical words and their definitions;—**glossarial** *adj*.—**glossarist** *n*.

glossary[2] *n* (*comput*) in word processing documents a glossary can be used to store phrases or styles that are commonly used.

glossitis *n* inflammation of the tongue.

glossography *n* the making of glossaries or glosses.—**glossographer** *n*.

glossolalia *see* **gift of tongues**.

glossy *adj* (**glossier, glossiest**) having a shiny or highly polished surface; superficial; (*magazines*) lavishly produced. * *n* (*pl* **glossies**) a magazine with many color pictures, printed on coated paper, esp a fashion magazine.—**glossily** *adv*.—**glossiness** *n*.

glottal *adj* of, pertaining to, or produced by the glottis.

glottis[1] *n* (**glottises, glottides**) the opening between the vocal cords in the larynx;—**glottidean** *adj*.

glottis[2] *n* (*mus*) reeds used in ancient woodwind instruments.

glove *n* a covering for the hand; a baseball player's mitt; a boxing glove. * *vt* to cover (as if) with a glove.

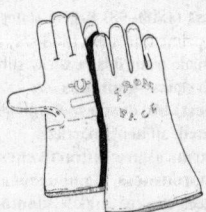

glover *n* a maker or seller of gloves.

Glover *n* **Jane** (1949–) British conductor and musicologist, appointed artistic director of the London Mozart Players (1984), conducted at Covent Garden (1988).

glow *vi* to shine (as if) with an intense heat; to emit a steady light without flames; to be full of life and enthusiasm; to flush or redden with emotion. * *n* a light emitted due to intense heat; a steady, even light without flames; a reddening of the complexion; warmth of emotion or feeling.

glower *vi* to scowl; to stare sullenly or angrily. * *n* a scowl, a glare.—**gloweringly** *adv*.

glow-worm *n* a beetle that emits light from the abdomen.

gloxinia *n* a tropical plant with showy bell-shaped flowers, cultivated as a houseplant.

glt. *abbr* = (*bookbinding*).gilt.

glucagon *n* a hormone important in maintaining the level of the body's blood sugar.

Gluck *n* **Christoph Willibald** (**von**) (1714–87) German composer of some 100 operas, best known for *Orfeo ed Euridice,* which revolutionized the Italian style of opera.

glucocorticosteroid *see* **corticosteroid**.

glucose *n* (*biochemistry*) a crystalline sugar occurring naturally in fruits, honey, etc.

glue *n* a sticky, viscous substance used as an adhesive. * *vt* (**gluing, glued**) to join with glue.—**gluer** *n*.

glue ear *or* **secretory otitis media** *n* a form of otitis, common in children, which occurs as an inflammation of the middle ear.

gluey *adj* (**gluier, glueist**) like glue, sticky.

glum *adj* (**glummer, glummest**) sullen; gloomy.—**glumly** *adv*.—**glumness** *n*.

glumaceous *adj* bearing or resembling glumes.

glume *n* the husk of corn or grasses.

glut *vt* (**glutting, glutted**) to over-supply (the market). * *n* a surfeit, an excess of supply.

gluteal *adj* pertaining to the buttocks.

gluten *n* a sticky elastic protein substance, esp of wheat flour, that gives cohesiveness to dough.—**glutenous** *adj*.

gluten enteropathy *see* **celiac disease**.

gluteus *n* (*pl* **glutei**) any of the three muscles that form the buttocks.

glutinous *adj* resembling glue, sticky.—**glutinousness, glutinosity** *n*.

glutton *n* a person who eats and drinks to excess; a person who has a tremendous capacity for something (e.g., for work); a wolverine.—**gluttonous** *adj*.

gluttony *n* the act or habit of eating and drinking to excess.

glyceride *n* an ester of glycerol.

glycerin, glycerine *n* the popular and commercial name for glycerol.

glycerol *n* (*biochemistry*) a colorless, syrupy liquid made from fats and oils, used in making skin lotions, explosives, etc.—**glyceric** *adj*.

glycogen *n* (*biochemistry*) a white insoluble starch-like substance obtained from the livers of animals and humans.—*also* **animal starch**.

glycol *n* a viscid liquid intermediate between glycerine and alcohol; antifreeze.

glycolysis *n* (*biochemistry*) a major metabolic process, occurring in the cytoplasm of virtually all living cells.

glycoprotein *see* **interferon**.

glycosuria *n* a disease marked by excess sugar in the urine.—**glycosuric** *adj*.

Glyndebourne *n* (*mus*) a small, but prestigious, English opera house established by John Christie (1882–1962) near Lewes. An annual opera festival has been held there since 1934.

glyph *n* a symbol (as on a road sign) that conveys information nonverbally; a hieroglyph; (*archit*) a perpendicular fluting.—**glyphic** *adj*.

glyptic *adj* pertaining to engraving on gems; figured. * *n* the art of engraving designs on precious stones, ivory, etc.

glyptography *n* the art of cutting designs or engraving on a gem.

gm *abbr* = gram(s).

g.m. *abbr* = general merchandise.

gm2 *abbr* = grams per square meter.

GM *abbr* = Geiger-Müller counter; George Medal; Grand Master; General Motors; general manager; guided missile.

GMA *abbr* = (*Brit*) Glasgow Mathematical Association; Gospel Music Association; Grocery Manufacturers of Australia.

GMAG *abbr* = Genetic Manipulation Advisory Group.

G-man *n* (*pl* **G-men**) (*inf*) an agent of the FBI.

gmb *abbr* = good merchantable brand.

GMB *abbr* = General, Municipal and Boilermakers Union; Grand Master of the Order of the Bath.

GMBE *abbr* = Grand Master of the Order of the British Empire.

GmbH *abbr* (*German*) = *Gesellschaft mit beschränkter Haftung*, "limited liability company."

GMC *abbr* = General Medical Council; General Management Committee.

GMFA *abbr* = Gay Men Fighting AIDS.

GMO *abbr* = genetically modified organism.

gmq *abbr* = good merchantable quality.

GMR *abbr* = ground-mapping radar.

GMS *abbr* = Grant-Maintained Status.

GMSC *abbr* = General Medical Services Committee.

GMST *abbr* = Grant-Maintained Schools Trust; Greenwich Mean Sidereal Time.

GMT *abbr* = Greenwich Mean Time.

GMusRNCM *abbr* = Graduate in Music of the Royal Northern College of Music (Hons).

g.m.v. *abbr* = gram-molecular volume.

GMW *abbr* = gram-molecular weight.

GMWU *abbr* = General and Municipal Workers Union.

gn. *abbr* = guinea; guineas.

gnarl *n* a knot on the trunk or branch of a tree.

gnarled *adj* (*tree trunks*) full of knots; (*hands*) rough, knobbly; crabby in disposition.

GNAS *abbr* = Grand National Archery Society.

gnash *vti* to grind (the teeth) in anger or pain. * *n* a grinding of the teeth.—**gnashingly** *adv*.

gnat *n* any of various small, two-winged insects that bite or sting.

gnathic, gnathial *adj* of or pertaining to jaws.

gnaw *vti* (**gnawing, gnawed**, *pp* **gnawed** *or* **gnawn**) to bite away bit by bit; to torment, as by constant pain.—**gnawable** *adj*.—**gnawer** *n*.

GNC *abbr* = General Nursing Council.

gneiss *n* (*geol*) a granite-like rock formed by layers of quartz, mica, etc.—**gneissic, gneissoid, gneissose** *adj*.

GNIS *abbr* = Geographic Names Information System.

GNMA *abbr* = Government National Mortgage Association.

gnocchi *npl* small dumplings made from flour, semolina, or potatoes.

gnome *n* (*folklore*) a dwarf who dwells in the earth and guards its treasure; a small statue of a gnome used as a garden decoration; a small and ugly person; (*sl*) an international banker or financier.—**gnomish** *adj*.

gnomic *adj* dealing in or containing pithy or sententious sayings; didactic.—**gnomically** *adv*.

gnomon *n* the indicator on a sundial that casts a shadow to indicate the time of day.—**gnomonic** *adj*.—**gnomonically** *adv*.

gnosis *n* (*pl* **gnoses**) higher knowledge, mysticism, or insight.

gnostic *adj* of, pertaining to, or having knowledge; (*with cap*) pertaining to the Gnostics or Gnosticism (—*also* **gnostical**). * *n* (*with cap*) a member of an early Christian sect seeking salvation by knowledge, not faith.

Gnosticism *n* the doctrine of the Gnostics.

GNP *abbr* = Gross National Product.

GNRS *abbr* = Great Northern Railway Society.

GNSM *abbr* = Graduate of the Northern School of Music.

GNTC *abbr* = Girls Nautical Training Corps.

gnu *n* (*pl* **gnus, gnu**) either of two large African antelopes with an ox-like head.—*also* **wildebeest**.

GNVQ *abbr* = General National Vocational Qualification.

go[1] *vb* (**going, went**, *pp* **gone**) *vi* to move on a course; to proceed; to work properly; to act, sound, as specified; to result; to become; to be accepted or valid; to leave, to depart; to die; to be allotted or sold; to be able to pass (through); to fit (into); to be capable of being divided (into); to belong; (*with about*) to handle (a task, etc) efficiently; to undertake (duties, etc); (*sailing*) to change tack; (*with into*) to enter; to become a member of; to examine or investigate; to discuss; (*with off*) to explode; to depart; (*food, etc*) to become stale or rotten; to fall asleep; to proceed, occur in a certain manner; to take place as planned; to stop liking (something or someone); (*with on*) to continue; to happen; to talk effusively; to nag; to enter on stage; (*with out*) to depart; (*light, fire, etc*) to become extinguished; to cease to be fashionable; to socialize; (*radio or TV show*) to be broadcast; to spend time with, esp a person of the opposite sex; (*with over*) to change one's loyalties (to); to be received or regarded in a certain way; to examine and repair (something); (*with round*) to circulate; to be sufficient for everyone; (*with slow*) to work at a slow rate as part of an industrial dispute; (*with through*) to continue to the end (with); to be approved; to use up completely; to experience (an illness, etc); to search thoroughly; (*with together*) to match, to be mutually suited; (*inf*) to associate frequently, esp as lovers; (*with up*) in the UK, to enter or return to college or university; (*with with*) to match; to accompany; to associate frequently, esp as lovers; (*with without*) to be deprived of or endure the lack of (something). * *vt* to travel along; (*inf*) to put up with. * *n* (*pl* **goes**) a success; (*inf*) a try; (*inf*) energy.

go[2] *n* a Japanese board game.

Go. *abbr* = Gothic.

g.o., GO *abbr* = Group Officer, general office; general order; (*army*) general orders; great or grand organ.

goa *n* an Asian gazelle, the male of which has horns that curve backwards.

goa *abbr* = gone on arrival.

goad *n* a sharp-pointed stick for driving cattle, etc; any stimulus to action. * *vt* to drive (as if) with a goad; to irritate, nag persistently.

go-ahead *n* (*inf*) permission to proceed. * *adj* (*inf*) enterprising, ambitious.

goal *n* the place at which a race, trip, etc is ended; an objective; the place over or into which the ball or puck must go to score in some games; the score made.

goalie *n* (*inf*) a goalkeeper.

goalkeeper *n* a player who defends the goal.—**goalkeeping** *n*.

"Go, Mississippi!" *n* the song of the American state, Mississippi.

goat *n* a mammal related to the sheep that has backward curving horns, a short tail, and usu straight hair; a lecherous man.

goatee *n* a small pointed beard.

goatherd *n* a person who looks after goats.

goatish *adj* pertaining to or like a goat; (*arch*) lustful; rank-smelling.—**goatishly** *adv.*—**goatishness** *n.*

goatsbeard, goat's-beard *n* a European grass-like plant with yellow flowers; an American plant with compound leaves and small white flowers.

goatskin *n* the skin of a goat; a bottle or garment made of this.

goatsucker *n* a nocturnal bird with dull mottled plumage.—*also* **nightjar**.

gob[1] *n* (*sl*) the mouth.

gob[2] *n* a lump or clot of something; (*inf*) spittle. * *vi* (**gobbing, gobbed**) (*inf*) to spit.

gob, g.o.b. *abbr* = good ordinary brand.

gobbet *n* a lump of something.

Gobbi *n* **Tito** (1915–84) Italian baritone who was one of the greatest singing actors of the 20th century, particularly impressive in Puccini's *Tosca* and Verdi's *Falstaff*.

gobble *vt* to eat greedily; (*often with* up) to take, accept, or read eagerly. * *vi* to make a throaty gurgling noise, as a male turkey.

gobbledygook, gobbledegook *n* (*sl*) nonsense, pretentious jargon.

gobbler *n* (*inf*) a turkey cock.

go-between *n* a messenger, an intermediary.

goblet *n* a large drinking vessel with a base and stem but without a handle.

goblin *n* an evil or mischievous elf.

goby *n* (*pl* **goby, gobies**) a sea fish with a large head and a long thin body.

GOC *abbr* = General Officer Commanding.

go-cart *n* a small cart for children to play in or pull; a stroller; a handcart.

GOC-in-C *abbr* = General Officer Commanding-in-Chief.

GOCO *abbr* = Government-owned, contractor-operated.

god *n* any of various beings conceived of as supernatural and immortal, esp a male deity; an idol; a person or thing deified; (*with cap*) in monotheistic religions, the creator and ruler of the universe.

GODA *abbr* = Guild of Drama Adjudicators.

Godard *n* **Jean-Luc** (1930–) F rench film director whose films include *Week-End* (1967).

godchild *n* (*pl* **godchildren**) the child a godparent sponsors.

goddaughter *n* a female godchild.

goddess *n* a female deity; a woman of superior charms or excellence.

Godefroy *n* **Maximilien** (1765–) F rench architect. His notable works include the Battle Monument, Baltimore.

Gödel *n* **Kurt** (1906–78) Austrian-born American logician and mathematician. "Gödel's theorem" shows the existence of undecidable elements in arithmetic systems.

godfather *n* a male godparent; the head of a Mafia crime family or other criminal organization.

god-fearing *adj* religious.

godforsaken *adj* desolate, wretched.

Godfred *n* (Crovan) (*d.* 1095) king of the Isle of Man (1079–1095). He founded a dynasty of Norse kings which ruled Orkney until 1265.

godhead *n* the divine nature, deity; God.

godhood *n* the quality or condition of being a god; divinity.

godless *adj* irreligious; wicked.—**godlessly** *adv.*—**godlessness** *n.*

godlike *adj* like a god, divine.

godly *adj* (**godlier, godliest**) religious; holy; devout; devoted to God.—**godliness** *n.*

godmother *n* a female godparent.

godown *n* in India and China, a warehouse or storeroom.

godparent *n* a person who sponsors a child, as at baptism or confirmation, taking responsibility for its faith.

God Save the Queen/King *n* (*mus*) the British national anthem; the authorship of both the tune and the words remains obscure.

godsend *n* anything that comes unexpectedly and when needed or desired.

godson *n* a male godchild.

Godspeed *n* success, good luck.

Godthåb (Nuuk) *n* capital city of Greenland.

Godwin *n* **Edward William** (1833–86) British architect who designed town halls and other buildings in a Gothic revival style.

godwit *n* any of a genus of wading birds with a long bill, related to the snipes but resembling curlews.

GOE *abbr* = General Ordination Examination.

Goebbels *n* **[Paul] Joseph** (1897–1945) German Nazi politician. He joined the Nazi Party in 1924, becoming head of its propaganda section in 1929 and was minister of enlightenment and propaganda (1933–45).

goer *n* a regular attender; something, as a car, that goes fast; an enthusiastic person.

Goes *n* **Hugo van der** (*d.* 1482) Flemish painter from Ghent. Important works include *The Adoration of the Magi* (1470) and *The Death of the Virgin* (1480).

Goethe *n* **Johann Wolfgang von** (1749–1832) German poet, dramatist, novelist, thinker, and statesman whose masterpiece is *Faust*.

GOETO *abbr* = Grand Order of European Tour Operators.

Goewin *n* (*Welsh Celtic myth*) the beautiful daughter of Pebin. Her beauty excited the admiration and love of Gilfaethwy.

Gofannon *n* (*Welsh Celtic myth*) a divine smith and the Welsh equivalent of the Irish Goibhniu. He is said to have struck the blow that killed his nephew Dylan Eil Ton, the son of Aranrhod.

gofer *n* (*inf*) a person who runs errands, as in an office.

Goff *n* **Bruce A** (1904–82) American architect. His notable works include Ford House, Aurora, Illinois.

goffer *vt* to make wavy or frilly with a hot iron, to crimp.—*also* **gauffer**.

GOFTA *abbr* = Golf Facilities Trades Association.

Gog and Magog *n* (*Bible*) "Gog of the land of Magog" is used by Ezekial to represent a symbolic enemy of Israel, and also "the nations which are at the four corners of the earth" whom Satan deceives and leads to battle.

Gogarty *n* **Oliver St John** (1878–1957) Irish poet and novelist remembered principally for being the model for the rumbustious Buck Mulligan in James Joyce's *Ulysses*, and for *As I was Going Down Sackville Street*, a memoir of Dublin's literary world.

go-getter *n* (*inf*) an ambitious person.

goggle *vi* to stare with bulging eyes. * *npl* large spectacles, sometimes fitting snugly against the face, to protect the eyes.

goggle-eyed *adj* with wide staring eyes.

Gogh *n* **Vincent Van** (1853–90) Dutch painter whose style was influenced by Degas and Gauguin.

go-go dancer *n* a scantily-clad dancer employed in a disco or nightclub.

Gogol *n* **Nikolai Vasilievich** (1809–52) Russian short-story writer, dramatist, and novelist whose work includes the novel *Dead Souls* (1854).

Goibhniu *n* (*Irish Celtic myth*) a smith god. He was a member of a triad of craft gods who were associated with the Tuatha De Danann, the other two being Creidhne and Luchta.

going *n* an act or instance of going, a departure; the state of the ground, e.g. for walking, horse-racing; rate of progress. * *adj* that goes; commonly accepted; thriving; existing.

going-over *n* (*pl* **goings-over**) (*inf*) a thorough inspection; (*sl*) a beating.

goings-on *npl* events or actions, esp when disapproved of.

goiter, goitre *n* an abnormal enlargement of the thyroid gland.—**goitrous** *adj*.

gold *n* a malleable yellow metallic element used esp for coins and jewelry; a precious metal; money, wealth; a yellow color. * *adj* of, or like, gold.

goldbeater's skin *n* a membrane prepared from the large intestine of an ox used to separate layers of gold in goldbeating.

goldbeating *n* the process of beating gold until it is very thin.—**goldbeater** *n*.

Goldberg *n* **Whoopi [Caryn Johnston]** (1949–) American actress whose films include *The Color Purple* (1985).

goldbrick *n* a brick that looks like gold but is worthless; something that gives a false appearance of value; a person (e.g., soldier) who shirks duty.—*also* **goldbricker**. * *vt* to cheat, swindle. * *vi* to avoid duty or responsibility.

gold card *n* a credit card that entitles the cardholder to extra benefits.

gold-digger *n* a person who mines gold; (*inf*) a woman who uses feminine charms to extract money or gifts from men.—**gold-digging** *adj*.

golden *adj* made of or relating to gold; bright yellow; priceless; flourishing.—**goldenly** *adv.*—**goldenness** *n*.

golden age *n* the fabled early age of innocence and perfect human happiness; the flowering of a nation's civilization or art.

golden calf *n* (*Bible*) a golden calf made by Aaron and worshipped by the Israelites; wealth worshipped as a god.

golden eagle *n* a large eagle of the Northern hemisphere.

golden fleece *n* (*Greek myth*) the ram's fleece in search of which Jason sailed with the Argonauts; an order of knighthood in Austria and Spain.

golden handcuffs *npl* financial incentives to induce an employee to remain in a particular job for an agreed period.

golden handshake *n* (*inf*) financial compensation awarded an employee for loss of employment.

golden hello *n* a payment made as an inducement to a person to take up an employment offer with a company.

Golden Horus Name *n* (*Egypt*) one of the five names making up ancient Egyptian royal titles, from the Twelfth Dynasty onwards. It characterized the king's personal qualities, as with Rameses II, "rich in years, great in victories."

golden mean *n* neither too much nor too little; moderation.

golden parachute *n* a clause in the employment contract of a director or senior executive of a company that provides for generous severance payments.

goldenrod *n* a tall plant of the aster family with yellow flowers.

golden rule *n* a guiding principle.

golden section *or* **golden mean** *n* (*art*) a proportion that has been observable since ancient times in most works of art in which the two divisions of a straight line are such that the smaller is to the larger as the larger is to the whole, a ratio of roughly 8:13. The same proportion applies to the two dimensions of a plane figure.

goldfield *n* a district containing gold deposits and diggings.

gold-filled *adj* coated with gold.

goldfinch *n* a common European finch with yellow and black wings.

Goldfinger *n* **Erno** (1902–87) Hungarian architect and designer who produced the first version of the *Safari* chair.

goldfish *n* (*pl* **goldfish, goldfishes**) a small gold-colored fish of the carp family, kept in ponds and aquariums.

goldilocks *n* any of various plants with yellow flowers, e.g. the buttercup; (*with cap*) a name for someone, usu female, with golden hair.

Golding *n* **Sir William [Gerald]** (1911–93) English novelist whose first novel was *The Lord of the Flies* (1954); winner of the 1983 Nobel prize for literature.

gold leaf *n* gold beaten into very thin sheets, used for gilding.

Goldman *n* 1. **Emma** (1869–1940) Russian-born American anarchist. She was imprisoned several times for agitating against employers and for advocating such measures as resistance to the draft. She was deported to the USSR in 1919 and returned in 1924. 2. **Jonathan** (1959–) American artist and per former.

gold mine *n* a mine where gold is extracted; (*inf*) a source of wealth.

Goldoni *n* **Carlo** (1707–93) Italian dramatist who wrote over 250 plays and some operas. About 150 of his plays are comedies, set in his native Venice and seen as adapting the form of *commedia dell'arte* to a more realistic approach.

gold plate *n* vessels of gold; a thin covering of gold.—**gold-plated** *adj*.

gold rush *n* a rush to a new gold field, as to the Yukon in 1897.

gold salts *or* **gold compound** *n* chemicals containing gold that are used in minute quantities to treat rheumatoid arthritis.

Goldschmidt *n* 1. **Richard Benedikt** (1878–1958) German-born American geneticist, noted for his theory that the pattern and chemical composition of the chromosome molecule determines heredity, rather than the qualities of the individual genes. 2. **Victor Moritz** (1888–1947) Swiss-born Norwegian geneticist. He drew on advances in geology, chemistry and mineralogy to create the modern discipline of geochemistry.

goldsmith *n* a worker in gold; a dealer in gold plate.

Goldsmith *n* **Oliver** (1728–74) Irish poet and essayist whose work includes the novel *The Vicar of Wakefield* (1766).

Goldsmiths' and Silversmiths' Company *n* British silversmiths, founded in London in 1898.

gold standard *n* a monetary standard in which the basic currency unit equals a specified quantity of gold.

Goldwyn *n* **Samuel [Samuel Goldfish]** (1882–1974) Polish-born American film producer who formed Metro-Goldwyn-Mayer with Louis B Mayer in 1924.

Goleuddydd *n* (*Welsh Celtic myth*) the wife of Cilydd and mother of Culhwch. While she was pregnant with him, she became mad and wandered aimlessly around the countryside.

golf *n* an outdoor game in which the player attempts to hit a small ball with clubs around a turfed course into a succession of holes in the smallest number of strokes.—**golfer** *n*.

golf ball *n* a hard dimpled ball used in golf; the spherical printing head in some typewriters.

golf club *n* a club with a wooden or metal head used in golf; a golf association or its premises.

golf course *or* **golf links** *n* a tract of land laid out for playing golf.

Golgi apparatus *n* (*biol*) a system of organelles within the cells of organisms, where enzymes and hormones are stored and moved.

Golgotha *n* (*Bible*) Aramaic name for the place where Jesus was crucified, meaning "skull"; the Latin name Calvaria has the same meaning.

Goliath *n* (*Bible*) Philistine giant whom David slew with a stone from his sling

Goll *n* (*Irish Celtic myth*) the son of the king of Magh Mell and the nephew of Fiachna. Goll abducted the wife of Fiachna and would not release her until Fiachna engaged the assistance of Laoghaire mac Crimthann.

Gollancz *n* **Sir Victor** (1893–1967) English publisher and philanthropist. He became a successful publisher in the 1930s, notably of crime fiction. A noted humanitarian, he campaigned for Jewish refugees before the war, and organized aid to Germany after it.

golliard *n* a medieval wandering jester or scholar.

golliwog, golliwogg *n* a cloth doll with a black face.

Goll mac Morna *n* (*Irish Celtic myth*) the leader of the Fianna before Fionn mac Cumhaill.

golly[1] *n* (*inf*) a golliwog.

golly[2] *interj* expressing surprise.

GOM *abbr* = Grand Old Man.

Gomorrah *see* **Sodom**.

gonad *n* a primary sex gland that produces reproductive cells, such as an ovary or testis.—**gonadal, gonadic** *adj*.

gonadotrophin, gonadotrophic hormone *n* hormones secreted by the anterior pituitary gland.

Gonaïves *n* a city in Haiti.

Gonder *n* a city in Ethiopia.

gondola *n* a long, narrow, black boat used on the canals of Venice; a cabin suspended under an airship or balloon; an enclosed car suspended from a cable used to transport passengers, esp skiers up a mountain; a display structure in a supermarket, etc.

gondolier *n* a person who propels a gondola with a pole.

Gondovin *n* **Jacques** (1737–) F rench architect. His notable works include the École de Chirurgie, Paris.

Gondwanaland *n* the hypothetical massive continent in the southern hemisphere that gave rise to parts of present day Africa, South America, India, Australia, New Zealand, and Antarctica.

gone[1] *see* **go**[1].

gone[2] *adj* departed; dead; lost; (*inf*) in an excited state; (*inf*) pregnant for a specified period.

goner *n* (*sl*) a person or thing that is ruined, dead, or about to die.

gonfalon *n* a banner, usu with streamers, hung from a crossbar, used in ecclesiastical processions; a military flag or standard with a pointed edge.

gong *n* (*mus*) a disk-shaped percussion instrument struck with a usu padded hammer; (*sl*) a medal. * *vi* to sound a gong.

Gongorism *n* (a passage of) a florid pedantic Spanish literary style resembling euphuism.

goniometer *n* an instrument for measuring solid angles; an instrument used to determine the location of a distant radio station.—**goniometry** *n*.

gonorrhea, gonorrhoea *n* a venereal disease causing a discharge of mucous and pus from the genitals.—**gonorrheal, gonorrhoeal, gonorrheic, gonorrhoeic** *adj*.

goo *n* (*sl*) sticky matter; sickly sentimentality.

goober *n* a peanut.

good *adj* (**better, best**) having the right or proper qualities; beneficial; valid; healthy or sound; virtuous, honorable; enjoyable, pleasant, etc; skilled; considerable. * *n* something good; benefit; something that has economic utility; (*with* the) good persons; (*pl*) personal property; commodities; (*pl*) the desired or required articles. * *adv* (*inf*) well; fully.—**goodish** *adj*.

goodbye *interj* a concluding remark at parting; farewell.—*also n*.

Gooden *n* **Robert Yorke** (1909–96) British architect who also designed hangings in Westminster Abbey for the coronation of Elizabeth II.

good faith *n* honesty of intention.

good-for-nothing *adj* useless, worthless. * a worthless person.

Good Friday *n* the Friday before Easter, commemorating the Crucifixion of Christ.

Goodhue *n* **Bertram G** (1869–1924) American architect. His notable works include Nebraska State Capitol, Lincoln.

good-humored *adj* genial, cheerful.—**good-humoredly** *adv*.—**good-humoredness** *n*.

good-looking *adj* handsome.

goodly *adj* (**goodlier, goodliest**) considerable; ample.—**goodliness** *n*.

goodman *n* (*pl* **goodmen**) (*formerly*) the master of a house, a husband; a man not born into the aristocracy.

Goodman *n* **Benny [Benjamin David]** (1909–86) American jazz clarinet player and bandleader.

good-natured *adj* amiable, easy-going.—**good-naturedly** *adv*.—**good-naturedness** *n*.

goodness *n* the state of being good; the good element in something; kindness; virtue. * *interj* an exclamation of surprise.

goods *npl* personal property; commodities; (*sl*) the desired or required articles; freight.

Good Samaritan *n* a person who helps those in distress (after the compassionate figure mentioned in the Bible.—Luke 10:33).

good turn *n* a favor; an act of kindness.

good-tempered *adj* having a pleasant and kindly nature.

goodwill *n* benevolence; willingness; the established custom and reputation of a business.

goodwoman *n* (*pl* **goodwomen**) (*formerly*) the mistress of a house, a wife; a woman not born into the aristocracy.

goody *n* (*pl* **goodies**) something pleasant or sweet; a goody-goody. * *interj* an expression (usu used by a child) signifying pleasure.

Goodyear *n* **Charles** (1800–60) American inventor of vulcanized rubber.

goody-goody *adj* insufferably virtuous. * *n* (*pl* **goody-goodies**) a goody-goody person.

gooey *adj* (**gooier, gooiest**) (*inf*) soft and sticky; sweet; sentimental.

goof *n* (*sl*) a stupid person; a blunder. * *vi* (*sl*) to bungle.

goofy *adj* (**goofier, goofiest**) (*sl*) silly, stupid.—**goofily** *adv*.—**goofiness** *n*.

googol *n* (*math*) the figure 1 followed by 100 zeroes (10^{100}).

G

googolplex *n* (*math*) the figure 1 followed by a googol of zeroes (10^{googol} or 10 100 100).

goon *n* (*sl*) a thug; a stupid person.

GOONS *abbr* = Guild of One-Name Studies.

goop *n* (*sl*) any sticky, semi-liquid substance; (*sl*) a rude person.

goosander *n* a web-footed migratory waterfowl.

goose[1] *n* (*pl* **geese**) a large, long-necked, web-footed bird related to swans and ducks; its flesh as food; a female goose as distinguished from a gander; (*inf*) a foolish person.

goose[2] *vt* (*sl*) to poke (a person) between the buttocks.

gooseberry *n* (*pl* **gooseberries**) the acid berry of a shrub related to the currant and used esp in jams and pies.

goose bumps, goose pimples, goose flesh *n* a roughening of the skin caused usu by cold or fear.

goose egg *n* (*sl*) a zero score in a game.

goosegrass *n* a species of creeping plant on which geese feed.

gooseneck *n* (*naut*) a bent iron fitted to the extremity of a boom or yard.

goose-step *vi* (**goose-stepping, goose-stepped**) to march in a stiff-legged manner using the goose step.

Goossens *n* 1. **Eugene** (1893–1962) English conductor and composer; his works include the operas *Judith* and *Don Juan de Manara*, as well as two symphonies and various pieces of incidental and chamber music. 2. **Robert** (1927–) French jewelry designer who produced his hallmark barrettes and earrings for Chanel, also working with Balenciaga and Yves Saint-Laurent.

GOP *abbr* = Grand Old Party, a rhetorical name for the Republican party.

Gopaleen *n* **Myles na** the pen name of the Irish journalist Flann O'Brien.

gopher *n* a North American burrowing, rat-like rodent; a ground squirrel; a burrowing tortoise; (*comput*) an early feature of the Internet; a means of searching for files using a particular set of menus.

gopherwood *n* the wood Noah's Ark is reputed to have been made from, possibly cypress; the yellowwood.

gopik *see* **manat**.

Gorbachev *n* **Mikhail Sergeevich** (1931–) Soviet Communist statesman who became general secretary of the Soviet Communist party in 1985, head of state in 1988 and "executive president" in 1990. He resigned following the break-up of the USSR in December 1991.

Gorboduc *n* (*Brit Celtic myth*) king of Britain who was supposed to be a descendant of Brutus. He was the husband of Judon and the father of Porrex and Ferrex.

Gordius *n* (*Greek myth*) a king who tied a knot so skillfully that an oracle declared that whoever should untie it would be ruler of all Asia. Alexander the Great cut the knot in two with his sword and applied the prophecy to himself; **to cut the Gordian knot** to solve a problem or end a difficulty in a vigorous or drastic way.

gore[1] *n* (clotted) blood from a wound.

gore[2] *n* a tapering section of material used to shape a garment, sail, etc.

gore[3] *vt* to pierce or wound as with a tusk or horns.

Gore *n* **Al[bert]** (1948–) American politician who became vice-president of the US under Clinton in 1992. He campaigned unsuccessfully for the presidency in 2000–01 against George W Bush.

gorge *n* a ravine. * *vt* to swallow greedily; to glut. * *vi* to feed gluttonously.—**gorgeable** *adj*.—**gorger** *n*.

gorgeous *adj* strikingly attractive; brilliantly colored; (*inf*) magnificent.—**gorgeously** *adv*.—**gorgeousness** *n*.

gorgheggi *n* (*mus*) (*Italian*) trills, quiverings.

Gorgon *n* (*Greek myth*) one of three female monsters with live snakes for hair whose looks turned the beholder to stone; (*without cap*) any ugly or formidable woman.

gorgonian *n* any of a genus of flexible branching coral.

Gorgonzola *n* a semi-hard blue-veined cheese with a rich flavor, originating in Italy.

Gorias *n* (*Irish Celtic myth*) Gorias was one of the four great cities of the Tuatha De Danann, the others being Falias, Finias and Murias. Lugh brought his invincible sword from Gorias.

gorilla *n* an anthropoid ape of western equatorial Africa related to the chimpanzee but much larger.

Göring, Goering *n* **Hermann [Wilhelm]** (1893–1946) German Nazi politician and military leader. He served Hitler as air minister (1933–45), organizing the rebuilding of the Luftwaffe.

Gorky *n* **Arshile [Vosdanig Manoog Adoian]** (1905–48) Armenian-born American painter.

Gorky, Gorki *n* **Maxim [Aleksey Maximovich Peshkov]** (1868–1936) Russian novelist, dramatist, and short-story writer whose works deal with the plight of the poor and society's outcasts in Czarist Russia and whose best-known works are *The Mother*, the autobiographical trilogy *Childhood*, *Among People*, and *My Universities*, and his great play, *The Lower Depths*.

gormand *see* **gourmand**.

gormandize *vti* to eat like a glutton.—**gormandizer** *n*.

gorse *n* a spiny yellow-flowered European shrub.

Gorton, Sir John Grey (1911–) Australian Liberal statesman. He was Liberal prime minister (1968–71), and resigned in 1971 following his defeat on a vote of confidence.

gory *adj* (**gorier, goriest**) bloodthirsty; causing bloodshed; covered in blood.—**gorily** *adv*.—**goriness** *n*.

gosba *n* (*mus*) an Arabian flute.

gosh *interj* an exclamation of surprise.

goshawk *n* any of several long-tailed hawks with short rounded wings.

Goshen *n* (*Bible*) area of Egypt where the shepherd clan of Jacob settled in the time of Joseph.

gosling *n* a young goose.

go-slow *n* a deliberate slowing of the work rate by employees as a form of industrial action.

gospel *n* the life and teachings of Christ contained in the first four books of the New Testament; (*with cap*) one of these four books; anything proclaimed or accepted as the absolute truth.

gospeller, gospeler *n* the reader of the gospel in a communion service; an evangelist.

gospel song *n* (*mus*) a type of popular religious song originated by African American slaves who sang hymns to pulsating blues rhythms. Such songs, which are still sung fervently today in religious services, were one of the originating forces of jazz.

Gossaert *n* **Jan [Jean de Mabuse]** (*c*.1478–1533) Flemish painter whose work is a curious yet dignified mixture of Flemish portraits and figures in classical poses, as in *St Luke* (1515) and *Danaë* (1527).

gossamer *n* very fine cobwebs; any very light and flimsy material. * *adj* light as gossamer.

gossip *n* one who chatters idly about others; such talk. * *vi* to take part in or spread gossip.—**gossiper** *n*. —**gossipingly** *adv*.—**gossipy** *adj*.

gossip column *n* a section of a newspaper or magazine devoted to gossip about celebrities.

gossipmonger *n* a gossip.

got *see* **get**.

Göteborg *n* a city in Sweden.

Goth *n* any member of a Germanic people that conquered most of the Roman Empire in the 3rd, 4th, and 5th centuries.

goth., Goth *abbr* = Gothic.

Gothic *adj* of a style of architecture with pointed arches, steep roofs, elaborate stonework, etc. * *n* German black letter type; a bold type style without serifs.—**Gothically** *adv*.

Gothic novel *n* a type of novel that was enormously popular in the late 18th century, combining elements of the supernatural, macabre, or fantastic, and often set in ruined abbeys or ancient castles.

goto *n* (*comput*) a programming phrase that directs the program logic to a part of the program in order to accomplish a specific function.

gotten *see* **get**.

Götterdämmerung *see* **Ring des Nibelungen, Der**.

Gottschalk *n* **Louis Moreau** (1829–69) American composer and pianist whose works include such memorable pieces as *The Aeolian Harp* and *The Dying Poet* for piano.

gouache *n* a method of painting with opaque watercolors —*also* **poster paint; body paint**.

Gouda *n* a type of large flat round Dutch cheese.

gouge *n* a chisel with a concave blade used for cutting grooves. * *vt* to scoop or force out (as if) with a gouge.

gouger *n* one who or that which gouges; a swindler.

Gough *n* **Piers** (1946–) British architect who designed the 1987 bent-and-folded-metal chaise longue for Aram Designs.

goujons *npl* narrow fried strips of fish or chicken in breadcrumbs.

goulash *n* a rich stew made with beef or veal seasoned with paprika.

Gould *n* 1. **Chester** (1900–85) American cartoonist, famous as the creator of Dick Tracy, the detective. 2. **Glenn** (1932–82) Canadian pianist with an international reputation and very broad repertoire, noted in particular for his interpretation on the piano of works by Bach. 3. **Morton** (1913–) American composer, conductor, and pianist, who composed a concerto for tap dancer and orchestra. He also wrote three symphonies, a ballet, *Fall River Legend*, and several musicals.

Gould's Belt *or* **the Local System** *n* (*astron*) an assemblage of young, hot, blue population I stars in the Milky Way.

Gounod *n* **Charles François** (1818–93) a French composer whose original ambition was to become a priest. He lived in England for a period and is best known for his opera *Faust*, although he wrote many other pieces, including cantatas, oratorios and symphonies.

gourami *n* (*pl* **gourami, gouramis**) an oriental fish cultivated for food.

gourd *n* any trailing or climbing plant of a family that includes the squash, melon, pumpkin, etc; the fruit of one species or its dried, hollowed-out shell, used as a cup, bowl, etc or ornament.

gourde *n* the standard monetary unit of Haiti.

gourmand *n* a person who likes good food and drink, often to excess.—*also* **gormand**.—**gourmandism** *n*.

gourmandise, gormandise *n* the (sometimes excessive) love of good food.

gourmet *n* a person who likes and is an excellent judge of fine food and drink.

gout *n* a disease causing painful inflammation of the joints; esp of the great toe.—**gouty** *adj.*—**goutiness** *n*.

gov., Gov. *abbr* = government; governor.

govern *vti* to exercise authority over; to rule, to control; to influence the action of; to determine.—**governable** *adj.*—**governability, governableness** *n*.

governance *n* the action, function, or power of government.

governess *n* a woman employed in a private home to teach and train the children.

government *n* the exercise of authority over a state, organization, etc; a system of ruling, political administration, etc; those who direct the affairs of a state, etc.—**governmental** *adj*.

governor *n* a person appointed to govern a province, etc; the elected head of any state of the US; the director or head of a governing body of an organization or institution; (*sl*) an employer; a mechanical device for automatically controlling the speed of an engine.—**governorship** *n*.

governor-general *n* (*pl* **governors-general, governor-generals**) a governor in charge of subgovernors; (*with caps*) the official representative of the British crown in a Commonwealth country.

Gov-Gen. *abbr* (*Brit*) = Governor-General.

govt, Govt *abbr* = government.

gowan *n* (*Scot*) the daisy.

gown *n* a loose outer garment, specifically a woman's formal dress, a nightgown, a long, flowing robe worn by clergymen, judges, university teachers, etc; a type of overall worn in the operating room. * *vt* to dress in a gown, to supply with a gown.

goy *n* (*pl* **goyim, goys**) (*sl*) Jewish for Gentile.

Goya y Lucientes *n* **Francisco de** (1746–1828) Spanish painter and printmaker with a strong, free-flowing technique and powerful pictorial style. Important later works include the etchings *Los Caprichos* (1799) and *Disasters of War* (1810–20).

GP *abbr* = Gallup Poll; (*Latin*) *Gloria Patri*, "Glory to the Father"; Government Property; Grand Prix; graduated pension; gross profit; (*med*) general paresis; general practitioner.

G.P. *abbr* (*mus*) = General Pause.

GPA *abbr* = Garden Products Association; Garlic Processors Association; Global Program of Action; Goat Producers Association.

GPALS *abbr* = Global Protection against Limited Strikes.

gpc *abbr* = good physical condition.

GPC *abbr* = General Purposes Committee.

gpd *abbr* = gallons per day.

GPDST *abbr* = Girls' Public Day School Trust.

gph *abbr* = gallons per hour.

GPh *abbr* = Graduate in Pharmacy.

GPHI *abbr* = Guild of Public Health Inspectors.

GPI *abbr* = general paralysis of the insane.

gpm *abbr* = gallons per minute.

GPMU *abbr* = Graphical, Paper, and Media Union.

GPO *abbr* = general post office; Government Printing Office.

GPP *abbr* = Guild of Pastoral Psychology.

gps *abbr* = gallons per second.

GPS *abbr* = Global Positioning System; Graduated Pension Scheme.

GPWM *abbr* = Guild for the Promotion of Welsh Music.

GQ *abbr* = general quarters.

gr. *abbr* = grain; grains; gram; grams; grammar; grammarian; grammatical; grand; great; gross; group.

g.r. *abbr* = gold rubles.

Gr. *abbr* = Grecian; Greece; Greek.

GR *abbr* = (*Latin*) *Georgius Rex*, "King George"; Green Realignment; (*Latin*) *Gulielmus Rex*, "King William"; gamma ray.

GRA *abbr* = Greyhound Racing Association.

grab *vt* (**grabbing, grabbed**) to take or grasp suddenly; to obtain unscrupulously; (*inf*) to catch the interest or attention of. * *n* a sudden clutch or attempt to grasp; a mechanical device for grasping and lifting objects.—**grabber** *n*.

grabber *n* (*comput*) a representation of the mouse pointer with which images, text or cells are selected by moving the pointer across the selection required.

grabble *vi* to feel about, to grope.—**grabbler** *n*.

graben *n* (*geol*) an area of land bounded by two or more faults with movements that result in a central block falling, relative to either side.

grace *n* beauty or charm of form, movement, or expression; good will; favor; a delay granted for payment of an obligation; a short prayer of thanks for a meal. * *vt* to decorate; to dignify.

Grace *n* **W[illiam] G[ilbert]** (1848–1915) English cricketer and physician. One of the first English cricketers to become a national institution, he began playing first-class cricket (for Gloucestershire) in 1864, and had scored a hundred centuries by 1895.

GRACE *abbr* = group routing and charging equipment.

grace and notice provision *n* a provision inserted in a loan agreement to avoid problems of seeming non-repayment caused by administrative error.

graceful *adj* having beauty of form, movement, or expression.—**gracefully** *adv.*—**gracefulness** *n*.

graceless *adj* unattractive; lacking sense of what is proper; clumsy.—**gracelessly** *adv.*—**gracelessness** *n*.

grace note *n* (*mus*) an ornamental note.

Graces *npl* (*Greek myth*) the three sister goddesses who are the givers of charm and beauty.

gracile *adj* slender.—**gracility** *n*.

gracious *adj* having or showing kindness, courtesy, etc; compassionate; polite to supposed inferiors; marked by luxury, ease, etc; *interj* an expression of surprise.—**graciously** *adv.*—**graciousness** *n*.

grackle *n* an Asian bird like a starling; an American bird with shiny black plumage; the crow blackbird.

grad *n* (*sl*) a graduate.

grad. *abbr* = graduate; graduated.

gradate *vti* to change or cause to change gradually from one stage, degree, color, etc to another; to arrange by grade or degree.

gradation *n* a series of systematic steps in rank, degree, intensity, etc; arranging in such stages; a single stage in a gradual progression; progressive change; (*mus*) by degrees of the scale.—**gradational** *adj*.

GradBHI *abbr* = Graduate of the British Horological Institute.

grade *n* a stage or step in a progression; a degree in a scale of quality, rank, etc; a group of people of the same rank, merit, etc; the degree of slope; a sloping part; a mark or rating in an examination, etc. * *vt* to arrange in grades; to give a grade to; to make level or evenly sloping.

grade crossing *n* a place where a road and rail line or two rail lines cross at the same level, a level crossing.

GradIAE *abbr* = Graduate of the Institution of Automobile Engineers.

GradIAP *abbr* = Graduate of the Institution of Analysts and Programmers.

GradIElecIE *abbr* = Graduate of the Institution of Electrical and Electronics Incorporated Engineers.

gradient *n* a sloping road or railway; the degree of slope in a road, railway, etc.

GradIISec *abbr* = Graduate of the Institute of Industrial Security.

GradIM *abbr* = Graduate of the Institute of Metals.

GradIMA *abbr* = Graduate Member of the Institute of Mathematics and its Applications.

GradIManf *abbr* = Graduate Member of the Institute of Manufacturing.

GradIMechIE *abbr* = Graduate Member of the Institution of Mechanical Incorporated Engineers.

GradIMF *abbr* = Graduate of the Institute of Metal Finishing.

GradIMS *abbr* = Graduate of the Institute of Management Specialists.

gradin, gradine *n* one of a tier of seats; a ledge at the back of an altar.

GradInstBE *abbr* = Graduate Member of the Institute of British Engineers.

GradInstNDT *abbr* = Graduate of the British Institute of Non-Destructive Testing.

GradInstP *abbr* = Graduate of the Institute of Physics.

GradInstPS *abbr* = Graduate of the Institute of Purchasing and Supply.

GradIOP *abbr* = Graduate of the Institute of Printing.

GradIPM *abbr* = Graduate of the Institute of Personnel Management.

GradIS *abbr* = Graduate Member of the Institute of Statisticians.

GradISCA *abbr* = Graduate of the Institute of Chartered Secretaries and Administrators.

GradPRI *abbr* = Graduate of the Plastics and Rubber Institute.

GradRSC *abbr* = Graduate of the Royal Society of Chemistry.

GradSE *abbr* = Graduate of the Society of Engineers.

GradStat *abbr* = Graduate Statistician.

gradual *adj* taking place by degrees.—**gradually** *adv.*—**gradualness** *n*.

graduate *n* a person who has completed a course of study at a school, college, or university; a receptacle marked with figures for measuring contents. * *adj* holding an academic degree or diploma; of or relating to studies beyond the first or bachelor's degree.—**graduator** *n*.

GraduateIEIE *abbr* = Graduate of the Institution of Electrical and Electronics Incorporated Engineers.

graduation *n* graduating or being graduated; the ceremony at which degrees are conferred by a college or university; an arranging or marking in grades or stages.

GradWeldI *abbr* = Graduate of the Welding Institute.

Graeae *npl* (*Greek myth*) two old women, gray-haired from birth.

Graeco- *see* **Greco-**.

graffiti *npl* (*sing* **graffito**) inscriptions or drawings, often indecent, on a wall or other public surface.

graft *n* a shoot or bud of one plant inserted into another, where it grows permanently; the transplanting of skin, bone, etc; the getting of money or advantage dishonestly—**grafter** *n*. —**grafting** *n*.

Graham *n* 1. **Billy [William Franklin Graham]** (1918–) American evangelist. 2. **Martha** (1893–1991) American dancer and choreographer regarded as a founder of modern dance.

Grahame *n* **Kenneth** (1859–1932) Scottish author whose masterpiece, *The Wind in the Willows* (1908), is a children's classic.

grail *n* in medieval legend, the dish or chalice that was used by Christ at the Last Supper, and the object of many knights' quests.—*also* **Holy Grail**.

grain *n* the seed of any cereal plant, as wheat, corn, etc; cereal plants; a tiny, solid particle, as of salt or sand; a unit of weight, 0.0648 gram; the arrangement of fibers, layers, etc of wood, leather, etc; the markings or texture due to this; natural disposition. * *vt* to form into grains; to paint in imitation of the grain of wood, etc. * *vi* to become granular.—**grainer** *n*.

Grainger *n* **Percy [Aldridge]** (1882–1961) Australian-born American pianist and composer.

Grainne *n* (*Irish Celtic myth*) beautiful daughter of Cormac mac Airt, a high king. She became betrothed to Fionn mac Cumhaill when he was already old but was in love with Diarmaid ua Duibhne..

grainy *adj* (**grainier, grainiest**) resembling grains in form or texture.—**graininess** *n*.

gram[1] *n* the basic unit of weight in the metric system, equal to one thousandth of a kilogram (one twenty-eighth of an ounce).

gram[2] *n* any of various leguminous plants grown for their edible seeds.

gram. *abbr* = grammar; grammatical.

grama (grass) *n* a low pasture grass of western and southwestern USA and South America.

gramarye, gramary *n* (*arch*) magic, necromancy.

gramercy *interj* (*arch*) an expression of great thanks; expressing great surprise.

gramineous *adj* of or like grass; grassy.

graminivorous *adj* feeding on grasses.

grammar *n* the study of the forms of words and their arrangement in sentences; a system of rules for speaking and writing a language; a grammar textbook; the use of language in speech or writing judged with regard to correctness of spelling, syntax, etc.

grammarian *n* one who studies grammar; the author of a grammar.

grammatical *adj* conforming to the rules of grammar.—**grammatically** *adv*.

gramophone *n* a record player, esp an old mechanical model with an acoustic horn.—*also* **phonograph**.

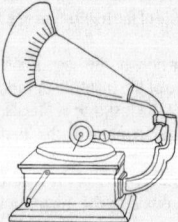

grampus *n* (*pl* **grampuses**) a marine mammal, as the blackfish or killer whale.

Gram's stain *n* a technique described by H C J Gram, the Danish bacteriologist, in 1884, which involves using a stain to differentiate between certain bacteria.

Gramsci *n* **Antonio** (1891–1937) Italian critic and founder of the Italian Communist Party.

Granada *n* a city in Nicaragua.

granadilla *n* another name for passion-fruit; the fruit of such a plant.

Granados *n* **Enrique** (1867–1916) Spanish composer, pianist and conductor, composer of seven operas and two symphonic poems.

granary *n* (*pl* **granaries**) a building for storing grain.

grand *adj* higher in rank than others; most important; imposing in size, beauty, extent, etc; distinguished; illustrious; comprehensive; (*inf*) very good; delightful; (*mus*) in complete classic form (sonata, symphony, or concerto); complete (orchestra); of the largest proportions, volume, and form (piano); of serious purport and sung throughout (opera). * *n* a grand piano; (*inf*) a thousand pounds or dollars.—**grandly** *adv*.—**grandness** *n*.

grand-aunt *n* a father's or mother's aunt.—*also* **great-aunt**.

grandchild *n* (*pl* **grandchildren**) the child of a person's son or daughter.

granddad *n* (*inf*) grandfather; an old man.

granddaughter *n* the daughter of a person's son or daughter.

grand duke *n* the ruler of a state or principality.

grande dame *n* a woman noted for her prestigious professional achievements.

grandee *n* a high-ranking person.

grandeur *n* splendor; magnificence; nobility; dignity.

grandfather *n* the father of a person's father or mother.

grandfather clock *n* a large clock with a pendulum in a tall, upright case.

grand jury *n* a jury in the US that examines evidence in a case to determine whether an indictment should be made.

grandiloquent *adj* using pompous words.—**grandiloquence** *n*.

grandiose *adj* having grandeur; imposing; pompous and showy.—**grandiosely** *adv*.—**grandiosity** *n*.

grandioso *adj,adv* (*mus*) (*Italian*) "in an imposing manner."

grandma, grandmama *n* (*inf*) grandmother.

grand mal *n* severe epilepsy.

grandmaster *n* an expert player (as of chess) who has scored consistently well in international competition.

grandmother *n* the mother of a person's father or mother.

grandnephew *n* a nephew's or niece's son.—*also* **great-nephew**.

grandniece *n* a nephew's or niece's daughter.—*also* **great-niece**.

grand opera *n* opera in which the whole text is set to music.

grand orchestre *n* (*mus*) (*French*) a full orchestra.

grand orgue *n* (*mus*) (*French*) a great organ (as opposed to a swell organ, etc) *See* **organ**.

grandpa, grandpapa *n* (*inf*) grandfather.

grandparent *n* a grandfather or grandmother; (*comput*) the oldest file in a grandparent, parent, son backup system.

grand piano *n* a large piano with a horizontal harp-shaped case.

Grand Prix *n* (*pl* **Grand Prix**) any of a series of formula motor races held in different countries throughout the season; an important contest in other sports, including horse racing, tennis, and athletics.

grand slam *n* (*tennis, golf*) a winning of all the major international championships in a season; (*bridge*) a bidding for and winning all the tricks in a deal; (*baseball*) a home run hit when there is a runner on each base.

grandson *n* the son of a person's son or daughter.

grandstand *n* the main structure for seating spectators at a sporting event.

grand tour *n* (*formerly*) a trip round Europe taken by the sons of wealthy Englishmen to complete their education; (*inf*) a sightseeing or educational tour.

Grand Turk *n* capital city of the Turks and Caicos Islands.

grand-uncle *n* a father's or mother's uncle.—*also* **great-uncle**.

grange *n* a country house with outbuildings etc; a local lodge of a powerful agricultural association; (*with* **the**) this association; (*formerly*) an outlying farm building where a monastery or local lord stored crops or tithes; (*arch*) a granary.

Grange *n* **Jacques** (1944–) F rench entrepreneur who worked for Yves Saint-Laurent in the 1970s and 1980s.

grangerize *vt* interleave (a book) with illustrations taken from other books; to remove illustrations, etc, from books for this purpose.—**grangerism** *n*.—**grangerization** *n*.

granite *n* a hard, igneous rock consisting chiefly of feldspar and quartz; unyielding firmness of endurance.—**granitic, granitoid** *adj*.

granivorous *adj* grain-eating; living on seeds.—**granivore** *n*.

Grannos *n* (*Gaulish Celtic myth*) a god of healing who possibly became assimilated with the classical god Apollo. He is often depicted in conjunction with Sirona, who is regarded as being his consort.

granny, grannie *n* (*pl* **grannies**) (*inf*) a grandmother; (*inf*) an old woman.

granny dumping *n* the practice of abandoning an elderly often confused person, usually by relatives, in an attempt to force the community care options to relieve responsibility from the family involved.

granny knot *n* a wrongly tied reef knot, which is insecure.

grant *vt* to consent to; to give or transfer by legal procedure; to admit as true. * *n* the act of granting; something granted, esp a gift for a particular purpose; a transfer of property by deed; the instrument by which such a transfer is made.

Grant *n* 1. **Cary [Archibald Alexander Leach]** (1904–86) English-born American film actor. 2. **Duncan** (1885–1978) Scottish painter who designed for Roger Fry's workshops and formed a close collaboration with Vanessa Bell. 3. **Ulysses S[impson]** (1822–85) American soldier and 18th US president (1869–77).

grantee *n* the person to whom property is transferred by deed, etc.

granter *n* one who grants.

grantor *n* one who transfers property by deed, etc.

granular *adj* consisting of granules; having a grainy texture.—**granularity** *n*.

granulate *vt* to form or crystallize into grains or granules. * *vi* to collect into grains or granules; to become roughened and grainy in surface texture.—**granulation** *n*.—**granulative** *adj*.—**granulator, granulater** *n*.

granulation *n* a technique of soldering particles of a metal together onto a surface, usually of the same metal, to produce a decorative effect.

granule *n* a small grain or particle.

Granville-Barker *n* **Harley** (1877–1946) English dramatist, producer, critic, and actor. His productions, especially those of Shakespeare, broke new ground in their concern for textual authenticity and non-elaborate sets.

grape *n* a small round, juicy berry, growing in clusters on a vine; a dark purplish red.—**grapey, grapy** *adj*.

grape fern *n* a fern with crescent-shaped fronds, moonwort.

grapefruit *n* (*pl* **grapefruit, grapefruits**) a large, round, sour citrus fruit with a yellow rind.

grape hyacinth *n* any of various small plants of the lily family bearing tight clusters of blue grape-like flowers.

grapeshot *n* cannon shot packed in layers, scattering when fired.

grapevine *n* a type of woody vine on which grapes grow; an informal means of communicating news or gossip.

graph *n* a diagram representing the successive changes in the value of a variable quantity or quantities. * *vt* to illustrate by graphs.

-graph   285   graylag

-graph *n suffix* a writing or recording device; something written, drawn or recorded.

-grapher *n suffix* denoting a person with specified skills; denoting a person who writes or draws in a certain way.

graphic, graphical *adj* described in realistic detail; pertaining to a graph, lettering, drawing, painting, etc.—**graphically** *adv*.—**graphicalness, graphicness** *n*.

graphical user interface *n* (*comput*) the part of the software program that communicates and interacts with the user by means of pull-down menus, dialog boxes and icons. * *abbr* GUI.

graphic arts *npl* the fine and applied arts involving design, illustration and printing.

graphics *n sing or pl* the use of drawings and lettering; the drawings, illustrations, etc used in a newspaper, magazine, television program, etc; information displayed in the form of diagrams, illustrations and animation on a computer monitor; **npl* (*comput*) a generic term used to describe anything to do with pictures as opposed to text. *See also* **bitmap; CAD**.

graphics files *n* (*comput*) files to do with pictures. Two types of graphic are used, namely **vector** or **raster** and some programs can use both and convert between them. The more versatile types of file format are the ones commonly found on the Internet or able to be downloaded from sites. Typical formats are: Tiff (.TIF), Bitmaps (.BMP), and Compuserve (*trademark*) (.GIF).

graphics tablet *n* (*comput*) an input device that uses a touch sensitive pad and a stylus to generate an electrical pulse that is recorded by the computer and translated into a digital form as a screen pixel.

graphite *n* a soft, black form of carbon used in pencils, for lubricants, etc.—**graphitic** *adj*.

graphology *n* the study of handwriting, esp as a clue to character.—**graphological** *adj*.—**graphologist** *n*.

graph paper *n* ruled paper for drawing graphs and diagrams.

-graphy *n suffix* denoting a form of writing, representation, or description.

grapnel *n* a small anchor with multiple claws.

Grappelli *n* Stéphane (1908–97) French jazz violinist; a member of the Hot Club de France quintet (1934–39); noted for his highly individual, sliding style.

grapple *vt* to seize or grip firmly. * *vi* to struggle hand-to-hand with; to deal or contend with. * *n* a grapnel; act of grappling, a wrestle; a grip.—**grappler** *n*.

grappling iron *or* **grappling hook** *n* an iron bar with claws at one end for anchoring a boat, securing a ship alongside or raising sunken objects.

GRAS *abbr* = generally recognized as safe.

grasp *vt* to grip, as with the hand; to seize; to understand. * *vi* to try to clutch, seize; (*with* **at**) to take eagerly. * *n* a firm grip; power of seizing and holding; comprehension.—**graspable** *adj*.—**grasper** *n*.

grasping *adj* greedy, avaricious.—**graspingly** *adv*.—**graspingness** *n*.

grass *n* any of a large family of plants with jointed stems and long narrow leaves including cereals, bamboo, etc; such plants grown as lawn; pasture; (*sl*) marijuana; (*sl*) an informer. * *vi* to cover with grass; (*sl*) to inform, betray.

Grass *n* Günter [Wilhelm] (1927–) German novelist, dramatist, and poet.

Grasset *n* Eugène (1845–1917) Swiss architect who also designed jewelry and textiles and was one of the founders of the Société des Artistes Decorateurs.

grasshopper *n* any of a group of plant-eating, winged insects with powerful hind legs for jumping.

grassland *n* land reserved for pasture; land, such as prairie, where grass dominates.

grass roots *npl* (*inf*) the common people, the ordinary members of a political or other organization; the basic level, the essentials.

grass snake *n* a small nonpoisonous European snake with a greenish body and yellow markings.

grass widow, grass widower *n* (*inf*) a person whose spouse is frequently absent.

grassy *adj* (**grassier, grassiest**) abounding in, covered with, or like, grass.—**grassiness** *n*.

grate[1] *n* a frame of metal bars for holding fuel in a fireplace; a fireplace; a grating.

grate[2] *vt* to grind into particles by scraping; to rub against (an object) or grind (the teeth) together with a harsh sound; to irritate. * *vi* to rub or rasp noisily; to cause irritation.

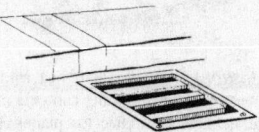

grateful *adj* appreciative; welcome.—**gratefully** *adv*.—**gratefulness** *n*.

grater *n* a metal implement with a jagged surface for grating food.

gratification *n* the act of gratifying; satisfaction; pleasure; (*arch*) a reward or recompense.

gratify *vt* (**gratifying, gratified**) to please; to indulge.—**gratification** *n*.—**gratifier** *n*.—**gratifyingly** *adv*.

grating[1] *n* a open framework or lattice of bars placed across an opening.

grating[2] *adj* harsh; irritating.—**gratingly** *adv*.

gratis *adj, adv* free of charge.

gratitude *n* a being thankful for favors received.

gratuitous *adj* given free of charge; done without cause, unwarranted.—**gratuitously** *adv*.—**gratuitousness** *n*.

gratuity *n* (*pl* **gratuities**) money given for a service, a tip.

Graun *n* Karl Heinrich (1704–59) German composer and singer. He wrote some 30 operas (e.g., *Montezuma*) as well as cantatas, church music and piano concertos. His brother, Johann Gottlieb, was also a noted composer and violinist.

grav *n* a unit of acceleration equal to standard free fall (1 grav = 9.8 meters (32 feet) per second).

gravamen *n* (*pl* **gravamens, gravamina**) the principal part of a legal complaint or accusation.

grave[1] *n* a hole dug in the ground for burying the dead; any place of burial, a tomb.

grave[2] *adj* serious, important; harmful; solemn, somber; (*sound*) low in pitch. * *n* an accent over a vowel.—**gravely** *adv*.—**graveness** *n*.

grave[3] *adj* (*mus*) (*Italian*) "slow" or "solemn."

grave goods *n* (*archeo*) artifacts included with a burial which may have been personal possessions of the deceased or items of religious significance.

gravel *n* coarse sand with small rounded stones. * *vt* (**graveling, graveled** *or* **gravelling, gravelled**) to cover or spread with gravel.—**gravelish** *adj*.

gravelly *adj* like gravel; (*voice*) deep and rough-sounding.

graven *adj* engraved; fixed indelibly.

graven image *n* an idol.

graver *n* an engraving tool. *See* **burin**.

Graves *n* 1. **Michael** (1934–) American architect. His notable works include P ublic Services Building, Portland, Oregon. 2. **Richard** (1715–1804) English clergyman and author of *The Spiritual Quixote*, an entertaining picaresque novel that describes the experiences of a dissenter traveling through England. 3. **Robert [von Ranke]** (1889–1985) English poet, novelist, and critic whose autobiography, *Goodbye to All That*, was one of the first accounts of World War I soldiering to make a major impact from an antiwar standpoint.

Graves' disease *n* (*med*) a disorder typified by thyroid gland overactivity, an enlargement of the gland, and protruding eyes. *See* **hyperthyroidism**.

gravestone *n* a stone marking a grave, usu inscribed with the name and details of the deceased.

Gravettian *adj* (*archeo*) relating to a stone tools industry belonging to the Upper Paleolithic period in France, dated *c*.25,000 BC.

graveyard *n* a burial-ground, cemetery.

gravid *adj* pregnant.—**gravidity, gravidness** *n*. —**gravidly** *adv*.

gravimeter *n* an instrument for measuring the specific gravity of liquid or solid bodies; an instrument for measuring gravity at particular geographical locations.—**gravimetry** *n*.

gravimetric, gravimetrical *adj* of or relating to measurement by weight; determined by weight.—**gravimetrically** *adv*.

gravitate *vi* to move or tend to move under the force of gravitation.—**gravitater** *n*.

gravitation *n* a natural force of attraction that tends to draw bodies together.—**gravitational** *adj*.—**gravitationally** *adv*.

gravitational collapse *n* a lower-energy state resulting from masses that are attracted together by gravitation collapsing, and released energy being transformed, usually into heat.

gravitational instability *n* a situation in which bodies acted on by gravity are in a stable position with respect to each other, but where a slight displacement destroys the stability.

gravitational redshift *n* the displacement of features in the spectra of astronomical bodies towards the longer wavelengths, i.e., shifted to the red.

gravitative *adj* pertaining to or determined by gravitation; likely to gravitate, causing something to gravitate.

gravity *n* (*pl* **gravities**) importance, esp seriousness; weight; the attraction of bodies toward the center of the earth, the moon, or a planet.

gravy *n* (*pl* **gravies**) the juice given off by meat in cooking; the sauce made from this juice; (*sl*) money easily obtained.

gravy boat *n* a small boat-shaped dish for holding and serving gravy or sauces.

gravy train *n* (*sl*) a source of easy money.

gray *n* any of a series of neutral colors ranging between black and white; something (as an animal, garment, cloth, or spot) of a gray color. * *adj* gray in color; having gray-colored hair; darkish; dreary; vague, indeterminate.—*also* **grey**.—**grayish** *adj*.—**grayness** *n*.

Gray *n* 1. **Milner Connorton** (1899–) British industrial designer whose propaganda exhibitions in World War II included the classic "Dig for Victory." 2. **Eileen Moray** (1878–1976) Paris-based Irish architect who also designed luxury furniture for society clients. 3. **Thomas** (1716–71) English poet. His "Elegy written in a country churchyard" (1751) is one of the most-quoted poems in the English language.

graybeard *n* an old man, esp one considered to be wise; an earthenware jug.—*also* **greybeard**.

gray economy *n* the term used to describe unofficial trading which is not accounted for in a country's official economic statistics.—*also* **grey economy**.

gray knight *n* in a situation involving a company takeover bid, a potential bidder whose intentions are undeclared and thus unknown. *See* **white knight**.

graylag (goose) *n* the common wild goose of Europe and Asia.

grayling *n* (*pl* **grayling, graylings**) a freshwater fish.

graymail *see* **greenmail**.

gray market *n* legal trading in goods of which there is a scarcity at a particular time; a market in shares that have not been issued, although they are due to be issued within a short time.

gray matter *n* gray-colored nerve tissue of the brain and spinal cord; (*inf*) brains, intelligence.

gray scale *n* (*comput*) the shades of gray from white to black that a computer can display.

gray squirrel *n* a common squirrel with gray fur orig from North America.

graywacke *n* a hard conglomerate rock of pebbles and sand.—*also* **greywracke**.

Graz *n* a city in Austria.

graze[1] *vi* to feed on growing grass or pasture. * *vt* to put (animals) to feed on growing grass or pasture.—**grazer** *n*.

graze[2] *vt* to touch lightly in passing; to scrape, scratch. * *n* an abrasion, esp on the skin, caused by scraping on a surface.—**grazingly** *adv*.

grazier *n* a person who grazes cattle and prepares them for the market.

grazing *n* pasture; the crops, plants, etc, growing on this for animals to feed from.

grazioso *adv* (*mus*) (*Italian*) "gracefully."

GRB *abbr* = Gas Research Board; gamma-ray burst.

GRBI *abbr* = Gardeners' Royal Benevolent Institution.

Gr. Br., Gr. Brit. *abbr* = Great Britain.

GRBS *abbr* = Gardeners' Royal Benevolent Society.

GRCM *abbr* = Graduate of the Royal College of Music.

grd. *abbr* = ground; guaranteed.

GRDF *abbr* = Gulf Rapid Deployment Force.

GRE *abbr* = Guardian Royal Exchange Assurance PLC.

grease *n* melted animal fat; any thick, oily substance or lubricant. * *vt* to smear or lubricate with grease.

greasepaint *n* make-up used by actors.

greaser *n* (*sl*) a mechanic; a motorcyclist, often a member of a gang; a member of the engine room crew on a commercial ship; (*derog*) an unpleasant, fawning person, (*derog*) a person from Latin America or Mexico.

greasy *adj* (**greasier, greasiest**) covered with grease; full of grease; slippery; oily in manner.—**greasily** *adv*.—**greasiness** *n*.

great *adj* of much more than ordinary size, extent, etc; much above the average; intense; eminent; most important; more distant in a family relationship by one generation; (*often with* **at**) (*inf*) skillful; (*inf*) excellent; fine. * *n* (*inf*) a distinguished person.—**greatly** *adv*.—**greatness** *n*.

great-aunt *n* a parent's aunt.—*also* **grand-aunt**.

great circle *n* any circle, e.g. the celestial equator, drawn on the celestial sphere.

Great C Major Symphony *n* the name given to Schubert's symphony no. 9; so called to distinguish it from his shorter 6th symphony, also in C major.

greatcoat *n* a large heavy coat.

Great Dane *n* a breed of very large smooth-haired dogs.

Great Dark Spot *n* an atmospheric feature on Neptune, possibly a whirling dust storm, situated in the southern hemisphere.

great divide *n* a watershed between major drainage systems; a significant point of division, esp death.

Great Ennead *n* (*Egypt*) the nine gods—Ra and the eight deities whom he formed: Shu, Tefnut, Geb, Nut, Seth, Nephthys, Osiris and Isis.

great-grandchild *n* the child of a person's grandchild.

great-grandparent *n* the parent of a person's grandparent.

great-nephew *n* a nephew's or niece's son.—*also* **grandnephew**.

great-niece *n* a nephew's or niece's daughter.—*also* **grandniece**.

Great Red Spot *n* an atmospheric feature on Jupiter first discovered by Hooke in 1664.

great stave *n* (*mus*) a stave created by pushing the stave with the treble clef and the stave with the bass clef closer together so that both clefs can be located on one exaggerated stave.

great tit *n* a common yellow, black and white Eurasian tit.

great-uncle *n* a parent's uncle.—*also* **grand-uncle**.

Great War *n* the First World War, 1914–18.

greave *n* armor for the lower leg.

greaves *npl* the sediment of melted tallow; (*often sing*) armor to protect the legs from the ankle to the knee.

grebe *n* any of a family of swimming and diving birds.

Grecian *adj* pertaining to Greece; in the Greek style; Greek. * *n* a native or inhabitant of Greece; a Greek scholar.

Grecism *n* a Greek idiom, phrase, spirit, or style; a reverent imitation of these, e.g. in architecture or literature.

Grecize *vti* to give a Greek form to; to imitate Greek.

Greco- *prefix* Greek.

Greco-Roman *adj* of or relating to the ancient Greeks and Romans.

Greece *n* a republic, also known as the Hellenic Republic, comprising of the southernmost portion of the Balkans Peninsula and more than 1,400 islands; (*Bible*) a country called Javan in the OT and Achaia in the NT. *See also* **Greek**.

greed *n* excessive desire, esp for food or wealth.

greedy *adj* (**greedier, greediest**) wanting more than one needs or deserves; having too strong a desire for food and drink.—**greedily** *adv*.—**greediness** *n*.

Greek *adj* of Greece, its people, or its language. * *n* a native of Greece; the language used by Greeks; (*inf*) something unintelligible.

Greek cross *n* a cross with four equal arms.

Greek fire *n* in ancient history, a weapon used in sea battles consisting of an unidentified substance that ignited on contact with water.

Greek (Orthodox) Church *n* the body of churches that split from the Western Church in the 11th century and that recognizes the authority of the Greek patriarch of Constantinople as opposed to the pope.

Greeley *n* **Horace** (1811–72) American journalist; founder (1841) and editor of the *New York Tribune*.

green *adj* of the color green; covered with plants or foliage; having a sickly appearance; unripe; inexperienced, naive; not fully processed or treated; concerned with the conservation of natural resources; (*inf*) jealous. * *n* a color between blue and yellow in the spectrum; the color of growing grass; something of a green color; (*pl*) green leafy vegetables, as spinach, etc; (*often with cap*) a person concerned with the future of the earth's environment; a grassy plot, esp the end of a golf fairway.—**greenish** *adj*.—**greenly** *adv*.—**greenness** *n*. —**greeny** *adj*.

Green *n* 1. **A Romney** (1872–1945) British craftsperson and sailor, a proponent of the arts and crafts movement in furniture. 2. **Henry [Henry Vincent Yorke]** (1905–73) English novelist whose strange, highly original novels, e.g. *Living*, *Loving*, and *Back*, have been much praised by his peers.

green audit *n* a review of a company's business activities in terms of the environmental consequences of these activities.

greenback *n* a legal-tender note of US currency.

green bean *n* any of various beans with narrow edible pods.

green belt *n* a belt of parkland, farms, etc surrounding a community, designed to prevent urban sprawl.

green card *n* an identity card issued to resident aliens in the US.

green currencies *npl* the currencies of members of the European Community using artificial rates of exchange for purposes of the Common Agricultural Policy.

Greene *n* 1. **[Henry] Graham** (1904–91) English novelist whose work includes *The Heart of the Matter* and *Brighton Rock*. 2. **Robert** (*c.*1558–92) English poet, dramatist, and pamphleteer whose tracts on the Elizabethan underworld are valuable for their descriptions of criminal life and language.

greenery *n* (*pl* **greeneries**) green vegetation.

green-eyed *adj* jealous.

green-eyed monster *n* jealousy.

greenfield project *n* a business project or scheme that starts from scratch, specifically the building of a factory on a site in the country that has not been built on before.

greenfinch *n* a European and Asian bird with yellow and green plumage.

green fingers *see* **green thumb**.

greenfly *n* (*pl* **greenflies**) an insect pest that infests garden plants and crops.

greengage *n* a small greenish sweet variety of plum.

greenheart *n* a tropical American tree that yields a dark durable timber; the timber.

greenhorn *n* an inexperienced person; a person easily duped.

greenhouse *n* a heated building, mainly of glass, for growing plants.

greenhouse effect *n* (*astron*) action of radiant heat from the sun passing through the glass of greenhouses etc., warming the contents inside, where such heat is thus trapped; application of the same effect to a planet's atmosphere.—*see* **global warming.**

greening[1] *n* a type of cooking apple that is green when ripe.

greening[2] *n* growing awareness of the environment.

Greenland *n* a self-governing region of Denmark. Greenland is the largest island in the world (discounting continental landmasses), lying mainly within the Arctic Circle, off the northeast coast of Canada.

green light *n* permission to proceed with a plan, etc.

greenmail *or* **graymail** *n* a situation that can arise in a company takeover bid in which a large block of shares is purchased by a potential takeover bidder, who then sells the shares back to the directors of the company at a premium over the market price of the shares, the directors acting in this way to avert the bid.

green pepper *n* the unripe fruit of the sweet pepper eaten raw or cooked.

greenroom *n* the actors' rest room in a theater, the room where they can receive visitors.

greensand *n* a green sandstone

greenshank *n* a large European wading bird with greenish legs and feet.

greenstick fracture *n* a fracture that occurs only in young children, whose bones are still soft and tend to bend.

greenstone *n* New Zealand jade; any green igneous rock that contains chlorite or epidote.

greensward *n* (*arch*) (a stretch of) turf.

green tea *n* a drink made from dried unfermented tea leaves.

green thumb *n* gardening expertise.—*also* **green fingers.**

Greenway *n* **Francis H** (1777–) English architect. His notable works include the Assembly Rooms, Bristol.

Greenwich Mean Time *or* **Universal Time** *n* the mean solar time defined on the Greenwich Meridian. * *abbrs* GMT *or* UT.

Greenwich Meridian *n* the imaginary line drawn over the surface of the Earth from pole to pole which cuts the equator at right angles and passes through a particular point at the Royal Greenwich Observatory.

greenwood *n* leafy woodland.

Greer *n* **Germaine** (1939–) Australian feminist, writer , and broadcaster who is best-known for her controversial work, *The Female Eunuch* (1970).

greet *vt* to address with friendliness; to meet (a person, event, etc) in a specified way; to present itself to.—**greeter** *n.*

greeting *n* the act of welcoming with words or gestures; an expression of good wishes; (*pl*) a message of regards.

gregarious *adj* (*animals*) living in flocks and herds; (*people*) sociable, fond of company.—**gregariously** *adv.*—**gregariousness** *n.*

Gregorian *adj* pertaining to or established by Gregory, the name of various popes.

Gregorian calendar *n* the reformed calendar introduced in 1582 by Pope Gregory XIII and currently in use.

Gregorian chant *n* (*mus*) a term that refers to the large collection of ancient solo and chorus plainsong melodies preserved by the Roman Catholic Church. They are named after Pope Gregory I (*c*.540-604) but date from about 800. Until recently they were sung at specific ceremonies, such as baptism.

Gregorian telescope *n* a type of telescope invented by James Gregory (1638–75) of Drumoak.

Gregory *n* 1. **Lady Augusta** (1852–1932) Anglo-Irish dramatist. She was a founder and director of the Abbey Theatre and a close friend of, and collaborator with, Yeats. 2. **Nazianzens** *n* Saint (*c*.330–390) a priest who was elected archbishop in Constantinople but he hated public life and led a solitary existence near Arianzus until he died. His feast day is January 2. 3. **Thaumaturgus** *n* Saint [Theodorus, **Gregory the Wonder-worker**] (*c*.210–270) bishop of Neocaesarea, in Pontus, whose work, *Ekthesis* or "Confession of Faith," is of value as a record of the state of theology at the middle of the 3rd century. His feast day is November 17.

Gregory I *n* Saint [Gregory the Great] (*c*. 540–604) pope (590–604). Gave up his position as prefect of Rome to become a monk; founded seven monasteries; elected pope in 590; strengthened papal authority and revised the liturgy. He sent St Augustine to convert the English. His feast day is September 3.

Gregory VII *n* Saint [Hildebrand] (*c*. 1020–85) pope (1073–85), born in Tuscany; believed that the welfare of the church and the regeneration of society were inseparable; reformed abuses in the church, established papal supremacy and abolished lay investiture. His feast day is May 25.

Gregory of Nyssa *n* Saint (331–95) the younger brother of Basil; a great speculative theologian, the most faithful to Origenistic views, and a zealous defender of Nicene doctrine. His feast day is March 9 .

Gregory of Tours *n* Saint (*c*. 540–94) Frankish bishop and theologian. We owe our exact knowledge of 6th-century Gaul to his *History of the Franks*. His feast day is November 17.

gremlin *n* an imaginary creature blamed for disruption of any procedure or of malfunction of equipment, esp in an aircraft.

Grenada *n* an independent state within the Commonwealth, comprising the most southerly of the Windward Islands chains in the Caribbean.

grenade *n* a small bomb thrown manually or projected (as by a rifle or special launcher).

grenadier[1] *n* a soldier of the British Grenadier Guards, the first regiment of the household infantry; (*formerly*) a foot soldier who threw grenades; (*formerly*) a company made up of the tallest and strongest soldiers in the regiment.

grenadier[2] *n* a sea fish with a large head and a long, narrow tail.

grenadine[1] *n* a gauze-like dress fabric.

grenadine[2] *n* a syrup made from pomegranates; a red-orange color.

Grenander *n* **Alfred** (1894–1956) German industrial designer, an early member of the Deutscher Werkbund.

Gresham *n* **Sir Thomas** (*c*.1519–79) English financier. He founded the Royal Exchange in London in 1568.

Gresley *n* **Herbert Nigel** (1876–1941) British engineer best-known for his designs of some of Britain's fastest and most powerful steam locomotives.

gressorial *adj* adapted for walking; (*birds*) having three toes of the feet forward, two of them connected, and one behind.

grew *see* **grow**.

grey *see* **gray**.

Grey *n* **Lady Jane** (1537–54) English Queen. The great-granddaughter of Henry VII, she was declared queen in 1553 in a move to ensure that the monarch served the Protestant interest, and reigned for ten days. Mary I was crowned queen, and Lady Jane imprisoned and subsequently executed.

greybeard *see* **graybeard**.

greyhound *n* any of a breed of tall and slender dogs noted for its great speed and keen sight.

greywacke *n* hard grey-green stone that can be polished to a fine very widely used in building and also in sculpture in ancient Egypt.

greywracke *see* **graywracke**.

GRI *abbr* (*Latin*) = *Georgius Rex Imperator*, "George, King and Emperor."

GRIC *abbr* = Graduate Membership of the Royal Institute of Chemistry.

grid *n* a gridiron, a grating; an electrode for controlling the flow of electrons in an electron tube; a network of squares on a map used for easy reference; a national network of transmission lines, pipes, etc for electricity, water, gas, etc.

GRID *abbr* = Global Resource Information Database; gay-related immunodeficiency.

griddle *n* a flat metal surface for cooking.

griddlecake *n* a pancake.

gridiron *n* a framework of iron bars for cooking; anything resembling this, as a field used for American football.

grid layout *n* (*archeo*) a technique used in excavation in which a site is divided into a grid of numbered squares, then alternate squares are excavated.

gridlock *n* a traffic jam that halts all traffic at a street crossing; the breakdown of an organization or a system.

grid plan *n* an urban area where equidistant parallel streets are crossed at right angles by other equidistant parallel streets. The layout of New York is a good example.

grid reference *n* a grid of horizontal and vertical lines on a map, numbered to show eastings and northings, whereby any point on the map can be pinpointed.

grief *n* extreme sorrow caused as by a loss; deep distress.

grief-stricken *adj* full of sorrow.

Grieg *n* **Edvard [Hagerup]** (1843–1907) Norwegian composer whose works include music for Ibsen's *Peer Gynt*.

Grierson *n* **John** (1898–1972) Scottish documentary film director and producer; the "father of British documentary."

grievance *n* a circumstance thought to be unjust and cause for complaint.

grieve *vti* to feel or cause to feel grief.—**griever** *n.* —**grieving** *adj, n.*

grievous *adj* causing or characterized by grief; deplorable; severe.—**grievously** *adv.*—**grievousness** *n.*

Griffes *n* **Charles Tomlinson** (1884–1920) American composer who was influenced by the impressionist movement. His works include the symphonic poem, *The Pleasure Dome of Kubla Khan*, and the dance drama, *The Kairn of Koridwen*.

griffin, griffon *n* (*myth*) a mythical animal with the body and tail of a lion and an eagle's beak and wings.—*also* **gryphon**.

Griffin *n* **Walter B.** (1876–1937) American architect. His notable works include the Capitol Theatre, Melbourne.

Griffith *n* 1. **Arthur** (1871–1922) Irish nationalist leader and first president of the Irish Free State. He founded Sinn Féin in 1905, and (with Michael Collins) signed the Anglo-Irish Treaty of 1921. 2. **D[avid] W[ark]** (1875–1948) American film director and producer; a co-founder of United Artists in 1919.

griffon *n* a small dog with a wire-haired coat; a large hawk with a pale body and black wings, found in Africa, Asia and warm parts of Europe.

grig *n* an extravagantly vivacious person; the sandeel; a young eel; a hen with short legs; heather.

grill *vt* to broil by direct heat using a grill or gridiron; (*inf*) to question relentlessly. * *n* a device on a cooker that radiates heat downward for broiling or grilling; a gridiron; broiled or grilled food; a grille; a grillroom.—**griller** *n.*

grillage *n* an arrangement of planks and crossbeams forming a foundation in loose or marshy soil.

grille, grill *n* an open grating forming a screen.

grillroom *n* a restaurant that specializes in grilled food.

grilse *n* (*pl* grilses, grilse) a young salmon returning from the sea to spawn for the first time.

grim *adj* (grimmer, grimmest) hard and unyielding, stern; appearing harsh, forbidding; repellent, ghastly in character.—**grimly** *adv.*—**grimness** *n.*

grimace *n* a contortion of the face expressing pain, anguish, humor, etc. * *vi* to contort the face in pain, etc.—**grimacer** *n.* —**grimacingly** *adv.*

G

grimalkin *n* an old she-cat; a spiteful, bad-tempered old woman.

grime *n* soot or dirt, rubbed into a surface, as the skin. * *vt* to dirty, soil with grime.

grimy *adj* (**grimier, grimiest**) dirty, soiled.—**griminess** *n*.

grin *vi* (**grinning, grinned**) to smile broadly as in amusement; to show the teeth in pain, scorn, etc. * *n* a broad smile.—**grinner** *n*.

grind *vb* (**grinding, ground**) *vt* to reduce to powder or fragments by crushing; to wear down, sharpen, or smooth by friction; to rub (the teeth) harshly together; to oppress, tyrannize; to move or operate by a crank. * *vi* to be crushed, smoothed, or sharpened by grinding; to jar or grate; to work monotonously; to rotate the hips in an erotic manner. * *n* the act or sound of grinding; hard monotonous work.

grinder *n* someone or something that grinds; a molar tooth.

grindstone *n* a circular revolving stone for grinding or sharpening tools.

gringo *n* (*pl* **gringos**) (*offensive*) among Hispanics, a foreigner, esp North Americans.

grip *n* a secure grasp; the manner of holding a bat, club, racket, etc; the power of grasping firmly; mental grasp; mastery; a handle; a small traveling bag. * *vt* (**gripping, gripped**) to take firmly and hold fast.

gripe *vt* to cause sharp pain in the bowels of; (*sl*) to annoy. * *vi* (*sl*) to complain.—**griper** *n*. —**gripingly** *adv*.

grippe *n* (*formerly*) influenza.

gripper *n* one who or that which grips; a mechanical device for seizing and holding.

Gris *n* **Juan [José Victoriano Gonzàlez]** (1887–1927) Spanish painter; an associate of Picasso and Braque and a leading cubist painter.

grisaille *n* a method of painting in grey tints so as to represent a solid body in relief; a decorative painting in grey monochrome, esp on glass.

griseofulvin *see* **ringworm**.

griseous *adj* bluish-grey.

grisette *n* a lively young French working girl, esp a flirtatious one; an edible toadstool.

griskin *n* the lean part of a loin of pork.

grisly *adj* (**grislier, grisliest**) terrifying; ghastly; arousing horror.—**grisliness** *n*.

grison *n* a carnivorous mammal of Central and South America, which resembles a weasel.

grist *n* grain that is to be or has been ground; matter forming the basis of a story or analysis.

gristle *n* cartilage, esp in meat.—**gristly** *adj*.—**gristliness** *n*.

gristmill *n* a mill for grinding grain.

grit *n* rough particles, as of sand; firmness of spirit; stubborn courage. * *vt* (**gritting, gritted**) to clench or grind together (e.g., the teeth); to spread grit on (e.g., an icy road).

grits *npl* oats, hulled and coarsely ground; coarsely ground maize, boiled in water or milk as a food (—*also* **hominy grits**).

gritty *adj* (**grittier, grittiest**) composed of, containing, or resembling, grit; courageous.—**grittily** *adv*.—**grittiness** *n*.

grivet *n* a green and white Ethiopian monkey with a long tail.

grizzle *vt* (*inf*) to fret; to complain. * *vti* to (cause to) become grey * *n* a grey color; hair that is, or is becoming, grey; a wig of grey hair.—**grizzled** *adj*.

grizzled *adj* streaked with grey; grey-haired.

grizzly *adj* (**grizzlier, grizzliest**) greyish; grizzled. * *n* (*pl* **grizzlies**) the grizzly bear.

grizzly bear *n* a large powerful bear of North America.

grm. *abbr* = gram.

GRN *abbr* = goods received note.

GRNCM *abbr* = Graduate of the Royal Northern College of Music.

gro. *abbr* = gross.

GRO *abbr* = General Register Office; Greenwich Royal Observatory.

groan *vi* to utter a deep moan; to make a harsh sound (as of creaking) under sudden or prolonged strain. * *n* a deep moan; a creaking sound.—**groaner** *n*. —**groaningly** *adv*.

groat *n* (*formerly*) a British silver coin worth fourpence; a trifling sum.

groats *npl* hulled grain broken into fragments, esp oats.

GROBDM *abbr* = General Register Office of Births, Deaths, and Marriages.

grocer *n* a dealer in food and household supplies.

grocery *n* (*pl* **groceries**) a grocer's shop; (*pl*) goods, esp from a grocer.

grog *n* rum diluted with water, often spiced and served hot.

groggy *adj* (**groggier, groggiest**) (*inf*) weak and unsteady, usu through illness, exhaustion, or alcohol.—**groggily** *adv*.—**grogginess** *n*.

grogram *n* a coarse cloth of silk or silk and mohair, or wool.

groin *n* (*archit*) the angle or edge created where two or more vaults intersect; (*biol*) the fold marking the junction of the lower abdomen and the thighs; the location of the genitals.

groined vault *n* (*archit*) a vault formed from two identical barrel vaults meeting at right angles. —*also* **cross vault**.

grommet *n* a plastic or rubber ring used to protect wire, a cable, etc passing through a hole; a ring formed of a strand of rope laid round, used in pipe joints or sails (—*also* **grummet**); (*formerly*) a cannon-wad made of rope, and rammed between the powder and the ball; (*med*) a small tube with a lip at either end which is inserted into the eardrum to permit fluid to drain from the middle ear in the treatment of secretory otitis media (glue ear).

gromwell *n* a herb of the borage family.

Gromyko *n* **Andrei Andreyevich** (1909–89) Soviet statesman and diplomat who adapted effortlessly to changing relations with the West, from the Cold War onwards. He was Soviet foreign minister (1957–85) and a Politburo member (1973–89).

Gronw Pebyr *n* (*Welsh Celtic myth*) the lover of Blodeuwedd. Together they tried to kill her husband, Lleu Llaw Gyffes. Lleu returned to kill Gronw. Blodeuwedd was transformed into an owl as a punishment.

groom *n* a person employed to care for horses; a bridegroom. * *vt* to clean and care for (animals); to make neat and tidy; to train (a person) for a particular purpose.—**groomer** *n*. —**grooming** *n*.

groomsman *n* (*pl* **groomsmen**) one who attends a bridegroom; a best man.

groove *n* a long, narrow channel; a spiral track in a gramophone record for the stylus; a settled routine. * *vt* to make a groove in.

grooved ware *n* (*archeo*) a characteristic form of late Neolithic pottery particularly associated with henges in southern and eastern England.

groovy *adj* (**groovier, grooviest**) (*sl*) excellent.

grope *vi* to search about blindly as in the dark; to search uncertainly for a solution to a problem. * *vt* to find by feeling; (*sl*) to fondle sexually. * *n* the act of groping.—**groper** *n*. —**gropingly** *adv*.

Gropius *n* **Walter** (1883–1969) German-born architect. He was a director of the Bauhaus school in Weimar and later a professor of architecture at Harvard. His notable works include the Bauhaus building in Dessau; the Pan Am Building in New York; the US Embassy in Athens. *See also* **Bauhaus**.

Gros *n* **Antoine Jean** (1771–1835) French painter who became Napoleon's official war painter. Travelling with Napoleon's armies, he recorded battle campaigns in a bold and vivid manner that won him great acclaim.

grosbeak *n* any finch-like bird of Europe or America with a large stout conical bill.

groschen *n* (*pl* **groschen**) a 10-pfennig coin used in Germany; a silver coin formerly current in Germany; in Austria, a coin with a value of one hundredth of a schilling. *See also* **Schilling**.

grosgrain *n* a stout double-corded silk; a fabric or ribbon of this.

gros point *n* a large needlepoint stitch covering two vertical and two horizontal threads; a piece of needlework done in this.

gross *adj* fat and coarse-looking; flagrant, dense, thick; lacking in refinement; earthy; obscene; total, with no deductions. * *n* (*pl* **grosses**) an overall total; (*pl* **gross**) twelve dozen. * *vt* to earn as total revenue.—**grossly** *adv*.—**grossness** *n*.

gross domestic product *n* the total value of goods and services produced by a country in one year.

gross income *n* the income of a person or organization before the deduction of any allowable expenses; income earned by a person or organization that is subject to tax but from which tax has not yet been deducted.

gross margin *or* **gross profit** *n* the difference between the sales revenue generated by a company and the cost of the products sold.

Grossmith *n* **George** (1847–1912) and **Weedon** (1852–1919) English theatricals and authors of *A Diary of a Nobody* (text by both, illustrations by Weedon), which first appeared in 1892.

gross national product *n* the gross domestic product plus income earned from abroad.

gross profit *see* gross margin.

gross receipts *npl* the total amount of money received before money is deducted to cover costs, taxation, etc.

Grosz *n* **George** (1893–1959) German painter, cartoonist, and illustrator who settled in the US in the 1930s and taught at the Art Students' League, New York.

groszy *n* a monetary unit of Poland, one hundredth of a zloty.

grot[1] *n* (*poet*) a grotto.

grot[2] *n* (*Brit sl*) unpleasant mess.—**grotty** *adj* (**grottier, grottiest**) nasty, unattractive; in bad condition; unsatisfactory.

grotesque *adj* distorted or fantastic in appearance, shape, etc; ridiculous; absurdly incongruous. * *n* a grotesque person or thing; a decorative device combining distorted plant, animal, and human forms; (*art*) a term for a style of ornamentation that began in Roman times and reached its height with rococo. It consisted of a series of figurative or floral ornaments in decorative frames that are linked by festoons. *See also* **arabesque**.—**grotesquely** *adv*.—**grotesqueness** *n*.

grotesquery, grotesquerie *n* (*pl* **grotesqueries**) *n* something that is fantastic or distorted in shape, etc.

grotto *n* (*pl* **grottoes, grottos**) a cave, esp one with attractive features.

grotty *see* grot.

grouch *vi* (*inf*) to grumble or complain. * *n* (*inf*) a grumble; a person who grumbles.—**groucher** *n*.

grouchy *adj* (**grouchier, grouchiest**) bad-tempered.—**grouchily** *adv*.—**grouchiness** *n*.

Groult *n* **André** (1884–1967) French furniture and textile designer whose signature piece was an anthropomorphic chest of drawers shown at the 1925 Paris Exposition.

ground *n* the solid surface of the earth; soil; the background, as in design; the connection of an electrical conductor with the earth; (*pl*) a basis for belief, action, or argument; the area about and relating to a building; a tract of land; sediment; (*art*) the first layer of color in a painting on which the others are worked; the primary of predominating color. * *vti* to set on the ground; to run aground or cause to run aground; to base, found, or establish; to instruct in the first principles of; to prevent (aircraft) from flying.

ground bass *n* (*mus*) a bass line that is constantly repeated throughout a composition, as a foundation for variation in the upper parts.

ground beef finely chopped beef.

ground control *n* the communications and tracking equipment and staff that monitor aircraft and spacecraft in flight and during takeoff and landing.

ground cover *n* low-growing shrubs, plants and other foliage on the ground.

ground crew *n* the technicians and engineers that service aircraft and spacecraft.

ground floor *n* the floor of a building on a level with the ground.

ground fog *n* fog in low-lying areas and valley floors caused the ground cooling quickly at night, chilling the lowest air layers to dew point.

ground frost *n* ice particles formed when the minimum temperature at ground level is less than 0°C, although the air temperature above may be higher than this.

ground hog *n* a woodchuck.

ground information *n* a term used in remote sensing referring to information obtained from data on the physical state of the Earth; e.g., maps, measurements of biomass, temperature, soil moisture content, etc.

grounding *n* basic general knowledge of a subject.

ground ivy *n* a trailing Eurasian plant with bluish-purple flowers.

groundless *adj* without reason.—**groundlessly** *adv*.

groundnut *n* a climbing plant of North America with an underground root; a peanut.

ground rule *n* a fundamental rule or principle.

groundsel *n* a weed of the aster family with yellow flowers.

groundsheet *n* a waterproof sheet placed on the ground in, or as part of, a tent.

groundsman *n* (*pl* **groundsmen**) a man who looks after a cricket pitch, football pitch, park, etc.

groundswell *n* a large rolling wave; a wave of popular feeling.

groundwater *n* water contained in the voids within rocks.

groundwork *n* foundation, basis.

group *n* a number of persons or things considered as a collective unit; a small musical band of players or singers; a number of companies under single ownership; two or more figures forming one artistic design; (*chem*) the vertical columns of elements in the periodic table. * *vti* to form into a group or groups.

groupie *n* a devoted fan.

group therapy *n* (*psychol*) the simultaneous treatment of patients with similar problems through mutual discussion and exchange of experiences.

groupware *npl* (*comput*) software that is created to increase the productivity of a group of workers in a team using a local area network.

grouse[1] *n* (*pl* **grouse**, **grouses**) a game bird; its flesh as food.

grouse[2] *vi* (*inf*) to complain.—**grouser** *n*.

grout *n* a thin mortar used as between tiles. * *vt* to fill with grout.—**grouter** *n*.

Grotius *n* **Hugo** (1583–1645) Dutch jurist, statesman, and theologian. His treatise on international law, *De Jura Belli et Pacis* (1625), is regarded as the main foundation of a system of international law, with its appeal to 'natural law' and to the social contract.

grove *n* a small wood, generally without undergrowth.

Grove *n* **George** (1820–1900) English scholar, editor, and writer on music; he edited *The Dictionary of Music and Musicians,* the authoritative music dictionary.

grovel *vi* (**groveling**, **groveled** *or* **grovelling**, **grovelled**) to lie and crawl in a prostrate position as a sign of respect, fear, or humility.—**groveller, groveler** *n*.—**grovellingly, grovelingly** *adv*.

Groves *n* **Charles** (1915–92) English conductor of outstanding merit, and a noted champion of British music.

grow *vb* (**growing**, **grew**, *pp* **grown**) *vi* to come into being; to be produced naturally; to develop, as a living thing; to increase in size, quantity, etc; (*with* **on**) to become more accustomed or acceptable to; (*with* **up**) to mature; to arise, develop. * *vt* to cause or let grow; to raise, to cultivate.—**growable** *adj*.—**grower** *n*.

growing pains *npl* muscular discomfort sometimes experienced by growing children; difficulties experienced in the early stages of a project.

growl *vi* to make a rumbling, menacing sound such as an angry dog makes. * *vt* to express in a growling manner. * *n* a growling noise; a grumble.—**growler** *n*.

growler *n* one who growls; (*arch*) a four-wheeled cab; a small iceberg; a beer jug or beer can.

grown-up *n* a fully grown person, an adult. * *adj* mature, adult; fit for an adult.

growth *n* the act or process of growing; progressive increase, development; something that grows or has grown; an abnormal formation of tissue, as a tumor; (*econ*) increase in the value of an asset; *same as* economic growth.

growth hormone, somatotrophin *or* **FH** *n* a hormone produced and stored by the anterior pituitary gland that controls protein synthesis in muscles and the growth of long bones in legs and arms. Low levels result in dwarfism in children. Overproduction produces gigantism in children, and acromegaly in adolescents.

groyne *n* a timber structure to stop the shifting of sand on a beach.

GRP *abbr* = glass-reinforced plastic (a plastic material that is made stronger by the addition of glass fibers, often incorrectly known as fiberglass).

grs. *abbr* = grains.

GRSC *abbr* = Graduate of the Royal Society of Chemistry.

GRSM, GRSM(Hons) *abbr* = Graduate of the Royal Schools of Music (Honours).

GRT *abbr* = gross registered tonnage.

grub *vb* (**grubbing, grubbed**) *vi* to dig in the ground; to work hard. * *vt* to clear (ground) of roots; to uproot. * *n* the worm-like larva of a beetle; (*sl*) food.

grubber *n* one who or that which grubs; a grub hoe.

grubby *adj* (**grubbier, grubbiest**) dirty.—**grubbily** *adv*.—**grubbiness** *n*.

Gruber *n* **Jacques** (1870–1936) French stained-glass artist who worked for Daum in Art Nouveau style.

grudge *n* a deep feeling of resentment or ill will. * *vt* to be reluctant to give or admit something.—**grudger** *n*. —**grudging** *adj*.—**grudgingly** *adv*.

gruel *n* a thin porridge cooked in water or milk.

grueling, gruelling *adj* severely testing, exhausting.

gruesome *adj* causing horror or loathing.

gruff *adj* rough or surly; hoarse.—**gruffly** *adv*.—**gruffness** *n*.

Gruffydd ap Cynan *n* (*b.* 1055) king of Gwynedd, Wales (1081–1137).

Gruffydd ap Llywelyn *n* (*d.* 1062) king of Gwynedd, Wales (1039–1063).

grugru *n* the larva of a South American weevil, cooked for food as a delicacy; the palm tree on which this lives.

grumble *vti* to mutter in discontent; to make a rumbling sound. * *n* a complaint; a grumbling sound.—**grumbler** *n*. —**grumblingly** *adv*.

Grumiaux *n* **Arthur** (1921–86) Belgian violinist of international repute whose playing was especially admired by fellow violinists for its classical purity.

grump *n* (*inf*) a bad-tempered person.

grumpy *adj* (**grumpier, grumpiest**) bad-tempered, peevish.—**grumpily** *adv*.—**grumpiness** *n*.

Grünewald *n* **Matthias** (*c.*1460–1528) German painter, whose few surviving works include religious paintings and altarpieces.

grunt *vi* to make a gruff guttural sound like a pig; to say or speak in such a manner. * *n* a low gruff sound; (*sl*) a US infantry man.

grunter *n* one who or that which grunts; an edible marine American fish; a pig; (*Austral sl*) a woman who is promiscuous.

grupetto *n* (*mus*) (*Italian*) literally, a "little group"; a general term used to describe various ornaments of one or more decorative notes.

Gruyère *n* a hard, pale yellow Swiss cheese usu with holes.

gr. wt. *abbr* = gross weight.

gry *abbr* = gross redemption yield.

gryphon *see* **griffin**.

gs *abbr* = ground speed.

g.s. *abbr* = general secretary; general service; (*army*) general staff.

GS *abbr* = General Staff/Secretary; Genetical Society; Grammar School.

GSA *abbr* = General Services Administration; Girls' School Association.

GSC *abbr* = General Staff Corps; gas-solid chromatography.

GSD *abbr* = General Supply Depot; Law Society Group for Solicitors with Disabilities.

GSG *abbr* = Guild of St Gabriel.

GSGB *abbr* = Geological Survey of Great Britain; Golf Society of Great Britain.

gsm *abbr* = grams per square meter; good sound merchantable.

GSM *abbr* = General Sales Manager; Guildhall School of Music and Drama.

GSMA *abbr* = Graduate of the Society of Sales Management Administrators.

GSNNA *abbr* = Graduate of the Society of Nursery Nursing Administrators.

GSO *abbr* = General Staff Officer.

GSOH *abbr* = good sense of humor.

GSP *abbr* = good service pension; glass fiber-strengthened polyester.

GSR *abbr* = galvanic skin response.

GSS *abbr* = Government Statistical Service; global surveillance system; geostationary satellite.

Gst. *abbr* = Gustav; Gustave; Gustavus.

GST *abbr* = Greenwich Sidereal Time.

G-string *n* a string on an instrument tuned to the note G; a string or strip worn round the waist and between the legs.

GSU *abbr* (*navy*) = general signals use.

G-suit *n* a (gravity) suit designed to counteract the physiological effects of acceleration on airmen and astronauts.

GSW *abbr* = gunshot wound.

gt. *abbr* = gilt; great; (*Latin*) *gutta*, "drop."

GT *abbr* = *Gran Turismo,* a sporty touring car; gas turbine; gas-tight; gross ton; gross tonnage.

GTA *abbr* = Gibraltar Teachers Association; Glass Textile Association; Gun Trade Association; gas-tungsten arc.

Gt. Br. or **Gt. Brit.** *abbr* = Great Britain.

GTC *abbr* = Government Training Center; General Teaching Council.

GTCL *abbr* (*Brit*) = Graduate of Trinity College of Music, London.

GTH *abbr* = gonadotrophic hormone.

GTI *abbr* (*Italian*) = *Gran Turismo,* "Grand Tourer, Injection."

GTM *abbr* = general traffic manager.

GTO *abbr* (*Italian*) = *Gran Turismo Omologato,* "certified Grand Tourer."

GTR *abbr* (*Italian*) = *Gran Turismo,* "Grand Tourer, Racing."

GTS *abbr* = gas-turbine ship; (*Italian*) *Gran Turismo,* "Grand Tourer Special/Sport"; Greenwich Time Signal.

gtt., Gtt. *abbr* (*pharm*) (*Latin*) = *gutta* or *guttae,* "a drop" or "drops."

G

GU *abbr* = genito-urinary; gastric ulcer.

guaco *n* (*pl* **guacos**) a tropical American plant, used as an antidote to snakebites.

Guadalajara *n* a city in Mexico.

Guadeloupe *n* a French overseas department comprising a small group of islands in the Caribbean lying in the middle of the Lesser Antilles Islands.

guaiacum *n* any of various tropical and West Indian shrubs or trees; the wood from these; a gum obtained from them, used medicinally and in the manufacture of varnishes.

Guam *n* an unincorporated territory of the USA comprising the most southerly and the largest of the Mariana Islands in the northwest Pacific Ocean.

guan *n* an American bird similar to a turkey.

guanaco *n* (*pl* **guanacos, guanaco**) the wild llama of South America.

Guangzhou *n* a city in China.

guanine *n* (*biol*) a nitrogenous base component of the nucleic acids, DNA and RNA, also found in guano.

guano *n* (*pl* **guanos**) dung of sea birds used as manure; a similar artificially produced fertilizer.

guar. *abbr* = guaranteed.

guarani *n* the standard monetary unit of Paraguay, made up of 100 centimos.

guarantee *n* a pledge or security for another's debt or obligation; a pledge to replace something if it is substandard, etc; an assurance that something will be done as specified; something offered as a pledge or security; a guarantor. * *vt* (**guaranteeing, guaranteed**) to give a guarantee for; to promise.

guarantor *n* a person who gives a guaranty or guarantee.

guaranty *n* (*pl* **guaranties**) (*law*) a guarantee.

guard *vt* to watch over and protect; to defend; to keep from escape or trouble; to restrain. * *vi* to keep watch (against); to act as a guard. * *n* defense; protection; a posture of readiness for defense; any device to protect against injury or loss; a person or group that guards; (*boxing, fencing, cricket*) a defensive attitude; a railway official in charge of a train; (*with cap: pl*) a regiment of British or European household troops.—**guardable** *adj*.—**guarder** *n*.

guarded *adj* discreet; cautious.—**guardedly** *adv*.—**guardedness** *n*.

guardhouse *n* a building used by a military guard when not walking a post; a military jail for temporary confinement.

Guardi *n* **Francesco** (1712–93) Venetian painter. He is known mainly for his views of Venice, painted in a free, expressive style in contrast to the detailed compositions of his older contemporary, Canaletto.

guardian *n* a custodian; a person legally in charge of a minor or someone incapable of taking care of their own affairs.—**guardianship** *n*.

guardrail *n* a railing, e.g. at the side of a road, to prevent falling; a short metal rod placed inside the rails to keep a train's wheels on the track.

guardsman *n* (*pl* **guardsmen**) an officer or solider of the US National Guard; an officer or soldier of the British Guards.

guard's van *n* the railway carriage where the guard travels, usu at the back of a train.—*also* **caboose**.

Guarneri *n* (*mus*) a famous family of violin-makers who were based in Cremona. The first member was Andrea who was a pupil of Amati (with Stradivari). The greatest was Giuseppe (1687–1744).

guart. *abbr* = guarantee.

Guatemala *n* a republic situated between the Pacific Ocean and the Caribbean Sea, where North America meets Central America.

Guatemala City *n* capital city of Guatemala.

guava *n* a tropical American shrubby tree widely cultivated for its sweet acid yellow fruit.

Guayaquil *n* a city in Ecuador.

gubernatorial *adj* pertaining to a governor or to his office.

gudgeon *n* a small edible freshwater fish; a fish used as bait in fishing; a person who is easily imposed upon; an iron pin or shaft on which a wheel revolves; (*naut*) one of the sockets into which a rudder is fixed.

guelder-rose *n* a cultivated variety of cranberry bush with large heads of sterile flowers.

Guelph, Guelf *n* a member of a powerful Italian political party in the Middle Ages, which supported the pope and sought the independence of Italy; a member of a secret society in 19th-century Italy, supporting Italian independence.

Guercino *n* **Il** (1591–1666) Italian baroque painter whose works are distinguished by their dramatic sense of light and color, soft, well-rounded forms, and excellent draughtsmanship.

guerdon *n* (*poet*) reward. * *vt* to reward, to recompense.

guernsey *n* a particular breed of dairy cattle orig from the island of Guernsey; a close-fitting knitted woolen jersey; (*Austral*) a woolen top worn by a football player.

guerrilla, guerilla *n* a member of a small force of irregular soldiers, making surprise raids.—*also adj*.

guess *vt* to form an opinion of or state with little or no factual knowledge; to judge correctly by doing this; to think or suppose. * *n* an estimate based on guessing.—**guessable** *adj*.—**guesser** *n*.

guesstimate *n* (*inf*) an estimate based mainly on guesswork.

guesswork *n* the process or result of guessing.

guest *n* a person entertained at the home, club, etc of another; any paying customer of a hotel, restaurant, etc; a performer appearing by special invitation; (*comput*) an access privilege in a local area network that allows an infrequent user to examine certain files on the network without having a password.

guesthouse *n* a private home or boarding-house offering accommodation.

guestroom *n* a room kept for guests.

Guevara *n* **Che [Ernesto Guevara]** (1928–67) Argentinean-born Communist revolutionary who joined Fidel Castro's forces in the Cuban revolution (1956–59) and subsequently led a guerrilla group in Bolivia, where he was killed.

guff *n* (*sl*) verbal nonsense.

guffaw *n* a crude noisy laugh. * *vi* to laugh boisterously.

gui *abbr* (*comput*) = graphics user interface.

GUI *abbr* = Golfing Union of Ireland.

Guilder *n* currency of the Netherlands.

guidance *n* leadership; advice, or counsel.

guide *vt* to point out the way for; to lead; to direct the course of; to control. * *n* a person who leads or directs others; a person who exhibits and explains points of interest; something that provides a person with guiding information; a device for controlling the motion of something; a book of basic instruction; a Girl Guide.—**guidable** *adj*.—**guider** *n*. —**guiding** *adj*, *n*.

guidebook *n* a book containing directions and information for tourists.

guide dog *n* a dog trained to guide a blind person.

guideline *n* a principle, or instruction which determines conduct or policy.

guided missile *n* a military missile whose course is controlled by radar or internal instruments, etc.

guidepost *n* a direction post; a guiding principle.

guidon *n* a forked or pointed military flag, used esp by troops of light cavalry.

guild *n* a club, society; an association of people with common interests formed for mutual aid and protection, as craftsmen in the Middle Ages.—*also* **gild**.

guilder *n* a coin of the Netherlands, or of Netherlands Antilles and Surinam; a gold or silver coin formerly in circulation in Germany, Austria and the Netherlands.— *also* **gilder, gulden**.

guildhall *n* the meeting place of a guild or corporation.

guile *n* craftiness, deceit.—**guileful** *adj*.—**guilefully** *adv*.—**guilefulness** *n*.

guileless *adj* without guile; ingenuous.—**guilelessly** *adv*.—**guilelessness** *n*.

guillemot *n* a small sea bird of the auk family.

guilloche *n* (*archit*) an ornament resembling braided ribbons.

guillotine *n* an instrument for beheading by a heavy blade descending between grooved posts; a device or machine for cutting paper; a rule for limiting time for discussion in a legislature. * *vt* to execute (someone) by guillotine.— **guillotiner** *n*.

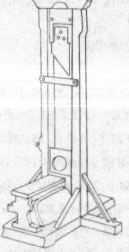

guilt *n* the fact of having done a wrong or committed an offence; a feeling of self-reproach from believing one has done a wrong.

guiltless *adj* innocent.

guilty *adj* (**guiltier, guiltiest**) having guilt; feeling or showing guilt.—**guiltily** *adv*.—**guiltiness** *n*.

Guimard *n* **Hector** (1867–1942) French architect whose signature pieces are the Castel Béranger apartment block and cast-iron details for the Paris Metro.

guimpe *n* a short blouse worn under a pinafore dress; a piece of cloth used to disguise a low-cut neckline; the starched cloth that covers the shoulders and front of a nun's habit; gimp.

guinea *n* a former English gold coin equal to 21 shillings (£1.05).

Guinea *n* a republic, formerly a French west African territory.

Guinea-Bissau *n* a republic located south of Senegal on the Atlantic coast of west Africa.

guinea fowl *n* a domestic African bird of the pheasant family.

Guinea franc *n* currency of Guinea.

guinea pig *n* a rodent-like animal commonly kept as a pet, and often used in scientific experiments; a person or thing subject to an experiment.

Guinness *n* **Sir Alec** (1914–2000) English stage and film actor whose films include *Kind Hearts and Coronets* (1949).

guipure (lace) *n* a coarse lace in which the pattern is supported by bars connecting the motifs rather than founded on a net base; a kind of gimp.

guise *n* an external appearance, aspect; an assumed appearance or pretence.

guitar *n* a stringed musical instrument with a long, fretted neck, and a flat body, which is plucked with a plectrum or the fingers.—**guitarist** *n*.

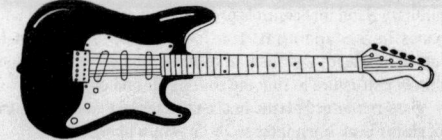

gulag *abbr* (*Russian*) = *Glavnoye Upravleniye Lagerei*, "Principal Administrative Camp" (a Soviet labor camp).

gular *adj* of, in, or pertaining to the gullet or throat.

Gulbenkian *n* 1. **Calouste Sarkis** (1869–1955) Turkish Armenian-born British financier, industrialist, diplomat, and philanthropist. He endowed the Gulbenkian Foundation. 2. **Nubar Sarkis** (1896–1972) son of Calouste Gulbenkian; Iranian diplomat and philanthropist.

gulch *n* a deep, narrow ravine.

gulden *see* **guilder**.

gules *n* (*her*) the color red, also indicated by vertical parallel lines.

gulf *n* a large area of ocean reaching into land; a wide, deep chasm; a vast separation.

Gulf Stream *n* a warm ocean current flowing from the Gulf of Mexico northward towards Europe.

gulfweed *n* brown seaweed with air bladders which floats in dense masses in warm Atlantic waters.—*also* **sargasso, sargasso weed**.

gull *n* any of numerous long-winged web-footed sea birds; a dupe; a gullible person. * *vt* to dupe, to cheat.

gullet *n* the esophagus; the throat.

gullible *adj* easily deceived.—**gullibility** *n*. —**gullibly** *adv*.

gully *n* (*pl* **gullies**) a narrow trench cut by running water after rain; (*cricket*) a fielding position between the slips and point. * *vt* (**gullying, gullied**) to make gullies in.

gulp *vt* to swallow hastily or greedily; to choke back as if swallowing. * *n* a gulping or swallowing; a mouthful.—**gulper** *n*. —**gulpingly** *adv*.

gum *n* the firm tissue that surrounds the teeth; a sticky substance found in certain trees and plants; an adhesive; chewing gum. * *vb* (**gumming, gummed**) *vt* to coat or unite with gum. * *vi* to become sticky or clogged; (*with* **up**) (*inf*) to mess up, prevent from working properly.

GUM *abbr* = genito-urinary medicine; (*Russian*) *Gosudarstvenni Universalni Magazin*, "Universal State Store."

gum ammoniac *n* a gum resin.—*also* **ammoniac**.

gum arabic or **acacia gum** *n* a white water-soluble powder that in natural form is obtained from some varieties of acacia trees.

gumbo *n* (*pl* **gumbos**) a rich soup thickened with okra.

gumboil *n* an abscess in the gum.

gumboot *n* a rubber, waterproof boot, a wellington.

gumma *n* (*pl* **gummas, gummata**) a syphilitic tumor.—**gummatous** *adj*.

gummy *adj* (**gummier, gummiest**) sticky; revealing the gums, toothless.—**gummily** *adv*.—**gumminess** *n*.

Gum nebula *n* (*astron*) the largest known nebula, located in the southern constellations Puppis and Vela.

gumption *n* (*inf*) shrewd practical common sense; initiative.

gum resin *n* a mixture of gum and resin exuded from certain plants and trees.

gumtree *n* a eucalyptus, or one of various other trees that yield gum.

gun *n* a weapon with a metal tube from which a projectile is discharged by an explosive; the shooting of a gun as a signal or salute; anything like a gun. * *vb* (**gunning, gunned**) *vi* to shoot or hunt with a gun; (*with* **for**) to search out in order to hurt or kill. * *vt* (*inf*) to shoot (a person); (*sl*) to advance the throttle of an engine.

gun. *abbr* = gunnery.

gunboat *n* a small armed ship.

gunboat diplomacy *n* the threat of force used to back diplomatic activity.

guncotton *n* a highly explosive substance formed by the action of nitric and sulfuric acid upon cotton or some other vegetable fiber.

Gundestrup Cauldron *n* a Celtic relic found in 1891 in a bog at Vesthimmerland in Jutland by a man cutting peat. Made of almost pure silver, it was probably originally gilded and would have been a ceremonial vessel.

gun dog *n* a dog trained to flush out or retrieve game shot by hunters.

gunfire *n* repeated and consecutive gunshots; the use of guns, etc, rather than other military options.

gung-ho *adj* enthusiastic; overeager.

gunk *n* (*inf*) dirty, greasy, matter; gunge.

gunman *n* (*pl* **gunmen**) an armed gangster; a hired killer.

gunmetal *n* bronze with a dark tarnish; its dark-grey color.

gunnel *see* **gunwale**.

gunner *n* a soldier, etc who helps fire artillery; a naval warrant officer in charge of a ship's guns.

gunnery *n* the science of the design and operation of large guns.

gunny *n* (*pl* **gunnies**) a strong coarse fabric made from jute used for sacking.

gunpoint *n* the muzzle of a gun; the threat of being shot.

gunpowder *n* an explosive powder used in guns, for blasting, etc.

gunrunning *n* the smuggling of firearms into a country.—**gunrunner** *n*.

gunship *n* an aircraft, esp a helicopter, equipped with rockets and machine guns.

gunshot *n* the range of a gun; the instance of shooting a gun or the shot fired from it.

gun-shy *adj* afraid of a loud noise; markedly distrustful.

gunslinger *n* (*sl*) a gunman or gunfighter.

gunsmith *n* a person skilled in making and repairing firearms.

gunstock *n* the wooden or metal mounting of a gun barrel.

gunwale *n* the upper edge of a ship's or boat's side.—*also* **gunnel**.

guppy *n* (*pl* **guppies**) a small vividly-colored fish of South America and the West Indies popular for aquariums.

Gurdjieff, Georgei Ivanovich (1877–1949) Russian mystic. He attracted disciples to his supposedly Sufi-based regime of spiritual enlightenment through physical discipline.

gurgitation *n* a whirling motion, a surging.

gurgle *vi* (*liquid*) to make a low bubbling sound; to utter with this sound. * *n* a bubbling sound.—**gurglingly** *adv*.

gurnard *n* (*pl* **gurnard, gurnards**) a spiny sea fish with an armored head.

Gurney *n* **Ivor Bertie** (1890–1937) English composer and poet who suffered terribly during World War I; composer of some memorable works, including the song-cycle *Ludlow and Teme*.

guru *n* (*pl* **gurus**) a Hindu or Sikh spiritual teacher; an influential leader or teacher, esp of a religious cult.

GUS *abbr* = Great Universal Stores.

gush *vi* to issue plentifully; to have a sudden flow; to talk or write effusively. * *vt* to cause to gush. * *n* a sudden outpouring.—**gushingly** *adv*.

gusher *n* an effusive person; an oil well from which oil spouts forth.

gushy *adj* (**gushier, gushiest**) expressing excessive admiration.—**gushily** *adv*.—**gushiness** *n*.

gusset *n* a small triangular piece of cloth inserted in a garment to strengthen or enlarge a part.

gust *n* a sudden brief rush of wind; a sudden outburst. * *vi* to blow in gusts.

gustation *n* the act of tasting; the ability to taste; taste.—**gustatory** *adj*.

gusto *n* great enjoyment, zest.

Guston *n* **Philip** (1913–80) American painter. His mature work includes some quite sinister pieces, notably his series on the Klu Klux Klan.

gusty *adj* (**gustier, gustiest**) windy; irritable.—**gustily** *adv*.—**gustiness** *n*.

gut *n* (*often pl*) the bowels or the stomach; the intestine; tough cord made from animal intestines; a narrow channel where a river joins an estuary or the sea; (*pl*) (*sl*) daring; courage. * *vt* (**gutting, gutted**) to remove the intestines from; to destroy the interior of.

Guthrie *n* 1. **Sir James** (1859–1930) Scottish painter and member of the Glasgow Boys. His works are subtle in tone and full of realism without sacrificing a good sense of decorative line and color. 2. **Sir [William] Tyrone** (1900–71) English actor and theatrical producer. 3. **Woody [Woodrow Wilson Guthrie]** (1912–67) American folksinger and writer whose songs influenced 1960s "protest" singers.

Guthrum *n* (*d*. 890) king of East Anglia (880–890).

gutless *adj* (*inf*) cowardly, lacking determination.—**gutlessness** *n*.

gutsy *adj* (**gutsier, gutsiest**) (*sl*) brave, courageous; passionate; greedy.

gutta *n* (*pl* **guttae**) (*archit*) a small loop-like ornament, esp in a Doric entablature; (*med*) (*formerly*) a drop.

gutta-percha *n* the flexible hardened juice of a tropical tree; one of several trees yielding this.

guttate, guttated *adj* (*plants*) spotted; drop-like.

gutter *n* a channel for carrying off water, esp at a roadside or under the eaves of a roof; a channel or groove to direct something (as of a bowling alley); the lowest condition of human life; (*comput*) an additional margin added to a word processing document or page layout document that allows space for a binder without obscuring the text. * *adj* marked by extreme vulgarity or indecency. * *vt* to provide with a gutter. * *vi* to flow in rivulets; (*candle*) to melt unevenly; (*candle flame*) to flutter.—**guttering** *n*.

guttering *n* the system of gutters, pipes, etc, on exterior walls for carrying off rainwater; material for making gutters.

gutter press *n* popular sensationalist newspapers.

guttersnipe *n* a dirty child who plays in the streets, esp in slum areas.

guttural *adj* formed or pronounced in the throat; harsh-sounding.—**gutturally** *adv*.—**gutturalness, gutturality, gutturalism** *n*.

gutturalize *vt* to form (a sound) in the throat; to speak in a harsh manner.—**gutturalization** *n*.

guy[1] *n* a rope, chain, etc, for fixing or steadying anything. * *vt* to fix or steady with a guy.

guy[2] *n* an effigy of Guy Fawkes made from old clothes stuffed with newspapers, etc burnt on the anniversary of the Gunpowder Plot (November 5); (*inf*) a man or boy; (*pl*) (*inf*) men or women; a shabby person. * *vt* to tease.

Guyana *n* a country in South America, situated on the northeast coast of the continent on the Atlantic Ocean.

Guyana Dollar *n* currency of Guyana.

guzzle *vti* to gulp down food or drink greedily.—**guzzler** *n*.

gv *abbr* = gravimetric volume.

GV *abbr* (*French*) = *grande vitesse*, "high speed."

GVA *abbr* = Gin and Vodka Association of Great Britain.

GVC *abbr* = Girls Venture Corps.

GVH *abbr* = graft-versus-host.

GVHD *abbr* = graft-versus-host disease.

GVS *abbr* = Goat Veterinary Society.

GVW *abbr* = gross vehicle weight.

GW *abbr* = gigawatt; gross weight.

Gwawl fab Clud *n* (*Welsh Celtic myth*) the suitor whom Rhiannon rejected to marry Pwyll.

Gwathmey *n* **Robert** (1903–88) American painter whose work is linear and colorful in a stylistically simplified style. A common theme is the life of southern African-American workers, as in *Workers on the Land* (1947).

G

Gwern *n* (*Welsh Celtic myth*) the son of Branwen and of Matholwch, king of Ireland.

Gweru *n* a city in Zimbabwe.

GWH *abbr* = gigawatt hour.

Gwion Bach *n* (*Welsh Celtic myth*) the son of Gwreang. According to legend, Taliesin was Gwion reincarnate.

GWIS *abbr* = German Wine Information Service.

GWP *abbr* = gross world product.

GWR *abbr* = Great Western Railway.

Gwreang *n* (*Welsh Celtic myth*) the father of Gwion Bach, who became Taliesin.

Gwreidawl *n* (*Welsh Celtic myth*) the father of Gwythyr.

Gwrhryr *n* (*Welsh Celtic myth*) one of the party formed to help Culhwch in his quest for Olwen. Gwrhryr was chosen because he could interpret the language of animals and so could ask them for directions.

Gwri *n* (*Welsh Celtic myth*) the name given to Pryderi by Teyrnon when the baby turned up on his doorstep.

GWS *abbr* = Great Western Society.

GWUCC *abbr* = Garment Workers Union Consultative Committee.

GWVA *abbr* = Great War Veterans' Association, Canada.

gwyddbwyll *see* **fidchell**.

Gwydion fab Don *n* (*Welsh Celtic myth*) a magician and a poet and the son of Don. He was the brother of Gilfaethwy and of Aranrhod.

Gwyn ap Nudd *n* (*Welsh Celtic myth*) a king of the Otherworld. He abducted Creiddylad, even although she was engaged to be married to another man.

Gwyn Dun Mane *n* (*Welsh Celtic myth*) Gwyn Dun Mane was a cow that Culhwch had to obtain for Yspaddaden.

gybe *vti* (*sail, boom*) to swing over from one side to the other; (*yacht*) to alter course in this way.—*also* **jibe**.

gym *n* (*inf*) a gymnasium.

gymkhana *n* a meeting featuring sports contests or athletic skills, esp horse-riding.

gymnasium *n* (*pl* **gymnasiums, gymnasia**) a room or building equipped for physical training and sports.

gymnast *n* a person skilled in gymnastics.

gymnastic *adj* pertaining to gymnastics.—**gymnastically** *adv*.

gymnastics *n sing* training in exercises devised to strengthen the body; (*pl*) gymnastic exercises; (*pl*) feats of dexterity or agility.

gymnosophist *n* one of a class of ancient Hindu philosophers who lived bare-footed and lightly clothed or naked.

gymnosperm *n* a plant whose seeds are not enclosed in a covering; a conifer or a conifer-like plant.—**gymnospermous** *adj*.

gynarchy *n* (*pl* **gynarchies**) gynecocracy.

gynecocracy, gynaecocracy *n* (*pl* **gynecocracies, gynaecocracies**) female rule or supremacy.—**gynecocratic, gynaecocratic** *adj*.

gynecol. *abbr* = gynecological; gynecology.

gynecology, gynaecology *n* the branch of medicine that deals with the diseases and disorders of the female reproductive system.—**gynecological, gynaecological, gynecologic, gynaecologic** *adj*.—**gynecologist, gynaecologist** *n*.

gynoecium *n* (*pl* **gynoecia**) (*bot*) the female organs of a flower.

gynopathy *n* the condition of feeling threatened by women.—**gynopathic** *adj*.

gynophore *n* the long stalk on which the pistil is situated, as in the passion flower.—**gynophoric** *adj*.

gyp *vt* (**gypping, gypped**) (*sl*) to cheat (someone). * *n* a swindle; a swindler; a college servant at Cambridge University; (*sl*) acute pain.—*also* **gip**.

gypsum *n* a chalk-like mineral used to make plaster of Paris and fertilizer.—**gypseous, gypsiferous** *adj*.

Gypsy *n* (*pl* **Gypsies**) a member of a travelling people, orig from India, now spread throughout Europe and North America; (*without cap*) a person who looks or lives like a Gypsy.—*also* **Gipsy** (*pl* **Gipsies**).

gyral *adj* rotatory, whirling; pertaining to a gyrus.

gyrate *vi* to revolve; to whirl or spiral.—**gyration** *n*. —**gyratory** *adj*.

gyre *vt* (*poet*) to gyrate. * (*poet*) a gyration.

gyrfalcon *n* a large northern falcon, often used for hunting.—*also* **gerfalcon**.

gyro *n* (*pl* **gyros**) (*inf*) a gyroscope; a gyrocompass.

gyrocompass *n* a compass mounted on a gyroscope to keep it stable.

gyroscope *n* a wheel mounted in a ring so that its axis is free to turn in any direction, so that when spinning rapidly it keeps its original plane of rotation.—**gyroscopic** *adj*.

gyrose *adj* (*bot*) turned round like a crook.

gyrostabilizer *n* a device of two or more gyroscopes to prevent rolling of a ship or aircraft.

gyrostat *n* a gyrostabilizer.

gyrus *n* (*pl* **gyri**) a convolution (of the brain).

gyve *vt* to fetter * *n* (*usu pl*) shackles.

H

h, H the eighth letter of the English alphabet.

H *symbol* = (*chem*) hydrogen (element); (*mus*) = B natural.

h *abbr* = hand; hecto- (hundred); (*phys*) Planck's constant.

h. *abbr* = harbor; hard; hardness; height; hence; high; honor; (*Latin*) *hora,* "hour"; (*shipping register*) hoy; hundred; husband; hydrant.

H *abbr* = (*pencil*) hard; (*cards*) hearts; (*phys, elec*) henry; heroin; (*phys*) horizontal component of the earth's magnetism; hospital; (*phys*) intensity of magnetic field; a Fraunhofer line produced by calcium.

H. *abbr* = Headquarters.

ha[1] *interj* used to express surprise, triumph, etc.—*also* **hah.**

ha[2] *abbr* = hectare(s); hardy annual; heir apparent; (*Latin*) *hoc anno,* "in this year."

HA *abbr* = Heavy Artillery; high altitude; (*gun*) high-angle; Historical Association.

HAA *abbr* = hepatitis-associated antigen; Historic Aircraft Association; Homeless Action and Accommodation Limited.

Haapi *n* (*Egypt*) god of the River Nile. He was believed to live above the first cataract and to be hermaphrodite.

Hab. *abbr* = Habakkuk.

hab. *abbr* = habitat.

HAB *abbr* = high-altitude bombing.

Habakkuk *n* (*OT*) writer of the book of Habakkuk; he may have been a musician of the Temple.

habanera *n* (*mus*) (*Spanish*) a dance of Cuban origin with a powerful, syncopated rhythm; it is, however, usu associated with Spain.

hab. corp. *abbr* (*Latin*) = *habeas corpus,* "may you have the body."

habeas corpus *n* a writ requiring that a prisoner be brought before a court, esp to ascertain the legality of his or her detention.

haberdasher *n* a dealer in sewing accessories; a dealer in men's clothing.— **haberdashery** *n.*

habergeon *n* a sleeveless coat of chain mail covering the neck and breast.

hab. fa. *or* **fac. poss.** *abbr* (*Latin*) = *habere facias possessionem.*

habile *adj* skillful.

habiliment *n* (*often pl*) clothing, attire.

habilitate *vi* to qualify for a post. * *vt* to provide working capital for (a mine).— **habilitation** *n.* —**habilitator** *n.*

habit *n* a distinctive costume, as of a nun, etc; a thing done often and hence easily; a usual way of doing things; an addiction, esp to narcotics. * *vt* to clothe.

habitable *adj* capable of being lived in.—**habitability** *n.* —**habitably** *adv.*

habitat *n* (*biol*) the normal environment of an animal or plant, specified by particular features, e.g., rivers, ponds, sea shore.

habitation *n* the act of inhabiting; a dwelling or residence.—**habitational** *adj.*

habited *adj* wearing a habit or a dress.

habit-forming *adj* addictive.

habitual *adj* having the nature of a habit; regular.—**habitually** *adv.*— **habitualness** *n.*

habituate *vt* to accustom.—**habituation** *n.*

habitude *n* a custom or tendency; familiarity.—**habitudinal** *adj.*

habitué *n* a frequent visitor to a place.

Habren *n* (*Brit Celtic myth*) the daughter of Locrinus and his mistress, Estrildis. She and her mother were drowned as an act of vengeance by Gwendolen, the estranged wife of Locrinus.

habt. *abbr* (*Latin*) = *habeat,* "let him have."

HAC *abbr* (*Brit*) = Honourable Artillery Company.

hachure *n* a short line on a map that indicates the direction and steepness of a slope but gives no indication of altitude.

hacienda *n* (in Spanish-speaking countries) a large estate or ranch; the main house on such an estate.

hack[1] *vti* to cut or chop (at) violently; to clear (vegetation) by chopping; (*comput*) (*with* **into**) to gain illegal access to confidential data. * *n* a gash or notch; a harsh, dry cough.

hack[2] *n* a riding horse for hire; an old worn-out horse; a mediocre or unexceptional writer; a coach for hire; (*inf*) a taxi. * *vti* to ride a horse cross-country. * *adj* banal, hackneyed.

hackbut *n* a type of arquebus.—*also* **hagbut.**

hacker *n* a person who hacks; (*inf*) (*comput*) a person who uses computers as a hobby, esp one who accesses other people's computers, usu with the aid of communications technology and without permission.

hacking *adj* (*cough*) short, dry, spasmodic.

hackles *npl* the hairs on the back of a dog, cat, etc, that stick out when the animal is angry or afraid.

Hackman *n* **Gene [Eugene Alden]** (1930–) American movie actor and winner of several Academy Awards, e.g., for his role in *The French Connection* (1971).

hackney *n* a horse for driving or riding; any of an English breed of high-stepping horses; a carriage or vehicle for hire.

hackneyed *adj* made trite or banal through over-use.

hacksaw *n* a fine-toothed saw for cutting metal.

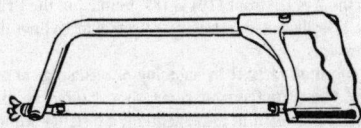

HACSG *abbr* = Hyperactive Children's Support Group.

HACT *abbr* = Housing Association Charitable Trust.

Hacular *n* an important lake settlement in southern Turkey, comparable to Çatal Hüyük.

had *see* **have.**

HAD *abbr* = high-altitude deterioration.

Hadan *n* (*mus*) the call to prayer chanted from the minarets by Mohammedan priests.

HADC *abbr* = Helen Arkell Dyslexic Centre.

haddock *n* (*pl* **haddocks, haddock**) an important Atlantic food fish related to the cod.

Hades *n* (*Greek myth*) the king of the underworld, afterwards called Pluto; the underworld; the home of the dead; (*inf*) hell.—**Hadean** *adj.*—*also* **hell.**

Hadfield *n* **George** (*b*.1763) English architect. His notable works include City Hall, Washington.

Hadith *n* (*pl* **Hadith, Hadiths**) the traditions surrounding Mohammed and his sayings; an appendix to the Koran

hadj *n* (*pl* **hadjes**) a pilgrimage to Mecca, required of all Muslims.—*also* **hajj** (*pl* **hajjes**).

hadji *n* (*pl* **hadjis**) a Muslim who has made the pilgrimage to Mecca.—*also* **haji, hajji** (*pl* **hajis, hajjis**).

hadn't = had not.

Hadrian *n* **[Publius Aelius Hadrianus]** (76–138) Roman soldier and emperor who spent his reign strengthening the boundaries of the Roman Empire. He built Hadrian's Wall.

Hadrian's Wall *n* a wall constructed across Northern England under the orders of the Roman Emperor Hadrian.

HAE *abbr* = Hire Association Europe.

Haemon *n* (*Greek myth*) a son of Pelasgus and father of Thessalus.

Haemus *n* ancient name for the range of mountains in Thrace, now called the **Balkans.**

Hafgan *n* (*Welsh Celtic myth*) "summer white," the rival and opponent of Arawn, king of Annw, with whom he is said to have taken part in an annual single combat contest.

hafiz *n* a Muslim who knows the Koran by heart; a title of respect; the guardian of the mosque.

hafnium *n* a silvery metallic element found in zirconium. *symbol* Hf.

HAFRA *abbr* (*Brit*) = Hat and Allied Feltmakers' Research Association.

haft *n* the handle of a weapon or tool.

hag *n* an ugly or unpleasant old woman; a witch.—**haggish** *adj.*—**haggishness** *n.*

Hag. *abbr* = Haggai.

Hagar *n* (*OT*) servant of Sarah, the wife of Abraham, who bore Abraham a son when Sarah was childless; when Sarah's son, Isaac, was born, Hagar and her child Ishmael were cast out to be wanderers in the desert. *See also* **Ishmael.**

Haggadah *n* (*pl* **Haggadoth**) (*Judaism*) a parable or illustration of a commentary on Scripture; a book containing the order for the traditional Passover feast; a narrative of the flight from Egypt that is the main part of the Passover feast.

Haggai *n* (*OT*) book of the Bible that is important for our knowledge of conditions in Palestine after the Exile.

haggard *adj* having an exhausted, untidy look.—**haggardly** *adv.*—**haggardness** *n*.

Haggard *n* Sir **H[enry] Rider** (1856–1925) English novelist, who wrote 34 adventure novels, the best known of which are *King Solomon's Mines* and *She*.

haggis *n* (*pl* **haggises, haggis**) a traditional Scottish dish made of minced offal with suet, onions, oatmeal, seasonings, etc.

haggle *vi* to bargain; barter; to dispute over terms; to cavil. * *n* the act of haggling.—**haggler** *n*.

hagiography *n* (*pl* **hagiographies**) the history or legends of the saints; an uncritical biography.—**hagiographer, hagiographist** *n*.—**hagriographic, hagiographical** *adj*.

Hag of Hell *n* (*Celtic myth*) a woman of supernatural powers who appears in the story of Culhwch and Olwen.

Hague *n* **The (s'Gravenhage)** seat of government of the Netherlands.

hah *see* **ha**.

ha-ha[1] *interj* an exclamation of mockery; an outburst of laughter.—*also* **haw-haw**.

ha-ha[2] *n* a fence sunk in the ground as a boundary of a park or garden.

Hahn *n* **Otto** (1879–1968) German physical chemist and winner of the 1944 Nobel Prize for Chemistry. With Meitner and others, he undertook research that led to the discovery of nuclear fission.

HAHP *abbr* = Health Action for Homeless People.

HAI *abbr* = Health Action International; Helicopter Association International; Help Age International; Historical Association of Ireland; hospital-acquired infection.

HAIA *abbr* = Hearing Aid Industry Association.

Haifa *n* a city in Israel.

Haig *n* **Douglas, 1st Earl** (1861–1928) British field marshal; commander in chief of British forces on the Western front (1915–18); founder of the British Legion.

haiku *n* (*pl* **haiku**) a 17-syllable sequential verse form of three lines devised by the Japanese poet Basho.

hail[1] *vt* to greet; to summon (a taxi) by shouting or signaling; to welcome with approval, to acclaim. * *vi* (*with* **from**) to come from. * *interj* an exclamation of tribute, greeting, etc. * *n* a shout to gain attention; a distance within which one can be heard calling.—**hailer** *n*.

hail[2] *n* (*meteor*) hard balls or pellets of ice usu associated with cumulonimbus cloud; something, as abuse, bullets, etc, sent forcefully in rapid succession. * *vti* to pour down like hail.

HAIL *abbr* = Hague Academy of International Law.

Haile Selassie *n* **[Ras Tafari Makonnen]** (1892–1975) emperor of Ethiopia (1930–36, 1941–74); focus of the Rastafarian cult. He helped establish the Organisation of African Unity in the 1960s and was deposed in a military coup.

Hail Mary *n* (*RC Church*) a prayer to the Virgin Mary beginning with these words.

"Hail! Minnesota" *n* the song of the American state, Minnesota.

"Hail, South Dakota" *n* the song of the American state, South Dakota.

hailstone *n* a pellet of hail.

hailstorm *n* a sudden storm of hail.

"Hail, Vermont" *n* the song of the American state, Vermont.

Haiphong *n* a city in Vietnam.

hair *n* a thread-like growth from the skin of mammals; a mass of hairs, esp on the human head; a threadlike growth on a plant.

haircut *n* a shortening and styling of hair by cutting it; the style of cutting.

hairdo *n* (*pl* **hairdos**) (*inf*) a particular style of hair after cutting, etc.

hairdresser *n* a person who cuts, styles, colors, etc, hair.—**hairdressing** *n*.

hairgrip *n* a clip for holding hair in position; a bobby pin.

hairless *adj* without hair; having little hair.

hairline *n* a very thin line; the outline of the hair on the head.

hairnet *n* a net used to keep the hair in place

hairpiece *n* a wig or toupee; an additional piece of hair attached to a person's real hair.

hairpin *n* a U-shaped pin used to hold hair in place.

hairpin bend *n* a sharply curving bend in a road, etc.

hair-raising *adj* terrifying, shocking.

hair's-breadth *n* a very small space or amount.

hairsplitting *adj* making petty distinctions; quibbling. * *n* the act of making petty distinctions. —**hairsplitter** *n*.

hairspring *n* a slender, hair-like coil spring, as in a watch.

hairstyle *n* the way in which hair is arranged.—**hairstylist** *n*.

hair transplant *n* the procedure of grafting hair strands to a bald area of the head.

hair trigger *n* a trigger on a firearm that responds to the slightest pressure.

hair-trigger *adj* reacting to the slightest stimulus.

hairweaving *n* the technique of attaching strands of false hair to the follicles of the head.

hairy *adj* (**hairier, hairiest**) covered with hair; (*inf*) difficult, dangerous.—**hairiness** *n*.

Haitink *n* **Bernard** (1929–) Dutch conductor with an international reputation and formidable repertoire, including, in particular, Mahler.

haji, hajji *see* **hadji**.

hake *n* (*pl* **hake, hakes**) a marine food fish related to the cod.

hakim *n* a judge, administrator or governor of an Islamic country; a Muslim physician.

Hal. *symbol* (*chem*) = halogen.

Halab *n* a city in the Syrian Arab Republic.

Halaf *n* an important archeological site, close to the Khabur river near the border of Turkey and Syria. It flourished *c*. 6000–5000 BC.

Halakah, Halacha *n* (*pl* **Halakoth, Halachoth**) (*Judaism*) traditional law containing minor precepts in addition to the Mosaic law; legal literature in general.

halal *n* meat from animals butchered according to Muslim law. * *adj* of or pertaining to such meat.—*also* **hallal**.

halala *n* a monetary unit of Saudi Arabia, equal to one hundredth of a riyal.

halation *n* (*photog, TV*) a halo-like appearance around an object, caused by light reflection.

halberd, halbert *n* a medieval ax-like weapon consisting of a long staff to which an ax with a spear-like point was affixed at right angles to its handle or haft.

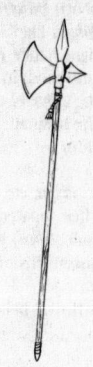

halberdier *n* a soldier armed with a halberd.

halcyon *adj* calm, gentle, peaceful. * *n* a fabled bird (probably the kingfisher) that nested at sea and calmed it.

hale *adj* healthy and strong.

Hale *n* **Nathan** (1755–1855) American Revolutionary War hero, who spied for the Americans behind British lines and was captured and hanged.

haler *n* a monetary unit of the Czech Republic and Slovakia, equal to one hundredth of a koruna.

Hale telescope *n* the 200-inch telescope at Mount Palomar Observatory, which took 15 years to build.

Halévy *n* **Jacques François** (1799–1862) French composer of operas and ballets, the most notable being *La Juive* (opera). He was also a teacher and instructed both Gounod and Bizet.

half *n* (*pl* **halves**) either of two equal parts of something; (*inf*) a half-price ticket for a bus, etc; (*inf*) half a pint. * *adj* being a half; incomplete; partial. * *adv* to the extent of a half; (*inf*) partly.

half-and-half *n* something half one thing and half another. * *adj* partly one thing and partly another. * *adv* in two equal parts.

halfback *n* (*football, hockey*) a player occupying a position between the forward and the fullbacks; a player in this position in other sports.

half-baked *adj* (*inf*) poorly planned or thought out; (*inf*) stupid.

half-brother *n* a brother through one parent only.

half-caste *n* a person whose parents are of different races.

half cock *n* the middle position of a gun's hammer; **at half cock** not prepared.—**half-cocked** *adj*.

half-hearted *adj* with little interest, enthusiasm, etc.—**half-heartedly** *adv.*—**half-heartedness** *n*.

half-height drive *n* (*comput*) a disk drive that occupies approximately 1.6 inches' height in a computer drive bay.

half-hitch *n* a knot made by passing the end of a piece of rope around an object, then across itself, and then through the resulting loop.

half-hour *n* 30 minutes; the point 30 minutes after the beginning of an hour.

half-life *n* (*phys*) the time taken for a radioactive isotope to lose exactly half of its radioactivity.

half-mast *n* the position to which a flag is lowered as a sign of mourning.

half-measure *n* (*often pl*) an inadequate action; a compromise.

half-moon *n* the moon at its phase when half the disk is illuminated; something shaped like this. * *adj* in the shape of a half-moon.

half-nelson *n* a wrestling hold, pinning the arm of an opponent behind the back from behind.

half note *n* (*mus*) a note, formerly the shortest in time value, with half the value of a whole note (semibreve).

halfpenny *n* (*pl* **halfpence**) a bronze coin worth two farthings in pre-decimal British currency.

half-pint *n* a dry or liquid measure equal to eight ounces; (*sl*) a small or unimportant person.

Halfdan *n* (Ragnarson) (*d.* 895) king of York (875–883). In 875 he founded the kingdom of York which had thirteen Norse rulers in eighty years.

half-sister *n* a sister through one parent only.

half-sole *n* a sole from the instep to the toe.

half step, half tone *n* (*mus*) a pitch interval halfway between two whole tones; the smallest interval regularly used in modern Western music.—*also* **semitone**.

half-term *n* (*Brit*) a short holiday in the middle of a school term.

half-time *n* (*sport*) an interval between two halves of a game.

half title *n* a short title on the page before the title page of a book; a bastard title.

halftone *n* an illustration printed from a relief plate, showing light and shadow by means of minute dots; (*comput*) the shading in an image created by use of dots of various sizes and densities.

half-track *n* a (military) vehicle with wheels in front but driven by Caterpillar tracks at the rear.

half-truth *n* a statement that is only partly true.

half volley *n* (*tennis, etc*) the striking of the ball the instant it bounces.

halfway *adj* midway between two points, etc.

halfway house *n* a place for helping people to adjust to normal society after being imprisoned, hospitalized, etc.

halfwit *n* a stupid or silly person.—**halfwitted** *adj.*—**halfwittedly** *adv.*—**halfwittedness** *n.*

halibut *n* (*pl* **halibut, halibuts**) a large marine flatfish used as food.

halide *n* (*chem*) a compound consisting of a halogen and another element.

halite *n* a common mineral in evaporite deposits, often associated with gypsum and anhydrite.— *also* **rock salt**.

halitosis *n* the condition of having bad breath, which may arise for a number of reasons, including the type of food recently eaten, disease of the teeth or infections of the throat, nose, and lungs.

hall *n* a public building with offices, etc; a large room for exhibits, gatherings, etc; the main house on a landed estate; a college building, esp a dining room; a vestibule at the entrance of a building; a hallway.

Hall *n* **1.** [Marguerite] Radclyffe (1883–1943) English novelist whose novel *The Well of Loneliness* (banned in the UK until 1949 but not in the USA) was one of the first works of fiction to describe lesbianism sympathetically. **2.** Sir **Peter [Reginald Frederick]** (1930–) English stage director and theater manager .

hallal *see* **halal**.

Hallé *n* **Charles** (1819–95) German-born conductor and pianist who settled in Manchester in 1848 and founded the internationally famous Hallé Orchestra in 1857.

Hallel *n* (*Judaism*) Psalms 113–118, chanted as part of morning services during Passover and other festivals.

hallelujah, halleluiah *interj* (*Bible*) an exclamation of praise to God. * *n* a praising of God; a musical composition having this as its theme.—*also* **alleluia**.

Halley *n* **Edmund** (1656–1742) English astronomer and mathematician, who calculated the orbit of the comet now named **Halley's Comet** and calculated the dates of its return; Astronomer Royal (1720–42) and a contemporary of Newton.

Halley's comet *n* the first-known periodic comet named after Edmund Halley, first seen in 1583. Halley predicted its return in 1758, 1835 and 1910.

halliard *see* **halyard**.

halling *n* (*mus*) a lively Norwegian dance, in 2/4 time, during which men leap high into the air.

hallmark *n* a mark used on gold, silver and platinum articles to signify a standard of purity, weight, date of manufacture; a mark or symbol of high quality; a characteristic feature. * *vt* to stamp with a hallmark.

hallo *see* **hello**.

hallow *vt* to make or regard as holy.—**hallowed** *adj.*—**hallowedness** *n.* —**hallower** *n.*

Hallowe'en, Halloween *n* October 31, All Hallows Eve , the eve of All Saints' Day. Traditionally associated with witches, who are said to roam around freely then. The equivalent of the ancient Celtic festival of Samhain.

Hallowmas *n* (*formerly*) All Saints' Day, November 1.

Hallstatt *n* a village in Upper Austria, situated by a lake in the region known as Salzkamergut "the place of good salt," whose capital is Salzburg "salt town." *adj of or denoting the final period of the Bronze Age and the first period of the Iron Age (9th–4th centuries BC).

Hallstatt Excavations *n* the uncovering of a vast prehistoric cemetery of two and a half thousand graves in 1846. The grave goods retrieved from the ancient cemetery at Hallstatt indicated a settlement of iron-using Celts.

hallucinate *vti* to have or cause to have hallucinations.—**hallucinator** *n.*

hallucination *n* the apparent perception of sights, sounds, etc that are not actually present; something perceived in this manner.—**hallucinational, hallucinative** *adj.*—**hallucinatory** *adj.*

hallucinogen *n* a substance or drug that causes hallucinations, e.g., mescaline and lysergic acid diethylamide.—**hallucinogenic** *adj.*

hallux *n* (*pl* **halluces**) the big toe; the first digit on the back foot of an amphibian, bird, mammal, or reptile.

halm *see* **haulm**.

halo *n* (*pl* **haloes, halos**) (*astron*) a bright ring of white or colored light that may be seen around a body such as the sun, the moon, a comet, globular cluster or galaxy, due to refraction of light by the crystals in high cirrus cloud; (*art*) a symbolic ring of light around the head of a saint in pictures; the aura of glory surrounding an idealized person or thing. * *vt* (**haloing, haloed**) to surround with a halo.

halo effect *see* **horns and halo effect**.

halogen *n* any of the five chemical elements, found in group 7 of the periodic table, that are the extreme form of the non-metals, i.e., fluorine, chlorine, bromine, iodine and astatine.—**halogenous** *adj.*

haloperidol *see* **tranquilizer**.

halophilic bacteria *npl* (*biol*) bacteria that can tolerate salt and live in the surface layers of the sea.

halophyte *n* (*bot*) a plant that can tolerate a high level of salt in the soil.

HALOW *abbr* (*Brit*) = Help and Advice Line for Offenders' Wives.

Hals *n* **Frans** (*c.*1581–1666) Dutch painter. His fresh, natural spontaneity and a sound understanding of the works of Caravaggio combine in the famous *Laughing Cavalier* (1624).

Halsey *n* **William F[rederick] Jnr** (1884–1959) American naval officer who distinguished himself in both World Wars and rose to the rank of fleet admiral.

Halstatt *n* an archeological site in Austria, 30 miles east of Salzburg, containing nearly 3000 burials and ancient extensive salt mines, mostly of Iron Age date.

halt[1] *n* a temporary interruption or cessation of progress; a minor station on a rail line. * *vti* to stop or come to a stop.

halt[2] *vi* to falter; to hesitate.—**halting** *adj.*

halter *n* a rope or strap for tying or leading an animal; a woman's dress or top tied behind the neck and waist leaving the back and arms bare. * *vt* to put a halter on (a horse, etc).

halve *vt* to divide equally into two; to reduce by half; (*golf*) to play one hole in the same number of strokes as one's opponent.

halves *see* **half**.

halyard *n* a line for hoisting or lowering a sail, yard or flag.—*also* **halliard**.

ham *n* the upper part of a pig's hind leg, salted, smoked, etc; the meat from this area; (*inf*) the back of the upper thigh; (*inf*) an actor who overacts; (*inf*) a licensed amateur radio operator. * *vti* (**hamming, hammed**) to speak or move in an exaggerated manner, to overact.

hamada *n* a flat, bare, rocky desert plateau left when the wind has blown away all loose material.

hamadryad *n* (*pl* **hamadryads, hamadryades**) (*Greek myth*) a wood nymph; a giant cobra, the king cobra.

hamadryas *n* a North African baboon, the male of which has a heavy mane of silvery hair.

hamal *n* a porter in several Muslim countries.—*also* **hammal, hammaul**.

Hamburg[1] *n* a city in Germany.

Hamburg[2] *n* a rich, black grape; a breed of black domestic fowl.

hamburger *n* ground beef; a cooked patty of such meat, often in a bread roll with pickle, etc.

Hamburgian *adj* relating to the earliest culture to emerge in the Netherlands, Belgium and North Germany, at the end of the last Ice Age.

hame[1] *n* either of two curved bars for the traces on the collar of a draught horse.

hame[2] *n, adv* (*Scot*) home.

ham-handed, ham-fisted *adj* (*inf*) clumsy.

Hamhung *n* a city in the Democratic People's Republic of Korea.

Hamilton[1] *n* **1.** a port in S Ontario, Canada. **2.** capital city and chief port of Bermuda. **3.** a a city in New Zealand. **3.** a town in S Scotland in South Lanarkshire.

Hamilton[2] *n* **1. Alexander** (1757–1804) American statesman and founder of the US Federal Bank. He was also the founder of the Federalist Party (1787) and first secretary of the Treasury (1789–95). **2. Gavin** (1723–98) Scottish painter. He settled permanently in Rome from 1775, where he was involved in the Neoclassical circle of Mengs. **3. Thomas** (1784–1858), Scottish architect. His notable works include the Royal High School, Edinburgh.

Hamite *n* a descendant of Ham, son of Noah; a member of the Hamitic race.

Hamitic *adj* relating to Ham, the races descended from him, or the languages they speak. * *n* any of a group of languages spoken in North Africa.

hamlet *n* a very small village.

hammal, hammaul *see* **hamal**.

Hammarskjöld *n* **Dag [Hjalmar Agne Carl]** (1905–61) Swedish Secretary General of the United Nations (1953–61). He was posthumously awarded the Nobel Peace Prize in 1961.

hammer *n* a tool for pounding, driving nails, etc, with a heavy head and a handle; a thing like this in shape or use, as the part of the gun that strikes the firing pin; (*anat*) a bone of the middle ear; (*sport*) a heavy metal ball attached to a wire thrown in athletic contests; (*mus*) that part of the piano mechanism which strikes the strings;(*mus*) mallet for playing the dulcimer; (*mus*) the clapper of bell; **hammer and tongs** with great force. * *vti* to strike repeatedly, as with a hammer; to drive, force, or shape, as with hammer blows; (*inf*) to defeat utterly.—**hammerer** *n.*

Hammer-god *n* a Gaulish Celtic god represented as bearded and as wearing a short belted tunic and a heavy cloak; connected with healing; associated with the sun and with earthly prosperity.

hammerhead *n* a shark with a mallet-shaped head.

Hammerstein *n* **Oscar (II)** (1895–60) American songwriter and librettist responsible for numerous musicals, in collaboration first with Jerome Kern, then with Richard Rodgers , e.g., *The Sound of Music* (1959).

hammer toe *n* condition similar to a bunion but involving the second toe, which becomes bent at the joint to resemble a hammer, because shoes or boots are too tight or pointed.

Hammett *n* [Samuel] **Dashiell** (1894–1961) American novelist whose best-known novels are *The Maltese Falcon* and *The Thin Man*.

hammock *n* a length of strong cloth or netting suspended by the ends and used as a bed.

Hammond organ *n* (*mus, trademark*) an electric organ first produced by the Hammond Organ Company, Chicago, in 1935.

hammy *adj* (**hammier, hammiest**) (*inf*) over-acting; exaggerated.

H

hamper¹ *vt* to hinder; to interfere with; to encumber.—**hamperer** *n*.

hamper² *n* a large, usu covered, basket for storing or transporting food, crockery, etc.

hamster *n* a small, short-tailed rodent with cheek pouches.

hamstring *n* any of the tendons at the back of the thigh that flex and rotate the leg and are responsible for the bending of the knee joint. * *vt* (**hamstringing, hamstrung**) to cripple by severing the hamstring of; to render useless, to thwart.

Hamsun *n* **Knut** (1859–1952) Norwegian novelist, poet, and dramatist, whose best-known novel is *Hunger*. He was awarded the Nobel Prize for Literature in 1920.

hamulus *n* (*pl* **hamuli**) a small hook-like projection at the end of the bones or between the fore and hind wings of a bee or bee-like insect.—**hamular** *adj*.

HANA *abbr* = Halibut Association of North America.

Hancock *n* **Tony [Anthony John]** (1924–68) English comedian, whose finest performances were in the British radio series *Hancock's Half Hour* and the TV series *Hancock*. He committed suicide.

hand *n* the part of the arm below the wrist, used for grasping; a side or direction; possession or care; control; an active part; a promise to marry; skill; one having a special skill; handwriting; applause; help; a hired worker; a source; one of a ship's crew; anything like a hand, such as a pointer on a clock; the breadth of a hand, four inches when measuring the height of a horse; the cards held by a player at one time; a round of card play; (*inf*) applause. * *adj* of, for, or controlled by the hand. * *vt* to give as with the hand; to help or conduct with the hand. * *vi* (*with* **on**) to pass to the next.

handax *n* (*archeo*) a stone tool, usu pear-shaped or oval, with a sharp cutting edge and a rounded portion that fitted into the palm of the hand.

handbag *n* (*Brit*) a purse.

handball *n* a game in which players bat a ball against a single wall or walled court with the hand; the small, hard, rubber ball used in this.

handbells *npl* (*mus*) bells, of various pitch, that are held in the hands of a group of performers and rung in sequence to create a tune.

handbill *n* a small printed notice to be passed out by hand.

handbook *n* a book containing useful instructions.

handbrake *n* a brake operated by hand.

h & c *abbr* = hot and cold (water).

handcart *n* a small cart pulled or pushed by hand.

handcuff *n* (*usu pl*) either of a pair of connected steel rings for shackling the wrists of a prisoner. * *vt* to manacle.

handed *adj* having or involving (a specified kind or number of) hands.

Handel *n* **George Frideric**, originally **Georg Friederich Handel** (1685–1759) German-born British composer. His works include operas, oratorios and orchestral pieces; he is probably most famous for *Water Music* and *The Messiah*.

h & f *abbr* = (*swimming pool*) heated and filtered.

handfast *vt* (*formerly*) to pledge or betroth; to grip with the hand. * *n* a contract of betrothal.

handful *n* as much as will fill the hand; a few; (*inf*) a person who is difficult to handle or control.

hand grenade *n* a grenade designed to be thrown by hand.

hand gun *n* a firearm that can be held and fired with one hand.

hand-held scanner *n* (*comput*) a scanning device that can be held in the hand. *See also* **bitmap, scanner**.

handicap *n* a mental or physical impairment; a contest in which difficulties are imposed on, or advantages given to, contestants to equalize their chances; such a difficulty or advantage; any hindrance. * *vt* (**handicaping, handicaped**) to give a handicap to; to hinder.—**handicaper** *n*.

handicaped *adj* mentally or physically disabled.

handicaper *n* a person who assigns handicaps to contestants; one who uses past records to predict the winners in horse races.

handicraft *n* a skill involving the hands, such as basketwork, pottery, etc; an item of pottery, etc made by hand.

handiwork *n* handmade work; something done by a person or thing.

h & j *abbr* = hyphenation and justification.

handkerchief *n* a small cloth for blowing the nose, etc.

handle *vt* to touch, hold, or move with the hand; to manage or operate with the hands; to manage, deal with; to buy and sell (goods). * *vi* to react in a specified way. * *n* a part of anything designed to be held or grasped by the hand; (*comput*) a small black square that surrounds a graphics image in an object-oriented program, allowing the user to change the size of the image or to reshape the image or to move the image around the screen.—**handleable** *adj*.—**handling** *n*.

handlebar *n* (*often pl*) the curved metal bar with a grip at each end, used to steer a bicycle, etc; a bushy mustache with curved ends.

handler *n* a person who trains or controls animals, such as a police dog.

handless *adj* awkward, clumsy.

handmade *adj* made by hand, carefully crafted.

handmaid(en) *n* a female servant.

hand-me-down *n* (*inf*) a used garment passed from one person to another; anything second-hand.

Hanoi *n* capital city of Vietnam.

hand-out *n* an item of food, clothing, etc given free to the needy; a statement given to the press to replace or supplement an oral presentation.

hand-picked *adj* carefully selected.

handrail *n* a narrow rail for gripping as a support.

handsaw *n* any saw that is used in one hand only.

handsel *n* (*formerly*) a good-luck gift on beginning something; a housewarming present; a New Year gift. * *vt* to give a handsel to; to inaugurate; to be first to use.

handset *n* a telephone earpiece and mouthpiece as a single unit.

handshake *n* a grasping and shaking of a person's hand as a greeting or when concluding an agreement.

handshaking *n* (*comput*) a signal between two devices, e.g., computer to printer, indicating that data transmission between them can proceed. *See also* **XON/XOFF**.

handsome *adj* good-looking; dignified; generous; ample.—**handsomely** *adv*.—**handsomeness** *n*.

hands-on *adj* involving active participation and operating experience.

handspike *n* an iron-shod bar or pipe used as a lever.

handspring *n* (*gymnastics*) a leaping forward or backward from a standing position into a handstand then back onto the feet.

handstand *n* the act of supporting the body on the hands with the feet in the air.

h & t *abbr* = hardened and tempered; hospitalization and treatment.

hand-to-hand *adj* (*fighting*) at close quarters.

hand-to-mouth *adj* having barely enough food or money to survive.—*also adv*.

H & W *abbr* = (*N Ireland*) Harland and Wolff, shipbuilders; (*Brit county*) Hereford & Worcester.

handwriting *n* writing done by hand; a style of such writing.—**handwritten** *adj*.

handy *adj* (**handier, handiest**) convenient, near; easy to use; skilled with the hands.—**handily** *adv*.—**handiness** *n*.

Handy *n* **W[illiam] C[hristopher]** (1873–1958) American composer known as "the father of the blues."

handyman *n* (*pl* **handymen**) a person who does odd jobs.

hang *vt* (**hanging, hung**) to support from above, esp by a rope, chain, etc, to suspend; to attach (a door, etc) by hinges to allow it to swing freely; to decorate with pictures, or other suspended objects; to stick (wallpaper) to a wall; to exhibit (works of art); to prevent (a jury) from coming to a decision; (*pt, pp* **hanged**) to execute or kill by suspending by the neck. * *vi* to be suspended, so as to dangle loosely; (*clothing, etc*) to fall or flow in a certain direction; to lean, incline, or protrude; to depend; to remain in the air; to be in suspense; to fall or droop; (*pt, pp* **hanged**) to die by hanging; (*with* **around**) to loiter; (*with* **back**) to hesitate, be reluctant; (*with* **out**) to meet regularly at a particular place. * *n* the way in which anything hangs; (*sl*) a damn.

hangar *n* a large shelter where aircraft are built, stored or repaired.—*also vt*.

hangbird *n* the Baltimore oriole; any North American bird that builds a hanging nest.

hangdog *adj* abject or ashamed in appearance or manner.

hanger *n* a device on which something is hung; one who hangs things.

hanger-on *n* (*pl* **hangers-on**) a sycophantic follower.

hang-glider *n* an unpowered aircraft consisting of a metal frame over which a lightweight material is stretched, with a harness for the pilot suspended below.—**hang gliding** *n*.

hanging *n* the act of executing a person by suspending him or her by the neck; something hung, as a picture; (*pl*) decorative draperies hung on walls. * *adj* suspended in the air; undecided; overhanging; situated on a steep slope.

hanging indent *n* (*comput*) the starting of the first line of text son the left margin, with the subsequent lines starting further to the right.

hanging valley *n* (*geog*) a tributary valley of a stream situated above the major river valley, possibly with a waterfall connecting the two.

hangman *n* (*pl* **hangmen**) a person who executes prisoners by hanging them.

hangnail *n* a thin strip of torn skin at the root of a fingernail.

hangout *n* a favorite meeting place.

hangover *n* the unpleasant after-effects of excessive consumption of alcohol; something surviving from an earlier time.

hang-up *n* an emotional preoccupation with something.

hank *n* a coiled or looped bundle of wool, rope, etc.

hanker *vi* (*with* **after** *or* **for**) to desire longingly.—**hankerer** *n*. —**hankering** *n*.

hanky, hankie *n* (*pl* **hankies**) (*inf*) a handkerchief.

hanky-panky *n* (*inf*) foolish behavior; dishonesty; illicit sexual relations.

Hannah *n* (*OT*) the mother of the prophet Samuel, who vowed that if God would give her a son she would "give him to the Lord all the days of his life." *See also* **Eli**.

Hannibal *n* (247–182 BC) Carthaginian general, who invaded Italy and crossed the Alps in 218 and was defeated in 204.

Hansard *n* the official, printed, verbatim reports of British parliamentary proceedings.

hanse *n* a medieval guild of merchants; a fee paid by new members of such a guild; (*with cap*) a town of the Hanseatic League; the Hanseatic League.—**hanseatic** *adj*.

Hanseatic League *n* a confederacy of merchants or commercial towns in Northern Germany and elsewhere, which lasted from the 14th to the 19th century.

Hansen *n* **Theophil von** (1813–91) Danish architect. His notable works include the Stock Exchange, Vienna.

hansom (cab) *n* a light two-wheeled covered horse-drawn carriage, with the driver's seat raised behind.

Hanson *n* **Duane** (1925–97) American sculptor famous for his realistically detailed figures modeled out of fiberglass resin, and using real garments and objects as props.

hao *n* a monetary unit of Vietnam, equal to one tenth of a dong.

hap *vi* (**happing, happed**) (*arch*) to happen or befall. * *vt* to cover up; to wrap up warmly. * *n* (*arch*) chance; luck; a fortunate accident; a covering of any kind.

HAPA *abbr* = Handicapped Adventure Playground Association.

haphazard *adj* not planned; random. * *adv* by chance.—**haphazardly** *adv*.—**haphazardness** *n*.

hapless *adj* unfortunate, unlucky.—**haplessness** *n*.

haploid *adj* (*genetics*) (*cell nucleus, organism*) possessing only half the normal number of chromosomes. * *n* a single set of unpaired chromosomes.

haply *adv* (*formerly*) by chance.

happen *vi* to take place; to be, occur, or come by chance.

happening *n* an occurrence; an improvisation.

happy *adj* (**happier, happiest**) fortunate; having, expressing, or enjoying pleasure or contentment; pleased; appropriate, felicitous.—**happily** *adv*.—**happiness** *n*.

happy-go-lucky *adj* irresponsible; carefree.

happy hour *n* a particular time of day when a bar, hotel, etc, sells drinks at reduced prices

happy medium *n* a middle course between extremes.

hapteron *n* (*pl* **haptera**) the tissue in seaweed and related plants that enables them to attach themselves to a host object.

haptic *adj* of or relating to the sense of touch.

Harakhte *n* (*Egypt*) a title of Horus, identifying him with Ra as god of the morning sun. The sun and moon were known as "the two eyes of Horus."

harakiri *n* ritual suicide by disembowelment.—*also* **harikari**.

Haran[1] *n* (*Bible*) city in northern Mesopotamia associated with Abraham, Isaac, Jacob and their kinsfolk.

Haran[2] *n* (*Bible*) name of a brother of Abraham and father of Lot.

harangue *n* a tirade; a lengthy, forceful speech. * *vti* to make a harangue, to address vehemently.—**haranguer** *n*.

Harare *n* capital city of Zimbabwe.

harass *vt* to annoy, to irritate; to trouble (an enemy) by constant raids and attacks.—**harasser** *n*. —**harassment** *n*.

Harbin *n* a city in China.

harbinger *n* a person or thing that announces or presages the arrival of another, a forerunner.

harbor *n* a protected inlet for anchoring ships; any place of refuge. * *vt* to shelter or house; to keep (a grudge, etc) in the mind secretly. * *vi* to take shelter.—**harborer** *n*.

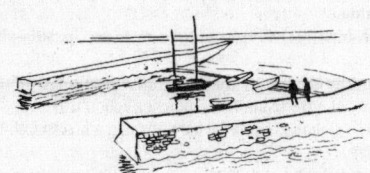

harborage *n* a port or anchorage for ships.

hard *adj* firm, solid, not easily cut or punctured; difficult to comprehend; difficult to accomplish; difficult to bear, painful; severe, unfeeling, ungenerous; indisputable, intractable; (*drugs*) addictive and damaging to health; (*weather*) severe; (*currency*) stable in value; (*news*) definite, not speculative; (*drink*) very alcoholic; (*water*) having a high mineral content that prevents lathering with soap; (*color, sound*) harsh; (*comput*) (*hyphen or page break*)inserted by the user in a word-processing, page layout or spread-sheet program, as opposed to a soft command inserted by the program. * *adv* with great effort or intensity; earnestly, with concentration; so as to cause hardness; with difficulty; with bitterness or grief; close, near by.—**hardness** *n*.

hardanger fiddle *n* (*mus*) a Norwegian violin used in folk music, somewhat smaller than an ordinary violin, and with four sympathetic strings.

hardback *n* a book bound with a stiff cover.—*also adj*.

hard-bitten *adj* (*inf*) tough, seasoned.

hardboard *n* a stiff board made of compressed wood chips.

hard-boiled *adj* (*eggs*) boiled until solid; (*inf*) unfeeling.

hard card *n* (*comput*) a printed circuit board that plugs into the expansion slot of a computer, containing a hard disk drive and controller circuitry.

hard cash *n* payment in coins and notes as opposed to check, credit card, etc.

hard copy *n* (*comput*) a document or file that is printed, as opposed to one that is stored in a computer's memory or stored on disk.

hard core *n* the stubborn inner group in an organization that is resistant to change; the heavy foundation material for a road.

hard-core *adj* of a hard core; utterly entrenched; (*pornography*) showing sexual acts in explicit detail.

hardcover *adj* (*books*) hardback. * *n* a hardback book.

hard currency *n* a currency that is commonly accepted throughout the world and so is valued because of its universal purchasing power.

hard disk *n* (*comput*) a fixed magnetic disk in a sealed unit that forms a storage medium within a computer.

harden *vti* to make or become hard.—**hardener** *n*.

hardhat *n* a protective helmet, esp as used by construction workers; a construction worker; a working-class person with conservative views.

hard-headed *adj* shrewd and unsentimental; practical.—**hard-headedly** *adv*.—**hard-headedness** *n*.

hardhearted *adj* unfeeling; cruel.—**hardheartedly** *adv*.—**hardheartedness** *n*.

hard-hitting *adj* forcefully effective.

Hardicanute *n* (1018–1042) king of England and Denmark. Reigned (England) from 1040–1042. The only son of Canute and Emma of Normandy. He was succeeded by Edward the Confessor.

Hardie *n* [**James**] **Keir** (1856–1915) Scottish Labour politician and the first leader of the British parliamentary Labour Party (1906–07).

Harding *n* **Warren G**[**amaliel**] (1865–1923) 29th president of the US who served as Republican president (1921–23).

hard labor *n* compulsory physical labor as punishment for convicted criminals.

hard line *n* an aggressive, unyielding policy.—**hard-line** *adj*.—**hardliner** *n*.

hardly *adv* scarcely; barely; with difficulty; not to be expected.

hard-nosed *adj* tough and stubborn or shrewd.

Hardovin-Mansart *n* **Jules** (*b.* 1646) French architect, whose notable works include extensions to Versailles.

hard pan *or* **hardpan** *n* a hard, water-resistant layer of clay in the soil, formed after soluble minerals have been leached out; a solid foundation.

hard sell *n* an aggressive selling technique.

hardship *n* something that causes suffering or privation.

hard shoulder *n* (*Brit*) a raised strip of land alongside a motorway for vehicles to make emergency stops.

hardtack *n* a hard, saltless biscuit formerly eaten by seamen.

hardtop *n* an automobile resembling a convertible but having a fixed metal top.

hard-up *adj* (*inf*) short of money.

hardware *n* articles made of metal, such as tools, nails, etc; (*comput*) the mechanical and electronic components that make up a computer system.

hardware interrupt *see* **interrupt**.

hardware platform *n* (*comput*) the physical equipment of a computer system, e.g., the central processing unit, disk drive(s), VDU and printer.

hard water *n* (*chem*) water that does not readily form a lather with soap, owing to dissolved compounds of calcium, magnesium and iron.

Hardwick *n* **Philip** (*b.* 1792) English architect, whose notable works include Euston Station, London.

hardwood *n* the close-grained wood of deciduous trees.

hardy *adj* (**hardier, hardiest**) bold, resolute; robust; vigorous; able to withstand exposure to physical or emotional hardship.—**hardily** *adv*.—**hardiness** *n*.

Hardy, Oliver *see* **Laurel, Stan**.

Hardy *n* **Thomas** (1840–1928) English novelist, short-story writer and poet, whose novels include *Far from the Madding Crowd*, *The Mayor of Casterbridge*, *Tess of the D'Urbervilles* and *Jude the Obscure*.

hare *n* (*pl* **hare, hares**) any of various timid, swift, long-eared mammals, resembling, but larger than, the rabbit.

Hare *n* 1. **David** (1917–91) American sculptor, whose best-known pieces are metalwork sculptures, such as *Juggler* (1950), which show his concern with linear and spatial forms. 2. **David** (1947–) English dramatist, whose plays include *Slag*, *Knuckle*, *Teeth 'n' Smiles* and *Plenty*.

harebell *n* the bluebell; the wild hyacinth.

harebrained *adj* flighty; foolish.

hare lip *or* **harelip** *n* a congenital developmental deformity of the upper lip in the form of a vertical fissure.—**harelipped** *adj*.

harem *n* the usu secluded part of a Muslim household where the women live; the women in a harem.

Hargeysa *n* major town in Somalia.

haricot *n* a type of French bean with an edible light-colored seed.

harikari *see* **harakiri**.

hark *vi* to listen; (*with* **back**) to retrace a course; to revert (to).

harken *see* **hearken**.

harlequin *n* (*usu* **Harlequin**) the performer in a pantomime who wears parti-colored garments and carries a wand. * *adj* fantastic or full of trickery; colorful.

harlequinade *n* a play or the part of a pantomime in which Harlequin plays a leading role; buffoonery.

harlot *n* (*formerly*) a prostitute.—**harlotry** *n*.

Harlow *n* **Jean** [**Harlean Carpentier**] (1911–37) American movie actress of the 1930s.

harm *n* hurt; damage; injury. * *vt* to inflict hurt, damage, or injury upon.—**harmer** *n*.

harmattan *n* a hot dust-laden wind that blows from the interior to the west coast of Africa.

harmful *adj* hurtful.—**harmfully** *adv*.—**harmfulness** *n*.

harmless *adj* not likely to cause harm.—**harmlessly** *adv*.—**harmlessness** *n*.

harmonic *adj* (*mus*) of or in harmony. * *n* an overtone; (*pl*) the science of musical sounds.—**harmonically** *adv*.

H

harmonica *n* a small wind instrument that produces tones when air is blown or sucked across a series of metal reeds.—*also* **mouth organ**.

harmonics *n* (*mus*) the sounds that can be produced on stringed instruments by lightly touching a string at one of its harmonic nodes, i.e., at a half-length of a string, quarter-length and so on.

harmonious *adj* fitting together in an orderly and pleasing manner; agreeing in ideas, interests, etc; melodious.—**harmoniously** *adv*.

harmonium *n* a keyboard musical instrument whose tones are produced by thin metal reeds operated by foot bellows.

harmonize *vi* to be in harmony; to sing in harmony. * *vt* to make harmonious.—**harmonization** *n*.

harmony *n* (*pl* **harmonies**) (*art*) a pleasing agreement of parts in color, size, etc; agreement in action, ideas, etc; (*mus*) the pleasing combination of musical tones in a chord; a collation of parallel narratives, esp of the Gospels, with a commentary.

harness *n* the leather straps and metal pieces by which a horse is fastened to a vehicle, plow, etc; any similar fastening or attachment, e.g., for a parachute, hang-glider. * *vt* to put a harness on; to control so as to use the power of.—**harnesser** *n*.

Harold I *n* (Harefoot) (1016–40) king of England (1035–40). The second son of Canute and Elgifu, he succeeded his father.

Harold II *n* (1020–66) king of England (reigned in 1066). The second son of Godwin, Earl of Kent, and Gytha, sister of Canute's Danish brother-in-law. Died on the field, supposedly killed by an arrow, with two of his brothers. His death ended England's 600 years of rule by Anglo-Saxon kings.

harp *n* a stringed musical instrument played by plucking. * *vi* (*with* **on**, **upon**) to talk persistently (on some subject).—**harpist, harper** *n*.

Harpies *npl* (*Greek myth*) ancient goddesses who were believed to be ministers of the vengeance of the gods.

harpoon *n* a barbed spear with an attached line, for spearing whales, etc. * *vt* to strike with a harpoon.—**harpooner** *n*.

harpsichord *n* a musical instrument resembling a grand piano, whose strings are plucked by a mechanism rather than struck.—**harpsichordist** *n*.

harpy *n* (*pl* **harpies**) a grasping, vicious person.

harquebus *see* **arquebus**.

harridan *n* a disreputable, shrewish, old woman.

harrier *n* a small breed of hound used for hunting hares; a cross-country runner.

Harriman *n* **W[illiam] Averell** (1891–1986) American diplomat, the main negotiator of the nuclear test-ban treaty of 1963 between the US, UK and USSR.

Harris *n* **Sir Arthur Travers** (1892–1984) English air-force officer, nicknamed "Bomber Harris" for his advocacy of the heavy bombing of German cities during World War II.

Harris *n* 1. **Frank** (1856–1913) Irish-born Anglo-American writer and editor, whose best-known work is his autobiography *My Life and Loves*, an entertaining, sexually explicit, and unreliable account of his life. 2. **Joel Chandler** (1848–1908) American writer whose Aesop-like "Uncle Remus" stories are based on a deep and sympathetic knowledge of the folklore of African Americans in the South. 3. **Roy** (1898–1979) American composer whose works include sixteen symphonies and works for chorus and orchestra. 4. **Thomas** (*c.* 1940–) American novelist whose work includes the gripping thrillers *Red Dragon*, *The Silence of the Lambs*, and *Hannibal*.

Harrisburg *n* the capital city of Pennsylvania, a state of the USA.

Harrison *n* 1. **Benjamin** (1833–1901) 23rd president of the US. A Republican, he served as president (1889–93). 2. **George** (1943–) English singer and songwriter , who played lead guitar in the Beatles (1962–70). 3. **Peter** (1716–75) American architect, whose notable works include Christ Church, Cambridge, Massachusetts. 4. **Thomas** (*b.* 1744) English architect, whose notable works include Chester Castle. 5. **Wallace K.** (1895–1981) American architect, whose notable works include the Rockefeller Center, New York. 6. **William Henry** (1773–1841) 9th president of the US. Elected in 1841, he died within weeks of assuming the presidency.

harrow *n* a heavy frame with spikes, spring teeth, or disks for breaking up and leveling plowed ground. * *vt* to draw a harrow over (land); to cause mental distress to.—**harrower** *n*. —**harrowing** *adj*,*.n*. —**harrowment** *n*.

harry *vt* (**harrying, harried**) to torment or harass.

harsh *adj* unpleasantly rough; jarring on the senses or feelings; rigorous; cruel.—**harshly** *adv*.—**harshness** *n*.

hart *n* (*pl* **hart, harts**) a male deer, especially the red deer, aged five years or more.

Hart *n* **Lorenz [Milton]** (1895–1943) American lyricist, best known for his collaborations with Richard Rodgers, e.g., *Pal Joey* (1940).

hartal *n* (*Hinduism*) the closing of shops as a sign of mourning or as a political gesture.

Harte *n* **[Francis] Bret[t]** (1836–1902) American poet and short-story writer, noted especially for his shrewdly observed stories of Californian gold miners in *The Luck of Roaring Camp and Other Stories,* and the best of whose humorous verse, e.g., "Plain Language from Truthful James," is still highly regarded.

hartebeest, hartbeest *n* the South African antelope.

Hartford *n* the capital city of Connecticut, a state of the USA.

Hartley *n* **L[eslie] P[oles]** (1895–1972) English novelist, whose works include *The Go-Between* (1953).

Hartley *n* **Marsden** (1877–1943) American abstract painter. Mature pieces include atmospheric, troubled landscapes dependent on mass and line, e.g., *Lobster Fishermen* (1940–41).

Hartmann's solution *n* a solution of salts given to replace lost fluid in cases of dehydration, acidosis, and after hemorrhage while awaiting cross-matched blood for transfusion.

hartshorn *n* the antler of a hart; sal volatile.

harum-scarum *adj* (*inf*) rash, reckless. * *n* a giddy, rash person.

haruspex *n* (*pl* **haruspices**) in ancient Rome, a soothsayer who foretold events by inspecting the entrails of sacrificial animals.

Harvard classification *n* (*astron*) a method of classifying the spectra of stars, in which stars are called O, B, A, F, G or K type stars.

harvest *n* (the season of) gathering in the ripened crops; the yield of a particular crop; the reward or product of any exertion or action. * *vti* to gather in (a crop). * *vt* to win by achievement.—**harvesting** *n*.

harvester *n* a person who harvests; a harvesting machine, esp a combine harvester.

harvest moon *n* the full moon nearest the time of the September equinox.

Harvey *n* **William** (1578–1657) English physician, who published his discovery of the circulation of the blood in 1628.

has *see* **have**.

HAS *abbr* (*Brit*) = Headmasters' Association of Scotland Health Advisory Service.

HASAWA *abbr* = Health and Safety at Work Act.

has-been *n* (*inf*) a person or thing that has lost its popularity or celebrity status.

Hasek *n* **Jaroslav** (1883–1923) Czech novelist and short-story writer, whose masterpiece is *The Good Soldier Svejk* (1925).

hash[1] *n* a chopped mixture of reheated, cooked meat and vegetables. * *vt* to chop up (meat or vegetables) for hash; to mix or mess up.

hash[2] *n* (*inf*) hashish.

hashish *n* resin derived from the leaves and shoots of the hemp plant, smoked or chewed as an intoxicant.

hasn't = has not.

hasp *n* a hinged fastening for a door, etc, esp a metal piece fitted over a staple and fastened by a bolt or padlock.

hassle *n* (*inf*) prolonged trouble; an argument; confusion; turmoil. * *vi* (*inf*) to argue, quarrel. * *vt* (*inf*) to cause annoyance or inconvenience to (a person).

hassock *n* a firm cushion used as a footstool or seat.

hast (*arch*) *the second person sing of* **have**, used with **thou**.

hastate *adj* (*leaf*) spear-shaped.

haste *n* quickness of motion; urgency. * *vi* (*poet*) to hasten.

HASTE *abbr* = Helicopter Ambulance Service to Emergencies.

hasten *vt* to accelerate; to cause to hurry. * *vi* to move or act with speed.—**hastener** *n*.

Hastings *n* **Warren** (1732–1818) British administrator in India; the first governor-general of Bengal (1773–85); founded the East India Company; impeached in 1788 for corruption.

hasty *adj* (**hastier, hastiest**) done in a hurry; rash, precipitate.—**hastily** *adv*.—**hastiness** *n*.

hat *n* a covering for the head. * *vt* (**hatting, hatted**) to cover with a hat.

HAT *abbr* = History of Advertising Trust; housing action trust.

hatband *n* a band or ribbon around the base of a hat; a black cloth band worn as a token of mourning.

hatbox *n* a box or case for a hat or hats.

hatch[1] *n* a small door or opening (as on an aircraft or spaceship); an opening in the deck of a ship or in the floor or roof of a building; a lid for such an opening; a hatchway.

hatch[2] *vt* to produce (young) from the egg, esp by incubating; to devise (a plot). * *vi* to emerge from the egg; to incubate.—**hatchable** *adj*.—**hatcher** *n*.

hatch[3] *vt* (*drawing, engraving*) to shade using closely spaced parallel lines or incisions.—**hatching** *n*.

hatchback *n* a sloping rear end on a car with a door; a car of this design.

hatchery *n* (*pl* **hatcheries**) a place for hatching eggs, esp of fish.

hatchet *n* a small ax with a short handle.

hatchet job *n* (*inf*) a devastating or malicious verbal or written criticism.

hatchet man *n* a person hired to perform unpleasant tasks; a critic specializing in invective.

hatchment *n* (*her*) a diamond-shaped tablet bearing a dead person's armorial bearings, placed on a house or tomb.

hatchway *n* an opening in a ship's deck or in a floor or roof; a passage giving access to an enclosed space (e.g., a cellar).

hate *vt* to feel intense dislike for. * *vi* to feel hatred; to wish to avoid. * *n* a strong feeling of dislike or contempt; the person or thing hated.—**hater** *n*.

hateful *adj* deserving or arousing hate.—**hatefully** *adv*.—**hatefulness** *n*.

hath (*arch*) *the third person sing of* **have**.

Hathor *n* (*Egypt*) a major Egyptian goddess, the Lady of Heaven, Earth and the Underworld. Portrayed as a cow or as a woman with the horned head of a cow, a goddess of pregnancy and childbirth.

HATIS *abbr* = Hide and Allied Trades Improvement Society.

HATRA *abbr* = Hosiery and Allied Trades Research Association.

hatred *n* intense dislike or enmity.

Hatshepsut *n* (*Egypt*) a female king of the Eighteenth Dynasty (ruled 1478–1458 BC). Daughter of the Pharaoh Thutmosis I and of the widow of Amenophis I, she married her half-brother who became king as Tuthmosis II.

hatter *n* a person who makes or sells hats.

hat trick *n* (*cricket*) the taking of three wickets with three successive bowls; the scoring of three successive goals, points, etc in any game.

hauberk *n* a coat of armor, often sleeveless, formed of chain mail, which reached below the knees.

haugh *n* (*Scot*) a small, low-lying riverside meadow.

Haughey *n* Charles [James] (1925–) Irish Fianna Fáil politician and prime minister of the Republic of Ireland (1979–81, 1982, 1988–92).

haughty *adj* (**haughtier, haughtiest**) having or expressing arrogance.—**haughtily** *adv*.—**haughtiness** *n*.

haul *vti* to move by pulling; to transport by truck, etc. * *n* the act of hauling; the amount gained, caught, etc, at one time; the distance over which something is transported.

haulage *n* the transport of commodities; the charge for this.

haulier *n* a person or business that transports goods by road.

haulm *n* the stalk of potatoes, peas, etc, esp after the crop has been gathered.—*also* **halm**.

haunch *n* the part of the body around the hips; the leg and loin of a deer, sheep, etc.—**haunched** *adj*.

haunt *vt* to visit often or continually; to recur repeatedly to. * *vi* to linger; to appear habitually as a ghost. * *n* a place often visited.—**haunter** *n*.

haunted *adj* supposedly visited by ghosts; obsessed; anxious, worried.

haunting *adj* constantly recurring in the mind; unforgettable.—**hauntingly** *adv*.

Hauptwerk *n* (*mus*) a great organ, as distinct from a swell organ etc. *See* **organ**.

Hausa *n* a member of a West African people living chiefly in Nigeria; the language of these people.

haust. *abbr* (*Latin*) = *haustus,* "a draft."

haustellum *n* (*pl* **haustella**) the tip of the proboscis of the housefly or similar insect, used for sucking foods.

hautbois, hautboy *n* (*pl* **hautbois, hautboy**) (*arch*) the oboe.

haute couture *n* high fashion.

haute cuisine *n* high-class cooking.

hauteur *n* arrogance, haughtiness.

HAV *abbr* = hepatitis A virus.

Havana *n* capital city of Cuba.

Havana (cigar) *n* a cigar rolled from Cuban tobacco.

have *vt* (**has, having,** *pp* **had**) to have in one's possession; to possess as an attribute; to hold in the mind; to experience; to give birth to; to allow or tolerate; to arrange or hold; to engage in; to cause, compel, or require to be; to be obliged; (*sl*) to have sexual intercourse with; to be pregnant with; (*inf*) to hold at a disadvantage; (*inf*) to deceive; to accept or receive; to consume food, drink, etc; to show some quality; to perplex.

Havel *n* Vàclav (1936–) Czech dramatist and statesman. He was elected Czchoslovakia's president in 1989 but resigned in 1992. He became president of the newly formed Czech Republic in 1993.

haven *n* a place where ships can safely anchor; a refuge.

haven't = have not.

haver *vi* (*Scot*) to talk foolishly or inconsequently; to dither. * *n* (*pl*) nonsense.

haversack *n* a canvas bag similar to a knapsack but worn over one shoulder.

Haversian canal *n* one of numerous small channels or cylindrical tubes that run through compact bone (the outer layer of bones) and contain blood vessels and nerves.

Haviland *n* John (1792–1852) American architect, whose notable works include Eastern Penitentiary, Philadelphia.

havoc *n* widespread destruction or disorder. * *vt* (**havocking, havocked**) to lay waste.

haw *n* (the berry of) the hawthorn.

Hawaii (HI) *n* a state of the United States of America (USA).

Hawaiian *adj* pertaining to Hawaii, its inhabitants or its language. * *n* an inhabitant of Hawaii; a Polynesian language spoken in Hawaii.

Hawaiian guitar *n* a style of guitar playing in which a steel bar is moved up and down the strings.

"Hawaii Ponoi" *n* the official song of the American state, Hawaii.

hawfinch *n* a rare European finch with a stout bill, brown plumage and black-and-white wings.

haw-haw *see* **ha-ha**[1].

hawk[1] *n* any of numerous birds of prey; a person who advocates aggressive or intimidatory action. * *vti* to hunt with a hawk; to strike like a hawk.—**hawkish** *adj*.—**hawkishly** *adv*.

hawk[2] *vti* to clear the throat (of) audibly. * *n* the sound of this.

hawk[3] *vt* to offer goods for sale, as in the street; to spread (gossip). * *vi* to peddle.

Hawke *n* Robert [James Lee] (1929–) Australian trade unionist and Labour statesman; prime minister of Australia (1983–92).

hawker *n* a person who goes about offering goods for sale; a person who hunts with a trained hawk.

hawk-eyed *adj* keen-sighted; vigilant.

Hawking *n* Stephen (William) (1942–) English physicist, regarded as perhaps the greatest physicist since Einstein. His research into the theory of black holes has been highly acclaimed.

Hawks *n* Howard (1896–1977) American movie director and producer, whose movies include *The Big Sleep* (1946).

Hawksmoor *n* Nicholas (*b.* 1661) English architect. His notable works include St George's Church, Bloomsbury.

hawkweed *n* a yellow-flowered plant of the aster family.

hawse *n* (*naut*) the part of a ship's bows where the hawseholes are situated; the distance from the bow of an anchored ship to the anchor. * *vi* (*naut*) to pitch violently when at anchor.

hawsehole *n* (*naut*) one of the two holes in the upper part of a ship's bows through which the anchor cables pass when the vessel is moored.

hawser *n* (*naut*) a heavy rope for towing, mooring, etc.

hawthorn *n* any of a genus of spring-flowering spiny shrubs or trees with white or pink flowers and red fruit.

Hawthorne *n* Nathaniel (1804–64) American novelist and short-story writer whose masterpiece is *The Scarlet Letter* (1850).

Hayashi track *or* **Hayashi line** *n* a particular path on the Hertzsprung-Russell diagram that is thought to represent the evolution of a young star as it joins the main sequence.

haybox *n* an airtight box packed with hay or any other natural insulating material used to keep partially cooked food warm and allow to cook by retained heat.

haycock *n* a conical pile of hay left in the fields to dry out.

Haydn *n* 1. [Franz] Joseph (1732–1809) Austrian composer, who established the form of both the symphony and the string quartet. His work includes symphonies, string quartets and the oratorio *The Creation*. 2. Johann Michael (1737–1806) Austrian composer, and the brother of Franz Joseph Haydn. His works include 24 Masses, two Requiem Masses and many miscellaneous compositions for orchestra.

Hayek *n* Friedrich August von (1899–1992) Austrian-born British economist, who shared the 1974 Nobel Prize for Economics with Myrdal.

Hayes *n* Rutherford B[irchard] (1822–93) 19th president of the US, who defeated Democrat candidate Samuel J Tilden to become president (1877–81).

Hayes command set *n* (*comput*) a standard set of instructions that have been developed to control communications through modems.

Hayes-compatible modem *n* (*comput*) a modem that recognizes the Hayes command set.

hay fever *n* an allergic reaction to pollen, causing irritation of the nose and eyes.

haymaker *n* one who lifts and spreads hay; either of two machines used in haymaking; a wild punch.

hayseed *n* grass seed or chaff shaken from cut hay; (*inf*) a simple person, a country bumpkin.

haystack, hayrick *n* a pile of stacked hay ready for storing.

haywire *adj* (*inf*) out of order; disorganized.

hazard *n* a risk; a danger; an obstacle on a golf course. * *vt* to risk; to venture.—**hazardable** *adj*.

hazardous *adj* dangerous; risky.—**hazardously** *adv*.—**hazardousness** *n*.

haze *n* a thin vapor of fog, smoke, etc. in the air; slight vagueness of mind. * *vti* to make or become hazy.

hazel *n* a tree with edible nuts; a light brown color. * *adj* light brown.

hazelnut *n* the edible nut of the hazel.

Hazlitt *n* William (1778–1830) English essayist and critic.

hazy *adj* (**hazier, haziest**) misty; vague.—**hazily** *adv*.—**haziness** *n*.

hb *abbr* = halfback; handbook; hardback; hardy biennial; homing beacon; human being.

Hb *abbr* = hemoglobin.

HB *abbr* = (*pencil*) hard black.

HbA *abbr* = adult hemoglobin.

HBAB *abbr* = hepatitis B antibody.

H

HBAg *abbr* = hepatitis B antigen.

HBC *abbr* = Historic Buildings Council; Hudson's Bay Company.

HBD *abbr* = has been drinking.

HBES *abbr* = Human Behavior and Evolution Society.

HbF *abbr* = fetal hemoglobin.

HBF *abbr* = hepatic blood flow.

HBJ *abbr* = Harcourt Brace Jovanovich.

HBLV *abbr* = human B-lymphotropic virus.

HBM *abbr* = His *or* Her Britannic Majesty.

HBO *abbr* = hyperbaric oxygen.

H-bomb *n* a hydrogen bomb.

HBP *abbr* = high blood pressure.

HBPF *abbr* = High Blood Pressure Foundation.

HbS *abbr* = sickle-cell hemoglobin.

HBS *abbr* = Harvard Business School; Hawaiian Botanical Society.

HBV *abbr* = hepatitis B virus.

HC *abbr* = Heralds' College; High Commission; High Commissioner; High Court; highly commended; Holy Communion; (*Brit*) House of Commons.

HCA *abbr* = Hypertrophic Cardiomyopathy Association.

HCAAS *abbr* = Homeless Children's Aid and Adoption Society.

hcd *abbr* = high-current density.

HC Deb. *abbr* (*Brit*) = House of Commons Debates.

hce *abbr* = human-caused error.

HCEC *abbr* = Hospital Committee of the European Community.

HCF *abbr* = highest common factor.

HCF *abbr* = high carbohydrate and fiber; Honorary Chaplain to the Forces.

HCFC *abbr* = hydrochlorofluorocarbon.

HCG *abbr* = human chorionic gonadotrophin.

HCH *abbr* = hexachlorocyclohexane.

HCI *abbr* = human-computer interaction *or* interface.

HCIL *abbr* = Hague Conference on International Law.

HCJ *abbr* = High Court of Justice; High Court Judge.

HCJA *abbr* = High Court Journalists' Association.

HCM *abbr* = His *or* Her Catholic Majesty.

HCO *abbr* = Higher Clerical Officer.

HCOPIL *abbr* = The Hague Conference on Private International Law.

HCP *abbr* = Healthy Cities Project.

HCPT *abbr* = Handicapped Children's Pilgrimage Trust.

HCT *abbr* = Herpetological Conservation Trust.

HCVD *abbr* = hypertensive cardiovascular disease.

hd. *abbr* = head.

Hd *abbr* (*Latin*) = *hora decubitus*, "at bedtime."

HD *abbr* = heavy duty; high density; Hodgkin's Disease; hydrodrome.

HDA *abbr* = Hodgkin's Disease Association; Hospital Doctors' Association.

HDATZ *abbr* = high-density air traffic zone.

HDC *abbr* = high-dose chemotherapy.

HDK *abbr* = husbands don't know.

HDL *abbr* = (*comput*) hardware description language; high-density lipoprotein.

HDLC *abbr* (*comput*) = High-level Data Link Control.

HDLC *abbr* = high-density lipoprotein cholesterol; high-level data-link control.

HDN *abbr* = hemolytic disease of the newborn.

hdqrs. *abbr* = headquarters.

HDR *abbr* = high dose rate.

HDU *abbr* = hemodialysis unit.

HDV *abbr* = heavy-duty vehicle.

he *pron* the male person or animal named before. * *n* a male person or animal.

He *symbol* (*chem*) = helium (element).

HE *abbr* = higher education; high explosive; His Eminence; His *or* Her Excellency.

HEA *abbr* = Health Education Authority; Higher Education Authority (Republic of Ireland).

head *n* the part of an animal or human body containing the brain, eyes, ears, nose and mouth; the top part of anything; the foremost part; the chief person; (*pl*) a unit of counting; the striking part of a tool; the mind; understanding; the topic of a chapter, etc; crisis, conclusion; freedom to act without restraint; pressure of water, steam, etc; the source of a river, etc; froth, as on beer; (*comput*) the device used by a disk drive to read a disk. * *adj* at the head, top or front; coming from in front; chief, leading. * *vt* to command; to lead; to cause to go in a specified direction; to strike (a football) with the head. * *vi* to set out; to travel (in a particular direction).—**headless** *adj*.

headache *n* a continuous pain in the head; (*inf*) a cause of worry or trouble.—**headachy** *adj*.

headband *n* a ribbon or band worn around the head; a narrow strip of cloth stitched to the top of the spine of a book for protection or decoration.

headboard *n* a board that forms the head of a bed, etc.

head crash *n* (*comput*) the physical impact of a disk head on the disk, possibly resulting in damage to its surface.

headdress *n* a decorative covering for the head.

headed *adj* having (a specified kind of) head; having a heading.

header *n* a dive with the head first; (*soccer*) the action of striking the ball with the head; (*comput*) text that is placed at the top of every page in a document; a beam placed between and at the top of two long beams; a brick laid across, not parallel to, a wall.

headfirst *adv* with the head in front; recklessly.—*also adj*.

headgear *n* a covering for the head, a hat, cap, etc.

head-hunt *vt* to cut off and preserve the heads of (enemies) as trophies; to recruit (executive personnel).—**head-hunter** *n*. —**head-hunting** *n*.

heading *n* something forming the head, top, or front; the title, topic, etc of a chapter, etc; the direction in which a vehicle is moving.

headlamp *or* **headlight** *n* a light at the front of a vehicle.

headland *n* a promontory; unplowed land at the ends of a furrow.

headless *adj* being without a head; leaderless.

headline *n* printed lines at the top of a newspaper article giving the topic; a brief news summary. * *vt* to give featured billing or publicity to.

headlock *n* (*wrestling*) a hold in which the arm encircles an opponent's head.

headlong *adv* with the head first; with uncontrolled speed or force; rashly.—*also adj*.

headman *n* (*pl* **headmen**) the chieftain or leader of a tribe; a foreman or overseer.

headmaster *or* **headmistress** *n* (*Brit*) the principal of a school.—**headmastership** *or* **headmistress-ship** *n*.

headmost *adj* foremost

head-on *adj, adv* with the head or front foremost; without compromise.

head over heels *adv* as if somersaulting; completely, utterly, deeply.

headphone *n* one of two radio receivers held to the head by a band.

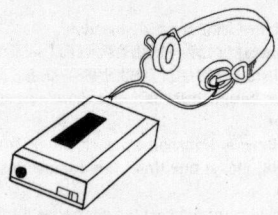

headquarters *n* the center of operations of a person or people in command, as in an army; the main office in any organization.

headrest *n* a support for the head.

headroom *n* space overhead, as in a doorway or tunnel.

headset *n* a set of headphones, usu with a microphone.

headshrinker *n* (*sl*) a psychiatrist.

headstall *n* the part of a bridle that fits around a horse's head.

headstand *n* (*gymnastics*) the feat of standing on one's head, usu with support from the hands.

head start *n* an early start; any other competitive advantage.

headstone *n* a marker placed at the head of a grave.

headstrong *adj* determined to do as one pleases; obstinate.

heads-up *adj* self-assured and excellent.

head voice *n* (*mus*) the upper register of a voice, so called because the sound seems to vibrate in the head of the singer. *Compare* **chest voice**.

head waiter *n* the head of the dining-room staff in a restaurant.

head wall *n* the steep back wall of a cirque.

headwaters *npl* the small streams that are the source of a river.

headway *n* forward motion; progress.

headwind *n* a wind blowing against the direction of a ship or aircraft.

headword *n* a term placed at the beginning (as of an entry in a dictionary).

headwork *n* mental work; the decoration on the keystone of an arch.

heady *adj* (**headier, headiest**) (*alcoholic drinks*) intoxicating; invigorating, exciting; impetuous.—**headily** *adv*.—**headiness** *n*.

heal *vti* to make or become healthy; to cure; (*wound, etc*) to repair by natural processes.—**healable** *adj*.—**healer** *n*. —**healingly** *adv*.

Healey *n* Denis [Winston] (1917–) British Labour politician; chancellor of the exchequer (1974–79); deputy leader of his party (1980–83).

health *n* physical and mental well-being; freedom from disease, etc; the condition of body or mind; a wish for one's health and happiness, as in a toast.

health farm *n* a residential establishment for improving health through a strict regime of diet and exercise.

health foods *npl* foods that are organically grown, unprocessed and additive-free.

healthful *adj* healthy.—**healthfully** *adv*.—**healthfulness** *n*.

health maintenance organization *n* a health-care organization that meets medical needs in return for a fee.

healthy *adj* (**healthier, healthiest**) having or producing good health; beneficial; sound.—**healthily** *adv*.—**healthiness** *n*.

Heaney *n* Seamus [Justin] (1939–) Irish poet and critic. He was winner of the 1995 Nobel Prize for Literature.

heap *n* a mass or pile of jumbled things; (*pl*) (*inf*) a large amount; (*comput*) a part of the computer's memory that is set aside for specific instructions that control such aspects as user input, menus and icons. * *vt* to throw in a heap; to pile high; to fill (a plate, etc) full or to overflowing.—**heaper** *n*.

hear *vt* (**hearing, heard**) to perceive by the ear; to listen to; to conduct a hearing of (a law case, etc); to be informed of; to learn. * *vi* to be able to hear sounds; (*with of or about*) to be told.—**hearable** *adj*.—**hearer** *n*.

hearing *n* the sense by which sound is perceived by the ear; an opportunity to be heard; the distance over which something can be heard, earshot.

hearing aid *n* a small electronic amplifier worn behind the ear to improve hearing.

hearing loss *see* **deafness**.

hearken *vi* to listen to.—*also* **harken**.—**hearkener** *n*.

hearsay *n* rumor, gossip.

hearse *n* a vehicle for transporting a coffin to a funeral.

Hearst *n* **William Randolph** (1863–1951) American newspaper publisher and politician and congressman for New York (1903–07). The inspiration for Welles' movie, *Citizen Kane*.

heart *n* the hollow, muscular organ that circulates the blood; the central, vital, or main part; the human heart as the center of emotions, esp sympathy, courage, etc; a conventional design representing a heart; one of a suit of playing cards marked with such a symbol in red.

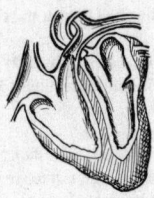

Heart *n* a city in Afghanistan.

heartache *n* sorrow or grief.

heart attack *n* a sudden instance of abnormal heart functioning, esp coronary thrombosis.

heart attack *see* **myocardial infarction**.

heartbeat *n* the rhythmic contraction and dilation of the heart.

heart block *n* a condition describing a failure in the conduction of electrical impulses from the natural pacemaker (the sinoatrial node) through the heart, which can lead to slowing of the pumping action.

heartbreak *n* overwhelming sorrow or grief.—**heartbreaker** *n*.

heartbreaking *adj* causing heartbreak; pitiful.—**heartbreakingly** *adv*.

heartbroken *adj* overcome by sorrow or grief.—**heartbrokenly** *adv*.—**heartbrokenness** *n*.

heartburn *n* a burning pain or discomfort felt in the region of the heart, caused by regurgitation of the stomach contents.

heartburn *n* a burning sensation in the lower chest.

hearten *vt* to encourage; to cheer up.—**hearteningly** *adv*.

heart failure *n* the inability of the heart to supply enough blood to the body; a cessation of heart activity leading to death.

heart failure *n* the inability of the heart to sustain effective circulation of the blood.

heartfelt *adj* deeply felt; sincere.

hearth *n* the floor of a fireplace and surrounding area; this as symbolic of house and home.

hearth *n* the site of an ancient open fire used for cooking.

hearthstone *n* a stone forming a hearth; soft stone used to whiten hearths, floors, steps, etc.

heartily *adv* in a vigorous or enthusiastic way; sincerely.

heartland *n* the central or most vital part of an area, region, etc.

heartless *adj* lacking compassion; unfeeling.—**heartlessly** *adv*.—**heartlessness** *n*.

heart-rending *adj* causing much mental anguish.

heartsease *n* the wild pansy.

heartsick *adj* extremely unhappy, despondent.—**heartsickness** *n*.

heartstrings *npl* deepest feelings.

heart-throb *n* (*inf*) the object of a person's infatuation; a heartbeat.

heart-to-heart *n* an intimate conversation. * *adj* intimate; candid.

heartwarming *adj* pleasing; inspiring sympathy; moving.

heartwood *n* the central older wood of a tree, usu harder and darker than the outer rings.—*also* **duramen**.

hearty *adj* (**heartier, heartiest**) warm and friendly; (*laughter, etc*) unrestrained; strong and healthy; nourishing and plentiful.—**heartiness** *n*.

heat *n* (*phys*) energy produced by molecular agitation.

heat *n* energy produced by molecular agitation; the quality of being hot; the perception of hotness; hot weather or climate; strong feeling, esp ardor, anger, etc; a single bout, round, or trial in sports; the period of sexual excitement and readiness for mating in female animals; (*sl*) coercion. * *vti* to make or become warm or hot; to make or become excited.

heated *adj* made hot; excited, impassioned.—**heatedly** *adv*.—**heatedness** *n*.

heater *n* a device that provides heat; (*sl*) a pistol.

heat exhaustion *n* (*med*) a physical state in which the body's normal cooling processes fail to operate as a result of increasing environmental temperature.

heat exhaustion *n* exhaustion and collapse as a result of overheating of the body and loss of fluid following unaccustomed or prolonged exposure to excessive heat.

heath *n* an area of uncultivated land with scrubby vegetation; any of various shrubby plants that thrive on sandy soil, e.g., heather.

Heath *n* **Edward [Richard George]** (1916–) British Conservative statesman and prime minister (1970–74).

heathen *n* (*pl* **heathens, heathen**) anyone not acknowledging the God of Christian, Jew, or Muslim belief; a person regarded as irreligious, uncivilized, etc. * *adj* of or denoting a heathen; irreligious; pagan.—**heathendom** *n*.

heathenish *adj* relating to or resembling a heathen or heathenish culture; rude, ignorant or uncultured.—**heathenishly** *adv*.—**heathenishness** *n*.

heathenism *n* ignorance of God; paganism; idolatry.

heather *n* a common evergreen shrub of northern and alpine regions with small sessile leaves and tiny usu purplish pink flowers.—**heathery** *adj*.

heating *n* a system of providing heat, as central heating; the warmth provided.

heat island *n* the area of higher temperature over a city caused by the reflection of the Sun's heat from buildings and streets and by the heat generated by industry, traffic, etc.

heat lightning *n* vivid flashes of distant lightning without thunder, esp at the end of a hot day.

heat pump *n* a device for warming or cooling by transferring heat.

heat rash *see* **prickly heat**.

heat stroke *n* a severe condition following exposure of the body to excessive heat, characterized by a rise in temperature and failure of sweating and temperature regulation.—*also* **hyperpyrexia**.

heat wave *n* a prolonged period of unusually hot weather.

heave *vb* (**heaving, heaved**) *vt* to lift or move, esp with great effort; to utter (a sigh, etc) with effort; (*inf*) to throw. * *vi* to rise and fall rhythmically; to vomit; to pant; to gasp; to haul; (**heaving, hove**) (*with* **to**) (*ship*) to come to a stop. * *n* the act or effort of heaving.—**heaver** *n*.

heaven *n* (*usu pl*) the visible sky; (*sometimes cap*) the dwelling place of God and his angels where the blessed go after death; any place or state of great happiness; (*pl*) *interj* an exclamation of surprise.

heaven *n* the sky where the sun shines by day and moon and stars by night;

Heaven *n* (*Bible*) the dwelling-place of the unseen, almighty, ever-present God or gods; the abode of the angels.

heavenly *adj* of or relating to heaven or heavens; divine; (*inf*) excellent, delightful.—**heavenliness** *n*.

heave offering *n* (*Bible*) sacrificial gift symbolically offered to God by being heaved or lifted up; later eaten by the priests as their share.

heavy *adj* (**heavier, heaviest**) hard to lift or carry; of more than the usual, expected, or defined weight; to an unusual extent; hard to do; stodgy, hard to digest; cloudy; (*industry*) using massive machinery to produce basic materials, as chemicals and steel; (*ground*) difficult to make fast progress on; clumsy; dull, serious. * *n* (*pl* **heavies**) (*theater*) a villain; (*sl*) a person hired to threaten violence, a thug.—**heavily** *adv*.—**heaviness** *n*.

heavy-duty *adj* made to withstand heavy strain or rough usage.

heavy-handed *adj* clumsy; tactless; oppressive.—**heavy-handedly** *adv*.—**heavy-handedness** *n*.

heavy metal *n* a type of rock music characterized by a heavy beat and reliance on loudly amplified instruments.

heavyset *adj* having a stout or stocky build.

heavy spar *see* **barium sulfate**.

heavy water *n* deuterium oxide, water in which the normal hydrogen content has been replaced by deuterium.

heavyweight *n* a professional boxer weighing more than 175 pounds (79 kg) or wrestler weighing over 209 pounds (95 kg); (*inf*) a very influential or important individual.

Heb. *or* **Hebr.** *abbr* = Hebrew(s).

HEBA *abbr* = Home Extension Building Association.

hebdomad *n* (*formerly*) seven; a group of seven; a week.

hebdomadal *adj* weekly.—**hebdomadally** *adv*.

Hebe *n* (*Greek myth*) the goddess of youth.

hebetate *vti* to make or become dull. * *adj* (*plant*) having a blunt or soft point.—**hebetation** *n*.

hebetude *n* mental dullness or lethargy.—**hebetudinous** *adj*.

Hebraic, Hebraical *adj* of or pertaining to the Hebrews, Jewish language or literature.—**Hebraically** *adv*.

Hebraism *n* a linguistic usage, custom or idiom borrowed from and characteristic of the Hebrew language, or the Jewish people or culture.

Hebraist *n* one who studies or is learned in the Hebrew language and culture.—**Hebraistic, Hebraistical** *adj*.—**Hebraistically** *adv*.

Hebrew *n* a member of an ancient Semitic people; an Israelite; a Jew; the ancient Semitic language of the Hebrews; its modern form. * *adj* pertaining to the Hebrew people; Jewish.

Hebrews *n* (*OT*) the people of Israel in early stories, e.g., in the accounts of Abraham, Joseph and Moses; the wandering Semitic tribes who came out of Arabia.

Hebrews, the Letter to the *n* (*Bible*) NT book, attributed to Paul, which is more a sermon than a letter; it is not known who the "Hebrews" were.

Hebron *n* ancient city of Canaan often mentioned in early OT history.

Hebrus *n* the ancient name of an important river in Thrace, now the boundary between Greece and Turkey.

HEBS *abbr* (*Brit*) = Health Education Board for Scotland.

HEC *abbr* = Health Education Council.

Hecabe *see* **Hecuba**.

Hecate *n* (*Greek myth*) a goddess of the underworld.

hecatomb *n* in ancient Greece, the ritual sacrifice of 100 oxen; any large sacrifice or slaughter.

Hecatoncheires *npl* (*Greek myth*) three giants each with 50 heads and 100 arms, Briareus, Gyes, and Cottus, who were kept in Tartarus as guardians of the Titans imprisoned there.

heck *interj* a mild expression of surprise or grief.

H

heckelphone *n* (*mus*) a double-reed instrument which is effectively a baritone oboe.

heckle *vti* to harass (a speaker) with questions or taunts.—**heckler** *n*.

hect- or **hecto-** *prefix* a hundred.

hectare *n* a metric measure of area, equivalent to 10,000 square meters (2.47 acres).

hectic *adj* involving intense excitement or activity.—**hectically** *adv*.

hectogram *n* a metric unit of mass equivalent to 100 grams (3.527 ounces).

hectograph *n* a process for copying a manuscript by transferring it onto a layer of gelatin coated with glycerin; the machine that uses this process. * *vt* to copy in this way.—**hectographic** *adj*.—**hectographically** *adv*.

hectol. *abbr* = hectoliter.

hectom. *abbr* = hectometer.

hector *vt* to bully; to annoy. * *n* a bully.

Hector *n* (*Greek myth*) Trojan commander whose exploits are celebrated in Homer's *Iliad*.

HECTOR *abbr* = heated experimental carbon thermal oscillator reactor.

Hecuba *n* (*Greek myth*) the wife of Priam, king of Troy.—*also* **Hecabe**.

he'd = he had; he would.

hedge *n* a fence consisting of a dense line of bushes or small trees; a barrier or means of protection against something, esp financial loss; an evasive or noncommittal answer or statement. * *vt* to surround or enclose with a hedge; to place secondary bets as a precaution. * *vi* to avoid giving a direct answer in an argument or debate.—**hedger** *n*. —**hedgy** *adj*.

hedgehog *n* a small insectivorous mammal with sharp spines on the back.

hedgerow *n* a line of shrubs or trees separating or enclosing fields.

hedging *n* the act of decreasing the degree of uncertainty about future price movements in commodities, securities and foreign currency.

hedging against inflation *n* an attempt to protect one's capital against depreciation by purchasing equities or making other investments that are likely to rise in value as the general level of prices rises.

hedonism *n* the doctrine that personal pleasure is the chief good.—**hedonistic** *adj*.—**hedonist** *n*.

heebie-jeebies *npl* (*sl*) nervousness, jitters.

heed *vt* to pay close attention to. * *n* careful attention.—**heeder** *n*.

heedful *adj* paying attention; mindful.—**heedfully** *adv*.—**heedfulness** *n*.

heedless *adj* inattentive; thoughtless.—**heedlessly** *adv*.—**heedlessness** *n*.

heehaw *n* (an imitation of) the bray of a donkey, a crude laugh. * *vi* to bray like a donkey.

heel[1] *n* the back part of the foot, under the ankle; the part covering or supporting the heel in stockings, socks, etc, or shoes; a solid attachment forming the back of the sole of a shoe; (*inf*) a despicable person. * *vt* to furnish with a heel; to follow closely; (*inf*) to provide with money, etc. * *vi* to follow along at the heels of someone.—**heelless** *adj*.

heel[2] *vti* to tilt or become tilted to one side, as a ship.

heelball *n* a black, waxy substance used to blacken the heels and soles of shoes; a waxy substance used in brass rubbing.

heeler *n* a person who works for a local political organization, esp a ward heeler; (*Austral*) a dog that herds cattle by snapping at their heels.

heeltap *n* a small layer of leather in the heel of a shoe; the dregs of an alcoholic drink left at the bottom of a glass.

HEF *abbr* = high-energy fuel.

HEFA *abbr* = Human Embryo and Fertilization Authority.

HEFC *abbr* = Higher Education Funding Council.

Hefeydd Hen *n* (*Welsh Celtic myth*) was the father of Rhiannon, the wife of Pwyll. He was known as Hen, meaning "old" or "ancient," in view of his advanced years.

heft *vt* to assess the weight of (an object) by holding it in the hand; to lift; to become used to. * *n* weight; the main part.

hefty *adj* (**heftier**, **heftiest**) (*inf*) heavy; large and strong; big.—**heftily** *adv*.—**heftiness** *n*.

Hegel *n* **Georg Wilhelm Friedrich** (1770–1831) German philosopher, whose work influenced Karl Marx.—**Hegelian** *adj*.—**Hegelianism** *n*.

hegemony *n* (*pl* **hegemonies**) leadership, domination, esp of one nation over others.—**hegemonic** *adj*.

Hegira *n* the flight of Mohammed from Mecca in AD 622, marking the start of the Muslim era.—*also* **Hejira**.

HEH *abbr* = His or Her Exalted Highness.

hei *abbr* = high-explosive incendiary.

HEI *abbr* = Health Effects Institute.

Heidegger *n* **Martin** (1889–1976) German philosopher, whose concepts, such as "angst," influenced the existentialists.

heifer *n* a young cow that has not calved.

Heifetz *n* **Jascha** (1901–87) Lithuanian-born American violinist.

height *n* the topmost point; the highest limit; the distance from the bottom to the top; altitude; a relatively great distance above a given level; an eminence; a hill.

heighten *vti* to make or come higher or more intense.—**heightener** *n*.

Heilyn *n* (*Welsh Celtic myth*) one of only seven Britons who survived the terrible war in Ireland between Matholwch and Bendigeid Vran.

Heimlich maneuver *n* a procedure to dislodge a foreign body that is blocking the larynx and causing choking.

Heine *n* **Heinrich** (1797–1856) German poet and critic, whose masterpiece is the *Book of Songs* (1827).

Heinin *n* (*Welsh Celtic myth*) the chief bard at the court of King Arthur at the time when Taliesin arrived.

heinous *adj* outrageously evil; wicked.—**heinously** *adv*.—**heinousness** *n*.

heir *n* a person who inherits or is entitled to inherit another's property, title, etc.—**heirless** *adj*.

heir app. *abbr* = heir apparent.

heirdom *n* succession by right of blood; inheritance.

heiress *n* a woman or girl who is an heir, esp to great wealth.

heirloom *n* any possession handed down from generation to generation.

heir pres. *abbr* = heir presumptive.

Heisenberg *n* **Werner Karl** (1901–76) German theoretical physicist and winner of the 1932 Nobel Prize for Physics for his work on quantum theory.

heist *n* (*sl*) a robbery. * *vt* (*sl*) to steal.—**heister** *n*.

HEIST *abbr* = Higher Education Information Services Trust.

Hejira *see* **Hegira**.

Hektor, **Hector** *n* a member of one of the two groups of asteroids that are in the same orbit as Jupiter around the Sun, known as the Trojan group.

HeLa *abbr* = Helen Lake (tumor cell line).

held *see* **hold**[1].

Heldentenor *n* (*mus*) a "heroic tenor," i.e., a tenor with a strong voice suitable for Wagnerian heroic roles.

Helen, **Helena** *n* (*Greek myth*) the most beautiful woman in Greece, carried off to Troy by Paris, for whose sake the Trojan War was fought.

Helena *n* the capital city of Montana , a state of the USA.

Helena *n* Saint (*c.* 248–327) mother of Constantine the Great, the first Christian emperor; became a Christian herself under the influence of her son. Helena gave large sums of money to the poor and secured the release of prisoners. Her feast day is 18 August.

Helenus *n* (*Greek myth*) a Trojan soothsayer, son of Priam and Hecuba.

heliacal *adj* emerging from or passing into the light of the sun.

heliacal rising *n* the rising of a star or planet which is visible just before sunrise.

heliacal setting *n* the setting of a star or planet coinciding with sunrise.

helianthus *n* any of a genus of plants with large yellow flowers, including the sunflower and Jerusalem artichoke.

helical *adj* like a helix, spiral.—**helically** *adv*.

helicoid *adj* resembling a flattened spiral. * *n* a spirally curved geometrical figure.

Helicon *n* ancient name of a mountain range of Greece, the seat of the Muses, now Sagara.

helicopter *n* a kind of aircraft lifted and moved, or kept hovering, by large rotary blades mounted horizontally.

heliculture *n* the rearing of snails for food.

Helig ap Glannowg *n* (*Welsh Celtic myth*) the ruler of a Welsh kingdom in the sixth century. It is said to have been situated about ten miles out to sea from Colwyn Bay.

helio- *prefix* sun.

heliocentric *adj* having the sun as the center; measured or viewed from the sun's center.—**heliocentrically** *adv*.—**heliocentricity**, **heliocentricism** *n*.

heliochrome *n* a photograph in natural colors.

Heliodorus *n* (*fl.* 3rd–4th century AD) Syrian-born Greek writer, whose romance *Aethiopica* is written in poetic prose.

heliograph *n* a signaling device using the sun's rays reflected by a mirror.—**heliographer** *n*. —**heliographic** *adj*.—**heliography** *n*.

heliogravure *n* photogravure, the process of photo-engraving or etching.

Heliopolis *n* (*Egypt*) now a suburb of Cairo, but once a great center of Egyptian religion, seat of the cult of the sun-god Ra and the center of the most widely accepted cosmology. The doctrine of Heliopolis spelled out how creation originally occurred, and the Ben-ben stone fetish in the temple was a symbol of that creation.

heliolatry *n* sun worship.

heliometer *n* a refracting telescope used to measure small angular distances between celestial bodies.

Helios *n* (*Greek myth*) the god of the sun, the Roman Sol.

heliosphere *n* a large region surrounding the sun, where the solar wind predominates.

heliostat *n* (*astron*) an astronomical instrument that enables study (both by photography and spectroscopy) of the sun to be made.

heliostat *n* an instrument that sends signals by reflecting the light of the sun in a constant direction.

heliotrope *n* a genus of plants whose flowers follow the course of the sun; a green-hued variety of chalcedony with small red spots; a bloodstone; the bluish-pink color of the flower heliotrope; an instrument used in geodetic surveying.

heliotropism *n* the movement of flowers or leaves toward the sun.—**heliotropic** *adj*.

heliport *or* **helipad** *n* a landing and takeoff place for a helicopter.

heli-skiing *n* the use of helicopters to take skiers to high, uncrowded, off-piste slopes.

helium *n* a light nonflammable gaseous element. *symbol He.

helium flash *n* a late stage in the life history of a star, in which the core collapses, giving rise to temperatures at which nuclear fusion reactions can occur.

helium star *n* hot, blue stars with surface temperatures near 14,000 K.

helix *n* (*pl* **helices**) **helix** *n* (*pl* **helices, helixes**) a spiral line, as a line coiled around; (*zool*) a snail or its shell; (*anat*) the folded rim of the external ear; (*archit*) a small volute on a capital; (*geom*) a curve in the form of a spiral, which encircles the surface of a cone or cylinder at a constant angle.

Helix Nebula *n* a nebula in the constellation Aquarius, and the largest of the planetary nebulae.

hell *n* (*Christianity*) the place of punishment of the wicked after death; the home of devils and demons; any place or state of supreme misery or discomfort; (*inf*) a cause of this. * *interj* (*inf*) an exclamation of anger, surprise, etc.

he'll = he will.

Helladic *adj* denoting the period of the Greek Bronze Age.

Hellas *n* the Greek name for Greece.—**Hellenic** *adj*.

hellbent *adj* (*inf*) rashly determined.

Helle *n* (*Greek myth*) sister of Phrixus, who fell into the strait between Europe and Asia, which was called Hellespont, "sea of Helle."

hellebore *n* any of a genus of mostly poisonous plants, including the Christmas rose.

Hellen *n* (*Greek myth*) founder of the four great branches of the Greek people, or Hellenes.

Hellene, Hellenian *n* a Greek.

Hellenic *adj* of or relating to classical Greece and the Greeks; relating to classical and modern Greeks and their language. * *n* a branch of the Indo-European family of languages made up of Greek and its dialects.

Hellenism *n* the national character of the Greeks; the ideals and principles of classical Greece; the love of Greek culture and art.

Hellenist *n* a non-Greek, especially a Jew, who spoke Greek in classical times; a student of Greek culture and language.

Hellenistic *adj* relating to or characteristic of classical Greece; relating to Greeks or to Hellenism.

Hellenize *vt* to adopt classical Greek culture or customs; to use or study the Greek language.—**Hellenization** *n*.—**Hellenizer** *n*.

Heller *n* 1. **Joseph** (1923–99) American novelist, whose most popular novel is *Catch-22* (1961). 2. **Stephen** (1813–88) Hungarian virtuoso pianist and composer, who traveled Europe giving recitals. He composed some 150 pieces for the piano, mainly using innovative techniques.

Hellespont *n* the ancient name for the Dardanelles, the strait between the Aegean Sea and the Sea of Marmara.

hellish *adj* of, pertaining to, or resembling hell; very wicked; (*inf*) very unpleasant.—**hellishly** *adv*.—**hellishness** *n*.

hello *interj* an expression of greeting. * *n* (*pl* **hellos**) the act of saying "hello."—*also* **hallo, hullo** (*pl* **hallos, hullos**).

helm[1] *n* (*naut*) the tiller or wheel used to steer a ship; any position of control or direction, authority. * *vt* to steer; to control.

helm[2] *n* (*arch*) a helmet. * *vt* to provide or cover with a helmet.

helmet *n* protective headgear worn by soldiers, policemen, divers, etc.—**helmeted** *adj*.

Helmholtz *n* **Hermann Ludwig Ferdinand von** (1821–94) German physiologist and physicist, who published highly important and influential books on sound theory. *On the Sensations of Tone* (1862) is the foundation of the modern theory of acoustics.

helminth *n* a worm, esp an intestinal one, a fluke.

helminthic *adj* pertaining to worms. * *n* a drug used to treat intestinal worms.

helminthoid *adj* worm-shaped.

helminthology *n* the study of parasitic worms

helmsman *n* (*pl* **helmsmen**) a man who steers.— **helmswoman** *nf* (*pl* **helmswomen**).

Héloïse *n* (*c.* 1101–64) pupil, mistress, and wife of Peter Abélard, who, after his castration, initiated by her uncle, became a nun.

helot *n* a serf or slave; (*with cap*) in ancient Sparta, a state-owned slave.

helotry *n* slavery or serfdom; the class of slaves or serfs.

help *vt* to make things better or easier for; to aid; to assist; to remedy; to keep from; to serve or wait on. * *vi* to give aid; to be useful.—*interj* used to ask for assistance. * *n* the action of helping; aid; assistance; a remedy; a person that helps, esp a hired person.—**helper** *n*.

HELP *abbr* = helicopter electronic landing path.

help file *n* (*comput*) a file built into a software program that provides assistance and information.

helpful *adj* giving help; useful.—**helpfully** *adv*.—**helpfulness** *n*.

helping *n* a single portion of food.

helpless *adj* unable to manage alone, dependent on others; weak and defenseless.—**helplessly** *adv*.—**helplessness** *n*.

helpmate, helpmeet *n* a helpful companion, esp a wife or husband.

Helsinki (Helsingfors) *n* capital city of Finland.

helter-skelter *adv* in confused haste. * *adj* disorderly. * *n* a tall spiral slide usu found in an amusement park.

helve *n* the handle of a tool.

Helvetia *n* the Latin name for Switzerland.

Helvetian *adj* of or relating to Helvetia; Swiss. * *n* a native or citizen of Switzerland.

Helvetii *n* a Celtic tribe who tried to migrate across Gaul to establish settlements on the Atlantic coast, having been driven out of their settlements in what is now Germany.

hem[1] *n* the edge of a garment, etc, turned back and stitched or fixed. * *vt* (**hemming, hemmed**) to finish (a garment) with a hem; (*with* **in**) to enclose, confine.—**hemmer** *n*.

hem[2] *n* a compound containing iron and composed of a pigment, known as a porphyrin, which confers color. It combines with a protein called globin in the blood to form hemoglobin.

hema- *or* **hemo-** *or* **hem-** *prefix* blood.

hemal *adj* of or relating to the blood, blood vessels or the part of the body that contains the heart.

he-man *n* (*pl* **he-men**) (*inf*) an excessively masculine or strongly built male.

hemangioma *n* a benign tumor of the blood vessels. It may be visible on the skin as a type of nevus (birthmark).

hemarthrosis *n* bleeding into a joint, which causes swelling and pain and may be the result of injury or disease.

hematemesis *n* vomiting of blood, which may occur for a number of different reasons.

hematic *adj* of, containing, acting on, or relating to blood. * *n* a drug that increases the level of hemoglobin in blood.

hematinic *n* a substance that increases the amount of hemoglobin in the blood, e.g., ferrous sulfate.

hematite *n* native ferric oxide, an important iron ore.

hematocele *n* leakage of blood into a cavity, causing a swelling.

hematoid *adj* relating to blood; blood-like.

hematology *n* the branch of medicine dealing with blood and its diseases.—**hematologic, hematological** *adj*.—**hematologist** *n*.

hematoma *n* a collection of blood forming a firm swelling or bruise that may occur as a result of injury, a clotting disorder of the blood or disease of the blood vessels.

hematuria *n* the presence of blood in the urine, which may have come from the kidneys, ureter, bladder or urethra.

Hemera *n* (*Greek myth*) the goddess of day; personification of day.

hemi- *prefix* half; partial.

hemicycle *n* a half-circle, semicircle.—**hemicyclic** *adj*.

hemidemisemiquaver *n* (*mus*) a 64th note.

hemihedral *adj* (*crystal*) having only half the normal number of faces.

Hemingway *n* **Ernest [Millar]** (1899–1961) American novelist and short-story writer, whose major novels include *For Whom the Bell Tolls* (1940). He was winner of the 1954 Nobel Prize for Literature.

hemiola *n* (*mus*) a rhythm in which two bars in triple time are played as though they were three bars in duple time.

hemiplegia *n* paralysis of one side of the body.—**hemiplegic** *adj, n*.

hemisphere *n* half of a sphere or globe; any of the halves (northern, southern, eastern, or western) of the earth.—**hemispheric, hemispherical** *adj*.—**hemispherically** *adv*.

hemistich *n* half of a line of verse.

hemline *n* the bottom edge of a skirt or dress.

hemlock *n* a poisonous plant with small white flowers; a poison made from this plant.

hemmer *n* one who stitches hems; a machine for hemming.

hemodialysis *n* the use of an artificial kidney to remove waste products from a person's blood using the principle of dialysis.

hemoglobin *n* the oxygen-carrying red coloring matter of the red blood corpuscles.

hemoglobinopathy *n* any of a number of inherited diseases in which there is an abnormality in the formation of hemoglobin.

hemoglobinuria *n* the presence of hemoglobin in the urine, caused by disintegration of red blood cells, conferring a dark red or brown color.

hemolysis *n* the destruction of red blood cells (erythrocytes), which may result from infection or poisoning or as an antibody response.

hemolytic disease of the newborn *n* a serious disease affecting fetuses and newborn babies, caused by incompatibility between the blood of the mother and that of the fetus.—*also* **hydrops fetalis**. *See* **Rhesus factor**.

hemophilia *n* a hereditary condition in which the blood fails to clot normally.—**hemophiliac, hemophile** *n*. —**hemophilic** *adj*.

H

hemophobia *n* a morbid or deep-seated fear of blood.—**hemophobic** *adj*.

hemopoiesis *n* formation of blood cells (particularly erythrocytes, the red blood cells) and platelets, which takes place in the bone marrow in adults but in a fetus occurs in the liver and spleen.

hemoptysis *n* the spitting or coughing up of blood or mucus containing blood.

hemorrhage *n* the escape of blood from a blood vessel; heavy bleeding. * *vi* to bleed heavily.—**hemorrhagic** *adj*.

hemorrhoids *npl* swollen or bleeding veins around the anus.—*also* **piles**.—**hemorrhoidal** *adj*.

hemostasis *see* **blood clotting**.

hemothorax *n* a leakage of blood into the pleural cavity of the chest, usu as a result of injury.

hemp *n* a widely cultivated Asian herb of the mulberry family; its fiber, used to make rope, sailcloth, etc; a narcotic drug obtained from different varieties of this plant (—*also* **cannabis, marijuana**).—**hempen** *adj*.

hemstitch *n* an ornamental stitch.—**hemstitcher** *n*.

hen *n* the female of many birds, esp the chicken.

henbane *n* a poisonous, sticky, hairy plant of the nightshade family.

hence *adv* from here; from this time; from this reason.

henceforth, henceforward *adv* from now on.

henchman *n* (*pl* **henchmen**) a trusted helper or follower.

hendecagon *n* an 11-sided plane figure.—**hendecagonal** *adj*.

hendecasyllable *n* a verse of 11 syllables.—**hendecasyllabic** *adj*.

hendiadys *n* the use of two connected words to express one idea, as "with might and main."

Hendrix *n* **Jimi [James Marshall Hendrix]** (1942–70) American rock guitarist, singer, and songwriter. He was the leader of the Jimi Hendrix Experience, and an influential figure in rock music.

henge *n* (*archeo*) a type of circular, ceremonial monument unique to the British Isles. It has a ditch with a bank normally thrown up outside it, with a diameter of 55–65 yards.

Hengest *or* **Hengist** *n* king of Kent (455–488). The first of the Jutish kings of Kent, he ruled jointly with his brother Horsa. His son, Aesc, succeeded him.

henhouse *n* a shelter for fowl.

Henie *n* **Sonja** (1912–69) Norwegian-born American ice skater, who was three times Olympic gold-medal winner for figure skating.

Henley *n* **W[illiam] E[rnest]** (1849–1903) English poet, critic and editor, with a talent for unusual rhymes and some of whose poems, e.g., "Invictus," will always retain their popularity, but who is best remembered as a mentor to younger writers, e.g., Kipling and Stevenson.

henna *n* a tropical plant; a reddish-brown dye extracted from its leaves, used to tint the hair or skin. * *vt* to dye with henna.

Hennebique *n* **François** (1842–1921) French architect, whose notable works include numerous concrete structures.

hennery *n* (*pl* **henneries**) a poultry farm.

henotheism *n* the worship of one god while recognizing the existence of others.—**henotheist** *n*, *adj*.—**henotheistic** *adj*.

henpeck *vt* to nag and domineer over (one's husband).—**henpecked** *adj*.

Henri *n* **Robert** (1865–1929) American painter; a leader of The Eight. The major import of his work is the social realism of his subject matter, based on a deeply held belief that artists should paint life around them as they saw it.

henry *n* (*pl* **henries, henrys**) a unit of electrical inductance.

Henry *n* 1. **George** (1858–1943) Scottish painter and member of the Glasgow School. One of his best-known paintings is *Galloway Landscape* (1889), illustrating a favorite theme of cattle in landscape. 2. **O** *see* **O Henry**.

Henry I *n* (1068–1135) king of England (1100–1135). Often surnamed "Beauclerk" (fine scholar). The youngest son of William the Conqueror and Matilda of Flanders.

Henry II *n* (1133–1189) king of England (1154–1189). The first of the Plantagenet line was born in Normandy the son of Geoffrey, Count of Anjou, and Matilda, daughter of Henry I.

Henry III *n* (1207–1272) king of England (1216–1272). The eldest son of John by Isabel of Angoulême, Married in 1236 to Eleanor of Provence.

Henry IV *n* (1366–1413) king of England and Wales (1399–1413). The eldest son of John of Gaunt, Duke of Lancaster, fourth son of Edward III, by Blanche of Lancaster, the daughter of Henry, Duke of Lancaster, great-grandson of Henry III.

Henry V *n* (1387–1422) king of England (1413–1422). The only surviving son of Henry IV and Mary de Bohun.

Henry VI *n* (1421–1471) king of England and Wales (1422–1461) and from 1470–1471. The only son of Henry V and Catherine of Valois.

Henry VII *n* (1457–1509) king of England (1485–1509). The first of the Tudor kings, Henry was the son of Edmund, Earl of Richmond, son of Owen Tudor and Catherine of France, widow of Henry V.

Henry VIII *n* (1491–1547) king of England and Ireland (from 1542) (1509–47). The second son of Henry VII and Elizabeth of York. His only son, by Jane Seymour, Edward VI, succeeded him.

Henry Draper Catalog *n* a catalog of stars, in which the stars are arranged according to the characteristics of their spectrum.

Henson *n* **Jim [James Maury Henson]** (1936–90) American puppeteer and movie producer, who created the Muppets.

hent *vt* (*arch*) to seize; to grasp. * *n* (*arch*) a clutching; intention; anything that has been gasped by the mind.

Hentrich *n* **Helmut** (*b.* 1905) German architect, whose notable works include University buildings, Bochum.

Henze *n* **Hans Werner** (1926–) German composer of extraordinarily diverse works. His works include *Boulevard Solitude, Raft of the Medusa* (dedicated to the revolutionary, Che Guevara), and *Voices,* which has a text partly written by Ho Chi Minh.

HEO *abbr* = Higher Executive Officer.

HEOS *abbr* = high-ecliptic-inclined-orbit satellite.

heparin *n* an anticoagulant substance naturally present in the body and produced by liver and some white blood cells.

hepat-, hepato- *prefix* liver.

hepatectomy *n* (*pl* **hepatectomies**) surgical removal of the whole or part of the liver.

hepatic *adj* of, like, or pertaining to the liver. * *n* a drug for treating the liver.

hepatic *adj* the term used to describe the liver.

hepatitis *n* inflammation of the liver.

hepatoma *n* a malignant tumor of the liver, which is rare in Western countries except among those with cirrhosis.

Hepburn *n* **Katharine** (1907–) American movie and stage actress, who was associated professionally and romantically with Spencer Tracy.

Hephaestus *or* **Hephaistos** *n* (*Greek myth*) the god of fire, and patron of all those who worked in iron and metals, identified by the Romans with their Vulcan.

heptad *n* a group of seven; the number seven; an atom or element with the valency of seven.

heptagon *n* a polygon of seven angles and seven sides.—**heptagonal** *adj*.

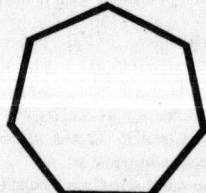

heptahedron *n* (*pl* **heptahedrons, heptahedra**) a solid figure with seven plane faces.—**heptahedral** *adj*.

heptameter *n* a verse line of seven metrical feet.

heptarchy *n* (*pl* **heptarchies**) government by seven rulers; a state divided into seven regions, each with its own ruler; the seven kingdoms of Anglo-Saxon England.

Heptateuch *n* (*Bible*) the first seven books of the Old Testament.

Hepworth *n* **Dame [Jocelyn] Barbara** (1903–75) English abstract sculptor.

her *pron* the objective and possessive case of the personal pronoun **she**. * *adj* of or belonging to a female.

her. *abbr* = heraldry.

Hera *n* (*Greek myth*) a goddess, identified by the Romans with their Juno, the sister and wife of Zeus.

Heracles *n* (*Greek myth*) a hero of superhuman strength and ability, called Hercules by the Romans. He performed tasks known as the 12 labors of Heracles, killed several monsters and did many other exploits among both humans and gods.

Heraclids, Heracleidae *npl* (*Greek myth*) the descendants of Heracles; a tribe who claimed descent from Heracles and joined the Dorians in the conquest of the Peloponnese.

Heraean Games *npl* in ancient Greece, games held specifically for women every four years at Olympia.

Herakleopolis *n* (*Egypt*) Egyptian settlement and nome capital situated to the south of the Faiyum region on a strategic north-south route. It was the home ground of the Herakleopolitan kings of the Ninth and Tenth Dynasties.

herald *n* a person who conveys news or messages; a forerunner, harbinger; (*Middle Ages*) an official at a tournament. * *vt* to usher in; to proclaim.

Herald *abbr* (*Brit*) = Highly-Enriched Reactor, Aldermaston.

heraldic *adj* of a herald or heraldry.—**heraldically** *adv*.

heraldry *n* the study of genealogies and coats of arms; ceremony; pomp.—**heraldist** *n*.

herb *n* any seed plant whose stem withers away annually; any plant used as a medicine, seasoning, etc.

herbaceous *adj* of or like herbs; green and leafy.

herbage *n* pasturage; the succulent parts of herbs.

herbal *adj* of herbs. * *n* a book listing and describing plants with medicinal properties.

herbalist *n* a person who practices healing by using herbs; a person who grows or deals in herbs.

herbarium *n* (*pl* **herbariums** *or* **herbaria**) a (place or container for a) systematic collection of dried plants.—**herbarial** *adj*.

herb Christopher *see* baneberry.

Herbert *n* 1. **George** (1593–1633) English Anglican priest and poet, whose poems were published posthumously as *The Temple: Sacred Poems and Private Ejaculations* and are among the great devotional poems in the English language. 2. **Victor** (1859–1924) an Irish-born composer, conductor and cellist who settled in the USA. He is best known for his operettas (e.g., *Babes in Toyland*) but he also wrote a cello concerto, a symphonic poem and various pieces of orchestral music.

herbicide *n* a substance for destroying plants.—**herbicidal** *adj*.

Herbig-Haro object *n* a small nebula of dust and gas that may represent early stages in star formation.

herbivore *n* a plant-eating animal.

herbivorous *adj* herb-eating; (*animals*) plant-eating.—**herbivorousness** *n*.

herb. recent. *abbr* (*Latin*) = *herbarum recentium* "of fresh herbs."

herby *adj* (**herbier, herbiest**) herb-like; rich in herbs.

herculean *adj* of extraordinary strength, size, or difficulty; (*with cap*) of or like the Roman god Hercules.

Hercules[1] *n* the Roman name for Heracles.

Hercules[2] *n* a northern sky constellation.

Hercules A *n* a strong radio source associated with a large elliptical galaxy.

herd *n* a large number of animals, esp cattle, living and feeding together. * *vi* to assemble or move animals together. * *vt* to gather together and move as if a herd; to tend, as a herdsman.—**herder** *n*.

herdsman *n* (*pl* **herdsmen**) a person who tends a herd of animals.

here *adv* at or in this place; to or into this place; now; on earth.

HERE *abbr* = Hotel Employees' and Restaurant Employees' International Union.

hereabout, hereabouts *adv* in this area.

hereafter *adv* after this, in some future time or state. * *n* (*with* **the**) the future, life after death.

hereat *adv* (*arch*) because of this.

hereby *adv* by this means.

hereditable *adj* that may be inherited, heritable.—**hereditability** *n*. — **hereditably** *adv*.

hereditament *n* (*law*) property capable of being inherited.

hereditary *adj* descending by inheritance; transmitted to offspring.—**hereditarily** *adv*.—**hereditariness** *n*.

heredity *n* (*pl* **heredities**) the transmission of genetic material that determines physical and mental characteristics from one generation to another.

Hereford. *abbr* (*Latin*) = *Herefordensis*, "of Hereford."

herein *adv* (*formal*) in this place, document, etc.

hereinafter *adv* (*formerly*) afterward of this.

hereof *adv* of this.

heresiarch *n* the leader or founder of a heretical movement or sect.

heresy *n* (*pl* **heresies**) a religious belief regarded as contrary to the orthodox doctrine of a church; any belief or opinion contrary to established or accepted theory.

heretic *n* a dissenter from an established belief or doctrine.—**heretical** *adj*.—**heretically** *adv*.

hereto *adv* (*formal*) to this matter, document, etc.

heretofore *adv* (*formal*) until now.

hereunder *adv* (*formal*) below.

hereupon *adv* (*formal*) on this matter, issue, etc; immediately after this.

"Here We Have Idaho" *n* the official song of the American state, Idaho.

herewith *adv* (*formal*) with this.

HERI *abbr* = Higher Education Research Institute.

Herihor *n* (*Egypt*) a high priest (first prophet) of Amun, in the reign of Rameses XI.

heriot *n* a tribute, usu cattle, paid to a feudal lord on the death of a tenant by his heir.

heritable *adj* able to be inherited, heritable.—**heritably** *adv*.

heritage *n* something inherited at birth; anything deriving from the past or tradition; historical sites, traditions, practices, etc, regarded as the valuable inheritance of contemporary society.

heritor *n* (*law*) one who inherits; a proprietor.

hermaphrodite *n* an animal or organism with both male and female reproductive organs; a plant with stamens and pistils in the same floral envelope.—**hermaphroditic** *adj*.—**hermaphroditically** *adv*.

hermaphrodite brig *n* a brig square-rigged forward and schooner-rigged aft.

hermaphroditism, hermaphrodism *n* the state of being an hermaphrodite.

Hermaphroditus *n* (*Greek myth*) a demigod who was joined with the nymph Salmacis to form a being half male and half female.

hermeneutics *n* (*sing*) the science of interpretation, esp of the Bible.—**hermeneutic, hermeneutical** *adj*.—**hermeneutically** *adv*

Hermes *n* (*Greek myth*) the messenger god, god of the lyre and dreams, often depicted with winged feet.

hermetic, hermetical *adj* perfectly closed and airtight; of alchemy, magical.—**hermetically** *adv*.

Hermione *n* (*Greek myth*) the daughter of Menelaus and Helen.

hermit *n* a person who lives in complete solitude, esp for religious reasons; a recluse.—**hermitic, hermitical** *adj*.—**hermitically** *adv*.

hermitage *n* the dwelling place of a hermit; a secluded retreat.

Hermopolis Magna *n* (*Egypt*) (Latin and Greek: "great city of Hermes," so called to distinguish it from the Delta town of the same name) a temple city 187 miles (300 kilometers) south of Cairo and source of the Hermopolitan cosmology. Here the god Shu was said to have raised the sky above the earth

Hermon *n* a range of mountains in Lebanon exceeding 9000 feet above sea level and covered with snow all year.

hern *n* (*arch*) the heron.

Herne the Hunter *n* (*Brit Celtic myth*) the name of a giant with antlers on his head who was probably connected with the Celtic cult of Cernunnos.

hernia *n* (*pl* **hernias, herniae**) the protrusion of an organ, esp part of the intestine, through an opening in the wall of the cavity in which it sits; a rupture.—**hernial** *adj*.—**herniated** *adj*.

hernioplasty *n* (*pl* **hernioplasties**) the surgical operation to repair a hernia.

hero *n* (*pl* **heroes**) a person of exceptional bravery; a person admired for superior qualities and achievements; the central male character in a novel, play, etc.

Hero *n* (*Greek myth*) a priestess of Aphrodite, who was loved by Leander. Every night he swam across the Hellespont to her, and after he was drowned Hero threw herself into the sea and died.

Herod *n* any of a large and much intermarried line of kings, governors and tetrarchs who ruled over parts of Palestine for 150 years.

Herodians *npl* a party of leading Jews who supported Herod Antipas, the ruler of Galilee 4 BC–AD 39.

Herodias *n* (*OT*) a granddaughter of Herod the Great; married Philip, Herod's son, and later Philip's brother, Herod Antipas. Her daughter, Salome, danced before Herod Antipas and Herodias suggested she ask for the head of John the Baptist

Herodotus *n* a Greek traveler and historian who visited Egypt and recorded his impressions during the second half of the 5th century BC.

Herod the Great *n* ruled from 37–4 BC; (*Bible*) the king mentioned in the birth stories of Jesus; cruel, and with a passion for building. *See also* **Herod**

heroic *adj* of, worthy of, or like a hero; having the qualities of a hero; daring, risky; (*poetry*) of or about heroes and their deeds, epic; (*language*) grand, high-flown. * *n* heroic verse; (*pl*) melodramatic talk or behavior.—**heroically** *adv*.

heroic age *n* the age in which the legendary heroes of a nation, esp ancient Greece and Rome, are fabled to have lived.

heroic couplet *n* a rhyming couplet in iambic pentameter, used in English heroic verse.

heroic verse *n* a verse form used in epic poetry, i.e., the hexameter in Greek and Latin poetry, the iambic pentameter in English, and the Alexandrine in French.

heroin *n* a powerfully addictive drug derived from morphine.

heroine *n* a woman with the attributes of a hero; the leading female character in a novel, movie or play.

heroism *n* the qualities or conduct of a hero; bravery.

heron *n* a slim wading bird with long legs and neck.

heronry *n* (*pl* **heronries**) a heron rookery; a breeding place for herons.

herp. *or* **herpet.** *abbr* = herpetology.

herpes *n* any of several virus diseases marked by small blisters on the skin or mucous membranes.—**herpetic** *adj*.

herpetology *n* the study of snakes and amphibians.—**herpetologist** *n*.

Herr *n* (*pl* **Herren**) a title, the German equivalent of Mister or Sir.

Herrick *n* **Robert** (1591–1674) English Anglican priest and poet.

herring *n* (*pl* **herrings, herring**) a small food fish of commercial importance.

herringbone *n* (*archit*) a zigzag pattern of bricks, tiles or stones achieved by laying alternate courses in diagonal lines in opposite directions.

herringbone *n* a kind of cross-stitch; a zigzag pattern used in brickwork; (*skiing*) a method of walking uphill with the skis pointing outward. * *vt* to work in cross-stitch; to decorate with a herringbone pattern. * *vi* to ascend a ski slope in herringbone fashion.

hers *pron* something or someone belonging to her.

herself *pron* the reflexive form of **she** or **her**.

hertz *n* (*pl* **hertz**) the unit of frequency equal to one cycle per second; (*comput*) a measure of the frequency at which electrical waves repeat each second, used to show the speed of a computer chip.

Hertzog *n* **James Barry Munnik** (1866–1942) South African statesman; founder of the Nationalist Party (1913) and the Afrikaner Party (1941); prime minister (1924–39).

H

Hertzsprung-Russell diagram *n* a form of graph that highlights important characteristics of stars and also groups them into categories, essentially a color-brightness diagram.

HERU *abbr* = Higher Education Research Unit.

Herzog *n* **Werner** (1942–) German movie director .

he's = he is; he has.

Hesiod *n* poet of ancient Greece, who lived probably in the 8h century BC, and composed the didactic poem "Works and Days" and "Theogony," an account of mythology.—**Hesiodic** *adj*.

Hesione *n* (*Greek myth*) a sister of Priam of Troy, who was chained to a rock to be eaten by wild animals, and rescued by Heracles.

hesitancy *n* (*pl* **hesitancies**) an act of hesitating; the state of being hesitant; indecision.

hesitant *adj* hesitating; indecisive; reluctant; shy.—**hesitantly** *adv*.

hesitate *vi* to be slow in acting owing to uncertainty or indecision; to be reluctant (to); to falter or stammer when speaking.—**hesitater** *n*. —**hesitatingly** *adv*.

hesitation *n* the act of hesitating; a pause in speech.

Hesperian *adj* of or relating to the Hesperides; western. * *n* a native or inhabitant of a western land.

Hesperides *n* (*Greek myth*) (*pl*) the nymphs who guarded the golden apples given by Gaia to Hera on her marriage to Zeus; (*sing*) the garden containing the golden apples.

Hesperus *n* the evening star, esp Venus.

Hess *n* 1. Dame **Myra** (1890–1965) English pianist. 2. **Victor Francis** (1883–1964) Austrian-born American physicist, who shared the 1936 Nobel Prize for Physics with the American physicist Carl David Anderson (1905–91) for his research into cosmic rays. 3. **[Walter Richard] Rudolf** (1894–1987) German Nazi politician and deputy leader of the Nazi party (1934–41).

Hesse *n* **Hermann** (1877–1962) German-born Swiss novelist, short-story writer, and poet, whose novels include *Steppenwolf, Narziss and Goldmund*, and *The Glass Bead Game*. He was awarded the Nobel Prize for Literature in 1946.

Hessian *adj* pertaining to the German state of Hesse. * *n* a native or inhabitant of Hesse; a mercenary soldier.

hest *n* (*arch*) a behest; a command.

Hestia *n* (*Greek myth*) the hearth and the goddess of the hearth. The equivalent Roman goddess was Vesta.

Heston *n* **Charlton [John Charlton Carter]** (1923–) American actor , famous for his roles in movie epics.

HET *abbr* = Heritage Education Trust; Holocaust Education Trust.

hetaera, hetaira *n* (*pl* **hetaerae, hetaeras, hetairai**) a female prostitute or courtesan, esp in ancient Greece.—**hetaeric, hetairic** *adj*.

heter- *or* **hetero-** *prefix* another; abnormal; different, other; unequal.

heterocercal *adj* (*fish*) having the upper lobe of the tail longer than the lower lobe.

heterochromatic *adj* of different colors.

heteroclite *n* an irregularly inflected or unusual word; an unusual person or thing. * *adj* irregular; deviating from the ordinary (—*also* **heteroclitic**).

heterocyclic compounds *npl* (*chem*) organic compounds forming a ring structure with the additional elements, e.g., oxygen, hydrogen, nitrogen and sulfur.

heterodox *adj* contrary to established beliefs or opinions; unorthodox; heretical.

heterodoxy *n* (*pl* **heterodoxies**) the state of being heterodox; an unorthodox doctrine or opinion; heresy.

heterodyne *vt* to impose (a radio-frequency wave) on a transmitting wave to produce pulsations of audible frequency. * *adj* having or produced by combining waves of different lengths.

heterogamous *adj* (*bot*) bearing two kinds of flowers that differ sexually.

heterogeneous *adj* opposite or dissimilar in character, quality, structure, etc; not homogeneous; disparate.—**heterogeneity** *n*. —**heterogeneously** *adv*.

heterogenesis *n* the production by certain organisms of offspring differing in structure and habit from the parent, but reverting in subsequent generations to the original type.—**heterogenetic** *adj*.

heterogenous *adj* (*biol*) originating outside of the body; foreign.—**heterogeny** *n*.

heterologous *adj* (*biol*) abnormal in type or structure; derived from a different species; consisting of the same elements in varying proportions.—**heterology** *n*.

heteromorphism *n* (*biol*) deviation from the natural form or structure.—**heteromorphic** *adj*.

heteronomous *adj* differing from the normal type; subject to external law, rule or authority.—**heteronomously** *adv*.

heteronym *n* a word spelled in the same way as another or others but having a different meaning, as *brake* (in a vehicle) and *brake* (fern).—**heteronymous** *adj*.

heterophony *n* (*mus*) (*Greek*) difference of sounds, i.e., two or more performers playing different versions of the same melody simultaneously.

heterophyllous *adj* (*plants*) having leaves of different forms on the same stem.—**heterophylly** *n*.

heterosexual *adj* sexually attracted to the opposite sex. * *n* a heterosexual person.—**heterosexuality** *n*. —**heterosexually** *adv*.

heterozygote *n* (*genetics*) an organism having two different alleles of the gene in question in all somatic cells.

HETMA *abbr* = Heavy Edge Tool Manufacturers' Association.

hetman *n* (*pl* **hetmen**) (*formerly*) a Cossack prince or general.

het-up *adj* (*inf*) agitated, annoyed.

HEU *abbr* = highly enriched uranium.

heulandite *n* a vitreous transparent brittle mineral.

Heuneberg *n* a hill-fort site in southwestern Germany.

heuristic *adj* assisting or leading to discovery or invention; (*comput*) denoting a method used by experts to solve problems using a rule of thumb rather than strict logic.—**heuristically** *adv*.

hew *vt* (**hewing, hewed**, *pp* **hewed** *or* **hewn**) to strike or cut with blows using an ax, etc; to shape with such blows. * *vi* to conform (to a rule, principle, etc).—**hewer** *n*.

hex *vt* to bewitch; to bring bad luck to. * *n* a magic spell; a curse; a witch.

Hex *abbr* = hexadecimal notation.

hex. *abbr* = hexachord; hexagon.

hex- *or* **hexa-** *prefix* six.

hexachord *n* (*mus*) a diatonic series of six notes with a semitone between third and fourth.

hexad *n* a group or series of six; the number or sum of six; a chemical element, atom, or radical that can be combined with, or replaced by, six atoms of hydrogen.—**hexadic** *adj*.

hexadecimal *adj* (*comput*) denoting a numbering system that uses a base of 16. *See also* **binary**.

hexagon *n* a polygon having six sides and six angles.—**hexagonal** *adj*.—**hexagonally** *adv*.

hexagram *n* a plane figure having six angles and six sides; a six-pointed star formed by two intersecting triangles; a group of six lines which may be combined into 64 different patterns in I Ching.

hexahedron *n* a solid bounded by six plane faces.—**hexahedral** *adj*

hexameter *n* a line of Greek or Latin verse consisting of six feet, the last usu being a spondee; a verse line consisting of six metric feet.—**hexametric** *or* **hexametrical** *adj*.

hexapod *n* any of a large class of arthropods; an animal with six legs; an insect. * *adj* having six legs (—*also* **hexapodous**).

Hexateuch *n* (*Bible*) the first six books of the Old Testament.

hey *interj* an expression of joy or surprise or to call attention.

heyday *n* a period of greatest success, happiness, etc.

Heyerdahl *n* **Thor** (1914–) Norwegian anthropologist.

Heywood *n* **Thomas** (*c*. 1574–1641) English dramatist whose two best-known plays are the domestic tragedy *A Woman Killed with Kindness* and the adventure comedy *The Fair Maid of the West*.

Hezekiah *n* (*Bible*) King of Judah, 716–687 BC; the son of Ahaz, regarded as an evil king because he indulged in heathen practices. *See also* **Isaiah, Siloam**.

Hf *symbol* (*chem*) = hafnium (element).

HF *abbr* = (*pencil*) hard firm.

HF *abbr* = high frequency.

hf. *abbr* = half.

hf. bd. *abbr* = half-bound.

HFC *abbr* = high frequency current; hydrofluorocarbon.

hf. cf. *Abbr* = (*bookbinding*) half-calf.

HFFF *abbr* = Hungarian Freedom Fighters' Federation.

HFH *abbr* = home from hospital.

hfm *abbr* = hold for money.

hf. mor. *abbr* = (*bookbinding*) half-morocco.

HFRA *abbr* = Honorary Fellow of the Royal Academy.

HFS *abbr* (*comput*) = Hierarchical File System; a disk storage system developed for organizing files on a hard disk.

Hg *symbol* (*chem*) = mercury (element)

hg. *abbr* = hectogram; heliogram.

HG *abbr* = Her *or* His Grace; High German; Home Guards; Horse Guards.

HGA *abbr* = Hop Growers of America.

HGCA *abbr* = Home Grown Cereals Authority.

HGDH *abbr* = His *or* Her Grand Ducal Highness.

HGG *abbr* = human gamma-globulin.

HGH *abbr* = human growth hormone.

hgt. *abbr* = height.

HH *abbr* = (*pencil*) double hard; His *or* Her Highness; His Holiness; His *or* Her Honor.

hha *abbr* = half-hardy annual.

hhb *abbr* = half-hardy biennial.

hhd. *abbr* = hogshead.

HHH *abbr* = (*pencil*) triple hard.

hhp *abbr* = half-hardy perennial.

HHW *abbr* = household hazardous waste.

hi *interj* an exclamation of greeting.

HI *abbr* = Hawaiian Islands; hearing-mpaired; (*Latin*) *hic iacet*, "here lies".

hia *abbr* = hold in abeyance.

Hiarbas *see* **Iarbas**.

hiatus *n* (*pl* **hiatuses** *or* **hiatus**) a break in continuity; a lacuna; (*med*) an aperture; (*phonetics*) the concurrence of two vowels in two successive syllables; (*geol*) a break in a succession of sedimentary rocks due to erosion or non-deposition.—**hiatal** *adj*.

HIB *abbr* = Herring Industry Board.

hibernaculum *n* (*pl* **hibernacula**) the winter quarters of a hibernating animal; the bud-scales of a winter bud.

hibernal *adj* of or happening in winter; wintry.

hibernate *vi* to spend the winter in a dormant condition like deep sleep; to be inactive.—**hibernation** *n.* —**hibernator** *n.*

Hibernian *adj* relating to Ireland. * *n* a native or inhabitant of Ireland.

hibiscus *n* any plant of a tropical or subtropical genus of plants with large, showy flowers.

HICAT *abbr* = high-altitude clear air turbulence.

hiccup, hiccough *n* a sudden involuntary spasm of the diaphragm followed by inhalation and closure of the glottis, producing a characteristic sound; (*inf*) a minor setback. * *vt* to have hiccups.

hic jacet *n* (*Latin*) "here lies" an inscription on tombstones.

hick *n* (*inf*) an unsophisticated person, esp from a rural area.

Hickok, Wild Bill *see* **Calamity Jane.**

hickory *n* (*pl* **hickories**) a North American tree of the walnut family; its wood; its smooth-shelled edible nut.

hid *see* **hide**[1].

hidalgo *n* (*pl* **hidalgoes**) a low-ranking Spanish nobleman.

HIDB *abbr* (*Brit*) = Highlands and Islands Development Board.

hidden *adj* concealed or obscured.

hidden code *n* (*comput*) an invisible code or instruction in a document that controls the appearance of the document when printed.

hidden file *n* (*comput*) a file whose attributes render it invisible.

hidden reserve *n* funds that are held in reserve by a company but do not appear on the balance sheet.

hide[1] *vt* (**hiding, hid,** *pp* **hidden** *or* **hid**) to conceal, put out of sight; to keep secret; to screen or obscure from view. * *vi* to conceal oneself. * *n* a camouflaged place of concealment used by hunters, bird-watchers, etc.—**hider** *n.*

hide[2] *n* the raw or dressed skin of an animal; (*inf*) the human skin.

hide[3] *n* an ancient English measure of land.

hide-and-seek *n* a children's game in which one player must find the others, who have hidden themselves.

hidebound *adj* obstinately conservative and narrow-minded; (*animals*) having a tight or contracted hide that impedes movement; (*trees*) having a tight bark that restricts growth.

hideous *adj* visually repulsive; horrifying.—**hideously** *adv.*—**hideousness** *n.*

hide-out *n* a hiding place, esp as used by outlaws.

hiding[1] *n* (*inf*) a thrashing, a beating.

hiding[2] *n* concealment.

hiding place *n* a place of concealment.

hidrosis *n* perspiration; any skin disease affecting the sweat glands.

hidrotic *adj* of or promoting perspiration. * *n* a drug that stimulates sweating.

hie *vti* (**hieing** *or* **hying, hied**) (*poet*) to speed; to hasten.

HIE *abbr* (*Brit*) = Highlands and Islands Enterprise.

hier- *or* **hiero-** *prefix* sacred.

Hierakonpolis *n* (*Egypt*) an ancient site in Upper Egypt, about 62 miles (100 kilometers) south of Thebes. Tomb finds here go back to the Gerza period, 400–3300 BC. It was here that two copper statues were discovered, of the Old Kingdom Pharaoh Pepy I and his heir, Merenra.

hierarch *n* the chief ruler of an ecclesiastical body; a person at a high level of hierarchy.

hierarchism *n* hierarchical principles; government by a hierarchy.—**hierarchist** *n.*

hierarchy *n* (*pl* **hierarchies**) a group of persons or things arranged in order of rank, grade, etc.—**hierarchical, hierarchic** *adj.*—**hierarchically** *adv.*

hieratic *adj* of or relating to priests; sacred; consecrated; of or relating to a cursive form of hieroglyphics used by priests in ancient Egypt. * *n* the Egyptian hieratic script.—**hieratically** *adv.*

hierocracy *n* (*pl* **hierocracies**) government by priests or ecclesiastics.

hieroglyph *n* a character used in a system of hieroglyphic writing.

hieroglyphic *n* a sacred character or symbol; (*pl*) the picture writings of the ancient Egyptians and others. * *adj* pertaining to hieroglyphs; emblematic.—**hieroglyphically** *adv.*

hierology *n* (*pl* **hierologies**) the sacred literature of people; a biography of a saint.

hierophant *n* in ancient Greece, a priest who initiated novices into the sacred mysteries; a person who explains arcane mysteries.

hifalutin *see* **highfalutin.**

hi-fi *n* (*inf*) high fidelity; equipment for reproducing high-quality musical sound.

Higgins *n* **George V[incent]** (1939–) American novelist and short-story writer, whose experiences as a reporter and assistant district attorney in Boston form the background to his highly acclaimed crime fiction, notably the novels *The Friends of Eddie Coyle* and *Impostors.*

higgle *vi* to dispute over trifling matters; to haggle.

higgledy-piggledy *adj, adv* (*inf*) in confusion; jumbled up.

high *adj* lofty, tall; extending upward a (specified) distance; situated at or done from a height; above others in rank, position, etc; greater in size, amount, cost, etc than usual; raised or acute in pitch; (*meat*) slightly bad; (*inf*) intoxicated; (*inf*) under the influence of drugs. * *adv* in or to a high degree, rank, etc. * *n* a high level, place, etc; an area of high barometric pressure; (*inf*) a euphoric condition induced by alcohol or drugs.

high and dry *adj* helpless; stranded; (*ship*) out of the water.

high and mighty *adj* (*inf*) arrogant.

highball *n* a cool drink with spirits, soda, etc, served in a tall glass.

highborn *adj* of noble birth.

highboy *n* a chest of drawers on legs; a tallboy.

highbrow *n* (*inf*) an intellectual. * *adj* (*inf*) interested in things requiring learning.

High Church *n* the part of the Anglican Church that attaches great importance to the authority of the Church, its sacraments and priesthood.—**High-Church** *adj.*

high-class *adj* of good quality; of or appropriate to the upper social classes.

high cross *n* (*Celtic*) an ancient cross with Celtic knotwork or spiral carvings constructed to indicate a meeting place; there are several examples of these situated in Britain and Ireland.

high density *n* (*comput*) a storage technique for floppy disks that can store over 1 megabyte of data on the disk (normally 1.44 megabytes).

higher *adj* more high. * *adv* in or to a higher position.

higher education *n* education at college or university level.

higher-up *n* (*inf*) a person of higher rank.

high explosive *n* a very powerful chemical explosive, such as gelignite.

highfalutin, highfaluting *adj* (*inf*) pretentious; pompous.—*also* **hifalutin.**

high fidelity *n* the high-quality reproduction of sound.

high-five *n* a form of greeting or congratulation when the hands of two people are joined, palms together, above their heads.

high-flown *adj* extravagantly ambitious; bombastic.

high-flyer, high-flier *n* an ambitious person; a person of great ability in any profession.—**high-flying** *adj.*

hill fort *n* an Iron Age settlement that enabled its inhabitants to observe the land below and to look out for any approaching danger, such as a marauding army.

high frequency *n* any radio frequency between 3 and 30 megahertz.

high-handed *adj* overbearing, arbitrary.—**high-handedly** *adv.*—**high-handedness** *n.*

high-hat *vti* (**high-hatting, high-hatted**) to affect superiority; to treat patronizingly. * *n* a person who behaves in this way.

highjack, highjacker *see* **hijack.**

high jinks *npl* (*inf*) mischievous sport or tricks.

high jump *n* an athletic event in which a competitor jumps over a high bar; (*inf*) (*with* the) a severe reprimand.

highland *adj* of or in mountains. * *n* a region with many hills or mountains; (*pl*) mountainous country; (*with cap*) the mountainous region occupying most of northern Scotland.

highlander *n* a person who lives in a highland area; (*with cap*) an inhabitant of the Scottish Highlands.

Highland fling *n* a lively Scottish dance by one person.

high-level programing language *n* (*comput*) a set of commands for computers that people can understand.

highlife *n* (*W Africa*) a style of jazz music combining American and African elements.

high life *n* fashionable society; its manner of living.—**high-life** *adj.*

highlight *n* the lightest area of a painting, etc; the most interesting or important feature; (*pl*) a lightening of areas of the hair using a bleaching agent. * *vt* to bring to special attention; to give highlights to; (*comput*) to select (an area of a document) in order to apply a command to that area or otherwise work with the selection.

highly *adv* very much; favorably; at a high level, wage, rank, etc.

highly strung *adj* nervous and tense; excitable; high-strung.

High Mass *n* (*RC Church*) a ceremonial mass, usu at the high altar, at which a deacon or subdeacon assists the celebrant.

high-minded *adj* having high ideals, etc.—**high-mindedness** *n.*

highness *n* the state or quality of being high; (*with cap and poss pron*) a title used in speaking to or of royalty.

high-pitched *adj* (*sound*) shrill; (*roof*) steep.

high-powered, high-power *adj* (*lens, etc*) producing great magnification; energetic; powerful; highly competent.

high pressure area *see* **anticyclone.**

high priest *n* a chief priest, esp the principal priest of the Jewish hierarchy; an unofficial leader of fashion, etc.

high-resolution *adj* (*comput*) denoting extra sharpness producing output with smooth curves and well-defined fonts with no jagged edges, measured in dots per inch or in the number of pixels that can be displayed.

high-rise *adj* (*building*) having multiple stories.* *n* a building of this kind.

highroad *n* a chief road, a highway; an easy course or method.

high roller *n* a gambler; an extravagant person; a leader of fashion.—**high rolling** *adj, n.*

high school *n* a school that children attend after elementary school or junior high school.

high seas *npl* open ocean waters outside the territorial limits of any nation.

high season *n* the busiest time of the year for a holiday resort, etc.

high sign *n* (*inf*) a secret warning signal.

hill sites *or* **tors** an ancient religious site, often man-made, possibly used because the sun played an important part in religious ritual. One of the best-known hill sites is Glastonbury Tor.

Highsmith *n* **Patricia** (1921–95) American novelist whose works include *The Talented Mr Ripley* (1956).

high-sounding *adj* imposing, pompous.

high-spirited *adj* courageous; lively.—**high-spiritedness** *n.*

high-strung *adj* strung to a high pitch; extremely sensitive.

hightail *vi* to leave in a great rush.

high-tech *adj* of or denoting specialized complex technology; *(fashion, design)* utilitarian.

high tide *n* the tide at its highest level; the time of this; an acme.

high time *adv* *(inf)* fully time. * *n* an especially good or enjoyable time.

high treason *n* treason against the ruler or state.

high-up *n* *(inf)* a person of high status or position.

high-velocity star *n* a very old star traveling at a high velocity relative to the sun.

high water *n* high tide.—**highwater** *adj*.

highwater mark *n* the highest point reached by a high tide; any maximum.

highway *n* a public road; a main thoroughfare.

highwayman *n* (*pl* **highwaymen**) one who robs travelers on a highway.

high wire *n* a high tightrope.

HIH *abbr* = His *or* Her Imperial Highness.

hijack *vt* to steal (goods in transit) by force; to force (an aircraft) to make an unscheduled flight. * *n* an act of hijacking.—*also* **highjack.**—**hijacker, highjacker** *n*.

hike *vi* to take a long walk. * *vt* *(inf)* to pull up, to increase. * *n* a long walk; a tramp.—**hiker** *n*.

hilarious *adj* highly amusing.—**hilariously** *adv*.—**hilariousness** *n*. — **hilarity** *n*.

Hilary of Arles *n* Saint (*c*. 403–49) bishop of Arles (429). He presided at Orange in 441, resulting in a serious controversy with Pope Leo I, who overturned his deposition of two bishops. His feast day was formerly 5 May.

Hilary of Poitiers *n* Saint (died 368) bishop of Poitiers; famous as a teacher and for his strenuous opposition to the Arians. Most of his episcopate was devoted to defending his faith. His feast day is 13 January.

Hilda *n* Saint (614–80) English abbess; founded a monastery at Whitby for men and women, which soon became famous as a school; a noted patron of learning. Her feast day is 17 November.

Hildebrandt *n* **Johann L von** (1668–1745) Austrian architect, whose notable works include Schloss Mirabell, Salzburg.

Hilkiah *n* (*Bible*) high priest of the Temple who found the book of the Law in the Temple and brought it to the king, who began the reformation of religion.

hill *n* a natural rise of land lower than a mountain; a heap or mound; an slope in a road, etc. *vt* to bank up; to draw earth around (plants) in mounds.

Hillary *n* **Sir Edmund [Percival]** (1919–) New Zealand explorer and mountaineer, who made the first ascent of Mount Everest in 1953 with Tibetan sherpa, Tenzing Norgay (1914–86).

hillbilly *n* (*pl* **hillbillies**) (*inf*) a person from the mountainous areas of southeastern US; country music.—*also adj*.

hill figure *n* (*archeo*) an ancient large figure, usu a horse or a human, cut into the slope of a chalk hillside in the downs of southern England.

hill fort *n* (*archeo*) a fortified structure built on the top of a hill and consisting of a ring of earthen banks with ditches outside them.

hillock *n* a small hill.—**hillocked, hillocky** *adj*.

hilly *adj* (**hillier, hilliest**) abounding with or characterized by hills; rugged.— **hilliness** *n*.

hilt *n* the handle of a sword, dagger, tool, etc.

hilum *n* (*pl* **hila**) a scar on the surface of a seed, indicating where it was attached to the seed grain; the nucleus of a starch grain.

him *pron* the objective case of **he**.

himation *n* (*pl* **himatia**) in ancient Greece, a square-shaped cloak draped around the body.

Himmler *n* **Heinrich** (1900–45) German Nazi leader. As head of the SS and the Gestapo, he organized repression in Germany and occupied Europe, and engineered the Nazi concentration-camp system and the genocide of the Jews.

Hims *n* a city in the Syrian Arab Republic.

himself *pron the reflexive* (he killed himself) *or emphatic* (he himself was lucky) *form of* **he, him.**

Himyaritic *n* an extinct language of the Semitic family of the Afro-Asian family; an Arabian dialect. * *adj* of or relating to the Himyarite people of Arabia or their language.

hind[1] *adj* (**hinder, hindmost** *or* **hindermost**) situated at the back; rear.

hind[2] *n* (*pl* **hinds, hind**) a female deer.

Hind. *abbr* = Hindu; Hindustan; Hindustani.

hindbrain *n* the part of the brain that consists of the medulla oblongata, pons, and cerebellum.

Hindemith *n* **Paul** (1895–1963) German composer and violist. The Nazis banned his works for their "impropriety," and he settled in the US in 1939.

Hindenburg *n* **Paul von Beneckendorff und von** (1847–1934) German field marshal and statesman. He shared command of the German forces in World War I (1916–18), and became president of Germany (1925–34).

hinder *vt* to obstruct, delay or impede. * *vi* to impose instructions or impediments. * *adj* belonging to or constituting the back or rear of anything.—**hinderer** *n*.

Hindi *n* the official language of India; a group of dialects of northern India.

hindmost *or* **hindermost** *adj* farthest behind.

hindquarters *npl* the hind legs and accompanying parts of a quadruped.

hindrance *n* the act of hindering; an obstacle, impediment.

hindsight *n* understanding an event after it has occurred.

Hindu *n* (*pl* **Hindus**) any of several peoples of India; a follower of Hinduism.

Hinduism *n* the dominant religion of India, characterized by an emphasis on religious law, a caste system and belief in reincarnation.

Hines *n* **Earl [Kenneth] "Fatha"** (1903–83) American jazz pianist, bandleader, and songwriter.

hinge *n* a joint or flexible part on which a door, lid, etc turns; a natural joint, as of a clam; a small piece of gummed paper for sticking stamps in an album. * *vti* to attach or hang by a hinge; to depend.

hinge joint *n* a joint allowing planar movement, e.g., the knee.

Hinnom *n* (*Bible*) a valley near Jerusalem, which was the scene of the sacrifice of children in Old Testament times; later it became a rubbish dump continually on fire, which suggested pictures of hell. *See also* **hell.**

hinny *n* (*pl* **hinnies**) the sterile offspring of a male horse and a female donkey or ass. * *vi* (**hinnying, hinnied**) to neigh.

hint *n* an indirect or subtle suggestion; a slight mention; a little piece of practical or helpful advice. * *vt* to suggest or indicate indirectly. * *vi* to give a hint.—**hinter** *n*.

hinterland *n* the land behind that bordering a coast or river; a remote area; the area served by a town or city.

hip[1] *n* either side of the body below the waist and above the thigh; (*archit*) the angle formed on the outside at the junction of two sloping roof surfaces.

hip[2] *n* the fruit of the wild rose.

hip[3] *interj* used as part of a cheer (*hip, hip, hurrah*).

hip[4] *adj* (*sl*) stylish, up-to-date.

HIP *abbr* = Homeless Information Project.

HIPA *abbr* = Honey Importers' and Packers' Association.

hip girdle *see* **pelvic girdle**.

hip joint *n* a "ball-and-socket" joint made up of the head of the femur, which rests inside a deep, cup-shaped cavity (the acetabulum) in the hip bone.

hippie, hippy *n* (*pl* **hippies**) (*sl*) a person who adopts an alternative lifestyle, e.g., involving mysticism, psychedelic drugs, or communal living, to express alienation from conventional society.

hippo *n* (*pl* **hippos**) (*inf*) a hippopotamus.

Hippocentaur *see* **Centaur**.

Hippocoön *n* (*Greek myth*) a king of Sparta, who refused to purify Heracles after he murdered Iphitus. In revenge Heracles killed Hippocoön and his twelve sons.

hippocras *n* an old English cordial of spiced wine.

Hippocratic oath *n* an oath taken by a doctor to observe the code of medical ethics derived from Hippocrates, a Greek physician of the 5th century BC.

Hippocrene *n* the Horse's Fountain, a spring on Mount Helicon in ancient Greece, sacred to the Muses, the waters of which gave poetic inspiration.

Hippodamia *n* (*Greek myth*) the beautiful daughter of king Oenomaus of Elis. She was married to Pelops, after he won the chariot race in a contest with her father.

hippodrome *n* a dance hall, music hall, etc; in ancient Greece, a stadium for horse and chariot races.

hippogriff *n* (*Greek myth*) a monster with a griffin's head, wings and claws, and the body of a horse.

Hippolyta *or* **Hippolyte** *n* (*Greek myth*) a queen of the Amazons who was killed by Heracles in pursuit of his ninth labor, to obtain the belt given to her by Ares.

Hippolytus *n* (*Greek myth*) son of Theseus, falsely accused of rape by Phaedra in revenge for his indifference to her love, and punished and killed by Poseidon. Hippolytus was restored to life by Aesculapius.

Hipponous *n* (*Greek myth*) the original name of the hero Bellerophon.

hippopotamus *n* (*pl* **hippopotamuses** *or* **hippopotami**) a large African water-loving mammal with thick dark skin, short legs, and a very large head and muzzle.

Hiram *n* (*Bible*) King of Tyre, on the coast of Palestine; a friend of David and Solomon, supplying them with timber and craftsmen for the new Jerusalem.

Hir Atrym *n* and **Hir Erwn** *n* (*Welsh Celtic myth*) feature in the legend of Culhwch and Olwen. They were two brothers who had absolutely insatiable appetites.

Hirayama family *n* a group of asteroids with very similar orbits; they may have originated in the break-up of a larger body.

hircine *adj* of or resembling a goat; smelling like a goat.

hire *vt* to pay for the services of (a person) or the use of (a thing). * *n* the payment for the temporary use of anything; the fact or state of being hired.—**hirable** *adj*.—**hirer** *n*.

hireling *n* a person who works only for money, esp for doing something unpleasant.

hire-purchase *n* a system by which a person takes possession of an article after paying a deposit and then becomes the owner only after payment of a series of installments is completed.

Hirohito *n* (1901–89) Japanese emperor (1926–89).

HIRS *abbr* = Health Information Resources Service

hirsute *adj* covered in hair; of or pertaining to hair.—**hirsuteness** *n*.

hirsutism *n* the growth of dark, coarse hair on the body of a female, on the face, chest, abdomen, and upper back.

his *poss pron* of or belonging to *him*.—*also adj*.

HIS *abbr* = (*Latin*) *hic iacet sepultus*, "here lies buried"; Hospital Infection Society; Hunters' Improvement and National Light Horse Breeding Society.

HISHA *abbr* (*Brit*) = Highlands and Islands Sheep Health Association.

Hispanic *adj* of or derived from Spain, Spanish or Spanish-speaking countries. * *n* a person of Hispanic descent, esp in the US.

Hispanicism *n* a word or expression borrowed from Spanish.

hispid *adj* bristly; covered with stiff hairs.—**hispidity** *n*.

hiss *vi* to make a sound resembling a prolonged *s*; to show disapproval by hissing. * *vt* to say or indicate by hissing. * *n* the act or sound of hissing.—**hisser** *n*.

Hiss *n* **Alger** (1904–96) American state department official who was jailed (1950–54) for spying for the USSR.

hist. *abbr* = historian; historical; history.

hist- *or* **histo-** *prefix* tissue.

histamine *n* a substance released by the tissues in allergic reactions, acting as an irritant.—**histaminic** *adj*.

histogenesis *n* the formation of organic tissue.—**histogenetic** *adj*.—**histogenetically** *adv*.

histogram *n* a statistical diagram representing frequency distribution in terms of columns.

histology *n* the study of the microscopic structure of animal and plant tissues.—**histologic** *or* **histological** *adj*.—**histologically** *adv*.—**histologist** *n*.

histolysis *n* (*biol*) the breakdown of a cell or tissue.

historian *n* a person who writes or studies history.

historic *adj* (potentially) important or famous in history.

historical *adj* belonging to or involving history or historical methods; concerning actual events as opposed to myth or legend; based on history.—**historically** *adv*.—**historicalness** *n*.

historical cost *n* a system of valuing units of stock or other assets by basing it on the original cost to the company.

historicity *n* historical authenticity; genuineness.

historiographer *n* a writer of history, esp an official historian.

historiography *n* the principles of historical writing, esp that based on the use of primary sources and techniques of research; the study of methods of historical research and writing.—**historiographic, historiographical** *adj*.—**historiographically** *adv*.

history *n* (*pl* **histories**) a record or account of past events; the study and analysis of past events; past events in total; the past events or experiences of a specific person or thing; an unusual or significant past; (*comput*) a listing on a Web browser of all recently-visited sites on the Internet.

history painting *n* a genre of painting that takes as its subject a scene from history (particularly ancient history), religious or mythological legend, or from great works of literature, e.g., by Dante or Shakespeare.

histrionic *or* **histrionical** *adj* of actors or the theater; melodramatic.—**histrionically** *adv*.

histrionics *n* (used as sing or pl) the art of theatrical representation; melodramatic behavior or tantrums to attract attention.

hit *vti* (**hitting, hit**) to come against (something) with force; to give a blow (to), to strike; to strike with a missile; to affect strongly; to arrive at; (*with* **on**) to discover by accident or unexpectedly. * *n* a blow that strikes its mark; a collision; a successful and popular song, movie, etc; (*inf*) an underworld killing; (*sl*) a dose of a drug.

HITA *abbr* = Hamper Industry Trade Association.

hit-and-run *n* an automobile accident in which the driver leaves the scene without stopping or informing the authorities.

hitch *vt* to move, pull, etc with jerks; to fasten with a hook, knot, etc; to obtain a ride by hitchhiking. * *vi* to hitchhike. * *n* a tug; a hindrance, an obstruction; a kind of knot used for temporary fastening; (*inf*) a ride obtained by hitchhiking.—**hitcher** *n*.

Hitchcock *n* **Sir Alfred** (1899–1980) English movie director, based in Hollywood from 1940, whose thrillers, e.g., *Psycho* (1960), are regarded as masterpieces.

hitchhike *vt* to travel by asking for free lifts from motorists along the way.—**hitchhiker** *n*.

Hite *n* **Shere [Shirley Diana Gregory]** (1943–) American feminist writer , whose best-known work is *The Hite Report: A Nationwide Study of Female Sexuality* (1976).

hither *adv* (*formal*) to or toward this place.

hitherto *adv* (*formal*) until this time.

Hitler *n* **Adolf** (1889–1945) Austrian-born German Nazi dictator; appointed chancellor by Hindenburg in 1933; became head of state in 1934; invaded Poland in 1939, beginning World War II. He committed suicide in Berlin in April 1945 as Germany faced defeat.

hit list *n* (*sl*) a list of people to be eliminated, etc.

hit man *n* a hired assassin.

HIT Scotland *abbr* (*Brit*) = Hospitality Industry Trust Scotland.

Hittite *n* a member of an ancient people of Asia Minor; the language of these people. * *adj* of or pertaining to the Hittite people or their language or inscriptions.

Hittorf *n* **Jakob I.** (1792–1867) German architect, whose notable works include St Vincent de Paul, Paris.

HIV *abbr* = human immunodeficiency virus, the virus that causes Aids.

hive *n* a shelter for a colony of bees; a beehive; the bees of a hive; a crowd of busy people; a place of great activity. * *vt* to gather (bees) into a hive. * *vi* to enter a hive; (*with* **off**) to separate from a group.

hives *n* (used as sing or pl) a rash on the skin often caused by an allergy; nettle rash.

Hivites *n* (*Bible*) inhabitants of Canaan before the Hebrew invasion.

hiya *interj* an exclamation of greeting.

HJ *abbr* (*Latin*) = *hic jacet*, "here lies."

HJS *abbr* (*Latin*) = *hic jacet sepultus*, "here lies buried."

HKCW *abbr* = Hong Kong Council of Women.

HKI *abbr* = Helen Keller International.

hl *abbr* = hectoliter(s).

HL *abbr* = (*Austral*) Homestead Lease; (*Brit*) House of Lords; (*Brit*) Honours List.

HLA *abbr* = human leukocyte antigen.

HLCas *abbr* (*Brit*) = House of Lords Cases.

HLDeb *abbr* (*Brit*) = House of Lords Debates.

HLE *abbr* = high-level exposure.

HLL *abbr* = high-level language.

HLNW *abbr* = high-level nuclear waste.

Hlothere *n* (*d.* 685) king of Kent (673–685). The younger brother of Egbert I.

HLPR *abbr* = Howard League for Penal Reform.

HLRW *abbr* = high-level radioactive waste.

HLS *abbr* = Harvard Law School.

hm *abbr* = hallmark; hectometer.

HM *abbr* = harbormaster; hazardous material; (*mus*) heavy metal; (*Brit*) His *or* Her Majesty('s).

HMA *abbr* = high-memory area.

HMAC *abbr* = His *or* Her Majesty's Customs.

HMCIC *abbr* (*Brit*) = His *or* Her Majesty's Chief Inspector of Constabulary.

HMD *abbr* (*Brit*) = His *or* Her Majesty's Destroyer.

HMF *abbr* (*Brit*) = His *or* Her Majesty's Forces.

HMG *abbr* (*Brit*) = His *or* Her Majesty's Government.

HMHS *abbr* (*Brit*) = His *or* Her Majesty's Hospital Ship.

HMI *abbr* = (*Brit*) His *or* Her Majesty's Inspectorate (of schools); human-machine interface.

HMML *abbr* (*Brit*) = His *or* Her Majesty's Motor Launch.

HMMS *abbr* (*Brit*) = His *or* Her Majesty's minesweeper.

HMP *abbr* = (*Brit*) His *or* Her Majesty's Prison; (*Latin*) *hoc monumentum posuit*, "erected this monument."

HMS *abbr* (*Brit*) = His *or* Her Majesty's Service; His *or* Her Majesty's Ship.

HMSO *abbr* = His *or* Her Majesty's Stationery Office.

HMT *abbr* = Her/His Majesty's Treasury.

HMV *abbr* = His Master's Voice.

HMW *abbr* = high molecular weight.

hn *abbr* (*Latin*) = *hac nocte* "tonight."

HNC *abbr* (*Brit*) = Higher National Certificate.

HND *abbr* (*Brit*) = Higher National Diploma.

hnRNA *abbr* = heterogeneous nuclear ribonucleic acid.

hnRNP *abbr* = heterogenerous nuclear ribonucleoprotein.

ho *interj* an exclamation used to attract attention.

ho. *abbr* = house.

Ho *symbol* (*chem*) holmium (element).

hoard *n* an accumulation of food, money, etc, stored away for future use. * *vti* to accumulate and store away.—**hoarder** *n*.

hoarding *n* a temporary screen of boards erected around a construction site; a billboard.

hoarfrost *n* a covering of minute ice crystals.—*also* **white frost**.

hoarse *adj* (*voice*) rough, as from a cold; (*person*) having a hoarse voice.—**hoarsely** *adv*.—**hoarseness** *n*.

hoary *adj* (**hoarier, hoariest**) white or gray with age; having whitish or grayish hairs; (*joke, etc*) ancient, hackneyed.—**hoarily** *adv*.

hoax *n* a deception; a practical joke. * *vt* to deceive by a hoax.—**hoaxer** *n*.

hob *n* a ledge near a fireplace for keeping kettles, etc hot; a flat surface on a cooker incorporating hot plates or burners.

Hoban *n* James (*b*. 1762) Irish architect. His notable works include White House, Washington.

Hobbes *n* Thomas (1588–1679) English philosopher, whose materialist views were strongly influential on his contemporaries and whose most notable work is *Leviathan*.

hobble *vi* to walk unsteadily, to limp. * *vt* to fasten the legs of (horses, etc) loosely together to prevent straying. * *n* a limp; a rope, etc used to hobble a horse.—**hobbler** *n*.

hobbledehoy *n* (*arch*) (*pl* **hobbledehoys**) an inexperienced and awkward young person.

hobby *n* (*pl* **hobbies**) a spare-time activity carried out for personal amusement; (*arch*) a hobbyhorse.—**hobbyist** *n*.

hobbyhorse *n* a child's toy comprising a stick with a horse's head; a rocking horse; a favorite topic for discussion.

hobgoblin *n* a mischievous goblin.

hobnail *n* a short nail with a wide head, used on the soles of heavy shoes.—**hobnailed** *adj*.

hobnob *vi* (**hobnobbing, hobnobbed**) to spend time with in a friendly manner.

hobo *n* (*pl* **hoboes, hobos**) a migrant laborer; a tramp.—**hoboism** *n*.

Ho Chi Minh *n* [**Nguyen That Tan**] (1890–1969) Vietnamese statesman; Marxist nationalist president of Vietnam (1945–54); became president of North Vietnam (1954–69) after the country's partition.

Ho Chi Minh City *n* a city in Vietnam.

hock[1] *vt* (*sl*) to give something in security for a loan.—**hocker** *n*.

hock[2] *n* the joint bending backward on the hind leg of a horse, etc.

hock[3] *n* a variety of German white wine.

hocket *n* (*mus*) the breaking up of a melody into very short phrases or single notes with rests in between them.

hockey *n* an outdoor game played by two teams of 11 players with a ball and clubs curved at one end (—*also* **field hockey**); ice hockey.

Hockney *n* David (1937–) English artist, whose versatility in the fields of painting, printmaking, photography and design makes it hard to confine him to any one category.

hockshop *n* (*inf*) a pawnshop.

HOCRE *abbr* = Home Office Central Research Establishment.

hocus *vt* (**hocusses, hocussing, hocussed** *or* **hocuses, hocusing, hocused**) to cheat or trick; to dupe; to doctor alcohol in order to stupefy a person so as to cheat him or her; to stupefy with a drug. * *n* a trick; drugged alcohol.

hocus-pocus *n* meaningless words used by a conjurer; sleight of hand; deception. * *vti* to play tricks (on).

hod *n* a trough on a pole for carrying bricks or mortar on the shoulder; a coal scuttle.

HoD *abbr* = Head of Department.

Hoddinott *n* Alun (1929–) Welsh composer and teacher, best known for his romantic, yet serious, operas (e.g., *The Magician* and *The Beach of Falesa*), symphonies, and the oratorio *Job*.

hodgepodge *n* a jumble.

Hodgkin *n* 1. Sir **Alan Lloyd** (1914–98) English physiologist, who shared the 1963 Nobel Prize for Physiology or Medicine with Sir Andrew Fielding Huxley and Sir John Carew Eccles for research into nerve impulses. 2. **Dorothy** [**Mary Crowfoot**] (1910–94) English chemist, and winner of the 1964 Nobel Prize for Chemistry for her work on the molecular structures of penicillin, insulin and vitamin B12.

Hodgkin's disease *n* a malignant disease affecting the lymphatic system, in which there is a gradual and increasing enlargement of lymph glands and nodes throughout the body.

hoe *n* a long-handled tool for weeding, loosening the earth, etc. * *vti* (**hoeing, hoed**) to dig, weed, till, etc, with a hoe.

Hoffman *n* Dustin (1937–) American actor distinguished for his versatility . He has won several awards including an Academy Award for his role in *Rain Man* (1988).

Hoffmanstahl *n* Hugo von (1874–1929) Austrian poet, dramatist, and librettist for six of Richard Strauss's operas, including *Electra* and *Rosenkavalier*.

Hofstadter, Robert *see* **Mossbauer, Rudolf Ludwig**.

hog *n* a domesticated male pig raised for its meat; (*inf*) a selfish, greedy, or filthy person. * *vt* (**hogging, hogged**) to take more than one's due; to hoard greedily.

Hogarth *n* William (1697–1764) English artist; an influential figure in painting, whose contribution to the development of satirical art is immeasurable.

hogfish *n* (*pl* **hogfish** *or* **hogfishes**) a fish with a bristled head of warm Atlantic waters; the wrasse.

Hogg *n* James (1770–1835) Scottish self-educated shepherd, novelist, and poet, who became a leading light of Edinburgh's literary world from 1810, and whose masterpiece is the macabre novel *The Private Memoirs and Confessions of a Justified Sinner*.

Hogmanay *n* (*Scot*) New Year's Eve.

hog's back *n* a steep, narrow ridge with symmetrical slopes, forming where the dip is almost vertical.

hogshead *n* a large cask or barrel; one of several measures of liquid capacity, esp one of 63 gallons (238.5 liters).

hogwash *n* swill fed to pigs; rubbishy or nonsensical writing or speech.

Hohokan *adj* relating to a farming culture with a settled way of life that developed in the arid regions of Arizona from *c* 300 BC.

HOI! *abbr* = Hands off Ireland!

hoi polloi *n* (*often derog*) the common people; the masses.

hoist *vt* to raise aloft, esp with a pulley, crane, etc. * *n* a hoisting; an apparatus for lifting to a higher floor; a lift, elevator.—**hoister** *n*.

hoity-toity *adj* arrogant or haughty. * *interj* an exclamation of surprise.

Hok-Braz *n* (*Celtic myth*) of the Gauls, Hok-Braz was a huge giant who dwelt on the coast of Brittany. He was a great danger to sailors as one of his habits was to swallow three-masted ships.

hokey-pokey *n* hocus-pocus; a cheap ice cream sold in slabs.

hol- *or* **holo-** *prefix* whole.

Holbein *n* Hans (**the Younger**) (*c*.1479–1543) German painter, whose most memorable religious painting is *The Death of Christ* (1521).

Holbrooke *n* Joseph (1878–1958) English composer, pianist, and conductor. His works include the trilogy of Celtic operas the *Cauldron of Annwen*, and the symphonic poem *The Raven*.

HOLC *abbr* = Home Owner's Loan Corporation.

hold[1] *vt* (**holding, held**) to take and keep in one's possession; to grasp; to maintain in a certain position or condition; to retain; to contain; to own, to occupy; to support, sustain; to remain firm; to carry on, as a meeting; to regard; to believe, consider; to bear or carry oneself; (*with* **back**) to withhold; to restrain; (*with* **down**) to restrain; (*inf*) to manage to retain one's job, etc; (*with* **forth**) to offer (e.g., an inducement); (*with* **off**) to keep apart; (*with* **up**) to delay; to hinder; to commit an armed robbery. * *vi* to go on being firm, loyal, etc; to remain unbroken or unyielding; to be true or valid; to continue; (*with* **back**) to refrain; (*with* **forth**) to speak at length; (*with* **off**) to wait, refrain; (*with* **on**) to maintain a grip; to persist; (*inf*) to keep a telephone line open. * *n* the act or manner of holding; a grip; a dominating force on a person.—**holdable** *adj*.

hold[2] *n* the storage space in a ship or aircraft used for cargo.

holdall *n* a portable container for miscellaneous articles.—*also* **carryall**.

holdback *n* a harness strap attached to the shaft of a horse-drawn vehicle that enables the horse to hold it back; a restraint, a hindrance; money retained to be paid on completion of a contract.

Holden *n* Charles (*b*. 1876) English architect, whose notable works include Bristol Public Library.

holder *n* one who holds; a device for holding things; a person who has control of something; one who is in possession of a financial document.

holdfast *n* a hook or clamp; the act of gripping strongly; the organ by which seaweed and related plants attach themselves to a host object.

holding *n* (*often pl*) legally held property, esp land, stocks, and bonds.

holding company *n* a company formed to hold the stock of other companies, which it then controls.

holding operation *n* a means of prolonging an existing situation.

holding pattern *n* the oval course taken by aircraft while waiting for clearance to land.

hold-up *n* a delay; an armed robbery.

hole *n* a hollow place; a cavity; a pit; an animal's burrow; an aperture; a perforation; a small, squalid, dingy place; (*inf*) a difficult situation; (*golf*) a small cavity into which the ball is hit; the tee, the fairway, etc leading to this. * *vti* to make a hole in (something); to drive into a hole; (*with* **up**) to hibernate; (*inf*) to hide oneself.

holey *adj* full of holes.

Holguin *n* a city in Cuba.

holiday *n* (*esp Brit*) a period away from work, school, etc for travel, rest or recreation, a vacation; a day of freedom from work, etc, esp one set aside by law. * *vi* to spend a holiday.—*also* **vacation**.

Holiday *n* Billie "**Lady Day**" [**Eleanora**] (1915–59) American jazz singer.

holiday-maker *n* (*Brit*) a vacationer.

holily *adv* in a holy manner.

holiness *n* sanctity; (*with cap and poss pron*) the title of the Pope.

holism *n* (*philos*) the creation by creative evolution of wholes that are greater than the sum of the parts; (*med*) consideration of the whole body in the treatment of disease.—**holistic** *adj*.—**holistically** *adv*.

Holl *n* Elias (1573–1646) German architect, whose notable works include Town Hall, Augsburg.

holland *n* an unbleached linen, either glazed or unglazed, used for furnishing.

Holland *n* Henry (*b.* 1745) English architect, whose notable works include Carlton House, London.

HOLLAND *abbr* = hope our love lasts and never dies.

hollandaise sauce *n* a rich sauce made with egg yolks, lemon juice, butter, etc.

Hollands *n* a kind of Dutch gin sold in stone bottles.

Hollein *n* Hans (*b.* 1934) Austrian architect, whose notable works include Abteilberg Museum, Mönchengladbach.

hollow *adj* having a cavity within or below; recessed, concave; empty or worthless. * *n* a hole, cavity; a depression, valley. * *vti* to make or become hollow.—**hollowly** *adv*.—**hollowness** *n*.

hollow-eyed *adj* with the eyes deep-set or sunken from tiredness, etc.

holly *n* (*pl* **hollies**) an evergreen shrub with prickly leaves and red berries.

Holly *n* Buddy [Charles Hardin Holley] (1936–59) American rock singer, songwriter, and guitarist.

hollyhock *n* a tall-stemmed plant with spikes of large flowers.

holm *n* a small islet, probably too small to be inhabited.

Holmes *n* Oliver Wendell (1809–94) American essayist, noted especially for the light, humorous discourses of *The Autocrat of the Breakfast Table* and its sequels.

HOLMES *abbr* = Home Office large major inquiry system (central crime-investigation computer).

holmium *n* a malleable white metallic element. *symbol Ho.

holoblastic *adj* wholly germinal.

holocaust *n* a great destruction of life, esp by fire; (*with cap and* **the**) the mass extermination of European Jews by the Nazis during World War II.—**holocaustal** or **holocaustic** *adj*.

hologram *n* an image made without the use of a lens on photographic film by means of interference between two parts of a laser beam, the result appearing as a meaningless pattern until suitably illuminated, when it shows as a three-dimensional image.

holograph *n* a document wholly in the handwriting of the author.

holographic storage *n* (*comput*) a storage technology that uses three-dimensional images created by light patterns projected and stored on photosensitive material.

holography *n* the technique of making or using holograms.—**holographic** *adj*.—**holographically** *adv*.

holohedral *adj* showing all the planes necessary for the perfect symmetry of the crystal system.

holophrastic *adj* (*linguistics*) describing the stage in language development where most utterances are single words; having the force of a whole phrase; polysynthetic.

holothurian *n* any echinoderm of the class that contains the sea cucumber. * *adj* of, related to, or belonging to the holothurians.

Holst *n* Gustav [Theodore] (1874–1934) English composer of Swedish descent, whose best-known composition is *The Planets* (1917).

holster *n* a leather case attached to a belt for a pistol.—**holstered** *adj*.

holt *n* an otter's den; the burrowed lair of any animal; (*poet*) a wood; a wooded hill.

Holub *n* Miroslav (1923–98) Czech poet, critic, and scientist, whose work combines a scientifically rigorous approach to observation with a vivid poetic imagination, and who published many volumes of verse and several important collections of essays, e.g., *The Dimension of the Present Moment and Other Essays*. His scientific works include *The Immunology of Nude Mice*.

holus-bolus *adv* (*inf*) at a gulp, all at once.

holy *adj* (**holier, holiest**) dedicated to religious use; without sin; deserving reverence. * *n* (*pl* **holies**) a holy place, innermost shrine.

Holy Communion *n* the celebration of the Eucharist.

Holy Ghost *n* (*Christianity*) the third person of the Trinity.

Holy Grail *n* in medieval legend, the dish or chalice that was used by Christ at the Last Supper, and the object of many knights' quests.

Holy Land *n* Palestine.

Holy Spirit *n* the Holy Ghost.

Holy Thursday *see* **Ascension Day**.

Holy Week *n* the week before Easter Sunday.

holystone *n* sandstone used by sailors to scour ships' decks. * *vt* to scrub a ship's deck with holystone.

hom- or **homo-** *prefix* same; like.

homage *n* a public demonstration of respect or honor toward someone or something.

hombre *n* (*sl*) a man.

homburg *n* a man's soft felt hat with a dented crown.

home *n* the place where one lives; the city, etc where one was born or reared; a place thought of as home; a household and its affairs; an institution for the aged, orphans, etc. * *adj* of one's home or country; domestic. * *adv* at, to, or in the direction of home; to the point aimed at. * *vi* (*birds*) to return home; to be guided onto a target; to head for a destination; to send or go home.

home banking *n* the carrying out of routine bank transactions by a customer by means of a home computer linked to the relevant bank's computer.

home computer *n* (*comput*) a computer that is designed or marketed for home use.

home economics *n* (*sing or pl*) the art and science of household management, nutrition, etc.

home-grown *adj* grown or produced at home or nearby; characteristic of a particular locale.

home key *n* (*comput*) a key on a keyboard that usu moves the cursor to the beginning of the current line, current paragraph or current document.

homeland *n* the country where a person was born.

homely *adj* (**homelier, homeliest**) simple, everyday; crude; not good-looking, plain.—**homeliness** *n*.

home-made *adj* made, or as if made, at home.

"Home Means Nevada" *n* the song of the American state, Nevada.

"Home On The Range" *n* the official song of the American state, Kansas.

homeopathy *n* the system of treating disease by small quantities of drugs that cause symptoms similar to those of the disease, based on the premise that "like cures like,"devised by Samuel Hahnemann (1755–1843).—**homeopath** or **homeopathist** *n*. —**homeopathic** *adj*.—**homeopathically** *adv*.

homeostasis *n* (*physiology*) the various physiological control mechanisms that operate within an organism to maintain the internal environment at a constant state.

home page *n* (*comput*) the opening page of a Web site, which is like the title and contents page, introducing the viewer to the company, service, etc. and showing what is contained on the site.

homer *n* (*baseball*) a home run; a homing pigeon; (*Brit inf*) work done on an informal basis, without declaring the earnings.

Homer[1] *n* (*c.*800 BC) Greek poet, best known as the author of *The Iliad* and *The Odyssey*.—**Homeric** *adj*. —**Homerically** *adv*.

Homer[2] *n* Winslow (1836–1910) American painter. Clear, bright paintings like *Breezing Up* (1876) are typical of his style and show the sea as a favorite theme.

home run *n* (*baseball*) a hit that allows the batter to touch all bases and score a run.

homesick *adj* longing for home.—**homesickness** *n*.

homespun *n* cloth made of yarn spun at home; coarse cloth like this.

homestead *n* a farmhouse with land and buildings.—**homesteader** *n*

home stretch or **home straight** *n* the part of a racetrack between the last turn and the finish line; the final part.

home truth *n* an unpleasant fact that a person has to face about himself or herself.

homeward *adj* going toward home. * *adv* toward home.

homework *n* work, esp piecework, done at home; schoolwork to be done outside the classroom; preliminary study for a project.

homeworking *n* work that is performed in the worker's own home.

homey, homeyness *see* **homy**.

homicidal *adj* characterized by homicide; likely to commit homicide.—**homicidally** *adv*.

homicide *n* the killing of a person by another; a person who kills another.

homiletic or **homiletical** *adj* of or relating to a homily or sermon; of or relating to homiletics.—**homiletically** *adv*.

homiletics *n sing* the art of writing or preaching sermons.

homily *n* (*pl* **homilies**) a sermon; moralizing talk or writing.—**homilist** *n*.

homing *adj* (*pigeon*) trained to fly home after being transported long distances; (*missile, etc*) designed to guide itself onto a target.

hominid *adj* of or relating to the zoological species that includes present-day man and his ancestors. * *n* a member of this species.

hominoid *adj* resembling man; of or belonging to primates.

hominy (grits) *n* ground maize boiled in water to make a thin porridge.

homo[1] *n* any member of the genus *Homo*, which includes modern man.

homo[2] *n* (*pl* **homos**) (*inf*) a male homosexual.

homocentric *adj* concentric; having the same center.

homogeneous *adj* composed of parts that are of identical or a similar kind or nature; of uniform structure.—**homogeneity** or **homogeneousness** *n*.

homogenize *vt* to break up the fat particles in (milk or cream) so they do not separate; to make homogeneous.—**homogenization** *n*. —**homogenizer** *n*.

homograph *n* a word spelled the same as another word but with a different meaning and derived from a different root.

homolog *n* something that exhibits homology.

homologous *adj* corresponding in relative position, structure, and descent; (*biol*) (*organs, structures*) having evolved from a common ancestor, regardless of present-day function.

homologous series *n* (*chem*) chemical compounds that are related by having the same functional groups but formulae that differ by a specific group of atoms.

homology *n* (*pl* **homologies**) a similarity often attributed to a common origin; affinity of structure.—**homological** *adj*.—**homologically** *adv*.

homonym *n* a word with the same spelling or pronunciation as another, but a different meaning.—**homonymic** *adj*.—**homonymy** *n*.

Homoousian *n* a Christian who believes that Jesus is of the same essence as God.

homophobia *n* fear and hatred of homosexuals; persecution of homosexuals.—**homophobe** *n*. —**homophobic** *adj*.

homophone *n* a letter or group of letters having the same sound as another letter or group of letters; one of a group of words with identical pronunciations but with different meanings or spellings or both.—**homophony** *n*.

homophonous *adj* alike in sound but different in meaning; relating to or denoting a homophone.

H

homophony *n* (*mus*) a term applied to music in which the parts move "in step" and do not have independent rhythms.

homoplastic *adj* similar in structure; derived from a donating individual of a tissue graft of the same species as the recipient.

Homo sapiens *n* the species designating mankind.

homosexual *adj* sexually attracted toward people of the same sex. * *n* a homosexual person.—**homosexuality** *n.* —**homosexually** *adv*.

homostadial *adj* (*archeo*) relating to archeological cultures, often in different geographical areas, that are at the same technological stage.

homotaxial *adj* (*archeo*) relating to objects in the same or a similar position in different sequences. This does not necessarily mean that they are contemporary in age.

homozygote *n* (*genetics*) an organism that has two identical alleles of the gene in question in all somatic cells.

homunculus *n* (*pl* **homunculi**) a dwarf; a miniature man.

homy *adj* (**homier, homiest**) cozy, home-like.—*also* **homey**.—**hominess, homeyness** *n*.

Homyel (Gomel) *n* a city in Belarus.

hon. *abbr* = honorary; honorable.

Hon. *abbr* = Honorable.

HonARAM *abbr* (*Brit*) = Honorary Associate of the Royal Academy of Music.

HonASTA *abbr* = Honorary Associate of the Swimming Teachers' Association.

Honble. *abbr* = Honorable.

hond. *abbr* = honored.

HonDrRCA *abbr* (*Brit*) = Honorary Doctorate of the Royal College of Art.

hone *n* a stone for sharpening cutting tools. * *vt* to sharpen (as if) on a hone.

Honecker *n* **Erich** (1912–94) East German Communist politician; appointed head of state in 1976; fell from power in 1989; charged in 1990 with treason and corruption following the re-unification of Germany.

Honegger *n* **Arthur** (1892–1955) Swiss composer, who spent most of his life in France. He achieved fame with his orchestral piece *Pacific 231*.

honest *adj* truthful; trustworthy; sincere or genuine; gained by fair means; frank, open.—**honestness** *n*.

honestly *adv* in an honest manner; really.

honesty *n* (*pl* **honesties**) the quality of being honest; a European plant with purple flowers that forms transparent seed pods.

honey *n* (*pl* **honeys**) a sweet, sticky, yellowish substance that bees make as food from the nectar of flowers; sweetness; its color; (*inf*) darling. * *adj* of, resembling honey; much loved.

honeybee *n* the common bee of the genus that produces honey.

honeycomb *n* the structure of six-sided wax cells made by bees to hold their honey, eggs, etc; anything arranged like this. * *vt* to fill with holes like a honeycomb.

honeydew *n* a sugary deposit on leaves secreted by aphids; a variety of melon with yellowish skin and pale greenish-white flesh.—**honeydewed** *adj*.

honeyed, honied *adj* flattering; of, containing, or resembling honey.—**honeyedly, honiedly** *adv*.

honeymoon *n* the vacation spent together by a newly married couple.—*also vi.*—**honeymooner** *n*.

honeysuckle *n* a climbing shrub with small fragrant flowers.

Hong Kong Dollar *n* currency of Hong Kong.

HonFBID *abbr* (*Brit*) = Honorary Fellow of the British Institute of Interior Design.

HonFBIPP *abbr* (*Brit*) = Honorary Fellow of the British Institute of Professional Photography.

HonFCP *abbr* = Charter Fellow of the College of Preceptors.

HonFEIS *abbr* (*Brit*) = Honorary Fellow of the Educational Institute of Scotland.

HonFHCIMA *abbr* = Honorary Fellow of the Hotel, Catering and Institutional Management Association.

HonFIEE *abbr* = Honorary Fellow of the Institution of Electrical Engineers.

HonFIGasE *abbr* = Honorary Fellow of the Institution of Gas Engineers.

HonFIIM *abbr* = Honorary Fellow of the Institution of Industrial Managers.

HonFIMM *abbr* = Honorary Fellow of the Institution of Mining and Metallurgy.

HonFIMarE *abbr* = Honorary Fellow of the Institute of Marine Engineers.

HonFIMechE *abbr* = Honorary Fellow of the Institution of Mechanical Engineers.

HonFInstD *abbr* = Honorary Fellow of the Institute of Directors.

HonFInstE *abbr* = Honorary Fellow of the Institute of Energy.

HonFInstMC *abbr* = Honorary Fellow of the Institute of Measurement.

HonFInstNDT *abbr* (*Brit*) = Honorary Fellow of the British Institute of Non-Destructive Testing.

HonFIQA *abbr* = Honorary Fellow of the Institute of Quality Assurance.

HonFIRSE *abbr* (*Brit*) = Honorary Fellow of the Institution of Railway Signal Engineers.

HonFIRTE *abbr* = Honorary Fellow of the Institute of Road Transport Engineers.

HonFPRI *abbr* = Honorary Fellow of the Plastics and Rubber Institute.

HonFRAM *abbr* (*Brit*) = Honorary Fellow of the Royal Academy of Music.

HonFRINA *abbr* (*Brit*) = Honorary Fellow of the Royal Institution of Naval Architects.

HonFRPS *abbr* (*Brit*) = Honorary Fellow of the Royal Photographic Society.

HonFSE *abbr* = Honorary Fellow of the Society of Engineers (Inc).

HonFSGT *abbr* = Honorary Fellow of the Society of Glass Technology.

HonFWeldI *abbr* = Honorary Fellow of the Welding Institute.

hong *n* (*formerly*) in China, a factory or warehouse, or a commercial establishment owned by a foreigner.

HonGSM *abbr* (*Brit*) = Honorary Member of the Guildhall School of Music and Drama.

Hong Kong *n* 1. a Special Administrative Region of China, formerly a British Crown Colony. 2. an Island in the Hong Kong region, containing the capital, Victoria.

Hong Kong Dollar *n* currency of Hong Kong.

Honiara *n* capital city of Solomon Islands.

honk *n* (a sound resembling) the call of the wild goose; the sound made by an old-fashioned motor horn. * *vti* to cry like a goose; to sound (a motor horn); (*sl*) to be sick.

honky, honkie *n* (*pl* **honkies**) (*offens*) a white person.

honky-tonk *n* a style of ragtime piano playing.

HonMInstNDT *abbr* (*Brit*) = Honorary Member of the British Institute of Non-Destructive Testing.

HonMRIN *abbr* (*Brit*) = Honorary Member of the Royal Institute of Navigation.

HonMWES *abbr* = Honorary Member of the Women's Engineering Society.

Honolulu *n* the capital city of Hawaii, a state of the USA.

honor *n* high regard or respect; glory; fame; good reputation; integrity; chastity; high rank; distinction; (*with cap*) the title of certain officials, as judges; cards of the highest value in certain card games. * *vt* to respect greatly; to do or give something in honor of; to accept and pay (a check when due, etc).—**honorer** *n*.

honorable *adj* worthy of being honored; honest; upright; bringing honor; (*with cap*) a title of respect for certain officials when addressing each other.—**honorably** *adv*.

honorable mention *n* a distinction awarded to an entry in a competition that is worthy of merit but not the top prizes.

honorarium *n* (*pl* **honorariums** or **honoraria**) a voluntary payment for professional services for which no fees are nominally due.

honorary *adj* given as an honor; (*office*) voluntary, unpaid.

Honored Ones *n* (*Egypt*) in ancient Egypt, the group forming a king's closest advisers.

honorific *adj* conferring honor.—**honorifically** *adv*.

HonRAM *abbr* (*Brit*) = Honorary Member of the Royal Academy of Music.

HonRCM *abbr* (*Brit*) = Honorary Member of the Royal College of Music.

HonRNCM *abbr* (*Brit*) = Honorary Member of the Royal Northern College of Music.

HonRSCM *abbr* (*Brit*) = Honorary Member of the Royal School of Church Music.

Honthorst *n* **Gerrit van** (1590–1656) Dutch painter; a prominent figure in the Utrecht School.

hooch *n* (*sl*) alcoholic liquor, esp when illicitly distilled or obtained.

Hooch, Hoogh *n* **Pieter de** (*c*. 1629–*c*. 1684) Dutch painter, whose still, peaceful interior and garden-figure compositions, e.g., *The Courtyard of a House in Delft* (1658), are absolutely typical of Dutch painting of the time.

hood[1] *n* a loose covering to protect the head and back of the neck; any hood-like thing, such as the (folding) top of an automobile, etc; the hinged metal covering over an automobile engine—*also* **bonnet**.

hood[2] *n* (*inf*) a hoodlum.

Hood *n* 1. **Raymond M.** (*b*. 1881) American architect, whose notable works include the McGraw-Hill Building, New York. 2. **Thomas** (1799–1845) English poet, whose humorous verses, e.g., *Odes and Addresses to Great People*, were very popular, and who is still recognized as a master of light, satirical, skillfully punning verse, as in "Faithless Sally Brown."

hoodlum *n* a gangster; a young hooligan.—**hoodlumism** *n*.

hood mold *n* (*archit*) a molding which projects from the wall above a doorway, etc to divert rainwater.—*also* **dripstone.**

hoodoo *n* (*pl* **hoodoos**) voodoo; a person or thing thought to bring bad luck. * *vt* (**hoodooing, hoodooed**) to bring ill luck to.—**hoodooism** *n*.

hoodwink *vt* to mislead by trickery.—**hoodwinker** *n*.

hooey *n* nonsense; humbug. * *interj* an exclamation of disbelief.

hoof *n* (*pl* **hoofs** *or* **hooves**) the horny covering on the ends of the feet of certain animals, such as horses, cows, etc.

hook *n* a piece of bent or curved metal to catch or hold anything; a fishhook; something shaped like a hook; a strike, blow, etc, in which a curving motion is involved; (*mus*) the black line attached to the stem of all notes of less value than a quarter note. * *vt* to seize, fasten, or hold, as with a hook; (*rugby*) to pass (the ball) backward from a scrum.

hookah *n* an oriental tobacco pipe with a long tube connected to a container of water, which cools the smoke as it is drawn through.

hook-and-ladder (truck) *n* a mobile fire-fighting apparatus carrying ladders and other essential equipment.

hooked *adj* shaped like a hook; (*sl*) addicted.—**hookedness** *n*.

hooker *n* (*sl*) a prostitute; (*rugby football*) a player in the scrum whose task is to hook the ball.

Hooker *n* 1. **John Lee** (1920–) American blues guitarist. 2. **Richard** (*c*.1554–1600) English divine, whose *Laws of Ecclesiastical Polity*, written in response to Puritan attacks on Anglican moderation, remains the most readable theological work of its size in English, thanks to his beautifully constructed prose and humane tolerance.

Hooke's law *n* (*phys*) the physical relationship between the size of the applied force on an elastic material and the resulting extension.

hookworm *n* a parasitic worm with hooked mouthparts that can bore through the skin and cause disease.

hooky *n* truancy from school.

hooligan *n* a lawless young person.—**hooliganism** *n*.

hoop *n* a circular band of metal or wood; an iron band for holding together the staves of barrels; anything like this, such as a child's toy or a ring in a hoop skirt. * *vt* to bind (as if) with hoops.—**hooped** *adj*.

hooper *n* a cooper; the wild swan.

hoopla *n* (*inf*) noise; bustle; misleading publicity.

hoopoe *n* a bird with a fanlike crest and pinkish-brown plumage.

hooray *or* **hoorah** *see* **hurrah**.

Hoosier *n* a nickname for a native or resident of Indiana.

hoot *n* the sound that an owl makes; a similar sound, as made by a train whistle; a shout of scorn; (*inf*) laughter; (*inf*) an amusing person or thing. * *vi* to utter a hoot; to blow a whistle, etc. * *vt* to express (scorn) of (someone) by hooting.—**hooter** *n*.

hootenanny *n* (*mus*) a small festival of folk music.

Hoover *n* 1. **Herbert [Clark]** (1874–1964) American Republican statesman and 31st president of the US (1929–33), who succeeded Coolidge as president in 1929. 2. **J[ohn] Edgar** (1895–1972) American public servant and founder of the Federal Bureau of Investigation (1924–1972).

hooves *see* **hoof**.

hop[1] *vi* (**hopping, hopped**) to jump up on one leg; to leap with all feet at once, as a frog, etc; (*inf*) to make a quick trip. * *n* a hopping movement; (*inf*) an informal dance; a trip, esp in an aircraft.

hop[2] *n* a climbing plant with small cone-shaped flowers; (*pl*) the dried ripe cones, used for flavoring beer.

hope *n* a feeling that what is wanted will happen; the object of this; a person or thing on which one may base some hope. * *vt* to want and expect. * *vi* to have hope (for).—**hoper** *n*.

Hope *n* **Bob [Leslie Townes Hope]** (1903–) English-born American comedian and movie actor.

HOPE *abbr* = Help Organise Peaceful Energy.

hopeful *adj* filled with hope; inspiring hope or promise of success. * *n* a person who hopes to or looks likely to be a success.—**hopefulness** *n*.

hopefully *adv* in a hopeful manner; it is hoped.

hopeless *adj* without hope; offering no grounds for hope or promise of success; impossible to solve; (*inf*) incompetent.—**hopelessly** *adv*.—**hopelessness** *n*.

Hopewell *adj* relating to a culture that flourished in the states of Illinois and Ohio in the USA from *c* 100 BC to the 6th century AD. It is one of the Woodland cultures.

Hopkins *n* 1. Sir **Frederick Gowland** (1861–1947) English biochemist, who shared the 1929 Nobel Prize for Physiology or Medicine with Eijkman for his discovery of vitamins. 2. **Gerard Manley** (1844–89) English Jesuit priest and poet. 3. **Michael** (*b*.1935) English architect, whose notable works include the Schlumberger Laboratories, Cambridge.

hoplite *n* in ancient Greece, a heavily armed foot soldier.

hopper *n* a hopping insect; a funnel-shaped container with an opening at the bottom from which its contents can be discharged into a receptacle.

Hopper *n* **Edward** (1882–1967) American artist, who is regarded as the foremost American realist painter.

Hoppner *n* **John** (1758–1810) English portrait painter. Among his works are portraits of the Prince of Wales and other members of the royal family.

hopsack *or* **hopsacking** *n* a loosely woven coarse fabric.

hopscotch *n* a children's game in which the players hop through a sequence of squares drawn on the ground.

hor. *abbr* = horizon; horizontal.

Horace *n* [**Quintus Horatius Flaccus**] (65–08 BC) Roman poet and satirist.

Horae *npl* (*Greek myth*) the goddesses of the seasons and the order of nature, Thallo, Carpo, and Auxo.

horary *adj* of or pertaining to or lasting an hour; noting the hours; hourly.

Horatian *adj* of or pertaining to the Roman poet Horace or his works.

Horatii *npl* (*Roman myth*) three brothers who were selected to fight three Alban brothers (the Curiatii), the champions of Alba Longa, in order to decide the supremacy between Rome and Alba.

Horatius Cocles *n* (*Roman myth*) a hero of ancient Rome and descendant of the surviving Horatii, who was one of the three who in 507 BC held the Sublician bridge against the army of Latium while the Romans broke it down behind them.

horde *n* a crowd or throng; a swarm.

hor. dec. *abbr* (*Latin*) = *hora decubitus*, "at bedtime."

Horeb *n* **Mt** (*Bible*) another name for Mt Sinai.

Horemheb *n* (*Egypt*) Egyptian New Kingdom pharaoh, the last king of the Eighteenth Dynasty (ruled 1323–1295 BC).

horizon *n* the apparent line along which the earth and sky meet; the limit of a person's knowledge, interest, etc; (*archeo*) a cultural trait or innovation, normally marked by a particular artefact, which is widely dispersed throughout a particular area; (*geol*) a plane within a series of rock layers, used to pinpoint changes in rock type; (*astron*) the great circle that marks out a horizontal plane where it meets the celestial sphere.

horizontal *adj* level; parallel to the plane of the horizon; (*math*) (*line*) being at right-angles with the vertical and parallel to the horizon.—**horizontally** *adv*.—**horizontalness** *n*.

horizontal marketing *n* a marketing system in which two or more companies in the same industry and at the same level join forces and resources to exploit a marketing opportunity.

hormone *n* a product of living cells formed in one part of the organism and carried to another part, where it takes effect; a synthetic compound having the same purpose.—**hormonal** *adj*.

hormone replacement therapy *n* a treatment for the menopause involving estrogen and progesterone, which is now generally recognized to be of great benefit. * *abbr* HRT.

horn *n* a bony outgrowth on the head of certain animals; the hard substance of which this is made; any projection like a horn; a wind instrument, esp the French horn or trumpet; a device to sound a warning; (*geol*) a pyramidal peak on a mountain left by a number of back to back cirques that have cut back toward each other. * *vt* to wound with a horn; (*with* **in**) to intrude.

hornbeam *n* a tree of the birch family.

hornbill *n* a tropical bird with a horny protuberance on its large beak.

hornblende *n* a dark mineral of silica with magnesium, lime, or iron.

hornbook *n* a framed child's primer made of a thin slab of wood or paper on which numbers, the alphabet, and the Lord's Prayer were printed and protected with a covering of transparent horn; any elementary primer.

horned *adj* having horns.

Hornel *n* **Edward Arthur** (1864–1933) Scottish painter, and member of the Glasgow School. A favorite theme was children playing in fields of flowers or by streams, usu painted in a rich colorful decorative impasto.

hornet *n* a large wasp with a severe sting.

hornpipe *n* a lively dance, formerly associated with British sailors; the music for such a dance; an obsolete wind instrument.

H

horns and halo effect *n* an effect that creates an unusually good or bad impression of an employee on an employer.

Horns of the Altar *npl* projections at the corners of the altar used for burnt offerings in the Tabernacle.

hornswoggle *vt* to deceive; to swindle.

horny *adj* (**hornier, horniest**) like horn; hard; callous; (*sl*) sexually aroused.—**hornily** *adv*.—**horniness** *n*.

horol. *abbr* = horology.

horologe *n* any instrument that tells the time; a timepiece.

horology *n* the science of measuring time; the art of making clocks, watches, etc.—**horologic** or **horological** *adj*.—**horologist** or **horologer** *n*.

horoscope *n* a chart of the zodiacal signs and positions of planets, etc, by which astrologers profess to predict future events, esp in the life of an individual.

Horowitz *n* **Vladimir** (1904–87) Russian-born pianist who settled in the USA in 1928. He was especially noted for his interpretation of music by Chopin and Scarlatti.

horrendous *adj* horrific; (*inf*) disagreeable.—**horrendously** *adv*.

horrible *adj* arousing horror; (*inf*) very bad, unpleasant, etc.—**horribleness** *n*. —**horribly** *adv*.

horrid *adj* terrible; horrible.—**horridly** *adv*.—**horridness** *n*.

horrific *adj* arousing horror; horrible.—**horrifically** *adv*.

horrify *vt* (**horrifying, horrified**) to fill with horror; to shock.—**horrification** *n*. —**horrifyingly** *adv*.

horripilation *n* gooseflesh; the bristling of the skin caused by chill or fright.

horror *n* the strong feeling caused by something frightful or shocking; strong dislike; a person or thing inspiring horror. * *adj* (*movie, story, etc*) designed to frighten.

Horsa *n* (*d.* 455) king of Kent (reigned in 455). With his brother Hengest he became joint ruler after being invited by Vortigern to help fight off raids from the north.

hors de combat *adj* excluded from competition; unrivaled; unequaled; disabled.

hors d'oeuvre *n* (*pl* **hors d'oeuvre, hors d'oeuvres**) an appetizer served at the beginning of a meal.

horse *n* a four-legged, solid-hoofed herbivorous mammal with a flowing mane and a tail, domesticated for carrying loads or riders, etc; cavalry; a vaulting horse; a frame with legs to support something.

horsebox *n* a trailer used for transporting a horse.

horse brass *n* a decorative brass ornament attached to a horse's harness.

horse chestnut *n* a large tree with large, palmate leaves and erect clusters of flowers.

horseflesh *n* horses; the flesh of a horse, esp for eating.

horsefly *n* (*pl* **horseflies**) any of many large flies, the female of which stings horses and other mammals, including humans.

horsehair *n* hair from the mane or tail of a horse, used for padding, etc.

Horsehead Nebula *n* a dark nebula in the constellation Orion.

horse latitude *n* either of two oceanic regions between 30 degrees north and 30 degrees south latitude, marked by calms.

horse laugh *n* a boisterous, usu derisive laugh.

horseleech *n* a large carnivorous leech; an insatiable person.

horseman *n* (*pl* **horsemen**) a person skilled in the riding or care of horses.—**horsemanship** *n*.

horseplay *n* rough, boisterous fun.

horsepower *n* (*pl* **horsepower**) a unit for measuring the power of engines, etc, equal to 746 watts or 33,000 foot-pounds per minute.

horseradish *n* a tall herb of the mustard family; a sauce or relish made with its pungent root.

horse sense *n* common sense.

horseshoe *n* a flat, U-shaped, protective, metal plate nailed to a horse's hoof; anything shaped like this.

horseshoe crab *n* any of several related marine arthropods with a fused head and thorax shaped like a broad crescent.—*also* **king crab**.

horsetail *n* a plant with jointed stems and whorls of small, dark, toothlike leaves; the tail of a horse, esp when used as a symbol of rank or as a standard.

horse-trade *n* a negotiation marked by shrewd bargaining and mutual concessions.—*also vi*.

horsewhip *n* a whip with a long thong, used on horses. * *vt* (**horsewhipping, horsewhipped**) to flog with a horsewhip.

horsewoman *n* (*pl* **horsewomen**) a woman skilled at riding.

horst *n* (*geol*) an area of land that is bounded by two or more faults with a central block that is raised.

horsy, horsey *adj* (**horsier, horsiest**) of or resembling a horse; preoccupied with horses, horse racing, etc.—**horsily** *adv*.—**horsiness** *n*.

hort. or **hortic.** *abbr* = horticultural; horticulture.

Horta *n* **V, Baron** (*b.* 1861) Belgian architect, whose notable works include Hôtel Tassel, Brussels.

hortatory or **hortative** *adj* exhorting; encouraging.—**hortatorily** *adv*.

horticulture *n* the art or science of growing flowers, fruits, and vegetables.—**horticultural** *adj*.—**horticulturally** *adv*.—**horticulturist** *n*.

HORU *abbr* = Home Office Research Unit.

Horus *n* (*Egypt*) Egyptian hawk-god, seen as the special protector of kings. Horus was normally incorporated into the king's name, and the hawk motif was widely used as a royal seal.

Horus lock *n* (*Egypt*) a long twist of hair in a single lock on an otherwise close-shaven scalp, worn by children of the nobility.

Horus name *n* (*Egypt*) the first of the royal set of names denoting a particular king; also the first in time. It associates the king with a particular aspect of the hawk-god.

Hos. *abbr* = Hosea.

hosanna, hosannah *interj* an exclamation of praise to God. * *n* the cry of hosanna; a shout of praise.

hose[1] *n* a flexible tube used to convey fluids. * *vt* to spray with a hose.

hose[2] *n* (*pl* **hose, hosen**) stockings, socks, and panty hose, collectively.

Hosea[1] *n* (*Bible*) an Old Testament book containing the oracles of the Hebrew prophet Hosea.

Hosea[2] *n* (*Bible*) a prophet in the northern kingdom of Israel in the second half of the 8th century BC.

hosier *n* a person who sells stockings, socks, etc.

hosp. *abbr* = hospital.

hospice *n* a home for the care of the terminally ill; a place of rest and shelter for travelers.

hospitable *adj* offering a generous welcome to guests or strangers; sociable.—**hospitableness** *n*. —**hospitably** *adv*.

hospital *n* an institution where the sick or injured are given medical treatment.

hospitaler *n* (*often cap*) a member of a medieval charitable religious order, esp one who worked in a hospital.

hospitality *n* (*pl* **hospitalities**) the act, practice, or quality of being hospitable.

hospitalize *vt* to place in a hospital.—**hospitalization** *n*.

hospital lien *n* (*law*) a claim against the property or assets of a person who has not paid any or all of the charges assessed him or her while receiving medical attention in a hospital.

host[1] *n* a person who receives or entertains a stranger or guest at his house; an animal or plant on or in which another lives; a compere on a television or radio show; the computer in a computer network that provides information, files, or programs to other computers or workstations on the network. * *vti* to act as a host (to a party, television show, etc).

host[2] *n* a very large number of people or things.

host[3] *n* the wafer of bread used in the Eucharist or Holy Communion.

HOST *abbr* = Hosting for Overseas Students.

hostage *n* a person given or kept as security until certain conditions are met.

hostel *n* a lodging place for the homeless, travelers, or other groups.—**hosteler** *n*. —**hosteling** *n*.

hostelry *n* (*pl* **hostelries**) (*formerly*) an inn.

hostess *n* a woman acting as a host; a woman who entertains guests at a nightclub, etc.

hostile *adj* of or being an enemy; unfriendly.—**hostilely** *adv*.

hostility *n* (*pl* **hostilities**) enmity, antagonism; (*pl*) deliberate acts of warfare.

hostler *see* **ostler**.

hot *adj* (**hotter, hottest**) of high temperature; very warm; giving or feeling heat; causing a burning sensation on the tongue; full of intense feeling; following closely; electrically charged; (*inf*) recent, new; (*inf*) radioactive; (*inf*) stolen. * *adv* in a hot manner.—**hotly** *adv*.—**hotness** *n*.

HOT *abbr* = Hawk and Owl Trust.

hot air *n* (*sl*) empty talk.

hotbed *n* a bed of heated earth enclosed by low walls and covered by glass for forcing plants; ideal conditions for the growth of something, esp evil.

hot-blooded *adj* easily excited.—**hot-bloodedness** *n*.

hotchpotch *n* a thick meat and vegetable stew; a hodgepodge.

hot desert *n* a desert found on the west coast of a land mass in tropical or subtropical latitudes, with average temperatures greater than 77°F and annual rainfall of less than 10 inches.

hot dog *n* a frankfurter served in a long soft roll.

hotel *n* a commercial establishment providing accommodations and meals for travelers, etc.

hotelier *n* the owner or manager of a hotel.

hotfoot *adv* with all speed; quickly.

hothead *n* an impetuous person.—**hot-headed** *adj*.—**hot-headedly** *adv*.—**hot-headedness** *n*.

hothouse *n* a heated greenhouse for raising plants; an environment that encourages rapid growth.

hot key *n* (*comput*) a keyboard key combination shortcut that gives access to a menu command or direct access to a program.

hot line *n* a direct telephone link between heads of government for emergency use.

hot link *n* (*comput*) a connection between two distinct documents that automatically copies information from one document (the source) to the other document (the target).

Hotol *abbr* = horizontal take-off and landing.

hotplate *n* a heated surface for cooking or keeping food warm; a small portable heating device.

hotpot *n* (*Brit*) a dish of meat cooked with potatoes in a tight-lidded pot.

hot potato *n* (*inf*) a problem that no one wants to handle.

hot rod *n* (*sl*) an automobile, usu an old model, modified and equipped with a supercharged engine.

hot seat *n* (*inf*) a dangerous position; (*sl*) the electric chair.

hot spring *n* a spring with a temperature of more than 98°F that flows continuously out of the ground.

Hottentot *n* (*pl* **Hottentots** *or* **Hottentot**) a member of a people of the Cape of Good Hope region of South Africa, with pale brown skin; any of the languages spoken by these people.

hot water *n* (*inf*) trouble.

Houdini *n* **Harry [Erich Weiss]** (1874–1926) Hungarian-born American illusionist and escape artist known as "The Great Houdini."

Houdon *n* **Jean-Antoine** (1741–1828) French sculptor, who established a reputation for portrait busts, examples of which are *Gluck* (1775), *Voltaire*, and *Benjamin Franklin* (1778).

Houelt Cross *n* Houelt Cross is an example of a Welsh Celtic high cross. It is situated at Llantwit Major.

houmous, houmus *see* **hummus**.

hound *n* a dog used in hunting; a contemptible person. * *vt* to hunt or chase as with hounds; to urge on by harassment.—**hounder** *n*.

hour *n* a period of 60 minutes, a 24th part of a day; the time for a specific activity; the time; a special point in time; the distance covered in an hour; (*pl*) the customary period for work, etc.

hour angle *n* the angle the Earth turns through in one hour (15°).

hour circle *n* a graduated circle on the equatorial mounting of an instrument such as a telescope, from which right ascension may be determined.

hourglass *n* an instrument for measuring time by trickling sand in a specified period.

houri *n* (*pl* **houris**) a beautiful woman of the Muslim paradise; a voluptuous young woman.

hourly *adj* occurring every hour; done during an hour; frequent. * *adv* at every hour; frequently.

house *n* a building to live in, esp by one person or family; a household; a family or dynasty including relatives, ancestors and descendants; the audience in a theater; a business firm; a legislative assembly; house music. * *vt* to provide accommodations or storage for; to cover, encase.

house arrest *n* detention in one's own house, as opposed to prison.

houseboat *n* a boat furnished and used as a home.

housebound *adj* confined to the house through illness, injury, etc.

housebreaker *n* a burglar; a person employed to demolish buildings.—**housebreaking** *n*.

house-broken *adj* (*dogs, cats, etc*) trained not to mess in the house; (*inf*) well-mannered.

housefly *n* (*pl* **houseflies**) a common fly found in houses, which is attracted by food and can spread disease.

household *n* all those people living together in the same house. * *adj* pertaining to running a house and family; domestic; familiar.

Household *n* **Geoffrey** (1900–88) English novelist and short-story writer, whose masterpiece is *Rogue Male*, in which the narrator sets out to assassinate Adolf Hitler.

householder *n* the person who owns or rents a house.

housekeeper *n* a person who runs a home, esp one hired to do so.

housekeeping *n* the daily running of a household; (*inf*) money used for domestic expenses; routine maintenance of equipment, records, etc in an organization; (*comput*) activities that are performed to reduce clutter on the computer desktop and disks and generally make for efficient use of the computer.

housel *n* (*formerly*) the Eucharist.

houseleek *n* a plant with a rosette of succulent leaves and pink flowers that grows on walls.

house lights *npl* lighting in the auditorium of a theater.

housemaid *n* a female servant employed to do housework.

housemaid's knee *n* a painful condition resulting from a swelling of the bursa (fluid-filled fibrous sac) in front of the kneecap.—*also* **bursitis.**

houseman *n* (*pl* **housemen**) an intern.

house martin *n* a type of swallow with a forked tail.

housemaster *n* a male teacher at a boarding school responsible for the pupils in his house.

house music *n* a style of dance music, using electronic bass and synthesizers, a fast hypnotic beat and sporadic vocals, that originated in Chicago.

House of Commons *n* the lower chamber of Parliament, as in Britain and Canada.

House of Lords *n* the upper chamber of the Parliament in Britain, composed of peers and bishops.

House of Representatives *n* the lower chamber of Congress in the US federal government and various state legislatures.

house party *n* a party, usu in a large house, where the guests stay over for several days; the guests themselves.

house plant *n* an indoor plant.

houseproud *adj* concerned with tidiness and cleanliness, often to excess.

Housesteads *npl* (Roman **Vercovicium** *or* **Burcovicium**) the site of an important Roman fort situated about halfway along Hadrian's Wall in Northern England.

house warming *n* a party given to celebrate moving into a new house.

housewife *n* (*pl* **housewives**) the woman who keeps house.—**housewifely** *adj*.—**housewifeliness** *n*.—**housewifery** *n*.

housework *n* the cooking, cleaning, etc, involved in running a home.—**houseworker** *n*.

housing *n* houses collectively; the provision of accommodations; a casing enclosing a piece of machinery, etc; a slot or groove in a piece of wood, etc, to receive an insertion.

Housman *n* **A[lfred] E[dward]** (1859–1936) English poet and neoclassical scholar, whose poetic output was small: *A Shropshire Lad*, *Last Poems*, and *More Poems*.

Houston *n* a city in the United States of America (USA).

HOV *abbr* = high-occupancy vehicle.

Hovd *n* a city in Mongolia.

hove *see* **heave**.

hovel *n* a small miserable dwelling. * *vt* to shelter in a hovel.

hover *vi* (*bird, etc*) to hang in the air stationary; to hang about, to linger.—**hoverer** *n*. —**hoveringly** *adv*.

hovercraft *n* a land or water vehicle that travels supported on a cushion of air.

Hovhaness *n* **Alan** (1911–2000) American composer, who has often relied on oriental subjects and instruments for inspiration. His most famous piece *And God Created Whales* is for a taped whale solo and orchestra.

how *adv* in what way or manner; by what means; to what extent; in what condition.

How *abbr* = howitzer.

HOW *abbr* = Hands off Our Water.

howbeit *conj* (*arch*) though; although.

howdah *n* a seat fixed on the back of an elephant or camel.

how-do-you-do, how-d'ye-do *n* (*inf*) a difficult situation, mess.

how do you do *interj* a formal greeting, esp when meeting for the first time.

howdy *n* (*inf*) how do you do; hello.

Howells *n* 1. **Herbert** (1892–1983) English composer, whose works include choral pieces (e.g., *Hymnus Paradisi*), organ and piano compositions, and chamber music. 2. **William Dean** (1837–1920) American novelist, critic, and editor who wrote 35 novels, of which the best known are *A Modern Instance*, *The Rise of Silas Lapham*, and *A Hazard of New Fortunes*.

however *adv* in whatever way or degree; still, nevertheless.

howitzer *n* a short cannon that fires shells at a steep trajectory.

howl *vi* to utter the long, wailing cry of wolves, dogs, etc; to utter a similar cry of anger, pain, etc; to shout or laugh in pain, amusement, etc. * *vt* to utter with a howl; to drive by howling. * *n* the wailing cry of a wolf, dog, etc; any similar sound.

howler *n* (*inf*) a stupid mistake.

howsoever *conj* still; nevertheless. * *adv* by whatever means; in whatever manner.

hoy *n* a coastal vessel; a freight barge. * *interj* a cry used to call attention.

hoya *n* a plant with pink, yellow, or white flowers.

hoyden *n* a tomboy; a wild girl.—**hoydenish** *adj*.

Hoyle *n* Sir **Fred** (1915–) English astronomer, mathematician, broadcaster, and writer.

hp *abbr* = half pay; hardy perennial; heir presumptive; horsepower; hybrid perpetual.

HP *abbr* = Handley Page; Hewlett Packard; High Priest; hire purchase; high pressure; horsepower; house physician; Houses of Parliament.

HPA *abbr* = Handley Page Association; Hen Packers' Association; Hospital Physicists' Association.

HPC *abbr* = Horticultural Policy Council; history of present complaint.

HPCC *abbr* = High Performance Computing and Communications

HPLC *abbr* = high-pressure liquid chromatography.

HPMA *abbr* = Heat Pump Manufacturers' Association.

HPPA *abbr* = Horses and Ponies Protection Association.

HPRU *abbr* = Handicapped Persons' Research Unit.

HPS *abbr* = Hardy Plant Society; Highland Pony Society; high-pressure steam.

HPTA *abbr* = High Pressure Technology Association; Hire Purchase Trade Association.

H

HPV *abbr* = human papilloma virus.

HQ *abbr* = headquarters.

hr *abbr* = hour(s).

Hr. *abbr* = Herr.

HR *abbr* = Highland Regiment; Home Rule; House of Representatives; human resources.

HRA *abbr* = Horse Rangers' Association.

HRC *abbr* = (*Brit*) Highland Regional Council; high-resolution chromatography.

HRCT *abbr* = high-resolution computerized tomography.

HRE *abbr* = Holy Roman Empire; Holy Roman Emperor.

HREM *abbr* = high-resolution electron microscopy.

HRG *abbr* = high-resolution graphics.

HRGB *abbr* (*Brit*) = Handbell Ringers of Great Britain.

HRGC *abbr* = high-resolution gas chromatography.

HRH *abbr* = His *or* Her Royal Highness.

HRIP *abbr* (*Latin*) = *hic requiescit in pace*, "here rests in peace."

HRMS *abbr* = high-resolution mass spectrometry.

HRP *abbr* = human remains pouch.

hrs. *abbr* = hours.

HRS *abbr* = Human Rights Society.

HRSA *abbr* = Health Resources and Services Administration.

HRT *abbr* = hormone replacement therapy.

HRW *abbr* = heated rear window.

hs *abbr* (*Latin*) = *hoc sensu*, "in this sense"; *hic sepultus*, "here is buried."

HS *abbr* = High School; Home Secretary; hospital ship; house surgeon.

HSA *abbr* = Hospital Saving Association; Humane Slaughter Association; Hunt Saboteurs' Association; human serum albumin.

HSBA *abbr* = Herdwick Sheep Breeders' Association.

HSBS *abbr* = Hunt Servants' Benefit Society.

HSC *abbr* = Health and Safety Commission; Higher School Certificate.

HSDU *abbr* = hospital sterilization and disinfection unit.

HSE *abbr* = Health and Safety Executive; (*Latin*) *hic sepultus est*, "here lies buried."

HSF *abbr* = Hospital Saturday Fund.

HSH *abbr* = His *or* Her Serene Highness.

HSI *abbr* = human-system interaction; human-system interface.

Hsia *n* the first dynasty in China, preceding the Shang. It existed earlier than 1500 BC.

HSLA *abbr* = (*steel*) hig-strength, low-alloy.

HSM *abbr* = His *or* Her Serene Majesty.

HSN *abbr* = Hysterectomy Support Network.

HSS *abbr* = Henry Sweet Society for the History of Linguistic Ideas.

HSSU *abbr* = hospital sterile supply unit.

HST *abbr* = high-speed train.

HSV *abbr* = herpes simplex virus.

ht *abbr* = half-time.

ht. *abbr* = height; heat.

HT *abbr* = heat-treated; heat treatment; high tension; high tide.

HTA *abbr* = Harris Tweed Association; Help the Aged; Horticultural Trades Association.

HTB *abbr* = high-tension battery.

HTC *abbr* = Higher Technical Certificate.

HTGR *abbr* = high-temperature gas-cooled reactor.

HTLV *abbr* = human T-cell lymphotrophic virus.

HTML *abbr* (*comput*) = HyperText Markup Language, a markup language, or text-description language, used for electronic publishing on the Internet, which enables links to be employed so that an interconnection can be generated between parts of a site, documents, words and documents, etc.

HTOL *abbr* = horizontal take-off and landing.

HTR *abbr* = high-temperature reactor.

Hts. *abbr* = heights.

HTS *abbr* = high-temperature superconductivity; high-temperature superconductor; high-tensile steel.

HTT *abbr* = heavy tactical transport.

HTTP *abbr* (*comput*) = HyperText Transfer Protocol, the structure used to connect the many servers on the Web, which allows pages in HTML format to be sent to the computer being used for browsing. *See* **hypertext**.

HTV *abbr* (*Brit*) = Harlech Television.

HU *abbr* = Harvard University.

Huambo *n* a city in Angola.

hub *n* the center part of a wheel; a center of activity; (*comput*) a device at the center of a computing system to which all the computers in a network are connected, allowing intercommunication.

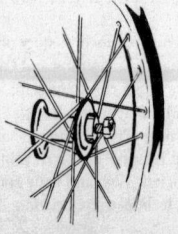

hubba *n* (*sl*) a piece of the drug crack.

hubba-hubba *interj* an exclamation of delight.

Hubbard *n* L[afayette] Ron[ald] (1911–86) American writer, and founder of the Church of Scientology (1954).

Hubble *n* Edwin Powell (1889–1953) American astronomer, whose discovery of galactic "red shift" and other research established the theory of the expanding universe.

hubble-bubble *n* a bubbling noise; confused talk; a hookah.

Hubble classification *n* (*astron*) a method of classifying the shapes of galaxies.

Hubble constant *n* (*astron*) a measure of the rate of expansion of the universe and its variation with distance.

Hubble constant *n* a constant found in cosmology, related to the age of the universe.

Hubble-Sandage variable *n* (*astron*) a hot supergiant variable star of very high luminosity.

Hubble Space telescope *n* a telescope put into orbit around the Earth in 1990; a 7.9-ft-diameter reflecting telescope for observing in the ultraviolet, visible, and infrared regions of the spectrum.

hubbub *n* a confused noise of many voices; an uproar.

hubby *n* (*pl* **hubbies**) (*inf*) a husband.

hubcap *n* a metal cap that fits over the hub of a car wheel.

hubris *n* arrogance, presumption.—**hubristic** *adj*.

huckaback *n* an absorbent linen or cotton fabric used for towels, etc.

huckleberry *n* (*pl* **huckleberries**) a North American shrub with dark blue berries; the fruit of this plant.

huckster *n* a person using aggressive or questionable methods of selling.—**hucksterism** *n*.

HUD *abbr* = Department of Housing and Urban Development

huddle *vti* to crowd together in a confined space; to curl (oneself) up. * *n* a confused crowd or heap.—**huddler** *n*.

Hudibrastic *adj* mock-heroic, in the style of "Hudibras," a poem by Samuel Butler (1612–80).

Hudson *n* W[illiam] H[enry] (1841–1922) Argentinian-born British novelist and naturalist, whose nonfiction works include *Idle Days in Patagonia* but whose masterpiece is the novel *Green Mansions*, a tale set in the Venezuelan jungle.

Hudson River School *n* a group of American landscape painters active in the mid-19th century, whose work was concerned with the beauty and mysticism of nature, expressed in romantic terms on a grand and noble scale.

hue *n* color; a particular shade or tint of a color.

Hué *n* a city in Vietnam.

hued *adj* having a color or hue as specified.

huff *n* a state of smoldering resentment. * *vi* to blow; to puff.

huffish *adj* prone to fits of anger or petulance.

huffy *adj* (**huffier, huffiest**) disgruntled, moody.—**huffily** *adv*.—**huffiness** *n*.

hug *vt* (**hugging, hugged**) to hold or squeeze tightly with the arms; to cling to; to keep close to. * *vi* to embrace one another. * *n* a strong embrace.—**huggable** *adj*.—**hugger** *n*.

huge *adj* very large, enormous.—**hugely** *adv*.—**hugeness** *n*.

huggermugger *n* secrecy, concealment; confusion. * *adj* secret, clandestine; confused, jumbled. * *adv* in confusion. * *vt* to conceal, hush up. * *vi* to muddle.

Hugh *n* (*Irish Celtic myth*) one of the four children of Lir who were turned into swans and destined to stay in that shape for nine hundred years.

Hughes *n* 1. **Howard [Robard]** (1905–76) American industrialist, aviator, and movie producer. He greatly extended his inherited wealth and made several epic flights before becoming an eccentric recluse. 2. **James Langston** (1902–67) American poet, who is best known as a chronicler of the sufferings of poor urban Blacks and whose works include *The Weary Blues* and *One-Way Ticket*. 3. **Ted [Edward James Hughes]** (1930–98) English poet, appointed British poet laureate in 1984.

Hugh of Avalon *n* Saint, also known as **Hugh of Lincoln** (*c*.1135–1200) English monk, prior of Witham, bishop of Lincoln, and a diligent and wise ruler of his huge diocese, who devoted much time to caring for the sick, especially lepers. His feast day is 17 November.

Hugo *n* Victor (1802–85) French novelist, dramatist, and poet whose novels include *Les Misérables* (1862). He was a leader of the French literary romantics.

Hugo *abbr* = Human Genome Organization.

hula *or* **hula-hula** *n* a Polynesian dance performed by men or women; the music for this.

hulk *n* the body of a ship, esp if old and dismantled; a large, clumsy person or thing.

hulking *or* **hulky** *adj* unwieldy, bulky.

hull *n* the outer covering of a fruit or seed; the framework of a ship. * *vt* to remove the hulls of; to pierce the hull of (a ship, etc).—**huller** *n*. —**hull-less** *adj*.

hullabaloo, hullaballoo *n* (*pl* **hullabaloos, hullaballoos**) a loud commotion, uproar.

hullo *see* **hello**.

hum *vi* (**humming, hummed**) to make a low, continuous, vibrating sound; to hesitate in speaking and utter an inarticulate sound; (*inf*) to be lively or busy; (*sl*) to stink. * *vt* to sing with closed lips. * *n* a humming sound; a murmur; (*sl*) a stink.

human *adj* of or relating to human beings; having the qualities of humans as opposed to animals; kind, considerate. * *n* a human being.—**humanness** *n*.

human being *n* a member of the races of *Homo sapiens*; a man, woman, or child.

humane *adj* kind, compassionate, merciful.—**humanely** *adv*.—**humaneness** *n*.

human immunodeficiency virus *n* either of two strains of a virus that inhibits the body from developing resistance to diseases and can lead to the development of AIDS. *abbr HIV.

human-interest *adj* (*newspaper story, etc*) appealing to the emotions.

humanism *n* belief in the promotion of human interests, intellect, and welfare.

humanist *n* one versed in the knowledge of human nature; a student of the humanities.—**humanistic** *adj*.

humanitarian *adj* concerned with promoting human welfare. * *n* a humanitarian person.—**humanitarianism** *n*. —**humanitarianist** *n*.

humanity *n* (*pl* **humanities**) the human race; the state or quality of being human or humane; philanthropy; kindness; (*pl*) the study of literature and the arts, as opposed to the sciences.

humanize *vti* to make or become human.—**humanization** *n*. —**humanizer** *n*.

humankind *n* the human species; humanity.

humanly *adv* in a way characteristic of humans; within the limits of human capabilities.

humanoid *adj* resembling a human being in appearance or character. * *n* a humanoid thing.

human resource management *n* the management of people so as to achieve a maximum individual performance from each worker that will add to the general overall effectiveness of a company.

human T-cell lymphocytotrophic virus *n* one of a group of viruses, including the HIV virus that causes Aids (HTLV III). *abbr HTLV.

humble *adj* having a low estimation of one's abilities; modest, unpretentious; servile. * *vt* to lower in condition or rank; to humiliate.—**humbleness** *n*. —**humbly** *adv*.

humblebee *n* the bumblebee.

humble pie *n* apology, usu under pressure.

Humboldt Current *n* a cold, nutrient-rich ocean current that flows northward along the west coast of South America to the coast of Peru until it meets the El Niño current.—*also* **Peru Current.**

humbug *n* fraud, sham, hoax; an insincere person; a peppermint-flavored candy. * *vt* (**humbugging, humbugged**) to cheat or impose on; to hoax.— **humbugger** *n*. —**humbuggery** *n*.

humdinger *n* (*inf*) a remarkable person or thing.

humdrum *adj* dull, ordinary, boring.—**humdrumness** *n*.

Hume *n* **David** (1711–76) Scottish philosopher, economist, and historian, whose works include *A Treatise of Human Nature*.

humerus *n* (*pl* **humeri**) the bone extending from the shoulder to the elbow.— **humeral** *adj*.

humid *adj* (*air*) moist, damp.—**humidly** *adv*.—**humidness** *n*.

humidifier *n* a device employed to increase the amount of water vapor in a room.

humidifier fever *n* a collection of symptoms, thought to be caused by micro-organisms found in humidifiers and including lethargy, headache and eye irritation, that affect those who work in totally air-conditioned buildings.—*also* **sick building syndrome**.

humidify *vt* (**humidifying, humidified**) to make humid.—**humidification** *n*. — **humidifier** *n*.

humidity *n* (a measure of the amount of) dampness in the air.

humidor *n* a humid cabinet or room where cigars are kept moist.

humiliate *vt* to cause to feel humble; to lower the pride or dignity of.—**humiliatingly** *adv*.—**humiliator** *n*. —**humiliatory** *adj*.

humiliation *n* the act of humiliation; the state of being humiliated; mortification; abasement.

humility *n* (*pl* **humilities**) the state of being humble; modesty.

Humint *abbr* = human intelligence.

Hummel *n* **Johann Nepomuk** (1778–1837) Austrian composer and pianist, who wrote nine operas and seven piano concertos, in addition to choral pieces.

hummingbird *n* a tiny, brightly colored tropical bird with wings that vibrate rapidly, making a humming sound.

hummock *n* a hillock.—**hummocky** *adj*.

hummus *n* a dip or appetizer of puréed chickpeas, sesame seeds, and garlic.—*also* **houmous, houmus.**

humor *n* the ability to appreciate or express what is funny, amusing, etc; the expression of this; temperament; disposition; state of mind; (*formerly*) any of the four fluids of the body (blood, phlegm, yellow bile, and black bile) that were thought to determine temperament. * *vt* to indulge; to gratify by conforming to the wishes of.—**humorful** *adj*.

humoresque *n* a light musical piece.

humorist *n* a person who writes or speaks in a humorous manner.— **humoristic** *adj*.

humorless *adj* done or said without humor; lacking a sense of humor.— **humorlessness** *n*.

humorology *n* the study of humor.

humorous *adj* funny, amusing; causing laughter.—**humorously** *adv*.— **humorousness** *n*.

hump *n* a rounded protuberance; a fleshy lump on the back of an animal (such as a camel or whale); a deformity causing curvature of the spine. * *vt* to hunch; to arch.

humpback *n* a hunchback.—**humpbacked** *adj*.

Humperdinck *n* **Engelbert** (1854–1921) German composer of operas, incidental music, and songs, who was for a time an assistant to Wagner. His best-known opera is *Hansel and Gretel*.

humph *interj* an exclamation of annoyance.

humus *n* dark brown or black organic matter in the soil, formed from partially decomposed leaves, plants, etc.

Humv *abbr* = human light vehicle.

Hun *n* one of the ancient Tartar races that overran Europe in the 4th and 5th centuries; a vandal; (*derog*) a German.

Hun. *abbr* = Hungarian; Hungary.

hunch *n* a hump; (*inf*) an intuitive feeling. * *vt* to arch into a hump. * *vi* to move forward jerkily.

hunchback *n* a person with curvature of the spine.

hunchbacked *adj* having an abnormal convex curvature of the thoracic spine.

hund. *abbr* = hundred(s).

hundred *adj, n* (*pl* **hundreds** *or* **hundred**) ten times ten; the symbol for this (100, C, c); the hundredth in a series or set.

hundredfold *adj, adv* one hundred times as great or many.

hundredth *adj* the last of a hundred.

hundredweight *n* (*pl* **hundredweight** *or* **hundredweights**) a unit of weight, equal to 110 pounds in US and 112 pounds in the UK.

hunebed *n* (*archeo*) circular and oval stone-built chamber tombs of mid-Neolithic date that are found in the Northern Netherlands and associated with the TRB culture.

hung *see* **hang**.

Hung. *abbr* = Hungarian; Hungary.

Hungarian *adj* pertaining to Hungary, its inhabitants, or language. * *n* an inhabitant of Hungary; the language spoken in Hungary.

Hungary *n* a land-locked republic sharing borders with Austria, Slovenia, Croatia, Yugoslavia, Romania, and Ukraine.

hunger *n* (a feeling of weakness or emptiness from) a need for food; a strong desire. * *vi* to feel hunger; to have a strong desire (for).

hunger strike *n* refusal to take food as a protest.

hung-over *adj* (*sl*) suffering from a hangover.

hungry *adj* (**hungrier, hungriest**) desiring food; craving for something; greedy.—**hungrily** *adv*.—**hungriness** *n*.

hunk *n* (*inf*) a large piece, lump, etc; (*sl*) a sexually attractive man.—**hunky** *adj*.

hunker *vi* to squat, crouch down. * *npl* the haunches or buttocks.

hunkydory *adj* first-rate.

hunt *vti* to seek out to kill or capture (game) for food or sport; to search (for); to chase. * *n* a chase; a search; a party organized for hunting.

Hunt *n* 1. **[James Henry] Leigh** (1784–1859) English poet and essayist, who produced some charming light verse, e.g., "Jenny Kissed Me," and the two ingenious sonnets "To a Fish" and "A Fish Replies." 2. **Richard M.** (1827–95) American architect, whose notable works include the Tribune building, New York. 3. **William Holman** (1827–1910) English painter, and a founder of the Pre-Raphaelite movement. 4. **William Morris** (1824–79) American painter, who studied in Paris and was associated with the Barbizon School.

hunter *n* a person who hunts; a horse used in hunting.—**huntress** *nf*.

Hunter *n* 1. **George Leslie** (1877–1931) Scottish painter and a member of the group referred to as the Scottish colorists. 2. **Rita** (1933–) English soprano with an international reputation, whose best-known role is that of Brunhilde in Wagner's *Ring Cycle*.

hunter-gatherers *npl* semi-nomadic bands of people whose subsistence is based on hunting animals for meat and gathering fruits, nuts, berries, etc.

hunth. *abbr* = hundred thousand.

hunting *n* the art or practice of one who hunts; a pursuit; a search.

Huntington's chorea *see* **chorea**.

huntsman *n* (*pl* **huntsmen**) a person who manages a hunt and looks after the hounds.

hurdle *n* a portable frame of bars for temporary fences or for jumping over by horses or runners; an obstacle; (*pl*) a race over hurdles.—**hurdler** *n*.

hurdy-gurdy *n* (*pl* **hurdy-gurdies**) a mechanical instrument such as a barrel organ.

Huridocs *abbr* = International Human Rights Information and Documentation System.

hurl *vt* to throw violently; to utter vehemently. * *n* a violent throw; (*Scot*) a ride in a car.—**hurler** *n*.

hurling *or* **hurley** *n* an Irish form of field hockey.

hurly-burly *n* (*pl* **hurly-burlies**) uproar; confusion.

hurrah *interj* an exclamation of approval or joy.—*also* **hooray, hoorah**.

Hurri *n* a group of people first identified as occupying the land to the southwest of the Caspian Sea *c* 2300 BC.

hurricane *n* a violent tropical cyclone with winds of at least 74 miles per hour.

hurried *adj* performed with great haste.—**hurriedly** *adv*.—**hurriedness** *n*.

hurry *n* (*pl* **hurries**) rush; urgency; eagerness to do, go, etc. * *vt* (**hurrying, hurried**) to cause to move or happen more quickly. * *vi* to move or act with haste.—**hurryingly** *adv*.

hurt *vt* (**hurting, hurt**) to cause physical pain to; to injure, damage; to offend. * *vi* to feel pain; to cause pain.—**hurter** *n*.

hurtful *adj* causing hurt, mischievous.—**hurtfully** *adv*.—**hurtfulness** *n*.

hurtle *vti* to move or throw with great speed and force.

Husat *abbr* = Human Science and Advanced Technology Research Institute.

husband *n* a man to whom a woman is married. * *vt* to conserve; to manage economically.—**husbander** *n*.

husbandman *n* (*pl* **husbandmen**) a farmer.

husbandry *n* management of resources; farming.

hush *vti* to make or become silent. * *n* a silence or calm.

hush-hush *adj* (*inf*) secret.

hush money *n* (*sl*) money paid to a person to keep a discreditable fact secret.

husk *n* the dry covering of certain fruits and seeds; any dry, rough, or useless covering. * *vt* to strip the husk from.—**husker** *n*.

husky[1] *adj* (**huskier, huskiest**) (*voice*) hoarse; rough-sounding; hefty, strong.—**huskily** *adv*.—**huskiness** *n*.

husky[2] *n* (*pl* **huskies**) an Arctic sled dog.

hussar *n* a member of any of various European light cavalry regiments, usu with an elegant dress uniform.

Hussein *n* 1. [**Ibn Talal**] (1935–99) king of Jordan; lost the West Bank of Jordan to Israel after the Six Day War of 1967; trod an uneasy diplomatic line between friendship with the West and his efforts in behalf of the Palestinians. 2. **Saddam** (1937–) Iraqi dictator; became president of Iraq in 1979; invaded Kuwait in 1990; forced to withdraw in the Gulf War (1991) by UN forces.

hussy *n* (*pl* **hussies**) an insolent woman; a promiscuous woman.

hustings *n* (*pl or sing*) the process of, or a place for, political campaigning.

hustle *vt* to jostle or push roughly or hurriedly; to force hurriedly; (*sl*) to obtain by rough or illegal means. * *vi* to move hurriedly. * *n* an instance of hustling.—**hustler** *n*.

Huston *n* John [**Marcellus**] (1906–87) American movie director whose last movie, *The Dead* (1987), starred his daughter, actress Anjelica Huston (1951–).

hut *n* a very plain or crude little house or cabin.

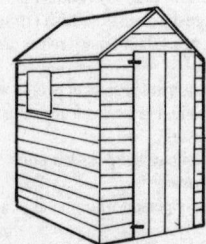

hutch *n* a pen or coop for small animals; a hut.

Hutton *n* Sir **Leonard** ("Len") (1916–90) English cricketer.

Huxley *n* 1. **Aldous [Leonard]** (1894–1963) author of *Brave New World* (1932) and brother of Sir Julian Huxley. 2. Sir **Andrew Fielding** *see* **Hodgkin**, Sir **Alan Lloyd**. 3. Sir **Julian [Sorell]** (1887–1975) English biologist, and the first director-general of UNESCO (1946–48). 4. **Thomas Henry** (1825–95) English biologist; grandfather of Sir Julian and Aldous Huxley; the most prominent scientific defender of Darwin's theory of evolution.

huzzah *interj* (*formerly*) hurrah.

HV *abbr* = Health Visitor; high velocity; high voltage.

HVAC *abbr* = heating, ventilation, and air conditioning; high-voltage alternating current.

HVACMA *abbr* = Heating, Ventilating & Air Conditioning Manufacturers' Association.

HVAR *abbr* = high-velocity aircraft rocket.

HVDC *abbr* = high-voltage direct current.

HVEM *abbr* = high-voltage electron microscope.

HVP *abbr* = hydrolyzed vegetable protein.

hw *abbr* = hot water.

HW *abbr* = hazardous waste.

Hwiccen *n* an ancient Celtic kingdom covering roughly the territory now covered by Gloucestershire and Worcestershire in England.

HWL *abbr* = high-water line.

HWLB *abbr* (*Brit*) = high water, London Bridge.

HWM *abbr* = high-water mark.

HWR *abbr* = heavy-water reactor.

HWS *abbr* = hot-water system.

Hwychdwn *n* (*Welsh Celtic myth*) the son of the brothers Gwydion fab Don and Gilfaethwy and the brother of Hydwn. Hwychdwn was born was born in the shape of a wild pig. He was turned into a human boy by Math fab Mathonwy.

hyacinth *n* a plant of the lily family with spikes of bell-shaped flowers; the orange gemstone jacinth; a light violet to moderate purple.—**hyacinthine** *adj*.

Hyacinth *or* **Hyacinthus** *n* (*Greek myth*) an extremely handsome young man, who was the first man to be loved by another man. He was accidentally killed by his lover Apollo and the flower that grew from his blood was called the hyacinth.

Hyades *npl* (*Greek myth*) five nymphs, the daughters of Atlas; the five stars in the constellation Taurus.

hyaline *adj* glassy; transparent.

hyaline membrane disease *see* **respiratory distress syndrome**.

Hy-Breasal *or* **Hy-Breasil** *or* **Hy-Brasil** *n* (*Irish Celtic myth*) an island off the west coast of Ireland that was visible above the water only once every seven years.

hybrid *n* the offspring of two plants or animals of different species; a mongrel. * *adj* crossbred.—**hybridism** *n*. —**hybridity** *n*.

hybridize *vti* to produce or cause to produce hybrids; to interbreed.—**hybridizable** *adj*.—**hybridization** *n*. —**hybridizer** *n*.

hyd. *abbr* = hydrostatics.

hydatid *n* a watery cyst in animal tissue; a large bladder containing the larvae of the tapeworm.—*also adj*.

Hyderabad *n* 1. a city in India. 2. a city in the Islamic Republic of Pakistan.

hydr- *or* **hydro-** *prefix* water, fluids.

hydra *n* (*pl* **hydras** *or* **hydrae**) (*usu with cap*) a legendary many-headed water serpent; any of numerous freshwater polyps having a mouth surrounded by tentacles.

Hydra *n* a constellation lying along the celestial equator.

Hydra A *n* a strong radio source associated with a large elliptical galaxy.

hydrangea *n* a shrub with large heads of white, pink, or blue flowers.

hydrant *n* a large pipe with a valve for drawing water from a water main; a fireplug.

hydrate *n* a chemical compound of water with some other substance. * *vt* to cause to combine with or absorb water.—**hydration** *n*. —**hydrator** *n*.

hydraul. *abbr* = hydraulics.

hydraulic *adj* operated by water or other liquid, esp by moving through pipes under pressure; of hydraulics.—**hydraulically** *adv*.

hydraulic action *n* the force that the water in a river or stream exerts on rocks in its path.

hydraulics *n sing* the science dealing with the mechanical properties of liquids, such as water, and their application in engineering.

hydric *adj* of or containing hydrogen; of or containing water.

hydride *n* any compound of hydrogen and another element.

hydriodic *adj* composed of hydrogen and iodine.

hydro *n* (*pl* **hydros**) a hotel or resort offering hydropathic treatment.

hydrocarbon *n* any organic compound containing only hydrogen and carbon.

hydrocele *n* an accumulation of fluid in a body cavity, esp in the scrotum.

hydrocephalus, hydrocephaly *n* an accumulation of fluid in the brain.—**hydrocephalic** *adj*.

hydrochloric *adj* composed of hydrogen and chlorine.

hydrochloric acid *n* a strong, highly corrosive acid that is a solution of the gas hydrogen chloride in water.

hydrocortisone *n* a steroid produced and released by the cortex of the adrenal glands (a corticosteroid).

hydrocyanic *adj* composed of hydrogen and cyanide.

hydrodynamics *n sing* the science of the mechanical properties of fluids.—*also* **hydromechanics**. —**hydrodynamic** *adj*.—**hydrodynamically** *adv*.

hydroelectricity *n* electricity generated by water power.—**hydroelectric** *adj*.

hydrofluoric *adj* composed of hydrogen and fluorine.

hydrofoil *n* a vessel equipped with vanes that lift the hull out of the water to allow fast cruising speeds.

hydrog. *abbr* = hydrographic; hydrography.

hydrogen *n* a flammable, colorless, odorless, tasteless, gaseous chemical element, the lightest substance known.

hydrogenate *vt* to combine with or treat with hydrogen.—**hydrogenation** *n*. — **hydrogenator** *n*.

hydrogen bomb *n* a powerful bomb that produces explosive energy through the fusion of hydrogen nuclei.

hydrogen peroxide *n* (*chem*) a strong, oxidizing and bleaching agent usu in the form of a solution in water.

hydrography *n* the study, surveying, and mapping of the oceans, seas, lakes, and rivers as on a chart.—**hydrographer** *n*. —**hydrographic** *or* **hydrographical** *adj*.

hydrokinetics *n sing* the branch of physics concerned with the study of fluids in motion.

hydrology *n* the science of the properties of water and its distribution on the earth and in the atmosphere.—**hydrologic** *or* **hydrological** *adj*.—**hydrologist** *n*.

hydrolysis *n* the chemical breakdown of organic compounds by interaction with water.

hydrolyze *vti* to decompose by hydrolysis.—**hydrolyzation** *n*. —**hydrolyzer** *n*.

hydromechanics *see* **hydrodynamics**.

hydromel *n* a mixture of honey and water that is fermented to make mead.

hydrometeor *n* (*meteorol*) a general term encompassing all forms of water vapor in the atmosphere that have condensed or sublimed.

hydrometer *n* a device for measuring the densities of liquids.—**hydrometric** *or* **hydrometrical** *adj*.—**hydrometry** *n*.

hydropathy *n* the use of water to treat diseases.—**hydropathic** *or* **hydropathical** *adj*.—**hydropathist** *or* **hydropath** *n*.

hydrophane *n* a partially opaque, white type of opal that becomes translucent in water.

hydrophobia *n* a morbid fear of water; rabies.—**hydrophobic** *adj*.

hydrophone *n* an instrument that detects sound through water.

hydrophyte *n* a plant that will grow only in water or sodden soil.—**hydrophytic** *adj*.

hydroplane *n* a light motor boat that skims through the water at high speed with its hull raised out of the water; a fin that directs the vertical movement of a submarine; an attachment to an aircraft that enables it to glide along the surface of water. * *vi* (of a boat) to rise out of the water in the manner of a hydroplane.

hydroponics *n sing* the growing of plants in chemical nutrients without soil.—**hydroponically** *adv*.

hydrops fetalis *see* **hemolytic disease of the newborn**.

hydros. *abbr* = hydrostatics.

hydroscope *n* any instrument that makes observations of underwater objects.

hydrosphere *n* the moisture-bearing envelope that surrounds the earth.

hydrostatics *n sing* the branch of physics concerned with the study of fluids at rest.—**hydrostatic** *adj*.

hydrotherapy *n* (*pl* **hydrotherapies**) the treatment of certain diseases and physical conditions by the external application of water.—**hydrotherapist** *n*.

hydrous *adj* containing water.

hydroxide *n* (*chem*) a compound derived from water through the replacement of one of the hydrogen atoms by another atom or group.

hydroxocobalamin *n* a cobalt-containing substance (cobalamin) used in the treatment of vitamin B12 deficiency, esp in pernicious anemia.

hydroxyl *n* (*chem*) the OH group comprising an oxygen and a hydrogen atom bonded together.

hydt. *abbr* = hydrant.

Hydwn *n* (*Welsh Celtic myth*) the son of the brothers Gwydion fab Don and Gilfaethwy. He was born as a fawn.

hyena *n* a nocturnal, carnivorous, scavenging mammal like a wolf.

Hygeia *n* (*Greek myth*) the goddess of health.

hygiene *n* the principles and practice of health and cleanliness.—**hygienic** *adj*.—**hygienically** *adv*.

hygienist *n* a person skilled in the practice of hygiene.

hygrometer *n* an instrument for measuring the humidity of the atmosphere.—**hygrometric** *adj*.—**hygrometrically** *adv*.—**hygrometry** *n*.

hygroscope *n* an instrument that shows changes in the humidity of the atmosphere.

hygroscopic *adj* readily absorbing and retaining moisture from the air.—**hygroscopically** *adv*.

Hyksos *npl* a dynasty of foreign rulers of Ancient Egypt from Asia, including peoples from the Hittite and Hurrian empires, who established themselves in the eastern Delta around 1600 BC and controlled Lower and Middle Egypt for 100 years until Egyptian rule from Thebes was re-established.

hylozoism *n* (*philos*) the doctrine that life is a property of matter; materialism.—**hylozoic** *adj*.—**hylozoist** *n*.

hymen *n* the mucous membrane partly closing the vaginal orifice.—**hymenal** *adj*.

Hymen *n* (*Greek myth*) the god of marriage.

hymeneal *adj* of marriage, nuptial.

hymenopteran *n* (*pl* **hymenopterans**, **hymenopterana**) any of a large order of insects that have two pairs of membranous wings.—**hymenopterous** *adj*.

hymn *n* a song of praise to God or other object of worship.

hymn book *or* **hymnal** *n* a book of hymns.

hymnology *n* the study of the composition of hymns.—**hymnologist** *n*.

hypostyle hall *n* (*Egypt*) a temple hall, supported by rows of columns, in which there were two levels of ceiling, supported by columns of different heights, creating a high central nave flanked by two lower aisles.

hyoid *adj* U-shaped; of or relating to the hyoid bone at the base of the tongue.

hyoscine *see* **scopolamine**.

hyp. *or* **hypoth.** *abbr* = hypothesis; hypothetical.

hyp- *or* **hypo-** *prefix* below; slightly.

hype[1] *n* (*sl*) deception; aggressive or extravagant publicity. * *vt* to publicize or promote a product, etc in this manner.

hype[2] *n* (*sl*) a hypodermic needle. * *vi* (*sl*) to inject a narcotic drug with a needle.

hyped-up *adj* aggressively publicized; (*sl*) stimulated as if by injection of a drug.

hyper- *prefix* above; too; exceeding.

hyperactive *adj* abnormally active.—**hyperactivity** *n*.

hyperadrenalism *n* a condition in which the adrenal glands are over-active, producing the symptoms of Cushing's syndrome.

hyperalgesia *n* an extreme sensitivity to pain.

hyperbola *n* (*pl* **hyperbolas**, **hyperbolae**) (*geom*) a curve formed by a plane intersecting a cone at a greater angle to its base than its side.

hyperbole *n* a figure of speech using absurd exaggeration.

hyperbolic *or* **hyperbolical** *adj* pertaining to or containing hyperbole, exaggerated; pertaining to or of the nature of a hyperbola.

hyperbolic paraboloid roof *n* (*archit*) a roof with a double curve formed from a rectangular shape folded across the diagonal.

hyperborean *adj* of or relating to the extreme north. * *n* an inhabitant of the extreme north; (*Greek myth*) (*with cap*) one of the people who lived in the sunny land beyond the north wind.

hypercard *n* (*comput*) an accessory program authored by Apple™.

hypercritical *adj* excessively critical.—**hypercritically** *adv*.—**hypercriticism** *n*.

hyperemesis *n* vomiting to excess.

hyperesthesia *n* increased sensitivity of any of the sense organs.—**hyperesthetic** *adj*.

hyperglycemia *n* the presence of excess sugar (glucose) in the blood, as in diabetes mellitus, caused by insufficient insulin to cope with carbohydrate intake.

hyperinflation *n* an extremely high rate of inflation.

Hyperion[1] *n* (*Greek myth*) a Titan, son of Uranos and Ge, and father of Helios, Selene and Eos.

Hyperion[2] *n* a satellite of Saturn discovered in 1848.

hyperlink *n* (*comput*) a link set up between objects. The link can be text, an icon, or a graphic. Pages on the Web commonly have links which may connect with other pages on that site or another site or may enable an e-mail to be sent.

Hyperlipidemia *or* **hyperlipemia** *n* the presence of an excess concentration of fat in the blood.

hypermarket *n* an enormous retail development offering a wide range of goods, usu situated on the outskirts of a town or city.

hypermedia *npl* (*comput*) the application of hypertext concepts to multimedia.

hypermetric *adj* beyond the normal meter of a line; having one syllable too many.

hyperparathyroidism *see* **parathyroidectomy**.

hyperplasia *n* increased growth in size and number of the normal cells of a tissue so that the affected part enlarges.

hyper-resonance *see* **resonance**.

hypersensitive *adj* extremely vulnerable; abnormally sensitive to a drug, pollen, etc.—**hypersensitivity** *n*.

hypersonic *adj* traveling at speeds at least five times faster than sound; of sound frequencies above 1000 megahertz.—**hypersonics** *n*.

hypertalk *n* (*comput*) a computer scripting language that is used to create instructions for hypercard programs.

hypertension *n* abnormally high blood pressure.—**hypertensive** *adj*.

hypertext *n* computer software/hardware that allows the user to pick up on one word in a document as a route to another area of the document or a different document.

hyperthermia *n* (*med*) an abnormally raised body temperature.—**hyperthermic** *adj*.

hyperthyroidism *n* the over-production of the thyroid hormone by the thyroid gland.—**hyperthyroid** *adj, n*.

hypertonic *adj* (*chem*) (*liquid*) having a higher osmotic pressure than another with which it is being compared.

hypertonicity *see* **spasticity**.

hypertrophy *n* (*pl* **hypertrophies**) abnormal enlargement of an organ or part.—**hypertrophic** *adj*.

hyperventilation *n* an abnormally fast breathing rate that may result in dizziness and nausea.— **hyperventilate** *vi*.

H

hypervitaminosis *n* the pathological condition that results from the excessive intake of vitamins.

hypethral *adj* (*archit*) lacking a roof and open to the sky.

hyphen *n* a punctuation mark (-) used to join two syllables or words, or to divide words into parts. * *vt* to hyphenate.

hyphenate *vt* to join by a hyphen.—**hyphenation** *n*.

Hypnos *n* (*Greek myth*) the god of sleep, called Somnos by the Romans; the personification of sleep.

hypnosis *n* (*pl* **hypnoses**) a relaxed state resembling sleep in which the mind responds to external suggestion.

hypnotherapy *n* the use of hypnosis in the treatment of emotional and psychological disorders.

hypnotic *adj* of or producing hypnosis; (*person*) susceptible to hypnosis. * *n* a drug causing sleep; a person susceptible to hypnosis.—**hypnotically** *adv*.

hypnotism *n* the act of inducing hypnosis; the study and use of hypnosis.—**hypnotist** *n*.

hypnotize *vt* to put in a state of hypnosis; to fascinate.—**hypnotizer** *n*.

hypo- *prefix* below; slightly.

hypocaust *n* the hot-air chamber under a Roman bath.

hypochondria *n* chronic anxiety about health, often with imaginary illnesses.

hypochondriac *n* a person suffering from hypochondria. * *adj* pertaining to or affected with hypochrondria.—**hypochondriacally** *adv*.

hypocorism *n* a diminutive pet name; a euphemism.—**hypocoristic** *or* **hypocoristical** *adj*.

hypocrisy *n* (*pl* **hypocrisies**) falsely pretending to possess virtues, beliefs, etc; an example of this.—**hypocritical** *adj*.—**hypocritically** *adv*.

hypocrite *n* a person who pretends to be what he or she is not.

hypocycloid *n* (*geom*) a curve traced by the point on the circumference of a circle, which rolls onto the inside of another circle.

hypodermic *adj* injected under the skin. * *n* a hypodermic needle, syringe, or injection.

hypodermic syringe *n* a syringe with a hollow (hypodermic) needle through which blood samples can be drawn.

hypogastrium *n* (*pl* **hypogastria**) the middle part of the lower region of the abdomen.

hypogeal *or* **hypogean** *or* **hypogeous** *adj* (*bot*) underground; occurring or living underground.

hypogene *adj* (*rocks*) formed under the surface of the ground.

hypogeum *n* (*pl* **hypogea**) (*archit*) a vault or chamber built underground.

hypoglycemia *n* an abnormal drop in the sugar content of the blood.—**hypoglycemic** *adj*.

hypoplasia *n* underdevelopment, which can occur in the teeth as a result of illness or starvation, marked by lines of brown enamel across the teeth.

hypostasis *n* (*pl* **hypostases**) the essential personality of a substance; (*Christianity*) any of the three persons of the Godhead which together make up the Holy Trinity; (*med*) an excess of blood in the organs as the result of poor circulation.—**hypostatic** *adj*.

hypostatize *vt* to regard as real; to embody or personify.—**hypostatization** *n*.

hypostyle *n* a roof supported by columns; a covered colonnade; a pillared hall or court.

hypotenuse *n* the side opposite to the right angle in a right-angled triangle .

hypothalamus *n* (*pl* **hypothalami**) an area of the forebrain that contains centers controlling vital processes, e.g., fat and carbohydrate metabolism, thirst, hunger, thermal regulation, sexual function, and the regulation of sleep.

hypothecate *vt* to pledge (a property) without delivery of title or possession.—**hypothecation** *n*.—**hypothecator** *n*.

hypothermia *n* (*med*) an abnormally low body temperature.—**hypothermic** *adj*.

hypothesis *n* (*pl* **hypotheses**) something assumed for the purpose of argument; a theory to explain some fact that may or may not prove to be true; supposition; conjecture.

hypothesize *vti* to form or assume as a hypothesis.

hypothetical *adj* based on hypothesis, conjectural.—**hypothetically** *adv*.

hypothyroidism *n* deficient activity of the thyroid gland.

Hypsipyle *n* (*Greek myth*) queen of Lemnos, who saved her father when the women of the island vowed to kill all the men.

hypsometry *n* the science of measuring altitude.—**hypsometric** *adj*

hyrax *n* (*pl* **hyraxes**, **hyraces**) a small African hamster-like mammal related to the elephant.

hyson *n* Chinese green tea.

hyssop *n* an aromatic plant with blue flowers, formerly used in medicine.

hysterectomy *n* (*pl* **hysterectomies**) surgical removal of the womb.

hysteresis *n* (*pl* **hystereses**) magnetic inertia.—**hysteretic** *adj*.

hysteria *n* a mental disorder marked by excitability, anxiety, imaginary organic disorders, etc; frenzied emotion or excitement.

hysteric *n* a hysterical person; (*pl*) fits of hysteria; (*inf*) uncontrollable laughter.

hysterical *adj* caused by hysteria; suffering from hysteria; (*inf*) extremely funny.—**hysterically** *adv*.

hysterotomy *n* (*pl* **hysterotomies**) a surgical incision into the womb.

hythergraph *n* a graph of monthly rainfall against monthly temperature throughout the year.

Hywel ab Idwal *n* (the Bad) king of Gwynedd (979–985). A descendant of Rhodi Mwar, he deposed his father Iago Iap Idwal.

Hywel Dda *n* (the Good) (*d.* 950) king of Gwynedd (904–950). A grandson of Rhodi Mwar.

Hz *abbr* = hertz.

Hzk. *abbr* (*OT*) = Hezekiah.

I

i, I *n* the ninth letter of the English alphabet.

I[1] *pron* the person who is speaking or writing, used in referring to himself or herself.

I[2] *symbol* (*chem*) iodine (element).

i. *abbr* = (*Latin*) *id*, "that"; incisor (*dentistry*); interest; intransitive; island.

I *abbr* = (*chem*) iso-; (*mech*) (moment of) inertia; (*astron*) inclination (of an orbit to the ecliptic); independence; institute; island.

I. *abbr* = Idaho; Independent; Iowa; Island; Isle(s).

Ia. *abbr* = Iowa.

IA *abbr* = Ileostomy Association of Great Britain; Import Administration; Incorporated Accountant; Indian Army; Institute of Actuaries; International Alert; International Ångström; infected area.

IAA *abbr* = International Advertising Association; International Aerosol Association; International Association for Aerobiology; Ireland-Australia Association; Irish Architectural Archive; indoleacetic acid.

IAAA *abbr* = Irish Amateur Athletic Association.

IAAAA *abbr* = Intercollegiate Association of Amateur Athletes of America.

IAAC *abbr* = International Antarctic Analysis Center.

IAAF *abbr* = International Agricultural Aviation Foundation; International Amateur Athletic Federation.

IAAI *abbr* = International Association of Arson Investigators.

IAAS *abbr* = Immigrant Appeals Advisory Service; Incorporated Association of Architects and Surveyors; Institute of Auctioneers and Apprentices in Scotland.

IAATM *abbr* = International Association for Accident and Traffic Medicine.

IAB *abbr* = Industrial Advisory Board; International Aquatic Board; Internet Architecture Board; Irish Association for the Blind.

IABA *abbr* = International Association of Aircraft Brokers and Agents; Irish Amateur Boxing Association.

IABSOIW *abbr* = International Association of Bridge, Structural and Ornamental Iron Workers.

IAC *abbr* = International Aerobatic Club; International Alpine Conference.

IACA *abbr* = Independent Air Carriers' Association; Irish American Cultural Association.

IACB *abbr* = International Advisory Committee on Bibliography.

Iacchus *n* (*Greek myth*) an obscure deity sometimes described as Demeter's son, sometimes as her husband, worshipped at the Eleusinian Mysteries with Demeter and Persephone.

IADR *abbr* = International Association for Dental Research.

IADRWG *abbr* = Interagency Alternative Dispute Resolution Working Group.

IAE *abbr* = International Association of Egyptologists.

IAEA *abbr* = International Atomic Energy Authority.

IAEGC *abbr* = Inter-Agency Electronic Grants Committee.

IAF *abbr* = Inter-American Foundation; International Archery Federation; International Association of Falconry and Conservation of Birds of Prey; International Astronautical Federation.

IAFF *abbr* = International Art Film Federation; International Association of Fire Fighters.

IAFT *abbr* = International Association of Forensic Toxicologists.

IAGLP *abbr* = International Association of Great Lakes Ports.

Iago I ab Idwal *n* (*d. c.*980) king of Gwynedd, Wales. He reigned from 950–979. Deposed by his son, Hywel ab Idwal.

Iago II ab Idwal *n* (*d. c.*1040) king of Gwynedd, Wales (1023–1039). The grandson of the first Iago and father of Gruffydd ap Cynan.

IAgrE *abbr* = Institution of Agricultural Engineers.

IAHM *abbr* = Incorporated Association of Headmasters.

IAI *abbr* = Institute of Architectural Ironmongers; International Apple Institute; International Association for Identification; Israel Aviation Authorities.

IAL *abbr* = International Algebraic Language.

Ialmenus *n* (*Greek myth*) one of the Argonauts, and a leader of 30 ships to the Trojan War.

Ialonus *n* (*Gaulish Celtic myth*) a deity associated with cultivated fields. He is thought also to have been associated with glades, since *ialo* means "glade."

IAM *abbr* = Institute of Administrative Management; Institute of Advanced Motorists.

IAMA *abbr* = International Abstaining Motorists Association; Irish Association of Municipal Authorities.

iamb, iambus *n* (*pl* **iambi, iambs, iambuses**) a metrical foot consisting of two syllables, the first short or unstressed and the second long or stressed.—**iambic** *adj*.

IAMPTH *abbr* = International Association of Master Penmen and Teachers of Handwriting.

IANA *abbr* = Internet Assigned Numbers Authority.

-iana, -ana *n suffix* sayings of, publications about, as *Shakespeariana*, etc.

I & D *abbr* = incision and drainage.

I & O *abbr* = intake and output.

I and R *abbr* = initiative and referendum.

IANE *abbr* = Institute of Advanced Nursing Education.

Ianuaria *n* (*Gaulish Celtic myth*) a female deity who was venerated at the sanctuary of Beire-le-Châtel in Burgundy.

IAOC *abbr* = International Athletic Olympic Committee.

IAP *abbr* = Institute of Animal Physiology; International Academy of Poets; International Association of Planetology.

IAPA *abbr* = Irish Airline Pilots Association.

Iapetus[1] *n* (*Greek myth*) a Titan and a son of Uranus and Ge, the father of Atlas, Menoetius, Prometheus, and Epimetheus.

Iapetus[2] *n* a satellite of Saturn, discovered by Cassini in 1671.

IAPP *abbr* = Irish Association of Pigmeat Producers.

IAPS *abbr* = Incorporated Association of Preparatory Schools.

IAPSC *abbr* = International Association of Pipe Smokers Clubs.

IAR *abbr* = instruction address register.

Iarbanel *n* (*Irish Celtic myth*) said to have been the ancestor of the Tuatha De Danann. He was one of the three sons of Nemedh who succeeded in escaping after the defeat and death of their father.

Iarbas *n* (*Greek myth*) a king of Numidia in North Africa, who sold the site of Carthage to Dido, and was Aeneas's rival for her love.—*also* **Hiarbas**.

IARU *abbr* = International Amateur Radio Union.

IARW *abbr* = International Association of Refrigerated Warehouses.

IAS *abbr* = immediate access store; instrument approach system; indicated air speed.

IASA *abbr* = International Air Safety Association.

Iasi *n* a city in Romania.

Iasion *n* (*Greek myth*) a demi-god loved by the goddess Demeter, who had a son, Plutus, by him.

IASMAL *abbr* = International Academy of Social and Moral Sciences, Arts, and Letters.

IASP *abbr* = International Association for the Study of Pain.

IASS *abbr* = International Association for Scandinavian Studies.

Iasus *n* (*Greek myth*) the father of Atalanta, who wanted only male children and left the child to die of exposure. She was suckled by a bear and rescued by hunters.

iat *abbr* = inside air temperature.

IATA *abbr* = International Air Transport Association.

IATEFL *abbr* = International Association of Teachers of English as a Foreign Language.

Iath n' Anann *n* (*Celtic myth*) an ancient name for Ireland and may be derived from *Anu* or *Ana*, an alternative form of Danu, a mother-goddess.

-iatric, -iatrical *adj* pertaining to doctors and medicine.

IAVS *abbr* = Irish Association for Victim Support.

iaw *abbr* = in accordance with.

IAWA *abbr* = International Animal Welfare Alliance; International Association of Wood Anatomists.

IAWCM *abbr* = International Association of Wiping Cloth Manufacturers.

IAWE *abbr* = International Association for Wind Engineering.

IAWM *abbr* (*Brit*) = Industrial Association of Wales and Monmouthshire.

IAWQ *abbr* = International Association on Water Quality.

IAWRT *abbr* = International Association of Women in Radio and Television.

ib. *abbr* (*Latin*) = *ibidem*, "in the same place."

IB *abbr* = in bond; inbound; incendiary bomb; Institute of Brewing; International Baccalaureate; Intervention Board; invoice book.

IBA *abbr* = (*Brit*) Independent Broadcasting Agency (now Independent Television Commission, the UK regulatory body for commercial radio and television); Institute of British Architects; International Banana Association; International Bartenders Association; International Bridge Academy; Irish Brewers Association.

Ibadan *n* a city in Nigeria.

Ibarruri [Gomez], Dolores ("La Pasionara") (1895–1989) Spanish Communist politician. A journalist, she was elected to parliament in 1936, and became world-famous for her slogan "They shall not pass" (borrowed from **Pétain**) during the Spanish Civil War. She lived in exile in the USSR (1939–77) and was re-elected to the Spanish parliament in 1977.

IBB *abbr* = Institute of British Bakers; International Bowling Board; Invest in Britain Bureau.

IBBA *abbr* = Irish Basket Ball Association; Irish Break Bakers' Association; Irish-Belgian Business Association.

Ibbetson *n* **Julius Caesar** (1759–1817) English painter. His work was essentially English and picturesque in style.

IBBR *abbr* = interbank bid-rate.

IBCAM *abbr* = Institute of British Carriage and Automobile Manufacturers.

IBCC *abbr* = International Bird Census Committee.

IBD *abbr* = inflammatory bowel disease.

IBDISFS *abbr* = Institute of British Detective, Investigative Security and Forensic Specialists.

IBE *abbr* = Institute of British Engineers; International Bureau of Education.

Iberian *adj* pertaining to Spain and Portugal; pertaining to Iberia, the ancient name of the southwest European peninsula now comprising Spain and Portugal.

Iberians *n* a group of people who inhabited the coastal areas of southeast and eastern Spain from *c*.1000 BC.

Ibert *n* **Jacques François Antoine** (1890–1962) French composer famed for his light and witty music, best known compositions include the *Ballad of Reading Jail* (after Wilde), *Le Roi d'Yvetot*, and *Escales*.

ibex *n* (*pl* **ibexes, ibices, ibex**) any of various wild mountain goats with large horns.

IBF *abbr* = International Badminton Federation; International Bandy Federation; International Bodysurfing Federation; International Boxing Foundation; Irish Bankers Federation.

IBFAN *abbr* = International Baby Food Action Network.

Ibhell *n* (*Irish Celtic myth*) the beautiful wife of Aed, the son of the king of Connacht. The king of Leinster fell in love with her, and Mongan used this as a way of taking revenge on the king of Leinster who had abducted Mongan's wife.

IBI *abbr* = invoice book, inward.

ibid. *abbr* (*Latin*) = *ibidem*, "in the same place."

Ibid *abbr* = international bibliographical description.

Ibiol *abbr* = Institute of Biology.

ibis *n* (*pl* **ibises, ibis**) a wading bird with a curved bill.

IBK *abbr* = Institute of Bookkeepers.

IBL *abbr* = International Brotherhood of Longshoremen.

IBM *abbr* = International Brotherhood of Magicians; Indian Bureau of Mines; (*trademark*) International Business Machines; intercontinental ballistic missile.

IBM personal computer (IBM PC) *n* (*comput*) a personal computer developed by IBM that was released in 1981.

IBMBR *abbr* = interbank market bid rate.

Ibn Saud *n* **Abdul Aziz** (1880–1953) king of Saudi Arabia. He negotiated terms with American oil companies after the discovery of oil in his country (1938).

Ibo *n* (*pl* **Ibo, Ibos**) a member of a negroid people of southern Nigeria; their language.

IBO *abbr* = invoice book, outward.

IBP *abbr* = Institute for Business Planning; Institute of British Photographers; initial boiling point.

IBRD *abbr* = International Bank for Reconstruction and Development.

IBS *abbr* = International Bible Students; irritable bowel syndrome.

IBSA *abbr* = International Blind Sports Association; International Board Sailing Association; Irish Building Societies Association.

Ibsen *n* **Henrik** (1828–1906) Norwegian dramatist whose plays fall into three groups: early verse dramas, e.g., *Peer Gynt*; plays of social realism, e.g., *A Doll's House*; and late symbolic plays, e.g., *The Wild Duck*, in which the realism of the middle period is mixed with an introspective, disturbing symbolism that draws upon folk traditions. *Hedda Gabler* marked a powerful return to realism in its depiction of the menace of intellectual arrogance.

IBTA *abbr* = International Baton Twirling Association of America and Abroad.

IBTS *abbr* = International Beer Tasting Society.

IBWM *abbr* = International Bureau of Weights and Measures.

i/c or I/c *abbr* = (*mil*) in charge, in command.

IC *abbr* = (*Latin*) *Iesus Christus*, "Jesus Christ"; index correction (of a sextant); Industrial Court; Institute of Carpenters; Intelligence Corps; International Chapters; integrated circuit; internal combustion.

ICA *abbr* = Ice Cream Alliance; Institute of Consumer Advisers; Institute of Contemporary Arts; International Caribbean Airways; International Chefs Association; International Claim Association; International Confederation of Accordionists; International Congress of Acarology; International Copper Association; Invalid Care Allowance; Irish Countrywomen's Association; Islamic Cement Association.

ICAN *abbr* = International Commission for Air Navigation; Invalid Children's Aid Nationwide.

ICAO *abbr* = International Civil Aviation Organization.

Icaria *n* an island in the Aegean Sea, where the mythical hero Icarus was said to be buried.

Icarius *n* (*Greek myth*) 1. brother of Tyndareus and father of Penelope. 2. an Athenian who was taught the art of vine culture by Dionysus, and who was honored after his death by certain rites in the grape festival.

Icarus[1] *n* (*Greek myth*) the son of Daedalus, who ignored his father's advice not to fly too near the sun by means of wings made of wax and feathers. The wax of his wings melted and he plunged into the sea south of Samos, an area called the Icarian Sea in his memory.

Icarus[2] *n* a small asteroid discovered in 1949 which comes within the orbit of Mercury to make the closest approach to the Sun of any object in the Solar System except for comets.

ICAS *abbr* = Institute of Chartered Accountants of Scotland; International Conference on Acoustics, Speech, and Signal Processing; International Council of Air Shows; International Council of Associations of Surfing.

ICBB *abbr* = International Commission for Bee Botany.

ICBBA *abbr* (*Brit*) = International Cornish Bantam Breeders Association.

ICBD *abbr* = International Council of Ballroom Dancing.

ICBM *abbr* = intercontinental ballistic missile.

ICBN *abbr* = International Code of Biological Nomenclature.

ICBP *abbr* = International Council for Bird Preservation.

ICC *abbr* = International Association of Cereal Science and Technology; International Chamber of Commerce; International Coffee Council; International Corrosion Council; International Cricket Conference; Interstate Commerce Commission; Inuit Circumpolar Conference; Irish Council of Churches.

ICCA *abbr* = International Corrugated Case Association.

ICCBC *abbr* = International Committee for Colorado Beetle Control.

ICCE *abbr* = International Commission on Continental Erosion.

ICCG *abbr* = International Conference on Crystal Growth.

ICCM *abbr* = International Committee for the Conservation of Mosaics.

ICCPR *abbr* = International Covenant on Civil and Political Rights.

ICCU *abbr* = International Cross-Country Union.

ICD *abbr* = International Classification of Diseases.

ICDA International Catholic Deaf Association.

ice *n* water frozen solid; a sheet of this; a portion of ice cream or water ice; (*sl*) diamonds; (*sl*) the drug methamphetamine packaged and sold as a stimulant in smokeable form. * *vti* (*often with* **up** *or* **over**) to freeze; to cool with ice; to cover with icing.

Ice. or **Icel.** *abbr* = Iceland; Icelandic.

ICE *abbr* = Institute for Consumer Ergonomics; Institution of Civil Engineers; International Congress of Ecology; International Cultural Exchange; internal combustion engine.

ice age *n* (*geol*) a period when much of the earth's surface was covered in glaciers; (with caps) the Pleistocene glacial epoch.

ICEATCA *abbr* = Icelandic Air Traffic Controllers Association.

ice barrier *n* a dam holding back the meltwaters of a glacier; the edge of the Antarctic ice sheet.

iceberg *n* (*geog*) a great mass of mostly submerged ice floating in the sea.

iceblink *n* a streak of whiteness on the horizon, caused by the reflection of light from masses of ice in the distance.

icebound *adj* (*ship, etc*) surrounded, and immobilized, by ice.

icebox *n* a compartment in a refrigerator for making ice.

icebreaker, iceboat *n* a powerful and reinforced vessel for breaking a channel through ice.

icecap *n* a mass of slowly spreading glacial ice.

ice cream *adj* a sweet frozen food, made from flavored milk or cream.

ICED *abbr* = Interprofessional Council on Environmental Design.

ice dance *n* a type of ballroom dancing by skaters on ice.

icefall *n* a steep part of a glacier, resembling a frozen waterfall.

ice field *n* an extensive field of floating ice.

ice floe *n* a sheet of floating ice.

ICEH *abbr* = International Center for Eye Health.

ice hockey *n* an indoor or outdoor hockey game played on ice by two teams of six skaters with curved sticks and a flat disk called a puck.

Iceland *n* a republic located in the North Atlantic Ocean about 298 kilometers or 186 miles east of Greenland and just south of the Arctic Circle.

Icelander *n* a native or inhabitant of Iceland.

Icelandic *adj* of or pertaining to Iceland or its language, literature and people. * *n* the language of Iceland.

Icelandic Króna *n* currency of Iceland.

Ice Man *n* (*archeo*) the oldest intact human body ever to be recovered, which was found in the Austrian Alps in 1991. Radiocarbon dates confirm that it is of late Neolithic date.

Iceni *n* an ancient British tribe and one of the leading tribes of the East Anglian area. It is particularly famous for one of its queens, Boudicca, the wife of Prasutagus.

ice pack *n* a field of broken and drifting ice, consisting of great masses packed together; a cloth or small bag filled with crushed ice for soothing sores and swellings on the body.

ICEPHEW *abbr* = Institution of Civil Engineers Panel for Historical Engineering Works.

ice pick *n* a pointed awl with a handle for chipping or breaking up ice.

ice plant *n* a type of plant with leaves that glisten as if covered with ice.

ICES *abbr* = International Council for the Exploration of the Sea.

ice sheet *n* a continuous sheet of thick ice, larger than an ice cap, that covers a land mass.

ice skate *n* a boot with a steel blade fixed to the sole for skating on ice.—*also vi.*—**ice skater** *n*.

ICET *abbr* = International Center for Earth Tides.

ICF *abbr* = Ice Cream Federation; Industrial Careers Foundation; Institute of Chartered Foresters; International Canoe Federation; International Chess Federation; International Crane Federation; International Cremation Federation; International Curling Federation.

ICFC *abbr* = International Council of Fan Clubs.

ICFG *abbr* = International Commission on Fungal Genetics.

ICFM *abbr* = Institute of Charity Fundraising Managers.

ICFPW *abbr* = International Confederation of Former Prisoners of War.

ICFS *abbr* = Ireland-Cuba Friendship Society.

ICFTU *abbr* = International Confederation of Free Trade Unions.

ICGA *abbr* = Imperial Continental Gas Association; International Carnival Glass Association; International Classic Guitar Association; Irish Craft and Giftware Association.

IchemE *abbr* = Institution of Chemical Engineers.

ichneumon *n* a North African mongoose.

ichneumon fly *n* an insect that lays its eggs in the bodies of other insects.

ichnite, ichnolite *n* a fossil footprint.

ichor *n* (*Greek myth*) the ethereal fluid believed to run, instead of blood, in the veins of the classical gods.—**ichorous** *adj*.

ichth. or **ich.** *abbr* = ichthyology.

ichtny-, icthyo- *prefix* fish.

ichthyic *adj* pertaining to fishes.

ichthyoid, ichthyoidal *adj* resembling a fish.

ichthyology *n* the study of fish.—**ichthyologic, ichthyological** *adj*.—**ichthyologist** *n*.

ichthyophagous *adj* fish-eating.—**ichthyophagy** *n*.

ichthyornis *n* an extinct species of toothed fish-eating bird.

ichthyosaur, ichthyosaurus *n* (*pl* **ichthyosaurs, ichthosauri**) a gigantic, extinct, marine reptile.

ichthyosis *n* a disease in which the skin becomes dry and scaly.

Ichthys *abbr* (*Greek*) = *Iesous Christos, Theou Uios, Soter*, "Jesus Christ, Son of God, Saviour" (persecuted members of the early Church used a drawing of a fish, *ichthys* in Greek, as a secret sign).

ICI *abbr* = Imperial Chemical Industries.

icicle *n* a hanging tapering length of ice formed when dripping water freezes.—**icicled** *adj*.

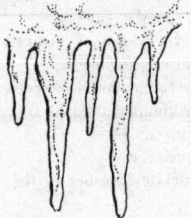

icily *adv* in an icy manner, coldly.

iciness *n* the state of being icy, coldness.

icing *n* a semi-solid sugary mixture used to cover cakes, etc.—*also* **frosting**.

ICJ *abbr* = International Commission of Jurists; International Court of Justice.

ICJW *abbr* = International Council of Jewish Women.

ICL *abbr* = International Computers Limited.

ICLA *abbr* = International Committee on Laboratory Animals.

ICLD *abbr* = International Commission on Large Dams.

ICLPA *abbr* = Irish Cream Liqueur Producers' Association.

ICM *abbr* = International Conference of Midwives.

ICMA *abbr* = International Christian Maritime Association; International City Management Association; International Congresses for Modern Architecture; Irish Cable Makers Association.

ICMR *abbr* = International Committee for Mountain Racing.

ICMSA *abbr* = Irish Creamery Milk Suppliers Association.

ICMT *abbr* = International Commission on Mycotoxicology.

ICMUA *abbr* = International Commission on the Meteorology of the Upper Atmosphere.

ICN *abbr* = (*Latin*) *in christi nomine*, "in the name of Christ"; International Communes Network; International Council of Nurses.

ICNAF *abbr* = International Council for North West Atlantic Fisheries.

ICNB *abbr* = International Code of Nomenclature of Bacteria.

ICNCP *abbr* = International Code of Nomenclature of Viruses.

ICO *abbr* = International Coffee Organization; International Commission on Oceanography; Irish Chiropodists Association; Islamic Circle Organization.

ICOBA *abbr* = International Confederation of Book Actors.

ICOM *abbr* = International Council of Museums.

ICOMOS *abbr* = International Council on Monuments and Sites.

icon[1] *n* an image; (*Eastern Church*) a sacred image, usu on a wooden panel.—*also* **ikon**.—**iconic, iconical** *adj*.

icon[2] *n* (comput) a symbol on screen that represents something or some process or function in the computer, used in a graphical user interface.

icon. *abbr* = iconographic; iconography.

Iconium *n* (*Bible*) city in the central plain of Asia Minor visited by Paul.

iconoclast *n* a person who attacks revered or traditional beliefs, opinions, etc.—**iconoclasm** *n*. —**iconoclastic** *adj*.—**iconoclastically** *adv*.

iconography *n* (*pl* **iconographies**) the art of representation by means of images (statues), pictures, or engravings; the study of this art.—**iconographer** *n*. —**iconographic, iconographical** *adj*.

iconolatry *n* the worship of images.

iconology *n* the study of icons.

icosahedron *n* (*pl* **icosahedrons, icosahedra**) (*geom*) a solid bounded by 20 plane faces.

ICOSI *abbr* = International Committee on Smoking Issues.

Icovellauna *n* (*Gaulish Celtic myth*) a deity who was worshipped in the area around Metz and Trier. She is associated with healing.

ICPL *abbr* = International Center for Protected Landscapes; International Committee of Passenger Lines.

ICPO *abbr* = International Criminal Police Organization.

ICPS *abbr* = International Cerebral Palsy Society; International Conference on the Properties of Steam.

ICR *abbr* = Institute of Cancer Research; International Collective Resistance; Irish Consumer Research Limited; intelligent character recognition.

ICRC *abbr* = International Committee of the Red Cross.

ICRF *abbr* = Imperial Cancer Research Fund.

ICRP *abbr* = International Commission on Radiological Protection.

ICRUM *abbr* = International Commission on Radiation Units and Measurements.

ICS *abbr* = Imperial College of Science and Technology; Institute of Chartered Shipbrokers; (*Brit*) Institute of Cornish Studies; Intensive Care Society; International Crocodilian Society; investors' compensation scheme.

ICSA *abbr* = Institute of Chartered Secretaries and Administrators; International Council of Securities Associations.

ICS/CI *abbr* = International Clarinet Society/ClariNetwork International.

ICSF *abbr* = Intermediate Certificate of the Society of Floristry.

ICSH *abbr* = interstitial-cell-stimulating hormone.

ICSLS *abbr* = International Convention for Safety of Life at Sea.

ICSU *abbr* = International Council of Scientific Unions.

ICT *abbr* = Institute of Clay Technology; Institute of Concrete Technology.

icterus *n* jaundice.—**icteric** *adj*.

ICTP *abbr* = International Center for Theoretical Physics.

ICTU *abbr* = Irish Congress of Trade Unions.

ictus *n* (*pl* **ictuses, ictus**) a stress in verse.

ICU *abbr* = International Code Use; intensive care unit.

ICUMSA *abbr* = International Commission for Uniform Methods of Sugar Analysis.

icw *abbr* = in connection with.

ICW *abbr* = (*radio*) interrupted continuous waves; Institute of Clayworkers; Institute of Clerks of Works of Great Britain.

ICWA *abbr* = Institute of Cost and Works Accountants; International Coil Winding Association.

icy *adj* (**icier, iciest**) full of, made of, or covered with ice; slippery or very cold; cold in manner.

ICYYLM *abbr* = International Commission on Yeasts and Yeast-like Microorganisms.

ICZN *abbr* = International Code of Zoological Nomenclature.

id *n* (*psychoanal*) the primitive psychological instincts in the unconscious which are the source of psychic activity.

id or i.d. *abbr* = inside diameter.

id. *abbr* = idem.

Id. *abbr* = Idaho.

I'd = I had; I should; I would.

ID *abbr* = identity; identity card; infectious diseases; information/Intelligence Department.

Ida[1] *n* 1. (d. c.568) king of Bernicia, Britain (547–568) 2. (*Greek myth*) a nymph of Mount Ida in Crete, who with her sister nursed the infant Zeus.

Ida[2] *n* 1. in ancient geography, the middle and highest summit of the mountain chain that divides the island of Crete from east to west, where Zeus was reared and educated. 2. in ancient geography, a mountain range in Asia Minor, extending from Phrygia through Mysia into the Troad, at the foot of which lay the city of Troy, modern Idhi.

Ida. *abbr* = Idaho.

IDA *abbr* = International Dark-Sky Association; International Desalination Association; International Development Association; International Drapery Association; International Drummers Association; Irish Diabetic Association; Israeli Dental Association.

Idaea *n* (*Greek myth*) a nymph of Mount Ida near Troy.

Idaean Mother *n* a name given to the goddess Cybele, who had a temple on Mount Ida near Troy.

Idaeus *n* (*Greek myth*) the herald of the Trojan forces at the time of the Trojan War.

Idaho (ID) *n* a state of the United States of America (USA) of which the capital is Boise.

IDAS *abbr* (*Brit*) = Implanted Defibrillator of Scotland.

IDB *abbr* = illicit diamond buyer/buying.

IDBRA *abbr* = International Drivers Behavior Research Association.

IDC *abbr* = International Dance Council; International Diamond Council; International Drycleaners Congress.

IDCA *abbr* = International Diving Coaches Association; International Dragon Class Association.

ID card *n* an identity card.

IDCCC *abbr* = International Dredging Conference Coordinating Committee.

IDD *abbr* = International Direct Dialing; Institute for Design and Disability (Eire); insulin-dependent diabetes.

IDDD *abbr* = International Direct Distance Dialing.

ide *n* a small European fish.

idea *n* a mental impression of anything; a vague impression, notion; an opinion or belief; a scheme; a supposition; a person's conception of something; a significance or purpose.

ideal *adj* existing in the mind or as an idea; satisfying an ideal, perfect. * *n* the most perfect conception of anything; a person or thing regarded as perfect; a standard for attainment or imitation; an aim or principle.—**ideally** *adv*.—**idealness** *n*.

idealism *n* the pursuit of high ideals; the conception or representation of things in their ideal form as against their reality.—**idealist** *n*. —**idealistic** *adj*.—**idealistically** *adv*.

ideality *n* (*pl* **idealities**) the quality of being ideal; the faculty to form ideals.

idealize *vt* to consider or represent as ideal.—**idealization** *n*. —**idealizer** *n*.

ideate *vti* to imagine.

idée fixe *n* (*pl* **idées fixes**) a fixed idea; an obsession.

IDE interface *n* (*comput*) a type of disk controller that is built into the hard disk drive, cutting out the need for a separate controller or adapter card.

idem *pron* (*Latin*) the same: used to indicate a reference to a book, article, etc, previously cited.

identical *adj* exactly the same; having the same origin.—**identically** *adv*.—**identicalness** *n*.

identical twins *npl* (*genetics*) two identical individuals that develop from a single fertilized egg that divides early on into two equal parts. *See* **monozygotic twins**.

identifiable *adj* able to be identified.—**identifiableness** *n*.

identification *n* the act of identifying; the state of being identified; that which identifies.

identify *vt* (**identifying, identified**) to consider to be the same, equate; to establish the identity of; to associate closely; to regard (oneself) as similar to another.—**identifier** *n*.

identity *n* (*pl* **identities**) the state of being exactly alike; the distinguishing characteristics of a person, personality; the state of being the same as a specified person or thing.

identity card *n* a card carrying personal details, a photograph, etc of an individual as carried by staff of an organization, journalists, etc.

ideogram, ideograph *n* a symbol, as in Chinese writing, used instead of a word to represent an idea or thing; a graphic sign.

ideography *n* the direct representation of ideas by symbols.—**ideographic, ideographical** *adj*.

ideologist, ideologue *n* one occupied with ideals or ideals; a theorist.

ideology *n* (*pl* **ideologies**) the doctrines, beliefs, or opinions of an individual, social class, political party, etc.—**ideological, ideologic** *adj*.

ides *n* the 15th day of March, May, July, or October, and the 13th day of any other month in the ancient Roman calendar.

IDF *abbr* = International Dairy Federation; International Dental Federation.

IDHS(GB) *abbr* = Irish Draught Horse Society (Great Britain).

IDI *abbr* = International Disaster Institute.

idiocy *n* (*pl* **idiocies**) mental deficiency; stupidity, imbecility; something stupid or foolish.

idiom *n* an accepted phrase or expression with a different meaning from the literal; the usual way in which the words of a language are used to express thought; the dialect of a people, region, etc; the characteristic style of a school of art, literature, etc—**idiomatic, idiomatical** *adj*.—**idiomatically** *adv*.

idiopathy *n* a disease whose cause is unknown.—**idiopathic** *adj*.

idiophone *n* (*mus*) any instrument in which sound is produced by the vibration of the instrument itself, e.g., cymbals, bells, castanets etc.

idiosyncrasy *n* (*pl* **idiosyncrasies**) a type of behavior or characteristic peculiar to a person or group; a quirk, eccentricity.—**idiosyncratic** *adj*.—**idiosyncratically** *adv*.

idiot *n* a severely mentally retarded adult; (*inf*) a foolish or stupid person.

idiot board *n* an autocue.

idiotic *adj* stupid; senseless.—**idiotically** *adv*.

idiot savant *n* (*pl* **idiots savants** *or* **idiot savants**) someone who, although suffering severe mental disability, such as autism, is able to perform unusual and often astonishing mental feats or who exhibits remarkable musical ability.

IDL *abbr* = International Date Line.

idle *adj* not employed, unoccupied; not in use; averse to work; useless; worthless. * *vt* to waste or spend (time) in idleness. * *vi* to move slowly or aimlessly; (*engine*) to operate without transmitting power.—**idleness** *n*. —**idler** *n*. —**idly** *adv*.

idler *n* someone who idles; a lazy person.

idle time n (*comput*) the time during which the computer is turned on but is not processing any instructions.

IDLG *abbr* = Infant Drinks Litigation Group.

Idmon *n* (*Greek myth*) one of the Argonauts, a seer who knew that if he joined the expedition he would not survive. He was killed by a boar on the southern shore of the Black Sea, where the city of Heracleia was later founded.

IDMS *abbr* = integrated data management system.

IDN *abbr* = (*Latin*) *in Dei nomine*, "in the name of God"; integrated data network.

idol *n* an image or object worshiped as a god; a person who is intensely loved, admired, or honored.

idolatry *n* the worship of idols; excessive admiration or devotion.—**idolatrous** *adj*.—**idolater** *n*.

idolize *vt* to make an idol of, for worship; to love to excess.—**idolization** *n*. —**idolizer** *n*.

Idomeneus *n* (*Greek myth*) a king of Crete who led a Cretan force of 80 ships to the Trojan War. He later sailed for Italy and settled in the part of the country which forms the "heel" of Italy, the Sallentine Plain.

IDP *abbr* = International Driving Permit; integrated data processing.

IDPM *abbr* = Institute of Data Processing Management.

IDPT *abbr* = International Donkey Protection Trust.

IDR *abbr* = Infantry Drill Regulations; International Dental Relief.

Idris *n* (*Welsh Celtic myth*) a giant who is said to have been skilled in poetry, astronomy and philosophy. His home was on the mountain of Cadair Idris in Gwynedd.

IDS *abbr* = Income Data Services; Industry Department for Scotland; International Dostoevsky Society; Irish Deaf Society.

IDSA *abbr* = Infectious Diseases Society of America; Irish Deaf Sports Association.

IDT *abbr* = Industrial Design Technology.

Idumea *n* (*Bible*) alternative for Edom.

Idwal Foel *n* (Idwal the Bald) king of Gwynedd, Wales (916–942). The son of Anarawd.

idyll, idyl *n* a short simple poem, usu evoking the romance and beauty of rural life; a romantic or picturesque event or scene; a romantic or pastoral musical composition.—**idyllist** *n*.

idyllic *adj* pertaining to or of the nature of an idyll, pastoral; romantic, picturesque.—**idyllically** *adv*.

i.e. *abbr* (*Latin*) = *id est*, "that is."

IE *abbr* = index error (of a sextant); Indo-European.

IEA *abbr* = International Emergency Action; International Energy Agency; International Entrepreneurs Association; International Ergonomics Association; Irish Epilepsy Association.

IEC *abbr* = International Egg Commission; International Everesters Club; Irish Equine Center.

IECA *abbr* = International Erosion Control Association.

IEE *abbr* = Institution of Electrical Engineers.

IEEE *abbr* = Institute of Earth Education; Institute of Electrical and Electronic Engineers; Institute of Explosives Engineers.

IEF *abbr* = International Eye Foundation; Irish Equine Foundation.

IEHO *abbr* = Institute of Environmental Health Officers.

IEM *abbr* = inborn error of metabolism.

IEng *abbr* = Incorporated Engineer.

IEngAMIMM *abbr* = Associate Member of the Institution of Mining and Metallurgy.

IERE *abbr* = Institution of Electronic and Radio Engineers.

IESBS *abbr* = Institute of Engineers and Ship Builders in Scotland.

if *n* (*comput*) a logical operator that tests a conditional statement and, if it is true, performs one task; if it is false, it performs another task.

if *conj* on condition that; in the event that; supposing that; even though; whenever; whether.

if *abbr* = information feedback.

i.f. *abbr* (*Latin*) = *ipse fecit*, "he did it himself."

I-f *abbr* = in flight.

IF *abbr* = Institute of Foresters; Institute of Fuel; intermediate frequency.

IFA *abbr* = Independent Film Makers Association; Institute of Field Archaeologists; Institute of Foresters of Australia; International Federation of Airworthiness; International Federation on Aging; International Florists Association; International Footprint Association; Irish Farmers Association.

IFAA *abbr* = Independent Financial Advisers Association.

IFAD *abbr* = International Fund for Agricultural Development.

IFAW *abbr* = International Fund for Animal Welfare.

IFB *abbr* = International Film Bureau; International Fire Buff Associates; invitation for bid.

IFBB *abbr* = International Federation of Body Builders.

IFC *abbr* = International Finance Corporation.

IFE *abbr* = Institute of Fence Engineers; Institute of Freshwater Ecology; Institution of Fire Engineers.

IFEAT *abbr* = International Federation of Essential Oils and Aroma Trades.

IFES *abbr* = International Flat Earth Society.

IFF *abbr* = Institute of Freight Forwarders.

iffy *adj* (*inf*) uncertain, unreliable.

IFHOH *abbr* = International Federation of the Hard of Hearing.

IFIP *abbr* = International Federation for Information Processing.

IFL *abbr* = Institute of Fluorescent Lighting; International Federation of Lithographers, Process Workers and Kindred Trades; International Friendship League.

IFLYO *abbr* (*Netherlands*) = International Lesbian and Gay Youth Organization.

IFM *abbr* = International Falcon Movement; International Federation of Musicians; International Fund for Monuments.

IFMA *abbr* = Independent Furniture Manufacturers' Association; International Farm Management Association.

IFMS *abbr* = International Federation of Magical Societies.

IFN *abbr* = International Feminist Network.

IFO *abbr* = International Farmers Organization.

IFOAD *abbr* = International Federation of Original Art Diffusers.

IFOG *abbr* = International Federation of Olive Growers.

IFR *abbr* = instrument flying regulations.

IFRB *abbr* = International Frequency Registration Board.

IFS *abbr* = Institute for Fiscal Studies; Irish Free State.

IFSA *abbr* = Instock Footwear Suppliers Association; International Federation of Sports Acrobatics; International Fuzzy Systems Association; Irish Federation of Sea Anglers.

IFSMP *abbr* = International Federation of Serious Music Publishers.

IFSSH *abbr* = International Federation of Societies for Surgery of the Hand.

IFST *abbr* = Institute of Food Science and Technology.

IFTU *abbr* = International Federation of Trade Unions.

Ig *abbr* = immunoglobulin.

IG *abbr* = Indo-Germanic; Inner Guard; Inside Guard *or* Guardian; Inspector General; Institution of Geologists; Irish Guards.

IGA *abbr* = International Gay Association; International Geographical Association; International Glaucoma Association; International Goat Association; International Gold Association; International Golf Association; Irish Grassland Association.

IG&GA *abbr* = International Grooving and Grinding Association.

IgasE *abbr* = Institute of Gas Engineers.

IGC *abbr* = Inspector General of Communications; Institute for Global Communications; International Garden Club; International Green Cross; International Guides Club.

IGD *abbr* = illicit gold dealer.

IGF *abbr* = International Gymnastic Federation.

IGLD *abbr* = International Grand Lodge of Druidism.

igloo *n* (*pl* **igloos**) an Inuit (Eskimo) house built of blocks of snow and ice.

IGM *abbr* = International Grand Master (chess).

ign. *abbr* = ignition; (*Latin*) *ignotus*, "unknown."

Ignatius of Antioch *n* Saint (*d.* 107) bishop of Antioch; possibly the child that Jesus showed to the disciples as a symbol of humility; condemned to be taken to Rome and thrown to wild beasts, he was devoured by two lions. His feast day is October 17.

Ignatius of Loyola *n* Saint (*c.*1495–1556) Spanish priest; founded the Society of Jesus (Jesuits) 1541 and elected the first general of the order; wrote *Spiritual Exercises*, the main text followed by Jesuits; founded orphanages, a house for converted Jews, and another for fallen women. His feast day is July 31.

igneous *adj* of fire; (*rocks*) produced by volcanic action or intense heat beneath the earth's surface.

igneous rock *n* (*geol*) one of the three main rock types that is formed by the forcing up of hot molten rock, from great depths, or lava flows on the surface associated with volcanoes.

ignite *vti* to set fire to; to catch fire; to burn or cause to burn.—**ignitable** *adj*.

ignition *n* an act or instance of igniting; the starting of an internal combustion engine; the mechanism that ignites an internal combustion engine.

ignoble *adj* dishonorable, despicable; base, of low birth.—**ignobly** *adv*.

ignominious *adj* bringing disgrace or shame; humiliating, degrading.— **ignominiously** *adv*.

ignominy *n* (*pl* **ignominies**) disgrace, dishonor; a cause of ignominy, a disgraceful act.

ignoramus *n* (*pl* **ignoramuses**) an ignorant person.

ignorance *n* the state of being ignorant; a lack of knowledge.

ignorant *adj* lacking knowledge; uninformed, uneducated; resulting from or showing lack of knowledge.—**ignorance** *n*. —**ignorantly** *adv*.

ignore *vt* to disregard; to deliberately refuse to notice someone.—**ignorable** *adj*.— **ignorer** *n*.

IGO *abbr* = intergovernmental organization.

I-GOOS *abbr* = IOC Committee for Global Oxean Observing System.

IGS *abbr* = Imperial General Staff; International Geoxtextile Society; International Glaciological Society; Israel Geographical Society.

iguana *n* any of a family of large lizards of tropical America.—**iguanian** *adj, n*.

iguanodon *n* a gigantic, extinct, herbivorous lizard.

IGY *abbr* = International Geophysical Year.

i.h. *abbr* (*Latin*) = *iacet hic*, "lies here."

IH *abbr* = Institute of Horticulture.

IHA *abbr* = Independent Hospitals Association; International H-Boat Association; International Horse Association; Issuing Houses Association.

IHBS *abbr* = Irish Hereford Breed Society.

IHC *abbr* = International Health Council; International Help for Children.

IHD *abbr* = ischaemic heart disease.

IHF *abbr* = International Hockey Federation; Irish Heart Foundation.

IHGS *abbr* = Institute of Heraldic and Genealogical Studies.

IHP, i.h.p., i. hp. *or* **ihp** *abbr* = indicated horsepower.

IHRA *abbr* = Indonesian Hotel and Restaurant Association; International Hot Rod Association.

ihram *n* the distinctive white robes worn by Muslims on pilgrimage to Mecca.

IHS *abbr* = Indian Health Service; International Headache Society; International Horn Society; International Hydrofoil Society.

IHSGB *abbr* = Icelandic Horse Society of Great Britain.

IHVE *abbr* = Institute of Heating and Ventilation Engineers.

II *abbr* = Ikebana International; Institute of Inventors.

IIA *abbr* = Information Industry Association; Institute of Industrial Archaeology; International Imagery Association; Irish Insurance Association.

IIBA *abbr* = Irish Indoor Bowling Association; Irish-Italian Business Association.

IID *abbr* = insulin-independent diabetes.

IIExE *abbr* = Associate Member of the Institution of Incorporated Executive Engineers.

IIHF *abbr* = International Ice Hockey Federation.

III *abbr* = Insurance Institute of Ireland; International Isocyanates Institute; Investors in Industry.

IIP *abbr* = International Ice Patrol; Irish Independence Party.

IIS *abbr* = Institute of Industrial Selling; International Institute of Stress; Institute of Information Scientists.

IIW *abbr* = Indian Institute of Welders; International Inner Wheel.

IJJF *abbr* = International Ju Jitsu Federation.

IJMA *abbr* = Indian Jute Mills Association.

IJS *abbr* = Institute of Jazz Studies.

IJVS *abbr* = International Jewish Vegetarian Society.

IKA *abbr* = International Kitefliers Association.

IKBS *abbr* = intelligent knowledge-based system.

ikebana *n* the Japanese art of flower arranging.

ikon *see* **icon**.

Il *symbol* (*chem*) illinium (element).

il *abbr* = inside leg.

il. *abbr* = illustrated; illustrations.

IL *abbr* = Independence League; Institute of Linguists; inside left.

ILA *abbr* = Independent Living Alternatives; Insolvency Lawyers Association; International Law Association; International Leprosy Association; International Longshoremen's Association; Israel Library Association.

ILAB *abbr* = Bureau of International Labor Affairs.

ILAE *abbr* = International League Against Epilepsy.

ILAM *abbr* = Institute of Leisure and Amenity Management.

ILAMA *abbr* = International Life-Saving Appliance Manufacturers Association.

ILC *abbr* = Inner Light Consciousness; International Life-Boat Conference.

ILCA *abbr* = International Lightning Class Association.

ILCS *abbr* = International Liquid Crystal Society.

ILCTA *abbr* = International League of Commercial Travelers and Agents.

ILD *abbr* = interstitial lung disease.

ILDA *abbr* = International Lutheran Deaf Association.

ILDAV *abbr* = International League of Doctors Against Vivisection.

ILE *abbr* = Institute of Legal Executives; Institution of Locomotive Engineers.

ILEA *abbr* (*Brit*) = Inner London Education Authority.

ileac, ileal *adj* (*anat*) pertaining to the ileum.

ileectomy *n* removal by surgery of all or part of the ileum.

ileitis *n* inflammation of the ileum.

ileostomy *n* a surgical procedure in which an opening is made in the abdominal wall through which the waste contents of the intestines are collected in a special bag.

ILESA *abbr* = International Law Enforcement Stress Association.

ileum *n* (*anat*) the lower part of the small intestine.

ileus *n* an obstruction of the intestine which may be mechanical or because of loss of the natural movement of the intestines (peristalsis).

ILF *abbr* = Industrial Leathers Federation; International Lifeboat Federation; International Loan Fund.

iliac arteries *npl* those arteries that supply blood to the lower limbs and pelvic region.

Iliad *n* a Greek epic poem describing the siege of Troy attributed to Homer. *See* **Homer**.—**illiadic** *adj*.

ilium (*pl* **ilia**) *n* the largest of the bones that form each half of the pelvic girdle.

Ilium *see* **Troy**.

ilk *n* a type or sort.

ill *adj* (**worse, worst**) not in good health; harmful; bad; hostile; faulty; unfavorable. * *adv* badly, wrongly; hardly, with difficulty. * *n* trouble; harm; evil.

ill. *abbr* = illustrated; illustration; (*Latin*) *illustrissimus*, "most distinguished."

I'll = I shall; I will.

Ill. *abbr* = Illinois.

ill-advised *adj* unwise.

ill at ease *adj* uneasy, embarrassed.

Illan *or* **Ullan** *n* (*Irish Celtic myth*) the husband of Tuireann, described as either the sister or sister-in-law of Fionn mac Cumhaill. Depicted as a king of Leinster who was thought to have led raids into Britain.

ill-bred *adj* bad-mannered.—**ill-breeding** *n*.

ill-considered *adj* lacking consideration; not thought out properly.

ill-disposed *adj* unfavorably inclined (towards).

illegal *adj* against the law.—**illegally** *adv*.—**illegality** *n*.

illegal character *n* (*comput*) a character that is not recognized by a command-driven operating system (*see* **event-driven program**) in a particular situation.

illegible *adj* impossible to read.—**illegibility, illegibleness** *n*. —**illegibly** *adv*.

illegitimate *adj* born of parents not married to each other; contrary to law, rules, or logic.—**illegitimacy, illegitimateness** *n*. —**illegitimately** *adv*.

ill-fated *adj* unlucky.

ill-favored, ill-favoured *adj* unattractive; unpleasant.

ill-founded *adj* not based on reliable facts; unsubstantiated.

ill-gotten *adj* illegally or dishonestly acquired.

ill-humored, ill-humoured *adj* bad tempered; sullen.—**ill-humor, ill humour** *n*.

illiberal *adj* narrow-minded; mean.—**illiberality, illiberalness** *n*.—**illiberally** *adv*.

illicit *adj* improper; unlawful.—**illicitly** *adv*.

illimitable *adj* limitless, infinite.—**illimitability** *n*.

Illinois (IL) *n* a state of the United States of America (USA) of which the capital is Springfield.

illiterate *adj* uneducated, esp not knowing how to read or write. * *n* an illiterate person.—**illiteracy** *n*. —**illiterately** *adv*.

ill-mannered *adj* rude.

Illmo. *abbr* = illustrissimo.

ill-natured *adj* spiteful.

illness *n* a state of ill-health; sickness.

illogical *adj* not logical or reasonable.—**illogicality, illogicalness** *n*. —**illogically** *adv*.

ills. *abbr* = illustrations.

ill-starred *adj* unlucky.

ill-timed *adj* occurring or done at an unsuitable time.

ill-treat *vt* to treat unkindly, unfairly, etc.—**ill-treatment** *n*.

illume *vt* (*poet*) to light up, illuminate.

illuminant *n* a substance or device that illuminates.

illuminate *vt* to give light to; to light up; to make clear; to inform; to decorate as with gold or lights.—**illumination** *n*. —**illuminative** *adj*.—**illuminator** *n*.

illuminated gospels *npl* gospels painstakingly decorated by Celtic monks over a long period of time, using natural pigments on velum. The three finest extant examples are respectively the Book of Kells and the gospel books of Lindisfarne and Durrow.

illuminati *npl* (*sing* **illuminato**) a name given to persons professing special spiritual or intellectual enlightenment.

illumination *n* a supply of light; the act of illuminating; the state of being illuminated; (*Brit, esp pl*) decorative colored lights used in public places.

illumine *vt* (*poet*) to illuminate.

illuminism *n* the belief in and profession of special spiritual and intellectual enlightenment.

illus. *or* **illust.** *abbr* = illustrated; illustration.

ill-usage *n* ill-use, abuse.

ill-use *vt* to treat badly, etc. * *n* abuse.

illusion *n* a false idea or conception; an unreal or misleading image or appearance.—**illusional, illusionary** *adj*.

illusionism *n* (*philos*) a disbelief in objective existence.

illusionist *n* a magician or conjuror.—**illusionism** *n*.

illusory, illusive *adj* deceptive; based on illusion.—**illusorily** *adv*.—**illusoriness** *n*.

illustrate *vt* to explain, as by examples; to provide (books, etc) with explanatory pictures, charts, etc; to serve as an example.—**illustratable** *adj*.—**illustrative** *adj*.—**illustrator** *n*.

illustration *n* the act of illustrating; the state of being illustrated; an example that explains or corroborates; a picture or diagram in a book, etc.—**illustrational** *adj*.

illustrious *adj* distinguished, famous. —**illustriousness** *n*.

ill-will *n* antagonism, hostility.

Illyria, Illyricum *n* a ancient name of a large area of country on the east side of the Adriatic, the ancient Illyrians being the ancestors of the modern Albanians.

ILMB *abbr* = Irish Livestock and Meat Board.

ILN *abbr* (*Brit*) = Illustrated London News.

ilo *abbr* = in lieu of.

ILO *abbr* = International Labor Organization.

"I Love New York" *n* the song of the American state, New York.

"I Love You California" *n* the official song of the American state, California.

ILP *abbr* = Independent Labor Party.

ILPH *abbr* = International League for the Protection of Horses.

ILR *abbr* = independent local radio.

ILRI *abbr* = International Institute for Land Reclamation and Improvement (Netherlands).

ILS *abbr* = Incorporated Law Society; Industrial Locomotive Society; International Latitude Service; International Lilac Society; International Lunar Society; Irish Literary Society; instrument landing system.

ILTTA *abbr* = International Light Tackle Tournament Association.

Ilus *n* (*Greek myth*) a king of Troy who gave his name to Ilium.

ILW *abbr* = intermediate-level waste.

ILWC *abbr* = International League of Women Composers.

Ilyushin, Sergei Vladimirovich (1894–1977) Russian aircraft designer. He designed many planes, notably bombers and passenger aircraft.

ILZSG *abbr* = International Lead and Zinc Study Group.

I'm = I am.

IM *abbr* = Institute of Metals; International Master (chess); International Missions; intramuscular/ly.

IMA *abbr* = Independent Midwives Association; Indonesian Mining Association; Industrial Marketing Association; International Magnesium Association; International Military Archives; International Mohair Association; International Music Association; Irish Medical Association.

image *n* a representation of a person or thing; the visual impression of something in a lens, mirror, etc; a copy; a likeness; a mental picture; the concept of a person, product, etc held by the public at large. * *vt* to make a representation of; to reflect; to imagine.

Image *n* Selwyn (1849–1930) British priest-turned-designer who formed the Century Guild with Arthur **Mackmurdo**.

image enhancement *n* (*comput*) the improvement of a graphics image.

image intensifier *n* any device whereby a faint received image can be made more visible or intensified.

image processing *n* (*comput*) any process that relates to manipulation of images from the initial digitizing to manipulating, saving, and printing the image.

imagery *n* (*pl* **imageries**) the work of the imagination; mental pictures; figures of speech; images in general or collectively.

image setter *n* (*comput*) a high quality, professional grade typesetting machine that creates images at resolutions of 1200 dots per inch or more.

imaginable *adj* able to be imagined.—**imaginably** *adv*.

imaginal *adj* pertaining to an image; pertaining to an imago.

imaginary *adj* existing only in the imagination.—**imaginarily** *adv*.

imagination *n* the image-forming power of the mind, or the power of the mind that modifies the conceptions, esp the higher form of this power exercised in art and poetry; creative ability; resourcefulness in overcoming practical difficulties, etc.

imaginative *adj* having or showing imagination; produced by imagination.—**imaginatively** *adv*.

imagine *vt* to form a mental image of; to believe falsely; (*inf*) to suppose; to guess. * *vi* to employ the imagination.—**imaginer** *n*.

imagism *n* a poetry movement of the early 20th century that advocated using everyday language and precise representation of the image of the subject discussed.

imagist *n* a member of a group of the poetry movement of imagism.

imago *n* (*pl* **imagoes, imagines**) an insect in its fully developed state; an idealized mental image of oneself or another.

imam *n* a leader of prayer in a mosque; a title given to various Muslim religious leaders.

imamate *n* a region controlled by an imam; the rank or term of office of an imam.

IMarE *abbr* = Institute of Marine Engineers.

imaret *n* a hostel in Turkey giving accommodation to pilgrims or travelers.

Imarsat International Maritime Satellite Organization.

IMAS *abbr* = International Marine and Shipping Conference.

IMASA *abbr* = Irish Match Angling and Surfcasting Association.

IMB *abbr* = Institute of Marine Biology.

IMBA *abbr* = Irish-Mexican Business Association.

imbalance *n* a lack of balance, as in proportion, emphasis, etc.

imbas forosnai *n* (*Irish Celtic myth*) a rite based on the fact that knowledge and sagacity could be imparted to someone who chewed the raw flesh of the thumb.

imbecile *n* an adult with a mental age of a three- to eight-year-old child; an idiotic person. * *adj* stupid or foolish.

imbecility *n* (*pl* **imbecilities**) mental or physical weakness.

imbed *vt* (**imbedding, imbedded**) to embed.

IMBEX *abbr* = International Mens and Boys Exhibition.

imbibe *vti* to drink, esp alcoholic liquor; to absorb mentally.—**imbiber** *n*.

imbibition *n* (*chem*) the process of a gel or solid absorbing a liquid; (*photog*) the process, used in color printing, of using gelatine to absorb dyes.

Imbolc *or* **Imbolg** *n* one of the four Celtic festivals (the others being Samhain, Beltane and Lughnasadh). It was celebrated on 1 February. It is associated with the lactation of ewes. The festival was also associated with the Irish goddess Brigid and is her feast day.

imbricate, imbricated *adj* (*tiles, leaves*) overlapping.—**imbrication** *n*.

Imbrium basin *or* **Mare Imbrium** (the sea of showers) *n* the site of an enormous impact crater, the largest on the Moon.

imbroglio *n* (*pl* **imbroglios**) a complicated, confusing situation; a confused misunderstanding.

imbrue *vt* (**imbruing, imbrued**) to wet or moisten; to soak; to drench, esp in blood.—*also* **embrue**.

IMC *abbr* = Institute of Measurement and Control; Institute of Motorcycling; International Mailbag Club; International Materials Conference; International Meteorological Committee; Irish Manuscripts Commission.

IMCO *abbr* = Intergovernmental Maritime Consultative Organization.

IMCoS *abbr* = International Map Collectors Society.

IMDA *abbr* = International Magic Dealers Association.

IME *abbr* = Institute of Medical Ethics.

IMechE *abbr* = Institute of Mechanical Engineers.

IMet *abbr* = Institute of Metals.

IMF *abbr* = International Monetary Fund.

Imgrand *n* **Max** (1908–69) French glass designer who was responsible for the illuminated glass fountain at the Rond Point, Avenue des Champs-Elysées, Paris.

IMH *abbr* = International Medical Help.

Imhotep *n* (*Egypt*) the vizier of the Third-Dynasty Pharaoh Djoser, credited with commissioning the first pyramid, the Step Pyramid at Saqqara.

IMI *abbr* = Imperial Metal Industries; Institute of Medical Illustrators; Institute of the Motor Industry.

IMinE *abbr* = Institution of Mining Engineers.

imit. *abbr* = imitative.

imitable *adj* able to be imitated.—**imitability, imitableness** *n*.

imitate *vt* to try to follow as a pattern or model; to mimic humorously, impersonate; to copy, reproduce.—**imitator** *n*.

imitation[1] *n* an act or instance of imitating; a copy; an act of mimicking or impersonation.—**imitational** *adj*.

imitation[2] *n* (*mus*) a device in counterpoint whereby a phrase is sung successively by different voices.

imitative *adj* imitating or inclined to imitate; characterized by imitation; copying an original, esp something superior.

IMLA *abbr* = International Maritime Lecturers Association.

IMLS *abbr* = Institute of Museum and Library Science.

IMM *abbr* = Institute of Massage and Movement; Institute of Master Mariners (Eire); Institution of Mining and Metallurgy.

immaculate *adj* spotless; flawless; pure, morally unblemished.—**immaculacy, immaculateness** *n*. —**immaculately** *adv*.

Immaculate Conception *n* (*RC Church*) the doctrine that the Virgin Mary was conceived without original sin.

immanent *adj* (*qualities*) inherent; (*God*) pervading the universe.—**immanence, immanency** *n*.

Immanuel *n* (*Bible*) alternative spelling of **Emmanuel**.

immaterial *adj* spiritual as opposed to physical; unimportant.—**immateriality, immaterialness** *n*.

immaterialism *n* (*philos*) the doctrine that matter has no existence independent of the mind.—**immaterialist** *n*.

immaterialize *vt* to make immaterial.

immature *adj* not mature.—**immaturity, immatureness** *n*.

immeasurable *adj* not able to be measured; immense, limitless.—**immeasurably** *adv*.

immediate *adj* acting or occurring without delay; next, nearest, without intervening agency; next in relationship; in close proximity, near to; directly concerning or touching a person or thing.—**immediacy, immediateness** *n*.

immediately *adv* without delay; directly; near, close by. * *conj* as soon as.

immemorial *adj* existing in the distant past, beyond the reach of memory.—**immemorially** *adv*.

immense *adj* very large in size or extent; limitless; (*inf*) excellent.—**immensely** *adv*.

immensity *n* (*pl* **immensities**) the character of being immense; immeasurableness; infinite space; vastness in extent or bulk.

immensurable *adj* immeasurable.

immerse *vt* to plunge into a liquid; to absorb or engross; to baptize by total submergence.—**immersible** *adj*.

immersion *n* the act of immersing; the state of being immersed; baptism by dipping the whole person into water; (*astron*) a phase in an eclipse when the eclipsed body is entering the shadow.

immesh *see* **enmesh**.

immethodical *adj* without method or order.

immigrant *n* a person who immigrates; a person recently settled in a country but not born there.

immigrate *vi* to come into a new country, esp to settle permanently.—**immigration** *n*. —**immigrator** *n*. —**immigratory** *adj*.

imminent *adj* about to happen; impending.—**imminence** *n*. —**imminently** *adv*.

immiscible *adj* incapable of being mixed.—**immiscbility** *n*.

immobile *adj* not able to be moved; motionless.—**immobility** *n*.

immobilize *vt* to make immobile.—**immobilization** *n*.

immoderate *adj* excessive, unrestrained.—**immoderately** *adv*.—**immoderation, immoderateness** *n*.

immodest *adj* lacking in modesty or decency.—**immodestly** *adv*.—**immodesty** *n*.

immolate *vt* to kill as a sacrifice.—**immolation** *n*. —**immolator** *n*.

immoral *adj* against accepted standards of proper behavior; sexually degenerate; corrupt; wicked.—**immorally** *adv*.

immorality *n* (*pl* **immoralities**) the quality of being immoral; an immoral act or practice.

immortal *adj* living for ever; enduring; having lasting fame. * *n* an immortal being or person; (*pl*) the gods of classical mythology.—**immortality** *n*. —**immortally** *adv*.

immortalize *vt* to render immortal; to bestow lasting fame upon.—**immortalization** *n*.

immortelle *n* a type of flower that retains its color when dried.

immotile *adj* (*biol*) not motile.— **immotility** *n*.

immovable *adj* firmly fixed; impassive, unyielding; (*property*) land, buildings, etc.—**immovability, immovableness** *n*. —**immovably** *adv*.

immram *n* the name given to the two main classifications of ancient Irish literature, the other being echtrai. Immram referred to a tale concerning a long voyage, usu a fantastic voyage to an island kingdom. The echtrai referred to a tale involving a journey made to a supernatural land either by crossing many tracts of water or by gaining entrance through a sidh or burial mound.

IMMRAN *abbr* = International Meeting of Marine Radio Aids to Navigation.

immune *adj* not susceptible to a specified disease through inoculation or natural resistance; conferring immunity; exempt from a certain obligation, tax, duty, etc.

immune gamma globulin *see* **gamma globulin**.

immune system *n* (*biol*) the natural defense system in the body of a vertebrate animal that helps to protect it against diseases caused by micro-organisms and parasites.

immunity *n* (*pl* **immunities**) the state of being immune.

immunize *vt* to make immune, esp against infection.—**immunization** *n*.

immuno- *prefix* immunity.

immunoglobulin *n* (*biol*) a protein, called an antibody, that is produced by special cells in the blood called B cells.

immunology *n* the branch of medical science dealing with immunity to disease.—**immunologic, immunological** *adj*.—**immunologist** *n*.

immunosuppression *n* the use of drugs (immuno-suppressives) that affect the body's immune system and lower its resistance to disease.

immunotherapy *n* the technique of developing the body's immunity to a disease by administering drugs or gradually increasing doses of the appropriate allergens, thereby modifying the immune response.

immure *vt* to enclose within walls; to shut up (in prison), confine.

immutable *adj* not capable of change; unalterable.—**immutability, immutableness** *n*. —**immutably** *adv*.

IMO *abbr* = International Maritime Organization; International Mennonite Organization; International Meteorological Organization; International Miners' Organization.

imp *n* a mischievous child; a little devil.

imp. *abbr* = imparted; imperative; imperfect; imperial; import, *or* imports; imported; importer; (*Latin*) *imprimatur*, "let it be printed"; imprimis (*geneal*); imprint.

Imp. *abbr* (*Latin*) = *Imperatrix*, "Empress"; *Imperator*, "Emperor."

IMPA *abbr* = International Maritime Pilots Association; International Master Printers Association; International Motor Press Association; International Myopia Prevention Association.

impact *n* violent contact; a shocking effect; the force of a body colliding with another. * *vt* to force tightly together. * *vi* to hit with force.—**impaction** *n*.

impact day *n* the day on which the terms of a new shares issue is announced.

impact printer *n* (*comput*) a printer that relies on contact with the paper and an ink ribbon to imprint the character.

impacted *adj* (*tooth*) unable to emerge through the gum because of an obstruction, esp proximity to another tooth; (*medical*) a descriptive term for things being locked or wedged together, or stuck in position.

impair *vt* to make worse, less, etc.—**impairer** *n*. —**impairment** *n*.

impala *n* (*pl* **impalas, impala**) a type of African antelope.

impale *vt* to fix on, or pierce through, with something pointed.—**impalement** *n*. —**impaler** *n*.

impalpable *adj* not able to be sensed by touch; difficult to apprehend or grasp with the mind.—**impalpability** *n*. —**impalpably** *adv*.

impanel *see* **empanel**.

imparity *n* (*pl* **imparities**) inequality; disproportion; disparity.

impart *vt* to give, convey; to reveal, disclose.—**imparter** *n*.

impartial *adj* not favoring one side more than another, unbiased.—**impartiality, impartialness** *n*. —**impartially** *adv*.

impartible *adj* (*law*) which cannot be partitioned.

impassable *adj* (*roads, etc*) incapable of being traveled through or over.—**impassability, impassableness** *n*. —**impassably** *adv*.

I

impasse *n* a situation from which there is no escape; a deadlock.

impassioned *adj* passionate; ardent.—**impassionedly** *adv*.

impassive *adj* not feeling or showing emotion; imperturbable.—**impassively** *adv*.—**impassiveness, impassivity** *n*.

impaste *vt* (*art*) to paint (onto canvas) in thick layers.—**impastation** *n*.

impasto *n* (*art*) the effect produced by applying thick layers of paint to a canvas; the technique of applying paint in thick layers.

impatiens *n* (*pl* **impatiens**) one of a genus of plants of this name, including balsam and touch-me-not.

impatient *adj* lacking patience; intolerant of delay, etc; restless.—**impatience** *n*.—**impatiently** *adv*.

impeach *vt* to question a person's honesty; to try (a public official) on a charge of wrongdoing.—**impeachable** *adj*.—**impeacher** *n*.—**impeachment** *n*.

impearl *vt* (*arch*) to adorn with pearls; to make like pearls.

impeccable *adj* without defect or error; faultless.—**impeccability** *n*.—**impeccably** *adv*.

impecunious *adj* having little or no money.—**impecuniousness, impecuniosity** *n*.

impedance *n* the total resistance in an electric circuit to the flow of alternating current.

impede *vt* to obstruct or hinder the progress of.—**impeder** *n*.—**impedingly** *adv*.

impediment *n* something that impedes; an obstruction; a physical defect, as a stammer that prevents fluency of speech.—**impedimental** *adj*.

impedimenta *npl* heavy items of baggage, esp military equipment.

impel *vt* (**impelling, impelled**) to urge or force into doing something; to propel.—**impeller** *n*.

impend *vi* to be imminent; to threaten.—**impending** *adj*.

impenetrable *adj* unable to be pierced or penetrated; incomprehensible; unable to be seen through.—**impenetrability** *n*.—**impenetrably** *adv*.

impenitent *adj* not sorry or feeling guilty; unrepentant.—**impenitence, impenitency** *n*.

imper. *abbr* = imperative.

imperative *adj* urgent, pressing; authoritative; obligatory; designating or of the mood of a verb that expresses a command, entreaty, etc. * *n* a command; (*gram*) the imperative mood of a verb.

imperator *n* (*ancient Rome*) a commander-in-chief; a title given to a victorious general; a title given to the head of state.

imperceptible *adj* not able to be detected by the mind or senses; slight, minute, gradual.—**imperceptibility** *n*.—**imperceptibly** *adv*.

impercipient *adj* lacking perception.

imperf. *abbr* = imperfect; imperforate.

imperfect *adj* having faults, flaws, mistakes, etc; defective; incomplete; (*gram*) designating a verb tense that indicates a past action or state as incomplete or continuous. * (*gram*) an imperfect tense.

imperfection *n* the state or quality of being imperfect; a defect, fault.

imperforate *adj* not perforated; (*anat*) without the normal opening.

imperial *adj* of an empire, emperor, or empress; majestic; of great size or superior quality; of the British non-metric system of weights and measures.—**imperially** *adv*.

imperialism *n* the policy of forming and maintaining an empire, as by subjugating territories, establishing colonies, etc.—**imperialist** *n*.—**imperialistic** *adj*.—**imperialistically** *adv*.

imperial system *n* a non-metric system of weights and measures established by statute in Britain.

imperil *vt* (**imperiling, imperiled** *or* **imperilling, imperilled**) to put in peril, to endanger.

imperioso *adv* (*mus*) (*Italian*) "imperiously."

imperious *adj* tyrannical; arrogant.—**imperiously** *adv*

imperishable *adj* indestructible, not subject to decay; permanently enduring.—**imperishability** *n*.

imperium *n* (*pl* **imperia**) supreme power; an empire.

impermanent *adj* not permanent.—**impermanence, impermanency** *n*.

impermeable *adj* not allowing fluids to pass through; impervious.—**impermeability** *n*.

impermissible *adj* not permissible.

impers. *abbr* = impersonal.

impersonal *adj* not referring to any particular person; cold, unfeeling; not existing as a person; (*verb*) occurring only in the third person singular, usu with "it" as subject.—**impersonality** *n*.—**impersonally** *adv*.

impersonate *vt* to assume the role of another person as entertainment or for fraud.—**impersonation** *n*.—**impersonator** *n*.

impertinent *adj* impudent; insolent; irrelevant.—**impertinence** *n*.—**impertinently** *adv*.

imperturbable *adj* not easily disturbed; calm; impassive.—**imperturbability** *n*.—**imperturbably** *adv*.—**imperturbation** *n*.

impervious *adj* incapable of being penetrated, as by water; not readily receptive (to) or affected (by).

impetigo *n* (*pl* **impetigos**) a contagious bacterial skin disease.—**impetiginous** *adj*.

impetrate *vt* to obtain by supplication, esp by prayer.—**impetration** *n*.

impetuoso *adv* (*mus*) (*Italian*) "impetuously."

impetuous *adj* acting or done suddenly with impulsive energy.—**impetuosity** *n*.—**impetuously** *adv*.

impetus *n* (*pl* **impetuses**) the force with which a body moves against resistance; driving force or motive.

impf. *abbr* = imperfect.

imp. gal. *abbr* = imperial gallon.

impiety *n* (*pl* **impieties**) want of piety; ungodliness; an act of irreverence or wickedness.

impinge *vi* (*with* **on, upon**) to have an impact; to encroach.—**impingement** *n*.—**impinger** *n*.

impious *adj* showing lack of reverence; wicked.—**impiously** *adv*.

impish *adj* of or like an imp.—**impishly** *adv*.—**impishness** *n*.

implacable *adj* not able to be appeased or pacified; inflexible, inexorable.—**implacability** *n*.—**implacably** *adv*.

implant *vt* to plant firmly; to fix (ideas, etc) firmly in the mind. * *n* something implanted in tissue surgically.—**implantation** *n*.—**implanter** *n*.

implantation[1] *n* the placing of an implant.

implantation[2] *n* (*medical*) the attachment of the blastocyst to the uterus wall during the very early stages of embryo development.

implausible *adj* not plausible.—**implausibility** *n*.—**implausibly** *adv*.

implead *vt* to sue, prosecute.

implement *n* something used in a given activity. * *vt* to carry out, put into effect.—**implemental** *adj*.—**implementation** *n*.—**implementer, implementor** *n*.

implicate *vt* to show to have a part, esp in a crime; to imply.—**implicative** *adj*.

implication *n* an implicating or being implicated; that which is implied; an inference not expressed but understood; deduction.

implicit *adj* implied rather than stated explicitly; unquestioning, absolute.—**implicitly** *adv*.—**implicitness, implicity** *n*.

implied terms *npl* the conditions of a contract that are not explicitly stated but are implicit, for example because the conditions are part of common law.

implode *vi* to collapse inwards.

implore *vt* to request earnestly; to plead, entreat.—**imploration** *n*.—**implorer** *n*.—**imploringly** *adv*.

imply *vt* (**implying, implied**) to hint, suggest indirectly; to indicate or involve as a consequence.

impolite *adj* not polite, rude.—**impolitely** *adv*.—**impoliteness** *n*.

impolitic *adj* contrary to good policy; unwise; injudicious; indiscreet.—**impoliticly** *adv*.

imponderable *adj* not able to be weighed or measured. * *n* something difficult to measure or assess.—**imponderability** *n*.—**imponderably** *adv*.

imponente *adj, adv* (*mus*) (*Italian*) "emphatic and pompous."

import[1] *vt* to bring (goods) in from a foreign country for sale or use; to mean; to signify. * *vi* to be of importance, to matter. * *n* something imported; meaning; importance.—**importable** *adj*.—**importer** *n*.

import[2] *vti* (*comput*) to open a file that has been created in one application in another application.

importance *n* the quality of being important; a high place in public estimation; high self-esteem.

important *adj* having great significance or consequence; (*person*) having power, authority, etc.—**importantly** *adv*.

importation *n* the act or business of importing; imported goods.

import deposit *n* a sum of money that is paid by an importer to the relevant government when goods arrive in a country prior to their sale.

import duty *n* a tax that is levied by a government on imported products.

imports *n* goods or services that are purchased from another country.

import surcharge *n* an extra tax that is imposed by a government on certain imports in addition to the usual import duty.

importunate *adj* persistent in asking or demanding.

importune *vt* to ask urgently and repeatedly.—**importuner** *n*.—**importuning** *n*.

importunity *n* (*pl* **importunities**) persistent solicitation or demand; incessant insistence; urgency.

impose *vt* to put (a burden, tax, punishment) on or upon; to force (oneself) on others; to lay pages of type or film and secure them. * *vi* (*with* **on** *or* **upon**) to take advantage of; to cheat or defraud.—**imposable** *adj*.—**imposer** *n*.

imposing *adj* impressive because of size, appearance, dignity, etc.—**imposingly** *adv*.

imposition *n* the act of imposing; something imposed, as a tax; an unfair burden; (*print*) the arrangement of pages of type or film in the correct order.

impossibility *n* (*pl* **impossibilities**) the character of being impossible; that which cannot be, or be supposed to be, done.

impossible *adj* not capable of existing, being done, or happening; (*inf*) unendurable, outrageous.—**impossibly** *adv*.

impost *n* a tax or duty, esp imposed by customs.

impostor, imposter *n* a person who acts fraudulently by impersonating another.

imposture *n* a fraud, deception.

impotent *adj* lacking in necessary strength, powerless; (*man*) unable to engage in sexual intercourse.—**impotence, impotency** *n*.—**impotently** *adv*.

impound *vt* to take legal possession of; to shut up (an animal) in a pound.—**impoundage, impoundment** *n*.—**impounder** *n*.

impoverish *vt* to make poor; to deprive of strength.—**impoverishment** *n*.

impr. *abbr* = improved.

impracticable *adj* not able to be carried out, not feasible.—**impracticability** *n.* —**impracticably** *adv.*

impractical *adj* not practical; not competent in practical skills.—**impracticality** *n.* —**impractically** *adv.*

imprecate *vti* to invoke evil (on); to curse or utter curses.—**imprecatory** *adv.*

imprecation *n* a curse.

imprecise *adj* not precise; ill-defined.—**imprecisely** *adv.*—**imprecision** *n.*

impregnable, impregnatable *adj* secure against attack, unyielding.—**impregnability** *n.* —**impregnably** *adv.*

impregnate *vt* to cause to become pregnant, to fertilize; to saturate, soak (with); to imbue, pervade.—**impregnation** *n.* —**impregnator** *n.*

impresario *n* (*pl* **impresarios**) the manager of an opera, a concert series, etc.

impress[1] *vt* to make a strong, usu favorable, impression on; to fix deeply in the mind; to stamp with a mark; to imprint. * *n* an imprint.—**impresser** *n.* —**impressible** *adj.*

impress[2] *vt* to coerce into military service.—**impressment** *n.*

Impressed Ware *n* (*archeo*) a form of pottery covered with an impressed form of ornamentation that has been found in the coastal areas of the western Mediterranean.

impression *n* the effect produced in the mind by an experience; a mark produced by imprinting; a vague idea, notion; the act of impressing or being impressed; a notable or strong influence on the mind or senses; the number of copies of a book printed at one go (—*also* **printing**); an impersonation or act of mimicry.—**impressional** *adj.*

impressionable *n* easily impressed or influenced.—**impressionability** *n.* —**impressionably** *adv.*

impressionism *n* painting, writing, etc in which objects are painted or described so as to reproduce only their general effect or impression without selection or elaboration of details; (*mus*) by analogy, atmospheric music, such as the music of Debussy and Ravel.—**impressionist** *adj, n.* —**impressionistic** *adj.*

impressive *adj* tending to impress the mind or emotions; arousing wonder or admiration.—**impressiveness** *n.*

impressment *n* the act of seizing (things) for public use or conscripting (people) into public service.

imprest *n* a sum of money advanced.

imprimatur *n* permission or license to publish a book, etc; an authoritative mark of approval; sanction.

imprint *vt* to stamp or impress a mark on, etc; to fix firmly in the mind. * *n* a mark made by imprinting; a lasting effect; a note in a book giving the facts of publication.—**imprinter** *n.*

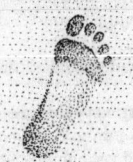

imprison *vt* to put in a prison; to confine, as in a prison.—**imprisoner** *n.* —**imprisonment** *n.*

improbable *adj* unlikely to be true or to happen.—**improbability** *n.* —**improbably** *adv.*

improbity *n* (*pl* **improbities**) wickedness, dishonesty.

impromptu *adj, adv* unrehearsed, unprepared. * *n* something impromptu, as a speech. * *n* (*mus*) a type of piano music that sounds as if it has been improvised.—*also* **adj.**

improper *adj* lacking propriety, indecent; incorrect; not suitable or appropriate.—**improperly** *adv.*

improper fraction *n* a fraction in which the numerator is greater than or equal to the denominator, as 4/3.

impropriety *n* (*pl* **improprieties**) the quality of being improper; indecency; an improper act, etc.

improve *vt* to make or become better.—**improvable** *adj.*—**improver** *n.* —**improvingly** *adj.*

improvement *n* the act of improving or being improved; an alteration that improves or adds to the value of something.

improvident *adj* lacking foresight or thrift; wanting care to provide for the future; careless.—**improvidence** *n.*

improvisation *n* the act of improvising; the act of composing poetry, music, etc, extemporaneously; an impromptu.—**improvisational** *adj.*

improvise *vti* to compose, perform, recite, etc without preparation; to make or do with whatever is at hand.—**improviser** *n.*

imprudent *adj* rash, lacking discretion; unwise.—**imprudence** *n.* —**imprudently** *adv.*

impudent *adj* disrespectfully bold; impertinent.—**impudence** *n.* —**impudently** *adv.*

impugn *vt* to oppose or challenge as false; to discredit.—**impugnation, impugnent** *n.* —**impugner** *n.*

impuissant *adj* powerless, weak.—**impuissance** *n.*

impulse *n* a sudden push or thrust; a stimulus transmitted through a nerve or a muscle; a sudden instinctive urge to act.

impulse buying *n* the purchase of a product by a consumer on impulse rather than because of planned intention.

impulsion *n* the act of impelling; the state of being impelled; impetus; an irrational urge, compulsion.

impulsive *adj* tending to act on impulse; forceful, impelling; acting momentarily.—**impulsively** *adv.*—**impulsiveness** *n.*

impunity *n* (*pl* **impunities**) exemption or freedom from punishment or harm.

impure *adj* unclean; adulterated.

impurity *n* (*pl* **impurities**) a being impure; an impure substance or constituent.

impute *vt* to attribute (esp a fault or misbehavior) to another.—**imputable** *adj.*—**imputation** *n.* —**imputative** *adj.*—**imputer** *n.*

imputed cost *n* a cost that is not actually incurred by a company but that is allowed for in management accounting records so that the costs that are incurred by operations that are not similar in all respects can be compared.

impv. *abbr* = imperative.

IMR *abbr* = infant mortality rate.

IMRA *abbr* = Irish Mountain Rescue Association.

IMRO *abbr* = Investment Management Regulatory Organization.

IMS *abbr* = Information Management System; Institute of Management Services; Institute of Museum Services; Institute on Man and Science; International Meditation Society; International Mountain Society; International Multihull Society.

IMU *abbr* = International Mathematical Union.

IMunE *abbr* = Institution of Municipal Engineers.

in *prep* inside; within; at; as contained by; during; at the end of; not beyond; affected by; being a member of; wearing; using; because of; into. * *adv* to or at a certain place; so as to be contained by a certain space, condition, etc; (*games*) batting, in play. * *adj* that is in power; inner; inside; gathered, counted, etc; (*inf*) currently smart, fashionable, etc.

In *symbol* (*chem*) indium.

in or **in.** *abbr* = inch (Imperial unit of length equal to 2.54 cm).

INA *abbr* = Institution of Naval Architects.

inability *n* (*pl* **inabilities**) lack of ability.

in absentia *adv* in the absence of.

inaccessible *adj* not accessible, unapproachable.—**inaccessibility** *n.* —**inaccessibly** *adv.*

inaccurate *adj* not accurate, imprecise.—**inaccuracy** *n.* —**inaccurately** *adv.*

Inachus the chief river of Argos, often personified as a god in Greek mythology.

inaction *n* idleness, inertia.

inactivate *vt* to make inactive.— **inactivation** *n.*

inactive *adj* not active.—**inactively** *adv.*—**inactivity** *n.*

inadequate *adj* not adequate; not capable.— **inadequacy** *n.* —**inadequately** *adv.*

inadmissible *adj* not admissible, esp as evidence.—**inadmissibility** *n.* —**inadmissibly** *adv.*

inadvertent *adj* not attentive or observant, careless; due to oversight.—**inadvertence, inadvertency** *n.* —**inadvertently** *adv.*

inadvisable *adj* not advisable; inexpedient.—**inadvisability** *n.* —**inadvisably** *adv.*

inalienable *adj* that cannot or should not be surrendered or transferred to another.—**inalienability** *n.* —**inalienably** *adv.*

in alt *see* alt.

inalterable *adj* unalterable.—**inalterability** *n.*

inamorata *n* (*pl* **inamoratas**) a woman with whom one is in love; a sweetheart.

inamorato *n* (*pl* **inamoratos**) a man who is in love, a lover.

inane *adj* lacking sense, silly.—**inanely** *adv.*

inanimate *adj* not animate; showing no signs of life; dull.—**inanimately** *adv.*—**inanimateness, inanimation** *n.*

inanition *n* emptiness; exhaustion from lack of nourishment.

inanity *n* (*pl* **inanities**) (*arch*) emptiness; silliness; frivolity; a silly action or remark.

inapplicable *adj* not applicable.—**inapplicability** *n.*

inapposite *adj* not apposite, unsuitable.—**inappositely** *adv.*

inappreciable *adj* not to be appreciated or estimated; of no consequence.

inappreciative *adj* unappreciative.

inapproachable *adj* not approachable, inaccessible.

inappropriate *adj* unsuitable.—**inappropriately** *adv.*—**inappropriateness** *n.*

inapt *adj* inappropriate; unfit, unskillful.—**inaptitude** *n.*

inarticulate *adj* not expressed in words; incapable of being expressed in words; incapable of coherent or effective expression of ideas, feelings, etc.—**inarticulately** *adv.*

inartistic *adj* not artistic; not appreciative of art.—**inartistically** *adv.*

inasmuch *adv* in like degree; (*with* **as**) seeing that; because.

inattentive *adj* not attending; neglectful.—**inattention** *n.*

inaudible *adj* unable to be heard.—**inaudibility** *n.* —**inaudibly** *adv.*

inaugural *n* of or pertaining to an inauguration; a speech made at an inauguration.

inaugurate *vt* to admit ceremonially into office; to open (a building, etc) formally to the public; to cause to begin, initiate.—**inauguration** *n.* —**inaugurator** *n.*

inauspicious *adj* ill-starred; unlucky; unfavorable; unfortunate.

inbd. *abbr* = inboard.

in between *prep* between two things.

in-between *adj* intermediate. * *n* an intermediate thing or person.

inboard *adv, adj* towards the center or within an aircraft, ship, etc.

inborn *adj* present from birth; hereditary.

inbred *adj* innate; produced by inbreeding.

inbreed *vti* (**inbreeding, inbred**) to breed by continual mating of individuals of the same or closely related stocks.

Inbucon *abbr* = International Business Consultants.

in-built *adj* built in.

inc. *abbr* = inclosure; included; including; inclusive; increase.

Inc or **Inc.** *abbr* = incorporated, esp after the names of business organizations.

INC *abbr* (*Latin*) = *in nomine Christi*, "in Christ's name."

Inca *n* (*pl* **Inca, Incas**) a member of an American Indian people of Peru before the Spanish conquest.— **Incaic, Incan** *adj*.

INCA *abbr* = Independent National Computing Association; International Committee for Andean Aid.

incalculable *adj* beyond calculation; unpredictable.—**incalculability** *n*. —**incalculably** *adv*.

incalescent *adj* (*chem*) increasing in heat.—**incalescence** *n*.

incalzando *vt* (*mus*) (*Italian*) "to press forward," i.e., to work up speed and force.

in camera *adv* in private; in a judge's chamber as opposed to open court.

incandesce *vi* to glow with heat.

incandescent *adj* glowing or luminous with intense heat.—**incandescence** *n*.

incantation *n* words chanted in magic spells or rites.—**incantational, incantatory** *adj*.

incapable *adj* lacking capability; not able or fit to perform an activity.— **incapability** *n*. —**incapably** *adv*.

incapacitate *vt* to weaken, to disable; to make ineligible.—**incapacitation** *n*.

incapacity *n* (*pl* **incapacities**) lack of power or strength, inability; ineligibility.

incarcerate *vt* to put in prison, to confine.—**incarceration** *n*. —**incarcerator** *n*.

incarnadine *adj* having the color of flesh; blood-red. * *n* the color of flesh or blood. * *vt* to make red.

incarnate *adj* endowed with a human body; personified. * *vt* to give bodily form to; to be the type or embodiment of.—**incarnation** *n*.

Incas *n* a people who established an empire in large parts of Ecuador, Peru, Bolivia, and Argentina, 1200–1572 AD.

incautious *adj* not cautious, reckless.—**incautiously** *adv*.—**incautiousness, incaution** *n*.

incendiarism *n* the act of burning illegally; arson.

incendiary *adj* pertaining to arson; (*bomb*) designed to start fires; tending to stir up or inflame. * *n* (*pl* **incendiaries**) a person that sets fire to a building, etc maliciously, an arsonist; an incendiary substance (as in a bomb); a person who stirs up violence, etc.

incense[1] *vt* to make extremely angry.

incense[2] *n* a substance that gives off a fragrant odor when burned; the fumes so produced; any pleasant odor.

incentive *n* a stimulus; a motive. * *adj* serving as a stimulus to action.

incept *vt* (*biol*) to ingest.

inception *n* the beginning of something.

inceptive *adj* noting a beginning, initial.

incertitude *n* doubt, uncertainty.

incessant *adj* never ceasing; continual, constant.—**incessancy** *n*. —**incessantly** *adv*.

incest *n* sexual intercourse between persons too closely related to marry legally.

incestuous *adj* involving incest; guilty of incest.

inch *n* a measure of length equal to $^1/_{12}$ foot (2.54 cm); a very small distance or amount. * *vti* to move very slowly, or by degrees.

inch. or **incho.** *abbr* = inchoative.

inchmeal *adv* inch by inch, gradually.

inchoate *adj* just begun; at a very early stage.—**inchoation** *n*.—**inchoative** *adj*.

incidence *n* the degree or range of occurrence or effect.

incident *adj* likely to happen as a result; falling upon or affecting. * *n* something that happens; an event, esp a minor one; a minor conflict.

incidental *adj* happening in connection with something more important; happening by chance. * *npl* miscellaneous items, minor expenses.

incidental music *n* background music for a film, play, etc.

incidentally *adv* in passing, as an aside.

incinerate *vt* to reduce to ashes.—**incineration** *n*.

incinerator *n* a furnace for burning refuse.

incipient *adj* beginning to be or appear; initial.—**incipience, incipiency** *n*.

incise *vt* to cut or carve into a surface; to engrave.—**incised** *adj*.

incision *n* incising; a cut made into something, esp by a surgeon into a body.

incisive *adj* keen, penetrating; decisive; biting.—**incisively** *adv*.—**incisiveness** *n*.

inciso *adj, adv* (*mus*) (*Italian*) "incisive," hence an instruction that a strong rhythm is required.

incisor *n* any of the front cutting teeth at the front of the mouth. *See* **tooth.**

incite *vt* to urge to action; to rouse.—**incitement** *n*. —**inciter** *n*. — **incitingly** *adv*.

incivility *n* (*pl* **incivilities**) lack of civility or courtesy; impoliteness.

incl. *abbr* = inclosure; including; inclusive.

inclement *adj* (*weather*) rough, stormy; lacking mercy; harsh.—**inclemency** *n*.

inclination *n* a propensity or disposition, esp a liking; a deviation from the horizontal or vertical; a slope; inclining or being inclined; a bending movement, a bow.— **inclinational** *adj*.

incline *vi* to lean, to slope; to be disposed towards an opinion or action. * *vt* to cause to bend (the head or body) forwards; to cause to deviate, esp from the horizontal or vertical. * *n* a slope.—**inclinable** *adj*.—**incliner** *n*.

inclined *adj* having a disposition or tendency; disposed to; having a gradient; leaning; making an angle with a line or plane.

inclinometer *n* an instrument used to measure the angle made by an aircraft with the horizontal.

include *vt* to enclose, contain; to comprise as part or a larger group, amount, etc.— **includable, includible** *adj*.—**inclusion** *n*.

inclusive *adj* comprehensive; including the limits specified.—**inclusively** *adv*.

incog. *abbr* = incognito.

incognito *adj, adv* under an assumed name or identity. * *n* (*pl* **incognitos**) a person appearing or living incognito; the name assumed by such a person.— **incognita** *nf* (*pl* **incognitas**).

incognizant *adj* (*usu with* **of**) unaware.—**incognizance** *n*.

incoherent *adj* lacking organization or clarity; inarticulate in speech or thought.— **incoherence, incoherency** *n*. —**incoherently** *adv*.

incombustible *adj* not able to be burned or ignited. * *n* an incombustible substance.—**incombustibility** *n*. —**incombustibly** *adv*.

income *n* the money etc received for labor or services, or from property, investments, etc.

income and expenditure account *nphr* an account that records the income and expenditure of an organization, such as a charity, whose main purpose is not the generation of profit.

income smoothing *n* the process undertaken by some companies of manipulating some items in their financial statements.

income tax *n* a tax levied on the net income of a person or business.

income tax allowance *n* an allowance that is deducted from a tax payer's gross income before the calculation of his or her income tax liability.

incomer *n* one who comes in; one who succeeds, as a tenant.

incoming *adj* coming; accruing. * *n* the act of coming in; that which comes in; income.

incommensurable *adj* not able to be measured or judged comparatively.— **incommensurability** *n*. —**incommensurably** *adv*.

incommensurate *adj* not commensurate; disproportionate; inadequate; incommensurable.

incommode *vt* to give inconvenience or trouble to; to disturb.— **incommodious** *adj*.

incommunicable *adj* not capable of being communicated.— **incommunicability** *n*. —**incommunicably** *adv*.

incommunicado *adj* not allowed to communicate with others.

incommunicative *adj* not disposed to give information, reserved.

incommutable *adj* which cannot be exchanged or commuted.

incomparable *adj* beyond comparison, matchless; not amenable to comparison.— **incomparability** *n*. —**incomparably** *adv*.

incompatible *adj* not able to exist together in harmony; antagonistic; inconsistent.— **incompatibility** *n*. —**incompatibly** *adv*.

incompetent *adj* lacking the necessary ability, skill, etc. * *n* an incompetent person.—**incompetence, incompetency** *n*. —**incompetently** *adv*.

incomplete *adj* unfinished; lacking a part or parts.—**incompletely** *adv*.— **incompleteness, incompletion** *n*.

incomprehensible *adj* not to be understood or grasped by the mind; inconceivable.—**incomprehensibility** *n*. —**incomprehensibly** *adv*.

incomprehension *n* failure to understand.

incompressible *adj* incapable of being reduced in volume by pressure; resisting pressure.—**incompressibility** *n*. —**incompressibly** *adv*.

incomputable *adj* incalculable, which cannot be reckoned.

inconceivable *adj* impossible to comprehend; (*inf*) unbelievable.— **inconceivably** *adv*.

inconclusive *adj* leading to no definite result; ineffective; inefficient.— **inconclusively** *adv*.—**inconclusiveness** *n*.

incondensable, incondensible *adj* which cannot be condensed or compressed.

inconformity *n* lack of conformity.

incongruity *n* (*pl* **incongruities**) unsuitableness of one thing to another, inconsistency; absurdity.

incongruous *adj* lacking harmony or agreement of parts; unsuitable; inappropriate.—**incongruously** *adv*.—**incongruousness, incongruence** *n*.

inconsequential, inconsequent *adj* not following logically; irrelevant.— **inconsequence** *n*. —**inconsequentiality** *n*. —**inconsequentially, inconsequently** *adv*.

inconsiderable *adj* trivial.—**inconsiderably** *adv*.

inconsiderate *adj* uncaring about others; thoughtless.—**inconsiderately** *adv*.— **inconsideration** *n*.

inconsistency *n* (*pl* **inconsistencies**) the quality of being inconsistent; incongruity.—**inconsistently** *adv*.

inconsistent *adj* not compatible with other facts; contradictory; irregular, fickle.

inconsolable *adj* not able to be comforted.—**inconsolability** *n*. —**inconsolably** *adv*.

inconsonant *adj* not in harmony or agreement.—**inconsonance** *n*.

inconspicuous *adj* not conspicuous.—**inconspicuously** *adv*.—**inconspicuousness** *n*.

inconstant *adj* subject to change; unstable; variable; fickle; capricious.—**inconstancy** *n*.

inconsumable *adj* which cannot be consumed or used up.

incontestable *adj* not admitting of question or doubt; incontrovertible.—**incontestability** *n*. —**incontestably** *adv*.

incontinent *adj* unable to control the excretion of bodily wastes; lacking self-restraint.—**incontinence** *n*.

incontrovertible *adj* not admitting of controversy; indisputable.—**incontrovertibility** *n*. —**incontrovertibly** *adv*.

inconvenience *n* want of convenience; unfitness; that which incommodes; disadvantage. * *vt* to put to inconvenience; to annoy.—**inconvenient** *adj*.

inconvertible *adj* incapable of being converted into or exchanged for something else.—**inconvertibility** *n*. —**inconvertibly** *adv*.

inconvincible *adj* unable or unwilling to be convinced.

incoordination *n* lack of coordination.

incor. *or* **incorp.** *abbr* = incorporated.

incorporate *vt* to combine; to include; to embody; to merge; to form into a corporation. * *vi* to unite into one group or substance; to form a corporation. * *adj* united; formed into a corporation.—**incorporation** *n*. —**incorporative** *adj*.—**incorporator** *n*.

incorporated *adj* joined in a single body; formed into a legal corporation.

incorporeal *adj* not corporeal, without substance; spiritual; (*law*) intangible, and existing only in contemplation of the law.—**incorporeally** *adv*.—**incorporeity**, **incorporeality** *n*.

incorrect *adj* faulty; inaccurate; improper.—**incorrectly** *adv*.—**incorrectness** *n*.

incorrigible *adj* not able to be corrected, reformed, or altered.—**incorrigibility** *n*. —**incorrigibly** *adv*.

incorrupt, incorrupted *adj* free from physical or moral taint; unimpaired; upright, esp above the influence of corruption or bribery; honest.

incorruptible *adj* incapable of physical corruption, decay, or dissolution; incapable of being bribed; not liable to moral perversion or contamination.—**incorruptibility** *n*. —**incorruptibly** *adv*.

Incpen *abbr* = Industry Committee for Packaging and the Environment.

incr. *abbr* = increased; increasing.

increase *vti* to make or become greater in size, quality, amount, etc. * *n* increasing or becoming increased; the result or amount by which something increases.—**increasable** *adj*.—**increaser** *n*. —**increasingly** *adv*.

increasing capital *n* an increase in the number of shares or in the value of shares in a company in order to augment the amount of its authorized share capital.

incredible *adj* unbelievable; (*inf*) wonderful.—**incredibility** *n*. —**incredibly** *adv*.

incredulity *n* skepticism; disbelief.

incredulous *adj* not able or willing to accept as true; unbelieving.—**incredulously** *adv*.—**incredulousness** *n*.

increment *n* (the amount of) an increase; an addition.—**incremental** *adj*.

incremental backup *n* (*comput*) a backup procedure that takes a copy of only the files on a disk that have been updated since the previous backup was taken. (*See also* **full backup**.)

increscent *adj* (*moon*) waxing, growing.

incriminate *vt* to involve in or indicate as involved in a crime or fault.—**incrimination** *n*. —**incriminator** *n*. —**incriminatory** *adj*.

incubation[1] *n* the act or process of incubating; the length of time for an infection to develop, from first exposure to manifestation of symptoms.—**incubational, incubative** *adj*.

incubation[2] *n* the time taken to start and grow microorganisms in culture media.

incubation[3] *n* the process of caring for and treating a premature baby in an incubator.

incubator[1] *n* the transparent box-like container in which a premature baby is kept in controlled, infection-free conditions.

incubator[2] *n* a heated container for growth of bacterial cultures in a laboratory.

incubus *n* (*pl* **incubi, incubuses**) an evil spirit believed in folklore to have intercourse with women as they sleep; something oppressive or disturbing, as a nightmare.

inculcate *vt* to teach by frequent repetition or urging.—**inculcation** *n*. —**inculcator** *n*.

inculpate *vt* to blame, censure; to incriminate.—**inculpation** *n*. —**inculpative, inculpatory** *adj*.

incumbency *n* (*pl* **incumbencies**) a duty or obligation; a term of office.

incumbent *adj* resting (on or upon) one as a duty or obligation; currently in office. * *n* the holder of an office, etc.

incunabulum *n* (*pl* **incunabula**) any book printed before 1500; the early stages of anything.—**incunabular** *adj*.

incur *vt* (**incurring, incurred**) to bring upon oneself (something undesirable).—**incurrable** *adj*.

incurable *adj* incapable of being cured; beyond the power of skill or medicine; lacking remedy; incorrigible. * *n* a person diseased beyond cure.—**incurability** *n*. —**incurably** *adv*.

incurious *adj* indifferent, heedless.—**incuriosity** *n*.

incursion *n* an invasion or raid into another's territory, etc.—**incursive** *adj*.

incurvate *vti* to curve inwards. * *adj* curved or bent inwards.—**incurvation** *n*.

incus *n* (*pl* **incudes**) a bone found in the middle ear.

incuse *n* a design stamped onto a coin.

ind *abbr* (*Latin*) = *in dies*, "each day."

ind. *abbr* = independent; index; indicative; indigo; induline; industrial.

Ind. *abbr* = India; Indian; Indiana; Indies.

IND *abbr* (*Latin*) = *in nomine Dei*, "in the name of God."

indebted *adj* in debt; obliged; owing gratitude.—**indebtedness** *n*.

indecency *n* (*pl* **indecencies**) lack of decency, modesty, or good manners; something indecent, vulgar, or obscene.

indecent *adj* offending against accepted standards of decent behavior.—**indecently** *adv*.

indecent assault *n* a sexual assault not involving rape.

indecent exposure *n* the offence of deliberately exposing one's genitals in public.

indeciduous *adj* (*bot*) not deciduous; evergreen.

indecipherable *adj* which cannot be deciphered; illegible.

indecision *n* not able to make a decision; hesitation.

indecisive *adj* inconclusive; irresolute.—**indecisively** *adv*.—**indecisiveness** *n*.

indeciso *adj* (*mus*) (*Italian*) "undecided," i.e., the pace of a piece of music can be varied according to the performer's feelings.

indecl. *abbr* = indeclinable.

indeclinable *adj* (*gram*) which cannot be declined, having no inflected forms.

indecorous *adj* violating decorum, or any accepted rule of conduct.—**indecorum** *n*.

indeed *adv* truly, certainly. * *interj* expressing irony, surprise, disbelief, etc.

indef. *abbr* = indefinite.

indefatigable *adj* tireless.—**indefatigability** *n*. —**indefatigably** *adv*.

indefeasible *adj* not to be defeated or made void, as a title.—**indefeasibility** *n*. —**indefeasibly** *adv*.

indefensible *adj* unable to be defended or justified.—**indefensibility** *n*. —**indefensibly** *adv*.

indefinable *adj* that cannot be defined.—**indefinably** *adv*.

indefinite *adj* not certain, undecided; imprecise, vague; having no fixed limits.—**indefinitely** *adv*.—**indefiniteness** *n*.

indefinite article *n* the word "a" or "an."

indefinite pronoun *n* a word, such as "any" or "some," that indicates a person, thing, quantity, etc, without being specific.

indehiscent *adj* (*bot*) not opening when mature.—**indehiscence** *n*.

indelible *adj* not able to be removed or erased; (*pen, ink, etc*) making an indelible mark.—**indelibility** *adv*.—**indelibly** *adv*.

indelicacy *n* (*pl* **indelicacies**) lack of delicacy; something offensive to modesty or refined taste.

indelicate *adj* improper; rough, crude; tactless.—**indelicately** *adv*.

indemnify *vt* (**indemnifying, indemnified**) to insure against loss, damage, etc; to repay (for damage, loss, etc).—**indemnification** *n*. —**indemnifier** *n*.

indemnity *n* (*pl* **indemnities**) compensation for damage or loss; insurance against future loss or injury.

indemonstrable *adj* which cannot be demonstrated or proved.

indent *vt* to make notches in; to begin (a line of text) farther in from the margin than the rest. * *vi* to form an indentation. * *n* a dent or notch.—**indentor** *n*.

indentation *n* a being indented; a notch, cut, inlet, etc; a dent; a spacing in from the margin (—*also* **indention, indent**).

indenture *n* a written agreement, a contract binding one person to work for another. * *vt* to bind by indentures.

independence *n* the state of being independent.

Independence Day *n* the anniversary of the adoption of the American Declaration of Independence on July 4 1776.

independency *n* (*pl* **independencies**) a self-governing political unit.

independent *adj* freedom from the influence or control of others; self-governing; self-determined; not adhering to any political party; not connected with others; not depending on another for financial support. * *n* a person who is independent in thinking, action etc.—**independently** *adv*.

independent variable *n* (*math*) a variable that may have any value, which does not depend upon the value of the other quantities present.

in-depth *adj* detailed, thorough.

indescribable *adj* unable to be described; too beautiful, horrible, intense, etc for words.—**indescribability** *n*. —**indescribably** *adv*.

indestructible *adj* not able to be destroyed.—**indestructibility** *n*. —**indestructibly** *adv*.

indeterminable *adj* which cannot be ascertained, settled, or classified.

indeterminate *adj* vague, uncertain; not defined or fixed in value; (*mus*) a term used by John Cage to describe music that does not follow a rigid notation and allows improvisation.—**indeterminacy, indetermination** *adv*.—**indeterminately** *adv*.

indeterminism *n* (*philos*) the doctrine that the will has a certain freedom, independent of motives.

index *n* (*pl* **indexes, indices**) an alphabetical list of names, subjects, items, etc mentioned in a printed book, usu listed alphabetically at the end of the text; a figure showing ratio or relative change, as of prices or wages; any indication or sign; a pointer or dial on an instrument; the exponent of a number. * *vt* to make an index of or for.—**indexer** *n*.

index arbitrage *see* **arbitrage**.

index file *n* (*comput*) a file in a database management program that keeps a list of the location of records using a pointer system.

index finger *n* the forefinger.

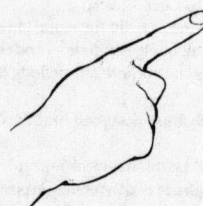

index number *n* a number showing the relative change in prices or wages in a given time with reference to a previous base period.

index-linked *adj* the term used to describe economic variables such as wages, social security benefits, etc, when these are related to a price index in some predetermined way.

India *n* a vast republic in South Asia, dominated in the extreme north by the Himalayas.

Indiaman *n* (*pl* **Indiamen**) (*formerly*) a commercial sailing vessel involved in trade with India.

Indian *n* a native of India; an American Indian, the original inhabitants of the continent of America.

Indiana (IN) *n* a state of the United States of America (USA) of which the capital is Indianapolis.

Indianapolis *n* the capital city of Indiana, a state of the USA.

Indian club *n* a bottle-shaped wooden or plastic club used by jugglers and gymnasts.

Indian corn *n* maize.

Indian file *n* single file.

Indian ink *n* a solid black pigment; a black ink made from this.—*also* **India ink**.

indiarubber *n* an elastic gummy substance obtained from the milky juice of several tropical trees and used for rubbing out pencil marks.

Indian summer *n* a period of unusually warm weather in the autumn.

indic. *abbr* = indicating; indicative; indicator.

Indic *adj* a term sometimes applied to the Indo-European languages of India, e.g., Sanskrit, Hindi, Bengali, etc.

indicant *n* something which indicates.

indicate *vt* to point out; to show or demonstrate; to be a sign or symptom of; to state briefly, suggest.—**indicatable** *adj*.—**indication** *n*. —**indicatory** *adj*.

indicative *adj* serving as a sign (of); (*gram*) denoting the mood of the verb that affirms or denies.

indicator[1] *n* a thing that indicates or points; a measuring device with a pointer, etc; an instrument showing the operating condition of a piece of machinery, etc; a device giving updated information, such as a departure board in a railway station or airport; a flashing light used to warn of a change in direction of a vehicle.

indicator[2] *n* (*chem*) a chemical substance, usu a large organic molecule, that is used to detect the presence of other chemicals in a solution.

indices *see* **index**.

indicia *npl* (*sing* **indicium**) distinguishing markings.

indict *vt* to charge with a crime; to accuse.

indictable *adj* subject to being indicted; making one liable to indictment.

indictment *n* a formal written statement framed by a prosecuting authority charging a person of a crime.

indifferent *adj* showing no concern, uninterested; unimportant; impartial; average; mediocre.—**indifference** *n*. —**indifferently** *adv*.

indifferentism *n* systematic indifference, esp with regard to religion.—**indifferentist** *n*.

indigen, indigene *n* a native (person, animal, etc).

indigenous *adj* existing naturally in a particular country, region, or environment; native.

indigent *adj* poor, needy.—**indigence** *n*.

indigestible *adj* difficult or impossible to digest.—**indigestibility** *n*.

indigestion *n* a pain caused by difficulty in digesting food. *See* **dyspepsia**.

indigestive *adj* pertaining to, or having, indigestion.

indign *adj* (*arch*) unworthy; disgraceful.

indignant *adj* expressing anger, esp at mean or unjust action.—**indignantly** *adv*.

indignation *n* anger at something regarded as unfair, wicked, etc.

indignity *n* (*pl* **indignities**) humiliation; treatment making one feel degraded, undignified.

indigo *n* (*pl* **indigos, indigoes**) a deep blue dye or color.

indirect *adj* not straight; roundabout; secondary; dishonest.—**indirectly** *adv*. **indirectness** *n*.

indirect costs *npl* costs that cannot be ascribed directly to a particular product or cost unit and thus are regarded as overheads.

indirect evidence *n* circumstantial or inferential evidence.

indirection *n* indirect means or procedure; lack of direction; deceit.

indirect labor *n* the part of a work force that is not directly involved in the manufacture of products or the provision of services. The indirect labor force includes clerical staff, cleaning staff, etc.

indirect materials *npl* materials that are not actually incorporated in a product but are a necessary part of the production process.

indirect object *n* (*gram*) a person or thing affected by a verb but less directly than the object.

indirect speech *n* reported speech.

indirect tax *n* a tax levied on goods and services (which increases prices) rather than directly on individuals or companies.

indiscernible *adj* not discernible.—**indiscernibly** *adv*.

indiscipline *n* lack of discipline.

indiscreet *adj* not discreet; tactless.—**indiscreetly** *adv*.

indiscrete *adj* not separated into distinct parts.

indiscretion *n* an indiscreet act; rashness.—**indiscretionary** *adj*.

indiscriminate *adj* not making a careful choice; confused; random; making no distinctions.—**indiscriminately** *adv*.—**indiscrimination** *n*. —**indiscriminative** *adj*.

indispensable *adj* absolutely essential.— **indispensability** *n*. —**indispensably** *adv*.

indispose *vt* to make unfit or unwell; to disincline.

indisposed *adj* ill or sick; reluctant; disinclined.

indisposition *n* disinclination; a slight illness.

indisputable *adj* unquestionable; certain.—**indisputability** *n*. —**indisputably** *adv*.

indissoluble *adj* permanent; not able to be dissolved or destroyed.—**indissolubility** *n*. —**indissolubly** *adv*.

indistinct *adj* not clearly marked; dim; not distinct.—**indistinctly** *adv*.—**indistinctness** *n*.

indistinctive *adj* not capable of making distinctions; lacking distinctive characteristics.—**indistinctiveness** *n*.

indistinguishable *adj* not distinguishable; lacking identifying characteristics.—**indistinguishability** *n*. —**indistinguishably** *adv*.

indite *vt* (*arch*) to write.

indium *n* a soft metallic element used in alloys and electronic circuitry.

individ. *abbr* = individual.

individual *adj* existing as a separate thing or being; of, by, for, or relating to a single person or thing. * *n* a single thing or being; a person.

individualist *n* a person who thinks or behaves with marked independence.—**individualism** *n*. —**individualistic** *adj*.—**individualistically** *adv*.

individuality *n* (*pl* **individualities**) the condition of being individual; separate or distinct existence; distinctive character.

individualize *vt* to mark as distinct, particularize; to distinguish individually.—**individualization** *n*.

individually *adv* in a distinctive manner; one by one; separately; personally.

individuate *vt* to individualize.—**individuation** *n*.

indivisible *adj* not divisible.—**indivisibility** *n*. —**indivisibly** *adv*.

indocile *adj* unteachable; intractable.—**indocility** *n*.

indoctrinate *vt* to systematically instruct in doctrines, ideas, beliefs, etc.—**indoctrination** *n*. —**indoctrinator** *n*.

Indo-European *adj* of a family of languages (including English) spoken in most of Europe and Asia as far east as northern India. —*also n*.

indolent *adj* idle; lazy.—**indolence** *n*. —**indolently** *adv*.

indomitable *adj* not easily discouraged or defeated.—**indomitability** *n*. —**indomitably** *adv*.

Indonesia *n* a republic made up of 13,677 islands scattered across the Indian and Pacific.

indoor *adj* done, used, or situated within a building.

indoors *adv* in or into a building.

indorse *see* **endorse**.

indraft *n* an inlet or inward current.

indrawn *adj* aloof; reserved; introspective.

indubitable *adj* not capable of being doubted.—**indubitability** *n*. —**indubitably** *adv*.

induc. *abbr* = induction.

induce *vt* to persuade; to bring on; to draw (a conclusion) from particular facts; to bring about (an electric or magnetic effect) in a body by placing it within a field of force.—**inducer** *n*. —**inducible** *adj*.

inducement *n* something that induces; a stimulus; a motive.

induct *vt* to place formally in an office, a society, etc; to enroll (esp a draftee) in the armed forces.

inductance *n* the property of an electric circuit by which an electromotive force is produced by a variation in the current in the same or a neighbouring circuit; the measure of inductance in an electric circuit.

inductile *adj* not ductile, not pliant.

induction[1] *n* the act or an instance of inducting, e.g., into office; reasoning from particular premises to general conclusions; the inducing of an electric or magnetic effect by a field of force.—**inductional** *adj*.

induction[2] *n* (*medical*) the commencement of labor by artificial means, either by administering drugs to produce uterine contractions or by amniotomy.

induction[3] *n* in anesthesia, the process prior to the required state of anesthesia, including premedication with a sedative.

inductive *adj* proceeding by or producing induction; operating by induction; susceptible to being acted on by induction.

inductor *n* one who inducts; (*elect*) that part of an apparatus that acts inductively.

indue *see* **endue**.

Indulf *or* **Indulph** *n* king of Scots (954–962). Succeeded his uncle Malcolm I to the throne and abdicated in 962 in favor of Dubf, Malcolm's son.

indulge *vt* to satisfy (a desire); to gratify the wishes of; to humor. * *vi* to give way to one's desire. —**indulger** *n*.

indulgence *n* indulging or being indulged; a thing indulged in; a favor or privilege; (*RC Church*) a remission of punishment still due for a sin after the guilt has been forgiven.

indulgent *adj* indulging or characterized by indulgence; lenient.—**indulgently** *adv*.

induline, indulin *n* a dark blue dye.

indult *n* (*RC Church*) a license from the Pope authorizing something not sanctioned by Church law.

induplicate, induplicated *adj* (*bot*) bent inwards.

indurate *vt* to make hard or callous. * *vi* to grow hard or callous.—**induration** *n*. —**indurative** *adj*.

Indus Valley Civilization *n* an ancient civilization that flourished 2600–2000 BC, centered on the Indus Valley, mainly in Pakistan.

indusium *n* (*pl* **indusia**) (*bot*) the covering of the growing spores in many ferns.—**indusial** *adj*.

industrial *adj* relating to or engaged in industry; used in industry; having many highly developed industries.—**industrially** *adv*.

industrial action *n* organized action that is undertaken by employees in order to bring pressure to bear on employers to get them to agree to their demands.

industrial arts *n sing* a subject taught in schools, which involves the use of tools and machines to develop manual skills.

industrial crop *n* a non-food crop grown as a raw material for industry.

industrial democracy *n* a system in which workers participate in some way in the management of an organization and/or share in its profits.

industrial design *n* the design of products to be manufactured.—**industrial designer** *n*.

industrial disease *see* **occupational disease**.

industrial dispute *n* a dispute between employees and employers, often involving industrial action.

industrial espionage *n* the act of spying illegally on the activities of a competitor in order to gain information about new products, sales strategy, etc.

industrial inertia *n* the survival of an industry in a location after the reasons for establishing it there no longer apply.

industrialism *n* social and economic organization characterized by large industries, machine production, urban workers, etc.

industrialist *n* a person who owns or manages an industrial enterprise.

industrial park *n* an area zoned for industrial and business use, usu on the outskirts of a city.

industrial relations *n* the relations between employees and employers.

industrial tribunal *n* a tribunal set up to adjudicate on a dispute between an employee and employer.

industrialize *vti* to make or become industrial.—**industrialization** *n*.

industrious *adj* hard-working.—**industriously** *adv*.—**industriousness** *n*.

industry[1] *n* (*pl* **industries**) organized production or manufacture of goods; manufacturing enterprises collectively; a branch of commercial enterprise producing a particular product; any large-scale business activity; the owners and managers of industry; diligence.

industry[2] *n* (*archeo*) a group or assemblage of a few similar artifacts that are in close association with one another and may be found at one or more sites.

indwelling *vti* (**indwelling, indwelt**) to dwell (in).

Indy *n* **Paul Marie Theodore Vincent d'** (1851–1931) French composer who also wrote music text books and important biographies of Beethoven and Franck. His compositions include the operas *Fervaal, L' Etranger,* and *La Legende de St Christophe,* symphonies, and pieces of chamber music.

Ine (*d. c.*728) *n* king of Wessex, England (688–726). One of the most powerful Wessex rulers. His greatest achievement, was the important law code he compiled between 690 and 693, which reveals a growing sophistication in the consideration of the concepts of kingship and royal authority.

inebriate *vt* to intoxicate, esp with alcoholic drink. * *n* a drunkard. * *adj* inebriated.—**inebriation** *n*.

inebriated *adj* drunken.

ined. *abbr* (*Latin*) = *ineditus,* "not made known," "unpublished."

inedible *adj* not fit to be eaten.—**inedibility** *n*.

inedited *adj* unpublished; not edited.

ineducable *adj* impossible to educate, esp due to mental deficiency.

INEEL *abbr* = Idaho National Engineering and Environmental Laboratory.

ineffable *adj* too intense or great to be spoken; unutterable; too sacred to be spoken.—**ineffability** *n*. —**ineffably** *adv*.

ineffaceable *adj* which cannot be effaced.—**ineffaceability** *n*.

ineffective *adj* not effective.—**ineffectively** *adv*.—**ineffectiveness** *n*.

ineffectual *adj* not effectual; futile.—**ineffectuality** *n*. —**ineffectually** *adv*.

inefficacious *adj* not having the power to produce a particular desired effect.—**inefficacy** *n*.

inefficiency *n* (*pl* **inefficiences**) the quality or condition of being inefficient; an instance of inefficiency or incompetence.

inefficient *adj* not efficient.—**inefficiently** *adv*.

inelastic *adj* not elastic; inflexible, unyielding.—**inelastically** *adv*.—**inelasticity** *n*.

inelegant *adj* ungraceful; lacking refinement or polish.—**inelegance** *n*.

ineligible *adj* not eligible.—**ineligibility** *n*.

ineluctable *adj* not possible to escape from or avoid.—**ineluctably** *adv*.

INEOA *abbr* = International Narcotic Enforcement Officers Association.

inept *adj* unsuitable; unfit; foolish; awkward; clumsy.—**ineptitude** *n*. —**ineptly** *adv*.

inequality *n* (*pl* **inequalities**) lack of equality in size, status, etc; unevenness.

inequitable *adj* unjust, unfair.—**inequitably** *adv*.

inequity *n* (*pl* **inequities**) lack of equity; injustice.

ineradicable *adj* which cannot be eradicated.

inert *adj* without power to move or to resist; inactive; dull; slow; with few or no active properties.—**inertly** *adv*.—**inertness** *n*.

inert gas *n* (*chem*) any of the unreactive gases that include helium, neon, argon, krypton, xenon, and radon.— *also* **noble gas**.

inertia *n* (*physics*) the tendency of matter to remain at rest (or continue in a fixed direction) unless acted on by an outside force; disinclination to act.

inertia selling *n* a form of selling in which goods are sent to people who have not ordered them in the hope that they will keep the goods and pay for them and not send them back.

inertial *adj* of, or pertaining to, inertia.

inescapable *adj* which cannot be escaped, inevitable.

inessential *adj* not essential.

inestimable *adj* not to be estimated; beyond measure or price; incalculable; invaluable.—**inestimably** *adv*.

inevitable *adj* sure to happen; unavoidable. * *n* something that is inevitable.—**inevitability** *n*. —**inevitably** *adv*.

inexact *adj* not strictly true or correct.—**inexactitude** *n*. —**inexactly** *adv*.

inexcusable *adj* without excuse; unpardonable.—**inexcusably** *adv*.

inexhaustible *adj* not to be exhausted or spent; unfailing; unwearied.—**inexhaustibility** *n*. —**inexhaustibly** *adv*.

inexorable *adj* unable to be persuaded by persuasion or entreaty, relentless.—**inexorability** *n*. —**inexorably** *adv*.

inexpedient *adj* unsuitable to circumstances; inadvisable.—**inexpedience, inexpediency** *n*.

inexpensive *adj* cheap.—**inexpensively** *adv*.

inexperience *n* want of experience or of the knowledge that comes by experience.

inexperienced *adj* lacking experience; unpracticed; unskilled; unversed.

inexpert *adj* unskilled; lacking the knowledge or dexterity derived from practice.

inexpiable *adj* which cannot be expiated.

inexplicable *adj* not to be explained, made plain, or intelligible; not to be interpreted or accounted for.—**inexplicability** *n*. —**inexplicably** *adv*.

inexplicit *adj* not clear.

inexpressible *adj* incapable of being expressed, uttered, or described.—**inexpressibly** *adv*.

inexpressive *adj* lacking expression or distinct significance.

inextensible *adj* which cannot be extended.—**inextensibility** *n*.

inextinguishable *adj* which cannot be extinguished, unquenchable.

in extremis *adv* close to death; in a very difficult situation.

inextricable *adj* that cannot be disentangled, solved, or escaped from.—**inextricably** *adv*.

in f. *abbr* = in fine.

inf. *abbr* = infinitive; information; (*Latin*) *infra,* "below"; (*Latin*) *infusum,* "infusion."

Inf. *abbr* = infantry.

INF *abbr* = intermediate-range nuclear forces, as named in the Intermediate Nuclear Forces Treaty; International Naturist Federation.

INFA *abbr* = International Federation of Aestheticians.

INFACT *abbr* = Irish National Federation Against Copyright Theft.

infallible *adj* incapable of being wrong; dependable; reliable.—**infallibility** *n*. —**infallibly** *adv*.

infamous *adj* having a bad reputation; notorious; causing a bad reputation; scandalous.

infamy *n* (*pl* **infamies**) ill fame; public disgrace; ignominy.

infancy *n* (*pl* **infancies**) early childhood; the beginning or early existence of anything.

I

infant *n* a very young child; a baby.

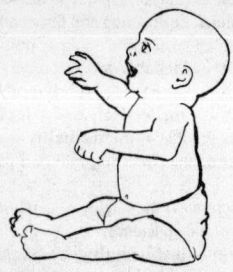

infanta *n* a title for a Spanish princess, not the heir apparent.

infante *n* a title for a Spanish prince, not the heir apparent.

infanticide *n* the killing of an infant; a person who does this.—**infanticidal** *adj*.

infantile *adj* of infants; like an infant, babyish.

infantile paralysis *n* poliomyletis.

infant mortality (rate) *n* a statistical measure of infant deaths, calculated as the number of deaths of infants under one year per 1,000 live births (in any given year).

infantry *n* (*pl* **infantries**) soldiers trained to fight on foot.

infantryman *n* (*pl* **infantrymen**) a soldier in an infantry regiment.

infarct, infarction *n* an area of dead tissue resulting from an interruption in blood flow to the affected region, as from a blood clot.

infatuate *vt* to inspire with intense, foolish, or short-lived passion.—**infatuated** *adj*.—**infatuatedly** *adv*.

infatuation *n* an extravagant passion.

infect *vt* to contaminate with disease-causing microorganisms; to taint; to affect, esp so as to harm.—**infective** *adj*.

infection[1] *n* an infecting or being infected; an infectious disease; a diseased condition.

infection[2] *n* (*comput*) the state of having a virus in a computer system.

infectious *adj* (*disease*) able to be transmitted; causing or transmitted by infection; tending to spread to others.—**infectiousness** *n*.

infectious hepatitis *n* an infectious disease which causes inflammation of the liver.

infectious mononucleosis *n* an infectious disease characterized by inflammation of the lymph glands.—*also* **glandular fever**.

infelicitous *adj* unfortunate; unhappy; inappropriate; ill-timed.

infelicity *n* (*pl* **infelicities**) misfortune; unhappiness; inappropriateness; an infelicitous act or expression.

infer *vt* (**inferring, inferred**) to conclude by reasoning from facts or premises; to accept as a fact or consequence.—**inferable** *adj*.—**inferrer** *n*.

inference *n* an inferring; something inferred or deduced; a reasoning from premises to a conclusion.—**inferential** *adj*.

inferior *adj* lower in position, rank, degree, or quality. * *n* an inferior person.—**inferiority** *n*.

inferiority complex *n* (*psychol*) an acute sense of inferiority expressed by a lack of confidence or in exaggerated aggression.

infernal *adj* of hell; hellish; fiendish; (*inf*) irritating, detestable.—**infernally** *adv*.

inferno *n* (*pl* **infernos**) hell; intense heat; a devastating fire.

infertile *adj* not fertile.—**infertility** *n*.

infest *vt* to overrun in large numbers, usu so as to be harmful; to be parasitic in or on.—**infestation** *n*. —**infester** *n*.

infidel *n* a person who does not believe in a certain religion; a person who has no religion.

infidelity *n* (*pl* **infidelities**) unfaithfulness, esp in marriage.

infield *n* (*cricket*) the area of the ground near the wicket; (*baseball*) the area of the field enclosed by the baselines.

infielder *n* (*baseball, cricket*) a player in an infield position.

infighting *n* (*boxing*) exchanging punches at close quarters; intense competition within an organization.—**infighter** *n*.

infiltrate *vti* to filter or pass gradually through or into; to permeate; to penetrate (enemy lines, etc) gradually or stealthily, e.g., as spies.—**infiltration** *n*. —**infiltrator** *n*.

infin. *abbr* = infinitive.

infinite *adj* endless, limitless; very great; vast.—**infinitely** *adv*.

infinitesimal *adj* immeasurably small.—**infinitesimally** *adv*.

infinitive *n* (*gram*) the form of a verb without reference to person, number, or tense.—**infinitival** *adj*.

infinitude *n* the condition or quality of being infinite; infinity.

infinity *n* (*pl* **infinities**) the condition or quality of being infinite; an unlimited number, quantity, or time period.

infirm *adj* physically weak, esp from old age or illness; irresolute.

infirmary *n* (*pl* **infirmaries**) a hospital or place for the treatment of the sick.

infirmity *n* (*pl* **infirmities**) being infirm; a physical weakness.

infix *vt* to fix or insert in.

in flagrante delicto *adv* in the very act of committing the crime, red-handed.—*also* **flagrante delicto**.

inflame *vti* to arouse, excite, etc, or to become aroused, excited, etc; to undergo or cause to undergo inflammation.—**inflamingly** *adv*.

inflammable *adj* able to catch fire, flammable; easily excited.—**inflammability** *n*.

inflammation *n* an inflaming or being inflamed; redness, pain, heat, and swelling in the body, due to injury or disease.

inflammatory *adj* rousing excitement, anger, etc; of or caused by inflammation.—**inflammatorily** *adv*.

inflatable *adj* able to be inflated.

inflate *vti* to fill or become filled with air or gas; to puff up with pride; to increase beyond what is normal, esp the supply of money or credit.—**inflatedly** *adv*.—**inflater, inflator** *n*.

inflation *n* an inflating or being inflated; an increase in the currency in circulation or a marked expansion of credit, resulting in a fall in currency value and a sharp rise in prices.

inflation accounting *n* an accounting system that aims to take account of inflation and so arrive at a statement of the true profitability of a company.

inflationary *adj* pertaining to or causing inflation.

inflationary universe *n* the theoretical idea that at a very early stage immediately after the Big Bang the expanding universe of that era suddenly inflated or experienced an accelerated expansion for a very short time.

inflationist *n, adj* (someone) in favor of a policy of an increased issue of money and availability of credit, with inflation as a consequence.

inflect *vt* to change the form (of a word) by inflection; to vary the tone of (the voice).—**inflective** *adj*.—**inflector** *n*.

inflected note *n* (*mus*) a note with an accidental placed before it, i.e., it is sharpened or flattened.

inflection *n* a bend; the change in the form of a word to indicate number, case, tense, etc; a change in the tone of the voice.—**inflectional** *adj*.

inflexible *adj* not flexible; stiff, rigid; fixed; unyielding.—**inflexibility** *n*. —**inflexibly** *adv*.

inflict *vt* to impose (pain, a penalty, etc) on a person or thing.—**inflicter, inflictor** *n*. —**infliction** *n*.

inflorescence *n* the producing of blossoms; the arrangement of flowers on a stem; a flower cluster; flowers collectively.—**inflorescent** *adj*.

inflow *n* something which flows in.

influence *n* the power to affect others; the power to produce effects by having wealth, position, ability, etc; a person with influence. * *vt* to have influence on.—**influenceable** *adj*.

influent *adj* flowing in.

influential *adj* having or exerting great influence.—**influentially** *adv*.

influenza *n* a contagious feverish virus disease marked by muscular pain and inflammation of the respiratory system.—**influenzal** *adj*.

influx *n* a sudden inflow of people or things to a place.

info *n* (*sl*) information.

inform *vt* to provide knowledge of something to. * *vi* to give information to the police, etc, esp in accusing another.

informal *adj* not formal; not according to fixed rules or ceremony, etc; casual.—**informally** *adv*.

informality *n* (*pl* **informalities**) the lack of regular, customary, or legal form; an informal act.

informal marriage license *n* (*law*) a marriage license created when a man and woman wish to declare that they are husband and wife and have been so since a date they name on the license. It is commonly referred to as a common law marriage, and it is recognized as a marriage even though no ceremony occurred.

informant *n* a person who gives information.

information *n* something told or facts learned; news; knowledge; data stored in or retrieved from a computer.—**informational** *adj*.

information superhighway *n* (*comput*) the global network of computers connected by satellites and telephone lines. (*See also* **internet**.)

information technology *n* (the study of) the collection, retrieval, use, storage, and communication of information using computers and microelectronic systems.

information theory *n* mathematical and statistical analysis of information communication systems.

informative, informatory *adj* conveying information, instructive.—**informatively** *adv*.

informer *n* a person who informs on another, esp to the police for a reward.

infra- *prefix* below; within; beneath; after.

infraction *n* a violation of a law, pact, etc.

infra dig. *abbr* (*Latin*) = *infra dignitatem*, "beneath one's dignity."

infrangible *adj* unbreakable; inviolable.—**infrangibility** *n*.

infrared *n* (*radiation*) having a wavelength longer than light but shorter than radio waves; of, pertaining to, or using such radiation.

infrared astronomy *n* observation of celestial objects by the infrared radiation they emit.

infrared galaxy *n* a galaxy emitting strongly in the infrared.

infrared photography *n* a remote sensing technique that uses infrared radiation to capture on special film an image of the subject being photographed.

infrared radiation *n* electromagnetic radiation lying in the electromagnetic spectrum between visible light and microwaves, most often generated by hot objects (black body radiation).

infrared sources *n* any hot body that emits infrared radiation, e.g. stars, galaxies, hot gas, and dust clouds.

infrared telescope *n* a telescope so constructed that it may be used with infrared radiation, in particular.

infrasonic *adj* (*soundwaves*) having a frequency below the audible range.—**infrasound** *n*.

infrastructure *n* the basic structure of any system or organization; the basic installations, such as roads, railways, factories, etc that determine the economic power of a country.

infrequent *adj* seldom occurring; rare.—**infrequence, infrequency** *n*. —**infrequently** *adv*.

infringe *vt* to break or violate, esp an agreement or a law.—**infringement** *n*.

infundibular, infundibulate *adj* funnel-shaped.

infuriate *vt* to enrage; to make furious.—**infuriating** *adj*.—**infuriatingly** *adv*.

infuse *vt* to instill or impart (qualities, etc); to inspire; to steep (tea leaves, etc) to extract the essence.—**infuser** *n*.

infusible[1] *adj* incapable of being fused or melted.—**infusibility** *n*.

infusible[2] *adj* capable of being infused.—**infusibility** *n*.

infusion *n* the act of infusing; something obtained by infusing.

infusorial earth *n* a siliceous deposit composed chiefly of the shells of microscopic vegetable organisms called diatoms, used as a polishing powder and in the manufacture of dynamite.

-ing[1] *vb suffix* used to form the present participle, as *coming*. * *adj suffix* forming adjectives not formed from verbs, as *swashbuckling*.

-ing[2] *n suffix* (*from verbs*) denoting action, process, or instance of an action or process, as *blessing, drawing*; (*from nouns*) used in, connected with, or involving, as *planking*.

-ing[3] *n suffix* denoting a thing or person of a particular kind or having a specific quality, as *whiting*.

Ingcel *n* (*Irish Celtic myth*) a monster with a single eye that contained three pupils, and he is said to have been the son of the king of Britain.

ingenious *adj* clever, resourceful, etc; made or done in an original or clever way.—**ingeniously** *adv*.—**ingeniousness** *n*.

ingénue *n* a naive young woman.

ingenuity *n* (*pl* **ingenuities**) skill in contriving or inventing; resourcefulness.

ingenuous *adj* naive, innocent; candid.—**ingenuously** *adv*.—**ingenuousness** *n*.

ingest *vt* to take (as food) into the body.—**ingestion** *n*. —**ingestive** *adj*.

ingestion[1] *n* the process of chewing and swallowing food and fluid that then go into the stomach.

ingestion[2] *n* (*medical*) the means whereby a phagocyte takes in cell debris, foreign particles, microorganisms, etc.

ingle *n* (*arch*) a fireplace.

inglenook *n* (a seat in) a recess by a large open fireplace.

inglorious *adj* disgraceful, shameful; obscure.

Ingo *abbr* = International non-governmental organization.

ingot *n* a brick-shaped mass of cast metal, esp gold or silver.

ingrain *vt* to make a deep impression upon; (*arch*) to dye.—*also* **engrain**.

ingrained *adj* (*habits, feelings, etc*) firmly established; (*dirt*) deeply embedded.—*also* **engrained**.

ingrate *adj* (*arch*) ungrateful. * *n* an ungrateful person.

ingratiate *vt* to bring oneself into another's favor.—**ingratiating, ingratiatory** *adj*.—**ingratiation** *n*.

ingratitude *n* absence of gratitude; insensibility to kindness.

ingredient *n* something included in a mixture; a component.

Ingres *n* **Jean Auguste Dominique** (1780–1867) French painter, one of the greatest exponents of neoclassical art. He strongly influenced Degas, Picasso, and Matisse through his excellent draughtsmanship.

ingress *n* entrance.

in-group *n* a group favoring its own members at the expense of members of other groups.

ingrowing *adj* (*toe nail, etc*) growing abnormally into the flesh.

inguinal *adj* of the groin or its vicinity.

ingurgitate *vt* to swallow greedily.—**ingurgitation** *n*.

inhabit *vt* to live in; to occupy; to reside.

inhabitable *adj* fit for habitation.—**inhabitability** *n*. —**inhabitation** *n*.

inhabitant *n* a person or animal inhabiting a specified place.—**inhabitancy, inhabitance** *n*.

inhalant *n* a medicine, etc that is inhaled.

inhalation, inspiration[1] *n* the act of drawing air into the lungs (*see* **respiration**).

inhalation[2] *n* the medication breathed in, whether in gas, vapor, or particulate form, to ensure contact with and/or treatment of conditions of the throat, bronchi, or lungs.

inhale *vti* to breathe in.

inhaler *n* a device that dispenses medicines in a fine spray for inhalation.

inharmonic, inharmonious *adj* lacking harmony; discordant.

inhere *vi* to be inherent.

inherent *adj* existing as an inseparable part of something.—**inherence, inherency** *n*. —**inherently** *adv*.

inherit *vt* to receive (property, a title, etc) under a will or by right of legal succession; to possess by genetic transmission. * *vi* to receive by inheritance; to succeed as heir.—**inheritor** *n*.

inheritable *adj* capable of being inherited.

inheritance *n* the action of inheriting; something inherited.

inheritance tax *n* a form of wealth tax that is payable on a proportion of assets when these are transferred to beneficiaries.

inhibit *vt* to restrain; to prohibit.—**inhibitor, inhibiter** *n*.

inhibition *n* an inhibiting or being inhibited; a mental process that restrains or represses an action, emotion, or thought.

inhibitor *n* (*chem, biol*) a substance that stops or slows down a chemical reaction.

inhospitable *adj* not hospitable; affording no shelter; barren; cheerless.—**inhospitably** *adv*.—**inhospitality** *n*.

in-house *adj* within an organization.

inhuman *adj* lacking in the human qualities of kindness, pity, etc; cruel, brutal, unfeeling; not human.

inhumane *adj* not humane; inhuman.

inhumanity *n* (*pl* **inhumanites**) the quality of being inhuman; cruelty.

inhume *vt* to bury, inter.—**inhumation** *n*. —**injumer** *n*.

inimical *adj* hostile; adverse, unfavorable.—**inimically** *adv*.

inimitable *adj* impossible to imitate; matchless.—**inimitably** *adv*.

in init. *abbr* (*Latin*) = *in initio* "in, or at, the beginning."

iniquitous *adj* marked by iniquity.

iniquity *n* (*pl* **iniquities**) wickedness; great injustice.

init *n* (*comput*) in the Macintosh operating system a utility file that is executed at start-up.

init. *abbr* = initial.

initial *adj* of or at the beginning. * *n* the first letter of each word in a name; a large letter at the beginning of a chapter, etc. * *vt* (**initialing, initialed** *or* **initialling, initialled**) to sign with initials.—**initialer, initialler** *n*. —**initially** *adv*.

initialize *vt* (*comput*) to format (a disk) to suit a particular processor.—**initialization** *n*. See also **format**.

initiate *vt* to bring (something) into practice or use; to teach the fundamentals of a subject to; to admit as a member into a club, etc, esp with a secret ceremony. * *n* an initiated person.—**initiator** *n*. —**initiatory** *adj*.

initiation *n* the act of initiating; a formal, often secret, ceremony of admission.

initiative *n* the action of taking the first step; ability to originate new ideas or methods.

initiator *n* (*chem*) a substance that starts a chemical reaction.

INJ *abbr* (*Latin*) = *in nomine Jesu*, "in the name of Jesus."

inject *vt* to force (a fluid) into a vein, tissue, etc, esp with a syringe; to introduce (a remark, quality, etc), to interject.—**injectable** *adj*.

injection *n* an injecting; a substance that is injected.—**injective** *adj*. See also **dosage; implant**.

injector *n* someone who, or something which, injects; a device for injecting fuel into an internal combustion engine; a device for filling the boiler of a steam engine with water.

injudicious *adj* not judicious; indiscreet; unwise.

injunction *n* a command; an order; a court order prohibiting or ordering a given action.—**injunctive** *adj*.

injure *vt* to harm physically or mentally; to hurt, do wrong to.—**injurer** *n*.

injurious *adj* causing injury.

injury *n* (*pl* **injuries**) physical damage; harm.

injury time *n* (*sport*) time added to compensate for stoppages through injuries to players.

injustice *n* the state or practice of being unfair; an unjust act.

ink *n* a colored liquid used for writing, printing, etc; the dark protective secretion of an octopus, etc. * *vt* to cover, mark, or color with ink.

inkhorn *n* (*formerly*) a container for ink.

inkjet printer *n* (*comput*) a printer type that forms an image by spraying ink on to a page from a matrix of tiny spray jets.

inkling *n* a hint; a vague notion.

inkstand *n* a stand for an ink bottle.

inkwell *n* a container for ink.

inky *adj* (**inkier, inkiest**) like very dark ink in color; black; covered with ink.—**inkiness** *n*.

INLA *abbr* = Irish National Liberation Army.

inlaid *see* **inlay**.

inland *adj* of or in the interior of a country. * *n* an inland region. * *adv* into or toward this region.—**inlander** *n*.

Inland Revenue the UK government department that is responsible for the assessing of the taxation liabilities of individuals and organizations and for the collection of money owed in taxation.

in-law *n* a relative by marriage.

inlay *vt* (**inlaying, inlaid**) to decorate a surface by inserting pieces of metal, wood, etc. * *n* inlaid work; material inlaid.—**inlaid** *adj*.

inlet *n* a narrow strip of water extending into a body of land; an opening; a passage, pipe, etc for liquid to enter a machine, etc. * *vt* (**inletting, inletted**) to inlay; to insert.

in loc. *abbr* (*Latin*) = *in loco*, "in its place."

I

in loc. cit *abbr* (*Latin*) = *in loco citato*, "in the place cited."

in loco parentis (*Latin*) in the place of a parent.

Inmarsat *abbr* = International Maritime Satellite.

inmate *n* a person confined with others in a prison or institution.

in mem. *abbr* (*Latin*) = *in memoriam*, "in memory of."

in memoriam (*Latin*) in memory of.

inmigration *n* the process of moving or settling into an area or community in large numbers.—**inmigrate** *vi*.

inmost *adj* farthest within; most secret.

inn *n* a small hotel; a restaurant or tavern, esp in the countryside.

INN *abbr* = International Negotiation Network.

innards *npl* (*inf*) the stomach and intestines, internal organs.

innate *adj* existing from birth; inherent; instinctive.—**innately** *adv*.

inner *adj* further within; inside, internal; private, exclusive. * *n* (*archery*) the innermost ring on a target.

inner city *n* the central area of a city, esp as affected by overcrowding and poverty.

inner ear *n* part of the ear lying within the temporal bone of the skull and containing the apparatus for hearing and balance.

innermost *adj* furthest within.

inner parts *n* (*mus*) the parts of a piece of music excluding the highest and lowest; e.g., in a work for soprano, alto, tenor, and bass, the alto and tenor roles are inner parts.

inner tube *n* the separate inflatable tube within a pneumatic tire.

innervation *n* the arrangement of nerve filaments in the body; special activity or stimulus in any part of the nervous system.

Inness *n* **George** (1825–94) American painter whose early landscapes were influenced by the Hudson River School, as in *The Delaware Valley* (1865).

inning *n* (*baseball*) a team's turn at bat

innings *n* (*cricket*) a turn at bat for a batsman or side; the number of runs scored at this time; an opportunity to demonstrate one's abilities.

innkeeper *n* a person who owns or manages an inn.

innocent *adj* not guilty of a particular crime; free from sin; blameless; harmless; inoffensive; simple, credulous, naive. * *n* an innocent person, as a child.—**innocence** *n*. —**innocently** *adv*.

innocuous *adj* harmless.—**innocuously** *adv*.—**innocuousness** *n*.

innominate *adj* without a name.

innominate artery *n* a branch of the aorta.—*also* **brachiocephalic trunk.**

In nomine *n* (*mus*) (*Latin*) "In the name [of the Lord]" a type of cantus firmus used by English composers of the 16th century. It was first used by Taverner in his setting of *In nomine Domini* for one of his Masses.

innovate *vi* to introduce new methods, ideas, etc; to make changes.—**innovation** *n*. —**innovative, innovatory** *adv*.

innovator *n* one who introduces, or seeks to introduce, new things.

innoxious *adj* harmless.

Innsbruck *n* a city in Austria.

innuendo *n* (*pl* **innuendos, innuendoes**) a hint or sly remark, usu derogatory; an insinuation.

Innuit *see* **Inuit.**

innumerable, innumerous *adj* too many to be counted; very numerous.—**innumerability** *n*. —**innumerably** *adv*.

innumerate *adj* lacking knowledge or understanding of mathematics and science; not numerate.—*also* *n*.

Ino *n* (*Greek myth*) a daughter of Cadmus, king of Thebes, who plotted to destroy her stepchildren Phrixus and Helle. They were saved by flying away on the miraculous ram with the golden fleece.

INO *abbr* = Irish Nurses Organization.

inobservance *n* inattention; failure to observe (law, etc).—**inobservant** *adj*.

inoculate *vt* to inject a serum or a vaccine into, esp in order to create immunity; to protect as if by inoculation.—**inoculative** *adj*. *See* **immunization; vaccination.**

inodorous *adj* without odor.

inoffensive *adj* harmless, not offensive.

inofficious *adj* contrary to moral duty.

inoperable *adj* not suitable for surgery.—**inoperability** *n*.

inoperative *adj* not working; producing no effect.

inopportune *adj* unseasonable; untimely.—**inopportuneness, inopportunity** *n*.

inordinate *adj* excessive.—**inordinately** *adv*.

inorg. *abbr* = inorganic.

inorganic *adj* not having the structure or characteristics of living organisms; denoting a chemical compound not containing carbon.—**inorganically** *adv*.

inorganic chemistry *n* (*chem*) the chemistry of all substances except those containing carbon.

inosculate *vti* (*anat, of blood vessels, fibers, etc*) to join closely, be closely joined.—**inosculation** *n*.

INPA *abbr* = International Newspaper Promotion Association.

inpatient *n* a patient being treated while remaining in hospital.

in perpetuum *adv* perpetually, forever.

in posse *adj, adv* having a possible but not an actual existence, potential.

in pr. *abbr* = in principio.

input *n* what is put in, as power into a machine, data into a computer, etc. * *vt* (**inputting, input** *or* **inputted**) to put in; to enter (data) into a computer.

input device *n* (*comput*) any peripheral device that provides a means of getting data into the computer e.g., keyboard, mouse, etc.

input tax *n* tax that is paid by a taxable person when purchasing goods or services.

input/output (I/O) *n* (*comput*) the general term for the equipment and system that is used to communicate with a computer.

inquest *n* a judicial inquiry held by a coroner, esp into a case of violent or unexplained death; (*inf*) any detailed inquiry or investigation.

inquietude *n* unease, disquiet.

inquiline *n* (*zool*) an animal which lives in the abode of another but does not harm it, e.g., a hermit crab.—**inquilinous** *adj*.

inquire *vi* to request information about; (*usu with* **into**) to investigate. * *vt* to ask about.—*also* **enquire.**—**inquirer, enquirer** *n*.

inquiry *n* (*pl* **inquiries**) the act of inquiring; a search by questioning; an investigation; a question; research.—*also* **enquiry.**

inquisition *n* a detailed examination or investigation; (*with cap and* **the**) (*RC Church*) formerly the tribunal for suppressing heresy.—**inquisitional** *adj*.

inquisitive *adj* eager for knowledge; unnecessarily curious; prying.—**inquisitively** *adv*.—**inquisitiveness** *n*.

inquisitor *n* a person who questions searchingly or forcefully; (*often cap*) a member of the Inquisition.

inquisitorial *adj* of or resembling an inquisitor; prying.—**inquisitorially** *adv*.

in re *prep* in the matter of.

INRI *abbr* (*Latin*) = *Jesus Nazarenus Rex Iudaeorum*, "Jesus of Nazareth, King of the Jews."

inroad *n* a raid into enemy territory; an encroachment or advance.

inrush *n* a sudden inward flow or influx.

ins. *abbr* = inches; inspector; insulated; insulator; insurance.

INS *abbr* = Immigration and Naturalization Service; International Neuromodulation Society; International News Service; inertial navigation system.

INSA *abbr* = International Shipowners' Association.

insalivate *vt* to mix (food) with saliva while chewing.—**insalivation** *n*.

insalubrious *adj* (*climate, place*) unhealthy.—**insalubrity** *n*.

insane *adj* not sane, mentally ill; of or for insane people; very foolish.—**insanely** *adv*.

insanitary *adj* unclean, likely to cause infection or ill-health.—**insanitariness, insanitation** *n*.

insanity *n* (*pl* **insanities**) derangement of the mind or intellect; lunacy; madness.

insatiable *adj* not easily satisfied; greedy.—**insatiability** *n*. —**insatiability** *adv*. **insatiably** *adv*.

insatiate *adj* insatiable.

INSCA *abbr* = International Sausage Casing Association.

INSCOM *abbr* = US Army Intelligence and Security Command.

inscr. *abbr* = inscription.

inscribe *vt* to mark or engrave (words, etc) on (a surface); to add (a person's name) to a list; to dedicate (a book) to someone; to autograph; to fix in the mind.—**inscribable** *adj*.

inscription *n* an inscribing; words, etc inscribed on a tomb, coin, stone, etc.—**inscriptional** *adj*.

inscrs. *abbr* = inscriptions.

inscrutable *adj* hard to understand, incomprehensible; enigmatic.—**inscrutability** *n*. —**inscrutably** *adv*.

insect *n* any of a class of small arthropods with three pairs of legs, a head, thorax, and abdomen, and two or four wings.

insectary *n* (*pl* **insectaries**) a place for keeping insects.

insecticide *n* a substance for killing insects.—**insecticidal** *adj*.

insectivore *n* an order of mammals that are small, nocturnal, and feed on insects or other invertebrates; any insect-eating plant or animal.—**insectivorous** *adj*.

insecure *adj* not safe; feeling anxiety; not dependable.—**insecurely** *adv*.

insecurity *n* (*pl* **insecurities**) the condition of being insecure; lack of confidence or sureness; instability; something insecure.

inselberg *n* a steep hill, usu of granite or some other resistant rock, rising abruptly from a plain, typical in tropical landscapes.

inseminate *vt* to fertilize; to impregnate.—**insemination** *n*. —**inseminator** *n*. *See also* **artificial insemination.**

insensate *adj* not feeling sensation; stupid; without regard or feeling; cold.

insensible *adj* unconscious; unaware; indifferent; imperceptible.—**insensibility** *n*. —**insensibly** *adv*.

insensitive *adj* not sensitive, unfeeling.

insentient *adj* inert; inanimate.

insep. *abbr* = inseparable.

inseparable *adj* not able to be separated; closely attached, as romantically.—**inseparability** *n*. —**inseparably** *adv*.

insert *vt* to put or fit (something) into something else. * *n* something inserted.—**insertion** *n*.

insertion *n* the act of inserting; something which is inserted.

insertion point *n* (*comput*) the point at which text can be entered into a document when typing.

insert mode *n* (*comput*) the input mode that allows input to be typed into a document at the cursor point.

in-service *adj* (*training*) given during employment.

insessorial *adj* (*ornithology*) adapted for perching.

inset *n* something inserted within something larger; an insert. * *vt* (**insetting, inset**) to set in, insert.—**insetter** *n*.

Inset *abbr* = in-service education and training.

inshore *adj, adv* near or towards the shore.

inshrine *see* enshrine.

inside *n* the inner side, surface, or part; (*pl: inf*) the internal organs, stomach, bowels. * *adj* internal; known only to insiders; secret. * *adv* on or in the inside; within; indoors; (*sl*) in prison. * *prep* in or within.

inside job *n* (*inf*) a crime committed with the help of someone connected with the victim or premises involved.

inside out *adj* reversed; with the inner surface facing the outside.

insider *n* a person within a place or group; a person with access to confidential information.

insider dealing *n* the dealing in financial securities by someone who has access to information that is not yet generally available and would affect the price of the securities, the aim being to exploit this knowledge to make a profit or avoid a loss.

inside track *n* (*athletics*) the inner curve of a running track which confers an advantage; a competitive advantage; an advantageous position.

insidious *adj* marked by slyness or treachery; more dangerous than seems evident.—**insidiously** *adv*.—**insidiousness** *n*.

insight *n* the ability to see and understand clearly the inner nature of things, esp by intuition; an instance of such understanding.—**insightful** *adj*.

insignia *n* (*pl* **insignias, insignia**) a mark or badge of authority; a distinguishing characteristic.

insignificant *adj* having little or no importance; trivial; worthless; small; inadequate.—**insignificance, insignificancy** *n*.—**insignificantly** *adv*.

insincere *adj* not sincere; hypocritical.—**insincerely** *adv*.—**insincerity** *n*.

insinuate *vt* to introduce or work in slowly, indirectly, etc; to hint.—**insinuator** *n*.

insinuation *n* the act of insinuating; an indirect or sly hint.

insipid *adj* lacking any distinctive flavor; uninteresting, dull.—**insipidity, insipidness** *n*.—**insipidly** *adv*.

insist *vi* (*often with* **on** *or* **upon**) to take and maintain a stand. * *vt* to demand strongly; to declare firmly.—**insister** *n*.

insistent *adj* insisting or demanding.—**insistence, insistency** *n*.—**insistently** *adv*.

in situ *adj* in the original or natural place or position.

insobriety *n* drunkenness.

in so far, insofar *adv* to such a degree or extent.

insolation *n* energy coming in from the Sun in the form of radiation.

insole *n* the inner sole of a shoe, etc; a thickness of material used as a inner sole.

insolent *adj* disrespectful; impudent, arrogant; rude.—**insolence** *n*.—**insolently** *adv*.

insoluble *adj* incapable of being dissolved; impossible to solve or explain.—**insolubility** *n*.—**insolubly** *adv*.

insolvent *adj* unable to pay one's debts; bankrupt.—**insolvency** *n*.

insomnia *n* abnormal inability to sleep.

insomniac *n* a person who suffers from insomnia.

insomuch *adv* (*with* **as** *or* **that**) to such an extent; (*with* **as**) inasmuch.

insouciant *adj* calm and unconcerned, carefree.—**insouciance** *n*.

insp. *abbr* = inspector.

Insp. Gen. *abbr* = Inspector General.

inspect *vt* to look at carefully; to examine or review officially.—**inspection** *n*.—**inspectional** *adj*.—**inspective** *adj*.

inspector *n* an official who inspects in order to ensure compliance with regulations, etc; a police officer ranking below a superintendent.—**inspectorate** *n*.—**inspectoral, inspectorial** *adj*.—**inspectorship** *n*.

inspectorate *n* the office, district, or rank of an inspector; a body of inspectors.

inspiration *n* an inspiring; any stimulus to creative thought; an inspired idea, action, etc.—**inspirational** *adj*.

inspiratory *adj* pertaining to inhalation. *See* **inhalation; respiration**.

inspire *vt* to stimulate, as to some creative effort; to motivate by divine influence; to arouse (a thought or feeling) in (someone); to cause.—**inspiring** *adj*.—**inspiringly** *adv*.

inspirit *vt* to put life into, invigorate; to animate, cheer.

inst. *abbr* = installment; instant (the present month); instantaneous; instrumental.

Inst. *abbr* = Institute; Institution.

instability *n* (*pl* **instabilities**) lack of stability; inconstancy.

Inst. Act. *abbr* = Institute of Actuaries.

install, instal *vt* (**installs** *or* **instals, installing, installed**) to formally place in an office, rank, etc; to establish in a place; to settle in a position or state.—**installer** *n*.

installation *n* the act of installing or being installed; machinery, equipment, etc that has been installed.

installation program *n* (*comput*) a utility program that is commonly supplied with application software with the purpose of assisting the user to install the software correctly on a hard disk.

installment, instalment *n* a sum of money to be paid at regular specified times; any of several parts, as of a magazine story or television serial.

installment plan *n* a method of paying for goods in regular installments.

instance *n* an example; a step in proceeding; an occasion. * *vt* to give as an example.

instant *adj* immediate; (*food*) concentrated or precooked for quick preparation. * *n* a moment; a particular moment.

instant replay *n* the immediate repetition of a piece of videotaped sporting action, often in slow motion.

instantaneous *adj* happening or done very quickly.—**instantaneously** *adv*.—**instantaneousness, instantaneity** *n*.

instanter *adv* (*law*) immediately.

instantly *adv* immediately.

instate *vt* to install in an office or rank.

Inst. C.E. *abbr* = Institution of Civil Engineers.

instead *adv* in place of the one mentioned.

Inst. E.E. *abbr* = Institution of Electrical Engineers.

instep *n* the upper part of the arch of the foot, between the ankle and the toes.

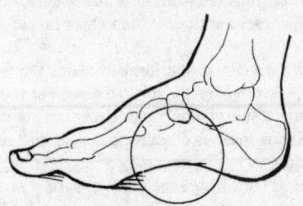

instigate *vt* to urge on, goad; to initiate.—**instigation** *n*.—**instigator** *n*.

instill, instil *vt* (**instills** *or* **instils, instilling, instilled**) to put (an idea, etc) in or into (the mind) gradually.—**instillation** *n*.—**instiller** *n*.

instinct *n* the inborn tendency to behave in a way characteristic of a species; a natural or acquired tendency; a knack.

instinctive, instinctual *adj* of, relating to, or prompted by instinct.—**instinctively, instinctually** *adv*.

institute *vt* to organize, establish; to start, initiate. * *n* an organization for the promotion of science, art, etc; a school, college, or department of a university specializing in some field.—**institutor, instituter** *n*.

institution *n* an established law, custom, etc; an organization having a social, educational, or religious purpose; the building housing it; (*inf*) a long-established person or thing.

institutional *adj* of or resembling an institution; dull, routine.

institutionalize *vt* to make or become an institution; to place in an institution; to make a person dependent on an institutional routine and unable to cope on their own.—**institutionalization** *n*.

Inst. M.E. *abbr* = Institution of Marine Engineers.

Inst. M.M. *abbr* = Institution of Mining and Metallurgy.

instn. *abbr* = institution.

Inst. n. A. *abbr* = Institution of Naval Architects.

instns. *abbr* = instructions.

instr. *abbr* = instructor; instrument; instruments; instrumental.

instruct *vt* to provide with information; to teach; to give instructions to; to authorize.—**instructible** *adj*.—**instructor** *n*.—**instructress** *nf*.

instruction *n* an order, direction; the act or process of teaching or training; knowledge imparted; (*comput*) a command in a program to perform a particular operation; (*pl*) orders, directions; detailed guidance.—**instructional** *adj*.

instructive *adj* issuing or containing instructions; giving information, educational.—**instructively** *adv*.

instructor *n* someone who instructs; a teacher.

instrument *n* a thing by means of which something is done; a tool or implement; any of various devices for indicating, measuring, controlling, etc; any of various devices producing musical sound; a formal document. * *vt* to orchestrate.

instrumental *adj* serving as a means of doing something; helpful; of, performed on, or written for a musical instrument or instruments.—**instrumentality** *n*.—**instrumentally** *adv*.

instrumentalist *n* a person who plays a musical instrument.

instrumentation *n* the arrangement of a musical composition for different instruments; the use or provision of tools or instruments. *See also* **orchestration**.

instrument panel *n* a panel in a vehicle or machine in which instruments monitoring speed, engine status, etc are mounted.

insubordinate *adj* not submitting to authority; rebellious.—**insubordination** *n*.

insubstantial *adj* unreal, imaginary; weak or flimsy.—**insubstantiality** *n*.—**insubstantially** *adv*.

insufferable *adj* intolerable; unbearable.—**insufferably** *adv*.

insufficient *adj* not sufficient.—**insufficiency, insufficience** *n*.—**insufficiently** *adv*.

insufflate *vt* to blow (air, powder) into or onto.—**insufflation** *n*.—**insufflator** *n*.

insula *n* (*archeo*) (*pl* **insulae**) strictly, an island, but in Roman town planning a block of buildings within a square formed by intersecting roads.

insular *adj* of or like an island or islanders; narrow-minded; illiberal.—**insularity, insularism** *n*.

insulate *vt* to set apart; to isolate; to cover with a nonconducting material in order to prevent the escape of electricity, heat, sound, etc.—**insulation** *n*. — **insulator** *n*.

insulation *n* the act of insulating; the material used for insulating.

insulator *n* something which insulates; a non-conductor of electricity, heat, or sound.

insulin *n* (*biochemistry*) a hormone that controls absorption of sugar by the body, secreted by islets of tissue in the pancreas.

insult *vt* to treat with indignity or contempt; to offend. * *n* an insulting remark or act.—**insulter** *n*.

insuperable *adj* unable to be overcome.—**insuperability** *n*. —**insuperably** *adv*.

insupportable *adj* unbearable, intolerable

insur. *abbr* = insurance.

insurable *adj* able to be insured.

insurance *n* insuring or being insured; a contract purchased to guarantee compensation for a specified loss by fire, death, etc; the amount for which something is insured; the business of insuring against loss.

insurance broker *n* a person or firm acting as an intermediary in bringing together clients seeking insurance cover and companies specializing in providing this cover.

insurance company *n* a financial institution that underwrites the risk of financial loss as a result of damage to or theft of property or loss of property or the risk of death or injury.

insurance policy *n* a document that formally states the terms of an insurance contract between the insurer and the insured person or company.

insurance premium *n* a sum of money paid either once or in regular installments to a company providing insurance against damage, theft, or loss of property or against death or injury.

insure *vt* to take out or issue insurance on; to ensure. * *vi* to contract to give or take insurance.

insurer *n* someone who insures, an underwriter; a company which sells insurance.

insurgent *adj* rebellious, rising in revolt. * *n* a person who fights against established authority, a rebel.—**insurgence** *n*. —**insurgency** *n*.

insurmountable *adj* which cannot be overcome, insuperable.

insurrection *adj* a rising or revolt against established authority.—**insurrectional** *adj*.—**insurrectionary** *n, adj*.—**insurrectionism** *n*. —**insurrectionist** *n*.

int. *abbr* = interest; interior; interjection; internal; international; interpreter; intransitive.

intact *adj* unimpaired; whole.

intaglio *n* (*pl* **intaglios**) a design carved or engraved below the surface; a printing technique using engraved surfaces.—**intagliated** *adj*.

intake *n* the place in a pipe, etc where a liquid or gas is taken in; a thing or quantity taken in, as students, etc; the process of taking in.

intangible *adj* that cannot be touched, incorporeal; representing value but without material being, as good will; indefinable. * *n* something that is intangible.—**intangibility** *n*. —**intangibly** *adv*.

intangible asset *n* an asset that cannot be touched or seen, e.g., copyright.

integer *n* (*math*) any member of the set consisting of the positive and negative whole numbers and zero, such as -5, 0, 5.

integral *adj* necessary for completeness; whole or complete; made up of parts forming a whole. * *n* the result of a mathematical integration.—**integrally** *adv*.

integral calculus *n* (*maths*) the determination of definite and indefinite integrals and their use in the solution of differential equations.

integrant *adj* component, making part of a whole.

integrate *vti* to make whole or become complete; to bring (parts) together into a whole; to remove barriers imposing segregation upon (racial groups); to abolish segregation; (*math*) to find the integral of.—**integration** *n*. —**integrative** *adj*.

integrated accounts *npl* company accounting records that are kept in one set of books so that the financial accounts and the cost accounts are together in an integrated form.

integrated circuit *n* (*comput*) a small electronic circuit assembled from microcomponents mounted on chips of semiconducting material.

integrated program *n* (*comput*) a group of software packages each with a logical relationship to the other components, and operating in a similar manner so that it is possible to transfer data between them.

integration *n* (*math*) a branch of the calculus using various types of formulae.

integrator *n* someone who, or something which, integrates.

integrity *n* honesty, sincerity; completeness, wholeness; an unimpaired condition; (*comput*) the quality associated with a file that is complete and uncorrupted.

integument *n* a natural covering as skin, a rind, a husk, etc.—**integumental, integumentary** *adj*.

Intel *n* (*comput, trademark*) a major manufacturing company that makes integrated chips.

intellect *n* the ability to reason or understand; high intelligence; a very intelligent person.—**intellective** *adj*.

intellection *n* thought.

intellectual *adj* of, involving, or appealing to the intellect; requiring intelligence. * *n* an intellectual person.—**intellectuality** *n*. —**intellectually** *adv*.

intellectualism *n* the use of the intellect; (*philos*) the theory that all knowledge is derived from the intellect; (*derog*) excessive emphasis on the value of the intellect.—**intellectualist** *n*.

intellectualize *vt* to make intellectual; to use the intellect on. * *vi* to become intellectual; to use the intellect.—**intellectualization** *n*.

intellectual property *n* the legal ownership of certain intangible assets, such as trademarks.

intelligence *n* the ability to learn or understand; the ability to cope with a new situation; news or information; those engaged in gathering secret, esp military, information.

intelligence quotient *n* a measure of a person's intelligence, calculated by dividing mental age by actual age and multiplying by 100.

intelligent *adj* having or showing intelligence; clever, wise, etc.—**intelligently** *adv*.

intelligentsia *n* intellectuals collectively.

intelligible *adj* able to be understood; clear.—**intelligibility** *n*. — **intelligibly** *adv*.

Intelsat *abbr* = International Telecommunications Satellite Organization.

intemperate *adj* indulging excessively in alcoholic drink; unrestrained; (*climate*) extreme.—**intemperance** *n*. —**intemperately** *adv*.

intend *vt* to mean, to signify; to propose, have in mind as an aim or purpose.—**intender** *n*.

intendancy *n* (*pl* **intendancies**) the rank or office of an intendant.

intendant *n* a superintendent or manager (esp under a monarch in France, Spain, and Portugal).

intended *adj* planned. * *n* (*inf*) a fiancé or fiancée.

intendment *n* the true meaning of something, as fixed by law.

intens. *abbr* = intensive.

intense *adj* very strong, concentrated; passionate, emotional.—**intensely** *adv*.

intensify *vti* (**intensifying, intensified**) to make or become more intense.—**intensification** *n*.

intensity *n* (*pl* **intensities**) the state or quality of being intense; density, as of a negative plate; the force or energy of any physical agent.

intensive *adj* of or characterized by intensity; thorough; denoting careful attention given to patients right after surgery, etc.—**intensively** *adv*.

intensive care *n* 24-hour monitoring and treatment of acutely ill patients in hospital; the specialized unit administering this.

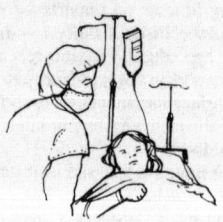

intensive distribution *n* a distribution strategy that is aimed at obtaining the maximum possible number of outlets for a product or products.

intent *adj* firmly directed; having one's attention or purpose firmly fixed. * *n* intention; something intended; purpose or meaning.—**intently** *adv*.—**intentness** *n*.

intention *n* a determination to act in a specified way; anything intended.

intentional *adj* done purposely.—**intentionality** *n*. —**intentionally** *adv*.

inter *vt* (**interring, interred**) to bury.

inter- *prefix* between, among.

interact *vi* to act upon each other.—**interaction** *n*. —**interactional** *adj*.

interacting galaxies *n* galaxies whose gravitational attraction to each other causes strong interactions with marked effects.

interactive *adj* interacting; allowing two-way communication between a device, such as a computer or compact video disc, and its user.—**interactivity** *n*.

interactive processing *n* (*comput*) a system in which the user can monitor the computer's processing directly on the computer screen and make any corrections to the process that are required. *See also* **batch processing.**

inter alia *adv* among other things.

interbank market *n* the section of the London money market in which banks lend to each other and to other large financial institutions.

interbreed *vti* (**interbreeding, interbred**) to breed within the same breed or family; to breed by crossing one species with another.

intercalary *adj* inserted into the calendar to harmonize it with the solar year, e.g., February 29 as inserted in the leap year.

intercalate *vt* to insert (an intercalary day) into the calendar.—**intercalation** *n*.

intercede *vi* to intervene on another's behalf; to mediate.—**interceder** *n*.

intercellular *adj* lying between cells.

intercept *vt* to stop or catch in its course. * *n* a point of intersection of two geometric figures; interception by an interceptor.—**interception** *n*. —**interceptive** *adj*.

interceptor, intercepter *n* a high-speed fighter aircraft used to intercept and destroy enemy aircraft.

intercession *n* the act of interceding, esp by prayer; mediation.—**intercessional, intercessory** *adj*.—**intercessor** *n*. —**intercessorial** *adj*.

interchange *vt* to give and receive one thing for another; to exchange, to put (each of two things) in the place of the other; to alternate. * *n* an interchanging; a junction on a freeway designed to prevent traffic intersecting.

interchangeable *adj* able to be interchanged.—**interchangeability** *n*. —**interchangeably** *adv*.

intercollegiate *adj* between or among colleges or universities.

intercolumniation *n* the distance between pillars; the spacing between pillars.— **intercolumniar** *adj*.

intercom *n* (*inf*) a system of intercommunicating, as in an aircraft.

intercommunicate *vi* to have mutual communication; to have passage to each other.—**intercommunicable** *adj*.—**intercommunication** *n*.

interconnect *vti* to connect by reciprocal links.—**interconnection** *n*.

intercontinental *adj* between continents.

intercostal *adj* (*anat*) lying between the ribs.

intercourse *n* a connection by dealings or communication between individuals or groups; sexual intercourse, copulation.

intercross *vti* to crossbreed.

intercurrent *adj* occurring at the same time; (*disease*) occurring during the course of another.—**intercurrence** *n*.

interdenominational *adj* relating to or involving more than one religious denomination.

interdependence, interdependency *n* dependence on each other.— **interdependent** *adj*.

interdict *vt* to prohibit (an action); to restrain from doing or using something. * *n* an official prohibition.—**interdiction** *n*. —**interdictory** *adj*.

interdisciplinary *adj* involving two or more different branches of knowledge.

interest *n* a feeling of curiosity about something; the power of causing this feeling; a share in, or a right to, something; anything in which one has a share; benefit; money paid for the use of money; the rate of such payment. * *vt* to excite the attention of; to cause to have a share in; to concern oneself with.

interested *adj* having or expressing an interest; affected by personal interest, not impartial.—**interestedly** *adv*.

interesting *n* engaging the attention.

interest rate *n* the amount that a borrower is required to pay for a loan, usu expressed as a percentage of the sum borrowed.

interface *n* a surface that forms the common boundary between two things; an electrical connection between one device and another, esp a computer. * *vt* (*elect*) to modify the input and output configurations of (devices) so that they may connect and communicate with each other; to connect using an interface; to be interactive (with).—**interfacial** *adj*.—**interfacially** *adv*. See also **user interface**.

interfacing *n* a layer of fabric between the neck, etc of a garment and its facing to give body.

interfere *vi* to clash; to come between; to intervene; to meddle; to obstruct.— **interfering** *adj*.

interference *n* an interfering; (*radio, TV*) the interruption of reception by atmospherics or by unwanted signals.

interferometer *n* (*physics*) an instrument used to measure the length of light waves by interference phenomena.

interferon *n* a protein, produced by cells in response to a virus, which then prevents the virus from growing.

interfluve *n* an area of ground separating two rivers that both run into the same drainage system.

interfuse *vti* to mix, blend.—**interfusion** *n*.

intergalactic *adj* occurring or existing between galaxies.

interglacial *adj* occurring between two glacial periods.

intergrade *vi* (*usu biol*) to change form gradually.—**intergradation** *n*.

interim *n* an intervening period of time. * *adj* provisional, temporary. * *adv* meanwhile.

interim dividend *n* a dividend that is paid to shareholders midway through a financial year.

interim report *n* a company financial statement that is issued for a period of less than a financial year, often half-yearly.

interior *adj* situated within; inner; inland; private. * *n* the interior part, as of a room, country, etc.

interior angle *n* the angle between two adjacent sides of a polygon.

interior design *n* the art or business of an interior designer—*also* **interior decoration.**

interior designer *n* a person whose profession is the planning of the decor and furnishings of the interiors of houses, offices, etc.—*also* **interior decorator.**

interior monologue *n* the term used by the novelist Dorothy Richardson for the stream of consciousness narrative technique.

interj. *abbr* = interjection.

interject *vt* to throw in between; to interrupt with.—**interjector** *n*. — **interjectory** *adj*.

interjection *n* an interjecting; an interruption; an exclamation.— **interjectional** *adj*.—**interjectionally** *adv*.

interlace *vti* to combine (as if) by lacing or weaving together.—**interlacement** *n*.

interlaced *adj* (*comput*) a VDU display technology that produces high resolution pictures but rapidly moving pictures may appear to flicker or streak.

interlard *vt* to insert something foreign into.

interleaf *n* (*pl* **interleaves**) an additional, blank leaf inserted into a book.

interleave *vti* to insert an extra page (usu blank) in a book.

interline *vt* to write between lines.—**interlinear** *adj*.—**interlineation** *n*.

interlining *n* an extra lining between the lining and the outer fabric of a garment, etc; the material for this.

interlink *vt* to link together.

interlock *vti* to lock or become locked together; to join with one another.

interlocution *n* dialogue, discussion.

interlocutor *n* a person who takes part in a conversation.—**interlocutress, interlocutrix** *nf*.

interlocutory *adj* conversational; (*law*) pronounced during legal proceedings.

interlope *vi* to intrude in a matter in which one has no real concern.

interloper *n* a person who meddles; an intruder.

interlude *n* anything that fills time between two events, as music between acts of a play.

interlunar *adj* coming between the old and the new moon.

intermarry *vi* (**intermarrying, intermarried**) (*different races, religions, etc*) to become connected by marriage; to marry within one's close family.— **intermarriage** *n*.

intermediary *n* (*pl* **intermediaries**) a mediator. * *adj* acting as a mediator; intermediate.

intermediate *adj* in the middle; in between.

intermediation *n* the role of a bank or other financial institution in acting as an intermediary between two parties in a business transaction.

interment *n* burial.

intermezzo *n* (*pl* **intermezzos, intermezzi**) a short musical composition between parts of an opera, play, etc; a movement between sections of an extended instrumental work; a similar composition intended as an independent work.

interminable *adj* lasting or seeming to last forever; endless.—**interminably** *adv*.

intermingle *vti* to mingle or mix together.

intermission *n* an interval of time between parts of a performance.

intermit *vb* (**intermitting, intermitted**) *vt* to cause to cease for a time; to suspend. * *vi* to cease for a time; to be suspended.

intermittent *adj* stopping and starting again at intervals; periodic.—**intermittence, intermittency** *n*. —**intermittently** *adv*.

intermix *vti* to mix together.

intermixture *n* the act of mixing together; a mixture.

intern[1] *vt* to detain and confine within an area, esp during wartime.— **internment** *n*.

intern[2] *n* a doctor serving in a hospital, usu just after graduation from medical school, a houseman.

intern[3], **interne** *n* an apprentice journalist, teacher, etc.

internal *adj* of or on the inside; of or inside the body; intrinsic; domestic.— **internality** *n*. —**internally** *adv*.

internal audit *n* an audit that is carried out in a company by members of its own staff, rather than by external auditors, in order to ascertain that the company's internal control system is operating effectively.

internal combustion engine *n* an engine producing power by the explosion of a fuel-and-air mixture within the cylinders.

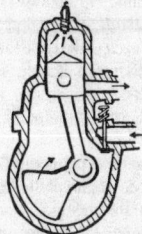

internal command *n* (*comput*) a DOS command that is always available at the DOS prompt.

internal ear *n* the inner ear.

internal growth *n* a method of business growth in a company that is self-generated, in that the growth is a result of the exploitation of the company's resources or new-product development.

internal hard disk *n* (*comput*) a hard disk that is located inside the personal computer's case.

internalize *vt* (*values, attitudes, etc*) to absorb into one's conscious or subconscious life through learning or socialization.

internal memory *n* (*comput*) another name given to RAM and ROM, which is where the computer stores information being used by a program or file.

internal modem *n* (*comput*) a modem that is located inside the personal computer's case and connected directly to the expansion slot.

internal revenue *n* government income derived from taxes etc within the country.

internat. *abbr* = international.

international *adj* between or among nations; concerned with the relations between nations; for the use of all nations; of or for people in various nations. * *n* a sporting competition between teams from different countries; a member of an international team of players.—**internationality** *n*. —**internationally** *adv*.

International Atomic Time *n* a standard time introduced in 1972, based on an atomic clock.

International Date Line *n* the line running north to south along the 180-degree meridian, east of which is one day earlier than west of it.

Internationale *n* (*mus*) the international Communist anthem. The words are by E Pottier and the music is by P Degeyter.

International Gothic *n* a predominant style in European art covering the period between the end of the Byzantine era and the beginning of the Renaissance, i.e., *c*.1375–*c*.1425, characterized by decorative detail and refined, flowing lines.

internationalism *n* an attitude, belief, or policy favoring the promotion of cooperation and understanding between nations.—**internationalist** *n*.

internationalization *see* globalization.

interne *see* **intern**[3].

internecine *adj* extremely destructive to both sides.

internee *n* a person who is interned.

Internet *n* the worldwide system of linked computer networks.

Internet *abbr* = International Network (of computers).

Internet address *see* **address**.

Internet domain name *see* **domain name**.

Internet Relay Chat *n* (*comput*) a type of "meeting to chat" facility on the Internet which runs in real time. Messages from a user are broadcast to anyone else who may be logged on, leading to discussions, potentially between a large group of people across the world.

Internet Service Provider *n* (*comput*) a company that allows people to connect up to the Internet through their own computer system.

internist *n* a physician who specializes in internal diseases.

internode *n* (*bot*) the space on a plant stem between two nodes or leaf joints.—**internodal** *adj*.

internuncial *adj* pertaining to an internuncio; (*anat*) transmitting nervous signals.

internuncio *n* a representative of the Pope.

interpellate *vt* to question (an official) about government policy or about personal conduct.—**interpellation** *n*. —**interpellator** *n*.

interpenetrate *vt* to penetrate thoroughly. * *vi* to penetrate each other.—**interpenetration** *n*. —**interpenetrative** *adj*.

interpersonal *adj* being, denoting, or involving relations between people.

interplanetary *adj* between or among planets.

interplanetary medium *n* the dust and solar wind to be found in the spaces between the planets.

interplay *n* the action of two things on each other, interaction.

interplead *vi* (**interpleading, interpleaded, interplead, interpled**) (*law*) to discuss a point incidentally arising, or concerning a third party.

interpleader *n* (*law*) the discussion of a point incidentally arising or concerning a third party.

Interpol (*acronym*) International Criminal Police Organization.

interpolate *vt* to change (a text) by inserting new material; to insert between or among others; (*math*) to estimate a value between two known values.—**interpolator** *n*. —**interpolation** *n*.

interpose *vti* to place or come between; to intervene (with); to interrupt (with).—**interposer** *n*. —**interposition** *n*.

interpret *vt* to explain; to translate; to construe; to give one's own conception of, as in a play or musical composition. * *vi* to translate between speakers of different languages.—**interpretational** *adj*.

interpretatio celtica *n* a term used to describe the fusion of the Celtic and Roman religious cults. As a result of this fusion, Roman gods to some extent were accepted into the Celts' own set of beliefs.

interpretation *n* an act or instance of interpreting; an explanation; a rendering (of a piece of music, theater, etc).

interpretatio romana *n* the converse of interpretatio celtica by which the Romans regarded some of the Celtic gods as part of the Roman culture.

interpreter *n* a person who translates orally for persons speaking in different languages; (*comput*) a program that translates an instruction into machine code. *See also* **compiler**.

interracial *adj* between or among races.

interregnum *n* (*pl* **interregnums, interregna**) the period between two reigns, governments, etc; a suspension of normal government; a pause in a continuous series.

interrelate *vti* to be or place in a mutually dependant or reciprocal relationship.—**interrelation** *n*. —**interrelationship** *n*.

interrog. *abbr* = interrogation; interrogative.

interrogate *vti* to question, esp formally.—**interrogation** *n*. —**interrogational** *adj*.—**interrogator** *n*.

interrogative *adj* asking a question. * *n* a word used in asking a question.—**interrogatively** *adv*.

interrogatory *adj* questioning. * *n* (*pl* **interrogatories**) examination by questions.—**interrogatorily** *adv*.

interrupt[1] *vt* to break into (a discussion, etc) or break in upon (a speaker, worker, etc); to make a break in the continuity of. * *vi* to interrupt an action, talk, etc.—**interrupter** *n*. —**interruptive** *adj*.

interrupt[2] *n*, *vti* (*comput*) a signal from the microprocessor that temporarily interrupts processing to allow another operation to take place.

interrupted ditch enclosure *see* **causewayed camp**.

interruption *n* the act of interrupting; a hindrance; a remark interposed in a conversation, etc.

intersect *vti* to cut or divide by passing through or crossing; (*lines, roads, etc*) to meet and cross each other.

intersection *n* an intersecting; the place where two lines, roads, etc meet or cross.—**intersectional** *adj*.

interspace *n* a space between things.

intersperse *vt* to scatter or insert among other things; to diversify with other things scattered here and there.—**interspersion** *n*.

interstate *adj* between or among different states of a federation.

interstellar *adj* between or among stars.

interstellar medium *n* the contents of the space between the stars, mainly gas and dust grains but also cosmic rays and magnetic fields as well as the whole gamut of electromagnetic radiation.

interstice *n* a crack; a crevice; a minute space.

interstitial *adj* occurring in interstices.

intertexture *n* the act or product of interweaving.

intertribal *adj* between or among tribes.

intertropical convergence zone *n* a narrow zone at low latitude where air masses from north and south of the Equator converge, often resulting in depressions, that may lead to hurricanes.

intertwine *vti* to twine or twist closely together.

interurban *adj* moving between urban centers. **interval** *n* a space between things; the time between events; (*mus*) the difference of pitch between two notes.

intervene *vi* to occur or come between; to occur between two events, etc; to come in to modify, settle, or hinder some action, etc.—**intervener, intervenor** *n*. —**intervention** *n*. —**interventional** *adj*.

interventionist *n* a person who favors intervention. * *adj* of or in favor of intervention. —**interventionism** *n*.

intervertebral disc *n* fibrous cartilaginous discs that connect adjacent vertebrae and permit rotational and bending movements.

interview *n* a meeting in which a person is asked about his or her views, etc, as by a newspaper or television reporter; a published account of this; a formal meeting at which a candidate for a job is questioned and assessed by a prospective employer. * *vt* to have an interview with.—**interviewer** *n*.

interviewee *n* a person who is interviewed.

interweave *vti* (**interweaving, interwove** or **interweaved**, *pp* **interwoven** or **interweaved**) to weave together, interlace; to intermingle.

interwind *vt* (**interwinding, interwound**) to wind together.

intestate *adj* having made no will. * *n* a person who dies intestate.—**intestacy** *n*.

intestinal flora *n* bacteria usu found in the intestine. Acidic surroundings are produced by the bacteria, and this helps lessen infection by pathogens unable to withstand the conditions.

intestine *n* the lower part of the alimentary canal between the stomach and the anus.—**intestinal** *adj*.

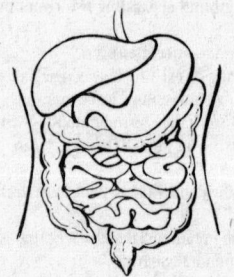

intifada *n* the Arabic word for "uprising," esp the uprising in Israel in 1987 of Palestinian inhabitants.

intimacy *n* (*pl* **intimacies**) close or confidential friendship; familiarity; sexual relations.

intimate *adj* most private or personal; very close or familiar, esp sexually; deep and thorough. * *n* an intimate friend. * *vt* to indicate; to make known; to hint or imply.—**intimately** *adv*.

intimation *n* the act of intimating; a notice, announcement.

intimidate *vt* to frighten; to discourage, silence, etc esp by threats.—**intimidation** *n*. —**intimidator** *n*.

intinction *n* (*Eastern Church*) the practice of administering both parts of Holy Communion at the same time by dipping the bread into the wine.

into *prep* to the interior or inner parts of; to the middle; to a particular condition; (*inf*) deeply interested or involved in.

intolerable *adj* unbearable.—**intolerably** *adv*.

intolerance *n* lack of toleration of the opinions or practices of others; inability to bear or endure; (*med*) the condition in which a patient is unable to metabolize a drug.—**intolerant** *adj*.

intolerant *adj* unwilling to tolerate others' beliefs, etc; bigoted; indisposed to endure; short-tempered.— **intolerantly** *adv*.

intonate *vti* to recite in a singing voice, chant.

intonation *n* intoning; variations in pitch of the speaking voice; an accent.—**intonational** *adj*.

intone *vti* to speak or recite in a singing tone; to chant.—**intoner** *n*.

in toto *adv* completely; as a whole; entirely.

intoxicant *n* something that intoxicates, esp a drug or an alcoholic drink.—*also adj*.

intoxicate *vt* to make drunken; to elate; to poison.—**intoxicatingly** *adv*.

intoxication *n* drunkenness; great excitement; poisoning.

intr. or **intrans.** *abbr* = intransitive.

intra- *prefix* within.

intracranial *adj* within the skull.

intracranial pressure *n* the pressure within the cranium maintained by all tissues: brain, blood, cerebrospinal fluid, etc.

intractable *adj* unmanageable, uncontrollable; (*problem, illness, etc*) difficult to solve, alleviate, or cure.—**intractability** *n*. —**intractably** *adv*.

intrados *n* (*pl* **intrados, intradoses**) the inner and lower curve of an arch.—*also* **soffit**.

intramural *adj* (*education*) within an institution or organization;

intramuscular *adj* a term meaning "within a muscle," e.g. an intramuscular injection.

intranet *n* (*comput*) a system that works in a similar way to the Internet, but which has limited access and is not generally available to the public.

in trans. *abbr* (*Latin*) = *in transitu*, "in transit."

intransigent *adj* unwilling to compromise, irreconcilable.—**intransigence** *n*. —**intransigently** *adv*.

intransitive *adj* (*gram*) denoting a verb that does not take a direct object.—**intransitively** *adv*.

intrauterine *adj* inside the uterus.

intrauterine device (**IUD**) *n* a small loop or coil inserted into the uterus as a contraceptive.

intravenous *adj* into a vein.—**intravenously** *adv*.

in-tray *n* a tray holding documents, etc, awaiting attention.

intrench *see* **entrench**.

intrepid *adj* bold; fearless; brave.—**intrepidity** *n*. —**intrepidly** *adv*.

Int. Rev. *abbr* = Internal Revenue.

intricate *adj* difficult to understand; complex, complicated; involved, detailed.—**intricacy** *n*. —**intricately** *adv*.

intrigue *n* a secret or underhand plotting; a secret or underhanded plot or scheme; a secret love affair. * *vb* (**intriguing, intrigued**) *vi* to carry on an intrigue. * *vt* to excite the interest or curiosity of.—**intriguer** *n*.

intrinsic *adj* belonging to the real nature of a person or thing; inherent.—**intrinsically** *adv*.

intro *n* (*pl* **intros**) (*inf*) introduction.

intro. *abbr* = introduction.

intro- *prefix* within, into.

introd. *abbr* = introduction; introductory.

introduce *vt* to make (a person) acquainted by name (with other persons); to bring into use or establish; to present (legislation, etc) for consideration or approval; to present a radio or television program; to bring into or insert.—**introducer** *n*.

introduction[1] *n* an introducing or being introduced; the presentation of one person to another; preliminary text in a book; a preliminary passage in a musical composition.

introduction[2] *n* a method of raising new share capital by issuing company shares at an agreed price to market makers and stockbrokers rather than directly to the public.

introductory *adj* serving as an introduction; preliminary.—**introductorily** *adv*.

introit *n* (*RC Church, Church of England*) a psalm or passage of scripture sung by the choir as the priest approaches the altar before Mass or Holy Communion.

intromission *n* insertion; introduction.

intromit *vt* to insert.—**intromittent** *adj*.

INTROP *abbr* = Information Center of Tropical Plant Protection.

introspect *vi* to examine one's own thoughts and feelings.

introspection *n* examination of one's own mind and feelings, etc.—**introspectional, introspective** *adj*.

introversion *n* the act of introverting; the state of being introverted; the direction of, or tendency to direct, one's thoughts and concerns inward.

introvert *vt* to turn or direct inward. * *vi* to produce introversion in. * *n* a person who is more interested in his or her own thoughts, feelings, etc than in external objects or events. * *adj* characterized by introversion.—**introversive** *adj*.

intrude *vti* to force (oneself) upon others unasked.—**intruder** *n*. —**intrudingly** *adj*.

intrusion *n* the act or an instance of intruding; the forcible entry of molten rock into and between existing rocks.—**intrusional** *adj*.

intrusive *adj* intruding; tending to intrude; (*rocks*) formed by intrusion.—**intrusively** *adv*.

intrust *see* **entrust**.

INTS *abbr* = International Nuclear Track Society.

intubate *vt* (*med*) to insert a tube into (the larynx, etc).—**intubation** *n*.

intuit *vt* to know by intuition.

intuition *n* a perceiving of the truth of something immediately without reasoning or analysis; a hunch, an insight.—**intuitional** *adj*.—**intutionally** *adv*.

intuitive *adj* perceiving or perceived by intuition.—**intuitively** *adv*.

intuitivism *n* the doctrine that ethical principles are matters of intuition.—**intuitivist** *n*.

intuitonism, intuitionalism *n* the doctrine that the immediate perception of truth is by intuition.—**intuitionist, intuitionalist** *n*.

intumescence, intumescency *n* a swelling up; a tumid state.—**intumescent** *adj*.

intussusception *n* (*med*) the protrusion of the upper part of the intestinal canal into the lower part; (*biol*) the expansion of a cell.

intwine *see* **entwine**.

INucE *abbr* = Institution of Nuclear Engineers.

Inuit *n* (*pl* **Inuit, Inuits**) an Eskimo from Greenland or North America.—*also* **Innuit**.

Inuktitut *n* the language of the Inuit.

inulin *n* a starchy constituent of many plants.

inunction *n* the act of applying ointment; the act of anointing or smearing with oil.

inundate *vt* to cover as with a flood; to deluge.—**inundation** *n*. —**inundator** *n*.

inure *vt* to accustom to, esp to something unpleasant.—*also* **enure**.—**inurement, enurement** *n*.

inurn *vt* to put (ashes) in an urn.

in utero *adj, adv* (*Latin*) in the uterus.

inutile *adj* useless.

inv. *abbr* = (*Latin*) *invenit*, "designed it"; invented; inventor; invoice.

in vacuo *adv* in a vacuum.

invade *vt* to enter (a country) with hostile intentions; to encroach upon; to penetrate; to crowd into as if invading.—**invader** *n*.

invaginate *vt* (*anat*) to fold back a part of a tubular organ on itself so that it is sheathed.

invagination *n* the process of invaginating; the state of being invaginated.

invalid[1] *adj* not valid.

invalid[2] *n* a person who is ill or disabled. * *vt* to cause to become an invalid; to disable; to cause to retire from the armed forces because of ill-health or injury.

invalidate *vt* to render not valid; to deprive of legal force.—**invalidation** *n*.

invalidity *n* (*pl* **invalidities**) a lack of validity; a state of illness or disability.

invaluable *adj* too valuable to be measured in money.—**invaluably** *adv*.

Invar *n* (*trademark*) an alloy of nickel and steel, used in scientific instruments because of its invariability.

invariable *adj* never changing; constant.—**invariability** *n*. —**invariably** *adv*.

invasion *n* the act of invading with military forces; an encroachment, intrusion; (*medical*) the state where bacteria enter the body or, more commonly, the process whereby malignant cancer cells move into nearby normal and deeper tissues and gain access to blood vessels.

invasive *adj* marked by military aggression; tending to spread; tending to infringe.

invective *n* the use of violent or abusive language or writing.

inveigh *vi* to speak violently or bitterly (against).—**inveigher** *n*.

inveigle *vt* to entice or trick into doing something.—**inveiglement** *n*. —**inveigler** *n*.

invent *vt* to think up; to think out or produce (a new device, process, etc); to originate; to fabricate (a lie, etc).—**inventible, inventable** *adj*.—**inventor** *n*.

invention[1] *n* something invented; inventiveness.—**inventional** *adj*.

invention[2] *n* (*mus*) a title used by Bach for his two-part keyboard pieces in contrapuntal form.

inventive *adj* pertaining to invention; skilled in inventing.—**inventiveness** *n*.

inventory *n* (*pl* **inventories**) an itemized list of goods, property, etc, as of a business; the store of such goods for such a listing; a list of the property of an individual or an estate. * *vt* (**inventorying, inventoried**) to make an inventory of; to enter in an inventory.—**inventoriable** *adj*.—**inventorial** *adj*.

inventory investment *n* investment in raw materials, work in progress, and finished stock.

inventory valuation *n* the valuation of raw materials, work in progress, and finished stock.

inveracity *n* (*pl* **inveracities**) untruthfulness.

Inverness *n* major Scottish city in United Kingdom of Great Britain and Northern Ireland (UK).

inverse *adj* reversed in order or position; opposite, contrary. * *n* an inverse state or thing.—**inversely** *adv*.

inverse square law *n* (*astron*) a relationship used to obtain the absolute magnitude of a star when its apparent magnitude and distance are known.

inversion[1] *n* an inverting or being inverted; something inverted.—**inversive** *adj*.

inversion[2] *n* (*mus*) a term which literally means turning upside down. It can refer to a chord, interval, theme, melody, or counterpoint. E.g., an inverted interval is an interval in which one note changes by an octave to the other side of the other note.

inversion[3] or **temperature inversion** *n* (*meteorology*) the situation in which temperature rises with height through the atmosphere, instead of falling as is normally the case.

invert *vt* to turn upside down or inside out; to reverse in order, position, or relationship.—**invertible** *adj*.

invertebrate *adj* without a backbone (—*also* **invertebral**). * *n* an animal without a backbone.

inverted comma *n* a quotation mark.

invest *vt* to commit (money) to property, stocks, and shares, etc for profit; to devote effort, time, etc on a particular activity; to install in office with ceremony; to furnish with power, authority, etc. * *vi* to invest money.

investigate *vti* to search (into); to inquire, examine.—**investigative, investigatory** *adj*.

investigation *n* the act of investigating; an inquiry; a search to uncover facts, etc.—**investigational** *adj*.

investigator *n* one who investigates, esp a private detective.

investiture *n* the act or right of giving legal possession; the ceremony of investing a person with an office, robes, title, etc.

investment *n* the act of investing money productively; the amount invested; an activity in which time, effort, or money has been invested.

investment grant *n* a grant that is made to a company by a government as an incentive to investment in plant, machinery, buildings, etc, as a means of encouraging new investment in an area.

investment income *n* a person's income that is derived from investments rather than from employment.

investment trust company *n* a limited company that invests its shareholders' funds in a variety of financial securities, the shares being bought and sold on the stock market.

investor *n* a person who invests money.

inveterate *adj* firmly established, ingrained; habitual.—**inveteracy** *n*. —**inveterately** *adv*.

invidious *adj* tending to provoke ill-will, resentment, or envy; (*decisions, etc*) unfairly discriminating.—**invidiously** *adv*.—**invidiousness** *n*.

invigorate *vt* to fill with vigor and energy; to refresh.—**invigorating** *adj*.—**invigoration** *n*. —**invigorative** *adj*.—**invigorator** *n*.

invincible *adj* unconquerable.—**invincibility** *n*. —**invincibly** *adv*.

inviolable *adj* not to be broken or harmed.—**inviolability** *n*. —**inviolably** *adv*.

inviolate *adj* not violated; unbroken, unharmed.—**inviolacy** *n*.

invisible *adj* unable to be seen; hidden.—**invisibility** *n*. —**invisibly** *adv*.

invisible assets *same as* intangible assets.

invisible earnings *npl* the earnings from abroad that contribute to a country's balance of payments as a result of transactions involving the sale of services relating to tourism, banking, insurance, etc, rather than to the sale of goods.

invisible exports *n* services rather than goods, such as insurance, advertising, or banking, that are sold abroad and therefore earn foreign currency.

invisible ink *n* a special ink that remains invisible on paper until exposed to a heat source.

invitation *n* a message used in inviting.

invite *vt* to ask to come somewhere or do something; to ask for; to give occasion for; to tempt; to entice. * *n* (*inf*) an invitation.

inviting *adj* attractive, enticing.—**invitingly** *adv*.

in vitro *adv, adj* (*biological experiments, etc*) occurring outside the living body and in an artificial environment.

in vitro fertilization (IVF) *n* the process of fertilizing an ovum outside the body. The first successful live birth using this technique was in 1978, when the phrase "test-tube baby" was coined.

in vivo *adv, adj* (*biological processes, etc*) occurring inside the living body.

invocation *n* the act of invoking; a formula used in invoking.—**invocatory** *adj*.

invoice *n* a document listing goods dispatched, usu with particulars of their price and quantity; to demand due settlement. * *vt* to submit an invoice for or to.

invoke *vt* to call on (God, etc) for help, blessing, etc; to resort to (a law, etc) as pertinent; to implore.

involucel *n* (*bot*) a bract around part of a flower head.

involucre *n* (*bot*) a ring of bracts around the base of a flower cluster.

involuntary *adj* not done by choice; not consciously controlled.—**involuntarily** *adv*.—**involuntariness** *n*.

involuntary muscle *n* a type of muscle not under voluntary or conscious control, such as those in the blood vessels, stomach, and intestines.

involute, involuted *adj* intricate; (*bot*) folded or rolled inwards (e.g., leaves, flowers); curled spirally.

involution *n* something which is involute; the act of involving; involvement, complication; (*anat*) the return of an organ or tissue to its normal size after distension; (*math*) the process of raising an arithmetical or algebraic quantity to a given power.

involve *vt* to affect or include; to require; to occupy, to make busy; to complicate; to implicate.—**involvement** *n*.

involved *adj* complicated; tangled; (*with* **with** *or* **in**) implicated or concerned; associated romantically or sexually.

invt. *abbr* = inventory.

invulnerable *adj* not capable of being wounded or hurt in any way.—**invulnerability** *n*. —**invulnerable** *adj*.

inward *adj* situated within or directed to the inside; relating to or in the mind or spirit. * *adv* inwards.

inwardly *adv* within; in the mind or spirit; towards the inside or center.

inwards *adv* towards the inside or interior; in the mind or spirit.

INWAT *abbr* = International Network of Women Against Tobacco.

inweave *vt* (**inweaving, inwove** *or* **inweaved,** *pp* **inwoven** *or* **inweaved**) to weave in.

Inwood *n* Henry W (*b*. 1794) English architect. His notable works include St Pancras Church, London.

inwrought *adj* worked into or onto (fabric, etc); adorned with figures or patterns.

Io[1] *n* (*Greek myth*) the daughter of Inachus, who was exiled by her father and was changed into a white heifer, wandering for many years throughout Greece and persecuted by Zeus's wife, Hera.

Io[2] *n* a satellite of Jupiter discovered by Galileo in 1610.

Io[3] *symbol* (*chem*) ionium (element).

Io. *abbr* = Iowa.

IO *abbr* = Intelligence Office.

I/O *abbr* (*comput*) *see* **input/output**.

IOB *abbr* = Institute of Brewing; Insurance Ombudsman Bureau.

IOC *abbr* = Indian Ocean Commission; Institute of Carpenters; International Olympic Committee; International Ornithological Congress; International Ozone Commission.

IOD *abbr* = Institute of Directors, injured on duty.

IODE *abbr* = Daughters of the Empire (*Canada*).

iodic *adj* pertaining to, or containing, iodine.

iodide *n* a compound of iodine.

iodine *n* a nonmetallic element, found in seawater and seaweed, whose compounds are used in medicine and photography.

iodism *n* poisoning caused by overdoses of iodine.

iodize *vt* to treat or combine with iodine.

iodoform *n* a compound of iodine, used as an antiseptic.

IoF *abbr* = Institute of Fuel.

IOF *abbr* = Independent Order of Foresters.

IOFB *abbr* = intraocular foreign body.

IOFGA *abbr* = Irish Organic Farmers and Growers Association.

IOGT *abbr* = Independent Order of Good Templars.

IoJ *abbr* = Institute of Journalists.

Iolcus *n* an ancient city of Magnesia in Thessaly, at the head of the gulf of Pagasae, associated with Jason and the Argonauts.

IOM *abbr* = International Organization for Migration; Isle of Man.

ion *n* an electrically charged atom or group of atoms formed through the gain or loss of one or more electrons.

Ion *n* (*Greek myth*) a son of Creusa, wife of Xuthus, who was taken to Delphi by Apollo and reunited by an oracle with his parents.

Iona *n* a Scottish Hebridean island, the site of a Celtic Christian community established by St Columba, having traveled there as a missionary from Ireland in AD 563.

Ionesco *n* Eugène (1912–94) Romanian-born French dramatist of the theater of the absurd whose plays include *The Bald Prima Donna, The Old Soprano, The Lesson,* and *Rhinoceros*.

Ionia *n* in ancient geography, part of Asia Minor which was inhabited by Ionian Greeks, founders of cities including Ephesus, Miletus, and Smyrna.—**Ionian** *adj*.

Ionian Islands *npl* a chain of Greek islands in the Ionian Sea, extending along the western and southern shores of Greece, including Corfu, Cephalonia, Zakinthos, Ithaca, and Paxos.

Ionian mode *n* (*mus*) a mode which, on the piano, uses the white notes from C to C.

Ionians *npl* a Greek-speaking people named after Ion, son of Xuthus or Apollo, who were driven out of the Peloponnese at the time of the Dorian invasion and migrated to Attica. Many later settled in the Cyclades and Asia Minor.

Ionian Sea *n* the sea that lies between southern Italy and Sicily on the west, and Greece, from Epirus to the Peloponnese, on the east.

ionic *adj* of or occurring in the form of ions.

Ionic *adj* of a Greek style of architecture that is characterized by ornamental scrolls on the tops of columns.

ionize *vti* to change or become changed into ions.—**ionization** *n*.

ionized layers *or* **ionosphere** *n* the series of ionized layers high in the stratosphere from which radio waves are reflected.—**ionospheric** *adj*.

IOOC *abbr* = International Olive Oil Council (Spain).

IOOF *abbr* = Independent Order of Odd Fellows.

IOOTS *abbr* = International Organization of Old Testament Scholars.

IoP *abbr* = Institute of Physics.

IOP *abbr* = intraocular pressure.

IOPC *abbr* = Institute of Paper Conservation.

IOPCW *abbr* = International Organization for the Prohibition of Chemical Weapons.

IOQ *abbr* = Institute of Quarrying.

IOR *abbr* = Independent Order of Rechabites; Institute of Roofing.

Ioruaidhe *n* (*Irish Celtic myth*) a kingdom, the ruler of which was the owner of a hound that could not be defeated in a fight.

IOS *abbr* = integrated office system.

Iosa Ghini *n* **Massimo** (1959–) Italian designer and illustrator and member of the Zak-Ark group.

iota *n* the ninth letter of the Greek alphabet; a very small quantity; a jot.

IOU *n* (*pl* **IOUs**) "I owe you"; a written note promising to pay a sum of money to the holder.

IOW *abbr* = Isle of Wight.

Iowa (IA) *n* a state of the United States of America (USA) of which the capital is Des Moines.

i.p. *abbr* = installment paid (stocks); intermediate pressure (cylinder).

IP *abbr* = india paper; in-patient; installment plan; International Pharmacopoeia; Internet Protocol.

i.p.a. *abbr* = including particular average.

IPA *abbr* = Independent Petroleum Association; Insolvency Practitioners Association; Institute of Practitioners in Advertising; India Pale Ale; International Association for the Child's Right to Play; International Peace Academy; International Peach Academy; International Phonetic Alphabet/Association; International Pinball Association; International Psychogeriatric Association; International Publishers' Association; Involvement and Participation Association.

IPAA *abbr* = International Prisoners' Aid Association.

IPARS *abbr* = International Programmed Airline Reservation System.

IPBA *abbr* = Irish Paper Box Association.

IPBM *abbr* = interplanetary ballistic missile.

IPC *abbr* = Indicative Planning Council; Institute of Pure Chiropractic; International Paralympic Committee; International Pepper Community; International Press Center; International Prison Commission; International Publishing Corporation.

IPCA *abbr* = International Petroleum Co-operative Alliance; International Postcard Collectors Association.

IPCC *abbr* = Intergovernmental Panel on Climatic Change; Irish Peatland Conservation Council.

IPCS *abbr* = Institution of Professional Civil Servants.

IPD *abbr* (*Latin*) = *in praesentia Dominorum*,"in the presence of the Lords [of Session]."

IPE *abbr* = Incorporated Plant Engineers.

ipecac, ipecacuanha *n* a South American plant, the root of which is made into a medicine used as an emetic and purgative.

IPF *abbr* = International Peace Forest; International Pen Friends (Ireland); International Powerlifting Federation; International Prayer Fellowship.

IPFA *abbr* = Member of Chartered Institute of Public Finance and Accountancy.

IPGS *abbr* = International Philatelic Golf Society.

IPGSA *abbr* = International Plant Growth Substance Association.

IPHC *abbr* = International Pacific Halibut Commission.

Iphicles, Iphiclus *n* (*Greek myth*) the son of Alcmene and Amphitryon, and twin and half-brother of Heracles, son of Alcmene and Zeus.

Iphigeneia, Iphigenia *n* (*Greek myth*) daughter of Agamemnon and Clytemnestra, sacrificed on the altar in order to obtain a fair wind for the Greek fleet, but miraculously conveyed in a cloud to Tauris (Crimea).

Iphis *n* (*Greek myth*) a king of Argos, who died in the war against Thebes.

IPI *abbr* = Institute of Patentees and Inventors; Institute of Professional Investigators; International Pesticide Institute; International Press Institute; Irish Planning Institute.

ipm *abbr* = inches per minute.

IPM *abbr* = Institute of Personnel Management; Institute of Psychosexual Medicine.

IPMI *abbr* = International Precious Metals Institute.

IPMS *abbr* = Institution of Professionals, Managers and Specialists.

IPO *abbr* = input, processing, output.

Ipoh *n* a city in Malaysia.

IPPA *abbr* = Indo-Pacific Prehistory Association (Australia); International Pediatric Pathology Association; International Peat Society; International Pectin Producers' Association; International Prisoners Aid Association; Irish Pre-School Playgroups Association.

IPPF *abbr* = International Planned Parenthood Federation.

ips *abbr* = inches/instructions per second.

IPS *abbr* = Incorporated Phonographic Society; Institute for Policy Studies; International Palm Society; International Planetarium Society; Intractable Pain Society of Great Britain and Northern Ireland.

ipso facto *adv* by the fact or act itself.

IPTPA *abbr* = International Professional Tennis Players' Association.

IPTS *abbr* = International Practical Temperature Scale.

IPU *abbr* = Interparliamentary Union.

i.q. *or* **iq** *abbr* (*Latin*) = *idem quod*, "the same as."

IQ *abbr* = Intelligence Quotient.

IQA *abbr* = Institute of Quality Assurance; Irish Quality Association.

Ir *symbol* (*chem*) iridium (element).

ir *abbr* = inside radius.

IR *abbr* = Industrial Relations; Internal Revenue; information retrieval; infra red.

Ir. *abbr* = Ireland; Irish.

IRA *abbr* = International Rodeo Association; Irish Republican Army.

Iráklion *n* a city in Greece.

Iran *n* an Islamic Republic lying across The Gulf from the Arabian Peninsula and stretching from the Caspian Sea to the Arabian Sea.

Iran. *abbr* = Iranian; Iranic.

Iranian *n* a native or inhabitant of Iran; a branch of the Indo-European group of languages including Persian; modern Persian.—*also adj*.

Iraq *n* a republic located in southwest Asia between The Gulf and Syria.

Iraqi Dinar *n* currency of Iraq.

IRASA *abbr* = International Radio Air Safety Association.

irascible *adj* easily angered; hot-tempered.—**irascibility** *n*. —**irascibly** *adv*.

IRATA *abbr* = Industrial Rope Access Trades Association.

irate *adj* enraged, furious.—**irately** *adv*.

Irbid *n* a city in the Hashemite Kingdom of Jordan.

IRBM *abbr* = intermediate range ballistic missile.

IRC *abbr* = Infantry Reserve Corps; International Red Cross; International Relations Club; International Rescue Committee; International Rubber Conference; Internet Relay Chat.

IRCS *abbr* = Irish Red Cross Society.

ire *n* anger; wrath.

Ireland *n* a republic covering four fifths of the island of Ireland, situated in the Atlantic Ocean, and is part of the British Isles.

Ireland *n* **John** (1897–1962) an English composer who was greatly influenced by French music and is best known for his orchestral works, e.g. The *Forgotten Rite*, *Mai-Dun*, and *Satyricon*.

Irenaeus of Lyons *n* Saint (*c*.130–*c*.200) missionary bishop of the Graeco-Gaulish Church of southern France; born near Smyrna, in Asia Minor; opposed the Gnostics. His feast day is June 28.

irenic, irenical *adj* aiming at peace.

IRF *abbr* = International Reform Federation; International Religious Fellowship; International Rowing Federation.

IRFB *abbr* = International Rugby Football Board.

Iribe *n* **Paul** (1883–1935) French jewelry designer for Chanel and illustrator for journals such as *Le Rirei*.

iridaceous *adj* (*bot*) of, or pertaining to, the iris family.

iridectomy *n* the surgical removal of part of the iris, often undertaken to correct the blockage of aqueous humor associated with glaucoma.

iridescent *adj* exhibiting a spectrum of shimmering colors, which change as the position is altered.—**iridescence** *n*.

iridium *n* a metallic element that is extraordinarily resistant to corrosion.

iridotomy *n* an incision into the iris.

iris[1] *n* (*pl* **irises, irides**) the round, pigmented membrane surrounding the pupil of the eye.

iris[2] *n* (*pl* **irises**) a perennial herbaceous plant with sword-shaped leaves and brightly colored flowers.

Iris *n* (*Greek myth*) the golden-winged messenger of the Olympian gods; the personification of the rainbow.

Irish *adj* of Ireland or its people. * *n* the Celtic language of Ireland.

irish bagpipe *n* (*mus*) the only bagpipe having a diatonic scale.

Irish bull *see* bull[3].

Irish coffee *n* coffee mixed with Irish whiskey and topped with fresh cream.

irish harp *n* (*mus*) a prototype of the Italian harp from which the modern instrument was developed.

Irish moss *see* carrageen.

Irish stew *n* a stew of mutton, onions, and potatoes.

iritis *n* (*med*) inflammation of the iris.

irk *vt* to annoy, irritate.

irksome *adj* tedious; tiresome.

IRL *abbr* = Institute of Rural Life at Home and Overseas.

IRLA *abbr* = Independent Record Labels Association; International Religious Liberty Association.

irlandais *n* (*mus*) (*French*) "in the Irish style."

IRLCOCSA *abbr* = International Red Locust Control Organization for Central and Southern Africa.

IRN *abbr* = Independent Radio News.

Irnan n (*Irish Celtic myth*) one of the three sorceress daughters of Conaran who were sent by their father to capture some members of the Fianna by spinning a magic web round them.

IRO *abbr* = Industrial Relations Officer; Inland Revenue Office; Institute of Rent Officers; Internal Revenue Office; International Refugee Organization.

iron *n* a metallic element, the most common of all metals; a tool, etc of this metal; a heavy implement with a heated flat underface for pressing cloth; (*pl*) shackles of iron; firm strength; power; any of certain golf clubs with angled metal heads. * *adj* of iron; like iron, strong and firm. * *vti* to press with a hot iron; (*with* **out**) to correct or settle a problem through negotiation or similar means.—**ironer** *n*.

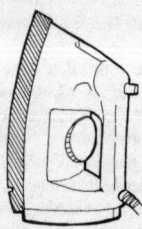

Iron Age *n* the period when most tools and weapons were made of iron, following the Bronze Age in around 1100BC.

ironbark *n* a type of eucalyptus tree.

ironbound *adj* bound with iron; unyielding.

ironclad *adj* covered in iron; difficult to change or break.

iron curtain *n* the name of the physical and ideological barrier which once separated the former Soviet Union and Communist Eastern Europe from the rest of Europe.

iron gray *adj* a slightly greenish dark gray.

iron hand *n* harsh, despotic control.— **ironhanded** *adj*.—**ironhandedly** *adv*.— **ironhandedness** *n*.

iron horse *n* a steam locomotive.

ironic, ironical *adj* of or using irony.—**ironically** *adv*.

ironing *n* the act of ironing; items of clothing, etc, for ironing.

ironing-board *n* a narrow flat surface to iron clothes on.

iron lung *n* a large respirator that encloses all of the body but the head.

iron maiden *n* a medieval instrument of torture consisting of a hinged coffin-like box fitted with spikes which was closed around the victim.

iron meteorite *n* a meteorite with an unusually high iron content.

ironmonger *n* a dealer in metal utensils, tools, etc; a hardware shop.— **ironmongery** *n*.

iron rations *npl* emergency food rations for military use.

Ironside, William Edmund, 1st Baron (1880–1959) Scottish soldier. His early adventurous exploits included dangerous secret service work in the Boer War (1899–1902). (John **Buchan** used him as the model for the adventurer Richard Hannay.) He became chief of the General Staff at the outbreak of World War II.

ironstone *n* a type of iron ore; a type of hardwearing earthenware.

ironwood *n* a name given to the timber of certain trees, which is of exceptional hardness and durability.

ironwork *n* articles made of iron, esp decorative railings, etc.

ironworks *n* (*pl or sing*) a factory where iron is smelted, cast, or wrought.

irony *n* (*pl* **ironies**) an expression in which the intended meaning of the words is the opposite of their usual sense; an event or result that is the opposite of what is expected.

Iroquois *n* (*pl* **Iroquois**) a member of a North American Indian confederacy of tribes formerly living in the eastern United States and Canada; any of their languages.— **Iroquoian** *adj*.

irradiance *n* the act of emitting rays of light; luster.

irradiant *adj* emitting rays of light; shining brightly.

irradiate *vt* to shine upon; to light up; to enlighten; to radiate; to expose to X-rays or other radiation. * *vi* to emit rays; to shine.—**irradiative** *adj*.—**irradiator** *n*.

irradiation *n* the act of irradiating; the condition of being irradiated; the apparent extension of the edges of an illuminated object seen against a dark background; the use of radiation in medicine.

irrational *adj* not rational, lacking the power of reason; senseless; unreasonable; absurd.—**irrationality** *n*. —**irrationally** *adv*.

irrational number *n* a real number (e.g.,) that cannot be expressed as the result of dividing one integer by another.

irreclaimable *adj* which cannot be reclaimed.

irreconcilable *adj* not able to be brought into agreement; incompatible.— **irreconcilability** *n*. —**irreconcilably** *adv*.

irrecoverable *adj* beyond recovery.—**irrecoverably** *adv*.

irrecusable *adj* which must be accepted.

irredeemable *adj* not able to be redeemed.—**irredeemably** *adv*.

irredentist *n* an advocate of the return of a country of neighbouring regions claimed by another on language and other grounds.—**irredentism** *n*.

irreducible *adj* unable to be reduced from one form, state, degree, etc to another.— **irreducibility** *n*. —**irreducibly** *adv*.

irrefragable *adj* irrefutable, unanswerable.

irrefrangible *adj* inviolable; (*physics*) which cannot be refracted.

irrefutable *adj* unable to deny or disprove; indisputable.—**irrefutability** *adv*.— **irrefutably** *adv*.

irreg. *abbr* = irregular; irregularly.

irregular *adj* not regular, straight, or even; not conforming to the rules; imperfect; (*troops*) not part of the regular armed forces.—**irregularly** *adv*.

irregularity *n* (*pl* **irregularities**) departure from a rule, order, or method; crookedness.

irrelative *adj* unconnected, unrelated.

irrelevant *adj* not pertinent; not to the point.—**irrelevance, irrelevancy** *n*. — **irrelevantly** *adv*.

irreligion *n* lack of religious belief; disregard for, or hostility towards, religion.

irreligious *adj* impious, irreverent.

irremediable *adj* which cannot be remedied.

irremissible *adj* unpardonable; (*obligation*) binding.

irremovable *adj* not removable.—**irremovability** *adv*.—**irremovably** *adv*.

irreparable *adj* that cannot be repaired, rectified, or made good.— **irreparably** *adv*.

irreplaceable *adj* unable to be replaced.—**irreplaceability** *n*.

irrepressible *adj* unable to be controlled or restrained.—**irrepressibly** *adv*.

irreproachable *adj* blameless; faultless.—**irreproachability** *adv*.— **irreproachably** *adv*.

irresistible *adj* not able to be resisted; overpowering; fascinating; very charming, alluring.—**irresistibility** *adv*.—**irresistibly** *adv*.

irresolute *adj* lacking resolution, uncertain, hesitating.—**irresolutely** *adv*.— **irresoluteness, irresolution** *n*.

irresolvable *adj* which cannot be resolved or solved.

irrespective *adj* (*with* **of**) regardless.—**irrespectively** *adv*.

irresponsible *adj* not showing a proper sense of the consequences of one's actions; unable to bear responsibility.—**irresponsibility** *n*. —**irresponsibly** *adv*.

irresponsive *adj* not responsive.

irretentive *adj* not retentive.

irretrievable *adj* that cannot be recovered; irreparable.—**irretrievability** *n*. — **irretrievably** *adj*.

irreverent, irreverential *adj* not reverent, disrespectful.—**irreverence** *n*. — **irreverently** *adv*.

irreversible *adj* not able to be reversed; unable to be revoked or altered.— **irreversibility** *n*. —**irreversibly** *adv*.

irrevocable *adj* unable to be revoked, unalterable.—**irrevocability** *n*. — **irrevocably** *adv*.

irrigate *vt* to supply (land) with water as by means of artificial ditches, pipes, etc; (*med*) to wash out (a cavity, wound, etc).—**irrigable** *adj*.—**irrigation** *n*. — **irrigative** *adj*.—**irrigator** *n*.

irrigation *n* the supply of water to dry land through canals, ditches, sprinklers or the flooding to facilitate plant growth; (*med*) the washing out of a wound or body cavity with a flow of water or other fluid.

irritable *adj* easily annoyed, irritated, or provoked; (*med*) excessively sensitive to a stimulus.—**irritability** *n*. —**irritably** *adv*.

irritable bowel syndrome *n* a condition caused by abnormal muscular contractions (or increased motility) in the colon, producing effects in the large and small intestines.

irritant *adj* irritating; causing irritation. * *n* something that causes irritation.

irritate *vt* to provoke to anger; to annoy; to make inflamed or sore.—**irritative** *adj*.—**irritator** *n*.

irritation *n* the act of irritating; the state of being irritated; someone who, or something which, irritates.

IRRS *abbr* = Irish Railway Records Society.

irrupt *vi* to enter forcibly or suddenly.—**irruption** *n*.

IRS *abbr* = Internal Revenue Service; International Rhinologic Society; information retrieval system.

IRSO *abbr* = Institute of Road Safety Officers.

IRTA *abbr* = International Reciprocal Trade Association; International Road Racing Teams Association (Switzerland).

IRU *abbr* = International Railway Union; International Rugby Union.

Irusan *n* (*Irish Celtic myth*) a huge cat that inhabited a cave near Knowth on the Boyne. The cat is said to have seized Seanchan Torpeist, the chief bard of Ireland, and to have run off with him.

Irving *n* **Washington** (1783–1859) American essayist and historian. Best-known stories are "Rip Van Winkle" and "The Legend of Sleepy Hollow."

is *see* **be**.

is. *abbr* = island; isle.

Is. *abbr* = Isaiah.

IS *abbr* = Industrial Society; International Socialists; International Society of Sculptors, Painters, and Gravers; information science; internal security.

Isa. *abbr* = Isaiah.

ISA *abbr* = Individual Savings Account; Instrument Society of America; International Schools Association; International Seaweed Association; International Settlement Authority; International Shakespeare Association; International Silk Association; International Skating Association; International Society of Arboriculture; International Sunflower Association; International Surfing Association; Irish Society for Archives.

Isaac *n* (*Bible*) son of Abraham, born to Sarah in her old age; Abraham arranged that he should marry Rebekah from Mesopotania since he did not want him to have a wife from Canaan; father of Esau and Jacob. *See also* **Rebekah**.

Isabella I of Castile *see* **Ferdinand V**.

Isaiah *n* (*Bible*) 8th century BC prophet who lived through the reigns of four kings of Judah including Hezekiah whom he advised to stand firm against the Assyrians *See also* **Hezekiah**.

Isaiah *n* **the Book of** (*Bible*) the first book of the Latter Prophets, the longest of the prophetic books of the OT and one of the greatest.

ISAM *abbr* = index sequential access method.

Isäus *n* **Magnus** (1841–90) Swedish architect who led the Renaissance revival in architecture during the 1880s.

ISB *abbr* = Institute of Small Business; International Society of Bassists; International Society of Biorheology.

ISBA *abbr* = Incorporated Society of British Advertisers; Independent Schools Bursars Association; International Seabed Authority; Irish-Swedish Business Association.

ISBN *abbr* = international standard book number.

ISBRA *abbr* = International Society for Biomedical Research on Alcoholism.

i.s.c. *abbr* = interstate commerce.

ISC *abbr* = Imperial Service College; Institute for the Study of Conflict; International Sculpture Center; International Society of Citriculture; International Sporting Commission; International Student Conference; International Supreme Council of World Masons; International Surfing Committee.

Iscariot *n* (*Bible*) the name applied to Judas the traitor, disciple of Jesus. *See also* **Judas**.

ISCh *abbr* = Incorporated Society of Chiropodists.

ischemic *n* relating to a decrease in blood supply to a part of the body or an organ, caused by a blockage or narrowing of the blood vessels.

ischium (*pl* **ischia**) *n* one of the three bones that comprise each half of the pelvis. It is the most posterior of the three and supports the weight of the body when sitting.

ISCM *abbr* = International Society for Contemporary Music.

ISD *abbr* = international subscriber dialing.

ISDD *abbr* = Institute for the Study of Drug Dependence.

ISDN *abbr n* (*comput*) = Integrated Services Digital Network. A means of transmitting data, voice, and video digitally over a telecommunications line. The line is quieter, and allows greater flexibility and capacity than conventional lines.

ISF *abbr* = International Science Foundation; International Shipping Federation; International Society for Fat Research; International Solidarity Fund; International Spiritualist Federation.

ISFL *abbr* = International Society of Family Law.

ISGA *abbr* = Irish Salmon Growers' Association.

Ishbosheth *n* (*Bible*) Saul's surviving son who plotted for power after his father was killed in battle at Mt Gilboa. However, he was killed in his sleep.

Isherwood *n* **Christopher [William Bradshaw]** (1904–86) English-born American novelist and dramatist whose best-known works are the novels *Mr Norris Changes Trains* and *Goodbye to Berlin*.

Ishimoto *n* **Fujiwo** (1941–) Japanese fabric designer who works in F inland and is known for his black-and-white palette.

Ishmael *n* (*Bible*) the son of Abraham and Hagar, Sarah's maidservant. Abraham later cast out Hagar and Ishmael to be desert wanderers, but Moslems still claim him as their forefather. *See also* **Hagar**, **Ishmaelites**, **Kedar**.

Ishmaelites *n* (*Bible*) desert traders who purchased Joseph from his brothers for twenty shekels of silver; also called Midianites. *See also* **Ishmael**, **Midionites**.

ISI *abbr* = International Statistical Institute; Iron and Steel Institute.

Isidore of Seville *n* **Saint**, also called Isidorus Hispalensis (*c.*560–636) Spanish ecclesiast and scholar; archbishop of Seville (590); wrote *Etymologies*, an encyclopedia. He was noted for his simplicity and goodness. His feast day is April 4.

isinglass *n* a gelatin prepared from fish bladders; mica, esp in thin sheets.

Isis *n* (*Egypt*) the prime goddess of the Egyptian pantheon, sister and wife of Osiris, mother of Horus and a potent divinity in her own right. She is normally depicted in human form.

ISIS *abbr* = Independent Schools Information Service.

isl. *abbr* = island.

Islam *n* the Muslim religion, a monotheistic religion founded by Mohammed; the Muslim world.—**Islamic** *adj*.

Islamabad *n* capital city of the Islamic Republic of Pakistan.

island *n* a land mass smaller than a continent and surrounded by water; anything like this in position or isolation.

island arc *n* a line of volcanoes on the continental side of a deep oceanic trench that marks the subduction of oceanic crust Earthquakes.

islander *n* a native or inhabitant of an island.

Islay *n* a Scottish Hebridean island, rich in evidence of Celtic culture from the megalithic and early Christian periods.

isle *n* an island, esp a small one.

islet *n* a small island.

islets of Langerhans *npl* clusters of cells within the pancreas, which are the endocrine part of the gland. The islets were named after Paul Langerhans, a German pathologist.

ISLEWTT *abbr* = International Post Conference Symposium on Low Cost and Energy Saving Wastewater Treatment Technologies.

isls. *abbr* = islands.

ISM *abbr* = Imperial Service Medal; Incorporated Society of Musicians; Institute of Spiritualist Mediums; International Society for Mesotherapy; Irish Sovereignty Movement.

-ism *n suffix* indicating a system or doctrine, as *Protestantism*; a state or condition, as *barbarism*; action, as *criticism*; a peculiarity or idiom, as *archaism*, *gallicism*; a morbid condition caused by abuse of drugs, as *alcoholism*.

Ismene *n* (*Greek myth*) a daughter of Oedipus, sister of Antigone.

ISMS *abbr* = International Society for Mushroom Science.

isn't = is not.

ISO *abbr* = Imperial Service Order; International Organization for Standardization.

ISO7 *abbr* = International Organization for Standardization 7-bit code.

ISOA *abbr* = International Support Vessel Owners' Association.

ISOB *abbr* = Incorporated Society of Organ Builders; International Society of Barristers.

isobar *n* a line on a map connecting places of equal barometric pressure.—**isobaric** *adj*.—**isobarism** *n*.

ISOC *abbr* = Internet Society.

isochromatic *adj* of the same color; (*photog*) giving equal intensity to different colors.

isochronal, isochronous *adj*

isoclinal, isoclinic *adj* having the same dip or inclination.

isodynamic *adj* having equal force.

isogon *n* (*geom*) a figure with equal angles.

isohel *n* a line on a map, linking places with the same hours of sunshine.

isohyet *n* a line on a map, linking places with the same rainfall.

Isola *n* **Maija** (1927–) F innish fabric designer whose bold printed textiles were widely admired in the 1950s and 1960s.

isolate *vt* to set apart from others; to place alone; to quarantine a person or animal with a contagious disease; to separate a constituent substance from a compound.—**isolator** *n*.

isolated *adj* lonely; remote; lacking social contact; unique; infrequent.

isolation *n* the state of being isolated; the act of isolating.

isolationism *n* a policy of refraining from involvement in international affairs.—**isolationist** *adj*, *n*.

isomer *n* any of two or more chemical compounds whose molecules contain the same atoms but in different arrangements.—**isomeric** *adj*.—**isomerism** *n*.

isometric, isometrical *adj* having equality of measure; relating to muscular contraction involving little shortening of the muscle; (*drawing*) projecting an image to scale in three dimensions with the axis equally inclined.—**isometrically** *adv*.

isometric exercises *n* exercises undertaken to build up muscle strength by increasing tension in the muscles without contract, e.g. by pushing against something that cannot move.

isometric projection *n* (*archit*) a method of projecting a scale drawing in three dimensions with vertical lines remaining vertical while other lines are drawn at an equal angle, usu 30°, to the horizontal.

isometrics *n* (*sing or pl*) physical exercises in which muscles are contracted against each other or in opposition to fixed objects.

isomorphism *n* (*biol*) similarity in form; (*chem*) the quality of having the same crystalline form despite being formed of different elements.—**isomorphic, isomorphous** *adj*.

isopod *n* a type of crustacean with seven pairs of equal legs, e.g., the woodlouse.

isorhythm *n* (*mus*) a term used to describe a short, rhythm pattern that is repeatedly applied to an existing melody which already has an distinct rhythm.

isosceles *adj* denoting a triangle with two equal sides.

isoseismic, isoseismal *adj* pertaining to points at which earthquake shock is of the same intensity. * *n* a line on a map, linking these points.

isotherm *n* a line on a map connecting points of the same temperature.—**isothermal** *adj*.

isotonic *adj* (*chem*) (*solutions*) having the same tone or tension; having the same osmotic pressure.—**isotonically** *adv*.—**isotonicity** *n*.

isotope *n* any of two or more forms of an element having the same atomic number but different atomic weights.—**isotopic** *adj*.—**isotopically** *adv*.

isotopic analysis *n* (*archeo*) a technique which examines the ratios of certain isotopes preserved in human bone to give an indication of the nature of the foods eaten.

Isozaki *n* **Arata** (1931–) One of Japan's best known architects of the last quarter of the century. Important buildings include the 1992 Guggenheim Museum, SoHo, New York.

ISP *abbr* = Internet Service Provider; Institute of Sales Promotion; Institute of Sewage Purification.

ISPA *abbr* = International Screen Publicity Association; International Skat Players Association; International Society of Parametric Artists; International Squash Players Association.

ISPCA *abbr* = Irish Society for the Prevention of Cruelty to Animals; Ironmaking and Steelmaking Plant Contractors Association.

ISPCAN *abbr* = International Society for Prevention of Child Abuse and Neglect.

ISQ *abbr* (*Latin*) = *in status quo*, "unchanged."

Isr. *abbr* = Israel.

ISR *abbr* = information storage and retrieval.

Israel[1] *n* **1** a republic situated in southwest Asia, on the southeast of the Mediterranean. **2**. (*Bible*) the ancient kingdom of the 12 Hebrew tribes at the SE end of the Mediterranean. **3**. (*Bible*) the name given to the ancient Northern Kingdom of ten tribes which broke away after the death of Solomon; destroyed by the Assyrians 721BC. **4**. (*Bible*) the most frequent use of the word in the Bible is its application in a religious rather than a political sense. The holy nation chosen by God to be his own people; (*inf*) the Jewish community throughout the world.

Israel² *n* (*Bible*) the name given to Jacob in the story of his wrestling with a messenger of God.

Israelite *n* (*Bible*) a descendant of the Hebrew patriarch Jacob.

ISRN *abbr* = Incorporated Society of Registered Naturopaths.

ISRS *abbr* = International Society for Reef Studies.

ISS *abbr* = Inn Sign Society; International Seaweed Symposium; International Social Services; International Society of Surgery; International Student Service; International Sunshine Society.

Issel *n* **Alberto** (1848–1926) Italian furniture designer who employed over 70 craftspeople in his Turin workshops.

Isselburg *n* **Peter** (*c*.1580–*c*.1630) German engraver who in 1625 published his handbook of grotesque patterns, bacchic subjects, and ornaments.

Issigonis *n* **Alec** (1906–88) Turkish-born auto designer whose successes were the Morris Minor in 1948 and the 1959 Mini.

ISSM *abbr* = Institute of Sterile Services Management.

ISSN *abbr* = International Standard Serial Number.

ISSO *abbr* = International Self-Service Organization; International Side-Saddle Organization.

ISSOL *abbr* = International Society for the Study of the Origin of Life.

issuable *adj* which can be issued.

issuance *n* the act of issuing.

issue *n* an outgoing; an outlet; a result; offspring; a point under dispute; a sending or giving out; all that is put forth at one time (an issue of bonds, a periodical, etc). * *vb* (**issuing, issued**) *vi* to go or flow out; to result (from) or end (in); to be published. * *vt* to let out; to discharge; to give or deal out, as supplies; to publish.

issue price *n* the price at which a new issue of shares is issued to the public.

issued share *n* a share that has been assigned by the directors of a company to an applicant and paid for in full.

issued share capital *n* the amount of the authorized share capital for which shareholders have subscribed.

issuing house *n* a financial house, such as a merchant bank, that arranges the issue of new stocks and shares for companies and organizes the flotation of private companies in the stock exchange.

IST *abbr* = insulin shock therapy.

-ist *n suffix* denoting a person concerned with something, as *environmentalist*; a member of a profession, as *anestheologist*; an advocate of a particular doctrine, as *atheist*; a person characterized by a particular habit, trait, etc, as *motorist, romanticist*; a person who is prejudiced about another social group, as *racist*. * *adj suffix* denoting a doctrine or belief, as *anarchist*; denoting prejudice against another social group, as *sexist* (—*also* **-istic, -istical**).

ISTA *abbr* = International School of Theater Anthropology; International Schools Theater; International Seed Testing Association; International Sight-Seeing and Tours Association; International Special Tooling Association.

Istanbul *n* a city in Turkey.

ISTC *abbr* = Institute of Scientific and Technical Communicators; Iron and Steel Trades Confederation.

isthmian *adj* of or pertaining to an isthmus.

isthmus *n* (*pl* **isthmuses, isthmi**) a narrow strip of land having water at each side and connecting two larger bodies of land.—**isthmoid** *adj*.

istle *n* a tough fiber made from a species of Mexican agave, used to make cord.—*also* **ixtle**.

ISTRA *abbr* = Interplanetary Space Travel Research Association.

ISTRC *abbr* = International Society for Tropical Root Crops.

ISTRO *abbr* = International Soil Tillage Research Organization.

IStructE *abbr* = Institution of Structural Engineers.

ISU *abbr* = Immigration Services Union; International Salvage Union; International Shooting Union; International Skating Union; International Stereoscopic Union.

ISV *abbr* = International Scientific Vocabulary.

ISVA *abbr* = Incorporated Society of Valuers and Auctioneers.

ISVBM *abbr* = International Society of Violin and Bow Makers.

ISVR *abbr* = Institute of Sound & Vibration Research.

ISWA *abbr* = International Science Writers Association; International Solid Wastes and Public Cleansing Association.

ISWG *abbr* = Imperial Standard Wire Gauge.

it *pron* the thing mentioned; the subject of an impersonal verb; a subject or object of indefinite sense in various constructions. * *n* the player, as in tag, who must catch another.

i.t. *abbr* = in transit.

It. or **Ital.** *abbr* = Italian; Italic; Italy.

IT *abbr* = Information Technology; Inner Temple; Institute of Trichologists; income tax; industrial tribunal.

ita *abbr* = initial teaching alphabet.

ITA *abbr* = Independent Television Authority; Indian Tea Association; Initial Teaching Alphabet Association; Institute of Transport Administration; Institute of Travel Agents; International Trade Administration; International Turquoise Association; International Twins Association; Ireland-Taiwan Association.

ITAI *abbr* = Institute of Traffic Accident Investigators.

ital. *abbr* = italic (type).

Italian *adj* of Italy or its people. * *n* a native of Italy; the Italian language.

Italianate *adj* Italian in style or character.

italiano or **italienne** *adj, adv* (*mus*) (*French*) "in the Italian style."

Italian sixth *see* **augmented sixth**.

italic *adj* denoting a type in which the letters slant upward to the right (*this is italic type*). * *n* (*usu pl*) italic type or handwriting.

Italic *adj* (*language*) of ancient Italy.

italicize *vi* to write in italics. * *vt* to underline a word to indicate italics.—**italicization** *n*.

Italy *n* a republic in southern Europe, comprising a large peninsula and the two main islands of Sicily (Sicilia) and Sardinia (Sardegna).

ITALY *abbr* = I trust and love you.

ITAR *abbr* = Information Telegraph Agency of Russia.

ITB *abbr* = Industry Training Board.

itc *abbr* = installation time and cost.

ITC *abbr* = Imperial Tobacco Company; Independent Television Commission; Independent Theater Council; Indian Tobacco Company; Industrial Training Council; Inland Transport Commission; International Tea Committee; International Thyroid Conference; International Trade Center; International Trade Commission; International Translations Center; International Tribology Council; International Trotsky Committee; International Typeface Corporation; Irish Timber Council.

itch *n* an irritating sensation on the surface of the skin causing a need to scratch; an insistent desire. * *vi* to have or feel an irritating sensation in the skin; to feel a restless desire.

itching *n* a skin condition or sensation prompting scratching to obtain relief.—*also* **pruritis**

itchy *adj* (**itchier, itchiest**) pertaining to or affected with an itch.—**itchiness** *n*.

-ite *n suffix* indicating a native or inhabitant, as *Israelite*; a follower or supporter of a particular movement, as *Luddite, Pre-Raphaelite*; a mineral or rock, as *graphite*; a fossil, as *ammonite*; a commercial product, as *ebonite*; (*biol*) a part of a body or organ, as *somite*.

item *n* an article; a unit; a separate thing; a bit of news or information.

itemize *vt* to specify the items of; to set down by items.—**itemization** *n*.

iterate *vt* to say or do again or repetitively.—**iteration** *n*. —**iterative** *adj*.

iteration *n* (*comput*) a command or program statement that is continually repeated until a particular condition is met.

ITF *abbr* = International Tennis Federation; International Trampoline Federation; Irish Textiles Federation.

ITG *abbr* = International Trumpet Guild.

Ith *n* (*Irish Celtic myth*) one of the Sons of Mil Espaine, who were the first human rulers of Ireland.

Ithaca *n* one of the Ionian Islands on the west of Greece, modern Ithaki.

ithyphallic *adj* (*poet*) in the manner of the rites or hymns to Bacchus.

ITI *abbr* = Indian Telephone Industries; Institute of Translation and Interpreting; International Theater Institute; International Thrift Institute; Irish Timber Industries.

itin. *abbr* = itinerant; itinerary.

itinerancy, itineracy *n* (*pl* **itinerancies, itineracies**) the act of traveling from place to place, esp to carry out an official duty.

itinerant *adj* traveling from place to place. * *n* a traveler.

itinerary *n* (*pl* **itineraries**) a route; a record of a journey; a detailed plan of a journey.

Itinierarium Cambriae *n* an important source book of Welsh legend written by the Norman-Welsh chronicler and cleric, Giraldus Cambrensis (*c*.1146–*c*.1223).

it'll = it will; it shall.

ITMA *abbr* = Imported Tire Manufacturers Association; Institute of Trade Mark Agents; Irish Transport Manufacturers Association (Eire); *It's That Man Again* (former British radio show).

ITN *abbr* = Independent Television News.

ITO *abbr* = International Trade Organization.

its *poss pron* relating to or belonging to **it**.

it's = it is; it has.

ITS *abbr* = Institute for Transport Studies; International Telecommunications Society; International Thespian Society; International Turfgrass Society; Irish Texts Society.

itself *pron* the reflexive and emphatic form of **it**.

ITT *abbr* = Institute of Travel and Tourism; International Telephone and Telegraph Corporation; insulin tolerance test.

Itten *n* **Johannes** (1888–1967) German theorist and teacher who was a founding member of the **Bauhaus** school.

ITTF *abbr* = International Table Tennis Federation.

ITTID *abbr* = International Trust for Terminal and Incurable Diseases.

ITU *abbr* = International Telecommunication Union; International Temperance Union; International Typographical Union; intensive therapy unit.

ITV *abbr* = Independent Television.

IU *abbr* = international unit.

IUA *abbr* = International Union of Advertising.

Iubdan *n* (*Irish Celtic myth*) the elfin king of Faylinn and husband of Queen Bebo.

IUC *abbr* = International Union of Crystallography.

IUCD *abbr* = intrauterine contraceptive device.

Iuchar *n* (*Irish Celtic myth*) the son of Tuirenn and the brother of Brian and Iucharba. The three brothers killed Cian whose son Lugh decided to take vengeance on them.

Iucharba *n* (*Irish Celtic myth*) the son of Tuirenn and the brother of Brian and Iuchar.

IUCW *abbr* = International Union for Child Welfare.

IUD *abbr* = intrauterine device.

IUGR *abbr* = intrauterine growth retardation.

IUHHA *abbr* = International Union of Historic House Associations.

IUI *abbr* = International Union of Interpreters.

IUMI *abbr* = International Union of Marine Insurance.

IUP *abbr* = intrauterine pressure.

IUPAC *abbr* = International Union of Pure and Applied Chemistry, an organization that regulates procedures, such as the nomenclature for naming substances.

IUPLAW *abbr* = International Union for the Protection of Literary and Artistic Works.

IUSF *abbr* = International Union of Societies of Foresters; International University Sports Federation.

IUT *abbr* = International Union of Tenants; intrauterine transfusion.

iv *abbr* = increased/invoice value.

i.v. *abbr* (*Latin*) = *in verbo, or in voce,* "under the word."

IV *abbr* = initial velocity; Institute of Valuers (South Africa); intravenous; intravenous(ly); intravenous drip.

IVA *abbr* = Independent Voters' Association; Invalidity Allowance; individual voluntary arrangement (concerning bankruptcy proceedings).

IVACL *abbr* = International Voluntary Action on Child Labor.

IVB *abbr* = Invalidity Benefit.

IVBA *abbr* = International Veteran Boxers Association.

IVBF *abbr* = International Volleyball Federation.

IVC *abbr* = Permanent Committee for the International Veterinary Congresses.

I've = I have

-ive *adj suffix* tending to, characteristic of, as *formative.*

Ives *n* **Charles Edward** (1874–1954) American composer best known for his orchestral pieces, e.g. *General Booth Enters into Heaven,* the *Unanswered Question,* and *Central Park in the Dark.*

IVF *abbr* = in vitro fertilization: a technique for helping infertile couples to have children, in which a woman's eggs are fertilized by the father's sperm in a laboratory and then re-implanted in the womb.

ivory *n* (*pl* **ivories**) the hard, creamy-white substance forming the tusks of elephants, etc; any substance like ivory; creamy white. * *adj* of or like ivory; creamy white.

ivory tower *n* a place or situation which excludes the realities of everyday life.— **ivory towered** *adj.*

IVR *abbr* = International Vehicle Registration.

IVS *abbr* = International Voluntary Service.

IVT *abbr* = International Visual Theater Research Community; intravenous transfusion.

IVU *abbr* = International Vegetarian Union.

ivy *n* (*pl* **ivies**) a climbing or creeping vine with a woody stem and evergreen leaves.— **ivied** *adj.*

IWA *abbr* = Inland Waterways Association; International Wheat Agreement; International Woodworkers of America; International Workers Aid; Irish Wheelchair Association.

Iwata *n* **Itako** (1922–) Japanese glass designer who was president of Awata Glass, Tokyo.

IWB *abbr* = International Waterpolo Board.

IWC *abbr* = Institute for World Concern; Interim Wilderness Committee; International Whaling Commission; International Wildlife Coalition; International Windglider Class; Irish Wildbird Conservancy.

IWCC *abbr* = International Women's Cricket Council; International Wrought Copper Council; International Wood Collectors Council.

IWCT *abbr* = International War Crimes Tribunal.

IWGA *abbr* = International World Games Association.

IWM *abbr* = Imperial War Museum; Institute of Wastes Management.

IWTF *abbr* = International Wheelchair Tennis Federation; Intractable Wastes Task Force.

IWW *abbr* = Industrial Workers of the World.

IX *abbr* (*Greek*) = *Iesous Christos,* "Jesus Christ" (the initial letters of the words in Greek capitals).

Ixion *n* (*Greek myth*) a king of the Lapiths in Thessaly and father of Perithous. He tried to seduce Hera, and was punished by being chained to a fiery wheel, which rolled forever in the sky.

ixtle *see* **istle.**

-ize *vb suffix* to cause to be, as *sterilize;* to make or become (like), as *crystallize;* to combine with, as *oxidize;* to engage in, as *soliloquize;* to act in a specified way, according to a principle, policy, etc, as *privatize;* to affect with or subject to, as *galvanize, anesthetize.*—**-ization** *n suffix.*

Izmir *n* a city in Turkey.

IZS *abbr* = insulin zinc suspension.

I

J

j, J the tenth letter of the English alphabet.

J *symbol* (*phys*) the mechanical equivalent of heat.

J *abbr* = joule(s), the SI unit of energy used in physics; Journal; Judge; Justice; (*math*) the Jacobian or Jacobian determinant.

Ja. *abbr* = January.

JA *abbr* = Joint Agent; Judge Advocate; Justice of Appeal.

j/a, J/A *abbr* = joint account.

JAA *abbr* = Joint Aviation Authorities.

JAAT *abbr* = joint air attack team.

jab *vti* (**jabbing, jabbed**) to poke or thrust roughly; to punch with short, straight blows. * *n* a sudden thrust or stab; (*inf*) an injection with a hypodermic needle.

jabber *vti* to speak or say rapidly, incoherently, or foolishly. * *n* such talk.— **jabberer** *n*.

Jabbok *n* a tributary of the Jordan; (*Bible*) the scene of the wrestling match between Jacob and a mysterious stranger; and also the place of the reunion with his brother Esau. *See also* **Jacob**.

Jabesh-Gilead *n* town in the east of Jordan; (*Bible*) where Saul and his sons fell in battle. *See also* **Ammonites; Saul**.

jabiru *n* a stork-like bird of tropical America; an Australian stork.

jaborandi *n* a tropical American plant that yields an alkoloid used to stimulate perspiration and as a diuretic.

jabot *n* an ornamental frill worn down the front of a blouse or shirt.

JAC *abbr* = Jewelry Advisory Center.

jacamar *n* a South American bird similar to a kingfisher.

jacana, jaçana *n* a small tropical wading bird.

jacaranda *n* a South American tree with purple flowers and hard, heavy wood; any one of several similar trees; the fragrant wood from such trees.

JACARI *abbr* = Joint Action Committee Against Racial Interference.

jacinth *n* a reddish-orange gem, a variety of zircon.

jack *n* any of various mechanical or hydraulic devices used to lift something heavy; a playing card with a knave's picture on it, ranking below the queen; a small flag flown on a ship's bow as a signal or to show nationality; a sailor; a socket that takes a plug at one end and attaches to an electrical circuit at the other; a small white ball used as a target in the game of bowls. * *vt* (*with* **in**) (*sl*) to abandon (an attempt at something); (*with* **up**) to raise (a vehicle) by means of a jack; to increase (prices, etc); (*sl*) to inject a narcotic drug.

Jack *n* **George Washington** (1855–1932) British architect, born in New York whose book *Wood Carving: Design and Workmanship* was published in 1903.

jackal *n* (*pl* **jackals, jackal**) any of various wild dogs of Africa and Asia.

jackanapes *n* a conceited or upstart person; a pert child; (*arch*) a monkey.

jackass *n* a male donkey; a fool.

jackboot *n* a leather military boot extending above the knee; authoritarian rule, oppression.

jackdaw *n* a black bird like the crow but smaller.

jackeroo, jackaroo (*pl* **jackeroos, jackaroos**) (*Austral*) (*sl*) a young person training to be a manager on a sheep or cattle station.

jacket *n* a short coat; an outer covering, as the removable paper cover of a book. * *vt* to cover with a jacket or cover.—**jacketed** *adj*.

jackfruit *n* an East Indian tree or its fruit, which is similar to breadfruit.

jack-in-the-box *n* a toy consisting of a box from which a figure on a spring pops out when the lid is lifted.

jackknife *n* (*pl* **jackknives**) a pocket-knife; a dive in which the diver touches his feet with knees straight and then straightens out. * *vi* to dive in this way; (*articulated truck*) to lose control so that the trailer and cab swing against each other.

jack-o'-lantern *n* a lantern made from a hollowed-out pumpkin with holes cut in it to resemble a face; a will-o'-the-wisp.

jack-of-all-trades *n* (*pl* **jacks-of-all-trades**) a person who does many different types of work.

jackpot *n* the accumulated stakes in certain games, e.g. poker; **hit the jackpot** (*sl*) to win; to gain an enormous amount.

jack rabbit *n* a large hare with long ears, common in North America.

jacksnipe *n* (*pl* **jacksnipes, jacksnipe**) a kind of small snipe; a sandpiper.

Jackson *n* 1. **Dakota** (1949–) American furniture designer whose first furniture commission was from Yoko Ono for John Lennon. 2. **Glenda** (1936–) English actress, who became a Labour member of parliament in 1992. 3. **Jesse** (1941–) American Democrat politician and a Baptist minister; one of Martin Luther King's aides. 4. **Michael [Joe]** (1958–) American pop singer . The youngest of the Jackson Five, he became a solo performer in the late 1970s.

Jackson *n* the capital city of Mississippi, a state of the USA.

jack-tar *n* (*inf*) a sailor.

JACNE *abbr* = Joint Advisory Committee on Nutritional Education.

Jacob *n* (*Bible*) grandson of Abraham and son of Isaac and Rebekah; considered the traditional ancestor of the children of Israel. *See also* **birthright; Esau; Rachel**.

Jacob *n* **Carl** (*c*.1925–) Danish furniture designer who produced the popular 1950 Jason stacking chairs.

Jacob, François *see* **Monod, Jacques-Lucien**.

Jacobean *adj* pertaining to the time or reign of James I of England and VI of Scotland. * *n* a person of this period, esp a poet.

Jacobean architecture *n* (*archit*) the style of building and decoration which occurred during the reign of James I of England and VI of Scotland (1603–25).

Jacobean tragedy *n* a development of revenge tragedy in the Jacobean period.

Jacobin *n* a French Dominican friar; a member of a violent democratic faction that exercised a powerful influence in the French Revolution; an extreme revolutionary.—**Jacobinic, Jacobinical** *adj*.—**Jacobinism** *n*.

Jacobite *n* a supporter of James II of England and VII of Scotland after his abdication or of his descendants.—*also adj*.—**Jacobitism** *n*.

Jacobs *n* **W[illiam] W[ymark]** (1863–1943) English novelist and short-story writer, particularly noted for the macabre story "The Monkey's Paw," in *The Lady of the Barge*.

Jacobsen *n* 1. **Arne** (1902–71) Danish architect and furniture designer whose buildings include St Catherine's College, Oxford. 2. **Jacob** (1901–1995) Norwegian lighting designer.

jaconet *n* a fine soft white cotton material resembling cambric.

jacquard *n* a loom for weaving patterns; a pattern woven on a jacquard loom.

JACT *abbr* = Joint Association of Classical Teachers.

jactation *n* boasting, bragging, ostentatious display; throwing.

jactitation *n* (*law*) a false claim of marriage, harmful to the interests of another; (*med*) extreme restlessness or tossing in bed, esp as a symptom of fever.—*also* **jactation**.

Jacuzzi (*trademark*) *n* a device that swirls water in a bath; a bath containing such a device.

jade *n* a hard, ornamental semiprecious green stone; its light green color.

jaded *adj* tired, exhausted; satiated.—**jadedly** *adv*.—**jadedness** *n*.

jadeite *n* a form of jade found in Burma.

jaeger *n* an American shore bird that steals the prey of other, weaker birds by scaring them away; a (German or Swiss) hunter; an Austrian or German military sharpshooter.

JAF *abbr* = Judge Advocate of the Fleet.

Jaffna *n* major city in Sri Lanka.

JAG *abbr* = Judge Advocate General.

jag[1] *n* a sharp, tooth-like notch or projection. * *vt* (**jagging, jagged**) to cut into notches; to prick.

jag[2] *n* (*sl*) intoxication from drugs or alcohol; (*sl*) a drinking spree.

jagged *adj* having sharp notches or projecting points; notched or ragged.—**jaggedly** *adv*.—**jaggedness** *n*.

Jagger *n* **Mick [Michael Philip Jagger]** (1943–) English singer, songwriter, and lead singer with the Rolling Stones. The other original members were guitarist Keith Richard (1943–), bass guitarist Bill Wyman (1936–), drummer Charlie Watts (1941–) and guitarist Brian Jones (1944-69).

jaggery, jaggary, jagghery *n* a coarse East Indian sugar made from palm sap.

jaggies *npl* (*comput*) the ragged edges that appear on computer graphics, caused by the square edges of pixels, which show up when a curve is drawn.—*also* **aliasing**.

jaggy *adj* (**jaggier, jaggiest**) jagged.

jaguar *n* (*pl* **jaguars, jaguar**) a large American black-spotted yellow wild cat similar to the leopard.

jail *n* a prison; imprisonment. * *vt* to send to or confine in prison.

jailbird *n* a person who is or has been confined in jail.

jailbreak *n* an escape from jail.

jailer, jailor *n* a person in charge of prisoners in a jail.

Jain *n* an adherent of Jainism. * *adj* pertaining to the Jains or their religious system.—*also* **Jaina, Jainist**.

Jainism *n* a Hindu religion of India similar to Buddhism.

Jairus *n* (*Bible*) the ruler of a synagogue whose dying daughter was healed by Jesus.

Jakarta *n* capital city of Indonesia.

JAL *abbr* = Japan Air Lines.

jalap, jalop *n* the root of a Mexican plant used formerly as a purgative; the plant itself or similar plants; the resin from the plant.—**jalapic** *adj*.

Jallot *n* 1. **Léon Albert** (1874–1967) French craftsman who was the first to react against the excesses of Art Nouveau. 2. **Maurice** (1900–) F rench furniture designer.

jalopy *n* (*pl* **jalopies**) an old battered vehicle.

jalousie *n* a blind with slats like a Venetian blind or a louvered shutter; a louver window.

jam session *n* (*mus*) (*sl*) an unrehearsed performance or imrpovisation by jazz, rock or other musicians, usu for their own enjoyment.

jam[1] *n* a preserve made from fruit boiled with sugar until thickened; (*inf*) something easy or desirable.—**jammy** *adj* (*sl*) lucky, crafty.

jam[2] *vb* (**jamming, jammed**) *vt* to press or squeeze into a confined space; to crowd full with people or things; to cause (machinery) to become wedged and inoperable; to cause interference to a radio signal rendering it unintelligible. * *vi* to become stuck or blocked; (*sl*) to play in a jam session. * *n* a crowded mass or congestion in a confined space; a blockage caused by jamming; (*inf*) a difficult situation.—**jammer** *n*.

Jam. *abbr* = Jamaica.

Jamaica *n* an island country in the Caribbean Sea about 150 kilometers or 93 miles south of Cuba.

Jamaican Dollar *n* currency of Jamaica.

jamb *n* (*archit*) the straight vertical side supports of a doorway, arch, window or fireplace.

jamboree *n* a large party or spree; a large, often international, gathering of Scouts.

James *n* (*Bible*) the son of Zebedee and brother of John, one of the twelve disciples of Jesus. *See also* **Boanerges**.

James I *n* (1394–1437) king of Scots (1406–1437). The son of Robert III by Annabella Drummond. His poem *The King's Quair* (or King's Book) entitles him to high rank among the followers of Chaucer. He was succeeded by his son James II.

James I of England *see* **James VI** of Scots.

James II *n* (1430–1460) king of Scots (1437–1460). The surviving twin son of James I and Queen Joan. By his wife, Mary of Gueldres, he had four sons and was succeeded by the eldest, James III.

James II *n* (1633–1701) king of Great Britain and Ireland (1685–1688). The second son of Charles I and Henrietta Maria of France.

James III *n* (1451–1488) king of Scots (1460–88).. The son of James II and Mary of Gueldres.

James IV *n* (1473–1513) king of Scots (1488–1513). The son of James III, married the daughter of Henry VII, Margaret. This was later to become the basis for Stuart rule in England. His heir, James V was barely more than a year old when James IV died.

James V *n* (1512–1542) king of Scots (1513–1542). Succeeded his father, James IV, who had fallen at Flodden when he was only eighteen months old. Father of Mary, who became Mary, Queen of Scots.

James VI *n* of Scots and **I** of England (1566–1625). Reigned (as James VI) from 1567–1625 and (as James I) from 1603–1625. The only son of Mary, Queen of Scots, and Henry Stuart, Lord Darnley.

James VI and I *n* (1566–1625) king of Scotland as James VI and king of England and Ireland as James I. The son of Mary, Queen Of Scots, he inherited the Scottish throne in 1567 and the English throne in 1603. A scholar, he was described by a contemporary as "the wisest fool in Christendom."

James VII and II *n* (1633–1701) king of Scotland as James VII and king of England and Ireland as James II. James had to flee to France after William III landed in England in 1688.

James *n* 1. **Henry** (1843–1916) American-born British novelist, short-story writer, and critic. 2. **M[ontague] R[hodes]** (1862–1936) English scholar and ghost-story writer. 3. **Dame P D [Phyllis Dorothy White]** (1920–) English author well known for her crime stories. 4. **William** (1842–1910) American philosopher and psychologist who coined the term "stream of consciousness."

James *n* Saint (*Bible*) also known as "James the Just," a brother of Jesus who appears in the Acts of the Apostles as an important leader of the early Church.

Jamesone *n* **George** (1581–1644) Scottish painter. He became famous as a portrait painter although he also painted historical pieces and landscape.

Jamestown *n* capital city of St Helena.

Jamnitzer *n* **Christoph** (1563–1618) German goldsmith.

jam-packed *adj* filled to capacity.

Jan. *abbr* = January.

Janácek *n* **Leos** (1854–1928) Czech composer, conductor and organist best known for his operas, e.g. the *Cunning Little Vixen*.

j & wo *abbr* = jettison and wash overboard.

JANE *abbr* = Journalists Against Nuclear Extermination.

JANET *abbr* = Joint Academic Network (computer network for scholars).

jangle *vi* to make a harsh or discordant sound, as bells. * *vt* to cause to jangle; to irritate. * *n* a harsh, discordant sound.

Janissary music *n* (*mus*) the music of Turkish military bands.

janitor *n* a person who looks after a building, doing routine maintenance, etc.—**janitorial** *adj*.

janizary, janissary (*pl* **janizaries, janissaries**) *n* (*formerly*) a foot-guard of the Turkish sultans; a Turkish infantryman.

JANSA *abbr* = Janatorial Supplies Association.

Jansenism *n* the doctrine of sovereign and irresistible grace, promulgated in the 17th century in opposition to the Jesuits; the religion based on these doctrines.—**Jansenist** *n*, *adj*.—**Jansenistic** *adj*.

jansky *n* the unit used for the measurement of the power received on Earth from a celestial radio source, named after Karl Jansky, a pioneer in the field.

Janssens *n* 1. **Abraham** (1575–1632) Flemish painter. His most memorable work is *Calvary* (*c*.1620). 2. **Cornelius [Cornelius Johnson]** (1593–1664) English-born painter of Dutch parentage. His work includes a portrait of the poet John Milton as a boy.

Januarius *n* Saint (*d.c.*305) Italian bishop of Benevento, martyred at Pozzuoli. His feast day is September 19.

January *n* (*pl* **Januaries**) the first month of the year, having 31 days.

Janus[1] *n* (*Roman myth*) a god depicted with two faces, one looking forward, the other backward, the protector of all doors, passages, and beginnings, and after whom the first month of the year was named.

Janus[2] *n* a small, irregular satellite of Saturn, in the same orbit as Epimetheus.

Jap *n* (*sl*) a Japanese.

Jap. *abbr* = Japan; Japanese.

japan *vt* (**japanning, japanned**) to cover with a hard black glossy lacquer.

Japan *n* a constitutional monarchy, comprising a series of over 1,000 islands in East Asia.

Japanese *adj* of Japan, its people or language. * *n* the language of Japan; an inhabitant of Japan.

jape *n* a joke, jest.—**japer** *n*.—**japery** *n*.

japonica *n* any of various species of Japanese plants, Japanese quince, pear, etc; the camellia.

Jaques-Dalcroze *n* **Emile** (1865–1950) Swiss composer and teacher who developed the concept of musical teaching through eurhythmics.

jar[1] *vb* (**jarring, jarred**) *vi* to make a harsh, discordant noise; to have an irritating effect (on one); to vibrate from an impact; to clash. * *vt* to jolt. * *n* a grating sound; a vibration due to impact; a jolt.

jar[2] *n* a short cylindrical glass vessel with a wide mouth; (*inf*) a pint of beer.

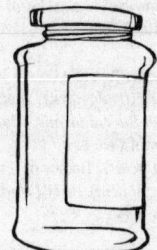

jar burial *n* a form of inhumation in which the body was buried within a large pottery jar.

jardiniere *n* an ornamental flower-stand of porcelain or metal; mixed diced vegetables stewed in a sauce and served around a meat dish.

jargon[1] *n* the specialized or technical vocabulary of a science, profession, etc; obscure and usu pretentious language. * *vi* to talk in jargon.—**jargonistic** *adj*.

jargon[2], **jargoon** *n* a translucent, colorless, yellowish, or smoky kind of zircon.

jargonize *vti* to put into or talk in jargon.—**jargonization** *n*.

jarl *n* an Old Norse chief, a noble.

Jarlshof *n* (*archeo*) a village site in Shetland, Scotland, dating from the Neolithic period.

Jarmo *n* an archeological site in northern Iraq. It is one of the oldest known examples to provide evidence of farming and dates from *c*.6500 BC.

Järnefelt *n* **Armas** (1869–1958) Finnish-born Swedish composer and conductor. His works include *Berceuse*.

Jarrell *n* **Randall** (1914–65) American poet, critic, and author of a satirical novel on academic life, *Pictures from an Institution*, an early example of the campus novel.

Jarry *n* **Alfred** (1873–1907) French dramatist of the theater of the absurd whose anarchic farce *Ubu Roi* is a savage and surreal version of *Macbeth*.

JAS *abbr* = Jamaica Agricultural Society; Japan Association of Shipbuilders; Junior Astronomical Society.

jasmine, jasmin *n* any of a genus of climbing shrubs with fragrant white, pink or yellow flowers.

Jason *n* (*Greek myth*) a hero who was given the task of bringing back the golden fleece to Iolcus, with the Argonauts, in their ship the *Argo*.

jasper *n* an opaque, many-shaded variety of quartz that, when polished, is made into a variety of ornamental articles and jewelry; a style of porcelain with a dull surface of green or blue.

JATCC *abbr* = Joint Aviation Telecommunications Coordination Committee.

JATO *abbr* = jet-assisted take-off.

Jaulmes *n* **Gustave-Louis** (1873–1959) Swiss architect who decorated the Champs Elysées and designed the Cenotaph.

jaundice *n* a condition characterized by yellowing of the skin, caused by excess of bile in the bloodstream; bitterness; resentment; prejudice.

jaundiced *adj* affected with jaundice; jealous, envious, disillusioned.

jaunt *n* a short journey, usu for pleasure. * *vi* to make such a journey.

jaunty *adj* (**jauntier, jauntiest**) sprightly or self-confident in manner.—**jauntily** *adv*.—**jauntiness** *n*.

JAVA *n* (*comput*) a programming language developed by Sun Microsystems (*trademark*) designed to have cross-platform compatibility.

Javan *n* Greece (OT).

Javanese *n* (*pl* **Javanese**) a native or inhabitant of Java; the language of Java.— *also adj* .

Javascript *n* (*comput*) created by Netscape(*trademark*), this uses the HTML as the interface and it resides within the Web page. It allows a variety of website features to be created.

javelin *n* a light spear, esp one thrown some distance in a contest.

jaw *n* one of the bones in which teeth are set; either of two movable parts that grasp or crush something, as in a vice; (*sl*) a friendly chat, gossip; argument. * *vi* (*sl*) to talk boringly and at length.

jawbone *n* a bone of the jaw, esp of the lower jaw.

jawbreaker *n* a machine for crushing rocks, etc; (*inf*) a word that is difficult to pronounce.

JAWC *abbr* = Joint Animal Welfare Council.

JAWG *abbr* = Joint Airmiss Working Group.

Jawlensky *n* **Alexei von** (1864–1941) Russian painter, associated with Kandinsky and the Blaue Reiter group.

jay *n* any of several birds of the crow family with raucous voices, roving habits, and destructive behavior to other birds.

jaycee *n* a young member of a Junior Chamber of Commerce.

jaywalk *vi* to walk across a street carelessly without obeying traffic rules or signals.—**jaywalker** *n*.

jazz *n* (*mus*) a general term for American popular music, characterized by syncopated rhythms and embracing ragtime, blues, swing, jive, and bebop; (*sl*) pretentious or nonsensical talk or actions. * *vt* (*with* **up**) (*inf*) to play (a piece of music) in a jazz style; to enliven, add color to.

jazzerati *npl* famous or accomplished jazz musicians.

jazzy *adj* (**jazzier, jazziest**) of or like jazz; (*sl*) lively.—**jazzily** *adj*.—**jazziness** *n*.

JB *abbr* (*Latin*) = *Jurum Baccalaureus*, "Bachelor of Laws."

JBIA *abbr* = Jewish Braille Institute of America.

jc *abbr* = junction.

JC *abbr* = Jesus Christ; Julius Caesar; Juvenile Court; Jurisconsult; Justice Clerk.

JCB *abbr* = Joseph Cyril Bamford (*trademark*), manufacturer of earth-moving machines; (*Latin*) *Juris Canonici Baccalaureus*, "Bachelor of Canon Law";*Juris Civilis Baccalaureus* , "Bachelor of Civil Law."

JCD *abbr* (*Latin*) = *Juris Civilis Doctor*, "Doctor of Civil Law."

JCL *abbr* = job-control language; (*Latin*) *Juris Canonici Lector* or *Licentiatus*, "Reader" or "Licentiate in Canon Law."

jct., jctn *abbr* = junction.

JD *abbr* = Junior Deacon; (*Latin*) *Juris Doctor*, "Doctor of Law"; *Jurum Doctor*, "Doctor of Laws"; juvenile delinquent.

JDC *abbr* = Jewish Documentation Centre.

JDM *abbr* (*med*) = juvenile diabetes mellitus.

jds *abbr* = job data sheet.

jealous *adj* apprehensive of or hostile toward someone thought of as a rival; envious of, resentful; anxiously vigilant or protective.—**jealously** *adv*.—**jealousness** *n*.

jealousy *n* (*pl* **jealousies**) suspicious fear or watchfulness, esp the fear of being supplanted by a rival.

jean *n* a hardwearing twilled cotton cloth; (*pl*) trousers made from this or denim.

Jeanneret *n* **Pierre** (1896–1967) Swiss architect and designer who collaborated with his cousin, Le Corbusier, on important furniture designs.

Jeannest *n* **Émile** (1813–57) French sculptor who designed the Minton majolica shown at the 1855 Paris Exposition.

Jeans *n* **Sir James [Hopwood]** (1877–1946) English physicist and astronomer. He made contributions to the study of quantum theory and stellar evolution.

Jebusites *n* (*Bible*) the original Canaanite inhabitants of Jerusalem.

Jeddah (Jiddah) *n* major city in Saudi Arabia.

jeep *n* a small robust vehicle with heavy duty tires and four-wheel drive for use on rough terrain, esp by the military.

jeer *vt* to laugh derisively. * *vi* to scoff (at). * *n* a jeering remark.—**jeerer** *n*. —**jeeringly** *adv*.

Jeffers *n* **[John] Robinson** (1887–1962) American poet. The dominant theme of his poetry is his doctrine of "Inhumanism." His works include *Roan Stallion* .

Jefferson City *n* the capital city of Missouri, a state of the USA.

Jefferson *n* **Thomas** (1743–1826) American statesman; the main creator of the Declaration of Independence in 1776; secretary of state (1790–93); 3rd president of the US (1801–9).

jehad *see* **jihad**.

Jehoiachin *n* (*Bible*) the second last king of Judah. He reigned for only three months. *See also* **Zerubbabel**.

Jehoiakim *n* (*Bible*) puppet king of the Pharaoh Neco of Egypt. *See also* **Jeremiah**.

Jehoida *n* (*Bible*) chief priest of the Temple in Jerusalem in the time of Queen Athaliah of Judah.

Jehoram *n* (*Bible*) king of Judah, son of Jehoshaphat.

Jehoshaphat *n* (*Bible*) the name of several men in the OT, in particular a ninth-century BC king of Judah.

Jehovah *n* (*Bible*) God.

Jehu *n* (*Bible*) army commander of Israel who destroyed the house of Ahab. *See also* **Ahab;Ahaziah; Baal.**

jejune *adj* lacking significance, dull; naïve; lacking in nourishment.—**jejunely** *adv*.—**jejuneness** *n*.

jejunum *n* (*anat*) the part of the small intestine lying before the ileum and after the duodenum.

jell *vti* to become or make into jelly; to crystallize, as a plan.—*also* **gel**.

jello *n* a sweet edible gelatin; jelly, jam.

jelly *n* (*pl* **jellies**) a soft, gelatinous food made from fruit syrup or meat juice; any substance like this. * *vt* (**jellying, jellied**) to turn into jelly, to congeal.—**jellied** *adj*.

jellyfish *n* (*pl* **jellyfish, jellyfishes**) a sea creature with a nearly transparent body and long tentacles.

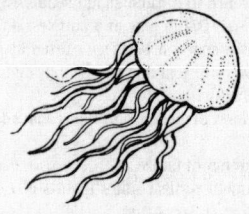

Jencks *n* **Charles A.** (1939–) American architect who designed limited-production furniture, including the 1984 Sun table.

Jenkins *n* **Roy [Baron Jenkins of Hillhead]** (1920–) W elsh Labour and Social Democrat politician; co-founder of the British Social Democratic Party.

Jenner *n* **Edward** (1749–1823) English physician who discovered that vaccination was efficacious in preventing smallpox.

jennet *n* a small Spanish horse; a female donkey.

jenny *n* (*pl* **jennies**) a machine for spinning; a female of some animals, e.g. a wren or donkey.

Jensen *n* 1. **Arthur Georg** (1866–1935) Danish metalworker who employed the best designers of the time, including Sigvaard Bernadotte. 2. **Jakob** (1926–) Danish industrial designer who designed audio equipment for Bang & Olufsen. 3.**Jens Jacob Herring Krog** (1895–1978) Danish ceramicist who worked for Rookwood Pottery. 4. **Jørgen** (1895–1966) Danish designer.

jeopardize *vt* to endanger, put at risk.

jeopardy *n* (*pl* **jeopardies**) great danger or risk.

Jephthah *n* (*Bible*) a mighty warrior.

jequirity *n* (*pl* **jequirities**) an Indian shrub with parti-colored seeds.

Jer. *abbr* = Jeremiah.

jerbil *see* **gerbil**.

jerboa *n* a small desert rodent with long hind legs and a long tail.

jeremiad *n* a long mournful lament or complaint.

Jeremiah *n* (*Bible*) a prophet whose life was bound up with the fate of Jerusalem. *See also* **Jehoiakim**.

Jeremiah *n* the Book of (*Bible*) 24th book of the OT.

Jericho *n*. **[Tell-es-Sultan]** a settlement north of the Dead Sea commanding the crossing of the River Jordan.

jerk[1] *n* a sudden sharp pull or twist; a sudden muscular contraction or reflex; (*inf*) a stupid person. * *vti* to move with a jerk; to pull sharply; to twitch.

jerk[2] *vt* to preserve (meat) by cutting it into long strips and drying it in the sun. * *n* jerked meat—*also* **jerky**.

jerkin *n* a close-fitting sleeveless jacket.

jerky[1] *see* **jerk**[2].

jerky[2] *adj* (**jerkier, jerkiest**) moving with jerks.—**jerkily** *adv*.—**jerkiness** *n*.

jeroboam *n* a huge bottle four times ordinary size, esp for champagne.

Jeroboam *n* 1. Israeli king; son of Nebat; committed heathen worship at the shrines at Bethel and Dan. 2. an eighth-century BC Samarian king who reigned for forty-one years.

Jerome *n* **Saint** (331–419) Christian monk and scholar born at Stridon. His greatest work was the Latin translation of the Bible, known as the *Vulgate*. His feast day is September 30.

Jerome *n* **Jerome K[lapka]** (1859–1927) English dramatist, essayist, and novelist whose most enduring work is *Three Men in a Boat*.

jerry can *n* a flat-sided container for liquids, esp fuel or water, with a capacity of about five gallons (25 liters).

jerry-built *adj* cheaply and flimsily constructed.—**jerry-builder** *n*. —**jerry-building** *n*.

jersey *n* (*pl* **jerseys**) any plain machine-knitted fabric of natural or artificial fibers; a knitted sweater.

Jerubbaal *n* (*Bible*) better known as Gideon.

Jerusalem *n* the capital of Israel ; this recognitionhas been withheld by several countries pending negotiations on Palestinian autonomy. A sacred city for Jews, Christians and Moslems. *See also* **Zion; temple**.

Jerusalem artichoke *n* (the edible tuber of) the North American sunflower.

Jerusalem cherry *n* a small South American shrub with reddish inedible fruit.

Jerusalem cross *n* a cross with equal arms which end in bars.

Jerusalem syndrome *n* the delusive identification with a religious figure by a visitor to Jerusalem.

Jes. *abbr* = Jesus.

jess, jesse *n* a short leather strap fixed to the leg of a hawk or falcon.

Jesse *n* (*Bible*) a prosperous farmer who had eight sons, the most famous of them being David.

JESSI *abbr* = Joint European Submicron Silicon Initiative.

jest *n* a joke; a thing to be laughed at. * *vi* to jeer; to joke.

jester *n* a person who makes jokes, esp an entertainer employed in a royal household in the Middle Ages.

Jesuit *n* a member of the Catholic Society of Jesus, founded by Ignatius Loyola in 1534; an insidious, crafty intriguer.—**Jesuitic, Jesuitical** *adj*.

Jesuitism, Jesuitry *n* (a following of) the principles, system, or practices of the Jesuits; subtle duplicity; disingenuousness.

Jesus Christ (*c*.6 BC–AD 30) founder of Christianity. He was born in Bethlehem, the son of Joseph and Mary, and was crucified at Cavalry. Christians believe he is the Son of God.

Jesus freak *n* (*sl*) a fervent Christian, esp a young member of an evangelical group.

jet[1] *n* a hard black compact mineral that can be polished and is used in jewelry; a lustrous black.—**jet-black** *adj*.

jet[2] *n* a stream of liquid or gas suddenly emitted; a spout for emitting a jet; a jet-propelled aircraft; (*astron*) a stream of moving matter found in observations of radio sources and quasars; the head of a comet evaporating under the Sun's radiation; movement of gas on the Sun's surface * *vti* (**jetting, jetted**) to gush out in a stream; (*inf*) to travel or convey by jet.

JET *abbr* = Joint European Torus.

jet engine *n* an engine, such as a gas turbine, producing jet propulsion.

Jethro *n* (*Bible*) the father of Zipporah, wife of Moses.

jet lag *n* fatigue caused by disruption of the daily bodily rhythms, associated with crossing time zones at high speed.—**jet-lagged** *adj*.

jet propulsion *n* propulsion of aircraft, boats, etc, by the discharge of gases from a rear vent.—**jet-propelled** *adj*.

jetsam *n* cargo thrown overboard from a ship in distress to lighten it, esp such cargo when washed up on the shore.

jet set *n* the wealthy and fashionable social elite who travel widely for pleasure.—**jetsetter** *n*.

jet stream *n* the jet of exhaust gases from a jet engine; (*meteorol*) high-altitude, high-speed westerly wind.

jettison *vt* to abandon, to throw overboard.

jetty *n* (*pl* **jetties**) a wharf; a small pier; (*archit*) the projection outwards of an upper story of a timber-framed building beyond the dimensions of the story below.

Jeune France *n* (*mus*) (*French*) "Young France," a group of French composers, including Jolivet and Messiaen, who identified their common aims in 1936.

Jew *n* a person descended, or regarded as descended, from the ancient Israelites; a person whose religion is Judaism.

jewel *n* a precious stone; a gem; a piece of jewelry; someone or something highly esteemed; a small gem used as a bearing in a watch. * *vt* (**jeweling, jeweled** *or* **jewelling, jewelled**) to adorn or provide with jewels.

Jewel Box cluster *n* (*astron*) an open star cluster situated close to the Southern Cross Galaxy.

jewel case *or* **jewel box** *n* a box or container for holding jewelry; the plastic, hinged container used to package a CD.

jeweler *n* a person who makes, repairs or deals in jewelry, watches, etc.

jewelry *n* jewels such as rings, brooches, etc, worn for decoration.

Jewish *adj* of or like Jews.

Jewry *n* (*pl* **Jewries**) the Jewish people.

jew's harp *n* a small metal musical instrument that makes a twanging sound when held between the lips and plucked.

Jezebel[1] *n* (*Bible*) wife of Ahab. She persecuted God's prophets. *See also* **Ahab; Baal; Naboth; Athaliah**.

Jezebel[2] *n* a woman of abandoned or licentious demeanor.

Jezreel *n* (*Bible*) fertile plain stretching from north of Mount Carmel to the River Jordan. *See also* **Megiddo**.

JFET *abbr* = junction field-effect transistor.

JFK *abbr* = John Fitzgerald Kennedy.

jg, j.g., JG *abbr* (*navy*) = junior grade.

jha *abbr* = job hazard analysis.

Jiang Jie Shi *see* **Chiang Kai-shek**.

Jiang Qing *see* **Chiang Ch'ing**.

jiao *n* a monetary unit of China, equal to one tenth of a yuan.

jib[1] *n* a triangular sail extending from the foremast in a ship. * *vti* (**jibbing, jibbed**) to pull (a sail) round to the other side; (*sail*) to swing round.—**jibber** *n*.

jib[2] *n* the projecting arm of a crane.

jib[3] *vi* to refuse to go on; to balk.

JIB *abbr* = Joint Intelligence Bureau.

jib door *n* (*archit*) a concealed door hidden in the surface of a wall.—*also* **gib door**.

jibe[1] (*sail, boom*) to swing over from one side to the other; (*yacht*) to alter course in this way.—*also* **jib, gybe**.

jibe[2] *vi* (*inf*) to be in accord or agreement with.

jiffy, jiff *n* (*pl* **jiffies, jiffs**) (*inf*) a very short time.

jig *n* a lively springing dance; the music for this; a device used to guide a tool. * *vt* (**jigging, jigged**) to dance in lively manner, as in a jig; to jerk up and down rapidly.

jigger[1] *see* **chigoe**.

jigger[2] *n* any of various mechanical devices that operate with a jigging motion; a small glass for spirits; a person or thing that jigs; (*naut*) small tackle, a small sail.

jiggermast *n* the stern mast in a two-masted sailing vessel; a small aftermost mast in a four-master.

jiggery-pokery *n* (*inf*) underhand work; trickery.

jiggle *vt* to jerk; to move (something) up and down lightly. * *n* a jerky movement.

jigsaw *n* a saw with a narrow fine-toothed blade for cutting irregular shapes. * *vt* to cut with a jigsaw.

jigsaw (puzzle) *n* a picture mounted on wood or stiff cardboard and then cut up into irregular pieces, which are then assembled for amusement.

jihad *n* a holy war waged by Muslims against nonbelievers; a crusade for or against a cause.—*also* **jehad**.

JII *abbr* = John Innes Institute.

jilt *vt* to discard (a lover) unfeelingly, esp without warning.—**jilter** *n*.

Jima *n* major city in Ethiopia.

jimjams *npl* (*sl*) delirium tremens; nervous jitters; (*inf*) pyjamas.

jimmy *n* (*pl* **jimmies**) a short crowbar used (esp by burglars) for forcing open doors and windows. * *vt* (**jimmying, jimmied**) to force open with a jimmy.—*also* **jemmy**.

jingle *n* a metallic tinkling sound like a bunch of keys being shaken together; a catchy verse or song with easy rhythm, simple rhymes, etc, often used in radio and television advertising. * *vti* (to cause) to make a light tinkling sound.—**jingler** *n*.

jingles *npl* (*mus*) an instrument consisting of a number of small bells or rattling objects on a strap, which are shaken to produce sound.

jingling johnny *n* (*mus*) an instrument, of Turkish origin, comprising a long stick with bells attached at one end.

jingly *adj* (**jinglier, jingliest**) tinkling.

jingo (*pl* **jingoes**) *n* a blustering patriot, a warmonger.

jingoism *n* advocacy of an aggressive foreign policy.—**jingoist** *adj, n*. — **jingoistic** *adj*.—**jingoistically** *adv*.

Jinja *n* major city in Uganda.

jink *n* a rapid swerve from side to side in order to dodge; (*pl*) high spirits. * *vti* to move nimbly; to dodge.

Jinnah *n* **Mohammed Ali** (1876–1948) Pakistani statesman who was the first governor-general of Pakistan (1947–48).

jinni *n* (*pl* **jinn**) (*fairy tales*) a spirit with supernatural powers that can fulfill your wishes.—*also* **genie**.

jinx *n* (*inf*) someone or something thought to bring bad luck.

Jiricná *n* **Eva** (1938–) Czech architect and interior designer .

JIT *abbr* = just-in-time.

jitney *n* (*pl* **jitneys**) (*sl*) a five-cent piece, a nickel; a small bus or other passenger vehicle, usu with inexpensive fares.

jitter *vi* (*inf*) to feel nervous or to act nervously. * *npl* (*inf*) (*with* **the**) an uneasy nervous feeling; fidgets.

jitterbug *n* a fast acrobatic dance for couples, esp popular in the 1940s. * *vi* (**jitterbugging, jitterbugged**) to dance the jitterbug.

jittery *adj* (*inf*) nervous.—**jitteriness** *n*.

JIU *abbr* = Joint Inspection Unit.

jive *n* improvised jazz played at a fast tempo; dancing to this music; (*sl*) foolish, exaggerated, or insincere talk. * *vti* to dance the jive.

JJ *abbr* = jaw jerk; judges; justices.

Jl. *abbr* = July.

JMB *abbr* = Joint Matriculation Board.

jn. *abbr* = junction.

JND *abbr* = just noticeable difference.

JNF *abbr* = Jewish National Fund.

jnr, Jnr *abbr* = Junior.

JNR *abbr* = Japanese National Railways.

Joab n (*Bible*) commander of David's army who slew David's son Absalom. *See also* **Abner; Absalom; Adonijah; David**.

Joachim n 1. **Christian** (1870–1943) Danish ceramicist who worked with Georg Jensen and Royal Copenhagen Porcelain. 2. **Joseph** (1831–1907) Hungarian violinist and composer.

Joan of Arc n **Saint** (*c*.1412–31) French patriot who was canonised in 1920. She helped raise the siege of Orléans in 1429 and brought Charles VII to Rheims to be crowned. Condemned for witchcraft by the English, she was burned at the stake.

Joash n (*Bible*) eighth king of Judah. *See also* **Jehoida**.

job n a piece of work done for pay; a task; a duty; the thing or material being worked on; work; employment; (*sl*) a criminal enterprise; (*inf*) a difficult task; (*comput*) an item of work performed by a computer, such as background printing of documents. * *adj* hired or done by the job. * *vti* (**jobbing, jobbed**) to deal in (goods) as a jobber; to sublet (work, etc).

Job n **the Book of** (*Bible*) the 18th book of the OT; a long poem with a prose prologue and epilogue on the subject of suffering.

job analysis n a research process involving the detailed analysis of a particular job.

jobber n a person who jobs; a person who buys and sells goods as a middleman; (*Brit*) a broker.

jobbery n profiting personally from a public office.

jobbing n a production process by which small numbers of a product are produced for individual customers. * *adj* working on a succession of small jobs.

job description n a detailed statement of the tasks and responsibilities that an employee is expected to carry out.

job design n the process of putting together the various elements that go together to form jobs.

jobless adj unemployed. * n unemployed people collectively.—**joblessness** n.

job lot n a miscellaneous collection of items sold as one lot; any miscellaneous collection of cheap items.

job number n a number that is assigned to a job for purposes of recording, costing, and invoicing.

job queue n (*comput*) a series of jobs that a computer is to perform in sequence.

job satisfaction n the sense of satisfaction and fulfillment experienced by people as a result of their work.

job security n the degree of certainty of continued employment in a particular position or place of work.

job share n **job sharing** n the sharing of a position of work between two part-time employees.

Jocasta n (*Greek myth*) the wife of Laius, king of Thebes, and mother of Oedipus, whom she married not knowing that he was her son.—*also* **Epicasta**.

jock n (*inf*) a jockey; a jockstrap; a male athlete; a disc jockey.

jockey n (*pl* **jockeys**) a person whose job is riding horses in races. * *vti* (**jockeying, jockeyed**) to act as a jockey; to maneuvre for a more advantageous position; to swindle or cheat.

jockstrap n a support for the genitals worn by men participating in sport.

jocose adj playful, humorous.—**jocosely** adv.—**jocoseness** n.

jocosity n (*pl* **jocosities**) the quality of being playful, jocose; a playful action; a humorous remark.

jocular adj joking; full of jokes.—**jocularity** n. —**jocularly** adv.

jocund adj merry, cheerful; jovial.—**jocundity** n. —**jocundly** adv.

JOD abbr (*med*) = juvenile onset diabetes.

jodhpurs npl riding breeches cut looser at the hips but close-fitting from knee to ankle.

Joel n (*Bible*) prophet named at the opening of the prophetic book as Joel.

Joel n **the Book of** (*Bible*) 29th book of the OT.

Joe Sixpack n a term used to describe an average blue-collar citizen – the name relating to an "average Joe" and "a sixpack of beer."

joey n (*pl* **joeys**) (*Austral inf*) a young kangaroo; any young animal or a small child.

jog vb (**jogging, jogged**) vt to give a slight shake or nudge to; to rouse, as the memory. * vi to move up and down with an unsteady motion; to run at a relaxed trot for exercise; (*borse*) to run at a jogtrot. * n a slight shake or push; a nudge; a slow walk or trot.—**jogger** n.

joggle vt (*archit*) to interlock two stones together by means of a projecting peg in one and notch in the other. * vti to move or shake slightly. * n a slight jolt.

jogtrot n a slow even-paced trot. * vi (**jogtrotting, jogtrotted**) to move at a slow even-paced trot.

Johannesburg n major city in South Africa.

john n (*sl*) a toilet; a prostitute's male customer; an easy prey.

John n 1. (*Bible*) father of Simon Peter. 2. (*Bible*) Son of Zebedee, with his brother James among the first chosen disciples of Jesus. *See also* **Boanerges**.

John n (1167–1216) king of England (1199–1216). The youngest son of Henry II, by Eleanor of Aquitaine.

John n 1. **Augustus [Edwin]** (1878–1961) Welsh painter. 2. **Elton [Reginald Kenneth Dwight]** (1947–) English pop and rock musician; particularly popular in the 1960s and 70s with hit songs such as "Daniel" and "Don't Go Breaking My Heart." 3. **Gwen** (1876–1939) English painter and elder sister of Augustus John.

John n **the Gospel of** (*Bible*) the last Gospel in the NT, attributed to John the Evangelist.

John n **the Letters of [1, 2 and 3]** n (*Bible*) books of the NT, attributed to John the Evangelist.

John Barleycorn n a personification of malt liquor.

John Chrysostom n **Saint** (*d*.407) Greek bishop and church reformer. His feast day is September 13.

John Dory n an edible yellow seafish, the dory.

John, King see **Richard I**.

johnnycake n a type of cornmeal bread.

John of Damascus n **Saint [Joannes Damascenus, John Chrysorrhoas]** (*c*.676–754) Syrian theologian. His feast day is December 4.

John of God n **Saint** (1495–1550) Portuguese soldier who became Christian; patron saint of hospitals, nurses and the sick. His feast day is March 8.

John of the Cross n **Saint** (1542–91) Spanish Carmelite friar and mystic. His feast day is December 14.

John Ogilvie n **Saint** (1579–1615) Scottish Jesuit martyr hanged in Glasgow for high treason. His feast day is March 10.

John Paul II n **[Karel Jozef Wojtyla]** (1920–) the first P olish pope and first non–Italian pope for 450 years (1978–).

Johns n **Jasper** (1930–) American painter , sculptor, and printmaker whose work was very influential on later pop artists.

Johnson n 1. **Amy** (1903–41) English aviator and the first woman to fly solo from England to Australia (1930). 2. **Andrew** (1808–75) 17th president of the US (1865–69). He was elected to the vice-presidency (1865) and then weeks later became president, following the assassination of Lincoln. 3. **Jack** (1878–1946) American boxer. He became the first African-American to win the world heavyweight title (1908–15). 4. **Lyndon B[aines]** (1908–73) American Democrat statesman who became the 36th president of the US (1963–69) following John F Kennedy's assassination. 5. **Magic [Earvin Johnson]** (1959–) American basketball player . He played with the Los Angeles Lakers (1979–91) and in the US Olympic team (1992). 6. **Philip** (1906–1995) New York-based American architect whose works include the New York State Theater. 7. **Dr Samuel** (1709–84) English critic, lexicographer, and poet whose works include the *Dictionary of the English Language* (1755). *See also* **Boswell**.

John the Baptist n **Saint** (*d.c.*29) (*Bible*) prophet, referred to as the forerunner of the Messiah. *See also* **Herodias; Salome**.

John the Evangelist n **Saint** (first century) (*Bible*) apostle; son of Zebedee. His feast day is December 27.

Johor Baharu n major city in Malaysia.

joie de vivre n great enjoyment of life.

join vti to bring and come together (with); to connect; to unite; to become a part or member of (a club, etc); to participate (in a conversation, etc); (*with* up) to enlist in the armed forces; to unite, connect. * n a joining; a place of joining; (*comput*) the combination of information from two separate data tables in a relational database, to create another data table containing summary information.

join. abbr = joinery.

joinder n the act of joining; (*law*) the coupling of two or more causes of action into the same declaration; the coupling of two issues or two parties.

joiner n a carpenter, esp one who finishes interior woodwork; (*inf*) a person who is involved in many clubs and activities, etc.

joinery n the trade of a joiner; the work of a joiner.

joint n a place where, or way in which, two things are joined; any of the parts of a jointed whole; the parts where two bones move on one another in an animal; a division of an animal carcass made by a butcher; (*geol*) a fracture in rock that can usu be related to tectonic stresses and the geometry of the rock body; (*sl*) a cheap bar or restaurant; (*sl*) a gambling or drinking den; (*sl*) a cannabis cigarette. * *adj* common to two or more; sharing with another. * *vt* to connect by a joint or joints; to divide (an animal carcass) into parts for cooking.

joint account n a bank account accessible to two or more people, for deposting or withdrawing funds.

joint and several liability n liability for a debt that is undertaken by a group.

jointed adj possessing a joint, or joints; divided into joints (animal carcass).

jointer n a tool for pointing; a kind of plane; someone or something that forms joints.

jointly adv in common; together.

joint stock n capital held in common and distributed as shares among the owners.

joint-stock company n a company whose capital is owned jointly by stockholders who may sell their individual shares.

jointure n landed estate or other property settled on a woman in consideration of her marriage, to be enjoyed by her after the death of her husband; the provision made to enable this; (*arch*) a joining or being joined.

joint venture n the sharing of expertise or commercial risk by two or more businesses, etc.

joist *n* any of the parallel beams supporting floorboards or the laths of a ceiling.

jojoba *n* a broad-leaved evergreen shrub with edible seeds yielding a valuable oil.

joke *n* something said or done to cause laughter; a thing done or said merely in fun; a person or thing to be laughed at. * *vi* to make jokes.—**jokingly** *adv*.

joker *n* a person who jokes; (*sl*) a person; an extra playing card made use of in certain games.

jokey, joky *adj* (**jokier, jokiest**) full, or fond, of jokes.

Jolivet *n* André (1905–74) French composer and a founder member of the *Jeune France* group.

jollify *vti* (**jollifying, jollified**) to make merry, esp with drink; to make jolly.—**jollification** *n*.

jollity *n* (*pl* **jollities**) the state of being jolly.

jolly *adj* (**jollier, jolliest**) merry; full of fun; delightful; (*inf*) enjoyable. * *vti* (**jollying, jollied**) (*inf*) to try to make (a person) feel good; to make fun of (someone).

Jolly Roger *n* a pirate's flag with a white skull and crossbones on a black background.

Jolson *n* Al [Asa Yoelson] (1886–1950) American actor and vaudeville singer who starred in the first talking movie, *The Jazz Singer* (1927).

jolt *vt* to give a sudden shake or knock to; to move along jerkily; to surprise or shock suddenly. * *n* a sudden jar or knock; an emotional shock.—**joltingly** *adv*.—**jolty** *adj*.

Jonah *n* (*Bible*) OT figure who was swallowed by a great fish.

JONAH *abbr* = Jews Organised for a Nuclear Arms Halt.

Jonah *n* **the Book of** (*Bible*) OT book, telling the story of Jonah.

Jonathan *n* (*Bible*) son of Saul; the first king of Israel.

Jones *n* 1. **Bobby [Robert Tyre Jones]** (1902–71) American golfer. Winner of many major championships, he is regarded as one of the greatest golfers of all time. 2. **Brian** *see* **Jagger, Mick.** 3. **Chuck [Charles Jones]** (1912–) American cartoon director who has won two Oscars. His most famous creation is Bugs Bunny. 4. **Inigo** (1573–1652) British theatre designer and architect whose works include the layout for Covent Garden, London. 5. **John Paul** (1747–92) Scots-born American naval officer who served with distinction in the Revolutionary War before joining the Russian navy.

jongleur *n* (*mus*) a medieval minstrel.

jonquil *n* a species of narcissus.

JONSIS *abbr* = Joint North Sea Information System.

Jonson *n* Ben[jamin] (*c*.1572–1637) English actor, dramatist, and poet whose works include *The Alchemist*. He was appointed the first English poet laureate in 1616.

jooal *see* **joual**.

Joplin *n* Scott (1868–1917) American pianist and composer of popular ragtime music, e.g. *Maple Leaf Rag*.

Joppa *n* Mediterranean seaport on the southern coast of Palestine.

Joram *n* (*Bible*) alternative name to Jehoram.

Jordaens *n* Jacob (1593–1678) Flemish painter, engraver, and designer.

Jordan[1] *n* a river that rises at the foot of Mount Hermon and flows through the Sea of Galilee into the Dead Sea.

Jordan[2] *n* a monarchy bounded by Saudi Arabia, Syria, Iraq and Israel.

Jordanian Dinar *n* currency of the Hashemite Kingdom of Jordan.

Jorn *n* Asger (1914–73) Danish painter and engraver. His paintings include *Green Bullet* (1960).

jorum *n* a large drinking vessel; its contents, esp punch.

Jos. *abbr* = Josiah.

Joseff of Hollywood *n* American costume jewelry company.

Joseph *n* Saint (first century) (*Bible*) husband of Mary the mother of Jesus; a carpenter from Nazareth.

Joseph *n* 1. (*Bible*) also called Barabbas, he was a follower of Jesus who accompanied the other disciples during his ministry. 2. (*Bible*) son of Jacob and his wife Rachel, whose dreams made his brothers jealous.

Joseph of Arimathea *n* Saint (*Bible*) a secret disciple of Jesus, who buried the body of Jesus in his own tomb.

Joses *n* (*Bible*) Greek form of Joseph.

josh *vi* (*sl*) to tease gently. * *n* (*sl*) friendly teasing; a teasing joke.—**josher** *n*.—**joshingly** *adv*.

Josh. *abbr* = Joshua.

Joshua *n* (*Bible*) successor of Moses as leader of the Jewish people.

Joshua *n* **the Book of** (*Bible*) sixth book of the OT.

Josiah *n* (seventh century BC) (*Bible*) king of Judah.

Josquin des Prez *n* [Desprez] (*c*.1440–1521) French-born Flemish composer.

joss *n* a Chinese god or idol.

joss stick *n* a stick of incense.

jostle *vti* to shake or knock roughly; to collide or come into contact (with); to elbow for position. * *n* a jostling; a push.

jot *n* a very small amount. * *vt* (**jotting, jotted**) to note (down) briefly.—**jotter** *n* a notebook.

jota *n* (*mus*) a Spanish dance from Aragon in 3/4 time usu accompanied by castanets.

Jotham *n* 1. (*Bible*) king of Judah. 2. (*Bible*) youngest son of Gideon.

jotting *n* something noted down, esp a memorandum.

joual *n* a French Canadian dialect also spoken in Maine that has nonstandard French grammar and pronunciation with English syntax and a substantial English vocabulary.—*also* **jooal**.

joule *n* (*physics*) a unit of energy equal to work done when a force of one newton acts over a distance of one meter.

jounce *vti* to bump; to jolt (someone or something). * *n* a bump, a jolt.

jour. *abbr* = journal, journeyman.

Jourdain *n* 1. **Francis** (1876–1958) French painter and designer, who exhibited with Cézanne and others in 1912. 2. **Frantz** (1847–1935) French architect. His notable works include the La Samaritaine department store, Paris.

journal *n* a daily record of happenings, as a diary; a newspaper or periodical; (*bookkeeping*) a book of original entry for recording transactions; that part of a shaft or axle that turns in a bearing.

journalese *n* a facile style of writing found in many magazines, newspapers, etc.

journalism *n* the work of gathering news for or producing a newspaper, magazine or news broadcast.

journalist *n* a person who writes for or edits a newspaper, etc; one who keeps a diary.—**journalistic** *adj*.—**journalistically** *adv*.

journalize *vt* to enter in a journal; to keep a daily record.—**journalization** *n*.—**journalizer** *n*.

journey *n* (*pl* **journeys**) a traveling or going from one place to another; the distance covered when traveling. * *vi* (**journeying, journeyed**) to make a journey.—**journeyer** *n*.

journeyman *n* (*pl* **journeymen**) a person whose apprenticeship is completed and who is employed by another; a reliable workman.

joust *n* a fight on horseback between two knights with lances. * *vi* to engage in a joust, to run at the tilt.—**jouster** *n*.

Jouve *n* Paul (1880–1973) French illustrator whose major work was Rudyard Kipling's *The Jungle Book*.

Jove *n* the Roman god Jupiter; **by Jove** a mild oath or exclamation of surprise.

jovial *adj* full of cheerful good humor.—**joviality** *n*.—**jovially** *adv*.

JOVIAL *abbr* (*comput*) = Jules' Own Version of International Algorithmic Language.

Jovian *adj* (*Roman myth*) of or like Jove or Jupiter.

Jovian planets *n* the four large outer planets: Jupiter, Saturn, Uranus, and Neptune.

jowl *n* the lower jaw; (*usu pl*) the cheek; the loose flesh around the throat; the similar flesh in an animal, as a dewlap.

jowly *adj* (**jowlier, jowliest**) having heavy jowls.—**jowliness** *n*.

joy *n* intense happiness; something that causes this; its expression.

Joyce *n* 1. **James [Augustine Aloysius]** (1882–1941) Irish novelist and short-story writer whose works include *Ulysses* (1922). 2. **William** (1906–46) American-born British traitor ("Lord Haw-Haw"), who broadcast Nazi propaganda to Britain during World War II and was executed for treason in 1946.

joyful *adj* filled with, expressing, or causing joy, glad.—**joyfully** *adv*.—**joyfulness** *n*.

joyless *adj* not occasioning joy, unhappy; bleak.—**joylessly** *adv*.—**joylessness** *n*.

joyous *adj* joyful, very happy.—**joyously** *adv*.—**joyousness** *n*.

joyride *n* (*inf*) a car ride, often in a stolen vehicle and at reckless speed, just for pleasure.—**joy-rider** *n*.—**joyriding** *n*.

joystick *n* (*inf*) the control lever of an aircraft; (*comput*) a device for controlling cursor movement on a monitor usu for computer games.

Joyner-Kersee *n* Jackie [Jacqueline] (1962–) American athlete, winner of several Olympic medals for track and field events.

jp *abbr* = jet propelled/propulsion.

JP *abbr* = Justice of the Peace.

JPEG *abbr* (*comput*) = Joint Photographic Experts Group. A file compression technique that is used to reduce the size of graphics files by close to 100 per cent.

jps *abbr* = jet propulsion system.

jpto *abbr* = jet propelled take-off.

jr, Jr *abbr* = Junior.

JR *abbr* (*Latin*) = *Jacobus Rex*, "King James."

JRA *abbr* = Japanese Red Army.

JRC *abbr* = Junior Red Cross.

JS *abbr* = judicial separation.

JSC *abbr* = Johnson Space Center

jt *abbr* = joint tenancy.

jt, jt., *abbr* = joint.

JTO *abbr* = jump take-off.

Ju. *abbr* = June.

J

Juan Carlos *n* (1938–) king of Spain (1975–). Nominated by Franco in 1969 as his successor, he moved towards democracy in Spain after Franco's death.

jubilant *adj* triumphant; expressing joy; rejoicing.—**jubilance** *n.* —**jubilantly** *adv.*

jubilate *vi* to exult, to show joy.—**jubilation** *n.*

Jubilate *n* (*Bible*) the 100th psalm, esp as a canticle in morning service; (*mus*) a setting of the 100th psalm.

jubilee *n* a 50th or 25th anniversary; a time of rejoicing.

Jubilee *n* (*Bible*) from the Hebrew *yobel* which means "a ram" or "a ram's horn blown as a trumpet."

jud. *abbr* (*law*) = judges; judgments; judicial.

JUD *abbr* (*Latin*) = *Juris Utriusque Doctor*, "Doctor of Both Laws," i.e. the Canon and the Civil Law.

Judah *n* (*Bible*) one of the tribes of Israel; the part of Canaan they occupied. *See also* **Israel**.

Judaic, Judaical *adj* of the Jews or Judaism.—**Judaically** *adv*

Judaism *n* the religion of the Jews, based on the Old Testament and the Talmud.—**Judaist** *n.* —**Judaistic** *adj*.

Judaize *vi, vt* to make or become Judaistic in belief, customs, precepts, etc.—**Judaization** *n.*

judas *n* a peephole, as in a cell door.

Judas *n* a traitor who pretends to be a friend.

Judas *n* **Saint** (*Bible*) the son or brother of James, one of the twelve disciples.

Judas *n* 1. (*Bible*) Christian disciple in whose home Saul of Tarsus stayed after his conversion on the Damascus road. 2. (*Bible*) also called Barsabbas, he was sent to Antioch with a letter from the apostles and elders of the Church in Jerusalem.

Judas Iscariot *n* (*Bible*) The man who betrayed Jesus.

Judas the Galilean *n* (*Bible*) a rebel mentioned by the Pharisee, Garnaliel.

Judd *n* **Donald** (1928–94) American conceptual artist and sculptor.

judder *vi* to vibrate violently. * *n* a spasmodic or rapid shaking.

Jude *n* **Saint [Thaddaeus]** (first century) disciple of Jesus and the writer of the Epistle of Jude. His feast day is October 28.

Judea *n* (*Bible*) Greek form of Judah, generally used in the NT.

Judean *adj* of, pertaining to, or from, the ancient region of Judaea.

Jude *n* **the Epistle of** (*Bible*) the 26th book of the NT, comprising a letter to the whole Church.

Judg. *abbr* = Judges.

judge *n* a public official with authority to hear and decide cases in a court of law; a person chosen to settle a dispute or decide who wins; a person qualified to decide on the relative worth of anything. * *vti* to hear and pass judgment (on) in a court of law; to determine the winner of (a contest) or settle (a dispute); to form an opinion about; to criticize or censure; to suppose, think.—**judgeable** *adj.*—**judgingly** *adv.*

Judges *n* the seventh book of the OT.

judgeship *n* the office of a judge; his or her jurisdiction.

judgment, judgement *n* a judging; a deciding; a legal decision; an opinion; the ability to come to a wise decision; censure.

judgmental, judgemental *adj* of or depending on judgment; tending to make moral or personal judgments.—**judgmentally, judgementally** *adv.*

judgment day *n* a final judgment; a day of reckoning.

Judgment Day *n* (*Christianity*) the time of God's final judgment of mankind.

judicable *adj* that may be judged; liable to be judged.

judicator *n* one who judges.

judicatory *n* (*pl* **judicatories**) a system of courts, a judiciary. * *adj* of or pertaining to the administration of justice.

judicature *n* a court or courts of justice; the power of dispensing justice by legal trial and judgment; jurisdiction; a body of judges; a tribunal.

judicial *adj* of judges, courts, or their functions.—**judicially** *adv.*

judiciary *adj* of judges or courts. * *n* (*pl* **judiciaries**) the part of government that administers justice; a system of courts in a country; judges collectively.

judicious *adj* possessing or characterized by sound judgment.—**judiciously** *adv.*—**judiciousness** *n.*

judo *n* a Japanese system of unarmed combat, adapted as a competitive sport from jujitsu.—**judoist** *n.*

Judon *n* (*Brit Celtic myth*) the wife of Gorboduc, a king of Britain who was said to be a descendant of Brutus. She was the mother of two sons, Ferrex and Porrex.

jug *n* a vessel for holding and pouring liquids, with a handle and curved lip; a pitcher; (*sl*) prison. * *vt* (**jugging, jugged**) to stew meat (esp hare) in an earthenware pot; (*sl*) to put into prison.—**jugful** *n.*

jugate *adj* coupled together; (*bot*) having leaflets in pairs.

Jugendstil *n* the German form of Art Nouveau. *See also* **Kirchner, Klinger**.

juggernaut *n* a terrible, irresistible force; a large heavy truck.

Juggernaut *n* a Hindu god; his idol, dragged annually in processional car, under whose wheels devotees formerly threw themselves.

juggle *vi* to toss up balls, etc and keep them in the air. * *vt* to manipulate skillfully; to manipulate so as to deceive. * *n* the act of juggling; manipulation.—**jugglery** *n.*

juggler *n* one who juggles, a conjurer; a manipulator, a cheat.

jugular *adj* (*anat*) of the neck or throat. * *n* a jugular vein.

jugular vein *n* (*anat*) any of the large veins in the neck carrying blood from the head.

juice *n* the liquid part of fruit, vegetables or meat; liquid secreted by a bodily organ; (*inf*) vitality; (*inf*) electric current; (*inf*) engine fuel.

juicer *n* a mechanical or electrical device for extracting juice from fruit and vegetables; (*sl*) a person who drinks to excess.

juicy *adj* (**juicier, juiciest**) full of juice; (*inf*) very interesting; (*inf*) highly profitable.—**juicily** *adv.*—**juiciness** *n.*

jujitsu *n* a traditional Japanese system of unarmed defence in which an opponent's strength is used against him.

Jujol *n* **Josep Maria** (1879–1949) Spanish architect whose work heralded the surrealist and expressionist movements.

juju *n* an object of superstitious worship in West Africa used as a fetish or charm; the magic attributed to this.—**jujuism** *n.*

jujube *n* a gelatinous, fruit-flavored lozenge; the fruit of any of several small trees of the buckthorn family; the trees themselves.

jukebox, juke box *n* a coin-operated automatic record or CD player.

JUL *abbr* (*Latin*) = *Juris Utriusque Licentiatus*, "Licentiate in Both Laws" (i.e. the Canon and Civil Law).

jul. *abbr* = julep.

Jul. *abbr* = July.

julep *n* a tall drink of bourbon or brandy and sugar over crushed ice, garnished with mint.

Julian *adj* of or pertaining to Julius Caesar or to the Julian calendar.

Juliana *n* **[Juliana Louise Emma Maria Wilhelmina]** (1909–) Queen of the Netherlands (1948–1980). She abdicated in favor of her daughter Beatrix.

Julian calendar *n* a calendar introduced in 46 BC by Julius Caesar, in which the year was made to consist of 365 days with a leap year of 366 days every fourth year.

Julian date *n* (*astron, comput*) a system for the consecutive numbering of days, irrespective of month and year.

Julian of Norwich *n* **Dame** (*c.*1342–1413) English mystic whose meditations were published as the *Revelations of Divine Love* .

julienne *adj* (*vegetables*) cut into very thin strips. * *n* a clear soup containing such vegetable.

Juliet *n* a small satellite of Uranus.

Jul. Per. *abbr* = Julian Period.

July *n* (*pl* **Julies**) the seventh month of the year, having 31 days.

jumble *vt* (*often with* **up**) to mix together in a disordered mass. * *n* items mixed together in a confused mass; articles for a jumble sale.—**jumbly** *adj.*

jumbo *n* (*pl* **jumbos**) something very large of its kind. * *adj* very large.

jumbo jet *n* a very large jet airliner.

jumbuck *n* (*Austral*) a sheep.

jump *vi* to spring or leap from the ground, a height, etc; to jerk; to pass suddenly, as to a new topic; to rise suddenly, as prices; (*sl*) to be lively; (*often with* **at**) to act swiftly and eagerly; (*with* **at**) to accept or agree too eagerly; (*with* **on**) (*inf*) to reprimand or criticize harshly. * *vt* to leap or pass over (something); to leap upon; to cause (prices, etc) to rise; to fail to turn up (for trial when out on bail); (*inf*) to attack suddenly; (*inf*) to react to prematurely; (*sl*) to leave suddenly; * *n* a jumping; a distance jumped; a sudden transition; an obstacle; a nervous start.

jumper *n* (*chiefly Brit*) a sweater; a knitted garment for the upper body; a sleeveless dress for wearing over a blouse, etc.

jumper cable *or* **jump lead** *n* one of two cables for transferring electric charge from one battery to another, used to start a car with a flat battery by using the battery of another vehicle.

jump jet *n* (*inf*) a jet aircraft that can take off and land vertically.

jump-off *n* the start of a race or military assualt; an extra round in a showjumping contest to decide the winner between competitors with equal points.

jump rope *n* a rope used for skipping

jump seat *n* a movable carriage-seat; a folding seat.

jump-start *vt* to start a motor vehicle by pushing it in low gear so the engine turns over or by using jump leads; (*inf*) to set (a sluggish system, etc) in motion.

jumpsuit *n* a one-piece garment, as worn by paratroopers.

jumpy *adj* (**jumpier, jumpiest**) moving in jerks, etc; apprehensive; easily startled.—**jumpily** *adv*.—**jumpiness** *n*.

jun., Jun. *abbr* = junior.

Jun. *abbr* = June.

Junc. *abbr* = junction.

junction *n* a place or point where things join; a place where roads or railway lines, etc meet, link or cross each other.—**junctional** *adj*.

juncture *n* a junction; a point of time; a crisis.

June *n* the sixth month of the year, having 30 days.

Juneau *n* the capital city of the state of the USA, Alaska.

Jung *n* **Carl Gustav** (1875–1961) Swiss psychiatrist whose theory of the "collective unconscious" has been influential.

jungle *n* an area overgrown with dense tropical trees and other vegetation, etc; any scene of wild confusion, disorder, or of ruthless competition for survival.

jungly *adj* (**junglier, jungliest**) pertaining to or covered with jungle.

Juni *n* **Juan de** (*c*.1510–77) Spanish sculptor who executed a large number of sculptures on religious themes.

junior *adj* younger in age; of more recent or lower status; of juniors. * *n* a person who is younger, of lower rank, etc; a young person employed in minor capacity in an office; a student in the third year of college or school.

Junior *n* (*inf*) the younger son, often used after the name if the same as the father's.

junior miss *n* a girl in her teens; a clothes size for girls and slim women.

juniper *n* an evergreen shrub that yields purple berries.

junk[1] *n* a flat-bottomed sailing vessel prevalent in the China Seas.

junk[2] *n* discarded useless objects; (*inf*) rubbish, trash; (*sl*) any narcotic drug, such as heroin. * *vt* (*inf*) to scrap. * *adj* cheap, worthless; showy but without substance.

junk bond *n* an interest-bearing certificate held without security, used in junk debt.

junk debt *n* a method of funding takeovers by lending money unsecured in return for a higher yield and other benefits.—*also* **mezzanine debt**.

junk e-mail *see* **spam**.

junker *n* (*sl*) a jalopy.

Junker *n* a member of the Prussian aristocracy known for its political conservatism and militarism.

Junkers *n* **Hugo** (1859–1935) German airplane designer and manufacturer, who designed and produced the first all-metal airplane and the first airplane passenger cabin.

junket *n* curdled milk, sweetened and flavoured; a picnic; an excursion, esp one by an official at public expense. * *vi* to go on a junket.

junketeer *n* to make a practice of going on free trips. * *vi* someone who does this.

junk food *n* a snack or fast food with little nutritional value.

junkie, junky *n* (*pl* **junkies**) (*sl*) an addict of a particular activity, food, etc; a drug addict.

junk mail *n* unsolicited mail, e.g. advertising leaflets.

Juno *n* (*Roman myth*) the queen of the gods, sister and wife of Jupiter, the equivalent of the Greek Hera; a queenly woman.—**Junoesque** *adj*.

junr., Junr. *abbr* = junior.

junta *n* a group of people, esp military, who assume responsibility for the government of a country following a coup d'état or revolution.

Jupiter *n* (*Roman myth*) the king of the gods, Jove; (*astron*) the largest planet in the solar system.

Jur. D. *abbr* (*Latin*) = *Juris Doctor*, "Doctor of Law."

jural *adj* of law; of moral rights and obligations.—**jurally** *adv*.

Jurassic *adj* (geol) of or pertaining to the middle system of the Mesozoic Era marked by the existence of dinosaurs and the appearance of birds and mammals. * *n* the Jurassic period.

jurat *n* (*law*) a record of the time, place, etc, of an affidavit.

juridical, juridic *adj* of judicial proceedings or law.—**juridically** *adv*.

jurisconsult *n* one learned in law, a jurist.

jurisdiction *n* the right or authority to apply the law; the exercise of such authority; the limits of territory over which such authority extends.—**jurisdictional** *adj*.—**jurisdictionally** *adv*.

jurisp. *abbr* (*law*) = jurisprudence.

jurisprudence *n* the science or philosophy of law; a division of law.—**jurisprudential** *adj*.—**jurisprudentially** *adv*.

jurisprudent *adj* skilled in law. * *n* a person skilled in law.

jurist *n* an expert on law; a judge.—**juristic** *adj*.—**juristically** *adv*.

juror *n* a member of a jury; a person who takes an oath.

jury[1] *n* (*pl* **juries**) a body of usu 12 people sworn to hear evidence and to deliver a verdict on a case; a committee or panel that decides winners in a contest.

jury[2] *adj* (*naut*) makeshift, temporary.

juryman *n* (*pl* **jurymen**) a male juror.

jury-rigged *adj* (*naut*) rigged in a temporary or makeshift way.

jurywoman *n* (*pl* **jurywomen**) a female juror.

jus., just. *abbr* = justice.

Jus. P. *abbr* = justice of the peace.

jussive *adj* (*gram*) imperative, expressing command. * *n* (*gram*) a jussive word, mood or form.

Jussow *n* **Heinrich C** (1754–) German architect. His notable works include Löwenburg Castle.

just *adj* fair, impartial; deserved, merited; proper, exact; conforming strictly with the facts. * *adv* exactly; nearly; only; barely; a very short time ago; immediately; (*inf*) really; justly, equitably; by right.—**justly** *adv*.—**justness** *n*.

justice *n* justness, fairness; the use of authority to maintain what is just; the administration of law; a judge.

justice of the peace *n* a magistrate who summarily tries minor cases within his or her jurisdiction.

justiciable *adj* subject to trial; able to be settled by law.—**justiciability** *n*.

justiciar *n* (*formerly*) in England, the administrator of justice, chief justice.

justiciary *n* (*pl* **justiciaries**) an officer who administers justice; a justiciar. * *adj* of or pertaining to the administration of justice.

justifiable *adj* capable of being justified or defended.—**justifiability** *n*. —**justifiably** *adv*.

justification[1] *n* the act of justifying; vindication or defence; a showing adequate reason; absolution.

justification[2] *n* (*print*) (*comput*) the spacing out of type to the full length of a line.

justify *vt* (**justifying, justified**) to prove or show to be just or right; to vindicate; to space out (a line of type) so that it fills the required length.

Justin the Martyr *n* Saint (*c*.100–165) Samarian philosopher coverted to Christianity; he wrote *Apologies for the Christians* . His feast day is June 1.

just-in-time *adj* pertaining to a method of inventory control in production industries, where components are delivered just before they are needed.

Justus of Ghent (*fl*.1460–80) Flemish artist. His work *The Communion of the Apostles* (1473–74) formed a link between the painting of Italy and the Netherlands.

jut *vti* (**jutting, jutted**) to project; to stick out. * *n* a part that projects.

jute *n* the fiber of either of two tropical plants used for making sacking, etc.

Juvarro *n* **Filippo** (1678–) Italian architect. His notable works include the chapel of the Venaria Reale, Turin.

juvenescent *adj* becoming young.—**juvenescence** *n*.

juvenile *adj* young; immature; of or for young persons. * *n* a young person.

juvenile delinquency *n* (*pl* **delinquencies**) antisocial or illegal behaviour by young people usu under 18.—**juvenile delinquent** *n*.

juvenile water *n* water that originates from a magma and has never been in the atmosphere.

juvenilia *npl* works produced in an artist's or author's youth.

juvenility *n* (*pl* **juvenilities**) the state of being juvenile; youthfulness; a childish act.

Juventas *n* (*Roman myth*) the goddess of youth, who was identified with the Greek goddess, Hebe.

juxtapose *vt* to place side by side, esp for comparison.—**juxtaposition** *n*.

JV *abbr* = jugular vein.

JW *abbr* = Jehovah's Witness.

JWB *abbr* = Jewish Welfare Board.

Jy. *abbr* = July.

J

K

k, K the eleventh letter of the English alphabet.

K *symbol* (*chem*) (*Latin*) *kalium,* potassium (element).

k *abbr* = (*elect*) capacity ; (*math*) constant ; (*meteorol*) cumulus; karat or carat; kilo or kilo-(one thousand); kingdom; kopeck(s); krone, kronen, or kroner.

K *abbr* = (*phys*) Kelvin(s); (*comput*) kilobyte; (*chess, cards*) king.

ka *n* (*Egypt*) a term used for the life force or spirit of an individual, which continued to reside inside the tomb. One of the five elements constituting the human being, its hieroglyphic is two raised arms.

ka. *abbr* (*elect*) = kathode, cathode.

KA *abbr* = King of Arms.

K/A *abbr* = Knights of the Altar International.

K & B *abbr* = kitchen and bathroom.

Kabalevsky *n* **Dmitri Borisovich** (1904–87) Russian composer of ballets, symphonies, piano pieces, and operas (e.g., *Invincible* and the *Sister*).

kabbala, kabala *see* **cabbala**.

kabuki *n* classical Japanese theater.

Kabul *n* capital city of Afghanistan.

Kabyle *n* (*pl* **Kabyles, Kabyle**) an Algerian Berber, or his dialect.

Kaddish *n* (*pl* **Kaddishim**) a Jewish daily prayer, used by mourners for the year following, and on the anniversary of, someone's death.

Kadesh *n* (*Bible*) desert oasis on the edge of the Negeb in southern Palestine.

Kaédi *n* major city in the Islamic Republic of Mauritania.

KAF *abbr* = Kenya Air Force.

Kaffir *n* (*pl* **Kaffirs**) (*S Africa*) (*offensive*) any Black African; a former name for a Xhosa language.

kaffir corn, kafir corn *n* a variety of sorghum with juicy stalks used as fodder.

Kafir *n* (*pl* **Kafirs, Kafir**) a member of the Nuristani people of ancient Iranian stock living in Afghanistan; (*Moslem*) (*derog*) an infidel.

Kafka *n* **Franz** (1883–1924) Czech-born German novelist and short-story writer. Several of his works are 20th century classics, notably the short story "Metamorphosis."

kaftan *see* **caftan**.

Kåge *n* **Algot Wilhelm** (1889–1960) Swedish ceramicist, known at first as a poster designer.

Kahn *n* **Louis I(sadore)** (1901–74) Estonian architect. Notable works include the Yale University Art Gallery.

kaiak *see* **kayak**.

kainite *n* a mineral fertilizer.

Kaiser *n* the title of the emperors of Germany and Austria.

kaka *n* a New Zealand parrot with a long beak.

kakapo *n* an owl-like parrot, a flightless nocturnal bird nesting in burrows in New Zealand.

kakemono *n* a Japanese hanging picture of paper or silk, mounted on rollers.

kaki *n* (*pl* **kakis**) *n* the Japanese persimmon.

Kalambo Falls *n* a site in Africa on the border between Tanzania and Zambia, remarkable both for its great antiquity and long period of occupancy.

Kaldor *n* **Nicholas [Baron]** (1908–86) Hungarian-born British economist who was highly influential in the 1960s. He was a notable critic of monetarism.

kale, kail *n* a variety of cabbage with crinkled leaves.

kaleidoscope *n* a small tube containing bits of colored glass reflected by mirrors to form symmetrical patterns as the tube is rotated; anything that constantly changes.—**kaleidoscopic** *adj.*—**kaleidoscopically** *adv.*

kalends *see* **calends**.

kaleyard, kailyard *n* (*Scot*) a kitchen garden.

Kali *n* (*Hindu myth*) the goddess of destruction.

Kalidasa *n* (*fl.* 5th century) Indian poet and dramatist, and one of the greatest of Indian dramatists, whose *Sakuntala* ("The Fatal Ring") aroused interest in Sanskrit literature in Europe.

kalif, khalif *see* **caliph**.

kalmia *n* the American mountain laurel.

Kalmuck, Kalmyk *n* (*pl* **Kalmucks, Kalmuck, Kalmyks, Kalmyk**) *n* a member of a Mongolian Buddhist people; a variety of the Mongolian language. * *adj* of or pertaining to the Kalmuck or their language.

kalong *n* a large Indonesian or tropical fruitbat; a flying fox.

kalpak *see* **calpac**.

kalsomine *see* **calcimine**.

Kamasutra *n* an ancient Hindu manual on erotic love.

Kamber *n* (*Brit Celtic myth*) the son of Brutus and brother of Locrinus and Albanactus. After his father died, he became king of Wales, Locrinus became king of England and Albanactus became king of Scotland.

kame[1] *n* (*geol*) a structure produced by glacial deposition, which occurs as a mound of sands and gravels, in layers, often slumping at the sides.

kame[2] *n* (*Scot*) a comb.

kami *n* (*pl* **kami**) a divinity or demigod in the Shinto religion of Japan, from whom the Japanese emperors were supposed to have been descended.

kamik *n* a knee-length sealskin moccasin.

kamikaze *n* (*World War II*) a Japanese aircraft packed with explosives for making a suicidal crashing attack; the pilot of such an aircraft.

Kampala *n* capital city of Uganda.

Kampong Cham *n* major city in Cambodia.

kamseen, kamsin *see* **khamsin**.

Kan *n* **Shiu-Kay** (1949–) British lighting designer , from Hong Kong, working in London.

Kan. *abbr* = Kansas.

Kananga *n* major city in the Democratic Republic of the Congo (DRC).

Kandahar *n* major city in Afghanistan.

Kandinsky *n* **Wassily** (1866–1944) Russian-born French painter; regarded as the first major abstract artist; one of the founders of the Blaue Reiter group in 1912.

Kandy *n* major city in Sri Lanka.

Kane *n* 1. **Bob [Robert Kahn]** (1915–98) American cartoonist who is best known as the creator of Batman (1939). 2. **Paul** (1810–71) Irish-born Canadian painter. He traveled in Canada in the late 1840s and used sketches made on his travels as a source for his bizarre paintings.

kangaroo court *n* an illegal court operated by an unauthorized body, which perverts the proper course of justice.

kangaroo *n* (*pl* **kangaroos**) an Australian marsupial with short forelegs and strong, large hind legs for jumping.

Kankan *n* major city in Guinea.

Kano *n* major city in Nigeria.

Kanpur *n* major city in India.

Kans. *abbr* = Kansas.

Kansas (KS) *n* a state of the United States of America (USA) of which the capital is Topeka.

Kant *n* **Immanuel** (1724–1804) German philosopher whose works include *The Critique of Pure Reason* (1781).

Kantian *adj* of the philosopher Immanuel Kant or his philosophy.

Kao-hsiung *n* major city in Taiwan.

Kaolack *n* major city in Senegal.

kaolin *n* a white powder form of aluminum silicate;a white clay used in porcelain, etc; China clay.

Kapellmeister *n* (*pl* **kapellmeister**) (*mus*) (*German*) "master of the chapel," i.e. director of music to a noble court or bishop.

Kapitza, Piotr Leonidovich (1894–1984) Russian physicist. He was awarded the 1978 Nobel prize for physics, and made notable contributions to the study of cryogenics.

KAPL *abbr* = Knolls Atomic Power Laboratory.

kapok *n* the silky fibers around the seeds of a tropical tree, used for stuffing cushions, etc.

Kaposi's sarcoma *n* a cancerous condition, found frequently in AIDS patients, involving malignant skin tumors that form from the blood vessels.

kappa *n* the tenth letter of the Greek alphabet.

Kaprow *n* **Allen** (1927–) American artist, famous as the inventor of "happenings."

kaput *adj* (*sl*) broken, ruined.

KAPWA *abbr* = Kite Aerial Photography Worldwide Association.

karabiner *n* (*mountaineering*) a spring-loaded hook for securing ropes.

Karachi *n* major city in the Islamic Republic of Pakistan.

Karajan *n* **Herbert von** (1908–89) Austrian conductor whose recordings, notably of Beethoven's symphonies, are held by some critics to be definitive.

karakul *n* a breed of sheep from the Bukhara region of central Asia; the wool of the karakul sheep.

karaoke *n* a CD music system that plays recordings of popular songs with the vocal part removed to allow amateurs to sing along. Songwords are displayed for the singer on a screen.

karat *n* a measure of weight for precious stones; a measure of the purity of gold.—*also* **carat.**

karate *n* a Japanese system of unarmed combat using sharp blows of the feet and hands.

Karen *n* (*pl* **Karens, Karen**) *n* a member of a Thai people in Burma; their language.

karma *n* (*Buddhism, Hinduism*) the sum of a person's actions during one of their existences, held to determine their destiny in the next; (*inf*) a certain aura that a person or place is felt to possess.—**karmic** *adj*.

Karnak *n* (*Egypt*) the site of a group of colossal temples, including the greatest of the Egyptian temples, that of Amun-Ra. The location is immediately north of Thebes, on the east bank of the Nile.

Karnagel *n* **Wolf** (1940–) German designer and teacher who worked as an associate designer with the Staatliche Porzellan-Manufaktur, Berlin.

karoo, karroo *n* (*pl* **karoos, karroos**) (*S Africa*) a tableland, usually barren except in the wet season; (*geol*) a system of strata in South Africa dating from the Triassic period.

kaross *n* a cloak made of skins as worn by various tribal peoples in South Africa.

Karpov *n* **Anatoly Yegenyevich** (1951–) Russian chess player. After Fischer refused to defend his title, Karpov became world champion by default (1975–85), being displaced by Kasparov in 1985, in the longest-ever world match (48 games over six months).

karst *n* (*geol*) a limestone landscape consisting of networks of furrows, sharp crests, and underground tunnels, caves, and streams.

kart *n* a small motorized vehicle used in racing.—*also* **go-kart.**

karting *n* kart racing.

karyo- *prefix* nucleus.

karyotype *n* (*biol, med*) the number, shapes, and sizes of the chromosomes within the cells of an organism.

KAS *abbr* = Kentucky Academy of Science.

Kas. *abbr* = Kansas.

Kasparov *n* **Gary [Gary Weinstein]** (1963–) Russian chess player. He became world champion in 1985 after defeating Karpov in a long, exhausting contest.

Kassites *n* a tribe who occupied Babylon after it fell to the Hittites in 1595 BC.

Kastholm *n* **Jørgen** (1931–) Danish architect and furniture designer whose signature piece is the 1962 *Scimitar Chair 63*.

katabatic wind *n* (*meteorol*) the sinking and downward movement of cold dense air beneath warmer lighter air.

Katavolos *n* **William** (1924–) American designer, in partnership with Ross Littell and Douglas Kelley.

Kathmandu *n* capital city of Nepal.

katydid *n* a large green North American insect like a grasshopper.

Kauffer *n* **Edward McKnight** (1890–1954) American graphic designer who worked in London for a number of important clients.

Kaufmann *n* **Angelica** (1741–1807) Swiss painter of portraits and scenes from Shakespeare and Homer as well as history paintings.

Kaunas *n* major city in Lithuania.

Kaunda *n* **Kenneth [David]** (1924–) Zambian politician. Became president of Zambia after independence (1964–91). Regarded as a relatively benign dictator by many in the West, his rule was shaken in the continent-wide wave of agitation for reform that followed the release of Mandela in 1990.

kauri (*pl* **kauris**) a New Zealand pine with oval leaves from which a resinous gum is extracted; the wood or gum from this tree.

kava *n* a Polynesian shrub; an intoxicating and narcotic drink made from it.

Kay *n* **John Illingworth** (1870–1950) Scottish designer who worked in London.

kayak *n* an Inuit canoe made of skins on a wooden frame.—*also* **kaiak.**

Kayes *n* town in Mali.

kayo *n* (*pl* **kayos**) (*boxing*) a knockout. * *vt* (**kayoing, kayoed**) to knock out; to stun with a blow.—*also* **k.o.**, **KO.**

Kazakhstan *n* a huge, central Asian republic.

Kazakov *n* **Matvey F** (1738–) Russian architect. Notable works include the Kremlin Senate building.

Kazann *n* **Elia [Elia Kazanjoglous]** (1909–) Turkish-born American film and stage director. His films include *On the Waterfront* (1954), *East of Eden* (1954), and *Splendour in the Grass* (1962).

Kazantzakis *n* **Nikos** (1885–1957) Greek novelist, poet, and dramatist. His best-known work is the novel *Zorba the Greek* (1946).

kazoo *n* (*mus*) a simple instrument consisting of a short tube through which the player hums, vibrating a membrane which covers a small hole in the side.

KB *abbr* (*chess*) = king's bishop.

KB, kbyte *abbr* (*comput*) = **kilobyte.**

KBD *abbr* = King's Bench Division.

KBE *abbr* = Knight (Commander of the Order) of the British Empire.

KBP *abbr* (*chess*) = king's bishop's pawn.

KBS *abbr* = knowledge-based system.

kc. *abbr* (*phys*) = kilocycle, kilocycles; kilocycles per second.

KC *abbr* = Kennel Club; King's College; King's Counsel.

Kcal *abbr* = kilocalorie.

KCB *abbr* = Knight Commander of the Order of the Bath.

KCC *abbr* = Kurdish Cultural Center.

K cell *abbr* (*biol*) = killer cell.

KCMG *abbr* = Knight Commander of the Order of St Michael and St George.

K-corona *n* the innermost region of the Sun's corona where free electrons scatter light from the photosphere, giving the white halo seen during solar eclipses.

kc/s *abbr* (*phys*) = kilocycles per second.

KCSJ *abbr* = Knight Commander of the Order of St John or St Jerusalem.

KCVC *abbr* = Knight Commander of the Royal Victorian Order.

kd, KD *abbr* = knocked down (disassembled).

K-Door *abbr* = Keep Death Off Our Roads.

KE *abbr* = kinetic energy.

keas *abbr* = knots equivalent airspeed.

Keaton *n* **Buster [Joseph Francis Keaton]** (1895–1966) American film comedian and director, famous for his "deadpan" expression and remarkable acrobatic skill; films include *The General* (1926).

Keats *n* **John** (1795–1821) English poet whose great poems include "The Eve of St Agnes" and "Ode To a Nightingale."

kebab *n* small cubes of grilled meat and vegetables, cooked on a skewer.

keck *vi* to make a sound as if about to vomit; to feel or express loathing.

Kedar *n* (*Bible*) wandering shepherd tribe of the desert to the east of ancient Damascus, said to be descended from Ishmael. *See also* **Ishmael.**

keddah *n* (*India, Burma*), an enclosure for catching wild elephants.

kedge *n* a small anchor for kedging a ship. * *vt* to move (a ship) by hauling on a cable attached to a kedge.

kedgeree *n* a dish containing fish, rice, and hard-boiled eggs.

keef *see* **kif.**

keek *vt* (*Scot*) to peep cheekily.

keel *n* one of the main structural members of a ship extending along the bottom from stem to stern to which the frame is attached; any structure resembling this. * *vti* (to cause) to turn over.

keelhaul *vt* (*formerly*) to drag under water beneath the bottom of a ship from one side to the other; to reprimand sternly.

keel molding *n* (*archit*) a curved molding reminiscent of the keel of a ship in profile.

keelson, kelson *n* a beam of timber laid on the middle of the floor timbers over the keel of a vessel to strengthen it.

keen[1] *adj* eager, enthusiastic; intellectually acute, shrewd; having a sharp point or fine edge; (*senses*) perceptive, penetrating; extremely cold and piercing; intense; (*prices*) very low so as to be competitive.—**keenly** *adv*.—**keenness** *n*.

keen[2] *n* a dirge or lament for the dead. * *vi* to lament the dead.

keep (**keeping, kept**) *vt* to celebrate, observe; to fulfill; to protect, guard; to take care of; to preserve; to provide for; to make regular entries in; to maintain in a specified state; to hold for the future; to hold and not let go; (*with* **at**) to harass (a person) into continuing (some task, etc); (*with* **back**) to refuse to disclose; to restrain; (*with* **down**) to repress; to subdue; (*with* **from**) to abstain or restrain from; to preserve as a secret (from someone); (*with* **to**) to cause to adhere strictly to; (*with* **up**) to persist in; to continue; to maintain in good condition. * *vi* to stay in a specified condition; to continue, go on; to refrain or restrain oneself; to stay fresh, not spoil; (*with* **at**) to persist; (*with* **away**) to prevent from approaching; (*with* **down**) to stay hidden; (*with* **on**) to talk or nag continuously; (*with* **to**) to (cause to) adhere strictly to; (*with* **up**) to maintain the same pace, level of knowledge, etc as another; to stay informed; to continue relentlessly. * *n* food and shelter; care and custody; the inner stronghold of a castle.

keeper *n* one who guards, watches, or takes care of persons or things.

keeping *n* care, charge; observance; agreement, conformity.

keepsake *n* something kept in memory of the giver.

kef *see* **kif.**

keg *n* a small barrel.

K

kegler *n* (*inf*) (*sports*) a bowler, the person who delivers the ball to a batter/batsman.

keister *n* (*sl*) a suitcase; the buttocks.

Keller *n* Helen [Adams] (1880–1968) American writer, deaf and blind from infancy who was taught to read and write by the partially sighted Anne Sullivan.

Kells, Book of *n* an illuminated Celtic Christian gospel; according to tradition, crafted by monks on Iona and taken to the monastery of Kells for preservation from the raids of the Vikings. Now located in the library of Trinity College Dublin.

Kelly *n* 1. Ellsworth (1923–) American painter and sculptor who became a leading figure among the "hard-edge" group of abstract painters. 2. **Gene [Eugene Curran Kelly]** (1912–96) American dancer, choreographer, and film director noted for his athleticism and witty dancing style. 3. **Grace [Patricia]** (1929–82) American film actress who married Prince Rainier III of Monaco in 1956.

keloid, cheloid *n* scar tissue that forms because of the growth of fibrous tissue over a burn or injury, creating a hard, often raised, patch with ragged edges.

kelp *n* a large brown algal seaweed found anchored to the sea bed below low tide level.

kelpie (*pl* **kelpies**) *n* in Scottish folklore, a malevolent water sprite, supposed to take the form of a horse.

Keltic *see* **Celtic**.

Keltoi *n* the name given by the Greeks and Romans to the northern tribes of barbarians who threatened them from parts of western and central Europe. The word may be the origin of the word Celt.

kelvin *n* the unit of measurement on the absolute or Kelvin temperature scale (one kelvin equals one degree Celsius).

Kelvin–Helmholtz contraction *n* the concept that a mass of gas would contract under its own gravity, the energy released would be transformed into heat, and this would form the source of energy for a star.

Kelvin scale *n* temperature on a scale where absolute zero (-273.15° Celsius) is taken as zero degrees.

Kemal *n* Yashar (1923–) Turkish (Kurdish) novelist and short-story writer whose works include *Memed, my Hawk* and *The Saga of a Seagull*.

Kemble *n* Fanny [Frances Anne Kemble] (1809–93) English writer and actress. Her writings include *Notes on Some of Shakespeare's Plays*.

ken *n* understanding; view; sight. * *vt* (**kenning, kenned** *or* **kent**) to know; to recognize at sight.

Ken. *abbr* = Kentucky.

kendo *n* a Japanese style of fencing with bamboo staves.

Kendrew *n* Sir John Cowdery (1917–97) English biochemist. With the Austrian-born British chemist Max Ferdinand Perutz, he shared the 1962 Nobel prize for biochemistry for work on the molecular structure of the protein myoglobin.

Keneally *n* Thomas (1935–) Australian novelist whose novels include *Schindler's List*.

Kenites *n* (*Bible*) Midianite tribe of Bedouin coppersmiths, whose fortunes were linked with the Hebrews during their desert wanderings and occupation of Canaan.

Kennedy *n* 1. **Edward [Moore]** (1932–) brother of J F Kennedy, he showed potential as a future president until the "Chappaquidick" incident of 1969. 2. **J[ohn] F[itzgerald]** (1917–63) American Democrat politician and 35th president of the US (1961–63). The first Roman Catholic president and the youngest man to be elected to the presidency, he was assassinated in Dallas. 3. **Robert Francis ["Bobby"]** (1925–68) brother of J F Kennedy; became attorney general (1961–64) and senator for New York (1965–68) assassinated in 1968.

kennel *n* a small shelter for a dog, a doghouse; (*often pl*) a place where dogs are bred or kept. * *vt* (**kenneling, kenneled**) to keep in a kennel.

Kennelly, Arthur Edwin *see* **Heaviside, Oliver**.

Kenneth I mac-Alpin *n* (d. 858) king of Scots (841 (Scots) and c.844 (Picts) to 858. The son of Alpin, the 34th king of Dalriadan Scots. He united the kingdoms of Scots and Picts. Succeeded by his brother, Donald I.

Kenneth II *n* (d. 995) king of Scots (971–995). The son of Dubf, he succeeded Cuilean in 971.

Kenneth III *n* (d. 1005) king of Scots (997–1005). He ruled jointly with his son, Giric II.

Kenniff cave *n* (*archeo*) a cave site in Queensland, Australia, the oldest levels of which are dated 14000–13000 BC.

keno *n* a game of chance, similar to bingo, played with numbered balls and cards.

kenosis *n* (*theology*) the self-limitation of Christ in laying aside his divinity and becoming man.—**kenotic** *adj*.

Kent *n* Rockwell (1882–1971) American painter and draughtsman, famous for his black and white book illustrations.

Kent *n* William (1684–1748) English architect; notable works include the Treasury, London.

Kentigern *n* Saint [Mungo ,"dear one"] (c.518–603) Celtic bishop, founder, and patron saint of Glasgow, Scotland. His feast day is January 13.

Kentish rag *n* (*archit*) a type of hard, weather-resistant limestone found in Kent, England and used for building.

kentledge *n* (*naut*) ballast of scrap metal.

Kentucky (KY) *n* a state of the United States of America (USA) of which the capital is Frankfort.

Kentucky bluegrass *see* **bluegrass**.

Kenya *n* a republic on the eastern side of the African continent.

Kenya Shilling *n* currency of Kenya.

Kenyatta *n* Jomo (c.1893–1978) Kenyan politician; jailed (1952–58) for leading the Mau-Mau rebellion; became prime minister of Kenya on independence in 1963 and president (1964–78).

kepi *n* (*pl* **kepis**) a French military peaked cap.

Kepler's Laws *n* three laws describing the motion of planets in their orbits derived from a long period of meticulous observation.

Kepler's star *or* **Kepler's Nova** *n* a supernova explosion observed by Kepler in 1604, one of only three known to have occurred in the Milky Way Galaxy.

kept *see* **keep**.

Ker *n* (*pl* **Keres**) (*Greek myth*) a spirit associated with death, which is often depicted as a woman with talons and fangs.

keratin *n* (*biochemistry*) a fibrous sulfur-rich protein consisting of coiled polypeptide chains, which occur in hair, hooves, horn, and feathers.

keratitis *n* inflammation of the cornea.

keratoplasty *see* **corneal graft**.

keratose *adj* having a horn-like skeleton (esp some varieties of sponges).

keratosis *n* a condition of the skin with a thickening and overgrowth of a horny layer (*stratum corneum*).

kerbstone *n* the stone edge of a path, curbstone.

kerchief *n* a piece of square cloth worn on the head.

Kerenski *n* Alexsandr Feodorovich (1881–1970) Russian revolutionary leader. He was prime minister of the Russian provisional government of 1917, but was deposed by Lenin's Bolsheviks.

kerf *n* a cut or slit made by a saw, etc.

Kerma *n* (*Egypt*) a site in Nubia, above the third cataract of the Nile, and centre of a local kingdom.

kermes *n* the dried bodies of female scale insects from which a dye of a deep cherry red color is obtained; an oak tree found in Europe and Asia, on which these insects live.

kermis *n* an open-air festival or fair.

kermit *n* (*comput*) an asynchronous communications protocol that is used for telephone communications.

kern[1], **kerne** *n* (*formerly*) a lightly armed Irish or Scottish medieval foot-soldier; a troop of these; (*arch*) a peasant.

kern[2] *n* (*print*) the part of a type or character that overhangs the following piece of type or character * *vt* (*comput*) to reduce or increase the space between two characters in a display font with the result of placing the characters in a pleasing style.

Kern *n* Jerome [David] (1885–1945) an American composer of musical comedies. His shows include *Show Boat*.

kernel *n* the inner edible part of a fruit or nut; the essential part of anything.

Kernig's sign *n* (*med*) the inability of someone with meningitis to straighten his or her legs at the knee when the thighs are at right angles to the body. It is symptomatic of the disease.

kerosene, kerosine *n* a thin fuel oil obtained during the fractional distillation of petroleum.

Kerouac *n* Jack [Jean-Louis Lebris de Kérouac] (1922–69) American novelist and poet who was a central figure of the Beat Generation. His most popular work is the semi-autobiographical novel *On the Road* (1957).

kersey *n* a coarse smooth-faced woolen cloth.

kerseymere *n* a twilled cloth of fine wool.

Kertesz *n* André (1894–1985) Hungarian-born American photographer, notable for his documentary photographs of Paris during the 1920s.

Kesey *n* Ken Elton (1935–) American writer whose works include *One Flew Over the Cuckoo's Nest* (1963).

kestrel *n* a type of small falcon.

ketch *n* a small two-masted sailing vessel.

ketchup *n* any of various thick sauces, esp one made from puréed tomato, for meat, fish, etc.—*also* **catchup, catsup**.

ketoaciduria *see* **ketonuria**.

ketogenesis *n* the normal production of ketones in the body because of metabolism of fats.

ketone *n* (*chem*) an organic compound that contains a carbonyl group within the compound rather than at either end of the compound.

ketone body *n* (*chem*) one of several compounds produced by the liver due to metabolism of fat deposits in the body.

ketonuria, acetonuria, *or* **ketoaciduria** *n* the presence of ketone bodies in the urine.

ketosis *n* the build-up of ketones in the body and bloodstream because of a lack of carbohydrates for metabolism.

kettle *n* a container with a handle and spout for boiling water.

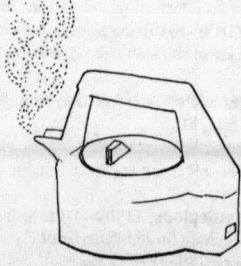

kettledrum *n* a musical instrument consisting of a hollow metal body with a parchment head, the tension of which controls the pitch and is adjusted by screws.—*also* **timpani**.

kettle hole *n* (*geol*) a hole or depression formed in glacial drift due to outwash material from glacier covering isolated masses of ice.

keV *abbr* (*elect*) = kiloelectronvolt.

kevel *n* (*naut*) a cleat for belaying ropes.

key[1] *n* a device for locking and unlocking something; a thing that explains or solves, as the legend of a map, a code, etc; a controlling position, person, or thing; one of a set of parts or levers pressed in a keyboard or typewriter, etc; (*comput*) a button on a keyboard; (*mus*) a system of related tones based on a keynote and forming a given scale; style or mood of expression; a roughened surface for improved adhesion of plaster, etc; an electric circuit breaker. * *vt* to furnish with a key; to bring into harmony. * *adj* controlling; important.

key[2] *n* a low island or reef.

KEY *abbr* = keep extending yourself.

keyboard *n* a set of keys in a piano, organ, microcomputer, etc.

key field *n* (*comput*) the field that is used as the one for sorting data.

keyhole *n* an opening (in a lock) into which a key is inserted.

keyhole surgery *n* surgery performed through small incisions in the body using fiber-optic tubes both for internal examination and as conduits for tiny surgical instruments.

Keyne *n* **Saint** (*c*.490) English virgin. Her feast day is October 8.

Keynes *n* **John Maynard [1st Baron]** (1883–1946) English economist. In his *General Theory of Employment, Interest and Money* (1936), he advocated the creation of employment through government schemes (which influenced Roosevelt's "New Deal" policies).

Keynesianism *n* the economic theories based on the works of the English economist John Maynard Keynes.—**Keynesian** *adj*.

keynote, key note *n* (*mus*) the basic note of a musical scale; the basic idea or ruling principle. * *vt* to give the keynote of; to give the keynote speech at.

keynote address, keynote speech *n* the opening speech at a (political) convention, which sets out the issues to be debated or discussed.

keypad *n* a small keyboard of numbered buttons used to tap in a telephone number, operate a calculator, etc; (*comput*) the group of numbers at the right-hand side of a keyboard.

keypunch *n* (*comput*) a device with a keyboard used to transfer data to punched cards or tape.—*also* **card punch**.

key signature *n* (*mus*) the sharps or flats printed on the stave, at the beginning of a piece of music, to indicate the key.

keystone *n* the middle stone at the top of an arch, holding the stones or other pieces in place.

keystroke *n* (*comput*) the action of pressing a key on the keyboard resulting in a character being entered or a command being initiated; the depressing of a key on a typewriter.

keyword *n* (*comput*) a word in a programming language which describes an action or operation that the computer recognizes.

Kf *abbr* = koruna.

KFA *abbr* = Keep Fit Association.

kg *abbr* = kilogram(s); keg.

KG *abbr* = Knight of the Order of the Garter.

KGB *abbr* (*Russian*) = *Komitet Gosudarstvennoi Bezopasnosti*, "Committee of State Security," formerly the secret police of the USSR.

kg-cal *abbr* = kilogram-calorie; kilogram-calories.

kgf *abbr* = kilogram-force.

kg-m *abbr* = kilogram-meter(s).

kgm. *abbr* = kilogram(s).

kgs. *abbr* = kegs.

Khachaturian *n* **Aram Ilich** (1903–78) a Russian Armenian composer. His works include the ballet *Spartacus*.

khaddar, khadi *n* an Indian homespun cotton cloth.

khaki *adj* dull yellowish-brown. * *n* (*pl* **khakis**) strong, twilled cloth of this color; khaki uniform or trousers.

khamsin, kamseen, kamsin *n* a hot southerly wind, esp in Egypt, that blows for about 50 days in spring.

khan *n* the title of a ruler, prince, or governor in Asia.

khanate *n* the rule or jurisdiction of a khan.

Khar'kov *n* major city in Ukraine.

Khartoum (El Khartum) *n* capital city of the Sudan.

Khartoum North *n* major city in the Sudan.

Khasekem *n* a warrior king of the Second Dynasty, conqueror of Nubia, *c*.2700 BC.

khedive *n* the title of the viceroy of Egypt (1867–1914).

Khephren *see* Chephren.

khet *n* (*Egypt*) a standard unit of measurement of area, 100 square cubits.

Kheti I *n* Egyptian King of the Ninth Dynasty.

Kheti II *n* Egyptian King of the Tenth Dynasty.

Kheti III *n* the last Egyptian king of the Tenth (Herakleopolitan) Dynasty in the First Intermediate Period (2200–2040 BC); an active and effective king who drove the Asiatic colonizers out of the Nile Delta, reintroduced nomes as local government districts and renewed irrigation systems.

Khnum *n* (*Egypt*) a ram-headed god whose cult was centered in the city of Elephantine. A potter, he was believed to have shaped the world and men upon his wheel.

Khomeini *n* **Ayatollah [Ruholla]** (1900–89) Iranian religious leader who established a theocratic dictatorship intent on spreading Shiite revolution throughout Islam.

Khonsu *n* (*Egypt*) a war-god of the later period, worshipped at Thebes, son of Amun and Mut.

khoraschot *n* the policy in the former USSR, initiated by President Gorbachev, of the decentralized economic accountability of managers in industrial production and other enterprises.

khoum *n* a monetary unit of Mauritania, equal to one fifth of an ouguiya.

Khrushchev *n* **Nikita Sergeyevich** (1894–1971) Soviet politician who was first secretary of the Communist Party (1953–64) and prime minister (1958–64). The Cuban Missile Crisis (1962) led to his decline and ultimate deposition in a coup in 1964.

Khufu *see* Cheops.

Khujand *n* major city in Tajikistan.

Khulna *n* major city in Bangladesh.

kHz *abbr* (*phys*) = kilohertz.

KIA *abbr* = killed in action.

kiang *n* a wild ass of Tibet.

kias *abbr* = knots indicated airspeed.

kibble[1] *vt* to grind coarsely.

kibble[2] *n* a raiseable bucket used in wells, mines etc.

kibbutz *n* (*pl* **kibbutzim**) a mainly agricultural commune in Israel.

kibbutznik *n* a person who lives in a kibbutz.

kibe *n* ulcerated chilblain, esp one on the heel.

kibitzer *n* (*inf*) a person who lingers, esp at a card game, offering unwanted advice.—**kibitz** *vt*.

kiblah, kibla *n* the point to which Muslims turn at prayer, Mecca.

kibosh *n* (*sl*) nonsense; something that checks or stops.—**to put the kibosh on** *vt* (*sl*) to veto.

kick *vt* to strike with the foot; to drive, force, etc as by kicking; to score (a goal, etc) by kicking; (*with about, around*) (*inf*) to abuse physically or mentally; to discuss or analyze (a problem, etc) in a relaxed unsystematic manner; (*with out*) (*inf*) to eject, dismiss; (*with up*) (*inf*) to cause (trouble, etc). * *vi* to strike out with the foot; to recoil, as a gun; (*inf*) to complain; (*with about, around*) (*inf*) to wander idly; to be unused or forgotten; (*with off*) (*football*) to give the ball the first kick to start play; (*inf*) to start. * *n* an act or method of kicking; a sudden recoil; (*inf*) a thrill; (*inf*) an intoxicating effect.—**kicker** *n*.

kickback *n* a recoil; (*inf*) a returning of part of a sum of money received in payment.

kickoff *n* (*football*) a kick putting the ball into play; the beginning or start of proceedings, e.g. a discussion.

kickshaw *n* a trifle, trinket; (*arch*) a small, light, fancy dish, a delicacy.

kickstand *n* a retractable stand for parking a bicycle or motorbike.

kick-start *vt* to start (a motorcycle engine, etc) by kicking a pedal downwards.—**kick-starter** *n*.

kid *n* a young goat; soft leather made from its skin; (*inf*) a child. * *vti* (**kidding, kidded**) (*inf*) to tease or fool playfully; (*goat*) to bring forth young.—**kidder** *n*.

kiddy, kiddie *n* (*pl* **kiddies**) (*inf*) a child.

kidnap *vt* (**kidnaping, kidnaped, or kidnapping, kidnapped**) to seize and hold to ransom, as of a person.—**kidnapper, kidnaper** *n*.

kidney *n* (*pl* **kidneys**) either of a pair of glandular organs excreting waste products from the blood as urine; an animal's kidney used as food.

kidney bean *n* any of various cultivated beans, esp a large dark red bean seed.

kidney stone *n* a hard mineral deposit in the kidney.

Kidron *n* (*Bible*) valley between Jerusalem and the Mount of Olives.

kidskin *n* a soft leather made from the skin of a young goat.

kids' stuff *n* something suited only for children; something simple and easy.

kief *see* kif.

Kieffer *n* 1. **Michel** (1916–) The son of René Kieffer. He developed his own bookbinding style,*décor cloisonné*. 2. **René** (1875–1964) French bookbinder noted for bright Art Nouveau designs.

Kienholz *n* **Edward** (1927–94) American sculptor. His works include *Portable War Memorial* (1968).

kier *n* a vat in which cloth is boiled for bleaching.

Kierkegaard *n* **Søren Aabye** (1813–55) Danish theologian and philosopher who is regarded as the founder of existentialism.

K

kieselguhr *n* mineral remains of algae, used for filtering and insulation purposes etc.

Kiev (Kiyev) *n* capital city of Ukraine.

kif *n* a drowsy state of well-being produced by marijuana; marijuana itself; any drug producing a similar state.—*also* **keef, kef, kief**.

KIF *abbr* = Knitting Industries Federation.

Kikutake *n* **K.** (1928–) Japanese architect. His notable works include the Miyakonoyo Town Hall.

Kigali *n* capital city of Rwanda.

kil. *abbr* = kilderkin; kilometer(s).

kild. *abbr* = kilderkin.

kill *vt* to cause the death of; to destroy; to neutralize (a color); to spend (time) on trivial matters; to turn off (an engine, etc); (*inf*) to cause severe discomfort or pain to. * *n* the act of killing; an animal or animals killed.—**killer** *n*.

Killaraus *n* (*Irish Celtic myth*) a mountain in County Kildare, Ireland from which Myrddin transported the ring of stones known as the Giant's Ring. He is said to have re-erected this at Stonehenge.

killer whale *n* a carnivorous black-and-white toothed whale.

killick, killock *n* (*naut*) a heavy stone used as an anchor; a small anchor.

killing *adj* (*inf*) tiring; very amusing; causing death, deadly. * *n* the act of killing; murder; (*inf*) a sudden (financial) success.—**killingly** *adv*.

killjoy *n* a person who spoils other people's enjoyment.

kiln *n* a furnace or large oven for baking or drying (pottery, bricks, etc).

kilo *n* (*pl* **kilos**) kilogram; kilometer.

kilo- *prefix* one thousand.

kilobyte *n* (*comput*) the basic unit of measurement for computer memory equal to 1,024 bytes.

kilocalorie *or* **Calorie** *n* (*phys*) a unit of heat used to express the energy value of food, equal to 1000 calories.

kilocycle *n* (*phys*) a kilohertz.

kilog. *abbr* = kilogram.

kilogram *n* a unit of weight and mass, equal to 1000 grams or 2.2046 pounds.

kilohertz *n* (*phys*) a measurement of sound waves, equal to one thousand cycles per second, 1000 hertz.

kilol. *abbr* = kiloliter.

kiloliter *n* 1000 liters.

kilom. *abbr* = kilometer.

kilometer *n* a unit of length equal to 1000 meters or 0.62 mile.—**kilometric** *adj*.

kiloton *n* a unit of explosive force equal to 1000 tons of TNT.

kilowatt *n* a unit of electrical power, equal to 1000 watts.

kilowatt-hour *n* a unit of energy equal to work done by one kilowatt in one hour.

kilt *n* a knee-length skirt made from tartan material pleated at the sides, worn as part of the Scottish Highland dress for men and women.

kilter *n* good working order; good condition.

Kim Il Sung *n* (1912–94) North Korean marshal and Communist politician; prime minister (1948–72) and president (1972–94) of the Democratic People's Republic of Korea (North Korea).

kimono *n* (*pl* **kimonos**) a loose Japanese robe.

kin *n* relatives; family.—*see* **kith**.

kina *n* the standard monetary unit of Papua New Guinea, made up of 100 toea.

kind[1] *n* sort; variety; class; a natural group or division; essential character.

kind[2] *adj* sympathetic; friendly; gentle; benevolent.—**kindness** *n*.

kindergarten *n* a class or school for very young children.

Kindertotenlieder *n* ["Songs on the Death of Children"] (*German*) a cycle of five songs for voice and orchestra by Mahler with words by F Ruckert.

kind-hearted *adj* benevolent; kind, warm.—**kind-heartedly** *adv*.

Kindia *n* major city in Guinea.

kindle *vt* to set on fire; to excite (feelings, interest, etc). * *vi* to catch fire; to become aroused or excited.

kindling *n* material, such as bits of dry wood, for starting a fire.

kindly *adj* (**kindlier, kindliest**) kind; gracious; agreeable; pleasant. * *adv* in a kindly manner; favorably.—**kindliness** *n*.

kindred *n* a person's family or relatives; family relationship; resemblance. * *adj* related; like, similar.

kine *n* (*pl*) (*arch*) cattle.

kinematic *adj* of pure motion, without reference to force etc.

kinematics *n* (*sing*) the science of pure motion.

kinescope *n* the cathode-ray tube in a TV monitor, etc, that reproduces the image; a TV program recorded on film.

kinesiology *n* the study of the anatomy and mechanics of human muscles.

kinesis *n* (*biol*) the response of an organism to a particular stimulus in which the response is proportional to the intensity of the stimulation.

Kineth *n* (*d.* 843) king of the Picts (842–843). The son of Uurad, he is thought to have killed his brother Bred to take the throne. He in turn was usurped and murdered by Brude, his nephew.

kinetic *adj* of or produced by movement.—**kinetically** *adv*.

kinetic art *n* sculpture, etc that moves or has moving parts.

kinetic energy *n* (*phys*) the energy possessed by a moving body by virtue of its mass and velocity.

kinetics *n* (*used as sing*) the science of the effects of forces in producing or changing motion; the study of the mechanisms and rates of chemical reactions.

kinfolk *npl* family and relatives.

king *n* the man who rules a country and its people; a man with the title of ruler, but with limited power to rule; man supreme in a certain sphere; something best in its class; the chief piece in chess; a playing card with a picture of a king on it, ranking above a queen; (*drafts*) a piece that has been crowned.

King *n* 1. **Billie Jean** (1943–) American tennis player and winner of twenty Wimbledon titles between 1965 and 1980. 2. **Jesse Marion** (1875–1949) British designer who was part of the Charles Rennie Mackintosh circle. 3. **Martin Luther [Jr]** (1929–68) American civil rights leader and Baptist minister. Over 200,000 people took part in his 'March on Washington' in 1963, when he made his 'I have a dream' speech. He was awarded the 1964 Nobel Peace Prize, and was assassinated in 1968. 4. **William Lyon Mackenzie** (1874–1950) Canadian Liberal statesman. He became leader of the Liberal party (1919–48) and prime minister (1921–26, 1926–30, 1935–48).

kingbolt *n* a main or large bolt in a mechanical structure; an iron rod in a roof used instead of a king post; a vertical bolt passing through the axle of a carriage, etc, and forming a pivot on which the axle swings in taking curves.

King Charles spaniel *n* a small breed of spaniel with black and brown markings.

king cobra *n* a large poisonous snake of Asia and the Philippines.—*also* **hamadryad**.

king crab *n* a horseshoe crab.

kingcup *or* **the marsh marigold** *n* any of various yellow-flowered, five-petaled plants, such as the buttercup or clematis.

kingdom *n* a country headed by a king or queen; a realm, domain; any of the three divisions of the natural world: animal: vegetable, mineral.

kingdom come *n* (*sl*) the next world; (*sl*) eternity.

Kingdoms, Old, Middle, and New *n* three major periods of advance in the culture of ancient Egypt, interspersed with phases of decline.

kingfisher *n* a short-tailed diving bird that feeds chiefly on fish.

King James Bible *or* **King James Version** *n* the version of the Bible published by the sanction of James I of England and VI of Scotland in 1611 and appointed to be read in churches.—*also* **Authorized Version**.

Kinglake *n* **Alexander William** (1809–91) English historian who wrote of the Crimean War in his monumental *History of the War in the Crimea*.

kinglet *n* a minor king; a small bird with a yellow crown found throughout North America.

king list *n* (*Egypt*) lists of pharaohs' names inscribed on temple walls, as at Karnak and Abydos, or on papyrus, as in the Turin Canon.

kingly *adj* (**kinglier, kingliest**) of, resembling, or fit for a king.—**kingliness** *n*.

king-of-arms *n* (*pl* **kings-of-arms**) chief officer of the Heralds' College.

kingpin *n* (*sl*) the chief person in a company, group, etc; the pin in a car, etc that attaches the stub axle to the axle beam and allows limited movement to the stub axle; the foremost pin in tenpin bowling; the central pin in ninepins; the crux of an argument.

king post *n* an upright post in the centre of a roof truss, extending from the ridge to the tie-beam.

Kings, 1 and 2 *n* (*Bible*) the 11th and 12th books of the OT.

kingship *n* the office or authority of a king; the art of ruling as king.

king-size, king-sized *adj* larger than standard size.

Kingsley *n* **Charles** (1819–75) English clergyman and novelist whose works include *Westward Ho!* and the children's story *The Water Babies*.

king snake *n* any of various nonvenomous snakes of the southern US with bright markings, which feeds on rodents.

Kingston *n* capital city of Jamaica.

Kingstown *n* capital city of St Vincent and the Grenadines.

kinin *n* one of a group of polypeptides that lower blood pressure through dilation of the blood vessels and cause smooth muscle to contract.

kink *n* a tight twist or curl in a piece of string, rope, hair, etc; a painful cramp in the neck, back, etc; a minor problem in some course of action; a personality quirk; (*Brit sl*) a sexual deviation; (*pl*) (*Scot*) a convulsive fit of laughter; a bright, original idea. * *vt* to form kinks.

kinkajou *n* nocturnal long-tailed quadruped of Central and Southern America similar to a racoon—*also* **honeybear**; a short-tailed primate with spiny protrusions from the neck —*also* **potto**.

kinky *adj* (**kinkier, kinkiest**) full of kinks; (*inf*) eccentric; (*inf*) sexually bizarre.— **kinkiness** *n*.

kinnikinnick, kinnikinic *n* a mixture of dried leaves and bark smoked by American Indians; any of the plants used for this.

kino (gum) *n* an astringent vegetable gum of a dark red color, used in medicine, tanning etc.

Kinsella *n* **Thomas** (1928–) Irish poet whose collections include *Peppercanister Poems: 1972–1978*.

Kinsey *n* **Alfred Charles** (1894–1956) American zoologist and sexologist whose controversial Kinsey Report, *Sexual behaviour in the Human Male*, was published in 1948.

kinsfolk *n* blood relations.

Kinshasa *n* capital city of the Democratic Republic of the Congo (DRC).

kinship *n* blood relationship; close connection.

kinsman, kinswoman *n* (*pl* **kinsmen, kinswomen**) a relative, esp by blood.

Kinsman *n* **Rodney** (1943–) British industrial designer who designed the *Omstack* chair.

KIO *abbr* = Kenya Information Office.

kiosk *n* a small open structure used for selling newspapers, confectionery, etc; a public telephone booth; (*Egypt*) a small, open-roofed chapel in which a god's statue was placed during a festival.

kip¹ *n* the standard monetary unit of Laos, made up of 100 at.

kip² *vi* (**kipping, kipped**) (*sl*) to sleep. * *n* (*sl*) sleep, a lodging.

Kipling *n* **[Joseph] Rudyard** (1865–1936) Indian-born English short-story writer, poet, and novelist, best known for his children's stories, e.g. *The Jungle Book*. He won the Nobel prize for literature in 1907.

kipper *n* a kippered herring, etc. * *vt* to cure (fish) by salting and drying, or smoking.

Kirbye *n* **George** (*c*.1565–1634) English composer of motets and madrigals.

Kirchner *n* **Ernst Ludwig** (1880–1938) German painter and engraver who was a leading figure in the German expressionist movement.

Kiribati *n* a republic in Micronesia that comprises three groups of coral atolls and one isolated volcanic island spread over a large expanse of the central Pacific.

kirk *n* (*Scot*) a church.

Kirkwood gaps *n* orbits that appear to be avoided in the asteroid belt.

kirsch, kirschwasser *n* a type of brandy made from cherries.

Kisangani *n* major city in the Democratic Republic of the Congo (DRC).

Kishon *n* (*Bible*) a small river in the plain of Jezreel, where Sisera's chariots were bogged down and the charioteers were routed. *See also* **Deborah**.

kismet *n* fate, destiny.

kiss *vti* to touch with the lips as an expression of love, affection, or in greeting; to touch the lips with those of another person as a sign of love or desire; to touch lightly. * *n* an act of kissing; a light, gentle touch.—**kissable** *adj*.

kissagram, kissogram *n* a celebratory telegram or message delivered with a kiss.

kiss-and-tell *adj* (*inf*) pertaining to the publication of memoirs that reveal hitherto secret details.

kisser *n* one who kisses; (*sl*) the mouth or face.

kissing cousin *n* a more or less distant relative with whom one is familiar enough to kiss on meeting; something or someone very like another.

Kissinger *n* **Henry [Alfred]** (1923–) German-born American statesman; secretary of state (1973–76). He shared the 1973 Nobel peace prize with North Vietnamese negotiator Le Duc Tho (1911–) for the treaty ending US involvement in Vietnam.

kiss of death *n* (*inf*) something or someone that causes failure or ruin.

kiss of life *n* mouth-to-mouth resuscitation.

kist *n* (*Scot*) a chest or box; (*arch*) a cist; (*S Africa*) a large chest or box used for storing linen, esp for a trousseau.

Kisumu *n* town in Kenya.

kit¹ *n* (*mus*) a miniature violin which was particularly popular with dancing masters of the 17th and 18th centuries.

kit² *n* clothing and personal equipment, etc; tools and equipment for a specific purpose; a set of parts with instructions ready to be assembled. * *vt* (**kitting, kitted**) (usu *with* out *or* up) to provide with kit.

kitchen *n* a place where food is prepared and cooked.

Kitchener of Khartoum *n* **[Horatio] Herbert [1st Earl]** (1850–1916) Anglo-Irish field marshal; commander in chief of the British forces during the Boer War (1901–2), and of the British forces in India (1902–9); British secretary for war in 1914.

kitchenette *n* a small kitchen.

kitchen garden *n* a garden where vegetables are grown for domestic use.

kitchen midden *n* (*archeo*) an ancient mound of domestic refuse and food remains, quite often consisting of large quantities of sea shells.

kite *n* a bird of prey with long narrow wings and a forked tail; a light frame covered with a thin covering for flying in the wind; (*inf*) an accommodation bill.

kith *n* friends and relations, now only in **kith and kin**.

kithara *see* **cithara**.

kit house *n* (*archit*) a type of industrialized building, usually a timber-framed house made up of prefabricated parts.

kitsch *n* art, literature, decor, etc regarded as pretentious, inferior, or in poor taste.— *also adj*.—**kitschy** *adj*.

kitten *n* a young cat; the young of other small mammals. * *vti* to give birth to kittens.

kittenish *adj* like a kitten, playful; (*woman*) flirtatious.

Kittim *n* (*Bible*) OT name for Cyprus.

kittiwake *n* either of two types of gull with black-tipped wings.

kittle *adj* (*Scot*) difficult to manage, capricious. * *vt* (*Scot*) to tickle; to cause (someone) to be puzzled or to bother someone.

kitty *n* (*pl* **kitties**) the stakes in a game of poker or other gambling game; a shared fund of money; affectionate name for a cat or kitten.

Kitwe *n* major city in Zambia.

kiwi fruit *n* a fruit of an Asian vine.—*also* **Chinese gooseberry**.

kiwi *n* (*pl* **kiwis**) a flightless bird of New Zealand; (*inf*) a New Zealander.

kj., kJ *abbr* = kilojoule.

KJ *abbr* = knee-jerk.

Kjaerholm *n* **Poul** (1929–80) Danish designer best-known for his chromium, wood, and leather furniture.

KJV *abbr* = King James Version (of the Bible).

KKK *abbr* = Ku Klux Klan.

KKt *abbr* (*chess*) = king's knight.

KKtP *abbr* (*chess*) = king's knight's pawn.

kl *abbr* = kiloliter.

Klaipeda *n* major city in Lithuania.

Klangfarbenmelodie *n* (*mus*) (*German*) "melody of tone colors"; a term used by Schoenberg to describe a form of composition in which the pitch does not change; "color" is achieved by adding or taking away instruments.

klavier *see* **clavier**.

klaxon *n* a type of old-fashioned motor horn.

Klebe *n* **Giselher** (1925–) German composer whose works include the opera *Die Rauber*.

Klee *n* **Paul** (1879–1940) Swiss painter and etcher; member of the Blaue Reiter group.

Kleenex *n* (*pl* **Kleenex, Kleenexes**) (*trademark*) a type of soft disposable paper tissue used as a handkerchief, etc.

Klein *n* 1. **Calvin Richard** (1942–) American fashion designer . 2. **Jacques** (1899–1963) French decorator and designer for the Galeries Lafayette store, Paris.

Klemperer *n* **Otto** (1885–1973) German-born conductor who became director of the Los Angeles Symphony Orchestra in 1936 and was director of the Budapest Opera (1947–50).

Klenze *n* **Leo von** (1784–1864) German architect. His notable works include the Propylaea, Münich.

kleptomania *n* an uncontrollable impulse to steal.—**kleptomaniac** *n*.

klieg light, kleig light *n* a carbon arc light used in filmmaking.

Klimt *n* **Gustav** (1862–1918) Austrian painter influenced by impressionism, symbolism, and Art Nouveau. He was a founder member of the Vienna Secession.

Kline *n* **Franz** (1910–62) American painter. Working mainly in black and white, his paintings include *Ninth Street* (1951).

Klinefelter's syndrome *n* (*med*) a genetic imbalance in males in which the physical manifestations are small testes, enlarged breasts, long thin legs, and little or no body hair.

Klinger *n* **Max** (1857–1920) German painter, sculptor, and illustrator. He is thought of primarily as a Jugendstil (German Art Nouveau) artist.

Klint *n* 1. **Ebsen** (1915–69) Danish industrial designer who is best-known for his 1947 folded-paper lighting fittings, inspired by origami. 2. **Kaare** (1888–1954) Danish architect and furniture designer.

klipspringer *n* a small South African antelope.

KLM *abbr* (*Dutch*) = *Koninklijke Luchtvaart Maatschappij*, "Royal Dutch Airlines."

kloof *n* a ravine, a deep narrow valley, in South Africa.

KLS *abbr* = kidney, liver, spleen.

klutz *n* (*sl*) a clumsy person; an idiot.— **klutziness** *n*. —**klutzy** *adj*.

klystron *n* an electronic device that generates and amplifies microwaves.

km, km. *abbr* = kilometer(s); kingdom.

KM *abbr* = Knight of Malta.

kn. *abbr* = kronen.

KN *abbr* (*chess*) = king's knight.

K.N. *abbr* = Know-Nothing.

knack *n* an ability to do something easily; a trick; a habit.

knacker *n* one who buys worn-out horses or old houses, ships, etc, for destruction.

knackwurst *n* a type of spicy German sausage.

knap (**knapping, knapped**) *vt* to break, snap, or hit something.

knapped flint *n* (*archit*) flints split in two and laid with the shiny black surface outward in the face of a wall.

knapsack *n* a bag for carrying equipment or supplies on the back.

knapweed *n* a purple-flowered weed.

knar *see* **knur**.

knave *n* (*arch*) a tricky or dishonest man; the jack in a pack of playing cards.— **knavish** *adj*.—**knavishly** *adv*.

K

knavery *n* (*pl* **knaveries**) dishonesty; fraud; deceit.

knead *vt* to squeeze and press together (dough, clay, etc) into a uniform lump with the hands; to make (bread, etc) by kneading; to squeeze and press with the hands.—**kneader** *n*.

knee *n* the joint between the thigh and the lower part of the human leg, former by the femur, patella, and tibia; anything shaped like a bent knee. * *vt* (**kneeing, kneed**) to hit or touch with the knee.

kneecap *n* the small bone covering and protecting the front part of the knee-joint.— also **patella** * *vt* (**kneecapping, kneecapped**) to maim by shooting into the kneecap.

knee-deep *adj* deep enough to cover the knees; deeply involved.

kneejerk, knee jerk *adj* responding automatically. *n* an involuntary jerk when the tendon below the knee is tapped. *See also* **reflex action**.

kneel *vi* (**kneeling, kneeled,** *or* **knelt**) to go down on one's knee or knees; to remain in this position.—**kneeler** *n*.

knell *n* the sound of a bell rung slowly and solemnly at a death or funeral; a warning of death, failure, etc. * *vi* (*bell*) to ring a knell; to summon, announce, etc (as if) by a knell.

knelt *see* **kneel.**

knew *see* **know.**

Knick. *abbr* = Knickerbocker.

Knickerbocker *n* a New Yorker; a descendant of the founders of the original city.

knickerbockers *npl* baggy breeches fastened by a band at the knee.

knickers *npl* plus fours; an undergarment covering the lower body and having separate leg holes, worn by women and girls.

knickknack *n* a small ornament or trinket.—*also* **nicknack.**

knife *n* (*pl* **knives**) a flat piece of steel, etc, with a sharp edge set in a handle, used to cut or as a weapon; a sharp blade forming part of a tool or machine. * *vt* to cut or stab with a knife.

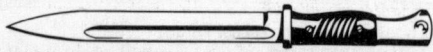

knife edge *n* the sharp edge of a knife; anything resembling this, such as the blade of an ice skate; a sharp wedge used as a pivot for a balance; a critical or precarious situation.

knight *n* a medieval mounted soldier; a man who for some achievement is given honorary rank entitling him to use "Sir" before his given name; a chessman shaped like a horse's head. * *vt* to make (a man) a knight.—**knightly** *adj*.— **knightliness** *n*.

Knight *n* **Dame Laura** (1877–1970) English painter known particularly for her paintings of the ballet, Gypsies, and the circus.

knight-errant *n* (*pl* **knights-errant**) a quixotic person; a medieaval knight who went in quest of adventure, to show his prowess, chivalry etc.

knight-errantry *n* the practices or customs of knights-errant; quixotic behavior.

knighthood *n* the character, rank, or dignity of a knight; the order of knights.

knit *vt* (**knitting, knitted,** *or* **knit**) to form (fabric or a garment) by interlooping yarn using knitting needles or a machine; to cause (e.g. broken bones) to grow together; to link or join together closely; to draw (the brows) together. * *vi* to make knitted fabric from yarn by means of needles; to grow together; to become joined or united. * *n* a knitted garment or fabric.—**knitter** *n*.

knitting *n* work being knitted.

knitting needle *n* a long thin eyeless needle, usu made of plastic or steel, used in knitting.

knitwear *n* knitted clothing.

knives *see* **knife.**

knob *n* a rounded lump or protuberance; a handle, usu round, of a door, drawer, etc.

knobby *adj* (**knobbier, knobbiest**) full of knobs.

knobkerrie *n* a round-headed stick used as a weapon in South Africa.

knock *vi* to strike with a sharp blow; to rap on a door; to bump, collide; (*engine*) to make a thumping noise; (*with* **off**) (*inf*) to finish work; (*with* **up**) (*tennis, etc*) to practise before a match. * *vt* to strike; (*inf*) to criticize; (*with* **about, around**) to wander around aimlessly; to treat roughly; (*with* **back**) (*inf*) to drink, swallow quickly; to reject, refuse; (*with* **down**) to indicate a sale at an auction; (*with* **down** *or* **off**) to hit so as to cause to fall; (*with* **off**) (*inf*) to do or make hastily and without effort; to reduce in price; to discontinue, esp work; (*sl*) to kill; (*sl*) to steal; (*with* **out**) to make unconscious or exhausted; to eliminate in a knockout competition; (*inf*) to amaze; (*with* **up**) (*inf*) to make or arrange hastily; (*cricket*) to score a certain number of runs; to rouse; (*sl*) to make pregnant. * *n* a knocking, a hit, a rap.

knockabout *adj* rough, boisterous.

knockdown *adj* cheap; (*furniture*) easy to dismantle.

knocker *n* a device hinged against a door for use in knocking; (*sl, usu pl*) a woman's breasts.

knock-for-knock agreement *n* an agreement between motor insurance companies by which they pay for any accident damage sustained by their own policyholders, irrespective of who was to blame for the accident.

knock-knee *n* an abnormal curvature of the legs so that when the knees are touching, the ankles are spaced apart.—*also* **genu valgum.**—**knock-kneed** *adj*.

knock-off *n* a copy that sells for less than the original.

knockout *n* a punch or blow that produces unconsciousness; a contest in which competitors are eliminated at each round; (*inf*) an attractive or extremely impressive person or thing.

knoll a low, rounded hill.

Knoll *n* a design company of international renown, founded by Florence and Hans Knoll.

Knossus *or* **Cnossus** *n* the greatest palace and settlement of the Minoans, situated on the northern coast of Crete.

knot *n* a lump in a thread, rope, etc, formed by a tightened loop or tangling; a fastening made by tying lengths of rope, etc; an ornamental bow; a small group, cluster; a hard mass of wood where a branch grows out from a tree, which shows as a roundish, cross-grained piece in a board; a unit of speed of one nautical mile (1.15 statute miles or 1.85 kilometers) per hour; something that ties closely, esp the bond of marriage. * *vti* (**knotting, knotted**) to make or form a knot (in); to entangle or become entangled.—**knotter** *n*.

knotgrass *n* a weed with a jointed stem and green flowers; any of various similar plants.

knothole *n* a hole in wood once filled by a knot.

knotting *n* a kind of lace work made with knots; a sealer applied to knots before priming wood as protection from sap.

knotty *adj* (**knottier, knottiest**) full of knots; hard to solve; puzzling.— **knottiness** *n*.

knotwork *n* one of the most common designs on Celtic crosses and other forms of sculpture. As the name suggests, it involved designs based on knots.

know *vt* (**knowing, knew,** *pp* **known**) to be well informed about; to be aware of; to be acquainted with; to recognize or distinguish.—**knowable** *adj*.

know-all *or* **know-it-all** *n* a person who acts as if they know about everything.

know-how *n* practical skill, experience.

knowing *adj* having knowledge; shrewd; clever; implying a secret understanding.— **knowingly** *adv*.—**knowingness** *n*.

knowledge *n* what one knows; the body of facts, etc accumulated over time; fact of knowing; range of information or understanding; the act of knowing.

knowledgeable *adj* having knowledge or intelligence; well-informed.—**knowledgeably** *adv*.

knowledge engineering *n* (*comput*) the process of extracting information from experts and expressing this knowledge in a form that an expert system can use.

known *see* **know.**

Knox *n* 1. **Archibald** (1864–1933) British silver designer whose refined silver pieces and Donegal carpets were amongst the most elegant of the age. 2. **John** (*c*.1513–72) Scottish Protestant reformer. 3. **Robert** (1791–1862) Scottish doctor and anatomist, who was supplied with bodies for dissection by the infamous murderers, William Burke and William Hare.

KNP *abbr* (*chess*) = king's knight's pawn.

knt. *abbr* = knight.

knuckle *n* a joint of the finger, esp at the roots of the fingers; the knee of an animal used as food.—*See also* **metacarpal bone**. * *vi* (*with* **down**) (*inf*) to apply oneself in earnest (to some task, duty, etc); (*with* **under**) to submit, to give in.

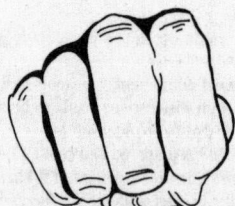

knuckle-duster *n* a metal device that fits over the knuckles, used for inflicting severe injury by punching.

knucklehead *n* (*inf*) a fool, idiot.—**knuckleheaded** *adj*.

knuckle sandwich *n* (*sl*) a punch with the fist.

knur, knurr *n* a knot either in a tree trunk or in wood; a hard lump.—*also* **knar.**

knurl *n* a small ridge, esp one of a series on a metal surface to prevent slippage.

k.o., KO *abbr* = kick-off; knockout.

KO *abbr* (*army*) (*sl*) = Commanding Officer.

koa *n* a Hawaiian tree; the hard wood it produces used in making furniture.

koala *n* an Australian tree-dwelling marsupial with thick, grey fur.

koan *n* an insoluble riddle used as a meditation exercise in Zen Buddhism.

kob *n* a South African water antelope.

Kobe *n* major city in Japan.

kobo *n* a monetary unit of Nigeria, equal to one hundredth of a naira.

kobold *n* a household goblin or elf; a spirit of mines and other underground places.

KOC *abbr* = Kuwait Oil Company.

Koch *n* Edward (1924–) American lawyer and Democrat politician, who became mayor of New York in 1978.

Köchel *n* Ludwig Alois Friedrich Ritter von (1800–77) Austrian scientist who catalogued Mozart's works, giving each one a Köchel or "K" number.

Kodály *n* Zoltán (1882–1967) Hungarian composer whose works include the comic opera *Hary Janos*.

Koechlin *n* Charles (1867–1950) French composer, and author of a treatise on Debussy.

Koehler *n* Florence (1861–1944) American artist and Art Nouveau jewelry designer.

Koestler *n* Arthur (1905–83) Hungarian-born British author and journalist whose masterpiece is *Darkness at Noon* (1940).

Kogoj *n* Oskar (1942–) Yugoslavian industrial designer, best-known for his 1968 *Red Object* plastic wagon.

Kohinoor, Koh-i-nor *n* a famous, very large Indian diamond, which has belonged to the British Crown since 1849.

kohl *n* a fine powder, as of antimony, used for darkening the eyelids.

Kohl *n* Helmut (1930–) German Christian Democrat statesman; chancellor of West Germany (1982–90); first chancellor of a reunited East and West Germany (1990).

Köhler, Wolfgang (1887–1967) Estonian-born German-American psychologist. With the German psychologist Kurt Koffka, he founded the Gestalt school of psychology.

kohlrabi *n* (*pl* kohlrabies) a variety of cabbage with a thick stem, used as a vegetable.

Kokoschka *n* Oskar (1886–1980) Austrian-born expressionist painter and dramatist.

kola nut *n* the seed of either of two tropical trees which has stimulant properties and is chewed or used in making sweet drinks.—*also* cola nut.

Kolff, Willem Johan (1911–) Dutch-born American physician who invented the kidney dialysis machine in 1943 and the artificial kidney in 1975. He also made significant contributions to cardiovascular surgery.

kolinsky *n* (*pl* kolinskies) an Asian mink; its fur.

kolkhoz *n* a collective farm in Russia.

Kollwitz *n* Käthe Schmidt (1867–1945) German engraver and sculptor.

Komintern *abbr* (*Russian*) = *Kommunisticheskii Internatsional*, "Communist International."

Komoi *n* Ray (1918–95) American graphic designer who moved into furniture design in 1949.

Komsomol *abbr* (*Russian*) = *Kommunisticheskii Soyuz Molodezhi*, "Communist Union of Youth."

koodoo *see* kudu.

kook *n* (*inf*) a person regarded as silly, eccentric, etc.

kookaburra *n* an Australian kingfisher with a harsh cry like loud laughter.

kooky, kookie *adj* (kookier, kookiest) (*inf*) crazy; eccentric.

Koons *n* Jeff (1955–) American sculptor.

kop *n* (*S Africa*) an isolated hill.

kop. *abbr* = kopeck(s).

Kópavogur *n* major city in Iceland.

kopeck, kopek *n* a Russian coin, one hundred of which comprise one rouble.

kopje *n* (*S Africa*) a hillock or small hill.

Köppen classification *n* (*meteorol*) a system of climatic classification, based on annual and monthly measurements of temperature and precipitation, and the major types of vegetation.

Koptos settlement on the River Nile, at the entrance to the Wadi Hammamet, with evidence of Old and Middle Kingdom temples. It was particularly a cult center of the fertility god Min.

Koran *n* the sacred book of the Muslims.—**Koranic** *adj*.

Kørbing *n* Kay (1915–1995) Danish designer of one of the earliest fibreglass chairs, in 1955.

Korda *n* Sir Alexander [Sandor Kellner] (1893–1956) Hungarian-born British film director and producer who produced one of the greatest of all films, Reed's and Welles' *The Third Man* (1949).

Kore *n* (*Greek myth*) a name given to Persephone, a goddess of the underworld.

Korea *or* **the Democratic People's Republic of Korea** *n* a socialist republic (formerly North Korea) occupying the northern half of the Korean Peninsula in eastern Asia.

Korea *n* **Republic of** a republic (formerly South Korea) occupying the southern half of the Korean Peninsula in eastern Asia.

Korean *n* a native or inhabitant of Korea; the language spoken in North and South Korea.* *adj* of or pertaining to Korea, its language or people.

Kornberg, Arthur (1918–) American biochemist. He shared the 1959 Nobel prize for physiology or medicine with Severo Ochoa for his discovery of the DNA enzyme, polymerase.

Korngold *n* Eric Wolfgang (1897–1957) Austrian-born American composer.

Koror *n* capital city of Palau.

Korsakoff's syndrome *n* (*med*) a neurological disorder caused primarily by alcoholism and a deficiency of thiamine (vitamin b), described by the Russian neuropsychiatrist, Sergei Korsakoff, in which the nerves and brain deteriorate.

koruna *n* standard monetary unit of the Czech Republic. *see* **haler**.

Kos *see* Cos.

kosher *adj* (*Judaism*) clean or fit to eat according to dietary laws; (*inf*) acceptable, genuine. * *n* kosher food.

Kosice *n* major city in the Slovak Republic.

Kosygin *n* Aleksei Nikolayevich (1904–80) Soviet statesman. A notable long-distance survivor in Soviet politics, he became prime minister (1964–80) of the Soviet Union after Khrushchev's overthrow.

Kotera *n* Jan (1871–1923) Czech architect who was influenced by Frank Lloyd Wright.

koto *n* (*pl* kotos) (*mus*) a Japanese musical instrument with silk strings, similar to a zither.

Koudougou *n* major city in Burkina Faso.

kowtow *vi* to show exaggerated respect (to) by bowing.

KP *abbr* = Knight of the Order of St Patrick; (*chess*) king's pawn.

KPD *abbr* (*German*) = *Kommunistische Partei Deutschland*, "German Communist Party."

kpg *abbr* = kilometers per gallon.

kph *abbr* = kilometers per hour.

kph *or* **km/h** *abbr* = kilometers per hour.

KPM *abbr* = King's Police Medal.

KPP *abbr* = Keeper of the Privy Purse.

KQC *abbr* = London University's King's College.

Kr *symbol* (*chem*) krypton (element).

kr, kr. *abbr* = kreutzer; krona; krone or kronen; kroner.

KR *abbr* = King's Regulations; (*chess*) king's rook.

kraal *n* an African village consisting of a group of huts surrounded by a pallisade; a sheepfold or cattle pen. * *vt* to pen sheep or cattle in a kraal.

kraft *n* a type of heavy brown wrapping paper made from wood pulp.

krait *n* a deadly Asian rock snake.

kraken *n* a gigantic fabled sea monster supposed to live in the sea off Norway.

Kraków *n* major city in Poland.

Kramer *n* Ferdinand (1898–1985) German architect who designed the 1925 *Kramer-Stove*.

Kranj *n* a major city in Slovenia.

Krebs *n* Sir Hans Adolf (1900–81) German-born British biochemist. He shared the 1953 Nobel prize for physiology or medicine with Fritz Lipmann for his work on metabolic cycles, particularly his discovery of the Krebs Cycle.

Kreisler *n* Fritz (1875–1962) Austrian-born American violinist and composer. Elgar's violin concerto was dedicated to him, and he became one of the most popular violinists of his day.

kremlin *n* a Russian citadel.

Kremlin *n* The citadel in Moscow, housing the former palace, cathedrals, and the Russian government; (formerly) the central government of Russia.

Krenek *n* Ernst (1900–91) Czech-born American composer, conductor, and pianist.

kriegspiel *n* (*mil*) a game with blocks or models representing the various sections of an army as if in actual warfare, used in training; a chess game for two players, each playing on their own board with their own pieces, unseen by the other, with the moves regulated by a third person also with a board unseen by either player.

krill *n* (*pl* krill) the tiny shrimp-like plankton eaten by many whales.

kris *n* a Malaysian or Indonesian knife or dagger with a wavy blade.—*also* **crease**, **creese**.

Krishna *n* a great deity of later Hinduism.—**Krishnaism** *n*.

Kristian *n* Roald (1893–) Norwegian artist.

Kristiansand *n* major city in the Kingdom of Norway.

KRL *abbr* = knowledge representation language.

krn. *abbr* (*Sweden*) = krona; kronor.

Krog *n* Arnold (1856–1931) Danish architect and artistic director of Royal Copenhagen Porcelain Factory.

Kroll *n* Boris (1913–91) American textile designer.

krona *n* (*pl* kronor) the standard monetary unit of Sweden.

króna *n* (*pl* krónur) the standard monetary unit of Iceland.

krone *n* (*pl* kroner) the standard monetary unit of Denmark and Norway.

Kronos *see* Cronos.

K

kroon *n* (*pl* **kroons** *or* **krooni**) the standard monetary unit of Estonia.

KRP *abbr* (*chess*) = king's rook's pawn.

Krugerrand *n* a South African coin containing one troy ounce of gold, used for investment only.

Krumhorn, Krummhorn *n* (*mus*) (*German*) a double-reed instrument, common in the 16th and early-17th centuries.

Krupp *n* **Alfred Alwin Felix** (1907–67) German industrialist. He took control of the Krupp industrial empire in 1943 by dispensation from Hitler. He was imprisoned (1947–51) for using slave labour in his factories. He subsequently helped develop Germany's postwar economy, and in 1959 he agreed to pay compensation to some of his ex-slave labourers.

krypton *n* a colorless, odorless gas used in fluorescent lights and lasers.

KS *abbr* = Kaposi's sarcoma; (*Brit*) King's Scholar; (*Brit*) King's School.

KSA *abbr* = Kitchen Specialists Association; Klinefelter's Syndrome Association.

KSC *abbr* = Kennedy Space Center

KSF *abbr* = Kashmiri Students Federation.

Kt *abbr* = Knight; (*chess*) knight.

kt., Kt. *abbr* = carat.

KT *abbr* (*Brit*) = Kingston-upon-Thames; Knight of the Order of the Thistle; Knight Templar.

KTL *abbr* = Keep the Link.

Ku *symbol* (*chem*) kurchatovium (element).

Kuala Belait *n* major city in Brunei.

Kuala Lumpur *n* capital city of Malaysia.

KUB *abbr* = kidney, ureter, bladder.

Kübler-Ross *n* **Elizabeth** (1926–) American doctor famous for her works on the emo - tional care of the terminally ill. Her publications include *On Death and Dying* (1969).

Kubrick *n* **Stanley** (1928–99) American film director and producer whose films include the innovative science fiction classic *2001: A Space Odyssey* (1968) and the still controversial *A Clockwork Orange* (1971).

kudos *n* (*used as sing*) (*inf*) fame, glory, prestige.

kudu *n* an African striped antelope with long spiral horns.—*also* **koodoo**.

Kue *n* (*Bible*) OT form of Cicilia.

Kufic *see* **Cufic**.

Kuhn *n* **Walt** (1877–1949) American painter. Favorite themes include circuses and clowns in bright colors; a typical work is *Clown with Black Wig* (1930).

Ku Klux Klan *n* a White American secret society hostile to African-Americans, Jews, Catholics, etc.

kulak *n* (*Russia*) an independent well-to-do peasant.

Kulli *n* (*archeo*) a culture and type of pottery discovered at sites in the south Baluchistan Mountains, on the border between Iran, Afghanistan and India.

Kumanovo *n* major city in the Former Yugoslav Republic of Macedonia (FYROM).

Kumasi *n* major city in Ghana.

kumiss *n* a spirit made in central Asia from fermented mare's milk and sometimes used as a medicine.

kümmel *n* a liqueur flavored with caraway seeds.

kumquat *n* a small fruit like an orange with a sweet rind.

kuna *n* the standard monetary unit of Croatia, made up of 100 lipas.

Kundera *n* **Milan** (1929–) Czech novelist whose masterpiece is *The Unbearable Lightness of Being* (1984).

kung fu *n* a Chinese system of unarmed combat.

Kuniyoshi *n* **Yasuo** (1893–1953) Japanese-born American painter. A typical work is *I'm Tired* (1938).

Kunmayr (Gyumri) *n* major city in Armenia.

Kupka *n* **Frank** (1871–1957) Czech painter whose notable works include *Working Steel* (1921–29).

Kurd *n* a native of Kurdistan, an area of plateaus and mountains covering eastern Turkey, northern Iraq, western Iran, and Armenia.

Kurdish *adj* pertaining to the Kurds or to their language. * *n* the language of the Kurds.

kurgan *n* (*archeo*) (*Russia*) a mound or barrow covering some form of burial. Kurgans first appeared in the Copper Age *c.*4000 BC.

Kurosawa *n* **Akira** (1910–) Japanese film director . His films include the samurai classics *The Seven Samurai* (1955) and *Yojimbo* (1961), (remade in the west as *The Magnificent Seven* and *A Fistful of Dollars*). Like John Ford, whom he much admired, Kurosawa was happiest with the epic form, and also had a "family" of actors he used regularly.

kuru *n* a monetary unit of Turkey, equal to one hundredth of a lira.

Kush *n* (*Egypt*) Egyptian term for Nubia.

Kuwait *n* a tiny Arab Emirate on The Gulf, comprising the city of Kuwait at the southern entrance of Kuwait Bay, a small desert wedged between Iraq and Saudi Arabia and nine small offshore islands.

Kuwait City (Al Kuwayt) *n* capital city of Kuwait.

Kuwaiti Dinar *n* currency of Kuwait.

Kuznets *n* **Simon** (1901–85) Russian-born American economist and statistician. He was awarded the 1971 Nobel prize for economics for his research into economic growth and social change.

kv., kV *abbr* (*elect*) = kilovolt(s).

kva, kVA, kv-a *abbr* (*elect*) = kilovolt-ampere.

kvass, kvas *n* a Russian rye beer that has stale bread as one of its ingredients.—*also* **quass**.

kw., kW *abbr* (*elect*) = kilowatt(s).

kwac *abbr* = keyword and context.

kwacha *n* the standard monetary unit of Malawi, made up of 100 tambala; the standard monetary unit of Zambia, made up of 100 ngwee.

kwanza *n* the standard monetary unit of Angola, made up of 100 lwei.

kwashiorkor *n* a disease, esp of children, caused by protein deficiency and characterized by a distended stomach and changes in skin pigmentation.

kwh, kWh, kw-hr *abbr* (*elect*) = kilowatt-hour(s).

kwic *abbr* = keyword in context.

kwoc *abbr* = keyword out of context.

Ky. *abbr* = Kentucky.

kyanize *vt* to preserve wood from dry rot by injecting corrosive sublimate.—**kyanization** *n*.

kyat *n* the standard monetary unit of Myanmar (Burma), made up of 100 pyas.

Kyd *n* **Thomas** (1558–94) English dramatist whose most important work is *The Spanish Tragedy*, which was influential on the work of Shakespeare and others.

kymograph *n* an instrument for recording pressure, oscillations, sound waves, etc, e.g., an apparatus for determining the pressure of blood, by means of a stylus on a continually rotating drum of paper; (*phonetics*) an instrument to measure muscular strength in the tongue, lips, etc; an instrument that records the angular oscillations of an aircraft in the air.—*also* **cymograph**.

Kyoto *n* major city in Japan.

kyphosis *n* an abnormal outward curvature of the spinal column causing the back to be hunched.

Kyrgyzstan *n* a central Asian republic which has been independent from the former USSR since 1991.

Kyrie (eleison) *n* (*mus*) (*Greek*) "Lord have Mercy," a prayer, part of a mass; a musical setting of this; the response in an Anglican communion service.

KZ *abbr* = killing zone.

L

l, L the twelfth letter of the English alphabet; something shaped like an L.

l, l. *abbr* = laevorotatory; lake; land; large; late; latitude; launch; law; leaf, leaves; league, leagues; leasehold; left; length; lex; (*Latin*) *liber*, "book"; liberal; (*Latin*) *libra*, "pound"; line, lines; lingual; link, links; (*Italian*) lira, lire; liter, liters; livre; loco; locus; low; lumen.

l- *or* **l.** *abbr* (*chem*) = levo-.

L *abbr* = 50 in Roman numerals; Lake; Latin; Liberal; Licentiate; Loch; Lough; (*elec*) inductance ; large (size in clothing); learner driver; longitude; lambert; (*phys*) length; (*astron*) (heliocentric) longitude; (*geog*) (terrestrial) longitude; (*elec*) coefficient of inductance.

L. *abbr* (*dynamics*) = kinetic potential.

L² *see* **el**.

la (lah) *n* (*mus*); the note A; in the tonic sol-fa, the sixth note or submediant, of the major scale.

La *symbol* (*chem*) lanthanum.

la *abbr* = low altitude.

la. *abbr* = last (the weight).

La. *abbr* = Louisiana.

LA *abbr* = Lard Association; Latin America/n; Law Agent; Lebanese Army; Legislative Assembly; Library Association; Licensing Act; Literate in Arts; Local Agent; Los Angeles; left atrium; local anaesthetic; local authority.

LAA *abbr* = light anti-aircraft.

laager *n* (*S Africa*) a camp in a circle of wagons.—*also* **lager**.

laari *n* a monetary unit of the Maldives that is worth one hundredth of a rufiyaa.

Laâyoune (El Aaiún) *n* capital city of Western Sahara.

lab *n* (*inf*) laboratory.

Lab. *abbr* = Labrador.

LAB *abbr* = Laboratory Animals Bureau; Latin America Board; Legal Aid Board; low-altitude bombing.

LABAC *abbr* = Licentiate Member of the Association of Business and Administrative Computing.

Laban *n* (*Bible*) a descendant of Nahor and wealthy shepherd; his sister, Rebekah, married Isaac.

labarum *n* (*pl* **labara**) a banner used in Christian processions.

LABBS *abbr* = Ladies' Association of British Barbershop Singers.

Labdacus *n* (*Greek myth*) a king of Thebes and father of Laius.

Labé *n* a city in Guinea.

label¹ *n* a slip of paper, cloth, metal, etc, attached to anything to provide information about its nature, contents, ownership, etc; a term of generalized classification. * *vt* (**labeling, labeled** *or* **labelling, labelled**) to attach a label to; to designate or classify (as).—**labeler, labeller** *n*.

label² *n* (*comput*) text in a spreadsheet program as opposed to a number or formula.

labeled compound *n* (*chem*) a compound used in radioactive tracing, where an atom of the compound is replaced by a radioactive isotope.

labellum *n* (*pl* **labella**) the lower petal of an orchid.

Labhraidh Loingsech (*Irish Celtic legend*) originally named Maon or Moen (meaning "dumb"), Labhraidh Loingsech was a king of Leinster who is supposed to have reigned around 268 BC.

labia *npl* (*sing* **labium**) the lips of the female genitals, comprising the outer pair (*labia majora*) and the inner pair (*labia minora*).

labial *adj* of the lips or labia.

labialize *vt* (*phonetics*) to pronounce (a sound) by rounding one's lips.—**labialization** *n*.

labiate *adj, n* (*bot*) (a plant) with the corolla or calyx divided into two parts, resembling lips.

labile *adj* (*chem*) unstable.

Labino *n* **Dominick** (*c*.1935–) American ceramicist and glassware designer who developed free-form techniques and layered pieces.

labiodental *adj* (*phonetics*) (*sound*) formed by the lips and teeth.

labionasal *adj* (*phonetics*) (*sound*) formed by the lips and nose.

labium *see* **labia**.

labor, labour *n* work, physical or mental exertion; a specific task; all wage-earning workers; workers collectively; the process of childbirth. * *vi* to work; to work hard; to move with difficulty; to suffer (delusions, etc); to be in childbirth. * *vt* to develop in unnecessary detail.

laboratory *n* (*pl* **laboratories**) a room or building where scientific work and research is carried out.

labor costs *npl* the cost of the wages paid to workers who are concerned with the manufacture of a product or the carrying out of a service.

Labor Day *n* the first Monday in September in US and Canada, a legal holiday honoring labor.

labored, laboured *adj* done with effort; strained.—**laboredly, labouredly** *adv*.

laborer, labourer *n* a person who labors, esp a person whose work requires strength rather than skill.

labor force *n* the total number of people who are employed by a firm in the manufacture of goods or the carrying out of services, or who are available to produce goods and carry out services.

labor-intensive *adj* the term used to refer to an industry or firm that employs a relatively high number of people and in which the labor costs are thus high, particularly in proportion to the cost of raw materials or capital equipment.

laborious *adj* requiring much work; hard-working; labored.—**laboriously** *adv*.—**laboriousness** *n*.

labor law *n* the body of legislation concerned with industrial relations and employment.

labor relations *same as* industrial relations.

labor-saving *adj* (*appliances, etc*) reducing or eliminating physical effort.

labor turnover rate *n* the proportion of the number of employees who leave a firm, organization or industry in a stated period in relation to the average number of employees working in the firm or industry during that period.

labor union, labour union *n* an organized association of employees of any trade or industry for the protection of their income and working conditions.

labour *see* **labor**.

Labraid Luathlam ar Cleb *n* (*Irish Celtic myth*) the ruler of Magh Mell and husband of Li Ban.

Labrador Current *n* an important cold ocean current that flows southwards from the Arctic along the west coast of Greenland until it meets the warm North Atlantic Drift on the Grand Banks, off Newfoundland.

labradorite *n* a type of feldspar.

Labrador retriever *n* a breed of large, usu smooth-coated sporting dog.

labret *n* a shell, etc, worn as an ornament in the lip.

labrum *n* (*pl* **labra**) the liplike shield of an insect's mouth.

laburnum *n* a small tree or shrub with hanging yellow flowers.

labyrinth¹ *n* a structure containing winding passages through which it is hard to find one's way; a maze.—**labyrinthine** *adj*.

labyrinth² *n* part of the inner ear, consisting of canals, ducts, and cavities, forming the organs of hearing and balance.

lac¹ *n* a resinous substance secreted by certain insects.

lac² *see* **lakh**.

LAC *abbr* = Landscape Advisory Committee; Library Association of China; Licentiate of the Apothecaries' Company.

Lacan *n* **Jacques** (1901–81) French psychoanalyst and advocate of structuralism who focused on the play between unconscious and conscious concepts.

lace *n* a cord, etc, used to draw together and fasten parts of a shoe, a corset, etc; a delicate ornamental fabric of openwork design using fine cotton, silk, etc. * *vt* to fasten with a lace or laces; to intertwine, weave; to fortify (a drink, etc) with a dash of spirits.

Lacedaemon *n* (*Greek myth*) a son of Zeus, king of Lacedaemon, whose capital was Sparta; the ancient name of Laconia.—**Lacedaemonian** *adj*.

laced windows *n* (*archit*) a decorative feature in which the vertical lines formed by the sides of a window are continued upwards and downwards, usu in brickwork of a different color, to join the windows above and below.

La Ceiba *n* a city in Honduras.

lacerate *vt* to tear jaggedly; to wound (feelings, etc).—**laceration** *n*.

laceration *n* a wound with jagged edges.

LACES *abbr* (*Brit*) = London Airport Cargo Electronic Processing Scheme.

Lachaise *n* **Gaston** (1882–1935) French sculptor who settled in the US in 1906. He was responsible for renewing enthusiasm for direct carving methods in American sculpture, and his work represented a move away from academic forms and strictures.

Lachenal *n* 1. **Edmond** (1855–1948) French sculptor who in 1890 perfected a partially dulled glaze and metallic luster glazes. 2. **Raoul** (1885–1956) French ceramicist, son of Edmond Lachenal.

laches *n* (*law*) undue delay in claiming one's rights, etc.

Lachesis *see* **Fates**.

Lachish *n* (*Bible*) double-walled fortress city in southern Judah about 30 miles from Jerusalem.

lachrimatory *n* (*pl* **lachrimatories**) a vessel used to hold tears, found in ancient Roman tombs.

lachrymal *adj* of tears; relating to the glands that secrete tears.—*also* **lacrimal**.

lachrymal gland *n* one of a pair of glands, situated above and to the side of each eye, that secrete saline and slightly alkaline tears.

lachrymose *adj* tending to shed tears; sad.—**lachrymosity** *n*.

laciniate, laciniated *adj* (*biol*) cut into narrow lobes, fringed.

lack *n* the fact or state of not having any or not having enough; the thing that is needed. * *vti* to be deficient in or entirely without.

lackadaisical *adj* showing lack of energy or interest; listless.—**lackadaisically** *adv*.

lackey *n* a male servant of low rank; a servile hanger-on.

lackluster, lacklustre *adj* lacking in brightness or vigor; dull.

LACMA *abbr* = Latin American and Caribbean Movers Association.

Lacombe *n* **Georges** (1886–1916) French carver who became a member of the Nabis artists' group.

Laconia *n* the southernmost part of the Peloponnese, whose principal city was Sparta or Lacedaemon.—**Laconian** *adj*.

laconic *adj* using few words; concise.—**laconically** *adv*.—**laconicism** *n*.

Lacoste *n* **Gerald** (1909–1995) British architect who designed decorative glass.

lacquer *n* a glossy varnish. * *vt* to coat with lacquer, to make glossy.

lacrimal *see* **lachrymal**.

lacrimoso *adj, adv* (*mus*) (*Italian*) tearful.

Lacroix *n* **Boris-Jean** (1902–84) French designer of wallpaper, lighting, bookbinding, and furniture.

lacrosse *n* a game played by two teams of 10 players with the aim of throwing a ball through the opponents' goal using a long stick topped with a netted pouch for catching and carrying the ball.

LACS *abbr* = League Against Cruel Sports.

lact-, lacto- *prefix* milk.

lactase *n* the enzyme that acts on milk sugar (lactose) to produce the simple sugars glucose and galactose.

lactate *vi* (*mammals*) to secrete milk.

lactation *n* the secretion of milk.—**lactational** *adj*.

lacteal *adj* pertaining to or resembling milk; (*anat*) conveying chyle.

lacteal vessels *npl* part of the lymphatic system, they occur as projections in the small intestine and take up digested fats as a milky fluid called chyle.

lactescent *adj* milky; (*plant, insect*) yielding a milky juice.—**lactescence** *n*.

lactic *adj* of or relating to milk; obtained from sour milk or whey; involving the production of lactic acid.

lactic acid *n* an organic acid normally present in sour milk.

lactiferous *adj* producing milk or a milky juice.

lacto-, lact- *prefix* milk.

lactometer *n* an instrument used for determining the quality of milk.

lactose *n* a sugar present in milk.

lacuna *n* (*pl* **lacunas, lacunae**) a gap, esp a missing portion in a text.—**lacunary** *adj*.

lacunar *adj* (*archit*) of or relating to the panels of a coffered ceiling or the ceiling itself.

lacustrine *adj* pertaining to lakes; growing by lakesides.

LACW *abbr* = Leading Aircraftswoman.

lacy *adj* (**lacier, laciest**) resembling lace.—**lacily** *adv*.—**laciness** *n*.

lad *n* a boy; a young man; a fellow, chap.

LAD *abbr* = language acquisition device.

ladar *abbr* = laser detection and ranging.

ladder *n* a portable metal or wooden framework with rungs between two vertical supports for climbing up and down; something that resembles a ladder in form or use.

ladder back chair *n* a type of chair with a tall slatted back.

laddie *n* a boy; a young lad.

lade *vt* (**lading, laded,** *pp* **laden** *or* **laded**) (*ship*) to load (with cargo); (*with* **with**) to burden; to spoon up (liquid), e.g. with a ladle.

Lade *n* **Jan** (1944–) Danish interior designer who founded Møre Designteam in 1970, with Sven Asbjørsen.

laden *adj* loaded with cargo; burdened.

la-di-da, la-de-da *adj* (*inf*) affected; foppish. * *n* an affected or foppish person.

ladies' room *n* a public lavatory for women.

lading *n* the act of loading; that which is loaded; cargo; freight.

ladle *n* a long-handled, cup-like spoon for scooping liquids; a device like a ladle in shape or use. * (*with* **out**) (*inf*) to give (money, etc) generously.—**ladleful** *n*.

Ladon *n* (*Greek myth*) a hundred-headed snake, which was immortal and helped the Hesperides to guard the apples in their garden.

Ladra *n* (*Irish Celtic myth*) the pilot who guided the ship of Cesair on its voyage to Ireland. One of only three men on an expedition that had fifty women in it. Ladra is said to have died of sexual excess.

LAdv *abbr* = Lord Advocate.

lady *n* (*pl* **ladies**) a polite term for any woman.

Lady *n* a title of honor given to various ranks of women in the British peerage.

ladybug, ladybird *n* a small, usu brightly colored beetle.

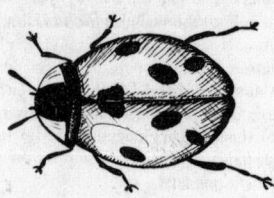

Lady Day *n* March 25, the feast of the Annunciation.

lady-in-waiting *n* (*pl* **ladies-in-waiting**) a female member of a royal household, who attends upon a queen or princess.

lady-killer *n* (*inf*) a man who is or thinks he is particularly attractive to women.

ladylike *adj* like or suitable for a lady; refined, polite.

ladylove *n* (*arch*) a sweetheart.

Ladyship *n* a title used in speaking to or of a woman with the rank of Lady.

lady-slipper *n* an orchid with flowers resembling slippers.

lady's-smock *n* a flowering plant, also known as the cuckooflower.

Laeg *or* **Loeg** *n* (*Irish Celtic myth*) charioteer to Cuchulainn.

Laertes *n* (*Greek myth*) king of Ithaca, father of Odysseus, and one of the Argonauts.

Laestrygonians, Laestrygones *npl* (*Greek myth*) cannibal giants who crushed several ships of Odysseus's fleet, and speared the sailors and ate them.

Laetoli *n* a site in Tanzania near Olduvai Gorge where a number of bones of *Australopithecus* have been discovered.

laevorotation *see* **levorotation**.

laevulose *see* **levulose**.

La Falaise *n* **Alexis de** (1948–) French farmer who designed furniture in oak, sycamore, and mahogany.

La Farge *n* **John Frederick Lewis Joseph** (1835–1910) American stained-glass artist whose methods – influenced by Burne-Jones, Brown, and Rossetti – changed the face of stained-glass design in America.

LAFU *abbr* = Ladies Amateur Fencing Union.

lag[1] *vi* (**lagging, lagged**) to fall behind, hang back; to fail to keep pace in movement or development; to weaken in strength or intensity. * *n* a falling behind; a delay.

lag[2] *vt* (**lagging, lagged**) to insulate (pipes, etc) with lagging.

lag[3] *n* (*sl*) a convict; a term of imprisonment.

LAG *abbr* = Legal Action Group.

lagan *n* goods or wreckage, lying on the seabed.—*also* **ligan**.

LAGB *abbr* = Linguistics Association of Great Britain.

lager[1] *n* a light beer that has been aged for a certain period.

lager[2] *see* **laager**.

laggard *n* a person who lags behind; a loiterer. * *adj* backward, slow.—**laggardly** *adv*.

lagging *n* insulating material used to lag pipes, boilers, etc.

lagniappe *n* a small item added to a purchase without charge; a gratuity.

lagoon[1] *n* shallow salt water almost cut off from the sea by a beach or reef.

lagoon[2] *n* the sheltered deep water within an atoll.

Lagoon Nebula *n* (*astron*) an ionized hydrogen nebula in the constellation Sagittarius.

Lagos *n* a city in Nigeria.

Lagrangian points *n* (*astron*) points in the neighborhood of two orbiting masses in which forces are balanced and in which a small mass can be in a stable position.

la Hale, la Halle *n* **Adam de** (1230–88) French composer and priest who wrote *La jeu de la feuillée*, first performed in Arras, France, in 1262, and *Le jeu de Robin et Marion*, first performed in Naples in 1285, which are now regarded as the earliest forms of comic opera.

Lahalle *n* **Pierre** (1877–1956) French architect and furniture designer whose simplified style reflected the change from Art Nouveau to Art Deco.

lahar *n* a mudflow developed on the flank of a volcano under the combined effects of eruption and torrential rainstorms, or melting of ice or snow.

Lahore *n* a city in the Islamic Republic of Pakistan.

lai *n* (*mus*) (*French*) a 13th and 14th-century French song usu consisting of 12 irregular stanzas sung to different musical phrases.

LAIA *abbr* = Latin American Integration Association.

laic, laical *adj* non-clerical; lay; secular.

laicize *vt* to make non-clerical or lay; to open to lay persons.—**laicization** *n*.

laid *see* **lay**[2].

laid-back *adj* relaxed, easy-going.

laid paper *n* paper impressed with fine lines from the wires on which the pulp is laid.

Laighin (*Irish Celtic myth*) 1. Galian was renamed Laighin before it became Leinster, in Ireland. Named after the Gauls who went to Ireland with Labhraidh Loingsech to recover his kingdom. 2. the Gailioin, one of the three companies who came from Greece and invaded Ireland. They named themselves Laighin because they settled in Leinster.

lain *see* **lie**[2].

Laing *n* R[onald] D[avid] (1927–89) Scottish psychiatrist who was influential in the 1960s for his revolutionary ideas about mental disorders.

lair *n* the dwelling or resting place of a wild animal; (*inf*) a secluded place, a retreat.

laird *n* (*Scot*) a landowner.

Lairgnen *n* (Irish Celtic legend) the son of a chief of Connacht. He was engaged to be married to Deoca, who asked him to capture four famous singing swans as a wedding present. This he did, but the swans were in fact the children of Lir.

laissez-faire, laisser-faire *n* the policy of non-interference with individual freedom, esp in economic affairs.—**laissez-faireism, laisser-faireism** *n*.

laity *n* laymen, as opposed to clergymen.

Laius *n* (*Greek myth*) a king of Thebes, husband of Jocasta, who was told by an oracle that a child of his would kill him. His son, Oedipus, killed his father and married his mother without knowing who they were.

lake[1] *n* a large inland body of water.

lake[2] *n* a purplish-red pigment, originally made from lac.

laker *n* a person or thing associated with a lake; a fish commonly found in lakes.

lake trout *n* any of various salmon and trout, esp a large gray trout found in the Great Lakes.

Lake Wobegon effect *n* a propensity to attribute quality to the average, from the novel by Garrison Keillor.

lakh *n* (*India*) 100,000, esp rupees.

Lalique *n* 1. **René** (1860–1945) French jeweler and glass designer who installed 200 decorative windows in the Coty building of Fifth Avenue, New York. 2. **Suzanne** (1899–1995) French painter and decorator, the daughter of René Lalique.

Lalo *n* **Victor Antoine Edouard** (1823–92) French composer of Spanish descent who is best known for his *Symphonie espagnole* for violin and orchestra.

lam[1] *vt* (**lamming, lammed**) (*inf*) to beat or thrash.

lam[2] *n* a sudden flight, esp to evade capture by the authorities.

Lam *n* **Izabel** (1948–) American fashion designer who took up industrial design in 1988.

lam. *abbr* = laminated.

Lam. *abbr* = Lamentations.

LAM *abbr* = (*Latin*) *Liberalium Artium Magister*, "Master of Liberal Arts"; London Academy of Music.

lama *n* a monk or priest of Lamaism.

La Mache *n* **Didier** (1945–) French designer who produces and sells his own lighting, furniture, and accessories.

Lamaism *n* a form of Buddhism in Tibet and Mongolia.—**lamaist** *n*. — **Lamaistic** *adj*.

Lamarck *n* **Jean [Baptiste Pierre Antoine de Monet, Chevalier de]** (1744–1829) French naturalist. In his *Philosophie Zoologique* (1809), he expounded his theory of the evolution of species through the acquisition of inherited characteristics. It is credited with preparing the ground for Darwin's theory of evolution.

LAMAS *abbr* = London and Middlesex Archaeological Society.

lamasery *n* (*pl* **lamaseries**) a monastery of lamas.

lamb *n* a young sheep; its flesh as food; (*inf*) an innocent or gentle person. * *vi* to give birth to a lamb; to tend (ewes) at lambing time.

Lamb *n* 1. **Charles** (1775–1834) English essayist and critic. His *Specimens of English Dramatic Poets* (1808) was an important contribution to the reassessment of Shakespeare's contemporary dramatists. 2. **Mary Anne** (1764–1847) sister of Charles Lamb with whom he wrote a prose version of Shakespeare's plays, *Tales from Shakespeare* (1807), which has retained its popularity. In 1796, in a fit of insanity, Mary killed their mother, and Charles looked after her until his death.

lambada *n* (the music for) a lively erotic dance of Brazilian origin, in which couples dance with their stomachs touching.

lambast, lambaste *vt* (*inf*) to beat or censure severely.

lambda *n* the Greek letter L.

lambdoid *adj* shaped like lambda.

lambeg drum *n* (*mus*) a large, double-headed bass drum from Northern Ireland.

lambent *adj* (*flame*) playing lightly over a surface; marked by radiance; brilliant.— **lambency** *n*.

lambert *n* a measure of brightness, the brightness of a surface radiating one lumen per square centimeter.

Lambert *n* **Saint** (*d*. 709) Dutch bishop of Tongres-Maastricht who set about the conversion of the pagans of the Campine; patron saint of surgeons. His feast day is September 17.

Lambert *n* **Constant** (1905–51) English composer, conductor, and critic who was commissioned by Diaghilev to write the music for the ballet *Romeo and Juliet*.

lambkin *n* a little lamb.

lambrequin *n* a short hanging over a door, mantelpiece, etc.

lambrusco *n* a sparkling red Italian wine.

lambskin *n* the skin of a lamb with the wool on or as leather, for making clothes, etc.

lamb's wool *n* fine, soft wool made from a young sheep's first shearing.—**lamb's-wool** *adj*.

LAMC *abbr* = Livestock Auctioneers Market Committee for England and Wales.

LAMDA *abbr* = London Academy of Music and Dramatic Art.

lame *adj* disabled or crippled, esp in the feet or legs; stiff and painful; weak, ineffectual. * *vt* to make lame.—**lamely** *adv*.—**lameness** *n*.

lamé *n* a fabric interwoven with metallic threads.

lame duck *n* a weak, ineffectual person; an elected official serving between the end of his or her term and the inauguration of a successor; an informal term used to describe a company that is experiencing trading problems and sustaining losses to the extent that its survival may be threatened.

lamella (*pl* **lamellae, lamellas**) a thin plate, scale, or film.—**lamellar, lamellate, lamellose** *adj*.

lamelliform *adj* lamella-shaped.

lament *vti* to feel or express deep sorrow (for); to mourn. * *n* a lamenting; an elegy, dirge, etc, mourning some loss or death.—**lamenter** *n*.

lamentable *adj* distressing, deplorable.—**lamentably** *adv*.

lamentation *n* a lamenting; a lament, expression of grief.

Lamentations *n* **The Book of** (*Bible*) consists of five short poems lamenting the downfall of the city of Jerusalem in 587 BC; incorrectly attributed to Jeremiah because they echo his words of doom concerning Jerusalem.

lamented *adj* grieved for.

lamentoso *adj, adv* (*mus*) (*Italian*) "mournfully."

lamia *n* (*pl* **lamias, lamiae**) (*myth*) a monster, half snake, half woman.

lamina *n* (*pl* **laminae, laminas**) a thin plate, scale, or layer; the expanded part of a foliage leaf.—**laminose** *adj*.

laminate *vt* to cover with one or more thin layers; to make by building up in layers. * *n* a product made by laminating. * *adj* laminated.—**laminator** *n*.

laminated *adj* built in thin sheets or layers; covered by a thin film of plastic, etc.

lamination *n* divisibility or division, into thin plates.

laminectomy *n* (*med*) the surgical procedure in which access is gained to the spinal cord by the removal of the arch of one or more vertebrae.

Lammas *n* (*RC Church*) a feast held on August 1; (*formerly*) a harvest festival celebrated on August 1.

lammergeier, lammergeyer *n* a vulture found in southern Europe, Africa and Asia, the bearded vulture.

L'Amour *n* **Louis** (1908–1988) America novelist who specialized in western fiction.

lamp *n* any device producing light, either by electricity, gas, or by burning oil, etc; a holder or base for such a device; any device for producing therapeutic rays.

lampas *n* a disease of horses, which causes swelling in the roof of the mouth; a type of flowered silk.

lampblack *n* fine charcoal or soot.

Lampedusa *n* **Giuseppe di** (1896–1957) Italian novelist whose most famous work is *The Leopard*, which describes the decline of aristocratic society in Sicily following the island's annexation by Garibaldi in 1860 during his unification of Italy.

lampion *n* a small lamp.

lamplighter *n* (*formerly*) someone who lit street lamps.

lampoon *n* a piece of satirical writing attacking someone. * *vt* to ridicule maliciously in a lampoon.—**lampooner** *n*. —**lampoonery** *n*.

lamppost *n* a post supporting a street lamp.

lamprey *n* (*pl* **lamprey, lampreys**) an animal resembling an eel but having a jawless, round sucking mouth.

lampshade *n* a shade used to soften or direct the light from a lamp.

LAMRTPI *abbr* = Legal Associate Member of the Royal Town Planning Institute.

LAN *abbr* (*comput*) = local area network.

lanate *adj* woolly.

Lancaster *n* **Sir Osbert** (1908–86) English cartoonist and author of several satirical studies of British architectural history, e.g. *Progress at Pelvis Bay* and *Draynfleete Revealed*.

lance corporal *n* in the US Marine Corps, a rank above private first class and below corporal; in the British army, a noncommissioned officer of the lowest rank.

lance *n* a long wooden spear with a sharp iron or steel head. * *vt* to pierce (as if) with a lance; to open a boil, etc with a lancet.

lancehead *n* a sharp point made of stone, bone, or metal attached to the end of a spear or lance.

lanceolate *adj* (*bot*) tapering to a point at either end.

lancer *n* a cavalry soldier formerly armed with a lance.

lancet *n* a small, usu two-edged, pointed surgical knife.

lancet arch *n* a sharply pointed arch.

lanceted *adj* (*archit*) with one or more lancet arches or windows.

L

lancet window *n* a tall narrow window with a lancet arch.

lancewood *n* a tough, elastic wood.

land *n* the solid part of the earth's surface; ground, soil; a country and its people; property in land. * *vt* to set (an aircraft) down on land or water; to put on shore from a ship; to bring to a particular place; to catch (a fish); to get or secure (a job, prize, etc); to deliver (a blow). * *vi* to go ashore from a ship; to come to port; to arrive at a specified place; to come to rest.

Land *n* **Edwin Herbert** (1909–91) American physicist and inventor of the Polaroid Land camera. Land is also noted for his research into the nature of vision, particularly of color.

landamman *n* (*Switzerland*) the chief official in some cantons.

land and sea breezes *n* air circulation along coasts during summer, developed when the overall pressure gradient is minimal.

landau *n* a four-wheeled horse-drawn carriage with a roof that folds down.

Landau *n* **Lev Davidovich** (1908–68) Russian physicist. He was awarded the 1962 Nobel prize for physics, for his research into theories of condensed matter.

landaulet, landaulette *n* a small landau.

Landberg *n* **Nils** (1907–1996) Swedish engraver and glassware designer who designed much tableware, architectural embellishments, and art pieces.

land bridge *n* a land connection between continents along which human beings and animals could migrate.

land classification *n* the classification of land according to its potential agricultural output, in terms of soil quality, elevation, rainfall, drainage, and susceptibility to erosion.

l & d, L and D *abbr* = loans and discounts; loss and damage.

landed *adj* consisting of land; owning land.

landfall *n* a sighting of land, esp from a ship at sea; the land sighted.

landfill *n* a large pit in which refuse is buried between layers of soil.—*also adj*.

landgrave *n* (*formerly*) a title given to certain counts in Germany.

landgravine *n* the wife of a landgrave; the title given to a woman landgrave.

landing *n* the act of coming to shore or to the ground; the place where persons or goods are loaded or unloaded from a ship; a platform at the end of a flight of stairs.

landing craft *n* a small military vessel designed for landing troops and equipment ashore.

landing gear *n* the undercarriage of an aircraft.

landing stage *n* a platform for landing goods or people from a ship.

landing strip *n* an airstrip.

Landini, Landino *n* **Francesco** (*c*.1335–97) Italian composer, organist and lute player who was blind from childhood. Among the most important musicians of his time, he composed numerous songs.

landlady *n* (*pl* **landladies**) a woman who owns and rents property; a woman who owns and runs a boarding house, pub, etc.

Ländler *n* (*mus*) a country dance in slow waltz time from Austria and Bavaria.

landlocked *adj* surrounded by land.

landlord *n* a man who owns and rents property; a man who owns and runs a boarding house, pub, etc.

landlubber *n* a person who has had little experience of the sea.

landmark *n* any prominent feature of the landscape distinguishing a locality; an important event or turning point.

landmass *n* a large expanse of land.

land mine *n* an explosive charge shallowly buried in the ground, usu detonated by stepping or driving on it.

Land of My Fathers *n* [**Hen Wlad fy Nhadau**] (*mus*) a song adopted by the Welsh as their national anthem whose words were written by Evan James and the tune by James James in 1860.

Landor *n* **Walter Savage** (1775–1864) English poet and essayist, noted for his classically inspired lyrics and epigrams and for his *Imaginary Conversations*, a collection of around 150 imagined dialogs.

landowner *n* a person who owns land.—**landowning** *adj*, *n*.

l. and r., L and R *abbr* = lake and rail.

LANDSAT *n* one of the series of unmanned NASA satellites that orbits the Earth specifically to acquire data about the Earth.

landscape *n* an expanse of natural scenery seen in one view; a picture of natural, inland scenery. * *vt* to make (a plot of ground) more attractive, as by adding lawns, bushes, trees, etc.

landscape architecture *n* the planning and management of land to fulfil functions in an aesthetically pleasing way.

landscape gardening *n* the decorative design and planting of gardens and grounds in imitation of natural scenery.—**landscape gardener** *n*.

landscape orientation *n* (*comput*) rotation of a page of text so that the wider edge becomes the base. *See also* **portrait orientation**.

landscapist *n* an artist who paints landscapes.

Landseer *n* **Sir Edwin Henry** (1802–73) English painter. Notable works include *The Monarch of the Glen* (1850) and the lions modeled for Trafalgar Square, London, in 1867.

landslide *n* the sliding of a mass of soil or rocks down a slope; an overwhelming victory, esp in an election.

landsman *n* (*pl* **landsmen**) a person who resides and works on land, as opposed to the sea.

Landsteiner *n* **Karl** (1868–1943) Austrian-born American pathologist. He discovered the major human blood groups (A, O, B, AB in 1901 and M and N in 1927), which resulted in the development of blood transfusions. He was awarded the 1930 Nobel prize for physiology or medicine.

Landtag *n* (*Germany, Austria*) the parliament of an individual state.

l & w *abbr* = living and well.

landward *adv*, *adj* towards the land.—**landwards** *adv*.

lane *n* a narrow road, path, etc; a path or strip specifically designated for ships, aircraft, cars, etc; one of the narrow strips dividing a running track, swimming pool, etc, for athletes and swimmers; one of the narrow passages along which balls are bowled in a bowling alley.

Lane *n* 1. **Sir Allen** (1903–70) English publisher who founded Penguin Books in 1935, which became one of the most successful—and most imitated—publishing concerns of the century. 2. **Danny** (1955–) American painter and designer who specialized in one-off architectural pieces in London. 3. **Edward William** (1801–76) British Arabic scholar who compiled an Arabic dictionary and promoted Islamic design.

Lang *n* 1. **Andrew** (1844–1912) Scottish scholar, essayist, and poet, remembered chiefly for his anthropological works, e.g. *Myth, Ritual and Religion*, which Freud drew from, and his fairy stories for children, e.g. *The Blue Fairy Book*. 2. **Fritz** (1890–1976) Austrian-born American film director, notable for three classic German films, *Metropolis* (1926), *M* (1931) and *The Testament of Dr Mabuse* (1932). He was offered the job of running the German film industry but fled to the USA in 1933 rather than work for the Nazis. He directed many fine films in the US, e.g. the grim film noir, *The Big Heat* (1953).

lang. *abbr* = language.

Lange *n* 1. **David Russell** (1942–) New Zealand Labour politician. He became leader of the Labour Party in 1983, and won the 1984 general election decisively on an anti-nuclear defense policy, which led to angry confrontations with other Western powers, notably France and the US. Lange was re-elected in 1987, but resigned, due to ill health, in 1989. 2. **Dorothea** (1895–1965) American photographer. Her uncompromising documentary studies of the poverty and suffering of migrant workers during the Depression in the 1930s were highly praised and brought the plight of her subjects into stark public focus.

Langenmayr *n* **Albert** (1951–) German furniture designer , based in Berlin, who is noted for the technical detail of his pieces.

Langhans *n* **Carl G** (1732–) German architect. His notable works include the Brandenburg Gate, Berlin.

Langland *n* **William** (*c*.1332–1400) English poet, about whom virtually nothing is known, and reputed author of the allegorical religious poem *Piers Plowman*, one of the great works in medieval literature, containing passages of great beauty.

langlauf *n* cross-country skiing.—**langläufer** *n*.

Langmuir *n* **Irving** (1881–1957) American chemist. He was awarded the 1932 Nobel prize for chemistry for his work on surface properties. He also developed the gas-filled tungsten lamp and the atomic hydrogen welding process.

langouste *n* the spiny lobster.

langoustine *n* a large prawn or small lobster.

langsam *adj, adv* (*mus*) (*German*) "slow."

langsyne *adv* (*Scot*) long ago.

Langtry *n* **Lily** [**Emilie Charlotte le Breton**] (1853–1929) English actress, nicknamed the "Jersey Lily." One of the great beauties of her day, she became the mistress of the Prince of Wales (later Edward VII). She published her (discreet) *Memoirs* in 1925.

language *n* human speech or the written symbols for speech; any means of communicating; a special set of symbols used for programming a computer; the speech of a particular nation, etc; the particular style of verbal expression characteristic of a person, group, profession, etc.

langue d'oc *n* a form of medieval French spoken in the South of France.

langue d'oïl *n* a form of medieval French spoken in the area north of the Loire river, the basis of modern French.

languid *adj* lacking energy or vitality; apathetic; drooping, sluggish.—**languidly** *adv*.—**languidness** *n*.

languido *adj, adv* (*mus*) (*Italian*) "languidly."

languish *vi* to lose strength and vitality; to pine; to suffer neglect or hardship; to assume a pleading or melancholic expression.—**languisher** *n*.—**languishment** *n*.

languor *n* physical or mental fatigue or apathy; dreaminess; oppressive stillness.—**languorous** *adj*.

langur *n* a long-tailed monkey, found in South Asia.

laniard *n see* **lanyard**.

laniary *n* (*pl* **laniaries**) a canine tooth.

Lanier *n* **Sidney** (1842–81) American poet noted for his study of the connection between music and poetry, *The Science of English Verse*, and for his verse collection, *Poems*, which experiments with metrical forms that resemble musical forms.

laniferous, lanigerous *adj* wool-bearing.

lank *adj* tall and thin; long and limp.—**lankly** *adv*.—**lankness** *n*.

lanky *adj* (**lankier, lankiest**) lean, tall, and ungainly.—**lankily** *adv*.—**lankiness** *n*.

LANL *abbr* = Los Alamos National Laboratory.

lanner *n* a falcon found in Mediterranean countries, North Africa, and South Asia; the female of this species.

Lanner *n* **Joseph** (1801–43) Austrian composer and conductor who was a contemporary of Johann Strauss the Elder, with whom he formed a quintet. He composed some 100 waltzes and many other dances.

lanneret *n* the male lanner falcon.

lanolin, lanoline *n* wool grease used in cosmetics, ointments, etc.

Lansbury *n* 1. **George** (1859–1940) English Labour politician, noted for his support for women's suffrage and pacifism. 2. **Angela** (1925–) daughter of George Lansbury. A film and television actress, she appeared in such films as *Gaslight* (1944), *The Manchurian Candidate* (1962), and *Bedknobs and Broomsticks* (1972) and in the TV series "Murder She Wrote."

Lansing *n* the capital city of Michigan, a state of the USA.

lantern¹ *n* a portable transparent case for holding a light; a structure with windows on top of a door or roof to provide light and ventilation; the light-chamber of a lighthouse.

lantern² *n* (*archit*) a small polygonal or circular turret on top of a roof or dome to let in air and light.

lantern jaw *n* a long thin jaw.

lanthanide *n* any of a series of related chemical elements with atomic numbers from 57 (lanthanum) to 71 (lutetium).

lanthanum *n* a metallic element.

Lantirn *abbr* = low-altitude navigation and targeting infrared system.

lanugo *n* a fine, downy hair that covers the fetus between the fifth and ninth month.

Lanvin *n* **Jeanne** (1867–1946) French fashion designer.

lanyard *n* a rope used for fastening things on board a ship; a cord worn round the neck to hold a knife, whistle, etc.

Laocoön¹ *n* (*Greek myth*) a Trojan priest who was killed by two enormous snakes sent by Apollo.

Laocoön² *n* an ancient Greek statue, discovered in 1506 in Rome. According to the Roman writer Pliny it was the work of the Rhodian artists Alesander, Polydorus, and Athenodorus, and it probably dates from a little before 100 BC.

Laodamas *n* (*Greek myth*) a king of Thebes in whose reign the Epigoni attacked Thebes. Laodamas led an army against them, but was killed by Alcmaeon.

Laodicea *n* (*Bible*) city of Asia Minor near Colossae; the home of one of the seven Churches of Asia mentioned in the book of Revelation.

laodicean *adj* indifferent, esp towards religion.

Laoghaire *n* (*c*.5th century AD) king of Ireland who was on the throne at the time that St Patrick arrived in Ireland.

Laoghaire mac Crimthann *n* (*Irish Celtic legend*) another of the name Laoghaire was Laoghaire mac Crimthann of Connacht. He assisted Fiachna mac Retach in the task of regaining his wife and daughter, who had been abducted by Goll of Magh Mell. He put Goll to death and married Der Greine, one of Fiachna's daughters.

Laomedon *n* (*Greek myth*) a king of Troy for whom Apollo and Poseidon built a wall round Troy. When he refused to pay them, they punished him by sending a plague and a sea monster to his land.

Laos *n* a landlocked people's republic in southeast Asia.

lap¹ *vti* (**lapping, lapped**) to take in (liquid) with the tongue; (*waves*) to flow gently with a splashing sound.

lap² *n* the flat area from waist to knees formed by a person sitting; the part of the clothing covering this.

lap³ *n* an overlapping; a part that overlaps; one complete circuit of a race track. * *vb* (**lapping, lapped**) *vt* to fold (over or on); to wrap. * *vi* to overlap; to extend over something in space or time.

LAP *abbr* = Labor Action for Peace.

laparoscope *n* a type of endoscope with a light source and a means of viewing the object that is inserted into the abdominal cavity through a small incision.

laparoscopy *n* (*med*) the use of a laparoscope to examine the organs in the abdominal cavity.

laparotomy *n* (*pl* **laparotomies**) (*med*) the operation of cutting the abdominal wall.

La Paz *n* administrative capital city of Bolivia.

lapdog *n* a dog small and docile enough to be held on the lap.

lapel *n* a part of a suit, coat, jacket, etc folded back and continuous with the collar.—**lapelled** *adj*.

LAPES *abbr* = low-altitude parachute extraction system.

lapidary *adj* of or relating to stones; inscribed on stone; concise, like an inscription. * *n* (*pl* **lapidaries**) a cutter or engraver of gems.—**lapidarian** *adj*.

lapidate *vt* to stone (to death).—**lapidation** *n*.

lapidify *vti* (**lapidifying, lapidified**) to turn to stone.

La Pietra *n* Ugo (1938–) Italian architect who has worked for all the major Italian manufacturers.

lapis lazuli *n* an azure, opaque, semi-precious stone.

Lapiths, Lapithae *npl* (*Greek myth*) a tribe of northern Thessaly famous for their battle against the Centaurs.

Laplace *n* **Pierre Simon, Marquis de** (1749–1827) French mathematician and astronomer. He formulated the nebular hypothesis in the 1790s, became (briefly) minister of the interior in 1803, and was created a marquis in 1817. He made important studies of the theory of probability.

La Plata *n* a city in Argentina.

lap of honor *n* a ceremonial circuit of the field by a winning person or team.

Laporte-Blairsy *n* Leo (1865–1923) French sculptor of great monumental pieces in the Art Nouveau style.

Lapp *n* a member of a nomadic people chiefly inhabiting northern Scandinavia, Finland, and the Kola Peninsula of northern Russia (—*also* **Laplander**); their language (—*also* **Lappish**).—**Lappish** *adj*.

lappet *n* a small, loose flap.

l'après-midi d'un faune *see* **Après-midi d'un Faune, Prelude a l'**.

lapse *n* a small error; a decline or drop to a lower condition, degree, or state; a moral decline; a period of time elapsed; the termination of a legal right or privilege through disuse. * *vi* to depart from the usual or accepted standard, esp in morals; to pass out of existence or use; to become void or discontinued; (*time*) to slip away.—**lapsable, lapsible** *adj*.—**lapser** *n*.

lapsus *n* (*pl* **lapsus**) a slip or error.

laptop *n* a small portable computer that can comfortably be used on the lap.

lapwing *n* a crested plover.

LAR *abbr* = limit address register.

LARA *abbr* = Land Access Rights Association.

LARAC *abbr* = Local Authority Recycling Advisory Council.

larboard *n* (*naut*) (*formerly*) the port or left side of a ship.

larceny *n* (*pl* **larcenies**) the theft of someone else's property.—**larcenist, larcener** *n*.—**larcenous** *adj*.

larch *n* a cone-bearing tree of the pine family.

Larche *n* **Françoise-Raoul** (1860–1912) French sculptor known for his monumental pieces.

Larcher *n* **Dorothy** (1884–1952) British textile designer who worked with Phyllis Barron.

lard *n* melted and clarified pig fat. * *vt* to insert strips of bacon or pork fat (in meat) before cooking; to embellish.

larder *n* a room or cupboard where food is stored.

Lardner *n* **Ring [Ringgold Wilmer Lardner]** (1885–1933) American journalist and short-story writer.

lares *npl* (*Roman myth*) the household gods.

lar familiaris *n* (*myth*) the deity worshiped by each Roman family as its founder.

largamente *adj, adv* (*mus*) (*Italian*) literally "broadly," meaning slowly and in a dignified manner.

large *adj* great in size, amount, or number; bulky; big; spacious; bigger than others of its kind; operating on a big scale.—**largeness** *n*.

large intestine *n* the section of the digestive system comprising the cecum, colon, and rectum.

largely *adv* much, in great amounts; mainly, for the most part.

largen *vt* to make larger, to enlarge.

large-scale *adj* drawn on a big scale to reveal much detail; extensive.

largess, largesse *n* the generous distribution of money, gifts, favors, etc; generosity.

larghetto *adj, adv* (*mus*) (*Italian*) slowly. * *n* (*pl* **larghettos**) a passage of music played in this way.

largish *adj* quite large.

largo *adv* (*mus*) (*Italian*) slow and dignified. * *n* (*pl* **largos**) a passage of music played in this way.

lari *n* the standard monetary unit of Georgia.

lariat *n* a rope for tethering grazing horses; a lasso.

Lárisa *n* a city in Greece.

Larissa *n* a small satellite of Neptune.

lark¹ *n* any of a family of songbirds.

lark² *n* a playful or amusing adventure; a harmless prank. * *vi* (*usu with* **about**) to have fun, frolic.—**larky** *adj*.

L

Larkin *n* Philip [Arthur] (1922–85) English poet, essayist, and novelist. Two important volumes, *The Whitsun Weddings* and *High Windows*, established him as the greatest of postwar English poets.

larkspur *n* an annual delphinium.

Larnaca *n* a city in Cyprus.

larnax *n* (*archeo*) a coffin made of terracotta.

Larnian *adj* (*archeo*) relating to a culture of the Mesolithic period, the type site for which is Larne in Northern Ireland.

larrigan *n* a knee-high leather boot worn by trappers.

larrikin *n* (*Austral sl*) a hooligan.

larrup *vt* (*dial*) to thrash, flog.

Larsen *n* Johannes (1912–) Danish civil engineer who took up industrial design in the 1960s.

Larsson *n* Lars-Erik (1908–86) Swedish composer, conductor, and critic who was influenced by Berg. His works include three symphonies, three concert overtures, a saxophone concerto, and film music.

larva *n* (*pl* **larvae**) the immature form of many animals after emerging from an egg before transformation into the adult state, e.g. a caterpillar.—**larval** *adj*.

laryngeal *adj* pertaining to or situated near the larynx.

laryngectomy *n* (*med*) surgical excision of all or part of the larynx.

laryngitis *n* inflammation of the larynx.—**laryngitic** *adj*.

laryngo-, laryng- *prefix* larynx.

laryngol. *abbr* = laryngological; laryngology.

laryngology *n* the medical study of the larynx.—**laryngologist** *n*.

laryngoscope *n* a medical instrument for examining the larynx.—**laryngoscopy** *n*.

laryngotomy *n* (*pl* **laryngotomies**) (*med*) the operation of cutting into the larynx.

laryngotracheobronchitis *n* an acute inflammation of the major parts of the respiratory tract, causing shortness of breath, a croup-like cough, and hoarseness.

larynx *n* (*pl* **larynxes, larynges**) the structure at the upper end of the windpipe, containing the vocal cords.

LAS *abbr* = Legal Aid Society; League of Arab States.

L.A.S. *abbr* = Licentiate of the Society of Apothecaries.

lasagna, lasagne *n* pasta formed in thin wide strips; a dish of lasagna baked in layers with cheese, minced meat, and tomato sauce.

lascar *n* an East Indian sailor.—*also* **lashkar**.

Lascaux *n* (*archeo*) a cave discovered in 1940 in the Dordogne region of France. Its Upper Paleolithic paintings date from *c*.18000 BC.

lascivious *adj* lecherous, lustful; arousing sexual desire.—**lasciviously** *adv*.—**lasciviousness** *n*.

Lasdun *n* Sir Denys Louis (1914–) English architect influenced by L e Corbusier. His buildings include the University of East Anglia (1968) and the National Theatre (1976).

lase *vi* (*gem, gas*) able to act as a laser.

laser *n* (acronym for Light Amplification by Stimulated Emission of Radiation) a device that produces an intense beam of light of one wavelength in which the waves are all in step with each other.

LASER *abbr* (*Brit*) = London and South East Advisory Council.

Laser-jet *n* (*trademark*) (*comput*) a laser printer manufactured by Hewlett-Packard (*trademark*).

laser printer *n* a computer printer that uses a laser beam and photoconductive drum to produce high quality text output.

laser surgery *n* the use of lasers in surgical operations.

lasertripsy *n* a medical procedure for removing kidney stones, etc, by the use of laser beams.

lash *vt* to strike forcefully (as if) with a lash; to fasten or secure with a cord, etc; to attack with criticism or ridicule. * *vi* to move quickly and violently; (*rain, waves, etc*) to beat violently against; (*with* out) to attack suddenly either physically or verbally; (*inf*) to spend extravagantly (on). * *n* the flexible part of a whip; an eyelash; a stroke (as if) with a whip.—**lasher** *n*.

lashkar *see* **lascar**.

LASI *abbr* = Licentiate of the Ambulance Service Institute; Licentiate of the Architects and Surveyors Institute.

Lasker *n* Emanuel (1868–1941) German chess player and world champion. His reign as world champion (1894–1921), is still a record.

Laski *n* Harold [Joseph] (1893–1950) English political scientist and socialist propagandist.

LASMO *abbr* = London and Scottish Marine Oil.

lass, lassie *n* (*Scot*) a young woman or girl.

LASSA *abbr* = Licensed Animal Slaughterers and Salvage Association.

Lassa fever *n* an infectious viral disease of Africa.

Lassaigne's test *n* (*chem*) a chemical test for the presence of nitrogen and also sulfur or halogens.

lassitude *n* weariness.

lasso *n* (*pl* **lassos, lassoes**) a long rope or leather thong with a running noose for catching horses, cattle, etc. * *vt* (**lassoes** *or* **lassos, lassoing, lassoed**) to catch (as if) with a lasso.—**lassoer** *n*.

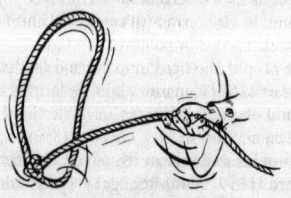

Lassus *n* Roland di (Orlando di Lasso) (1532–94) Flemish composer who experimented with a wide range of musical forms, his compositions include Masses, motets, madrigals, and many other choral pieces.

last[1] *n* a shoemaker's model of the foot on which boots and shoes are made or repaired. * *vt* to shape with a last.

last[2] *vi* to remain in existence, use, etc; to endure. * *vt* to continue during; to be enough for.

last[3] *adj* being or coming after all the others in time or place; only remaining; the most recent; least likely; conclusive. * *adv* after all the others; most recently; finally. * *n* the one coming last.

last-ditch *adj* being a final effort to avoid disaster.

last hurrah *n* a final appearance; a swan song.

lasting *adj* enduring.—**lastingly** *adv*.

lastly *adv* at the end, in the last place, finally.

last-minute *adj* at the last possible time when something can be done.

last name *n* a surname.

Last Post, The *n* a bugle call of the British Army to signal the end of the day at 10 p.m. It is also played at military funerals.

last quarter *n* a phase of the Moon or other body: as seen from the Earth, the dividing line between dark and light on the Moon would be a straight line running over the moon's disk.

last resort *n* the last available course of action.

last rites *npl* the sacraments prescribed for a person near death.

last straw *n* a final addition to one's burdens that results in collapse or defeat.

last word *n* the final remark in an argument; a definitive statement; the latest fashion.

László *n* Paul (1900–93) Hungarian architect who also decorated houses for movie stars, including Cary Grant.

lat *n* the currency of Latvia.

lat. *abbr* = latitude.

Lat. *abbr* = Latin.

LAT *abbr* = local apparent time.

LATA *abbr* = London Amenity and Transport Association.

LATCC *abbr* = London Air Traffic Control Centre.

latch *n* a fastening for a door, gate, or window, esp a bar, etc, that fits into a notch. * *vti* to fasten with a latch.

latchet *n* (*arch*) a strap or lace for fastening a shoe.

latchkey *n* the key of an outer door.

latchkey child *n* a child that returns home after school to an empty house because both parents are still at work.

lat. dol. *abbr* (*Latin*) (*pharm*) = *lateri dolenti*, "to the painful side."

late *adj, adv* after the usual or expected time; at an advanced stage or age; near the end; far on in the day or evening; just prior to the present; deceased; not long past; until lately; out of office.—**lateness** *n*.

latecomer *n* a person or thing that arrives late.

lateen *n* a triangular sail used on boats in the Mediterranean.—**lateenrigged** *adj*.

lately *adv* recently, in recent times.

La Tène *adj* of or pertaining to Celtic culture between the 5th and 1st centuries BC (up to the time of the Roman occupation, the second stage of the Iron Age). * *n* the site, at the eastern end of Lake Neuchâtel in Switzerland, from which the second stage of the Iron Age in Europe is named. *See also* **Hallstatt**

latent *adj* existing but not yet visible or developed.—**latency** *n*. —**latently** *adv*.

latent heat *n* (*physics*) the measurement of heat energy involved when a substance changes state.

later *adv* subsequently; afterwards.—*also compar of* **late**.

lateral *adj* of, at, from, towards the side.—**laterally** *adv*.

lateral erosion *n* this occurs when a river erodes its banks, and is most marked in a meander, where the faster flow of water undercuts the outside.

lateral line *n* (*zool*) the sensory system of fish and aquatic amphibians, which consists of sensory cells called neuromast organs in a line along the body.

lateral moraine *n* rock debris created by a glacier, that accumulates at the margin of a valley glacier, caused by transport and reworking of rocks from the valley sides.

lateral thinking *n* a solving of problems by employing unorthodox thought processes.

latest *adj* most recent or fashionable. * *n* (*inf*: *with* the) the most up-to-date fashion, news, etc.—*also superl of* **late**.

latex *n* (*pl* **latexes, latices**) the milky juice produced by certain plants, used in the manufacture of rubber.

lath *n* (*pl* **laths**) a thin narrow strip of wood used in constructing a framework for plaster, etc.

lathe *n* a machine that rotates wood, metal, etc, for shaping.

lather *n* a foam made by soap or detergent mixed with water; frothy sweat; a state of excitement or agitation. * *vti* to cover with or form lather.—**lathery** *adj*.

lathi *n* a long, heavy stick, carried by policemen in India.

Latians *n* an Iron Age people who lived in the area called Latium south of Rome. They were the ancestors of the Romans.

Latin *adj* of ancient Rome, its people, their language, etc; denoting or of the languages derived from Latin (Italian, Spanish, etc), the peoples who speak them, their countries, etc. * *n* a native or inhabitant of ancient Rome; the language of ancient Rome; a person, as a Spaniard or Italian, whose language is derived from Latin.

Latinate *adj* of, resembling or derived from Latin.

Latin cross *n* a cross, the lowest arm of which is longer than the others.

Latinist *n* a Latin scholar.

Latinity *n* Latin style.

Latinize *vt* to translate into Latin; to give Latin characteristics to.—**Latinization** *n*. —**Latinizer** *n*.

Latino *n* a person of Latin American origin living in the US.

Latins, Latini *npl* the ancient inhabitants of Latium in Italy.

Latinus *n* (*Roman myth*) king of Laurentum, after whom the area of Latium was named. He was defeated by Aeneas, who married his daughter Lavinia, and succeeded as king of Laurentum.

latish *adj* somewhat late.

latitude *n* the distance from north or south of the equator, measured in degrees; a region with reference to this distance; extent; scope; freedom from restrictions on actions or opinions.—**latitudinal** *adj*.—**latitudinally** *adv*.

latitudinarian *adj* claiming or showing freedom of thought, esp regarding religion. * *n* a person with such an outlook.—**latitudinarianism** *n*.

Latium *n* the ancient name of a district of central Italy on the Tyrrhenian Sea, extending between Etruria and Campania.

Latona *n* the Roman name for the Greek goddess Leto.

La Tour *n* **Georges** (1593–1652) French painter whose works are possessed of a more classical serenity than the late mannerist paintings of his contemporaries.

latria *n* (*RC Church*) supreme worship, offered to God alone.

latrine *n* a lavatory, as in a military camp.

Latrobe *n* **Benjamin H** (1764–1820) Moravian architect. His notable works include the Bank of Pennsylvania.

-latry *n suffix* worship, esp excessively.

lats *n* the standard monetary unit of Latvia, which is made up of 100 santims.

latter *adj* later; more recent; nearer the end; being the last mentioned of two.

latter-day *adj* present-day; modern.

latterly *adv* recently.

lattermost *adj* last.

lattice[1] *n* a network of crossed laths or bars.—**latticed** *adj*.

lattice[2] *n* (*physics*) the particular arrangement of atoms in a crystal structure.

lattice window *n* (*archit*) a window with diagonal glazing bars in which are set rectangular or diamond-shaped leaded lights.

latticework *n* a lattice, lattices collectively.

Latv. *abbr* = Latvia.

Latvia *n* a republic in northeastern Europe that shares borders with Estonia, Russia, Belarus, and Lithuania.

Latvian *n* a native or inhabitant of Latvia; an official language of Latvia (—*also* **Lettish**).— *also adj*.

laud *vt* to praise; to extol.

Lauda *n* **Niki [Nikolas Andreas Lauda]** (1949–) Austrian racing driver and world champion in 1975, 1977, and 1984, who suffered dreadful injuries in the 1976 German Grand Prix. He retired in 1985.

laudable *adj* praiseworthy.—**laudability** *n*. —**laudably** *adv*.

laudanum *n* (*formerly*) any of various opium preparations; a solution of opium in alcohol.

laudation *n* praise.

laudatory, laudative *adj* expressing praise.

Lauder *n* **Sir Harry [Hugh MacLennan]** (1870–1950) Scottish music-hall comedian and singer of international repute – one of the last great music-hall stars in Britain.

laugh *vi* to emit explosive inarticulate vocal sounds expressive of amusement, joy, or derision. * *vt* to utter or express with laughter; (*with* **off**) to dismiss as of little importance, make a joke of. * *n* the act or sound of laughing; (*inf*) an amusing person or thing.—**laugher** *n*. —**laughing** *adj, n*. —**laughingly** *adv*.

laughable *adj* causing laughter; ridiculous.—**laughably** *adv*.

laughing gas *n* nitrous oxide.

laughing stock *n* an object of ridicule.

laughter *n* the act or sound of laughing.

Laughton *n* **Charles** (1899–1962) English-born American stage and film actor, renowned for his larger-than-life performances in films such as *The Private Life of Henry VIII* (1932), *Mutiny on the Bounty* (1935) and *The Hunchback of Notre Dame* (1939).

LAUK *abbr* = Library Association of the United Kingdom.

launch[1] *vt* to throw, hurl or propel forward; to cause (a vessel) to slide into the water; (*rocket, missile*) to set off; to put into action; to put a new product onto the market; (*comput*) to start an application or program. * *vi* to involve oneself enthusiastically. * *n* the act or occasion of launching.

launch[2] *n* an open or partly enclosed motor boat.

launch pad, launching pad *n* a platform from which a spacecraft is launched.

launder *vti* to wash and iron clothes. * *vt* to legitimize (money) obtained from criminal activity by passing it through foreign banks, or investing in legitimate businesses, etc.—**launderer** *n*.

launderette *n* an establishment equipped with coin-operated washing machines and driers for public use.

laundress *n* a woman who earns her living by doing laundry.

Laundromat *n* (*trademark*) a launderette.

laundry *n* (*pl* **laundries**) a place where clothes are washed and ironed; clothes sent to be washed and ironed.

laureate *adj* crowned with laurel leaves as a mark of honor. * *n* the recipient of an honor or distinction; a poet laureate.—**laureateship** *n*.

laurel *n* an evergreen shrub with large, glossy leaves; the leaves used by the ancient Greeks as a symbol of achievement.

Laurel *n* **Stan [Arthur Stanley Jefferson]** (1890–1965) American comedian who formed a partnership (Laurel and Hardy) with fellow-American comedian Oliver Hardy in 1929. Their films include *Another Fine Mess* (1930).

Lauren *n* **Ralph [Ralph Lipschitz]** (1939–) American fashion designer .

Lauricocha *n* (*archeo*) a group of three caves situated in the Andes of Peru in which a series of levels indicate a long period of occupancy.

Lausanne *n* a city in Switzerland.

LAUTRO *abbr* = Life Assurance and Unit Trust Regulatory Organization.

LAV *abbr* = light-armored vehicle.

lava *n* (*geol*) molten rock flowing from a volcano; the solid substance formed as this cools.

lavabo *n* (*pl* **lavaboes, lavabos**) (*RC Church*) the ritual washing of the celebrant's hands at the Eucharist; a washbasin.

lavage *n* the washing out of a hollow organ with water for medical or therapeutic reasons.

Laval *n* **Pierre** (1883–1945) French statesman and prime minister (1931–32, 1935–36, 1942–44). He sided openly with the Germans and was executed for treason in 1945 by the Free French.

lavation *n* the act of washing.

lavatory *n* (*pl* **lavatories**) a sanitary device for the disposal or feces and urine; a room equipped with this.—*also* **bathroom; toilet**.

lavender *n* the fragrant flowers of a perennial shrub dried and used in sachets; a pale purple color.

laver *n* an edible seaweed.

Laverne *n* **1. Erwine** (1909–1995) and **2. Estelle** (1915–) American designers who established Laverne Originals.

Lavery *n* **Sir John** (1856–1941) Irish-born Scottish painter and member of the Glasgow Boys. His well-draughted compositions are light and relaxed in atmosphere, e.g. *The Tennis Party* (1885).

Laves *n* **Georg L F** (1788–) German architect. His notable works include the Wagenheim Palace.

Lavinia *n* (*Roman myth*) the daughter of Latinus, wife of Aeneas.

Lavinium *n* an ancient city south of Rome, according to tradition built by Aeneas and named after his wife, Lavinia.

lavish *vt* to give or spend freely. * *adj* abundant, profuse; generous; extravagant.—**lavishly** *adv*.—**lavishness** *n*.

Lavoisier *n* **Antoine Laurent** (1743–94) French chemist, regarded as the founder of modern chemistry, who discovered oxygen and established its role in combustion and respiration.

law *n* all the rules of conduct in an organized community as upheld by authority; any one of such rules; obedience to such rules; the study of such rules, jurisprudence; the seeking of justice in courts under such rules; the profession of lawyers, judges, etc; (*inf*) the police; a sequence of events occurring with unvarying uniformity under the same conditions; any rule expected to be observed.

L

Law *n* 1. **Andrew Bonar** (1858–1923) Canadian-born Scottish Conservative statesman. He became a Conservative MP in 1900, party leader in 1911, leader of the House (1916–21) and prime minister shortly afterwards (1922–23). 2. **David** (1937–) American designer who co-founded the Design Planning Group and was a prolific designer of graphics, packaging, furniture, products, and interiors during the 1970s and 1980s.

LAW *abbr* = Land Authority for Wales; Legal Action for Women; Loyalist Association of Workers.

law-abiding *adj* obeying the law.

law-and-order *adj* advocating strong measures to keep order and reduce crime and violence.

lawbreaker *n* a person who violates the law.—**lawbreaking** *adj, n.*

Lawes *n* **Henry** (1596–1662) English composer who composed the coronation anthem *Zadok the Priest* for Charles II.

lawful *adj* in conformity with the law; recognized by law.—**lawfully** *adv.*—**lawfulness** *n.*

lawgiver *n* a maker of a code of laws.

lawless *adj* not regulated by law; not in conformity with law, illegal.—**lawlessly** *adv.*—**lawlessness** *n.*

lawmaker *n* a maker of laws, a legislator.

lawn[1] *n* a fine sheer cloth of linen or cotton.—**lawny** *adj.*

lawn[2] *n* land covered with closely cut grass, esp around a house.

lawn bowling *n* a bowling game played on a green with balls that are rolled at a jack.

lawn darts *n* an outdoor game of darts using a lawn as a board, at which are fired foot-long metal darts.

lawn mower *n* a hand-propelled or power-driven machine to cut lawn grass.

lawn tennis *n* tennis played on a grass court.

law of averages *n* the belief that an event will occur with a frequency approximating its probability.

law of the sea *see* sea, law of the.

Lawrence *n* **Saint** (*d.* 258) Christian martyr. Patron saint of cooks. An archdeacon of Rome, he was roasted on a gridiron and is said to have said, "Turn me, I am done on this side!" His feast day is August 10.

Lawrence *n* 1. **D[avid] H[erbert]** (1885–1930) English novelist, poet, and short-story writer whose novels include the controversial *Lady Chatterley's Lover* (1928). 2. **Ernest Orlando** (1901–58) American physicist, awarded the 1939 Nobel prize for physics for his important contributions to modern physics, including the invention of the cyclotron in 1929. 3. **Gertrude [Gertrud Alexandra Dagmar Lawrence-Klasen]** (1898–1952) English actress. 4. **Jacob** (1917–) American painter whose works include the series *The Migration of the Negro* (1941). 5. **T[homas] E[dward]** (1888–1935) Welsh-born Anglo-Irish soldier and author who was known as "Lawrence of Arabia." 6. **Sir Thomas** (1769–1830) mainly self-taught English painter. His work rises out of 18th-century traditions but with a fluidity and sparkle that anticipates the romanticism of the 19th century.

lawrencium *n* a radioactive metallic element.

lawsuit *n* a suit between private parties in a law court.

lawyer *n* a person whose profession is advising others in matters of law or representing them in a court of law.

lax *adj* slack, loose; not tight; not strict or exact.—**laxly** *adv.*—**laxness** *n.*

laxative *n* a substance that promotes emptying of the bowels.—*also adj. See also* **purgative**.

laxity *n* the state or quality of being lax, laxness.

lay[1] *see* lie[2].

lay[2] *vt* (**laying, laid**) to put down; to allay or suppress; to place in a resting position; to place or set; to place in a correct position; to produce (an egg); (*sl*) to have sexual intercourse with; to devise; to present or assert; to stake a bet; (*with* **down**) to put down; to surrender, relinquish; to begin to build; to establish (guidelines, rules, etc); to record tracks in a music studio; (*with* **in**) to store, to stockpile; (*with* **off**) to suspend from work temporarily or permanently; (*with* **on**) to supply, provide; to install (electricity, etc); (*with* **out**) to plan in detail; to arrange for display; to prepare (a corpse) for viewing; (*inf*) to spend money, esp lavishly; (*with* **up**) to store for future use; to disable or confine through illness. * *vi* (*inf*) to leave (a person or thing) alone; (*with* **into**) to attack physically or verbally. * *n* a way or position in which something is situated; (*sl*) an act of sexual intercourse; a sexual partner.

lay[3] *n* a simple narrative poem, esp as intended to be sung; a ballad.

lay[4] *adj* of or pertaining to those who are not members of the clergy; not belonging to a profession.

layabout *n* a loafer, lazy person.

lay-by *n* a deposit payment system that reserves an article for a purchaser until full settlement; (*Brit*) a pull-in place for motorists to stop at the side of a main road.—**lay by** *vt* to set aside or save for future needs.

lay clerk *n* (*mus*) an adult male member of an Anglican cathedral choir.

layer *n* a single thickness, fold, etc; the runner of a plant fastened down to take root; a hen that lays; (*comput*) an on-screen sheet on which text or graphic images are placed. * *vti* to separate into layers; to form by superimposing layers; to (cause to) take root by propagating a plant shoot still attached to its parent.

layette *n* a complete set of clothes, equipment and accessories for a newborn baby.

lay figure *n* a jointed model of the human body used by artists for hanging drapery on; a person regarded as a puppet or nonentity.

laying *n* a sitting of eggs; the first coat of plaster.

layman *n* (*pl* **laymen**) a person who is not a member of the clergy; a non-specialist, someone who does not possess professional knowledge.—**laywoman** *nf* (*pl* **laywomen**).

layoff *n* a period of involuntary unemployment.

layout[1] *n* the manner in which anything is laid out, esp arrangement of text and pictures on the pages of a newspaper or magazine, etc; the thing laid out; (*comput*) the process of arranging text or graphics on a page in programs such as word processing or database management systems.

layover *n* a stop on a journey.

lazar *n* (*arch*) a leper.

lazaretto, lazaret, lazarette *n* (*pl* **lazarettos, lazarets, lazarettes**) (*naut*) a part of a ship's hold; (*formerly*) a hospital for people suffering from infectious diseases.

Lazarus *n* (*Bible*) 1. the beggar in Jesus' parable about a rich man and a poor man. 2. the brother of Mary and Martha; Jesus raised Lazarus from the dead after his body had been in the tomb for four days.

laze *vti* to idle or loaf.

lazulite *n* an azure blue mineral.

lazy *adj* (**lazier, laziest**) disinclined to work or exertion; encouraging or causing indolence; sluggishly moving.—**lazily** *adv.*—**laziness** *n.*

lazybones *n* a lazy person.

lb *abbr* = (*football*) left back; (*cricket*) leg bye; (*Latin*) *libra*, "pound" (an Imperial measure of weight approximating to 454g).

l.b. *abbr* (*Latin*) = *lectori benevolo*, "to the kind reader."

LB *abbr* = (*Latin*) *Lit(t)erarum Baccalaureus*, "Bachelor of Letters"; Local Board; (*wine*) late bottled.

lb. ap. *abbr* = apothecaries' pound.

LBdr *abbr* = Lance Bombardier.

lbf *abbr* = pound force.

LBF *abbr* = liver blood flow.

lb-ft *abbr* = pound foot.

LBH *abbr* = length, breadth, height.

LBL *abbr* = lymphoblastic lymphoma.

LBO *abbr* = leveraged buy-out.

lbs. *abbr* = pounds.

l.b.s. *abbr* (*Latin*) = *lectori benevolo salutem*, "to the kind reader, greeting."

lbw *abbr* (*cricket*) = leg before wicket.

lc, l.c. *abbr* = (*Latin*) *loco citato*, "in the place cited"; (*print*) lower case; left center.

LC *abbr* = Lance Corporal; Library of Congress; Lord Chamberlain/Chancellor; Lower Canada; Lutheran Council of Great Britain; landing craft.

l/c., L/C *abbr* = letter of credit.

LCB *abbr* = Lord Chief Baron.

LCCC *abbr* = Library of Congress Catalogue Card.

lcd *abbr* = lowest common denominator.

LCD *abbr* = liquid-crystal display.

LChir (*Latin*) *Licentiatus Chirurgiae*, "Licentiate in Surgery."

LCJ *abbr* = Lord Chief Justice.

LCL *abbr* = Licentiate of Civil Law; London College of Music.

l.c.m., LCM *abbr* = lowest or least common multiple.

l. corp. *abbr* = lance corporal.

LCP *abbr* = Licentiate of the College of Preceptors; last complete program.

LCpl *abbr* = lance corporal.

LCPS *abbr* = Licentiate of the College of Physicians and Surgeons.

l. cr. *abbr* (*French*) = *lettre de crédit*, "letter of credit."

LCS *abbr* = London Co-operative Society.

ld. *abbr* = limited.

l.d. *abbr* = (*Latin*) *litera dominicalis*, "dominical letter"; low door; (*Latin*) *lepide dictum*, "elegantly said."

LD *abbr* = (*Latin*) *Laud Deso*, "Praise be to God"; Lady Day; Low Dutch; lethal dosage; low density.

L/D *abbr* = letter of deposit.

ldc *abbr* = long-distance call.

LDC *abbr* = less developed country.

ldg. and dely. *abbr* = landing and delivery.

ld. gt. *abbr* = land grant.

LDiv *abbr* = Licentiate in Divinity.

LDL *abbr* = low-density lipoprotein.

LDN *abbr* = less developed nation.

LDP *abbr* = long-distance path.

LDPAS *abbr* = Long Distance Paths Advisory Service.

LDS *abbr* = (*Latin*) *Laus Deo semper*, "Praise be to God always"; Latter-Day Saints; Licentiate in Dental Surgery.

LDSc *abbr* = Licentiate in Dental Science.

lea[1] *n* (*poet*) a meadow, grassland.

lea[2] *n* a measure of yarn, varying from 80 yards (approx 73 meters) for wool to 300 yards (approx 274 meters) for linen.

lea. *abbr* = league; leather.

LEA *abbr* = Local Education Authority.

Leabhar Gabhala Eireann *n* a mythical history of Ireland also known as the *Book of Invasions*.

leach *vt* to wash (soil, ore, etc) with a filtering liquid; to extract (a soluble substance) from some material. * *vi* to lose soluble matter through a filtering liquid.—**leacher** *n*.

Leach *n* **Bernard Howell** (1887–1979) English potter (born in Hong Kong), who revolutionized the production of pottery by creating reasonably priced, attractively designed studio pottery for use in everyday life.

leaching *n* the percolation of water down through the soil, dissolving out humus and soluble salts and depositing them in the underlying layers of soil.

lead[1] *vb* (**leading, led**) *vt* to show the way, esp by going first; to direct or guide on a course; to direct by influence; to be head of (an expedition, orchestra, etc); to be ahead of in a contest; to live, spend (one's life); (*with* **on**) to lure or entice, esp into mischief. * *vi* to show the way, as by going first; (*with* **to**) to tend in a certain direction; to be or go first. * *n* the role of a leader; first place; the amount or distance ahead; anything that leads, as a clue; the leading role in a play, etc; the right of playing first in cards or the card played.

lead[2] *n* a heavy, soft, bluish-gray, metallic element; a weight for sounding depths at sea, etc; bullets; a stick of graphite, used in pencils; (*print*) a thin strip of metal used to space lines of type. * *adj* of or containing lead. * *vt* (**leading, leaded**) to cover, weight, or space out with lead.

LEAD *abbr* = Linking Education and Disability.

Leadbelly *see* **Ledbetter, Huddy.**

leaded light *n* (*archit*) a diamond-shaped or rectangular pane of glass in a lattice window.

leaden *adj* made of lead; very heavy; dull gray; gloomy.—**leadenly** *adv*.

leader *n* the person who goes first; the principle first violin-player in an orchestra; the conductor of an orchestra; the director of an orchestra; the inspiration or head of a movement, such as a political party; a person whose example is followed; the leading editorial in a newspaper; the leading article.

leadership *n* the act of leading; the ability to be a leader; the leaders of an organization or movement collectively.

lead glass *n* flint glass.

lead-in *n* introductory material; the connection between a radio transmitter or receiver with an aerial or transmission cable.

leading[1] *adj* capable of guiding or influencing; principal; in first position.

leading[2] *n* a covering of lead; (*print*) the body of a type, larger than the size, giving space.

leading and lagging *n* methods used at the end of a company's financial year to improve the cash position. Leading is the arrangement of the acceleration of the settlement of outstanding financial obligations and lagging is the delaying of these.

leading article *n* an article in a newspaper stating editorial opinion on a given subject; the leader.

leading light *n* the most important member of a group or organization.

leading motif *see* **leitmotiv**.

leading note *n* (*mus*) the seventh note of the scale; it is so called because it "leads to" the tonic, a semitone above.

leading question *n* a question worded so as to suggest the desired answer.

leadsman *n* (*pl* **leadsmen**) a sailor who heaves the lead.

lead time *n* the period between the design of a product and its manufacture.

leaf *n* (*pl* **leaves**) any of the flat, thin (usu green) parts growing from the stem of a plant; a sheet of paper; a very thin sheet of metal; a hinged or removable part of a table top. * *vi* to bear leaves; (*with* **through**) to turn the pages of.

leafage *n* foliage.

leaf-and-dart *n* (*archit*) a type of ovolo molding consisting of alternating leaf and dart shapes.

leafless *adj* without leaves.

leaflet *n* a small or young leaf; a sheet of printed information (often folded), esp advertising matter distributed free. * *vi* to distribute leaflets (to).

leaf mold *n* compost or soil composed of decaying leaves and other vegetable matter; any of various fungal diseases of plants.

leafy *adj* (**leafier, leafiest**) having many or broad leaves; resembling leaves.—**leafiness** *n*.

league[1] *n* an association of nations, groups, etc for promoting common interests; an association of sports clubs that organizes matches between members; any class or category. * *vti* (**leaguing, leagued**) to form into a league.

league[2] *n* (*formerly*) a varying measure of distance, averaging about three miles (5km).

Leah *n* (*Bible*) the elder daughter of Laban, the wealthy shepherd of Mesopotamia; through her father's trickery, Leah became Jacob's first wife.

leak *n* a crack or hole through which liquid or gas may accidentally pass; the liquid or gas passing through such an opening; confidential information made public deliberately or accidentally. * *vi* to (let) escape though an opening; to disclose information surreptitiously.—**leaker** *n*.

leakage *n* the act of leaking; that which enters or escapes by leaking.

Leakey *n* 1. **Louis Seymour Bazett** (1903–72) Kenyan-born British archaeologist and anthropologist who together with his wife made several important discoveries about humanity's origins in East Africa. 2. **Mary Douglas** (1913–96) English archaeologist, married (1936) to Louis Leakey. 3. **Richard Erskine Frere** (1944–) son of Mary and Louis and also a prominent (Kenyan) archaeologist.

leaky *adj* (**leakier, leakiest**) leaking or likely to leak.—**leakiness** *n*.

leal *adj* (*Scot*) loyal.

lean[1] *adj* thin, with little flesh or fat; spare; meager. * *n* meat with little or no fat.—**leanness** *n*.

lean[2] *vb* (**leaning, leaned** *or* **leant**) *vi* to bend or slant from an upright position; to rest supported (on or against); to rely or depend for help (on). * *vt* to cause to lean.

Lean *n* **Sir David** (1908–91) English film director whose highly acclaimed films include *Brief Encounter* (1946), *Great Expectations* (1946), and the epics *Bridge on the River Kwai* (1957), *Lawrence of Arabia* (1962) and *Dr Zhivago* (1970).

Leander *see* **Hero**.

leaning *n* inclination, tendency.

leant *see* **lean**[1].

lean-to *n* (*pl* **lean-tos**) a building whose rafters rest on another building.

leap *vb* (**leaping, leaped** *or* **leapt**) *vi* to jump; (*with* **at**) to accept something offered eagerly. * *vt* to pass over by a jump; to cause to leap. * *n* an act of leaping; bound; space passed by leaping; an abrupt transition.—**leaper** *n*.

LEAP *abbr* = Life Education for the Autistic Person.

leap year *n* a year with an extra day (February 29) occurring every fourth year.

leapfrog *n* a game in which one player vaults over another's bent back. * *vi* (**leapfrogging, leapfrogged**) to vault in this manner; to advance in alternate jumps.

Lear *n* **Edward** (1912–88) English poet and painter who is particularly noted for his ingenious and amusing nonsense verse, esp in limerick form, e.g. "The Owl and the Pussycat."

learn *vti* (**learning, learned** *or* **learnt**) to gain knowledge of or skill in; to memorize; to become aware of, realize.—**learner** *n*.

learned *adj* having learning; erudite; acquired by study, experience, etc.—**learnedly** *adv*.

learning *n* a gaining of knowledge; the acquiring of knowledge or skill through study.

learning curve *n* the process by which the labor force and management of a company gain experience in a new technology or new production process from cumulative contact and so become more efficient and cost-effective.

learning disability *n* any of various conditions that are thought to involve the nervous system and that interfere with the ability to master reading and writing.

lease *n* a contract by which an owner lets land, property, etc to another person for a specified period. * *vt* to grant by or hold under lease.—**leaseable** *adj*.—**leaser** *n*. *See also* **lessee** and **lessor**.

lease-back *n* the process of selling an asset, esp a building, and then renting it.

leasehold *n* the act of holding by lease; the land, buildings, etc held by lease.—**leaseholder** *n*.

leash *n* a cord, strap, etc by which a dog or animal is held in check. * *vt* to hold or restrain on a leash.

L

leasing *n* the hiring of an asset, such as a vehicle or piece of equipment, by one firm from another rather than purchasing it.

least *adj* smallest in size, degree, etc; slightest. * *adv* to the smallest degree. * *n* the smallest in amount.

least common denominator *see* **lowest common denominator**.

least common multiple *see* **lowest common multiple**.

leastways *adv* at least.

leat *n* an artificial channel to carry water to a reservoir or for some industrial purpose.

leather *n* material made from the skin of an animal prepared by removing the hair and tanning; something made of leather. * *vt* to cover with leather; to thrash.

leatherback *n* the largest existing sea turtle, having a flexible shell.

Leatherette *n* (*trademark*) an imitation leather.

leatherjacket *n* a tropical fish with a leathery skin; the larva of the cranefly.

leathern *adj* (*arch*) made of or resembling leather.

leatherneck *n* (*sl*) a member of the US Marine Corps.

leathery *adj* like leather; tough and flexible.

leave[1] *n* permission to do something; official authorization to be absent; the period covered by this.

leave[2] *vb* (**leaving, left**) *vt* to depart from; to cause or allow to remain in a specified state; to cause to remain behind; to refrain from consuming or dealing with; to have remaining at death, to bequeath; to have as a remainder; to allow to stay or to continue doing without interference; to entrust or commit to another; to abandon. * *vi* to depart; (*with off*) to stop, desist.—**leaver** *n*.

leave[3] *vi* (**leaving, leaved**) to put forth foliage, to leaf.

leaven *n* a substance to make dough rise, esp yeast; something that changes or enlivens. * *vt* to raise with leaven; to modify, to enliven.—**leavening** *n*.

leaves *see* **leaf**.

leave-taking *n* a departure, farewell.

leavings *npl* leftovers; remnants; refuse.

Leavis *n* F[rank] R[aymond] (1895–1978) English literary critic, who, with his wife, Q[ueenie] D[orothy] Leavis, made a major impact on literary criticism from the early 1930s on, through such works as *New Bearings in English Poetry* and *The Great Tradition*.

Lebanon[1] *n* a small republic in the eastern Mediterranean.

Lebanon[2] *n* (*Bible*) a chain of mountains 100 miles long and rising to 10,000 feet, parallel to the coast of Palestine and forming the northern boundary of the promised land; the forests of Lebanon were famous for their mighty cedars.

Lebanese Pound *n* currency of the Lebanon.

Lebbaeus *n* (*Bible*) ancient version of Thaddeus.

leben *n* a food made from soured milk, eaten in North Africa and the Levant.

Lebensraum *n* a piece of territory claimed by another country on the basis that it is needed to accommodate the country's expanding population.

Le Blond *n* **Jean-Baptiste Alexandre** (1679–1719) French architect who worked in Russia on the Peterhof Palace in St Petersburg, and introduced the French rococo style.

Lebrun *n* **Charles** (1619–90) French painter. He was a fine draughtsman and portraitist, and was court painter to Louis XIV from 1661. He was responsible for much of the decor at Versailles.

LEC *abbr* (*Brit*) = Launceston Environment Centre.

Le Carré *n* **John [David John Moore Cornwell]** (1931–) English novelist whose novels are sombre, anti-romantic narratives of Cold War espionage, e.g. *The Spy Who Came in from the Cold* (1963).

lech *vt* (*sl*) to lust after.

lecher *n* a lecherous man.

lecherous *adj* characterized by or encouraging lechery.

lechery *n* (*pl* **lecheries**) unrestrained sexuality; debauchery.

lecithin *n* any of a group of fatty compounds found in plant and animal tissues, used as an emulsifier and antioxidant.

Leclair *n* **Jean-Marie** (1697–1764) French composer and violinist, who wrote the opera *Scylla et Glaucus*, ballets and many pieces for violin.

Le Corbusier *n* **[Charles Edouard Jeanneret]** (1887–1965) Swiss-born French architect and town planner. An influential architect of the 20th century, his work features reinforced concrete and modular units of construction. His notable works include the Unité de'Habitation, Marseilles, Swiss House, Paris, and the Museum of Modern Art, Tokyo.

lect. *abbr* = lecture.

lectern *n* a reading stand in a church; any similar reading support.

lection *n* a reading from scripture for a particular day; a variant reading of a text.

lectionary *n* (*pl* **lectionaries**) a book listing lessons from scripture to be read at religious services on particular days.

lector *n* a lecturer or reader at a university.

lecture *n* an informative talk to a class, etc; a lengthy reprimand. * *vti* to give a lecture (to); to reprimand.—**lecturer** *n*.

lectureship *n* the position of lecturer.

led *see* **lead**[1].

led. *abbr* = ledger.

LED *abbr* (*comput*) = light emitting diode. A small light used by various computer devices to communicate information about the status of the device.

Leda[1] *n* (*Greek myth*) the wife of the Spartan king Tyndareus, mother of Castor and Pollux by Zeus, who came to her in the form of a swan.

Leda[2] *n* the smallest satellite of Jupiter.

Ledbetter *n* **Huddy [Leadbelly]** (1885–1949) African-American blues singer, composer, twelve-string guitarist and piano player whose most famous songs include *Goodnight Irene* and *Fannin Street*. He led a violent life and reputedly earned his nickname from the number of lead bullets that remained in his body.

Lederberg *n* **Joshua** (1925–) American geneticist who shared the 1958 Nobel prize for physiology or medicine with George Beadle and Edward Tatum for his bacterial research.

lederhosen *npl* leather shorts with braces worn by men in Austria and Bavaria.

ledge *n* a narrow horizontal surface resembling a shelf projecting from a wall, rock face, etc; an underwater ridge of rocks; a rock layer containing ore.—**ledgy,** *adj*.

ledger *n* a book in which a record of debits, credits, etc is kept.

ledger line *n* a short line added above or below a musical staff to extend its range.— *also* **leger line**.

Le Douanier *see* **Rousseau, Henri Julien**.

Ledoux *n* **Claude Nicolas** (1736–1806), French architect. His notable works include the Château de Bénouville, Paris.

Ledru *n* 1. **Auguste** (1860–1902) French glassmaker who was one of the first designers to use the female form in Art Nouveau design. 2. **Léon** (1855–1926) French glassmaker who was innovative in technique, color and design.

Le Duc, Tho *see* **Kissinger, Henry**.

lee *n* a shelter; the side or part away from the wind.

LEEA *abbr* = Lifting Equipment Engineers' Association.

leech *n* a blood-sucking worm; a person who clings to or exploits another.

Leeds *n* major English city in United Kingdom of Great Britain and Northern Ireland (UK).

leek *n* a vegetable that resembles a greatly elongated green onion.

Lee Kuan Yew *n* (1923–) Singapore's first prime minister (1959–), he established a strict regime noted for its economic achievements and Cromwellian authoritarianism.

leer *n* a sly, oblique or lascivious look. * *vi* to look with a leer.—**leeringly** *adv*.

leery *adj* (**leerier, leeriest**) (*with of*) suspicious, wary.

lees *npl* sediment in the bottom of a wine bottle, etc.

lee shore *n* the shore towards which the wind is blowing.

leeward *adj, n* (*naut*) (in) the quarter towards which the wind blows.

leeway *n* the distance a ship or aircraft has strayed sideways of its course; freedom of action as regards expenditure of time, money, etc.

left[1] *see* **leave**[2].

left[2] *adj* of or on the side that is towards the west when one faces north; worn on the left hand, foot, etc. * *n* the left side; (*often cap*) of or relating to the left in politics; the left hand; (*boxing*) a blow with the left hand.

left-hand *adj* of or towards the left side of a person or thing; for use by the left hand.

left-handed *adj* using the left hand in preference to the right; done or made for use with the left hand; ambiguous, backhanded. * *adv* with the left hand.—**left-handedly** *adv*.—**left-handedness** *n*.

left-hander *n* a left-handed person; a blow delivered with the left fist.

leftist *adj* tending to the left in politics. * *n* a person tending towards the political left.—**leftism** *n*.

left-luggage office *n* a checkroom.

leftovers *npl* unused portions of something, esp uneaten food.

leftward *adj, adv* on or toward the left.—**leftwards** *adv*.

left-wing *adj* of or relating to the liberal faction of a political party, organization, etc.—**left-winger** *n*.

lefty *n* (*pl* **lefties**) (*inf*) a left-winger; (*sl*) a left-handed person.

leg *n* one of the limbs on which humans and animals support themselves and walk; the part of a garment covering the leg; anything shaped or used like a leg; a branch or limb of a forked object; a section, as of a trip; any of a series of games or matches in a competition.

leg. *abbr* = legal; legate; (*mus*) (*Italian*) legato, "smooth" or "joined"; legend; legislation; legislative; legislature; (*Latin*) *legit*, "he reads"; (*Latin*) *legunt*, "they read."

legacy *n* (*pl* **legacies**) money, property, etc left to someone in a will; something passed on by an ancestor or remaining from the past.

legal *adj* of or based on law; permitted by law; of or for lawyers.—**legally** *adv*.

legalese *n* legal language as used in documents.

legal holiday *n* a holiday established by legal authority.

legalism *n* observance of the letter rather than the spirit of the law, red tape.—**legalist** *n*. —**legalistic** *adj*.—**legalistically** *adv*.

legality *n* (*pl* **legalities**) conformity with the law.

legalize *vt* to make lawful.—**legalization** *n*.

legal reserve *n* the minimum amount of money that insurance companies, etc, must hold by law as security in the interests of their customers.

legal tender *n* a currency which a creditor is legally bound to accept in payment of a debt.

legate *n* an envoy, esp from the Pope; an official emissary.—**legatine** *adj*.

legatee *n* a person to whom a legacy is bequeathed.

legation *n* a diplomatic minister and staff; the headquarters of a diplomatic minister.—**legationary** *adj*.

legato *adj, adv* (*mus*) smoothly and evenly.

leg before wicket *n* (*cricket*) the dismissal of a batsman for illegally preventing the ball from hitting the wicket by obstructing it with his or her leg.

leg bye *n* (*cricket*) a run made when the ball touches any part of the batsman except the hand.

legend *n* a story handed down from the past; a notable person or the stories of his or her exploits; an inscription on a coin, etc; a caption; an explanation of the symbols used on a map; (*comput*) the key on a graph that shows the meaning of the different colors or shades.—**legendary** *n*.

legendary *adj* of, based on, or presented in legends; famous, notorious.

Léger *n* **Fernand** (1881–1955) French painter. His early paintings and most of his figurative works involve simplifications of form and structure resulting in static, rather tubular figure forms, as in *Nude in the Forest* (1909–10).

legerdemain *n* trickery, sleight of hand.

leger line *see* **ledger line**.

legg. *abbr* (*mus*) (*Italian*) = leggiero.

legged *adj* having legs.

leggiero *adj, adv* (*mus*) (*Italian*) light.

leggings *npl* protective outer coverings for the lower legs; a leg-hugging garment for women.

leggy *adj* (**leggier, leggiest**) having long and shapely legs.—**legginess** *n*.

leghorn *n* fine plaited straw; a hat made of this; (*with cap*) a breed of domestic fowl.

legible *adj* able to be read.—**legibility** *n*. —**legibly** *adv*.

legion *n* an infantry unit of the ancient Roman army; a large body of soldiers; a large number, a multitude.

legionary *adj* of a legion. * *n* (*pl* **legionaries**) a member of a legion; a soldier in a legion of the ancient Roman army.

legionnaire *n* a member of certain military forces or associations.

Legionnaire's disease *n* a serious and sometimes fatal bacterial infection which causes symptoms like pneumonia (first identified after an outbreak at an American Legion convention in 1976).

Legis. *abbr* = Legislature.

legislate *vi* to make or pass laws * *vt* to bring about by legislation.

legislation *n* the act or process of law-making; the laws themselves.

legislative *adj* of legislation or a legislature; having the power to make laws.

Legislative Assembly *n* the bicameral assembly in various US states; the unicameral legislature in most Canadian provinces; the lower chamber in a bicameral legislature, as in Australia.

Legislative Council *n* the upper chamber of certain bicameral legislatures, as in most Australian states; the unicameral legislature of certain colonies and dependencies; a committee of both houses of a US state legislature that discusses problems and proposes legislative solutions.

legislator *n* a member of a legislative body.

legislature *n* the body of people who have the power of making laws.

legist *n* someone versed in the law.

legit *adj* (*sl*) legitimate.

legitimate *adj* lawful; reasonable, justifiable; conforming to accepted rules, standards, etc; (*child*) born of parents married to each other.—**legitimacy** *n*. —**legitimately** *adv*.

legitimatize *vt* to legitimize.

legitimist *n* a supporter of a hereditary title to a monarchy.—**legitimism** *n*.

legitimize *vt* to make or declare legitimate.—**legitimization** *n*.

legman *n* a reporter who gathers information; a subordinate who delivers messages and runs errands.

legno *n* (*mus*) (*Italian*) wood: *col legno* is a direction to a violinist to turn the bow over and to tap the strings "with the wood."

legroom *n* space for stretching out the legs when seated.

Le Guin *n* **Ursula K[roeber]** (1929–) American novelist and short-story writer who is regarded as one of the leading 20th-century science fiction and fantasy authors. Her *Earthsea* trilogy for children has become a modern classic.

legume *n* any of a large family of plants having seeds growing in pods, including beans, peas, etc; the pod or seed of such a plant used as food.

leguminous *adj* (*bot*) belonging to a family of flowering and pod-bearing plants.

legwork *n* (*inf*) work that involves a lot of walking.

Lehár *n* **Franz** (1870–1948) Hungarian composer and conductor, noted for his operettas, e.g. *The Merry Widow* (1905).

Lehmann *n* **Rosamond [Nina]** (1901–90) English novelist whose *The Ballad and the Source*, a study of adult sexuality, is generally regarded as her masterpiece.

Lehmbruck *n* **Wilhelm** (1881–1919) German sculptor and illustrator who played an influential role in the revival of sculpture in Germany at the beginning of the 20th century.

lei *n* a garland of flowers worn around the neck, given as a token of affection in Hawaii.

Leibnitz, Leibniz *n* **Gottfried Wilhelm** (1646–1716) German philosopher and mathematician, he developed a calculus system at the same time as Newton, and made important contributions to many different scientific fields.

Leigh *n* 1. **Vivien [Vivien Mary Hartley]** (1913–67) Indian-born English stage and film actress who starred in *Gone With the Wind* (1939) with Clark Gable. 2. **Walter** (1905–42) English composer best known for his operettas, e.g. *The Jolly Roger*.

Leighton *n* **John** (1822–1912) British designer of the title page of *The Art-Journal Catalogue of the Great Exhibition*, 1851 and a founder member of the Photographers' Society of Great Britain.

Leinster *n* (*Irish Celtic myth*) one of the five provinces into which the **Fir Bholg** divided Ireland. *See* **Laighin**.

Leipzig *n* a city in Germany.

Leischner *n* **Margaret** (1908–70) German-born textile designer who designed Tintawn sisal carpeting in 1959.

leise *adj* (*mus*) (*German*) "soft" or "gentle."

leishmaniasis *n* a common tropical and subtropical disease (in Africa, Asia, South America, and the Mediterranean) caused by the parasitic protozoa *Leishmania*, which are transmitted by the bites of sandflies.

leister *n* a pronged spear used for catching salmon.

leisure *n* ease, relaxation, esp freedom from employment or duties. * *adj* free and unoccupied.—**leisured** *adj*.

leisurely *adj* relaxed, without hurry.

leitmotif, leitmotiv *n* a dominant theme.

lek *n* the standard monetary unit of Albania, being made up of 100 qindar.

Leleu *n* **Jules-Emile** (1883–1961) French sculptor who also designed decor and furniture for over 20 passenger liners.

Lely *n* **Sir Peter** (1618–80) Dutch-born English portrait painter. He set a trend for society portrait styles that continued for nearly a century.

Lem *n* **Stanislaw** (1921–) Polish novelist, critic, and scientist whose critically acclaimed science fiction novels include *Cyberiad* and *Solaris*.

LEM *abbr* = lunar excursion module.

lemma *n* (*pl* **lemmas, lemmata**) (*logic*) a premise believed to be true.

Lemmen *n* **Georges** (1865–1916) Belgian painter who revived interest in the decorative arts.

lemming *n* a small arctic rodent; one of a group willfully heading on a course for destruction.

Lemmon *n* **Jack [John Uhler]** (1925–) American actor whose films include *The China Syndrome* (1979).

Lemnos *n* the most northerly island of the Greek Archipelago, between the Hellespont and Mount Athos. It was sacred to Hephaestus and was said to contain a volcano which was his workshop.—**Lemnian** *adj*.

lemon *n* (a tree bearing) a small yellow oval fruit with an acid pulp; pale yellow; (*sl*) a person or thing considered disappointing or useless.—**lemony** *adj*.

lemonade *n* a lemon-flavored drink.

lemon grass *n* a tropical grass with lemon-scented leaves used in cooking and which yields an aromatic oil.

lempira *n* the standard monetary unit of Honduras, being made up of 100 centavos.

lemur *n* a Madagascan arboreal primate related to the monkey.

lemures *npl* (*myth*) Roman spirits of the dead, honored in the festival of Lemuria.

lemuroid, lemurine *adj* pertaining to, or resembling, a lemur.

Lenci *n* **Fabio** (1935–) Italian designer who set up a store in 1966 to sell his contemporary furniture, which was made of recently developed plastics.

lend *vb* (**lending, lent**) *vt* to give the use of something temporarily in expectation of its return; to provide (money) at interest; to give, impart. * *vi* to make loans.—**lender** *n*.

lender of last resort *n* the central bank of a country, which is in control of its banking system.

L'Enfant *n* **Pierre C** (1754–) French architect. His notable works include old City Hall, New York.

length *n* the extent of something from end to end, usu the longest dimension; a specified distance or period of time; something of a certain length taken from a larger piece; a long expanse; (*often pl*) the degree of effort put into some action.

lengthen *vti* to make or become longer.

lengthwise, lengthways *adv* in the direction of the length.

lengthy *adj* (**lengthier, lengthiest**) long, esp too long.—**lengthily** *adv*.—**lengthiness** *n*.

lenient *adj* not harsh or severe; merciful.—**leniency, lenience** *n*.—**leniently** *adv*.

Lenin *n* **Vladimir Ilyich [Vladimir Ilyich Ulyanov]** (1870–1924) Russian revolutionary leader and Marxist philosopher; instigator of the Bolshevik October Revolution and leader of the Bolsheviks in the Russian Civil War (1918–21).

lenitive *adj* easing pain.

lenity *n* (*pl* **lenities**) clemency, mercy; leniency.

Lennon *n* **John [Winston]** (1940–80) English guitarist, singer, and songwriter who formed the Beatles with Paul McCartney, George Harrison and Ringo Starr; married Yoko Ono; pursued a solo career after 1969; assassinated outside his apartment in New York.

Lennox *n* **Charlotte** (1720–1804) American-born English novelist and dramatist whose best-known work is the novel *The Female Quixote*, a comedy modeled on Cervantes' great novel, that was very popular in its day.

leno *n* (*pl* **lenos**) a way of weaving fabric; a fabric woven in this way.

Lenoble *n* **Émile** (1875–1940) French ceramicist who worked in earthenware and later in stoneware.

lens *n* a curved piece of transparent glass, plastic, etc used in optical instruments to form an image; any device used to focus electromagnetic rays, sound waves, etc; a similar transparent part of the eye that focuses light rays on the retina.

lent *see* **lend**.

Lent *n* the forty weekdays from Ash Wednesday to Easter, observed by Christians as a period of fasting and penitence.—**Lenten** *adj*.

Lenta *abbr* = London Enterprise Agency.

lentamente *adv* (*mus*) (*Italian*) slowly.

lenticular *adj* doubly convex.

lenticular galaxy *n* a galaxy in the shape of a converging lens, as if a sphere had been compressed along a diameter.

lentigo *n* (*pl* **lentigines**) a freckle.

lentil *n* any of several leguminous plants with edible seeds; their seed used for food.

lento *adj, adv* (*mus*) (*Italian*) slow, slowly. * *n* (*pl* **lentos**) a piece of music played in this way.

L

Leo *n* (*astrol*) the fifth sign of the zodiac, in astrology operative July 22–August 21; (*astron*) the Lion, a constellation in the northern hemisphere.

LEO *abbr* = Lyons Electronic Office.

León *n* a city in Mexico; major city in Nicaragua.

Leonard *n* **Saint** (*d*. *c*.560) Frankish monk; godson of Clovis I, king of the Franks; founded a monastery, the abbey of Noblac, where the town of Saint-Leonard was established later; patron saint of women in labor. His feast day is November 6 .

Leonard *n* **Sugar Ray** (1956–) American boxer and world welter weight champion (1981).

Leonardo da Vinci *n* (1452–1519) Florentine painter, draughtsman, engineer, musician, and thinker who was a genius of his time. His paintings include the *Mona Lisa* (*c*.1505).

Leoncavallo *n* **Ruggiero** (1858–1919) Italian composer who started his musical career as a café pianist. He is best known for his opera, *I Pagliacci,* although he composed several others.

leone *n* the standard monetary unit of Sierra Leone, being made up of 100 cents.

Leoni *n* **Giacomo** (1686–) Italian architect. His notable works include Queensbury House, London.

Leonid *n* (*pl* **Leonids, Leonides**) (*astron*) one of the meteors that fall in showers during the November of certain years, their chief point being in the constellation of Leo.

leonine *adj* of or like a lion.

Leoninus, Léonin *n* (12th century) a French composer and organist of whom little is known. He is thought to have been one of the first musicians to use time-values.

leopard *n* a large tawny feline with black spots found in Africa and Asia.—*also* **panther**.—**leopardess** *nf*.

leotard *n* a skintight one-piece garment worn by dancers and others engaged in strenuous exercise.

Lepape *n* **Georges** (1887–1971) French painter who became a theater set designer and then movie set designer.

Le Pautre *n* **Jean** (1618–82) French engraver and designer who introduced a lighter design style for chimney-pieces.

Le Pen *n* **Jean-Marie** (1928–) F rench politician. He founded the right-wing National Front in 1972, a party identified by most observers as crypto-fascist with its crude anti-immigrant policies.

leper *n* a person with leprosy.

lepidopteran *n* (*pl* **lepidopterans, lepidoptera**) any of a large order of insects, such as moths or butterflies, that as adults have four wings covered with minute, often colored, scales and that as larvae are caterpillars.—**lepidopterous** *adj*.

lepidopterist *n* an expert on moths and butterflies.

lepidosiren *n* an eel-like mudfish found in South America

leporine *adj* pertaining to hares; hare-like.

Lepra *abbr* = Leprosy Relief Association.

leprechaun *n* (*Irish folklore*) a fairy.

leprosy *n* a chronic infectious bacterial disease of the skin, often resulting in disfigurement.—**leprous** *adj*.

lepta *n* a standard monetary unit of Greece, equal to one hundredth of a drachma.

leptomeningitis *n* inflammation of two of the three meninges surrounding the brain and spinal cord.

lepton *n* (*phys*) any of various elementary particles, such as electrons and muons, that participate in weak interactions with other elementary particles.

leptospirosis *n* an acute influenza-type infectious disease caused by bacteria of the genus *Leptospira*. One particular species *L. icterohaemorrhagiae*, transmitted by rats, is responsible for the most severe form called Weil's disease.

Lepus *n* (*astron*) a southern constellation with no very bright stars.

Lermontov *n* **Mikhail Yurievich** (1814–41) Russian novelist and poet whose masterpiece is the novel *A Hero of our Time* (1840).

lesbian *n* a female homosexual. * *adj* of or characteristic of lesbians.— **lesbianism** *n*.

Lesbos *n* a Greek island of the Aegean group.—**Lesbian** *adj*.

Les Cayes *n* major city in Haiti.

Lescaze *n* **William** (1896–1969) Swiss architect who worked widely in Europe and America.

lèse-majesté, lese-majesty *n* high treason; a crime against royalty.

lesion *n* any change in an organ or tissue caused by injury or disease; an injury.

Lesotho *n* a small, landlocked kingdom entirely surrounded by the Republic of South Africa.

less *adj* not so much, not so great, etc; fewer; smaller. * *adv* to a smaller extent. * *n* a smaller amount. * *prep* minus.

LESS *abbr* = least-cost estimating and scheduling.

lessee *n* a person who holds property under a lease.

lessen *vti* to make or become less.

lesser *adj* less in size, quality, or importance.

Lessing *n* 1. **Doris [May]** (1919–) English novelist and short-stor y writer whose most famous work is the seminal feminist novel, *The Golden Notebook*. 2. **Gotthold Ephraim** (1729–81) German dramatist and critic whose critical work was significant in the development of German romanticism.

lesson *n* something to be learned or studied; something that has been learned or studied; a unit of learning or teaching; (*pl*) a course of instruction; a selection from the Bible, read as a part of a church service.

lessor *n* a person who lets property on a lease.

lest *conj* in order, or for fear, that not; that.

Les Vingt *n* a group of 20 Belgian painters who exhibited together in Brussels for ten years from 1884.

let[1] *n* a stoppage; (*tennis*) a minor obstruction of the ball that requires a point to be replayed.

let[2] *vb* (**letting, let**) *vt* to allow, permit; to rent; to assign (a contract); to cause to run out, as blood; as an auxiliary in giving suggestions or commands (*let us go*); (*with* **down**) to lower; to deflate; to disappoint; to untie; to lengthen; (*with* **off**) to allow to leave (a ship, etc); to cause to explode or fire; to release, excuse from (work, etc); to deal leniently with, refrain from punishing; to allow (gas, etc) to escape; (*with* **out**) to release; to reveal; to rent out; to make a garment larger; (*with* **up**) to relax; to cease. * *vi* to be rented; (*with* **on**) (*inf*) to pretend; (*inf*) to reveal (a secret, etc); to pretend. * *n* the letting of property or accommodation.

let-down *n* a disappointment.

Lethaby *n* **William Richard** (1857–1931) British architect and theorist whobecame the first professor of design at the Royal College of Art, London (1900).

lethal *adj* deadly.—**lethality** *n*. —**lethally** *adv*.

lethal gene *n* (*genetics*) a gene that, if expressed, will cause the death of the individual.

lethargy *n* (*pl* **lethargies**) an abnormal drowsiness; sluggishness; apathy.—**lethargic** *adj*.—**lethargically** *adv*.

Lethe *n* (*Greek myth*) the River of Oblivion, one of the streams of the underworld, whose water had the power of making those who drank of it forget the whole of their former existence.

Leto *n* (*Greek myth*) the mother of Apollo and Artemis.

Letopolis *n* a settlement in Lower Egypt, a nome capital on the west bank of the Rosetta arm of the Nile, an early source of the Horus legend. Its deity was a mummified falcon.

let's = let us.

Lett *n* a Latvian.

letter *n* a symbol representing a phonetic value in a written language; a character of the alphabet; a written or printed message; (*pl*) literature; learning; knowledge; literal meaning. * *vt* to mark with letters.

letter bomb *n* an explosive device concealed in an envelope and sent through the post.

letter box *n* a slit in the doorway of a house or building through which letters are delivered; a postbox.

letter carrier *n* a person who delivers mail.

lettered *adj* literate; highly educated; marked with letters.

letterhead *n* a name, address, etc printed as a heading on stationery; stationery printed with a heading.

lettering *n* the act or process of inscribing with letters; letters collectively; a title; an inscription.

letter of credit *n* a letter issued by a bank authorizing the bearer to draw funds up to a specified limit.

letter of intent *n* a letter in which a person formally indicates his or her serious intention to do something, such as buy property, etc.

letter-perfect *adj* accurate in the tiniest detail; word-perfect.

letterpress *n* a method of printing; the printed matter of a book, as opposed to the illustrations.

letter quality *n* (*comput*) a style of print that matches the quality of impact printing on a typewriter.

letters of administration *n* an order that authorizes the named person to distribute the property of a deceased person in cases where the latter has not appointed anyone else to carry out this task.

letters patent *npl* official documentation conferring a right, patent or privilege.

Lettish *see* **Latvian**.

lettuce *n* a plant with succulent leaves used in salads.

letup *n* a relaxation of effort.

leu *n* the standard monetary unit of Moldova.

LEU *abbr* = London Ecology Unit.

leucocyte, leukocyte *n* a white blood cell, so called because it contains no hemoglobin, that differs from red blood cells (erythrocytes) in having a nucleus.

leucocytosis *n* an abnormal and temporary increase in the number of white blood cells in the blood, except during pregnancy, menstruation, and exercise.

leucoplast *n* (*bot*) a colorless object that contains reserves of starch and is found in some plant cells.

leucorrhea, leukorrhea *n* a discharge of white or yellow-colored mucus from the vagina which may be a normal condition, increasing before and after menstruation, but a large discharge probably indicates an infection somewhere in the genital tract.

leukemia, leukaemia *n* a chronic disease characterized by an abnormal increase in the number of white blood cells in body tissues and the blood.

leukocyte *n* a white blood cell.

leukoma *n* a white, opaque scar on the cornea of the eye.

leukotomy *n* (*pl* **leukotomies**) the severing of nerve fibers in the frontal lobes of the brain formerly used to relieve certain severe mental disorders.

lev *n* (*pl* **leva**) the monetary unit of Bulgaria.

lev *see* **stotinka**.

Lev., Levit. *abbr* = Leviticus.

LEV *abbr* = lunar excursion vehicle.

levadopa, l-dopa *n* a drug used to treat Parkinsonism. *See* **dopa**.

Levalloisian *n* (*archeo*) a method of preparing a flint core in order to produce a flake of a particular shape and size.

levanter *n* an easterly wind in the Mediterranean.

Levanti *n* Giovanni (1956–) Italian designer of the 1987 *Nastassia* chair and 1987 *Alfonso* leather and metal bench for Memphis.

levantine *n* a kind of reversible silk cloth.

levator *n* (*anat*) a muscle that serves to raise a part of the body.

Le Vau *n* **Louis** (1612–70) French architect. His notable works include the Collège des Quatres Nations, Paris.

leveche *n* a hot, dry, dust-laden wind blowing from the Sahara into Spain.

levee[1] *n* a reception of visitors formerly held by a sovereign or other important person on rising from bed; a reception usu in honor of a particular person.

levee[2] *n* an embankment beside a river.

Léveillé *n* André (1880–1962) French artist and designer of jewelry and industrial textiles.

level *n* a horizontal line or plane; a position in a scale of values; a flat area or surface; an instrument for determining the horizontal. * *adj* horizontal; having a flat surface; at the same height, rank, position, etc; steady. * *vti* (**leveling, leveled** *or* **levelling, levelled**) to make or become level; to demolish; to raise and aim (a gun, criticism, etc).—**levelly** *adv*.

level crossing *n* a grade crossing.(*Brit*) a place where a road crosses a railway line on the same level esp where gates or barriers close the road to allow trains to pass.

leveler, leveller *n* one who levels; an advocate of social equality.

level-headed *adj* having an even temper and sound judgment.—**level-headedly** *adv*.

lever *n* a bar used for prising or moving something; a means to an end; a device consisting of a bar turning about a fixed point; any device used in the same way, e.g., to operate machinery. * *vt* to raise or move (as with) a lever.

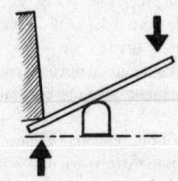

leverage *n* the action of a lever; the mechanical advantage gained by the use of a lever; power, influence.

leveraged buy-out *n* the buy-out of one company by another by means of borrowed funds.

leveret *n* a hare less than a year old.

Levi *n* (*Bible*) 1. third son of Jacob and Leah, regarded as the ancestor of the Levites, the priesthood of Judaism. *See also* **Levites**. 2. (*Bible*) tax collector called by Jesus to follow him, but his name does not appear in the list of 12 disciples.

Levi *n* Primo (1919–87) Italian novelist, short-story writer, and poet. A survivor of Auschwitz, his deeply moving writings on the subject, e.g. the first volume of his autobiography, are among the key texts of the 20th century.

leviable *adj* subject to a levy; (*goods*) which may be levied upon or seized.

leviathan *n* something huge.

levigate *vt* to grind to a fine powder.

levigation *n* (*archeo*) a method of cleaning and separating clay according to grain size by placing it in water and allowing the heavier grains to fall to the bottom.

Levis *n* (*trademark*) jeans made from (blue or black) denim.

Lévi-Strauss *n* Claude (1908–) French anthropologist and advocate of structuralism.

levitate *vti* to rise or cause to rise into the air and float without support.—**levitation** *n*.

Levites *n* (*Bible*) tribe said to be descended from Levi, the son of Jacob; by ancient tradition they were set apart to minister to the priests of the Tabernacle. *See also* **Aaron; Levi; priest**.

Leviticus *n* (*Bible*) third book of the Pentateuch or "five books of Moses." Leviticus is entirely made up of rules and regulations, most of which are religious; it is here that the words "you shall love your neighbor as yourself" occur.

levity *n* (*pl* **levities**) excessive frivolity; lack of necessary seriousness.

levodopa, l-dopa *see* **dopa**.

levorotation *n* left-handed or counterclockwise rotation.—*also* **laevorotation.**—**levorotatory** *adj*.

levulose *n* a fruit found in sugar.—*also* **laevulose**.

levy *vt* (**levying, levied**) to collect by force or authority, as a tax, fine, etc; an amount levied; to enroll or conscript troops; to prepare for or wage war. * *n* (*pl* **levies**) a levying; the amount levied.—**levier** *n*.

Lévy *n* Claude (1895–1942) French painter who worked for the Primavera decorating department of the Au Printemps store in Paris.

Lévy-Dhurmer *n* Lucien (1865–1953) French ceramicist who rediscovered the metallic luster glaze technique used in Middle East ceramics from the 9th century.

lewd *adj* indecent; lustful; obscene.—**lewdly** *adv*.—**lewdness** *n*.

Lewes, George Henry *see* **Eliot, George**.

lewis *n* an appliance for lifting heavy blocks of stone.

Lewis *n* 1. C[live] S[taples] (1898–1963) English novelist and critic best remembered for his Narnia stories, e.g. *The Lion, the Witch and the Wardrobe*. 2. David (1939–) British designer who designed the 1979 *Gori* boat propeller, the 1982 Odontoson range of dental instruments and the 1989 Multimec switch. 3. Jerry Lee (1935–) American rock singer and pianist noted for his flamboyant playing and primitive rock and roll lyrics. 4. Norman (1914–) English novelist and travel writer whose travel books include two modern classics of the genre, *A Dragon Apparent*, on Vietnam, and his book on Burma, *Golden Earth*. 5. [Harry] Sinclair (1885–1951) American novelist and the first American to win the Nobel prize for literature (1930). 6. [Percy] Wyndham (1884–1957) English painter, novelist, and critic.

Lewis and Clark expedition *n* an expedition that would make its way along the Missouri River and go farther west to try to discover a link between the Mississippi and the Pacific, so called because the leaders of the expedition were Captain Meriwether Lewis (1774–1809) and William Clark (1770–1838).

lewisite *n* a blistering liquid obtained from arsenic and acetylene, used in gas form in chemical warfare.

Lewitt *n* Sol (1928–) American sculptor whose work centers on the infinite variety of combinations of simple geometric forms.

lex *n* (*pl* **leges**) law.

lex. *abbr* = lexicon.

Lexell's Comet *n* a lost comet that came close to the Earth in 1770 and was never seen again.

lexical *adj* of or pertaining to words in a language; of a lexicon or dictionary.—**lexically** *adv*.

lexicog. *abbr* = lexicographical; lexicography; lexicographer.

lexicographer *n* a person skilled in lexicography.

lexicography *n* the process of writing or compiling a dictionary; the principles and practices of dictionary making.—**lexicographic, lexicographical** *adj*.—**lexicographically** *adv*.

lexicology *n* the branch of linguistics dealing with the meaning and use of words.—**lexicological** *adj*.—**lexicologist** *n*.

lexicon *n* a dictionary; a special vocabulary, as of a specific language, branch of knowledge, etc.

lexigraphy *n* a writing system in which signs represent words.

lexis *n* the total of words or vocabulary in a language.

ley, ley-line *n* a straight line joining two landmarks, supposedly of prehistoric origin.

Leyden *n* Lucas van (1494–1533) Dutch painter and engraver. He was a child prodigy, producing maturé, accomplished works from the age of 14, e.g., *Mohammed and the Murdered Monk* (1508).

LF *abbr* = low frequency; line feed.

LFA *abbr* = Licentiate of the Institute of Financial Accountants; less favored area; local freight agent.

lfc *abbr* = low-frequency current.

LFC *abbr* = Lutheran Free Church.

LFCS *abbr* = Licentiate of the Faculty of Secretaries.

LFD *abbr* = least fatal dose; low fat diet.

LFr *abbr* = Law French.

l.g. *abbr* = large grain.

LG *abbr* = Life Guards; Low German.

LGCM *abbr* = Lesbian and Gay Christian Movement.

LGr, L. Gr. *abbr* = Late Greek.

LGR *abbr* = leasehold ground rent.

lgth. *abbr* = length.

lg. tn. *abbr* = long ton.

LGU *abbr* = Ladies' Golf Union.

lh, l.h. *abbr* = left hand; left-half.

LH *abbr* = luteinizing hormone.

L/H *abbr* = leasehold.

LHA *abbr* = Lord High Admiral; local health authority.

lhb *abbr* = left half-back.

lhd *abbr* = left-hand drive.

LHD *abbr* (*Latin*) = *Litterarum Humaniorum, In Litteris Humanioribus,* "Doctor of Humanities."

LHS *abbr* = left-hand side.

li *n* the Chinese equivalent of a mile, equivalent to approximately 590 yards (500 meters).

Li *symbol* (*chem*) lithium.

li. *abbr* (*meas*) = link.

LI *abbr* = Landscape Institute; Liberty International; Lincoln's Inn; light infantry.

L.I. *abbr* = Licentiate of Instruction; Long Island.

Lia *n* (*Irish Celtic myth*) lord of Luachar in Connacht. He was treasurer of the Fianna and keeper of the hereditary treasures that had passed to them from the Tuatha De Danann.

liability *n* (*pl* **liabilities**) a being liable; something for which one is liable; (*inf*) a handicap, disadvantage; (*pl*) debts, obligations, disadvantages.

liable *adj* legally bound or responsible; subject to; likely (to).

Liadov *n* **Anatol Konstantinovich** (1855–1914) a Russian composer, teacher, and conductor who was a pupil of Rimsky-Korsakov. His most famous works are the symphonic poems *Baba Yaga, The Enchanted Lake*, and *Kikimora*.

Liaigre *n* **Christian** (1943–) French interior designer who furnished the Lloyds Building in the City of London, as well as French embassies in New Delhi, Warsaw, and Ottawa.

liaise *vi* to form a connection and retain contact with. French

liaison *n* intercommunication as between units of a military force; an illicit love affair; a thickening for sauces, soups, etc, as egg yolks or cream.

liana, liane *n* a climbing plant found in tropical forests.

liar *n* a person who tells lies.

Lias *n* (*geol*) the lowest division of rocks of the Jurassic system.—**Liassic** *adj*.

lib *n* (*inf*) liberation.

lib. *abbr* = (*Latin*) *liber*, "book"; librarian; library.

Lib. *abbr* = Liberal.

Li Ban *n* (*Irish Celtic myth*) Li Ban was the wife of Labraid Luath-lam ar Cleb and sister of Fand. She invited Cuchulainn to help slay three Fomorii, promising him Fand as a lover in return.

libation *n* the act of pouring wine or oil on the ground, as a sacrifice; the liquid so poured out; a drink.

libations *npl* (*astron*) the oscillation of a satellite, e.g. the moon, when viewed from Earth.

Libby *n* **Willard Frank** (1908–80) American chemist. He was awarded the 1960 Nobel prize for chemistry for his role in developing the Carbon–14 radioactive method of dating.

libel *n* any written or printed matter tending to injure a person's reputation unjustly; (*inf*) any defamatory or damaging assertion about a person. * *vt* (**libeling, libeled** *or* **libelling, libelled**) to utter or publish a libel against.— **libeler, libeller** *n*.—**libelous, libellous** *adj*.

Liber *n* (*Roman myth*) an ancient god of fertility.

Libera *n* (*Greek myth*) an ancient goddess of fertility.

Liberia *n* a republic in West Africa.

Liberian Dollar *n* currency of Liberia.

liberal *adj* ample, abundant; not literal or strict; tolerant; (*education*) contributing to a general broadening of the mind, non-specialist; favoring reform or progress. * *n* a person who favors reform or progress.—**liberally** *adv*.

liberal arts *npl* fine art, language, literature, philosophy, social sciences, etc, as opposed to science and technology; educational courses promoting general knowledge in contrast to specific vocational and professional studies.

liberalism *n* liberal opinions, principles, or politics.

liberality *n* (*pl* **liberalities**) generosity; breadth of mind.

liberalize *vti* to make or become less strict.—**liberalization** *n*.

liberamente *adj, adv* (*mus*) (*Italian*) "freely," i.e. as the performer wishes.

liberate *vt* to set free from foreign occupation, slavery, etc.—**liberator** *n*.

liberation *n* the act of liberating; the state of being liberated; the pursuit of social, political, or economic equality by or on behalf of those being discriminated against.

liberation priest *n* a priest who is active in working for social and political justice.

liberation theology *n* the belief that Christianity requires commitment to social and political change, as well as faith, esp in South America.

libertarian *n* a person who advocates liberty, esp in conduct or thought; a believer in free will.—**libertarianism** *n*.

liberticide *n* a destroyer of liberty; the destruction of liberty.

libertine *n* a dissolute person; a freethinker. * *adj* unrestrained, morally or socially; licentious.—**libertinism, libertinage** *n*.

Libertines *n* (*Bible*) the word means "freedmen" and probably refers to Jews descended from captives sent to Rome by Pompey and later liberated.

liberty *n* (*pl* **liberties**) freedom from slavery, captivity, etc; the right to do as one pleases, freedom; a particular right, freedom, etc granted by authority; an impertinent attitude; authorized leave granted to a sailor.

Liberty *n* **Arthur Lasenby** (1843–1917) British design entrepreneur who founded the eponymous store in Regent Street, London. Such was the influence of the company that, in Italy, Art Nouveau was known as Lo Stile Liberty.

Libid *abbr* = London Inter-Bank Bid Rate.

libidinous *adj* lustful, lascivious.

libido *n* (*pl* **libidos**) the sexual urge.—**libidinal** *adj*.

Libor *abbr* = London Inter-Bank Offered Rate.

Libra *n* (*astrol*) the 7th sign of the zodiac, operative September 24–October 23; a constellation represented as a pair of scales.—**Libran** *n, adj*.

librarian *n* a person in charge of a library or trained in librarianship.

librarianship *or* **library science** *n* the profession of organizing collections of books, etc for reference by others.

library *n* (*pl* **libraries**) a collection of books, tapes, records, photographs, etc for reference or borrowing; a room, building, or institution containing such a collection; (*comput*) a set of, usu general purpose, programs or subroutines for use in programming.

librate *vi* to waver; to balance.—**libratory** *adj*.

libration *n* the act of oscillating; the act of balancing; an apparent irregularity in the motion of the moon or a satellite.

librettist *n* a writer of a libretto.

libretto *n* (*pl* **libretti, librettos**) the text to which an opera, oratorio, etc is set.— **librettist** *n*.

Libreville *n* capital city of Gabon.

Librium *n* a minor tranquillizer used in the treatment of anxiety.

Libya *n* a socialist people's republic in north Africa.

Libyan *n* a native or inhabitant of Libya.—*also adj*.

Libyan Dinar *n* currency of Libya.

LicAc *abbr* = Licentiate of Acupuncture.

lice *see* **louse**.

license *n* a formal or legal permission to do something specified; a document granting such permission; freedom to deviate from rule, practice, etc; excessive freedom, an abuse of liberty (—*also* **licence**). *vt* to grant a license to or for; to permit.—**licenser, licensor** *n*.

licensee *n* a person who is granted a license.

license plate *n* a plate on the front or rear of a motor vehicle that displays its registration number.—*also* **numberplate**.

licentiate *n* a person holding a certificate of competence in a profession; a degree between that of bachelor and doctor in some universities; one licensed to preach.— **licentiateship** *n*.

licentious *adj* morally unrestrained; lascivious.—**licentiousness** *n*.

licenza *n* (*mus*) (*Italian*) "license" or "freedom"; *con alcuna licenza* means "with some freedom."

lichee *see* **litchi**.

lichen *n* any of various small plants consisting of an alga and a fungus living in symbiotic association, growing on stones, trees, etc. *See* **symbiosis**.

lichenology *n* the study of lichens.

lich gate *n* (*Brit*) a roofed gate of a churchyard, under which a coffin can be rested.— *also* **lych gate**.

lichi *see* **litchi**.

Lichtenstein *n* **Roy** (1923–97) American painter and sculptor, and the leading pop art painter of the 1960s.

LicIQA *abbr* = Licentiate of the Institute of Quality Assurance.

licit *adj* lawful.—**licitly** *adv*.

lick *vt* to draw the tongue over, esp to taste or clean; (*flames, etc*) to flicker around or touch lightly; (*inf*) to thrash; (*inf*) to defeat. * *vi* (*sl*) to take the drug crack. * *n* a licking with the tongue; (*inf*) a sharp blow; (*inf*) a short, rapid burst of activity.

lickerish *adj* (*arch*) lustful; greedy.

lickety-split *adv* very fast.

licking *n* (*inf*) a severe beating; a defeat.

lickspittle *n* a servile flatterer.

Lic. Med. *abbr* = Licentiate in Medicine.

licorice *n* a black extract made from the root of a European plant, used in medicine and confectionery; a licorice-flavored sweet.—*also* **liquorice**.

lictor *n* an official serving a magistrate in ancient Rome.

LICW *abbr* = Licentiate of the Institute of Clerks of Works of Great Britain Incorporated.

lid *n* a removable cover as for a box, etc; an eyelid.—**lidded** *adj*.

Lidar *abbr* = light detection and ranging.

Liddell *n* **Eric Henry** (1902–45) Scottish athlete and missionary who refused to run on a Sunday during the 1924 Olympics and was the inspiration for the film *Chariots of Fire*.

Liddell Hart *n* **Sir Basil Henry** (1895–1970) English soldier and military historian.

lido *n* (*pl* **lidos**) an open air swimming pool and recreational complex for public use.

LIDPM *abbr* = Licentiate of the Institute of Data Processing Management.

lie[1] *n* an untrue statement made with intent to deceive; something that deceives or misleads. * *vi* (**lying, lied**) to speak untruthfully with an intention to deceive; to create a false impression.

lie[2] *vi* (**lying, lay,** *pp* **lain**) to be or put oneself in a reclining or horizontal position; to rest on a support in a horizontal position; to be in a specified condition; to be situated; to exist. * *n* the way in which something is situated.

LIE *abbr* = loss of independent existence.

Liebermann *n* **Max** (1847–1935) German painter and graphic artist. He was influential in promoting new impressionist ideas in German art although he finally came to represent the formal traditionalism that artists, such as those of Die Brücke, later reacted against.

Liebknecht, Karl *see* **Luxembourg, Rosa**.

Liechtenstein *n* Principality of a constitutional monarchy sandwiched between Switzerland in the north, west, and south, and Austria in the east.

lied *n* (*pl* **lieder**) a German song or ballad.

lie detector *n* a polygraph device used by police and security services that monitors sharp fluctuations in involuntary physiological responses as evidence of stress, guilt, etc when deliberately lying.

lief *adv* (*arch*) willingly.

liege *n* (*feudalism*) a lord or sovereign (—*also* **liege lord**); a subject or vassal.

Liège *n* a city in Belgium.

lien *n* (*law*) a right to keep another's property pending payment of a debt due to the holder.

lien affidavit *n* (*law*) a sworn statement of claims against property by a person, firm, or corporation for the purpose of satisfying a debt.

Liepaja *n* a city in Latvia.

lierne *n* (*archit*) a cross-rib or branch rib in vaulting.

lierne vault *n* (*archit*) a ribbed vault with extra ribs called lierne.

lieu *n* place; stead (esp *in lieu of*, in place of, instead of).

Lieut. *abbr* = Lieutenant.

Lieut. Col. *abbr* = Lieutenant Colonel.

lieutenant *n* a commissioned army officer ranking below a captain; a naval officer next below a lieutenant commander; a deputy, a chief assistant to a superior.—**lieutenancy** *n*.

Lieut. Gen. *abbr* = Lieutenant General.

Lieut. Gov. *abbr* = Lieutenant Governor.

life *n* (*pl* **lives**) that property of plants and animals (ending at death) that enables them to use food, grow, reproduce, etc; the state of having this property; living things collectively; the time a person or thing exists; one's manner of living; one's animate existence; vigor, liveliness; (*inf*) a life sentence; a biography. * *adj* of animate being; lifelong; using a living model; of or relating to or provided by life insurance.

life annuity *n* an annuity that ceases to be paid on the death of a specified person.

life assurance *n* a form of insurance by which a specified amount of money is paid on the death of the person whose life is assured.

life assured *n* the person who is named on a life assurance policy and on whose death the insurance company makes a payment.

life-belt *n* an inflatable ring to support a person in the water; a safety belt.

lifeblood *n* the blood necessary to life; a vital element.

lifeboat *n* a small rescue boat carried by a ship; a specially designed and equipped rescue vessel that helps those in distress along the coastline.

life buoy *n* a ring-shaped buoyant device to keep a person afloat.

life cycle *n* a sequence of stages through which a living being passes during its lifetime

life expectancy *n* the statistically computed average number of years an individual can be expected to live.

lifeguard *n* an expert swimmer employed to prevent drownings.

life history *n* the succession of stages between the earliest development and death of an organism; the life cycle.

life insurance *n* insurance that pays a specified sum to a nominated beneficiary on the death of the insured party.—*also* **life assurance**.

life jacket *n* a sleeveless jacket or vest of buoyant material to keep a person afloat.

lifeless *adj* dead; unconscious; dull.—**lifelessly** *adv*.—**lifelessness** *n*.

lifelike *adj* resembling a real life person or thing.

lifeline *n* a rope for raising or lowering a diver; a rope for rescuing a person, e.g., as attached to a lifebelt; a vitally important channel of communication or transport.

lifelong *adj* lasting one's whole life.

life peer *n* a British peer whose title lapses with death.

life preserver *n* a lifebelt or life jacket. (*Brit*) a club used as a weapon of self-defense.

lifer *n* (*sl*) a person sentenced to prison for life.

life raft *n* a raft kept on board ship for use in emergencies.

lifesaving *adj* something (as drugs) designed to save lives. * *n* the skill or practice of saving lives, esp from drowning.—**lifesaver** *n*.

life science *n* a science dealing with living organisms and life processes, such as biology, zoology, etc.

life sentence *n* imprisonment for life, or a long period, as punishment for a grave offence.

life-size, life-sized *adj* of the size of the original.

life span *n* the extent of the life of a person or thing.

lifestyle *n* the particular attitudes, living habits, etc of a person.

life-support system *n* equipment that preserves life in an hostile environment or under adverse circumstances by providing oxygen, food, water, etc.

lifetime *n* the length of time that a person lives or something lasts.

LIFFE *abbr* (*Brit*) = London International Financial Futures Exchange.

LIFMA *abbr* = Leather Importers, Factors, and Merchants Association.

LIFO *abbr* = last in, first out.

lift *vt* to bring to a higher position, raise; to raise in rank, condition, etc; (*sl*) to steal; to revoke. * *vi* to exert oneself in raising something; to rise; to go up; (*fog, etc*) to disperse; (*with* off) (*rocket, etc*) to take off. * *n* act or fact of lifting; distance through which a thing is lifted; elevation of mood, etc; elevated position or carriage; a ride in the direction in which one is going; help of any kind; (*Brit*) an elevator; upward air pressure maintaining an aircraft in flight.—**lifter** *n*.

liftoff *n* the vertical thrust of a spacecraft, etc at launching; the time of this.

ligament *n* a band of tissue connecting bones; a unifying bond.

ligan *see* **lagan**.

ligand *n* (*chem*) any molecule or atom capable of forming a bond with another molecule by donating an electron pair to form a complex ion; (*biol*) any molecule capable of binding with a specific antibody.

ligate *vt* to tie up (with a ligature).—**ligation** *n*.

ligature[1] *n* a tying or binding together; a tie, bond, etc; two or more printed letters joined together, as æ; a thread used to suture a blood vessel, etc in surgery.

ligature[2] *n* (*mus*) a 12th-century form of notation for a group of notes; a slur indicating that a group of notes must be sung to one syllable; the tie used to link two notes over a bar line.

ligature[3] *n* the metal band fixing the reed to the mouthpiece of a clarinet, etc.

Ligeti *n* **Gyorgy Sándor** (1923–) Hungarian composer renowned for composing sophisticated yet easy-to-listen-to pieces such as *Atmospheres* and *Lontano* for orchestra.

light[1] *n* the agent of illumination that stimulates the sense of sight; electromagnetic radiation such as ultraviolet, infrared or X-rays; brightness, illumination; a source of light, as the sun, a lamp, etc; daylight; a thing used to ignite something; a window; knowledge, enlightenment; aspect or appearance. * *adj* having light; bright; pale in color. * *adv* palely. * *vt* (**lighting, lit** *or* **lighted**) to ignite; to cause to give off light; to furnish with light; to brighten, animate.

light[2] *adj* having little weight; not heavy; less than usual in weight, amount, force, etc; of little importance; easy to bear; easy to digest; happy; dizzy, giddy; not serious; moderate; moving with ease; producing small products. * *adv* lightly. * *vi* (**lighting, lit** *or* **lighted**) to come to rest after travelling through the air; to dismount, to alight; to come or happen on or upon; to strike suddenly, as a blow.—**lightly** *adv*.—**lightness** *n*.

light[3] *n* (*archit*) the opening between the upright posts or mullions of a window.

light-emitting diode *n* (*comput*) *see* **LED**.

lighten[1] *vti* to make or become light or lighter; to shine, flash.—**lightener** *n*.

lighten[2] *vti* to make or become lighter in weight; to make or become more cheerful; to mitigate.—**lightener** *n*.

lightening *n* (*medical*) a sensation experienced by many pregnant women when the fetus settles lower in the pelvis. This lessens the pressure on the diaphragm and breathing becomes easier.

lighter[1] *n* a small device that produces a naked flame to light cigarettes.

lighter[2] *n* a large barge used in loading or unloading larger ships.

lighterage *n* the transport of goods by lighter; the price paid for the service; lighters collectively.

light-fingered *adj* thievish.

light-footed *adj* stepping lightly; nimble.— **light-footedly** *adv*.—**light-footedness** *n*.

light-headed *adj* dizzy; delirious.—**light-headedly** *adv*.

light-hearted *adj* carefree.—**light-heartedly** *adv*.

light-heavyweight *n* a professional boxer weighing not more than 175 pounds (79.38 kg); an amateur boxer weighing not more than 178 pounds (80.7 kg).

lighthouse *n* a tower with a bright light to guide ships.

lighting *n* the process of giving light; equipment for illuminating a stage, television set, etc; the distribution of light on an object, as in a work of art.

lightning *n* a discharge or flash of electricity in the sky. * *adv* fast, sudden.

lightning conductor *or* **rod** *n* a metal rod placed high on a building and grounded to divert lightning from the structure.

light opera *n* an operetta.

light pen *n* a pen-shaped photoelectric device used to communicate with a computer by pointing at the monitor; a similar device used for reading bar codes.

light reactions *npl* (*biochemistry*) the biochemical processes that generate oxygen and other products during photosynthesis, in the presence of light.

light reflex *n* the mechanism whereby the pupil of the eye opens in response to direct light.

light show *n* a spectacular display of lighting and laser effects, esp during a pop concert.

lights out *n* (a signal indicating) the time prescribed for retiring to bed, as in a military barracks.

lightship *n* a ship equipped with a warning beacon and moored at a place dangerous to navigation.

lightsome *adj* (*arch, poet*) carefree; graceful, nimble.

lightweight *adj* of less than average weight; trivial, unimportant. * *n* a person or thing of less than average weight; a professional boxer weighing 130-135 pounds (59-61 kg); a person of little importance or influence.

light-year *n* the distance light travels in one year.

lignaloes *see* **eaglewood**.

ligneous *adj* of or like wood.

ligniform *adj* resembling wood.

lignify *vti* (**lignifies, lignifying, lignified**) (*bot*) to make or become wood, or woody.—**lignification** *n*.

lignin *n* a woody fiber.

lignite *n* a soft brownish-black coal with the texture of the original wood.—**lignitic** *adj*. *See also* **brown coal**.

lignocaine *n* a commonly used local anesthetic given by injection for minor surgery and dental treatment.

L

lignum vitae *n* the heavy hard wood of the South American guaiacum tree.

ligroin *n* a solvent distilled from petroleum.

ligulate *adj* (*bot*) strap-shaped.

ligule *n* (*bot*) a membranous appendage at the top of a sheathing petiole in grasses; one of the rays of a composite plant.

Liisberg *n* 1. **Carl Frederick** (1860–1909) Danish ceramicist who innovated the use of slip in porcelain painting, adding relief to the image. 2. **Hugo** (1896–1958) Danish jewelry designer for the Georg **Jensen** Silverworks, in the 1940s.

LIIST *abbr* = Licentiate of the International Institute of Sports Therapy.

likable, **likeable** *adj* attractive, pleasant, genial, etc.—**likably, likeably** *adv*.

like[1] *adj* having the same characteristics; similar; equal. * *adv* (*inf*) likely. * *prep* similar to; characteristic of; in the mood for; indicative of; as for example. * *conj* (*inf*) as; as if. * *n* an equal; counterpart.

like[2] *vt* to be pleased with; to wish. * *vi* to be so inclined.

-like *adj suffix* similar to, as *lifelike*; having the characteristics of, as *godlike*.

likelihood *n* probability.

likely *adj* (**likelier, likeliest**) reasonably to be expected; suitable; showing promise of success.* *adv* probably.—**likeliness** *n*.

like-minded *adj* sharing the same tastes, ideas, etc.—**likemindedness** *n*.

liken *vt* to compare.

likeness *n* a being like; something that is like, as a copy, portrait, etc; appearance, semblance.

likewise *adv* the same; also.

liking *n* fondness; affection; preference.

likuta (*plural* **makuta**) *n* a monetary unit of the Democratic Republic of Congo (formerly Zaire), equivalent to one hundredth of a zaire.

lilac *n* a shrub with large clusters of tiny, fragrant flowers; a pale purple. * *adj* lilac colored.

LILAM *abbr* = Licentiate of the Institute of Leisure and Amenity Management.

lilangeni *n* the standard monetary unit of Swaziland, made up of 100 cents.

Lilburn *n* **Douglas** (1915–) New Zealand's most famous composer , who studied in England for a period, best known for his more conservative works, which include three symphonies and his *Aotearoa Overture*.

Lilliputian *adj* tiny; petty. * *n* a tiny person, a midget.

Lillo *n* **George** (1693–1739) English dramatist who wrote seven plays, the most important of which is *The London Merchant*, or *The History of George Barnwell*, a domestic tragedy that had great influence throughout Europe.

Li-Lo *n* (*pl* **Li-Los**) (*trademark*) an inflatable rubber or plastic mattress.

LILO *abbr* = last in, last out.

Lilongwe *n* capital city of Malawi.

lilt *n* a light rhythmic song or tune; a springy motion. * *vi* (*mus, song*) to have a lilt; to move buoyantly.—**lilting** *adj*.

lily *n* (*pl* **lilies**) a bulbous plant having typically trumpet-shaped flowers; its flower.

lily-livered *adj* cowardly.

lily of the valley *n* a small plant of the lily family with white bell-shaped flowers.

lily pad *n* a floating leaf of a water lily.

lily-white *adj* pure white; (*inf*) pure, incorruptible.

Lim. *abbr* = limited (company).

LIM *abbr* = Licentiate of the Institute of Metals.

Lima *n* capital city of Peru.

LIMA *abbr* = Licentiate of the Institute of Mathematics and its Applications.

lima bean *n* a kind of bean that produces flat, edible pale green seeds; its edible seed.

Limassol *n* a city in Cyprus.

limb *n* a projecting appendage of an animal body, as an arm, leg, or wing; a large branch of a tree; a participating member, agent; an arm of a cross; (*geol*) the areas between hinges in folded rocks; (*astron*) the rim of a heavenly body that has a visible disk, e.g., sun or moon.—**limbless** *adj. See also* **fold**.

limbate *adj* (*bot*) with a border of a different color.

limber[1] *adj* flexible, able to bend the body easily. * *vt* to make limber. * *vi* to become limber; (*with* **up**) to stretch and warm the muscles in readiness for physical exercise.

limber[2] *n* the detachable wheeled section of a gun carriage.

Limbert *n* **Charles P**. (1854–1923) American furniture designer and manufacturer who started the Holland Dutch Arts and Crafts company.

limbo[1] *n* (*pl* **limbos**) (*Christianity*) the abode after death assigned to unbaptized souls; a place for lost, unwanted, or neglected persons or things; an intermediate stage or condition between extremes.

limbo[2] *n* (*pl* **limbos**) a West Indian dance that involves bending over backwards and passing under a horizontal bar that is progressively lowered.

lime[1] *n* a white calcium compound used for making cement and in agriculture. * *vt* to treat or cover with lime.

lime[2] *n* a small yellowish-green fruit with a juicy, sour pulp; the tree that bears it; its color.

lime[3] *n* the linden tree.

limekiln *n* a furnace for making lime.

limelight *n* intense publicity; a type of lamp, formerly used in stage lighting, in which lime was heated to produce a brilliant flame.

limen *n* (*pl* **limens, limina**) (*psychol*) the point at which the effect of a stimulus is just discernible.

limerick *n* a type of humorous verse consisting of five lines.

Limerick *n* a city in the Republic of Ireland.

limestone *n* a type of rock composed mainly of calcium carbonate.

limey *n* (*pl* **limeys**) (*sl*) a British person.

LIMF *abbr* = Licentiate of the Institute of Metal Finishing.

limit *n* a boundary; (*pl*) bounds; the greatest amount allowed; (*inf*) as much as one can tolerate. * *vt* to set a limit to; to restrict.—**limitable** *adj*.

limitary *adj* restrictive; restricted.

limitation *n* the act of limiting or being limited; a hindrance to ability or achievement.

limitations of actions *npl* statutory rules that put a limit on the period of time within which a civil legal action can be brought.

limited *adj* confined within bounds; lacking imagination or originality.

limited company *n* a company in which the liability of its members with reference to the debts of the company is limited.

limited edition *n* an edition of a book, print, etc, that is issued in only a certain number of copies.

limited liability *n* in UK, responsibility for the debts of a company only to the extent of the amount of capital stock held.

limiter *n* an electronic circuit producing an output signal, the amplitude of which is flattened above a predetermined peak value.

limitless *adj* boundless, immense.—**limitlessly** *adv*.—**limitlessness** *n*.

limn *vt* to paint or draw.—**limner** *n*.

limnology *n* the scientific study of freshwater bodies (e.g., lakes and ponds) in terms of their support for plant and animal life, physical geography, chemical composition, etc.

limo *n* (*inf*) **limousine**.

Límon *n* a city in Costa Rica.

Limoges *n* French factory at Limoges, which was established in 1736 for the production of domestic ceramics.

limousine *n* (*sl*) a large luxury car.

limp[1] *vi* to walk with or as with a lame leg. * *n* a lameness in walking.—**limper** *n*. —**limpingly** *adv*.

limp[2] *adj* not firm; lethargic; wilted; flexible.—**limply** *adv*.—**limpness** *n*.

limpet *n* a mollusk with a low conical shell that clings to rocks.

limpid *adj* perfectly clear; transparent.—**limpidity** *n*.

limpkin *n* a kind of American wading bird.

limy *adj* (**limier, limiest**) containing, or resembling, lime.

lin. *abbr* = lineal; linear.

Lin *n* **Maya Ying** (1959–) American architect and designer of the Vietnam Veterans Memorial, Washington DC (1982).

Linac *abbr* = linear accelerator.

linage *n* the number of written or printed lines on a page.

linchpin *n* a pin passed through an axle to keep a wheel in position; a person or thing regarded as vital to an organization, project, etc.

Lincoln *n* the capital city of Nebraska, a state of the USA.

Lincoln *n* **Abraham** (1809–65) American statesman; 16th president of the United States (1861–65); declared emancipation for slaves in 1863; led the Union to victory before his assassination in 1865 by **John Wilkes Booth** (1839–65) while attending the theater.

Lincoln. *abbr* (*Latin*) = *Lincolniensis*, "of Lincoln."

linctus *n* a medicine, particularly to treat coughs, that is thick and syrup-like.

Lind *n* **Jenny** (1820–87) Swedish soprano who made her début at the age of ten. Her voice was remarkable for its power and flexibility, and gained her the nickname "The Swedish Nightingale."

Lindbergh *n* **Charles Augustus** (1902–74) American aviator who was the first man to fly the Atlantic solo and nonstop (1927) in the monoplane *Spirit of St Louis*.

linden *n* a tree with deciduous heart-shaped leaves and small fragrant yellow flowers.

Linden *n* a city in Guyana.

Lindfors *n* **Stefan** (1962–) Finnish sculptor.

Lindh *n* **Richard** (1929–) Finnish ceramicist whose work has been widely exhibited.

Lindinger-Loewy *n* **Lone** (1956–) Danish industrial designer who works with her husband, **Gideon Loewy** (1952–).

Lindow Man *n* part of a human body uncovered in August 1984 in a peat bog at Lindow Moss in Cheshire, England, probably placed in the bog around the 4th century BC, thought to be evidence of the Celtic practice of human sacrifice. *See* **Tollund Man**.

line[1] *vt* (**lining, lined**) to put, or serve as, a lining in.

line[2] *n* a length of cord, rope, or wire; a cord for measuring, making level; a system of conducting fluid, electricity, etc; a thin threadlike mark; anything resembling such a mark, as a wrinkle; edge, limit, boundary; border, outline, contour; a row of persons or things, as printed letters across a page; a succession of persons, lineage; a connected series of things; the course a moving thing takes; a course of conduct, actions, etc; a whole system of transportation; a person's trade or occupation; a field of experience or interest; (*inf*) glib, persuasive talk; a verse; the forward combat position in warfare; fortifications, trenches, or other defenses used in war; a stock of goods; a piece of information; a short letter, note; (*pl*) all the speeches of a character in a play; (*sl*) a measure of the drug cocaine laid in a strip, ready for sniffing. * *vb* (**lining, lined**) *vt* to mark with lines; to form a line along; to cover with lines; to arrange in a line. * *vi* to align.

lineage *n* direct descent from an ancestor; ancestry.

lineal¹ *adj* hereditary; direct; linear.—**lineally** *adv*.

lineal² *n* (*archeo*) a thin sheet of decorative gold, in the form of a crescent, worn by people belonging to the Food Vessel Culture in Scotland and Ireland.

lineament¹ *n* (*usu pl*) a facial feature.

lineament² *n* (*geol*) a long structural or volcanic feature on the Earth's surface.

line and staff management *n* a system of management used in some large organizations in which there are two separate hierarchies of management, **line managers** and **staff managers**. Line managers are involved in the achieving of the company's primary policy goals and in the running of the organization's main activities. Staff managers are responsible for providing advice and support services, such as personnel management.

linear *adj* of, made of, or using a line or lines; narrow and long; in relation to length only.—**linearity** *n*. —**linearly** *adv*.

linear A and B *n* (*archeo*) a form of writing used by the Minoan and Mycenaean civilizations of Greece and Crete during the Bronze Age.

linear accelerator *n* a device for accelerating elementary particles in a straight line by successively activating electric fields at regular intervals along their path.

linear development *see* **ribbon development**.

linear earthwork *n* (*archeo*) single or multiple earth mounds and ditches running across country in a relatively straight line that can be many miles long.

linear equation *n* (*math*) a mathematical term used to describe any equation containing two variables and of the general form $y = mx + c$, where x and y are the variables, m is the slope of the line and c is the intercept or the point where the curve crosses the y-axis.

linear measure *n* a measure or a system of measures of length.

line art *n* (*comput*) a computer drawing that consists of only black and white areas.

lineate *adj* marked with lines.

lineation *n* the drawing, or arrangement, of lines.

linebacker *n* (*football*) a defensive player directly behind the line.

line drawing *n* a drawing made with solid lines.

line drive *n* (*tennis, baseball, etc*) a ball hit in a straight line parallel to the ground.

line engraving *n* an engraving with fine lines; the art of this type of engraving.

line feed *adj* (*comput*) *see* **feed**.

line graph *n* (*comput*) a style of graph using lines to show the relationship between the variables being plotted.

line judge *n* (*football*) a linesman whose duties include being official timekeeper.

lineman *n* (*pl* **linemen**) a person who installs, maintains, and repairs telephone or electricity power lines; a person who maintains and repairs railroad tracks; (*football*) a player in the line.

linen *n* thread or cloth made of flax; household articles (sheets, cloths, etc) made of linen or cotton cloth.

line of balance chart *n* a chart used in production scheduling that supplies data on the agreed delivery dates of products and data on the availability of the component parts that are required to manufacture the products.

line of fire *n* the flight path of a projectile such as a bullet or missile.

line of sight *n* the straight line along which an observer looks.

line of sight velocity *n* (*astron*) the velocity at which a heavenly body approaches or recedes from the Earth.

line-out *n* (*Rugby Union*) the method of restarting a game after the ball has been put into touch, the forwards forming two opposing parallel lines at right angles to the touch-line and jumping for the ball that is thrown in.

line printer *n* a high-speed computer printer that prints each line as a single unit instead of character by character.

line production *or* **mass production** *n* a type of manufacturing process in which large volumes of identical, or very similar, products are made in a set sequence of operations.

liner *n* a large passenger ship or aircraft traveling a regular route.

line score *n* (*baseball*) a score giving the runs, hits, and errors by each team.

linesman *n* (*pl* **linesmen**) an official in certain games who assists the referee in deciding when the ball is out of play, etc.

line spacing *n* (*comput*) the space between lines of text in a word processing document or page layout program.

line spectrum *n* a spectrum consisting of bright lines, an emission spectrum or a continuous spectrum crossed by dark lines, an absorption spectrum.

lineup *n* an arrangement of persons or things in a line, e.g., for inspection.

ling¹ *n* a type of heather.

ling² *n* (*pl* **ling, lings**) a sea fish of northern waters used as food.

ling. *abbr* = linguistics.

linger *vi* to stay a long time; to delay departure; to dawdle or loiter; to dwell on in the mind; to remain alive though on the point of death.—**lingerer** *n*. —**lingering** *adj*.—**lingeringly** *adv*.

lingerie *n* women's underwear and nightclothes.

lingo *n* (*pl* **lingoes**) (*inf*) a dialect, jargon, etc.

lingua franca *n* (*pl* **lingua francas, linguae francae**) a language used for communication between speakers of different languages.

lingual *adj* of, or pronounced with, the tongue.—**lingually** *adv*.

linguiform *adj* tongue-shaped.

linguist *n* a person who is skilled in speaking foreign languages.

linguistic *adj* of or pertaining to language or linguistics.—**linguistically** *adv*.

linguistics *n* (*used as sing*) the science of language.

lingulate *adj* tongue-shaped.

liniment *n* a soothing medication, usu applied to the skin.

lining *n* a material used to cover the inner surface of a garment, etc; any material covering an inner surface.

link¹ *n* a single loop or ring of a chain; something resembling a loop or ring or connecting piece; a person or thing acting as a connection, as in a communication system, machine, or organization. * *vti* to connect or become connected.

link² *or* **hyperlink** *n* the means whereby connections to other pages (on a Website) or other Websites are embedded in web pages. Also, to establish a connection between two computers (as in a network) or two programs or two files. *See also* **hyperlink**.

LINK *abbr* = Let's Increase Neurofibromatosis Knowledge.

linkage *n* a linking; a series or system of links; (*genetics*) the association between two or more genes situated on the same chromosome.

linkboy *n* (*formerly*) someone who guided others through dark streets with a torch.

linkman *n* (*pl* **linkmen**) (*radio, TV*) a presenter who links items, reports, etc, esp on a sports program.

Linköping *n* a city in Sweden.

links *npl* (*also used as sing*) flat sandy soil; a golf course, esp by the sea.

linkup *n* a linking together.

Linley *n* 1. **Thomas** (1733–95) an English composer and teacher who wrote incidental music for plays, including Sheridan's *The Duenna* and *School for Scandal*. He also wrote madrigals, songs and cantatas. 2. His daughter **Elizabeth Ann**, (1754–92) a noted soprano who married Sheridan. 3. His son, also **Thomas** (1756–78), was a violinist and friend of Mozart, and also composed songs before his accidental death by drowning.

linn *n* (*Scot*) a waterfall; the pool beneath a waterfall; a ravine.

Linn. *abbr* = Linnaean; Linnaeus.

Linnaean, Linnean *adj* pertaining to the Swedish naturalist Linnaeus or to his system of classification.

linnet *n* a small brown or gray songbird.

lino *n* (*inf*) (*pl* **linos**) linoleum.

linocut *n* a design cut in relief on a piece of linoleum; a print made from this.

linoleic, linolenic *see* **essential fatty acid**.

linoleum *n* a floor covering of coarse fabric backing with a smooth, hard decorative coating.

Linotype *n* (*trademark*) a typesetting machine that casts lines in one piece.

linsang *n* a type of civet, found in Indonesia and Borneo.

linseed *n* the seed of flax, from which linseed oil is made.

linseed oil *n* oil made from flax seeds, used in paint and varnish.

linsey-woolsey *n* a sturdy coarse fabric of linen or cotton and wool mixed.

LInstBA *abbr* = Licentiate of the Institute of Business Administration.

LInstBB *abbr* = Licentiate of the Institute of British Bakers.

LInstBCA *abbr* = Licentiate of the Institute of Burial and Cremation Administration.

linstock *n* (*formerly*) a staff holding a match, used to light a cannon.

LInstP *abbr* = Licentiate of the Institute of Physics.

lint *n* scraped and softened linen used to dress wounds; fluff.

lintel *n* the horizontal crosspiece spanning a doorway or window.

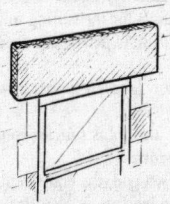 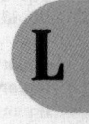

lintwhite *n* (*Scot, arch*) a linnet.

Linus *n* (*Greek myth*) the personification of a dirge or lamentation.

Linz *n* a city in Austria.

lion *n* a large, flesh-eating feline mammal with a shaggy mane in the adult male; a person of great courage or strength.—**lioness** *nf*.

lionhearted *adj* extremely brave.

lionize *vt* to treat as or make famous.—**lionization** *n*. —**lionizer** *n*.

lion's share *n* the largest portion.

lip *n* either of the two fleshy flaps that surround the mouth; anything like a lip, as the rim of a jug; (*sl*) insolent talk. * *vt* (**lipping, lipped**) to touch with the lips; to kiss; to utter.

LIP *abbr* = life insurance policy.

lipa *see* **kuna**.

lipase *n* (*biochemistry*) any enzyme capable of breaking down fat to form fatty acids and glycerol.

Lipchitz *n* **Jacques** (1891–1973) Lithuanian-born sculptor, of Polish-Jewish parentage, resident in France from 1909 and in the US from 1941. Notable works include *Sacrifice* (1948).

lipid *n* an organic compound in fats, which is soluble in solvents but insoluble in water.

Lipmann, Fritz *see* **Krebs, Sir Hans Adolf**.

lipo-, lip- *prefix* fat, fatty.

lipoid, lipoidal *adj* fatty, resembling fat. * *n* a fat-like substance.

lipolysis *n* the breakdown of lipids into fatty acids via the action of the enzyme lipase.

lipoma *n* a benign tumor, made up of fat cells, that can occur in the fibrous tissues of the body, often beneath the skin.

lipoprotein *n* (*biochemistry*) any protein that has a fatty acid as a side chain.

liposarcoma *n* a malignant tumor of fat cells that is very rare, particularly under the age of 30. It occurs in the buttocks or thighs.

liposome *n* a spherical droplet of microscopic size comprising fatty membranes around an aqueous vesicle.

liposuction *n* cosmetic surgery involving the removal of fat from under the skin of the thighs, stomach, etc using a suction device inserted through an incision.

lipped *adj* having lips or rounded edges.

Lippi *n* 1. **Filippino** (1457–1504) Florentine painter, son of Filippo Lippi. His most outstanding works are his frescoes, in particular *The Life of St Thomas Aquinas* (1488–93) for Santa Maria sopra Minerva in Rome. 2. **Fra Filippo** (c.1406–69) Florentine painter whose son, Filippino Lippi also became a painter.

Lippincott *n* **J. Gordon** (1909–) American industrial designer who set up his studio in 1935.

lip-read *vt* (**lip-reading, lip-read**) to understand another's speech by watching their lip movements.

LIPS *abbr* = logical inferences per second.

lip service *n* support expressed but not acted upon.

lipstick *n* a small stick of cosmetic for coloring the lips; the cosmetic itself.

lip-sync, lip-synch *vt* to move the lips in time with a prerecorded soundtrack (of dialogue or music) on film or television.

LIPT *abbr* = Ladies' International Polo Tournament.

liq. *abbr* = liquid; liquor.

liquate *vt* to melt (metals) to separate or purify them.—**liquation** *n*.

liquefacient *adj* serving to liquefy. * *n* something that liquefies.

liquefy *vti* (**liquefying, liquefied**) to change to a liquid.—**liquefaction** *n*. — **liquefier** *n*.

liquescent *adj* becoming liquid.

liqueur *n* a sweet and variously flavored alcoholic drink.

liquid *n* a substance that, unlike a gas, does not expand indefinitely and, unlike a solid, flows readily. * *adj* in liquid form; clear; limpid; flowing smoothly and musically, as verse; (*assets*) readily convertible into cash.—**liquidity** *n*.

liquid assets *npl* assets that are held either in the form of cash or in the form of something that can readily be converted into cash.

liquidate *vt* to settle the accounts of; to close a (bankrupt) business and distribute its assets among its creditors; to convert into cash; to eliminate, kill.

liquidation *n* the act of liquidating or paying off; the settlement of the affairs of a bankrupt person or business.

liquidator *n* an official who winds up a business.

liquid crystal display *n* an electronic display using a liquid with crystalline properties that changes its reflectivity when a signal is applied.

liquidity *n* the possession by a company of enough liquid assets to discharge its debts and carry out its business.

liquidize *vt* to make liquid.

liquidizer *n* a domestic appliance for liquidizing and blending foods.

liquid measure *n* a unit or units for measuring volumes of liquid.

liquid paraffin *n* an oily distillate of petroleum used as a laxative.—*also* **mineral oil**.

liquor *n* an alcoholic drink; any liquid, esp that in which food has been cooked.

liquorice *n* *see* **licorice**.

liquor store *n* a place where alcohol is sold for consumption off the premises.—*also* **off-licence, package store**.

Lir *n* (*Irish Celtic myth*) the sea-god, the equivalent of the Welsh god Llyr. He was the father of Manannan who became in turn the sea-god. He married Aobh and the children whom he had by her were turned into swans for nine hundred years by Aoife[1], his second wife, because she was jealous of Lir's love for them.

LIR *abbr* = Licentiate of the Institute of population Registration.

lira *n* (*pl* **lire, liras**) the monetary unit of Italy and Turkey.

lira da braccio *n* Italian stringed instrument of the 15th and 16th centuries. It had seven strings and was played like a violin.

lira da gamba *n* Italian stringed instrument of the 15th and 16th centuries. It was a bass instrument, played between the knees, and had anything up to sixteen strings.

lira organizzata *n* (*mus*) a type of hurdy-gurdy that included a miniature organ.

LIS *abbr* = Lesbian Information Service; List and Index Society.

Lisbon (Lisboa) *n* capital city of Portugal.

LISC *abbr* = Library and Information Services Council.

lisente *n* the standard monetary unit of Lesotho, equal to one hundredth of a loti.

lisle *n* a fine tightly-twisted cotton thread.

LISM *abbr* = Licentiate of the Incorporated Society of Musicians.

lisp *vi* to substitute the sounds *th* (as in *thin*) for *s* or *th* (as in *then*) for *z*; a speech defect or habit involving such pronunciation; to utter imperfectly. * *vt* to speak or utter with a lisp.—*also n.* —**lisper** *n*.

LISP *abbr* (*comput*) = LISt Processing. A high-level programming language used to a great extent in the development of artificial intelligence.

lis pendens *n* (*law*) a notice that a suit has been filed in a court of law and that property owned may be liable to a judgment.

lissom *adj* lithe; supple; agile, etc.—**lissomeness** *n*.

list[1] *n* a series of names, numbers, words, etc written or printed in order. * *vt* to make a list of; to enter in a directory, etc.

list[2] *vti* to tilt to one side, as a ship. * *n* such a tilting.

list box *n* (*comput*) a box that appears as part of a dialog box and lists various options from which the user can make a choice.

LISTD *abbr* = Licentiate of the Imperial Society of Teachers of Dancing.

listed *adj* (*company, etc*) having its shares quoted on a stock exchange; (*building*) of architectural interest and protected from demolition or alteration without permission.

listed building *n* in UK, a building officially designated as of historic or architectural interest and protected from alteration or demolition.

listed company *n* a company the shares of which are traded on the main market in the London Stock Exchange.

listen *vi* to try to hear; to pay attention, take heed; (*with* **in**) to intercept radio or telephone communications; to tune into a radio broadcast; to eavesdrop.

listener *n* a person who listens; a person listening to a radio broadcast.

listeriosis *n* chronic food poisoning caused by the bacteria *Listeria*.

l'istesso tempo *n* (*mus*) (*Italian*) "the same tempo."

listing *n* a list, or an individual entry therein; the act of making a list; (*pl*) a guide giving details of events, e.g., music, theater, taking place in a particular area, published in a newspaper or magazine.

listing requirements *npl* the conditions that require to be satisfied before the shares of a company can be traded on the main market of the London Stock Exchange.

listless *adj* lacking energy or enthusiasm because of illness, dejection, etc; languid.—**listlessly** *adv*.—**listlessness** *n*.

list price *n* the retail price of a consumer article as recommended by the manufacturer and shown on the price list; the price entered on an invoice by a supplier to a retailer or wholesaler before the deduction of any discounts.

Liszt *n* **Ferencz (Franz)** (1811–86) Hungarian composer and pianist. His principal compositions include: the Faust and *Dante* symphonies; 12 *Etudes d'Execution Transcendante* and 20 *Hungarian Rhapsodies* for piano; several choral pieces; and 12 symphonic poems.

lit *see* **light**[1], **light**[2].

lit. *abbr* = literal; literally; literary; literature; liter.

Lit. *abbr* (*Italian*) = *lire Italiane*, "Italian lire."

litany *n* (*pl* **litanies**) a type of prayer in which petitions to God are recited by a priest and elicit set responses by the congregation; any tedious or automatic recital.

litas *n* the standard monetary unit of Lithuania.

Lit.B. or Litt. B. *abbr* (*Latin*) = *Litterarum Baccalaureus*, "Bachelor of Letters", "Bachelor of Literature."

litchi *n* a fruit consisting of a soft, sweet white pulp in a thin brown shell; the tree that bears this fruit.—*also* **lichee, lichi**.

Lit.D. or Litt. D. *abbr* (*Latin*) = *Literarum Doctor*, "Doctor of Letters," "Doctor of Literature."

-lite *n suffix* stone; mineral; fossil.

liter, litre *n* a measure of liquid capacity in the metric system, equivalent to 1.76 pints.

literacy *n* the ability to read and write.

literal *adj* in accordance with the exact meaning of a word or text; in a basic or strict sense; prosaic, unimaginative; real.—**literalness, literality** *n*. —**literally** *adv*.

literalism *n* adherence to the literal sense of a word or saying.—**literalist** *n*.

literary *adj* of or dealing with literature; knowing much about literature.—**literarily** *adv*.—**literariiness** *n*.

literate *adj* able to read and write; educated.—*also n*.

literati *npl* educated people.

literatim *adv* letter for letter.

literature *n* the writings of a period or of a country, esp those valued for their excellence; of style or form; all the books and articles on a subject; (*inf*) any printed matter.

lith. or litho. or lithog. *abbr* = lithograph; lithography.

Lith. *abbr* = Lithuania; Lithuanian.

-lith *n suffix* stone or rock.

litharge *n* an oxide of lead.

lithe *adj* supple, flexible.—**litheness** *n*.

lithesome *adj* lithe, supple.

lithia *n* an oxide of lithium.

lithic *adj* of or pertaining to stone.

lithification *n* (*geol*) the processes that change unconsolidated sediment into rock, including cementation of the grains.

lithium *n* the lightest metallic element.

litho *n* (*pl* **lithos**) a lithograph; lithography.

lithograph *n* a print, etc made by lithography.—**lithographic** *adj*.—**lithographically** *adv*.

lithography *n* printing from a flat stone or metal plate, parts of which have been treated to repel ink.—**lithographer** *n*.

lithoid, lithoidal *adj* stonelike.

lithol. *abbr* = lithology.

lithology *n* the study of rocks and their physical characteristics.—**lithologic, lithological** *adj*.

lithophyte *n* a stony polyp; a plant which grows on a rocky surface.

lithosphere *n* the solid outer part of the earth.

lithotomy *n* (*pl* **lithotomies**) (*med*) the operation of cutting into the bladder to remove a stone.—**lithotomic** *adj*.

lithotripter, lithotriptor *n* an instrument that fragments kidney or bladder stones, etc by ultrasound without the need for invasive surgery.

lithotrity *n* (*pl* **lithotrities**) (*med*) the operation of crushing a stone in the bladder.

Lithuania *n* a republic bounded by Latvia, Belarus, Poland, and Russia (Kaliningrad) with a Baltic Sea coastline to the west.

lit. hum. *abbr* (*Latin*) = *litterae humaniores*, "more humane letters" (Oxford honors degree in Ancient History, Philosophy, Latin, and Greek).

litigant *n* a person engaged in a lawsuit.

litigate *vti* to bring or contest in a lawsuit.—**litigator** *n*.

litigation *n* the act or process of carrying on a lawsuit; a judicial contest.

litigious *adj* of or causing lawsuits; fond of engaging in lawsuits; contentious.—**litigiousness** *n*.

litmus *n* a coloring material obtained from certain lichens that turns red in acid solutions and blue in alkaline solutions.

litotes *n* (*pl* **litotes**) (*rhetoric*) understatement for effect.

litre *see* **liter**.

litt. *abbr* = litterateur.

Littell *n* **Ross** (1924–) American designer for **Laverne** Originals.

litter *n* rubbish scattered about; young animals produced at one time; straw, hay, etc used as bedding for animals; a stretcher for carrying a sick or wounded person. * *vt* to make untidy; to scatter about carelessly.

littérateur *n* a writer.

litterbug *n* a person who drops refuse in public places.

Litt.L. *abbr* (*Latin*) = *Litterarum Licentiatus*, "Licentiate in Letters."

little *adj* not great or big, small in size, amount, degree, etc; short in duration; small in importance or power; narrow-minded. * *n* small in amount, degree, etc. * *adv* less, least, slightly; not much; not in the least.

little finger *n* the smallest finger, at the edge of the hand.

Little Ice Age *n* a period of climatic cooling between about 1550 and 1850. Glaciers in the northern hemisphere advanced several miles down their valleys and temperatures were much colder than at present.

little people *npl* (*folklore*) supernatural beings such as fairies, elves, and leprechauns.

Little Rock *n* the capital city of Arkansas, a state of the USA.

Little's disease *n* cerebral palsy on both sides of the body that affects the legs more than the arms.

little theater *n* a small theater for low-cost drama productions.

Littlewood *n* **Joan** (1914–) English theater director . Her theater company, Theatre Workshop, formed in 1945, became one of the major left-wing theater companies in the British theater.

littoral *adj* of or along the seashore.

littoral zone the area between high and low water marks during ordinary spring tides water to a depth of 200 meters.

liturgics *n* (*sing*) the study of liturgies.

liturgist *n* someone who studies or composes liturgies.

liturgy *n* (*pl* **liturgies**) the prescribed form of service of a church.—**liturgical** *adj*.—**liturgically** *adv*.

livable *adj* worth living; suitable for living in.

live[1] *vi* to have life; to remain alive; to endure; to pass life in a specified manner; to enjoy a full life; to reside; (*with* **in, out**) (*employee*) to reside at (or away from) one's place of work; (*with* **together**) (*unmarried couple*) to cohabit. * *vt* to carry out in one's life; to spend; pass; (*with* **down**) to survive or efface the effects of (a crime or mistake) by waiting until it is forgotten or forgiven.

live[2] *adj* having life; of the living state or living beings; of present interest; still burning; unexploded; carrying electric current; broadcast during the actual performance.

liveable *see* **livable**.

live-in *adj* resident; (*sexual partner*) cohabiting.

livelihood *n* employment; a means of living.

livelong *adj* of the whole length of (the day).

lively *adj* (**livelier, liveliest**) full of life; spirited; exciting; vivid; keen. * *adv* in a lively manner.—**liveliness** *n*.

liven *vti* to make or become lively.—**livener** *n*.

liver *n* the largest glandular organ in vertebrate animals, which secretes bile, etc and is important in metabolism; the liver of an animal used as food; a reddish-brown color.

liveried *adj* wearing a livery.

liverish *adj* suffering from liver disorder; peevish.

Liverpool *n* major English city in United Kingdom of Great Britain and Northern Ireland (UK).

liverwort *n* a cryptogamous plant, found in wet places.

liverwurst *n* sausage made with liver.

livery *n* (*pl* **liveries**) an identifying uniform, as that worn by a servant.

liveryman *n* (*pl* **liverymen**) a keeper of a livery stable; a member of a livery company.

lives *see* **life**.

livestock *n* (farm) animals raised for use or sale.

live wire *n* (*inf*) a lively, energetic person.

livid *adj* (*skin*) discolored, as from bruising; grayish in color; (*inf*) extremely angry.—**lividly** *adv*.—**lividness, lividity** *n*.

living *adj* having life; still in use; true to life, vivid; of life, for living in. * *n* a being alive; livelihood; manner of existence.

living room *n* a room in a house used for general entertainment and relaxation.

living wage *n* a wage sufficient to maintain a reasonable standard of comfort.

Livingstone *n* **David** (1813–73) Scottish missionary and explorer who discovered Lake Ngami (1849) and the Victoria Falls (1855). He encountered the Welsh-American adventurer **Henry Morton Stanley** (1841–1904) on his last trip, in search of the source of the Nile.

lixiviate *vt* to wash (soil, ore, etc) with a filtering liquid; to extract (a soluble substance) from some material.—**lixiviation** *n*.

lizard *n* a reptile with a slender body, four legs, and a tapering tail.

IJ *abbr* = Lord Justice.

IJA *abbr* = Lady Jockeys Association; (*Brit*) London Jute Association.

Ljubljana *n* capital city of Slovenia.

l.l. *abbr* (*Latin*) = *loco laudato*, "in the place cited"; loose leaf.

ll. *abbr* = lines; leaves.

LL *abbr* = Lord Lieutenant.

LL. *abbr* = Late Latin; Law Latin; (*Latin*) *leges*, "laws"; Low Latin.

llama *n* a South American animal, related to the camel, used for carrying loads and as a source of wool.

llano *n* (*pl* **llanos**) one of the vast, level plains of South America.

Llassar Llaesgynewid *n* (*Welsh Celtic myth*) the husband of **LLB** or **LL.B.** *abbr* (*Latin*) = *Legum Baccalaureus*, "Bachelor of Laws."

LLCM *abbr* (*Brit*) = Licentiate of the London College of Music.

LLCM(TD) *abbr* (*Brit*) = Licentiate of the London College of Music (Teacher's Diploma).

LLD or **LL.D.** *abbr* (*Latin*) = *Legum Doctor*, "Doctor of Laws."

Llefelys *n* (*Welsh Celtic myth*) the son of Beli and brother of Lludd. He was the ruler of Gaul and helped his brother, who was ruler of Britain, to get rid of the three plagues.

Llefelys *n* (*Welsh Celtic myth*) the son of Beli and brother of Lludd. He was the ruler of Gaul and helped his brother, who was ruler of Britain, to get rid of the three plagues.

Lleu Llaw Gyffes *n* (*Welsh Celtic myth*) a warrior god who may have some form of association with the Irish god Lugh. His mother, Aranrhod, was annoyed when he was born because she was hoping to get a post as foot-holder at the court of Math Fab Mathonwy, a post that could be held only by a virgin.

LLG *abbr* = Labor Life Group; Landcare Liaison Group.

lli *abbr* = latitude and longitude indicator.

LLL *abbr* = Labor Left Liaison; low-level logic.

LL.L. *abbr* (*Latin*) = *Legum Licentiatus*, "Licentiate in Laws."

LLM or **LL.M.** *abbr* (*Latin*) = *Legum Magister*, "Master of Laws."

LLNL *abbr* = Lawrence Livermore National Laboratory.

LLNW *abbr* = low level nuclear waste.

Lloyd George *n* **David [1st Earl Lloyd George of Dwyfor]** (1863–1945) Welsh Liberal statesman; chancellor of the exchequer (1908–15); British Prime Minister (1916–22).

Lloyd *n* 1. **Clive Hubert** (1944–) Guyanian-born W est Indian cricketer. 2. **Harold [Clayton]** (1893–1971) American film comedian noted for his dangerous stunts.

L

3. **Marshall Burns** (1858–1927) American furniture manufacturer who invented a method of manufacturing bedsprings and mattresses, and patented a system for producing wicker products.

Lloyd's (of London) *n* a corporation that is involved in underwriting of insurance. Lloyd's does not itself perform any underwriting insurance business, its member brokers and insurers either acting individually or acting together on a consortium or syndicate basis.

Lloyd Webber *n* **Sir Andrew** (1948–) English composer . He composed several musicals, e.g., *Jesus Christ Superstar* (1970), with the librettist Tim Rice (1944–).

LLRW *abbr* = low level radioactive waste.

LLSPT *abbr* (*Brit*) = Licentiateship of the London School of Polymer Technology.

Lludd Llaw Ereint *n* (*Welsh Celtic myth*) the equivalent of Nuada. He was the father of Creiddylad, and it has been suggested that she was the inspiration for Cordelia, the daughter of King Lear in Shakepeare's play of the same name. *See* **Llyr**.

Lludd *n* (*Welsh Celtic myth*) the son of Beli and the brother of Llefelys. He ruled Britain while Llefelys ruled Gaul, and during that time three plagues beset Britain.

LLW *abbr* = low level waste.

Llwyd *n* (*Welsh Celtic myth*) the son of Cil Coed and the friend of Gwawl. To avenge Pwyll's treatment of Gwawl, Llwyd put a curse on the Dyfed and took Rhiannon and her son Pryderi prisoner.

Llyn Cerrig Bach *n* a lake on the island of Anglesey, Wales, that was sacred to the Celts. Metal votive gifts dating from between the second century BC and the first century AD have been recovered there.

Llyr *n* (*Welsh Celtic myth*) cognate with the Irish god Lir. He is thought to have been the original of Shakespeare's King Lear.

Llywelyn ap Gruffydd *n* (Llywelyn the Last) (*d.* 1282) Prince of Wales (*c.*1260–1282). The eldest son of Gruffydd, he styled himself "Prince of Wales" and received recognition from Henry III of England in 1267.

Llywelyn ap Iorwerth *n* (Llwelyn the Great) (*d.* 1240) king of Gwynedd (1202–1240). He reunited the formerly divided kingdom of Gwynedd in 1202 and came to dominate all other Welsh princes.

lm *abbr* = lumen.

l.m. *abbr* = long meter.

LM *abbr* = Licentiate in Medicine, or in Midwifery; Lord Mayor.

LMC *abbr* (*Brit*) = London Mennonite Centre.

LMCA *abbr* = Long-Term Medical Conditions Alliance; Lorry Mounted Crane Association.

LMD *abbr* = long meter double.

LME *abbr* (*Brit*) = London Metal Exchange.

LMN *abbr* = Live Music Now!

LMP *abbr* = last menstrual period.

LMPA *abbr* = Qualified Member of the Master Photographers Association.

LMRCP *abbr* = Licentiate in Midwifery of the Royal College of Physicians.

LMRTPI *abbr* = Legal Member of the Royal Town Planning Institute.

LMS *abbr* = Latin Mass Society; (*Brit*) London Medieval Society; (*Brit*) London Missionary Society; local management of schools.

LMSR *abbr* (*Brit*) = London, Midland and Scottish Railway.

LMSSA *abbr* = Licentiate in Medicine and Surgery of the Society of Apothecaries.

LMSSALond *abbr* (*Brit*) = Licentiate in Medicine, Surgery and Midwifery of the Society of Apothecaries of London.

LMT *abbr* = local mean time; length, mass, time.

LMusLCM *abbr* (*Brit*) = Licentiate in Music of the London College of Music.

LMusTCL *abbr* (*Brit*) = Licentiate in Music, Trinity College of Music, London.

LMX *abbr* (*Brit*) = London Market Excess of Loss (insurance).

ln *abbr* (*Latin*) = *logarithmus naturalis*, "natural logarithm."

LNCP *abbr* = Licentiate Member of the National Council of Psychotherapists.

LNER *abbr* (*Brit*) = London and North-Eastern Railway.

LNG *abbr* = liquefied natural gas.

LNHS *abbr* (*Brit*) = London Natural History Society.

LNLC *abbr* = Ladies' Naval Luncheon Club.

LNS *abbr* = land navigation system.

lo *interj* behold!, see!

LO *abbr* = liaison officer.

loa *abbr* = length overall.

LOA *abbr* = leave of absence.

loach *n* an edible freshwater fish.

load *n* an amount carried at one time; something borne with difficulty; a burden; (*often pl*) (*inf*) a great amount. * *vt* to put into or upon; to burden; to oppress; to supply in large quantities; to alter, as by adding a weight to dice or an adulterant to alcoholic drink; to put a charge of ammunition into (a firearm); to put film into (a camera); (*comput*) to install a program in memory. * *vi* to take on a load.—**loader** *n*.

loaded *adj* (*sl*) having plenty of money; drunk; under the influence of drugs.

loading *n* burden; weight; stress; an amount added to something.

loadstar *see* **lodestar**.

loadstone *see* **lodestone**.

loaf[1] *n* (*pl* **loaves**) a mass of bread of regular shape and standard weight; food shaped like this; (*sl*) the head.

loaf[2] *vi* to pass time in idleness.—**loafer** *n*.

loam *n* rich and fertile soil.

loamy *adj* (**loamier, loamiest**) consisting of or full of loam.—**loaminess** *n*.

loan *n* the act of lending; something lent, esp money. * *vti* to lend.—**loanable** *adj*.—**loaner** *n*.

loan account *n* an account that is opened by a bank for a customer who has taken out a bank loan rather than taking advantage of an overdraft facility.

loan capital *or* **debt capital** *n* money used in the financing of a company that has been borrowed from an external source for a set period of time and that is subject to payment of interest over the period of time for which the loan has been granted.

loan shark *n* (*inf*) a person who loans money illegally at exorbitant rates of interest.

LOAS *abbr* = Loyal Order of Ancient Shepherds.

loath *adj* unwilling.—*also* **loth**.—**loathly** *adv*.

loathe *vt* to dislike intensely; to detest.—**loather** *n*. —**loathing** *n*.

loathsome *adj* giving rise to loathing; detestable.—**loathsomeness** *n*.

loaves *see* **loaf**[1].

lob *vti* (**lobbing. lobbed**) to toss or hit (a ball) in a high curve. * *n* a high-arching throw or kick.

LOB *abbr* = Location of Offices Bureau.

Lobamba *n* town in Swaziland.

lobar *adj* of or relating to a lobe.

lobate *adj* having lobes; lobelike.

lobby *n* (*pl* **lobbies**) an entrance hall of a public building; a person or group that tries to influence legislators. * *vti* (**lobbying, lobbied**) to try to influence (legislators) to support a particular cause or take certain action.

lobbyist *n* someone employed to lobby.

lobe *n* a rounded projection, as the lower end of the ear; any of the divisions of the lungs or brain.

lobectomy *n* the removal of a lobe of an organ, e.g., lung or brain.

lobelia *n* a genus of garden plants, usu with blue flowers.

Lobito *n* a city in Angola.

loblolly *n* (*pl* **loblollies**) a type of American pine tree; (*naut*) gruel.

lobotomy *n* (pl **lobotomies**) surgical incision into the lobe of an organ; a leukotomy.

lobscouse *n* a sailor's dish of meat, vegetables, and ship's biscuit.

lobster *n* (*pl* **lobsters, lobster**) any of a family of edible sea crustaceans with four pairs of legs and a pair of large pincers.

lobster pot *n* a basket used to trap lobsters.

lobule *n* a small lobe.—**lobular, lobulate** *adj*.

loc *abbr* = lines of communication.

LOC *abbr* = Library of Congress.

local *adj* of or belonging to a particular place; serving the needs of a specific district; of or for a particular part of the body. * *n* an inhabitant of a specific place; (*Brit inf*) a pub serving a particular district.—**locally** *adv*.—**localness** *n*.

local anesthetic *n* an anesthetic that affects only a restricted area of the body.

local area network (often abbreviated to **LAN**) *n* (*comput*) a network of microcomputers connected together in a localized area such as an office building.

local bus *n* (*comput*) a high speed expansion slot that allows high speed transmission of information to travel between the computer processor and a peripheral device such as a monitor.

loc. cit. *abbr* (*Latin*) = *loco citato*, "in the place cited".

local color *n* a description of the features and inhabitants of a specific locality in writing.

loc. cur. *abbr* = local currency.

local drive *n* (*comput*) a built-in disk drive in a networked workstation, as opposed to the server drive or remote drive.

locale *n* a place or area, esp in regard to the position or scene of some event.

Local Group of galaxies *or* **Local Cluster of galaxies** *n* approximately 20 galaxies in the neighborhood of the Milky Way Galaxy, sufficiently close to be substantially influenced by each other's gravitational attraction.

localism *n* a word, idiom, or custom restricted to a particular locality; narrowness of outlook.

locality *n* (*pl* **localities**) a neighborhood or a district; a particular scene, position, or place; the fact or condition of having a location in space and time.

localize *vt* to limit, confine, or trace to a particular place.—**localization** *n*.

Local Supercluster *n* the cluster of clusters of galaxies (of which the Milky Way Galaxy is one) containing more than 50,000 galaxies all of which experience mutual gravitational attraction.

locate *vt* to determine or indicate the position of something; to set in or assign to a particular position.

location *n* a specific position or place; a locating or being located; a place outside a studio where a film is (partly) shot; (*comput*) an area in memory where a single item of data is stored.

locative *adj, n* (a grammatical case) indicating place.

loch *n* (*Scot*) a lake.

Loch *n* (*Irish Celtic myth*) the son of Mofebais. He was a champion warrior of Connacht who refused to fight Cuchulainn because he did not wish to fight a youth without a beard..

lochan (*Scot*) the Scottish term for a small, freshwater loch, similar to a cirque lake.

lochia *n* the material discharged through the vagina from the uterus after childbirth for a few weeks.

loci *see* **locus**.

LOCIG *abbr* = Limited Overs Cricket Information Group.

LOCIS *abbr* = Library of Congress Information System.

lock[1] *n* a fastening device on doors, etc, operated by a key or combination; part of a canal, dock, etc in which the level of the water can be changed by the operation of gates; the part of a gun by which the charge is fired; a controlling hold, as used in wrestling. * *vt* to fasten with a lock; to shut; to fit, link; to jam together so as to make immovable. * *vi* to become locked; to interlock.—**lockable** *adj*.

lock[2] *n* a curl of hair; a tuft of wool, etc.

lock[3] *vti* (*comput*) to protect a file being altered or changed either accidentally or deliberately.

lockage *n* a system of canal locks; the act of going through a lock; the fee paid for so doing.

Locke *n* 1. **John** (1632–1704) English empiricist philosopher whose theory of "natural law" was influential. 2. **Matthew** (*c*.1630–77) English composer who was employed by Charles II. His works include incidental music for Shadwell's *The Tempest*, several anthems and many pieces for the recorder.

locker *n* a small cupboard, chest, etc that can be locked, esp one for storing possessions in a public place.

locker room *n* room equipped with lockers for storing possessions in a public place.

locket *n* a small ornamental case, usu holding a lock of hair, photograph or other memento, hung from the neck.

lockjaw *n* tetanus.

lockout *n* the exclusion of employees from a workplace by an employer, as a means of coercion during an industrial dispute.

locksmith *n* a person who makes and repairs locks and keys.

lockstep *n* a way of marching in which each person stays as close as possible to the one in front; mindless routine.

lockup *n* a jail; a garage, or storage room.

loco[1] *adj* (*sl*) crazy.

loco[2] *n* (*mus*) (*Italian*) literally, "place." It is used in music to indicate that a passage is to be played at normal pitch, after a previous, contrary instruction, i.e., the music reverts to its original "place" on the stave.

locoism *n* a disease of livestock resulting in paralysis caused by poisoning by locoweed.

locomotion *n* motion, or the power of moving, from one place to another.

locomotive *n* an electric, steam, or diesel engine on wheels, designed to move a railway train. * *adj* of locomotion.

locomotor *adj* of or pertaining to locomotion; locomotive.

locomotor ataxia *n* a late symptom of syphilis that progressively destroys sensory nerves.—*also* **tabes dorsalis**.

loco price *n* a price quoted for goods that does not include loading or transport charges but is simply the price for them in the place where they are located.

locoweed *n* any of various perennial plants of North America that cause locoism in livestock.

loc. primo cit. *abbr* (*Latin*) = *loco primo citato*, "in the place first cited."

Locrinus (*Brit myth*) a son of Brutus and brother of Albanactus and Kamber. After his father died, he became the ruler of England and Albanactus became ruler of Scotland.

locular, loculate *adj* (*biol*) split into compartments.

loculus, locule *n* (*pl* **loculi, locules**) (*biol*) a small cavity or cell.

locum *n* (*inf*) a locum tenens.

locum tenens *n* (*pl* **locum tenentes**) a person who stands in for a professional colleague, esp for a doctor, chemist, or clergyman.

locus *n* (*pl* **loci**) a place; (*math*) the path of a point or curve, moving according to some specific rule; the aggregate of all possible positions of a moving or generating element; (*biol*) the region of a chromosome occupied by a particular gene.

locust *n* a type of large grasshopper often traveling in swarms and destroying crops; a type of hard-wooded leguminous tree.

locution *n* a word, phrase, or expression; an act or mode of speaking.

Lodan *n* (*Irish Celtic myth*) the son of Lir, the father of Sinend and the brother of Manannan mac Lir.

lode *n* an ore deposit.

lodestar *n* a star, usu the North Star, used to guide navigation.—*also* **loadstar**.

lodestone *n* a magnetic oxide of iron; a piece of this oxide, used as a magnet or a crude compass.—*also* **loadstone**.

lodge *n* a small house at the entrance to a park or stately home; a country house for seasonal leisure activities; a resort hotel or motel; the local chapter or hall of a fraternal society; a beaver's lair. * *vt* to house temporarily; to shoot, thrust, etc firmly (in); to bring before legal authorities; to confer upon. * *vi* to live in a place for a time; to live as a paying guest; to come to rest and stick firmly (in).

Lodge *n* **David** (1935–) English novelist and critic whose best-known novels are entertaining satires on academic life, *Changing Places* and *Small World*.

lodger *n* a person who lives in a rented room in another's home.

lodging *n* a temporary residence; (*pl*) accommodation rented in another's house.

lodgment, lodgement *n* the act of lodging; the state of being lodged; an accumulation of something deposited; (*mil*) a foothold in enemy territory.

Lódz *n* a city in Poland.

Loeffler *n* **Charles Martin** (1861–1935) Alsatian-born composer and violinist who settled in the USA. He is best known for the orchestral pieces *La Morte de Tintagiles*, *A Pagan Poem*, and *The Canticle of the Sun* (with voice).

loess *n* a light brown deposit of fine silt and clay found in Asia, Europe and America.—**loessial, loessal** *adj*,

Loewe *n* 1. **Frederick** (1904–88) Austrian-born composer who became an American citizen. In collaboration with the lyricist **Alan Jay Lerner**, he created many famous musicals including *Paint Your Wagon, My Fair Lady* (from Shaw's *Pygmalion* and *Camelot*.) He also wrote, with Lerner, the songs for the film *Gigi*. 2. **Johann Karl Gomried** (1796–1869) German composer, conductor, pianist, and singer who was the son of a noted musician of the same name. He wrote some 500 songs, five operas, 18 oratorios, and many other pieces.

Loewy *n* **Raymond** (1893–1986) French designer who settled in New York, in 1919.

LOFA *abbr* = Leisure and Outdoor Furniture Association.

L of C *abbr* = Library of Congress; line of communications.

Loffler *n* **Berthold** (1874–1960) Austrian designer, who founded Wiener Keramik with Michael Powolny, and also designed distinctive posters between 1910 and 1920.

LOFIT *abbr* (*Brit*) = London's Organised Fraud Investigation Team.

L of N *abbr* = League of Nations.

loft *n* a space under a roof; a storage area under the roof of a barn or stable; a gallery in a church or hall. * *vt* to send into a high curve.

Loft *abbr* = low-frequency radio telescope.

lofty *adj* (**loftier, loftiest**) (*objects*) of a great height, elevated; (*person*) noble, haughty, superior in manner.—**loftily** *adv*.—**loftiness** *n*.

log[1] *n* a section of a felled tree; a device for ascertaining the speed of a ship; a record of speed, progress, etc, esp one kept on a ship's voyage or aircraft's flight. * *vb* (**logging, logged**) *vt* to record in a log; to sail or fly (a specified distance). * *vi* (*with* **on, off**) (*comput*) to establish or disestablish communication with a mainframe computer from a remote terminal in a multi-user system.—**logger** *n*.

log[2] *n* a logarithm.

loganberry *n* (*pl* **loganberries**) a hybrid developed from the blackberry and the red raspberry.

logarithm *n* the exponent of the power to which a fixed number (the base) is to be raised to produce a given number, used to avoid multiplying and dividing when solving mathematical problems.—**logarithmic** *adj*.—**logarithmically** *adv*.

logbook *n* an official record of a ship's or aircraft's voyage or flight; an official document containing details of a vehicle's registration.

loge *n* a box in a theater.

loggerhead *n* (*arch*) a blockhead; (*pl*) a dispute, confrontation (*to be at loggerheads with someone*); (*zool*) a type of turtle.

loggia *n* (*pl* **loggias, loggie**) a covered open gallery or balcony on the side of a building.

logging *n* the business of cutting down timber.

loggorhea *n* excessive or incoherent talkativeness.

logic *n* correct reasoning, or the science of this; way of reasoning; what is expected by the working of cause and effect.—**logician** *n*.

logical *adj* conforming to the rules of logic; capable of reasoning according to logic.—**logically** *adv*.—**logicality** *n*.

logical drive *n* (*comput*) *see* **physical drive**.

logical operator *n* (*comput*) a special word (e.g., AND, OR, NOT) used in a programming statement that expands or limits a search.

logician *n* someone versed in logic.

logistics *n* (*used as sing*) the science of the organization, transport, and supply of military forces; the planning and organization of any complex activity.—**logistic** *adj*.—**logistically** *adv*.

log jam *n* a blockage of logs floating in a watercourse; a deadlock, standstill.

logo[1] *n* (*pl* **logos**) (*inf*) a logotype.

logo[2] *n* (*comput*) a high-level programming language that is commonly used in education to teach programming concepts.

logo- *prefix* word, speech.

log off *vi* (*comput*) to end a session working at a computer terminal or system.

logogram, logograph *n* a sign or letter representing a word or phrase.

logographer *n* an annalist or writer of speeches in ancient Greece.

logography *n* a method of printing in which a type represents a word instead of a letter.

logogriph *n* a word puzzle based on an anagram.

logomachy *n* (*pl* **logomachies**) a dispute over words.

log on *vi* (*comput*) to begin working at a computer terminal or system.

Logos *n* (*Christianity*) the Divine Word; the second person of the Trinity, Jesus Christ.

logotype *n* a printed symbol representing a corporation, product, etc; a trademark, emblem.

logrolling *n* the undemocratic trading of votes between politicians to ensure the passage of legislation of mutual interest.

-logue, -log *n suffix* indicating a particular type of speech or writing, as in monologue, travelogue.

logwood *n* a wood of a deep-red color, used in dyeing.

logy *adj* (**logier, logiest**) dull, sluggish.

-logy *n suffix* science, theory or doctrine of, e.g., *astrology*; type of writing or discourse, e.g., *phraseology*.

LOI *abbr* = Loyal Orange Institution.

loin *n* (*usu pl*) the lower part of the back between the hipbones and the ribs; the front part of the hindquarters of an animal used for food.

loincloth *n* a cloth worn around the loins.

loiter *vi* to linger or stand about aimlessly.—**loiterer** *n*.

Lola *abbr* = library on-line acquisition.

loll *vi* to lean or recline in a lazy manner, to lounge; (*tongue*) to hang loosely.—**loller** *n*.

lollapalooza, lollapaloosa *n* (*sl*) something or someone exceptional.

Lollard *n* (*hist*) a follower of the 14th-century English religious reformer, John Wycliff.

lollipop *n* a flat boiled sweet at the end of a stick.

lollop *vi* to run or walk with an ungainly, bouncing rhythm.

lolly *n* (*pl* **lollies**) (*inf*) a lollipop; (*Brit sl*) money.

Lomazzi *n* **Paolo** (1936–) Italian designer whose best-known work with Gionatan De Pas and Donato D'Urbino included the 1967 *Blow* clear plastic inflatable chair.

Lombard Street *n* the street in the City of London that is the center of the money market.

Lombardo *n* **Pietro** (*c*.1435–1515) Venetian sculptor, father of Tullio (*c*.1455–1532) and Antonio (*d*. 1516), with whom he ran a family workshop producing decorations and monuments for chapels in Venice, Padua, and Treviso.

Lomé *n* capital city of Togo.

loment *n* a plant pod that breaks at maturity into single-seeded joints.

lon. or **long.** *abbr* = longitude.

Lon. or **Lond.** *abbr* = London.

Londin. *abbr* (*Latin*) = *Londiniensis*, 'of London'.

London *n* capital city of United Kingdom of Great Britain and Northern Ireland (UK).

London *n* **Jack** (1876–1916) American novelist and short-story writer who led an adventurous early life before becoming a writer and whose best-known works are the dog stories *The Call of the Wild* and *White Fang*.

London Acceptance Credit *n* a method by which a UK exporter of goods can be supplied with immediate cash.

London Interbank Offered Rate (commonly abbreviated to **LIBOR**) *n* the rate of interest charged on interbank loans. It is the most important interest rate for international banks and is used as a yardstick for lending to bank customers.

London International Financial Futures and Options Exchange (**LIFFE**) *n* a futures market opened in London in 1982 and now based in the City of London.

London Pride *n* a type of saxifrage plant with pink flowers.

London Stock Exchange *n* the market in London that deals in securities.

lone *adj* by oneself; isolated; without companions, solitary.—**loneness** *n*.

lonely *adj* (**lonelier, loneliest**) isolated; unhappy at being alone; (*places*) remote, rarely visited.—**loneliness** *n*.

loner *n* a person who avoids the company of others.

lonesome *adj* having or causing a lonely feeling.—**lonesomely** *adv*.

long[1] *adj* measuring much in space or time; having a greater than usual length, quantity, etc; tedious, slow; far-reaching; well-supplied. * *adv* for a long time; from start to finish; at a remote time.

long[2] *vi* to desire earnestly, esp for something not likely to be attained.

long. *abbr* = longitude.

longanimity *n* long-suffering, forbearance.

longboat *n* the largest boat carried aboard a ship.

longbow *n* a large hand-drawn bow.

longcloth *n* a fine cotton fabric.

long-dated gilts *or* **longs** *npl* gilt-edged securities not redeemable for 15 years or more.

long-distance *adj* traveling or communicating over long distances.

long division *n* arithmetic division with the details of the calculations written down.

longe *see* **lunge**[2].

longeron *n* the principal longitudinal spar of an aircraft's fuselage.

longevity *n* long life.

Longfellow *n* **Henry Wadsworth** (1807–82) American poet, several of whose poems, e.g., "The Wreck of the Hesperus," "The Village Blacksmith," and "Excelsior!" were among the most popular poems of the 19th century and whose narrative poems on American legends and folk tales, e.g., *Evangeline* and *The Song of Hiawatha*, were also extremely popular.

long green *n* (*sl*) paper money.

long-hair *n* (*inf*) a highbrow; an artistically gifted person; a lover of the arts; a hippie. * *adj* (*inf*) of intellectuals or intellectual tastes (—*also* **long-haired**).

longhand *n* ordinary handwriting, as opposed to shorthand.

long-headed *adj* shrewd.

Longhena *n* **Baldassare** (*b*. 1597) Italian architect. His notable works include numerous palaces.

longhorn *n* a breed of long-horned cattle.

longhouse *n* a long low dwellinghouse built of stone and timber, introduced into Britain by the Norse invaders.

longicorn *n* a type of beetle with long antennae.

longing *n* an intense desire.—**longingly** *adv*.

longitude *n* distance east or west of the prime meridian, expressed in degrees or time.

longitudinal *adj* of or in length; running or placed lengthways; of longitude.—**longitudinally** *adv*.

longitudinal wave *n* (*physics*) the classification for a wave that is produced when the vibrations occur in the same direction as the direction of travel for that wave.

long johns *npl* (*inf*) warm underpants with long legs.

long jump *n* an athletic event consisting of a horizontal running jump.

long-lived *adj* having or tending to live a long time.

long-playing *adj* of or relating to an LP record.

long position *n* a situation in which the holdings of a dealer in securities, commodities, currencies, etc, exceed his or her sales, often because he or she is expecting prices to rise.

long-range *adj* reaching over a long distance or period of time.

longs *see* long-dated gilts.

longshore *adj* found on, or pertaining to, the shore.

longshore drift *n* the movement of sand and shingle along the shore by a current parallel to the shoreline.

longshoreman *n* (*pl* **longshoremen**) a person who loads and unloads ships at a port.

long shot *n* a wild guess; a competitor, etc who is unlikely to win; a project that has little chance of success.

long-sighted *adj* only seeing distant objects clearly.—**long-sightedly** *adv*.

long-standing *adj* having continued for a long time.

long-suffering *adj* enduring pain, provocation, etc patiently.

long suit *n* (*cards*) more than four of a suit in a hand; (*inf*) a quality or talent.

long-term *adj* of or extending over a long time.

long-term liability *n* a sum of money that is owed but does not have to be repaid within the next accounting period of a company.

long ton *n* a unit of weight equal to 2240 tons, the UK ton.

longueur *n* a tedious period of time.

long wave *n* a radio wave of a frequency less than 300 kHz.

longways, longwise *adv* in the direction of the length (of something), lengthways.

long-winded *adj* speaking or writing at great length; tiresome.—**long-windedly** *adv*.—**long-windedness** *n*.

Lonrho *abbr* (*Brit*) = London and Rhodesian Mining and Land Company Limited.

Lonsdale *n* **Dame Kathleen** (1903–71) Irish physicist, noted for innovative work in X-ray crystallography; the first woman member to be elected a fellow of the Royal Society (1945).

lontano *adj* (*mus*) (*Italian*) "distant."

loo *n* (*pl* **loos**) (*Brit inf*) a lavatory, a toilet.

looby *n* (*pl* **loobies**) a clumsy, stupid person.

loofah *n* the fibrous skeleton of a type of gourd used as a sponge for scrubbing.—*also* **luffa**.

look *vi* to try to see; to see; to search; to appear, seem; to be facing in a specified direction; (*with* **in**) to pay a brief visit; (*with* **up**) to improve in prospects. * *vt* to direct one's eyes on; to have an appearance befitting. * *n* the act of looking; a gaze, glance; appearance; aspect; (*with* **after**) to take care of; (*with* **over**) to examine; (*with* **up**) to research (for information, etc) in book; to visit.

look-alike *n* a person that looks like another.

looker *n* (*inf*) an attractive woman.

looker-on *n* (*pl* **lookers-on**) a spectator.

look-in *n* a brief visit.

looking glass *n* a mirror.

lookout *n* a place for keeping watch; a person assigned to watch.

look-see *n* (*inf*) a brief inspection.

look-up function *n* (*comput*) in programming, a procedure in which the program consults a pre-defined data list (**look-up table**) to obtain information or for comparison purposes.

loom[1] *n* a machine or frame for weaving yarn or thread. * *vt* to weave on a loom.

loom[2] *vi* to come into view indistinctly and often threateningly; to come ominously close, as an impending event.

loon[1] *n* a large fish-eating diving bird.

loon[2] *n* (*sl*) a clumsy or stupid person; a crazy person.

loony, looney *n* (*pl* **loonies**) (*sl*) a lunatic. * *adj* (**loonier, looniest**) (*sl*) crazy, demented.—**looniness** *n*.

loop *n* a figure made by a curved line crossing itself; a similar rounded shape in cord, rope, etc crossed on itself; anything forming this figure; (*comput*) a set of instructions in a program that are executed repeatedly; an intrauterine contraceptive device; a segment of film or magnetic tape. * *vt* to make a loop of; to fasten with a loop. * *vi* to form a loop or loops.

looper *n* a caterpillar that crawls by arching itself into loops.

loophole *n* a means of evading an obligation, etc; a slit in a wall for looking or shooting through.

loopy *adj* (**loopier, loopiest**) (*inf*) slightly mad, cracked.

Loos *n* **Adolph** (1870–1933) Moravian architect and influential theorist who argued against the excesses of **Jugendstil**.

loose *adj* free from confinement or restraint; not firmly fastened; not tight or compact; not precise; inexact; (*inf*) relaxed. * *vt* to release; to unfasten; to untie; to detach; (*bullet*) to discharge. * *vi* to become loose.—**loosely** *adv*.—**looseness** *n*.

loose cannon *n* a person who acts independently and often obstreperously.

loose-leaf *adj* having pages or sheets that can easily be replaced or removed.

loosen *vti* to make or become loose or looser.—**loosener** *n*.

loosestrife *n* a kind of plant with golden or purple flowers.

loot *n* goods taken during warfare, civil unrest, etc; (*sl*) money. * *vti* to plunder, pillage.—**looter** *n*.

lop *vt* (**lopping, lopped**) to sever the branches or twigs from a tree; to cut off or out as superfluous.

lope *vi* to move or run with a long bounding stride.—*also n.*—**loper** *n*.

lop-eared *adj* having drooping ears.

lophobranchiate *adj* (*fish*) with gills arranged in tufts.

lopsided *adj* having one side larger in weight, height, or size than the other; badly balanced.—**lopsidedly** *adv*.—**lopsidedness** *n*.

loq. *abbr* (*Latin*) = *loquitor*, "he/she speaks."

loquacious *adj* talkative.—**loquaciously** *adv*.—**loquacity** *n*.

loquat *n* an evergreen tree found in China and Japan; its edible fruit.

loquitur (*theater*) (*formerly*) he or she speaks (as a stage direction).

Lor. *abbr* = Lorenz, Lorenzo.

loran *n* a long-range navigation system in which pulses emitted by pairs of widely spaced radio transmitters are used by ships and aircraft to determine their geographical position.

Lorca *n* **Federigo Garcia** (1899–1936) Spanish poet and dramatist whose masterpiece is his trilogy of tragedies on the frustrated and oppressed life of Spanish women, *Blood Wedding*, *Yerma*, and *The House of Bernarda Alba*.

lord *n* a ruler, master, or monarch; a male member of the nobility; (*with cap and the*) God; a form of address used to certain peers, bishops, and judges.

lordling *n* a young or minor lord.

lordly *adj* (**lordlier, lordliest**) noble; haughty; arrogant.—**lordliness** *n*.

Lord Mayor *n* the mayor of the City of London and certain other UK boroughs and towns—*also* **Lord Provost** in Scotland.

lordosis *n* forward curvature of the spine.

Lord Privy Seal *n* a British cabinet minister without specific responsibilities.

Lord Provost *see* **Lord Mayor**.

Lord's Day *n* (*with the*) Sunday.

lordship *n* the rank or authority of a lord; rule, dominion; (*with **his** or **your***) a title used in speaking of or to a lord.

Lord's Prayer *n* (*with the*) the prayer taught by Jesus to His disciples beginning "Our Father."

lords spiritual *npl* the bishops and archbishops who are members of the British House of Lords.

Lord's Supper *n* (*Bible*) NT name for the Eucharist or Holy Communion, based on the last meal Jesus shared with his disciples before his death.

lords temporal *npl* the peers other than bishops and archbishops in the British House of Lords.

lore *n* knowledge; learning, esp of a traditional nature; a particular body of tradition.

Loren *n* **Sophia** [Sophia Scicoloni] (1934–) Italian actress. A strikingly beautiful woman, she starred in films as diverse as the comedy *The Millionairess* (1960) and the grim war drama *Two Women* (1961).

Lorenz *n* **Konrad** [Zacharias] (1903–89) Austrian ethologist and zoologist who shared the 1973 Nobel prize for physiology or medicine with Niko Tinbergen and Karl von Frisch for his work on animal behavior.

lorgnette *n* a long-handled opera glass; a pair of spectacles fixed to a long handle, into which they fold.

lorica *n* (*pl* **loricae**) the hard outer shell of certain animals.—**loricate, loricated** *adj*.

lorikeet *n* a small, brightly colored parrot.

loris *n* (*pl* **loris**) a small, nocturnal, climbing primate, found in South and South-East Asia.

lorn *adj* (*poet*) forsaken; forlorn.

Lorre *n* **Peter** [Laszlo Lowenstein] (1904–64) Hungarian stage and film actor whose films include *M* (1931), *Casablanca* (1942), *The Maltese Falcon* (1941), and *The Raven* (1963).

lorry *n* (*pl* **lorries**) (*esp Brit*) a large motor vehicle for transporting heavy loads.—*also* **truck**.

Lortzing *n* **Albert** (1801–51) German composer, singer and conductor, best known for his comic operas which he wrote to his own libretti, e.g., *Zar und Zimmermann*.

lory *n* (*pl* **lories**) a small parrot with brilliant plumage.

LOS *abbr* = line of sight; loss of signal.

Los Angeles *n* a city in the United States of America (USA).

lose *vb* (**losing, lost**) *vt* to have taken from one by death, accident, removal, etc; to be unable to find; to fail to keep, as one's temper; to fail to see, hear, or understand; to fail to have, get, etc; to fail to win; to cause the loss of; to wander from (one's way, etc); to squander. * *vi* to suffer (a) loss.—**losable** *adj*.—**loser** *n*.

losel *n* (*dial*) a worthless person.

loser *n* one who or that which loses; (*inf*) a person or thing that appears destined to fail; a person who takes loss (of a game) in a particular way; (*sl*) one who is found guilty of a crime a particular number of times.

Losey *n* **Joseph** (1909–84) American film director whose films include *The Go-Between* (1971). Blacklisted during the McCarthy era, he came to work in England.

losing *adj* that which loses or results in loss; (*business*) unprofitable; (*game*) played with little success; (*team*) in the process of being defeated. * *n* the action of losing; (*pl*) losses, esp at gambling.

loss *n* a losing or being lost; the damage, trouble caused by losing; the person, thing, or amount lost.

loss adjuster *n* a person who is appointed by an insurance company to investigate and produce a report on an insurance claim made by a policy holder.

loss leader *n* an item sold at a price below its value in order to attract customers.

lossy compression *n* (*comput*) an image compression technique that achieves very considerable compression and therefore much smaller files, but which on decompression and restoration back to the original does not restore the image 100%.—*see also* **JPEG**.

lost *adj* no longer possessed; missing; not won; destroyed or ruined; having wandered astray; wasted.

lost generation *n* a term coined by Gertrude Stein to describe the many expatriate American writers and artists in 1920s' Paris, including Hemingway.

lost wax process *n* a bronze-casting technique that uses as a mould a wax model that melts in the process.—*also* **cire perdue**.

lot *n* an object, such as a straw, slip of paper, etc drawn from others at random to reach a decision by chance; the decision thus arrived at; one's share by lot; fortune; a plot of ground; a group of persons or things; an item or set of items put up for auction; (*often pl*) (*inf*) a great amount; much; (*inf*) sort. * *vt* (**lotting, lotted**) to divide into lots.

Lot *n* (*Bible*) accompanied his uncle, Abraham, to Canaan, but there was insufficient land for their flocks; Lot chose the Jordan valley but had to flee the fire and brimstone that fell on Sodom and Gomorrah. *See also* **Sodom**.

lota, lotah *n* a brass or copper water pot.

loth *see* **loath**.

Lothario *n* (*pl* **Lotharios**) a libertine.

loti *n* the standard monetary unit of Lesotho, made up of 100 lisente.

lotion *n* a liquid for cosmetic or external medical use.

lottery *n* (*pl* **lotteries**) a system of raising money by selling numbered tickets that offer the chance of winning a prize; an enterprise, etc which may or may not succeed.

lotto *n* a game of chance based on the drawing of prize numbers.

Lotto *n* **Lorenzo** (*c*.1480–1556) Venetian painter. His best works are probably his portraits, which have a disturbing quality of intensity and unusual modes of color and composition, e.g., *Young Man in his Study* (*c*.1528).

lotus *n* a type of waterlily; (*Greek legend*) a plant whose fruit induced contented forgetfulness.

lotus position *n* an erect sitting position in yoga with the legs crossed close to the body.

lotus-eater *n* a person dedicated to a life of idle pleasure.

louche *adj* untrustworthy, shady.

loud *adj* characterized by or producing great noise; emphatic; (*inf*) obtrusive or flashy.—**loudly** *adv*.—**loudness** *n*.

louden *vi* to grow louder. * *vt* to make louder.

loudmouth *n* (*inf*) a person who boasts or talks offensively and excessively loudly.—**loudmouthed** *adj*.

loudspeaker *n* a device for converting electrical energy into sound.

lough *n* (*Irish*) a lake; an arm of the sea.

louis, louis d'or *n* (*pl* **louis, louis d'or**) (*formerly*) a French gold coin, with a value of 20 francs.

Louis *n* 1. **Joe** [Joseph Louis Barrow] (1914–81) US boxer nicknamed the "Brown Bomber." He was world heavyweight champion for 12 years. 2. **Morris** (1912–62) American painter. He pioneered techniques in color stain painting. His major works were series paintings, notably the *Veil* series and the *Unfurled* series. 3. **Victor** (b. 1731) French architect. His notable works include Bordeaux theater.

Louisiana (LA) *n* a state of the United States of America (USA) of which the capital is Baton Rouge.

Louis Philippe *see* **Daumier, Honoré**.

Louis IX *n* **Saint**, known as **Saint Louis** (1215–70) king of France (1226–70); he led a crusade to the Holy Land (1243); taken prisoner (1250); led another crusade (1270) but died at Tunis. His feast day is August 25.

Louis XIV *n* (1638–1715) king of France. Known as the "Sun King," he inherited the throne at the age of five and became absolute ruler in 1661, after which he declared "*L'état c'est moi*." He also pursued territorial claims throughout Europe, and established the French army as the most powerful in Europe. He was also a noted patron of the arts.

Louis XVI *n* (1754–93) king of France. While still dauphin, he married **Marie Antoinette** (1755–93) in 1770 and inherited the throne in 1774. Although inclined to reform and initially popular with the people, Louis was unable to prevent the revolutionaries dictating the course of events that led to himself and Marie being guillotined during the Revolution.

L

lounge *vi* to move, sit, lie, etc in a relaxed way; to spend time idly. * *n* a room with comfortable furniture for sitting, as a waiting room at an airport, etc; a comfortable sitting room in a hotel or private house.

lounger *n* a comfortable couch or chair for relaxing on; a person who lounges.

lour *vi* to look sullen; to become dark, gloomy, threatening.—*also* **lower**.—**louringly, loweringly** *adv.*

loure *n* (*mus*) a type of bagpipe played in northern France, esp Normandy.

louse *n* (*pl* **lice**) any of various small wingless insects that are parasitic on humans and animals; any similar but unrelated insects that are parasitic on plants; (*inf*) (*pl* **louses**) a mean, contemptible person.

lousy *adj* (**lousier, lousiest**) infested with lice; (*sl*) disgusting, of poor quality, or inferior; (*sl*) well supplied (with).—**lousily** *adv*,—**lousiness** *n.*

lout *n* a clumsy, rude person.—**loutish** *adj.*

louver, louvre *n* one of a set of slats in a door or window set parallel and slanted to admit air but not rain.—**louvered, louvred** *adj.*

lovable *adj* easy to love or feel affection for.—**lovability** *n.* —**lovably** *adv.*

lovage *n* a European herb used as a seasoning in food.

love *n* a strong liking for someone or something; a passionate affection for another person; the object of such affection; (*tennis*) a score of zero. * *vti* to feel love (for).

Love *n* the Magician *see* **Amor Brujo, El**.

love affair *n* a romantic or sexual relationship between two people.

lovebird *n* any of various small parrots.

love child *n* an illegitimate child.

love-in-a-mist *n* a flowering garden plant, fennelflower.

love knot *n* an intricate knot used as an emblem of love.

Lovelace *n* **Richard** (1618–*c*.1658) English Cavalier poet whose witty and graceful "To Althea" is perhaps the most loved of the Cavalier poems.

loveless *adj* without love; not feeling or receiving love.—**lovelessly** *adv.*

lovelock *n* a curl worn on the forehead.

lovelorn *adj* pining from love.

lovely *adj* (**lovelier, loveliest**) beautiful; (*inf*) highly enjoyable. * *n* (*pl* **lovelies**) a lovely person.—**loveliness** *n.*

lovemaking *n* sexual activity, esp intercourse, between lovers.

love nest *n* a place where lovers live or meet, esp illicitly.

lover *n* a person in love with another person; a person, esp a man, having an extramarital sexual relationship; (*pl*) a couple in love with each other; someone who loves a specific person or thing.

love seat *n* a chair or small sofa for two.

lovesick *adj* languishing through love.—**lovesickness** *n.*

lovey-dovey *adj* (*sl*) displaying affection in an excessive or exaggerated manner.

loving *adj* affectionate.—**lovingly** *adv.*—**lovingness** *n.*

loving cup *n* a large cup with two or more handles passed round a group for all to drink from.

low[1] *n* the sound a cow makes, a moo. * *vi* to make this sound.

low[2] *adj* not high or tall; below the normal level; less in size, degree, amount, etc than usual; deep in pitch; depressed in spirits; humble, of low rank; vulgar, coarse; not loud. * *adv* in or to a low degree, level, etc. * *n* a low level, degree, etc; a region of low barometric pressure.

lowborn, lowbred *adj* of humble birth.

lowboy *n* a table with drawers.

lowbrow *n* (*inf*) a person regarded as uncultivated and lacking in taste.—*also adj.*

low comedy *n* comedy reliant on farce or physical slapstick.

lowdown *n* (*sl: with* **the**) the true, pertinent facts.

low-down *adj* (*inf*) mean, contemptible.

Lowei, Otto *see* **Dale, Sir Henry Hallett**.

Lowell *n* 1. **Amy** (1874–1925) American poet and critic who became an enthusiastic member of the imagist school of poetry and whose volumes of poetry include *Sword Blades and Poppy Seed* and *Men, Women, and Ghosts*. 2. **James Russell** (1819–91) American poet, essayist, and diplomat whose best-known work, inspired by his fervent abolitionism, is contained in *The Biglow Papers*. 3. **Robert [Traill Spence]** (1917–77) American poet whose verse is intensely personal, notable volumes including his first, *Land of Unlikeness*, and *Life Studies*, and *Near the Ocean*.

lower[1] *adj* below in place, rank, etc; less in amount, degree, etc. * *vt* to let or put down; to reduce in height, amount, etc; to bring down in respect, etc. * *vi* to become lower.—**lowerable** *adj.*

lower[2] *see* **lour**.

lower case *n* small letters (not capitals) used for printing.

lower class *n* the class of people having the lowest status in society.

lower deck *n* the deck above the hold of a ship; (*inf*) the petty officers and men of a ship collectively.

lower house, lower chamber *n* one of the two chambers in a bicameral legislature, such as the US House of Representatives or the British House of Commons.

lowermost *adj* lowest.

lowest common denominator *n* the smallest integer that is a multiple of each of the denominators of a set of fractions (—*also* **least common denominator**); (*inf*) that which is acceptable to the greatest number of people.

lowest common multiple *n* the smallest number or amount that is a multiple of two or more numbers or amounts.— *also* **least common multiple**.

low frequency *n* a radio frequency between 300 and 30 kilohertz.

low-key, low-keyed *adj* of low intensity, subdued.

lowland *n* low-lying land; (*pl*) a flat region. * *adj* of or pertaining to lowlands.—**lowlander** *n.*

low-level language *n* (*comput*) a programming language that corresponds more to machine language than human language.

lowlife *n* (*pl* **lowlifes**) (*sl*) a criminal.

lowly *adj* (**lowlier, lowliest**) humble, of low status; meek.—**lowliness** *n.*

Low Mass *n* a Mass without music or elaborate ritual.

low profile *n* a position intended to attract the least attention.

low resolution *adj* (*comput*) screen or printer output that is of low quality, having few dots per inch.

low-rise *adj* (*building*) having only one or two storeys.—*also n.*

Lowry *n* 1. **L[aurence] S[tephen]** (1887–1976) English painter whose paintings have a distinctive naïve style. 2. **[Clarence] Malcolm** (1909–57) English novelist and poet whose novels, e.g., *Ultramarine* and *Under the Volcano*, often feature thinly veiled accounts of incidents from his own adventurous life.

low spirited *adj* unhappy, depressed.

low-tech *adj* of or involving low technology.

low technology *n* unsophisticated technology limited to the provision of basic human needs.

low tension *adj* using, conveying, or operating at a low voltage.

low tide *n* (the time of) the tide when it is at its lowest level; a low point.

low water *n* low tide.

low water mark *n* the level of low tide; the lowest or most degrading point.

lox[1] *n* a type of smoked salmon.

lox[2] *n* liquid oxygen.

loyal *adj* firm in allegiance to a person, cause, country, etc, faithful; demonstrating unswerving allegiance.—**loyally** *adv.*—**loyalty** *n.*

loyalist *n* a person who supports the established government, esp during a revolt.—**loyalism** *n.*

Loyola *n* **Saint Ignatius** (1491–1556) Spanish saint and founder of the Society of Jesus (the Jesuits) in 1534.

lozenge *n* a four-sided diamond-shaped figure; a cough drop, sweet, etc, originally diamond-shaped.

l.p. *abbr* = large paper, *or* post; long primer; low pressure.

LP *abbr* = Labour Party; Lady/Lord Provost; Liberal Party; (*Brit*) London Philharmonia; long playing (record); life policy; low pressure.

LPA *abbr* = Liberal Party of Australia; Loyalist Prisoners Aid.

LPG *abbr* = liquefied petroleum gas.

lpi *abbr* = lines per inch.

lpm *abbr* = lines per millimeter/minute.

LPM *abbr* = long particular meter.

LPS *abbr* = Lord Privy Seal.

LPU *abbr* = Low Pay Unit.

LQ *abbr* = letter quality.

lr. *abbr* = lira; lire.

Lr *symbol* (*chem*) lawrencium (element).

LR *abbr* = Land Registry; Lloyd's Register.

LRBM *abbr* = long range ballistic missile.

ls *abbr* = left side; lump sum.

l.s. *abbr* = land service; (*Latin*) locus sigilli, "place of the seal"; left side; letter signed.

LS *abbr* = Law Society; long shot; loudspeaker.

LSB *abbr* = least significant bit.

lsc *abbr* (*Latin*) = loco supra citato, "in the place cited above."

LSCS *abbr* = lower segment Caesarian section.

lsd *abbr* = least significant digit.

LSD *abbr* = (*Latin*) librae, solidi, denarii, "pounds, shillings, pence."

LSD *n* a powerful hallucinary drug (lysergic acid diethylamide).

LSE *abbr* (*Brit*) = London Stock Exchange.

LSG *abbr* = League of St George.

LSgt *abbr* = Lance Sergeant.

LSI *abbr* = Labor and Socialist International; large-scale integration.

LSO *abbr* (*Brit*) = London Symphony Orchestra.

l.s.s. *abbr* = life-saving (service) station.

LSS *abbr* = life support system.

lt *abbr* = local time.

l.t. *abbr* = long ton.

Lt *abbr* = lieutenant.

LT *abbr* = lira Turca (Turkish pound).

Lt. Col. *abbr* = Lieutenant Colonel.

Lt. Comdr. or **Lt.-Comm.** abbr = Lieutenant Commander.

Lt. Gen. abbr = Lieutenant General.

Lt. Gov. abbr = Lieutenant Governor.

Lt. Inf. abbr = Light Infantry.

LTA abbr = lighter than air.

Ltd or **ltd.** abbr = limited liability (used by private companies only).

Ltge. abbr = lighterage.

LTH abbr = luteotropic hormone.

LTM abbr = long-term memory.

ltng. arr. abbr = lightning arrester.

Ltr. abbr = lighter.

LtRN abbr = Lieutenant, Royal Navy.

LTUA abbr = Lawn Tennis Umpires Association.

LU symbol (chem) lutetium (element).

Luanda n capital city of Angola.

Luang Prabang n a city in Laos.

luau n a sumptuous feast in Hawaii; a warm welcome; an unexpected source of wealth; a bonanza.

Lubango n a city in Angola.

lubber n a clumsy person.

Lubetkin n **Berthold** (1901–95) Russian architect best-known for his enclosures at London zoo. His austere detailing was influential in the 1930s.

lubricant n a substance that lubricates.

lubricate vt to coat or treat (machinery, etc) with oil or grease to lessen friction; to make smooth, slippery, or greasy. * vi to act as a lubricant.—**lubrication** n.

lubricator n person who or thing that lubricates; a device used for oiling machines.

lubricious, lubricous n slippery, oily; lewd, lecherous.—**lubriciously** adv.

lubricity n slipperiness; evasiveness; lewdness.

Lubumbashi n a city in the Democratic Republic of the Congo (DRC).

lucarne n a dormer window, esp in a spire.

Lucci n **Roberto** (1942–) Italian designer of household and decorative goods.

lucent adj bright, shining.—**lucency** n.

lucerne see **alfalfa**.

Luchta or **Luchtaine** or **Luchtar** n (Irish Celtic myth) one of a triad of craft gods, Luchta being a wright or carpenter. With the other two, Goibhniu and Creidhne, he made and repaired the weapons of the Tuatha De Danann.

Lucian n **Saint** (c.240–311) Syrian theologian and priest; revised the text of the Greek version of the OT and that of the four Gospels; tortured by having his legs dislocated at the hip and being left to starve to death. His feast day is January 7.

Luciano n **Lucky** [**Charles Luciano**] (1897–1962) Italian-born American gangster and Mafia leader.

lucid adj easily understood; sane.—**lucidly** adv.—**lucidity** n.

Lucifer n Satan.

Lucina n (Roman myth) goddess of light, a title given to Diana as the goddess who presided over childbirth.

Lucino n **Ennio** (1934–) Italian pack aging designer.

luck n chance; good fortune.

luckless n unfortunate, unlucky.—**lucklessly** adv.—**lucklessness** n.

lucky adj (**luckier, luckiest**) having or bringing good luck.—**luckily** adv.—**luckiness** n .

lucrative adj producing wealth or profit; profitable.—**lucratively** adv.—**lucrativeness** n.

lucre n (derog) riches, money.

Lucretia n (Roman myth) the wife of Tarquinius Collatinis, who initiated a revolution by which the dynasty of Tarquins was expelled and a republic formed.

lucubrate vi to study, esp by night.—**lucubrator** n.

lucubration n study, esp nocturnal; (often pl) a literary composition produced as the result of protracted study.

Lucy n **Saint** (d.c.304) Sicilian virgin martyr; a suitor betrayed her as a Christian; condemned to death by having a sword thrust down her throat. Her feast day is December 13.

Ludeca n king of Mercia. Reigned in 827. An ealdorman who succeeded Beornwulf, he reigned briefly before being killed in battle along with five of his earls.

Lüderitz n a city in Namibia.

ludicrous adj absurd, laughable.—**ludicrously** adv.

luff n (naut) the part of ship towards the wind. * vti (naut) to turn (a ship) into the wind.

luffa see **loofah**.

Luftwaffe n the German Air Force.

lug¹ vt (**lugging, lugged**) to pull or drag along with effort.

lug² n an ear-like projection by which a thing is held or supported.

Lugansk n a city in Ukraine.

luge n a small one-person toboggan.

luggable adj (comput, inf) a personal computer that is too big to be described as portable but is small enough to be transported easily from place to place.

luggage n the suitcases and other baggage containing the possessions of a traveler.

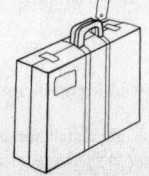

lugger n a small vessel rigged with one or more lugsails.

Lugh n (Irish Celtic myth) one of the more important of the Celtic gods. He was associated with light and the sun, and was also the god of arts and crafts. He is cognate with the British and Gaulish god Lugus and the Welsh god Lludd.

Lughnasadh n the Celtic harvest festival held on 1 August and was the Celtic festival. It was so called because it was the feast of the god Lugh. Later it became the Christian festival of Lammas. The other three major festivals were Samhain, Imbolc and Beltane.

lugsail n a square sail, with no boom or lower yard, which hangs nearly at right angles to the mast.

lugubrious adj mournful, dismal.—**lugubriously** adv.

Lugus n (Brit and Gaulish Celtic myth) a god who gave his name to Lyons and Leiden. He is cognate with the Irish god Lugh and the Welsh Lludd and is associated with the Roman god Mercury.

lugworm n a marine worm used as bait.

Lukács n **Georg** or **György** (1885–1971) Hungarian philosopher who wrote works on literary criticism and Marxist politics.

Luke n **Saint** (1st century) Greek evangelist; author of the third Gospel; a disciple of St Paul; in the Acts of the Apostles, Luke follows the sequence of events after Jesus' Ascension. His feast day is October 18. **Luke** n the Gospel of (Bible) set out like a history, to inform other non-jews of the words and events on which the Christian faith is based, and to commend that faith to the authorities of the Roman Empire.

lukewarm adj barely warm, tepid; lacking enthusiasm.

Luks n **George Benjamin** (1867–1933) American painter and graphic artist; a member of The Eight. His style is flamboyant and vigorous, and his subject matter is concerned with social and urban realism.

Lulach n (1032–1058) king of Scots (1057–1058). Installed as king on the death of Macbeth, his stepfather. Killed by Malcolm III at Strathbogie.

lull vt to soothe, to calm; to calm the suspicions of, esp by deception. * n a short period of calm.

lullaby n (pl **lullabies**) a song to lull children to sleep.

Lully n **Jean-Baptiste** (originally Giambattista Lulli) (1632–87) French composer of Italian origin who worked in the court of Louis XIV. He composed many comedy-ballets (e.g., Le Marriage Forcé, Le Sicilien), in which he acted and danced himself.

lulu n (inf) a wonderful or remarkable person or thing.

LUM abbr = lunar excursion model.

lumbago n rheumatic pain in the lower back.

lumbar adj of or in the loins.

lumbar puncture n the procedure wherein a hollow needle is inserted into the spinal canal in the lumbar region to obtain a sample of cerebrospinal fluid.

lumbar vertebrae n the five vertebrae between the sacrum and the thoracic vertebrae at the lowest part of the back.

lumber¹ n timber, logs, beams, boards, etc, roughly cut and prepared for use; articles of unused household furniture that are stored away; any useless articles. * vi to cut down timber and saw it into lumber. * vt to clutter with lumber; to heap in disorder.

lumber² vi to move heavily or clumsily.—**lumberer** n.

lumbering¹ adj moving clumsily and heavily.—**lumberingly** adv.

lumbering² n the cutting down and sawing of trees into timber as a business.

lumberjack n a person employed to fell trees and transport, and prepare timber.

lumbrical adj wormlike.

lumen n (pl **lumina, lumens**) the SI unit of light flux; (anat) a duct within a tubular organ.

Lumière n **Auguste Marie Louis Nicolas** (1862–1954) and **Louis Jean Lumière** (1864–1948) French chemists and cinematographers who invented the cine camera and projector and a color photography process.

luminary n (pl **luminaries**) a body that gives off light, such as the sun; a famous or notable person.

luminescent adj emitting light but not heat.—**luminescence** n.

luminosity n (pl **luminosities**) the quality of being luminous; something luminous; (astron) the degree of light emitted by a star when compared with the sun.

luminous adj emitting light; glowing in the dark; clear, easily understood.—**luminously** adv.

lump n a small, compact mass of something, usu without definite shape; an abnormal swelling; a dull or stupid person. * adj in a lump or lumps. * vt to treat or deal with in a mass. * vi to become lumpy.

lumpectomy n the surgical removal of a tumor with the tissue immediately around it but leaving intact the bulk of the tissue and the lymph nodes.

lumper n a docker.

L

lumpfish *n* (*pl* **lumpfish, lumpfishes**) a sea fish found in the North Atlantic, with horny spines and a sucker with which it clings to objects.

lumpish *adj* like a lump; heavy; dull, stupid.

lump sum *n* a sum of money (esp cash) paid as a whole and not in installments.

lumpy *adj* (**lumpier, lumpiest**) filled or covered with lumps.—**lumpily** *adv*.—**lumpiness** *n*.

Lumumba *n*Patrice (1925–61) Congolese statesman. First prime minister of the former Belgian Congo in 1960.

Luna *n* (*Roman myth*) the goddess of the moon, equivalent of the Greek Selene.

lunacy *n* (*pl* **lunacies**) insanity; utter folly.

lunar *adj* of or like the moon.

lunar day *n* 24 hours 50 minutes, is the time taken by the Moon to make two successive crossings of the same meridian on Earth.

lunar eclipse *n* an eclipse when the earth passes between the sun and the moon.

lunar month *n* a month measured by the complete revolution of the moon, 29.5 days.

lunar phases *n* phases of the Moon, as seen from Earth when the Sun illuminates different amounts of the Moon's surface.

lunar year *n* a year of twelve lunar months, 354.33 days.

lunate, lunated *adj* crescent-shaped.

lunatic *adj* insane; utterly foolish. * *n* an insane person.

lunatic fringe *n* the members of an organization regarded as being fanatical or extreme.

lunation *n* a lunar month, the time taken for the moon to revolve once around the earth.

Lunation *adj* relating to a Bronze Age culture which can be recognized by *c.*1500 BC in Poland, the Czech Republic, and eastern Germany.

lunch *n* a light meal, esp between breakfast and dinner; **out to lunch** (*sl*) crazy; eccentric. * *vi* to eat lunch.—**luncher** *n*.

luncheon *n* lunch, esp a formal lunch.

luncheonette *n* a small restaurant serving light lunches.

luncheon meat *n* processed meat in tins ready to eat.

lunchroom *n* a luncheonette; a room in an office, etc, where lunches can be brought from home and eaten.

Lundin *n* Ingeborg (1921–) Swedish glassware designer who worked at Or refors Glasbruk, from 1947 to 1971.

lune *n* (*geom*) a figure formed on a plane or sphere by two intersecting arcs of circles.

Luned *n* (*Welsh Celtic myth*) a girl who rescued Owain from prison and who gave him a ring to make him invisible. Later, Owain saved her life when she was about to be burnt alive.

lunette *n* anything shaped like a crescent; an arched opening in a vaulted roof to admit light.

lung *n* either of the two sponge-like breathing organs in the chest of vertebrates.

lunga pausa *n* (*mus*) (*Italian*) a "long pause."

lunge[1] *n* a sudden forceful thrust, as with a sword; a sudden plunge forward. * *vti* to move, or cause to move, with a lunge.—**lunger** *n*.

lunge[2] *n* a long halter for training a horse; the use of this in training horses. * *vt* to train with a lunge.—*also* **longe**.

lungfish *n* (*pl* **lungfish, lungfishes**) a freshwater fish with lungs as well as gills.

lungi *n* a long piece of cloth worn as a skirt or loincloth by Indian men.

lungwort *n* a Eurasian plant with dark-colored leaves spotted with white.

lunisolar *adj* pertaining to the sun and moon; produced by the sun and moon in unison.

lunula, lunule *n* (*pl* **lunulae, lunules**) the white crescent-shaped part near the root of the fingernail.

lupine[1] *n* a garden plant of the pea family.

lupine[2] *adj* of or resembling a wolf.

Lupu *n* Radu (1945–) a Romanian pianist, cur rently living in Britain, who has a worldwide reputation as a virtuoso performer.

lupulin *n* a powder, obtained from hops, used as a sedative.

lupus *n* any of several diseases marked by lesions of the skin.

lur *n* (*mus*) a primitive Scandinavian bronze instrument, similar to a bugle. Lurs came in pairs and resembled the horns of a ram.

Lurçat *n* 1. **André** (1894–1970) French architect noted for his furniture designs. 2. **Jean** (1892–1966) French painter who often decorated the buildings of his brother, **André Lurçat**. He also designed tapestries that were produced by his mother.

lurch *vi* to lean or pitch suddenly to the side. * *n* a sudden roll to one side.—**lurchingly** *adv*.

lurdan *adj* (*arch*) stupid. * *n* a stupid person.

lure *n* something that attracts, tempts, or entices; a brightly colored fishing bait; a device used to recall a trained hawk; a decoy for wild animals. * *vt* to entice, attract, or tempt.—**luringly** *adv*.

lurid *adj* vivid, glaring, shocking; sensational.—**luridly** *adv*.—**luridness** *n*.

Lurie *n* Alison (1926–) American novelist and P ulitzer prizewinner for *Foreign Affairs* (1984).

lurk[1] *vi* to lie hidden in wait; to loiter furtively.—**lurker** *n*.

lurk[2] *n* (*archeo*) a bronze horn in a bent s-shape of late Bronze Age date.

LURS (*Brit*) *abbr* = London Underground Railway Society.

Lusaka *n* capital city of Zambia.

luscious *adj* delicious; richly sweet; delighting any of the senses.—**lusciously** *adv*.—**lusciousness** *n*.

lush[1] *adj* tender and juicy; of or showing abundant growth.—**lushly** *adv*.—**lushness** *n*.

lush[2] *n* (*sl*) an alcoholic.

lusingando *adv* (*mus*) (*Italian*) literally, "flattering," i.e., in a cajoling manner.

lust *n* strong sexual desire (for); an intense longing for something. * *vi* to feel lust.—**lustful** *adj*.—**lustfully** *adv*.

luster, lustre *n* gloss; sheen; brightness; radiance; brilliant beauty or fame; glory; a chandelier with pendants of cut glass; a fabric with a lustrous surface; a substance used to give luster to an object; a metallic glaze on pottery; the quality and intensity of light reflected from the surface of minerals.—**lusterless** *adj*.—**lustrous** *adj*.

lusterware, lustreware *n* earthenware decorated with luster.

lustral *adj* of or relating to ceremonial purification; of or relating to a lustrum.

lustrate *vt* to purify by sacrifice or ceremonial washing.—**lustration** *n*.

lustrum *n* (*pl* **lustrums, lustra**) a period of five years.

lusty *adj* (**lustier, lustiest**) strong; vigorous; healthy.—**lustily** *adv*.—**lustiness** *n*.

lute[1] *n* an old, round-backed stringed musical instrument plucked with the fingers.

lute[2] *n* clay or cement used to make joints airtight, etc.

lutenist, lutist *n* a lute player.

luteous *adj* greenish-yellow.

lutetium *n* a metallic element.

Luther *n* Martin (1483–1546) German Christian reformer. He proclaimed justification by faith and a break with Rome. The Lutheran Reformation, aided by reformers such as **Philipp Melanchthon** (1497–1560) spread rapidly throughout Germany.

Lutheran *adj* pertaining to Martin Luther 1483–1546), the German religious reformer, or to the Lutheran Church and its doctrines. * *n* a follower of Martin Luther; a member of the Lutheran Church.—**Lutheranism** *n*.

Lutheran Church *n* the Protestant church founded by Martin Luther in Germany in the 16th century.

Luthersson *n* Petur B (1936–) Iceland's most important furniture designer .

Luthuli, Lutuli *n* Chief Albert John (1898–1967) South African nationalist; president of the African National Congress (1952–60); awarded the 1961 Nobel peace prize for his advocacy of nonviolent resistance to apartheid.

lutienizing hormone *see* **progesterone**.

Lutoslawski *n* Witold (1913–94) a Polish composer who is renowned for his avante-garde pieces, e.g., *Funeral Music for Strings*.

Lutyens *n* Sir Edwin Landseer (1869–1944) English architect, most noted for his monumental buildings in New Delhi, India and the Roman Catholic Cathedral in Liverpool, England.

LUV *abbr* = Land Use Volunteer Service.

lux *n* (*pl* **lux**) a unit of illumination.

luxate *vt* to put out of joint.—**luxation** *n*.

Luxembourg City *n* capital city of the Grand Duchy of Luxembourg.

Luxembourg, Grand Duchy of *n* a constitutional monarchy, which is entirely landlocked, bounded by France in the south, Belgium in the west and Germany in the east.

Luxembourg Franc *n* currency of the Grand Duchy of Luxembourg.

Luxemburg *n* Rosa (1871–1919) Polish-born German revolutionary and socialist theorist. With **Karl Liebknecht** (1871–1919) she founded the Spartacus League in Berlin in 1914 and later the German Communist Party.

Luxor *n* a site in Upper Egypt, on the east bank of the Nile, immediately south of, and often equated with, Thebes.

luxuriant *adj* profuse, abundant; ornate; fertile.—**luxuriance** *n*.

luxuriate *vi* to enjoy immensely, to revel (in).—**luxuriation** *n*.

luxurious *adj* constituting luxury; indulging in luxury; rich, comfortable.—**luxuriously** *adv*.—**luxuriousness** *n*.

luxury *n* (*pl* **luxuries**) indulgence and pleasure in sumptuous and expensive food, accommodation, clothes, etc; (*often pl*) something that is costly and enjoyable but not indispensable. * *adj* relating to or supplying luxury.

lv *abbr* = low voltage.

lv. *abbr* = leave; legal volt; livres; licensed victualer.

LV *abbr* = left ventricle; luncheon voucher.

LVA *abbr* = Licensed Victualers' Association.

LVECC *abbr* = Light Vehicles Energy Consumption Committee.

LVS *abbr* = Licentiate in Veterinary Science.

LW *abbr* = lightweight; long wave (radio wavelength of over 1000m/3300 ft); low water.

LWA *abbr* (*Brit*) = London Weighting Allowance; London Welsh Association.

lwb *abbr* = long wheel base.

LWC *abbr* (*Brit*) = London Women's Centre.

lwei *n* a monetary unit of Angola, equal to one hundredth of a kwanza.

LWL *abbr* = length at waterline; load waterline.

LWM *abbr* = low-water mark.

LWP *abbr* = load water plane.

LWR *abbr* = light-water reactor.

LWT *abbr* (*Brit*) = London Weekend Television; London Wildlife Trust.

lx *abbr* (*phys*) = lux.

LX *abbr* = electrical; electrics; technical staff working on sound and lighting.

lxxx *abbr* = love and kisses (prior to signature on a letter).

-ly *adj suffix* (*from nouns*) having the qualities of, like, as *princely*; recurring at intervals, as *weekly*. * *adv suffix* (*from adjectives*) in a specified manner, as *quietly*: to a specified degree, as *wholly*; at a specified time interval, as *hourly*; from a specific point of view, as *personally*; in a serial position, as *firstly*.

lycanthrope *n* a werewolf; (*med*) a sufferer from lycanthropy.

lycanthropy *n* the supposed power of changing from a human being into a werewolf; (*med*) a form of mental illness in which the sufferer believes himself or herself to be a wolf.

Lycaon *n* (*Greek myth*) a king of Arcadia, the father of a large number of sons, either 50 or 22.

lycée *n* (*pl* lycées) a state secondary school in France.

lyceum *n* a public lecture hall.

lych gate *see* **lich gate**.

lychee *see* **litchi**.

lychnis *n* a genus of flowering plants, including the ragged robin and campion.

Lycia *n* an ancient maritime province in the south of Asia Minor, bounded by Caria on the west, Pamphylia on the east, and Pisidia and Phrygia on the north.—**Lycian** *adj*.

lycopod *n* a kind of moss, also known as the club moss.

lycopodium *n* any of a genus of perennial plants, the club mosses; an inflammable yellow powder in the spore cases of certain species, used in fireworks.

Lycra *n* (*trademark*) an elastic synthetic material used for tight-fitting garments, such as bicycle shorts and swimwear.

Lycurgus *n* (*Greek myth*) a king of the Edonians of Thrace, punished by the gods for driving out Dionysus.

Lydda *n* (*Bible*) town in the plain of Sharon where Peter healed a paralyzed man named Aeneas; by tradition it is also the place where St George slew the dragon.

lyddite *n* a powerful explosive, composed chiefly of picric acid.

Lydia[1] *n* (*Bible*) the first known Christian convert in Europe; Lydia listened to Paul and was baptized, along with her household.

Lydia[2] *n* an ancient and powerful kingdom of Asia Minor, which extended eastward from the Aegean and comprised Paphlagonia (Black Sea littoral), Bithynia, Mysia (at the Hellespont), Lydia Proper, Lycia, Phrygia, and part of Cappadocia. Sardis was the capital.—**Lydian** *adj*.

Lydian mode *n* (*mus*) a scale used in ancient Greek music, the equivalent of the white notes on a piano from C to C; from the Middle Ages onwards, the equivalent of a scale on the white notes on a piano from F to F.

lye *n* an alkaline solution.

lying *see* **lie**[1], **lie**[2].

lying-in *n* (*pl* lyings-in, lying-ins) childbirth.

Lyly *n* John (*c*.1554–1606) English dramatist and prose romance writer whose works were highly popular in Elizabethan times and had some influence on the development of the English novel.

Lyman series *n* a set of spectral lines of specific wavelengths absorbed or given off by hydrogen gas when excited; it lies in the ultraviolet.

Lyme disease *n* an infectious disease, carried by ticks, that produces fever, pains in the joints and a rash, and can result in paralysis or chronic fatigue, and, rarely, death.

lymph *n* a clear, yellowish body fluid, found in intercellular spaces and the lymphatic vessels.

lymphadenectomy *n* removal of lymph nodes, e.g., when a node has become cancerous.

lymphadenitis *n* inflammation of the lymph nodes, which become enlarged, hard, and tender.

lymphangiography *n* the technique of injecting a radio-opaque substance into the lymphatic system to render it visible on an X-ray.

lymphatic *adj* of, relating to, or containing lymph; sluggish. * *n* a vessel that contains or conveys lymph.

lymphatic system, lymphatics *n* the network of vessels that carry lymph from the tissues to the bloodstream and help maintain the internal fluid environment of the body.

lymphedema *n* the build-up of lymph in soft tissues, causing swelling. It may be the result of obstruction of the vessels by parasites, tumor, or inflammation.

lymph node *n* any of numerous nodules of tissue distributed along the course of lymphatic vessels that produce lymphocytes.

lympho- *prefix* lymph; lymph tissue; lymphatic system.

lymphocyte *n* a white blood cell formed in the lymph nodes, which helps to protect against infection.—**lymphocytic** *adj*.

lymphocytosis *n* a condition where the blood contains an increased number of lymphocytes, as during lymphocytic leukaemia.

lymphography *see* **lymphangiography**.

lymphoid *adj* relating to lymph glands; resembling lymph.

lymphoid tissue *n* tissues that are involved in the formation of lymph, such as the spleen, thymus, and lymph nodes.

lymphoma *n* (*pl* lymphomata) a tumor of the lymphoid tissue.

lymphosarcoma *n* a tumor of the lymphatic system resulting in enlargement of the glands, spleen, and liver.

lyncean *adj* pertaining to or resembling the lynx; sharp-eyed.

Lynceus *n* (*Greek myth*) husband of Hypermnestra, daughter of Danaus, who alone among her sisters, spared her husband's life.

lynch *vt* to murder (an accused person) by mob action, without lawful trial, as by hanging.—**lyncher** *n*. — **lynching** *n*.

lynchet *n* (*archeo*) a naturally occurring buildup of earth on the downward edge of an ancient sloping field, caused by plowing.

lynch law *n* trial and punishment of a person without due process of law, as by a mob.

lynx *n* (*pl* lynxes, lynx) a wild feline of Europe and North America with spotted fur.

lynx-eyed *adj* keen-sighted.

Lyon *n* a city in France.

lyonnaise *adj* (*cooking*) with onions.

Lyonesse *n* (*Brit Celtic myth*) said to have been a land off the south coast of Cornwall, famous for housing the remnants of the court of Arthur after the death of the king. The sea is said to have rushed over the land to prevent people following his knights.

Lyot *n* inventor of the coronagraph, an instrument for producing an artificial eclipse of the Sun, enabling study of the corona.

Lyra *n* The Lyre, a constellation, the lyre being that used by Orpheus.

lyrate, lyrated *adj* lyre-shaped.

lyre *n* an ancient musical instrument of the harp family.

lyrebird *n* an Australian bird with a tail shaped like a lyre.

lyric *adj* denoting or of poetry expressing the writer's emotion; of, or having a high voice with a light, flexible quality. * *n* a lyric poem; (*pl*) the words of a popular song.

lyrical *adj* lyric; (*inf*) expressing rapture or enthusiasm.—**lyrically** *adv*.

lyricism *n* lyrical quality or expression.

lyricist *n* a person who writes lyrics, esp for popular songs.

Lyrids *n* a meteor shower which appears to radiate from a point in the constellation Lyra, first recorded by Chinese astronomers in 687 BC.

lyrist *n* a lyric poet; a lyre player.

Lysanias *n* (*Bible*) the name of the ruler said to have been tetrarch (governor) of Abilene in the time of Jesus. *See also* **Abilene**.

Lysenko *n* **Trofim Denisovich** (1898–1976) Russian geneticist and agronomist. His doctrinal approach to genetics did severe damage to the development of Soviet biology and agronomy. His influence gradually waned after Stalin's death.

lysergic acid *see* **LSD**.

lysin *n* a substance, esp an antibody, that kills living cells or bacteria.

lysine *n* an amino acid formed by the digestion of dietary protein.

lysis *n* (*pl* lyses) (*biol*) the process of destroying cells with a lysin; (*med*) the gradual abatement of an acute disease.

-lysis *n suffix* disintegration; decomposition.

Lysithea *n* a small satellite of Jupiter.

Lysol *n* (*trademark*) a solution of phenol compounds in water, used as an antiseptic and disinfectant.

lysozyme *n* (*biochemistry*) an enzyme that is present in tears and nasal secretions and on the skin and has an antibacterial action.

Lystra *n* (*Bible*) Roman colony in Asia Minor visited by Paul and Barnabas on their first missionary journey.

-lyte *n suffix* denoting a substance able to be disintegrated or decomposed.

-lytic *adj suffix* indicating a disintegration or decomposition.

L

M

m, M the thirteenth letter of the English alphabet.

M *n* (*astron*) a short-hand way of referring to a celestial object listed in the Messier Catalog of 1774, often given alongside the numbers in the New General Catalog (NGC).

m (me) *symbol* (*mus*) in tonic sol-fa, the third note (or mediant) of the major scale.

m, m. *abbr* = (*cricket*) maiden over; male; (*Latin*) *manipulus* "handful"; manual; mare; (*currency*) mark or marks; (*ordn*) mark; married; martyr; masculine; mass; measure; medicine; medium; member; meridian; *meridies* (*Latin*) "noon"; meter(s); middle; mile(s); militia; mill; *mille* (*French*) "thousand"; milli- (thousandth); million(s); minim (liquid measure); minute; (*Latin*) *misce* "mix"; (*Latin*) *mistura* "mixture"; modulus; (*dentistry*) molar; month; moon; morning; mountain; (*anat*) muscle; muster; myopia.

M *abbr* = 1000 in Roman numerals; Master; mega- (million); Messier's catalog of nebulas; moment; Monday; (*magnetism*) strength of pole; Manitoba; March; (*chem*) *in formulas*, metal; Monsieur (*French*) "Mr"; Member; motorway; medium (garment size); metronome (with pulse value).

m- *abbr* (*chem*) = meta-.

3M *abbr* = Minnesota Mining and Manufacturing Company.

ma *n* (*inf*) mother.

Ma *symbol* (*chem*) masurium.

ma. *abbr* (*mus*) = major.

m/a *abbr* (*bookkeeping*) = my account.

mA. *abbr* = milliangstrom.

Ma. *abbr* = milliampere.

MA *abbr* = *Magister Artium* (*Latin*) "Master of Arts"; Massachusetts; Mathematical Association; menstrual age; mental age; Mountain Artillery.

MAA *abbr* = Manufacturers Agents Association of Great Britain and Ireland; Master at Arms; Money Advice Association; Motor Agents' Association.

MAAC *abbr* = Mastic Asphalt Advisory Council.

ma'am *n* madam (used as a title of respect, esp when addressing royalty).

MA(Architectural Studies) *abbr* = Master of Arts (Architectural Studies).

Maastricht Treaty *n* an agreement between the member countries of the European Union, signed in 1991, with the aim of providing closer unification of the economic and political systems of the member countries.

Maat *n* the Egyptian goddess of truth.

MAAT *abbr* = Member of the Association of Accounting Technicians.

MAB *abbr* = Memorial Advisory Bureau; monoclonal antibody.

MABAC *abbr* = Member of the Association of Business and Administrative Computing.

MABE *abbr* = Member of the Association of Business Executives.

MABIC *abbr* = Movement Against Bats in Churches.

Mabinogion *n* one of the most important source texts of Welsh Celtic myths. It is based on two earlier manuscripts, *The White Book of Rhydderch* (1300–25) and *The Red Book of Hergest* (1375–1425).

Mabon *n* (*Welsh Celtic myth*) the son of Modron. Abducted from his mother when he was three days old and incarcerated at Caer Loyw, which in the legend was synonymous with the Otherworld. Culhwch rescued him from captivity.

MABP *abbr* = mean arterial blood pressure.

Mabuse, Jean de *see* **Gossaert, Jan**.

m/a/c *abbr* = money of account.

MAC *abbr* = Market Access and Compliance; Martial Arts Commission; Mobile Advice Center; Museums Association of Canada; maximum allowable concentration; multiplex analog components.

MAcA *abbr* = Master of the Acupuncture Association and Register.

macabre *adj* gruesome; grim; of death.

macaco *n* (*pl* **macacos**) one of various lemurs, esp the ruffled lemur and the ring-tailed lemur.

macadam *n* a road surface composed of successive layers of small stones compacted into a solid mass.

macadamia *n* an Australian tree bearing white flowers and an edible seed (**macadamia nut**).

macadamize *vt* to surface (a road) with macadam.—**macadamization** *n*.

Macao or **Macau,** *n* a special administrative region under Chinese sovereignty; the capital city of Macao or Macau.

macaque *n* a short-tailed monkey of Asia and Africa.

macaroni *n* (*pl* **macaronis, macaronies**) a pasta made chiefly of fine wheat flour and made into tubes; an 18th-century dandy who copied continental mannerisms etc.

macaronic *adj* (*verse*) using words from more than one language, or a mixture of everyday words and Latin words or words with Latin endings. *n* (*often pl*) macaronic verse.

macaroon *n* a small cake or biscuit made with sugar, egg whites and ground almonds or coconut.

MacArthur *n* **Douglas** (1880–1964) American general and supreme Allied commander in the southwest Pacific in 1942. He accepted the Japanese surrender in 1945 and commanded the UN forces in the Korean War (1950–51), being dismissed his command by Truman.

Macaulay *n* 1. [Dame] **Rose** (1881–1958) English novelist, essayist, and travel writer whose post-World War I novels, e.g. *Dangerous Ages*. After a spiritual conversion she wrote what is held to be her best novel, *The Towers of Trebizond*. 2. **Thomas Babington** [1st Baron] (1800–1859) English essayist and historian, whose writings were very popular in Victorian times, e.g. in *Essays Critical and Historical* (1834).

macaw *n* a large parrot with brightly colored plumage.

Macbeth *n* (1005–1057) king of Scots (1040–1057). A nephew of Malcolm II, he was one of three kings who came to dominate 11th-century Scotland. The legends round the name of Macbeth were collected by John of Fordun and Hector Boece, and reproduced by Holinshed in his *Chronicle*, where they were found by Shakespeare.

Macbeth *n* **Ann** (1875–1944) Scottish designer who wrote several influential textbooks.

Macc. or **Mac.** *abbr* = Maccabees.

MAcc *abbr* = Master of Accountancy.

MACC *abbr* = military aid to the civilian community.

McCabe *n* **John** (1939–) English composer and pianist who has specialized in performing 20th-century pieces and works by Haydn. His compositions include *The Play of Mother Courage, Mary, Queen of Scots*.

Maccabean *adj* pertaining to the Maccabees, a family of Jewish patriots who led a successful revolt against the Syrians, or to its most famous member, Judas Maccabaeus.

maccaboy *n* a kind of snuff, usu rose-scented.

McCarthy *n* 1. **Joseph R[aymond]** (1908–57) American politician. Became a Republican senator in 1946 and carried on a bizarre crusade against supposed communist sympathizers in public life (1950–54). McCarthy's wide and increasingly bizarre accusations against innocent people came to an end shortly after being accused, during a televised hearing, of having no shame. 2. **Mary** (1912–89) American novelist, short-story writer, and critic whose most famous novel, *The Group*, created some controversy due to its open, matter-of-fact treatment of upper-middle-class female sexuality.

McCartney *n* **Sir Paul** (1942–) British guitarist, singer and songwriter, and founder member of the group The Beatles (1961–70). In partnership with John Lennon, and on his own, he is one of the world's most successful songwriters.

Mac Cecht *n* (*Irish Celtic myth*) one of the Tuatha De Danann at the time of the invasion of Ireland by the Sons of Mil Espaine, who defeated the Tuatha. A son of Oghma, he was the husband of the goddess Fotla or Fodla. He was killed by Eremon.

Macchi-Cassia *n* **Antonio** (1937–) Italian industrial designer and consultant to Olivetti.

MacCunn *n* **Hamish** (1868–1916) Scottish composer and conductor whose best-known work is the concert overture *Land of the Mountain and the Flood*.

Mac Da Tho *n* (*Irish Celtic myth*) a king of Leinster who owned a huge pig and a hunting dog that was so fast it could run all around Leinster in a single day.

MacDiarmid *n* **Hugh [Christopher Murray Grieve]** (1892–1978) Scottish nationalist poet and critic. He was expelled from the Scottish Nationalist Party in the 1930s for Communist sympathies, and expelled shortly after from the Communist Party for Nationalist sympathies. His poetic masterpiece is *A Drunk Man Looks at the Thistle* (1926), a triumphant allegory of awakening Scottish consciousness. More broadly influential was his *First Hymn to Lenin* (1931), the first great leftist poem of the decade.

MacDonald *n* 1. **Frances** (1874–1921) British artist, the sister of Margaret **Macdonald** and the wife of J Herbert **MacNair**. 2. **George** (1824–1905) Scottish novelist and poet, remembered chiefly for his children's stories, *At the Back of the North Wind* and *The Princess and the Goblin*, and for two adult fantasy novels, *Phantastes* and *Lilith*. 3. **[James] Ramsay** (1866–1937) Scottish statesman; the first British Labour prime minister (1924, 1929–31); prime minister of a coalition government (1931–35). 4. **Margaret** (1865–1933) British artist, and the wife of Charles Rennie **Mackintosh**, with whom she collaborated after their marriage in 1900.

Macdonald-Wright *n* **Stanton** (1890–1973) American painter; a co-founder of synchronism, a movement in color abstraction along similar lines to orphism.

MacDowell *n* **Edward Alexander** (1861–1908) an American composer who studied in Europe, where he met Liszt. He is remembered for his piano pieces and symphonic poems.

mace¹ *n* a club with a spiked metal head (esp in the Middle Ages); a staff used as a symbol of authority by certain institutions.

mace² *n* an aromatic spice made from the external covering of the nutmeg.

Mace *n* (*trademark*) an irritant liquid that causes temporary immobilization when sprayed onto a victim, used in riot control and carried in aerosol form by women, etc, as protection against attack. * *vt* to use Mace.

MACE *abbr* = Member of the Association of Conference Executives.

macédoine *n* a dish of mixed fruits, served hot or cold; a dish of diced vegetables, usu in jelly or syrup; any mixture.

Macedonia *n* part of northern Greece which came into importance under Philip of Macedon and his son Alexander the Great; (*Bible*) in *NT* times it was a Roman province, which Paul visited.

Macedonia, Former Yugoslav Republic of (FYROM), *n* a landlocked republic sharing its borders with Albania, Bulgaria, Greece and Yugoslavia.

macerate *vti* to soften or become soft or separated through soaking; to make or become thin.—**maceration** *n*.—**macerator** *n*.

MacGonagall *n* **William** (*c*.1830–*c*.1902) Scottish poet renowned for his memorably awful doggerel poems which were published posthumously in *Poetic Gems* and *More Poetic Gems.*

Mac Greine *n* (*Irish Celtic myth*) one of the Tuatha De Danann rulers at the time of the invasion of Ireland by the Sons of Mil Espaine. A son of Oghma and the husband of the goddess Eriu, who gave her name to Eire or Ireland.

Mach, Mach number *n* the ratio of the speed of a body in a particular medium to the speed of sound in the same medium. Mach 1 is equal to the speed of sound.

mach. or **machin.** *abbr* = machine; machinery; machinist.

Macha *n* (*Irish Celtic myth*) a goddess who is sometimes taken to be one deity and sometimes taken to be three. Associated with war, fertility and the prosperity of Ireland, and is also associated with horses.

machair *n* (*Brit*) the white shell sand found in western Scotland, esp in the Western Isles, forming a light, easily worked soil.

Machaut *n* **Guillaume de** (*c*.1304–77) French composer, poet and diplomat. He composed many motets and madrigals, several using his own poems. One of his most important works is his Mass, *Messe de Notre Dame*, for four voices.

Machen *n* **Arthur [Llewellyn]** (1863–1947) Welsh writer of supernatural and horror stories, representative collections including *The Great God Pan* and *The Three Imposters.*

machete *n* a large knife used for cutting, or as a weapon.

Machiavelli *n* **Niccolò** (1469–1527) Italian statesman and political theorist. His treatise, *The Prince* (1513) sees humanity as essentially corrupt and therefore best ruled by whatever method ensures the stability of the state, even if the method entails merciless cruelty.

Machiavellian *adj* cunning; deceitful.

machicolation *n* (*archit*) a projecting parapet on an outside wall of a castle, supported on corbels with openings in the floor through which missiles could be dropped.—**machicolated** *adj.*

machinate *vti* to scheme, plan, esp to do harm.—**machinator** *n.*

machination *n* (usu *pl*) an artifice; an intrigue; a plot; the act of plotting or intriguing.

machine *n* a structure of fixed and moving parts, for doing useful work; an organization functioning like a machine; the controlling group in a political party; a device, as the lever, etc that transmits, or changes the application of energy. * *vt* to shape or finish by machine-operated tools. * *adj* of machines; done by machinery.

machine code *or* **machine language** *n* (*comput*) programming instructions in binary or hexadecimal code, the basic 1s and 0s a computer processor uses as its instructions.

machine gun *n* an automatic gun, firing a rapid stream of bullets.—*also vt.*

machine-readable *adj* directly usable by a computer.

machinery *n* machines collectively; the parts of a machine; the framework for keeping something going.

machine shop *n* a workshop where machine tools are used for machining and assembling objects.

machine tool *n* a mechanized tool for cutting or shaping metals, wood, etc.

machinist *n* one who makes, repairs, or operates machinery.

machismo *n* strong or assertive masculinity; virility.

macho *n* (*pl* **machos**) an exaggeratedly masculine man. * *adj* demonstrating or marked by machismo; domineering.

Machutus *n* **Saint**, also known as **Malo** (died 627) Welsh evangelist who also built churches and founded monasteries; went to Brittany and became bishop of Aleth (Saint-Servan) and made many converts. His feast day is 15 November.

McIndoe *n* **Sir Archibald [Hector]** (1900–60) New Zealand plastic surgeon. He became one of the world's leading plastic surgeons through his ingenious and caring rebuilding of the faces of badly burned RAF crews at his East Grinstead hospital during World War II.

McIntire *n* **Samuel** (1757–1811) American architect. His notable works include Salem Court House (now demolished).

Macintosh *n* (*comput, trademark*) the first GUI computers, designed and manufactured by Apple Computer.

Mack *n* **Daniel** (1947–) Canadian writer and broadcaster who also played a major part in the revival of 19th-century rustic furniture.

Macke *n* **August** (1887–1914) German painter and founder member of *Der Blaue Reiter*. Macke's works had a powerful influence on Paul Klee.

Mackenzie *n* 1. Sir **[Edward Montague] Compton** (1883–1972) English novelist whose best-known novels are the semi-autobiographical *Sinister Street,* an account of a privileged young man's life at Oxford University and in the London slums, and his series of comic novels set in the Scottish Western Isles, e.g. *Whisky Galore* and *Rockets Galore.* 2. **Henry** (1745–1831) Scottish lawyer and novelist whose most famous work is *The Man of Feeling.*

mackerel *n* (*pl* **mackerel, mackerels**) a common oily food fish.

mackerel sky *n* (*meteorology*) a cloud pattern made up of wavy cirrocumulus or altocumulus with holes, suggesting the markings of a mackerel.

McKim *n* **Charles F.** (1847–1909) American architect. His notable works include Columbia University, New York.

Mackinaw (coat) *n* a short, double-breasted coat made of a heavy woolen plaid material.

mackintosh *n* a waterproof raincoat.

Mackintosh *n* **Charles Rennie** (1868–1928) Scottish architect, designer, and painter. In 1894, he and his wife, Margaret Macdonald, with J Herbert MacNair and his wife, Frances Macdonald, organized an exhibition of furniture, jewelry, metalwork, and book illustration. They melded the styles of the arts and crafts movement, Pre-Raphaelites, Celtic, and Japanese revival styles into the "Glasgow School." His major works include the Glasgow School of Art, Willow Tea Rooms and Hill House, Helensburgh.

mackle *n* (*printing*) a blurred or imprecise impression, which produces the effect of a double printing.—*also* **macule.**

Mackmurdo *n* **Arthur Heygate** (1851–1942) British architect who spearheaded the neo-**Gothic** revival.

macle *n* a type of crystal in two parts, containing carbon impurities, sometimes used as a gemstone.

McLaughlin *n* **Mary Louise** (1847–1939) American pottery and porcelain decorator who was a pioneer of china painting in America.

Maclean *n* 1. **Donald** *see* Burgess, Guy. 2. **Sorley** [Somhairle Macgill-Eain] (1911–96) Scottish Gaelic poet who is widely regarded as one of the leading Scottish poets of the 20th century.

Macleish *n* 1. **Archibald** (1892–1982) American poet and dramatist who was one of the lost generation of American poets in 1920s' Paris, and whose works include *The Pot of Earth, Conquistador, Frescoes for Mr Rockefeller's City,* and *New Found Land.* 2. **Minnie** (b.1876) Scottish textile designer who worked with Charles Rennie **Mackintosh** and Constance Irving.

Macleod *n* 1. **Fiona** [William Sharp] (1855–1905) Scottish writer of Celtic fantasy tales set in the Scottish Western Isles. The identity of "Fiona Macleod" was kept secret during Sharp's lifetime. 2. **George** [Baron MacLeod of Fuinary] (1895–1991) Scottish clergyman. Founded the Iona Community, restoring the old cathedral and establishing the Community as an international and ecumenical place of worship. 3. **John** *see* Banting, Sir Frederick.

Mac Liammóir *n* **Micheál** (1899–1978) Irish actor, writer and painter. His one-man shows included *The Importance of Being Oscar* (1960), a tribute to Oscar Wilde.

McLuhan *n* **Marshall** (1911–80) Canadian critic whose studies of mass culture and communication include *The Gutenberg Galaxy* and *The Medium is the Message.*

Macmillan *n* 1. **Sir Kenneth** (1929–92) Scottish choreographer. He became the Royal Ballet's principal choreographer in 1977. He was also director of the Royal Ballet (1970–77) in succession to Ashton. 2. **Sir [Maurice] Harold [1st Earl of Stockton]** (1894–1986) English Conservative statesman. He became prime minister (1957–63) in succession to Eden.

McMurtry *n* **Larry Jeff** (1936–) American novelist whose novels include *The Last Picture Show* (1966).

MacNair *n* **J Herbert** (1870–1945) Scottish architect Together with his wife, Frances **Macdonald**, and Charles Rennie Mackintosh and his wife, they formed the group known as The Four, practicing in the arts and crafts and Pre-Raphaelite styles.

MacNeice *n* **[Frederick] Louis** (1907–63) Irish poet and classical scholar who was one of the leading Auden generation poets and whose collections include *Letters From Iceland* (written in collaboration with Auden) and *Autumn Journal.*

Mac OS *n* (*comput, trademark*) the version of the disk operating system written by Apple™ that is packaged with their Macintosh™ computers.

MACP *abbr* = Member of the Association of Computer Professionals.

Macpherson *n* **James** (1736–96) Scottish poet whose supposed translations of early Scottish Gaelic verse, *Fragments of Ancient Poetry, Fingal,* and *Temora,* the latter two allegedly by an ancient bard called Ossian, achieved extraordinary popularity.

macramé *n* (the art of) knotting or weaving coarse thread to produce ornamental work.

macro *n* (*comput*) a record of commands used regularly in an application that can be activated by a keystroke.

M

macro- *prefix* = long, large.

macrobiotic *adj* (*diet*) composed of an extremely restricted range of foods, usu organic vegetables and whole grains.

macrobiotics *npl* the theory that health and longevity are promoted by eating a macrobiotic diet of organic cereal grains and fruit.

macrocephalic *adj* having an unusually large skull.—*also* **megacephalic** *adj*.—**macrocephaly** *n*.

macrocephaly *n* an abnormal enlargement of the head when compared with the rest of the body. *See* **microcephaly; hydrocephalus**.

macroclimate *n* the general climate of a large area, from a country to a continent.

macrocosm *n* the universe; any complex system.—**macrocosmic** *adj*.

macrocyte *n* (*physiology*) a red blood cell (erythrocyte) that is abnormally large.

macrocytosis *n* (*physiology*) a condition in which abnormally large red blood cells (erythrocytes) are present in the blood.

macroeconomics *n* (*used as sing*) the study of the economy in terms of total national income, production and investment; the study of large-scale economic issues — **macroeconomic** *adj*.

macron *n* a mark placed over a letter to indicate a stressed or long vowel (ˉ).

macrophage *n* (*physiology*) a large scavenger cell (phagocyte), numbers of which are found in various tissues and organs of the body including the liver, spleen, bone marrow, lymph nodes, and connective tissue. It forms part of the immune system of vertebrates.

macropterous *adj* (*zool*) large-winged.

macroscopic *adj* visible to the naked eye; regarded in terms of large elements.

macrospore *see* **megaspore**.

Macsen Wledig *n* the Welsh Celtic name for the Roman emperor Maximus.

McTaggart *n* William (1835–1910) Scottish painter, renowned for having painted mainly out of doors and in all weathers. His works are freely and powerfully painted, conveying the breathtaking shock of strong winds, and stormy seas and skies.

macula (*physiology*) (*pl* **maculae**), **macule** *n* a spot of small pigmented area in the skin, which may be thickened; a colored area near the retina, where vision is esp sharp.—**macular** *adj*.—**maculation** *n*.

macule *see* **mackle**.

mad *adj* (**madder, maddest**) insane; frantic; foolish and rash; infatuated; (*inf*) angry.

mad *abbr* = maintenance, assembly and disassembly.

Mad. or **Madm.** *abbr* = Madam.

MAD *abbr* = major affective disorder; mutual assured destruction, this is the basis of the theory that to possess nuclear weapons is a deterrent; magnetic anomaly destruction.

Madagascar *n* a republic comprising an island in the Indian Ocean lying off the southeast coast of Africa.

madam *n* a polite term of address to a woman; a woman in charge of a brothel; (*inf*) a precocious little girl.

madame *n* (*pl* **mesdames**) the title of a married French woman; used as a title equivalent to Mrs.

madcap *adj* reckless, impulsive.—*also n*.

mad cow disease *n* an informal name for bovine spongiform encephalopathy (BSE).

madden *vti* to make or become insane, angry, or wildly excited.—**maddening** *adj*.—**maddeningly** *adv*.

madder[1] *see* **mad**.

madder[2] *n* a plant of the genus from whose root a red dye and pigment are extracted; the red dye so obtained; a synthetic pigment used in paints and inks.

madding *adj* (*arch*) raging; furious; causing (someone or something) to be raging.

made *see* **make**.

Madeira *n* a rich, strong, white wine made in the North Atlantic island of Madeira.

madeleine *n* a small sponge cake with a coating of red jam covered with coconut.

Madeleine Sophie Barat *n* Saint (1779–1865) French nun; mother superior and director of the Society of the Sacred Heart, for the education of girls. She was canonized in 1925. Her feast day is 25 May.

mademoiselle *n* (*pl* **mesdemoiselles**) the title of an unmarried French girl or woman; used as a title equivalent to Miss; a French teacher or governess.

Maderna *n* Bruno (1920–73) Italian composer and conductor. He composed piano, flute and oboe pieces and also favored electronic instruments as in his *Musica su due dimensioni* (for flute, percussion instruments and electronic tape). As a conductor, he was a renowned interpreter of contemporary music.

made-to-measure *adj* (*clothing*) made to individual requirements.

made-to-order *adj* produced to a customer's specifications; being ideally suited for a particular purpose.

made-up *adj* invented, fabricated, false; (*type*) put together; (*person*) having make-up on; (*road*) surfaced with tarmac, etc.

madhouse *n* (*inf*) as mental institution; a state of uproar or confusion.

Madison *n* the capital city of Wisconsin, a state of the USA.

Madison *n* James (1751–1836) American politician and 4th president of the US (1809–17).

madly *adv* in an insane manner; at great speed, force; (*inf*) excessively.

madman *n* (*pl* **madmen**) an insane person.

mad money *n* money saved for spending on small luxuries or frivolous items; a small amount of money carried to maintain independence of movement, esp by a woman on a date.

madness *n* insanity; foolishness; excitability.

MADO *abbr* = Member of the Association of Dispensing Opticians.

Madonna[1] *n* the Virgin Mary, esp as seen in pictures or statues.

Madonna[2] *n* [Madonna Louise Veronica Ciccone] (1958–) American singer and film actress who made her first recording as a solo singer in 1982. One of the world's most successful female recording artists.

madras *n* a strong cotton or silk material, usu striped.

Madras *n* major city in India.

madrepore *n* any of several corals, often forming tropical coral reefs. —**madreporic** *adj*.

Madrid *n* capital city of Spain.

madrigal *n* (*mus*) 14th-century Italian song derived from a pastoral poem; 16th-century love song or pastoral poem in the form of an unaccompanied part-song; in the 17th century they were superseded by cantatas —**madrigalist** *n*.

maduro *adj* (*cigar*) dark and full-flavored. * *n* (*pl* **maduros**) such a cigar.

madwoman *n* (*pl* **madwomen**) an insane person.

madwort *n* a small herb with yellow or white flowers, formerly reputed to cure madness; a type of small, low-growing, flowering plant with hairy leaves and blue flowers.

MaE. *abbr* = Master of Engineering.

MAE *abbr* = (*Brit*) Manchester Association of Engineers; Maritime Advisory Exchange.

Maeander, Maeandrus *n* (*Greek mythology*) a son of Oceanus and Tethys, and the god of the winding River Maeander in Phrygia.

MA(Econ) *abbr* = Master of Arts in Economic and Social Studies.

MA(Ed) *abbr* = Master of Arts in Education.

Mael Sechnaill I *n* (*d.* 862) high king of Ireland. Succeeded by Aed.

Mael Sechnaill II *n* (*d.* 1023) high king of Ireland (1002–1023 (interrupted). He abdicated in favor of Brian Boru in 1014 following his defeat at the Battle of Clontarf. Boru was killed in his tent shortly after the battle, however, and he was able to regain the title.

maelstrom *n* a whirlpool; a state of turbulence or confusion.

Maelzel *n* Johann Nepomuk (1772–1828) a German-born inventor who settled in Vienna where he constructed various mechanical instruments. He is best known for patenting the first clockwork metronome.

maenad *n* (**maenads, maenades**) (*Greek myth*) a female adherent of Dionysus; a frantic, agitated woman.—*also* **menad**.

Maes Howe *n* the site of a well-preserved passage grave in Orkney, Scotland.

Maes *n* Nicolaes (1634–93) Dutch portrait painter. His work had a strong influence on succeeding generations of portrait painters.

maest., maestoso *abbr* = (*mus*) (*Italian*) *maestoso*, "majestic" or "dignified."

maestà *adj* used in art to denote a depiction of the Virgin and Child enthroned in majesty and surrounded by angels or saints.

maestro *n* (*pl* **maestros**) a master of an art, esp a musical composer, conductor, or teacher.

Maeterlinck *n* [Count] Maurice (1862–1949) Belgian poet, writer and playwright. His masterpiece is *Pelléas et Mélisande* (1892), the basis for the opera by Debussy (1902). He was awarded the Nobel prize for literature in 1911.

Maeve *see* **Medb**.

mae west *n* (*inf*) an inflatable life jacket.

MAF *abbr* = Missionary Aviation Fellowship.

MAFF *abbr* = (*Brit*) Ministry of Agriculture, Fisheries and Food.

Mafia *n* a secret society composed chiefly of criminal elements, originating in Sicily.

mafioso *n* (*pl* **mafiosos, mafiosi**) a member of the Mafia.

MAG *abbr* = Motorcycle Action Group.

mag. *abbr* = magazine; magnet; magnetic; magnetism; magnitude (of a star).

magazine *n* a military store; a space where explosives are stored, as in a fort; a supply chamber, as in a camera, a rifle, etc; a periodical publication containing articles, fiction, photographs, etc.

Magdala *n* town on the shore of the Sea of Galilee.

magdalen, magdalene *n* a reformed prostitute; (*rare*) an institution for housing and reforming prostitutes.

Magdalenian *adj* relating to a widespread western European culture named after the archeological site of La Madeleine in the Dordogne region of France

Magellanic Clouds *npl* (*astron*) two separate galaxies (the Large Magellanic Cloud or Nebucula Major and the Small Magellanic Cloud, Nebucula Minor), detached from the Milky Way, which appear, from the southern hemisphere, as patches of light

magenta *n* a purplish-red dye; purplish red.—*also adj*.

maggiore *n* (*mus*) (*Italian*) "major mode."

maggot *n* a worm-like larva, as of the housefly.—**maggoty** *adj*.—**maggotiness** *n*.

magi, magian *see* **magus**.

magic *n* the use of charms, spells, etc to supposedly influence events by supernatural means; any mysterious power; the art of producing illusions by sleight of hand, etc. * *adj* of or relating to magic; possessing supposedly supernatural powers; (*inf*) wonderful. * *vt* (**magicking, magicked**) to influence, produce or take (away) by or as if by magic.—**magical** *adj*.—**magically** *adv*.

magician *n* one skilled in magic; a conjurer.

magic realism a term often applied with particular reference to the work of certain South American novelists, notably Mario Vargas Llosa and Gabriel Garcia Marquez, whose work combines deadpan description of the everyday world with excursions into fantasy.

magisterial *adj* of, or suitable for a magistrate; authoritative.—**magisterially** *adv*.

magistracy *n* (*pl* **magistracies**) the office, jurisdiction or dignity of a magistrate; magistrates collectively.

magistral *adj* of or pertaining to a master or teacher, magisterial; (*med*) specially prescribed; (*fortification*) in a strategic position.

magistrate *n* a public officer empowered to administer the law.—**magistrateship**, **magistrature** *n*.

Magistretti *n* **Vico** (1920–) Italian architect who designed the distinctive 1963 chair which bears his name.

Maglemosian *adj* relating to the earliest Mesolithic culture of northern Europe, which emerged *c* 8000 BC, in the post-glacial period.

maglev *abbr* = magnetically levitated; magnetic levitation.

magma *n* (*pl* **magmas**, **magmata**) (*geol*) the fluid rock beneath the earth's surface, that solidifies to form lava.

Magna Carta, Magna Charta *n* in England, the Great Charter, forming the basis of civil liberty, granted by King John to the barons, church and freemen in 1215.

magnanimity *n* (*pl* **magnanimities**) generosity.

magnanimous *adj* noble and generous in conduct or spirit, not petty.—**magnanimously** *adv*.

magnate *n* a very wealthy or influential person.

magnesia *n* a magnesium compound used as a mild laxative.

Magnesia *n* in ancient Greece, a coastal area of eastern Thessaly which contains Mount Pelion and was the home of the Centaurs.

magnesium *n* a white metallic element that burns very brightly.

magnet *n* any piece of iron or steel that has the property of attracting iron; anything that attracts.

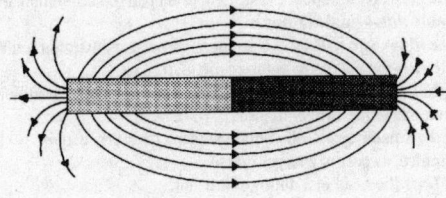

magnetic *adj* of magnetism or a magnet; producing or acting by magnetism; having the ability to attract or charm people.—**magnetically** *adv*.

magnetic bubble *n* (*comput*) a portion of computer memory which consists of a small region in a material such as garnet, which is magnetized in one direction.

magnetic declination *n* deviation of the magnetic needle from true north; the measure of this.

magnetic deviation *n* the angle through which a compass has to be corrected to compensate for the effects of magnetic fields in its immediate surroundings.

magnetic dip or **magnetic inclination** *n* the angle at which lines of magnetic force caused by the earth's magnetic field appear to enter the earth's surface.

magnetic disk *n* (*comput*) a secondary storage device that consists of a plastic disk coated with magnetically sensitive material.

magnetic equator *n* the imaginary point near the equator where the magnetic needle has no dip, the aclinic line.

magnetic field *n* (*astron*) the region of space in which a magnetic body exerts its force; (*comput*) a force surrounding electrical devices that can have an adverse effect on data stored on magnetic media; any space in which there is an appreciable magnetic force.

magnetic head *n* an electromagnet used in recording, retrieving or erasing information on magnetic tape, as in tape recorders and computer disks.

magnetic media *n* (*comput*) any of a wide variety of disks or tapes, coated or impregnated with magnetic material, on which information can be recorded and stored.

magnetic meridian *n* an imaginary line joining the positions of the magnetic poles.

magnetic needle *n* a thin piece of magnetized iron, steel, etc, used in a compass and other instruments, that indicates the direction of a magnetic field.

magnetic north *n* the northerly direction of the earth's magnetic field, as pointed to by a compass needle.

magnetic pole *n* the points where the lines of magnetic force of the earth's magnetic field are vertical.

magnetic recording *n* the process of recording information by producing variations in the arrangement of magnetic particles on magnetic tape, disk, etc.

magnetic resonance imaging *n* a method of viewing the body's internal organs by the use of radio waves.

magnetics *n sing* the science of magnetism.

magnetic stars *n* (*astron*) stars in which the magnetic field is sufficiently strong to produce very significant effects, classified in the Babcock Catalog as magnetic stars.

magnetic storm *n* (*meteorology*) a temporary disturbance in the earth's magnetic field, thought to be caused by charged particles emanating from sun spots, solar flares, etc.

magnetic tape *n* a thin plastic ribbon with a magnetized coating for recording sound, video signals, computer data, etc.

magnetic variation *see* **magnetic declination**.

magnetism *n* (*physics*) the effective force that originates within the earth and that behaves as if there were a powerful magnet at the center of the earth, producing a magnetic field; the property, quality, or condition of being magnetic; the force to which this is due; personal charm.

magnetize *vt* to make magnetic; to attract strongly.—**magnetization** *n*.—**magnetizer** *n*.

magneto *n* (*pl* **magnetos**) a small generator with permanent magnets for generating high voltages, esp the ignition spark in an internal combustion engine.

magnetoelectricity *n* electric phenomena produced by magnetism.

magnetometer *n* a piece of equipment used for measuring the strength of the magnetic field of the earth at any given point.

magneton *n* one of two units of magnetic moment.

magnetosphere *n* (*astron*) the space around the earth and other planets with a magnetic field in which charged particles are affected by the magnetic field of that planet rather than of the sun.

magnet school *n* a school in which resources are devoted to developing excellence in one particular field, e.g. science.

Magnificat *n* (*mus*) (*Latin*) the canticle of the Virgin Mary sung at Roman Catholic Vespers and Anglican Evensong. Usu chanted, but many composers, such as Bach, have set it to their own music; (*without cap*) any hymn of praise.

magnification *n* magnifying or being magnified; the degree of enlargement of something by a lens, microscope, etc.

magnificence *n* grandeur of appearance; splendor; pomp.

magnificent *adj* splendid, stately or sumptuous in appearance; superb, of very high quality.—**magnificently** *adv*.

magnifico *n* (*pl* **magnificoes**) a person of importance or high rank; (*formerly*) a title of a Venetian nobleman.

magnify *vt* (**magnifying**, **magnified**) to exaggerate; to increase the apparent size of (an object) as (with) a lens.—**magnifiable** *adj*.—**magnifier** *n*.

magnifying glass *n* a lens that produces an enlarged image.

magniloquent *adj* pompous in style or speech, bombastic.—**magniloquence** *n*.—**magniloquently** *adv*.

magnitude *n* (*physics*, *math*) the absolute value or length of a physical or mathematical quantity; (*astron*) a relative measure of the apparent brightness of stars; greatness of size, extent, etc; importance;.

magnolia *n* a spring-flowering shrub or tree with evergreen or deciduous leaves and showy flowers.

magnum *n* (*pl* **magnums**) a wine bottle that holds twice the normal quantity.

magnum opus *in* (*pl* **magna opera**) the great or chief work of an artist or author.

Magnussen *n* 1. **Erik** (1884–1961) Danish metalworker whose best-known work was the 1927 *Lights and Shadows of Manhattan* silver coffee set. 2. **Gunnar** (1933–) Icelandic designer who specializes in furnishing public spaces.

Magog *see* **Gog**.

magpie *n* a black and white bird of the crow family; a person who chatters; an acquisitive person.

MAgr *abbr* = Master of Agriculture.

Magritte *n* **René** (1898–1967) Belgian painter. His early styles included impressionism and cubism, but later he became interested in surrealism, devising a style dubbed "magic realism."

MAgrSc *abbr* = Master of Agricultural Science.

maguey *n* any of several species of a tropical American plant, esp one from which fiber is obtained or that is used in the production of alcoholic drinks; the fiber from such a plant.

magus *n* (*pl* **magi**) a Zoroastrian priest; (*with cap*) any of the three wise men who paid homage to Christ at His birth; a magician, sorcerer.—**magian** *adj*, *n*.

Magyar *adj* pertaining to the Hungarian or Magyar race or language; (*sleeve*) cut as part of the bodice, with no armhole seam.

Mahabharata *n* a great Hindu epic that narrates the dynastic wars of ancient India.

Mahajanga *n* major city in Madagascar.

Mahalapye *n* major city in Botswana.

maharajah, maharaja *n* the former title of an Indian prince.

maharani, maharanee *n* the wife of a maharajah.

maharishi *n* a Hindu spiritual leader and teacher.

mahatma *n* (*Hinduism*, *Buddhism*) a wise man, a sage; (*with cap*) (*Hinduism*) a title or respect for a man of great spirituality.

Maher *n* **George Washington** (1864–1926) American furniture designer, whose first pieces were monumental and ornate.

M

Mahfouz *n* **Naguib** (*c.*1911–) Egyptian novelist and short-story writer, the most important modern Arab novelist, whose novels include the controversial and allegorical *Awlad Haritna* and *Miramar*. He was awarded the Nobel prize for literature in 1988.

Mahican *see* **Mohican**.

Mahilyov *n* major city in Belarus.

mahi-mahi *n* (*biol*) either of two dolphin fish (genus *Coryphaena*) of the Pacific Ocean, a food fish.

mahjong, mah-jongg *n* an *orig* Chinese game for four people played with decorative tiles.

Mahler *n* **Gustav** (1860–1911) Austrian composer and conductor; his principal works include: ten symphonies (the 10th was unfinished); the song cycles *Lieder eines fahrenden Gesellen* (Songs of the Wayfarer) and kindertotenlieder; the song symphony *Das Lied von der Erde* (The Song of the Earth); and numerous individual songs.

mahlstick, maulstick *n* a stick used by painters to steady and support the hand while working.

mahogany *n* (*pl* **mahoganies**) the hard, reddish-brown wood of a tropical tree; a reddish-brown color.

Mahometan *see* **Muhammedan**.

mahout *n* (*India*) an elephant driver.

MAI *abbr* = *Magister in Arte Ingeniaria* (*Latin*) "Master of Engineering"; Medical Aid for Iraq; Music Association of Ireland.

Maia *n* (*Greek mythology*) the oldest of the Pleiades, the mother of Hermes.

Maiakkovskaia *n* **Ludmilla** (1884–1963) Russian textile designer whose designs were shown at the 1925 Paris Exhibition.

MAIB *abbr* = Marine Accident Investigation Board.

maid *n* a maiden; a woman servant.

maiden *n* a girl or young unmarried woman. * *adj* unmarried or virgin; untried; first.—**maidenhood** *n*.

Maiden Castle *n* the site of an important Iron Age hill fort just outside Dorchester, England.

maidenhair (fern) *n* a delicate-leafed fern with small light green leaflets.

maidenhead *n* the hymen.

maidenly *adj* like or suitable to a maiden; modest; gentle.—**maidenliness** *n*.

maiden name *n* the surname of a woman before marriage.

maid of honor *n* the principal unmarried attendant of a bride; a small almond-flavored tart.

maiden over *n* (*cricket*) an over during which no runs are scored.

maidservant *n* a female servant.

Maidum *n* (*Egypt*) a site on the west bank of the Nile, about 30 miles (50 kilometers) south of Saqqara, where the Pharaoh Snofru of the Fourth Dynasty erected a pyramid.

MAIE *abbr* = Member of the British Association of Industrial Editors.

maieutic *adj* of the Socratic method of teaching by means of questions.

mail[1] *n* a body armor made of small metal rings or links.

mail[2] *n* letters, packages, etc transported and delivered by the post office; a postal system. * *vt* to send by mail.—**mailable** *adj*.

Mail *or* **Mael Fothartaig** *or* **Fhothartaig** *n* (*Irish Celtic myth*) Mail Fothartaig was the son of Ronan and a very handsome man. His stepmother fell in love with him and made advances towards him, which he rejected. She accused him of rape. Reluctantly Ronan believed her and had him killed.

mailbag *n* a shoulder bag or large sack for carrying mail.

mailbox *n* a public box for depositing mail; a box near a house for the occupant's mail; (*comput*) within the electronic mail system, a disk file or memory area in which messages for a particular destination (or person) are placed.

mail drop *n* a receptacle for mail; a specified location used for transferring secret communications.

Mail Duin *or* **Mael Duin** *n* (*Irish Celtic myth*) the central character of one of the immram or invasion tales. He was the son of a nun who, according to legend, was raped by his father, Ailill, who was said to have come from Aran.

mailer *n* a container for mail, as a cardboard tube; an advertisement sent by mail.

Mailer *n* **Norman Kingsley** (1923–) American journalist and writer whose first novel, *The Naked and the Dead*, based on his experiences in World War II, was highly successful. Subsequent novels include *The Deer Park*, the semi-autobiographical *An American Dream*, and *Ancient Evenings*. His nonfiction works include *The Executioner's Song*.

mail gateway *n* (*comput*) an electronic path that allows electronic mail to be sent between different mail services or direct to a computer on the internet.

Maillart *n* **Robert** (1872–1940) Swiss architect. His notable works include Tavenasa Bridge.

Maillol *n* **Aristide** (1861–1944) French sculptor, designer, and painter. He is best remembered for his sculptures of the female nude in the classical and dignified style of Greek and Roman sculpture.

maillot *n* a woman's one-piece swimsuit; a similar garment worn by gymnasts, ballet dancers, etc.

mailman *n* (*pl* **mailmen**) a person who collects or delivers mail.—*also* **postman**.

mail merge *vt* (*comput*) to merge two or more files for the purpose of creating a mail shot. * *n* the process of merging two or more files.

mail order *n* a means of selling products directly to customers through the postal service by means of catalogs.

mail server *n* (*comput*) a computer in a network (*see*, e.g., **local area network**) that acts as a mail "sorting office." It stores mail for onward distribution to computers on the network.

mail shot *n* sales or advertising material that is sent by post to a large number of people regarded as potential customers.

maim *vt* to cripple; to mutilate.

main[1] *n* (*mus*) (*French*) "hand," so *main droite* means "right hand" (particularly in piano music).

main[2] *adj* chief in size, importance, etc; principal. * *n* (*often pl but used a sing*) a principal pipe in a distribution system for water, gas, etc; the essential point.

Maine (ME) *n* a state of the United States of America (USA) of which the capital is Augusta.

mainframe *n* (*comput*) any large computer that can handle multiple tasks concurrently.

mainland *n* the principal land mass of a continent, as distinguished from nearby islands.

mainline *n* the principal road, course, etc. * *vt* (*sl*) (*drugs*) to inject directly into a vein.

mainly *adv* chiefly, principally.

main market *n* the premier market for trading in equities on the London Stock Exchange.

mainmast *n* (*naut*) the principal mast of a sailing ship with more than one mast.

main memory *n* (*comput*) *see* **RAM**.

mainsail *n* (*naut*) the principal lowermost sail on the mainmast.

main sequence *n* (*astron*) a region on the Hertzsprung–Russell diagram representing the longest period in a star's life, and giving an indication of the masses and colors that stars may have.

main sequence star *n* (*astron*) a star occupying a place on the main sequence of the Hertzsprung–Russell diagram.

mainsheet *n* (*naut*) one of the ropes by which the mainsail is extended and fastened, controlling its angle.

mainspring *n* the principal spring in a clock, watch, etc; the chief incentive, motive, etc.

mainstay *n* a chief support.

MAInstCF *abbr* = (*Brit*) Master Fitter of the National Institute of Carpet Fitters.

mainstream *n* a major trend, line of thought, etc.—*also adj*.

maintain *vt* to preserve; to support, to sustain; to keep in good condition; to affirm.—**maintainable** *adj*.—**maintainer** *n*.

maintenance *n* upkeep; (*financial*) support, esp of a spouse after a divorce.

maintop *n* (*naut*) the platform on top of the mainmast.

Mairet *n* **Ethel** (1872–1952) British weaver who introduced traditional Indian weaving methods to the British market.

maisonette *n* a small house; self-contained living quarters, usu on two floors with its own entrance, as part of a larger house.

maitre d' *n* (*inf*) the head of a dining-room staff.

maître d'hôtel *n* (*pl* **maîtres d'hôtel**) a head waiter; a hotel manager or owner; a house steward.

MAIU *abbr* = Marine Accident Investigation Unit.

maize *n* corn; a light yellow color.

Maj. *abbr* = (*mil*) Major, major.

majestic *adj* dignified; imposing.—**majestically** *adv*.

majesty *n* (*pl* **majesties**) grandeur; (*with cap*) a title used in speaking to or of a sovereign.

Maj. Gen. *abbr* = (*mil*) Major General.

majolica *n* a fine, soft, enameled kind of pottery of Italian origin, with a glaze of bright metallic oxides.

major *adj* greater in size, importance, amount, etc; (*surgery*) very serious, life-threatening; (*mus*) higher than the corresponding minor by half a tone. * *vi* to specialize (in a field of study). * *n* in US, an officer ranking just above a captain, in UK, a lieutenant-colonel; (*mus*) a major key, chord or scale.

major axis *n* (*astron*) in an ellipse, the line joining the two foci and extended to reach the ellipse.

major-domo *n* (*pl* **major-domos**) a head steward; a butler.

majorette *n* one of a group of girls who march in formation and twirl batons.

major histocompatibility complex *see* **MHC**.

majority *n* (*pl* **majorities**) the greater number or part of; the excess of the larger number of votes cast for a candidate in an election; full legal age; the military rank of a major.

majority rule *n* the political principle that a decision made by an organized group constituting 51 per cent of the members will be binding on the whole group.

Major *n* **John** (1943–) English Conservative politician, foreign secretary, chancellor of the exchequer (1989–90), and prime minister (1990–97).

major league *n* a league of the highest level in professional baseball, basketball, hockey, etc; the top rank of an enterprise or activity.

major planet *n* (*astron*) any of the larger bodies orbiting the Sun in the Solar System: Mercury, Venus, Earth, Mars, Jupiter, Saturn, Uranus, Neptune and Pluto.

major scale *n* (*mus*) a scale with half steps between the third and fourth, and the seventh and eighth, tones.

majuscule *n* a capital letter used in printing or in writing. * *adj* of, pertaining to or written in such letters.—**majuscular** *adj*.

Makarios III *n* [Mikhail Khristodoulou Mouskos] (1913–77) Cypriot archbishop and statesman. Archbishop of the Orthodox Church in Cyprus, he became first president of Cyprus (1959–77) after independence, with a brief hiatus in 1974 when he was removed from office after a coup by Greek Cypriot extremists forced him to flee to London.

make *vt* (**making, made**) to cause to exist, occur, or appear; to build, create, produce, manufacture, etc; to prepare for use; to amount to; to have the qualities of; to acquire, earn; to understand; to do, execute; to cause or force; to arrive at, reach; (*with* **believe**) to imagine, pretend; (*with* **good**) to make up for, pay compensation; (*with* **out**) to write out; to complete (a form, etc) in writing; to attempt to understand; to discern, identify; (*with* **up**) to invent, fabricate, esp to deceive; to prepare; to make complete; to put together; to settle differences between. * *vi* (*with* **do**) to manage with what is available; (*with* **for**) to go in the direction of; to bring about; (*with* **good**) to become successful or wealthy; (*with* **off**) to leave in haste; (*with* **out**) to pretend; to fare, manage; (*with* **up**) to become reconciled; to compensate for; to put on make-up for the stage. * *n* style, brand, or origin; manner of production.—**maker** *n*.

make-believe *adj* imagined, pretended.—*also n*.

Makepeace *n* John (1939–) British furniture designer who established the Parnham Trust and School for Craftsmen in Wood in 1977.

makeshift *adj* being a temporary substitute.—*also n*.

make-up *n* the cosmetics, etc used by an actor; cosmetics generally; the way something is put together, composition; nature, disposition.

makeweight *n* something added to make up the required weight; anything of little value added to fill a lack.

make-work *adj* (*project, job, etc*) having no purpose other than to give an idle person something to do.

making *n* the act or process of making, creation; (*pl*) earnings; (*pl*) potential; (*pl*) (*sl*) the materials for rolling a cigarette.

Makkah *see* **mecca**.

makuta *see* **likuta, zaire**.

Mal. *abbr* = Malayan.

mal- *prefix* = bad or badly, wrong, ill.

Malabo *n* capital city of Equatorial Guinea; the capital city of Eritrea.

malabsorption syndrome *n* (*med*) a group of diseases in which there is a reduction in the normal absorption of digested food materials in the small intestine.

malac. *abbr* = malacology.

malacca *n* the tough stem of a species of climbing palm, rattan; a brown walking stick made of this (*also* **malacca cane**).

Malachi, the Book of *n* (*Bible*) an anonymous work from about 460 BC; its main theme is to rebuke priests and worshippers for their casual indifference to religious matters.

malachite *n* copper carbonate occurring as a green mineral; used as an ore, for making ornaments, as a cosmetic for the eyes and as a natural insecticide.

Malachy *n* Saint (*c.* 1095–1148) Irish priest; abbot of Bangor (1125); archbishop of Armagh (1132); papal legate for Ireland; canonized by Clement IV. His feast day is 3 November.

malacology *n* the science of mollusks.—**malacological** *adj*.—**malacologist** *n*.

malacostracan *adj* (*crustacean*) soft-shelled.

maladjusted *adj* poorly adjusted, esp to the social environment.—**maladjustment** *n*.

maladministration *n* corrupt or incompetent management of public affairs.—**maladminister** *vt*.

maladroit *adj* clumsy.—**maladroitness** *n*.

malady *n* (*pl* **maladies**) a disease, illness.

Malaga *n* major city in Spain; a sweet, white, dessert wine from the Spanish port of Malaga.

Malagasy *n* (*pl* **Malagasy, Malagasies**) a native of Madagascar; the language of Madagascar. * *adj* pertaining to Madagascar, its language or people.

malagueha *n* (*mus*) a Spanish dance 3/4 or 3/8 time, named after the town of Malaga. The tune is often sung as it is danced.

malaise *n* a feeling of discomfort or of uneasiness.

Malamud *n* Bernard (1914–86) American novelist and short-story writer whose best-known work is *The Fixer*, a tragic tale of anti-Semitism in Czarist Russia. Other works include the novels *The Natural*, *The Assistant*, *Dublin's Lives*, and the short-story collection *The Magic Barrel*.

malamute *n* a powerful Alaskan dog with a dense gray coat used to pull sledges.—*also* **malemute**.

Malan *n* Daniel F[rançois] (1874–1959) South African politician. He became prime minister (1948–54).

malanders *n sing* a disease in horses, the main symptom of which is an eczema-like patch on the horse's leg.

malapert *adj* (*arch*) impudent; pert; saucy.

malapropism *n* a ludicrous misuse of words.—**malapropian** *adj*.

malapropos *adj* out of place, ill-timed. * *adv* in an inappropriate way; unseasonably.

malar *adj* of or relating to the cheek or cheekbone. * *n* the cheekbone.

malaria *n* (*med*) an infectious disease caused by the presence of minute parasitic organisms of the genus *Plasmodium* in the blood transmitted to humans by the *Anopheles* mosquito (common in subtropical and tropical regions), and characterized by recurring attacks of fevers and chills.—**malarial** *adj*.

malarkey *n* (*inf*) nonsense; foolish talk.

Malawi *n* a republic lying along the southern and western shores of the third largest lake in Africa, Lake Malawi.

Malaysia *n* a federal constitutional monarchy which lies in the South China Sea in southeast Asia.

Malchus *n* (*Bible*) the name of the high priest's slave whose right ear Simon Peter cut off with his sword in the garden where Jesus was arrested.

Malcolm I *n* (d. 954) king of Scots (943–954). The son of Donald II, he succeeded to the throne on the abdication of his cousin Constantine I.

Malcolm II *n* (*c.*954–1034) king of Scots (1005–1034). The son of Kenneth II, he ascended the throne after killing his cousin, Kenneth III. On his death Duncan I became king of all Scotland.

Malcolm III Canmore *n* (1031–1093) king of Scots (1058–1093). Canmore means "big head" or "chief." Married Margaret, sister of the Anglo-Saxon Prince Edgar the Aetheling, who had fled the Norman invasion with her brother. Margaret had six sons by Malcolm, three of whom became kings: Edgar, Alexander I and David I.

Malcolm IV *n* (the Maiden) (1141–1165) king of Scots (1153–1165). The grandson of David I and eldest of the three sons of Henry, the Earl of Northumberland.

Malcolm X *n* [Malcolm Little] (1925–65) American black separatist leader. He abandoned his "slave" surname of Little in the early 1950s, by which time he had become a convert to Elijah Muhammad's Nation of Islam while in jail for burglary. An advocate of violent response to racism, he was murdered by fellow black Muslims in a feud.

malcontent *adj* discontented and potentially rebellious.—*also n*.

MA(LD) *abbr* = Master of Arts (Landscape Design).

mal de mer *n* seasickness.

Maldives, the, *n* a republic comprising 1,200 low-lying coral islands grouped into 12 atolls, lying 640 kilometers or 398 miles southwest of Sri Lanka in the Indian Ocean.

male *adj* denoting or of the sex that fertilizes the ovum; of, like, or suitable for men and boys; masculine. * *n* a male person, animal or plant.—**maleness** *n*.

Malé *n* capital city of Maldives.

male chauvinist *n* a man who believes women are inferior.—**male chauvinism** *n*.

malediction *n* a curse, an imprecation; a denunciation of evil; a slander.—**maledictory** *adj*.

malefactor *n* a criminal, an evildoer.—**malefaction** *n*.

maleficent *adj* harmful, causing evil; mischief-making.—**maleficently** *adv*.—**maleficence** *n*.

malemute *see* **malamute**.

Malenkov *n* Georgi Maksimilianovich (1902–88) Soviet politician. He became *de facto* prime minister of the USSR after Stalin's death (whose private secretary he had been in the 1920s). He was deposed by Khrushchev.

Malevich *n* Kasimir Severinovich (1878–1935) Russian painter of Polish origins. He pioneered Suprematist ideas of purely abstract art, sometimes anticipating the minimalist art of the 1960s.

malevolent *adj* ill-disposed toward others; spiteful, malicious.—**malevolence** *n*.—**malevolently** *adv*.

malfeasance *n* (*law*) an illegal action, official misconduct.—**malfeasant** *adj, n*.

malformation *n* faulty or abnormal formation of a body or part.—**malformed** *adj*.

malfunction *n* faulty functioning. * *vi* to function wrongly.

malgré lui *adv* (*French*) against one's wishes, despite oneself.

Mali *n* a landlocked republic in west Africa.

malic acid *adj* a colorless crystalline acid derived from fruit, esp apples.

malice *n* active ill will, intention to inflict injury upon another.—**malicious** *adj*.—**maliciously** *adv*.—**maliciousness** *n*.

malign *adj* harmful; evil. * *vt* to slander; to defame.—**malignity** *n*.—**malignly** *adv*.

malignant *adj* (*med*) a term used to describe a tumor that proliferates rapidly, destroys surrounding healthy tissue and can spread via the lymphatic system and bloodstream to other parts of the body; having a wish to harm others; injurious; —**malignancy** *n*.—**malignantly** *adv*.

malignant pustule *see* **anthrax**.

malignity *n* (*pl* **malignities**) the state of being malignant or deadly; (*often pl*) (an act of) malice; virulence.

malinconia *n* (*mus*) (*Italian*) "melancholy."

malinger *vi* to feign illness in order to evade work, duty.—**malingerer** *n*.

Malinowski *n* Arno (1899–1976) Danish sculptor who designed the medal that was worn by thousands of Danes during WWII as a symbol of resistance.

Malipiero *n* Gian Francesco (1882–1973) Italian composer-who is best known for his operas (e.g. *Julius Caesar, Antony and Cleopatra*, oratorios, piano pieces, and songs.

malison *n* (*arch*) a curse, execration.

mall *n* a shaded avenue, open to the public; a shopping street for pedestrians only; an enclosed shopping center.

mallard *n* (*pl* **mallard, mallards**) a common wild duck, the ancestor of domestic breeds of duck.

M

Mallarmé *n* **Stéphane** (1842–98) French symbolist poet whose impressionistic free-verse works include *Afternoon of a Faun*, which was set to suitably sensuous music by Claude Debussy.

malleability *n* (*physics*) the property of metals and alloys that enables them to be changed in shape by hammering or rolling into thin sheets.

malleable *adj* pliable; capable of being shaped.—**malleability** *n*.

mallee *n* a dwarf eucalyptus found in Australia; (*with* **the**) a sparsely populated area in Australia, the bush.

mallemuck *n* any of various sea birds, *incl* the fulmar and petrel.

malleolar *adj* pertaining to the ankle.

mallet *n* a small, usu wooden-headed, short-handled hammer; a long-handled version for striking the ball in the games of polo and croquet.

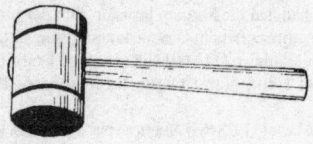

Mallet-Stevens *n* **Robert** (1886–1945) French architect who reacted against the excesses of **art nouveau**.

malleus *n* small bone, the "hammer," of the middle ear.

mallow *n* any of a widely found genus of plants with pink flowers and palm-shaped leaves; a similar plant, e.g. marshmallow.

malm *n* soft friable limestone rock; a loamy soil derived from this; a clay and chalk mixture used as an ingredient in brickmaking.

Malmö *n* major city in Sweden.

malmsey *n* (*pl* **malmseys**) a strong, full-flavored sweet wine *orig* from Greece but now also made in Madeira, Spain, etc.

Malmsten *n* **Carl** (1888–1972) Swedish furniture designer whose austere designs anticipated Modern Scandinavian design.

malnourished *adj* suffering from malnutrition.

malnutrition *n* (*med*) a condition caused either by an unbalanced diet or by an inadequate food intake (subnutrition), which can lead to starvation; lack of nutrition.

Malo, Saint *see* **Machutus**.

malocclusion *n* (*dentistry*) abnormal occlusion, resulting in incorrect alignment of the teeth when the jaw is closed.

malodorous *adj* having a foul smell, bad-smelling.—**malodorously** *adv*.—**malodorousness** *n*.

Maloof *n* **Sam** (1916–) American furniture designer who started out doing in-store design for Bullock's, Los Angeles.

Malory *n* **Sir Thomas** (*fl*. 15th century) translator, largely from French sources, of *Le Morte d'Arthur* (printed by Caxton, 1485), a collection of Arthurian legends. The work includes several episodes, e.g. the quest for the Holy Grail, that have been recycled by generations of authors. The author has traditionally (and doubtfully) been identified with a rather violent Warwickshire knight of that name.

Malpighian *adj* (*anat*) pertaining to various structures, such as the capillary system, discovered by the Italian anatomist Marcello Malpighi (1628-94).

malposition, malpresentation *n* the situation in which the head of an unborn baby before and near delivery is not in the usual (occipitoanterior) position.

malpractice *n* professional misconduct, esp by a medical practitioner.

Malraux *n* **André** (1901–76) French novelist, art historian and politician. His active life had a great influence on his novels, which include *La Condition humaine* (1933).

malt *n* a cereal grain, such as barley, which is soaked and dried and used in brewing; (*inf*) malt liquor, malt whisky * *vt* to make into malt; to combine with malt. * *vi* to become malt; to make grain into malt.—**malty** *adj*.

Malta *n* a republic situated in the Mediterranean Sea approximately 288 kilometers or 180 miles east of North Africa (Tunisia) and 93 kilometers or 58 miles south of Sicily. Malta is an archipelago of three large inhabited islands and two small uninhabited ones.

malted milk *n* a powder made from malted cereals; a hot drink made from this mixed with milk.

Maltese Pound *n* currency of Malta.

maltha *n* a natural black bitumen; a mineral wax.

Malthusian *adj* of or pertaining to the British political economist Thomas Malthus (1766-1834) or his theory, which maintains that population tends to outgrow its means of subsistence and should be checked by means of birth control. * *n* an advocate of this theory.—**Malthusianism** *n*.

maltose *n* a sugar obtained from starch by the action of diatase or malt and used in bacteriological cultures and baby foods.

maltreat *vt* to treat roughly or badly.—**maltreatment** *n*.

maltster *n* a maker of or dealer in malt.

malvoisie *n* a French dessert wine similar to malmsey.

MAM *abbr* = Medical Association of Malta.

mama *n* (*inf*) mother.—*also* **mamma**.

MAMA *abbr* = Meet-a-Mum Association.

MAMAA *abbr* = Mothers Against Murder and Aggression.

mamba *n* a partly tree-living green or black poisonous snake of tropical and southern Africa.

Mameluke *n* (*formerly*) a member of the ruling classes in Egypt.

Mamet *n* **David** (1947–) American dramatist and film director whose plays, e.g. *American Buffalo* and *House of Games*, are engrossing and highly ingenious studies of bluff and double-cross among low-life characters.

mamma¹ *see* **mama**.

mamma² *n* (*pl* **mammae**) (*biol*) the milk-secreting organ of female mammals, such as the udder of a cow, or breast of a woman.—**mammary** *adj*.

mammal *n* (*biol*) any member of a class of warm-blooded vertebrates that suckle their young with milk.—**mammalian** *adj*.

mammalogy *n* (*zool*) the branch of zoology involving the study of mammals.—**mammalogical** *adj*.—**mammalogist** *n*.

mammary gland *n* (*biol*) the gland in female mammals that produces milk.

mammee *n* a tropical American tree with edible fruit; the large red-skinned fruit from this tree (—*also* **mamee apple**).

mammiferous *adj* having breasts.

mammilla *n* (*pl* **mamillae**) (*biol*) a nipple; a nipple-shaped thing.

mammillary *adj* of or like the breast or a nipple.

mammock *vt* (*inf*) to break in pieces; to shred. * *n* a small piece.

mammogram *n* (*med*) an X-ray photograph of the breast.

mammography *n* (*med*) a special X-ray technique used to determine the structure of the breast, useful in the early detection of tumors.

mammon *n* riches regarded as an object of worship and greedy pursuit; (*with cap*) (*Bible*) in the NT, mammon is personified as a god which men worship; modern versions of the Bible translate Mammon as money.—**mammonism** *n*.—**mammonist** *n*.

mammoplasty *n* plastic surgery of the breasts to decrease or increase size and alter shape.

mammoth *n* an extinct elephant with long, curved tusks. * *adj* enormous.

mammy (*pl* **mammies**) *n* (*inf*) mother, as used by a child; (*offensive*) a black nurse to white children.

MAMS *abbr* = Member of the Association of Medical Secretaries, Practice Administrators and Receptionists.

M.Am.Soc.M.E. *abbr* = Member of the American Society of Mechanical Engineers.

MA(MUS) *abbr* = Master of Arts (Music).

man *n* (*pl* **men**) a human being, esp an adult male; the human race; an adult male with manly qualities, e.g. courage, virility; a male servant; an individual person; a person with specific qualities for a task, etc; an ordinary soldier, as opposed to an officer; a member of a team, etc; a piece in games such as chess, checkers, etc; a husband. * *vt* (**manning, manned**) to provide with men for work, defense, etc.

man. *abbr* = manège; *manipulus* (*Latin*, "handful"); manual.

Man. *abbr* = Manila (paper); Manitoba.

MANA *abbr* = Musicians Against Nuclear Arms.

manacle *n* (usu *pl*) a handcuff. * *vt* to handcuff; to restrain.

manage *vt* to control the movement or behavior of; to have charge of; to direct; to succeed in accomplishing. * *vi* to carry on business; to contrive to get along.—**manageable** *adj*.

management *n* those carrying out the administration of a business; the managers collectively; the technique of managing or controlling.

management accounting *n* the process of collecting and processing information relevant to accounting within an organization with a view to ensuring effective financial planning and control.

management buy-in *n* the acquisition of a company or of a division of a company by a small group of shareholders, often ex-managers of the company, who then form part of a new management team, the buy-in often being backed by venture capital.

management buy-out *n* the acquisition of a company or a division of a company by members of its existing management team.

management by exception *n* a management system by which only important variations from plan or budget are brought to the attention of senior management, routine decisions being made further down the line.

management by walking around *n* a management system that involves managers spending time walking around the factory or office, thereby having the opportunity to communicate regularly with the staff on an informal basis.

management consultant *n* a professional adviser who specializes in giving advice to organizations on ways of improving their business efficiency and profitability.

manager *n* a person who manages a company, organization, etc; an agent who looks after the business affairs of an actor, writer, etc; a person who organizes the training of a sports team; a person who manages efficiently.

manageress *n* a woman who manages a business, shop, etc.

managerial *adj* of or pertaining to a manager or management.—**managerially** *adv*.

managing director *n* the director in a company who has the responsibility for the day-to-day running of the company.

Managua *n* capital city of Nicaragua.

manakin *n* any of a genus of small South American birds with bright plumage and short beaks; a manikin.

Manama (Al Manamah) *n* capital city of Bahrain.

mañana *adv* tomorrow; by and by. * *n* an unspecified time in the future.

Manannan mac Lir *n* (*Irish Celtic myth*) the son of Lir. Like his father, he was a sea-god and is associated with sea journeys to the Otherworld. The first king of the Isle of Man.

Manasseh *n* (*Bible*) the elder son of Joseph and therefore ancestor of one of the tribes of Israel.

manat *n* the standard monetary unit of Azerbaijan and Turkmenistan, made up of 100 gopik.

man-at-arms *n* (*pl* men-at-arms) *n* an armed soldier, esp of medieval times.

manatee *n* a large aquatic animal resembling a whale found in tropical seas, the sea cow.

Manawydan fab Lyr *n* (*Welsh Celtic myth*) the son of Llyr. He may be the Welsh equivalent of Manannan mac Lir; said to have been the brother of Bendigeid Vran and Branwen, and possibly a cousin of Pryderi. He is also said to have been the husband of Rhiannon.

mancando *n* (*mus*) (*Italian*) "fading away."

Manchester *n* major English city in United Kingdom of Great Britain and Northern Ireland (UK).

Manchester School *n* (*mus*) the name applied to a group of British composers who studied music at the Royal Manchester College during the 1950s. They include Harrison Birtwistle and Peter Maxwell Davies, among others.

manchineel *n* a poisonous tropical American tree.

manciple *n* in UK, a catering official or steward, esp in a monastery, college, or Inn of Court.

Mancunian *adj* of Manchester. * *n* a citizen of Manchester.

mand. *abbr* (*law*) (*Latin*) = *mandamus*, "we send" (type of writ).

mandala *n* a circular figure used as a symbol of the universe in various religions.

Mandalay *n* major city in the Union of Myanmar.

mandamus *n* (*pl* mandamuses) (*law*) (*formerly*) a writ issued by a superior court directing the person or inferior court to whom it is issued to perform some specified act or public duty.

mandarin *n* (*formerly*) a high-ranking bureaucrat of the Chinese empire; any high-ranking official, esp one given to pedantic sometimes obscure public pronouncements; (*with cap*) the Beijing dialect that is the official pronunciation of the Chinese language; the fruit of a small spiny Chinese tree that has been developed in cultivation (—*also* **tangerine**).

mandarin collar *n* a narrow, stand-up collar, open in front.

mandatary *n* (*pl* mandataries) a person or nation to whom a mandate is given.

mandate *n* an order or command; the authority to act on the behalf of another, esp the will of constituents expressed to their representatives in legislatures. * *vt* to entrust by mandate.

mandatory *adj* of, containing, or having the nature of a mandate; required by mandate; compulsory; (*nation*) holding a mandate. * *n* a mandatary.—**mandatorily** *adv*.

M & B *abbr* = May and Baker; Mills and Boon.

M & E *abbr* = music and effects.

Mandela *n* 1. Nelson [Rolihlahla] (1918–) South African lawyer and nationalist leader; imprisoned as leader of the African National Congress (1964–90); became president following the end of apartheid (1994–99). 2. His second wife, **Winnie** (1934–) was convicted in 1991 of complicity in the murder of a young black activist, with few observers expecting her to go to prison. They separated in 1992.

Mandelstam *n* Osip (1891–1938) Russian poet, associated with Akhmatova in the Acmeist group, whose collections are *Stone*, *Tristia*, and *Poems*. In 1934 he and his wife, **Nadezhda Mandelstam** (1899–1980), were exiled to Siberia where he died. Nadezhda's two books describing her husband's life and work, *Hope Against Hope* and *Hope Abandoned*, affirm the resilience of the human spirit.

Mandeville *n* Sir **John** (*fl*.14th century) supposed English author of *The Travels of Sir John Mandeville*, an eventful and thoroughly mendacious travel book that has charmed countless readers since its first appearance in the 14th century.

M & G *abbr* = Mercantile and General.

mandible *n* (*biol*) the lower jaw of a vertebrate; the mouth parts of an insect; either jaw of a beaked animal.—**mandibular** *adj*.

mandolin *n* mandoline a stringed instrument, similar to the lute, but smaller and usu played with a plectrum. It has four pairs of strings and has occasionally been used as an orchestral instrument.

m & r *abbr* = maintenance and repairs.

mandragora *n* (*poet*) mandrake; a narcotic obtained from it.

mandrake *n* a plant of the nightshade family with narcotic properties that, in folklore, shrieked when uprooted; the May apple.

mandrel, mandril *n* the shank of a lathe, to which work is fixed while turned; the revolving arbor of a circular saw or other machine tool; the spindle that drives the headstock of a lathe.

mandrill *n* a large baboon of West Africa, the male having a red and blue backside.

m & s *abbr* = maintenance and supply.

M & S *abbr* = Marks and Spencer PLC.

manducate *vt* (*poet*) to chew, eat.

mane *n* long hair that grows on the back of the neck of the horse, lion, etc.

man-eater *n* an animal that eats human flesh.

manège, manege *n* a school for training horses and teaching horsemanship; the movements of a trained horse.

manes *n* (*npl*:*often cap*) (*Roman mythology*) the souls or ghosts of the dead, who were offered sacrifices at funerals and at the Parentalia, or Fralia, commemorative ceremonies held by the Romans in February.—*also* **dimanes** (*sing*) the spirit of a dead person.

Manet *n* Edouard (1832–83) French painter. Some of his paintings, such as *Le Déjeuner sur l'Herbe* (1863) and *Olympia* (1863), initially caused outrage due to his direct approach and fresh, painterly style, but over time his paintings won increasing acceptance, and he was awarded the Légion d'Honneur in 1881.

Manetho *n* (*Egypt*) an Egyptian priest from the time of Greek rule (around 250 BC), who compiled a kind of history of Egypt together with a list of kings and dynasties.

maneuver *n* a planned and controlled movement of troops, warships, etc; a skillful or shrewd move; a stratagem. * *vti* to perform or cause to perform maneuvers; to manage or plan skillfully; to move, get, make, etc by some scheme.—*also* **manoeuvre.**—**maneuverable, manoeuvrable** *adj*.—**maneuverer, manoeuvrer** *n*.

manful *adj* showing courage and resolution.—**manfully** *adv*.

mangabey *n* (*pl* mangabeys) a large, slender, arboreal, African monkey.

manganate *n* a salt of manganic acid.

manganese *n* a hard brittle metallic element; its oxide.

manganese star *n* (*astron*) an unusual star with a spectrum showing a remarkable excess of manganese, with gallium, yttrium and often mercury.

manganic *adj* pertaining to, resembling, or containing manganese in the trivalent state.

mange *n* a skin disease affecting mainly domestic animals, which causes itching.

mangel-wurzel *n* a variety of beet used as cattle-fodder.

manger *n* a trough in a barn or stable for livestock fodder.

mangle[1] *vt* to crush, mutilate; to spoil, ruin.

mangle[2] *n* a machine for drying and pressing sheets, etc between rollers. * *vt* to smooth through a mangle.

mango *n* (*pl* mangoes) a yellow-red fleshy tropical fruit with a firm central stone.

mangonel *n* an ancient military engine for hurling stones.

mangosteen *n* a tropical Indian tree; its red-brown, sweet, juicy fruit about the size of an orange.

mangrove *n* a tropical tree or shrub with root-forming branches.

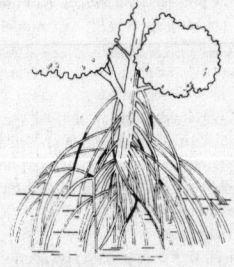

mangy *adj* (**mangier, mangiest**) having mange; scruffy, shabby.—**manginess** *n*.

manhandle *vt* to handle roughly; to move by human force.

manhole *n* a hole through which one can enter a sewer, drain, etc.

manhood *n* the state or time of being a man; virility; courage, etc.

man-hour *n* the time unit equal to one hour of work done by one person.

manhunt *n* a hunt for a fugitive.—**manhunter** *n*.

mania *n* (*med*) a mental illness characterized by great excitement and euphoria which then gives way to irritability as in manic depressive psychosis; great excitement or enthusiasm; a craze.

maniac *n* a madman; a person with wild behavior; a person with great enthusiasm for something.—**maniacal** *adj*.

manic *adj* affected with, characterized by, or relating to mania.

manic depressive psychosis *n* (*med*) a form of severe mental illness in which there are alternating bouts of mania and severe depression. * *n* a person suffering from this.

Manichaeism, Manicheism *n* the doctrine of the Manicheans, who held the dualistic theory of two eternal equal beings or principles, light (God), the author of all good, and darkness (Evil or Satan), the author of all evil, locked in a constant struggle for ascendancy; any similar doctrine.—**Manichaean, Manichean** *n*, *adj*.

Manichee *n* one of the sect of Manicheans.

manicure *n* trimming, polishing etc of fingernails.—*also vt*.—**manicurist** *n*.

M

manifest *adj* obvious, clearly evident. * *vt* to make clear; to display, to reveal. * *n* a list of a ship's or aircraft's cargo; a list of passengers on an aircraft.—**manifestation** *n*.—**manifestly** *adv*.

manifestation *n* the act of manifesting; the state of being manifested; the demonstration of the reality or existence of a quality, person, etc; the form of revelation of an idea, divine being, etc.

manifesto *n* (*pl* **manifestoes, manifestos**) a public printed declaration of intent and policy issued by a government or political party.

manifold *adj* having many forms, parts, etc; of many sorts. * *n* a pipe (e.g. in an engine) with many inlets and outlets. * *vt* to make copies of.—**manifolder** *n*.

manikin *n* a little man, a dwarf; an anatomical model of the body; a mannequin.—*also* **mannikin**.

manila, manilla *n* a strong, buff-colored paper originally made from hemp from the Philippines.

Manila *n* capital city of Philippines.

MAnimSc *abbr* = Master of Animal Science.

man in the moon *n* an imaginary resemblance between the moon's surface and the face of a man.

man in the street *n* an average person as opposed to an expert.

manioc *n* cassava, a tropical plant from the roots of which tapioca and cassava are prepared.

maniple *n* (*formerly*) a band worn on the left arm by a priest at mass; a company of a Roman legion.

manipulate *vt* to work or handle skillfully; to manage shrewdly or artfully, often in an unfair way.—**manipulation** *n*.—**manipulative** *adj*.—**manipulator** *n*.

manipulation *n* the act or process of manipulating; the state of being manipulated; the movement of bones, etc, by a physiotherapist; shrewd or knowing management of others for one's own ends.—**manipulatory** *adj*.

Manit. *abbr* = Manitoba.

manitou, manitu (*pl* **manitous, manitus, manitou, manitu**) *n* an American Indian spirit of good or evil.

Mankayane *n* town in Swaziland.

mankind *n* the human race.

Manley *n* **Michael [Norman]** (1924–97) Jamaican statesman; leader of the socialist People's National Party in 1969; prime minister (1972–80, 1989–92). He is regarded as a spokesman for the Third World.

manly *adj* (**manlier, manliest**) appropriate in character to a man; strong; virile.—**manliness** *n*.

man-made *adj* manufactured or created by man; artificial, synthetic.

Mann *n* **Thomas** (1875–1955) German novelist, critic, and essayist whose preoccupation was the role of the artist and artistic creation in modern society. Representative works include the novella *Death in Venice*, and the novels *The Magic Mountain*, *Mario and the Magician*, *Lotte in Weimar*, and *The Confessions of the Confidence Trickster Felix Krull*. He was awarded the Nobel prize for literature in 1929 and fled Nazi Germany in 1933.

Manna *n* (*Bible*) a sweet, sticky substance produced by insects which feed on the tamarisk bushes; the drops evaporate in the heat and lie on the ground from where they can be gathered in the cool of the morning and eaten; the food miraculously given to the ancient Israelites in the wilderness; any help that comes unexpectedly.

manned *adj* performed by a person; (*spacecraft, etc*) having a human crew.

mannequin *n* a model in a fashion show; a life-size model of the human body, used to fit or display clothes.

manner *n* a method of way of doing something; behavior; type or kind; habit; (*pl*) polite social behavior.

mannered *adj* full of mannerisms; artificial, stylized, etc.

mannerism *n* an idiosyncracy; an affected habit or style in dress, behavior or gesture; (*with cap*) a post-Reformation movement in art that held that beauty should be represented as an ideal and used exaggeration and distortion of naturalistic forms to attain this.—**mannerist** *adj, n*.

mannerless *n* rude, bad-mannered.

mannerly *adj* polite; respectful. * *adv* politely; respectfully.—**mannerliness** *n*.

mannikin *see* **manikin**.

mannish *adj* like or pertaining to a man; (*woman*) masculine, aping men.—**mannishly** *adv*.—**mannishness** *n*.

mano *n* (*Italian*) "hand."

Manoah *n* (*Bible*) the father of Samson, whose wife was told by an angel that she would bear a son who would begin to deliver Israel from the Philistines.

manoeuvre *see* **maneuver**.

man of the cloth *n* a clergyman.

man of the world *n* a man with wide experience of life.

man-of-war *n* (*pl* **men-of-war**) a (sailing) warship.

manometer *n* an instrument for measuring the pressure of gases and liquids.—**manometric, manometrical** *adj*.

man. op. *abbr* = manually operated.

manor *n* a landed estate; the main house on such an estate; (*sl*) a police district.—**manorial** *adj*.

manor house *n* (*archit*) an unfortified country mansion house of the late Middle Ages.

manpower *n* power furnished by human strength; the collective availability for work of people in a given area.

man. pr. *abbr* = *mane primo* (*Latin*) "first thing in the morning."

manqué *adj* potential; unsuccessful, failed.

MANS *abbr* = Member of the Academy of Natural Sciences.

mansard (roof) *n* (*archit*) a roof with a break in its slope, the lower part being steeper than the upper.

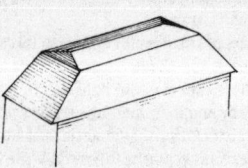

Mansart *n* 1. **François** (1598–1666) French architect. His notable works include Maisons Lafitte, Paris. 2. **Jules Hardouin** (1646–1708) French architect. His notable works include Dôme des Invalides, Paris.

manse *n* a nonconformist clergyman's house; (*Scot*) the house of a minister, esp a Church of Scotland parish minister; (*archit*) a large house.

manservant *n* (*pl* **menservants**) a male servant, esp a valet.

Mansfield *n* **Katherine** [Kathleen Mansfield Beauchamp] (1888–1923) New Zealand-born English short-story writer who is widely recognized as one of the masters of the short-story form. Her story collections are *In a German Pension*, *Bliss*, *The Garden Party*, *The Dove's Nest*, and *Something Childish*.

Manship *n* **Paul Howard** (1885–1966) American sculptor who designed the Paul J. Rainey memorial gateway of the New York Zoological Park, the epitome of the Streamline style.

-manship *suffix* skill in a particular field or activity, as *craftsmanship*; the art of maneuvering to gain tactical advantage, as *gamesmanship*.

mansion *n* a large, imposing house.

manslaughter *n* the killing of a human being by another, esp when unlawful but without malice.

mansuetude *n* (*arch*) gentleness, mildness.

manta (ray) *n* a very large fish with a flattened body and wing-like fins.

Manta *n* major city in Ecuador.

Mantegna *n* **Andrea** (*c*.1430–1506) Italian painter and prominent figure of the early Renaissance. A proficient draftsman, he had the rare ability for that time of being skilled in the use of perspective.

mantel *n* the facing above a fireplace; the shelf above a fireplace.—*also* **mantelpiece**.

mantelet *n* a woman's short cape of the mid-19th century; a movable, protective screen, formerly used by besiegers, gunners, pioneers, etc (—*also* **mantlet**).

mantelpiece *n* the surrounding structure of a fireplace made of wood, stone, marble or brick.

mantic *adj* of, having the power of, or pertaining to divination.

manticore *n* a fabulous beast with a human head, the body of a lion, and the tail of a scorpion.

mantilla *n* a scarf, usu of lace, worn as a headdress in Spain and South America; a woman's light cloak or hood.

mantis *n* (*pl* **mantises, mantes**) an insect that preys on other insects.—*also* **praying mantis**.

mantissa *n* (*math*) the decimal part of a logarithm.

mantle *n* (*geol*) that layer of the earth between the crust and core. a loose cloak; anything that envelops or conceals; a fine mesh cover on a gas or oil lamp that emits light by incandescence. * *vt* to cover as with a mantle. * *vi* to be or become covered.

mantlet *see* **mantelet**.

man-to-man *adj* with frankness and honesty.

Mantoux test *n* (*med*) a test for the presence of a measure of immunity to tuberculosis.

mantra *n* (*Hinduism, Buddhism*) a devotional incantation used in prayer, meditation and in certain forms of yoga.

mantua *n* a woman's loose gown of the 17th and 18th centuries, worn with the front of the skirt caught up or back to show an underskirt.

manual *adj* of the hands; operated, done, or used by the hand; involving physical skill or hard work rather than the mind. * *n* a handy book for use as a guide, reference, etc; a book of instructions; (*mus*) a keyboard on an organ or harpsichord; organs may have four manuals, named Solo, Swell, Great, and Choir.—**manually** *adv*.

manuf. *abbr* = manufactory; manufacture; manufacturer; manufacturing.

manufactory *n* (*pl* **manufactories**) *n* (*obs*) a factory, workshop.

manufacture *vt* to make, esp on a large scale, using machinery; to invent, fabricate. * *n* the production of goods by manufacturing.—**manufacturer** *n*.

manumit *vt* (**manumitting, manumitted**) to release from slavery; to free.—**manumission** *n*.—**manumitter** *n*.

manure *n* animal dung used to fertilize soil. * *vt* to spread manure on.

manus *n* (*pl* **manus**) (*zool*) the hand or that part of the anatomy corresponding to the hand; in ancient Roman law, the fact of a woman's legal subjugation to her husband.

manuscript *n* a book or document that is handwritten or typewritten as opposed to printed; an author's original handwritten or typewritten copy as submitted to a publisher before typesetting and printing.

many *adj* (**more, most**) numerous. * *n* a large number of persons or things.

manyplies *n sing* a ruminant's third stomach, the omasum.

many-sided *adj* with many aspects; versatile.—**many-sidedness** *n*.

Manzini *n* town in Swaziland.

Manzó *n* **Pio** (1939–69) Italian designer who designed autos, taxis and tractors for Fiat, packaging for Olivetti, and the Parentisi lamp.

MAO *abbr* = Master of Arts, Obstetrics, Master of Obstetric Art; monoamine oxidase.

Maori *n* (*pl* **Maoris, Maori**) a member of the indigenous peoples of New Zealand; their language.—*also adj.*

Mao Tse-tung, Mao Ze Dong *n* (1893–1976) Chinese Communist statesman, Marxist philosopher and founder of the Chinese Communist Party (1922); established his People's Republic (1949) following civil war; notorious for the murderous "Cultural Revolution" (1966–69) of his dictatorship.

map *n* a representation of all or part of the earth's surface, showing either natural features as continents and seas, etc or man-made features as roads, railways etc; (*law*) document which sets aside certain property within the county for certain purposes. * *vt* (**mapping, mapped**) to make a map of.

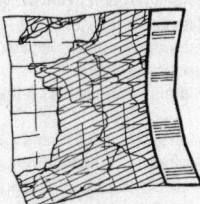

MAP *abbr* = mean arterial pressure; medical aid post.

maple *n* a tree with two-winged fruits, grown for shade, wood, or sap; its hard light-colored wood; the flavor of the syrup or sugar made from the sap of the sugar maple.

MAppArts *abbr* = Master in Applied Arts.

Mappin and Webb *n* British silversmiths founded in 1863.

map projection *n* a system for depicting the features of the earth onto a flat sheet of paper.

MAppSc *abbr* = Master in Applied Science.

map reference *see* **grid reference**.

MAPSAS *abbr* = Member of the Association of Public Service Administrative Staff.

Maputo *n* capital city of Mozambique.

maquette *n* a small preliminary model, as used by a sculptor, architect, etc.

maquis *n* low, evergreen, shrub vegetation characteristic of the northern coast of the Mediterranean Sea.

mar *vt* (**marring, marred**) to blemish, to spoil, to impair.

mar. *abbr* = maritime.

Mar. *abbr* = March.

MAr *abbr* = Master of Architecture.

MAR *abbr* = memory address register.

marabout[1]**, marabou** *n* a large African stork with handsome feathers and a short neck; its down, used as trimming, etc; a material produced from a fine raw silk.

marabout[2] *n* in North Africa, a Muslim hermit or saint; the shrine or burial place of a marabout.

Maracaibo *n* major city in Venezuela.

maracas *n* (*mus*) a pair of Latin-American percussion instruments made from gourds filled with seeds, pebbles or shells. Sound is produced by shaking the gourds.

MArAd *abbr* = Master of Archive Administration.

MARAD *abbr* = Maritime Administration

Maradi *n* major city in Niger.

maraschino *n* a strong sweet liqueur made from a type of wild cherry.

maraschino cherry *n* a cherry preserved in maraschino.

marasmus *n* emaciation or atrophy, esp in babies, when it is usu caused by defective feeding.—**marasmic** *adj.*

Marat *n* **Jean Paul** (1743–93) French revolutionary and journalist; a prominent supporter of Danton and Robespierre.

marathon *n* a foot race of 26 miles, 385 yards (42.195 km); any endurance contest.

Marathon *n* a town of ancient Greece in Attica, northeast of Athens; in Greek mythology, the eponymous hero of the Attic town of Marathon.

Maratti *n* **Carlo** (1625–1713) Italian portrait painter whose best works were influenced by the calm, classical tradition of Raphael, in contrast to the baroque dynamism of his contemporaries.

maraud *vi* to roam in search of plunder.—**marauder** *n.*—**marauding** *adj.*

MArb *abbr* = Master of Arboriculture.

Marbeck, John *see* **Merbecke, John**.

marble *n* (*geol*) a limestone that has been metamorphosed and recrystallized due to the action of heat, and that takes a high polish; a block or work of art made of marble; a little ball of stone, glass, etc; (*pl*) a children's game played with such balls; (*pl*) (*sl*) wits. * *adj* of or like marble.—**marbly** *adj.*

marbled *adj* veined or mottled like marble; (*meat*) streaked with fat.

marc *n* (*winemaking*) the refuse from pressed fruit; a brandy derived from this.

marc *abbr* = machine-readable cataloguing.

Marc *n* **Franz** (1880–1916) German expressionist painter; one of the leading members, with Kandinsky, of *Der Blaue Reiter* group of expressionist artists.

MA(RCA) *abbr* = (*Brit*) Master of Arts, Royal College of Art (Photography).

marcasite *n* (*geol*) white iron pyrites; a white metal, esp steel, cut and polished for use in jewelry.

Marceau *n* **Marcel** (1923–) French mime artist. Regarded as the world's leading mime artist. His films include *Silent Movie* (1976), in which his is the only speaking part.

marcel (wave) *n* a style of artificially waving the hair, popular in the 1920s and 1930s. * *vt* (**marcelling, marcelled**) to style in regular waves.

Marcello *n* **Benedetto** (1686–1739) an Italian composer, librettist and writer on music who was also a lawyer. He is known for his cantatas, psalm settings, oratorios and concertos. His brother, Alessandro, was also a composer of worth.

marcescent *adj* (*bot*) withering without falling off.—**marcescence** *n.*

march *vi* to walk with regular steps, as in military formation; to advance steadily. * *vt* to make a person or group march. * *n* a steady advance; a regular, steady step; the distance covered in marching; (*mus*) a piece of music with a strongly accented rhythm for marching.—**marcher** *n.*

March *n* the third month of the year having 31 days.

MArch *abbr* = Master in, or of, Architecture.

MArchE *abbr* = Master of Architectural Engineering.

marching orders *npl* official orders for infantry to move to a particular destination; (*inf*) a notice of dismissal.

marchioness *n* the wife or widow of a marquess; a woman of the rank of marquess.

marcia *n* (*mus*) (*Italian*) "march," so *alla marcia* means "in a marching style."

Marciano *n* **Rocky** [Rocco Francis Marchegiano] (1923–69) American boxer. He became world heavyweight champion (1952–56), and never lost a professional fight.

Marconi *n* **Guglielmo, Marchese** (1874–1937) Italian physicist and electrical engineer. He shared the 1909 Nobel prize for physics for his development of wireless telegraphy. He sent signals across the English Channel in 1898, and across the Atlantic in 1901, and later developed short-wave radio transmissions.

Marcos *n* **Ferdinand** [Edralin] (1917–89) Filipino politician. President of the Philippines (1965–86). He declared martial law in 1972, after which he ruled by oppressive and idiosyncratic decree. He was deposed in 1986 and lived in exile in Hawaii with his wife, **Imelda**, who, after his death, returned to the Philippines and was sued by the Philippines' government for corruption.

Marcuse *n* **Herbert** (1898–1979) German-born American philosopher. He became prominent in the 1960s as a theorist of the New Left. His works include *Eros and Civilisation* (1955) and *Soviet Marxism* (1958).

Mar del Plata *n* a city in Argentina.

Mardi gras *n* the last day before Lent, Shrove Tuesday, a day of carnival in some cities, esp New Orleans.

mare[1] *n* (*astron*) (*pl* **maria**) a large impact crater on the Moon's surface which was later filled with lava.

mare[2] *n* a mature female horse, mule, donkey.

Mare *n* **André** (1887–1932) French painter who also designed furniture in radical Cubist style.

mare clausum *n* (*law*) a body of water under one country's jurisdiction and closed to foreign ships.

mare liberum *n* (*law*) a body of water open to ships of all countries.

maremma *n* (*pl* **maremme**) an unhealthy marshy coastal district, esp in Italy.

Marenzio *n* **Luca** (1553–99) Italian composer who worked in Poland as well as in Rome. He is most famous for his madrigals, the style of which was influential.

mare's-tail *n* (*bot*) an aquatic plant with tiny flowers and tapering leaves; a wisp of trailing alto-cirrus cloud indicating strong winds at high altitude.

Marfan's syndrome *n* (*med*) an inherited disease of the connective tissue, producing defects in the skeleton, heart, and eyes. The person is abnormally tall and thin, has spindly, elongated fingers and toes, deformities of the spine and chest, and weak ligaments

marg. *abbr* = margin; marginal.

Margaret *n* (Maid of Norway) (1283–90) queen of Scotland (1286–1290). The daughter of Erik II of Norway and Margaret, daughter of Alexander III. Margaret was declared heiress to the Scottish throne in 1284 whilst still an infant.

Margaret of Antioch *n* **Saint** (date unknown) Syrian martyr; said to have been the daughter of a pagan priest of Antioch in Pisidia; tortured and beheaded for her Christianity. Joan of Arc believed that she, with St Catherine, appeared to her constantly. Her feast day until 1969 was 20 July.

Margaret of Scotland *n* **Saint** (c. 1045–93) Hungarian (?) queen of Scotland; daughter of the exiled Atheling Edward (son of Edmund Ironside, king of England in 1016); wife of the Scottish king, Malcolm Canmore; did much to assimilate the Celtic church to the rest of Christendom, built a church at Dunfermline and established Benedictine monks there, and re-founded Iona; canonized in 1250. Her feast day is 16 November.

margaric *adj* pertaining to, or like, a pearl.

margarine *n* a butter substitute made from vegetable and animal fats, etc.

margarite *n* (*geol*) a pearly translucent mineral related to mica; a bead-like rock formation.

margay *n* a South American tiger cat.

margin *n* a border, edge; the blank border of a printed or written page; an amount beyond what is needed; provision for increase, error, etc; (*commerce*) the difference between cost and selling price.

marginal *adj* written in the margin; situated at the margin or border; close to the lower limit of acceptability; very slight, insignificant; (*Brit politics*) denoting a constituency where the sitting MP has only a small majority. * *n* a marginal constituency.—**marginally** *adv.*

marginalia *npl* notes written in the margin of a book, etc.

M

marginalize *vt* to transfer someone away from the center of affairs in order to render them powerless.

marginal land *n* poor quality land that is difficult to cultivate and unlikely to be profitable, used mostly for rough grazing.

marginal revenue *n* the extra revenue that is obtained by a firm from the sale of an additional unit of production.

marginate *adj* (*biol*) having a margin. * *vt* to border something with a margin.— **margination** *n*.

Margold *n* **Emanuel Josef** (1889–1962) Austrian architect who became assistant to Josef **Hoffmann** at the **Wiener Werkstatte**.

margrave *n* (*formerly*) a German nobleman, one rank above a count.

margraviate, margravate *n* the domain or jurisdiction of a margrave.

margravine a female margrave; a margrave's wife or widow.

marguerite *n* a large daisy with white or yellow flowers.

Mari *n* (*Bible*) early civilization in Mesopotania *see also* **Mesopotania**.

Mari *n* **Enzo** (1932–) Italian designer whose wooden puzzles were put into production by Danese.

maria *npl* (*astron*) the "seas" on the surface of the moon.

mariachi *n* (*mus*) (*Spanish*) a Mexican folk group of variable size; it normally includes violins and guitars.

Marian *adj* pertaining to the Virgin Mary, or to Mary, Queen of England, or to Mary, Queen of Scots. * *n* one who worships the Virgin Mary; a partisan of Mary, Queen of England or Mary, Queen of Scots.

Maria Theresa[1] *n* (1717–80) Queen of Hungary and Bohemia and archduchess of Austria . She married the Holy Roman Emperor Francis I (1708–65) in 1736.

Maria Theresa[2] or **Maria Theresia** *n* the nickname for Haydn's symphony no. 48 in C. It is so called because it was written when Empress Maria Theresa visited Haydn's patron, Prince Esterhazy (1773).

Maribor *n* a a city in Slovenia.

Marie Antoinette *n* (1755–93) queen of France (1774–93) by marriage to Louis XVI of France. *See* **Louis XVI**.

Mariette *n* **Auguste** (1821–81) French Egyptologist who became Keeper of Monuments to the Egyptian government. He excavated the Sphinx and uncovered many other monuments.

marigold *n* (*bot*) a plant with a yellow or orange flower.

marijuana, marihuana *n* a narcotic obtained by smoking the dried flowers and leaves of the hemp plant.—*also* **cannabis, pot**.

marimba *n* (*mus*) a Latin American instrument which may have originated in Africa. It is similar to a large xylophone and can be played by up to four people at the same time.

marina *n* a small harbor with pontoons, docks, services, etc for yachts and pleasure craft.

marinade *n* a seasoning liquid in which meat, fish, etc is soaked to enhance flavor or to tenderize it before cooking. * *vt* to soak in a marinade.—*also* **marinate**.

marine *adj* of, in, near, or relating to the sea; maritime; nautical; naval. * *n* a soldier trained for service on land or sea; naval or merchant ships.

mariner *n* a seaman, sailor.

Marinetti *n* **Filipo** (1876–1944) Italian poet whose *Futurist Manifesto* was the founding document of futurism, calling, in literature, for the destruction of traditional sentence construction.

Mariolatry *n* the exaggerated worship of the Virgin Mary.

marionette *n* a little jointed doll or puppet moved by strings or wires.

Mariscal *n* **Javier** (1950–) Spanish designer of a wide range of products, from posters to furniture, comic strips to textiles.

marital *adj* of marriage, matrimonial.

maritime *adj* on, near, or living near the sea; of navigation, shipping, etc.

maritime climate *n* the climate of areas in mid-latitudes that is moderated by the influence of the sea; cool and wet winters, warm and moist summers.

marjoram *n* (*bot*) a fragrant herb used in cooking and salads.

mark[1] *n* a spot, scratch, etc on a surface; a distinguishing sign or characteristic; a cross made instead of a signature; a printed or written symbol, as a punctuation mark; a brand or label on an article showing the maker, etc; an indication of some quality, character, etc; a grade for academic work; a standard of quality; impression, influence, etc; a target; (*sl*) a potential victim for a swindle.* *vt* to make a mark or marks on; to identify as by a mark; to show plainly; to heed; to grade, rate; (*Brit football*) to stay close to an opponent so as to hinder his play; (*with* **down**) to reduce the price of (goods, etc); to make a note of; to designate as a victim or target.

mark[2] *n* the basic monetary unit of Germany.

Markarian galaxy *n* (*astron*) a galaxy that emits particularly strongly in the ultraviolet, usu from the nucleus, occasionally from a more extended region.

markdown *n* a selling at a reduced price; the amount of reduction.

marked *adj* having a mark or marks; noticeable; obvious.—**markedly** *adv*.

Markelius *n* **Sven G** (1889–1972) Swedish architect. His notable works include Vällingby (suburb of Stockholm).

marker *n* one that marks; something used for marking.

market *n* a meeting of people for buying and selling merchandise; a space or building in which a market is held; the chance to sell or buy; demand for (goods, etc); a region where goods can be sold; a section of the community offering demand for goods. * *vti* to offer for sale; to sell, buy domestic provisions.—**marketability** *n*.—**marketable** *adj*.

market challenger *n* a firm that is ranked second in terms of the market share of a product and that may be in a position to challenge the position of the market leader by the mounting of an aggressive campaign.

market development *n* a sales strategy undertaken by a firm that aims at extending the sales of existing products in new markets.

market economy *n* an economic system based on the free operation of the forces of demand and supply.

market forces *npl* the forces of supply and demand that in a free market determine such things as the price at which a product is offered.

market garden *n* an area where fruit and vegetables are grown for the market.— **market gardener** *n*.

marketing *n* act of buying or selling; the process relating to the various steps involved in identifying and satisfying customers' needs.

marketing audit *n* a review of a firm's marketing capabilities by assessing its strengths and weaknesses.

marketing mix *n* the factors that are important to a firm in marketing its products to consumers.

marketing strategy *n* a strategy employed by a firm in order to identify and achieve its marketing objectives.

market leader *n* the seller of a product that has the largest share of a market.

market-maker *n* a dealer on the London Stock Exchange who buys and sells securities as a principal.

market-making *n* the activity of buying and selling stocks, shares, bonds, securities, etc.—**market-maker** *n*.

marketplace *n* a market in a public square; the world of economic trade and activity; a sphere in which ideas, opinions, etc compete for acceptance.

market price *n* the current price available in the market.

market research *n* the gathering of factual information from consumers concerning their preferences for goods and services.

market segment *n* a part of a market that differs from other parts in terms of customer profile, buying pattern, etc, and therefore can be targeted by separate marketing campaigns, etc.

market segmentation *n* the division of a market into market segments.

market share *n* the proportion of total sales of a product in a market that is achieved by one brand or company.

market-skimming pricing *n* a pricing policy that involves the setting of a relatively high price for a product in order to make high profit margins.

market value *n* the amount obtainable for goods and services on the open market.

Markiewicz *n* [**Constance Georgine**] **Countess** (1868–1927) Irish nationalist; a member of Sinn Féin involved in the Easter Rising of 1916; the first woman to be elected to the British Parliament in 1918, but refused to take her seat.

marking *n* the conferring of a mark or marks; the characteristic arrangement of marks, as on fur or feathers.

marking-up *n* the raising of prices by market-makers on the London Stock Exchange in expectation of an increased demand for a particular security.

markka *n* the standard monetary unit of Finland, made up of 100 pennia.

Markova *n* **Dame Alicia** [Lilian Alicia Marks] (1910–) English ballerina. She became a member of Diaghilev's Ballet Russe (1924–29) and then of the Vic–Wells Ballet, where she became prima ballerina (1933–35).

Mark *n* 1. **Saint** (*Bible*) (first century) evangelist; writer of the second Gospel, probably between AD 65 and 70; considered to be esp the historian of the Resurrection. His feast day is 25 April. 2. **the Gospel of** (*Bible*) Mark did not set out to write a straightforward chronological life of Jesus; instead he concentrates on the supreme importance of the suffering and death of Christ – a "Gospel for martyrs."

marksman *n* (*pl* **marksmen**) one who is skilled at shooting.—**marksmanship** *n*.

Marks *n* **Simon** [1st Baron Marks of Broughton] (1888–1964) English businessman. He inherited the Marks and Spencer chain of shops, and, with Israel (later Lord) Seiff, built the chain into one of the most respected retail empires in the world.

markup *n* the amount by which the cost of goods or services is increased when the selling price is established; the amount of increase.—*also vt*.

markup language *n* (*comput*) an internet text description language; a mechanism to identify structures in an electronic document or data format. *See* **SGML, XML** and **HTML**.

marl[1] *n* a mixture of clay and carbonate of lime, used as a manure. * *vt* to manure with marl.—**marly** *adj*.

marl[2] *vt* (*naut*) to wind with marlines, securing with a hitch at each turn.

Marley *n* **Bob** [Robert Nesta Marley] (1945–81) Jamaican singer and songwriter and devout Rastafarian. With his group, the Wailers, he became the world's leading reggae singer. His songs include "No Woman, No Cry," and "I Shot the Sheriff ."

marlin *n* (*pl* **marlin**, **marlins**) any of various long-nosed marine fishes hunted as game and used for food.

marline, marlin, marling *n* (*naut*) a two-stranded cord, often tarred, used for winding round ropes, splicing, etc.

marlinespike, marlinspike, marlingspike *n* a pointed piece of iron used for opening the strands of a rope in splicing, etc.

Marlowe *n* **Christopher** (1564–93) English dramatist and poet; one of the first English dramatists to use blank verse to great dramatic and poetic effect in his plays, the most famous of which are *Tamburlaine the Great* and his masterpiece, *Doctor Faustus*. He also wrote some very fine classically inspired poetry, e.g. *Hero and Leander*.

marmalade *n* a jam-like preserve made from oranges, sugar and water.

Marmara, Marmora *n* the sea separating Asia Minor from Europe.

marmoreal, marmorean *adj* of or like marble.

marmoset *n* a small monkey of South and Central America.

marmot *n* a widely distributed rodent with rough fur, a bushy tail and short legs.

maroon[1] *n* a dark brownish red (—*also adj*); a type of distress rocket.

maroon[2] *vt* to abandon alone, esp on a desolate island; to leave helpless and alone.

marque *n* a brand of a product, esp a car.

marquee *n* a large tent used for entertainment; a canopy over an entrance, as to a theater.

marquess *n* in UK, a title of nobility ranking between a duke and an earl.

marquetry, marqueterie *n* (*pl* **marquetries, marqueteries**) decorative inlaid veneers of wood, ivory, etc used esp in furniture.

Marquez *n* **Gabriel Garcia** (1928–) Colombian novelist whose masterpiece is *One Hundred Years of Solitude* and who is generally regarded as the greatest practitioner of magic realism. He was awarded the Nobel prize for literature in 1982.

marquis *n* (*pl* **marquises, marquis**) (*Europe*) a nobleman equivalent in rank to a British marquess.

Marquis *n* **Don[ald Robert Perry]** (1878–1937) American newspaper columnist and author of several books, e.g. *archys life of mehitabel*, narrated by a cockroach, Archy, who cannot use the shift keys, and often featuring an alley cat called Mehitabel and with a minor cast drawn from all parts of the animal kingdom.

marquisate *n* the estate, dignity, or lordship of a marquis.

marquise *n* a marchioness; a gemstone or ring setting cut in an oval pointed form.

Marrakech *n* a city in Morocco.

marram grass *n* one of the commonest plants found on sand dunes with roots that stabilize the dunes.

marriage *n* the legal contract by which a woman and man become wife and husband; a wedding, either religious or civil; a close union.

marriageable *adj* of an age to marry.—**marriageability** *n*.

marriage license *n* (*law*) a document declaring that two people did in fact get married on the date and by the person indicated on the license.

Marriner *n* **Neville** (1924–..) an English conductor and pianist who founded the famous Academy of St Martin-in-the-Fields in 1956.

marron glacé *n* (*pl* **marrons glacés**) *n* a cooked chestnut coated with sugar.

marrow *n* (*anat*) the fatty tissue in the cavities of bones; the best part or essence of anything; a widely grown green fruit eaten as a vegetable.

marrowbone *n* a bone containing marrow used in cooking.

marrowfat, marrow pea *n* a late variety of pea that has large seeds; the seed of one of these.

marry[1] *vt* (**marrying, married**) to join as wife and husband; to take in marriage; to unite. * *vi* to get married.

marry[2] *interj* (*arch*) indeed, forsooth.

Mars *n* (*astron*) the fourth planet in the solar system and, after earth, the outermost of the terrestrial planets; (*Roman myth*) the god of war and of agriculture, identified with the Greek Ares; (*alchemy*) iron.

Marsala *n* a sweet fortified wine from Sicily.

Marseillaise *adj* pertaining to the city of Marseilles in France or to its inhabitants.

Marseillaise, La *n* the French national anthem which was composed by Rouget de Lisle in 1792 and is so called because it was sung by men from Marseille as they entered Paris in the same year.

Marseille *n* a city in France.

marsh *n* an area of boggy, poorly drained land, often containing small stretches of open water.—**marshiness** *n*.—**marshy** *adj*.

Marsh *n* **Reginald** (1898–1954) American painter. He worked as an illustrator for *Harper's Bazaar* and *The New Yorker* and painted seriously from about 1923. Typical works include *The Park Bench* (1933) and *Pip and Flip* (1932).

marshal *n* in some armies, a general officer of the highest rank; an official in charge of ceremonies, parades, etc. * *vt* (**marshaling, marshaled** *or* **marshalling, marshalled**) (*ideas, troops*) to arrange in order; to guide.—**marshaller** *n*.

Marshall *n* 1. **Alfred** (1842–1924) English economist. His works, e.g., *Principles of Economics* (1890) and *Industry and Trade* (1919), have been of great influence on modern economics. He devised concepts such as "elasticity," "consumer surplus" and "time analysis." 2. **George C[atlett]** (1880–1959) American general and statesman; US army chief of staff in World War II; winner of the 1953 Nobel peace prize for his work as secretary of state on the Marshall Aid Plan.

Marshall Islands *n* an archipelago of over 1,000 atolls and islets in eastern Micronesia to the northwest of Kiribati in the western Pacific Ocean. The Marshall Islands are a republic in free association with the USA.

marsh gas *n* a mostly methane gas formed by the decomposition of organic materials.

Mars Hill *see* **Areopagus**.

marsh mallow, marshmallow *n* (*bot*) a perennial plant with a pink flower and a mucilaginous root used in confectionery and medicine; a soft spongy confection made of sugar, gelatin, etc; (*formerly*) a sweet paste made from the root of the marsh mallow.

marsupial *adj* (*zool*) of an order of mammals that carry their young in a pouch. * *n* an animal of this kind, as a kangaroo, opossum.

marsupium *n* (*pl* **marsupia**) (*zool*) in female marsupials, an external pouch for carrying and nurturing young.

mart *n* a market.

Mart. *abbr* = Martyrology.

martagon *n* (*bot*) a variety of lily with purple-red flowers found in Europe and Asia; a Turk's-cap lily.

martelé *n* (*mus*) (*French*) *see* **martellato**.

martellato *n* (*mus*) (*Italian*) literally, "hammered"; a term used mainly in music for strings to indicate that notes should be played with short, sharp strokes of the bow. The term is also occasionally used in guitar and piano music.

Martello tower *n* (*archit*) (*formerly*) a type of low, round, fort used for coastal defense and with a flat roof on which guns were mounted.

marten *n* (*zool*) (*pl* **martens, marten**) a carnivorous tree-dwelling weasel-like mammal.

Martha *n* (*Bible*) sister of Mary and Lazarus, friends of Jesus, who lived at Bethany. Martha welcomed Jesus to their home but complained that Mary was not helping sufficiently; Jesus rebuked her for over-anxiety.

martial *adj* warlike; military.—**martially** *adv*.

martial arts *npl* systems of self-defense, usu from the Orient, practiced as sports, as karate or judo.

martial law *n* rule by military authorities over civilians, as during a war or political emergency.

Martian *adj* of or relating to the planet Mars. * *n* an inhabitant of Mars.

martin *n* one of various types of bird similar to the swallow, with a characteristic shape of tail; the house martin.

Martin *n* **Saint** (*d*. 401) born in Pannonia (now Hungary); a disciple of St Hilary of Poitiers; founded a monastery in Genoa, the first in Gaul; bishop of Tours (371); patron saint of France. His feast day is 11 November.

Martin *n* 1. **Camille** (1861–98) French painter who designed bookbindings. 2. **Dean [Dion Paul Crocetti]** (1917–95) American singer and actor famous for his "crooning" singing style. 3. **Frank** (1890–1974) Swiss composer, pianist and harpsichordist who settled in Holland; best known for his operas ballets, orchestral pieces, incidental pieces and choral works. 4. **Sir Leslie** (1908–) English architect. His notable works include Roehampton housing estate.

martinet *n* one who exerts strong discipline.—**martinetish, martinettish** *adj*.

martingale, martingal *n* a broad strap passing from the noseband to the girth of a horse between its forelegs to keep its head down and prevent it from rearing; a gambling system of doubling successive stakes; (*naut*) a short spar under the bowsprit used as a lower stay for the jib boom or flying jib boom.

martini *n* (*trademark*) (*often with cap*) Italian vermouth; a cocktail of gin and vermouth.

Martinique *n* one of the larger Windward Islands in the Lesser Antilles group in the southern Caribbean, administered as an overseas department of France.

Martinmas *n* St Martin's Day, November 11, a Christian festival; one of the Scottish quarter days.

Martinu *n* **Bohuslav** (1890–1959) Czech composer who wrote thirteen operas (e.g., *Comedy on the Bridge, The Greek Passion*) six symphonies, choral works, ballets, sonatas and many pieces of chamber music.

martlet *n* (*arch*) a martin; (*her*) a bird without legs or beak.

MArt/RCA *abbr* = (*Brit*) Master of Arts, Royal College of Art.

martyr *n* a person tortured for a belief or cause; a person who suffers from an illness. * *vt* to kill as a martyr; to make a martyr of.—**martyrdom** *n*.

martyrize *vt* to martyr.

martyrology *n* (*pl* **martyrologies**) *n* a register or history of martyrs; the study of the lives of the martyrs.—**martyrological, martyrologic** *adj*.—**martyrologist** *n*.

martyry *n* (*pl* **martyries**) *n* a shrine in honor of a martyr.

marv *abbr* = maneuvrable re-entry vehicle.

marvel *n* anything wonderful; a miracle. * *vti* (**marveling, marveled** *or* **marvelling, marvelled**) to become filled with wonder, surprise, etc.—**marvelous, marvellous** *adj*.

MARVEL *abbr* = Machine Assisted Realization of the Virtual Electronic Library

Marvell *n* **Andrew** (1621–78) English poet and passive supporter of Parliament during the English Civil War, whose metaphysical poems, e.g. "The Garden" and "Upon Appleton House," display an enormous talent for symbolism and metaphor,

M

and whose poem celebrating Cromwell's suppression of the Irish Rebellion, "An Horatian Ode upon Cromwell's Return from Ireland," remains one of the great political poems.

Marx *n* 1. **Brothers** an American comedy group of brothers (of German parents), consisting of **Arthur Marx (Harpo)** (1893–1964), **Milton (Gummo)** (1894–1977), **Herbert Marx (Zeppo)** (1901–79), **Julius Marx (Groucho)** (1895–1977) and **Leonard Marx (Chico)** (1891–1961). Their films, without Gummo, include *Monkey Business* (1932), *Duck Soup* (1933) and *A Night at the Opera* (1937). 2. **Enid Crystal Dorothy** (1902–93) British textile and graphic designer who set up her own workshop in 1927. 3. **Karl** (1818–83) German philosopher, communist, and influential political thinker whose theories on class struggle dominated 20th-century politics from the Bolshevik Revolution of 1917 to the collapse of the Communist regimes in Eastern Europe in 1989–90. His works include *Das Kapital*, his study of the economics of capitalism, and, with Engels, *The Communist Manifesto*.

Marxian *n* a student or advocate of Marxism.—*also adj.*

Marxism *n* the theory and practice developed by Karl Marx and Friedrich Engels advocating public ownership of the means of production and the dictatorship of the proletariat until the establishment of a classless society.—**Marxist** *adj*, *n*.

Mary[1] *n* 1. (*d.* ?AD 63) (*Bible*) also called the Virgin Mary, the Blessed Virgin, Saint. Wife of Joseph and mother of Jesus Christ. The feast of the Assumption, on 15 August, is the traditional date of her death and is her feast day. 2. (*Bible*) wife of Clopas and mother of James (the younger) and Joseph (Joses), disciples of Jesus. She was among the women who witnessed his Crucifixion from afar, and who went to the tomb early in the morning of the third day. 3. (*Bible*) mother of John Mark, in whose house Jesus' followers met for prayer; traditionally the house in which in which the Last Supper was held.

Mary[2] *n* a a city in Turkmenistan.

Mary I (1516–58) Queen of England. The daughter of Catherine of Aragon and Henry VIII, she inherited the throne in 1553 after her half-brother **Edward VI** (1537–53) died and after Lady Jane Grey was deposed. She gradually reintroduced Roman Catholicism into England and married Philip II in 1554.

Mary II *n* (1662–1694) queen of England, Scotland and Ireland (1689–1694). The elder daughter of James, Duke of York, afterwards James II, by his wife, Anne Hyde, daughter of Lord Clarendon. Married in 1677 to her cousin William, Prince of Orange (later William III).

Maryland (MD) *n* a state of the United States of America (USA) of which the capital is Annapolis.

"Maryland, My Maryland" *n* the song of the American State, Maryland.

Mary Magdalene *n* Saint (first century) (*Bible*) a woman of Magdala, near the Sea of Galilee, from whom Jesus cast out seven devils. The tradition that identifies her with the repentant prostitute who anointed Jesus' feet has been repudiated by the Church. However, she is the patron saint of penitent sinners and repentant prostitutes. Her feast day is 22 July.

Mary of Bethany *n* (*Bible*) sister of Martha and Lazarus; Luke mentions her as sitting at Jesus' feet listening to his teaching, while her sister was distracted with much serving; Jesus praised Mary for her devotion.

Mary, Queen of Scots *n* (1542–87) queen of Scotland. The daughter of James V by Mary of Lorraine, a princess of the family of Guise. She was married to: **Francis II** (1544–60), king of France (1559–60); **Henry Stewart, Lord Darnley** (1545–67); **James Hepburn, 4th Earl of Bothwell** (1535–78). A Roman Catholic, Mary saw increasing religious strife during her reign as Protestant reformers made their mark. The marriage to Bothwell sealed her fate, and she was forced to abdicate in favor of her son (*see* **James VI and I**) and to flee to England in 1567, where she was eventually executed on Elizabeth I's orders.

marziale *n* (*mus*) (*Italian*) "warlike."

marzipan *n* a paste made from ground almonds, sugar and egg white, used to coat cakes or make confectionery.

mas. or **masc.** *abbr* = masculine.

MAS *abbr* = Manchester Astronomical Society; Master of Applied Science; Medical Advisory Service; Microbeam Analysis Society; Money Advice Scotland.

Masaccio *n* (1401–*c.*1428) Florentine painter, a key figure of the early Renaissance. His most important surviving masterpieces include the Pisa polyptych (1426), and the *Trinity* fresco (*c.*1428) in Santa Maria Novella, Florence.

Masaki *n* **Yuri** (1950–) Japanese glass designer, president of the Masaki Glass and Art Studio.

Masaryk *n* 1. **Tomás [Garrigue]** (1850–1937) Czech statesman who founded (with Benes) the modern state of Czechoslovakia in 1918, and became the country's first president (1918–35). His works include *Russia and Europe* (1913). 2. His son, **Jan [Garrigue] Masaryk** (1886–1948); also a Czech statesman. He became foreign minister of the Czech government in exile in 1941. He returned to Czechoslovakia (with Benes). It is assumed that either he killed himself in grief at the Communist takeover of his country, or he was murdered by the Communists.

masc *abbr* = masculine (used in grammar).

MASc *abbr* = Master of Agricultural Science; Master of Applied Scienc.

Mascagni *n* **Pietro** (1863–1945) Italian composer best known for his outstanding early work, the opera *Cavalleria Rusticana*. He was a confirmed fascist, as his opera *Nerone* shows.

mascara *n* a cosmetic for darkening the eyelashes.

mascle *n* (*her*) a lozenge perforated with a lozenge shape; a voided lozenge.

mascon *n* (*astron*) a local concentration of mass at the lunar surface associated with the maria.

mascot *n* a person, animal or thing thought to bring good luck.

masculine *adj* having characteristics of or appropriate to the male sex; (*gram*) of the male gender.—**masculinity** *n*.

Masefield *n* **John [Edward]** (1878–1967) English poet whose *Salt-Water Ballads* includes his best-known poem, "I must go down to the sea again." He was appointed poet laureate in 1930.

maser *n* (acronym for Microwave Amplification by Stimulated Emission of Radiation) a microwave amplifier/oscillator working in a similar way to the laser.

Maseru *n* capital city of Lesotho.

mash *n* any soft, pulpy mass; crushed malt and hot water for brewing; (*inf*) mashed potatoes. * *vt* to crush into a mash.

MASH *abbr* = Mobile Army Surgical Hospital.

Mashhad *n* a city in Islamic Republic of Iran.

masher[1] *n* a kitchen utensil for mashing potatoes and other vegetables.

masher[2] *n* (*sl*) a man who forces his attentions on women.

mashie *n* (*formerly*) an iron golf club with a deep, short blade, more or less lofted.

MASI *abbr* = Member of the Architects and Surveyors Institute.

mask[1] *n* a covering to conceal or protect the face; a molded likeness of the face; anything that conceals or disguises; a respirator placed over the nose and mouth to aid or prevent inhalation of a gas; (*surgery*) a protective gauze placed over the nose and mouth to prevent the spread of germs; (*photog*) a screen used to cover part of a sensitive surface to prevent exposure by light. * *vt* to cover or conceal as with a mask; to disguise one's intentions or character.—**masked** *adj*.

mask[2] *see* **masque**.

masker *n* a masked person; a participant in a masque or masquerade.—*also* **masquer**.

MASME *abbr* = Member of the American Society of Mechanical Engineers.

masochism *n* abnormal pleasure, esp sexual, obtained from having physical or mental pain inflicted on one by another person.—**masochist** *n*.—**masochistic** *adj*.

MA(SocSci) *abbr* = Master of Arts (Social Science).

mason *n* a person skilled in working or building with stone; (*with cap*) a Freemason.

Mason *n* 1. **Daniel Gregory** (1873–1953) American composer and writer on music. His works include three symphonies (e.g., A *Lincoln Symphony*). 2. **James** (1909–84) English stage and film actor. His films include *A Star is Born* (1954), *Georgy Girl* (1966) and his last film, *The Shooting Party* (1984). 3. **Lowell** (1792–1872) grandfather of Daniel Gregory; American organist and influential teacher. 4. **William** (1829–1908), son of Lowell Mason; American concert pianist, composer and writer.

masonic *adj* (*often cap*) relating to Freemasonry.

masonry *n* (*pl* **masonries**) the craft carried out by masons of building with stone; stonework.

Masora, Masorah *n* a critical work in Hebrew by the rabbis of the 6th-10th centuries, indicating how the verbal text of the Bible is to be written in accordance with ancient rules; the critical notes and commentaries of this.—**Masoretic** *adj*.

MASP *abbr* = Member of the Association of Sales Personnel.

Maspero *n* **Gaston** (1846–1916). French Egyptologist, discoverer of the pyramid texts.

masque *n* (*mus*) a spectacular court entertainment that was especially popular during the 17th century. It combined poetic drama with pageantry, pantomime, dance, song, etc; the words and music for one of these; a masquerade.—*also* **mask**.

masquer *see* **masker**.

masquerade *n* a ball or party at which fancy dress and masks are worn; a pretence, false show. * *vi* to take part in a masquerade; to pretend to be what one is not.—**masquerader** *n*.

mass *n* (*pl* **masses**) a quantity of matter of indefinite shape and size; a large quantity or number; bulk; size; the main part; (*physics*) the measure of the quantity of matter that a substance possesses; (*pl*) the common people, esp the lower social classes. * *adj* of or for the masses or for a large number. * *vti* to gather or form into a mass.

Mass *n* (*RC Church*) the celebration of the Eucharist; (*mus*) the setting to music of the Latin Ordinary of Mass (those parts of the Mass that do not vary). The five parts are the kyrie eleison, gloria, credo, sanctus with benedictus, and agnus dei.

Mass. *abbr* = Massachusetts.

Massachusetts (MA) *n* a state of the United States of America (USA) of which the capital is Boston.

massacre *n* the cruel and indiscriminate killing of many people or animals. * *vt* to kill in large numbers.

massage *n* a kneading and rubbing of the muscles to stimulate the circulation of the blood. * *vt* to give a massage to.

Massari *n* **Giorgio** (born 1687) Italian architect. His notable works include Palazzo Grassi, Venice.

mass defect *n* in nuclear fusion and nuclear fission reactions, the difference between the total mass of the reacting nuclei and the total mass of the nuclei produced.

Massenet *n* **Jules Emile Frederic** (1842–1912) French composer and teacher who was much influenced by Wagner, but whose music is considered rather more sweet and melodious. He wrote 27 operas (e.g., *Le Roi de Lahore, Manon, Don Quichotte*), ballets, oratorios and some 200 songs.

massé shot *n* in billiards, a stroke with the cue held upright, usu to cause the ball to curve round another ball before it hits the intended ball.

masseur *n* a man who gives a massage professionally.—**masseuse** *nf*.

mass hysteria *n* a condition that affects a group, esp those gathered together under conditions of emotional excitement. A number of people may suffer from giddiness, vomiting, and fainting, which run through the whole crowd.

Massier *n* **Clément** (1844–1917) French ceramicist who learned pottery in his father's workshop, before setting up on his own in 1864.

massif *n* (*geol*) a clearly defined mountainous area that has a uniform appearance and geology and is distinct from the surrounding area.

massive *adj* big, solid, or heavy; large and imposing; relatively large in comparison to normal; extensive.—**massively** *adv*.—**massiveness** *n*.

mass-luminosity relation *n* (*astron*) an observed relationship between the mass of a star and its luminosity.

mass media *npl* newspapers, radio, television, and other means of communication with large numbers of people.

mass number *n* (*physics*) the total number of protons and neutrons in the nucleus of any atom.

Masson *n* **André** (1896–1987) French painter; one of the circle of surrealists that included Breton, Miró and Ernst.

mass production *n* quantity production of goods, esp by machinery and division of labor; see line production.

massy *adj* (**massier massiest**) (*arch*) massive.

mast *n* (*naut*) a tall vertical pole used to support the sails on a ship; a vertical pole from which a flag is flown; a tall structure supporting a television or radio aerial.

MASTA *abbr* = Medical Advisory Service for Travellers Abroad.

mastaba, mastabah *n* (*hist*) the forerunners of the pyramids in ancient Egypt, being an early Egyptian tomb with a flat roof.

Matagalpa *n* a city in Nicaragua.

mastalgia *n* (*med*) pain in the breast.

Mata-Uru *n* capital city of the Wallis and Futuna Islands.

mast cell *n* (*biol*) a large, blood-borne cell that has a fast-acting role in the body's immune system in fighting inflammation.

mastectomy *n* (*pl* **mastectomies**) (*med*) the removal of a breast by surgery, usu performed because of the presence of a tumor.

master *n* a man who rules others or has control over something, esp the head of a household; an employer; an owner of an animal or slave; the captain of a merchant ship; a male teacher in a private school; an expert craftsman; a writer or painter regarded as great; an original from which a copy can be made, esp a phonograph record or magnetic tape; (*with cap*) a title for a boy; one holding an advanced academic degree. * *adj* being a master; chief; main; controlling. * *vt* to be for become master of; (*in art, etc*) to become expert.—**mastership** *n*.

master-at-arms *n* (*pl* **masters-at-arms**) a ship's chief petty officer with responsibility for policing, administration, etc.

masterful *adj* acting the part of a master; domineering; expert; skillful.—**masterfully** *adv*.—**masterfulness** *n*.

master key *n* a key that opens all the locks of a set.

masterly *adj* expert; skillful.—**masterliness** *n*.

mastermind *n* a very clever person, esp one who plans or directs a project. * *vt* to be the mastermind of.

master of ceremonies *n* a person who presides at a public occasion, making announcements, introducing guests, etc; a television compere.

Master of Flemalle *see* **Campin, Robert**.

Master of the Queen's Musick *n* (*mus*) an honorary position (in Britain) awarded to a prominent musician of the time; it is his (or her) duty to compose anthems etc. for royal occasions.

masterpiece *n* a work done with extraordinary skill; the greatest work of a person or group.

mastersingers *n* (*mus*) (*German, Meistersinger*) musicians or minstrels who operated in German cities from the 14th century until the 19th century. Usu craftsmen or tradesmen who composed poems and music and they formed themselves into powerful guilds.

masterstroke *n* brilliant stroke of policy, skill, etc.

masterwork *n* a masterpiece.

mastery *n* control as by a master; victory; expertise.

masthead *n* (*naut*) the top of a mast; the title and ownership details, etc of a newspaper or periodical printed on the front page.

mastic *n* an aromatic resin from mastic trees used chiefly in varnishes; a type of putty used for sealing wood, plaster, etc.

masticate *vt* to chew food before swallowing; to reduce to a pulp.—**mastication** *n*.—**masticator** *n*.

mastication *n* the chewing of food in the mouth, the first stage in the digestive process (*see* digestion).

masticatory *adj* adapted for, or pertaining to, chewing. * *n* (*pl* **masticatories**) (*med*) something chewed in order to promote the flow of saliva.

mastiff *n* a breed of large, thickset dogs used chiefly as watchdogs.

mastitis *n* (*med*) an inflammation of a female breast or an udder.

mastodon *n* (*zool*) any of an extinct genus of mammals allied to the elephant.—**mastodonic** *adj*.

mastoid, mastoid process, *n* (*anat*) a projection of the temporal bone of the skull, which contains numerous air spaces (mastoid cells) and is situated behind the ear. See **mastoiditis**.

mastoidectomy *n* (*med*) the surgical removal of the inflamed cells in (and the drainage of) the mastoid process.

mastoiditis *n* (*med*) inflammation of the mastoid cells and mastoid atrium, usu caused by bacterial infection that spreads from the middle ear. See **mastoid process; mastoidectomy**.

Mastroianni *n* **Marcello** (1924–96) Italian actor. His films include Visconti's *White Nights* (1957) and Fellini's *La Dolce Vita* (1960).

MAstS *abbr* = Member of the Astronomical Society.

masturbate *vi* to manually stimulate one's sexual organs to achieve orgasm without sexual intercourse.—**masturbation** *n*.

mat[1] *n* a piece of material of woven fibers, etc, used for protection, as under a vase, etc, or on the floor; a thick pad used in wrestling, gymnastics, etc; anything interwoven or tangled into a thick mass. * *vti* (**matting, matted**) to cover as with a mat; to interweave or tangle into a thick mass.

mat[2] *adj* without luster, dull.—*also* **matt**.

mat. *abbr* = matins.

matador *n* the bullfighter who kills the bull with a sword.

Mata Hari *n* [Margarethe Geertruida Zelle] (1876–1917) Dutch spy. A dancer in Paris with many lovers, she became a German spy and was shot for treason.

match[1] *n* a thin strip of wood or cardboard tipped with a chemical that ignites under friction.

match[2] *n* any person or thing equal or similar to another; two persons or things that go well together; a contest or game; a mating or marriage. * *vt* to join in marriage; to put in opposition (with, against); to be equal or similar to; (*one thing*) to suit to another. * *vi* to be equal, similar, suitable, etc.

MATCH *abbr* = Mothers Apart from their Children.

matchboard *n* one of a number of thin planks tongued and grooved to fit together, used for paneling, etc.

matchbook *n* a small cardboard folder containing rows of paper matches.

matchbox *n* a small box for holding matches.

matchless *adj* unequaled.—**matchlessly** *adv*.

matchlock *n* (*hist*) a mechanism containing a slow match used to ignite the powder in a gun; a gun with such a mechanism.

matchmaker *n* a person who arranges marriages for people; one who schemes to bring about the marriage of two others; a maker of matches.

match play *n* (*golf*) scoring by the number of holes won as opposed to strokes played.

match point *n* (*tennis, badminton, etc*) the situation where the winner of the next point wins the match.

matchwood *n* wood suitable for making matches; wood splinters or fragments.

mate[1] *n* an associate or colleague; (*inf*) a friend; one of a matched pair; a marriage partner; the male or female of paired animals; an officer of a merchant ship, ranking below the master. * *vti* to join as a pair; to couple in marriage or sexual union.

mate[2] *vt* to checkmate.

maté *n* (*bot*) an evergreen South American shrub, related to holly; an infusion of its dried leaves which makes a mildly stimulating tea,.—*also* **Paraguay tea**.

matelote *n* a stew of fish cooked with wine, etc.

mater *n* (*sl*) mother.

materfamilias *n* (*pl* **matresfamilias**) the mother of a family or mistress of a household.

material *adj* of, derived from, or composed of matter, physical; of the body or bodily needs, comfort, etc, not spiritual; important, essential, etc. * *n* what a thing is, or may be made of; elements or parts; cloth, fabric; (*pl*) tools, etc needed to make or do something; a person regarded as fit for a particular task, position, etc.

materialism *n* concern with money and possessions rather than spiritual values; the doctrine that everything in the world, including thought, can be explained only in terms of matter.—**materialist** *n*.—**materialistic** *adj*.

materiality *n* (*pl* **materialities**) the quality or state of being material; material existence; substance.

materialize *vt* to give material form to. * *vi* to become fact; to make an unexpected appearance.—**materialization** *n*.

materially *adv* physically; to a great extent; substantially.

materials cost *n* the money that is spent by a firm on its direct materials or indirect materials.

materials management *n* the administration and control of the materials used by a firm in a production process.

materialsmen's lien *n* (*law*) a legal claim created on real property by a person, firm, or corporation for materials furnished for improvements to be made upon property.

materia medica *n* (*med*) the science of substances used in medicine *incl* pharmacology, pharmacy, etc; a substance employed as a medicine or in making drugs.

materiel, matériel *n* the baggage, munitions, and provisions of an army or of any other organization.

maternal *adj* of, like, or from a mother; related through the mother's side of the family.—**maternally** *adv*.

maternity *n* motherhood; motherliness. * *adj* relating to pregnancy.

matey *n* a crony or companion (often used when directly addressing such). * *adj* (**matier, matiest**) (*inf*) friendly, sociable.—**mateyness, matiness** *n*.—**matily** *adv*.

math, maths *n* (*inf*) mathematics.

math. *abbr* = mathematical; mathematician; mathematics.

math coprocessor *n* (*comput*) a chip used for performing floating point calculations.

M

mathematical, mathematic *adj* of, like or concerned with mathematics; exact and precise.—**mathematically** *adv*.

mathematics *n* (*used as sing*) the science dealing with quantities, forms, space, etc and their relationships by the use of numbers and symbols; (*sing or pl*) the mathematical operations or processes used in a particular problem, discipline, etc.—**mathematician** *n*.

MA(Theol) *abbr* = Master of Arts in Theology.

Math fab Mathonwy *n* (*Welsh Celtic myth* the son of Mathonwy. He was supposed to have to keep his level of vitality charged by constantly placing his feet in a virgin's lap. He had great powers of magic. He may also have been associated with fertility.

Mathias *n* **William** (1934– 92) Welsh composer and pianist, and a pupil of Lennox Berkeley, who has written a broad variety of work, including a symphony, concertos, choral and chamber music.

Mathieu *n* **Paul** (1950–) French designer who worked in collaboration with the American designer Michael Ray.

Matholwch *n* (*Welsh Celtic myth*) a king of Ireland who married Branwen in an attempt to promote good relations between Ireland and Wales, and who received a magic cauldron from Branwen's brother, Bendigeid Vran or Bran the Blessed.

Mathsson *n* **Bruno** (1907–1995) Swedish architect best-known for the 1934 *Eva* chair.

Matilda *n* (Empress Maud) (1102–1167) queen of England. Reigned in 1141 (uncrowned). The daughter of Henry I of England and Matilda (Edith), the daughter of Malcolm III of Scotland. She married Henry V, the Holy Roman Emperor, at the age of twelve.

matin, matinal *adj* of or pertaining to the morning or to matins.

matinée *n* a daytime, esp an afternoon performance of a play, etc.

Matins, matins *n* (*sing or pl*) (*mus*) the name given to the first of the "Canonical Hours" of the Roman Catholic Church. The term also refers to Morning Prayer in the Anglican Church; (*poet*) a bird's morning song.

Matisse *n* **Henri** (1869–1954) French painter and sculptor. In the period before World War I he became the leading painter of the group mockingly dubbed *Fauves* ("wild beasts").

Matrah n a city in the Sultanate of Oman.

matriarch *n* a woman who heads or rules her family or tribe.—**matriarchal, matriarchic** *adj*.

matriarchy *n* (*pl* **matriarchies**) form of social organization in which the mother is the ruler of the family or tribe and in which descent is traced through the mother.

matrices *see* **matrix**.

matricide *n* a person who kills his (her) mother; the killing of one's mother.—**matricidal** *adj*.

matriculate *vti* to enrol, esp as a student.—**matriculation** *n*.

matrimony *n* (*pl* **matrimonies**) the act or rite of marriage; the married state.—**matrimonial** *adj*.—**matrimonially** *adv*.

matrix *n* (*pl* **matrices, matrixes**) the place, substance, etc from which something originates; a mold; the connective intercellular substance in bone, cartilage, or other tissue; (*math*) an array of elements, i.e., numbers or algebraic symbols, set out in rows and columns.

matrix organization *n* an organization structure in a firm in which some employees report to managers in more than one department.

matron *n* a wife or widow, esp one of mature appearance and manner; a woman in charge of domestic and nursing arrangements in a school, hospital or other institution.—**matronal** *adj*.

matronly *adj* pertaining to or suitable for a matron; sedate, dignified; (*figure*) plump.—**matronliness** *n*.

matron of honor *n* a married woman acting as chief attendant to a bride.

matronymic *see* **metronymic**.

Matsunaga *n* **Naoki** (1936–) Japanese designer who works in Milan, designing tables, seating, luggage and other domestic products.

matt *see* **mat²**.

Matta (1911–) *n* Chilean furniture designer, born Roberto Sebastien Matto Echaurren.

matter *n* (*physics*) any substance that occupies space and has mass: the material of which the universe is made; what a thing is made of; material; any specified substance; content of thought or expression; a quantity; a thing or affair; significance; trouble, difficulty; pus. * *vi* to be of importance.

matter of course *n* an event or process that is inevitable.—**matter-of-course** *adj*.

matter-of-fact *adj* relating to facts, not opinions, imagination, etc.

Matthew 1. *n* (*Bible*) **Saint** (first century) Jewish tax gatherer for the Romans. Matthew appears in the lists of the twelve chosen disciples of Jesus, the writer of the Gospel of Matthew. His feast day is 21 September. 2. **the Gospel of** (*Bible*) the Gospel is one of the Synoptic Gospels meaning that, together with those of Mark and Luke, it presents a common pattern in telling of the story of Jesus; it was not the first gospel to be written.

Matthew *n* **Sir Robert Hogg** (1906-) English architect. His notable works include York University.

Matthews *n* **Sir Stanley** (1915– 2000) English footballer. An outstanding player, he was nicknamed the "Wizard of Dribble." Regarded as one of the greatest wingers of all time, he won 54 international caps in a career that spanned 22 years.

Matthias *n* (*Bible*) **Saint** (first century) chosen by lot to replace Judas Iscariot as the twelfth disciple and to be a witness of the Resurrection. His feast day is 14 May.

matting *n* a coarse material, such as woven straw or hemp, used for making mats.

mattock *n* a pick with one head like an ax, the other like an adz.

mattress *n* a casing of strong cloth filled with cotton, foam rubber, coiled springs, etc, used on a bed.

matts *abbr* = multiple airborne target trajectory system.

maturate *vti* (*med*) to discharge pus, to fester; (*arch*) to bring or come to maturation.—**maturative** *adj*.

maturation *n* the process of ripening or coming to maturity; (*biol*) the progressive generation of cells already present in the ovary and testis, mitosis; (*rare*) the act of discharging pus, suppuration.

mature *adj* mentally and physically well-developed, grown-up; (*fruit, cheese, etc*) ripe; (*bill*) due; (*plan*) completely worked out. * *vti* to make or become mature; to become due.—**maturely** *adv*.—**matureness** *n*.

maturity *n* the state of being mature; full development; the date a loan becomes due.

maturity date *n* the date on which a bond, bill of exchange, insurance policy, etc, becomes due for payment.

matutinal *adj* of, happening during, or pertaining to the morning; early.—**matutinally** *adv*.

MATV *abbr* = master antenna television.

matzo, matzoh *n* (*pl* **matzos, matzohs** *or* **matzoth**) a wafer of unleavened bread eaten esp during Passover.

maud *n* (*Scot*) a gray-striped woolen plaid worn by shepherds.

maudlin *adj* foolishly sentimental; tearfully drunk.

Maugham *n* 1. **Syrie** (1879–1955) British interior and furniture designer whose use of white influenced a generation of interior and movie designers. 2. **W[illiam] Somerset** (1874–1965) physician, novelist, dramatist, and short-story writer whose best-known novels are *Of Human Bondage*, *The Moon and Sixpence* (based on the life of the painter Paul Gauguin), and the satirical comedy *Cakes and Ale*. He was a British secret agent during World War I, and his experiences then form the basis of his spy novel, *Ashenden* (1928).

maul *vt* to bruise or lacerate; to paw.

maulstick *n* a long stick used by painters as a rest for the hand while painting.—*also* **mahlstick**.

maund *n* any of various Asian units of weight, varying from 25 pounds (11 kilograms) to 82 pounds (37 kilograms), according to locality.

maunder *vi* to speak, act or move listlessly or purposelessly.—**maunderer** *n*.

Maundy Thursday *n* the Thursday before Good Friday, in remembrance of the Last Supper.

Maurer *n* **Alfred Henry** (1868–1932) American painter. His early paintings are in the impressionist style but from 1908 he began to experiment more under the influence of Fauvism, and his late works show an interest in cubism. He exhibited in the Armory Show of 1913.

Mauritania or the Islamic republic of Mauritania *n* a republic located on the west coast of Africa.

Mauritian rupee *n* currency of Mauritius.

Mauritius *n* an island republic lying in the Indian Ocean some 800 kilometers or 497 miles east of Madagascar.

Mauryan empire *n* an empire in India that was established after the Greeks, led by Alexander the Great, had upset the old balance of power.

mausoleum *n* (*pl* **mausoleums, mausolea**) a large tomb.

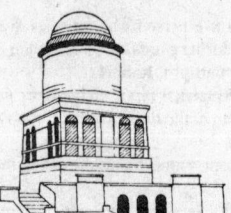

mauve *n* any of several shades of pale purple. * *adj* of this color.

Mauve *n* **Anton** (1838–88) Dutch painter, prominent leader of The Hague School. He painted small, delicately lit landscapes which show the influence of Corot and Millet.

maven, mavin *n* (*inf*) an expert; a connoisseur.

maverick *n* an independent-minded or unorthodox individual; an unbranded animal, e.g. a stray calf.

mavis *n* the song thrush.

mavourneen, mavournin *n* (*Irish*) "my darling."

maw *n* the stomach, crop or throat of animals, esp those who require large quantities of food; (*inf*) the throat and stomach of a person who eats food indiscriminately and in large quantities.

MAW *abbr* = medium assault weapon.

mawkish *adj* maudlin; insipid.—**mawkishly** *adv*.—**mawkishness** *n*.

max. *abbr* = maximum.

max. cap. *abbr* = maximum capacity.

maxi *n* (*pl* **maxis**) a skirt, dress or coat that reaches to the ankle.

maxi- *prefix* maximum; of greater than usual extent, length, scope, etc.

maxilla *n* (*anat*) (*pl* **maxillae, maxillas**) the upper jawbone; in some insects, any of several parts of the mouth used as a secondary jaw.—**maxillar, maxillary** *adj*.

maxim *n* a concise rule of conduct; a precept.

maxima *see* **maximum**.

maximal *adj* of, consisting of, or pertaining to a maximum; (*math*) last in order. * *n* (*math*) in an ordered set, the member last in order.—**maximally** *adv*.

maximalist *n* one who insists on maximum demands without compromise; (*often with cap*) one who advocates direct action as a means of accomplishing something, esp social and political ends.

maximize *vt* to increase to a maximum.—**maximization** *n*.

maximum *n* (*pl* **maxima, maximums**) the greatest quantity, number, etc. * *adj* highest; greatest possible reached.

maxixe *n* a Brazilian round dance similar to the tango, and like the two-step in rhythm.

maxwell *n* a unit of magnetic flux in the cgs system.

Maxwell (*n*) **[Ian] Robert** [Robert Hoch] (1923–91) Czech-born British newspaper proprietor, publisher and politician. His mysterious death by drowning off the Canary Islands was followed by revelations of his mishandling of his companies' assets, particularly the pension funds.

Maxwell Montes *n* a very prominent mountain found on Venus by radar surveys.

may *vb aux* (*past* **might**) expressing possibility; permission; wish or hope.

May *n* the fifth month of the year having 31 days.

May *n* **Hugh** (*b.* 1621) English architect. His notable works include Eltham Lodge, London.

maya *n* (*Hinduism*) illusion, esp that of the world as experienced by the senses as non-material.

Maya *n* a highly advanced civilization that began to emerge *c* 2500–1800 BC in Yucatan, Belize, Guatemala and western Honduras.

Mayakovsky *n* **Vladimir** (1893–1930) Russian poet who led the Russian variant of futurism and whose curious love affair with the Soviet dictatorship ended with his suicide.

Mayan calendar *n* the starting or zero date for this has been calculated as 13th August, 3113 BC, in the Julian calendar.

May apple *n* (*bot*) an American plant with an egg-shaped edible fruit; its fruit.

maybe *adv* perhaps.

MAYC *abbr* = Methodist Association of Youth Clubs.

Mayday *n* the international radio-telephone signal indicating a ship or aircraft in distress.

May Day *n* the first day of May, celebrated as a traditional spring festival; observed in many countries as a labor holiday.

Mayekawa *n* **Kunio** (1905–) Japanese architect. His notable works include Tokyo Metropolitan Festival Hall.

Mayer *n* **Louis B[urt] [Eliezer Mayer]** (1885–1957) Russian-born American film producer who joined with Goldwyn to form Metro-Goldwyn-Mayer in 1924. He became one of the most powerful of the Hollywood moguls, producing such films as *Ben Hur* (1926), and fostering the "star system."

mayhem *n* violent destruction, confusion.

mayn't = may not.

Mayodon *n* **Jean** (1893–1967) French painter who also produced pottery heavily influenced by Persian pottery.

mayonnaise *n* a salad dressing made from egg yolks whisked with oil and lemon juice or vinegar.

mayor *n* the chief administrative officer of a municipality.—**mayoral** *adj.*—**mayorship** *n.*

mayoralty *n* (*pl* **mayoralties**) the office or term of office of a mayor.

mayoress *n* the wife of a mayor; a female mayor.

maypole *n* a flower-decked pole hung with ribbons around which May Day festivities are held.

Mazar-e-Sharif *n* a city in Afghanistan.

Mazdaism *n* Zoroastrianism.

maze *n* a confusing, intricate network of pathways, esp one with high hedges in a garden; a labyrinth; a confused state.—*adj* **maze like**.

mazer *n* (*arch*) a large drinking cup of hard wood or metal.

mazuma *n* (*sl*) money.

mazurka, mazourka *n* (*mus*) a Polish folk dance of the 17th century for up to twelve people. The music can vary in speed and is often played on bagpipes. Chopin, amongst other composers, was influenced by the music and wrote some 55 "mazurkas" for piano.

mazy, mazier, maziest *adj* intricate, winding; perplexing.—**mazily** *adv.*—**maziness** *n.*

Mazza *n* **Sergio** (1931–) Italian interior architect who is best-known for his work in plastics.

mb *abbr* = millibar.

MB *abbr* = *Medicinae Baccalaureus* (*Latin*) "Bachelor of Medicine"; *Musicae Baccalaureus* (*Latin*) "Bachelor of Music"; (*Brit*) Maternity Benefit.

MB, mbyte *abbr* (*comput*) *see* **megabyte**.

MB, BCh *or* **MB, BChir** *or* **MB, BS** *abbr* = conjoint degree of Bachelor of Medicine, Bachelor of Surgery.

MBA *abbr* = Master in, *or* of, Business Administration.

Mbabane *n* capital city of Swaziland.

MBAE *abbr* = Member of the British Academy of Experts; Member of the British Association of Electrolysis.

Mbale *n* a city in Uganda.

mbc *abbr* = maximum breathing capacity.

MB, ChB *abbr* = conjoint degree of Bachelor of Medicine, Bachelor of Surgery.

MBCM *abbr* = *Baccalaureus Medicinae Chirurgiae Magister* (*Latin*) "Bachelor of Medicine, Master of Surgery."

MBD *abbr* = minimal brain dysfunction.

MBE *abbr* = Member of the Order of the British Empire.

MBI *abbr* = management buy-in.

MBK *abbr* = missing, believed killed.

MBL *abbr* = menstrual blood loss.

MBM *abbr* = Thousands [of feet] board measure.

MBP *abbr* = mean blood pressure.

MBR *abbr* = memory buffer register.

MBT *abbr* = main battle tank.

Mbuji-Mayi *n* a city in the Democratic Republic of the Congo (DRC).

m.c. *abbr* = marked capacity (freight cars).

MC *abbr* (*phys chem*) = millicurie; *Magister Chirurgiae* (*Latin*) "Master of Surgery"; magistrates' court; Master Commandant; Master of Ceremonies; Member of Congress, or of Council; metric carat; Medical Corps; Military Cross.

M/C *abbr* = (*bank*) marginal credit; (*marine ins*) metaling clause.

McArthur *n* **Warren** (1885–1961) American designer and manufacturer who patented the early use of aluminum in furniture design in 1930.

mcb *abbr* = miniature circuit breaker.

MCB *abbr* = Mastership in Clinical Biochemistry; Metric Conversion Board; memory control block.

MCC *abbr* = Marylebone Cricket Club; Maxwell Communications Corporation; Motor Caravanners' Club.

MCCA *abbr* = Minor Counties Cricket Association.

MCCC *abbr* = Marie Curie Cancer Care.

McClelland *n* **Nancy Vincent** (1877–1959) American designer who set up the first design studio in a store, Au Quatriéme at Wanamaker's.

MCCN *abbr* = Marine and Coastal Community Network.

McCobb *n* **Paul** (1917–69) American furniture designer who popularized modular furniture and moveable walls.

McConnico *n* **Hilton** (1943–) American fashion designer who worked for Ted Lapidus, Yves Saint-Laurent and Jacques Heim, later turning to movie set design.

MCCU *abbr* = mobile coronary care unit.

McCullers *n* **Carson** (1917–67) American novelist and short-story writer whose works, which usu center on loners and misfits, include *The Heart is a Lonely Hunter*, *Reflections in a Golden Eye*, and the short-story collection *The Ballad of the Sad Café*.

MCE *abbr* = Master of Chemical Engineering; Master of Civil Engineering.

McEnroe *n* **John Patrick** (1959–) American tennis player; winner of several major titles and famed for temperamental outbursts during matches.

MCES *abbr* = Member of the Faculty of Executive Secretaries.

MCGA *abbr* = multicolor graphics array.

McGill *n* **Donald** [Fraser Gould] (1875–1962) English comic postcard artist, renowned for his slightly risqué seaside greeting cards.

MCGPIrel *abbr* = Member of the Irish College of General Practitioners.

McGrath *n* **Raymond** (1903–77) Australian architect who worked in London.

McGugan *n* **Steve** (1960–) Canadian industrial designer who designed the widely publicized 1985 *Form 2* earphones for Bang & Olufsen.

Mch *abbr* = March.

MCh *abbr* = *Magister Chirurgiae* (*Latin*) "Master of Surgery."

MCH *abbr* = mean corpuscular hemoglobin.

MCHC *abbr* = mean corpuscular hemoglobin concentration.

MChD *abbr* = *Magister Chirurgiae Dentalis* (*Latin*) "Master of Dental Surgery."

MChE *abbr* = Master of Chemical Engineering.

MChemEng *abbr* = Master of Chemical Engineering.

MChir *abbr* = *Magister Chirurgiae* (*Latin*) "Master of Surgery."

MChOrth *abbr* = *Magister Chirurgiae Orthopaedicae* (*Latin*) "Master of Orthopedic Surgery."

MChS *abbr* = Member of the Society of Chiropodists.

MCIT *abbr* = Member of the Chartered Institute of Transport.

MCPO *abbr* = Master Chief Petty Officer.

MCPS *abbr* = Member of the College of Physicians and Surgeons.

MCR *abbr* = Middle Common Room; mobile control room.

Mcs *abbr* = Marcus.

Mc/s *abbr* = megacycles per second.

MCS *abbr* = Marine Conservation Society; Master of Commercial Science; missile control system.

MCU *abbr* = medium close-up (photography); Motor Cycle Union.

MCV *abbr* = mean corpuscular volume.

MCW *abbr* = modulated continuous wave.

MCYW *abbr* = Member of the Community and Youth Work Association.

md, m.d. *abbr* = (*mus*) *mano destra* (*Italian*) or *main droite* (*French*) "right hand"; memorandum of deposit.

Md *symbol* (*chem*) mendelevium.

MD *abbr* = malicious damage; Managing Director; Maryland; *Medicinae Doctor* (*Latin*) "Doctor of Medicine"; (*mil*) Medical Department; mentally deficient; Middle Dutch; muscular dystrophy; musical director.

M/D or **M/d** or **m/d.** *abbr* = months' date, *or* months after date.

mda *abbr* = monochrome display adaptor.

Mdent, MDentSc *abbr* = Master of Dental Science.

MDes *abbr* = Master of Design.

MDes(RCA) *abbr* = Master of Design, Royal College of Art.

MDF *abbr* = medium density fiberboard.

Mdlle. *abbr* = Mademoiselle.

Mdm. *abbr* = Madam.

MDMA *abbr* = methylene dioxymethamphetamine, a synthetic drug used as the stimulant Ecstasy.

Mdme. *abbr* = Madame.

MDR *abbr* = memory data register; minimum daily requirement.

mdse. *abbr* = merchandise.

MDU *abbr* = Medical defence Union.

Mdx. *abbr* = Middlesex.

me *pers pron* the objective case of I; **n* (*mus*) in the tonic sol-fa, the third note (or mediant) of the major scale. *See also* **mi**.

m.e. *abbr* (*bookbinding*) = marbled edges.

Me *abbr* (*chem*) = methyl, an organic chemical group of carbon and hydrogen (CH_3).

Me. *abbr* = Maine; maitre.

ME *abbr* = Maine: Master of Engineering; Methodist Episcopal; Middle East; Middle English, the English language from 1050 to 1550; mechanical engineer; Military, *or* Mining, *or* Mechanical Engineer; myalgic encephalomyelitis.

mea culpa *n* (*Latin*) "my fault": a formal acknowledgment of guilt.

mead *n* a wine made from a fermented solution of honey and spices.

Mead *n* **Margaret** (1901–78) American anthropologist. Her works, which include *Coming of Age in Samoa* (1928) and *Growing up in New Guinea* (1930), argue that cultural conditioning shapes personality, rather than heredity. The validity of much of her research is still debated.

meadow *n* a piece of land where grass is grown for hay; low, level, moist grassland.

meadowlark *n* one of two North American yellow-breasted songbirds related to the Baltimore oriole; any of several birds of South, Central and North America.

meadowsweet *n* a fragrant white-flowered plant of Europe and Asia.

meager, meagre *adj* thin, emaciated; lacking in quality or quantity.—**meagerly, meagrely** *adv*.—**meagerness, meagreness** *n*.

meal[1] *n* any of the times for eating, as lunch, dinner, etc; the food served at such a time.

meal[2] *n* any coarsely ground edible grain; any substance similarly ground.— **mealiness** *n*.—**mealy** *adj*.

meal ticket *n* (*sl*) a person, thing, or situation that is a source of income.

mealy-mouthed *adj* not outspoken and blunt; euphemistic; devious in speech.

mean[1] *adj* selfish, ungenerous; despicable; shabby; bad-tempered; (*sl*) difficult; (*sl*) expert.—**meanly** *adv*.—**meanness** *n*.

mean[2] *adj* halfway between extremes; average. * *n* what is between extremes.

mean[3] *vt* (**meaning, meant**) to have in mind; to intend; to intend to express; to signify. * *vi* to have a (specified) degree of importance, effect, etc.

mean anomaly *n* (*astron*) the angle that would result if an elliptically orbiting body were to move round the ellipse at constant speed, resulting in an average or mean motion.

mean daily motion *n* (*astron*) the angle a celestial body moves through in one day, assuming uniform orbital motion.

meander *n* (*geog*) the side to side wandering of a stream/river channel, which is best developed in river deposits on the flood plain; a winding path esp a labyrinth. * *vi* (*river*) to wind; to wander aimlessly.—**meandering** *adj*.

meanie *n* (*inf*) one who is mean, selfish, etc.—*also* **meanie** *pl* **meanies**).

meaning *n* sense; significance; import. * *adj* significant.—**meaningful** *adj*.— **meaningless** *adj*.

mean motion *n* (*astron*) the average of the earth's actual motion round the sun, i.e. assuming that the earth moves round a fictitious body, the mean sun, at a constant speed.

means *npl* that by which something is done; resources; wealth.

mean sea level (MSL) *n* the average level of the surface of the sea.

mean solar day *n* (*astron*) the average value of the interval between successive returns of the sun to the meridian.

meant *see* **mean**[3].

meantime, meanwhile *adv* in or during the intervening time; at the same time. * *n* the intervening time.

meany *see* **meanie**.

meas. *abbr* = measure.

measles *n* (*used as sing*) an extremely infectious disease of children caused by a virus and characterized by the presence of a rash.

measly *adj* (**measlier, measliest**) (*inf*) slight, worthless; having measles.

measure *n* the extent, dimension, capacity, etc of anything; a determining of this, measurement; a unit of measurement; any standard of valuation; an instrument for measuring; a definite quantity measured out; a course of action; a statute, law; (*mus*) a **rhythmical unit, a bar.** * *vt* to find out the extent, dimensions etc of, esp by a standard; to mark off by measuring; to be a measure of. * *vi* to be of specified measurements.—**measurable** *adj*.—**measurably** *adv*.

measured *adj* set or marked off by a standard; rhythmical, regular; carefully planned or considered.

measured day work *n* a system of calculating wages in which a daily wage is agreed on the basis of a set daily production target.

measureless *adj* infinite, without limit.—**measurelessly** *adv*.

measurement *n* a measuring or being measured; an extent or quantity determined by measuring; a system of measuring or of measures.

measuring cup, measuring jug *n* a standard cup or jug marked off to show lesser quantities for measuring cooking ingredients.

meat *n* animal flesh; food as opposed to drink; the essence of something.

meatball *n* a small ball of ground meat usu mixed with breadcrumbs and spices; (*inf*) a stupid or foolish person.

meatus *n* (*pl* **meatuses, meatus**) any passage in the body, e.g. the ear canal.

meaty *adj* (**meatier, meatiest**) full of meat; full of substance.

MEc *abbr* = Master of Economics.

MEC *abbr* = Master of Engineering Chemistry; Member of the Executive Council; Methodist Episcopal Church; minimum effective concentration.

mecca *n* a place of pilgrimage or a goal of aspiration; a resort or attraction that is visited by a large number of people.

Mecca *n* Islam's holiest city, the birthplace of Muhammed (*c.* AD 570) (—*also* **Makkah**).

MECh *abbr* = Methodist Episcopal Church.

mech. *abbr* = mechanical; mechanics; mechanism.

mechanic *n* a person skilled in maintaining or operating machines, cars, etc.

mechanical *adj* of or using machinery or tools; produced or operated by machinery; done as if by a machine, lacking thought or emotion; of the science of mechanics.—**mechanically** *adv*.

mechanical drawing *n* a scale drawing of a machine, component, etc, from which precise measurements can be taken.

mechanical engineer *n* a person skilled in the design, construction and repair of machines.—**mechanical engineering** *n*.

mechanical instruments *n* (*mus*) instruments that can play complex music through the programming of their mechanism (e.g., by punched paper or pins on a spindle) when supplied with power (through foot pedals, clockwork, steam power, electricity etc.)

mechanician, *n* a person skilled in mechanics or machinery; a technician; a mechanist.

mechanics *n* (*used as sing*) the science of motion and the action of forces on bodies; knowledge of machinery; (*pl*) the technical aspects of something.

mechanic's lien *n* (*law*) a legal right to make a claim on property by a person or contractor for labor performed upon the property if the work is not paid for.

mechanism *n* the working parts of a machine; any system of interrelated parts; any physical or mental process by which a result is produced.

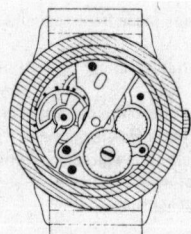

mechanist *n* an expert in mechanics, a mechanician; an advocate of mechanistic philosophy.

mechanistic *adj* of or pertaining to mechanics; of or relating to mechanism; attributing phenomena to physical or biological causes.—**mechanistically** *adv*.

mechanize *vt* to make mechanical; to equip with machinery or motor vehicles.— **mechanization** *n*.—**mechanized** *adj*.

MechE *abbr* = Mechanical Engineer.

MECI *abbr* = Member of the Institute of Employment Consultants.

MEcon *abbr* = Master of Economics.

meconium *n* the first stools (feces) of a newborn baby which are dark green and slimy and contain bile pigments, mucus, and debris from cells, and are passed during the first two days after birth; the juice of the poppy; opium.

med. *abbr* = medalist; medical; medicine; medieval; medium.

MEd *abbr* = Master of Education.

MED *abbr* = Master of Elementary Didactics; minimum effective dose.

medal *n* a small, flat piece of inscribed metal, commemorating some event or person or awarded for some distinction.—**medallic** *adj*.

medalist, medallist n one awarded a medal.

medallion n a large medal; a design, portrait, etc shaped like a medal; a medal worn on a chain around the neck.

Medan n a city in Indonesia.

Medawar n **Sir Peter Brian** (1915–87) Brazilian-born British zoologist. He shared the 1960 Nobel prize for physiology or medicine with the Australian virologist **Sir Frank Macfarlane Burnet** (1899–1985) for his work on immunological tolerance.

Medb n (*Irish Celtic myth*) sometimes anglicized as **Maeve**, a goddess-queen of Connacht. Her name means "she who intoxicates" and is related to the word "mead." She is said to have been the wife of nine Irish kings, and only someone who was her mate could be a true king of Ireland. She is said to have been killed by a sling-shot and a lump of cheese.

meddle vi to interfere in another's affairs.—**meddler** n.—**meddlesome** adj.

Mede n an inhabitant of Media, an ancient country in southwest Asia to the south of the Caspian Sea.—**Median** n, adj.

Medea, Medeia n (*Greek myth*) daughter of Aeètes, king of Colchis. When Jason, the leader of the Argonauts, came in search of the golden fleece, she fell in love with him, helped him to obtain the fleece, and fled with him. When he abandoned her in favor of Glauce (or Creusa), she killed her rival and then killed her own children by Jason.

Med(EdPsych) abbr = Master of Education (Educational Psychology).

Medellin n a city in Colombia.

Medes n (*Bible*) Media lay in north-east Mesopotamia between the Black Sea and the Caspian Sea; a tribe of people connected to the Persians, who established an empire in northern Iran.

media (*pl* **mediae**) n (*medical*) the middle layer of a tissue or organ. *See also* **medium.**

mediaeval *see* **medieval.**

mediaevalism, mediaevalist *see* **medievalism.**

medial adj of or in the middle; mean, average; (*math*) pertaining to or denoting an average; median; (*phonetics*) denoting a sound made by using an average amount of muscular tension, neither strongly vocalized nor gently pronounced.

median adj middle; intermediate. * n a median number, point, line, etc.

mediant n (*mus*) the third note in a major or minor scale above the tonic (lowest note), e.g. E in the scale of C major. —*also* adj.

mediastinum n (*pl* **mediastina**) (*anat*) a membranous partition, esp that between the lungs; the space in the chest cavity between the two lungs, which contains the heart, aorta, esophagus, trachea, thymus gland, and phrenic nerves.—**mediastinal** adj.

mediate vt to intervene (in a dispute); to bring about agreement. * vi to be in an intermediate position; to be an intermediary. * adj involving an intermediary, not direct or immediate.—**mediately** adv.—**mediative** adj.

mediation n the act of mediating; reconciliation; intervention, esp by a neutral nation seeking a settlement between warring nations.

mediatize vt to annex (a state) while leaving its ruler his title.—**mediatization** n.

mediator n one who or that which mediates; a person who acts as an intermediary; an intercessor.—**mediatory** adj.

medic n (*inf*) a medical student; (*inf*) a physician or surgeon.

medicable adj potentially curable.

medical adj relating to the practice or study of medicine. * n (*inf*) a medical examination.—**medically** adv.

medicament n a medicine or healing application.

medicate vt to treat with medicine; to impregnate (soap, shampoo, etc) with medication.—**medicative** adj.

medication n any substance introduced into or on the body for the purposes of medical treatment, e.g. drugs and medicated dressings.

Medici[1] n an Italian family, political rulers of Florence in the 15th century and dukes of Tuscany from the 16th century to 1737. They were important patrons of the arts.

Medici[2] n **Lorenzo de'** (1449–92) Florentine aristocrat and statesman. Styled "The Magnificent," he was a poet and a noted patron of the arts. His tomb in Florence was designed by Michelangelo.

medicine n any substance used to treat or prevent disease; the science of preventing, treating or curing disease.—**medicinal** adj.—**medicinally** adv.

medicine ball n a heavy leather ball used in physical exercises.

medicine chest n a box for holding medicines.

medicine dance n a dance performed by a medicine man to invoke supernatural healing powers.

medicine lodge n a wooden house used by certain North American Indian peoples for religious or magic ceremonies.

medicine man n a person believed to possess supernatural healing powers, esp among North American Indian peoples.

medicine show n a traveling show with entertainments to attract crowds of people, among whom quack remedies are peddled.

medico n (*inf*) a doctor or medical student.

medieval adj of or like the Middle Ages.—*also* **mediaeval.**

medievalism n the spirit, esp in religion and art, customs, etc, characteristic of the Middle Ages; a study of these; any one of these extant since the Middle Ages, or a contemporary imitation of it.—*also* **mediaevalism.**—**medievalist, mediaevalist** n.

medigap n health insurance taken out by an individual to pay for treatment excluded by government schemes.

medina n (*often with cap*) the ancient part of a North African city.

Medina (Al Madinah) n a city in Saudi Arabia.

Medinet Habu n in Egypt, the site of numerous temples on the west bank of the Nile, facing Thebes, and in the vast funerary region that includes Malqata and Deir el Bahri.

mediocre adj average; ordinary; inferior.—**mediocrity** n.

Medit. abbr = Mediterranean.

meditate vi to think deeply; to reflect; to empty the mind in order to concentrate on nothing or on one thing, esp as a religious exercise.—**meditator** n.

meditation n the act of meditating; contemplation of spiritual or religious matters.

meditative adj expressing or characterized by meditation; thoughtful.—**meditatively** adv.—**meditativeness** n.

Mediterranean n the Mediterranean Sea. * adj of, or relating to (the area around) the Mediterranean Sea; denoting a subdivision of the Caucasian race characterized by a slender build and dark complexion.

Mediterranean climate n hot, dry summers and warm, wet winters, experienced on the western edges of continents between latitudes 30° and 40° north and south of the Equator.

medium n (*pl* **media, mediums**) the middle state or condition; a substance for transmitting an effect; any intervening means, instrument, or agency; a material used in art, e.g. oil in painting, pencil in drawing, or bronze in sculpture. The term is also used to denote a method, e.g. painting as opposed to sculpture; (*pl* **media**) a means of communicating information (e.g. newspapers, television, radio); (*pl* **mediums**) a person claiming to act as an intermediary between the living and the dead. * adj midway; average.

medium frequency n a radio frequency between 3000 and 300 kilohertz.

Medjay n a desert tribe from whom the Egyptians recruited soldiers, including internal guards: an early application of the principle that a district should not provide its own policemen.

medlar n a small fruit tree of Europe and Asia; its apple-like fruit; any one of several trees similar to this; the fruit from one of these.

Medlars abbr = Medical Literature Analysis and Retrieval System.

medley n (*pl* **medleys**) a miscellany; a musical piece made up of various tunes or passages.

Médoc n a red wine from the Bordeaux region of France.

MedPAC abbr = Medicare Payment Advisory Commission

Med RC abbr = Medical Reserve Corps.

MEdStud abbr = Master of Educational Studies.

medulla n (*pl* **medullas, medullae**) (*anat*) the marrow of bones; inner tissue; (*bot*) the pith of plants.—**medular, medullary** adj.

medulla oblongata n (*pl* **medulla oblongatas, medullae oblongatae**) the nervous tissue of the lower part of the cranium, which governs respiration, the action of the heart, etc. It extends through the foramen magnum to become the upper part of the spinal cord.

medusa n (*pl* **medusas, medusae**) (*biol*) a jellyfish; one of two coelenterate life cycles, when it has a sac-like, umbrella-shaped body that is capable of moving freely in water (—*also* **medusan, medusoid**).—**medusan** adj.

Medusa *see* **Gorgons.**

MEE abbr = Master of Electrical Engineering.

meed n (*poet*) recompense, reward.

meek adj patient, long-suffering; submissive.—**meekly** adv.—**meekness** n.

meerschaum n a creamy claylike silicate of magnesium from which pipe bowls and building stones are made; a tobacco pipe with a bowl made of this.

meet[1] vt (**meeting, met**) to encounter, to come together; to make the acquaintance of; to contend with, deal with; to experience; to be perceived by (the eye, etc); (*demand, etc*) to satisfy; (*bill, etc*) to pay. * vi to come into contact with; to be introduced. * n a meeting to hunt or for an athletics competition.

meet[2] adj (*arch*) fit, suitable.

meeting n a coming together; a gathering.

mega- prefix great, large; a million of; (*inf*) greatest.

megabyte (MB, mbyte) n (*comput*) one million bytes (characters) of information. The common storage measurement for memory and hard disks, e.g. 4 megabytes of RAM, with a 210-megabyte hard disk drive.

megacephalic *see* **macrocephalic.**

megacycle n a megahertz.

Megaera n (*Greek myth*) one of the three Furies, the others being Alecto and Tisiphone.

megahertz (MHz) n (*comput*) a unit of frequency equal to one million hertz.

megalith n a huge stone, esp part of a prehistoric monument.—**megalithic** adj.

megalithic yard n (*archeo*) a measurement of 33 inches (92.5 cm) that may have been the unit used to plan the stone circles of the British Isles and Brittany.

megaloblast n an abnormally large form of any of the cells that go on to produce erythrocytes (red blood cells).

megalomania n a form of insanity in which a person suffers from delusions of grandeur about his or her greatness and power; (*inf*) a lust for power.—**megalomaniac** n, adj.—**megalomaniacal** adj.

megalopolis n any conurbation of more than 10 million inhabitants.

Megapenthes n (*Greek myth*) a son of Proteus, king of Argos, who exchanged his dominion for that of Perseus so that the latter received Tiryns instead of Argos, and afterwards killed Perseus.

M

megaphone *n* a device to amplify and direct the voice.

megapode *n* any of a family of birds of Australia and the South Pacific that builds mounds of sand, etc, to incubate its eggs.

Megara *n* the principal ancient city on the Isthmus of Corinth.—**Megarian** *adj*.

Megaris *n* a small mountainous state of ancient Greece, between Attica and the Isthmus of Corinth. Its capital was Megara.

megaron *n* (*archeo*) a rectangular hall with a porch at one end which forms the entrance. Palaces each built around a megaron were found at Troy dating from *c.* 4000 BC.

megaspore *n* (*bot*) the protective covering containing the embryo in flowering plants (—*also* **macrospore**); the larger spore of certain mosses, ferns and fungi, which forms the female gametophyte.

megass, megasse *n* a type of paper produced from the residue left after the extraction of sugar from cane.

megastream *n* (*comput*) a name used by British Telecom for its high speed digital communication lines.

megathere *n* a huge extinct animal allied to the sloth.—**megatherian** *adj*.

megaton *n* a unit of explosive force equivalent to one million tons of TNT.

megavolt *n* a million volts.

megawatt *n* one million watts.

Megiddo *n* (*Bible*) ancient city of strategic importance in northern Palestine, and proverbial symbol of war. *See also* **Armageddon**, **Jezreel**.

megilp *n* a mixture of linseed oil and mastic varnish or turpentine, used as a base in oil colors.

megohm *n* a million ohms.

megrim *n* (*arch*) a sick or neuralgic headache, usu of one side of the head, a migraine; a whim, caprice; (*pl*) a disease of horses or cattle, characterized by vertigo, the staggers.

Mehta *n* **Zubin** (1936–) an Indian conductor, violinist and pianist. He is best known as a conductor and has worked with most of the world's leading orchestras, notably the New York Philharmonic Orchestra.

Meiche *n* (*Irish Celtic myth*) the son of Morrigan. He was killed by Dian Cecht because it was prophesied that he would bring disaster to Ireland. When he was dead, his body was cut open to reveal three hearts each of which had a serpent growing in it.

Meier *n* 1. **Otto** (1910–82) Swiss architect who, with Ernst Mumenthaler, developed the modular furniture system 3M-Möbel. 2. **Richard Alan** (1934–) American architect whose buildings reflected the ideas of **Le Corbusier**.

Meier-Graefe *n* **Julius** (1867–1935) Romanian writer, art critic and entrepreneur. He was one of the first people to promote the stained glass and enamels of Louis Comfort **Tiffany**.

Meinhoff *n* **Ulrike** (1934–76) German terrorist. With **Andreas Baader** (1943–77) and others, she founded the "Red Army Faction" in 1970, an ultra-leftist terrorist organization dedicated to using violence to bring about the collapse of West German "capitalist tyranny." She and Baader died in prison, apparently having committed suicide.

Meinzer *n* **Manfred** (1943–) German industrial designer whose first important design was the 1967 Revox stereo tape recorder.

meiosis *n* (*pl* **meioses**) *n* (*biol*) the process of cell division where a nucleus splits into four, each new nucleus having half the number of chromosomes that the *orig* one had; a rhetorical understatement, esp one where a negative is used instead of its opposite, e.g. "a not inconsiderable amount" instead of "a large amount"; litotes; (*rare*) any division or separation.—**meiotic** *adj*.—**meiotically** *adv*.

Meir *n* **Golda** (1898–1978) Russian-born Israeli stateswoman active in the fight for a Jewish state who became Israel's first female prime minister (1969–74).

Meistersinger *n* (*German*) (*pl* **Meistersinger, Meistersingers**) a member of one of the various guilds in German cities of the 14th-16th centuries, which instituted the development of poetry and music by establishing competitive standards.

Meitner *n* **Lise** (1878–1968) Austrian-born Swedish physicist; discovered protactinium (1918) with Otto Hahn; discovered the process of nuclear fission (1930s) with Otto Frisch and others.

melamine *n* a resinous material used for adhesives, coatings, and laminated products.

Melampus *n* (*Greek myth*) one of the great seers, who could understand the language of birds and animals, and brother of Bias.

melancholy *n* gloominess or depression; sadness. * *adj* sad; depressed.—**melancholia** *n*.—**melancholic** *adj*.

mélange *n* a (confused) mixture; a medley; (*geol*) a hotchpotch of variously shaped rocks of different periods and sizes.

melanin *n* (*biol*) a dark brown pigment found in the skin, hair, and eyes of humans and animals.

Melanippus *n* (*Greek myth*) a Theban champion in the war against Argos, who killed two of the Seven against Thebes.

melanism, melanosis *n* dark coloration of the skin in pale-skinned people or dark-colored feathers, etc, in birds and animals, caused by abnormal deposits of black or dark pigment in skin tissue, the opposite of albinism.—**melanistic, melanotic** *adj*.

melanocyte *see* **melanoma**.

melanoma *n* (*pl* **melanomas, melanomata**) an extremely malignant tumor of the melanocytes, the cells in the skin that produce melanin.

Melantheus, Melanthius *n* (*Greek myth*) the chief goatherd of Odysseus, who sided with the suitors of Penelope even after his master returned. He was mutilated and left to die as a punishment.

Melba *n* **Dame Nellie** [Helen Porter Mitchell] (1861–1931) Australian soprano. One of the world's leading prima donnas in the late 1880s. She chose her stage name, Melba, in tribute to the city of Melbourne.

Melbourne *n* a city in Australia.

Melchizedek *n* (*Bible*) priest-king of Salem encountered by Abraham during his wanderings.

meld[1] *vti* to merge or become merged.

meld[2] *vt* (*card games*) to declare or lay down cards that score points. * *vi* to declare a card or sequence of cards as a meld. * *n* the act of melding; a sequence of cards for melding.

Meleager *n* (*Greek myth*) the hero who killed the Calydonian Boar. During the hunt he quarreled with some of his uncles, and as a result his mother brought about his death.

melee, mêlée *n* a confused, noisy struggle.

Melia *n* (*Greek myth*) a nymph who was carried off by Apollo and gave birth to Ismenius and the seer Tenerus.

melic *adj* (*poem*) meant to be sung, often used of ancient Greek lyric poetry.

melilot *n* a species of sweet-scented trefoil or clover, with clusters of small yellow or white flowers.—*also* **sweet clover**.

melinite *n* a high explosive similar to lyddite.

meliorate *vti* to improve; to grow better; to make (something) better.—**meliorable** *adj*.—**meliorative** *adj*, *n*.—**meliorator** *n*.

melioration *n* the process of improving; the state of being improved; an improvement.

meliorism *n* the doctrine that in nature there is a tendency to gradual improvement and this may be accelerated by human effort.

Melisseus *n* (*Greek myth*) an ancient king of Crete, the father of the nymphs Adrasteia and Ida, to whom Rhea entrusted the infant Zeus to be raised.

Melita *n* (*Bible*) the island of Malta where Paul was shipwrecked.

melliferous *adj* forming or yielding honey.

mellifluous, mellifluent *adj* (*voice, sounds*) sweetly flowing, smooth.—**mellifluously** *adv*.—**mellifluousness** *n*.

Mellor *n* **David** (1930-) British metalworker, manufacturer and retailer who established himself as a major retailer in London.

mellow *adj* (*fruit*) sweet and ripe; (*wine*) matured; (*color, light, sound*) soft, not harsh; kind-hearted and understanding. * *vti* to soften through age; to mature.—**mellowness** *n*.

Melo *n* a city in Uruguay.

melodeon *n* a kind of accordion; a small reed organ.

melodic *adj* pertaining to or having melody.—**melodically** *adv*.

melodica *n* (*mus*) (*Italian*) a free-reed instrument which was developed from the harmonica. It is box-shaped and has a small keyboard; the player blows down a tube and plays notes by pressing the keys.

melodic minor scale *see* **scale**.

melodic sequence *see* **sequence**.

melodious *adj* full of melody, tuneful, musical; sweet-sounding.—**melodiously** *adv*.—**melodiousness** *n*.

melodist *n* a singer; a composer of melodies.

melodize *vti* to make (something) melodious; to compose a melody (for something); to sing a melody.

melodrama *n* a form of drama that seems to have arisen in 18th-century France and that contained elements of music, spectacle, sensational incidents, and sentimentalism, reaching its peak in the popular theater of the 19th-century. From this, the word has come to mean an exaggeratedly dramatic or sensational play, film, etc., filled with overdramatic emotion and action; drama of this genre; sensational events or emotions.—**melodramatic** *adj*.—**melodramatically** *adv*.—**melodramatist** *n*.

melody *n* (*pl* **melodies**) (*mus*) a succession of notes, of varying pitch, that create a distinct and identifiable musical form. Melody, harmony and rhythm are the three essential ingredients of music. The criteria of what constitutes a melody change over time; a tune; a pleasing series of sounds.—**melodic** *adj*.—**melodious** *adj*.

melon *n* the large juicy many-seeded fruit of trailing plants, as the watermelon, cantaloupe.

Melpomene *n* (*Greek myth*) the Muse who presides over tragedy.

melt *vti* (**melting, melted**, *pp* **molten**) to make or become liquid; to dissolve; to fade or disappear; to soften or be softened emotionally.—**melting** *adj*.—**meltingly** *adv*.

meltdown *n* the melting of the fuel core of a nuclear reactor; the drastic collapse of almost anything.

melting point *n* (*physics*) the temperature at which a substance is in a state of equilibrium between the solid and liquid states, e.g., ice/water.

melting pot *n* a place, situation, or product of mixing many different races, traditions, cultures, etc.

melton *n* a kind of thick woolen cloth, with a surface nap, often used for overcoats.

meltwater *n* water derived from the melting of snow or ice.

Melville *n* **Herman** (1819–91) American novelist, short-story writer and poet. His masterpiece is the novel *Moby Dick* (1851). Other notable works include the story "Bartleby the Scrivener," and the short novel *Billy Budd, Foretopman* (published posthumously in 1924).

mem. *abbr* = member; *mementor* (*Latin*) "remember"; memoir; memoranda; memorandum; memorial.

Mém. *abbr* = mémoire.

MEMA *abbr* = Marine Engine and Equipment Manufacturers' Association.

member *n* a person belonging to a society or club; a part of a body, such as a limb; a representative in a legislative body; a distinct part of a complex whole.

member bank *n* a bank that belongs to a clearing system or central banking system.

membership *n* the state of being a member; the number of members of a body; the members collectively.

membrane *n* (*biol, medical*) a thin, pliable, composite, layer of lipoprotein surrounding an individual cell, or of fibrous tissue surrounding an organ, lining a cavity or tube or separating tissues and organs within the body —**membranous, membranaceous** *adj.*

membrane keyboard *n* (*comput*) a style of keyboard covered by a touch sensitive material to prevent liquid or dirt entering the keyboard circuits.

membranophone *n* (*mus*) the generic term for all instruments in which sound is produced by the vibration of a skin or membrane, e.g. drum, kazoo.

memento *n* (*pl* **mementos, mementoes**) a reminder, esp a souvenir.

memento mori *n* (*pl* **memente mori**) (an object that serves as) a reminder of death.

Memling *or* **Memlinc** *n* **Hans** (*c*.1430–94) German-born Dutch painter, probably a pupil of Rogier van der Weyden. Notable works include *Tommaso Portinari and his Wife* (*c*.1468).

Memnon *n* (*Greek myth*) a hero who assisted Priam at the siege of Troy, and who was killed by Achilles, but made immortal by Zeus.

memo *n* (*pl* **memos**) (*law*) a memorandum stating facts, e.g., a memorandum of lease.

memoir *n* an historical account based on personal experience; (*pl*) an autobiographical record.

memorabilia *npl* (*sing* **memorabile**) things worthy of remembrance or record; clothing, letters, manuscripts, notes, etc, once belonging to or written by famous people or connected with famous events and thought worthy of collection.

memorable *adj* worth remembering; easy to remember.—**memorably** *adv.*

memorandum *n* (*pl* **memorandums**) an informal written communication as within an office; (*pl* **memoranda**) a note to help the memory.

memorial *adj* serving to preserve the memory of the dead. * *n* a remembrance; a monument.

Memorial Day *n* a legal holiday in the US (the last Monday in May in most states) in memory of dead servicemen of all wars.

memorialist *n* one who prepares, signs or presents a memorial; one who writes memoirs.

memorialize *vt* to commemorate; to honor by means of a memorial.—**memorialization** *n.*—**memorializer** *n.*

memorize *vt* to learn by heart, to commit to memory.—**memorization** *n.*

memory *n* (*pl* **memories**) the function of the brain that enables past events to be stored and remembered; the sum of things remembered; an individual recollection; commemoration; remembrance; (*comput*) the circuitry and devices that are capable of storing data as well as programs (—*also* **store**).

memory address *n* (*comput*) a code or name that refers to a specific location where data is stored in a computer's RAM.

memory cache *n* (*comput*) *see* **cache**.

memory management *n* (*comput*) the process of efficiently using a computer's memory.

memory map *n* (*comput*) a map that shows how the operating system utilizes the RAM.

memory resident program *n* (*comput*) a program that remains in RAM memory ready for use at any time.

Memphis *n* the ancient city of Egypt, on the left bank of the Nile, at the apex of the Delta; in Egyptian mythology, daughter of the god Nile, who married Epaphis who founded the city of Memphis, named after her.

memsahib *n* (*formerly*) a form of address for a European married woman in India.

men *see* **man**.

menace *n* a threat; (*inf*) a nuisance. * *vt* to threaten.—**menacing** *adj.*—**menacingly** *adv.*

menad *see* **maenad**.

ménage *n* a household.

ménage à trois *n* (*pl* **ménages à trois**) a relationship in which a married couple and a lover of one of them live together.

menagerie *n* a place where wild animals are kept for exhibition; a collection of wild animals.

Menander *n* (*c*.342–*c*.292 BC) Greek dramatist whose comedies were known only from small fragments and through adaptations by the Roman dramatists Terence and Plautus until the 20th century when a complete play, *The Misanthropist*, was discovered in Egypt.

menarche *n* the onset of menstruation in puberty.

Mencap *abbr* = (*Brit*) Royal Society for Mentally Handicapped Children and Adults.

mend *vt* to repair; (*manners, etc*) to reform, improve. * *vi* to become better. * *n* the act of mending; a repaired area in a garment, etc.

mendacity *n* (*pl* **mendacities**) telling lies; a falsehood.—**mendacious** *adj.*—**mendaciously** *adv.*

Mendel *n* **Gregor Johann** (1822–84) Austrian monk, biologist and botanist. By experimenting with generations of pea plants, Mendel discovered that traits such as color or height had two factors (hereditary units) and that these factors do not blend but can be either dominant or recessive. With no knowledge of genes or cell division, he developed two laws of genetics.

mendelevium *n* an artificially produced radioactive metallic element.

Mendelism *n* the theories of the Austrian monk and geneticist Gregor Mendel (1822–84) respecting heredity, as set out in Mendel's laws with later modifications.—**Mendelian** *adj.*

Mendelsohn *n* **Erich** (1887–1953) German architect. His notable works include Potsdam Observatory; Columbushaus, Berlin.

Mendelssohn *n* **Felix** (Jakob Ludwig Felix Mendelssohn-Bartholdy) (1809–47) a German Romantic composer, organist, pianist and conductor whose principal works include: five symphonies (e.g., the *Scottish Reformation* and *Italian* symphonies); overtures (e.g., *The Hebrides* ("Fingal's cave"), *Calm Sea and Prosperous Voyage);* oratorios (e.g. *St Paul, Elijah, Christus);* and numerous pieces for organ, piano and chamber orchestra.

Mendes *n* in Egypt, a site on the southern side of the Delta, nome capital and capital of the Thirtieth Dynasty kings.

Mendès-France *n* **Pierre** (1907–82) French statesman. He was appointed minister of the national economy by De Gaulle in 1945, but resigned and joined the opposition the following year. He became prime minister (1954–55), and negotiated the peace treaty that ended the Vietnamese war.

mendicant *adj* begging; (*religious orders*) reliant on alms. * *n* a mendicant friar.—**mendicancy, mendicity** *n.*

mending *n* garments requiring to be repaired.

Mendoza *n* a city in Argentina.

Menelaus *n* (*Greek myth*) a son of Atreus, younger brother of Agamemnon and husband of the beautiful Helen, with whom he received the kingdom of Sparta or Lacedaemon. His wife having been abducted by Paris, son of Priam, king of Troy, he summoned the Greek princes to war and himself led sixty ships to the siege of Troy.

MEng *abbr* = Master of Engineering; Mechanical, *or* Mining, Engineer.

Mengistu *n* **Mariam Haile** (1937–) Ethiopian dictator who participated in the 1974 coup that toppled Haile Selassie. He established a relentlessly brutal dictatorship. In 1991, as secessionists closed in on Addis Ababa, he fled to Kenya.

Mengs *n* **Anton Raffael** (1728–1779) German painter prominent in the neoclassical movement.

Mengshoel *n* **Hans Christian** (1946–) Norwegian furniture designer, who, with Peter **Ospvik**, designed the 1979 ergonomic chairs in the Balans series.

menhaden *n* (*pl* **menhadens, menhaden**) (*biol*) an inedible American fish, yielding a valuable oil.

menhir *n* a tall, monolithic obelisk, sometimes crudely carved, dating from the Bronze Age. Menhirs are found in the British Isles, Ireland, and the Breton region of France.

menial *adj* consisting of work of little skill; servile. * *n* a domestic servant; a servile person.

Ménière's disease *n* a (*med*) disease first described by the French physician Prosper Ménière in 1861, which affects the inner ear, causing deafness and tinnitus (ringing in the ears), vertigo, vomiting, and sweating.

meningeal sarcoma *see* **meningioma**.

meninges *npl* (*sing* **meninx**) (*physiology*) the three membranes covering and protecting the brain and the spinal cord.—**meningeal** *adj.*

meningioma *n* (*med*) a slow-growing tumor affecting the meninges of the brain or spinal cord that exerts pressure on the underlying nervous tissue.

meningitis *n* (*med*) inflammation of the meninges (membranes) enveloping the brain (cerebral meningitis) or spinal cord (spinal meningitis), or the disease may affect both regions.

meniscus *n* (*pl* **menisci, meniscuses**) (*physics*) a crescent; the crescent-shaped surface of a liquid contained in a tube; a lens convex on one side and concave on the other; (*anat*) the cartilage between the bones of joints, esp at the knee.

meno *n* (*mus*) (*Italian*) "less," so **meno mosso** means "slower" (less moved).

Menoetius *n* (*Greek myth*) one of the Titans, who was killed by Zeus with a flash of lightning in the fight of the Titans and thrown into Tartarus.

menology *n* (*pl* **menologies**) an ecclesiastical calendar; a calendar of saints, esp in the Orthodox Church.

menopause *n* the time in a woman's life, usu between 45 and 55, when the ovaries no longer release an egg cell every month and menstruation ceases permanently.—**menopausal** *adj. See also* **climacteric**

menorrhagia *n* an excessive menstrual flow.

Menotti *n* **Gian Carlo** (1911–) Italian-born composer who emigrated to the USA in 1928. He is best known for his operas, e.g., *Amelia goes to the Ball, The Telephone, The Saint of Bleeker Street, Amahl and the Night Visitors* and *Help, help, the Globolinks.* He has also written ballets and various pieces for orchestra.

M

menses *n* (*pl* **menses**) menstruation; the monthly discharge of blood, etc, from the uterus; the days during which this occurs.

Menshevik *n* (*pl* **Mensheviks, Mensheviki**) (*hist*) a member of the more moderate Russian socialist party (1903-17) or of a liberal opposition party set up after the Revolution.—**Menshevism** *n*.—**Menshevist** *adj, n*.

menstrual cycle, menstruation *n* the cyclical nature of the reproductive life of a sexually mature female.

menstruation *n* the monthly discharge of blood from the uterus.—**menstrual** *adj*.—**menstruate** *vi*.

menstruum *n* (*pl* **menstruums, menstrua**) a solvent, esp if used in making drugs.

mensur. *abbr* = mensuration.

mensurable *adj* measurable; (*mus*) of a fixed rhythm.—**mensurability** *n*.

mensuration *n* the science of measurement; the act or process of measuring or taking the dimensions of anything; measurement.

mental *adj* of, or relating to the mind; occurring or performed in the mind; having a psychiatric disorder; (*inf*) crazy, stupid.—**mentally** *adv*.

mental age *n* a measure used in psychological testing that expresses mental attainment in terms of the number of years it takes the average child to reach the same level.

mental block *n* a temporary loss of memory or intellectual function.

mental cruelty *n* the infliction of emotional suffering on another, used legally as grounds for divorce.

mental deficiency *n* mental retardation.

mental hospital *n* an institution for the care of mentally ill patients.

mentalism *n* (*philos*) the doctrine that the mind is the fundamental reality and external objects are essentially aspects of consciousness; (*psychol*) the belief in the importance of subjective data in the study of behavior.—**mentalistic** *adj*.

mentality *n* (*pl* **mentalities**) intellectual power; disposition, character.

mental retardation *n* congenital lowness of intelligence.

menthol *n* peppermint oil.—**mentholated** *adj*.

mention *n* a brief reference to something in speech or writing; an official recognition or citation. * *vt* to refer to briefly; to remark; to honor officially.—**mentionable** *adj*.

mentor *n* a wise and trusted adviser.

Mentuhotpe II *n* Egyptian king of the Eleventh Dynasty (ruled 2040–2009 BC) and first king of the Middle Kingdom, who came to the throne of the Theban kingdom and later extended his kingship over all Egypt.

Mentuhotpe III *n* Egyptian king of the Eleventh Dynasty (ruled 2009–1997 BC). The son of Mentuhotpe II.

Mentuhotpe IV *n* (*d.* 1991 BC) Egyptian king of the Eleventh Dynasty.

menu *n* the list of dishes served in a restaurant; (*comput*) a list of commands or options that are available to the computer user on a monitor or VDU.

menu bar *n* (*comput*) the area of a screen that is given over to the listing of menu items.

menu-driven program *n* (*comput*) a program that proceeds to the next step only when the user responds to a menu prompt.

Menuhin *n* **Yehudi** (1916–99) American-born violinist and conductor who settled in England after the Second World War. He was a child prodigy and achieved international fame. In 1963 he founded the Menuhin School of Music for musically gifted children. He was knighted in 1965.

Menzies *n* 1. **Sir Robert Gordon** (1894–1978) Australian Liberal statesman. He became prime minister (1939–41, 1949–66) and a respected arbiter in international affairs, e.g. during the Suez crisis. 2. **William Cameron** (1896–1957) American movie set designer who became the most famous designer and art director of the 1920s and 1930s.

meow *n* the cry of a cat; a spiteful remark.—*also vi*.

mep, m.e.p. *abbr* = mean effective pressure.

MEP *abbr* = Member of the European Parliament.

Mephistophelean, Mephistophelian *adj* pertaining to or like Mephistopheles, the devil of the Faust legend; fiendish, cynical; diabolic.

mephitis *n* a noxious gas emitted from the ground; a foul stench.—**mephitic, mephitical** *adj*.

mer, mer. *abbr* = meridian; meridional.

Mer, La (*The Sea*) *n* three symphonic sketches for orchestra by Debussy, inspired by the sea (1905).

Merak *or* **Beta Ursae Majoris** *n* (*astron*) a second magnitude star in the constellation Ursa Major or the Great Bear.

Merbecke *or* **Marbeck** *n* **John** (1510–85) English composer and organist who was the first person to set the English (as distinct from the Latin) liturgy to music.

merc. *abbr* = mercurial; mercury.

mercantile *adj* of merchants or trade.

mercantilism *n* a theory popular in 17th and 18th century Europe suggesting that the wealth of a nation increases in proportion to the level of the foreign trade surplus, therefore trade and commerce with other countries, the founding of colonies, a merchant navy etc should be encouraged; (*rare*) commercialism—**mercantilist** *n, adj*.

mercaptopurine *n* (*med*) a type of antimetabolite, cytotoxic drug that prevents the proliferation of malignant cancer cells.

Mercator's projection *n* (*geog*) a system of map projection that is frequently used in atlases, distorts and enlarges land areas towards the poles.

mercenary *adj* working or done for money only. * *n* (*pl* **mercenaries**) a soldier hired to fight for a foreign army.—**mercenarily** *adv*.—**mercenariness** *n*.

mercer *n* a dealer in textiles, esp silk and velvet.

mercerize *vt* to treat cotton thread so as to strengthen it and make it resemble silk.—**mercerization** *n*.

merchandize *n* commercial goods. * *vti* to sell, to trade; to promote sales by display or advertising.—**merchandiser** *n*.

merchandizing, merchandising *n* the in-store promotion by a retailer of selected products; the exploitation of a fictional character, pop group, etc, by the production of goods with their image, name, etc.

merchant *n* a trader; a retailer; (*sl*) a person fond of a particular activity.

merchantable *adj* marketable.

merchant bank *n* a bank that originally specialized in the provision of finance for merchants, often being involved in foreign trade. In recent times, however, the merchant banks have diversified and now offer a whole range of financial services to clients.

merchantman *n* (*pl* **merchantmen**) a trading ship.

merchant marine, merchant navy *n* commercial shipping.

merciful *adj* compassionate, humane.—**mercifulness** *n*.

mercifully *adv* in a merciful way; (*inf*) thank goodness.

merciless *adj* cruel, pitiless; without mercy.—**mercilessly** *adv*.—**mercilessness** *n*.

Mercouri *n* **Melina** (1923–94) Greek actress and politician. Her best-known film is *Never on Sunday* (1960). She became an MP in 1974 after the fall of the military junta, which she had bravely criticized and which had forced her into exile, and was appointed minister for culture and science in 1981.

mercurial *adj* of, containing, or caused by mercury; lively, sprightly; volatile.—**mercurially** *adv*.

mercuric *adj* (*chem*) of or containing bivalent mercury.

mercurochrome *n* (*trademark*) a crystalline compound used in solution as a tropical antiseptic.

mercurous *adj* (*chem*) of or containing monovalent mercury.

mercury *n* (*chem*) a heavy, silvery-white, liquid, metal element (and the only liquid metal element at room temperature) which occurs naturally as the ore cinnabar, used in thermometers etc.

Mercury *n* (*astron*) the smallest and first planet of the solar system and nearest to the Sun; (*Roman myth*) the god of traders, thieves and moneymaking, the messenger of Jupiter, and identified in later times with the Greek Hermes.

mercy *n* clemency; compassion; kindness; pity.

mere[1] (*Brit*) *n* a small, shallow lake.

mere[2] *adj* nothing more than; simple, unmixed.

Meredith *n* **George** (1828–1909) English novelist and poet whose novels, e.g. *The Ordeal of Richard Feverel* and *The Egoist*, are complex studies of human relationships.

merely *adv* simply; solely.

meretricious *adj* tawdry, superficially attractive; insincere.

merganser *n* (*pl* **mergansers, merganser**) *n* a large, diving fish-eating duck with a long narrow bill with serrated edges; a sawbill.

merge *vti* to blend or cause to fuse together gradually; to (cause to) combine, unite. * *vt* (*comput*) to draw two pieces of information or records together to create a new file.

merger *n* a combining together, esp of two or more commercial organizations.

meridian *n* an imaginary circle on the earth's surface connecting the geographic poles; (*astron*) the great circle cutting the celestial sphere at its poles and which cuts the observer's horizon at the north and south points.

meridional *adj* of a meridian; of the south.—**meridionally** *adv*.

Merimde *n* a very ancient site in the Nile delta in Egypt that was occupied *c.* 5000 BC.

meringue *n* a mixture of egg whites beaten with sugar and baked; a small cake or shell made from this, filled with cream.

merino *n* (*pl* **merinos**) a breed of sheep with fine silky wool; the wool or the cloth made from it.

merit *n* excellence; worth; (*pl*) (*of a case*) rights and wrongs; a deserving act. * *vt* to be worthy of, to deserve.

meritocracy *n* (*pl* **meritocracies**) rule by those most skilled or talented; a social system or government based on this; the most talented group in a society.

meritorious *adj* deserving of merit or honor.—**meritoriously** *adv*.—**meritoriousness** *n*.

merkhet *n* (*Egypt*) a surveying instrument used by the Egyptians in laying out the ground for a temple or pyramid.

merle *n* (*Scot*) a blackbird. * *adj* (*dog*, esp *a collie*) having blue-gray fur with black tinges or streaks.

merlin *n* a small dark-colored falcon, often used in falconry.

Merlin *n* (*Welsh Celtic myth*) a wizard who played a major part in the Arthurian legends. The Welsh form of his name was Myrddin, and a character of this name played a part in Welsh mythology. Geoffrey of Monmouth describes Merlin and his exploits in *Li-bellus Merline* (Little Book of Merlin) which was written around AD 1135 and incorporated into his *Historia*.

MERLIN *abbr* = Multi-Element Radio-Linked Interferometer Network.

merlon *n* (*archit*) a raised portion of a parapet or battlement between two embrasures.

mermaid *n* (*legend*) a woman with a fish's tail.—**merman** *nm* (*pl* **mermen**).

meroblastic *adj* (*biol*) (*fertilized egg*) of or pertaining to the splitting of cells in the white only and not the entire ovum.

Merope *n* (*Greek myth*) a daughter of Atlas and one of the Pleiades.

Merovingian *adj* pertaining to the first Frankish dynasty of French kings (*c*.500–751). * *n* a member or adherent of this dynasty.

mer. rect. *abbr* = mercury rectifier.

merry *adj* (**merrier, merriest**) cheerful; causing laughter; lively; (*inf*) slightly drunk.—**merrily** *adv*.—**merriment** *n*.

merry-go-round *n* a revolving platform of hobbyhorses, etc, a carousel.

merrymaking *n* festivity, fun.—**merrymaker** *n*.

merrythought *n* (*rare*) the forked bone of a chicken's breast, the wishbone.

MERU *abbr* = Maharishi European Research University.

merv. *abbr* = merveilleux, a silk fabric.

Merz *n* **Johann Georg** (1649–1762) German engraver of table designs and copies of other works.

mes-, meso- *prefix* middle.

mesa *n* (*geol*) a steep-sided tableland, found where layers of sedimentary strata have a hard, resistant top layer, thought to be a stage in the denudation of a plateau.

mésalliance *n* a misalliance; a marriage with one of lower social position.

MESc *abbr* = Master of Engineering Science.

mescaline *n* a hallucinogenic drug derived from the mescal cactus.

mesdames *see* **madame**.

mesdemoiselles *see* **mademoiselle**.

mesembryanthemum *n* one of a genus of flowering, succulent plants with thick and fleshy leaves and showy flowers.

mesencephalon *n* the part of the brain that connects the pons and cerebellum with the cerebrum.—*also* **mid-brain**.

mesentery *n* (*pl* **mesenteries**) (*anat*) a double layer of the peritoneal membrane (peritoneum) attached to the back wall of the abdomen which supports a number of abdominal organs, including the stomach, small intestine, spleen, and pancreas.

mesh *n* an opening between cords of a net, wires of a screen, etc; a net; a network; a snare; (*geared wheels, etc*) engagement. * *vt* to entangle, ensnare. * *vi* to become entangled or interlocked.

MeSH *abbr* = Medical Subject Headings

mesial *adj* (*anat*) in or toward the middle line of the body.—**mesially** *adv*.

Mesmer *n* **Friedrich Anton** *or* **Franz** (1734–1815) Austrian physician and founder of mesmerism. Believed in a power called "Animal Magnetism" and caused a sensation in Paris in 1778 seemingly curing diseases at seances with an early method of hypnotism. Denounced as a fraud in 1785.

mesmerism *n* hypnotism.—**mesmerist** *n*.

mesmerize *vt* to hypnotize; to fascinate.—**mesmeric** *adj*.—**mesmerizer** *n*.

mesne *adj* (*law*) intervening, intermediate.

meso-, mes- *prefix* middle.

mesoblast *n* (*biol*) the middle germinal layer of an ovum, the basis of muscles, bones, blood etc.—*also* **mesoderm**.

mesocarp *n* (*bot*) the middle layer of the seed vessel of a fruit.

mesocephalic *adj, n* (*person*) with a head or skull of medium proportions.

mesoderm *see* **mesoblast**.

mesogastrium *n* (*biol*) the membrane that supports the embryonic stomach.—**mesogastric** *adj*.

Mesolithic *adj* (*or* **Middle Stone Age**) relating to the transitional period between the Old (Paleolithic) and New (Neolithic) Stone Age. It began *c* 8000 BC.

mesomorph *n* a person of compact and muscular physical build.—**mesomorphic** *adj*.

meson *n* (*physics*) an unstable elementary particle having a mass between that of proton and an electron, belonging to a group called hadrons.

mesophyll *n* (*bot*) the internal tissues of a leaf that are between the upper and lower epidermal layers and contain chlorophyll.—**mesophyllic, mesophyllous** *adj*.

mesophyte *n* (*bot*) a plant requiring an average water supply.—**mesophytic** *adj*.

Mesopotamia, Mesopotania (Iraq) *n* (*hist*) the country lying between the two great rivers, the Tigris and Euphrates, that saw the dawning of some of the most ancient civilizations, such as those of Sumer, Assyria and the Amorites.

mesosphere *n* the atmospheric layer between the stratosphere and the thermosphere.

mesothelioma *n* (*med*) a malignant tumor of the pleura of the chest cavity and also of the pericardium or peritoneum.

mesothorax *n* (*biol*) (*pl* **mesothoraxes, mesothoraces**) *n* the middle ring of an insect's thorax, with the second pair of walking legs and the front pair of wings.

Mesozoic *adj* pertaining to the era of geological time lasting from about 248 to 65 million years ago. * *n* this era.

mesquite, mesquit *n* (*bot*) a small pod-bearing tree of the southwest US whose pods are used as fodder.

mess *n* a state of disorder or untidiness, esp if dirty; a muddle; an unsightly or disagreeable mixture; a portion of soft and pulpy or semi-liquid food; a building where service personnel dine; a communal meal. * *vti* to make a mess (of), bungle; to eat in company; to potter (about).

message *n* any spoken, written, or other form of communication; the chief idea that the writer, artist, etc seeks to communicate in a work.

Messel *n* **Oliver** (1904–78) British theater, movie and interior designer.

messenger *n* a person who carries a message.

Messenia *n* an ancient state of Greece in the southern part of the Peloponnese, whose capital was Messene. —**Messenian** *adj*.

Messerschmitt *n* **Willy** [Wilhelm Messerschmitt] (1898–1978) German aircraft designer and manufacturer. His planes include two notable fighters, the ME–109, a version of which won the world speed record in 1939, and the first jet combat aircraft, the ME–262.

Messiaen *n* **Olivier** (1908–92) French composer and organist. His rhythmically complex works, often influenced by birdsong, include *Quartet for the End of Time* (1941, performed before fellow prisoners in a German POW camp) and the massive Hindu-influenced *Turangallia* symphony (1946).

Messiah *n* the promised savior of the Jews; Jesus Christ. —**Messianic** *adj*.

Messier Catalog *n* (*astron*) a listing of 108 galaxies, star clusters and nebulae drawn up by the French comet hunter Charles Messier in 1770.

messieurs *see* **monsieur**.

Messmer *n* **Otto** (1894–1985) American cartoonist. His "Felix the Cat" first appeared in *Feline Follies* (1920) and became the first cartoon superstar. "Felix kept on walking" became an international catchphrase.

Messrs *abbr* = messieurs, (*French*) "sirs" or "gentlemen"; *pl* of Mr; used when writing formally to a group of people or organization.

messuage *n* (*law*) a dwelling house with its adjacent buildings and land for the use of the household.

messy *adj* (**messier, messiest**) dirty; confused; untidy.—**messily** *adv*.—**messiness** *n*.

mestizo *n* (*pl* **mestizos, mestizoes**) a person of mixed parentage, esp the child of a Spanish American and an American Indian.

mesto *adj* (*mus*) (*Italian*) "sad."

met *see* **meet**.

met. *abbr* = metaphor; metaphysical; metaphysics; metronome; metropolitan.

meta-, met- *prefix* after, with, or implying change.

metabolism *n* (*biol*) all the chemical and physical processes which occur in living organisms and that maintain life and growth. —**metabolic** *adj*.

metabolize *vt* to process by metabolism; to assimilate.

metacarpal *adj* (*anat*) pertaining to the metacarpus. * *n* a bone of the metacarpus.

metacarpal bone (*anat*) n one of the five bones of the middle of the hand, between the phalanges of the fingers and the carpal bones of the wrist forming the metacarpus. The heads of the metacarpal bones form the knuckles.

metacarpus *n* (*pl* **metacarpi**) (*anat*) the bones of that part of the hand that is between the wrist and the fingers, or the corresponding part in other animals.

metacenter, metacentre *n* the point in a floating body where the verticals intersect when the body is tilted and on the position of which its equilibrium or stability depends.—**metacentric** *adj*.

metage *n* the official weighing or measuring of the contents of something; the fee paid for this.

metagenesis *n* the alternation of sexual and asexual generations.—**metagenetic** *adj*.—**metagenetically** *adv*.

metal *n* any of a class of chemical elements which are often lustrous, ductile solids, and are good conductors of heat, electricity, etc, such as gold, iron, copper, etc; any alloy of such elements as brass, bronze, etc; anything consisting of metal.—**metalled** *adj*.

metal. *abbr* = metallurgical; metallurgy.

metallic *adj* of, relating to, or made of metal; similar to metal.

metalliferous *adj* yielding metal or metallic ores.

metalline *adj* metallic; impregnated with or yielding metal.

metallize, metalize *vt* to give metallic qualities to; to coat or treat with metal.

metallo *adj* (*mus*) (*Italian*) "metal," so *bel metallo di voce*, "ringing quality of voice."

metallography *n* the science or description of the structure of metals and alloys; (*print*) lithography using metal plates to print an image.

metalloid *n* a nonmetallic element that possesses some of the chemical properties associated with metals and some associated with non-metals. * *adj* of or having the properties of a metalloid; resembling a metal (—*also* **metalloidal**).

metallophone *n* (*mus*) an instrument that is similar to a xylophone but has metal bars (usu bronze).

metallurgy *n* the science of separating metals from their ores and preparing them for use by smelting, refining, etc.—**metallurgical** *adj*.—**metallurgist** *n* .

metalwork *n* the art of working in metal; objects crafted in metal.

metamere *n* (*zool*) a segment of a body, as in earthworms, crayfish, etc.

metameric *adj* (*zool*) of or having metameres; (*chem*) having the same elements and molecular weight but different properties.—**metamerism** *n*.

metamorphic rock *n* (*geol*) one of the three main rock types, formed by the alteration or recrystallization of existing rocks by the application of heat, pressure or change in volatiles (gases and liquids).

metamorphism *n* (*geol*) the change in the structure of rocks through heat, pressure, etc.

metamorphosis *n* (*pl* **metamorphoses**) a complete change of form, structure, substance, character, appearance, etc; (*myth*) the transformation of human beings into animals, stones, trees, fire, water, etc.; (*zool*) the period of change in form of an organism from the larval to the adult state. —**metamorphic** *adj*.—**metamorphose** *vi*.

M

metaph. *abbr* = metaphor; metaphorical; metaphorically; metaphysics.

metaphase *n* (*biol*) a stage of cell division in mitosis or meiosis.

metaphor *n* a figure of speech in which a word or phrase is used for another of which it is an image.—**metaphoric, metaphorical** *adj.*—**metaphorically** *adv.*

metaphrase *n* a word-for-word translation, the opposite of paraphrase. * *vt* to alter the wording of something, esp to alter the meaning; to translate literally.

metaphrast *n* one who alters text, esp one who changes the form, as from verse to prose.—**metaphrastic, metaphrastical** *adj.*

metaphysical *adj* of or pertaining to metaphysics; abstruse, abstract; supernatural; (*poetry*) fantastic or over-subtle in style.—**metaphysically** *adv.*

metaphysical painting *n* an art movement begun in Italy in 1917 by Carrà and de Chirico. By the early 1920s, both artists had developed other interests.

metaphysical poetry *n* a poetry movement of the 17th century, noted for intense feeling, extended metaphor, and striking, elaborate imagery, often with a mystical element.

metaphysics *n sing* (*philos*) the branch of philosophy that seeks to explain the nature of being and reality; speculative philosophy in general.—**metaphysician** *n.*

metaplasia *n* (*med*) an abnormal change that has taken place within a tissue, e.g., myeloid metaplasia, where elements of bone marrow develop within the spleen and liver.

metaplasm *n* (*biol*) that part of the contents of a cell consisting of inert matter; (*gram*) a change in a word by the adding or dropping of a letter.—**metaplasmic** *adj.*

metapsychology *n* (*psychol*) the study of the operation of the mind beyond what can be verified experimentally.— **metapsychological** *adj.*

metasomatism *n* (*geol*) the introduction of chemical constituents in a gaseous or liquid phase into a rock (or their removal from it) thus altering the overall composition of the rock.

metastable *adj* (*physics*) denoting a group of minerals created under high temperature and/or pressure, or a supersaturated that appears to be stable but, in fact, will react or change if disturbed.

metastasis *n* (*pl* **metastases**) *n* (*med*) a change or shift in the location of a disease, often used of the spreading of cancer cells from the affected tissue to create secondary areas of growth in other tissues of the body; a transformation or change; (*rare*) metabolism—**metastatic** *adj.*

metatarsal *adj* pertaining to the metatarsus. * *n* one of the bones of the metatarsus.

metatarsal bone *n* (*anat*) one of the five bones in the foot, lying between the toes and the tarsal bones of the ankle, together forming the metatarsus.

metatarsus *n* (*pl* **metatarsi**) (*anat*) in humans, the instep, the middle part of the foot between the tarsus and the toes; in other animals, the part corresponding to this.

metathesis *n* (*pl* **metatheses**) the transposition of the letters or syllables of a word; (*chem*) a reaction between two compounds in which the first and second parts of one unite with the second and first parts of the other.—**metathetic, metathetical** *adj.*

metathorax *n* (*pl* **metathoraxes, metathoraces**) (*zool*) the hindmost segment of an insect's thorax, with the third pair of walking legs and the second pair of wings.

metazoan *n* (*zool*) an animal belonging to a division of the animal kingdom in which the body is made up of a large number of cells, i.e., all animals except sponges and protozoans.

mete *vt* to allot; to portion (out).

Met. E. *abbr* = Metallurgical Engineer.

metempsychosis *n* (*pl* **metempsychoses**) the belief that the souls of the dead are reborn in the bodies of other men or animals.

meteor *n* (*astron*) a small particle of matter which travels at great speed through space and becomes luminous through friction as it enters the earth's atmosphere and burns up; a shooting star.

meteor. *abbr* = meteorology.

meteoric *adj* (*astron*) of or relating to a meteor; dazzling, transitory.

meteoric water *n* (*meteorology*) water originating in the atmosphere, e.g., as rain and snow.

meteorite *n* (*astron*) a meteor that has fallen to earth without being completely vaporized.—**meteoritic** *adj.*

meteorograph *n* (*meteorology*) an instrument for recording various meteorological conditions simultaneously.

meteoroid *n* (*astron*) a small body moving through space, often orbiting the Sun, that on entering the earth's atmosphere is heated by friction and leaves a bright trail, a meteor.

meteorol. *abbr* = meteorological; meteorology.

meteorology *n* a study of the earth's atmosphere, particularly weather and climate.—**meteorological** *adj.*—**meteorologist** *n.*

meteor shower *n* (*astron*) a group of meteors that appear to come from one point on the celestial sphere.

meter[1] *n* a device for measuring and recording a quantity of gas, water, time, etc supplied; a parking meter. * *vt* to measure using a meter.

meter[2] *n* rhythmic pattern in verse, the measured arrangement of syllables according to stress; rhythmic pattern in music.—*also* **metre**.

meter[3] *n* the basic unit of length in the metric system, consisting of 100 centimeters and equal to 39.37 inches.—*also* **metre**.

-meter *suffix* denoting a device for measuring; meter(s) in length.

Meth. *abbr* = Methodist.

methadone *n* (*med*) a powerful, narcotic drug used in pain relief, as a cough suppressant, and as a morphine or heroin substitute.

methane *n* (*chem*) a colorless, odorless, flammable gas, which is the main constituent of coal gas and is a by-product of any decaying vegetable matter.

methinks *vt* (*pt* **methought**) (*arch*) it appears or seems to me.

method *n* the mode or procedure of accomplishing something; orderliness of thought; an orderly arrangement or system.

method acting *n* a style of acting, developed by Lee Strasberg from the theories of Stanislavsky, that requires an actor to immerse himself in the inner life of the character he is playing, and, using the insights gained in this study, to convey to the audience the hidden reality behind the words.

methodical *adj* orderly, systematic.—**methodically** *adv.*

Methodist *n* a member of a Christian denomination founded by John Wesley.—**Methodism** *n.*

Methodius *n* Saint *see* **Cyril and Methodius**.

methodize *vt* to reduce to method; systematize.

methodology *n* (*pl* **methodologies**) the methods and procedures used by a science or discipline; the philosophical analysis of method and procedure.

method study *n* the analysis and recording of ways of carrying out tasks with a view to maximizing the efficiency of these methods.

methought *see* **methinks**.

meths *n* (*inf*) methylated spirit.

Methuselah *n* a wine bottle eight times the size of an ordinary bottle; (*OT*) a patriarch reputed to have been 969 years old when he died; a very old person.

methyl *n* a compound composed of organic material and metals in which metal groups are bound directly to a metal atom.

methylated spirit *n* a form of alcohol, adulterated to render it undrinkable, used as a solvent.

methyldopa *n* (*med*) a drug that is used to reduce high blood pressure, esp in pregnancy.

methylene *n* a bivalent organic radical found in unsaturated hydrocarbons; an inflammable liquid obtained from the distillation of wood.

metical *n* the currency of Mozambique. *See* **centavo**.

meticulous *adj* very precise about small details.—**meticulously** *adv.*—**meticulousness** *n.*

métier *n* a person's calling or trade, esp if that person has a natural leaning toward it; a strong point, forte.

métis *n* (*pl* **métis**) *n* (*often cap*) an offspring of mixed parentage; in Canada, one who is the child or a descendant of a French Canadian and an American Indian; one of a group of such people forming a political and national entity, who settled in Manitoba and Saskatchewan.—**métisse** *nf.*

Metis *n* 1. (*Greek myth*) the personification of prudence, a daughter of Oceanus and Tethys, the first wife of Zeus, who conceived Athena but was eaten by Zeus before the birth; 2. the innermost satellite of Jupiter

met'l *abbr* = meteorological.

m et n *abbr* = *mane et nocte* (*Latin*) "morning and night."

Metol *n* (*trademark*) a colorless, soluble organic substance used as a photographic developer.

meton. *abbr* = metonymy.

metonymy *n* (**metonymies**) a figure of speech in which a thing is replaced by its attribute, e.g. "the pen is mightier than the sword."—**metonym** *n.*—**metonymical, metonymic** *adj.*

metope *n* (*archit*) the space between two triglyphs of a Doric frieze.

metric *adj* based on the meter as a standard of measurement; of, relating to, or using the metric system.

metrical *adj* of, relating to, or composed in rhythmic meter.—**metrically** *adv.*

metrication *n* conversion of an existent system of units into the metric system.

metrics *n sing* the study of verse form; the art of composing verse.

metric system *n* a decimal system of weights and measures based on the meter, liter and the kilogram.

metric ton *n* 1000 kilograms.—*also* **tonne**.

metritis *n* (*med*) inflammation of the uterus.

metro *n* (*pl* **metros**) an urban underground railway system, such as in Paris and other cities.

metrol. *abbr* = metrological; metrology.

metrology *n* (*pl* **metrologies**) *n* the science of weights and measures or units of measurement; any of the various systems of units.

metronome *n* (*mus*) an instrument that produces regular beats and can therefore be used to indicate the pace at which a piece of music should be played. .—**metronomic** *adj.*

metronymic *adj* (*name*) derived from one's mother or a female ancestor. * *n* such a name.—*also* **matronymic**.

metrop. *abbr* = metropolitan.

metropolis *n* a large city together with its suburbs. —**metropolitan** *adj*.

Metropolitan Opera House, **New York** *n* the home of the prestigious Metropolitan Opera Company which was formed in 1883. The opera house is part of the Lincoln Center for the Performing Arts and is affectionately called "The Met."

metsat *abbr* = meteorological satellite.

mettle *n* courage, spirit.

mettled *adj* mettlesome.

mettlesome *adj* high-spirited, full of courage.

meunière *adj* (*fish*) coated with flour, cooked in butter and served with parsley and lemon juice.

MeV *abbr* = mega-electron-volt; million electron-volts.

MEW *abbr* = microwave early warning system.

mew[1] *vi* (*cat*) to emit a high-pitched cry. * *n* the cry of a cat.

mew[2] *n* a gull found in northern areas.

mew[3] *n* a cage for hawks. * *vti* (*hawk*) to shed (feathers), to moult; to put in a mew, to confine.

mewl *vi* (*baby*) to cry feebly, to whimper; to mew. * *n* a whimper.

mews *n sing or pl* a yard or road at the back of town houses formerly used as stables and later converted into living accommodation.

Mex. *abbr* = Mexican; Mexico.

Mexican peso *n* currency of Mexico.

Mexico *n* a federal republic bounded in the north by its long border with the USA and in the south with Guatemala and Belize.

Mexico City *n* capital city of Mexico.

Meyer *n* **Daniel** (1576–1630) German son of a glass painter who published a book of architectural ornaments in 1609.

Meyerbeer *n* **Giacomo** (1791–1864) German-born composer whose best known works, written for the Paris Opera, include *Robert le Diable, Les Huguenots* and *L'Africaine*.

Meyerhold *n* **Vsevolod** (1874–1940) Russian theatrical producer and director who was the most prominent exponent of avant-garde ideas and productions on the Russian stage, introducing futurism and constructivist theater.

Meynell *n* **Alice** (1847–1922) English poet and essayist who converted to Roman Catholicism, carrying her beliefs into her writings, and who befriended Francis Thompson and rescued him from opium addiction.

mezzanine *n* (*archit*) a lower story flanked by two higher ones; a theater balcony. —*also* **entresol**

mezzanine debt *see* **junk debt**.

mezzo *adj* (*mus*) (*Italian*) literally "half," so *mezzo-soprano* means a voice between soprano and contralto. * *adv* (*mus*) moderately; quite. * *n* (*pl* **mezzo-sopranos**) a mezzo-soprano.

mezzo-relievo *n* (*pl* **mezzo-relievos**) a carving in half-relief, where the figures project in neither high relief nor low relief from the background.

mezzotint *n* a method of engraving on copper or steel in imitation of drawing in Indian ink, the lights being scraped and burnished out of a prepared dark ground; a print so made. * *vt* to engrave a copper plate using this method.

mf *adj, adv* (*mus*) *mezzo forte* (*Italian*) "moderately loud."

mf. *abbr* = microfarad; millifarad.

MF *abbr* = machine, *or* mill, finish; medium frequency.

MFA *abbr* = Master of Fine Arts; Metal Finishing Association; Multi-Fiber Arrangement.

MFARCS *abbr* = (*Brit*) Member of the Faculty of Anaesthetists of the Royal College of Surgeons.

MFBA *abbr* = Member of the Faculty of Business Administrators.

MFC *abbr* = Mastership in Food Control.

MFCM *abbr* = Member of the Faculty of Community Medicine.

mfd. *abbr* = manufactured; microfarad.

MFD *abbr* = minimum fatal dose.

MFDO *abbr* = Member of the Faculty of Dispensing Opticians.

mfg *abbr* = manufacturing.

MFH *abbr* = Master of Foxhounds; mobile field hospital.

MFHom *abbr* = Member of the Faculty of Homoeopathy.

MFlem *abbr* = Middle Flemish.

mflops *abbr* = million floating-point operations per second.

MFM *abbr* = modified frequency modulation.

MFMI *abbr* = Men for Missions International (USA).

MFN *abbr* = most favored nation.

MFP *abbr* = Mothers for Peace.

MFPA *abbr* = Mouth and Foot Painting Artists.

MFPC *abbr* = Man-made Fibres Producers' Committee.

MFPHM *abbr* = Member of the Faculty of Public Health Medicine.

mfr, mfr. *abbr* = manufacture; manufacturer.

MFr *abbr* = Middle French.

mft, m.ft. *abbr* = (*pharm*) *mistura fiat* (*Latin*) "let a mixture be made"; thousand feet.

MFTCom *abbr* = Member of the Faculty of Teachers in Commerce.

mfv *abbr* = motor fleet vehicle.

mg *abbr* (*mus*) *main gauche* (*French*) "left hand"; milligram(s); motor generator.

Mg (*symbol*) (*chem*) magnesium; megagram.

MG *abbr* = Major-General; Morris Garages; machine gun.

MGAGB *abbr* = Mounted Games Association of Great Britain.

mgawd *abbr* = make good all works disturbed.

MGC *abbr* = machine-gun company *or* corps; (*Brit*) Museums and Galleries Commission.

m.g.d., mgd million gallons per day.

MGDSRCSEd *abbr* = Membership in General Dental Surgery, Royal College of Surgeons of Edinburgh.

MGDSRCSEng *abbr* = Membership in General Dental Surgery, Royal College of Surgeons of England.

MGM *abbr* = Metro Goldwyn Meyer; mobile guided missile.

MGN *abbr* = (*Brit*) Mirror Group Newspapers.

mgr. *abbr* = milligram; milligrams.

Mgr *abbr* = manager; Monseigneur; Monsignor, as used in the Roman Catholic Church; Monsignore.

MGr *abbr* = Medieval Greek.

mh, mH *abbr* = millihenry.

m.h. *abbr* (*shipping*) = main hatch.

MH *abbr* = marital history; Master of Horse; Master of Horticulture or of Hygiene; Master of Hounds;.

MHA *abbr* = Member of the House of Assembly; Methodist Homes for the Aged.

MHC (major histocompatibility complex) *n* a group of genes located on the chromosomes.

MHD *abbr* = magnetic hydrodynamic.

MHE *abbr* = Master of Home Economics.

MHF *abbr* = medium high frequency.

MHFS *abbr* = Member of the Council of Health Fitness & Sports Therapists.

MHG *abbr* = Middle High German.

MHK *abbr* = Member of the House of Keys.

MHLG *abbr* = Ministry of Housing and Local Government.

MHM *abbr* = Mental Health Media.

MHort(RHS) *abbr* = National Diploma in Horticulture, Royal Horticultural Society.

MHortSc *abbr* = Master of Horticultural Science.

MHR *abbr* = Member of the House of Representatives.

MHRA *abbr* = Modern Humanities Research Association.

mhs *abbr* = medical history sheet; message handling system.

MHS *abbr* = Malta Heraldic Society; Meat Hygiene Service; Military Historical Society.

MHTGR *abbr* = modular high-temperature gas-cooled reactor.

MHW *abbr* = mean high water.

MHy *abbr* = Master of Hygiene.

MHz *abbr* = megahertz.

mi *n* (*mus*) the third note of a major scale in the diatonic system.—*also* **me**.

mi. *abbr* = mile, or miles; mill, or mills; minute; minor (*music*).

m.i. *abbr* = malleable iron.

MI *abbr* = Michigan; Military Intelligence (state security and anti-espionage service in the UK); medical inspection; myocardial infarction; Mounted Infantry.

MI5 *abbr* = Military Intelligence 5 (UK anti-espionage and state security service, officially ceased since 1964).

MI6 *abbr* = Military Intelligence 6 (UK anti-espionage and state security service, officially ceased since 1964).

MIA *abbr* = Maldive International Airlines; Malleable Ironfounders' Association; Music Industries Association; missing in action.

MIAA & S *abbr* = Member of the Incorporated Institute of Auctioneers and Surveyors.

MIAB *abbr* = Member of the International Association of Book-keepers.

MIAEA *abbr* = Member of the Institute of Automotive Engineer Assessors.

MIAgrE *abbr* = Member of the Institution of Agricultural Engineers.

MIAP *abbr* = Member of the Institution of Analysts and Programmers.

miasma *n* (*pl* **miasmas, miasmata**) an unwholesome, foreboding atmosphere; an unpleasant vapor, as from decaying swamp matter.—**miasmal, miasmatic, miasmic** *adj*.

MIAT *abbr* = Member of the Institute of Animal Technology; Member of the Institute of Asphalt Technology.

MIB *abbr* = Metal Information Bureau; Motor Insurers' Bureau; Mustard Information Bureau (USA).

MIBC *abbr* = Member of the Institute of Building Control.

MIBCM *abbr* = Member of the Institute of British Carriage and Automobile Manufacturers.

MIBCO *abbr* = Member of the Institution of Building Control Officers.

MIBF *abbr* = Member of the Institute of British Foundrymen.

MIBiol *abbr* = Member of the Institute of Biology.

Mic. *abbr* = Micah.

MIC *abbr* = Magnesium Industry Council; Millinery Information Centre.

mica *n* a mineral that crystallizes in thin, flexible layers, resistant to heat.— **micaceous** *adj*.

Micah *n* 1. (*Bible*) eighth century BC prophet who spoke against the oppression of the poor by the rich "who tear the skin from off my people, and their flesh from off their bones; who abhor justice and pervert all equity." 2. **Micah, the Book of** (*Bible*) Micah's oracles are concerned with the daily hardships of the small farmer, but include the famous prophecy concerning Bethlehem as the birthplace of the coming Messianic ruler.

mice *see* **mouse**.

MICE *abbr* = Member of the Institution of Civil Engineers.

M

Mich. *abbr* = Michaelmas; Michigan.

Michael *n* **Saint** one of the three archangels who stand before the throne of God, St Michael is described in the Book of Revelations as the leader of the heavenly armies; the protector of Christians in general and soldiers in particular; patron saint of grocers. His feast day is 29 September.

Michaelmas *n* a church festival commemorating the archangel Michael, celebrated on September 29.

Michelangelo Buonarotti *n* (1475–1564) Florentine painter, sculptor, draftsman, architect, and poet. An outstanding figure of the Italian Renaissance, his masterpiece was the ceiling paintings for the Sistine Chapel (1508–12).

Michelozzo *n* **Bartolommeo di** (*b*. 1396) Italian architect. His notable works include Portinari chapel, Milan.

Michelson interferometer *n* a device using the interference of light to make very accurate measurements of lengths.

MIChemE *abbr* = Member of the Institution of Chemical Engineers.

Michigan (MI) *n* a state of the United States of America (USA) of which the capital is Lansing.

"Michigan, My Michigan" *n* the song of the American State, Michigan.

Michs. *abbr* = Michaelmas.

MICM *abbr* = Associate Member of the Institute of Credit Management.

MICO *abbr* = Member of the Institute of Careers Officers.

MICorr *abbr* = Member of the Institute of Corrosion.

MICR *abbr* = magnetic ink character recognition.

micra *see* **micron**.

micro *n* (*pl* **micros**) a microwave oven; (*comput*) a microcomputer, a microprocessor.

Micro *abbr* = Multinational Initiative for the Use of Computers in Research Organizations.

micro-, micr- *prefix* small.

microbe *n* a microscopic organism such as a bacillus or disease-causing bacterium.—**microbial, microbic** *adj*.

microbiology *n* the biology of bacteria and other microorganisms and their effects.—**microbiological, microbiologic** *adj*.—**microbiologically** *adv*.—**microbiologist** *n*.

microburin *n* (*archeo*) a small, residual flake of stone which was snapped off during the manufacture of a microlith.

microbus *n* (*pl* **microbuses, microbusses**) a station wagon that resembles a small bus.

microcephalic, microcephalous *adj* having an unusually small head.—**microcephaly** *n*.

microcephaly *n* the condition in which there is abnormal smallness of the head compared to the rest of the body. *See also* **macrocephaly**.

microchip *n* (*comput*) a small wafer of silicon, etc, containing electronic circuits. *See also* **chip; microprocessor.**

microcircuit *n* a miniature electronic circuit, esp an integrated circuit.—**microcircuitry** *n*.

microclimate *n* the climate of a restricted specific place within an area as opposed to the climate of the area.—**microclimatic** *adj*.

micrococcus *n* (**micrococci**) a round bacterium, a source of fermentation and of zymotic disease.—**micrococcal** *adj*.

microcomputer *n* (*comput*) now a small computer or small computer system, but originally one whose central processing unit was a microprocessor.

microcosm *n* a miniature universe or world.—**microcosmic, microcosmical** *adj*.—**microcosmically** *adv*.

microcyte *n* (*biol*) an unusually small red blood corpuscle, often present in disease.—**microcytic** *adj*.

microdensitometer *n* (*astron*) a device for determining in a quantitative manner the density, or degree of blackening, of a photographic plate, used to convert the image of a star into a measurement of its brightness.

microdot *n* a photographic reproduction of a document, plan, etc reduced to a tiny dot, esp for reasons of espionage.

microeconomics *n sing* (*econ*) the branch of economics concerned with the activities of consumers, firms, and commodities.—**microeconomic** *adj*.

microelectronics *n sing* the design, production and use of microchips and microcircuits.

microfiche *n* (*pl* **microfiche, microfiches**) a sheet of microfilm containing pages of printed matter.—*also* **film card**.

microfilm *n* film on which documents, etc, are recorded in reduced scale. * *vt* to record on microfilm.

microfloppy *n* (*comput*) (*pl* **microfloppies**) a floppy disk of 3.5 inches (8.7 cm) diameter contained in a hard covering.

micrograph *n* a photograph of something as seen through a microscope; a device for executing minute engraving or writing.

micrography *n* the description, study or representation of microscopic objects; the process of writing in miniature.—**micrographic** *adj*.

microhabitat *n* (*ecol*) the smallest life-supporting environment in an ecosystem.

microlith *n* (*archeo*) a Mesolithic flint tool usu set in bone or a wooden haft.—**microlithic** *adj*.

micrometeorite *n* a very small meteoritic particle that loses its energy before burning up in the earth's atmosphere, and then falls to the surface as dust.

micrometer[1] *n* any instrument used for the accurate measurement of minute objects, distances, angles, thicknesses, or apparent diameters, sometimes used with a microscope.

micrometer[2], **micrometre** *n* a unit of length of one thousandth of a millimeter, a micron.

micrometry *n* the measurement of tiny objects, distances, etc, by a micrometer.—**micrometric, micrometrical** *adj*.—**micrometrically** *adv*.

micron *n* (*pl* **microns, micra**) one millionth of a meter, a micrometer.

Micronesia, Federated States of, *n* a self-governing republic comprising around 600 islands in the Caroline Islands Archipelago which lies scattered across the western Pacific Ocean roughly 4,025 kilometers or 2,500 miles southwest of Hawaii.

micronutrient *n* a nutrient required in tiny quantities by a plant or animal.

microorganism *n* (*biol*) an organism visible only through a microscope.

microphone *n* an instrument for transforming sound waves into electric signals, esp for transmission, or recording.—**microphonic** *adj*.

microphotograph *n* a photograph taken through a microscope or of microscopic size, in which the details cannot be distinguished by the naked eye; a photomicrograph.—**microphotographic** *adj*.—**microphotography** *n*.

microphysics *n* the physics of elementary particles.—**microphysical** *adj*.—**microphysically** *adv*.

microphyte (*biol*) *n* a microscopic vegetable growth, esp a parasitic one.—**microphytic** *adj*.

microprocessor or **microchip** *n* (*comput*) an electronic device (integrated circuit) that has been programmed to follow a set of logic-driven rules.

micros. *abbr* = microscopist; microscopical; microscopy.

microscope *n* an optical instrument for making magnified images of minute objects by means of a lens or lenses.

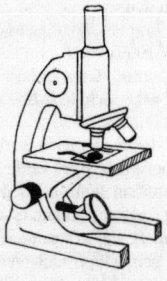

microscopic *adj* of, with, like, a microscope; visible only through a microscope; very small.—**microscopically** *adv*.

microscopy *n* (*pl* **microscopies**) the use of microscopes; microscopic investigation.—**microscopist** *n*.

microsecond (µs) *n* (*comput*) one millionth of a second.

microseism *n* a faint earth tremor, probably not related to earthquakes.—**microseismic** *adj*.

Microsoft™ *n* (*comput*) the world's largest software company.

microsurgery *n* (*med*) surgery performed on cells and tissues using microscopes and miniaturized precision instruments.

microtome *n* an instrument for cutting thin sections for microscopic examination, used particularly in biology.

microtones *n* (*mus*) intervals that are smaller than a semitone in length, e.g., the quarter-tone.

microtubule *n* (*biol*) a long hollow fiber of protein that is found in all higher plant and animal cells.

microwave *n* an electromagnetic wave 0.4–39 ins (1–100 cm) in length; (*inf*) a microwave oven. * *vt* to cook (food) in a microwave oven.—**microwavable, microwaveable** *adj*.

microwave background *n* (*astron*) a weak radio signal that is thought to be the remains of the big bang with which the universe began.

microwave oven *n* a cooker in which food is cooked or heated by microwaves.

microwave therapy *n* (*medical*) the use of very short wavelength electromagnetic waves in the procedure known as diathermy.

MICS *abbr* = Member of the Institute of Chartered Shipbrokers.

micturate *vi* to urinate.—**micturition** *n*.

micturition *n* the act of urination.

MICU *abbr* = mobile intensive care unit.

MICW *abbr* = Member of the Institute of Clerks of Works of Great Britain Incorporated.

MID *abbr* = minimum infective dose.

mid *adj* middle. * *prep* amid.

mid. *abbr* = middle; midshipman.

mid- *prefix* middle.

midair *adj* in the air, somewhere above the ground. * *n* any point not in touch with the ground.

Midas[1] *n* (*Greek myth*) king of Phrygia, whose request that whatever he touched should turn to gold was granted by Dionysus.

Midas[2] *abbr* = Missile Defence Alarm System.

Midavaine *n* **Louis** (1888–1978) French designer who learned the skill of lacquering whilst a prisoner in WWI.

midbrain *n* the part of the brain that develops from the middle section of the embryonic neural tube. *See* **mesencephalon**.

midday *n* the middle of the day, noon.

midden n a dunghill, a refuse heap; (archeo) a mixed layer or heap of refuse which was discarded and built up through time at the site of a human settlement.

middle adj halfway between two given points, times, etc; intermediate; central. * n the point halfway between two extremes; something intermediate; the waist. * vt to put in the middle; (naut) to fold (a sail) in the middle.

middle age n the time between youth and old age, c.40-60.—**middle-aged** adj.

Middle Ages npl the period of European history between about AD 500 and 1500.

middle C n (mus) the note C which occupies the first ledger line below the treble staff, the first ledger line above the bass staff, and is indicated by the C clef.

middle class n the class between the lower and upper classes, mostly composed of professional and business people.—**middle-class** adj.

middle ear n (anat, physiology) the central, air-filled cavity of the ear behind the drum that is linked to the pharynx via the Eustachian tube.

Middle East n a general term applied currently to an area extending from the eastern Mediterranean to the Gulf of Arabia; (formerly) that part of Southern Asia from the Tigris and Euphrates to Burma.

Middle Egypt n (Egypt) a geographical term applied to the Nile Valley between Asyut and Cairo.

middleman n (pl **middlemen**) a person or firm that acts as an intermediary between the producer or seller of goods or services and the buyer of these goods and services, the middleman making a profit in the process.

middle management n management at a level between supervisory staff and senior policy makers.

middle name n the name between one's first and last name.

middle-of-the-road adj avoiding extremes, esp political extremes.—**middle-of-the-roader** n.

middle price n the price of a security, commodity or currency that lies halfway between the offer price or selling price and the bid price or buying price.

Middleton n Thomas (c.1570–1627) English dramatist. His two powerful tragedies, The Changeling (1622) and Women Beware Women (1627), are now highly regarded. His other works include the satirical comedy A Trick to Catch the Old One (1608) and a political satire, A Game at Chesse (1624).

middleweight n a professional boxer weighing 154–160 pounds (70–72.5 kilograms); a wrestler weighing usu 172–192 pounds (78–87 kilograms).

middling adj of medium quality, size, etc; second-rate. * adv moderately.—**middlingly** adv.

middy n (pl **middies**) n (naut) inf) a midshipman; a middy blouse; (Austral) a glass of beer, usu containing half a pint.

middy blouse n a loose blouse with a sailor collar.

midge n a small gnat-like insect with a painful bite.

midget n a very small person, a dwarf; something small of its kind.—also adj.

Midhir n (Irish Celtic myth) was married to Fuamnach but fell in love with Etain, and Oenghus helped him to bring her home as his new bride.

midi n a coat or skirt that reaches to mid calf.

MIDI abbr = (comput) musical instrument digital interface (manufacturer's standard permitting different digital musical equipment to be freely connected when composing or recording).

Midianites n (Bible) nomadic clans from the Arabian desert who frequently raided Canaan in the days of Israelite settlement; their ancestor was said to be a son of Abraham.

midland n the middle part of a country; (pl) (with cap) central England; the industrial and manufacturing area of that part of England. * adj of or in midland; inland.

midlife n (pl **midlives**) middle age.—also adj.

midmost adj in or nearest the middle. * adv in the middle.

midnight n twelve o'clock at night.

mid-oceanic ridge n (geol) long, linear, volcanic ridges throughout the oceans where new oceanic crust is created through the spreading of the plates and outpouring of basalt.

MIDPM abbr = Member of the Institute of Data Processing Management.

Midrash n (pl **Midrashim**) a critical exposition of or a sermon on the Jewish scriptural law or some portion of it; one of the various collections of these originating between AD 400 and 1200.

midrib n (bot) the principal central vein of a leaf.

midriff n (anat) the middle part of the torso between the abdomen and the chest.—also adj.

midship adj (naut) of or pertaining to the middle part of a ship.

midshipman n (naut) (pl **midshipmen**) in some navies, a noncommissioned officer ranking immediately below a sublieutenant; this naval rank; (formerly) a naval cadet officer; (biol) an American fish with light-producing organs.

midships adv (naut) at, near or toward the middle of a ship, amidships.

midst n middle. * prep amidst, among.

midsummer n the middle of summer.—also adj.

Midsummer Day n June 24, celebrated as the summer solstice or in commemoration of the birth of St John the Baptist.

Midsummer Eve n the day before Midsummer Day, June 23.

MIDTA abbr = Member of the International Dance Teachers' Association.

midterm n (an exam at) the middle of the academic term; the middle of a term of office.—also adj.

midway adv halfway. * n a middle course of action; the area of a carnival where the sideshows are.

midwife n (pl **midwives**) a person trained to assist women before, during, and after childbirth.—**midwifery** n.

midwifery n the profession devoted to the care of mothers during pregnancy and childbirth, and of mothers and babies during the period after delivery. A member of the profession is known as a midwife.

MIED abbr = Member of the Institution of Engineering Designers.

MIEE abbr = Member of the Institution of Electrical Engineers.

MIEIE abbr = Corporate Member of the Institution of Electrical and Electronics Incorporated Engineers.

MIEM abbr = Master Member of the Institute of Executives and Managers.

mien n the expression of the face; demeanor.

Mies van der Rohe n Ludwig (1886–1969) German-born American architect with an austere style. Notable works are his German pavilion for the 1929 International Exhibition in Barcelona , and the New York Seagram Tower. One of the most influential architects in America and a major figure in the development of 20th century modern architecture.

MIEx abbr = Member of the Institute of Export.

MIEx(Grad) abbr = Graduate Member of the Institute of Export.

MIExpE abbr = Member of the Institute of Explosives Engineers.

MIF abbr = Miners' International Federation; migration inhibition factor.

MIFA abbr = Member of the Institute of Field Archaeologists.

miff n (inf) a petty quarrel, a tiff; a sulky mood. * vti to take offence; to offend.

MIFF abbr = Member of the Institute of Freight Forwarders Ltd.

miffy adj (**miffier, miffiest**) (inf) touchy, huffy; over-sensitive.—**miffiness** n.

MIFireE abbr = Member of the Institution of Fire Engineers.

MIFST abbr = Member of the Institute of Food Science and Technology.

MiG abbr = Mikoyan and Gurevich (designers of Soviet warplane).

MIG abbr = mortgage indemnity guarantee.

MIGA abbr = Multilateral Investment Guarantee Agency

MIGD abbr = Member of the Institute of Grocery Distribution.

MIGeol abbr = Member of the Institute of Geologists.

might[1] see **may**.

might[2] n power, bodily strength.

mightn't = might not.

mighty adj (**mightier, mightiest**) powerful, strong; massive; (inf) very.—**mightily** adv.—**mightiness** n.

mignonette n a (bot) sweet-scented plant with spikes of small green- white flowers; a grayish-green color; a delicate bobbin lace.

migraine n (med) a very severe throbbing headache, usu on one side of the head, which is often accompanied by disturbances in vision, nausea, and vomiting.

migrant n a person or animal that moves from one region or country to another; an itinerant agricultural laborer. * adj migrating.

migrate vi to settle in another country or region; (biol) (birds, animals) to move to another region with the change in season; (comput) to move from using one computer platform to another or from one software application to another.—**migration** n.—**migratory** adj.

migration n (biol) the seasonal movement of animals, esp birds, fish and some mammals (e.g., porpoises).

mikado n (sl **mikados**) (arch) (often with cap) the Japanese emperor.

mike n (inf) a microphone. * vt to provide with a microphone; to transmit by microphone.

Miklos n Gustave (1888–1967) Hungarian sculptor who worked for Jacques Doucet's house in Paris.

mil n a unit of length of one thousandth of an inch; (gunnery) an angle of one sixty-four-hundredth of a circumference; a milliliter.

Mil n (Irish Celtic myth) the ancestor of the first human rulers of Ireland, who were known as the Sons of Mil Espaine. He was the brother or nephew of Ith, who led an invasion expedition from Spain to Ireland but was killed by the Tuatha De Danann.

mil. abbr = military; militia.

MIL abbr = Member of the Institute of Linguists.

milady n (pl **miladies**) n (formerly) a word used in Europe for an aristocratic Englishwoman.

milage see **mileage**.

MILAM abbr = Member of the Institute of Leisure and Amenity Management.

Milan (Milano) n a city in Italy.

Mil. Att. abbr = military attaché.

milch adj yielding milk, used esp of cattle.

milch cow n a cow from which milk is obtained for human consumption; a ready source of gain.

mild adj (temper) gentle; (weather) temperate; bland; feeble.—**mildly** adv.—**mildness** n.

mildew n a fungus that attacks some plants or appears on damp cloth, etc as a whitish coating. * vti to affect or be affected with mildew.—**mildewy** adj.

mile[1] n a unit of linear measure equal to 5,280 feet (1.61 km).

mile[2] n the geographical mile, which is the distance of 1 minute along the Equator (1.852 kilometers).

mile[3] n the British nautical mile measures 1 minute of arc at latitude 48°. Other nations define the nautical mile as 1 minute of arc at 45°. One British nautical mile equals 1.00064 international nautical miles.

mileage n total miles traveled; an allowance per mile for traveling expenses; the average number of miles that can be traveled, as per liter of fuel.—also **milage**.

M

Mil Espaine, Sons of *or* **Milesians** *n* (*Irish Celtic myth*) the sons and descendants of **Mil**. They landed in Ireland under the leadership of Amhairghin. The invaders defeated the Tuatha De Danann. In the end, the two sides decided to divide the land between them, the Tuatha De Danann getting the underground part. The part above ground went to the Sons of Mil Espaine.

milestone *n* a stone marking the number of miles to a place; an important event in life, history, etc.

Miletus *n* an ancient city of Caria, Asia Minor, one of the most important Greek cities of Asia Minor; in Greek mythology, a son of Apollo who built the town in Caria which he called after his own name.—**Miletan** *adj*.

milfoil *n* (*bot*) a yarrow plant; one of various pond plants with feather-like leaves and small flowers.

Milhaud *n* **Darius** (1892–1974) French composer and pianist, of Jewish ancestry, who became a member of the group known as "*Les Six.*" His works, mostly polytonal and often influenced by jazz, include the ballets *The Creation of the World* and *The Ox on the Roof,* the operas *Cristophe Colomb* and *David,* and the orchestral piece *Saudades do Brasil.*

miliaria *n* (*med*) a skin disease resulting from blocked sweat glands and characterized by an acute itchiness, heat rash.—**miliarial** *adj.* *See* **prickly heat**.

miliary *adj* (*med*) (*growth, lesion*) very small; (*skin disease*) marked by small lesions resembling millet seeds.

milieu *n* (*pl* **milieus, milieux**) environment, esp social setting.

milime *see* **dinar**.

milit. *abbr* = military.

militant *adj* ready to fight, esp for some cause; combative.—*also n.*—**militance, militancy** *n.*—**militantly** *adv*.

militarism *n* military spirit; a policy of aggressive military preparedness.

militarist *n* a believer in militarism; a student of military science.—**militaristic** *adj.*—**militaristically** *adv*.

militarize *vt* to equip and prepare for war.—**militarization** *n*.

military *adj* relating to soldiers or to war; warlike. * *n* (*pl* **militaries**) the armed forces.

military band *n* (*mus*) a band in the armed forces that plays military music, usu for marching. There are many different types of military band, and the number of players can vary. Most bands comprise a mixture of brass, woodwind and percussion instruments.

military discharge *n* (*law*) *see* **DD214**.

military intelligence *n* the intelligence gathering section of the armed services; information gathered by military intelligence.

military police *n* a corps that performs policing duties within the army.

militate *vt* to have influence or force; to produce an effect or change.

militia *n* an army composed of civilians called out in time of emergency.—**militiaman** *n* (*pl* **militiamen**).

milk *n* (*biol*) a white nutritious liquid secreted by female mammals for feeding their young. * *vt* to draw milk from; to extract money, etc, from; to exploit.—**milker** *n*.

milkmaid *n* a girl or woman who milks cows or works in a dairy.

milkman *n* (*pl* **milkmen**) a person who sells or delivers milk to homes.

milk run *n* (*sl*) a routine journey.

milk toast *n* toasted bread soaked in warm milk, often eaten by babies and invalids.

milk tooth *n* (*dent*) any of the first teeth of a mammal.

milksop *n* a weak cowardly man or boy.—**milksoppy** *adj*.

milkweed *n* (*bot*) a plant found mainly in North America yielding a milky sap and with pointed pods containing tufted seeds; any plant with a milky sap.—*also* **silkweed**.

milkwort *n* a kind of plant with small blue, pink or white flowers.

milky *adj* (**milkier, milkiest**) of, filled with, consisting of, yielding, or resembling milk; timid.—**milkily** *adv*.—**milkiness** *n*.

Milky Way *n* (*with* **the**) (*astron*) the galaxy to which the earth belongs; the system of stars, nebulae, etc, that can be seen in the night sky as a trailing ribbon of light and forms part of the galaxy. *See* **galaxy**.

Mill *n* **John Stuart** (1806–73) English philosopher and economist. A follower of Bentham, he elaborated the philosophy of the "greater good" in his philosophy of utilitarianism, as expounded in *Utilitarianism* (1861). His other works include *On Liberty* (1859), in which he asserts the freedom of the individual, *Principles of Political Economy* (1848), and his remarkable *Autobiography* (1873), which describes his forced education by his father, the Scottish philosopher **James Mill** (1773–1836).

mill[1] *n* an apparatus for grinding by crushing between rough surfaces; a building where grain is ground into flour; a factory. * *vt* to produce or grind in a mill; (*coins*) to put a raised edge on. * *vi* to move around confusedly.—**miller** *n*.

mill[2] *n* a unit of money equal to one tenth of a cent.

Millais *n* **Sir John Everett** (1829–96) English painter. Along with Holman Hunt and Rossetti he founded the Pre-Raphaelite Brotherhood. Millais gradually shed his Pre-Raphaelite style, becoming president of the Royal Academy in 1896. His works include *The Boyhood of Raleigh* (1870) and the notoriously sentimental *Bubbles* (1870).

Millay *n* **Edna St Vincent** (1892–1950) American poet whose early collections, e.g., *Renascence and Other Poems* and *A Few Figs from Thistles,* established her reputation as a Bohemian-style New Woman.

millboard *n* a thick pasteboard, often black or gray, that forms the front and back covers and spine of a book, usu covered by the book binding.

millenarian *adj* consisting of or pertaining to a thousand years; pertaining to the millennium or to millenarianism. **n a believer in the millennium; an advocate of millenarianism.

millenarianism *n* (*Christianity*) the belief that the Second Coming of Christ will be preceded or followed by a thousand years of holiness.

millenary *adj* of or pertaining to a thousand; millenarian. * *n* (*pl* **millenaries**) a thousandth anniversary; one thousand as a total, esp one thousand years; a millenarian.

millennium *n* (*pl* **millennia, millenniums**) a period of a thousand years; (*Christianity*) a period of a thousand years of holiness preceding or following the Second Coming of Christ; a coming time of happiness.—**millennial** *adj*.—**millennially** *adv*.

millepede *see* **millipede**.

millepore *n* (*biol*) a tropical coelenterate resembling a coral, with a smooth surface perforated with very small pores.

miller *n* one who or that which mills; an owner of a mill; a moth with a floury appearance.

Miller *n* 1. **[Alton] Glenn** (1904–44) American composer, bandleader, and trombonist whose dance band became one of the most popular in the world, with tunes such as "Moonlight Serenade" and "In the Mood." The airplane which was carrying Miller and his band to play for the troops disappeared over the English Channel in 1944. 2. **Arthur** (1915–) American dramatist whose tragedies include three classics: *Death of a Salesman,* describing the destruction of a salesman by the false values of everyday society; *The Crucible,* in which the Salem witchcraft trials are used to comment on McCarthyism, and *A View from the Bridge,* a successful combination of naturalism with the conventions of Greek drama. He was married to Marilyn Monroe (1955–61) and wrote the screenplay for her last film, *The Misfits*. 3. **Henry** (1891–1980) American novelist, notorious for his graphic descriptions of his numerous sexual experiences in such works as *Tropic of Cancer* and *Tropic of Capricorn*. He was a strong influence on the Beat Generation.

Milles *n* **Carl** (1875–1955) Swedish sculptor influenced by Rodin. Notable works include the Peace Monument (1936) and the Orpheus Fountain (1930–36).

millesimal *adj* pertaining to a thousandth. * *n* a thousandth.

millet *n* (*bot*) a cereal grass used for grain and fodder.

Millet *n* **Jean-François** (1814–75) French painter who initially earned his living by portraiture. He was labeled a social-realist although his works had no political motive. From the 1860s, he painted more direct landscapes.

Millett *n* **Kate** (1934–) American feminist. Her works, notably *Sexual Politics* (1969), are cornerstones of feminist fundamentalism, arguing that society is constructed for the benefit of "male patriarchy," which uses the family as a device for repressing women.

milli- *prefix* a thousandth part.

millibar *n* a unit of measurement of atmospheric pressure equal to one thousandth of a bar. One millibar is a pressure of 1000 dynes per cm^2 or 100 Newtons per m^2.

Milligan *n* **Spike [Terence Allan Milligan]** (1918–) Indian-born, Anglo-Irish comedian and writer. In collaboration with **Peter Sellers**, Welsh comedian and singer **Harry Secombe** (1921–2001) and Anglo-Peruvian comedian **Michael Bentine** (1921–96), he wrote and performed in the highly influential the radio comedy series *The Goon Show* (1951–59). Milligan's books include the novel *Puckoon* (1963) and several autobiographies, e.g., *Adolf Hitler, My Part in his Downfall* (1971).

milligram *n* a thousandth of a gramme.

Millikan *n* **Robert Andrews** (1868–1953) American physicist. He was awarded the 1923 Nobel prize for physics for his determination of the charge on the electron, and did significant research on cosmic rays.

milliliter, millilitre *n* a thousandth (.001) of a liter.

millimeter, millimetre *n* a thousandth (.001) of a meter.

milliner *n* a designer or seller of women's hats.—**millinery** *n*.

milling *n* the act of grinding in or passing through a dressing mill; the process of making a serrated edge on a coin, etc; the serrated edge of such a coin; a stratagem to stop cattle stampeding.

million *n* (*pl* **million, millions**) a thousand thousands, the number one followed by six zeros: 1,000,000; (*inf*) a very large number.—**millionth** *adj*.

millionaire *n* a person who owns at least a million of money; one who is extremely rich.

millipede *n* a wormlike arthropod with many legs and a segmented body.—*also* **millepede**.

millisecond (**ms**) *n* (*comput*) one thousandth of a second.

Millo *n* (*Bible*) rampart at the north end of "the city of David," which David strengthened and made part of his enlarged fortress city of Jerusalem.

millpond *n* a reservoir of water for driving a mill; any stretch of calm water.

millrace *n* a current of water that drives a mill; the channel in which this flows.

Mills *n* **Robert** (1781–1855) American architect. His notable works include Washington Monument, Washington.

millstone *n* a stone used for grinding corn; a heavy burden.

millwright *n* a person who designs, builds, and repairs mills or mill parts.

Milne *n* **A[lan] A[lexander]** (1882–1956) English writer and dramatist. His children's books, e.g. *When We Were Very Young* (1924), *Winnie-the-Pooh* (1926) and *The House at Pooh Corner* (1928), are much loved classics of children's literature.

milord *n* (*formerly*) a word used in Europe for an aristocratic or rich Englishman.

milquetoast *n* a weak ineffectual person.

milt n (biol) the sperm of a male fish; its reproductive glands when filled with this; the spleen of some animals. * vt to fertilize (the roe of female fish), esp artificially.

milter n a male fish in the breeding season.

Milton n **John** (1608–74) English poet. His most famous prose work is the tract Areopagitica, a defence of the liberty of free speech. His masterpiece is the epic poem on the Fall of Man, Paradise Lost. Other notable works include the verse drama Samson Agonistes. Some of his sonnets are among the greatest ever written.

Miltonic, Miltonian adj pertaining to, characteristic of, or resembling the writings of the English poet John Milton (1608–74).

Mimas n a satellite of Saturn, found by Herschel in 1789.

mime n a theatrical technique using action without words; a mimic. * vi to act or express using gestures alone; (singers, musicians) to perform as if singing or playing live to what is actually a prerecorded piece of music.—**mimer** n.

MIME n (comput) abbrev = Multipurpose Internet Mail Extensions. The commonest form in which attachments are sent with e-mails. MIME encodes the file for transmission and then decodes it at the receiving end.

MIMechE abbr = Member of the Institution of Mechanical Engineers.

MIMechIE abbr = Member of the Institution of Mechanical Incorporated Engineers.

mimeograph n a machine for making multiple copies of a letter, drawing, etc, by means of a stencil fixed to an inked drum, and masking the non-printing areas; a copy produced from this machine; * vti to produce copies (of something) by using this machine.

mimesis n (art, literature, etc) the realistic representation of objects, people, everyday life, etc; (biol) mimicry; (med) a condition characterized by symptoms that occur in other diseases but that cannot be found by objective medical testing; a disease that mimics the symptoms of another disease.

mimetic adj of or given to imitation or mimicry; (biol) pertaining to or having the ability to mimic.—**mimetically** adv.

mimic n a person who imitates, esp an actor skilled in mimicry. * adj related to mimicry; make-believe; sham. * vt (**mimicking, mimicked**) to imitate or ridicule.—**mimicker** n.

mimicry n (pl **mimicries**) practice, art, or way of mimicking; (biol) the resemblance of an animal to its environment, another animal, etc, to provide protection from predators, mimesis.

mimosa n (bot) any of a genus of leguminous plants, usu with clustered yellow flowers, whose leaves and stems fold when touched or when exposed to light; the sensitive plant; any of several related or similar plants.

Min n (Egypt) a fertility god whose cult center was Koptos, he was portrayed as a rotund figure with a large penis.

min. abbr = mineralogical; mineralogy; minim; minimum; minima; mining; minister; minor; minute; minutes.

Min. abbr = Minister; Ministry.

mina[1] n (pl **minas, minae**) a weight and coin, current in ancient Anatolia, equal to one sixtieth of a talent.

mina[2] see **myna**.

minaret n (archit) a tall, slender turret with one or more balconies from which the Muezzin calls the people to prayer in the mosque.

minatory, minatorial adj threatening.—**minatorily** adv.

mince vt to chop or cut up into small pieces; to diminish or moderate one's words. * vi to speak or walk with affected daintiness.—**mincer** n.—**mincing** adj.—**mincingly** adv.

mincemeat n a mixture of chopped apples, raisins, etc, used as a pie filling; finely chopped meat.

mind n the faculty responsible for intellect, thought, feelings, speech; memory; intellect; reason; opinion; sanity. * vt to object to, take offence to; to pay attention to; to obey; to take care of; to be careful about; to care about. * vi to pay attention; to be obedient; to be careful; to object.

mind-bending adj (inf) (drugs, etc) unbalancing the mind; (inf) stretching credibility to the limits.—**mind-bender** n.—**mind-bendingly** adv.

mind-blowing adj (inf) (drugs) hallucinatory.

mind-boggling adj (inf) astonishing, bewildering.—**mind-boggler** n.

minded adj disposed, inclined; (in compounds) having a mind as described, e.g., small-minded.—**mindedness** n.

minder n a person who looks after or protects another.

mind-expanding adj producing awareness; psychedelic, distorting.

mindful adj heedful, not forgetful.—**mindfully** adv.—**mindfulness** n.

mindless adj unthinking, stupid; requiring little intellectual effort.—**mindlessly** adv.—**mindlessness** n.

mind reader n a person who claims to be able to discern another's thoughts.—**mind reading** n.

mindset n attitude, esp when fixed or rigid; a habit.

mind's eye n the visual memory or imagination.

mine[1] poss pron belonging to me.

mine[2] n an excavation from which minerals are dug; (mil) an explosive device concealed in the water or ground to destroy enemy ships, personnel, or vehicles that pass over or near them; a rich supply or source. * vt to excavate; to lay explosive mines in an area. * vi to dig or work a mine.

Min. E. abbr = Mining Engineer.

mine detector n a device for indicating the whereabouts of explosive mines.—**mine detection** n.

minefield n an area sown with explosive mines; a situation containing hidden problems.

minelayer n a ship or aircraft for laying mines.

miner n a person who works in a mine.

mineral n an inorganic substance, found naturally in the earth; (chem) a substance with a definite and certain chemical composition and usu with a crystalline structure and certain physical properties, including hardness, luster, cleavage, color, fracture and relative density; any substance neither vegetable nor animal. * adj relating to or containing minerals.

mineral. abbr = mineralogical; mineralogy.

mineralize vt to convert (something) into a mineral; to impregnate (something) with mineral matter; to change something into a fossil-like object. * vi (gases, etc, in molten rock) to transform a metal into an ore.—**mineralization** n.

mineral kingdom n the group of natural substances that consist of only inorganic matter.

mineralogy n the study of any chemical element or compound extracted from the earth.—**mineralogical** adj.—**mineralogically** adv.—**mineralogist** n.

mineral springs n springs that produce water that contains a high concentration of dissolved mineral salts.

mineral water n water containing mineral salts or gases, often with medicinal properties.

Minerva n (Roman myth) the goddess of all arts and trades, the protector of warriors in battle, and the inventor of numbers and musical instruments, esp wind instruments. She was sometimes identified with the Greek goddess Athena.

minestrone n a soup of vegetables with pieces of pasta.

minesweeper n a ship for clearing away explosive mines.—**minesweeping** n.

mingle vti to mix; to combine.—**mingler** n.

mingy adj (**mingier, mingiest**) (inf) meager in quantity; miserly, mean.

mini n (pl **minis**) something smaller than others of its type; a miniskirt.

mini- prefix small.

miniature adj minute, on a small scale. * n a painting or reproduction on a very small scale.—**miniaturist** n.

miniaturize vt to greatly reduce the size of.—**miniaturization** n.

minibar n a small refrigerator in a hotel bedroom, stocked with alcoholic drinks.

minibike n a small single-passenger motorcycle.

minibus n (pl **minibuses, minibusses**) a small bus for carrying up to twelve passengers.

minicab n a saloon car used as a taxi, which can be booked by telephone but not hailed.

minicar n a very small car.

minicomputer n (comput) a computer system, usu smaller than a mainframe but larger than a microcomputer, designed for many users.

minim n (mus) (Brit) a note, formerly the shortest in time-value, with half the value of a whole note (semibreve); the equivalent of a **half-note** in US terminology; a unit of fluid measure of one sixtieth of a fluid dram (0.0616ml) in the US and one twentieth of a scruple (0.592ml) in the UK.

minima see **minimum**.

minimal adj very minute; least possible.—**minimality** n.—**minimally** adv.

minimalism n a style in the creation of art, music, etc, that uses the fewest possible elements to achieve the greatest effect.—**minimalist** n, adj.

minimize vt to reduce to or estimate at a minimum.—**minimization** n.

minimum n (pl **minimums, minima**) the least possible amount; the lowest degree or point reached.

minimum lending rate see **bank rate**.

mining n the act, process, or industry of excavating from the earth; (mil) the laying of explosive mines.

minion n a servile flatterer or dependant; an obsequious person acting on behalf of or carrying out the wishes of another. * adj dainty, graceful.

miniseries n (pl **miniseries**) (TV) the dramatization of a novel, etc, shown in several episodes; (sport) a short series.

miniskirt n a very short skirt.

minister n a clergyman serving a church; an official heading a government department; a diplomat. * vi to serve as a minister in a church; to give help (to).—**ministerial** adj.—**ministerially** adv.

ministrant adj serving as a minister. * n a person who ministers.

ministration n the act or process of giving aid; the act of ministering religiously.

ministry n (pl **ministries**) the act of ministering; the clergy; the profession of a clergyman; a government department headed by a minister; the building housing a government department.

mini tower n (comput) a small tower style computer system designed to sit on a desk rather than the floor where a normal tower system would sit.

minium n red oxide of lead, used as a pigment in paints; red lead.

miniver n a white fur, orig from the Siberian squirrel, used as a trimming on ceremonial robes, etc.

mink n (pl **mink, minks**) any of several carnivorous weasel-like mammals valued for its durable soft fur.

Minn. abbr = Minnesota.

Minnelli n **Liza May** (1946–) American singer and actress ; daughter of director Vincente Minelli and Judy Garland; her most celebrated role is as Sally Bowles in the film version of Cabaret (1972) for which she won an Academy Award. See also **Garland, Judy**.

Minnesingers n (mus) the poet-musicians of Germany in the 12th and 13th centuries, who were of noble birth, like the troubadours of France, and who produced

M

minnelieder, or love songs. Wagner's *Tannhäuser* is a minnesinger. They were succeeded by the meistersingers.

Minnesota (MN) *n* a state of the United States of America (USA) of which the capital is St Paul.

minnow *n* (*pl* **minnow, minnows**) a small, slender freshwater fish.

Minoans *n* a Bronze Age people who emerged on Crete between 2400 and 1400 BC.

minor *adj* lesser in size, importance, degree, extent, etc; (*mus*) (*Latin*) "less" or "smaller." Minor intervals contain one semitone less than major. The minor third is characteristic of scales in the minor mode * *n* (*law*) a person under full legal age; (*education*) a secondary area of study requiring fewer credits; (*sport*) a minor league, esp in baseball. * *vi* (*with* in) to take a subject requiring fewer credits.

Minorite, Minorist *n* a Franciscan friar, esp one of the order of Friars Minor.

minority *n* (*pl* **minorities**) the smaller part or number; a political or racial group smaller than the majority group; the state of being under age.

minor scale *n* (*mus*) a scale having intervals of a semitone between the second and third, fifth and sixth, and seventh and eighth degrees.

Minos *n* (*Greek myth*) a ruler of Crete, famous as a wise lawgiver and a lover of justice, and after his death one of the judges of the underworld.

Minotaur *n* (*Greek myth*) a monster with the body of a man and the head of a bull, who ate human flesh. Minos imprisoned him in the labyrinth where he was killed by Theseus with the help of Ariadne.

Minsk *n* capital city of Belarus.

MInstBE *abbr* = Member of the Institute of British Engineers.

minster *n* a large and important church, often with cathedral status; any monastic community or its church.

minstrel *n* (*mus*) a professional, traveling entertainer or musician of medieval times, often employed by a royal court or aristocratic family; a performer in a minstrel show.

minstrel show *n* a variety show with performers singing and dancing wearing black face make-up.

minstrelsy *n* (*pl* **minstrelsies**) the art or occupation of minstrels; minstrels collectively; a collection of ballad poetry.

mint[1] *n* the place where money is coined; a large amount of money; a source of supply. * *adj* unused, in perfect condition. * *vt* (*coins*) to imprint; to invent.—**minter** *n*.

mint[2] *n* (*bot*) an aromatic plant whose leaves are used for flavoring.—**minty** *adj*.

mintage *n* a coin, etc, produced in a mint; the process of producing coins, etc, in a mint; the fee paid to a mint for coining gold or silver; an official mark on a coin.

mint julep *n* a tall drink of bourbon or brandy and sugar over crushed ice, garnished with mint.

Minton *n* British design company founded when Thomas Minton bought a pottery in 1793, later employing a number of well-known decorators.

Minton *n* **John Francis** (1917–57) influential British painter and designer, with a high reputation as a teacher at all the London art colleges.

minuend *n* (*math*) the number from which another number is to be subtracted.

minuet *n* (*mus*) a French rural dance in 3/4 time that was popular during the 17th and 18th centuries. It remained popular and was incorporated into classical sonatas and symphonies as a regular movement; (the music for) a slow, graceful dance in triple time.

minus *prep* less; (*inf*) without. * *adj* involving subtraction; negative; less than. * *n* a sign (-), indicating subtraction or negative quantity.

minute[1] *n* the sixtieth part of an hour or a degree of latitude or longitude; a moment; (*pl*) an official record of a meeting. * *vt* to record or summarize the proceedings (of).

minute[2] *adj* tiny; detailed; exact.—**minuteness** *n*.

minute hand *n* the long hand of a clock or watch that marks out the minutes.

minutely[1] *adj* occurring every minute. * *adv* every minute.

minutely[2] *adv* in a minute manner; precisely.

minuteman *n* (*pl* **minutemen**) (*sometimes cap*) a member of the militia in the American Revolution, ready to fight at a minute's notice.

minutiae *npl* (*sing* **minutia**) small or unimportant details.

minx *n* a pert, forward girl; (*arch*) a prostitute.—**minxish** *adj*.

MIOC *abbr* = Member of the Institute of Carpenters.

Miocene *adj* (*geol*) pertaining to the middle division of the Tertiary formation after the Olicene and before the Pliocene eras, marked by the appearance of grasses and grazing mammals. * *n* this division or rock formation.

Miodchaoin *n* (*Irish Celtic myth*) a warrior who lived on a hill and friend of Cian. He was placed under a bond never to permit anyone to shout from the summit of the hill.

MIOFMS *abbr* = Member of the Institute of Financial and Management Studies.

MIOP *abbr* = Member of the Institute of Printing.

MIOSH *abbr* = Member of the Institution of Occupational Safety and Health.

miosis *n* (*med*) abnormal contraction of the pupil of the eye.—*also* **myosis**.—**miotic** *adj*, *n*.

mip *abbr* = mean indicated pressure.

m.i.p. *abbr* = marine insurance policy.

mips *abbr* = millions of instructions per second.

Mir *n* the Russian space station.

M.Ir. *abbr* = Middle Irish.

MIR *abbr* = mortgage interest relief.

Mira *or* **Mira Ceti** *n* (*astron*) a binary star in the constellation Cetus, which lies across the celestial equator.

miracle *n* an extraordinary event attributed to the supernatural; an unusual or astounding event; a remarkable example of something; (*religion*) a marvelous event due to some special act of God; miracles of the *OT* are more properly called "signs"; in the *NT*, the Gospel writers all declare that Jesus did certain things which were "mighty works."

miraculous *adj* supernatural; wonderful; able to work miracles.—**miraculously** *adv*.—**miraculousness** *n*.

mirage *n* an optical illusion caused by the reflection and refraction of light. A mirage is seen wherever there is calm air with varying temperatures near the earth's surface; anything illusory or fanciful.

Miralles *n* **Pedro** (1955–) Spanish architect who worked in the office of fashion designer Jesus del Pozo.

Miranda *n* a satellite of Uranus, discovered in 1948.

MIRAS *abbr* = mortgage interest relief at source.

mire *n* an area of wet, soggy, or muddy ground. * *vt* to sink in mire; to dirty; to embroil in difficulties.

Miriam *n* (*Bible*) sister of Moses and Aaron, who appears in the tale of the baby Moses in the reeds by the river of Egypt where she watched over the child.

mirk *see* **murk**.

mirky *see* **murky**.

mirliton *n* (*mus*) (*France*) any wind instrument in which a thin membrane is made to vibrate and make a noise when the player blows, hums or sings into it. It is now known as the Kazoo.

Miró *n* **Joan** (1893–1983) Spanish painter, sculptor, and designer.

mirror *n* a highly polished, regular surface, coated with a material to reflect light strongly; a faithful depiction. * *vt* (**mirroring, mirrored**) to reflect or depict faithfully.

mirror music *n* (*mus*) any piece of music that sounds the same when played backwards.

mirth *n* merriment, esp with laughter.

mirthful *adj* full of merriment.—**mirthfully** *adv*.—**mirthfulness** *n*.

mirthless *adj* lacking laughter; miserable.—**mirthlessly** *adv*.—**mirthlessness** *n*.

MIRV *abbr* = multiple independently targeted re-entry vehicle, as used in nuclear warfare.

MIS *abbr* (*comput*) = Management Information Systems. The current name given to the subject of data processing; Member of the Institute of Statisticians; Mining Institute of Scotland; Mobility Information Service.

mis-[1] *prefix* wrong(ly); bad(ly); no, not.

mis-[2] *see* **miso-**.

misadventure *n* an unlucky accident; bad luck.

misalliance *n* an unsuitable alliance, usu by marriage with a person of lower social status; a mésalliance.

misandry *n* (*rare*) hatred of and hostility toward men.—**misandrist** *n*.

misanthrope, misanthropist *n* a person who hates or distrusts mankind.

misanthropic *adj* of or characterized by hatred of his or her fellow human beings.—**misanthropically** *adv*.—**misanthropy** *n*.

misapply *vt* (**misapplying, misapplied**) to apply mistakenly or wrongly.—**misapplication** *n*.

misapprehend *vt* to misunderstand; to misconceive.—**misapprehension** *n*.

misappropriate *vt* to appropriate wrongly or dishonestly; to use illegally; to embezzle.—**misappropriation** *n*.

misbehave *vi* to behave badly. * *vt* to behave (oneself) badly.—**misbehavior, misbehaviour** *n*.

misc., miscl. *abbr* = miscellaneous; miscellany.

MISC *abbr* (*comput*) = Minimum Instruction Set Chip. The basis of the next generation of computer chips, advancing the concept of RISC chips.

miscalculate *vti* to calculate wrongly.—**miscalculation** *n*.

miscarriage *n* the spontaneous expulsion of a fetus prematurely; mismanagement or failure. See **abortion**.

miscarry *vi* (**miscarrying, miscarried**) to spontaneously expel a fetus from the uterus; to be unsuccessful; to fail.

miscegenation *n* interbreeding between races, esp with different colors of skin.

miscellaneous *adj* consisting of various kinds; mixed.—**miscellaneously** *adv*.—**miscellaneousness** *n*.

miscellany *n* (*pl* **miscellanies**) a mixed collection; a book comprising miscellaneous writings, etc.

mischance *n* bad luck; an unlucky event.

mischief *n* wayward behavior; damage.

mischievous *adj* harmful, prankish.—**mischievously** *adv*.—**mischievousness** *n*.

miscible *adj* (*chem*) (*liquids*) capable of being mixed.—**miscibility** *n*.

misconceive *vt* to conceive wrongly; to misjudge; to misapprehend; to misunderstand.—**misconceiver** *n*.

misconception *n* a mistaken idea; misunderstanding.

misconduct *n* dishonest management; improper behavior. * *vt* to conduct (oneself) badly; to manage dishonestly.

misconstrue *vt* (**misconstruing, misconstrued**) to misinterpret.—**misconstruction** *n*.

miscreant *n* an unscrupulous villain; (*arch*) a heretic. * *adj* unscrupulous; (*arch*) heretical.

miscue *n* (*billiards, snooker*) to mishit or miss the ball with the cue; (*inf*) a blunder. * *vi* (**miscuing, miscued**) to make a miscue; (*theater*) to miss one's cue.

MISD *abbr* = multiple instruction, single data stream.

misdeal *vi* (**misdealing, misdealt**) to deal cards out incorrectly. * *n* a mistake in dealing cards.

misdeed *n* a wrong or wicked act; crime; sin; etc.

misdemeanor, misdemeanour *n* (*law*) a minor offence, a misdeed.

misdiagnose *vt* to diagnose incorrectly.— **misdiagnosis** *n*.

misdial *vt* (**misdialed, misdialing** *or* **misdialled, misdialling**) to dial (a telephone number) incorrectly.

misdirect *vt* to give (someone) the wrong directions; to address a letter, etc, incorrectly.

mise en scène *n* (*pl* **mise en scènes**) the arrangement of scenery in a play; a stage setting; the setting of an event.

miser *n* a greedy, stingy person who hoards money for its own sake.

miserable *adj* wretched; unhappy; causing misery; bad, inadequate; pitiable.— **miserableness** *n*.—**miserably** *adv*.

miserere *n* a misericord in a choir stall.

misericord, misericorde *n* a small ledge, often carved, on the underside of a folding seat in the stall of a church against which a worshipper can lean when standing; in the Middle Ages, a small dagger for giving a death thrust to a seriously wounded person, esp a knight; (*Christianity*) the relaxation of monastic rules for elderly or infirm monks or nuns; a room in a monastery for those with such a dispensation.

miserly *adj* like a miser; tending to hoard; very mean.—**miserliness** *n*.

misery *n* (*pl* **miseries**) extreme pain, unhappiness, or poverty; a cause of such suffering.

misfeasance *n* (*law*) the wrong performance of something that is itself legal.— **misfeasor** *n*.

misfire *vi* (*engine, etc*) to fail to ignite, start; to fail to succeed.—*also n*.

misfit *n* something that fits badly; a maladjusted person.

misfit stream *see* **underfit stream**.

misfortune *n* ill luck; trouble; a mishap; bad luck.

misgiving *n* a feeling of misapprehension, mistrust.

misguided *adj* foolish; mistaken.—**misguidedly** *adv*.

mishap *n* an unfortunate accident.

Mishima *n* Yukio (1925–70) Japanese novelist and short-story writer whose work, e.g. the novel *The Temple of the Golden Pavilion*, is dominated by the themes of homosexuality, beauty, and death. He committed suicide in public while exhorting his followers to perform a military coup.

mishmash *n* a confused mixture, hotchpotch.

Mishnah, Mishna *n* (*Judaism*) the oral law; the written form of this, which was collected in the 2nd century and forms the text of the earlier part of the Talmud.

misinform *vt* to supply with wrong information.—**misinformant, misinformer** *n*.—**misinformation** *n*.

misinterpret *vt* to interpret incorrectly or badly.—**misinterpretation** *n*.— **misinterpreter** *n*.

misjudge *vt* to judge wrongly, to form a wrong opinion.—**misjudgment** *n*.

Miskolc *n* a city in Hungary.

mislay *vt* (**mislaying, mislaid**) to lose something temporarily; to put down or install improperly.—**mislayer** *n*.

mislead *vt* (**misleading, misled**) to deceive; to give wrong information to; to lead into wrongdoing.—**misleader** *n*.

misleading *adj* deceptive; confusing.—**misleadingly** *adv*.

mismatch *vt* to match unsuitably, as in marriage.— *also n*.

misnomer *n* an incorrect or unsuitable name or description.—**misnomered** *adj*.

miso-, mis- *prefix* hatred of.

misogamy *n* hatred of marriage.—**misogamic** *adj*.—**misogamist** *n*.

misogynist *n* a hater or distruster of women. * *adj* of or characterized by hatred of women.—**misogynistic** *adj*.

misogyny *n* hatred of women.—**misogynic** *adj*.

misology *n* hatred of argument or reasoning.— **misologist** *n*.

misplace *vt* to put in a wrong place; (*trust, etc*) to place unwisely.—**misplacement** *n*.

misprint *vt* to print incorrectly. * *n* an error in printing.

misprision *n* (*law*) the concealment of a seriously criminal act; the knowledge of the commission of treason and the failure to report this; (*arch*) contempt; the disparagement or undervaluing of something

mispronounce *vt* to pronounce wrongly.—**mispronunciation** *n*.

misquote *vt* to quote wrongly.—**misquotation** *n*.

Misrātah *n* a city in Libya.

misread *vt* (**misreading, misread**) to read or to interpret wrongly.

misrepresent *vt* to represent falsely; to give an untrue idea of.—**misrepresentation** *n*.—**misrepresentative** *adj*.

misrule *n* bad government. * *vt* to govern badly; to govern in an inhumane manner or with injustice.

miss[1] *n* (*pl* **misses**) a girl; (*with cap*) a title used before the surname of an unmarried woman or girl.

miss[2] *vt* to fail to reach, hit, find, meet, hear; to omit; to fail to take advantage of; to regret or discover the absence or loss of. * *vi* to fail to hit; to fail to be successful; to misfire, as an engine. * *n* a failure to hit, reach, obtain, etc.

miss. *abbr* = mission; missionary.

Miss. *abbr* = Mississippi.

Missa *n* (*mus*) (*Latin*) "Mass," so *missa brevis* means "short mass," and *missa cantata* means "sung mass."

missal *n* a book containing the prayers for Mass.

misshapen *adj* badly shaped; deformed.

missile *n* an object, as a rock, spear, rocket, etc, to be thrown, fired, or launched.

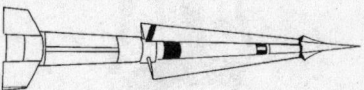

missing *adj* absent; lost; lacking.

missing link *n* something required to complete a series; a hypothetical animal supposedly intermediate between the anthropoid apes and man.

mission *n* a group of people sent by a church, government, etc to carry out a special duty or task; the sending of an aircraft or spacecraft on a special assignment; a vocation. * *adj* of a mission; (*archit*) of a style of church building established by Spanish missioners in the southwest USA.

missionary *n* (*pl* **missionaries**) a person who tries to convert unbelievers to his or her religious faith, esp abroad; one sent on a mission. * *adj* .of a religious mission; tending to propagandize.

missionary position *n* (*inf*) a position for sexual intercourse with the partners face to face and the man on top.

mission control *n* a command center that controls space flights from the ground.

missioner *n* a missionary; a person in charge of a parochial mission.

mission statement *n* a formal statement of the aims of a firm.

missis *n* (*inf*) (usu *with* **the**) one's wife; (*inf*) a name used when directly addressing a woman.—*also* **missus**.

Mississippi (MS) *n* a state of the United States of America (USA) of which the capital is Jackson.

missive *n* (*formal*) a letter or message, often official. * *adj* (*rare*) sent specially, or intended to be sent.

Missouri (MO) *n* a state of the United States of America (USA) of which the capital is Jefferson City.

"Missouri Waltz" *n* the song of the American State, Missouri.

misspent *adj* wasted, frittered away.

missus *see* **missis**.

mist *n* (*meteorology*) water droplets in suspension, that reduce visibility to not less than 1 kilometer (1093 yards); something that dims or obscures. * *vti* to cover or be covered, as with mist.

mist. *abbr* = *mistura* (*Latin*) "mixture."

MIST *abbr* = (*Brit*) Music in Scotland Trust.

mistake *vt* (**mistaking, mistook**, *pp* **mistaken**) to misunderstand; to misinterpret; * *vi* to make a mistake. * *n* a wrong idea, answer, etc; an error of judgment; a blunder; a misunderstanding.—**mistakable** *adj*.—**mistakably** *adv*.

mistaken *adj* erroneous, ill-judged.—**mistakenly** *adv*.

mister *n* (*inf*) sir; (*with cap*) the title used before a man's surname.

misterioso *n* (*mus*) (*Italian*) "mysteriously."

mistime *vt* to do or say at the wrong time; to time wrongly.

mistletoe *n* an evergreen parasitic plant with white berries used as a Christmas decoration.

mistral *n* (*France*) the cold, dry winter wind that blows strongly down the Rhône valley from the Alps to the Mediterranean Sea.

mistreat *vt* to treat wrongly or badly.—**mistreatment** *n*.

mistress *n* a woman who is head of a household; a woman with whom a man is having a prolonged affair; a female schoolteacher; (*with cap*) the title used before a married woman's surname.

mistrial *n* (*law*) a trial made void due to an error in procedure.

MIStructE *abbr* = Member of the Institution of Structural Engineers.

mistrust *n* lack of trust. * *vti* to doubt; to suspect.—**mistrustful** *adj*. — **mistrustfully** *adv*

misty *adj* (**mistier, mistiest**) full of mist; dim, obscure.—**mistily** *adv*.—**mistiness** *n*.

misunderstand *vt* (**misunderstanding, misunderstood**) to fail to understand correctly.

misunderstanding *n* a mistake as to sense; a quarrel or disagreement.

misunderstood *adj* not fully understood; not appreciated properly.

misura *n* (*mus*) (*Italian*) "measure"; equivalent to a bar.

misuse *vt* to use for the wrong purpose or in the wrong way; to ill-treat, abuse. * *n* improper or incorrect use.

mit. *abbr* = (*pharm*) *mitte* (*Latin*) "send."

m.i.t. *abbr* = milling, *or* milled, in transit.

Mitanni *n* a kingdom that flourished for just over one century, between 1500 and 1370 BC, in the hill country between the Rivers Tigris and Euphrates.

M

Mitchell *n* **R[eginald] J[oseph]** (1895–1937) English aircraft designer. He designed the Supermarine Spitfire (1934–36), dying just after its acceptance by the RAF.

MITD *abbr* = Member of the Institute of Training and Development.

mite *n* any of numerous very small parasitic or free-living insects; (*money, etc*) a very small amount.

miter, mitre *n* the headdress of a bishop; a diagonal joint between two pieces of wood to form a corner. * *vt* to join with a miter corner.—**miterer** *n*.

miter box *n* a device that guides a handsaw at the correct angle for making miter joints.

mitigate *vti* to become or make less severe.—**mitigable** *adj*.—**mitigation** *n*.—**mitigator** *n*.

mitobronitol *n* (*med*) a type of drug, used in the treatment of leukemia, that prevents the growth of cancer cells.

mitochondrion (*pl* **mitochondria**) *n* (*biol*) a tiny rodlike structure, numbers of which are present in the cytoplasm of every cell.

mitosis *n* (*pl* **mitoses**) *n* (*biol*) the type of cell division undergone by most body cells by means of which the growth and repair of tissues can take place. *Compare* **meiosis**.—**mitotic** *adj, adv*.

mitral *adj* of or like a miter; (*anat*) pertaining to the mitral valve.

mitral incompetence, mitral regurgitation *n* (*med*) a condition in which the mitral valve of the heart is defective and allows blood to leak back from the left ventricle into the left atrium.

mitral stenosis *n* (*med*) a condition in which the opening between the left atrium and left ventricle of the heart is narrowed because of scarring and adhesion of the mitral valve.

mitral valve *n* (*anat*) (formerly known as the bicuspid valve) a valve that is located between the atrium and ventricle of the left side of the heart, attached to the walls at the opening between the two.

mitre *see* **miter**.

MITSA *abbr* = Member of the Institute of Trading Standards Administration.

Mitsamiouli *n* a city in Comoros.

mitt *n* a glove covering the hand but only the base of the fingers; (*sl*) a hand; a boxing glove; a baseball glove.

mitten *n* a glove with a thumb but no separate fingers.

Mitterrand *n* **François [Maurice Marie]** (1916–96) French statesman. A member of the Resistance during World War II, he became leader of the Socialist Party in 1971 and the first socialist president of France (1981–95).

mitts *abbr* = minutes of telecommunications traffic.

MIWEM *abbr* = Member of the Institution of Water and Environmental Management.

MIWPC *abbr* = Member of the Institute of Water Pollution Control.

mix *vt* to blend together in a single mass; to make by blending ingredients, as a cake; to combine; (*with* **up**) to make into a mixture; to make disordered; to confuse or mistake. * *vi* to be mixed or blended; to get along together. * *n* a mixture.—**mixable** *adj*.

mixed *adj* blended; made up of different parts, classes, races, etc; confused.

mixed bag *n* (*inf*) a collection of diverse things or people.

mixed blessing *n* something that has both advantages and disadvantages.

mixed cultivation *n* the growing of two crops in a field to create shade or to reduce soil erosion.

mixed economy *n* (*econ*) a country's economy in which some goods and services are produced by means of state-owned organizations and some by private enterprise firms.

mixed farming *n* the type of agriculture where stock rearing and crop production take place on the same farm.

mixed marriage *n* a marriage between persons of different races or religions.

mixed number *n* (*math*) a number that is a combination of an integer and a fraction.

mixed-up *adj* (*inf*) perplexed, mentally confused.

mixer *n* a device that blends or mixes; a person considered in terms of their ability (good or bad) to get on with others; a soft drink added to an alcoholic beverage.

Mixolydian mode *n* (*mus*) the set of notes, in ancient Greek music, which are the equivalent of the white notes on a piano from B to B; in church music of the Middle Ages onwards, the equivalent of the white notes on a piano from G to G.

mixt. *abbr* = mixture.

Mixtec *n* a group of people who lived in the upland regions of Oaxaca in Mexico, who possibly shared a common ancestry with the Zapotec people.

mixture *n* the process of mixing; a blend made by mixing; (*mus*) an organ stop that brings into play a number of pipes that produce harmonics above the pitch corresponding to the actual key which is played.

mix-up *n* a mistake; confusion, muddle; (*inf*) a fight.

Mizar *or* **Zeta Ursae Majoris** *n* (*astron*) a second magnitude multiple star in the constellation Ursa Major.

mizzen, mizen *n* (*naut*) the lowest sail on the mizzenmast of a vessel; the mizzenmast. * *adj* pertaining to something used with the mizzenmast.

mizzenmast, mizenmast *n* (*naut*) the aftermost mast when there are three masts on a ship; the aftermast on other ships.

mizzle *vi* to rain in very minute drops, to drizzle. * *n* a very fine rain.

MJ *abbr* = megajoule.

MJur *abbr* = Master of Jurisprudence.

mk. *abbr* = mark.

MK *abbr* = mark (numbering of car design variants).

mkd. *abbr* = marked.

m-kg *abbr* = meter-kilogram.

mks *abbr* = meter-kilogram-second.

mks. *abbr* = marks (*coin*).

mksa *abbr* = meter-kilogram-second-ampere.

MK system *or* **MKK system** *n* (*astron*) a star classification system based on spectral type and luminosity.

mkt *abbr* = market.

ml *abbr* = mile; milliliter.

ml. *abbr* = mail; milliliter.

ML *abbr* = *Magister Legum* (*Latin*) "Master of Laws"; Maoriland; *Medicinae Licentiatus* (*Latin*) "Licentiate in Medicine"; Medieval, *or* Middle, Latin.

MLA *abbr* = Member of the Legislative Assembly; Modern Language Association; Music Library Association.

MLC *abbr* = Maori Language Commission; mixed lymphocyte culture.

MLCOM *abbr* = Member of the London College of Osteopathic Medicine.

MLD *abbr* = Master of Landscape Design; (*or* **m.l.d.**) (*med*) mean/minimum lethal dose.

MLF *abbr* = multilateral force.

MLG *abbr* = Middle Low German.

MLibSc *abbr* = Master of Library Science.

MLing *abbr* = Master of Languages.

M.Lit(t). *abbr* = (*Latin*) *Magister Lit(t)erarum*, "Master of Letters."

Mlle(s) *abbr* = mademoiselle, mesdemoiselles.

m.l.r. *abbr* = muzzle-loading rifle.

MLR *abbr* = minimum lending rate; mixed lymphocyte reaction.

MLRS *abbr* = multiple launch rocket system.

MLV *abbr* = murine leukemia virus.

mm *abbr* = (*Latin*) *matrimonium* "matrimony"; (*Latin*) *millia*, "thousands"; millimeter(s).

mm. *abbr* = millimeter(s).

m.m. *abbr* = machinist's mate; mercantile marine; motor mechanics.

mM *abbr* = millimole.

MM *abbr* = Master Mechanic; *Messieurs* (*French*) "Sirs"; Military Medal; mucus membrane.

MMA *abbr* = Master of Management and Administration.

MMath *abbr* = Master of Mathematics.

MMC *abbr* = Monopolies and Mergers Commission.

Mme. *abbr* = madame.

Mmes. *abbr* = mesdames.

MMF *or* **m.m.f.** *or* **mmf** *abbr* = magnetomotive force.

mmfds. *abbr* = microfarads.

MMG *abbr* = medium machine gun.

mmHg *abbr* = millimeter of mercury.

MMI *abbr* = man-machine interface.

MMM *abbr* = International Association of Margaret Morris Method; Medical Missionaries of Mary.

MMMA *abbr* = Metalforming Machinery Makers Association.

mmol *abbr* = millimole.

MMP *abbr* = International Organisation of Masters, Mates and Pilots; Military Mounted Police.

MMQ *abbr* = minimum manufacturing quantity.

MMR *abbr* = measles, mumps and rubella; mass miniature radiography.

MMR vaccine *n* a vaccine, introduced in 1988, that protects against measles, mumps, and German measles (rubella) normally given to children during their second year.

MMS *abbr* = Massachusetts Medical Society; Methodist Missionary Society.

MMus *abbr* = Master of Music.

MMusArt *abbr* = Master of Musical Arts.

Mmus, RCM *abbr* = (*Brit*) Degree of Master of Music, Royal College of Music.

MMWR *abbr* = Morbidity and Mortality Weekly Report

m/n *abbr* = moneda national.

Mn *symbol* (*chem*) manganese (element).

MN *abbr* = Master of Nursing; Merchant Navy; Minnesota.

MNAD *abbr* = Multinational Airborne Division (NATO).

MNC *abbr* = multinational company.

MND *abbr* = motor neurone disease.

MNDA *abbr* = Missionary Sisters of Our Lady of the Angels; Motor Neurone Disease Association.

mnemonic *adj* of or aiding memory.—*n* a device to aid the memory.—**mnemonically** *adv*.

mnemonics *n sing* a technique of assisting the memory by using formulae to remember things.

Mnemosyne *n* (*Greek myth*) the goddess of memory and mother of the nine Muses.

Mngr *abbr* = Monseigneur; Monsignor.

MNP *abbr* (*comput*) = **Microcom Network Protocol**. A standard developed by the communications company Microcom™, aimed at error detection and correction between communications devices.

MNR *abbr* = marine nature reserve.

MNT *abbr* = Mononitrotoluene.

MNurs *abbr* = Master of Nursing.

m.o. *abbr* = money order; municipal ownership.

Mo *symbol* (*chem*) molybdenum.

Mo. *abbr* = Missouri; Monday; month.

MO *abbr* = mass observation; Master of Obstetrics; Master of Oratory; Medical Officer; Meteorological Office; Missouri; *modus operandi* (*Latin*) "way of working"; money order.

moa *n* (*zool*) any one of several extinct species of large, wingless birds of New Zealand.

MOA *abbr* = memorandum of agreement.

Moab *n* (*Bible*) part of Palestine lying east of the Dead Sea, well-watered and fertile.

Moabite *adj* pertaining to the ancient kingdom of Moab, now part of Jordan. * *n* an inhabitant of Moab.

moan *n* a low mournful sound as of sorrow or pain. * *vti* to utter a moan; to complain.—**moaner** *n*.—**moaningly** *adv*.

moat *n* a deep ditch surrounding a fortification or castle, usu filled with water.

mob *n* a disorderly or riotous crowd; a contemptuous term for the masses; (*sl*) a gang of criminals. * *vt* (**mobbing, mobbed**) to attack in a disorderly group; to surround.—**mobbish** *adj*.

MOB *abbr* = money-order business.

mobcap *n* a plain cap, usu surrounded with a frill, worn indoors by women in the 18th century.

mobile *adj* movable, not fixed; easily changing; characterized by ease in change of social status; capable of moving freely and quickly; (*inf*) having transport. * *n* a suspended structure of wood, metal, etc with parts that move in air currents.—**mobility** *n*. *See* **Calder, Alexander.**

mobiliary art *n* the earliest Paleolithic art, executed on small artifacts made from bone, antler, stone or ivory.

mobilize *vt* to prepare for action, esp war by readying troops for active service; to organize for a particular reason; to put to use.—**mobilization** *n*.

mobocracy *n* (*pl* **mobocracies**) political rule or ascendancy of the mob; a ruling mob.—**mobocrat** *n*.—**mobocratic** *adj*.—**mobocratically** *adv*.

MOBS *abbr* = multiple orbit bombardment system.

mobster *n* (*sl*) a gangster.

MObstG *abbr* = Master of Obstetrics and Gynaecology.

Mobuto *n* **Sese Seko Kuku Ngbendu Wa Za Banga [Joseph Désiré Mobuto]** (1930–) Zairean dictator. He assumed complete power over the Congo in 1965, renaming it Zaire in 1971, and was deposed in 1997. His notoriously corrupt regime was backed by the Western powers for its supposedly anti-communist virtues.

moccasin *n* a flat shoe based on Amerindian footwear; any soft, flexible shoe resembling this.

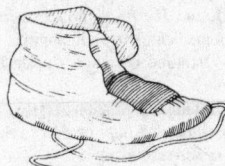

mocha *n* a type of coffee, orig from Arabia; a flavoring made from coffee and chocolate.—*also adj*.

Moche *adj* (or **Mochica**) relating to a Peruvian culture originally centered on the valleys of Moche and Chicama. It emerged in the first centuries AD and lasted until 600 or 700 AD.

mock *vt* to imitate or ridicule; to behave with scorn; to defy; (*with* **up**) to make a model of. * *n* ridicule; an object of scorn. * *adj* false, sham, counterfeit.—**mocker** *n*.—**mockingly** *adv*.

mockery *n* (*pl* **mockeries**) derision, ridicule, or contempt; imitation, esp derisive; someone or something that is mocked; an inadequate person, thing, or action.

mock-heroic *adj* parodying the heroic style of literature or, particularly, poetry, esp when the subject matter is unheroic. * *n* a burlesque imitation of an epic poem or of the heroic style in general.—**mock-heroically** *adv*.

mockingbird *n* a gray American bird with the ability to imitate with exactness the call of other birds.

mockup, mock-up *n* a full-scale working model of a machine, etc.

mod *n* (*often with cap*) a member of a British youth group of the mid-1960s who wore highly fashionable clothes and opposed the rockers, another youth group; a member of a revival of this group, in the late 1970s and early 1980s, whose opposition was to skinheads.

mod. *abbr* = moderate; *moderato* (*Italian*) (*mus*) "moderate"; modern.

Mod. *abbr* (*ordnance*) = modification.

MOD *abbr* = Ministry of Defence; mail order department.

modal *adj* of mode or form, not substance; (*gram*) expressing mood; (*philos*) asserting with qualification; (*mus*) of or composed in a mode.—**modality** *n*.—**modally** *adv*.

mode *n* a way of acting, doing or existing; a style or fashion; form; (*comput*) the state of operation of a computer; (*mus*) any of the scales used in composition; (*statistics*) the predominant item in a series of items; (*gram*) mood.

mode indicator *n* (*comput*) a message displayed on screen that indicates the mode of operation in which the computer is set, e.g., edit mode, insert mode, etc.

model *n* a pattern; an ideal; a standard worth imitating; a representation on a smaller scale, usu three-dimensional; a person who sits for an artist or photographer; a person who displays clothes by wearing them. * *adj* serving as a model; representative of others of the same style. * *vt* (**modeling, modeled** *or* **modelling, modelled**) (*with* **after, on**) to create by following a model; to display clothes by wearing. * *vi* to serve as a model for an artist, etc.—**modeller, modeler** *n*.

modem *abbr* (*comput*) = MOdulator/DEModulator. A device for converting a computer's digital signals into analog signals that can be transmitted down a telephone line.

moderate *vti* to make or become moderate; to preside over. * *adj* having reasonable limits; avoiding extremes; mild, calm; of medium quality, amount, etc. * *n* a person who holds moderate views.—**moderately** *adv*.—**moderateness** *n*.

moderation *n* moderateness; freedom from excess; equanimity.

moderato *n* (*mus*) (*Italian*) "moderate" (in terms of speed).

moderator *n* a mediator; (*physics*) a substance that slows the speed of neutrons in a nuclear reactor; (*Presbyterian Church*) a minister who presides at a court, assembly, synod, etc.

modern *adj* of the present or recent times; up-to-date.—**modernity** *n*.—**modernly** *adv*.

Modern architecture *n* (*archit*) the architectural style developed in many countries since the First World War, using industrialized building techniques and materials such as steel, glass and concrete.

modernism *n* modern view, methods or usage; the theory or practice of modern art, literature, etc; (*Christianity*) rationalistic theology.—**modernist** *adj*, *n*.—**modernistic** *adj*.—**modernistically** *adv*.

Modernism *n* (*archit*) rebelling against the florid excesses of art nouveau, Modernism sought to strip away unnecessary ornament and decoration in architecture and associated design.

modernize *vti* to make or become modern.—**modernization** *n*.

modes *n* (*mus*) the various sets of notes or scales which were used by musicians until the concept of the key was accepted (*c.*1650). Modes were based on what are now the white notes of the piano.

modest *adj* moderate; having a humble opinion of oneself; unpretentious.—**modestly** *adv*.

modesty *n* (*pl* **modesties**) the quality or state of being modest; propriety of behavior or manner; diffidence; moderation.

modicum *n* (*pl* **modicums, modica**) a small quantity.

modification *n* a modifying or being modified; the result of this; a modified form; an adjustment, alteration; (*law*) affects a previously filed document and modifies the terms of that document; (*biol*) a change in an organism caused by environmental factors but not passed on.—**modificator** *n*.—**modificatory, modificative** *adj*.

modifier *n* one who or that which modifies; (*gram*) a word, clause or phrase that qualifies or limits the meaning of another word, etc, a qualifier.

modify *vt* (**modifying, modified**) to lessen the severity of; to change or alter slightly; (*gram*) to limit in meaning, to qualify.—**modifiable** *adj*.—**modifiability** *n*.

Modigliani *n* **Amedeo** (1884–1920) Italian painter and sculptor. His paintings, mainly portraits, were influenced by Cézanne and Picasso and reached a peak of simplification of form and refinement of line and color in the last decade of his life. His best-known works are his African-influenced sculptures of elongated figures.

modillion *n* (*archit*) an ornamental bracket under a cornice in the Corinthian order.

modiolus (*pl* **modioli**) *n* (*anat*) the pillar of the cochlea of the internal ear.

modish *adj* fashionable, stylish.—**modishly** *adv*.—**modishness** *n*.

modiste *n* a person who makes fashionable dresses or hats.

Modron *n* (*Welsh Celtic myth*) meaning "mother," the mother of Mabon. Her name is thought to be a form of the Gaulish Matrona, and she is considered to have been one of the mother-goddesses.

Mods. *abbr* (*univ*) = moderations.

modular design *n* (*archit*) a design based on modules producing buildings of fixed proportions usu using pre-fabricated parts.

modulate *vti* to adjust; to regulate; to vary the pitch, intensity, frequency, etc, of.—**modulator** *n*.—**modulatory** *adj*.

modulation *n* a modulating or being modulated; a change in pitch or intensity of the voice; (*gram*) inflection, esp to change meaning; (*mus*) the gradual changing of key during the course of a part of a composition by means of a series of harmonic progressions. Modulation is *diatonic* when it is accomplished by the use of chords from relative keys; *chromatic* when by means of non-relative keys; *enharmonic* when effected by the alteration of notation; *final*, or complete, when a new tonality is established; and *partial*, or passing, when the change of key is only transient; (*electronics*) the variation of amplitude, frequency or phase of a signal or wave in response to another signal or wave, esp in the transfer to carrier waves.

module *n* a unit of measurement; a self-contained unit, esp in a spacecraft; (*education*) one of a set of learning units making up a course of study; (*archit*) a unit of measurement which regulates the proportions of a building; (*comput*) part of a program or set of programs capable of functioning on its own. —**modular** *adj*.

M

modulor *n* (*archit*) a system of measurement devised by the Swiss architect Le Corbusier, based upon the proportions of the parts of the male body.

modulus *n* (*pl* **moduli**) a quantity expressing the measure of some function or property, e.g. elasticity; (*math*) the measure of the value quantity regardless of its sign

modus operandi *n* (*pl* **modi operandi**) a method of operating, procedure.

modus vivendi *n* (*pl* **modi vivendi**) a compromise, as between two parties in dispute; a way of living.

Moeran *n* **Ernest John** (1894-1950) English composer of Irish ancestry. His compositions include a symphony, violin and cello concertos, miscellaneous orchestral pieces, songs, and works for chamber orchestra.

mofette, moffette *n* (*geol*) a fissure in an almost extinct volcano from which carbon dioxide and other gases issue; the gases.

M of M *abbr* = Ministry of Munitions.

Mogadishu (Muqdisho) *n* capital city of Somalia.

Moggeridge *n* **Bill** (1943–) British industrial designer whose studio, ID2, in California, was responsible for the design of the first portable computer.

Mogollon *adj* relating to a culture of agricultural people that emerged in New Mexico and southern Arizona *c*.100 BC.

mogul, moghul[1] *n* (*inf*) an important person, a magnate; (*with cap*) a ruler of the former Moghul Empire in India.

mogul[2] *n* a small mound or bump on a ski slope

MOH *abbr* = Medical Officer of Health; Master of Otter Hounds.

mohair *n* the long, fine hair of the Angora goat; the silk cloth made from it.

Moham. *abbr* = Mohammedan.

Mohammed *or* **Muhammad** *n* (*c*.570–*c*.632) Arab prophet and founder of Islam. Born in Mecca, the son of a merchant, he began having revelations, sometime after 600, that he was the last prophet of Allah and His channel of communication with the world. He gathered together a band of followers and established himself at Medina in 622, from where, after several battles, his forces conquered Mecca in 629, and shortly after all Arabia. He died after making a pilgrimage to Mecca.

Mohammedan *n, adj* a former word for Muslim.

Mohave *n* (*pl* **Mohaves, Mohave**) one of a North American Indian people who occupied the land along the Colorado river.—*also* **Mojave**.

Mohawk *n* (*pl* **Mohawks, Mohave**) one of a North American Indian people who occupied the area from the St Lawrence to the Mohawk river. * *n* the language of the Mohawk people.

Mohenjo-daro *n* one of the two capitals of the Indus Valley Civilization. Its buildings were constructed from hard-baked bricks.

mohican *n* a hairstyle in which the sides of the head are shaved, leaving a central band of hair, often dyed or in spikes, from the forehead to the nape of the neck.

Mohican *n* one of a confederation of North American Indian peoples who lived in the upper Hudson River valley; the language of the Mohicans.—*also* **Mahican**.

Moholy-Nagy *n* **László** (1895–1946) Hungarian painter, photographer, movie-maker, sculptor and stage designer who opened the New Bauhaus in Chicago in 1937. His importance lies in his pioneering experimentation and in his influence as a teacher

Mohorovicic discontinuity *or* **Moho** *n* (*geol*) a major seismic discontinuity (a break in rock properties at depth) discovered in 1909 from a study of the seismograms of the Yugoslav earthquake that occurred that year.

moidore *n* an ancient Portuguese gold coin.

moiety *n* (*pl* **moieties**) one of two parts or shares; a half.

Moirai *npl* (*Greek myth*) the Greek name for the Fates.

moiré *n* a fabric, silk, that has a surface pattern suggesting rippling water; such a pattern impressed on a fabric; (*comput*) a type of graphic distortion seen as flickering on the screen caused by placing several high contrast line patterns too close to one another.

moiré effect *n* a pattern created when the same pattern is superimposed on another version of itself.

moist *adj* damp; slightly wet.—**moistly** *adv*.—**moistness** *n*.

moisten *vti* to make or become moist.—**moistener** *n*.

moisture *n* liquid in a diffused, absorbed, or condensed state.

moisturize *vt* (*skin, air, etc*) to add moisture to.—**moisturizer** *n*.

Mojave *see* **Mohave**.

moke *n* (*sl*) a boring person; (*Brit*) a donkey; (*Austral*) a horse not of the top class.

mol. *abbr* = molecular; molecule.

molar[1] *n* (*dent*) a type of tooth situated at the back of the jawbone, used for grinding food. *See* **tooth**.

molar[2] *adj* of or in the whole mass of matter as distinguished from the properties or motions of atoms or molecules.

MOLARA *abbr* = Motoring Organizations Land Access & Rights Association.

molarity *n* (*chem*) the number of moles of a substance dissolved in one liter of solution.

molasses *n* (*pl* **molasses**) the thick brown sugar that is produced during the refining of sugar; treacle.

mold[1] *n* a fungus producing a furry growth on the surface of organic matter. * *vi* to become moldy.—*also* **mould**.

mold[2] *n* a hollow form in which something is cast; a pattern; something made in a mold; distinctive character. * *vt* to make in or on a mold; to form, shape, guide.—*also* **mould**.—**moldable** *adj*.—**molder** *n*.

molder *vi* to decay to rot, to crumble to dust.

molding *n* anything made in a mold; a shaped strip of wood or plaster, as around the upper walls of a room.—*also* **moulding**.

Moldova (Moldavia) *n* a landlocked republic in southeast Europe bordered by Romania in the west and bounded on all other sides by Ukraine.

moldy *adj* (**moldier, moldiest**) containing or covered with mold; musty, stale; antiquated; (*sl*) dull, boring.—*also* **mouldy**.—**moldiness** *n*.

mole[1] *n* (*chem*) the amount of substance that contains the same number of elementary particles as there are in 0.4 oz of carbon.

mole[2] *n* a spot on the skin, usu dark-colored and raised.

mole[3] *n* (*zool*) a small burrowing insectivore with soft dark fur; a spy within an organization.

mole[4] *n* a large breakwater.

Molech *n* (*Bible*) a pagan Semitic god whose worship involved child-sacrifice; although forbidden by Hebrew Law, the sacrifice of first-born children continued for centuries in Canaanite custom and was copied by the Israelites.

molecular *adj* of or inherent in molecules.

molecular biology *n* (*biol*) the branch of biology dealing with the molecular basis of heredity and of protein synthesis.

molecular electronics *n* the use of molecular materials in electronics and opto-electronics.

molecular formula *n* (*chem*) the chemical formula that indicates both the number and type of any atom present in a molecular substance.

molecular weight *n* the total of the atomic weights of all the atoms present in a molecule; the average mass per molecule of any substance relative to one-twelfth the mass of an atom of carbon-12.

molecule *n* (*chem*) the smallest chemical unit of an element or compound that can exist independently; a small particle.

mole fraction *n* (*chem*) the ratio of the number of moles of a substance to the total moles present in a mixture.

molehill *n* a mound of earth thrown up by a burrowing mole.

Molepolole *n* a city in Botswana.

moleskin *n* the fur of a mole; a twilled cotton cloth with a soft surface resembling a mole's fur, used for work clothes; (*pl*) pants made of moleskin.

molest *vt* to annoy; to attack or assault, esp sexually.—**molestation** *n*.—**molester** *n*.

Molesworth *n* **Thomas** (1890–1977) American furniture designer who perfected the "Wild West" look originated by Colonel William F. (Buffalo Bill) Cody.

Molière *n* [pseud. of Jean-Baptiste Poquelin] (1622–73) French dramatist whose great comedies, e.g. *Tartuffe* (a satire on religious hypocrisy), *The Misanthrope* (a study of a cynic in love), and *The Imaginary Invalid* (a hilarious depiction of hypochondria and quack medicine), are still popular.

Molinis *n* **Luigi** (1940–) Italian designer who designed televisions and hi-fi equipment for Zanussi.

MOLIS *abbr* = Minority On-Line Information Service

moll *adj* (*sl*) a female partner of a thief or other criminal; a prostitute; (*mus*) (*German*) "minor" (as opposed to major).

mollify *vt* (**mollifying, mollified**) to make less severe or violent; to soften.—**mollification** *n*.—**mollifier** *n*.—**mollifyingly** *adv*.

Mollino *n* **Carlo** (1905–73) Italian architect influenced by the organic forms of sculptors such as Henry Moore.

mollusk, mollusc *n* (*biol*) an invertebrate animal usu enclosed in a shell, as oysters, etc.—**molluscan, molluskan** *adj, n*.

mollycoddle *vti* to care for someone in an indulgent way; to coddle, pamper. * *n* someone so treated.—**mollycoddler** *n*.

moloch *n* (*zool*) a spiny Australian lizard with a horned head, found in desert areas; (*with cap*) (*OT*) an ancient Semitic fire god to whom children were offered as a sacrifice.

Molotov *n* **Vyacheslav Mikhailovich [Vyacheslav Mikhailovich Scriabin]** (1890–1986) Russian statesman. One of the few leading Bolsheviks to survive Stalin's purges, he negotiated the non-aggression pact with Nazi Germany, attended the founding conference of the UN in 1945 and became minister for foreign affairs (1953–56).

molt *vi* to shed hair, skin, horns, etc prior to replacement of new growth. * *n* a molting.—*also* **moult**.—**molter** *n*.

molten *adj* melted by heat.

molto *adj* (*mus*) (*Italian*) "very," so *allegro molto* means "very fast."

moly *n* (*pl* **molies**) (*Greek myth*) a magical herb, with a black root and a white flower, given by Hermes to Odysseus, which he used as an antidote to the charms of Circe.

molybdenum *n* (*chem*) a metallic element used in alloys, esp strengthening steel.—**molybdous, molybdic** *adj*.

mom *n* (*inf*) mother.

MOMA *abbr* = Museum of Modern Art.

Mombasa *n* town in Kenya.

moment *n* an indefinitely brief period of time; a definite point in time; a brief time of importance; (*physics*) a measure of the turning effect of a force about a point and the force multiplied by the perpendicular distance from the point.

momenta *see* **momentum**.

momentarily *adv* for a short time; in an instant; at any moment.

momentary *adj* lasting only for a moment.—**momentariness** *n*.

moment of truth *n* a time when a person or thing is put to the ultimate test; the conclusion of a bullfight, when the matador dispatches the bull.

momentous *adj* very important.—**momentously** *adv*.—**momentousness** *n*.

momentum *n* (*pl* **momenta, momentums**) (*physics*) the impetus of a moving object, equal to the product of its mass and its velocity.

MOMI *abbr* = Museum of the Moving Image.

MOMIMTS *abbr* = Military & Orchestral Musical Instrument Makers' Trade Society.

momma *n* mama.

mommy *n* (*pl* **mommies**) (*inf*) mother.

Mon. *abbr* = Monday; Monmouthshire; Monsignor; Montana.

mon-, mono- *prefix* alone, sole, single.

monachism *n* monasticism; the monastic life or system.—**monachal** *adj*.

Monaco *n* a tiny principality situated on the French Riviera; capital city of Monaco

monad *n* a unit, number one; (*philos*) the ultimate unit of being or evolution in Leibniz's theory; (*chem*) a radical or atom with a valency of one; (*biol*) a single-celled organism.—**monadic, monadical** *adj*.—**monadically** *adv*.

monadelphous *adj* (*bot*) having stamens in one bundle of filaments wrapped around the style.

monadism *n* (*philos*) the theory, esp as propounded by Leibniz, that the real universe is composed of monads.

monandrous *adj* having only one husband or male partner at a time; (*bot*) (*flowers*) having one stamen only; (*plants*) having flowers with only one stamen.—**monandry** *n*.

monarch *n* a sovereign who rules by hereditary right; a powerful or dominant thing or person.—**monarchal, monarchic, monarchical** *adj*.—**monarchically** *adv*.

monarchism *n* the principles of, or devotion to, monarchy.—**monarchist** *n, adj*.—**monarchistic** *adj*.

monarchy *n* (*pl* **monarchies**) a government headed by a monarch; a kingdom.

monastery *n* (*pl* **monasteries**) the residence of a group of monks, or nuns.—**monasterial** *adj*.

monastic, monastical *adj* of monks or monasteries. * *n* a monk; a recluse.—**monastically** *adv*.—**monasticism** *n*.

Mond. *abbr* = Monday.

Monday *n* the second day of the week.

mondial *adj* encompassing the whole world; worldwide.

Mondrian *n* Piet [Pieter Cornelis Mondriaan] (1872–1944) Dutch painter; a leading member of de Stijl. He developed a style of painting based on grids of lines against strong colors, e.g., *Composition in Yellow and Blue* (1929).

Mondsee *n* an Austrian culture dated to the Copper Age.

monecious *see* **monoecious**.

Monet *n* Claude Oscar (1840–1926) French Impressionist painter. His *Impression: Sunrise* gave its name to the movement. From 1862–63 he studied in Paris, where he met Renoir and Sisley and together they began the direct studies of nature and changing light that was to characterize their works. Manet was an early influence on Monet, but Monet was more interested in experiment with light and color, e.g., *Women in a Garden* (1867). Other works include the *Haystacks* (1891) and *Rouen Cathedral* (1894) series.

monetarism *n* (*econ*) the theory that control of the money supply is the key to achieving low inflation and economic growth.—**monetarist** *n, adj*.

monetary *adj* of the coinage or currency of a country; of or relating to money.—**monetarily** *adv*.

monetary control *n* the employment of a central bank of a country by the government of that country to control the money supply.

monetary system *n* the system that is used by a country to implement its monetary policy, to provide money for internal use and to control the exchange of its own currency with the currencies of foreign countries; a system used to control the exchange rate of a group of countries, as in the European Monetary System.

monetary unit *n* the standard unit of currency in a particular country.

monetize *vt* to convert into money; to give a standard of current value to.—**monetization** *n*.

money *n* (*pl* **moneys, monies**) coins or paper notes authorized by a government as a medium of exchange; property; wealth.

moneychanger *n* one who changes money into other coinage at fixed rate; a machine that dispenses coins.

moneyed *adj* rich.—*also* **monied**.

money-grubbing *adj* (*inf*) greedy and grasping.—**money-grubber** *n*.

moneylender *n* a person who lends money for interest, esp as a business.—**moneylending** *n*.

money market *n* a market that is engaged in the short-term lending and borrowing of money, and that links the various financial institutions and the government.

money order *n* an order issued by a bank or post office for payment of a specified sum at any of their branches.

money supply *n* the stock of money that is in a country's economy, often the quantity of money issued by a country's central bank.

Mongan *n* 1. (*Irish Celtic myth*) the son of the sea-god Manannan mac Lir. Said to be a reincarnation of Fionn mac Cumhaill, and parallels have been drawn between the legend of Mongan and the Arthurian legend. 2. Irish king who ruled at Moylinny on Lough Neagh and died around AD 625.

monger *n* a dealer.

mongo *n* a Mongolian monetary unit equal to one hundredth of a tugrik.

Mongolia *n* a large, central Asian republic which shares a long northern border with Russia and is surrounded on all other sides by China.

mongoose *n* (*pl* **mongooses**) a small predatory mammal of Africa and Asia.

mongrel *n* an animal or plant of mixed or unknown breed, esp a dog. * *adj* of mixed breed or origin.—**mongrelism** *n*.—**mongrelly** *adj*.

mongrelize *vt* to render mongrel.—**mongrelization** *n*.

Monica *n* Saint (*d.* 388) best known as the mother of St Augustine of Hippo; she converted her husband Patricius and his mother to Christianity; she eventually converted Augustine in 386. Her feast day is 27 August.

monied *see* **moneyed**.

monies *see* **money**.

moniker, monicker *n* (*sl*) a name; a nickname.

moniliform *adj* (*biol*) shaped like a necklace.

monism *n* (*philos*) the theory that there is only one kind of being and that matter and mind are ultimately identical.—**monist** *n, adj*.—**monistic** *adj*.—**monistically** *adv*.

monition *n* an admonition; a formal notice from an ecclesiastical court to an offender; a summons; a warning.

monitor *n* a student chosen to help the teacher; any device for regulating the performance of a machine, aircraft, etc; a screen for viewing the image being produced by a television camera; (*comput*) another name for display, screen or VDU; * *vti* (*TV or radio transmissions, etc*) to observe or listen to for political or technical reasons; to watch or check on; to regulate or control, a machine, etc.—**monitorial** *adj*.

monitory *adj* conveying a warning. * *n* (*pl* **monitories**) a letter containing an admonition or warning, esp a papal letter.

monk *n* a male member of a religious order living in a monastery.

Monk *n* 1. John Lawrence (1936–) American industrial designer, based in Milan. 2. Thelonius [Sphere] (1920–82) American jazz pianist and composer. He became a member of Dizzy Gillespie's band in 1946 and formed his own band in 1947, which later included many talented saxophonists, e.g., Coltrane. His compositions include "Round Midnight."

monkey *n* any of the primates except man and the lemurs, esp the smaller, long-tailed primates; a mischievous child; (*sl*) $500 or £500. * *vi* (**monkeying, monkeyed**) (*inf*) to play, trifle, or meddle.

monkey business *n* (*inf*) mischief; underhand dealings.

monkeyshine *n* (*sl*) a prank.

monkey suit *n* (*inf*) evening dress.

monkey wrench *n* a large wrench with an adjustable jaw.

monkfish *n* (*pl* **monkfish, monkfishes**) an angelfish.

monkhood *n* the character or condition of a monk; monks collectively.

monkish *adj* pertaining to or resembling a monk; monastic.—**monkishly** *adv*.—**monkishness** *n*.

monkshood, monk's-hood *n* (*bot*) a poisonous plant, aconite.

mono *adj* (*inf*) monophonic. * *n* (*pl* **monos**) (*inf*) monophonic sound.

mono-, mon- *prefix* alone, sole, single.

monobasic *adj* (*chem*) having one base or atom of a base.

monobasic acid *n* (*chem*) an acid that contains only one replaceable hydrogen atom per molecule.

monocarp *n* (*bot*) a monocarpic plant.

monocarpic, monocarpous *adj* (*bot*) bearing fruit only once.

Monoceros *n* (*astron*) a constellation running across the celestial equator.

monochord *n* (*mus*) a one-stringed musical instrument with a sound box for determining musical intervals.

monochromatic *adj* consisting of one color.—**monochromatically** *adv*.

monochrome *n* a painting, drawing, or print in a single color; (*comput*) a type of monitor that displays only black and white pixels (or black with green or another color); * *adj* in one color or shades of one color; black and white—**monochromic** *adj*. *See also* **grisaille**.

monocle *n* a single eyeglass held in place by the face muscles.—**monocled** *adj*.

monocline *n* (*geol*) a geological formation in which the strata are tilted one way only.—**monoclinal** *adj*.

monoclonal antibody *n* (*biol*) a particular antibody produced by a cell or cells derived from a single parent cell, i.e., a clone (with each cell being monoclonal).

monocoque *n* a type of design for a fuselage or body shell in which all or most of the structural loads are carried by the skin; a type of vehicle construction that integrates the chassis and the body; the hull of a boat built in one piece.

monocotyledon *n* (*bot*) the subclass of flowering plants that have a single seed leaf (cotyledon) and three-part flowers, incl grasses, lilies and orchids.—**monocotyledonous** *adj*..

monocrat *n* one who governs alone; an advocate of autocracy or monarchy.—**monocracy** *n*.

monocular *adj* pertaining to, for, or with one eye only; adapted for use with one eye.

monoculture *n* the growing of a single crop by a farmer.

monocyte *n* (*physiology*) the largest type of white blood cell (leucocyte) that is capable of motion and ingests foreign bodies such as bacteria and tissue particles.

Monod *n* Jacques-Lucien (1910–76) French biochemist. He shared the 1965 Nobel prize for physics with **François Jacob** (1920–) for their work on clusters of genes ("operons") round chromosomes.

monodrama *n* a dramatic piece for one actor.—**monodramatic** *adj*.

monody *n* (*pl* **monodies**) in Greek tragedy, a lyrical poem sung by one actor alone; a plaintive poem or song for one voice, a dirge, an elegy; (*mus*) a type of accompanied solo song which was developed during the late-16th and early 17th cents. It contained dramatic and expressive embellishments and devices, and consequently had an influence on opera.—**monodic, monodical** *adj*.—**monodist** *n*.

monoecious *adj* (*bot*) having stamens and pistils on the same plant but on different flowers; (*zool*) hermaphroditic.—*also* **monecious**.—**monoeciously** *adv*.

monogamy *n* the practice of being married to only one person at a time.—**monogamist** *n*.—**monogamous** *adj*.

monogenesis *n* (*biol*) derivation from a single cell, resulting in an organism like the adult of the species; asexual reproduction from a single cell; the supposed descent of all organisms from one *orig* cell; the supposed descent of all human beings from one *orig* pair.—**monogenous** *adj*.

monogenetic *adj* pertaining to or having the property of monogenesis; (*animals*) born, living and dying on a single host; (*rocks*) originating from a single source or by a single process.

monogr. *abbr* (*cataloguing*) = monograph.

monogram *n* the embroidered or printed initials of one's name on clothing, stationery, etc.—**monogrammed** *adj*.—**monogrammatic** *adj*.

monograph *n* a learned paper written on one particular subject. * *vt* to write such a paper on.—**monographer** *n*.—**monographic** *adj*.—**monographically** *adv*.

monolingual *adj* speaking or understanding only one language; written or expressed in only one language. * *n* a monolingual person.

monolith *n* a single, large, block of stone, erected as a monument or column; any massive, unyielding structure.—**monolithic** *adj*.—**monolithically** *adv*.

monologue, monolog *n* a long speech; a soliloquy, a skit, etc for one actor only.—**monologuist, monologist** *n*.

monomania *n* an irrational obsession with a single subject, object, idea, etc.—**monomaniac** *n*.—**monomaniacal** *adj*.

monomer *n* (*chem*) a simple molecule that is the basic unit of polymers.

monometallic *adj* containing only one metal; of monometallism.

monometallism *n* the use of a single metal, often gold or silver, as a standard of currency; the economic system underpinning such a standard.—**monometallist** *n*.

monomial *n* (*math*) an expression consisting of one term; (*biol*) a taxonomic classification consisting of one term.—*also adj*.

monomorphic, monomorphous *adj* (*species*) of one type or structure or with parts that have only one type or structure; (*individual organism*) unchanging in shape throughout its life cycle; (*chem*) denoting a chemical compound with a single crystalline form.

mononucleosis *see* **glandular fever**.

monopetalous *adj* (*bot*) (*flowers*) having the corolla in one piece; possessing a single petal.

monophobia *n* an overwhelming fear of being alone.—**monophobic** *adj*.

monophonic *adj* (*sound reproduction*) using one channel only for transmission.—**monophonically** *adv*.

monophthong *n* a simple single vowel sound; two different written vowels pronounced as a single sound.—**monophthongal** *adj*.

monoplane *n* an airplane with a single pair of wings.

monoplegia *n* paralysis affecting one limb or one group of muscles only.—**monoplegic** *adj*, *n*.

monopolize *vt* to get, have, or exploit a monopoly of; to get full control of.—**monopolization** *n*.—**monopolizer** *n*.

monopoly *n* (*pl* **monopolies**) exclusive control in dealing in a particular commodity or supplying a service; exclusive use or possession; that which is exclusively controlled; such control granted by a government.—**monopolism** *n*.—**monopolist** *n*.—**monopolistic** *adj*.—**monopolistically** *adv*.

monopsony *n* a market in which there is only a single buyer.

monopteral *n* (*archit*) a temple without walls, the roof of which is supported by a series of columns.

monorail *n* a single track railway, often with suspended carriages.

monosaccharide *n* (*chem*) a sugar that cannot be further broken down into simpler sugars by hydrolysis.

monosepalous *adj* (*bot*) (*flowers*) having the calyx undivided; possessing a single sepal.

monosodium glutamate *n* a chemical additive used to give food a meaty taste.

monospace *n* (*comput*) a font type that uses an equal amount of space for each character in the font family.

monospermous, monospermal *adj* (*bot*) (*plants*) one-seeded.

monostich *n* a poem in one line.—**monostichic** *adj*.

monosyllabic *adj* (*word*) having one syllable; characterized by or made up of one syllable; terse; curt.—**monosyllabically** *adv*.

monotheism *n* the doctrine of or belief in the existence of only one God.—**monotheist** *n*.—**monotheistic** *adj*.—**monotheistically** *adv*.

monothematic *n* (*mus*) a piece of music that is developed from a single musical idea.

monotone *n* an utterance or musical tone without a change in pitch; a tiresome sameness of style, color, etc.—**monotonic** *adj*.—**monotonically** *adv*.

monotonous *adj* unvarying in tone; with dull uniformity, wearisome.—**monotonously** *adv*.—**monotonousness** *n*.

monotony *n* (*pl* **monotonies**) lack of variety; irksome sameness.

monotreme *n* (*zool*) one of a primitive order of Australian egg-laying mammals, with a single vent for digestive, urinary and genital organs.—**monotrematous** *adj*.

monotype *n* (*print*) one print from a metal or glass plate with a painted image; (*biol*) a genus or species that has only a single type.—**monotypic** *adj*.

Monotype *n* (*trademark*) a hot-metal typesetting machine that casts each character separately; type so cast.

monovalent *adj* (*chem*) with a valency of one; univalent.—**monovalence, monovalency** *n*.

monoxide *n* an oxide with one oxygen atom in each molecule.

monozygotic twins, identical twins *npl* (*genetics*) twin children who are derived from a single fertilized egg which then divides into two separate embryos.

Monroe *n* 1. **James** (1758–1831) American statesman and 5th president of the US (1817–25). 2. **Marilyn [Norma Jean Baker, Mortenson]** (1926–62) American film actress and sex symbol in films such as *Gentleman Prefer Blondes* (1953), *Bus Stop* (1956), and *Some Like It Hot* (1959). Her last film, *The Misfits* (1961), was written by her third husband, Arthur Miller.

Monrovia *n* capital city of Liberia.

Mons. *abbr* = Monsieur.

Monseigneur *n* (*pl* **Messeigneurs**) a French title given to princes, prelates and bishops.

monsieur *n* (*pl* **messieurs**) the French equivalent of sir in address and of Mr with a name.

Monsig. *abbr* = Monseigneur; Monsignor.

Monsignor *n* (*pl* **Monsignors, Monsignore**) (*RC Church*) a title given, usu by the Pope, to some prelates or officers.

monsoon *n* (*meteorology*) winds that blow in opposite directions during different seasons of the year, with features that are associated with widespread temperature changes over land and water in the subtropics; the rainy season.

mons pubis *n* (*pl* **montes pubis**) (*anat*) the fleshy area in human males where the pubic bones meet.

monster *n* any greatly malformed plant or animal; an imaginary beast; a very wicked person; a very large animal or thing. * *adj* very large, huge.

monstrance *n* (*RC Church*) a transparent vessel, usu set in a gold or silver frame, in which the consecrated Host is carried in procession or exhibited.

monstrosity *n* (*pl* **monstrosities**) the state or quality of being monstrous; an ugly, unnatural or monstrous thing or person.

monstrous *adj* abnormally developed; enormous; horrible.—**monstrously** *adv*.—**monstrousness** *n*.

mons veneris *n* (*pl* **montes veneris**) (*anat*) the fleshy area in human females where the pubic bones meet.

Mont. *abbr* = Montana.

montage *n* a rapid sequence of film shots, often superimposed; the art or technique of assembling various elements, esp pictures or photographs; such an assemblage.

Montagnac *n* **Pierre-Paul** (1883–1962) French painter and architect who designed furniture and interiors in the classical tradition.

Montagu *n* **Mrs Elizabeth** (1720–1800) English author and "bluestocking" whose *Essay on the Writings and Genius of Shakespeare*, a reply to Voltaire's criticisms of Shakespeare's work, was highly acclaimed by her contemporaries.

Montaigne *n* **Michel Eyquem de** (1553–92) French essayist who established the essay as a literary form and whose self-examination of his reflections on incidents in his life and on his favorite authors has had a wide and lasting influence. Shakespeare used a translation of his essays as one of the sources for *The Tempest*.

Montana (MT) *n* a state of the United States of America (USA) of which the capital is Helena.

"Montana" *n* the song of the American State, Montana.

montane *adj* of or inhabiting mountains or mountainous terrain.

Montañés *n* **Juan Martinez** (1568–1694) Spanish sculptor who lived and worked in Seville, where he carved and painted wooden statues of great dignity and grace.

Monte Albán *n* the great capital city of the Zapotecs, which was founded in 600 BC and came to dominate the whole of the valley of Oaxaca, Mexico.

monte (bank) *n* a gambling card game *orig* played with dice or cards in Spain.

Montego Bay *n* major town in Jamaica.

Monterrey *n* a city in Mexico.

Montessori *n* **Maria** (1870–1952) Italian educationalist; the first woman in Italy to be awarded a medical degree. Her book *The Montessori Method* (1912), which set out her educational method of encouraging the child to learn at her or his own pace, was very influential on modern pedagogy.

Montessori Method *n* a system of educating very young children, through play, based on free discipline, with each child developing at his or her own pace.

Monteverdi (Monteverde) *n* **Claudio Giovanni Antonio** (1567–1643) Italian composer from Cremona working in Mantua and Venice, who composed many religious works (e.g., Masses, Vespers, Magnificats) but also numerous secular works. Unfortunately, only three of his twelve operas survive in their complete state (*Orfeo, Il Ritorno d'Ulisse in Patria* and *l'Incoronazione De Poppea*). Monteverdi's role in the development of music has been compared to Shakespeare's in literature.

Montevideo *n* capital city of Uruguay.

Montgomery *n* the capital city of Alabama, a state of the USA.

Montgomery of Alamein *n* **Bernard Law, 1st Viscount** (1887–1976) English soldier who commanded the 8th Army in Egypt in 1942 and won the Battle of Alamein later that year against Rommel's forces, a victory recognized by Churchill as a turning point in the war. He later commanded the Allied land forces on D-Day, and accepted Germany's surrender on Luneburg Heath.

month *n* a period of time determined by the time the moon takes to complete one orbit of the earth; any of the twelve divisions of the year; a calendar month.

monthly *adj* continuing for a month; done, happening, payable, etc every month. * *n* a monthly periodical. * *adv* once a month; every month.

monticule *n* a hillock; a small mound resulting from a volcanic eruption.

Montpelier *n* the capital city of Vermont, a state of the USA.

Montréal *n* a city in Canada.

Montserrat *n* a British overseas territory and one of the Leeward Islands in the Caribbean Sea.

Montu *n* (*Egypt*) the tutelary god of Thebes, later overshadowed and absorbed by Amun-Ra.

monument *n* an obelisk, statue or building that commemorates a person or an event; an exceptional example.

monumental *adj* of, like, or serving as a monument; colossal; lasting.— **monumentality** *n*.—**monumentally** *adv*.

moo *n* the long deep sound made by a cow. * *vi* (*cattle*) to low; to make a deep long noise like a cow.

mooch *vt* (*sl*) to wander around aimlessly; (*sl*) to cadge, steal.—**moocher** *n*.

mood *n* a temporary state of mind or temper; a gloomy feeling; a predominant feeling or spirit; (*gram*) that form of a verb indicating mode of action; (*mus*) mode.

moody *adj* (**moodier, moodiest**) gloomy; temperamental.—**moodily** *adv*.— **moodiness** *n*.

moolah *n* (*sl*) money.

moon, Moon *n* (*astron*) the earth's one satellite, which orbits around the earth at an average distance of 238,600 miles (384,400 km) and shines by reflected sunlight; any natural satellite of another planet; something shaped like the moon. * *vi* to behave in an idle or distracted way.

moonbeam *n* a ray of moonlight.

mooncalf *n* (*pl* **mooncalves**) a born fool; an idler; (*arch*) a monster.

moonflower *n* (*bot*) any of a family of climbing or creeping plants with trumpet-shaped flowers that bloom at night; a tropical plant, *orig* found in Mexico, with white flowers that bloom at night.

moonlight *n* the light of the moon. * *vi* (*inf*) to have a secondary (usu night-time) job.—**moonlighter** *n*.

moonlit *adj* lit by the moon.

moonraker, moonsail *n* (*naut*) a small sail carried above a skysail.

moonshine *n* moonlight; (*inf*) nonsense, foolish talk; (*sl*) illegally distilled spirits.

moonshiner *n* (*sl*) a distiller of illicit whiskey; a whiskey smuggler.

moonstone *n* a translucent yellowish or yellowish-white stone that exhibits pearly blue-tinged reflections, used as a gemstone.

moonstruck, moonstricken *adj* besotted with love or sentiment; demented.

moonwort *n* a fern with crescent-shaped fronds, grape fern; honesty.

moony *adj* (**moonier, mooniest**) of or like the moon; crescent-shaped; round; listless, dreamy; absent-minded.

moor[1] *n* a tract of open wasteland, usu covered with heather and often marshy.

moor[2] *vti* (*a ship*) to secure or be secured by cable or anchor.

Moor *n* a North African Muslim of mixed Arab and Berber ancestry.

moorage *n* the act of mooring a vessel; a place or charge for mooring.

moorcock *n* the male red grouse.

Moore *n* 1. **Brian** (1921–99) Irish-born Canadian novelist whose works, e.g. *Black Robe, The Color of Blood*, and *Catholics*, place him in the first rank of modern writers, and who also had a gift for blending supernatural events in the commonplace patterns of everyday life, as in *Cold Heaven*. 2. **Charles W.** (born 1925) American architect. His notable works include Kresge College, Santa Cruz. 3. **Douglas Stuart** (1893–1969) American composer and teacher. His works include operas (e.g. *The Devil and Daniel Webster, The Ballad of Baby Doe)*, and orchestral and choral pieces. 4. **Edward Chandler** (1827–91) American silversmith known for his fine craftsmanship. 5. **George [Augustus]** (1852–1933) Irish novelist whose novels, e.g., *Esther Waters* and *The Brook Kerith*, were heavily influenced by Balzac and Zola. He was a friend of Yeats, and played a leading role in the founding of the Abbey Theatre. 6. **G[eorge] E[dward]** (1873–1958) English philosopher. A strong influence on his fellow student Bertrand Russell, Moore became one of the leading philosophers of his day with the publication of his *Principia Ethica* (1903), an analysis of the non-analyzable nature of good and of the value of friendship. 7. **Henry** (1898–1986) British sculptor. Moore was responsible for reviving the popularity of direct carving methods, disliking the accepted methods of modeling and casting pieces of sculpture. African and Mexican art had a profound influence on his work. 8. **Marianne [Craig]** (1887–1972) American poet, noted for sophisticated and witty verse in volumes such as *Selected Poems*. 9. **Thomas** (1779–1852) Irish poet whose *Irish Melodies*, songs of his own composition (e.g., "Believe me, if all those Endearing Young Charms," "The Last Rose of Summer") set to traditional Irish airs, achieved great popularity and are still loved and sung.

moorfowl *n* (*arch*) red grouse collectively.

moorhen *n* an aquatic dark-colored bird with a red bill and a characteristic red mark above the bill, found in ponds and lakes; the female red grouse.

mooring *n* the act of mooring; the place where a ship is moored; (*pl*) the lines, cables, etc by which a ship is moored.

Moorish *adj* pertaining to the Moors; denoting a Spanish architectural style of the 13th-16th centuries, one of the distinguishing features of which is the horseshoe arch.

moorland *n* a stretch of moors.

moose *n* (*pl* **moose**) the largest member of the deer family, native to North America.

moot *adj* debatable; hypothetical. * *vt* (**mooting, mooted**) to propose for discussion.

mop *n* a rag, sponge, etc fixed to a handle for washing floors or dishes; a thick or tangled head of hair. * *vt* (**mopping, mopped**) to wash with a mop; (*with* **up**) to wipe as with a mop; (*mil*) to clear isolated pockets of remaining enemy resistance after occupying an area; (*inf*) to finish; to make a large profit.

m.o.p. *abbr* = mother of pearl.

MOPA *abbr* = Mail Order Publishers' Authority.

mope *vi* to be gloomy and apathetic. * *n* a person who mopes, a moper.—**moper** *n*.—**mopey** *adj*.—**mopingly** *adv*.

moped *n* a light, motor-assisted bicycle.

moppet *n* a pet name for a small child, esp a girl; (*arch*) a rag doll.

Mopti *n* town in Mali.

mop-up *n* a military clearing operation.

moquette *n* a material with short velvety pile used for carpets and upholstery.

mor. *abbr* = (*mus*) morendo (*Italian*) "dying"; (*bookbinding*) morocco

MOR *abbr* = middle-of-the-road (of music that is broadcast).

moraine *n* (*geol*) ridges of rock debris deposited by glaciers, and marking present or former ice margins. —**morainal, morainic** *adj*.

moral *adj* of or relating to character and human behavior, particularly as regards right and wrong; virtuous, esp in sexual conduct; capable of distinguishing right from wrong; probable, although not certain; psychological, emotional. * *n* a moral lesson taught by a fable, event, etc; (*pl*) principles; ethics.

morale *n* moral or mental condition with respect to courage, discipline, confidence, etc.

moralism *n* moralizing; a moral attitude or maxim; the practice of or belief in a system of morals independent of religion.

moralist *n* a teacher or student of morals; one for whom morality needs no religious sanction; one concerned with the morals of others.—**moralistic** *adj*.—**moralistically** *adv*.

morality *n* (*pl* **moralities**) virtue; moral principles; a particular system of moral principles.

morality play *n* a medieval allegorical play.

M

moralize, moralise *vt* to explain or interpret morally; to give a moral direction to. * *vi* to make moral pronouncements.—**moralization, moralisation** *n.*—**moralizer, moraliser** *n.*

morally *adv* in a moral manner, ethically; virtually, practically.

moral philosophy *n* ethics.

Moral Rearmament *n* an international evangelical movement, founded in the US by Frank Buchman (1938), that seeks moral and spiritual revival following conservative Christian principles.—*also* **Buchmanism**.

Morandi *n* **Riccardo** (1902-) Italian architect. His notable works include Maracaibo bridge, Venezuela.

Morandini *n* **Marcello** (1940-) Italian designer who designed ceramics for **Rosenthal**, as well as the façade of their offices in Selb.

Morann *n* (*Irish Celtic myth*) a druid at the court of Conchobar mac Nessa.

morass *n* a bog, marsh.

moratorium *n* (*pl* **moratoria, moratoriums**) a legally authorized delay in the payment of money due; an authorized delay or suspension of any activity.—**moratory** *adj.*

Moratuwa *n* a city in Sri Lanka .

moray *n* (*pl* **morays**) any of various brilliantly colored marine coastal eels that can inflict sharp bites.

morbid *adj* diseased, resulting as from a diseased state of mind; gruesome.—**morbidly** *adv.*—**morbidness** *n.*

morbid anatomy *n* (*anat*) the branch of anatomy dealing with the structure and analysis of diseased organs.

morbidity *n* (*medical*) the state of being diseased, the morbidity rate being expressed as the number of cases of a disease occurring within a particular number of the population.

morbido *n* (*mus*) (*Italian*) "soft" or "gentle."

morbific *adj* causing or producing disease.

morceau *n* (*pl* **morceaux**) a small piece, a morsel; (*mus*) (*French*) a "piece" (of music).

Mørch *n* **Ibi Trier** (1910–1994) Danish architect who specialized in the design of glass and silver.

mordacious *adj* biting; sarcastic; cutting.—**mordaciously** *adv.*—**mordacity** *n.*

mordant *adj* biting, caustic; corrosive. * *n* (*chem*) a chemical fixative that is used in dyeing when the dye will not fix directly onto the fabric; a corrosive substance.—**mordancy** *n.*—**mordantly** *adv.*

mordent *n* (*mus*) a musical ornament, a trill created by one note rapidly alternating with another one degree below it; this is indicated by a sign over the note.

more *adj* (*superl* **most**) greater; further; additional (—*also compar of* **many, much**). * *adv* to a greater extent or degree; again; further.

More *n* 1. **Hannah** (1745–1833) English writer and a member of the "bluestocking" circle gravitating around Dr Johnson, whose works include *Bas Bleu*, tragedies, e.g., *Percy*, and many poems. 2. **Henry** (1614–87) English philosopher and leading light of a small group of Anglican divines known as the Cambridge Platonists. They were much influenced by humanist thinkers such as Erasmus, Hooker and Sir Thomas More. His works include *Psychozoia Platonica* and *Divine Dialogs*. 3. **Sir Thomas** (1478–1535) English humanist, reformer, statesman and Roman Catholic saint who was Henry VIII's Lord Chancellor, and whose refusal to recognize the annulment of Henry's marriage to Catherine of Aragon and declaration of supremacy over the Church of England led to his execution for treason. More's greatest work is his fantasy of a supposedly ideally organized state, *Utopia*. More was canonized in 1835.

moreen *n* a stout woolen fabric used esp for furnishings, often embossed or figured with a watered pattern.

morel[1] *n* an edible mushroom with a brownish cap.

morel[2] *n* a nightshade, esp the black nightshade.

morello *n* (*pl* **morellos**) a small dark-red cherry with a tart flavor.

morendo *n* (*mus*) (*Italian*) "dying," i.e., decreasing in volume.

moreover *adv* in addition to what has been said before; besides.

mores *npl* customs so fundamentally established that they have the force of law.

moresca *n* (*mus*) (*Italian*) a sword dance dating from the 15th and 16th centuries. It has been included in operas, often to a marching rhythm.

Moresque *adj* (*archit*) Moorish style. * *n* an example of such decoration or architecture; a design in this style.

Moretti *n* **Carlo** (1934-) and **Giovanni** (1936-) Italian grandsons of Vicenzo Moretti, who established a glass and bead factory at the end of the last century.

Moreux *n* **Jean-Charles** (1889–1956) French architect and furniture designer who created massive, but elegant pieces.

Morfessa *n* (*Irish Celtic myth*) one of the wizards who taught the Tuatha De Danann their magic skills before they went to Ireland.

Morgan *n* 1. **David** (1951-) British industrial designer specializing in lighting design. 2. **Edwin George** (1920-) Scottish poet and translator, best known for his witty, experimental verse, e.g., the much anthologized "The First Men on Mercury," and for his poems on Scottish life, e.g., *Glasgow Sonnets*. 3. **Thomas Hunt** (1866–1945) American geneticist and biologist and winner of the 1933 Nobel prize for physiology or medicine for his research into chromosomes and heredity.

morganatic *adj* (*marriage*) between a royal person and one of lower rank the children of which are legitimate but neither they nor the morganatic wife or husband share royal rank or property.—**morganatically** *adv.*

Morgen *n* (*Welsh Celtic myth*) a druidic goddess who had nine sisters and may have associations with Modron. She is thought to have been the original of the Morgan Le Fay of the Arthurian legend.

morgue *n* a place where the bodies of unknown dead or those dead of unknown causes are temporarily kept prior to burial; (*inf*) a collection of reference materials, e.g., newspaper clippings.

MORI *abbr* = Market and Opinion Research Institute.

moribund *adj* in a dying state; near death.—**moribundity** *n.*

morion *n* a 16th-century hat-shaped helmet without beaver or visor.

Morison *n* **Stanley Arthur** (1889–1967) British typographer who designed the font, Times New Roman, in 1932.

Morisot *n* **Berthe** (1841–95) French impressionist painter. Typical works include *The Cradle* (1873) and *Jeune Femme au Bal* (1880).

Morley *n* **Thomas** (1557–*c*.1602) English composer who was given the patent to print song-books by Elizabeth I. As well as publishing his own works, he also published works of his contemporaries and educational booklets. He is considered to be the father of the English madrigal and he also wrote ballets and pieces for the lute.

Mormon *n* a member of the Church of Latter-Day Saints whose authority is the Bible and the Book of Mormon, revelations to Joseph Smith in 1827.—**Mormonism** *n.*

morn *n* (*poet*) dawn, morning; (*Scot*) tomorrow.

morn. *abbr* = morning.

mornay *n* a white sauce flavored with cheese. * *adj* (*eggs, etc*) cooked with this sauce.

morning *n* the part of the day from midnight or dawn until noon; the early part of anything. * *adj* of or in the morning.

morning coat *n* a tailcoat, usu grey, with a cutaway front.

morning-glory *n* (*pl* **morning-glories**) any of various twining plants with showy blue bell-shaped flowers.

morning sickness *n* vomiting and nausea, most common during the first three months of pregnancy. *See also* **hyperemesis**.

morning star *n* (*astron*) a planet (usu Venus or possibly Mercury), seen to the east in the sky around sunrise.

morning suit *n* a man's formal suit of a morning coat and striped trousers.

morning watch *n* (*naut*) a watch on board ship from 4 am to 8 am.

Moro *n* **Aldo** (1916–78) Italian Christian democrat statesman. He was prime minister (1963–68, 1974–76) and brought the Communist Party into close cooperation with his center-left coalition shortly before his abduction and murder by the Red Brigade.

Moroccan dirham *n* currency of Western Sahara.

morocco *n* (*pl* **moroccos**) a fine kind of grained leather of goatskin or sheepskin, used in bookbinding and for shoes.

Morocco *n* a constitutional monarchy in northwest Africa.

moron *n* an adult mentally equal to a 8 to 12-year-old child; (*inf*) a very stupid person.—**moronic** *adj.*—**moronically** *adv.*—**moronism, moronity** *n.*

Moroni *n* capital city of Comoros.

morose *adj* sullen, surly; gloomy.—**morosely** *adv.*—**moroseness** *n.*

morph. or **morphol.** *abbr* = morphology.

morpheme *n* the smallest meaningful unit of language as a base, prefix or suffix.—**morphemic** *adj.*—**morphemically** *adv.*

Morpheus *n* (*Greek myth*) the god of dreams and of sleep.

morphine *n* (*chem*) a crystalline alkaloid occurring in opium; (*med*) a very strong analgesic drug used for the relief of severe pain, but tolerance and dependence may occur leading to addiction.—**morphinic** *adj.*

morphing *n* (*comput*) a technique that appears to melt one image into another image to create a special effect.

morphinism *n* (*med*) addiction to morphine; poisoning caused by the excessive use of morphine.

morphogen *n* (*biol*) that substance in an embryo that determines what the structure will become.

morphology *n* (*biol*) a branch of biology dealing with the form and structure of organisms; the study of word formation in a language.—**morphological** *adj.*—**morphologist** *n.*

morphosis *n* (*pl* **morphoses**) (*biol*) a development in an organism or its parts marked by structural change.—**morphotic** *adj.*

Morrigan *n* (*Irish Celtic myth*) one of a group of Irish war-goddesses who can be thought of as a single goddess or as a triple goddess..

morris (dance) *n* a traditional English dance accompanied by tambourines, bells, castanets, violin, concertina, etc, and usu performed by men in costumes representing the Robin Hood legend or other characters from English folklore.

Morris *n* 1. **Desmond [John]** (1928-) English zoologist. His studies of animal and human behavior, *The Naked Ape* (1967) and *The Human Zoo* (1968), popularized versions of the theories of behaviorists such as Lorenz and Tinbergen and were bestsellers in the late 1960s and 70s. 2. **May** (1862–1938) British designer, embroiderer and professor, trained by her father William **Morris**, and a founder member of the Women's Guild of Arts. 3. **Robert Lee** (1948-) American jewelry designer who designed sculptured pieces in Minimal style, and branched out into leatherware and cosmetic design. 4. **Roger** (1695–1749) English architect. His notable works include White Lodge, Richmond. 5. **Talwin** (1865–1911) British designer and metalworker who was a member of the Glasgow School with Charles Rennie **Mackintosh**. 6. **William** (1834–96) British designer, craftsman, writer poet and political activist who set up a co-operative of leading designers and artists of the day, including Burne-Jones, Rossetti and Ford Madox **Brown**. He was instrumental in founding the Arts and Crafts Movement;

Morrison *n* 1. **Herbert Stanley**, Baron Morrison of Lambeth (1888–1965) English Labour politician. He became home secretary (1940–45) in Churchill's World War II cabinet and is credited with having written much of the manifesto that took Labour to power after the war when he became leader of the House of Commons (1945–51). 2. **Jasper** (1959–) British designer of wittily understated furniture and architectural ironmongery. 3. **Jim** (1943–71) American rock singer and songwriter. His band, The Doors became a huge cult after his death (from alcohol and drug abuse). 4. **Toni** [**Chloe Anthony, née Wofford**] (1931–) American novelist and winner of the 1993 Nobel prize for literature whose novels, including *Tar Baby, Beloved, Jazz* and *Paradise*, strongly reflect Afro-American community life.

morrow *n* (*arch, poet*) morning; the following day.

morse *n* a jeweled clasp on a cope.

Morse code *n* a code in which letters are represented by dots and dashes or long and short sounds, and are transmitted by visual or audible signals.

morsel *n* a small quantity of food; a small piece of anything.

mor. sol. *abbr* = *more solito* (*Latin*) "in the usual way."

mort[1] *n* a note or notes sounded on a hunting horn to notify a kill.

mort[2] *n* (*dial*) a great amount or number (of).

mort[3] *n* a salmon in its third year.

mort. *abbr* = mortuary.

mortal *adj* subject to death; causing death, fatal; hostile; very intense. * *n* a human being.—**mortally** *adv*.

mortality *n* (*pl* **mortalities**) state of being mortal; death on a large scale, as from war; number or frequency of deaths in a given period relative to population.

mortality rate *n* the yearly proportion of deaths to population.—*also* **death rate**.

mortar *n* a mixture of cement or lime with sand and water applied wet between stones, bricks etc to bind them together; (*mil*) an artillery piece that fires shells at low velocities and high trajectories; a bowl in which substances are pounded with a pestle.

mortarboard *n* a small square board for holding mortar; a square black college or university cap with a tassel.

mortgage *n* (*law*) a conveyance of property to a creditor as security, usu for the purpose of buying the property; the deed for this transaction; the rights conferred by it. * *vt* to place something under a mortgage; to make over as a security or pledge; to put an advance claim on.

mortgagee *n* one to whom a mortgage is made or given.

mortgagor, mortgager *n* one who grants a mortgage.

MOrthRCSEng *abbr* = Membership in Orthodontics, Royal College of Surgeons of England.

mortician *n* a person who manages funerals.

Mortier *n* **Michel** (1925–) French furniture designer who worked in the interiors department of the Au Bon Marché department store, Brussels.

mortification *n* the act of mortifying; gangrene; (*Christianity*) subjugation of passions and appetite by abstinence; humiliation; vexation, chagrin caused by something that injures one's pride; (*Scots law*) a charitable bequest of lands.

mortify *vti* (**mortifying, mortified**) to subdue by repression or penance; to humiliate or shame; to become gangrenous.—**mortifier** *n*.—**mortifyingly** *adv*.

mortise, mortice *n* a hole in a piece of wood to receive a projection of another piece made to fit.

mortise and tenon *n* (*archit*) a joint fixing together two beams by means of a projecting piece of peg (tenon) from one beam which fits into a slot (mortise) in the other.

mortise lock *n* a lock fitted into a mortise in the frame of a door.

mortmain *n* (*law*) a tenure of land held by a corporation, ecclesiastical or other, which cannot transfer ownership.

Morton *n* 1. **Alistair** (1910–63) British textile designer and manufacturer, son of Sir James Morton, Chairman of Morton Sundour Fabrics. 2. **Ferdinand ("Jelly Roll")** (1885–1941) African American jazz pianist, singer and composer who helped to establish jazz as a genuine art form. One of the founders of New Orleans jazz, his band, the Red Hot Peppers, became one of the most popular jazz bands of the mid–1920s, between the ragtime and swing eras.

mortuary *n* (*pl* **mortuaries**) a place of temporary storage for dead bodies.

mortuary house *n* (*archeo*) a building constructed out of wood or stone, made to resemble a dwelling house but used as a tomb.

mortuary temple *n* (*Egypt*) the temple in which the religious cult of a dead Egyptian king was celebrated.

morula *n* (*pl* **morulas, morulae**) (*biol*) the spherical mass of cells produced by the splitting of the ovum in its primary stage.—**morular** *adj*.

mos. *abbr* = months.

MOS *abbr* = metal oxide semiconductor.

mosaic *n* a surface decoration made by inlaying small pieces (of colored glass, stone, marble, or other substances) to form figures or patterns; a design made in mosaic. * *adj* of or made of mosaic. * *vt* (**mosaicking, mosaicked**) to adorn with or make into mosaic.—**mosaicist** *n*.

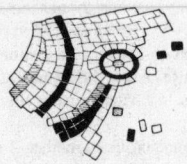

Mosaic, Mosaical *adj* pertaining to Moses, the lawgiver of the Bible, or to the law, institutions, etc, given through him, or to his writings.

Mosbrugger *n* **Caspar** (*b.* 1656) Swiss architect. His notable works include Einsiedeln abbey church.

moschatel *n* (*bot*) a plant with a pale-green flower and a musky smell.

Moscow (**Moskva**) *n* capital city of the Russian Federation.

Moseley *n* **Henry Gwyn-Jeffries** (1887–1915) English physicist. His research in radioactivity using X-rays led to the discovery of what he called the "atomic numbers" of the elements.

Moselle, Mosel *n* a German dry white wine from the Moselle valley.

Moser *n* **Koloman** (Kolo) (1868–1918) Austrian painter and designer who was one of the founders of the Vienna Secession in 1897 and the **Wiener Werkstatte** in 1903.

Moses *n* 1. (*Bible*) forever associated in Hebrew memory and Jewish writing with the Exodus, giving the Law, making the Covenant; he shaped the nation who were to possess Canaan as the land of promise. *See also* **Nebo**. 2. **Grandma** (1860–1961) entirely self-taught American painter. Her works are a romantic and unsophisticated record of country life in her native New York State.

mosey *vi* (*inf*) (*often with* **along, on down**) to go, to saunter, to amble.

Moslem *see* **Muslim**.

Mosley *n* 1. **Sir Nicholas** [3rd Baron Ravensdale] (1923–) English novelist whose novels include *Accident, Impossible Object*, and *Hopeful Monsters*. He also wrote *Rules of the Game* and *Beyond the Pale*, a damning two-volume biography of his father, Sir Oswald Mosley. 2. **Sir Oswald** (1896–1980) English politician who founded the British Union of Fascists in 1932.

mosque *n* a place of worship for Muslims.

mosquito *n* (*pl* **mosquitoes, mosquitos**) a small two-winged bloodsucking insect.

moss *n* (*bot*) a very small green plant that grows in clusters on rocks, moist ground, etc.

mossback *n* (*sl*) a turtle or a crab, lobster, oyster, etc, that is so old that it has moss growing on its back; (*inf*) an out-of-date or provincial person.

Mossbauer *n* **Rudolf Ludwig** (1929–) German physicist who shared the 1961 Nobel prize for physics with American physicist Robert Hofstadter (1915–) for his discovery of the "Mossbauer effect," involving gamma radiation in crystals.

Mössbauer spectroscopy *n* an analytical technique that examines the iron compounds in pottery, measuring the gamma radiation absorbed by the nuclei of the particles.

mosso *n* (*mus*) (*Italian*) "moved," so *piu mosso* means "more moved," i.e., quicker.

mosstrooper *n* one of a gang of marauders that ravaged the borderland of England and Scotland in the mid-17th century.

mossy *adj* (**mossier, mossiest**) overgrown with, or like, moss.—**mossiness** *n*.

most *adj* (*compar* **more**) greatest in number; greatest in amount or degree; in the greatest number of instances (—*also superl* of **many, much**). * *adv* in or to the greatest degree or extent. * *n* the greatest amount or degree; (*with pl*) the greatest number (of).

-most *adj suffix* forming a superlative, e.g., *hindmost*.

Mostar *n* a city in Bosnia-Herzegovina.

mostly *adv* for the most part; mainly, usually.

mot. *abbr* = motor.

MOT *abbr* = Ministry of Transport.

mot juste *n* (*pl* **mots justes**) exactly the right word.

mote[1] *n* a very small particle, a speck (of dust); a mite.

mote[2] *vi* (*arch*) might, must.

motel *n* a hotel for motorists with adjacent parking.

motet *n* (*mus*) a musical setting of sacred words for solo voices or choir, with or without accompaniment. The first motets were composed in the 13th century.

moth *n* a four-winged chiefly night-flying insect related to the butterfly.

mothball *n* a small ball of camphor or naphthalene used to protect stored clothes from moths.

moth-eaten *adj* eaten into by moths; dilapidated; outmoded.

mother *n* a female who has given birth to offspring; an origin or source. * *adj* of or like a mother; native. * *vt* to be the mother of or a mother to.

motherboard *n* (*comput*) the main printed circuit board in a computer, containing the main processor chips, the display controllers, sound chips, etc.

motherhood *n* the state of being a mother; the qualities of feelings of being a mother; mothers collectively.

mother-in-law *n* (*pl* mothers-in-law) the mother of one's spouse.

motherland *n* a person's native land or the country of a person's forebears.

mother liquor *n* (*chem*) the solution that remains after a substance has crystallized out of that solution.

motherly *adj* of, proper to a mother; like a mother.—**motherliness** *n*.

mother-of-pearl *n* the iridescent lining of the shell of the pearl oyster.

Motherwell *n* Robert (1915–91) American painter whose work is mainly in the abstract expressionist tradition. Notable works include the series *Elegies to the Spanish Republic* begun in 1949.

motif (motive) *n* a repeated theme, subject, or figure, e.g., in a design; (*mus*) a small group of notes which create a melody or rhythm, e.g., the first four notes of Beethoven's 5th symphony form a motif.

motile *adj* (*zool, bot*) the ability to move without outside aid; exhibiting movement. * *n* (*psychol*) a person whose perception of the material world comprises, to a very strong degree, the imagery of movement, esp his own.—**motility** *n*.

motion *n* activity, movement; a formal suggestion made in a meeting, law court, or legislative assembly; evacuation of the bowels; (*mus*) the upward or downward progress of a melody. * *vti* to signal or direct by a gesture.

motionless *adj* not moving, still.—**motionlessness** *n*.

motion picture *n* a film, movie.

motion sickness *n* symptoms of vomiting, nausea, and headache caused by travel via car, boat or airplane.—*also* **travel sickness**.

motivate *vt* to supply a motive to; to instigate.—**motivator** *n*.

motivation *n* a motivating or being motivated; incentive; (*psychol*) the mental function or instinct that produces, sustains and regulates behavior in humans and animals.—**motivational** *adj*.

motive *n* something (as a need or desire) that causes a person to act; a motif in music. * *adj* moving to action; of or relating to motion.—**motiveless** *adj*.—**motivity** *n*.

motley *adj* multicolored; composed of diverse elements.

motmot *n* any of various tropical American blue and brownish-green, long-tailed birds similar to the jay, of the same family as the kingfisher.

moto *n* (*mus*) (*Italian*) "motion," so *con moto* means "with motion" or quickly.

motor *n* anything that produces motion; a machine for converting electrical energy into mechanical energy; a motor car. * *adj* producing motion; of or powered by a motor; of, by or for motor vehicles; of or involving muscular movements. * *vi* to travel by car.

motorbike *n* a motorcycle.

motorboat *n* a boat propelled by an engine or motor.

motorbus *n* (*pl* motorbuses, motorbusses) a bus driven by a motor engine.

motorcade *n* a procession of motor vehicles.

motorcar *n* a usu four-wheeled vehicle powered by an internal combustion engine.—*also* **automobile**.

motorcycle *n* a two-wheeled motor vehicle.—**motorcyclist** *n*.

motorist *n* a person who drives a car.

motorize *vt* to equip with a motor; to equip with motor vehicles.—**motorization** *n*.

motorman *n* (*pl* motormen) the driver of a tram or an underground train, or other vehicle powered by electricity; a person who operates a motor.

motor nerve *n* (*physiology*) a nerve, containing motor neurone fibers, that carries electrical impulses outwards from the central nervous system to a muscle or gland to bring about a response there.

motor neuron *n* (*physiology*) one of the units or fibers of a motor nerve. An upper motor neuron is contained within the central nervous system, a lower motor neuron has its cell body in the spinal cord or brain stem.

motor-neurone disease *n* (*med*) a disease that most commonly occurs in middle age and is a degenerative condition affecting elements of the central nervous system causing increasing paralysis.

motor pool *n* a group of motor vehicles available for use by employees of a government agency, large corporation, etc.

motor scooter *n* a small-wheeled motorcycle with an enclosed engine.

motorway *n* (*Brit*) a road with controlled access for fast-moving traffic.—*also* **freeway**.

MOTT *abbr* = Men of the Trees.

Motte *n* Joseph-Andre (1925–) French furniture designer who worked for the Au Bon Marché store in Paris.

mottle *vt* to mark with colored blotches or spots, to variegate. * *n* a pattern of colored blotches of spots, as on marble; one of the colored blotches in such a pattern.

mottled *adj* marked with blotches of various colors.

motto *n* (*pl* mottoes, mottos) a short saying adopted as a maxim or ideal; a slogan on a heraldic crest; a quotation prefixed to a book, etc; verses, etc, in a Christmas cracker.

motto theme *n* (*mus*) a short theme that recurs during the course of a composition.

MOU *abbr* = memorandum of understanding.

mouflon, moufflon *n* (*pl* mouflons, mouflon, moufflons, moufflon) a wild large-horned sheep with a short fleece, found in Corsica and Sardinia.

Mougin *n* Joseph (1876–1961) and **Pierre** (1879–1955) French ceramicists who set up a pottery with their sculptor friend Lemarquier, and received notable commissions.

mouillé *adj* softened in sound, palatalized, e.g., *gl* in *seraglio*.

moujik *see* **muzhik**.

mould[1] *n* (*archeo*) a structure made from pottery, stone, clay or metal, containing some form of hollowed-out shape into which molten metal was poured.

mould[2] *see* mold[1], mold[2].

moulder *see* **molder**.

moulding *n* (*archit*) a molded surface given to projecting parts of a building either as ornamental or protective features. *See* **molding**.

mouldy *see* **moldy**.

moulin *n* (*geol*) a deep crack in a glacier through which water and debris drain.

Moulmein *n* a city in the Union of Myanmar.

moult *see* **molt**.

mound *n* an artificial bank of earth or stones; a heap or bank of earth. * *vt* to form into a mound.

Moundou *n* a city in Chad.

mount[1] *n* a high hill.

mount[2] *vi* to increase. * *vt* to climb, ascend; to get up on (a horse, platform, etc); to provide with horses; (*a jewel*) to fix on a support; (*a picture*) to frame. * *n* a horse for riding; (*for a picture*) a backing.—**mountable** *adj*.—**mounter** *n*.

mountain *n* a hill more than 2000 feet (600 meters) in height; a vast number or quantity. * *adj* of or in mountains.

mountain ash *n* any of various trees of the rose family with red or orange fruits.

mountain dew *n* (*sl*) illegally distilled liquor, moonshine.

mountaineer *n* one who climbs mountains.

mountaineering *n* the technique of climbing mountains.

mountain goat *n* any wild goat living in mountainous regions.

mountain lion *n* a cougar.

mountainous *adj* having many mountains; very high; huge.—**mountainously** *adv*.—**mountainousness** *n*.

mountain range *n* a group of mountains, connected geographically or geologically.

Mountain Standard Time *n* the 7th time zone west of Greenwich that includes the Rocky Mountain states of the US.

Mountbatten *n* Louis [Francis Victor Albert Nicholas], [1st Earl Mountbatten of Burma] (1900–79) British naval commander and statesman. As viceroy of India (1947), he oversaw the transfer of power to the independent governments of India and Pakistan. Murdered by an IRA bomb while sailing off Ireland.

Mount Carmel *n* a hill in Palestine whose caves have yielded stone tools spanning the whole of the Paleolithic period.

mountebank *n* (*formerly*) an itinerant quack doctor; a boastful pretender, a charlatan, an impostor.

mounted *adj* seated on horseback or on a bicycle, etc; serving on horseback, as a policeman; placed on a suitable support.

Mount of Olives *see* Olives, Mount of.

Mourgue *n* 1. Olivier (1939–) French designer, the brother of Pascal **Mourgue**, whose 1965 *Djinn Chaise Longue*, featured in the 1968 movie *2001: A Space Odyssey*. 2. **Pascal** (1943–) French interior designer who created furniture ranges for Mobilier International and **Knoll**.

mourn *vti* (*someone dead*) to grieve for; (*something regrettable*) to feel or express sorrow for.—**mourner** *n*.

mournful *adj* expressing grief or sorrow; causing sorrow.—**mournfully** *adv*.—**mournfulness** *n*.

mourning *adj* grieving. * *n* the expression of grief; dark clothes worn by mourners.

MOUS *abbr* = multiple occurrence of unexplained symptoms.

mousaka *see* **moussaka**.

mouse *n* (*pl* mice) a small rodent with a pointed snout, long body and slender tail; a timid person; (*comput*) a hand-held device used to position the cursor and control software on a computer screen.

MOUSE *abbr* = minimum orbital unmanned satellite of the earth.

mouser *n* an animal that is skilled at catching mice, esp a cat.

moussaka, mousaka *n* a Greek dish comprising aubergines, minced lamb and tomatoes topped with a cheese or white sauce.

mousse *n* a chilled dessert made of fruit, eggs, and whipped cream; a similar savory dish made with meat or fish; a foamy substance applied to the hair to help it keep its style.

mousseline *n* a sheer fabric resembling muslin, made of rayon or silk; mousseline sauce.

mousseline sauce *n* a white sauce to which whipped cream or the white of an egg has been added.

Moussorgsky, Modest *see* **Mussorgsky, Modest**.

moustache *see* **mustache**.

Mousterian *adj* (*archeo*) types of flint implements associated with Neanderthal peoples, typically flakes worked to produce triangular points, handaxes and scrapers.

mousy, mousey *adj* (**mousier, mousiest**) mouse-like; gray-brown in color; quiet, stealthy; timid, retiring.—**mousily** *adv*.—**mousiness** *n*.

mouth *n* (*pl* **mouths**) the opening that forms the beginning of the alimentary canal and through which food enters the digestive process; the opening through which sound is uttered or words spoken; the lips; opening, entrance, as of a bottle, etc. * *vt* to say, esp insincerely; to form words with the mouth without uttering sound. * *vi* to utter pompously; to grimace.—**mouther** *n*.

mouthful *n* (*pl* **mouthfuls**) as much (food) as fills the mouth; a word or phrase that is difficult to say correctly; (*sl*) a pertinent remark.

mouth organ *n* (*mus*) a harmonica.

mouthpiece *n* (*mus*) the part of a musical instrument placed in the mouth; a person, periodical, etc that expresses the views of others.

mouth-to-mouth resuscitation *n* a method of artificial respiration in which air is forced into the victim's lungs by blowing into the mouth.

mouthwash *n* a flavored, often antiseptic liquid for rinsing the mouth.

mouthwatering *adj* appetizing; tasty.

mouton *n* sheepskin shorn and processed to resemble beaver or seal.

mov. *abbr* = (*mus*) *movimento* (*Italian*) "motion."

movable, moveable *adj* that may be moved. * *npl* personal property.—**movably** *adv*.—**movability** *n*.

movable feast *n* a church festival that varies in date from year to year, esp Easter.

move *vt* (**moving, moved**) to shift or change place; to set in motion; to rouse the emotions; to put (a motion) formally. * *vi* to go from one place to another; to walk, to carry oneself; to change place; to evacuate the bowels; to propose a motion as in a meeting; to change residence; (*chess, draughts, etc*) to change the position of a piece on the board. * *n* the act of moving; a movement, esp in board games; one's turn to move; a premeditated action.

Move *abbr* = Men over Violence (counselling, etc, for wife-beaters).

movement *n* act of moving; the moving part of a machine, esp a clock; the policy and activities of a group; a trend, e.g., in prices; (*mus*) a self-contained section of a larger instrumental composition, such as a symphony; tempo.

mover *n* one who moves; (*inf*) a driving force, an innovator; a proposer of a motion.

movie *n* a cinema film, motion picture; (*pl*) the showing of a motion picture; the motion-picture medium or industry.

moving *adj* arousing the emotions; changing position; causing motion.—**movingly** *adv*.

moving cluster *n* (*astron*) a form of open cluster in which the stars are close enough to earth for their proper motion to be determined.

mow *vti* (**mowing, mowed**, *pp* **mowed** *or* **mown**) (*grass, etc*) to cut with a sickle or lawn mower; (*with* **down**) to cause to fall like cut grass.—**mower** *n*.

MOW *abbr* = Movement for the Ordination of Women.

moxa *n* down obtained from plants, used in Oriental medicine as a counterirritant or for cauterizing by burning on the skin; any plant that yields such down.

moxie *n* (*sl*) energy; courage; expertise.

Mozambique *n* a republic located in southeast Africa.

Mozart *n* **Wolfgang Amadeus** (1756–91) Austrian composer, keyboard player, violinist, violist and conductor. An infant prodigy, he composed his first pieces for harpsichord when he was five and later helped to establish the classical style of composition. One of the most lyrical of all composers, his principal compositions include: the operas, *Idomeneo, The Marriage of Figaro, Don Giovanni, Cosi Fan Tutte* and *The Magic Flute;* 41 symphonies; 27 piano concertos; 23 string quartets; 17 piano sonatas; and 18 Masses. He never finished his last work *The Requiem.* The theory that he was poisoned by his rival, **Salieri**, has never been proved.

Mozer *n* **Jordan** (1959–) American interior and furniture designer, responsible for several restaurants in Chicago.

mozzarella *n* a moist curd cheese noted for its elasticity when melted.

mp *abbr* = (*mus*) *mezzo piano* (*Italian*) "moderately quiet";

m.p., mp *abbr* = (*chem*) melting point.

MP *abbr* = Master of Painting; Member of Parliament, *or* of Police; Methodist Protestant; Metropolitan/Military Police; Mounted Police; Municipal Police.

M/P *abbr* = mail payment.

MPA *abbr* = Major Projects Association; Master of Public Administration; Modern Poetry Association; Mortar Producers Association.

MPAA *abbr* = Motion Picture Association of America.

MPAGB *abbr* = Modern Pentathlon Association of Great Britain.

MPAS *abbr* = Mobile Projects Association Scotland.

MPB *abbr* = male pattern baldness.

MPC *abbr* = Member of Parliament, (*Canada*); Metropolitan Police Commissioner.

MPd *abbr* = Master of Pedagogy.

MPD *abbr* = maximum permissible dose.

MPE *abbr* = Master of Physical Education; maximum permissible exposure (to radiation); maximum possible error.

mpg *abbr* = miles per gallon.

mph or **m.p.h.** *abbr* = miles per hour.

MPh *abbr* = Master of Philosophy.

MPH *abbr* = Master of Public Health.

MPharm *abbr* = Master of Pharmacy.

MPhil *abbr* = Master of Philosophy.

MPhil(Eng) *abbr* = Master of Philosophy in Engineering.

mphps *abbr* = miles per hour per second.

MPhys *abbr* = Master of Physics.

MPI *abbr* = Max Planck Institute; maximum permissible intake.

MPL *abbr* = Master of Patent Law; maximum permissible level.

mpm *abbr* = meters per minute.

MPP *abbr* = Member of the Provincial Parliament.

MPPS *abbr* = Master of Public Policy Studies.

MPRI *abbr* = Member of the Plastics and Rubber Institute.

MProfBTM *abbr* = Member of Professional Business and Technical Management.

mps *abbr* = meters per second.

MPS *abbr* = Member of the Pharmaceutical Society; Member of the Philological Society.

Mpsych, MPsychol *abbr* = Master of Psychology.

MPsychMed *abbr* = Master of Psychological Medicine.

mpu *abbr* = microprocessor unit.

MPU *abbr* = Medical Practitioners Union.

MPV *abbr* = multipurpose vehicle.

mr. *abbr* = millier.

Mr *abbr* = (*pl* **Messrs**) (*title*) Mister (the title used before a name if the person is male, formerly Master).

MR *abbr* = Master of the Rolls; magnetic resonance; map reference; mental retardation; metabolic rate; mill run; mine run; motivational research.

MRA *abbr* = moral rearmament.

MRad MRad(D) *abbr* = Master of Radiology (Radiodiagnosis) or (Radiotherapy).

MRAeS *abbr* = Member of the Royal Aeronautical Society.

MRAF *abbr* = Marshal of the Royal Air Force.

MRAS *abbr* = Member of the Royal Astronomical Society; Member of the Royal Asiatic Society.

MRBM *abbr* = medium-range ballistic missile.

MRC *abbr* = Medical Research Council; Medical Reserve Corps.

MRCA *abbr* = multirole combat aircraft.

MRCGP *abbr* = Member of the Royal College of General Practitioners.

MRCOG *abbr* = Member of the Royal College of Obstetricians and Gynaecologists.

MRCP *abbr* = Member of the Royal College of Physicians.

MRCPath *abbr* = Member of the Royal College of Pathologists.

MRCPIrel *abbr* = Member of the Royal College of Physicians of Ireland.

MRCPsych *abbr* = Member of the Royal College of Psychiatrists.

MRCP(UK) *abbr* = Member of the Royal College of Physicians of the United Kingdom.

MRCSEng *abbr* = Member of the Royal College of Surgeons of England.

MRCVS *abbr* = Member of the Royal College of Veterinary Surgeons.

MRD *abbr* = minimal residual disease.

MRE *abbr* = Master of Religious Education; Microbiological Research Establishment; meals ready to eat.

MREHIS *abbr* = Member of the Royal Environmental Health Institute of Scotland.

MRG *abbr* = Minority Rights Group.

MRGS *abbr* = Member of the Royal Geographical Society.

MRI *abbr* = magnetic resonance imaging.

MRICS *abbr* = Member of the Royal Institution of Chartered Surveyors.

MRIN *abbr* = Member of the Royal Institute of Navigation.

MRINA *abbr* = Member of the Royal Institution of Naval Architects.

MRIPHH *abbr* = Member of the Royal Institute of Public Health and Hygiene.

MRM *abbr* = mechanically removed meat.

mRNA *abbr* = messenger ribonucleic acid.

MRO *abbr* = Member of the Register of Osteopaths.

mrp *abbr* = manufacturer's recommended price.

MRPharms *abbr* = Member of the Royal Pharmaceutical Society of Great Britain.

mrrp *abbr* = manufacturer's recommended retail price.

Mrs *abbr* = (*pl* **Mrs** *or* **Mesdames**) (*title*) Mistress, the title used before a married woman's name. The title Ms can also be used but it does not denote marital status.

MRSC *abbr* = Member of the Royal Society of Chemistry.

MRSH *abbr* = Member of the Royal Society of Health.

MRSM *abbr* = Member of the Royal Society of Medicine.

MRTPI *abbr* = Member of the Royal Town Planning Institute.

MRUA *abbr* = Mobile Radio Users Association.

MRV *abbr* = multiple re-entry vehicle.

ms *abbr* = millisecond.

ms. *abbr* = (*org. chem*) meso- ; manuscript.

m/s *abbr* = meters per second.

Ms *abbr* = (*title*) the title used before a woman's name, which can be used for either married or single women. It was introduced in the 1970s as an equivalent to Mr.

MS *abbr* = Mammal Society; Manpower Society; Master of Surgery; Master of Science; Media Society; Movement for Survival; Multiple Sclerosis Society of Great Britain and Northern Ireland; (*also* **m.s.**) (*mus*) *mano sinistra* (*Italian*) "left hand"; manuscript (*pl* **MSS**); mass spectrometry; mean square; *memoriae sacrum* (*Latin*) "sacred to the memory"; multiple sclerosis.

M/S *abbr* = (*com*) months after sight; (*also* **M.S.**) motor ship.

MSA *abbr* = Marine Safety Agency; Master of Agricultural Science; Master of Science and Arts, *or* of Scientific Agriculture; Metropolitan Statistical Area; Modern Studies Association; Motor Schools Association of Great Britain; motorway service area.

MSAgr. *abbr* = Master of Scientific Agriculture.

M

MSAPP *abbr* = Member of the Society of Advanced Psychotherapy Practitioners.
MSArch *abbr* = Master of Science in Architecture.
MSB *abbr* = most significant bit.
MSBA *abbr* = Master of Science in Business Administration.
MSBP *abbr* = Member of the Society of Business Practitioners.
MSBT *abbr* = Member of the Society of Business Teachers.
MSBTH *abbr* = Member of the Society of Health and Beauty Therapists.
MSBus *abbr* = Master of Science in Business.
msc *abbr* = moved, seconded and carried.
MSc *abbr* = Master of Science.
MSC *abbr* = Manpower Services Commission.
MScAg *abbr* = Master of Science in Agriculture.
MScChemE *abbr* = Master of Science in Chemical Engineering.
MSCD *abbr* = Master of Dental Science.
MSCE *abbr* = Master of Science in Civil Engineering.
MSc(Econ) *abbr* = Master of Science in Economics.
MSc(Ed) *abbr* = Master of Science in Education.
MSc(Eng) *abbr* = Master of Science in Engineering.
MSCI Index *abbr* = Morgan Stanley Capital International World Index.
MScMed *abbr* = Master of Medical Science.**MSCT** *abbr* =
MSc(Mgt) *abbr* = Master of Science in Management.
Member of the Society of Cardiological Technicians.
MScTech. *abbr* (*Latin*) = *Magister Scientiae Technicae* "Master of Technical Science."
MSD. *abbr* = Master of Scientific Didactics.
MS-DOS *n* (*comput*) the disk operating system of Microsoft™.
MSE *abbr* = Member of the Society of Engineers.
MSEcon *abbr* = Master in Faculty of Economic and Social Studies.
MSEL *abbr* = Materials Science and Engineering Library
MSF *abbr* = Manufacturing, Science and Finance Union; Master of Science in Forestry; Médécins sans Frontières; Multiple Shops Federation; medium standard frequency.
MSG *abbr* = monosodium glutamate.
Msgr, Msgr. *abbr* = Monseigneur; Monsignor.
MSHA *abbr* = Mine Safety and Health Administration
MSHR *abbr* = Missionary Sisters of the Holy Rosary.
MSI *abbr* = Marie Stopes International; medium-scale integration.
MSIAD *abbr* = Member of the Society of Industrial Artists and Designers.
MSIE *abbr* = Master of Science in Industrial Engineering.
MS in CE *abbr* = Master of Science in Civil Engineering.
MS in ChE *abbr* = Master of Science in Chemical Engineering.
MS in EE *abbr* = Master of Science in Electrical Engineering.
MS in ME *abbr* = Master of Science in Mechanical Engineering.
m.s.l., MSL *abbr* = mean sea level.
MSM *abbr* = Meritorious Service Medal.
MSN *abbr* = Master of Science in Nursing.
MSocSc *abbr* = Master of Social Science.
m.-sopr. *abbr* = mezzo-soprano.
MSPB *abbr* = Merit Systems Protection Board
MSRG *abbr* = Mediaeval Settlement Research Group; Moated Site Research Group.
MSS *abbr* = Master of Social Science; mass storage system.
MSS,mss. *abbr* = manuscripts.
MSSc *abbr* = Master of Social Science; Master of Surgical Science.
MSSCH *abbr* = Member of the School of Surgical Chiropody.
MSST *abbr* = Member of the Society of Surveying Technicians.
MSt *abbr* = Master of Studies.
MST *abbr* = Mountain Standard Time; mean survival time.
MSTA *abbr* = Member of the Swimming Teachers' Association.
Ms-Th *abbr* (*chem*) = mesothorium.
MSU *abbr* = Migrant Support Unit; mid-stream specimen of urine.
msv *abbr* = millisievert.
MSW *abbr* = Master in Social Work; Medical Social Worker; magnetic surface wave.
MSY *abbr* = maximum sustainable yield.
mt *abbr* = megaton; metric ton; mountain.
Mt *abbr* = meitnerium (chemical element).
Mt. or mt. *abbr* = mount; mountain.
MT *abbr* = Mechanical Transport; Middle Temple; machine translation; mean time; metric ton; Montana.
MTA *abbr* = Master Tanners Association; Mica Trades Association.
MTB *abbr* = motor torpedo-boat.
MTBF *abbr* (*comput*) = Mean Time Between Failures. A measure of the reliability of a computer or of the reliability of a component used in the manufacture of the computer.
MTD *abbr* = Master of Transport Design; maximum tolerated dose; moving target detector.
MTech *abbr* = Master of Technology.
MTFCI *abbr* = Model T Ford Club International.
mtg. *abbr* = meeting; mortgage.
mtgd. *abbr* = mortgaged.
mtge. *abbr* = mortgage.
mth. *abbr* = month.
MTh, MTheol *abbr* = Master of Theology.
MTI *abbr* = moving target indicator.
mtl. *abbr* = material.

MTM *abbr* = methods time measurement.
mtn. *abbr* = mountain.
MTP *abbr* = Master of Town and Country Planning.
MTPI *abbr* = Master of Town Planning.
Mt. Rev. *abbr* = Most Reverend.
MTropMed *abbr* = Master of Tropical Medicine.
mts. *abbr* = mountains.
MTTR *abbr* = mean time to repair.
M-type asteroid *n* (*astron*) an asteroid with a spectrum containing metallic lines.
mu *n* the 12th letter of the Greek alphabet (M, μ).
Mu *abbr* = (*chem*) murium.
MU *abbr* = Mothers' Union; Musicians' Union.
MUA *abbr* = Machinery Users Association; Mail Users Association.
much *adj* (*compar* more, *superl* most) plenty. * *adv* considerably; to a great extent.
Mucha *n* **Alfons** (1860–1939) Czech painter, designer, and graphic artist famous for his Art Nouveau posters for the actress Sarah Bernhardt in the 1890s in Paris.
muchness *n* (arch) bulk, greatness; **much of a muchness** just about the same.
mucilage *n* a adhesive prepared for use; a sticky substance obtained from some plants.—**mucilaginous** *adj*.
muck *n* moist manure; black earth with decaying matter; mud, dirt, filth. * *vt* to spread manure; to make dirty; (*with* out) to clear of muck. * *vi* to move or load muck; (*with* about, around) to engage in useless activity.
mucker *n* (*mining*) a person who clears broken rocks or other waste; (*Brit sl*) a friend; (*US sl*) a coarse person.
muckrake *vi* to investigate corruption and scandal, esp in government.— **muckraker** *n*.
muckworm *n* a grub or larva bred in manure or mud; (*inf*) a skinflint, a hoarder.
mucky *adj* (**muckier, muckiest**) of or like muck; muddy; filthy.—**muckily** *adv*.— **muckiness** *n*.
mucosa *n* another term for mucous membrane.
mucous *adj* slimy, sticky; like mucus. —**mucosity.**
mucous membrane *n* (*anat*) a moist membrane, lubricated with mucous, that is found as a layer lining cavities in the body that connect with the exterior, e.g., gut, respiratory tracts, etc.
mucus *n* a slimy substance that may contain enzymes, secreted by mucous membranes as a lubricant.
mud *n* soft, wet earth. * *vt* (**muds, mudding, mudded**) to muddy, to throw mud at; to vilify.
mud bath *n* a bath of heated mud for medicinal purposes; a mucky occasion.
mud brick *see* **adobe.**
mud cat *n* any of various catfishes that live in muddy water.
muddle *vt* to confuse; to mix up. * confusion, mess.
muddleheaded *adj* silly; confused; absent-minded. —**muddleheadedness** *n*.
muddy *adj* (**muddier, muddiest**) like or covered with mud; not bright or clear; confused. * *vti* (**muddying, muddied**) to make or become dirty or unclear. — **muddily** *adv*. —**muddiness** *n*.
mud flat *n* an area of muddy land exposed at low tide.
mudguard *n* a screen on a wheel to catch mud splashes.
mudlark *n* (*formerly*) a person who worked or dabbled in mud, esp a scavenger on the banks of tidal rivers; (*arch sl*) a mischievous, poorly dressed child who frequented city streets. (*Austral sl*) a horse that performs well on wet, muddy ground.
mudslinger *n* a person who makes malicious accusations against another, esp during a political campaign.— **mudslinging** *n*.
muesli *n* a mixture of rolled oats, dried fruit, nuts, etc eaten with milk.
muezzin *n* a Muslim official who proclaims from the minaret of a mosque the hour of prayer, and summons the faithful to worship.
MUF *abbr* = maximum usable frequency.
muff[1] *n* a warm, soft, fur coveer for warming the hands.
muff[2] *n* a bungling performance; failure to hold a ball when trying to catch it. * *vti* to bungle.
muffin *n* a baked yeast roll.
muffle *vt* to wrap up for warmth or to hide; (*sound*) to deaden by wrapping up.
muffled drum *n* (*mus*) a drum with a piece of cloth or toweling draped over the vibrating surfaces. It produces a somber tone when struck, and is usu associated with funeral music.
muffler *n* a long scarf; any means of deadening sound; a device for reducing the noise of a vehicle exhaust. —also **silencer.**
mufti *n* civilian dress worn by a naval or military officer when off duty.
Mufti *n* (*pl* **Muftis**) an official expounder or Muslim law.
MUFTI *abbr* = minimum use of force tactical intervention.
Mufulira *n* a city in Zambia.
mug *n* a cylindrical drinking cup, usu of metal or earthenware; its contents; (*sl*) the face; (*sl*) a fool. * (**mugging, mugged**) *vt* to assault, usu with intent to rob.

Mugabe *n* Robert [**Gabriel**] (1924–) Zimbabwean statesman. He was imprisoned for ten years (1964–74) for his opposition to white rule in Rhodesia (as Zimbabwe then was), being released under Ian Smith's amnesty of 1974. He became leader of the Zimbabwe African National Union and became prime minister (1980–) following the end of white minority rule. A Roman Catholic and a Marxist, Mugabe merged his ruling party with the Zimbabwe African People's Union in 1988 to form a one-party state.

mugger[1] *n* a person who assaults with intent to rob.

mugger[2], **muggar, muggur** *n* a broad-snouted Asian crocodile that lives in marshes and pools.

muggins *n* an idiot. * *pron* oneself (used deprecatingly).

muggy *adj* (**muggier, muggiest**) (*weather*) warm, damp and close. — **mugginess** *n*.

mugwump *n* an independent in politics; (*formerly*) a chief, a bigwig.

Muir *n* 1. **Edwin** (1887–1959) Scottish poet, translator, and critic, who, with his wife, Willa, produced what are still the standard English translations of Kafka's novels in the 1930s. His volumes of elegiac poetry include *The Labyrinth* and *One Foot in Eden*. 2. **John** (1838–1914) Scottish-born American environmentalist. Regarded as one of the main founders of environmentalism, his vigorous campaign for a national park in California led to the establishment of Yosemite National Park in 1890. His books include *My First Summer in the Sierra* (1911).

Mujibur Rahman *n* Sheik (1920–75) Bangladeshi politician. He became the first prime minister of Bangladesh (1972–75) following the bloody civil war and secession from Pakistan in 1972, and was subsequently elected president (1975). He assumed dictatorial powers and was assassinated during a military coup.

mujik *see* **muzhik**.

mulatto *n* (*pl* **mulattos, mulattoes**) a person with one black parent and one white parent.

mulberry *n* (*pl* **mulberries**) a tree on whose leaves silkworms feed; its berry.

mulch *n* loose, organic, strawy dung providing a protective covering around the roots of plants. * *vt* to spread mulch.

mulct *vt* to punish with a fine; to acquire money, etc, by fraud or deception; * *n* a fine, esp for some misdemeanor.

Muldoon *n* Sir **Robert** [**David**] (1921–92) New Zealand statesman. He became National Party prime minister (1975–84), and held several important international posts, notably with the International Monetary Fund and the World Bank.

mule[1] *n* the offspring of a male donkey and a female horse; a machine for spinning cotton; an obstinate person.

mule[2] *n* a slipper without a heel.

mule[3] *n* (*sl*) someone used to smuggle drugs.

mule deer *n* a long-eared deer native to northwestern America.

muleskinner, muleteer *n* a person who drives mules.

muleteer *n* a mule driver.

muliebrity *n* (*formal*) womanhood; the qualities of womanhood.

mulish *adj* like a mule; stubborn, intractable, wilful. —**mulishly** *adv*. —**mulishness** *n*.

mull[1] *n* (*Brit*) a Scottish term for a headland.

mull[2] *n* the humus produced by decomposition of grass or forest litter.

mull[3] *vti* (*inf*) to ponder (over).

mull[4] *vt* (*wine, etc*) to heat, sweeten and spice. —**mulled** *adj*.

mullah, mulla (*formerly*) a Muslim theologian or teacher; a Muslim title of respect.

muller *n* a flat-bottomed pestle for grinding (drugs, paints) on a slab.

Müller *n* 1. **Albin** (1871–1941) German architect who became the leading architect at the Darmstadt artists' colony of the Grand Duke Louis IV of Hesse-Darmstadt. 2. **Karl** (1888–1972) German silversmith who taught at Halle, producing more commercial pieces than the **Bauhaus**.

Müller-Munk *n* Peter (1904–67) German metalworker who established the first degree course in industrial design to be offered in America.

mullet *n* (*pl* **mullets, mullet**) any of various types of food fish.

mulligatawny *n* a curry-flavored meat soup.

Mulliken, Robert Sanderson (1896–1986) American chemist and physicist. He was awarded the 1986 Nobel prize for chemistry for his work on molecular structure and on chemical bonding.

mullion *n* (*archit*) a vertical dividing bar or division between the panes of a window or the panels of a screen, etc, esp in a Gothic arch; (*geol*) a projecting ridge on a rock face. * *vt* to provide with or divide by mullions.

mullock *n* (*Austral*) a rock containing no gold or from which gold has been extracted, rubbish; (*dial*) disorder.

mult-, multi. *prefix* = much, many.

multangular, multiangular *adj* many-angled.

multeity *n* multiplicity.

multi *abbrev* = many.

multiband camera *n* a remote sensing camera used in aerial photography to distinguish objects with different reflective abilities from each other.

multicolored, multicoloured *adj* many-colored.

multicultural *adj* of, relating to, or comprising many different cultures or ethnic groups.—**multiculturally** *adv*.

multidimensional *adj* of or involving more than three dimensions.— **multidimensionality** *n*.— **multidimensionally** *adv*.

multidisciplinary *adj* of or involving many different fields of study.

multifaceted *adj* (*gem*) having many facets; (*person*) having many abilities.

multifarious *adj* multiform; diversified, of great variety; manifold. — **multifariously** *adv*. —**multifariousness** *n*.

multifid, multifidous *adj* (*bot*) cleft into many parts or lobe-like elements.

multifoil *n* (*archit*) an ornament with over five leaf-like divisions. —*also adj*.

multiform *adj* having many shapes; of many kinds. —**multiformity** *n*.

multilateral *adj* having many sides; with several nations or participans. —**multilaterally** *adv*.

multilateral netting *n* a financial arrangement under which two or more associated companies may offset their receipts and payments with each other and thus arrive at a single net intercompany payment or receipt balance.

multilingual *adj* able to speak more than two languages. —**multilingually** *adv*.

multimedia *npl* (*comput*) the process of combining computer data, sound and video images to create an environment similar to television.

multimillionaire *n* a person with two or more millions of money.

multinational *n* a business operating in several countries. —*also adj*.

multinational enterprise *n* a corporation that has production centers in more than one country.

multinomial *n* (*math*) an expression that consists of the sum of several terms, a polynomial. —*also adj*.

multipara *n* (*pl* **multiparas, multiparae**) a woman who has given birth at least once; one who is about to give birth for a second or subsequent time.— **multiparous** *adj*.

multiplane *n* an airplane with two or more pairs of wings.

multiple *adj* of many parts; manifold; various; complex. * (*math*) a number exactly divisible by another.

multiple births *n* twins, triplets, quadruplets, quintuplets, and sextuplets born to one mother.

multiple-choice *adj* (*question*) offering several different solutions from which the correct one must be chosen.

multiple exchange rate *n* an exchange rate that has more than one value, depending on what the relevant currency is to be used for.

multiple fruit *n* a single fruit formed from several flowers, as the pineapple.

multiple sclerosis *n* (*med*) a disease of the brain and spinal cord that affects the myelin sheaths of nerves and disrupts their function, leading to loss of muscular coordination, etc.

multiple star *n* (*astron*) a star system that contains three or more stars revolving around a common center of gravity and held in position by their gravitational forces.

multiple-unit pricing a pricing system under which more than one unit of a product is sold at a price that is lower than the total price of the individual units.

multiplex *adj* (*radio, telecommunications*) the use of a single channel of communication to transmit more than one signal; (*map-making*) the use of three or more cameras so that the end product appears to be rendered in three dimensions; manifold, multiple. * *vt* to transmit messages or send signals in a multiplex system. * *vt* to send (several signals) simultaneously on one frequency.

multiplexing *n* (*comput*) a technique that is used in local area networks to allow several signals to pass along the cables at one time so that several computers can access the network simultaneously.

multipliable, multiplicable *adj* able to be multiplied.

multiplicand *n* a number to be multiplied by another.

multiplicate *adj* (*rare*) consisting of many.

multiplication *n* the act of multiplying; the process of repeatedly adding a quantity to itself a certain number of times, or any other process which has the same result. —**multiplicational** *adj*.

multiplication table *n* (*math*) a list of multiples of a particular number.

multiplicative *adj* relating to the mathematical operation of multiplication; tending to multiply; able to multiply.

multiplicity *n* (*pl* **multiplicities**) a great number or variety (of).

multiplier *n* a thing or person that multiplies; the number by which another is to be multiplied; (*econ*) a term used in economics to describe the increased effect of an action on an area's economy.

multiply *vti* (**multiplying, multiplied**) to increase in number, degree, etc; to find the product (of) by multiplication.

multipurpose *adj* having several purposes or uses.

multiracial *adj* involving different racial groups.—**multiracially** *adv*.

multispectral scanner *n* in remote sensing, a sensor in a satellite or aircraft that simultaneously records images of the earth's surface in various wavebands.

multisync monitor *n* (*comput*) a color monitor that automatically adjusts to the input frequency of the adapter card that is used by the computer (VGA, super VGA, etc).

multitasking *n* (*comput*) where a computer processor can undertake more than one task or operation at a time, e.g. printing and saving.

multithreading *n* (*comput*) the procedure used to describe when a program splits itself into separate tasks or threads.

multitude *n* a large number (of people).

multitudinous *adj* of a multitude; very many; having innumerable elements. — **multitudinousness** *n*.

multiuser system *n* (*comput*) a system that allows more than one user to operate the system at any one time.

multivallate *adj* having two or several ramparts.

mum[1] *n* (*inf*) mother.

mum² *adj* silent, not speaking. * *n* silence; * *vi* (**mumming, mummed**) to act as a mummer (—*also* **mumm**).

mumble *vti* to speak indistinctly, mutter. * *n* a mumbled utterance. —**mumbler** *n*. —**mumblingly** *adv*.

mumbo jumbo *n* (*pl* **mumbo jumbos**) meaningless ritual, talk, etc.

mumchance *adj* (*arch*) silent; tongue-tied.

mumm *see* **mum²**.

mummer *n* a person who acts in a play without words; an actor.

mummery *n* (*pl* **mummeries**) performance by mummers; ridiculous ceremonial, pretentious display.

mummify *vt* (**mummifying, mummified**) to embalm (a body) as a mummy; to shrivel, to desiccate. —**mummification** *n*.

mummy¹ *n* (*pl* **mummies**) (*inf*) mother.

mummy² *n* (*pl* **mummies**) a carefully preserved dead body; (*archeo*) the embalmed body of a person or animal from ancient Egypt.

mumps *n* (*med*) an acute, contagious, viral disease that produces inflammation and swelling of the salivary glands. The infection may spread to the pancreas and, in 15-30 per cent of males, to the testicles.

mun. *abbr* = municipal.

Munari *n* **Bruno** (1907–1995) Italian artist who began showing in Futurist exhibitions in the late 1920s.

munch *vti* to chew steadily. —**muncher** *n*.

Munch *n* **Edvard** (1863–1944) Norwegian expressionist painter. Much of his painting reflects a morbid obsession with sickness and isolation. His best-known work, *The Scream* (1893), is typical of his most creative period.

Munchausen's syndrome *n* (*med*) a rare mental disorder in which a person tries to obtain hospital treatment for a nonexistent illness.

Münchner Sezession *n* In 1892 a group of over 100 artists broke away from the Munich Society of Visual Artists. The group grew enormously and became known as the Münchner Sezession.

mundane *adj* routine, everyday; banal; worldly. —**mundanely** *adv*.

Mundy *n* **John** (c.1566-1630) an English organist and composer who was taught by his composer father, William. His works include madrigals and pieces for viols.

mungo *n* (*pl* **mungos**) a cheap woolen material made from cloth waste.

Mungo, Saint *see* **Kentigern**.

Munich (München) *n* a city in Germany.

municipal *n* of or concerning a city, town, etc or its local government. —**municipally** *adv*.

municipality *n* (*pl* **municipalities**) a city or town having corporate status and powers of self-government; the governing body of a municipality.

municipalize *vt* to bring under municipal control; to constitute a place as a municipality.

munificent *adj* extremely generous, bountiful. —**munificence** *n*. —**munificently** *adv*.

muniment *n* (*rare*) a defence, a fortification; (*pl*) (*law*) deeds, charters, and other papers for proving title to land.

munition *vt* to equip with arms. * (*pl*) war supplies, esp weapons and ammunition.

MUniv *abbr* = Master of the University (Honorary).

Munro *n* 1. **Alice** (1931–) Canadian novelist and short-story writer whose stories, e.g., *Dance of the Happy Shades* and *Something I've Been Meaning to Tell You*, are set in the fictional town of Jubilee, Ontario. 2. **Hector Hugh**, known as **Saki** (1870–1916) Burmese-born Scottish short-story writer, noted for his satirical short stories, e.g., *The Chronicles of Clovis* and *Beasts and Super-Beasts*. He was killed in the trenches during World War I.

Munthe *n* **Axel [Martin Frederik]** (1857–1949) Swedish physicist and psychiatrist. His autobiographical book, *The Story of San Michele* (1929), describing his experiences while practicing medicine, became a world bestseller.

Munthe-Kaas *n* **Herman** (1890–1977) Norwegian architect and one of the early exponents of tubular steel furniture in Norway.

muntjac, muntjak *n* any of various small, brown, Asian deer with small antlers and a cry similar to that of a dog.

muon *n* (*physics*) an unstable elementary particle with a mass about 200 times that of an electron.

mural *n* a picture or design painted directly onto a wall, a practice that began in very early times. *See also* **encaustic painting, fresco**; * *adj* relating to a wall. —**muralist** *n*.

murder *n* the intentional and unlawful killing of one person by another; (*inf*) something unusually difficult or dangerous to do or deal with. * *vti* to commit murder (upon), to kill; to mangle, to mar. —**murderer** *n*. —**murderess** *nf*.

murderous *adj* capable of or bent on murder; deadly. —**murderously** *adv*. —**murderousness** *n*.

Murdoch *n* 1. **Dame Iris** (1919–99) Irish-born English novelist whose novels, e.g., *A Severed Head* and *The Sea, the Sea*, are intellectual sex comedies, with complex symbolism and a strong dash of the macabre. 2. **[Keith] Rupert** (1931–) Australian-born American newspaper tycoon. He inherited an Australian newspaper group from his father and subsequently expanded into Britain, where he turned the *Sun* into Britain's bestselling "sex and sleaze" tabloid. He later bought *The Times* and *The Sunday Times* and the publisher Collins, and established the satellite television network, Sky Television, in 1989. The immense losses from the latter enterprise were alleviated by tapping into the reserves of other parts of his empire. His expansion into the US market from the late 1970s necessitated his acquisition of US citizenship in 1985. 3. **Peter** (1940–) British furniture designer who specializes in children's designs.

murex *n* (*pl* **murices, murexes**) (*biol*) any of a genus of marine gasteropods, one species of which yields a purple dye used in ancient Greece and Rome.

Murias *n* (*Irish Celtic myth*) one of the four great cities of the Tuatha De Danann.

Murillo *n* **Bartolomé Esteban** (1618–82) Spanish painter who painted religious and genre scenes popular for their pretty sentimentality. Large selections of his work are in the Prado, Madrid, and the Museo de Belles Artes, Seville.

murine *adj* pertaining to or resembling a mouse or rate; affected, caused or transmitted by rats or mice. * *n* any animal belonging to the same family as rats and mice.

murk *n* indistinct gloom, darkness. * *adj* (*arch*) dark, obscured by fog or mist. —*also* **mirk**.

murky *adj* (**murkier, murkiest**) dark, gloomy; darkly vague or obscure. —*also* **mirky**. —**murkily** *adv*. —**murkiness** *n*.

murmur *n* a continuous, low, indistinct sound; a mumbled complaint; (*med*) a characteristic sound, which can be heard using a stethoscope, caused by uneven blood flow through the heart or blood vessels when these are diseased or damaged. * *vti* to make a murmur; to say in a murmur. —**murmurer** *n*. —**murmurous** *adj*.

murphy *n* (*pl* **murphies**) (*inf*) a potato.

murrain *n* any infectious disease of cattle, such as foot-and-mouth disease; (*arch*) a plague.

Murray *n* **John** 1. (1778–1843) English publisher whose authors included Jane Austen, Thomas Moore, Byron, Crabbe, and Coleridge. He was renowned for his hospitality and generous assistance to authors, and his premises became a common meeting ground for many of the literary figures of the day. 2. **Keith Day Pearce** (1892–1981) New Zealand architect who worked at Wedgwood, producing pieces in a **Modernist** style.

murrhine, murrine *n* of or pertaining to an unknown substance (possibly jade or porcelain) used to make delicate pottery in ancient Rome. * *n* this substance (—*also* **murra**).

murther *n* (*arch*) murder. —**murtherer** *n*.

mus. *abbr* = museum; music; musical; musician.

MusB, MusBac *abbr* = *Musicae Baccalaureus* (*Latin*) "Bachelor of Music."

muscadine *n* a type of woody plant that produces a grape used to make wine.

muscat *n* any of various types of sweet, white, grapes used to make wine; muscatel.

Muscat (Masqat) *n* capital city of the Sultanate of Oman.

muscatel, muscadel *n* a sweet wine made from muscat grapes

muscle *n* (*anat*) fibrous tissue that contracts and relaxed, producing bodily movement; strength; brawn; power. * *vi* (*inf*) to force one's way (in).

muscle-bound *adj* having some of the muscles abnormally enlarged and lacking in elasticity as from too much exercise; inflexible, rigid.

muscle cramp *see* **cramp**.

muscle fatigue *n* fatigue resulting from hard exercise caused by a build-up of lactic acid.

muscle relaxant *n* a substance or drug that causes muscles to relax.

muscovado, muscavado *n* raw sugar left after the molasses has evaporated from sugar cane.

muscovite *n* (*geol*) a type of mica often found in granite and sedimentary rocks.

Muscovite *n* a person who lives in, or originates from, Moscow; (*arch*) a Russian. * *adj* (*arch*) Russian.

Muscovy (duck) *n* a green-brown duck with white markings and a characteristic red, fleshy, growth on its beak. —*also* **musk duck**.

muscular *adj* of or done by a muscle; having well-developed muscles; strong, brawny. —**muscularity** *n*. —**muscularly** *adv*.

muscular dystrophy, myopathy *n* (*med*) any of a group of genetic diseases that produce a progressive deterioration of the muscles.

musculature *n* the entire system of muscles in a living thing; the system of muscles in an organ or a part of this system.

MusD, MusDoc, MusDoct, MusDr *abbr* = *Musicae Doctor* (*Latin*) "Doctor of Music."

muse *vti* to ponder, meditate; to be lost in thought. * *n* a fit of abstraction. —**muster** *n*.

Muses *npl* (*Greek myth*) the daughters of Zeus and Mnemosyne, the divinities who inspired and presided over poetry, the sciences, and the arts. There were nine of them: Clio, Euterpe, Thalia, Melpomene, Terpsichore, Erato, Polyhymnia, Urania, and Calliope.

musette *n* (*mus*) (*French*) (1) a type of bagpipe popular at the French court in the 17th and 18th centuries. (2) an air in 2/4, 3/4 or 6/8 time that imitates drone of the bagpipe.

museum *n* a building for exhibiting objects of artistic, historic, or scientific interest.

Musgrave *n* **Thea** (1928–) Scottish composer best known for her operas (e.g., *The Decision, The Voice of Ariadne)*, and her ballets *Beauty and the Beast* and *A Tale for Thieves.* She has also written choral and orchestral works.

mush *n* a thick porridge of boiled meal; any thick, soft, mass; (*inf*) sentimentality.

mushroom *n* a fleshy fungus with a capped stalk, some varieties of which are edible. * *vi* to gather mushrooms; to spread rapidly, to increase.

mushy *adj* (**mushier, mushiest**) soft, pulpy; (*sl*) sentimental, soppy. —**mushily** *adv.* —**mushiness** *n*.

music *n* the art of combining tones into a composition having structure and continuity; vocal or instrumental sounds having rhythm, melody or harmony; an agreeable sound.

musica ficta *n* (*mus*) (*Latin*) literally, "feigned music"; it is a term for accidentals used in mode music.

musical *n* (*mus*) a type of play or film in which music plays an important part and the actors occasionally sing, e.g., *My Fair Lady, West Side Story.* * *adj* of or relating to music or musicians; having the pleasant tonal qualities of music; having an interest in or talent for music. —**musicality** *n*. —**musically** *adv*.

musical comedy *n* (*mus*) a term used between 1890 and 1930 to describe a humorous play with light music and singing in it.

musicale *n* a musical party.

music box, musical box *n* (*mus*) a clockwork mechanical instrument in which a drum studded with small pins plays a tune by plucking the teeth of a metal comb.

musician *n* one skilled in music, esp a performer. —**musicianly** *adj.* —**musicianship** *n*.

musicology *n* (*mus*) the scientific study of music.

music stand *n* an adjustable metal frame for holding sheet music during a performance.

Musil *n* **Robert [Elder von]** (1880–1942) Austrian novelist and dramatist whose masterpiece is his huge unfinished novel, *The Man Without Qualities*, a psychological study of a purposeless drifter in pre–1914 Vienna.

musing *adj* meditative; lost in thought. —**musingly** *adv*.

musique concrète *n* (*mus*) a term coined by the French composer Pierre Schaffer in 1948 to describe a type of music in which taped sounds are distorted or manipulated by the composer. The term electronic music is now more generally used.

musk *n* an animal secretion with a strong odor, used in perfumes; the odor of musk; a plant with a similar odor.

musk duck *see* **Muscovy.**

muskeg *n* a spongy swamp or bog formed by moss, leaves and other decayed vegetation.

muskellunge *n* (*pl* **muskellunges, muskellunge**) a large, North American game fish similar to the pike.

musket *n* (*mil*) a long-barreled, smoothbore shoulder gun formerly used by infantrymen.

musketeer *n* (*mil*) (*formerly*) a soldier armed with a musket.

musketry *n* (*mil*) small-arm fire; practice in this; muskets or musketeers collectively.

muskmelon *n* any of several varieties of widely cultivated melon with a netted or ribbed skin and sweet, light-colored or green flesh and a musky smell; any one of several types of melon related to the honeydew and cantaloupe.

muskrat *n* (*pl* **muskrats, muskrat**) a large, North American aquatic rodent, related to the vole, that emits a musky secretion; the fur from this. —*also* **musquash**

musky *adj* (**muskier, muskiest**) like or smelling of musk; sweet-smelling. —**muskiness** *n*.

Muslim *n* an adherent of Islam. * *adj* of Islam, its adherents and culture. —*also* **Moslem.**

muslin *n* a fine, cotton cloth.

MusM *abbr* = *Musicae Magister* (*Latin*) "Master of Music."

MusM(Comp) *abbr* = Master of Music (Composition).

MusMPerf *abbr* = Master of Music (Performance).

musquash *n* the fur of the muskrat; the muskrat.

muss *vt* (*often with* **up**) (*inf*) to disarrange, to rumple. * *n* a state of disorder.

mussel *n* (*biol*) an edible, marine bivalve shellfish.

Mussolini *n* **Benito [Amilcare Andrea]** (1883–1945) Italian dictator. Originally a socialist, he founded his fascist "Blackshirt" party in 1919, and was elected to parliament in 1921, establishing himself as dictator ("Il Duce") in 1922 following a march on Rome. He formed the Axis with Hitler in 1937 and declared war on the Allies in 1940. He was deposed in 1943 and rescued by German paratroops, but was later executed by partisans.

Mussorgsky (Moussorgsky, Musorgsky) *n* **Modest Petrovich** (1839-81) Russian composer who gave up a military career to write music. A chronic alcoholic, he lived in a state of poverty and left much of his work unfinished. His best-known works include the Operas *Boris Godunov* and *Sorochintsy Fair* (unfinished), the piano piece "Pictures At An Exhibition," and many songs.

must [1] *aux vb expressing*: necessity; probability; certainty. * *n* (*inf*) something that must be done, had, etc.

must [2] *n* newly pressed grape juice, unfermented or partially fermented wine; the pulp and skin of crushed grapes.

must [3] *see* **musth**.

must [4] *see* **musty**.

mustache *n* the hair on the upper lip. —*also* **moustache.**

mustachio *n* (*pl* **mustachios**) (*often pl*) a moustache, usu. bushy or shaped.

mustang *n* a small, hardy, semi-wild horse of the American prairies.

mustard *n* the powdered seeds of the mustard plant used as a condiment; a brownish-yellow color; (*sl*) zest.

mustard gas *n* an oily liquid that emits an irritant and vesicant gas, used in warfare.

muster *vt* to assemble or call together, as troops for inspection or duty; to gather. * *vi* to be assembled, as troops. * *n* gathering; review; assembly.

musth, must *n* a state of sexual frenzy in the males of elephants and certain other large mammals. * *adj* denoting an animal in musth.

musty *adj* (**mustier, mustiest**) moldy, damp; stale. —**mustily** *adv.* —**mustily** *adv.* —**mustiness, must** *n*.

Mut *n* (*Egypt*) wife to Amun-Ra, the goddess-mother, a vulture-headed goddess local to Thebes and so given this elevated status and provided there with a splendid temple but little worshipped elsewhere.

mut. *abbr* = mutilated; mutual.

mutable *adj* able or tending to change or be changed; fickle, inconstant. —**mutability** *n*. —**mutably** *adv*.

mutagen *n* any substance or agent that increases the rate of mutation in body cells, examples being various chemicals, viruses, and radiation.

mutant *n* a mutation; an organism whose structure has undergone mutation. * *adj* mutating.

Mutare *n* a city in Zimbabwe.

mutate *vti* to experience or cause to experience change or alteration.

mutation *n* the act or process of mutating; alteration; (*biol*) a sudden change in some inheritable characteristic of a species due to a change that takes place in the DNA (the genetic material) of the chromosomes of a cell, caused by faulty replication of the cell's genetic material at cell division; (*linguistics*) a change in the vowel sound when assimilated with another, esp an umlaut. —**mutational** *adj*.

mutation stops *n* (*mus*) organ stops that produce sound usu a harmonic which is different from the normal or octave pitch corresponding to the key which is depressed.

mutatis mutandis (*Latin*) "with the necessary changes."

mute *adj* silent; dumb; (*color*) subdued. * *n* a person who is unable to speak; (*mus*) any device used to soften or reduce the normal volume, or alter the tone, of an instrument. * *vt* to lessen the sound of a musical instrument. —**mutely** *adv.*—**muteness** *n*.

Muti *n* **Riccardo** (1941–) Italian conductor with an international reputation.

mutilate *vt* to maim; to damage by removing an essential part of. —**mutilation** *n*. —**mutilative** *adj.* —**mutilator** *n*.

mutineer *n* a person who takes part in a mutiny.

mutinous *adj* threatening mutiny, rebellious; taking part in a mutiny. —**mutinously** *adv*.

mutiny *vi* (**mutinying, mutinied**) to revolt against authority, esp in military service. * *n* (*pl* **mutinies**) a rebellion against authority, esp by soldiers and sailors against officers.

mutism *n* the refusal or inability to speak, which may result from brain damage or psychological factors.

Mutsamudu *n* a city in Comoros.

mutt *n* (*sl*) a fool; a mongrel dog.

mutter *vti* to utter in a low tone or indistinctly; to grumble. —**mutterer** *n*. —**mutteringly** *adv*.

mutton *n* the edible flesh of sheep.

muttonchops *n* whiskers on the side of the face, narrow at thetop, broad at the bottom.

mutual *adj* given and received in equal amount; having the same feelings one for the other; shared in common. —**mutuality** *n*. —**mutually** *adv*.

mutual fund *n* a company that invests shareholders' funds in a portfolio of securities of other companies.

mutule *n* (*archit*) a square projecting block of stone under the soffit of the cornice of a Greek Doric cornice.

Muzak *n* (*trademark*) a system for playing recorded music in public places; (*without cap*) bland background music.

muzhik *n* a peasant in pre-Revolutionary Russia. —*also* **mujik, moujik.**

Muzorewa, Bishop Abel *see* **Smith, Ian.**

muzz *vt* (*inf*) to make (anything) muzzy.

muzzle *n* the projecting nose or mouth or an animal; a strap fitted over the jaws to prevent biting; the open end of a gun barrel. * *vt* to put a muzzle on; to silence or gag. —**muzzler** *n*.

muzzy *adj* (**muzzier, muzziest**) confused, dazed; dizzy; blurred; dull. —**muzzily** *adv.* —**muzziness** *n*.

mv *abbr* = market value; mean variation; merchant/motor vessel; (*mus*) *mezzo voce* (*Italian*) "half the power of voice"; muzzle velocity.

mV, mv *abbr* = millivolt.

MV *abbr* = *Medicus Veterinarius* (*Latin*) "Veterinary Physician"; megavolt.

M

MVM *abbr* = Master of Veterinary Medicine.

MVRG *abbr* = Mediaeval Villages Research Group.

MVSc *abbr* = Master of Veterinary Science.

MVT *abbr* = Military Vehicle Trust.

MW *abbr* = medium wave; megawatt.

mW *abbr* = milliwatt.

MWA *abbr* = Modern Woodmen of America; Mystery Writers of America.

Mwanza *n* town in Tanzania.

MWeldI *abbr* = Member of the Welding Institute.

MWES *abbr* = Member of the Women's Engineering Society.

MWF *abbr* = Medical Women's Federation.

MWG *abbr* = music-wire gauge.

MWGM *abbr* = Most Worshipful Grand Master (freemasonry).

MWh *abbr* = megawatt hour.

MWV *abbr* = Mexican War Veteran.

Mx *abbrev* = maxwell

MX *abbr* = missile experimental.

mxd. *abbr* = mixed.

my¹ *poss adj* of or belonging to me.

my² *abbr* = million years.

My. *abbr* = May.

myalgia *n* (*med*) pain, stiffness or cramp in the voluntary muscles or in one muscle.

myalgic encephalomyelitis (ME) *n* (*med*) a disorder characterized by muscular pain, fatigue, general depression, and loss of memory and concentration.—*also* **post-viral fatigue syndrome**, **post-viral syndrome**.

Myanmar, Union of, *n* a republic (formerly Burma) in southeast Asia.

myasthenia gravis *n* (*med*) a serious and chronic condition of uncertain cause, which may be an autoimmune disease.

mycelium *n* (*pl* **mycelia**) a cellular spawn of fungi.

Mycenae *n* a very ancient city of Argolis, the home of Agamemnon, in whose reign it was the most important city in Greece.—**Mycenaean** *adj*.

Mycenaeans *n* people who lived in the region of southern Greece during the late Bronze Age.

Mycerinus *or* **Menkaure** a Fourth-Dynasty (2625–2510 BC) pharaoh, builder of the smallest of the three pyramids of Giza.

mycetoma *n* (*pl* **mycetomas, mycetomata**) a fungoid disease, usu of feet, often caused by a wound.

mycol. *abbr* = mycological; mycology.

mycology *n* the science of fungi or mushrooms; the fungi found in a particular area. —**mycologist** *n*.

mycoplasma *n* (*biol*) a microorganism of the *Mycoplasma* genus, several species of which cause disease.

mycosis *n* (*pl* **mycoses**) (*med*) any disease caused by a parastic fungus, e.g., thrush.

MYD *abbr* = Member of the Youth Development Association.

mydriasis *n* excessive dilatation of the pupil of the eye.

mydriatic *adj* causing mydriasis. * *n* a drug that induces mydriasis.

myelin *n* a sheath of liposome and protein that surrounds the axons of some neurons.

myelin sheath *n* (*anat, physiology*) a fatty substance that surrounds axons in the central nervous system of vertebrates and functions as an insulating layer.

myelitis *n* (*med*) inflammation of the spinal cord or of the bone marrow. *See* **osteomyelitis**.

myeloblast *see* **leukemia**.

myelocyte *n* (*physiology*) a cell that is an immature type of granulocyte responsible for the production of white blood cells.

myelofibrosis *n* (*med*) a disease in which fibrosis takes place within the bone marrow, and immature red and white blood cells appear in the circulation because of the resultant anemia.

myelography *n* (*med*) a specialized X-ray technique involving the injection of a radio-opaque dye into the central canal of the spinal cord in order to distinguish the presence of disease. The X-rays are called myelograms.

myeloid *adj* a term meaning like or relating to bone marrow or like a myelocyte.

myeloma *n* (*med*) a malignant disease of the bone marrow in which tumors are present in more than one bone at the same time.

myg. *abbr* = myriagram.

myl. *abbr* = myrialiter.

Mylne *n* **Robert** (born 1733) Scottish architect. His notable works include Blackfriars Bridge, London.

mylonite *n* (*geol*) a rock type produced in zones of faulting and shearing.

mym. *abbr* = myriameter.

myna (bird) *n* any of several Asian birds resembling the starling, some species of which can imitate speech. —*also* **mina (bird)**.

Mynheer *n* a Dutch title used before a name, as "Mister" as a term of respect.

myob *abbr* = mind your own business.

myocardial infarction *n* (*med*) necrosis of part of the myocardium, usu as a result of a coronary thrombosis.

myocarditis *n* (*med*) inflammation of the muscle in the wall of the heart.

myocardium *n* (*anat, physiology*) the middle of the three layers of the heart wall, which is the thick, muscular area. —**myocardial** *adj*.

myoglobin *n* (*physiology*) an iron-containing pigment that is similar to hemoglobin and occurs in muscle cells.

"My Old Kentucky Home" *n* the song of the American State, Kentucky.

myology *n* (*med*) a branch of medicine concerned with studying the muscles or the diseases affecting them.

myoma *n* (*med*) a benign tumor in muscle, often in the uterus (womb).

myomectomy *n* (*med*) surgical removal of fibroids from the muscular wall of the uterus.

myometrium *n* (*anat, physiology*) the muscular tissue of the uterus, composed of smooth muscle and surrounding the endometrium.

myopathy *see* **muscular dystrophy**.

myope *n* a short-sighted person.

myopia *n* short-sightedness, which is corrected by wearing spectacles with concave lenses. —**myopic** *adj*. —**myopically** *adv*.

myosin *n* (*biochemistry*) a large protein found originally with actin in muscles but occurring in most eukaryotic cells.

myosis *see* **miosis**.

myosotis, myosote *n* any of various small plants with blue, pink, or white flowers, *incl* the forget-me-not.

Myrdal *n* **[Karl] Gunnar** (1898–1987) Swedish economist. He shared the 1974 Nobel prize for economics with Hayek, largely for his work on the application of economic theory to the economies of the Third World.

Myrddin *n* (*Welsh Celtic myth*) the original Welsh name of Merlin, who was the wizard in the Arthurian legends.

myriad *n* a great number of persons or things. * *adj* innumerable.

myriapod *n* (*zool*) an arthropod with many legs and a segmented body, *incl* millipedes and centipedes. —**myriapodan** *adj, n*. —**myriapodous** *adj*.

myrica *n* the root bark of the candleberry or wax myrtle.

myrmecology *n* the scientific study of ants. —**myrmecological** *adj*. —**myrmecologist** *n*.

myrmecophagous *adj* (*biol*) feeding on ants; (*jaws, etc*) adapted for eating ants.

Myrmidon *n* (*pl* **Myrmidons, Myrmidones**) (*Greek myth*) one of a tribe of Thracian warriors formed by Zeus from an anthill who accompanied Achilles to the Trojan war; a brutal, unprincipled or unquestioning follower or subordinate. —*also adj*.

myrobalan *n* any of several tropical trees containing tannin and bearing a fruit that, when dried, was used medicinally and in dyeing and tanning; the dye from such a fruit.

myrrh *n* a fragrant gum resin used in perfume, incense etc; (*Bible*) gift offered by the wise men at the birth of Jesus.

Mysia *n* in ancient geography, a country in the extreme northeast corner of Asia Minor, on the modern Aegean, Hellespont and Sea of Marmara.—**Mysian** *adj*.

myrtaceous *adj* of the myrtle family, *incl* eucalyptus, clove and guava, with leaves that secrete oil.

myrtle *n* an evergreen shrub with fragrant leaves; a trailing periwinkle.

myself *pron* emphatic and reflexive form of I; in my normal state.

myst. *abbr* = mysteries.

mystagogue *n* an initiator into or interpreter of mysteries—**mystagogic** *adj*. —**mystagogy** *n*.

Mysteries *npl* rites and ceremonies of ancient Greece and Rome, known only to, and practiced by, congregations of certain initiated people at appointed times and in strict seclusion.

mysterious *adj* difficult to understand or explain, obscure; delighting in mystery. —**mysteriously** *adv*. —**mysteriousness** *n*.

mystery *n* (*pl* **mysteries**) something unexplained and secret; a story about a secret crime, etc; secrecy.

mystic *n* one who seeks direct knowledge of God or spiritual truths by self-surrender. * *adj* **mystical**.

mystical *adj* having a meaning beyond normal human understanding; magical. —**mystically** *adv*.

mysticism *n* the beliefs or practices of a mystic; belief in a reality accessible by intuition, not the intellect; obscurity of thought or doctrine.

mystify *vt* (**mystifying, mystified**) to puzzle, bewilder, to confuse. —**mystification** *n*. —**mistifier** *n*. —**mistifyingly** *adv*.

myth *n* a fable; a fictitious event; a traditional story of gods and heroes, taken to be true. —**mythic** *adj*.

myth., mythol. *abbr* = mythology; mythological.

mythical *adj* imaginary, unreal, untrue; having to do with myths, mythic. —**mythically** *adv*.

mythicize *vt* to treat as myth; to interpret mythically; to turn (something) into myth.

mythologist *n* a student of myths; a writer of myths.

mythology *n* (*pl* **mythologies**) myths collectively; the study of myths. —**mythological** *adj*.

mythopoeic *adj* producing or creating myths. —**mythopoeia, mythopoeisis** *n*.

myxedema, myxoedema *n* (*med*) a disease caused by underactivity of the thyroid gland (hypothyroidism), leading to physical and mental degeneration.

myxomycete *n* (*biol*) any of various organisms forming a network of creamy filaments on decaying wood, leaves, etc, and displaying characteristics of both plants and animals.

N

n, N *n* the 14th letter of the English alphabet; an indefinite number.

N *symbol* (*chem*) nitrogen (element).

n *abbr* = en; née; (*math*) indefinite number; name; nano-; (*Latin*) *natus*, "born"; navigation; navy; nephew; neuter; new; nominative; noon; note; noun; (*phys*) refractive index.

n. *abbr* = nimbus; (*Latin*) *nomen*, "name"; (*eccles*) nones; noon; (*chem*) normal (strength solution); (*Latin*) *novus*, "new".

N *abbr* = national; navy; (*elect*) neutral; newton; Norse; (*phys*) (Avogadro) number.

N, N. *abbr* = North, Northern; Nationalist; Norse; (*law*) Novellae; November.

na. *abbr* = nail; nails.

n.a. *abbr* (*micros*) = numerical aperture.

n/a *abbr* = no account; not applicable; not available.

Na *symbol* (*chem*) (*Latin*) *natrium*, "sodium" (element).

NA *abbr* = Napoleonic Association; Narcotics Anonymous; National Academician or Academy; National Army; Nautical Almanac; North America.

N/A *abbr* (*bank*) = no advice.

NAA *abbr* = National Aeronautic Association; National Artists' Association; Neckware Association of America; North Atlantic Assembly.

NAAFI *abbr* = Navy, Army and Air Force Institutes.

Naaman *n* (*Bible*) a commander of the Syrian army in the days of war with Israel.

NAAS *abbr* = National Agricultural Advisory Scheme.

NAAW *abbr* = National Association of Amateur Winemakers.

nab *vt* (**nabbing, nabbed**) (*sl*) to catch, arrest.

Nabataeans *n* a group of people who are first mentioned in 647 BC. Their territory included northern Saudi Arabia and the Negev Desert of Israel.

NABBA *abbr* = National Amateur Body Building Association.

NABC *abbr* = National Association of Boys' Clubs.

NABD *abbr* = National Association of Blood Donors.

Nabis *n* a group of French artists formed in 1888, who opposed the naturalism of impressionism.

NABISCO *abbr* = National Biscuit Company.

nabob *n* in India, a deputy or administrator under the Mogul Empire; one who has amassed wealth in India; a very wealthy man.

Nabokov *n* **Vladimir** (1899–1977) Russian-born American novelist whose most famous novel is *Lolita* (1955).

Naboth *n* (*Bible*) a man of Jezreel who refused to sell his vineyard to King Ahab of Israel. *See also* **Ahab; Elijah; Jezebel.**

NAC *abbr* = National Amusements Council; National Anglers Council; National Association for the Childless.

NACA *abbr* = National Athletic and Cycling Association.

NACAB *abbr* = National Association of Citizens' Advice Bureaux.

NACAM *abbr* = National Association of Corn and Agricultural Merchants.

nacelle *n* the car of an aircraft.

nacho *n* a Mexican snack consisting of a tortilla chip often served grilled with melted cheese, chili, etc.

NACIC *abbr* = National Counterintelligence Center.

NACLE *abbr* = National Association of Chimney Lining Engineers.

NACM *abbr* = National Association of Charcoal Manufacturers; National Association of Cider Makers; National Association of Colliery Manufacturers.

NACODS *abbr* = National Association of Colliery Overmen, Deputies and Shotfirers.

nacre *n* mother-of-pearl; the shellfish that yields it.

nacreous *adj* having an iridescent luster; resembling mother of pearl.

nacreous clouds *npl* (*meteorol*) a cloud formation at a great height before sunrise or after sunset, when its coloring is similar to mother of pearl.

NACRO *abbr* = National Association for the Care and Resettlement of Offenders.

NACT *abbr* = National Association of Clinical Tutors; National Association of Cycle Traders.

NAD *abbr* = National Academy of Design; National Association of the Deaf; (*med*) no abnormality detected; no appreciable difference; not on active duty.

NADECT *abbr* = National Association for Drama in Education and Children's Theater.

Nader *n* **Ralph** (1934–) American lawyer and consumer protectionist.

nadir *n* the point opposite the zenith; the lowest point; the depths of despair; the lowest point reached by an object in orbit.

Nadir *n* (*astron*) the pole that is vertically below the observer in the celestial sphere.

NADJ *abbr* = National Association of Disc Jockeys.

NADW *abbr* = National Association of Disabled Writers.

NAEA *abbr* = National Association of Estate Agents.

naevus *see* **nevus**.

NAEW *abbr* = Nato Airborne Early Warning.

N. Af. *abbr* = North Africa.

NAFB & AE *abbr* = National Association of Farriers, Blacksmiths & Agricultural Engineers.

NAFBRC *abbr* = National Association of Family Based Respite Care.

NAFD *abbr* = National Association of Funeral Directors.

NAFO *abbr* = National Association of Fire Officers; Northwest Atlantic Fisheries Organization.

NAFSCA *abbr* = National Automatic Sprinkler and Fire Control Association.

NAFSO *abbr* = National Association of Field Study Officers.

NAFTA *abbr* = North American Free Trade Agreement; North American Free Trade Area.

nag[1] *vti* (**nagging, nagged**) to scold constantly; to harass; to be felt persistently. * *n* a person who nags.

nag[2] (*inf*) a horse.

nag *abbr* = net annual gain.

NAG *abbr* = National Acquisitions Group; Nystagmus Action Group.

Naga *n* (*pl* **Nagas, Naga**) (*Hindu myth*) a deified serpent, esp the cobra; a member of the Naga tribes; a class of mendicant Hindus. * *adj* pertaining to an ancient race who invaded India about the 6th century BC, or to certain Burmese border tribes.

nagana *n* a disease caused by the tsetse-fly.

Nagari *n* the name of the Sanskrit alphabet.

NAGC *abbr* = National Association of Gifted Children.

NAGCS *abbr* (*Brit*) = National Association for Gifted Children in Scotland.

nagelflue *n* a peculiar alpine conglomerate rock, interspersed with nail-like pebbles.

nagor *n* a Senegal antelope.

Nagoya *n* a city in Japan.

NAGS *abbr* = National Allotments and Gardens Society.

Nagy *n* **Imre** (1896–1958) Hungarian statesman. He was prime minister from 1953 to 1955 and again in 1956, but was replaced after the Soviet invasion of that year.

Nah. *abbr* = Nahum.

NAHT *abbr* = National Association of Head Teachers.

Nahum *n* one of the prophetical books of the Old Testament.

NAI *abbr* = non-accidental injury.

naiad *n* (*pl* **naiads, naiades**) a water nymph; (*pl*) an order of aquatic plants; a family of freshwater bivalves.

Naiad *n* the smallest and innermost satellite of Neptune.

naiant *adj* (*her*) representing fishes swimming in a horizontal position.

NAIBD *abbr* = National Association of Industries for the Blind and Disabled.

NAICS *abbr* = North American Industry Classification System.

naif, naïf *adj* naive.

nail *n* a horny plate covering the end of a human finger or toe; a thin pointed metal spike for driving into wood as a fastening or hanging device. * *vt* to fasten with nails; to fix, secure; (*inf*) to catch or hit; (*inf*) to arrest.

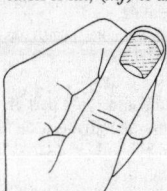

nail-biting *n* the habit or process of biting one's fingernails. * *adj* inducing suspense or anxiety.

nailfile *n* a small metal file or strip of cardboard coated with emery used for trimming and shaping the nails.

nail polish *n* a lacquer for giving a clear or colored shiny surface to fingernails.

Nain *n* (*Bible*) a town in Galilee where Jesus brought a widow's son back to life.

nainsook *n* a kind of closely woven muslin, originally Indian.

Naipaul *n* **V[idiadhar] S[urajprasad]** (1932–) Trinidad-born English novelist whose works include *A House for Mr Biswas*.

naira *n* the monetary unit of Nigeria, made up of 100 kobo.

Nairobi *n* capital city of Kenya.

NAIRU *abbr* = non-accelerating inflation rate of unemployment.

naissant *adj* (*her*) issuing forth or rising from some ordinary, and showing only the foreparts of the body.

NAITA *abbr* = National Association of Independent Travel Agents.

naive, naïve *adj* inexperienced; unsophisticated; (*argument*) simple.— **naively, naïvely** *adv*.

naive art *n* work by untrained artists whose style is noted for its innocence and simplicity.

naive quantitative methods *npl* methods that are used to obtain a forecast of future trends of some kind.

naiveté, naïveté, naivety *n* natural, unaffected simplicity or ingenuousness.

NAIWC *abbr* = National Association of Inland Waterway Carriers.

Nakashima *n* **George** (1905–1990) American woodworker influenced by Shaker and Japanese craftsmanship.

naked *adj* bare, without clothes; without a covering; without addition or ornament; (*eye*) without optical aid.—**nakedness** *n*.

naked-eye object *n* (*astron*) any celestial body which can be seen without the use of an optical device such as binoculars, telescope, etc.

naker *n* (*mus*) the medieval English name for a small kettledrum (often with snares) of Arabic origin, from which timpani developed.

Nakhon Ratchasima *n* a city in Thailand.

Nakuru *n* a town in Kenya.

NAL *abbr* = National Agricultural Library.

NALC *abbr* = National Association of Laryngectomy Clubs; National Association of Lawyers for Children.

NALGO *abbr* (*Brit*) = National and Local Government Officers' Association.

NALHF *abbr* = National Association of League of Hospital Friends.

NALI *abbr* = National Association of the Launderette Industry.

NALM *abbr* = National Association of Lift Makers.

NALSAT *abbr* = National Association of Land Settlement Association Tenants.

N. Am. *abbr* = North America.

NAMB *abbr* = National Association of Master Bakers, Confectioners and Caterers.

namby-pamby *adj* weakly sentimental or affectedly pretty or fine. * *n* (*pl* **namby-pambies**) an affected person.

NAMCW *abbr* = National Association for Maternal and Child Welfare.

name *n* a word or term by which a person or thing is called; a title; reputation; authority. * *vt* to give a name to; to call by name; to designate; to appoint to an office; (a date, price, etc) to specify.

NAME *abbr* = National Association of Marine Enginebuilders; New American Music in Europe.

name-calling *n* verbal abuse, esp in place of reasoned debate.

name-dropping *n* the practice of mentioning the names of famous or important people as if they were friends, in order to impress others.—**name-dropper** *n*.

nameless *adj* without a name; obscure; anonymous; unnamed; indefinable; too distressing or horrifying to be described.

namely *adv* that is to say.

nameplate *n* a small plate on a door of a room, house, etc, displaying the name of the occupant.

namesake *n* a person or thing with the same name as another.

NAMG *abbr* = National Association of Multiple Grocers.

NAMHO *abbr* = National Association of Mining History Oranisations.

Namibia *n* a republic situated on the Atlantic coast of southwest Africa.

Namibian Dollar *n* the currency of Namibia.

Namier *n* **Sir Lewis Bernstein** (1888–1960) Polish-born British historian. His works include *The Structure of Politics at the Accession of George III* (1929).

NAMM *abbr* = National Association of Master Masons.

Nampula *n* a major town in Mozambique.

nan bread, naan bread *n* a type of slightly leavened Indian bread in a flattened oval shape.

nance *n* (*derog*) an effeminate man.

N & Q *abbr* = notes and queries.

n & v *abbr* = nausea and vomiting.

nankeen, nankin *n* a buff-colored cotton cloth, originally from China.

nanny *n* (*pl* **nannies**) a child's nurse.

nanny goat *n* a female domestic goat.

nano- *prefix* one thousand millionth (10^{-9}) part of, e.g. *nanosecond*.

nanometer *n* a unit of measurement that is used for extremely small objects.

nanosecond *n* (*comput*) one billionth of a second, used to indicate the speed of operation of a computer chip.

nanotechnology *n* (*comput*) the study of how to make computers smaller and more efficient.

Nansen *n* **Fridtjof** (1861–1930) Norwegian explorer, scientist, and statesman; almost reached the North Pole in 1895; became commissioner for refugees for the League of Nations (1920–22) ; won the 1922 Nobel peace prize.

Nantes *n* a city in France.

Nantosvelta *n* (*Gaulish Celtic myth*) a goddess often associated with prosperity and abundance, she also has connections with death.

NAO *abbr* = National Audit Office.

Naoise *n* (*Irish Celtic myth*) one of the three sons of Uisnech. He attracted the attention and love of Deirdre, who had been told by friends that he had the physical attributes that she sought—black hair, white skin and red cheeks.

Naomi *n* (*Bible*) Ruth's mother-in-law.

naos *n* (*Egypt*) a shrine or niche in the innermost part of a temple or chapel, where a divine statue was placed.

nap[1] *n* a short sleep, doze. * *vi* (**napping, napped**) to take a nap.

nap[2] *n* a hairy surface on cloth or leather; such a surface.

NAP *abbr* = National Association of the Paralyzed.

napalm *n* a substance added to petrol to form a jelly-like compound used in firebombs and flame-throwers. * *vt* to attack or burn with napalm.

Napata *n* (*Egypt*) capital city of Nubia, situated just below the third cataract of the Nile.

nape *n* the back of the neck.

napery *n* household linen, esp for the table.

NAPF *abbr* = National Association of Pension Funds.

NAPGC *abbr* = National Association of Public Golf Courses.

Naphtali *n* (*Bible*) second son of Jacob and Bilhah; the ancestor of one of the twelve tribes.

naphtha *n* (*chem*) a clear, volatile, inflammable bituminous liquid hydrocarbon exuding from the earth or distilled from coal tar, etc; rock oil.

naphthalene *n* a white crystalline hydrocarbon distilled from coal tar, used in making dyes, explosives and in mothballs.

napiform *adj* turnip-shaped.

napkin *n* a square of cloth or paper for wiping fingers or mouth or protecting clothes at table, a serviette.

Naples, Napoli *n* a city in Italy.

NAPO *abbr* = National Association of Probation Officers.

napoleon *n* a gold coin formerly current in France, value 20 francs.

Napoleon I *n* [**Napoleon Bonaparte**] (1769–1821) emperor of France (1804–15); established an empire throughout Europe until his defeat at Leipzig in 1813. His return to France for the "Hundred Days" campaign (1815) resulted in defeat at Waterloo and banishment to St Helena.

Napoleonic *adj* of or like Emperor Napoleon I.

NAPP *abbr* = National Association for Patient Participation; National Association for the Protection of Punters.

nappe[1] *n* (*geol*) a large-scale geological structure occurring as a sheet of rock that has been pushed over a fault plane or thrust at the base.

nappe[2] *n* the sheet of water flowing over a dam or weir.

nappy[1] *adj* (**nappier, nappiest**) covered with nap or pile.

nappy[2] *n* (*pl* **nappies**) a diaper.

NAPR *abbr* = National Association of Pram Retailers.

NAPS *abbr* = National Association for Premenstrual Syndrome; National Association of Personal Secretaries; Nationwide Association of Preserving Specialists.

NAPT *abbr* = National Association of Percussion Teachers.

NAPV *abbr* = National Association of Prison Visitors.

NARA *abbr* = National Archives and Records Administration.

Narayan *n* **R[asipuram] K[rishnaswami]** (1906–) Indian novelist whose works include *The World of Nagaraj*.

Narayanganj *n* a city in Bangladesh.

narc, nark *n* (*sl*) a drugs law enforcement agent.

narceine *n* an alkaloid obtained from opium and used as a sedative.

N. Arch. *abbr* = Naval Architect.

narcissism *n* excessive interest in one's own body or self.

narcissistic *adj* full of admiration for oneself.

narcissus *n* (*pl* **narcissi, narcissuses**) a spring-flowering bulb plant, esp the daffodil.

Narcissus *n* (*Greek myth*) a beautiful but vain boy who fell in love with his own reflection and was transformed into a flower.

narco- *prefix* indicating torpor or narcotics.

narcodollars *npl* (*sl*) US dollars earned by a country by the export of illegal drugs.

narcolepsy *n* a disease characterized by uncontrollable fits of deep sleep.—**narcoleptic** *adj, n*.

narcosis *n* (*pl* **narcoses**) a state of unconsciousness or drowsiness produced by narcotics.

narcotic *adj* inducing sleep. * *n* a drug, often addictive, used to relieve pain and induce sleep.

narcotism *n* a morbid dependence on narcotics.

narcotize *vt* to use a narcotic upon.—**narcotization.**

nard *n* spikenard, an aromatic plant; an aromatic unguent prepared from it.

Nardini *n* **Pietro** (1722–93) Italian violinist and composer.

nardoo *n* a genus of Australian acotyledonous aquatic plants, Australian pillwort, the spore cases of which are used as bread.

nares *npl* (*sing* **naris**) the nostrils.—**narial** *adj*.

Nares *n* **James** (1715–83) an English organist and composer, who is best known for his church music and songs.

NARFE *abbr* = National Association of Retired Federal Employees.

narghile *n* a small hookah pipe.

nark[1] *n* (*Brit sl*) an informer.— also *vti*.

nark[2] *see* **narc**.

NARO *abbr* = Naval Aircraft Repair Organization.

NARPS *abbr* = National Association of UK River Protection Societies.

narrate *vt* (*a story*) to tell, relate; to give an account of; (*film, TV*) to provide a spoken commentary for.

narration *n* the act of narrating; a statement, written or verbal.

narrative *n* a spoken or written account of a sequence of events, experiences, etc; the art or process of narration.—*also adj*.

narrator *n* one who narrates.

narrow *adj* small in width; limited; with little margin; prejudiced or bigoted. * *n* (*usu pl*) the narrow part of a pass, street, or channel. * *vti* to make or grow narrow; to decrease; to contract.—**narrowly** *adv*.—**narrowness** *n*.

narrow gauge *adj* denoting the distance of less than standard gauge (4 feet, 8.5 inches/1.44 meters) between rail metals.

narrow-minded *adj* prejudiced, bigoted; illiberal.—**narrow-mindedness** *n*.

NARSIS *abbr* = National Association for Road Safety Instruction in Schools.

narthex *n* in Early Christian churches the western portico, railed off for catechumens and penitents.

Narva *n* a city in Estonia.

narwhal *n* an Arctic whale, the male of which has a long spiral tusk.

nary = never a, ne'er a.

NAS *abbr* = National Academy of Sciences; National Adoption Society; Nautical Archaeology Society; Noise Abatement Society.

NASA *abbr* = National Aeronautics and Space Administration.

nasal *adj* of the nose; sounded through the nose. * *n* a sound made through the nose.—**nasally** *adv*.

nasal cavity *n* one of two cavities in the nose, divided by a septum, which lie between the roof of the mouth and the floor of the cranium.

NASC *abbr* = National Aviation Security Committee.

Nasca, Nazca *adj* relating to a culture that evolved out of that of Paracas in southern Peru and flourished *c* 200 BC–AD 600.

nascent *adj* just starting to grow or develop.

NASE *abbr* = National Academy of Stationary Engineers.

naseberry *n* (*pl* **naseberries**) sapodilla plum tree.

Nash *n* 1. **Ogden [Frederick]** (1902–71) American humorous poet whose verse includes *You Can't Get There from Here*. 2. **Paul** (1889–1946) British painter who was an official war artist in World War I and World War II.

NASH *abbr* = National Association of Specimen Hunters.

Nashe *n* **Thomas** (1567–1601) English writer and author of the first major English picaresque novel, *The Unfortunate Traveller*.

Nashville *n* capital city of Tennesse, a state of the USA.

NASM *abbr* = National Air and Space Museum.

Nasmyth *n* **Alexander** (1758–1840) Scottish painter of landscapes and portraits.

naso- *prefix* nose.

nasogastric *adj* (*anat*) pertaining to the nose and stomach.

nasogastric tube *n* (*med*) a tube of small diameter that is passed through the nose into the stomach for purposes of introducing food or drugs or removing fluid.

NASPM *abbr* = National Association of Seed Potato Merchants.

NASS *abbr* = National Agricultural Statistics Service; National Ankylosing Spondylitis Society; National Association of Semen Suppliers; National Association of Steel Stockholders.

Nassau *n* capital city of the Bahamas.

Nasser *n* **Gamal Abdel** (1918–70) Egyptian soldier and statesman who took a leading part in the coup that deposed King Farouk (1920–65) in 1952. He became prime minister (1954) and then president (1956–70).

nasturtium *n* an ornamental garden plant with bright flowers, a pungent odor, and edible leaves.

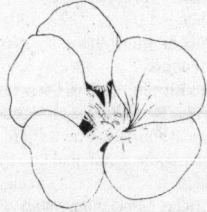

nasty *adj* (**nastier, nastiest**) unpleasant; offensive; ill-natured; disagreeable; (*problem*) hard to deal with; (*illness*) serious or dangerous.—**nastily** *adv*.—**nastiness** *n*.

NAS/UWT *abbr* = National Association of Schoolmasters/Union of Women Teachers.

nat. *abbr* = national; native; natural; (*Latin*) *natus*, "born."

Nat. *abbr* = Nationalist.

natal *adj* pertaining to one's birth or birthday; indigenous.—**natality** *n*.

natant *adj* swimming; (*her*) (*fish*) floating on the surface.

natation *n* the act or art of swimming.—**natational** *adj*.

natatorial, natatory *adj* swimming or adapted for swimming.

Natchrantal *n* (*Irish Celtic myth*) a Connacht champion in Medb's army. He fought with Cuchulainn and gave Medb the excuse to push far into Ulster in order to take the Donn Cuailgne.

NATCOL *abbr* = Natural Food Colors Association.

NATD *abbr* = National Association of Teachers of Dancing.

nates *npl* (*sing* **natis**) the buttocks.

NATFHE *abbr* = National Association of Teachers in Further and Higher Education.

Nathan *n* (*Bible*) a prophet at the court of David. *See also* **Bathseba; David; Uriah**.

Nathanael *see* **Bartholemew**.

nat. hist. *abbr* = natural history.

nation *n* people of common territory, descent, culture, language, or history; people united under a single government.

national *adj* of a nation; common to a whole nation, general. * *n* a citizen or subject of a specific country.—**nationally** *adv*.

national anthem *n* a patriotic song or hymn adopted officially by a nation for ceremonial and public occasions.

national bank *n* a US commercial bank established by means of a federal charter, which requires it to be a member of the Federal Reserve System.

national debt *n* the total money currently on loan to the government of a nation.

National Guard *n* state militia that can be called into federal service.

national income *n* the total monetary value of the income brought in by a country's economic activity over one year.

national income accounts *npl* a financial statement of the total income that is generated in a country's economy over a set period of time, usually one year.

national insurance contributions *npl* (*Brit*) payments made by employers and employees to the UK government to finance benefits such as retirement pensions.

nationalism *n* patriotic sentiments, principles, etc; a policy of national independence or self-government; fanatical patriotism, chauvinism.—**nationalist** *n*. —**nationalistic** *adj*.

nationality *n* (*pl* **nationalities**) the status of belonging to a nation by birth or naturalization; a nation or national group.

nationalization *n* the process of bringing the assets of a company under the control of the state.

nationalize *vt* to make national; to convert into public or government property.

national park *n* an area designated by a government as of important scenic, historical, or environmental value.

nation-state *n* a sovereign state containing a relatively homogeneous population.

nationwide *adj* extending across the nation.

native *adj* inborn; natural to a person; innate; (*language, etc*) of one's place of birth; relating to the indigenous inhabitants of a country or area; occurring naturally. * *n* a person born in the place indicated; a local inhabitant; an indigenous plant or animal; (*formerly*) an indigenous inhabitant, esp a non-White under colonial rule.

native file format *n* (*comput*) the format in which a particular program saves a file.

nativism *n* (*philos*) the doctrine of innate ideas; the advocacy of the claim of native as opposed to that of naturalized Americans.—**nativist** *adj, n*. —**nativistic** *adj*.

nativity *n* (*pl* **nativities**) birth; a horoscope at the time of one's birth; (*with cap*) the birth of Christ.

natl. *abbr* = national.

Natlas *abbr* = National Testing Laboratory Accreditation Scheme.

NATMA *abbr* = National Association of Teachers of Marketing and Advertising.

NATO *abbr* = North Atlantic Treaty Organization.

nat. phil. *abbr* = natural philosophy.

natrolite *n* a hydrated silicate of aluminum and soda.

natron *n* (*Egypt*) a mineral and an important element in mummification, in the manufacture of faience and glassware, and in soldering metal. It was used with salt to preserve meat, and, when mixed with oil and scented unguents, produced a kind of soap.

Nats. abbr = Nationalists.

Natsopa *abbr* = National Society of Operative Printers, Graphical and Media Personnel (previously Printers and Assistants).

NATT *abbr* = National Association of Teachers of Travellers.

natter *vi* (*inf*) to chat, talk aimlessly.—*also n*.

NATTKE *abbr* = National Association of Television, Theatrical and Kinematographic Employees.

natty *adj* (**nattier, nattiest**) tidy, neat, smart.—**nattily** *adv*.—**nattiness** *n*.

Natufian *adj* (*archeo*) relating to a transitional culture in Palestine, spanning the late Mesolithic to early Neolithic period.

natural *adj* of or produced by nature; not artificial; innate, not acquired; true to nature; lifelike; normal; at ease; (*mus*) not flat or sharp. * *n* (*inf*) a person or thing considered to have a natural aptitude (for) or to be an obvious choice (for); (*inf*) a certainty; (*mus*) a natural note or a sign indicating one.—**naturalness** *n*.

natural childbirth *n* giving birth using techniques of relaxation, controlled breathing, etc, rather than with anesthetics.

natural gas *n* gas trapped in the earth's crust, a combustible mixture of methane and hydrocarbons extracted for fuel.

natural history *n* the study of nature, esp the animal, mineral, and vegetable world.

naturalism *n* (*art, literature*) the theory or practice of describing nature, character, etc in realistic detail; (*philos*) a theory of the world based on scientific as opposed to spiritual or supernatural explanations.—**naturalistic** *adj*.

naturalist *n* a person who studies natural history; a person who advocates or practises naturalism.

naturalization *n* the act of investing a foreigner with the rights and privileges of a natural-born citizen.

naturalize *vt* to confer citizenship upon (a person of foreign birth); (*plants*) to become established in a different climate. * *vi* to become established as if native.

natural language *n* (*comput*) a human language such as English, as opposed to an artificial language such as BASIC or COBOL.

natural law *n* law based on innate moral sense.

naturally *adv* in a natural manner, by nature; of course.

natural number *n* any of the whole numbers starting with 1.

natural philosophy *n* physics.

natural resource *n* a naturally occurring source of wealth as in land, oil, coal, water power, etc.

natural science *n* the study of material things.

natural selection *n* the principle that evolution is determined by the survival of the fittest.

natural theology *n* knowledge of God derived from empirical observation and fact rather than from divine revelation.

natural wastage *n* the process by which a firm or organization can decrease in size without the necessity of resorting to redundancy.

nature *n* the phenomena of physical life not dominated by man; the entire material world as a whole, or forces observable in it; the essential character of anything; the innate character of a person, temperament; kind, class; vital force or functions; natural scenery.

nature morte *n* (*French*) "still life."

nature worship *n* the worship of the deified forces of nature.

naturism *n* nudism.

N

naturist *n* nudist.—*also adj.*

NatVALA *abbr* (*Brit*) = National Viewers & Listeners Association.

NatWest *abbr* = National Westminster Bank PLC.

naught *see* **nought**.

naughty *adj* (**naughtier, naughtiest**) mischievous or disobedient; titillating.— **naughtily** *adv*.—**naughtiness** *n*.

naumachia, naumachy *n* (*pl* **naumachias** *or* **naumachiae, naumachies**) a sea fight; a show representing a sea fight.

Nauplia *n* a port near the head of the Gulf of Argolis in Greece.

Nauplius *n* (*Greek myth*) a son of Poseidon and founder of the town of Nauplia.

Nauru *n* the smallest of the states in Oceania and one of the smallest republics in the world, occupying just over 8 square miles (21 square km) in the central Pacific.

Nauru n capital city of Nauru.

nausea *n* a desire to vomit; disgust.

nauseate *vti* to arouse feelings of disgust; to feel nausea or revulsion.—**nauseating** *adj*.

nauseous *adj* causing nausea; disgusting.—**nauseously** *adv*.—**nauseousness** *n*.

Nausicaä *n* (*Greek myth*) daughter of Alcinous and Arete.

naut. *abbr* = nautical.

nautch *n* in India, a dance performed by girls; a dancing exhibition.

nautical *adj* of ships, sailors, or navigation.

nautically *adv* in a nautical manner.

nautical mile *n* an international unit of measure for air and sea navigation equal to 6,075 feet (1.85 km).

nautilus *n* (*pl* **nautiluses, nautili**) a genus of cephalopods, including those furnished with a chambered spinal univalve shell; a shellfish with webbed arms once supposed to sail upon the sea; a kind of diving bell.

nav. *abbr* = naval; navigable; navigation.

NAV *abbr* = net asset value.

NAVA *abbr* = National Audio-Visual Association.

naval *adj* of the navy; of ships.

Navarre *n* Henri (1885–1970) French monumental sculptor.

Nav. Const. *abbr* = Naval Constructor.

Navdotoli *n* an archeological site in central India on the Narbada river dating from the Chalcolithic period, beginning *c.*2000 BC.

nave[1] *n* the central space of a church, distinct from the chancel and aisles.

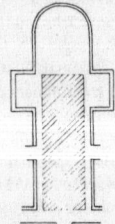

nave[2] *n* the central block of a wheel, the hub.

navel *n* the small scar in the abdomen caused by severance of the umbilical cord; a central point.

Naver *n* Kim (1940–) Danish weaver and designer who designed jewelry for Georg Jensen.

naveta *n* a form of Megalithic chamber tomb unique to the island of Minorca, dating from the early Bronze Age, *c.*2000–1500 BC.

NAVGRA *abbr* = Navy and Vickers Gearing Research Association.

NAVH *abbr* = National Association of Voluntary Hostels.

navig. *abbr* = navigation; navigator.

navigability *n* the quality or state of being navigable.

navigable *adj* (*rivers, seas*) that can be sailed upon or steered through.—**navigably** *adv*.

navigate *vti* to steer or direct a ship, aircraft, etc; to travel through or over (*water, air, etc*) in a ship or aircraft; to find a way through, over, etc, and to keep to a course.

navigation *n* the act, art or science of navigating; the method of calculating the position of a ship, aircraft, etc.—**navigational** *adj*.

navigator *n* one who navigates; one skilled in the science of navigation.

NAVL *abbr* = National Anti-Vaccination League.

NAVM *abbr* = Nurses Anti-Vivisection Movement.

Navratilova *n* Martina (1956–) Czech-born American tennis player and winner of nine Wimbledon singles championships.

NAVS *abbr* = National Anti-Vivisection Society.

navsat *abbr* = navigational satellite.

navvy *n* (*pl* **navvies**) (*Brit*) a laborer, esp one who works on roads or railways.

navy blue *n* an almost black blue.

navy *n* (*pl* **navies**) (*often with cap*) the warships of a nation; a nation's entire sea force, including ships, men, stores, etc; navy blue.

NAW *abbr* = National Assembly of Women; National Association of Widows.

nawab *n* an Indian viceroy; a nabob.

NAWB *abbr* = National Association of Wine and Beermakers; National Association of Workshops for the Blind.

NAWPU *abbr* = National Association of Water Power Users.

Naxos *n* the largest and most important island of the Cyclades group, in the Aegean Sea.

nay *adv* (*arch*) no; not only so; yet more; or rather, and even. * *n* a refusal or denial.

NAYC *abbr* = Youth Clubs UK (previously National Association of Youth Clubs).

NAYPIC *abbr* = National Association of Young People in Care.

NAYT *abbr* = National Association of Youth Theatres.

Nazarene *n* a native of Nazareth, applied to Jesus Christ, his followers, and the early Christians as a term of contempt; in the early Church, one of a sect of Judaising Christians.

Nazarenes *n* an art movement based on the Brotherhood of St Luke formed in Vienna in 1809.

Nazareth *n* (*Bible*) home town of Joseph and Mary where Jesus was brought up.

Nazarite, Nazirite *n* a native of Nazareth; a Jew devoted by vow to God to a life of abstinence and purity.

Nazi *n* (*pl* **Nazis**) a member of the German National Socialist Party (1930s).—*also adj.*

Nb *symbol* (*chem*) niobium (element).

nb *abbr* = no ball.

n.b., NB *abbr* (*Latin*) =*nota bene*, "note well."

Nb. *abbr* = nimbus.

NB *abbr* = New Brunswick.

NBA *abbr* = National Basketball Association; National Blood Authority; National Braille Association; Net Book Agreement.

NBAC *abbr* = National Bioethics Advisory Commission.

NBC *abbr* = National Broadcasting Corporation; nuclear, biological and chemical (as in warfare).

NbE *abbr* = north by east.

nbg *abbr* = no bloody good.

NBI *abbr* = National Benevolent Institution.

NBII *abbr* = National Biological Information Infrastructure.

NBL *abbr* = National Book League; New Brunswick Laboratory.

n-body problem *n* (*astron*) the orbital motions of an unspecified number, *n*, of bodies under their mutual gravitation.

NBR *abbr* = National Buildings Record.

NBRI *abbr* = National Building Research Institute.

NBS *abbr* = National Bureau of Standards.

NBTS *abbr* = National Blood Transfusion Service.

nbv *abbr* = net book value.

NbW *abbr* = north by west.

nc *abbr* = numerical/ly control/led.

n.c. *abbr* = nitrocellulose.

n/c *abbr* = no charge.

NC *abbr* = Navy-Curtiss seaplane; North Carolina.

nca *abbr* = no copies available.

NCA *abbr* = National Cemetery Administration; National Coffee Association of the USA; National Council of Aviculture.

NCB *abbr* = National Children's Bureau; National Cooperative Bank; no-claims bonus.

NCBI *abbr* = National Center for Biotechnology Information.

NCBW *abbr* = nuclear, chemical and biological warfare.

NCC *abbr* = National Consumer Council; National Curriculum Council; Nature Conservancy Council.

NCCA *abbr* = National Club Cricket Association; National Cotton Council of America.

NCCL *abbr* = National Council for Civil Liberties.

ncd *abbr* = no can do.

NCD *abbr* = National Council on Disability.

NCDC *abbr* = National Climatic Data Center.

NCES *abbr* = National Center for Education Statistics.

NCF *abbr* = National Clayware Federation; National Coaching Foundation; National Cooperage Federation.

NCFE *abbr* = Northern Council for Further Education.

NCI *abbr* = National Cancer Institute.

NCIS *abbr* = Naval Criminal Investigative Service.

NCJRS *abbr* = National Criminal Justice Reference Service.

NCL *abbr* = National Carriers Limited.

NCO *abbr* = noncommissioned officer.

NCP *abbr* = National Council of Psychotherapists; New Communist Party.

NCPS *abbr* = non-contributory pension scheme.

ncr *abbr* = no carbon required.

NCRR *abbr* = National Center for Research Resources.

NCS *abbr* = National Corrosion Service.

NCSS *abbr* = National Council for School Sports.

NCT *abbr* = National Center for Tribology; National Chamber of Trade.

NCTR *abbr* = National Center for Toxicological Research.

NCTU *abbr* = Northern Carpet Trades Union.

NCU *abbr* = National Communications Union; National Cyclists' Union.

NCUA *abbr* = National Credit Union Administration.

NCUMC *abbr* = National Council for the Unmarried Mother and her Child.

ncup *abbr* = no commission until paid.

ncv *abbr* = no commercial value.

NCVO *abbr* = National Council for Voluntary Organizations.

NCVQ *abbr* (*Brit*) = National Council for Vocational Qualifications.

Nd *symbol* (*chem*) neodymium (element).

nd *abbr* = no date; not dated/drawn; nothing doing.

n.d. *abbr* = no date.

Nd *abbr* (*chem*) = neodymium (element).

ND abbr = North Dakota; National Debt.

NDA *abbr* = National Dairymen's Association; National Development Association.

N. Dak. *abbr* = North Dakota.

NDBL *abbr* = National Deaf Blind League.

NDD *abbr* = National Diploma in Design.

NDE *abbr* = near-death experience.

NDF *abbr* = National Diploma in Forestry.

N'Djamena *n* capital city of Chad.

Ndola *n* a city in Zambia.

NDP *abbr* = net domestic product.

NDT *abbr* = non-destructive testing.

NDU *abbr* = National Defense University.

Ne *symbol* (*chem*) neon (element).

ne *abbr* = not essential; not exceeding.

n/e *abbr* = new edition; not entered; (*bank*) no effects.

NE *abbr* = Naval Engineer; Nebraska; New England; northeast, northeastern.

N/E *abbr* (*bank*) = no effects.

NEA *abbr* = National Education Association; National Endowment for the Arts; National Exhibitors Association; Neighbourhood Energy Action; Northern Examination Association.

NEAC *abbr* = New English Art Club.

Neagle *n* **Richard** (1922–) American industrial designer.

Neanderthal *adj* denoting or characteristic of Neanderthal man; primitive.

Neanderthal man *n* a type of primitive human inhabiting Europe in Paleolithic times.

neap *adj* of either of the lowest high tides in the month. * *n* a neap tide.

Neapolitan *adj* pertaining to Naples or to its inhabitants.

Neapolitan ice cream *n* brick ice cream in layers of different colors and flavors.

near *adj* (**nearer, nearest**) close, not distant in space or time; closely related, intimate; approximate, (*escape, etc*) narrow. * *adv* to or at a little distance; close by; almost. * *prep* close to. * *vti* to approach; to draw close to.—**nearness** *n*.

nearby *adj* neighbouring; close by in position.

Near East *n* Southeast Europe; (formerly) included Turkey, the Balkans and the area of the Ottoman Empire.

near letter quality *n* (*comput*) a mode of operation for dot matrix printers that produces characters at typewriter quality.

nearly *adv* almost, closely.

near miss *n* a bomb, mortar, etc that just fails to hit the target; any type of shot that misses its target; a situation in which two aircraft narrowly avoid a midair collision.

near-sighted *adj* short-sighted, myopic.—**near-sightedness** *n*.

neat[1] *adj* clean and tidy; skillful; efficiently done; well made; (*alcoholic drink*) undiluted; (*sl*) nice, pleasing, etc.—**neatly** *adv*.—**neatness** *n*.

neat[2] *n* cattle of the bovine genus. * *adj* pertaining to bovine animals.

neaten *vt* to make tidy and neat.

neath *prep* (*poet*) beneath.

neb *n* (*Scot*) a bird's beak; a mouth; a nose or snout; a projecting part, a point.

Neb., Nebr. *abbr* = Nebraska.

NEB *abbr* = New English Bible; National Enterprise Board.

NEbE *abbr* = northeast by east.

NEbN *abbr* = northeast by north.

Nebo *n* (*Bible*) a high mountain in Moab from which Moses viewed the promised land. *See also* **Moses.**

Nebraska *n* a state of the USA, of which the capital is Lincoln.

Nebuchadrezzar or Nebuchadnezzar *n* (*Bible*) emperor of Babylon who took Jerusalem in 587 BC.

nebula[1] *n* (*pl* **nebulae, nebulas**) (*astron*) a gaseous mass or star cluster in the sky appearing as a hazy patch of light.—**nebular** *adj*.

nebula[2] (*pl* **nebulae**)*n* (*med*) a slight opacity or scar of the cornea that does not obstruct vision but may create haziness; a liquid applied in a fine spray.

nebular hypothesis *n* the theory that the solar system in its primal condition existed in the form of a nebula, from which the sun, planets, and satellites were produced by condensation.

nebulizer *n* a device for producing a fine spray.

nebulosity *n* (*pl* **nebulosities**) the state or quality of being nebulous.

nebulous *adj* indistinct; formless.

nec *abbr* = not elsewhere classified.

NEC *abbr* = National Emergency Council; National Executive Committee.

necessarily *adv* as a natural consequence.

necessary *adj* indispensable; required; inevitable. * *n* (*pl* **necessaries**) something necessary; (*pl*) essential needs.

necessitarianism *n* (*philos*) the doctrine of necessity, or that man cannot control his actions by his own free will; fatalism.—**necessitarian** *n*.

necessitate *vt* to make necessary; to compel.

necessitous *adj* urgent; pressing; needy.

necessity *n* (*pl* **necessities**) a prerequisite; something that cannot be done without; compulsion; need.

Necho I *n* Egyptian king of the 26th Dynasty; ruled 672–644 BC; a descendant of Tefnakht; father of Psammetichus I.

Necho II *n* Egyptian king of the 26th Dynasty; ruled 610–595 bc; succeeded by Psammetichus II.

Nechta Scene *n* (*Irish Celtic myth*) a monstrous being whose three sons, Foill, Fannell and Tuachell, were killed by Cuchulainn.

Nechton *n* (*d. c.*724) king of Picts, Scotland (706–724). The brother of Bridei IV, he embraced Christianity and abdicated, leaving four rivals to contest the succession.

neck *n* the part of the body that connects the head and shoulders; that part of a garment nearest the neck; (*med*) the narrow part of a bone or organ; (*mus*) the narrow projecting part of a stringed instrument that supports the finger-board; a neck-like part, esp a narrow strip of land; the narrowest part of a bottle; a strait. * *vti* (*sl*) to kiss and caress.

neckerchief *n* a cloth square worn around the neck.

necking *n* (*archit*) a narrow convex molding between the base of a capital and the shaft of a column.

necklace *n* a string or band, often of precious stones, beads, or pearls, worn around the neck.

neckline *n* the line traced by the upper edge of a garment below the neck.

necktie *n* a man's tie.

Neco, Nechoh *n* (*Bible*) Pharaoh of Egypt who defeated King Josiah of Judah at Megiddo.

NE Code *abbr* = National Electrical Code.

necro-, necr- *prefix* corpse.

necrobiosis *n* the decay of living tissue.—**necrobiotic** *adj*.

necrology *n* (*pl* **necrologies**) a register or account of the dead.—**necrological** *adj*.

necromancer *n* one who practises necromancy; a conjurer; a wizard.

necromancy *n* predicting the future by alleged communication with the dead; sorcery.—**necromantic** *adj*.

necrophagous *adj* (*animal*) feeding on carrion.

necrophilia *n* erotic interest in or copulation with corpses.—*also* **necromania.**

necrophile, necrophiliac *n* a person who has an erotic interest in corpses.

necrophobia *n* fear of corpses or of death.— **necrophobe** *n*.—**necrophobic** *adj*.

necropolis *n* (*pl* **necropolises, necropoleis**) a cemetery.

necropsy *n* (*pl* **necropsies**) a post-mortem examination.

necrosis *n* mortification and death of a bone; gangrene; a disease in plants, characterized by small black spots.—**necrotic** *adj*.

necrotizing fasciitis *n* (*med*) a progressive infection that causes the destruction of soft tissue just below the skin.

NECSR *abbr* = North East Coast Ship Repairers.

Nectanebo I *n* (*Egypt*) a pharaoh (ruled 380–362 bc) of the final dynastic period, the 30th Dynasty, whose reign was dominated by efforts to keep the Persians from reclaiming Egypt as a satrapy.

Nectanebo II *n* (*Egypt*) the last Egyptian-born king of ancient Egypt (ruled 360–343 BC). Displaced by the Second Persian Occupancy, he retreated southwards and eventually took refuge in Nubia, where he maintained a government in exile for few years.

nectar *n* a sweetish liquid in many flowers, used by bees to make honey; any delicious drink.

nectareous, nectarous *adj* producing, or sweet, like nectar.

nectarine *n* a smooth-skinned peach.

nectary *n* (*pl* **nectaries**) that part of a flower which secretes a saccharine fluid.

NEDC or Neddy *abbr* = National Economic Development Council.

NEDL *abbr* = National Equine Defence League.

NEDO *abbr* = National Economic Development Office.

nee, née *adj* (*literally*) born: indicating the maiden name of a married woman.

need *n* necessity; a lack of something; a requirement; poverty. * *vt* to have a need for; to require; to be obliged.

needful *adj* necessary, required, vital. * *n* (*inf*) what is required, esp money.—**needfulness** *n*.

Needham *n* **Joseph** (1900–95) English biochemist and historian. His works include *The Sceptical Biologist*.

needle *n* a small pointed piece of steel for sewing; a larger pointed rod for knitting or crocheting; a stylus; the pointer of a compass, gauge, etc; the thin, short leaf of the pine, spruce, etc; the sharp, slender metal tube at the end of a hypodermic syringe; a pointed spire of rock, detached from a mountain rockface or sea cliff. * *vt* to goad, prod, or tease.

needlepoint *n* a type of embroidery worked on canvas; point lace.

needless *adj* not needed, unnecessary; uncalled for, pointless.—**needlessly** *adv*.—**needlessness** *n*.

needlework *n* sewing, embroidery.

needn't *abbr* = need not.

needs *adv* necessarily; indispensably.

needy *adj* (**needier, neediest**) in need, very poor.

neep *n* (*Scot*) a turnip.

ne'er *adv* (*poet*) never.

ne'er-do-well *adj* good-for-nothing; improvident; lazy. * *n* an irresponsible person.

NEF *abbr* = National Energy Foundation.

NEFA *abbr* = North East Forest Alliance.

nefarious *adj* wicked, evil.

Neferefre, Neferirkare *n* (*Egypt*) a pharaoh of the Old Kingdom, Fifth Dynasty (2510–2460 BC).

N

Nefertari *n* Egyptian Queen of the 18th Dynasty; married Ahmosis, her brother; succeeded by her son, Amenophis I, in 1526 BC.

Nefertiti *n* (14th century BC) queen consort of Akhenaten by whom she had six children.

neg. *abbr* = negative(ly).

negate *vt* to nullify; to deny.

negation *n* a negative statement, denial; the opposite or absence of something; a contradiction.

negative *adj* expressing or meaning denial or refusal; lacking positive attributes; (*math*) denoting a quantity less than zero, or one to be subtracted; (*photog*) reversing the light and shade of the original subject, or having the colors replaced by complementary ones; (*elect*) of the charge carried by electrons; producing such a charge. * *n* a negative word, reply, etc; refusal; something that is the opposite or negation of something else; (*in debate, etc*) the side that votes or argues for the opposition; (*photog*) a negative image on transparent film or a plate. * *vt* to refuse assent, contradict; to veto.—**negatively** *adv*.

negative cash flow *n* a cash flow in which the outgoings exceed the income.

negative income tax *n* a form of taxation aimed at improving the lot of the less well off.

negative painting *n* a method of decorating pottery using wax or wet clay to protect parts of the surface, then blackening the rest.

negativism *n* a tendency to be overly critical; skepticism.—**negativist** *n, adj.*—**negativistic** *adj.*

Negeb *n* (*Bible*) an area to the south of Judah from Beersheba to the Arabian Desert.

Neg. Ins. *abbr* = negotiable instrument.

neglect *vt* to pay little or no attention to; to disregard; to leave uncared for; to fail to do something. * *n* disregard; lack of attention or care.

neglectful *adj.*careless; heedless; slighting.—**neglectfully** *adv.*

negligee *n* a woman's loosely fitting dressing gown.

negligence *n* lack of attention or care; an act of carelessness; a carelessly easy manner.

negligent *adj* careless, heedless.—**negligently** *adv.*

negligible *adj* that need not be regarded; unimportant; trifling.

negotiable *adj* able to be legally negotiated; (*bills, drafts, etc*) transferable.—**negotiability** *n.*

negotiate *vti* to discuss, bargain in order to reach an agreement or settlement; to settle by agreement; to obtain or give money value for (a bill); to overcome (an obstacle, etc).

negotiation *n* the act of negotiating or transacting business; a treaty.

negotiator *n* one who negotiates.

Negrillo *n* (*pl* **Negrillos, Negrilloes**) one of a pigmy Negroid race found in Africa.

Negrito *n* (*pl* **Negritos, Negritoes**) one of a diminutive Negroid race of the Philippines and Polynesia.

negritude *n* the quality or condition of being a Negro; awareness of, or commitment to, Negro culture.

Negro *n* (*pl* **Negroes**) a member of the dark-skinned, indigenous peoples of Africa; a member of the Negroid group; a person with some Negro ancestors.—*also adj.*—**Negress** *nf.*

Negroid *adj* denoting, or of, one of the major groups of humankind, including most of the peoples of Africa south of the Sahara.

negus *n* (*pl* **neguses**) a beverage of hot water and wine, sweetened and spiced.

Negus *n* (*pl* **Neguses**) a title of the ruler of Ethiopia.

Neh. *abbr* = Nehemiah.

NEH *abbr* = National Endowment for the Humanities.

Nehemiah *n* (*Bible*) an exiled Jew who returned to Jerusalem to rebuild the wall. *See also* **Artaxerxes; Tobiah.**

Nehemiah *n* the Book of (*Bible*) the 16th book of the OT.

Nehru *n* **Jawaharlal** (1889–1964) Indian nationalist leader and statesman, son of Motilal Nehru ("Pandit" Nehru) (1861–1931), he became the first prime minister of India (1947–64) following independence and partition.

n.e.i. *abbr* (*Latin*) = *non est inventus.*

NEIC *abbr* = National Earthquake Information Center.

neigh *vi* (**neighing, neighed**) to whinny; to make a sound like the cry of a horse. * *n* the cry of a horse; a whinny.

neighbor, neighbour *n* a person who lives near another; a person or thing situated next to another; a fellow human being. * *vt* to be near, to adjoin.

neighborhood, neighbourhood *n* a particular community, area, or district; the people in an area.

neighboring, neighbouring *adj* adjoining, nearby.

neighborly, neighbourly *adj* characteristic of a neighbour, friendly. * *adv* in a neighbourly or social manner.—**neighborliness, neighbourliness** *n.*

Neill *n* **A[lexander] S[utherland]** (1883–1973) Scottish educationalist and founder of Summerhill School.

Neit *see* **Net.**

Neith *n* an Egyptian goddess of the 26th Dynasty and a huntress.

neither *adj, pron* not one or the other (of two); not either. * *conj* not either; also not.

nek *n* (S Africa) a depression or pass in a mountain range.

nekton *n* a collective term for minute forms of organic life found at various depths in seas and lakes.—**nektonic** *adj.*

NEL *abbr* = National Engineering Laboratory.

Neleus *n* (*Greek myth*) a king of Pylus; brother of Pelias and father of Nestor.

nelson *n* (*wrestling*) a type of hold in which the arms are placed under an opponent's arms from behind so that pressure can be exerted by the palms on the back of the opponent's neck.

Nelson *n* 1. **George** (1907–1986) American industrial designer who promoted modernism and pioneered pedestrian malls. 2. **Horatio [Viscount Nelson]** (1758–1805) English naval commander; became rear-admiral in 1797; defeated the French at the Battle of the Nile in 1798; killed at Trafalgar in 1805.

NEMA *abbr* = National Early Music Association.

Nemain, Nemhain *n* (*Irish Celtic myth*) a war-goddess like Macha and Morrigan. She was the wife of Net.

nemato-, nemat- *prefix* thread, fiber.

nematode *adj* thread-like * *n* a threadworm.

nem. con. *abbr* (*Latin*) = *nemine contradicente,* "with no one opposing."

nem. diss. *abbr* (*Latin*) = *nemine dissentiente,* "with no one dissenting."

Nemea *n* a city in northern Argolis in Greece.—**Nemean** *adj.*

Nemean Games *npl* ancient Greek games held in the valley of Nemea in Argolis.

Nemean Lion *n* (*Greek myth*) a monster which was killed by Heracles as the first of his labors.

Nemedh, Nemed *n* (*Irish Celtic myth*) the leader of the third invasion of Ireland. When Nemedh died, his people were defeated and subjugated by the Fomorii.

Nemedians *n* (*Irish Celtic myth*) the followers of Nemedh.

nemes headdress *n* (*Egypt*) a royal headdress, made of cloth, knotted at the back and with two prominent side lappets.

nemesis *n* (*pl* **nemeses**) retribution; just punishment; an agent of defeat.

Nemesis *n* (*Greek myth*) the personification of the righteous anger and retribution of the gods.

nemeton *n* (*Celtic*) a sacred grove, the Celts having a special veneration for woodlands.

Nemetona *n* (*Roman-Celtic myth*) a goddess associated with groves, her name being formed from nemeton. An association between her and Nemain has been suggested.

Nemhain *see* **Nemain.**

NEMS *abbr* (*Brit*) = North of England Museums Service.

NEMSA *abbr* = (*Brit*) North of England Mule Sheep Association.

N. Eng. *abbr* = New England.

neo- *prefix* new, newly.

neoclassicism, neo-classicism *n* (*mus*) a 20th-century musical movement which reacted against the overtly romantic forms of the late-19th century; (*art*) movement in art and architecture in the late 18th and early 19th centuries. *See also* **classicism.**

neodymium *n* a silvery-white metallic element used in alloys, etc.

neo-impressionism *n* (*art*) development of impressionism pioneered by the pointillist painters Seurat, Signac and Pissarro.

Neolithic *adj* of the later Stone Age, marked by the use of polished stone implements.

neologism *n* a new word; the coining of new words, neology; the introduction of new doctrines.—**neologistic, neologistical** *adj.*

neologist *n* an innovator in language or religion, esp one who holds doctrinal views opposed to the orthodox interpretation of revealed religion.

neologize *vt* to introduce new words, phrases, or religious doctrines.

neology *n* neologism; doctrines or rationalistic theological interpretation at variance with orthodox belief.

neomycin *n* an antibiotic, usually applied as a cream, effective against a wide spectrum of bacteria.

neon *n* an inert gaseous element that gives off a bright orange glow, used in lighting and advertisements.

neonatal *adj* a term meaning "relating to the first 28 days of life."

neonate *n* a newborn child, esp one less than a month old.

neophyte *n* a novice; one recently baptised; a convert. * *adj* recently entered.

neoplasm *n* a new and abnormal growth of cells, i.e. a tumor, which may be benign or malignant.

neoplastic *adj* newly formed.

neoplasty *n* the restoration of tissue by plastic surgery.

NeoPlatonism *n* a system of eclectic philosophy combining the doctrines of Plato with Oriental mysticism in the 3rd century.—**NeoPlatonist** *n.*

neoprene *n* a durable synthetic rubber used in waterproof products.

Neoptolemus *n* (*Greek myth*) a son of Achilles; he fought bravely in the Trojan War and was one of the Greeks who hid in the wooden horse.—*also* **Pyrrhus.**

neoteric *adj* recent in origin; newfangled, modern.—**neoterically** *adv.*

Neotropical *adj* of tropical or South America.

Neozoic *adj* (*geol*) denoting rocks from the Trias to the present time.

Nepalese *n, adj* of Nepal.

Nepalese Rupee *n* currency of Nepal.

Nepali *n* (*pl* **Nepali, Nepalis**) a native or inhabitant of Nepal; the language of Nepal.—*also adj.*

nepenthe *n* a drug supposed by the ancient Greeks to have the power of causing forgetfulness of sorrow.—**nepenthean** *adj.*

Nephele *n* (*Greek myth*) the first wife of Athamas and mother of Phrixus and Helle.

nephew *n* the son of a brother or sister.

nephology *n* the study of clouds.—**nephological** *adj.*—**nephologist** *n.*

nephralgia *n* pain or disease in the kidneys.—**nephralgic** *adj.*

nephrectomy *n* surgical removal of the kidney (radical) or part of the kidney (partial).

nephrite *n* jade.

nephritic *adj* of or pertaining to the kidneys or kidney disease; affected with disease of the kidneys.

nephritis *n* inflammation of the kidneys.

nephro-, nephr- *prefix* kidney; kidneys.

nephroblastoma *see* **Wilm's tumor.**

nephrology *n* study of the kidneys.

nephron *n* a renal tubule and blood vessel which filters blood under pressure, reabsorbing water and other substances.

nephrotomy *n* (*pl* **nephrotomies**) incision into the kidney.

Nephthys *n* (*Egypt*) an ancient but relatively unimportant Egyptian goddess, sister and wife of Seth but nevertheless devoted to both Osiris and Isis.

ne plus ultra *n* (*Latin*) the farthest attainable point; the acme, the perfect state.—*also* **non plus ultra**.

nepotism *n* undue favoritism shown to relatives, esp in securing jobs.

NEPRA *abbr* = National Egg Producers Retail Association.

Neptune[1] *n* (*astron*) the eighth planet of the solar system with its orbit between that of Uranus and Pluto.

Neptune[2] *n* (*Roman myth*) the god of the sea, identified with the Greek, Poseidon.

Neptunian *adj* pertaining to the classical deity Neptune, god of the sea, or to the sea; deposited by the agency of the sea.

neptunium *n* a radioactive metallic element.

Nera *n* (*Irish Celtic myth*) an attendant of Ailill who went on an adventure to the Otherworld, where he married and had a son.

NERA *abbr* = National Emergency Relief Administration.

NERC *abbr* = Natural Environment Research Council.

nerd *n* (*sl*) a boring, straight-laced person; a creep.

Nereid[1] *n* (*pl* **Nereids, Nereides**) (*Greek myth*) a sea nymph.

Nereid[2] *n* the outermost satellite of Neptune.

nereis *n* (*zool*) a sea worm.

Nereus *n* (*Greek myth*) a god of the sea, the father of the Nereides.

NERIS *abbr* = National Educational Resources Information Service.

neritic zone *n* (*ecology*) the zone of shallow water near the seashore.

Nernst *n* **Walther Hermann** (1864–1941) German physical chemist; winner of the 1920 Nobel prize for chemistry for his proposal of the heat theorem, which was formulated as the third law of thermodynamics.

Nero *n* (37–68) Roman emperor who succeeded Claudius in 54 and became infamous for his debauchery.

neroli *n* the essential oil of orange flowers.

NERSC *abbr* = National Energy Research Scientific Computing Center.

Neruda *n* 1. **Jan** (1834–91) Czech writer whose plays and prose, e.g. *Tales of the Little Quarter*, are highly regarded. 2. **Pablo [Ricardo Neftali Reyes]** (1904–73) Chilean poet and diplomat. He was awarded the Nobel prize for literature in 1971.

Nerval *n* **Gerard de** (1808–55) French writer who influenced both the symbolism and surrealism movements.

nervate *adj* (*bot*) ribbed.

nervation *n* (*bot*) the arrangement of veins, venation.

nerve *n* any of the fibers or bundles of fibers that transmit impulses of sensation or of movement between the brain and spinal cord and all parts of the body; courage, coolness in danger; (*inf*) audacity, boldness; (*pl*) nervousness, anxiety. * *vt* to give strength, courage, or vigor to.

nerve block *n* the technique of blocking sensory nerves sending pain impulses to the brain, thus creating anesthesia in that part of the body.—*also* **conduction anesthesia.**

nerve cell *n* a cell transmitting impulses in nerve tissue.—*also* **neuron, neurone.**

nerve center, nerve centre *n* a group of closely connected cells; (*mil*) a centre of control from which instructions are sent out.

nerve gas *n* a poison gas that affects the nervous system.

nerve impulse *n* the transmission of information along a nerve fiber by electrical activity.

nerve injury *n* damage to a nerve, either by severing or pressure.

nerveless *adj* calm, cool; weak, feeble.—**nervelessly** *adv*.

nerve-racking, nerve-wracking *adj* straining the nerves, stressful.

Nervi *n* **Pier Luigi** (1891–1979) Italian architect of monumental buildings who introduced the use of reinforced concrete.

nervous *adj* excitable, highly strung; anxious, apprehensive; affecting or acting on the nerves or nervous system.

nervous breakdown *n* a (usu temporary) period of mental illness resulting from severe emotional strain or anxiety.

nervous system *n* the brain, spinal cord, and nerves collectively.

nervure *n* the veins of leaves; the horny ribs supporting the membranous wings of an insect.

nervy *adj* (**nervier, nerviest**) (*inf*) anxious, agitated; (*inf*) impudent, cheeky.

nes, NES *abbr* = not elsewhere specified.

NES *abbr* = National Eczema Society; Numerical Engineering Society Limited.

Nesbit *n* **E[dith]** (1858–1924) English writer of children's books such as *The Railway Children*.

nescience *n* ignorance; agnosticism.—**nescient** *adj*.

NESDIS *n* = National Environmental Satellite, Data, and Information Service.

ness *n* a headland or cape, a promontory.

-ness *suffix* state, quality of being.

Nessa *n* (*Irish Celtic myth*) the mother of Conchobar mac Nessa, either by her husband, Fachta, or by the druid Cathbad. She was the lover of Fergus mac Roth.

Nessus *n* (*Greek myth*) a centaur who was expelled from Arcadia by Heracles, and who was the ultimate cause of the death of Heracles.

nest *n* a structure or place where birds, fish, mice, etc, lay eggs or give birth to young; a place where young are nurtured; a swarm or brood; a lair; a cosy place; a set of boxes, tables, etc of different sizes, designed to fit together. * *vi* to make or occupy a nest.

nest egg *n* money put aside as a reserve or to establish a fund.

nestle *vti* to rest snugly; to lie snugly, as in a nest; to lie sheltered or half-hidden.

nestling *n* a young bird that has not left the nest.

Nestor *n* (*Greek myth*) a Greek sage of the Trojan war; a wise old man.

Nestorianism *n* the fifth-century doctrine of Nestorius, Bishop of Constantinople, who taught that there were two natures in Christ, one human and one divine, which did not unite and form one person; also that the Virgin Mary was not the Mother of God.—**Nestorian** *n, adj*.

net[1] *n* an openwork material of string, rope, or twine knotted into meshes; a piece of this used to catch fish, to divide a tennis court, etc; a snare; (*comput*) the Internet. * *vti* (**netting, netted**) to snare or enclose as with a net; to hit (a ball) into a net or goal.

net[2], **nett** *adj* clear of deductions, allowances or charges. * *n* a net amount, price, weight, profit, etc. * *vt* (**netting, netted**) to clear as a profit.

net, Net *abbr* = not earlier than; the Internet.

Net, Neit *n* (*Irish Celtic myth*) a war-god. He was the husband of Nemain.

net assets *npl* the assets of a company, including fixed assets and net current assets, or working capital, less current liabilities.

net asset value *n* the value of a share in a company.

net book value *n* the value at which an asset appears in the financial records of a firm, usually as at the date of the last balance sheet.

net current assets *npl* the current assets of a company less its current liabilities.

net dividend the dividend that a company pays to its shareholders after the exclusion of the tax credit received by the shareholders.

net domestic product *n* the gross domestic product after the deduction of capital consumption.

Neth. *abbr* = Netherlands.

nether *adj* lower or under.

Netherlands *n* [Holland] a constitutional monarchy forming one of the Benelux or Low Countries along with Belgium and Luxembourg.

Netherlands Antilles *n* a self-governing Dutch territory comprising two sets of islands, the Southern Netherlands Antilles and the Northern Netherlands Antilles.

Netherlands Antilles Guilder *n* the currency of the Netherlands Antilles.

nethermost *adj* lowest.

nether world *n* the underworld, hell.

net income *n* a person's income after income tax has been deducted; the income of a person or organization that remains after the deduction of the expenses that have had to be met in earning it.

net interest *n* the interest that is paid into a bank or other savings account after tax has been deducted at source.

netizen *n* (*comput*) literally "net citizen," someone who uses the Internet.

NETL *abbr* = National Energy Technology Laboratory.

n et m *abbr* (*Latin*) = *nocte et mane*, "night and morning."

net national product *n* the amount that remains after the capital consumption (i.e., the total depreciation in the value of capital goods) has been deducted from the gross national product, being equal to the amount of money that is available in a country's economy for expenditure on goods and services.

net present value *n* in discounted cash flows, the difference between the present value of the cash outflow and that of the cash inflow.

net price *n* the price that a purchaser pays for goods after the deduction of any discounts.

net profit *n* the profit that a company makes after all running costs and expenses have been taken into account; the final profit that a company makes after all relevant taxes have been deducted from net profit above.

net realizable value *n* the amount for which the stock of a company can be sold, less the costs likely to be involved in carrying out the sale.

net receipts *npl* the total amount of money received by a company or in a business transaction after the deduction of costs, raw materials, relevant taxation, etc.

net return *n* the profit that is made on any form of investment after the deduction of all expenses.

Netscape *n* (*trademark*) (*comput*) a company founded in 1994 which produces software for the Web and the popular browser, Navigator.

netsuke *n* a Japanese ornamental toggle for fastening the front of a garment.

netting *n* netted fabric.

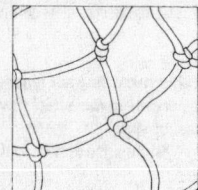

nettle *n* a wild plant with stinging hairs. * *vt* to irritate, annoy.

nettle rash *n* a cutaneous skin eruption resembling the effects of a nettle sting. *See* **urticaria**.

network *n* an arrangement of intersecting lines; a group of people who cooperate with each other; a chain of interconnected operations, computers, etc; (*radio, TV*) a group of broadcasting stations connected to transmit the same programme simultaneously. * *vt* to broadcast on a network; (*comput*) to interconnect systems so that information, software, and peripheral devices, such as printers, can be shared.

N

network administrator *n* (*comput*) the individual who manages a local area network.

network analysis/modeling *n* a method of planning, scheduling and controlling complex projects that involves various interrelated but distinct elements of work known as activities.

networking *n* the making of contacts and trading information as for career advancement; the interconnection of computer systems.

network interface card *n* (*comput*) an adapter card that allows networking cable to be connected directly to the computer.

Network Neighborhood *n* (*trademark*) (*comput*) a feature of Windows (*trademark*) that appears as an icon and shows, when double-clicked, the extent of the network available through the computer being used. It will show whatever computers, printers, etc. are linked to the network.

network operating system *n* (*comput*) the operating system that is used as a controller for all network components.

network server *n* (*comput*) *see* **file server; server**.

net worth *n* the value of a company when its liabilities have been deducted from its assets.

Neue Sachlichkeit *n* an exhibition of postwar figurative art planned in 1923 by Gustave Hartlaub; any art concerned with objective representation of real life.

Neumann *n* **Johann** (1687–) German architect. His notable works include the pilgrimage church of Vierzehn Heiligen.

neume *n* (*mus*) a sign used in musical notation from the 7th to 14th centuries. It gave an indication of pitch.

neur-, neuro- *prefix* nerve.

neural *adj* of or pertaining to the nerves.

neuralgia *n* pain along a nerve.

neuralgic *adj* pertaining to neuralgia.

neurasthenia *n* brain and nerve exhaustion, as from influenza, etc.

neurectomy *n* (*pl* **neurectomies**) excision of a nerve.

neuritis *n* inflammation of a nerve.

neuroendocrine system *n* one of a number of dual control systems regulating bodily functions through the action of nerves and hormones.

neurofibromatosis *see* **von Recklinghausen's disease**.

neuroglia *n* the delicate connective tissue between the nerve fibers of the brain and spinal cord.

neurohormone *n* a hormone that is secreted by the nerve endings of specialized nerve cells and not by an endocrine gland.

neurohypophysis *see* **pituitary gland**.

neuroleptic *n* any drug that induces neurolepsis, i.e. reduced activity, some indifference to the surroundings, and possibly sleep.

neurology *n* the branch of medicine studying the nervous system and its diseases.—**neurological** *adj*.—**neurologist** *n*.

neuroma *n* (*pl* **neuromas, neuromata**) a fibrous tumor occuring in nerve tissue.

neuromuscular blockade *n* the blocking of impulses at the neuromuscular junction to paralyze a part of the body for surgery. *See also* **nerve block**.

neuromuscular junction *n* the area of membrane between a muscle cell and a motor neuron, forming a synapse between the two.

neuron, neurone *n* a nerve cell, vital in the transmission of nerve impulses.

neuropathic *adj* pertaining to, or suffering from, nervous disease; affecting the nerves.—**neuropath** *n*.—**neuropathically** *adv*.

neuropathology *n* the study of diseases of the nervous system.—**neuropathologist** *adj*.

neuropathy *n* disease of the nervous system.

neuropteran *n* (*pl* **neuropterans**) any of an order of insects characterized by four transparent, finely reticulated, membranous wings. * *adj* with four wings marked with a network of nerves (—*also* **neuropterous**).

neurosecretory cell *see* **neurohormone**.

neurosis (*pl* **neuroses**) *n* a mental disorder in which the patient retains a grasp on reality (unlike psychosis) which may be caused by anxiety, depression, phobia, hysteria, or hypochrondria.

neurosurgery *n* the branch of surgery dealing with the brain and the nervous system.—**neurosurgical** *adj*.

neurotic *adj* suffering from neurosis; highly strung; of or acting upon the nerves. * *n* someone with neurosis.

neurotomy *n* (*pl* **neurotomies**) dissection of the nerves.

neurotransmitter *n* a chemical by which nerves cells communicate with each other or with muscles.

neut. *abbr* = neuter.

neuter *adj* (*gram*) of gender, neither masculine nor feminine; (*biol*) having no sex organs; having undeveloped sex organs in the adult. * *n* a neuter person, word, plant, or animal. * *vt* to castrate or spay.

Neutra *n* **Richard Josef** (1892–1970) Austrian architect. His notable works include Lovell Health House, Los Angeles.

neutral *adj* nonaligned; not taking sides with either party in a dispute or war; having no distinctive characteristics; (*color*) dull; (*chem*) neither acid nor alkaline; (*physics*) having zero charge. * *n* a neutral state, person, or color; a position of a gear mechanism in which power is not transmitted.

neutrality *n* the state of being neutral.

neutralization *n* (*chem*) a reaction that either increases the pH of an acidic solution, or decreases the pH of an alkaline solution, to neutral seven.

neutralize *vt* to render ineffective; to counterbalance; to declare or render neutral.—**neutralization** *n*.—**neutralizer** *n*.

neutrally *adv* in a neutral manner.

neutrino *n* (*pl* **neutrinos**) (*phys*) a stable elementary particle with almost zero mass and spin 1/2.

neutron *n* a subatomic elementary particle with no electric charge and the same mass approximately as a proton.

neutron activation analysis *n* (*archeol*) a scientific technique for the analysis of trace elements present in a sample of a metal or pottery.

neutron bomb *n* a nuclear bomb with a small blast that releases neutrons, destroying life but leaving property undamaged.

neutron number *n* the number of neutrons in the nucleus of an atom.

neutron star *n* a star composed solely of densely packed neutrons that has collapsed under its own gravity.

Nev., NV *abbr* = Nevada.

Nevada *n* a state of the USA, of which the capital is Carson City.

névé *n* the granular compressed snow that forms glacier ice. *See* also **firn**.

Nevelson *n* **Louise** (1899–1988) Russian-born American sculptor. Her works include *An American Tribute to the British People* (*Gold Wall*) (1959).

never *adv* at no time, not ever; not at all; in no case; (*inf*) surely not.

nevermore *adv* never again.

never-never *adj* imaginary, ideal.

nevertheless *adv* all the same, notwithstanding; in spite of, however.

Nevinson *n* **Christopher Richard Wynne** (1889–1946) English painter; a leading figure in British futurism.

nevus *n* (*pl* **nevi**) a birthmark, a mole.—*also* **naevus**.—**nevoid** *adj*.

new *adj* recently made, discovered, or invented; seen, known, or used for the first time; different, changed; recently grown, fresh; unused; unaccustomed; unfamiliar; recently begun. * *adv* again; newly; recently.

New Amsterdam *n* a city in Guyana.

Newbery *n* **John** (1713–67) English publisher who became the first to specialize in selling books written for children.

new blood *n* a recent arrival in an organization expected to bring new ideas and revitalize the system.

Newbolt *n* **Sir Henry [John]** (1862–1938) English poet whose patriotic naval poems, e.g. "Drake's Drum," were popular at the end of the 19th century.

newborn *adj* newly born; reborn.

New Caledonia *n* a French overseas territory, also known as Nouvelle Calédonie, which is the most southerly of the Melanesian countries in the Pacific Ocean.

newcomer *n* a recent arrival.

New Deal *n* the economic and social measures introduced into the USA by President Roosevelt in 1933 to combat the economic crisis that began in 1929.

New Delhi *n* capital city of India.

New Dinar *n* the currency of Yugoslavia (FRY).

New Dong *n* the currency of Vietnam.

newel *n* the central pillar of a spiral staircase; the end post of a banister.

New England *n* the six northeastern states of the USA.

Newf. *abbr* = Newfoundland.

newfangled *adj* (*contemptuous*) new; novel, very modern.

Newfoundland *n* a large variety of dog, originally from Newfoundland.

New Hampshire *n* a state of the USA, of which the capital is Concord.

Newill *n* **Mary J.** (1860–1947) British designer and embroider; a founder member of the Arts and Crafts Exhibition Society.

New Israeli Shekel *n* the currency of Israel and of the West Bank and Gaza Strip.

new issue *n* a share that is being offered for sale on a stock exchange for the first time.

New Jersey *n* a state of the USA, of which the capital is Trenton.

New Kingdom *n* (Egypt) from around 1552–1070 BC, the period of the 18th to the 29th Dynasties of ancient Egypt.

New Kip n the currency of Laos.

newly *adv* recently, lately.

newlywed *n* a recently married person.

New M. *abbr* = New Mexico.

Newman *n* 1. **Barnett** (1905–70) American painter; pioneer of abstract expressionism along with Rothko and Motherwell. 2. Cardinal **John Henry** (1801–90) English theologian, whose spirited defence of his faith, *Apologia pro vita sua*, created a deep impression on believers and nonbelievers alike. 3. **Paul** (1925–) American film actor whose films include *The Color of Money* (1986) for which he won an Oscar.

New Mexico *n* a state of the USA, of which the capital is Santa Fe.

new moon *n* the moon when first visible as a crescent.

news *npl* current events; recent happenings; the mass media's coverage of such events; a program of news on television or radio; information not known before.

news agency *n* an organization that gathers news for newspapers and other news media such as television and radio.— *also* **press agency**.

newscast *n* radio or television news broadcast.—**newscaster** *n*.

newsdealer, newsagent *n* a retailer of newspapers, magazines, etc.

newsflash *n* an important news item broadcast separately and often interrupting other programmes.

newsgroup *n* (*comput*) a group of people who use an on-line service to discuss interactively topics of mutual interest.

newsletter *n* a bulletin regularly distributed among the members of a group, society, etc, containing information and news of activities, etc.

new sol *n* the standard monetary unit of Peru, which is made up of 100 cents.

Newson *n* **Mark** (1962–) Australian industrial designer who is best-known for his 1985 *Lockheed Lounge* steel chaise.

newspaper *n* a printed periodical containing news published daily or weekly.

newspeak *n* the convoluted and often misleading language used by politicians and bureaucrats.

newsprint *n* an inexpensive paper on which newspapers are printed.

newsreel *n* a short film presenting news of current events with a commentary.

newsroom *n* the department of a newspaper or broadcasting system that prepares news for publication or broadcasting; a room, etc, where newspapers, magazines, etc, may be read.

newsstand *n* a stand, often portable, from which newspapers, etc, are sold.

New Style calendar *n* the Gregorian or present style of computing the calendar, which replaced the Julian calendar.

newsworthy *adj* timely and important or interesting.

newt *n* any of various small amphibious lizard-like creatures.

New Taiwan Dollar *n* the currency of Taiwan.

New Test. *abbr* = New Testament.

New Testament *n* the second part of the Bible including the story of the life and teachings of Christ.

newton *n* the SI unit of force that when acting for 1 second on a mass of 1 kilogram imparts an acceleration of 1 meter per second.

Newton *n* Sir Isaac (1642–1727) English scientist, philosopher, and mathematician who discovered the law of gravity.

Newtonian *adj* pertaining to, discovered by, or invented by, Sir Isaac Newton, the philosopher, or to his system.

Newtonian telescope *n* (*astron*) a type of telescope in which the image is reflected from a main mirror into an eyepiece on the side of the tube.

new town *n* in UK, any of various towns built since 1946 as planned units sponsored by government to house overspill population from nearby cities, aid urban redevelopment, etc.

New World *n* the Americas.

New Year's (Day) *n* the first day of a new year; 1 January, a legal holiday in many countries.

New Year's Eve *n* the evening of the last day of the year; 31 December.—*also* **Hogmanay.**

New York *n* a state of the USA, of which the capital is Albany.

New York *n* a city in the USA.

New Zealand *n* a constitutional monarchy lying over 1,242 miles or 2,000 kilometers southeast of Australia in the South Pacific. It comprises two major islands—North Island and South Island—Stewart Island, the Chatham Islands, and many smaller islands.

New Zealand Dollar *n* the currency of New Zealand.

next *adj* nearest; immediately preceding or following; adjacent. * *adv* in the nearest time, place, rank, etc; on the first subsequent occasion.

neXT *n* (*comput*) a computer workstation designed by Steve Jobs, combining the UNIX operating system with a graphic user interface.

next-door *adj* living or situated in the adjoining house, apartment, room, etc; nearby. * *adv*.

next of kin *n* the nearest relative of a person.

nexus *n* (*pl* **nexus, nexuses**) a connecting principle or link.

n/f. *abbr* (*bank*) = no funds.

NF *abbr* = (pharm)National Formulary ; Newfoundland; Norman/Northern French; no funds; noise factor.

N.F. *abbr* = Newfoundland.

nfa *abbr* = no further action.

NFA *abbr* = National Federation of Anglers; National Film Archive; National Food Authority; National Fire Academy.

NFAC *abbr* = National Federation of Aerial Contractors.

NFAS *abbr* = National Field Archery Society.

NFBPM *abbr* = National Federation of Builders' and Plumbers' Merchants.

NFBPWC *abbr* = National Federation of Business and Professional Women's Clubs.

nfc *abbr* = not favourably considered.

NFC *abbr* = National Freight Consortium; Northern Fisheries Committee.

NFCA *abbr* = National Foster Care Association.

NFCF *abbr* = National Federation of Cemetery Friends.

NFER *abbr* = National Foundation for Educational Research.

NFF *abbr* = National Farers' Federation; National Federation of Fishmongers.

NFFC *abbr* = National Film Finance Corporation.

NFFPOW *abbr* = National Federation of Far-Eastern Prisoners of War Clubs.

NFFPT *abbr* = National Federation of Fruit and Potato Trades.

NFFQO *abbr* = National Federation of Freestone Quarry Owners.

Nfld. *abbr* = Newfoundland.

NFMS *abbr* = National Federation of Music Societies.

NFPA *abbr* = National Foster Parents Association.

NFPS *abbr* = Norse Film & Pageant Society.

nfr *abbr* = no further requirements.

NFRC *abbr* = National Freight Rail Corporation.

NFRS *abbr* = National Fancy Rat Society.

nfs *abbr* = not for sale.

NFS *abbr* = National Federation of Shopmobility.

NFS & MC *abbr* = National Federation of Sailing and Motor Cruising Schools.

NFSC *abbr* = National Federation of Football Supporters' Clubs.

NFSE *abbr* = National Federation of Self-Employed and Small Businesses.

NFSS *abbr* = National Federation of Sea Schools.

NFT *abbr* (*Brit*) = National Film Theatre.

NFTS *abbr* = National Film and Television School.

NFU *abbr* (*Brit*) = National Farmers' Union.

NFWI *abbr* (*Brit*) = National Federation of Women's Institutes.

NFYFC *abbr* = National Federation of Young Farmers' Clubs.

ng, n.g. *abbr* = no good; not given.

Ng. *abbr* = Norwegian.

NG *abbr* = National Gallery.

N.G. *abbr* = National Guard; New Granada; (*bank*) not good.

NGA *abbr* = National Graphical Association.

NGAC *abbr* = National Greenhouse Advisory Committee.

N galaxy or **N-type galaxy** *n* a galaxy with a pronounced star-like nucleus having a faint surrounding haze.

NGBF *abbr* = National Grocers' Benevolent Fund.

NGC *abbr* = National Gypsy Council; New General Catalog.

NGCAA *abbr* = National Golf Clubs Advisory Association.

NGDC *abbr* = National Geophysical Data Center.

n. gen. *abbr* = new genus.

NGNP *abbr* = nominal gross national product.

NGO *abbr* = non-governmental organization.

N.Gr. *abbr* = New Greek.

NGRC *abbr* = National Greyhound Racing Club.

NGS *abbr* = National Gardens Scheme; National Geographic Society.

NGU abbr = non-gonococcal urethritis.

ngultrum *see* **chetrum.**

Ngultrum *n* currency of Bhuta.

NGVA *abbr* = Natural Gas Vehicle Association.

ngwee *n* a monetary unit of Zambia that is worth one hundredth of a kwacha.

NH *abbr* = New Hampshire; New Hebrides.

NHA *abbr* = National Housewives Association.

NHBRC *abbr* = National House-Builders' Registration Certificate/Council.

NHBS *abbr* = National Horse Brass Society.

NHC *abbr* = National Hyperbaric Centre.

NHeb. *abbr* = New Hebrew.

NHF *abbr* = National Hairdressers' Federation.

NHG *abbr* = New High German.

NHGRI *abbr* = National Human Genome Research Institute.

NHI *abbr* = National Health Insurance; National Highway Institute.

NHLBI *abbr* = National Heart, Lung and Blood Institute.

NHLS *abbr* = National Hedge-Laying Society.

NHM *abbr* = Natural History Museum.

NHMF *abbr* = National Heritage Memorial Fund.

nhp, NHP *abbr* = nominal horsepower.

NHPRC *abbr* = National Historical Publications and Records Commission.

NHR *abbr* (*Brit*) = National Hunt Rules.

NHS *abbr* = National Health Service.

NHTSA *abbr* = National Highway Traffic Safety Administration.

Ni *symbol* (*chem*) nickel (element).

NI *abbr* = National Insurance; Nautical Institute; Northern Ireland.

niacin *n* nicotinic acid.

NIAID *abbr* = National Institute for Allergy and Infectious Diseases.

Niall of the Nine Hostages or **Niall Noigiallach** *n* (*d.* 405) high king of Ireland (379–405); a semi-legendary figure who gained his name by holding nine members of different ruling dynasties hostage at the same time in order to secure his position as high king.

Niamey *n* capital city of Niger.

Niamh *n* (*Irish Celtic myth*) 1. the daughter of Manannan mac Lir, she became the lover of Oisin. 2. wife of Conall Cernach and the lover of Cuchulainn. She begged him not to attack the sons of Calatin for she knew that this would lead to his death. 3. the daughter of Celtchar, who married Conganchas mac Daire, a warrior whom no one could slay. She learned the secret of his invulnerability and revealed it to her father, who killed the warrior.

NIAS *abbr* = Northern Ireland Archery Society.

nib *n* a pen point. * *vt* (**nibbing, nibbed**) to furnished with a nib; to cut or insert a pen nib.

nibble *vti* to take small bites at (food, etc); to bite (at) lightly and intermittently.—**nibbler** *n*.

Nibelungenlied *n* a medieval German epic poem.

niblick *n* a golf club with a heavy head, used for lofting.

nic *abbr* = newly industrialised country; not in contract.

NIC *abbr* = National Institute of Corrections; (*Brit*) National Insurance Contributions.

nicad *adj* of nickel and cadmium. * *n* a nickel and cadmium battery.

Nicar. *abbr* = Nicaragua.

Nicaragua *n* a republic in central America.

nice *adj* pleasant, attractive, kind, good, etc; particular, fastidious; delicately sensitive.—**nicely** *adv*.

Nice *n* a city in France.

NICEC *abbr* = National Institute for Careers, Education and Counselling.

NICEIC *abbr* = National Inspection Council for Electrical Installation Contracting.

nice-looking *adj* pretty, handsome.

N

Nicene Creed *n* the creed, one of the three held by the Anglican Church, drawn up by the Ecumenical Council of the Early Christian Church at the Council of Nicaea in Asia Minor in AD 325, with additions made at the Council of Constantinople 381.

niceness *n* the state or quality of being nice; delicacy of perception or touch.

nicety *n* (*pl* **niceties**) a subtle point of distinction; refinement.

niche *n* (*archit*) a small recess set into a wall for a statue, etc; a place, use, or work for which a person or thing is best suited;(*ecology*) all the environmental factors that affect an organism and its community.

niche marketing *n* a form of marketing that involves a comparatively small segment of a market with its own distinctive customer profile and buyer characteristics.

Nicholas *n* **Saint** (*d. c.*326) patron saint of Russia, and of pawnbrokers, sailors, and children; the custom of giving presents in his name originated among the Protestant Dutch. His feast day is December 6.

Nicholas II (1868–1918) Russian tsar (1895–1917) who was deposed and murdered with his family by the Bolsheviks.

Nicholls *n* **David Shaw** (1959–) British furniture designer who has worked mostly in Milan and New York.

Nicholson *n* 1. **Ben** (1894–1982) largely self-taught English artist; notable later works include *Tuscan Relief* (1967). 2. **Jack** (1937–) American film actor who won Oscars for *One Flew Over the Cuckoo's Nest* (1975) and *Terms of Endearment* (1983). 3. **Roger** (1922–) British painter.

nick *n* a small cut, chip, etc, made on a surface; (Brit sl) a police station, prison. * *vt* to make a nick in; to wound superficially; (*Brit sl*) to steal; (*Brit sl*) to arrest.

nickel *n* a silvery-white metallic element used in alloys and plating; a US or Canadian coin worth five cents.

nickel-and-dime *adj* (*inf*) offering little money; insignificant. * *vti* (*inf*) to pay close attention to petty spending; to treat stingily.

nickel cadmium battery *or* **NiCad battery** *n* (*comput*) a type of rechargeable battery used in notebook and laptop computers.

nickel metal hydride battery *n* (*comput*) a rechargeable battery that is more powerful than the nickel cadmium battery.

nickelodeon *n* an early type of jukebox.

nickel silver *n* an alloy of nickel, copper and zinc.—*also* **German silver**.

nicker *vi* to neigh, to snigger.—*also n.*

Nicklaus *n* **Jack [William]** (1940–) American golfer and winner of more major tournaments than any other player in history.

nicknack *see* **knickknack**.

nickname *n* a substitute name, often descriptive, given in fun; a familiar form of a proper name. * *vt* to give as a nickname.

Nicodemus *n* (*Bible*) the man who helped Joseph of Arimathea lay Jesus' body in the tomb after the Crucifixion.

Nicolai *n* **Carl Otto Ehrenfried** (1810–49) German composer and conductor whose most famous work is the comic opera *The Merry Wives of Windsor*.

Nicolson *n* **Sir Harold [George]** (1886–1968) English diplomat, essayist, and literary critic.

Nicosia *n* capital city of Cyprus.

nicotiana *n* any of the *Nicotiana* genus of plants of Australia and America, e.g. tobacco.

nicotine *n* a poisonous alkaloid present in tobacco.

nicotinic acid *n* a vitamin of the B complex derived from milk, liver and yeast.—*also* **niacin**.

NICSA *abbr* (*Brit*) = Northern Ireland Countryside Staff Association.

nictitate, nictate *vi* to wink.—**nictitation, nictation** *n.*

nictitating membrane *n* a membrane that can be drawn over the eye beneath the eyelid present in many birds, reptiles, fish and some mammals.

NICU *abbr* = neonatal intensive care unit.

NIDA *abbr* = National Institute on Drug Abuse.

NIDCR *abbr* = National Institute of Dental and Craniofacial Research.

NIDDK *abbr* = National Institute of Diabetes and Digestive and Kidney Disease.

NIDFA *abbr* = National Independent Drama Festivals Association.

nidificate *vi* to build a nest.

nidification *n* the act of building a nest, rearing young, etc.

nidify *vi* (**nidifying, nidified**) to nidificate.

nidus *n* (*pl* **nidi, niduses**) the developing place of spores, seeds, germs, insects' eggs, etc; an accumulation of eggs, tubercles, etc; a nest or hatching place.

Niebuhr *n* 1. **Helmut Richard** (1894–1962) American theologian. His works on Protestant theology include *Radical Monotheism and Western Culture* (1960). 2. **Reinhold** (1892–1971) Protestant theologian, and brother of Helmut, whose works include *Moral Man and Immoral Society* (1932).

niece *n* the daughter of a brother or sister.

NIEHS *abbr* = National Institute of Environmental Health Sciences.

niello *n* (*pl* **nielli, niellos**) an ornamental engraving in black on silver, gold, brass, etc; a black alloy used in this. * *vt* (**nielloing, nielloed**) to engrave or decorate with niello.

Nielsen *n* 1. **Carl August** (1865–1931) Danish composer, violinist, and conductor whose works include the opera *Saul and David*. 2. **Erik** (1857–1947) Danish ceramicist who collaborated with Arnold Krog on one-off ceramics.

Niemeyer *n* **Oscar** (1907–1995) Brazilian architect of the United Nations Building in New York.

Niemöller *n* **Martin** (1892–1984) German Lutheran pastor; an opponent of Hitler; president of the World Council of Churches (1961–68).

niente *n* (*mus*) (*Italian*) "nothing"; used in *quasi niente,* "almost nothing," indicating a very soft tone.

Nies-Friedlaender *n* **Cordula Kianga** (1958–) German industrial designer based in London.

NIESR *abbr* = National Institute of Economic and Social Research.

Nietzsche *n* **Friedrich Wilhelm** (1844–1900) German philosopher and poet whose written works include *Thus Spake Zarathustra* (1883–92).

nifedipine *n* a drug used in the treatment of angina and high blood pressure.

Niflheim *n* (*Scandinavian myth*) the region of eternal mist and cold.

nifty *adj* (**niftier, niftiest**) (*sl*) neat, stylish.—**niftily** *adv.*—**niftiness** *n.*

Niger *n* a landlocked republic in west Africa, just south of the Tropic of Cancer.

Nigeria *n* a large federal republic in west Africa which extends from the Gulf of Guinea north to the border with Niger.

niggard *adj* meanly covetous; parsimonious; miserly; niggardly. * *n* one who is meanly covetous; a stingy person, a miser.

niggardliness *n* the state of being niggardly; stinginess.

niggardly *adj* giving grudgingly, ungenerous, * *adv* like a niggard.

nigger *n* (*offensive*) a Negro, Black person; a dark-skinned person.

niggle *vi* to waste time on petty details; to be finicky.

niggler *n* one who trifles at handiwork.

niggling *adj* finicky, fussy; petty; gnawing, irritating.—**nigglingly** *adv.*

nigh *adj*, *adv*, *prep* near.

night *n* the period of darkness from sunset to sunrise; nightfall; a specified or appointed evening.

night blindness *see* **nyctalopia**.

nightcap *n* a cap worn in bed; (*inf*) an alcoholic drink taken just before going to bed.

nightclothes *npl* clothes for wearing in bed, as a nightgown, pyjamas, etc.

nightclub *n* a place of entertainment for drinking, dancing, etc, at night.

nightdress *n* a loose garment worn in bed by women and girls.

nightfall *n* the close of the day.

nightflower *n* a flower that opens at night.

nightglass *n* a short telescope for night use.

nightgown *n* a nightdress.

nightie *n* (*inf*) a nightdress, nightgown.—*also* **nighty**.

nightingale *n* a songbird celebrated for its musical song at night.

nightjar *n* a nocturnal bird with dull mottled plumage.

night life *n* social entertainment at night, esp in towns.

night-light *n* a dim light kept burning at night.

nightlong *adj* lasting through the night.

nightly *adj*, *adv* done or happening by night or every night.

nightmare *n* a frightening dream; any horrible experience.—**nightmarish** *adj.*

night owl *n* (*inf*) a person who stays up late at night.

night school *n* an educational institution where classes are held in the evening.

nightshade *n* a flowering plant related to the potato and tomato, esp deadly nightshade (belladonna).

nightshirt *n* a long shirt for sleeping in.

night soil *n* human excrement used as fertilizer.

nightspot *n* (*inf*) a nightclub.

nightstick *n* (*US*) a short club carried by a policeman or policewoman; a truncheon.

night table *n* a small bedside table.

nightwalker *n* a person who wanders about at night, esp with criminal intent.

night watch *n* a watch by night or the person keeping it.

night watchman *n* the person who guards a building at night.

nighttime *n* night.

nighty *n* (*pl* **nighties**) (*inf*) a nightie.

NIGMS *abbr* = National Institute of General Medical Sciences.

nigrescent *adj* blackish, growing black.—**nigrescence** *n.*

NIH *abbr* = National Institutes of Health.

nihil *n* (*Latin*) nothing, nil.

nihil ad rem *adj* (*Latin*) irrelevant.

nihilism *n* the belief that nothing has real existence, scepticism; the rejection of customary beliefs in morality, religion, etc.

nihilist *n* a supporter of nihilism.—**nihilisitic** *adj.*

nihility *n* nonexistence.

NII *abbr* = Nuclear Installations Inspectorate.

NIJ *abbr* = National Institute of Justice.

Nijinsky *n* **Vaslav** (1890–1950) Russian ballet dancer and choreographer.

Nike *n* (*Greek myth*) the goddess of victory. In Roman mythology, she is called Victoria.

Nikkei Index *n* a Japanese share index by which changes in the aggregate value of a particular "basket" of company shares are measured.

nil *n* nothing.

nil basis *n* the basis on which the earnings per share of a company is worked out, taking into account only the constant elements in the tax charge of the relevant company.

Nile *n* Egyptian river, whose Blue Nile branch rises in the mountains of Equatorial Africa, and whose longer White Nile branch rises in Lake Victoria, south of the Equator. It flows for some 4,000 miles (6,500 kilometers) to reach the Mediterranean Sea through its many streamed Delta.

nilgai, nilgau *n* (*pl* **nilgai, nilgais, nilgau, nilgaus**) a large short-horned Indian antelope.

Nilometer *n* a graduated pillar for measuring the rise of water in the river Nile during its floods; a river gauge.

Nilotic *adj* pertaining to the River Nile.

Nilsson *n* **Birgit** (1918–) Swedish soprano who is particularly famous for her role as Brunnhilde in Wagner's *Ring* cycle.

NIMA *abbr* = National Imagery and Mapping Agency.

nimble *adj* agile; quick.—**nimbly** *adv*.

nimbostratus *n* (*meteorology*) a gray layer of cloud that obscures the sun and produces continuously falling rain or snow.

nimbus *n* (*pl* **nimbi, nimbuses**) (*art*) the halo or cloud of light surrounding the heads of divinities, saints, and sovereigns; a rain cloud.

nimby *abbr* = not in my back yard.

NIMH *abbr* = National Institute of Medical Herbalists; National Institute of Mental Health.

niminy-piminy *adj* mincing, prim.

NIMR *abbr* = National Institute for Medical Research.

Nimrod *n* a distinguished hunter, from Nimrod, "the mighty hunter" (Genesis 10.9).

Nimrud *n* **[ancient Kalhu]** called Calah in the Bible, the ancient military capital of Assyrai, near Mosul in southern Iraq.

Nin *n* **Anais** (1903–77) French-born American novelist and essayist who is best known for her diaries, depicting literary life in Paris and New York in the 1930s.

nincompoop *n* a stupid, silly person.

NINDS *abbr* = National Institute of Neurological Disorders and Stroke.

nine *adj, n* one more than eight. * *symbol* 9, IX, ix; the ninth in a series or set; something having nine units as members.

nine days' wonder *n* someone or something that is temporarily famous.

ninefold *adj* having nine units or members; being nine times as great or as many.

nine iron *n* a golf club with a heavy head, used for lofting; a niblick.

ninepins *see* **skittles**.

nineteen *adj, n* one more than eighteen. * *symbol* 19, XIX, xix.—**nineteenth** *adj*.

nineteenth *adj* being one of 19 equal parts.* *n* a nineteenth part.

nineteenth hole *n* (*golf*) (*sl*) the bar in the clubhouse.

ninetieth *adj* next after 89. * *n* a ninetieth part.

nine to five *n* typical office hours.—**nine-to-five** *adj, adv*.

ninety *adj, n* nine times ten. * *symbol* 90, XC, xc; (in pl) nineties; the numbers from 90 to 99; the same numbers in a life or century.

Nineveh *n* city on the banks of the Tigris and capital of Assyria in ancient times; (*Bible*) regarded as a symbol of Assyrian oppression in the OT.

Ninian *n* **Saint [Ringan]** (c. 360–432) Scottish monk who evangelized the Southern Picts. His feast day is August 26 .

ninja *n* a Japanese warrior trained in ninjutsu.—*also adj*.

ninjutsu *n* an ancient Japanese martial art which practises techniques of stealth or invisibility, orig for the purpose of espionage and political assassination.

ninny *n* (*pl* **ninnies**) a person of weak character or mind, a simpleton.

ninon *n* a light silk material.

ninth *adj, n* next after eighth; one of nine equal parts of a thing; * *n* (*mus*) an interval of nine notes, in which both the first and last notes are counted.

Niobe *n* an inconsolable bereaved woman; (*Greek myth*) a heroine who was turned to stone while weeping for her slain children.—**Niobean** *adj*.

niobic *adj* of or containing pentavalent niobium.

niobium *n* a metallic element used in alloys.

NIOSH *abbr* = National Institute for Occupational Safety and Health.

nip[1] *vt* (**nipping, nipped**) to pinch, pinch off; to squeeze between two surfaces; (*dog*) to give a small bite; to prevent the growth of; (*plants*) to have a harmful effect on because of cold. * *n* a pinch; a sharp squeeze; a bite; severe frost or biting coldness.

nip[2] *n* a small drink of spirits. * *vti* (**nipping, nipped**) to drink in nips.

nipa *n* an East Indian palm.

NIPA *abbr* = National Income and Product Accounts.

NIPC *abbr* = National Infrastructure Protection Center.

nipper *n* a person or thing that nips; the pincer of a crab or lobster; (*pl*) pliers, pincers, etc; (*Brit inf*) a small child.

nipple *n* the small protuberance on a breast or udder through which the milk passes, a teat; a teat-like rubber part on the cap of a baby's bottle; a projection resembling a nipple.

nippy *adj* (**nippier, nippiest**) (*weather*) frosty; (*Brit inf*) quick, nimble.

ni. pri. *abbr* (*Latin*) (*law*) = *nisi prius*, "unless previously."

NIR *abbr* = Northern Ireland Railways.

NIRA *abbr* = National Industrial Recovery Act.

NIRC *abbr* = National Industrial Relations Court.

Nirex *abbr* = Nuclear Industry Radioactive Waste Executive.

nirvana *n* (*Buddhism*) the highest religious state, when all desire of existence and worldly good is extinguished, and the soul is absorbed into the Deity.

nis *abbr* = not in stock.

Nis *n* a city in Yugoslavia (FRY).

nisi *adj* (*decree, order, rule, etc*) valid unless cause is shown be the contrary by a fixed date, at which it is made absolute.

Nisien *n* (*Welsh Celtic myth*) the brother of Efnisien and half-brother of Bran, Branwen and the other children of Llyr. He was a peacemaker and mediator.

nisi prius *n* (*law*) a writ, beginning with these words, directing a sheriff to empanel a jury; the name of certain courts for the trial of civil actions in the counties; a trial of civil causes by judges of assize.

NIST *abbr* = National Institute of Standards and Technology.

NISTIR *abbr* = National Institute of Standards and Technology Interagency Report.

nit *n* the egg of a louse or other parasitic insect.

NIT *abbr* = negative income tax.

niter *n* potassium nitrate, saltpeter.—*also* **nitre**.

Nitocris *n* (*Egypt*) the first example in Egyptian history of a female king, i.e. a ruling queen. She is shown on Manetho's list and in the Turin Canon as a king.

niton *n* a gaseous radioactive element, radon.

nit-picking n (inf) concern with petty details in order to find fault.—*also adj*.

nitr-, nitro- *prefix* containing nitrogen; made with nitric acid.

Nitra *n* a city in the Slovak Republic.

nitrate *n* (*chem*) a salt of nitric acid; a fertilizer made of this.—**nitration** *n*.

nitration *n* (*chem*) the addition of the nitro group to organic compounds.

nitre *see* **niter**.

nitric *adj* containing nitrogen.

nitric acid *n* (*chem*) a corrosive, caustic liquid used to make explosives, fertilizers, etc.

nitride *n* (*chem*) a compound of nitrogen with a metal, also with phosphorus, silicon or boron.

nitrification *n* (*chem*) the process of converting into niter.

nitrify *vti* (**nitrifying, nitrified**) (*chem*) to make or become nitrous.

nitrite *n* a salt of nitrous acid.

nitro-, nitr- *prefix* (*chem*) containing nitrogen; made with nitric acid.

nitrogen *n* (*chem*) a colorless odorless gas that exists as a molecule containing two atoms and forms almost 80% of the atmosphere by volume.

nitrogenase *n* (*chem*) the enzyme that catalyzes the production of nitrogenous compounds from free nitrogen in the process of nitrogen fixation. *See* **catalyst**.

nitrogen cycle *n* (ecology) the regular circulation of nitrogen due to the activity of organisms.

nitrogen fixation *n* (*biol*) the process by which free (available) nitrogen is extracted from the atmosphere by certain bacteria.

nitrogenize *vt* to impregnate with nitrogen.—**nitrogenization** *n*.

nitrogenous *adj* pertaining to, or containing, nitrogen.

nitroglycerin, nitroglycerine *n* a powerful explosive made by adding glycerine to a mixture of nitric and sulphuric acids.

nitrous *adj* resembling, obtained from, or impregnated with, niter.

nitrous acid *n* a compound of four volumes of nitrogen and one of oxygen.

nitrous oxide *n* a compound of one volume of oxygen and two volumes of nitrogen; laughing gas.

nitty-gritty *n* (*sl*) basic elements; harsh realities; practical details.

nitwit *n* (*inf*) a stupid person.

nival *adj* of or pertaining to snow.

Niven *n* **David [James David Graham Nevins]** (1909–83) Scottish film actor who starred in many Hollywood productions.

niveous *adj* resembling snow, snow-like.

nix[1] *n* (*German myth*) a water sprite; (*Scot*) a kelpie.—**nixie** *nf*.

nix[2] *n* (*sl*) nothing. * *interj* (*sl*) look out! be careful!

Nixon *n* **Richard Milhous** (1913–94) American Republican politician and 37th president of the US (1969–74); the first president to resign from office (1974), following the Watergate Scandal. While in office, he ended the Vietnam war and established rapprochement with China.

nizam *n* (*with cap*) a title of the ruler of Hyderabad, India; a Turkish army soldier.

Nizhniy Novgorod *n* a city in the Russian Federation.

Nizzoli *n* **Marcello** (1887–1969) Italian designer who became the most influential product designer at Olivetti.

NJ *abbr* = New Jersey.

NJAC *abbr* = National Joint Council.

NJCC *abbr* = National Joint Consultative Committee of Architects, Quantity Surveyors and Builders.

NJFA *abbr* = National Jazz Foundation Archive.

NJNC *abbr* = National Joint Negotiating Committee.

Nkrumah *n* **Kwame** (1909–72) Ghanaian statesman and the first president of Ghana (1957–66) after independence.

n.l. *abbr* = new line; (*Latin*) (*law*) *non licet*, "illegal"; (*Latin*) (*law*) *non liquet*, "unclear"; (*Latin*) (*law*) *non longe*, "not far."

NL *abbr* = north latitude; New Latin.

N. Lat. *abbr* = north latitude.

NLB *abbr* = National Labor Board.

NLB & D *abbr* = National League of the Blind and Disabled.

NLCB *abbr* = National Lottery Charities Board.

NLE *abbr* = National Library of Education.

NLF *abbr* = National Liberation Front.

NLL *abbr* (*Eire*) = National Land League.

NLM *abbr* = National Library of Medicine.

nln *abbr* = no longer needed.

N

NLP *abbr* = natural language processing.

NLQ *abbr* = (*comput*) near letter quality.

NLRB *abbr* = National Labor Relations Board.

nlt *abbr* = not later than; not less than.

NLW *abbr* (*Brit*) = National Library of Wales.

nm *abbr* = nanometre; nautical mile.

n/m *abbr* = (*com*) no mark; not married.

NM, N. Mex *abbr* = New Mexico.

NMA *abbr* = National Museum of Australia; Needlemakers Association.

NMB *abbr* = National Mediation Board.

nmc *abbr* = no more credit.

NMC *abbr* = National Museum of Canada.

NMFS *abbr* = National Marine Fisheries Service

NMHRA *abbr* = National Mobile Homes Residents Association.

NMR *abbr* = nuclear magnetic resonance.

NMS *abbr* = Natural Medicines Society.

nmt *abbr* = not more than.

NMTF *abbr* = National Market Traders' Federation.

NN, N.N. *abbr* = names.

nnd *abbr* = neonatal death.

NNE, N.N.E., n.n.e. *abbr* = north-northeast.

NNEB *abbr* (*Brit*) = National Nursery Examination Board.

NNHT *abbr* (*Brit*) = Nuffield Nursing Homes Trust.

NNI *abbr* = Noise and Number Index (aircraft noise).

NNP *abbr* = net national product.

N.N.R. *abbr* (*med*) = New and Nonofficial Remedies.

NNT *abbr* = nuclear non-proliferation treaty.

NNW, N.N.W., n.n.w. *abbr* = north-northwest.

no *adv* (*used to express denial or disagreement*) not so, not at all, by no amount. * *adj* not any; not a; not one, none; not at all; by no means. * *n* (*pl* noes, nos) a denial; a refusal; a negative vote or voter.

No, Noh *n* (*pl* No, Noh) Japanese classic dance-drama.

No *symbol* (*chem*) nobelium (element).

no *abbr* = not out, as in cricket.

no., No. *abbr* = number.

No. *abbr* = Noah; north; northern.

NO *abbr* = natural order; New Orleans.

N/O *abbr* (*bank*) = no orders.

NOAA *abbr* = National Oceanic and Atmospheric Administration.

Noachian, Noachic *adj* pertaining to the patriarch Noah, the deluge, or his times.

Noah *n* (*Bible*) hero of the story of the Flood. *See also* **ark; flood.**

NOAH *abbr* = National Office of Animal Health Limited.

nob¹ *n* a knob; (*sl*) the head.

nob² *n* (*at cribbage*) knave of suit of turn-up card.

nob³ *n* (*Brit sl*) a member of the upper classes; a wealthy person.

nobble *vt* (*Brit sl*) to tamper with (a racehorse) to prevent its winning; to obtain (money) by dishonest means; to suborn (a juror, etc) by bribes or threats; to defeat by underhand methods; to steal; to kidnap.

Nobel *n* **Alfred Bernhard** (1833–96) Swedish chemist and philanthropist who invented dynamite.

nobelium *n* a radioactive metallic element.

Nobel prize *n* an annual international prize, endowed by Alfred Nobel, given for distinction in one of six areas: physics, chemistry, physiology or medicine, economics, literature, and promoting peace.

nobile *adj* (*Italian*) "noble."–**nobilmente** *adv*.

nobility *n* (*pl* nobilities) nobleness of character, mind, birth, or rank; the class of people of noble birth.

noble *adj* famous or renowned; excellent in quality or character; of high rank or birth. * *n* a person of high rank in society.

noble gases *npl* (*chem*) the elements comprising group 8 of the periodic table: helium, neon, argon, krypton, xenon and radon.

nobleman *n* (*pl* noblemen) a peer.—**noblewoman** *nf* (*pl* noblewomen).

noble metals *npl* (*chem*) metals, e.g. platinum, silver and gold, that are highly resistant to corrosion.

nobleness *n* the state of quality of being noble.

noble savage *n* an idealized view of primitive man.

noblesse *n* nobility.–**noblesse oblige** (*French*) "rank has its obligations."

nobly *adv* in a noble manner; of noble rank.

nobody *n* (*pl* nobodies) a person of no importance. * *pron* no person.

NOC *abbr* = National Olympic Committee.

nock *n* a notch in a bow or arrow for the string; (*naut*) the forward upper corner of some sails. * *vt* to fit (an arrow) to string.

no-claim bonus *n* a discount given on premiums to policy-holders by insurance companies as a reward for not claiming on their insurance.

noctambulism, noctambulation *n* sleepwalking.— **noctambulist** *n*.

nocti-, noct- *prefix* night.

noctiluca *n* (*pl* noctilucae) a phosphorescent animalcule.

noctilucent cloud *n* (*meteor*) a rare form of cloud of ice crystals or meteoric dust, often brightly colored, forming at about 50 miles above earth's surface, higher than any other clouds.

noctule *n* the largest British kind of bat.

nocturn *n* (*eccles*) a part of matins.

nocturnal *adj* of, relating to, night; active by night.—**nocturnally** *adv*.

nocturnal emission *n* the emission of semen while asleep.

nocturne *n* a picture of a night scene; a musical composition appropriate to the night; a lullaby.

Nocturnes *n* **The** pieces of music by Field and Chopin; the title of three orchestral pieces by Debussy.

nocuous *adj* hurtful.

nod *vti* (**nodding, nodded**) to incline the head quickly, esp in agreement or greeting; to let the head drop, be drowsy; to indicate by a nod; (*with* off) (*inf*) to fall asleep. * *n* a quick bob of the head; a sign of assent or command.

NOD *abbr* = Naval Ordnance Department.

nodal *adj* pertaining to nodes.

NODC *abbr* = National Oceanographic Data Center.

noddy *n* (*pl* noddies) a simpleton; a tropical sea bird; a four-wheeled carriage with a door at the back.

node¹ *n* a knob; a knot; a point of intersection; (*med*) a swelling; (*bot*) the joint of a stem and leaf or leaves; (*math*) the point at which a curve crosses itself; the point of rest in a vibrating body.

node² *n* (*astron*) one of two points diametrically opposite each other, in which the orbit of a celestial body cuts the ecliptic on the celestial sphere.

nodical *adj* (*astron*) pertaining to nodes.

nodose *adj* having knots or nodes, knotty, knobbed.—**nodosity** *n*.

nodular, nodulose, nodulous *adj* pertaining to, or like, a nodule.

nodule *n* a small lump or tumor; (*bot*) a small swelling or structure on a plant, especially the root, which is due to nitrogen-fixing bacteria.—**nodular** *adj*.

nodus *n* (*pl* nodi) a knotty point, a complication in the plot of a story, etc.

NOE *abbr* = not otherwise enumerated.

noel, noèl *n* Christmas, esp in carols.

noetic *adj* pertaining to, performed by, or originating in, the mind or intellect, intellectual, abstract. * *n* the science of the intellect.—also **noemics**.

no-fault *adj* (*insurance*) providing damages without blame being fixed; (*divorce*) concluded without blame being charged.

nog¹ *n* a wooden peg or block; a stump. * *vt* (**nogging, nogged**) to secure with nogs.

nog² *n* an East Anglian strong beer.

nog³ *n* (an) eggnog.

noggin *n* a small quantity of alcoholic drink; (*inf*) the head.

nogging *n* a partition formed of timber scantlings filled up with bricks.

no-go area *n* an area that certain individuals or groups are forbidden to enter.

Noguchi *n* 1. **Isamu** (1904–1988) American sculptor who made a major contribution to all aspects of industrial and stage design. 2. **Yone [Jiro]** (1875–1947) Japanese poet and essayist whose works are regarded as forming an important bridge between Japanese and Western culture.

Noh *see* **No.**

nohow *adv* in no way, by no means.

nohp, NOHP *abbr* (*com*) = not otherwise herein provided.

NOIBN *abbr* (*com*) = not otherwise indexed by name.

noil *n* a short wool-combing.

NOIL *abbr* = Naval Ordnance Inspection Laboratory.

noire *n* (*mus*) (*French*), "black," a crotchet or quarter note.

noise *n* a sound, esp a loud, disturbing or unpleasant one; a din; (*elect, comput*) unwanted fluctuations in a transmitted signal; (*pl*) conventional sounds, words, etc made in reaction, such as sympathy. * *vt* to make public.

noiseless *adj* making no sound, silent.—**noiselessly** *adv*.—**noiselessness** *n*.

noise pollution *n* persistent noise levels that are annoying or that threaten physical harm.

noisette *n* a small round piece of meat.

noisome *adj* harmful, noxious; foul-smelling.

noisy *adj* (**noisier, noisiest**) making much noise; turbulent, clamorous.—**noisily** *adv*.—**noisiness** *n*.

nok *abbr* = next of kin.

Nolan *n* **Sir Sidney [Robert]** (1917–92) Australian painter; almost completely self-taught; noted for surreal figurative works on Australian themes.

Nolde *n* **Emil** (1867–1956) German expressionist painter whose notable works include *Dance around the Golden Calf* (1910).

nolens volens *adv* (*Latin*), "willingly or unwillingly," willy-nilly.

noli me tangere *n* (*Latin*) a warning not to meddle; an erosive ulcer, lupus; a wild cucumber; a picture of Christ as he appeared to Mary Magdalen at the sepulchre.

nolle prosequi *n* (*Latin*) (*Eng law*), "do not continue," a term indicating the plaintiff's abandonment of his suit.

nolo episcopari *n* (*Latin*), "I do not wish to be bishop," i.e., unwillingness to accept office.

nol. pros. *abbr* (*Latin*) = nolle prosequi, "do not continue."

nom. *abbr* = nomenclature; nominal; nominative, as used in grammar.

nomad *n* one of a people or tribe who move in search of pasture; a wanderer.—**nomadic** *adj*.

nomadic *adj* wandering; leading a wandering life; pastoral.—**nomadically** *adv*.

no-man's-land *n* an unclaimed piece of land; a strip of land, esp between armies, borders; an ambiguous area, subject, etc.

nomarch *n* in ancient Egypt the governor of a nome, or province, a leader of a provincial aristocracy, with power as administrator, judge and high priest of the nome's own local deity; the senior administrator in a Greek nomarchy.

nomarchy *n* any of the provinces of modern Greece.

nombril *n* (*her*) the centre of an escutcheon.

nom de guerre *n* (*pl* **noms de guerre**) (*French*) a pseudonym, an assumed name.

nom de plume *n* (*pl* **noms de plume**) (*French*) a pseudonym.

nome *n* a province of modern Greece; a territorial division in ancient Egypt.

nomen *n* one of the five names in an ancient Egyptian king's formal set of titles; an ancient Roman's second name.

nomenclator *n* an ancient Roman slave who named persons met; one who gives names to things, an inventor of names.

nomenclature *n* a system of names, terminology, used in a science, etc, or for parts of a device, etc.

nomin. *abbr* = nominative.

nominal *adj* of or like a name; existing in name only; having minimal real worth, token.

nominal accounts *npl* ledger accounts that do not bear the name of an individual or organization but relate to concepts, such as rents from properties received by a company.

nominalism *n* (*philos*) the doctrine that general notions exist only in the mind or in name, opposite to realism.

nominalist *n* one who holds the doctrine of nominalism.—**nominalistic** *adj*.

nominal ledger *n* the ledger that is used to record nominal accounts as distinct from personal ledgers.

nominally *adv* in name only.

nominal value *n* the par value (of a note, coin, share, etc).

nominate *vt* to appoint to an office or position; (*candidate*) to propose for election.—**nominator** *n*.

nomination *n* the act or right of nominating; the state of being nominated.

nominative *adj* (*gram*) denoting the case of the subject of a verb; appointed, not elected. * *n* (*gram*) the nominative case or a word in it.

nominee *n* a person who is nominated.

nomo-, nom- *prefix* law.

nomography *n* (*pl* **nomographies**) the art of drawing up laws.—**nomographic, nomographical** *adj*.

nomology *n* the science of the laws of the mind.—**nomological** *adj*.—**nomologist** *n*.

nomothetic, nomothetical *adj* legislative, founded on a system of laws.

nom. nov. *abbr* (*Latin*) = *nomen novum*.

nom. nud. *abbr* (*Latin*) = *nomen nudum*.

-nomy *n suffix* denoting a science or the laws governing it, as *astronomy, economy*.

non. *abbr* (*Latin*) = *nonae*, "nones."

non- *prefix* not, reversing the meaning of a word.

nona- *prefix* nine.

nonage *n* minority, legal infancy; an early stage.

nonagenarian *n* a person who is in his or her nineties.

nonagon *n* a plane figure with 9 sides and 9 angles.—**nonagonal** *adj*.

nonalcoholic *adj* (*drinks, etc*) containing little or no alcohol.

nonaligned *adj* not in alliance with any side, esp in power politics.

nonallergenic *adj* not capable of inducing an allergy.

nonce *n* **for the nonce** for this time only.

nonce word *n* a word coined for one occasion.

nonchalance *n* coolness; indifference.

nonchalant *adj* calm; cool, unconcerned, indifferent.—**nonchalantly** *adv*.

noncom. *abbr* = noncommissioned officer.

noncombatant *n* a member of the armed forces whose duties do not include fighting, as a doctor or chaplain; a civilian during wartime.

noncommissioned officer *n* (*mil*) a subordinate officer, as a corporal, sergeant, etc, appointed from the ranks.

noncommittal *adj* not revealing one's opinion.—**noncommittally** *adv*.

non compos mentis *adj* (*Latin*) of unsound mind, not responsible.

nonconductor *n* a substance that will not conduct electricity or heat.

nonconformist *n* a person who does not conform to prevailing attitudes, behavior, etc; (with cap) in Britain, a Protestant who does not belong to the established church.—*also adj*.

nonconformity *n* (with cap) refusal to conform to the established church; a want of conformity, irregularity.

noncooperation *n* refusal to cooperate, esp with government decree, etc.—**noncooperative** *adj*.

non. cul. *abbr* (*Latin*) (*law*) = *non culpabilis*, "not guilty."

nondescript *adj* hard to classify, indeterminate; lacking individual characteristics. * *n* a nondescript person or thing.

none *pron* no one; not anyone; (*pl verb*) not any; no one. * *adv* not at all.

noneffective *adj* not effective; (*soldier, sailor*) not qualified for active service.—*also n*.

nonentity *n* (*pl* **nonentities**) a person or thing of no significance.

nones *npl* in the ancient Roman calendar the ninth day before the Ides, reckoned inclusively, ie 7th of March, May, July, October, and the 5th of the other months; (*eccles*) the devotional office for the ninth hour.

nonesuch *n* an unrivaled person or thing, a nonpareil; a plant like clover used for fodder.—*also* **nonsuch**.

nonet *n* a group of nine connected objects or people; (*mus*) a piece for nine players.

nonetheless *conj* nevertheless.

nonevent *n* an event or experience that is unexpectedly disappointing.

nonexecutive director *n* a member of the board of directors of a company who is not employed by the company.

nonexistent *adj* not existing.—**nonexistence** *n*.

nonfeasance *n* (*law*) the omission of an obligatory act.

nonferrous *adj* containing no iron.

nonfiction *n* literature that is not fiction.— **nonfictional** *adj*.

nonflammable *adj* not easily set on fire.

nonidentical *adj* not identical.

nonillion *n* in the US and France, tenth power of a thousand (1 followed by 30 ciphers); in Britain, the ninth power of one million (1 followed by 54 ciphers).—**nonillionth** *adj*.

non-impact printer *n* (*comput*) a printer that produces text on paper without contact between the printing mechanism and the paper, e.g. inkjet, bubblejet, or laser printers.

nonintervention *n* the policy of refusing to interfere in the affairs of others, esp nations.—**noninterventionist** *adj*.

non-ionic detergents *npl* (*chem*) detergents which do not ionize in water.

nonjuror *n* one who refused to take the oath of allegiance to William and Mary in 1689.

non-lethal *adj* pertaining to foreign aid given to provide medicine, clothing or food rather than weapons.

nonmetal *n* a chemical element, e.g. carbon, that is not a metal.

nonmoral *adj* unconcerned with morality; without moral standards.

no-no *n* (*pl* **no-nos, no-noes**) (*inf*) something that is completely unacceptable or useless.

non obst. *abbr* (*Latin*) = *non obstante*.

Nono *n* Luigi (1924–90) Italian composer who is considered a champion of "modern" music. His works include the opera *Intolleranza* (1960).

no-nonsense *adj* sensible, straightforward; not tolerating excess, strict.

nonpareil *adj* without an equal; (*person or thing*) unrivaled, matchless, unsurpassed. * *n* unequaled excellence; (*print*) a 6-point type; a variety of apple; a kind of bird, moth, wheat, etc.

nonpartisan *adj* not aligned to one particular political party.

nonparty *adj* free from party obligations.

nonplus *vt* (**nonpluses, nonplusing, nonplused** *or* **nonplusses, nonplussing, nonplussed**) to cause to be so perplexed that one cannot, go, speak, act further. * *n* (*pl* **nonpluses**) a state of perplexity, a standstill.

non plus ultra *see* **ne plus ultra**.

non-profit *adj* (*organization*) not conducted for the purpose of making money.

nonproliferation *n, adj* (placing) restriction on the acquisition or production of, esp nuclear weapons.

non pros. *abbr* (*Latin*) = *non prosequitur*.

non-recourse finance *n* a bank loan in which the bank issuing the loan is entitled to repayment only from the profits of the scheme that the loan is being used to finance and not from any other resources of the borrower.

nonrenewable *adj* not able to be replenished.

non rep. *abbr* (*Latin*) = *non repetatur*, "let it not be repeated."

nonrepresentational *adj* (*art*) abstract.

nonresident *adj* not living in a particular place; (*job*) not requiring the holder to live at the place of work; (*comput*) requiring to be loaded into memory before use. * *n* a nonresident person.—**nonresidence** *n*.—**nonresidential** *adj*.

nonreturnable *adj* not needing or requiring to be returned.

nonsense *n* words, actions, etc, that are absurd and have no meaning.—*also adj*.

nonsensical *adj* absurd; unmeaning.—**nonsensically** *adv*.

non seq. *abbr* (*Latin*) = *non sequitur*, "it does not follow logically."

non sequitur *n* a statement that has no relevance to what has preceded it.

nonsmoker *n* a person who does not smoke; a place where smoking is not permitted.

nonsoc. *abbr* = nonsociety.

nonstarter *n* a person who is unlikely to succeed; (*horse, racing car, etc*) withdrawn at the last moment.

non-statutory accounts *npl* a balance sheet or profit and loss account that does not form part of the statutory accounts.

non-steroidal anti-inflammatory drugs *n* a large group of drugs used to relieve pain and also inhibit inflammation.

nonstick *adj* (*saucepans*) coated with a surface that prevents food from sticking.

nonstop *adj* (*train, plane, etc*) not making any intermediate stops; not ceasing. * *adv* without stopping or pausing.

nonsuch *see* **nonesuch**.

nonsuit *n* the withdrawal of a suit during trial either voluntarily or by judgment of the court on the discovery of error or defect in the pleadings. * *vt* to pronounce a nonsuit against.

non-thermal radiation *n* any electromagnetic radiation not generated by a hot body.

nonunion *adj* not belonging to a trade union.

nonviolence *n* the abstaining from physical force to achieve civil rights.—**nonviolent** *adj*.

nonvoting shares *or* **A shares** *npl* ordinary shares in a company, the holders of which do not have any voting rights.

noodle[1] *n* (often *pl*) pasta formed into a strip.

noodle[2] *n* (*inf*) a foolish person; (*sl*) the head.

nook *n* a secluded corner, a retreat; a recess.

noon *n* midday; twelve o'clock in the day. * *adj* pertaining to noon.

noonday, noontide, noontime *adj* pertaining to noon, or midday. * *n* noon.

no one *pron* nobody.

noose *n* a loop of rope with a slipknot, used for hanging, snaring, etc. * *vt* to tie in a noose; to make a noose in or of.

N

nop, n.o.p. *abbr* = not otherwise provided.

NOP *abbr* = National Opinion Poll.

nopal *n* an American cactus, the food of the cochineal insect.

no-par *adj* a term used to describe a security that has no par value.

no-par value stock *n* shares that have "no-par value" printed on the share certificate.

nope *adv* (*sl*) no.

NOPWC *abbr* = National Old People's Welfare Council.

nor *conj* and not; not either.

nor. *abbr* = north; northern.

Nor, Nor. *abbr* = Norman; Norway; Norwegian; north; .

Nordic *adj* (*physical type*) characterized by tall stature, long head, light skin and hair, and blue eyes; (*skiing*) including cross-country runs and jumping.

norepinephrine *n* a neurotransmitter of the sympathetic nervous system similar to adrenaline, secreted by nerve endings and also the adrenal glands.

Norf. *abbr* = Norfolk.

Norfolk jacket *n* a man's loose jacket with a belt.

Nor. Fr. *abbr* = Norman-French.

noria *n* a water-raising apparatus in Spain, etc, a waterwheel.

norm *n* a standard or model, esp the standard of achievement of a large group.—**normative** *adj*.

Norm. *abbr* = Norman.

NORMAC *abbr* = Northern Prawn Fishery Management Committee.

normal[1] *adj* regular; usual; stable mentally. * *n* anything normal; the usual state, amount, etc.—**normalcy** *n*.—**normality** *n*.—**normally** *adv*.

normal[2] *n* (*geom*) a line perpendicular to the tangent of a curve or contact point of a line or plane.

normal fault *n* (*geol*) a fault where the direction of dip is towards the side that has been moved down.

normalize *vti* to make or become normal.—**normalization** *n*.

normal salt *n* (*chem*) any salt formed by an acid, which loses more than one hydrogen ion per molecule during a neutralization reaction.

normal school *n* a school for the training of teachers for elementary schools.

Norman *n* any of the people of Normandy who conquered England in 1066; a native or inhabitant of Normandy in France. * *adj* pertaining to the Normans or Normandy; (*archit*) of a style introduced into England by the Normans, characterized by rounded arches and massive square towers (—*also* **Normanesque**).

Norman *n* **Jessye** (1945–) American opera singer who has been outstanding in many diverse roles.

Normandie *n* French ocean liner, commissioned in 1935.

Norn *n* (*Scand myth*) one of the three fates, representing the past, the present and the future.

Norris *n* [Benjamin] Frank[lin] (1870–1902) American novelist whose novels include *McTeague* (1899).

Norse *adj* of ancient Scandinavia or its inhabitants; of Norway. * *n* the language of Norway.

Norseman *n* (*pl* **Norsemen**) any of the ancient Scandinavian people, the Vikings.

north *n* one of the four points of the compass, opposite the sun at noon, to the right of a person facing the sunset; the direction in which a compass needle points; (*often with cap*) the northern part of one's country or the earth. * *adj* in, of, or towards the north; from the north. * *adv* in or towards the north.

North *n* 1. **Frederick [8th Lord North, 2nd Earl of Guilford]** (1732–92) English statesman. As prime minister (1770–82) during the reign of George III, he implemented the king's policy which led to the loss of the American colony. 2. **Oliver** (1943–) American soldier. He resigned from the National Security Council over the Iran–Contra affair (1986) and was found guilty (1989) on charges relating to it, but charges were dropped in 1991. 3. **Sir Thomas** (*c*.1535–1601) English author whose translations of works such as Plutarch's *Lives* exerted a strong influence on Elizabethan writers, notably Shakespeare.

north. *abbr* = northern.

North America Nebula *n* a nebula in the constellation Cygnus which vaguely resembles the North American continent.

North American Free Trade Agreement *n* a free trade agreement signed in 1989 by the USA and Canada and extended to include Mexico in 1994.

North Carolina *n* a state of the USA, of which the capital is Raleigh.

North Dakota *n* a state of the USA, of which the capital is Bismarck.

"North Dakota Hymn, the" *n* song of the American state, North Dakota.

Northants. *abbr* (*Brit*) = Northamptonshire.

North Atlantic Drift *see* **Gulf Stream**.

northeast *adj, n* (of) the direction midway between north and east.

northeaster *n* a northeast wind.

northeasterly *adj* towards or coming from the northeast. * *n* (*pl* **northeasterlies**) a northeast wind or storm.

northeastern *adj* belonging to the northeast, or in that direction.

northeastward *adj* towards or in the northeast.—*also adv*.—**northeastwards** *adv*.

norther *n* a wind or storm from the north, esp a strong gale that prevails in the Gulf of Mexico from September to March.

northerly *adj* in, from, or towards the north. * *n* (*pl* **northerlies**) a northerly wind.

northern *adj* of or in the north.

Northern Hemisphere *n* the half of the earth north of the Equator.

northern lights *npl* the aurora borealis.

Northern Mariana Islands *n* a commonwealth in union with the USA, situated in the northwest Pacific Ocean.

northerner *n* a native or inhabitant of the north.

northernmost *adj* farthest north.

northing *n* distance northward.

north polar distance *n* the angular distance of a celestial object on the celestial sphere measured from the north celestial pole to the object along a meridian.

North Pole *n* the northern end of the axis of the earth at a latitude of 90 degrees north.

north star *n* the polar star.

Northum(b). *abbr* (*Brit*) = Northumberland.

northward *adj* towards or in the north.—*also adv*.—**northwards** *adv*.

northwest *adj, n* (of) the direction midway between north and west.

northwester *n* a northwest wind.

northwesterly *adj* towards or coming from the northwest. * *n* (*pl* **northwesterlies**) a northwest wind or storm.

northwestern *adj* belonging to the northwest, or in that direction.

northwestward *adj* towards or in the northwest.—*also adv*.—**northwestwards** *adv*.

Norvic. *abbr* (*Latin*) = *Norvicensis*, "of Norwich."

Norw. *abbr* = Norway; Norwegian.

Norway *n* **Kingdom of** a constitutional monarchy occupying the western part of the Scandinavian Peninsula in northern Europe.

Norwegian *adj, n* (of or relating to) the language, people, etc, of Norway.

Norwegian Krone *n* currency of Norway.

Norwich *n* English city in the UK.

nos., Nos. *abbr* = numbers.

NOS abbr = **not otherwise** specified.

nose *n* the part of the face above the mouth, used for breathing and smelling, having two nostrils; the sense of smell; anything like a nose in shape or position. * *vt* to discover as by smell; to nuzzle; to push (away, etc) with the front forward. * *vi* to sniff for; to inch forwards; to pry.

nosebag *n* a bag containing fodder hung from a horse's head.

noseband *n* the part of a bridle that covers the horse's nose.

nosebleed *n* a bleeding from the nose.

nose dive *n* a swift downward plunge of an aircraft, nose first; any sudden sharp drop, as in prices.—**nose-dive** *vi*.

nosegay *n* a bouquet.

nosewheel *n* the landing wheel under the nose of an aircraft.

nosey *see* **nosy**.

nosh *n* (*sl*) food, a meal. * *vt* to chew. * *vi* to eat.

nosing *n* the rounded edge of a step, etc, or the metal shield for it.

nose job *n* (*sl*) cosmetic plastic surgery to reshape the nose.

noso- *prefix* disease.

nosography *n* the systematic description of diseases.

nosology *n* the classification of the diseases of animals and plants.—**nosological** *adj*.—**nosologically** *adv*.—**nosologist** *n*.

nostalgia *n* yearning for past times or places.

nostalgic *adj* feeling or expressing nostalgia; longing for one's youth.—**nostalgically** *adv*.

nostology *n* the study of senility or ageing, gerontology.—**nostologic** *adj*.

Nostradamus *n* [Michel de Notredame] (1503–66) French astrologer and physician whose two books of cryptic prophecies, *Centuries*, were published in English in 1672.

no-strike agreement *n* an agreement between employer and labor union by which the labor union undertakes not to instigate or support strike action by employees.

nostril *n* one of the two external openings of the nose for breathing and smelling.

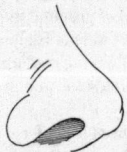

nostro account *n* a bank account that is conducted by a UK bank in another country, usually in the currency of that country.

nostrum *n* a quack remedy, patent medicine.

nosy *adj* (**nosier, nosiest**) (*inf*) inquisitive, snooping.—**nosily** *adv*.—**nosiness** *n*.—*also* **nosey**.

nosy parker *n* (*inf*) a prying person, busybody.

not *adv* expressing denial, refusal, or negation.

NOT *see* **logical operator**.

nota bene (*Latin*), "note well."

nota cambiata *see* **changing note**.

notabilia *npl* things worthy of note.

notability *n* (*pl* **notabilities**) the quality of being notable; a notable person or thing.

notable *adj* worthy of being noted or remembered; remarkable, eminent. * *n* an eminent or famous person.—**notably** *adv*.

notandum *n* (*pl* **notanda**) a thing to be noted.

notarial *adj* pertaining to, or done by, a notary.

notary *n* (*pl* **notaries**) a notary public.

notary public *n* (*pl* **notaries public**) a public official authorized to certify deeds, contracts, etc.

notation *n* a system of symbols or signs to represent quantities, etc, esp in mathematics, music, etc.

NOTB *abbr* = National Ophthalmic Treatment Board.

notch *n* a V-shaped cut in an edge or surface; (*inf*) a step, degree; a narrow pass with steep sides. * *vt* to cut notches in.

note[1] *n* a brief summary or record, written down for future reference; a memorandum; a short letter; notice, attention; an explanation or comment on the text of a book.

note[2] *n* a musical sound of a particular pitch; a sign representing such a sound; a piano or organ key; the vocal sound of a bird. * *vt* to notice, observe; to write down; to annotate.

notebook *n* a book with blank pages for writing in.

notebook computer *n* (*comput*) a small computer that is generally more compact than a laptop.

noted *adj* celebrated, well-known.

notepad *n* a small pad of paper for making notes on.

note paper *n* paper for writing letters.

noteworthy *adj* outstanding; remarkable.

nothing *n* no thing; not anything; nothingness; a zero; a trifle; a person or thing of no importance or value. * *adv* in no way, not at all.

nothingness *n* the state of being nothing; unconsciousness; worthlessness.

notice *n* an announcement; a warning; a placard giving information; a short article about a book, play, etc; attention, heed; a formal warning of intention to end an agreement at a certain time. * *vt* to observe; to remark upon. * *vi* to be aware of.

noticeable *adj* easily noticed or seen.—**noticeably** *adv*.

notice board *n* a board on which notices are posted.

notifiable *adj* (*infectious diseases*) that must be reported to health authorities.

notifiable diseases *n* diseases that must be reported to the health authorities to enable rapid control and monitoring to be undertaken.

notification *n* the act of notifying; a notice or paper bearing it.

notify *vt* (**notifying**, **notified**) to inform; to report, give notice of.

notion *n* a general idea; an opinion; a whim.

notional *adj* hypothetical, abstract; imaginary.

notional income *n* income that is not actually received, although it is a possibility that it might be deemed to be so for income tax purposes.

notions *npl* small useful articles, as thread, needles, etc; haberdashery.

noto- *prefix* back.

notochord *n* the rudimentary form of the vertebral column; a band forming the basis of the spinal column.—**notochordal** *adj*.

notoriety *n* the state of being notorious; disrepute, infamy; public exposure.

notorious *adj* widely known, esp unfavorably.—**notoriously** *adv*.

notornis *n* the gigantic short-winged coot of New Zealand.

nototherium *n* (*pl* **nototheria**) an extinct gigantic marsupial of Australia.

Notts *abbr* (*Brit*) = Nottinghamshire.

Notus *n* (*Greek myth*) the south wind, a brother of Boreas and Zephyrus.

notwithstanding *prep* in spite of. * *adv* nevertheless. * *conj* although.

Nouadhibou *n* a city in the Islamic Republic of Mauritania.

Nouakchott *n* capital city of the Islamic Republic of Mauritania.

nougat *n* a chewy sweet consisting of sugar paste with nuts.

nought *n* nothing; a zero. * *adv* in no degree.—*also* **naught**.

noughts and crosses *see* **tick-tack-toe**.

Noumea *n* capital city of New Caledonia or Nouvelle Calédonie.

noumenon *n* (*pl* **noumena**) an object of purely intellectual intuition; (*philos*) the substance or real existing under the phenomenal.—**noumenal** *adj*.

noun *n* (*gram*) a word that names a person, a living being, an object, action etc; a substantive.

nourish *vt* to feed; to encourage the growth of; to raise, bring up.

nourishing *adj* containing nourishment; health-giving; beneficial.

nourishment *n* food; the act of nourishing.

nous *n* pure intellect; common sense.

nouveau riche *n* (*pl* **nouveaux riches**) the new rich, a parvenu.—*also adj*.

nov. *abbr* = novelist.

Nov. *abbr* = novellae; November.

nova *n* (*pl* **novas**, **novae**) a new star that explodes into bright luminosity before subsiding.

Novalis *n* [Friedrich Leopold von Hardenberg] (1772–1801) German poet and novelist who was called the "Prophet of Romanticism" in Germany.

Novatian *adj* pertaining to the doctrines of the Novatians, a 3rd-century sect who held that the Church should not re-admit the lapsed, and that second marriages were of the nature of sin.

novation *n* (*law*) the replacement of one legal agreement by another, subject to the agreement of the parties involved.

novel *n* a relatively long fictional prose narrative. * *adj* new and unusual.

novelette *n* a short novel.—**novelettish** *adj*.

novelist *n* a writer of novels.

novelize *vt* to turn (a play, film, etc) into a novel.—**novelization** *n*.

novella *n* (*pl* **novellas**, **novelle**) a short novel.

Novello *n* 1. **Clara Anastasia** (1808–1908) Welsh soprano. 2. **Ivor** [Ivor Novello Davies] (1893–1951) Welsh songwriter, composer, and actor. 3. **Vincent** (1781–1861) London-based editor, organist and composer who founded the music publishing firm of Novello.

novelty *n* (*pl* **novelties**) a novel thing or occurrence; a new or unusual thing; (*pl*) cheap, small objects for sale.

November *n* the eleventh month, having 30 days.

Novembergruppe *n* an association of radical artists, founded in Berlin in 1918.

novena *n* (*pl* **novenae**) (*eccles*) a prayer made for nine days to obtain a request through intercession of the Virgin or saint.

novice *n* a person on probation in a religious order before taking final vows; a beginner.

Novi Sad *n* a city in Yugoslavia (FRY).

novitiate, **noviciate** *n* a probationary period, initiation; a novice; a place where novices live.

Novocaine *n* (*trademark*) the anesthetic procaine.

Novosibirsk *n* a city in the Russian Federation.

Nov. Sc. *abbr* = Nova Scotia.

now *adv* at the present time; by this time; at once; nowadays. * *conj* since; seeing that. * *n* the present time. * *adj* of the present time.

nowadays *adv* in these days; at the present time.

noway *adv* not at all. * *interj* (**no way**) used to express emphatic denial or refusal.

nowhere *adv* not in, at, or to anywhere.

no-win *adj* (*policy, situation, etc*) not having any chance of success.

nowise *adv* not in any manner or degree.

noxious *adj* harmful, unhealthy.—**noxiously** *adv*.—**noxiousness** *n*.

noyade *n* execution by drowning, esp that system of capital punishment for political offenders employed by the French revolutionists of 1789.

noyau *n* (*pl* **noyaux**) a liqueur flavored with bruised bitter almonds.

Noyes *n* 1. **Alfred** (1880–1958) English poet whose work includes the epic poem *Drake*. 2. **Eliot Fette** (1910–77) American architect.

nozzle *n* the spout at the end of a hose, pipe, etc.

Np *symbol* (*chem*) neptunium (element).

np *abbr* = net profit; new paragraph; (*Latin*) *nisi prius*, "unless previously"; (*Latin*) *nomen proprium*, "its own name."

np. *abbr* (*naut*) = neap.

n.p. *abbr* (*print*) = new paragraph ; no paging (of books so printed); no place (of publication).

n/p *abbr* = net proceeds.

N.P. *abbr* = (*Latin*) (*law*) *nisi prius*, "unless previously"; (*bank*) no protest; Notary Public; National Park.

NPA *abbr* = National Pawnbrokers' Association; Newspaper Publishers' Association.

NPC *abbr* = National Packaging Confederation; National Peace Council; National Population Council; (law) nisi prius cases.

NPD *abbr* = North Polar Distance.

npf *abbr* = not provided for.

NPG *abbr* = National Portrait Gallery.

npo *abbr* (*Latin*) = *nil per os*, "nothing by mouth."

n. p. or d. *abbr* = no place or date (*bibliography*).

n.p.t., **NPT** *abbr* = normal pressure and temperature.

npv, **NPV** *abbr* = net present value.

nr. *abbr* = near.

Nr. *abbr* = number.

nra *abbr* = never refuse anything.

NRA *abbr* = National Rifle Association.

NRDS *abbr* = neonatal respiratory distress syndrome.

NREM *abbr* = non-rapid eye movement.

nrv, **NRV** *abbr* = net realizable value.

ns *abbr* = nanosecond; near side; non-smoker; not significant/specified.

n.s. *abbr* = nickel steel; not specified.

n/s *abbr* = news sheet; not sufficient.

NS *abbr* = New Style; Nova Scotia; new series.

N/S, NSF *abbr* (*bank*) = not sufficient (funds).

N-S *abbr* (*French*) = *Notre-Seigneur*, "Our Lord."

NSA *abbr* = Nuclear Stock Association.

NSA/CSS *abbr* = National Security Agency/Central Security Service.

NSAID *abbr* = non-steroidal anti-inflammatory drug.

NSB *abbr* = National Savings Bank.

NSC *abbr* = National Safety Council; National Security Council.

NSCR *abbr* = National Society for Cancer Relief.

NSD *abbr* = nominal standard dose; (*med*) normal spontaneous delivery.

nsf *abbr* = not sufficient funds.

NSF *abbr* = National Science Foundation; National Squash Federation.

NSFGB *abbr* = National Ski Federation of Great Britain.

NSG *abbr* (*Brit*) = nonstatutory guidelines (concerning the National Curriculum).

NSGT *abbr* = Non-Self-Governing Territory.

NSI (*or* **J**) **C** *abbr* (*Latin*) = *Noster Salvator Iesus*, or *Jesus, Christus*, "Our Saviour Jesus Christ."

NSPCA *abbr* = National Society for the Prevention of Cruelty to Animals.

NSPCC *abbr* = National Society for the Prevention of Cruelty to Children.

nspf, n.s.p.f ., **NSPF** *abbr* = not specifically provided for.

nstd. *abbr* = nested.

NSTL *abbr* = National Space Technology Laboratories.

NSU *abbr* = non-specific urethritis.

NSW *abbr* = New South Wales.

NSWA *abbr* = National Small Woods Association.

nsw-bty *name see* **pre-nomen**.

n.t. *abbr* = net ton; new terms (*grain trade*).

N

Nt *abbr* (*chem*) = niton.

NT *abbr* = National Theatre; National Trust; New Testament; Northern Territory; no trumps (cards).

-n't = not.

nth *adj* (*maths*) of or having an unspecified number; (*inf*) utmost, extreme.

NTIS *abbr* = National Technical Information Service.

ntp, n.t.p. *abbr* = normal temperature and pressure; no title page.

NTVLRO *abbr* = National Television Licence Records Office.

nt. wt. *abbr* = net weight.

nu *n* the 13th letter of the Greek alphabet.

n.u. *abbr* = name unknown.

NU *abbr* = name unknown; number unobtainable.

Nuada Airegetlamh *n* (*Irish Celtic myth*) a leader of the Tuatha De Danann. He lost an arm in the first battle of Magh Tuiredh, even although he owned a sword from which no one could escape.

nuance *n* (*mus*) a subtle difference in speed, tone, color, meaning etc.

nub *n* a lump or small piece; (*inf*) the central point or gist of a matter.

nubbin *n* a small or imperfect ear of maize; undeveloped fruit.

nubecula *n* (*pl* **nubeculae**) the Magellanic clouds, a small galaxy; cloudy appearance; a light film on the eye.

Nubia *n* the region ranging from the south of the first cataract of the River Nile at Aswan to Khartoum in the Sudan.

nubile *adj* (*girl*) marriageable; attractive.

nuclear *adj* of or relating to a nucleus; using nuclear energy; having nuclear weapons.

nuclear bomb *n* a bomb whose explosive power derives from uncontrolled nuclear fusion or fission.

nuclear chemistry *n* (*chem*) the study of reactions involving the changes from one type of atom to another due to a nuclear reaction.

nuclear energy *n* energy released as a result of nuclear fission or fusion.

nuclear family *n* father, mother and children.

nuclear fission *n* the splitting of a nucleus of an atom either spontaneously or by bombarding it with particles.

nuclear-free zone *n* an area free of nuclear weapons or reactors.

nuclear fusion *n* (*phys*) the combining of two nuclei into a heavier nucleus, releasing energy in the process.

nuclear magnetic resonance *n* an analytical technique based upon the absorption of electromagnetic radiation resulting in a change in orientation of the nuclei.

nuclear power *n* electrical or motive power produced by a nuclear reactor.

nuclear reaction *n* any reaction in which the nuclei of atoms take direct part.

nuclear reactor *n* a device in which nuclear fission is maintained and harnessed to produce energy.

nuclear waste *n* radioactive waste.

nuclear winter *n* the blocking of sunlight and resultant catastrophic drop in temperatures predicted as a consequence of a nuclear explosion.

nucleate *adj* having a nucleus.

nucleic acid *n* (*biochem*) a linear molecule composed of four nucleotides that occurs in two forms: DNA (deoxyribonucleic acid) and RNA (ribonucleic acid).

nucleo-, nucle- *prefix* nucleus; nucleic acid.

nucleolus *n* (*pl* **nucleoli**) (*biol*) an object enclosed by a membrane found within the nucleus.

nucleon *n* either a proton or a neutron, the ordinary components of a nucleus.

nucleonics *n* (*used as sing*) the physics and technology of the applications of nuclear energy.

nucleophile *n* (*chem*) a reactive molecule that will readily "donate" its unshared pair of electrons.

nucleosynthesis *n* (*astron*) nuclear fission reactions occurring in stars and supernova explosions that produce elements other than hydrogen and helium.

nucleotide *n* (*biochem*) a molecule that acts as the basic building block of the nucleic acids, DNA and RNA.

nucleus *n* (*pl* **nuclei, nucleuses**) the central part of core around which something may develop, or be grouped or concentrated; the centrally positively charged portion of an atom; the part of an animal or plant cell containing genetic material.

NUCPS *abbr* = National Union of Civil and Public Servants.

nude *adj* naked; bare; undressed. * *n* a naked human figure, esp in a work of art; the state of being nude.—**nudity** *n*.

nudge *vt* to touch gently with the elbow to attract attention or urge into action; to push slightly. * *n* a gentle touch, as with the elbow.

nudibranch *n* any of the order Nudibranchia of shell-less molluscs with naked gills.

nudism *n* the practice of going nude, esp in groups at designated places and times.

nudist *n* one who believes in going nude.—*also adj*.

nudity *n* (*pl* **nudities**) nakedness.

Nuevo Sol *n* currency of Peru.

Nuffield *n* **William Richard Morris [1st Viscount]** (1877–1963) English car manufacturer and philanthropist.

nugatory *adj* trifling, worthless; inoperative, not valid; useless.

nugget *n* a small lump, esp of gold in its natural state.

NUGMW *abbr* = National Union of General and Municipal Workers.

NUI *abbr* (*Brit*) = National University of Ireland.

nuisance *n* a person or thing that annoys or causes trouble.

NUIW *abbr* = National Union of Insurance Workers.

NUJ *abbr* = National Union of Journalists.

NUJMB *abbr* = Northern Universities Joint Matriculation Board.

nuke *vt* (*sl*) to attack and destroy with a nuclear weapon; (*sl*) to cook or heat (food) in microwave oven. * *n* a nuclear weapon.

Nuku'alofa *n* capital city of Tonga.

Nukus *n* a city in Uzbekistan.

null *adj* without legal force; invalid.

null modem cable *n* (*comput*) a cable used to connect two computers without using a modem.

nullah *n* a watercourse in India that is filled after monsoons but dry at other times.

nulla-nulla *n* (*Australia*) a hard wooden club.

nullifier *n* one who nullifies.

nullify *vt* (**nullifying, nullified**) to make null, to cancel out.—**nullification** *n*.

nullipara *n* (*pl* **nulliparae**) a woman who has never given birth to a child, esp if not a virgin.—**nulliparous** *adj*.

nullipore *n* a marine coral-like plant with calcareous fronds.

nullity *n* (*pl* **nullities**) the state of being null; a legally invalid document or act; something ineffectual, worthless, etc.

num, num. *abbr* = number; numeral.

Num., Numb. *abbr* = Numbers (*OT*).

NUM *abbr* = National Union of Mineworkers.

Numa Pompilius *n* in the legendary history of Rome, its second king.

Numast *abbr* = National Union of Marine, Aviation and Shipping.

numb *adj* deadened; having no feeling (due to cold, shock, etc). * *vt* to make numb.—**numbness** *n*.

number *n* a symbol or word indicating how many; a numeral identifying a person or thing by its position in a series; a single issue of a magazine; a song or piece of music, esp as an item in a performance; (*inf*) an object singled out; a total of persons or things; (*gram*) the form of a word indicating singular or plural; a telephone number; (*pl*) arithmetic; (*pl*) numerical superiority. * *vti* to count; to give a number to; to include or be included as one of a group; to limit the number of; to total.

number one *n* the first in a list, series, etc; (*inf*) oneself or one's own interests; (*inf*) the most important person or thing; (*inf*) a best-selling pop record. * *adj* most important, urgent, etc.

numbered account *n* a bank account that is identified only by a number rather than by a name and number.

numberless *adj* too many to count.

numberplate *n* (*Brit*) a license plate.

Numbers *n* (*Bible*) fourth book of the OT.

Number Ten *n* 10 Downing Street, the London residence of the British prime minister.

numbles *npl* humbles, entrails, esp of a deer.

numbskull *see* **numskull**.

numerable *adj* countable.—**numerably** *adv*.

numeraire *n* a monetary unit that is used to value international transactions in goods and services and intergovernmental financial settlements on a common basis.

numeral *n* a symbol or group of symbols used to express a number (e.g. two = 2 or II, etc).

numerate *adj* having a basic understanding of arithmetic. * *vt* to reckon or enumerate; to point or read, as figures.

numerati *npl* people, esp financiers, who are proficient at arithmetic.

numeration *n* the act of numbering; the art of reading in words numbers expressed by symbols.

numerator *n* (*math*) the number or quantity to be divided by the denominator of a fraction.

numerical, numeric *adj* of or relating to numbers; expressed in numbers.

numerical forecasting *n* (*meterol*) weather forecasting that relies on numerous observations and measurements both "on the ground" and in the atmosphere and the subsequent calculation of what should follow.

numerical value *n* (*math*) the absolute value of a number.

numeric format *n* (*comput*) in a spreadsheet, the way a number can be displayed is controlled by use of the numeric format command.

numeric keypad *n* (*comput*) a section of the keyboard that allows numbers to be entered in an easy format. *See* **keypad**.

numerology *n* the study of the supposed occult meaning of numbers.

numerous *adj* many, consisting of many items.

numis., numism. *abbr* = numismatic, numismatics; numismatology.

numismatics *n* (*used as sing*) the study of coins, medals, etc.—*also* **numismatology.**—**numismatic** *adj*.

numismatist *n* one skilled in numismatics; a student of coins.

Numitor *n* in the legendary history of Rome, a king of Alba Longa.

num lock key *n* (*comput*) a keyboard key that when pressed fixes the keypad to numeric format rather than the optional controls or characters.

nummular *adj* pertaining to, or like, coins.

nummulite *n* a many-chambered fossil foraminifer resembling a coin.—**nummulitic** *adj*.

numskull *n* a dolt, a blockhead.—*also* **numbskull**.

nun *n* a woman belonging to a religious order.

Nun *n* (*Egypt*) the pre-Creation, a primordial shapeless ocean out of which the sun-god Ra emerged.

Nunet *n* (*Egypt*) the consort of Nun.

nunatak *n* (*geol*) a rock mountain peak that protrudes above the ice in an area undergoing glaciation.

Nunc Dimittis *n* (*mus*) (*Latin*) The Song of Simeon ("Lord, now lettest Thy Thou servant depart in peace), a canticle which is sung at evening church services.

nunciature *n* the office of a nuncio; the tenure of it.

nuncio *n* (*pl* **nuncios**) the pope's ambassador at a foreign court.

nuncupate *vt* to declare, to make a will verbally, not in writing.

nuncupative *adj* (*law*) verbal, not written; nominal.

Nunna *n* king of Sussex, England (*c*.710–725); an under-king of Ine of Wessex.

nunnery *n* (*pl* **nunneries**) a convent of nuns.

NUPE *abbr* (*Brit*) = National Union of Public Employees.

nuptial *adj* relating to marriage. * *npl* a wedding ceremony; marriage.

NUR *abbr* (*Brit*) = National Union of Railwaymen.

nuraghe *n* a construction of one or more defensive towers built of cyclopean masonry and unique to the island of Sardinia.

Nureyev *n* **Rudolf** (1939–93) Russian ballet dancer and choreographer. The successor to Nijinsky, he partnered Fonteyn in 1962.

nurse *n* a person trained to care for the sick, injured or aged; a person who looks after another person's child or children. * *vt* to tend, to care for; (*baby*) to feed at the breast; (*hatred*) to foster; to tend with an eye to the future.

nursemaid *n* a woman in charge of children, a nanny.

nursery *n* (*pl* **nurseries**) a room set aside for children; a place where children may be left in temporary care; a place where young trees and plants are raised for transplanting.

nurseryman *n* (*pl* **nurserymen**) a person who owns or works in a plant nursery.

nursery rhyme *n* a (usually traditional) short verse or song for children.

nursery school *n* a school for young children, usu under five.

nursery slope *n* a gently inclined slope for novice skiers.

nurse shark *n* any of various sharks with a furrow on each side of the head between the mouth and nose.

nursing *n* the profession of a nurse.

nursing home *n* an establishment providing care for convalescent, chronically ill, or disabled people.

nursling, nurseling *n* an infant; one who is nursed.

nurture *vt* to feed; to bring up, educate. * *n* the act of bringing up a child; nourishment.

NUS *abbr* = National Union of Seamen; National Union of Students.

nut[1] *n* a kernel (sometimes edible) enclosed in a hard shell; a usu metallic threaded block screwed on the end of a bolt; (*sl*) a mad person; (*sl*) a devotee, fan. * *vt* (**nutting, nutted**) to gather nuts.

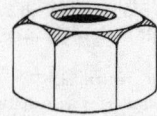

nut[2] *n* (*mus*) the part of the bow of a stringed instrument which holds the horsehair and which incorporates a screw that tightens the tension of the hairs; the hardwood ridge at the peg-box end of a stringed instrument's finger-board that raises the strings above the level of the finger-board.

NUT *abbr* = National Union of Teachers.

Nut *n* (*Egypt*) the sky goddess, paired in the original group of eight with the earth-god, Geb. Nut came later to be fused with Hathor.

nutant *adj* (*bot*) having the top bent downward.

nutation *n* nodding; the periodic vibratory movement of the axis of the earth; (*bot*) the turning of flowers towards the sun.—**nutational** *adj*.

nut-brown *adj* colored like a ripe hazelnut.

nut case *n* (*sl*) a crazy or foolish person.

nutcracker *n* (usu *pl*) a tool for cracking nuts; a bird with speckled plumage.

NUTG *abbr* = National Union of Townswomen's Guilds.

nuthatch *n* a small climbing bird feeding on nuts.

nuthouse *n* (*sl*) a mental hospital.

nutmeg *n* the aromatic kernel produced by a tree, grated and used as a spice.

nutria *n* the fur or skin of the coypu, a South American beaver.

nutrient *n* a substance that nourishes. * *adj* promoting growth.

nutriment *n* nourishing food, nourishment.

nutrition *n* the act or process by which plants and animals take in and assimilate food in their systems; the study of the human diet.—**nutritional** *adj*.

nutritionist *n* a specialist who studies and advises on the human diet.

nutritious *adj* efficient as food; health-giving, nourishing.

nutritive *adj* serving as good. * *n* an article of food.—**nutritively** *adv*.

nuts *adj* (*inf*) very keen (on); (*inf*) crazy.

nuts and bolts *npl* (*inf*) the basic facts or details.

nutshell *n* the hard covering of a nut; a tiny receptacle; a compact way of expression.

nutting *n* nut-gathering.

nutty *adj* (**nuttier, nuttiest**) tasting of or containing nuts; (*sl*) very enthusiastic; (*sl*) crazy, mad, etc.

NUWW *abbr* = National Union of Women Workers.

nux vomica *n* the fruit of an East Indian plant (*Strychnos Nux vomica*), which yields the deadly poison strychnine.

nuzzle *vti* to push (against) or rub with the nose or snout; to nestle, snuggle.

nv *abbr* = non-voting.

n/v *abbr* = non-vintage.

NV *abbr* = Nevada; (*Bible*) New Version; non-vintage.

NVALA *abbr* = National Viewers' and Listeners' Association.

nvd *abbr* = no value declared.

NVM *abbr* = Nativity of the Virgin Mary.

NVQ *abbr* = National Vocational Qualification.

n.w., NW *abbr* = northwest, northwestern.

NWAF *abbr* = National Women's Aid Federation.

NWbN *abbr* = northwest by north.

NWbW *abbr* = northwest by west.

NWC *abbr* = National War College.

NWCAF *abbr* = North West Councils Against Fluoridation.

NWEB *abbr* = North Western Electricity Board.

NWML *abbr* = National Weights and Measures Laboratory.

NWRAC *abbr* = North Western Regional Advisory Council for Further Education.

NWS *abbr* = National Weather Service.

NWT *abbr* = Northwest Territories.

NWTRB *abbr* = Nuclear Waste Technical Review Board.

NY *abbr* = New York.

NYA *abbr* = National Youth Agency.

nyala *n* (*pl* **nyala, nyalas**) a southern African antelope with spiral horns.

NYAM *abbr* = New York Academy of Music.

nybble *see* **nibble**.

NYC *abbr* = New York City.

nyct-, nycti-, nycto- *prefix* indicating night or darkness.

nyctalopia *n* poor vision in near darkness; the inability to see clearly in dim light.—also **night blindness**.

Nycteus *n* (*Greek myth*) a king of Thebes.

Nyctimene *n* (*Greek myth*) a daughter of Epopeus, king of Lesbos, who was turned into an owl by Athena.

nyctitropism *n* (*bot*) the so-called sleep of plants, turning in a certain direction at night.—**nyctitropic** *adj*.

nyctophobia *n* fear of the dark.—**nyctophobic** *adj*.

NYD *abbr* = not yet diagnosed.

Nyerere *n* **Julius [Kambarage]** (*c*.1922–) Tanzanian statesman; became president (1962–85); negotiated the union of Tanganyika and Zanzibar (1964) which formed Tanzania. His invasion of Uganda in 1978 ended Idi Amin's dictatorship.

NYHS *abbr* = New York Historical Society.

nylon *n* any of numerous strong, tough, elastic, synthetic materials used esp in plastics and textiles; (*pl*) stockings made of nylon.

Nymex *abbr* = New York Mercantile Exchange.

nymph *n* (*myth*) a spirit of nature envisaged as a maiden; (*poet*) a lovely young maiden; the chrysalis of an insect.—**nymphean** *adj*.

nymphet *n* a sexually desirable pre-adolescent girl.

nympho *n* (*pl* **nymphos**) (*inf*) a nymphomaniac.

nympholepsy *n* (*pl* **nympholepsies**) frenzy caused by desire of the unattainable.

nympholept *n* one inspired by violent enthusiasm for an ideal.—**nympholeptic** *adj*.

nymphomania *n* uncontrollable sexual desire in women.—**nymphomaniac** *adj, n.*—**nymphomaniacal** *adj*.

NYO *abbr* = National Youth Orchestra.

nystagmus *n* a condition of the eye, with spasmodic movement of the eyeballs.—**nystagmic** *adj*.

Nyx *n* (*Greek myth*) night and the goddess of night, called Nox by the Romans.

NZ, N. Zeal. *abbr* = New Zealand.

NZAA *abbr* = New Zealand Archaeological Association.

NZGA *abbr* = New Zealand Grassland Association.

NZRFU *abbr* = New Zealand Rugby Football Union.

N

O

o, O *n* the 15th letter of the English alphabet; something shaped like the letter O; naught, nothing, zero.

O *interj* an exclamation of wonder, pain, etc.

o *symbol* (*mus*) when placed over a note in a musical score for strings, indicates that the note must be played on an open string or as a harmonic.

O *symbol* (*chem*) oxygen (element).

o *abbr* = ohm; (*mus*) (*Italian*) *ottava*, "octave."

O *abbr* = Office; Order (of nuns, etc); ordinary.

o. *abbr* = occidental; octavo; old; only; order; oriental; (*anat*) (*Latin*) *os*, "bone"; (*pharm*) (*Latin*) *octarius*, "pint"; off; only; (*Latin*) *optimus*, "best."

O. *abbr* = Ocean; October; Ohio; Ontario; (*eccl*) (*Latin*) *Ordo*, "Order"; Oregon.

o' *prep* (*inf, arch*) short for *of* or *on*.

O' *prefix* (in Irish surnames) descendant of.

o- *abbr* (*chem*) = ortho-.

-o *n, adj suffix* (*inf*) indicating a diminutive, *cheapo*; (*inf*) forming an interjection, *cheerio*.

oa *abbr* = overall.

OA *abbr* = Office of Administration; Officers Association; Overeaters Anonymous; office automation; operations analysis; osteoarthritis.

o.a. *abbr* = on account; overall.

O/a *or* o/a *abbr* = on account of; our account.

OAA *abbr* = Obstetric Anesthetists Association; Opticians Association of America; Outdoor Advertising Association of Great Britain.

OAC *abbr* = Oceanic Affairs Committee; Office of Antiboycott Compliance.

OAD *abbr* = obstructive airways disease.

oaf *n* (*pl* oafs) a loutish or stupid person.—oafish *adj*.—oafishly *adv*.

OAIT *abbr* = Office of American Indian Trust.

oak *n* a tree with a hard durable wood, having acorns as fruits.

oak apple *n* a spongy excrescence growing on the leaves or young branches of the oak, caused by the gallfly.

oaken *adj* made of or consisting of oak.

oakum *n* a loose fiber obtained by unpicking old rope and used for caulking.

OALJ *abbr* = Office of Administrative Law Judges.

o & c *abbr* = onset and course.

O & C *abbr* (*Brit*) = Oxford and Cambridge.

O & G *abbr* = obstetrics and gynecology.

O & M *abbr* = organization and method(s).

o. and r. *abbr* (*transp*) = ocean and rail.

oao *abbr* = off and on; one and only.

OAP *abbr* (*Brit*) = old age pensioner, senior citizen.

OAPEC *abbr* = Organization of Arab Petroleum Exporting Countries.

oar *n* a pole with a flat blade for rowing a boat; an oarsman.

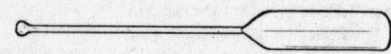

OAR *abbr* = Office of Oceanic and Atmospheric Research.

oarlock *n* a rowlock.

oarsman *n* (*pl* oarsmen) a person who rows a boat.—oarsmanship *n*.

OAS *abbr* = Organization of American States; Secret Army Organization (Algeria); on active service.

oasis *n* (*pl* oases) a fertile place in a desert; a refuge.

oast *n* a kiln for drying hops or barley.

OAT *abbr* = outside air temperature.

oatcake *n* a thin broad cake of oatmeal.

oaten *adj* made of oats.

Oates *n* Joyce Carol (1938–) American novelist and poet whose work includes *A Garden of Earthly Delights* and *A Bloodsmoor Romance*.

OATG *abbr* = outside air temperature gauge.

oath *n* (*pl* oaths) a solemn declaration to a god or a higher authority that one will speak the truth or keep a promise; a swear word; a blasphemous expression; (*law*) an instrument indicating that a person is giving a statement in which they will perform certain duties or meet certain obligations.

oatmeal *n* ground oats; a porridge of this; a pale grayish-brown color.

oats *npl* a cereal grass widely cultivated for its edible grain; the seeds.

OAU *abbr* = Organization of African Unity.

ob. *abbr* = (*Latin*) *obiit*, "died"; (*Latin*) *obiter* , "incidentally"; oboe; obolus.

Ob., Obad *abbr* = Obadiah.

OB *abbr* = obstetrics; old boy; outside broadcast; (*bank*) ordered back.

o/b *abbr* = on or before.

ob- *prefix* before, against, toward, in front of, reversed.

Obadiah, the Book of *n* (*Bible*) the shortest OT book with one chapter of twenty-one verses, comprising a few poetic oracles against the people of Edom, by tradition descendants of Esau and enemies of the children of Israel.

Obanian *adj* relating to a culture of Mesolithic date named after the town of Oban on the west coast of Scotland.

obb. *abbr* (Italian) = *obbligato* , "essential."

obbligato *n* (*mus*) (*Italian*) obligatory; a term that refers to a part which cannot be dispensed with in a performance (some parts can be optional). However, some 19th-century composers used the word to mean the exact opposite, i.e., a part that was optional. * *n* (*pl* obbligatos, obbligati) an indispensable instrumental part or accompaniment written especially for the instrument named.—*also* obligato (*pl* obligatos, obligati).

OBC *abbr* = on-board computer; Old Bottle Club of Great Britain.

obcordate *adj* (*bot*) inversely cordate.

OBD *abbr* = organic brain disease.

obdt. *abbr* = obedient.

obdurate *adj* hard-hearted; unyielding, stubborn.—obduracy *n*.—obdurately *adv*.

OBE *abbr* = (*Brit*) Officer of the Order of the British Empire; out-of-the-body experience.

obeah *see* obi².

obedience *n* the condition of being obedient; observance of orders, instructions, etc; respect for authority.

obedient *adj* obeying; compliant; submissive to authority, dutiful.—obediently *adv*.

obeisance *n* a bow or curtsey; an act of reverence or homage.

obelisk *n* a four-sided tapering pillar esp with a pyramidal top; a reference mark used in printing (†) (—*also* dagger).

obelize *vt* to mark with an obelus.

obelus *n* (*pl* obeli) a mark (— *or* ÷ *or* †) used in old MSS to indicate a doubtful or spurious reading; in modern writing, a break (—).

OBEMLA *abbr* = Office of Bilingual Education and Minority Languages Affairs.

Oberon *n* the outermost and second largest satellite of Uranus, discovered by Herschel in 1787.

Oberwerk *n* (*mus*) (*German*) a swell organ. *See* organ.

obese *adj* very fat.—obesity *n*.

obesity *n* the accumulation of excess fat in the body, mainly in the subcutaneous tissues, caused by eating more food than is necessary to produce the required energy for each day's activity.

obey *vti* (obeying, obeyed) to carry out (orders, instructions); to comply (with); to submit (to).

obfuscate *vt* to bewilder or confuse, to darken.—obfuscation *n*.

OB-GYN *abbr* = obstetrician and gynecologist.

obi¹ *n* (*pl* obis, obi) a Japanese woman's sash.

obi² *n* (*pl* obis) in the West Indies and Africa, a system of secret sorcery or magical rites.—*also* obeah.

obit *n* (*inf*) an obituary.

obiter dictum *n* (*pl* obiter dicta) (*Latin*) a casual remark or opinion expressed incidentally, as by a judge or writer.

obituary *n* (*pl* obituaries) an announcement of a person's death, often with a short biography.—obituarist *n*.

obj. *abbr* = object; objection; objective.

object *n* something that can be recognized by the senses; a person or thing toward which action, feeling, etc, is directed; a purpose or aim; (*gram*) a noun or part of a sentence governed by a transitive verb or a preposition. * *vti* to state or raise an objection; to oppose; to disapprove.—**objector** *n*.

object ball *n* (*billiards*) the ball meant to be hit by the cue ball.

objectify *vt* (**objectifying, objectified**) to render objective; to embody; to materialize.—**objectification** *n*.

objection *n* the act of objecting; a ground for, or expression of, disapproval.

objectionable *adj* causing an objection; disagreeable.—**objectionably** *adv*.

objective *adj* relating to an object; not influenced by opinions or feelings; impartial; having an independent existence of its own, real; (*gram*) of, or appropriate to an object governed by a verb or a preposition. * *n* the thing or placed aimed at; (*gram*) the objective case; (*astron*) the front lens in a refracting telescope which forms the first image of the object under examination.—*also* **objective lens, object glass.**—**objectively** *adv*.

objective and task method *n* a method of managing and budgeting that involves the formulation of specific objectives and the setting out of and costing of the tasks, which have to be completed in order to meet these objectives.

objective prism *n* (*astron*) a glass prism of small refracting angle used with a telescope to form a small spectrum from all of the stars in the field of view.

objectivism *n* (*philos*) the doctrine that the knowledge of the non-ego is anterior to that of the ego; (*art, literature*) the representation of persons and incidents as they really appear.—**objectivist** *adj, n.*—**objectivistic** *adj*.

objectivity *n* the state or quality of being objective; in accounting terms a principle that seeks to minimize any subjectivity or personal judgment affecting the recording and summarizing of financial transactions on the part of the person undertaking the preparation of the records.

object lesson *n* a convincing practical illustration of some principle.

object linking and embedding (OLE) *n* (*comput*) a set of standards designed to allow links to be created between documents and applications.

object oriented graphics *n* (*comput*) graphics that are created by a program that creates an image by a mixture of lines, rectangles, ovals, etc, which can be moved independently.

object oriented programming system *n* (*comput*) a programming environment that consists of a range of objects that have their own programming code.

object program *n* (*comput*) a computer program derived from the conversion of a source program into machine code by a compiler or assembler.

objet d'art *n* (*pl* **objets d'art**) a small decorative object.

objet trouvé *see* **found object**.

objurgate *vt* to chide or reprove, to scold.—**objurgation** *n*.

objurgatory *adj* containing reproof or censure.

obl. *abbr* = oblique; oblong.

OBL *abbr* = Office of Business Liaison.

oblanceolate *adj* (*bot*) lanceolate in the reversed order.

oblate[1] *n* (*RC Church*)a secular priest who has devoted himself and his property to the monastery he has entered. *adj* dedicated to a monastic or religious life.

oblate[2] *adj* (of a spheroid) slightly flattened at the poles, as is the Earth; orange-shaped.

oblateness *n* (*astron*) the measure of the difference between the actual shape of a celestial body and a perfect sphere.

oblation *n* an offering or sacrifice; anything presented in religious worship, esp the Eucharist.—**oblatory, oblational** *adj*.

obligate *vt* to bind by a contract, promise, sense of duty, etc.

obligation *n* the act of obligating; a moral or legal requirement; a debt; a favor; a commitment to pay a certain amount of money; the amount owed under such an obligation.

obligato *see* **obbligato**.

obligatory *adj* binding, not optional; compulsory.

oblige *vt* to compel by moral, legal, or physical force; to make (someone) grateful for some favor; to do a favor for.

obligee *n* (*law*) a person in whose favor a bond is made; a creditor.

obliging *adj* ready to do favors, agreeable.—**obligingly** *adv*.

obligor *n* (*law*) a person who is bound by a bond; a debtor.

oblique *adj* slanting, at an angle; diverging from the straight; indirect, allusive. * *n* an oblique line.—**obliquely** *adv*.

oblique angle *n* (*math*) any angle that does not equal 90º (right angle) or any multiple of 90º.

oblique case *n* (*gram*) any case except the nominative and vocative.

oblique motion *n* (*mus*) two parallel melody lines, or parts: one moves up or down the scale while the other stays on a consistent note.

obliquity *n* (*pl* **obliquities**) obliqueness; a slanting direction; deviation from a moral code.

obliquity of the ecliptic *n* the angle between the plane of the earth's equator and the plane of the ecliptic (the plane containing its orbit).

obliterate *vt* to wipe out, to erase, to destroy.—**obliteration** *n*.

oblivion *n* a state of forgetting or being forgotten; a state of mental withdrawal.

oblivious *adj* forgetful, unheeding; unaware (of).

oblong *adj* rectangular. * *n* any oblong figure.

obloquy *n* (*pl* **obloquies**) reproachful language, detraction; calumny; slander, disgrace.

obnoxious *adj* objectionable; highly offensive.—**obnoxiously** *adv*.—**obnoxiousness** *n*.

oboe *n* (*mus*) a woodwind instrument with a conical bore and a double reed. The instrument has a history dating back to ancient Egyptian times. Shawms evolved from these Egyptian predecessors and became known as "hautbois" (high-wood) instruments in the 17th and 18th centuries. The modern oboe (the word is a corruption of "hautbois") dates from the 18th century. The established variations of the instrument are: the oboe (treble), the cor anglais (alto), the bassoon (tenor), and the double bassoon (bass).—**oboist** *n*.

obolus, obol *n* (*pl* **oboli, obols**) an ancient Greek silver coin; a modern Greek weight = $^1/_{10}$th of a gram.

Obote *n* [Apollo] Milton (1924–) Ugandan politician. Uganda's first prime minister (1962–66) after independence, and president (1966–71). He was deposed by Amin and became president again (1980–85) after Amin's overthrow.

obovate *adj* (*bot*) inversely ovate.

Obrecht (Hobrecht) *n* Jacob (1450–1505) Flemish composer who traveled extensively in Europe and was one of the foremost musicians of his era. He is remembered for writing 24 Masses, 22 motets, and many songs.

O'Brien *n* 1. **Conor Cruise** (1917–) Irish statesman, critic, historian, and dramatist. A strong opponent of the IRA. His works include a collection of political and literary essays, *Passion and Cunning* (1988). 2. **Edna** (1932–) Irish novelist and short-story writer whose novels include *The Country Girls, The Lonely Girl*, and *Girls in their Married Bliss*. 3. **Flann** [Brian O'Nolan or O Nuallain] (1911–66) Irish novelist and journalist whose regular column in the *Irish Times* established him as one of the major Irish satirists. His novels include *The Dalkey Archive*.

Obrist *n* **Hermann** (1862–1927) One of the most important Swiss designers of **Jugendstil**, and a founder of **Munchner Werkstatte**.

obs. *abbr* = observation; obsolete.

obscene *adj* indecent, lewd; offensive to a moral or social standard.—**obscenely** *adv*.

obscenity *n* (*pl* **obscenities**) the state or quality of being obscene; an obscene act, word, etc.

obscurant *adj* (of a person) opposed to enlightenment, reactionary.—*also n.*—**obscurantism** *n.*—**obscurantist** *adj, n.*

obscure *adj* not clear; dim; indistinct; remote, secret; not easily understood; inconspicuous; unimportant, humble. * *vt* to make unclear, to confuse; to hide.—**obscurely** *adv*.

obscurity *n* (*pl* **obscurities**) the state or quality of being obscure; an obscure thing or person.

obsequies *npl* (*sing* **obsequy**) funeral rites, a funeral.

obsequious *adj* subservient; fawning.—**obsequiously** *adv*.

observable *adj* worthy of observation; remarkable.—**observably** *adv*.

observance *n* the observing of a rule, duty, law, etc; a ceremony or religious rite.

observant *adj* watchful; attentive, mindful.—**observantly** *adv*.

observation *n* the act or faculty of observing; a comment or remark; careful noting of the symptoms of a patient, movements of a suspect, etc, prior to diagnosis, analysis, or interpretation.—**observational** *adj.*—**observationally** *adv*.

observatory *n* (*pl* **observatories**) a building for astronomical observation; an institution whose primary purpose is making such observations.

observe *vt* to notice; to perceive; to keep to or adhere to (a law, etc); to arrive at as a conclusion; to examine scientifically. * *vi* to take notice; to make a comment (on).—**observable** *adj*.

observed time *n* the time taken by an operator to perform a task when under observation as part of a time and motion study.

observer *n* a person who observes; a delegate who attends a formal meeting but may not take part; an expert analyst and commentator in a particular field.

obsess *vt* to possess or haunt the mind of; to preoccupy.—**obsessive** *adj, n.*—**obsessively** *adv*.

obsession *n* a fixed idea, often associated with mental illness; a persistent idea or preoccupation; the condition of obsessing or being obsessed.

obsidian *n* (*geol*) a dark gray or black translucent volcanic glass, formed by the rapid cooling of a molten rock with a composition of granite; it was highly prized in the ancient world for tool making.

obsidian hydration dating *n* (*archeo*) a method of dating based on the amount of water absorbed by the surface of obsidian.

obsoles. *abbr* = obsolescent.

obsolescence *n* a reduction in the value of a fixed asset because of its age.

obsolescent *adj* becoming obsolete, going out of date.

obsolete *adj* disused, out of date.

ob. s. p. *abbr* (*Latin*) = *obiit sine prole*, "died without issue."

obstacle *n* anything that hinders something; an obstruction.

obstacle course *n* a course filled with fences, ditches, etc, that have to be negotiated, esp as used for military training.

obstet. *abbr* = obstetrical.

obstetrics *n sing* the branch of medicine concerned with the care and treatment of women during pregnancy, childbirth, and the period immediately after birth. *See* **midwifery.**—**obstetric, obstetrical** *adj.*—**obstetrician**.

obstinate *adj* stubborn, self-willed; intractable; persistent.—**obstinacy** *n.*—**obstinately** *adv*.

obstreperous *adj* unruly, turbulent, noisy.

O

obstruct *vt* to block with an obstacle; to impede; to prevent, hinder; to keep (light, etc) from.

obstruction *n* that which obstructs; the act or an example of obstructing; a hindrance, obstacle.

obstructionism *n* the systematic hindering of political business, etc.—**obstructionist** *adj, n*.

obstructive *adj* tending to obstruct; preventing, hindering.—**obstructively** *adv*.—**obstructiveness** *n*.

obt. *abbr* = obedient; (*Latin*) *obiit*, "died."

obtain *vt* to get, to acquire, to gain. * *vi* to be prevalent, hold good.—**obtainable** *adj*.—**obtainment** *n*.

obtect *adj* (of a pupa) protected by a hard outer case.

obtrude *vti* to push (an opinion, oneself) on others uninvited; to intrude.—**obtruding** *adj*.

obtrusion *n* the act of obtruding; an unwelcome intrusion.

obtrusive *adj* apt to obtrude, pushy; protruding, sticking out.—**obtrusively** *adv*.—**obtrusiveness** *n*.

obtund *vt* (*med*) to blunt, to deaden.

obturate *vt* to stop, to block or seal up; (of a gun breech) to close.—**obturation** *n*.—**obturator** *n*.

obtuse *adj* mentally slow; not pointed; dull, stupid; (*geom*) greater than a right angle but less than 180°.—**obtusely** *adv*.—**obtuseness** *n*.

obtuse angle *n* (*geom*) any angle that lies between but does not equal 90° and 180°.

obverse *n* the front or top side; (of a coin) the head; a counterpart. * *adj* facing the viewer; with the top wider than the base.—**obversely** *adv*.

obversion *n* (*logic*) the immediate inference by which we deny the opposite of anything affirmed.

obvert *vt* (*logic*) to infer by obversion; to turn toward, to face.

obviate *vt* to make unnecessary; (of danger, difficulty) to prevent, clear away.—**obviation** *n*.

obvious *adj* easily seen or understood; evident.—**obviously** *adv*.—**obviousness** *n*.

obvolute *adj* arranged so as to overlap, as the margins of an organ or part of a plant.

oc *abbr* = office copy; only child.

OC *abbr* = Officer Commanding; Officer in Charge; Official Classification; Old Carthusian; oral contraceptive; original cover (in stamp collecting).

Oc. or **oc.** *abbr* = ocean.

o.c. *abbr* (*Latin*) = *opere citato*, "in the work cited."

o/c *abbr* = old charter, *or* crop; overcharge.

oc- *prefix* the form of *ob-* before *c*.

O. Cart. *abbr* (*Latin*) = *Ordo Cartusiensis*, "Carthusian Order."

O'Casey *n* Sean (1880–1964) Irish dramatist whose three early plays, *The Shadow of a Gunman*, *Juno and the Paycock*, and *The Plough and the Stars*, focussed on the patriotism that followed the 1916 Easter Rising.

Ochain *n* (*Irish Celtic myth*) the magic shield belonging to Conchobar mac Nessa. When its owner was in danger, it gave out a moaning sound.

o'clock *adv* indicating the hour; indicating a relative direction or position, twelve o'clock being directly ahead or above.

O'Connell *n* Daniel (1775–1847) Irish nationalist. Founded the Catholic Association in 1823 to campaign for Roman Catholic emancipation and for repeal of the Union.

O'Connor *n* 1. [Mary] Flannery (1925–64) American novelist and short-story writer whose masterpiece is *Wise Blood*. 2. Frank [Michael Francis O'Donovan] (1903–66) Irish short-story writer and critic best known for his portraits of Irish life in such short-story collections as *Bones of Contention* and *Domestic Relations*.

ocarina *n* (*mus*) a small, egg-shaped wind instrument, often made of clay, which is played in a way similar to a recorder. It was invented in the mid-19th century and is still made, mainly as a toy.

occasion *n* a special occurrence or event; a time when something happens; an opportunity; reason or grounds; a subsidiary cause. * *vt* to cause; to bring about.

occasional *adj* infrequent, not continuous; intermittent; produced for an occasion; (of a cause) incidental.

occasionalism *n* (*philos*) the Cartesian theory of occasional causes, that bodily actions are caused and controlled by divine agency and not by the human will.

occasionally *adv* intermittently; now and then; infrequently.

occident *n* the west; (*with cap*) specifically Europe and America; the countries west of Asia and Turkey in Europe.—**occidental, Occidental** *adj*.

occipital *adj* of or pertaining to the occiput.

occipital bone *n* a bone of the skull, which is shaped like a saucer and forms the back of the cranium and part of its base.

occipitoanterior *see* **malposition**.

occiput *n* (*pl* occipita, occiputs) (*anat*) the back part of the skull or head.

occlude *vti* to shut out or in; to stop up, close; (*chem*) to absorb and retain.

occluded front *n* (*meteorol*) the phenomenon formed by a cold front overtaking a warm front and lifting the warm air above the earth's surface.

occlusion *n* the act of occluding; (*dent*) the position of the teeth when the jaws are closed; (*med*) the closing or blocking of an organ or duct; an occluded front.

occult *adj* supernatural, magical; secret; (*med*) not easily seen, not visible to the naked eye.—*also n*.

occultation *n* (*astron*) the blocking of the light from a distant star or other celestial body by the movement of a nearer object across its line of sight, as the eclipse of a star or planet by the moon, etc.

occulted *adj* (*astron*) hidden from view, as a star, etc.

occultism *n* mysticism, spiritualism, theosophy, etc.—**occultist** *n*.

occult sciences *npl* magic, alchemy, and astrology.

occupancy *n* (*pl* occupancies) the act of taking and holding in possession; the time of possession.

occupant *n* a person who occupies, resides in, holds a position or place, etc.

occupation *n* the act of occupying; the state of being occupied; employment or profession; a pursuit.—**occupational** *adj*.

occupational disease *or* **industrial disease** *n* a disease that is specific to a particular occupation and to which workers are prone.

occupational pension *n* a pension scheme that is operated by employers and to which employees and employees both make regular contributions, the employee on retirement receiving a pension in relation to the amount of his or her contributions.

occupational therapy *n* therapy by means of work in the arts and crafts, to aid recovery from disease or injury.—**occupational therapist** *n*.

occupier *n* an occupant.

occupy *vt* (occupying, occupied) to live in; to take up or fill (a room, office); to hold (a position); to engross (one's mind); to take possession of (a city, etc).

occur *vi* (occurring, occurred) to happen; to exist; to come into the mind of.

occurrence *n* a happening, an incident, an event; the act or fact of occurring.

OCD *abbr* = obsessive compulsive disorder.

ocean *n* a large stretch of sea, esp one of the earth's five oceans; technically, a body of water that occupies the ocean basin; more generally all the water on the Earth's surface, excluding lakes and inland seas; a huge quantity or expanse. * *npl* (*geog*) those bodies of water that occupy the ocean basins, which begin at the edge of the continental shelf.

oceanarium *n* (*pl* oceanariums, oceanaria) a large seawater aquarium for displays of marine life.

ocean currents *n* fast-moving large-scale flows of water in the oceans, formed by the rotation of the earth, prevailing winds, and differences in temperature and sea water densities.

oceangoing *adj* (*vessel*) designed and equipped for traveling on the open ocean.

Oceania *n* the Pacific islands.—**Oceanic** *adj*.

oceanic *adj* of or relating to the ocean; formed or found in the ocean.

Oceanid *n* (*pl* Oceanids, Oceanides) (*Greek myth*) a nymph of the great ocean which flows around the earth, daughter of Oceanus.

oceanography *n* study of all aspects of the oceans, from their structure and composition to the life within and the movements of the water.—**oceanographer** *n*.

Oceanus *n* (*Greek myth*) the eldest of the Titans, regarded as the god of the ocean.

ocellate, ocellated *adj* marked with small spots or eyes.

ocellus *n* (*pl* ocelli) the facet of a compound eye; an eye-like spot, as on a peacock's tail, etc.

ocelot *n* a medium-sized spotted wildcat of North and South America.

OCF *abbr* = Officiating Chaplain to the Forces.

och *interj* (*Scot, Irish*) expressing surprise, contempt, disagreement, disappointment, etc.

ocher, ochre *n* a yellow to orange-colored clay used as a pigment. It was used by Paleolithic peoples for cave art and probably as body paint.

ochlo-, ochl- *prefix* mob.

ochlocracy *n* (*pl* ochlocracies) mob rule.—**ochlocrat** *n*.—**ochlocratic** *adj*.

Ochoa, Severo *see* **Kornberg, Arthur**.

OCIMF *abbr* = Oil Companies International Marine Forum.

Ockeghem (Okeghem, Ockenheim) *n* Johannes (Jan) (*c*.1430–*c*.1495) Flemish composer of considerable originality, who achieved fame with his motets, Masses and songs.

Ocnus *n* (*Greek myth*) one of the damned in Hades. His punishment was continually to braid a rope of straw that was eaten by a she-ass as rapidly as Ocnus could braid it.

OCR *abbr* (*comput*) = optical character reader; optical character recognition.

OCS *abbr* = Office of Community Services; Office of the Chief Scientist; Oriental Ceramic Society.

OCSC *abbr* (*Brit*) = Office of the Civil Service Commissioners.

OCSE *abbr* = Office of Child Support Enforcement.

oct. *abbr* = octavo.

Oct. *abbr* = October.

Octa *n* (*d*. *c*.540) king of Kent (*c*.512–*c*.540). The grandson of Hengest, he succeeded his father, Aesc.

octa- *prefix* eight.

octachord *n* an eight-stringed musical instrument; a series of eight notes, diatonic scale.—**octachordal** *adj*.

octad *n* a group of eight; the number eight; (*chem*) an element or radical with a valence of eight.—**octadic** *adj*.

octagon *n* a plane figure having eight equal sides.—**octagonal** *adj*.

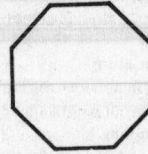

octahedral *adj* having eight equal sides.

octahedron *n* (*geom*) a geometrical solid that consists of eight equilateral triangular faces.

octal *n* (*comput*) a number system with 8 as its base, one digit being equivalent to three bits.

octameter *n* an eight-foot verse.

octane *n* a hydrocarbon found in petrol.

octane number *or* **octane rating** *n* a measure of the anti-knock quality of a liquid motor fuel expressed as a percentage.

octant *n* the eighth part of a circle; an instrument for measuring angles; (*astron*) an aspect of two planets, etc, when 45° apart.

octave *n* (*mus*) an interval of eight notes, inclusive of the top and bottom notes, e.g., C to C; the interval of eight degrees between a tone and either of its octaves, or the series of tones within this interval.

octavo *n* (*pl* **octavos**) a sheet of printing paper folded in eight leaves or 16 pages (8vo); this size, average 9 $\frac{1}{2}$ x 6 ins. * *adj* having eight leaves or 16 pages to the sheet.

octennial *adj* recurring every eighth year; continuing eight years.—**octennially** *adv*.

octet *n* (*mus*) a group of eight (instruments, performers, lines of a sonnet); a composition for eight instruments or voices. ·

octillion *n* in the US and France, the ninth power of a thousand (1 with 27 ciphers); (*Brit*) the eighth power of a million (1 with 48 ciphers).—**octillionth** *adj*.

octo- *prefix* eight.

octobass *n* (*mus*) a huge kind of three-stringed double bass, some 4 meters in height, which incorporated pedal-operated levers to stop the immensely thick strings. It was invented by J B Vuillaume in Paris in 1849, but proved impractical.

October *n* the tenth month of the year, having 31 days.

October surprise *n* a political act aimed at generating voting support prior to a November election.

octodecimo *adj* consisting of 18 leaves or 36 pages to a sheet. * *n* (*pl* **octodecimos**) a book of such size (18mo).

octogenarian *n* a person who is in his or her eighties.

octopod *n* an animal with eight feet; an eight-armed mollusc.—*also adj*.

octopus *n* (*pl* **octopuses**, **octopi**) a mollusc having a soft body and eight tentacles covered with suckers.

octoroon *n* the offspring of a white person and a quadroon.

octosyllable *n* a word or verse of eight syllables.—**octosyllabic** *adj*.

octroi *n* in France and Belgium, a tax levied upon articles brought into the gates of a city; duty on goods.

OCTU *abbr* (*Brit*) = Officer Cadet Training Unit.

octuple *adj* eight-fold.

ocular *adj* of, by, or relating to the eye; resembling an eye in form or function.

ocularist *n* a person skilled in making and fitting artificial eyes.

oculist *n* (*formerly*) an ophthalmologist.

oculomotor nerve *n* either of a pair of cranial nerves that are involved in eye movements, including movement of the eyeball and alterations in the size of the pupil and lens.

oculus *n* (*archit*) a circular opening in the top of a roof dome or in a wall.

od *n* a hypothetical natural force once used to explain magnetism, mesmerism, etc.

od *abbr* = outer diameter.

OD *n* (*inf*) an overdose of a drug, esp a narcotic. * *vi* (**OD'ing**, **OD'd**) to take an overdose.

OD *abbr* = Officer of the Day; Old Dutch; ordinary seaman; Ordnance Datum; Ordnance Department; overdose; overdraft; overdrawn.

o/d *abbr* = on demand.

/d *or* **o/d.** *abbr* = on demand.

o.d. *abbr* = olive drab.

ODA *abbr* (*Brit*) = Offa's Dyke Association; Overseas Development Administration.

odalisque, odalisk *n* a female slave or concubine in the harem of a sultan; (*art*) a painting of a reclining female nude figure often wearing the baggy trousers of a Middle Eastern female slave. Matisse painted a series of odalisques.

ODan. *abbr* = Old Danish.

ODC *abbr* = Order of Discalced Carmelites.

odd *adj* eccentric; peculiar; occasional; not divisible by two; with the other of the pair missing; extra or left over. * *npl* probability; balance of advantage in favor of one against another; excess of one number over another, esp in betting; likelihood; disagreement; strife; miscellaneous articles, scraps.—**oddly** *adv*.—**oddness** *n*.

oddball *n* (*sl*) an eccentric person. * *adj* bizarre.

Odd Fellow (*Brit*) *n* a member of the order of the benevolent society of the Odd Fellows, a friendly society similar to freemasons.

oddity *n* (*pl* **oddities**) the state of being odd; an odd thing or person; peculiarity.

odd lot *n* a block of stock of fewer than 100 shares.

odd man out *n* a person left when others pair off.

oddment *n* an odd piece left over, esp of fabric.

odds and ends *npl* miscellaneous articles, scraps.

odds-on *adj* (of a horse, etc) (judged to be) having a better than even chance of winning; likely to happen, succeed, win, etc.

ode *n* a lyric poem marked by lofty feeling and dignified style; in Ancient Greece, originally a poem intended to be sung; now loosely applied to any elaborate lyric poem.

Odense *n* a city in Denmark.

odeon *n* (*archit*) a small, roofed classical theater.

Odessa *n* a city in Ukraine.

Odets *n* Clifford (1906–63) American dramatist whose masterpiece is *Waiting for Lefty*, a play about a taxi-drivers' strike that ends in a mass meeting (in which the audience is invited to participate) calling for a strike.

odeum *n* (*pl* **odeums, odea**) a hall for musical performances.

ODI *abbr* = Open Door International for the Economic Emancipation of the Woman Worker.

odious *adj* causing hatred or offence; disgusting.—**odiously** *adv*.—**odiousness** *n*.

odium *n* general dislike.

odometer *n* an instrument attached to the axle of a vehicle to measure the distance it travels.

odonto-, odont- *prefix* tooth.

odontoglossum *n* a tropical orchid.

odontoid *adj* tooth-shaped, tooth-like.

odontology *n* dental science.—**odontological** *adj*.—**odontologist** *n*.

odor *n* smell; scent; aroma; a characteristic or predominant quality.— *also* **odour**.

odoriferous *adj* diffusing fragrance; (*sl*) smelly.

odorless *adj* without odor.

odorous *adj* having or emitting a scent; smelly; fragrant.

odour *see* **odor**.

ODSBA *abbr* (*Brit*) = Oxford Down Sheep Breeders Association.

Odysseus *n* (*Greek myth*) king of the island of Ithaca and one of the Greek heroes who engaged in the war against Troy; called Ulysses in Roman mythology. His voyage home took twenty years, in the course of which he had many adventures, related in Homer's *Odyssey*.

odyssey *n* (*pl* **odysseys**) a long adventurous journey; an intellectual or spiritual quest.

Odyssey *see* **Homer**.

Oe (*symbol*) oersted.

OE *abbr* = Old English; (*Brit*) Old Etonian.

o.e. *abbr* = omissions excepted.

OECD *abbr* = Organisation for Economic Co-operation and Development.

oecumenical *adj* a rare spelling of **ecumenical**.

OED *abbr* (*Brit*) = *Oxford English Dictionary*.

OEDA *abbr* = Occupational and Environmental Diseases Association.

oedema *see* **edema**.

Oedipus complex *n* (*psychoanal*) a complex arising from the relationship of a son to his parents.

Oedipus, Oedipodes *n* (*Greek myth*) son of the Theban King Laius and his queen Jocasta. He unknowingly killed his father and married his mother, in fulfillment of an oracle that he had tried to evade.

oeil de boeuf *n* a small round or oval window in the roof or frieze of a large building.

oeillade *n* a suggestive glance or ogle.

OEM *abbr* (*comput*) = Original Equipment Manufacturer. A business that makes a piece of hardware.

Oeneus *n* (*Greek myth*) a king of Calydon and father of Meleager, to whom Dionysus gave the gift of vine culture.

Oenghus *or* **Aenghus** *n* (*Irish Celtic myth*) a god of love. He was a son of the Daghda, his mother being Boann. Because his mother conceived him in the course of an illicit affair, her pregnancy was concealed by the sun standing still for nine months. Oenghus was thus supposedly conceived and born on the same day.

Oengus *n* (*d*. 761) king of Picts, Britain (728–761). He claimed the throne during the civil war which erupted after Nechtan abdicated in 724.

oeno-, oen- *prefix* wine.

oenology *see* **enology**.

Oenomaus *n* (*Greek myth*) a king of Pisa in Elis and father of Hippodamia, who killed all his daughter's suitors until he himself was killed by Pelops.

o'er *prep, adv* (*poet*) over.

OERI *abbr* = Office of Educational Research and Improvement.

oersted *n* the cgs unit of magnetic field strength.

OES *abbr* = optical emission spectrometry.

OESE *abbr* = Office of Elementary and Secondary Education.

oesophagus *see* **esophagus**.

oestrogen *see* **estrogen**.

oestrus *see* **estrus**.

oeuvre *n* (*pl* **oeuvres**) a work of art, literature, music, etc; the life's work of an artist, writer or composer.

of *prep* from; belonging or relating to; concerning; among; by; during; owing to.

OF *abbr* = Oddfellow; Old French; Operation Friendship; oil-fired.

of- *prefix* the form of *ob-* before *f*.

o.f. *abbr* = oxidizing flame.

OFA *abbr* = Office of Family Assistance.

"O, Fair New Mexico" *n* the song of the American state, New Mexico.

O'Faolain *n* Sean (1900–91) Irish novelist and short-story writer whose stories, like those of Frank O'Connor, focus on the constricting patterns of

O

provincial Irish life but from a more edgily critical perspective. His *Collected Stories* were published in 1981. His vigorous campaign against censorship is a prominent theme in his autobiography, *Vive-Moi!*

OFC *abbr* = Overseas Food Corporation.

OFCCP *abbr* = Office of Federal Contract Compliance Programs.

off *adv* away, from; detached, gone; unavailable; disconnected; out of condition; entirely. * *prep* away from; not on. * *adj* distant; no longer operating; canceled; (*food or drink*) having gone bad; on the right-hand side; (*runners, etc*) having started a race.

off. *abbr* = offered; officer; official; officinal.

Off. *abbr* = Office.

Offa *n* 1. (*d.* 796) king of Mercia, Britain (757–796). A descendant of Penda's younger brother, he defeated his rival claimants to the throne of Mercia in the civil war that followed the death of Ethelbald. 2. (*d. c.*720) king of Essex, Britain (reigned in 709). The son of Sigeherd.

offal *n* the entrails of an animal eaten as food.

off and on *adv* intermittently; occasionally.

off-balance *adj* unbalanced.

off-balance sheet financing *n* a method of financing a company's business activities so that some of the finance and assets do not appear on the balance sheet. The payment for the use of a piece of equipment by hiring or leasing it rather than buying it outright can be regarded as an example.

offbeat *adj* unconventional, eccentric.

off-Broadway *adj* denoting a type of small scale, experimental and generally non-commercial theater situated outside theatrical Broadway in New York.

off-center, off-centered *adj* not exactly in the center.

off chance *n* a remote possibility.

off-color *adj* unwell; risqué.

Offenbach *n* **Jacques** (1819-80) German-French composer, conductor, and cellist, the son of a Jewish cantor. Of his 90 operettas, *Orpheus in the Underworld* and *The Tales of Hoffmann* are the most famous.

offend *vt* to affront, displease; to insult. * *vi* to break a law.—**offender** *n*.

offense, offence *n* an illegal action, crime; a sin; an affront, insult; a cause of displeasure or anger.

offensive *adj* causing offence; repulsive, disagreeable; insulting; aggressive. * *n* an attack; a forceful campaign for a cause, etc.—**offensively** *adv*.—**offensiveness** *n*.

offer *vt* to present for acceptance or rejection; to show willingness (to do something); to present for consideration; to bid; (*a prayer*) to say. * *vi* to present itself; to declare oneself willing. * *n* something offered; a bid or proposal.

Offer *abbr* = Office of Electricity Regulation.

offer by prospectus *n* an offer of a new issue of shares by a company made directly to the public by means of a prospectus which sets out details of the company, such as its past trading record and its capital structure.

offer for sale *n* a method of raising new share capital by offering and issuing new shares to members of the general public.

offering *n* a gift, present; a sacrifice.

offertory *n* (*pl* **offertories**) (*Anglican Church*) the sentences read in the Communion service during the collection of the alms; the alms collecting; (*RC Church*) an anthem chanted during Mass while the priest prepares the elements.

offhand *adv* impromptu; without thinking. * *adj* inconsiderate; curt, brusque; unceremonious.

office *n* a room or building where business is carried out; the people there; (*with cap*) the location, staff, of authority of a Government department, etc; a task or function; a position of authority; a duty; a religious ceremony, rite.

office hours *npl* the normal business day.

officer *n* an official; a person holding a position of authority in a government, business, club, military services, etc; a policeman.

official *adj* of an office or its tenure; properly authorized; formal. * *n* a person who holds a public office.—**officially** *adv*.

officialdom *n* a body of officials.

officialese *n* the jargon of official documents or as expressed by officials.

Official List *n* (*Brit*) a list of all the securities traded on the main market of the London Stock Exchange; a list prepared daily by the London Stock Exchange which records all the sales in listed securities which have taken place during the day and gives prices and dividend dates.

official receiver *n* (*Brit*) an officer of the court who is appointed by the government to act as a receiver in bankruptcy and winding-up cases. *See* **receivership**.

officiant *n* an officiating priest, clergyman, etc.

officiary *n* (*pl* **officiaries**) (a group or body of) officers or officials. * *adj* (of a title) attached to or derived from an office held; (of a person) having a title or rank derived from an office.

officiate *vi* to conduct a ceremony; to act in an official capacity; to perform the functions of a priest, minister, rabbi, etc.

officious *adj* interfering, meddlesome; offering unwanted advice.—**officiously** *adv*.—**officiousness** *n*.

offing *n* the near or foreseeable future.

offish *adj* (*inf*) distant, stiff.

off-key *adj* sung or played in the wrong key; out of tune; out of step.

off-licence *n* (*Brit*) a licence to sell alcohol for consumption off the premises; a place so licensed (—*also* **liquor store, package store**).

off-limits *adj* out of bounds.

off-line *adj* (*comput*) not connected to the central processor; disconnected.

off-line reader *n* a computer program that allows users to be connected to an on-line computing system and to download any e-mail messages to their own machine.

off-load *vt* to unload; to get rid of.

off. nom. *abbr* = official nomenclature.

off-piste *adj* pertaining to skiing in areas away from the normal runs.

offprint *n* a separately printed copy or part of a publication.

off-putting *adj* discouraging, daunting.

off-roading *n* the sport or hobby of driving on dirt tracks or other rugged terrain.—**off-roader** *n*.

offscourings *npl* refuse, dregs.

off-screen *adj* not visible to the cinema or television audience; in private life.

off-season *n* a period of the year when business is reduced. * *adj* of, for, or during the off-season.

off-set *n* (*archit*) a sloping or horizontal surface in the face of a wall caused by a reduction in thickness in the upper part.

offset *vt* (**offsetting, offset**) to compensate for, counterbalance. * *n* compensation; a method of printing in which an image is transferred from a plate to a rubber surface and then to paper; a sloping ledge on the face of a wall; a code on the magnetic strip of a plastic card which, in conjunction with a **personal identification number** (PIN), acts as verification that the person who is using it has the right to do so; the right of a bank to seize any bank-account balances of a debtor or guarantor who has failed to meet loan obligations; (*comput*) similar to gutter, the space added to a left margin to allow for the document binding.—*also adj*.

offset printing *n* printing in which the impression is transferred from a plate to a rubber surface and then to paper.

offshoot *n* a branch or shoot growing from the main stem; something derivative.

offshore *adv* at sea some distance from the shore.

offshore banking *n* banking services in places which offer non-residents tax advantages in a legal way. They are informally known as tax havens.

offshore fund *n* a fund held by a financial institution which has its registered office in a tax haven.

offside *adj, adv* (*sport*) illegally in advance of the ball.

offspring *n* a child, progeny; a result.

offstage *adj, adv* out of sight of the audience; behind the scenes.

off-the-cuff *adj* (of remarks) unrehearsed, spontaneous.

off-the-peg *adj* (*Brit*) (of clothes) made ready to wear in standard sizes.

off-the-rack *adj* (*clothes*) made ready to wear in standard sizes.

off-the-record *adj* (of remarks) not for publication.

off-the-shelf *adj* in stock, not custom-built.

off the shelf software *n* (*comput*) a software application that is mass-marketed and serves a general purpose, rather than custom software, which is developed for a specific customer. *See also* **packaged software**.

off-the-wall *adj* (*sl*) innovative, unusual, unexpected.

off-track *adj, adv* (of betting, etc) not at the racetrack.

off-white *n, adj* (a) white tinged with yellow or gray.

off year *n* a year of reduced economic activity, etc; a year without a major election.—**off-year** *adj*.

OFG *abbr* = Organic Farmers and Growers Limited.

Ofgas *abbr* (*Brit*) = Office of Gas Supply.

OFHEO *abbr* = Office of Federal Housing Enterprise Oversight.

O'Flaherty *n* **Liam** (1897–1984) Irish novelist and short-story writer whose works include the novel *The Informer* and collections of short stories, e.g., *Spring Sowing*.

OFM *abbr* = Office of Financial Management; (*Latin*) *Ordo Fratrum Minorum*, "Order of Minor Friars," Franciscans.

OFR *abbr* = Office of the Federal Register.

O.Fr. *abbr* = Old French.

OFris *abbr* = Old Friesian.

OFS *abbr* = Orange Free State, South Africa.

Ofsted *abbr* (*Brit*) = Office for Standards in Education.

OFT *abbr* (*Brit*) = Office of Fair Trading.

oft *adv* (*poet*) often.

Oftel *abbr* (*Brit*) = Office of Telecommunications.

often *adv* many times, frequently.

oftentimes, oftimes *adv* often, frequently.

OFW *abbr* = Opportunities For Women.

Ofwat *abbr* (*Brit*) = Office of Water Services.

og *abbr* = original gravity (strength of beer); (*philately*) original gum; own goal.

Og *n* (*Bible*) a giant; king of Bashan, defeated by the Israelites. *See also* **Bashan**.

OG *abbr* = Officer of the Guard; ogee; Openly Gay; Outer Guard; Outside Guard, or Guardian.

OGA *abbr* = Organic Growers Association.

Ogam *or* **Ogham** *n* a form of Celtic script carved on stone consisting of a series of short parallel strokes that either met or intersected a base line.

Ogbomosho *n* a city in Nigeria.

ogdoad *n* eight, a set of eight; (*Egypt*) a group of eight deities. The most famous is the Hermopolitan, comprising four pairs of male frogs and female snakes, personifying the primeval forces of creation.

Ogdon *n* **John** (1937–89) English pianist and composer who was a member of the "Manchester School."

OGE *abbr* = Office of Government Ethics.

ogee *n* (*archit*) a line with a double curve formed by a concave and convex portion as in an S or backward S.

Ogen melon *n* a type of small melon similar to a cantaloupe with sweet orange flesh.

Ogham *n* the earliest form of Irish writing. The script takes the form of a series of lines or notches. Legend has it that it was the invention of Oghma. Developed in the third and fourth centuries AD, although there have been claims that it was in use as early as the first century BC. Sometimes known as the Tree Alphabet because each letter takes the name of a tree.

Oghma or **Ogma** *n* (*Irish Celtic myth*) the god of eloquence and literature. He was given the titles of Grianainech, referring to the fact that he had a sunny countenance, and Cermait, referring to the fact that he had a honeyed mouth.

ogive *n* (*archit*) a pointed arch; a diagonal groin of a vault.—**ogival** *adj*.

ogle *vti* (**ogling, ogled**) to gape at; to make eyes at; to look at lustfully.—**ogler** *n*.

OGM *abbr* = Ordinary General Meeting.

Ogmios *n* (*Gaulish Celtic myth*) the equivalent of the Irish Celtic god **Oghma**.

Ogpu *n* the secret police of Soviet Russia (1923–34).

ogre *n* a man-eating giant; a hideous person.

Ogygia *n* (*Greek myth*) the name given by Homer in the *Odyssey* to the island inhabited by the nymph Calypso.

oh *interj* expressing surprise, delight, pain, etc.

oh *abbr* = office hours; (*Latin*) *omni hora*, "every hour."

OH *abbr* = Ohio.

O'Hara *n* **John [Henry]** (1905–70) American novelist and short-story writer whose tough, satirical works on "sophisticated" life, e.g., the novels *Butterfield 8* and *Pal Joey*, were very popular in the 1930s and 1940s.

OHG *abbr* = Old High German.

Ohio (OH) *n* a state of the United States of America (USA) of which the capital is Columbus.

ohm *n* a unit of electrical resistance.

ohmmeter *n* an instrument for measuring electrical resistance.

OHMS *abbr* (*Brit*) = On Her/His Majesty's Service.

oho *interj* an exclamation of surprise.

ohp *abbr* = overhead projector.

Ohr *n* **George Edgar** (1857–1918) eccentric American potter, dubbed "the mad potter of Biloxi."

Ohrid *n* a city in the Former Yugoslav Republic of Macedonia (FYROM).

OHS *abbr* = Occupational Health Service.

OIC *abbr* = Optical Information Council.

-oid *suffix* like, as in *spheroid*.

OIEO *abbr* = offers in excess of.

OIG *abbr* = Office of the Inspector General.

oil *n* any of various greasy, combustible liquid substances obtained from animal, vegetable, and mineral matter; petroleum; an oil painting; (*pl*) paint mixed by grinding a pigment in oil. * *vt* to smear with oil, lubricate.—**oiled** *adj*.

OILC *abbr* = Offshore Industry Liaison Committee.

oilcake *n* a cattle food made of linseed.

oilcan *n* a container with a long spout for releasing oil for lubricating in individual drops.

oilcloth *n* a waterproof fabric impregnated with oil or synthetic resin.

oil color *n* a color in which oil is used as a vehicle for pigment.

oiler *n* an oilcan; a greaser.

oil field *n* an area on land or under the sea that produces petroleum.

oilman *n* (*pl* **oilmen**) a dealer in oils.

oil paint *n* (*art*) a paint made by mixing color pigments with oil (generally linseed oil) to produce a slow-drying, malleable sticky substance.

oil painting *n* a painting in oils; the art of painting in oils.

oil palm *n* an African palm whose fruit yields an edible oil.

oilpan *n* a section of the crankcase under an internal combustion engine for the oil to drain into to form a reservoir.—*also* (*Brit*) **sump**.

oil rig *n* a drilling rig for extracting oil or natural gas.

oils *npl* greasy liquid substances obtained from animal or vegetable matter or mineral sources.

oil sand *n* sandstone rock that yields petroleum.

oil shale *n* a type of rock (as shale) from which oil can be extracted.

oilskin *n* fabric made waterproof by treatment with oil; a waterproof garment of oilskin or a plastic-coated fabric.

oil slick *n* a mass of oil floating on the surface of water.

oil well *n* a well from which petroleum is extracted.

oily *adj* (**oilier, oiliest**) like or covered with oil; greasy; too suave or smooth, unctuous.—**oiliness** *n*.

oink *n* (*inf*) the grunt of a pig.—*also vi*.

ointment *n* a fatty substance used on the skin for healing or cosmetic purposes; a salve.

O.Ir. *abbr* = Old Irish.

Oireachtas *n* the legislature of Ireland, consisting of the president, the Dáil Eireann (the Chamber of Deputies) and the Seanad Eireann (the Senate).

OIRO *abbr* = offers in the region of.

Oisin or **Ossian** *n* (*Irish Celtic myth*) *n* a legendary Celtic hero and bard of the 3rd century. The son of Fionn mac Cumhaill and Sadb and the father of Oscar. He is said to have grown up to be a great warrior and a great poet. *See also* **Macpherson**.

Oistrakh *n* 1. **David** (1908–74) a Russian violinist who gained international recognition after the Second World War. 2. his son **Igor** (1931–) also a celebrated violinist and a conductor.

O.It. *abbr* = Old Italian.

OJJDP *abbr* = Office of Juvenile Justice and Delinquency Prevention.

Ojocs *abbr* = (*horse-racing*) overnight declaration of jockeys.

OJP *abbr* = Office of Justice Programs.

OK, okay *adj*, *adv* (*inf*) all right; correct(ly). * *n* (*pl* **OK's, okays**) approval. * *vt* (**OK'ing, OK'ed** *or* **okaying, okayed**) to approve, sanction as OK.

OK *abbr* = Oklahoma.

okapi *n* (*pl* **okapis, okapi**) an African animal related to the giraffe but smaller and with a shorter neck.

O'Keefe *n* **Georgia** (1887–1986) American painter. Most of her art concerns precisionist abstraction of observed forms, often using the technique of isolating one detail in close-up.

Okeghem, Johannes *see* **Ockeghem, Johannes**.

Okla. *abbr* = Oklahoma.

Oklahoma (OK) *n* a state of the United States of America (USA) of which the capital is Oklahoma City.

"Oklahoma!" *n* the song of the American state, Oklahoma.

Oklahoma City *n* the capital city of Oklahoma, a state of the USA.

okra *n* a tall annual plant yielding long seedpods used as a vegetable.

Oktoberfest *n* a festival held in the fall in Munich, southern Germany, to drink beer; any similar festival.

ol. *abbr* = oleum.

Ol. *abbr* = Olympiad.

OL *abbr* = Old Latin; on-line; (*sport*) outside left; (*elect*) overload.

OLA *abbr* = Organic Living Association.

Olaf *n* Saint (995–1030) king of Norway and the country's patron saint; converted to Christianity in 1013 and worked to convert Norway. His feast day is July 29.

Olaf Guthfrithson *n* (*d.* 941) king of Dublin. He was an ally of the Scots under Constantine II at the Battle of Brunanburgh in 937.

Olaf the Red *n* (*b. c.*920) king of Dublin (*c.*945–980).

Olaf the White *n* (*d. c.*854) king of Dublin (853–*c.*854).

Olbers' paradox *n* a paradox expressed by Heinrich Olbers in 1826 in the question "Why is the sky dark at night?": in an infinitely large universe full of stars and galaxies, the night sky ought to be at least as bright as the surface of the sun, yet it is not.

Olbrich *n* **Josef Maria** (1867–1908) Austrian architect who was a founder member of the Vienna Secession. His notable works include the Tietz department store, Düsseldorf.

old *adj* aged; elderly, not young; having lived or existed for a long time; long used, not new; former; of the past, not modern; experienced; worn out; of long standing.

Old *n* **Maxime** (1910–94) French decorator and furniture designer who furnished liners.

Old Bailey *n* the central criminal court of England.

old boy *n* (*Brit*) a former pupil of a school; (*inf*) a friendly form of address; an old person.—**old girl** *nf*.

old boy network *n* (*inf*) the monopoly of power by a privileged elite who attended the best public schools and universities.

Old Catholic *n* one of a body of Roman Catholics who refused to accept the dogma of papal infallibility (1870).

Old Copper *adj* relating to a culture that emerged *c.*4000 BC around the Great Lakes of Canada and the USA. The people mined and used copper in its native form.

Old Cordilleran *adj* relating to a culture that emerged in the states of Washington and Oregon in the USA between 9000 and 4000 BC.

old country *n* the birthplace of an immigrant or an immigrant's ancestors.

Old Crow *adj* relating to Pleistocene deposits along the Porcupine and Old Crow rivers of Canada in which bones of extinct animals were found along with possible human artifacts.

olden *adj* relating to a bygone era.

Oldenburg *n* **Claes** (1929–) Swedish-born American sculptor, one of the originators of pop art.

Old English *n* the English language during the 7th to the 11th centuries.—*also* Anglo-Saxon.

Old English sheepdog *n* a breed of sheepdog with an extremely long shaggy coat.

old-fashioned *adj* out of date; in a fashion of an older time.

old fogey *n* a dull, conservative-minded person.

"Old Folks At Home" *n* the official song of the American state, Florida.

Old French *n* the French language from the 7th to the early 14th centuries.

Old Glory *n* the Stars and Stripes.

old gold *adj* of the color of tarnished gold.

old guard *n* the (original) conservative elements within a political party or other organization.

old hand *n* a very experienced person.

old hat *adj* old-fashioned, clichéd.

oldie *n* (*inf*) an old joke, song, etc; an elderly person.

old lady *n* (*inf*) wife, mother.

old-line *adj* well-established, respectable; traditional, conservative.

old maid *n* (*derog*) a woman, esp an older woman who has never married; a prim, prudish, fussy person.

old man *n* (*inf*) father, husband; (*inf*) someone in charge, esp the captain of a ship.

old master *n* a painting by one of the best painters working in Europe in the 16th and 17th centuries; one of these painters.

"Old New Hampshire" *n* the song of the American state, New Hampshire.

Old Nick *n* (*inf*) the Devil.

"Old North State, The" *n* the song of the American state, North Carolina.

old school *n* supporters of traditional or conservative values and practices.

old school tie *n* a distinctive tie which indicates which school one attended; the elitism and solidarity associated with British public schools and their products.

Old Style *n* the old mode of reckoning time according to the Julian year of 365 and a quarter days.

Old Test. *abbr* = Old Testament.

Old Testament *n* the Christian designation for the Holy Scriptures of Judaism, the first of the two general divisions of the Christian Bible.

old-time *adj* of an earlier period; old-fashioned.

old-timer *n* an old man; a veteran; a person who has been in the same job, position, etc, for many years.

Olduvai gorge *n* an important site in northern Tanzania, Africa, from which very ancient hominid remains and stone tools have been recovered.

old wives' tale *n* a belief sustained by tradition, not accuracy.

old-world *adj* traditional, quaint; antiquated.

Old World *n* Europe, Asia, and Africa.

OLE *see* **object linking and embedding**.

olé *interj* an exclamation of approval or triumph.

oleaginous *adj* oily; unctuous.

oleander *n* a poisonous evergreen shrub with handsome fragrant flowers.

oleaster *n* the wild olive; a yellow-flowered shrub like it.

oleate *n* a salt of oleic acid.

olefin, olefine *n* a hydrocarbon containing two atoms of hydrogen and one atom of carbon.—**olefinic** *adj*.

oleic *adj* obtained from oil.

oleic acid *n* an oily acid obtained from the saponification of linseed and other oils, or in the making of soap.

olein *n* the pure liquid part of oil or fat.

oleo *abbr* = oleomargarine.

oleo- *prefix* oil.

oleograph *n* a lithograph in oil colors.

olfaction *n* the sense of smell. *See* **nose**.

olfactory *adj* relating to the sense of smell. * *n* (*pl* **olfactories**) (*esp pl*) an organ of smell.

olfactory nerve *n* one of a pair of sensory nerves for smell.

OLG *abbr* = Office of Local Government; Old Low German.

olibanum *n* a gum resin used in incense; the frankincense of the ancients.

oligarch *n* a member of an oligarchy.

oligarchy *n* (*pl* **oligarchies**) government by a small group of people; the members of such a government; a state ruled in this way.—**oligarchic, oligarchical** *adj*.

oligo-, olig- *prefix* few, small.

Oligocene *n* (*geol*) a term used to denote certain strata intermediate between the Eocene and Miocene.

oligopoly *n* a kind of market structure in which relatively few sellers supply the needs of a large number of buyers; the domination of an industry by a few firms.

oligotrophic *adj* a term that describes water low in nutrients and therefore able to support only a limited range of aquatic life.

olio *n* (*pl* **olios**) a hotchpotch, a stew; a miscellany.

Oliphant *n* **Margaret** [née Wilson] (1828–97) Scottish novelist and author of almost 100 published novels, the best known of which are the five novels of *The Chronicles of Carlingford*. She also wrote biographies, e.g., of Cervantes and Sheridan, and other non-fiction works.

Olitzki *n* **Jules** (1922–) Russian-born American painter. From 1960 he began to experiment with color staining and with spray-gun techniques. A typical work is *Pink Alert* (1966).

olivaceous *adj* olive-green.

olivary *adj* olive-shaped, oval.

olive *n* an evergreen tree cultivated for its edible hard-stoned fruit and oil; its fruit; a yellow-green color. * *adj* of a yellow-green color.

olive branch *n* a gesture of reconciliation or desire to make peace.

olive drab *n* the color of the US service uniform.

olive green *n* a brighter, deeper green than that of a normal olive.—**olive-green** *adj*.

olive oil *n* an edible yellow oil obtained from the fruit of the olive by pressing.

Olives, Mount of *n* (*Bible*) the line of hills east of Jerusalem across the Kidron valley.

Olivetti *n* **Camillo** (1868–1943) Italian engineer and industrialist who founded the Olivetti office machinery company in 1908.

Olivier *n* **Laurence** [**Kerr**] [**Baron Olivier of Brighton**] (1907–89) English stage and film actor and director, noted for his major roles in plays by Shakespeare.

olivine *n* a rock-forming mineral, a variety of chrysolite, that occurs in igneous rocks that do not contain much silica.

olla podrida *n* a mixed stew or hash of meat and vegetables, a favorite Spanish dish; any incongruous mixture.

Ollav Fola *n* king of Ireland (reigned *c*.1000 BC) the only king of Ireland said to have reached the highest rank of the druids. The eighteenth ruler of Ireland.

Olmec *adj* relating to a civilization that arose around the Gulf Coast of Mexico *c*.1400 BC.

OLML *abbr* = Our Lady's Missionary League.

OLMS *abbr* = Office of Labor Management Standards.

ology *n* (*pl* **ologies**) (*sl*) a branch of knowledge, a science.

Olomouc *n* a city in the Czech Republic.

OLRT *abbr* = on-line real time.

Olwen *n* (*Welsh Celtic myth*) meaning "white track" ; four white trefoils are said to have sprung up wherever she walked, was the daughter of the chief giant, Yspaddaden.

Olym. *abbr* = Olympiad.

Olympia *n* a locality in Greece, the scene of the Olympic Games, in the ancient district of Elis, in the western part of the Peloponnese; the capital city of Washington, a state of the USA.—**Olympian, Olympic** *adj*

Olympiad *n* in ancient Greece, the interval (four years) between the celebration of the Olympic games; a system of chronology reckoning from the first Olympiad, 776 BC.

Olympian *adj* of Olympus, home of the Greek gods; Olympic; stately; condescending. * *n* a great person.

Olympians *npl* (*Greek myth*) the gods and goddesses who occupied Olympus.

Olympic *adj* pertaining to Olympia in Elis, where the Olympic games were celebrated.

Olympic Games *n sing or pl* an ancient athletic contest, originally held at Olympia, revived in 1896 as an international meeting held every four years in a different country.—*also* **Olympics**.

Olympus *n* the highest mountain in ancient Greece, regarded as the chief home of the gods.

om *n* (*Hinduism*) the mystic name of the supreme being uttered when invoking Brahma; (*modern occultism*) spiritual essence, supreme truth and virtue.

om *abbr* (*Latin*) = *omni mane*, "every morning."

OM *abbr* = Order of Merit.

OMA *abbr* = Overall Manufacturers Association of Great Britain.

-oma *n suffix* indicating a tumor.

Oman *or* **the Sultanate of Oman** *n* an oil-rich state in the southern Arabian Peninsula.

omasum *n* (*pl* **omasa**) the third stomach of ruminant animals.

OMB *abbr* = Office of Management and Budget.

omber, ombre *n* an old card game for three players.

ombudsman *n* (*pl* **ombudsmen**) an official appointed to investigate citizens' or consumers' complaints.

ombudsman *n* an official in charge of a body which is responsible for settling disputes between suppliers of services of goods and those who use them.

omc *abbr* = operation and maintenance costs.

Omdurman *n* a city in the Sudan.

omega *n* the last letter of the Greek alphabet; (*with cap*) (*Bible*) this letter used with Alpha to express the greatness and completeness of God. *See also* **Alpha**.

Omega Nebula *n* an emission nebula in the constellation Sagittarius which radiates radio wavelengths as well as visible light.

Omega Workshops *n* a British cooperative for the production of furniture, furnishings, ceramics and textiles, set up in 1913 by Roger **Fry**. Artists who took part included Vanessa Bell, Duncan Grant, Wyndham Lewis, and Paul Nash.

omelet, omelette *n* eggs beaten and cooked flat in a pan.

omen *n* a sign or warning of impending happiness or disaster.

omentum *n* (*pl* **omenta, omentums**) (*anat*) the caul or adipose membrane attached to the stomach.

omerta *n* a conspiracy of silence, esp as practiced by the Mafia.

omicron *n* the 15th letter of the Greek alphabet.

OMIG *abbr* = Opencast Mining Intelligence Group.

ominous *adj* relating to an omen; foreboding evil; threatening.—**ominously** *adv*.

omission *n* something that has been left out or neglected; the act of omitting.

omit *vt* (**omitting, omitted**) to leave out; to neglect to do, leave undone.

OMM *abbr* = Offshore Minerals Management Program.

omni- *prefix* all; universally.

omnibus *n* (*pl* **omnibuses**) (*formal*) a bus; a book containing several works esp by one author.

omnibus research *n* a method of market research based on questionnaires with several parts which are sent out on a regular basis to a panel of people who fill them in.

omnifarious *adj* of all kinds.

omnipotent *adj* all-powerful, almighty; having very great power.—**omnipotence** *n*.

omnipresent *adj* present everywhere, ubiquitous.—**omnipresence** *n*.

omniscient *adj* knowing all things.—**omnisciently** *adv*.—**omniscience** *n*.

omnium-gatherum *n* a miscellaneous collection of persons or things.

omnivore *n* (*biol*) any organism that eats both plant and animal tissue.

omnivore *n* an omniverous animal or person.

omnivorous *adj* eating any sort of food; taking in everything indiscriminately.

omo- *n* one-man operation (buses).

Omo *adj* relating to localities along the Omo river in East Africa at which ancient Australopithecus and Homo fossils have been found.

omophagic, omophagous *adj* eating raw flesh.—**omophagia** *n*.

Omphale *n* (*Greek myth*) a queen of Lydia, who bought Heracles when he was sold into slavery.

omphalos *n* center, hub; (*ancient Greece*) a boss on a shield; (*Greek myth*) a sacred stone at Delphi supposed to mark the center of the world.

OMR *abbr* = optical mark reader.

Omri *n* (*Bible*) commander of the Israeli army during civil war; he seized power and made himself the sixth king of Israel 876–869 BC; a powerful king who kept peace with Judah and made an alliance with Phoenicia.

OMRS *abbr* (*Brit*) = Orders and Medals Research Society.

oms *abbr* = output per man shift.

OMS *abbr* = Oriental Missionary Society International.

on *prep* in contact with the upper surface of; supported by, attached to, or covering; directed toward; at the time of; concerning, about; using as a basis, condition, or principle; immediately after; (*sl*) using; addicted to. * *adv* (so as to be) covering or in contact with something; forward; (of a device) switched on; continuously in progress; due to take place; (of an actor) on stage; on duty. * *adj* (*cricket*) designating the part of the field on the batsman's side in front of the wicket. * *n* (*cricket*) the on side.

on *abbr* (*Latin*) = *omni nocte*, "every night."

ONA *abbr* = Office of National Assessments.

onager *n* (*pl* **onagri, onagers**) the wild ass.

onanism *n* masturbation; coitus interruptus.—**onanist** *n, adj*.

onboard *adj* on or in a vehicle, ship or aircraft.

ONC *abbr* (*Brit*) = Ordinary National Certificate.

once *adv* on one occasion only; formerly; at some time. * *conj* as soon as. * *n* one time.

once-over *n* a preliminary survey.

onco- *prefix* swelling, tumor.

oncogene *n* (*med*) any gene directly involved in cancer, whether in viruses or in an individual.

oncogenic *adj* pertaining to any factor that gives rise to tumors.

oncology *n* the branch of medicine dealing with the study and treatment of tumors, including medical and surgical aspects and treatment with radiation.—**oncologist** *n*.

oncoming *adj* approaching.

OND *abbr* = (*Brit*) Ordinary National Diploma; other neurological disorders.

Ondes Martenot (Ondes Musicales) *n* (*mus*) an electronic instrument patented by Maurice Martenot in 1922. It was used by such composers as Messiaen.

one *adj* single; undivided, united; the same; a certain unspecified (time, etc). * *n* the first and lowest cardinal number; an individual thing or person; (*inf*) a drink; (*inf*) a joke. * *pron* an indefinite person, used to apply to many people; someone.

one and all everyone.

one-armed bandit *n* (*inf*) a slot machine for gambling, operated by pulling down a lever on its side.

one by one *adv* one at a time; in order.

one-horse *adj* (*sl*) paltry.

O'Neill *n* Eugene [Gladstone] (1885–1923) American dramatist whose greatest plays are *Mourning Becomes Electra*, *The Iceman Cometh*, and *Long Day's Journey into Night*. He was winner of the 1936 Nobel prize for literature and three times a Pulitzer prizewinner.

oneiro- *prefix* dream.

oneirology *n* the study and interpretation of dreams.

one-liner *n* (*inf*) a brief joke or witty comment.

one-man *adj* performed, produced or operated by one person; involving one person.

oneness *n* unity, singleness, concord.

one-night stand *n* a performance given for one night only in a certain place; (*inf*) (a partner in) a sexual liaison that lasts one night only.

one-off *n, adj* (*Brit*) (something) performed or made only once.

one-piece *adj* (*garment*) made in a single piece.

onerous *adj* oppressive, burdensome; troublesome.

oneself *pron reflex form of* one.

one-sided *adj* favoring one side; unequal.

one-step *n* a ballroom dance involving quick short steps, similar to, but earlier than, the foxtrot; the music for this. * *vi* (**one-stepping, one-stepped**) to dance the one-step.

one-time *adj* sometime, former.

one-to-one *adj* with one member of one group pairing identically with a member of another group; denoting a relationship involving only one other person.

one-track *adj* with a single line of rails; with room for only one idea at a time.

one-up *adj* (*inf*) having a particular advantage. * *vt* (**one-upping, one-upped**) to gain or have an advantage over.

one-upmanship *n* the skill of being one jump ahead of or going one better than someone or something else.

one-way *adj* (*traffic*) restricted to one direction; requiring no reciprocal action or obligation.

ongoing *adj* progressing, continuing.

Onitsha *n* a city in Nigeria.

onion *n* an edible bulb with a pungent taste and odor.

Onion Portage *n* a site in Alaska with evidence of a very long period of occupancy, beginning *c.*9000 BC.

onionskin *n* a think, strong, translucent lightweight paper.

on-line *adj* referring to equipment that is connected to and controlled by the central processor of a computer.

online *adj* (*comput*) switched on and ready to receive data.

on-line help *n* (*comput*) a utility associated with a particular application that provides a help system for reference while the application is being operated.

on-line information service *n* (*comput*) a profit-making organization, such as America On-line™ or Compuserve™, that makes information available to its members or subscribers via telephone services.

online services (*see also* **Internet service provider**) *n* (*comput*) the term given to a number of companies that provide access to the Internet and e-mail facilities, as do Internet service providers, but also provide additional services.

onlooker *n* a spectator.

only *adj* alone of its kind; single, sole. * *adv* solely, merely; just; not more than. * *conj* except that, but.

ono *abbr* = or near(est) offer.

Ono, Yoko *see* **John Lennon**.

onoma- *prefix* name.

onomastic *adj* of or pertaining to a name or names.

onomasticon *n* (*pl* **onomastica**) (*Egypt*) a categorized list of hieroglyphic words, listing animals, towns, plants, etc.

onomastics *n sing* the study of proper names.

onomatopoeia *n* the formation of a word to imitate a sound.—**onomatopoeic** *adj*.

ONR *abbr* = Office of Naval Research.

onrush *n* a powerful rushing forwards.

ONS *abbr* = Offshore North Sea Technology Conference; Oriental Numismatic Society.

onset *n* a beginning; an assault, attack.

onshore *adj, adv* towards the land; on land, not the sea.

onslaught *n* a fierce attack.

onstage *adj, adv* on the stage and in view of the audience.

Ont. *abbr* = Ontario.

on-the-job *adj* (of training, etc) learned or acquired while working in a particular occupation.

onto *prep* to a position on.

onto- *prefix* being.

ontogeny *n* (*biol*) the complete development of an individual to maturity.

ontogeny, ontogenesis *n* (*biol*) the history of the evolution of individual organisms.—**ontogenic, ontogenetic** *adj*.

ontology *n* (*philos*) the logic of pure being or reality; metaphysics.—**ontological** *adj*.—**ontologically** *adv*.

ONTR *abbr* (*med*) = orders not to resuscitate.

onus *n* (*pl* **onuses**) responsibility, duty; burden.

onward *adj* advancing, forward. * *adv* to the front, ahead, forward.

onwards *adv* onward.

"On Wisconsin" *n* the song of the American state, Wisconsin.

onyx *n* a limestone similar to marble with layers of color.

OO *abbr* = Ordnance Officer.

o/o *abbr* = on order; offers over.

oo- *prefix* egg.

oocyte *n* (*biol*) a cell in the ovary that undergoes meiosis to produce an ovum, the female reproductive cell. *See* **ovulation**.

oodles *npl* (*sl*) an abundance.

oogamous *adj* heterogamous.

oogenesis *n* the formation of an ovum.—**oogenetic** *adj*.

ooh *interj* expressing surprise, delight, pain, etc.

oolite *n* a limestone composed of grains like the roe of a fish.—**oolitic** *adj*.

oology *n* the scientific study of birds' eggs; a treatise on birds' eggs.—**oological** *adj*.—**oologist** *n*.

oolong *n* a Chinese black tea the flavor of which resembles green tea.

oomiak *see* **umiak**.

oompah *n* an imitation of the deep sound of a brass instrument such as the tuba.

oomph *n* (*inf*) energy, verve; sex appeal.

oop *abbr* = out of pocket (expenses, etc).

oops *interj* expressing surprise or apology, esp when making a mistake.

Oort Cloud *or* **Öpik-Oort Cloud** *n* a cloud of cometary nuclei thought to be in orbits at the fringes of the solar system, perhaps from the time of its origin.

Oort's constants *n* quantities introduced by Oort in his study of the proper motions of stars.

oosperm *n* a fertilized ovum.

Oostende *n* a city in Belgium.

oot *abbr* = out of town.

ootheca *n* (*pl* **oothecae**) the egg case of certain mollusks and insects containing the eggs.—**oothecal** *adj*.

ooze *vti* to flow or leak out slowly; to seep; to exude. * *n* soft mud or slime; (*marine biol*) a deep sea mud made up of clays and the calcareous or siliceous remains of certain organisms, e.g., diatoms.

op *abbr* = open-plan; out of print; over proof.

op. *abbr* = opera; operation; operator; optical; opposite; (*mus*) opus.

o.p. *abbr* = observation post or posts; open policy.

OP *abbr* = (*Latin*) *Ordo Praedicatorum*, "Order of Preachers"; (*theat*) opposite prompt (an actor's position on stage); outpatient.

op- *prefix* form of *ob-* before *p*.

OPA *abbr* = Oil and Pipelines Agency.

opacity *n* (*pl* **opacities**) the state of being opaque; obscurity; (*astron*) a quantity expressing the amount of absorption or scattering of electromagnetic radiation in its passage through material, most often dust, gas-clouds, or plasmas.

opah *n* a bright-colored sea fish like the mackerel, the kingfish.

opal *n* a white or bluish stone with a play of iridescent colors.

opalescent *adj* resembling opal in its reflection of light, iridescent.—**opalescence** *n*.

opaline *adj* pertaining to or resembling the opal.

opaque *adj* not letting light through; neither transparent nor translucent.—**opaquely** *adv*.—**opaqueness** *n*.

op art, optical art *n* abstract art that uses precise, hard-edged patterns in strong colors that dazzle the viewer and make the image appear to move.

OPB *abbr* (*Brit*) = Occupational Pensions Board.

OPCA *abbr* (*Austral*) = Ornamental Plant Collections Association.

op. cit. *abbr* (*Latin*) = *opere citato*, "in the work cited"; *opus citatum*, "the work cited."

OPCS *abbr* (*Brit*) = Office of Population, Censuses and Surveys.

OPD *abbr* = Outpatient Department.

OPE *abbr* = Office of Postsecondary Education.

OPEC *abbr* = Organization of Petroleum Exporting Countries.

open *adj* not closed; accessible; uncovered, unprotected; not fenced; free from trees; spread out, unfolded; public; lacking reserve; (of a person) forthcoming; generous; readily understood; liable (to); unrestricted; (of a syllable) ending with a vowel; (of a consonant) made without stopping the stream of breath. * *vti* to make or become accessible; to unfasten; to begin; to expand, unfold; to come into view. * *n* a wide space; (*sport*) a competition that any player can enter.—**openness** *n*.

open *vt* (*comput*) to access a file with its associated application in order, e.g., to edit the file or print a hard copy of it.

open air *n* outdoors.

open-and-shut *adj* easily solved; straightforward.

open book *n* a person or thing that is easily understood.

open bus system *n* (*comput*) a design of the motherboard where the expansion bus has slots into which expansion boards can be fixed.

opencast mining *n* a system of mining in which the top layers of rock are removed and the mineral ores removed. *See* **strip mining.**

open chain *n* (*chem*) an organic compound with an open chain, not a ring structure, as in aliphatic compounds, e.g., alkanes, alkenes, and alkynes, and compounds formed from them.

open cluster *n* (*astron*) a group of stars which are relatively close together and move through space in association, but are only loosely bound by gravitation to each other and are subject to gravitational effects from the galaxy and other clusters.

open door *n* unrestricted access; a policy of free trade and immigration.—**open-door** *adj*.

open-ended *adj* with no fixed limit of time or amount.

opener *n* a device for opening cans or bottles.

open-eyed *adj* vigilant.

open-faced *adj* having a frank expression; (of a watch) having no glass or lid; (of a sandwich) without a top layer of bread.

openhanded *adj* generous.—**openhandedness** *n*.

open harmony *see* **harmony.**

open-heart surgery *n* surgery on the heart whilst its function is performed temporarily by a heart-lung machine.

openhearted *adj* responsive to emotional appeal, frank.—**openheartedness** *n*.

open house *n* a party with hospitality to all visitors; a house, apartment, or institution open for inspection.

opening *n* a gap, aperture; a beginning; a chance; a job opportunity. * *adj* initial.

open letter *n* a letter addressed to an individual but published in a newspaper for all to see.

openly *adv* frankly; publicly.

open market *n* a market with unrestricted access for buyers and sellers.

open-market operations *npl* the buying or selling of government bonds and treasury bills as a means of controlling the money supply.

open-market value *n* the value of an asset, equal to the amount of money that a willing purchaser would be prepared to pay a willing seller at a particular time.

open-minded *adj* unprejudiced.—**open-mindedness** *n*.

open-mouthed *adj* having the mouth open in surprise; gaping, expectant.

open-pricing agreement *n* an agreement among firms operating in an oligopoly by which a list of prices and intended price changes is circulated to those firms involved with a view to avoiding a price war.

open season *n* a period when hunting game, etc, is unrestricted by law.

open secret *n* a supposed secret which is actually widely known.

open sesame *n* a way of getting into something usually inaccessible.

open shop *n* an establishment where membership of a labor union is not a condition for employment.

open string *n* (*mus*) any string on an instrument that is allowed to vibrate along its entire length without being stopped.

open universe *n* a model in cosmology in which the universe is without bounds, of infinite extent, as opposed to a closed universe.

openwork *n* a pattern with interstices.

opera *n* (*mus*) a dramatic work in which all or most of the text is sung to orchestral accompaniment. The word stands for *opera in musica* (*Italian*), meaning a "musical work."

opera *n pl* of **opus.**

operable *adj* capable of being put into action, practicable; (*med*) capable of being operated upon.

opéra-bouffe *n* (*mus*) (*French*) a comic opera, i.e., an opera with lightweight music and a lightweight libretto.—*also* (*Italian*) **opera buffa.**

opéra-comique *n* (*mus*) (*French*) a comic opera.

opera glasses *n* a small binocular telescope used in theaters, etc.

opera hat *n* a man's collapsible top hat.

opera house *n* a theater for opera.

opera seria *n* (*mus*) (*Italian*) "serious opera," as usu applied to work of the 17th and 18th centuries.

operate *vi* to work, to function; to produce a desired effect; to carry out a surgical operation. * *vt* to work or control (a machine); to carry on, run.

operatic *adj* of or relating to opera; exaggerated, overacting.

operating budget *n* a forecast of the financial needs of a company or organization required for its future trading over a fixed period, usu a year.

operating environment *see* **environment.**

operating lease *n* a form of lease under which a fixed asset is hired out to an individual or firm for a period of time that is considerably shorter than the likely length of its useful economic life.

operating system *n* (*comput*) a suite of computer programs (systems software) that control the overall operation of a computer.

operation *n* a method of operating; a procedure; a military action; a surgical procedure.

operational *adj* of or relating to an operation; functioning; ready for use; involved in military activity.—**operationally** *adv*.

operational research *n* a method of tackling industrial and commercial problems or issues using scientific and mathematical techniques.

operations research, operational research *n* the application of mathematical techniques to the analysis of business methods.

operative *adj* functioning; in force, effective; of, by surgery. * *n* a mechanic; a secret agent; a private detective.

operator *n* a person who operates or works a machine, esp a telephone switchboard; a person who owns or runs a business; a person who manipulates.

operculum *n* (*pl* **opercula, operculums**) (*biol*) a cap, lid, or cover; the plate closing the orifice of a univalve; a shell; the gill cover of a fish.—**opercular, operculate** *adj*.

operetta *n* (*mus*) a light opera; an opera with some spoken dialogue, and a romantic plot with a happy ending.

Opet Festival *n* (*Egypt*) the annual processional journey of Amun-Ra, down-river from Thebes to Luxor and back again.

OPFS *abbr* (*Brit*) = One Parent Families Scotland.

Ophelia *n* (*astron*) a small satellite of Uranus.

Opheltes *n* (*Greek myth*) a son of Lycurgus, king of Nemea, who as a child was put on the ground by his nurse and killed by a snake, and in whose honor the Nemean Games were later founded.

ophicleide *n* (*mus*) the largest member of the now redundant key-bugle family (bugles with keys).

ophidian *n* any of the Ophidia, an order of reptiles including the snakes.—*also adj* .

ophiology *n* that branch of natural history which treats of snakes.—**ophiological** *adj*.—**ophiologist** *n*.

Ophir *n* (*Bible*) a country on the south-west coast of Arabia, the modern Yemen.

ophite *n* serpentine marble.

Ophiuchus *n* a constellation, usu regarded as of the northern sky, but cutting across the celestial equator.

OPHS *abbr* = Office of Public Health and Science.

ophthalmia *n* inflammation of the eye.

ophthalmic *adj* of, relating to, or situated near, the eye.

ophthalmic nerve *see* **trigeminal nerve.**

ophthalmo-, ophthalm- *prefix* eye or eyeball.

ophthalmology *n* the branch of medicine dealing with the structure of the eye, its function, associated diseases, and treatment.—**ophthalmologist** *n*.

ophthalmoplegia *n* paralysis of the muscles serving the eye, which may be internal (affecting the iris and ciliary muscle) or external (those muscles moving the eye itself).

ophthalmoscope *n* an instrument with a light source for examining the interior of the eye.

ophthalmoscopy *n* examination of the eye.—**ophthalmoscopic** *adj*.

-opia *n suffix* indicating a visual defect.

opiate *n* a narcotic drug that contains opium, such as morphine or codeine; something that induces sleep or calms feelings.

OPIC *abbr* = Overseas Private Investment Corporation.

opine *vt* to hold or express the opinion (that).

opinicus *n* (*her*) a fabulous winged animal with the head and wings of a griffin, the body of a lion, and the tail of a camel.

opinion *n* a belief that is not based on proof; judgment; estimation, evaluation; a formal expert judgment; professional advice.

opinionated *adj* unduly confident in one's opinions, dogmatic.

opinionative *adj* fond of preconceived ideas; self-conceited.—**opinionatively** *adv*.

opinion poll *n* a testing of public opinion by questioning a representative sample on an issue.

opisthodomus *n* (*archit*) the small room, usu a treasury, found at the back of the naos in a Greek temple.

opium *n* a narcotic drug produced from an annual Eurasian poppy; a milky liquid extracted from the unripe seed capsules of the poppy *Papaver somniferum*, containing 10 per cent of anhydrous morphine. Opium is a narcotic and analgesic.

OPKA *abbr* (*Brit*) = Original Pearly Kings and Queens Association.

OPM *abbr* = Office of Personnel Management.

OPMA *abbr* = Overseas Press and Media Association.

opossum *n* (*pl* **opossums**, **opossum**) a small nocturnal and arboreal marsupial.

opp. *abbr* = opposed; opposite.

Oppenheimer *n* J[ulius] **Robert** (1904–67) American nuclear physicist who resigned from the Los Alamos atom bomb project after the bombing of Hiroshima and Nagasaki, and argued for cooperation with the USSR on nuclear weapons control.

oppidan *adj* urban, town-dwelling.

oppilate *vt* (*med*) to block up, to obstruct.—**oppilation** *n*.

opponent *n* a person who opposes another; an adversary, antagonist. * *adj* opposing.

opportune *adj* well-timed; convenient.—**opportunely** *adv*.

opportuneness *n* seasonableness.

opportunist *n* a person who forms or adapts his or her views or principles to benefit from opportunities; one who seizes opportunities as they may arise.—**opportunism** *n*.

opportunistic *adj* relating to opportunism; (*med*) relating to an infection that is contracted by someone with a lowered resistance.

opportunity *n* (*pl* **opportunities**) chance; a favorable combination of circumstances.

opportunity cost *n* a term used in economics to describe cost in terms of the sacrificed alternative; the financial advantage that is foregone if a firm opts for one form of action or activity rather than another using the same resources.

opposable *adj* that may be opposed.—**opposability** *n*.—**opposably** *adv*.

oppose *vt* to put in front of or in the way of; to place in opposition; to resist; to fight against; to balance against.—**opposer** *n*.

opposite *adj* placed on opposed sides of; face to face; diametrically different; contrary. * *n* a person or thing that is opposite; an antithesis. * *prep*, *adv* across from.

opposite number *n* a person in a corresponding position on the other side; a counterpart.

opposition *n* the act of opposing or the condition of being opposed; resistance; antithesis; hostility; a political party opposing the government; (*astron*) the diametrically opposite position of two heavenly bodies, when 180° apart.

oppress *vt* to treat unjustly; to subjugate; to weigh down in the mind.—**oppressor** *n*.

oppression *n* the act of oppressing; the state of being oppressed; persecution; physical or mental distress.

oppressive *adj* tyrannical; burdensome; (of weather) sultry, close.—**oppressively** *adv*.—**oppressiveness** *n*.

opprobrious *adj* abusive; infamous.

opprobrium *n* a reproach with disdain or contempt; disgrace, ignominy.

OPPS *abbr* (*Brit*) = Oxford Project for Peace Studies.

oppugn *vt* to reason against, to controvert; to resist.—**oppugnant** *adj*, *n*.—**oppugner** *n*.

OPS *abbr* = Ophthalmic Photographers Society.

Ops *n* (*Roman myth*) a goddess of plenty, equated with the Greek goddess Rhea and with Cybele.

OPSIS *abbr* (*Brit*) = National Association for the Education, Training and Support of Blind and Partially Sighted People.

opsonin *n* a chemical agent in blood serum, which makes bacteria vulnerable to phagocytic activity.—**opsonic** *adj*.

Opsvik *n* **Peter** (1939–) Norwegian furniture designer who collaborated with Christian **Mengshoel** on the development of ergonomic seating.

opt *vi* to choose, to exercise an option; (*with* **in**) to choose to participate in something; (*with* **out**) to choose not to participate in something.

opt. *abbr* = optative; optic; optical; optician; optics; optimal; (*Latin*) *optime* ("excellently"); optimum; optional.

Opt.D. *abbr* = Doctor of Optometry.

optative *adj* (*gram*) expressing a desire or wish. * *n* an optative mood or form of a verb.

optic *adj* relating to the eye or sight. * *n* (*inf*) the eye; a device for dispensing a standard measure of spirits, etc.

optical *adj* of or relating to the eye or light; optic; aiding or correcting vision; visual.—**optically** *adv*.

optical character reader *n* a device that allows printed characters, figures, etc, to be scanned and input to a computer, by a process of optical character recognition.

optical character recognition (OCR) *n* (*comput*) an information processing technology that can convert readable (scanned) text into computer data.

optical dating *n* a method for dating minerals in sedimentary deposits such as quartz by exposing a sample to light of a certain wavelength and measuring the luminescence.

optical disk *n* (*comput*) a type of disk that uses light to write data to the disk and read the data from the disk.

optical emission spectrometry (OES) *n* a method of determining the composition of a sample by heating it so that its electrons emit light of a particular wavelength appropriate to each element present.

optical fiber *n* (*comput*) a thin glass filament that is used to transmit data or light.

optical instrument *n* any apparatus or instrument used for the study of light or for the investigation of bodies or phenomena by means of light.

optical isomerism *n* (*chem*) the existence of two chemical compounds that are isomers, each being the mirror image of the other.

optical mouse *n* (*comput*) an input device that is connected to a computer by light beams rather than wires.

optic atrophy *n* a deterioration and wasting of the optic disk as a result of degeneration of fibers in the optic nerve.

optic chiasma *or* **optic commissure** *n* the cross-shaped structure formed from a crossing over of the optic nerve running back from the eyeballs to meet beneath the brain in the midline.

optic disk *n* an oval area on the retina where the optic nerve enters the eyeball.

optician *n* a person who makes or sells optical aids.

optic nerve *n* a sensory nerve that sends messages from the retina to the brain. *See also* **optic chiasma**.

optics *n sing* the branch of physics dealing with the study of light, usu extended to include non-visible regions of the electromagnetic spectrum; also used more loosely to refer to the lenses, mirrors, prisms, gratings, etc, as used in optical instruments.

optimal *adj* optimum.—**optimally** *adv*.

optimism *n* a tendency to take the most cheerful view of things; hopefulness; the belief that good must ultimately prevail.—**optimist** *n*.—**optimistic** *adj*.—**optimistically** *adv*.

optimize *vt* to make the best possible advantage of. * *vi* to be optimistic.—**optimization** *n*.

optimized production technology *n* a computer-based system for planning production and the assigning of resources.

optimum *n* (*pl* **optima**, **optimums**) the best, most favorable condition.—*also adj*.

option *n* the act of choosing; the power to choose; a choice; the right to buy, sell or lease at a fixed price within a specified time; (*comput*) a choice that the user faces when operating a computer, e.g., print, cancel, etc.

optional *adj* left to choice; not compulsory.—**optionally** *adv*.

optional extra *n* a feature that can be added to a product to enhance its appearance or performance but is not part of the basic or standard model.

option to purchase *n* a right that is given to shareholders to buy shares in certain companies under certain circumstances at a reduced price; a right that is purchased by or given to a person at a specified price on or before an arranged date with the undertaking that the seller will not sell it to anyone else or withdraw it from sale before that date.

optometer *n* an instrument for measuring the limits of distinct vision.

optometrist *n* a person qualified to test eyesight and to prescribe glasses or contact lenses.

optometry *n* the profession of testing eyesight and prescribing corrective lenses.—**optometric**, **optometrical** *adj*.

opulent *adj* wealthy; luxuriant.—**opulence** *n*.

opuntia *n* any of a genus of cacti; the Indian fig.

opus *n* (*mus*) (*Latin*) work; a term used by composers (or their catalogers) to indicate the chronological order of their works. It is usu abbreviated to **op.** and is followed by the cataloged number of the work.

opus incertum *n* (*archit*) Roman walling of random rubble construction.

opus listatum *n* (*archit*) Roman walling in which courses of brick and small stone blocks alternate with one another.

opus quadratum *n* (*archit*) Roman walling using shaped squared stones.

opus reticulatum *n* (*archit*) Roman walling using worked squared stones arranged diagonally to form a diamond-shaped mesh pattern.

OPV *abbr* = oral poliomyelitis vaccine.

or[1] *conj denoting* an alternative; the last in a series of choices.

or[2] *n* (*her*) gold, denoted by small engraved dots.

OR *abbr* = Odinic Rite; Official Receiver; operating room; operational research; other ranks; Order of the Road; Oregon; (*comput*) *see* **formula**; **logical operator**.

Or. *abbr* = Oregon; oriental.

o.r. *abbr* (*transp*) = owner's risk.

ora *see* **os**[1].

ora. *abbr* = oratorio.

ORACBA *abbr* = Office of Risk Assessment and Cost-Benefit Analysis.

orach, orache *n* mountain spinach.

oracle *n* (*myth*) the response delivered by a deity or supernatural being to a worshiper or inquirer; the place where the response was delivered; a wise adviser; sage advice.—**oracular** *adj*.

ORACLE *abbr* = optional reception of announcements by coded line electronics.

oracle bones *n* animal bones used by mystics in ancient China for divination. These are particularly a feature of the Shang period.

oral *adj* of the mouth; spoken, not written; (*drugs*) taken by mouth. * *n* a spoken examination.—**orally** *adv*.

oral contraceptive *see* **contraceptive**.

oral history *n* the history of past events as recorded from interviews with people living at the time.

Oran[1] *n* a city in Algeria.

Oran[2] *n* the brother of St Columba. He is said to have volunteered to die so that Columba could consecrate with a burial the ground on which he wished to build his chapel.

orange *n* a round, reddish-yellow, juicy, edible citrus fruit; the tree bearing it; its color. * *adj* orange-colored.

orange stick *n* a small thin pointed stick, *orig* orangewood, used in manicuring the nails.

orangeade *n* a drink made with the juice of oranges.

Orangeman *n* (*pl* **Orangemen**) a member of an Irish protestant political party named after William of Orange.

orangery *n* (*pl* **orangeries**) a hothouse for the cultivation of oranges; an orange garden.

orangutan, orangoutang *n* a large, long-armed, herbivorous anthropoid ape.

Oranian *adj* relating to an Upper Paleolithic culture concentrated mainly along the Mediterranean coastal areas of Morocco, Algeria, and Tunisia.

Oranjestad *n* capital city of Aruba.

orate *vi* to make an oration; (*inf*) to hold forth.

oration *n* a formal or public speech.

orator *n* an eloquent public speaker.—**oratorical** *adj*.

oratorio *n* (*mus*) the musical setting of a religious or epic libretto for soloists, chorus, and orchestra, performed without the theatrical effects of stage and costumes, etc.

oratory *n* (*pl* **oratories**) the art of public speaking; eloquence; a place for prayer.

orb *n* a sphere or globe; an ornamental sphere surmounted by a cross, esp as carried by a sovereign at a coronation.

o.r.b. *abbr* (*transp*) = owner's risk of breakage.

orbicular, orbiculate, orbiculated *adj* orb-shaped, spherical.—**orbicularity** *n*.

orbit *n* (*astron*) a curved path along which a planet or satellite moves, under the influence of all other bodies in space principally by their gravitational attraction; a field of action or influence; the eye socket; (*physics*) the path of an electron around the nucleus of an atom. * *vti* to put (a satellite, etc) into orbit; to circle round.—**orbital** *adj*.

orbital elements *n* six quantities essential to specify the motions of celestial bodies.

orc *n* a grampus; the killer whale; a sea monster.

ORC *abbr* = Officers' Reserve Corps.

o.r.c. *abbr* (*transp*) = owner's risk of chafing.

Orcagna *n* (1343–68) Florentine painter, sculptor, and architect. His masterpiece and only certain dated work is the altarpiece, *The Redeemer with the Madonna and Saints* (1354–57), in the Church of Santa Maria Novella.

orch. *abbr* = orchestra.

orchard *n* an area of land planted with fruit trees.

orchestra *n* a group of musicians playing together under a conductor; their instruments; the space (or pit) in a theater where they sit; the stalls of a theater; (*archit*) a central circular space in the Classical Greek theater.—**orchestral** *adj*.

orchestrate *vt* to arrange music for performance by an orchestra; to arrange, organize to best effect.—**orchestrator** *n*.

orchestration *n* (*mus*) the art of writing and arranging music for an orchestra.

orchestrion *n* a large automatic barrel organ.

orchid *n* a plant with unusually shaped flowers in brilliant colors comprising three petals of uneven size.

orchidectomy *n* removal of one or both testicles (castration), usu to treat a malignant growth.

orchidopexy *n* the operation performed to bring an undescended testicle into the scrotum.

orchil *n* a red or violet dye obtained from lichen; the lichen.—*also* **archil**.

orchis *n* a genus of wild orchid with curiously shaped roots and flowers.

Orchomenus *n* the principal ancient city of northern Boeotia in Greece.

orcinol, orcin *n* a substance obtained from lichens yielding dye.

Orcus *n* (*Roman myth*) a name for Pluto and for his kingdom.

ord. *abbr* = ordained; order; ordinal; ordinance; ordinary; ordnance.

o.r.d. *abbr* (*transp*) = owner's risk of damage.

ordain *vti* to confer holy orders upon; to appoint; to decree; to order, to command.—**ordainer** *n*.—**ordainment** *n*.

ordeal *n* a severe trial or test; an exacting experience.

order *n* arrangement; method; relative position; sequence; an undisturbed condition; tidiness; rules of procedure; an efficient state; a class, group, or sort; a religious fraternity; a style of architecture; an honor or decoration; an instruction or command; a rule or regulation; (*law*) a legal document, generally issued by a court of law or a governing body, ordering a particular party or agency to perform a certain act; a state or condition, esp with regard to functioning; a request to supply something; the goods supplied; (*zool*) a division between class and family or genus. * *vti* to put or keep (things) in order; to arrange; to command; to request (something) to be supplied.

ordered *adj* marked by regularity and discipline; being arranged or identifiable according to a rule; being labeled by ordinal numbers.

orderly *adj* in good order; well-behaved; methodical. * *n* (*pl* **orderlies**) a hospital attendant; a soldier attending an officer.—**orderliness** *n*.

order of business *n* the order of the items to be dealt with on the agenda of a business meeting.

order of magnitude *n* (*math*) the approximate size of an object or quantity usu expressed in powers of 10.

Orders *n* the Roman architectural writer, Marcus Vitruvius Pollio, whose works detailed the orders of ancient architecture comprising columns with their bases, capitals and entablatures.

o.r.det. *abbr* (*transp*) = owner's risk of deterioration.

ordinal *adj* showing position in a series. * *n* an ordinal number.

ordinal number *n* (*math*) 1st, 2nd etc., rather than 1, 2 etc (cardinal numbers).

ordinal scale *n* (*statistics*) a statistical scale that arranges the data in order of rank in the absence of a numerical scale with regular intervals.

ordinance *n* a decree, a law; a rite.

ordinary *adj* normal, usual; common; plain, unexceptional.* *n* (*pl* **ordinaries**) a meal for all comers at fixed charges and a fixed time, an inn providing this; archbishop in province, bishop in diocese; prescribed form of service; an ecclesiastical judge; a prison chaplain; (*her*) that part of the escutcheon contained between straight and other lines, one of the simple charges.—**ordinarily** *adv*.

ordinary seaman *n* a seaman of the lowest rank, below able-bodied seaman.

ordinary share *n* a unit of the share capital of a company.

ordinary shareholders *npl* those who hold ordinary shares.

ordinate *n* (*geom*) one of the coordinates of a point; a straight line in a curve terminated on both sides by the curve and bisected by the diameter; the vertical or *y*-axis in a geometrical diagram for Cartesian co-ordinates.

ordination *n* the act of ordaining or being ordained; admission to the ministry.

ordn *abbr* = ordnance.

ordnance *n* military stores; artillery.

ordnance datum *see* **mean sea level**.

Ordovices *n* one of the tribes that supported Caratacus against the Roman invaders was a northern Welsh tribe known as Ordovices.

Ordovician *adj* (*geol*) of the period between the Cambrian and Silurian.

ordure *n* excrement; dung.

ore *n* any naturally occurring substance that contains commercially useful metals or other compounds.

öre *n* (*pl* **öre**) a monetary unit in Sweden. *See* **krona**.

øre *n* (*pl* **øre**) a monetary unit in Denmark and Norway. *See* **krone**.

Ore. *or* **Oreg.** *abbr* = Oregon.

oread *n* a mountain nymph (Greek).

Örebro *n* a city in Sweden.

oregano *n* an aromatic herb whose leaves, either fresh of dried, are used to flavor food.

Oregon (OR) *n* a state of the United States of America (USA) of which the capital is Salem.

"Oregon, My Oregon" *n* the song of the American state, Oregon.

Orestes *n* (*Greek myth*) the son of Agamemnon and Clytemnestra. When his father was murdered, he was saved from a similar fate by his sister, Electra.

o.r.f. *abbr* (*transp*) = owner's risk of fire *or* freezing.

Orff *n* Carl (1895–1982) German composer whose best-known work is *Carmina Burana* (1937).

ORG *abbr* (*Brit*) = Oxford Research Group.

org. *abbr* = organic; organized.

organ *n* a large and complex musical wind instrument with pipes, stops, and a keyboard; (*biol*) a part of an animal or plant consisting of two or more types of tissue that performs a vital or natural function, such as the liver, kidney, heart, and brain; the means by which anything is done; a medium of information or opinion, a periodical.

organdy, organdie *n* (*pl* **organdies**) a light transparent, esp stiffened cotton fabric.

organelle *n* (*biol*) any structure that is bound by a membrane to separate it from the other cell constituents and which has a particular function within the cell e.g. a mitochondrion.

organ grinder *n* the player of a barrel organ.

organic *adj* of or relating to bodily organs; (of disease) affecting a bodily organ; of, or derived from, living organisms; systematically arranged; structural; (*chem*) of the class of compounds that are formed from carbon; (of vegetables, etc) grown without the use of artificial fertilizers or pesticides.—**organically** *adv*.

organic chemistry *n* (*chem*) the branch of chemistry that is concerned with the study of carbon compounds.

organism *n* (*biol*) any living creature, including micro-organisms, plants, and animals; any living thing; an organized body.

organist *n* a person who plays an organ.

organistrum *see* **hurdy-gurdy**.

organization *n* the act or process of organizing; the state of being organized; arrangement, structure; an organized body or association.

organization chart *n* a chart or diagram that illustrates the structure and chain of responsibility of a company.

Organization of the Petroleum Exporting Countries (often abbreviated to **OPEC**) *n* an organization that was founded in 1960 to coordinate the petroleum policies of the member countries and to protect their individual and collective interests.

organize *vt* to arrange in an orderly way; to establish; to institute; to persuade to join a cause, group, etc; to arrange for.—**organizer** *n*.

organogenesis *n* organic development.—**organogenetic** *adj*.—**organogenetically** *adv*.

organography *n* a scientific description of the organs of animals or plants.—**organographic** *adj*.

organology *n* the branch of physiology that treats of animal organs.—**organological** *adj*.—**organologist** *n*.

organon *n* (*pl* **organa**, **organons**) a body of rules for regulating scientific or philosophical investigation; a method of thought, a logical system.

organotherapy *n* the treatment of disease with organic extracts.

organzine *n* a strong silk thread of a very fine texture; a fabric made from it.

orgasm *n* the climax of sexual arousal which, in men, coincides with ejaculation and comprises a series of involuntary muscle contractions. In women, there are irregular contractions of the vaginal walls.—**orgasmic** *adj*.

orgeat *n* a drink made of barley water flavored with almonds.

orgies *npl* secret rites or customs connected with the worship of some Greek gods, such as the mystery religion of Demeter and the festival of Dionysus, which were conducted with many customs of mystic symbolism and much license.

Org. Res. *abbr* = Organized Reserves.

orgy *n* (*pl* **orgies**) a wild party or gathering of people, with excessive drinking and indiscriminate sexual activity; over-indulgence in any activity.—**orgiastic** *adj*.

ORHP *abbr* = Office of Rural Health Policy.

oriel *n* a projecting angular recess with a window; the window.

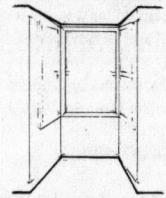

orient *n* the east; eastern regions or lands; (*with cap*) the East, or Asia, esp the Far East; the Eastern Hemisphere; the countries of Asia.

orient, **orientate** *vti* to adjust (oneself) to a particular situation; to arrange in a direction, esp in relation to the points of the compass; to face or turn in a particular direction.

oriental *adj* (*often cap*) of the Orient, its people or languages.

Oriental rug *n* a handwoven one-piece rug made in the Orient.

Orientalism *n* an idiom or custom characteristic of the East.

Orientalist *n* an expert in Oriental languages, history, etc.

orientation *n* arrangement; alignment; position relative to a compass direction; one's way of thinking or direction of interest; (*print*) page format (vertical or portrait orientation, horizontal or landscape orientation).

orienteering *n* the sport of racing on foot over difficult country using a map and compass.

orifice *n* an opening or mouth of a cavity.

oriflamme *n* the ancient royal standard of France, a red flag split at one end and forming flame-shaped streamers; a party symbol; a blaze of color.

orig. *abbr* = origin; original; originally.

origami *n* the Japanese art of paper folding to make complicated shapes.

origin *n* the source or beginning of anything; ancestry or parentage; (*math*) in a graph, the point of intersection of the horizontal (*x*) and the vertical (*y*) axes.

original *adj* relating to the origin or beginning; earliest, primitive; novel; unusual; inventive, creative. * *n* an original work, as of art or literature; something from which copies are made; a creative person; an eccentric.—**originality** *n*.—**originally** *adv*.

original goods *npl* natural products that have no commercial value until they have been subjected to some kind of production process.

original sin *n* the inherent tendency of mankind to sin, derived from Adam and imputed to his descendants.

originate *vti* to initiate or begin; to bring or come into being.—**origination** *n*.—**originator** *n*.

orinasal *adj* (of a vowel) sounded with both the mouth and nose.—*also n*.

oriole *n* a kind of yellow, black-winged bird.

Orion *n* (*Greek myth*) a giant who was a hunter and is said to have been extremely beautiful. After his death he was placed in the sky as the constellation on the celestial equator which bears his name.

Orion arm *n* the spiral arm of the Milky Way Galaxy in which the Sun lies.

Orionids *n* a meteor shower seen in October which appears to come from a radiant in the Orion constellation.

Orion Nebula *n* an emission nebula (M42 or NGC 1976) in the constellation Orion, also known as the Great Nebula in Orion.

orison *n* (*arch*) a prayer.

ORL *abbr* = otorhinolaryngology (treatment of the ear, nose, and throat).

Orl. *abbr* = Orlando.

o.r.l. *abbr* (*transp*) = owner's risk of leakage.

orle *n* (*her*) an ordinary in the form of a fillet round a shield; (*archit*) a fillet under the capital of a column.

Orley *n* **Bernard van** (*c*.1488–1541) Dutch painter and designer; known as "Raphael of the Netherlands" because of the influence of the art of Raphael on his work.

Orlon *n* (*trademark*) an acrylic fiber.

orlop *n* the lowest deck of a ship with three or more decks.

Ormandy *n* **Eugene** (1899–1985) Hungarian-born conductor who was a child prodigy on the violin. He moved to the USA in 1921 and conducted many of the world's leading orchestras.

ormer *n* a mollusc, sea ear.

ormolu *n* an imitation gold made of copper and tin alloy, used to decorate fireplaces, furniture, and marble and stone surfaces, esp during the 18th century.

Orna *see* **Oghma**.

ornament *n* anything that enhances the appearance of a person or thing; a small decorative object. * *vt* to adorn, to decorate with ornaments.

ornamental *adj* serving as an ornament; decorative, not useful.—**ornamentally** *adv*.

ornamentation *n* the act or process of ornamenting; something that decorates.

ornaments and graces *n* (*mus*) embellishments to the notes of a melody, indicated by symbols or small notes. They were used frequently in the 17th and 18th centuries.

ornate *adj* richly adorned; (of style) highly elaborate.—**ornately** *adv*.—**ornateness** *n*.

ornery *adj* (*sl*) of a bad disposition, hard to manage.

ornith. *or* **ornithol.** *abbr* = ornithological; ornithology.

ornitho-, ornith- *prefix* bird.

ornithology *n* the study of birds.—**ornithological** *adj*.—**ornithologically** *adv*.—**ornithologist** *n*.

ornithopter *n* an aircraft with flapping wings.

ornithorhynchus *n* an Australian genus of monotremes, including the platypus.

ORNL *abbr* = Oak Ridge National Laboratory.

oro- *prefix* mountain.

orogeny *n* (*geol*) a period of mountain building, each lasting for millions of years.—*also* **orogenesis**.—**orogenic, orogenetic** *adj*.

orographic rainfall *see* **relief rainfall**.

orography, orology *n* the geography of mountains and mountain systems, their mapping, etc.—**orographic, orological** *adj*.

oroide *n* a gold-colored alloy of tin and copper.

O'Rorke *n* **Brian** (1901–74) New Zealand architect who studied at Cambridge University and practiced in Britain.

orotund *adj* (of the voice) full, resonant; (of style) pompous, high-flown.

Orozco *n* **José Clemente** (1883–1949) Mexican painter commissioned to paint a large number of murals and frescos, of which *An Epic of American Civilization* (1932–4) is a notable example.

Orpen *n* **Sir William** (1878–1931) Irish-born English painter who established himself as a successful society portraitist in the fashion of Sargent, though his own costume self-portraits and his group portraits are generally works of better quality and insight.

orphan *n* a child whose parents are dead. * *vt* to cause to become an orphan.—*also adj*.

orphanage *n* a residential institution for the care of orphans.

Orphean *adj* of or pertaining to Orpheus, the celebrated bard of Classic mythology, or his music; melodious, enchanting.

Orpheus *n* (*Greek myth*) a hero and legendary singer, the chief representative of the art of song, and the founder of a religious sect. He played the lyre so well so that he moved not only people and animals, but the woods and rocks with its melody.

Orphic *adj* of Orpheus or his cult; mystical.

orphism *n* brief but influential art movement developed out of cubist principles by the artists Delaunay, Léger, Picabia, Duchamp, and Kupka.—*also* **orphic cubism**.

orphrey *n* an embroidered band or bands of gold or silver on the front of an ecclesiastical vestment from the neck downward, esp on a cope.

orpiment *n* a yellow compound of arsenic, used as a pigment.

orpine *n* a succulent plant with fleshy leaves and purple flowers.

ORR *abbr* = Office of Refugee Resettlement.

ORRA *abbr* = Oriental Rug Retailers of America.

orrery *n* (*pl* **orreries**) a moving model of the solar system, often driven by clockwork, which illustrates by balls mounted on rods the motions, magnitudes, and positions of the planets.

orris *n* a kind of iris.

orrisroot *n* the dried roots of the Florentine orris, used in perfumery and medicine.

o

o.r.s. *abbr* (*transp*) = owner's risk of shifting.

ORT *abbr* = oral rehydration therapy.

Ortega *n* **Daniel** (1945–) Nicaraguan politician; leader of the Sandinista resistance movement; president (1985–90); defeated in the 1989 election.

Ortega y Gasset *n* **José** (1883–1955) Spanish philosopher whose best-known work is *The Revolt of the Masses* (1929).

ortho- *prefix* straight, right, true.

orthocephalic, orthocephalous *adj* (*anat*) with a skull of medium proportions, between brachycephalic and dolichocephalic.

orthochromatic *adj* (*photog*) giving the correct relative tones to colors, isochromatic.

orthoclase *n* potash feldspar.

orthodontics *n* a part of dentistry dealing with development of the teeth and the treatment of (or prevention of) any disorders or irregularities.—**orthodontic** *adj.*—**orthodontist** *n.*

orthodox *adj* conforming with established behavior or opinions; not heretical; generally accepted, conventional;

Orthodox *adj* (*with cap*) of or relating to a conservative political or religious group.

orthodoxy *n* (*pl* **orthodoxies**) the state or quality of being orthodox; an orthodox practice or belief.

orthoepy *n* the science of correct pronunciation.—**orthoepic** *adj.*—**orthepist** *n.*

orthogenesis *n* evolution following a definite line, determinate variation.—**orthogenetic** *adj.*

orthognathous *adj* having an upright jaw, neither receding nor protruding.—**orthognathism** *n.*

orthogonal *adj* rectangular.—**orthogonally** *adv.*

orthography *n* (*pl* **orthographies**) the art of spelling and writing words with grammatical correctness; a map projection with a point of sight supposedly infinitely distant.—**orthographer** *n.*—**orthographic, orthographical** *adj.*

orthopedics *n* the branch of medicine concerned with the study and surgical treatment of the skeletal system and the joints, muscles, etc.—**orthopedic** *adj.*—**orthopedist** *n.*

orthopnea *n* a severe difficulty in breathing that is so bad that a person cannot lie down and has to sleep in a sitting position.

orthopteran *n* (*pl* **orthopterans, orthoptera**) any of the Orthoptera order of insects, having their two outer wings overlapping at the top when shut, as in grasshoppers.—**orthopterous** *adj.*

orthoptic *adj* of correct seeing. * *n* the peep-sight of a rifle.

orthostat *n* (*archeo*) a large, vertical stone that is part of some other structure.

orthotropism *n* vertical growth in plants.—**orthotropic** *adj.*—**orthotropous** *adj.*

ortolan *n* a small bird, allied to the bunting, much esteemed for its flesh.

Orton *n* **Joe** [John] (1933–67) English dramatist whose best known plays are *Entertaining Mr Sloane*, *Loot*, and the *What the Butler Saw*.

ORTPA *abbr* = Oven-Ready Turkey Producers Association.

Oruro *n* a city in Bolivia.

o.r.w. *abbr* (*transp*) = owner's risk of becoming wet.

Orwell *n* **George** [Eric Arthur Blair] (1903–50) Indian-born English novelist and essayist whose novels include *Nineteen Eighty-Four* (1949).

oryx *n* (*pl* **oryxes, oryx**) a straight-horned African antelope.

os[1] *n* (*pl* **ossa**) (*anat*) bone.

os[2] *n* (*pl* **ora**) (*anat*) the mouth.

Os *symbol* (*chem*) osmium.

os *abbr* = only son.

OS *abbr* = Oceanography Society; Old Saxon; Old Style; Omnibus Society; operating system; Ordinary Seaman; (*Brit*) Ordnance Survey; outsize.

o.s. *abbr* = (*comput*) on spot.

O.S. *abbr* = Old School; Old Series; Old Side; Outside Sentinel.

o/s *abbr* = out of stock; outstanding.

O/s or **o/s** *abbr* = *oro sellado*.

OS/2 *n* (*comput*) an operating system created by IBM™.

OSA *abbr* = Official Secrets Act; (*Latin*) *Ordo Sancti Augustini* ("Order of St Augustine").

OSAC *abbr* = Overseas Security Advisory Council.

Osaka *n* a city in Japan.

o.s. and d. *abbr* (*transp*) = over, short, and damaged.

OSB *abbr* (*Latin*) = *Ordo Sancti Benedicti*, "Order of St Benedict."

Osbald *n* (*d.* 796) king of Northumbria (reigned in 796). He was one of the conspirators who killed Ethelred in 796 but only reigned for a few weeks before being ousted by Eardwulf.

Osbert *n* (*d.* 867) king of Northumbria (850–865). Expelled in favor of his brother, Aelle.

Osborne *n* **John** [James] (1929–94) English dramatist whose first play, *Look Back in Anger*, was an immediate and influential success. The best known of his later plays are *The Entertainer* and *Luther*.

OSBP *abbr* = Office of Small Business Programs.

OSC *abbr* = Office of Special Counsel.

osc. *abbr* = oscillating; oscillator.

Oscar[1] *n* (*Irish Celtic myth*) the son of Oisin. A mighty warrior who distinguished himself by killing a huge boar that many others had failed to catch.

Oscar[2] *n* any of several small statuettes awarded annually by the US Academy of Motion Picture Arts and Sciences for outstanding achievements.

OSCAR *abbr* (*Brit*) = Organisation for Sickle Cell Anaemia Research.

OSCE *abbr* = Office of Child Support Enforcement.

OSCH *abbr* = off-peak storage central heating.

oscillate *vi* to swing back and forth as a pendulum; to waver, vacillate between extremes of opinion, etc.

oscillation *n* (*physics*) the regular fluctuation of an object whether by means of a cycle, vibration, or rotation.

oscillator *n* (*mus*) an electronic instrument that converts electrical energy into audible sound; (*physics*) a circuit or device that produces an alternating current or voltage of a specific frequency as its output signal.

oscillatory *adj* swinging; vibrating.

oscilloscope *n* a device for viewing oscillations on a display screen of a cathode-ray tube.

osculate *vti* (of species) to have features in common; (*geom*) to make contact (with); (*humorous*) to kiss, to touch.—**osculation** *n.*

osculatory *adj* pertaining to kissing. * *n* a tablet or board on which a picture of Christ or the Virgin Mary is painted for worshippers to kiss.

OSDBU *abbr* = Office of Small and Disadvantaged Business Utilization.

-ose *suffix* full of.

OSF *abbr* = Office of Space Flight; (*Latin*) *Ordo Sancti Francisci* "Order of St Francis."

OSFC *abbr* (*Latin*) = *Ordo Sancti Francisci Cappuchinorum* ("Cappuchin Order of St Francis").

OSGB *abbr* = Orchid Society of Great Britain.

Osh *n* a city in Kyrgyzstan.

OSHA *abbr* = Occupational Safety and Health Administration.

OSHRC *abbr* = Occupational Safety and Health Review Commission.

OSI *abbr* = Open Systems Interconnection.

OSIC *abbr* = Overseas Spinning Investment Company.

osier *n* a willow, the twigs of which are used in basket-making.

Osijek *n* a city in Croatia.

Osiris *n* the best loved of the Egyptian gods, husband of Iris and father of Horus.

-osis *n* *suffix* indicating a particular state, esp a diseased condition, *thrombosis*; increase, development of, *fibrosis*.

Oslo *n* capital city of the Kingdom of Norway.

OSM *abbr* = Office of Surface Mining; (*Latin*) *Ordo Servorum Beatae Virginis Mariae* ("Order of the Servants of the Blessed Virgin Mary").

Osmanli *adj* of or pertaining to the Ottoman Empire.—*also n.*

osmium *n* a hard bluish-white metallic element used in alloys.

osmometry *n* the measurement of smells.

osmosis *n* (*pl* **osmoses**) (*biol, chem*) the process in which solvent molecules move through a semi-permeable membrane to the more concentrated solution.—**osmotic** *adj.*—**osmotically** *adv.*

Osmund *n* king of Sussex (*c.*765–770). An under-king of the powerful Offa of Mercia who annexed the kingdom in 772.

osmunda, osmund *n* the flowering fern of the genus Osmunda.

osnaburg *n* a coarse linen cloth.

Osorkon *n* last Egyptian king of the Libyan Dynasty, Twenty-fifth Dynasty (747–656 BC).

osp *abbr* = (*Latin*) *obiit sine prole*, "died without issue"; off-street parking.

osprey *n* (*pl* **ospreys**) a large fish-eating bird of prey.

Osred I *n* (*d.* 716) king of Northumbria (705–716). The young successor of Aldfrith in 705, he earned a reputation as a tyrant and was murdered.

Osred II *n* king of Northumbria (788–790). A nephew of Elfwold, he was imprisoned by Ethelred I and later escaped to the Isle of Man.

Osric *n* (*d.* 729) king of Northumbria (718–729). He was succeeded by his nephew, Ceolwulf.

Ossa *n* the ancient name of a mountain in Magnesia in northern Greece; in Greek mythology, the seat of the Centaurs and Giants, and one of the three mountains that Otus and Ephialtes piled up to form a structure that would enable them to storm heaven.

ossa *see* **os**[2].

OSSC *abbr* (*Canada*) = Oil Spill Service Centre.

ossein *n* gelatinous tissue in bone.

osseous *adj* pertaining to, consisting of, or like, bone.

ossia *n* (*mus*) (*Italian*) "or"; used to indicate an alternative passage of music.

Ossian *see* **Oisin**.

ossicle *n* a little bone, esp of the middle ear, e.g., the incus, malleus, and stapes; (*pl*) hard structures of small size, as the calcareous plates of the starfish.—**ossicular** *adj.*

ossiferous *adj* producing or containing bone.

ossification *n* bone formation, which occurs in several stages via special cells called osteoblasts.—*also* **osteogenesis.**

ossification *n* conversion of soft animal tissue into bone.

ossifrage *n* an old name for the osprey or lammergeier.

ossify *vti* (**ossifying, ossified**) *vt* to convert into bone or into a bone-like substance; to harden. * *vi* to become bone; to grow rigid and unprogressive.

ossuary *n* (*pl* **ossuaries**) (*archeo*) a receptacle for holding the bones of a dead person.

OST *abbr* = Office of Science and Technology; Office of the Secretary of Transportation.

o.s.t. *abbr* = ordinary spring tides.

Østberg *n* **Ragnar** (1866–1945) Swedish architect. His notable works include Stockholm City Hall.

osteal *adj* osseous.

osteclast *see* **osteosclerosis**.

osteitis *n* inflammation of the bone, caused by damage, infection, or bodily disorder.

osteitis deformans *see* **Paget's disease of bone**.

ostensible *adj* apparent; seeming; pretended.—**ostensibly** *adv*.

ostensive *adj* showing, exhibiting.

ostentation *n* a showy, pretentious display.—**ostentatious** *adj*.—**ostentatiously** *adv*.

osteo-, oste- *prefix* bone.

osteoarthritis *n* a form of arthritis involving degeneration of the joint cartilage with accompanying changes in the associated bone; painful inflammation of the joints, esp the hips, knees, and others that bear weight.—**osteoarthritic** *adj*.

osteoblast *n* a specialized cell responsible for the formation of bone.

osteochondritis *n* inflammation of bone and cartilage.

osteochondrosis *n* a disease affecting the ossification centers of bone in children.

osteocyte *n* a bone cell formed from an osteoblast that is no longer active and has become embedded in the matrix of the bone.

osteogenesis *see* **ossification**.

osteogenesis imperfecta *n* a hereditary disease that results in unusually fragile and brittle bones.—*also* **brittle bone disease.**

osteology *n* that part of anatomy treating of bones, their structure, etc; a bony structure.—**osteological** *adj*.—**osteologist** *n*.

osteoma *n* (*pl* **osteomas, osteomata**) a bone tumor.

osteomalacia *n* a softening of the bones and the adult equivalent of rickets, which is caused by a lack of vitamin D.

osteomyelitis *n* an infectious disease causing inflammation of the bone marrow.

osteopathy *n* the treatment of disease by manipulation of the bones and muscles, often as an adjunct to medical and surgical measures.—**osteopath** *n*.

osteophyte *n* an abnormal bony projection that occurs near a joint or intervertebral disk where cartilage has degenerated or been destroyed.—**osteophytic** *adj*. *See* **osteoarthritis**.

osteoplasty *n* (*pl* **osteoplasties**) surgery involving bone replacement and grafting.—**osteoplastic** *adj*.

osteoporosis *n* a loss of bone tissue because of its being resorbed, resulting in bones that become brittle and likely to fracture.—**osteoporotic** *adj*.

osteosarcoma *n* the commonest and most malignant tumor of the bone found most commonly in older children.

osteosclerosis *n* a condition in which the density of bone tissue increases abnormally.

osteotome *n* an instrument used in dissecting bones.—**osteotomy** *n*.

Østergaard *n* **Steen** (1935–) Danish designer who designed the first plastic chair to be produced by a single-extrusion process.

OSTI *abbr* = Office of Scientific and Technical Information.

ostiary *n* (*pl* **ostiaries**) (*RC Church*) a church door-keeper.

ostinato *n* (*mus*) (*Italian*) "obstinate"; a short phrase or other pattern that is repeated over and over again during the course of a composition.

OStJ *abbr* = Officer of the Order of St John of Jerusalem.

ostler *n* (*formerly*) a man who attended to horses at an inn, a hostler.

OSTP *abbr* = Office of Science and Technology Policy.

ostracize *vt* to exclude, banish from a group, society, etc.—**ostracism** *n*.

ostracon *n* (*archeo*) (*pl* **olstraca**) a piece of pottery that was used as a surface for writing.

Ostrava *n* a city in the Czech Republic.

ostrich *n* (*pl* **ostriches, ostrich**) a large, flightless, swift-running African bird.

Ostrogoth *n* an eastern Goth.

Oswald *n* (St Oswald) (?605–641) king of Northumbria, Britain (634–641). The brother of Enfrith. He was a devout Christian and gave Bishop Aiden the island of Lindisfarne. Killed by Penda of Mercia. He was the first Anglo-Saxon king to be canonized. His feast day is August 5.

Oswald *n* **Lee Harvey** (1939–63) American alleged assassin of President Kennedy. Arrested shortly after Kennedy's murder, he was shot dead by Jack Ruby (1911–64) before he could come to trial.

Oswin *n* (*d.* 651) king of Deira, Britain (642–651). The son of Oswald.

Oswini *n* (*d.* 690) king of Kent, Britain. Ruled jointly from 688–690 with Suaebhard.

Oswulf *n* (*d.* 759) king of Northumbria, Britain. (reigned in 759). The son and successor of Eadbert.

Oswy *n* (602–670) king of Northumbria, Britain (651–670). The brother of Oswald, his time as ruler saw the peak of Northumbrian power. His daughter Alchfled married Peada of Mercia only after he was persuaded to convert to Christianity.

OT *abbr* = Old Testament; occupational therapy; operating theatre; overtime.

o.t. *abbr* = (*transp*) on track.

OTA *abbr* = Office of Technology Assessment.

otalgia *n* earache.

OTC *abbr* = Officers' Training Camp, or Corps; over the counter.

OTDOGS *abbr* = Opposition to Destruction of Open Green Space.

OTE *abbr* = on-target earnings; or the equivalent.

OTG *abbr* = outside temperature gauge.

other *adj* second; remaining; different; additional. * *pron* the other one; some other one.

other-directed *adj* guided primarily by the influence or example of others.

otherness *n* diversity.

otherwhere *adv* (*arch*) elsewhere.

otherwhile *adv* (*arch*) at another time.

otherwise *adv* if not, or else; differently.

Otherworld *n* (*Celtic myth*) a name for the place where people's souls went after death to be reborn, it being part of the Celtic doctrine to believe in the immortality of the soul; also the land of the gods; (*Welsh Celtic myth*) the Otherworld was known as Annw.

otherworldly *adj* spiritual; unworldly.—**otherworldliness** *n*.

otic *adj* of the ear.

otiose *adj* superfluous, serving no practical purpose; futile; at leisure.—**otiosity** *n*.

otitis *n* inflammation of the ear.

oto- *prefix* ear.

otolith *n* a chalky concretion in the ear.—**otolithic** *adj*.

otology *n* the branch of medicine concerned with the ear, its disorders, diseases, and their treatment.—**otological** *adj*.—**otologist** *n*.

otosclerosis *n* a hereditary condition of deafness in which there is overgrowth of bone in the inner ear, which restricts and then stops sound reaching the inner ear from the middle ear.

otoscope *n* an instrument for examining the interior of the ear.

OTS *abbr* = Office of Thrift Supervision; Officers Training School.

OTT *abbr* = Office of Transportation Technologies; over the top.

ott. *abbr* (*music*) = ottava.

Ottawa *n* capital city of Canada.

ottava *n* (*mus*) (*Italian*) octave.

ottava rima *n* (*poet*) an Italian stanza of eight lines of five accents each with three rhymes, the seventh and eighth forming a couplet; a stanza of eight five-foot lines rhyming abababcc.

otter *n* (*pl* **otters, otter**) a fish-eating mammal with smooth fur and a flat tail.

Otto *n* **Frei** (*b.* 1925) German architect whose notable works include the German Pavilion, Montreal.

ottoman *n* an upholstered, backless chair or couch. * *adj* (*with cap*) of or relating to a former Turkish dynasty and empire; Turkish.

OTU *abbr* = operational training unit.

Otus and Ephialtes *n* (*Greek myth*) twin giants, who were very arrogant and unruly. They tried to storm heaven by heaping Mount Ossa on Mount Olympus and Mount Pelion on Mount Ossa.

Otway *n* **Thomas** (1652–85) English dramatist, remembered chiefly for one work, the great tragedy *Venice Preserved*, a penetrating study of treason and loyalty.

OU *abbr* (*Brit*) = the Open University; Oxford University.

OUA *abbr* = Order of United Americans.

Ouagadougou *n* capital city of Burkina Faso.

OUAM *abbr* = Order of United American Mechanics.

oubliette *n* (*archit*) a concealed dungeon in a medieval castle, accessed by a trapdoor through which the prisoner was dropped, in which prisoners condemned to perpetual imprisonment or secret death were confined.

ouch[1] *interj* an exclamation of pain or annoyance.

ouch[2] *n* a clasp, a jewel; the setting of a gem.

OUDS *abbr* (*Brit*) = Oxford University Dramatic Society.

ought *aux vb* expressing obligation or duty; to be bound, to be obliged (to); a variant spelling of **aught**.

ouguiya *n* the standard monetary unit of Mauritania, being made up of 5 khoums.

Ouija *n* (*trademark*) a board with letters and symbols used to obtain messages at seances.

ounce[1] *n* a unit of weight, equal to one sixteenth of a pound or 28.34 grams; one sixteenth of a pint, one fluid ounce.

ounce[2] *n* the snow leopard; (*poet*) the lynx or an animal like it.

OUP *abbr* = Oxford University Press.

our *poss adj, pron* relating or belonging to us.

"Our Delaware" *n* the official song of the American state, Delaware.

ours *pron* belonging to us.

ourselves *pron* emphatic and reflexive form of we.

-ous *suffix* full of, as in *joyous*; (*chem*) containing in lower proportion, as in *ferrous* as opposed to *ferric*.

ousel *see* ouzel.

oust *vt* to eject, expel, esp by underhand means; to remove forcibly.

out *adv* not in; outside; in the open air; to the full extent; beyond bounds; no longer holding office; ruled out, no longer considered; loudly and clearly; no longer included (in a game, fashion, etc); in error; on strike; at an end; extinguished; into the open; published; revealed; (*radio conversation*) transmission ends. * *prep* out of; out through; outside. * *adj* external; outward. * *n* an exit; means of escape.

out- *prefix* out, outside, away from; external; separate; more, longer.

outage *n* a quantity of something lost during transport or after storage; an interruption (in production, etc) due to power failure.

out-and-out *adj* thoroughgoing; absolute; complete.

outback *n* a remote area inland, esp in Australia.

outbalance *vt* to exceed in weight.

outbid *vt* (**outbidding, outbid**, *pp* **outbidden** *or* **outbid**) to bid higher than.

outboard *adj* (*engine*) outside a ship, etc. * *n* an engine attached to the outside of a boat.

outbound *adj* outward bound.

outbrave *vt* to excel in bravery; to defy.

outbreak *n* a sudden eruption (of disease, strife, etc).

outbuilding *n* a detached subsidiary building.

outburst *n* a bursting out; a spurt; an explosion of anger, etc.

outcast *n* a person who is rejected by society.—*also adj*.

outcaste *n* one who has lost caste, a pariah. * *vt* to expel from a caste.

outclass *vt* to surpass or excel greatly.

outcome *n* the result, consequence.

outcrop *n* (*geol*) exposure at the Earth's surface of part of a rock formation. * *vi* (**outcropping, outcropped**) to crop out at the surface.

outcry *n* (*pl* **outcries**) protest; uproar.

outdated *n* obsolete, old-fashioned.

outdistance *vt* to get well ahead of.

outdo *vt* (**outdoing, outdid**, *pp* **outdone**) to surpass, to do more than, to excel.

outdoor *adj* existing, taking place, or used in the open air.

outdoors *adv* in or into the open air; out of doors. * *n* the open air, outside world.

outdoorsman *n* (*pl* **outdoorsmen**) a person who works, or spends a lot of time, in the open air.— **outdoorswoman** *nf* (*pl* **outdoorswomen**).

outer *adj* further out or away.

outer ear *n* a cartilage and skin structure (auricle or pinna) that is not actually essential to hearing in humans.

outermost *adj* furthest out; most distant.

outer planets *or* **giant planets** *or* **major planets** *or* **non-terrestrial planets** *n* the planets beyond the asteroid belt: Jupiter, Saturn, Uranus, Neptune, and Pluto.

outer space *n* any region of space beyond the earth's atmosphere.

outface *vt* to stare down or out of countenance; to defy.

outfall *n* the lower end of a watercourse; a point of discharge.

outfield *n* the outer part of a cricket or baseball field.

outfit *n* the equipment used in an activity; clothes worn together, an ensemble; a group of people associated in an activity. * *vt* (**outfitting, outfitted**) to provide with an outfit or equipment.

outfitter *n* a supplier of equipment or clothes.

outflank *vt* to get round the side of (an enemy); to circumvent.

outflow *n* a flowing out; something that flows out.

outfox *vt* to outwit by superior cunning.

outgeneral *vt* to outdo in strategy.

outgo *vt* (**outgoing, outwent**, *pp* **outgone**) to go beyond; to surpass.

outgoing *adj* departing; retiring; sociable, forthcoming. * *n* an outlay; (*pl*) expenditure.

outgrow *vt* (**outgrowing, outgrew**, *pp* **outgrown**) to become too big for; to grow taller than; to grow out of.

outgrowth *n* an offshoot.

outguess *vt* to anticipate correctly another's meaning or intention.

outgun *vt* (**outgunning, outgunned**) to defeat by greater firepower; (*inf*) to surpass.

outhouse *n* a shed, etc, adjoining a main house.

outing *n* a pleasure trip; an excursion.

outlandish *adj* unconventional; strange; fantastic.

outlast *vt* to endure longer than.

outlaw *vt* to declare illegal. * *n* an outlawed person; a habitual or notorious criminal.

outlay *n* a spending (of money); expenditure.

outlet *n* an opening or release; a means of expression; a market for goods or services.

outlier *n* a part of a rock or stratum detached at some distance from the principal mass.

outline *n* a profile; a general indication; a rough sketch or draft.—*also vt*.

outline font *n* (*comput*) a font for printer and screen in which each character is generated from a mathematical formula, producing a smooth outline to a character. *See also* **bitmap** and **truetype**.

outline utility *n* (*comput*) a utility program where the user can outline his or her projects, as if on a scratchpad.

outlive *vt* to live longer than, outlast; to live through; to survive.

outlook *n* mental attitude; view; prospect.

outlying *adj* detached; remote, distant.

outmaneuver, outmanoeuvre *vt* to outwit in tactics.

outmatch *vt* to be more than a match for.

outmoded *adj* old-fashioned.

outmost *adj* outermost.

outnumber *vt* to exceed in number.

out of bounds *adj* not to be entered by (a specified person, group, etc); outside the stated limits or boundaries.— *also adv*.

out-of-date *adj* no longer valid, unfashionable; outmoded.

out-of-pocket *adj* (of expenses) paid for in cash; having lost money.

out-of-the-way *adj* uncommon; secluded.

outpatient *n* a person treated at, but not resident in, a hospital.

outperform *vt* to do better than; to surpass.— **outperformance** *n*.

outplay *vt* to play better than.

outpoint *vt* to accumulate more points than.

outport *n* a part of harbor at some distance from the chief port.

outpost *n* (*mil*) a post or detachment at a distance from a main force.

outpour *vti* to pour out.

outpouring *n* an effusion, an emotional speech.

output *n* the quantity (of goods, etc) produced, esp over a given period; (*comput*) data produced, e.g., screen images, printouts, or information sent to a storage device; (*elect*) the useful voltage, current, or power delivered.—*also vt*.

output device *n* (*comput*) any device that produces a usable form of output from the computer.

output tax *n* the tax that is added by a trader to the price of the goods or services that he or she supplies.

outrage *n* an extremely vicious or violent act; a grave insult or offence; great anger, etc, aroused by this.—*also vt*.

outrageous *adj* flagrant; atrocious; violent; excessive.—**outrageously** *adv*.—**outrageousness** *n*.

outrank *vt* to be of a higher rank than; to be of a higher priority.

outré *adj* outraging decorum; eccentric, unconventional; extravagant.

outreach *vt* to reach further than; to surpass. * *vi* to reach out; to go too far. * *n* the act of reaching out; the extent or length of reaching out; the extent of an organization's activities or influence in the surrounding community, esp a social agency.

outride *vt* (**outriding, outrode**, *pp* **outridden**) to ride faster or farther than; to keep afloat through (a storm).

outrider *n* a mounted escort who goes in advance of a automobile, carriage, etc.

outrigger *n* a projecting spar for a sail, etc; a projection with a float extending from a canoe to prevent capsizing; a canoe of this type; a projecting frame to support the elevator or tail of an aircraft or the rotor of a helicopter.

outright *adj* complete, downright, direct. * *adv* at once; without restrictions.

outrun *vt* (**outrunning, outran**, *pp* **outran**) to run faster than; to exceed, to go beyond; to escape by running.

outsell *vt* (**outselling, outsold**) to sell more than; to be sold in greater quantities than; to excel in salesmanship.

outset *n* the start, beginning.

outshine *vt* (**outshining, outshone**) to outdo in brilliance, ability; to shine longer and brighter than.

outshoot *vti* (**outshooting, outshot**) *vt* to surpass in shooting or shoot further than; to score more points than another player, team, etc. * *vi* to protrude, shoot out. * *n* something that shoots out.

outside *n* the outer part or surface, the exterior. * *adj* outer; outdoor; (*chance, etc*) slight. * *adv* on or to the outside. * *prep* on or to the exterior of; beyond.

outside broker *n* a stockbroker who is not a member of the stock exchange but is an intermediary between a member of the public and a broker who is a member of the stock exchange.

outsider *n* a person or thing not included in a set, group, etc, a non-member; a contestant, esp a horse, not thought to have a chance in a race.

outsize *adj* of a larger than usual size.

outskirts *npl* districts remote from the center, as of a city.

outsmart *vt* to outwit.

outsourcing *n* the buying-in by a company of components, finished products, services, etc, from an external source rather than supplying these internally.

outspan *vt* (**outspanning, outspanned**) (*S Africa*) to unyoke ox teams from a wagon; to encamp. * *n* a halting place.

outspoken *adj* candid in speech, frank, blunt.

outspread *vti* (**outspreading, outspread**) to spread out; to expand. * *adj* stretched out; scattered. * *n* a spreading out.

outstanding *adj* excellent; distinguished, prominent; unpaid; unresolved, still to be done.

outstare *vt* to beat in staring; to discomfort by staring.

outstation *n* a distant post or station.

outstay *vt* to stay longer than or too long.

outstretch *vt* to reach out or stretch out; to stretch or extend further than.

outstrip *vt* (**outstripping, outstripped**) to surpass; to go faster than.

outtake *n* an unreleased section of a music, video, television, etc, recording.

outtalk *vt* to talk down.

outvote *vt* to defeat by a higher number of votes.

outward *adj* directed toward the outside; external; clearly apparent. * *adv* toward the outside.

Outward Bound movement *n* (*Brit*) an educational scheme to promote youth adventure training.

outwardly *adv* externally.

outwards *adv* outward.

outwash fan *n* (*geol*) a fan-shaped deposit of sands and gravel laid down by glacial meltwater at the margin of boulder clay derived from the glacier.

outwear *vt* (**outwearing, outwore,** *pp* **outworn**) to outlast; to wear out.

outweigh *vt* to count for more than, to exceed in value, weight, or importance.

outwent *see* outgo.

outwit *vt* (**outwitting, outwitted**) to get the better of, defeat, by wit or cunning.

outwork *n* a defense constructed beyond the main body of a fort, etc; work that is carried out on the worker's own premises rather than those of the company for whom he or she is working.

ouzel *n* a kind of small bird; a blackbird.—*also* **ousel**.

ouzo *n* a Greek aniseed-flavored spirit.

o.v. *abbr* = oil of vitriol; over voltage.

ova *see* ovum.

OVAC *abbr* = Overseas Visual Aids Centre.

OVAE *abbr* = Office of Vocational and Adult Education.

oval *adj* egg-shaped; elliptical. * *n* anything oval.

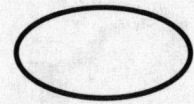

ovarian cyst *n* a sac filled with fluid that develops in the ovary.

ovariotomy *n* (*pl* **ovariotomies**) the surgical operation of removing an ovary or an ovarian tumor.

ovaritis *n* inflammation of the ovary.

ovary *n* (*pl* **ovaries**) one of the two female reproductive organs producing eggs (ova) and hormones (mainly oestrogen and progesterone).—**ovarian** *adj*.

ovate *adj* (*bot*) oval, egg-shaped.

ovation *n* enthusiastic applause or public welcome.

ovc *abbr* = other valuable consideration.

OVC *abbr* = Office for Victims of Crime.

oven *n* an enclosed, heated compartment for baking or drying; a stove.

ovenbird *n* a kind of bird with a dome-shaped nest; a fowl for cooking.

ovenproof *adj* (*kitchen ware*) designed to withstand the heat of an oven.

oven-ready *adj* (*food*) prepared for immediate cooking in the oven.

ovenware *n* attractive heat-resistant dishes in which food can be cooked and served.

over *prep* higher than; on top of; across; to the other side of; above; more than; concerning. * *adv* above; across; in every part; completed; from beginning to end; up and down; in addition; too. * *adj* upper; excessive; surplus; finished; remaining. * *n* (*cricket*) the number of balls bowled before changing ends.

over- *prefix* in excess, too much; above.

overabundant *adj* in excessive quantity or supply.— **overabound** *vi*.—**overabundance** *n*.

overachieve *vi* to do better than expected, esp educationally. * *vt* to exceed in achieving (one's stated goals).—**overachievement** *n*.—**overachiever** *n*.

overact *vti* to act in an exaggerated manner, to overdo a part.

overactive *adj* abnormally or excessively active.—**overactivity** *n*.

overage *adj* over a certain age. * *n* a surplus.

overall *adj* including everything. * *adv* as a whole; generally. * *n* a loose protective garment; (*pl*) a one-piece protective garment covering body and legs.

overarch *vti* to form an arch (over).

overarm *adj, adv* (*sport*) bowled, thrown, performed, etc, with the arm raised above the shoulder.

overawe *vt* to restrain by awe, daunt.

overbalance *vti* to fall over; to upset; to outweigh. * *n* a surplus.

overbear *vt* (**overbearing, overbore,** *pp* **overborne**) to dominate, to repress, to bear down.

overbearing *adj* domineering; overriding.—**overbearingly** *adv*.

overbite *n* the projection of the teeth of the upper jaw over those in the lower with the mouth closed.

overblown *adj* excessive, pretentious.

overboard *adv* over the side of a ship, etc; (*inf*) to extremes of enthusiasm.

overbook *vti* to sell tickets (for) in excess of the available seats or space.

overburden *vt* to load too heavily. * *n* (*geol*) within a sequence of sediment, the strata that lie over and therefore compress those beneath; superficial material that overlies solid rock.

overcall *vti* (*bridge*) to bid more on (a hand) than it is worth; to take a bid away from (a partner).

overcame *see* overcome.

overcapacity *n* (of a firm or industry) more capacity for production than is called for by market demand.

overcapitalize *vt* to float (a company) with too great a capital.—**overcapitalization** *n*.

overcast *adj* clouded over.

overcharge *vt* (*battery*) to overload; to fill to excess; to demand too high a price (from). * *n* an excessive or exorbitant charge or load.

overcloud *vti* to cover or become covered with clouds; to make or become dark or depressed.

overcoat *n* a warm, heavy topcoat.

overcome *vti* (**overcoming, overcame,** *pp* **overcome**) to get the better of, to prevail; to render helpless or powerless, as by tears, laughter, emotion, etc; to be victorious; to surmount obstacles, etc.

overcompensation *n* (*psychoanal*) an excess of compensation, often resulting in an overbearing manner.—**overcompensatory** *adj*.

overcrop *vt* (**overcropping, overcropped**) to exhaust (land) by excessive cultivation.

overcrowd *vti* to make or become too crowded.

overdevelop *vt* to develop excessively; (*bodybuilding*) to develop the muscles disproportionately; (*photography*) to immerse in developing solution for too long.—**overdevelopment** *n*.

overdo *vt* (**overdoing, overdid,** *pp* **overdone**) to do to excess; to overact; to cook (food) too much.—**overdone** *adj*.

overdose *n* an excessive dose.—*also vti*.

overdraft *n* (*bank*) a form of credit facility that allows the holder of a bank checking account to let the account go into debit up to an agreed limit, interest being charged on the daily debit balance; an overdrawing, an amount overdrawn.

overdraw *vti* (**overdrawing, overdrew,** *pp* **overdrawn**) to draw in excess of a credit balance; to exaggerate in describing; to make an overdraft.

overdress *vti* to dress too warmly, too showily, or too formally.

overdrive *n* a high gear in a motor vehicle to reduce wear for traveling at high speed. * *vt* (**overdriving, overdrove,** *pp* **overdriven**) to drive too hard, overtax.

overdub *vt* (**overdubbing, overdubbed**) to add (new sounds) to an existing recording. * *n* the production of combined sounds in one recording using this method.

overdue *adj* past the time for payment, return, performance, etc; in arrears; delayed.

overeat *vi* (**overeating, overate,** *pp* **overeaten**) to eat too much.

overestimate *vt* to set too high an estimate on or for. * *n* an excessive estimate.—**overestimation** *n*.

overexpose *vt* (*photog*) to expose (a film) to light for too long.—**overexposure** *n*.

overflow *vti* (**overflowing, overflowed,** *pp* **overflown**) to flow over, flood; to exceed the bounds (of); to abound (with emotion, etc). * *n* that which overflows; surplus, excess; an outlet for surplus water, etc.

overgrow *vti* (**overgrowing, overgrew,** *pp* **overgrown**) to cover with growth; to grow too big or fast (for); to outgrow.—**overgrowth** *n*.

overgrown *adj* grown beyond the normal size; rank; ungainly.

overhand *adj, adv* (*sport*) bowled, thrown, performed, etc, with the hand above the shoulder.

overhang *n* (*archit*) a part of a building which projects outwards over a lower part.

overhang *vti* (**overhanging, overhung**) to hang or project over. * *n* a projecting part.

overhaul *vt* to examine for, or make, repairs; to overtake.—*also n*.

overhead *adj, adv* above the head; in the sky. * *n* (often *pl*) the general, continuing costs of a business, as of rent, light, etc; a cost that is not directly related to the materials or labor directly concerned with a product.—*also* **overhead cost**.

overhead-cost variance *n* the difference between the actual overhead cost of a product and that which was budgeted for by the company.

overhear *vt* (**overhearing, overheard**) to hear without the knowledge of the speaker.

overheat *vti* to make or become excessively hot; to stimulate unduly.

overjoyed *adj* highly delighted.

overkill *n* the capability to employ more weapons, etc, than are necessary to destroy an enemy; excess capacity for a task.

overland *adj, adv* by, on, or across land.

overlap *vt* (**overlapping, overlapped**) to extend over (a thing or each other) so as to coincide in part.—*also n*.

overlay *vt* (**overlaying, overlaid**) to cover with a coating, to spread over. * *n* a coating.

overleaf *adv* on the other side of the leaf of a book.

overlie *vt* (**overlying, overlay,** *pp* **overlain**) to lie on top of; to stifle thus.

overload *vt* to put too great a burden on; (*elect*) to charge with too much current.

O

overlong *adj, adv* too long.

overlook *vt* to fail to notice; to look at from above; to excuse.

overlord *n* a lord ranking above other lords; an absolute or supreme ruler.

overly *adv* too; excessively.

overman *vt* (**overmanning, overmanned**) to supply with too many workers.

overmaster *vt* to dominate wholly, to overpower.

overmuch *adj, adv* too much.

overnice *adj* too particular.

overnight *adv* for the night; in the course of the night; suddenly. * *adj* done in the night; lasting the night.

overnight bag *n* a small bag for clothing, toiletries, etc, for an overnight trip.

overpass *n* a road crossing another road, path, etc, at a higher level; the upper level of such a crossing. * *vt* (**overpassing, overpassed,** *pp* **overpast**) to pass beyond, to overstep; to surpass.

overplay *vt* to place too much emphasis on; to behave in an exaggerated or affected manner.

overplus *n* a surplus, an excess.

overpopulated *adj* having an excessive population damaging to the environment.— **overpopulation** *n*.

overpower *vt* to overcome by superior force, to subdue; to overwhelm.

overpowering *adj* overwhelming; compelling; unbearable.

overprint *vt* to print additional matter on a printed surface. * *n* the added printed matter.

overproduction *n* supply in excess of the demand.

overproof *adj* containing more alcohol than proof spirit.

overprotect *vt* to be too protective of.— **overprotective** *adj*.

overqualified *adj* having more qualifications or experience than required for a particular job.

overrate *vt* to value or assess too highly.

overreach *vt* to extend beyond; to circumvent, outwit; to fail by trying too much or being too subtle.

overreact *vi* to show an excessive reaction to something.

override *vt* (**overriding, overrode,** *pp* **overridden**) to ride over; to nullify; to prevail.

overripe *adj* (of fruit, etc) past its best and beginning to decay; decadent.

overrule *vt* to set aside by higher authority; to prevail over.

overrun *vt* (**overrunning, overran,** *pp* **overrun**) to attack and defeat; to swarm over; to exceed (a time limit, etc).

overseas *adj, adv* across or beyond the sea; abroad.

Overseas Development Administration *n* (*Brit*) (*formerly*) the government department that dealt with the administration of financial and technical aid to overseas countries.

oversee *vt* (**overseeing, oversaw,** *pp* **overseen**) to supervise; to superintend. * *n* **overseer** *n*.

oversell *vt* (**overselling, oversold**) to sell more than can be delivered, esp stocks.

oversensitive *adj* overly sensitive; easily offended.

overset *vti* (**oversetting, overset**) to upset, to disturb; to overthrow.

oversew *vt* (**oversewing, oversewed,** *pp* **oversewn**) to stitch over again to reinforce; to stitch over an edge to prevent fraying.

overshadow *vt* to throw a shadow over; to appear more prominent or important than.

overshoe *n* a galosh.

overshoot *vt* (**overshooting, overshot**) to shoot or send beyond (a target, etc); (of aircraft) to fly or taxi beyond the end of a runway when landing or taking off.—*also n*.

oversight *n* a careless mistake or omission; supervision.

oversimplify *vt* (**oversimplifying, oversimplified**) to distort the truth (of a problem, situation, etc) by stating it in too simple terms.— **oversimplification** *n*.

oversize, oversized *adj* of larger than average size.

overslaugh *n* (*mil*) the passing over of an ordinary duty because of a special one.

oversleep *vi* (**oversleeping, overslept**) to sleep beyond the intended time.

overspend *vt* (**overspending, overspent**) to spend more than necessary; to wear out, tire. * *vi* to spend more than one can afford.

overstate *vt* to state too strongly, to exaggerate.—**overstatement** *n*.

overstay *vt* to remain longer than or beyond the limits of.

overstep *vt* (**overstepping, overstepped**) to exceed; to step beyond (a limit).

overstock *vt* to lay in too large a stock of or for, to glut.—*also n*.

overstrung *adj* too highly strung; too sensitive.

oversubscribe *vt* to apply for more shares in (an issue) than can be allotted.

oversubscription *n* a new share issue resulting in there being more applications for the shares than there are shares available.

oversupply *vt* (**oversupplying, oversupplied**) to supply excessively. * *n* an excessive supply.

overt *adj* openly done, unconcealed; (*law*) done with evident intent, deliberate.— **overtly** *adv*.

overt. *abbr* (*mus*) = overture.

overtake *vt* (**overtaking, overtook,** *pp* **overtaken**) to catch up with and pass; to come upon suddenly.

overtax *vt* to make too great demands on; to tax too heavily.

over-the-counter *adj* (of securities) not traded through or listed on the stock exchange; (of drugs) available legally without prescription.

overthrow *vt* (**overthrowing, overthrew,** *pp* **overthrown**) to throw over, overturn; to bring down (a government, etc) by force.—*also n*.

overtime *adv* beyond regular working hours. * *n* extra time worked; payment for this.

overtone *n* an additional subtle meaning; an implicit quality; (*mus*) a harmonic; the color of light reflected (as by a paint).

overtook *see* **overtake**.

overtop *vt* (**overtopping, overtopped**) to be higher than, to tower above.

overtrading *n* a trading situation in which a company expands its production and sales beyond the resources of its working capital and which can lead to liquidity problems.

overtrain *vti* to train too hard.

overtrump *vt* to play a higher trump than (the card that has trumped another).

overture *n* an initiating of negotiations; a formal offer, proposal; (*mus*) a piece of music that introduces an opera, oratorio, ballet, or other major work. A concert overture is often an independent piece, written for performance in a concert hall.

overturn *vti* to upset, turn over; to overthrow.

overtype mode *see* **insert mode**.

overview *n* a general survey.

overweening *adj* arrogant, presumptuous, conceited.

overweight *adj* weighing more than the proper amount. * *n* excess weight.

overwhelm *vt* to overcome totally; to submerge; to crush; to overpower with emotion.

overwhelming *adj* irresistible; uncontrollable; vast; vastly superior; extreme.

overwork *vti* to work or use too hard or too long.

overwrite *vt* (**overwriting, overwrote, overwritten**) to write in an overly elaborate style; to write too much; (*comput*) to save a file onto a disk under a file name that already exists, deleting the original file.

overwrought *adj* over-excited; too elaborate.

ovi- *prefix* egg.

Ovid *n* [**Publius Ovidius Naso**] (43 BC–AD *c*.17) Roman poet. His best-known work is the *Metamorphoses*, a long poem that relates mythological tales involving transformations.

oviduct *n* the tube which conducts the ovum from the ovary to the uterus.

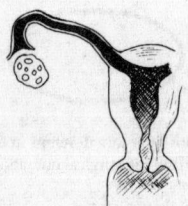

oviferous *adj* egg-carrying.

oviform *adj* egg-shaped.

ovine *adj* pertaining to sheep.

oviparous *adj* producing young by eggs.—**oviparity** *n*.

oviposit *vi* to lay or deposit eggs.—**oviposition** *n*.

ovipositor *n* the organ in certain insects by which its eggs are deposited.

ovisac *n* the cavity in the ovary which contains the ovum.

ovno *abbr* = or very near offer.

ovoid *adj* egg-shaped.

ovolo *n* (*pl* **ovoli**) (*archit*) a round or convex egg-shaped molding.

ovolo molding *n* (*archit*) a rounded convex molding, usu having a cross section in the form of a quarter of a circle.

ovotestis *see* **hermaphrodite**.

ovoviviparous *adj* producing eggs containing the young in a living state, as certain animals; relating to the development of offspring within the body of the female where there is no development of a placenta.—**ovoviviparity** *n*.

ovulate *vi* to discharge or produce eggs from an ovary.

ovulation *n* the release of an egg from an ovary which then moves down the Fallopian tube to the uterus.

ovule *n* the germ borne by the placenta of a plant which develops into a seed after fertilization.—**ovular** *adj*.

ovum (*pl* **ova**) *n* the mature, unfertilized female egg cell, which is roughly spherical with an outer membrane and a single nucleus.

OWA *abbr* = One World Action.

Owain *n* (*fl*. AD 593) Welsh warrior, was the son of Urien. (*Welsh Celtic myth*) said to have been the son of Urien and Arthur's sister, Morgan Le Fay. Legend has it that he defeated the Black Knight

Owain Gwynedd *n* (1100–1170) king of Gwynedd, Britain (1137–1170). He united the kings in the south to resist Henry II's advances into Wales in 1165.

OWBO *abbr* = Office of Women's Business Ownership.

OWC *abbr* = Order of Woodcraft Chivalry.

OWCP *abbr* = Office of Workers' Compensation Programs.

owe *vti* to be in debt; to be obliged to pay; to feel the need to give, do, etc, as because of gratitude.

Owen *n* (the Bald) (*d. c*.1018) king of Strathclyde, Britain. Probably the last king of Strathclyde.

Owen *n* 1. **David** [**Anthony Llewellyn**] (1938–) English politician; founder of the Social Democratic Party; UN peace negotiator in the Bosnian conflict of the 1990s. 2. **Robert** (1771–1858) Welsh social reformer, educationist, and industrialist. He transformed the cotton mills in New Lanark, Scotland, into a model industrial community. He founded several cooperatives in Britain and America.

Owens *n* Jesse [James Cleveland Owens] (1913–80) African-American athlete who won four gold medals in the 1936 Berlin Olympics, one of the finest athletes of his generation.

Oxford *n* an English city in United Kingdom of Great Britain and Northern Ireland (UK).

owing *adj* due, to be paid; owed; (*with* **to**) because of, on account of.

owl *n* a nocturnal bird of prey with a large head and large eyes; a person of nocturnal habits, solemn appearance, etc.—**owlish** *adj*.

owlet *n* a young owl.

own *vti* to possess; to acknowledge, admit; to confess to. * *adj* belonging to oneself or itself, often used reflexively (*my own, their own*).

own-brand product *n* a product that is sold under a retailer's or distributor's own name or trademark.

owner *n* one who owns, a possessor, a proprietor.—**ownership** *n*.

own shares purchase *n* the buying by a company of its own shares.

OWTC *abbr* (*Brit*) = Orkney Water Test Centre.

ox *n* (*pl* **oxen**) a cud-chewing mammal of the cattle family; a castrated bull.

oxalate *n* a salt of oxalic acid.

oxalic acid *n* a poisonous acid obtained from oxalis.

oxalis *n* wood sorrel.

oxbow *n* a horseshoe loop in a stream; the U-shaped collar of a yoke.

oxbow lake *n* the development of meanders into large loops cut off from original river. Eventually the "neck" between a looped meander is cut and the river straightens its course, leaving a cut-off loop or oxbow lake.

Oxbridge *n, adj* (*Brit*) (of) the universities of Oxford and Cambridge.

oxen *see* **ox**.

oxeye *n* a kind of flower; a large eye.

Oxfam *abbr* (*Brit*) = Oxford Committee for Famine Relief.

oxford *n* a type of laced shoe with a low heel; a soft lightweight cotton or synthetic fabric used for men's shirts.

Oxford Group *n* (*Brit*) a former name of Moral Rearmament.

Oxford movement *n* (*Brit*) an Anglican high-church movement begun in Oxford in 1833.

oxidation *n* (*chem*) any chemical reaction that is characterized by the gain of oxygen or the loss of electrons from the reactant; the operation of converting into an oxide.

oxide *n* (*chem*) a compound formed by the combination of oxygen with another element, with the exception of the inert gases.

oxidize *vti* to cause to undergo a chemical reaction with oxygen; to rust.—**oxidization** *n*.

oxidizing agent *n* (*chem*) any substance that will gain electrons during a chemical reaction.

oxlip *n* a variety of primula; a hybrid between primrose and cowslip.

Oxon. *abbr* (*Brit*) (*Latin*) = *Oxonia*, "Oxford," as used in the county abbreviation; *Oxoniensis* , "of Oxford," used with bishop's signature and in university degrees.

Oxonian (*Brit*) *adj* pertaining to Oxford. * *n* a graduate or member of Oxford University.

oxtail *n* the tail of an ox, esp skinned and used for stews, soups, etc.

oxy- *prefix* sharp; oxygen.

oxyacetylene *n* a mixture of oxygen with acetylene used in a blowtorch to cut or weld metal.—*also adj*.

oxygen *n* (*chem*) a colorless, odorless, tasteless, highly reactive gas, which occurs as the molecule made up of two atoms, essential for the respiration of most life forms. It is the most abundant of all the elements, forming 20 per cent by volume of the atmosphere, about 90 per cent by weight of water, and 50 per cent by weight of rocks in the Earth's crust.—**oxygenic, oxygenous** *adj*.

oxygenate *vt* to combine or supply with oxygen.—**oxygenation** *n*.

oxygenator *n* a machine for oxygenating blood outside the body. During heart surgery the patient's blood is pumped through the machine.

oxygenize *vt* to oxygenate.—**oxygenizer** *n*.

oxygen mask *n* a face mask used for dispensing oxygen for breathing.

oxygen tent *n* a canopy over a hospital bed, etc, within which a supply of oxygen is maintained.

oxyhemoglobin, oxyhaemoglobin *n* a loose compound of oxygen and hemoglobin.

oxyhydrogen *n* a mixture of oxygen with acetylene and hydrogen, as in a blowtorch, by which an intense heat is produced by the combination of gases.

oxymoron *n* (*pl* **oxymora**) a figure of speech combining contradictory words, e.g., "faith unfaithful kept him falsely true."

oxytocin *n* a hormone from the pituitary gland that causes the uterus to contract during labor, and prompts lactation because of contraction of muscle fibers in the milk ducts of the breasts.

oxytone *adj* (*linguistics*) having an acute sound; having the last syllable accented. * *n* an acute sound; a word with the acute accent on the last syllable.

OYC *abbr* (*Brit*) = Ocean Youth Club.

oyez, oyes *interj* the introductory cry of an official or public crier demanding attention or silence.

oyster *n* an edible marine bivalve shellfish.

oyster bed, oyster bank *n* an area of the seabed where oysters grow naturally or are bred artificially.

oystercatcher *n* a wading sea bird.

Oz *n* (*Austral sl*) Australia.

Oz *n* Amos (1939–) Israeli novelist, essayist, and short-story writer, regarded as one of the most important Israeli writers, whose novels include *My Michael*, *To Know a Woman*, and *The Third Condition*.

oz *abbr* = ounce(s).

oz. av. *abbr* = avoirdupois ounce.

Ozenfant *n* Amédée (1886–1966) French painter who founded the journal *L'Elan* with Pablo **Picasso** and Guillaume Apollinaire.

Ozma Project *n* (*astron*) an (unsuccessful) attempt to detect artificial radio signals from two nearby stars, Tau Ceti and Epsilon Eridani, where there is some reason to suppose a planetary system exists.

ozokerite, ozocerite *n* a waxy fossil resin used for candles.

ozone *n* (*chem*) a condensed form of oxygen that exists not with the usual two atoms of oxygen, but with three atoms per molecule; (*inf*) bracing seaside air.—**ozonic, ozonous** *adj*.

ozone *n* a denser form of oxygen that exists as three atoms per molecule (O_3). Ozone is a more reactive gas than the more common diatomic molecule (O_2), and can react with some hydrocarbons in the presence of sunlight to produce toxic substances that are irritants to the eyes, skin and lungs. Minute quantities of O_3 are found in sea water. It forms the Earth's ozone layer, 15 to 30 kilometers (9 to 18 miles) above the Earth's surface.

ozone *n* a molecule consisting of three oxygen atoms, O_3, produced when ordinary oxygen molecules, O_2, are subjected to ultraviolet radiation or electrical strains.

ozone layer *n* a layer of ozone in the stratosphere that absorbs ultraviolet rays from the sun but has harmful effects in excess.—*also* **ozonosphere.**

ozonize *vt* to charge with ozone.—**ozonization** *n*.—**ozonizer** *n*.

ozs. *abbr* = ounces.

oz T *abbr* = troy ounce.

O

P

P *symbol* (*chem*) phosphorus (element).

p *abbr* = (*organ*) pedal; penny, pence.

p or **p.** *abbr* = page; (*mus*) (*Italian*) *piano*, "softly."

p. *abbr* = paragraph; part; participle; (*Latin*) *partim*, "in part"; passive; past; pastor; (*Latin*) *pater*, "father"; (*chess*) pawn; penny; (*Latin*) *per*, "by"; (*fuse*) percussion; (*French*) *père*, "father"; (*Latin*) *perpetuus*, "uninterrupted"; peseta; peso; pico; (*coin*) (*India*) pie; pint; (*Latin*) *pius*, "holy"; pole; (*Latin*) *pondere*, "by weight"; pontifex; population; (*Latin*) *populus*, "people"; positive; (*Latin*) *post*, "after"; power; president; priest; (*Latin*) *primus*, "first"; prince; (*Latin*) *pro*, "for," "in favor of"; (*court*) probate; proconsul; professional; (*theat*) prompter; proton; purl.

p- *abbr* = para-.

P *abbr* = Paris; parking; (*chess*) pawn; (*elec*) power; (*logic*) predicate; President; (*phys*) pressure; (*Bible*) Priestly Code, Law of Holiness.

pa *n* (*inf*) father, papa.

p.a. *abbr* = participial adjective; (*Latin*) per annum, "yearly"; (*Latin*) pro anno, "for the year."

p/a or **P/A** *abbr* (*bookkeeping*) = private account.

P/A or **p.a.** *abbr* (*marine ins*) = particular average.

Pa *symbol* (*chem*) protactinium (element).

Pa *abbr* = (*unit of pressure*) pascal.

Pa. *abbr* = Pennsylvania.

PA *abbr* = Panama; Pennsylvania; personal assistant; Press Agent; Press Association; public address system.

PA or **P/A** *abbr* = power of attorney.

pa'anga *n* the standard monetary unit of Tonga, made up of 100 seniti.

PABA *abbr* = para-aminobenzoic acid, an ingredient in sunscreen ointment.

PABLA *abbr* = problem analysis by logical approach.

Pabst *n* Daniel (1826–1910) German furniture designer who produced Renaissance revival style pieces for all the major stores in America.

PABX *abbr* = private automatic branch exchange.

Pac. or **Pacif.** *abbr* = Pacific.

paca *n* a burrowing rodent found in Central and South America.

PACC *abbr* = Pesticides and Agricultural Chemicals Committee.

pace[1] *n* a single step; the measure of a single stride; speed of movement. * *vti* to measure by paces; to walk up and down; to determine the pace in a race; to walk with regular steps.—**pacer** *n*.

pace[2] *prep* with the permission of; with due respect to.

PACE *abbr* = performance and cost evaluation; Protestant and Catholic Encounter.

pacemaker *n* a person who sets the pace in a race; the part of the heart that regulates the beat, the sinoatrial node; an electronic device inserted in the heart, used to regulate heartbeat.

pacer *n* a horse trained to pace; a pacemaker.

pacha *see* **pasha**.

Pacheco *n* Francisco (1564–1654) Spanish painter, poet, and writer. His most important contribution to Spanish art history is his book, *The Art of Painting* (1649), and his finest work is *The Immaculate Conception* (c.1621).

Pachelbel *n* 1. **Johann** (1653–1706) German organist and composer who wrote motets, concertos and cantatas, and is now mainly known for his Canon and Gigue in D major. 2. **Wilhelm Hieronymus** (1685–c.1764), son of the above, an organist and composer, who succeeded his father as organist at the Nuremberg Sebalduskirche and who composed preludes and fugues, as well as variations for the organ or the harpsichord.

Pacher *n* Michael (c.1645–98) Austrian painter and sculptor whose masterpiece is the *Wolfgang Altarpiece* (1481). Another notable work is *The Four Doctors of the Church* (c.1483).

pachinko *n* a Japanese variation on pinball.

pachisi *n* an Indian game, similar to backgammon.

pachouli *see* **patchouli**.

pachyderm *n* any large thick-skinned mammal, esp an elephant.—**pachydermatous** *adj*.

pachymeninx *see* **meninges**.

pacific *adj* promoting peace; mild, conciliatory.—**pacifically** *adv*.

Pacific Standard Time *n* the 8th time zone west of Greenwich that includes the west coast of the US.

Pacific-type coast *see* **concordant coast**.

pacifier *n* a person or thing that pacifies; a small rubber or plastic nipple for a baby to suck or chew on.

pacifism *n* opposition to the use of force under any circumstances, specifically the refusal to participate in war.—**pacifist** *n*.

pacify *vt* (**pacifying, pacified**) to soothe; to calm; to restore peace to.—**pacification** *n*.

pack *n* a load or bundle (esp one carried on the back); a set of playing cards; a group or mass; a number of wild animals living together; an organized troop (as of Cub Scouts); a compact mass (as of snow); a small package used as a container for goods for sale. * *vt* to put together in a bundle or pack; (*suitcase*) to fill; to crowd; to press tightly so as to prevent leakage; to carry in a pack; to send (off); (*sl: gun, etc*) to carry; (*sl: punch*) to deliver with force; (*comput*) to compress a file. * *vi* (*snow, ice*) to form into a hard mass; to assemble one's belongings in suitcases or boxes. * *adj* used for carrying packs, loads, etc.—**packer** *n*.

package *n* a parcel, a wrapped bundle; several items, arrangements, etc offered as a unit. * *vt* to make a parcel of; to group together several items, etc.—**packager** *n*.

package deal *n* a proposal involving separate items offered as a complete unit.

packaged software *n* (*comput*) software that is mass-produced, marketed, and sold.—*also* **off the shelf software**.

package store *n* a place where alcohol is sold for consumption off the premises.—*also* **liquor store**.

package tour *n* a vacation or tour with all the fares, accommodation, food, etc, arranged for an all-inclusive price.

packaging *n* the wrapping round a product offered for sale; the presentation of a product.

pack animal *n* an animal, such as a mule or camel, used for carrying loads.

packed out *adj* (*inf*) crowded.

packet *n* a small box or package; (*sl*) a considerable sum; a vessel carrying mail, etc, between one port and another.

packet switching *n* (*comput*) a technology used in networking in which a message is broken up into small segments or packets prior to transmission to addresses in a wide area network.—*also* **circuit switching**.

packhorse *n* a horse used for carrying goods.

pack ice *n* sea ice formed into a mass by the crushing together of floes, etc.

packing *n* material for protecting packed goods or for making airtight or watertight; the act of filling a suitcase, box, etc.

packing house *n* a meat processing plant where livestock is slaughtered, butchered, and packaged for consumption.

packsack *n* a canvas carrying bag with shoulder straps used when hiking.

PACSA *abbr* = People Against Child Sex Abuse.

packsaddle *n* a saddle for carrying goods.

pact *n* an agreement or treaty.

pad[1] *n* the dull sound of a footstep. * *vi* (**padding, padded**) to walk, esp with a soft step.

pad[2] *n* a piece of a soft material or stuffing; several sheets of paper glued together at one edge; the cushioned thickening of an animal's sole; a piece of folded absorbent material used as a surgical dressing; a flat concrete surface; (*sl*) one's own home or room. * *vt* (**padding, padded**) to stuff with soft material; to fill with irrelevant information.

PAD *abbr* = packet assembler/disassembler; payable after death.

padding *n* stuffing; anything unimportant or false added to achieve length or amount.

paddle[1] *vi* to wade about or play in shallow water.

paddle[2] *n* a short oar with a wide blade at one or both ends; a implement shaped like this, used to hit, beat, or stir. * *vti* (*canoe, etc*) to propel by a paddle; to beat as with a paddle; to spank.—**paddler** *n*.

paddle boat *n* a vessel propelled by a paddle wheel.

paddle wheel *n* a wheel with boards round the circumference for propelling a vessel.

paddock *n* an enclosed field in which horses are exercised.

paddy[1] *n* (*pl* **paddies**) threshed unmilled rice; a rice field.

paddy[2] *n* (*pl* **paddies**) (*sl*) rage, a fit of temper.

Paddy *n* (*pl* **Paddies**) (*derog*) a nickname for an Irishman.

paddy wagon *n* (*sl*) a police patrol truck for carrying prisoners.

pademelon, paddymelon *n* (*Austral*) a small wallaby.

Paderewski *n* Ignace Jan (1860–1941) Polish pianist, composer, and statesman. Widely regarded as the greatest pianist of his day, he served as prime minister for ten months in 1919. He became president of the Polish government in exile in 1940.

PADI *abbr* = Professional Association of Diving Instructors.

padlock *n* a detachable lock used to fasten doors etc. * *vt* to secure with a padlock.

padre *n* a military chaplain.

padrone *n* an innkeeper, esp in Italy.

PADT *abbr* = Public Art Development Trust.

paduasoy *n* a silk fabric.

p. ae. *abbr* (*Latin*) = *partes aequales*, "equal parts."

paean *n* a song of triumph or thanks; praise.—*also* **pean**.

Paean *n* (*Greek myth*) a god of healing, later identified with Apollo.

paeon *n* a four-syllabled metrical foot, comprising, in any order, three short and one long syllable.

PAF *abbr* = Public Art Forum.

pagan *n* a heathen; a person who has no religion.* *adj* irreligious; heathen, non-Christian.—**paganism** *n*.—**paganist** *adj*, *n*.

Paganini *n* Niccolò (1782–1840) Italian violinist and composer, who delighted in composing complicated and difficult pieces for himself. He wrote five violin concertos and several pieces for the guitar.

paganize *vt* to make pagan. * *vi* to become pagan.

Pagano *n* Giuseppe (1896–1945) Italian architect and Fascist leader who in World War II reacted and joined the resistance movement.

PAGB *abbr* (*Brit*) = Poultry and Egg Producers' Association of Great Britain.

page[1] *n* a boy attendant at a formal function (as a wedding); a uniformed boy employed to run errands. * *vt* to summon by messenger, loudspeaker, etc.

page[2] *n* a sheet of paper in a book, newspaper etc. * *vt* (*a book*) to number the pages of (—*also* **paginate**).

Page *n* James (*fl.* 1840) one of the earliest influential designers and design educators.

pageant *n* a spectacular procession or parade; representation in costume of historical events; a mere show.

pageantry *n* (*pl* **pageantries**) grand or formal display; pomp.

pageboy *n* a page; a medium-length hairstyle with the ends of the hair turned under.

page break *n* (*comput*) a mark in a document that indicates the end of one page and the start of the next.

page description language, PDL *n* (*comput*) a programing language that tells a printer how to print out a page of text or graphics.

page feed *see* **feed**.

page layout program *n* (*comput*) an application that allows the user to mix text and graphics in a document of virtually any page size and almost unlimited extent.

page preview *n* (*comput*) a feature of many programs that shows the user the way a full page will appear in print.

pager *n* a device carried on a person so that he or she can be summoned.—*also* **bleeper**.

pages per minute, ppm *n* (*comput*) a measurement of the number of pages that a printer can output per minute.

Paget's disease of bone *n* a chronic bone disease, particularly of the long bones (e.g. the femur), skull, and spine, that results in them becoming thickened and soft, causing them to bend.—*also* **osteitis deformans.**

paginal *adj* consisting of pages; page for page.

paginate *see* **page**[2].

pagination *n* the act of numbering the pages of a book; the arrangement and number of pages; (*comput*) the process of dividing a document into pages and numbering the pages ready for printing.

pagoda *n* an oriental temple in the form of a tower.

Pago Pago *n* capital city of American Samoa.

Pahlavi *n* the Persian dialect in which Zoroastrian scriptures were written.

Pahlavi *n* Mohammed Reza (1919–80) shah of Iran, who came to power in 1941 and established a dictatorship which was undermined by religious fundamentalists led by Khomeini. He fled from Iran in 1979.

Pahlmann *n* William (1900–88) American interior designer who was noted for his colorful rooms at Lord and Taylor's store on Fifth Avenue, New York.

PAHO *abbr* = Pan American Health Organization.

paid *see* **pay**.

pail *n* a bucket.

paillasse *n* a straw mattress.—*also* **palliasse**.

pain *n* physical or mental suffering; hurting; (*pl*) trouble, exertion. * *vt* to cause distress to.

PAIN *abbr* = Parents Against Injustice; Prisoners Advice and Information Network.

Paine *n* 1. James (*b.* 1717) English architect, whose notable works include Wardour Castle. 2. Thomas (1737–1809) English-born American political theorist and pamphleteer. His pamphlet *Common Sense* (1776) was recognized by Washington as a significant contribution to the Revolution. He also wrote *The Rights of Man* and *The Age of Reason*.

pained *adj* hurt, offended.

painful *adj* giving pain, distressing.—**painfully** *adv*.—**painfulness** *n*.

painkiller *n* a drug that relieves pain.

painless *adj* without pain.—**painlessly** *adv*.

painstaking *adj* very careful, laborious.—**painstakingly** *adv*.

paint *vt* (*a picture*) to make using oil pigments, etc; to depict with paints; to cover or decorate with paint; to describe. * *vi* to make a picture. * *n* a coloring pigment; a dried coat of paint.

paint. *abbr* = painting.

paintbrush *n* a brush used for painting.

painter[1] *n* a person who paints, esp an artist.

painter[2] *n* a bow rope for tying up a boat.

painting *n* the act or art of applying paint; a painted picture.

paint program *n* (*comput*) an application that allows the user to create pictures or drawings on the computer by selecting the individual pixels that make up the screen display.

pair *n* a set of two things that are equal, suited, or used together; any two persons or animals regarded as a unit. * *vti* to form a pair (of); to mate.

pair bond *n* (*people*) a monogamous relationship; (*animals, birds*) a long-term relationship between male and female during breeding.—**pair bonding** *n*.

pair production *n* the simultaneous conversion, within an atomic nucleus, of a gamma-ray high-energy photon into an electron and positron.

paisa *n* a monetary unit of India, Nepal, and Pakistan, equal to one-hundredth of a rupee; a monetary unit of Bangladesh, equal to one hundredth of a taka.

paisley *n* an intricate pattern of curved shapes; a soft woolen fabric with this design; a shawl made of this material. * *adj* of this pattern or material.

Paisley *n* Ian [Richard Kyle] (1926–) Northern Ireland Protestant clergyman and Unionist politician, a strident opponent of Irish nationalism and Roman Catholicism.

pajamas *npl* a loosely fitting sleeping suit of jacket and pants.—*also* **pyjamas**.

pakeha *n* (*New Zealand*) a non-Maori, esp a white person.

Pakistan *n* a Federal Islamic Republic lying just north of the Tropic of Cancer with the Arabian Sea as its southern border.

Pakistan Rupee *n* currency of the Islamic Republic of Pakistan.

Paksé *n* a city in Laos.

pal *n* a close friend. * *vi* (**palling, palled**) (*with* **up**) (*inf*) to make friends (with).

pal. *abbr* = paleontology.

Pal. *abbr* = Palestine.

PAL *abbr* = (*color TV system*) phase alternation line.

palace *n* the official residence of a sovereign, president, or bishop; a large stately house or public building.

paladin *n* a knight-errant, esp of the court of Charlemagne.

palaeo- *see* **paleo-**.

palaeobotany *see* **paleobotany**.

palaeography *see* **paleography**.

Palaeolithic *see* **Paleolithic**.

Palaeozoic *see* **Paleozoic**.

palaeozoology *see* **paleozoology**.

palatable *adj* (*taste*) pleasant; (*fig*) pleasant or acceptable.—**palatability** *n*.—**palatably** *adv*.

palate *n* the roof of the mouth; taste; mental relish.

palatial *adj* of or like a palace.—**palatially** *adv*.—**palatialness** *n*.

Palau *n* a small republic in the Pacific Ocean, formerly called Belau or Beleu, which gained its independence from US trusteeship in 1994. It consists of a small number of volcanic islands and numerous coral atolls in the Caroline Group about 900 kilometers or 625 miles equidistant from New Guinea to the south and the Philippines to the west.

palaver *n* idle chatter; flattery; cajolery. * *vt* to flatter, cajole. * *vi* to talk idly.

Palazzetti *n* Sergio (1949–) Italian furniture designer and manufacturer who started with one showroom in New York in 1981.

pale[1] *n* a fence stake; a boundary; (*her*) a vertical stripe in the middle of a shield.

pale[2] *adj* (*complexion*) with less color than usual; (*color, light*) faint, wan, dim. * *vti* to make or become pale.—**palely** *adv*.—**paleness** *n*.

paleface *n* (*derog*) a term for a white person, supposedly used by Native Americans.

Palembang *n* a city in Indonesia.

paleo- *prefix* old; ancient; prehistoric.

paleob. *or* **paleobot.** *abbr* = paleobotany.

paleobotany *n* the study of fossil plants.—*also* **palaeobotany**.

paleog. *abbr* = paleography.

paleogeography *n* (*geog*) the study of the physical geography at periods in the past.—*also* **palaeogeography**.

paleography *n* the study of ancient writing and manuscripts.—*also* **palaeography**.—**paleographic, paleographical** *adj*.—**paleographer** *n*.

Paleolithic *adj* pertaining to the early Stone Age.—*also* **Palaeolithic**.

paleontol. *or* **paleon.** *or* **paleont.** *abbr* = paleontology.

paleontology *n* the scientific study of fossils.—*also* **palaeontology**.—**paleontological** *adj*.—**paleontologist** *n*.

paleopathology *n* the study of ancient human bones, teeth, or cadavers in order to discover evidence of disease or injury.—*also* **palaeopathology.**

Paleozoic *adj* pertaining to the geological period in which fossils of the earliest forms of life appear which began 600 million years ago and ended 225 million years ago.—*also* **Palaeozoic**.

paleozoology *n* the study of fossil animals.—*also* **palaeozoology**.—**paleozoological** *adj*.—**paleozoologist** *n*.

Palermo *n* a city in Italy.

Palermo stone *n* a slab of black basalt on which a record of the kings of Egypt during the first five dynasties was inscribed in hieroglyphic writing.

Palestine *n* an ancient historic region on the eastern shore of the Mediterranean Sea, which is also known as The Holy Land because of its symbolic importance for Christians, Jews, and Muslims.

Palestrina *n* Giovanni Pierluigi da (*c.* 1525–94) Italian polyphonic composer who wrote noted Masses (e.g., *Missa Papae Marcelli*), motets, and other religious works, notably a great Stabat Mater.

palette *n* a small, wooden board on which colored paints are mixed; (*comput*) the menu of colors, brush styles, or patterns that can be chosen to create an image in graphics programs.

palette knife *n* (*pl* **palette knives**) a thin knife used for mixing colors; a round-ended, flexible knife used in cookery.

Paley *n* **Albert** (1944–) American metalworker who became known for architectural metalwork.

palfrey *n* (*arch*) a saddle horse, esp for a woman.

Palikir *n* capital city of the Federated States of Micronesia.

palimony *n* (*inf*) the payment of alimony from one partner in a formal long-term sexual relationship to the other.

palimpsest *n* a manuscript which has been written on more than once, the former writing being still discernible in spite of erasure.

palindrome *n* a word or sentence reading the same forwards as backwards, e.g. "Able was I ere I saw Elba."—**palindromic** *adj*.

paling *n* a row of stakes in a fence; a railing.

palingenesis *n* (*pl* **palingeneses**) (*theology*) spiritual rebirth through baptism.—**palingenetic** *adj*.

palinode *n* a poem retracting a former poem.

palisade *n* a fence made of pointed stakes driven into the ground; a pointed stake used in a fence of this kind.

palish *adj* somewhat pale.

pall[1] *n* a heavy cloth over a casket; (*of smoke*) a mantle.

pall[2] *vi* to become boring; to become satiated.

Palladian *adj* (*archit*) in the pseudo-classical style of the architect Andrea Palladio (1508–80).

Palladio *n* **Andrea** (1508–80) Italian architect whose notable works include Teatro Olimpico, Vicenza and churches of S. Giorgio Maggiore and Il Redentore, Venice.

palladium *n* a rare grayish-white metal found with platinum.

Palladium *n* (*Greek myth*) a wooden image of Pallas Athene which is said to have fallen from heaven and to have been preserved in Troy.

Pallas[1] *n* (*Greek myth*) the epithet most commonly applied to Athena, as Pallas Athene, thought to be an early Greek word for girl.

Pallas[2] *n* (*astron*) a carbonaceous asteroid and the second to be discovered in 1802.

pallbearer *n* someone who carries the casket at a funeral.

pallet[1] *n* a portable platform for lifting and stacking goods.

pallet[2] *n* a straw bed.

palletize, palletise *vt* to stack, transport, or store on pallets.—**palletization, palletisation** *n*.

palliate *vt* to extenuate, to excuse; to alleviate without curing.—**palliation** *n*.—**palliator** *n*.

palliative *adj* alleviating without curing; excusing, extenuating. * *n* a thing that palliates.

pallid *adj* wan, pale.—**pallidness** *n*.

pallium *n* (*pl* **pallia, palliums**) a white woolen scarf worn by an archbishop; (*anat*) the cerebral cortex and surrounding matter; (*zool*) a mollusk's outer fold of skin.

pallor *n* paleness, esp of the face.

Pallucco *n* **Paolo** (1950–) Italian architect who established the Pallucco company.

pally *adj* (**pallier, palliest**) friendly with; intimate.

palm[1] *n* the underside of the hand between fingers and wrist. * *vt* to conceal in or touch with the palm; (*with* **off**) to pass off by fraud, foist.

palm[2] *n* a tropical branchless tree with fan-shaped leaves; a symbol of victory.

palm oil *n* an oil obtained from the fruits of various palms, used in soap, etc.

Palm Sunday *n* the Sunday before Easter.

palmaceous *adj* of the palm family.

palmar *adj* of or in the palm of the hand.

palmate, palmated *adj* like an open hand; (*bot*) having leaves with lobes radiating from a common point; (*zool*) web-footed.—**palmation** *n*.

palmer *n* (*formerly*) a pilgrim returning from the Holy Land, carrying a palm branch as a token of the pilgrimage.

Palmer *n* **Samuel** (1805–81) English painter and engraver. He painted pastoral landscapes, and *A Hilly Scene* (*c*.1826) is typical of his most intensely creative period.

palmette *n* (*archit*) a fan-shaped decorative motif resembling a palm leaf or honeysuckle flowers.

palmetto *n* (*pl* **palmettos, palmettoes**) a species of small palm tree.

palmistry *n* foretelling the future from lines of the hand.—**palmist** *n*.

Palmqvist *n* **Sven Ernst Robert** (1906–84) Swedish glassware designer who invented a new technique for forming glass bowls.

palm-top *n* a portable computer small enough to fit in the palm of the hand.

palmy *adj* (**palmier, palmiest**) abounding in palm trees; (*fig*) flourishing, prosperous.

palmyra *n* a palm found in Asia, the leaves of which are used for matting and thatching.

palomino *n* (*pl* **palominos**) a horse with a golden or cream-colored coat and a white mane and tail.

palp, palpus *n* (*pl* **palps, palpi**) a jointed feeler attached to the mouth parts of an insect.

palpable *adj* tangible; easily perceived, obvious.—**palpability** *n*.—**palpably** *adj*.

palpate *vt* to examine by touch, esp medically.—**palpation** *n*.

palpebral *adj* of the eyelids.

palpitate *vi* (*heart*) to beat abnormally fast; to tremble, flutter.—**palpitation** *n*.

palstave *n* a particular type of European Bronze Age ax.

palsy *n* (*pl* **palsies**) paralysis; a condition marked by an uncontrollable tremor of a part of the body. * *vt* (**palsying, palsied**) to paralyze; to make helpless.

palter *vi* to be insincere.

Palterer *n* **David** (1949–) Israeli designer and teacher who established a design and manufacturing firm with Borek Sipek in Amsterdam in 1983.

paltry *adj* (**paltrier, paltriest**) almost worthless; trifling.—**paltrily** *adv*.—**paltriness** *n*.

palynology *n* (*biol*) the study of pollen, spores, and some other microfossils.

pam. or **pamph.** *abbr* = pamphlet.

PAM *abbr* = pulse-amplitude modulation.

pambe *n* a small Indian drum.

pampas *npl* the treeless, grassy plains of South America.

pampas grass *n* a tall-stemmed South American grass growing in thick tussocks.

pamper *vt* to overindulge; to coddle, spoil.—**pamperer** *n*.

pampero *n* (*pl* **pamperos**) a cold south or south west wind which blows across the pampas.

pamphlet *n* a thin, unbound booklet, esp one attacking or advocating a cause, etc; a brochure.—**pamphleteer** *n*.

PAMR *abbr* = Public Access Mobile Radio.

pan[1] *n* a wide metal container, a saucepan; (*of scales*) a tray; a depression in the earth filled with water; severe criticism; the bowl of a lavatory. * *vi* (**panning, panned**) (*with* **out**) (*inf*) to turn out, esp to turn out well; to succeed. * *vt* to wash gold-bearing gravel in a pan; (*inf*) to disparage, find fault with.

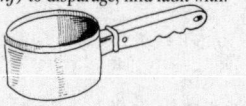

pan[2] *n* a betel leaf; a mixture of betel nuts and lime wrapped in a betel leaf used for chewing.

pan[3] *vti* (**panning, panned**) (*film camera*) to move horizontally to follow an object or provide a panoramic view.—*also n*.

Pan *n* (*Greek myth*) the god of woods and fields, depicted with two horns, pointed ears, and a goat's beard, tail, and feet.—**Pandean** *adj*.

Pan. *abbr* = Panama.

PAN *abbr* = Pesticides Action Network.

pan- *prefix* all; general.

panacea *n* a cure-all, universal remedy.—**panacean** *adj*.

panache *n* flair; sense of style.

panada *n* (*cooking*) bread boiled to a pulp and flavored, used as a sauce base or as stuffing.

Panaftel *abbr* = Pan-African Telecommunications Network.

PanAm *abbr* = Pan-American World Airways Incorporated.

panama *n* a hat of a fine, straw-like material.

Panama *n* a narrow, S-shaped isthmus that links central America and South America. Panama is a republic, which is heavily dependent on income from the Panama Canal.

Panama City *n* capital city of Panama.

Pan-American *adj* of or pertaining to North, South, and Central America collectively; advocating unity among American countries.

panatella *n* a long, slim cigar.

pancake *n* a round, thin cake made from batter and cooked on a griddle; a thing shaped thus. * *vi* (*aircraft*) to descend vertically in a level position.

PanCan *abbr* = Panama Canal.

panchromatic *adj* (*photog*) sensitive to light of all colors.

Pancras *n* **Saint** (*d*. 304) a Phrygian of noble birth who was brought to Rome on the death of his father by his uncle Dionysius. They were both baptized by the pope and were martyred by Diocletian. He is said to be the special enemy of those who swear falsely. His feast day is May 12.

pancreas *n* a large gland secreting a digestive juice into the intestine and also producing insulin.—**pancreatic** *adj*.

pancreatectomy *n* surgical removal of the pancreas (or part of it) to deal with tumors or chronic pancreatitis.

pancreatin *n* a clear fluid secreted by the pancreas, often extracted from animals and used in medicine.

pancreatitis *n* inflammation of the pancreas, occurring in several forms but often associated with gallstones or alcoholism.

panda *n* a large black and white bear-like herbivore (*also* **giant panda**); a related reddish-brown raccoon-like animal with a ringed tail (—*also* **lesser panda**).

Pandean *adj* pertaining to the god Pan.

pandemic *adj* epidemic over a large region, universal.

pandemonium *n* (*pl* **pandemoniums**) uproar; chaos.

pander *n* a go-between in sexual liaisons; a pimp. * *vi* (*usu with* **to**) to gratify or exploit a person's desires or weaknesses, etc.—**panderer** *n*.

P & G abbr = Procter and Gamble.

P & GWA abbr = Pottery and Glass Wholesalers Association.

Pandion n (Greek myth) a son of Erichthonius, the king of Athens, the father of Procne and Philomela and of the twins Erechtheus and Butes.

pandit see **pundit**.

p & l, P & L, P and L abbr = profit and loss.

P & O abbr = Peninsular and Oriental Steamship Navigation Company.

pandora n (mus) a plucked stringed instrument of the Cittern family. It was particularly popular in England during the 16th century.

Pandora[1] n (Greek myth) the first woman on earth, made from clay by Hephaestus, and sent by Zeus to humankind in vengeance for Prometheus's theft of heavenly fire. Each of the gods gave her some gift fatal to man.

Pandora[2] n (astron) a small elongate satellite of Saturn.

Pandora's box n a source of many troubles.

p & p abbr = postage and packing.

P & S abbr = Pike & Shot Society.

P and S abbr = (College of) Physicians and Surgeons (New York City).

pane n a sheet of glass in a frame of a window, door, etc; (comput) a term used for each section of a split screen window.—**paned** adj.

panegyric n an ovation or eulogy in praise of a person or event.—**panegyrical** adj.—**panegyrist** n.

panegyrize vti to compose a panegyric (about); to praise highly.

panel n a usu rectangular section or division forming part of a wall, door, etc; a board for instruments or controls; a lengthwise strip in a skirt, etc; a group of selected persons for judging, discussing, etc. * vt (**paneling, paneled** or **panelling, panelled**) to decorate with panels.

paneling, panelling n panels collectively; sheets of wood, plastic, etc used for panels.

panelist, panellist n a member of a panel.

panelology n the collection of comic books as a hobby.

pang n a sudden sharp pain or feeling.

Pangaeus n a mountain in western Thrace where, in Greek mythology, Lycurgus was torn to pieces by horses when his treatment of the maenads brought famine to the land.

pangenesis n (formerly) the theory that reproductive cells contain particles from all parts of the parents.—**pangenetic** adj.

pangolin n an insectivorous mammal, also known as the spiny anteater, found in Africa and Asia.

panhandle[1] n a narrow, projecting tongue of land.

panhandle[2] vi (inf) to beg, esp from passers-by. * vt (inf) to obtain by begging.

panic n a sudden overpowering fright or terror.—also adj. * vti (**panicking, panicked**) to affect or be affected with panic.—**panicky** adj.

panic button n a switch for setting off an alarm; (sl) a frenzied response.

panicle n (bot) an irregularly bunched flower cluster.

panic-stricken, panic-struck adj affected by panic.

paniculate, paniculated adj (bot) arranged in panicles.

panjandrum n a pompous official.

Pankhurst n **Emmeline** (1857–1928) English suffragette and feminist. With her daughter Dame Christabel Harriette Pankhurst (1880–1958), she founded the Women's Social and Political Union in 1903. Her daughter Estelle Sylvia Pankhurst (1882–1960) was also a suffragette.

Pankok n **Bernhard** (1872–1943) German designer and founder member of the Muncher Werkstatte.

panne n a soft, velvet-like fabric.

pannier n a large basket for carrying loads on the back of an animal or the shoulders of a person; a bag or case slung over the rear wheel of a bicycle or motorcycle.

pannikin n a small metal drinking-cup.

panoply n (pl **panoplies**) a complete array; a full suit of armor.—**panoplied** adj.

panorama n a complete view in all directions; a comprehensive presentation of a subject; a constantly changing scene.—**panoramic** adj.—**panoramically** adv.

panpipes npl a wind instrument consisting of short hollow tubes of different lengths, originally of reed, bound together.

pansy n (pl **pansies**) a garden flower of the violet family, with velvety petals; (sl) an effeminate boy or man.

pant vi to breathe noisily, gasp; to yearn (for or after something). * vt to speak while gasping.

pantalets, pantalettes npl a woman's long ruffled drawers.

pantaloon n (pantomine) a foolish old man on whom the clown plays tricks.

pantaloons npl (hist) a man's tight breeches fastened at the calf or the foot; (inf) baggy pants.

pantheism n the doctrine that the universe in its totality is God; willingness to worship all, or several gods.—**pantheist** n.—**pantheistic, pantheistical** adj.

pantheon n a temple to all the gods; a building in which the famous dead of a nation are buried or remembered; a group of famous persons.

panther n (pl **panther, panthers**) a leopard, esp one with a black unspotted coat; a puma.

panties npl (inf) short underpants.

pantihose n women's tights.—also **panty hose**.

pantile n a roof tile with an S-shaped cross-section.

panto n (pl **pantos**) (Brit inf) a pantomime.

pantograph n an instrument for copying drawings, maps, etc, to scale.

pantomime n (Brit) a Christmas theatrical entertainment with music and jokes; a drama without words, using only actions and gestures; mime. * vti to mime.—**pantomimic** adj.

pantomimist n a person who performs in a pantomime; one who composes a pantomime.

Panton n **Verner** (1926–) Danish architect whose best-known design is the 1960 Stacking Chair.

pantonality see **atonal**.

Pantone n (trademark) a system that allocates numbers to a range of colors in order that the exact color match is made.

pantoum n a verse form of four-lined rhyming stanzas.

pantry n (pl **pantries**) a small room or cupboard for storing cooking ingredients and utensils, etc.

pants npl trousers; underpants.

panty hose see **pantihose**.

Panufnik n **Andrzej** (1914–91) Polish composer and conductor who settled in England in 1954. Noted pieces, including the ballet Miss Julie, and the orchestral pieces Sinfonia Rustica and Sinfonia Sacra.

panzer adj (division) armored. * n a tank, or other armored vehicle, from a panzer division; (pl) armored troops.

Paolo n **Veneziano** (1321–62) Venetian painter who executed a number of important state commissions, including the cover for the Pala d'Oro in the Church of San Marco (1345).

Paolozzi n **Sir Eduardo Luigi** (1924–) Scottish sculptor and printmaker of Italian parentage. Works include The City of the Circle and the Square (1963–66).

pap n soft, bland food for infants, invalids, etc; any oversimplified or insipid writing, ideas, etc.

pap. abbr = paper.

PAP abbr = Profesional Association of Partners.

papa n (inf) father.

papacy n (pl **papacies**) the office or authority of the pope; papal system of government.

papal adj of the pope or the papacy.—**papally** adv.

Papandreou n **Andreas George** (1919–96) Greek socialist politician and Greece's first socialist prime minister (1981–89).

Papanicolaou test see **Pap test**.

paparazzo n (pl **paparazzi**) a freelance photographer who pursues celebrities for sensational or candid shots for publication in newspapers and magazines.

papaveraceous adj (bot) pertaining or belonging to the poppy family.

papaw n (the small edible fruit of) a North American tree of the custard-apple family.—also **pawpaw**.

papaya n (a West Indian tree bearing) an elongated melon-like fruit with edible yellow flesh and small black seeds.

Papeete n capital city of French Polynesia.

paper n the thin, flexible material made from pulped rags, wood, etc which is used to write on, wrap in, or cover walls; a single sheet of this; an official document; a newspaper; an essay or lecture; a set of examination questions; (pl) personal documents. * adj like or made of paper. * vt to cover with wallpaper.

paperback n a softback book bound in a flexible paper cover. * adj pertaining to such a book or the publication of such books.

paper boy, paper girl n a boy or girl who delivers or sells newspapers.

papering n the process of covering with paper; paper so used.

paperknife n (pl **paperknives**) a blunt knife for opening letters or cutting folded paper.

paperless office n (comput) an office in which paper is no longer used or generated.

paper money n bills; paper currency authorized by a government as representing value.

paper profit n a profit that is indicated by the financial records of a company but that may not in fact be a realizable profit, such as when the value of an asset falls below its book value.

paper tiger n something that appears dangerous but is in reality weak and harmless.

paperweight n a small heavy object for keeping papers in place.

paperwork n clerical work of any kind.

papery adj like paper in appearance or consistency.—**paperiness** n.

papeterie n a case containing paper and writing materials.

Paphos n two ancient cities in Cyprus: Old Paphos, on a hill near the southwestern coast, and New Paphos (modern Baffa), to the northwest and on the shore.

papier-mâché n a substance made of paper pulp mixed with size, glue, etc and molded into various objects when moist.

papilla n (pl **papillae**) a small, nipple-like protuberance.—**papillary, papillate, papillose** adj.

papilloma (pl **papillomata**) n a usually benign growth on the skin surface or mucous membrane, e.g. warts.

papist n (derog) a Roman Catholic.—**papistic** adj.—**papistry** n.

papoose n an American Indian young child.

pappus n (pl **pappi**) (bot) the feathery substance on the seeds of some plants, e.g., dandelion, thistle.

pappy adj (**pappier, pappiest**) semi-liquid, like pap.

paprika n a mild red condiment ground from the fruit of certain peppers.

Pap test, Pap smear n a technique for the early detection of cancer by examining specially stained cells from the cervix, etc.—also **Papanicolaou test**.

Papua New Guinea n a republic in the southwest Pacific comprising the eastern half of the island of New Guinea and a number of archipelagos and islands.

papule, papula n (pl **papules, papulae**) a small, solid elevation of the skin.—**papular** adj.

Papworth n **John** (b. 1775) English architect, whose notable works include Lansdown Crescent, Cheltenham.

papyrology *n* the study of papyri.—**papyrologist** *n*.

papyrus *n* (*pl* **papyri, papyruses**) an aquatic plant; paper made from this plant, as used in ancient times.

par *n* the standard or normal level; the established value of a currency in foreign-exchange rates; the face value of stocks, shares, etc; (*golf*) the score for a hole required by an expert player; equality.

par *abbr* (*wood*) = planed all round.

par. *abbr* = paragraph; parallel; parenthesis; parish.

PAR *abbr* = precision approach radar.

par-, para- *prefix* beside; against; irregular; abnormal; associated in a subsidiary or accessory capacity.

para[1] *n* (*pl* **paras**) (*inf*) a paragraph; a paratrooper.

para[2] *n* a monetary unit of Bosnia-Herzegovina and Serbia, equal to one hundredth of a dinar.

Para. *abbr* = Paraguay.

parabasis *n* (*pl* **parabases**) (*classical Greek comedy*) an address to the audience by the chorus.

parable *n* a short story used to illustrate a religious or moral point.—**parabolist** *n*.

parabola *n* (*pl* **parabolas**) (*maths*) the curve formed by the cutting of a cone by a plane parallel to its side; (*astron*) an orbit shape (open curve) which may be assumed by a body moving around a central gravitational force, e.g., a comet moving around the Sun.

parabolic[1] *adj* of or like a parabola; parabolical.

parabolic[2], **parabolical** *adj* of or expressed in a parable.—**parabolically** *adv*.

paraboloid *n* (*geom*) a solid formed by the revolution of a parabola on its axis.

Paracas *n* a site in southern Peru where the extremely arid climate has led to the excellent preservation of ancient materials such as textiles.

paracentesis *n* the procedure of tapping or taking off (excess) fluid from the body by means of a hollow needle or cannula.

paracetamol *n* a drug that has analgesic effects and also reduces fever.

parachronism *n* an error in chronology, esp in postdating an event.

parachute *n* a fabric umbrella-like canopy used to retard speed of fall from an aircraft. * *vti* to drop, descend by parachute.—**parachutist** *n*.

paraclete *n* a mediator.

parade *n* a ceremonial procession; an assembly of troops for review; ostentatious display; public walk, promenade. * *vti* to march or walk through, as for display; to show off; to assemble in military order.

paradigm *n* a pattern or model; a list of grammatical inflexions of a word.—**paradigmatic** *adj*.—**paradigmatically** *adv*.

paradise *n* heaven; (*Bible*) the Garden of Eden; any place of perfection.

paradisiacal, paradisiac *adj* like, or pertaining to, paradise.

paradox *n* a self-contradictory statement that may be true; an opinion that conflicts with common beliefs; something with seemingly contradictory qualities or phases.—**paradoxical** *adj*.—**paradoxically** *adv*.

par. aff. *abbr* (*Latin*) = *pars affecta*, "the injured part."

paraffin *n* a white waxy tasteless substance obtained from shale, wood, etc; a distilled oil used as fuel, kerosene.—**paraffinic** *adj*.

paragenesis, paragenesia *n* (*geol*) the sequence of formation of the various minerals in a mass of rock—**paragenetic** *adj*.

paragoge, paragogue *n* (*linguistics*) the addition of a letter or a syllable to a word.

paragon *n* a model of excellence or perfection.

paragraph *n* a subdivision in a piece of writing used to separate ideas, marked by the beginning of a new line; a brief mention in a newspaper. * *vt* to divide into paragraphs.—**paragraphic** *adj*.—**paragraphically** *adv*.

Paraguay *n* a small landlocked republic in central South America.

Paraguay tea *n* an infusion of the dried leaves of maté, which makes a mildly stimulating tea.—*also* **yerba maté**.

parainfluenza viruses *npl* a group of viruses affecting infants and young children that cause respiratory tract infections with usually mild influenza-like symptoms.

parakeet *n* a small parrot.

paraldehyde *n* a colorless liquid used as a sedative.

paralegal *adj* of or relating to a person who assists a lawyer.—*also n*.

paraleipsis, paralipsis *n* (*pl* **paraleipses, paralipses**) (*rhetoric*) drawing attention to something by deliberately understating it.

parallax *n* the apparent angular shifting of an object caused by a change in position of the observer; (*astron*) the difference in the apparent position of a heavenly body and its true place.

parallel *adj* equidistant at every point and extended in the same direction; side by side; never intersecting; similar, corresponding. * *n* a parallel line, surface, etc; a likeness, counterpart; comparison; a line of latitude. * *vt* (**paralleling, paralleled**) to make or be parallel; to compare.

parallel bars *npl* a set of horizontal bars raised above the floor on posts used by gymnasts.

parallel columns *npl* (*comput*) a feature of word processing or page layout programs that sets two or more columns side by side.

parallel communication *see* **serial communication**.

parallelepiped *n* a regular solid figure bounded by six parallelograms, of which the opposite pairs are equal and parallel.

parallelism *n* the state or quality of being parallel.

parallelogram *n* a four-sided plane figure whose opposite sides are parallel.

parallel port *n* (*comput*) a slot on the back of a computer that is used to transmit high speed synchronous data streams, an extension of a computer's internal data bus used primarily for connection to printers.

parallel printer *n* (*comput*) a printer designed to be connected to a parallel port.

parallel processing *n* (*comput*) the use of two processors combined to undertake one task.

paralogism *n* (*logic*) a fallacy in reasoning made unconsciously by the reasoner.

paralysis *n* (*pl* **paralyses**) a partial or complete loss of voluntary muscle function or sensation in any part of the body; a condition of helpless inactivity.—**paralytic** *adj*, *n*.

paralyze, paralyse *vt* to affect with paralysis; to bring to a stop.—**paralyzation** *n*.

Paramaribo *n* capital city of Suriname.

paramatta *n* a light fabric of cotton and wool.—*also* **parramatta**.

paramecium *n* (*pl* **paramecia, parameciums**) any of a genus of ciliate oval-bodied protozoa with a ventral feeding groove.

paramedic *n* a a person trained to provide emergency medical treatment and to support professional medical staff.

paramedical *adj* (*services*) supplementing and assisting the work of professional medical staff.

parameter *n* (*math*) an arbitrary constant, the value of which influences the content but not the structure of an expression; (*inf*) a limit or condition affecting action, decision, etc; (*mus*) a limit placed esp on electronic music with regard to volume, etc; (*comput*) a step in any program sequence that will cause the program to take a specific course of action.—**parametric** *adj*.—**parametrically** *adv*.

paramilitary *adj* (*forces*) organized on a military pattern and ancillary to military forces.

paramo *n* (*pl* **paramos**) a high bleak plateau in the Andes.

paramount *adj* of great importance.

paramour *n* an illicit lover.

parang *n* a heavy Malay sheath knife.

paranoia *n* a mental illness characterized by delusions of grandeur and persecution; (*inf*) unfounded fear, suspicion.—**paranoiac** *adj*, *n*.

paranoid *adj* of or like paranoia; (*inf*) highly suspicious or fearful.—*also n*.

paranormal *adj* beyond the scope of normal experience or scientific explanation.—**paranormally** *adv*.

parapet *n* a low, protective wall along the edge of a roof, balcony, or bridge, etc.—**parapeted** *adj*.

paraph *n* a mark or flourish after a signature.

paraphernalia *npl* personal belongings; accessories; (*law*) what a wife possesses in her own right.

paraphimosis *n* constriction of the penis because of retraction of an abnormally tight foreskin, which contracts on the penis behind the glans and cannot be easily moved.

paraphrase *n* expression of a passage in other words in order to clarify meaning. * *vt* to restate.—**paraphrastic** *adj*.

paraplegia *n* paralysis of the lower half of the body.—**paraplegic** *adj*.

parapsychology *n* the study of mental phenomena, e.g. telekinesis, beyond what can be explained by ordinary psychology.—**parapsychological** *adj*.—**parapsychologist** *n*.

parasailing *n* the sport of gliding through the air attached to an open parachute and towed by a speedboat.—**parasailer, parasailor** *n*.

parascending *n* a form of parachuting in which participants wearing open parachutes are towed into the air by a vehicle or speedboat and then released to glide to the ground.—**parascender** *n*.

paraselene *n* (*pl* **paraselenae**) (*astron*) a bright spot on a lunar halo.

parasite *n* an organism that lives on and feeds off another without rendering any service in return; a person who sponges off another.—**parasitic** *adj*.—**parasitically** *adv*.

parasiticide *n* a substance which kills parasites.

parasitism *n* the parasite-host relationship; the state or behavior of a parasite.

parasitize *n* to infest with parasites.

parasitology *n* the study of parasites.—**parasitologist** *n*.

parasol *n* a lightweight umbrella used as a sunshade.

parasympathetic nervous system *n* one of the two parts of the autonomic nervous system, which acts antagonistically with the sympathetic nervous system.

parasynthesis *n* (*gram*) derivation from a compound plus affix, e.g. faint-hearted, which is made up from faint + heart + -ed.

parataxis *n* (*gram*) use of successive clauses without connecting words.

parathyroid *adj* (*anat*) lying near the thyroid gland. * *n* a gland near the thyroid that secretes a hormone that regulates the body's calcium levels.

parathyroidectomy *n* removal of the parathyroid glands, usually in treatment of hyperparathyroidism (hyperactivity of one or all of the glands).

paratroops *npl* troops dropped by parachute into the enemy area.—**paratrooper** *n*.

paratyphoid fever *n* a bacterial infection caused by *Salmonella paratyphi* A, B, or C. Symptoms resemble those of typhoid fever and include diarrhea, a rash, and mild fever.

paravane *n* a device shaped like a torpedo, with serrated teeth for destroying the moorings of sea mines.

paraxial *adj* aligned close to the optical axis of a lens or similar system.

parboil *vt* to boil briefly as a preliminary cooking procedure.

par bond *n* a financial security that is bought and sold at face value and not at a discount or premium.

parbuckle *n* a rope sling for raising or lowering casks.

PARC *abbr* = Parallel Algorithm Research Center.

parcel *n* a tract or plot of land; a wrapped bundle; a package; a collection or group of persons, animals, or things. * *vt* (**parceling, parceled** *or* **parcelling, parcelled**) to wrap up into a parcel; (*with* **out**) to apportion.

parcenary *n* joint heirship.

parcener *n* a coheir.

parch *vti* to make or become hot and dry, thirsty; to scorch, roast.—**parched** *adj*.

parchment *n* the skin of a sheep, etc prepared as a writing material; paper like parchment.

parclose *n* (*archit*) a screen in a church separating off a shrine or chapel.

pard *n* (*arch*) a leopard.

pardon *vt* to forgive; to excuse; to release from penalty. * *n* forgiveness; remission of penalty.—**pardonable** *adj*.—**pardonably** *adv*.

pardoner *n* one who pardons; (*hist*) a person licensed to sell papal indulgences.

pare *vt* to cut or shave; to peel; to diminish.

paregoric *n* (*formerly*) an opium-based drug used to treat diarrhea and coughs.

paren. *abbr* = parenthesis.

parenchyma *n* (*bot*) the soft cellular tissue or pith of plants; (*anat*) the soft tissue of the glandular organs of the body.—**parenchymatous, parenchymal** *adj*.

parens. *abbr* = parentheses.

parent *n* a father or a mother; an organism producing another; a source.—**parental** *adj*.—**parentally** *adv*.—**parenthood** *n*.

Parent *n* **Guillame** (1961–) French furniture designer who designed furniture for Musée Carnavalet, Paris.

parentage *n* descent, extraction from parents.

parenteral nutrition *n* provision of nutrition by any means other than by the mouth.

parent file *n* (*comput*) the second oldest file in a series of three backups of a file.

parentheses *npl* (*math, logic*) the curved brackets ( ) used to group terms or as a sign of aggregation in a mathematical or logical expression.

parenthesis *n* (*pl* **parentheses**) an explanatory comment in a sentence contained within brackets and set in a sentence, independently of grammatical sequence.—**parenthetic, parenthetical** *adj*.—**parenthetically** *adv*.

parenthesize, parenthesise *vt* to insert as a parenthesis; to enclose in parentheses.

parenting *n* the act of being a parent; the role of a parent in relation to a child; that role in relation to someone who is not the child of a parent; (*business*) the manner in which senior management of a company manage their subsidiary companies.

parent material *n* the substrate from which and on which a soil is formed.

paresis *n* partial or slight paralysis.—**paretic** *adj*.

paresthesia *n* (*med*) an abnormal tickling sensation on the skin.—*also* **paraesthesia**.—**paresthetic** *adj*.

Pareto *n* **Vilfredo** (1848–1923) Italian economist and sociologist. A highly influential economist, his work is regarded as anticipatory of both Fascist and modern welfare economics. His best-known work is *Mind and Society* (1916).

Paret y Alcazar *n* **Luis** (1746–99) Spanish painter of versatile talent, who painted historical, mythical, and religious scenes as well as landscapes and still lifes.

par excellence *adv* pre-eminently; to the highest degree.

parfait *n* a rich iced dessert of whipped cream, eggs, etc served in a tall glass; layers of ice cream served in a tall glass.

parget *n* a type of plaster. * *vt* to cover with parget.

pargeting *n* (*archit*) any type of coarse plaster work applied to the outside walls of an early Medieval building; the decorative panels of plasterwork on the external walls of a timber-framed building.

parhelion *n* (*pl* **parhelia**) a bright spot on a solar halo.

pariah *n* a social outcast; a member of a low caste in southern India and Burma.

parietal *adj* (*anat*) pertaining to the wall of a cavity of the body; pertaining to the large lateral bones of the skull.

parietal art *n* ancient art on the walls of rock shelters or caves, cliffs, or enormous blocks of stone.

pari-mutuel *n* (*pl* **pari-mutuels, paris-mutuels**) a mechanical betting system in which the losers' stakes, less a deduction for the management, are divided among the winners.

paring *n* the act of paring; what is pared off, rind.

pari passu *adv* (*law*) (*Latin*) "with equal pace," together; in equal degree.

Paris[1] *n* capital city of France.

Paris[2] *n* (*Greek myth*) a son of Priam and Hecuba of Troy, who took Menelaus' wife Helen, which led to the siege of Troy.—*also* **Alexander**.

parish *n* an ecclesiastical area with its own church and clergy; the inhabitants of a parish.

parishioner *n* an inhabitant of a parish.

parish register *n* a book that lists births, baptisms, marriages, and deaths in a parish.

Parish *n* **Sister** (1910–) doyenne of American interior designers, well known in the 1960s through her work for the Kennedys.

Paris Opéra *n* the most important opera house in France, opened in 1671, usu referred to as "L' Opéra." Its official title is the "Académie de Musique."

Paris Symphonies *npl* a set of six symphonies by Haydn which were commissioned by the "Concert de la Loge Olympique," a Masonic concert society based in Paris.

parisyllabic *adj* (*inflected noun or verb*) having an equal number of syllables in all or most inflected forms.

parity *n* (*pl* **parities**) equality; equality of value at a given ratio between different kinds of money, etc; being at par.

parity bit *n* (*comput*) an extra bit added to transmitted data that allows checking for communications errors.

park *n* land kept as a game preserve or recreation area; a piece of ground in an urban area kept for ornament or recreation; an enclosed stadium, esp for ball games; a large enclosed piece of ground attached to a country house. * *vti* (*vehicle*) to leave in a certain place temporarily; to maneuver into a parking space; (*comput*) to remove the read/write head from a hard disk to an area of the disk that contains no data, to protect files during transportation.

parka *n* a warm hooded garment, often of fur, for wear in arctic conditions.

Parker *n* 1. **Charlie "Bird" [Christopher]** (1920–55) American jazz alto and tenor saxophonist who was the leading exponent of "bop" jazz in the 1940s. 2. **Dorothy [Rothschild]** (1893–1960) American journalist, poet, and short-story writer, noted especially for her sharply ironic satires, many of which were published in *The New Yorker* magazine. 3. **Horatio William** (1863-1919) American organist and composer who wrote several oratorios, including *Hora Novissima*, two operas, choral works, and pieces for piano and organ.

parking lot *n* an area reserved for parking motor vehicles.

parking meter *n* a coin-operated machine that registers the purchase of parking time for a motor vehicle.

Parkinson's disease *n* a progressive nervous disease resulting in tremor, muscular rigidity, partial paralysis and weakness.—*also* **Parkinsonism**.

Parkinson's Law *n* any of various humorous observations on human behavior framed as economic laws, esp the notion that work expands to fill the time available for its completion (named after the English writer C. *n*. Parkinson 1909-93).

parkway *n* an open landscaped highway.

parl. *abbr* = parliament; parliamentary.

Parl. Agt. *abbr* = Parliamentary Agent.

parlance *n* a manner of speech, idiom.

parlay *n* a type of bet in which the winnings of an initial wager are automatically risked on subsequent wagers. * *vt* to bet in parlay; to maneuver to an advantage.

parley *n* a conference, esp with an enemy. * *vi* to discuss, esp with an enemy with a view to bringing about a peace.

parliament *n* a legislative assembly made up of representatives of a nation or part of a nation; (*with cap*) the supreme governing and legislative body of various countries, esp the UK.

parliamentarian *n* a skilled parliamentary debater; an expert on parliamentary rules; (*with cap*) (*hist*) a supporter of the English Parliament against Charles I.

parliamentary *adj* of, used in, or enacted by a parliament; conforming to the rules of a parliament; having a parliament.

parlor *n* a room in a house used primarily for conversation or receiving guests; a room or a store used for business.

parlor game *n* a game usually played indoors.

parlous *adj* (*arch*) dangerous; shrewd.—**parlously** *adv*.—**parlousness** *n*.

parmales *n* any of the order Parmales of single-celled algae found in the polar regions.

Parmesan *n* a hard cheese with a sharp flavor used, esp grated, as a garnish.

Parmigianino *n* (1503–40) Italian mannerist painter and etcher of precocious talent. An early masterpiece is *The Vision of St Jerome* (1526–7) and his best-known mature piece is *The Madonna of the Long Neck* (c.1535).

Parnassus *n* a mountain of Greece, situated in Phocis, northwest of Athens. It has two prominent peaks, the higher of which in ancient times was dedicated to the worship of Dionysus. All the rest of the mountain was sacred to Apollo and the Muses.

Parnell *n* **Charles Stewart** (1846–91) Irish politician and ardent Home Ruler.

Pärnu *n* a city in Estonia.

parochial *adj* of or relating to a parish; narrow; provincial in outlook.—**parochially** *adv*.

parochialism *n* narrow-mindedness.

parody *n* (*pl* **parodies**) a satirical or humorous imitation of a literary or musical work or style. * *vt* (**parodying, parodied**) to make a parody of.—**parodic** *adj*.—**parodist** *n*.

paroicous, paroecious *adj* (*bot*) with the two sexes developing in close proximity.

parole *n* word of honor; the release of a prisoner before his sentence has expired, on condition of future good behavior. * *vt* to release on parole.

parolee *n* a person on parole.

paronomasia *n* a pun or play on words.

paronym *n* (*gram*) a paronymic word.

paronymic, paronymous *adj* (*gram*) with the same derivation; with the same sound but different spelling and meaning.

parotid *adj* (*anat*) situated near the ear. * *n* a parotid gland.

parotid gland *n* one of a pair of salivary glands situated in front of each ear and opening inside on the cheek near the second-last molar of the upper jaw.

parotitis, parotiditis *n* inflammation of the parotid gland which, as epidemic or infectious parotitis, is called mumps.

paroxysm *n* a sudden attack of a disease; a violent convulsion of pain or emotion; an outburst of laughter.—**paroxysmal** *adj*.

parquet *n* an inlaid hard wood flooring; the stalls of a theater below the balcony. * *vt* to furnish (a room) with a parquet floor.

parquetry *n* mosaic woodwork used to cover floors.

parr *n* (*pl* **parrs, parr**) a young salmon.

parramatta *see* **paramatta**.

parricide *n* a person who murders their father, mother, or other close relative; the act of doing this.— **parricidal** *adj*.

parrot *n* a tropical or subtropical bird with brilliant plumage and the ability to mimic human speech; one who repeats another's words without understanding. * *vt* to repeat mechanically.

parrotfish *n* (*pl* **parrotfish, parrotfishes**) a brightly colored tropical fish, with mouth parts resembling a parrot's beak.

parry *vt* (**parrying, parried**) to ward off, turn aside. * *n* (*pl* **parries**) a defensive movement in fencing.

Parry *n* [Charles] Hubert [Hastings] (1848–1918) English composer, teacher, and musical historian who is remembered for his choral works (e.g., *Blest Pair of Sirens, Ode on St Cecilia's Day*), motets (e.g., *Songs of Farewell*), and many orchestral works. His most famous piece is his setting of Blake's "Jerusalem."

pars. *abbr* = paragraphs.

parse *vti* (*words*) to classify; (*sentences*) to analyze in terms of grammar; to give a grammatical description of a word or group of words.

parsec *n* (*astron*) a unit of measure for stellar distances equal to 3.26 light years, approx 19 million miles.

Parsee *n* an Indian adherent of the Zoroastrian religion.—**Parseeism** *n*.

parsimony *n* extreme frugality; meanness, stinginess.—**parsimonious** *adj*.

parsley *n* a bright green herb used to flavor or garnish some foods.

parsnip *n* a biennial plant cultivated for its long tapered root used as a vegetable.

parson *n* an Anglican clergyman in charge of a parish; (*inf*) any, esp Protestant, clergyman.

parsonage *n* the house provided for a parson by his church.

Parsons *n* 1. Frank Alvah (*d.* 1930) American teacher of interior design who had a profound influence on students at the Parsons School of Design in New York. 2. Talcott (1902–79) American sociologist whose writings formed the basis for the functionalist school of sociology. His works include *The Structure of Social Action* (1937) and *Social Structure and Personality* (1964).

part *n* a section; a portion (of a whole); an essential, separable component of a piece of equipment or a machine; the role of an actor in a play; a written copy of his/her words; (*mus*) one of the melodies of a harmony; the music for it; duty, share; one of the sides in a conflict; a parting of the hair; (*pl*) qualities, talent; the genitals; a region, land or territory. * *vt* to separate; to comb the hair so as to leave a parting. * *vi* to become separated; to go different ways.

part. *abbr* = participle; particular; particularly.

Pärt *n* Arvo (1935–) Estonian composer whose work, marked by its simplicity and purity, includes *Fratres* (1977) scored for a solo violin and piano, and *Tabula Rasa* (1977).

part. adj. *abbr* = participial adjective.

part. aeq. *abbr* (*Latin*) = *partes aequales*, "equal portions."

partake *vi* (**partaking, partook**; *pp* **partaken**) to participate (in); (*food or drink*) to have a portion of.

partan *n* (*Scot*) a crab.

part and parcel *n* an essential part.

Partch *n* Harry (1901–1974) American composer who experimented with musical ideas and invented his own instruments. Many of his instruments can be regarded as sculptures.

parte *n* (*mus*) (*Italian*) "part," as in *colla parte* "with the part."

parterre *n* an ornamental flower garden; the area of a ground floor of a theater that lies underneath the balconies.

parthenocarpy *n* (*bot*) the formation of fruit without seeds having been formed or fertilized.

parthenogenesis *n* reproduction without sexual union; virgin birth.—**parthenogenetic** *adj*.

Parthenon *n* the temple of Athena at Athens, situated on the Acropolis.

Partholan or **Parytholon** *n* (*Irish Celtic myth*) said to have been the son of Sera and the leader of one of the invasions of Ireland. Partholan is credited with bringing civilization to Ireland.

partial *adj* incomplete; biased, prejudiced; (*with* **to**) having a liking or preference for.—**partially** *adv*.

partial fractions *npl* (*math*) the simple fractions into which a larger fraction may be separated so that the sum of the simpler fractions equals the original fraction.

partiality *n* (*pl* **partialities**) biased judgment; (*with* **for**) liking, fondness.

partial release *n* (*law*) a legal document affecting a previously filed lien releasing some part of the lien.

partible *adj* able to be divided or separated.

participant *n* one who participates; a sharer.

participate *vi* to join in or take part with others (in some activity).—**participator** *n*.—**participatory** *adj*.

participation *n* the act of participating; the state of being related to a larger whole.

participle *n* (*gram*) a verb form used in compound forms or as an adjective.—**participial** *adj*.—**participially** *adv*.

particle *n* a tiny portion of matter; a speck; a very small part; (*gram*) a word that cannot be used alone, a prefix, a suffix.

particle accelerator *n* (*physics*) a machine for increasing the speed (and therefore the kinetic energy) of charged particles such as protons, electrons, and helium nuclei by accelerating them in an electric field.

particle horizon *n* the extremity of the universe from which light has reached us since expansion of the universe commenced, the "visible universe."

particle size or **grain size** *n* (*geol*) the diameter of the grains in a sedimentary rock.

parti-colored *adj* differently colored in different parts, variegated.

particular *adj* referring or belonging to a specific person or thing; distinct; exceptional; careful; fastidious. * *n* a detail, single item; (*pl*) detailed information.

particularism *n* exclusive devotion to one party or sect; the principle of political freedom for each state in a federation; the theological doctrine that salvation is only for the elect.—**particularist** *n*.

particularity *n* (*pl* **particularities**) the quality of being particular, as distinguished from universal; exactness; fastidiousness.

particularize *vt* to describe in detail; to mention one by one.—**particularization** *n*.

particularly *adv* very; especially; in detail.

particulate *adj* made up of separate particles. * *n* material in this form.

parting *n* a departure; a breaking or separating; a dividing line in combing hair. * *adj* departing, esp dying; separating; dividing.

partisan, partizan *n* a strong supporter of a person, party, or cause.—*also adj.*—**partisanship, partizanship** *n*.

partite *adj* (*bot*) divided almost to the base.

partition *n* division into parts; that which divides into separate parts; a dividing wall between rooms; (*comput*) a section of a hard disk that is created for a particular purpose. * *vt* to divide; (*comput*) to divide a disk into several parts.

partitive *adj* (*gram*) denoting a part or partition. * *n* a partitive word.

partizan *see* **partisan**.

partly *adv* in part; to some extent.

partner *n* one of two or more persons jointly owning a business who share the risks and profits; one of a pair who dance or play a game together; either member of a married or non-married couple. * *vt* to be a partner (in or of); to associate as partners.

partnership *n* a contract between two or more people involved in a joint business venture; the state of being a partner.

part of speech *n* each of the categories (e.g. verb, noun, adjective) into which words are divided according to their grammatical and semantic functions.

Parton *n* Dolly (1946–) American country and western singer, songwriter, and actress. A performer of enduring popularity, her songs include "I Will Always Love You."

partook *see* **partake**.

partridge *n* (*pl* **partridge, partridges**) a stout-bodied game bird of the grouse family.

part song *n* a song with two or more voice parts.

part-time *adj* working fewer than the full number of hours.—**part-timer** *n*.—**part time** *adv*.

parturient *adj* pertaining to childbirth; about to give birth, in labor.

parturition *n* the act of childbirth.

party *n* (*pl* **parties**) a group of people united for political or other purpose; a social gathering; a person involved in a contract or lawsuit; a small company, detachment; a person consenting, accessory; (*inf*) an individual. * *vi* (**partying, partied**) to attend social parties. * *vt* to give a party for. * *adj* of or for a party.

party line *n* a telephone line shared by two or more subscribers; the policies of a political body.

party politics *npl* politics involving the rivalry between different parties.

party-pooper *n* (*sl*) a person who spoils other people's fun.

PARU *abbr* = post-anesthetic recovery unit.

par value *n* the face value of a share, coin, etc.

parvenu *n* someone regarded as vulgar or an upstart, following a rise in his social or economic status.—**parvenue** *nf*.

PARVO *abbr* = Professional and Academic Regional Visits Organization.

pas *n* (*pl* **pas**) (*ballet*) (*French*) a step or series of steps; a dance sequence.

pas *abbr* = power assisted steering.

PAS *abbr* = public address system.

pascal *n* the SI unit of pressure; the force of one newton acting on one square meter.

Pascal *n* Blaise (1623–62) French theologian, mathematician, and physicist who made important discoveries in hydraulics and invented a calculating machine.

PASCAL *n* a high-level computer programing language used esp for teaching.

Pascal's triangle *n* (*math*) an array of numbers in the shape of a pyramid starting with one, such that each number is the sum of the two numbers in the row directly above it.

pas de deux *n* (*pl* **pas de deux**) (*ballet*) (*French*) a ballet sequence for two dancers.

pasha *n* a Turkish title given to a high official; (*formerly*) a provincial governor in the Ottoman Empire.—*also* **pacha**.

Pasini *n* Gianni (1941–) Italian designer who began his professional career in 1965 with clients such as Olivetti, Magneti Marelli, and Crinospital.

Pasiphaè *n* (*Greek myth*) the wife of Minos and mother by the Cretan Bull of the Minotaur.

Pasmore *n* Victor (1908– 98) English painter, a founding member of the Euston Road School in 1937. The bulk of his mature work is strictly geometric abstraction, although he later incorporated more organic forms.

Pasolini *n* Pier Paolo (1922–75) Italian movie director, poet, novelist, and critic, whose movies include *The Gospel According to St Matthew* (1964).

pasque-flower *n* a type of anemone which flowers around Easter.

Pasqui *n* **Sandro** (1937–) Italian industrial designer who in 1974 with Gianni Pasini set up the partnership Pasqui e Pasini.

pasquinade *n* a lampoon or rude satire.

pass *vi* (**passing, passed**) to go past; to go beyond or exceed; to move from one place or state to another; (*time*) to elapse; to go; to die; to happen; (*with* **for**) to be considered as; (*in exam*) to be successful; (*cards*) to decline to make a bid; (*law*) to be approved by a legislative assembly. * *vt* to go past, through, over, etc; (*time*) to spend; to omit; (*law*) to enact; (*judgment*) to pronounce; to excrete; (*in test, etc*) to gain the required marks; to approve. * *n* a narrow passage or road; a permit; (*in a test, etc*) success; transfer of (a ball) to another player; a gesture of the hand; (*inf*) an uninvited sexual approach.

pass. *abbr* = passenger; (*Latin*) *passim*, "here and there"; passive.

passable *adj* fairly good, tolerable; (*a river, etc*) that can be crossed.—**passably** *adv*.

passacaglia *n* (*mus*) (*Italian*) a slow and stately dance originating in Spain, for which keyboard music was written in the 17th century. It has come to mean a work in which such a theme recurs again and again.

passage *n* act or right of passing; transit; transition; a corridor; a channel; a route or crossing; a lapse of time; a piece of text or music.

passage grave *n* (*archeo*) a type of chamber tomb in which there is a distinct narrow passage leading into the burial chamber.

passageway *n* a narrow way, esp flanked by walls, that allows passage; a corridor.

passage work *n* (*mus*) a piece of music that provides an opportunity for virtuoso playing.

passamezzo *n* (*mus*) (*Italian*) "half-step," a quick Italian dance in duple time that became popular throughout Europe in the late 16th century.

passbook *n* a bankbook.

passé *adj* past its best; outdated.

passementerie *n* a decorative trimming of gold or silver lace, braid, beads, etc.

passenger *n* a traveler in a public or private conveyance; one who does not pull his/her weight.

passe-partout *n* a frame for a picture in which the picture, glass, and backing are held together by gummed paper; a master key.

passepied *n* (*mus*) (*French*) a French dance in triple time, like a quick Minuet, that is thought to have originated in Brittany. It was incorporated into French ballets of the mid-17th century.

passer-by *n* (*pl* **passers-by**) one who happens to pass or go by.

passerine *adj* pertaining to the order of birds which perch.—*also n*.

passim *adv* here and there; throughout.

passing *adj* transient; casual. * *n* departure, death.

passing note *n* (*mus*) a note that is dissonant with the prevailing harmony but which is nevertheless useful in making the transition from one chord or key to another.

passion *n* compelling emotion, such as love, hate, envy; ardent love, esp sexual desire; (*with cap*) the suffering of Christ on the cross; the object of any strong desire.—**passionless** *adj*.

passional *adj* pertaining to passion; due to passion.

passionate *adj* moved by, showing, strong emotion or desire; intense; sensual.—**passionately** *adv*.

passionflower *n* a chiefly tropical climbing vine.

passion fruit *n* the edible fruit of a passion flower.

Passion music *n* the setting to music of the story of Christ's Passion (the story of the crucifixion taken from the gospels).

Passion play *n* a play representing Christ's Passion.

Passion Sunday *n* the second Sunday before Easter.

passive *adj* acted upon, not acting; submissive; (*gram*) denoting the voice of a verb whose subject receives the action.—**passively** *adv*.—**passivity** *n*.

passive glacier *n* a glacier that flows extremely slowly and which has a constant bulk, occurring in the interior of continents or ice sheets where precipitation is low.

passive immunity *n* (*physiology*) the ability of an individual to resist disease using antibodies that have been donated by another individual rather than by producing its own antibodies.

passive matrix display *n* (*comput*) a form of LCD screen display used for laptop and notebook computers.

passive remote-sensing system *n* a sensor that does not transmit electromagnetic radiation but detects radiation from the Earth's surface.

passive resistance *n* nonviolent noncooperation with the authorities.

passive smoking *n* the involuntary inhalation of smoke from others' cigarettes.

pass laws *npl* the former laws restricting the movements of South African black people.

pass off *vti* (*usu with* **as**) to misrepresent or cause to be misrepresented fraudulently. * *vi* (*feelings, etc*) to disappear gradually. * *vt* to occur, take place; to set aside, disregard.

pass out *vi* to become unconscious. * *vt* to distribute.

pass over *vt* to overlook, omit, or ignore; to deliberately disregard (a person's rightful claims to something).

Passover *n* (*Judaism*) a spring holiday, celebrating the liberation of the Israelites from slavery in Egypt.

passport *n* an official document giving the owner the right to travel abroad; something that secures admission or acceptance.

pass up *vt* (*inf*) (*an opportunity, etc*) to reject or ignore.

password *n* a secret term by which a person is recognized and allowed to pass; any means of admission; a sequence of characters required to access a computer system.

password protection *n* (*comput*) a means of protecting files from unauthorized use, using a password.

past *adj* completed; ended; in time already elapsed. * *adv* by. * *prep* beyond (in time, place, or amount). * *n* time that has gone by; the history of a person, group, etc; a personal background that is hidden or questionable.

past participle *n* a participle verb form used to express completed action used in the formation of perfect tenses in the active voice and all tenses in the passive voice.

past perfect *n* a verb tense usu used with "had" relating past events where the action had already been completed before a past time mentioned.

pasta *n* the flour paste from which spaghetti, noodles, etc are made; any dish of cooked pasta.

paste *n* a soft plastic mixture; flour and water forming dough or adhesive; a fine glass used for artificial gems. * *vt* to attach with paste; (*comput*) to insert text that has just been cut from somewhere else; (*sl*) to beat, thrash.

pasteboard *n* a stiff board made from sheets of paper pasted together. * *adj* flimsy.

pastel *n* a dried mixture of chalk, pigments, and gum used for drawing; a drawing made with such; a soft, pale color. * *adj* delicately colored.

pastelist *n* an artist who uses pastels.

pastern *n* the part of a horse's foot between the fetlock and the hoof.

Pasternak *n* **Boris** [**Leonidovich**] (1890–1960) Russian poet and novelist whose most famous work is *Dr Zhivago* (1958). He was forced by the Soviet authorities to decline the Nobel prize for literature.

paste-up *n* a document prepared for printing consisting of different elements (e.g. type and graphics) pasted onto a backing.

Pasteur *n* **Louis** (1822–95) French chemist who developed the process of pasteurization to destroy microorganisms, and developed immunization against rabies and anthrax.

pasteurization *n* the sterilization of food by heating it to a certain temperature to destroy potentially harmful bacteria.

pasteurize *vt* (*milk, etc*) to sterilize by heat or radiation to destroy harmful organisms.—**pasteurization** *n*.

Pasteur treatment *n* (*med*) a method of inoculation against rabies by successive injections of vaccine.

pasticchio *n* (*mus*) (*Italian*) a selection of pieces from various composers' works.

pastiche *n* (*pl* **pastiches**) a literary, musical, or artistic work in imitation of another's style, or consisting of pieces from other sources.—*also* **pasticcio** (*pl* **pasticci**).

pastille, pastil *n* an aromatic or medicated lozenge.

pastime *n* a hobby; recreation, diversion.

pastor *n* a clergyman in charge of a congregation.

pastoral *adj* of shepherds or rural life; pertaining to spiritual care, esp of a congregation.—**pastorally** *adv*.

pastorale *n* a musical composition with a pastoral subject; a stage entertainment based on a pastoral subject.

pastorate *n* the office or jurisdiction of a pastor; a collective term for pastors.

pastrami *n* highly seasoned smoked beef.

pastry *n* (*pl* **pastries**) dough made of flour, water, and fat used for making pies, tarts, etc; (*pl*) baked foods made with pastry.

pasturage *n* the right to graze animals; pasture.

pasture *n* land covered with grass for grazing livestock; the grass growing on it. * *vt* (*cattle, etc*) to put out to graze in a pasture.

pasty[1] *n* (*pl* **pasties**) meat, etc enclosed in pastry and baked.

pasty[2] *adj* (**pastier, pastiest**) like paste; pallid and unhealthy in appearance.—**pastily** *adv*.—**pastiness** *n*.

pat[1] *vti* (**patting, patted**) to strike gently with the palm of the hand or a flat object; to shape or apply by patting. * *n* a light tap, usu with the palm of the hand; a light sound; a small lump of shaped butter.

pat[2] *adj* apt; exact; glib.—*also adv*.

pat. *abbr* = patent; patented; pattern.

PAT *abbr* = planned actvities time.

pataca *n* the standard monetary unit of Macao, made up of 100 avos.

patagium *n* (*pl* **patagia**) (*zool*) the wing membrane of a bat.

patch *n* a piece of cloth used for mending; a scrap of material; a shield for an injured eye; a black spot of silk, etc worn on the face; an irregular spot on a surface; a plot of ground; a bandage; an area or spot; (*comput*) an addition to a computer software program that is released after the launch of the main product and which serves to correct a fault (bug) or enhances the running of the program. * *vt* to repair with a patch; to piece together; to mend in a makeshift way.—**patchable** *adj*.—**patcher** *n*.

patchouli, patchouly *n* an Asian plant which yields an essential oil from which a perfume is made.

patch test *n* a test undertaken to identify the substances causing a person's allergy.

patchwork *n* needlework made of pieces sewn together; something made of various bits.

patchy *adj* (**patchier, patchiest**) irregular; uneven; covered with patches.—**patchily** *adv*.—**patchiness** *n*.

patd. *abbr* = patented.

pate *n* the head.

pâté *n* a rich spread made of meat, fish, herbs, etc.

pâté de foie gras *n* (*pl* **pâtés de foie gras**) (*French*) a rich paste made from goose liver.

patella *n* (*pl* **patellae**) (*anat*) the kneecap.—**patellar** *adj*.

patellar reflex *see* **reflex action**.

paten *n* (*Christian Church*) a plate used for the bread at the Eucharist.

patency *n* the quality or state of being obvious; (*med*) the state of being unobstructed.

patent *adj* plain; apparent; open to public inspection; protected by a patent. * *n* a government document, granting the exclusive right to produce and sell an invention, etc for a certain time; the right so granted; the thing protected by such a right. * *vt* to secure a patent for.—**patentable** *adj*.

patentee *n* a holder of a patent.

patent leather *n* leather with a hard, glossy finish.

patently *adv* obviously, openly.

patent medicine *n* a medicine made and sold under patent and available without a prescription.

patent office *n* an office which issues patents.

patentor *n* the grantor of a patent.

patent right *n* a right established by a patent, esp the right to manufacture and market an invention exclusively.

Pater *n* **Walter [Horatio]** (1839–84) English essayist and critic, noted esp for his ornate prose style, in particular for his essays *Studies in the History of the Renaissance*. He was a strong influence on the esthetic movement.

paterfamilias *n* (*pl* **patresfamilias**) the (male) head of a family.

paternal *adj* fatherly in disposition; related through the father.—**paternally** *adv*.

paternalism *n* a system that provides for human needs but allows no individual responsibility.—**paternalist** *adj, n*.—**paternalistic** *adj*.—**paternalistically** *adv*.

paternity *n* fatherhood; origin or descent from a father.

paternity suit *n* a lawsuit to determine whether a particular man is the father of a particular child.

paternity test *n* a blood test to establish whether a man is or is not the father of a particular child.

paternoster *n* the Lord's Prayer in Latin; every eleventh bead in a rosary; a fishing line with hooks at intervals; an elevator consisting of a continuously revolving belt of linked compartments.

paternoster lakes *n* a series of elongated lakes in a glacial valley, connected by a river, resembling the beads on a rosary.

path *n* (*pl* **paths**) a way worn by footsteps; a track for people on foot; a direction; a course of conduct; (*comput*) the means of pointing to the exact location of a file on a computer disk.

path. *or* **pathol.** *abbr* = pathological; pathology.

-path *n suffix* denoting an expert in a specific area of medicine; denoting a person suffering from a specified disorder.

pathetic *adj* inspiring pity; (*sl*) uninteresting, inadequate.—**pathetically** *adv*.

pathetic fallacy *n* the attribution of human emotions to inanimate objects.

pathfinder *n* a person who discovers a way; a person who explores untraversed regions to mark out a new route; a person or thing that marks a spot; a radar device for homing on to a target or navigating.—**pathfinding** *n*.

patho- *prefix* disease.

pathogen *n* an agent, such as a microorganism, that causes disease.—**pathogenic** *adj*.

pathogenesis, pathogeny *n* the origin and development of a disease.—**pathogenetic** *adj*.

pathognomonic *adj* characteristic of a particular disease.

pathological, pathologic *adj* of pathology; of the nature of, caused or altered by disease; (*inf*) compulsive.—**pathologically** *adv*.

pathologist *n* a medical specialist who diagnoses by interpreting the changes in tissue and body fluid caused by a disease.

pathology *n* (*pl* **pathologies**) the branch of medicine that deals with the nature of disease, esp its functional and structural effects; any abnormal variation from a sound condition.

pathos *n* a quality that excites pity or sadness; an expression of deep feeling.

pathway *n* a path; (*chem*) a sequence of enzyme-catalyzed reactions.

-pathy *n suffix* feeling; disease; medical treatment.

patience *n* the capacity to endure or wait calmly; a card game for one (—*also* **solitaire**).

patient *adj* even-tempered; able to wait or endure calmly; persevering. * *n* a person receiving medical, dental, etc treatment.—**patiently** *adv*.

patina *n* a green incrustation on old bronze; a surface appearance of something grown beautiful by age or use; a superficial covering or exterior.

patio *n* (*pl* **patios**) an inner, usu roofless, courtyard; a paved area adjoining a house, for outdoor lounging, dining, etc.

patisserie *n* a pastry store; pastries.

Patmos *n* a barren island in the Aegean Sea off the coast of Asia Minor.

Pat. Off. *abbr* = Patent Office.

patois *n* (*pl* **patois**) a dialect.

Paton *n* 1. **Alan [Stewart]** (1903–88) South African novelist whose best-known work is *Cry, the Beloved Country*, a moving study of the hideous consequences of South Africa's race laws. 2. **Sir Joseph Noel** (1821–1901) Scottish painter who specialized in allegorical, historical, and biblical scenes. He worked in a style similar to that of the Pre-Raphaelite Brotherhood.

Patrae *n* the ancient name of Patras, a seaport of Greece, in the northwest of the Morea, on the gulf of the same name.

Patras (Patrai) *n* a city in Greece.

patriarch *n* the father and head of a family or tribe; a man of great age and dignity; (*with cap*) name given to the early forefathers of the Hebrew people.—**patriarchal** *adj*.

patriarchate *n* the office, rank, or jurisdiction of a patriarch; people ruled by a patriarch.

patriarchy *n* (*pl* **patriarchies**) government by the head of a family, tribe, etc; a community ruled in this way.

patrician *n* (*ancient Rome*) a member of the nobility. * *adj* aristocratic; oligarchic.

patricide *n* the unlawful killing of one's father; a person who kills his or her father.—**patricidal** *adj*.

Patrick *n* **Saint** (*d.* 463) British monk who became a missionary in Ireland. He became the patron saint of Ireland. His feast day is March 17.

patrimony *n* (*pl* **patrimonies**) an estate or right inherited from a father or one's ancestors; an ecclesiastical endowment or estate.—**patrimonial** *adj*.

patriot *n* one who strongly supports and serves his or her country.—**patriotic** *adj*.—**patriotically** *adv*.

patriotism *n* love for or loyalty to one's country.

patristic, patristical *adj* pertaining to the theology and writings of the fathers of the early Christian church.

Patroclus *n* (*Greek myth*) the friend of Achilles, whom he accompanied to the Trojan War.

patrol *vti* (**patrolling, patrolled**) to walk around a building or area in order to watch, guard, inspect. * *n* the act of going the rounds; a unit of persons or vehicles employed for reconnaissance, security, or combat; a subdivision of a Scout or Guide group.—**patroller** *n*.

patrolman *n* (*pl* **patrolmen**) a policeman who patrols a particular area.

patron *n* a regular client or customer; a person who sponsors and supports the arts, charities, etc; a protector.—**patronal** *adj*.

patronage *n* the support given or custom brought by a patron; clientele; business; trade; the power to grant political favors; such favors.

patronize *vt* to treat with condescension; to sponsor or support; to be a regular customer of.—**patronization** *n*.

patronizing *adj* condescending.—**patronizingly** *adv*.

patron saint *n* a saint regarded as the sponsor or guardian of an individual, nation, etc.

patronymic *adj* derived from the name of an ancestor. * *n* a name derived from an ancestor.

patsy *n* (*pl* **patsies**) (*sl*) a gullible person; a sucker.

patten *n* a wooden shoe on a metal ring, worn as a protection from the damp.

patter[1] *vi* to make quick tapping sounds, as if by striking something; to run with light steps. * *n* the sound of tapping or quick steps.

patter[2] *vi* to talk rapidly and glibly; to mumble (prayers, etc) mechanically. * *vt* to repeat speech mechanically, to gabble. * *n* rapid speech, esp that of a salesman, comedian, etc; glib speech; chatter; jargon.

pattern *n* a decorative arrangement; a model to be copied; instructions to be followed to make something; a regular way of acting or doing; a predictable route, movement, etc. * *vt* to make or do in imitation of a pattern.—**patterned** *adj*.

patter song *n* a kind of comic song which has a string of tongue-twisting syllables, usu sung quickly to minimal accompaniment. It is often found in opera.

Patti *n* 1. **Adelina** (1843–1919) Spanish soprano of Italian parentage, who made her début in New York in 1859. A natural coloratura, she also sang lyric and dramatic roles, becoming the most successful singer of her age. 2. **Carlo** (1842–73) brother of the above, a violinist and conductor. 3. **Carlotta** (1840–89), sister of the above, a soprano who retired from operatic performances in 1863 because of lameness, and appeared with success in concert work and became a teacher in Paris.

Patton *n* **George S[mith]** (1885–1945) American general and commander of the Allied invasion of North Africa (1942–43). He led US forces across France and Germany to the Czech border (1944–45).

patty *n* (*pl* **patties**) a small pie; a flat cake of ground meat, fish, etc, usu fried.

patulous *adj* (*bot*) spreading, extended.

PAU *abbr* = Pan American Union.

paucity *n* fewness; lack of; scarcity.

Paul *n* **Saint** (*d. c.*67 AD) also known as Saul of Tarsus, Christian apostle and missionary to the Gentiles, writer of many of the Epistles in the New Testament.

Paul VI *n* **[Giovanni Battista Montini]** (1897–1978) Italian pope (1963–78), elected in succession to John XXIII, who continued the trend towards reforms instituted by his predecessor and the Second Vatican Council. His encyclical *Humanae Vitae* (1968), however, reaffirmed the total opposition of the Church towards abortion and 'artificial' methods of contraception.

Pauli *n* **Wolfgang** (1900–58) Austrian-born American physicist. He was awarded the 1945 Nobel prize for physics for his discovery of the "exclusion principle" in 1924, and postulated the existence of the neutrino (later established by Fermi).

Pauling *n* **Linus Carl** (1901–94) American chemist and winner of the 1954 Nobel prize for physics for his research into chemical bonding and molecular structure, and winner of the 1962 Nobel peace prize for his campaigns against nuclear testing.

Paulinus of York *n* **Saint** (*d.* 644) English bishop, who converted Edwin, the pagan king of Northumbria, to Christainity. His feast day is October 10.

paulownia *n* a member of a Japanese genus of trees, with heart-shaped leaves and purple flowers.

paunch *n* the belly, esp a potbelly.

paunchy *adj* (**paunchier, paunchiest**) having a big belly.—**paunchiness** *n*.

pauper *n* a very poor person; (*formerly*) a person dependent on charity.—**pauperism** *n*.

pauperize, pauperise *vt* to reduce to pauperism.

pausa *n* (*mus*) (*Italian*) "rest."

pause *n* a temporary stop, esp in speech, action or music. * *vi* to cease in action temporarily, wait; to hesitate.

P/Av. *abbr* = particular average.

pavage *n* a tax paid for paving streets.

pavane, pavan *n* (the music for) an old stately dance.

Pavarotti *n* **Luciano** (1935–) Italian tenor and one of the most powerful tenor singers of the modern era.

pave *vt* (*a road, etc*) to cover with concrete to provide a hard level surface; **pave the way** to prepare a smooth easy way; to facilitate development.—**paving** *n*.

pavement *n* (*Brit*) sidewalk, flat slabs, tiles, etc forming a surface, esp on a public thoroughfare.

pavilion *n* an annex; a temporary building for exhibitions; a large ornate tent; (*archit*) a part of a building projecting from the main block, often square with a domed roof.

pavillon *n* (*mus*) (*French*) the bell of a brass instrument.

Pavlov *n* **Ivan Petrovich** (1849–1936) Russian physiologist, who was awarded the 1904 Nobel prize for physiology or medicine for his work on the physiology of digestion, and conducted experiments on the conditioning of reflexes.

Pavlova *n* **Anna** (1885–1931) Russian ballerina. Fokine choreographed *The Dying Swan* for her. She also worked with Diaghilev.

Pavlovian *adj* of or relating to the work of the Russian physiologist Ivan Petrovich Pavlov on conditioned reflexes in animals.

pavonine *adj* pertaining to peacocks; resembling a peacock.

paw *n* a foot of a mammal with claws; (*sl*) a hand. * *vti* to touch, dig, hit, etc with paws; to maul; to handle clumsily or roughly.

pawky *adj* (**pawkier, pawkiest**) (*Scot*) having a dry sense of humor.

pawn[1] *n* the piece of lowest value in chess; a person used to advance another's purpose.

pawn[2] *vt* to deposit an article as security for a loan; to wager or risk. * *n* a thing pawned; the state of being given as a pawn.—**pawner** *n*.

pawnbroker *n* a person licensed to lend money at interest on personal property left with him as security.—**pawnbroking** *n*.

pawnshop *n* a pawnbroker's store.

pawpaw *see* papaw.

pax *abbr* = per annum exclusive.

PAX *abbr* = private automatic exchange.

Paxton *n* **Sir Joseph** (1803–65) English architect. His notable works include the Crystal Palace.

paxwax *n* a strong tendon in an animal's neck.

pay *vti* (**paying, paid**) to give (money) to in payment for a debt, goods or services; to give in compensation; to yield a profit; to bear a cost; to suffer a penalty; (*homage, attention*) to give. * *n* payment for services or goods; salary, wages.—**paying** *adj*.—**payer** *n*.

payable *adj* that must be paid, due; to be paid on a specified date.

payback period *n* the period of time that is required for a project to repay its original capital outlay.

paycheck *n* a check made in payment of wages or a salary.

payday *n* the regular day when wages or salaries are paid.

pay differential *n* the difference between the rates of pay of different groups of workers.

pay dirt *n* soil, gravel, etc worth mining for minerals; (*inf*) a source of wealth.

PAYE *abbr* = pay-as-you-earn; the deduction of income tax from wages or salaries at source; pay as you enter.

payee *n* one to whom money is paid.

payload *n* cargo that earns revenue; the total load of an aircraft, spacecraft, satellite, etc.

paymaster *n* a person in charge of paying wages and salaries.

payment *n* the act of paying; amount paid; reward.

payment by results *n* a system of paying workers in which wages are directly related to performance or output.

paynim *n* (*arch*) a heathen; a Muslim.

pay off *vt* to dismiss after paying all due wages; to take revenge on; (*inf*) to bribe. * *vi* (*inf*) to be successful; to yield a large profit. * *n* (**payoff**) a final payment or reckoning; (*inf*) the climax; (*inf*) a bribe.

payola *n* a bribe paid for the clandestine promotion of a product, esp one paid to a disc jockey to play a particular record; a system of such bribes.

PAYP *abbr* = pay as you play (of golf clubs, etc, membership).

payphone *n* a coin-operated telephone.

Payr. *abbr* = Paymaster.

payroll *n* a list of employees and their wages; the actual money for paying wages.

payt. *abbr* = payment.

Payton *n* **Walter** (1954–99) American footballer nicknamed "Sweetness" who played for the Chicago Bears (1975–87).

PAYV *abbr* = pay as you view.

Paz *n* **Octavio** (1914–98) Mexican poet and critic whose important works include *The Violent Season* and *Configurations The Labyrinth of Solitude* and *Eagle or Sun*. He was awarded the Nobel prize for literature in 1990.

Pb *symbol* (*chem*) lead (element).

pb *abbr* = paperback.

p/b *abbr* = purpose-built; push-button.

PB *abbr* = passbook; Pharmacopoeia Brittanica; (*Latin*) *Philosophiae Baccalaureus*, "Bachelor of Philosophy"; Plymouth Brethren; Prayer Book.

PBI *abbr* = Peace Brigades International; (*inf*) poor bloody infantry.

PBM *abbr* = permanent benchmark.

pbr *abbr* = payment by results.

PBS *abbr* = Prayer Book Society; Public Broadcasting System; Public Buildings Service.

pbt *abbr* = profit before tax.

PBT *abbr* = President of the Board of Trade.

PBX *abbr* = private branch exchange.

pc *abbr* = parsec; (*pharm*) (*Latin*) *post cibum* "after meals."

pc or **p.c.** *abbr* = per cent; postcard.

pc. *abbr* = piece; prices.

p/c *abbr* = petty cash; prices current.

P/C *abbr* = per cent.

PC *abbr* = Panama Canal; Past Commander; (*Latin*) *Patres Conscripti*, "conscript fathers," those enrolled as Roman senators; Peace Corps; Perpetual Curate; (*comput*) personal computer; Police Constable; political correctness; politically correct; postcard; Post Commander; Press Council; Principal Chaplain; Principal Conductor; Printmakers' Council.

PCA *abbr* = (*Netherlands*) Permanent Court of Arbitration

pcb *abbr* = petty cash book; printed circuit board.

p.c.b. *abbr* = petty cashbook.

PCB *abbr* = polychlorinated biphenyl; post-coital bleeding; printed circuit board; *see also* **hard card**.

PCC *abbr* = Pacific Conference of Churches; Panama Canal Commission.

PC card *see* **PCMCIA**.

PCCS *abbr* = Primate Captive Care Society.

PCD or **P.C. Dept.** *abbr* = Panama Canal Department.

PC DOS *abbr* (*comput*) = the version of the disk operating system written by Microsoft™ Corporation that is packaged by IBM™ with their personal computers.

pcf *abbr* = pounds per cubic foot.

PCGG *abbr* = Primary Care Group in Gynecology.

pci *abbr* = pounds per cubic inch.

PCI *abbr* (*comput*) = Peripheral Component Interconnect (a standard created by Intel™ dealing with the process of communicating directly between peripheral devices and the computer processor).

PCIFC *abbr* = Permanent Commission of the International Fisheries Convention.

PCIJ *abbr* = Permanent Court of International Justice.

PCJ *abbr* = (Sisters of the) Poor Child Jesus.

PCL *abbr* = printer control language.

pcm *abbr* = per calendar month; pulse code modulation.

PCMCIA *abbr* (*comput*) = Personal Computer Memory Card International Association. A group of manufacturers that has set a standard for credit card-sized peripheral devices such as memory cards, fax modems, sound cards, etc.

PCN *abbr* = personal communications network.

PCOD *abbr* = polycystic ovary disease.

P. Comdr. *abbr* = Post Commander.

PCP *abbr* = pentachlorophenol; phencyclidine (*also* **angel dust**); Pneumocystis carinii pneumonia.

PCR *abbr* = polymerase chain reaction.

pcs. *abbr* = pieces.

pct. *abbr* = per cent.

PCV *abbr* = passenger-carrying vehicle.

P Cygni *n* (*astron*) a recurrent nova in the constellation Cygnus.

PCZ *abbr* = Panama Canal Zone.

Pd *symbol* (*chem*) palladium (element).

pd *abbr* = postage due; post-dated.

pd. or **pd** *abbr* = paid.

p.d. or **pd** *abbr* = (*Latin*) *per diem*, "by the day."

p.d. *abbr* = pitch diameter; (*elec*) potential difference.

p/d *abbr* = price dividend.

PD *abbr* = preventive detention; (*Latin*) *Philosophiae Doctor*, "Doctor of Philosophy."

PD or **P.D.** *abbr* = Police Department.

P.D. *abbr* = public domain.

PDA *abbr* = Packaging Distributors Association; Photographic Dealers Association; *see also* **personal digital assistant**.

PdB, Pd.B. *abbr* (*Latin*) = *Pedagogiae Baccalaureus*, "Bachelor of Pedagogy."

PdD, Pd. D. *abbr* (*Latin*) = *Pedagogiae Doctor*, "Doctor of Pedagogy."

PDF *abbr* (*comput*) = Portable Document Format.

pdi *abbr* = pre-delivery inspection.

PDL *abbr* = page description language.

PdM, Pd.M. *abbr* (*Latin*) = *Pedagogiae Magister*, "Master of Pedagogy."

PDN *abbr* = public data network.

p.d.q., pdq *abbr* = (*inf*) pretty damn quick.

pdr. *abbr* = pounder (as 12-pdr.).

PDRA *abbr* = postdoctoral research assistant.

PDS *abbr* = Parkinson's Disease Society.

pe *abbr* = personal estate; plastic explosive.

p.e. *abbr* = pinion end; pulley end.

p/e *abbr* = price earnings.

PE *abbr* = phase-encoded; physical education; Prince Edward Island; (*statistics*) probable error; Protestant Episcopal.

pea *n* the edible, round, green seed of a climbing leguminous annual plant.

PEA *abbr* = Physical Education Association of Great Britain and Northern Ireland.

PEAB *abbr* = Professional Engineers' Appointments Bureau.

peace *n* tranquility, stillness; freedom from contention, violence or war; a treaty that ends a war.

peaceable *adj* inclined to peace.—**peaceably** *adv*.—**peaceableness** *n*.

Peace Corps *n* a government organization that sends volunteers to work on social, educational, agricultural, etc projects in developing countries.

peace dividend *n* the increase in funds for domestic civil expenditure from a reduction in the defense budget.

peaceful *adj* having peace; tranquil; quiet.—**peacefully** *adv*.—**peacefulness** *n*.

peacemaker *n* one who makes or restores peace; one who reconciles enemies.—**peacemaking** *adj*, *n*.

peace offering *n* a conciliatory gift.

peace officer *n* a civil servant empowered to maintain law and order, a police officer.

peace pipe *n* a tobacco pipe smoked by American Indians as a sign of peace.

peace process *n* the sequence or progress of negotiations towards the settlement of conflict.

peach *n* a round, sweet, juicy, downy-skinned stone-fruit; the tree bearing it; a yellowish pink color; (*sl*) a well-liked person or thing.

peachy *adj* (**peachier, peachiest**) of or resembling a peach; (*inf*) great, excellent.—**peachily** *adv*.—**peachiness** *n*.

peacock *n* (**peacocks, peacock**) a male peafowl with a large brilliantly colored fan-like tail; a person who is a show-off.

Peacock *n* **Thomas Love** (1785–1866) English novelist, essayist, and poet, whose novels (*Headlong Hall*, *Nightmare Abbey*, *Crotchet Castle*, and *Gryll Grange*) consist mostly of witty dialog between characters modeled on his friends and contemporaries, e.g. Byron and Shelley.

Peada *n* (*d*. 656) king of Middle Anglia, Britain (653–656). The youngest son of Penda, he was made an under-king of Middle Anglia.

peafowl *n* (**peafowls, peafowl**) a peacock or a peahen.

pea-green *adj* bright green.

peahen *n* a female peafowl.

peak *n* the summit of a mountain; the highest point; the pointed end of anything; maximum value; the eyeshade of a cap, visor. * *vti* (*politician, actor, etc*) to reach or cause to reach the height of power, popularity; (*prices*) to reach and stay at the highest level.

Peake *n* **Mervyn [Laurence]** (1911–68) English artist, novelist, and poet whose best-known work is the *Gormenghast* trilogy. An official war artist during World War II, his visit to Belsen concentration camp in 1945 profoundly affected him.

peaked *adj* pointed; having a peak; peaky.

peaky *adj* (**peakier, peakiest**) drawn, emaciated; sickly; peaked.

peal *n* a reverberating sound as of thunder, laughter, bells, etc; a set of bells; the changes rung on them. * *vti* to sound in peals, ring out.

Peale *n* 1. **Charles Willson** (1741–1827) American portrait painter. Famous works include *The Exhumation of the Mastodon* (1806) and *Staircase Group* (1795). 2. **Raphaelle** (1774–1825) son of Charles Willson Peale; a gifted still-life painter, his best-known work being *After the Bath* (1823). 3. **Rembrandt** (1778–1860) son of Charles Willson Peale; a portrait painter like his father. 4. **Titian Ramsay** (1799–1885) son of Charles Willson Peale; a painter of natural history.

pean *see* **paean**.

peanut *n* a leguminous plant with underground pods containing edible seeds; the pod or any of its seeds; (*pl*) (*sl*) a trifling thing or amount.

peanut butter *n* a food paste made by grinding roasted peanuts.

pear *n* a common juicy fruit of tapering oval shape; the tree bearing it.

Pearce *n* **Sir Edward L** (*b*. 1699) Irish architect whose notable works include Parliament House, Dublin.

pearl *n* the lustrous white round gem produced by oysters; mother-of-pearl; anything resembling a pearl intrinsically or physically; one that is choice and precious; a bluish medium gray. * *vti* to fish for pearls; to form drops (on), to bespangle.—**pearler** *n*.—**pearliness** *n*.

pearl button *n* a button covered with mother-of-pearl.

pearl diver *n* a person who dives for pearl oysters.

pearl oyster *n* any of various marine bivalve mollusks that yield pearls.

pearly *adj* (**pearlier, pearliest**) clear, lustrous, like a pearl; covered with pearls; bluish gray. * *n* (*pl* **pearlies**) (*pl*) a London costermonger's dress covered with pearl buttons.

Pearly Gates *npl* (*inf*) the gates of Heaven.

pearmain *n* a variety of apple.

Pears *n* **Sir Peter** (1910–86) English tenor. He was closely associated with Britten, who wrote parts with his voice in mind. He was also famed for singing pieces by Bach and Schubert.

Pearsall *n* **Robert Lucas de** (1795–1856) English composer who revived the polyphonic style and who is most famous for his madrigals, part-songs, and religious pieces.

Pearse *n* **Patrick** *or* **Padraic [Henry]** (1879–1916) Irish revolutionary. A prominent spokesman for the Gaelic cultural revival, he joined the Irish Revolutionary Brotherhood in 1915 and was executed for his part in the 1916 Easter Rising.

Pearson *n* 1. **John** (*b*. 1817) English architect whose notable works include Truro Cathedral. 2. **Lester B[owles]** (1897–1972) Canadian Liberal statesman. He became prime minister (1963–68) and was awarded the 1957 Nobel Peace Prize for his role as mediator during the Suez Crisis.

Peary *n* **Robert Edwin** (1856–1920) American naval commander and Arctic explorer credited with being the first man to reach the North Pole (1909).

peasant *n* (*inf*) a countryman or countrywoman; an agricultural laborer; (*derog*) a lout.

peasantry *n* peasants as a class.

pease *n* (*arch*) a pea.

peashooter *n* a toy blowpipe through which peas, etc, are blown.

peasouper *n* (*sl*) a thick yellow fog.

peat *n* decayed vegetable matter from bogs, which is dried and cut into blocks for fuel or used as a fertilizer.—**peaty** *adj*.

peavey *n* (*pl* **peaveys**) a type of cant hook.

PeB, Pe.B. *abbr* (*Latin*) = *Pediatriae Baccalaureus*, "Bachelor of Pediatrics."

pebble *n* a small rounded stone; an irregular, grainy surface.—**pebbled** *adj*.—**pebbly** *adj*.

pebble tool *n* (*archeo*) the most ancient form of human tool, formed from striking off a number of flakes from the top of a pebble to produce a haphazard sharpened edge.

pec *abbr* = photoelectric cell.

PEC *abbr* = Protestant Episcopal Church.

pecan *n* a hickory tree widely grown in the US and Mexico for its edible nuts; its wood; its thin-shelled nut.

peccable *adj* liable to sin.—**peccability** *n*.

peccadillo *n* (*pl* **peccadilloes, peccadillos**) a trifling misdeed, indiscretion.

peccary *n* (*pl* **peccaries, peccary**) an American wild piglike mammal.

peccavi *n* (*pl* **peccavis**) a confession of guilt.

pe. cen. *abbr* = per cent.

Peche *n* **Dagobert** (1887–1923) Austrian designer of ceramics and carpets for industry in a highly distinctive style.

peck *vt* to strike with the beak or a pointed object; to pick at one's food; (*inf*) to kiss lightly; to nag.—*also n*.

pecker *n* something, esp a bird, that pecks; (*sl*) penis.

pecking order *n* a social hierarchy in groups of some birds (e.g. hens), characterized by the pecking of those lower in the scale and submitting to being pecked by those higher; any social hierarchy.

peckish *adj* (*inf*) hungry; irritable.—**peckishly** *adv*.—**peckishness** *n*.

Pécs *n* a city in Hungary.

pecten *n* (*pl* **pectens, pectines**) (*zool*) a comblike membrane on the eyes of birds and some reptiles.

pectin *n* a carbohydrate found in fruits and vegetables, yielding a gel that is used to set jellies.—**pectic** *adj*.

pectoral *adj* of or relating to the breast, chest. * *n* the muscle in the chest; something worn on the breast.

pectoral girdle *n* the skeletal structure to which the bones of the upper limbs are attached—*also* **shoulder girdle**.

peculate *vt* to appropriate money entrusted to one's care, to embezzle.—**peculation** *n*.—**peculator** *n*.

peculiar *adj* belonging exclusively (to); special; distinct; characteristic; strange.—**peculiarly** *adv*.

peculiar galaxy *n* any galaxy that does not easily fit into the standard classification schemes.

peculiarity *n* (*pl* **peculiarities**) an idiosyncrasy; a characteristic; an oddity.

peculiar motion *n* (*astron*) the movement of a specific star with respect to a nearby group of stars.

peculiar star *n* (*astron*) any star that exhibits unusual features in its spectrum when contrasted with most stars in its spectral type.

pecuniary *adj* of or consisting of money.—**pecuniarily** *adv*.

ped. *abbr* = pedal; pedestal.

PED *abbr* = Emergency Preparedness and Disaster Relief Co-ordination Office.

pedagog *n* a schoolteacher.—**pedagogic, pedagogical** *adj*.

pedagogy *n* the art or science of teaching.

pedal¹ *n* a lever operated by the foot. * *vt* (**pedaling, pedaled** *or* **pedalling, pedalled**) to operate or propel by pressing pedals with the foot.—**pedaler, pedaller** *n*.

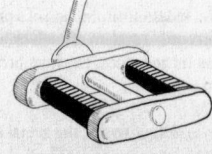

pedal² *adj* (*zool*) pertaining to the foot or feet.

pedalo *n* (*pl* **pedalos**) a small pedal-operated pleasure boat.

pedant *n* a person who attaches too much importance to insignificant details.

pedantic *adj* of, relating to, or being a pedant; narrowly learned.—**pedantically** *adv*.

pedantry *n* (*pl* **pedantries**) an ostentatious display of learning; the state of being a pedant.

pedate *adj* (*bot*) having lateral sections divided into lobes; (*zool*) having, or resembling, feet.

PedB, Ped.B. *abbr* (*Latin*) = Pedagogiae Baccalaureus, "Bachelor of Pedagogy."

PedD, Ped.D. *abbr* (*Latin*) = Pedagogiae Doctor, "Doctor of Pedagogy."

peddle *vt* to go from place to place selling small items; to sell (drugs, etc) illegally.

peddler *n* a person who peddles goods; a person who sells drugs illegally.

pederast *n* a person who practices pederasty.

pederasty *n* sex between a man and a boy.

pedestal *n* the base that supports a column, statue, etc. * *vt* to set on a pedestal; to serve as a pedestal for.

pedestrian *adj* on foot; dull, commonplace. * *n* a person who walks.

pedestrianism *n* walking, or a fondness for walking; the quality of being dull or commonplace.

pedestrianize *vti* to convert (an area) for use by pedestrians only.—**pedestrianization** *n*.

pediatrics *n sing* the branch of medicine dealing with children and their diseases.—*also* **paediatrics**.—**pediatric** *adj*.—**pediatrician** *n*.

pedicab *n* a pedal-driven rickshaw.

pedicle *n* (*med*) a narrow neck of tissue connecting a tumor to its tissue of origin.

pedicular, pediculous *adj* pertaining to lice; infested with lice.—**pediculosis** *n*.

pedicure *n* cosmetic care of the feet, toes, and nails; a person trained to care for feet in this way.

pediform *adj* foot-shaped.

pedigree *n* a line of descent of an animal; a recorded purity of breed of an individual; a genealogy; lineage; derivation. * *adj* having a known ancestry.—**pedigreed** *adj*.

pediment *n* a triangular ornament crowning the front of a classical building, esp a Greek temple; (*geog*) a gentle slope at the foot of a mountain that extends at a low grade towards a river.—**pedimental, pedimented** *adj*.

pedo- *prefix* child.—*also* **paedo-**.

pedology¹ *n* the study of children.—*also* **paedology.**—**pedologic, pedological** *adj*.—**pedologically** *adv*.—**pedologist** *n*.

pedology² *n* the study of soils, their composition, occurrence, and formation.

pedometer *n* an instrument for measuring the distance walked by recording the number of steps taken.

pedophilia *n* sexual attraction towards children.—*also* **paedophilia.**—**pedophiliac, pedophilic** *adj*.—**pedophile** *n*.

Pedubastis *n* (*Egypt*) 1. a local Egyptian Delta king during the turbulent period of the Assyrian war, who opposed and was executed by Assurbanipal. 2. a Twenty-third-Dynasty pharaoh of the same name.

peduncle *n* a flower stalk; (*zool*) the stalk by which certain organisms, such as brachiopods, anchor themselves to the substrate.—**peduncular** *adj*.

pedunculate, pedunculated *adj* having, or growing upon, a peduncle.

Peduzzi *n* Richard (1943–) French painter who restored the library and museum of the Paris Opéra.

pee *vi* (*sl*) to urinate. * *n* urination; urine.

peek *vi* to look quickly or furtively.—*also n*.

peekaboo *n* a child's game in which one person hides behind his or her hands then peeps out suddenly, shouting, "peekaboo!"

peel *vt* to remove skin or rind from; to bare. * *vi* to flake off, as skin or paint. * *n* rind, esp that of fruit and vegetables.—**peeling** *n*.

Peel *n* Sir Robert (1788–1850) British statesman who was twice prime minister (1834–35, 1841–46). He founded the Metropolitan police (nicknamed "Peelers" or "bobbies").

peeler *n* a device for peeling; (*sl*) a stripteaser.

peen *n* the pointed or thin end of a hammer-head.

peep¹ *vi* to make shrill noises as a young bird. * *n* a peeping sound.

peep² *vi* to look hastily or furtively; to look through a slit or narrow opening; to be just showing. * *n* a furtive or hurried glance, a glimpse; (*of day*) the first appearance.

peeper *n* one who peeps; (*sl*) the eye; (*sl*) a private detective.

peephole *n* a small hole, esp in a door, to spy through.

peeping Tom *n* a person who peeps furtively, a voyeur.

peepshow *n* a small show, esp of erotic pictures, viewed through a hole with a lens; a live show with a nude model, viewed from a booth.

peepul *n* an Indian fig tree, sacred to Buddhists.—*also* **pipal**.

peer¹ *vi* to look closely; to look with difficulty; to peep out.

peer² *n* an equal in rank, ability, etc; a nobleman.—**peeress** *nf*.

peerage *n* the rank or title of a peer; peers collectively; a book with a list of peers.

peer group *n* a group of people of the same age, background, education, interests, etc.

peerless *adj* having no equal, matchless.

peer to peer *n* (*comput*) a style of local area network where all the computers are connected to one another and have access to all the information in the network.

peeve *vt* (*inf*) to annoy.

peeved *adj* annoyed, resentful.

peevish *adj* fretful, irritable.—**peevishly** *adv*.—**peevishness** *n*.

peewee *n* a pewit; (*inf*) something small, esp a small child.

peewit *see* **pewit**.

PEF *abbr* = European Pentecostal Fellowship.

PEFC *abbr* = Paper Exporters Freight Committee.

peg *n* a tapered piece (of wood) for securing or hanging things on, for marking position; a predetermined level at which (a price) is fixed; (*mus*) one of the movable parts for tuning the string of an instrument. * *vti* (**pegging, pegged**) to fasten or mark with a peg; (*a price*) to keep steady; (*with* **away at**) to work steadily, persevere.

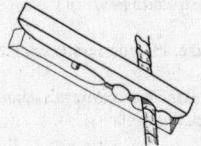

Pegasus¹ *n* (*Greek myth*) the winged horse ridden by Bellerophon.

Pegasus² *n* a large constellation near Cygnus in the northern hemisphere distinguished by a square of its brightest stars.

pegboard *n* a board with small holes for pegs used in cribbage and other games.

peg-box *n* (*mus*) the part of a stringed instrument which houses the pegs that anchor and tune the strings.

pegging *n* the fixing of the value of a country's currency on foreign exchange markets; the fixing by government order of wages or prices at their existing level in order to prevent them rising excessively during a period of inflation.

Pegu *n* a city in the Union of Myanmar.

Pei *n* I. M. (1917–) American architect. His notable works include the John F Kennedy Library, the John Hancock Tower, Boston, and Place Ville-Marie, Montreal.

PEI *abbr* = Prince Edward Island.

Peierls *n* Sir Rudolf Ernst (1907–95) German-born British physicist. With Otto Frisch, he demonstrated the feasibility of an atom bomb during World War II.

peignoir *n* a woman's dressing gown.

Peirithous *n* (*Greek myth*) a king of the Lapiths, who waged a war against the Centaurs and helped Theseus carry off the Amazon Antiope and later Helen.

pejorative *adj* (*word, etc*) disparaging, derogatory. * *n* a disparaging word.—**pejoratively** *adv*.

peke *n* (*sl*) a Pekingese dog.

Pekingese, Pekinese *n* (*pl* **Pekingese, Pekinese**) a breed of small dog with long, silky hair, short legs, and a pug nose.

pekoe *n* a scented black Chinese tea.

PEL *abbr* = Priests' Eucharistic League.

pelage *n* the hair, wool, or fur of an animal.

pelagian *adj* (*marine life*) of or inhabiting the open sea.—*also n.*—**pelagic** *adj*.

pelargonium *n* a member of a widely cultivated genus of flowering plants, including geraniums.

Pelasgians *npl* the earliest inhabitants of Greece and the islands, who were succeeded by the Hellenes.

Pelasgus *n* (*Greek myth*) the ancestor of the Pelasgians.

Pelé [Edson Arantes do Nascimento] (1940–) Brazilian soccer player, recognized as one of the most skillful and entertaining soccer players of all time.

Pel-Epstein fever *see* **Hodgkin's disease**.

pele tower *n* (*archit*) a small fortified building constructed in the border regions of England and Scotland.—*also* **peel tower**.

Peleus *n* (*Greek myth*) a king of Phthia in Thessaly.

pelf *n* (*derog*) money, wealth.

Pelias *n* (*Greek myth*) a king of Iolcus, who was killed by Jason after tricking him into going on the quest for the golden fleece.

pelican *n* a large fish-eating waterbird with an expandable pouched bill.

Pelion *n* a mountain of ancient Greece, in Thessaly, which according to myth the Titans piled upon Mount Ossa to aid them in climbing to Olympus.

pelisse *n* a woman's long cloak, usu trimmed with fur.

pelitic rock *n* (*geol*) a metamorphic rock formed by the metamorphism of shales and mudstones.

pellagra *n* a disease affecting the skin and nervous system caused by a deficiency of nicotinic acid.—**pellagrous** *adj*.

pellet *n* a small ball of paper, bread, etc; a pill; a small ball of hair, bones, etc regurgitated by a bird of prey; a piece of shot. * *vt* to form into pellets.

pellicle *n* a thin skin or film.—**pellicular** *adj*.

pellitory *n* (*pl* **pellitories**) a European flowering plant, growing in walls.

pell-mell *adv, adj* in a disorderly rush; confusedly; headlong.

Pellonia *n* (*Roman myth*) a goddess who was believed to assist mortals in warding off their enemies.

pellucid *adj* (*water, etc*) transparent; (*speech, writing, etc*) clear, lucid.—**pellucidity, pellucidness** *n*.

pelmet *n* a canopy for a window frame to hide a curtain rail, etc; a valance.

Peloponnese, Peloponnesus *n* the peninsula which forms the southern part of Greece.—**Peloponnesian** *adj*.

Pelops *n* (*Greek myth*) son of Tantalus, king of Lydia, who married Hippodamia, a daughter of the king of Elis, and succeeded his father-in-law in that kingdom by conquering him in a chariot race. The Peloponnese received its name from him.

pelorus *n* a navigational instrument resembling a compass used for taking bearings.

pelota *n* a Basque ball game similar to tennis, played with basket-shaped rackets against a wall.

pelt[1] *vt* to throw missiles, or words, at. * *vi* (*rain*) to fall heavily; to hurry, rush. * *n* a rush.—**pelter** *n*.

pelt[2] *n* a usu undressed skin of an animal with its hair, wool, or fur.

peltry *n* (*pl* **peltries**) a collective term for the pelts of animals.

Pelusium *n* (*Egypt*) a strategic town in the eastern Delta region, one of the first to face any invader from Asia, and the location of several sieges and battles in the Late Period.

pelvic girdle *n* the skeletal structure to which the bones of the lower limbs are attached.—*also* **hip girdle**.

pelvic inflammatory disease, PID *n* an acute or chronic infection of the uterus, ovaries, or Fallopian tubes.

pelvis *n* (*pl* **pelvises, pelves**) the bony cavity that joins the lower limbs to the body; the bones forming this.—**pelvic** *adj*.

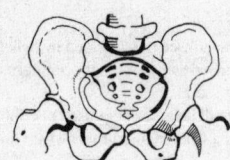

pemmican, pemican *n* a cake of dried lean meat formerly used by North American Indians; a mixture of beef and suet used as emergency rations.

pemphigus *n* a rare skin disease, characterized by watery blisters.—**pemphigoid, pemphigous** *adj*.

pen[1] *n* an implement used with ink for writing or drawing. * *vt* (**penning, penned**) to write, compose.

pen[2] *n* a small enclosure for cattle, poultry, etc; a small place of confinement. * *vt* (**penning, penned**) to enclose in a pen, shut up.

pen[3] *n* a female swan.

pen[4] *n* (*sl*) a penitentiary.

Pen. *or* **pen.** *abbr* = peninsula; penitent; penitentiary.

PEN *abbr* = (International Association of) Poets, Playwrights, Editors, Essayists, and Novelists.

penal *adj* relating to, liable to, or prescribing punishment; punitive.—**penally** *adv*.

penal code *n* a code of laws concerning crimes and offenses and their punishment.

penalize *vt* to impose a penalty; to put under a disadvantage.—**penalization** *n*.

penalty *n* (*pl* **penalties**) a punishment attached to an offense; suffering or loss as a result of one's own mistake; a disadvantage imposed for breaking a rule as in sports; a fine.

penalty area *n* (*soccer*) the area in front of goal in which a foul by a defending player results in the award of a penalty kick.

penalty box *n* (*ice hockey*) an area of the ice where players are sent as a penalty.

penance *n* voluntary suffering to atone for a sin; a sacramental rite consisting of confession, absolution, and penance. * *vt* to impose a penance on.

Penardun *n* (*Welsh Celtic myth*) said to have been the daughter of Don and the wife of Llyr. One legend has it that she was the mother of Manawydan fab Lyr, Branwen and Bendigeid Vran.

penates *npl* (*Roman religion*) gods of the storeroom and kitchen, whose images were kept in the central part of every house, each family having its own penates and the state its public penates.—*also* **di penates**.

pence *see* penny.

penchant *n* inclination, strong liking (for).

pencil *n* a pointed rod-shaped instrument with a core of graphite or crayon for writing, drawing, etc; a set of convergent light rays or straight lines; a fine paintbrush. * *vt* (**penciling, penciled** *or* **pencilling, pencilled**) to write, draw, or color with a pencil; (*with* **in**) to commit tentatively.—**penciler, penciller** *n*.

pen computer *n* a style of computer that can recognize handwriting as a method of input.

Penda *n* (577–655) king of Mercia, Britain (626–655). The son of Pybba, he features heavily in Bede's *Ecclesiastical History*, where he is portrayed as an anti-hero pagan warrior-king.

pendant, pendent *n* a hanging ornament, esp a jewel on a necklace, bracelet, etc; a light-fitting suspended from a ceiling. * *adj* (*usu* **pendent**) hanging; projecting; undecided.—**pendency** *n*.

Pendaran Dyfed *n* (*Welsh Celtic myth*) a swineherd who is the foster father of Pryderi.

pendentive *n* (*archit*) a portion of a dome supported by a single pillar.

Penderecki *n* **Krzysztof** (1933–) Polish composer who has experimented with many unconventional sounds. His compositions include *Threnody to the Victims of Hiroshima*, the operas *The Devils of Loudon* and *Paradise Lost*, pieces for chorus and orchestra (such as *St Luke Passion)*, and many orchestral works.

pending *adj* undecided; unfinished; imminent. * *prep* during; until, awaiting.

pendragon *n* (*hist*) a chief of the ancient Britons or Welsh.

pendulous *adj* hanging downwards and swinging freely.—**pendulously** *adv*.

pendulum *n* a weight suspended from a fixed point so as to swing freely; such a device used to regulate the movement of a clock; something that swings to and fro.

penecontemporaneous *adj* (*geol*) (*process*) happening in a rock soon after its formation.

Penelope *n* (*Greek myth*) the wife of Odysseus and mother of Telemachus.

peneplain, peneplane *n* (*geol*) a tract of land which is almost a plain.

penetrable *adj* able to be penetrated.—**penetrability** *n*.

penetralia *npl* the inner parts of a temple, etc; mysteries.

penetrant *adj* penetrating. * *n* something which, or someone who, penetrates.

penetrate *vti* to thrust, force a way into or through something; to pierce; to permeate; to understand.—**penetrator** *n*.—**penetrative** *adj*.

penetrating *adj* acute, discerning; (*voice*) easily heard through other sounds.—**penetratingly** *adv*.

penetration *n* the capability, act, or action of penetrating; acute insight.

penguin *n* a flightless, marine bird with black and white plumage, usu found in the Antarctic.

penicillate *adj* (*biol*) having, or forming, small tufts.

penicillin *n* an antibiotic produced naturally and synthetically from molds.

penile *adj* of, like, or affecting the penis.

peninsula *n* a piece of land almost surrounded by sea.—**peninsular** *adj*.

penis *n* (*pl* **penises, penes**) the male copulative and urinary organ in mammals.

penitence *n* sorrow for committing a sin, repentance.

penitent *adj* feeling regret for sin, repentant, contrite. * *n* a person who atones for sin.—**penitently** *adv*.

penitential *adj* of or expressing penance; being penitent.—**penitentially** *adv*.

penitentiary *n* (*pl* **penitentiaries**) a state or federal prison. * *adj* pertaining to penance; pertaining to the reformatory treatment of prisoners.

penknife *n* (*pl* **penknives**) a small knife, usu with one or more folding blades, that fits into the pocket.

penman *n* (*pl* **penmen**) a writer.

penmanship *n* the art, or style, of writing.

Penn, Penna, Penn., Penna. *abbr* = Pennsylvania.

pen name *n* a literary pseudonym.—*also* **nom de plume**.

pennant *n* a long tapering flag used for identifying vessels and for signaling; such a flag symbolizing a championship.

penni *n* a monetary unit of Finland, equal to one hundredth of a markka.

penniless *adj* having no money; poor.—**pennilessly** *adv*.—**pennilessness** *n*.

pennon *n* a small, pointed, or swallow-tailed flag of a medieval knight; a long tapering streamer on a ship.

Pennsylvania (PA) *n* a state of the United States of America (USA) of which the capital is Harrisburg.

Pennsylvania *n* the song of the American state, Pennsylvania.

penny *n* (*pl* **pence** *denoting sum*, **pennies** *denoting separate coins*) a one-cent coin; (*UK*) a coin worth one hundredth of a pound; a monetary unit of the Republic of Ireland, equal to one hundredth of a punt.

penny arcade *n* an amusement arcade with coin-operated machines.

penny dreadful *n* (*inf*) a cheap crime or adventure novel..

penny-pinching *adj* frugal; miserly. * *n* a penny-pinching person.—**penny pincher** *n*.

pennyroyal *n* an aromatic plant of the mint family.

pennyweight *n* a weight, equivalent to 24 grains or $^1/_{20}$ of an ounce (troy).

penny-whistle *see* **tin whistle**.

pennywort *n* a kind of round-leafed plant, growing variously in walls or in marshes.

pennyworth *n* a penny's worth (of a purchase); a small amount.

penology *n* the study of the punishment and prevention of crime.—*also* **poenology**.—**penological** *adj*.—**penologist** *n*.

pen pal *n* a friend with whom one is in contact only through correspondence.

pensile *adj* suspended; pendulous.

pension *n* a payment received by people who have retired from employment or who have reached a certain age.

pension[1] *n* a periodic payment to a person beyond retirement age, or widowed, or disabled; a periodic payment in consideration of past services. * *vt* to grant a pension to; (*with* **off**) to dismiss or retire from service with a pension.—**pensionable** *adj*.

pension[2] *n* a boarding-house or small hotel in continental Europe, esp France.

pensionary *adj* by way of pension. * *n* (*pl* **pensionaries**) a pensioner.

pensioner *n* a person who receives a pension; a senior citizen.

pension fund *n* money from state and private pension contributions that is invested so as to obtain as high a return as possible to provide the funds from which pensions are paid.

pensive *adj* thoughtful, musing; wistful, melancholy.—**pensively** *adv*.—**pensiveness** *n*.

penstemon *n* a flowering garden plant of the family including the beard-tongues.—*also* **pentstemon**.

penstock *n* a sluice gate for regulating (water) flow; a water pipe.

Pent. *abbr* = Pentecost.

pent-, penta- *prefix* five.

pentacle *see* **pentagram**.

pentad *n* a group of five; the number five; (*meteorology*) a period of five days, which is used in meteorological records because it is a fraction of a normal year.

pentadactyl *adj* (*zool*) having five fingers or toes.

pentagon *n* (*geom*) a polygon with five sides; (*with cap*) the pentagonal headquarters of the US defense establishment; the US military leadership collectively.—**pentagonal** *adj*.

pentagram *n* a five-pointed star, often used as a magic symbol.—*also* **pentacle**.

Pentagram *n* British industrial and graphic design consultancy which grew out of the firm Forbes, Fletcher and Gill.

pentahedron *n* (*pl* **pentahedrons, pentahedra**) a solid figure with five faces.

pentamerous *adj* (*bot, zool*) with five parts.

pentameter *n* a verse of five metrical feet.

pentangle *n* a pentagram.

Pentateuch *n* the collective name for the first five books of the Old Testament.

pentathlon *n* an athletic contest involving participation by each contestant in five different events.—**pentathlete** *n*.

pentatonic *adj* (*mus*) of five notes.

pentatonic scale *n* (*mus*) a scale composed of five notes in an octave. It is found in various types of folk music from Scottish to Chinese.

pentavalent *adj* (*chem*) with a valency of five.

Pentecost *n* a Christian festival on the seventh Sunday after Easter; Whit Sunday; the Jewish festival held on the fiftieth day after Passover.

Pentecostal *adj* denoting a mainly Protestant Christian movement, now with various organized forms, emphasizing the immediate presence of God in the Holy Spirit; of Pentecost or the influence of the Holy Spirit. * *n* a member of a Pentecostal church.—**Pentecostalist** *adj, n*.

Pentheus *n* (*Greek myth*) a king of Thebes, who refused to worship Dionysus and was pulled to pieces by his mother and her sisters, who in a fit of insanity thought he was a wild boar.

penthouse *n* an apartment on the roof or in the top floor of a building.

pentimento *n* (*art*) part of a painting that has been painted over by the artist but later faintly reappears.

Pentium *n* (*comput*) (*trademark*) the name of a microprocessor chip from Intel™. The Pentium is a RISC and operates much faster than its predecessors. —*See also* **power PC**.

pent-up *adj* (*emotion*) repressed, confined.

penult *n* the penultimate syllable of a word. * *adj* last but one.

penultimate *adj* last but one.—*also adj*.

penumbra *n* (*pl* **penumbrae, penumbras**) a shaded region around the shadow of an opaque object, esp the shadow of the moon or earth in an eclipse; the lighter outer part of a sunspot; (*art*) the boundary of light and shade in a picture.—**penumbral** *adj*.

penurious *adj* grudging with money, stingy; poor; scanty.—**penuriously** *adv*.—**penuriousness** *n*.

penury *n* (*pl* **penuries**) extreme poverty; want.

peon *n* a Spanish American laborer; (*formerly*) a Spanish American laborer compelled to work to pay off debts.

peonage, peonism *n* the condition of being a peon; the system of compelling someone to work for a creditor to pay off debts.

peony *n* (*pl* **peonies**) a plant with large, showy, red, pink, or white flowers.

people *n* the body of enfranchised citizens of a state; a person's family, relatives; the persons of a certain place, group, or class; persons considered indefinitely; human beings; (*pl*) all the persons of a racial or ethnic group, typically having a common language, institutions, homes, and culture. * *vt* to populate with people.

Peoples of the Sea *npl* a group of people of diverse origins who came by sea and invaded Egypt and some surrounding regions, *c.*1300–1200 BC.—*also* **Sea Peoples**.

pep *n* (*inf*) energy, vigor; bounce. * *vt* (**pepping, pepped**) (*usu with* **up**) to enliven by injecting with pep.

PEP *abbr* = personal equity plan; political and economic planning.

Peploe *n* **Samuel John** (1871–1935) Scottish painter, known for his still lifes of flowers.

pepper *n* a sharp, hot condiment made from the fruit of various plants; capsicum, the fruit of the pepper plant, which can be red, yellow, or green, sweet or hot, and is eaten as a vegetable. * *vt* to sprinkle or flavor with pepper; to hit with small shot; to pelt; to beat.

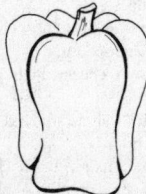

peppercorn *n* a dried pepper berry.

pepper mill *n* hand mill for grinding peppercorns.

peppermint *n* a pungent and aromatic mint plant; its oil used for flavoring; a sweet flavored with peppermint.

pepperoni *n* a spicy beef and pork sausage.

pepperwort *n* a form of aquatic or marsh fern; a type of cress.

peppery *adj* of, like, full of, pepper; fiery; hot-tempered.—**pepperiness** *n*.

peppy *adj* (**peppier, peppiest**) full of bounce; lively.—**peppiness** *n*.

pepsin, pepsine *n* a digestive enzyme contained in gastric juice.

pep talk *n* (*inf*) a vigorous talk made with the intention of arousing enthusiasm, increasing confidence, etc.

peptic *adj* of or promoting digestion; of, producing, or caused by the action of the digestive juices.

peptic ulcer *n* an ulcer of the stomach lining or duodenum.

peptide *n* an organic compound made up of two or more amino acids and collectively named by the number of amino acids. A dipeptide therefore contains two, and a polypeptide many.

peptide bond *n* (*biochemistry*) a covalent linkage formed when two amino acids join together.

peptone *n* a product of the action of pepsin on proteins.

peptonize *vt* to convert into peptone.

Pepusch *n* **Johann Christoph** (1667–1752) German-born composer, conductor, organist, and teacher who settled in London in 1700. His works include odes, motets, masques, and cantatas and he wrote the overture to John Gay's *The Beggar's Opera*.

Pepy I *n* (*Egypt*) an Old Kingdom pharaoh of the Sixth Dynasty.

Pepy II *n* (*Egypt*) an Old Kingdom pharaoh of the Sixth Dynasty. He is believed to have reigned for longer than any other king of Egypt, and may have attained the age of a hundred.

Pepys *n* **Samuel** (1633–1703) English diarist and Admiralty official. His diary (written in code) was first published in 1825. The full uncensored version was published in 11 volumes (1970–83), and includes much fascinating detail of life in 17th-century London.

per *prep* for or in each; through, by, by means of; (*inf*) according to.

per. *abbr* = period; person.

PER *abbr* = Professional and Executive Recruitment; Professional Employment Register.

PERA *abbr* = Production Engineering Research Association (of Great Britain).

peradventure *adv* (*arch*) by chance; perhaps.

perambulate *vti* to walk around.—**perambulation** *n*.—**perambulatory** *adj*.

perambulator *n* one who or that which perambulates; (*Brit formal*) a baby carriage.

per an. or per ann. *abbr* = per annum.

per annum *adv* yearly; each year.

percale *n* a cotton fabric, often used for sheets.

per capita *adj, adv* of or for each person.

perceive *vt* to become aware of, apprehend, through the senses; to recognize.—**perceivable** *adj*.—**perceivably** *adv*.

per cent, percent *adv* in, for each hundred. * *n* a percentage.

percentage *n* rate per hundred parts; a proportion; (*inf*) profit, gain.

percentage of sales method *n* a rule-of-thumb method of establishing a company's promotion budget in which the budgeted amount is a set percentage of the past sales or projected sales of the relevant product.

percept *n* something which is perceived.

perceptible *adj* able to be perceived; discernible.—**perceptibility** *n*.—**perceptibly** *adv*.

perception *n* the act or faculty of perceiving; discernment; insight; a way of perceiving, view.—**perceptional** *adj*.

perceptive *adj* able to perceive; observant.—**perceptively** *adv*.—**perceptivity, perceptiveness** *n*.

perch[1] *n* (*pl* **perch, perches**) a spiny-finned chiefly freshwater edible fish.

perch[2] *n* a pole on which birds roost or alight; an elevated seat or position. * *vti* to alight, rest, on a perch; to balance (oneself) on; to set in a high position.

perchance *adv* (*arch*) by chance; perhaps.

perched water table *n* (*geol*) an aquifer that lies on top of impermeable rock, which is above the level of the normal water table of the area.

Percheron *n* a sturdy breed of drafthorse.

Percier *n* **Charles** (1764–1838) French architect who became a designer.

percipient *adj* perceiving; perceptive. * *n* a person who perceives.—**percipience** *n*.

percolate *vt* (*liquid*) to pass through a filter or pores; to brew coffee. * *vi* to ooze through; to spread gradually.—**percolation** *n*.

percolation *n* (*geol*) the process by which water moves downwards through soil and through the joints, cracks, and pores in rocks.

percolator *n* a coffeepot in which boiling water is forced through ground coffee beans.

percuss *vt* to tap sharply; (*med*) to tap (the patient's body) gently to find out the condition of an internal organ by sound.

percussion *n* impact, collision; musical instruments played by striking with sticks or hammers, e.g. cymbals, drums, etc; such instruments regarded as a section of an orchestra; (*med*) tapping the body to discover the condition of an organ by the sounds.—**percussive** *adj*.

percussionist *n* a person who plays a percussion instrument.

percutaneous *adj* (*med*) done through the skin.

perd. *abbr* (*mus*) (*Italian*) = *perdendosi*, "vanishing."

perdendosi *n* (*mus*) (*Italian*) "vanishing," i.e. dying away (of sound).

per diem *adv, adj* every day. * *n* a daily allowance, as for expenses.

perdition *n* utter loss of the soul; eternal damnation; (*arch*) total destruction, ruin.

Peredur *n* (*Welsh Celtic myth*) the son of Efrawg. He is the model of Percival of the Arthurian legends, who went on quests to find the Holy Grail.

peregrinate *vti* to travel, roam about.—**peregrinator** *n*.—**peregrination** *n*.

peregrine *n* a type of falcon common to most areas of the world.

Perelman *n* **S[idney] J[oseph]** (1904–79) American humorist who wrote the sceenplays for some of the Marx Brothers' movies, and published several collections of articles, including *The Road to Milltown* and *Under the Spreading Atrophy*.

peremptory *adj* urgent; absolute; dogmatic; dictatorial.—**peremptorily** *adv*.—**peremptoriness** *n*.

perennial *adj* perpetual; lasting throughout the year. * *n* (*bot*) a plant lasting more than two years.—**perennially** *adv*.

perestroika *n* the Russian word for "reform, reconstruction," applied to the policy, initiated by President Gorbachev of the former USSR, of dismantling the monolithic state institutions and replacing them with democratic forms of legislation and administration.—**perestroikan** *adj*.

perf. *abbr* = perfect; perforated; performer.

perfect *adj* faultless; exact; excellent; complete. * *n* (*gram*) a verb form expressing completed action or designating a present state that is the result of an action in the past. * *vt* to improve; to finish; to make fully accomplished in anything.—**perfecter** *n*.—**perfectness** *n*.

perfectible *adj* capable of being made perfect.—**perfectibility** *n*.

perfect interval *see* **interval**.

perfection *n* the act of perfecting; the quality or condition of being perfect; great excellence; faultlessness; the highest degree; a perfect person or thing.

perfectionist *n* one who demands the highest standard.—**perfectionism** *n*.

perfectly *adv* thoroughly, completely; quite well; in a perfect manner.

perfecto *n* (*pl* **perfectos**) a large cigar, tapered at both ends.

perfervid *adj* (*arch*) very fervid, ardent.

perfidious *adj* treacherous, faithless; deceitful.—**perfidiously** *adv*.—**perfidiousness** *n*.

perfidy *n* (*pl* **perfidies**) breach of faith; treachery.

perfoliate *adj* (*bot*) with a stalk which apparently passes through the leaf.

perforate *vt* to pierce; to make a hole or row of holes, by boring through. * *adj* perforated.—**perforatory** *adj*.—**perforator** *n*.

perforation *n* the act of perforating; the condition of being perforated; a hole; a row of holes to facilitate tearing; (*medical*) a hole that forms in a hollow organ, tissue, or tube, e.g. the stomach, eardrum, etc.

perforce *adv* (*arch*) by necessity.

perform *vti* to carry out, do; to put into effect; to act; to execute; to act before an audience; to play a musical instrument.—**performable** *adj*.—**performing** *adj*.

performance *n* the act of performing; a dramatic or musical production; an act or action; (*inf*) a fuss; the capabilities of a vehicle, aircraft, etc. * *adj* high-performance.

performance appraisal *n* the process of evaluating the performance of an employee by management.

performer *n* a person who performs, esp one who entertains an audience.

performing arts *npl* arts, such as drama, music, and dance, that require theatrical presentation.

perfume *n* a pleasing odor; fragrance; a mixture containing fragrant essential oils and a fixative. * *vt* to scent; to put perfume on.—**perfumer** *n*.

perfumery *n* (*pl* **perfumeries**) a place where perfume is sold; perfume in general.

perfunctory *adj* superficial, hasty; done merely as a matter of form, half-hearted; performed carelessly; indifferent.—**perfunctorily** *adv*.—**perfunctoriness** *n*.

perfuse *vt* (*with* **with**) to suffuse, permeate.—**perfusion** *n*.—**perfusive** *adj*.

pergola *n* an arbor or walk arched by a latticework structure supporting climbing plants.

Pergolesi *n* 1. **Giovanni Battista** (1710–36) Italian composer, violinist, and organist who became famous for his comic intermezzos, *La Serva Padrona* and *Livietta e Tracollo*. He also wrote church music and sonatas. 2. **Michelangelo** (*fl*.1765–1800) Italian decorator, probably brought to England by Robert Adam.

perh. *abbr* = perhaps.

perhaps *adv* possibly, maybe.

peri., perig. *abbr* = perigee.

peri- *prefix* around; near.

Peri *n* **Jacopo** (1561–1633) Italian composer and singer. He is credited with writing the music for *Eurydice* (1600), the first opera for which the complete music is extant. He wrote other operas as well as madrigals and ballets.

perianth *n* the outer part of a flower, comprising the calyx and corolla together.

periapt *n* an amulet.

periastron *n* (*astron*) (in a binary star system) the point in the orbits where the two stars are closest to each other.

pericarditis *n* inflammation of the pericardium.

pericardium *n* (*pl* **pericardia**) the membrane enclosing the heart.—**pericardiac, pericardial** *adj*.

pericarp *n* the part of a fruit developed from the wall of the ovary.—**pericarpial** *adj*.

pericenter *n* (*astron*) in an orbit, the point that is nearest the center of mass of the whole system.

perichondrium *n* (*pl* **perichondria**) the membrane covering a cartilage.

periclase *n* magnesium oxide as a mineral in crystal or grain form.

pericranium *n* (*pl* **pericrania**) the membrane surrounding the cranium.

peridot *n* a pale green semi-precious form of olivine.

perigee *n* the point of the moon's, or a planet's, orbit, when it is nearest the earth.—**perigean** *adj*.

perihelion *n* (*pl* **perihelia**) the point of a planet's or comet's orbit when it is nearest the sun.

peril *n* danger, jeopardy; risk, hazard.

perilous *adj* dangerous.—**perilously** *adv*.

perilymph *n* the fluid that separates the bony labyrinth and the membranous labyrinth of the ear.

perimeter *n* a boundary around an area; (*math*) the curve or line bounding a closed figure; the length of this.—**perimetric** *adj*.—**perimetry** *n*.

perinatal mortality *n* fetal deaths after week 28 of pregnancy and newborn deaths during the first week or two of life.

perineum *n* the area between the genitals and the anus.—**perineal** *adj*.

period *n* a portion of time; menstruation; an interval of time as in an academic day, playing time in a game, etc; an age or era in history, epoch; a stage in life; (*gram*) the punctuation mark at the end of a sentence, a full stop (.); (*astron*) a planet's time of revolution; (*physics*) the time taken for a body to complete one full oscillation, which can involve a vibration, rotation, or harmonic motion; (*chem*) a horizontal row in the periodic table, e.g. those elements between an alkali metal and the next inert gas; (*geol*) the second order of geological time, e.g. the Carboniferous Period. * *interj* an exclamation used for emphasis.

period bill *n* a bill of exchange that is payable on a specified date rather than on demand.

periodic *adj* relating to a period; recurring at regular intervals, cyclic; intermittent.—**periodically** *adv*.—**periodicity** *n*.

periodical *adj* periodic. * *n* a magazine, etc issued at regular intervals.

periodic table *n* a list of chemical elements tabulated by their atomic number.

Period–luminosity relation *n* (*astron*) a graphical plot of luminosity against time for stars of the Cepheid variable type (pulsating variable yellow giants).

period of grace *n* the time that is usually allowed for certain bills of exchange after they mature.

periodontics *n sing* the branch of dentistry dealing with disorders of the gums and tissues around the teeth.—**periodontal** *adj*.—**periodontist** *n*.

periosteum *n* (*pl* **periostea**) the membrane covering the bones.

periostitis *n* inflammation of the periosteum.

peripatetic *adj* itinerant; (*teacher*) traveling from one school to another.—*also n*.

peripheral *adj* incidental, superficial; relating to a periphery; (*equipment*) for connection to a computer. * *n* a device such as a printer, scanner, etc used with a computer.—**peripherally** *adv*.

peripheral nervous system *n* those parts of the nervous system excluding the central nervous system (brain and spinal cord).

peripheral neuritis *n* inflammation of the nerves of the peripheral nervous system.

periphery *n* (*pl* **peripheries**) the outer surface or boundary of an area; the outside surface of anything.

periphrasis *n* (*pl* **periphrases**) a roundabout way of speech; circumlocution.

periphrastic *adj* using periphrasis; circumlocutory.—**periphrastically** *adv*.

peripteral *adj* (*archit*) with a row of columns on every side.

periscope *n* a device with mirrors that enables the viewer to see objects above or around an obstacle or above water, as from a submarine.

periscopic *adj* (*lens*) with a view around; of a periscope.—**periscopically** *adv*.

perish *vi* to be destroyed or ruined; to die, esp violently; (*rubber, etc*) to deteriorate, rot. * *vt* to cause to rot or perish.

perishable *adj* liable to spoil or decay. * *n* something perishable, esp food.—**perishability** *n*.

peristalsis *n* (*physiology*) the wave-like contraction and relaxation of muscles in the esophagus and intestines that move ingested food gradually along the alimentary canal.

peristalth *n* (*archeo*) an encircling curb of stones that was sometimes placed around a barrow or cairn.

peristyle *n* (*archit*) a series of columns surrounding a court, cloister, or open space.

peristyle court *n* (*Egypt*) a temple or palace courtyard with a pillared arcade on all four sides.

peritoneum *n* (*pl* **peritoneums, peritonea**) a membrane that lines the walls of the abdomen.—**peritoneal** *adj*.

peritonitis *n* inflammation of the peritoneum.—**peritonitic** *adj*.

peritonsillar abscess *see* **quinsy**.

periwinkle[1] *n* any of various edible small marine gastropods with spiraled shells.

periwinkle[2] *n* any of various evergreen trailing plants with blue or white flowers.

perjure *vt* to commit perjury, swear falsely.—**perjurer** *n*.

perjury *n* (*pl* **perjuries**) (*law*) the crime of giving false witness under oath, swearing to what is untrue.

perk[1] *n* (*usu pl*) (*inf*) a perquisite.

perk[2] *vti* (*usu with* **up**) to recover self-confidence; to become lively or cheerful; to prick up, as of a dog's ears; to smarten up.

perky *adj* (**perkier, perkiest**) pert, cheeky; lively, jaunty.—**perkily** *adv*.—**perkiness** *n*.

Perlman *n* **Itzhak** (1945–) Israeli violinist who has been a soloist with many famous orchestras.

perm *n* a straightening or curling of hair by use of chemicals or heat lasting through many washings. * *vt* (*hair*) to give a perm to.—*also* **permanent wave**.

permafrost *n* subsoil that is permanently frozen.

permanence *n* the condition or quality of being permanent.

permanency *n* (*pl* **permanencies**) permanence; a person or thing that is permanent.—**permanently** *adv*.

permanent *adj* lasting, or intended to last, indefinitely.

permanent interest-bearing share *n* a fixed-interest security that is non-redeemable and that pays interest at a fixed rate at issue.

permanent magnet *n* a magnet that retains its magnetic properties after being removed from the energizing magnetic field.

permanent press *n* a process for treating a fabric so that it holds its shape permanently and resists wrinkling; material treated by this process.

permanent wave *n* a perm.

permanganate *n* a salt of an acid of manganese, esp permanganate of potash.

PERME *abbr* = Propellants, Explosives, and Rocket Motor Establishment.

permeable *adj* admitting the passage of a fluid.—**permeability** *n*.—**permeably** *adv*.

permeate *vti* to fill every part of, saturate; to pervade, be diffused (through); to pass through by osmosis.—**permeation** *n*.

permissible *adj* allowable.—**permissibility** *n*.

permission *n* authorization; consent.

permission to deal *n* (*UK*) permission granted by the London Stock Exchange to deal in the shares of a newly floated company.

permissive *adj* allowing permission; lenient; sexually indulgent.—**permissively** *adv*.—**permissiveness** *n*.

permit *vti* (**permitting, permitted**) to allow to be done; to authorize; to give opportunity. * *n* a license.—**permitter** *n*.

permutation *n* any radical alteration; a change in the order of a series; any of the total number of groupings within a group; an ordered arrangement of a set of objects.—**permutational** *adj*.

permute *vt* to put into a different order.

pernicious *adj* destructive; very harmful.—**perniciously** *adv*.—**perniciousness** *n*.

pernicious anemia *n* a type of anemia caused by vitamin deficiency, which in turn results in a lack of red blood cell (erythrocyte) production and megaloblasts in the bone marrow.

pernickety *see* **persnickety**.

Perón *n* **Juan Domingo** (1895–1974) Argentinian dictator, who became president (1946–55) and was deposed by the army and exiled, until his re-election as president (1973–74). His success owed much to his wife Eva [Duarte] Perón (1919–52) an ex-actress nicknamed "Evita."

perorate *vi* to speak at length.

peroration *n* the final part of a speech or discourse.

Pérotin *or* **Petronius** *n* **Magnus** (*c*.1160–1220) French composer, one of the first to be known by name. He wrote church music and motets.

peroxide *n* hydrogen peroxide; a colorless liquid used as an antiseptic and as a bleach.

perpendicular *adj* upright, vertical; (*geom*) at right angles (to). * *n* a perpendicular line, position or style.—**perpendicularity** *n*.—**perpendicularly** *adv*.

perpetrate *vt* (*something evil, criminal, etc*) to do; (*a blunder, etc*) to commit.—**perpetration** *n*.—**perpetrator** *n*.

Perpetua *n* **Saint** (*d*. 203) Christian martyr. Aged twenty-two and the mother of a young baby, she was killed at Carthage, along with another female martyr, Felicitas, by the gladiators' swords. Their feast day is March 7.

perpetual *adj* continuous; everlasting; (*plant*) blooming continuously throughout the season.—**perpetually** *adv*.

perpetual canon *n* (*mus*) a canon so constructed that it may be repeated perpetually without break in time or rhythm.

perpetual inventory *n* a system of continuous stock control in which an account is kept of each item of stock.

perpetuate *vt* to cause to continue; to make perpetual.—**perpetuation** *n*.—**perpetuator** *n*.

perpetuity *n* (*pl* **perpetuities**) endless duration, eternity; perpetual continuance; an annuity payable forever.

perpetuum mobile *n* (*mus*) (*Latin*) "perpetually in motion," a short piece of music with a repetitive note-pattern that is played quickly without any pauses.

perplex *vt* to puzzle, bewilder, confuse; to complicate.

perplexity *n* (*pl* **perplexities**) bewilderment, a being at a loss; a perplexing thing, a dilemma.

per pro *or* **per proc.** *abbr* (*Latin*) = *per procurationem*, "by the agency of" (used when signing correspondence on behalf of someone else).

perquisite *n* an expected or promised privilege, gain, or profit incidental to regular wages or salary; a tip, gratuity; something claimed as an exclusive right.—*also* **perk**.

Perriand *n* **Charlotte** (1903–89) French designer who worked closely with Le Corbusier.

perron *n* a flight of steps outside a building, leading to the first floor.

perry *n* (*pl* **perries**) a cider-like drink made from pears.

Perry *n* **Fred[erick John]** (1909–95) English-born American tennis and table-tennis player. He became the world champion table-tennis player in 1929, and became one of the most successful lawn tennis players of the 1930s, winning every major tournament.

pers. *abbr* = person; personal; personally.

per se *adv* by itself; by its very nature, intrinsically.

persecute *vt* to harass, oppress, esp for reasons of race, religion, etc; to worry persistently.—**persecutor** *n*.

persecution *n* a persecuting or being persecuted; unfair or cruel treatment for reasons of race, religion, etc; a time of persecution.

Perseids *n* (*astron*) an annual meteor shower which peaks on August 12.

Persephone *n* (*Greek myth*) a goddess of the underworld, the daughter of Zeus and Demeter, who was abducted by Hades and had to remain a third of the year with Hades and the rest of the year with her mother. In Roman mythology, she is called Proserpine.

Persepolis *n* the capital city of the Achaemenid (Persian) empire, which was established in 518 BC by King Darius I.

Perses *n* (*Greek myth*) a son of Perseus and Andromeda who is described as the founder of the Persian nation.

Perseus[1] *n* (*Greek myth*) king of Mycenae and Tiryns, who brought the head of the Gorgon Medusa to King Polydectes.

Perseus[2] *n* a large constellation in the northern hemisphere lying in the Milky Way, and containing the variable star Algol.

Perseus Arm *n* one part of the spiral arm of the Milky Way reaching from beyond the galactic center to the region beyond the Sun.

perseverance *n* persisting efforts of belief, esp in the face of opposition; steadfastness; (*Christianity*) continuance in grace.—**perseverant** *adj*.

persevere *vi* to persist, maintain effort, steadfastly, esp in face of difficulties.—**perseveringly** *adv*.

Persia *n* ancient name for Iran. The Persian Empire lasted from the emperor Cyrus to the rise of Alexander the Great (550–334 BC), and at its mightiest extended from India to the Aegean Sea, including Mesopotamia, Palestine, and Egypt. *See also* **Cyrus**, **Darius**.

Persians *npl* a tribe of Indo-European origin from Turkestan, who settled in the northern part of Iran *c*. 2000 BC.

persiennes *npl* outside window shutters with horizontal louvers.

persiflage *n* frivolous talk, banter.

persimmon *n* one of a species of tropical American trees; the fruit of such a tree.

persist *vi* to continue in spite of obstacles or opposition; to persevere; to last.—**persister** *n*.

persistence, persistency *n* a persisting; tenacity of purpose.

persistent *adj* persevering; stubborn.—**persistently** *adv*.

persnickety *adj* (*inf*) fussy, fastidious; over-attentive to detail.—*also* **pernickety**.

person *n* (*pl* **persons**) a human being, individual; the body (including clothing) of a human being; (*in a play*) a character; one who is recognized by law as the subject of rights and duties; (*gram*) one of the three classes of personal pronouns and verb forms, referring to the person(s) speaking, spoken to, or spoken of.

persona *n* (*pl* **personae**) a person; a character in a play, etc; (*pl*) public role or image.

personable *adj* pleasing in personality and appearance.—**personableness** *n*.—**personably** *adv*.

personage *n* a distinguished person.

persona grata *n* (*pl* **personae gratae**) (*Latin*) a person who is acceptable or welcome, esp a diplomat to a foreign government.

persona non grata *n* (*pl* **personae non gratae**) (*Latin*) a person who is not acceptable or welcome, esp to a foreign government.

personal *adj* concerning a person's private affairs, or his or her character, habits, body, etc; done in person; (*law*) of property that is movable; (*gram*) denoting person.

personal account *n* an account in a company's ledger that carries the name of an individual or organization and records the state of indebtedness of the person or organization to the company or the state of indebtedness of the company to the individual or organization, whichever is relevant.

personal column *n* a newspaper column devoted to private messages and advertisements.

personal computer *n* a microcomputer that can be programed to perform a variety of tasks for home and office.—*also* **PC**.

personal digital assistant *or* **PDA** *n* (*comput*) a portable battery-powered computer, slightly larger than the palm of a hand, for note-taking, addresses etc.

personal effects *npl* items such as clothing, keys, etc, normally worn or carried on the person.

personal information manager *n* (*comput*) a database management program designed specifically to emulate a diary, address book, and notebook.

personality *n* (*pl* **personalities**) one's individual characteristics; excellence or distinction of social and personal traits; a person with such qualities; a celebrity.

personalize *vt* to mark with name, initials, etc; to endow with personal characteristics; to take personally; to personify.—**personalization** *n*.

personally *adv* in person; in one's own opinion; as though directed to oneself.

personal pronoun *n* a pronoun such as *I, we, you, them*, used to denote a definite person or thing.

personalty *n* (*pl* **personalties**) (*law*) personal property.

personate *vt* to play the part of (in a play etc); (*law*) to pretend to be (someone else) for fraudulent purposes.—**personation** *n*.—**personator** *n*.

person-hour *see* **man-hour**.

personification *n* representation of an abstract idea or a thing as a person; an embodiment, a type; a perfect example.

personify *vt* (**personifying, personified**) to think of, represent, as a person; to typify.—**personifier** *n*.

personnel *n* the employees of an organization or company; the department that hires them.

personnel management *n* human resource management.

persp. *abbr* = perspective.

perspective *n* objectivity; the art of drawing so as to give an impression of relative distance or solidity; a picture so drawn; relation, proportion, between parts of a subject; vista, prospect. * *adj* of or in perspective.

perspicacious *adj* of clear understanding; shrewd; discerning.—**perspicaciously** *adv*.—**perspicacity** *n*.

perspicuous *adj* clearly expressed, lucid.—**perspicuity** *n*.

perspiration *n* the salty fluid excreted on to the surface of the skin, sweat; the act of perspiring.

perspire *vti* to excrete (moisture) through the pores of the skin to cool the body, to sweat.—**perspiringly** *adv*.

persuadable, persuasible *adj* able to be persuaded.—**persuadability, persuasibility** *n*.

persuade *vt* to convince; to induce by argument, reasoning, advice, etc.—**persuader** *n*.

persuasion *n* the act of persuading; a conviction or opinion; a system of religious beliefs; a group adhering to such a system.

persuasive *adj* able to persuade; influencing the mind or emotions.—**persuasively** *adv*.—**persuasiveness** *n*.

pert *adj* impudent, cheeky; sprightly.—**pertly** *adv*.—**pertness** *n*.

pert. *abbr* = pertaining.

PERT *abbr* = program evaluation and review technique.

pertain *vi* to belong to; to be appropriate to; to have reference to.

Perth *n* a city in Australia.

Perthes' disease *n* a hip condition in children between the ages of four and ten, which is self-healing.

pertinacious *adj* persistent; unyielding; obstinate.—**pertinacity, pertinaciousness** *n*.

pertinent *adj* relevant, apposite; to the point.—**pertinence** *n*.—**pertinently** *adv*.

perturb *vt* to trouble; to agitate; to throw into confusion; (*astron*) to cause to undergo perturbation.—**perturbable** *adj*.—**perturbably** *adv*.—**perturbingly** *adv*.

perturbation *n* the state of being troubled, mental agitation; (*astron*) an irregularity or deviation in a regular orbit produced by some additional force.

pertussis *see* **whooping cough.**

Peru *n* a republic located just south of the Equator, on the Pacific coast of South America.

Peru Current *see* **Humboldt Current.**

Perugino *n* **Pietro** (*c*.1445–1523) Italian painter, who painted the fresco *The Giving of the Keys to St Peter* (*c*.1481) in the Sistine Chapel, Rome. A peaceful serenity pervades his work, as in the gentle and graceful *Virgin and Child*.

peruse *vt* to read carefully, to examine.—**perusal** *n*.

Peruv. *abbr* = Peruvian.

Peruzzi *n* **Baldassare** (*b*. 1481) Italian architect whose notable works include Palazzo Massimo alle Colonne, Rome.

pervade *vt* to permeate or spread through; to be rife among.—**pervasion** *n*.

pervasive *adj* able or tending to pervade.—**pervasively** *adv*.—**pervasiveness** *n*.

perverse *adj* deviating from right or truth; persisting in error; wayward; contrary.—**perversely** *adv*.—**perverseness** *n*.

perversion *n* an abnormal way of obtaining sexual gratification, e.g. sadism; a perverted form or usage of something.

perversity *n* (*pl* **perversities**) a being perverse; a disposition to thwart or annoy; a perverse act.

pervert *vt* to corrupt; to misuse; to distort. * *n* a person who is sexually perverted.—**perverter** *n*.—**pervertible** *adj*.

perverted *adj* wrong; harmful; unnatural; sexually deviant.—**pervertedly** *adv*.

pervious *adj* giving passage, permeable; open to new ideas.

pes. *abbr* = peseta.

pesade *n* (*dressage*) a position in which the horse is standing on its hind legs and raises its forelegs.

pesante *adj* (*mus*) (*Italian*) "heavy," "ponderous," or "solid."

Pesce *n* **Gaetano** (1939–) Italian architect and founding member of Gruppo *n*.

PESD *abbr* = Private and Executive Secretary's Diploma (London Chamber of Commerce and Industry).

peseta *n* the unit of currency in Spain.

pesewa *n* a monetary unit of Ghana, equal to one hundredth of a cedi.

PESGB *abbr* = Petroleum Exploration Society of Great Britain.

pesky *adj* (**peskier, peskiest**) (*inf*) troublesome, annoying.

peso *n* (*pl* **pesos**) a unit of currency in several Latin American countries and the Philippines.

Peso Uruguayos *n* currency of Uruguay.

pessary *n* (*pl* **pessaries**) (*med*) a surgical appliance or suppository inserted into the vagina.

pessimism *n* a tendency to see in the world what is bad rather than good; a negative outlook that always expects the worst.—**pessimist** *n*.—**pessimistic** *adj*.—**pessimistically** *adv*.

pest *n* anything destructive, esp a plant or animal detrimental to man as rats, flies, weeds, etc; a person who pesters or annoys.

PEST *abbr* (*Brit*) = Pressure for Economic and Social Toryism.

pester *vt* to annoy or irritate persistently.—**pesterer** *n*.

pesticide *n* any chemical for killing pests.—**pesticidal** *adj*.

pestiferous *adj* spreading infection; (*fig*) physically or morally noxious.

pestilence *n* an outbreak of a fatal epidemic disease; anything regarded as harmful.

pestilent *adj* irritating; likely to cause a fatal epidemic.—**pestilently** *adv*.

pestilential *adj* of the nature of or conveying pestilence; harmful; annoying.—**pestilentially** *adv*.

pestle *n* a usu club-shaped tool for pounding or grinding substances in a mortar. * *vt* to beat, pound, or pulverize with a pestle.

pet *n* a domesticated animal kept as a companion; a person treated as a favorite. * *adj* kept as a pet; spoiled, indulged; favorite; particular. * *vti* (**petting, petted**) to stroke or pat gently; to caress; (*inf*) to kiss, embrace, etc, in making love.

PET *abbr* = polyethylene terephthalate; pre-eclamptic toxaemia.

PETA *abbr* = People for the Ethical Treatment of Animals; Postal Equipment Trade Association.

Pétain *n* **Henri Philippe Omer** (1856–1951) French soldier and statesman. He headed the collaborationist Vichy government (1940–44) and was sentenced to death (commuted to life imprisonment) at the end of World War II.

petal *n* any of the leaf-like parts of a flower's corolla.—**petaline** *adj*.—**petalled** *adj*.

petard *n* (*formerly*) a small bomb used to blow in a door, etc.

peter *vi* (*with out*) to come to an end; to dwindle to nothing.

Peter *n* **Saint** (*d*. *c*.67) a disciple of Jesus Christ (also known as Simon Bar-Jona) and Christian apostle who played a prominent role in establishing Christianity after the crucifixion. He is regarded by Roman Catholics as the first pope.

Peter *n* **the First Letter of** (*Bible*) NT book, a letter addressed to the universal Church rather than to a particular group; scholars disagree about its author or date of writing, but it is unlikely to be by Peter the apostle.

Peter *n* **the Second Letter of** (*Bible*) NT book, whose opening words suggest it is by Peter the apostle, but he was not regarded as the author even in the early traditions of the Church; it is dated about the first quarter of the second century AD.

petersham *n* a thick corded ribbon used in dressmaking as a stiffening; a thick woolen fabric used for overcoats, etc.

Peterson *n* **Oscar [Emmanuel]** (1925–) Canadian jazz pianist and composer, a virtuoso pianist in the mode of his friend Art Tatum. The Oscar Peterson Trio became one of the best known small jazz groups of the 1950s.

Peter's Pence *n* (*RC Church*) voluntary contributions to the papal treasury; (*formerly*) in England, an annual tax, until its abolishment by Henry VIII, of one penny levied on every house and paid to the Pope.

pethidine *n* a drug with analgesic and mild sedative action for relief of moderate pain.

Pethuel *n* (*Bible*) father of Joel.

petiolate *adj* (*bot*) growing on a petiole.

petiole *n* (*bot*) a leaf stalk.

petit *adj* (*esp law*) of lesser importance.

Petit *n* **Roland** (1924–) French dancer and choreographer, highly influential on contemporary dance. His works include a *Carmen* (1949) and dance sequences in several movies, e.g. *Daddy Longlegs* (1955, starring Fred Astaire).

petite *adj* (*woman*) small and trim in figure.

petition *n* a formal application or entreaty to an authority; a written demand for action by a government, etc, signed by a number of people. * *vti* to present a petition to; to ask humbly.—**petitionary** *adj*.—**petitioner** *n*.

petit larceny *n* the theft of property below a legal minimum.—*also* **petty larceny.**

petit mal *n* a mild form of epilepsy.

petit point *n* a fine stitch used in needlepoint.

petnap *vt* (**petnaping, petnaped** *or* **petnapping, petnapped**) to capture a domestic pet and hold it to ransom.—**petnapper** *n*.

Petrarch *n* **[Francesco Petrarca]** (1304–74) Italian lyric poet, regarded as the first major poet of the Renaissance, whose sonnets, madrigals, and songs, inspired by his love for "Laura," were strongly influential on Tudor and Elizabethan writers and poets. His work popularized the sonnet form.

Petras *abbr* = Polytechnic Educational Resources Advisory Service.

Petrassi *n* **Goffredo** (1904–) Italian composer whose works include the operas *The Tapestry* and *Death in the Air*, ballets, and orchestral and choral pieces.

petrel *n* a dark-colored sea bird capable of flying far from land.

Petriburg. *abbr* (*Latin*) = *Petriburgensis*, "of Peterborough."

Petri dish *n* a shallow dish with a lid used in a laboratory for growing cultures of bacteria and other microorganisms.

Petrie *n* **Sir William Flinders** (1853–1942) British Egyptologist, Surveyor of the Pyramids and temples of Giza, and author of many books on ancient Egypt.

petrifaction, petrification *n* the process of changing animal or vegetable material into stone.

petrify *vti* (**petrifying, petrified**) to turn or be turned into stone; to stun or be stunned with fear, horror, etc.

petro- *prefix* rock, stone; petroleum.

petrochemical *n* any chemical obtained from natural gas or petroleum.

petrodollar *n* a notional unit of money earned by the export of petroleum.

petrog. *abbr* = petrography.

petroglyph *n* a rock carving or drawing.

petrography *n* the scientific description and classification of rocks.—**petrographer** *n*.—**petrographic, petrographical** *adj*.

petrol *n* (*chiefly Brit*) gasoline.

petrol. *abbr* = petrology.

petrolatum *n* a greasy, jelly-like substance obtained from petroleum and used for ointments, etc.—*also* **petroleum jelly.**

petroleum *n* a crude oil consisting of hydrocarbons occurring naturally in certain rock strata and distilled to yield petrol, kerosene, etc.

petrology *n* (*pl* **petrologies**) the study of rocks and their structure.

Petronius *n* **[Gaius Petronius Arbiter]** (*d*. *c*.66) Roman courtier and satirist whose most famous work is the *Satyricon*.

petrous *adj* of, or like, rock.

petticoat *n* an underskirt; a slip; (*inf*) woman.

pettifog *vi* to be, or behave like, a pettifogger.

pettifogger *n* an inferior or crooked lawyer; someone who quibbles over details.

pettish *adj* peevish, sulky.

pettitoes *npl* pig's trotters, esp as food.

petty *adj* (**pettier, pettiest**) trivial; small-minded; minor.—**pettily** *adv*.—**pettiness** *n*.

petty cash *n* a small amount of cash used for minor expenses.

petty larceny *see* **petit larceny**.

petty officer *n* a noncommissioned officer in the navy.

petulant *adj* showing impatience or irritation; bad-humored.—**petulance** *n*.—**petulantly** *adv*.

petunia *n* a plant with funnel-shaped purple or white flowers.

petuntse *n* a fine white clay used with kaolin in the manufacture of porcelain.

Pevsner *n* 1. **Antoine** (1886–1962) Russian-born French painter and sculptor, a leading constructivist artist, whose notable works include *Torso* (1924–26) and *Development Column* (1942). 2. **Sir Nikolaus Bernhard** (1902–83) influential German-born art historian and critic, whose major work is his *Buildings of England* series.

pew *n* a wooden, bench-like seat in a church, often enclosed; (*sl*) a chair.

pewit *n* the lapwing.—*also* **peewit**.

pewter *n* an alloy of tin and lead with a silvery-gray color; dishes, etc, made of pewter.—**pewterer** *n*.

peyote *n* mescal.

pf *abbr* = (*mus*) (*Italian*) *piano e forte*, "soft and then loud"; public funding.

pf. *abbr* = perfect; pfennig; pianoforte; preferred.

p.f. *or* **pf** *abbr* = (*mus*) (*Italian*) *più forte*, "louder"; power factor.

pF *abbr* = picofarad.

PF *abbr* = (*Zimbabwe*) Patriotic Front; Police Federation.

PFAS *abbr* = President of the Faculty of Architects and Surveyors.

PFB *abbr* = preformed beam.

pfc *abbr* = passed flying college.

PFC *abbr* = polychlorinated fluorocarbon; private first class.

pfd. *abbr* = preferred.

pfennig *n* (*pl* **pfennigs, pfennige**) a unit of currency in Germany worth one hundredth of a Deutschmark.

pfg. *abbr* = pfennig.

Pfister *n* **Charles** (1939–90) American interior and furniture designer.

PFM *abbr* = pulse frequency modulation.

PFPUT *abbr* = Pension Fund Property Unit Trust.

PFR *abbr* = prototype fast reactor.

PFSA *abbr* (*French*) = *pour faire ses adieux*, "to say goodbye."

pfte. *abbr* = pianoforte.

PFV *abbr* (*French*) = *pour faire visite*, "to make a call."

Pg. *abbr* = Portugal; Portuguese.

PG *abbr* = (*movie classification*) parental guidance: denoting a motion-picture suitable for all ages, but advising parental guidance; (*ceramics*) Paris granite; paying guest; postgraduate.—*see also* **prostaglandin**.

Pg.B. *abbr* (*Latin*) = *Pedagogiae Baccalaureus*, "Bachelor of Pedagogy."

PGCE *abbr* = Postgraduate Certificate in Education.

PGDipLCM *abbr* = Postgraduate Diploma of the London College of Music.

PGDRS *abbr* = psychogeriatric dependency rating scale.

PGF *abbr* = polypeptide growth factor.

PGG *abbr* = Professional Gardeners' Guild.

PGL *abbr* = persistent generalised lymphadenopathy.

PGM *abbr* = Past Grand Master; precision guided missile.

pgt *abbr* = per gross ton.

Ph *symbol* (*chem*) phenyl (element).

ph. *abbr* = phase.

pH *abbr* = potential of hydrogen ions (in an aqueous solution, a measure of acidity).

Ph. *abbr* = Philadelphia.

PH *abbr* = public health.

PHAB *abbr* = Physically Handicapped and Able Bodied.

Phaeacians *npl* (*Greek myth*) a seafaring people who lived on the island of Scherie or Drepane.

Phaedra *n* (*Greek myth*) a daughter of Minos, king of Crete, whose unrequited love for Hippolytus, son of Theseus, led to his death and her suicide.

Phaestos, Phaistos *n* a Minoan palace on the island of Crete that was built *c.* 1900 BC over an earlier site.

Phaethon[1] *n* (*Greek myth*) a son of the sun-god Helios, who tried to drive his father's chariot. The horses bolted and, approaching too near Earth, almost set it on fire. Phaethon was struck down by a thunderbolt.

Phaethon[2] *n* an asteroid discovered in 1983, which may be the nucleus of a former comet.

phaeton *n* a light, open, four-wheeled horse-drawn carriage.

phage *n* a short form of bacteriophage.

phagocyte *n* a white corpuscle which devours harmful micro-organisms and other foreign bodies.

phagocytosis *n* the process by which a phagocyte devours foreign bodies.

phalange *see* **phalanx**.

phalangeal *adj* (*anat*) of or pertaining to a phalanx.

phalanger *n* a small tree-living marsupial of Australasia, with a long tail and bushy fur.

phalanx *n* (*pl* **phalanxes, phalanges**) a massed body or rank of people; (*pl* **phalanges**) a bone of a finger or toe.

phalarope *n* a small wading bird, with a straight bill and webbed feet.

phallic *adj* pertaining to, or resembling, a phallus.

phallicism, phallism *n* the worship of the phallus as the emblem of the generative power in nature.

phallus *n* (*pl* **phalli, phalluses**) the male reproductive organ.

phanerogam *n* (*bot*) a flowering plant.—**phanerogamic, phanerogamous** *adj*.

Phantasie *see* **fantasia**.

phantasm *n* a phantom; a vision of an absent person.

phantasmagoria, phantasmagory *n* a series of shifting images, like those seen in a dream.—**phantasmagoric, phantasmagorical** *adj*.

phantom *n* a specter or apparition. * *adj* illusionary.

phantom limb *n* the feeling that a limb or part of a limb is still attached to the body after it has been amputated.

Phar. *or* **Pharm.** *abbr* = pharmaceutical; pharmacopeia; pharmacy.

pharaoh *n* (*also with cap*) the title of the kings of ancient Egypt.—**pharaonic** *adj*.

Phar.B., PharB, Pharm.B. *or* **PharmB** *abbr* (*Latin*) = *Pharmaciae Baccalaureus*, "Bachelor of Pharmacy."

Phar.D., PharD, Pharm.D. *or* **PharmD** *abbr* (*Latin*) = *Pharmaciae Doctor*, "Doctor of Pharmacy."

Pharisaic, Pharisaical *adj* pertaining to, or characteristic of, the Pharisees; (*fig*) hypocritical.

Pharisee *n* a member of a Jewish religious sect, characterized by its strict observance of the letter of the law; (*fig*) a self-righteous person, a hypocrite.

Phar.M., PharM, Pharm.M. *or* **PharmM** *abbr* (*Latin*) = *Pharmaciae Magister*, "Master of Pharmacy."

pharmaceutical *adj* of, relating to pharmacy or drugs. * *n* a medicinal drug.

pharmaceutics *n sing* the science of pharmacy.

pharmacist *n* one licensed to practice pharmacy.

pharmacol. *abbr* = pharmacology.

pharmacology *n* the science dealing with the effects of drugs on living organisms.—**pharmacological** *adj*.—**pharmacologist** *n*.

pharmacopeia, pharmacopoeia *n* a book containing a list of drugs with directions for their use.—**pharmacopeial** *adj*.

pharmacy *n* (*pl* **pharmacies**) the preparation and dispensing of drugs and medicines; a drugstore.

pharyngeal, pharyngal *adj* pertaining to, or situated near, the pharynx.

pharyngectomy *n* surgical excision of part of the pharynx.

pharyngitis *n* inflammation of the pharynx.

pharyngology *n* the medical study of the pharynx.

pharyngoscope *n* an instrument used for looking at the pharynx.

pharyngotomy *n* (*pl* **pharyngotomies**) the surgical operation of making an incision into the pharynx.

pharynx *n* (*pl* **pharynges, pharynxes**) the cavity leading from the mouth and nasal passages to the larynx and esophagus.

phase *n* (*pl* **phases**) an amount of the moon's or a planet's surface illuminated at a given time; a characteristic period in a regularly recurring sequence of events or stage in a development; (*chem*) a part of a system that is chemically uniform but that occurs in a different form. * *vt* to do by stages or gradually; (*with* **out**) (*making, using, etc*) to stop gradually.—**phasic** *adj*.

phase angle *n* (*astron*) the angle created between two lines, one of which joins the Sun to a planet, the other joining the Earth to the planet.

Ph.B. *or* **PhB** *abbr* = Bachelor of Physical Culture; (*Latin*) *Pharmaciae Baccalaureus*, "Bachelor of Pharmacy"; (*Latin*) *Philosophiae Baccalaureus* "Bachelor of Philosophy."

ph. bz. *abbr* = phosphor bronze.

Ph.C. *abbr* = Pharmaceutical Chemist; Philosopher of Chiropractic.

PHC *abbr* = pharmaceutical chemist; primary health care.

Ph.D., PhD *abbr* (*Latin*) = *Pharmaciae Doctor*, "Doctor of Pharmacy"; *Philologiae Doctor*, "Doctor of Philology"; *Philosophiae Doctor*, "Doctor of Philosophy."

PHD(RCA) *abbr* = Doctor of Philosophy (Royal College of Art).

pheasant *n* a richly colored game bird.

phellem *n* (*bot*) cork.

phenacetin *n* a drug used for the relief of pain and fever.

Phenobarbital *n* (*trademark*) a crystalline barbiturate used as a hypnotic and sedative.

phenobarbitone *n* a widely used long-acting barbiturate

phenocryst *n* (*geol*) a large well-formed crystal among a mass of smaller crystals in an igneous rock.

phenol *n* carbolic acid.

phenology *n* the study of the influence of climate on certain recurrent phenomena of animal and plant life.

phenomenal *adj* perceptible through the senses; remarkable; outstanding.—**phenomenally** *adv*.

phenomenalism *n* (*philos*) the doctrine that all knowledge is derived from sense impressions.—**phenomenalist** *n*.

phenomenon *n* (*pl* **phenomena, phenomenons**) anything perceived by the senses as a fact; a fact or event that can be scientifically described; a remarkable thing or person.

phenotype *n* (*biol*) the detectable characteristics of an organism, i.e., its appearance which is determined by the interaction between its genotype and the environment in which the organism develops.

phenyl *n* the hydrocarbon radical of phenol.

phenylketonuria *n* a genetic disorder that results in the deficiency of an enzyme that converts phenylalanine, an essential amino acid, to tyrosine.

Pherae *n* an ancient city of Thessaly, which, under the rule of tyrants, became a controlling power of the whole of Thessaly.

pheromone *n* a molecule that functions as a chemical communication signal between individuals of the same species.

phew *interj* an exclamation of relief, surprise, etc.

Ph.G. *abbr* = Graduate in Pharmacy.

phi *n* the 21st letter of the Greek alphabet.

PHI *abbr* = permanent health insurance.

phial *n* a small glass bottle; a vial.

Phi Beta Kappa *n* (a member of) the oldest college fraternity.

phil. *abbr* = philosopher; philosophical; philosophy.

Phil. *abbr* = Philadelphia; (*Bible*) Philemon; (*Bible*) Philippians; Philippine.

phil-, philo- *prefix* loving.

Phila. *abbr* = Philadelphia.

Philadelphia *n* a city in the United States of America (USA).

Philae *n* (*Egypt*) a site on the Nile, just north of Elephantine, center of the cult of Isis. The Philae temples have been resited in modern times on the island of Agilkia because of the building of the Aswan High Dam.

philander *vi* (*man*) to flirt with women for amusement.—**philanderer** *n*.

philanthropist *n* a person who tries to benefit others.

philanthropy *n* (*pl* **philanthropies**) love of mankind, esp as demonstrated by benevolent or charitable actions.—**philanthropic, philanthropical** *adj*.—**philanthropically** *adv*.

philatelist *n* a person who collects or studies stamps.

philately *n* the study and collecting of postage and imprinted stamps; stamp collecting.—**philatelic** *adj*.—**philatelically** *adv*.

Philby *n* **Kim [Harold Adrian Russell]** (1911–88) English diplomat, journalist, and double agent. He became a Soviet agent in 1933 and was recruited to the British Secret Service in 1940, working in Washington DC. He fled to the USSR in 1963.

Philem. *abbr* = Philemon.

Philemon *n* (*Bible*) NT book, a letter written by Paul to a Christian in Colossae of the same name.

philharmonic *adj* loving music.

philhellene *n* a lover or supporter of Greece.

Philip *n* **[Prince] [Duke of Edinburgh]** (1921–) Greek-born British naval officer and prince consort. The nephew of Mountbatten, he married the then Princess Elizabeth in 1947.

Philip *n* **Saint** (1st cent) the first of the Apostles whom Jesus called to follow him. Tradition says that St Philip carried the Gospel into Scythia and Phrygia. His feast day is May 3.

Philip II *n* (1527–98) king of Spain. He inherited the Spanish throne in 1556, was the husband (1554–58) of Mary I and became Philip I of Portugal (1580–98). A devout Roman Catholic, he strongly supported the Counter-Reformation and launched the disastrous Armada invasion against Elizabeth I in 1588.

Philip Neri *n* **Saint** (1515–95) Italian priest, who tried to make religion attractive, especially to the young. During carnival or in vacations he instituted musical entertainments and religious dramas. He was canonized in 1622. His feast day is May 26.

Philippi *n* a city of Macedonia and an important trade center. The first place in Europe to which Paul brought the Christian Gospel.

Philippians, the Letter of Paul to the *n* (*Bible*) NT book, the letter to the Christians of the first Christian Church in Europe, founded by Paul at Philippi.

philippic *n* a bitter denunciation, an invective.

Philippine Peso *n* currency of Philippines.

Philippines *n* a republic comprising a group of 7,107 islands and islets in the western Pacific which are scattered over a great area and form the northernmost group of the Malay Archipelago.

Philips *n* 1. **Ambrose** (1671–1749) English poet who was ridiculed by Swift and Pope. He also wrote three tragedies: *The Distrest Mother*, *The Briton*, and *Humphrey, Duke of Gloucester*. 2. **John** (1676–1708) English poet whose works include *The Splendid Shilling*, a burlesque poem in blank verse, *Blenheim*, a poem in celebration of the Duke of Marlborough's victory, and *Cyder*, a work in imitation of Virgil's *Georgics*.

3. **Katherine** (1631–64) English poet whose work was much admired by her contemporaries, e.g. Cowley and Dryden, among whom she was known as the "Matchless Orinda."

philistine *n* a person with no feeling for culture; an uncultured, conventional person; (*with cap*) a member of a warlike race hostile to ancient Israel. * *adj* uncultured.—**philistinism** *n*.

Phil.L.D. *abbr* (*Latin*) = *Philologiae Lituanicae Doctor*, "Doctor of Lithuanian Philology."

Philoctetes *n* (*Greek myth*) a famous archer, the friend and armor-bearer of Heracles, who was abandoned on the island of Lemnos because of a stinking wound to his foot. He was healed by Aesculapius at Troy.

philogyny *n* fondness for women.—**phylogynous** *adj*.—**phylogynist** *n*.

philol. *abbr* = philological; philologist; philology.

philology *n* the study, esp comparative, of languages and their history and structure.—**philological** *adj*.—**philologist, philologer** *n*.

philomel *n* (*poet*) a nightingale.

Philomela, Philomena *n* (*Greek myth*) a daughter of Pandion and Zeuxippe who, after being raped by her brother-in-law Tereus, was metamorphosed into a nightingale.

philos. *abbr* = philosopher; philosophical; philosophy.

philosopher *n* a person who studies philosophy; a person who acts calmly and rationally.

philosophical, philosophic *adj* of, relating to, or according to philosophy; serene; temperate; resigned.—**philosophically** *adv*.

philosophize *vi* to reason like a philosopher; to speculate, moralize.—**philosophizer** *n*.

philosophy *n* (*pl* **philosophies**) the study of the principles underlying conduct, thought, and the nature of the universe; general principles of a field of knowledge; a particular system of ethics; composure; calmness.

Phil. Soc. *abbr* = Philological, or Philosophical, Society.

philter, philtre *n* a love potion.

Philyra *n* (*Greek myth*) a daughter of Oceanus and Tethys, whom Zeus turned into a linden tree after she gave birth to a child with the body of a horse from the waist down, named Chiron and later king of the Centaurs.

phimosis *n* a condition in which the edge of the foreskin is narrowed and cannot be drawn back over the glans of the penis.

pH index *n* a scale for expressing how acidic or alkaline a solution is.

Phineus *n* (*Greek myth*) a blind king who had his food snatched away by the Harpies every time he tried to eat.

PHJC *abbr* = Poor Handmaids of Jesus Christ.

PhL *abbr* = Licentiate in Pharmacy; Licentiate in Philosophy.

phlebectomy *n* removal of a vein, or part of a vein, sometimes undertaken in the treatment of varicose veins.

phlebitis *n* (*med*) an inflammation of a vein.—**phlebitic** *adj*.

phlebothrombosis *n* the obstruction of a vein by a blood clot, common in the deep veins of the leg (in particular the calf).—*also* **deep vein thrombosis**.

phlebotomize *vti* (*med*) to practice phlebotomy (on).

phlebotomy *n* (*pl* **phlebotomies**) a surgical incision into a vein to let blood.—**phlebotomist** *n*.

phlegm *n* a thick mucus discharged from the throat, as during a cold; sluggishness; apathy.

phlegmatic, phlegmatical *adj* unemotional, composed; sluggish.—**phlegmatically** *adv*.

Phlegyas *n* (*Greek myth*) a son of Ares and a very warlike leader.

phloem *n* (*bot*) the tissue which carries food around a plant.

phlogiston *n* (*chem*) an inflammable element once believed to exist in all combustible bodies.

phlox *n* (*pl* **phlox, phloxes**) a North American flowering plant.

PHLS *abbr* = Public Health Laboratory Service.

PHLSB *abbr* = Public Health Laboratory Service Board.

PhM *abbr* (*Latin*) = *Philosophiae Magister*, "Master of Philosophy."

PhmB *abbr* (*Latin*) = *Pharmaciae Baccalaureus*, "Bachelor of Pharmacy."

PhmG *abbr* = Graduate in Pharmacy.

Phnom-Penh *n* capital city of Cambodia.

phobia *n* an irrational, excessive, and persistent fear of some thing or situation.—**phobic** *adj, n*.

Phobos *n* one of the two small satellites of Mars discovered in 1877.

Phocis *n* one of the original states of ancient Greece, west of Boeotia in northern Greece.—**Phocian** *adj*.

Phoebe[1] *n* (*Greek myth*) a female Titan, a daughter of Uranus and Ge, and the mother of Leto and Asteria by her brother Coeus.

Phoebe[2] *n* the outermost of Saturn's satellites.

Phoebus *n* (*Greek myth*) a name given to the god Apollo, referring both to the youthful beauty of the god and to the radiance of the sun.

Phoenicians *npl* a seafaring and trading people who were descended from the Canaanites. They occupied the coastal strip of Lebanon and Syria.

phoenix *n* a mythical bird that set fire to itself and rose from its ashes every 500 years; a symbol of immortality.

Phoenix[1] *n* the capital city of Arizona, a state of the USA.

Phoenix[2] *n* (*Greek myth*) a king of the Dolopians, who was guardian of the young Achilles, and later accompanied Achilles to the Trojan War.

phon *n* a unit of loudness.

phon. *abbr* = phonetics; phonology.

phonate *vi* to utter vocal sounds.—**phonation** *n*.

phone *n*, *vti* (*inf*) (to) telephone.

phone book *n* (*inf*) telephone directory.

phone-in *n* a radio program in which questions or comments by listeners are broadcast.

phoneme *n* any of the sound units of a language that distinguish one word from another.

phonet. *or* **phon.** *abbr* = phonetics.

phonetic *adj* relating to, or representing, speech sounds.—**phonetically** *adv*.

phonetic alphabet *n* a set of symbols used to transcribe words phonetically; a code identifying letters of the alphabet in voice communication.

phonetician *n* a student of, or expert in, phonetics.

phonetics *n sing* the science concerned with pronunciation and the representation of speech sounds.

phonetist *n* a phonetician; an advocate of phonetic spelling.

phoney *see* **phony**.

phonics *n sing* a phonetics-based method of teaching reading.—**phonic** *adj*.

phonog. *abbr* = phonography.

phonogram *n* (*phonetics*) a written character representing a particular sound.

phonograph *n* a device for reproducing sounds from a vinyl disk.

phonography *n* spelling based on pronunciation; a system of shorthand writing based on sound.

phonol. *abbr* = phonology.

phonology *n* (*pl* **phonologies**) the study of speech sounds and their development, and of the sound systems of language.—**phonological** *adj*.—**phonologist** *n*.

phony, phoney *adj* (**phonier, phoniest**) (*inf*) not genuine. * *n* (*pl* **phonies, phoneys**) a fake; an insincere person.—**phoniness, phoneyness** *n*.

phooey *interj* (*inf*) a exclamation of disgust or ridicule.

Phorcys *n* (*Greek myth*) a sea-god, a son of Pontus and Ge, and the father of a series of monsters, such as the Gorgon Echidna and Ladon the snake.

phosgene *n* a poisonous gas used in chemical warfare and in industry.

phosphate *n* a compound of phosphorus.—**phosphatic** *adj*.

phosphene *n* the sensation of luminous rings seen when a closed eye is pressed.

phosphide *n* a compound of phosphorus with another element.

phosphite *n* a salt of phosphorous acid.

phospholipids *npl* (*biochemistry*) biological compounds that resemble fats.

phosphorescence *n* the property of giving off light without noticeable heat, as phosphorus does; such light.—**phosphorescent** *adj*.

phosphorous *adj* containing phosphorus in lower or higher proportions.

phosphorus *n* a highly reactive, poisonous nonmetallic element; a phosphorescent substance or body, esp one that glows in the dark.

phot. *or* **photog.** *abbr* = photograph, or photographs; photographic; photography.

photic *adj* of, or pertaining to, light.

photic zone *n* the uppermost layer of a lake or sea where there is adequate light to allow photosynthesis to proceed.

photo *n* (*pl* **photos**) a photograph.

photo- *prefix* light; a photographic process.

photobiology *n* (*biol*) the study of the effect of light on living organisms.

photocell *n* a photoelectric cell.

photochemical *adj* of or relating to the effect of radiant energy, esp light.

photochemical fog *n* a haze, often incorrectly called smog, produced when sunlight reacts with vehicle emissions in hot, dry, calm conditions.

photochemistry *n* the branch of chemistry concerned with the effect of radiant energy in producing chemical changes; photochemical properties or processes.

photochromics *npl* materials which are sensitive to light.

photocontour map *n* a map that shows the surface features of an area, obtained from information acquired by aerial photography.

photocopy *n* (*pl* **photocopies**) a photographic reproduction of written or printed work. * *vt* (**photocopying, photocopied**) to copy in this way.—**photocopier** *n*.

photoelectric cell *n* a cell whose electrical properties are affected by light; any device in which light controls an electric circuit that operates a mechanical device, as for opening doors.—*also* **photocell**.

photoengraving *n* any photomechanical process of making printing plates.

photo finish *n* the finish of a race where the decision on the winner has to be determined by a photograph as the contestants are so close; any race where the winning margin is small.

photogenic *adj* likely to look attractive in photographs; (*biol*) generating light.—**photogenically** *adv*.

photogrammetry *n* the use of a series of photographs to produce an accurate scaled plan of an archeological site.

photograph *n* an image produced by photography.—*also* **photo**.

photographic *adj* of or like a photograph; minutely accurate like a photograph; (*memory*) capable of retaining facts, etc, after reading for only a brief time.—**photographically** *adv*.

photography *n* the art or process of recording images permanently and visibly by the chemical action of light on sensitive material, producing prints, slides, or film.—**photographer** *n*.

photogravure *n* a printing process using an intaglio plate photographically produced; printed matter so produced.

photojournalism *n* a form of news reporting in which the story is presented mainly through photographs.—**photojournalist** *n*.

photolithograph *n* a picture produced by photolithography.

photolithography *n* (*print*) lithography using plates made from photographs.

photolysis *n* chemical decomposition caused by light or other electromagnetic radiation.—**photolytic** *adj*.

photom. *abbr* = photometrical; photometry.

photomap *n* a quickly made map obtained by adding place names, boundary lines, etc, to a mosaic of aerial photographs.

photomechanical *adj* of or relating to a printing process that utilizes photography in plate-making.—**photomechanically** *adv*.

photometer *n* an instrument for measuring the intensity of light.

photometry *n* the area of physics concerned with the measurement of light; the use of a photometer; (*astron*) the measurement of a star's magnitude (brightness) within certain wavelength bands, and the variation over time.

photomicrograph *n* a photograph taken through a microscope.—**photomicrography** *n*.

photomultiplier *n* a device used in photometry which consists of a photocathode (an electrode that emits electrons when struck by electromagnetic radiation) that gives off electrons when light falls on it.

photon *n* (*physics*) a quantum or packet of energy that is a basic part of all electromagnetic waves.

photophobia *n* (*med*) oversensity (of the eyes) to light; (*psychol*) fear or, or aversion to, sunlight.

photoreception *n* perception of light waves in the visible spectrum; vision.

photoreceptor *see* **cone**.

photosphere *n* the surface of a star, esp the sun.

Photostat *n* (*trademark*) a device for making photographic copies of documents, etc; a copy made in this way. * *vt* (*often without cap*) to copy in this way.—**Photostatic** *adj*.

photosynthesis *n* (*bot*) the process by which a green plant manufactures sugar from carbon dioxide and water in the presence of light.—**photosynthetic** *adj*.—**photosynthetically** *adv*.

photosynthesize *vti* (*plants, etc*) to produce by or carry on photosynthesis.

phototaxis *n* (*biol*) the movement or reaction of an organism in response to light.

phototelegraphy *n* the telegraphic transmission of photographs and drawings.

phototropism *n* (*biol*) a growth movement shown by parts of plants in response to the effect of light

php *abbr* = pounds per horsepower.

phr. *abbr* = phrase.

phrasal *adj* of or consisting of a phrase or phrases.—**phrasally** *adv*.

phrasal verb *n* (*gram*) a usu simple verb that combines with a preposition or adverb, or both, to convey a meaning more than the sum of its parts, e.g. *come out*.

phrase *n* a group of words that does not contain a finite verb but which expresses a single idea by itself; a pointed saying; a high-flown expression; (*mus*) a short, distinct musical passage. * *vt* to express orally, put in words; (*mus*) to divide into melodic phrases.

phrase book *n* a book containing idiomatic expressions of a foreign language and their translations.

phraseogram *n* a shorthand symbol representing a phrase.

phraseology *n* (*pl* **phraseologies**) mode of expression, wording; phrases used by a particular group.—**phraseological** *adj*.

phrasing *n* the wording of a speech or a piece of writing; (*mus*) the division of a melodic line, etc, into musical phrases.

phren. *or* **phrenol.** *abbr* = phrenological; phrenology.

phrenetic *see* **frenetic**.

phrenic *adj* (*anat*) of, or pertaining to, the diaphragm.

phrenic nerve *n* the nerve to the muscles of the diaphragm, arising from the 3rd, 4th, and 5th cervical spinal nerves.

phrenology *n* the belief that intelligence and ability may be judged from the shape of a person's skull; study of the shape of the skull based on this belief.—**phrenological** *adj*.—**phrenologist** *n*.

PHRG *abbr* = Parliamentary Human Rights Group.

Phrixus *n* (*Greek myth*) the brother of Helle, who escaped with her on a ram with a golden fleece. In Colchis Phrixus hung the golden fleece on a sacred oak tree and it became the object of Jason's quest.

Phrygia *n* in ancient geography, a country in Asia Minor, stretching along the shores of the Hellespont and Troad.—**Phrygian** *adj*.

Phrygians *npl* a people who occupied Anatolia in Turkey after the conquest of the Hittites, *c*.1000 BC. They established their capital city at Gordium (Yassihöyük) under King Midas (750–680 BC).

PHS *abbr* = Presbyterian Historical Society; Public Health Service

PHSA *abbr* = Provincial Hospital Services Association.

Ph. Soc. *abbr* = Philological Society.

Phthia *n* in ancient Greece the principal city of Achaea in southern Thessaly.—**Phthian** *adj*.

Phthiotis *n* in ancient Greece, the southeast corner of Thessaly and the home of Achilles.

phthisis *n* a wasting disease, esp tuberculosis of the lungs.

PHWR *abbr* = pressurised heavy water reactor.

phycology *n* the study of algae.

phylactery *n* (*pl* **phylacteries**) (*Judaism*) a small case containing Hebrew texts, worn by Jewish men during prayers.

phyletic *adj* relating to the racial development of an animal or plant type.

Phyleus *n* (*Greek myth*) king of Dulichium, who was exiled from his native Elis and later had the throne of Elis restored to him by Heracles.

Phyllis *n* (*Greek myth*) a daughter of the Thracian king, Sithon.

phyllode *n* (*bot*) a flattened petiole with the functions of a leaf.

phyllotaxy, phyllotaxis *n* (*pl* **phyllotaxies, phyllotaxes**) (*bot*) the arrangement of leaves on a stem.

phylloxera *n* (*pl* **phylloxeras, phylloxerae**) an insect which attacks vines.

phylogeny, phylogenesis *n* (*pl* **phylogenies, phylogeneses**) (*biol*) the racial evolution of an animal or plant type.—**phylogenic, phylogenetic** *adj*.

phylum *n* (*pl* **phyla**) a major division of the animal or plant kingdom.

phys. *abbr* = physical; physician; physics; physiological; physiology.

physic *vt* (**physicking, physicked**) (*arch*) to administer medicine to.

physical *adj* relating to the world of matter and energy, the human body, or natural science. * *n* a general medical examination.—**physically** *adv*.

physical capital *n* items that are used in the production of goods and services, as opposed to financial capital.

physical chemistry *n* the branch of chemistry concerned with the effect of chemical structure on physical properties and of physical changes brought about by chemical reactions.

physical drive *n* (*comput*) the hardware that is used as the storage device for a computer.

physical education *n* education in fitness and cure of the body, stressing athletics and hygiene.

physical examination *n* the medical examination of the body and bodily functions.

physical science *n* any of the sciences dealing with inanimate objects, such as physics, astronomy, geography.

physical therapy *n* the treatment of disorders and disease by physical and mechanical means (as massage, exercise, water, heat, etc).—*also* **physiotherapy**.

physician *n* a doctor of medicine.

physicist *n* a specialist in physics.

physics *n* the branch of science concerned with matter and energy and their interactions in the fields of mechanics, acoustics, optics, heat, electricity, magnetism, radiation, atomic structure, and nuclear phenomena; the physical processes and phenomena of a particular system.

physio- *prefix* nature.

physiocrat *n* a supporter of the doctine of government according to a natural order based on land as the sole form of wealth.

physiognomy *n* (*pl* **physiognomies**) the art of judging character from facial features; facial expression, face; physical features generally.—**physiognomic, physiognomical** *adj*.—**physiognomist** *n*.

physiography *n* the study of the earth's natural features, physical geography.—**physiographer** *n*.

physiol. *abbr* = physiological; physiologist; physiology.

physiology *n* the science of the functioning and processes of living organisms.—**physiological** *adj*.—**physiologist** *n*.

physiotherapy *n* physical therapy.—**physiotherapist** *n*.

physique *n* bodily structure and appearance; build.

phytochemistry *n* (*chem*) the study of the chemical make-up of plants.

phytogenesis, phytogeny *n* the study of plant evolution.

phytogeog. *abbr* = phytogeography.

phytogeography *n* the study of the geographical distribution of plants.

phytoliths *n* minute grains of silica, present in plants, that are extremely resistant to decay and survive when all other traces of organic material have disappeared.

phyton *n* (*bot*) the smallest unit of a plant capable of growing into a new plant.

phytoplankton *n* plankton in plant form.

pi[1] *n* the 16th letter of the Greek alphabet; (*math*) the Greek letter ( ) used as a symbol for the ratio of the circumference to the diameter of a circle, approx. 3.14159.

pi[2] *n* (*pl* **pis**) (*print*) a jumble of type; any disorder. * *vt* to mix, disarrange (type). * *vi* to become mixed up.—*also* **pie**.

Pi. *or* **pias.** *abbr* = piaster or piasters.

PI *abbr* = parainfluenza virus; Philippine Islands; Privacy International; programed instruction.

PIA *abbr* = Personal Investment Authority; Photographic Importers Association; Pilots International Association.

PIAC *abbr* = Petroleum Industry Advisory Council.

piacere *n* (*mus*) (*Italian*) "pleasure," as in *a piacere*, "at (the performer's) pleasure."

piacevole *adv* (*mus*) (*Italian*) "pleasantly."

piacular *adj* expiatory; sinful.

Piaf *n* **Edith [Giovanna Gassion]** (1915–63) French singer and songwriter nicknamed "Little Sparrow" whose songs include "Non, je ne regrette rien."

piaffe *n* (*dressage*) a slow trot.

Piaget *n* **Jean** (1896–1980) Swiss psychologist who pioneered the study of the cognitive functions of children.

pia mater *n* (*anat*) the inner membrane enclosing the brain.

piangevole *adv* (*mus*) (*Italian*) "sadly."

pianissimo *adv* (*mus*) (*Italian*) very softly.

pianist *n* a person who plays the piano.

Piankhy *n* (*Egypt*) a pharaoh of the Twenty-fifth Dynasty (ruled 747–716 BC). King of Nubia. His court and society at Napata set out to follow the example of the Egyptian capital, including the construction of pyramids and mortuary temples.

piano *n* (*pl* **pianos**) a large stringed keyboard instrument in which each key operates a felt-covered hammer that strikes a corresponding steel wire or wires.

Piano *n* **Renzo** (1937–) Italian architect, whose notable works include Pompidou Center, Paris.

piano accordion *see* **accordion**.

pianoforte *n* (*pl* **pianofortes**) a piano.

piano nobile *n* (*archit*) the main floor of a house in which the reception rooms are situated.

piaster, piastre *n* a unit of currency in Egypt, Lebanon, Sudan, Syria, and South Vietnam.

piazza *n* in Italy, a public square; a covered walkway or gallery; a veranda.

PIB *abbr* = Petroleum Information Bureau.

pi bond *n* (*chem*) the covalent bond formed when two atoms join to form a molecule.

Pibor *abbr* = Paris Interbank Offered Rate.

pibroch *n* a kind of music composed for Scottish bagpipes.

PIBS *abbr* = permanent interest-bearing share.

PIC *abbr* = programable interrupt controller.

pica[1] *n* (*print*) a standard measurement, equal to 12 points.

pica[2] *n* (*med*) an abnormal desire to eat non-food substances such as soap, chalk, glue, clay, etc.

Picabia *n* **Francis** (1879–1953) French painter. His early works are in an impressionist style but he took a more avant-garde direction from 1912 and was involved with the Section d'Or group. Notable works include *I see again in memory my dear Udnie* (1914).

PICAGB *abbr* = Police Insignia Collectors Association of Great Britain.

picaresque *adj* pertaining to a genre of fiction describing the exploits of rogues.

picaroon *n* (*arch*) a robber, pirate, or marauder.

Picasso *n* 1. **Pablo** (1881–1973) Spanish painter, sculptor, designer, and illustrator. In 1906–7, he painted *Les Demoiselles d'Avignon*, which was to herald cubism and represents a major turning point in modern art. A further development is represented by the painting *Guernica* (1937), in response to the bombing of the Basque capital by German planes during the Spanish Civil War. 2. **Paloma** (1949–) French fashion and furnishings designer, the daughter of Pablo Picasso.

picayune *adj* (*inf*) of little value.

PICC *abbr* = Provisional International Computation Center.

piccalilli *n* a kind of pickle made with cauliflower, onions, etc.

piccaninny *n* (*pl* **piccaninnies**) (*offensive*) a black baby or child.

Piccinni *n* **Niccolò** (1728–1800) Italian composer who was also a notable opera producer. He wrote some 120 operas including *Iphigenie en Tauride*, for which settings were commissioned from both Piccinni and Gluck, *Pénélope*, and *La Buona Figola*.

piccolo *n* (*pl* **piccolos**) a small shrill flute.

pick *n* a heavy tool with a shaft and pointed crossbar for breaking ground; a tool for picking, such as a toothpick or icepick; a plectrum; right of selection; choice; best (of). * *vti* to break up or remove with a pick; to pluck at; to nibble (at), eat fussily; to contrive; to choose; (*fruit, etc*) to gather; to steal from a pocket; (*lock*) to force open; (*with* up) to lift; to acquire; to call for; to recover; (*inf*) to make the acquaintance of casually; to learn gradually; to resume; to give a lift to; to increase speed.

Pick *n* **Frank** (1878–1941) British design theorist who was a founding member of the British Design and Industries Association.

pickaback *see* **piggyback**.

pickaninny *n* (*pl* **pickaninnies**) varient spelling of **piccaninny**.

pickaxe, pickax *n* (*pl* **pickaxes**) a pick with a long pointed head for breaking up hard ground, etc.

pickerel *n* (*pl* **pickerel, pickerels**) a North American freshwater fish of the pike family.

picket *n* a pointed stake; a patrol or group of men selected for a special duty; a person posted by strikes outside a place of work to persuade others not to enter. * *vt* (**picketing, picketed**) to tether to a picket; to post as a military picket; to place pickets, or serve as a picket (at a factory, etc).

picket fence *n* a fence made of pickets driven into the ground.

picket line *n* a line held by military pickets; a line of people acting as pickets.

Pickford *n* **Mary [Gladys Mary Smith]** (1893–1979) Canadian-born American movie star and co-founder of the United Artists studio (1919) with Charlie Chaplin and D W Griffith.

pickings *npl* gleanings, perquisites.

pickle *n* vegetables preserved in vinegar; (*inf*) a plight, mess. * *vt* to preserve in vinegar.

pickled *adj* preserved in pickle; (*sl*) drunk.

picklock *n* an instrument for picking locks; someone, esp a thief, who picks locks.

pick-me-up *n* a tonic.

pickpocket *n* a person who steals from pockets.

pick-up *n* the act of picking up; a person or thing picked up; (*elect*) a device for picking up current; the power to accelerate rapidly; the balanced arm of a record player; a pickup truck.

pickup truck *n* a light truck with an enclosed cab and open body.

picky *adj* (**pickier, pickiest**) fussy.— **pickily** *adv*.—**pickiness** *n*.

picnic *n* a usu informal meal taken on an excursion and eaten outdoors; an outdoor snack; the food so eaten; an easy or agreeable task. * *vi* (**picnicking, picnicked**) to have a picnic.—**picnicker** *n*.

pico- *prefix* denoting one trillionth (10^{-12}).

picot *n* a small loop of thread used as an edging to lace.

picotee *n* a type of small carnation.

picric acid *n* a toxic acid used as a dye and an explosive.

PICT *abbr* (*comput*) = picture. An object oriented graphics file format developed by Apple™ for the MacDraw™ program.

pictograph *n* a picture representing a word or idea.

pictorial *adj* relating to pictures, painting, or drawing; containing pictures; expressed in pictures; graphic.—**pictorially** *adv*.

Picts *npl* the "painted people" described by the Romans in the 3rd century AD, who occupied the northern part of Britain and were conquered by the kingdom of Dalriada in 843 AD.—**Pictish** *adj*.

picture *n* drawing, painting, photography, or other visual representation; a scene; an impression or mental image; a vivid description; a cinema film. * *vt* to portray, describe in a picture; to visualize.

picturesque *adj* striking, vivid, usually pleasing; making an effective picture.—**picturesquely** *adv*.—**picturesqueness** *n*.

PICUTPC *abbr* = Permanent and International Committee of Underground Town Planning and Construction.

PICV *abbr* = Permanent International Commission of Viticulture.

PID *abbr* = pelvic inflammatory disease; personal identification device; prolapsed intervertebral disk (slipped disk).

piddle *vt* to squander. * *vi* (*inf*) to idle; to urinate.

piddling *adj* (*inf*) trifling, insignificant.

piddock *n* a bivalve, boring, shellfish.

pidgin *n* a jargon for trade purposes, using words and grammar from two or more different languages.

PIDS *abbr* = primary immune deficiency syndrome.

pie[1] *n* a baked dish of fruit, meat, etc, with an under or upper crust of pastry, or both.

pie[2] *see* **pi**[2].

piebald *adj* covered with patches of two colors. * *n* a piebald horse, etc.

pièce de résistance *n* (*pl* **pièces de résistance**) (*French*) the most important item or dish.

piece *n* a distinct part of anything; a single object; a literary, dramatic, artistic, or musical composition; (*sl*) a firearm; a man in chess or checkers; an opinion, view; a short distance. * *vt* to fit together, join.—**piecer** *n*.

piecemeal *adv* gradually; bit by bit.

piecework *n* work paid for according to the quantity produced.

pie chart *n* a circular graph divided into segments in proportion to the relative quantities.—*also* **pie graph**.

pied *adj* of mixed colors, mottled

pied-à-terre *n* (*pl* **pieds-à-terre**) (*French*) an apartment for occasional use; a second home.

piedmont glacier *n* an extension of ice from a valley glacier, which projects beyond its valley walls onto the adjacent flat plain at the foot of the mountains.

piedmont gravels *npl* (*geol*) coarse deposits of pebbles, etc, found on the flat lowlands (piedmont).

pier *n* a structure supporting the spans of a bridge; a structure built out over water and supported by pillars, used as a landing place, promenade, etc; a heavy column used to support weight.

pierce *vt* to cut or make a hole through; to force a way into; (*fig*) to touch or move. * *vi* to penetrate.

Pierce *n* **Franklin** (1804–69) American Democrat statesman and 14th president of the US (1853–57).

piercing *adj* penetrating; keen; (*cold, pain*) acute.—**piercingly** *adv*.

Pieria *n* in ancient Greece the region around Mount Olympus, associated with the Muses.—**Pierian** *adj*.

Piero della Francesca *n* (*c*.1416–92) Italian early Renaissance painter. From *c*.1460 he worked at the Urbino court, where he painted some of his finest works, e.g. *The History of the True Cross* and *The Resurrection*.

Piero di Cosimo *n* (1462–1521) Florentine painter who painted mainly scenes featuring mythological creatures and figures, and depicting animals in a sympathetic manner. Notable works include *Cephalus and Procris* and *Mythological Subject*.

Pierre *n* the capital city of South Dakota, a state of the USA.

Pierrot *n* (*pantomime*) a male character, usu in a loose white costume with a whitened face; a clown in such a costume.

Pierrot Lunaire *n* a melodrama for voice and instruments by Schoenberg. It is a setting of 21 poems by Albert Giraud, translated from French into German by O E Hartleben. It was first performed in 1912.

Pierus *n* (*Greek myth*) a king of Pella in Macedonia.

pietà *n* a picture or sculpture of the Virgin mourning over the dead Christ.

piety *n* (*pl* **pieties**) religious devoutness; the characteristic of being pious.

piezoelectricity *n* the production of electricity in certain types of crystal through the application of mechanical stress.—**piezoeletric, piezoelectrical** *adj*.—**piezoelectrically** *adv*.

PIF *abbr* (*comput*) = Program Information File. A file containing information about DOS applications that assists Microsoft Windows™ in running the application.

PIFA *abbr* = Packaging and Industrial Films Association; Practitioner of the Institute of Field Archaeologists.

piffle *n* (*inf*) silly stuff, nonsense. * *vi* to talk nonsense.

pig *n* a domesticated animal with a broad snout and fat body raised for food; a hog; a greedy or filthy person; an oblong casting of metal poured from the smelting furnace; (*sl*) a policeman. * *vi* (**pigging, pigged**) (*sow*) to give birth; (*inf*) to live in squalor.

Pigalle *n* **Jean-Baptiste** (1714–85) French sculptor and painter. Notable monumental works include the tomb for Maurice of Saxony. A technically accomplished and naturally versatile artist, he also painted brilliant portraits, including *Self Portrait* (1780) and *Voltaire* (1770–76).

pigeon *n* a bird with a small head and a heavy body; (*inf*) a person who is easily conned.

pigeonhole *n* a small compartment for filing papers, etc; a category usu failing to reflect actual complexities. * *vt* to file, classify; to put aside for consideration, shelve.

pigeon-toed *adj* having the toes turned inward.

piggery *n* (*pl* **piggeries**) a place where pigs are reared; a pigsty.

piggish *adj* greedy, dirty, selfish, like a pig.—**piggishly** *adv*.—**piggishness** *n*.

Piggott *n* **Lester [Keith]** (1935–) English jockey. Regarded as one of the finest flat-racing jockeys of modern times, he won the Derby nine times.

piggy *n* (*pl* **piggies**) a child's name for a young or little pig. * *adj* (**piggier, piggiest**) piggish.

piggyback *n* a ride on the shoulders or back of a person. * *adv* carried on the shoulders or back; transported on top of a larger object.—*also* **pickaback**.

piggy bank *n* a container for coins, often shaped like a pig.

pigheaded *adj* stupidly stubborn.—**pigheadedly** *adv*.—**pigheadedness** *n*.

pig iron *n* crude iron directly from a blast furnace.

piglet *n* a young pig.

pigment *n* paint; a naturally occurring substance used for coloring.—**pigmentary** *adj*.

pigmentation *n* (*biol*) coloration of the tissues of plants and animals caused by pigment; the depositing of pigments by cells.

pigmy *see* **pygmy**.

pignut *n* an earthnut.

pigpen *n* a pen for pigs; any messy or untidy place.

pigskin *n* leather made from the skin of a pig.

pigsticker *n* a person who goes pigsticking.

pigsticking *n* the hunting of wild boar with a spear, usu on horseback.

pigsty *n* (*pl* **pigsties**) a pen for pigs; a dirty hovel.

pigtail *n* a tight braid of hair.—**pigtailed** *adj*.

PIH *abbr* = Paintings in Hospitals; pregnancy-induced hypertension.

Pijper *n* **Willem** (1894–1947) Dutch composer, pianist, and author. He is often considered to be the father of modern Dutch music and his works include three symphonies, numerous pieces of chamber music, and the opera *Halewijn*.

pik *abbr* = payment in kind.

pike[1] *n* a sharp point or spike; the top of a spear. * *vt* to pierce or kill with a pike.

pike[2] *n* (*pl* **pike, pikes**) a long-snouted fish, important as a food and game fish.

pike perch *n* (**pike perch, pike perches**) any of various fishes of the perch family resembling the pike.

pikestaff *n* the shaft of a pike.

pil *abbr* = payment in lieu.

pil. *abbr* (*pharm*) (*Latin*) = *pilula*, "pill."

PIL *abbr* = Pest Infestation Laboratory.

pilaf, pilaff *n* a dish of spiced rice cooked in stock with, optionally, meat or fish.—*also* **pilau**.

pilaster *n* a rectangular pillar, usu set in a wall.

Pilate *n* **[Pontius]** Roman governor of Judea from AD 26–36, who according to the Gospels sentenced Jesus to be crucified.

pilch *n* (*arch*) a triangular flannel wrap for a baby.

pilchard *n* a fish of the herring family.

pile[1] *n* a heap or mound of objects; a large amount; a lofty building; a pyre; (*sl*) a fortune. * *vt* (*with* **up, on**) to heap or stack; to load; to accumulate. * *vi* to become heaped up; (*with* **up, out, on**) to move confusedly in a mass.

pile[2] *n* a vertical beam driven into (the ground) as a foundation for a building, etc. * *vt* to support with piles; to drive piles into.

pile[3] *n* the nap of a fabric or carpet; soft, fine fur or wool.

pileate, pileated *adj* (*biol*) crested.

piledriver *n* a machine for driving in piles.

pile dwelling *n* (*archeo*) a house that was built on boggy ground near the edge of a lake, supported on wooden posts.

piles *npl* hemorrhoids.

pile-up *n* an accumulation of tasks, etc; (*inf*) a collision of several vehicles.

pilfer *vti* to steal in small quantities.—**pilferage** *n*.—**pilferer** *n*.

pilgrim *n* a person who makes a pilgrimage.

pilgrimage *n* a journey to a holy place as an act of devotion; any long journey; a life's journey.

piliferous *adj* (*esp bot*) hairy.

piliform *adj* (*bot*) in the form of or like a hair.

pill *n* medicine in round balls or tablet form; (*with cap*) an oral contraceptive.

PILL *abbr* = programed instruction language learning.

pillage *n* looting, plunder. * *vti* to plunder, esp during war.—**pillager** *n*.

pillar *n* a slender, vertical structure used as a support or ornament; a column; a strong supporter of a cause.

pillar box *n* (*UK*) a mailbox in the shape of a pillar.

pillar crosses *n* Celtic standing stones with designs carved on them. They gradually evolved over several hundred years into the great intricate high crosses.

pillbox *n* a box for pills, esp a decorative one; a small round hat without a brim; (*mil*) a small, fortified, concrete shelter.

pillion *n* a seat behind the driver for a passenger on a motorcycle, etc.

pillory *n* (*pl* **pillories**) (*formerly*) stocks in which criminals were put as punishment. * *vt* (**pillorying, pilloried**) to expose for public scorn and ridicule.

pillow *n* a cushion that supports the head during sleep; something that supports to equalize or distribute pressure. * *vti* to rest on, serve as, a pillow.

pillowcase, pillowslip *n* a removable cover for a pillow.

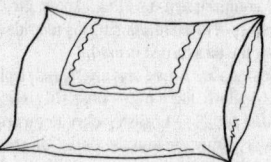

pillow lava *n* subaqueous, basaltic lava flows, characterized by pillow structure, each rarely more than four feet in diameter but often forming a sequence hundreds of yards thick through branching and budding.

Pilon *n* **Germain** (1527–90) French sculptor. His early works are decorative in the mannerist style, while a much more moving naturalism is expressed in the tomb of the king and his queen, Catherine de' Medici, at St Denis (1563–70).

pilose *adj* (*biol*) hairy.

pilot *n* a person who operates an aircraft; one who directs ships in and out of harbor; a guide; a television show produced as a sample of a proposed series. * *vt* to direct the course of, act as pilot; to lead or guide.

pilotage *n* the work or fee of a pilot.

pilot balloon *n* (*meteorol*) a small hydrogen-filled balloon used to determine wind speed and direction at high altitude.

pilot fish *n* a small fish marked with vertical stripes that often swims along with sharks.

pilot light *n* a burning gas flame used to light a larger jet; an electric indicator light.

Pilsudski *n* **Józef Klemens** (1867–1935) Polish soldier and statesman. He became provisional president (1918–21) and, as marshal of Poland, held the Bolshevik army's advance into Polish territory in 1920. He was prime minister (1926–28, 1930).

Piltdown *n* place in England where some animal bones and a human skull were found in the early 20th century. These were accepted by many as the "missing link" between apes and man, but were later proved to be part of a hoax.

pilule *n* a small pill.—**pilular** *adj*.

pilus (*pl* **pili**) *n* a hair or a structure like a hair.

PIM *abbr* = personal information manager.

PIME *abbr* (*RC Church*) (*Latin*) = *Pontificium Institutum pro Missionibus Externis*, "Pontifical Institute for Foreign Missions."

pimento *n* (*pl* **pimentos**) allspice; a pimiento.

pimiento *n* a sweet red pepper (capiscum) used in salads and cooked dishes.

pimp *n* a prostitute's agent.—*also vt*.

pimpernel *n* a primulaceous plant with small scarlet, blue, or white flowers.

pimple *n* a small, raised, inflamed swelling of the skin.—**pimpled** *adj*.—*also* **papule**.

pimply *adj* (**pimplier, pimpliest**) covered with pimples.

PIMS *abbr* = profit impact of market strategy.

pin *n* a piece of metal or wood used to fasten things together; a small piece of pointed wire with a head; an ornament or badge with a pin or clasp for fastening to clothing; (*bowling*) one of the clubs at which the ball is rolled. * *vt* (**pinning, pinned**) to fasten with a pin; to hold, fix; (*with* **down**) to get (someone) to commit himself or herself as to plans, etc; (*a fact, etc*) to establish.

PIN *abbr* = personal identification number (issued by a bank to a customer to validate electronic transactions).

pinafore *n* a sleeveless garment worn over a dress, blouse, etc.

pinaster *n* a Southern European pine tree.

pinball *n* a game in which a small metal ball is shot through a maze containing various electronic gates and switches that score points when hit.

Pinc *abbr* = property income certificate.

pince-nez *n* (*pl* **pince-nez**) eyeglasses clipped to the nose by a spring.

pincers *npl* a tool with two handles and jaws used for gripping and drawing out nails, etc; a grasping claw, as of a crab.

pinch *vti* to squeeze or compress painfully; to press between the fingers; to nip; (*sl*) to steal; (*sl*) to arrest. * *n* a squeeze or nip; what can be taken up between the finger and thumb, a small amount; a time of stress; an emergency.

pinchbeck *n* a copper and zinc alloy, used as imitation gold.

pinched *adj* appearing to be squeezed; drawn by cold or stress.

pinch-hit *vi* (**pinch-hitting, pinch-hit**) to bat in place of another in an emergency; to serve as a replacement. * *n* a hit made by a pinch hitter.—**pinch hitter** *n*.

pincushion *n* a pad for holding pins.

Pindar *n* (c.522–c.443 BC) Greek lyric poet noted for his odes celebrating victories in the Greek games. His elaborate poems became influential in late 17th-cent England.

Pindaric *adj* (*ode*) associated with the poet Pindar.

pine[1] *n* an evergreen coniferous tree with long needles and well-formed cones; a tree of the pine family; its wood.

pine[2] *vi* to languish, waste away through longing or mental stress; (*with* **for**) to yearn.

pineal gland *n* a pea-sized gland in the brain.

pineapple *n* a tropical plant; its juicy, fleshy, yellow fruit.

pine tar *n* tar distilled from pine wood and used in roofing, paint, and various medicines.

pin feed *adj* (*comput*) (paper) inserted into a printer by means of holes, similar to tractor feed.

pinfold *n* a pound for stray cattle. * *vt* to shut into, or as if into, such a pound.

ping *n* a high-pitched ringing sound. * *vti* to strike with a ping, emit a ping.—**pinger** *n*.

pingo *n* (*Inuit*) a dome-shaped hill with a core of ice.

ping-pong *n* a name for table tennis; (*with caps*) (*trademark*) table tennis equipment.

pinhead *n* the head of a pin; something very small; (*inf*) a stupid or foolish person.—**pinheaded** *adj*.—**pinheadedness** *n*.

pinion[1] *n* the outer joint of a bird's wing; a wing feather. * *vt* to cut off a pinion; to bind arms to sides, restrain.

pinion[2] *n* a cogwheel.

pink[1] *n* any of various garden plants with a fragrant flower, including carnations; a pale red color; a huntsman's red coat; the highest type. * *adj* pink-colored; (*inf*) radical in political views.

pink[2] *vt* to stab, pierce; (*cloth, etc*) to cut a zigzag edge on; to perforate with pinking shears.

Pinkerton *n* **Allan** (1819–84) Scots-born American detective and founder of the Pinkerton National Detective Agency in Chicago (1850).

pinkeye *n* an inflammation of the conjunctiva, affecting animals and humans.

pinkie, pinky *n* (*pl* **pinkies**) the little finger on the human hand.

pinking shears *npl* shears with notched edges for pinking edges of cloth.

pin money *n* money given to a woman by her husband for personal expenses.

pinna[1] *n* (*pl* **pinnae, pinnas**) (*biol*) the fin of a fish; the feather or wing of a bird; the leaflet of a pinnate leaf.

pinna[2] *see* **ear**.

pinnace *n* (*naut*) a small light schooner-rigged vessel with oars; an eight-oared small boat belonging to a warship.

pinnacle *n* a slender tower crowning a roof, etc; a rocky peak of a mountain; the highest point, climax.

pinnate, pinnated *adj* shaped like a feather; (*leaf*) divided into leaflets.

Pinner *n* (*Brit Celtic myth*) a king of England who was defeated and killed by Molmotius, who was set on expanding the kingdom of Cornwall, which he had inherited from his father.

pinniped *adj* (*zool*) with fin-like feet or flippers.

pinny *n* (*pl* **pinnies**) (*sl*) a pinafore.

Pinochet [Ugarte] *n* **Augusto** (1915–) Chilean general and dictator. He led the 1973 coup that deposed Allende and became president (1974–90), ruthlessly suppressing dissent.

pinochle, pinocle *n* a card game.—*also* **pinuchle**.

Pinodjem I *n* Egyptian king of the Twenty-first Dynasty (ruled 1054–1042 BC).

pinpoint *vt* to locate or identify very exactly.

pinprick *n* a small puncture as made by a pin; a trivial annoyance.

pins and needles *npl* a tingling feeling in the fingers, toes, etc, caused by impeded blood circulation returning to normal; (*with* on) in an anxious or expectant state.

pinstripe *n* a very narrow stripe in suit fabrics, etc.

pint *n* a liquid measure equal to half a quart or one eighth of a gallon (0.47 liters); (*inf*) a drink of beer.

pintadera *n* (*archeo*) a pottery stamp that may have been used to apply dyes to the skin.

pintail *n* (*pl* **pintails, pintail**) a type of duck.

Pinter *n* **Harold** (1930–) English dramatist whose works incude *The Caretaker*.

Pinteresque *adj* (*of dialog*) halting, menacing, and punctuated by sinister pauses.

pintle *n* a bolt or pin esp comprising a pivot.

pinto *n* (*pl* **pintos**) a piebald horse.

pinuchle *see* **pinochle**.

pin-up *n* (*sl*) a photograph of a naked or partially naked person; a person who has been so photographed; a photograph of a famous person.

pinx. *abbr* (*Latin*) = *pinxit*, "painted it."

pioneer *n* a person who initiates or explores new areas of enterprise, research, etc; an explorer; an early settler; (*mil*) one who prepares roads, sinks mines, etc. * *vti* to initiate or take part in the development of; to act as a pioneer (to); to explore (a region).

pious *adj* devout; religious; sanctimonious.—**piously** *adv*.—**piousness** *n*.

pip[1] *n* the seed in a fleshy fruit, e.g. apple, orange.

pip[2] *n* a spot with a numerical value on a playing card, dice, etc; (*inf*) insignia on a uniform showing an officer's rank; a signal on a radar screen.

pip[3] *vi* (**pipping, pipped**) (*bird*) to chirp, to peep; (*hatching bird*) to pierce (its shell).

pipal *see* **peepul**.

pipe *n* a tube of wood, metal, etc, for making musical sounds; (*pl*) the bagpipes; a stem with a bowl for smoking tobacco; a long tube or hollow body for conveying water, gas, etc. * *vt* to play on a pipe; (*gas, water, etc*) to convey by pipe; to lead, summon with the sound of a pipe(s); to trim with piping. * *vi* (*sl*) to take the drug crack.

pipeclay *n* a white clay, used to make tobacco pipes and to whiten leather, etc. * *vt* to whiten using pipeclay.

pipe dream *n* an impossible plan, hope or fantasy.

pipeline *n* a pipe (often underground) used to convey oil, gas, etc; a direct channel for information; the processes through which supplies pass from source to user.

pipe organ *n* a musical organ.

piper *n* a person who plays a pipe, esp bagpipes.

Piper *n* **John** (1903–92) British painter who was an official war artist in World War II and designed for the stage.

pipette, pipet *n* a hollow glass tube into which liquids are sucked for measurement.

pipe wrench *n* a wrench that grips a pipe when turned in one direction only.

piping *n* a length of pipe, pipes collectively; a tube-like fold of material used to trim seams; a strip of icing, cream, for decorating cakes, etc; the art of playing a pipe or bagpipes; a high-pitched sound. * *adj* making a high-pitched sound.

piping hot *adj* very hot.

pipistrelle, pipistrel *n* a small brown bat.

pipit *n* a type of songbird.

pipkin *n* a small earthenware pot.

pippin *n* one of several types of eating apple.

pipsqueak *n* (*inf*) a contemptible or insigificant person.

piquant *adj* strong-tasting; pungent, sharp; stimulating.—**piquancy** *n*.—**piquantly** *adv*.

piqué *n* a corded cotton fabric.

pique *n* resentment, ill-feeling. * *vt* (**piquing, piqued**) to cause resentment in; to offend.

piquet *n* a card game for two.

PIRA *abbr* = Paper and Board, Printing and Packaging Industries Research Association.

piracy *n* (*pl* **piracies**) robbery at sea; the hijacking of a ship or aircraft; infringement of copyright; unauthorized use of patented work; (*comput*) the unauthorized copying of software.

Piraeus (Piraiévs) *n* a city in Greece.

piragua *see* **pirogue**.

Piramesse *n* a site in Egypt in the eastern Delta, selected as capital by Rameses II and used until the end of the Ramessid era, about 200 years later. Its monumental buildings were later used as quarries to extend the new capital at nearby Tanis.

Pirandello *n* **Luigi** (1867–1936) Italian dramatist, short-story writer, and novelist whose two best-known plays are *Six Characters in Search of an Author* and *Henry IV*, both of which are influential experimental plays. He was awarded the Nobel prize for literature in 1934.

Piranesi *n* **Giovanni [Battista]** (1720–78) Italian artist whose work profoundly influenced the first generation of neo-classical designers.

piranha *n* a small voracious freshwater fish of tropical America with sharp teeth and a strong jaw.

pirate *n* a person who commits robbery at sea; a hijacker; one who infringes copyright. * *vti* to take by piracy; to publish or reproduce in violation of a copyright.—**piratical, piratic** *adj*.

Piretti *n* **Giancarlo** (1940–) Italian designer who produced innovative furniture.

pirogue *n* a dugout canoe.—*also* **piragua**.

pirouette *n* a spin on the toes in ballet.—*also vi*.

Pisanello *n* (*c*.1395–1455/6) Italian painter. His decorative and detailed works are rich in color and texture. Excellent draftsmanship is evident in carefully observed drawings of birds and animals and in the accuracy of his portraits.

Pisano *n* 1. **Giovanni** (*c*.1265–1314) one of the leading Italian sculptors of his time. His works are expressive and elegant in the Gothic tradition. 2. **Nicola** (*c*.1225–84) father of Giovanni Pisano. A sculptor famous for the pulpits in the Baptistry at Pisa (1260) and the Cathedral at Siena (1265–8).

piscatorial, piscatory *adj* of, or pertaining to, fish or fishing.

Pisces *n* the Fishes, in astrology the twelfth sign of the zodiac, operative from February 19 – March 20.—**Piscean** *adj, n*.

pisciculture *n* the controlled rearing and breeding of fish.—**piscicultural** *adj*.—**pisciculturist** *n*.

piscina *n* (*pl* **piscinae, piscinas**) (*RC Church*) a basin with a drain in a church wall, used for rinsing sacred vessels after Mass.

piscine *adj* pertaining to fish.

piscivorous *adj* fish-eating.

pisé *or* **terre pisée** *n* (*archeo*) (*French*) a building constructed from layers of mud built up on the site without being first made into bricks.

pisiform *adj* pea-shaped.

pismire *n* an ant.

piss *vi* (*vulg*) to urinate. * *n* urine.

Pissarro *n* 1. **Camille** (1830–1903) West Indian-born French impressionist painter. 2. **Lucien** (1863-1744) painter son of Camille Pissarro, who experimented with pointillism before establishing his neo-impressionist style.

pissed *adj* (*sl*) very angry; depressed (—*also* **pissed-off**); (*Brit sl*) drunk.

pistachio *n* (*pl* **pistachios**) a tree found in Mediterranean countries and West Asia; the edible nut of this tree.

piste *n* a ski trail of packed snow; (*fencing*) the rectangular area where a bout takes place.

pistil *n* the seed-bearing part of a flower.

pistillate *adj* (*bot*) having a pistil; with a pistil but no stamens.

pistol *n* a small, short-barreled handgun. * *vt* (**pistoling, pistoled** *or* **pistolling, pistolled**) to shoot with a pistol.

pistole *n* (*formerly*) a gold coin used in Europe.

piston *n* a disk that slides to and fro in a close-fitting cylinder, as in engines, pumps.

Piston *n* **Walter** (1894–1976) American composer, teacher, and author. His works, in traditional tonal style, include the ballet *The Incredible Flautist*, eight symphonies and many pieces of chamber music.

pit *n* a deep hole in the earth; a (coal) mine; a scooped-out place for burning something; a sunken or depressed area below the adjacent floor area; a space at the front of the stage for the orchestra; the area in a securities or commodities exchange in which members do the trading; the scar left by smallpox, etc; the stone of a fruit; a place where racing cars refuel. * *vti* (**pitting, pitted**) to set in competition; to mark or become marked with pits; to make a pit stop.

pit-a-pat *adv* with quick, light steps or beats. * *n* quick, light steps or beats. * *vi* (**pit-a-patting, pit-a-patted**) to make quick, light steps or beats.

PITB *abbr* = Petroleum Industry Training Board.

Pitcairn Islands *n* a British overseas territory situated in the southeast Pacific Ocean.

pitch[1] *vti* (**tent, etc**) to erect by driving pegs, stakes, etc, into the ground; to set the level of; (*mus*) to set in key; to express in a style; to throw, hurl; to fall heavily, plunge, esp forward. * *n* a throw; height, intensity; a musical tone; a place where a street trader or performer works; distance between threads (of a screw); amount of slope; a sound wave frequency; a sports field; (*cricket*) the area between the wickets; sales talk; (*comput*) a measurement of the number of characters that a printer prints in a linear inch.

pitch[2] *n* the black, sticky substance from distillation of tar, etc; any of various bituminous substances. * *vt* to smear with pitch.

pitch-black *adj* black, or extremely dark.

pitchblende *n* a black mineral, composed largely of uranium oxide, that also yields radium.

pitch-dark *adj* completely dark.

pitcher *n* a large water jug; (*baseball*) the player who pitches the ball.

pitchfork *n* a long-handled fork for tossing hay, etc. * *vt* to lift with this; to thrust suddenly or willy-nilly into.

pitch pipe *n* a small pipe used to set the pitch for musical instruments or singing.

pitchy *adj* (**pitchier, pitchiest**) resembling, or smeared with, pitch.

piteous *adj* arousing pity; heart-rending.—**piteously** *adv*.—**piteousness** *n*.

pitfall *n* concealed danger; unexpected difficulty.

pith *n* the soft tissue inside the rind of citrus fruits; the gist, essence; importance.

pithos *n* (*archeo*) a large pottery container for holding grain or oil that was occasionally used as a receptacle for a dead body in a jar burial.

pithy *adj* (**pithier, pithiest**) like or full of pith; concise and full of meaning.—**pithily** *adv*.—**pithiness** *n*.

pitiable *adj* deserving pity, lamentable, wretched.—**pitiableness** *n*.—**pitiably** *adv*.

pitiful *adj* causing pity, touching; contemptible, paltry.—**pitifully** *adv*.—**pitifulness** *n*.

pitiless *adj* without pity, ruthless.—**pitilessly** *adv*.—**pitilessness** *n*.

pitman *n* (*pl* **pitmen**) a miner.

Pitman *n* **Benn** (1822–1910) British-born teacher and pioneer of the phonetic shorthand system, named after his brother, Isaac Pitman, who invented it.

pitsaw *n* a handsaw used by two people to cut logs into planks, one standing in a pit and the other above the log.

pit stop *n* a stop in the pits by a racing car; a stop for rest, food, fuel, etc, during a long journey.

Pitt *n* 1. **William [the Elder, 1st Earl of Chatham]** (1707–88) English statesman and prime minister, who led Britain to victory in the Seven Years War (1756–63) with France. He resigned in 1761 and served again in 1766–68. 2. **William [the Younger]** (1759–1806) son of William Pitt the Elder, who became prime minister in 1783. He instituted important social and political reforms, worked for good relations with America, and formed a European coalition against Napoleon.

pittance *n* a very small quantity or allowance of money.

Pittoni *n* **Giovanni Battista** (1520–83) Italian designer who published plates of strapwork.

pituitary *adj* of or pertaining to the pituitary gland; (*arch*) of or secreting mucus. * *n* (*pl* **pituitaries**) the pituitary gland.

pituitary gland *n* a ductless gland at the base of the brain that affects growth and sexual development.—*also* **hypophysis**.

pity *n* (*pl* **pities**) sympathy with the distress of others; a cause of grief; a regrettable fact. * *vt* (**pitying, pitied**) to feel pity for.—**pityingly** *adv*.

pityriasis *n* (*pl* **pityriases**) a skin disease characterized by scaly, pink eruptions.

piu *adv* (*mus*) (*Italian*) "more", as in *piu allegro*, "faster."

Pius V *n* **Saint** (1504–72) Italian Dominican monk, bishop of Sutri and Nepi (1556) and cardinal (1557), canonized by Clement XI in 1712. Inquisitor-general for Lombardy, he strove to enforce the disciplinary decrees of the Council of Trent. He excommunicated Elizabeth I of England (1570). His feast day is April 30.

Pius X *n* **Saint** (1835–1914) Italian ecclesiastic, elected pope in 1903, who was known for the simplicity of his life and sympathy with the poor. He was conservative in theology and condemned modernism. His feast day is August 21.

Pius XII *n* **[Eugenio Pacelli]** (1876–1958) Italian pope. He preserved the neutrality of the Church during World War II, in which he maintained diplomatic relations with both Axis and Allies. He pursued a strong anti-communist policy after the war.

Piva *n* **Paolo** (1950–) Italian designer who designed kitchen units, seating, and travel goods for clients.

pivot *n* a pin on which a part turns, fulcrum; a key person upon whom progress depends; a cardinal point or factor. * *vt* to turn or hinge (on) a pivot; to attach by a pivot. * *vi* to run on, or as if on, a pivot.—**pivotal** *adj*.

pixel *n* any of the tiny units that form an image (as on a television screen, computer monitor).

pixie, pixy *n* (*pl* **pixies**) a fairy or elf.

pixilated *adj* acting as if influenced by pixies; unconventional, eccentric, whimsical; (*sl*) drunk.

pizazz, pizzazz *n* (*sl*) vitality, energy, glamor.—**pizazzy, pizzazzy** *adj*.

pizz., pizza. *abbr* (*mus*) (*Italian*) = *pizzicato*, "plucked."

pizza *n* a baked dough crust covered with cheese, tomatoes, etc.

pizzeria *n* a pizza restaurant.

Pizzetti *n* **Ildebrando** (1880–1968) Italian composer and academic. He is best known for his operas, including *Deborah e Jaele, Vianna Lupa*, and *Murder in the Cathedral*. His other works include orchestral pieces and compositions for piano.

pizzicato *n* (*pl* **pizzicati, pizzicatos**) (*mus*) a note or passage played by plucking the string of a violin or other bowed instrument.—*also adj*.

pizzle *n* (*arch*) the penis of an animal, esp a bull.

PJ *abbr* = police justice; presiding judge; probate judge.

pk *abbr* = psychokinesis.

pk. *abbr* = pack; park; peak; peck.

pkg. *abbr* = package, packages.

pks. *abbr* = pecks.

pkt. *abbr* = packet.

pkts. *abbr* = packets.

PKU *abbr* = phenylketonuria.

pl. *abbr* = place; plate; plural.

p.l. *abbr* = pamphlet laws; (*ins*) partial loss; proportional logarithm; public laws.

PL *abbr* = Poet Laureate; Primrose League; Public Library; (*scouting*) patrol leader.

P/L *abbr* = profit and loss.

PL/1 *abbr* = Programing Language 1.

PLA *abbr* = Para Legal Association; Private Libraries Association; programable logic array.

placable *adj* easily to placate.—**placability** *n*.

placard *n* a poster or notice for public display.

placate *vt* to appease; to pacify.—**placation** *n*.—**placatory** *adj*.

place *n* a locality, spot; a town or village; a building, residence; a short street, a square; space, room; a particular point, part, position, etc; the part of space occupied by a person or thing; a position or job; a seat; rank, precedence; a finishing position in a race. * *vt* to put; to put in a particular place; to find a place or seat for; to identify; to estimate; to rank; (*order*) to request material from a supplier. * *vi* to finish second or among the first three in a race.

place mat *n* a small mat serving as an individual table cover for a person at a meal.

place name *n* the name of a geographical locality.

placebo *n* (*pl* **placebos, placeboes**) something harmless given by a doctor to fool a patient into thinking he is undergoing treatment.

placement *n* a placing or being placed; location or arrangement.

placenta *n* (*pl* **placentas, placentae**) the organ in the uterus of a female mammal that nourishes the fetus.—**placental** *adj*.

placenta previa *n* the condition when the placenta is situated in the bottom part of the uterus next to or over the cervix and a Cesarean section is necessary for delivery.

placer *n* a deposit containing a valuable mineral found in a river, etc.

placid *adj* calm, tranquil.—**placidity** *n*.—**placidly** *adv*.

placing *n* (*finance*) a method of raising new share capital by issuing shares in a company to a selected group of investors rather than to the public.

placket *n* a slit at the waist of a dress or skirt to make it easy to put on or take off.

placoid *adj* platelike.

plafond *n* a ceiling, esp one of elaborate design; a card game.

plagal *adj* (*musical composition*) having its principal notes between the fifth of the key and its octave.

plagiarism *n* the act of stealing from another author's work, literary theft; that which is plagiarized.—**plagiarist** *n*.—**plagiaristic** *adj*.

plagiarize *vt* to appropriate writings from another author.—**plagiarizer** *n*.

plague *n* a highly contagious and deadly disease; (*inf*) a person who is a nuisance. * *vt* (**plaguing, plagued**) to afflict with a plague; (*inf*) to annoy, harass.

plaguy, plaguey *adj* (*arch*) (*inf*) troublesome, vexatious.

plaice *n* (*pl* **plaice, plaices**) any of various flatfishes, esp a flounder.

plaid *n* a long wide piece of woolen cloth used as a cloak in Highland dress; cloth with a tartan or checkered pattern.

plain *adj* level, flat; understandable; straightforward; manifest, obvious; blunt; unadorned; not elaborate; not colored or patterned; not beautiful; ugly; pure; unmixed. * *n* a large tract of level country.—**plainness** *n*.

plain clothes *npl* ordinary clothes, not uniform, as worn by a policeman on duty.—*also adj*.

plain sailing *n* easy progress over an unobstructed course.

plainly *adv* clearly, intelligibly.

plainsman *n* (*pl* **plainsmen**) an inhabitant of a plain.

plainsong *n* an old, plain kind of church music chanted in unison.

plain-spoken *adj* frank, outspoken.

plaint *n* (*poet*) lamentation, sad song; (*law*) formal statement of grievance.

plaintiff *n* (*law*) a person who brings a civil action against another.

plaintive *adj* sad, mournful.—**plaintively** *adv*.—**plaintiveness** *n*.

plait *n* intertwined strands of hair, straw, etc; a braid. * *vti* (**plaiting, plaited**) to twist strands (of hair) together into a braid.

plan *n* a scheme or idea; a drawing to scale of a building; a diagram, map; any outline or sketch. * *vti* (**planning, planned**) to make a plan of; to design; to arrange beforehand, intend; to make plans.

planar *adj* of or located in a plane; flat.

planarian *n* a type of flatworm.

planchet *n* a plain metal disc from which a coin is made.

planchette *n* a heart-shaped board on wheels, holding a pencil which is supposed to write automatically, giving messages from spirits, when a hand is rested upon it.

Planck *n* **Max [Karl Ernst Ludwig]** (1858–1947) German physicist who formulated the quantum theory and was awarded the 1918 Nobel prize for physics.

Planck's constant *n* the ratio of the energy and frequency of a photon, symbol *h*.—*also* **constant of proportionality**.

plane[1] *n* a tall tree with large broad leaves.

plane[2] *n* a tool with a steel blade for smoothing level wooden surfaces. * *vt* to smooth with a plane.

plane[3] *n* any level or flat surface; a level of attainment; one of the main supporting surfaces of an airplane; an airplane. * *adj* flat or level. * *vi* to fly while keeping the wings motionless; to skim across the surface of water; to travel by airplane.

planet *n* a celestial body that orbits the sun or other star. The nine planets are: Mercury, Venus, Earth, Mars, Jupiter, Saturn, Uranus, Neptune, and Pluto.

planetarium *n* (*pl* **planetariums, planetaria**) a machine used to exhibit the planets, their motions around the sun and their relative distances and magnitudes; a building for housing this instrument; a model of the solar system.

planetary *adj* (*astrol*) under the influence of one of the planets; terrestrial; wandering, erratic.

planetary nebula *n* (*astron*) a layer of glowing gas produced by and surrounding an evolved star and representing a late stage in star evolution.

planetary rings *n* the ring-like structures composed of dust particles and small bodies that surround the four large planets: Jupiter, Saturn, Uranus, and Neptune.

planetoid *n* an asteroid.

Planets, The a suite for orchestra, organ and female chorus by Holst. It was first performed in 1918.

planet X *n* the planet in the Solar System which as yet exists only in theory, thought to be beyond Pluto and indicated by discrepancies in orbits of the outer planets.

plangent *adj* (*sound*) loud and deep; resounding.—**plangency** *n*.

planimeter *n* an instrument for measuring the area of an irregular plane figure.

planimetry *n* the measurement of plane figures.

planish *vt* (*metal*) to smooth and flatten with a hammer or between rollers.

planisphere *n* a sphere projected on a plane or a map of the heavens.

plank *n* a long, broad, thick board; one of the policies forming the platform of a political party. * *vt* to cover with planks.

planking *n* planks collectively; the act of laying boards.

plankton *n* the microscopic organisms that float on seas, lakes, etc.

planner *n* a person who plans; (*UK*) an official who plans architectural development and land use.—**planning** *n*.

planning blight *n* the difficulty that is experienced in selling, leasing, or developing a building or site owing to the fact that the building or site is affected by some kind of government or local authority projected development plan.

planoconcave *adj* (*lens*) with one side flat and the other concave.

planoconvex *adj* (*lens*) with one side flat and the other convex.

plant *n* a living organism with cellulose cell walls, which synthesizes its food from carbon dioxide, water and light; a soft-stemmed organism of this kind, as distinguished from a tree or shrub; the machinery, buildings, etc of a factory, etc; (*sl*) an act of planting; (*sl*) something or someone planted. * *vt* (*seeds, cuttings*) to put into the ground to grow; to place firmly in position; to found or establish; (*sl*) to conceal something in another's possession in order to implicate.

plantain[1] *n* a low-growing weed with tough leaves.

plantain[2] *n* a tropical broad-leaved tree yielding an edible fruit similar to the banana.

plantar *adj* (*anat*) pertaining to the sole of the foot.

plantation *n* a large cultivated planting of trees; an estate where tea, rubber, cotton, etc, is grown, cultivated by local labor.

planter *n* a person who owns or runs a plantation; a machine that plants; a decorative container for plants.

plantigrade *adj* (*zool*) walking on the sole of the foot. * *n* a plantigrade animal.

plaque *n* an ornamental tablet or disk attached to or inserted in a surface; a film of mucus on the teeth that harbors bacteria.

plash *n* a splash; a marshy pool or puddle.—**plashy** *adj* (**plashier, plashiest**).

plasm *n* a kind of protoplasm; plasma.

plasma *n* the colorless liquid part of blood, milk, or lymph; a collection of charged particles resembling gas but conducting electricity and affected by a magnetic field.

plasma display *n* (*comput*) a type of display screen that uses charged gas particles to illuminates the screen.

plasmasphere *n* a region of cold plasma lying around the Earth, within the magnetosphere and above the ionosphere.

plasmid *n* (*biol*) a structure consisting of DNA (with just a few genes) that exists outside the chromosome in a prokaryotic cell and is able to replicate independently.

plasmodium *n* (*pl* **plasmodia**) (*biol*) a mass of protoplasm formed by the union of single-cell organisms; (*med*) any of a genus of parasitic protozoa which cause malaria.

plasmolysis *n* (*biol*) the shrinkage of the protoplasm of a plant cell occurring as a result of loss of water.

plasmolyze *vt* to subject to plasmolysis.

plaster *n* an adhesive dressing for cuts; a mixture of sand, lime, and water that sets hard and is used for covering walls and ceilings. * *vt* to cover as with plaster; to apply like a plaster; to make lie smooth and flat; to load to excess.—**plasterer** *n*.

plaster cast *n* a rigid dressing of gauze impregnated with plaster of Paris; a sculptor's model in plaster of Paris.

plasterboard *n* a thin board formed by layers of plaster and paper, used in wide sheets for walls, etc.

plastered *adj* (*sl*) intoxicated.

plaster of Paris *n* gypsum and water made into a quick-setting paste.

plastic[1] *adj* able to be molded; pliant; made of plastic; (*art*) relating to modeling or molding. * *n* any of various nonmetallic compounds, synthetically produced, that can be molded, cast, squeezed, drawn, or laminated into objects, films, or filaments.—**plastically** *adv*.

plastic[2] *n* colloquial term for charge cards, store cards, credit cards, etc, used to pay for goods and services instead of cash.

plastic explosive *n* a powerful explosive substance that is pliable like putty.

plasticity *n* the ability to be molded or altered; the ability to retain a shape attained by pressure deformation.

plastic surgery *n* surgery to repair deformed or destroyed parts of the body.

plastron *n* a breastplate; a trimming on a dress front; a shirt front; a bony plate on the underside of a tortoise or turtle.

plat *n* a small plot of ground; a map, esp of land divided into lots for building. * *vt* (**platting, platted**) to make a map of.

plat. *abbr* = platoon.

platan *n* a plane tree.

plate *n* a flat sheet of metal on which an engraving is cut; an illustration printed from it; a full-page illustration separate from text; a sheet of metal photographically prepared with text, etc, for printing from; a sheet of glass with sensitized film used as a photographic negative; a trophy as prize at a race; a coating of metal on another metal; utensils plated in silver or gold; plated ware; a flat shallow dish from which food is eaten; a helping of food; the part of a denture that fits the palate; (*inf*) a denture; (*geol*) any of the layers of the earth's lithosphere. * *vt* (*a metal*) to coat with a thin film of another metal; to cover with metal plates.

plateau *n* (*pl* **plateaus, plateaux**) a flat, elevated area of land; a stable period; a graphic representation showing this.

plated *adj* coated with metal, esp silver or gold.

plateful *n* as much as a plate can hold.

plate glass *n* rolled, ground, and polished sheet glass.

platelet *n* a small disk-shaped cell in the blood involved in the process of blood clotting.—*also* **thrombocyte**.

platen *n* the roller on a typewriter; (*print*) a plate which presses the paper against the type.

plater *n* someone who, or something which, plates; a mediocre racehorse.

plate tectonics *n* the study of the features and processes of the Earth's crust that seeks to account for continental drift, sea-floor spreading, volcanic and earthquake activity, and crustal structure.

platform *n* a raised floor for speakers, musicians, etc; a stage; a place or opportunity for public discussion; the raised area next to a railroad line where passengers board trains; a statement of political aims.

platform independent *adj* (*comput*) of a network that allows computers using different operating systems to be present.

Plath *n* **Sylvia** (1932–63) American poet and novelist who married Ted Hughes and settled in England. She published only two books in her lifetime: a volume of poems, *Colossus*, and a novel, *The Bell Jar*. She took her own life.

plating *n* the act or process of plating; a thin coating of metal; a coating of metal plates.

platinize *vt* to coat with platinum.

platinum *n* a valuable, silvery-white metal used for jewelry, etc.

platinum-blond *adj* (*hair*) silvery blond. * *n* someone with hair of this color.—**platinum-blonde** *nf*.

platinum metals *npl* (*chem*) a block of six transition elements with similar properties: ruthenium, rhodium, palladium, osmium, iridium, and platinum.

platitude *n* a dull truism; a commonplace remark.—**platitudinous** *adj*.

platitudinize *vi* to utter platitudes.

Platner *n* **Warren** (1919–) American architect who designed furniture for Knoll and the Windows on the World restaurant in the World Trade Center, New York.

Plato (*c*.427–347 BC) Greek philosopher and founder of Western philosophy, a pupil of Socrates and tutor of Aristotle, whose works include *The Republic*.

PLATO *abbr* = Programed Logic for Automatic Teaching Operation.

platonic *adj* (*love*) spiritual and free from physical desire; (*with cap*) relating to Plato, the Greek philosopher, or his teachings.—**platonically** *adv*.

Platonism *n* the teachings of Plato whose *Theory of Forms* postulates that objects as we perceive them are distinguished from the idea of the objects.

platoon *n* a military unit divided into squads or sections.

platter *n* an oval flat serving dish.

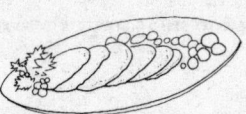

platy- *prefix* flat.

platyhelminth *n* a type of flatworm.

platypus *n* (*pl* **platypuses**) a small aquatic egg-laying mammal of Australia and Tasmania, with webbed feet, a bill like a duck's, dense fur, and a broad flat tail.—*also* **duck-billed platypus**.

platyrrhine, platyrrhinian *adj* (*zool*) broad-nosed.

plaudit *n* (*usu pl*) a commendation; a round of applause.

plausible *adj* apparently truthful or reasonable.—**plausibility** *n*.—**plausibly** *adv*.

Plautus *n* **Titus Maccius** (*c*.254–*c*.184 BC) Roman dramatist whose comedies were adaptations of lost Greek originals, notably by Menander. He wrote about 130 plays, of which 20 are extant.

play *vi* to amuse oneself (with toys, games, etc); to act carelessly or trifle (with somebody's feelings); to gamble; to act on the stage or perform on a musical instrument; (*light*) to flicker, shimmer; (*water*) to discharge or direct on. * *vt* to participate in a sport; to be somebody's opponent in a game; to perform a dramatic production; (*instrument*) to produce music on; (*hose*) to direct; (*fish*) to give line to; to bet on. * *n* fun, amusement; the playing of, or manner of playing, a game; the duration of a game; a literary work for performance by actors; gambling; scope, freedom to move.—**playable** *adj*.

playact *vi* to behave affectedly or overdramatically; to make believe, pretend; to act in a play.—**playacting** *n*.—**playactor** *n*.

playback *n* the act of reproducing recorded sound or pictures, esp soon after they are made; a mechanism in an audio or video recorder for doing this.—*also vt*.

playbill *n* a poster advertising a theatrical performance.

playboy *n* a person who lives for pleasure.

player *n* a person who plays a specified game or instrument; an actor.

player piano *n* a mechanical piano.

Playfair *n* **William H** (*b*. 1790) Scottish architect whose notable works include the Royal Scottish Academy.

playfellow *see* **playmate**.

playful *adj* full of fun; humorous; sportive; fond of sport or amusement.—**playfully** *adv*.—**playfulness** *n*.

playgoer *n* a person who goes to the theater, esp one who attends frequently or regularly.—**playgoing** *adj*, *n*.

playground *n* an area outdoors for children's recreation.

playhouse *n* a theater.

playing card *n* one of a set of 52 cards used for playing games, each card having an identical pattern on one side and its own symbol on the reverse.

playing field *n* a place for playing sport.

playlet *n* a short play.

playmate *n* a friend in play.—*also* **playfellow**.

playpen *n* a portable usu collapsible enclosure in which a young child may be left to play safely.

playroom *n* a child's or family's recreation room.

playschool *n* a kindergarten for pre-school children.

plaything *n* a toy; a thing or person treated as a toy.

playtime *n* a time for recreation, esp at a school.

playwright *n* a writer of plays.

plaza *n* a public square in a town or city; an area for the parking and servicing of cars.

PLC *or* **plc** *abbr* = public limited company.

PLCW & TWU *abbr* = Power Loom Carpet Weavers' and Textile Workers' Union.

plea *n* (*law*) an answer to a charge, made by the accused person; a request; an entreaty.

plea bargaining *n* an arrangement between a prosecutor and a defendant in which the defendant is allowed to plead guilty to a lesser charge.

plead *vti* (**pleading, pleaded, plead** *or* **pled**) to beg, implore; to give as an excuse; to answer (guilty or not guilty) to a charge; to argue (a law case).—**pleadable** *adj*.—**pleader** *n*.

pleading *n* advocacy of a cause in a court of law; one of the allegations and counter allegations made alternately, usu in writing, by the parties in a legal action; the act or instance of making a plea; a sincere entreaty. * *adj* begging, imploring.—**pleadingly** *adv*.

pleasant *adj* agreeable; pleasing.—**pleasantly** *adv*.—**pleasantness** *n*.

pleasantry *n* (*pl* **pleasantries**) a polite or amusing remark.

please *vti* to satisfy; to give pleasure to; to be willing; to have the wish. * *adv* as a word to express politeness or emphasis in a request; an expression of polite affirmation.

pleased *adj* gratified.

pleasing *adj* giving pleasure; agreeable.—**pleasingly** *adv*.

pleasurable *adj* gratifying, delightful.—**pleasurably** *adv*.

pleasure *n* enjoyment, recreation; gratification of the senses; preference.

pleat *n* a double fold of cloth, etc pressed or stitched in place. * *vt* to gather into pleats.

pleb *n* a plebeian; (*sl*) a common person.

plebeian *adj* relating to the common people; base, vulgar. * *n* a commoner of ancient Rome; a vulgar, coarse person.—**plebeianism** *n*.

plebiscite *n* a direct vote of the electorate on a political issue such as annexation, independent nationhood, etc.

plectrum *n* (*pl* **plectra, plectrums**) a thin piece of metal, etc, for plucking the strings of a guitar, etc.

pledge *n* a solemn promise; security for payment of a debt; a token or sign; a toast. * *vt* to give as security; to pawn; to bind by solemn promise; to drink a toast to.

pledgee *n* someone to whom a pledge is given.

pledget *n* a small pad of lint, etc, used to apply pressure to wounds.

pleiad *n* a brilliant group (of people).

Pleiades[1] *npl* (*Greek myth*) the seven daughters of Atlas and the nymph Pleione, placed in the sky as a constellation: Electra, Maia, Taÿgete, Alcyone, Celaeno, Sterope (the invisible star), and Merope.

Pleiades[2] *npl* a cluster of seven stars visible to the naked eye in the constellation Taurus; an open cluster of many hundred stars in the constellation Taurus.

plein-air *adj* (*art*) depicting the effects of light and atmosphere outdoors.

Pleistocene *adj* (*geol*) pertaining to the earliest division of the Quaternary Period. The oldest known hominids (Australopithecus) appeared during this period, which possibly began around 3.5 million years ago.

plen. *abbr* = plenipotentiary.

plenary *adj* full, complete; (*assembly, etc*) attended by all the members.—**plenarily** *adv*.

plenipotentiary *adj* possessing full powers. * *n* (*pl* **plenipotentiaries**) an envoy with authority to act at his own discretion.

plenitude *n* abundance.

plenteous *adj* abundant.

plentiful *adj* abundant, copious.—**plentifully** *adv*.—**plentifulness** *n*.

plenty *n* an abundance; more than enough; a great number. * *adv* (*sl*) quite.

plenum *n* (*pl* **plenums, plena**) a full assembly; a space filled with matter.

pleonasm *n* (*rhetoric*) the use of unnecessary words, e.g. "he is blind and cannot see."—**pleonastic** *adj*.

plesiosaurus, plesiosaur *n* a large, extinct, long-necked swimming reptile.

plessor *see* **plexor**.

plethora *n* overabundance, glut; (*med*) an excess of red corpuscles in the blood.—**plethoric** *adj*.

pleura *n* (*pl* **pleurae**) the membrane enclosing the lungs.—**pleural** *adj*.

pleural cavity *n* the small space between the pleurae when they slide over each other as a person breathes in and out.

pleurectomy *n* removal, by surgery, of part of the pleura to overcome pneumothorax or to excise diseased areas.

pleurisy *n* inflammation of the membranes enclosing the lungs.—**pleuritic** *adj*.

pleuropneumonia *n* an inflammation of both the pleura and the lung.

Plexiglas *n* (*trademark*) a transparent thermoplastic.

plexor *n* (*med*) a small hammer used in percussion and for testing reflexes.—*also* **plessor**.

plexus *n* (*pl* **plexuses, plexus**) a network, esp of nerves or blood vessels.

Pleyel *n* **Ignaz Joseph** (1757–1831) Austrian pianist, violinist, and composer who founded a piano-manufacturing company in Paris. His compositions include 29 symphonies, piano sonatas, and songs.

plf. or **plff.** *abbr* = plaintiff.

pliable *adj* easily bent or molded; easily influenced.—**pliability** *n*. —**pliably** *adv*.

pliant *adj* easily bent or influenced; supple; flexible, yielding.—**pliancy** *n*.—**pliantly** *adv*.

plicate, plicated *adj* pleated; folded in the form of a fan.

pliers *npl* a tool with hinged arms and jaws for cutting, shaping wire.

plight[1] *n* a dangerous situation; a predicament.

plight[2] *vt* to pledge, vow solemnly. * *n* a pledge; an engagement.—**plighter** *n*.

Plimsoll line *n* a system of markings on the hull of ships to ensure there is no overloading and that cargo is balanced.—*also* **load line**.

plimsolls, plimsoles *npl* (*Brit*) rubber-soled canvas shoes, sneakers.

plinth *n* (*archit*) the base of a pedestal, usually slightly larger than the dado and molded around the top.

Pliocene *adj* (*geol*) pertaining to the latest division of the Tertiary Period.

PLLI *abbr* = (National Institute on) Postsecondary Education, Libraries, and Lifelong Learning.

PLO *abbr* = Palestine Liberation Organization.

plod *vi* (**plodding, plodded**) to walk heavily and slowly, to trudge; to work or study slowly and laboriously.—**plodder** *n*.—**ploddingly** *adv*.

Ploiesti *n* a city in Romania.

plop *vti* (**plopping, plopped**) to fall into water without a splash. * *n* the sound of this. * *adv* with a plop.

plot *n* a small piece of land; a secret plan or conspiracy; the story in a play or novel, etc. * *vt* (**plotting, plotted**) to conspire; (*route*) to mark on a map; (*points*) to mark (on a graph) with coordinates; (*comput*) to create an image using lines rather than a series of dots.—**plotter** *n*.

Plotinus (*c*.205–*c*.270) Egyptian-born Roman philosopher who was the main figure behind Neoplatonism.

plotter *n* (*comput*) a hardware device that creates drawings by moving a series of pens across a page.

Plough *n* **the** (*astron*) the big Dipper, a group of the brightest stars in the constellation Ursa Major.

Plovdiv *n* a city in Bulgaria.

plover *n* a wading bird with a short tail and a straight bill.

plow, plough *n* a farm implement for turning up soil; any implement like this, as a snowplough. * *vt* to cut and turn up with a plough; to make a furrow (in), to wrinkle; to force a way through; to work at laboriously; (*with* **into**) to run into; (*with* **back**) to reinvest; (*sl*) to fail an examination.—**plowable** *adj*.—**plower** *n*.

plowed-back profit *see* **retained profit**.

plowman *n* (*pl* **plowmen**) one who ploughs; a farmworker.

plowshare *n* the part of a plow which cuts the soil.

plowshare vault *n* (*archit*) a vault in which the diagonal ribs arise at a lower level than the wall ribs, producing a pattern like a plowshare.—*also* **stilted vault**.

ploy *n* a tactic or maneuvre to outwit an opponent; an occupation or job; an escapade.

PLP *abbr* = Parliamentary Labour Party.

PLR *abbr* = public lending right.

pls. *abbr* = plates.

Pl. Sgt *abbr* = platoon sergeant.

PLSS *abbr* = portable life-support system.

plts. *abbr* = plates.

plu. *abbr* = plural.

pluck *vt* to pull off or at; to snatch; to strip off feathers; (*fruit, flowers, etc*) to pick; (*person*) to remove from one situation in life and transfer to another. * *vi* to make a sharp pull or twitch. * *n* a pull or tug; heart, courage; dogged resolution.—**plucker** *n*.

plucky *adj* (**pluckier, pluckiest**) brave, spirited.—**pluckily** *adv*.—**pluckiness** *n*.

plug *n* a stopper used for filling a hole; a device for connecting an appliance to an electricity supply; a cake of tobacco; a kind of fishing lure; (*inf*) a free advertisement usu incorporated in other matter; (*seismology*) the cylinder-like remnant of a volcano that is formed by the cooling and solidification of magma within the main feeder of the volcano (—*also* **neck**). * *vti* (**plugging, plugged**) to stop up with a plug; (*sl*) to shoot or punch; (*inf*) to seek to advertise by frequent repetition; (*with* **at**) (*inf*) to work doggedly.

plug and play *n* (*comput*) a technology that allows a peripheral device to be connected to a computer and then used without further setting of dip switches.

plum *n* an oval smooth-skinned sweet stone-fruit; a tree bearing it; a reddish-purple color; a choice thing.

plum pudding *n* a rich boiled or steamed pudding with suet, dried fruit, spices, etc.

plumage *n* a bird's feathers.

plumb *n* a lead weight attached to a line, used to determine how deep water is or whether a wall is vertical; any of various weights. * *adj* perfectly vertical. * *adv* vertically; in a direct manner; (*inf*) entirely. * *vt* to test by a plumb line; to examine minutely and critically; to weight with lead; to seal with lead; to supply with or install as plumbing. * *vi* to work as a plumber.

plumbago *n* (*pl* **plumbagos**) graphite; one of a genus of flowering plants.

plumber *n* a person who installs and repairs water or gas pipes.

plumbing *n* the system of pipes used in water or gas supply, or drainage; the plumber's craft.

plumbism *n* lead poisoning.

plume *n* a large or ornamental bird's feather; a feathery ornament or thing; something resembling a feather in structure or density. * *vt* (*feathers*) to preen; to adorn with feathers; to indulge (oneself) with an obvious display of self-satisfaction.

Plumet *n* **Charles** (1861–1928) French architect who was chief architect of the 1925 Paris Exposition.

plummet *n* a plumb. * *vi* (**plummeting, plumeted**) to fall in a perpendicular manner; to drop sharply and abruptly.

plummy *adj* (**plummier, plummiest**) like, full of, plums; (*inf*) rich, desirable; (*inf*) (*voice*) deep, drawling, rich-sounding.

plump¹ *adj* rounded, chubby. * *vti* to make or become plump; to swell.—**plumply** *adv*.—**plumpness** *n*.

plump² *vti* to fall, drop or sink, or come into contact suddenly and heavily; (*someone, something*) to favor or give support. * *n* a sudden drop or plunge or the sound of this. * *adv* straight down, straight ahead; abruptly; bluntly.

plumule *n* (*zool*) a down feather; (*bot*) the embryonic stem of a plant.

plumy *adj* (**plumier, plumiest**) feathery; feathered.

plunder *vt* to steal goods by force, to loot. * *n* plundering; booty.—**plunderer** *n*.

plunge *vti* to immerse, dive suddenly; to penetrate quickly; to hurl oneself or rush; (*horse*) to start violently forward.

plunger *n* a solid cylinder that operates with a plunging motion, as a piston; a larger rubber suction cup used to free clogged drains.

plunk *vt* (*mus*) to pluck. * *vti* to throw or fall heavily. *n* the sound produced by something being plucked, or falling in this way.

plup. or **plupf.** *abbr* = pluperfect.

pluperfect *adj, n* (*gram*) (a tense) denoting an action completed before a past point of time.

plur. *abbr* = plural; plurality.

plural *adj* more than one; consisting of or containing more than one kind or class. * *n* (*gram*) the form referring to more than one person or thing.—**plurally** *adv*.

pluralism *n* the simultaneous holding of more than one office or benefice; a theory that reality is composed of a plurality of entities; a theory that there are at least two levels of ultimate reality; the coexistence in society of people of distinct ethnic, cultural, or religious groups, each preserving their own traditions; a doctrine or policy advocating this condition.—**pluralist** *n*.—**pluralistic** *adj*.—**pluralistically** *adv*.

plurality *n* (*pl* **pluralities**) being plural; a majority; a large number; another term for pluralism.

plus *prep* added to; in addition to. * *adj* indicating addition; positive. * *n* the sign (+) indicating a value greater than zero; an advantage or benefit; an extra.

plush *n* a velvet-like fabric with a nap. * *adj* made of plush; (*inf*) luxurious.

Pluto¹ *n* (*Greek myth*) the god of the underworld who ruled the spirits of the dead.

Pluto² *n* (*astron*) the ninth and smallest planet in the solar system, and the one that lies farthest away from the sun, discovered in 1930.

plutocracy *n* (*pl* **plutocracies**) government or rule by the wealthy; a wealthy class.—**plutocratic** *adj*.—**plutocratically** *adv*.

plutocrat *n* a person who has power through wealth; a rich person.

Plutonian *adj* pertaining to Pluto or the underworld; infernal.

plutonic *adj* (*geol*) formed from magma cooling beneath the earth's surface.

plutonium *n* a highly toxic transuranic element used as fuel in nuclear power stations and in nuclear weapons.

Plutus *n* (*Greek myth*) a god of wealth, depicted as a boy carrying a cornucopia.

pluvial *adj* caused by the action of rain; rainy.

pluviometer *n* an instrument used to measure rainfall.—*also* **rain gauge**.

PLWA *abbr* (*Canada*) = People Living With AIDS.

ply¹ *vti* (**plying, plied**) to work at diligently and energetically; to wield; to subject to persistently; (*goods*) to sell; to go to and fro, run regularly; to keep busy.

ply² *n* (*pl* **plies**) a layer or thickness, as of cloth, plywood, etc; any of the twisted strands in a yarn, etc. * *vt* (**plying, plied**) to twist together.

Plymouth *n* capital city of Montserrat.

plywood *n* a building material consisting of several thin layers of wood glued together.

Plzen *n* a city in the Czech Republic.

Pm *symbol* (*chem*) promethium (element).

p.m. *abbr* (*Latin*) = post meridiem, "after noon."

p.m. *abbr* = post mortem.

pm. *abbr* = pamphlet; (*dentistry*) premolar.

Pm. *abbr* = premium.

PM *abbr* = Pacific Mail; Past Master; Past Midshipman; Paymaster; Pontifex Maximus; Police Magistrate; Postmaster; post meridiem; post mortem; Prime Minister.

PMA *abbr* = Pacific Maritime Association; paramethoxyamphetamine (an hallucinogenic drug); Personal Managers Association; Property Managers Association.

PMG *abbr* = Paymaster General; Postmaster General.

pmh *abbr* = per man-hour.

PMH *abbr* = previous medical history.

pmk *abbr* = postmark.

P. mks. *abbr* = Polish marks.

PMO *abbr* = Principal Medical Officer.

p.m.r. *abbr* = (of a curve) point of minimum radius.

PMS *abbr* = premenstrual syndrome.

PMT *abbr* = photomechanical transfer; premenstrual tension.

pn, p.n. or **P/N** *abbr* = promissory note.

PN *abbr* = postnatal.

PNA *abbr* = Psychiatric Nurses' Association.

PND *abbr* = postnatal depression.

PNdb *abbr* = perceived noise decibel.

pneum. *abbr* = pneumatic; pneumatics.

pneumatic *adj* concerning wind, air, or gases; operated by or filled with compressed air.—**pneumatically** *adv*.

pneumatics *n sing* the science dealing with the mechanical properties of air.

pneumatology *n* the theological study of the Holy Spirit.

pneumatometer *n* an instrument for measuring the amount of air exhaled in one breath.

pneumatophore *n* the breathing organ of a marsh plant.

pneumoconiosis *n* a general term for a chronic form of lung disease caused by inhaling dust while working.

pneumonectomy *n* the surgical removal of a lung.

pneumonia *n* acute inflammation of the lungs.—**pneumonic** *adj*.

pneumonitis *n* inflammation of the lungs by chemical or physical agents.

pneumothorax *n* air in the pleural cavity, which enters via a wound in the chest wall or lung.

png *abbr* (*Latin*) = persona non grata, "unacceptable person."

pnr *abbr* = prior notice required.

PNS *abbr* = parasympathetic nervous system.

pnxt. *abbr* = pinxit.

Po *symbol* (*chem*) polonium (element).

po *abbr* (*Latin*) = per os, "through the mouth."

po. *abbr* = point; pole.

p.o. *abbr* = petty officer; postal order; post office; public office; public officer.

PO *abbr* = Personnel Officer; Petty Officer; Pilot Officer; post office; postal order; (*Latin*) Professor Ordinarius, "Ordinary Professor."

POA *abbr* = Prison Officers' Association.

poach¹ *vt* to cook (an egg without its shell, fish, etc) in or over boiling water.

poach² *vti* to catch game or fish illegally; to trespass for this purpose; to encroach on, usurp another's rights, etc; to steal another's idea, employee, etc.—**poaching** *n*.

poacher¹ *n* a pan with shallow cups for poaching eggs; a dish for poaching fish, etc.

poacher² *n* a person who poaches another's property.

p.o.b. *abbr* = post-office box.

p.o.c. *abbr* = port of call.

pochard *n* (*pl* **pochards, pochard**) a red-headed European duck.

pock *n* an eruptive pustule on the skin, esp as a result of smallpox.

pocket money *n* money for occasional expenses; a child's allowance.

pocket *n* a small bag or pouch, esp in a garment, for carrying small articles; an isolated or enclosed area; a deposit (as of gold, water, or gas). * *adj* small enough to put in a pocket. * *vt* to put in one's pocket, to steal; (*ball*) to put in a pocket; to envelop; to enclose; (*money*) to take dishonestly; to suppress.

pocketbook *n* a small folder or case for letters, money, credit cards, etc; a woman's wallet, a purse; monetary resources; a small esp softback book.

pocketful *n* (*pl* **pocketfuls**) as much as a pocket holds.

pocketknife *n* (*pl* **pocketknives**) a small knife with one or more blades that fold into the handle.

pockmark *n* a small skin depression or scar caused by acne, chicken pox, smallpox, etc; something resembling a pockmark. * *vt* to scar with pockmarks.

poco *adv* (*mus*) (*Italian*) a little.

pococurante *n, adj* (someone who is) indifferent.

pod¹ *n* a dry fruit or seed vessel, as of peas, beans, etc; a protective container or housing; a detachable compartment on a spacecraft. * *vi* (**podding, podded**) to remove the pod from.

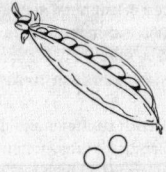

pod² *n* a group of animals, as whales or seals; a flock of birds.

pod³ *n* the socket for a drill bit; a groove or channel in boring tools.

p.o.d. *abbr* = pay on delivery.

POD *abbr* = pay on delivery; point of debarkation.

podagra *n* gout, esp in the feet.—**podagral, podagric, podagrous** *adj*.

podgy *adj* (**podgier, podgiest**) short and fat, squat.—*also* **pudgy.**—**podginess** *n*.

podium *n* (*pl* **podiums, podia**) a platform used by lecturers, etc; a low wall around the arena of an amphitheater; a continuous base supporting a series of columns.

podophyllin *n* a purgative resin obtained from the root of the May apple and mandrake.

podsol or **podzol** *n* a soil with minerals leached from its surface layers into lower layers.

POE *abbr* = port of embarkation; port of entry.

Poe *n* Edgar Allan (1809–49) American short-story writer, poet, and critic who wrote macabre, highly Gothic horror stories, including *Tales of the Grotesque and Arabesque*. His detective stories, e.g. "The Murders in the Rue Morgue," are influential early examples of the form.

poem *n* an arrangement of words, esp in meter, often rhymed, in a style more imaginative than ordinary speech; a poetic thing.

poesy *n* (*pl* **poesies**) the art of writing poetry.

poet *n* the writer of a poem; a person with imaginative power and a sense of beauty.—**poetess** *nf*.

poet. *abbr* = poetic; poetical; poetry.

poetaster *n* an inferior poet.

poetic justice *n* an outcome in which vice is punished and virtue rewarded in an appropriate manner.

poetic license *n* latitude allowed to a poet in grammar, facts, etc.

poetic, poetical *adj* of poets or poetry; written in verse; imaginative, romantic, like poetry.—**poetically** *adv*.

poetics *n sing* the theory, or study, of poetry.

poetize *vt* to make poetic; to compose poetry about. * *vi* to compose poetry.

poet laureate *n* (*pl* **poets laureate**) a poet officially appointed by the British sovereign to write poems celebrating national events, etc.

poetry *n* the art of writing poems; poems collectively; poetic quality or spirit.

POEU *abbr* = Post Office Engineering Union.

P of H *abbr* = patrons of husbandry.

pogo stick *n* a stilt with a powerful spring used to hop along the ground.

pogrom *n* an organized extermination of a minority group.

poi *n* (*mus*) (*Italian*) "then," as in *scherzo da capo, poi la coda*, "repeat the scherzo, then play the coda."

poignant *adj* piercing; incisive; deeply moving.—**poignancy** *n.*—**poignantly** *adv.*

Poillerat *n* Gilbert (1902–88) French metal engraver.

Poilly *n* 1. **François de** (1622–93) French engraver who worked for Louis XIV. 2. **Nicolas de** (1626–96) French designer of six plates of artisan designs.

poinsettia *n* a South American plant, widely cultivated as a house plant for its red bracts, which resemble petals.

point *n* a dot or tiny mark used in writing or printing (e.g. a decimal point, a full stop); a location; a place in a cycle, course, or scale; a unit in scoring or judging; the sharp end of a knife or pin; a moment of time; one of 32 divisions of the compass; a fundamental reason or aim; the tip; a physical characteristic; a railroad switch; a unit of size in printing equal to one seventy-second of an inch; a unit used in quoting the prices of stocks, bonds, and commodities; a headland or cape. * *vti* to give point to; to sharpen; to aim (at); to extend the finger (at or to); to indicate something; to call attention (to).

point and click *vi* (*comput*) to use a device that points, such as a mouse or trackball, to select a command.

point-blank *adj* aimed straight at a mark; direct, blunt.—*also adv.*

point d'orgue *n* (*mus*) (*French*) "organ point," a harmonic pedal (a note sustained under changing harmonies); the sign for a pause; a cadenza in a concerto.

Pointe-à-Pitre *n* a city in Guadelope.

pointed *adj* having a point; pertinent; aimed at a particular person or group; conspicuous.—**pointedly** *adv.*—**pointedness** *n.*

Pointe-Noire *n* a city in the Congo.

pointer *n* a rod or needle for pointing; an indicator; a breed of hunting dog.

Pointers *npl* **the** two stars in the Big Dipper which, when joined by a line, point towards the Pole star.

pointillism *n* in painting, the practice of applying small strokes or dots of color to a surface so that from a distance they blend together; (*mus*) a style of music in which notes seem to be isolated as "dots" rather than as sequential parts of a melody.—**pointillist** *n, adj.*

pointing *n* mortar applied between the joints of bricks, masonry or stone.

pointless *adj* without a point; irrelevant, aimless.—**pointlessly** *adv.*—**pointlessness** *n.*

point of sale *n* the place where a consumer makes a purchase.

point of sale display *n* promotional material for a product displayed in the retail outlet where the product is to be sold.

point of view *n* (*pl* **points of view**) a position from which something is observed; an attitude, standpoint.

Poiret *n* Paul (1879–1944) French couturier and design entrepreneur whose costumes for the actress Sarah Bernhardt brought him fame.

poise[1] *vt* to balance; to hold supported without motion; (*the head*) to hold in a particular way; to put into readiness. * *vi* to become drawn up into readiness; to hover. * *n* a balanced state; self-possessed assurance of manner; gracious tact; bearing, carriage.

poise[2] *n* a centimeter-gram-second unit of viscosity equivalent to one dyne-second per square meter.

poison *n* a substance that through its chemical action usu destroys or injures an organism; any corrupt influence; an object of aversion or abhorrence. * *vt* to administer poison in order to kill or injure; to put poison into; to influence wrongfully—**poisoner** *n.*

poison gas *n* a poisonous gas, or a liquid or solid giving off poisonous vapors, used in warfare.

poison ivy *n* a climbing plant with ivory-colored berries and an acutely irritating oil that causes an intensely itchy skin rash; the rash caused by poison ivy.

poison oak *n* a type of poison ivy.

poisonous *adj* being or containing poison; toxic; having a harmful influence; (*inf*) unpleasant.—**poisonously** *adv.*—**poisonousness** *n.*

poison-pen letter *n* an abusive, spiteful letter, usu written anonymously.

poke *vt* to thrust (at), jab or prod; (*bole, etc*) to make by poking; (*sl*) to hit. * *vi* to jab (at); to pry or search (about or around). * *n* a jab; a prod or nudge; a thrust.

poker[1] *n* a metal rod for poking or stirring fire.

poker[2] *n* a card game in which a player bets that the value of his hand is higher than that of the hands held by others.

poker face *n* an expressionless face, concealing a person's thoughts or feelings.—**poker-faced** *adj.*

poky, pokey *adj* (**pokier, pokiest**) small and uncomfortable.—**pokily** *adv.*—**pokiness** *n.*

pol *abbr* = problem-oriented language.

pol. *abbr* = political; politics.

Pol. *abbr* = Poland; Polish.

POL *abbr* = Patent Office Library; petrol, oil, and lubricants.

polacca *see* **polonaise**.

Poland *n* a republic situated on the North European Plain with a Baltic Sea coastline.

polar *adj* of or near the North or South Pole; of a pole; having positive and negative electricity; directly opposite.

polar air mass *n* a mass of air that forms in latitudes 40°–60° north or south of the Equator.

polar angle *n* the angle between the positive (polar) axis and the radius vector in polar coordinates.

polar axis *n* (*math*) the diameter of a sphere which passes through both poles.

polar bear *n* a large creamy-white bear that inhabits arctic regions.

polar caps *n* a circular area around the pole region of a planet.

polar coordinates *npl* either of a pair of coordinates that determine the position of points in space by measuring their distance along a fixed line from the origin or other given point and their angle, which lies between the fixed line and a single axis.

polar high *n* an area of semi-permanent high pressure, anticyclone, that forms over the North and South Poles.

polarimeter *n* an instrument for measuring the polarization of light.

Polaris *n* (*astron*) the brightest star in the Ursa Minor constellation, also known as the Pole Star.

polariscope *n* an instrument used to detect polarized light.

polarity *n* (*pl* **polarities**) the condition of being polar; the magnet's property of pointing north; attraction towards a particular object or in a specific direction; (*elect*) the state, positive or negative, of a body; diametrical opposition; an instance of such opposition.

polarization *n* the production or acquirement of polarity; (*optics*) the process of causing light waves to vibrate in a uniform circular, elliptical or linear pattern; (*elect*) the separation of positive and negative charges; the grouping about opposing factions.

polarize *vt* (*light waves*) to cause to vibrate in a definite pattern; to give physical polarity to; to break up into opposing factions; to concentrate.—**polarizable** *adj.*—**polarizer** *n.*

Polaroid *n* (*trademark*) a transparent material used esp in sunglasses and lamps to prevent glare; a camera that produces a print in seconds.

polder *n* (*Netherlands*) a piece of land reclaimed from the sea.

pole[1] *n* a long slender piece of wood, metal, etc; a flagstaff. * *vt* to propel, support with a pole.

pole[2] *n* either end of an axis, esp of the earth; either of two opposed forces, parts, etc, as the ends of a magnet, terminals of a battery, etc; either of two opposed principles.

poleax, poleaxe *n* a long-handled battle ax; a type of ax used to slaughter cattle. * *vt* to hit or knock down with, or as if with, such an ax.

pole bean *n* a climbing plant that produces long green edible pods, a runner bean.

polecat *n* (*pl* **polecats, polecat**) a small, dark-brown animal, found in Europe, North Africa, and Asia, related to the weasel and known for its unpleasant smell.

Pol. Econ. *or* **Polit. Econ.** *abbr* = political economy.

polemic *n* a controversy or argument over doctrine; strong criticism; a controversialist. * *adj* involving dispute; controversial (—*also* **polemical**).—**polemically** *adv.*—**polemicist** *n.*

polemics *n sing* the art of controversial debate. * *adj* disputatious, controversial.

polenta *n* an Italian porridge of maize, barley, or chestnut meal.

pole vault *n* a field event in which competitors jump over a high bar using a long flexible pole.—**pole-vault** *vi.*—**pole-vaulter** *n.*

Polglase *n* Van Nest (*b.* 1898) American movie set designer whose ideas influenced interior design of the 1920s and 1930s.

police *n* the government department for keeping order, detecting crime, law enforcement, etc; (*pl*) the members of such a department; any similar organization. * *vt* to control, protect, etc with police or a similar force.

police dog *n* a dog trained for police work.

policeman *n* (*pl* **policemen**) a member of a police force.—**policewoman** *nf* (*pl* **policewomen**).

police officer *n* a policeman or policewoman.

police state *n* a totalitarian state controlled by a repressive political police.

police station *n* a local police headquarters.

policy[1] *n* (*pl* **policies**) a written insurance contract.

policy[2] *n* (*pl* **policies**) political wisdom, statecraft; a course of action selected from among alternatives; a high-level overall plan embracing the general principles and aims of an organization, esp a government.

policyholder *n* a person who has an insurance policy.

policymaking *n* the formulation of policy, esp at the highest levels of government.—**policymaker** *n.*

polio *n* poliomyelitis.

poliomyelitis *n* an acute infectious virus disease marked by inflammation of nerve cells in the spinal cord, causing paralysis.—*also* **infantile paralysis**.

POLIS *abbr* = Parliamentary On-Line Information Service.

police officer *n* a policeman or policewoman.

police state *n* a totalitarian state controlled by a repressive political police.

police station *n* a local police headquarters.

polish *vti* to make or become smooth and shiny by rubbing (with a cloth and polish); to give elegance or culture to; (*with* **off**) (*inf*) to finish completely. * *n* smoothness; elegance of manner; a finish or gloss; a substance, such as wax, used to polish.—**polisher** *n.*

Polish *adj* of or pertaining to Poland, its inhabitants, language, or culture. * *n* the Slavic language of Poland.

polished *adj* accomplished; smoothly or professionally done or performed; (*rice*) having had the husk removed.

polit. *abbr* = political; politics.

polite *adj* courteous; well-bred; refined.—**politely** *adv*.—**politeness** *n*.

politesse *n* (excessively) formal politeness.

politic *adj* expedient; shrewdly tactful; prudent.

political *adj* relating to politics or government; characteristic of political parties or politicians.—**politically** *adv*.

political asylum *n* protection for a political refugee from another country.

political correctness *n* a movement aimed at removing discrimination against women, ethnic minorities, gays and lesbians, etc, by combating sexist and racist language or policies in education, the arts, media, and government.—**politically correct** *adj*.

political economy *n* the former name for the science of economics.

political prisoner *n* a person imprisoned for their political beliefs or actions.

political science *n* the study of government systems and institutions.—**political scientist** *n*.

politician *n* a person engaged in politics, often used with implications of seeking personal or partisan gain, scheming, etc.

politico *n* (*sl*) a politician.

politics *n* (*sing or pl*) the science and art of government; political activities, beliefs, or affairs; factional scheming for power.

polity *n* (*pl* **polities**) the form or constitution of the government of a state; a constitution.

Polk *n* **James K[nox]** (1795–1849) American Democrat statesman and 11th president of the US (1845–49).

polka *n* a lively dance; the music for this. * *vi* to dance the polka.

polka dot *n* any of a pattern of small round dots forming a pattern on cloth.

poll *n* a counting, listing, etc of persons, esp of voters; the number of votes recorded; an opinion survey; (*pl*) a place where votes are cast. * *vti* to receive the votes (of); to cast a vote; to canvass or question in a poll.—**poller** *n*.

pollack *n* (*pl* **pollacks, pollack**) a type of food fish.—*also* **pollock** (*pl* **pollocks, pollock**).

Pollaiuolo *n* **Antonio del** (1431–98) Florentine artist who ran a workshop with his brother Piero (1441–96). Although they collaborated on many works, including *The Martyrdom of St Sebastian*, Antonio's superior talent is evident in his outstanding pen drawings.

Pollak *n* 1. **Leopoldo** (*b.* 1751) Austrian architect whose notable works include Villa Belgioso Reale. 2. **Mihály** (*b.* 1773) Hungarian architect whose notable works include the Theater and Assembly Rooms, Budapest.

pollan *n* an Irish freshwater fish.

pollard *n* a tree with its branches pruned to encourage growth; an animal which has cast its horns or antlers, or had them removed.

pollen *n* the yellow dust, containing male spores, that is formed in the anthers of flowers.—**pollinic** *adj*.

Pollen *n* **John Hungerford** (1820–1902) British clergyman who took to painting in the 1840s.

pollen count *n* an index of the amount of pollen in the air, useful for sufferers of hay fever and asthma.

pollex *n* (*pl* **pollices**) a thumb or similar first digit.

pollinate *vti* to fertilize by uniting pollen with seed.—**pollinator** *n*.

pollination *n* the transfer of pollen from the anthers of a flower to the stigma, esp by insects.

Pollini *n* **Gino** (1903–1993) Italian architect of the Olivetti building in Ivrea and designer of early experimental all-electric kitchens.

Pollitzer *n* **Sigmund** (1913–) British painter and decorative glass designer who worked on the Marble Arch Corner House, London.

polliwog, pollywog *n* a tadpole.

pollock *see* **pollack**.

Pollock *n* **[Paul] Jackson** (1912–56) American painter and leading exponent of action painting.

pollster *n* a person who conducts a poll or compiles data obtained from a poll.

poll tax *n* a tax of a fixed amount per person levied on adults.

pollutant *n* something that causes pollution, esp a chemical.

pollute *vt* to contaminate with harmful substances; to make corrupt; to profane.—**polluter** *n*.

pollution *n* the act of polluting; the state of being polluted; contamination by chemicals, noise, etc.

pollution dome *n* the mass of warm, polluted air that accumulates over a city in calm weather when there is a layer of colder air preventing it from rising (*see* **heat island**).

pollution plume *n* the air of a pollution dome when blown away by the wind.

Pollux[1] *see* **Castor and Pollux**.

Pollux[2] or **Beta Geminorum** *n* the brightest star, an orange giant, in the constellation Gemini.

polo *n* a game played on horseback by two teams, using a wooden ball and long-handled mallets.

polo shirt *n* a sports shirt made of a knitted fabric.

polonaise *n* a slow, stately dance in three-four time; the music for such a dance; an outfit with a one-piece bodice and a skirt looped up at the sides.

polonium *n* a radioactive element.

Pol Pot *n* **[Saloth Sar]** (1929–97) Cambodian communist politician whose Maoist dictatorship cost millions of lives. His Khmer Rouge regime was overthrown by the Russian-backed Vietnamese invasion of 1979.

poltergeist *n* a spirit believed to move heavy objects about and to make noises.

poltroon *n* (*arch*) a coward.

poly- *prefix* many.

polyandry *n* the practice of a woman having more than one husband at the same time.—**polyandrous** *adj*.

polyanthus *n* (*pl* **polyanthuses**) a hybrid garden primrose; a narcissus with small yellow or white flowers in clusters.

polyatomic *adj* with more than two atoms in the molecule.

polybasic *adj* (*chem*) having more than two bases or atoms of a base.

Polybus *n* (*Greek myth*) a king of Corinth, who was the foster-father of Oedipus.

Polycarp *n* **Saint** (*d. c.*155) bishop who was an immediate disciple of the Apostles and was established by St John as bishop of Smyrna. He is noted for his letter to the church at Philippi. His feast day is February 23.

polychaete, poltchete *n* a type of marine worm. * *adj* pertaining to this type of worm (—*also* **polychaetous**).

polychromatic, polychromic, polychromous *adj* having many colors; exhibiting a play of colors; (*physics*) (*light, etc*) having a mixture of wavelengths.—**polychromatism** *n*.

polychrome *adj* made with, or decorated in, many colors. * *n* a work of art in several colors; a painted statue.

polyclinic *n* a general hospital.

polydactyl *n, adj* (an animal or person) with more than the normal number of fingers or toes.

polydactyly *n* the condition in which there are extra fingers or toes.

Polydectes *n* (*Greek myth*) a king of Seriphos, who was turned to stone by Perseus.

polydipsia *n* an intense abnormal thirst.

polyester *n* any of a number of synthetic polymeric resins used for adhesives, plastics, and textiles.

polyethylene *n* a light, plastic, multipurpose synthetic material resistant to moisture and chemicals.—*also* **polythene**.

polygamist *n* a person who advocates or practices polygamy.

polygamy *n* the practice of being married to more than one person at a time; (*bot*) the condition of having staminate, pistillate, and hermaphrodite flowers on one plant; (*zool*) the practice of having more than one mate.—**polygamous** *adj*.—**polygamously** *adv*.

polygenesis *n* the derivation of a species or race from many origins.—**polygenetic** *adj*.

polyglot *adj* having command of many languages; composed of numerous languages; containing matter in several languages; composed of elements from different languages. * *n* a person who speaks several languages.

polygon *n* a closed plane figure bound by three or more straight lines.—**polygonal** *adj*.

polygonum *n* one of a family of flowering plants including knotgrass.

polygraph *n* an instrument for detecting and measuring involuntary changes in blood pressure, breathing, etc, often used as a lie detector.—**polygraphic** *adj*.

polygyny *n* the practice of a man having more than one wife at the same time.—**polygynous** *adj*.

polyhedron *n* (*pl* **polyhedrons, polyhedra**) a solid with many (usu more than six) plane faces.—**polyhedral** *adj*.

polymath *n* someone learned in many subjects.

polymer *n* (*chem*) a compound that has large molecules composed of many simpler molecules.—**polymeric** *adj*.—**polymerism** *n*.

polymerize *vti* to (cause to) form a polymer.

polymorph *n* a polymorphous organism.

polymorphous, polymorphic *adj* having, or assuming, many different forms.

polyneuritis *see* **neuritis**.

Polynices, Polyneices *n* (*Greek myth*) brother of Eteocles, with whom he was meant to rule Thebes in alternate years. Eteocles refused to relinquish the throne, and in the war of the Seven against Thebes, Polynices and Eteocles killed each other.

polynomial *n* (*math*) an expression consisting of a sum of terms each of which is a product of a constant and one or more variables raised to a positive or zero integral power; (*biol*) a species name of more than two terms. * *adj* composed of or expressed as one or more polynomials.

polyp *n* a small water animal with tentacles at the top of a tube-like body; a growth on mucous membrane.—**polypoid** *adj*.

polypeptide *n* (*biochemistry*) a single linear molecule that is formed from many amino acids joined by peptide bonds.

polyphagous *adj* voracious; (*zool*) feeding on various kinds of food.

Polyphemus *n* (*Greek myth*) the most famous of the Cyclops, a cannibal giant with one eye in his forehead, who lived in a cave of Mount Etna.

polyphone *n* (*linguistics*) a polyphonic letter or symbol

polyphonic *adj* many-voiced; (*mus*) contrapuntal; (*phonetics*) representing more than one sound.

polyphony *n* (*pl* **polyphonies**) being polyphonic; using polyphones; (*mus*) counterpoint.

polypod *n, adj* (an animal) with many legs.

polypod bowl *n* a pottery bowl supported on four small feet that was characteristic of some late Neolithic cultures in central Europe, particularly the Beaker People.

polypody *n* (*pl* **polypodies**) a type of fern.

polyptych *n* a painting, usu an altarpiece, consisting of two or more paintings within a decorative frame. *See also* **diptych, triptych**.

polypus *n* (*pl* **polypi**) (*med*) a tumor with branching roots, found in the nose or womb.

polystyrene *n* a rigid plastic material used for packing, insulating, etc.

polysyllable *n* a word of many syllables.—**polysyllabic** *adj*.—**polysyllabically** *adv*.

polytechnic *n* an institution that provides instruction in many applied sciences and technical subjects.

polytheism *n* belief in many gods, or more than one god.—**polytheist** *n*.—**polytheistic** *adj*.

polythene *see* **polyethylene**.

polytonality *n* (*mus*) the use of two or more keys at the same time.

polyunsaturated *adj* denoting any of certain plant and animal fats and oils with a low cholesterol content.

polyurethane *n* any of various polymers that are used esp in flexible and rigid foams, resins, etc.

polyuria *n* the passing of a larger than normal quantity of urine, which is also usually pale in color.

pom. *or* **pomol.** *abbr* = pomological.

POM *abbr* = prescription-only medicine.

pomace *n* crushed apples for making cider; the crushed apples left after making cider.

pomaceous *adj* pertaining to pomes.

pomade *n* a scented ointment for the hair.

pomander *n* an aromatic ball or powder formerly carried for its pleasant smell or as protection against infection; a container for this.

pome *n* the stoneless fruit of the apple and related plants.

pomegranate *n* an edible fruit with many seeds; the widely cultivated tropical tree bearing it.

Pomeranian *n* a breed of small dog.

pomiculture *n* fruit growing.

pommel *n* the rounded, upward-projecting front part of a saddle; a knob on the hilt of a sword. * *vt* (**pommeling, pommeled** *or* **pommelling, pommelled**) to pummel.

pommy, pommie *n* (*pl* **pommies**) (*Austral sl*) a British person.

pomology *n* the study of fruit growing.—**pomological** *adj*.—**pomologist** *n*.

Pomona *n* (*Roman myth*) the goddess of fruit trees.

pomp *n* stately ceremony; ostentation.

pompadour *n* an 18th century hairstyle.

Pomp and Circumstance *n* a set of five military marches for orchestra by Elgar. A C Benson's words, "Land of Hope and Glory," were later set to the finale of the first march for the *Coronation Ode*, sung at Edward VII's coronation in 1902.

pompano *n* (*pl* **pompano, pompanos**) an edible American sea fish.

Pompe *n* **Antoine** (1873–1980) Belgian architect and designer who designed silver flatware and hollow-ware.

Pompeii *n* ancient city in Italy southwest of Naples buried by the eruption of Mount Vesuvius 79 AD.

Pompey *n* (106–48 BC) Roman general and statesman.

Pompidou *n* **Georges [Jean Raymond]** (1911–74) French statesman, prime minister (1962–68), and president (1969–74).

pom-pom *n* a quick-firing automatic anti-aircraft gun.

pompon, pompom, *n* an ornamental ball or tuft of fabric strands used on clothing as an ornament; a small tufted flower on some varieties of chrysanthemum and dahlia.

pomposity *n* (*pl* **pomposities**) the state of being pompous; self-importance; a pompous utterance or act.

pompous *adj* stately; self-important.—**pompously** *adv*.—**pompousness** *n*.

poncho *n* (*pl* **ponchos**) a blanket-like cloak with a hole in the center for the head.

pond *n* a body of standing water smaller than a lake.

Pond *n* **Edward** (1929–) British designer of textiles and wallpapers for clients in Britain and abroad.

ponder *vti* to think deeply; to consider carefully.

ponderable *adj* capable of being evaluated; capable of being weighed.—**ponderability** *n*.

ponderous *adj* heavy; awkward; dull; lifeless.—**ponderously** *adv*.—**ponderousness** *n*.

pone *n* corn pone; maize bread.

pong *n* (*Brit sl*) an unpleasant smell. * *vi* (*Brit sl*) to stink.

pongee *n* a thin, unbleached, Chinese silk.

pons *n* (*pl* **pontes**) (*med*) tissue that joins parts of an organ, e.g. the pons Varolii, a part of the brain stem that links various parts of the brain stem, including the medulla oblongata, and thalamus.

Ponti *n* **Gio** (1891–1979) Italian architect who designed enamels, mosaics, printed fabrics, ceramics, and automobile bodies from the 1930s.

ponticello *n* (*mus*) (*Italian*) "bridge" (of a stringed instrument).

pontifex *n* (*pl* **pontifices**) (*ancient Rome*) a pontiff or high priest.

pontiff *n* the Pope; a bishop; a pontifex.

pontifical *adj* of a pontiff; pompous. * *npl* a bishop's robes.—**pontifically** *adv*.

pontificate *vi* to speak sententiously, pompously, or dogmatically; to officiate at a pontifical mass.—**pontificator** *n*.

pontoon[1] *n* a boat or cylindrical float forming a support for a bridge.

pontoon[2] *n* a card game.

Pontormo *n* (1494–1557) Italian painter whose works are characterized by vivid colors and a graceful dynamism conveying a strong spiritual feeling and sense of grandeur. A notable work is *The Deposition* (c.1526–28).

Pontus[1] *n* Roman province in the north of Asia Minor on the shores of the Black Sea.

Pontus[2] *n* (*Greek myth*) a personification of the sea and described as a son of Ge.

pony *n* (*pl* **ponies**) a small horse, a bronco, mustang, etc; (*inf*) a racehorse.

pony express *n* a postal system that was operated across the western US (1860–61) by relays of horses and riders.

ponytail *n* a style of arranging hair to resemble a pony's tail.

poodle *n* a breed of dog of various sizes with a curly coat.

pool[1] *n* a small pond; a puddle; a small collection of liquid; a swimming pool.

pool[2] *n* a game played on a billiards table with six pockets; a combination of resources, funds, supplies, people, etc for some common purpose; the parties forming such a combination. * *vti* to contribute to a common fund, to share.

poolroom *n* a room where pool is played; a room used by bookmakers, a betting shop.

pool table *n* a billiards table for playing pool.

poop[1] *n* (*naut*) the stern of a ship; the raised deck in the stern of a ship.

poop[2] *vti* (*sl*) (to cause) to become tired.

poor *adj* having little money, needy; deserving pity, unfortunate; deficient; disappointing; inferior. * *n* those who have little.—**poorness** *n*.

poorhouse *n* (*formerly*) a public institution housing poor people.

poorly *adv* insufficiently, badly. * *adj* not in good health.

pop[1] *n* a short, explosive sound, a shot; any carbonated, nonalcoholic beverage. * *vti* (**popping, popped**) to make or cause a pop; to shoot; to go or come quickly (in, out, up); (*corn, maize*) to roast until it pops; to put suddenly; (*eyes*) to bulge.

pop[2] *adj* in a popular modern style. * *n* pop music; pop art; pop culture.

pop[3] *n* (*inf*) father; (*inf*) a name used to address an old man.

pop *abbr* = plaster of Paris.

pop. *abbr* = popular; popularly; population.

POP *abbr* = point of purchase.

POPA *abbr* = Property Owners' Protection Association.

pop art *n* a realistic art style using techniques and subjects from commercial art, comic strips, posters, etc.

popcorn *n* a kind of corn or maize, which when heated pops or puffs up.

pope *n* the bishop of Rome, head of the RC Church.—**popedom** *n*.

Pope *n* **Alexander** (1688–1744) English poet who wrote *Essay on Criticism*, a poetic manifesto of neoclassical principles, and the poem *The Rape of the Lock*. He translated Homer's *Iliad* and *Odyssey*, and compiled an edition of Shakespeare. His mastery of the rhymed couplet, his satirical powers, and gift for sustaining a metaphor place him as one of the most important English poets.

popedom *n* the office, dignity or jurisdiction of the pope.

popery *n* (*derog*) Roman Catholicism.

pop-eyed *adj* with bulging eyes; (*fig*) astonished.

popgun *n* a toy gun firing pellets with a popping noise.

Popin *abbr* = Population Information Network.

popinjay *n* a conceited person.

popish *adj* (*derog*) pertaining to Roman Catholicism.

Poplab *abbr* = (International) Program of Laboratories for Population Statistics.

poplar *n* a slender, quick-growing tree of the willow family.

poplin *n* a sturdy corded fabric.

Pöppelmann *n* **Matthaus D** (1662–1736) German architect whose notable works include the Zwinger, Dresden.

Popper *n* **Sir Karl [Raimund]** (1902–94) Austrian-born British philosopher who established the concept of "falsifiability." His books, *The Open Society and its Enemies* (1945) and *The Poverty of Historicism* (1957), examine the totalitarian implications of political thought from Plato to Marx.

poppet *n* a term of endearment.

poppet valve *n* a valve opened by being lifted from its seat.

poppy *n* (*pl* **poppies**) an annual or perennial plant with showy flowers, one of which yields opium; a strong reddish color.

poppycock *n* (*inf*) nonsense.

poppy head *n* (*archit*) a finial at the top of the bench end of a pew, usually in the form of an animal or human figure, foliage, or *fleur de lis*.

POPS *abbr* = Partners of Prisoners and Families Support Group.

populace *n* the common people; the masses; all the people in a country, region, etc.

popular *adj* of the people; well liked; pleasing to many people; easy to understand.—**popularly** *adv.*

popularity *n* the condition or quality of being popular.

popularize *vt* to make popular; to make generally accepted or understood.—**popularization** *n.*—**popularizer** *n.*

populate *vt* to inhabit; to supply with inhabitants.

population *n* all the inhabitants or the number of people in an area.

Population I and II *n* (*astron*) two divisions of stars and clusters introduced in 1944 by W Baade. Population I stars are thought to be relatively young and occur in the spiral arms of galaxies. Population II stars are relatively old and are found in a halo around the galactic center.

Population III *n* (*astron*) a theoretical third class of stars comprising supermassive stars that might have predated formation of the galaxies.

populism *n* any movement based on belief in the rights, wisdom, or virtue of the common people.

populist *n* an advocate of populism; one who claims to represent the people; (*with cap*) a member of the Populist or People's Party in the US (1891–1904) aiming at public control of utilities, etc.

populous *adj* densely inhabited.—**populously** *adv.*—**populousness** *n.*

pop-up *adj* (*toaster*) having a mechanism that partially ejects the toast when ready; (*book, card, etc*) containing three-dimensional figures, diagrams, etc, that rise as the page is opened; (*baseball*) a high-flying ball.

pop up menu *n* (*comput*) a menu of command options that appears on the screen when the user points and clicks a particular part of the screen or uses a second mouse button. (*See also* **pull down menu.**)

por, POR *abbr* = pay(able) on receipt; pay(able) on return.

porbeagle *n* a type of shark.

porcelain *n* a hard, white, translucent variety of ceramic ware. * *adj* made of porcelain.—**porcellaneous** *adj.*

porch *n* a covered entrance to a building; an open or enclosed gallery or room on the outside of a building.

porcine *adj* of, relating to, or resembling swine.

porcupine *n* a large rodent covered with protective quills.

Porden *n* **William** (*c*.1755–1822) British architect who designed Eaton Hall, Cheshire for Lord Grosvenor.

pore[1] *n* a tiny opening, as in the skin, plant leaves, stem, etc, for absorbing and discharging fluids.

pore[2] *vti* (*with* over) to look with steady attention; to study closely.

porgy *n* (*pl* porgy, porgies) an edible sea fish.

pork *n* the flesh of a pig used as food.

pork barrel *n* (*inf*) a government scheme that brings funds and employment, etc, to a district and enhances the standing of local politicians.—**pork-barreling** *n.*

porker *n* a pig, esp a fattened one.

porkpie hat *n* a hat with a flat crown and a brim turned up (or down) all round.

porky *adj* (porkier, porkiest) of or like pork; (*sl*) impertinent; (*sl*) obese, fat.—**porkiness** *n.*

porno *n* (*sl*) pornography—*also* **porn.** * *adj* pornographic.

pornography *n* writings, pictures, movies, etc, intended primarily to arouse sexual desire.—**pornographer** *n.*—**pornographic** *adj.*—**pornographically** *adv.*

porosity *n* (*geol*) the ratio of the volume of space in a rock to its total volume.

porous *adj* having pores; able to absorb air and fluids, etc.—**porously** *adv.*—**porousness** *n.*

porphyrin *n* (*biochemistry*) a naturally occurring pigment, such as chlorophyll.

porphyry *n* (*pl* porphyry) a reddish igneous rock, containing crystals of feldspar.

porpoise *n* (*pl* porpoise, porpoises) any of several small whales, esp a black blunt-nosed whale of the north Atlantic and Pacific; any of several bottle-nosed dolphins.

Porrex *n* (*Brit Celtic myth*) a prince of Britain. According to Geoffrey of Monmouth, he was a descendant of Brutus and was the son of Gorboduc and Judon.

porridge *n* a thick food, usu made by boiling oats or oatmeal in water or milk.

porringer *n* a small dish for porridge, etc.

Porsche *n* **Ferdinand Alexander "Butzi"** (1935–) German designer, grandson of the founder of the Porsche auto company, and responsible for the celebrated *911*.

port[1] *n* a harbor; a town with a harbor where ships load and unload cargo; airport; a place where goods may be cleared through customs.

port[2] *n* a porthole; an opening, as in a valve face, for the passage of steam, etc; a hole in an armored vehicle for firing a weapon; a circuit in a computer for inputting or outputting data.

port[3] *n* the left of an aircraft or ship looking forward.—*also adj.*

port[4] *n* a strong, sweet, fortified dark red wine.

port. *abbr* = portrait.

Port. *abbr* = Portugal; Portuguese.

Porta *n* **Guglielmo della** (1485–1577) Italian sculptor who become Keeper of the Papal Seal.

portable *adj* capable of being carried or moved about easily.—**portability** *n.*

portable computer *n* (*comput*) a computer that can be packed up and moved to a different location. (*See also* **notebook computer.**)

Portable Document Format *n* (*comput*) a file transfer system developed by Adobe™. It retains the layout of the page and contains all the features such as graphics, color, and typefaces used.

portage *n* a carrying of boats and supplies overland between navigable rivers, lakes, etc; any route over which this is done. * *vti* (*boats, etc*) to carry over a portage.

portal *n* an impressive gate or doorway.

portal dolmen *n* (*archeo*) an Irish form of Megalithic chamber tomb dating from *c*.4000 BC. Similar structures also occur in Cornwall and Wales.

portal vein *n* a vein that carries blood to the liver from other abdominal organs (stomach, spleen, intestine, etc).

portamento *n* (*mus*) (*Italian*) a continuous glide from one note to another.

Port-au-Prince *n* capital city of Haiti.

portcullis *n* a grating that can be lowered to bar entrance to a castle.

Port Elizabeth *n* a city in South Africa.

portend *vt* to give warning of, to foreshadow.

portent *n* an omen, warning.

portentous *adj* ominous; pompous, self-important.—**portentously** *adv.*—**portentousness** *n.*

porter[1] *n* a doorman or gatekeeper.

porter[2] *n* a person who carries luggage, etc, for hire at a station, airport, etc; a railroad attendant for passengers; a dark brown beer.

Porter *n* **Cole [Albert]** (1893–1964) American popular songwriter and composer whose songs include "Begin the Beguine" and "Night and day."

porterage *n* the hire of a porter; the charge for this.

porterhouse *n* a choice cut of beef steak; (*formerly*) an eating place.

portfolio *n* (*pl* portfolios) a flat case for carrying papers, drawings, etc; a collection of work or products; a list of stocks, shares, etc; a collection of financial securities that is held by an investor; the office of a cabinet minister or minister of state.

Port Gentil *n* a city in Gabon.

Porthault *n* **Madeleine** (1905–79) French producer of household linens whose clients included the Rothschilds, the Shah of Iran, and the Kennedys.

porthole *n* an opening (as a window) with a cover or closure esp in the side of a ship or aircraft; a port through which to shoot; an opening for intake or exhaust of a fluid.

porthole slab *n* (*archeo*) a large slab, usu protecting the entrance of a chamber tomb, with a hole cut into the middle of it for access.

Portia *n* one of the small satellites of Uranus, discovered in 1986.

portico *n* (*pl* porticoes, porticos) a covered walkway with columns supporting the roof.

portière *n* a heavy curtain over a door or doorway.

portion *n* a part, a share, esp an allotted part; a helping of food; destiny. * *vt* to share out.

Port Louis *n* capital city of Mauritius.

portly *adj* (portlier, portliest) dignified; stout.—**portliness** *n.*

portmanteau *n* (*pl* portmanteaus, portmanteaux) a large oblong traveling case with two compartments.

portmanteau word *n* a word combining the sound and sense of two other words, e.g. brunch.

Port Moresby *n* capital city of Papua New Guinea.

port of call *n* a port where a ship docks; any stopping-place on a journey.

Porto *n* a city in Portugal.

Porto Alegre *n* a city in Brazil.

Port of Spain *n* capital city of Trinidad and Tobago.

Porto Novo *n* capital city of Benin.

portrait *n* a painting, photograph, etc, of a person, esp of the face; (*of person*) a likeness; a vivid description.

portrait orientation *n* (*comput*) a description of the normal way of printing a page of text, with the page longer than it is wide.

portraitist *n* a maker of portraits by painting, photography, etc.

portraiture *n* the drawing of portraits; a portrait; a description in words; portraits collectively.

portray *vt* to make a portrait of; to depict in words; to play the part of in a play, movie, etc.—**portrayable** *adj.*—**portrayer** *n.*

portrayal *n* the act or process of portraying; a description; a representation.

portress *n* a female porter.

Port Said *n* a city in Egypt.

Port Sudan *n* a city in the Sudan.

Portugal *n* a republic in the southwest corner of Europe, making up about 15 per cent of the Iberian Peninsula including the island groups of Madeira and the Azores in the Atlantic.

Portzamparc *n* **Christian de** (1944–) French architect and furniture designer responsible for the Café Beaubourg in Paris.

pos. *abbr* = positive; possession; possessive.

POS *abbr* = point of sale.

POSAS *abbr* = Patent Office Search and Advisory Service.

pose *n* a position or attitude, esp one held for an artist or photographer; an attitude deliberately adopted for effect. * *vti* to propound, assert; to assume an attitude for effect; to sit for a painting, photograph; to set oneself up (as).

Poseidon *n* (*Greek myth*) god of the sea, earthquakes, and horses. The Roman equivalent was Neptune.

poser *n* a person who poses; a difficult problem.

poseur *n* an affected, insincere person.

posh *adj* (*inf*) elegant; fashionable.

posit *vt* to assume as fact, postulate.

position *n* place, situation; a position occupied; posture; a job; state of affairs; point of view. * *vt* to place or locate.

positional *adj* related to, or fixed by position; involving little movement; dependent on context, environment or position.

position angle *n* (*astron*) the angle which states the orientation of one celestial body with respect to another.

positive *adj* affirmative; definite; sure; marked by presence, not absence, of qualities; expressed clearly, or in a confident manner; constructive; empirical; (*elect*) charged with positive electricity; (*math*) greater than zero, plus; (*gram*) of adjective or adverb, denoting the simple form; (*photog*) having light, shade, color as in the original. * *n* a positive quality or quantity; a photographic print made from a negative.

positively *adv* in a positive way; decidedly.

positiveness *n* the condition or quality of being positive; confidence; certainty.

positivism *n* a philosophy recognizing only matters of fact and experience; the quality of being positive.—**positivist** *n*, *adj*.—**positivistic** *adj*.—**positivistically** *adv*.

positron *n* (*physics*) a particle of the same size as an electron, but with a positive charge.

posology *n* the area of medicine dealing with evaluation of doses.

poss. *abbr* = possession; possessive; possibly.

posse *n* a body of people summoned by a sheriff to assist in keeping the peace, etc; (*sl*) a group of criminals, usu of Jamaican origin and in New York.

possess *vt* to own, have, keep; to dominate or control the mind of.—**possessor** *n*.—**possessory** *adj*.

possessed *adj* owned; controlled as if by a demon.

possession *n* ownership; something possessed; (*pl*) property.

possessive *adj* of or indicating possession; (*gram*) denoting a case, form or construction expressing possession; having an excessive desire to possess or dominate.—**possessively** *adv*.—**possessiveness** *n*.

posset *n* a hot drink of milk curdled with wine or ale.

possetting *adj* the normal habit of babies to regurgitate small amounts of a recently eaten meal.

possibility *n* (*pl* **possibilities**) the state of being possible; a possible occurrence, a contingency.

possible *adj* that may be or may happen; feasible, practicable.—**possibly** *adv*.

possum *n* (*inf*) an opossum; a phalanger; **play possum** to pretend to be asleep or dead; to remain silent.

post[1] *n* a piece of wood, metal, etc, set upright to support a building, sign, etc; the starting or finishing point of a race. * *vt* (*poster, etc*) to put up; to announce by posting notices; (*name*) to put on a posted or published list.

post[2] *n* a fixed position, esp where a sentry or group of soldiers is stationed; a position or job; a trading post; a settlement. * *vt* to station in a given place.

post[3] *n* (*Brit*) the official conveyance of letters and parcels, mail; letters, parcels, etc, so conveyed; collection or delivery of post, mail. * *vt* (*Brit*) to send a letter or parcel; to keep informed; (*comput*) to add data to a record in a database management program or similar program, e.g. for keeping accounting records.—**postal** *adj*.

Post *n* 1. **George B** (1837–1913) American architect whose notable works include New York Times building. 2. **Pieter** (1608–69) Dutch architect whose notable works include Town Hall, Maastricht.

POST[1] *abbr* = point-of-sale terminal.

POST[2] *abbr* (*comput*) = Power On Self Test. A test that a computer carries out on start-up to ensure that the main components are working correctly.

post- *prefix* after.

postage *n* the charge for sending a letter, etc, as represented by stamps.

postage meter *n* a machine that imprints postal indicia on mail; a franking machine.

postage stamp *n* an adhesive or imprinted stamp issued or authorized by a government and used on mail as evidence of prepayment of postage.

postal card *n* a card with a stamp issued by the government for mailing at low rates; a post card.

postbellum *adj* denoting a period after a war, used esp for the period after the American Civil War.

postcard *n* a card, usu decorative, for sending messages by post; a postal card.

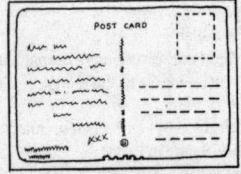

post chaise *n* (*formerly*) a light, closed, horse-drawn carriage used for carrying both mail and passengers.

postcode *n* (*UK*) zip code.

postdate *vt* to write a future date on a letter or check.

postdiluvian, postdiluvial *adj* occurring after the Flood (of the Old Testament).

postdoctoral *adj* relating to studies, research, degrees, etc, beyond the doctoral level.

poste restante *n* the department of a post office that will hold mail until it is called for, general delivery.

poster *n* a usu decorative or ornamental printed sheet for advertising.

poster paint *see* **gouache**.

posterior *adj* later in time or order; at the rear. * *n* the buttocks.—**posteriorly** *adv*.

posterity *n* future generations; all of a person's descendants.

postern *n* a back or side entrance; a small private door.

postfix *vt* to append as a suffix. * *n* a suffix.

post-free *adj* (*UK*) with the postage paid in advance; free of postal charge.

postglacial *adj* existing after a glacial period.

postgraduate *n* a person pursuing study after graduating from a high school or college. * *adj* (*study*) continued after the taking of a degree.

posthaste *adv* with all possible speed.

post hoc *n* (*logic*) (*Latin*) the fallacy of assuming that because event B followed A, therefore A *caused* B.

posthorn *n* (*mus*) a simple (valveless) brass instrument similar to a bugle, but usu coiled in a circular form.

posthumous *adj* (*child*) born after its father's death; (*award, etc*) given after one's death.—**posthumously** *adv*.

postiche *adj* artificial; superfluous; inappropriate. * *n* an ornament added, esp inappropriately, to finished work; a wig; an imitation.

postilion, postillion *n* someone who rides one of the horses drawing a carriage and guiding the team.

postimpressionism *n* a 19th-century school of painting which sought to express the artist's conception of things rather than their outward appearance.—**postimpressionist** *n*, *adj*.

postliminium, postliminy *n* (*law*) the right of a prisoner of war or exile to resume his or her former privileges on return to his or her own country.

postlude *n* (*mus*) a closing movement.

postman *n* (*pl* **postmen**) a mailman.

postmark *n* the post office mark canceling the stamp on a letter by showing the date, place of posting.

postmaster *n* the manager of a post office.

postmeridian *adj* of or taking place in the afternoon.

post meridiem = p.m. (Latin for *after noon*).

Post-Modernism *n* (*archit*) an architectural revolt against the ideas of modernism which first became current in the 1940s and later in the 1960s and 70s.

postmortem *n* an examination of a cadaver to determine the cause of death; an autopsy.—*also adj*.

postnatal *adj* occurring immediately after birth.

post-obit *adj* (*law*) after death. * *n* a bond in which a borrower undertakes to repay a loan on the death of someone from whom he or she expects to receive a legacy.

post office *n* the building where postage stamps are sold and other postal business conducted; a public department handling the transmission of mail.

post office box *n* a private numbered area in a post office where mail is lodged until collected in person.

postpaid *adj* with a charge for postage, post free.

postpartum *adj* denoting the period after parturition.

postpone *vt* to put off, delay to a future date.—**postponable** *adj*.—**postponement** *n*.—**postponer** *n*.

postprandial *adj* after-dinner.

poststructuralism *see* **deconstruction**.

postscript *n* a note added to a letter after completion.

Postscript *n*, *trademark* (*comput*) an example of a page description language for printing, created by Adobe™.

post-testing *n* testing that is undertaken after the appearance of an advertisement to try to establish whether the objectives set for it have been met.

post time *n* the official starting time for a horse race.

postulant *n* someone making a request; a candidate for admission to a religious order.

postulate *vt* to assume to be true; to demand or claim. * *n* a position taken as self-evident; (*math*) an unproved assumption taken as basic; an axiom.—**postulation** *n*.

posture *n* a pose; a body position; an attitude of mind; an official stand or position. * *vti* to pose in a particular way; to assume a pose.—**postural** *adj*.—**posturer** *n*.

post-viral syndrome *n* the viral condition myalgic encephalomyelitis that affects the nervous system.

posy *n* (*pl* **posies**) a small bunch of flowers.

pot[1] *n* a deep, round cooking vessel; an earthenware or plastic container for plants; a framework for catching fish or lobsters; (*inf*) a large amount (as of money); (*inf*) all the money bet at a single time. * *vb* (**potting, potted**) *vt* to put or preserve in a pot. * *vi* to take a pot shot, shoot.

pot[2] *n* (*sl*) cannabis.

pot. *abbr* = potential.

potable *adj* drinkable.

potash *n* potassium carbonate.

potassium *n* a soft silvery-white metallic element.—**potassic** *adj*.

potassium-argon dating *or* **K-A dating** *n* a method which involves measuring the amount of the potassium isotope K^{40} which has decayed to $Argon^{40}$.

potation *n* the act of drinking; a draft or drink.

potato chip *n* a thin slice of fried potato; (*Brit*) a chip; a crisp.

potato *n* (*pl* **potatoes**) a starchy, oval tuber eaten as a vegetable.

potbelly *n* (*pl* **potbellies**) a protruding belly.—**potbellied** *adj*.

potboiler *n* an inferior literary or artistic work done simply to earn money.

potboy *n* (*formerly*) in UK, an assistant in a public house.

poteen *n* (*Irish*) illicitly distilled whiskey.

potency *n* (*pl* **potencies**) the quality or condition of being potent; power; strength.

potent *adj* powerful; influential; intoxicating; (*a male*) able to have sexual intercourse.—**potently** *adv*.

potentate *n* a person with great power; a ruler; a monarch.

potential *adj* possible, but not yet actual. * *n* the unrealized ability to do something.—**potentially** *adv*.

potential difference *n* (*physics*) the work done in driving a unit of electric charge (one coulomb) from one point to another in a current-carrying circuit.

potentiality *n* (*pl* **potentialities**) latent capacity for development or growth; something with this.

potentiate *vt* to make possible; to give power to.

potentilla *n* a flowering plant of the rose family.

pother *n* a bustle or turmoil; a turmoil.

potholder *n* a padded cloth for handling hot pots and pans.

pothole *n* a hole worn in a road by traffic; (*geol*) a deep hole or cave in rock caused by the action of water.

pothouse *n* (*formerly*) in UK, a public house.

pothunter *n* someone who hunts for the sake of the game caught, not for the sport.

potion *n* a mixture of liquids, such as poison.

pot luck *n* whatever food is available without special preparation; whatever is available at the time.

Potosi *n* a city in Bolivia.

potpourri *n* (*pl* **potpourris**) a mixture of scented, dried flower petals; a collection; a medley or miscellany.

potsherd, potshard *n* a piece of broken earthenware.

pot shot *n* a random or easy shot.

Pott *n* **Carl Hugo** (1906–85) German metalworker who abandoned decoration for simple lines.

pottage *n* a thick broth.

potted *adj* in a pot; preserved (in a pot); (*version, history*) abridged.

potter[1] *n* a person who makes earthenware vessels.

potter[2] *vi* to busy oneself idly; to putter.—**potterer** *n*.

pottery *n* (*pl* **potteries**) earthenware vessels; a workshop where such articles are made.

potto *n* (*pl* **pottos**) a West African lemur; a kinkajou.

potty[1] *adj* (**pottier, pottiest**) (*inf*) slightly crazy; trivial, petty.—**pottiness** *n*.

potty[2] *n* (*pl* **potties**) (*inf*) a chamber pot.

pouch *n* a small bag or sack; a bag for mail; a sacklike structure, as that on the abdomen of a kangaroo, etc, for carrying young.—**pouched** *adj*.

pouf, pouffe *n* a large firm cushion for sitting on; a woman's hairstyle in which the hair is piled in soft rolls, fashionable in the 18th century; a decorative puff on a dress.

Poulenc *n* **Francis** (1899–1963) French composer and pianist who became a member of the group known as *Les Six*. His works include the operas *Les Mamelles de Tiresias* and *Dialogues des Carmelites*, ballets, concertos, chamber music, choral works, and compositions for piano.

poult *n* a young fowl.

poultice *n* a hot moist dressing applied to a sore part of the body.

poultry *n* domesticated birds kept for meat or eggs.

POUNC *abbr* (*Brit*) = Post Office Users' National Council.

pounce *vi* to swoop or spring suddenly (upon) in order to seize; to make a sudden assault or approach.—*also n*.

pound[1] *n* a unit of weight equal to 16 ounces; a unit of money in the UK and other countries, symbol £.

pound[2] *vt* to beat into a powder or a pulp; to hit hard. * *vi* to deliver heavy blows repeatedly (at or on); to move with heavy steps; to throb; (*with* **away**) to work hard and continuously.—**pounder** *n*.

pound[3] *n* a municipal enclosure for stray animals; a depot for holding impounded personal property until claimed; a place or condition of confinement.

Pound *n* **Ezra [Weston Loomis]** (1885–1972) American poet and critic who lived in Italy from 1925 and broadcast propaganda against the Allies during World War II. His main work is the unfinished sequence of poems entitled *Cantos*.

poundage *n* a charge per pound of weight; weight in pounds; the act of impounding; the state of being impounded.

poundal *n* a unit of force, giving to a mass of one pound an acceleration of one foot per second per second.

Pound Sterling *n* currency of United Kingdom of Great Britain and Northern Ireland (UK).

pour *vti* to cause to flow in a stream; to flow continuously; to rain heavily; to serve tea or coffee.—**pourer** *n*.

pourboire *n* a tip or gratuity.

Poussin *n* **Nicolas** (1594–1665) French painter noted for his carefully composed pictures in a classical style.

pout *vti* to push out (the lips); to look sulky. * *n* a thrusting out of the lips; (*pl*) a fit of pique.—**poutingly** *adv*.

pouter *n* someone who pouts; a breed of pigeon with a prominent crop.

pov *abbr* = point of view; privately owned vehicle.

poverty *n* the condition of being poor; scarcity.

poverty-stricken *adj* very poor, impoverished.

Povey *n* **Albert John Stephen** (1951–) British furniture and interior designer who became known for clever re-interpretations of classic British styles.

POW *abbr* = prisoner of war.

powder *n* any substance in tiny, loose particles; a specific kind of powder, esp for medicinal or cosmetic use; fine dry light snow. * *vti* to sprinkle or cover with powder; to reduce to powder.—**powderer** *n*.

powdered *adj* sprinkled or covered with powder; reduced to power.

powdered sugar *n* finely ground granulated sugar.

powder room *n* women's restroom.

powdery *adj* like powder; easily crumbled.

Powell *n* 1. **Anthony [Dymoke]** (1905–2000) English novelist, noted particularly for his sequence of 12 novels entitled *A Dance to the Music of Time*. 2. **David Harman** (1933–) British designer who became the first tutor in molded plastics at the Royal College of Art, London, in 1968. 3. **Powell** *n* **[John] Enoch** (1912–98) English Conservative politician and an outspoken opponent of immigration into Britain. 4. **Michael** (1905–90) English movie producer and director who made several important movies, e.g. *The Life and Death of Colonel Blimp*, with screenwriter Emeric Pressburger (1902–88).

power *n* ability to do something; political, social or financial control or force; a person or state with influence over others; legal force or authority; physical force; a source of energy; (*math*) the result of continued multiplication of a quantity by itself a specified number of times. * *adj* operated by electricity, a fuel engine, etc; served by an auxiliary system that reduces effort; carrying electricity. * *vt* to supply with a source of power.—**powered** *adj*.

power broker *n* a person, such as a politician, who exerts power because of the votes, etc, they control.

power down *vi* (*comput*) to turn off a computer.

powerful *adj* mighty; strong; influential.—**powerfully** *adv*.—**powerfulness** *n*.

powerhouse *n* a power station; (*inf*) a strong or energetic person, team, etc.

powerless *adj* without power; helpless; feeble.—**powerlessly** *adv*.—**powerlessness** *n*.

power notation *n* (*math*) the use of a small number (an exponent) placed next to an ordinary number to show how many times the ordinary number is multiplied by itself.

power of attorney *n* (a document conferring) legal authority to act for another in specified matters.

power PC *n* (*comput*) a microprocessor chip used by IBM™ and Apple™, using RISC technology. (*See also* **Pentium**.)

power station, power plant *n* a building where electric power is generated.

power-striding *n* brisk walking as a means of improving fitness.

power supply *n* (*comput*) a device in a computer that converts the AC mains supply to DC current used by a computer.

power up *vi* (*comput*) to switch on a computer and load the operating system ready for use.

power user *n* (*comput*) a computer user who is able to use all the advanced features of a program or series of programs.

POW/MP *abbr* = Prisoner of War/Missing Personnel

powwow *n* an American Indian ceremony (as for invoking victory in war); (*inf*) any conference or get-together. * *vi* to confer, chat.

Powys *n* 1. **J[ohn] C[owper]** (1872–1963) English novelist, essayist, and poet whose novels include *Wolf Solent, Weymouth Sands*, and his masterpiece, *A Glastonbury Romance*. 2. **T[heodore] F[rancis]** (1875–1953) brother of the above, writer of novels and stories in the same West Country setting, the most notable of which is the remarkable fantasy novel *Mr Weston's Good Wine*. 3. **Llewellyn** (1884–1939), brother of the above, journalist and essayist, whose *Skin for Skin* is an account of his fight against tuberculosis.

pox *n* a virus disease marked by pustules; (*arch*) smallpox; syphilis; a plague; a curse.

Poynting–Roberston effect *n* small interplanetary particles that orbit the Sun, absorb solar radiation, and then radiate energy back out in all directions. The effect of this process is to reduce the kinetic energy of the particles and they move in ever decreasing orbits around the Sun, spiraling in to the center.

Poznan *n* a city in Poland.

pozzuolana, pozzolana *n* volcanic ashes used in hydraulic cement.

pp *abbr* = past participle; (*Latin*) *per procurationem* (*see* **per pro**); (*mus*) (*Italian*) *pianissimo*, "very soft"; planning permission; post paid; (*pharm*) (*Latin*) *post prandium*, "after meal"; privately printed.

pp or PP *abbr* (*mus*) (*Italian*) = *pianissimo*, "very soft."

pp. *abbr* = pages; participle past; privately printed.

p.p. *abbr* = parcel post; parish priest; past participle; percussion primer; (*Latin*) *per procurationem* (*see* **per pro**); play or pay; postpaid.

PP *abbr* = parish priest; past president; (*Latin*) *Patres*, "Fathers"; Phonographic Performance.

p.p.a. *abbr* = per power of attorney.

PPA *abbr* = Piano Publicity Association; Pipeline Protection Association; Potato Processors Association; Pre-School Playgroups Association.

PPARC *abbr* = Particle Physics and Astronomy Research Council.

ppb *abbr* = paper, printing, and binding; parts per billion.

ppc *abbr* = progressive patient care.

PPC *abbr* (*French*) = *pour prendre congé*, "to take leave."

ppd. *abbr* = prepaid.

PPE *abbr* = Philosophy, Politics, and Economics.

PPFAS *abbr* = Past President of the Faculty of Architects and Surveyors.

PPG *abbr* = Player Piano Group.

pph. *abbr* = pamphlet.

PPH *abbr* = post-partum hemorrhage.

ppi *abbr* (*radar*) = plan-position indicator.

PPI *or* **p.p.i.** *abbr* (*marine ins*) = policy proof of interest.

PPITB *abbr* = Printing and Publishing Industry Training Board.

PPL *abbr* = Private Pilot's License.

ppm *abbr* = (*comput*) pages per minute; (*chem*) parts per million.

PPM *abbr* = peak program meter.

PPMA *abbr* = Plastic Pipe Manufacturers Association; Produce Packaging and Marketing Association.

PPN *abbr* = public packet network.

Ppoton–proton chain *n* a primary source of energy in stars. Through a series of nuclear fusion reactions hydrogen is converted into helium with the release of energy which maintains the core temperature.

ppp *abbr* (*mus*) (*Italian*) = *pianississimo*, "extremely quietly."

PPP *abbr* = personal pension plan; (*comput*) Point-to-Point Protocol. A method for connecting computers to the internet via telephone lines and a modem, similar to SLIP.

pppm *abbr* = per person per month.

pppn *abbr* = per person per night.

p. pr., ppr. *abbr* = participle present.

PPR *abbr* = printed paper rate.

PPRA *abbr* (*Brit*) = Past President of the Royal Academy.

p. pro. *abbr* (*Latin*) = per procurationem. *See* **per pro**.

PPS *or* **p.p.s.** *abbr* = pelvic pain syndrome; (*Latin*) *post postscriptum*, "additional postscript."

PPSG *abbr* = Protein and Peptide Science Group.

ppt. *abbr* (*chem*) = precipitate.

PPU *abbr* = Peace Pledge Union.

p.q. *abbr* = previous question.

PQ *abbr* = Province of Quebec.

Pr *symbol* (*chem*) praseodymium (element).

pr *abbr* (*pharm*) (*Latin*) = *per rectum*, "by way of the rectum."

pr. *abbr* = pair; pairs; pounder (as 12-pr.); power; (*stock*) preferred; present; price; priest; prince; printing paper; pronoun; proposition.

p.r. *or* **PR** *abbr* = prize ring.

Pr. *abbr* = Provençal.

PR *abbr* (*Latin*) *Populus Romanus*, "Roman people"; press release; proportional representation; public relations; Puerto Rico.

PRA *abbr* = Paint Research Association; (*Canada*) Prairie Rail Authority; Psychiatric Rehabilitation Association.

practicable *adj* able to be practiced; possible, feasible.—**practicability** *n.*—**practicably** *adv.*

practical *adj* concerned with action, not theory; workable; suitable; trained by practice; virtual, in effect.

practical joke *n* a prank intended to embarrass or to cause discomfort.

practicality *n* (*pl* **practicalities**) the condition of being practical; a practical feature or aspect.

practically *adv* in a practical manner; virtually.

practice[1] *n* action; habit, custom; repetition and exercise to gain skill; the exercise of a profession.

practice[2] *vti* to repeat an exercise to acquire skill; to put into practice; to do habitually or frequently; (*profession*) to work at.

practiced *adj* acquired by practice; proficient; experienced.

practitioner *n* a person who practices a profession.

praedial *adj* pertaining to land or landed property.—*also* **predial**.

praetor *n* (*ancient Rome*) a magistrate, ranking next to a consul.

pragmatic *adj* practical; testing the validity of all concepts by their practical results.—**pragmatically** *adv.*

pragmatics *n sing* the study of the relationship of signs and symbols and their use; (*linguistics*) the study of meaning derived from context.

pragmatism *n* the judging of events or actions by their results, esp in politics; pragmatic behavior; (*philos*) a theory that judges the truth of a doctrine by the conduct resulting from belief in it.—**pragmatist** *n.*—**pragmatistic** *adj.*

Prague (Praha) *n* capital city of the Czech Republic.

Praia *n* capital city of Cape Verde.

prairie *n* a large area of level or rolling land predominantly in grass; a dry treeless plateau.

prairie chicken, prairie hen *n* either of two types of North American grouse with mottled brownish plumage.

prairie dog *n* a burrowing rodent related to the marmot.

prairie wolf *n* the coyote.

praise *vt* to express approval of, to commend; to glorify, to worship. * *vi* to express praise. * *n* commendation; glorification.—**praiser** *n.*

praiseworthy *adj* deserving praise; commendable.—**praiseworthily** *adv.*—**praiseworthiness** *n.*

praline *n* a confection made of nuts and sugar.

prance *vi* (*horse*) to spring on the hind legs, bound; (*person*) to walk or ride in a showy manner; to swagger. * *n* a prancing; a caper.—**prancer** *n.*—**prancingly** *adv.*

Prandtauer *n* **Jakob** (1660–1726) Austrian architect whose notable works include Melk Abbey.

prank[1] *n* a mischievous trick or joke; a ludicrous act.—**prankster** *n.*

prank[2] *vti* to adorn, to deck; to dress up showily.

prase *n* a green, transparent form of quartz.

praseodymium *n* a silvery-white metallic element.

Prasutagus *n* (d. 60) king of the Iceni, Britain. He ruled the tribal kingdom as a client of the Romans but when he died his lands were seized, his daughters raped and his wife, Boadicea, flogged. Boadicea led a rebellion against the Romans which was eventually quashed.

prate *vti* to chatter, talk idly.—**prater** *n.*

pratincole *n* a bird resembling a swallow.

Pratt *n* **Sir Roger** (1620–84) English architect whose notable works include Clarendon House, London (now destroyed).

prattle *vti* to talk in a childish manner; to babble. * *n* empty chatter.—**prattler** *n.*

prawn *n* a shrimp, an edible marine crustacean. * *vi* to fish for prawns.—**prawner** *n.*

praxis *n* (*pl* **praxises, praxes**) practice; an example, or set of examples, for an exercise.

pray *vti* to offer prayers to God; to implore.

prayer[1] *n* supplication, entreaty, praise or thanks to God; the form of this; the act of praying; (*pl*) devotional services; something prayed for.

prayer[2] *n* one who prays.

prayerful *adj* given to prayer; devout.—**prayerfully** *adv.*

praying mantis *n* a mantis.

PRB *abbr* = Pre-Raphaelite Brotherhood.

PRC *abbr* = People's Republic of China; (*Latin*) *post Romam conditam*, "after the foundation of Rome."

pre- *prefix* before, beforehand; previous to; surpassingly.

preach *vi* to advocate in an earnest or moralizing way. * *vt* to deliver a sermon; (*patience, etc*) to advocate.

preacher *n* one who preaches, esp a Protestant clergyman.

preachify *vi* (*inf*) to hold forth tediously.—**preachification** *n.*

preachy *adj* (**preachier, preachiest**) (*inf*) fond of moralizing or preaching.

pre-acquisition *n* the retained profit of a company before its acquisition or takeover.

preamble *n* an introductory part to a document, speech, or story, stating its purpose.—**preambulary** *adj.*

prearrange *vt* to arrange beforehand.—**prearrangement** *n.*

preb. *abbr* = prebend; prebendary.

prebend *n* a stipend granted to a canon or member of the chapter by a cathedral.—**prebendal** *adj.*

prebendary *n* (*pl* **prebendaries**) someone who holds a prebend.

prec. *abbr* = preceding; precentor.

Precambrian *adj* (of or relating to) the earliest geological time period, from the formation of the earth to the beginnings of life.—*also n.*

precancerous *adj* likely to become cancerous.

precarious *adj* dependent on chance; insecure; dangerous.—**precariously** *adv.*—**precariousness** *n.*

precatory, precative *adj* suppliant, expresssing a wish.

precaution *n* a preventive measure; care taken beforehand; careful foresight.—**precautionary** *adj.*

precede *vti* to be, come or go before in time, place, order, rank, or importance.

precedence *n* priority; the right of higher rank; (*comput*) the order in which arithmetic operations are performed.

precedent *n* a previous and parallel case serving as an example; (*law*) a decision, etc, serving as a rule. * *adj* preceding; previous.—**precedented** *adj.*—**precedently** *adv.*

precedential *adj* serving as a precedent; having precedence.

preceding *adj* coming or going before; former.

precentor *n* the leader of a choir in a cathedral or church.

precept *n* a rule of moral conduct; a maxim; an order issued by a legally constituted authority to a subordinate.

preceptive *adj* of or using precepts; didactic.—**preceptively** *adv.*

preceptor *n* an instructor or teacher.—**preceptress** *nf.*

precession[1] *n* going before, in advance of—**precessional** *adj.*

precession[2] *n* (*astron*) the westward motion of the equinoxes caused mainly by the attraction of the Sun and Moon on the equatorial bulge of the Earth. The time period involved is almost 26,000 years.

precessional motion *n* (*physics*) the type of motion shown by a gyroscope.

precinct *n* (*usu pl*) an enclosure between buildings, walls, etc; a limited area; an urban area where traffic is prohibited; (*pl*) environs; a police district or a subdivision of a voting ward.

preciosity *n* (*pl* **preciosities**) excessive attention to detail; fastidiousness.

precious *adj* of great cost or value; beloved; very fastidious; affected; thoroughgoing. * *adv* (*sl*) very.—**preciously** *adv.*—**preciousness** *n.*

precious metal *n* gold, silver, or platinum.

precious stone *n* a diamond, emerald, ruby, sapphire, pearl, and sometimes black opal; a gem.

precipice *n* a cliff or overhanging rock face.

precipitant *adj* falling headlong; hasty, impetuous. * *n* (*chem*) a substance causing precipitation.—**precipitance, precipitancy** *n.*

precipitate *vti* to throw from a height; to cause to happen suddenly or too soon; (*chem*) to separate out; to rain; to fall as rain, snow, dew, etc.—**precipitately** *adv.*—**precipitateness** *n.*—**precipitator** *n.*

precipitation *n* the act of precipitating; undue haste; rain, snow, etc; the amount of this; (*chem*) the formation of an insoluble substance (precipitate) in a reaction between two solutions.

precipitato, precipitoso *adv* (*mus*) (*Italian*) precipitately, impetuously.

precipitous *adj* of or like a precipice; sheer, steep.—**precipitously** *adv*.—**precipitousness** *n*.

précis *n* (*pl* **précis**) a summary or abstract. * *vt* to make a précis of.

Precis *abbr* = preserved context index system.

precise *adj* clearly defined, exact; accurate; punctilious; particular.—**precisely** *adv*.—**preciseness** *n*.

precision *n* the quality of being precise; accuracy. * *adj* (*machines*) having a high degree of accuracy.

preclude *vt* to rule out in advance; to make impossible.—**preclusion** *n*.—**preclusive** *adj*.

precocious *adj* prematurely ripe or developed.—**precociously** *adv*.—**precociousness** *n*.

precocity *n* the condition of being precocious, precociousness; early development, esp of a child's mind.

precognition *n* the supposed extrasensory perception of a future event; clairvoyance.—**precognitive** *adj*.

pre-Columbian *adj* of or originating in the Americas before their discovery by Christopher Columbus.

preconceive *vt* to form an idea or opinion of before actual experience.

preconception *n* the act of preconceiving; an opinion formed without actual knowledge.

precondition *n* a requirement that must be met beforehand, a prerequisite. * *vt* (*an organism, a patient*) to prepare to behave or react in a certain way under certain conditions.

precook *vt* to cook completely or partially in advance.

precursor *n* a predecessor; a substance from which another substance is formed.—**precursory** *adj*.

pred. *abbr* = predicate.

predacious, predaceous *adj* living on prey.—**predaciousness, predaceousness, predacity** *n*.

predate *vt* to antedate.

predator *n* a person who preys, plunders, or devours; a carnivorous animal.

predatory *adj* living on prey, of or relating to a predator; characterized by hunting or plundering.—**predatorily** *adv*.—**predatoriness** *n*.

predatory pricing *n* a pricing strategy that prices goods or services at such a low level that other firms are unable to compete and so get out of the market.

predecease *vt* to die before (another).

predecessor *n* a former holder of a position or office; an ancestor.

predella *n* (*pl* **predelle**) (*Italian*) a platform for, or shelf upon, an altar; a painting, or sculpture, on such a platform or shelf.

predestinarian *adj* pertaining to predestination. * *n* someone who believes in the doctrine of predestination.

predestinate *adj* predestined. * *vt* to predestine.

predestination *n* a predestining or being predestined; destiny; (*theol*) the doctrine that God has from all eternity decreed the salvation or damnation of each soul.

predestine *vt* to foreordain; to destine beforehand.

predeterminate *adj* predetermined.

predetermine *vt* to decide beforehand.—**predetermination** *n*.

predicable *adj* which can be predicated.

predicament *n* a difficult or embarrassing situation.

predicant *adj* pertaining to preaching. * *n* a preaching friar, esp a Dominican.

predicate *vt* to state as a quality or attribute; to base (on facts, conditions etc). * *n* (*gram*) that which is stated about the subject.—**predication** *n*.

predicative *adj* (*gram*) (*adjective, etc*) making a statement about the subject of a verb. * *n* a predicative construction.

predicatory *adj* of or given to preaching.

predict *vt* to foretell; to state (what one believes will happen).—**predictor** *n*.

predictable *adj* able to be predicted or anticipated; lacking originality.—**predictability** *n*.—**predictably** *adv*.

prediction *n* the act of predicting; that which is predicted; a forecast or prophecy.—**predictive** *adj*.—**predictively** *adv*.

predigest *vt* to treat (food) artificially to make easily digestible.

predilection *n* partiality, liking for.

predispose *vt* to incline beforehand; (*disease, etc*) to make susceptible to.—**predisposition** *n*.

predominant *adj* ruling over, controlling; influencing.—**predominance, predominancy** *n*.

predominantly *adv* mainly.

predominate *vt* to rule over; to have influence or control over; to prevail; to be greater in number, intensity, etc.—**predomination** *n*.—**predominator** *n*.

pre-eclampsia *n* the development of high blood pressure in pregnancy, sometimes with edema, which, unless treated, may result in eclampsia.

pre-eminent, preeminent *adj* distinguished above others; outstanding.—**pre-eminence, preeminence** *n*.—**pre-eminently, preeminently** *adv*.

pre-empt, preempt *vt* to take action to check other action beforehand; to gain the right to buy (public land) by settling on it; to seize before anyone else can; to replace; (*in bridge*) to bid highly to exclude bids from opponents.—**pre-emptor, preemptor** *n*.—**pre-emptory, preemptory** *adj*.

pre-emption, preemption *n* a pre-empting or being pre-empted; a buying or the right to buy before the opportunity is given to others; such a purchase.

pre-emptive, preemptive *adj* (*bridge*) denoting a high bid to exclude bids from the opposition.—**pre-emptively, preemptively** *adv*.

preen *vti* (*birds*) to clean and trim the feathers; to congratulate (oneself) for achievement; to groom (oneself); to gloat.—**preener** *n*.

pref. *abbr* = preface; prefaced; prefatory; preference; preferred; prefix; prefixed.

prefab *n* (*inf*) a prefabricated part or building.

prefabricate *vt* (*house, etc*) to build in standardized sections for shipment and quick assembly; to produce artificially.—**prefabrication** *n*.—**prefabricator** *n*.

preface *n* an introduction or preliminary explanation; a foreword or introduction to a book; a preamble. * *vt* to serve as a preface; to introduce.—**prefacer** *n*.

prefatory *adj* of or pertaining to a preface; introductory.—**prefatorily** *adv*.

prefect *n* a person placed in authority over others; a student monitor in a school; in some countries, an administrative official.—**prefectorial** *adj*.

prefecture *n* the office, district, residence, or tenure of a prefect.—**prefectural** *adj*.

prefer *vt* (**preferring, preferred**) to like better; to promote, advance; to put before a court, etc, for consideration.—**preferrer** *n*.

preferable *adj* deserving preference; superior; more desirable.—**preferably** *adv*.

preference *n* the act of preferring, choosing, or favoring one above another; that which is chosen or preferred; prior right; advantage given to one person, country, etc, over others.

preferential *adj* giving or receiving preference.—**preferentialism** *n*.—**preferentially** *adv*.

preferment *n* advancement; promotion to a higher post.

preferred stock *n* a share in a company that pays a fixed rate of interest rather than a variable dividend.

prefiguration *n* the act of prefiguring.—**prefigurative** *adj*.

prefigure *vt* to suggest in advance, foreshadow; to imagine beforehand.

prefix *vt* to put at the beginning of or before; to put as an introduction. * *n* a syllable or group of syllables placed at the beginning of a word, affecting its meaning.—**prefixal** *adj*.—**prefixally** *adv*.

preglacial *adj* existing before a glacial period.

pregnable *adj* capable of being attacked and captured.

pregnancy *n* (*pl* **pregnancies**) the state of being pregnant; the period of this.

pregnancy test *n* any of various tests used to check for pregnancy, most of which are based on the presence of chorionic gonadotrophic hormone in the urine.

pregnant *adj* having a fetus in the womb; significant, meaningful; imaginative; filled (with) or rich (in).—**pregnantly** *adv*.

preheat *vt* to heat in advance.

prehensile *adj* capable of grasping, esp by wrapping around.—**prehensility** *n*.

prehension *n* grasping; the ability to grasp.

prehistoric, prehistorical *adj* of the period before written records began; (*inf*) old-fashioned.—**prehistorically** *adv*.

prehistory *n* (*pl* **prehistories**) events that took place before recorded history; the study of prehistoric events; the history of the earlier background of an incident, etc.—**prehistorian** *n*.

prejudge *vt* to pass judgment on before a trial; to form a premature opinion.—**prejudger** *n*.—**prejudgment, prejudgement** *n*.

prejudice *n* a judgment or opinion made without adequate knowledge; bias; intolerance or hatred of other races, etc; (*law*) injury or disadvantage due to another's action. * *vt* to affect or injure through prejudice.—**prejudiced** *adj*.

prejudicial *adj* causing prejudice; detrimental, damaging.—**prejudicially** *adv*.

prelacy *n* (*pl* **prelacies**) the office or status of a prelate; prelates collectively; church government by prelates.

prelate *n* a church dignity with episcopal authority.—**prelatic** *adj*.

prelature *n* the office or status of a prelate.

prelim. *abbr* = preliminary.

preliminary *adj* preparatory; introductory. * *n* (*pl* **preliminaries**) an event preceding another; a preliminary step or measure; (*in school*) a preparatory examination.—**preliminarily** *adv*.

preliminary expenses *npl* the initial costs that are involved in the setting up of a company.

prelims *npl* the front matter of a book, before the main text; preliminary university exams.

prelude *n* an introductory act or event; an event preceding another of greater importance; (*mus*) a movement which acts as an introduction; (*mus*) a self-contained piano piece in one movement. * *vti* to serve as a prelude to, to usher in; to play a prelude.—**preludial** *adj*.—**prelusion** *n*.—**prelusive, prelusory** *adj*.

prem. *abbr* = premium.

premarital *adj* (*sex*) taking place before marriage.

premature *adj* occurring before the expected or normal time; too early, hasty.—**prematurely** *adv*.—**prematurity** *n*.

premature birth *n* a birth occurring before the end of the normal full term of pregnancy.

premed *n* a premedical student or course of study.— *also adj*.

premedical *adj* of or relating to medical studies required to enter medical school.

premedication *n* a sedative drug given to a patient before an operation in which an anesthetic will be used.

premeditate *vt* (*crime, etc*) to plan in advance.—**premeditatedly** *adv*.—**premeditative** *adj*.—**premeditator** *n*.

premeditation *n* deliberation or thought before doing something; (*law*) the plotting of a crime beforehand, demonstrating intent to commit it.

premenstrual syndrome *n* symptoms, such as nervous tension, irritability, and aggression, that may be experienced in the days before menstruation begins.—*also* **premenstrual tension, PMT**.

premier *adj* principal; first. * *n* the head of a government, a prime minister.—**premiership** *n*.

premiere, première *n* the first public performance of a play, movie, etc. * *vt* to give a premiere of. * *vi* to have a first performance; to appear for the first time as a star performer.

premise *n* a proposition on which reasoning is based; something assumed or taken for granted (—*also* **premiss**); (*pl*) a piece of land and its buildings. * *vt* to state as an introduction; to postulate; to base on certain assumptions.

premium *n* a reward, esp an inducement to buy; a periodical payment for insurance; excess over an original price; something given free or at a reduced price with a purchase; a high value or value in excess of expectation. * *adj* (*goods*) high quality.

premolar *adj* situated in front of a molar tooth. * *n* any of the eight teeth in adult humans present in pairs between each of the four canine teeth and each first molar.

premonition *n* a foreboding; a feeling of something about to happen.—**premonitory** *adj*.

prenatal *adj* before birth.

prenatal diagnosis *see* **amniocentesis**.

pre-nomen *n* (*Egypt*) one of the five names making up the king's formal title. Written inside a cartouche, it is also known as the *nsw-bty* name, from the accompanying phrase meaning "He of the Sedge and the Bee," or *neb tawy* name "Lord of the Two Lands," both expressing the dual kingship.

Prenzell *n* **Robert** (1866–1941) Austrian-born potter who produced pieces in the "Gumnut Nouveau" style, a sophisticated Australian version of Art Nouveau.

preoccupation *n* a concern that prevents thought of other things; mental absorption; business that takes precedence; preoccupancy.

preoccupied *adj* absent-minded, lost in thought; (*with* **with**) having one's attention completely taken up by.

preoccupy *vt* (**preoccupying, preoccupied**) to take possession of beforehand; to engross, fill the thoughts of.

preordain *vt* to ordain beforehand.—**preordination** *n*.

prep *abbr* = preparatory school; preparation; preparatory; prepare; preposition.

PREP *abbr* = post-registration education and practice (nursing).

prepaid *see* **prepay**.

preparation *n* the act of preparing; a preparatory measure; something prepared, as a medicine, cosmetic, etc.

preparative *adj* preparatory. * *n* something that prepares the way.—**preparatively** *adv*.

preparatory *adj* serving to prepare; introductory. * *adv* by way of preparation; in a preparatory manner.—**preparatorily** *adv*.

preparatory school *n* a private school that prepares students for an advanced school or college.—*also* **prep** (**school**).

prepare *vt* to make ready in advance; to fit out, equip; to cook; to instruct, teach; to put together. * *vi* to make oneself ready.—**preparedly** *adv*.

prepared *adj* subjected to a special process or treatment.

preparedness *n* the state of being prepared, esp for waging war.

prepay *vt* (**prepaying, prepaid**) to pay in advance.—**prepayment** *n*.

prepense *adj* premeditated.

preponderant *adj* being greater in number, amount, importance, weight, etc; predominant.—**preponderance, preponderancy** *n*.—**preponderantly** *adv*.

preponderate *vi* to be greater in number, amount, influence, etc; to predominate, prevail; to weigh more.—**preponderation** *n*.

preposition *n* a word used before a noun or pronoun to show its relation to another part of the sentence.—**prepositional** *adj*.

prepositive *adj, n* (*gram*) (a particle or word) which can be attached as a prefix to a word.

prepossess *vt* to impress favorably; to prejudice.

prepossessing *adj* impressing favorably; attractive.—**prepossessingly** *adv*.

prepossession *n* a prepossessed state; a preconceived opinion or judgement.

preposterous *adj* ridiculous; laughable; absurd.—**preposterously** *adv*.—**preposterousness** *n*.

prepotency *n* the state of being prepotent; (*biol*) a dominant hereditary influence.

prepotent *adj* very or more powerful; (*biol*) having a dominant hereditary influence.

preppy, preppie *n* (*pl* **preppies**) a person who attends or has graduated from an expensive preparatory school; a person who acts or dresses in the style of a preppy. * *adj* (**preppier, preppiest**) of or like a preppy; expensive, classically fashionable.—**preppiness** *n*.

prep school *see* **preparatory school**.

prepuce *n* the loose skin at the end of the penis.—*also* **foreskin**.

pre-Raphaelite *adj, n* (a member) of a 19th-century school of artists who imitated the Italian style of painting before Raphael, using brilliant color and minute detail.

Pre-Raphaelite Brotherhood *n* the pre-Rapaelite movement founded in 1848 by Holman Hunt, Millais, and Rossetti.

prerecord *vt* (*radio, TV program*) to record in advance for later broadcasting.—**prerecorded** *adj*.

prerequisite *n* a condition, etc, that must be fulfilled prior to something else. * *adj* required beforehand.

prerogative *n* a privilege or right accorded through office or hereditary rank.

pres. *abbr* = present; presidency.

Pres. *abbr* = President.

presage *n* a foreboding or presentiment; an omen. * *vt* to foretell; to have a presentiment of.

Presb. *or* **Presbyt.** *abbr* = Presbyterian.

presbyopia *n* a condition of long-sightedness, usu progressing with age, in which near objects are seen indistinctly, caused by a change in the refractive power of the eye due to the flattening of the lens.

presbyter *n* in the Presbyterian Church, an elder; in the Episcopal Church, a priest or pastor.—**presbyterial** *adj*.

presbyterian *adj* of or denoting government by presbyteries; (*with cap*) of a Presbyterian Church. * *n* a member of a Presbyterian Church.—**Presbyterianism** *n*.

presbytery *n* (*pl* **presbyteries**) in a Presbyterian Church a court composed of pastors and one elder from each church within a district; a district so represented; the eastern part of the chancel of a church; a Roman Catholic priest's house.

preschool *adj* of or for a child between infancy and school age.

prescience *n* foreknowledge.—**prescient** *adj*.

prescind *vt* to cut off, separate. * *vi* (*usu with* **from**) to withdraw one's attention.

prescribe *vt* to designate; to ordain; (*rules*) to lay down; (*medicine, treatment*) to order, advise.—**prescriber** *n*.

prescript *n* an ordnance or decree. * *adj* prescribed, directed.

prescription *n* act of prescribing; (*med*) a written instruction by a physician for the preparation of a drug; (*law*) establishment of a right or title through long use.

prescriptive *adj* prescribing, ordering, advising; based on long use, traditional.—**prescriptively** *adv*.

preselect *vt* to select beforehand, usu according to a particular criterion.—**preselection** *n*.—**preselective** *adj*.

presence *n* being present; immediate surroundings; personal appearance and bearing; impressive bearing, personality, etc; something (as a spirit) felt or believed to be present.

presence of mind *n* readiness of resource in an emergency, etc; the ability to say the right thing.

present[1] *adj* being at the specified place; existing or happening now; (*gram*) denoting action or state now or action that is always true. * *n* the time being; now; the present tense.

present[2] *n* a gift.

present[3] *vt* to introduce someone, esp socially; (*a play, etc*) to bring before the public, exhibit; to make a gift or award; to show; to perform; (*law*) to lay a charge before a court; (*weapon*) to point in a particular direction. * *vi* to present a weapon; to become manifest; to come forward as a patient.

presentable *adj* of decent appearance; fit to go into company.—**presentability** *n*.—**presentably** *adv*.

presentation *n* act of presenting; a display or exhibition; style of presenting; something offered or given; a description or persuasive account; (*med*) the position of a fetus in the uterus.—**presentational** *adj*.

presentative *adj* (*of benefice*) admitting presentation by patron; (*philos*) able to be apprehended directly by the mind

present-day *adj* happening now, current; modern.

presenter *n* a person who presents someone or something; (*radio, TV*) a person who introduces a show, an announcer.

presentient *adj* having a presentiment.

presentiment *n* a premonition, apprehension, esp of evil.

presently *adv* in a short while, soon.

presentment *n* the act of presenting; something which is presented; a representation or delineation; the laying of a formal statement before a court or authority.

present tense *n* (*gram*) the tense expressing an action or state happening now or habitually performed.

preservation *n* the act of preserving or securing; a state of being preserved or repaired.

preservationist *n* someone who undertakes or advocates preservation (as of a biological species or a historic landmark).

preservative *adj* preserving. * *n* something that preserves or has the power of preserving, esp an additive.

preserve *vt* to keep safe from danger; to protect; (*food*) to can, pickle, or prepare for future use; to keep or reserve for personal or special use. * *vi* to make preserves; to raise and protect game for sport. * *n* (*usu pl*) fruit preserved by cooking in sugar; an area restricted for the protection of natural resources, esp one used for regulated hunting, etc; something regarded as reserved for certain persons.—**preservable** *adj*.—**preserver** *n*.

preset *vt* (**presetting, preset**) to set (the controls of an electrical device) in advance.

preshrunk *adj* (*fabric*) treated during manufacture so that it does not shrink in use.

preside *vi* to take the chair or hold the position of authority; to take control or exercise authority.—**presider** *n*.

presidency *n* (*pl* **presidencies**) the office, dignity, term, jurisdiction, or residence of a president.

president *n* the head of state of a republic; the highest officer of a company, club, etc.—**presidential** *adj*.—**presidentially** *adv*.

president-elect *n* a president who has been elected to office but has not yet taken up the post.

presidio *n* (*pl* **presidios**) (*Spain*) a fort or military establishment.

presidium *n* (*pl* **presidiums, presidia**) a presiding committee in a communist organization.

Presley *n* **Elvis [Aaron]** (1935–77) American rock singer and one of the most popular singers in the world in the mid-1950s.

press *vt* to act on with steady force or weight; to push against, squeeze, compress, etc; to squeeze the juice, etc from; (*clothes, etc*) to iron; to embrace closely; to force, compel; to entreat; to emphasize; to trouble; to urge on; (*record*) to make from a matrix. * *vi* to weigh down; to crowd closely; to go forward with determination. * *n* pressure, urgency, etc; a crowd; a machine for crushing, stamping, etc; a machine for printing; a printing or publishing establishment; the gathering and distribution of news and those who perform these functions; newspapers collectively; any of various pressure devices; an upright closet for storing clothes.

press. *abbr* = pressure.

press agency *see* **news agency**.

press agent *n* a person employed to generate favorable publicity in the press.

press box *n* an area reserved for reporters, as in a stadium.

Pressburger, Emeric *see* **Powell, Michael**.

press conference *n* a group interview given to members of the press by a politician, celebrity, etc.

press gallery *n* a gallery for reporters, as in a legislative assembly.

pressing *adj* urgent; calling for immediate attention; importunate. * *n* a number of records made at one time from a master.—**pressingly** *adv*.

pressman *n* (*pl* **pressmen**) a journalist; an operator of a printing press.

pressmark *n* a number showing a book's place in a library.

press officer *n* an employee of a business, government department, etc, who liaises with the press.

press release *n* an official statement intended for publication.

press run *n* (the number of copies produced by) a continuous run of a printing press.

press secretary *n* a person officially in charge of relations with the press for a usu prominent public figure.

press-up *n* an exercise involving raising and lowering the body with the arms.

pressure *n* the act of pressing; a compelling force; a moral force; compression; urgency; constraint; (*physics*) force per unit of area. * *vt* to exert pressure on; to attempt to compel, press.

pressure cooker *n* a strong, sealed pan in which food can be cooked quickly by steam under pressure; (*inf*) a situation beset with emotional or social pressure.

pressure flaking *n* (*archeo*) a method of manufacturing stone implements in which fine flakes were removed by applying pressure by means of a tool.

pressure group *n* a group of people organized to alert public opinion, legislators, etc, to a particular area of interest.

pressure point *n* a point on the body where a blood vessel can be compressed to check bleeding.

pressure sores *see* **bed sores**.

pressure system *n* a body of moving air above or below normal atmospheric pressure.

pressurize *vt* to keep nearly normal atmospheric pressure inside an airplane, etc, as at high altitudes; to pressure.—**pressurization** *n*.—**pressurizer** *n*.

presswork *n* the operation of, or material produced by, a printing press.

Prest. *abbr* = President.

prestidigitation *n* sleight of hand.—**prestidigitator** *n*.

prestige *n* standing in the eyes of people; commanding position in people's minds.

prestigious *adj* imparting prestige or distinction.

prestissimo *adj, adv* (*mus*) (*Italian*) very fast.

presto *adj, adv* (*mus*) (*Italian*) quick; immediately. * *n* (*pl* **prestos**) (*mus*) a lively passage.

presumable *adj* that may be presumed or taken to be true.

presumably *adv* as may be presumed.

presume *vt* to take for granted, suppose. * *vi* to assume to be true; to act without permission; to take liberties; (*with* **on**, **upon**) to take advantage of.—**presumedly** *adv*.—**presumer** *n*.

presuming *adj* venturing without permission; presumptuous.—**presumingly** *adv*.

presumption *n* a supposition; a thing presumed; a strong probability; effrontery.

presumptive *adj* assumed in the absence of contrary evidence; probable.—**presumptively** *adv*.

presumptuous *adj* tending to presume; bold; forward.—**presumptuously** *adv*.—**presumptuousness** *n*.

presuppose *vt* to assume beforehand; to involve as a necessary prior condition.—**presupposition** *n*.

pret. *abbr* = preterit.

pretence *see* **pretense**.

pretend *vti* to claim, represent, or assert falsely; to feign, make believe; to lay claim (to).

pretended *adj* feigned; ostensible; untrue; insincerely asserted or claimed.—**pretendedly** *adv*.

pretender *n* a person who makes a pretense; a claimant to a title.

pretense *n* the act of pretending; a hypocritical show; a fraud, a sham.—*also* **pretence**.

pretension *n* a false claim; affectation; assumption of superiority.

pretentious *adj* claiming great importance; ostentatious.—**pretentiously** *adv*.—**pretentiousness** *n*.

preterit, preterite (*gram*) *adj* denoting past action. * *n* the past tense.

preterition *n* omission; (*theology*) the doctrine of the passing over of the non-elect by God.

preternatural *adj* out of the regular course of things, abnormal.

pretext *n* a pretended reason to conceal a true one; an excuse.

Pretoria *n* administrative capital city of South Africa.

prettify *vt* (**prettifying, prettified**) to make pretty.—**prettifaction** *n*.

pretty *adj* (**prettier, prettiest**) attractive in a dainty, graceful way. * *adv* (*inf*) fairly, moderately. * *n* (*pl* **pretties**) (*inf*) a pretty or pleasing person or thing. * *vt* (**prettying, prettied**) (*with* **up**) (*inf*) to make pretty.—**prettily** *adv*.—**prettiness** *n*.

pretzel *n* a hard, brittle, salted biscuit, often formed in a loose knot.

prevail *vi* to overcome; to predominate; to be customary or in force.

prevailing *adj* generally accepted, widespread; predominant.—**prevailingly** *adv*.

prevailing wind *n* the wind direction most often recorded at a given location.

prevalent *adj* current; predominant; widely practiced or experienced.—**prevalence** *n*.—**prevalently** *adv*.

prevaricate *vi* to make evasive or misleading statements.—**prevarication** *n*.—**prevaricator** *n*.

prevenient *adj* preceding; anticipating; aiming at prevention.

prevent *vt* to keep from happening; to hinder.—**preventable, preventible** *adj*.—**preventably, preventibly** *adv*.—**preventer** *n*.

preventative maintenance *n* a planned system of maintenance that aims to minimize or eliminate breakdown in equipment and machinery by a program of regular inspection and repairs.

prevention *n* a preventing or being prevented; a hindrance; a preventive.

preventive, preventative *adj* serving to prevent, precautionary. * *n* something used to prevent disease.—**preventively** *adv*.—**preventiveness** *n*.

preventive medicine *n* the branch of medicine that seeks to prolong life by prophylaxis or by early diagnosis (e.g. cervical smear), or to prevent the occurrence of a disease by encouraging a healthy lifestyle.

preview *n* an advance, restricted showing, as of a movie; a showing of scenes from a movie to advertise it. * *vt* to view or show in advance of public presentation; to give a preliminary survey.

Previn *n* **André** (1929–) American (German-born) conductor, pianist, and composer, esp of movie scores for which he won four Oscars. A highly respected jazz pianist, his compositions include concertos for violin, sitar, and guitar, and many pieces for piano.

previous *adj* coming before in time or order; prior, former.—**previously** *adv*.—**previousness** *n*.

prewar *adj* before a war.

prey *n* an animal killed for food by another; a victim. * *vi* (*with* **on**, **upon**) to seize and devour prey; (*person*) to victimize; to weigh heavily on the mind.

PRF *abbr* = pulse repetition frequency.

PRG *abbr* = Producer Responsibility Group.

PRI *abbr* = Penal Reform International.

Priam *n* (*Greek myth*) king of Troy at the time of the Trojan War, husband of Hecuba, and father of Hector, Paris, Helenus, Troilus, Creusa, and Cassandra.

priapism *n* (*med*) abnormally prolonged penile erection.

Priapus *n* (*Greek myth*) a Phrygian god of fertility, represented as being very ugly and satyr-like with huge genitals.—**priapic** *adj*.

PRIBA *abbr* (*Brit*) = President of the Royal Institute of British Architects.

price *n* the amount, usu in money, paid for anything; the cost of obtaining some benefit; value, worth. * *vt* to set the price of something; to estimate a price; (*with* **out of the market**) to deprive by raising prices excessively.

price competition *n* competition between rival companies that is based on price.

price control *n* government regulation of the maximum or minimum price levels of basic goods and services.

price discrimination *n* the practice of selling the same products at different prices to different buyers.

price index *n* an index number relating the change in the prices of a group of commodities with reference to a chosen base period.

priceless *adj* very expensive; invaluable; (*inf*) very amusing, odd, or absurd.—**pricelessly** *adv*.

price support *n* government intervention to maintain prices (e.g. of raw materials) at a certain level.

price war *n* a period of commercial competition marked by repeated cutting of prices among competitors.

pricey *adj* (**pricier, priciest**) (*inf*) expensive.—*also* **pricy**.

prick *n* a sharp point; a puncture or piercing made by a sharp point; the wound or sensation inflicted; a qualm (of conscience); (*vulgar*) penis; (*offensive*) a spiteful person usu with authority. * *vti* to affect with anguish, grief, or remorse; to pierce slightly; to cause a sharp pain to; to goad, spur; (*the ears*) to erect; (*with* **out**) to transfer seedlings.

pricker *n* a thing that pricks, esp a prickle or thorn.

pricket *n* a buck in its second year.

prickle *n* a thorn, spine or bristle; a pricking sensation. * *vti* to feel or cause to feel a pricking sensation.

prickly *adj* (**pricklier, prickliest**) having prickles; tingling; irritable.—**prickliness** *n*.

prickly heat *n* a skin eruption caused by inflammation of the sweat glands.

prickly pear *n* (the pear-shaped fruit of) any of various cactuses with flattened spiny joints native to arid regions of America.

pride *n* feeling of self-worth or esteem; excessive self-esteem; conceit; a sense of one's own importance; a feeling of elation due to success; the cause of this; splendor; a herd (of lions). * *vti* (*reflex*) (*with* **in** *or* **on**) to be proud of; to take credit for.—**prideful** *adj*.

priedieu *n* a desk with a low rest for kneeling upon while working or praying.

prier *n* one who pries.—*also* **pryer**.

priest *n* in various churches, a person authorized to perform sacred rites; an Anglican, Eastern Orthodox, or Roman Catholic clergyman ranking below a bishop.

priestcraft *n* the work of a priest and its related skills; (*derog*) the schemes used by priests to get power and wealth.

priestess *n* a priest who is a woman; a woman regarded as a leader (as of a movement).

priesthood *n* the office of priest; priests collectively.

Priestley *n* **J[ohn] B[oynton]** (1891–1984) English novelist and dramatist whose huge output includes the novels *The Good Companions* and *Angel Pavement*, and the plays *Time and the Conways* and the much staged mystery *An Inspector Calls*.

priestly *adj* (**priestlier, priestliest**) of or befitting a priest.—**priestliness** *n*.

prig *n* a smug, self-righteous person.—**priggery, priggism** *n*.

priggish *adj* tiresomely precise; strait-laced.—**priggishly** *adv*.—**priggishness** *n*.

prim *adj* (**primmer, primmest**) proper, formal, and precise in manner; demure. * *vti* (**primming, primmed**) to make prim; to assume a prim expression.—**primly** *adv*.—**primness** *n*.

prim. *abbr* = primary; primate; primitive.

prima ballerina *n* (*pl* **prima ballerinas**) the principal female dancer in a ballet company.

primacy *n* (*pl* **primacies**) the office of primate; the state of being first.

prima donna *n* (*pl* **prima donnas**) the leading female singer in an opera; (*inf*) a temperamental person.

prima facie *adv* (*Latin*) at first sight. * *adj* true, valid, or sufficient at first impression; self-evident; legally sufficient to establish a fact unless disproved.

prima gravida *n* (*med*) a woman in her first pregnancy.

primal *adj* primeval; original; primitive; fundamental.

primarily *adv* mainly.

primary *adj* first; earliest; original; first in order of time; chief; elementary. * *n* (*pl* **primaries**) a person or thing that is highest in rank, importance, etc; a preliminary election at which candidates are chosen for the final election.

primary color *n* one of the three colors from which all others except black can be obtained: red, blue, and yellow.

primary document *see* **client document**.

primary school *n* a school for children up to the third or fourth grade of elementary school and sometimes kindergarten.

primary storage *n* (*comput*) a computer's main RAM or ROM, unlike secondary storage such as hard disks, compact disks, and optical disks.

primate[1] *n* any of the highest order of mammals, including man.—**primatial** *adj*.

primate[2] *n* an archbishop or the highest ranking bishop in a province, etc.—**primateship** *n*.

prime[1] *adj* first in rank, importance, or quality; chief; (*math*) of a number, divisible only by itself and 1. * *n* the best time; the height of perfection; full maturity; full health and strength.—**primeness** *n*.

prime[2] *vt* to prepare or make something ready; to pour liquid into (a pump) or powder into (a firearm); to paint on a primer.

prime costs *see* **direct costs**.

prime focus *n* the point at which incident light from the primary mirror in a reflecting telescope focuses.

prime meridian *n* the circle of zero longitude on a planet.

prime minister *n* the head of the government in a parliamentary democracy.

primer[1] *n* a simple book for teaching; a small introductory book on a subject.

primer[2] *n* a detonating device; a first coat of paint or oil.

prime rate *n* the lowest interest rate available to a bank's trusted creditors.

prime time *n* (*radio, TV*) the hours when the largest audience is available.

primeval *adj* of the first age of the world; primitive.

primeval fireball *n* an early phase of the universe which was swamped with high-energy radiation.

priming *n* a preliminary coating (of paint); a powder used to explode a charge.

primip. *abbr* = primipara.

primipara *n* (*pl* **primiparas, primiparae**) (*obstetrics*) a woman due to give birth to her first child, or who has given birth to only one child.—**primiparous** *adj*.

primitive *adj* of the beginning or the earliest times; crude; simple; basic; (*art*) belonging to the pre-Renaissance period. * *n* a primitive person or thing.—**primitively** *adv*.—**primitiveness** *n*.

primo *n* (*pl* **primos, primi**) (*mus*) the leading part in a duet or ensemble.

primogenitor *n* an ancestor or forefather; an earliest ancestor.

primogeniture *n* the condition of being the first-born child; (*law*) the right of inheritance of the eldest child.—**primogenitary** *adj*.

primordial *adj* earliest; primeval; fundamental; primitive.—**primordially** *adv*.

primp *vti* to dress (oneself) up.

primrose *n* a perennial plant with pale yellow flowers.

primrose path *n* the path of self-indulgence and (sensual) pleasure.

primula *n* any of a genus of plants that includes the primrose, cowslip, etc.

primum mobile *n* the first movement or cause of motion; (*astron*) the tenth and outermost of the imaginary spheres in the Ptolemaic system, which was supposed to revolve from East to West once every 24 hours, carrying the other spheres with it.

prin. *abbr* = principal; principally; principle; principle; principles.

prince *n* the son of a sovereign; a ruler ranking below a king; the head of a principality; any pre-eminent person.—**princedom** *n*.

princeling *n* a young prince; a petty ruler.

princely *adj* (**princelier, princeliest**) of or like a prince; lavish, generous; regal.—**princeliness** *n*.

princess *n* a daughter of a sovereign; the wife of a prince; one outstanding in a specified respect.

principal *adj* first in rank or importance; chief. * *n* a principal person; a person who organizes; the head of a college or school; the leading player in a ballet, opera, etc; (*law*) the person who commits a crime; a person for whom another acts as agent; a capital sum lent or invested; a main beam or rafter.—**principalship** *n*.

principality *n* (*pl* **principalities**) the position of responsibility of a principal; the rank and territory of a prince.

principally *adv* mainly.

principal subject *n* (*mus*) the first subject in a sonata form or a rondo.

principle *n* a basic truth; a law or doctrine used as a basis for others; a moral code of conduct; a chemical constituent with a characteristic quality; a scientific law explaining a natural action; the method of a thing's working.

principled *adj* having, or acting in line with, moral principles.

prink *vti* to dress (oneself) up; to preen oneself.

print *vti* to stamp (a mark, letter, etc) on a surface; to produce (on paper, etc) the impressions of inked type, etc; to produce (a book, etc); to write in letters resembling printed ones; to make (a photographic print). * *n* a mark made on a surface by pressure; the impression of letters, designs, etc, made from inked type, a plate, or block; an impression made by a photomechanical process; a photographic copy, esp from a negative.

print. *abbr* = printing.

printable *adj* able or fit to be printed.—**printability** *n*.

printed circuit *n* an electronic circuit whose connections are printed on metal-coated board.

printer *n* a person engaged in printing; a machine for printing from; a device that produces printout.

printer font *n* (*comput*) a font that a printer keeps in memory and uses to produce output on a page.

printer port *n* (*comput*) a port or slot on the computer to which a printer is connected.

printing *n* the activity, skill, or business of producing printed matter; a style of writing using capital letters; the total number of books, etc, printed at one time (—*also* **impression**).

printing press *n* a machine used for printing.

printmaking *adj* the art or craft of making print or prints.—**printmaker** *n*.

printout *n* the printed output of a computer.

print queue *n* (*comput*) a list of files to be printed that are temporarily held by a print spooler.

print run *n* a single printing of a book or other printed material.

print spooler *n* (*comput*) a utility program that maintains a queue of files waiting to be printed.

prior[1] *adj* previous; taking precedence (as in importance).

prior[2] *n* the superior ranking below an abbot in a monastery; the head of a house or group of houses in a religious community.—**prioress** *nf*.

Prior *n* **Matthew** (1664–1721) English poet, diplomat, and spy whose first important work, *The Hind and Panther Transvers'd*, was a satire on Dryden's defense of Roman Catholicism.

priorate *n* the office or status of a prior.

prior charges *npl* interest payments on debentures and loan stock that must be paid by a company before any of its shareholders can be paid dividend payments.

priority *n* (*pl* **priorities**) precedence in rank, time, or place; preference; something requiring specified attention.

priory *n* (*pl* **priories**) a religious house under a prior or prioress.

Prisca *n* **Saint** (*d.* 265) also known as Priscilla, a Roman girl and Christian martyr. Aged thirteen, she was thrown to a lion, which lay down at her feet and licked them. She had her flesh torn by hooks and pincers and later was beheaded. Her feast day is January18.

Priscilla *n* (*Bible*) wife of Aquila and a leader of the early Church. *See also* **Aquila**.

prise *vt* to pry, to force (open, up) with a lever, etc.

prism *n* (*geom*) a solid whose ends are similar, equal, and parallel plane figures and whose sides are parallelograms; a transparent body of this form usu with triangular ends used for dispersing or reflecting light.

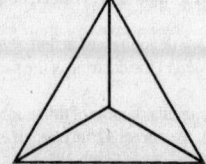

prismatic *adj* of or like a prism; (*colors*) formed by a prism; brilliant.—**prismatically** *adv*.

prismatic astrolabe *n* an instrument used to determine accurately the positions of stars.

prison *n* a building used to house convicted criminals for punishment and suspects remanded in custody while awaiting trial; a penitentiary or jail.

prisoner *n* a person held in prison or under arrest; a captive; a person confined by a restraint.

prisoner of conscience *n* a person imprisoned for their political beliefs.

prisoner of war *n* a member of a military force taken prisoner by the enemy during combat.

prissy *adj* (**prissier, prissiest**) (*inf*) fussy; prim, prudish.—**prissily** *adv*.—**prissiness** *n*.

Pristina *n* a city in Yugoslavia (FRY).

pristine *adj* pure; in an original, unspoiled condition.

Pritchard *n* **Jack** (1899–1993) British designer and manufacturer of plywood furniture.

Pritchett *n* **Sir V[ictor] S[awdon]** (1900–97) English short-story writer, novelist, essayist, and critic who is best known for his excellent short stories. His critical works, e.g. *The Living Novel*, have been highly praised for their shrewd insights into the creative process.

prithee *interj* (*arch*) pray, please (= "I pray thee").

priv. *abbr* = privative.

privacy *n* (*pl* **privacies**) being private; seclusion; secrecy; one's private life.

private *adj* of or concerning a particular person or group; not open to or controlled by the public; for an individual person; not holding public office; secret. * *n* (*pl*) the genitals; an enlisted man of the lowest military rank in the army.—**privately** *adv*.

private bill *n* a bill presented to a legislature on behalf of a private individual or corporation.

private detective *n* a person engaged privately to investigate crime or make inquiries.

privateer *n* a privately owned ship commissioned by a government to seize and plunder enemy vessels; a captain or crew member of such a ship.

private enterprise *n* an economic system in which business activity is operated by private individuals or companies under private not state control.

private income *n* income from sources (e.g. investments) other than employment.

private ledger *n* a ledger that contains confidential accounts and to which access is restricted to a few authorized personnel.

private limited company *see* **limited company**.

private parts *npl* the genitals.

private school *n* a school operated independently of state control, usu financed by fees.

private sector *n* economic activity independent of direct state control.

privation *n* being deprived; want of comforts or necessities; hardship.

privative *adj* depriving; denoting the absence of something.

privatization *n* the transference of a publicly owned company or industry from the state to the private sector. *See also* **nationalization**.

privatize *vt* to restore private ownership by buying back publicly owned stock in a company.

privet *n* a white-flowered evergreen shrub used for hedges.

privilege *n* a right or special benefit enjoyed by a person or a small group; a prerogative. * *vt* to bestow a privilege on.

privileged *adj* having or enjoying privileges; not subject to disclosure in a court of law.

privity *n* (*pl* **privities**) private knowledge; (*law*) a legally recognized relationship.

priv. pr. *abbr* = privately printed.

privy *adj* private; having access to confidential information. * *n* (*pl* **privies**) a latrine; (*law*) a person with an interest in an action.—**privily** *adv*.

Prix *n* **Wolf-Dieter** (1942–) Austrian architect who designed most of the furniture for the Coop Himmelblau, in Vienna.

prize *n* an award won in competition or a lottery; a reward given for merit; a thing worth striving for. * *adj* given as, rewarded by, a prize. * *vt* to value highly.

prizefight *n* a professional boxing match.—**prizefighter** *n*.

prm *abbr* = personal radiation monitor.

prn, PRN *abbr* (*Latin*) = *pro re nata*, "as the situation may require."

pro[1] *adv*, *prep* in favor of. * *n* (*pl* **pros**) an argument for a proposal or motion.

pro[2] *adj* professional. * *n* (*pl* **pros**) a professional.

pro. *abbr* = progressive.

pro- *prefix* acting; vice-; favoring; before; forth; according to.

PRO *abbr* = public relations officer.

proa *n* a long, narrow, Malay boat propelled by oars and sails.

pro-am *adj* (*sports events*) involving professionals and amateurs.

pro and con *see* **pros and cons**.

prob. *abbr* = probable; probably; problem.

probability *n* (*pl* **probabilities**) that which is probable; likelihood; (*math*) the ratio of the chances in favor of an event to the total number.

probable *adj* likely; to be expected.

probable cause *n* a good reason for believing that a criminal charge is justified.

probably *adv* without much doubt.

probang *n* (*med*) a flexible rod with a sponge at the end, used to clear obstructions from, or apply medication to, the gullet.

probate *n* the validating of a will; the certified copy of a will; matters within the jurisdiction of a probate court.

probation *n* testing of character or skill; release from prison under supervision by a probation officer; the state or period of being on probation.—**probationary, probational** *adj*.

probation officer *n* an official who watches over prisoners on probation.

probationer *n* a person (as a newly admitted student nurse or teacher) whose fitness is being tested during a trial period; a convicted offender on probation.

probe *n* a flexible surgical instrument for exploring a wound; a device, as an unmanned spacecraft, used to obtain information about an environment; an investigation. * *vt* to explore with a probe; to examine closely; to investigate.—**prober** *n*.

probity *n* honesty, integrity, uprightness.

problem *n* a question for solution; a person, thing or matter difficult to cope with; a puzzle; (*math*) a proposition stating something to be done; an intricate unsettled question.

problematical, problematic *adj* presenting a problem; questionable; uncertain.—**problematically** *adv*.

proboscidian, proboscidean *adj* pertaining to the class of mammals which includes the elephant. * *n* an animal with a proboscis.

proboscis *n* (*pl* **proboscises, proboscides**) an elephant's trunk; a long snout; an insect's sucking organ; (*humorous*) a (large) nose.

proc. *abbr* = proceedings; process; proctor.

procaine *n* a synthetic compound used as a local anesthetic.

procedure *n* an established mode of conducting business, esp in law or in a meeting; a practice; a prescribed or traditional course; a step taken as part of an established order of steps.—**procedural** *adj*.—**procedurally** *adv*.

proceed *vi* to go on, esp after stopping; to come from; to continue; to carry on; to issue; to take action; to go to law.

proceeding *n* an advance or going forward; (*pl*) steps, action, in a lawsuit; (*pl*) published records of a society, etc.

proceeds *npl* the total amount of money brought in; the net amount received.

process *n* a course or state of going on; a series of events or actions; a method of operation; forward movement; (*law*) a court summons; the whole course of proceedings in a legal action; (*med*) a protuberance or projecting part of a bone or other part. * *vt* to handle something following set procedures; (*food, etc*) to prepare by a special process; (*law*) to take action; (*film*) to develop.

process-focused layout *or* **process-oriented layout** *n* a factory or office layout in which all the production operations of a similar kind are grouped together in the same part of the factory or department.

processing *n* (*comput*) the normal operation of the computer acting upon the input data according to the instructions of the program in use.

procession *n* a group of people marching in order, as in a parade.

processional *adj* pertaining to, or used in, processions. * *n* a processional hymn or hymn book.

processor *n* one who or that which processes; (*comput*) a central processing unit.

pro-choice *adj* supporting a woman's right to choose whether or not to have an abortion.

proclaim *vt* to announce publicly and officially; to tell openly; to praise.—**proclaimer** *n*.

proclamation *n* the act of proclaiming; an official notice to the public.—**proclamatory** *adj*.

proclitic *n, adj* (a word) so closely connected with the following word as to lose its accent.

proclivity *n* (*pl* **proclivities**) a tendency or inclination.

Procne *n* (*Greek myth*) a daughter of King Pandion of Athens and wife of Tereus, who was changed into a swallow.

proconsul *n* a governor of a colony or province.—**proconsular** *adj*.—**proconsulate, proconsulship** *n*.

Procopé *n* **Ulla** (1921–68) Finnish ceramicist who produced many designs for Arabia.

procrastinate *vti* to defer action, to delay.—**procrastination** *n*.—**procrastinator** *n*.

procreate *vt* to bring into being, to engender offspring.—**procreation** *n*.—**procreant, procreative** *adj*.—**procreator** *n*.

Procrustean *adj* compelling uniformity by violent means.

Procrustes *n* (*Greek myth*) the Stretcher, a robber who put travelers in a bed, either stretching them to death if they were short, or if they were too tall, cutting off their feet or legs.

proctology *n* the branch of medicine dealing with the rectum.—**proctologic, proctological** *adj*.—**proctologist** *n*.

proctor *n* a person who supervises dormitories and examinations in a school.—**proctorial** *adj*.

procumbent *adj* lying face down, prone; (*bot*) trailing.

procuration *n* procuring; (*law*) the authorization to act on behalf of someone else.

procurator *n* an agent; (*ancient Rome*) a provincial governor or treasurer.

procuratory *n* (*law*) the authorization to act on another person's behalf.

procure *vt* to obtain by effort; to get and make available for sexual intercourse; to bring about. * *vi* to procure women.—**procurable** *adj*.—**procurement** *n*.

procurer *n* one who procures, esp one who supplies prostitutes.—**procuress** *nf*.

Procyon *or* **Alpha Canis Minoris** *n* the brightest star of the Canis Minor constellation, the fifth brightest star in the sky.

prod *vt* (**prodding, prodded**) to poke or jab, as with a pointed stick; to rouse into activity. * *n* the action of prodding; a sharp object; a stimulus.—**prodder** *n*.

prod. *abbr* (*mus, drama*) = produced.

prodigal *adj* wasteful; extravagant; open-handed. * *n* a wastrel; a person who squanders money.—**prodigally** *adv*.

prodigality *n* (*pl* **prodigalities**) the state or quality of being prodigal; extravagance, wastefulness; lavishness.

prodigious *adj* enormous, vast; amazing.—**prodigiously** *adv*.—**prodigiousness** *n*.

prodigy *n* (*pl* **prodigies**) an extraordinary person, thing or act; a gifted child.

produce *vt* to bring about; to bring forward, show; to yield; to cause; to manufacture, make; to give birth to; (*play, movie*) to put before the public. * *vi* to yield something. * *n* that which is produced, esp agricultural products.—**producible** *adj*.—**producibility** *n*.

producer *n* someone who produces, esp a farmer or manufacturer; a person who finances or supervises the putting on of a play or making of a movie; an apparatus or plant for making gas.

producer goods *npl* capital goods.

product *n* a thing produced by nature, industry or art; a result; an outgrowth; (*math*) the number obtained by multiplying two or more numbers together; (*business*) goods and services that are purchased by consumers.

product costs *npl* the total costs of making a product, including direct costs and indirect costs or overheads.

product development *n* a business strategy undertaken by a company to increase sales and profitability.

product differentiation *n* the means by which a supplier's product is distinguished from a similar product made by a competitor.

product diversification *n* a business strategy undertaken by a company to increase sales and profitability and consisting of developing new products for new consumers or markets.

product-focused layout *or* **product-oriented layout** *n* a factory or office layout in which the position of the work stations, equipment, etc, is arranged to suit the needs of the product, the machinery being arranged in the same order and sequence as the operations necessary for production of the product.

product liability *n* the legal liability that manufacturers or others carry for defective products.

product life cycle *n* the course of a product's life from its development and its introduction to the market to its eventual decline when demand falls or it is displaced by a new product.

product line *n* a group of closely related versions of a product, for example a number of versions of a particular make of automobile.

product portfolio *n* a collection of products that are marketed by one company.

production *n* the act of producing; a thing produced; a work presented on the stage or screen or over the air.—**productional** *adj*.

production cost center *n* the part of an organization where production is carried out.

production line *n* a method of production in which a product is manufactured by passing it through a number of operations.

productive *adj* producing or capable of producing; fertile.—**productively** *adv*.—**productiveness** *n*.

productivity *n* the state of being productive; the ratio of the output of a manufacturing business to the input of materials, labor, etc.

productivity agreement *n* an agreement reached between an employer and employees or between employers and unions by which an increase in wages is related to an increase in productivity.

proem *n* a preface or introduction.

Proetus *n* (*Greek myth*) twin brother of Acrisius, who was defeated and expelled by his brother in a dispute for the kingdom of Argos but was finally restored and accepted the city of Tiryns.

Proetz *n* Miroslav (1896–1954) American designer who devised the entire furnishings for the John Lohman House in Connecticut.

Prof., prof. *abbr* = professor.

profane *adj* secular, not sacred; showing no respect for sacred things; irreverent; blasphemous; not possessing esoteric or expert knowledge. * *vt* to desecrate; to debase by a wrong, unworthy or vulgar use.—**profanation** *n*.—**profanely** *adv*.—**profaneness** *n*.—**profaner** *n*.

profanity *n* (*pl* **profanities**) irreverence; a profane act; blasphemy, swearing.

profess *vt* to affirm publicly, declare; to claim to be expert in; to declare in words or appearance only.

professed *adj* openly acknowledged.—**professedly** *adv*.

profession *n* an act of professing; avowal, esp of religious belief; an occupation requiring specialized knowledge and often long and intensive academic preparation; the people engaged in this; affirmation; entry into a religious order.

professional *adj* of or following a profession; conforming to the technical or ethical standards of a profession; earning a livelihood in an activity or field often engaged in by amateurs; having a specified occupation as a permanent career; engaged in by persons receiving financial return; pursuing a line of conduct as though it were a profession. * *n* one who follows a profession; a professional sportsman; one highly skilled in a particular occupation or field.—**professionally** *adv*.

professionalism *n* the methods of professionals; the pursuit of an activity, e.g. a sport, for financial gain.

professor *n* a teacher of the highest rank at an institution of higher education; a teacher.—**professorial** *adj*.—**professorship** *n*.

professoriate, professorate *n* a body of professors.

proffer *vt* to offer, usu something intangible.

proficiency *n* (*pl* **proficiencies**) a being proficient; competence; skill.

proficient *adj* skilled, competent.—**proficiently** *adv*.

profile *n* a side view of the head as in a portrait, drawing, etc; a biographical sketch; a graph representing a person's abilities; (*archit*) the outline of a molding or any part or the whole of a building. * *vt* to represent in profile; to produce (as by writing, drawing, etc) a profile of.

profit *n* gain; the excess of returns over expenditure; the compensation to entrepreneurs resulting from the assumption of risk; (*pl*) the excess returns from a business; advantage, benefit. * *vti* to be of advantage (to), benefit; to gain.—**profitless** *adj*.

profitable *adj* yielding profit, lucrative; beneficial; useful.—**profitably** *adv*.—**profitability** *n*.

profit and loss *n* a statement at the end of an accounting period that summarizes the revenue and expenditure of a business and shows the consequent profit or loss.

profiteer *vi* to make exorbitant profits, esp in wartime. * *n* a person who profiteers.—**profiteering** *n*.

profitless *adj* without profit; useless.

profit margin *n* the difference between the selling price of a product and the costs of producing and selling it.

profit sharing *n* a system by which employees share in the profits of a business.—**profit-sharing** *adj*.

profligate *adj* dissolute; immoral; extravagant. * *n* a profligate person, a libertine.—**profligacy** *n*.—**profligately** *adv*.

pro forma *adj* made or carried out as a formality; provided in advance to prescribe form or describe items.

pro forma invoice *n* an invoice that is sometimes sent to a customer in advance of a transaction before some of the invoice details are known.

profound *adj* at great depth; intellectually deep; abstruse, mysterious.—**profoundly** *adv*.—**profoundness** *n*.

Profumo *n* **John Dennis** (1915–) English Conservative politician and secretary of state for war (1960–63), who resigned after misleading the House of Commons about a sexual affair.

profundity *n* (*pl* **profundities**) great depth of place, knowledge, skill, etc; a profound or abstruse thing.

profuse *adj* abundant; generous; extravagant.—**profusely** *adv*.—**profuseness** *n*.

profusion *n* an abundance.

prog., Prog. *abbr* = progressive.

progenitive *adj* able to bear offspring.

progenitor *n* an ancestor.

progeny *n* (*pl* **progenies**) offspring; descendants; outcome.

progesterone *n* a steroid hormone that is vital in pregnancy. It is produced by the corpus luteum of the ovary when the lining of the uterus is prepared for the implanting of an egg cell.

prognathous, prognathic *adj* having projecting lower jaw.—**prognathism** *n*.

prognosis *n* (*pl* **prognoses**) a prediction; (*med*) a forecast of the course of a disease.

prognostic *adj* predictive (of); foretelling. * *n* a prediction; an omen; a forewarning symptom.

prognostic chart *n* (*meteor*) a weather forecast chart specifying the expected meteorological conditions.

prognosticate *vt* to predict; to presage.—**prognostication** *n*.—**prognosticator** *n*.

progradation *n* the situation that occurs when the beach budget is upset and more material is deposited than is removed.

program *n* a printed list containing details of a ceremony, of the actors in a play, etc; a scheduled radio or television broadcast; a curriculum or syllabus for a course of study; a plan or schedule; a sequence of instructions fed into a computer. * *vti* (**programing, programed** *or* **programming, programmed**) to prepare a plan or schedule; to prepare a plan or schedule to feed a program into a computer; to write a program.—**programable** *adj*.—**programer, programmer** *adj*.—**programatic** *adj*.

programing *n* (*comput*) the procedure involved in writing instructions that the computer will follow to perform a specific task.

programing language *n* (*comput*) a language that is used by computer programmers to write computer routines, e.g. COBOL, BASIC, FORTRAN, Pascal, C, Visual Basic.

program music *n* music which attempts to tell a story or evoke an image. The term was first used by Liszt to describe his symphonic poems. Parts of Beethoven's pastoral symphony can be described as program music.

progress *n* a movement forwards or onwards, advance; satisfactory growth or development; a tour from place to place in stages. * *vi* to move forward, advance; to improve. * *vt* (*project*) to take to completion.

progression *n* progress; advancement by degrees; (*math*) a series of numbers, each differing from the succeeding according to a fixed law; (*mus*) a regular succession of chords.—**progressional** *adj*.

progressive *adj* advancing, improving; proceeding by degrees; continuously increasing; aiming at reforms; (*with cap*) denoting a broadly liberal Progressive Party. * *n* a person who believes in moderate political change, esp social improvement by government action; (*with cap*) a member of a Progressive Party.—**progressively** *adv*.—**progressiveness** *n*.—**progressivism** *n*.

progressive tax *n* a tax, such as income tax, that increases with increases in the base tax.

prohibit *vt* to forbid by law; to prevent.

prohibition *n* the act of forbidding; an order that forbids; a legal ban on the manufacture and sale of alcoholic drinks; (*with cap*) the period (1920–33) when there was a legal ban of alcohol in the US.

prohibitionist *n* an advocate of legally prohibiting the sale of alcohol; (*with cap*) a member of the Prohibition Party.

prohibitive, prohibitory *adj* forbidding; so high as to prevent purchase, use, etc, of something.—**prohibitively** *adv*.

project *n* a plan, scheme; an undertaking; a task carried out by students, etc, involving research. * *vt* to throw forward; (*light, shadow, etc*) to produce an outline of on a distant surface; to make objective or externalize; (*one's voice*) to make heard at a distance; (*feeling, etc*) to attribute to another; to imagine; to estimate, plan, or figure for the future. * *vi* to jut out; to come across vividly; to make oneself heard clearly.

projectile *n* a missile; something propelled by force. * *adj* throwing forward; capable of being thrown forward.

projection *n* the act of projecting or the condition of being projected; a thing projecting; the representation on a plane surface of part of the earth's surface; a projected image; an estimate of future possibilities based on a current trend; a mental image externalized; an unconscious attribution to another of one's own feelings and motives.—**projectional** *adj*.

projectionist *n* a person who operates a projector.

projective *adj* (*geom*) pertaining to projection.

projector *n* an instrument that projects images from transparencies or film; an instrument that projects rays of light; a person who promotes enterprises.

prokaryote, procaryote *n* (*biol*) any organism that lacks a true-membrane nucleus and is either a bacterium or a blue-green alga.

Prokofiev *n* **Sergei Sergeyevich** (1891–1953) Russian composer and pianist whose works include the well-known *Peter and the Wolf* (1936).

prolapse *vi* (*med*) to fall or slip out of place. * *n* a prolapsed condition.

prolapsed intervertebral disk *n* loss of cushioning for the brain and spinal cord usu provided by the intervertebral disks, causing pain (commonly lumbago or sciatica).—*also* **slipped disk**.

prolate *adj* extended; (*spheroid*) elongated at the poles.

prolegomenon *n* (*pl* **prolegomena**) a critical introduction to a text.

proletariat *n* the lowest social or economic class of a community; wage earners; the industrial working class.—**proletarian** *adj, n*.

proliferate *vi* to grow or reproduce rapidly.—**proliferation** *n*.—**proliferative** *adj*.

proliferous *adj* reproducing by budding; producing many offshoots.

prolific *adj* producing abundantly; fruitful.—**prolificacy** *n*.—**prolifically** *adv*.

prolix *adj* verbose, long-winded, tedious.—**prolixity, prolixness** *n*.

prolocutor *n* a chairman or speaker at a convocation, esp of the Anglican Church.

Prolog *abbr* (*comput programing langauge*) = Programing in Logic.

prolog, prologue *n* the introductory lines of a play, speech, or poem; the reciter of these; a preface; an introductory event. * *vt* (**prologing, prologed** *or* **prologuing, prologued**) to provide with a prolog; to usher in.

prolong *vt* to extend or lengthen in space or time; to spin out.—**prolonger** *n*.

prolongation *n* the act of prolonging; an extension or continuation.

prolusion *n* a preliminary essay or article.—**prolusory** *adj*.

prom *n* a dance for a high school or college class.

prom. *abbr* = promontory.

PROM *abbr* (*comput*) = programable read-only memory.

promenade *n* an esplanade; a ball or dance; a leisurely walk. * *vti* to take a promenade (along or through).—**promenader** *n*.

Promenade Concerts *npl* an annual season of concerts given in London's Royal Albert Hall.

Promethean *adj* (*myth*) pertaining to Prometheus[1]; life-giving.

Prometheus[1] *n* (*Greek myth*) one of the Titans, brother of Atlas and Epimetheus, who brought fire from heaven to humans, and was punished by being chained to a rock, where his liver was torn by an eagle.

Prometheus[2] *n* (*astron*) a satellite of Saturn that was discovered in 1980 with another, Pandora.

promethium *n* a radioactive metallic element present in nuclear waste, (*chem symbol*) Pm.

prominence, prominency *n* the state of being prominent; a projection; relative importance; celebrity, fame; (*astron*) a cloud or flame-like structure in the Sun's corona or chromosphere.

prominent *adj* jutting, projecting; standing out, conspicuous; widely and favorably known; distinguished.—**prominently** *adv*.

promiscuity *n* (*pl* **promiscuities**) the state of being promiscuous; promiscuous sexual behavior; an indiscriminate mixture.

promiscuous *adj* indiscriminate, esp in sexual liaisons.—**promiscuously** *adv*.—**promiscuousness** *n*.

promise *n* a pledge; an undertaking to do or not to do something; an indication, as of a successful future. * *vti* to pledge; to undertake; to give reason to expect.—**promiser** *n*.

promisee *n* (*law*) someone to whom a promise is made.

promising *adj* likely to turn out well; hopeful.

promisor *n* (*law*) someone who makes a promise.

promissory *adj* of the nature of or containing a promise.

promissory note *n* a signed note containing a written promise to pay a stated amount at some future date to a specified individual or the bearer.

promo *n* (*pl* **promos**) (*inf*) something used for advertising or publicity, as a pop video or movie trailer.

promontory *n* (*pl* **promontories**) a peak of high land that juts out into a body of water.

promontory fort *n* (*archeo*) a defensive structure built on a promontory.

promote *vt* to encourage; to advocate; to raise to a higher rank; (*employee, student*) to advance from one grade to the next higher grade; (*product*) to encourage sales by advertising, publicity, or discounting.—**promotable** *adj*.

promoter *n* a person who promotes, esp one who organizes and finances a sporting event or pop concert; a substance that increases the activity of a catalyst.

promotion *n* an elevation in position or rank; the furtherance of the sale of merchandise through advertising, publicity, or discounting.—**promotional** *adj*.

prompt *adj* without delay; quick to respond; immediate; of or relating to prompting actors. * *vt* to urge; to inspire; (*actor*) to remind of forgotten words, etc (as in a play). * *n* something that reminds; a time limit for payment of an account; the contract by which this time is fixed; (*comput*) a symbol or message that informs the user that the computer is ready to accept data or input of some form.—**promptly** *adv*.

prompt day *or* **prompt date** *n* the day or date on which payment becomes due for the purchase of goods; the date on which a contract commodity exchange matures.

prompter *n* one that prompts, esp a person who sits offstage and reminds actors of forgotten lines.

promptitude *n* quickness of decision and action; readiness; alacrity; punctuality.

promptness *n* alacrity in action or decision; quickness; punctuality.

promulgate *vt* to publish, spread abroad; to put (a law) into effect; to proclaim as coming into force.—**promulgation** *n*.—**promulgator** *n*.

pron. *abbr* = pronominal; pronoun; pronounced; pronunciation.

pronaos *n* (*archit*) an area behind the portico and in front of the naos, in a Greek temple.

pronate *vt* (*hand, arm*) to turn so that the palm is downwards.—**pronation** *n*.

pronator *n* a pronating muscle.

prone *adj* face downwards; lying flat, prostrate; inclined or disposed (to).—**pronely** *adv*.—**proneness** *n*.

prong *n* a spike of a fork or other forked object.—**pronged** *adj*.

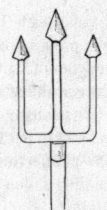

pronghorn *n* a small-horned ruminant mammal of the deserts of North America that resembles an antelope.

pro. no. *abbr* (*accounts*) = progressive number.

pronom. *abbr* = pronominal.

pronominal *adj* pertaining to pronouns; acting as a pronoun.

pronoun *n* a word used to represent a noun (e.g. *I, he, she, it*).

pronounce *vt* to utter, articulate; to speak officially, pass (judgment); to declare formally.—**pronounceable** *adj*.—**pronouncer** *n*.

pronounced *adj* marked, noticeable.—**pronouncedly** *adv*.

pronouncement *n* a formal announcement, declaration; a confident assertion.

pronto *adv* (*inf*) quickly.

pronunciation *n* articulation; the way a word is pronounced.

proof *n* evidence that establishes the truth; the fact, act, or process of validating; test; demonstration; a sample from type, etc, for correction; a trial print from a photographic negative; the relative strength of an alcoholic liquor. * *adj* resistant; impervious, impenetrable. * *vt* to make proof against (water).

proof spirit *n* a mixture of alcohol and water in fixed proportions used as a standard of strength.

proofread *vti* (**proofreading, proofread**) to read and correct (printed proofs).—**proofreader** *n*.

prop[1] *vt* (**propping, propped**) to support by placing something under or against. * *n* a rigid support; a thing or person giving support.

prop[2] *see* **property**.

prop[3] *n* a propeller.

prop. *abbr* = properly; property; proposition.

PROP *abbr* = Preservation of the Rights of Prisoners.

propaedeutic *adj* pertaining to propaedeutics, the preliminary knowledge or instruction necessary for the study of any art or science.

propagable *adj* which can be propagated.

propaganda *n* the organized spread of ideas, doctrines, etc, to promote a cause; the ideas, etc, so spread.—**propagandism** *n*.—**propagandist** *n, adj*.

propagandize *vt* to spread by propaganda; to use propaganda among. * *vi* to spread propaganda; to use propaganda.

propagate *vti* to cause (a plant or animal) to reproduce itself; (*plant or animal*) to reproduce; (*ideas, customs, etc*) to spread.—**propagation** *n*.—**propagative** *adj*.

propagator *n* a device consisting of a box with a ventilated lid, used to regulate growing conditions for seeds and young plants.

propane *n* a colorless flammable gas obtained from petroleum and used as a fuel.

pro patria (*Latin*) for one's country.

propel *vt* (**propelling, propelled**) to drive or move forward.

propellant, propellent *n* a thing that propels; an explosive charge; rocket fuel; the gas that activates an aerosol spray.

propeller, propellor *n* a mechanism to impart drive; a device having two or more blades in a revolving hub for propelling a ship or aircraft.

propensity *n* (*pl* **propensities**) a natural inclination; disposition, tendency.

proper *adj* own, individual, peculiar; appropriate, fit; correct, conventional; decent, respectable; in the most restricted sense; (*sl*) thorough.

proper motion *n* (*astron*) the combination of the true motion of a star in space and the relative motion of the Solar System to produce an apparent motion for the star across the celestial sphere.

proper noun *n* the name of a particular person, place, etc.

properly *adv* in the right way; justifiably; (*sl*) thoroughly.

property *n* (*pl* **properties**) a quality or attribute; a distinctive feature or characteristic; one's possessions; real estate, land; a movable article used in a stage setting (—*also* **prop**).

property bond *n* a bond that is issued by a life-assurance company, the premiums for which are invested in a property-owning fund.

prophase *n* (*biol*) the first stage of meiosis or mitosis in cells of eukaryotes.

prophecy *n* (*pl* **prophecies**) a message of divine will and purpose; prediction.

prophesy *vti* (**prophesying, prophesied**) to predict with assurance or on the basis of mystic knowledge; to foretell.—**prophesier** *n*.

prophet *n* a religious leader regarded as, or claiming to be, divinely inspired; one who predicts the future.—**prophetess** *nf*.

prophetic, prophetical *adj* of a prophet or prophecy; prophesying events.—**prophetically** *adv*.

prophylactic *adj* guarding against disease. * *n* a medicine which guards against disease; a condom.

prophylaxis *n* preventive treatment.

propinquity *n* nearness of time, place or relationship.

propitiate *vt* to appease, conciliate.—**propitiation** *n*.—**propitiator** *n*.

propitious *adj* favorable, encouraging; auspicious, opportune.—**propitiously** *adv*.—**propitiousness** *n*.

propolis *n* a resin from tree buds, collected by bees.

proponent *n* someone who makes a proposal, or proposition.

Propontis *n* the ancient name of the Sea of Marmara.

proportion *n* the relationship between things in size, quantity, or degree; ratio; symmetry, balance; comparative part or share; (*math*) the equality of two ratios; a share or quota; (*pl*) dimensions. * *vt* to put in proper relation with something else; to make proportionate (to).—**proportionment** *n*.—**proportionable** *adj*.

proportional *adj* of proportion; aiming at due proportion; proportionate.—**proportionality** *n*.—**proportionally** *adv*.

proportional representation *n* an electoral system arranged so that minorities are represented in proportion to their strength.

proportional sizing *n* (*comput*) the process by which the user changes the size of a graphics object without altering the relative dimensions of the image.

proportional spacing *n* (*comput*) a font in which each letter takes up space relative to the size of that letter.

proportionate *adj* in due proportion, corresponding in amount. * *vt* to make proportionate.—**proportionately** *adv*.

proposal *n* a scheme, plan, or suggestion; an offer of marriage.

propose *vt* to present for consideration; to suggest; to intend; to announce the drinking of a toast to; (*person*) to nominate; to move as a resolution. * *vi* to make an offer (of marriage).—**proposer** *n*.

proposed dividend *n* a dividend that has been recommended to be paid by the directors of a company but that has not yet been paid.

proposition *n* a proposal for consideration; a plan; a request for sexual intercourse; (*inf*) a proposed deal, as in business; (*inf*) an undertaking to be dealt with; (*math*) a problem to be solved.—**propositional** *adj*.

propound *vt* to put forward (a question, suggestion, etc).

propr. *abbr* = proprietor.

proprietary *adj* characteristic of a proprietor; privately owned and managed and run as a profit-making organization; (*drug*) made and distributed under a tradename; (*comput*) (technology) developed and owned by a person or company who restricts the use of the technology.. * *n* (*pl* **proprietaries**) proprietors collectively; a drug protected by secrecy, patent, or copyright against free competition.

proprietor *n* one with legal title to something; an owner.—**proprietorial** *adj*.—**proprietorially** *adv*.

propriety *n* (*pl* **proprieties**) correctness of conduct or taste; fear of offending against rules of behavior, esp between the sexes; (*pl*) the customs and manners of polite society.

Propst *n* **Bob** (1921–) American designer who designed the 1968 Action Office system for Herman Miller.

proptosis *n* (*pl* **proptoses**) (*med*) a prolapse, esp of the eyeball.

propulsion *n* the act of propelling; something that propels.—**propulsive, propulsory** *adj*.

propylaeum, propylon *n* (*pl* **propylaea, propylons** *or* **propyla**) a porch or entrance to a temple.

pro rata *adj, adv* in proportion.

prorate *vti* to divide or distribute proportionately.

prorogue *vt* to terminate a session (of a parliament, etc) without dissolving it.

pros. *abbr* = prosody.

prosaic *adj* commonplace, matter-of-fact, dull.—**prosaically** *adv*.—**prosaicness** *n*.

prosaism *n* the quality of being prosaic; a word, saying, etc demonstrating this.

pros and cons *npl* considerations for and against an action, cause, idea, etc.

Pros. Atty. *abbr* = prosecuting attorney.

proscenium *n* (*pl* **prosceniums**) the part of a stage in front of the curtain.

proscribe *vt* to outlaw; to denounce; to prohibit the use of.—**proscriber** *n*.

proscription *n* the act of proscribing; the condition of being proscribed; outlawry; interdiction.—**proscriptive** *adj*.—**proscriptively** *adv*.

prose *n* ordinary language, as opposed to verse. * *adj* in prose; humdrum, dull. * *vti* to talk tediously; to turn into prose.

prose poem *n* a prose work of poetic style.

prosecute *vt* to bring legal action against; to pursue. * *vi* to institute and carry on a legal suit or prosecution.—**prosecutable** *adj*.

prosecution *n* the act of prosecuting, esp by law; the prosecuting party in a legal case.

prosecutor *n* a person who prosecutes, esp in a criminal court.

proselyte *n* a convert, esp to Judaism. * *vti* to proselytize.

proselytize *vti* to try to make a convert (of).—**proselytizer** *n*.

prosenchyma *n* (*bot*) tissue of elongated cells with little protoplasm.—**prosenchymatous** *adj*.

Proserpina *n* the Roman name of Persephone.

prosody *n* the study of verse forms and metrical structure; a particular style, system, or theory of versification.—**prosodic** *adj*.—**prosodically** *adv*.—**prosodist** *n*.

prosopopeia, prosopopoeia *n* (*rhetoric*) a figure of speech in which an absent, dead, or inanimate figure is represented as present and speaking.

prospect *n* a wide view, a vista; (*pl*) measure of future success; future outlook; expectation; a likely customer, candidate, etc. * *vti* to explore or search (for).

prospective *adj* likely; anticipated, expected.—**prospectively** *adv*.

prospector *n* one who prospects for gold, etc.

prospectus *n* (*pl* **prospectuses**) a printed statement of the features of a new work, enterprise, issue of shares, etc; something (as a condition or statement) that forecasts the course or nature of a situation.

prosper *vi* to thrive; to flourish; to succeed.

prosperity *n* (*pl* **prosperities**) success; wealth.

prosperous *adj* successful, fortunate, thriving; favorable.—**prosperously** *adv*.

prostaglandin, PG *n* any of a group of compounds, derived from essential fatty acids, that act in a way that is similar to hormones.

prostate *n* (*also* **prostate gland**) a gland situated around the neck of a man's bladder.—**prostatic** *adj*.

prostatectomy *n* surgical excision of the prostate gland.

prostatitis *n* inflammation of the prostate gland as a result of bacterial infection.

prosthesis *n* (*pl* **prostheses**) (*med*) the replacement of a lost limb, tooth, etc with an artificial one; (*gram*) the addition of a letter or syllable at the beginning of a word.—**prosthetic** *adj*.

prostitute *n* a person who has sexual intercourse for money; (*fig*) one who deliberately debases his or her talents (as for money). * *vt* to offer indiscriminately for sexual intercourse, esp for money; to devote to corrupt or unworthy purposes.—**prostitutor** *n*.

prostitution *n* the act or activity of being a prostitute; sexual intercourse for money, etc.

prostrate *adj* lying face downwards; helpless; overcome; lying prone or supine. * *vt* to throw oneself down; to lie flat; to humble oneself.—**prostration** *n*.

prostyle *adj* (*archit*) with columns in front. * *n* a building, esp a temple, with columns in front.

prosy *adj* (**prosier, prosiest**) like prose; dull, dry, tedious.—**prosily** *adv*.—**prosiness** *n*.

Prot. *abbr* = Protestant.

protactinium *n* a rare radioactive element similar to uranium.

protagonist *n* the main character in a drama, novel, etc; a supporter of a cause.

protasis *n* (*pl* **protases**) (*gram*) an introductory clause of a conditional sentence.

protean *adj* able to assume many shapes, versatile; variable.

protease *n* (*biochemistry*) a group of enzymes that act as catalysts in the breaking up of proteins into peptides and amino acids.

protect *vt* to defend from danger or harm; to guard; to maintain the status and integrity of, esp through financial guarantees; to foster or shield from infringement or restriction; to restrict competition through tariffs and trade controls.

protection *n* the act of protecting; the condition of being protected; something that protects; shelter; defense; patronage; the taxing of competing imports to foster home industry; the advocacy or theory of this (—*also* **protectionism**); immunity from prosecution or attack obtained by the payment of money.

protectionist *n* a person who advocates the protection of home trade by taxing competitive imports. * *adj* serving to protect.—**protectionism** *n*.

protective *adj* serving to protect, defend, shelter.—**protectively** *adv*.—**protectiveness** *n*.

protector *n* a person or thing that protects; (*with cap*) (*formerly*) a regent who ruled during the minority, absence, or illness of a monarch.

protectorate *n* the administration of a weaker state by a powerful one; a state so controlled; a regency; (*with cap*) the English government under Oliver and Richard Cromwell (1653–9).

protégé *n* a person guided and helped in his career by another person.—**protégée** *nf*.

protein *n* a complex organic compound containing nitrogen that is an essential constituent of food.

proteinuria *n* the condition in which protein (usu albumin) is found in the urine.

pro tem, pro tempore *adv* for the time being.

proteolysis *n* the disintegration of protein, esp during digestion.—**proteolytic** *adj*.

proteose *n* a compound substance formed by proteolysis.

protest *vi* to object to; to remonstrate. * *vt* to assert or affirm; to execute or have executed a formal protest against; to make a statement or gesture in objection to. * *n* public dissent; an objection; a complaint; a formal statement of objection.—**protester, protestor** *n*.—**protestingly** *adv*.

Protestant *n* a member or adherent of one of the Christian churches deriving from the Reformation; a Christian not of the Orthodox or Roman Catholic Church, who adheres to the principles of the Reformation.—**Protestantism** *n*.

protestation *n* a solemn declaration; a strong protest.

Proteus[1] *n* (*Greek myth*) a minor sea-god, sometimes called the old man of the sea, who could change himself into various shapes, such as a lion, a leopard, and a snake.—**protean** *adj*.

Proteus[2] *n* (*astron*) Neptune's second largest satellite, discovered in 1989.

prothalamion *n* (*pl* **prothalamia**) a bridal song, sung before a marriage ceremony.

prothonotary *n* (*pl* **prothonotaries**) (*formerly*) the principal clerk in certain courts.—*also* **protonotary** (*pl* **protonotaries**).

prothorax *n* (*pl* **prothoraxes, prothoraces**) the first segment of an insect's thorax.

prothrombin *see* **thrombin**.

protist *n* a single-celled organism, neither animal nor plant.

protocol *n* a note, minute, or draft of an agreement or transaction; the ceremonial etiquette accepted as correct in official dealings, as between heads of state or diplomatic officials; the formatting of data in an electronic communications system; the plan of a scientific experiment or treatment.

protogalaxy *n* a gas cloud that condenses in the initial stages of evolution of a galaxy.

proton *n* an elementary particle in the nucleus of all atoms, carrying a unit positive charge of electricity.

protonotary *see* **prothonotary**.

protoplanet *n* a body in the process of evolving into a planet by means of accretion.

protoplasm *n* a semi-fluid viscous colloid, the essential living matter of all plant and animal cells.—**protoplasmic** *adj*.

protostar *n* one of the earliest stages seen in star formation, when it is fragmenting and condensing from an interstellar gas cloud.

prototype *n* an original model or type from which copies are made.—**prototypal, prototypic, prototypical** *adj*.

protozoan, protozoon *n* (*pl* **protozoans, protozoa**) a microscopic animal consisting of a single cell or a group of cells.

protozoology *n* the study of protozoans.

protract *vt* to draw out or prolong; to lay down the lines and angles of with scale and protractor; to extend forwards and outwards.—**protractible** *adj*.—**protraction** *n*.

protracted *adj* extended, prolonged; long-drawn-out.—**protractedly** *adv*.—**protractedness** *n*.

protractile *adj* (*zool*) able to be extended.—**protractility** *n*.

protractive *adj* delaying; protracted.

protractor *n* an instrument for measuring and drawing angles; a muscle that extends a limb.

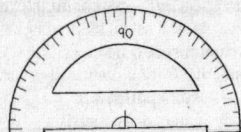

protrude *vti* to thrust outwards or forwards; to obtrude; to jut out, project.

protrusile *adj* (*zool*) which can be thrust forward.

protrusion *n* the act of protruding; something that protrudes; a bulge, a lump; a projection.

protrusive *adj* tending to protrude; bulging out; unduly conspicuous; obtrusive; (*arch*) thrusting or impelling forward.—**protrusively** *adv*.—**protrusiveness** *n*.

protuberance, protuberancy *n* (*pl* **protuberance, protuberancies**) something that protrudes; a swelling, prominence.

protuberant *adj* bulging out, prominent.—**protuberantly** *adv*.

proud *adj* having too high an opinion of oneself; arrogant, haughty; having proper self-respect; satisfied with one's achievements.—**proudly** *adv*.—**proudness** *n*.

Proust *n* **Marcel** (1871–1922) French novelist, essayist and critic known for his long work *A la recherche du temps perdu*.

Prouvé *n* 1. **Jean** (1901–1984) French metalworker, engineer, and furniture designer who published *Le Decor d'Aujourd'hui*. 2. **Victor** (1858–1943) French painter and sculptor who worked with Émile Galle and later assumed the leadership of the Ecole de Nancy.

prov. *abbr* = provident; province; provincial; provisional; provost.

Prov. *abbr* = Provençal; Proverbs.

prove *vti* (**proving, proved** *or* **proven**) to try out, test, by experiment; to establish or demonstrate as true using accepted procedures; to show (oneself) to be worthy or capable; to turn out (to be), esp after trial or test; to rise.—**provable** *adj*.—**provably** *adv*.—**prover** *n*.

provenience *n* place of origin, source.—*also* **provenance**.

provender *n* dry fodder for cattle; any food.

proverb *n* a short traditional saying expressing a truth or moral instruction; an adage.

proverbial *adj* of or like, a proverb; generally known.—**proverbially** *adv*.

Proverbs *n* **the Book of** (*Bible*) OT book, a collection of wise sayings, mainly concerned with the moral education of the young.

provide *vti* to arrange for; to supply; to prepare; to afford (an opportunity); to make provision for (financially).—**provider** *n*.

provided, providing *conj* on condition (that).

providence *n* foresight, prudence; God's care and protection.

Providence *n* the capital city of Rhode Island, a state of the USA.

provident *adj* providing for the future; far-seeing; thrifty.—**providently** *adv*.

providential *adj* arranged by providence; very opportune or lucky.—**providentially** *adv*.

province *n* an administrative district or division of a country; the jurisdiction of an archbishop; (*pl*) the parts of a country removed from the main cities; a department of knowledge or activity.

provincial *adj* of a province or provinces; having the way, speech, etc of a certain province; country-like; rustic; unsophisticated. * *n* an inhabitant of the provinces or country areas; a person lacking sophistication.—**provinciality** *n*.—**provincially** *adv*.

provincialism *n* provincial speech, phrases, or point of view; narrowness.

provision *n* a requirement; something provided for the future; a stipulation, condition; (*business*) an amount that is allotted from profits in a company's accounts either in respect of a known liability or in respect of the reduction in value of an asset; (*pl*) supplies of food, stores. * *vt* to supply with stores.—**provisioner** *n*.

provisional, provisionary *adj* temporary; conditional.—**provisionally** *adv*.

proviso *n* (*pl* **provisos, provisoes**) a condition, stipulation; a limiting clause in an agreement, etc.

provisory *adj* conditional; making provision; temporary.—**provisorily** *adv*.

provocation *n* the act of provoking or inciting; a cause of anger, resentment, etc.

provocative *adj* intentionally provoking, esp to anger or sexual desire; (*remark*) stimulating argument or discussion.—**provocatively** *adv*.—**provocativeness** *n*.

provoke *vt* to anger, infuriate; to incite, to arouse; to give rise to; to irritate, exasperate.

provoking *adj* annoying, exasperating.—**provokingly** *adv*.

provost *n* a high executive official, as in some churches, colleges, or universities; in Scotland, a mayor.

prow *n* the forward part of a ship, bow.

prowess *n* bravery, gallantry; skill.

prowl *vi* to move stealthily, esp in search of prey.—*also n*.

prowler *n* one that moves stealthily, esp an opportunist thief.

prox. *abbr* (*Latin*) = *proximo* (*mense*), "next month."

prox. acc. *abbr* (*Latin*) = *proxime accessit*, "came closest" (to the winner in a competition, etc).

Proxima Centauri *n* (*astron*) the star nearest to the sun and a member of the constellation Centaurus.

proximal *adj* (*anat*) at the inner end, towards the center of the body.

proximate *adj* nearest, next; approximate.

proximity *n* nearness in place, time, series, etc.

proximo *adv* (*Latin*) next month.

prox. luc. *abbr* (*Latin*) = *proxima luce*, "on the preceding day."

proxy *n* (*pl* **proxies**) the authority to vote or act for another; a person so authorized.—*also adj*.

PRP *abbr* = performance related pay.

PRR *abbr* = pulse repetition rate.

prs. *abbr* = pairs.

PRS *abbr* = Pattern Recognition Society; Performing Rights Society; Pre-Raphaelite Society; Protestant Reformation Society.

PRT *abbr* = Prison Reform Trust.

prude *n* a person who is overly modest or proper in behavior, speech, attitudes to sex, etc.—**prudery** *n*.

prudence *n* the quality of being prudent; caution; discretion; common sense.

prudent *adj* cautious; sensible; managing carefully; circumspect.—**prudently** *adv*.

prudential *adj* marked by prudence.—**prudentially** *adv*.

prudish *adj* over-correct in behavior.—**prudishly** *adv*.—**prudishness** *n*.

pruinose *adj* (*bot*) covered with a whitish dust or bloom.

prune[1] *n* a dried plum.

prune[2] *vti* (*plant*) to remove dead or living parts from; to cut away what is unwanted or superfluous.—**pruner** *n*.

prunella *n* a strong silk or worsted fabric, used in shoes.

prurient *adj* tending to excite lust; having lewd thoughts.—**prurience** *n*.—**pruriently** *adv*.

prurigo *n* a skin disease causing violent itching.

pruritus *n* a strong sensation of itching.

Prus. *abbr* = Prussia; Prussian.

Prussian blue *n* a deep blue.

prussic acid *n* a solution of hydrogen and cyanide that makes a deadly poison.

p.r.v. *abbr* (*French*) = *pour rendre visite*, "to return a call."

Prydein *n* (*Brit Celtic myth*) said to have been a king of Cornwall who conquered the rest of Britain after Porrex's death. Some sources indicate that Britain may be named after him.

p.s. *abbr* = (*Latin*) *post scriptum*, "postscript"; (*theat*) prompt side; public sale.

p.t. *abbr* = privilege ticket; (*grain trade*) private terms; (*Latin*) *pro tempore*, "for the time being"; pupil teacher.

pry[1] *vi* (**prying, pried**) to snoop into other people's affairs; to inquire impertinently. * *n* (*pl* **pries**) close inspection; impertinent peeping; a highly inquisitive person.

pry[2] *vt* (**prying, pried**) to raise with a lever, to prise.

pryer *see* **prier**.

ps- *abbr* (*chem*) = pseudo-.

ps. *abbr* = pieces; pseudonym; pseudonymous.

Ps. or **Psa.** *abbr* = Psalm; Psalms.

PS *abbr* = Pastel Society; Philippine Scouts; Philological Society; Physical Society; Planetary Society; Police Sergeant; Polite Society; (*Latin*) *post scriptum*, "after writing," postscript; private secretary; (*theat*) prompt side.

PSA *abbr* = Pakistan Sociological Association; Passenger Shipping Association; Peace Studies Association; Poultry Science Association; Prices Surveillance Authority; Property Services Authority; Public Services Authority.

PSAC *abbr* = Production Statistics Advisory Committee.

psalm *n* a sacred song or hymn, esp one from the Book of Psalms in the Bible.

Psalmanazar *n* **George** (*c.*1679–1763) French-born English literary hoaxer who arrived in London in 1703, claiming to be a "Formosan," for which country he invented a language and to which he published a travel guide. After years as a hack writer, he eventually renounced his imposture and became a respected literary figure.

psalmist *n* a writer of psalms.

psalmody *n* (*pl* **psalmodies**) the art or practice of singing psalms or hymns.— **psalmodic** *adj*.—**psalmodist** *n*.

Psalms *n* **the Book of** (*Bible*) OT book of sacred songs and poems.

Psalter, psalter *n* the Book of Psalms, esp as found in a prayer book.

psaltery *n* (*pl* **psalteries**) an ancient stringed musical instrument.

Psammetichus I *n* Egyptian king of the Twenty-sixth Dynasty in the Late Period. At this time Egypt was under Assyrian domination, and Psammetichus began his rule by permission of Assurbanipal as a client king.

Psammetichus II *n* Egyptian king of the Twenty-sixth Dynasty in the Late Period (ruled 595–589 BC).

Psammetichus III *n* Egyptian king of the Twenty-sixth Dynasty in the Late Period (ruled 526–525 BC).

PSBR *abbr* = Public Sector Borrowing Requirement.

psc *abbr* = passed staff college.

PSC *abbr* = Program Support Center

PSDA *abbr* = Paper Sack Development Association.

PSDR *abbr* = Public Sector Debt Repayment.

PSE *n* = psychological stress evaluator (similar to a lie detector).

pseud. *abbr* = pseudonym.

Pseudepigrapha *npl* spurious writings falsely ascribed to Biblical figures or times; Jewish writings of the first century BC and first century AD, allegedly by various prophets and kings of the Hebrew scriptures.

pseudo *adj* false, pretended.

pseudocarp *n* (*bot*) a fruit formed from parts other than the ovary.

pseudo-dipteral *n* (*archit*) a Greek temple in which the peristyle is formed from a double colonnade except around the naos where there is only a single row of columns.

pseudomorph *n* (*geol*) a mineral with the crystalline shape of another mineral.— **pseudomorphic, pseudomorphous** *adj*.—**pseudomorphism** *n*.

pseudonym *n* a false name adopted as by an author.—**pseudonymity** *n*.

pseudonymous *adj* written or writing under an assumed name.— **pseudonymously** *adv*.

pseudo-peripteral *n* (*archit*) typically referring to a Roman temple, in which half columns are attached all round the external wall of the cella, in line with those of the portico at the front.

pseudopodium *n* (*pl* **pseudopodia**) (*biol*) the temporary projection from the body of certain cells.

psf *abbr* = per square foot.

pshaw *interj* an exclamation of disgust, disbelief, etc.

psi *abbr* = pounds per square inch.

PSI *abbr* = Policy Studies Institute.

PSIF *abbr* = Prison Service Industries and Farms.

psittacine *n* pertaining to parrots.

psittacosis *n* a contagious parrot disease transmissible to humans, in whom it causes pneumonia.

psk *abbr* = phase shift keying.

PSL *abbr* = Polish Peasant Party; private sector liquidity; public sector loan.

PSM *abbr* = product sales manager.

PSMA *abbr* = Pressure Sensitive Manufacturers Association.

PSN *abbr* = packet switching network; Poor Sisters of Nazareth.

PSO *abbr* = principal scientific officer.

psoas *n* a muscle in the loin.

psoriasis *n* a chronic skin disease marked by red scaly patches.—**psoriatic** *adj*.

PSPS *abbr* = Paddle Steamer Preservation Society.

Pss *abbr* = Psalms.

PSS *abbr* = packet switching system; (*Latin*) *postscripta*, "postscripts."

PST *abbr* = Pacific Standard Time.

pstn *abbr* = public switched telephone network.

PSU *abbr* = power supply unit.

Psusennes I *n* Egyptian king of the Twenty-first Dynasty (1039–993 BC).

PSV *abbr* = public service vehicle.

PSW *abbr* = psychiatric social worker.

PSWMRL *abbr* = Pasture Systems and Watershed Management Research Lab.

psych *vt* (*inf*) (*usu with* **up**) to prepare oneself mentally for a performance, ordeal, etc; (*with* **out**) to analyze psychologically, esp for one's own ends; to intimidate psychologically; to subject to psychoanalysis.

psyche *n* the spirit, soul; the mind, esp as a functional entity governing the total organism and its interactions with the environment.

Psyche *n* (*Greek myth*) a beautiful woman whose unknown lover was Eros, whose face she was forbidden to look at. One night she looked at him and he fled, leaving her inconsolable. Eventually she was overcome by a deathlike sleep and Zeus made her immortal and married her to Eros.

psychedelic *adj* of or causing extreme changes in the conscious mind; of or like the auditory or visual effects produced by drugs (as LSD). * *n* a psychedelic drug.— **psychedelically** *adv*.

psychiatrist *n* a specialist in psychiatric medicine.

psychiatry *n* the branch of medicine dealing with disorders of the mind, including psychoses and neuroses.—**psychiatric** *adj*.—**psychiatrically** *adv*.

psychic *adj* of the soul or spirit; of the mind; having sensitivity to, or contact with, forces that cannot be explained by natural laws (—*also* **psychical**). * *n* a person apparently sensitive to nonphysical forces; a medium; psychic phenomena.

psychoanalysis *n* a method of treating neuroses, phobias, and some other mental disorders by analyzing emotional conflicts, repressions, etc.—**psychoanalytic, psychoanalytical** *adj*.

psychoanalyst *n* a specialist in psychoanalysis.

psychoanalyze, psychoanalyse *vt* to analyze and treat by psychoanalysis.

psychodynamics *n sing* the study of interaction of thoughts, motives, etc within an individual.—**psychodynamic** *adj*.

psychogeriatrics *n* the branch of psychiatry dealing with mental ill-health in old people.

psychokinesis *n* (*parapsychology*) the movement of physical objects by pure thought.— **psychokinetic** *adj*.—**psychokinetically** *adv*.

psychol. or **psych.** *abbr* = psychological; psychologist; psychology.

psychological *adj* of or relating to psychology; of, relating to or coming from the mind or emotions; able to affect the mind or emotions.—**psychologically** *adv*.

psychologist *n* a person trained in psychology.

psychology *n* (*pl* **psychologies**) the science that studies the human mind and behavior; mental state.

psychometrics *n sing* the scientific measurement and testing of mental powers.— **psychometric, psychometrical** *adj*.—**psychometrician, psychometrist** *n*.

psychomotor *adj* denoting a physical action induced by a mental condition.

psychoneurosis *n* (*pl* **psychoneuroses**) neurosis.

psychopath *n* a person suffering from a mental disorder that results in antisocial behavior and lack of guilt.—**psychopathic** *adj*.

psychopathology *n* the study of mental disorders.

psychopathy *n* mental disorder or disease.

psychophysiology *n* the study of the relation between psychological and physiological processes.—**psychophysiological** *adj*.—**psychophysiologist** *n*.

psychosis *n* (*pl* **psychoses**) a mental disorder in which the personality is very seriously disorganized and contact with reality is usu impaired.

psychosomatic *adj* of physical disorders that have a psychological or emotional origin.—**psychosomatically** *adv*.

psychotherapy *n* the treatment of mental disorders by psychological methods.—**psychotherapeutic** *adj*.—**psychotherapist** *n*.

psychotic *adj* of or like a psychosis; having a psychosis. * *n* a person suffering from a psychosis.—**psychotically** *adv*.

psychotropic drug *n* a drug that affects the mind and its moods, e.g. antidepressants, sedatives, and stimulants.

psychrometer *n* a type of hygrometer with both a wet and a dry bulb.

psychrophilic *adj* (*biol*) thriving in the cold.

Pt *symbol* (*chem*) platinum (element).

pt *abbr* = past tense; pint; (*Latin*) *pro tempore*, "for the time being."

pt. *abbr* = part; payment; pint; pints; point; port.

Pt. *abbr* = point (in place names).

PT *abbr* = Pacific Time; part time; physical training; physiotherapist.

PTA *abbr* = Parent-Teacher Association; prior to admission.

Ptah *n* (*Egypt*) the local god of Memphis, Egypt. When Memphis became a royal capital during the First and Second Dynasties, Ptah's status grew accordingly. The Memphis priesthood developed a cult of Ptah, which claimed he was the oldest god and had himself created Ra-Atum by pure thought. All other gods and created things were similarly the product of the mind of Ptah.

Ptahhotep *n* (*Egypt*) a hereditary royal official of the Pharaoh Wenis (Fifth dynasty), grandson of a vizier of the same name. He is credited with the authorship of a celebrated set of *Maxims*, setting out rules for leading a well-ordered and balanced life.

ptarmigan *n* (*pl* **ptarmigans, ptarmigan**) a species of grouse.

ptas. *abbr* = pesetas.

PT boat *n* a patrol torpedo boat, a highspeed motorboat equipped with torpedoes and other weaponry.

PTBT *abbr* = partial test-ban treaty.

PTC *abbr* = Pacific Telecommunications Council; Peace Tax Campaign.

PTD *abbr* = permanent total disability.

Pte. *abbr* = private (soldier).

PTE *abbr* = Passenger Transport Executive.

pteridology *n* the study of ferns.

pterodactyl *n* an extinct flying reptile with batlike wings.

pteroma *n* (*archit*) a passageway around a Greek temple between the peristyle and the walls of the naos.

pteropod *n* a small swimming mollusk with winglike lobes on its foot.

pterosaur *n* an extinct flying reptile.

pterygoid *adj* (*anat*) of or pertaining to either of the two processes in the skull attached like wings to the spheroid bone.

PTES *abbr* = People's Trust for Endangered Species.

PTFE *abbr* = polytetrafluoroethene, a thermosetting plastic produced by the polymerization of tetrafluoroethene.

ptg. *abbr* = printing.

Ptg. *abbr* = Portugal; Portuguese.

PTH *abbr* = parathyroid hormone.

PTI *abbr* = public tool interface.

PTIA *abbr* = Pet Trade and Industry Association.

PTM *abbr* = pulse-time modulation.

PTN *abbr* = public telephone network.

PTO *or* **p.t.o.** *abbr* = please turn over.

Ptolemaic *adj* of or pertaining to the Macedonian dynasty that ruled Egypt (323–30 BC); of or pertaining to the ancient astronomer Ptolemy

Ptolemaic Period *n* (323–30 BC) the period of rule of Egypt by the Macedonian dynasty of the Ptolemies, from the death of Alexander the Great (323 BC) to the suicide of Cleopatra (30 BC) Egypt.

Ptolemaic system *n* (*astron*) an early model of planetary motion within the Solar System described by Ptolemy, a Greek astronomer, during the second century.

Ptolemy I *n*, called Ptolemy Soter (*c*. 367–283 BC) king of Egypt (323–246 BC).

Ptolemy II *n*, called Philadelphus (309–246 BC) the son of Ptolemy I, (ruled 285–246 BC).

Ptolemy *n* 1. family name of the last independent rulers of Egypt (323–30 BC). 2. **Claudius Ptolemaeus** (2nd century AD) Greek astronomer, mathematician, and geographer. His system of astronomy remained undisputed till the Copernican system.

ptomaine, ptomain *n* a kind of alkaloid, often poisonous, found in decaying matter.

ptomaine poisoning *n* (*arch*) food poisoning.

ptosis *n* (*pl* **ptoses**) drooping of the eyelid.

pts. *abbr* = parts; pints.

PTS *abbr* = Philatelic Traders' Society; Protestant Truth Society.

PTSD *abbr* = post-traumatic stress disorder.

PTU *abbr* = Plumbing Trades Union.

PTUF *abbr* = Professional Tennis Umpires' Federation.

ptw *abbr* = per thousand words.

PTx *abbr* = parathyroidectomy.

Pty. *abbr* = proprietary.

ptyalin *n* an enzyme found in saliva.

ptyalism *n* excessive salivation.

P-type asteroid *n* a common type of asteroid thought to have organic-rich surfaces.

Pu *symbol* (*chem*) plutonium (element).

PU *abbr* = passed urine; peptic ulcer; polyurethane; processing unit.

PUA *abbr* = Pacific Union Association.

pub *n* (*Brit*) a bar, a public house, an inn.

pub. *abbr* = public; published; publisher; publishers; publishing; publication.

Pub. Doc. *abbr* = Public Document; Public Documents.

puberty *n* the stage at which the reproductive organs become functional.— **pubertal** *adj*.

pubescent *adj* arriving at or having reached puberty; of or relating to puberty; covered with fine soft short hairs.—**pubescence** *n*.

pubic *adj* related to or situated near the pubis.

pubis *n* (*pl* **pubes**) the front part of the bones composing either half of the pelvis.

publ. *abbr* = published; publisher.

public *adj* of, for, or by the people generally; performed in front of people; for the use of all people; open or known to all; acting officially for the people. * *n* the people in general; a particular section of the people, such as an audience, body of readers, etc; open observation.

public-address system *n* a system using microphones and loudspeakers to enable groups of people to hear clearly in an auditorium or out of doors.

publican *n* a person who keeps a public house; in ancient Rome, a collector of taxes.

publication *n* public notification; the printing and distribution of books, magazines, etc; something published as a periodical, book, etc.

public defender *n* a lawyer appointed by the state to defend a person who cannot afford private representation.

public domain *n* the status of non-copyright or out-of-copyright published material.

public domain software *n* (*comput*) a computer program that the author has decided to distribute free to users.

public health *n* the practice and science of protecting and improving community health by organized effort including sanitation, preventive medicine, etc.

public holiday *n* a legal vacation.

public issue *n* a method of issuing a new issue of shares, loan stocks, etc, in which members of the public apply for shares at a fixed price.

publicist *n* a person who publicizes, esp one whose business it is; a political journalist.

publicity *n* any information or action that brings a person or cause to public notice; work concerned with such promotional matter; notice by the public.

publicize *vt* to give publicity to.

public limited company *n* a limited company whose shares are available to the public on the open market.

publicly *adv* in a public manner; openly; by the public; with the consent of the public.

public opinion *n* views held among the general population.

public prosecutor *n* a district attorney, an official who prosecutes important legal cases on behalf of the state.

public relations *n* relations with the general public of a company, institution, etc, as through publicity.

public school *n* a school maintained by public money and supervised by local authorities; in England, a private secondary school, usu boarding.

public sector *n* economic activity dependent on or controlled by government.—**public-sector** *adj*.

public-sector borrowing requirement (often abbreviated to **PSBR**) *n* the amount of money that the government requires to borrow in order to make up for a budget deficit.

public servant *n* a government official or employee.

public service *n* the supply of a commodity (gas, water, etc) or a service (transport, etc) to the community; a service in the public interest; employment in a government department, esp the civil service.

public speaking *n* the art, science or process of making speeches.—**public speaker** *n*.

public works *npl* the construction of community buildings, roads, facilities, etc, financed by government for the use of the public.

publish *vt* to make generally known; to announce formally; (*book*) to issue for sale to the public. * *vi* to put out an edition; to have one's work accepted for publication.— **publishable** *adj*.

publisher *n* a person or company that prints and issues books, magazines, etc.

publishing *n* the business of the production and distribution of books, magazines, recordings, etc.

PUC *abbr* = Public Utilities Commission.

Puccini *n* **Giacomo** (1858–1924) Italian composer whose operas include *Madame Butterfly*.

puce *n*, *adj* (a) purplish brown.

puck *n* a hard rubber disk used in ice hockey.

Puck *n* (*astron*) an almost spherical satellite of Uranus, discovered in 1985.

pucker *vti* to draw together in creases, to wrinkle; (*with* **up**) to contract the lips ready to kiss. * *n* a wrinkle or fold.

puckish *adj* impish, irresponsible.—**puckishly** *adv*.—**puckishness** *n*.

pud *abbr* = pick-up and delivery.

pudding *n* a dessert; a steamed or baked dessert; a suet pie.

puddle *n* a small pool of water, esp stagnant, spilled, or muddy water; a rough cement of kneaded clay. * *vti* to dabble in mud, to make muddy; to make or line with puddle; to stir (molten iron) to free it from carbon.—**puddler** *n*.

pudency *n* modesty, sense of shame.

pudendum *n* (*pl* **pudenda**) (*usu pl*) the external reproductive organs, esp of a woman.—**pudendal** *adj*.

pudgy *adj* (**pudgier, pudgiest**) short and fat, squat.—**pudginess** *n*.

Puebla *n* a city in Mexico.

pueblo *n* an Indian settlement in Mexico and the South West United States.

puerile *adj* juvenile; childish.—**puerilely** *adv*.—**puerility** *n*.

puerilism *n* a psychiatric condition of adults characterized by infantile or childish behavior.

puerperal *adj* pertaining to, or following, childbirth.

puerperal fever *n* an infection, now rare in developed countries, that occurs within two or three days of childbirth when a mother is susceptible to disease.

Puerto Armuelles *n* a city in Panama.

Puerto Barrios *n* a city in Guatemala.

Puerto Cortés *n* a city in Honduras.

Puerto Rico *n* the most easterly of the Greater Antilles Islands lying in the Caribbean Sea between the Dominican Republic and the US Virgin Islands. It is a self-governing commonwealth in association with the USA. —**Puerto Rican** *adj*.

PUFA *abbr* = polyunsaturated fatty acids.

puff *n* a sudden short blast or gust; an exhalation of air or smoke; a light pastry; a pad for applying powder; a flattering notice, advertisement. * *vti* to emit a puff; to breathe hard, pant; to put out of breath; to praise with exaggeration; to swell; to blow, smoke, etc, with puffs.

puffball *n* a round fungus which emits dustlike spores when broken.

puffer *n* someone who, or something which puffs; a tropical fish with a spiny body which can be puffed up to form a globe.

puffin *n* a sea bird that has a short neck and a brightly colored laterally compressed bill.

puffiness *n* the state of being puffy or swollen.

puffy *adj* (**puffier, puffiest**) inflated, swollen; panting.—**puffily** *adv*.

pug *n* a breed of small dog with a face and nose like a bulldog. * *vt* (**pugging, pugged**) to mix (clay) for making bricks; to fill (a space) with clay or mortar.

pug nose *n* a nose having a slightly concave bridge and flattened nostrils.—**pug-nosed** *adj*.

pugilism *n* the practice of fighting with the fists; boxing; skill in doing this.

pugilist *n* a boxer; a prizefighter.—**pugilistic** *adj*.—**pugilistically** *adv*.

Pugin *n* **Augustus Charles** (1769–1832) French-born architect whose books were a vital source for designers and architects working in the Gothic style.

pugnacious *adj* fond of fighting, belligerent.—**pugnacity, pugnaciousness** *n*.

puisne *adj* (*judge*) lower in rank.

puissance *n* (*arch*) power; (*showjumping*) an event in which a horse attempts particularly large jumps.—**puissant** *adj*.

puke *vti* (*inf*) to vomit.—*also n*.

pukka *adj* (*Anglo-Indian*) genuine, real; reliable, sound.

pul *n* an Afghan monetary unit, equal to one hundredth of an afghani.

pula *n* the standard monetary unit of Botswana, made up of 100 thebes.

pulchritude *n* beauty.

pule *vi* to whine, whimper.

Pulitzer *n* **Joseph** (1847–1911) Hungarian-born American journalist and lawyer who built up a newspaper-owning business and endowed the Pulitzer prizes.

Pulitzer prize *n* any of a group of annual prizes for journalism, literature, and music founded by the American newspaper proprietor Joseph Pulitzer (1847–1911).

pull *vt* to tug at; to pluck; to move or draw towards oneself; to drag; to rip; to tear; (*muscle*) to strain; (*inf*) to carry out, perform; (*inf*) to restrain; (*inf: gun, etc*) to draw out; (*inf*) to attract; (*with out*) to extract, withdraw; to withdraw troops; (*with up*) to remove by the roots; to stop (a vehicle) suddenly; to criticize. * *vi* to carry out the action of pulling something; to be capable of being pulled; to move (away, ahead, etc); (*with out*) (*vehicle*) to move off from the side of the road; to overtake; to abandon; to level off from a dive; (*with over*) to steer a vehicle to the side of the road; to move aside to let another pass; (*with through*) to survive a dangerous situation; (*with up*) (*vehicle*) to stop suddenly; (*racer, etc*) to draw level or ahead. * *n* the act of pulling or being pulled; a tug; a device for pulling; (*inf*) influence; (*inf*) drawing power.

pullback *n* a moving back or withdrawal, esp of military forces.

pull down menu *n* (*comput*) a selection of sub-options related to a command name on the main menu bar.

pullet *n* a young hen.

pulley *n* a wheel with a grooved rim for a cord, etc, used to raise weights by downward pull or change of direction of the pull; a group of these used to increase applied force; a wheel driven by a belt.

Pullman *n* (*pl* **Pullmans**) a train carriage offering luxury accommodation, usu with sleeping berths.

pullout *n* the act of pulling out; withdrawal; something intended to be pulled out, as a supplement in a magazine.

pullover *n* a buttonless garment with or without sleeves pulled on over the head.

pullulate *vi* to sprout, grow; to multiply quickly; to spring up.—**pullulation** *n*.

pulmonary *adj* of, relating to or affecting the lungs; having lungs; denoting the artery that conveys deoxygenated blood directly to the lungs from the right ventricle of the heart.

pulmonary edema *n* gathering of fluid in the lungs.

pulmonary embolism *n* a condition involving the blocking of the pulmonary artery or a branch of it by an embolus (usu a blood clot).

pulmonary hypertension *n* an increase in blood pressure in the pulmonary artery because of increased resistance to the flow of blood.

pulmonary stenosis *n* a narrowing of the outlet from the heart to the pulmonary artery via the right ventricle.

pulmonary vein *n* one of the four veins that carry oxygenated blood from the lungs to the left atrium of the heart.

pulp *n* a soft, moist, sticky mass; the soft, juicy part of a fruit or soft pith of a plant stem; the center of a tooth containing blood vessels and nerve fibers and connected with the dentine by means of fine cellular processes; ground-up, moistened fibers of wood, rags, etc, used to make paper; a book or magazine printed on cheap paper and often dealing with sensational material. * *vti* to make or become pulp or pulpy; to produce or reproduce (written matter) in pulp form.

pulpit *n* a raised enclosed platform, esp in a church, from which a clergyman preaches; preachers as a group.

pulpitum *n* (*archit*) a stone screen in a large church or cathedral, dividing the chancel from the nave.

pulpy *adj* (**pulpier, pulpiest**) consisting of or like pulp; soft.—**pulpiness** *n*.

pulque *n* a Mexican alcoholic drink made from the fermented juice of the agave.

pulsar *n* any of several very small stars that emit radio pulses at regular intervals.

pulsate *vi* to beat or throb rhythmically; to vibrate, quiver.—**pulsative** *adj*.

pulsating star *n* a variable star that pulsates, periodically dimming and brightening, due to internal instability.

pulsation *n* a pulsating; a single beat or throb; rhythmic throbbing.

pulsatory *adj* pertaining to pulsation; pulsating.

pulse[1] *n* a rhythmic beat or throb, as of the heart; a place where this is felt; the regular expansion and contraction of an artery as a fluid wave of blood passes along, originating with the contraction of the heart muscle and blood leaving the left ventricle; an underlying opinion or sentiment or an indication of it; a short radio signal. * *vti* to throb, pulsate.

pulse[2] *n* the edible seeds of several leguminous plants, such as beans, peas and lentils; the plants producing them.

pulsimeter, pulsometer *n* (*med*) an instrument used to measure pulse rate and strength.

Pult *n* (*mus*) (*German*) "desk," the music stand that two orchestral players share.

pulv. *abbr* (*Latin*) = *pulvis*, "powder."

pulverize *vti* to reduce to a fine powder; to demolish, smash; to crumble.—**pulverization** *n*.—**pulverizer** *n*.

pulverulent *adj* covered with dust; powdery; crumbling to dust.

pulvin *n* (*archit*) a dosseret with a convex, rounded, pillow-like shape.

pulvinate, pulvinated *adj* (*archit*) curved convexly; (*bot*) having a cushionlike pad or swelling.

puma *n* a mountain lion.

pumice *n* a light, porous volcanic rock, used for scrubbing, polishing, etc.—**pumiceous** *adj*.

pummel *vt* (**pummeling, pummeled** or **pummelling, pummelled**) to strike repeatedly with the fists, to thump.

pump[1] *n* a device that forces a liquid or gas into, or draws it out of, something. * *vti* to move (fluids) with a pump; to remove water, etc, from; to drive air into with a pump; to draw out, move up and down, pour forth, etc, as a pump does; (*inf*) to obtain information through questioning.

pump[2] *n* a light low shoe or slipper; a rubber-soled shoe.

pumped storage scheme *n* a system frequently used in hydroelectricity generation, whereby water used during the day to turn the generators is pumped back up to the reservoir during the night when demand for electricity is low.

pumpernickel *n* a coarse rye bread.

pumpkin *n* a large, round, orange fruit of the gourd family widely cultivated as food.

pums *abbr* = permanently unfit for military service.

PUMS *abbr* = Public Use Microdata Samples.

pun *n* a play on words of the same sound but different meanings, usu humorous. * *vi* (**punning, punned**) to make a pun.—**punningly** *adv*.

pun. *abbr* (*wine measure*) = puncheon.

punch[1] *vt* to strike with the fist; to prod or poke; to stamp, perforate with a tool; (*cattle*) to herd. * *n* a blow with the fist; (*inf*) vigor; a machine or tool for punching.

punch[2] *n* a hot, sweet drink made with fruit juices, often mixed with wine or spirits.

punchbowl *n* a bowl for mixing punch; a bowl-shaped hollow.

punch card, punched card *n* in data processing, a card with a series of holes representing data.

punch line *n* the last line of a joke or story, that conveys its humor or point.

punch-drunk *adj* stupified (as if) from repeated blows to the head.

puncheon *n* a large cask holding between 70 and 120 gallons.

Punchinello *n* the figure of the clown in Italian puppet theater; a grotesque character.

punching bag *n* a stuffed suspended bag used by boxers for training and exercise.

punctate, punctated *adj* marked with dots or points.—**punctation** *n*.

punctilio *n* (*pl* **punctilios**) a fine point of etiquette; petty formality.

punctilious *adj* very formal in conduct; scrupulously exact.

punctual *adj* being on time; prompt.—**punctuality** *n*.—**punctually** *adv*.

punctuate *vt* to use certain standardized marks in (written matter) to clarify meaning; to interrupt; to emphasize. * *vi* to use punctuation marks.—**punctuator** *n*.

punctuation *n* the act of punctuating; the state of being punctuated; a system of punctuation.

punctuation mark *n* one of the standardized symbols used in punctuation, as the period, colon, semicolon, comma, etc.

puncture *n* a small hole made by a sharp object; the deflation of a tire caused by a puncture. * *vt* to make useless or ineffective as if by a puncture; to deflate. * *vi* to become punctured.—**puncturable** *adj*.

pundit *n* a learned person; an expert; a critic, esp one who writes in a daily newspaper.—*also* **pandit**.

pung *n* a horse-drawn sleigh.

pungent *adj* having an acrid smell or a sharp taste; caustic; bitter.—**pungency** *n*.—**pungently** *adv*.

punish *vt* to subject a person to a penalty for a crime or misdemeanor; to chastise; to handle roughly.—**punisher** *n*.

punishable *adj* liable to legal punishment.—**punishability** *n*.

punishing *adj* causing retribution; (*inf*) arduous, gruelling, exhausting.—**punishingly** *adv*.

punishment *n* a penalty for a crime or misdemeanor; rough treatment; the act of punishing or being punished.

punitive, punitory *adj* involving the inflicting of punishment.—**punitively** *adv*.—**punitiveness** *n*.

punk *adj* (*sl*) inferior, of low quality. * *n* a young gangster; a follower of punk rock.

punk rock *n* an aggressive form of rock music usu performed in a coarse, offensive way.

punka, punkah *n* a palm-leaf fan; (*Anglo-Indian*) a large swinging fan suspended from the ceiling of a room and worked by an attendant.

punster, punner *n* a person who makes puns.

punt[1] *n* a long flat-bottomed square-ended river boat usu propelled with a pole. * *vti* to propel or convey in a punt.

punt[2] *vt* to kick a dropped ball before it reaches the ground. * *n* such a kick.

punt[3] *vi* in some gambling games, to bet against the bank; to bet, gamble.

punt[4] *n* the standard monetary unit of the Republic of Ireland, made up of 100 Pighne (pence).

punta *n* (*mus*) (*Italian*) "point," as in *a punta d'arco*, "at the point of the bow," indicating that only the tip of the bow should be used to play the strings.

Puntarenas *n* a city in Costa Rica.

punter *n* a person who gambles; (*sl*) a consumer; a customer.

punty *n* (*pl* **punties**) an iron rod used in glass-blowing.

puny *adj* (**punier, puniest**) of inferior size, strength, or importance; feeble.—**puniness** *n*.

PUO *abbr* = pyrexia of uncertain/unknown origin.

pup *n* a young dog, a puppy; a young fox, seal, rat, etc. * *vi* (**pupping, pupped**) to give birth to pups.

pupa *n* (*pl* **pupae, pupas**) an insect at the quiescent stage between the larva and the adult.—**pupal** *adj*.

pupate *vi* (*entomology*) to become a pupa.—**pupation** *n*.

pupil[1] *n* a child or young person taught under the supervision of a teacher or tutor; a person who has been taught or influenced by a famous or distinguished person.

pupil[2] *n* the round, dark opening in the center of the iris of the eye through which light passes.

pupilage, pupillage *n* the state of being a pupil; the period of time during which someone is a pupil.

pupillary *adj* pertaining to a pupil, or to a legal ward.

pupiparous *adj* (*entomology*) producing young in the pupal state.

puppet *n* a doll moved by strings attached to its limbs or by a hand inserted in its body; a person controlled by another. * *adj* of or relating to puppets; acting in response to the controls of another while appearing independent.

puppeteer *n* a person who controls and entertains with puppets.

puppetry *n* the art of making and entertaining with puppets; stilted presentation.

puppy *n* (*pl* **puppies**) a young domestic dog less than a year old.—**puppyhood** *n*.—**puppyish** *adj*.

puppy love *n* a brief adolescent infatuation with another person.

pup tent *n* a low small tent for two persons.

Purana *n* a book of Hindu scriptures, written in Sanskrit.

Purbeck marble *n* (*archit*) a type of dark limestone that takes a high polish, used as a marble in construction and sculpture.

purblind *adj* half-blind; (*fig*) obtuse, dull.

Purcell *n* Henry (*c*.1659–95) English composer whose works include the operas *The Fairy Queen* and *Dido and Aeneas*.

purchase *vt* to buy; to obtain by effort or suffering. * *n* the act of purchasing; an object bought; leverage for raising or moving loads; means of achieving advantage.—**purchasable** *adj*.—**purchaser** *n*.

purchase ledger *n* the ledger in which are recorded the personal accounts of a company's suppliers.

purchasing agent *n* a person who makes purchases on behalf of another.

purchasing power *n* the amount a person has to spend; the real value of a currency.

purdah *n* the custom among Muslims and some Hindus of secluding women from public observation.

pure *adj* clean; not contaminated; not mixed; chaste, innocent; free from taint or defilement; mere; that and that only; abstract and theoretical; (*mus*) not discordant, perfectly in tune.—**pureness** *n*.

purebred *adj* having an impeccable pedigree. * *n* a purebred animal or plant.

purée *n* cooked food sieved or pulped in a blender; a thick soup of this. * *vt* (**puréeing, puréed**) to prepare food in this way.

purely *adv* in a pure way; solely, entirely.

purgation *n* a purging or purifying.

purgative *adj* purging, cleansing; * *n* a drug or agent that purges the bowels.

purgatorial *adj* of, relating to or like purgatory; serving to purify of sin.

purgatory *n* a place of suffering or purification; (*with cap: RC church*) the intermediate place between death and heaven, where venial sins are purged.

purge *vt* to cleanse, purify; (*nation, party, etc*) to rid of troublesome people; to clear (oneself) of a charge; to clear out the bowels of. * *n* the act or process of purging; a purgative; the removal of persons believed to be disloyal from an organization, esp a political party.—**purger** *n*.

purificator *n* (*Christian Church*) a cloth used to wipe the chalice during Holy Communion.

purify *vti* (**purifying, purified**) to make or become pure; to cleanse; to make ceremonially clean; to free from harmful matter.—**purification** *n*.—**purificatory** *adj*.—**purifier** *n*.

Purim *n* a Jewish holiday celebrated yearly in February or March, to commemorate the deliverance of the Jews from massacre at the hands of Haman.

purine *n* a white crystalline compound found in uric acid.

purism *n* insistence on correctness in language, form, style, etc.

purist *n* someone who is a stickler for correctness in language, style, etc.—**purism** *n*.—**puristic** *adj*.—**puristically** *adv*.

puritan *adj* a person who is extremely strict in religion or morals; (*with cap*) an extreme English Protestant of Elizabethan or Stuart times. * *adj* of or like a puritan; (*with cap*) of the Puritans.—**puritanism, Puritanism** *n*.

puritanical *adj* rigorously strict in religious or moral matters; (*with cap*) of the Puritans or Puritanism.—**puritanically** *adv*.—**puritanicalness** *n*.

purity *n* the state of being pure.

purl *vt* to knit a stitch by drawing its base loop from front to back of the fabric. * *n* a stitch made in this way.

purlieu *n* (*usu pl*) adjacent or outlying areas.

purlin, purline *n* a piece of lumber lying horizontally to support rafters.

purloin *vt* to steal.—**purloiner** *n*.

purple *n* a dark, bluish red; crimson cloth or clothing, esp as a former emblem of royalty. * *adj* purple-colored; royal; (*writing style*) over-elaborate. * *vti* to make or become purple.

Purple Heart *n* a US military decoration awarded to all those wounded or killed in action against an enemy.

purport *vt* to claim to be true; to imply; to be intended to seem. * *n* significance; apparent meaning.—**purportedly** *adv*.

purpose *n* objective; intention; aim; function; resolution, determination. * *vti* to intend, design.

purposeful *adj* determined, resolute; intentional.—**purposefully** *adv*.—**purposefulness** *n*.

purposeless *adj* lacking purpose; pointless.—**purposelessly** *adv*.—**purposelessness** *n*.

purposely *adv* deliberately; on purpose.

purposive *adj* having or serving a purpose.—**purposively** *adv*.

purpura *n* a blood disease causing the eruption of small purple spots.

purr *vi* (*cat*) to make a low, murmuring sound of pleasure.—**purring** *n*.

purse *n* a woman's handbag; a small pouch or bag for money; finances, money; a sum of money for a present or a prize. * *vt* to pucker, wrinkle up.

purser *n* an officer on a passenger ship in charge of accounts, tickets, etc; an airline official responsible for the comfort and welfare of passengers.

purslane *n* a flowering plant with fleshy leaves, used in salads.

pursuance *n* the pursuing or performance of an action.

pursuant *adj* (*law*) according; (*arch*) pursuing.

pursue *vb* (**pursuing, pursued**) *vt* to follow; to chase; to strive for; to seek to attain; to engage in; to proceed with. * *vi* to follow in order to capture.—**pursuer** *n*.

pursuit *n* the act of pursuing; an occupation; a pastime.

pursuivant *n* a low-ranking officer of the British College of Heralds; (*formerly*) an attendant or state messenger.

purulent *adj* pertaining to pus.—**purulence, purulency** *adj*.—**purulently** *adv*.

purvey *vti* to procure and supply (provisions).

purveyance *n* the procuring of provisions; the provisions provided; (*formerly*) the right accorded to royalty to buy up provisions without the owner's consent.

purveyor *n* a person who, or an organization which, supplies provisions.

purview n the scope or range of an action, document, statute, etc; the extent or range of outlook.

pus[1] abbr = permanently unfit for service.

pus[2] n a yellowish fluid produced by infected sores.

PUS abbr = Pharmacopoeia of the United States.

Pusan n a city in the Republic of Korea.

push vti to exert pressure so as to move; to press against or forward; to impel forward, shove; to urge the use, sale, etc, of; (inf) to approach an age; (inf) to sell drugs illegally; to make an effort * n a thrust, shove; an effort; an advance against opposition; (inf) energy and drive.

push button n a knob that activates an electrical switch which opens or closes a circuit to operate a radio, bell, etc.

pushcart n a barrow or cart pushed by hand.

pushchair n (Brit) a wheeled metal and canvas chair for a small child.—also **stroller**.

pusher n that which pushes; (inf) a person who sells illegal drugs.

pushing adj go-ahead, energetic; ambitious; assertive.

Pushkin n Aleksandr Sergeyevich (1799–1837) Russian poet, novelist, and dramatist, widely regarded as Russia's greatest poet, whose novels include Eugene Onegin (1828).

pushover n (inf) something easily done, as a victory over an opposing team; (inf) a person easily taken advantage of.

pushrod n a metal rod in an internal combustion engine that opens and closes the valves.

pushy adj (**pushier, pushiest**) (inf) assertive; forceful; aggressively ambitious.—**pushily** adv.—**pushiness** n.

pusillanimous adj faint-hearted, cowardly.—**pusillanimity** n.

puss[1] n (inf) a cat; (sl) a girl.

puss[2] n (sl) the mouth; the face.

pussy[1] n (pl **pussies**) (inf) a cat, a pussycat; (vulg sl) the female genitalia; a contemptuous term for a woman; sex with a woman.

pussy[2] adj (pl **pussier, pussiest**) like or containing pus.

pussycat n (inf) a cat; an amiable person.

pussyfoot vi to move stealthily; to be evasive.—**pussyfooter** n.

pussy willow n a willow with long, furry catkins.

pustule n a blister or swelling containing pus.—**pustular** adj.—**pustulation** n.

put vti (**putting, put**) to place, set; to cast, throw; to apply, direct; to bring into a specified state; to add (to); to subject to; to submit; to estimate; to stake; to express; to translate; to propose; (a weight) to hurl; (with **about**) to change the course of (a ship); to worry; (with **across**) to effect successfully; (with **away**) to remove; to lay by; (sl) to consume; (arch) to divorce; (with **back**) to replace; to return to land; (with **by**) to thrust aside; to store up; (with **down**) to suppress; to silence; to kill or have killed; to write or enter; to reckon; to assign; (sl) to belittle or humiliate; (with **forth**) to exert; to bud or shoot; to set out; (with **in**) to interpose; to spend (time); to apply (for); to call (at); (with **off**) to doff, discard; to postpone; to evade; to get rid of; to discourage, repel; to foist (upon); to leave shore; (with **on**) to don; to assume, pretend; to increase; to add; to advance; to stage (a play, etc); (sl) to hoax; (with **out**) to eject; to extend; to exert; to dislocate; to quench; to publish; to place (money) at interest; to disconcert, to anger; to leave shore; (baseball) to retire a batter or runner; (with **over**) to succeed in, to carry through; to postpone; (with **through**) to carry out; to cause to do or undergo; (with **up**) to rouse; to offer (prayer); to propose as a candidate; to pack; to sheathe; to lodge; to build; to provide (money); to arrange (hair) on top; (inf) to incite some action; (with **up with**) to endure, to tolerate; (with **upon**) to impose upon; (with **wise**) to disabuse, to enlighten. * adj fixed.

putative adj reputed, supposed.—**putatively** adv.

putdown n (sl) a humiliation; a cutting remark.

Putman n Andrée (1925–) French interior and furniture designer noted for her black-and-white interiors, such as the 1985 Morgan Hotel in New York.

put-on adj pretended. * n (sl) a hoax.

putout n (baseball) a play in which the runner or batter is put out or retired.

putrefy vti (**putrefying, putrefied**) to make or become putrid; to rot, decompose.—**putrefaction** n.—**putrefactive** adj.—**putrefier** n.

putrescent adj decaying, rotting.—**putrescence** n.

putrid adj rotten or decayed and foul-smelling.—**putridity** n.—**putridly** adv.

putrid fever n (arch) typhus fever.

Putsch n an uprising or revolt.

putt vti (golf) to hit (a ball) with a putter. * n in golf, a stroke to make the ball roll into the hole.

puttee n a legging made from a strip of cloth wound spirally from the ankle to the knee.

putter[1] n (golf) a straight-faced club used in putting.

putter[2] vi to busy oneself idly; to spend time, to potter.—**putterer** n.

putter[3] n one who or that which puts; an athlete who puts the shot.

putting green n (golf) the area of smooth grass surrounding the hole.

putto n (pl **putti**) (art) a figure of cupid and representations of children.—also **amoretto, amorino**.

putty n (pl **putties**) a soft, plastic mixture of powdered chalk and linseed oil used to fill small cracks, fix glass in window frames, etc. * vt (**puttying, puttied**) to fix or fill with putty.

PUVA abbr = psoralen plus ultra-violet A (treatment for psoriasis).

Puvis de Chavannes n (1824–98) French symbolist painter. His chaste, timeless allegorical works, such as The Inspiring Muses (1893–95), were extremely popular and highly influential.

Puzo n Mario (1920–99) American novelist whose most famous work is The Godfather (1969).

puzzle vt to bewilder; to perplex. * vi to be perplexed; to exercise one's mind, as over a problem. * n bewilderment; a difficult problem; a toy or problem for testing skill or ingenuity; a conundrum.—**puzzlement** n.—**puzzler** n.

puzzling adj perplexing, bewildering, inexplicable.—**puzzlingly** adv.

pv abbr (pharm) (Latin) = per vaginam, "by way of the vagina."

PVA = polyvinyl acetate, a plastic produced by the polymerization of vinyl acetate.

PVC = polyvinyl chloride or polychloroethene, the most widely used of the vinyl plastics formed by polymerization of vinyl chloride.

PVD abbr = peripheral vascular disease.

PVFS abbr = post-viral fatigue syndrome.

PVOA abbr = Passenger Vehicle Operators' Association.

PVS abbr = persistent vegetative state; post-viral syndrome.

pvt abbr = pressure, volume, temperature.

Pvt. abbr = Private.

pw abbr = per week.

PW abbr = Policewoman; Positively Women.

PW or **p.w.** abbr (transp) = packed weight.

PWA abbr = person with AIDS.

PWBA abbr = Pension and Welfare Benefits Administration.

PWC abbr = Pakistani Workers' Association; People's World Convention; Postwar Credits.

PWD abbr = Public Works Department.

PWG abbr = Permanent Working Group (of European Junior Hospital Doctors).

PWI abbr = Permanent Way Institution.

PWLB abbr = Public Works Loan Board.

PWM abbr = pulse with modulation.

PWPS abbr = Pure Water Preservation Society.

PWR abbr = pressurised water reactor.

pwt. abbr = pennyweight.

px abbr = part exchange.

PX abbr = physical examination; please exchange; Post Exchange; private exchange.

pxt. abbr (Latin) = pinxit, "he (or she) painted it."

Py symbol (chem) pyridyl; pyridine (element).

pya n a monetary unit of Myanmar (Burma), worth one hundredth of a kyat.

Py.B. abbr = Bachelor of Pedagogy.

pycnometer n an instrument for measuring densities or specific gravities.

pyelitis n inflammation of part of the kidney, the renal pelvis.

pyemia, pyaemia n blood poisoning.—**pyemic** adj.

Pygmalion n (Greek myth) a king of Cyprus, who fell in love with a statue of a girl, which Aphrodite brought to life for him.

pygmy n (pl **pygmies**) an undersized person.—also **pigmy** (pl **pigmies**).

pyjamas see pajamas.

Pylades n (Greek myth) faithful friend of Orestes, who helped Orestes to murder Clytemnestra.

Pwyll n (Welsh Celtic myth) a lord of Dyfed, Wales whose chief court was at Arbeth.

Pybba n (d. c.606) king of Mercia, Britain (c.593–c.606). He is thought to have been the son of Creoda, the first king of the Mercians. His family of three sons and two daughters founded the Mercian dynasty.

pylon n transmission tower, a structure supporting electric power lines; (archit) one of a pair of short towers with a rectangular base and pyramidal shape, set on either side of a gateway to an Egyptian temple.

pyloric stenosis n a narrowing of the pylorus which limits the movement of food from the stomach to the duodenum, resulting in vomiting.

pylorus n (pl **pylori**) (anat) the opening from the stomach into the intestine.

Pylos n ancient town of the Peloponnese in Greece, one of the most important palaces and settlements of the Mycenaeans and among the best preserved.

Pylos decay n a method of dating which involves measuring the amount of decay in a chemical element. (See **radiocarbon dating**).

Pym n Barbara (1913–80) English novelist whose works, including Excellent Women and A Glass of Blessings, are gently satirical, occasionally melancholic, comedies of middle-class life.

pymt. abbr = payment.

Pynchon n Thomas (1937–) American novelist, whose huge and complex books employ black humor to portray his vision of humanity's struggle against technology and whose best-known novels are V and Gravity's Rainbow.

PYO abbr = pick your own.

Pyongyang n capital city of the Democratic People's Republic of Korea.

pyorrhea, pyorrhoea n inflammation of the gums and tooth sockets.

pyracantha n a small, flowering, evergreen shrub.

pyramid n (geom) a solid figure having a polygon as base, and whose sides are triangles sharing a common vertex; a huge structure of this shape, as a royal tomb of ancient Egypt; an immaterial structure built on a broad supporting base and narrowing gradually to an apex. * vi to speculate (as on a commodity exchange) by using paper profits as margin for additional transactions; to build up, as in a pyramid. * vt to use (as profits) in speculative pyramiding; to increase the impact of price to the consumer by treating an assessed tax as a cost subject to markup.—**pyramidal, pyramidical, pyramidic** adj.—**pyramidally, pyramidically** adv.

pyramidion n (Egypt) the pyramid-shaped apex of an obelisk. It represents the Benben stone: the rays of the sun caught in stone, set on the primeval mound that rose from the waters.

pyramid selling *n* the process of selling goods to agents who then sell batches to other distributors at a higher price, and so on.

pyramid texts *n* (*Egypt*) texts engraved on the passage walls of Fifth and Sixth-Dynasty pyramids at Saqqara, concerned with securing entry into the afterlife for the deceased.

Pyramus and Thisbe *n* (*myth*) young Assyrian lovers whose love was forbidden by their parents. When they tried to meet, Thisbe was frightened away by a lioness, and Pyramus thought that she had been killed and killed himself with his sword. Thisbe returned and also killed herself.

pyre *n* a pile of wood for cremating a dead body.

pyrethrum *n* a type of chrysanthemum with showy flowers; an insecticide made from this plant.

pyretic *adj* pertaining to, or causing, fever.

Pyrex *n* (*trademark*) heat-resistant glassware.

pyrexia *n* fever.—**pyrexial, pyrexic** *adj*.

pyrheliometer *n* an instrument for measuring the sun's heat.

pyrimidine *n* (*chem*) one of the two different structures that form the base components of DNA and RNA.

pyrites *or* **pyrite** *n* (*pl* **pyrites**) a sulfide of a metal, esp iron.

pyroclastic rocks *npl* (*geol*) rocks, such as pumice, that are formed by the violent expulsion of rock and lava from volcanic vents.

pyroelectric *adj* becoming electric as a result of heat.

pyrogen *n* any substance that causes a rise in temperature of the body.

pyrogenic, pyrogenous *adj* caused by, or causing, heat, or fever.

pyrolisis *n* decomposition by heat.

pyromania *n* (*psychol*) an uncontrollable urge to set things on fire.

pyrometer *n* an instrument used to measure very high temperatures.—**pyrometry** *n*.

pyrope *n* a deep red variety of garnet.

pyrophoric *adj* igniting when exposed to air.

pyrosis *n* heartburn.

pyrotech. *abbr* = pyrotechnics.

pyrotechnics *n sing* the art of making or setting off fireworks; (*sing or pl*) a fireworks display; a brilliant display of virtuosity.—**pyrotechnic, pyrotechnical** *adj*.

pyroxenes *npl* (*geol*) an important group of rock-forming minerals that are silicates of iron, magnesium and calcium, sometimes with aluminum.

pyroxylin, pyroxyline *n* a substance derived from cellulose, used in making plastics.

Pyrrhic *adj* (*victory*) so costly as to be equal to defeat.

pyrrhic *n* a metrical foot of two syllables.

Pyrrhus *n* 1. (319–271 BC) king of Epirus (306–272 BC) 2. another name for **Neoptolemus**.

Pythagoras *n* (?580–500 bc) Greek philosopher and mathematician.

Pythagoras' theorem *n* (*geom*) the theorem that states that in any right-angled triangle, the square of the hypotenuse is equal to the sum of the squares of the two shorter sides.—*also* **Pythagorean theorem**.

Pythagorean *adj* pertaining to, or characteristic of, the Greek philosopher Pythagoras.

python *n* a large, nonpoisonous snake that kills by constriction.—**pythonic** *adj*.

Python *n* (*Greek myth*) a dragon that guarded the oracle of Delphi.

pythoness *n* a priestess in the temple of Apollo at Delphi, in ancient Greece; a (female) soothsayer; a witch.

pyuria *n* (*med*) the discharge of pus into the urine.

pyx *n* (*Christian Church*) a container in which consecrated bread is kept.

pyxidium *n* (*pl* **pyxidia**) (*bot*) a pyxis.

pyxis *n* (*pl* **pyxides**) a seed capsule with a lid that falls off to release the seeds.

Q

q, Q *n* the 17th letter of the alphabet.

q *abbr* = quark; quart/er; query; quintal; quire.

q. *abbr* = quart; quarter (of a hundredweight); quarterly; quarto; quasi; queen; query; question; quintal; quire; squall.

Q *abbr* = Quarto (early Shakespeare text); Quebec; Queen; Queensland; quality; quantity; quartermaster; (*cards, etc*) queen; question.

Q. *abbr* = Quebec (province); Queensland.

qa *abbr* = quick assembly.

QA *abbr* = quality assurance; quarters allowance.

QAA *abbr* = Quality Ash Association.

QAB *abbr* = Queen Anne's Bounty.

Qaddafi, Moammar al- *see* Gaddafi, Moammar al-.

QADS *abbr* = quality assurance data system.

QAIMNS *abbr* (*Brit*) = Queen Alexandra's Imperial Military Nursing Service.

QALY *abbr* = quality-adjusted life year (concerned with the cost–benefit assessment of possible treatment).

Q & A *abbr* = question and answer.

Qantas *abbr* = Queensland and Northern Territory Aerial Service (Australian airline).

QARANC *abbr* (*Brit*) = Queen Alexandra's Royal Army Nursing Corps.

QARNNS *abbr* (*Brit*) = Queen Alexandra's Royal Naval Nursing Service.

Qatar *n* an oil-rich emirate which lies halfway along the coast of The Gulf. Qatar is an absolute monarchy.

Qatar Riyal *n* currency of Qatar.

q.b. *abbr* = quick break.

QB *abbr* = (*Brit*) Queen's Bench; (*chess*) queen's bishop.

QBC *abbr* = Quality British Celery Association.

QBD *abbr* (*Brit*) = Queen's Bench Division.

Q-boat *abbr* = query-boat (ship with hidden guns and so of uncertain status).

QBP *abbr* = (*chess*) queen's bishop's pawn.

qc *abbr* = quality control.

QC *abbr* (*Brit*) = Queen's Counsel.

QCA *abbr* = Quaker Concern for Animals.

QCD *abbr* = quantum chromodynamics.

QCE *abbr* = quality control engineering.

QCGA *abbr* (*Austral*) = Queensland Cane Growers' Association.

QCT *abbr* = quality control technology.

q.d. *abbr* (*Latin*) = *quasi dicat*, "as if he should say."

q.d.a. *abbr* = quantity discount agreement.

qds *abbr* (*Latin*) = *quater die sumendus*, "to be taken four times a day."

q.e. *abbr* (*Latin*) = *quod est*, "which is."

QE2 *abbr* = Queen Elizabeth the Second (ship).

QED *abbr* = quantum electrodynamics; (*Latin*) *quod erat demonstrandum*, "which was to be proved."

QEF *abbr* (*Latin*) = *quod erat faciendum*, "which was to be done."

QEH *abbr* (*Brit*) = Queen Elizabeth Hall.

QEI *abbr* (*Latin*) = *quod erat inveniendum*, "which was to be found out."

QF *abbr* = quick-firing.

QFD *abbr* = quantum flavor dynamics.

Q fever *n* an infectious disease that produces symptoms resembling pneumonia, including a severe headache, high fever, and breathing problems. *See* rickettsiae.

QFSM *abbr* (*Brit*) = Queen's Fire Service Medal.

QG *abbr* = Quartermaster General.

QGM *abbr* (*Brit*) = Queen's Gallantry Medal.

qh *abbr* (*Latin*) = *quaque hora*, "every hour."

QI *abbr* = quartz-iodine.

QIB *abbr* = Qatar Islamic Bank.

qid *abbr* (*Latin*) = *quater in die*, "four times a day."

qindar *see* lek.

QISAM *abbr* = queued indexed sequential access method.

QKOA *abbr* = Quarantine Kennel Owners' Association.

QKt *abbr* = (*chess*) queen's knight.

QKtP *abbr* = (*chess*) queen's knight's pawn.

ql. *abbr* = quintal.

q.l., q. lib. *abbr* (*Latin*) = *quantum libet*, "as much as you please."

QL *abbr* = query language.

QLA *abbr* = Quantum Leap Society.

qlty. *abbr* = quality.

qm *abbr* (*Latin*) = *quaque mane*, "each morning."

qm. *abbr* (*Latin*) = *quo modo*, "in what way."

QM *abbr* = Quartermaster; quantum mechanics.

QMC *abbr* = Quartermaster Corps.

Qmess *abbr* (*Brit*) = Queen's Messenger.

QMG, Q. M. Gen. *abbr* = Quartermaster-General.

QMORC *abbr* = Quartermaster Officers' Reserve Corps.

QMP *abbr* = Quality Milk Producers.

QMS *abbr* = Quartermaster-Sergeant.

QMW *abbr* (*Brit*) = Queen Mary and Westfield College, University of London.

qn *abbr* (*Latin*) = *quaque nocte*, "each night."

QN *abbr* = (*chess*) queen's knight.

QNI *abbr* (*Brit*) = Queen's Nursing Institute.

QNP *abbr* = (*chess*) queen's knight's pawn.

qns *abbr* = quantity not sufficient.

QP *abbr* = (*chess*) queen's pawn.

QP, q. pl. *abbr* (*Latin*) = *quantum placet*, "as much as you wish."

QPM *abbr* (*Brit*) = Queen's Police Medal.

QPR *abbr* (*Brit*) = Queen's Park Rangers (soccer team).

QPS *abbr* = Quaker Peace and Service.

qq. *abbr* = questions.

Qq *abbr* = quartos.

qq. hor. *abbr* (*Latin*) = *quaque hora*, "each hour."

qq.v. *abbr* (*Latin*) = *quae vide*, "which [things] see."

qr. *abbr* = quarter; quire.

QR *abbr* = (*chess*) queen's rook.

QRA *abbr* = quick reaction alert.

QRP *abbr* = (*chess*) queen's rook's pawn.

QRPG *abbr* = Quebec Rubber and Plastic Group (Canada).

qrs. *abbr* = quarters; quires.

qs *abbr* = quadraphonic stereo.

q.s. *abbr* = (*Latin*) *quantum sufficit*, "enough"; quarter section (of land).

QS *abbr* (*Brit*) = Queen's Scholar; quarter sessions.

QSO *abbr* = quasi-stellar object.

QSS *abbr* = quasi-stellar radio source.

QST *abbr* (*Brit*) = Quality Scottish Trout.

QSTOL *abbr* = quiet short take-off and landing.

qt. *abbr* = quantity; quart.

QT *abbr* (*inf*) = quiet (such as "on the QT," meaning surreptitiously).

qto. *abbr* = quarto.

QTOL *abbr* = quiet take-off and landing.

qtr. *abbr* = quarter.

qts. *abbr* = quarts.

qty *abbr* = quantity.

Q-type asteroid *n* a rare asteroid type with similarities to meteorites known as chondrites.

qu. *abbr* = quart; quarter; queen; query; question.

qu., quar., quart. *abbr* = quarter; quarterly.

qua *prep* as, in the character of, because.

quack[1] *n* the cry of a duck. * *vi* to make a sound like a duck.

quack[2] *n* an untrained person who practices medicine fraudulently; a person who pretends to have knowledge and skill he does not have.—*also adj*.

quackery *n* (*pl* quackeries) pretence of medical or other skill; imposture.

quacksalver *n* (*arch*) a quack who deals in ointments, etc; a charlatan.

quad *n* quadrangle; quadruplet.

quadr-, quadri-, quadru- *prefix* four.

quadragenarian *n* (a person) forty to forty-nine years old. * *adj* relating to such a person.

Quadragesima (Sunday) *n* the first Sunday in Lent.

Quadragesimal *adj* pertaining to, or used in, Lent.

quadrangle *n* (*archit*) a large oblong or square courtyard surrounded by buildings on all sides.

quadrangle *n* (*geom*) a plane figure with four sides and four angles, a rectangle; a court enclosed by buildings.—quadrangular *adj*.

quadrant *n* (*geom*) a quarter of the circumference of a circle; an arc of 90 degrees; an instrument with such an arc for measuring angles, altitudes, or elevations; a curved street.—quadrantal *adj*.

Quadrantids *n* a meteor shower with its radiant in the constellation Boötes that occurs annually early in January.

quadrant method *n* (*archeo*) a method for the excavation of a circular structure by digging away two alternate quarters.

quadraphonic *adj* using four channels to record and reproduce sound.—quadraphonics, quadraphony *n*.

quadrat *n* an area in which a sample is surveyed.

quadrate *adj* (*zool*) of or pertaining to one of a pair of bones found in the skulls of fishes, reptiles, and some birds; (*anat*) of or pertaining to the middle bone of the middle ear in mammals; (*arch*) square or rectangular. * *vt* to square or make rectangular; (*often with* **with**) to cause to conform; to correspond. * *n* a quadrate bone; a square or cube.

quadratic *adj* square; (*math*) involving the square but no higher power. * *n* a quadratic equation.

quadratic equation *n* an equation in which the highest power of the unknown is the square.

quadratics *n sing* the branch of algebra dealing with quadratic equations.

quadrature *n* the act of squaring; the reduction of a figure to a square, exactly or approximately; (*astron*) the position of a heavenly body when distant 90 degrees from another, usu the earth, said esp of the position of the moon from the sun; (*math*) the finding of a square with an area exactly equal to a circle or other figure or a surface; (*electronics*) the state between two waves being 90 degrees out of phase.

quadrennial *adj* lasting or occurring every four years.—**quadrennially** *adv*.

quadricentennial *n* a four hundredth anniversary.—*also adj*.

quadriceps *n* the large thigh muscle, which is divided into four distinct parts and is responsible for movements of the knee joint.

quadrifid *adj* with four parts, four-cleft.

quadrifrons *n* (*archit*) a Roman structure with four arches, placed at a cross-roads.

quadriga *n* (*pl* **quadrigas, quadrigae**) an ancient Roman two-wheeled chariot drawn by four horses abreast; (*archit*) a large sculpture of a chariot drawn by a row of four horses, placed on top of a building façade or monument.

quadrilateral *n* (*geom*) any geometric shape that has four sides, e.g., a rectangle, square, kite, parallelogram, or rhombus; a combination or group that involves four parts or individuals. * *adj* having four sides.

quadrille *n* a square dance for four or more couples; the music for this.

quadrillion *n* in Europe, the fourth power of a million, i.e., 1 with 24 zeros; in the US, the fifth power of a thousand, i.e., 1 with 15 zeros.—*also adj*.—**quadrillionth** *adj*.

quadrinomial *n* an algebraic expression consisting of four terms.

quadripartite *adj* of four parts; shared by four.

quadripartite vault *n* (*archit*) a vault with the bay divided into four compartments by two ribs crossing diagonally.

quadriplegia *n* paralysis of all four limbs.—**quadriplegic** *adj, n*.

quadrivalent *adj* (*chem*) with four valences; with a valence of four, tetravalent.—**quadrivalence, quadrivalency** *n*.

quadrivial *adj* pertaining to a quadrivium; (*roads, etc*) leading in four ways; coming from four directions and meeting at the same point.

quadrivium *n* (*pl* **quadrivia**) a medieval course of study comprising arithmetic, geometry, astronomy, and music.

quadroon *n* the child of one White and one half-Negro parent, a person one quarter Black.

quadrumanous, quadrumanal *adj* (*monkeys, apes*) having four hands that can grasp.

quadruped *n* a four-footed animal.—**quadrupedal** *adj*.

quadruple *adj* four times as much or as many; made up of or consisting of four; having four divisions or parts. * *vti* to make or become four times as many.

quadruplet *n* one of four children born at one birth; (*mus*) a group of four notes of equal value played in the time of three.

quadruple time *n* (*mus*) (common time) the time of four quarter notes (crotchets) in a bar; it is indicated by the time-signature 4/4 or C.

quadruplicate *vt* to multiply by four; to make four copies of. * *adj* fourfold.—**quadruplication** *n*.

quadruplicity *n* (*pl* **quadruplicities**) fourfold nature.

quad spin CD ROM *n* (*comput*) a CD ROM that spins at a rate four times faster than the original CD ROM drives.

quaestor, questor *n* in ancient Rome, the public treasurer, or sometimes one of the other public officials.

quaff *vti* to take large drinks (of), drain.—**quaffer** *n*.

quagga *n* (*pl* **quaggas, quagga**) an extinct striped South African animal like a sand-colored zebra.

quaggy *adj* (**quaggier, quaggiest**) of or like a bog or marsh.

quagmire *n* a bog that is so soft and wet that the surface moves up and down when walked on.

quagmire *n* soft, wet ground; a difficult situation.

quahog *n* an edible North American clam, found on the Atlantic coast.

quail[1] *vi* to cower, to shrink back with fear.

quail[2] *n* (*pl* **quails, quail**) a small game bird.

quaint *adj* attractive or pleasant in an odd or old-fashioned style.—**quaintly** *adv*.—**quaintness** *n*.

quake *vi* to tremble or shiver, esp with fear or cold; to quiver. * *n* a shaking or tremor; (*inf*) an earthquake.

Quaker *n* a popular name for a member of the Society of Friends, a religious sect advocating peace and simplicity.—**Quakerism** *n*.

quaky *adj* (**quakier, quakiest**) shaky; trembling; unstable.—**quakily** *adv*.—**quakiness** *n*.

qualgo *abbr* = quasi-autonomous local government organization.

qualifiable *adj* that may be qualified.

qualification *n* qualifying; a thing that qualifies; a quality or acquirement that makes a person fit for a post, etc; modification; limitation; (*pl*) academic achievements.

qualifier *n* one that qualifies; an adjective or adverb.

qualify *vti* (**qualifying, qualified**) to restrict; to describe; to moderate; to modify, limit; to make or become capable or suitable; to fulfill conditions; to pass a final examination; (*gram*) to limit the meaning of.—**qualificatory** *adj*.—**qualifyingly** *adv*.

qualitative *adj* of or depending on quality; determining the nature, not the quality, of components.—**qualitatively** *adv*.

qualitative analysis *n* (*chem*) the chemical examination of a sample to discover what substances are present.

quality *n* (*pl* **qualities**) a characteristic or attribute; degree of excellence; high standard. * *adj* of high quality.

quality control *n* a system of assessing and maintaining the quality of manufactured products by periodically sampling the output and comparing it to the original specification.

qualm *n* a doubt; a misgiving; a scruple; a sudden feeling of faintness or nausea.—**qualmish** *adj*.

quandary *n* (*pl* **quandaries**) a predicament; a dilemma.

quango *abbr* (*Brit*) = quasi-autonomous non-governmental organization, an executive body that, although not a government agency as such, is often ultimately responsible to a government minister and is appointed to oversee a specified area of public-sector activity and expenditure.

quant *n* (*Brit*) a long pole, used in punting, with a disk on the end to prevent it from sinking when pushed into mud etc in a river. * *vt, vi* to punt with a quant.

Quant *n* **Mary** (1934–) English fashion designer and designer of the miniskirt, which became the symbol of "swinging sixties" London.

quant. suff. *abbr* (*Latin*) = *quantum sufficit* ("just enough").

quantify *vt* (**quantifying, quantified**) to express as a quantity; to determine the amount of.—**quantifiable** *adj*.—**quantification** *n*.

quantitative *adj* capable of being measured; relating to size or amount.—**quantitatively** adv.

quantitative analysis *n* (*chem*) the examination of a sample to discover the amounts of the substances present.

quantity *n* (*pl* **quantities**) an amount that can be measured, counted, or weighed; a large amount; the property by which a thing can be measured; a number or symbol expressing this property.

quantity discount *n* a price reduction to buyers who purchase a product in large quantities.

quantum *n* (*pl* **quanta**) a quantity, share or portion; a fixed, elemental unit of energy; (*physics*) a small amount or unit of electromagnetic radiation that can be thought of as a particle of energy. * *adj* large, significant.

quantum gravity *n* an as yet undeveloped theory to combine *Grand Unified Theory* (i.e. a single theory of nuclear and electromagnetic forces) with a theory of gravitational interaction.

quantum leap *n* an abrupt transition from one energy state to another; a sudden or noticeable change or increase.—*also* **quantum jump**.

quantum numbers *n* a set of four numbers used to describe atomic structures.

Quantz *n* **Johann Joachim** (1697–1773) German composer and flautist. He composed some 300 flute concertos and many other works for the instrument. He also wrote an important treatise on flute playing.

quaquaversal *adj* (*geol*) pointing in every direction.

quar. *abbr* = quart; quarterly.

quarantine *n* a period of isolation imposed to prevent the spread of disease; the time or place of this. * *vt* to put or keep in quarantine.

Quarenghi *n* **Giacomo** (*b*. 1744), Italian architect. His notable works include the Academy of Sciences, St Petersburg.

quark *n* (*physics*) a hypothetical elementary particle; any of the theoretical building blocks that participate in the strong interactive forces between elementary particles.

Quarles *n* **Francis** (1592–1644) English poet whose most popular work was *Emblems*, a set of devotional poems. His other poetry includes *Divine Poems*, *Divine Fancies*, and *Argalus and Parthenia* (1629). His prose works include *Enchiridion*.

In the English Civil War he wrote pamphlets, e.g., *The Loyal Convert*, in the royalist cause.

quarrel[1] *n* an argument; an angry dispute; a cause of dispute. * *vi* (**quarreling, quarreled** *or* **quarrelling, quarrelled**) to argue violently; to fall out (with); to find fault (with).—**quarreler, quarreller** *n*.

quarrel[2] *n* (*archit*) a pane of glass, usu diamond-shaped, in a medieval leaded window.—*also* **quarry**.

quarrelsome *adj* contentious; apt to quarrel.

quarrier, quarryman *n* (*pl* **quarriers, quarrymen**) one who works in a quarry.

quarry[1] *n* (*pl* **quarries**) an excavation for the extraction of stone, slate, etc; a place from which stone is excavated; a source of information, etc. * *vti* (**quarrying, quarried**) to excavate (from) a quarry; to research.

quarry[2] *n* (*pl* **quarries**) a hunted animal, prey.

quart *n* a liquid measure equal to a quarter of a gallon or two pints; a dry measure equal to two pints.

quartan *adj* recurring every fourth day, said of a fever, esp malaria.

quartan fever *n* the recurrent fever, which usu occurs every fourth day, associated with malaria.

quarter *n* a fourth of something; one fourth of a year; one fourth of an hour; 25 cents, or a coin of this value; any leg of a four-legged animal with the adjoining parts; a particular district or section; (*pl*) lodgings; a particular source; an unspecified person or group; a compass point other than the cardinal points; mercy; (*her*) any of four quadrants of a shield. * *vti* to share or divide into four; to provide with lodgings; to lodge; to range over (an area) in search (of). * *adj* constituting a quarter.

quarterage *n* a quarterly payment; (*rare*) a shelter.

quarterback *n* (*football*) a player directly behind forwards and the center, who directs play. * *vt* to direct the attacking play of (a football team); to manage, direct. * *vi* to play quarterback.

quarterbound *adj* a book bound on the spine only in leather, or another material more expensive than the rest of the binding.

quarterdeck *n* the stern area of the upper deck of a ship.

quartered *adj* divided into four quarters; sawn along two diameters, said of logs; (*her*) a shield divided into four parts, each with different arms, or with two sets of arms repeated at diagonally opposite corners; stationed or billeted, said esp of soldiers in civilian lodgings.

quarterfinal *n* one of four matches held before the semifinals in a tournament.—*also adj*.

quarter horse *n* a breed of muscular horse valued for its speed and endurance over short distances, esp a quarter of a mile.

quartering *n* the assignment of quarters to soldiers etc; (*her*) the division of a shield that contains several coats, often denoting a family's alliances and intermarriages; any coat of arms so treated.

quarterlight *n* a usu triangular section within the window of a car.

quarterly *adj* occurring, issued, or spaced at three-month intervals; (*her*) divided into quarters. * *adv* once every three months; (*her*) in quarters. * *n* (*pl* **quarterlies**) a publication issued four times a year.

quartermaster *n* (*mil*) an officer in charge of stores; (*naut*) a petty officer in charge of steering, etc.

quarter note *n* (*mus*) a note having one fourth the duration of a whole note.

quarters *npl* lodgings, esp for soldiers; action stations, esp used in reference to each member of the crew of a battleship; in India, accommodation provided by an employer or by the government; (*sl used by soldiers*) (*sing*) a quartermaster.

quarterstaff (*pl* **quarterstaves**) *n* a staff 6 to 8 feet long and shod with iron, formerly used as a two-handed weapon of defense; the use of one of these.

quarter tone *n* (*mus*) half a semitone, which is the smallest interval traditionally used in Western music.

quartet, quartette *n* a set or group of four; a group of four performers or a composition for such a group; a piece of music composed for four instruments or voices; a group of four instrumentalists or voices.

Quarti *n* **Eugenio** (1867–1931) Italian furniture designer who furnished the Palazzo Castiglioni in Milan.

quartic *adj* (*math*) pertaining to the fourth power, biquadratic. * *n* the fourth power, arising from the multiplication of a square number or quantity by itself.

quartile *n* (*statistics*) (*astrol*) one of three values of a variable that separates its distribution into four sets with equal frequencies. * *adj* (*statistics*) pertaining, or referring, to a quartile; (*astrol*) referring to an aspect of planets separated by 90 degree longitude.

quarto *n* (*pl* **quartos**) a page size, *approx* 9 by 12 inches; a book of this size of page.

Quarton *n* **Enguerrand** (*c*.1410–66) French medieval painter. His works are characterized by strong light and powerful draftsmanship, richly illuminated. Only two of his authenticated works have survived.

quartz *n* one of the most widely distributed rock-forming minerals, silicon dioxide, which occurs in all kinds of rocks; in its various crystalline forms and with certain impurities, it forms semi-precious stones, e.g. amethyst and agate.

quartzite *n* a very hard quartz rock; a light-colored quartz sandstone.

quasar *n* a distant "*quasi*-stel*lar*" object that emits an enormous amount of energy, mainly as infrared radiation.

quash *vt* to put down (a rebellion, etc); to suppress; to make void.

quasi *n* (*mus*) (*Italian*) literally, "as if" or "nearly"; so *quasi niente* means "almost nothing", or as softly as possible. * *adv* seemingly; as if. * *prefix* almost, apparently.

quasi-contract *n* an obligation that one party is deemed by a court to have to another, although there is no formal contract between the parties.

quassia *n* a South American tree yielding bark and wood of excessive bitterness; the bark and wood from a tree of the same family, used to make furniture; formerly a bitter tonic drug obtained from this, which is now used as an ingredient in insecticides.

quat. *abbr* (*Latin*) = *quattuor* ("four").

quatercentenary *n* (*pl* **quatercentenaries**) a 400th anniversary, or the entire year of celebrations etc of a 400th anniversary.

quaternary *adj* consisting of, arranged in, or by, fours; of the number 4; (*chem*) an atom bound to four other atoms or groups, or containing such an atom; (*math*) with four variables; (*geol, with cap*) denoting strata more recent than the Upper Tertiary, i.e., the most recent geological period, of less than 1 million years ago. * *n* (*pl* **quaternaries**) (*with* **the**) this geological rock system, consisting of Pleistocene and Holocene (recent) epochs.

quaternion *n* the number 4; a set of 4; (*math*) a calculus or method of mathematical investigation using a generalized complex number with four components.

quaternity *n* (*pl* **quaternities**) four persons regarded as one, esp in relation to God.

quatrain *n* a four-line stanza, rhymed alternately.

quatrefoil *n* a four-leaved plant, such as certain clovers; an ornamental figure in architectural tracery divided by cusps into four leaves.

quattrocento *n* the fifteenth century, esp in connection with Italian art and literature.

quaver[1] *n* (*mus*) (*Brit*) eighth note; a note which is half the length of a quarter note and the eighth of a whole note.

quaver[2] *vi* to tremble, vibrate; to speak or sing with a quivering voice. * *n* a trembling sound or note; (*mus*) (*Brit*) an eighth note.—**quaveringly** *adv*.—**quavery** *adj*.

quay *n* a loading wharf or landing place for vessels.

quayage *n* an interconnected network of quays; quay dues.

Quayle *n* 1. **Sir [John] Anthony** (1913–89) English actor and director. 2. **Dan [James Danforth]** (1947–) American Republican politician. Elected a congressman for Indiana (1977) and senator (1981), Bush selected him as his presidential running mate (1988) and he was elected vice-president of the USA (1989–93). 3. **Sir [John] Anthony** (1913–89) English actor and director. He worked with the Shakespeare Memorial Theatre (1948–56), now the Royal Shakespeare Company, helping to establish its international standing. He appeared in several films, e.g., *Woman in a Dressing Gown* (1957) and *The Guns of Navarone* (1961), but was principally a stage actor, founding his own classical touring company, Compass (1982).

QUB *abbr* (*Brit*) = Queen's University of Belfast.

Que. *abbr* = Quebec.

queasy *adj* (**queasier, queasiest**) nauseous; easily upset; over-scrupulous.—**queasily** *adv*.—**queasiness** *n*.

Quebec *n* a province in east Canada.

Québec City *n* a city in Canada.

quebracho *n* (*pl* **quebrachos**) one of two types of South American tree with a hard timber rich in tannin, and used in tanning and dyeing; the medicinal bark of a South American tree, the alkaloids from the bark of which are also used in tanning; the wood or bark from any of these trees; any South American tree yielding a hard wood.

queen *n* a female sovereign and head of state; the wife or widow of a king; a woman considered pre-eminent; the egg-laying female of bees, wasps, etc; a playing card with a picture of a queen; (*chess*) the most powerful piece; (*sl*) a male homosexual, esp one who ostentatiously takes a feminine role. * *vi* (*with* **it**) to act like a queen, esp to put on airs. * *vt* to promote (a pawn) to a queen in chess.—**queendom** *n*.

queencake *n* a small currant cake.

queenly *adj* (**queenlier, queenliest**) like or having the character or attributes of a queen; regal.—**queenliness** *n*.

queen mother *n* a queen dowager who is the mother of a ruling sovereign.

Queensberry *n* **David, Marquess of** (1930–) British glassware and ceramics designer whose notable pieces include the 1963 *Harlequin* range of cut glass for Webb Corbett.

queer *adj* strange, odd, curious; (*inf*) eccentric; (*sl*) homosexual. * *n* a (male) homosexual. ******vt* (*sl*) to spoil the success of.—**queerness** *n*.

Queirolo *n* **Francesco** (1704–62) Italian sculptor. The intricacy of his work is evident in his *Allegory of Deception Unmasked* (1750s), which is of outstandingly high quality.

quell *vt* to suppress; to allay.—**queller** *n*.

Quellin *n* **Artus I** (1609–68) Flemish sculptor. He established his reputation as a classical sculptor in his decoration of Amsterdam Town Hall (1650–64).

quench *vt* to satisfy or slake (thirst); to put out, extinguish (fire); to cool (steel); to suppress.—**quenchable** *adj*.—**quencher** *n*.

quenelle *n* a ball of savory cooked meat, formed into various shapes and boiled in stock or fried.

Quercia *n* **Jacopo della** (*c.*1375–1438) Italian sculptor. His last major commission was for the relief scenes of *Genesis* and *The Birth of Christ* at San Petronio in Bologna, the energetic directness and strength of which were admired by Michelangelo.

quercine *adj* of the oak.

querist *n* one who asks questions.

quern *n* a grinding stone for pounding grains of corn into flour.

querulous *adj* complaining, fretful, peevish.—**querulously** *adv*.

query *n* (*pl* **queries**) a question; a question mark; doubt; (*comput*) a focused search request used in a database management program. * *vti* (**querying, queried**) to question; to doubt the accuracy of.

ques. *abbr* = question.

quest *n* a search, seeking, esp involving a journey. * *vti* to search (about) for, seek.—**quester** *n*.—**questingly** *adv*.

question *n* an interrogative sentence; an inquiry; a problem; a doubtful or controversial point; a subject of debate before an assembly; a part of a test or examination. * *vti* to ask questions (of); to interrogate intensively; to dispute; to subject to analysis.—**questioner** *n*.

questionable *adj* doubtful; not clearly true or honest.—**questionability** *n*. —**questionably** *adv*.

question mark *n* a punctuation mark (?) used at the end of a sentence to indicate a question, or to express doubt about something; something unknown.

questionnaire *n* a series of questions designed to collect statistical information; a survey made by the use of questionnaire.

questor *see* **quaestor**.

quetzal *n* a large brilliantly colored Central or Southern American bird, the male having long tail feathers; the standard monetary unit of Guatemala, made up of 100 centavos.

queue (*Brit*) *n* a line of people, vehicles, etc awaiting a turn; (*comput*) two or more files waiting, e.g., to print.* *vi* (**queuing, queued**) to wait in turn; *vti* (*comput*) (of files) to wait, e.g., to print.

Quezaltenango *n* a city in Guatemala.

Quezon City *n* a city in Philippines.

quibble *n* (*esp Brit*) a minor objection or criticism. * *vi* to argue about trifling matters.—**quibbler** *n*.—**quibblingly** *adv*.

quiche *n* a savory tart filled with various ingredients, e.g., onions, and a cheese and egg custard.

quick *adj* rapid, speedy; nimble; prompt; responsive; alert; eager to learn. * *adv* (*inf*) in a quick manner. * *n* the sensitive flesh below a fingernail or toenail; the inmost sensibilities.—**quickly** *adv*.—**quickness** *n*.

quicken *vti* to speed up or accelerate; to make alive; to come to life; to invigorate.—**quickener** *n*.

quickening *n* (*med*) the first movements of a baby in the womb (uterus), which are perceived by the mother usu around the fourth month of pregnancy.

quickie *n* (*inf*) anything done rapidly or in haste.

quicklime *n* calcium oxide.

quicksand *n* an unstable stretch of super-saturated sand that cannot bear weight.

quicksilver *n* mercury.

quickstep *n* a ballroom dance in quick time; the music for this. * *vi* (**quickstepping, quickstepped**) to do this dance.

quick-tempered *adj* easily angered.

quick-witted *adj* mentally alert; quick in repartee.—**quick-wittedness** *n*.

quid *n* (*pl* **quid**) (*Brit sl*) a pound (sterling).

quiddity *n* (*pl* **quiddities**) (*philos*) the essence of a thing; captious subtlety, a quibble.

quidnunc *n* one who is curious to know everything that happens; a gossip, a busybody.

Quidor *n* **John** (1801–81) American painter who drew his imagery from literary sources, e.g., *The Return of Rip van Winkle* (1829), but his lively and humorous genre paintings were generally unappreciated.

quid pro quo *n* (*pl* **quid pro quos**) something equivalent given in exchange for something else.

quiescent *adj* dormant, inactive, inert; silent.—**quiescence** *n*.

quiet *adj* silent, not noisy; still, not moving; gentle, not boisterous; unobtrusive, not showy; placid, calm; monotonous, uneventful; undisturbed. * *n* stillness, peace, repose; an undisturbed state. * *vti* to quieten.—**quietly** *adv*.—**quietness** *n*.

quieten *vti* to make or become quiet; to calm, soothe.

quietism *n* a mental tranquillity and passive attitude towards life; a form of religious mysticism, founded in 17th–century Spain, in which the cultivation of this attitude with reference to God's will is to be attained.

quietize, quietise *vt* to insulate something from sound; to soundproof.

quietness *n* repose.

quiet Sun *n* the term applied to the Sun when its sunspot cycle is at its minimum.

quietude *n* repose; tranquillity.

quietus *n* (*pl* **quietuses**) death; the final settlement or discharge of debts etc; anything that results in death or annihilation.

quiff *n* (*Brit*) a curl plastered up above the forehead.

quill *n* the hollow stem of a feather; anything made of this, as a pen; a stiff, hollow spine of a hedgehog or porcupine.

Quiller-Couch *n* **Sir Arthur Thomas** (1863–1944) British author and critic whose career began with the novel *Dead Man's Rock*. He wrote a series of novels set in Cornwall, written under the pseudonym "Q." He edited some anthologies, e.g., *The Oxford Book of English Verse*. As a critic, his works include *On the Art of Writing*, *Shakespeare's Workmanship*, and *On the Art of Reading*.

quilt *n* a thick, warm bedcover; a bedspread; a coverlet of two cloths sewn together with padding between. * *vti* to stitch together like a quilt; to make a quilt.—**quilter** *n*.—**quilting** *n*.

Quilter *n* **Roger** (1877–1953) English composer who studied in Germany for a time. He is best known for his songs. His work also includes the light opera *Julia*, and the orchestral work *A Children's Overture*.

quin *n* a quintuplet.

quinary *adj* consisting of, or arranged in, fives; having five parts. * *n* (*pl* **quinaries**) a number system with a base of the number 5; the fifth member of something.

quinate *adj* (*bot*) with five leaflets on a petiole; said of a digitate leaf.

quince *n* a hard-fleshed yellow Asian fruit used in preserves; the tree it grows on.

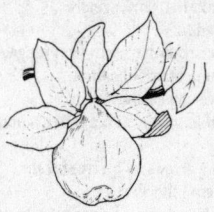

quincentenary *n* (*pl* **quincentenaries**) a 500th anniversary, or the entire year of celebration, etc, of the 500th anniversary.

quincunx *n* an arrangement of five things in the form of four corners and the center of a square; (*bot*) such an arrangement of petals or sepals in bud; (*astrol*) two planets with an aspect of 150 degrees.

quindecagon *n* a plane figure with 15 angles and 15 sides.

Quine, Willard van Orman (1908–) American philosopher and logician. Noted for his criticisms of empiricism, his works include *Set Theory and its Logic* (1963) and *Word and Object* (1961).

Quinet *n* **Jacques** (1918–94) French interior architect who was a master cabinetmaker, designing the architectural interior and decoration of the 1953 liner *La Bourdonnais*.

quinine *n* a colorless bitter crystalline alkaloid, derived from the bark of certain (cinchona) trees, which is a strong antiseptic and esp effective against the malarial parasite.

quinqu-, quinque- *prefix* five.

quinquagenarian *n* (a person) fifty to fifty-nine years old; relating to such a person. * *adj* relating to such a person.

Quinquagesima (Sunday) *n* the Sunday before Lent.

quinquennial *adj* lasting five years or occurring every five years.—**quinquennially** *adv*.

quinquennium *n* (*pl* **quinquennia**) a period of five years.

quinquepartite *adj* of five parts; shared by five.

quinquereme *n* in ancient Rome, a galley with five banks of oars on each side.

quinquevalent *adj* (*chem*) having a valence of five, pentavalent.—**quinquevalence, quinquevalency** *n*.

quinsy *n* a complication of tonsillitis, when a pus-filled abscess occurs near the tonsil, causing great difficulty in swallowing.—*also* **peritonsillar abscess**.

quint *n* a quintuplet.

quintain *n* a post with a sandbag on a pivot, or other object, used for practicing the medieval sport of tilting; tilting at this.

quintal *n* a measure of weight, 100 lb; a measure of weight of 100 kilograms.

quintan *adj* said of an intermittent fever which recurs every fifth day.

quintessence *n* the purest form or most typical representation of anything, the embodiment.

quintessential *adj* most typical; fundamental.—**quintessentially** *adv*.

quintet, quintette *n* a set or group of five; a piece of music composed for five instruments or voices; a group of five instrumentalists or voices.

Quintilian [Marcus Fabius Quintilianus] (AD *c.*35–100) Roman rhetorician and critic, born in Spain, whose fame rests on his major work *De Institutione Oratoria*, a manual for the training of orators.

quintillion *n* (*pl* **quintillions, quintillion**) in North America, the sixth power of a thousand, known as a trillion in Britain; in Western Europe, a million raised to the fifth power, known in North America as a nonillion. —**quintillionth** *adj*.

quintuple *adj* fivefold; having five divisions or parts; five times as much or as many. * *vti* to multiply by five. * *n* a number five times greater than another.

quintuplet *n* one of five offspring produced at one birth.

quintuple time *n* (*mus*) five beats, usu quarter notes, in a bar, i.e., 5/4 time.

quintuplicate *vt* to multiply by five; to make five copies of. * *adj* fivefold. * *n* a set of five objects.—**quintuplication** *n*.

quip *n* a witty remark; a gibe. * *vt* (**quipping, quipped**) to make a clever or sarcastic remark.—**quipster** *n*.

quire *n* a set of 24 sheets of paper; one twentieth of a ream; a section of folded sheets sewn together in bookbinding.

Quirinalia *n* a festival in honor of Romulus, held annually on the thirteenth day before the calends of March, that is, 17th February.

Quirinus *n* (*Roman myth*) a surname of Romulus after he had been raised to the rank of a divinity.

quirk *n* an unexpected turn or twist; a peculiarity of character or mannerism.

quirky *adj* (**quirkier, quirkiest**) odd or unusual in character, behavior, or appearance.—**quirkily** *adv*.—**quirkiness** *n*.

quirt *n* a riding whip of plaited leather with a leather thong at the end. * *vt* to lash with this.

quisling *n* a traitor who aids an invading enemy to regularize their conquest of his or her country; a collaborator.

Quisling *n* **Vidkun** (1887–1945) Norwegian Fascist leader installed as prime minister (1942–45) by the Nazis, and executed for treason after the war.

quit *vti* (**quitting, quitted** *or* **quit**) to leave; to stop or cease; to resign; to free from obligation; to admit defeat; (*comput*) to exit from a program. * *adj* free from; released from.

quitch (grass) *n* couchgrass.

quit claim deed *n* (*law*) an instrument conveying the title of real estate from one individual, who is quitting any claim that he or she has, to another party.

quite *adv* completely; somewhat, fairly; really.

Quito *n* capital city of Ecuador.

quits *adj* even; on equal terms by payment or revenge.

quittance *n* a release from debt or obligation.

quitter *n* a person who gives up easily.

quiver[1] *vi* to shake; to tremble, shiver. * *n* a shiver, vibration.—**quiveringly** *adv*.—**quivery** *adj*.

quiver[2] *n* a case for holding arrows.—**quiverful** *n*.

qui vive *n* **on the qui vive** on the alert.

quixotic, quixotical *adj* chivalrous or romantic to extravagance; unrealistically idealistic.—**quixotically** *adv*.

quixotism, quixotry *n* romantic or extravagant notions or schemes; quixotic conduct or ideals.

quiz *n* (*pl* **quizzes**) a form of entertainment where players are asked questions of general knowledge; a short written or oral test. * *vt* (**quizzing, quizzed**) to interrogate; to make fun of.—**quizzer** *n*.

quizmaster *n* a person who puts the questions to a contestant in a quiz show.

quiz show *n* an entertainment program on television or radio in which contestants answer questions to win prizes.

quizzical *adj* humorous and questioning.—**quizzicality** *n*.—**quizzically** *adv*.

QUNG *abbr* = Quaker United Nations Group.

quod erat demonstrandum (*Latin*) that which was to be proved.

quodlibet *n* a subtle or moot point, esp as part of a theological argument; (*mus*) a light musical medley.—**quodlibetical** *adj* **quodlibetically** *adv*.

quoin *n* a wedge of wood or metal used to support and steady something (esp formerly a gun or cannon); a keystone; (*archit*) an external angle of a building; the dressed stone forming this, the cornerstone; a wedge-shaped wooden block to tighten the pages of type within a chase.

quoit *n* a ring of metal, plastic, etc thrown in quoits; (*pl*) a game in which rings are thrown at or over a peg.

quondam *adj* that was, former.

quorum *n* the minimum number that must be present at a meeting or assembly to make its proceedings valid.

quot. *abbr* = quotation.

quota *n* a proportional share; a prescribed amount; a part to be contributed; a restriction on the trade in, or in the production of, a particular product imposed, for example, by a government or supplier.

quotable *adj* worthy or fit to be quoted.—**quotability** *n*.

quotation *n* the act of quoting; the words quoted; an estimated price.

quotation[1] *n* the price and terms on which a tradesman, company, etc, is prepared to provide a service or goods; the official price of a security or commodity.

quotation[2] *n* permission from the regulatory authority of a stock market for the shares of a company to be traded in that market.

quotation mark *n* a punctuation mark to indicate the beginning (" *or* ') and the end (" *or* ') of a quoted passage.

quote *vt* to cite; to refer to; to repeat the words of a novel, play, poem, speech, etc, exactly; to adduce by way of authority; to set off by quotation marks; to state the price of (something). * *n* (*inf*) something quoted; a quotation mark.

quoted company *same as* **listed company**.

quoth *vt* (*arch*) said, used with nouns and all pronouns except thou and you.

quotid. *abbr* (*Latin*) = *quotidie* ("daily").

quotidian *adj* daily; recurring every day, occurring every day; belonging to each day; commonplace, routine, everyday, trivial. * *n* a fever, esp malaria, recurring every day.

quotient *n* (*math*) the result arrived at when a mathematical quantity is divided by another quantity –the "answer."

quotient rule *n* (*math*) a mathematical method used in calculus.

quo warranto *n* (*law*) a proceeding set in motion to determine the authority by which someone claims an office or privilege; (*formerly*) the title of a writ issued to a person to try the question of title to any public office or privilege.

q.v. *abbr* (*Latin*) = *quantum vis* ("as much as you wish"); *quod vide* ("which see").

q.v. *abbr* = quantum vis; quod vide.

qwerty, QWERTY *adj* (*comput*) the standard computer keyboard, denoted by the letters on the top line of characters.

qwl *abbr* = quality of working life.

qy. *abbr* = query.

R

r, R *n* the 18th letter of the English alphabet.

r *abbr* = radius; rear, recto, right; rises (of the Sun); run.

r. *abbr* = (*chem*) racemic; railroad; railway; (*surveying*) range; rare; (*comput*) received; recipe; rector; redactor; (*dyeing*) reddish; reserve (troops); resides; retired; river; road; rod *or* rods; rood *or* roods; rubber; (*law*) rule; (*navy*) run (deserted).

R *abbr* = Rabbi; (*chem*) radical, esp. hydrocarbon radical; Réaumur (temperature scale); (*church service*) respond *or* response; (*elect*) resistance; (*math*) radius, radius (vector), rank, ratio; (*org chem*) with names of oleofines, the isomeric cyclic hydrocarbons, as *R*-propylene; (*phys chem*) gas constant; Rector; (*Latin*) *Regina*, "Queen"; Republican; (*Latin*) *Rex* , "King"; Réaumur; (*paper*) retree; River; Röntgen; (*chess*) rook; Royal; railway; (*Latin*) *recipe* , "take"; reply; return (train ticket, etc); reverse; ring; ruble; runic; rupee.

R18 *abbr* = Restricted 18 (classification by which a film can be shown or distributed only from premises where no one under that age is allowed).

Ra *or* **Re** *n* (*Egypt*) the oldest and one of the greatest of the Egyptian gods. He is also known as Atum, or Ra-Atum. A sky-god identified with the sun, he arose out of Nun, the primeval water, and through his own creation created the elements to sustain life on Earth, with Shu the air-god, Nut the sky-god, Geb the earth-god, Tefnut, the goddess of moisture, Nephthys, Osiris and Isis.

Ra *symbol* (*chem*) radium.

RA *abbr* = (*Brit*) Racecourse Association; (*Brit*) Ramblers' Association; Rear Admiral; Referees' Association; Refugee Action; Regular Army; Religious of the Assumption; (*Latin*) *Reverendus admodum*, "Very Reverend"; (*Brit*) Rice Association; (*astron*) right ascension; (*Brit*) Royal Academician; (*Brit*) Royal Academy of Art, London; (*Brit*) Royal Artillery; Rural Action; rheumatoid arthritis; right atrium.

R/A *abbr* (*comput*) = refer to acceptor.

Ra-A, **Ra-B** etc *symbol* (*chem*) radium A, radium B, etc.

RAA *abbr* = Regional Arts Association; Rice Growers' Association of Australia; (*Brit*) Royal Academy of Arts.

Ra-Ac, **Ra-Act** *symbol* (*chem*) radioactinium.

RAAF *abbr* = Royal Australian Air Force; (*Brit*) Royal Auxiliary Air Force.

Raamses *n* store city on the Nile delta built by the Hebrews when they worked as slaves for the Pharaoh.

RAAS *abbr* = Racial Adjustment Action Society; Royal Amateur Arts Society.

Rabat *n* capital city of Morocco.

rabb. *abbr* = rabbinical.

rabbet *n* (*archit*) a rectangular step-like recess or groove cut in a piece of wood or stone into which another piece fits. * *vt* to cut a rabbet in; to join (pieces of wood, etc) using a rabbet. —*also* **rebate.**

rabbi *n* (*pl* **rabbis**) the religious and spiritual leader of a Jewish congregation; (Hebrew) master or teacher; a Jewish title of respect.

rabbinate *n* the position or tenure of a rabbi; rabbis collectively.

rabbinical *adj* of or pertaining to rabbis, their office, writings, etc.—**rabbinically** *adv*.

rabbit *n* a small burrowing mammal of the hare family with long ears, a short tail, and long hind legs; their flesh as food; their fur.

rabbit punch *n* a sharp blow to the back of the neck.

rabbit's foot *n* the foot of a rabbit worn as a lucky charm.

rabble *n* a disorderly crowd, a mob; the common herd.

rabble-rouser *n* a person who excites a mob to violent action; a demagogue.

RABDF *abbr* = Royal Association of British Dairy Farmers.

Rabelais *n* **François** (*c.*1494–1553) French monk, physician, and satirist, noted for his huge, rambling prose fantasy *Gargantua and Pantagruel*, which includes many fascinating insights into the intellectual currents of the age.

Rabelaisian *adj* of, pertaining to, or resembling the coarse, satirical humor of François Rabelais; denoting language that is robustly bawdy.

RABI *abbr* (*Brit*) = Royal Agricultural Benevolent Institution.

rabid *adj* infected with rabies; raging; fanatical.

rabies *n* an acute, infectious, viral disease affecting the central nervous system, which occurs in dogs, wolves, cats, and other animals. Human beings are infected through the bite of a rabid animal, usu a dog.—*also* **hydrophobia.**

Rabin *n* **Yitzhak** (1922–95) Israeli politician and prime minister (1974–77, 1992–95) who was a signatory of the Israeli–Palestinian Peace Accord in 1994, along with Yasser Arafat. He was assassinated by a Jewish extremist.

RAC *abbr* = (*Brit*) Royal Agricultural College; (*Brit*) Royal Armoured Corps; (*Brit*) Royal Automobile Club; Rubber Association of Canada.

raccoon *n* a small nocturnal carnivore of North America that lives in trees; its yellowish gray fur.

race[1] *n* any of the divisions of humankind distinguished esp by color of skin; any geographical, national, or tribal ethnic grouping; a subspecies of plants or animals; distinctive flavor or taste.

race[2] *n* a contest of speed, as in running, swimming, cycling, etc; a rapid current or channel of water. * *vi* to run at top speed or out of control; to compete in a race; (of an engine) to run without a working load or with the transmission disengaged. * *vt* to cause to race; to contest against.

Race *n* **Ernest** (1913–64) British designer whose first success was the BA3 chair – more than 250,000 were produced.

RACE *abbr* = rapid automatic checkout equipment.

racecourse *n* a track over which races are run, esp an oval track for racing horses.—*also* **racetrack**.

racehorse *n* a horse bred and trained for racing.

raceme *n* (*bot*) an arrangement of flowers directly on a main stem, as in the lily of the valley.

racer *n* a person who races; a machine used for racing, esp a bicycle; a kind of American snake.

race relations *npl* the relationship between different races in a community or nation; the sociological study of such relations.

racetrack *see* **racecourse.**

Rachel *n* (*Bible*) younger daughter of Laban and beloved wife of Jacob; she became Jacob's wife after he had served Laban seven years for Leah, her elder sister, and another seven for her. *See also* **Jacob.**

rachis, rhachis *n* (*pl* **rachises, rhachises** *or* **rachides, rhachides**) the main stem of a plant's flower-head; the shaft of a feather; the spinal column.

rachitis *n* rickets.

Rachmaninov *n* **Sergei Vassilievich** (1873–1943) Russian composer and pianist whose principal compositions include: three operas (such as *The Miserly Knight*); three symphonies; pieces for piano and orchestra (such as *Rhapsody on a theme by Paganini*); choral pieces; numerous piano pieces; and songs.

racial *adj* of or relating to any of the divisions of humankind distinguished by color, etc.

Racine *n* **Jean** (1639–99) French dramatist, regarded as the finest of the French tragedians. Several of his plays, e.g., *Andromaque* and *Phèdre*, have been performed in English translations from the late 17th century onwards.

Racinet *n* **Albert Charles August** (1825–93) French draftsman and chromolithographer, who published his *L'Ornement Polychrome* in 1869.

racism, racialism *n* a belief in the superiority of some races over others; prejudice against or hatred of other races; discriminating behavior towards people of another race.—**racist** *n*.

rack[1] *n* a framework for holding or displaying articles; an instrument for torture by stretching; the triangular frame for setting up balls in snooker; a toothed bar to engage with the teeth of a wheel pinion or worm gear; extreme pain or anxiety. * *vt* (*person*) to stretch on a rack; to arrange in or on a rack; to torture, torment; to move parts of machinery with a toothed rack.

rack[2] *n* a thin broken mass of cloud driven by the wind. * *vi* (of clouds) to be blown by the wind.

rack[3] *n* a cut of lamb that includes 8 or 9 pairs of ribs.—*also* **rack of lamb**.

racket[1] *n* a bat strung with nylon, for playing tennis, etc; (*pl*) a game for two or four players played in a four-walled court.—*also* **racquet**.

racket[2] *n* noisy confusion; din; an obtaining of money illegally; any fraudulent business.

racket[3] *n* (*mus*) a woodwind instrument with a double reed used between the late-16th and early-18th centuries. It came in four sizes (soprano, tenor, bass, double bass) and created a distinctive buzzing sound.—*also* **rackett, ranket.**

racketeer *n* a person who extorts money by threat or engages in an illegal profit-making enterprise.

rack railway *see* **cog railway**.

rack-rent *n* an extortionate rent.—*also vt.*—**rack-renter** *n*.

racloir *n* (*archeo*) a large scraper that was often used also as a knife.

raconteur *n* a person who excels in relating anecdotes.

racquet *see* **racket**[1].

racy *adj* (**racier, raciest**) lively, spirited; risqué.—**racily** *adv*.

rad[1] *n* a unit of absorbed dose of ionizing radiation.

rad[2] *symbol* radian.

rad. *abbr* = radical; radix.

RAD *abbr* = (*Brit*) Royal Academy of Dancing; (*Brit*) Royal Association in Aid of Deaf People; reflex anal dilatation.

Rad. Sec. *abbr* = radio section.

RADA *abbr* (*Brit*) = Royal Academy of Dramatic Art.

radar *abbr* = Radio Detection And Ranging, a system or device for detecting objects such as aircraft by using the reflection of radio waves.

RADAR *abbr* (*Brit*) = Royal Association for Disability and Rehabilitation.

radar astronomy *n* the transmission of high-frequency radio signals to bodies within the Solar System.

radar beacon *n* a fixed radio transmitter that sends out a signal which allows a ship or an aircraft to determine its own position.

radarscope *n* a cathode-ray oscilloscope which displays radar signals.

RADC *abbr* (*Brit*) = Royal Army Dental Corps.

Radcliffe *n* **Mrs Ann** (1764–1823) English novelist whose Gothic novels, e.g., *A Sicilian Romance* and *The Mysteries of Udolpho*, were very popular in their day but are now largely remembered as part-sources for Jane Austen's satire on the Gothic novel, *Northanger Abbey*.

RADD *abbr* (*Brit*) = Royal Association in Aid of the Deaf and Dumb.

Radhakrishnan *n* **Sir Sarvepalli** (1888–1975) Indian philosopher and statesman. His works, which stress the similarities between Western and Hindu culture, include *The Hindu View of Life* (1926) and *An Idealist View of Life* (1932).

radial *adj* pertaining to a radius; branching from a common center.

radial ply *adj* (of a tire) having the fabric cords of the outer casing lying radial to the hub for greater flexibility.

radial symmetry *n* the state of having similar parts arranged symmetrically around a common axis.

radial velocity or **line-of-sight velocity** *n* the velocity of a star or similar object along the observer's line of sight.

radian *n* an alternative to the degree when measuring angles; the angle subtended at the center of a circle by an arc that is equal in length to the radius.

radiance *n* the condition of being radiant; brilliant light; dazzling beauty.

radiant *adj* shining; beaming with happiness; sending out rays; transmitted by radiation. * *n* the apparent origin of meteor showers on the celestial sphere.—**radiantly** *adv*.

radiant energy *n* energy in the form of electromagnetic radiation, such as heat or light.

radiant heat *n* heat conveyed by electromagnetic radiation rather than conduction or convection.

radiate *vt* (of light, heat, etc) to emit in rays; to give forth (happiness, love, etc). * *vi* to spread out as if from a center; to shine; to emit rays.

radiation *n* (*physics*) the giving out of energy from a source, which may be in the form of electromagnetic waves (radio, light, X-rays, infrared rays, etc), particles, or sound waves; radiant particles emitted as energy; rays emitted in nuclear decay; (*med*) treatment using a radioactive substance.

radiation belt *n* the region around a planet in which charged particles (electrons and protons) are trapped.

radiation pressure *n* the pressure created by photons (such as light or other electromagnetic radiation) on a surface.

radiation sickness *n* an illness caused by excessive exposure to radiation from radioactive materials.

radiator *n* an apparatus for heating a room; a cooling device for a vehicle engine.

radical *adj* of or relating to the root or origin; fundamental; favoring basic change. * *n* a person who advocates fundamental political or social change; (*chem*) a group of atoms within a compound, which are not able to exist on their own and are not changed when the substance is involved in chemical reactions.—**radicalism** *n*.

radically *adv* fundamentally.

radical sign *n* the symbol placed before a number to show that the square root (or a higher root denoted by an index number over the sign) is to be extracted.

radical treatment *n* (*med*) treatment aimed at the complete cure of a condition rather than the alleviation of symptoms. In contrast, conservative treatment is directed towards the minimum interference necessary to keep a condition under control.

radicchio *n* (*pl* **radicchios**) a type of Italian chicory with white-veined purple leaves eaten raw in salads.

radices *see* **radix**.

radicle *n* the part of a seed that develops into a root; a root-like subdivision of a nerve or vein.

radii *see* **radius**.

radio *n* the transmission of sounds or signals by electromagnetic waves through space, sending information in the form of sound, pictures, and digital data, without wires, to a receiving set; such a set; broadcasting by radio as an industry, entertainment, etc. * *adj* of, using, used in, or sent by radio. * *vti* to transmit, or communicate with, by radio.

radio- *prefix* radial; radio; using radiant energy.

radioactive *adj* giving off radiant energy in the form of particles or rays caused by the disintegration of atomic nuclei.—**radioactivity** *n*.

radioactive decay *n* the disintegration of a nucleus as the result of electron capture.

radioactive waste *n* any waste products that contain radioactive materials.—*also* **nuclear waste**.

radioactivity *n* (*physics*) the giving out of particles (known as a or b particles and g rays) by unstable substances that are disintegrating.

radio astronomy *n* (*physics*) the recording and study of radio waves given out by many bodies in space including the sun, stars and quasars.

radio beacon *n* a radio transmitter that sends out signals as an aid to navigation.

radio button *n* (*comput*) a round button that allows the user to choose one of a range of options in a dialog box.

radiocarbon *n* a radioisotope of carbon used in carbon dating.

radiocarbon dating *n* a method of dating organic material based on the radioactive decay of carbon-14. It can be used over the time range 400 to 50,000 years ago.—*also* **carbon dating**.

radiochemistry *n* (*chem*) the scientific study and purification of radioactive materials.

radio compass *n* a navigational device which can determine the direction of radio waves from a specific radio beacon.

radio control *n* remote control using radio signals.—**radio-controlled** *adj*.

radioelement *n* a radioactive chemical element.

radio frequency *n* a frequency intermediate between audio frequencies and infrared frequencies used esp in radio and television transmission.

radio galaxy *n* a galaxy that is the origin of radio emissions from electrons that are traveling close to the speed of light.

radiogram *n* (*Brit*) a combined radio and record player.

radiograph *n* an image produced on sensitive photographic film or plate by radiation other than light, esp X-rays.

radiography *n* (*physics*) the method or process of making an image of an object on photographic film (or on a fluorescent screen), using X-rays (or similar rays such as gamma rays); the diagnostic technique used to examine the body using X-rays; the production of X-ray photographs for use in medicine, industry, etc.—**radiographer** *n*.

radio-immuno assay *n* a technique of protein analysis that can be applied to tissues and fossils, based on the detection of a reaction to antibodies.

radio interferometer *n* a type of radio telescope in which an object is observed by more than one antenna.

radioisotope *n* a radioactive isotope.

radiologist *n* a doctor specializing in the interpretation of X-rays and other diagnostic records.

radiology *n* the branch of medicine concerned with the use of radiant energy (as X-rays and radium) in the diagnosis and treatment of disease.

radiometer *n* a device for measuring the electromagnetic radiation from an object, whether infrared radiation or radio emissions.

radiometer *n* an instrument for measuring radiant energy.—**radiometric** *adj*.

radiometric dating *n* (*physics*) a precise method of dating rocks that measures the amounts of certain radioactive elements present in their original and decayed states.

radiopaging *n* a system for alerting a person using a small radio transmitter which beeps in response to a signal from a distance.

radiosonde *n* (*meteorol*) a small radio transmitter, carried by a probe, that sends back data on successive atmospheric levels for the measurement of temperature, humidity, and pressure.

radio source *n* any celestial object that emits radio waves (e.g., the Sun, Jupiter, quasars).

radio spectrum *n* that range of frequencies, between 10 kHz and 300,000 MHz, used in radio transmission.

radiotelegraphy *n* telegraphy that uses radio waves to transmit messages.—**radiotelegraph** *n*.—**radiotelegraphic** *adj*.

radiotelephone *n* a device for transmitting telephone messages using radio waves. * *vt* to transmit by radiotelephone, * *vi* to operate a radiotelephone.—**radiotelephony** *n*.

radio telescope *n* (*astron*) an instrument used to detect and analyze electromagnetic radiation coming from various sources in space.

radiotherapy *n* the medical treatment of disease, esp cancer, by X-rays or other radioactive substances.—**radiotherapist** *n*.

radio wave *n* an electromagnetic wave with frequencies in the radio range of the spectrum.

radish *n* a pungent root eaten raw as a salad vegetable.

radium *n* a highly radioactive metallic element that occurs naturally and emits alpha, beta, and gamma rays as it decays.

radium therapy *n* the treatment of cancer by exposure to radiation from radium.

radius (*pl* **radii**) *n* (*anat*) the shorter outer bone of the forearm; (*geom*) a straight line joining the center of a circle or sphere to its circumference; a thing like this, a spoke; a sphere of activity.

radix *n* (*pl* **radices, radixes**) (*math*) a number that is the base of a number system or for computation of logarithms.

RAdm *abbr* = Rear Admiral.

radmon *abbr* = radiological monitoring.

radome *n* a protective housing for a radar antenna constructed from material which is transparent to radio waves.

radon *n* a gaseous radioactive element produced when radium decays. Radon seeds are small, sealed capsules that are used in radiotherapy for cancer.—*also* **niton**.

radula *n* (*pl* **radulae**) a horny strip covered with minute teeth on the tongue of certain mollusks.

RAE *abbr* (*Brit*) = Royal Aerospace Establishment.

RAeC *abbr* (*Brit*) = Royal Aero Club of the United Kingdom.

RAEC *abbr* (*Brit*) = Royal Army Educational Corps.

RAeS *abbr* (*Brit*) = Royal Aeronautical Society.

RAF *abbr* (*Brit*) = Royal Air Force.

RAFA *abbr* (*Brit*) = Royal Air Forces Association.

RAFBF *abbr* (*Brit*) = Royal Air Force Benevolent Fund.

RAFES *abbr* (*Brit*) = Royal Air Force Educational Service.

raffia *n* a kind of palm; fiber from its leaves used in basket-making, etc.

raffish *adj* untidy, disreputable, rakish; vulgarly flashy.

raffle *n* a lottery with prizes. * *vt* to offer as a prize in a raffle.

RAFGSA *abbr* (*Brit*) = Royal Air Force Gliding and Soaring Association.

RAFMS *abbr* (*Brit*) = Royal Air Force Medical Services.

RAFR *abbr* (*Brit*) = Royal Air Force Regiment.

RAFRO *abbr* (*Brit*) = Royal Air Force Reserve Officers.

RAFSC *abbr* (*Brit*) = Royal Air Force Staff College; Royal Air Force Strike Command.

raft *n* a platform of logs, planks, etc, strapped together to float on water.

RAFT *abbr* (*Brit*) = Restoration of Appearance and Function Trust.

rafter *n* a sloping roof beam running from the eave to the ridge to support the roof covering.

RAFVR *abbr* (*Brit*) = Royal Air Force Volunteer Service.

rag[1] *n* a torn or waste scrap of cloth; a shred; (*inf*) a sensationalist newspaper; (*pl*) tattered or shabby clothing.

rag[2] *vt* (**ragging, ragged**) to tease; (*Brit*) to play practical jokes on. * *n* (*Brit*) a practical joke; a series of boisterous stunts staged by students to raise money for charity.

rag[3] *n* ragtime music.

RAG *abbr* = Rainforest Action Group.

raga *n* (*mus*) a composition based on any of various conventional melodic or rhythmic patterns in Indian music used as the basis for improvisation; a type of Indian scale or a type of melody based on such a scale. Each raga is associated with a mood and with particular times of the day and year.

ragamuffin *n* an unkempt dirty person, esp a child.

rag and bone man *n* (*Brit*) a junk dealer.

ragbag *n* a bag for scraps; a miscellaneous collection, jumble.

rag doll *n* a doll made of bits of cloth, often stuffed.

rage *n* violent anger; passion; frenzy; fashion, craze. * *vi* to behave with violent anger; to storm; to spread rapidly; to be prevalent.

RAGE *abbr* = Radiotherapy Action Group Exposure.

ragged *adj* jagged; uneven; irregular; worn into rags; tattered.—**raggedly** *adv*.—**raggedness** *n*.

ragged robin *n* a Eurasian plant of the pink family with tattered looking pink or white flowers.

raggedy *adj* (*inf*) tattered.

raggle *n* (*archit*) a horizontal groove in a wall, esp. to hold the edge of a roof or a flashing.

ragi, raggee *n* a cereal grass cultivated in Asia and Africa.

raging *adj* violent; intense.

raglan *n* a type of loose sleeve cut in one piece with the shoulder of a garment.

ragout *n* a stew of meat and vegetables, highly seasoned.

RAGS *abbr* (*Brit*) = Recycling Advisory Group Scotland.

ragstone *n* (*archit*) a hard coarse stone used in masonry.

ragtime *n* (*mus*) a style of syncopated popular dance music, dating from the late 19th century. The combination of ragtime and the blues led to the development of jazz. Scott Joplin was a famous ragtime piano player.

ragweed *n* any of various weedy composite herbs native to North America.

ragwork *n* (*archit*) the use of ragstone, often laid flat with a thick layer of mortar in between then plastered and roughcast.

ragwort *n* a European composite plant with yellow flowers.

rah *interj* hurrah.

RAH *abbr* (*Brit*) = Royal Albert Hall.

Rahab *n* (*Bible*) a harlot in Jericho who hid spies sent by Joshua and secretly let them down by a rope through her window; Rahab and those in her house were the only persons spared when Jericho fell to the invading Israelites.

RAI *abbr* = Reading Association of Ireland; Restaurants Association of Ireland; (*Brit*) Royal Anthropological Institute; (*Brit*) Royal Archaeological Institute.

RAIC *abbr* = Russian-American Industrial Corporation.

raid *n* a sudden attack to assault or seize. * *vt* to make a raid on; to steal from.

raider *n* an individual or organization that makes a habit of initiating hostile takeover bids.

rail[1] *n* a horizontal bar extending from one post to another, as in a fence, etc; one of a pair of parallel steel lines forming a track for the wheels of a train; a railroad.

rail[2] *vi* to speak angrily.

railhead *n* the furthest point reached by the tracks of an uncompleted railway; a terminus.

railing *n* a fence of rails and posts; rails collectively.

raillery *n* (*pl* **railleries**) good-humored banter, mockery.

railroad *n* a track of parallel steel rails along which carriages are drawn by locomotive engines; a complete system of such tracks. * *vt* to force unduly; (of a bill, etc) to push forward fast; to imprison hastily, esp unjustly.

rail-splitter *n* a person who splits logs to make fences.

railway *n* (*Brit*) a railroad.

railway station *see* **train station.**

raiment *n* (*poet*) clothing.

rain *n* water that falls from the clouds in the form of drops; (*meteorol*) the condensation of water vapor into droplets when moist air is cooled below its dewpoint; a shower; a large quantity of anything falling like rain; (*pl*) the rainy season in the tropics. * *vti* (of rain) to fall; to fall like rain; (of rain, etc) to pour down.

rainboot *n* one of a pair of waterproof boots.

rainbow *n* (*meteorology*) the characteristic display of colors formed by the refraction and reflection of sunlight by raindrops in the air. * *adj* many-colored.

rainbow trout *n* a large freshwater trout of Europe and North America with bright markings.

rain check *n* a ticket stub allowing future admission to an event in the case of its being rained off; the postponement of acceptance of an offer or invitation.

raincoat *n* a waterproof coat.

raindrop *n* a drop of rain.

Raine *n* **Kathleen [Jessel]** (*b*. 1908) Anglo-Scottish poet and critic whose work reflects her life-long mystical vision of the world. Her works include *Collected Poems* and three autobiographical volumes, *Farewell Happy Fields*, *The Land Unknown*, and *The Lion's Mouth*.

rainfall *n* a fall of rain; the amount of rain that falls on a given area in a specified time.

rain forest *n* a dense, evergreen forest in a tropical area with much rainfall.

rain gauge *n* (*meteorol*) an apparatus for measuring rainfall, sometimes made of a funnel leading into a collecting bottle.

Rainier *n* **Priaulx** (1903–86) South African composer and violinist who won a scholarship to study in England and remained there for the rest of her life. Her works include orchestral pieces (e.g., *Sinfonia da Camera*), chamber music, compositions for piano, and many songs.

rainmaking *n* the process of attempting to produce rain by artificial means.—**rainmaker** *n*.

rainout *n* interruption or postponement caused by rain; radioactive fallout carried by rain.

rainproof *adj* rain-resisting.

rain shadow the leeward side of a hill or mountain where the rain is relatively lighter.

rainwater head *n* (*archit*) a metal box-like structure fixed to the top of a down-pipe to collect water from the gutter.

rainy *adj* (**rainier, rainiest**) full of rain; wet.

rainy day *n* a future need, esp financial.

RAIS *abbr* (*Brit*) = Royal Air International Service.

raise *vt* to elevate; to lift up; to set or place upright; to stir up, rouse; to increase in size, amount, degree, intensity, etc; to breed, bring up; to put forward (a question, etc); to collect or levy; to abandon (a siege). * *n* a rise in wages.

raised beach *n* (*geol*) an ancient beach that is now above the level of the shoreline, often because there has been a fall in sea level.

raisin *n* a sweet, dried grape.

raison d'être *n* (*pl* **raisons d'être**) reason for existence; justification.

raj *n* the period of British rule in India.

rajah, raja *n* (*formerly*) an Indian ruler; an Indian or Malayan chief or prince.

Rajar *abbr* (*Brit*) = Radio Joint Audience Research.

rake[1] *n* a tool with a row of teeth and a handle for gathering together, scraping (leaves, hay, etc) or for smoothing gravel, etc. * *vt* to scrape, gather as with a rake; to sweep with gaze or gunshot; (*with* **in**: of money, etc) to gather a great amount rapidly; (*with* **up**) to bring to light (past misdemeanors, etc).

rake[2] *n* the incline or slope of a mast, stern, etc.

rake[3] *n* a dissolute, debauched man, a libertine.

Rakhmaninov *see* **Rachmaninov, Sergei Vassilievich.**

raki, rakee *n* a strong aromatic spirit distilled from grain in Turkey.

rakish *adj* jaunty, dashing; dissolute.—**rakishly** *adv*.—**rakishness** *n*.

rale *n* a wheezing rattle detectable with a stethoscope in the chest of patients with lung disorders.

Raleigh[1] *n* the capital city of North Carolina, a state of the USA.

Raleigh[2] *n* **Sir Walter** (1552–1618) English courtier, poet, and explorer who organized unsuccessful attempts to colonize Virginia with English settlers in the 1580s.

rall. *abbr* (mus) (Italian) = *rallentando*.

rallentando *adv* (*mus*) (*Italian*) gradually slower.

rally *vti* (**rallying, rallied**) to bring or come together; to recover strength, revive; to take part in a motor rally; (*with* **round**) to help (a person); to support financially or morally. * *n* (*pl* **rallies**) a large assembly of people for a political purpose; a recovery (after illness); (*stock exchange*) a sharp increase in price after a decline; (*tennis*) a lengthy exchange of shots; a competitive test of driving and navigational skills.

ram *n* a male sheep; a battering device; a piston; (*with cap*) Aries, the first sign of the zodiac. * *vt* (**ramming, rammed**) to force or drive; to crash; to cram; to thrust violently.

ram *abbr* = relative atomic mass.

RAM *abbr* = (*Brit*) Royal Academy of Music; (*comput*) Random Access Memory: the **main memory** or **internal memory** that is altered in normal computer operations, allowing modification of the file in use until it is ready for storage permanently on disk.

Ramadan *n* the ninth month of the Islamic year; the great fast during it.

Ramah *n* (*Bible*) height or hill town; a common place name in Old Testament times.

Raman *n* **Sir Chandrasekhara Venkata** (1888–1970) Indian physicist who was awarded the 1930 Nobel prize for physics for his discovery of the Raman effect during his researches into the diffusion of light.

Ramanujan *n* **Srinivasa** (1887–1920) Indian mathematician. A self-taught prodigy with considerable intuitive powers, he sent a large number of theorems to Godfrey Hardy, who arranged for him to study at Cambridge University. He became the first Indian to be elected a Fellow of the Royal Society (1919).

Ramases *n see* **Raamses**.

Rambert *n* **Dame Marie [Cyvia Rambam]** (1888–1982) Polish-born ballet dancer, teacher, and producer; after working with Diaghilev and Nijinsky she settled in Britain in 1917. She formed the Ballet Club in 1931, which, renamed the Ballet Rambert in 1935, became the most influential ballet company in Britain.

ramble *vi* to wander or stroll about for pleasure; (of plants) to straggle; to write or talk aimlessly. * *n* a leisurely walk in the countryside.

rambler *n* a person who rambles; a climbing rose.

rambling *adj* spread out, straggling; circuitous; disconnected; disjointed.

Ramboesque *adj* in the aggressive, mindless style of the fictional character Rambo, an indestructible one-man army who featured in several violent action films in the 1980s.

rambunctious *adj* (*inf*) boisterous, unruly.—**rambunctiously** *adv*.—**rambunctiousness** *n*.

rambutan *n* (a Malaysian tree bearing) a hairy red edible fruit.

RAMC *abbr* (*Brit*) = Royal Army Medical Corps.

RAM cache *n* (*comput*) a part of the RAM that is set aside to store data and programs in order that the computer can operate more speedily. *See also* **cache**.

RAM disk *n* (*comput*) an area of RAM set aside by a utility program that is formatted to act like a disk drive.

Rameau *n* **Jean Philippe** (1683–1764) French composer, organist, and harpsichordist. His major works include the operas *Hippolyte et Aricie, Castor et Pollux,* and *Dardanus;* the opera-ballets *Les Indes galantes* and *Les Fêtes d'Hebe;* pieces of chamber music; church music and trio sonatas; and works for harpsichord.

Rameses I *n* the first Egyptian pharaoh of the Nineteenth Dynasty in the New Kingdom.

Rameses II *n* an Egyptian pharaoh of the Nineteenth Dynasty (ruled 1279–1212 BC) in the New Kingdom.

ramekin *n* a baked dish of cheese, breadcrumbs, etc; the small pot in which this is cooked.

ramification *n* a branching out; an offshoot; a consequence.

ramify *vti* to (cause to) divide into branches or constituent parts.

ramjet *n* (an aircraft having) a type of jet engine that uses compressed air from the forward movement to burn the fuel.

ramose *adj* composed of or having branches.—**ramosely** *adv*.

ramp *n* a sloping walk or runway joining different levels; a wheeled staircase for boarding a plane; a sloping runway for launching boats, as from trailers.

ramp *abbr* = rampion.

rampage *n* angry or violent behavior. * *vi* to rush about in an angry or violent manner.

rampant *adj* dominant; luxuriant, unrestrained; violent; rife, prevalent; (*her*) (of a beast) standing on its hind legs.

rampart *n* (*archit*) a defensive wall around a castle, fortified city, etc, built of earth, stone or brick.

Ramphal *n* **Sir Shridath Surrendranath, "Sonny"** (*b.* 1928) Guyanan statesman. As secretary-general of the Commonwealth (1975–89), he took an active and influential role in world affairs.

rampion *n* a Eurasian plant with bell-shaped red or purple flowers whose root is sometimes used in salads.

ramrod *n* a rod for ramming home a charge in a muzzle-loading gun. * *adj* denoting a stiff, inflexible person.

ramshackle *adj* dilapidated.

RAN *abbr* = Royal Australian Navy.

ran *see* **run**.

RANA *abbr* (*Brit*) = Royal Animal Nursing Auxiliary.

ranch *n* a large farm for raising cattle, horses, or sheep; a style of house with all the rooms on one floor. * *vi* to own, manage, or work on a ranch.—**rancher** *n*.

rancherie *n* a settlement of North American Indians in a reserve in British Columbia, Canada.

rancid *adj* having an unpleasant smell and taste, as stale fats or oil.—**rancidity, rancidness** *n*.

rancor, rancour *n* bitter hate or spite.—**rancorous** *adj*.—**rancorously** *adv*.

rand *n* the standard monetary unit of South Africa and Namibia, divided into 100 cents.

R & A *abbr* (*Brit*) = Royal and Ancient (Scottish golf club).

R & B *abbr* = rhythm and blues.

r. and c. *abbr* (*transp*) = rail and canal.

r & cc *abbr* = riot and civil commotion.

R & D *abbr* = research and development.

R&DSoc *abbr* = Research and Development Society.

R & E *abbr* = research and engineering.

R & I *abbr* (*Latin*) = *Regina et Imperatrix* ("Queen and Empress"); *Rex et Imperator* ("King and Emperor").

r. and l. *abbr* (*transp*) = rail and lake.

r & m *abbr* = reliability and marketing; reports and memoranda.

r. and o. *abbr* (*transp*) = rail and ocean.

random *adj* haphazard; left to chance.

random access *adj* (*comput*) the random retrieval of information without going through a series of locations to reach the desired point; direct access to data in any desired order.

random access memory *see* **RAM**.

randomize *vt* to arrange (e.g., a survey, samples) in a random way to obtain unbiased statistical results.—**randomization** *n*.—**randomizer** *n*.

random rubble *see* **rubble walling**.

R & R *abbr* = rescue and resuscitation; rest and recreation; rock and roll.

R & VA *abbr* = Rating and Valuation Association.

r. and w. *abbr* (*transp*) = rail and water.

randy *adj* (**randier, randiest**) (*Brit*) (*sl*) lustful, sexually aroused; horny.

ranee *see* **rani**.

rang *see* **ring**[2].

range *n* a row; a series of mountains, etc; scope, compass; the distance a ship, aircraft, or motor vehicle can travel without refueling; the distance a gun, etc, can fire, a projectile can be thrown, or from gun to target; fluctuation; a large open area for grazing livestock; a place for testing rockets in flight; a place for shooting or golf practice; a cooking stove; (*comput*) a cell or a group of contiguous cells in a spreadsheet program. * *vt* to place in order or a row; to establish the range of; (*livestock*) to graze on a range. * *vi* to be situated in a line; to rank or classify; (*gun*) to point or aim; to vary (inside limits).

range finder *n* an instrument for determining the range of a target.

ranger *n* a forest or park warden.

Rangoon (Yangon) *n* capital city of the Union of Myanmar.

rangy *adj* (**rangier, rangiest**) tall and slim; long-limbed.—**ranginess** *n*.

rani, ranee *n* in India, a queen or princess; the wife of a rajah.

Ranjitsinhji [Vibhaji] *n* **Prince [Kumar Shri]** (1872–1933) Indian maharajah and cricketer; nicknamed the "Black Prince" of cricket, he batted for Sussex (with C B Fry) and England. After service in World War I commanding Indian troops, he became maharajah of Nawanagar in 1918, and was noted for his progressive rule.

rank[1] *n* a line of objects; a line of soldiers standing abreast; high standing or position; status; (*pl*) ordinary members of the armed forces. * *vti* to arrange in a line; to have a specific position in an organization or on a scale; to outrank; (*with* **with**) to be counted among.

rank[2] *adj* growing uncontrollably; utter, flagrant; offensive in odor or flavor.

rank and file *n* ordinary soldiers; ordinary members, as distinguished from their leaders.

ranket *see* **racket**[3].

ranking *n* a listing of things or people in order of importance. * *adj* of the highest rank; outstanding.

rankle *vi* to fester; to cause continuous resentment or irritation.

ransack *vt* to plunder; to search thoroughly.

ransom *n* the release of a captured person or thing; the price paid for this. * *vt* to secure the release of by payment.

Ransom *n* **John Crowe** (1888–1974) American poet and critic whose poetic output, e.g., *Poems about God* and *Two Gentlemen in Bonds*, was small but highly regarded, as are his literary studies, *God without Thunder* and *The New Criticism*.

Ransome *n* **Arthur** (1884–1967) English novelist and journalist whose first popular success was as a popularizer of Russian folk tales, with his *Old Peter's Russian Tales*, but who is best remembered for his classic children's adventure novels, the first three of which were *Swallows and Amazons*, *Swallowdale*, and *Peter Duck*.

Ranson *n* **Pierre** (1736–86) French painter and designer who was the nephew of the great Gobelins flower painter Louis Tessier.

rant *vi* to speak loudly or violently; to preach noisily. * *n* loud, pompous talk.

ranunculus *n* (*pl* **ranunculuses, ranunculi**) a common genus of usu yellow-flowered plants including the buttercup.

RAOB *abbr* = Royal Antediluvian Order of Buffaloes.

RAOC *abbr* (*Brit*) = Royal Army Ordnance Corps.

rap[1] *n* a sharp blow; a knock; (*inf*) talk, conversation; (*sl*) arrest for a crime; (*sl*) rap music. * *vti* (**rapping, rapped**) to strike lightly or sharply; to knock; (*sl*) to criticize sharply; (*with* **out**) to utter abruptly; (*sl*) to speak in a fast and rhythmic manner to a musical backing.

rap[2] *n* a style of popular music in which (usu rhyming) words and phrases are spoken in a rhythmic chant over an instrumental backing.—**rapper** *n*.

RAP *abbr* = Radical Alternatives to Prison; Refugee Arrival Project; rupees, annas, pies.

rapacious *adj* grasping; extortionate.—**rapaciously** *adv*.—**rapacity** *n*.

RAPC *abbr* (*Brit*) = Royal Army Pay Corps.

rape[1] *n* the act of forcing a person to have sexual intercourse against his or her will; the plundering (of a city, etc) as in warfare. * *vti* to commit rape (upon).

rape[2] *n* a bright yellow plant of the mustard family grown for its leaves and oily seeds.

Raphael [Raffaello Sanzio] (1483–1520) Italian painter and architect from Urbino, a leading figure of the High Renaissance. His notable architectural works include the Palazzo Pandolfini, Florence.

rapid *adj* at great speed; fast; sudden; steep. * *npl* a part of a river where the gradient steepens and flow is fast and turbulent.—**rapidity** *n*.—**rapidly** *adv*.

RAPID *abbr* = Register for the Ascertainment and Prevention of Inherited Diseases.

rapid eye movement sleep *see* **REM sleep**.

rapid transit *n* a fast urban transport system, usu of electric trains.

rapier *n* a straight, two-edged sword with a narrow pointed blade.

rapine *n* plunder, pillage.

rapist *n* a person who commits rape.

rappel *vi* to abseil.

rapport *n* a sympathetic relationship; accord.

rapprochement *n* re-establishment of cordial relations; reconciliation.

rapscallion *n* a rascal.

rapt *adj* carried away, enraptured; absorbed, intent.

raptor *n* a bird of prey.

raptorial *adj* of or pertaining to birds of prey; (of birds' feet) adapted for seizing prey.

rapture *n* the state of being carried away with love, joy, etc; intense delight, ecstasy.—**rapturous** *adj*.—**rapturously** *adv*.

rara avis *n* a rare or unique person or thing.

RARDE *abbr* (*Brit*) = Royal Armament Research and Development.

rare[1] *adj* unusual; seldom seen; exceptionally good; (of a gas) of low density, thin.—*adv*.—**rareness** *n*.

rare[2] *adj* not completely cooked, partly raw; underdone.

rare earth *n* (an oxide of) any of the lanthanide series of chemical elements.

rarefy *vti* (**rarefying, rarefied**) to make or become less dense; to thin out; to expand without the addition of matter; to make more spiritual, abstruse or refined.—**rarefied** *adj*.

rare gas *n* an inert gas.

rarely *adv* almost never, seldom; exceptionally, unusually.

raring *adj* (*inf*) eager, enthusiastic.

rarity *n* (*pl* **rarities**) rareness; a rare person or thing.

RARO *abbr* = Regular Army Reserve of Officers.

RAS *abbr* = Recruitment and Assessment Services; (*Brit*) Royal Agricultural Society; (*Brit*) Royal Aeronautical Society; (*Brit*) Royal Asiatic Society; (*Brit*) Royal Astronomical Society.

Ras Algethi *or* **Alpha Herculis** *n* a binary star, the brightest in the constellation Hercules, comprising a red supergiant.

Ras al Khaymah *n* a city in the United Arab Emirates (UAE).

rasbora *n* any of various small brightly-colored tropical fishes popular for aquariums.

RASC *abbr* (*Brit*) = Royal Army Service Corps.

rascal *n* a rogue; a villain; a mischievous person.

Rasch *n* **Heinz** (*b*. 1902) **and Bodo** (*b*. 1903) German architects and designers who specialized in chair design.

rase *see* **raze**.

rash[1] *adj* reckless; impetuous.—**rashly** *adv*.—**rashness** *n*.

rash[2] *n* a skin eruption which is usu short-lived and consists of a reddened, perhaps itchy, area or raised red spots.

rasher *n* (*Brit*) a thin slice of bacon or ham.

RASNZ *abbr* = Royal Astronomical Society of New Zealand.

rasp *n* a coarse file; a grating sound. * *vt* to scrape with a rasp. * *vi* to produce a grating sound.

raspberry *n* (*pl* **raspberries**) a shrub with white flowers and red berry-like fruits; the fruit produced; (*inf*) a sound of dislike or derision.

Rasputin *n* **Grigori Efimovich** (*c*.1871–1916) Russian monk who was a cult figure among the Russian aristocracy, and an influential member of the royal household. He was assassinated in 1916.

Rastafarian, Rasta *n* a member of a largely Jamaican religious and political movement that worships Ras Tafari, the former Emperor of Ethiopia, Haile Selassie, as God.—*also adj*.

raster *n* a grid of lines scanned by an electron beam to make up an image, esp on a television screen; (*comput*) a form of computer-graphic composed of a matrix of dots or pixels. Otherwise known as bitmaps, or bitmapped images, there are several file formats that use raster graphics, including TIF, BMP, PCX.

rat *n* a long-tailed rodent similar to a mouse but larger; (*sl*) a sneaky, contemptible person, esp an informer; a scab. * *vi* (**ratting, ratted**) to hunt or catch rats; to betray or inform on someone; to work as a scab.

ratafia *n* a liqueur flavored with fruit kernels, such as cherry, peach, or almond; a sweet biscuit flavored with coconut and almond.

ratatouille *n* a dish consisting of a thick stew of roughly chopped vegetables such as onions, peppers, zucchini, eggplant, and tomatoes.

rat-bite fever *n* two types of infectious disease that are contracted following the bite of a rat. The first type is caused by bacteria, the second by a fungus.

ratchet *n* a device with a toothed wheel that moves in one direction only.

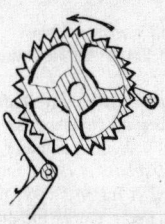

RATD *abbr* (*Brit*) = Register of Apparel and Textile Designers.

rate *n* the amount, degree, etc, of something in relation to units of something else; price, esp per unit; degree. * *vt* to fix the value of; to rank; to regard or consider; (*sl*) to think highly of. * *vi* to have value or status.

Rateau *n* **Armand-Albert** (1882–1938) French furniture designer and woodcarver who was director of the Avaloine interior decoration firm in 1905.

ratel *n* a carnivorous nocturnal mammal of Africa and Asia resembling the badger.

rate of exchange *n* the amount of one currency that may be exchanged for another; exchange rate.

rate of return *n* the annual amount of income that is derived from an investment.

ratepayer *n* a person who pays rates, a householder.

rath *n* (*archeo*) a small ring fort or ringwork up to 65 yards in diameter, usu enclosed by a bank and outer ditch.

Ra-Th *symbol* (*chem*) radiothorium.

rather *adv* more willingly; preferably; somewhat; more accurately; on the contrary; (*inf*) yes, certainly.

Ratia *n* **Armi** (1912–79) Finnish textile designer who set up a weaving store in Vyborg.

ratification *n* (*law*) an instrument filed by an individual who is confirming certain items or facts, or giving formal approval or sanction to an action.

ratify *vt* (**ratifying, ratified**) to approve formally; to confirm.

rating *n* an assessment; an evaluation, an appraisal, as of credit worthiness; classification by grade, as of military personnel; (*radio*, *TV*) the relative popularity of a program according to sample polls.

ratio *n* (*pl* **ratios**) the number of times one thing contains another; the quantitative relationship between two classes of objects; proportion.

ratiocinate *vi* to reason or argue systematically.—**ratiocination** *n*.

ration *n* (*food*, *petrol*) a fixed amount or portion; (*pl*) food supply. * *vt* to supply with rations; to restrict the supply of (food, petrol).

rational *adj* of or based on reason; reasonable; sane.—**rationally** *adv*.

rationale *n* the reason for a course of action; an explanation of principles.

rationalism *n* dependence on reason and rejection of intuition or the supernatural to justify ideas and beliefs, esp with regard to religion; the belief that reason can supply knowledge independently of personal experience.

rationality *n* (*pl* **rationalities**) the condition of being rational; the practice of being reasonable.

rationalization *n* the reorganization of an organization or industry with the intention of increasing efficiency and profitability.

rationalize *vti* to make rational; to justify one's reasons for an action; to cut down on personnel or equipment; to substitute a natural for a supernatural explanation.

rational number *n* a number that can be expressed as the ratio of two integers.

ratline *n* any of the short ropes fastened between the shrouds of a sailing ship to form rungs.

RATO *abbr* = rocket-assisted take-off.

ratoon, rattoon *n* a new shoot sprouting from the root of a perennial plant, esp sugarcane, after it has been cut back. * *vt* to encourage growth in this way.

rat race *n* continual hectic competitive activity.

rattan *n* a climbing palm with a jointed stem; cane made of this.

Rattigan *n* Sir **Terence [Mervyn]** (1911–77) English dramatist, many of whose plays, e.g., *French Without Tears, The Browning Version,* and *The Deep Blue Sea,* have become firm repertory favorites. Another notable play is *Ross,* a psychological study of T E Lawrence.

rattle *vi* to clatter. * *vt* to make a series of sharp, quick noises; to clatter; to recite rapidly; to chatter; (*inf*) to disconcert, fluster. * *n* a rattling sound; a baby's toy that makes a rattling sound; a voluble talker; the rings on the tail of a rattlesnake; (*mus*) a type of percussion instrument which traditionally consists of a hollowed-out gourd filled with seeds which rattle when shaken.

Rattle *n* **Simon** (1955–) English conductor of international standing and principal conductor of the City of Birmingham Symphony Orchestra. He is esp noted for his interpretation of 20th-century music.

rattlebrain *n* an overly talkative person; a careless or thoughtless person.

rattler *n* a rattlesnake.

rattlesnake *n* a venomous American snake with a rattle in its tail.

rattling *adj* brisk, vigorous; first-rate. * *adv* to an extreme degree; very.

rattrap *n* a trap for rats; a dilapidated dwelling; a dead-end situation.

ratty *adj* (**rattier, rattiest**) like or full of rats; (*sl*) angry, irritable, snappish.

raucous *adj* hoarse and harsh-sounding; loud and rowdy.

raunchy *adj* (**raunchier, raunchiest**) (*sl*) coarse, earthy; careless, slovenly; cheap, inferior.

rauwolfia *n* a tropical flowering shrub of Southeast Asia; an extract from the root of this used in various drugs.

ravage *vt* to ruin, destroy; to plunder, lay waste. * *n* destruction; ruin; (*pl*) the effects of this.

RAVC *abbr* (*Brit*) = Royal Army Veterinary Corps.

rave *vi* to speak wildly or as if delirious; (*inf*) to enthuse. * *n* enthusiastic praise.— **raving** *adj*.

ravel *vti* (**raveling, raveled** *or* **ravelling, ravelled**) to entangle or disentangle; to fray; to unwind; to make or become complicated.

Ravel *n* **Maurice** (1875–1937) French composer and pianist, whose principal works include: the ballets *Daphnis et Chloé* and *Ma Mère l'Oye;* the operas *L'Heure Espagnole, L'Enfant et les Sortilèges;* pieces for orchestra (such as *Boléro);* chamber music; many pieces for piano; and numerous songs. Influenced by Fauré and Debussy, he became one of the leading impressionist composers of his time.

raven *n* a large crow-like bird with glossy black feathers. * *adj* of the color or sheen of a raven.

ravenous *adj* famished; voracious.—**ravenously** *adv*.

Ravenscroft *n* **Thomas** (*c.*1590–1633) English composer and publisher of many collections of rounds, catches, canons, and popular songs of the time. He also composed instrumental works.

Ravilious *n* **Eric William** (1903–42) British wood engraver and ceramics decorator.

ravine *n* a deep, narrow valley, bigger than a gully, the sides of which slope more than in a gorge.

ravioli *n* small cases of pasta filled with highly seasoned chopped meat or vegetables.

ravish *vt* to violate; to rape; to enrapture.

ravishing *adj* charming, captivating.

raw *adj* uncooked; unrefined; in a natural state, crude; untrained, inexperienced; sore, skinned; damp, chilly; (*inf*) harsh or unfair.—**rawness** *n*.

RAW *abbr* (*Brit*) = Reality at Work Scotland.

Rawalpindi *n* a city in the Islamic Republic of Pakistan.

RAWC Radioactive Waste Co-ordinating Committee.

rawhide *n* (a whip made from strips of) untanned leather.

raw material *n* a basic material, such as wood, iron ore, or wool, out of which a finished article is made; something with a potential for development, improvement, etc.

Rawsthorne *n* **Alan** (1905–71) English composer and pianist whose works include three symphonies, two piano concertos, three string quartets, pieces of chamber music, and many songs.

RAX *abbr* = rural automatic exchange.

ray[1] *n* a beam of light that comes from a bright source; any of several lines radiating from a center; a beam of radiant energy, radioactive particles, etc; a tiny amount.

ray[2] *n* any of various fishes with a flattened body and the eyes on the upper surface.

ray[3] *n* (*mus*) in the tonic sol-fa, the second note of the major scale.—*also* re.

Ray *n* 1. **Man** (1890–1976) American photographer and painter, a founder (with Duchamp) of New York Dadaism. He moved to Paris in 1921, where he became a leading exponent of surrealist photography. 2. **Satyajit** (1921–92) Indian film director. His films, popular in art houses the world over, include the *Apu* trilogy of life in rural India, *Pather Panchali* (1955), *Aparajito* (1956), and *Apu Sansar* (1959), and *The Chess Players* (1977).

rayon *n* a textile fiber made from a cellulose solution; a fabric of such fibers; the term applied formerly to "artificial silk," but now to two man-made cellulose fibers, viscose and cellulose acetate rayon.

raze *vt* to demolish; to erase; to level to the ground.—*also* **rase**.

razor *n* a sharp-edged instrument for shaving.

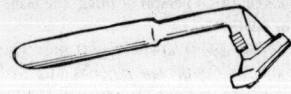

razorbill *n* a North Atlantic auk with a flattened sharp-edged bill.

razor clam, razor-shell *n* any of various bivalve marine mollusks with curved sharp shells.

razz *vt* (*inf*) to deride, heckle.

razzle-dazzle, razzmatazz *n* (*inf*) exciting, exuberant or colorful activity or atmosphere.

Rb *symbol* (*chem*) rubidium.

rb *abbr* (*sport*) = right back.

rb. *abbr* = ruble.

RB *abbr* = Rifle Brigade; Royal Ballet; reconnaissance bomber.

RBA *abbr* = (*Brit*) Refined Bitumen Association; (*Brit*) Retail Book, Stationery and Allied Trades Employees Association; Royal Bhutanese Army; (*Brit*) Royal Society of British Artists.

RBC *abbr* = red blood cell.

RBE *abbr* = relative biological effectiveness (concerning radiation treatment).

RBG *abbr* (*Brit*) = Royal Botanic Gardens (Kew).

RBL *abbr* (*Brit*) = Royal British Legion.

RBLS *abbr* (*Brit*) = Royal British Legion Scotland.

RBNA *abbr* (*Brit*) = Royal British Nurses' Association.

RBOA *abbr* = Residential Boat Owners' Association.

RBPF *abbr* = Royal Bahamas Police Force.

RBS *abbr* = Rare Breeds Society; (*Brit*) Royal Ballet School; (*Brit*) Royal Botanical Society; (*Brit*) Royal Society of British Sculptors; Rural Business-Cooperative Service.

RBST *abbr* (*Brit*) = Rare Breeds Survival Trust.

RBT *abbr* = random breath-testing.

rc *abbr* = reinforced concrete.

r.c. *abbr* = release clause; relief claim; right center.

RC *abbr* = Red Cross; Reserve Corps; Rifle Club; Roman Catholic; Royal Commission; red cell; red corpuscle; (*telephone*) reversed charge.

R/C *abbr* = reconsigned.

RCA *abbr* = (*Brit*) Race Course Association; Radio Corporation of America; Reformed Church in America; Reinforced Concrete Association; Residential Care Association; (*Brit*) Royal College of Art; (*Brit*) Royal Company of Archers; Rural Crafts Association.

RCAF *abbr* = Royal Canadian Air Force.

r. c. and l. *abbr* (*transp*) = rail, canal, and lake.

RCC *abbr* = Revolutionary Conservative Caucus; Roman Catholic Church.

RCCC *abbr* (*Brit*) = Royal Caledonian Curling Club.

RCCh *abbr* = Roman Catholic Church.

RCD *abbr* = residual current device.

rcd. *abbr* = received.

RCDS *abbr* (*Brit*) = Royal College of Defence Studies.

RCF *abbr* (*Brit*) = Redundant Churches Fund.

RCGP *abbr* (*Brit*) = Royal College of General Practitioners.

RCHM *abbr* (*Brit*) = Royal Commission on Historical Manuscripts/Monuments.

rci *abbr* = radar coverage indicator.

RCI *abbr* (*Brit*) = Radiochemical Inspectorate.

RCJ *abbr* (*Brit*) = Royal Courts of Justice.

RCM *abbr* = (*Brit*) Royal College of Midwives; (*Brit*) Royal College of Music; radar countermeasures.

r.c.m. *abbr* = regimental court-martial.

RCMP *abbr* = Royal Canadian Mounted Police.

RCN *abbr* = Royal Canadian Navy; (*Brit*) Royal College of Nursing.

RCNR *abbr* = Royal Canadian Naval Reserve.

RCO *abbr* (*Brit*) = Royal College of Organists.

RCOG *abbr* (*Brit*) = Royal College of Obstetricians and Gynaecologists.

RCP *abbr* = Revolutionary Communist Party; (*Brit*) Royal College of Physicians; (*Brit*) Royal College of Preceptors.

RCPath *abbr* (*Brit*) = Royal College of Pathologists.

RCPB *abbr* = Revolutionary Communist Party of Great Britain.

RCPsych *abbr* (*Brit*) = Royal College of Psychiatrists.

RCR *abbr* (*Brit*) = Royal College of Radiologists.

RCRP *abbr* = Rape Counselling and Research Project.

RCS *abbr* = Rainforest Conservation Society; (*Brit*) Royal Choral Society; (*Brit*) Royal College of Science; (*Brit*) Royal College of Surgeons; (*Brit*) Royal Commonwealth Society; (*Brit*) Royal Corps of Signals; (*Australia*) Rural Counselling Service.

RCSC *abbr* = Radio Components Standardization Committee.

RCSE *abbr* (*Brit*) = Royal College of Surgeons of England.

RCSEd *abbr* (*Brit*) = Royal College of Surgeons of Edinburgh.

RCT *abbr* = (*Brit*) Royal Corps of Transport; randomized clinical trial; regimental combat team; remote-control transmitter.

rctg. *or* **rctg** *abbr* = recruiting.

RCU *abbr* = remote control unit.

RCVS *abbr* (*Brit*) = Royal College of Veterinary Surgeons.

rd. *abbr* = round.

Rd *abbr* = road.

RD *abbr* = Regional Director; (*Spanish*) República Dominicana (Dominican Republic); Reserve Decoration; Rural Dean.

R/D *abbr* (*bank*) = refer to drawer.

RDA *abbr* = (*Brit*) Revolving Doors Agency; (*Brit*) Riding for the Disabled Association; recommended daily/dietary allowance.

Rd-Ac *symbol* (*chem*) radioactinium.

rd & d *abbr* = research, development, and demonstration.

rd & e *abbr* = research, development, and engineering.

RDAT *abbr* = rotary-head digital audio tape.

RDBMS *abbr* = relational database management system.

RDC *abbr* = (*Brit*) Red Deer Commission (Scotland); Rural Development Commission; Rural District Council.

r.d.c. *abbr* (*marine ins*) = running-down clause.

RDCC *abbr* (*Brit*) = Royal Dutch Cattle Company.

rdd *abbr* = required delivery date.

RDF *abbr* = radio direction-finding; rapid deployment force; refuse-derived fuel.

rDNA *abbr* = recombinant deoxyribonucleic acid.

RDS *abbr* = (*Brit*) Railway Development Society; (*Brit*) Research Defence Society; (*Brit*) Royal Drawing Society; Royal Dublin Society (Eire); radio data system; respiratory distress syndrome.

rdt & e *abbr* = research, development, testing, and engineering.

Rd-Th *symbol* (*chem*) radiothorium.

RDX *abbr* = Research Department Explosive (cyclonite).

RDZ *abbr* = radiation danger zone.

re[1] *prep* concerning, with reference to.

re[2] *n* the second note of a major scale in solmization.—*also* ray.

Re[1] *see* Ra.

Re[2] *symbol* (*chem*) rhenium.

Re. *abbr* = rupee.

RE *abbr* = Real Estate; Reformed Episcopal; (*Brit*) Royal Engineers; (*Brit*) Royal Exchange; (*Brit*) Royal Society of Painter-Printmakers (*formerly* Royal Society of Painter-Etchers and Engravers); religious education.

re- *prefix* again, anew; back.

reach *vti* to arrive at; to extend as far as; to make contact with; to pass, hand over; to attain, realize; to stretch out the hand; to extend in influence, space, etc; to carry, as sight, sound, etc; to try to get. * *n* the act or power of reaching; extent; mental range; scope; a continuous extent, esp of water; a narrow inlet of the sea; a straight stretch of a river between bends or locks.

REACH *abbr* (*Brit*) = Retired Executives Action Clearing House.

react *vi* to act in response to a person or stimulus; to have a mutual or reverse effect; to revolt; (*chem*) to undergo a chemical reaction.

React *abbr* (*Brit*) = Research, Education and Aid for Children with Potentially Terminal Illness.

react. *abbr* = reactance.

reaction *n* an action in response to a stimulus; a revulsion of feeling; exhaustion after excitement, etc; opposition to new ideas; (*chem*) an action set up by one substance in another.

reactionary *adj, n* (a person) opposed to political or social change.

reactive *adj* of or relating to reaction; reacting to stimuli; caused by stress.

reactor *n* a person or substance that undergoes a reaction; (*chem*) a vessel in which a reaction occurs; a nuclear reactor.

read *vti* (**reading, read**) to understand something written; to speak aloud (from a book); to study by reading; to interpret, divine; to register, as a gauge; to foretell; (*comput*) to retrieve information stored on magnetic media and transfer it to the memory of the computer; (*sl*) to hear and understand (a radio communication, etc); (*with* **about, of**) to learn by reading; to be phrased in certain words. * *adj* well-informed.

readable *adj* legible; pleasantly written.

readdress *vt* to address again; (*letter*) to change the address when forwarding.

reader *n* a person who reads; one who reads aloud to others; a proofreader; a person who evaluates manuscripts; a textbook, esp on reading; a unit that scans material for computation or storage; a senior lecturer.

readership *n* all the readers of a certain publication, author, etc.

readily *adv* in a ready manner; willingly, easily.

reading *n* the act of one who reads; any material to be read; the amount measured by a barometer, meter, etc; a particular interpretation of a play, etc.

readjust *vt* to adjust again.

read.me file *n* (*comput*) a text file that is often included with program disks and contains up-to-date information about the program, etc.

read only attribute *n* (*comput*) an attribute ensuring a file cannot be changed in any way.

read only memory *see* **ROM**.

read-out *n* the retrieval of information from a computer memory; the information retrieved.

read/write head *n* (*comput*) the electromechanical means whereby information stored on magnetic media can be retrieved and transferred to the memory of the computer.

read/write head alignment *n* (*comput*) the alignment of a disk drive such that a disk may be read correctly. Incorrect alignment may be caused by jolting the computer during transport.

ready *adj* (**readier, readiest**) prepared; fit for use; willing; inclined, apt; prompt, quick; handy. * *n* the state of being ready, esp the position of a firearm aimed for firing. * *vt* (**readying, readied**) to make ready.—**readiness** *n*.

ready-made *adj* made in standard sizes, not to measure.

ready-mix *adj* (*food, concrete, etc*) having some or all of the ingredients already mixed together.

ready-to-wear *adj* (*clothes*) manufactured in standard sizes. * *n* ready-made clothing.

Reagan *n* Ronald [Wilson] (1911–) American film actor, Republican statesman and 40th president of the US (1981–89). 2. his second wife, the actress **Nancy Davis** (1923–), whom he married in 1952, is often credited with transforming the liberal trade unionist into a conservative.

reagent *n* (*chem*) a chemical substance or solution that is used to detect, measure, or react with other substances.

real *adj* existing, actual, not imaginary; true, genuine, not artificial; (*law*) immovable, consisting of land or houses. * *adv* (*sl*) very; really.

REAL *abbr* = Road Emulsion Association Limited.

real estate *n* property; land.

real estate broker *n* a person who deals in property.

realgar *n* a reddish mineral composed of arsenic sulfide.

realign *vti* to align again; (*politics, diplomacy*) to readjust alliances, policies, etc.—**realignment** *n*.

real interest rate *n* the actual interest rate less whatever the current rate of inflation is standing at.

realism *n* practical outlook; (*art, literature*) the ability to represent things as they really are without concealment, a true and faithful representation of reality; (*philos*) the doctrine that the physical world has an objective existence; the doctrine that general ideas have an objective existence.—**realist** *n*.

realistic *adj* matter-of-fact, not visionary; lifelike; of or relating to realism.—**realistically** *adv*.

reality *n* (*pl* **realities**) the fact or condition of being real; an actual fact or thing; truth.

realization *n* the action of realizing; something comprehended or achieved.

realize *vt* to become fully aware of; to make (an ambition, etc) happen; to cause to appear real; to convert into money, be sold for.

really *adv* in fact, in reality; positively, very. * *interj* indeed.

realm *n* a kingdom, country; domain, region; sphere.

real number *n* (*math*) any rational or irrational number.

real tennis *n* an early form of tennis played in a walled indoor court.

real time *n* (*comput*) the near-instantaneous processing of data and feedback, used in, e.g., flight simulator games, on-line chat forums.

real-time *adj* involving the continual processing, manipulation, and presentation of data by a computer as it is generated.

realtor *n* a person whose business is selling and leasing property, a real estate agent.

realty *n* real estate.

ream *n* a quantity of paper varying from 480 to 516 sheets; (*pl, inf*) a great amount.

reap *vti* to harvest; to gain (a benefit).

reaper *n* a person or a machine that reaps.

rear[1] *n* the back part or position, esp of an army; (*sl*) the rump. * *adj* of, at, or in the rear.

rear[2] *vt* to raise; to bring up (children); to educate, nourish, etc. * *vi* (*horse*) to stand on the hind legs.

Rear-Adm. *abbr* = Rear-Admiral.

rear admiral *n* a naval officer next below in rank to a vice admiral.

rear arch *n* (*archit*) the arch which spans a window or doorway on the inside of a wall.

rear guard *n* a military detachment assigned to guard the rear of a body of troops. * *adj* relating to determined defensive resistance.

rear light, rear lamp *n* (*Brit*) a taillight.

rearm *vti* to arm or become armed again, esp with better weapons.—**rearmament** *n*.

rearview mirror *n* a mirror in a motor vehicle that allows the driver to see following traffic.

rearward *adj, adv* at or towards the rear.—**rearwards** *adv*.

Rea Silvia *n* (*Roman myth*) the mother of twin boys, Romulus and Remus.

reason *n* motive or justification (of an action or belief); the mental power to draw conclusions and determine truth; a cause; moderation; sanity; intelligence. * *vti* to think logically (about); to analyze; to argue or infer.

reasonable *adj* able to reason or listen to reason; rational; sensible; not expensive; moderate, fair.—**reasonableness** *n*.—**reasonably** *adv*.

reasoned *adj* convincingly argued.

reassure *vt* to hearten; to give confidence to; to free from anxiety.—**reassurance** *n*.

Réaum. *abbr* = Réaumur.

reaves *n* (*archeo*) Bronze Age stone boundary walls on Dartmoor, England.

rebate[1] *n* a refund of part of an amount paid; discount.

rebate[2] *see* **rabbet**.

rebec (**rebeck**) a small instrument with a pear-shaped body and three strings, which was played with a bow. It developed from the Arabian *rebab* and was used in Europe from the 16th century.

Rebekah *n* (*Bible*) sister of Laban, who became the wife of Isaac and mother of Esau and Jacob. *See also* **Isaac**.

rebel *n* a person who refuses to conform with convention. * *vi* (**rebeling, rebeled** *or* **rebelling, rebelled**) to rise up against the authorities or the government; to dissent.

rebellion *n* armed resistance to an established government, insurrection; defiance of authority.

rebellious *adj* of or engaged in rebellion; tending to rebel; stubborn.—**rebelliously** *adv*.

rebirth *n* a second or new birth; a revival, renaissance; spiritual regeneration.

reboot *vti* (*comput*) to restart the computer without turning off the power. *See also* **bootstrapping**.

rebop *see* **bebop**.

rebound *vi* to spring back after impact; to bounce back; to recover. * *n* a recoil; an emotional reaction.

rebounder *n* a small trampoline used for keep-fit exercises.

rebuff *vt* to snub, repulse; to refuse unexpectedly.—*also n*.

rebuke *vt* to reprimand, chide. * *n* a reproof, reprimand.

rebus *n* (*pl* **rebuses**) a puzzle using images to represent the sound of words or syllables.

rebut *vt* (**rebutting, rebutted**) to disprove or refute by argument, etc.—**rebuttal** *n*.

rec *abbr* = receipt; recipe; record.

rec. *abbr* = *recensuit*; receptacle; recorded; recorder; recording.

REC *abbr* = regional electricity company.

recalcitrant *adj* refusing to obey authority, etc; actively disobedient.—**recalcitrance** *n*.

recalculation method *n* (*comput*) the method chosen to recalculate a spreadsheet after the values in a cell or number of cells have been changed.

recalculation order *n* (*comput*) the sequence that a spreadsheet program uses to calculate a spreadsheet.

recall *vt* to call back; to bring back to mind, remember; to revoke. * *n* remembrance; a summons to return; the removal from office by popular vote.

recall test *n* a test that is used in advertising research to try to establish how well people can remember the details of an advertisement that they have seen.

recant *vti* to repudiate or retract a former opinion, declaration, or belief.—**recantation** *n*.

recap[1] *vti* (**recapping, recapped**) to recapitulate. * *n* (*inf*) recapitulation.

recap[2] *vt* (**recapping, recapped**) to put a new tread on (a tire), to retread. * *n* a tire that has been recapped, a retread.

recapitulate *vt* to restate the main points of, to summarize.—**recapitulation** *n*.

recapitulation *see* **sonata form**.

recapture *vt* to capture again; to discover anew, regain (a lost feeling, etc). * *n* the act of recapturing; a thing or feeling recaptured.

recd, rec'd *abbr* = received.

RECD *abbr* = Rural Economic & Community Development.

recede *vi* to move back; to withdraw, retreat; to slope backwards; to grow less; to decline in value.

receding *adj* sloping backwards; disappearing from view; (of hair) ceasing to grow at the temples.

receipt *n* the act of receiving; a written proof of this; (*pl*) the amount received from business. * *vt* to acknowledge and mark as paid; to write a receipt for.

RECEIPT Number 00124

Received the sum of _____
from _____
on (date) _____

Signed _____

receive *vt* to acquire, be given; to experience, be subjected to; to admit, allow; to greet on arrival; to accept as true; (*stolen goods*) to take in; to transfer electrical signals. * *vi* to be a recipient; to convert radio waves into perceptible signals.

received *adj* accepted, recognized.

Received Pronunciation *n* the unlocalized accent of British English, regarded as standard.

receiver *n* a person who receives; equipment that receives electronic signals, esp on a telephone; (*law*) a person appointed to manage or hold in trust property in bankruptcy or pending a lawsuit.

receivership *n* the status of a business in the hands of a receiver.

receiving blanket *n* a small blanket for wrapping an infant.

receiving line *n* a line of people who welcome each guest with a kiss or handshake, as at a wedding reception.

recent *adj* happening lately, fresh; not long established, modern.—**recently** *adv*.

receptacle *n* a container.

reception *n* the act of receiving or being received; a welcome; a social gathering, often to extend a formal welcome; a response, reaction; the quality of the sound or image produced by a radio or television set.

receptionist *n* a person employed to receive visitors to an office, hotel, hospital, etc.

receptive *adj* able or quick to take in ideas or impressions.

receptor *n* a sensory nerve ending that changes stimuli into nerve impulses to the brain. *See also* **nervous system**.

recess *n* a temporary halting of work, a vacation; a hidden or inner place; an alcove or niche. * *vti* to place in a recess; to form a recess in; to take a recess.

recession *n* the act of receding; a downturn in economic activity, a fall or marked slowing-down in the rate of growth of the gross domestic product; an indentation.

recessive allele *n* (*genetics*) a gene form that is not expressed (that is, it does not show as a feature in the organism) and will therefore not affect the phenotype of the organism unless the organism is homozygous for that particular recessive allele.

recessive gene *n* a gene the character of which will only be expressed if paired with a similar gene (allele).

Rechabite *n* (*Bible*) a member of a family that practiced asceticism. Rechabites did not cultivate the land; they lived in tents long after other tribes had settled in towns and villages, and drank no wine; this was a protest against a settled, farming civilization with its heathen gods.

recharge *vi* to renew the electric charge in (a battery, etc); to recover one's energies.

recherché *adj* uncommon, choice; refined, precious.

recidivism *n* inevitable relapse into crime.—**recidivist** *n*.

Recife *n* a city in Brazil.

recipe *n* a list of ingredients and directions for preparing food; a method for achieving an end.

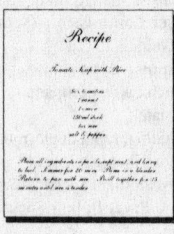

recipient *n* a person who receives.

reciprocal *adj* done by each to the other; mutual; complementary; interchangeable; (*gram*) expressing a mutual relationship. * *n* (*math*) an expression so related to another that their product is 1; the inverse of a fraction.—**reciprocally** *adv*.—**reciprocity** *n*.

reciprocate *vti* to give in return; to repay; (*mech*) to move alternately backwards and forwards.—**reciprocating** *adj*.—**reciprocation** *n*.

recit. *abbr* (*mus*) = (*Italian*) *recitando*.

recital *n* the act of reciting; a detailed account, narrative; a statement of facts; (*mus*) a public concert given by just one or two people, e.g., a singer with piano accompaniment.

recitando (*Italian*) reciting, i.e., speaking rather than singing.

recitation *n* the act of reciting; something recited, as a poem, etc.

recitative *n* (*mus*) a narrative part of an opera sung in the rhythms of ordinary speech; a way of singing (usu on a fixed note) in which the rhythm and lilt are taken from the words and there is no tune as such. It is commonly used in opera and oratorio.

recite *vti* to repeat aloud from memory, declaim; to recount, enumerate; to repeat (a lesson).

reciting note *n* (*mus*) in plainsong, the note on which the first few words of each verse of a psalm are sung.

reckless *adj* rash, careless, incautious.—**recklessly** *adv*.—**recklessness** *n*.

reckon *vti* to count; to regard or consider; to think; to calculate; (*with* **with**) to take into account.

reckoning *n* a calculation; the settlement of an account.

reclaim *vt* to recover, win back from a wild state or vice; to convert (wasteland) into land fit for cultivation; (of plastics, etc) to obtain from waste materials.—**reclaimable** *adj*.—**reclamation** *n*.

recline *vti* to cause or permit to lean or bend backwards; to lie down on the back or side.—**reclinable** *adj*.

recluse *n* a person who lives in solitude; a hermit.

recognition *n* the act of recognizing; identification; acknowledgment, admission; the sensing and encoding of printed and written data by a machine.

recognizance *n* (*law*) a bond by which a person undertakes before a court to observe some condition; the sum pledged as surety for this.

recognize *vt* to know again, identify; to greet; to acknowledge formally; to accept, admit.—**recognizable** *adj*.

recoil *vti* to spring back, kick, as a gun; to shrink or flinch. * *n* the act of recoiling, a rebound.

recollect *vti* to recall; to remind (oneself) of something temporarily forgotten; to call something to mind.

recollection *n* the act of recalling to mind; a memory, impression; something remembered; tranquillity of mind; religious contemplation.

recombinant DNA *n* (*genetics*) a new DNA sequence formed by the insertion of a foreign DNA fragment into another DNA molecule.

recombination *n* (*physics*) the process whereby a free electron combines with an ion in an ionized gas and energy is released as electromagnetic radiation; (*genetics*) the combination of genetic material from different sources.

recommend *vt* to counsel or advise; to commend or praise; to introduce favorably.—**recommendable** *adj*.—**recommendation** *n*.

recommended retail price (often abbreviated to **RRP**) *n* the price that a manufacturer or supplier recommends that his or her products should be sold at.

recompense *n* to reward or pay an equivalent; to compensate. * *n* reward; repayment; compensation.

reconcile *vt* to re-establish friendly relations; to bring to agreement; to make compatible; to resolve; to settle; to make resigned (to); (*financial account*) to check with another account for accuracy.—**reconcilable** *adj*.—**reconciliation** *n*.

recondite *adj* needing specialized training or knowledge; complex, obscure.

recondition *vt* to repair and restore to good working order.

reconnaissance *n* a survey of an area, esp for obtaining military information about an enemy.

reconnoiter, reconnoitre *vti* to make a reconnaissance (of).

REconS *abbr* (*Brit*) = Royal Economic Society.

reconsider *vt* to consider afresh, review; to modify.—**reconsideration** *n*.

reconstitute *vt* (of a dried or condensed substance) to constitute again, esp to restore to its original form by adding water.—**reconstitution** *n*.

reconstruct *vt* to build again; to build up, as from remains, an image of the original; to supply missing parts by conjecture.—**reconstruction** *n*.

record *vt* to preserve evidence of; to write down; to chart; to register, enroll; to register permanently by mechanical means; to register (sound or visual images) on a disk, tape, etc, for later reproduction; (*comput*) to store data on a disk; to celebrate; to make a recording. * *vi* to record something. * *adj* being the best, largest, etc. * *n* a written account; a register; a report of proceedings; the known facts about anything or anyone; an outstanding performance or achievement that surpasses others previously recorded; a grooved vinyl disc for playing on a record player; (*comput*) data in machine-readable form.

recorder *n* an official who keeps records; a machine or device that records; a tape recorder; (*mus*) a straight, end-blown flute, as opposed to a side-blown (concert) flute. Notes can be played by opening or closing eight holes in the instrument with the fingers. Recorders come in consorts (families): descant, treble, tenor, and bass.

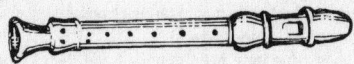

recording *n* what is recorded, as on a disk or tape; the record.

recordist *n* a person who records sound.

record player *n* an instrument for playing records through a loudspeaker.

recount[1] *vt* to narrate the details of; to narrate.

recount[2] *vt* to count again * *n* a second counting of votes at an election.

recoup *vti* to make good (financial losses); to regain; to make up for something lost.

recourse *n* a resort for help or protection when in danger; that to which one turns when seeking help.

recover *vti* to regain after losing; to reclaim; to regain health or after losing emotional control. * *vt* (*comput*) to restore lost or damaged files from, e.g., a backup copy.—**recoverable** *adj*.

re-cover *vt* to put a new cover on.

recovery *n* (*pl* **recoveries**) the act or process of recovering; the condition of having recovered; reclamation; restoration; a retrieval of a capsule, etc, after a space flight.

recovery room *n* a hospital room where patients are kept for close observation or care following surgery.

recovery stock *n* stock that has fallen in value but is thought to have the potential to recover its original value.

recpt. *abbr* = receipt.

recreate *vt* to create over again, esp mentally.

recreation *n* relaxation of the body or mind; a sport, pastime, or amusement.—**recreational** *adj*.

recreational vehicle *n* a vehicle for camping out, such as a motor home, camper, etc.

recreation room *n* a room used for relaxation, recreation, or social activities, esp in a hospital, etc.

recriminate *vi* to return an accusation, make a counter-charge.—**recrimination** *n*.—**recriminatory** *adj*.

recrudesce *vi* (esp *of disease*) to reappear again.—**recrudescence** *n*.

recrudescent *adj* (*med*) relating to a disease (e.g., hepatitis) that appears again after a period of abatement.

recruit *n* a soldier newly enlisted; a member newly joined; a beginner. * *vti* to enlist (military personnel); to enlist (new members) for an organization; to increase or maintain the numbers of; to restore, reinvigorate.—**recruitment** *n*.

Rec. Sec. or **rec. sec.** *abbr* = recording secretary.

rect. *abbr* = receipt; rector; rectory.

rectal *adj* of, for, or near the rectum.

rectangle *n* a parallelogram with all its angles right angles.

rectangular *adj* having the shape of a rectangle; crossing, meeting, or lying at a right angle; having faces or surfaces shaped like right angles.

rectifier *n* (*elect*) a device that converts alternating current into direct current.

rectify *vt* (**rectifying, rectified**) to put right, correct; to amend; (*chem*) to refine by repeated distillation; (*elect*) to convert to direct current.—**rectifiable** *adj*.

rectilinear, rectilineal *adj* of or bounded by straight lines; straight.

rectitude *n* moral uprightness; probity; a being correct in judgment or procedure.

recto *n* (*pl* **rectos**) the right-hand page of an open book.

rector *n* a pastor; in some churches, a clergyman in charge of a parish; the head of certain schools, colleges, etc.—**rectorial** *adj*.

rectory *n* (*pl* **rectories**) the house of a minister or priest.

rectrix *n* (*pl* **rectrices**) any of the tail feathers of a bird, used for controlling the direction of flight.

rectum *n* (*pl* **rectums, recta**) the final portion of the large intestine between the sigmoid colon and anal canal in which feces are stored prior to elimination.

rectus *n* (*pl* **recti**) any of various straight muscles, esp of the abdomen.

recumbent *adj* leaning, resting; lying down.

recuperate *vti* to get well again; to recover (losses, etc).—**recuperation** *n*.

recur *vi* (**recurring, recurred**) to be repeated in thought, talk, etc; to occur again or at intervals.—**recurrence** *n*.—**recurrent** *adj*.

recurrent nova *n* a star that undergoes an explosive event, producing dramatic and sudden increases in brightness, and which shows periodic outbursts.

recycle *vti* (of a substance) to pass through a process again; to process (used matter) to regain re-usable material; to save from loss and restore to usefulness.—**recyclable** *adj*.

red *adj* (**redder, reddest**) of the color of blood; politically left-wing. * *n* the color of blood; any red pigment; a communist.

red. *abbr* = reduction.

redact *vt* to edit (a manuscript, etc) for publication.—**redaction** *n*.—**redactor** *n*.

red admiral *n* a common butterfly of Europe and North America with black and red markings.

red alert *n* an alert that precedes imminent attack; a state of readiness for crisis or attack.

redback *n* (*Austral*) a poisonous spider with red spots on its back.

red blood cell *n* any blood cell containing hemoglobin that conveys oxygen to the tissues.

red blood cell *see* **erythrocyte**.

red-blooded *adj* (*inf*) vigorous, virile.

Red Branch *n* (*Irish Celtic myth*) the collective name given to the group of heroic warriors at the court of Conchobar mac Nessa.

redbreast *n* a robin.

redbrick *adj, n* (a British university) founded after 1945.

redcap *n* (*US*) a porter at a train station or airport; (*Brit*) a military policeman.

red card *n* (*soccer*) a red card held up by the referee indicating that a player is to be sent off.

red carpet *n* a strip of red carpet for dignitaries to walk on; a grand or impressive welcome or entertainment.

red cedar *n* (the reddish wood of) a North American juniper tree.

red cent *n* (*inf*) a trivial quantity of money.

red corpuscle *n* a red blood cell.

Red Crescent *n* the Red Cross in Muslim countries.

Red Cross *n* a red cross on a white ground, the symbol of the International Red Cross, a society for the relief of suffering in time of war and disaster.

red deer *n* a large deer with a reddish brown coat.

redden *vti* to make or become red; to blush.

reddish *adj* tinged with red.—**reddishness** *n*.

red dwarf *n* a main-sequence star which is cooler and smaller than the Sun and which generates a magnetic field; a star with a relatively small mass and low luminosity.

redeem *vt* to recover by payment; to regain; to deliver from sin; to pay off; to restore to favor; to make amends for.—**redeemable** *adj*.—**redeemer** *n*.

redeemable shares *npl* shares that the issuing company has the right to redeem under certain terms that are stipulated when the shares are issued.

redemption *n* the act of redeeming or the state of being redeemed; recovery; repurchase; salvation.

redemption date *n* the date on which a redeemable financial security has to be repaid.

redeploy *vt* to assign (troops, workers) to new positions or activities.—**redeployment** *n*.

redeye *n* (*sl*) cheap whiskey.

red flag *n* a symbol of communism or revolution; a sign of danger.

Redford *n* [Charles] Robert (*b*. 1937) American actor and director whose films include *All the President's Men* (1976).

red fox *n* the common European fox with reddish fur.

red giant *n* (*astron*) a giant aging star with a relatively low surface temperature that emits a red glow. Having expanded greatly and used up about 10% of its hydrogen, its outer layers have become cooler than the hot center and it therefore appears red.

Redgrave *n* 1. **Lynn** (1944–)English stage, film and TV actress; daughter of Sir Michael Redgrave; notable films include Georgy Girl (1966), The Virgin Soldiers (1969). 2. **Richard** (1804–88) British designer and administrator. 3. **Sir Michael [Scudamore]** (1908–85) English stage and film actor, one of the finest actors of his generation; husband of actress **Rachel Roberts** (*b*. 1910). His stage roles included Hamlet (1949–50) and Uncle Vanya (1963). His films include *The Lady Vanishes* (1938), *The Browning Version* (1951), and *The Go-Between* (1971). 4. **Vanessa** (1937–), eldest daughter of Michael; a highly successful stage and film actress, winning an Oscar for *Julia* (1977).

red-handed *adj* caught in the act of committing a crime.

redhead *n* a person having red hair.—**redheaded** *adj*.

red herring *n* a herring cured to a dark brown color; something that diverts attention from the real issue.

red-hot *adj* glowing with heat; extremely hot; very excited, angry, etc; very new.

redirect *vt* to change the direction or course of; to readdress.—**redirection** *n*.

rediscounting *n* the discounting of a bill of exchange or bond that has already been discounted, usu by a discount house.

red lead *n* a poisonous red oxide of lead used as a pigment.

red-letter *adj* of special significance.

red light *n* a warning signal, a cautionary sign; a deterrent.

red-light *adj* (of a district) containing brothels.

redlining *n* (*comput*) the process of marking changes or additions to the text of a document when comparing different versions.

red mullet *n* a food fish of European waters, a goatfish.

redneck *n* (*derog*) a poor white farm laborer in the South. * *adj* racist, reactionary.

redo *vt* (**redoing, redid**, *pp* **redone**) to do again; to redecorate.

red ochre *n* any of several types of reddish earth used as pigments.

redolent *adj* having a strong scent, fragrant; reminiscent (of).—**redolence** *n*.

redouble *vti* to double again; to make or become twice as much.

redoubt *n* a detached outpost of a fortification.

redoubtable *adj* formidable.

redound *vi* to have a directly positive or negative effect (on); to rebound (on or upon).

redox potential *n* (*chem*) a method for evaluating the reduction or oxidation potential of a reactant.

redox reaction *n* (*chem*) a chemical reaction in which both reduction and oxidation are involved.

red pepper *n* a variety of pepper grown for its spicy red fruit, capsicum; its fruit; the fruit of the sweet pepper when ripe and red; cayenne pepper.

redress *vt* to put right, adjust; to compensate, make up for. * *n* remedy; compensation.

red salmon *n* any salmon with pinkish flesh, esp the sockeye.

redshank *n* a type of large European sandpiper.

red shift *n* (*astron*) a displacement of spectral lines towards the red end of the spectrum of light, as observed from certain galaxies.

red squirrel *n* a squirrel with reddish-brown fur of Europe, North America, and Asia.

red tape *n* rigid adherence to bureaucratic routine and regulations, causing delay.

reduce *vt* to diminish or make smaller in size, amount, extent, or number; to lower in price; to simplify; to make thin; to subdue; to bring or convert (to another state or form).—**reducible** *adj*.

reducing agent *n* (*chem*) any substance that will lose electrons during a chemical reaction.

reductio ad absurdum *n* (*logic*) a proof of the falsity of a proposition by demonstrating the absurdity of its logical consequences.

reduction *n* the act or process of reducing or being reduced; something reduced; the amount by which a thing is reduced; (*math*) the conversion of a fraction into decimal form; (*chem*) any chemical reaction that is characterized by the loss of oxygen or by the gain of electrons from one of the reactants.—**reductional** *adj*.—**reductive** *adj*.

redundancy *n* the termination of a person's employment when it ceases to be required by the employer, whether because of rationalization, downsizing, etc.

redundant *adj* surplus to requirements; (*Brit*) deprived of one's job as being no longer necessary; excessive, wordy; (of words) unnecessary to the meaning.—**redundancy** *n*.

redup. *abbr* = reduplication.

reduplicate *vt* to make double, to repeat; (*gram*) to repeat (a syllable or letter), to form (a word) thus. * *adj* doubled, repeated.—**reduplication** *n*.—**reduplicative** *adj*.

Redwald *n* king of East Anglia (*c*.593–*c*.617). The pagan ship burial site at Sutton Hoo near Ipswich, England is thought to commemorate his death.

red wine *n* wine made from black grapes with the skins left on.

redwood *n* an important timber tree of California that can reach a height of 360 feet; any of various trees yielding a red dye or reddish wood.

REE *abbr* = rare earth element(s).

reebok *n* a small southern African antelope with pointed horns.—*also* **rhebok**.

reed *n* a tall grass found in marshes; (*mus*) a thin piece of cane or metal in many blown instruments that vibrates when air is blown across it; a person or thing too weak to rely on; one easily swayed or overcome.

Reed *n* **Sir Carol** (1906–76) English film director whose films include *The Third Man* (1949), written by Graham Greene and starring Orson Welles, a bleak thriller set in postwar Vienna that is one of the most highly praised films ever made. Other films include the spy comedy (from a Greene novel) *Our Man in Havana* (1959).

reedbird *see* **bobolink**.

reeding *n* (*archit*) a decoration comprising touching parallel convex moldings.

reed-organ *n* (*mus*) the generic term for a number of instruments which have no pipes and use free reeds to produce their notes. Examples are the accordion and the harmonium.

reed-pipe *n* (*mus*) an organ pipe with a metal reed in the mouthpiece which vibrates when air is passed over it.

re-educate, reeducate *vt* to educate again in order to adapt to changing circumstances.—**re-education, reeducation** *n*.

reedy *adj* (**reedier, reediest**) filled with reeds; resembling a reed; shrill, piping, as in the sound of a reed.—**reedily** *adv*.—**reediness** *n*.

reef *n* a ridge of rocks, sand, or coral at or just below the surface of water; a coral reef that may form an atoll; a hazardous obstruction; a lode or vein of ore bearing gold or other precious metal, esp in South Africa.

reefer *n* a thick double-breasted jacket, formerly worn by sailors; (*inf*) a cigarette containing cannabis.

reef knot *n* a symmetrical double knot.

reek *n* a strong smell. * *vi* to give off smoke, fumes or a strong or offensive smell.

reel[1] *n* a winding device; a spool or bobbin; thread wound on this; a length of film, about 300 m (1000 ft). * *vt* to wind on a reel; (*with* **in**) to draw in by means of a reel; (*with* **off**) to tell, write, etc, with fluency; (*with* **out**) to unwind from a reel.

reel[2] *vi* to stagger or sway about; to be dizzy or in a whirl. * *n* a staggering motion.

reel[3] *n* (*mus*) a lively Scottish or Irish dance, usu in quick 4/4 time and in regular four-bar phrases; the music for it. * *vi* to dance a reel.

re-enter *vti* to enter again.

re-entry *n* (*pl* **re-entries**) the act of entering or possessing again; the return of a spacecraft to the earth's atmosphere.

re-exports *npl* goods that have been imported and then exported again without having been subjected to any process while in the country that imported them. *See* **entrepot trade**.

ref *n* (*inf*) a referee.

ref. *abbr* = referee; reference, with reference to; referred; reformation; reformed; reformer.

REF *abbr* (*Brit*) = Railway Engineers Forum.

Ref. Ch. *abbr* = Reformed Church.

refectory *n* (*pl* **refectories**) the dining hall of a monastery, college, etc.

refer *vti* (**referring, referred**) to attribute, assign (to); (*with* **to**) to direct, have recourse (to); to relate to; to mention or allude to; to direct attention (to).—**referable** *adj*.

referee *n* an adjudicator, arbitrator; an umpire; a judge.

reference *n* the act of referring; a mention or allusion; a testimonial; a person who gives a testimonial; a direction to a passage in a book; a passage in a book referred to.

reference book *n* a book for reference rather than general reading, e.g., a yearbook, directory.

reference library *n* a library whose books may be consulted but not borrowed.

referendum *n* (*pl* **referendums, referenda**) the submission of an issue directly to the vote of the electorate, a plebiscite.

referral *n* the act of referring or instance of being referred.

referred pain *n* pain felt in a part of the body at a distance from the site at which it might be expected, e.g., certain heart conditions cause pain in the left arm and fingers.—*also* **synalgia**.

refer to drawer (*abbr* **R/D** *or* **rd**) a phrase written on a check to indicate that a bank will not honor it.

refg. *or* **refrig.** *abbr* = refrigerating; refrigeration.

refill *vt* to fill again. * *n* a replacement pack for an empty permanent container; a providing again.

refinancing *n* the process of repaying part or all of the loan capital of a company by acquiring new loans.

refine *vti* to purify; to make free from impurities or coarseness; to make or become cultured.

refined *adj* polished, cultured; affected.

refinement *n* fineness of manners or taste; an improvement; a fine distinction.

refinery *n* (*pl* **refineries**) a plant where raw materials, e.g., sugar, oil, are refined.

refit *vti* (**refitting, refitted**) to make or become functional again by repairing, re-equipping, etc.—*also n*.

refitting *n* (*archeo*) (*or* **conjoining**) the process of fitting back together stone tools and flakes that originally formed the parts of one piece of stone.

refl. *abbr* = reflection; reflective; reflectively; reflex; reflexive; reflexively.

reflation *n* the restoration of deflated prices to a desirable level; a government fiscal policy that is aimed at expanding the output of the economy.—**reflationary** *adj*.

reflect *vt* to throw back (light, heat, etc); to bend aside or back; to show an image of, as a mirror; to express. * *vi* to reproduce to the eye or mind; to mirror; to meditate; (*with* **upon**) to ponder; (*with* **on**) to discredit, disparage.

reflected *adj* thrown or cast back; mirrored; bent or folded back.

reflecting telescope *n* (*astron*) a telescope that uses a series of mirrors to focus light rays.

reflection *n* a reflecting back, turning aside; the action of changing direction when a ray strikes and is thrown back; (*physics*) the property of certain surfaces whereby rays of light (or other wave motion) striking the surface are returned (reflected) in accordance with definite laws; reflected heat, light, or color; a reflected image; meditation, thought; reconsideration; reproach.—*also* **reflexion**.

reflection nebula *n* a cloud of interstellar gas and dust that is close to a star and reflects and scatters light from the star, creating the effect of the cloud being luminous.

reflective *adj* meditative; concerned with ideas.—**reflectively** *adv*.—**reflectiveness** *n*.

reflector *n* a disk, instrument, strip, or other surface that reflects light or heat.

reflex *n* an involuntary response to a stimulus. * *adj* (*geom*) (of an angle) of more than 180°; (*camera*) with a full-size viewfinder using the main lens.

reflex action *n* an unconscious movement caused by relatively simple nervous circuits in the central nervous system. Examples are the knee-jerk reflex and the pupil light reflex.

reflex camera *n* a camera in which the image from the lens is conveyed by an angled mirror to a viewfinder for composition and focusing.

reflexion *see* **reflection.**

reflexive *adj* (of a pronoun or verb) referring back to the subject.—**reflexively** *adv*.

reflexology *n* (*alternative med*) a technique of applying pressure to specific points on the hands and feet to stimulate the blood supply to other areas of the body and help relieve stress.—**reflexologist** *n*.

reform *vti* to improve; to make or become better by the removal of faults; to amend; to abolish abuse. * *n* improvement or transformation, esp of an institution; removal of social ills.—**reformed** *adj*.

re-form *vti* to form again.

reformat *vti* (*comput*) to repeat a formatting operation on a disk or to proceed with a formatting operation on a disk that has already been formatted; to change the arrangement or style of the text.

reformation *n* the act of reforming or the state of being reformed; improvement; (*with cap*) the 16th-century religious revolt that resulted in the formation of Protestant churches.

reformatory *adj* reforming; * *n* (*pl* **reformatories**) an institution for reforming young criminals; a prison for women.

reformer *n* a person who advocates or works for reform; (*chem*) an apparatus for changing the molecular structure of a hydrocarbon to form specialized products.

reform school *n* a reformatory for young people.

refract *vt* to cause (a ray of light, etc) to undergo refraction.

refracting telescope *n* (*astron*) a telescope that uses lenses to focus light rays.

refraction *n* (*physics*) the bending of, most commonly, a light ray when it travels from one medium to another, e.g., air to water.

refractive index *n* (*physics*) the ratio of the sine of the angle of incidence to the sine of the angle of refraction, when light is refracted from a vacuum into the medium.

refractory *adj* obstinate; (*med*) relating to a condition that is resistant to treatment; (*muscle*) unresponsive to stimuli; able to withstand high temperatures. * *n* (*pl* **refractories**) a heat-resistant material.

refractory period *n* the time taken for a nerve or muscle cell to recover after an electrical impulse or after contraction.

refrain[1] *vi* to abstain (from).

refrain[2] *n* recurring words in a song or poem, esp at the end of a stanza; a chorus.

refrangible *adj* able to be refracted.

refresh *vt* to revive; to give new energy to; to make cool; to take a drink; (*comput*) to update the image on the computer screen.

refresher *n* something that refreshes, esp a drink; a reminder; a training course to renew one's skill or knowledge.

refresher course *n* a course designed to keep professionals informed of recent developments in their field of knowledge or expertise.

refreshing *adj* invigorating, reviving; pleasing because unsophisticated.

refreshment *n* the act of refreshing; a restorative; (*pl*) food and drink; a light meal.

refresh rate *n* (*comput*) the speed at which the monitor updates its display.

refrigerate *vti* to make, become, or keep, cold; to preserve by keeping cold.—**refrigeration** *n*.

refrigerator *n* something that refrigerates; a chamber for keeping food, etc, cool; an apparatus for cooling.—*also* **fridge, icebox.**

refuel *vti* (**refueling, refueled** *or* **refuelling, refuelled**) to supply with or take on fresh fuel.

refuge *n* a protection or shelter from danger; a retreat, sanctuary.

refugee *n* a person who flees to another country to escape political or religious persecution.

refulgent *adj* producing radiant light; beaming; brilliant.—**refulgence** *n*.

refund *vti* to repay; to reimburse. * *n* a refunding or the amount refunded.

refurbish *vt* to renovate or re-equip.—**refurbishment** *n*.

refusal *n* the act or process of refusing; the choice of refusing or accepting.

refuse[1] *n* (*Brit*) garbage, waste, rubbish.

refuse[2] *vt* to decline, reject; to withhold, deny. * *vi* (of a horse) to decline to jump.

refute *vt* to rebut; to disprove.—**refutable** *adj*.—**refutably** *adv*.—**refutation** *n*.

reg. *abbr* = regent; regiment; (*Latin*) *regina* ("queen"); region; register; registered; registrar; registry; regular, regularly; regulation; regulator.

regain *vt* to get back, recover; to reach again.

regal *adj* royal; relating to a king or queen. * *n* (*mus*) a portable reed-organ of the 16th and 17th centuries.

regale *vt* to entertain, as with a feast; to delight.

regalia *npl* royal insignia or prerogatives; the insignia of an order, office, or membership; finery.

regard *vt* to gaze at, observe; to hold in respect; to consider; to heed, take into account. * *n* a look; attention; reference; respect, esteem; (*pl*) good wishes, greetings.

regarding *prep* with reference to, about.

regardless *adj* having no regard to. * *adv* (*inf*) in spite of everything; without heeding the cost, consequences, etc.

regatta *n* a meeting for yacht or boat races.

regd. *abbr* = registered.

regency *n* (*pl* **regencies**) the status or authority of a regent; a regent's period of office; a body entrusted with the duties of a regent; rule; (*with cap*) in British history, the period 1810–20.

regenerate *vti* to renew, give new life to; to be reborn spiritually; to reorganize; to produce anew.

regeneration *n* (*biol*) the repair or regrowth of the bodily parts of an organism that have been damaged and have been subsequently lost.

regent *n* a person who rules or administers a country during the sovereign's minority, absence, or incapacity; a member of a governing board (as of a university).

Reger *n* Max (1873–1916) German composer, pianist, organist, conductor, and teacher. He was opposed to program music and claimed to be a progressive composer, while in fact he was musically a conservative. His works include many pieces for organ and piano, several orchestral pieces, and compositions for chamber orchestra.

reggae *n* (*mus*) a strongly accented West Indian musical form with four beats to the bar, a heavy and pronounced rhythm, and strongly accented upbeat.

Reg. Gen. *abbr* = Registrar General.

regicide *n* the killer or the killing of a king.

regime, régime *n* a political or ruling system.

regimen *n* (*med*) a course of treatment that usu involves several elements, including drugs, diet, and lifestyle, such as the taking of exercise, aimed at curing a disease or promoting good health; a regular course of training.

regiment *n* a military unit, smaller than a division, consisting usu of a number of battalions. * *vt* to organize in a strict manner; to subject to order or conformity.—**regimental** *adj*.

regimentation *n* the act of regimenting; excessive orderliness.

Regina *n* a reigning queen.

region *n* a large, indefinite part of the earth; one of the zones into which the atmosphere is divided; an administrative area of a country; a part of the body.—**regional** *adj*.

regionalism *n* identification with, or loyalty to, a particular region; regional policy; a characteristic feature of a particular area, esp a word or custom; something that evokes the characteristics of an area.—**regionalist** *n*, *adj*.—**regionalistic** *adj*.

register *n* an official list; a written record, as for attendance; the book containing such a record or list; a tone of voice; a variety of language appropriate to a subject or occasion; (*comput*) a device in which data can be stored and operated on; (*print*) exact alignment; a device for indicating speed, etc; a plate regulating draught; (*mus*) a set of organ pipes which are controlled by a single stop; a part of a singer's vocal compass, e.g., chest register, head register etc. The term is also applied to certain instruments, e.g., the Chalumeau register of the clarinet. * *vti* to record; to enter in or sign a register; to correspond exactly; to entrust a letter to the post with special precautions for safety; to express emotion facially; to make or convey an impression.

registered *adj* recorded officially; qualified formally or officially.

registered company *n* (*Brit*) a company registered under the Companies Act. Such a company has to be registered with the Registrar of Companies.

registered name *n* (*Brit*) the name under which a company is registered in the United Kingdom.

registered office *n* (*Brit*) the official address of a company in the United Kingdom to which all official correspondence must be sent.

register of charges *n* (*Brit*) a list of the charges on its assets that a company must keep; a register that is kept by the Registrar of Companies on which companies must register certain charges against its assets of the kind set out in the Companies Act.

register of members *n* (*Brit*) a list of the shareholders of a company that must be kept at the company's registered office or head office.

registrar *n* a person who keeps records, esp one in an educational institution in charge of student records; a hospital doctor below a specialist in rank.

Registrar of Companies *n* (*Brit*) a government official responsible for maintaining a record of companies that operate in the United Kingdom and for undertaking duties connected with the registering of companies.

registration *n* the act of registering; the condition of having registered.

registry *n* (*pl* **registries**) registration; a place where records are kept; an official record book.

regius professor *n* in UK, a person appointed to a university chair founded by the Crown.

regnal *adj* pertaining to a sovereign or reign, esp designating a year of a reign calculated from the date of accession.

regolith *n* (*astron*) a fine powdery covering on the moon (and other planets and asteroids), created by meteoritic impact.

regr. *abbr* = registrar.

regress *vi* to move backwards; to revert to a former condition.—**regressive** *adj*.—**regressively** *adv*.

regression *n* the act of regressing; a relapse, reversion; a return to an earlier time or stage; (*med*) the stage in the course of a disease when symptoms cease and the patient recovers; (*psychoanal*) a retreat of the personality, a reversion to a more immature form of behavior; (*math*) the connection between the expected value of a random variable and the values of one or more possibly related variables; (*biol*) the tendency to an average state from an extreme one.

regressive tax *n* a form of tax in which the rate of tax, such as indirect tax, decreases as income increases.

regret *vt* (**regretting, regretted**) to feel sorrow, grief, or loss; to remember with longing; (*with that*) to repent of. * *n* disappointment; sorrow; grief; (*pl*) polite refusal.—**regretful** *adj*.—**regretfully** *adv*.

regrettable *adj* to be regretted; deserving reproof.—**regrettably** *adv*.

regroup *vti* to group again; (*mil*) to reorganize (troops, etc) following action.

regt. *abbr* = regent; regiment.

regular *adj* normal; habitual, not casual; at fixed intervals; according to rule, custom, or the accepted practice; uniform, consistent; symmetrical; fully qualified; belonging to a standing army; (*inf*) thorough, complete; (*inf*) pleasant, friendly. * *n* a professional soldier; (*inf*) a person who attends regularly.—**regularity** *n*.—**regularly** *adv*.

regular army *n* a permanent army; (*with caps*) the United States Army.

regular coarsed rubble *see* **rubble walling**.

regularize *vt* to make regular or correct.—**regularization** *n*.

regulate *vt* to control according to a rule; to cause to conform to a standard or needs; to adjust so as to put in good order.—**regulatory** *adj*.

regulation *n* the act of regulating or state of being regulated; a prescribed rule, ordinance. * *adj* normal, standard.

regulator *n* one that regulates; a regulating device; a lever in a watch that adjusts its speed.

Regulus *or* **Alpha Leonis** *n* a triple star, the brightest in the constellation Leo.

regurgitate *vti* to pour back, cast up again, esp from the stomach to the mouth.

regurgitation *n* (*med*) the backward flow of blood in the heart if one or more valves is diseased and defective; the bringing up of swallowed undigested food from the stomach to the mouth. *See also* **possetting**.

rehabilitate *vt* to help (a prisoner, etc) adapt to society after a stay in an institution; to put back in good condition; to restore to rights or privileges; to help (a sick person, etc) to adjust to normal conditions after illness.

rehabilitation *n* the process of restoring (as far as possible) back to normal life a person who has been disabled by injury or physical and/or mental illness.

rehash *n* old materials put in a new form. * *vt* to dish up again.

rehearse *vti* to practice repeatedly before public performance; to recount, narrate in detail.—**rehearsal** *n*.

REHIS *abbr* (*Brit*) = Royal Environmental Health Institute of Scotland.

rehoboam *n* a wine bottle that holds six times the amount of a standard bottle.

Rehoboam *n* (*Bible*) son and successor of King Solomon; faced with a revolt he answered: "my father chastised you with whips, but I will chastise you with scorpions"; the outcome was the break-up of his kingdom.

REHVA *abbr* = Representatives of European Heating and Ventilating Associations.

Reiber *n* Émile Auguste (1826–93) French architect, born in Alsace, who founded the influential pattern-book periodical *L'Art Pour Tous* in 1861 and defined renaissance revival designs.

Reich *n* 1. Lilly (1885–1947) German architect and furniture designer whose career is closely interwoven with Ludwig **Mies Van Der Rohe**, who claimed title to many of her designs. 2. **Steve** (*b.* 1936) American composer, a pupil of Milhaud, whose work is marked by the use of repetition progressing through gradual change, and shows the influence of non-European music. His compositions include *Music for Eighteen Musicians* and *Music for Large Ensemble*.

reify *vt* (**reifying, reified**) to make (something abstract) real or concrete.

reign *n* the rule of a sovereign; the period of this; influence; domination. * *vi* to rule; to prevail.

reimburse *vt* to repay; to refund (for expense or loss).—**reimbursable** *adj*.—**reimbursement** *n*.

rein *n* the strap of a bridle for guiding or restraining a horse; (*pl*) a means of control or restraint. * *vt* to control with the rein; to restrain.

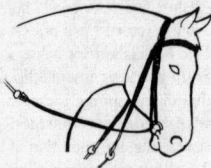

reincarnation *n* the incarnation of the soul after death in another body.—**reincarnate** *adj*, *vt*.

reindeer *n* a large deer with branched antlers found in northern regions.

reindeer moss *n* a lichen of northern regions that provides food for reindeer.

reinforce *vt* to strengthen (an army, etc) with fresh troops; to add to the strength of (a material).

reinforced concrete *n* (*archit*) concrete containing steel reinforcement to accommodate the tensile stresses created upon loading.

reinforcement *n* the act of reinforcing; additional support; (*pl*) additional troops.

Reinhardt *n* Django [Jean Baptiste Reinhardt] (1910–53) Belgian jazz guitarist of gypsy origin who, with Stephane Grapelli, led the quintet the Hot Club de France (1934–9). He lost the use of two fingers, which caused him to develop his highly individual technique and style.

reinstate *vt* to restore to a former position, rank, or condition.—**reinstatement** *n*.

reinstatement agreement *n* (*law*) an instrument which gives something back to a party that had something taken away.

REInstCF *abbr* = Registered Fitter of the National Institute of Carpet Fitters.

reinterpret *vt* to interpret again; to give a new explanation of.—**reinterpretation** *n*.

REIS *abbr* = Regional Economic Information System (Searchable REIS)

reissue *vt* to issue again; to republish. * *n* a new issue; a reprint.

reiterate *vt* to repeat; to say or do again or many times.—**reiteration** *n*.

Reiter's syndrome *n* a disease of unknown cause that affects men and produces symptoms of urethritis, conjunctivitis, and arthritis.

Reith, John Charles Walsham [1st Baron Reith of Stonehaven] (1889–1971) Scottish engineer, who was appointed first manager of the British Broadcasting Company (later Corporation) in 1922. He did much to shape the BBC into an institution of great influence.

reject *vt* to throw away, to discard; to refuse to accept, to decline; to rebuff. * *n* a thing or person rejected.—

rejection *n* (*med*) in transplantation, failure of the immune system of the recipient individual to accept an organ or tissue grafted from a donor.

rejoice *vi* to feel joyful or happy.

rejoin *vt* to join again; to return to.

rejoinder *n* a retort, a reply.

rejuvenate *vt* to give youthful vigor to.—**rejuvenation** *n*.

rel. *abbr* = relating; relative; relatively; released; religion; religious; (*Latin*) *reliquiae* ("relics").

relapse *vi* to fall back into a worse state after improvement; to return to a former vice, to backslide. * *n* the recurrence of illness after apparent recovery.

relapsing fever *n* a disease caused by spirochaete bacteria of the genus *Borrelia*, which is transmitted to humans by lice and ticks.

relate *vt* to narrate, recount; to show a connection (between two or more things). * *vi* to have a formal relationship (with).

related *adj* connected, allied; akin.

related keys *see* **modulation**.

relation *n* the way in which one thing stands in respect to another, footing; reference, regard; connection by blood or marriage; a relative; a narration, a narrative; (*pl*) the connections between or among persons, nations, etc; (*pl*) one's family and in-laws.

relational database *n* (*comput*) a type of database management program in which data are stored in two-dimensional tables that are indexed for cross-reference.

relational operator *n* (*comput*) a sign that is used to specify the relationship between values, e.g., = (equal to), > (less than), etc.

relationship *n* the tie or degree of kinship or intimacy; affinity; (*inf*) an affair.

relative *adj* having or expressing a relation; corresponding; pertinent; comparative, conditional; respective; meaningful only in relationship; (*gram*) referring to an antecedent. * *n* a person related by blood or marriage.—**relatively** *adv*.

relative cell reference *n* (*comput*) a reference to a cell in a spreadsheet that refers to its position with regard to another cell rather than an absolute reference.

relative dating *n* (*archeo*) putting artifacts, deposits, sequences, etc, in order of date, relative to one another.

relative humidity *n* the amount of water vapor in the air compared to the maximum amount of water vapor which that volume of air at the same temperature could carry, expressed as a percentage.

relative major, relative minor *n* (*mus*) the connection between a major key and a minor key that share the same key signature, e.g., A minor is the relative key of C major.

relative molecular mass *n* (*chem*) the total of the atomic weights of all the atoms present in a molecule; the average mass per molecule of any substance relative to one-twelfth the mass of an atom of carbon-12.—*also* **molecular weight**.

relative pronoun *n* a pronoun that is used to connect a dependent clause to a main clause and that refers to a noun in the main clause.

relativistic *adj* the term applied to anything traveling at a velocity close to that of light.

relativity *n* the state of being relative; the relation between one thing and another; (*physics*) the theory of the relative, rather than absolute, character of motion, velocity, mass, etc, and the interdependence of time, matter, and space derived by Albert Einstein. Establishes the concept of a four-dimensional space–time continuum where there is no clear line between three-dimensional space and independent time, hence space and time are considered to be bound together. The *special theory of relativity* states that the speed of light is the same for all observers, whatever their speed. The *general theory of relativity* states that matter in space causes space to curve so as to set up a gravitational field and gravitation becomes a property of space.

relaunch *n* the reintroduction of a product or service into a market after some alterations have been made to it to increase its market appeal.

relax *vti* to slacken; to make or become less severe or strict; to make (the muscles) less rigid; to take a rest.

relaxant *n* a drug that relieves muscular tension.

relaxation *n* the act of relaxing; the condition of being relaxed; recreation.

relay n a team of fresh horses, men, etc, to relieve others; a race between teams, each member of which goes a part of the distance; (elect) a device for enabling a weak current to control others; a relayed broadcast. * vt (**relaying, relayed**) to spread (news, etc) in stages; to broadcast signals.

relay race n a race between teams in which each member does part of the distance.

release vt to set free; to let go; to relinquish; (film, etc) to issue for public exhibition; (information) to make available; (law) to make over to another. * n a releasing, as from prison, work, etc; a device to hold or release a mechanism; a news item, etc, released to the public; (law) an instrument which fully surrenders a right to real or personal property; a written surrender of a claim.

release number n (comput) the decimal number that is used to identify an improvement in a version of a software program.

relegate vt to move to an inferior position; to demote; to banish.—**relegation** n.

relent vi to soften in attitude; to become less harsh or severe.

relentless adj pitiless; unremitting.

relevant adj applying to the matter in hand, pertinent; to the point.—**relevance, relevancy** n.

reliable adj dependable, trustworthy.—**reliability** n.—**reliably** adv.

reliance n trust; dependence; a thing relied on.—**reliant** adj.

relic n an object, fragment, or custom that has survived from the past; part of a saint's body or belongings; (pl) remains of the dead.

relief n the sensation following the easing or lifting of discomfort or stress; release from a duty by another person; a person who takes the place of another on duty; that which relieves; aid; assistance to the needy or victims of a disaster; the projection of a carved design from its ground; the shape of the land surface of the Earth; distinctness, vividness. * adj providing relief in disasters, etc.

relief map n a map in which topographic relief is represented by shading, colors, etc.

relief rainfall or **orographic rainfall** n rain that occurs when moisture-laden clouds are forced to rise in order to cross mountains.

relieve vt to bring relief or assistance to; to release from obligation or duty; to ease; (with oneself) to empty the bladder or bowels. * vi to give relief; to break the monotony of; to bring into relief, to stand out.

relieved adj having or showing relief, esp from anxiety or repressed emotions.

religion n a belief in God or gods; a system of worship and faith; a formalized expression of belief.

religiosity n the condition of being religious, esp excessively or sentimentally so.—**religiose** adj.

religious adj of or conforming to religion; devout, pious; scrupulously and conscientiously faithful.—**religiously** adv.

relinquish vt to give up; to renounce or surrender.—**relinquishment** n.

reliquary n (pl **reliquaries**) a container or shrine for sacred relics.

relish n an appetizing flavor; a distinctive taste; enjoyment of food or an experience; a spicy accompaniment to food; gusto, zest. * vt to like the flavor of; to enjoy, appreciate.

relocate vti to set up in a new place; to place (an employee) in a different job; (business) to move to a new location.

relocation n the transference from one place of work to another.

rel. pron. abbr = relative pronoun.

reluctant adj unwilling, loath; offering resistance.—**reluctance** n.—**reluctantly** adv.

rely vi (**relying, relied**) to depend on; to trust.

rem. abbr = remark, or remarks; remittance.

REM abbr = rapid eye movement.

REM sleep n a phase of sleep when the eyeballs move rapidly behind closed eyelids. This appears to be the phase during which dreaming occurs.

remain vi to stay behind or in the same place; to continue to be; to survive, to last; to be left over. * npl anything left after use; a corpse.

remainder n what is left, the rest; (math) the result of subtraction; the quantity left over after division; unsold stock, esp of books; (law) the residual interest in an estate.

remake vt (**remaking, remade**) to make again. * n a new version of an old film.

remand vt to send back into custody for further evidence.—also n.

remark vti to notice; to observe; to pass a comment (upon). * n a brief comment.

remarkable adj unusual; extraordinary; worthy of comment.—**remarkably** adv.

remaster vt to make a new (digital) master recording from an original (analog) recording to provide improved sound quality on vinyl records or compact discs.

Rembrandt [Rembrandt Harmensz van Rijn] (1606–69) Dutch painter, draftsman, and etcher. Notable works include The Anatomy Lesson of Dr Tulp (1632), The Blinding of Samson, and Supper at Emmaus (1648). He also produced a remarkable series of self-portraits, painted over 40 years.—**Rembrandtesque** adj.

REMC abbr = Radio and Electronics Measurements Committee.

REME abbr (Brit) = Royal Electrical and Mechanical Engineers.

remedial adj providing a remedy; corrective; relating to the teaching of people with learning difficulties.

remedy n a medicine or any means to cure a disease; anything that puts something else to rights. * vt (**remedying, remedied**) to cure; to put right.

remember vti to recall; to bear in mind; to mention (a person) to another as sending regards; to exercise or have the power of memory.

remembrance n a reminiscence; a greeting or gift recalling or expressing friendship or affection; the extent of memory; an honoring of the dead or a past event.

Remembrance Day n (Canada) November 11, on which the dead of the two world wars are commemorated.

Remembrance Sunday n (Brit) the Sunday nearest November 11, on which the dead of the two world wars are commemorated.

Remigius n **Saint** (d. 530) Gaulish bishop famous throughout the church for his outstanding holiness, ability, and eloquence. He set about converting the Franks to Christianity. His feast day is October 1.

remind vt to cause to remember.

reminder n a thing that reminds, esp a letter from a creditor.

reminisce vi to think, talk, or write about past events.

reminiscence n the recalling of a past experience; (pl) memoirs.

reminiscent adj reminding, suggestive (of); recalling the past.

remiss adj negligent, slack.

remission n the act of remitting; the reduction in length of a prison term; the lessening of the symptoms of a disease; a period during the course of a disease when symptoms have lessened or disappeared; pardon, forgiveness.

remit vti (**remitting, remitted**) to forgive; to refrain from inflicting (a punishment) or exacting (a debt); to abate, moderate; to send payment (by post); (law) to refer to a lower court for reconsideration. * n the act of referring; an area of authority.

remittance n the sending of money or a payment (by post); the payment or money sent.

remix vt to adjust the balance and separation of a recording.—also n.

remnant n a small remaining fragment or number; an oddment or scrap; a trace; an unsold or unused end of piece goods.

remodel vt (**remodeling, remodeled** or **remodelling, remodelled**) to fashion afresh; to recast.

remonstrate vi to protest, to make a complaint (against).—**remonstrance** n.

remorse n regret and guilt for a misdemeanor; compassion.—**remorseful** adj.—**remorsefully** adv.

remorseless adj ruthless, cruel; relentless.—**remorselessly** adv.—**remorselessness** n.

remote adj far apart or distant in time or place; out of the way; not closely related; secluded; aloof; vague, faint.—**remotely** adv.

remote control n the control of a device or activity from a distance, usu by means of an electric circuit or the making or breaking of radio waves.

remote sensing n the collection of a variety of information without contact with the object of study; (archeo) using satellite images to study surface features; using geophysical methods to locate underground features or objects.

removable storage n (comput) any secondary storage system where the storage medium can be extracted and taken away from the computer, e.g., floppy disks.

removal n the act of removing; a change of home or office; dismissal; (law) an instrument which removes a person's privileges, responsibilities, or duties to perform a certain act.

remove vti to take away and put elsewhere; to dismiss, as from office; to get rid of; to kill; to go away. * n a stage in gradation; a degree in relationship.—**removable** adj.

removed adj remote; separated by a specified degree, as of relationship; of a younger or older relationship.

remunerate vt to pay for a service; to reward.

remuneration n money paid in the form of wages, salary, or fees for work done or services rendered.

Remus see **Romulus and Remus**.

renaissance n a rebirth or revival; (with cap) the revival of European art and literature under the influence of classical study during the 14th–16th centuries, as a result of the rediscovery of the writing of the great classical writers, notably the works of Plato and Aristotle.—also adj.

Renaissance man, Renaissance woman n a person with wide knowledge, interests, and accomplishments.

renal adj relating to or near the kidneys.

rename vt (comput) to change the name of a file, directory, or disk.

renascent adj becoming active again, reviving.

rend vti (**rending, rent**) to tear, to wrench (apart); to be torn apart.

render vt to submit (payments, accounts, etc), as for approval; to give back; to pay back; to perform; to represent as by drawing; to translate, interpret; to cause to be; to melt down (fat).

rendering n interpretation, translation; (archit) plastering with render, a mortar, or similar mix.

rendezvous n (pl **rendezvous**) an arranged meeting; a place to meet; a popular haunt; the process of bringing two spacecraft together. * vi to meet by appointment.

rendition n an interpretation; performance.

renegade n a deserter; a person who is faithless to a principle, party, religion, or cause.

renege vti to go back on, or fail to keep, a promise or agreement.

renegotiate vti to negotiate again, esp to improve the terms of a contract.—**renegotiable** adj.—**renegotiation** n.

Renenutet n (Egypt) a cobra-headed goddess, a protector of households and the harvest. Traces of her worship have been found at Deir el Medina.

renew vti to restore to freshness or vigor; to begin again; to make or get anew; to replace; to grant or obtain an extension of.—**renewable** adj.—**renewal** n.

renewable resource n a resource that keeps replacing itself, e.g., wind, tide, or heat from the Sun.

renewal notice n a communication from an insurance company inviting a policyholder to renew the policy when it is about to expire.

R

rennet *n* an extract from the stomach of calves, etc, used to curdle milk.

Rennie *n* **John** born 1761, Scottish architect. His notable works include Southwark, Waterloo, and London Bridges and Plymouth breakwater.

Renoir *n* 1. **Pierre Auguste** (1841–1919) French impressionist painter. Notable works include *The Bathers* (*c*.1884–7), *Mme Charpentier and her Children* (1876) and *Moulin de la Galette* (1876). 2. **Jean** (1894–1979) French film director, the son of the impressionist painter Pierre Auguste Renoir. His films, often described as "humanist" for their compassion and sense of humanity's unity, include two classics of the cinema, *La Grande illusion* (1937) and *La Règle du jeu* (1939). He fled the German occupation of France to the US in 1941.

renounce *vt* to abandon formally; to give up; to disown.

renovate *vt* to renew; to restore to good condition; to do up, repair.—**renovation** *n.*—**renovator** *n.*

renown *n* fame, celebrity.

renowned *adj* famous, illustrious.

rent[1] *see* **rend**.

rent[2] *n* regular payment to another for the use of a house, machinery, etc. * *vti* to occupy as a tenant; to hire; to let for rent.

rent-a-car *n* the system of renting cars; a rented car.

rental *n* an amount paid or received as rent; a house, car, etc, for rent; an act of renting; a business that rents something.

rent boy *n* a young male prostitute.

rent control *n* legal regulation of rents; the powers of eviction possessed by landlords.

renunciation *n* the act of renouncing; formal abandonment; repudiation; the surrender to someone else of shares offered to someone in a rights issue.

Renwick *n* 1. **James** (1818–95) English architect whose notable works include the Smithsonian Institute, Washington. 2. **William Crosby** (1814–92) American industrial designer who designed the seminal 1953 *Bubble Lamp*.

reopen *vti* to open again; to resume.

reorder level *n* a pre-arranged level to which stocks of a product must drop before an order for more of the product is placed.

reorganize *vti* to organize again; to bring about a reorganization.—**reorganization** *n*.

rep *abbr* = repeat; report; reporter.

Rep. *abbr* = Representative; Republic; Republican.

repaginate *vt* (*comput*) to change the number of pages in a document according to the quantity of text in it.

repair[1] *vt* to mend; to restore to good working order; to make amends for. * *n* the act of repairing; a place repaired; condition as to soundness.

repair[2] *vi* to go to, to resort; to haunt. * *n* (*arch*) the act of repairing to; a haunt.

repairman *n* (*pl* **repairmen**) a person who repairs things for a living.

reparable *adj* capable of being repaired.

reparation *n* amends; (*pl*) compensation, as for war damage.

repartee *n* a witty reply; skill in making such replies.

repast *n* a meal.

repatriate *vt* to send back or restore to one's country of origin or citizenship.—**repatriation** *n*.

repay *vt* (**repaying, repaid**) to pay back; to refund.—**repayable** *adj*.—**repayment** *n*.

repeal *vt* to annul, to rescind; to revoke.—*also n.*

repeat *vti* to say, write, or do again; to reiterate; to recite after another or from memory; to reproduce; to recur. * *n* a repetition, encore; anything said or done again, as a re-broadcast of a television program; (*mus*) a passage to be repeated; the sign for this.—**repeatable** *adj*.

repeated *adj* frequent; done, seen, etc, again.

repeatedly *adv* many times, over and over again.

repeater *n* a clock or watch with a striking mechanism; a device for receiving and amplifying electronic communication signals; a firearm that has a repeating mechanism for reloading; a habitual violator of the laws.

repeating firearm *n* a firearm designed to load cartridges from a magazine.

repeat rate *n* (*comput*) the rate at which a character will be typed on the screen when a particular key is kept depressed.

repel *vt* (**repelling, repelled**) to drive back; to beat off, repulse; to reject; to hold off; to cause distaste; to be resistant to (water, dirt).

repellent *adj* distasteful, unattractive; capable of repelling; impermeable. * *n* a substance that repels, esp a spray for protection against insects.

repent *vi* to wish one had not done something; to feel remorse or regret (for); to regret and change from evil ways.—**repentant** *adj*.

repentance *n* penitence; contrition.

repercussion *n* a rebound; a reverberation; a far-reaching, often indirect reaction to an event.

repertoire *n* the stock of plays, songs, etc, that a company, singer, etc, can perform.

repertory *n* (*pl* **repertories**) a repertoire; the system of alternating several plays through a season with a permanent acting group.

repet. *abbr* (*Latin*) = *repetatur* ("let it be repeated").

repetiteur *n* (*mus*) (*French*) a person hired to teach musicians or singers, particularly opera singers, their parts.

repetition *n* the act of repeating; something repeated, a copy.—**repetitive** *adj*.

repetitious *adj* full of repetition; boring.—**repetitiously** *adv*.—**repetitiousness** *n*.

repetitive strain injury *see* **tendinitis**.

rephrase *vt* to phrase (a statement) in a different way.

replace *vt* to put back; to take the place of, to substitute for; to supersede.—**replaceable** *adj*.

replacement *n* the act or process of replacing; a person or thing that replaces another.

replacement cost *n* the cost of replacing a fixed asset or item of stock, either in its present form or in an equivalent form.

replenish *vt* to stock again, refill.—**replenishment** *n*.

replete *adj* filled, well provided; stuffed, gorged.

repletion *n* complete fullness; satisfaction.

replica *n* an exact copy; a reproduction; (*mus*) (*Italian*) "repeat"; *senza replica*, "without repetition."

replication *n* (*biol*) the duplication of genetic material, generally before cell division.

reply *vti* (**replying, replied**) to answer, respond; to give as an answer. * *n* an answer.

repo-man *n* (*pl* **repo-men**) (*sl*) a person who repossesses (e.g., a motor car).

report *vti* to give an account of; to tell as news; to take down and describe for publication; to make a formal statement of; to complain about or against; to inform against; to present oneself (for duty). * *n* an account of facts; the formal statement of the findings of an investigation; a newspaper, radio, or television account of an event; a rumor; a sharp, loud noise, as of a gun; (*comput*) a presentation of information in print.

reportage *n* the art of reporting on current events; an accurate, observant, and well-written account of an event.

report card *n* a report on a pupil or student that is periodically given to his or her parent; an evaluation of performance.

reportedly *adv* as reported, not directly.

reporter *n* a person who gathers and reports news for a newspaper, radio, or television; a person authorized to make statements concerning law decisions or legislative proceedings.

repose *n* rest, sleep; stillness, peace; composure, serenity. * *vti* to lie down or lay at rest; to place (trust, etc) in someone; to rest; to lie dead.

reposition *vt* to place in a different or new position.

repositioning *n* the altering of the design, packaging, brand name, brand image, etc, of a product in order to change its position in the market in relation to its competitors as perceived by consumers.

repository *n* (*pl* **repositories**) a receptacle; a storehouse, warehouse; a confidant.

repossess *vt* to possess again; to restore possession of (property), esp for nonpayment of debt.—**repossession** *n*.

repossession *n* the process of taking back something that is being paid for by installments or by a mortgage system when the contracted regular payments have not been met.

repoussé *n* a method of decorating sheet metal in which projections are hammered out from the back.

repr. *abbr* = representing; reprinted.

reprehend *vt* to rebuke, to find fault with, to criticize.

reprehensible *adj* blameworthy, culpable.

reprehension *n* blame, censure.

represent *vt* to portray; to describe; to typify; to stand for, symbolize; to point out; to perform on the stage; to act as an agent for; to deputize for; to serve as a specimen, example, etc, of.—**representable** *adj*.

re-present *vt* to present again.

representation *n* the act of representing or being represented, as in a parliamentary assembly; a portrait, reproduction; (*pl*) a presentation of claims, protests, views, etc.

representative *adj* typical; portraying; consisting of or based on representation of the electorate by delegates. * *n* an example or type; a person who acts for another; a delegate, agent, salesman, etc.

representative fraction *n* the ratio of one unit of length on a map to the distance represented by that unit on the ground.

repress *vt* to suppress, restrain; to keep (emotions) under control; to exclude involuntarily from the conscious mind.—**repressive** *adj*.—**represser, repressor** *n*.

repression *n* the act of repressing; the condition of being repressed; domination, tyranny.

reprieve *vt* to postpone or commute the punishment of; to give respite to.—*also n.*

reprimand *n* a formal rebuke. * *vt* to reprove formally.

reprint *vt* to print again. * *n* a book or article that has appeared in print before.

reprisal *n* an act of retaliation for an injury done; (*mus*) a musical repetition often found in musical comedies when songs heard in one act are repeated in another.

reprise *n* (*mus*) the repetition of an earlier theme or passage.—*also vt.*

reproach *vt* to accuse of a fault; to blame. * *n* a reproof; a source of shame or disgrace.—**reproachful** *adj*.

reprobate *n* a depraved person; a hardened sinner; a scoundrel.

reproduce *vti* to make a copy, duplicate, or likeness of; to propagate; to produce offspring; to multiply.

reproduction *n* the act of reproducing; (*biol*) the production of new individuals of the same species either by asexual or sexual means; a copy or likeness; a representation.—**reproductive** *adj*.

reproductive system *n* the name given to all the organs involved in reproduction. In males, these comprise the testicles, vasa deferentia, prostate gland, seminal vesicles, urethra, and penis. In females, the reproductive system consists of the ovaries, Fallopian tubes, uterus, vagina, and vulva.

reprography *n* the process of reproducing printed material, as by photocopying.—**reprographic** *adj*.

reproof *n* a rebuke, blame.

reprove *vt* to rebuke, censure.—**reprovingly** *adv*.

rept. *abbr* = receipt; report.

reptile *n* any of a class of coldblooded, air-breathing vertebrates with horny scales or plates, as turtles, crocodiles, snakes, lizards, etc; a groveling or despised person.—**reptilian** *adj*.

Repub. *abbr* = Republic; Republican.

republic *n* a government in which the people elect the head of state, usu called president, and in which the people and their elected representatives have supreme power; a country governed in this way; a body of persons freely engaged in a specified activity.

republican *adj* of, characteristic of, or supporting a republic. * *n* an advocate of republican government; (*with cap*) a member of the US Republican party.—**republicanism** *n*.

republish *vt* to publish again; to issue a new edition of (a book).—**republication** *n*.

repudiate *vt* to reject, disown; to refuse to acknowledge or pay; to deny; (a treaty, etc) to disavow.—**repudiation** *n*.

repugnant *adj* distasteful, offensive; contradictory; incompatible.—**repugnance** *n*.

repulse *vt* to drive back; to repel; to reject. * *n* a rebuff, rejection; a defeat, check.

repulsion *n* a feeling of disgust; aversion; (*physics*) the tendency of bodies to repel each other.

repulsive *adj* disgusting; loathsome; exercising repulsion.—**repulsively** *adv*.

reputable *adj* of good repute, respectable.—**reputably** *adv*.

reputation *n* the estimation in which a person or thing is held; good name, honor.

repute *vt* to consider to be, to deem. * *n* reputation.

reputed *adj* generally reported; supposed, putative.

reputedly *adv* in common estimation; by repute.

req. *abbr* = required; requisition.

request *n* an asking for something; a petition; a demand; the thing asked for. * *vt* to ask for earnestly.

request stop *n* a place where a bus, etc, stops only if signaled to do so.—*also* **flag stop**.

Requiem *n* (*mus*) a Mass for the dead in the Roman Catholic Church, so called because of the opening words *Requiem aeternam dona eis, Domine* ("Grant them eternal rest, O Lord)"; music for this.

require *vt* to demand; to need, call for; to order, command.

requirement *n* a need or want; an essential condition.

requisite *adj* needed; essential, indispensable. * *n* something required or indispensable.

requisition *n* a formal request, demand, or order, as for military supplies; the taking over of private property, etc, for military use. * *vt* to order; to take by requisition.

reredos *n* a screen or partition separating the altar from the choir.

rerun *vt* to run (a race, etc) again; to show a television program, film, etc, again.—*also n*.

res. *abbr* = research; reserve; residence; resides; resigned; resistance; resistor.

RES *abbr* (*Brit*) = Royal Economic Society; Royal Entomological Society.

resale *n* the selling again (of something) usu to a new buyer; a repeat sale to a customer; a second-hand sale.

RESCARE *abbr* (*Brit*) = National Society for Mentally Handicapped People in Residential Care.

reschedule *vt* (of debt) to postpone or extend repayment terms.

rescind *vt* to annul, cancel.

rescue *vt* to save (a person, thing) from captivity, danger, or harm; to free forcibly from legal custody.—*also n*.—**rescuer** *n*.

RESCUE *abbr* (*Brit*) = Rescue Trust for British Archaeology.

research *n* a diligent search; a systematic and careful investigation of a particular subject; a scientific study. * *vi* to carry out an investigation; to study.—**researcher** *n*.

research and development (often abbreviated to **R & D**) *n* the department of a company and the portion of its resources that are concerned with research into potential new products, and the process of modification of such research aimed at their ultimate development as commercially viable products.

resection *n* (*med*) a surgical operation in which part of an organ, or any body part, is removed.

resemble *vt* to be like, to have a similarity to.—**resemblance** *n*.

resent *vt* to be indignant about; to begrudge; to take badly.—**resentful** *adj*.—**resentfully** *adv*.—**resentment** *n*.

reserpine *n* an alkaloid extracted from the roots of a rauwolfia, used to treat high blood pressure and as a sedative.

reservation *n* the act of reserving; (of tickets, accommodation, etc) a holding until called for; a limitation or proviso; (*pl*) doubt, skepticism; land set aside for a special purpose.

reserve *vt* to hold back for future use; to retain; to have set aside; to book (a ticket, hotel room, etc). * *n* something put aside for future use; land set aside for wild animals; (*sport*) a substitute; (*mil*) a force supplementary to a regular army; a restriction or qualification; reticence of feelings; caution.

reserved *adj* set apart, booked; uncommunicative, lacking cordiality.—**reservedly** *adv*.

reserve price *n* the lowest price that a seller is willing to accept for an article offered for sale to the public at auction.

reserves *n* resources that can be developed economically.

reservist *n* a member of a military reserve force.

reservoir *n* a tank or artificial lake for storing water; an extra supply or store.

reservoir rock *n* (*geol*) a porous and permeable rock which can hold oil, gas or water.

reset[1] *vt* (**resetting, reset**) to set (a bone, gem, type) over again; to place in a new setting; to change the reading of.

reset[2] *vt* (**resetting, reset**) (*Scots law*) to receive (stolen goods).—*also n*.

reset button *n* (*comput*) a button on a computer that allows the user to perform a warm boot or restart of the computer. *See also* **bootstrapping**.

reshape *vti* to shape anew.

reside *vi* to live in a place permanently; to be vested or present in.

residence *n* the act of living in a place; the period of residing; the house where one lives permanently; the status of a legal resident; a building used as a home.

residency *n* (*pl* **residencies**) a usually official place of residence, e.g., of a governor; a period of advanced training in medicine.

resident *adj* residing; domiciled; living at one's place of work. * *n* a permanent inhabitant; a doctor who is serving a residency.

residential *adj* of or relating to residence; used for private homes.

residual *adj* left over; remaining as a residue. * *n* (*astron*) the discrepancy between an observed valve or quantity (such as the position of a comet) and the predicted, calculated value.

residual deposits *npl* (*geol*) the production of rock waste (from clays to boulders) due to weathering, or the weathered material remaining after soluble components have been dissolved out.

residuary *adj* of or relating to the residue of an estate.

residue *n* a remainder; a part left over; what is left of an estate after payment of debts and legacies.

resign *vti* to give up (employment, etc); to relinquish; to yield to; to reconcile (oneself).

resignation *n* the resigning of office, etc; the written proof of this; patient endurance.

resigned *adj* submissive, acquiescent; accepting the inevitable.

resilience, resiliency *n* the quality of being resilient; physical or mental stamina.

resilient *adj* elastic, springing back; buoyant; (of a person) capable of carrying on after suffering hardship.

resin *n* a sticky substance exuded in the sap of trees and plants and used in medicines, varnishes, etc; (*biol*) an organic compound secreted by a plant or animal; (*chem*) any synthetic plastic material produced by polymerization; rosin; a similar synthetic substance used in plastics.—**resinous** *adj*.

resist *vti* to fight against; to be proof against; to oppose or withstand.

resistance *n* the act of resisting; the power to resist, as to ward off disease; (*med*) the degree of natural immunity that an individual possesses against disease, or the degree to which a disease or disease-causing organism can withstand treatment with drugs, such as a course of antibiotics; opposition, esp to an occupying force; hindrance; (*elect*) non-conductivity, opposition to a steady current; (*psychoanal*) a process by which the ego opposes the conscious recall of unpleasant experiences.

resistant *adj* capable of resisting; (*with* **to**) immune to.

resister *n* a person who resists, esp an opponent of government policy.

resistivity *n* (*physics*) resistance to the passage of an electrical current; the reciprocal of a material's conductivity, giving the resistance in terms of its dimensions.

resistor *n* (*physics*) a component of electric circuits, used to provide a known resistance.

Resnais *n* Alain (*b*. 1922) French film director who is among the best known of the French "New Wave" directors. His films include *Hiroshima mon amour* (1959) and *Last Year in Marienbad* (1961).

resolute *adj* determined; firm of purpose, steadfast.—**resolutely** *adv*.—**resoluteness** *n*.

resolution *n* the act of resolving or the state of being resolved; determination; a fixed intention; the formal decision or opinion of a meeting; analysis, disintegration; (*med*) the dispersion of a tumor, etc; the picture definition in a TV; (*mus*) the relieving of a discord by a following concord; (*physics*) the process or capability of making distinguishable closely adjacent optical images or sources of light; (*astron*) a measure of the smallest detail that can be distinguished with a telescope or other imaging instrument; (*comput*) a measurement of the sharpness of an image generated by a printer or VDU. *See also* **dot pitch, high resolution, low resolution**.

resolve *vt* to break into component parts, dissolve; to convert or be converted (into); to analyze; to determine, make up one's mind; to solve, settle; to vote by resolution; to dispel (doubt); to explain; to conclude; (*med*) to disperse (a tumor); (*mus*) to convert (discord) into concord. * *n* a fixed intention; resolution; courage.

resolving power *n* the ability of a microscope or telescope to produce distinct images of objects in close proximity.

resonance *n* resounding quality; vibration; (*astron*) the phenomenon responsible for commensurable orbits and the divisions in the rings of Saturn.

resonant *adj* ringing; resounding, echoing.

resonator *n* a device that produces or increases sound by resonance.

resort *n* a popular holiday location; a source of help, support, etc; recourse. * *vi* to have recourse to; to turn (to) for help, etc.

resound *vti* to echo; to reverberate; to go on sounding; to be much talked of; to spread (fame).

resounding *adj* echoing; notable; thorough.

resource *n* source of help; an expedient; the ability to cope with a situation; a means of diversion; (*pl*) wealth; assets; raw materials.

resourceful *adj* able to cope in difficult situations; ingenious.—**resourcefulness** *n*.

resp. *abbr* = respective; respectively; respiration; respondent.

respect *n* esteem; consideration; regard; (*pl*) good wishes; reference; relation. * *vt* to feel or show esteem or regard to; to treat considerately.

respectable *adj* worthy of esteem; well-behaved; proper, correct, well-conducted; of moderate quality or size.—**respectability** *n*.—**respectably** *adv*.

respectful *adj* deferential.—**respectfully** *adv*.

respecting *prep* concerning.

respective *adj* proper to each, several.

respectively *adv* in the indicated order.

Respighi *n* **Ottorino** (1879–1936) Italian composer, violinist, conductor, pianist, and teacher. He studied composition with Rimsky-Korsakov, who influenced him greatly, and then taught composition himself in Rome. His works include operas (such as *Belfagor*); a ballet (*La Boutique fantastique*, which was adapted from music by Rossini); orchestral compositions, notably *The Fountains of Rome* and *The Pines of Rome*; and pieces for voice and orchestra.

respiration *n* the act or process of breathing; (*biol*) the process by which living cells of an organism release energy by breaking down complex organic compounds into simpler ones using enzymes.

respirator *n* an apparatus to maintain breathing by artificial means; a device or mask to prevent the inhalation of harmful substances.

respiratory *adj* of or for respiration.

respiratory distress syndrome *n* a condition usu arising in newborn babies, usu those who are premature, characterized by rapid shallow labored breathing.—*also* **hyaline membrane disease**.

respiratory syncitial virus, RS virus *n* the main cause of bronchiolitis and pneumonia in babies under the age of six months.

respiratory system, respiratory tract *n* all the organs and tissues involved in respiration, including the nose, pharynx, larynx, trachea, bronchi, bronchioles, lungs, and diaphragm.

respire *vti* to breathe.

respite *n* a temporary delay; a period of rest or relief; a reprieve.

resplendent *adj* dazzling, shining brilliantly; magnificent.

respond *vti* to answer; to reply; to show a favorable reaction; to be answerable; (*with* **to**) to react. * *n* (*archit*) a half-pier bonded into a wall and carrying one end of an arch.

respondent *n* a defendant, esp in a divorce suit; one who answers.

response *n* an answer; a reaction to stimulation.

responses *n* (*mus*) the plainsong replies of a choir or congregation to solo chants sung by a priest.

responsibility *n* (*pl* **responsibilities**) being responsible; a moral obligation or duty; a charge or trust; a thing one is responsible for.

responsible *adj* having control (over); (*with* **for**) accountable (for); capable of rational conduct; trustworthy; involving responsibility.—**responsibly** *adv*.

responsive *adj* responding; sensitive to influence or stimulus; sympathetic.

rest home *n* an old people's home; a convalescent home.

rest mass *n* the mass of a particle at rest, usu measured in megaelectron volts.

rest[1] *n* stillness, repose, sleep; inactivity; the state of not moving; relaxation; tranquillity; a support or prop; a pause in music, meter, etc; a place of quiet. * *vti* to take a rest; to give rest to; to be still; to lie down; to relax; to be fixed (on); to lean, support or be supported; to put one's trust (in); to dwell; (of land) to lie fallow or unworked.

rest[2] *n* the remainder; the others. * *vi* to remain.

restate *vt* to state over again; to put differently.—**restatement** *n*.

restaurant *n* a place where meals can be bought and eaten.

restaurateur *n* the keeper of a restaurant.

restful *adj* peaceful.—**restfully** *adv*.—**restfulness** *n*.

restitution *n* the restoring of something to its owner; a reimbursement, as for loss.

restive *adj* impatient; fidgety; refractory, stubborn; balky.—**restively** *adv*.—**restiveness** *n*.

restless *adj* unsettled; agitated; never still or motionless, as the sea.—**restlessly** *adv*.—**restlessness** *n*.

restoration *n* the act of restoring; reconstruction; renovation; (*with cap*) the re-establishment of the monarchy in Britain in 1660 under Charles II; the period of Charles II's reign (1660–85). *adj* (*with cap*) (of literature of the period) characterized by wit, salaciousness, and religious and philosophical questioning.

restorative *adj* tending to restore health and strength. * *n* a medicine or food that reinvigorates.

restore *vt* to give or put back; to re-establish; to repair; to renovate; to bring back to the original condition; (*comput*) to recreate the previous conditions or state of a disk, file, or program before an error or event occurred to destroy or corrupt the data.—**restorer** *n*.

restrain *vt* to hold back; to restrict; to deprive (a person) of freedom.

restrained *adj* moderate; self-controlled; without exuberance.

restraint *n* the ability to hold back; something that restrains; control of emotions, impulses, etc.

restrict *vt* to keep within limits, circumscribe.

restricted *adj* affected by restriction; limited; not generally available.

restriction *n* restraint; limitation; a limiting regulation; (*law*) a restriction on a piece of real estate for certain purposes.—**restrictive** *adj*.

restrictive trade practices *npl* agreements between traders relating to restrictions on prices, terms, conditions of sale, etc, which are not held to be in the interests of the public and may be detrimental to other suppliers.

restroom *n* a room equipped with toilets, washbowls, etc, for the use of the public.

result *vi* to have as a consequence; to terminate in. * *n* a consequence; an outcome; a value obtained by mathematical calculation; (*sport*) the final score; (*pl*) a desired effect.

resultant *adj* derived from or resulting from something else.

resultant tone *see* **combination tone**.

resume *vti* to begin again; to continue after a stop or pause; to proceed after interruption.—**resumption** *n*.

résumé *n* a summary, esp of employment experience; a curriculum vitae.

resurgence *n* a revival; a renewal of activity.—**resurgent** *adj*.

resurrect *vt* to bring back into use; to revive (a custom); to restore to life.

resurrection *n* a revival; a rising from the dead; (*with cap*) the rising of Christ from the dead.

resuscitate *vti* to revive when apparently dead or unconscious.—**resuscitation** *n*.

resuscitation *n* the reviving of a person in whom heartbeat and breathing have ceased. *See* **artificial respiration; cardiac massage**.

resuscitator *n* an apparatus for forcing oxygen into the lungs; a person who resuscitates.

ret. *abbr* = retired; returned.

retable *n* a step or ledge behind the altar of a church, slightly raised above it for the reception of lights, flowers, and other symbolical ornaments.

retail *n* selling directly to the consumer in small quantities. * *adv* at a retail price. * *vti* to sell or be sold by retail.—*also adj*.—**retailer** *n*.

retailer *n* an individual or company that stocks a particular type of product or a range of products for sale to consumers, as opposed to a wholesaler.

retail outlet *n* business premises where products are sold to consumers.

retain *vt* to keep possession of; to keep in the mind, to remember; to keep in place, support; to hire the services of.

retained profit *n* the amount of profit that remains after tax has been deducted and after dividends have been paid to shareholders and is reinvested in the company.

retainer *n* that which retains; (*formerly*) a servant to a family, a dependant; a fee to retain the services of.

retaining wall *n* (*archit*) a wall that is constructed to hold back earth or water.—*also* **revetment**.

retake *vt* (**retaking, retook**, *pp* **retaken**) to capture again; to shoot a film scene again. * *n* a scene that has been reshot.

retaliate *vti* to revenge oneself, usu by returning like for like; to strike back; to cast back (an accusation).—**retaliation** *n*.—**retaliatory** *adj*.

retard *vti* to slow down, to delay; to make slow or late.—**retardation** *n*.

retardant *n* a substance that retards, esp a chemical reaction. * *adj* retarding.

retardation *n* the slowing down of an activity or a process, often referring to mental subnormality or "backwardness"; (*mus*) a suspension in which a discordant note is resolved upwards by one step rather than downwards.

retarded *adj* slow in physical or mental development.

retch *vi* to heave as if to vomit.

retd. *abbr* = retained; returned.

Ret'dABID *abbr* (*Brit*) = Retired Associate of the British Institute of Interior Design.

Ret'dFBID *abbr* (*Brit*) = Retired Fellow of the British Institute of Interior Design.

Ret'dMBID *abbr* (*Brit*) = Retired Member of the British Institute of Interior Design.**retention** *n* the act of retaining; the capacity to retain; memory; (*med*) the abnormal retaining of fluid in a body cavity.

retentive *adj* capable of retaining; keeping, holding. * *n* one who retains.—**retentiveness** *n*.

rethink *vt* (**rethinking, rethought**) to consider or think about again, esp with a change in mind.

R et I *abbr* (*Latin*) = *Regina et Imperatrix* ("Queen and Empress"); *Rex et Imperator* ("King and Emperor").

reticent *adj* reserved in speech; uncommunicative.—**reticence** *n*.

reticle *n* a network of fine wires, threads, etc, placed in the focal plane of an optical instrument.

reticulate *adj* resembling a network.—*also* **reticular**. * *vti* to arrange or be arranged into a network.—**reticulation** *n*.

reticulated *adj* having a net-like feature in a decoration or element of a building. *See* **tracery**.

retina *n* (*pl* **retinas, retinae**) the layer that lines the interior of the eye and receives light directed onto its surface by the lens.

retinue *n* a body of attendants.

retire *vi* to give up one's work when pensionable age is reached; to withdraw; to retreat; to go to bed. * *vt* (*troops*) to withdraw from use; to compel to retire from a position, work, etc.

retirement *n* the act of retiring or the state of being retired; seclusion; privacy.

retirement age *n* the age of retirement as stipulated in law.

retiring *adj* unobtrusive; shy.

retort *vi* to reply sharply or wittily. * *n* a sharp or witty reply; a vessel with a funnel bent downwards used in distilling; a receptacle used in making gas and steel.

retouch *vt* to improve or change (a photograph, etc) by touching up; to color (new growth of hair) to match other hair.

RETRA *abbr* (*Brit*) = Radio, Electrical and Television Retailers' Association.

retrace *vt* to go back over; to trace back to a source.—**retraceable** *adj*.

retract *vti* to draw in or back; to withdraw (a statement, opinion, etc); to recant.—**retractable** *adj*.—**retraction** *n*.

retractor *n* one of a number of different surgical instruments designed to pull apart the cut edges of an incision to allow greater operating access.

retread *vt* (**retreading, retreaded**) to put a new tread on a worn tire. * *n* a retreaded tire.

re-tread *vt* (**re-treading, re-trod,** *pp* **re-trodden** *or* **re-trod**) to tread (a path) again.

retreat *vi* to withdraw, retire; to recede. * *n* a withdrawal, esp of troops; a sign for retiring; a quiet or secluded place, refuge; seclusion for religious devotion.

retrench *vti* to cut down (esp expenses); to economize.—**retrenchment** *n*.

retrial *n* a second trial.

retribution *n* deserved reward; something given or exacted in compensation, esp punishment.

retrieve *vt* to recover; to revive; (*a loss*) to make good; (*comput*) to obtain information from data stored in a computer. * *vi* (of dogs) to retrieve game.—**retrievable** *adj*.—**retrieval** *n*.

retriever *n* any of several breeds of dogs capable of being trained for retrieving.

retro *n* (*pl* **retros**) a retrorocket. * *adj* denoting a fashion or style (in music, clothes, etc) that pays homage to the past.

retro- *prefix* backwards; behind.

retroactive *adj* having an effect on things that are already past.

retroflexion *n* (*med*) the bending backwards of a part of an organ, particularly the upper portion of the uterus.

retrog. *abbr* = retrogressive.

retrogradation *n* erosion of a shoreline by the sea so that it retreats inland.

retrograde *adj* going backwards; passing from better to worse. * *n* (*astron*) the east–west movement of an object on the celestial sphere or clockwise movement (when viewed from the north) in an orbit or around an axis within the Solar System.

retrograde motion *n* (*mus*) a term for music that is played backwards.

retrogression *n* going backwards, usu a return to a former, less complex, level of development.

retrorocket *n* a small rocket on an aircraft or spacecraft that produces thrust in the opposite direction to the line of flight to slow it down.

retrospect *n* a looking back; a mental review of the past.—**retrospection** *n*.

retrospective *adj* looking backwards; relating to the past. * *n* an exhibition of an artist's lifetime work.—**retrospectively** *adv*.

retroussé *adj* turned upwards (esp of the nose).

retroversion *n* the act of turning or state of being turned backwards; (*med*) an abnormal position of the uterus in which the whole organ is tilted backwards instead of forwards, as is normally the case.—**retroverted** *adj*.

Retrovir *n* (*trademark*) AZT.

retrovirus *n* any of various viruses that use RNA to synthesize DNA, reversing the normal process in cells of transcription from DNA to RNA, which includes HIV.

retsina *n* a Greek white wine flavored with resin.

return *vi* to come or go back; to reply; to recur. * *vt* to give or send back; to repay; to yield; to answer; to elect. * *n* something returned; a recurrence; recompense; the income derived from an investment, frequently expressed as a percentage of its original cost; (*archit*) the point at which a wall, molding, etc, continues at an angle to the original orientation; (*comput*) a command key on the keyboard that is used to initiate a chosen command; (*pl*) yield, revenue; a form for computing (income) tax.

returnable *adj* required to be returned; capable of being returned (for reuse).

return ticket *n* (*Brit etc*) a ticket whose price includes the cost of the journey to and back from a destination.

Reuben *n* (*Bible*) eldest son of Jacob and Leah, and forefather of one of the twelve tribes of Israel.

Reubke *n* **Julius** (1834–58) German pianist and composer who studied under Liszt. He is best known for his organ sonata *The Ninety-fourth Psalm*.

Reuel *n* (*Bible*) an alternative name for Jethro.

reunion *n* a meeting following separation; a social gathering of former colleagues.

Réunion *n* a French overseas department in the Indian Ocean, south of Mauritius.

reunite *vt* to unite again; to reconcile. * *vi* to become reunited.

reusable *adj* able to be used again; renewable.

rev *vt* (**revving, revved**) (*inf*) (*with* **up**) to increase the speed of an engine. * *n* revolution per minute.

rev. *abbr* = revenue; reverse; review; revise; revised; revision; revolution; revolving.

Rev *abbr* = Revelation; Reverend.

Rév. *abbr* = révue.

rev. A/C *abbr* (*bank*) = revenue account.

revaluate *vt* to reassess the value of; to change (esp increase) the exchange value of (a currency).

revamp *vt* to renovate, to rework, remodel; to transform. * *n* the process of revamping; something revamped.

revanchism *n* (support for) a policy aimed at regaining lost territory or possessions.—**revanchist** *n, adj*.

Revd. *abbr* = reverend.

reveal *vt* (*something hidden or secret*) to make known; to expose; to make visible. * *n* (*archit*) the part of the jamb, in a door or window opening, that is not covered by the frame.

reveille *n* a morning bugle call to wake soldiers.

revel *vi* (**reveling, reveled** *or* **revelling, revelled**) (*with* **in**) to take pleasure or delight in; to make merry. * *n* (*pl*) merrymaking; entertainment.—**reveler, reveller** *n*.

revelation *n* the act of revealing; the disclosure of something secret; a communication from God to man; an illuminating experience.

Revelation of John, the, The Book of Revelation *n* (*Bible*) the last book of the New Testament.

revelry *n* (*pl* **revelries**) the act of reveling; noisy festivity.

revenant *n* a person who returns from the dead or from a prolonged absence.—*also adj*.

revenge *vt* to inflict punishment in return for; to satisfy oneself by retaliation; to avenge. * *n* the act of revenging; retaliation; a vindictive feeling.—**revenger** *n*.

revengeful *adj* keen for revenge; vindictive.

revenge tragedy a dramatic genre that appeared in the late 16th century, heavily influenced by the bloodthirsty language and plots of Seneca's plays, in which revenge, often for the death of a son or father, is the prime motive.

revenue *n* the total income produced by taxation; gross income from a business or investment.

revenue expenditure *n* any expenditure that is written off entirely in the profit-and-loss account in the financial year to which it is relevant.

reverb *n* (*mus*) an electronic device for producing an artificial echo.

reverberate *vi* to rebound, recoil; to be reflected in; to resound, to echo.—**reverberation** *n*.

revere *vt* to regard with great respect or awe; to venerate.

reverence *n* profound respect; devotion; a gesture of respect (such as a bow). * *vt* to hold in respect.

reverend *adj* worthy of reverence; of or relating to the clergy; (*with cap*) a title for a member of the clergy.

reverent *adj* feeling or expressing reverence.—**reverently** *adv*.

reverie *n* a daydream; (*mus*) a dreamy piece.—*also* **revery** (*pl* **reveries**).

revers *n* (*pl* **revers**) a lapel, esp on a woman's garment.

reversal *n* the act or process of reversing.

reverse *vti* to turn in the opposite direction; to turn outside in, upside down, etc; to move backwards; (*law*) to revoke or annul. * *n* the contrary or opposite of something; the back, esp of a coin; a setback; a mechanism for reversing. * *adj* opposite, contrary; causing movement in the opposite direction.

REVERSE
REVERSE

REVERSE
REVERSE

reverse takeover *n* a takeover by a company that has a lower stock valuation than the firm that is the object of the takeover; the takeover of a public company by a private company.

reverse video *n* (*comput*) a technique for highlighting on a computer monitor by reversing the normal text and background colors.

reversible *adj* with both sides usable; wearable with either side out; able to undergo a series of changes either backwards or forwards. * *n* a reversible cloth or article of clothing.

reversible reaction *n* (*chem*) a chemical reaction that can proceed in either direction.

reversion *n* return to a former condition or type; right to future possession; the return of an estate to the grantor or his heirs.—**reversionary** *adj*.

revert *vi* to go back (to a former state); to take up again (a former subject); (*biol*) to return to a former or primitive type; (*law*) to go back to a former owner or his or her heirs.—**revertible** *adj*.

revery *see* reverie.

revetment *n* (*archit*) a retaining wall; the cladding fixed to a wall constructed of a different material.

review *n* an evaluation; a survey; a reconsideration; a critical assessment, a critique; a periodical containing critical essays; an official inspection of ships or troops. * *vt* to re-examine; to inspect formally; to write a critique on.

reviewer *n* a person who writes a review, esp for a newspaper, a critic.

revile *vti* to use abusive language (to or about).

revise *vt* to correct and amend; to prepare a new, improved version of; to study again (for an examination).—**revision** *n*.

revitalize *vt* to put new life into.—**revitalization** *n*.

revival *n* the act of reviving; recovery from a neglected or depressed state; renewed performance (of a play); renewed interest in; religious awakening.

revivalist *n* a person who encourages religious practice.—**revivalism** *n*.

revive *vti* to return to life; to make active again; to take up again.—**reviver** *n*.

revivify *vt* to put new life into; to reanimate; to revive.—**revivification** *n*.—**revivifier** *n*.

revocation *n* (*law*) an instrument which takes away certain powers or privileges of an individual.

revoke *vt* to cancel; to rescind. * *vi* (*cards*) to fail to follow suit.—**revocable** *adj*.—**revocation** *n*.

revol. *abbr* = revolutions.

revolt *vt* to rebel; to overturn; to shock. * *vi* to feel great disgust. * *n* rebellion; uprising; loathing.

REVOLT *abbr* (*Brit*) = Rural England Versus Overhead Live Transmissions.

revolting *adj* extremely offensive.—**revoltingly** *adv*.

revolution *n* the act of revolting; a motion round a center or axis; a single completion of an orbit or rotation; a great change; an overthrow of a government, social system, etc.

revolutionary *adj* of or advocating revolution; radically new. * *n* a person who takes part in, or favors, revolution.

revolutionize *vt* to cause a complete change in.

revolve *vti* to travel or cause to travel in a circle or orbit; to rotate.

revolver *n* a handgun with a magazine that revolves to reload.

revolving credit *n* a letter authorizing credit that can be used repeatedly within the limits of a fixed sum.

revolving door *n* a door of two or four panels rotating around a central axis within a round chamber and operated electrically or manually.

revolving fund *n* a fund established for certain purposes, which stipulates that repayments to the fund can be used for the same purposes.

rev/s *abbr* = revolutions per second.

Revs. *abbr* = Reverends.

revs. per min. *abbr* = revolutions per minute.

Rev. Stat. *abbr* = Revised Statutes.

revue *n* a musical show with skits, dances, etc, often satirizing recent events.

revulsion *n* disgust; aversion; a sudden change or reversal of feeling, esp withdrawal with a sense of utter distaste.

Rev. Ver. *abbr* = Revised Version.

reward *n* something that is given in return for something done; money offered, as for the capture of a criminal. * *vt* to give a reward.

rewarding *adj* (of an experience, activity, etc) pleasing, profitable.

rewind *vt* to wind again; to wind (an audiotape, etc) back to the beginning. * *n* the act of rewinding.

rewire *vt* to put new wiring into an electrical system.

reword *vt* to change the wording of.

rework *vt* to use again in a different form; to rewrite; to remodel.

rewrite *vt* to write again; to revise. * *n* something rewritten; revision.

Rex *n* a reigning king.

Reye's syndrome a rare disorder, causing brain damage, that affects children and seems to follow on from a viral infection such as chickenpox, often manifesting itself during the recovery phase.

Reykjavík *n* capital city of Iceland.

Reynolds *n* 1. **Albert** (*b.* 1933) Irish politician and Fianna Fáil member who until 1991 held several posts under Charles Haughey, whom he succeeded as *taoiseach* (prime minister) in 1992. 2. **Sir Joshua** (1723–92) English painter and art theorist. As first president of the British Royal Academy he set high standards in portraiture.

Reznicek *n* **Emil Nikolaus von** (1860–1945) an Austrian composer and conductor who worked in Germany. His works include operas (e.g., *Donna Diana, Till Eulenspiegel*), four symphonies, choral pieces, and many songs.

Rf *symbol* (*chem*) = rutherfordium.

rf *abbr* = radio frequency; range finder; rapid fire, rapid firing.

rf, rfz *abbr* (*mus*) (*Italian*) = rinforzando.

rf. *abbr* = (of paper) rough finish.

RF *abbr* = representative fraction; Rockefeller Foundation; Rural Forum; rugby football.

RFA *abbr* (*Brit*) = Royal Fleet Auxiliary; Rugby Fives Association.

RFAC *abbr* (*Brit*) = Royal Fine Art Commission.

RFBPA *abbr* = Raw Fat and Bone Processors Association.

RFC *abbr* = (*comput*) request for comment; (*Brit*) Royal Flying Corps; (*Brit*) Rugby Football Club.

RFD *abbr* = radio frequency device; reporting for duty.

RFG *abbr* = rapid-fire gun.

rfg. *abbr* = refunding.

RFH *abbr* (*Brit*) = Royal Festival Hall.

RFI *abbr* = radio-frequency interference.

RFL *abbr* (*Brit*) = Rugby Football League.

RFR *abbr* (*Brit*) = Royal Fleet Reserve.

RFS *abbr* (*Brit*) = Registry of Friendly Societies; Royal Forestry Society.

RFSU *abbr* (*Brit*) = Rugby Football Schools Union.

RFTF *abbr* (*Brit*) = Retail Fruit Trade Federation.

RFU *abbr* (*Brit*) = Rugby Football Union.

rfz. *abbr* (*music*) = rinforzando.

RGB *abbr* = red-green-blue (color transmission system).

RGG *abbr* (*Brit*) = Royal Grenadier Guards.

RGN *abbr* (*Brit*) = Registered General Nurse.

RGNP *abbr* = real gross national product.

RGO *abbr* (*Brit*) = Royal Greenwich Observatory.

RGOF *abbr* (*Brit*) = Royal Gardeners' Orphan Fund.

RGS *abbr* (*Brit*) = Royal Geographical Society.

Rgt *abbr* = Regiment.

RGV *abbr* = remote guidance vehicle.

Rh *symbol* (*chem*) = rhodium.

rh *abbr* = (*soccer*) right half; right-hand.

Rh *abbr* = rhesus (blood group).

RH *abbr* = (*mus*) right hand; (*Brit*) Royal Highness.

RHA *abbr* = Regional Health Authority; (*Brit*) Road Haulage Association; (*Brit*) Royal Horse Artillery.

rhachis *see* **rachis**.

RHACT *abbr* (*Brit*) = Red Hot AIDS Charitable Trust.

Rhadamanthus, Rhadamanthys *n* (*Greek myth*) the brother of Minos, king of Crete, a man of inflexible integrity, who became one of the three judges of the underworld.

rhap. *abbr* (*music*) = rhapsody.

rhapsodize *vi* to speak or write (about) with enthusiasm or emotion.—**rhapsodist** *n.*

rhapsody *n* (*pl* **rhapsodies**) an enthusiastic speech or writing; (*mus*) an irregular instrumental composition of an epic, heroic, or national character; (*mus*) the title commonly given by 19th and 20th-century composers to an instrumental composition in one continuous movement.

RHAS *abbr* (*Brit*) = Rider Haggard Appreciation Society.

RHB *abbr* = Regional Hospital Board.

RHD *abbr* = right-hand drive.

rhea *n* any of several large flightless birds of South America resembling ostriches but smaller.

Rhea *n* the second largest satellite of Saturn, with a heavily cratered and icy surface.

Rhea, Rheia *n* (*Greek myth*) one of the female Titans, sister and wife of Cronos, and mother of Hestia, Demeter, Hera, Hades, Poseidon, and Zeus, known as Mother of the Gods or Great Mother, and later identified with Cybele.

rhebok *see* **reebok**.

Rheingold, Das *see* **Ring des Nibelungen, Der**.

RHEL *abbr* (*Brit*) = Rutherford High Energy Laboratory.

rhenium *n* a hard heat-resistant metallic element.

rheo. *abbr* = rheostat, *or* rheostats.

rheo- *prefix* flow, current.

rheology *n* the physics of the flow and deformation of matter.—**rheologist** *n.*—**rheological** *adj*.

rheostat *n* (*physics*) a device that regulates electric current by varying the resistance to it.—**rheostatic** *adj*.

Rhesus *n* (*Greek myth*) a king of Thrace and an ally of the Trojans against the Greeks, who after his death became an oracular spirit living in caves in Thrace.

rhesus factor, Rh factor *n* an antigen usu present in the red blood cells of humans and higher animals.

rhesus monkey *n* a type of southern Asian macaque with light brown fur.

rhesus negative *adj* lacking the rhesus factor in the blood.

rhesus positive *adj* containing the rhesus factor in the blood.

rhet. *abbr* = rhetoric; rhetorical.

rhetoric *n* the art of effective speaking and writing; skill in using speech; insincere language.

rhetorical *adj* of or relating to rhetoric; high-flown, bombastic.—**rhetorically** *adv*.

rhetorical question *n* a question asked for effect, to which no answer is expected.

rheum *n* a watery discharge from the mucous membranes of the nose, eyes, etc.—**rheumy** *adj*.

rheumatic *adj* of, relating to or suffering from rheumatism. * *n* a person who has rheumatism.

rheumatic fever *n* a severe disease characterized by inflammation and pain in the joints, affecting children and young adults, a complication of upper respiratory tract infection with *Hemolytic streptococci* bacteria.

rheumatism *n* a disorder causing pain in muscles and joints.

rheumatoid *adj* of or like rheumatism.

rheumatoid arthritis *n* a common form of usu chronic joint disease, characterized by inflammation, pain, and swelling, which often affects the feet, ankles, fingers, and wrists. The condition varies greatly in its degree of severity, but at its worst can be progressive and seriously disabling. *See also* **osteoarthritis**.

rheumatology *n* the branch of medicine concerned with diseases of the joints and associated tissues and structures.—**rheumatologist** *n*.

RHF *abbr* (*Brit*) = Royal Highland Fusiliers.

RHG *abbr* (*Brit*) = Royal Horse Guards.

RHHI *abbr* (*Brit*) = Royal Hospital and Home for Incurables.

Rhiannon *n* (Welsh Celtic myth) the daughter of Hefeydd Hen and extremely beautiful. Her name means "great queen," and she became the wife of Pwyll.

rhinal *adj* of or pertaining to the nose.

Rhine *n* **Joseph Banks** (1895–1980) American psychologist. He founded parapsychology, the study of ESP and related mental phenomena, such as telekinesis. His works include *New Frontiers of the Mind* (1937).

rhinestone *n* a colorless imitation precious stone made from paste, glass, or quartz.

Rhine wine *n* any of several wines from the valley of the River Rhine in Germany; a light dry wine from the Rhine valley or elsewhere.

rhinitis *n* inflammation of the mucous membrane of the nose, such as occurs with colds and allergic reactions.

rhino *n* (*pl* **rhinos, rhino**) (*inf*) a rhinoceros.

rhino-, rhin- *prefix* nose.

rhinoceros *n* (*pl* **rhinoceroses**, **rhinoceros**) a large, thick-skinned mammal with one or two horns on the nose.

rhinology *n* the branch of medicine dealing with the nose.—**rhinologist** *n*.

rhinophyma *see* **rosacea**.

rhinoplasty *n* plastic surgery of the nose.—**rhinoplastic** *adj*.

RHistS *abbr* (*Brit*) = Royal Historical Society.

rhizo-, rhiz- *prefix* root.

rhizome *n* (*bot*) a stem on or below ground that produces roots below and shoots above; a rootstock.

RHM *abbr* (*Brit*) = Rank Hovis McDougall.

Rh negative *see* **rhesus negative**.

rho *n* (*pl* **rhos**) the 17th letter of the Greek alphabet.

Rhoda *n* (*Bible*) name of a girl in the house of Mary the mother of John Mark.

Rhode, Rhodos *n* (*Greek myth*) a nymph who gave her name to the island of Rhodes.

Rhode Island *n* a state of the United States of America (USA) of which the capital is Providence.

"Rhode Island" *n* the song of the American State, Rhode Island.

Rhode Island Red *n* an American breed of domestic fowl with reddish-brown plumage.

Rhodes *n* an island in the Aegean Sea, off the southwest coast of Turkey.—**Rhodian** *adj*.

Rhodes scholarship *n* any of the 72 scholarships founded by Cecil Rhodes (1853–1902), which are awarded to Commonwealth and US students to study at Oxford University in England.

Rhodi Mawr *n* (the Great) king of Gwynedd, Wales (844–878). He resisted several attacks by the Vikings and came to dominate Powys and Deheubarth in south Wales.

rhodium *n* a hard white metallic element similar to platinum.

rhododendron *n* an evergreen shrub with large flowers.

Rhodope *n* a range of mountains situated on the border between Greece and Bulgaria.

rhomb *n* a rhombus.

rhombohedron *n* (*pl* **rhombohedrons**, **rhombohedra**) a six-sided solid figure whose sides are rhombuses.—**rhombohedral** *adj*.

rhomboid *n* a parallelogram whose adjacent sides are unequal and whose angles are not right angles.—*also adj*.

rhombus *n* (*pl* **rhombuses**, **rhombi**) a diamond shape.

Rhone *n* a European river that rises in Switzerland and flows through southern France to the Mediterranean.

rhp *abbr* = rate horsepower.

Rh positive *see* **rhesus positive**.

RHQ *abbr* = regimental headquarters.

RHR *abbr* (*Brit*) = Royal Highland Regiment.

rhs *abbr* = right-hand side; round headed screw.

RHS *abbr* = (*Brit*) Robin Hood Society; (*Brit*) Royal Highland Show; (*Brit*) Royal Historical Society; (*Brit*) Royal Horticultural Society; (*Brit*) Royal Humane Society; Rural Housing Service; Russian Heraldry Society.

RHT *abbr* (*Brit*) = Railway Heritage Trust; Rural Housing Trust.

rhubarb *n* a plant with large leaves and edible (when cooked) pink stalks; (*inf*) a noisy quarrel.

rhumb *n* an imaginary line crossing all meridians at the same angle; a course navigated by a ship or aircraft that maintains a fixed compass bearing.—*also* **rhumb line**.

RHV *abbr* (*Brit*) = Registered Health Visitor.

rhyme *n* the repetition of sounds usu at the ends of lines in verse; such poetry or verse; a word corresponding with another in end sound. * *vti* to form a rhyme (with); to versify, put into rhyme.

rhyming slang *n* a type of slang that substitutes the original (often indecent) word with a word or phrase that rhymes with it, e.g., *loaf of bread* = *head*.

rhythm *n* a regular recurrence of beat, accent or silence in the flow of sound, esp of words and music; a measured flow; cadence; (*mus*) the aspect of music that is concerned with time. In notation, rhythm is determined by the way in which notes are grouped together into bars, the number and type of beats in a bar (as governed by the time signature), and the type of emphasis (accent) that is given to the beats. Along with melody and harmony, it is one of the essential characteristics of music.—**rhythmic, rhythmical** *adj*.—**rhythmically** *adv*.

rhythm and blues *n* a type of music that fuses elements of folk, blues, and rock.

rhythm method *n* a method of contraception that relies on abstinence from sexual intercourse during the period when ovulation is most likely to occur.

rhythm-names *see* **time-names**.

rhythm section *n* (*mus*) those instruments in a jazz band or group whose main role is to supply the rhythm, such as the double bass and drums.

rhyton *n* a slim, deep vessel typical of the Minoans, Mycenaeans, Achaemenids, and classical Greeks that was used for liquid offerings to the gods and spirits.

ri *abbr* = refractive index.

RI *abbr* = (*Brit*) Railway Inspectorate; (*Latin*) *Regina et Imperatrix* ("Queen and Empress"); Religious Instruction; (*Latin*) *Rex et Imperator* ("King and Emperor"); Rhode Island; Rotary International; (*Brit*) Royal Institute of Painters in Water Colours; (*Brit*) Royal Institution.

ria *n* a coastal river valley or estuary that has been flooded as a result of a rise in sea level, usu found on discordant coasts.

RIA *abbr* = Royal Irish Academy.

rial *n* the standard monetary unit of Iran, made up of 100 dinars; the standard monetary unit of Oman, made up of 100 baizas.

rib *n* one of the curved bones of the chest attached to the spine; any rib-like structure; a leaf vein; a vein of an insect's wing; a ridge or raised strip, as of knitting; a ridge of a mountain; (*archit*) a band, on a ceiling or vault, which is raised and may be structural and/or decorative. * *vt* (**ribbing**, **ribbed**) to provide with ribs; to form vertical ridges in knitting; (*inf*) to tease or ridicule.

RIB *abbr* = Racing Information Bureau.

RIBA *abbr* (*Brit*) = Royal Institute of British Architects.

ribald *adj* irreverent; humorously vulgar.

riband *n* a ribbon.

Ribbentrop *n* **Joachim von** (1893–1946) German Nazi diplomat, who served Hitler as foreign minister (1938–45), signing the German-Soviet treaty with Molotov. He was convicted and hanged for war crimes at Nuremberg.

ribbon *n* silk, satin, velvet, etc, woven into a narrow band; a piece of this; a strip of cloth, etc, inked for use, as in a typewriter; (*pl*) torn shreds.

ribbon development or **linear development** *n* the development, often only one plot deep, running along a main route away from a city center.

rib cage *n* the bony framework of ribs enclosing the wall of the chest.

Ribera *n* **Pedro de** (*b*. 1683) Spanish architect whose notable works include Toledo bridge.

riboflavin *n* a factor of the vitamin B complex found in milk, eggs, fruits, etc.

ribonuclease *n* any of several enzymes that act as catalytic triggers of RNA hydrolysis.

ribonucleic acid *n* (*biochemistry*) a complex nucleic acid, present mainly in the cytoplasm of cells but also in the nucleus, essential to protein development.—**RNA** *abbr*. *See also* **DNA**.

ribose *n* a sugar occurring in RNA and riboflavin.

ribosomal RNA *n* (*biochemistry*) one of the three major classes of RNA, which is transcribed from DNA in a structure of eukaryotic nuclei called the nucleolus.

ribosome *n* (*biochemistry*) any of the tiny particles containing RNA and protein in cells where protein synthesis takes place; the structure within the cell that is the site of protein synthesis in all eukaryotic and prokaryotic cells.—**ribosomal** *adj*.

ribs *npl* 12 pairs of thin, slightly twisted and curved bones that form the thoracic rib cage, which protects the lungs and heart. At the backbone, the head of each rib articulates with one of the 12 thoracic vertebrae. *See also* **floating rib**.

RIC *abbr* = (*Brit*) Radio Industry Council; Railway Industry Council; Rice Improvement Conference; (*Brit*) Royal Institute of Chemistry; (*Brit*) Royal Institution of Cornwall; Royal Irish Constabulary.

RICA *abbr* = (*Brit*) Research Institute for Consumer Affairs.

ricasso *n* the blunting of a sword's cutting edge below the hilt so that the user can hold it without injury.

rice *n* an annual cereal grass cultivated in warm climates; its starchy food grain.

Rice, Tim *see* **Lloyd Webber, Andrew**.

RICE *abbr* = (*Brit*) Research Institute for the Care of the Elderly.

ricebird *see* **bobolink**.

rice paper *n* a delicate paper prepared from pith.

rich *adj* having much money, wealthy; abounding in natural resources, fertile; costly, fine; (*food*) sweet or oily, highly flavored; deep in color; (*inf*) full of humor. * *n* wealthy people collectively; (*pl* **riches**) wealth, abundance.—**richly** *adv*.—**richness** *n*.

Richard I *n* (the Lionheart) (1157–1199) king of England (1189–1199). The third son of Henry II by Eleanor of Aquitaine.

Richard II *n* (1367–1400) king of England and Wales (1377–1399). The second and only surviving son of Edward the Black Prince and Joan of Kent and the grandson of Edward III.

Richard III *n* (1452–1485) king of England and Wales (1483–1485). The last of the Yorkist kings was the youngest son of Richard Plantagenet, Duke of York, and Lady Cecily Neville.

Richard *n* **Cliff** [Harry Roger Webb] (1940–) Indian-born English pop singer and film actor. An institution in British popular music. His films include the musicals *The Young Ones* (1961) and *Summer Holiday* (1962), and the satirical *Expresso Bongo* (1959).

Richard, Keith *see* **Jagger, Mick**.

Richards *n* 1. **Viv** (*b*. 1952) Antiguan-born West Indian cricketer. He was captain of the West Indies (1985–91), and was regarded as one of the best batsmen and fielders in modern cricket. 2. **Sir Gordon** (1904–86) English jockey. He rode 4,870 winners and was champion jockey 26 times.

Richardson *n* 1. **Dorothy [Miller]** (1873–1957) English novelist, noted for her stream-of-consciousness interior monologue which anticipated Joyce's use of the technique. Her best-known work is the *Pilgrimage* sequence of novels. 2. **Samuel** (1689–1761) English novelist, all of whose novels were written in epistolary form. The first was *Pamela; or Virtue Rewarded*, which was attacked by Fielding in *Shamela* for its dubious morality, followed by *Clarissa Harlowe* and *Sir Charles Grandison*. 3. **Henry Hobson** (1838–86) American architect whose notable works include Austin Hall, Harvard. 4. **Sir Ralph [David]** (1902–83) English stage and film actor. One of the finest British actors of the 20th century. Notable films include *Richard III* (1955), *Our Man in Havana* (1960), and his role as God in*Time Bandits* (1981).

Richmond *n* the capital city of Virginia, a state of the USA.

RICHS *abbr* = Rural Information Center Health Service.

Richter scale *n* (*geol*) the scale ranging from 1 to 10 used to measure the intensity of earthquakes that uses the amplitude of seismic waves, which depends on the depth of the earthquake focus.

rich text format *n* (*comput*) a standard text file format which allows files to be transported between applications without loss of the format of the text.

Richthofen, Manfred, Baron von (1882–1918) German fighter pilot, nicknamed the "Red Baron." He commanded the 11th Chasing Squadron ("Richthofen's Flying Circus") in World War I, and was credited with shooting down 80 allied aircraft. He was killed in action, probably by ground fire.

rick[1] *n* a stack or large pile of hay, etc, in the open.

rick[2] *vt* (*Brit etc*) to sprain or strain slightly. * *n* such an injury.—*also* **wrick**.

rickets *n* a children's disease marked by softening of the bones, caused by vitamin D deficiency.

Ricketts *n* **Charles de Sousy** (1866–1931) Swiss illustrator who worked in Britain in the **art nouveau** style.

rickettsia *n* (*pl* **rickettsiae, rickettsias**) any of a genus of microorganisms that inhabit mites, ticks, etc, and cause serious diseases, such as typhus.—**rickettsial** *adj*.

rickety *adj* shaky, unsteady.

Rickman *n* **Thomas** (1776–1841), English architect. His notable works include New Court, St John's Cambridge.

rickrack *n* a zigzag braid for trimming clothing.

rickshaw, ricksha *n* a light, two-wheeled man-drawn vehicle, *orig* used in Japan.

ricochet *vi* (**ricocheting, ricocheted** *or* **ricochetting, ricochetted**) (of a bullet) to rebound or skip along ground or water. * *n* a rebound or glancing off; a hit made (by a bullet) after ricocheting.

ricotta *n* a mild-flavored soft white cheese made from sheep's milk.

RICS *abbr* (*Brit*) = Royal Institution of Chartered Surveyors.

RICSS *abbr* (*Brit*) = Royal Institution of Chartered Surveyors in Scotland.

rictus *n* (*pl* **rictus, rictuses**) the gap in an open mouth or beak; a fixed grimace, esp in horror.—**rictal** *adj*.

rid *vt* (**ridding, rid** *or* **ridded**) to free from; to dispose (of).

riddance *n* clearance; disposal.

ridden *vti pp of* **ride**. * *adj* oppressed by; full of.

riddle[1] *n* a puzzling question; an enigma; a mysterious person or thing.

riddle[2] *n* a coarse sieve. * *vt* to sieve or sift; to perforate with holes; to spread through, permeate.

ride *vti* (**riding, rode**, *pp* **ridden**) to be carried along or travel in a vehicle or on an animal, bicycle, etc; to be supported or move on the water; to lie at anchor; to travel over a surface; to move on the body; (*inf*) to continue undisturbed. * *vt* to sit on and control (a horse, bicycle, etc); to oppress, dominate; (*inf*) to torment. * *n* a trip or journey in a vehicle or on horseback, on a bicycle, etc; a thing to ride at a fairground.

rider *n* a person who rides; an addition to a document, amending a clause; an additional statement; something used to move along another piece.

ridge *n* a narrow crest or top; the ploughed earth thrown up between the furrows; a line where two slopes meet; (of land, etc) a raised strip or elevation; a range of hills. * *vti* to form into ridges, wrinkle.—**ridged** *adj*.

ridge of high pressure *n* an elongated area of high pressure between two depressions, bringing a short spell of fine weather.

ridgepole *n* the horizontal pole along the top of a tent.

ridge rib *n* (*archit*) the main rib along the ridge of a vault which may run along either the length or the width.

ridgeway *n* (*archeo*) an ancient route that follows the line of a ridge.

ridicule *n* mockery, derision. * *vt* to make fun of, to mock.

ridiculous *adj* deserving ridicule; preposterous, silly.—**ridiculously** *adv*.—**ridiculousness** *n*.

Riding *n* **Laura Jackson** (1901–91) American poet, who lived with Robert Graves from 1927 to 1939.

Rie *n* **Lucie** (1902–95) Austrian ceramicist who designed sophisticated domestic wares with Hans **Coper**.

RIE *abbr* = recognized investment exchange.

riel the standard monetary unit of Cambodia, made up of 100 sen.

Riesling *n* (the grape that produces) a dry white wine.

RIF *abbr* = reduction in force.

rife *adj* widespread; prevalent.

riff *n* (*jazz, rock*) a musical phrase played repeatedly, esp as the background to an extended solo improvisation.—*also vi*.

riffle *vt* to leaf or flick rapidly through (pages, files, etc); to shuffle cards by dividing the deck and then flicking the corners together with the thumbs. * *vi* to flick cursorily (through). * *n* (the sound of) an act or instance of riffling; a ripple in a stream or the small obstruction causing this; grooves, etc, at the bottom of a sluice to trap gold particles.

riffraff *n* disreputable persons; trash, rubbish.

rifle range *n* a place for rifle practice.

rifle[1] *n* a shoulder gun with a spirally grooved bore.

rifle[2] *vti* to steal; to look through (a person's papers or belongings).

rifling *n* (the cutting of) spiral grooves in the bore of a firearm that spin the projectile.

rift *n* a split; a cleft; a fissure. * *vti* to split.

rift valley *n* (*geol*) a narrow valley caused by land subsiding between two parallel faults.

Rift Valley fever *n* a disease, caused by a virus, that mainly affected domestic animals and rarely human beings in sub-Saharan Africa. A widespread outbreak in Egypt in 1977, however, caused many fatalities, and it now poses a threat to people throughout the Middle East.

rig *vt* (**rigging, rigged**) (*naut*) to equip with sails and tackle; to set up in working order; to manipulate fraudulently. * *n* the way sails, etc, are rigged; equipment or gear for a special purpose, such as oil drilling; a type of truck.

Riga *n* capital city of Latvia.

rigaudon (rigadoon) *n* (*mus*) a jaunty dance from the South of France that has two or four beats to the bar. It was used in French ballets and operas, and became popular in England in the late-17th century.

Rigel *or* **Beta Orionis** *n* (*astron*) a supergiant and luminous star (type B) that is the brightest in the constellation Orion.

rigging *n* the ropes for supporting masts and sails; (*theat*) a network of ropes and pulleys to support and maintain scenery.

right *adj* correct, true; just or good; appropriate; fit, recovered; opposite to left; conservative; designating the side meant to be seen. * *adv* straight; directly; completely, exactly; correctly, properly; to or on the right side. * *n* that which is just or correct; truth; fairness; justice; privilege; just or legal claim; (*pl*) the correct condition. * *vti* to set or become upright; to correct; to redress.—**rightness** *n*.

right angle *n* (*math*) an angle of 90º.

right ascension *n* (*astron*) a coordinate used, with others, in specifying positions on the celestial sphere, equivalent to longitude on Earth.

righteous *adj* moral, virtuous.—**righteously** *adv*.—**righteousness** *n*.

rightful *adj* legitimate; having a just claim.—**rightfully** *adv*.—**rightfulness** *n*.

right-hand *adj* of or towards the right side of a person or thing; for use by the right hand.

right-handed *adj* using the right hand; done or made for use with the right hand. * *adv* with the right hand.

right-hand man *n* a person's most trusted and valuable assistant.

rightist *adj* politically conservative. * *n* a person belonging to or supporting a conservative political party.

right justification *n* (*comput*) the alignment of text in a word processing document along the right margin of the document.

rightly *adv* in truth; in the right; with good reason; properly.

right-minded *adj* having principles in accordance with standard notions of what is right.

right of way *n* a public path over private ground; the right to use this; precedence over other traffic.

right of way deed *n* (*law*) an instrument which transfers the title of property to a party for the purpose of gaining access to property.

right-on *adj* (*inf*) fashionable, trendy.

rights issue *n* a method by which companies raise new capital by the issue of new shares.

right-thinking *adj* holding generally acceptable views.

right-to-life *adj* opposed to abortion.—**right-to-lifer** *n*.

right-wing *adj* of or relating to the conservative faction of a political party, organization, etc.—**right-winger** *n*.

rigid *adj* stiff, inflexible; severe, strict.—**rigidity** *n*.—**rigidly** *adv*.—**rigidness** *n*.

rigidity *n* stiffness in a limb, esp one that is being moved passively, which is a symptom of Parkinson's disease. See **Parkinsonism**.

rigmarole *n* nonsense; a foolishly involved procedure.

rigor *n* harsh inflexibility; severity; strictness; a sudden bout of shivering and feeling of coldness that often accompanies the start of a fever.—*also* **rigour**.

rigor mortis *n* the stiffening of the body that occurs usu within eight hours of death as a result of chemical and enzyme reactions in the muscles.

rigoroso *n* (*mus*) (*Italian*) "rigorously," i.e., in exact time.

rigorous *adj* stern, severe, strict.—**rigorously** *adv*.—**rigorousness** *n*.

rigour *see* **rigor**.

RIGS *abbr* (*Brit*) = regionally important geological site.

RIIA *abbr* (*Brit*) = Royal Institute of International Affairs.

Rijeka *n* a city in Croatia.

RILC *abbr* = Racing Industry Liaison Committee.

rile *vt* (*inf*) to irritate, to annoy, to anger.

Riley *n* **Terry** (*b*. 1935) American composer and saxophonist. He is best known for his unconventional compositions which take on a comprehensible form only during rehearsals. His works include *Poppy Nogood and the Phantom Band* and *Rainbow in Curved Air*.

Rilke, Rainer Maria (1875–1926) Prague-born Austrian poet. His lyrical, mystical poems, in, e.g., *Duino Elegies* (1922) and *Sonnets to Orpheus* (1923), are regarded as amongst the finest religious verse of the 20th century.

RILKO *abbr* = Research into Lost Knowledge Organization.

rill *n* a small, narrow, steep-sided stream that is often dry but can carry enough water after storms to cause soil erosion.

rim *n* a border or raised edge, esp of something circular; the outer part of a wheel. * *vt* (**rimming, rimmed**) to supply or surround with a rim; to form a rim.

Rimbaud *n* **Arthur** (1854–91) French poet who was an early symbolist but stopped writing poetry at the age of 19 after a torrid affair with Verlaine, described in *Une Saison en enfer* (*A Season in Hell*). Some of the pieces in his collection of hallucinatory, vivid prose poems, *Les Illuminations*, were set to music by Benjamin Britten.

rimless *adj* lacking a rim; (of eyeglasses) without a frame.

Rimnet *abbr* (*Brit*) = Radioactive Incident Monitoring Network.

Rimsky-Korsakov *n* **Nikolay Andreyevich** (1844–1908) Russian composer whose works include operas, symphonies, and orchestral pieces. His principal compositions include: sixteen operas (e.g., *The Snow Maiden*, *The Tsar's Bride*, *The Golden Cockerel*); three symphonies; numerous orchestral pieces (such as *Sheberazade*, *Capriccio*, and Es*pagnol*); many pieces for chamber orchestra; and over 80 songs.

Rinaldi *n* **Gastone** (*b*. 1920) Italian furniture designer who specializes in metal furniture.

rind *n* crust; peel; bark.

rinderpest *n* an acute viral disease of cattle.

rinf. *abbr* (*mus*) (*Italian*) = *rinforzando*.

rinforzando *adj* (*mus*) (*Italian*) "reinforcing," i.e., a sudden strong accent on a note or chord.

ring[1] *n* a circular band, esp of metal, worn on the finger, in the ear, etc; a hollow circle; a round enclosure; an arena for boxing, etc; a group of people engaged in secret or criminal activity to control a market, etc. * *vt* (**ringing, ringed**) to encircle, surround; to fit with a ring.

ring[2] *vti* (**ringing, rang** or **rung**, *pp* **rung**) to emit a bell-like sound; to resound; to peal; to sound a bell; to telephone; (*with* **up**) to total and record esp by means of a cash register; to achieve. * *n* a ringing sound; a resonant note; a set of church bells.

Ringan *n* Saint *see* **Ninian.**

ring back system *n* (*comput*) a security system for communications over telephone lines whereby the receiver confirms the identity of the remote computer and returns the call using a pre-stored telephone number.

ring binder *n* a loose-leaf binder with split metal rings that open for the insertion of perforated paper.

ringdove *n* a wood pigeon.

ringed *adj* wearing rings; forming rings; having ring-like markings; surrounded by.

ringer *n* a person that rings bells; (*sl*) a person or thing closely resembling another; a horse entered into a race under a false name, weight, etc.

Ringer's solution *n* a physiological solution of sodium chloride, potassium chloride, and calcium chloride that is injected intravenously in people suffering from dehydration, and is also used to bathe and maintain organs that have been removed for transplantation operations.

ring finger *n* the third finger, esp of the left hand, on which a wedding ring is traditionally worn.

ring galaxy *n* a very rare galaxy that is shaped like a ring, sometimes with a nucleus situated off-center.

ringgit or **Malaysian Dollar** *n* currency of Malaysia. *See* **sen.**

ringhals *n* a poisonous African snake that spits venom at its victims.

ringleader *n* a person who takes the lead in mischievous or unlawful behavior.

ringlet *n* a curling lock of hair.

ringmaster *n* a master of ceremonies in a circus.

Ring nebula *n* (*astron*) a bright ring-shaped planetary nebula in the constellation Lyra.

ringworm *n* a highly contagious infection caused by various species of fungus, known medically as tinea. The infection is slightly raised, itchy, and has a ring-like appearance. The commonest form is athlete's foot.

rink *n* an expanse of ice for skating; a smooth floor for roller skating; an alley for bowling.

Rinne's test *n* a hearing test that uses a vibrating tuning fork and helps to determine whether deafness is perceptive (nervous) or conductive (indicating an obstruction within the ear).

rinse *vt* to wash lightly; to flush under clean water to remove soap. * *n* the act of rinsing; a preparation for tinting the hair.

Rio de Janeiro *n* a city in Brazil.

rioja *n* a type of Spanish red or white wine.

RIOP *abbr* (*Brit*) = Royal Institute of Oil Painters.

riot *n* violent public disorder; uproar; unrestrained profusion; (*inf*) something very funny. * *vi* to participate in a riot.—**rioter** *n*.—**rioting** *n*.

riotous *adj* disorderly, tumultuous, seditious; luxurious, wanton.—**riotously** *adv*.—**riotousness** *n*.

rip[1] *vti* (**ripping, ripped**) to cut or tear apart roughly; to split; (*with* **off, out**) to remove in a violent or rough manner; (*inf*) to rush, speed; (*with* **into**) to attack, esp verbally. * *n* a tear; a split.

rip[2] *n* a turbulent area of sea water where strong tidal currents meet, or where a tidal current meets wind-driven waves head on.

rip. *abbr* (*mus*) (*Italian*) = *ripieno*.

RIP *abbr* (*Latin*) = *requiescat* or *requiescant in pace* ("may he/she/ they rest in peace").

RIPA *abbr* (*Brit*) = Royal Institute of Public Administration.

rip cord *n* a cord for releasing a parachute.

rip current *n* a strong, swift current that has been deflected seaward by an obstruction such as a headland or spit.

ripe *adj* ready to be eaten or harvested; fully developed; mature.—**ripely** *adv*.—**ripeness** *n*.

ripen *vt* to grow or make ripe.

RIPHH *abbr* (*Brit*) = Royal Institute of Public Health and Hygiene.

ripieno *adj* (*mus*) (*Italian*) literally, "full"; a term used to describe passages that are to be played by the whole Baroque orchestra, rather than only a soloist.

rip-off *n* (*sl*) the act or a means of stealing; plagiarizing, cheating, etc.

riposte, ripost *n* a counterstroke; a retort; a retaliatory maneuver. * *vi* to make a riposte.

ripple *n* a little wave or undulation on the surface of water; the sound of this. * *vti* to have or form little waves on the surface (of).

ripple marks *npl* (*geol*) the preservation of ripples in sandstone, which may exhibit small cross-laminations reflecting current movement.

rip-roaring *adj* (*inf*) exuberant, boisterous, thrilling.

RIPS *abbr* (*Brit*) = Radiotherapy Injured Patients Support.

ripsaw *n* a handsaw for cutting wood in the direction of the grain.

riptide *n* a powerful current flowing outwards from the shore.

RIR *abbr* = Royal Irish Regiment.

RIS *abbr* = Research Information Service.

RISC (*abbr*) (*comput*) reduced instruction set computer: a computer with advanced yet simplified internal circuitry that allows a significant increase in processing speed over standard designs.

rise *vi* (**rising, rose**, *pp* **risen**) to get up; to stand up; to ascend; to increase in value or size; to swell; to revolt; to be provoked; to originate; to tower; to slope up; (of the voice) to reach a higher pitch; to ascend from the grave; (of fish) to come to the surface. * *n* an ascent; origin; an increase in price, salary, etc; an upward slope; (*archit*) the vertical distance between the level of the springing line and the soffit of the crown of an arch or vault.

risible *adj* tending to laugh; provoking laughter, derisory.—**risibility** *n*.

rising *n* a revolt, insurrection. * *adj* ascending; approaching.

risk *n* chance of loss or injury; hazard; danger, peril. * *vt* to expose to possible danger or loss; to take the chance of.

risk capital *n* venture capital; any business capital that is invested in a project when there is a significant element of risk of loss in the event of the project's failing.

risk premium *n* an additional return on an investment that is given to an investor in order to compensate him or her for the possibility of losing the investment in the event of the project's failing.

risky *adj* (**riskier, riskiest**) dangerous; uncertain; not secure.

risoluto *n* (*mus*) (*Italian*) "resolute" or "in a resolute manner."

risotto *n* (*pl* **risottos**) a dish of onions, rice, butter, etc, cooked in meat stock.

risqué *adj* verging on indecency; slightly offensive.

rissole *n* a fried cake of minced meat, egg, and breadcrumbs.

rit. or **ritard.** *abbr* (*mus*) (*Italian*) = *ritardando*.

rit. or **riten.** *abbr* (*mus*) (*Italian*) = *ritenuto*.

RIT *abbr* = Rorschach Inkblot Test.

ritardando *adj, adv* (*mus*) (*Italian*) "becoming gradually slower."

rite *n* a ceremonial practice or procedure, esp religious.

riten. *abbr* (*mus*) (*Italian*) = *ritenuto*.

ritenuto *adj* (*mus*) (*Italian*) "held back" (in tempo), i.e., slower.—*also adv*.

rite of passage *n* a ritual indicating a change in an individual's status, as at puberty or marriage.

ritmico *adj*. (*mus*) (*Italian*) rhythmic.

ritmo *n* (*mus*) (*Italian*) rhythm.

ritornello *n* (*mus*) (*Italian*) a small repetition; a short passage for the whole orchestra in a Baroque aria or concerto, during which the soloist is silent; a short instrumental piece, played between scenes in early opera.

ritual *adj* relating to rites or ceremonies. * *n* a fixed (religious) ceremony.—**ritually** *adv*.

ritzy *adj* (**ritzier, ritziest**) (*sl*) luxurious, smart.

riv. *abbr* = river.

rival *n* one of two or more people, organizations or teams competing with each other for the same goal. * *adj* competing; having comparable merit or claim. * *vt* (**rivaling, rivaled** or **rivalling, rivalled**) to strive to equal or excel; to be comparable to; to compete.

rivalry *n* (*pl* **rivalries**) emulation; competition.

river *n* a large natural stream of fresh water flowing into an ocean, lake, etc; a copious flow.

river basin *n* land drained by a river and its tributaries.

riverbed *n* the channel formed by a river.

river capture *n* the capture or diversion of one river into a more powerful adjacent river, often at a sharp change of stream direction.

riverfront *n* the land or an area along a river.

riverine *adj* of, like, or produced by a river; living or located on the banks of a river.

rivers *n* streams of water that flow into the sea, lakes, or swamps.

riverside *n* the bank of a river.

river terrace a raised flat area running along and parallel to valley walls. It is part of a former flood plain, left behind as the river cut down through the valley floor.

rivet *n* a short metal bolt for holding metal plates together, the headless end being hammered flat. * *vt* to join with rivets; to fix one's eyes upon immovably; to engross one's attention.

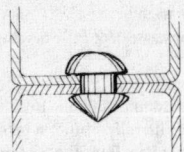

riveter *n* a person who rivets; a machine that rivets.

Riviera *n* the coast of the northern Mediterranean from southeast France to northwest Italy.

rivulet *n* a little stream.

Riyadh (Ar Riyād) *n* capital city of Saudi Arabia.

riyal *n* the standard monetary unit of Saudi Arabia, made up of 100 halala; the standard monetary unit of Qatar, made up of 100 dirhams; the standard monetary unit of Yemen, made up of 100 fils.

RJDip *abbr* (*Brit*) = Diploma for Retail Jewellers.

RJE *abbr* = remote job entry.

RJET *abbr* = remote job entry terminal.

RK *abbr* = religious knowledge.

RL *abbr* = (*math*) right line; Rugby League; reference library.

RLAF *abbr* = Right Livelihood Awards Foundation.

r. l. and r. *abbr* (*transp*) = rail, lake, and rail.

RLC *abbr* (*Brit*) = Refugee Legal Centre; Royal Logistic Corps.

RLF *abbr* (*Brit*) = Royal Literary Fund.

RLLMA *abbr* = Red Lead and Litharge Manufacturers' Association.

RLO *abbr* = Returned Letter Office.

RLPS *abbr* (*Brit*) = Royal Liverpool Philharmonic Society.

RLSS *abbr* (*Brit*) = Royal Life Saving Society.

rm. *abbr* = ream.

r.m. *abbr* = ring micrometer.

RM *abbr* = Registered Midwife; Resident Magistrate; (*Brit*) Royal Mail; (*Brit*) Royal Marines.

RMA *abbr* = Risk Management Agency; (*Brit*) Royal Military Academy; (*Brit*) Royal Musical Association.

RMAG *abbr* = Rocky Mountain Association of Geologists.

RMCM *abbr* (*Brit*) = Royal Manchester College of Music.

RMCS *abbr* (*Brit*) = Royal Medical and Chirurgical Society; Royal Military College of Science.

RMetS *abbr* (*Brit*) = Royal Meteorological Society.

RMFVR *abbr* (*Brit*) = Royal Marine Forces Volunteer Reserves.

RMN *abbr* (*Brit*) = Registered Mental Nurse.

RMO *abbr* = Resident Medical Officer.

RMP *abbr* (*Brit*) = Royal Marine Police; Royal Military Police.

RMR *abbr* (*Brit*) = Royal Marines Reserve.

rms *abbr* = root mean square.

rms. *abbr* = rooms.

RMS *abbr* = Railway Mail Service; (*Brit*) Records Management Society; (*Brit*) Royal Medical Society; (*Brit*) Royal Microscopical Society; (*Brit*) Royal Society of Miniature Painters, Sculptors and Gravers.

RMSchMus *abbr* (*Brit*) = Royal Military School of Music.

RMT *abbr* (*Brit*) = National Union of Rail, Maritime and Transport Workers.

Rn *symbol* (*chem*) radon.

rn *abbr* = reception nil.

RN *abbr* = Registered Nurse; (*Brit*) Royal Navy.

RNA *abbr* = ribonucleic acid; (*Brit*) Romantic Novelists' Association; (*Brit*) Royal Naval Association.

RNAA *abbr* (*Brit*) = Royal Norfolk Agricultural Association.

RNAS *abbr* (*Brit*) = Royal Naval Air Service.

r'n'b *abbr* = rhythm and blues.

RNBS *abbr* (*Brit*) = Royal Naval Benevolent Society.

RNBT *abbr* (*Brit*) = Royal Naval Benevolent Trust.

RNBWS *abbr* (*Brit*) = Royal Naval Bird Watching Society.

RNC *abbr* (*Brit*) = Royal Naval College.

RNCC *abbr* (*Brit*) = Royal Northern & Clyde Yacht Club.

RNCM *abbr* (*Brit*) = Royal Naval College of Music.

RNEC *abbr* (*Brit*) = Royal Naval Engineering College.

RNHA *abbr* (*Brit*) = Registered Nursing Home Association.

RNHU *abbr* (*Brit*) = Royal National Homing Union.

RNIB *abbr* (*Brit*) = Royal National Institute for the Blind.

RNID *abbr* (*Brit*) = Royal National Institute for the Deaf.

RNLI *abbr* (*Brit*) = Royal National Lifeboat Institution.

RNMDSF *abbr* (*Brit*) = Royal National Mission to Deep Sea Fishermen.

RNMH *abbr* (*Brit*) = Registered Nurse for the Mentally Handicapped.

RNMS *abbr* (*Brit*) = Royal Naval Medical School.

r'n'r *abbr* = rock and roll.

RNR *abbr* (*Brit*) = Royal Naval Reserve.

RNRS *abbr* (*Brit*) = Royal National Rose Society.

RNS *abbr* (*Brit*) = Royal Numismatic Society.

RNSA *abbr* (*Brit*) = Royal Naval Sailing Association.

RNSC *abbr* (*Brit*) = Royal Naval Staff College.

RNSR *abbr* (*Brit*) = Royal Naval Special Reserve.

RNSS *abbr* (*Brit*) = Royal Naval Scientific Service.

RNT *abbr* (*Brit*) = Royal National Theatre.

RNTE *abbr* (*Brit*) = Royal Naval Training Establishment.

RNTU *abbr* (*Brit*) = Royal Naval Training Unit.

RNVR *abbr* (*Brit*) = Royal Naval Volunteer Reserve.

RNXS *abbr* (*Brit*) = Royal Naval Auxiliary Service.

RO *abbr* = Receiving Office; Regimental Order *or* Orders; Returning Officer; (*Brit*) Royal Observatory.

ro *abbr* = run out (cricket).

ro. *abbr* = recto; roan; rood.

Ro. *abbr* = ruble.

ROA *abbr* = (*Brit*) Racehorse Owners' Association; Record of Achievement; return on assets.

roach[1] *n* a small silvery freshwater fish.

roach[2] *n* (*inf*) a cockroach; (*sl*) the butt of a marijuana cigarette.

road *n* a track, surfaced with tarmac or concrete, made for traveling; a highway; a street; a way or route; (*naut*) an anchorage for ships (*also* **roadstead**).

road block *n* a barrier erected across a road to halt traffic.

road hog *n* a car driver who obstructs other vehicles by encroaching on the others' traffic lane.

roadhouse *n* a tavern usu outside city limits providing meals, etc.

roadie *n* (*inf*) a person with responsibility for transporting and setting up stage equipment for a rock group, etc, on tour.

road map *n* a map for motorists that gives information on the roads of a particular area.

road metal *n* broken stone and cinders used in making roads and railbeds.

road movie *n* a film genre in which the main characters are on a journey, both in a real and figurative sense.

road runner *n* a long-tailed, swift-running, terrestrial North American cuckoo.

roadshow *n* a group of touring entertainers; a radio or television show presented from a touring outside-broadcasting unit.

roadside *n* the border of a road.—*also adj*.

road-test *vt* to test (a vehicle) under practical operating conditions.—**road test** *n*.

Road Town *n* capital city of the British Virgin Islands.

roadway *n* the strip of land over which a road passes; the main part of a road, used by vehicles.

roadwork *n* conditioning for an athletic contest consisting mainly of long runs.

roam *vti* to wander about, to rove.

roan *adj* having a base color thickly sprinkled with white or gray. * *n* a horse with a roan coat, esp when the base color is red.

roar *vti* to make a loud, full, growling sound, as a lion, wind, fire, the sea; to utter loudly, as in a rage; to bellow; to guffaw.—*also n*.

ROAR *abbr* = right of admission reserved.

roaring *adj* boisterous, noisy; brisk.

roaring forties *n* the westerly gales that are a feature of the oceans $40°$–$50°$ south where there are no land masses either to break up heavy seas or to interrupt the wind.

roast *vti* to cook (meat, etc) with little or no moisture, as before a fire or in an oven; to process (coffee, etc) by exposure to heat; to expose to great heat; (*inf*) to criticize severely; to undergo roasting. * *n* roasted meat; a cut of meat for roasting; a picnic at which food is roasted.

rob *vti* (**robbing, robbed**) *vt* to seize forcibly; to steal from; to plunder. * *vi* to commit robbery.—**robber** *n*.

Robards *n* **Jason** (1922–2000) American actor and Oscar winner for his role in *All the President's Men* (1976).

Robbe-Grillet *n* **Alain** (*b*. 1922) French novelist whose works, e.g., *Topology of a Phantom City* and the screenplay *Last Year in Marienbad*, are regarded as antinovels.

robbery *n* (*pl* **robberies**) theft from a person by intimidation or by violence.

Robbins *n* 1. **Frederick Chapman** (*b*. 1916) American pediatrician who was awarded the 1954 Nobel prize for physiology or medicine for his studies on the cultivation of viruses, in particular the polio virus. 2. **Harold [Frances Kane]** (1916–97) American novelist whose books include *The Carpetbaggers* (1961).

robe *n* a long flowing outer garment; the official dress of a judge, academic, etc; a bathrobe or dressing gown; a covering or wrap; (*pl*) ceremonial vestments. * *vti* to put on or dress in robes.

Robert I *n* **the Bruce** (1274–1329) king of Scots (1306–29) (1306–1329). Considered to be the greatest of the Scottish kings, Robert de Bruce VIII, eldest son of Robert de Bruce (1253–1304). His son David succeeded him.

Robert II *n* (1316–1390) king of Scots (1371–1390). The son of Marjory, daughter of Robert I the Bruce, and of Walter, Steward of Scotland, Robert II was the first of the Steward (later changed to Stuart) kings.

Robert III *n* (1337–1406) king of Scots (1390–1406). The eldest son of Robert II and Elizabeth Mure. He was succeeded by his son James I.

Robertson *n* **Alexander W.** (1840–1925) British ceramicist who worked in America.

Robeson *n* **Paul [Le Roy]** (1898–1976) American bass singer and actor who qualified as a lawyer before becoming a highly popular stage actor in the 1920s. His notable performances include *Showboat* (1927) and *Othello* (1940). A noted advocate of civil rights for African Americans.

Robespierre *n* **Maximilien Marie Isidore de** (1758–94) French lawyer and revolutionary. Elected to the National Assembly (1789), he became leader of the Jacobin group and launched the infamous "Reign of Terror." He was guillotined in 1794.

robin *n* a songbird with a dull-red breast.

Robinson *n* 1. **Brooks** (*b*. 1937) American baseball player and a fifteen-times winner of the Golden Glove (1960–74). 2. **Edwin Arlington** (1869–1935) American poet whose early poems are mostly concerned with New England small-town characters, e.g., *The Children of the Night*. His later verse includes a trilogy on the Arthurian legend. 3. **Mary** (*b*. 1944) Irish barrister, politician, and president (1990–97) of the Republic of Ireland. Notably liberal in her policies, she won wide support from parties opposed to her conservative Fianna Fáil opponent. 4. **"Sugar" Ray** [Walker Smith] (1920–89) American boxer. A highly skilled boxer, he was world welterweight champion (1946–51) and world middleweight champion five times from 1951 to 1960. 5. **Joan Violet** (1903–83) English economist. She became one of the leading theorists of the "Cambridge School" of economists, and developed, following Keynes, macroeconomic theories of growth and distribution. Her works include *Introduction to Modern Economics* (1973). 6. **John [Arthur Thomas]** (1919–83) English Anglican prelate and theologian. His best-selling book, *Honest to God* (1963), inspired by the thinking of (predominantly German) theologians, created much public controversy with its portrayal of God as an inner presence rather than an external "father in the sky." 7. **Sir Robert** (1886–1975) English chemist awarded the 1947 Nobel prize for chemistry for his work on plant extracts. He also made significant contributions to the study of plant pigments.

robot *n* a mechanical device that acts in a seemingly human way; a mechanism guided by automatic controls; (*comput*) an electromechanical device that may perform programmed tasks.

robotics *n* (used as sing) the science of designing and using robots.

Robsjohn-Gibbings *n* **Terence Harold** (1905–76) British designer who in the 1930s became a successful interior designer in the **neo-classical** vein.

Robson *n* **Dame Flora** (1902–84) English stage and film actress. She was esp noted for her historical roles, e.g., as Queen Elizabeth in the highly patriotic film *Fire over England* (1937).

robust *adj* strong, sturdy; vigorous.—**robustly** *adv*.—**robustness** *n*.

roc *n* (*Arabian legend*) a giant bird of enormous strength.

Roc *n* (*Irish Celtic myth*) steward of Oenghus, the love god. The wife of Donn had a son by Roc, and Donn was so enraged that he killed the child by crushing it to death.

ROC *abbr* = (*Brit*) Royal Observer Corps; return on capital.

Roche *n* **Eamonn K** (*b*. 1922) Irish architect whose notable works include the United Nations Plaza Hotel, New York.

Roche limit *n* (*astron*) the minimum distance between a body and a satellite at which the satellite can stay in equilibrium and remain stable.

Roche lobes *n* (*astron*) two drop-shaped surfaces that meet at their points to resemble an hourglass, and are found in binary star systems.

Rochester *n* **John Wilmot, 2nd Earl of** (1647–80) English poet and courtier, renowned (and feared) for his savage wit and supposedly limitless depths of depravity, whose verse is among the most sexually explicit in English.

rock[1] *n* a large stone or boulder; a person or thing providing foundation or support; (*geol*) a natural mineral deposit including sand, clay, etc; a hard sweet; (*inf*) a diamond, ice; (*sl*) the drug crack.

rock[2] *vti* to move to and fro, or from side to side; to sway strongly; to shake. * *n* a rocking motion; rock and roll; (*mus*) a type of pop music that evolved from rock 'n' roll during the 1960s. It mixes country and western with rhythm and blues, and is usu played loudly on electric instruments.

rockabilly *n* a type of fast-paced rock and country music originating in the South in the 1950s.

rock-and-roll *n* popular music that incorporates country and blues elements and is usu played on electronic instruments with a heavily accented beat.

rock bottom *n* the lowest or most fundamental part or level. * *adj* very lowest.

Rock Cornish (hen) *n* (*Brit*) a domestic fowl produced by crossing Cornish and Plymouth Rock breeds.

rock crystal *n* transparent colorless quartz used in electronic and optical equipment.

rocker *n* a rocking chair; a curved support on which a cradle, etc, rocks.

rockery *n* (*pl* **rockeries**) a garden among rocks for alpine plants.—*also* **rock garden**.

rocket *n* any device driven forward by gases escaping through a rear vent, such as a firework, distress signal, or the propulsion mechanism of a spacecraft. * *vi* to move in or like a rocket; to soar.

rocket launcher *n* a device for launching rockets; an aircraft or motor vehicle equipped to launch rockets.

rocketry *n* the science of building and launching rockets.

rock garden *see* **rockery**.

rock house *n* (*sl*) a place where the drug crack is made available by dealers.

rocking chair *n* a chair mounted on rockers.

rocking horse *n* a toy horse fixed on rockers or springs.

rock-'n'-roll *n* rock-and-roll.

rock salt *n* common salt in solid form or in large crystals.

rocks *n* aggregates of minerals or organic matter, which can be divided into three types, based on the way they are formed: igneous, sedimentary, and metamorphic.

rock shelter *n* (*archeo*) a naturally formed shelter in a rock face that is not deep enough to be classed as a cave.

rock tombs *n* (*Egypt*) Fourth Dynasty Egyptian tombs, cut in the rock of the Giza plateau. Their layout was similar to that of the mastaba, with anteroom, chapel and serdab.

rocky *adj* (**rockier, rockiest**) having many rocks; like rock; rugged, hard; shaky, unstable.

Rocky Mountain sheep *n* the wild sheep of the Rocky Mountains, the bighorn.

Rocky Mountain spotted fever *n* an acute rickettsial fever caused by a bite from an infected tick.

rococo *adj* elaborately ornate, as in an architectural style of 18th-century Europe typified by graceful light ornamentation and the use of asymmetrical and often abstract motifs. * *n* the highly decorative, florid style of architecture and painting typical of the 18th century; music from the same period.

rod *n* a stick; a thin bar of metal or wood; a staff of office; a wand; a fishing rod; one of the two types of light-sensitive cell present in the retina of the eye; (*sl*) a pistol.

rode *see* **ride**.

rodent *n* any of several relatively small gnawing mammals with two strong front teeth.

rodent ulcer *n* a slow-growing malignant ulcer that occurs on the face in elderly people, usu near the lips, nostrils or eyelids.

rodeo *n* (*pl* **rodeos**) the rounding up of cattle; a display of cowboy skill.

Rodgers *n* **Richard [Charles]** (1902–79) American composer of musicals. With Lorenz Hart as his librettist, he created such shows as *The Boys from Syracuse* and *Pal Joey;* with Oscar Hammerstein as librettist, he wrote *Oklahoma* and *South Pacific*, both of which were turned into memorable films.

Rodin *n* **Auguste** (1840–1917) French sculptor who came to prominence with *The Age of Bronze* (1875–6), a male nude figure that he was accused of casting from life. His most famous pieces are *The Thinker* and *The Kiss*.

Rodrigo *n* **Joaquin** (1902–99) Spanish composer, blind from the age of three, who composed many outstanding works, such as *Concierto de Aranjuez* (for guitar and orchestra) and *Concierto Heroico* (for piano and orchestra).

Rodriguez Tizon *n* **Ventura** (*b*. 1717) Spanish architect whose notable works include Pamplona Cathedral.

roe[1] *n* the eggs of fish.

roe[2] *n* a small reddish brown graceful deer of European and Asian woodlands (*also* **roe deer**); the female red deer.

ROE *abbr* = (*Brit*) Royal Observatory, Edinburgh; return on equity.

roebuck *n* the male roe deer.

roe deer *see* **roe**[2].

roentgen *n* the unit of measuring X-rays or gamma rays.—*also* **röntgen**.

Roentgenol. *abbr* = roentgenological; roentgenology.

ROF *abbr* (*Brit*) = Royal Ordnance Factory.

Roffen. *abbr* (*Latin*) = *Roffensis* ("of Rochester").

roger *interj* used in radio communications, etc, to indicate message received and understood.

Rogers *n* 1. **Isaiah** (*b*. 1800) American architect whose notable works include the Bank of America, New York. 2. **Richard** (1933–) Italian-born English architect whose notable works include the Lloyd's building (1979) in London, a steel and glass confection that typifies the controversial nature of his frontiersmanship approach to architectural technology. 3. **William Harry** (1825–75) British woodcarver, the son of the celebrated carver William Gibbs Rogers. 4. **Ginger** *see* **Astaire, Fred**. 5. **Will[iam Penn Adair]** (1879–1935) American humorist and actor, nicknamed the "cowboy philosopher." A highly skilled rodeo performer, he came to exemplify, for many Americans, the common man in rhetorical arms against injustice and governmental stupidity. He appeared in several John Ford movies, most notably *Judge Priest* (1934).

rogue *n* a scoundrel; a rascal; a mischievous person; a wild animal that lives apart from the herd.—**roguish** *adj*.—**roguishly** *adv*.

rogues' gallery *n* a collection of portraits of criminals kept by the police for identification purposes.

ROH *abbr* (*Brit*) = Royal Opera House (Covent Garden).

ROI *abbr* = (*Brit*) Royal Institute of Oil Painters; return on investment.

role, rôle *n* a part in a film or play taken by an actor; a function.

role model *n* a person who inspires others to emulate him or her.

role-playing *n* (*psychol*) a technique in which participants take on and act out roles in order to rehearse a situation or resolve a conflict.

role reversal *n* the adoption of a role quite different from one's usual role.

Rolfing *n* a form of massage used as physical and emotional therapy.

roll *n* a scroll; anything wound into cylindrical form; a list or register; a turned-over edge; a rolling movement; a small cake of bread; a trill of some birds; an undulation; the sound of thunder; the beating of drumsticks. * *vi* to move by turning over or from side to side; to move like a wheel; to curl; to move in like waves; to flow. * *vt* to cause to roll; to turn on an axis; to move on wheels; to press with a roller; (*dice*) to throw; to beat rapidly, as a drum.

roll bar *n* a bar that reinforces the frame of a racing or sports car to protect the driver should the vehicle overturn.

roll call *n* the reading aloud of a list of names to check attendance.

roller *n* a revolving cylinder used for spreading paint, flattening surfaces, moving paper, etc; a large wave.

roller coaster *n* an elevated amusement ride in which small cars move on tracks that curve and dip sharply.—*also* **big dipper**.

roller skate *n* a four-wheeled skate strapped on to shoes.—**roller skating** *n*.

roller-skate *vi* to skate on roller skates.— **roller skater** *n*.

roller towel *n* a towel without ends on a roller.

rolling pin *n* a wooden, plastic, or stone cylinder for rolling out pastry.

rolling stock *n* all the vehicles of a railroad.

rolling stone *n* a person who cannot settle in one place; a free spirit.

rollmop *n* a fillet of herring rolled up and pickled in brine or spiced vinegar.

roll-on *adj* (of deodorant) applied to the body using a rolling ball at the end of the container. * *n* a deodorant of this type.

roll-on/roll-off *adj* pertaining to a cargo ship or passenger ferry designed so that vehicles can be driven straight on and off.

Rolls *n* **Charles Stewart** (1877–1910) English automobile manufacturer and aviator who joined Henry Royce in 1906. He made the first nonstop double flight across the English Channel in 1910, shortly before his death in a plane crash.

roll-top desk *n* a writing desk with a flexible sliding cover of slats.

roly-poly *n* (*pl* **roly-polies**) (*Brit*) a pudding of pastry covered with jam and rolled up; a round and plump person.

r.o.m. *abbr* = run of mine (coal).

Rom. *abbr* = Roman; Romance; Romans.

ROM *abbr* = (*comput*) Read Only Memory, the part of a computer's internal memory that can be read but not altered, containing the essential system programs; (*obstetrics*) rupture of membranes.

romaine (lettuce) *n* a variety of lettuce with long leaves forming the head.—*also* **cos**.

Romalpa clause *n* a clause in a contract of sale by which the seller of the goods retains the right to their ownership until the goods have been paid for.

roman *adj* ordinary type, not italic.

Roman *adj* of or relating to the city of Rome or its ancient empire, or the *Latin* alphabet; Roman Catholic. * *n* an inhabitant or citizen of Rome; a Roman Catholic.

Roman *n* **Johan Helmich** (1694–1758) Swedish composer, often referred to as the "father of Swedish music." He wrote some twenty symphonies and many violin and piano sonatas.

Roman architecture *n* (*archit*) the architecture of ancient Rome, characterized by the use of rounded elements such as domes, vaults, and arches.

Roman candle *n* a type of cylindrical firework that emits colored sparks.

Roman Catholic *adj* belonging to the Christian church that is headed by the Pope.—*also n*.

romance *n* a prose narrative; a medieval tale of chivalry; a series of unusual adventures; a novel dealing with this; an atmosphere of awe or wonder; a love story; a love affair; a picturesque falsehood. * *vi* to write romantic fiction; to exaggerate.

Romanesque *adj* (*archit*) in the style of round-arched and vaulted architecture prevalent in Europe *c*.1050 to 1200, between the Classical and Gothic periods.—*also n*.

Roman holiday *n* a holiday or entertainment at the expense of others' suffering.

Romania *n* a republic located in southeast Europe and bordered by Ukraine, Moldova, Bulgaria, Serbia, and Hungary.

Roman nose *n* a nose with a slender prominent ridge.

Roman numerals *n* the letters I, V, X, L, C, D, and M used to represent numbers in the manner of the ancient Romans.

Romans, Letter of Paul to the *n* (*Bible*) considered to be the most authentic of Paul's writings, the one that most clearly sets forth his faith and teaching; it is addressed not only to Christians in Rome but to the whole world of Jews and Gentiles.

romantic *adj* of or given to romance; strange and picturesque; imaginative; sentimental; (*art, literature*) preferring passion and imagination to proportion and finish, subordinating form to content.—**romantically** *adv*.

romanticism *n* a 19th-century philosophical and cultural movement characterized by the desire to bring nature and man into unity through the shaping power of the imagination; denoting any movement in the arts that emphasizes feeling and content as opposed to form and order; romantic approach, quality, or ideals.

romanticize *vt* to imbue (a person, concept, etc) with a romantic character. * *vi* to have romantic ideas.—**romanticization** *n*.

romantic music *n* (*mus*) music dating from the so-called Romantic Era, *c*.1820–*c*.1920. During this phase music tended to be more poetic, subjective, and individualistic than in the previous Classical Era. Lyricism, drama, and often nationalistic feeling were characteristic of romantic music.

Romany *n* a Gypsy; the Indic language of Gypsies.

Romberg *n* 1. **Andreas Jakob** (1767–1821) German violinist and composer whose works include operas, choral works and symphonies. 2. his cousin **Bernhard** (1767–1841), a cellist who greatly increased the capability of the cello by careful study of its technique. He also became a notable composer, writing many works for the solo cello, a cello concerto, chamber music, and operas.

Rom. Cath. *abbr* = Roman Catholic.

Rome *n* the capital city of Italy situated on the River Tiber. Founded, according to tradition, by Romulus, it became the center of a great civilization.—**Roman** *adj*.

Romero y Galdames *n* **Oscar Arnulfo** (1917–80) Salvadorean Roman Catholic prelate. Appointed archbishop in 1977. Became an outspoken opponent of the murderous campaigns of the El Salvador government's semi-official death squads, for which he was assassinated.

Rommel *n* **Erwin** (1891–1944) German soldier who, after distinguished service in World War I, became a Nazi supporter in the 1920s. During World War II he commanded the Afrika Korps in North Africa, but was defeated at El Alamein by Montgomery's troops. He committed suicide after the discovery of his complicity in an assassination attempt on Hitler.

romp *vi* to play boisterously. * *n* a noisy game; a frolic; an easy win.

rompers *npl* a child's one-piece garment; a jumpsuit.

Romulus and Remus *n* (*Roman myth*) the twin sons of Mars and Rea Silvia, put in a basket on the River Tiber so that they would die. They were suckled by a wolf and rescued, and built a city which was named Rome after Romulus.

Ronan *n* (*Irish Celtic myth*) a king of Leinster. He was the father of Mail Fhothartaig and the husband of Ethne.

rondo *n* (*pl* **rondos**) (*mus*) a form of instrumental music which incorporates a recurring theme, either in an independent piece or (more usu) as part of a movement.

röntgen *see* **roentgen**.

rood *n* (*archit*) a cross, usu wooden, often placed on a beam at the entrance to the chancel of a church.

rood loft *n* (*archit*) a gallery, reached by stairs, above the rood screen for the purpose of carrying the rood.

rood screen *n* (*archit*) a screen surmounted by the rood which shuts off the chancel from the main part of the church.

roof *n* (*pl* **roofs**) the upper covering of a building; the top of a vehicle; an upper limit. * *vt* to provide with a roof, to cover.

roof garden *n* a garden on a flat roof or balcony; a top floor decorated as a garden, esp if used as a restaurant.

roofing *n* materials for a roof.

rook[1] *n* a crow-like bird.

rook[2] *n* (*chess*) a piece with the power to move horizontally or vertically, a castle.

rookery *n* (*pl* **rookeries**) a colony of rooks; a breeding ground or haunt of other birds or mammals; a crowded place.

rookie *n* (*sl*) an inexperienced army recruit; any novice.—*also adj*.

room *n* space; unoccupied space; adequate space; a division of a house, a chamber; scope or opportunity; those in a room; (*pl*) lodgings. * *vi* to lodge.

room and board *n* accommodation and food, usu for a fixed price.

room clerk *n* a receptionist in a hotel who books in guests and allocates rooms, etc.

rooming house *n* a house with individual rooms to let.

roommate *n* a person with whom one shares a room or rooms.

room service *n* the serving of food or drink to guests in their hotel bedrooms.

room temperature *n* the average comfortable temperature of a living room, about 20 °C (68 °F).

roomy *adj* (**roomier, roomiest**) having ample space; wide.—**roominess** *n*.

Roosevelt *n* 1. **Theodore** (1858–1919) American Republican statesman and 26th president of the US (1901–9). A notably bellicose figure who organized a corps of irregular soldiers, dubbed "Roosevelt's Rough Riders," during the Spanish-American War (1898), he legislated against big business monopolies, intervened forcefully during the Panama civil war to protect the construction of the Panama Canal, and won the 1906 Nobel peace prize for mediating the end of the Russo-Japanese war. He split the Republican presidential vote in 1912 by standing as a Progressive (letting in Woodrow Wilson). 2. **Franklin D[elano]** (1882–1945) American Democrat statesman and 32nd president of the US (1933–45). He instituted far-reaching "New Deal" economic reforms, e.g., his massive Public Works Administration program of public spending and establishment of basic social security measures. He was a popular and highly effective leader during World War II, dying shortly after the Yalta summit meeting with Churchill and Stalin. 3. His wife, **[Anna] Eleanor Roosevelt** (1884–1962), an active and popular First Lady, who supported her husband during his illness with polio and wrote several books, e.g., *It's Up to the Women* (1933) and *The Moral Basis of Democracy* (1940). After his death she worked with the UN as US representative to the General Assembly (1946–52) and as chairman of the Human Rights Commission (1947–51).

roost *n* a bird's perch or sleeping-place; a place for resting. * *vi* to rest or sleep on a roost; to settle down, as for the night.

rooster *n* an adult male domestic fowl, a cockerel.

root[1] *n* the part of a plant, usu underground, that anchors the plant, draws water from the soil, etc; the embedded part of a tooth, a hair, etc; a supporting or essential part; something that is an origin or source; (*math*) the factor of a quantity which multiplied by itself gives the quantity; (*mus*) the lowest or fundamental note of a chord; (*pl*) plants with edible roots. * *vti* to take root; to become established; (*with* **out**) to tear up, to eradicate.

root[2] *vti* to dig up with the snout; to search about, rummage; (*with* **for**) (*inf*) to encourage a team by cheering.

root beer *n* a carbonated drink flavored with extracts of certain roots and barks.

root crop *n* a crop, such as turnips, sugar beet, cultivated for its edible roots.

root directory *n* (*comput*) the top level or first directory on a disk in which subdirectories are created.

rooted *adj* firmly fixed; planted.

root mean square *n* the square root of the average of the squares of a set of numbers.

rootstock *n* an underground stem, rhizome; a stock for grafting, having a root or a piece of root.

rope *n* a thick cord made of twisted fibers or wires; a string or row of things braided, intertwined, or threaded together; a viscous thickening in a liquid. * *vt* to tie, bind, divide or enclose with a rope; to lasso; (of liquid) to become ropy.—**ropy** *adj*.

Roquefort *n* a French blue-veined cheese with a strong flavor.

RORC *abbr* (*Brit*) = Royal Ocean Racing Club.

ro-ro *abbr* = roll-on/roll-off (ferry).

rorqual *n* any of several large whalebone whales with dorsal fins and deep furrows on the skin of the throat and chest.—*also* **finback**.

Rorschach test *n* (*psychol*) a personality test using inkblots on paper that are presented to a subject for interpretation.

Rory *n* **O'Connel** or **Roderic O'Connor** (*d.* 1198) high king of Ireland (1116–86).

rosacea *n* a disease of the skin of the face characterized by a red, flushed appearance and enlargement of the sebaceous glands in the skin. The nose may also enlarge and look red and lumpy (rhinophyma).

rosaceous *adj* of or belonging to the large family of plants that includes the rose; resembling a rose; rose-colored.

Rosario *n* a city in Argentina.

rosary *n* (*pl* **rosaries**) a string of beads for keeping count of prayers; a series of prayers.

ROSCO *abbr* (*Brit*) = Road Operators' Safety Council.

rose[1] *see* **rise**.

rose[2] *n* a prickly-stemmed plant with fragrant flowers of many delicate colors; its flower; a rosette; a perforated nozzle; a pinkish red or purplish red.

rosé *n* a pink wine made from skinless red grapes or by mixing white and red wine.

Rose *n* **Joseph** (1745–99) British head of a dynasty of decorative plasterers.

ROSE *abbr* = Research Open Systems in Europe.

Roseau *n* capital city of Dominica.

rose-colored *adj* rosy; overly optimistic.

rosehip *n* the small round fruit of the rose plant.

rosemary *n* a fragrant shrubby mint used in cookery and perfumery.

Rosenberg *n* **Isaac** (1890–1918) English poet and artist who had established a reputation as a promising poet by 1914, the year he enlisted in the British Army; he was killed in action. His war poems have a more objective tone than those of contemporaries such as Owen and Sassoon, although they are no less grim (e.g., "Dead Man's Dump").

Rosenthal *n* a German ceramics manufacturer founded by Philip Rosenthal in 1880.

roseola *n* any rose-colored rash such as accompanies various infectious diseases, e.g., measles.

Rosetta Stone *n* an inscribed slab of black basalt found at Rosetta (now Rashid) in Egypt in 1799 by Napoleon's expedition. Carries the text of a decree of Ptolemy V

Epiphanes, in Greek, demotic Egyptian and hieroglyphics. The Rosetta Stone is in the British Museum in London.

rosette *n* a rose-shaped bunch of ribbon; a carving, etc, in the shape of a rose.

Rose-Waaler test *n* a diagnostic blood test that is used to detect rheumatoid arthritis.

rosewater *n* water scented with rose petals.

rose window *n* (*archit*) a circular window ornamented with foils of patterned tracery giving a rose-like pattern.

rosewood *n* (any of various tropical trees yielding) a fragrant dark wood used in making furniture.

rosin *n* a pine-wood resin, esp in solid form, used in varnishes, etc, and for waxing the bows of stringed instruments.

ROSL *abbr* (*Brit*) = Royal Overseas League.

Rosmerta *n* (*Gaulish and Brit Celtic myth*) a goddess associated with material wealth and prosperity. Her name means "great provider." She was the patron saint of merchants.

RoSPA *abbr* (*Brit*) = Royal Society for the Prevention of Accidents.

Rossby waves *n* (*meteorol*) the wave patterns formed by the wind in the mid- to upper troposphere as they travel at the edge of a polar front.

Rossetti *n* 1. **Christina Georgina** (1830–94) English poet noted for her reflective, occasionally melancholic religious poems. She also wrote verses for children, and the remarkable verse fairy story *Goblin Market*. 2. her brother, **Dante Gabriel** (1828–82), poet and artist, one of the founders of the Pre-Raphaelite Brotherhood. His most famous poems are "The Blessed Damozel" and the fine sonnet sequence "The House of Life," the complete version of which is in *Ballads and Sonnets*.

Rossi *n* 1. **Angelo** (1670–1742) Italian painter who worked as a decorative artist in Venice. 2. **Giovanni A. de'** (*b.* 1616) Italian architect whose notable works include the Palazzo Altieri, Rome. 3. **Karl I.** (*b.* 1775) Russian architect whose notable works include the New Michael Palace, St Petersburg. 4. **Pucci de** (1947–) Italian furniture designer who works in New York and Paris.

Rossini *n* **Gioacchino Antonio** (1792–1868) Italian composer whose major works were operas (38 in all), including *The Italian Girl in Algiers*, *The Barber Of Seville*, *William Tell*, and *The Thieving Magpie*. He also wrote songs, piano pieces and instrumental quartets.

Ross the Red *n* (*Irish Celtic myth*) a king of Leinster. He is thought by some to have given his epithet to the Red Branch. He married Maga, daughter of Oenghus, and she bore him a son, a giant called Fachtna.

Rostand *n* **Edmond** (1868–1918) French dramatist and poet whose best-known work is his verse drama *Cyrano de Bergerac*.

roster *n* a list or roll, as of military personnel; a list of duties.

Rostropovich *n* 1. **Mstislav Leopoldovich** (1927–) Russian cellist, pianist, and conductor, possibly the greatest cellist of the 20th century. Many composers, notably Prokofiev, Britten, and Shostakovich, wrote pieces for him. He made public his support of Solzhenitsyn in 1970, and left the USSR in 1975. 2. His wife, the soprano **Galina Vishnevskaya** (1926–).

rostrum *n* (*pl* **rostrums**, **rostra**) a platform or stage for public speaking.

Rosualt *n* (*Irish Celtic myth*) a sea monster that was washed up on the Plain of Murrish in County Mayo.

rosy *adj* (**rosier**, **rosiest**) of the color of roses; having pink, healthy cheeks; optimistic, hopeful.

rot *vti* (**rotting**, **rotted**) to decompose; to decay; to become degenerate. * *n* decay; corruption; several different diseases affecting timber or sheep; (*inf*) nonsense.

rot. *abbr* = rotating; rotation.

ROT *abbr* = registered occupational therapist; rule of thumb.

rota *n* (*Brit*) a turn in succession; a list or roster of duties.

rotary *adj* revolving; turning like a wheel.

Rotary Club *n* a club belonging to an international organization of business people for promoting community service.—**Rotarian** *n*.

rotate *vti* to turn around an axis like a wheel; to follow a sequence.

rotation *n* the action of rotating; one complete turn of a body about its axis; a regular succession, as of crops to avoid exhausting the soil; (*astron*) the spinning of a galaxy or bodies held together by gravity.

rotation curve *n* (*astron*) the graphical plot showing the velocity of rotation of a galaxy against the distance from the center.

rotation of the Earth *n* the motion of the Earth from west to east as it rotates on its axis.

rotavirus *n* one of a number of viruses that commonly cause gastroenteritis and diarrhea in children under the age of six.

ROTC *abbr* = Reserve Officers' Training Corps *or* Camp.

rote *n* a fixed, mechanical way of doing something.

rotgut *n* (*sl*) a cheap or inferior whiskey or other spirit.

Roth *n* **Philip Milton** (*b.* 1933) American novelist and short-story writer, much of whose fiction is concerned with the problems (often sexual) of Jewish family life, e.g., the novella *Goodbye Columbus* and *Portnoy's Complaint*. His novel *Deception* is an intriguing semi-autobiographical work.

Rothko *n* **Mark [Marcus Rothkovitch]** (1903–70) Russian-born American painter. Having passed through Expressionism and Surrealism, in the late 1940s he adopted the Abstract Expressionist style of painting for which he became famous.

Rothschild *n* **[Nathaniel Mayer] Victor, 3rd Baron** (1910–90) English zoologist and banker. A member of the Rothschild dynasty of bankers and intellectuals. After service in British Intelligence during World War II, he became a scientist and served on various government committees. His works include *A Classification of Living Animals* (1961).

rotisserie *n* a large rotating spit on which poultry is roasted; a place where such food is prepared.

rotor *n* a rotating part of a machine or engine.

rototill *vt* to till the soil with a cultivator, with rotary blades.—**rototiller** *n*.

rotten *adj* decayed, decomposed; corrupt; (*inf*) bad, nasty.—**rottenness** *n*.

Rotterdam *n* a city in the Netherlands.

rotund *adj* rounded; spherical; plump.

rotunda *n* (*archit*) a circular building or room, often domed and surrounded by a colonnade.

rouble *n* the standard monetary unit of the Russian Federation, Belarus, the Ukraine, and Tajikistan, made up of 100 kopecks.—*also* **ruble**.

rouge *n* a red cosmetic for coloring the cheeks; a red powder for polishing jewelry, etc. * *vti* to color (the face) with rouge.

Rouget de Lisle *n* **Claude Joseph** (1760–1836) French royalist soldier and composer, best remembered for writing the words and music for the Marseillaise.

rough *adj* uneven; not smooth; ill-mannered; violent; rude, unpolished; shaggy; coarse in texture; unrefined; violent, boisterous; stormy; wild; harsh, discordant; crude, unfinished; approximate; (*inf*) difficult. * *n* rough ground; (*golf*) any part of a course with grass, etc, left uncut; a first sketch. * *vt* to make rough; to sketch roughly; (*with* **up**) (*inf*) to injure violently, beat up. * *adv* in a rough manner.—**roughly** *adv*.—**roughness** *n*.

roughage *n* rough or coarse food or fodder, as bran, etc; dietary fiber necessary to maintain the healthy function of the bowels and to prevent constipation and diverticulosis.

rough-and-ready *adj* unfinished but sufficient; prepared hastily.

rough-and-tumble *n* a scuffle; confusion.

roughcast *n* a mixture of lime and gravel for coating buildings; a rough surface finish. * *vt* (**roughcasting, roughcast**) to coat with roughcast.—*also* (*Brit*) **pebbledash**.

rough-cut *n* an early version of a film with the scenes edited together in sequence and a soundtrack added.

roughen *vti* to make or become rough.

roughhouse *n* (*sl*) (an instance of) noisy, boisterous or violent behavior.

roughneck *n* (*sl*) a coarse person.

roughshod *adj* marked by force without consideration.

rough stuff *n* (*inf*) violent behavior.

rough trade *n* (*sl*) a homosexual partner who is tough and possibly violent.

roulade *n* food in the shape of a roll, such as cheese or meat; (*mus*) a run of notes on one syllable.

roulette *n* a gambling game played with a revolving disk and a ball; a toothed wheel for making dots or perforations; a wheel with cogs that is rolled over a clay pot before it hardens to create impressions in the surface.

Roum. *abbr* = Roumania; Roumanian.

round *adj* circular, spherical, or cylindrical in form; curved; plump; (*math*) expressed to the nearest ten, hundred, etc, not fractional; considerable; candid; (of style) flowing, balanced; (of a vowel) pronounced with rounded lips. * *adv* circularly; on all sides; from one side to another; in a ring; by indirect way; through a recurring period of time; in circumference; in a roundabout way; about; near; here and there; with a rotating movement; in the opposite direction; around. * *prep* encircling; on every side of; in the vicinity of; in a circuit through; around. * *n* anything round; a circuit; a volley (of shots); a unit of ammunition; a series or sequence; a bout, turn; (*golf*) a circuit of a course; a stage of a contest; (*mus*) a kind of canon. * *vt* to make or become round or plump; (*math*) to express as a round number; to complete; to go or pass around. * *vi* to make a circuit; to turn; to reverse direction.—**roundly** *adv*.—**roundness** *n*.

roundabout *adj* indirect, circuitous. * *n* a circuitous route; a merry-go-round; (*Brit*) a traffic circle.

round dance *n* (*mus*) a dance in which partners start opposite each other and subsequently form a ring.

rounded *adj* curved or round; flowing, not angular.

roundhouse *n* a circular building for repairing and servicing railway locomotives.

round robin *n* a document with signatures in a circle to conceal their order.

round-shouldered *adj* with bent shoulders; stooping.

round-table conference *n* a conference with all the parties on an equal footing.

round trip *n* a journey to a place and back again.

round-trip ticket *n* a ticket whose price includes the cost of the journey to and back from a destination.

roundup *n* a driving together of livestock; (*inf*) the detention of several prisoners; a summary, as of news.

roundworm *n* a nematode parasitic in people and pigs.

Roupert *n* **Louis** (*fl.* 1660s) German goldsmith and designer who published his suite of designs in 1668.

Rous *n* **Francis Peyton** (1879–1970) American pathologist. With the Canadian-born surgeon **Charles Brenton Huggins** (*b.* 1901), he shared the 1966 Nobel prize for physiology or medicine for his innovative cancer research. Much of his work, e.g., his discovery of the Rous Sarcoma Virus, had been done over fifty years previously.

rouse *vti* to provoke; to stir up; to awaken; to wake up; to become active.

rousing *adj* stirring; vigorous.

Rousseau *n* 1. **Clément** (1872–1950) French sculptor who designed idiosyncratic pieces of furniture for wealthy clients. 2. **Henri Julien ["Le Douanier"]** (1844–1910) French painter. He defied conventions of color and perspective in his exotic imaginary landscapes and painted dreams, e.g., *The Dream* (1910). 3. **Jean-**

Jacques (1712–78) Swiss-born French philosopher. His most notable fictional works are the novels *Julie, or the New Héloïse* and *Émile*. These works and others, notably the political tract *The Social Contract* (1762), were profoundly influential on the intellectual ferment that led to the French Revolution. His 12 volumes of autobiography, *Confessions*, were published posthumously from 1781–88.

Roussel *n* **Albert** (1869–1937) French composer who was influenced by Chinese and Indian music. His works include four symphonies, the opera-ballet *Padmavati*, ballets (such as *Bacchus and Ariadne*), chamber music, and many songs.

rout[1] *n* a noisy crowd, a rabble; a disorderly retreat. * *vt* to defeat and put to flight.

rout[2] *vti* to grub up, as a pig; to search haphazardly; to gouge out or make a furrow in (as wood or metal); to cause to emerge, esp from bed; to come up with; to uncover.

route *n* a course to be taken; the roads traveled on a journey. * *vt* (**routing, routed**) to plan the route of; to send (by a specified route).

route sheet *or* **routing sheet** *n* a document that shows in detail the sequence of operations through which a product or component passes and often the tools and equipment required.

routine *n* a procedure that is regular and unvarying; a sequence of set movements, as in a dance, skating, etc.—*also adj*.

roux *n* a mixture of equal quantities of flour and melted fat used as the basis for sauces.

ROV *abbr* = remotely operated vehicle.

rove *vti* to wander about, roam (over).

rover *n* a wanderer; a fickle person; (*Brit*) (*formerly*) a senior Scout.

row[1] *n* a line of persons or things; a line of seats (in a theater, etc); (*comput*) a horizontal block of cells that extends from the left to the right of a spreadsheet.

row[2] *vti* to propel with oars; to transport by rowing. * *n* an act or instance of rowing.—**rower** *n*.

row[3] *n* a noisy quarrel or dispute; a scolding; noise, disturbance. * *vi* to quarrel; to scold.

ROW *abbr* = Rights of Women; right of way.

rowan *n* a tree producing white flowers followed by small red berries.

rowboat, rowing boat *n* a small boat made for rowing.

rowdy *adj* (**rowdier, rowdiest**) rough and noisy, disorderly. * *n* (*pl* **rowdies**) a rowdy person, a hooligan.—**rowdiness, rowdyism** *n*.

Rowe *n* **Nicholas** (1674–1718) English dramatist and poet whose best-known plays are *Tamerlane* and *Jane Shore*. His translation of the Roman poet Lucan's *Pharalia* was much admired by Dr Johnson, and he also produced an important edition of Shakespeare. He was poet laureate from 1715.

rowel *n* a spiked revolving disk at the end of a spur.

row house *n* a house in a row of similar houses joined by shared walls.

rowing machine *n* an exercise machine with oars and a sliding seat that simulates a rowing action.

Rowlandson, Thomas (1756–1827) English caricaturist and printmaker. His popular series of engravings included *The Comforts of Bath* (1798) and *The Tour of Dr Syntax in Search of the Picturesque* (1812, 1820, and 1821).

rowlock *n* a fitting on the side of a boat that holds an oar in place and serves as its fulcrum.

royal *adj* relating to or fit for a king or queen; regal; under the patronage of a king or queen; founded by a king or queen; of a kingdom, its government, etc. * *n* a type of topsail; a stag with a head of twelve points; (*inf*) a member of a royal family.—**royally** *adv*.

Royal Albert Hall *n* (*mus*) a purpose-built, domed concert hall in central London at the southern edge of Hyde Park, renowned for its good acoustics. Conceived by Prince Albert, it was built in his memory following his death in 1861, and was opened in 1871.

royal blue *n, adj* deep blue.

Royal Copenhagen Porcelain Manufactury (Den Kongelige Porcelaensfabric) *n* The first pottery in Copenhagen, which was established in 1755 under the patronage of King Frederick V.

Royal Festival Hall *n* (*mus*) a concert hall in London which was opened in 1951 as part of the Festival of Britain.

royal flush *n* (*poker*) a straight flush headed by an ace.

royalist *n* a person who advocates monarchy.

royal jelly *n* a nutritious secretion of the honeybee which is fed to larvae, esp those destined to become queens; a preparation of this sold as a health product.

royal palm *n* any of various palms of tropical America with tall trunks and large feathery fronds.

royalty *n* (*pl* **royalties**) the rank or power of a king or queen; a royal person or persons; a share of the proceeds from a patent, book, song, etc, paid to the owner, author, composer, etc.

Royce *n* **Sir [Frederick] Henry** (1863–1933) English engineer who founded the Rolls-Royce automobile manufacturer in 1906 in partnership with Charles Rolls.

rp *abbr* = reception poor.

r-p. *abbr* = reprinting.

RP *abbr* = Received Pronunciation; Reformed Presbyterian; Registered Plumber; Regius Professor; (*Brit*) Royal Society of Portrait Painters; recommended price; reply paid; reprint; (*Latin*) *respublica* ("republic"); retinitis pigmentosa; (*Latin*) *Reverendus Pater* ("Reverend Father").

RPA *abbr* = Radio Paging Association; (*Brit*) Rationalist Press Association; Record of Personal Achievement; (*Brit*) Registered Plumbers Association; Rural Pharmacists Association; Rural Preservation Association.

RPB *abbr* = recognized professional body.

RPD *abbr* (*Latin*) = *Rerum Politicarum Doctor* ("Doctor of Political Science").

RPE *abbr* = Reformed Protestant Episcopal.

RPI *abbr* (*Brit*) = retail price index.

rpm *abbr* = revolutions per minute.

RPRA *abbr* = (*Brit*) Royal Pigeon Racing Association; Rubber and Plastics Reclamation Association.

r-process *n* (*astron*) a nucleosynthetic process which is rapid (hence r-process) and occurs in supernova explosions when there is a high flux of neutrons.

rps *abbr* = revolutions per second.

RPS *abbr* (*Brit*) = Racial Preservation Society; Rare Poultry Society; Royal Philatelic Society; Royal Philharmonic Society; Royal Photographic Society.

rpt. *abbr* = report.

RPT *abbr* (*Brit*) = Reptile Protection Trust.

RPV *abbr* = remotely piloted vehicle.

RQ *abbr* = respiratory quotient.

RR *abbr* = railroad; Right Reverend.

RRA *abbr* = (*Brit*) Road Roller Association; Rubber Research Association (Israel).

RRB *abbr* = Railroad Retirement Board.

-rrhagia *n suffix* denoting an abnormal discharge.

-rrhea, -rrhoea *n suffix* a flow.

RR Lyrae stars *n* a group of pulsating variable stars found mainly in globular clusters.

RRP *abbr* = recommended retail price.

RRQ *abbr* = request for quotation.

rs *abbr* = right side.

Rs *or* **rs.** *abbr* = rupees.

RS *abbr* = recording secretary; Recruiting Service; Reformed Spelling; Revised Statutes; (*Brit*) Royal Society.

RSA *abbr* = (*Brit*) Racket Sports Association; (*Brit*) Refined Sugar Association; (*Brit*) Relay Services Association of Great Britain; Republic of South Africa; (*Brit*) Royal Scottish Academy of Painting, Sculpture and Architecture; (*Brit*) Royal Society of Arts; Royal Society of Australia; Rehabilitation Services Administration.

RSABI *abbr* (*Brit*) = Royal Scottish Agricultural Benevolent Institution.

RSAI *abbr* = Royal Society of Antiquaries of Ireland.

RSAS *abbr* (*Brit*) = Royal Surgical Aid Society.

RSBA *abbr* (*Brit*) = Royal Society of British Artists.

RSBEI *abbr* = Registered Student of the Institution of Body Engineers.

RSC *abbr* (*Brit*) = Refugee Support Centre; Royal Shakespeare Company; Royal Society of Chemistry.

RS Canum Venaticorum Star *n* a variable binary star that exhibits high activity such as flares, star-spots and coronae.

RSCDS *abbr* (*Brit*) = Royal Scottish Country Dance Society.

RSCN *abbr* (*Brit*) = Registered Sick Children's Nurse.

RSDA *abbr* (*Brit*) = Road Surface Dressing Association.

RSE *abbr* (*Brit*) = Royal Society of Edinburgh.

RSFS *abbr* (*Brit*) = Royal Scottish Forestry Society.

RSM *abbr* = Regimental Sergeant Major; (*Brit*) Royal School of Mines; (*Brit*) Royal Society of Musicians.

RSMG *abbr* (*Brit*) = Rubber Stamp Manufacturers Guild.

RSN *abbr* (*Brit*) = Royal Society of Needlework.

RSPA *abbr* = Research and Special Programs Administration.

RSPB *abbr* (*Brit*) = Royal Society for the Protection of Birds.

RSPCA *abbr* (*Brit*) = Royal Society for the Prevention of Cruelty to Animals.

RSPCC *abbr* (*Brit*) = Royal Society for the Prevention of Cruelty to Children.

RSPS *abbr* (*Brit*) = Royal Scottish Pipers Society.

RSR *abbr* (*Brit*) = Royal Sailors' Rests.

RSRC *abbr* (*Brit*) = Rural Studies Research Centre.

RSRIGS *abbr* (*Brit*) = Royal Society for the Relief of Indigent Gentlewomen of Scotland.

RSS *abbr* (*Brit*) = Remote Sensing Society; Robert Simpson Society; Royal Statistical Society.

R star *n* (*astron*) a spectral type of red giant star which is now included in the carbon stars.

RSTMH *abbr* (*Brit*) = Royal Society of Tropical Medicine and Hygiene.

RSV *abbr* = Revised Standard Version (of the Bible).

RSVP *abbr* (*French*) = *répondez s'il vous plaît* ("please reply").

rt. *abbr* = right.

RTA *abbr* = (*Brit*) Racehorse Transporters Association; Road Transport Association; Roofing Tile Association; (*Brit*) Rose Trade Association.

RTB *abbr* = Rural Telephone Bank.

RTCS *abbr* (*Brit*) = Round Tower Churches Society.

rtd. *abbr* = returned.

rte. *abbr* = route.

Rt Hon *abbr* = Right Honourable (title used by British members of Parliament).

RTI *abbr* = Round Table International; respiratory tract infection.

RTITB *abbr* (*Brit*) = Road Transport Industry Training Board.

RTK *abbr* = right to know.

RTL *abbr* (*comput*) = real time language.

RTO *abbr* = Railway Transport Officer.

RTOL *abbr* = reduced take-off and landing.

RTP *abbr* = room temperature and pressure.

RTPI *abbr* (*Brit*) = Royal Town Planning Institute.

RTR *abbr* (*Brit*) = Royal Tank Regiment.

Rt Rev *abbr* = Right Reverend.

Rts. *abbr* (*stocks*) = rights.

RTS *abbr* = Religious Tract Society; Risk Theory Society; (*Brit*) River Thames Society; (*Brit*) Royal Television Society; (*Brit*) Royal Toxophilite Society.

RTSA *abbr* = Retail Standards Association.

RTTC *abbr* (*Brit*) = Road Time Trials Council.

rtu *abbr* = returned to unit.

rtw *abbr* = (of clothing) ready to wear.

RTYC *abbr* (*Brit*) = Royal Thames Yacht Club.

R-type asteroid *n* a rare type of asteroid with quite high albedo.

RTZ *abbr* = Rio Tinto Zinc Corporation Limited.

Ru *symbol* (*chem*) ruthenium.

ru. *abbr* = runic.

RU *abbr* = Rugby Union.

RUA *abbr* (*Brit*) = Royal Ulster Academy.

Ruadan *n* (*Irish Celtic myth*) a son of Bres and the goddess Brigid. He wounded the smith god Goibhniu at the second Battle of Magh Tuiredh, but was mortally wounded in combat by the smith god with one of his magical weapons.

Ruadh *n* (*Irish Celtic myth*) a son of Rigdonn; on a sailing expedition, perhaps to Norway, when the ships suddenly became completely becalmed, even although the sails were still filled with wind.

rub *vti* (**rubbing, rubbed**) to move (a hand, cloth, etc) over the surface of with pressure; to wipe, scour; to clean or polish; (*with* **away, off, out**) to remove or erase by friction; to chafe, grate; to fret; to take a rubbing of; (*with* **along**) to manage somehow; (*with* **down**) to rub vigorously with a towel; to smooth down. * *n* the act or process of rubbing; a drawback, difficulty.

rubato *n* (*mus*) (*Italian*) literally, "robbed," i.e., the taking of time from one note or passage and passing it on to another note or passage.

rubber[1] *n* an elastic substance made synthetically or from the sap of various tropical plants; an eraser; (*pl*) galoshes.

rubber[2] *n* a group of three games at whist, bridge, etc; the deciding game.

rubber check *n* (*sl*) a check returned by a bank because the account holder has insufficient funds.

rubberize *vt* to coat with rubber to make waterproof.

rubberneck *n* (*sl*) a person who gapes, esp intrusively; a sightseer.—*also vi.*

rubber plant *n* an Asian plant related to the fig with shiny leaves, popular as a houseplant.

rubber-stamp *vt* (*inf*) to give automatic approval without investigation.

rubber tree *n* a tree native to South America and widely cultivated in the tropics as a source of latex to make rubber.

rubbing *n* an impression of an inscribed brass plate, etc, obtained by rubbing a wax substance on paper laid over it.

rubbish *n* refuse; garbage, trash; nonsense. —**rubbishy** *adj.*

rubble *n* rough broken stone or rock; builders' rubbish.

rubble walling *n* (*archit*) a style of coarse walling generally consisting of rough stones of irregular size.

Rubbra *n* (**Charles**) **Edmund** (1901–86) English composer who studied under Vaughan Williams and Holst. A traditionalist composer, Rubbra found much of his inspiration in English lyric poetry, and in his religious beliefs (originally an Anglican, he converted to Roman Catholicism in 1948). His works include symphonies, concertos, Masses, motets, and modern-day madrigals.

rubdown *n* a brisk rubbing down of the body.

rubella *n* a mild contagious viral disease that may cause damage to an unborn child; German measles.

rubella *see* **German measles**.

Rubenesque *adj* of, like, or pertaining to the art of the Florentine painter Peter Paul Rubens (1577–1640); opulent, colorful; (of a woman's figure) full-figured and shapely.

Rubens *n* **Sir Peter Paul** (1577–1640) Flemish painter and diplomat. He became court painter to the Spanish viceroys in Antwerp in 1609. He was already famous when he painted his masterpiece, the triptych *Descent from the Cross* (1611–14). In 1629 he was sent to England to negotiate peace with Charles I, who knighted him, and while there he painted *Peace and War*.

rubidium *n* a soft radioactive metallic element.

Rubinstein *n* 1. **Anton Gregoryevich** (1821–94) Russian virtuoso pianist and composer who flew against the wind by composing Western as opposed to Russian (nationalistic) music. Most of his works have not survived the test of time, but his songs and piano pieces are still occasionally performed. 2. **Artur** (1887–1982) Polish-born pianist who became an American citizen in 1946. One of the greatest interpreters of piano music of the 20th century, he was esp noted for his performance of works by Brahms, Chopin, Beethoven, Schubert, and Schumann.

ruble *see* **rouble**.

rubric *n* a heading or line marked out in red; any rule, explanatory comment, etc.

RUBSSO *abbr* (*Brit*) = Rossendale Union of Boot, Shoe and Slipper Operatives.

ruby *n* (*pl* **rubies**) a deep red, transparent, valuable precious stone. * *adj* of the color of a ruby.

ruby orange *n* an orange with red juice.

Ruby, Jack *see* **Oswald, Lee Harvey**.

RUC *abbr* (*Brit*) = Royal Ulster Constabulary.

ruche *vt* to pleat, gather, or flute fabric for use as a trimming. * *n* ruched fabric.

rucksack *n* (*Brit*) a backpack.

RUCR *abbr* (*Brit*) = Royal Ulster Constabulary Reserve.

ruction *n* (*inf*) a disturbance, a row, uproar.

rudder *n* a flat vertical piece of wood or metal hinged to the stern of a ship or boat or the rear of an aircraft to steer by; a guiding principle.

ruddy *adj* (**ruddier, ruddiest**) reddish pink; (of the complexion) of a healthy, red color.

rude *adj* uncivil, ill-mannered; uncultured, coarse; harsh, brutal; crude, roughly made; in a natural state, primitive; vigorous, hearty.—**rudely** *adv.*—**rudeness** *n*.

rudiment *n* a first stage; a first slight beginning of something; an imperfectly developed organ; (*pl*) elements, first principles.

rudimentary *adj* elementary; imperfectly developed or represented only by a vestige.

rue *vti* (**rueing, rued**) to feel remorse for (a sin, fault, etc); to regret (an act, etc). * *n* (*arch*) sorrow.

r.u.e. *abbr* (*theat*) = right upper entrance.

rueful *adj* regretful; dejected; showing good-humored self-pity.—**ruefully** *adv.*

ruff *n* a pleated collar or frill worn round the neck; a fringe of feathers or fur round the neck of a bird or animal.

ruffian *n* a brutal lawless person; a villain.

ruffle *vti* to disturb the smoothness of, disarrange; to irritate; to agitate; to upset; to swagger about; to be quarrelsome; to flutter. * *n* pleated material used as a trim; a frill; a bird's ruff; a dispute, quarrel.

rufiyaa *n* the standard monetary unit of the Maldives, made up of 100 laari.

rug *n* a thick heavy fabric used as a floor covering; a thick woolen wrap or coverlet.

RUG *abbr* (*comput*) = restricted users group.

rugby *n* a football game for two teams of 15 players played with an oval ball.

rugged *adj* rocky; rough, uneven; strong; stern; robust.—**ruggedly** *adv.*—**ruggedness** *n*.

rugger *n* (*Brit inf*) rugby.

Ruggles *n* **Carl** (1876–1971) American composer and painter who experimented with various forms of music and helped to establish an "American" style of "modern" composition. His works include *Angels* (for muted trumpets and trombones), and various pieces for assorted instruments. *Sun-Treader* is his most notable work.

Ruhlmann *n* **Jacques Émile** (1879–1933) French designer and craftsman whose best-known piece was the 1930 *Soleil* bed.

ruin *n* destruction; downfall, wrecked state; the cause of this; a loss of fortune; (*pl*) the remains of something destroyed, decayed, etc. * *vti* to destroy; to spoil; to bankrupt; to come to ruin.

ruinous *adj* in ruins, tumbledown; causing ruin, disastrous.

Ruisdael *or* **Ruysdael** *n* 1. **Jacob van** (*c*.1628–82) Dutch landscape painter. His atmospheric landscapes, e.g., *Landscape with Ruins*, and seascapes are outstanding. 2. his uncle **Salomon van Ruysdael** (*c*.1600–70), also a landscape painter, was possibly his tutor.

RUKBA *abbr* (*Brit*) = Royal United Kingdom Beneficent Association.

"Rule Britannia" *n* (*mus*) a patriotic British song with words (possibly) by James Thomson and music by Arne, first performed in a masque called *Alfred* in 1740.

rule *n* a straight-edged instrument for drawing lines and measuring; government; the exercise of authority; a regulation, an order; a principle, a standard; habitual practice; the code of a religious order; a straight line. * *vti* to govern, to exercise authority over; to manage; to draw (lines) with a ruler; (*with* **out**) to exclude, to eliminate; to make impossible.

rule of thumb *n* a rough commonsense approach as opposed to a precise or theoretical one.

ruler *n* a person who governs; a strip of wood, metal, etc, with a straight edge, used in drawing lines, measuring, etc; (*comput*) in a word-processing environment, a bar at the top of the page to assist the user in setting margins and tab stops.

Ruler of the Synagogue *n* a Jewish elder responsible for day-to-day administration of the worship and work of the synagogue.

ruling *adj* governing; reigning; dominant. * *n* an authoritative pronouncement.

rum *n* a spirit made from sugar cane.

Rum. *abbr* = Rumania; Rumanian.

rumba *n* (*mus*) a fast dance of Afro-Cuban origin with a complex rhythm. * *vi* to dance the rumba.

rumble *vti* to make a low heavy rolling noise (as thunder); to move with such a sound; (*sl*) to see through, find out. * *n* the dull deep vibrant noise of thunder, etc.

rumbustious *adj* unruly, boisterous.

rumen *n* (*pl* **rumens, rumina**) the first compartment of the stomach of a ruminant mammal.

ruminant *n* a cud-chewing animal, such as cattle, deer, camels, etc; (*zool*) any mammal that has three or four compartments in the stomach to aid the digestion of large amounts of plant material. * *adj* chewing the cud; thoughtful.

ruminate *vi* to regurgitate food after it has been swallowed, chew cud; to ponder deeply, muse (on).

rummage *n* odds and ends; a search by ransacking. * *vti* to search thoroughly; to ransack; to fish (out).

rummage sale *n* a sale of second-hand clothes, books, etc, to raise money for charity.—*also* (*Brit*) **jumble sale**.

rummy *n* a card game whose object is to form sets and sequences.

rumor, rumour *n* hearsay, gossip; common talk not based on definite knowledge; an unconfirmed report, story. * *vt* to report by way of rumor.

rump *n* the hindquarters of an animal's body; the buttocks; the back end.

rumple *n* a crease or wrinkle. * *vti* to crease; to disarrange, tousle.

rumpus *n* (*pl* **rumpuses**) a commotion; a din.

run *vi* (**running, ran** *or* **run,** *pp* **run**) to go by moving the legs faster than in walking; to hurry; to flee; to flow; to operate; to be valid; to compete in a race, election, etc; (of colors), to merge; (*with* **across**) to meet by accident; (*with* **around** *vi* (*inf*) to associate (with); to behave evasively or promiscuously; (*with* **away** *vi* to take flight, escape; to go out of control; (*with* **away with**) to abscond, elope; to steal; to win easily; (*with* **down**) (of an engine, etc) to cease to operate through lack of power; to become tired or exhausted; (*with* **off**) to leave hastily; to decide (a race) with a run-off; (*with* **through**) to use up (money, etc) completely; to read quickly. * *vt* to drive (a car, etc); to manage (a business, etc); to publish (a story) in a newspaper; to suffer from (a fever, etc); (*comput*) to initiate or execute (a program); (*with* **down**) to knock down with a moving vehicle; to collide with and cause to sink; to chase and capture; to tire, exhaust; to investigate, find; to criticize persistently; to allow (an engine, etc) to gradually lose power; to reduce in quantity; (*with* **in**) to run a new car engine gently to start with; (*inf*) to arrest; (*with* **off**) to compose and talk glibly; to produce quickly, as copies on a photocopier; to drain off; (*with* **out**) to exhaust a supply; (*inf*) to desert; (*with* **over**) (of a vehicle) to knock down a person or animal; to overflow; to exceed a limit; to rehearse quickly; (*with* **through**) to pierce with a sword or knife; to rehearse; (*with* **up**) to incur or amass. * *n* an act of running; a trip; a flow; a series; prevalence; a trend; an enclosure for chickens, etc; free and unrestricted access to all parts; (in tights, etc) a hole.

Run *n* (*d. c*.878) king of Strathclyde. He married a daughter of Kenneth mac-Alpin, the Scots king, and their son, Eocha, followed Constantine and Aed to the throne.

run-around *n* deceitful or evasive behavior towards someone.

runaway *n* a person or thing that runs away; a fugitive. * *adj* out of control; (of inflation) rising uncontrollably; (of a race, etc) easily won.

runaway star *n* (*astron*) a young star that has an unusually high velocity through space.

rundown *n* a brief summary; the process of going into a decline.

run-down *adj* dilapidated; ill; tired.

rune *n* a letter of a primitive Teutonic alphabet comprising angular characters, first seen in the 3rd century in Denmark and Schleswig; a magic mark or sign.—**runic** *adj*.

rung[1] *see* **ring**[2].

rung[2] *n* the step of a ladder; the crossbar of a chair.

run-in *n* (*inf*) a quarrel.

runner *n* an athlete; a person who runs; a smuggler; a groove or strip on which something glides.

runner bean *n* (*Brit*) a pole bean.

runner-up *n* (*pl* **runners-up**) the competitor who finishes second in a race, contest, etc.

running *n* the act of moving swiftly; that which runs or flows; a racing, managing, etc. * *adj* moving swiftly; kept for a race; being in motion; continuous; discharging pus. * *adv* in succession.

running commentary *n* a verbal description on TV or radio of an event as it happens, esp sport.

running costs *npl* the costs that are incurred in the operation of a company or fixed asset, such as expenditure on power in a factory.

running mate *n* the candidate in a US election standing for the less important of two positions in a linked office.

runny *adj* (**runnier, runniest**) tending to flow.

runoff *n* the water that leaves a drainage area, usu estimated as the rainfall minus any water lost by evaporation; a final deciding race, contest, etc.

run-of-the-mill *adj* average, mediocre.

runt *n* an unusually small animal, esp the smallest of a litter of pigs; (*derog*) a person of small stature.

run-through *n* a rehearsal; a cursory reading.

run time version *n* (*comput*) a special version of an interpreter that allows one application only to be run.

run-up *n* a preliminary period.

runway *n* a landing strip for aircraft.

Runyon *n* **[Alfred] Damon** (1884–1946) American short-story writer noted for his humorous, racy short stories about New York low life and the seamier side of Broadway, e.g., *Guys and Dolls*.

rupee *n* the standard monetary unit of India, Pakistan, and Nepal, made up of 100 paise; the standard monetary unit of Sri Lanka, Mauritius, and the Seychelles, made up of 100 cents.

rupiah *n* (*pl* **rupiah, rupiahs**) the standard currency unit of Indonesia, made up of 100 sen.

rupture *n* a breach; a severance, quarrel; the act of bursting or breaking; (*med*) the bursting open of an organ, tissue, or structure, a hernia. * *vti* to cause or suffer a rupture.

RUR *abbr* (*Brit*) = Royal Ulster Regiment.

rural *adj* relating to the country or agriculture, rustic.—**rurally** *adv*.

Rural *abbr* (*Brit*) = Society for the Responsible Use of Resources in Agriculture and on the Land.

Rury *n* (*Irish Celtic myth*) the son of Partholan. A lake is said to have sprung forth from Rury's grave and became known as Lake Rury.

Rus. *or* **Russ.** *abbr* = Russia; Russian.

RUS *abbr* = Rural Utilities Service.

ruse *n* a trick or stratagem.

Ruse *n* a city in Bulgaria.

rush[1] *vti* to move, push, drive, etc, swiftly or impetuously; to make a sudden attack (on); to do with unusual haste; to hurry. * *adj* marked by or needing extra speed or urgency. * *n* a sudden surge; a sudden demand; a press, as of business, requiring unusual haste; an unedited film print.

rush[2] *n* a marsh plant; its slender pithy stem; a worthless thing.

Rushdie *n* [Ahmed] **Salman** (*b*. 1947) Indian-born British novelist. His first major success was *Midnight's Children* (1981). After the publication of *Satanic Verses* (1988), Ayatollah Khomeini of Iran pronounced a death sentence on him for blasphemy which led to a worldwide debate on free speech. In 1998 the Iranian government withdrew its support of the fatwa.

rush hour *n* the time at the beginning and end of the working day when traffic is at its heaviest.

RUSI *abbr* (*Brit*) = Royal United Services Institute for Defence Studies.

rusk *n* a sweet or plain bread sliced and rebaked until dry and crisp.

Rusk *n* [David] **Dean** (1909–94) US secretary of state (1961–69). Notable for being a firm Cold Warrior and a strong supporter of the Vietnam War, which he saw as a crusade against communism, he served under Kennedy and Johnson.

Ruskin *n* **John** (1819–1900) English writer, artist, and influential art critic whose *Modern Painters* championed the works of Turner. Other works include *The Seven Lamps of Architecture*, *The Stones of Venice*, *Unto this Last*, and *Sesame and Lilies*. He was an enthusiast for Gothic art, the Pre-Raphaelite movement, and Turner, and was, like Carlyle, a strong critic of the values and ugliness of Industrial England.

RUSM *abbr* (*Brit*) = Royal United Service Museum.

russ. *abbr* (*bookbinding*) = Russia leather.

Russell *n* 1. **Bertrand Arthur William [3rd Earl Russell]** (1872–1970) British philosopher, mathematician, and political reformer who made notable contributions to mathematical and philosophical theory and won the 1950 Nobel prize for literature. Notable works include: *Principles of Mathematics* (1903); with Whitehead, *Principia Mathematica* (1910–13); *Problems of Philosophy* (1912); and *A History of Western Philosophy* (1945). 2. **Gordon** (1892–1980) British furniture maker and designer who, from 1939, was influential in British furniture design, through his involvement with the Utility Scheme. 3. **Ken** (1927–) English film director. He is esp noted for his film biographies of musicians, which began with a film for television on Elgar (1962) and (on Delius) *A Song of Summer* (1968), and progressed through increasingly bizarre works such as (on Tchaikovsky) *The Music Lovers* (1970) to the lunatic *Lisztomania* (1975).

russet *adj* reddish-brown. * *n* a russet color; a winter apple with a rough russet skin; a homespun russet cloth.

Russia *or* **the Russian Federation** *n* the largest single country in the world, extending from the Gulf of Finland in the west to the shores of the Pacific Ocean in the east and from the Arctic Ocean in the north to the Caucasus in the south.

Russian *n* a native or inhabitant of Russia; the Slavonic language of Russians.— *also adj*.

Russian roulette *n* an act of bravado in which the cylinder of a revolver loaded with a single bullet is spun and the muzzle then pointed at the head and fired.

Russo- *prefix* Russia; Russian.

rust *n* a reddish oxide coating formed on iron or steel when exposed to moisture; a reddish brown color; a red mold on plants; the fungus causing this. * *vti* to form rust (on); to deteriorate, as through disuse.

rustic *n* pertaining to or characteristic of the country; rural; simple, unsophisticated. * *n* a person from the country; a simple country dweller.

rusticated *adj* of a type of decoration on pots where the surface is covered with marks made by a stick, the tips of the fingers, or something similar.

rustication *n* (*archit*) massive textured blocks of masonry divided by deep joints and used to give a striking effect to exterior walls.

rustle *n* a crisp, rubbing sound as of dry leaves, paper, etc. * *vti* to make or move with a rustle; to hustle; to steal (cattle); (*with up*) (*inf*) to collect or get together.

rustler *n* a person who steals livestock, esp cattle; a hustler.

rusty *adj* (**rustier, rustiest**) coated with rust; rust-colored, faded; out of practice; antiquated.—**rustiness** *n*.

rut[1] *n* a track worn by wheels; an undeviating mechanical routine. * *vt* (**rutting, rutted**) to mark with ruts.

rut[2] *n* the seasonal period of sexual excitement in male ruminants, such as deer. * *vi* (**rutting, rutted**) to be in rut.

rutabaga *n* a swede.

Ruth *n* (*Bible*) a Moabite widow who came with her mother-in-law to Bethlehem, where she was befriended by Boaz, a wealthy farmer who eventually married her. *See also* **Boaz**.

Ruth *n* **Babe** [George Herman Ruth] (1895–1948) American baseball player. Regarded as the finest all-rounder in the history of baseball, as pitcher with the Boston Red Sox (1914–19) and batter for New York Yankees (1920–34), his total of 714 home runs was unsurpassed until 1974. He finished his career as coach for the Brooklyn Dodgers.

Ruth, the Book of *n* (*Bible*) the story of Ruth.

ruthenium *n* a rare metallic element of the platinum group.

Rutherford *n* 1. **Ernest [1st Baron Rutherford of Nelson]** (1871–1937) New Zealand physicist and winner of the 1908 Nobel prize for chemistry for his work in the radioactive transformation of atoms. In 1911 he deduced the existence of the atom's structure, and was the first scientist to split the atom. 2. **Dame Margaret** (1892–1972) English actress. Notable for her engaging portrayal of eccentrics, she portrayed Agatha Christie's Miss Marple in several films in the 1960s.

ruthless *adj* cruel; merciless.—**ruthlessly** *adv*.—**ruthlessness** *n*.

Rutulians, Rutuli *npl* (*Roman myth*) a tribe living in Latium who went to war against Aeneas and his Trojan companions.

Ruysdael *see* **Ruisdael**.

rv *abbr* = rendezvous.

RV *abbr* = recreational vehicle; Reformed Version; Revised Version (translation of the Bible); ratable value; right ventricle.

RVA *abbr* = Returned Volunteer Action.

RVC *abbr* (*Brit*) = Royal Veterinary College.

RVSVP *abbr* (*French*) = *répondez vite s'il vous plaît* ("please reply at once").

RV Tauri star *n* one of a group of yellow giants, pulsating variable stars.

r/w *abbr* (*comput*) = read/write.

Rw. *abbr* = railway.

RW *abbr* = Right Worshipful; Right Worthy; runway.

RWA *abbr* (*Brit*) = Race Walking Association.

Rwanda *n* a small landlocked republic in the heart of central Africa.

Rwanda Franc *n* currency of Rwanda.

RWAS *abbr* (*Brit*) = Royal Welsh Agricultural Society.

rwd *abbr* = rear wheel drive.

RWD *abbr* = radioactive waste disposal.

RWF *abbr* (*Brit*) = Royal Welsh Fusiliers.

RWIC *abbr* = Rioja Wine Information Center.

RWM *abbr* = radioactive waste management.

RWMAC *abbr* (*Brit*) = Radioactive Waste Management Advisory Committee.

RWS *abbr* (*Brit*) = Royal Society of Painters in Water Colours.

Rwy. *abbr* = railway.

Rx. *abbr* (*Latin*) = *recipe*, "take".

rxb. *abbr* = Roxburgh (bookbinding).

Ry. *abbr* = Railway.

RYA *abbr* (*Brit*) = Royal Yachting Association.

rye *n* a hardy annual grass; its grain, used for making flour and whiskey; a whiskey made from rye.

Ryle *n* **Gilbert** (1900–76) English philosopher. He became one of the leading "linguistic" philosophers of his generation. His works include *The Concept of Mind* (1949) and *Plato's Progress* (1966). 2. **Sir Martin** (1918–84) English astronomer. He was awarded the 1974 Nobel prize for physics for his work in the field of radio astronomy, which, in the 1960s, led to the conclusion that the universe is not in a "steady state." He was astronomer royal (1972–82).

RYS *abbr* (*Brit*) = Royal Yacht Squadron.

RZS *abbr* (*Brit*) = Royal Zoological Society.

S

S, s *n* the 19th letter of the English alphabet; something shaped like an S.

S *symbol* (*chem*) = sulfur (element).

s *abbr* = second(s); section; semi-; series; sets (of the sun); shilling (former Brit monetary unit); singular; sister; son; suit; symmetrical.

s. *abbr* = (*anat*) sacral; saint; school; scribe; (*phys, chem*) secondary (rays); see; (*Latin*) *senatus*, "senate"; sign; (*Latin*) *signa*, "write" (esp. directions to a patient concerning medicine); signed; silver; sire (*pedigree*); socialist; society; solidus; solo; soprano; sou; southern; spherical; steel; stem; stere; stratus; substantive; succeeded; sun; surplus.

S *abbr* = Sabbath; Saint; Saturday; (*math*) scalar; school; (*Italian*) *segno*, "sign"; September; (*Latin*) *signa* (imperative), "write"; (*Italian*) *Signor*, "Mr"; slow; Society; small; South; Southern; (*cards*) spades; square; summer; sun; Sunday.

S- *abbr* = denoting attachment to sulfur (as, *S*-methyl-thiophenol).

sa *abbr* = (*Latin*) *secundum artem*, "in the standard way"; semiannual.

s.a. *abbr* = (*Latin*) *sine anno*, "without year".

s/a *abbr* = subject to acceptance *or* approval.

Sa. *abbr* = sable; Saturday.

SA *abbr* = Salvation Army; Saudi Arabia; South Africa; South America; South Australia.

SAA *abbr* = South African Airways; Systems Application Architecture (software operating system).

SAAA *abbr* (*Brit*) = Scottish Agricultural Arbiters' Association; Scottish Amateur Athletic Association.

Saab *abbr* (*Swedish*) = *Svensk Aeroplan Aktiebolag*, "Swedish Aeroplane Company" (car and aircraft manufacturer).

SAAD *abbr* = small arms ammunition depot.

Saarinen *n* 1. **Eero** (1910–61) Finnish-born American architect, whose most notable building was the TWA Terminal at Kennedy Airport, New York. 2. (**Gottlieb**) **Eliel** (1873–1950) Finnish-born American architect, whose notable works include Railroad Station, Helsinki.

Sab. *abbr* = Sabbath.

SAB *abbr* = Scientific Advisory Board; soprano, alto, bass.

Saba *see* **Sheba**[1].

Sabbatarian *n* a strict observer of the sabbath.—**Sabbatarianism** *n*.

Sabbath *n* a day of rest and worship observed on a Saturday by Jews, Sunday by Christians and Friday by Muslims.

sabbatical *n* a year's leave from a teaching post, often paid, for research or travel.

Sabbatical *adj* of, pertaining to, or resembling the Sabbath.

Sabattini *n* **Lino** (1925–) Italian metalsmith and designer, whose early work is exemplified by the 1950 teapot for W. Wolff in Germany.

Sabean *see* **Sheba**.

Sabeca *n* (*Hebrew*) probably a large harp, although translated in the Revised Version of the Bible as "sackbut."

Sabena *abbr* (*French*) = *Société Anonyme Belge d'Exploitation de la Navigation Aérienne*, "Belgian Company for the Development of Air Travel."

saber *n* a cavalry sword with a curved blade; a light fencing sword.

saber-rattling *n* (*inf*) a conspicuous display of military power or aggression.

saber-toothed tiger *n* an extinct species of large cat with long curved upper canine teeth.

sabin *n* (*phys*) a unit of acoustic absorption.

Sabin *n* **Albert Bruce** (1906–93) Polish-born American microbiologist, who developed the Sabin polio vaccine in the mid–1950s.

Sabine *n* a member of an ancient people who lived in the central Apennines in Italy.—*also adj*.

Sabin vaccine *n* an oral vaccine for poliomyelitis.

sabkha *n* (*geog*) a flat coastal belt situated between desert dunes and a lagoon or the sea.

sable *n* a carnivorous mammal of arctic regions valued for its luxuriant dark brown fur; its fur.

sabot *n* a shoe made from a single piece of wood; a shoe with a wooden sole and cloth upper.

sabotage *n* deliberate damage of machinery, or disruption of public services, by enemy agents, disgruntled employees, etc, to prevent their effective operation. * *vt* to practice sabotage on; to spoil, disrupt.

saboteur *n* a person who engages in sabotage.

sac *n* a bag-like part or cavity in a plant or animal.

saccate *adj* in the shape of a sac or pouch.

saccharide *n* a sugar.

saccharimeter *n* an instrument for measuring the concentration of sugar solutions.

saccharin *n* a non-fattening sugar substitute.

saccharine *adj* containing sugar; excessively sweet.

saccharo- *or* **sacchar-** *prefix* sugar.

sacerdotal *adj* relating to priests or the priesthood.—**sacerdotalism** *n*.—**sacerdotally** *adv*.

sachem *n* an Native American chief of certain tribes; a political boss.

sachet *n* a sealed envelope or packet; a small perfumed bag or pad used to perfume clothes.

SACHR *abbr* = Standing Advisory Commission on Human Rights.

sack[1] *n* a large bag made of coarse cloth used as a container; the contents of this; a loose-fitting dress or coat; (*baseball*) a bag serving as a base; (*sl: with* **the**) dismissal. * *vt* to put into sacks; (*sl*) to dismiss.

sack[2] *n* the plunder or destruction of a place. * *vt* to plunder or loot.

sackbut *n* a type of medieval trombone.

sackcloth *n* a coarse fabric for sacks, etc; penitential clothing.

sacking *n* the coarse cloth used for sacks; the storming and plundering of a place.

sack race *n* a jumping race in which the participants' legs and lower bodies are enclosed in sacks.

Sackville-West *n* **Vita** [**Hon. Victoria Mary**] (1892–1962) English poet and novelist, who is best known for her novels *The Edwardians* and *All Passion Spent*, and her poem *The Land*.

SACP *abbr* = South African Communist Party.

sacra *see* **sacrum**.

sacral nerves *npl* nerves that serve the legs, anal, and genital region and originate from the sacral area of the spinal column.

sacral vertebrae *npl* the five vertebrae that are fused together to form the sacrum.

sacrament *n* a religious ceremony forming an outward and visible sign of inward and spiritual grace, esp baptism and the Eucharist; the consecrated elements in the Eucharist, esp the bread; a sacred symbol or pledge.

sacramental *adj* of, pertaining to, or like a sacrament. * *n* (*RC Church*) a rite recognized as similar to a sacrament, e.g., the use of holy water.—**sacramentally** *adv*.

Sacramento *n* the capital city of California, a state of the USA.

sacred *adj* regarded as holy; consecrated to a god or God; connected with religion; worthy of or regarded with reverence, sacrosanct.

sacred cow *n* (*inf*) a person or thing regarded as above criticism.

sacrifice *n* the act of offering ceremonially to a deity; the slaughter of an animal (or person) to please a deity; the surrender of something valuable for the sake of something more important or worthy; loss without return; something sacrificed, an offering. * *vt* to slaughter or give up as a sacrifice; to give up for a higher good; to sell at a loss.—**sacrificial** *adj*.

sacrilege *n* violation of anything holy or sacred.

sacrilegious *adj* guilty of sacrilege; irreverent.—**sacrilegiously** *adv*.—**sacrilegiousness** *n*.

sacristan *n* a person in charge of the contents of a church; a sexton.

sacristy *n* (*pl* **sacristies**) a room in a church where the sacred vessels, etc are kept

sacrosanct *adj* inviolable; very holy.

sacrum *n* (*pl* **sacra**) a compound bone at the base of the spine forming the back of the pelvis.

SACS *abbr* = Senior Aircraftwoman.

sad *adj* (**sadder, saddest**) expressing grief or unhappiness; sorrowful; deplorable.—**sadly** *adv*.—**sadness** *n*.

SAD *abbr* = (*Brit*) Scottish Action on Dementia; (*Brit*) Scottish Association for the Deaf; seasonal affective disorder.

Sadat *n* [**Mohammed**] **Anwar El** (1918–81) Egyptian statesman, who succeeded Nasser as president in 1970. He signed a peace treaty with Begin (for which both were awarded the 1978 Nobel Peace Prize) and was assassinated by Islamic fundamentalists.

Sadb *or* **Saar** *or* **Sabia** *n* (*Irish Celtic myth*) turned into a fawn by a druid. Fionn mac Cumhaill came across her when he was out hunting. Sadb took on her mortal form and became Fionn's mistress or wife.

sadden *vti* to make or become sad.

saddle *n* a seat, usu of leather, for a rider on a horse, bicycle, etc; a ridge connecting two mountain peaks; a joint of mutton or venison consisting of the two loins; **in the saddle** mounted on a saddle; in control. * *vt* to put a saddle on; to burden, encumber.

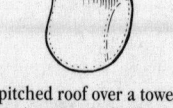

saddleback roof *n* (*archit*) a pitched roof over a tower.

saddlebag *n* a bag hung from the saddle of a horse or bicycle.

saddlebow *n* the arched front of a saddle.

saddlecloth *n* a piece of cloth placed under a horse's saddle to prevent chafing.

saddler *n* a person who makes or sells saddles, harness, etc.

saddlery *n* (*pl* **saddleries**) articles made by a saddler; the business or premises of a saddler.

saddle soap *n* an oily soap for cleaning and preserving leather.

saddletree *n* the frame of a saddle.

Sadducees *npl* (*NT*) a Jewish party comprising priests of the Temple and aristocratic families. They were conservative in politics and religion and resisted changes which might weaken their control over the Temple.

Sade *n* **Donatien Alphonse François**, Marquis de (1740–1814) French soldier and novelist, whose licentious works include the novel *Justine*.

sadhu, saddhu *n* a Hindu holy man.

SADI *abbr* = Society of Approved Driving Instructors.

sadism *n* sexual pleasure obtained from inflicting cruelty upon another; extreme cruelty.—**sadist** *n*.—**sadistic** *adj*.—**sadistically** *adv*.

Sadler's Wells *n* (*mus*) a theater in London, dating originally from the 17th century, which was famed for its opera, ballet, and dance companies. The opera company became the English National Opera in 1974.

sadomasochism *n* sexual pleasure obtained from inflicting cruelty upon oneself and receiving it from another.—**sadomasochist** *n*.—**sadomasochistic** *adj*.

s.a.e. *abbr* = self-addressed envelope; stamped addressed envelope.

SAE *abbr* = Society of Automotive Engineers.

Saebert *n* (*d*. 606) king of Essex (605–616). He was succeeded by his sons, Sexred and Saeward.

SAEF *abbr* = Stock Exchange Automatic Execution Facility.

Saelred *n* (*d*. 746) king of Essex (709–746). He was descended from Sigeberht the Good.

SAEMA *abbr* = Suspended Access Equipment Manufacturers' Association.

Saeward *n* (*d*. 616) king of Essex (reigned in 616). The son of Saebert.

SAF *abbr* = (*Brit*) Scottish Athletic Federation; Singapore Air Force; Society of American Florists; South African Foundation; Sports Aid Foundation.

SAFA *abbr* (*Brit*) = Scottish Amateur Football Association.

safari *n* (*pl* **safaris**) a journey or hunting expedition, esp in Africa.

safari jacket *n* a belted shirt-style jacket with pleated pockets.

safari suit *n* a safari jacket and matching pants or skirt made from denim or similar hard-wearing material.

Safdie *n* **Moshe** born 1938, Israeli architect, whose notable works include Yeshivat Porat Yosef Rabbinical College.

safe *adj* unhurt; out of danger; reliable; secure; involving no risk; trustworthy; giving protection; prudent; sure; incapable of doing harm. * *n* a locking metal box or compartment for valuables.—**safely** *adv*.

SAFE *abbr* = Struggle Against Financial Exploitation; Sustainable Agriculture, Food, and Environment.

safe-conduct *n* written permission for the holder to travel safely through hostile country.

safecracker *n* a person who opens and robs safes.—*also* **safe-breaker**.—**safecracking** *n*.

safe-deposit *adj* (*box, room, etc*) designed for the protective storage of valuables, deeds, etc. * *n* a building with safes for renting—*also* **safety deposit**.

safeguard *n* anything that protects against injury or danger; a proviso against foreseen risks. * *vt* to protect.

safekeeping *n* the act or process of keeping safely; protection.

safe house *n* a refuge for victims of domestic violence, sexual abuse, etc run by social welfare organizations; a clandestine place used by intelligence services, terrorists, etc as a refuge.

safe period *n* the time in a woman's menstrual cycle when she is least likely to conceive.

safe seat *n* (*Brit*) a parliamentary constituency in which the sitting MP enjoys a substantial majority and can be assured of re-election.

safe sex *n* sex in which precautions are taken to lessen the risk of catching AIDS and other sexually transmitted diseases.

safety *n* (*pl* **safeties**) freedom from danger; the state of being safe.

safety belt *n* a belt worn by a person working at a great height to prevent falling; a seatbelt.

safety curtain *n* a fireproof curtain that can be lowered to separate a theater stage from the auditorium.

safety deposit *see* **safe-deposit**.

safety glass *n* shatterproof glass.

safety lamp *n* a miner's lamp in which the flame is enclosed by a protective gauze to prevent it igniting combustible gases.

safety match *n* a match that will only ignite on a particular surface.

safety net *n* a net suspended beneath acrobats, etc; any protection against loss.

safety pin *n* a pin with a guard to cover the point.

safety razor *n* a razor with a guard that covers the blade to protect the skin from accidental cuts.

safety valve *n* an automatic valve for relieving excess pressure of steam, etc; a harmless outlet for emotion.

saffian *n* a brightly dyed leather made from the skin of goats or sheep.

safflower *n* (a red dye and oil derived from) a thistle-like plant with large orange or red flowers.

saffron *n* a crocus whose bright yellow stigmas are used as a food coloring and flavoring; an orange-yellow color.

S. Afr. *abbr* = South Africa; South African.

SAFrD *abbr* = South African Dutch (Afrikaans).

SAFU *abbr* (*Brit*) = Scottish Amateur Fencing Union.

sag *vi* (**sagging**, **sagged**) to droop downward in the middle; to sink or hang down unevenly under pressure.

SAG *abbr* = Scandinavian Society of Geneticists; Steroid Action Group.

saga *n* a long story of heroic deeds.

SAGA *abbr* = (*Brit*) Scottish Amateur Gymnastics' Association; Society of American Graphic Artists.

sagacious *adj* mentally acute, shrewd; wise.—**sagaciously** *adv*.—**sagaciousness** *n*.

sagacity *n* (*pl* **sagacities**) readiness of apprehension; discriminating intelligence; acute practical judgment.

sagamore *n* a Native American chief of certain tribes.

SAGB *abbr* (*Brit*) = Schizophrenia Association of Great Britain; Shellfish Association of Great Britain; Skibob Association of Great Britain; Spiritualist Association of Great Britain.

sage[1] *adj* wise through reflection and experience. * *n* a person of profound wisdom.—**sagely** *adv*.—**sageness** *n*.

sage[2] *n* a herb with leaves used for flavoring food; sagebrush.

sagebrush *n* a low shrub of the alkaline plains of North America.

SAGGA *abbr* = Scout and Guide Graduate Association.

sagger, saggar *n* a fireproof clay case in which porcelain is put for baking.

Sagitta *or* **The Arrow** *n* the third smallest constellation lying in the Milky Way in the northern hemisphere near to Cygnus.

Sagittarius *n* the Archer, ninth sign of the zodiac in astrology, operative November 22–December 20.—**Sagittarian** *adj, n*.

Sagittarius A *n* the overall name for a complex of radio sources associated with the center of the galaxy, with Sagittarius A being one of these sources.

sagittate *adj* (*leaf*) shaped like an arrowhead.

sago *n* (*pl* **sagos**) a type of Asian palm; its starchy pith used in puddings.

SAGTA *abbr* = School and Group Travel Association.

saguaro *n* (*pl* **saguaros**) a large cactus of North American and Mexican desert areas bearing white flowers and edible fruit.

SAH *abbr* = subarachnoid hemorrhage; Supreme Allied Headquarters.

Saha equations *npl* a set of equations derived by M N Saha, an Indian physicist, which are useful in the study of star spectra and atmospheres.

SAHC *abbr* (*Brit*) = Scottish Association of Health Councils.

Sahel *n* the narrow belt of semi-desert that stretches across Africa from Senegal to the Red Sea.

SAHGB *abbr* (*Brit*) = Society of Architectural Historians of Great Britain.

sahib *n* a form of polite address formerly used by Indians to European men.

SAHR *abbr* = Society of Army Historical Research.

SAI *abbr* = Scout Association of Ireland.

SAIC *abbr* (*Brit*) = Scottish Agricultural Improvement Council.

said *see* **say**.

Saidpur *n* a city in Bangladesh.

SAIF *abbr* = Society of Allied & Independent Funeral Directors; South African Institute of Forestry.

saiga *n* a stocky antelope of the Russian steppes.

sail *n* a piece of canvas used to catch the wind to propel or steer a vessel; sails collectively; anything like a sail; an arm of a windmill; a voyage in a sailing vessel; **to set sail** to spread the sails; to begin a voyage; **under sail** with the sails set; under way. * *vt* to navigate (a vessel); to manage (a vessel). * *vi* to be moved by sails; to travel by water; to glide or pass smoothly; to walk in a stately manner.

sailboard *n* a type of large surfboard with a sail used in windsurfing.

sailboat *n* a sailing boat.

sailcloth *n* canvas used for sails; a strong, durable fabric for clothing.

sailer *n* a sailing vessel.

sailfish *n* (*pl* **sailfish** *or* **sailfishes**) a large game fish of tropical waters with a long sail-like dorsal fin.

sailing *n* the act of sailing; the motion or direction of a ship, etc on water; a departure from a port.

sailing boat *n* a boat that is propelled by a sail or sails.

sailor *n* a person who sails; one of a ship's crew.

sailoring *n* a sailor's life.

sailplane *n* a type of light glider. * *vi* to fly a sailplane.

sain *vt* (*arch*) to make the sign of the cross on; to bless in order to protect from evil.

sainfoin *n* a Eurasian leguminous plant with pink flowers, grown for fodder.

saint *n* a person who is very patient, charitable, etc; a person who is canonized by the Roman Catholic Church; one of the blessed in heaven.—**sainthood** *n*.

Saint-Aubin *n* **Gabriel Jacques** (1724–80) French painter, who published engravings in the baroque style.

Saint Bernard *n* a breed of large dog with a reddish-brown coat, often used as a rescue dog.

St Denis *n* capital city of Réunion.

sainted *adj* canonized; holy; dead; much admired.

St George's *n* capital city of Grenada.

St Helena *n* volcanic island in the southeast Atlantic; a British colony of which the capital is Jamestown.

St Helena Pound *n* currency of St Helena.

St John's *n* capital city of Antigua and Barbuda.

St Kitts and Nevis *n* a sovereign democratic federal state with the British monarch as head of state, lying in the Leeward Islands in the eastern Caribbean Sea.

St Louis *n* a city in Senegal.

St Lucia *n* a constitutional monarchy comprising one of the Windward Islands in the eastern Caribbean.

saintly *adj* (**saintlier, saintliest**) of, like, or relating to a saint.—**saintliness** *n*.

Saint Patrick's Day *n* March 17, observed by the Irish in honor of the patron saint of Ireland.

St Paul *n* the capital city of Minnesota, a state of the USA.

St Petersburg (Sankt Peterburg) *n* a city in the Russian Federation.

Saint-Saëns *n* Charles Camille (1835–1921) French composer and pianist, whose output includes operas, symphonies, pieces for piano duet and orchestra, and many works for individual piano.

saint's day *n* a day in the church calendar which is devoted to the commemoration of a particular saint.

Saint Vitus' dance *n* the former name for **Sydenham's chorea**.

Saipan *n* capital city of Northern Mariana Islands.

Sais *n* (*Egypt*) a settlement and nome capital in the eastern Delta region of Egypt, center of the cult of Neith and the source of two of the later dynasties, the brief Twenty-fourth and the more splendid Twenty-sixth.

SAISSA *abbr* (*Brit*) = Scottish Amateur Ice Speed Skating Association.

Saite *n* (*mus*) a string.

SAJ *abbr* = Shipbuilders' Association of Japan; Sumo Association of Japan.

sake[1] *n* behalf; purpose; benefit; interest.

sake[2]**, saké, saki** *n* a Japanese alcoholic drink made from fermented rice and drunk warm.

Sakharov *n* Andrei Dimitrievich (1921–89) Russian physicist and dissident, who developed the Russian hydrogen bomb in the 1950s and subsequently campaigned for international nuclear weapons control. He won the 1975 Nobel Peace Prize.

Saki *n* the pen name of Hector Hugh **Munro**.

sal *n* (*chem*) a salt.

Sala *n* 1. **Bienvenue** (1869–1939) Spanish glassmaker, who settled in Paris in 1905. 2. **Jean** (1895–1976) Spanish glassmaker and designer, who designed vessels and chandeliers for the Cristalleries de Saint-Louis. 3. **Pierre** (1948–89) French furniture and stage designer, who founded the Marie Stuart Theatre in Paris.

salaam *n* a form of ceremonial greeting in Muslim countries. * *vti* to make a salaam (to).

salable *adj* marketable; in good demand.

salacious *adj* lustful; obscene.—**salaciously** *adv*.—**salaciousness** *n*.

salad *n* a dish, usu cold, of vegetables, fruits, meat, eggs, etc; lettuce, etc, used for this.

salad bar *n* a buffet in a restaurant at which diners choose their own salads.

salad days *npl* a time of youth and inexperience.

salad dressing *n* a cooked or uncooked sauce of oil, vinegar, spices, etc, to put on a salad.

salade niçoise *n* a salad of various ingredients, including tomatoes, hard-boiled eggs, and anchovy fillets or tuna.

Saladin *n* [Salah al-Din al-Ayyubi] (1137–93) sultan of Egypt and Syria and the leader of the Arab world during the Crusades.

Salalah *n* a city in the Sultanate of Oman.

Salam, Abdus *see* **Weinberg, Steven**.

salamander *n* any of various lizard-like amphibians; a mythical lizard-like creature that was supposedly impervious to fire.

salamanie *n* (*mus*) an oriental flute.

salami *n* a highly seasoned Italian sausage.

Salamis *n* an island of Greece, in the Gulf of Aegina, close to the shore of Attica.

salaried *adj* receiving a salary.

salary *n* (*pl* **salaries**) fixed, regular payment for non-manual work, usu paid monthly.

sala terrena *n* (*archit*) a feature of palaces in the 17th and 18th centuries in which a room opened onto a garden.

Salazar, António de Oliveira (1889–1970) Portuguese dictator. A former professor of economics, he was prime minister (1932–68), during which time he gradually assumed dictatorial powers. He retired in 1968.

salchow *n* (*ice-skating*) a jump incorporating turns in the air.

sale *n* the act of selling; the exchange of goods or services for money; the market or opportunity of selling; an auction; the disposal of goods at reduced prices; the period of this.

sale and leaseback *n* an agreement by which the owner of an asset sells it to a purchaser and immediately purchases from the new owner the right to use the asset under a lease arrangement.

sale and repurchase agreement *n* an agreement by which the owner of an asset sells it to a purchaser on condition that the original owner is allowed to repurchase the asset under certain circumstances.

sale as seen *n* a selling process in which the purchaser inspects the goods before the purchase and carries out the purchase solely on the basis of this inspection.

Salem *n* the capital city of Oregon, a state of the USA.

sale or return *n* a selling process in which a seller agrees to take back from the purchaser any goods that remain unused or unsold, usu within a certain period of time.

salep *n* (food made from) the starchy dried roots of various orchidaceous plants.

saleratus *n* sodium bicarbonate, used in cooking.

saleroom *n* a salesroom; an auction room.

sales analysis *n* a detailed survey of the information relating to a company's sales in order to evaluate the efficiency and profitability of this.

salesclerk *n* a person who sells goods in a store.

sales forecasting *n* the process by which a company tries to estimate the likely volume of future sales and the extent of future sales revenue.

sales invoice *n* a document that is sent by a seller of goods or services to the purchaser indicating the amount of payment due.

sales ledger *n* a company ledger that records the personal accounts of the company's customers.

salesman *n* (*pl* **salesmen**) a person who sells either in a given territory or in a store.—**saleswoman** *nf* (*pl* **saleswomen**).

salesmanship *n* the art or skill of selling.

salesperson *n* (*pl* **salespeople**) a salesman or saleswoman.

sales promotion *n* a process that is designed to increase the sales of a company's goods or services.

sales quota *n* a target that is set by the management of a company for its sales representatives.

sales representative *n* a person who travels to sell within a given territory.

salesroom *n* a place where goods are displayed for sale; a saleroom.

sales talk *n* talk aimed at selling something; any talk to persuade.

sales tax *n* a tax levied (usu as a percentage) on the price of an object bought by a consumer.

Salic *adj* of or pertaining to the Franks; relating to the Salic law.

salicin *n* a bitter compound obtained from the bark of willows and poplars, used in medicine.

Salic law *n* the law of the Franks excluding females from the succession to the French throne.

salient *adj* projecting outward; conspicuous; noteworthy; leaping, gushing.—**salience** *or* **saliency** *n*.—**saliently** *adv*.

Salieri *n* Antonio (1750–1825) Italian composer, conductor and teacher, who taught Beethoven, Liszt, and Schubert but is more often remembered for his jealousy of Mozart. His works include some 40 operas, and many pieces of church and piano music.

salify *vt* (**salifying, salified**) to make salty; (*chem*) to convert into a salt.—**salification** *n*.

salimeter *n* a device for measuring the amount of salt in a solution.

saline *adj* of or impregnated with salt or salts; salty. * *n* a solution of salt and water.—**salinity** *n*.

Salinger *n* J[erome] D[avid] (1919–) American novelist, whose novel *The Catcher in the Rye* (1951) achieved enormous popularity with teenage readers.

salinization *n* the process whereby soils tend to become salty when there is a high rate of evaporation from the surface.

saliva *n* the liquid secreted by glands in the mouth that aids digestion.—**salivary** *adj*.

salivary glands *npl* three pairs of glands that produce saliva.

salivate *vi* to secrete saliva, esp excessively.—**salivation** *n*.

Salk *n* Jonas Edward (1914–95) American physician and microbiologist, who developed the Salk vaccine against polio.

Salk vaccine *n* a vaccine against poliomyelitis developed in 1954 by J E Salk. It is administered by injection.

sallenders *npl* an eczematous rash on a horse's hock.

sallet *n* a light helmet of the 15th century.

sallow *adj* (*complexion*) of an unhealthy yellow color, a pale brown color.—**sallowness** *n*.

sally *n* (*pl* **sallies**) a sudden attack; an outburst; a lively remark, quip. * *vi* (**sallying, sallied**) to make a sally; to go (forth).

sally-port *n* (*archit*) the entrance of a subterranean passage which joins parts of a castle or palace.

salmagundi *n* a mixed dish of chopped meat, anchovies, eggs, vegetables, etc; a miscellany.

salmi *n* (*pl* **salmis**) a casserole of game birds in a rich wine sauce.

salmon *n* (*pl* **salmon** *or* **salmons**) a large silvery edible fish that lives in salt water and spawns in fresh water; salmon pink.

salmonella *n* (*pl* **salmonellae** *or* **salmonella** *or* **salmonellas**) any of a genus of bacteria that causes food poisoning and diseases of the genital tract.

salmon ladder *n* a series of steps (e.g., in a waterfall or dam) to allow salmon to swim upstream to their breeding grounds.

salmon of knowledge *n* (*Irish and Welsh Celtic myth*) the salmon was a symbol of wisdom and knowledge, supposed to have acquired its gift of knowledge from having eaten the nuts of hazel trees that grew at the bottom of the sea. Finegas the druid caught it and gave it to Fionn mac Cumhaill to cook. While he was cooking the fish, Fionn burnt his thumb on the fish and put it into his mouth to cool down and instantly received the gift of knowledge and wisdom.

salmon-pink *adj* a yellowish-pink color.

salmon trout *n* a large trout resembling a salmon.

Salome *n* (*Bible*) 1. the daughter of Herodias, who danced before Herod, who promised to give her whatever she asked; at her mother's suggestion Salome asked for the head of John the Baptist. *See also* **Herodias**, **John the Baptist**. 2. a woman who witnessed the Crucifixion in the company of other women from Galilee and accompanied them to the tomb early on the morning of the Resurrection.

Salomon *n* Johann Peter (1745–1815) German-born violinist and composer, who settled in England. He became an influential advocate of Haydn and Mozart. He was a notable concert promoter.

salon *n* a large reception hall or drawing room for receiving guests; the shop of a hairdresser, beautician, or couturier; an art gallery.

saloon n a large reception room; a large cabin for the social use of a ship's passengers; a four-seater car with a boot; a place where alcoholic drinks are sold and consumed.

saloon bar n a comfortably furnished bar.

salopettes npl thick quilted pants with shoulder straps, worn for skiing.

Saloth Sar see **Pol Pot**.

salpingectomy n (pl **salpingectomies**) the surgical excision of a Fallopian tube, the removal of both of which produces sterilization.

salpingitis n inflammation of a Fallopian tube by bacterial infection.

salpingostomy n (pl **salpingostomies**) the clearing of a blocked Fallopian tube in which the blocked part is removed surgically.

SALRC abbr = Society for Assistance to Ladies in Reduced Circumstances.

salsa n (the music for) a type of Puerto Rican dance; a spicy tomato sauce.

salsify n (pl **salsifies**) a purple-flowered plant with an edible root.

salt n a white crystalline substance (sodium chloride) used as a seasoning or preservative; piquancy, wit; (chem) a compound of an acid and a base; (pl) mineral salt as an aperient. * adj containing or tasting of salt; preserved with salt; pungent. * vt to flavor, pickle, or sprinkle with salt; to give flavor or piquancy to (as a story); (with away) to hoard; to keep for the future.

SALT abbr = (Brit) Scottish Association for Language Teaching; Strategic Arms Limitation Talks or Treaty.

Salta n a city in Argentina.

saltando n (mus) leaping (an instruction to the string player to bounce the bow lightly off the string). — also **sautille**.

saltarello n (mus) a festive Italian folk dance in 3/4 or 6/8 time.

saltation n the process of moving particles such as sand by water or wind that are too heavy to remain in suspension.

saltbush n a shrub-like plant which provides grazing in dry regions.

salt cellar n a vessel for salt at the table; a saltshaker.

salt dome n a plug-shaped body, either circular or elongated, that is formed by the upward movement of lighter evaporitic sediments into the overlying, denser rocks.

salt flat n the flat, dried-out bed of a former salt lake.

saltine n a thin crisp cracker sprinkled with salt.

saltire n an X-shaped cross dividing a shield, flag, etc, into four compartments.

salt lake n a lake containing water that has become very salty because of a high rate of evaporation.

Salt Lake City n the capital city of Utah, a state of the USA.

salt lick n an area where animals go to lick salt residue; a block of salt for animals to lick.

salt marsh n an area regularly flooded by seawater.

Salto n a city in Uruguay.

saltpan n a hollow or depression where salt is deposited by evaporating seawater.

saltpeter n a white powder (potassium nitrate) used in making gunpowder, etc.

Salt Sea n Dead Sea.

saltshaker n a container for salt with a perforated top.

saltwater adj of or living in salt water or the sea.

salty adj (**saltier, saltiest**) of, containing, or tasting of salt; witty, earthy, coarse.

salubrious adj health-giving; wholesome.—**salubriously** adv.—**salubriousness** n.

saluki n a breed of tall, slender hounds with long, silky coats.

salutary adj beneficial, wholesome.—**salutarily** adv.—**salutariness** n.

salutation n a greeting; the words used in it.

salute n a gesture of respect or greeting; (mil) a motion of the right hand to the head, or to a rifle; a discharge of guns, etc, as a military mark of honor. * vti to make a salute (to); to greet; to kiss; to praise or honor.

salvable adj able to be salvaged.

Salvador n a city in Brazil.

salvage n the rescuing of a ship or property from loss at sea, by fire, etc; the reward paid for this; the thing salvaged; waste material intended for further use. * vt to save from loss or danger.—**salvageable** adj.—**salvager** n.

salvation n the act of saving or the state of being saved; in Christianity, the deliverance from evil; a means of preservation.—**salvational** adj.

Salvation Army n an international religious and charitable group organized on military lines, founded by William Booth in 1865.—**Salvationist** n.

Salvatore n Carlo see **Cherubini, (Maria) Luigi**.

salve[1] n a healing ointment or balm; a soothing influence. * vt to apply ointment to; to smooth over; to soothe.

salve[2] vt to salvage; (arch) to save.

salver n a small tray.

salvia n any of a genus of plants or small shrubs with red or purple flowers.

Salvin n Anthony (b. 1799) English architect, whose notable works include Peckforton Castle, Cheshire.

salvo[1] n (**salvoes, salvos**) a firing of several guns or missiles simultaneously; a sudden burst; a spirited verbal attack.

salvo[2] n (pl **salvos**) an exception or reservation.

sal volatile n a solution of ammonium carbonate in alcohol used as a remedy for faintness.

salvor n a person or vessel effecting a salvage at sea.

Salzburg n a city in Austria.

Salzburg Festival n an annual festival of music and drama, established in 1920 to celebrate the works of Mozart, who was born in Salzburg. Today many other composers' works are also performed.

SAm abbr = South America or American.

S. Am. or **S. Amer.** abbr = South America or American.

SAM abbr = (Brit) Scottish AIDS Monitor; (Brit) Scottish Airline Museum; (Brit) Scottish Association for Metals; South Australian Museum; surface-to-air missile.

SAMA abbr = (Brit) Scottish Agricultural Machinery Association; (Brit) Scottish Amateur Music Association; Shock Absorber Manufacturers' Association; South African Museums' Association.

samara n a dry winged single-seeded fruit produced by the ash, elm, etc.

Samara n a city in the Russian Federation.

Samaria n (Bible) capital of the northern kingdom of Israel, which fell in 721 BC to the Assyrians; 27,290 Israelites were deported; in New Testament times the city was rebuilt by Herod the Great and renamed Sebaste.

Samaritan n a native or inhabitant of Samaria; a compassionate person; a Good Samaritan; a member of a voluntary organization that helps people in distress or despair.

samarium n a silvery metallic element used in lasers and alloys. * symbol Sm.

Samarkand n a city in Uzbekistan.

SAMB abbr (Brit) = Scottish Association of Master Bakers; Scottish Association of Master Blacksmiths.

samba n a Brazilian dance of African origin; the music for this. * vi to dance the samba.

sambaquí n (archeo) shell middens of very different ages found along the coast of Brazil.

same adj identical; exactly similar; unchanged; uniform, monotonous; previously mentioned. * pron the same person or thing. * adv in like manner.

sameness n the state of being the same; monotony.

SAMH abbr (Brit) = Scottish Association for Mental Health.

Samhain n celebrated on 1 November and on the night that preceded it, one of the four major Celtic festivals. In terms of time the equivalent of the modern Halloween.

Samhair n (Irish Celtic myth) the daughter of Fionn mac Cumhaill. She was the wife of Cormac Cas, who is recorded as living in the third century AD.

SAMHSA abbr = Substance Abuse and Mental Health Services Administration

Samian n a native or inhabitant of the Aegean island of Samos in Greece. * adj of or pertaining to Samos or its people.

Samian ware n a type of red or black pottery from Samos.

samisen n a Japanese guitar-like instrument with three strings.

samite n a medieval heavy silken fabric.

samizdat n in the former Soviet Union, a system for the clandestine printing and distribution of banned literature.

Sammartini (San Martini) n **Giovanni Battista** (c. 1698–1775) Italian composer and organist, who may have instructed Gluck. He composed a large body of work, including operas, symphonies, violin concertos, and over 200 chamber works. His brother, **Giuseppe**, was also a famous composer of the time.

Samoan n a native or inhabitant of Samoa, a group of islands in the South Pacific; the Polynesian language of Samoa.* adj of or pertaining to Samoa, its people, or language.

Samos n a mountainous Greek island in the Aegean Sea, near the coast of Turkey.— **Samian** adj.

samosa n (pl **samosas** or **samosa**) an Indian savory pasty with a spicy meat or vegetable filling.

Samothrace n a mountainous Greek island in the north of the Aegean Sea.

samovar n a metal urn with an internal element used for boiling water for tea, esp in Russia.

Samoyed n a member of a people of the northern Urals; the language of these people; a breed of sled-dog with a thick creamy coat and a tightly curled tail.— **Samoyedic** adj.

sampan n a small flat-bottomed Chinese river boat.

samphire n a Eurasian coastal rock plant with edible fleshy leaves.

sample n a specimen; a small part representative of the whole; an instance. * vt (food, drink) to taste a small quantity of; to test by taking a sample.

sampler n a person who takes samples; something containing a representative selection, such as a CD or book; an assortment; a piece of ornamental embroidery showing different stitches and patterns as an example of skill.

sampling n (mus industry) the practice of extracting phrases from several recorded songs and putting them together electronically to make a new one; (archeo) investigation of part of a site, or one of a number of sites, then making generalizations and predictions from the information gathered.

Sampras n **Pete** (1971–) American tennis player and winner of many major championships.

SAMSA abbr = Silica and Moulding Sands Association.

Samson n (OT) the first Israelite leader to do battle against the invading Philistines; a popular hero who used his strength to discomfort the Philistines but was betrayed by a woman. See also **Manoah**, **Nazarites**.

sämtlich n (mus) complete, as in sämtliche Werke (complete works).

Samuel n (OT) Hebrew judge and prophet, who anointed Saul to "reign over the people of the Lord" and save them from their enemies; after Saul's disobedience, Samuel sought out and anointed David as the future king of Israel. See also **Hannah**.

Samuel 1 and 2 n (Bible) two books of the Old Testament that tell of the beginning of kingship in Israel, the chief characters being Samuel, Saul, and David.

samurai n (pl **samurai**) a member of an ancient Japanese warrior caste.

samurai bond n a financial bond issued in yen by a non-Japanese company.

SAN abbr = Science Association of Nigeria; Society for Ancient Numismatists.

-san *n suffix* a Japanese title of respect similar to Mr, Mrs, etc.

San'a *n* capital city of Yemen.

SANA *abbr* (*Brit*) = Scottish Anglers' National Association.

sanatorium *see* **sanitarium**.

San. C. *abbr* = Sanitary Corps.

San Carlo *n* **Teatro di** one of Italy's leading opera houses, in Naples. It was built in 1737.

sancta *see* **sanctum**.

sanctified *adj* hallowed; consecrated; sanctimonious.

sanctify *vt* (**sanctifying, sanctified**) to make holy; to purify from sin or evil; (*the Church*) to give official approval.—**sanctification** *n*.—**sanctifier** *n*.

sanctimonious *adj* pretending to be holy; hypocritically pious or righteous.—**sanctimoniously** *adv*.—**sanctimoniousness** *n*.

sanctimony *n* self-righteousness; hypocrisy.

sanction *n* express permission, authorization; a binding influence; a penalty by which a law is enforced, esp a prohibition on trade with a country that has violated international law. * *vt* to permit; to give authority.—**sanctionable** *adj*.

sanctity *n* (*pl* **sanctities**) the condition of being holy or sacred; inviolability.

sanctuary *n* (*pl* **sanctuaries**) a sacred place; the part of a church around the altar; a place where one is free from arrest or violence, an asylum; a refuge; an animal reserve.

sanctum *n* (*pl* **sanctums** *or* **sancta**) a holy place; a private room where one is not to be disturbed.

Sanctus *n* (*Christianity*) the hymn "Holy, holy, holy" used in communion; an orchestral setting of this.

sand *n* very fine rock particles; (*pl*) a desert; a sandy beach. * *vt* to smooth or polish with sand or sandpaper; to sprinkle with sand. * *adj* reddish-yellow.

SAND *abbr* (*Brit*) = Scotland Against Nuclear Dumping.

sandal[1] *n* a shoe consisting of a sole strapped to the foot; a low slipper or shoe.—**sandaled** *adj*.

sandal[2] *n* sandalwood.

sandalwood *n* the yellow, scented wood of an Asian tree; the tree.

sandbag *n* a bag of sand used for ballast or to protect against floodwater. * *vt* (**sandbagging, sandbagged**) to protect by laying sandbags; to hit with a sandbag; (*inf*) to coerce; (*sl*) to deceive.—**sandbagger** *n*.

sandbag tactics *npl* tactics adopted by the management of a company that is the unwilling target of a takeover bid.

sandbank *n* a sand bar; a large deposit of sand forming a hill or mound.

sand bar *n* a ridge of sand built up in a river, a lake, or coastal waters by currents.

sandblast *vt* to clean (a building) by blasting with sand at high velocity.—*also n*.

sand box *n* a small enclosure filled with sand for children to play in.—*also* **sandpit**.

Sandburg *n* **Carl** (1878–1967) American poet, and a Pulitzer Prize winner (1950) for *Complete Poems*.

s. and c. *abbr* = shipper and carrier; (*paper*) sized and calendered.

sand castle *n* a model of a castle molded from damp sand, as made on the beach by children.

s & d *abbr* = search and destroy; song and dance.

sand dollar *n* any of various flat circular sea urchins that live in shallow water.

sand dune *n* a hill that is formed by wind-blown sand.

sander *n* a power-driven tool for sanding wood or other surfaces.

sanderling *n* a small wading bird.

s & f *abbr* = stock and fixtures.

s & fa *abbr* = shipping and forwarding agents.

sandfly fever *n* a short-lived viral infection occurring in the tropics and subtropics during the warmer months, that is passed to humans through the bite of a sandfly.—*also* **bartonellosis**.

sandglass *n* an instrument that measures time by the running of sand through a narrow aperture.

s & h *abbr* = shipping and handling.

San Diego *n* a city in the United States of America (USA).

S & L *abbr* = savings and loan association.

s & m *abbr* = sausages and mash; stock and machinery.

S & M *abbr* = sadomasochism.

sandman *n* (*pl* **sandmen**) (*folklore*) an imaginary being who sends children to sleep by sprinkling sand in their eyes.

sand martin *n* a small European songbird that nests in holes in sandy riverbanks, etc.

Sandor *n* **Gyorgy** (1912–) Hungarian-born pianist, who has lived in the USA since 1939. He specializes in performing works by Bartok and Prokofiev.

sand painting *n* a ceremonial design made by the Navaho and the Pueblo using various types of colored sand.

sandpaper *n* a paper coated on one side with sand or another abrasive, used to smooth or polish. * *vt* to rub with sandpaper.

sandpiper *n* any of numerous small wading birds.

sandpit *see* **sand box**.

SANDS *abbr* = Stillbirth and Neonatal Death Society.

s. and s. c. *abbr* = sized and supercalendered (*paper*).

sandstone *n* a sedimentary rock of compacted sand.

sandstorm *n* a windstorm in a desert carrying clouds of sand.

s & t *abbr* = supply and transport.

S and T *abbr* = signaling and telecommunications.

S & TA *abbr* = Salmon and Trout Association.

sand trap *n* (*golf*) a pit of sand forming an obstacle on a golf course, a bunker.

sand wedge n (*golf*) a club for hitting the ball out of a sand trap.

sandwich *n* two slices of bread with meat, cheese, or other filling between; anything in a sandwich-like arrangement. * *vt* to place between two things or two layers; to make such a place for.

sandwich board *n* two hinged boards hanging from the shoulders, one in front and one at the back, carried by a sandwich man.

sandwich man *n* a person who advertizes by wearing a sandwich board.

sandy *adj* (**sandier, sandiest**) of, like, or sprinkled with sand; yellowish-gray.—**sandiness** *n*.

sane *adj* mentally sound, not mad; reasonable, sensible.—**sanely** *adv*.—**saneness** *n*.

SANE *abbr* = Schizophrenia: A National Emergency.

San Fernando *n* town in Trinidad and Tobago.

Sanforized *adj* (*trademark*) (*fabrics*) preshrunk by a patented industrial process.—**Sanforize** *vt*.

SANFP *abbr* (*Brit*) = Scottish Association for Natural Family Planning.

San Fran. *abbr* = San Francisco.

San Francisco *n* a city in the United States of America (USA).

sang *see* **sing**.

Sangallo *n* 1. **Antonio da** (1483–1546) Italian architect, whose notable works include Palazzo Farnese, Rome. 2. **Giuliano da** (*b*. 1445) Italian architect, whose notable works include Palazzo Gondi, Florence.

Sanger, Frederick *n* (1918–) English biochemist, who was awarded two Nobel Prizes for chemistry (1958, 1980), the first for his work on protein structure and the sequence of amino acids, the second for his work on the structure of nucleic acids.

sangfroid *n* coolness in danger, imperturbability.

Sangreal *n* the Holy Grail.

sangria *n* a Spanish drink made with red wine, orange juice, and fresh fruit laced with brandy.

sanguinary *adj* accompanied by bloodshed; bloodthirsty.—**sanguinarily** *adv*.

sanguine *adj* confident, hopeful; blood-red; (*complexion*) ruddy.—**sanguineness** *n*.

sanguinely *adv* confidently, hopefully.

sanguineous *adj* of or relating to blood; (*med*) containing blood; (*med*) covered or stained with blood; full-blooded; blood-red; sanguinary; sanguine.

Sanhedrin *n* (*Bible*) a Hebrew word for Council.

sanies *n* a watery mixture of blood and pus discharged from a sore or wound.—**sanious** *adj*.

sanitarian *adj* hygienic. * *n* a specialist in matters of public health.

sanitarium *n* (*pl* **sanitariums** *or* **sanitaria**) an establishment for the treatment of convalescents or the chronically ill.—*also* **sanatorium**.

sanitary *adj* relating to the promotion and protection of health; relating to the supply of water, drainage, and sewage disposal; hygienic.—**sanitarily** *adv*.—**sanitariness** *n*.

sanitary cordon *n* a cordon sanitaire.

sanitary engineering *n* the design, construction, and installation of water and sewage systems.—**sanitary engineer** *n*.

sanitary napkin *n* an absorbent pad worn externally during menstruation.

sanitation *n* the science and practice of achieving hygienic conditions; drainage and disposal of sewage.

sanitize *vt* to clean or sterilize; to make (language, etc) more respectable or acceptable.

sanity *n* the condition of being sane; mental health; common sense.

San José *n* capital city of Costa Rica.

San Juan *n* the capital city of Puerto Rico, an autonomous commonwealth of the USA.

sank *see* **sink**.

Sanka *n* (*trademark*) a decaffeinated coffee.

San Marino *n* a tiny landlocked republic in central Italy, lying in the eastern foothills of the Apennine Mountains; capital city of San Marino.

Sanmicheli *n* **Michele** (*b*. 1484) Italian architect, whose notable works include Porta Palio, Verona.

San Miguel *n* a city in El Salvador.

sannup *n* a Native American warrior, a brave.

San Pedro de Macoris *n* a city in the Dominican Republic.

San Pedro Sula *n* a city in Honduras.

sanrs *abbr* = subject to approval - no risks.

sans *prep* without.

Sans. *abbr* = Sanskrit.

San Salvador *n* capital city of El Salvador.

sansculotte *n* in the French Revolution, a man without breeches, a term of contempt applied to a revolutionary who wore pantaloons instead of knee breeches; any revolutionary.

sans doute *adv* (*French*) doubtless; certainly.

Sansk. *abbr* = Sanskrit.

Sanskrit *n* the ancient language used in Indian and Hindu sacred literature.—**Sanskrit** *adj*.—**Sanskritic** *adj*.

sans-serif *or* **sanserif** *n* (*print, comput*) a character or typeface with no serifs.—*also adj*.

sans souci *adj* (*French*) free from care.

Santa *n* Santa Claus. * *adj* sainted, holy.

Santa Ana *n* a city in El Salvador.

Santa Clara *n* a city in Cuba.

Santa Claus *n* a legendary fat, white-bearded old man who brings presents to children at Christmas.—*also* **Father Christmas**.

Santa Cruz *n* a city in Bolivia.

Santa Fe *n* the capital city of New Mexico, a state of the USA.

Santayana *n* **George** (1863–1952) Spanish-born American philosopher, critic, and poet, whose works include *The Life of Reason* (1905–1906) and *Realms of Being* (1927–40).

Santiago[1] *n* capital city of Chile.

Santiago[2] *n* a city in the Dominican Republic.

Santiago de Cuba *n* a city in Cuba.

santim *see* **lats**.

Santo Domingo *n* capital city of the Dominican Republic.

São Paulo *n* a city in Brazil.

SAO star catalog *n* the Smithsonian Astrophysical Observatory Star Catalog, listing 259,000 stars, which was published in 1966.

São Tomé *n* capital city of São Tomé and Príncipe.

São Tomé and Príncipe *n* a republic comprising volcanic islands that lie off the west coast of Africa.

sap[1] *n* the vital juice of plants; energy and health; (*inf*) a fool. * *vt* (**sapping, sapped**) to drain of sap; to exhaust the energy of.

sap[2] *n* a narrow or covered siege trench; the digging of this, undermining. * *vti* (**sapping, sapped**) to attack by or dig a sap; to undermine insidiously.

s.a.p. *abbr* = semi-armor-piercing; soon as possible.

s. ap. *abbr* (*apothecaries' weight*) = scruple.

SAPC *abbr* (*Brit*) = Scottish Accident Prevention Council.

SAPCT *abbr* (*Brit*) = Scottish Association of Painting Craft Teachers.

saphead *n* (*sl*) a fool, a stupid person.

sapid *adj* having a pleasing flavor; agreeable.—**sapidity** *n*.

sapient *adj* (*often ironical*) wise, discerning.—**sapience** *n*.—**sapiently** *adv*.

Sapir, Edward *see* **Whorf, Benjamin Lee**.

sapling *n* a young tree; a youth.

saponification *n* (*chem*) a process in which esters are hydrolyzed by the action of acids, alkalis, boiling with water, or superheated steam.

saponify *vt* (**saponifying, saponified**) (*chem*) to convert (fat, oil, etc) into soap by combination with an alkali. * *vi* to undergo this process.—**saponification** *n*.—**saponifier** *n*.

sapor *n* taste, flavor.

sapper *n* one who or that which saps; a soldier who lays, detects, or disarms mines.

Sapper *n* **Richard** (1932–) German industrial designer, best known for his high-technology products.

sapphire *n* a transparent blue precious stone; a deep pure blue.—*also adj*.

Sappho *n* (*b. c.* 650 BC) Greek poet, who was regarded by the Greeks as one of the greatest of all lyric poets.

Sapporo *n* a city in Japan.

sapro- *or* **sapr-** *prefix* dead or decaying matter.

Saprogenic *or* **saprogenous** *adj* producing or caused by putrefaction.

saprolite *n* weathered rock in its place of origin, best formed under tropical conditions.

saprophagous *adj* feeding on decaying matter.

saprophyte *n* a plant or fungus that grows on dead organic matter.—**saprophytic** *adj*.

saprotroph *n* (*biol*) an organism that obtains its nutrition from dead and decaying organic matter.

SAPT *abbr* (*Brit*) = Scottish Association for Public Transport.

Saqqara *n* (*Egypt*) a major funerary site of the Old Kingdom of Egypt, at the southern end of the vast funerary district that extends from Giza, on the west bank of the Nile, south of Cairo.

sar *abbr* = search and rescue.

Sar. *abbr* = Sardinia; Sardinian.

SAR *abbr* = Sons of the American Revolution; South African Railways; synthetic aperture radar.

SARA *abbr* = (*Brit*) Scottish Amateur Rowing Association; (*Brit*) Scottish Anti-Racist Alliance; Society of American Registered Architects.

sarabande *n* (*mus*) a slow dance in 3/2 or 3/4 time, which came to Italy from Spain.

Saracen *n* a member of a nomadic people of the Syrian desert; a Muslim at the time of the Crusades. * *adj* of or pertaining to Saracens.—**Saracenic** *adj*.

Sarah *n* (*OT*) the wife of Abraham, who grew old but was still childless. An angel told Abraham that Sarah would bear a son; she overheard this and laughed, but the prophesy came true. Her son was called Isaac.

Sarai *n* (*OT*) alternative form of **Sarah**.

Sarajevo *n* capital city of Bosnia-Herzegovina.

sarcasm *n* a scornful or ironic remark; the use of this.—**sarcastic** *adj*.—**sarcastically** *adv*.

sarco- *or* **sarc-** *prefix* flesh.

sarcoma *n* (*pl* **sarcomas** *or* **sarcomata**) a malignant tumor of connective tissue.—**sarcomatous** *adj*.

sarcophagus *n* (*pl* **sarcophagi** *or* **sarcophaguses**) a large stone coffin or tomb; (*Egypt*) the chest, made of stone or wood and equipped with a lid, in which the coffin of a mummified corpse was laid.

sard *n* an orange-red variety of chalcedony.

SARDA *abbr* = Search and Rescue Dog Association.

sardine *n* (*pl* **sardines** *or* **sardine**) a small, edible seafish.

sardonic *adj* (*smile, etc*) derisive, mocking, maliciously jocular.—**sardonically** *adv*.

sardonyx *n* an onyx with alternate layers of white chalcedony and orange sard.

saree *see* **sari**.

sargasso *n* (*pl* **sargassos**) a large mass of floating sargassum.

sargassum *n* any of a genus of tropical seaweed with air bladders that form to float in large masses.

sarge *n* (*sl*) sergeant.

Sargent *n* 1. **John Singer** (1856–1925) American painter, particularly noted for his portraits. 2. **Sir (Harold) Malcolm (Watts)** (1895–1967) English conductor, who began as a pianist and composer. He will always be remembered for his performances as conductor-in-chief of the London promenade concerts for 16 years.

Sarh *n* a city in Chad.

sari, saree *n* a Hindu woman's principal garment, consisting of a long piece of cloth wrapped around the waist and across the shoulder.

sark *n* (*Scot*) a shirt.

SARM *abbr* (*Brit*) = Scottish Anti-Racist Movement.

saroh *n* (*mus*) an Indian bow instrument.

sarong *n* a long strip of cloth wrapped around the lower body, worn esp in the Malay archipelago and the Pacific Islands.

Sarpedon *n* (*Greek myth*) a brother of Minos, king of Crete, who became king of the Lycians, and lived for three generations.

SARS *abbr* = Safety and Reliability Society; (*Brit*) Scots Ancestry Research Society.

sarsaparilla *n* any of various tropical American trailing plants; the dried roots of these used as a flavoring and (formerly) in medicine; a soft drink flavored with these roots.

SARSAT *abbr* = Search and Rescue Satellite (for maritime disasters).

sarsens *npl* sandstone blocks of Tertiary age which were used by the builders of Stonehenge, Avebury and a number of Megalithic chamber tombs.

sartorial *adj* of or relating to the making of men's clothing.—**sartorially** *adv*.

sartorius *n* (*pl* **sartorii**) a muscle that helps flex the knee.

Sartre *n* **Jean-Paul** (1905–80) French philosopher, novelist, and dramatist, whose attempts at reconciling existentialist philosophy with Marxism are now of historical interest. His novels include *Nausea* (1938).

SAS *abbr* = (*Brit*) Scottish Australian Society; (*Italian*) *Società in accomandita semplice*, "Limited"; (*Latin*) *Societatis Antiquariorum Socius*, "Fellow of the Society of Antiquaries"; Society for Armenian Studies; Special Air Service; Surfers Against Sewage.

SASA *abbr* = (*Brit*) Scottish Amateur Snooker Association; (*Brit*) Scottish Amateur Swimming Association; South African Sugar Association.

SASE *abbr* = self-addressed stamped envelope.

SASF *abbr* = Salvation Army Students' Fellowship.

sash[1] *n* a band of satin or ribbon worn around the waist or over the shoulder, often as a badge of honor.

sash[2] *n* a frame for holding the glass of a window, esp one that slides vertically.

sashay *n* (*inf*) to walk in a casual manner, saunter; to swagger.

sash cord *n* a cord used to attach a sash weight to a sash.

sashimi *n* a Japanese dish of thin strips of raw fish.

sash weight *n* a weight used to balance a sliding sash in an open position.

sash window *n* a window with sliding sashes.

Sask. *abbr* = Saskatchewan.

SASLI *abbr* (*Brit*) = Scottish Association of Sign Language Interpreters for the Deaf.

SASMA *abbr* = Silk and Art Silks Mills Association (India).

SASO *abbr* = Senior Air Staff Officer.

SASR *abbr* = Special Air Service Regiment.

sass *n* (*inf*) rudeness, impudence. * *vt* to talk rudely or impudently to.

SASS *abbr* = (*Brit*) Scottish Agricultural Statistics Service; Sir Arthur Sullivan Society.

sassafras *n* a North American tree of the laurel family; the aromatic dried root of this, used as a flavoring.

Sassanians *npl* a dynasty established in Persia *c.* 220 AD after the end of Parthian rule.

Sassenach *n* (*Scot, Irish*) an English person.

Sassoon *n* **Siegfried [Lorraine]** (1886–1967) English poet and novelist, whose work established him as one of the major poets of World War I. His trilogy of novels, *Memoirs of a Fox-Hunting Man*, *Memoirs of an Infantry Officer*, and *Sherston's Progress*, describes the progress of a young man from sports-loving boyhood through the horrors of trench warfare.

sassy *adj* (**sassier, sassiest**) (*sl*) rude; impertinent.

SASV *abbr* (*Brit*) = Scottish Association for the Speaking of Verse.

sat *see* **sit**.

Sat *abbr* = Saturday; Saturn.

SAt *abbr* = South Atlantic.

SAT *abbr* = Senior Member of the Association of Accounting Technicians; South Australia Time; Standard Assessment Task.

Satan *n* the devil, the adversary of God.

satang *n* a monetary unit of Thailand, equal to one hundredth of a baht.

satanic *or* **satanical** *adj* of or relating to Satan, devilish; marked by viciousness or cruelty.—**satanically** *adv*.

Satanism *n* the worship of Satan; the perversion of Christian ceremonial forms associated with this.—**Satanist** *n*.

satay, saté *n* an Indonesian dish of cubed chicken, beef, etc served with a piquant peanut sauce.

SATB *abbr* = soprano, alto, tenor, bass.

SATC *abbr* = Students' Army Training Corps.

satchel *n* a bag with shoulder straps for carrying school books, etc.

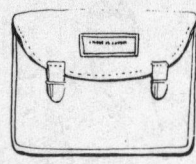

SATCO *abbr* = signal automatic air-traffic-control system.

sate *vt* to satisfy to repletion, to satiate.

sateen *n* a closely woven fabric with a glossy surface made in imitation of satin.

satellite *n* a planet orbiting another; a man-made object orbiting the earth, moon, etc, to gather scientific information or for communication; a nation economically dependent on a more powerful one.

satellite broadcasting *or* **satellite television** *n* the transmission of television programs via an orbiting satellite to subscribers in possession of a receiving satellite-dish antenna.

satellite galaxy *n* a small galaxy that orbits a large massive one.

satellite town *n* a town that relies upon a larger center nearby for facilities such as hospitals.

sati *see* **suttee**.

satiable *adj* able to be satiated or sated.—**satiability** *n*.—**satiably** *adv*.

satiate *vt* to provide with more than enough so as to weary or disgust; to gorge.—**satiation** *n*.

Satie *n* Erik [Alfred Leslie] (1866–1925) French composer.

satiety *n* the state of being sated; a feeling of having had too much.

satin *n* a fabric of woven silk with a smooth, shiny surface on one side. * *adj* of or resembling satin.

satinwood *n* a smooth, yellowish-brown hard wood; a tree that yields such wood.

satiny *adj* smooth and lustrous, like satin.

SATIPS *abbr* = Society of Assistant Teachers in Preparatory Schools.

satire *n* a literary work in which folly or evil in people's behavior are held up to ridicule; trenchant wit, sarcasm.—**satirical** *adj*.—**satirically** *adv*.

satirist *n* a writer of satires.

satirize *vt* to attack with satire.—**satirizer** *n*.

satisfaction *n* the act of satisfying or the condition of being satisfied; that which satisfies; comfort; atonement, reparation.

satisfactory *adj* giving satisfaction; adequate; acceptable; convincing.—**satisfactorily** *adv*.—**satisfactoriness** *n*.

satisfy *vi* (**satisfying, satisfied**) to be enough for; to fulfill the needs or desires of. * *vt* to give enough to; (*hunger, desire etc*) to appease; to please; to gratify; to comply with; (*creditor*) to discharge, to pay in full; to convince; to make reparation to; (*guilt, etc*) to atone for.

Sato Eisaku *n* (1901–75) Japanese Liberal-Democrat prime minister (1964–72). He was awarded the 1974 Nobel Peace Prize for his opposition to the nuclear-arms race.

satori *n* (*Zen Buddhism*) a state of intuitive enlightenment.

SATRA *abbr* = Shoe and Allied Trades Research Organization.

satrap *n* the governor of an administrative province of the Achemenid empire.

SATRO *abbr* = Science and Technology Regional Organization.

satsuma *n* a loose-skinned, seedless, small orange; (*with cap*) a glazed yellow Japanese pottery.

saturate *vt* to soak thoroughly; to fill completely.—**saturator** *n*.

saturated *adj* (*chem*) absorbing the maximum amount possible of a substance; pure in color.

saturated compound *n* (*chem*) a group of organic compounds with no double or triple bonds.

saturated solution *n* (*chem*) a solution of a substance (solute) that exists in equilibrium with excess solute present.

saturation *n* the act of saturating or the condition of being saturated; the supplying of a market with all the goods it will absorb; an overwhelming concentration of military power.

saturation point *n* the point at which no more can be absorbed or accepted.

Saturday *n* the seventh and last day of the week.

Saturn *n* (*Roman myth*) the god of agriculture; (*astron*) the second largest planet in the solar system, with three rings revolving about it.—**Saturnian** *adj*.

Saturnalia *n* (*pl* **Saturnalias** *or* **Saturnalia**) in ancient Rome, a festival held in December in honor of Saturn; (*without cap*) a wild, unrestrained celebration.—**Saturnalian** *n*.

saturnine *adj* sullen, morose.—**saturninely** *adv*.

satyagraha *n* the principle and practice of passive resistance as adopted by Mahatma Gandhi in opposition to British colonial rule in India.

satyr *n* (*Greek myth*) a woodland god in human form but with goat's ears, tail, and legs; a man with strong sexual appetites; a man with satyriasis.—**satyric** *adj*.

satyriasis *n* excessive sexual desire in men.

Satz *n* (*mus*) a movement, piece of music.

sauce *n* a liquid or dressing served with food to enhance its flavor; stewed or preserved fruit eaten with other food or as a dessert; (*inf*) impudence. * *vt* to season with sauce; to make piquant; (*sl*) to be impertinent to.

saucepan *n* a deep cooking pan with a handle and lid.

saucer *n* a round, shallow dish placed under a cup; a shallow depression; a thing shaped like a saucer.

saucy *adj* (**saucier, sauciest**) rude, impertinent; sprightly.—**saucily** *adv*.—**sauciness** *n*.

Saudi Arabia *n* a monarchy whose government and laws are based on the sacred teachings of Islam, occupying over 80 per cent of the Arabian Peninsula.

sauerkraut *n* a German dish of chopped pickled cabbage.

Saul *n* 1. (*OT*) the first king of Israel. Saul and his sons waged war against the Philistines but were eventually defeated at Mt Gilboa. Saul's sons were slain and Saul fell upon his sword. *See also* **Gilboa, Jabesh-Gilead**. 2. [Saul of Tarsus] (*NT*) Christian missionary and theologian, dramatically converted to Christianity on the road to Damascus, where saw a light and heard a voice; changed his name to Paul. *See also* **Paul**.

sauna *n* exposure of the body to hot steam, followed by cold water; the room where this is done.

saunter *vi* to walk in a leisurely or idle way. * *n* a stroll.—**saunterer** *n*.

-saur *n suffix* (*scientific*) reptiles.

saurian *adj* of or resembling a lizard. * *n* (*formerly*) a lizard.

sauro- *prefix* lizard.

saury *n* (*pl* **sauries**) an Atlantic fish with a long body and elongated jaws.

SAus *abbr* = South Australia *or* Australian.

sausage *n* minced seasoned meat, esp pork, packed into animal gut or other casing.

Saussure *n* **Ferdinand de** (1857–1913) Swiss linguist, who pioneered the use of structuralism in linguistics.

sauté *adj* fried quickly and lightly. * *vt* (**sautéing, sautéed**) to fry in a small amount of oil or fat. * *n* a sautéed dish.

sautille *see* **saltando**.

sauve qui peut *n* a precipitate flight, a general stampede.

SAV *abbr* = sale at valuation; stock at valuation.

savage *adj* fierce; wild; untamed; uncivilized; ferocious; primitive. * *n* a member of a primitive society; a brutal, fierce person or animal.—**savagely** *adv*.—**savageness** *n*.

Savage *n* **Michael Joseph** (1872–1940) Australian-born New Zealand Labour politician. He became the first Labour prime minister of New Zealand (1935–40).

savagery *n* (*pl* **savageries**) the state of being a savage; an act of violence or cruelty; an uncivilized state.

savanna, savannah *n* a treeless plain; an area of tropical or subtropical grassland.

savant *n* a person with extensive knowledge, esp in a certain discipline.

savate *n* a form of boxing using both the fists and the feet.

save¹ *vt* to rescue from harm or danger; to keep, to accumulate; to set aside for future use; to avoid the necessity of; (*energy, etc*) to prevent waste of; (*theol*) to deliver from sin; (*comput*) to transfer (the contents of a computer's RAM) to a less volatile memory such as a hard disk or floppy disk. * *vi* to avoid waste, expense, etc; to economize; to store up money or goods; (*sports*) to keep an opponent from scoring or winning. * *n* (*sports*) the act of preventing one's opponent from scoring.—**savable** *adj*.

save² *conj*, *prep* except, but.

Save *abbr* = Save Britain's Heritage.

SAVE *abbr* = Systematic Alien Verification for Entitlement.

saveloy *n* a type of highly seasoned smoked sausage.

saver *n* a person who saves money in a bank or building society.

savin, savine *n* a small Eurasian juniper bush with dark fruit the oil from which was once used medicinally.

saving¹ *adj* thrifty, economical; (*clause*) containing a reservation; redeeming. * *n* what is saved; (*pl*) money saved for future use.

saving² *prep* except; with apology to.

savings account *n* a bank account that earns interest.

savings and loan association *n* a company that pays interest on deposits and issues loans to enable people to buy their own houses, a building society.

savings bank *n* a bank receiving small deposits and holding them in interest-bearing accounts.

savior *n* a person who saves another from harm or danger; (*with cap*) Jesus Christ.

savoir-faire *n* the skill of knowing the right thing to do; tact.

savor *n* the flavor or smell of something; a distinctive quality. * *vti* to season; to enjoy; to have a specified taste or smell; to smack (of); to appreciate critically.—**savorer** *n*.

savory¹ *adj* having a good taste or smell; spicy, not sweet; reputable. * *n* (*pl* **savories**) a savory dish at the beginning or end of dinner; (*pl*) snacks served with drinks.—**savorily** *adv*.—**savoriness** *n*.

savory² *n* (*pl* **savories**) any of various Mediterranean aromatic plants used as herbs for flavoring.

savoy (cabbage) *n* a variety of cabbage with wrinkled, dark green leaves.

Savoy Operas *npl* (*mus*) a name for the light operas written by Gilbert and Sullivan, which were first performed at the Savoy Theatre in London by the D'Oyly Carte company.

SAVS *abbr* (*Brit*) = Scottish Anti-Vivisection Society.

savvy *vti* (**savvying, savvied**) (*sl*) to understand. * *n* (*sl*) understanding, know-how. * *adj* (**savvier, savviest**) (*sl*) shrewd.

saw[1] *see* **see**[1].

saw[2] *n* a tool with a toothed edge for cutting wood, etc. * *vti* (**sawing, sawed**, *pp* **sawed** *or* **sawn**) to cut or shape with a saw; to use a saw; to make a to-and-fro motion.—**sawer** *n*.

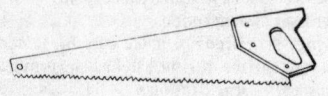

saw[3] *n* a wise saying, a proverb.

SAW *abbr* = (*Brit*) Scottish Association of Writers; (*Brit*) Society of Architects in Wales; surface acoustic wave.

SAWA *abbr* (*Brit*) = Scottish Amateur Wrestling Association; Scottish Asian Women's Association.

sawbill *n* a large, diving, fish-eating duck with a long narrow bill with serrated edges.

sawbones *n* (*sl*) a doctor or surgeon.

sawbuck *n* a sawhorse.

sawdust *n* fine particles of wood caused by sawing.

sawed-off *see* **sawn-off**.

sawfish *n* (*pl* **sawfish** *or* **sawfishes**) a large ray with a serrated snout.

sawfly *n* (*pl* **sawflies**) any of various insects with a saw-like ovipositor.

SAWGU *abbr* = South African Wattle Growers' Union.

sawhorse *n* a trestle, etc on which wood is laid for sawing.

SAWJ *abbr* (*Brit*) = Scottish Association of Watchmakers and Jewellers.

sawmill *n* a mill where timber is cut into logs or planks.

sawn *see* **saw**[2].

sawn-off *adj* (*shotgun*) having the barrel shortened to aid concealment; (*person*) (*sl*) small.—*also* **sawed-off**.

saw set *n* an instrument for setting the teeth of a saw by bending each tooth to the left or right alternately.

sawyer *n* a person employed to saw timber.

sax *n* saxophone.

Sax *n* Adolphe (1814–94) a Belgian instrument-maker, who invented the saxophone and the saxhorn.

saxatile *adj* saxicolous.

saxe blue *n* a light grayish-blue.—*also adj*.

saxhorn *n* a brass musical instrument resembling a tuba.

saxicolous *or* **saxicoline** *adj* living among or on rocks.

saxifrage *n* any of a genus of plants with small flowers and tufted leaves, popular in rock gardens.

Saxon *adj*, *n* (of) a member of a North German people that settled the southern part of Britain in the 5th-6th century.

saxony *n* a fine wool; cloth made from it.

saxophone *n* a brass wind instrument with a single reed and about 20 finger keys.—**saxophonic** *adj*.—**saxophonist** *n*.

say *vt* (**says, saying, said**) to speak, utter; to state in words; to affirm, declare; to recite; to estimate; to assume. * *vi* to tell; to express in words. * *n* (*pl* **says**) the act of uttering; the right or opportunity to speak; a share in a decision. * *adv* for example. * *interj* expressing admiration, surprise, etc.

SAYC *abbr* (*Brit*) = Scottish Association of Youth Clubs.

SAYE *abbr* (*Brit*) = save as you earn.

saying *n* a common remark; a proverb or adage.

Saynshand *n* a city in Mongolia.

say-so *n* (*inf*) an unfounded assertion; an authorization; the right to authorize.

sayyid, sayid *n* a Muslim title of respect applied to descendants of Mohammed's daughter Fatima.

Sb (*chem*) *symbol* = antimony (element).

sb *abbr* = single-breasted.

sb. *abbr* = substantive.

s.b. *abbr* = southbound.

SB *abbr* = Savings Bank; School of Business Administration; (*Latin*) *Scientiae Baccalaureus*, "Bachelor of Science"; selection board; Shipping Board; sick bay; simultaneous broadcast; smooth bore; stillbirth; Special Branch (police); (*transp*) statement of billing; Sugar Bureau.

SBA *abbr* = (*Brit*) Scottish Basketball Association; (*Brit*) Scottish Beekeepers Association; (*Brit*) Scottish Bonsai Association; (*Brit*) Scottish Bowling Association; Small Business Administration; Smaller Businesses Association; Society of Botanical Artists; Steam Boat Association of Great Britain; sick bay attendant.

SBAC *abbr* = Society of British Aerospace Companies.

SBBA *abbr* (*Brit*) = Scottish Boat Builders' Association.

SBBC *abbr* = Shell Better Britain Campaign.

SBBNF *abbr* = Ship and Boat Builders' National Federation.

SBC *abbr* = single-board computer; Stamp Bug Club; Swiss Broadcasting Corporation.

SbE *abbr* = south by east.

SBGI *abbr* (*Brit*) = Society of British Gas Industries.

SBH *abbr* (*Brit*) = Scottish Board of Health.

SBKKV *abbr* = space-based kinetic kill vehicle (a system of missiles launched from a satellite).

SBL *abbr* = Society of Biblical Literature; Society of Black Lawyers.

'sblood *interj* (*obs*) God's blood.

SBN *abbr* = Standard Book Number.

SBP *abbr* = systolic blood pressure.

SBPR *abbr* = Society for Back Pain Research.

SBR *abbr* = strict bed rest.

SBS *abbr* = (*Brit*) Save British Science Society; sick building syndrome; Special Boat Service.

SBSA *abbr* = (*Brit*) Scottish Board Sailing Association; Standard Bank of South Africa.

SBSB *abbr* = (*Brit*) Society of British Snuff Blenders.

SBTD *abbr* = (*Brit*) Society of British Theatre Designers.

SBU *abbr* = (*Brit*) Scottish Badminton Union; strategic business unit.

SbW *abbr* = south by west.

Sc (*chem*) *symbol* = scandium (element).

sc. *abbr* = scale; scene; science; scilicet; screw; (*weight*) scruple; (*print*) small capitals.

s/c *abbr* = self-catering; self-contained; (*French*) = *son compte*, "his *or* her account."

Sc. *abbr* = Scandinavia; Scandinavian; Scotland; Scots; Scottish.

SC *abbr* = sailing club; Sanitary Corps; Schools Council; Security Council (UN); Signal Corps; Social Club; South Carolina; Special Circular; Special Constable; Sports Club; Staff College; Staff Corps; standing committee; structural change; subcutaneous; Supreme Court.

SCA *abbr* = (*Brit*) Scottish Canoe Association; (*Brit*) Scottish Cashmere Association; (*Brit*) Scottish Chess Association; (*Brit*) Scottish Council on Alcohol; (*Brit*) Scottish Croquet Association; Sea Cadet Association; Social Care Association; Specialist Cheesemakers' Association; Sprayed Concrete Association; Steel Cladding Association; Suez Canal Authority; sickle-cell anemia.

SCAARF *abbr* (*Brit*) = Scottish Combined Action Against Racism and Fascism.

scab *n* a dry crust on a wound or sore; a plant disease characterized by crustaceous spots; a worker who refuses to join a strike or who replaces a striking worker. * *vi* (**scabbing, scabbed**) to form a scab; to be covered with scabs; to work as a scab.—**scabby** *adj*.

scabbard *n* a sheath for a sword or dagger. * *vt* to sheathe.

scabies *n* a contagious, itching skin disease.

scabiosa *n* any of a genus of Mediterranean plants with tightly clustered blue, red, or white flowers.—*also* **scabious**.

scabious[1] *adj* covered with scabs; of or resembling scabies.

scabious[2] *see* **scabiosa**.

scabrous *adj* (*surface*) rough, scaly; indecent, offensive; intractable, difficult to manage.—**scabrously** *adv*.—**scabrousness** *n*.

SCAFA *abbr* (*Brit*) = Scottish Child and Family Alliance.

scaffold *n* a raised platform for the execution of a criminal; capital punishment; scaffolding.

scaffolding *n* a temporary framework of wood and metal for use by workmen constructing a building, etc; materials for a scaffold.

scagliola *n* (*archit*) an imitation marble consisting of gypsum, isinglass, glue, and sometimes marble dust.

SCAHT *abbr* (*Brit*) = Scottish Churches Architectural Heritage Trust.

Scala *n* La (Teatro alla Scala) Milan's, and Italy's, premier opera house, which was opened in 1778.

scalable *adj* able to be scaled or climbed.

scalable font *n* (*comput*) a font that can be reduced or enlarged to any size required without distorting the font shape.

scalar *adj* (*math*) having magnitude but not direction. * *n* a scalar quantity, e.g., time, mass.

scalar product *n* a scalar produced by multiplying together the magnitudes of two vectors and the cosine of the angle between them.

scalawag *n* (*inf*) a rascal; a scamp; a Southern white who supported the Republicans after the American Civil War.—*also* **scallawag, scallywag**.

scald *vt* to burn with hot liquid or steam; to heat almost to boiling point; to immerse in boiling water to sterilize. * *n* an injury caused by hot liquid or steam.

scale[1] *n* (*pl*) a machine or instrument for weighing; one of the pans or the tray of a set of scales; (*pl*) (*with cap*) Libra, the seventh sign of the zodiac. * *vti* to weigh in a set of scales; to have a specified weight on a set of scales.

scale[2] *n* one of the thin plates covering a fish or reptile; a flake (of dry skin); an encrustation on teeth, etc. * *vti* to remove the scales from; to flake off.

scale[3] *n* a graduated measure; an instrument so marked; (*math*) the basis for a numerical system, 10 being that in general use; (*mus*) a series of tones from the keynote to its octave, in order of pitch; the proportion that a map, etc bears to what it represents; a series of degrees classified by size, amount, etc; relative scope or size. * *vt* (*wall*) to go up or over; (*model*) to make or draw to scale; to increase or decrease in size.

scaled *adj* (*reptile, etc*) covered with or having scales.

scalene *adj* (*geom*) having three sides of unequal length. * *n* a scalene triangle.

scallawag, scallywag see **scalawag**.

scallion *n* a young onion with a small bulb and long shoots eaten raw in salads, a spring onion or shallot.

scallop *n* an edible shellfish with two fluted, fan-shaped shells; one of a series of curves in an edging. * *vt* to cut into scallops.—**scalloped** *adj*.

scalp *n* the skin covering the skull, usu covered with hair. * *vti* to cut the scalp from; to criticize sharply; (*inf*) (*tickets, etc*) to buy and resell at higher prices.

scalpel *n* a short, thin, very sharp knife used esp for surgery.

scaly *adj* (**scalier, scaliest**) (*reptile etc*) like or covered with scales.—**scaliness** *n*.

scaly anteater *n* a pangolin.

scam *n* (*sl*) a swindle, a fraud. * *vt* (**scamming, scammed**) (*sl*) to swindle or defraud.

Scamander or **Scamandrus** *n* a river rising on Mount Ida and crossing the Plain of Troy.

Scamozzi *n* Vincenzo (1552–1616) Italian architect, whose notable works include Villa Rocca Pisana, Lonigo.

scamp *n* a rascal; a mischievous child.

SCAMP *abbr* (*Brit*) = Scottish Association of Magazine Publishers.

scamper *vi* to run away quickly or playfully. * *n* a brisk or playful run or movement.

scampi *n* a dish of large shrimps or prawns cooked in breadcrumbs or prepared with a flavored dressing.

scan *vt* (**scanning, scanned**) (*page etc*) to look through quickly; to scrutinize; (*med*) to examine with a radiological device; (*TV*) to pass an electronic beam over; (*radar*) to detect with an electronic beam; (*poem*) to conform to a rhythmical pattern; to check for recorded data by means of a mechanical or electronic device; (*human body*) to make a scan of in a scanner. * *vi* to analyze the pattern of verse. * *n* the act of scanning or an instance of being scanned.

Scan. or **Scand.** *abbr* = Scandinavia; Scandinavian.

SCAN *abbr* = suspected child abuse and neglect.

scandal *n* a disgraceful event or action; talk arising from immoral behavior; a feeling of moral outrage; the thing or person causing this; disgrace; malicious gossip.

scandalize *vt* to shock the moral feelings of; to defame.—**scandalization** *n*.—**scandalizer** *n*.

scandalmonger *n* a person who spreads scandal or malicious gossip.—**scandalmongering** *n*.

scandalous *adj* causing scandal; shameful; spreading slander.—**scandalously** *adv*.—**scandalousness** *n*.

scandal sheet *n* a newspaper or magazine that contains mainly malicious gossip.

Scandinavian *adj* of or pertaining to Scandinavia, the region comprising Norway, Sweden, and Denmark, and sometimes Iceland, or its people. * *n* a native or inhabitant of Scandinavia.

scandium *n* a rare metallic element present in small quantities in various minerals. *symbol Sc.

s. c. and s. *abbr* (*transp*) = strapped, corded, and sealed.

scan. mag. *abbr* = scandalum magnatum.

SCANN *abbr* = South Coast Against Nuclear Energy.

scanner *n* a person or thing that scans; an electronic device that monitors or scans; a device for receiving or transmitting radar signals; a device for scanning the human body to obtain an image of an internal part; (*comput*) a piece of hardware that copies an image or page into a computer by creating a digital image.

scanning electron microscope *n* an electron microscope which scans an object to produce a three-dimensional image.

scansion *n* the analysis of verse to show its meter.

scant *adj* limited; meager; insufficient; scanty; grudging.

scantling *n* a small piece of timber; the dimensions of timber and stone for a building or of a component for a ship or aircraft; a small quantity.

scanty *adj* (**scantier, scantiest**) barely adequate; insufficient; small.—**scantily** *adv*.—**scantiness** *n*.

scapegoat *n* a person who bears the blame for others; one who is the object of irrational hostility.

scapegrace *n* a graceless, hare-brained person; an incorrigible scamp.

scaphoid bone *n* a bone of the wrist, the outside one on the thumb side of the hand.

s. caps. *abbr* = small capitals.

scapula *n* (*pl* **scapulae**) the shoulder blade.

scapular *adj* of or relating to the scapula. * *n* a monastic robe worn in various Christian religious orders, consisting of a wide piece of cloth worn over the shoulders and hanging down at the front and back; any of the feathers along the base of a bird's wing.

scar[1] *n* a mark left after the healing of a wound or sore; a blemish resulting from damage or wear. * *vti* (**scarring, scarred**) to mark with or form a scar.

scar[2] *n* a protruding or isolated rock; a precipitous crag; a rocky part of a hillside.

SCAR *abbr* = Scientific Committee on Antarctic Research.

scarab *n* a dung-beetle held to be sacred in ancient Egypt; a gem or seal in the shape of this.

scarabaeid *n* any of a family of beetles including the dung beetle.—*also adj*.

scarce *adj* not in abundance; hard to find; rare.—**scarceness** *n*.

scarcely *adv* hardly, only just; probably not or certainly not.

scarcity *n* (*pl* **scarcities**) the state of being scarce; a dearth, deficiency.

scare *vti* to startle; to frighten or become frightened; to drive away by frightening. * *n* a sudden fear; a period of general fear; a false alarm.

scarecrow *n* a wooden figure dressed in clothes for scaring birds from crops; a thin or tattered person; something frightening but harmless.

scaremonger *n* a person who causes fear or panic by spreading rumors; an alarmist.

scarf *n* (*pl* **scarves**) a rectangular or square piece of cloth worn around the neck, shoulders, or head for warmth or decoration.

SCARF *abbr* = Sickle Cell Anemia Research Foundation.

scarfskin *n* the outer layer of skin; cuticle.

scarify *vt* (**scarifying, scarified**) to make cuts in, to scratch; to criticize savagely; to loosen the surface of (soil); to hasten germination by softening the wall of (a hard seed).—**scarification** *n*.

scarlatina *n* scarlet fever.

Scarlatti *n* 1. Alessandro (1660–1725) Italian composer, who was instrumental in developing opera when it was in its formative years. He composed some 115 operas, of which only 70 or so survive. He also wrote 150 oratorios and hundreds of cantatas. 2. (Giuseppe) Domenico (1685–1757) Italian composer and harpsichordist, who was the son of Alessandro Scarlatti. He devised new techniques of playing keyboard instruments and was as influential as his father. He wrote some 550 pieces for the harpsichord.

scarlet *n* a bright red with a tinge of orange; scarlet cloth or clothes. * *adj* scarlet-colored; immoral or sinful.

scarlet fever *n* an acute contagious disease marked by a sore throat, fever, and a scarlet rash.

scarlet pimpernel *n* a plant with red, purple, or white flowers that close in dull weather.

scarlet runner *n* a climbing bean plant with scarlet flowers and elongated edible pods.—*also* **runner bean**.

scarlet tanager *n* an American songbird, the male of which has a scarlet body and black wings.

scarlet woman *n* (*arch*) a prostitute.

scarp *n* a low steep slope; the inner face of a ditch in a fortification.

scarp-and-vale terrain *n* the undulating pattern formed by a series of cuestas and valleys where the sedimentary rock is tilted gently.

scarper *vi* (*inf*) to run away.

scar tissue *n* the connective tissue forming a scar.

scarves see **scarf**.

scary *adj* (**scarier, scariest**) frightening, alarming.—**scariness** *n*.

SCAS *abbr* = Signal Corps Aviation School; Society for Companion Animal Studies.

scat[1] *vi* (**scatting, scatted**) (*inf*) to leave hastily.

scat[2] *n* (*jazz*) a form of improvised singing without words. * *vi* (**scatting, scatted**) to sing in this way.

Scathach *n* (*Irish Celtic myth*) a prophetess and great warrior. She is supposed to have run a kind of military school at which she passed on her skills in war to her pupils. One of her pupils was Cuchulainn.

scathing *adj* bitterly critical; cutting, withering.—**scathingly** *adv*.

scatology *n* the scientific study of fossil and human excrement; a preoccupation with excrement or obscenity.—**scatological** *adj*.

scatter *vti* to throw loosely about; to sprinkle; to dissipate; to put or take to flight; to disperse; to occur at random. * *n* a scattering or sprinkling.

scatterbrain *n* a frivolous, heedless person.—**scatterbrained** *adj*.

scattered *adj* dispersed widely, spaced out; straggling.

scattering *n* a small amount spread over a large area; a dispersion; (*phys*) the dispersal of waves or particles upon impact with matter.

scatter rug *n* a rug that can be placed (usu with others) in different parts of a room to achieve various decorative effects or to hide blemishes.

scatty *adj* (**scattier, scattiest**) (*inf*) thoughtless, absentminded, crazy.—**scattily** *adv*.—**scattiness** *n*.

scaup (duck) *n* a diving duck of Europe and America.

scavenge *vi* to gather things discarded by others; (*animal*) to eat decaying matter.—**scavenger** *n*.

ScB *abbr* = Bachelor of Science.

SCB *abbr* = (*Brit*) Solicitors' Complaints Bureau; Speedway Control Board (motorcycle racing).

SCBU *abbr* = Special Care Baby Unit.

scc *abbr* = single column centimeter.

SCC *abbr* = Scandinavian Collectors' Club; Science Council of Canada; (*Brit*) Scottish Churches Council; (*Brit*) Scottish Consumer Council; Sea Cadet Corps; Silhouette Collectors Club; Society of Cheese Connoisseurs; Structural Concrete Consortium; Sylvac Collectors' Club.

SCCA *abbr* = (*Brit*) Scottish Consumer Credit Association; Society of Company and Commercial Accountants.

SCCL *abbr* = (*Brit*) Scottish Council for Civil Liberties.

ScD *abbr* = Doctor of Science.

SCD *abbr* = Doctor of Commercial Science; (*Brit*) Scottish Council on Disability.

SCDC *abbr* = Schools Curriculum Development Committee.

SCE *abbr* = (*Brit*) Scottish Certificate of Education.

SCEC *abbr* = (*Brit*) Scottish Community Education Council.

scenario *n* (*pl* **scenarios**) an outline of events, real or imagined; the plot or script of a movie, etc.

scene *n* the place in which anything occurs; the place in which the action of a play or a story occurs; a section of a play, a division of an act; the stage of a theater; a painted screen, etc, used on this; an unseemly display of strong emotion; a landscape; surroundings; a place of action; (*inf*) an area of interest or activity (e.g., *the music scene*).

scene dock *n* (*theat*) a storage area for scenery near the stage.

scenery *n* (*pl* **sceneries**) painted screens, etc, used to represent places, as in a play, movie, etc; an aspect of a landscape, esp of beautiful or impressive countryside.

scenic *adj* relating to natural scenery; picturesque; of or used on the stage.—**scenically** *adv*.

scenic railway *n* (*Brit*) a miniature railroad at an amusement park, etc.

scent *n* a perfume; an odor left by an animal, by which it can be tracked; the sense of smell; a line of pursuit or discovery. * *vt* to recognize by the sense of smell; to track by smell; to impart an odor to, to perfume; to get wind of, to detect.

scented *adj* perfumed.

scepter *n* the staff of office held by a monarch on a ceremonial occasion; sovereignty.

scf *abbr* = standard cubic foot (*or* feet).

SCF *abbr* = (*Brit*) Save the Children Fund; Spanish Cycling Federation; Standing Committee on Fishing.

scfd *abbr* = standard cubic feet per day.

scfh *abbr* = standard cubic feet per hour.

SCGB *abbr* = (*Brit*) Ski Club of Great Britain.

sch. *abbr* = scholium; school; schooner.

Scharoun *n* **Hans** (1893–1972) German architect, whose notable works include the German Embassy, Brasilia.

Schawinsky *n* **Alexander** (1904–79) Swiss designer for Olivetti and Motta, in Italy from 1933.

sched. *abbr* = schedule.

schedule *n* a list, inventory, or tabulated statement; a timed plan for a project; a timetable. * *vt* to make a schedule; to plan.

scheelite *n* a mineral consisting of calcium tungstate.

schema *n* (*pl* **schemata**) a plan or diagram.

schematic *adj* of or like a scheme or diagram.—**schematically** *adv*.

schematize *vt* to form into or express as a scheme.—**schematization** *n*.

scheme *n* a plan; a project; a systematic arrangement; a diagram; an underhand plot. * *vti* to devise or plot.—**schemer** *n*.

scheming *adj* cunning; intriguing.

scherzando *adj*, *adv* (*mus*) to be performed lightheartedly. * *n* (*pl* **scherzandi**) a piece of music played in this manner.

scherzetto *n* (*mus*) (*Italian*) a short scherzo.

scherzo *n* (*pl* **scherzos** *or* **scherzi**) a lively musical passage or movement, usu in triple time.

Schickhardt *n* **Heinrich** (1558–1635) German architect, whose notable works include a wing of the Schloss, Stuttgart (now destroyed).

schilling *n* the standard monetary unit of Austria.

Schindler *n* **Rudolph M.** (1887–1953) German architect, whose notable works include Beach House, Newport beach.

Schinkel *n* **Karl F.** (1781–1841) German architect, whose notable works include the Old Museum, Berlin.

schism *n* a division or separation into two parties, esp of a Church; the sin of this; discord, disharmony.

schismatic *or* **schismatical** *adj* of or creating schism. * *n* a person who creates schism or supports schism.—**schismatically** *adv*.

schist *n* a type of crystalline rock in thin layers.—**schistose** *adj*.

schistosity *n* (*geol*) the planar fabric formed in a schist due to the alignment of minerals, predominantly micas, but also amphiboles.

schistosome *n* any of a genus of parasitic worms that infest the blood vessels of humans and animals.

schistosomiasis *n* a disease caused by infestation with schistosomes.

schizo *n* (*pl* **schizos**) (*inf*) a schizophrenic person. * *adj* schizophrenic.

schizo- *or* **schiz-** *prefix* split, division.

schizocarp *n* a dry fruit that splits into single-seeded parts.

schizoid *adj* mildly schizophrenic.—*also n*.

schizomycete *n* any microscopic organism such as a bacterium.

schizophrenia *n* a mental disorder characterized by withdrawal from reality and deterioration of the personality; the presence of mutually contradictory qualities or parts.—**schizophrenic** *adj*, *n*.

Schlesinger *n* **John [Richard]** (1926–) English movie director, whose movies include *Billy Liar* (1963), *Midnight Cowboy* (1969), and *Sunday, Bloody Sunday* (1971).

Schlick *n* **Moritz** (1882–1936) German philosopher. One of the founders of the "Vienna Circle" logical positivist school, his works include *Problems of Ethics* (1930). He was murdered by one of his students.

schlieren *n* (*phys*) visible streaks in a transparent medium caused by variations in its density.

schmaltz, schmalz *n* overly sentimental music, art, movies, etc.—**schmaltzy, schmalzy** *adj*.

Schmidt *n* 1. **Franz** (1874–1939) Austrian composer, cellist, organist, and pianist, whose works include two operas, the oratorio *The Book of the Seven Seals*, four

symphonies, and chamber music. 2. **Helmut [Heinrich Waldemar]** (1918–) West German Social Democrat statesman and chancellor. A former leader in the Hitler Youth, he won the Iron Cross during the war. He succeeded Willy Brandt as chancellor (1974–82) and fostered relations with East Germany, resigning from politics in 1983.

Schmied *n* **François-Louis** (1873–1941) Swiss illustrator and designer, who came to note through his illustrations for Rudyard Kipling's *Jungle Book*.

Schnabel *n* **Artur** (1882–1951) Austrian pianist and composer, who settled in the USA from 1939 after the Nazi seizure of Austria.

schnapps *n* (*pl* **schnapps**) a Dutch spirit distilled from potatoes; (*German*) any strong spirit.

schnauzer *n* an orig German breed of terrier with a short wiry coat.

schnell *adj* (*mus*) quick.

schnitzel *n* a cutlet of veal.

schnorkel *see* **snorkel**.

schnozzle *n* (*sl*) nose.

Schoenberg, Schönberg *n* **Arnold [Franz Walter]** (1874–1951) Austrian-born composer and US citizen from 1941.

schol. *abbr* = scholium.

scholar *n* a student; a learned person; the holder of a scholarship.

scholarly *adj* learned, erudite, academic.

scholarship *n* an annual grant to a student, usu won by competitive examination; learning, academic achievement.

scholastic *adj* of or relating to schools, scholars, or education; academic.—**scholastically** *adv*.

Scholastica *n* **Saint** (*d*. 548) Italian nun, the sister of St Benedict. Her feast day is 10 February.

school[1] *n* an educational establishment; its teachers and students; a regular session of teaching; formal education, schooling; a particular division of a university; a place or means of discipline; a group of thinkers, artists, writers, holding similar principles. * *vt* to train; to teach; to control or discipline.

school[2] *n* a shoal of porpoises, whales, or other aquatic animals of one kind swimming together.

schoolboy *n* a boy who attends school.

schoolchild *n* (*pl* **schoolchildren**) a child who attends school.

schoolgirl *n* a girl who attends school.

schoolhouse *n* a building used as a school.

schooling *n* instruction in school.

schoolmaster *n* a man who teaches in school.

schoolmate *n* a companion at school.—*also* **schoolfellow**.

schoolmistress *n* a woman who teaches in school.

schoolroom *n* a room in which pupils are taught, as in a school.

schoolteacher *n* a person who teaches in school.

schooner *n* a sailing ship with two or more masts rigged with fore-and-aft sails; a large drinking glass for sherry or beer.

Schopenhauer *n* **Arthur** (1788–1860) German philosopher, renowned for his pessimistic outlook on life.

schottische *n* (music for) a type of slow dance resembling a polka.

schr. *abbr* = schooner.

Schrammel quartet *n* (*mus*) a Viennese ensemble, usu comprising two violins, a guitar, and an accordion, or the music composed for such an ensemble. It takes its name from Joseph Schrammel (1858–93), who wrote waltzes for such a group.

Schreiber *n* **Gaby** (1912–) Austrian designer, who was general consultant designer for the 1965 liners *Queen Elizabeth II* and *Cunarder*.

Schreiner *n* **Olive** (1855–1920) South African novelist, remembered chiefly for one work, *The Story of an African Farm*, based on her own childhood on a South African farm.

Schreker *n* **Franz** (1878–1934) an Austrian avant-garde composer and conductor, whose works include operas (e.g., *Der ferne Klang*), orchestral pieces, and songs.

Schrödinger, Erwin *n* (1887–1961) Austrian physicist. He shared the 1933 Nobel Prize for Physics with Dirac for his formulation of his wave equation, which was the starting point for the study of wave mechanics in quantum theory. He fled from Germany to Britain in 1933 when the Nazis came to power.

Schrödinger equation *n* (*phys*) the basic equation used in wave mechanics, which describes the behavior of a particle in a force field.

Schubert *n* **Franz Peter** (1797–1828) Austrian composer, famous for his songs, some 600 in all, but he also composed operas, nine symphonies, chamber music, piano music, and Masses.

Schumacher *n* **Ernst Friedrich** (1911–77) German-born British economist, whose book *Small is Beautiful* (1973) became a founding text of the conservationist movement.

Schuman *n* **William Howard** (1910–92) American composer of distinctively American music, whose works include nine symphonies, concertos for piano and violin, ballets, and the opera *The Mighty Casey*, which is about a baseball player.

Schumann *n* 1. **Clara Josephine** (née **Wieck**) (1819–96) German pianist and composer, who married Robert Schumann in 1840. 2. **Robert (Alexander)** (1810–56) German composer of symphonies, songs, and piano music.

Schuschnigg *n* **Kurt von** (1897–1977) Austrian statesman. A staunch opponent of Adolf Hitler, he became chancellor in 1934 and was imprisoned by the Nazis (1938–45).

schuss *n* (*skiing*) a fast straight downhill run. * *vi* to ski down this.

Schütz *n* **Heinrich** (1585–1672) German composer and organist, who was possibly the greatest German composer of his era. His works include many religious pieces, which married Lutheran philosophy to contemporary Italian musical styles, as well as three impressive Passions.

Schwanzer *n* **Karl** (1918–75) Austrian furniture designer, whose chairs were intended for mass production.

Schwarzkopf *n* 1. **Dame Elisabeth** (1915–) German soprano, who is recognized as being one of the great singers of the 20th century. She had a very wide repertoire, which included in particular Mozart, Richard Strauss, and Wolf. 2. **Norman** (1935–) American general, who commanded Operation Desert Shield and Desert Storm against Iraqi forces in Kuwait during the Gulf War (1990). He was nicknamed "Stormin' Norman."

Schweitzer, Albert (1875–1965) Alsatian medical missionary, theologian, musician, and philosopher. In 1913, he founded a missionary hospital at Lambaréné, Gabon, which attracted worldwide interest for Schweitzer's avowed aim of helping Africa in the spirit of "atonement" rather than benevolence. He was awarded the 1952 Nobel Peace Prize. His works include *The Quest of the Historical Jesus* (1906) and *On the Edge of the Primeval Forest* (1922).

sci *abbr* = single column inch.

sci. *abbr* = science; scientific.

SCIAF *abbr* (*Brit*) = Scottish Catholic International Aid Fund.

Sciascia *n* **Leonardo** (1921–89) Italian novelist, short-story writer, and essayist, whose work, whether fictional or non-fictional, is concerned with the endemic public corruption at the heart of Italian society. Notable examples of his work include *Sicilian Uncles*, *Candido*, and *The Moro Affair*.

sciatic *adj* of the hip.

sciatica *n* pain along the sciatic nerve, esp in the back of the thigh; (*loosely*) pain in the lower back or adjacent parts.

sciatic nerve *n* a long nerve running from the pelvic region to the back of the thigh.

SCID *abbr* = (*Brit*) Scotland's Campaign Against Irresponsible Drivers; severe combined immunodeficiency disease.

science *n* knowledge gained by systematic experimentation and analysis, and the formulation of general principles; a branch of this; skill or technique.

science fiction *n* highly imaginative fiction typically involving actual or projected scientific phenomena.

science park *n* an area where scientific discoveries are translated into commercial products and applications.

scientific *adj* of or concerned with science; based on or using the principles and methods of science; systematic and exact; having or showing expert skill.—**scientifically** *adv*.

scientism *n* the use of scientific methods; the inappropriate use of or reliance on scientific methods.

scientist *n* a specialist in a branch of science, as in chemistry, etc.

Scientology *n* (*trademark*) a cult movement founded in 1951.

sci. fa. *abbr* = scire facias.

sci-fi *n* science fiction.

scil. *abbr* = scilicet.

scilicet *adv* namely, that is to say.

scilla *n* any of a genus of plants with small pink, blue, or white flowers grown from bulbs.

scimitar *n* an Oriental curved sword, broadest near the point.

scintigraphy *n* the production of images of internal body parts by detecting high-energy particles from a radioactive tracer administered to a patient.

scintilla *n* an iota, tiny amount.

scintillate *vti* to give off sparks; to sparkle.

scintillating *adj* sparkling; amusing.

scintillation *n* (*phys*) small light flashes caused by ionizing radiations striking substances that luminesce; (*astron*) the twinkling of stars, due to deflection by the Earth's atmosphere.

scintillation counter *n* an instrument for registering the intensity of a radioactive source by recording the flashes of light produced by the impact of emitted photons on a phosphor.

scioltamente *adv* with ease or freedom.

scion *n* a shoot for grafting; a young member of a family, a descendant.

Scipio *see* **Hannibal**.

scirocco *see* **sirocco**.

scirrhus *n* (*pl* **scirrhi** *or* **scirrhuses**) a cancerous tumor consisting of fibrous tissue.

scission *n* the act of cutting or dividing; a cut, divide, or split.

scissor *vt* to cut with scissors, to clip. * *npl* a tool for cutting paper, hair, etc, consisting of two fastened pivoted blades whose edges slide past each other; a gymnastic feat in which the leg movements resemble the opening and closing of scissors.

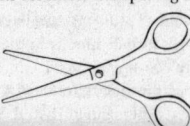

scissors kick *n* (*swimming*) a kick in which the legs move from the hip in a scissoring motion.

sciurine *adj* of or resembling a family of rodents which include squirrels and marmots.

SCIVU *abbr* = Scientific Council of the International Vegetarian Union.

SCL *abbr* = (*Brit*) Scottish Central Library; Society for Caribbean Linguistics; Society of Construction Law; Student of Civil Law.

SCLC *abbr* = (*Brit*) Scottish Child Law Centre; Southern Christian Leadership Conference.

sclera *n* the opaque outer covering of the eyeball excluding the cornea.

sclerenchyma *n* a tissue forming the hard fibrous parts of plants.

scleritis *n* inflammation of the white of the eye

sclero- *or* **scler-** *prefix* hardness.

scleroderma *n* (*med*) a chronic disease in women causing thickening and hardening of the skin.

sclerodermatous *adj* (*zool*) covered with a hard layer of tissue, e.g., scales.

scleroproteins *npl* (*biochemistry*) insoluble proteins that form the skeletal parts of tissues.

sclerosis *n* a pathological hardening of body tissue; a disease marked by this.

sclerotherapy *n* a treatment for varicose veins.

sclerotic *adj* pertaining to the sclera; of or affected by sclerosis. * *n* the sclera.

sclerous *adj* hard, bony.

s.c.m. *abbr* = summary court-martial.

ScM *abbr* (*Latin*) = *Scientiae Magister*, "Master of Science."

SCM *abbr* = Society of Coal Merchants; State Certified Midwife; Student Christian Movement.

SCMA *abbr* = (*Brit*) Scottish Carpet Manufacturers' Association; (*Brit*) Scottish Cement Merchants' Association; (*Brit*) Scottish Childminding Association; Stilton Cheese Manufacturers' Association.

SCMAC *abbr* (*Brit*) = Scottish Catholic Marriage Advisory Council.

SCMM *abbr* = Sisters of Charity of Our Lady Mother of Mercy.

SCNI *abbr* (*Brit*) = Sports Council for Northern Ireland.

SCO *abbr* (*Brit*) = Scottish Committee of Optometrists.

Scobec *abbr* (*Brit*) = Scottish Business Education Council.

scoff[1] *vti* to jeer (at) or mock. * *n* an expression or object of derision; mocking words, a taunt.

scoff[2] *vt* (*sl*) to eat quickly and greedily.

SCOLAG *abbr* (*Brit*) = Scottish Legal Action Group.

scold *vti* to reprove angrily; to tell off.

scolding *n* a harsh reprimand.

scolia *n* (*mus*) short Greek songs sung during banquets, formerly by the whole assemblage, afterward by each guest alone, holding in his or her hand a myrtle branch.

scoliosis *n* (*med*) lateral curvature of the spine.

scollop *see* **scallop**.

scombroid *n* any member of a suborder of spiny-finned marine fishes used for food, such as the mackerel and tuna.—*also adj*.

sconce[1] *n* a bracket on a wall for holding candles or electric lights.

sconce[2] *n* a defensive fortification, a bulwark.

scone *n* a small, round cake made from flour and fat that is baked and spread with butter, etc.

SCONUL *abbr* = Standing Conference of National and University Libraries.

scoop *n* a small shovel-like utensil, as for taking up flour, ice cream, etc; the bucket of a dredge, etc; the act of scooping or the amount scooped up at one time; (*inf*) a piece of exclusive news; (*inf*) the advantage gained in being the first to publish or broadcast this. * *vt* to shovel, lift, or hollow out with a scoop; (*inf*) to obtain as a scoop; (*inf: rival newspaper etc*) to forestall with a news item.

scoot *vti* to run quickly; to hurry (off).

scooter *n* a child's two-wheeled vehicle with a footboard and steering handle; a motor scooter.

scope *n* the opportunity to use one's abilities; extent; range; an instrument for viewing.

SCOPE *abbr* = Scientific Committee on Phosphates in Europe; (*Brit*) Scottish Council for Opportunities in Play Experience.

scopolamine *n* an alkaloid extracted from certain plants, used as a sedative and for travel sickness.—*also* **hyoscine**.

scorbutic *adj* of, suffering from, or resembling scurvy.—**scorbutically** *adv*.

scorch *vti* to burn or be burnt on the surface; to wither from over-exposure to heat; to singe; (*inf*) to drive or cycle furiously.

scorcher *n* (*inf*) a very hot day.

scorching *adj* (*inf: weather*) very hot; scathing.

scordatura *n* (*mus*) mistuning (tuning stringed instruments to abnormal notes, so as to produce special effects).

score *n* the total number of points made in a game or examination; a notch or scratch; a line indicating deletion or position; a group of 20; a written copy of a musical composition showing the different parts; the music composed for a movie; a grievance for settling; a reason or motive; (*inf*) the real facts; a bill or reckoning; (*pl*) an indefinite large number. * *vt* to mark with cuts; (*mus*) to arrange in a score, to orchestrate; to gain or record points, as in a game; to evaluate in testing. * *vi* to make points, as in a game; to keep the score of a game; to gain an advantage, a success, etc; (*sl*) to be successful in seduction; (*with* **off**) to get the better of someone.—**scorer** *n*.

scoreboard *n* a large, manually or electronically operated board showing the score in a game or match.

scorecard *n* (*golf, etc*) a card on which scores are recorded.

scorn *n* extreme contempt or disdain; the object of this. * *vt* to treat with contempt, to despise; to reject or refuse as unworthy.—**scornful** *adj*.—**scornfully** *adv*.

Scorpio *n* the Scorpion, eighth sign of the zodiac in astrology, operative October 23–November 21.—**Scorpionic** *adj*.

scorpion *n* a small, tropical, insect-like animal with pincers and a jointed tail with a poisonous sting.

scorpion fish *n* any of a genus of fish with poisonous spines on the dorsal fins.

Scorpius *or* **the Scorpion** *n* an extensive, prominent, and bright zodiac constellation lying partly in the Milky Way and within the southern hemisphere.

Scorpius-x-1 *n* the first stellar X-ray source to be discovered (in 1962) and also the brightest, lying in the constellation of Scorpius in the southern hemisphere.

Scorsese *n* **Martin** (1942–) American movie director, whose movies include *Taxi Driver* (1976), *Raging Bull* (1980), and *Goodfellas* (1990).

Scot *n* a native or inhabitant of Scotland; a member of a Celtic people from Ireland who settled in northern Britain in the 5th–6th centuries.

Scot. *abbr* (*Brit*) = Scotland; Scottish.

SCOT *abbr* (*Brit*) = Scottish Confederation of Tourism.

scotch *vt* to stamp out (a rumor).

Scotch *n* whisky made in Scotland.

Scotch broth *n* a thick soup made from beef or mutton with vegetables and pearl barley.

Scotch egg *n* a hard-boiled egg enclosed in sausagemeat, coated in breadcrumbs, and fried.

Scotchman *n* (*pl* **Scotchmen**) a Scotsman.—**Scotchwoman** *nf* (*pl* **Scotchwomen**).

Scotch mist *n* a dense, wet mist; fine drizzle.

Scotch pine *n* a Scots pine.

Scotch snap *n* (*mus*) the name for a rhythm which leaps from a short note to a longer note, which is found in many Scottish folk tunes.

Scotch tape *n* (*trademark*) a transparent adhesive tape.

Scotch terrier *n* a Scottish terrier.

scoter *n* (*pl* **scoters** *or* **scoter**) a large sea duck with black plumage.

scot-free *adj* without penalty or injury.

scotia *n* (*archit*) a deep, concave molding often used in the base of columns.

Scotland Yard *n* the headquarters of the Metropolitan Police Force in London.

scotoma *n* (*pl* **scotomas** *or* **scotomata**) a blind spot in the visual field.

Scots *adj* of or pertaining to Scotland, its law, money, and people, and the Scots language. * *n* the dialect of English developed in Lowland Scotland.

Scotsman *n* (*pl* **Scotsmen**) a native or inhabitant of Scotland.—**Scotswoman** *nf* (*pl* **Scotswomen**).

Scots pine *n* (the wood of) a European pine with needle-like leaves.

Scott *n* 1. **C[harles] P[restwich]** (1846–1932) English journalist, who became editor of *The Manchester Guardian* in 1872. He was a Liberal MP (1895–1906) and a strong opponent of the Boer War. 2. **Cyril Meir** (1879–1970) English composer and poet, who was nicknamed "the English Debussy." His works include the opera *The Alchemist,* many pieces for piano, and several orchestral compositions. 3. **Sir George Gilbert** (1811–78) English architect, whose notable works include the St Pancras Hotel, London and St Nicholas's Church, Hamburg. 4. **Sir Giles Gilbert** (1880–1960) English architect, whose notable works include Liverpool Cathedral and Waterloo Bridge, London. 5. **Isaac Elwood** (1845–1920) American furniture designer and wood carver. 6. **Lady John Douglas** (originally **Alicia Ann Spottiswoode**) (1810–1900) Scottish poet and song-writer who composed "Annie Laurie" and other Scottish songs. 7. **Sir Peter [Markham] Scott** (1909–89) English naturalist and artist, whose books include an autobiography, *The Eye of the Wind* (1961). 8. **Robert Falcon** (1868–1912) English explorer, who led two Antarctic expeditions (1901–1904, 1910–12) and died on his last expedition, which reached the South Pole. He was the father of Sir Peter Scott. 9. **Sir Walter** (1771–1832) Scottish novelist and poet, whose early narrative poems, e.g., *The Lady of the Lake,* established his popularity. His historical novels, e.g., *Waverley* (1814), were enormously influential. 10. **William Bell** (1811–1900) British painter, who was a minor member of the Pre-Raphaelite circle.

Scotticism *n* a Scottish word or idiom.

Scottie *n* (*inf*) a Scotsman; a Scottish terrier.

SCOTTIE *abbr* = Society for the Control of Troublesome and Toxic Industrial Emissions.

Scottish *adj* of or relating to Scotland and its people.

Scottish deerhound *n* a large rough-haired greyhound, a deerhound.

Scottish National Party *n* a political party seeking independence for Scotland.

Scottish terrier *n* a small terrier with short legs and a wiry coat.

scoundrel *n* a rascal; a dishonest person.

scour[1] *vt* to clean by rubbing with an abrasive cloth; to flush out with a current of water; to purge. * *n* the act or process of scouring; a place scoured by running water; scouring action (as of a glacier); damage done by scouring action.

scour[2] *vt* to hasten over or along; to range over, esp in search or pursuit; to cause erosion in (a place) by a current of water.

scourge *n* a whip; a means of inflicting punishment; a person who harasses and causes widespread and great affliction; a pest. * *vt* to flog; to punish harshly.

Scouse *n* (*inf*) a person from Liverpool, England; the dialect of Liverpool.—*also adj* .

scout *n* a person, airplane, etc, sent to observe the enemy's strength, etc; a person employed to find new talent or survey a competitor, etc; (*with cap*) a member of the Scouting Association, an organization for young people. * *vti* to reconnoiter; to go in search of (something).

scouting *n* the act of one who scouts; (*with cap*) the activities of the Scouting Association.

Scouting Association *n* (*formerly* **Boy Scouts**, **Girl Guides**) an organization to develop in young people self-reliance and initiative, moral and physical courage, and a courteous spirit.

scoutmaster *n* (*formerly*) the adult leader of a troop of Scouts.

scow *n* an unpowered, flat-bottomed boat for carrying freight, refuse, etc.

scowl *n* a contraction of the brows in an angry or threatening manner; a sullen expression. * *vi* to make a scowl; to look sullen.

scp. *abbr* = script.

SCP *abbr* = (*Brit*) Scottish Communist Party; single-cell protein; Society of Christian Philosophers.

SCPA *abbr* = Scottish Cashmere Producers' Association; (*Brit*) Scottish Clay Pigeon Association.

SCPL *abbr* (*Brit*) = Senior Commercial Pilot's Licence.

SCPS *abbr* = (*Brit*) Scottish Centre for Pollen Studies; Society of Civil and Public Servants.

SCR *abbr* = (*Brit*) senior combination room (Cambridge colleges); (*Brit*) senior common room (Oxford colleges); sequence control register.

scr. *abbr* = scruple.

scrabble *vi* to scratch or grope about; to struggle; to scramble. * *n* a repeated scratching or clawing; a scramble; a scribble.

Scrabble *n* (*trademark*) a game in which words are formed from individual lettered tiles on a grid.

scrag *n* a scrawny person or animal; the lean end of a neck of mutton or veal; (*loosely*) neck.

scraggly *adj* (**scragglier**, **scraggliest**) untidy, uneven.

scraggy *adj* (**scraggier**, **scraggiest**) thin and bony, gaunt.

scram *vi* (**scramming**, **scrammed**) (*sl*) to get out, to go away at once.

SCRAM *abbr* = (*Brit*) Scottish Campaign to Resist the Atomic Menace.

scramasax *n* a knife or dagger that was often buried with Anglo-Saxon men.

scramble *vi* to move or climb hastily on all fours; to scuffle or struggle for something; to move with urgency or panic. * *vt* to mix haphazardly; to stir (slightly beaten eggs) while cooking; (*transmitted signals*) to make unintelligible in transit. * *n* a hard climb or advance; a disorderly struggle; a rapid emergency take-off of fighter planes; a motorcycle rally over rough ground.—**scrambler** *n*.

scrap[1] *n* a small piece; a fragment of discarded material; (*pl*) bits of food. * *adj* in the form of pieces, leftovers, etc; used and discarded. * *vt* (**scrapping**, **scrapped**) to discard; to make into scraps.

scrap[2] *n* (*inf*) a fight or quarrel. * *vi* (**scrapping**, **scrapped**) to have a scrap.

scrapbook *n* a book for pasting clippings, etc, in; (*comput*) a utility program that can be used to retain frequently used images, pictures, or text.

scrape *vt* to rub with a sharp or abrasive object so as to clean, smooth or remove; to eke out or to be economical; to amass in small portions; to draw along with a grating or vibration; to get narrowly past, to graze; to draw back the foot in making a bow; (*with* **together**) to save or collect with difficulty. * *vi* (*with* **through**) to manage or succeed with difficulty or by a slim margin. * *n* the act of scraping; a grating sound; an abrasion, scratch; an awkward predicament.

scraper *n* an instrument for scraping; a grating or edge for scraping mud from boots; a tool made of stone or flint and used for scraping hides and skins; (*mus*) a percussion instrument in which sound is produced by scraping a stick over a series of notches cut into a piece of wood or bone.

scraperboard *n* a board with a black surface which can be scraped off with a special tool to form a design.

scrapheap *n* a pile of discarded material or things.

scraping *n* a piece scraped off.

scrappy *adj* (**scrappier**, **scrappiest**) disjointed; fragmentary; full of gaps.—**scrappily** *adv*.—**scrappiness** *n*.

scratch *vt* to mark with a sharp point; to scrape with the nails or claws; to rub to relieve an itch; to chafe; to write awkwardly; to strike out (writing, etc); to withdraw from (a race, etc). * *vi* to use nails or claws to tear or dig. * *n* the act of scratching; a mark or sound made by this; a slight injury; a starting line for a race; a scribble. * *adj* taken at random, haphazard, impromptu; without a handicap.

scratch pad *n* a notebook.

scratch video *n* a collage of images from existing television or motion-picture film.

scratchy *adj* (**scratchier**, **scratchiest**) making a scratching noise; uneven, ragged.—**scratchily** *adv*.—**scratchiness** *n*.

scrawl *n* careless or illegible handwriting; a scribble. * *vti* to draw or write carelessly.

scrawny *adj* (**scrawnier**, **scrawniest**) skinny; bony.—**scrawniness** *n*.

SCRE *abbr* (*Brit*) = Scottish Council for Racial Equality; Scottish Council for Research in Education.

scream *vti* to utter a piercing cry, as of pain, fear, etc; to shout; to shriek. * *n* a sharp, piercing cry; (*inf*) a very funny person or thing.

Scream *abbr* (*Brit*) = Society for the Control and Registration of Estate Agents and Mortgage Brokers.

scree *n* loose shifting stones; a slope covered with these.

screech *n* a harsh, high-pitched cry. * *vti* to utter (with) a screech, to shriek.

screech owl *n* a small North American owl with reddish or grayish plumage; (*Brit*) a barn owl.

screed *n* a long, tedious letter or speech; an informal piece of writing.

screen *n* a movable partition or framework to conceal, divide, or protect; a shelter or shield from heat, danger or view; an electronic display (as in a television set, computer terminal, etc); a surface on which movies, slides, etc are projected; the movie industry; a coarse wire mesh over a window or door to keep out insects; a sieve. * *vt* to conceal or shelter; to grade by passing through a screen; to separate according to skill, etc; to show (a movie) on a screen.

screen capture *n* (*comput*) a snapshot of the screen at a particular moment.—*also vt.*

screen dump *n* (*comput*) a printed output of a snapshot of the screen.

screen font *n* (*comput*) a font that is used by a program to display text.

screening *n* a showing of a movie; a metal or plastic mesh, as for window screens; the refuse matter after sieving.

screening test *n* a program of tests carried out on a large number of apparently healthy people to find those who may have a particular disease.

screenplay *n* a story written in a form suitable for a movie.

screen saver *n* (*comput*) a utility program designed to prolong the life of a screen by preventing a static image from being burnt onto it, either by switching it off or replacing it with a moving image.

screens passage *n* (*archit*) a corridor-like space in a medieval hall separated from the hall by a decorated screen.

screen test *n* an audition for a role in a movie.

screenwriter *n* a person who writes screenplays.

screw *n* a metal cylinder or cone with a spiral thread around it for fastening things by being turned; any spiral thing like this; a twist or turn of a screw; a twist of paper; pressure; a propeller with revolving blades on a shaft. * *vt* to fasten, tighten, etc with a screw; to oppress; to extort, to cheat out of something due; (*sl, vulg*) to have sexual intercourse with; (*with* up) to gather (courage, etc). * *vi* to go together or come apart by being turned like a screw; to twist or turn with a writhing movement; (*sl, vulg*) to have sexual intercourse; (*with* up) to bungle.

screwball *n* (*sl*) an odd or eccentric person. * *adj* whimsical, zany.

screwdriver *n* a tool like a blunt chisel for turning screws; a drink of vodka and orange juice.

screwed *adj* (*sl*) drunk.

screw pine *n* any of various tropical plants with slender stems and clusters of spiral leaves.

screw propeller *n* an early form of propeller based on the Archimedes screw.

screw top *n* a cap that screws onto the top of a bottle or other container; a bottle, etc having this.

screwy *adj* (**screwier, screwiest**) (*sl*) eccentric, odd.—**screwiness** *n.*

Scriabin, Skryabin *n* **Alexander Nikolayevich** (1872–1915) Russian composer and pianist.

scribble *vti* to draw or write hastily or carelessly, to scrawl; to be a writer. * *n* hasty writing, a scrawl.—**scribbler** *n.*

scribe *n* a person who copies documents; an author or journalist; (*Bible*) an expounder of Jewish law. * *vt* to draw a line on by cutting with a pointed instrument.

scriber *n* a pointed tool used to score or mark lines (e.g., on metal) as guides for cutting.

scrim *n* a light, open-weave fabric used in upholstery, lining, and theater sets.

scrimmage *n* a confused struggle; a skirmish; (*football*) the period between the ball entering play and it being declared dead. * *vi* to engage in a scrimmage.

scrimp *vti* to be sparing or frugal (with); to make too small, skimp.

scrimshank *vi* (*inf*) to shirk work, esp military duties.

scrimshaw *n* carvings made from shells, whalebone, ivory, etc, usu by sailors; the art of producing such carvings.

scrip *n* a written list; a certificate entitling the holder to a share of company stock.

scrip issue *n* the issue of new share certificates to existing shareholders without any further capital being required to be paid.

script *n* handwriting; a style of writing; the text of a stage play, screenplay, or broadcast; a plan of action; (*print*) type that resembles handwriting; (*comput*) a list of instructions that automatically perform a task within an application program. * *vt* to write a script for.

Script. *abbr* = Scriptural; Scripture(s).

scriptural *adj* of or based on the Bible or Scripture.

scripture *n* any sacred writing; (*with cap, often pl*) the Jewish Bible, or Old Testament; the Christian Bible, or Old and New Testaments. * *adj* contained in or quoted from the Bible.

scriptwriter *n* a writer of screenplays for movies, TV, etc; a screenwriter — **scriptwriting** *n.*

scrofula *n* tuberculosis of the lymph glands in the neck.—**scrofulous** *adj.*

scroll *n* a roll of parchment or paper with writing on it; an ornament like this; (*her*) a ribbon with a motto; a list; (*mus*) the decorative end of the peg-box of a violin or other stringed instrument, which may be carved into a curl resembling a scroll, or an animal head. * *vti* (*comput*) to move (text) across a screen; to decorate with scrolls.

scroll saw *n* a thin saw for cutting intricate designs.

Scrooge *n* (*also without cap*) a miserly, miserable person (after the character in *A Christmas Carol* by Charles Dickens).

scrotum *n* (*pl* **scrota** *or* **scrotums**) the pouch of skin containing the testicles.

scrounge *vti* (*inf*) to seek or obtain (something) for nothing.—**scrounger** *n.*

scrub[1] *n* an arid area of stunted trees and shrubs; such vegetation; anything small or mean. * *adj* small, stunted, inferior, etc.

scrub[2] *vti* (**scrubbing, scrubbed**) to clean vigorously, scour; to rub hard; (*inf*) to remove, cancel. * *n* the act of scrubbing.

scrubber *n* a person or thing that scrubs; (*sl*) a promiscuous woman.

scrubby *adj* (**scrubbier, scrubbiest**) stunted; paltry; unkempt.—**scrubbily** *adv.*—**scrubbiness** *n.*

scrub typhus *n* a disease prevalent in Southeast Asia, caused by a parasitic microorganism, *Rickettsia*, which is transmitted from rodents to humans by the bite of mites.

scruff[1] *n* the back of the neck, the nape.

scruff[2] *n* (*inf*) a shabbily dressed person.

scruffy *adj* (**scruffier, scruffiest**) shabby; unkempt.—**scruffily** *adv.*—**scruffiness** *n.*

scrum *n* a scrummage.

scrum half *n* (*rugby*) (the position held by) the player who puts the ball into the scrum.

scrummage *n* (*rugby*) a play consisting of a tussle between rival forwards in a compact mass for possession of the ball. * *vi* to form a scrum(mage).

scrump *vt* (*Brit, dial*) to steal (apples) from an orchard or garden.

scrum-pox *n* a bacterial (impetigo) or viral (herpes simplex) infection of the face that is common in rugby players, occurring probably through facial contact in the scrum or communal changing facilities.

scrumptious *adj* (*inf*) delicious; very pleasing.—**scrumptiously** *adv.*—**scrumptiousness** *n.*

scrunch *vti* to crumple (esp the hair) when drying; to crunch or be crumpled or crunched. * *n* a crunching sound; the act of scrunching.

scruple *n* (*usu pl*) a moral principle or belief causing one to doubt or hesitate about a course of action. * *vt* to hesitate owing to scruples.

scrupulous *adj* careful; conscientious; thorough.—**scrupulously** *adv.*—**scrupulousness** *n.*

scrutineer *n* a person who scrutinizes, esp an inspector of ballot papers.

scrutinize *vti* to look closely (at), to examine narrowly; to make a scrutiny of.—**scrutinizer** *n.*

scrutiny *n* (*pl* **scrutinies**) a careful examination; a critical gaze; an official inspection of votes cast in an election.

scs. *abbr* = scales.

SCS *abbr* = (*Brit*) Scottish Crime Squad; Singapore Civil Service; Society of Cosmetic Scientists; Swiss Cooks' Society.

SCSA *abbr* = (*Brit*) Scottish Cold Storage Association; Strip Curtain Suppliers' Association.

SCSI *abbr* = small computer systems interface.

SCTA *abbr* = (*Brit*) Scottish Clay Target Association.

SCU *abbr* = (*Brit*) Scottish Cricket Union; (*Brit*) Scottish Crofters' Union; (*Brit*) Scottish Cyclists' Union; Special Care Unit.

SCUA *abbr* = (*Brit*) Scottish Conservative and Unionist Association; Suez Canal Users' Association.

scuba *n* a diver's apparatus with compressed-air tanks for breathing underwater.

scud *vti* (**scudding, scudded**) to go along swiftly; to be driven before the wind. * *n* an act of scudding; light clouds, etc, driven by wind; a type of missile.

scuff *vti* to drag (the feet), to shuffle; to wear or mark the surface of by doing this.

scuffle *n* a confused fight; the sound of shuffling. * *vi* to fight confusedly; to move by shuffling.

scull *n* an oar worked from side to side over the stern of a boat; a light rowing boat for racing. * *vti* to propel with a scull.

scullery *n* (*pl* **sculleries**) a room for storage or kitchen work, such as washing dishes, etc.

sculp. *abbr* = sculptor; sculptural; sculpture.

sculpt *vt* to carve, sculpture.

sculpt. *abbr* = sculptor; sculptural; sculpture.

sculptor *n* a person skilled in sculpture.

Sculptor *or* **the Sculptor's workshop** *n* a faint constellation lying in the southern hemisphere near Grus (the Crane), which is not readily detectable.

sculptress *n* a woman skilled in sculpture.

sculpture *n* the art of carving wood or forming clay, stone, etc, into figures, statues, etc; a three-dimensional work of art; a sculptor's work. * *vt* to carve, adorn, or portray with sculptures; to shape, mold, or form like sculpture.—**sculptural** *adj.*

scum *n* a thin layer of impurities on top of a liquid; refuse; despicable people.

scumbag *n* (*sl*) a disgusting or despicable person.

scumble *vt* to soften the lines or colors of (a painting) by applying a thin coat of opaque color. * *n* the upper layer of color applied for this purpose.

scunner *n* (*Scot*) disgust. * *vti* to cause to feel disgust.—**scunnered** *adj*

scupper n a hole in a ship's side that lets water run from the deck into the sea. * vt (sl) to sink deliberately; to disable.

scurf n small flakes of dead skin, such as dandruff; any scaly coating.

scurrilous adj abusive; grossly offensive.

scurry vi (**scurrying**, **scurried**) to hurry with quick, short steps, scamper. * n (pl **scurries**) a bustle; a flurry (as of snow).

scurvy n a disease caused by a deficiency of vitamin C. * adj base; contemptible.

scut n the short tail of certain animals, such as the deer or hare.

scute or **scutum** n an external scale or plate on the bodies of animals such as the armadillo, turtle, etc.

scutellum n (pl **scutella**) any of the small horny scales or plates on a plant or animal.

scuttle[1] vi to run quickly; to hurry away. * n a short, swift run; a hurried pace.

scuttle[2] n a bucket with a lip for storing coal.

scuttle[3] n (naut) a hatchway, a hole with a cover in a ship's deck or side. * vt to sink (a ship) by making holes in the bottom.

scuttlebut n (formerly) a cask containing drinking water on the deck of a ship; (sl) gossip.

Scutum or **the Shield** n a small constellation lying in the Milky Way in the southern hemisphere, near Sagittarius.

scuzzy adj (**scuzzier**, **scuzziest**) (sl) filthy, squalid.

SCV abbr = Sons of Confederate Veterans; (Italian) Stato della Città del Vaticano, "Vatican City State."

SCW abbr = Society of Colonial Wars.

Scylla and Charybdis n two rocks in the Strait of Messina between Italy and Sicily, which in ancient times were very dangerous to navigators. Scylla was believed to be a monster who barked like a dog, and had six long necks and mouths, each of which contained three rows of sharp teeth. Charybdis, three times every day, swallowed the waters of the sea and threw them up again.

Scyros or **Scyrus** n modern Skiros, an island in the Aegean Sea, and one of the northern Sporades.

scythe n a two-handed implement with a large, curved blade for cutting grass, etc. * vti to cut with a scythe; to mow down.

Scythians npl a nomadic race that occupied land north of the Black Sea around the 8th century BC.

sd abbr = semi-detached; (Latin) sine die, "without a day"; special delivery; stage door.

sd. abbr = said (i.e., aforesaid); sewed.

s.d. abbr = sine die; solid-drawn; (mil) special duty; (statistics) standard deviation.

SD abbr = (Latin) salutem dicit, "he sends greeting"; (Latin) Scientiae Doctor, "Doctor of Science"; senile dementia; Senior Deacon; South Dakota; (mil) Southern Department.

S/D abbr = (grain trade) sea-damaged; sight draft.

SDA abbr = (Brit) Scottish Darts Association; (Brit) Scottish Decorators' Association; (Brit) Scottish Development Agency; Seventh Day Adventists' General Conference.

S. Dak. abbr = South Dakota.

SD&BBA abbr = Soft Drink and Beer Bottlers' Association (Republic of Ireland).

SDASA abbr (Brit) = Scottish Deaf Amateur Sports Association.

SDAT abbr = senile dementia of the Alzheimer type.

S-DAT abbr = stationary digital audio tape.

SDC abbr = Society of Designer-Craftsmen; (Brit) Society of Dyers and Colourists; Sustainable Development Commission.

SDCGB abbr (Brit) = Square Dance Callers of Great Britain.

SDD abbr (Brit) = Scottish Development Department; subscriber direct dialling.

SDG abbr (Latin) = soli Deo gloria, "glory be to God alone."

sdg. abbr = siding.

SDHBS abbr (Brit) = South Devon Herd Book Society.

SDI abbr = Strategic Defense Initiative.

SDLP abbr (Brit) = Social Democratic and Labour Party (in n. Ireland).

SDMJ abbr = September, December, March, June (re quarterly payments).

SDO abbr = senior duty officer.

SDP abbr = (Brit) Social Democratic Party; (motor insurance) social domestic and pleasure.

SDR abbr = special dispatch rider; special drawing right.

SDSA abbr (Brit) = Scottish Down's Syndrome Association.

SDT abbr = Society of Dairy Technology.

SDTA abbr (Brit) = Scottish Dance Teachers' Alliance.

SDTU abbr = Sign and Display Trades Union.

SDUK abbr = Society for the Diffusion of Useful Knowledge.

Se symbol (chem) = selenium (element).

se abbr = standard error.

s.e. abbr = (theat) second entrance.

SE abbr = (Brit) Scottish Enterprise; Society of Engineers; Stock Exchange; southeast(ern).

sea n the ocean; a section of this; a vast expanse of water; a heavy wave, the swell of the ocean; something like the sea in size; the seafaring life; **law of the sea** an agreement between most maritime nations for administering the seas that recognizes and defines areas and rights. * adj marine, of the sea.

SEA abbr = Shipbuilding Exports Association; Slag Employers' Association; Society for Electronic Access; Southeast Asia.

sea anchor n a device dragged behind a vessel to slow the rate of drifting or keep it heading into the wind.

sea anemone n any of various solitary brightly colored polyps with a ring of petal-like tentacles surrounding the mouth.

sea bass n any of numerous American marine fishes with a long body and a spiny dorsal fin.

seaboard n, adj (land) bordering on the sea.

seaborne adj conveyed by the sea; carried on a ship.

sea bream n any of numerous marine food fishes of European seas.

sea breeze n a wind that blows from the sea to the land.

SEAC abbr = Schools Examinations and Assessment Council; Southeast Asia Command.

sea change n a radical transformation.

Seachran n (Irish Celtic myth) a giant who became a friend of Fionn mac Cumhaill.

seacock n a valve in the hull of a vessel through which water can pass in or out.

sea cow see **dugong**.

sea cucumber n an echinoderm with an elongated body, leathery skin, and an oral ring of tentacles at one end.

sea dog n an old sailor.

sea eagle n any of various fish-eating eagles.

seafarer n a sailor; a person who travels by sea.

seafaring n traveling by sea, esp the work of a sailor.—also adj.

sea-floor spreading n (geol) the theory that the ocean floor is created at ridges running along the centers of the ocean floors and that these are the margins of new tectonic plates.

seafood n edible fish or shellfish from the sea.

sea front n the waterfront of a seaside town.

Seaga n Edward (1930–), American-born Jamaican politician. He became prime minister (1980–89) when his Labour Party defeated Michael Manley's National Party in the 1980 general election, and lost power to Manley's party in 1989.

seagoing adj (ship) made for use on the open sea.

sea-green adj, n (a) pale bluish-green.

seagull n a gull.

sea holly n a European coastal plant with blue flowers.

sea horse n a small, bony-plated fish with a horse-like head and neck and a long tail that swims in an upright position; in fable, a horse with the tail of a fish.

sea kale n a European coastal plant with fleshy leaves and edible shoots.

seal[1] n an engraved stamp for impressing wax, lead, etc; wax, lead, etc, so impressed; that which authenticates or pledges; a device for closing or securing tightly. * vt to fix a seal to; to close tightly or securely; to shut up; to mark as settled, to confirm.

seal[2] n an aquatic mammal with four webbed flippers; the fur of some seals; a dark brown. * vi to hunt seals.

SEAL abbr = Society of English and American Lawyers; Southeast Adult Learning.

sea lane n a route for ships.

sealant n a thing that seals, such as wax, etc; a substance for stopping a leak, making watertight, etc.

sea lavender n any of a genus of coastal plants with white, pink, or purple flowers.

sealed-beam adj (car headlight) having the reflector incorporated in the lamp.

sea legs npl (inf) the ability to walk steadily on a moving ship and to be free from seasickness.

sealer n a person or a ship whose business is hunting seals.

sea level n the level of the surface of the sea in relation to the land.

sea lily n an echinoderm with a thin, elongated body topped by petal-like tentacles.

sealing wax n a resinous compound that is plastic when warm and used for sealing letters, etc.

SEALION abbr = Sea Level Instrumentation and Observation Network.

sea lion n a large seal of the Pacific Ocean that has a loud roar and, in the male, a mane.

sealskin n the fur of a seal; a coat of this.

Sealyham terrier n a breed of wire-haired terrier with short legs and a longish, usu white, coat.

seam n the line where two pieces of cloth are stitched together; (geol) a stratum of coal, oil, etc, between thicker ones; a line or wrinkle. * vt to join with a seam; to furrow.

seaman n (pl **seamen**) a sailor; a naval rank.

seamanship n the skill of handling, working, and navigating a ship.

seamark n a mark indicating tidal limit; an elevated signal serving as a guide for mariners.

sea mile n a nautical mile.

sea mouse n a marine worm with a broad body covered in hair-like bristles.

seamstress n a woman who sews for a living.

seamy adj (**seamier**, **seamiest**) unpleasant or sordid.

seance, séance n a meeting of spiritualists to try to communicate with the dead.

sea otter n a large marine otter of North Pacific coasts that feeds on shellfish.

S

Sea Peoples *see* **Peoples of the Sea**.

sea pink *n* the plant thrift.

seaplane *n* an airplane with floats that allow it to take off from and land on water.

seaport *n* a port, harbor or town accessible to oceangoing ships.

SEAQ *abbr* = Stock Exchange Automated Quotations.

sear *vt* to burn or scorch the surface of; to brand with a heated iron; to wither up.

Searbhan *n* (*Irish Celtic myth*) a one-eyed giant who was sent to guard a magic rowan tree that had grown from a berry that had accidentally been let fall by one of the Tuatha De Danann.

search *vi* to look around to find something; to explore. * *vt* to examine or inspect closely; to probe into. * *n* the act of searching; an investigation; a quest.—**searcher** *n* .

search engine *n* (*comput*) a facility or tool that is used to look for and retrieve information on the Web.

searching *adj* keen, piercing; examining thoroughly.—**searchingly** *adv*.

searchlight *n* a powerful ray of light projected by an apparatus on a swivel; the apparatus.

search party *n* a group of people organized to locate a missing person or thing.

search warrant *n* a legal document that authorizes a police search.

Searle *n* **Ronald [William Fordham]** (1920–) English cartoonist and writer and creator of the St Trinian's schoolgirls, e.g., in *Back to the Slaughterhouse* (1951). Regarded, particularly in the US and France, as one of the finest graphic artists of the 20th century. His haunting book *To the Kwai—and Back: War Drawings 1939–45* (1986), is a record of his experiences as a Japanese prisoner of war.

SEASAT *n* an artificial satellite, launched in 1978 with the object of collecting information on the oceans using remote sensing techniques.

seascape *n* a picture of a scene at sea.

Sea Scout *n* a member of a Scout troop specializing in sailing, canoeing, diving, etc.

sea serpent *n* a legendary sea-dwelling monster resembling a snake or dragon.

seashell *n* the discarded or empty shell of a marine mollusk.

seashore *n* land beside the sea or between high and low water marks; the beach.

seasick *adj* affected with nausea brought on by the motion of a ship.—**seasickness** *n*.

seaside *n* seashore.

sea snail *n* a spiral-shelled marine mollusk, such as a whelk; a small slimy fish with pelvic fins formed into a sucker.

sea snake *n* a venomous snake of tropical waters with an oar-shaped tail.

season *n* one of the four equal parts into which the year is divided: spring, summer, autumn, or winter; a period of time; a time when something is plentiful or in use; a suitable time; (*inf*) a season ticket. * *vt* (*food*) to flavor by adding salt, spices, etc; to make mature or experienced; (*wood*) to dry until ready for use. * *vi* to become experienced.

seasonable *adj* suitable for the season; timely, opportune.—**seasonableness** *n*.—**seasonably** *adv*.

seasonal *adj* of or relating to a particular season.—**seasonally** *adv*.

seasonal affective disorder *n* a state of depression that affects some people in the winter months, thought to be caused by a lack of sunlight.

seasoning *n* salt, spices, etc, used to enhance the flavor of food; the process of making something fit for use.

Seasons *n* **The** (*Die Jahreszeiten*) an oratorio by Haydn to a libretto by Van Swieten, which was based on a poem of the same name by James Thomson and which was first performed in Vienna in 1801. It was Haydn's last important work.

season ticket *n* a ticket or set of tickets valid for a number of concerts, games, journeys, etc, during a specified period.

seat *n* a piece of furniture for sitting on, such as a chair, bench, etc; the part of a chair on which one sits; the buttocks, the part of the pants covering them; a way of sitting (on a horse, etc); the chief location, or centere; a part at or forming a base; the right to sit as a member; a parliamentary constituency; a large country house. * *vt* to place on a seat; to provide with seats; to settle.

seatbelt *n* an anchored strap worn in a car or airplane to secure a person to a seat.

seated *adj* provided with a seat or seats; fixed, confirmed; located.

seating *n* the arrangement or provision of seats.

SEATO *abbr* = Southeast Asia Treaty Organization.

sea trout *n* a marine variety of brown trout that migrates to fresh water to spawn.

sea urchin *n* a small marine animal with a round body enclosed in a shell covered with sharp spines.

sea wall *n* a barrier or embankment to prevent erosion by the sea.

seaward *adj* toward the sea. * *adv* toward or in the direction of the sea.

seaway *n* an ocean traffic lane; a waterway for seagoing traffic to an inland port.

seaweed *n* a mass of plants growing in or under water; a sea plant, esp a marine alga.

seaworthy *adj* fit to go to sea; able to withstand sea water, watertight.—**seaworthiness** *n*.

SEB *abbr* = Society for Experimental Botany.

sebaceous *adj* of, secreting, containing, or producing oily or fatty matter.

sebaceous cyst *n* a cyst formed in the duct of a sebaceous gland of the skin.

sebaceous glands *npl* the small skin glands that secrete sebum onto the skin surface.

Sebaste *n* (*Bible*) Samaria.

Sebastian *n* **Saint** (*d*. 303) martyr born at Narbonne in France and brought up in Milan; entered the army of Emperor Carinus in order to give secret help to the victims of the persecution. Diocletian made Sebastian captain of a company of guards. He was discovered to be a Christian, pierced with arrows, beaten to death with cudgels, and thrown into a sewer. His feast day is 20 January.

Sebbi *n* king of Essex (665–695). A joint ruler with his nephew Sighere.

SEbE *abbr* = southeast by east.

Sebek *n* an Egyptian deity associated with Seth. Crocodile-headed, his cult was in the Faiyum region.

seborrhea *n* the excessive secretion of sebum.—**seborrheic** *adj*.

SEbS *abbr* = southeast by south.

sebum *n* a fatty substance secreted by the sebaceous glands to lubricate the hair and skin.

sec¹ *adj* (*wine*) dry; (*champagne*) medium-sweet.

sec² *n* (*inf*) a second.

sec. *abbr* = secant; secondary; second(s); secretary; section(s); sector; secundum; (*bank*) security.

sec-1 *abbr* = per second.

sec-2 *abbr* = per second per second.

SEC *abbr* = (*Brit*) Scottish Evangelistic Crusade; Secondary Examinations Council; Securities and Exchange Commission; Space Environment Center

Secam *abbr* (*French*) = *Séquentiel Couleur à Mémoire*, "color sequence by memory" (Russian and French color television system).

secant *n* a trigonometrical function that is the reciprocal of the cosine; a straight line that intersects a curve.

secateurs *npl* a pair of small shears with curved blades for pruning, etc.

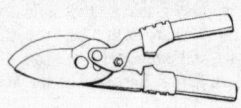

secede *vi* to withdraw formally one's membership from a society or organization.—**seceder** *n*.

secession *n* the act or an instance of seceding; a breaking away.—**secessional** *adj*.

sec.-ft. *abbr* = second-foot.

sech *abbr* = hyperbolic secant.

Sec. Leg. *abbr* = Secretary of Legation.

seclude *vt* to keep (a person, etc) separate from others; to remove or screen from view.

secluded *adj* private; sheltered; kept from contact with other people.

seclusion *n* the state of being secluded; privacy, solitude.

Secombe, Sir Harry *see* **Milligan, Spike**.

second *adj* next after first; alternate; another of the same kind; next below the first in rank, value, etc. * *n* a person or thing coming second; another; an article of merchandise not of first quality; an aid or assistant, as to a boxer, duelist; the gear after low gear; one sixtieth of a minute of time or of an angular degree; (*pl*) (*inf*) another helping of food. * *adv* in the second place, group, etc. * *vt* to act as a second to; to support (a motion, resolution, etc); (*mil*) to place on temporary service elsewhere.

secondary *adj* subordinate; second in rank or importance; in the second stage; derived, not primary; relating to secondary school. * *n* (*pl* **secondaries**) that which is secondary; a delegate, a deputy.—**secondarily** *adv*.

secondary cell *n* a battery that can convert chemical energy to electrical energy by reversible chemical reactions and so be recharged.

secondary color *n* a color formed by mixing two primary colors.

secondary emission *n* (*phys*) the emission of secondary electrons from a solid surface due to bombardment by a beam of primary electrons or other elementary particles.

secondary school *n* a school between elementary or primary school and college or university.

secondary sexual characteristic *n* an attribute of a human being or animal that is characteristic of a particular sex but is not directly concerned with reproduction.

secondary storage *or* **auxiliary storage** *n* (*comput*) a form of permanent storage of data on disk drives, e.g., hard disks, CD ROMs, etc.

second best *adj* next to the best; inferior. * *adv* in second place. * *n* next to the best; an inferior alternative.

second chamber *n* the upper house in a legislative assembly with two chambers.

second childhood *n* dotage, senility.

second class *n* the class next to the first in a classification. * *adj* (**second-class**) relating to a second class; inferior, mediocre; (*seating, accommodation*) next in price and quality to first class; (*mail*) less expensive and handled more slowly than first class.

Second Coming *n* (*Christianity*) the return to earth of Christ at the Last Judgment as prophesied.

second cousin *n* a child of the first cousin of one's parent.

second-degree burn *n* a burn which causes blistering of the skin.

second fiddle *n* (the musical part for) a second violin in an orchestra or string quartet; (*inf*) a person of secondary importance.

second-generation *adj* denoting a native-born citizen of a country whose grandparents or parents were immigrants; (*comput*) denoting computers in which transistors replaced vacuum tubes (in the early 1960s).

second-guess *vt* to predict by guessing, to outguess; to explain or criticize with hindsight.—**second-guesser** *n*.

second-hand *adj* bought after use by another; derived, not original.—*also adv.*

second hand *n* the moving pointer in a clock or watch that indicates the seconds.

secondly *adv* in the second place.

second mortgage *n* a mortgage taken out on a property that is already mortgaged in order to raise loan capital.

second nature *n* a long-established habit, etc, deeply fixed in a person's nature.

second person *n* that form of a pronoun (as *you*) or verb (as *are*) that refers to the person spoken to.

second-rate *adj* of inferior quality.

second sight *n* the supposed faculty of seeing events before they occur.

second string *n* a reserve or substitute player in a team.

second thought *n* a change in thought or decision after consideration.

second wind *n* a return to regular breathing after a bout of exercise; renewed energy or enthusiasm.

secrecy *n* (*pl* **secrecies**) the state of being secret; the ability to keep secret.

secret *adj* not made public; concealed from others; hidden; private; remote. * *n* something hidden; a mystery; a hidden cause.

secret agent *n* a spy.

secretaire *n* a writing desk with an upper section for books and documents.

secretariat *n* an administrative office or staff, as in a government.

secretary *n* (*pl* **secretaries**) a person employed to deal with correspondence, filing, telephone calls of another or of an association; the head of a state department.—**secretarial** *adj.*

secretary bird *n* a large, long-legged African bird of prey that eats mostly snakes.

secretary-general *n* (*pl* **secretaries-general**) the chief administrator of a large organization (e.g., the United Nations).

Secretary of State *n* in the US, the minister in charge of foreign affairs; in the UK, any of various ministers in charge of government departments.

secrete *vt* to conceal; to hide; (*cell, gland, etc*) to produce and release (a substance) out of blood or sap.

secretin *n* a polypeptide hormone produced by the lining of the duodenum and jejunum in response to acid from the stomach.

secretion *n* the process of secreting; a substance secreted by an animal or plant.

secretive *adj* given to secrecy; uncommunicative, reticent.—**secretively** *adv.*—**secretiveness** *n.*

secretly *adv* in a secret way; unknown to others.

secretory *adj* having the function of secreting, as a gland.

secretory otitis media *see* **glue ear**.

secret police *n* a police force that operates covertly to suppress political dissent rather than criminal activity.

secret service *n* a government agency that gathers intelligence, infiltrates terrorist or subversive organizations, conducts espionage, etc in the interests of national security.

secs. *abbr* = seconds; sections.

sect *n* a religious denomination; a group of people united by a common interest or belief; a faction.

sect. *abbr* = section.

sectarian *adj* of or confined to a religious sect; bigoted. * *n* a member or adherent of a sect.

sectarianism *n* devotion to a sect; religious narrowness.

section *n* the act of cutting; a severed or separable part; a division; a distinct portion; a slice; a representation of anything cut through to show its interior; (*geom*) the cutting of a solid by a plane; a plane figure formed by this. * *vti* to cut or separate into sections; to represent in sections; to become separated or cut into parts.

sectional *adj* of a section; made up of several sections; local rather than general in character.—**sectionally** *adv.*

sector *n* (*geom*) a space enclosed by two radii of a circle and the arc they cut off; a distinctive part (as of an economy); a subdivision; (*mil*) an area of activity; (*comput*) a storage area on a disk.

secular *adj* having no connection with religion or the church; worldly; changing or continuing over an extended period of time.—**secularly** *adv.*

secular acceleration *n* the gradual apparent increase in the velocity of the orbit of the moon around the Earth, which has been measured as 10.3 arc seconds every century.

secularize *vt* to change from religious to civil use or control.—**secularization** *n.*

secular parallax *n* the ongoing increase in the angular displacement of stars over a period of time due to the movement of the sun through space.

secure *adj* free from danger, safe; stable; firmly held or fixed; confident, assured (of); reliable. * *vt* to make safe; to fasten firmly; to protect; to confine; to fortify; to guarantee; to gain possession of; to obtain.—**securely** *adv.*

security *n* (*pl* **securities**) the state of being secure; a financial guarantee, surety; a pledge for repayment, etc; a protection or safeguard; a certificate of shares or bonds; (*comput*) the method of protecting files or programs so that unauthorized people cannot copy or access them.

security blanket *n* a blanket, soft toy, etc, carried by a child for security; (*inf*) any familiar object that provides reassurance; a policy of temporary secrecy imposed by the authorities in the interests of security.

Security Council *n* the principal council of the United Nations charged with maintaining world peace.

security guard *n* a person employed to protect public buildings, banks, offices, etc and to transport large sums of money.

security police *n* a police force whose function is to prevent espionage; the military police of an air force.

security risk *n* a person or thing regarded as a potential threat to security.

secy. *abbr* = secretary.

SED *abbr* (*Brit*) = Scottish Education Department.

SEDAC *abbr* = Socioeconomic Data and Applications Center

sedan *n* an automobile with no division between driver and passengers; a covered chair for one person with poles carried by two bearers.

Sedanta *see* **Setanta**.

sedate¹ *adj* calm; composed; serious and unemotional.—**sedately** *adv.*—**sedateness** *n.*

sedate² *vti* to calm or become calm by the administration of a sedative.

sedation *n* the act of calming or the condition of being calmed, esp by sedatives; the administration of sedatives to calm a patient.

sedative *n* a drug with a soothing, calming effect. * *adj* having a soothing, calming effect.

Seddon *n* John P[ollard] (1827–1906) British architect, whose notable works include a hotel (now a university), Aberystwyth, Wales.

sedentary *adj* requiring a sitting position; inactive; not migratory.

Seder *n* a Jewish ceremonial meal held on the first night of Passover.

Sed Festival *n* (*Egypt*) a king's jubilee festival, supposedly held to mark thirty years of rule but often held after a much shorter time.

sedge *n* a grass-like plant that grows in marshes or beside water; (*Egypt*) the lily emblem of Upper Egypt. The king of the two lands was known, in the allusive style preferred by the Egyptians, as "He of the sedge and the bee."

sedge warbler *n* a European songbird that inhabits marshy areas.

sedile *n* (*archit*) a seat, found particularly in churches, usu made of stone and set into the wall.

sediment *n* matter that settles at the bottom of a liquid; (*geol*) matter deposited by water or wind.

sedimentary *adj* relating to or formed by sediment.

sedition *n* incitement to rebel against the government.—**seditious** *adj.*—**seditiously** *adv.*

Sedley *n* Sir **Charles** (1639–1701) English poet and dramatist, whose three plays are the tragedy *Antony and Cleopatra*, and two comedies, *The Mulberry Garden* and *Bellamira*. His lyrics include the magical "Love still has something of the sea".

seduce *vt* to lead astray; to corrupt; to entice into unlawful sexual intercourse.—**seducer** *n.*

seduction *n* the act of seducing; temptation; attraction.

seductive *adj* tending to seduce; enticing, alluring.—**seductively** *adv.*—**seductiveness** *n.*

sedulous *adj* diligent; persevering.—**sedulously** *adv.*—**sedulousness** *n.*

see¹ *vt* (**seeing, saw,** *pp* **seen**) to perceive with the eyes; to observe; to grasp with the intelligence; to ascertain; to take care (that); to accompany; to visit; to meet; to consult; to receive (guests); (*with* **through**) to persist or endure to the end; to assist (e.g., a friend) during a crisis, difficulty, etc. * *vi* to have the faculty of sight; to make inquiry; to consider, reflect; to understand; (*with* **about**) to deal with; to consider in detail; (*with* **off**) to be present when someone leaves on a journey, etc; (*inf*) to repel, get rid of; (*with* **through**) to recognize the true character of.

see² *n* the diocese of a bishop.

SEE *abbr* (*Brit*) = Save Eyes Everywhere (British Council for the Prevention of Blindness).

seed *n* the small, hard part (ovule) of a plant from which a new plant grows; such seeds collectively; the source of anything; sperm or semen; descendants; (*tennis*) a seeded tournament player. * *vti* to sow (seed); to produce or shed seed; to remove seeds from; (*tennis*) to arrange (a tournament) so that the best players cannot meet until later rounds.

seedbed *n* a nursery bed for a plant; a place or source of growth or development.

seed cake *n* a sweet cake flavored with aromatic (usu caraway) seeds.

seed capital *n* a small amount of capital that is needed to pay for any research and development that has to be carried out before the setting up of a new business.

seed coral *n* small pieces of coral used in jewelry.

seed corn *n* corn reserved for sowing; assets promising future earning potential.

seedless *adj* without seeds.

seedling *n* a young plant raised from seed, not from a cutting; a young tree before it is a sapling.

seed money *n* money used to start a new project or enterprise.

seed oyster *n* a young oyster ready for transplantation to a new bed.

seed pearl *n* a very small pearl.

seed potato *n* a potato tuber ready for planting.

seed vessel *n* a pericarp.

seedy *adj* (**seedier, seediest**) full of seeds; out of sorts, indisposed; shabby; rundown.—**seedily** *adv.*—**seediness** *n.*

S

seeing *n* vision, sight; (*astron*) the quality of the conditions for viewing an astronomical object at the time of observation. * *adj* having sight; observant. * *conj* in view of the fact that; since.

Seeing Eye dog *n* (*trademark*) a guide dog for the blind.

seek *vti* (**seeking**, **sought**) to search for; to try to find, obtain, or achieve; (*comput*) to locate (a file) on a disk; to resort to; (*with* **to**) to try, endeavor; (*with* **out**) to search for and locate (a person or thing); to try to secure the society of.—**seeker** *n*.

seem *vi* to appear (to be); to give the impression of; to appear to oneself.

seeming *adj* that seems real, true; ostensible, apparent.—**seemingly** *adv*.

seemly *adj* (**seemlier**, **seemliest**) proper, fitting.—**seemliness** *n*.

seen *see* see[1].

seep *vi* to ooze gently, leak through.

seepage *n* the act of seeping; the liquid that has seeped.

seer *n* a person who sees visions, a prophet.

seersucker *n* a light, usu cotton, fabric with a puckered surface.

seesaw *n* a plank balanced across a central support so that it is tilted up and down by a person sitting on each end; an up-and-down movement like this; vacillation. * *vi* to move up and down; to fluctuate. * *adj, adv* alternately rising and falling.

seethe *vi* to be very angry inwardly; to swarm (with people).

SEF *abbr* = (*Brit*) Scottish Environmental Forum; Shipbulding Employers' Federation.

SEFA *abbr* = Southeast Forest Alliance.

SEG *abbr* = socioeconomic grade.

segment *n* a section; a portion; one of the two parts of a circle or sphere when a line is drawn through it. * *vti* to cut or separate into segments.—**segmentation** *n*.

Ségou *n* town in Mali.

Segovia *n* **Andrés** [Marquis of Salobreña] (1894–1987) Spanish guitarist, who initiated a revival of interest in the classical guitar.

segregate *vti* to set apart from others, to isolate; to separate (racial or minority groups).

segregation *n* the act of segregating or the condition of being segregated; the policy of compelling racial groups to live apart.

segue *vi* (**segueing**, **segued**) to continue from one piece of music to another without a pause. * *n* an uninterrupted transition in this manner.

seguidilla *n* (the music for) a lively Spanish dance in triple time.

seiche *n* an undulation of the surface of a lake, caused by earth tremors or changes in barometric pressure.

seigneur *n* a feudal lord.

seigneury *n* (*pl* **seigneuries**) the estate or authority of a seigneur.

Seilenus *n* **Silenus** *n* (*Greek myth*) the foster-father and constant companion of Dionysus, and a leader of the satyrs.

seine *n* a large fishing net that hangs vertically by means of floats along the top and weights along the bottom. * *vi* to catch fish with this.

SEIS *abbr* = submarine escape immersion suit.

seismic *adj* of or caused by earthquakes.—**seismically** *adv*.

seismic survey *n* a technique used to investigate the nature of underground rocks, especially those that may contain valuable ores, minerals, or oil.

seismo- *or* **seism-** *prefix* earthquake.

seismograph *n* an instrument for recording the direction, intensity, and time of an earthquake.—**seismographer** *n*.—**seismographic** *adj*.—**seismography** *n*.

seismol. *abbr* = seismological; seismology.

seismology *n* the scientific study of earthquakes.—**seismologic** *or* **seismological** *adj*.—**seismologist** *n*.

seize *vt* to grasp; to capture; to take hold of suddenly or forcibly; to attack or afflict suddenly. * *vi* (*machinery*) to become jammed.—**seizable** *adj*.

seizure *n* the act of seizing; what is seized; a sudden attack of illness, an apoplectic stroke.

Sekhmet *n* (*Egypt*) the lion-headed goddess of war and sickness, originally associated with Memphis and a figure to be placated.

Sekondi-Takoradi *n* a city in Ghana.

sel. *abbr* = selected; selection.

selah *n* (*OT*) a mysterious Hebrew word that occurs over 70 times in the Psalms.

seldom *adv* not often, rarely.

select *vti* to choose or pick out; (*comput*) to choose (a portion of a document or database) in which to perform a particular task. * *adj* excellent; choice; limited (e.g., in membership); exclusive.

select committee *n* a parliamentary committee established to investigate and report on a particular subject.

selection *n* the act of selecting; what is or are selected; the process by which certain animals or plants survive while others are eliminated, natural selection.

selective *adj* having the power of selection; highly specific in activity or effect.—**selectively** *adv*.—**selectiveness** *n*.

Selene *n* (*Greek myth*) the goddess of the moon, also called Phoebe, and in later times identified with Artemis.

selenium *n* a nonmetallic solid chemical element with semiconductive and photoconductive properties, which has various uses in electronics. * symbol Se.

seleno- *or* **selen-** *prefix* the moon.

selenography *n* the study and mapping of the physical features of the moon.—**selenographer** *n*.—**selenographic** *adj*.

selenology *n* the scientific and geological study of the moon.

Seles *n* **Monica** (1973–) Serbian-born American tennis player, and winner of several major titles.

Seleucia *n* seaport of the city of Antioch in Syria.

self *n* (*pl* **selves**) the identity, character, etc, of any person or thing; one's own person as distinct from all others; one's own interests or advantage. * *adj* (*color*) matching, uniform.

self- *prefix* of itself or oneself; by, for, in relation to, itself or oneself; automatic.

self-abnegation *n* denial of one's own interests or desires in favor of those of others.

self-absorption *n* preoccupation with one's own interests and welfare.

self-abuse *n* masturbation.

self-acting *adj* automatic.

self-addressed *adj* addressed to return to the sender; intended for oneself.

self-aggrandizement *n* acting to increase one's own power and importance at the expense of others.—**self-aggrandizing** *adj*.

self-approbation *n* satisfaction with one's own actions or accomplishments, esp to excess.

self-assertion *n* the act of asserting one's own opinions, ideas, or rights, esp determinedly.—**self-assertive** *adj*.

self-assessment *n* (*Brit*) a taxation system by which taxpayers assess their own income-tax liabilities and capital-gains liabilities for the tax year.

self-assured *adj* confident.—**self-assurance** *n*.

self-catering *adj* catering for oneself.

self-centered *adj* preoccupied with one's own affairs.—**self-centeredly** *adv*.—**self-centeredness** *n*.

self-colored *adj* of a single color.

self-confessed *adj* according to one's own testimony.

self-confident *adj* sure of one's own powers.—**self-confidence** *n*.—**self-confidently** *adv*.

self-conscious *adj* embarrassed or awkward in the presence of others, ill at ease.—**self-consciously** *adv*.—**self-consciousness** *n*.

self-contained *adj* complete in itself; showing self-control; uncommunicative.—**self-containment** *n*.

self-control *n* control of one's emotions, desires, etc, by the will.—**self-controlled** *adj*.

self-deception *n* the act or state of deceiving oneself.

self-defense *n* the act of defending oneself; (*law*) a plea for the justification of the use of force.

self-denial *n* abstention from pleasure, etc; unselfishness.

self-determination *n* free will; the choice of action without compulsion; the right of a nation to choose its own form of government.

self-discipline *n* the act of disciplining oneself, with regard to feelings, desires and willpower.

self-dissociation *n* (*chem*) the splitting of the molecules of certain highly polar liquids into ions.

self-drive *adj* (*hired vehicle*) driven by the hirer.

self-educated *adj* educated without benefit of formal instruction; educated at one's own expense.

self-effacement *n* the act of making oneself or one's actions inconspicuous, due to modesty or timidity.

self-employed *adj* earning one's living in one's own business or profession, not employed by another; working freelance.

self-esteem *n* confidence and respect for oneself; an exaggerated opinion of oneself.

self-evident *adj* evident without proof or explanation.—**self-evidently** *adv*.

self-examination *n* the scrutiny of one's own actions; the physical examination of oneself, e.g., for tumors.—**self-examining** *adj*.

self-explanatory *adj* easily understood without explanation.

self-expression *n* the expression of one's own personality, as in creative art.

self-financing *adj* referring to a company that is able to fund its capital expenditure from its undistributed profits rather than from loans.

self-governing *adj* autonomous; (*colony, etc*) having an elective legislation.—**self-government** *n*.

selfheal *n* a herbaceous plant with tightly clustered violet flowers.—*also* **allheal**.

self-help *n* the provision of means to help oneself, instead of relying on others.

self-image *n* one's sense of oneself or one's importance.

self-importance *n* an exaggerated estimate of one's own worth; pompousness.—**self-important** *adj*.

self-induced *adj* brought on by oneself or itself.

self-induction *n* the production of an electromotive force in a circuit by a variation in the electric current in the same circuit.

self-indulgence *n* undue gratification of one's desires, appetites, or whims.—**self-indulgent** *adj*.

self-inflicted *adj* (*wound, etc*) caused to a person by himself or herself.

self-interest *n* regard to one's own advantage.

selfish *adj* chiefly concerned with oneself; lacking in consideration for others.—**selfishly** *adv*.—**selfishness** *n*.

self-justification *n* the act or instance of making excuses for one's actions, etc.

selfless *adj* with no thought of self, unselfish.—**selflessly** *adv*.—**selflessness** *n*.

self-liquidating[1] *adj* denoting a loan in which the money loaned is used to fund a project that is expected to yield enough money to repay the loan and any interest payable on the loan and leave a profit; denoting an asset that earns back its original cost out of income over a set period of time; denoting a sales-promotion offer that is expected to make enough money in increased sales to pay for the money spent on the offer.

self-loading *adj* (*firearm*) semiautomatic.—**self-loader** *n*.

self-love n conceit; selfishness.

self-made adj having achieved status or wealth by one's own efforts.

self-opinionated adj conceited; stubborn.

self-pity n pity for oneself.—**self-pitying** adj.

self-pollination n the transfer of pollen from the anther to the stigma in the same flower.

self-portrait n an artist's or author's painting or account of himself or herself.

self-possessed adj cool and collected.

self-preservation n the instinct to protect oneself from injury or death.

self-propelled adj (vehicle) moving under its own power.

self-realization n the understanding or achievement of one's own potential or desires.

self-regard n concern for one's own interests; respect for oneself.

self-reliant adj relying on one's own powers; confident.—**self-reliance** n.

self-reproach n the act of blaming oneself.

self-respect n proper respect for oneself, one's standing and, dignity.—**self-respecting** adj.

self-righteous adj thinking oneself better than others; priggish.—**self-righteousness** n.

self-rising adj (flour) containing a rising agent.

self-rule n self-government.

self-sacrifice n the sacrifice of one's own interests, welfare, etc, to secure that of others.

selfsame adj identical, the very same.

self-satisfied adj smugly conceited.

self-seeking adj preoccupied with securing one's own well-being or interest; selfish.—**self-seeker** n.

self-service adj serving oneself in a cafe, store, service station, etc.

self-serving adj always seeking to protect or further one's own interests.

self-sown adj (plants) grown from seeds that were planted or deposited naturally without intervention by humans or animals.

self-starter n an electric device for starting an engine; a motivated employee who requires little supervision.

self-styled adj called by oneself; pretended.

self-sufficient adj independent; supporting oneself (e.g., in growing food) without the help of others.—**self-sufficiency** n.

self-supporting adj able to manage without help from others; able to stand unaided.

self-will n fixed adherence to one's own desires, intentions, etc; obstinacy.

self-winding adj (watch) wound automatically by an internal mechanism.

sell vt (**selling, sold**) to exchange (goods, services, etc) for money or other equivalent; to offer for sale; to promote; to deal in; (with up) to sell all the goods of (a debtor) to clear the debt. * vi (with off) to clear out stock at bargain prices; (with out) to sell off, to betray someone for money or reward; (inf) to disappoint or trick someone; to make sales; to attract buyers; (with up) to sell one's house, business, etc. * n an act or instance of selling; (inf) a disappointment, a trick, a fraud.—**seller** n.

Sellers n **Peter** (1925–80) English actor and comedian. One of the founders of The Goon Show with **Spike Milligan**, he starred as Inspector Clouseau in such movies as The Pink Panther (1963). Other, better, films include , The Lady Killers (1955), I'm all Right Jack (1959), Lolita (1962), Dr Strangelove (1963), and Being There (1979).

seller's market n a market in which demand exceeds supply, allowing sellers to set high prices.

Sellotape n (trademark) (Brit) a transparent adhesive tape; Scotch tape. * vt to seal or stick (something) using adhesive tape.

sellout n a show, game, etc, for which all the tickets are sold; (inf) a betrayal.

Selmersheim n **Pierre** (1869–1941) French architect and decorator.

seltzer n a naturally sparkling mineral water originally from Germany; an artificially carbonated mineral water.

selva n thick tropical rain forest.

selvage, selvedge n the edge of cloth so finished as to prevent unraveling.

selves see **self**.

sem abbr = semester; semicolon.

se(m) abbr = standard error (of the mean).

Sem abbr = Seminary; Semitic.

SEM abbr = scanning electron microscope.

SEMA abbr = Spray Equipment Manufacturers' Association; Storage Equipment Manufacturers' Association.

semantic adj relating to the meaning of words. * npl the study of word meanings and changes.

semaphore n a system of visual signaling using the operator's arms, flags, etc; a signaling device consisting of a post with movable arms.

Semarang n a city in Indonesia.

sematic adj (animal coloration) warning of danger.

semblance n likeness, resemblance; an outward, sometimes deceptive appearance.

Semele n (Greek myth) the mother of Dionysus by Zeus, who came to her accompanied by lightning and thunderbolts, which killed her.

semen n the fluid that carries sperm in men and male animals.

semester n an academic half-year.

SEMG abbr = Spring Makers' Export Group.

semi n (pl **semis**) (inf) a semi-detached house; a semifinal.

semi- prefix half; not fully; twice in a specified period.

semiannual adj happening twice a year, or lasting for six months.—also **semiyearly**.

semiautomatic adj partly automatic; (firearm) self-loading but discharging in single shots only as the trigger is pulled.

semibreve n (Brit, mus) a whole note.

semichorus n (mus) a passage to be sung by only a section of the chorus.

semicircle n half of a circle.—**semicircular** adj.

semicircular canal n any of the three fluid-filled tubes in the inner ear concerned with maintaining balance.

semicolon n the punctuation mark (;), of intermediate value between a comma and a full stop.

semiconductor n a substance in a transmitter, e.g., silicon, used to control the flow of current.

semiconscious adj not fully conscious.—**semiconsciousness** n.

semidemisemiquaver n (Brit, mus) a sixty-fourth note.

semi-detached adj (house) with another joined to it on one side.—also n.

semi-diurnal tide n high tide and low tide occurring twice in each lunar day, governed by the position of the moon and the configuration of the land.

semifinal adj, n (the match or round) before the final in a knockout tournament.—**semifinalist** n.

semifluid adj having qualities between those of a fluid and those of a solid; viscous.

semiliterate adj barely able to read or write.

semilunar adj in the shape of a crescent.

semilunar valve n either one of the two crescent-shaped valves in the heart.

seminal adj of, relating to, or containing semen; promising or contributing to further development; original, influential.—**seminally** adv.

seminar n a group of students engaged in study or research under supervision; any group meeting to pool and discuss ideas.

seminary n (pl **seminaries**) a training college for priests, ministers, etc; a school for young women.

seminiferous adj producing or containing semen; (plants) bearing seeds.

seminiferous tubule see **testicle**.

semiology n the study of signs and symbols.—**semiologic** or **semiological** adj.—**semiologist** n.

Semion n (Irish Celtic myth) the son of Stariat. The Fir Bholg are said to have been descended from him.

semiotics n sing the study of signs and symbols, esp their use in language and relationship to the world of things and ideas; the study of the symptoms of disease.—**semiotic** or **semiotical** adj.—**semiotician** n.

semiprecious adj denoting gems of lower value than precious stones.

semiprivate adj of, pertaining to, or providing hospital services that are better than those for ward patients but inferior to those for private patients.

semiprofessional adj taking part in sport for pay, but not on a full-time basis.—**semiprofessionally** adv.

semiquaver n (Brit, mus) a sixteenth note.

semiquaver rest n (Brit, mus) **a** stop rest the length of a semiquaver (sixteenth note).

semiregular variables or **SR variables** npl a class of vast, pulsating variable stars which have variations in brightness, usu in the order of one to two magnitudes.

semirigid adj (airship) having a flexible gas container attached to a rigid keel.

semiskilled adj partly skilled or trained.

semiskimmed adj (Brit) (milk) having the cream partially removed, low-fat.

semisolid adj having the properties between that of a liquid and that of a solid; extremely viscous.

Semite n a member of the group of peoples including Arabs and Jews.

Semitic adj of or belonging to Semites; Jewish.

Semitism n any political or economic policy relating to Jews.

semitone n (mus) an interval equal to half a tone.

semitrailer n a trailer that has wheels at the back but is supported at the front by the towing vehicle.

semivowel n (phon) a consonant that sound like a vowel (e.g., y), a glide.

semiyearly see **semiannual**.

semolina n coarse particles of grain left after the sifting of wheat.

semp. abbr (Italian) = sempre, "always."

Semper n **Gottfried** (1803–79) German architect, whose notable works include the Opera, Dresden.

semplice adv (mus) in a simple manner.

sempre adv (mus) always.

sen n a monetary unit of Cambodia, equal to one hundredth of a riel; a monetary unit of Malaysia, equal to one hundredth of a ringgit; a former monetary unit of Japan, equal to one hundredth of a yen.

Sen abbr = senate; senator; senior.

SEN abbr = Special Educational Needs; (Brit) State Enrolled Nurse.

Senach n (Irish Celtic myth) a warrior against whom Cuchulainn did battle and won.

senate n a legislative or governing body; (with cap) the upper branch of a two-body legislature in France, the US, etc; the governing body of some universities.

senator n a member of a senate.—**senatorial** adj.

SenAWeldI abbr = Senior Associate of the Welding Institute.

Sencha n (Irish Celtic myth) the chief judge and poet of Ulster at the time of Conchobar mac Nessa.

S

send *vti* (**sending, sent**) to cause or enable to go; to have conveyed, dispatch (a message or messenger); to cause to move, propel; to grant; to cause to be; (*sl*) to move (a person) to ecstasy; (*with* **down**) (*Brit*) to expel from university; (*with* **for**) to order to be brought, to summon; (*with* **up**) (*inf*) to send to prison; to imitate or make fun of.—**sender** *n*.

Sen. Doc. *abbr* = Senate Document.

send-off *n* a friendly demonstration at a departure; a start given to someone or something.

sene *n* a monetary unit of Western Samoa, equal to one hundredth of a tala.

Seneca *n* [Lucius Annaeus Seneca] (*c.* 4 BC–AD 65) Roman dramatist and Stoic philosopher.

Senefru *see* Snofru.

Senegal *n* a republic, formerly a French colony, in west Africa, extending from the most western point in Africa (Cape Verde) to the border with Mali.

senescent *adj* growing old.—**senescence** *n*.

seneschal *n* (*hist*) a steward in the house of a feudal lord.

SEng, FinstSMM *abbr* = Qualified Sales Engineer of the Institute of Sales and Marketing Management.

Senghor *n* Léopold Sédar (1906–) Senegalese politician and poet. He became the president of Senegal (1960–80).

senile *adj* of or relating to old age; weakened, esp mentally, by old age.—**senility** *n*.

senile dementia *n* an organic mental disorder of the elderly involving generalized atrophy of the brain.

senior *adj* higher in rank; of or for seniors; longer in service; older (when used to distinguish between father and son with the same first name). * *n* one's elder or superior in standing; a person of advanced age; a student in the last year of college or high school.

senior citizen *n* an elderly person, esp a retired one.

senior common room *n* a staffroom in a British college or university.

seniority *n* (*pl* **seniorities**) the condition of being senior; status, priority, etc, in a given job.

seniti *n* a monetary unit of Tonga, equal to one hundredth of a pa'anga.

SenMWeldI *abbr* = Senior Member of the Welding Institute.

SENNAC *abbr* = Special Educational Needs National Advisory Council.

Sennacherib *n* king of Assyria, 705–681 BC. He appears in the Biblical account of the Assyrian attack on Judah and siege of Jerusalem.

Sennett *n* Mack [Michael Sinnott] (1880–1960) Canadian-born American movie director and producer of the Keystone Kops comedies, and Charlie Chaplin's first movies.

señor *n* (*pl* **señors** *or* **señores**) the title of a Spanish-speaking man, equivalent to Mr or sir.

señora *n* (*pl* **señoras**) the title of a Spanish-speaking married woman, equivalent to Mrs or madam.

señorita *n* (*pl* **señoritas**) the title of a Spanish-speaking unmarried woman, equivalent to Miss or madam.

Senr., senr. *abbr* = senior.

sensation *n* awareness due to stimulation of the senses; an effect on the senses; a thrill; a state of excited interest; the cause of this.

sensational *adj* of or relating to sensation; exciting violent emotions; melodramatic.—**sensationally** *adv*.

sensationalism *n* the use of sensational writing, language, etc; the doctrine that all knowledge is obtained from sense impressions.—**sensationalist** *adj*.

sense *n* one of the five human and animal faculties by which objects are perceived: sight, hearing, smell, taste, and touch; awareness; moral discernment; soundness of judgment; meaning, intelligibility; (*pl*) conscious awareness. * *vt* to perceive; to become aware of; to understand; to detect.

SENSE *abbr* (*Brit*) = Scottish Environmental Network for a Sustainable Economy; The National Deafblind and Rubella Association.

senseless *adj* stupid, foolish; meaningless, purposeless; unconscious.—**senselessly** *adv*.—**senselessness** *n*.

sense organ *n* a bodily structure that reacts to stimuli and transmits them to the brain as nerve impulses.

sensibility *n* (*pl* **sensibilities**) the capacity to feel; over-sensitiveness; susceptibility; (*pl*) sensitive awareness or feelings.

sensible *adj* having good sense or judgment; reasonable; practical; perceptible by the senses, appreciable; conscious (of); sensitive.—**sensibleness** *n*.—**sensibly** *adv*.

sensitive *adj* having the power of sensation; feeling readily and acutely, keenly perceptive; (*skin*) delicate, easily irritated; (*wound etc*) still in a painful condition; easily hurt or shocked, tender, touchy; highly responsive to slight changes; sensory; (*photog*) reacting to light.—**sensitively** *adv*.—**sensitiveness** *n*.

sensitive plant *n* a tropical American plant whose leaves and stems fold when touched.

sensitivity *n* (*pl* **sensitivities**) the condition of being sensitive; awareness of changes or differences; responsiveness to stimuli or feelings, esp to excess; (*med*) in a screening test, the proportion of people with the disease who are identified by the test; (*phys*) the smallest signal that can be detected above background noise in recording equipment.

sensitize *vt* to make sensitive; (*person*) to render sensitive to an antigen, etc; (*photog: paper etc*) to render sensitive to light.—**sensitization** *n*.—**sensitizer** *n*.

sensitometer *n* a device for measuring the sensitivity to light of a photographic medium.

sensor *n* a device for detecting, recording, or measuring physical phenomena, such as heat, pulse, etc; a sense organ.

sensorium *n* (*pl* **sensoriums** *or* **sensoria**) the area of the brain regarded as responsible for receiving and processing external stimuli; the body's entire sensory apparatus.

sensory *adj* of or relating to the senses, sensation, or the sense organs; conveying nerve impulses to the brain.

sensual *adj* bodily, relating to the senses rather than the mind; arousing sexual desire.—**sensuality** *n*.—**sensually** *adv*.

sensuous *adj* giving pleasure to the mind or body through the senses.—**sensuously** *adv*.—**sensuousness** *n*.

sent *see* send.

sentence *n* a court judgment; the punishment imposed; (*gram*) a series of words conveying a complete thought. * *vt* (*a convicted person*) to pronounce punishment on; to condemn (to).

sententious *adj* terse, pithy; making frequent use of axioms and maxims; exhibiting a pompous, moralizing tone.—**sententiously** *adv*.—**sententiousness** *n*.

sentient *adj* making use of the senses, conscious.—**sentiently** *adv*.

sentiment *n* a feeling, awareness, or emotion; the thought behind something; an attitude of mind; a tendency to be swayed by feeling rather than reason; an exaggerated emotion.

sentimental *adj* of or arising from feelings; foolishly emotional; nostalgic.—**sentimentally** *adv*.

sentimentality *n* (*pl* **sentimentalities**) the quality or state of being sentimental; an affected or extreme tenderness.

sentinel *n* a sentry or guard.

sentry *n* (*pl* **sentries**) a soldier on guard to give warning of danger and to prevent unauthorized access.

sentry box *n* a shelter for a sentry.

senza *prep* (*mus*) without.

SEO *abbr* = Senior Executive Officer; Senior Experimental Officer; Society of Education Officers.

seoo *abbr* (*French*) = *sauf erreurs ou omissions*, "errors and omissions excepted."

Seoul (Soul) *n* capital city of the Republic of Korea.

S E ou O *abbr* (*French*) = *sauf erreur ou omission*, "errors and omissions excepted."

sep. *abbr* = sepal; separate.

Sep. *abbr* = September; Septuagint.

SEPA *abbr* (*Brit*) = Scottish Environment Protection Agency.

sepal *n* any of the individual parts of the calyx of a flower.

separable *adj* able to be separated or parted.—**separability** *n*.—**separably** *adv*.

separate *vt* to divide or part; to sever; to set or keep apart; to sort into different sizes. * *vi* to go different ways; to cease to live together as man and wife. * *adj* divided; distinct, individual; not shared. * *n* (*pl*) articles of clothing designed to be interchangeable with others to form various outfits.—**separately** *adv*.—**separateness** *n*.

separation *n* the act of separating or the state of being separate; a formal arrangement of husband and wife to live apart; (*astron*) the angular distance, measured in arc seconds, between two stars in an optical double or visual binary star system.

separatist *n* a person who advocates or practices separation from an organization, Church, or government; a person who advocates racial or political separation.—*also adj*.—**separatism** *n*.

separator *n* one who separates; a machine that separates liquids from solids or liquids of different specific gravities.

SEPFA *abbr* = Southeast Professional Fishermen's Association.

Sephardi *n* (*pl* **Sephardim**) a Jew of Spanish, Portuguese, or North African descent.—**Sephardic** *adj*.

sepia *adj, n* (a) dark reddish-brown.

sepoy *n* (*formerly*) an Indian soldier employed by the British.

seppuku *n* harakiri.

sepsis *n* a septic state or agency; blood poisoning.

Sept. *abbr* = September; Septuagint.

septa *see* septum.

septal defect *n* a hole in the septum or partition between the left and right sides of the heart, whether in the atrium or ventricle, a congenital disorder caused by an abnormal development of the fetal heart.

September *n* the ninth month of the year, having 30 days.

septennial *adj* occurring every, or lasting, seven years. * *n* a seven-year period.—**septennially** *adv*.

septet *n* a set of seven singers or players; a musical composition for seven instruments or voices.

septic *adj* infected by micro-organisms; causing or caused by putrefaction.—**septically** *adv*.—**septicity** *n*.

septicemia *n* a disease caused by poisonous bacteria in the blood.—**septicemic** *adj*.

septic shock *n* a form of shock that occurs because of septicemia when the toxins cause a drastic fall in blood pressure as a result of tissue damage and blood clotting.

septic tank *n* an underground tank in which sewage is decomposed by the action of bacteria.

septuagenarian *n* a person in the age range 70–79.

Septuagesima *n* the third Sunday before Lent.

Septuagint *n* the Greek version of the Old Testament including the Apocrypha (said to have been translated by 70 scholars).

septum *n* (*pl* **septa**) a dividing membrane between two bodily cavities or parts.—**septal** *adj*.

septuplet *n* one of seven offspring produced at one birth.

sepulcher *n* a tomb, a burial vault.

sepulchral *adj* of or like a sepulcher; dismal, funereal; (*sound*) deep and hollow.

seq. *abbr* = sequel.

seq. luce *abbr* (*Latin*) = *sequenti luce*, "on the following day."

seqq. *abbr* (*Latin*) = *sequentes* or *sequentia,* "the following."

sequel *n* something that follows, the succeeding part; a consequence; the continuation of a story begun in an earlier literary work, movie, etc.

sequela *n* (*pl* **sequelae**) (*med*) a condition arising from an existing disease; any complication of a disease or injury.

Sequena *n* (*Gaulish Celtic myth*) the goddess of the source of the River Seine, which takes its name from her.

sequence *n* order of succession; a series of succeeding things; a single, uninterrupted episode, as in a movie; the repetition of a short passage of music in a different pitch; (*mus*) a form of hymn in Latin used in the Roman Catholic Mass, such as "Dies Irae" or "Stabat Mater."

sequential *adj* arranged in a sequence; following in sequence; consecutive.—**sequentially** *adv*.

sequential access *n* (*comput*) the method of reading data files from beginning to end, as opposed to by random-access means.

sequester *vt* to place apart; to retire in seclusion; (*law*) to remove from one's possession until the claims of one's creditors are satisfied.

sequestrate *vt* to sequester.—**sequestration** *n*.

sequin *n* a shiny, round piece of metal or foil sewn on clothes for decoration.

sequoia *n* a lofty coniferous Californian tree.

ser. *abbr* = series; sermon.

sera *see* **serum**.

Sera *n* (*Irish Celtic myth*) the father of Partholan. According to some sources, it was not Partholan but Sera who was the husband of Dealgnaid.

sérac *n* a pinnacle or tower-shaped mass of ice among the crevasses of a glacier.

seraglio *n* (*pl* **seraglios**) a harem in a Muslim household or palace.

Serapeum *n* the underground galleries at Saqqara, Egypt where the sacred Apis bulls were buried, from the Eighteenth Dynasty onwards. The name comes from the ground-level temple of Serapis, a composite deity who combined aspects of Osiris and Apis.

seraph *n* (*pl* **seraphs** or **seraphim**) (*theol*) a member of the highest order of angels.—**seraphic** *adj*.

Serb or **Serbian** *n* a native or inhabitant of Serbia; the Serbo-Croatian language of Serbia.—*also adj*.

Serbo-Croatian or **Serbo-Croat** *n* the Slavonic language of the Serbs and Croatians.—*also adj*.

SERC *abbr* = Science and Engineering Research Council; = Smithsonian Environmental Research Center.

serdab *n* (*Egypt*) (from the Arabic word for cellar) a tomb chamber in which statues of the deceased were placed.

serenade *n* music sung or played at night beneath a person's window, esp by a lover. * *vt* to entertain with a serenade.

serenata *n* (*mus*) an 18th-century form of secular cantata or a short opera composed for a patron.

serendipity *n* the faculty of making fortunate finds by chance.

serene *adj* calm; untroubled; tranquil; clear and unclouded; (*with cap*) honored (used as part of certain royal titles).—**serenely** *adv*.—**serenity** *n*.

serf *n* (*pl* **serfs**) a laborer in feudal service who was bound to, and could be sold with, the land he worked; a drudge.—**serfdom** *n*.

Serf, Saint *see* **Kentigern**.

serge *n* a hard-wearing twilled woolen fabric.

sergeant *n* a non-commissioned officer ranking above a corporal in the army, air force, or marine corps; a police officer ranking above a constable.

sergeant-at-arms *n* (*pl* **sergeants-at-arms**) an official in various legislative assemblies responsible for enforcing discipline.

sergeant major *n* a non-commissioned officer in the army, air force, or marine corps serving as chief administrative assistant in a headquarters.

Sergt. *abbr* = Sergeant.

Seria *n* a city in Brunei.

serial *adj* of or forming a series; published, shown or broadcast by installments at regular intervals. * *n* a story presented in regular installments with a connected plot.

serial communication *n* (*comput*) a method of transferring data over a single wire, one bit at a time.

serialism *n* (*mus*) the use of the twelve notes of the chromatic scale in a fixed order in a composition.

serialize *vt* to arrange, publish, or broadcast in serial form.—**serialization** *n*.

serial killer *n* a person who murders people one at a time over a period of time.

serial mouse *n* (*comput*) an input pointing device that is connected to a serial port on the computer as opposed to the bus mouse, which is connected to the main processor board.

serial number *n* one of a series of numbers given for identification.

serial port *n* (*comput*) a port on the back of a computer that is set up to allow serial communications between the computer and another device.

serial printer *n* (*comput*) a printer that connects to a serial port of the computer.

seriatim *adv* consecutively.

seriation *n* (*archeo*) the ordering of assemblages of artifacts by similarities of shape to indicate their relative position over time.

sericeous *adj* (*bot*) covered in fine hairs.

sericulture *n* the breeding of silkworms to produce raw silk.—**sericultural** *adj*.—**sericulturist** *n*.

series *n* (*pl* **series**) a succession of items or events; a succession of things connected by some likeness; a sequence, a set; a radio or television serial whose episodes have self-contained plots; a set of books issued by one publisher; (*math*) a progression of numbers or quantities according to a certain law; (*geol*) a major part of a system, with reference to the rock formed during one epoch.

serif *n* (*print, comput*) a small line at the top or the bottom of the main stroke of a letter.

serigraph *n* a print made using the silk-screen technique.—**serigraphy** *n*.

serin *n* any of various small European finches related to the canary.

seriocomic *adj* combining humor and seriousness.—**seriocomically** *adv*.

serious *adj* grave, solemn, not frivolous; meaning what one says, sincere, earnest; requiring close attention or thought; important; critical.—**seriously** *adv*.—**seriousness** *n*.

Seriphos or **Seriphus** *n* a small island of the Greek Cyclades, where, in myth, Danaè and Perseus were washed ashore.

serj. or **serjt.** *abbr* = serjeant.

SERL *abbr* = Services Electronics Research Laboratory.

Serling *n* Rod (1924–75) American television dramatist, whose TV plays include the much-acclaimed *Requiem for a Heavyweight* (1956, broadcast live). He also created and introduced the innovative fantasy series *The Twilight Zone* (1959–64).

sermon *n* a speech on religion or morals, esp by a clergyman; a long, serious talk of reproof, esp a tedious one.

sermonize *vt* to compose sermons; to preach at length.—**sermonizer** *n*.

Sermon on the Mount *n* (*NT*) part of Jesus' teaching, giving the new law of the kingdom of God to his chosen followers. *See also* **Beatitudes**, **Lord's Prayer**.

sero- *prefix* serum.

serology *n* the scientific study of serums.—**serological** *adj*.—**serologist** *n*.

seropositive *adj* having a particular disease (e.g., AIDS) for which one's blood has been tested.

serositis *n* inflammation of a serous membrane.

serotonin *n* a substance occurring in various body tissues that induces vasoconstriction.

serous *adj* of or producing serum.

serous membrane *n* a thin membrane lining a body cavity that secretes a thin lubricant.

Serpens or **the Serpent** *n* a constellation which is unique in being split into two parts: Serpens Caput (the Serpent's Head) lying near Corona Borealis (the Northern Crown) in the northern hemisphere; and Serpens Canda (the Serpent's Body) lying in the southern hemisphere and partly within the Milky Way, near Scorpius.

serpent *n* a snake; a venomous or treacherous person; an obsolete bass woodwind instrument with several curves, used during the 16th century in church orchestras and military bands.

serpentine *adj* like a serpent; twisting, tortuous; crooked, treacherous.

serpigo *n* a spreading skin complaint such as ringworm or herpes.

SERPS *abbr* (*Brit*) = State Earnings-Related Pension Scheme.

Serravalle *n* town in San Marino.

serrate *adj* (*leaves, etc*) having toothed edges; notched like a saw. * *vt* to make serrate.

serrated *adj* having an edge notched like the teeth of a saw.

serration *n* the state of being serrated; a saw-like edge; a single notch in a serrated edge.

serried *adj* packed closely, in compact order.

serum *n* (*pl* **serums** or **sera**) the watery part of bodily fluid, esp liquid that separates out from the blood when it coagulates; such fluid taken from the blood of an animal immune to a disease, used as an antitoxin.

serum albumin *n* the principal blood protein.

serum hepatitis *n* a viral disease, characterized by acute inflammation of the liver and jaundice, transmitted by contact with infected blood.

serum sickness *n* a hypersensitive reaction that occasionally occurs several days after injection of foreign serum, producing rashes, joint pains, fever, and swelling of the lymph nodes.

serv. *abbr* (*Latin*) = *serva*, "preserve"; servant.

serval *n* (*pl* **servals** or **serval**) an African cat with long legs and a tawny coat with black spots.

servant *n* a personal or domestic attendant; one in the service of another.

serve *vt* to work for; to do military or naval service for; to be useful to; to meet the needs of, suffice; to wait on (a customer); to hand roun (food, etc); to undergo (a sentence); (*a male animal*) to copulate with; (*law*) to deliver (a summons, etc); (*naut*) to bind (a rope) with thin cord to prevent fraying; (*tennis*) to put (the ball) into play. * *vi* to be employed as a servant; to be a soldier, sailor, etc; to be enough. * *n* the act of serving in tennis, etc.

server *n* one who serves, esp at tennis; something used in serving food and drink; a person who serves legal processes on others; the celebrant's assistant at Mass; a computer used in a local area network that is the main source of programs or shared data and controls the use of peripherals such as printers or modems.

service *n* the act of serving; the state of being a servant; domestic employment; a department of state employ; the people engaged in it; military employment or duty; work done for others; use, assistance; attendance in a hotel, etc; a facility providing a regular supply of trains, etc; a set of dishes; any religious ceremony; an overhaul of a vehicle; (*tennis*) the act or manner of serving; (*pl*) friendly help or professional aid; a system of providing a utility, such as water, gas, etc. * *vt* to provide with assistance; to overhaul.

serviceable *adj* useful; durable.—**serviceably** *adv*.—**serviceableness** *n*.

service area *n* (*Brit*) a place offering a range of services such as restaurants, toilet facilities, and fuel.

service charge *n* a sum added to a restaurant or hotel bill, etc for service.

service industry *n* the section of industry that is concerned with the provision of a service rather than goods.

serviceman *n* (*pl* **servicemen**) a member of the armed services; a person whose work is repairing something.—**servicewoman** *nf* (*pl* **servicewomen**).

service provider *n* (*comput*) a company that provides a connection to the Internet in return for a monthly subscription and a charge per hour of use.

service road *n* a minor road beside a main route that provides access to local housing, etc.

service station *n* a place selling fuel, etc, for motor vehicles; a place at which some service is offered.

serviette *n* (*Brit*) a table napkin.

servile *adj* of or like a slave; subservient; submissive; menial.—**servilely** *adv*.—**servility** *n*.

serving *n* a portion of food or drink.

servitude *n* slavery, bondage; work imposed as punishment for a crime.

Servius Tullius *n* the sixth king of Rome, who, according to legend, was the son of a slave and married the daughter of King Tarquinius.

servo *n* (*pl* **servos**) (*inf*) a servomotor or servomechanism. * *adj* activated by a servomechanism.

servomechanism *n* an automatic device that uses small amounts of power to control a system of much greater power.

servomotor *n* a motor that supplies power to a servomechanism.

servt. *abbr* = servant.

SES *abbr* = Scientific Exploration Society; (*Brit*) Scottish Equipment Suppliers; socioeconomic status; Solar Energy Society.

sesame *n* an Asian plant that yields oil-bearing seeds; its seeds, also used for flavoring.

sesamoid *adj* of or pertaining to the small bones or lumps of cartilage in a tendon.

Sesostris I *n* Egyptian pharaoh of the Middle Kingdom, Twelfth Dynasty (ruled 1962–1928 BC). An energetic ruler who went farther beyond Egypt's bounds than any predecessor, invading Nubia as far as the third cataract, acquiring much gold and territory.

Sesostris II *n* Egyptian pharaoh of the Middle Kingdom, Twelfth Dynasty (ruled 1895–1878 BC).

Sesostris III *n* Egyptian pharaoh of the Middle Kingdom, Twelfth Dynasty (ruled 1878–1842 BC).

sesqui- *prefix* one and a half; (*chem*) a ratio of two to three.

sesquicentennial *n* a period of 150 years; (the celebration of) a 150th anniversary.—also *adj*.

sesquih. *abbr* (*Latin*) = *sesquihora*, "an hour and a half."

sess. *abbr* = session.

sessile *adj* (*leaves*) without a stalk; permanently attached; (*med*) (*tumor, growth*) having no stalk.

session *n* the meeting of a court, legislature, etc; a series of such meetings; a period of these; a period of study, classes, etc; a university year; a period of time passed in an activity.

Sessions *n* **Roger** (1896–1985) American composer, whose works include operas (e.g., *The Trial of Lucullus*), symphonies, chamber music, and pieces for piano.

sesterce *or* **sestertius** *n* in ancient Rome, a coin worth a quarter of a denarius.

sestet *n* a poem or stanza of six lines, esp the last six lines of a sonnet.

set *vt* (**setting, set**) to put in a specified place, condition, etc; to fix (a trap for animals); to adjust (a clock, etc); to arrange (a table) for a meal; to fix (hair) in a desired style; to put (a bone) into normal position, etc; to make settled, rigid, or fixed; to mount (gems); to direct; to furnish (an example) for others; to fit (words to music or music to words); (*type*) to arrange for printing; (*with* **against**) to weigh up, compare; to cause to be opposed to; (*with* **aside**) to discard; to reserve for a particular reason; (*with* **down**) to place (something) on a surface; to record, put in writing; to regard; to attribute (to); to allow to alight from (a vehicle); (*with* **out**) to present or display; to explain in detail; to plan, lay out. * *vi* to become firm, hard, or fixed; to begin to move (out, forth, off, etc); (*sun*) to sink below the horizon; (*with* **about**) to begin; to abuse physically or verbally; (*with* **in**) to stitch (a sleeve) within a garment; to become established; (*with* **off**) to show up by contrast; to set in motion; to cause to explode; (*with* **on**) to urge (e.g., a dog) to attack or pursue; to go on, advance; (*with* **out**) to begin a journey, career, etc; (*with* **to**) to start working, esp eagerly; to start fighting; (*with* **up**) to erect; to establish, to found; to install (a piece of hardware or software) into a computer system so that it works with the system; (*with* **upon**) to attack, usu with violence. * *adj* fixed, established; intentional; rigid, firm; obstinate; ready. * *n* a number of persons or things classed or belonging together; a group, a clique; the way

in which a thing is set; direction; the scenery for a play, movie, etc; assembled equipment for radio or television reception, etc; (*math*) the totality of points, numbers, or objects that satisfy a given condition; (*tennis*) a series of games forming a unit of a match; a rooted cutting of a plant ready for transplanting; a badger's burrow (—also **sett**).

SET *abbr* = selective employment tax; Society for Experimental Therapy.

seta *n* (*pl* **setae**) a bristle or similar appendage of an animal or plant.

SETA *abbr* (*Brit*) = Scottish Egg Trade Association.

Setanta *or* **Sedanta** *n* (*Irish Celtic myth*) the boyhood name of Cuchulainn. While he still bore this name he performed his first noted heroic deed when he defeated all fifty youths who were in the service of Conchobar mac Nessa.

set-aside *n* (*Brit*) a government grant to a farmer in an EU country so that the farmer will take land out of agriculture production for an agreed period of time; (*Brit*) the land that has been taken out of production in exchange for a set-aside grant.

setback *n* misfortune; a reversal.

Seth *n* (*Egypt*) one of the principal Egyptian gods, murderer of his brother, Osiris, identified with the dry desert areas to east and west of the Nile Valley. Seth has sometimes been seen as a Satan figure, but this is incorrect. He was also a war god.

Sethnakhte *n* Egyptian pharaoh of the New Kingdom, Twentieth Dynasty (ruled 1188–1186 BC). Father of Rameses III.

Sethos I *n* (*Egypt*) Egyptian pharaoh of the New Kingdom, Nineteenth Dynasty (ruled 1294–1279 BC). A military leader and former vizier, he rewrote the king lists in order to provide himself with a pharaonic pedigree.

SETI *abbr* = search for extra-terrestrial intelligence.

setline *n* a long fishing line with hooked shorter lines attached at regular intervals.

set-off *n* (*archit*) a feature whereby a wall or element is reduced in thickness creating a planar ledge, often sloping, between the two thicknesses.

set piece *n* a formal or elaborate performance, esp of a work of art, music, etc; an elaborate fireworks display; (*sport*) a carefully rehearsed team move usu aimed at gaining the ball when play resumes.

setscrew *n* a screw that when tightened prevents parts of a machine from moving relative to each other.

set-square *n* a flat, triangular instrument for drawing angles.

settee *n* a sofa.

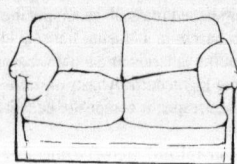

setter *n* a large breed of gundog trained to stand rigid when spotting game.

set theory *n* the branch of mathematics concerned with the relations and properties of sets.

setting *n* a background, scene, surroundings, environment; a mounting, as for a gem; the music for a song, etc.

settle *vti* to put in order; to pay (an account); to clarify; to decide, come to an agreement; to make or become quiet or calm; to make or become firm; to establish or become established in a place, business, home, etc; to colonize (a country); to take up residence; to come to rest; (*dregs*) to fall to the bottom; to stabilize; to make or become comfortable (for resting); (*bird*) to alight; to bestow legally for life; (*with* **for**) to be content with.

settlement *n* the act of settling; a sum settled, esp on a woman at her marriage; an arrangement; the conclusion of an industrial dispute or civil litigation as a result of a voluntary agreement between the parties involved; a small village; a newly established colony; subsidence (of buildings).

settler *n* a person who settles; an early colonist.

set-to *n* (*inf*) a squabble, fight.

Setúbal *n* a city in Portugal.

set-up *n* the plan, makeup, etc, of equipment used in an organization; the details of a situation, plan, etc; (*inf*) a contest, etc, arranged to result in an easy win.

set-up time *n* the time that is taken in setting up a machine or operation to carry out a production task.

Seurat *n* **Georges** (1859–91) French painter and a leading neo-impressionist.

Sevastopol (in the Crimea) *n* a city in Ukraine.

seven *adj, n* one more than six. * *n* the symbol for this (7, VII, vii); the seventh in a series or set; something having seven units as members.

Seven against Thebes *npl* (*Greek myth*) a group of champions who attacked Thebes with the aim of getting the throne back for Polynices from his brother Eteocles. They were Adrastus, Mecisteus, Capaneus, Amphiaraus, Hippomedon, Eteoclus, and Parthenopaeus.

sevenfold *adj* having seven units or members; being seven times as great or as many.

seven seas *npl* all the world's oceans.

seventeen *adj, n* one more than sixteen. * *n* the symbol for this (17, XVII, xvii).—**seventeenth** *adj*.

seventh *adj, n* next after sixth; one of seven equal parts of a thing. * *n* (*mus*) an interval of seven diatonic degrees; the leading note.

seventh heaven *n* perfect happiness.

seventy *adj, n* seven times ten. * *n* the symbol for this (70, LXX, lxx); (*pl*) the numbers 70 to 79; the same numbers in a life or century.—**seventieth** *adj*.

sever *vti* to separate, divide into parts; to break off.—**severance** *n*.

several *adj* more than two but not very many; various; separate, distinct; respective. * *pron* (*with pl vb*) a few. * *n* (*with pl vb*) a small number (of).

severe *adj* harsh, not lenient; very strict; stern; censorious; exacting, difficult; violent, not slight; (*illness*) critical; (*art*) plain, not florid.—**severely** *adv*.—**severity** *n*.

severy *n* (*pl* **severies**) (*archit*) a bay of a vault.

Sevilla *n* a city in Spain.

sevillana *n* (*mus*) a Spanish folk dance similar to the seguidilla, originally from the city of Seville.

Seville orange *n* (an orange tree bearing) a fruit with bitter flesh used to make marmalade.

Sèvres *n* a type of fine porcelain made in France.

sew *vti* (**sewing, sewed,** *pp* **sewn** *or* **sewed**) to join or stitch together with needle and thread; to make, mend, etc, by sewing; (*with* **up**) to get full control of; (*inf*) to make sure of success in.—**sewing** *n*.

sewage *n* waste matter carried away in a sewer.

sewage farm *n* a place where sewage is treated for use as manure.

sewer[1] *n* one who sews.

sewer[2] *n* an underground pipe or drain for carrying off liquid waste matter, etc; a main drain.

sewerage *n* a system of drainage by sewers; sewage.

sewing machine *n* a machine for sewing or stitching, usu driven by an electric motor.

sewn *see* **sew**.

sex *n* the characteristics that distinguish male and female organisms on the basis of their reproductive function; either of the two categories (male and female) so distinguished; males or females collectively; the state of being male or female; the attraction between the sexes; (*inf*) sexual intercourse.

sex- *prefix* six.

sexagenarian *n* a person in the age range 60–69.—*also adj*.

Sexagesima *n* the second Sunday before Lent.

sexagesimal *adj* of or based on the number 60.

sex appeal *n* what makes a person sexually desirable.

sex chromosome *n* a chromosome that determines the sex of an animal.

sexed *adj* having a certain amount of sex or sexuality.

sex hormone *n* a hormone affecting the development of sexual organs and characteristics.

sexism *n* exploitation and domination of one sex by the other, esp of women by men.—**sexist** *adj, n*.

sexless *adj* without sexual intercourse; sexually unappealing.—**sexlessly** *adv*.—**sexlessness** *n*.

sex-linked disorder *n* a condition produced because the genes controlling certain characteristics are carried in sex chromosomes, usu the X-chromosome. *See* **hemophilia**.

sex object *n* a person regarded solely in terms of his or her sexual attractiveness.

sexology *n* the study of human sexuality.—**sexologist** *n*.—**sexological** *adj*.

sexpartite vault *n* (*archit*) a vault in which a bay of a quadripartite vault is further divided into two by a transverse division.

Sexred *n* (*d*. 616) king of Essex (reigned in 616). The son of Saebert, he reigned jointly with his brother, Saeward.

sex shop *n* a store specializing in sex aids, pornographic magazines, etc.

Sextans *or* **the Sextant** *n* a faint and inconspicuous constellation lying in the southern hemisphere near Leo.

sextant *n* a navigator's instrument for measuring the altitude of the sun, etc to determine position at sea.

sextet *n* a set of six singers or players; a musical composition for six instruments or voices.

sexton *n* an officer in charge of the maintenance of church property.

sextuple *adj* having six units or members; being six times as much or as many.—*also n*.

sextuplet *n* one of six offspring produced at one birth; (*mus*) a group of six notes to be performed in the time of four notes.

sexual *adj* of sex or the sexes; having sex.—**sexually** *adv*.

sexual harassment *n* frequent unwelcome attention from the opposite sex in the form of suggestive remarks, fondling, etc.

sexual intercourse *n* the act of copulating.

sexuality *n* sexual activity; expression of sexual interest, esp when excessive.

sexually transmitted disease *n* any of various diseases, such as syphilis or HIV/AIDS, transmitted by sexual contact.—*also* **venereal disease**.

sexual reproduction *n* (*biol*) the production of progeny that have initially arisen from the fusion of male and female gametes in a process called fertilization.

sexy *adj* (**sexier, sexiest**) (*inf*) exciting, or intending to excite, sexual desire; attractive, entertaining; fashionable or stylish and as a result worthwhile.—**sexily** *adv*.—**sexiness** *n*.

Seychelles *npl* a republic comprising a group of volcanic islands that lie in the western Indian Ocean about 746 miles from the coast of east Africa.

Seychelles rupee *n* currency of Seychelles.

Seyfert galaxy *n* (*astron*) a small category of galaxy that exhibits a bright nucleus and weak spiral arms.

Seyfert galaxy spiral *n* a type of galaxy, first described in 1943 by Carl Seyfert, which has an extremely bright nucleus, a significant source of non-thermal radiation.

Seymour *n* 1. **Jane** (?1509–37), third wife of Henry VIII; mother of Edward VI. 2. **Richard** (1953–) British industrial designer, who formed the Seymour-Powell consultancy with Dick Powell in 1983.

sf *abbr* = sforzando; sinking fund; (*Latin*) *sub finem*, "toward the end".

SF *abbr* = science fiction; Senior Fellow; signal frequency; Sinn Féin; Society of Friends; Stone Federation.

SFA *abbr* = Scientific Film Association; (*Brit*) Scottish Football Association; Securities and Futures Authority; (*Brit*) Shetland Fishermen's Association; Small Farmers' Association; sweet Fanny Adams.

Sfax *n* a city in Tunisia.

SFBIU *abbr* (*Brit*) = Scottish Farm Buildings Investigation Unit.

SFBMS *abbr* = Small Farm Business Management Scheme.

SFC *abbr* = (*Brit*) Scottish Film Council; specific fuel consumption.

SFD *abbr* = small for dates.

SFF *abbr* (*Brit*) = Scottish Fishermen's Federation; Scottish Flag Fund.

SFHEA *abbr* (*Brit*) = Scottish Further and Higher Education Association.

SFInstE *abbr* = Senior Fellow of the Institute of Energy.

SFL *abbr* = (*Brit*) Scottish Football League; sequenced flashing lights (on runway).

SFLA *abbr* = Solicitors' Family Law Association.

sfm *abbr* = surface feet per minute.

SFMA *abbr* (*Brit*) = Scottish Flour Millers' Association.

SFO *abbr* = Senior Flag Officer; Serious Fraud Office.

sforzando *or* **sforzato** *adv* (*mus*) with vigor at the start. * *n* a notation indicating this.

SFSA *abbr* (*Brit*) = Scottish Federation of Sea Anglers; Scottish Field Studies Association.

SFSR *abbr* = Socialist Federation of Soviet Republics.

SFU *abbr* = suitable for upgrade (on airline tickets).

sfz *abbr* = sforzando.

sg *abbr* = specific gravity; steel girder.

SG *abbr* = Seaman Gunner; Secretary General; (*Brit*) Showmen's Guild of Great Britain; Siege Group; Society of Genealogists; Solicitor General; Surgeon General.

SGA *abbr* = Sand and Gravel Association; (*Brit*) Scottish Games Association; (*Brit*) Scottish Glass Association; Society of Graphic Artists; small for gestational age.

Sgathach *n* (*Irish Celtic myth*) the daughter of Eanna. Fionn mac Cumhaill offered to marry Sgathach for a year and a day. Eanna and his wife agreed to this temporary marriage, but the girl was not in favor. While Fionn and his men were asleep, she played a tune on her magical harp, and next morning Fionn and his men found themselves far away.

SGBI *abbr* (*Brit*) = Schoolmistresses' and Governesses' Benevolent Institution.

SgC *abbr* = Surgeon Captain.

sgd *abbr* = signed.

sgdg *abbr* (*French*) = *sans garantie du gouvernement*, "without government guarantee" (on French patents).

Sgeimh Solais *n* (*Irish Celtic myth*) "light of beauty"; the daughter of Cairbre, a high king. A son of the king of the Desi tribe became betrothed to her. The betrothal led to the Fianna asking Cairbre to pay a tribute. Cairbre's refusal led to the battle of Gabhra. This was to lead to the end of the supremacy of the Fianna in Ireland.

Sgeolan *or* **Sceolan** *n* (*Irish Celtic myth*) one of the two faithful hounds of Fionn mac Cumhaill, the other one being Bran[2]. They were the sons of Tuireann, sister of Fionn mac Cumhaill, who was made to change shapes and gave birth when she was still in the form of a wolfhound.

SGF *abbr* (*Brit*) = Scottish Grocers' Federation.

SGHWR *abbr* = steam-generating heavy water reactor.

Sgilti *n* (*Welsh Celtic myth*) one of the group of followers who were formed to help Culhwch find Olwen; was so light-footed that he could run across the ends of branches of trees.

SGlam *abbr* (*Brit*) = South Glamorgan.

SgLCr *abbr* = Surgeon Lieutenant-Commander.

SGLI *abbr* = Servicemembers' Group Life Insurance

SGM *abbr* = Sea Gallantry Medal; Sergeant Major.

SGMA *abbr* = Soup and Gravy Manufacturers' Association.

SGML *abbr* = Standardized Generalized Mark-up Language.

SGPA *abbr* = Stained Glass Professionals Association.

SgRA *abbr* = Surgeon Rear Admiral.

sgraffito *n* (*pl* **sgraffiti**) (an example of) a technique in ceramic or mural design in which the surface layer of glaze, plaster, etc is scraped away to expose a contrasting background.

Sgt *abbr* = sergeant

SGT *abbr* = Society of Glass Technology.

Sgt Maj *abbr* = sergeant major.

SGTS *abbr* (*Brit*) = Scottish Gaelic Texts Society.

SGU *abbr* (*Brit*) = Scottish Gliding Union; Scottish Golf Union.

SgVA *abbr* = Surgeon Vice-Admiral.

sh *interj* used to command silence.

sh *abbr* = scrum half; second-hand.

sh. *abbr* = (*bookbinding*) ; sheet; shunt.

s/h *abbr* = shorthand.

SH *abbr* = sexual harassment; southern hemisphere.

SHA *abbr* = (*Brit*) Scottish Hockey Association; Secondary Heads' Association; Society of Heraldic Arts; Special Health Authority; Swiss Hotel Association.

shabby *adj* (**shabbier, shabbiest**) (*clothes*) threadbare, worn, or dirty; run-down, dilapidated; (*act, trick*) mean, shameful.—**shabbily** *adv*.—**shabbiness** *n*.

shabti *n* (*Egypt*) a small figure in the form of a mummy, made of stone, wood or pottery. They were placed in tombs, and their function was to work for the deceased in the afterlife, performing necessary tasks like dredging silt from waterways.

SHAC *abbr* = Shelter Housing Aid Centre; Society for the History of Alchemy and Chemistry.

shack *n* a small, crudely built house or cabin; a shanty. * *vi* (*with* **up**) (*sl*) to cohabit (with); to spend the night (with), esp a person of the opposite sex.

shackle *n* a metal fastening, usu in pairs, for the wrists or ankles of a prisoner; a staple; anything that restrains freedom; (*pl*) fetters. * *vt* to fasten or join by a shackle; to hamper, to impede.

Shackleton *n* **Sir Ernest Henry** (1874–1922) Anglo-Irish explorer, who served in Robert Scott's Antarctic expedition, and led two further expeditions (1908–1909, 1914–16).

SHACT *abbr* (*Brit*) = Scottish Housing Associations' Charitable Trust.

shad *n* (*pl* **shad** *or* **shads**) any of various fishes of the herring family used as food.

shade *n* relative darkness; dimness; the darker parts of anything; shadow; a shield or screen protecting from bright light; a ghost; a place sheltered from the sun; degree of darkness of a color, esp when made by the addition of black; a minute difference; a blind; (*pl*) the darkness of approaching night; (*pl: sl*) sunglasses. * *vti* to screen from light; to overshadow; to make dark; to pass by degrees into another color; to change slightly or by degrees.

shade temperature *n* (*meteorol*) the temperature of the air recorded inside a Stevenson screen, away from direct sunlight or other radiation.

shading *n* the fine gradations of color, line, tone, etc, creating light and dark in a painting, etc; a shielding against light; nuances.

shadow *n* a patch of shade; darkness, obscurity; the dark parts of a painting, etc; shelter, protection; the dark shape of an object produced on a surface by intercepted light; an inseparable companion; a person (such as a detective) who shadows; an unsubstantial thing, a phantom; a mere remnant, a slight trace; gloom, affliction. * *vt* to cast a shadow over; to cloud; to follow and watch, esp in secret. * *adj* having an indistinct pattern or darker section; (*opposition party*) matching a function or position of the party in power.

shadow bands *npl* a phenomenon sometimes observed if the sky is very clear, immediately before and after a total eclipse of the sun: narrow bands or patches of light and shadow moving erratically over the Earth's surface.

shadow-box *vi* (*boxing*) to practice blows against an invisible opponent.

shadowy *adj* full of shadows; dim, indistinct; unsubstantial.

shaduf *n* (*Egypt*) the ancient Egyptian device for raising water from one level to a higher one by means of a pole set on a pivot, with a leather bucket at one end and a stone counterweight to balance it at the other.

Shadwell *n* **Thomas** (*c*. 1642–92) English dramatist and poet in the best of whose 17 plays, the comedies, he gives a lively and often satirical account of contemporary life, e.g. *The Virtuoso*. He replaced Dryden as poet laureate in 1689.

shady *adj* (**shadier, shadiest**) giving or full of shade; sheltered from the sun; (*inf*) of doubtful honesty, disreputable.

SHAEF *abbr* = Supreme Headquarters, Allied Expeditionary Forces.

shaft *n* a straight rod, a pole; a stem, a shank; the main part of a column; an arrow or spear, or its stem; anything hurled like a missile; a ray of light, a stroke of lightning; a revolving rod for transmitting power, an axle; one of the poles between which a horse is harnessed; a hole giving access to a mine; a vertical opening through a building, as for a lift; a critical remark or attack; (*sl*) harsh or unfair treatment.

shaft grave *n* (*archeo*) a rectangular shaft used for burial.

shag *n* a coarse tobacco cut into long pieces; a rough mop of hair, etc; a crested cormorant. * *adj* (*carpet*) having long, thick, woolen threads.

shaggy *adj* (**shaggier, shaggiest**) (*hair, fur, etc*) long and unkempt; rough; untidy.—**shagginess** *n*.

shaggy-dog story *n* (*inf*) a long joke with a punchline that is a deliberate anticlimax.

shagreen *n* the rough skin of certain sharks and rays; a type of leather with a gritty surface made from the hides of certain animals.

shah *n* the title of the former ruler of Iran.

Shak. *abbr* = Shakespeare.

shake *vti* (**shaking, shook,** *pp* **shaken**) to move to and fro with quick short motions, agitate; to tremble, vibrate; to jar, jolt; to brandish; to make or become unsteady; to weaken; to unsettle; to unnerve or become unnerved; to clasp (another's hand) as in greeting; (*with* **down**) to cause to subside by shaking; to obtain makeshift accommodations; (*sl*) to extort money from; (*with* **off**) to get rid of; (*with* **out**) to empty by shaking; to spread (a sail); (*with* **up**) to shake together, mix; to upset. * *n* the act of shaking or being shaken; a jolt; a shock; a milkshake; (*mus*) a trill; (*inf*) a deal; (*pl: inf*) a convulsive trembling.

shakedown *n* a makeshift or improvised bed; (*sl*) an extortion of money, as by blackmail; a thorough search.

shaker *n* a container for holding condiments; a container in which cocktail ingredients are mixed.

Shaker *adj* denoting an austere style of furniture design, produced by the Shaker sect on the east coast of America.

shakers *see* **movers and shakers.**

Shakers *npl* an American sect, who were an offshoot of the Quakers, founded in 1747. They got their name from their ecstatic shaking style of worship.

Shakespeare *n* **William** (1564–1616) English dramatist and poet, whose plays include *Romeo and Juliet, Julius Caesar, Hamlet, Othello, King Lear*, and *Macbeth*. His other major works are the narrative poems *Venus and Adonis* and *The Rape of Lucrece*, and his magnificent *Sonnets*.

Shakespearean, Shakespearian *adj* of, pertaining to, or characteristic of William Shakespeare or his works.

shake-up *n* an extensive re-organization.

shako *n* (*pl* **shakos** *or* **shakoes**) a cylindrical military cap with a high crown and tall plume.

shaky *adj* (**shakier, shakiest**) unsteady; infirm; unreliable.—**shakily** *adv*.—**shakiness** *n*.

shale *n* a kind of clay rock like slate but softer.

shall *vb aux* (*pt* **should**) used formally to express the future in the 1st person and determination, obligation or necessity in the 2nd and 3rd person; the more common form is **will.**

shallot *n* a small onion.

shallow *adj* having little depth; superficial, trivial. * *n* a shallow area in otherwise deep water.—**shallowness** *n*.

shalt (*arch*) *the 2nd person sing of* **shall.**

sham *n* a pretense; a person or thing that is a fraud. * *adj* counterfeit; fake.

shaman *n* a priest of shamanism believed to possess magical powers which allow him to communicate with and influence the spirit world.

shamanism *n* a religion of northern Asia that views the world as being dominated by good and evil spirits that can be influenced only by the shamans.

shamateur *n* (*sport*) a player, athlete, etc who is officially classed as an amateur but who accepts payment.

shamble *vi* to walk with an ungainly stumbling gait.—*also n*.

shambles *npl* a scene of great disorder; a slaughterhouse.

shambolic *adj* (*inf*) disorganized; utterly confused.

shame *n* a painful emotion arising from guilt or impropriety; modesty; disgrace, dishonor; the cause of this; (*sl*) a piece of unfairness. * *vti* to cause to feel shame; to bring disgrace on; to force by shame (into); to humiliate by showing superior qualities.

shamefaced *adj* bashful or modest; sheepish; showing shame; ashamed.—**shamefacedly** *adv*.—**shamefacedness** *n*.

shameful *adj* disgraceful; outrageous.—**shamefully** *adv*.—**shamefulness** *n*.

shameless *adj* immodest; impudent, brazen.—**shamelessly** *adv*.—**shamelessness** *n*.

shamisen *n* a Japanese long-necked lute with three strings. It has no frets and is plucked with a plectrum.

shammy (leather) *see* **chamois leather.**

shampoo *n* a liquid cleansing agent for washing the hair; the process of washing the hair or a carpet, etc. * *vt* to wash with shampoo.—**shampooer** *n*.

shamrock *n* a three-leaved clover-like plant, the national emblem of Ireland.

shanai *n* (*mus*) a double-reed instrument from India, similar to a shawm.

shandy *n* (*pl* **shandies**) beer diluted with a non-alcoholic drink such as lemonade.

Shang dynasty *n* a Chinese dynasty between the Hsia and the Chou dynasties. It lasted *c*. 1500–1050 BC.

Shanghai *n* a city in China.

shanghai *vt* (**shanghaiing, shanghaied**) to force (a sailor, etc) to join a ship's crew, esp by kidnapping or drugging; to trick or force (a person) into doing something.—**shanghaier** *n*.

Shangri-la *n* an imaginary utopia.

shank *n* the leg from the knee to the ankle, the shin; a shaft, stem, or handle.

Shankar *n* **Ravi** (1920–) Indian sitar player who, more than anyone, has been responsible for popularizing the instrument and Indian music in the West. He regularly tours the world giving recitals.

Shankly *n* **Bill [William Shankly]** (1913–81) Scottish soccer player and manager of Liverpool Football Club.

shanks's pony, shanks's mare *n* one's own legs as used for walking.

shan't = shall not.

shantung *n* a coarse kind of silk.

shanty[1] *n* (*pl* **shanties**) a crude hut built from corrugated iron or cardboard.

shanty[2] *n* (*pl* **shanties**) (*formerly*) a song sung by sailors in the rhythm of their work, a chantey.

shantytown *n* a community of poor people living in shanties.

shape *n* the external appearance, outline or contour of a thing; a figure; a definite form; an orderly arrangement; a mold or pattern; (*inf*) condition. * *vt* to give shape to; to form; to model, mold; to determine; (*with* **up**) to develop to a definite or satisfactory form.

SHAPE *abbr* = Supreme Headquarters Allied Powers Europe.

shapeless *adj* lacking definite form; baggy.—**shapelessly** *adv*.—**shapelessness** *n*.

shapely *adj* (**shapelier, shapeliest**) well-proportioned.—**shapeliness** *n*.

shard *n* a fragment or broken piece, esp of pottery.

share *n* an allotted portion, a part; one of the parts into which a company's capital stock is divided, entitling the holder to a share of profits. * *vti* to distribute, to apportion (out); to have or experience in common with others; to divide into portions; to contribute or receive a share of; to use jointly.

share capital *n* the part of the capital of a company that derives from the issue of shares.

share certificate *n* a document that is issued to provide evidence of the ownership of shares in a company.

sharecropper *n* a tenant farmer who hands over a portion of the crop as rent.—**sharecrop** *vi*.

share-for-share offer *n* a form of takeover bid in which the directors of the company seeking to make such a bid for another company offer shares in their own company in payment for shares in the target company.

shareholder *n* a holder of shares in a property, esp a company.

share issue *n* the process of issuing shares in a company.

share option *n* an option open to employees to buy shares in the company they work for.

share premium *n* the amount of money paid for shares issued by a company, the price of which is higher than the nominal value of the shares.

share register *n* a record of the shareholders of a company, which lists the names and addresses of the shareholders, the extent of their shareholding, and the class of shares that they hold.

share shop *n* (*Brit*) a financial intermediary, such as a stockbroker or bank, that is appointed by the government to deal with applications for shares issued in connection with the privatization of an organization.

share split *n* the division of the share capital of a company into smaller units, in which the number of shares is increased and the nominal value of the shares is reduced.

shareware *n* (*comput*) software that can be obtained on a trial basis but that requires a fee to be paid to the author for continuing use of the program.

share warehousing *n* the practice of accumulating a holding of the shares in a company that is the target of a takeover bid, the shares being gradually bought in the name of several nominees and kept until the prospective takeover bidder has built up a significant number of shares in the target company.

share warrant *n* a document that gives the holder the right to buy a security at a particular price at a particular date in the future.

Sharjah *n* a city in the United Arab Emirates (UAE).

shark *n* a large voracious marine fish; an extortioner, a swindler; (*sl*) an expert in a given activity.

sharkskin *n* a rayon fabric with a smooth, shiny finish.

Sharon, Plain of *n* (*Bible*) a plain on the coast of west Israel, between the Mediterranean and the hills of Samaria.

sharp *adj* having a keen edge or a fine point; pointed, not rounded; clear-cut; distinct; intense, piercing; cutting, severe; keen, biting; clever, artful; alert, mentally acute; (*mus*) raised a semitone in pitch; out of tune by being too high; (*sl*) smartly dressed. * *adv* punctually; quickly; (*mus*) above the right pitch. * *n* (*mus*) a note that is a semitone higher than the note denoted by the same letter; the symbol for this (#).—**sharply** *adv*.—**sharpness** *n*.

Sharp *n* **Cecil James** (1859–1924) collector of English and American folk music, who founded the English Folk Dance Society. His endeavors spurred a revival of interest in folk song and dance.

SHARP *abbr* = (*Brit*) Self Help Addiction Recovery Programme; Society for the History of Authorship, Reading, and Publishing.

sharpen *vti* to make or become sharp or sharper.

sharpener *n* something that sharpens.

sharpshooter *n* a marksman.

sharp-tongued *adj* sarcastic; quick to criticize.

sharp-witted *adj* thinking quickly and effectively.—**sharp-wittedly** *adv*.—**sharp-wittedness** *n*.

shatter *vti* to reduce to fragments suddenly; to smash; to damage or be damaged severely.

shatterproof *adj* resistant to shattering.

shave *vti* to remove facial or body hair with a razor; to cut away thin slices, pare; to miss narrowly, graze. * *n* the act or process of shaving; a narrow escape or miss; a paring.

shaven *adj* shaved.

shaver *n* one who shaves; an instrument for shaving, esp an electrical one.

Shavian *adj* of, relating to, or resembling the works of George Bernard Shaw.

shaving *n* the act of using a razor or scraping; a thin slice of wood, metal, etc, shaved off.

Shaw *n* 1. **George Bernard** (1856–1950) Anglo-Irish dramatist and critic, whose plays include *Man and Superman* (1903) and *Pygmalion* (1913). He was the winner of the 1925 Nobel Prize for Literature. 2. **[Richard] Norman** (1831–1912) Scottish-born architect, who employed Sir Edward Burne-Jones.

shawabti *n* a small statue buried with the dead in ancient Egypt in order to see to the needs of the person.

shawl *n* a large square or oblong cloth worn as a covering for the head or shoulders or as a wrapping for a baby.

shawm *n* a medieval woodwind instrument resembling an oboe.

she *pron* (*obj* **her**, *poss* **her, hers**) the female person or thing named before or in question. * *n* a female person or animal.

s/he *pron* he or she.

S/HE *abbr* = Sundays and holidays excepted.

shea *n* a tropical African tree with seeds that yield a butter-like fat used as food.

sheaf *n* (*pl* **sheaves**) a bundle of reaped corn bound together; a collection of papers, etc, tied in a bundle.

shear *vti* (**shearing, sheared,** *pp* **sheared** *or* **shorn**) to clip or cut (through); to remove (a sheep's fleece) by clipping; to divest; (*metal*) to break off because of a heavy force or twist. * *n* a stress acting sideways on a rivet and causing a break, etc; a machine for cutting metal; (*pl*) large scissors; (*pl*) a tool for cutting hedges, etc.

shearling *n* (the fleece of) a sheep after its first shearing.

shearwater *n* any of various seabirds that often glide close to the water.

shear zone *n* (*geol*) a zone which is usu narrow compared to its length, in which there is intense deformation due to the relative movement of two adjacent undeformed blocks of rock.

sheath *n* a close-fitting cover, esp for a blade; a condom; a close-fitting dress usu worn without a belt.

sheathe *vt* to put into a sheath; to encase; to protect with a casing; (*cat*) to withdraw (its claws).

sheath-knife *n* a knife with a fixed blade covered by a sheath.

sheave¹ *vt* to gather into sheaves.

sheave² *n* a grooved wheel, esp in a pulley.

sheaves *see* **sheaf**.

Sheba¹ *or* **Saba** *n* the ancient kingdom of the Sabeans; country on the southwest coast of Arabia, famous in Old Testament times for its trade in frankincense, gold, and precious stones.

Sheba² *n* Queen of (*OT*) the legendary Sheba, queen of the Sabeans, who came with a caravan to visit Solomon.

shebang *n* (*inf*) affair, business.

shebeen *n* an unlicensed or illegal drinking den.

Shechem *n* important town in the hill country of Canaan, mentioned in the stories of Abraham, Jacob, and Joseph, remembered as one of the most significant centers of early Jewish history.

shed¹ *n* a hut for storing garden tools; a large roofed shelter, often with one or more sides open; a warehouse.

shed² *vt* (**shedding, shed**) (*tears*) to let fall; (*skin, etc*) to lose or cast off; to allow or cause to flow; to diffuse, radiate. * *n* a parting in the hair.

she'd = she had; she would.

sheen *n* a gloss, luster; brightness.

sheep *n* (*pl* **sheep**) a cud-chewing four-footed animal with a fleece and edible flesh called mutton; a bashful, submissive person.

sheepcote *n* a sheepfold.

sheep-dip *n* a liquid disinfectant or insecticide into which sheep are plunged to destroy parasites.

sheepdog *n* a dog trained to tend, drive, or guard sheep.

sheepfold *n* an enclosure for sheep.

sheepish *adj* bashful, embarrassed.—**sheepishly** *adv*.—**sheepishness** *n*.

sheep's eyes *npl* (*arch*) amorous glances.

sheepshank *n* a knot in a rope to shorten it temporarily.

sheepskin *n* the skin of a sheep, esp with the fleece; a rug, parchment, or leather made from it; a garment made of or lined with sheepskin.

sheepwalk *n* an area of pasture for sheep.

sheer¹ *adj* pure, unmixed; downright, utter; perpendicular, extremely steep; (*fabric*) delicately fine, transparent. * *adv* outright; perpendicularly, steeply.

sheer² *vti* to deviate or cause to deviate from a course; to swerve. * *n* the act of sheering; the upward curve of a deck toward bow or stern; a change in a ship's course.

sheerlegs *n sing* a hoisting device comprising two or more upright poles crossed at the top from which lifting gear is suspended.

sheet[1] *n* a broad, thin piece of any material, such as glass, plywood, or metal; a large rectangular piece of cloth used as inner bedclothes; a single piece of paper; (*inf*) a newspaper; a broad, flat expanse; a suspended or moving expanse (as of fire or rain).

sheet[2] *n* a rope that controls the angle of a sail in relation to the wind.

sheet anchor *n* a large anchor used only in emergencies; a support in extremity.

sheet bend *n* a knot for joining ropes of different thicknesses.

sheet feeder *n* (*comput*) a device that feeds individual pages of paper into a printer or a scanner.

sheet glass *n* glass made in large sheets directly from the furnace or by making a cylinder and then flattening it.

sheeting *n* fabric for sheets.

sheet lightning *n* lightning that has the appearance of a broad sheet due to reflection and diffusion by the clouds and sky.

sheet metal *n* metal rolled out in the form of a thin sheet.

sheet music *n* music printed on unbound sheets of paper.

SHEFC *abbr* (*Brit*) = Scottish Higher Education Funding Council.

Sheffield. *abbr* (*Latin*) = *Sheffieldensis*, "of Sheffield."

sheikh *n* an Arab chief.

sheila *n* (*Austral, NZ sl*) a girl or woman.

shekel *n* the unit of money in Israel; an old Jewish weight or silver coin; (*pl: sl*) money.

shelduck *or* **sheldrake** *n* any of several Old World brightly plumaged ducks.

shelf *n* (*pl* **shelves**) a board fixed horizontally on a wall or in a cupboard for holding articles; a ledge on a cliff face; a reef, a shoal.

shelf ice *n* a mass of ice extending from a glacier into coastal waters.

shelf life *n* the length of time for which something may be stored without deterioration.

shell *n* a hard outside covering of a nut, egg, shellfish, etc; an explosive projectile; an external framework; a light racing boat; outward show; a cartridge; (*comput*) a utility program that operates as an interface between the user and an operating system that is regarded as difficult to use. * *vt* to remove the shell from; to bombard with shells; (*with* **out**) (*inf*) to pay out (money).

she'll = she will.

shellac, shellack *n* a resin usu produced in thin, flaky layers or shells; a thin varnish containing this and alcohol.

shell company *n* a company that is no longer trading but may have a listing on the Stock Exchange and may be used for various company maneuvers; a company that has ceased to trade and that is sold to new owners for a small fee.

Shelley *n* 1. **Mary Wollstonecraft** (1797–1851) English novelist, whose masterpiece is *Frankenstein, or the Modern Prometheus* (1818). 2. **Percy Bysshe** (1792–1822) English Romantic poet, whose works include "Prometheus Unbound" and "To a Skylark" (both 1820).

shellfire *n* the firing of artillery shells.

shellfish *n* an aquatic animal, esp an edible one, with a shell.

shellproof *adj* impervious to artillery shells, rockets, and bombs.

shell shock *n* a nervous disorder caused by the shock of being under fire.—**shellshocked** *adj*.

shell star *n* (*astron*) a star surrounded by a layer of luminous gas.

shelter *n* a structure that protects, esp against weather; a place giving protection, a refuge; protection. * *vti* to give shelter to, shield, cover; to take shelter.

sheltie, shelty *n* (*pl* **shelties**) a Shetland pony or Shetland sheepdog.

shelve *vti* to place on a shelf; to defer consideration, put aside; to slope gently, incline.

shelves *see* **shelf**.

shelving *n* material for making shelves; shelves collectively.

shemozzle *n* (*inf*) a scene of confusion; a brawl.

shenanigan *n* (*often pl*) trickery, deception; mischief, boisterous high spirits.

shendyr kilt *or* **skirt** *n* (*Egypt*) the pleated linen kilt-like garment seen on many representations of kings, with a flat central tab.

sheng *n* a sophisticated Chinese mouth organ, dating back some 3000 years.

shepherd *n* a person who looks after sheep; a pastor. * *vt* to look after, as a shepherd; to maneuver or marshal in a particular direction.—**shepherdess** *nf*.

shepherd dog *n* a sheepdog.

shepherd satellites *npl* small moons or satellites of a planet, which exert a sufficiently great gravitational pull to keep particles in a ring around the planet.

shepherd's pie *n* a dish of ground meat covered with a mashed potato crust.

shepherd's purse *n* an annual plant with small, white flowers and heart-shaped seed pods.

Sheppard *n* **Richard** (*b*. 1910) English architect, whose notable works include Churchilll College, Cambridge.

Shepseskaf *n* the last Egyptian king of the Fourth Dynasty (between 2625 and 2510 BC).

shequel *n* the standard monetary unit of Israel, equal to 100 agorot.

sherbet *n* a fruit-flavored powder that can be used to make a slightly sparkling drink; a sorbet.

Sheridan *n* **Richard Brinsley** (1751–1816) Irish dramatist and politician.

sheriff *n* in the US, the chief law-enforcement officer of a county; in Scotland, a judge in an intermediate law court; in England and Wales, the chief officer of the Crown, a ceremonial post.

sheriff court *n* (*Scot*) the court dealing with the majority of criminal and civil cases.

Sheringham *n* **George** (1884–1937) British interior and textile designer, who designed numerous sets and costumes for the Lyric Theatre, Hammersmith, London.

Sherpa *n* (*pl* **Sherpas** *or* **Sherpa**) a member of a people living on the southern slopes of the Himalayas, on the borders of Nepal and Tibet.

Sherrington *n* Sir **Charles Scott** (1857–1952) English physiologist, who shared the 1932 Nobel Prize for Physiology or Medicine for his research into reflex action. His works include *The Integrative Action of the Nervous System* (1906).

sherry *n* (*pl* **sherries**) a fortified wine originally made in Spain.

she's = she is; she has.

Shetland pony *n* a breed of small, sturdy pony with a shaggy mane.

Shetland sheepdog *n* a breed of dog resembling a collie but smaller.

Shevardnadze *n* **Eduard Ambrosievich** (1928–) Soviet politician, foreign minister (1985–91).

shewbread *n* sacred loaves of hot, fresh, unleavened bread laid on a table in the shrines of Israel and later in the Temple "before the face of God."

SHEx *abbr* = Sundays and holidays excepted.

SHF, shf *abbr* = superhigh frequency.

SHGF *abbr* (*Brit*) = Scottish Hang-Gliding Federation.

SHHD *abbr* (*Brit*) = Scottish Home and Health Department.

Shiah, Shia *n* a member of the main branch of Islam who acknowledge Muhammad's cousin Ali and his successors as the true imams.—*also adj*.

shibboleth *n* a slogan or catchword, esp that regarded as outmoded or identified with a particular group or culture; a custom or linguistic usage which identifies members of a particular group, party, class, etc.

Shibboleth *n* (*Bible*) a Hebrew word used by Jephthah at the fords of Jordan to test fleeing Ephraimites. Unable to pronounce "sh," they said "Sibboleth" and were thus detected and slain.

shied *see* **shy**[1], **shy**[2].

shield *n* a broad piece of armor carried for defense, usu on the left arm; a protective covering or guard; a thing or person that protects; a trophy in the shape of a shield; (*geol*) a stable area of the crust. * *vti* to defend; to protect; to screen.

Shield *n* **William** (1748–1829) an English composer, whose works include some 50 operas (e.g., *Rosina*), songs, and trio sonatas.

shier, shiest *see* **shy**[1].

shift *vti* to change position (of); to contrive, manage; to remove, transfer; to replace by another or others; to change the arrangement of (gears). * *n* a change in position; an expedient; a group of people working in relay with others; the time worked by them; a change or transfer; a straight dress; (*mus*) changing the position of the hands when playing on string instruments.

shift key *n* (*comput*) a key on a keyboard that allows the user to select an alternative range of characters such as upper-case letters, brackets, pound signs, etc.

shiftless *adj* incapable; feckless.—**shiftlessly** *adv*.—**shiftlessness** *n*.

shifty *adj* (**shiftier, shiftiest**) artful, tricky; evasive.—**shiftily** *adv*.—**shiftiness** *n*.

shigella *n* any of a genus of rod-shaped bacteria causing dysentery in humans and animals.

Shiite *or* **Shiah** *n* a follower of Shiah.—*also adj*.

shillelagh *n* an Irish club or cudgel.

shilling *n* a former unit of currency of the UK and other countries, worth one twentieth of a pound; the standard monetary unit of Kenya, Somalia, Tanzania, and Uganda, equal to 100 cents.

shillyshally *vi* (**shillyshallying, shillyshallied**) to vacillate, hesitate. * *n* (*pl* **shillyshallies**) the inability to make up one's mind.

Shiloh *n* (*Bible*) an important religious center in the early days of the Israelite conquest of Canaan.

shim *n* a thin washer or spacer used to tighten or space out joints, etc. * *vt* (**shimming, shimmed**) to space out, etc using shims.

shimmer *vi* to glisten softly, glimmer.—*also n*.—**shimmery** *adj*.

shimmy *n* (*pl* **shimmies**) a jazz dance involving rapid movements of the upper body; an abnormal vibration in a vehicle or aircraft. * *vi* (**shimmying, shimmied**) to dance a shimmy; to vibrate.

shin *n* the front part of the leg from the knee to the ankle; the shank. * *vi* (*with* **up**) to climb (a pole, etc) by gripping with legs and hands.

Shinar *n* (*Bible*) Babylonia, the cradle of Hebrew civilization. *See also* **Babylon**.

shinbone *n* the tibia.

shindig *n* (*inf*) a lively, noisy celebration; an uproar.

shine *vti* (**shining, shone**) to emit light; to be bright, glow; to be brilliant or conspicuous; to direct the light of; to cause to gleam by polishing; * *n* a luster, a gloss; (*sl*) a liking.

shiner *n* (*inf*) a black eye.

shingle[1] *n* a thin, wedge-shaped roof tile; a small signboard.

shingle[2] *n* waterworn pebbles, as on a beach; an area covered with these.—**shingly** *adj*.

shingles *npl* a virus disease marked by a painful rash of red spots on the skin.

Shinto *n* the indigenous religion of Japan, involving veneration of the emperor, and the worship of ancestors and various natural deities.—**Shintoism** *n*.—**Shintoist** *n*.

shinty *n* a game similar to hockey and hurling, played with a ball and curved sticks.

shiny *adj* (**shinier, shiniest**) glossy, polished; worn smooth.

ship *n* a large vessel navigating deep water; its officers and crew; a spacecraft. * *vti* (**shipping, shipped**) to transport by any carrier; to take in (water) over the side; to lay (oars) inside a boat; to go on board; to go or travel by ship.

shipboard *n* the side of a ship.

shipbuilder *n* a person or company that designs or constructs ships.—**shipbuilding** *n*.

ship chandler *n* an individual or business that provides essential supplies for ships.

shipload *n* as much as a ship can carry.

shipmaster *n* the captain or master of a ship.

shipmate *n* a fellow sailor.

shipment *n* goods shipped; a consignment.

ship of the line *n* (*formerly*) a warship large enough to fight in the first line of battle.

shipowner *n* a person who owns or has shares in a ship.

shipper *n* an individual or company that ships goods.

shipping *n* the business of transporting goods; ships collectively.

ship's biscuit *n* a type of hard cookie that was formerly part of a sailor's diet.

shipshape *adj* in good order, tidy.

ship-to-shore *adj* (*communications*) linking a ship with the shore.

shipworm *n* any of a genus of worm-like mollusks that burrow in submerged wood.

shipwreck *n* the loss of a vessel at sea; the remains of a wrecked ship; ruin, destruction. * *vti* to destroy by or suffer shipwreck; to ruin or be ruined.

shipwright *n* a person skilled in constructing and repairing ships.

shipyard *n* a yard or shed where ships are built or repaired.

shire *n* in the UK, a county; a large powerful breed of draft horse.

Shire *n* **Peter** (1947–) American designer, who designed eccentric furniture in Pop Art colors and kinetic shapes.

shirk *vti* to neglect or avoid work; to refuse to face (duty, danger, etc).—**shirker** *n*.

shirr *vt* to gather (fabric) with parallel threads run through it; to bake (eggs) in buttered dishes.

shirring *n* a gathering made in cloth by drawing the material up on parallel rows of short stitches.

shirt *n* a sleeved garment of cotton, etc, for the upper body, typically having a fitted collar and cuffs and front buttons; (*inf*) one's money or resources.

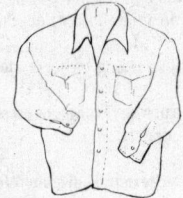

shirtdress *n* a long shirt worn as a dress.

shirting *n* a fabric suitable for men's shirts.

shirtsleeve *n* the sleeve of a shirt.

shirt-tail *n* the flap of material at the back of a shirt below the waist.

shirtwaister *or* **shirtwaist** *n* a woman's dress tailored in front, in style similar to a shirt.

shirty *adj* (**shirtier, shirtiest**) (*sl*) irritable, rude.

Shishak *see* **Rehoboam**.

shish kebab *n* a kebab.

shit *or* **shite** *n* (*vulg*) waste matter from humans or animals; excrement; heroin. * *vti* to defecate (on). * *interj* (*sl*) an expression of strong disgust or disapproval.

shivaree *see* **charivari**.

shiver[1] *n* a small fragment, a splinter.

shiver[2] *vi* to shake or tremble, as with cold or fear, shudder.—*also n.*—**shivery** *adj*.

Shkodèr *n* a city in Albania.

SHLTA *abbr* = Skin, Hide, & Leather Traders' Association.

shm *abbr* = simple harmonic motion.

SHMIS *abbr* (*Brit*) = Society of Headmasters and Headmistresses of Independent Schools.

SHNC *abbr* (*Brit*) = Scottish Higher National Certificate.

SHND *abbr* (*Brit*) = Scottish Higher National Diploma.

SHO *abbr* (*Brit*) = Senior House Officer.

shoal[1] *n* a large number of fish swimming together; a large crowd. * *vi* to form shoals.

shoal[2] *n* a submerged sandbank, esp one that shows at low tide; a shallow place; a hidden danger. * *vti* to come to a less deep part; to become shallower.

shock[1] *n* a shaggy mass of hair.

shock[2] *n* a violent jolt or impact; a sudden disturbance to the emotions; the event or experience causing this; the nerve sensation caused by an electrical charge through the body; a disorder of the blood circulation, produced by displacement of body fluids (due to injury); (*sl*) a paralytic stroke. * *vt* to outrage, horrify. * *vi* to experience extreme horror, outrage, etc.

shock absorber *n* a device, as on the springs of an automobile that absorbs the force of bumps and jars.

shocker *n* a sensational novel, play, etc; anything that shocks; (*sl*) a very bad specimen.

shocking *adj* revolting; scandalous, improper; very bad.—**shockingly** *adv*.

shock-jock *n* a DJ at a radio station who is deliberately provocative in presentation, particularly when airing controversial issues.

Shockley *n* **William Bradford** (1910–89) American physicist, who shared the 1956 Nobel Prize for Physics (for his development of the junction transistor) with John Bardeen and Walter Brattain.

shockproof *adj* capable of withstanding shock without damage.

shock therapy *or* **shock treatment** *n* the treatment of certain mental illnesses by inducing convulsions using drugs or by passing electricity through the brain.

shock troops *npl* a highly disciplined force trained to lead an attack.

shock wave *n* the violent effect in the vicinity of an explosion caused by the change in atmospheric pressure; the compressed wave built up when the speed of a body or fluid exceeds that at which sound can be transmitted in the medium in which it is traveling.

shod, shodden *see* **shoe**.

shoddy *adj* (**shoddier, shoddiest**) made of inferior material; cheap and nasty, trashy.—**shoddily** *adv*.—**shoddiness** *n*.

shoe *n* an outer covering for the foot not enclosing the ankle; a thing like a shoe, a partial casing; a horseshoe; a drag for a wheel; a device to guide movement, provide contact, or protect against wear or slipping; a dealing box that holds several decks of cards. * *vt* (**shoeing, shod** *or* **shoed**, *pp* **shod, shoed**, *or* **shodden**) to provide with shoes; to cover for strength or protection.

shoehorn *n* a curved piece of plastic, metal, or horn used for easing the heel into a shoe.

shoelace *n* a cord that passes through eyelets in a shoe and is tied to keep the shoe on the foot.

shoemaker *n* a person who makes or mends shoes.

shoestring *n* a shoelace; (*inf*) a small amount of money.

shoetree *n* a block of wood, plastic, or metal for preserving the shape of a shoe.

shofar, shophar *n* (*mus*) an ancient Jewish wind instrument, made from a ram's horn, which is still used in synagogues.

shogun *n* the hereditary commander of the army in feudal Japan.

Sholokhov *n* **Mikhail** [**Alexandrovich**] (1905–84) Russian novelist, whose *And Quiet Flows the Don* presents a panorama of Don Cossack life before and during the Bolshevik Revolution and has been hailed as a masterpiece although there have been persistent rumors that the work is not entirely his own. He was awarded the Nobel Prize for Literature in 1965.

shone *see* **shine**.

shoo *interj* used to frighten animals or people away. * *vt* (**shooing, shooed**) to frighten away (as if) by shouting "shoo." * *vi* to cry "shoo."

shoo-in *n* (*inf*) a person or thing certain to win or succeed.

shook *see* **shake**.

shoot *vt* (**shooting, shot**) to discharge or fire (a gun, etc); to hit or kill with a bullet, etc; (*rapids*) to be carried swiftly over; to propel quickly; to thrust out; (*bolt*) to slide home; to variegate (with another color, etc); to photograph (a movie scene); (*sport*) to kick or drive (a ball, etc) at goal; (*with* **down**) to disprove (an argument); (*with* **up**) to grow rapidly, rise abruptly. * *vi* to move swiftly, dart; to emit; to put forth buds, sprout; to attack or kill indiscriminately; (*sl*) to inject a narcotic into a vein. * *n* a contest, a shooting trip, etc; a new growth or sprout.

shooting *n* the act of firing a gun or letting off an arrow.

shooting gallery *n* an indoor range with targets for rifle practice.

shooting script *n* the final version of a movie script with scenes arranged together for convenience of shooting; the final script of a television show.

shooting star *n* a meteor.

shooting stick *n* a spiked stick with a handle that folds out into a small seat.

shop *n* a store; a factory; a workshop; the details and technicalities of one's own work, and talk about these. * *vti* (**shopping, shopped**) to visit stores to examine or buy; (*sl*) to inform on (a person) to the police; (*with* **around**) to hunt for the best buy.

shop assistant *n* (*Brit*) a salesclerk.

shop ballad *see* **ballad**.

shop floor *n* (*Brit*) the part of a factory where goods are manufactured; the work force employed there, usu unionized.

shopkeeper *n* a person who owns or runs a shop.—**shopkeeping** *n*.

shoplifting *n* stealing from a store during shopping hours.—**shoplifter** *n*.

shopper *n* a person who shops; (*Brit*) a bag for carrying shopping.

shopping *n* the act of shopping; the goods bought.—*also adj*.

shopping center *n* a complex of stores, restaurants, and service establishments, with a common parking area.—*also* **shopping plaza**.

shopping mall *n* a large, enclosed shopping center.

shopsoiled *adj* (*Brit*) shopworn.

shop steward *n* an employee of a company who represents the interests of his or her colleagues in negotiations with management.

shoptalk *n* the specialized vocabulary of those in the same line of work or sharing an area of interest; talk about work after hours.

shopwalker *n* (*Brit*) a person employed in large shop who oversees salesclerks, helps customers, etc.

shopworn *adj* faded, etc, from being on display in a store.

shoran *abbr* = short-range navigation.

shore[1] *n* land beside an ocean or a large body of water; beach.

shore[2] *n* a prop or beam used for support. * *vt* to prop (up), to support with a shore.

shoreline *n* the edge of an expanse of water.

shore platform *n* the gentle slope extending from the base of a cliff toward the sea.

shorn *see* **shear**.

short *adj* not measuring much; not long or tall; not great in range or scope; brief; concise; not retentive; curt; abrupt; less than the correct amount; below standard; deficient, lacking; (*pastry*) crisp or flaky; (*vowel*) not prolonged, unstressed;

(*drink*) undiluted, neat. * *n* something short; (*pl*) pants not covering the knee; (*pl*) an undergarment like these; a short circuit. * *adv* abruptly; concisely; without reaching the end. * *vti* to give less than is needed; to short-change; to short-circuit.—**shortness** *n*.

shortage *n* a deficiency.

short bill *n* a bill of exchange that is payable within a very short time, either on demand, at sight, or within ten days.

shortbread *n* a rich, crumbly cake or cookie made with much shortening.

short-change *vt* to give back less than the correct change; (*sl*) to cheat.

short-circuit *n* the deviation of an electric current by a path of small resistance; an interrupted electric current. * *vti* to establish a short-circuit in; to cut off electric current; to provide with a short cut.

shortcoming *n* a defect or inadequacy.

shortcrust pastry *n* a firm but crumbly pastry made with half as much fat as flour.

short cut *n* a shorter route; any way of saving time, effort, etc.

shortcut key *n* (*comput*) a key or a key combination that allows the user to bypass the normal menu selection process by pressing a key or keys simultaneously.

short-dated gilts *or* **shorts** *npl* gilt-edged securities that are redeemable in less than five years.

shorten *vt* to make or become short or shorter; to reduce the amount of (sail) spread; to make (pastry, etc) crisp and flaky by adding fat.

shortening *n* the act of shortening; the state of becoming shortened; a fat used for making pastry, etc, crisp and flaky.

shortfall *n* (the amount or degree of) a deficit or deficiency.

shorthand *n* a method of rapid writing using signs or contractions.—*also adj*.

short-handed *adj* not having the usual number of assistants.

shorthand typist *n* (*Brit*) a stenographer.

short head *n* (*horse racing*) a distance less than a horse's head.

shorthorn *n* one of a breed of large heavy cattle with short, curved horns.

short-list *vt* to place (a person) on a short list.

short list *n* a selected list of qualified applicants from which a choice must be made.

short-lived *adj* not lasting or living for long.

shortly *adv* soon, in a short time; briefly; rudely.

short order *n* an order for food that can be quickly prepared.—**short-order** *adj*.

short-period comet *n* (*astron*) a comet with an orbit inside the solar system and a period of under 150 years, e.g., Halley's Comet.

short position *n* a situation in which a dealer or market-maker in a particular security, commodity, or foreign currency is selling more than he or she is buying or holding in expectation of prices falling.

short-range *adj* having a limited range in time or distance.

shorts *see* **short-dated gilts.**

short shrift *n* curt, dismissive treatment.

short sight *see* **myopia.**

short-sighted *adj* not able to see well at a distance; lacking foresight.—**short-sightedly** *adv*.—**short-sightedness** *n*.

short story *n* a piece of narrative fiction shorter than a novel.

short-tempered *adj* easily annoyed.

short-term *adj* of or for a limited time.

short time *n* a reduction in working hours due to recession, etc.

shortwave *n* a radio wave 60 meters or less in length.

short-winded *adj* easily becoming breathless; (*speech, writing*) brief, to the point

Shoshenq *n* Libyan king of Egypt (Biblical Shishank) of the Twenty-Second Dynasty. Reigned from 945 BC. His descendants reigned until 825 BC.

Shostakovich *n* **Dimitri Dimitriyevich** (1906–75) Russian composer, whose works include symphonies, string quartets, and song cycles.

shot[1] *see* **shoot.**

shot[2] *n* the act of shooting; range, scope; an attempt; a solid projectile for a gun; projectiles collectively; small lead pellets for a shotgun; a marksman; a photograph or a continuous film sequence; a hypodermic injection, as of vaccine; a drink of alcohol.

shotgun *n* a smooth-bore gun for firing small shot at close range.

shotgun wedding *n* (*inf*) an enforced wedding, usu because the woman is pregnant.

shot put *n* a field event in which a heavy metal ball is propelled with an overhand thrust from the shoulder.—**shot-putter** *n*.

shotten *adj* (*fish*) having spawned recently.

should *vb aux* used to express obligation, duty, expectation, or probability, or a future condition.—*also pt of* **shall.**

shoulder *n* the joint connecting the arm with the trunk; a part like a shoulder; (*pl*) the upper part of the back; (*pl*) the capacity to bear a task or blame; a projecting part; the strip of land bordering a road. * *vti* to place on the shoulder to carry; to assume responsibility; to push with the shoulder, jostle.

shoulder blade *n* the large, flat, triangular bone on either side of the back part of the human shoulder.

shoulder girdle *see* **pectoral girdle.**

shoulder strap *n* a strap over the shoulders to hold up a garment, bag, etc.

shouldn't = should not.

shout *n* a loud call; a yell. * *vti* to call loudly, yell; (*with* **down**) to drown out or silence (a person speaking) by shouting.

shove *vti* to drive forward; to push; to jostle; (*with* **off**) to push (a boat) off from the shore; (*inf*) to depart, leave. * *n* a forceful push.

shove-halfpenny *n* a game in which coins or disks are slid across a board marked with a scoring grid.

shovel *n* a broad tool like a scoop with a long handle for moving loose material. * *vt* to move or lift with a shovel.

shoveler *n* any of several pond and marsh ducks with a broad beak.

shovelhead *n* a breed of shark with a shovel-shaped head.

show *vti* (**showing, showed,** *pt* **showed** *or* **shown**) to present to view, exhibit; to demonstrate, make clear; to prove; to manifest, disclose; to direct, guide; to appear, be visible; to finish third in a horse race; (*inf*) to arrive; (*with* **off**) to display to advantage; to try to attract admiration; to behave pretentiously; (*with* **up**) to put in an appearance, arrive; to expose to ridicule. * *n* a display, an exhibition; an entertainment; a theatrical performance; a radio or television show; third place at the finish (as a horse race).

show business *or* **show biz** *n* the entertainment industry.

showcase *n* a glass case or cabinet for displaying items in a store or museum; a setting or situation designed to exhibit something to best advantage.—*also vt*.

showdown *n* (*inf*) a final conflict; a disclosure of cards at poker.

shower *n* a brief period of rain, hail, or snow; a similar fall, as of tears, meteors, arrows, etc; a great number; a method of cleansing in which the body is sprayed with water from above; a wash in this; a party for the presentation of gifts, esp to a bride. * *vt* to pour copiously; to sprinkle; to bestow (with gifts). * *vi* to cleanse in a shower.

showgirl *n* a young woman who appears in a chorus line, variety act, etc.

show house *n* (*Brit*) a house on a new housing development used as a sample for prospective buyers.

showjumping *n* the competitive riding of horses to demonstrate their skill in jumping.

showman *n* (*pl* **showmen**) a man who manages or presents a theatrical show, circus, etc; a person skilled in presentation.

shown *see* **show.**

showpiece *n* an exhibit; a perfect example of something.

showplace *n* a place (e.g., a tourist attraction, historic site) regarded as being of exemplary interest or beauty.

showroom *n* a room where goods for sale are displayed.

show stopper *n* a performance that receives prolonged applause; someone or something of arresting beauty, excellence, etc.—**show-stopping** *adj*.

showy *adj* (**showier, showiest**) bright, colorful; ostentatious.—**showily** *adv*.—**showiness** *n*.

shp *abbr* = shaft horsepower; single-flowered hardy perennial (rose).

shpt. *abbr* = shipment.

SHQ *abbr* = supreme headquarters.

shr. *abbr* = share(s).

shrank *see* **shrink.**

shrapnel *n* an artillery shell filled with small pieces of metal that scatter on impact.

shred *n* a strip cut or torn off; a fragment, a scrap. * *vt* (**shredding, shredded**) to cut or tear into small pieces.

shrew *n* a small, brown, nocturnal mouse-like animal with a long snout; a bad-tempered, nagging woman.

shrewd *adj* astute, having common sense; keen, penetrating.—**shrewdly** *adv*.—**shrewdness** *n*.

shrewish *adj* sharp-tongued, nagging.

SHRG *abbr* (*Brit*) = Scottish Homosexual Rights Group.

shriek *n* a loud, shrill cry, a scream. * *vti* to screech, scream.

shrieval *adj* of or pertaining to a sheriff.

shrievalty *n* (*pl* **shrievalties**) the office, term of office, or jurisdiction of a sheriff.

shrike *n* a bird with a hooked beak that impales its prey, mainly insects and small animals, on thorns.

shrill *adj* high-pitched and piercing in sound; strident.

shrimp *n* a small, edible shellfish with a long tail; (*sl*) a small or unimportant person. * *vt* to fish for shrimp.

shrine *n* a container for sacred relics; a saint's tomb; a place of worship; a hallowed place.

shrink *vti* (**shrinking, shrank** *or* **shrunk,** *pp* **shrunk** *or* **shrunken**) to become smaller, contract as from cold, wetting, etc; to recoil (from), flinch; to cause (cloth, etc) to contract by soaking. * *n* (*sl*) a psychiatrist.—**shrinkable** *adj*.

shrinkage *n* contraction; diminution; goods that are no longer in a retail outlet but have not been recorded as having been sold.

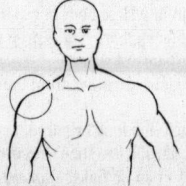

shrinking violet *n* a very shy or unassuming person.

shrink-wrap *vt* (**shrink-wrapping, shrink-wrapped**) (*book, etc*) to wrap in plastic film that is then shrunk by heat to form a tightly fitting package.

shrive *vt* (**shriving, shrived** or **shrove**, *pp* **shriven** or **shrived**) (*arch*) to hear the confession of; to impose penance on and absolve. * *vi* to confess, do penance, and receive absolution.

shrivel *vti* to dry up or wither and become wrinkled; to curl up with heat, etc.

shroud *n* a burial cloth; anything that envelops or conceals; (*naut*) a supporting rope for a mast. * *vt* to wrap in a shroud; to envelop or conceal.

shrove *see* **shrive**.

Shrovetide *n* the three days before Ash Wednesday.

Shrove Tuesday *n* the last day before Lent.

shrub *n* a woody plant smaller than a tree with several stems rising from the same root; a bush.—**shrubby** *adj*.

shrubbery *n* (*pl* **shrubberies**) an area of land planted with shrubs.

shrug *vti* (**shrugging, shrugged**) to draw up and contract (the shoulders) as a sign of doubt, indifference, etc; (*with* **off**) to brush aside; to shake off; (*a garment*) to remove by wriggling out. * *n* the act of shrugging.

shrunk *see* **shrink**.

shrunken *adj* shriveled, pinched; reduced.

SHS *abbr* (*Latin*) = *Societatis Historicae Socius*, "Fellow of the Historical Society."

sht *abbr* = single-flowered hybrid tea (rose).

shtg. *abbr* = shortage.

sh. tn. *abbr* = short ton.

shtoom *adj* (*sl*) silent, dumb.

Shu *n* (*Egypt*) in the cosmology of Heliopolis, Shu was the air-god (dry), a member of the original ogdoad, whose partner was Tefnut, goddess of moisture.

shuck *n* a husk, pod, or shell. * *vt* to remove the shucks from.

shucks *interj* used to express disappointment, irritation, etc.

shudder *vi* to tremble violently, shiver; to feel strong repugnance. * *n* a convulsive shiver of the body; a vibration.

shuffle *vt* to scrape (the feet) along the ground; to walk with dragging steps; (*playing cards*) to change the order of, mix; to intermingle, mix up; (*with* **off**) to get rid of.—*also n*.

shuffleboard *n* a game in which players propel plastic or wooden disks into numbered scoring areas marked on a large, flat surface.

shufty, shufti *n* (*pl* **shufties**) (*sl*) a peek, a glance.

Shultz *n* **George Pratt** (1920–) American politician and secretary of state (1982–89).

shun *vt* (**shunning, shunned**) to avoid scrupulously; to keep away from.

shunt *vti* to move to a different place; to put aside, shelve; (*trains*) to switch from one track to another; (*sl*) to collide.—*also n*.

shush *interj* used to demand silence; peace, silence. * *vt* to demand silence (as if) by saying "shush."

shut *vti* (**shutting, shut**) to close; to lock, fasten; to close up parts of, fold together; to bar; (*with* **down**) to (cause to) stop working or operating; (*with* **in**) to confine; to enclose; to block the view from; (*with* **off**) to check the flow of; to debar; (*with* **out**) to exclude; (*with* **up**) to confine; (*inf*) to stop talking; (*inf*) to silence.

shutdown *n* a stoppage of work or activity, as in a factory.

shuteye *n* (*inf*) sleep.

shutter *n* a movable cover for a window; a flap device for regulating the exposure of light to a camera lens.

shuttle *n* a device in a loom for holding the weft thread and carrying it between the warp threads; a bus, aircraft, etc, making back-and-forth trips over a short route. * *vti* to move back and forth rapidly.

shuttlecock[1] *n* a cork stuck with feathers, or a plastic imitation, hit with a racket in badminton.

shuttlecock[2] *see* **battledore**.

shv *abbr* (*Latin*) = *sub hac voce*, "under this word."

SHW *abbr* = safety, health, and welfare.

shy[1] *adj* (**shyer, shyest** or **shier, shiest**) very self-conscious, timid; bashful; wary, suspicious (of); (*sl*) lacking. * *vi* (**shying, shied**) to move suddenly, as when startled; to be or become cautious, etc. * *n* (*pl* **shies**) a sudden movement.—**shyly** *adv*.—**shyness** *n*.

shy[2] *vt* (**shying, shied**) to throw (something). * *n* (*pl* **shies**) a throw; (*inf*) an attempt, try.

shyster *n* (*inf*) a person, esp a lawyer, who is manipulative and disreputable.

si *n* (*mus*) ti.

SI *n* (Système International d'Unités) the universally used system of units based on the meter, second, kilogram, ampere, kelvin, candela, siemens, tesla, weber, and mole.

Si *symbol* (*chem*) = silicon (element).

si *abbr* = sum insured.

SI *abbr* = seriously ill; Smithsonian Institution; Socialist International; Society of Indexers; Staten Island (NY); statutory instrument; Survival International; (*French*) *Système International d'Unités*, "International Units System."

SIA *abbr* = Securities Industry Association; Service Innovation Action; Singapore International Airlines; Society of Investment Analysts; Solvents Industry Association; Spinal Injuries Association.

SIAD *abbr* = Society of Industrial Artists and Designers.

sial *n* the outer layer of the Earth's crust, composed mostly of rock rich in silicon and aluminum.

Siamese cat *n* a breed of domestic short-haired cat with a fawn or gray coat, darker ears, paws, tail, and face, and blue eyes.

Siamese fighting fish *n* an aggressive, brightly colored freshwater fish.

Siamese twins *npl* twin babies born with the bodies joined together at some point, esp the hip.

Siauliai *n* a city in Lithuania.

sib *n* a sibling.

Sib. *abbr* = Siberia; Siberian.

SIB *abbr* = Securities and Investments Board; self-injurious behavior; Shipbuilding Industry Board; Society of Independent Businesses; Special Investigations Branch.

SIBA *abbr* = (*Brit*) Scottish Indoor Bowling Association; Services Insurance Brokers' Association.

Sibelius *n* **Jean** (1865–1957) Finnish composer.

Siberia *n* Umberto Giordano's three-act opera, to a book by Luigi Illica, first performed in 1903 in Milan; in Genoa and other Italian cities the same year.

Siberian high *n* a persistent anticyclone that forms over central and northern Asia during the winter, associated with extremely low temperatures.

SIBH *abbr* = Society for the Interpretation of Britain's Heritage.

sibilant *adj* hissing. * *n* a sibilant letter, e.g., *s, z*.—**sibilance** *n*.

sibling *n* a brother or sister.

SIBOR *abbr* = Singapore Inter-Bank Offered Rate.

sibyl *n* in ancient Greece and Rome, a female prophet or oracle.

sic *adv* as written (used in text to indicate that an error or doubtful usage is reproduced from the original).

sic. *abbr* (*Latin*) = *siccus*, "dry."

Sic. *abbr* = Sicilian; Sicily.

SIC *abbr* = Standard Industrial Classification.

SICAV *abbr* (*French*) = *Société d'Investissement à Capital Variable*, "unit trust."

siciliano *n* (*mus*) a slow dance from Sicily in 6/8 or 12/8 time, with a characteristic lilting rhythm.

Sicily *n* the large, triangular island at the southwestern extremity of Italy, from which it is separated by the narrow strait of Messina.—**Sicilian** *adj, n*.

sick *adj* unhealthy, ill; having nausea, vomiting; thoroughly tired (of); disgusted by or suffering from an excess; (*inf*) (*humor*) sadistic, gruesome.—**sickness** *n*.

sick bay *n* an area in a ship used as a hospital or dispensary; a room used for the treatment of the sick.

sickbed *n* the bed where one lies sick.

sick building syndrome *n* a collection of symptoms, thought to be caused by microorganisms found in humidifiers and including lethargy, headache, and eye irritation, that affect those who work in totally air-conditioned buildings.—*also* **humidifier fever**.

sicken *vti* to make or become sick or nauseated; to show signs of illness.

sickening *adj* disgusting.—**sickeningly** *adv*.

sickle *n* a tool with a crescent-shaped blade for cutting tall grasses; anything shaped like this.

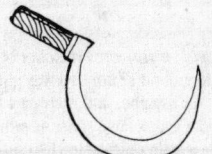

sick leave *n* absence from work due to illness.

sickle cell anemia *n* a form of anemia that is hereditary and marked by the presence of sickle-shaped red blood cells.

sick list *n* a list of employees, soldiers, etc who are absent due to sickness.

sickly *adj* (**sicklier, sickliest**) inclined to be ill; unhealthy; causing nausea; mawkish; pale, feeble.—**sickliness** *n*.

sick-making *adj* (*inf*) nauseating, galling.

sick pay *n* wages or salaries paid to an employee while he or she is off sick.

sickroom *n* the room to which a patient is confined while sick.

Sicyon *n* one of the most ancient cities of Greece.

sid *abbr* = sudden ionospheric disturbance.

side *n* a line or surface bounding anything; the left or right part of the body; the top or underneath surface; the slope of a hill; an aspect, a direction; a party or faction; a cause; a team; a line of descent; (*sl*) conceit. * *adj* toward or at the side, lateral; incidental. * *vi* to associate with a particular faction.

side arms *npl* weapons (e.g., a pistol, dagger) worn in a belt or holster at the side of the waist.

sideboard *n* a long table or cabinet for holding cutlery, crockery, etc; (*pl*) two strips of hair growing down a man's cheeks.—*also* **sideburns**.

sidecar *n* a small car attached to the side of a motorcycle; a cocktail of brandy, liqueur, and lemon juice.

sided *adj* having sides of a specified number or kind.

side dish *n* food accompanying a main course at a meal.

side drum *n* a small, double-headed drum with snares, carried, and played at the side.

side effect *n* a secondary and usu adverse effect, as of a drug or medical treatment.

side-glance *n* a look directed to one side; a slight reference.

sidekick *n* (*sl*) a confederate; a partner; a close friend.

sidelight *n* light coming from the side; a light on the side of an automobile, etc; incidental information.

sideline *n* a line marking the side limit of a playing area; a minor branch of business; a subsidiary interest.

sidelong *adj* oblique, not direct. * *adv* obliquely.

sideman *n* (*pl* **sidemen**) a member of a jazz band or orchestra other than the leader.

Sideng *n* (*Irish Celtic myth*) the daughter of Mongan. According to legend, she gave Fionn mac Cumhaill a flat stone to which a golden chain was attached. When Fionn whirled this stone round his head he was able to cut his opponents in half.

sidereal *adj* of or by reference to stars and constellations.

sidereal day *n* (*astron*) the time taken for the Earth to make one complete rotation upon its axis with reference to the fixed stars

sidereal month *n* (*astron*) the time taken by the moon to complete one orbit of the Earth.

sidereal period *n* (*astron*) the period taken by the moon and planets to reach the identical successive positions, relative to the line joining the Earth to the sun.

sidereal rate *n* the speed at which an equatorially mounted telescope must be driven around its polar axis, to keep it fixed upon one particular point in the sky allowing exactly for the rotation of the Earth.

sidereal time *n* (*astron*) the measurement of time using the rotation of the Earth with reference to distant stars.

sidereal year *n* (*astron*) the period in which the sun appears to make one revolution with reference to the fixed stars.

siderite *n* a mineral composed mainly of ferrous carbonate, used as a source of iron.

sidero- *or* **sider-** *prefix* iron.

siderosis *n* a lung disease caused by inhalation of iron or other types of metallic particles.

side-saddle *n* a saddle that enables a rider to sit with both feet on the same side of a horse. * *adv* as if sitting on a side-saddle.

sideshow *n* a minor attraction at a fair, etc; a subsidiary event.

sidesman *n* (*pl* **sidesmen**) (*Anglican Church*) an officer assisting the churchwardens.

side-splitting *adj* uproariously funny.

sidestep *vti* to take a step to one side; to avoid or dodge.—*also n*.

sidestroke *n* (*swimming*) a stroke used while swimming on one's side.

sideswipe *n* a glancing blow; (*inf*) an incidental jibe or criticism.

sidetrack *vt* to prevent action by diversionary tactics; to shunt aside, shelve. * *n* a railroad siding.

sidewalk *n* a path, usu paved, at the side of a street.

sidewall *n* either of the sides of a pneumatic tire.

sideward *adj, adv* sideways.

sideways, sideway *adj, adv* toward or from one side; facing to the side.

side whiskers *n* sideboards, sideburns.

sidewinder *n* a North American rattlesnake that moves in a twisting sideways motion.

sidewise *adv* sideways.

sidh *n* (*pl* **sidhe**) (*Irish Celtic myth*) each member of the Tuatha De Danann was assigned part of the underground realm that was given to them when they were defeated by the Sons of Mil Espaine, and each part was called a *sidh*, the word meaning a mound or hill; a god; a fairy, sprite or other supernatural being.

siding *n* a short line beside a main railroad track for use in shunting; a covering, as of boards for the outside of a frame building.

sidle *vi* to move sideways, esp to edge along.

Sidney *n* **Sir Philip** (1554–86) English poet, soldier, and courtier.

Sidon (Saïda) *n* a city in the Lebanon; (*Bible*) an ancient seaport on the northern coast of Palestine and a city, along with Tyre, of the kingdom of Phoenicia.

SIDP *abbr* = Society of Infectious Diseases Pharmacists.

SIDS *abbr* = sudden infant death syndrome.

SIE *abbr* = Society of Industrial Engineers.

SIEDip *abbr* = Securities Industry Examination Diploma.

siege *n* the surrounding of a fortified place to cut off supplies and compel its surrender; the act of besieging; a continued attempt to gain something.

siemens *n* (*pl* **siemens**) the SI unit of electrical conductance.

sienna *n* an earthy pigment, either yellowish-brown (raw sienna) or reddish-brown (burnt sienna).

sierra *n* a range of mountains with jagged peaks.

Sierra Leone *n* a republic on the Atlantic coast of west Africa.

SIES *abbr* = Office of Strategic Industries & Economic Security.

siesta *n* a midday nap, esp in hot countries.

sieve *n* a utensil with a meshed-wire bottom for sifting and straining; a person who cannot keep secrets. * *vt* to put through a sieve, sift.

SIF *abbr* = Society for Individual Freedom; Society of Irish Foresters.

sift *vti* to separate coarser parts from finer with a sieve; to sort out; to examine critically; to pass as through a sieve.

Sig., sig. *abbr* = signature; (*Italian*) *Signor*, "Mr."

SIG *abbr* = special interest group.

SIGBI *abbr* (*Brit*) = Soroptimist International of Great Britain and Ireland.

Sig C, Sig. C. *abbr* = Signal Corps.

Sigeberht I *n* (the Little) (*d.* 653) king of Essex (617–653). Succeeded by his son, also Sigeberht.

Sigeberht II *n* (the Good) king of Essex (653–660). After his baptism he restored Christianity to the kingdom after a generation of paganism.

Sigeberht *n* (*d.* 759) king of Wessex (756–757).

Sigeberht *n* (*d. c.*634) king of East Anglia (631–634). A half-brother of Eorpwald.

Sigeherd *n* (*d. c.*709) king of Essex (695–709). Succeeded his father Sebbi and became joint ruler with his brother, Swalfred.

Sigered *n* (*d.* 825) king of Essex (798–825). The last king of Essex before the kingdom became absorbed by Wessex.

Sigeric *n* king of Essex (758–798). Ruled as an under-king of Mercia before abdicating.

sigh *vti* to draw, deep audible breath as a sign of weariness, relief, etc; to make a sound like this; to pine or lament (for); to utter with a sigh.—*also n*.

Sighere *n* (*d. c.*695) king of Essex (665–695). Son of Swithelm, he shared the throne with his uncle, Sebbi. He married a Mercian princess.

sight *n* the act or faculty of seeing; what is seen or is worth seeing, a spectacle; a view or glimpse; range of vision; a device on a gun etc to guide the eye in aiming it; aim taken with this; (*inf*) anything that looks unpleasant, odd, etc. * *vti* to catch sight of; to aim through a sight.

sight deposit *n* a bank deposit that can be withdrawn on demand without notice.

sight draft *n* a bill of exchange that is payable on sight, no matter when it was drawn.

sighted *adj* having sight, esp of a particular character, e.g., short-sighted.

sightless *adj* without sight, blind.—**sightlessly** *adv*.—**sightlessness** *n*.

sightly *adj* (**sightlier, sightliest**) pleasing to the eye; comely.—**sightliness** *n*.

sight-read *vt* (**sight-reading, sight-read**) to play or sing from (a piece of printed music) without previous preparation. * *vi* to read at sight.

sightseeing *n* the viewing or visiting of places of interest.—**sightseer** *n*.

sigill. *abbr* (*Latin*) = *sigillum*, "seal."

sigint *abbr* = signal intelligence.

sigma *n* the 18th letter of the Greek alphabet; (*math*) the symbol S, indicating summation.

sigmoid *or* **sigmoidal** *adj* curved like the letter S.

sigmoid colon *n* the end part of the colon, which is S-shaped.

sigmoidectomy *n* (*pl* **sigmoidectomies**) surgical excision of the sigmoid colon, performed usu for tumors.

sigmoidoscopy *n* (*pl* **sigmoidoscopies**) the examination of the sigmoid colon and rectum with a special viewing device. *See also* **fiberoptic endoscopy**.

sign *n* a mark or symbol; a gesture; an indication, token, trace, or symptom (of); an omen; (*math*) a conventional mark used to indicate an operation to be performed; a board or placard with publicly displayed information. * *vi* to append one's signature; to ratify something thus. * *vt* to engage by written contract; to write one's name on; to indicate by a sign; to signal; to communicate by sign language; (*with* **away**) to relinquish by signing a deed, etc; (*with* **on**) to accept employment; to register; (*with* **off**) to complete a broadcast.

signal *n* a sign, device or gesture to intimate a warning or to give information, esp at a distance; a message so conveyed; a semaphore system used by railroads; in radio, etc, the electrical impulses transmitted or received; a sign or event that initiates action. * *vti* to make a signal or signals (to); to communicate by signals. * *adj* striking, notable.—**signaler** *n*.

signalize *vt* to point out; to distinguish.—**signalization** *n*.

signally *adv* remarkably; notably.

signalman *n* (*pl* **signalmen**) a person who works signals or transmits signals.

signatory *n* (*pl* **signatories**) a party or state that has signed an agreement or treaty; the person who signs in behalf of his or her government.

signature *n* a person's name written by himself or herself; the act of signing one's own name; a characteristic mark; (*mus*) the flats and sharps after the clef showing the key; (*print*) a mark on the first pages of each sheet of a book as a guide to the binder; such a sheet when folded.

signature tune *n* a tune associated with a performer or a TV or radio show, etc.

signboard *n* a board with a sign or inscription in front of a business, store, etc.

signet *n* a small seal, esp one set in a ring; an official seal used in lieu of a signature in authenticating documents; the impression made by this.

signet ring *n* a ring with a seal set in it.

significant *adj* full of meaning, esp a special or hidden one; momentous, important; highly expressive; indicative (of).—**significance** *n*.—**significantly** *adv*.

significant figures *npl* (*math*) the digits in a number that contribute to its value.

signify *vti* (**signifying, signified**) to mean; to be a sign of; to indicate; to represent; to matter, be important; to make a sign.—**signification** *n*.

sign language *n* a system of manual signs and gestures for conveying meaning, used esp by hearing-impaired people.

sig. nom. pro. *abbr* (*Latin*) = *signa nomine proprio*, "label with the correct title."

signor *or* **signior** *n* (*pl* **signors** *or* **signori**) the title of an Italian man, equivalent to Mr or sir.

signora *n* (*pl* **signoras, signore**) the title of an Italian married woman, equivalent to Mrs or madam.

signore *n* (*pl* **signori**) the title of an Italian man, equivalent to Mr or sir.

signorina *n* (*pl* **signorinas, signorine**) the title of an Italian unmarried woman, equivalent to Miss or madam an unmarried Italian woman.

signpost *n* a post with signs on it to direct travelers; a beacon, a guide.—*also vt*.

SigO *abbr* = Signals Officer.

SIH *abbr* = Society for Italic Handwriting.

Sihanouk *n* **Prince Norodom** (1922–) Cambodian statesman formerly (elected) king of Cambodia (1941–55). He became head of state (1960–70) and again (1975–76) in alliance with the Khmer Rouge, until he was deposed by Pol Pot.

Sikasso *n* town in Mali.

Sikh *n* a member of an Indian sect, founded in the 16th century, that teaches monotheism and rejects idolatry and caste. * *adj* of or pertaining to the Sikhs or their beliefs.

Sikorski *n* **Wladyslaw** (1881–1943) Polish general and statesman; premier of the Polish government in exile during World War II and commander in chief of the Free Polish armed forces.

Sikorsky *n* **Igor Ivan** (1889–1972) Russian-born American aeronautical engineer who built the first four-engined aircraft in 1913 and the first successful helicopter in 1939.

Sil. *abbr* = Silesia.

silage *n* green fodder preserved for the winter in a silo.

Silas *n* (*Bible*) a leader of the Church in Jerusalem, sent to Antioch with Paul and Barnabas to announce the findings of the council of apostles and elders concerning relationships between Jewish and Christian believers.

sild *n* (*pl* **silds** *or* **sild**) a young herring, esp when canned in Norway.

silence *n* absence of sound; the time this lasts; refusal to speak or make a sound; secrecy. * *vt* to cause to be silent. * *interj* be silent!

silencer *n* (*Brit*) a device for reducing the noise of a vehicle exhaust or gun, a muffler.

silent *adj* not speaking; taciturn; noiseless; still.—**silently** *adv*.

silent majority *n* those who rarely assert their views but are presumed to be moderates.

silent partner *n* a partner in a business who takes no part in its management.

Silenus *see* **Seilenus**.

silhouette *n* the outline of a shape against light or a lighter background; a solid outline drawing, usu in solid black on white, esp of a profile. * *vt* to show up in outline; to depict in silhouette.

silica *n* a hard mineral, a compound of oxygen and silicon, found in quartz and flint.

silica gel *n* (*geol*) the hard amorphous form of hydrated silica, which is chemically inert, but highly hygroscopic.

silicate *n* a salt containing silicon.

siliceous, silicious *adj* of or containing silica.

silicon *n* a metalloid element occuring in silica and used extensively in transistors, etc, and as a compound in glass, etc; (*comput*) the material from which computer chips are made. * *adj* of an area in which there are a number of computer software and hardware companies.

silicon chip *n* a microchip.

silicone *n* an organic polymer compound with good lubricating and insulating properties, used widely as a repellent, resin, etc.

Silicon Valley *n* an industrial area in the Santa Clara Valley in California that has a high concentration of information technology industries.

silicosis *n* a disease of the lungs caused by prolonged inhalation of silica particles.

silk *n* a fiber produced by silkworms; lustrous textile cloth or thread or a garment made of silk; (*pl*) silk garments; (*pl*) the colors of a racing stable, worn by a jockey, etc. **adj* of, relating to, or made of silk.

silk cotton *n* kapok.

silken *adj* made of or like silk; silky.

silk hat *n* a top hat covered in silk.

silk screen *n* a stencil method of printing a color design through the meshes of a fabric, such as silk; a print so produced.—**silk-screen** *vt*.

silkweed *see* **milkweed**.

silkworm *n* a caterpillar of various moths that feeds on mulberry leaves and produces a strong fiber to construct its cocoon.

silky *adj* (**silkier, silkiest**) soft and smooth like silk; glossy; suave.—**silkiness** *n*.

sill *n* a heavy, horizontal slab of wood or stone at the bottom of a window frame or door; (*geol*) an igneous intrusion that pushes into the surrounding rocks and often takes advantage of weaknesses by bedding planes.

sillabub *see* **syllabub**.

silly *adj* (**sillier, silliest**) foolish, stupid; frivolous; lacking in sense or judgment; being stunned or dazed. * *n* (*pl* **sillies**) a silly person.—**silliness** *n*.

silo *n* (*pl* **silos**) an airtight pit or tower for storing fodder in a green, compressed state; a deep pit for storing cement, coal, etc; an underground structure from which a missile can be fired.

Siloam *n* (*Bible*) a tunnel through solid rock, which carried water more than 1700 feet from the spring Gihon in the Kidron valley below Jerusalem to a pool inside the city. The supply was vital to Jerusalem in time of siege.

silt *n* a fine-grained sandy sediment carried or deposited by water. * *vti* to fill or choke up with silt.

Silurian *adj* (*geol*) of or pertaining to the division of Paleozoic rocks between Ordovician and Devonian. * *n* this period.

Silvanus, Sylvanus *n* (*Roman myth*) a god of the fields and forests, who is also called the protector of the boundaries of fields.

silver *n* a ductile, malleable, grayish-white metallic element used in jewelry, cutlery, tableware, coins, etc; a lustrous, grayish white. * symbol Ag. * *adj* made of or plated with silver; silvery; (*hair*) gray; marking the 25th in a series * *vt* to coat with silver or a substance resembling silver; to make or become silvery or gray.

silver birch *n* a Eurasian birch tree with silvery bark.

silver fox *n* (the pelt of) a red fox in a color phase when its fur is black with silver-tipped hairs.

silver gilt *n* gilded silver.

silver lining *n* a more favorable aspect of an otherwise hopeless situation.

silver paper *n* a metallic paper coated or laminated to resemble silver, tinfoil.

silver plate *n* a plating of silver; domestic utensils made of silver or of silver-plated metal.—**silver-plate** *vt*.

silver screen *n* (*inf*) (*with* **the**) the movie industry; the screen on which a movie is projected.

silver service *n* (*in restaurants*) a manner of serving food using a spoon and fork in one hand.

silverside *n* a joint of beef cut from the upper haunch.

silversmith *n* a worker in silver.

silver-tongued *adj* plausible, eloquent.

silverware *n* items, such as serving plates, flatware, etc made from silver or silver plate.

silver wedding *n* the 25th anniversary of a marriage.

silverweed *n* any of various plants with silvery leaves or hairs.

silvery *adj* white and lustrous like silver; covered with silver; resembling silver in color; (*sound*) soft and clear.

silviculture *n* the branch of forestry dealing with the care and development of forests.

SIM *abbr* = self-inflicted mutilation.

SIMA *abbr* (*Brit*) = Scientific Instrument Manufacturers' Association of Great Britain.

Simca *abbr* (*French*) = Société Industrielle de Mécanique et Carrosserie Automobiles, "Car Engine and Coachbuilding Company."

simd *abbr* = single instruction, multiple data.

Simeon *n* (*Bible*) 1. a form of the name Simon, used by Simon Peter. 2. a member of the Church at Antioch, who was a prophet and teacher. 3. an old man who was in the Temple when Mary and Joseph brought their son there according to the Law. Simeon took the child Jesus in his arms and gave thanks to God. 4. the second son of Jacob and Leah; ancestor of one of the tribes of Israel.

Simeon Stylites *n* **Saint** (died 460) Greek monk. At the monastery of Heliodorus, his mortifications were so severe that he was dismissed as a warning to the monks to avoid extremes. In 423, began to live on a pillar at Telanissus; over the years its height was increased to about 60 feet; he spent the remaining years of his life there. His feast day is 5 January.

simian *adj* of or like an ape or monkey.

simian immunodeficiency virus *n* a virus, similar to human immunodeficiency virus, that interferes with the ability of the immune system of monkeys to resist disease.

similar *adj* having a resemblance to, like; nearly corresponding; (*geom*) corresponding exactly in shape if not size.—**similarity** *n*.—**similarly** *adv*.

similar motion *n* (*mus*) the simultaneous progression of two or more parts in the same direction.

Simias *n* (*Irish Celtic myth*) a wizard from the mythical city of Murias. He was one of the four wizards (the other three being Esias, Morfessa and Uscias) who taught the Tuatha De Danann their magic skills before they invaded Ireland.

simile *n* a figure of speech likening one thing to another by the use of "like," "as," etc.

similitude *n* the state of being similar; guise, likeness.

SIMM *abbr* = single in-line memory module.

simmer *vti* to boil gently; to be or keep on the point of boiling; to be in a state of suppressed rage or laughter; (*with* **down**) to abate. * *n* the state of simmering.

simnel cake *n* a rich fruit cake with marzipan and decorations, traditionally eaten during Lent or Easter.

Simon[1] *n* (*Bible*) 1. a brother of Jesus. 2. a leper in Bethany in whose house a woman anointed Jesus' head with precious ointment. 3. a magician in Samaria who was converted by Philip the evangelist and baptized. 4. a man of Cyrene, who was ordered to carry Jesus' cross on the way to Calvary. 5. a tanner in Joppa with whom Peter stayed for many days. 6. one of the twelve chosen disciples of Jesus, called "Simon the Cananaean" in the Gospels of Matthew and Mark, and "Simon who was called the Zealot" in the Gospel of Luke and the Acts of the Apostles. 7. Simon Peter; *see* **Peter**. 8. the father of Judas Iscariot.

Simon[2] *n* **[Marvin] Neil** (1927–) American dramatist, whose very popular New-York based comedies of manners include *Barefoot in the Park* and *The Odd Couple*.

simony *n* the buying and selling of ecclesiastical offices.

simoom *or* **simoon** *n* a strong, hot, dry wind of the Arabian and North African deserts.

simpatico *adj* (*inf*) agreeable, sympathetic.

simper *vi* to smile in a silly or self-conscious way.—*also n*.

simple *adj* single, uncompounded; plain, not elaborate; clear, not complicated; easy to do, understand, or solve; artless, not sophisticated; weak in intellect; unsuspecting, credulous; sheer, mere.—**simpleness** *n*.

simple fraction *n* a fraction in which both the numerator and denominator are whole numbers.

simple harmonic motion *n* (*phys*) motion that is characteristic of many systems that vibrate or oscillate.

simple-hearted *adj* sincere, honest.

simple interest *n* interest paid on the principal of a loan only.

simple interval *n* (*mus*) any interval that is an octave or less. Compare **compound interval**.

simple-minded *adj* foolish; mentally retarded.

simple time *see* **compound time**.

simpleton *n* a foolish, weak-minded person.

simplicity *n* (*pl* **simplicities**) the quality or state of being simple; absence of complications; easiness; lack of ornament, plainness, restraint; artlessness; directness; guilelessness, openness, naivety.

simplification *n* the act or result of making less complicated.

simplified financial statements *npl* simplified versions of the annual accounts of a company.

simplify *vt* (**simplifying, simplified**) to make simple or easy to understand.

simplistic *adj* over-simplified; uncomplicated.—**simplistically** *adv*.

simply *adv* in a simple way; plainly; merely; absolutely.

Simpson, Wallis *see* **Windsor, Duke of.**

simulacrum *n* (*pl* **simulacra**) a likeness or representation, esp a superficial one.

simulate *vt* to pretend to have or feel, to feign; to reproduce (conditions) in order to conduct an experiment; to imitate.—**simulation** *n*.

simulator *n* a device that simulates specific conditions in order to test actions or reactions.

simulcast *n* a simultaneous radio and television broadcast.—*also vt*.

simultaneous *adj* done or occurring at the same time.—**simultaneity** *n*.—**simultaneously** *adv*.

simultaneous equations *npl* (*math*) two or more equations with two or more unknown variables, which may have a unique solution.

sin[1] *n* an offense against a religious or moral principle; transgression of the law of God; a wicked act, an offense; a misdeed, a fault. * *vi* (**sinning, sinned**) to commit a sin; to offend (against).

sin[2] *abbr* = sine.

SINA *abbr* = (*Brit*) Scottish Independent Nurseries Association; Shellfish Institute of North America.

Sinai *n* (*Bible*) Mt Horeb, the sacred mountain where Moses saw the burning bush and heard God speak; also the place of thunder and lightnings, smoke, and flame where the Law was given. *See also* **Covenant**.

Sinai Peninsula *n* the peninsula to the northeast of Egypt.

Sinan *n* (*b.* 1489) Turkish architect, whose notable works include mosques at Edirne and Istanbul.

Sinatra *n* **Frank [Francis Albert Sinatra]** (1915–98) American singer and movie actor, who became a highly popular "crooner" of romantic songs in the 1940s, and won an Oscar for his part in *From Here to Eternity* (1952). He is regarded as one of the finest modern popular singers, with a finely tuned jazz-like sense of phrasing.

sin bin *n* (*ice hockey, etc*) (*sl*) an enclosure off the playing area where players guilty of fouls are temporarily sent.

since *adv* from then until now; subsequently; ago. * *prep* during, or continuously from then until now; after. * *conj* from the time that; because, seeing that.

sincere *adj* genuine, real, not pretended; honest, straightforward.—**sincerely** *adv*.

sincerity *n* the quality or state of being sincere; genuineness, honesty, seriousness.

sinciput *n* (*pl* **sinciputs** or **sincipita**) the front part of the skull; forehead.

Sinclair *n* 1. **Clive** (1940–) British electronics engineer, who produced the first pocket calculator. 2. **Upton [Beall]** (1878–1968) American novelist, the best-known of whose works are *The Jungle*, which features a no-holds-barred account of the Chicago meat trade, and the "Lanny Budd" sequence of political novels, e.g., *World's End* and *The Return of Lanny Budd*.

Sinding *n* **Christian** (1856–1941) Norwegian composer and pianist, who studied in Leipzig. His works include operas, four symphonies, and many songs. However, he is best remembered for his piano piece *The Rustle of Spring*.

sine *n* (*trig*) a function that in a right-angled triangle is equal to the ratio of the length of the side opposite the angle to that of the hypoteneuse.

sinecure *n* a position or office that provides an income without involving duties.

sine die *adv* without a date, indefinitely.

sine qua non *n* an essential condition, a necessity.

sine tone *n* (*mus*) an electronically produced note that is entirely "pure."

sinew *n* a cord of fibrous tissue, a tendon; (*usu pl*) the chief supporting force, a mainstay; (*pl*) muscles, brawn.

sinewy *adj* having a lean body and strong muscles; tough, stringy.

sinfonia *n* (*pl* **sinfonie** or **sinfonias**) a symphony.

sinfonietta *n* a short symphony; a small orchestra.

sinful *adj* guilty of sin, wicked.—**sinfully** *adv*.—**sinfulness** *n*.

sing *vti* (**singing, sang**, *pp* **sung**) to utter (words) with musical modulations; to perform (a song); to hum, ring; to write poetry (about); to praise; (*with* **out**) to shout, call out.—**singer** *n*.—**singing** *n*.

sing. *abbr* = singular.

Singapore *n* a small island republic located just off the southern tip of the Malay Peninsula in Southeast Asia; capital city of Singapore.

Singapore dollar *n* currency of Singapore.

singe *vt* (**singeing, singed**) to burn slightly; to scorch, esp to remove feathers, etc.—*also n*.

Singer *n* **Isaac Bashevis** (1904–91) Polish-born American Yiddish writer, and winner of the 1978 Nobel Prize for Literature.

Singhalese *see* **Sinhalese.**

singing *n* the art or an act of singing.

singing telegram *n* (a service that provides) a greetings message delivered in song, usu by a person in fancy dress.

single *adj* one only, not double; individual; composed of one part; alone, sole; separate; unmarried; for one; with one contestant on each side; simple; whole, unbroken; (*tennis*) played between two persons only; (*ticket*) for the outward journey only. * *n* a single ticket; a game between two players; a hit scoring one; a CD with one tune on each side. * *vt* (*with* **out**) to pick out, select.

single-breasted *adj* (*suit, etc*) fastening in the center with a single row of buttons.

single blessedness *n* the unmarried state.

single chant *see* **Anglican chant.**

single cream *n* cream with a low fat content.

single currency *n* a unified currency proposed for the use of all member states of the European Union when economic and monetary union takes place.

single-decker *n* (*Brit*) a bus with only one level of passenger accommodation.

single-density *adj* (*comput*) denoting an obsolete disk-storage technology.

single entry *n* (*book-keeping*) a system in which transactions are kept in one account only.

single figures *npl* the numbers less than 10, i.e., 1 to 9.

single file *n* a single column of persons or things, one behind the other.

single-handed *adj*, *adv* without assistance, unaided.—**single-handedly** *adv*.—**single-handedness** *n*.

single in-line package *n* (*comput*) a small circuit board similar to a SIMM. * *abbr* SIP.

single-lens reflex *n* a camera whose lens allows the photographer to see the same image as it exposes.

single market *n* an association of countries trading without restrictions, especially the countries of the European Union.

single-minded *adj* having only one aim in mind.—**single-mindedly** *adv*.—**single-mindedness** *n*.

singles bar *n* a bar or social club for single people only.

single-sided disk *n* (*comput*) an old type of storage disk that allows only one side to be used to read or write data.

singlestick *n* fencing with wooden sticks instead of swords; the stick used for this.

singlet *n* (*Brit*) an undershirt.

single ticket *n* a ticket for a one-way journey only.

singleton *n* a playing card that is the only one of its suit in a hand.

singly *adv* alone; one by one.

singsong *n* a droning monotonous utterance; a verse with a regular, marked rhythm and rhyme; (*inf*) a party where everyone sings. * *adj* having a regular or monotonous rhythm.

singular *adj* remarkable; exceptional; unusual; eccentric, odd; (*gram*) referring to only one person or thing. * *n* (*gram*) the singular number or form of a word.

singularity *n* (*pl* **singularities**) the state of being singular; uniqueness; an odd trait, a peculiarity; (*math*) a point or region where time and space become absolutely distorted and ordinary laws of physics no longer apply.

singularly *adv* unusually; exceptionally.

sinh *abbr* = hyperbolic sine.

Sinhalese *n* a member of a people who form the largest community in Sri Lanka; the language of these people.—*also adj*.—*also* **Singhalese**.

Siniann *see* **Sionan.**

sinister *adj* inauspicious; ominous; ill-omened; evil-looking; malignant; wicked; left; (*her*) on the left side of the shield.

sinistral *adj* of or on the left; left-handed.—**sinistrally** *adv*.

sinistro, sinistra *adj* (*mus*) (*Italian*) left, as in *mano sinistra*, meaning "left hand."

sink *vti* (**sinking, sank** or **sunk**, *pp* **sunk**) to go under the surface or to the bottom of a liquid; to submerge in water; to go down slowly; (*wind*) to subside; to pass to a lower state; to droop, decline; to grow weaker; to become hollow; to lower, degrade; to cause to sink; to make by digging out; to invest; (*with* **in**) to penetrate; to thrust into; (*inf*) to be understood in full. * *n* a basin with an outflow pipe, usu in a kitchen; a cesspool; an area of sunken land.—**sinking** *n*.

sinker *n* a weight used to submerge a fishing line.

sinkhole *n* a hole in rock strata, esp limestone, though which water sinks or runs underground; a hole into which foul waste matter is discharged.

sinking fund *n* money put aside for gradual payment of a debt.

sinner *n* a person who sins.

Sinn Fein *n* a republican party in Ireland that is the political wing of the IRA.

Sino- *prefix* Chinese.

sinoatrial node *n* the natural heart pacemaker, which consists of specialized muscle cells in the right atrium that contract and initiate contractions in the muscles of the heart.

Sinology *n* the study of Chinese language, history, society, etc.—**Sinologist** *n*.—**Sinological** *adj*.

Sinon *n* (*Greek myth*) a Greek hero who fought at Troy, allowed himself to be taken prisoner by the Trojans, and opened the wooden horse.

Sinope *n* one of the small moons or satellites of Jupiter, first recorded in 1914.

Sino-Tibetan *n* a family of languages that includes all the Chinese languages, Burmese, and Tibetan.—*also adj*.

sinsemilla *n* (a plant which produces) a highly potent type of marijuana.

SInstBB *abbr* (*Brit*) = Student of the Institute of British Bakers.

SInstPet *abbr* = Student of the Institute of Petroleum.

sinter *n* a white silicious deposit formed by the evaporation of hot mineral waters. * *vt* to form (metal or glass powder) into lumps by the application of heat and pressure.

sinuate *adj* (*leaf*) having a wavy edge.—**sinuately** *adv*.

Sinuhe *n* (*Egypt*) *The Story of Sinuhe*, dating from the reign of Sesostris I, became one of the most widely copied Egyptian texts, much used in the schools for scribes during the New Kingdom period.

sinuous *adj* curving; winding; tortuous.—**sinuously** *adv*.—**sinuousness** *n*.

sinus *n* (*pl* **sinuses**) an air cavity in the skull that opens in the nasal cavities.

sinusitis *n* inflammation of a sinus.

sio *abbr* = serial input/output.

Sion *see* **Zion**.

Sionan *or* **Sinainn** *n* (*Irish Celtic myth*) the daughter of Lodan, who was a son of Lir. She is associated with the River Shannon, Co. Cavan, Ireland, which is said to be named after her.

Siouan *n* a family of North American Indian languages.

Sioux *n* (*pl* **Sioux**) a member of various Native American peoples who speak Siouan.

sip *vti* (**sipping**, **sipped**) to drink in small mouthfuls. * *n* the act of sipping; the quantity sipped.

siphon *n* a bent tube for drawing off liquids from a higher to a lower level by atmospheric pressure; a bottle with an internal tube and tap at the top for aerated water. * *vti* to draw off, or be drawn off, with a siphon.—*also* **syphon**.

siphon bottle *n* a soda siphon.

sipo *abbr* = serial in, parallel out.

SIPS *abbr* = side impact protection system.

sir *n* a title of respect used to address a man in speech or correspondence; (*with cap*) a title preceding the first name of a knight or baronet. * *vt* to address as "sir."

sire *n* a father; a male ancestor; the male parent of an animal; a form of address to a king. * *vt* (*animal*) to beget.

siren *n* a device producing a loud wailing sound as a warning signal; a fabled sea nymph who lured sailors to destruction with a sweet song; a seductive or alluring woman.

sirenian *n* a member of an order of plant-eating mammals that live in water, comprising the dugong and the manatee.—*also adj*.

Sirius *or* **the Dog Star** *or* **Alpha Canis Majoris** *or* **CMa** *n* a brilliant visual binary star with a magnitude of −1.46 which is one of the closest to Earth at a distance of 8.7 light years.

sirloin *n* the upper part of a loin of beef.

sirocco, scirocco *n* a hot, oppressive wind that blows across southern Europe from North Africa.

Sirona *n* (*Gaulish Celtic myth*) a goddess whose name means "star," although there is no evidence that she played any kind of celestial part in Celtic belief. She was associated with regeneration and fertility as well as with healing.

SIRP *abbr* = Society of Independent Roundabout Proprietors.

sirree *interj* (*inf*) sir, used for emphasis, esp after *yes* or *no*.

sis *n* (*inf*) sister.

SIS *abbr* = Satellite Information Services; Scientific Instrument Society; Secret Intelligence Service.

SISA *abbr* (*Brit*) = Scottish Ice Skating Association; Scottish Industrial Sports Association.

sisal *n* (a tropical agave plant whose leaves yield) a tough fiber used to make rope.

SISD (*Brit*) = Scottish Information Service for the Disabled.

Sisera *n* (*Bible*) Canaanite commander whose charioteer army oppressed the Israelites; he was defeated by Barak *See also* **Deborah**.

siskin *n* a Eurasian songbird with greenish plumage related to the goldfinch.

Sisley *n* **Alfred** (1839–99) French painter of English extraction. Influenced by the impressionists, he painted mainly landscapes.

sissy *n* (*pl* **sissies**) an effeminate, feeble, or cowardly boy or man.—*also adj*.

sist. *abbr* = sister.

sister *n* a female sibling, a daughter of the same parents; a female member or associate of the same race, creed, trade union, etc; a member of a religious sisterhood; one of the same kind, model, etc; a senior nurse. * *adj* (*ship, etc*) belonging to the same type.

SISTER *abbr* = Special Institutions for Scientific and Technical Education and Research.

sisterhood *n* a female religious or charitable order; the state of being a sister.

sister-in-law *n* (*pl* **sisters-in-law**) the sister of a husband or wife; the wife of a brother.

sisterly *adj* like a sister, kind, affectionate.

sistrum *n* (*pl* **sistra**) an ancient Egyptian metal rattle used as a percussion instrument.

Sisyphus *n* (*Greek myth*) a king of Corinth, who was eternally punished in the underworld, by having to roll a heavy stone to the top of a hill, on reaching which it would always roll back again.—**Sisyphean** *adj*.

sit *vti* (**sitting, sat**) to rest oneself on the buttocks, as on a chair; (*bird*) to perch; (*hen*) to cover eggs for hatching; (*legislator, etc*) to occupy a seat; (*court*) to be in session; to pose, as for a portrait; to ride (a horse); to press or weigh (upon); to be located; to rest or lie; to take an examination; to take care of a child, pet, etc, while the parents or owners are away; to cause to sit; to provide seats or seating room for; (*with* **down**) to take a seat; (*with* **for**) to represent in parliament; (*with* **in**) to attend a discussion or a musical session; to participate in a sit-in; (*with* **on**) to hold a meeting to discuss; to delay action on; (*inf*) to suppress; to rebuke; (*with* **out**) to sit through the whole; to abstain from dancing; (*with* **up**) to straighten the back while sitting; not to go to bed; (*inf*) to be astonished.

s.i.t. *abbr* (*transp*) = stopping in transit.

sitar *n* an Indian musical instrument similar to a lute with a long neck.

SITC *abbr* = Standard International Trade Classification.

sitcom *see* **situation comedy**.

sit-down strike *n* a form of industrial action in which the workers arrive at their place of work but refuse either to work or to leave the workplace.

site *n* a space occupied or to be occupied by a building; a situation; the place or scene of something. * *vt* to locate, place.

site license *n* an agreement between the authors of a computer program and a user of the program that allows the user to run the program on an agreed number of computers at one time.

SITES *abbr* = Smithsonian Institution Traveling Exhibition Service

sit-in *n* a strike in which the strikers refuse to leave the premises; civil disobedience in which demonstrators occupy a public place and refuse to leave voluntarily.

sitka spruce *n* a tall North American spruce tree.

Sitpro *abbr* = Simpler Trade Procedures Board (originally Simplification of International Trade Procedures).

sitter *n* a person who looks after a child, dog, house, etc, while the parents or owners are away.

sitting *n* the state of being seated; a period of being seated, as for a meal, a portrait; a session, as of a court; a clutch of eggs. * *adj* that is sitting; being in a judicial or legislative seat; used in or for sitting; performed while sitting.

Sitting Bull *n* [Tatanka Iyotake] (1834–90) Native American leader. Chief of the Dakota Sioux, he led the Native American warriors at the Battle of the Little Big Horn (1876), at which Custer was killed.

sitting duck *or* **sitting target** *n* (*inf*) a person or thing that is an easy target for attack, criticism, etc.

sitting room *n* a room other than a bedroom or kitchen; a parlor.

sitting tenant *n* a tenant in occupation of a property.

situate *vt* to place in a site, situation, or category.

situated *adj* having a site, located; placed; provided with money, etc.

situation *n* a place, a position; a state of affairs, circumstances; a job or post.

situation comedy *n* a comic television or radio series made up of episodes involving the same group of characters.—*also* **sitcom**.

situla *n* an Iron Age pottery or sheet-bronze vessel.

sit-up *n* an exercise of sitting up from a prone position without using hands or legs.

Sitwell *n* 1. Dame **Edith Louisa** (1887–1964) English poet and critic, whose works include *Facade*, an "entertainment" consisting of jazz-influenced abstract verses, first performed in 1923 with music by William Walton, and several fine elegiac poems, e.g. "Still Falls the Rain" (on the "total war" of World War II). 2. her brother, Sir **Osbert** (1892–1969), English writer, whose six-volume autobiography, from *Left Hand, Right Hand* to *Tales My Father Taught Me*, provides a remarkable portrait of upper-class English life in the 20th century. 3. his brother, **Sacheverell** (1897–1988) English poet and writer on art and travel, whose volumes of poetry include *Doctor Donne and Gargantua* and *Sacred and Profane Love*.

Siugmall *n* (*Irish Celtic myth*) the grandson of Midhir and Fuamnach. One legend has it that he helped his grandmother to dispose of Edain Echraidhe, and as a result was killed with her.

SIV *abbr* = simian immunodeficiency virus.

SIW *abbr* = self-inflicted wound.

SIWA *abbr* (*Brit*) = Scottish Inland Waterways Association.

six *adj, n* one more than five. * *n* the symbol for this (6, VI, vi); the sixth in a series or set; something having six units as members.

Six, les *npl* (*French*) "the Six," the name given in 1920 to six young French composers by the poet and music critic H Collet who, with another of their champions, Jean Cocteau, was passionately anti-Wagner. The six were Auric, Durey, Honegger, Milhaud, Poulenc, and Tailleferrey.

sixer *n* a leader of a group of six Brownie Guides or Cub Scouts.

sixfold *adj* having six units or members; being six times as great or as many.

six-pack *n* a pack of six units, e.g., cans of beer, etc, sold together.

sixpence *n* (*formerly*) a British coin worth six old pennies.

six-shooter *n* (*inf*) a six-chambered revolver.

sixteen *adj, n* one more than fifteen. * *n* the symbol for this (16, XVI, xvi).—**sixteenth** *adj*.

sixteenth note *n* a musical note with a sixteenth the time value of a whole note.

sixth *n* one of six equal parts of a thing; (*mus*) an interval of six diatonic degrees; the sixth tone of a diatonic scale.—*also adv*. * *adj* next after fifth.—**sixthly** *adv*.

sixth sense *n* intuitive power.

sixty *n* six times ten. * *n* (*pl* **sixties**) the symbol for this (60, LX, lx); (*pl*) the numbers 60 to 69; the same numbers in a life or century.—**sixtieth** *adj*.

sixty-fourth note. *n* a musical note with the time value of one sixty-fourth of a whole note.

sixty-nine *n* soixante-neuf.

Sizable *adj* of some size; large.—**sizably** *adv*.—**sizableness** *n*.

size[1] *n* magnitude; the dimensions or proportions of something; a graduated measurement, as of clothing or shoes. * *vt* to sort according to size; to measure; (*with* **up**) (*inf*) to make an estimate or judgment of; to meet requirements.

size[2] *n* a thin pasty substance used to glaze paper, stiffen cloth, etc. * *vt* to treat with size.

sized *adj* having a specified size.

sizzle *vti* to make a hissing spluttering noise, as of frying; to be extremely hot; to be very angry; to scorch, sear, or fry with a sizzling sound. * *n* a hissing sound.

sj *abbr* (*Latin*) = *sub judice*, "under trial."

SJ *abbr* = Society of Jesus.

SJAA *abbr* = St John Ambulance Association.

SJAB *abbr* = St John Ambulance Brigade.

sjambok *n* (*in S Africa*) a heavy whip made from rhinoceros hide.

SJBI *abbr* (*Brit*) = Scottish Joint Breast-Feeding Initiative.

SJC *abbr* = standing joint committee; Supreme Judicial Court.

SJCRE *abbr* (*Brit*) = Scottish Joint Committee on Religious Education.

SJD *abbr* (*Latin*) = *Scientiae Juridicae Doctor*, "Doctor of Juridical Science."

SJF *abbr* (*Brit*) = Scottish Judo Federation.

SJH *abbr* = Society of Jewellery History.

SJJA *abbr* (*Brit*) = Scottish Ju-Jitsu Association.

Sjögren's syndrome *n* dryness of the mouth and eyes as a result of the destruction of the salivary glands and lacrimal glands associated with rheumatoid arthritis.

sk. *abbr* = sack.

SK *abbr* = Saskatchewan; Sealed Knot.

ska *n* a form of West Indian pop music, a precursor of reggae.

SKA *abbr* (*Brit*) = Scottish Knitwear Association.

Skalkottas *n* **Nikos** (1904–49) Greek composer and violinist, who was a disciple of Schoenberg but who later incorporated Greek folk music into his compositions. His works include *Greek Dances* for orchestra, much chamber music, and pieces for piano.

Skara Brae *n* a Neolithic village (*c.* 3000 BC) in Orkney, Scotland.

skate[1] *n* a steel blade attached to a boot for gliding on ice; a boot with such a runner; a roller skate. * *vi* to move on skates; (*with* **over**) to avoid dealing with (an issue, problem, etc) directly.—**skater** *n*.

skate[2] *n* (*pl* **skate** *or* **skates**) an edible fish of the ray family with a broad, flat body and short, spineless tail.

skateboard *n* a short, oblong board with two wheels at each end for standing on and riding.—*also vi.*

SKC *abbr* (*Brit*) = Scottish Kennel Club; Scottish Knitwear Council.

skean-dhu *n* (*Scot*) a dagger worn in the stocking as part of Highland dress.

skedaddle *vi* (*inf*) to run away.—*also n.*

skeet *n* a type of clay-pigeon shooting in which clay targets are hurled into range at varying speeds and trajectories from two traps.

skein *n* a folded coil of yarn, thread, etc; a tangle; a flight of wild fowl, esp geese.

skeleton *n* the bony framework of the body of a human, an animal, or a plant; the bones separated from flesh and preserved in their natural position; a supporting structure, a framework; an outline, an abstract; a very thin person; something shameful kept secret. * *adj* (*staff, crew, etc*) reduced to the lowest possible level.—**skeletal** *adj*.

skeleton key *n* a key with a slender bit that can open many simple locks.

Skena *or* **Scena** *n* (*Irish Celtic myth*) the wife of Amhairghin, one of the Sons of Mil Espaine. She died on the voyage to Ireland and was buried when the expedition arrived in Ireland.

skeptic *n* a person who questions opinions generally accepted; a person who doubts religious doctrines, an agnostic; an adherent of skepticism.

skeptical *adj* doubting; questioning..—**skeptically** *adv*.

skepticism *n* an attitude of questioning criticism, doubt; (*philos*) the doctrine that absolute knowledge is unattainable.

skerry *n* (*pl* **skerries**) a rocky isle or reef.

sketch *n* a rough drawing, quickly made; a preliminary draft; a short literary piece or essay; a short humorous item for a revue, etc; a brief outline; (*mus*) a short piano or instrumental piece. * *vti* to make a sketch (of); to plan roughly.

sketchy *adj* (**sketchier, sketchiest**) incomplete; vague; inadequate.—**sketchily** *adv*.—**sketchiness** *n*.

skew *adj* slanting, oblique, set at an angle. * *adv* at a slant. * *vti* to slant or set at a slant; to swerve. * *n* (*archit*) a part set at an angle to the rest of the structure; (*archit*) the stone at the bottom of a gable that supports coping stones above.

skewbald *adj* marked with patches of white and another color other than black. * *n* an animal, esp a horse, with such markings.

skewer *n* a long wooden or metal pin on which pieces of meat and vegetables are cooked. * *vt* to pierce and fasten on a skewer; to transfix.

skewwhiff *adj* (*inf*) askew, not straight.

SKFA *abbr* (*Brit*) = Scottish Keep Fit Association.

ski *n* (*pl* **skis**) a long, narrow runner of wood, metal, or plastic that is fastened to a boot for moving across snow; a water-ski. * *vi* (**skiing, skied**) to travel on skis.—**skier** *n*.

skibob *n* a snow vehicle similar to a bicycle with a low seat and a steering handle mounted on two skis instead of wheels.

skid *vti* (**skidding, skidded**) to slide without rotating; to slip sideways; (*vehicle*) to slide sideways out of control; to cause (a vehicle) to skid. * *n* the act of skidding; a drag to reduce speed; a ship's fender; a movable support for a heavy object; a runner on an aircraft's landing gear.

skid row *or* **skid road** *n* (*sl*) a shabby district where vagrants, etc, live.

skied *see* **ski**.

skiff *n* a small, light boat for rowing.

skiffle *n* a type of music using guitars and makeshift instruments (e.g., washboards) which became popular in the 1950s.

ski jump *n* a long ramp surmounting a slope from which skiers jump in competition.—**ski-jump** *vi*.

ski lift *n* any of various devices for conveying skiers up a slope, such as a chair lift.

skill *n* proficiency; expertness, dexterity; a developed aptitude or ability; a type of work or craft requiring specialist training.

skilled *adj* fully trained, expert.

skillet *n* a frying pan.

skillful *adj* having skill; proficient, adroit.—**skillfully** *adv*.—**skillfulness** *n*.

skim *vti* (**skimming, skimmed**) to remove (cream or scum) from the surface of; to glide lightly over, brush the surface of; to read superficially.

skimmer *n* that which skims, esp a perforated utensil for skimming milk.

skimmia *n* any of a genus of evergreen shrubs with red berries.

skim milk *n* milk from which the cream has been removed.

skimp *vti* to give scant measure (of), stint; to be sparing or frugal (with).

skimpy *adj* (**skimpier, skimpiest**) small in size; inadequate, scant, meager.—**skimpily** *adv*.—**skimpiness** *n*.

skin *n* the tissue forming the outer covering of the body; a hide; the rind of a fruit; an outer layer or casing; a film on the surface of a liquid; a vessel for water, etc, made of hide. * *vti* (**skinning, skinned**) to remove the skin from, peel; to injure by scraping (the knee, etc); to cover or become covered with skin; (*inf*) to swindle.

skin-deep *adj* superficial.

skin diving *n* the sport of swimming under water with scuba equipment.—**skin-diver** *n*.

skinflick *n* (*sl*) a pornographic movie.

skinflint *n* a stingy person.

skinful *n* (*pl* **skinfuls**) (*sl*) as much alcoholic drink as one can take.

skin graft *n* a piece of skin taken from one part of the body to replace damaged skin elsewhere.

skinhead *n* a British or American youth with cropped hair, large boots, and suspenders, often belonging to an aggressive gang.

skink *n* a small lizard of tropical Asia and Africa.

skinned *adj* having skin of a specified kind.

Skinner *n* **B[urrhus] F[rederic]** (1904–90) American psychologist, who developed various techniques of behavioral psychology to illustrate his theory of "learning laws." His works include *Beyond Freedom and Dignity* (1971).

Skinner box *n* an animal cage, devised by B F Skinner and used for psychological conditioning, which has various levers operated to obtain food or receive punishment.

skinny *adj* (**skinnier, skinniest**) very thin; emaciated.—**skinniness** *n*.

skinny-dip *vi* (**skinny-dipping, skinny-dipped**) to swim naked. * *n* a swim in the nude.— **skinny-dipper** *n*.

skint *adj* (*sl*) having no money.

skintight *adj* (*clothing*) fitting tightly; clinging.

skip[1] *vti* (**skipping, skipped**) to leap or hop lightly over; to keep jumping over a jump rope as it is swung under one; to make omissions, pass over, esp in reading; (*inf*) to leave (town) hurriedly, to make off; (*inf*) to miss deliberately. * *n* a skipping movement; a light jump.

skip[2] *n* a large, metal container for holding building debris; a cage or bucket for hoisting workers or materials in a mine, quarry, etc.

ski pants *npl* fashion pants worn tight with a strap that fits under the foot.

skipjack *n* (*pl* **skipjack** *or* **skipjacks**) any of various food fishes including two varieties of tuna, one striped (skipjack) and the other spotted (black skipjack).

skiplane *n* a light aircraft fitted with skis for taking off and landing on snow.

skipper *n* the captain of a boat, aircraft, or team. * *vt* to act as skipper of; to captain.

skipping rope *n* (*Brit*) a light rope, often with a handle at each end, that is swung over the head and under the feet while jumping, a jump rope.

skirl *n* (*Scot*) the shrill, wailing sound characteristic of bagpipes.—*also vi.*

skirmish *n* a minor fight in a war; a conflict or clash. * *vi* to take part in a skirmish.

skirt *n* a woman's garment that hangs from the waist; the lower part of a dress or coat; an outer edge, a border; (*sl*) a woman. * *vti* to border; to move along the edge (of); to evade.

skirting *n* a border, an edging; fabric for skirts.

skirting board *n* a narrow panel of wood at the foot of an interior wall.

skit *n* a short humorous sketch, as in the theater.

skitter *vti* to move or cause to move quickly or to skim across a surface.

skittish *adj* (*animal*) frisky, easily frightened; (*person*) playful, frivolous, lively.—**skittishly** *adv*.—**skittishness** *n*.

skittles *n* (*Brit*) a bowling game in which a wooden or plastic bottle-shaped pin is knocked down by a ball.—*also* **ninepins**.

skive *vi* (*Brit, inf*) to avoid work or duties because of laziness.

skivvy[1] *n* (*pl* **skivvies**) (*pl*) men's underwear; (*sl*) a man's short-sleeved, lightweight undershirt (—*also* **skivvy shirt**).

skivvy[2] *n* (*pl* **skivvies**) (*Brit*) a female domestic servant. * *vi* (**skivvying, skivvied**) (*Brit*) to perform menial domestic duties.

skol, skoal *interj* good health, cheers (*used in a toast*).

Skopje *n* capital city of the Former Yugoslav Republic of Macedonia (FYROM).

Skr. *abbr* = Sanskrit.

Skryabin *see* **Scriabin**.

sks. *abbr* = sacks.

Skt. *abbr* = Sanskrit.

skua *n* any of various large predatory seabirds with dark plumage.

skulduggery, skullduggery *n* (*inf*) deceit, underhand dealing.

skulk *vi* to move in a stealthy manner; to lurk.

skull *n* the bony casing enclosing the brain; the cranium.

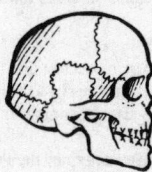

skull and crossbones *n* (*pl* **skulls and crossbones**) an image of a human skull and crossed thighbones used as a warning of danger.

skunk *n* a small, black-and-white mammal that emits a foul-smelling liquid when frightened; its fur; (*sl*) an obnoxious or mean person.

sky *n* (*pl* **skies**) the apparent vault over the earth; heaven; the upper atmosphere; weather, climate.

sky-blue *adj, n* (of) a bright pure blue, azure.

sky-diving *n* the sport of parachute jumping involving free-fall maneuvers.—**sky-diver** *n*.

Skye terrier *n* a breed of short-legged terrier with long hair and a long body.

sky-high *adj, adv* very high; in an enthusiastic manner; extremely expensive.

skyjack *vt* to hijack (an aircraft).

skylark *n* a lark famous for its song as it soars.

skylight *n* a window in the roof or ceiling.

skyline *n* the visible horizon; the outline, as of mountains, buildings, etc, seen against the sky.

skyrocket *n* a rocket. * *vi* to rise rapidly (e.g., in price, status, etc).

skyscraper *n* a very tall building.

skyward *adj, adv* toward the sky.

skywriting *n* (the act of creating) writing in the sky formed by smoke or vapor emitted from an aircraft.

s.l. *abbr* = seditious libeler; sergeant-at-law; (*Latin*) *sine loco*, "without place"; solicitor at law; south latitude; (*Latin*) *suo loco*, "in its place."

SL *abbr* = sea level; Squadron Leader.

SLA *abbr* = Scaffold Lashings Association; School Libraries Association; (*Brit*) Scottish Library Association; Sleep-Learning Association; Small Landowners' Association.

slab *n* a flat, broad, thick piece (as of stone, wood, or bread, etc); something resembling this. * *vt* to cut or form into slabs; to cover or support with slabs; to put on thickly.

SLAC *abbr* = Stanford Linear Accelerator Center

slack *adj* loose, relaxed, not tight; (*business*) slow, not brisk; sluggish; inattentive, careless. * *n* the part of a rope, etc that hangs loose; a dull period; a lull; the period of still water between ebb and flow currents; the portion of a river current that moves more slowly, often on the inside of a bend; the hollow between coastal sand dunes; (*pl*) pants for casual wear. * *vti* to neglect (one's work, etc), be lazy; (*with* **off**) to slacken (a rope, etc).—**slackness** *n*.

slacken *vti* to make or become less active, brisk, etc; to loosen or relax, as a rope; to diminish, abate.—**slackening** *n, adj*.

slacker *n* a lazy person; a person who shirks.

slack water *n* the turn of the tide; a slow-moving stretch of water.

SLADE *abbr* = Society of Lithographic Artists, Designers, Engravers, and Process Workers.

slag *n* the waste product from the smelting of metals; volcanic lava.

slain *see* **slay**.

slake *vt* to quench or satisfy (thirst, etc); to mix (lime) with water.

slalom *n* downhill skiing in a zigzag course between upright markers; (*skiing, canoeing, etc*) a timed race over a slalom course. * *vi* to move over a zigzag course.

slam *vti* (**slamming, slammed**) to shut with a loud noise, bang; to throw (down) violently; (*inf*) to criticize severely. * *n* a sound or the act of slamming, a bang; (*inf*) severe criticism; (*bridge*) the taking of 12 or 13 tricks.

SLAM *abbr* = stand-off land-attack missile.

slammer *n* (*sl*) a jail.

s.l.a.n. *abbr* (*Latin*) = *sine loco, anno, vel nomine*, "without place, year, or name."

slander *n* a false and malicious statement about another; the uttering of this. * *vt* to utter a slander about, defame.—**slanderous** *adj*.

slang *n* words or expressions used in familiar speech but not regarded as standard English; jargon of a particular social class, age group, etc. * *adj* relating to slang.

slant *vti* to incline, slope; to tell in such a way as to have a bias. * *n* a slope; an oblique position; a bias, a point of view. * *adj* sloping.—**slantly** *adv*.

slanted *adj* prejudiced, biased; sloping.

slantwise *adv* at a slant.

slap *n* a smack with the open hand; an insult; a rebuff. * *vt* (**slapping, slapped**) to strike with something flat; to put, hit, etc, with force. * *adv* directly, full.

slapdash *adj* impetuous; hurried; careless; haphazard. * *adv* carelessly.

slaphappy *adj* (**slaphappier, slaphappiest**) casually or cheerfully irresponsible; giddy, punch-drunk.

slapstick *n* boisterous humor of a knockabout kind.

slap-up *adj* (*inf*) (*meals, entertainment*) lavish, luxury.

SLAR *abbr* = side-looking airborne radar.

SLAS *abbr* = (*Brit*) Scottish Law Agents' Society; Society for Latin American Studies.

slash *vti* to cut gashes (in), slit; to strike fiercely (at) with a sword, etc; to reduce (prices) sharply. * *n* a cutting blow; a long slit, a gash.

SLASH *abbr* (*Brit*) = Scottish Local Authorities' Special Housing Group.

slash and burn *n* a destructive method of agriculture in which ground for planting is claimed from forest.

slat *n* a thin, flat, narrow strip of wood, etc.

S. Lat. *abbr* = South Latitude.

slate[1] *vt* to criticize or punish severely.

slate[2] *n* a fine-grained rock easily split into thin layers; a flat plate of this or other material used in roofing; a tablet (as of slate) for writing on; a list of proposed candidates. * *adj* of the color of slate, a deep bluish-gray color; made of slate. * *vt* to cover with slates; to suggest as a political candidate.

slater *n* a person trained in roofing with slates; a wood louse.

slatted *adj* having slats.

slattern *n* a slovenly woman; a slut.

slaughter *n* the butchering of animals for food; a wholesale killing, a massacre.—*also vt*.—**slaughterer** *n*.

slaughterhouse *n* a place where animals are slaughtered, an abattoir.

Slav *n* any person who speaks a Slavonic language.

Slav. *abbr* = Slavic; Slavonian; Slavonic.

slave *n* a person without freedom or personal rights, who is legally owned by another; a person under domination, esp of a habit or vice; a person who works like a slave, a drudge. * *vti* to toil hard, as a slave.

slave driver *n* a supervisor of slaves at work; a hard taskmaster.

slaveholder *n* a person who owns slaves.

slaver[1] *n* a person engaged in the buying and selling of slaves.

slaver[2] *vti* to dribble, cover with saliva; to fawn (upon), flatter.

slavery *n* the condition of being a slave; bondage; drudgery; slave-owning as an institution.

slave ship *n* a ship used in the slave trade.

Slave State *n* (*hist*) any of the Southern states of the US where slavery was legal until the Civil War.

slave trade *n* commercial traffic in slaves, esp the transport of Black Africans to Europe and America in the 16th to 19th centuries.

Slavic *see* **Slavonic**.

slavish *adj* servile, abject; unoriginal.—**slavishly** *adv*.—**slavishness** *n*.

Slavonic *or* **Slavic** *adj* of or characteristic of the Slavs. * *n* a branch of the Indo-European family of languages, including Russian, Bulgarian, Polish, and Czech.

slaw *n* coleslaw.

slay *vti* (**slaying, slew,** *pp* **slain**) to kill in great numbers; to murder; (*sl*) to overwhelm, affect in a powerful way.—**slayer** *n*.

SLBM *abbr* = submarine-launched ballistic missile.

SLC *abbr* = (*Brit*) Scottish Land Court; (*Brit*) Scottish Law Commission; Secretarial Language Certificate; Surgeon Lieutenant-Commander.

SLCM *abbr* = sea-launched cruise missile.

SLD *abbr* = Secretarial Language Diploma; self-locking device; Social and Liberal Democrats.

sld. *abbr* = sailed; sealed.

SLDP *abbr* = Social and Liberal Democratic Party.

SLdr *abbr* = Squadron Leader.

SLE *abbr* = systemic lupus erythematosus.

sleaze *n* (*inf*) sleaziness.

sleazy *adj* (**sleazier, sleaziest**) disreputable, squalid.—**sleaziness** *n*.

sled *n* a framework on runners for traveling over snow or ice; a toboggan; a sleigh. * *vti* (**sledding, sledded**) to go or convey by sled.

Sledda *n* (d. *c.*605) king of Essex (587–605). He married a sister of Ethelbert I of Kent.

sledgehammer *n* a large, heavy hammer for two hands.

sleek *adj* smooth, glossy; having a prosperous or well-groomed appearance; plausible.

sleep *n* a natural, regularly recurring rest for the body, with little or no consciousness; a period spent sleeping; a state of numbness followed by tingling. * *vti* (**sleeping, slept**) to rest in a state of sleep; to be inactive; to provide beds for; (*with* **around**) (*inf*) to be sexually promiscuous; (*with* **in**) to sleep on the premises; to sleep too long in the morning; (*with* **on**) to have a night's rest before making a decision; (*with* **off**) to get rid of by sleeping; (*with* **over**) to pass the night in someone else's house; (*with* **with**) to have sexual relations with.

sleeper *n* a person or thing that sleeps; a horizontal beam that carries and spreads a weight; a sleeping car; something that suddenly attains prominence or value.

sleeper wall *n* (*archit*) a wall that carries the joists of a wooden first floor.

sleeping bag *n* a padded bag for sleeping in, esp outdoors.

sleeping car *n* a train carriage with berths.

sleeping partner *n* a partner in a business who takes no part in its management.

sleeping pill *n* a pill that induces sleep.

sleeping sickness *n* a serious infectious disease marked by lethargy, coma.

sleepless *adj* without sleep; unable to sleep.

sleepwalker *n* a person who walks while asleep, a somnambulist.—**sleepwalking** *n*.

sleepy *adj* (**sleepier, sleepiest**) drowsy; tired; lazy, not alert.—**sleepily** *adv*.—**sleepiness** *n*.

sleepyhead *n* a tired or lazy person.

sleet *n* snow or hail mixed with rain. * *vi* to rain in the form of sleet.

sleeve *n* the part of a garment enclosing the arm; (*mech*) a tube that fits over a part; an open-ended cover, esp a paperboard envelope for a phonograph record.

sleeveless *adj* (*garment*) without sleeves.

sleigh *n* a light vehicle on runners for traveling over snow; a sled.

sleigh bells *npl* (*mus*) small metal bells with steel balls inside that are mounted together in groups to produce a richly textured, jingling sound. They are traditionally hung on sleighs, but are occasionally used in orchestras to create special effects.

sleight of hand *n* manual dexterity, e.g., in conjuring or juggling; a deception.

slender *adj* thin; slim; slight; scanty.—**slenderly** *adv*.—**slenderness** *n*.

slept *see* **sleep**.

s. l. et a. *abbr* (*Latin*) = *sine loco et anno*, "without place and year."

sleuth *n* (*inf*) a detective.

sleuthhound *n* a bloodhound; (*inf*) a detective.

slew[1] *see* **slay**.

slew[2], **slue** *vti* to twist or be twisted sideways.

slew[3], **slue** *n* (*inf*) a great quantity.

slf *abbr* = straight line frequency.

SLF *abbr* (*Brit*) = Scottish Landowners' Federation.

SLG *abbr* = Socialist Labour Group; Socialist Lesbian Group.

SLGA *abbr* (*Brit*) = Scottish Ladies' Golfing Association.

slice *n* a thin, flat piece cut from something (as bread, etc); a wedge-shaped piece (of cake, pie, etc); a portion, a share; a broad knife for serving fish, cheese, etc; (*golf*) a stroke that makes the ball curl to the right. * *vti* to divide into parts; to cut into slices; to strike (a ball) so that it curves.—**slicer** *n*—**slicing** *adj, n*.

slick *adj* clever, deft; smart but unsound; insincere; wily; (*inf*) smooth but superficial, tricky, etc. * *n* a patch or area of oil floating on water. * *vt* to make glossy; (*with* **up**) (*inf*) to make smart, neat, etc.

slicker *n* a loose, waterproof coat.

slide *vti* (**sliding, slid**) to move along in constant contact with a smooth surface, as on ice, glide; to coast over snow and ice; to pass gradually (into); to move (an object) unobtrusively. * *n* the act of sliding, a glide; a strip of smooth ice for sliding on; a chute; the glass plate of a microscope; a photographic transparency; a landslide.

slide rule *n* a ruler with a graduated sliding part for making calculations.

slide show *n* (*comput*) a pre-set list of graphic presentations that are displayed on a screen in a pre-defined order.

slide trombone *see* **trombone**.

slide trumpet *n* an early form of trumpet that had a slide similar to that used in the trombone, which became obsolete when the valve trumpet was invented.

sliding scale *n* a schedule for automatically varying one thing (e.g., wages) according to the fluctuations of another thing (e.g., cost of living); a flexible scale.

slier, sliest *see* **sly**.

slight *adj* small, inconsiderable; trifling; slim; frail, flimsy. * *vt* to disregard as insignificant; to treat with disrespect, snub. * *n* intentional indifference or neglect, discourtesy.

slighting *adj* disparaging; hurtful.

slightly *adv* to a small degree; slenderly.

slightness *n* frailness or slenderness; lack of weight, solidity, importance, or thoroughness.

slim[1] *adj* slender, not stout; small in amount, degree, etc; slight. * *vti* (**slimming, slimmed**) to make or become slim; to reduce one's weight by diet, etc.—**slimness** *n*.

slim[2] *n* the name used in Africa for AIDS.

slime *n* a sticky, slippery, half-liquid substance; a glutinous mud; mucus secreted by various animals (e.g., slugs).

slimmer *n* a person who controls his or her diet to lose weight.

slimming *n* the process of losing weight by dieting.

slimy *adj* (**slimier, slimiest**) like or covered with slime; repulsive; fawning.—**sliminess** *n*.

sling[1] *n* a loop of leather with a string attached for hurling stones; a rope for lifting or hoisting weights; a bandage suspended from the neck for supporting an injured arm. * *vt* (**slinging, slung**) to throw, lift, or suspend (as) with a sling; to hurl.

sling[2] *n* a drink of sweetened water mixed with a spirit such as gin.

slingback *n* a shoe whose back consists of a strap.

slingshot *n* a contraption with elastic for shooting small stones, a catapult.

slink *vi* (**slinking, slinked** *or* **slunk**) to move stealthily or furtively, sneak.

slinky *adj* (**slinkier, slinkiest**) (*inf*) sinuous in line or movement; (*clothes*) hugging the figure.

slip[1] *vti* (**slipping, slipped**) to slide, glide; to lose one's foothold and slide; to go or put quietly or quickly; to let go, release; to escape from; (*with* **up**) to make a slight mistake. * *n* the act of slipping; a mistake, a lapse; a woman's undergarment; a pillowcase; a slipway.

slip[2] *n* a small piece of paper; a young, slim person; a long seat or narrow pew; a shoot for grafting, a cutting; a descendant, an offspring.

slip[3] *n* a mixture of watery clay used for coating or decorating pottery.

SLIP *abbr* (*comput*) = Serial Line Internet Protocol.

slipcase *n* a protective case for one or more books with an open end to reveal the spines.

slipknot *n* a knot that slips along the rope around which it is tied; a knot that can be undone at a pull.

slip-on *adj* (*garment, shoe*) easy to put on or take off.—*also n*.

slippage *n* a slipping, as of one gear past another.

slipped disk *n* a ruptured cartilaginous disk between vertebrae.

slipper *n* a light, soft shoe worn in the house.

slippery *adj* so smooth as to cause slipping; difficult to hold or catch; evasive, unreliable, shifty.

slippy *adj* (**slippier, slippiest**) slippery.

slip road *n* (*Brit*) a road that gives access to a main road or freeway.

slipshod *adj* having the shoes down at heel; slovenly, careless.

slip stitch *n* a concealed stitch used for hemming; an unworked stitch in knitting.—**slipstitch** *vti*.

slipstream *n* a stream of air driven astern by the engine of an aircraft; an area of forward suction immediately behind a rapidly moving racing car.

slip-up *n* (*inf*) an error, a lapse.

slipway *n* an inclined surface for launching or repairing ships; a sloped landing stage.

slit *vt* (**slitting, slit**) to cut open or tear lengthways; to slash or tear into strips. * *n* a long cut, a slash; a narrow opening.—**slitter** *n*.

slither *vi* to slide, as on a loose or wet surface; to slip or slide like a snake.—**slithery** *adj*.

slit trench *n* a narrow trench to provide shelter during battle.

sliver *n* a small, narrow piece torn off, a splinter; a thin slice.

slivovitz, slivowitz *n* plum brandy.

SLLA *abbr* (*Brit*) = Scottish Ladies' Lacrosse Association.

SLM *abbr* = ship-launched missile.

SLMC *abbr* (*Brit*) = Scottish Ladies' Mountaineering Club.

SLO *abbr* = senior liaison officer.

SLOA *abbr* = Steam Locomotive Operators' Association.

slob *n* (*sl*) a coarse or sloppy person.

slobber *vti* to drool; to run at the mouth; to smear with dribbling saliva or food. * *n* dribbling saliva; maudlin talk.

sloe *n* (the dark fruit of) the blackthorn.

sloe-eyed *adj* having almond-shaped, dark or black eyes.

sloe gin *n* a gin flavored with sloes.

slog *vti* (**slogging, slogged**) to hit hard and wildly; to work laboriously; to trudge doggedly. * *n* a hard, boring spell of work; a strenuous walk or hike; a hard, random hit.—**slogger** *n*.

slogan *n* a catchy phrase used in advertizing or as a motto by a political party, etc.

sloop *n* a small sailing vessel with one mast and a jib.

slop *n* a puddle of spilled liquid; unappetizing semi-liquid food; (*pl*) liquid kitchen refuse. * *vti* (**slopping, slopped**) to spill or be spilled; (*with* **out**) (*prisoners*) to empty slop from chamber pots in the morning.

slope *n* rising or falling ground; an inclined line or surface; the amount or degree of this. * *vti* to incline, slant; (*inf*) to make off, go.

sloppy *adj* (**sloppier, sloppiest**) slushy; (*inf*) maudlin, sentimental; (*inf*) careless, untidy.—**sloppily** *adv*.—**sloppiness** *n*.

slosh *n* watery snow, slush; (*inf*) a heavy blow; the sound of liquid splashing. * *vi* to walk (through) or splash (around) in liquid, mud, etc; (*liquid*) to splash. * *vt* to throw or splash (liquid, etc) at someone or something; (*inf*) to hit (somebody).

sloshed *adj* (*inf*) drunk.

slot *n* a long, narrow opening in a mechanism for inserting a coin, a slit; (*comput*) *see* **expansion slot**. * *vt* (**slotting, slotted**) to fit into a slot; to provide with a slot; (*inf*) to place in a series.

sloth *n* laziness, indolence; a slow-moving South American animal.—**slothful** *adj*.

slot machine *n* a machine operated by the insertion of a coin, used for gambling or dispensing drinks, etc.

slouch *vti* to sit, stand, or move in a drooping, slovenly way. * *n* a drooping slovenly posture or gait; the downward droop of a hat brim; (*inf*) a poor performer, a lazy or incompetent person.

slouch hat *n* a hat with a soft, wide brim that can be pulled down to cover the ears.

slough[1] *n* a bog; deep, hopeless dejection.

slough[2] *n* the dead, outer skin of a snake. * *vti* to cast off, as a dead skin.

Slovak *n* a native or inhabitant of Slovakia; the language of Slovakia.—*also adj*.

Slovakia *or* **the Slovak Republic** *n* a small, landlocked central European republic that came into being as a new independent nation in January 1993, following the dissolution of the 74-year-old Federal Republic of Czechoslovakia.

Slovak Koruna *n* currency of the Slovak Republic.

Slovene *n* a native or inhabitant of Slovenia; the Slavonic language of Slovenia.—*also adj*.

Slovenia *n* a small republic that prior to 1991 was part of the former Yugoslavia, bounded by Croatia in the southwest, Hungary in the east, Austria in the north, and Italy in the west.

slovenly *adj* untidy, dirty; careless.—**slovenliness** *n*.

slow *adj* moving at low speed, not fast; gradual; not quick in understanding; reluctant, backward; dull, sluggish; not progressive; (*clock*) behind in time; tedious, boring; (*surface*) causing slowness. * *vti* (*also with* **up, down**) to reduce the speed (of).—**slowly** *adv*.—**slowness** *n*.

slowcoach *n* (*inf*) a person who moves, works, or thinks slowly.

slowdown *n* a reduction in speed, production, etc; a go-slow.

slow handclap *n* slow regular clapping expressive of audience dissatisfaction.

slow match *or* **slow fuse** *n* a slow-burning match or fuse for igniting explosives.

slow-motion *adj* moving slowly; denoting a filmed or taped scene with the original action slowed down.

slowpoke *see* **slowcoach**.

slow virus *n* one of several viruses that show their effects some time after infection. Such a virus causes scrapie in sheep and bovine spongiform encephalopathy in cows. In humans, a slow virus is thought to be the cause of Creutzfeldt-Jakob disease and a type of meningitis.

slowworm *n* a legless European lizard with a grayish, elongated body and very small eyes.

slp *abbr* (*Latin*) = *sine legima prole,* "without legitimate issue."

SLP *abbr* = (*Brit*) Scottish Labour Party; Serbian Liberal Party.

SLR *abbr* = single-lens reflex; self-loading rifle.

SLRS *abbr* = Sexual Law Reform Society.

SLS *abbr* = (*Brit*) Scots Language Society; Society of Landscape Studies; Stephenson Locomotive Society.

SLSDC *abbr* = Saint Lawrence Seaway Development Corporation.

SLTA *abbr* = (*Brit*) Scottish Lawn Tennis Association; (*Brit*) Scottish Licensed Trade Association; Sri Lanka Tourist Association.

slub *n* a lump in a piece of yarn or thread.

sludge *n* soft mud or snow; sediment; sewage.

slue *see* **slew**[2].

slug[1] *n* a mollusk resembling a snail but with no outer shell.

slug[2] *n* a small bullet; a disk for inserting into a slot machine; a line of type; (*inf*) a hard blow; a drink of spirits. * *vt* (**slugging, slugged**) (*inf*) to hit hard with a fist or a bat.

sluggard *n* a lazy person. * *adj* lazy.

sluggish *adj* slow, inactive; unresponsive.—**sluggishly** *adv.*—**sluggishness** *n.*

sluice *n* a gate regulating a flow of water; the water passing through this; an artificial water channel. * *vti* to draw off through a sluice; to wash with a stream of water; to stream out as from a sluice.

slum *n* a squalid, rundown house; (*usu pl*) an overcrowded area characterized by poverty, etc. * *vi* (**slumming, slummed**) to make do with less comfort.

slumber *vi* to sleep. * *n* a light sleep.

slump *n* a sudden fall in value or slackening in demand; (*sport*) a period of poor play. * *vi* to fall or decline suddenly; to sink down heavily; to collapse; to slouch.

slung *see* **sling**.

slunk *see* **slink**.

slur *vti* (**slurring, slurred**) to pronounce or speak indistinctly; to run (letters or words) together; (*mus*) to produce by gliding without a break; to make disparaging remarks about. * *n* the act of slurring; a stigma, an imputation of disgrace; (*mus*) a curved line over notes to be slurred.

slurp *vti* (*sl*) to drink or eat noisily. * *n* a loud sipping or sucking sound.

slurry *n* (*pl* **slurries**) a liquid mixture of insoluble matter (as mud, lime, etc).

slush *n* liquid mud; melting snow; (*inf*) sentimental language.—**slushy** *adj.*

slush fund *n* a fund of money used secretly to bribe, etc.

slut *n* a slovenly or immoral woman.—**sluttish** *adj.*

SLV *abbr* = Society of Licensed Victuallers; space launch vehicle; standard launch vehicle.

sly *adj* (**slyer, slyest** *or* **slier, sliest**) secretively cunning, wily; underhand; knowing.—**slyly** *adv.*—**slyness** *n.*

slype *n* (*archit*) a covered passage in a cathedral from the cloisters and between the transept and chapterhouse.

Sm *symbol* (*chem*) = samarium (element).

SM *abbr* = master of science; sadomasochist; sales manager; sergeant major; short meter; stage manager; State Militia; Stipendiary Magistrate; stage manager; Surgeon Major; strategic missile; systolic murmur.

S/M, S-M *abbr* = sadomasochism.

SMA *abbr* = Saint Mungo Association; Salt Manufacturers' Assocation; Sheffield Metallurgical Association; (*Brit*) Society for Mediaeval Archaeology; Society of Miniaturists; Society of Motor Auctions; (*Brit*) Society of Museum Archaeologists; Stage Management Association; Survey & Mapping Alliance.

SMAC *abbr* = Standing Medical Advisory Committee.

smack[1] *n* a taste; a distinctive smell or flavor; small quantity, a trace. * *vi* to have a smell or taste (of); to have a slight trace of something.

smack[2] *vt* to strike or slap with the open hand; to kiss noisily; to make a sharp noise with the lips.—*also n.*

smack[3] *n* a small fishing vessel used in coastal waters.

smacker *n* (*sl*) a noisy kiss; (*sl*) a pound note or dollar bill.

small *adj* little in size, number, importance, etc; modest, humble; operating on a minor scale; young; petty. * *adv* in small pieces. * *n* the narrow, curving part of the back.

small arms *npl* portable firearms, such as handguns.

small beer *n* (*inf*) people or things regarded as trivial.

small cap *or* **small capital** *n* (*comput*) a capital letter that is smaller than a normal capital.

small change *n* coins of low value.

small estate affidavit *n* (*law*) a document the purpose of which is to distribute the assets of a deceased party, whose estate is valued at less than $50,000.

small fry *npl* people or things of little significance.

smallholding *n* (*Brit*) a small piece of agricultural land, usu between one and 50 acres.—**smallholder** *n.*

small hours *npl* the period between midnight and dawn.

small intestine *n* the section of the alimentary canal between the stomach and the colon.

small-minded *adj* intolerant, narrow-minded; mean, vindictive.—**small-mindededly** *adv.*—**small-mindedness** *n.*

smallpox *n* an acute contagious viral disease, now rare, causing the eruption of pustules which leave the skin scarred and pitted.

small print *n* small type that is difficult to read in a contract or other document, esp conditions and limitations made deliberately inconspicuous.

small screen *n* a television.

small-scale *adj* small in size or scope.

small talk *n* light, social conversation.

small-time *adj* (*inf*) unimportant.

smalt *n* a blue pigment used in coloring glass and ceramics.

smarmy *adj* (**smarmier, smarmiest**) (*inf*) obsequious, unpleasantly smooth and flattering.

smart *n* a sudden, stinging pain. * *vi* to have or cause a sharp, stinging pain (as by a slap); to feel distress. * *adj* stinging; astute; clever, witty; fashionable; neatly dressed; (*equipment, etc*) capable of seemingly intelligent action through computer control; (*bombs, missiles*) guided to the target by lasers ensuring pinpoint accuracy.—**smartly** *adv.*—**smartness** *n.*

Smart *n* 1. **Christopher** (1722–71) English poet, whose best-known works are his highly idiosyncratic religious poems "A Song to David" and "Jubilate Agno," a wonderfully original celebration of God's creation written while Smart was confined in a lunatic asylum (1759–63). 2. **Elizabeth** (1913–86) Canadian author of two short novels, *By Grand Central Station I Sat Down and Wept,* inspired by her love for the poet George Barker, and *The Assumption of the Rogues and Rascals.* Her journal for 1933–40 was published in 1991 under the title *Necessary Secrets.*

smart aleck *n* (*inf*) an annoyingly clever person, a know-all.

smart card *n* a credit card containing a memory chip that records transactions made with the card.

smarten *vti* to make or become smart.

smart money *n* money invested or bet by experienced gamblers or financiers; money paid to secure release from an unpleasant situation, or obligation, esp military service.

smart set *n sing or pl* fashionable people or society.

smart terminal *n* (*comput*) a computer terminal that has its own processor and secondary storage.

SMAS *abbr* (*Brit*) = Saint Margaret of Scotland Adoption Society.

smash *vti* to break into pieces with noise or violence; to hit, collide, or move with force; to destroy or be destroyed. * *n* a hard, heavy hit; a violent, noisy breaking; a violent collision; total failure, esp in business; (*inf*) a popular success.

smashed *adj* (*sl*) drunk or under the influence of drugs.

smasher *n* (*inf*) an attractive or excellent person or thing.

smashing *adj* (*inf*) excellent.

smash-up *n* (*inf*) a serious collision, a crash.

smattering *n* a slight superficial knowledge; a small number.

SMATV *abbr* = satellite master antenna television.

SMBF *abbr* (*Brit*) = Scottish Musicians' Benevolent Fund.

SMBG *abbr* = self-monitoring of blood glucose.

SMC *abbr* = School Meals Campaign; (*Brit*) Scottish Mountaineering Club; (*Brit*) Scottish Museums Council.

sm. c. *or* **sm. cap.** *abbr* = small capital(s).

sm. caps. *abbr* = small capitals.

SMD *abbr* = senile macular degeneration; surface-mounted device.

SME *abbr* (*Latin*) = *Sancta Mater Ecclesia,* "Holy Mother Church."

smear *vt* to cover with anything greasy or sticky; to make a smudge on; to slander. * *n* a smudge; a slanderous attack; a deposit of blood, secretion, etc on a glass slide for examination under a microscope.

smear test *n* microscopic analysis of a smear of bodily cells, esp from the cervix, for cancer.—*also* **Pap smear, Pap test, cervical smear**.

smegma *n* a sebaceous secretion which accumulates as solid matter in the folds of the skin, esp under the foreskin.

smell *n* the sense by which odors are perceived with the nose; a scent, odor, or stench; a trace. * *vti* (**smelling, smelt** *or* **smelled**) to have or perceive an odor.—**smelly** *adj.*

smelling salts *npl* a preparation of ammonia used as a stimulant in cases of faintness, etc.

smelt[1] *vt* to extract ore from (metal) by melting.

smelt[2] *n* any of various small marine or freshwater food fishes related to the salmon.

smelt[3] *see* **smell**.

Smendes *n* first Egyptian king of the Twenty-first Dynasty (ruled 1069–1043 BC).

Smetana *n* **Bedrich** (1824–84) Czech composer, who studied in Prague, his most famous work is the opera *The Bartered Bride.* He also wrote nine operas (the last, *Viola,* was unfinished), piano pieces, chamber music, and symphonic poems (such as *Richard III*).

SMetO *abbr* = Senior Meteorological Officer.

SMG *abbr* = sub-machine gun.

SMGC *abbr* (*Brit*) = Scottish Marriage Guidance Council.

smidgen, smidgin *n* (*inf*) a small amount.

smilax *n* any of a genus of climbing plants bearing red berries that includes the sarsaparilla; an African vine cultivated for its decorative green leaves.

smile *vi* to express amusement, friendship, pleasure, etc, by a slight turning up of the corners of the mouth. * *n* the act of smiling; a bright aspect.—**smilingly** *adv*.

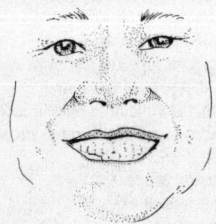

smirch *vt* to dishonor; to soil, stain, or sully. * *n* a stain on reputation; a smudge, a smear.

Smirgat *n* (*Irish Celtic myth*) the wife of Fionn mac Cumhaill towards the end of his life. She is said to have prophesied that he would die if he should ever drink from a horn. For that reason he was always extremely careful always to drink from a cup, goblet or bowl.

smirk *vi* to smile in an expression of smugness or scorn. * *n* a smug or scornful smile.—**smirkingly** *adv*.

Smirke *n* Sir Robert (*b.* 1780) English architect, whose notable works include the British Museum, London.

smite *vt* (**smiting, smote**, *pp* **smitten** *or* **smote**) (*arch*) to strike hard; to kill or injure; to have a powerful affect on. * *vi* to strike, beat, or come down (on) with force.—**smiter** *n*.

smith *n* a person who works in metal; a blacksmith.

Smith *n* 1. **Adam** (1723–90) Scottish economist and philosopher, whose *Inquiry into the Nature and Causes of the Wealth of Nations* (1776) was influential in the development of modern capitalist societies. 2. **Bessie** (1895–1937) American jazz singer, nicknamed the "Empress of the Blues" for the emotional intensity of her singing. She made many recordings with such people as Louis Armstrong. 3. **Ian [Douglas]** (1919–) Zimbabwean politician; prime minister of Rhodesia (1964–79); declared UDI (unilateral declaration of independence) from Britain in 1965 to maintain White minority rule (majority rule came in 1979). 4. **John Moyr** (1864–94) British decorative artist, who published his *Ornamental Interiors, Ancient and Modern*, in 1887. 5. **John Stafford** (1750–1836) English composer and organist, who wrote church music and songs, including "Anacreon in Heaven," the tune of which was adapted for the American national anthem, "The Star-Spangled Banner." 6. **Stevie [Florence Margaret]** (1902–71) English poet and novelist, who wrote graceful, melancholic, and occasionally fiercely funny verse. As well as the superb collection *Not Waving but Drowning*, she also wrote three novels, *Novel on Yellow Paper*, *Over the Frontier*, and *The Holiday*.

smithereens *npl* (*inf*) fragments.

smithery *n* the trade of a blacksmith.

smithy *n* (*pl* **smithies**) a blacksmith's workshop.

smitten *see* **smite**.

sml *abbr* = small, medium, large (range of sizes).

SML *abbr* = Science Museum Library.

SMM *abbr* (*Latin*) = *Sancta Mater Maria*, "Holy Mother Mary."

SMMB *abbr* (*Brit*) = Scottish Milk Marketing Board.

SMMT *abbr* = Society of Motor Manufacturers and Traders.

SMO *abbr* = Senior Medical Officer; Society of Museum Officers.

smock *n* a loose shirt-like outer garment to protect the clothes.

smocking *n* ornamental stitching in a honeycomb pattern.

smog *n* a mixture of fog and smoke; polluted air.—**smoggy** *adj*.

smoke *n* a cloud or plume of gas and small particles emitted from a burning substance; any similar vapor; an act of smoking tobacco, etc; (*inf*) a cigar or cigarette. * *vi* to give off smoke; to (habitually) draw in and exhale the smoke of tobacco, etc. * *vt* to fumigate; to cure (food) by treating with smoke; to darken (e.g., glass) using smoke; (*with* **out**) to flush out using smoke; to bring into public view.—**smokable** *adj*.

smoke and mirrors *n phr* a presentation, demonstration, or explanation seen to be unclear and deceptive, involving an intent to confuse.

smoke detector *n* an electrical device that sets off an alarm when smoke is detected.

smokehouse *n* a building used for curing meat or fish by smoking.

smokeless *adj* giving off little or no smoke.

smoker *n* a person who habitually smokes tobacco; a smoking car; (*formerly*) a gathering of men to smoke.

smoke screen *n* dense smoke used to conceal military movements, etc; something designed to obscure, conceal, or disguise the truth.

smokestack *n* a tall chimney or funnel which discharges smoke or exhaust gases into the air.

smoking car *n* a train compartment where smoking is permitted.

smoking jacket *n* a man's comfortable loose-fitting jacket for wearing around the house.

smoky *adj* (**smokier, smokiest**) emitting smoke, esp excessively; filled with smoke; resembling smoke in appearance, flavor, smell, color, etc.—**smokily** *adv*.—**smokiness** *n*.

smoky quartz *n* cairngorm.

smolder *vi* to burn slowly or without flame; (*feelings*) to linger on in a suppressed state; to have concealed feelings of anger, jealousy, etc.

Smollett *n* Tobias [George] (1721–71) Scottish surgeon and novelist, whose novels include *The Expedition of Humphrey Clinker*.

smolt *n* a young salmon, about two years old, at the stage where it migrates to the sea for the first time.

smooch *vi* (*sl*) to kiss and cuddle, esp while dancing as a couple. * *n* (*sl*) a long kiss, an embrace.—**smoochy** *adj*.

smooth *adj* having an even or flat surface; silky; not rough or lumpy; hairless; of even consistency; calm, unruffled; gently flowing in rhythm or sound. * *vti* to make smooth; to calm; to make easier.—**smoothly** *adv*.—**smoothness** *n*.

smooth muscle *n* a muscle capable of regular involuntary contractions, as in the walls of the stomach and gut.

smoothbore *adj* (*firearm*) not rifled. * *n* such a gun.

smoothen *vti* to make or become smooth.

smooth-faced *adj* shaven; having a smooth surface; hypocritical.

smoothie *n* (*sl*) a person, esp a man, who is excessively suave and self-assured in speech and appearance.

smooth-tongued *adj* persuasive in speech.

smoothy *n* (*pl* **smoothies**) (*sl*) a smoothie.

smorgasbord, smörgåsbord *n* a type of buffet or hors d'œuvres of various cold dishes of cheese, fish, salads, etc, served in Scandinavia; a restaurant specializing in this.

smorzando *adj* (*mus*) fading or dying away, i.e., becoming softer and slower.

smote *see* **smite**.

smother *vt* to stifle, suffocate; to put out a fire by covering it to remove the air supply; to cover over thickly; to hold back, suppress. * *vi* to undergo suffocation.—*also n*.

smp *abbr Latin* = *sine mascula prole*, "without male issue."

SMP *abbr* = Society of Mural Painters; Statutory Maternity Pay.

SMPA *abbr* (*Brit*) = Scottish Master Patternmakers' Association.

SMR *abbr* = standard metabolic rate; standard mortality rate.

SMRC *abbr* = (*Brit*) Scottish Motor Racing Club; Society of Miniature Rifle Clubs.

SMRE *abbr* = Safety in Mines Research Establishment.

SMS *abbr* = Shipwrecked Mariners' Society; (*Brit*) Socialist Movement Scotland; Society of Master Saddlers; Society of Model Shipwrights.

SMSR *abbr* = Society of Master Shoe Repairers.

SMTA *abbr* (*Brit*) = Scottish Motor Trade Association.

SMTF *abbr* (*Brit*) = Scottish Milk Trade Federation.

SMTP *abbr* (*comput*) = Simple Mail Transport Protocol.

SMTWTFS *abbr* = Sunday, Monday, Tuesday, Wednesday, Thursday, Friday, Saturday.

smudge *n* a dirty or blurred spot or area; a fire made to produce dense smoke. * *vt* to make a smudge on; to smear; to blur; to produce smoke in (a place) to protect against insects, etc. * *vi* to become smudged.

smudgy *adj* blurred or dirty, smeared.—**smudgily** *adv*.—**smudginess** *n*.

smug *adj* (**smugger, smuggest**) complacent, self-satisfied.—**smugly** *adv*.—**smugness** *n*.

smuggle *vt* to import or export (goods) secretly without paying customs duties; to convey or introduce secretly.—**smuggler** *n*.

smut *n* a speck or smudge of dirt, soot, etc; indecent talk, writing, or pictures; a fungal disease of crop plants that covers the leaves in sooty spores. * *vti* (**smutting, smutted**) to stain or become stained with smut; (*crops, etc*) to infect or become infected with smut.

smut disease *n* a disease of wheat caused by fungi.

Smuts *n* Jan [Christian] (1870–1950) South African statesman and philosopher; commander of the Boer forces during the Boer War; prime minister (1919–24, 1939–48).

smutty *adj* (**smuttier, smuttiest**) soiled with smuts; obscene, filthy.—**smuttily** *adv*.—**smuttiness** *n*.

SMWBA *abbr* (*Brit*) = Scottish Master Wrights' and Builders' Association.

SMWS *abbr* (*Brit*) = Scottish Malt Whisky Society.

Smyrna *n* important ancient city of Asia Minor, on the Gulf of Smyrna.

Smyth *n* Ethel Mary (1858–1944) English composer and writer, who studied music in Germany. Her works include operas (such as *The Wreckers* and *The Boatswain's Mate*), chamber music, and choral works.

Sn *symbol* (*chem*) tin (element).

sn *abbr* (*Latin*) = *secundum naturam*, "according to nature"; *sine nomine*, "without name"; *sub nomine*, "under the name."

s/n *abbr* = serial number; service number; signal-to-noise (ratio).

Sn. *abbr* = sanitary; (*Latin*) *sine*, "without."

SN *abbr* = shipping note.

SNA *abbr* (*Brit*) = Scottish Netball Association.

snack *n* a light meal between regular meals.

SNACMA *abbr* (*Brit*) = Snack, Nut, and Crisp Manufacturers' Association.

snaffle *n* a jointed bit for a bridle (—*also* **snaffle bit**). * *vt* (*inf*) to snatch or steal for oneself.

snafu *n* (*sl*) (*situation normal all fucked up*) a state of utter confusion. * *adj* confused, chaotic. * *vt* (**snafuing, snafued**) to cause a state of confusion or chaos.

snag *n* a sharp point or projection; a tear, as in cloth, made by a snag, etc; an unexpected or hidden difficulty. * *vti* (**snagging, snagged**) to tear, etc, on a snag; to clear of snags.

snail *n* a mollusk having a worm-like body and a spiral protective shell; a slow-moving or sluggish person or thing.

snail mail *n* (*comput: inf*) the postal service, as it is much slower than electronic mail.

snail-paced *adj* moving very slowly.

snail's pace *n* a very slow speed or rate of progress.

snake *n* a limbless, scaly reptile with a long, tapering body and with salivary glands often modified to produce venom; a sly, treacherous person. * *vt* to twist along like a snake. * *vi* to crawl silently and stealthily.

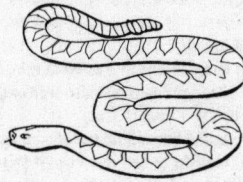

snake charmer *n* a person who entertains by appearing to mesmerize venomous snakes by playing music.

snake-eyes *n* (*sl*) a toss of the dice totaling two.

snakeroot *n* any of various North American plants whose roots have been used to treat snakebites.

snakes and ladders *n* a British board game in which counters are moved on a grid of squares, some of which have ladders leading nearer the finish, and others snakes leading back toward the start.

snakeskin *n* the skin of a snake as used to make purses, shoes, etc.

snakestone *n* an ammonite twisted like a ram's horn.

snakeweed *n* a herb with twisted roots, bistort.

snaky *adj* (**snakier, snakiest**) like or full of snakes; treacherous-looking.—**snakily** *adv*.—**snakiness** *n*.

snap *vti* (**snapping, snapped**) to break suddenly; to make or cause to make a sudden, cracking sound; to close, fasten, etc with this sound; (*with* **at**) to bite or grasp suddenly; to speak or utter sharply. * *adj* sudden. * *n* a sharp, cracking sound; a fastener that closes with a snapping sound; a crisp cookie; a snapshot; a sudden spell of cold weather; (*inf*) vigor, energy.

SNAP *abbr* = (*Brit*) Shelter Neighbourhood Action Project; systems for auxiliary nuclear power.

snapdragon *n* any of several plants of the figwort family with showy white, red, or yellow flowers shaped like small jaws.

snap fastener *n* a snap.

snapper *n* one who or that which snaps; (*pl* **snapper** *or* **snappers**) any of various sea fishes used as food; a snapping turtle.

snapping turtle *n* a large North American turtle with powerful jaws, a snapper.

snappy *adj* (**snappier, snappiest**) speaking sharply; brisk; lively; smart, fashionable.—**snappily** *adv*.—**snappiness** *n*.

snapshot *n* a photograph taken casually with a simple camera.

snare *n* a loop of string or wire for trapping birds or animals; something that catches one unawares, a trap; a loop of gut wound with wire stretched around a snare drum that produces a rattling sound. * *vt* to trap using a snare.

snare drum *n* a double-headed drum with snares.

snarl[1] *vi* to growl with bared teeth; to speak in a rough, angry manner. * *vt* to express in a snarling manner. * *n* the act of snarling; the sound of this.

snarl[2] *vti* to make or become entangled or complicated. * *n* a tangle; disorder.

snarl-up *n* (*inf*) an instance or state of blockage or disorder, esp in traffic.

snatch *vt* to seize or grasp suddenly; to take as opportunity occurs. * *n* the act of snatching; a brief period; a fragment; (*inf*) a robbery.

snazzy *adj* (**snazzier, snazziest**) (*inf*) stylish, fashionable; flashy.

SNB&RTU *abbr* = Screw, Nut, Bolt, & Rivet Trade Union.

SNBTS (*Brit*) *abbr* = Scottish National Blood Transfusion Service.

SNC (*Brit*) *abbr* = Scottish National Certificate.

SND *abbr* = (*Brit*) Scottish National Diploma; Sisters of Notre Dame; static no delivery.

sneak *vti* (**sneaking, sneaked** *or* (*sl*) **snuck**) to move, act, give, put, take, etc, secretly or stealthily. * *n* a person who acts secretly or stealthily; (*inf*) a person who tells or informs on others. * *adj* without warning.

sneaker *n* one who or that which sneaks; a shoe with a cloth upper and soft rubber sole, worn informally.

sneaking *adj* underhand; secret; (*suspicion, admiration, etc*) felt or thought, but not openly expressed.—**sneakingly** *adv*.

sneak preview *n* a special showing of a movie, play, exhibition, etc, to a private audience before opening to the general public.

sneaky *adj* (**sneakier, sneakiest**) like a sneak; furtive; underhand.—**sneakily** *adv*.—**sneakiness** *n*.

sneer *vi* to show scorn or contempt by curling up the upper lip. * *n* a derisive look or remark.—**sneerer** *n*.—**sneeringly** *adv*.

sneeze *vi* to expel air through the nose violently and audibly. * *n* the act of sneezing.—**sneezy** *adj*.

sneezing *n* the involuntary reflex expulsion of air via the nose and mouth caused by irritating particles in the nose, e.g. pollen

Snellen chart *n* the chart commonly used for testing distant vision, comprising rows of capital letters that become progressively smaller.

SNF *abbr* = solids, non-fat.

SNFU *abbr* (*Brit*) = Scottish National Farmers' Union.

SNG *abbr* = synthetic natural gas.

SNH *abbr* (*Brit*) = Scottish Natural Heritage.

snick *n* a tiny cut or notch; (*cricket*) a stroke of the edge of the bat. * *vt* to make a tiny cut or notch in; to hit (a ball) with a snick.

snicker *vi* to laugh furtively and slyly, to snigger; to neigh, whinny. * *n* a half-suppressed laugh, a giggle.—**snickeringly** *adv*.

snide *adj* malicious; superior in attitude; sneering.—**snidely** *adv*.—**snideness** *n*.

sniff *vti* to inhale through the nose audibly; to smell by sniffing; to scoff; (*with* **at**) to express dislike or contempt for. * *n* the act of sniffing; the sound of this; a smell.—**sniffer** *n*.

sniffer dog *n* a police dog trained to locate hidden drugs or explosives by smell.

sniffle *vi* to sniff repeatedly. * *n* the act or sound of sniffling.

sniffy *adj* (**sniffier, sniffiest**) (*inf*) disdainful, dismissive.—**sniffily** *adv*.—**sniffiness** *n*.

snifter *n* a glass with a wide body and narrow top to preserve the aroma of brandy or other spirits; (*inf*) a small amount of alcoholic drink.

snig *abbr* = sustainable non-inflationary growth.

snigger *vt* to laugh disrespectfully, snicker.—*also n*.

snip *vti* (**snipping, snipped**) to cut or clip with a single stroke of the scissors, etc. * *n* a small piece cut off; the act or sound of snipping; (*inf*) a bargain; (*inf*) a certainty, cinch.

snipe *n* (*pl* **snipes, snipe**) any of various birds with long straight flexible bills. * *vi* to shoot snipe; to shoot at individuals from a hidden position; to make sly criticisms.—**sniper** *n*.

snippet *n* a scrap of information.

snitch *vi* (*sl*) to inform, betray. * *vt* (*sl*) to steal, pilfer. * *n* (*sl*) an informer; the nose.—**snitcher** *n*.

snivel *vi* to whine or whimper; to have a runny nose.—**sniveler** *n*.

SNLA *abbr* (*Brit*) = Scottish National Liberation Army.

snlr *abbr* = services no longer required.

SNLV *abbr* = strategic nuclear launch vehicle.

SNMA *abbr* (*Brit*) = Scottish Net Manufacturers' Association.

SNNEB *abbr* (*Brit*) = Scottish Nursery Nurses' Examination Board.

SNO *abbr* = (*Brit*) Scottish National Orchestra; Senior Naval *or* Nursing Officer.

snob *n* a person who wishes to be associated with those of a higher social status, while acting condescendingly to those whom he or she regards as inferior.

snobbery *n* (*pl* **snobberies**) snobbish behavior or attitude; a snobbish act.

snobbish *adj* pertaining to, characteristic of, or like a snob.—**snobbishly** *adv*.—**snobbishness** *n*.

SNOBOL *n* (*comput*) *String Orientated Symbolic Language*: a programming language used for text (i.e., strings of characters) retrieval and manipulation

Sno-cat *n* (*trademark*) a vehicle designed for traveling on snow.

Snofru *or* **Senefru** *n* (*Egypt*) Egyptian king of the Fourth Dynasty (2625–2510 BC). He is the first king, and one of the few from the Old Kingdom, of whom some personal characteristics were preserved. He is said to have been a genial and popular figure.

snog *vi* (**snogging, snogged**) (*sl*) to kiss and cuddle.—*also n*.

snood *n* a small net or fabric pouch for holding a woman's hair at the back of the head; (*Scot*) a ribbon around the hair formerly worn by unmarried girls.

snook *n* (*sl*) a gesture of contempt with the thumb to the nose and fingers spread.

snooker *n* a game played on a billiard table with 15 red balls, 6 variously colored balls, and a white cue ball; a position in the game where a ball lies directly between the cue ball and target ball. * *vt* to place in a snooker; (*inf*) to obstruct, thwart.

snoop *vi* (*inf*) to pry about in a sneaking way. * *n* an act of snooping; a person who pries into other people's business.—**snooper** *n*.

snooperscope *n* an infrared night-vision device used by the police and military services.

snoot *n* (*sl*) the nose.

snooty *adj* (**snootier, snootiest**) haughty, snobbish.—**snootily** *adv*.—**snootiness** *n*.

snooze *vi* (*inf*) to sleep lightly. * *n* (*inf*) a nap.

snore *vi* to breathe roughly and noisily while asleep. * *n* the act or sound of snoring.

snorkel *n* a breathing tube extending above the water, used in swimming just below the surface. * *vi* (**snorkeling, snorkeled**) to swim using a snorkel.—*also* **schnorkel**.—**snorkeler** *n*.

snort *vi* to exhale noisily through the nostrils, esp as an expression of contempt or scorn. * *vt* to inhale (a drug) through the nose.

snorter *n* (*sl*) something remarkable for its size, strength, difficulty, etc.

snot *n* (*sl*) nasal mucus; (*sl*) a snotty person.

snotty *adj* (**snottier, snottiest**) covered with snot; (*sl*) irritatingly unpleasant; snobbish.—**snottily** *adv*.—**snottiness** *n*.

snout *n* the nose or muzzle of an animal.

snow *n* frozen water vapor in the form of white flakes; a snowfall; a mass of snow; (*sl*) cocaine or heroin. * *vi* to fall as snow. * *vt* to deceive with smooth talk.

snowball *n* snow pressed together in a ball for throwing; (*Brit*) a drink made with advocaat and lemonade. * *vi* to throw snowballs; to increase rapidly in size.

snowberry *n* (*pl* **snowberries**) any of various shrubs bearing white berries.

snow-blind *adj* temporarily blinded or dazzled by the intense glare of sunlight reflected from snow.—**snow-blindness** *n*.

snowblower *n* a machine for clearing snow from roads by sucking it up and blowing it off to the side.

snowboard *n* a board shaped like a large ski which a person can stand on to slide across snow.

snowbound *adj* trapped by or covered in snow.

snowcap *n* a covering of snow, as on a mountain peak.—**snowcapped** *adj*.

snowdrift *n* a bank of drifted snow.

snowdrop *n* a Eurasian plant of the daffodil family with white flowers that appears in early spring.

snowfall *n* a fall of snow; the amount of snow in a given time or area.

snow fence *n* a slatted fence used to protect a railroad track or road from drifting snow.

snowflake *n* a fragile cluster of ice crystals.

snow goose *n* a large white North American goose with black-tipped wings.

snow job *n* (*sl*) a determined effort to persuade by flattery or deception.

snow leopard *n* a large cat of the central Asian mountains with a tawny coat that becomes white in winter.

snow line *or* **snow limit** *n* the lowest limit in altitude of permanent snow.

snowman *n* (*pl* **snowmen**) snow piled into the shape of a human figure.

snowmobile *n* a motor vehicle for traveling at speed over snow.

snowplow *n* a vehicle designed for clearing away snow.

snowshoe *n* an item of footwear in the shape of a racket-like frame with thongs for walking on soft snow. * *vi* (**snowshoeing, snowshoed**) to walk on snow using snowshoes.

snowshoe rabbit *or* **snowshoe hare** *n* a large rabbit of North America with large furry feet and brown fur that turns white in winter.

snowstorm *n* a storm with heavy snow.

snow tire *n* a heavy tire with deep treads for improved traction on snow and ice.

snow-white *adj* pure white.

snowy *adj* (**snowier, snowiest**) covered with snow; white or pure, like snow.—**snowily** *adv*.—**snowiness** *n*.

snowy owl *n* a large owl with white plumage of northern regions.

SNP *abbr* = (*Brit*) Scottish National Party; Society for Natural Philosophy.

Snr, snr *abbr* = senior.

Snr. *abbr* = Senhor.

SNR *abbr* = signal-to-noise ratio; Society for Nautical Research.

Snra. *abbr* = Senhora.

SNSC *abbr* (*Brit*) = Scottish National Ski Council.

SNSPRCS *abbr* (*Brit*) = Scottish National Sweet Pea, Rose, and Carnation Society.

SNSS *abbr* = School Natural Science Society.

SNU *abbr* = Spiritualists' National Union.

snub *vt* (**snubbing, snubbed**) to insult by ignoring or making a cutting remark. * *n* the act of snubbing; an intentional slight.

snub-nosed *adj* having a short, upturned nose; (*pistol*) having a very short barrel.

snuck *see* **sneak**.

snuff[1] *n* a powdered preparation of tobacco inhaled through the nostrils.

snuff[2] *n* the charred portion of a wick. * *vt* to extinguish (a candle flame).

snuffbox *n* a small box for snuff.

snuffer *n* a cone-shaped device for putting out a candle.

snuffle *vi* to make sniffing noises, as when suffering from a cold or crying. * *n* the act of snuffling; (*pl*) a form of catarrh.

snuff movie *n* a pornographic movie which ends by depicting the brutal murder of an unsuspecting participant.

snug *adj* (**snugger, snuggest**) cozy; warm; close-fitting.—**snugly** *adv*.—**snugness** *n*.

SNUG *abbr* (*Brit*) = Scottish Network Users' Group.

snuggle *vi* to nestle, cuddle. * *vt* to cuddle.

so[1] *adv* in this way; as shown; as stated; to such an extent; very; (*inf*) very much; therefore; more or less; also, likewise; then.

so[2] *n* (*Brit, mus*) sol.

s.o. *abbr* = seller's option; (*com*) shipping order; (*com*) ship's option; special order; sub-office.

So. *abbr* = South; southern.

SO *abbr* = (*Brit*) Scottish Office; Signal *or* Staff Officer; special *or* standing order; Stationery Office; sub-office; symphony orchestra.

soa *abbr* = state of the art.

SoA *abbr* = Society of Authors.

SOA *abbr* (*Brit*) = Scottish Orienteering Association.

soak *vt* to submerge in a liquid; to take in, absorb; (*sl*) to extract large amounts of money from. * *vi* to become saturated; to penetrate. * *n* the act or process of soaking.

so-and-so *n* (*pl* **so-and-sos**) an unspecified person or thing; (*inf*) (*euphemism*) an unpleasant or disliked person or thing.

Soane *n* Sir **John** (*b*. 1753, English architect), whose notable works include the Bank of England and St Peter's, Walworth.

soap *n* a substance used with water to produce suds for washing; the sodium or potassium salts of the fatty acids, stearic, palmitic and oleic acid; (*inf*) a soap opera. * *vt* to rub with soap.—**soapy** *adj*.

SOAPA *abbr* (*Brit*) = Scottish Old Age Pensions Association.

soapberry *n* (*pl* **soapberries**) any of various tropical American trees bearing fruit which are rich in saponin.

soapbox *n* a temporary platform from which to deliver informal speeches.

soap opera *n* (*inf*) a daytime radio or television serial melodrama.

soapstone *n* a type of soft gray-green stone with a soapy texture.—*also* **steatite**.

soapwort *n* a Eurasian herbaceous plant of the pink family whose leaves form a soapy lather with water.

soapy *adj* (**soapier, soapiest**) like or full of soap; flattering, unctuous.—**soapily** *adv*.—**soapiness** *n*.

soar *vi* to rise high in the air; to glide along high in the air; to increase; to rise in status.—**soarer** *n*.

SOAS *abbr* = School of Oriental and African Studies.

soave *adj* (*mus*) soft or gentle.

sob *vi* (**sobbing, sobbed**) to weep with convulsive gasps. * *vt* to say while sobbing.

sob *abbr* = son of a bitch.

SOB *abbr* = shortness of breath.

Sobekneferu *n* Egyptian female king. She ruled at the end of the Twelfth Dynasty, around 1790–1785 BC. Sister and perhaps also wife of the Pharaoh Ammenemes IV, her titles announce her as a woman king.

sober *adj* not drunk; serious and thoughtful; realistic, rational; subdued in color. * *vti* (*often with* **up** *or* **down**) to make or become sober.—**soberly** *adv*.—**soberness** *n*.

Sobers *n* **Gary** [Sir **Garfield St Auburn**] (1936–) West Indian cricketer.

SOBHD *abbr* (*Brit*) = Scottish Official Board of Highland Dancing.

sobriety *n* soberness; temperance; seriousness.

sobriquet *n* a nickname.—*also* **soubriquet**.

SOBS *abbr* = Society of Bookbinders.

sob story *n* (*inf*) a tale of distress intended to arouse sympathy.

Soc., soc. *abbr* = socialist; society.

SOC *abbr* (*Brit*) = Scottish Ornithologists' Club; Specialised Oceanographic Centre.

soca *n* (*mus*) a type of powerful, rhythmic dance music from the English-speaking islands of the Caribbean. It evolved from soul (hence "so") and calypso ("ca").

so-called *adj* commonly named or known as.

soccer *n* a football game played on a field by two teams of 11 players with a round, inflated ball, association football.

SOCGPA *abbr* = Seed, Oil, Cake, and General Produce Association.

sociable *adj* friendly; companionable.—**sociability** *n*.—**sociably** *adv*.

social *adj* living or organized in a community, not solitary; relating to human beings living in society; of or intended for communal activities; sociable. * *n* an informal gathering of people, such as a party.—**socially** *adv*.

social anthropology *n* the branch of anthropology that studies social and cultural systems and beliefs.

social audit *n* a survey of the non-financial aspects of a company's performance, the object being to enable the company to assess its performance in relation to society.

social climber *n* a person who strives to attain a higher social position.

social contract *or* **social compact** *n* a tacit agreement between individuals in society and between individuals and the government, which defines the rights and duties of each.

Social Democratic Party *n* a political party that advocates the transition from capitalism to socialism in a gradual manner.—**Social Democrat** *n*.—**Social Democratic** *adj*.

social disease *n* a sexually transmitted disease.

social insurance *n* compulsory contributions from government and employers to provide financial support for people in the event of illness or unemployment and for old age.

socialism *n* (a system based on) a political and economic theory advocating state ownership of the means of production and distribution.—**socialist** *n*, *adj*.—**socialistic** *adj*.—**socialistically** *adv*.

socialist realism *n* a genre in literature that bears no relation to realism, the term usu denoting any form of fiction, within a socialist dictatorship, that is written to serve the interests of the ruling clique of that state by lauding its achievements.

socialite *n* a person active or prominent in fashionable society.

socialize *vi* to meet other people socially.—**socialization** *n*.—**socializer** *n*.

socialized medicine *n* medical services financed by government from taxation.

social realism *n* a form of realism in which an artist's political viewpoint (usually on the left) affects the content of his or her work.

social register *n* a listing of socially prominent people in a community.

social science *n* the study of human social organization and relationships using scientific methods.

social security *n* financial assistance for the unemployed, the disabled, etc to alleviate economic distress.

social service *n* a welfare service provided by the state, such as housing, education, and health.—**social-service** *adj*.

social studies *n sing* the study of society and social relationships, as in politics, economics, human geography, and sociology.

social work *n* any of various professional welfare services to aid the underprivileged in society.—**social worker** *n*.

societal marketing *n* a form of marketing that seeks to meet the needs of consumers without damaging the environment or wasting natural resources.

society *n* (*pl* **societies**) the social relationships between human beings or animals organized collectively; the system of human institutional organization; a community with the same language and customs; an interest group or organization; the fashionable or privileged members of a community; companionship.—**societal** *adj*.

Society of Friends *n* the official name for the Quakers.

Society of Jesus *n* the Roman Catholic religious order of the Jesuits.

socio- *prefix* society; social.

sociobiology *n* the study of human and animal social behavior.—**sociobiological** *adj*.—**sociobiologist** *n*.

socioeconomic *adj* of or involving social and economic aspects.

sociol. *abbr* = sociological; sociology.

sociolinguistics *n sing* the study of the social and cultural context of language.—**sociolinguist** *n*.

sociology *n* the study of the development and structure of society and social relationships.—**sociological** *adj*.—**sociologically** *adv*.—**sociologist** *n*.

sociometry *n* the study of social relations within small groups.—**sociometric** *adj*.

sociopath *n* a person suffering from a mental disorder that results in antisocial behavior and lack of guilt.—**sociopathic** *adj*.

sociopolitical *adj* of or involving social and political aspects.

Soc. Is. *abbr* = Society Islands.

sock[1] *n* a kind of short stocking covering the foot and lower leg.

sock[2] *vt* (*sl*) to punch hard. * *n* a blow.

socket *n* a hollow part into which something is inserted, such as an eye, a bone, a tooth, an electric plug, etc.

sockeye *n* a Pacific salmon valued as a food fish.—*also* **red salmon**.

SOCO *abbr* = scene-of-crime officer.

Socrates *n* (470–399 BC) Greek philosopher, and tutor of Plato.

Socratic *adj* of or relating to Socrates or his methods. * *n* an adherent of Socrates or his philosophy.

Socratic irony *n* feigning ignorance when posing questions to expose the real ignorance of the person responding.

Socratic method *n* philosophical instruction by means of question and answer.

socy. *abbr* = society.

sod[1] *n* a lump of earth covered with grass; turf. * *vt* (**sodding, sodded**) to cover with turf.

sod[2] *n* (*sl*) an obnoxious person; (*loosely*) a person or a man. * *vi* (**sodding, sodded**) (*Brit sl*) to damn; (*with off*) (*sl*) to go away.—*also interj*.

soda *n* sodium bicarbonate; sodium carbonate; soda water.

soda bread *n* bread made with baking soda instead of yeast.

soda fountain *n* a counter selling soft drinks, ice cream, snacks, etc; a device that dispenses soda water.

soda siphon *n* a pressurized container that dispenses soda water.

soda water *n* a fizzy drink made by charging water with carbon dioxide under pressure.

sodden *adj* completely soaked through.—**soddenly** *adv*.

Soddy *n* Frederick (1877–1956) English chemist, who was awarded the 1921 Nobel Prize for Chemistry for his discovery of isotopes during his research in radioactivity.

sodium *n* a metallic element. * symbol Na.

sodium bicarbonate *n* a white soluble alkaline powder used in baking powder, fire extinguishers, and in antacid medicines.

sodium chloride *n* salt.

sodium hydroxide *n* a white alkaline solid used in the manufacture of soap, paper, and rayon.

sodium nitrate *n* a white crystalline compound used in fertilizers, matches, and explosives, and as a food preservative.

sodium-vapor lamp *n* an electric lamp using sodium vapor through which a current is passed to produce an orange light, esp used for street lighting.

Sodom *n* (*Bible*) a wicked city destroyed by God; a wicked and depraved place.

sodomite *n* a person who practices sodomy.

sodomy *n* anal sexual intercourse.

SOE *abbr* = Special Operations Executive (WW II).

SOED *abbr* = (*Brit*) Scottish Office Education Department; Shorter Oxford English Dictionary.

Soekarno *see* **Suharto**.

SOF *abbr* = share of freehold; Society of Floristry.

sofa *n* an upholstered couch or settee with fixed back and arms.

Sofiya n capital city of Bulgaria.

soffit *n* the underside of a structural element, such as an arch, stairway, balcony, etc.

S of M *abbr* = Society of Metaphysicians.

S of S *abbr* = Secretary of State; Song of Solomon *or* Song of Songs.

S of Sol *abbr* = Song of Solomon.

soft *adj* malleable; easily cut, shaped, etc; not as hard as normal, desirable, etc; smooth to the touch; (*drinks*) non-alcoholic; mild, as a breeze; lenient; (*sl*) easy, comfortable; (*color, light*) not bright; (*sound*) gentle, low; (*drugs*) non-addictive; (*comput*) denoting punctuation, etc inserted by a program, as opposed to a hard command inserted by the user.—**softly** *adv*.—**softness** *n*.

S of T *abbr* = Sons of Temperance.

softball *n* a game similar to baseball, but played with a larger, softer ball.

soft-boiled *adj* (*egg*) boiled so that the white hardens while the yolk remains soft.

soft-core *adj* (*pornography*) not sexually explicit.

softcover *adj* paperback. * *n* a paperback book.

soft drink *n* a non-alcoholic drink.

soften *vti* to make or become soft or softer.—**softener** *n*.

soft-focus *adj* (*lens*) designed to produce a slightly blurred image.

soft furnishings *npl* items such as curtains, carpets, rugs, etc.

soft goods *npl* textile and clothing products.

softheaded *adj* stupid, feeble-minded.—**softheadedly** *adv*.—**softheadedness** *n*.

softhearted *adj* kind; sentimental.—**softheartedly** *adv*.—**softheartedness** *n*.

soft landing *n* a landing by a spacecraft that leaves the vehicle and occupants undamaged.

soft loan *n* a loan that has an interest-rate charge that is much lower than the market rate of interest.

soft option *n* the easiest choice in a range of alternatives.

soft palate *n* the fleshy area at the back of the roof of the mouth.

soft paste *n* a type of translucent porcelain made from refined clay, ground glass, bone ash, etc.

soft-pedal *n* a pedal on a piano for muting the tone. * *vt* (*inf*) to avoid direct reference to (esp something embarrassing or unpleasant).

soft porn *n* (*inf*) soft-core pornography.

soft sell *n* selling by gentle persuasion.—**soft-sell** *adj*.

soft soap *n* a type of semisolid or liquid soap; (*inf*) flattery.

soft-soap *vt* (*inf*) to flatter.—**soft-soaper** *n*.

soft spot *n* a sentimental fondness (for).

soft touch *n* (*inf*) a person who is easily persuaded or exploited.

software *n* the programs used in computers.

software piracy *n* (*comput*) the illegal, unauthorized copying of software.

software publisher *n* (*comput*) the company that writes, markets, sells, and distributes a computer program.

softwood *n* the wood of any coniferous tree.

softy *n* (*pl* **softies**) (*inf*) a person regarded as sentimental or physically weak.

S of V *abbr* = Sons of Veterans.

soggy *adj* (**soggier, soggiest**) soaked with water; moist and heavy.—**soggily** *adv*.—**sogginess** *n*.

soh *n* (*Brit, mus*) sol.

SOH *abbr* = sense of humor.

soi-disant *adj* self-styled.

soigné, soignée *adj* well-groomed; elegant.

soil[1] *n* the ground or earth in which plants grow; territory.

soil[2] *vt* to make or become dirty or stained.

soil pipe *n* a sewage or waste-water pipe.

soiree, soirée *n* an evening party of music in a private house.

soixante-neuf *n* a sexual position that facilitates mutual cunnilingus and fellatio.—*also* **sixty-nine**.

sojourn *n* a temporary stay. * *vi* to stay for a short time.—**sojourner** *n*.

Sokodé *n* a city in Togo.

sol[1] *n* (*mus*) the fifth note of the diatonic scale.

sol[2] *n* liquid in which a colloid is dissolved or suspended.

Sol[1] *see* **Helios**.

Sol[2] *n* (*Welsh Celtic myth*) one of the members of the group that was formed to help Culhwch in his quest for Olwen. He was selected to be part of the group because he could stand on one foot all day.

sol. *abbr* = soluble; solution.

Sol. *abbr* = Solicitor.

solace *n* comfort in misery; consolation. * *vt* to bring solace to.

solar *adj* of or from the sun; powered by light or heat from the sun; reckoned by the sun. * *n* (*archit*) a private room on the second or third floor of a house, particularly in the 14th to 16th centuries, to which the family could retire and view the proceedings in the great hall below.

solar activity *n* a collective term for various phenomena connected with the sun that take place within a regular cycle but vary in frequency and magnitude.

solar cell *n* a cell that converts the sun's rays into electricity.

solar constant *n* the quantity of the sun's energy radiated onto a given area of the Earth's surface in a prescribed period; (*phys*) the energy received on the Earth's surface, allowing for any losses due to the atmosphere.

solar corona *n* (*astron*) the outer layer of the sun's atmosphere, which reaches temperatures of two million K.

solar cycle *n* the cycle of solar activity, particularly relating to sunspots, which lasts for about eleven years.

solar day *n* the period of time during which the Earth makes a complete revolution relative to the sun.

solar energy *n* (*phys*) energy of any form that is derived from the Sun.

solar flare *n* a sudden brief eruption of intense energy from the sun's surface.

Solari *n* Santino (*b.* 1576) Italian architect, whose notable works include Salzburg Cathedral.

solarium *n* (*pl* **solariums** *or* **solaria**) a glass-enclosed room for sunbathing or exposure to the sun for medical treatment.

solar month *n* the period of time taken for the moon to make one complete revolution around the Earth (approx. 27 days).

solar panel *n* a large, thin panel that absorbs energy from sunlight and regenerates it.

solar plexus *n* the network of nerves behind the stomach; (*inf*) the pit of the stomach.

solar pond *n* a shallow artificial pond of salt water covered by fresh water, which absorbs heat from the sun's rays and converts it to electricity.

solar power *n* energy derived from the heat of the sun.

solar radiation *n* the heat, light, X-rays, gamma rays, and ultraviolet rays emitted by the sun.

solar spectrum *n* the spectrum of the sun extending from gamma ray to radio wavelengths.

solar system *n* the sun and those bodies moving about it under the attraction of gravity.

solar units *npl* the physical properties of a star or other body in relation to those of the sun.

S

solar wind *n* the constant flow of charged particles from the sun into outer space.

solar year *n* the period of time taken for the Earth to make one revolution around the sun.

sold *see* **sell.**

solder *n* a metal alloy used when melted to join or patch metal parts, etc. * *vti* to join or be joined with solder.

soldering iron *n* an electrically heated tool for melting and applying solder.

soldier *n* a person who serves in an army, esp a non-commissioned officer or a private. * *vi* to serve as a soldier; (*with* **on**) to continue regardless of difficulties or dangers.—**soldierly** *adj.*

soldier of fortune *n* a man in constant search of military adventure; a mercenary.

soldiery *n* (*pl* **soldieries**) soldiers collectively; a body of soldiers; the profession of being a soldier.

sole[1] *n* the underside of the foot or shoe. * *vt* to put a new sole on (a shoe).

sole[2] *n* (*pl* **sole** *or* **soles**) a type of flatfish used as food.

sole[3] *adj* only, being the only one; exclusive.—**solely** *adv.*

solecism *n* an error in speech or writing; a breach of etiquette or good manners.

solemn *adj* serious; formal; sacred; performed with religious ceremony.—**solemnly** *adv.*—**solemnness** *n.*

solemnis *adj* (*mus*) (*Latin*) solemn, as in *Missa Solemnis* (Solemn Mass).

solemnity *n* (*pl* **solemnities**) solemnness; a formal rite.

solenne *or* **solennelle** *adj* (*mus*) solemn.

solenoid *n* a coil of wire that produces a magnetic field when an electric current is passed through it.—**solenoidal** *adj.*

Soleri *n* **Paolo** (*b.* 1919) Italian architect, whose notable works include Solimene ceramics factory, Salerno.

sole structure *n* (*geol*) a sedimentary structure found on the base of beds formed primarily by the scouring of a current or the movement of an object over the sediment surface.

sol-fa *see* **tonic sol-fa.**

sol-fa syllable *n* any of the syllables (*do, re, mi,* etc) used to represent the notes of the musical scale in tonic sol-fa or solmization

solfatara *n* a volcanic outlet that emits only sulfurous gases and water vapors.

solfeggio *n* (*pl* **solfeggi** *or* **solfeggios**) (singing using) the application of the sol-fa syllables to musical scales or melody.

Sol. Gen. *abbr* = Solicitor General.

solicit *vti* to make a request or application to (a person for something); (*prostitute*) to offer sexual services to (somebody) for money.—**solicitation** *n.*

solicitor *n* (*Brit*) a lawyer.

solicitous *adj* showing concern or attention.—**solicitously** *adv.*—**solicitousness** *n.*

solicitude *n* the state of being solicitous; concern; anxiety; carefulness.

solid *adj* firm; compact; not hollow; strongly constructed; having three dimensions; neither liquid nor gaseous; unanimous. * *n* a solid substance (not liquid or gas); a three-dimensional figure.—**solidly** *adv.*—**solidness** *n.*

solidarity *n* (*pl* **solidarities**) unity of interest and action.

solid geometry *n* geometry of three-dimensional figures.

solidi *see* **solidus.**

solidify *vti* (**solidifying, solidified**) to make or become solid, compact, hard, etc.—**solidification** *n.*

solidity *n* the state of being solid; density; compactness; stability; truth; moral firmness.

solid-state *adj* (*electronic devices*) using components, such as transistors, in which the current flow is through solid materials as opposed to a vacuum; of or relating to solids or their properties and characteristics.

solid-state physics *n sing* the physics of the properties of solids.

solidus *n* (*pl* **solidi**) an oblique stroke (/) used to separate items of text as in dates, alternative words, lists, or the terms of fractions.

solifluction *n* the downhill movement of water-saturated regolith, the layer of unconsolidated and weathered material that lies over solid rock and is particularly prevalent in the humid conditions of the tropics.

soliloquize *vt* to utter a soliloquy. * *vi* to talk to oneself.—**soliloquist** *n.*

soliloquy *n* (*pl* **soliloquies**) the act of talking to oneself; an act or speech in a play that takes this form.

solipsism *n* (*philos*) the theory that the only possible true knowledge is of self-existence.—**solipsistic** *adj.*—**solipsist** *n.*

solitaire *n* a single gemstone, esp a diamond; a card game for one.

solitary *adj* alone; only; single; living alone; lonely. * *n* (*pl* **solitaries**) a recluse.—**solitarily** *adv.*—**solitariness** *n.*

solitary confinement *n* isolation of a prisoner by confinement in a special cell as punishment.

solitude *n* the state of being alone; lack of company; a lonely place.—**solitudinous** *adj.*

solmization *n* (*mus*) the use of syllables to name the notes or degrees of a musical scale.

solo *n* (*pl* **solos**) a musical composition for one voice or instrument; a flight by a single person in an aircraft, esp a first flight; a single bill of exchange of which no other copies are in circulation. * *vi* to perform by oneself. * *adv* alone. * *adj* unaccompanied.—**soloist** *n.*

Solomon *n* (*Bible*) the youngest son of David and Bathsheba, and one of the most famous kings of Israel, remembered for his wisdom, his political shrewdness, and the magnificence of his court. *See also* **Bathsheba, Jeroboam.**

solomonic column *n* (*archit*) a column which is fluted or shaped in a spiral fashion.

Solomon Islands *npl* an archipelago of several hundred islands in the southwest Pacific Ocean.

Solomon Islands dollar *n* currency of Solomon Islands.

Solomon's Porch *n* (*Bible*) a colonnade that ran along the east side of the outer court of Herod's Temple in Jerusalem.

Solon *n* **Léon Victor** (1872–1957) French designer, who decorated the Philadelphia Museum of Fine Arts.

so long *interj* (*inf*) goodbye, farewell.

solo organ *n* (*mus*) a manual on an organ with strong, distinctive stops, used for individual effect.

solo pitch *n* (*mus*) tuning an instrument higher than the regular pitch, to obtain a more brilliant tone.

solo whist *n* a form of whist in which any player may bid independently to win or lose a prescribed number of tricks.

solstice *n* either of the two times in the year at which the sun is farthest from the equator (June 21 and December 21).—**solsticial** *adj.*

Solti *n* **Sir Georg** (1912–97) Hungarian-born British conductor.

soluble *adj* capable of being dissolved (usu in water); capable of being solved or answered.—**solubility** *n.*—**solubly** *adv.*

solute *n* a dissolved substance in a solution.

solution *n* the act or process of answering a problem; the answer found; the dispersion of one substance in another, usu a liquid, so as to form a homogeneous mixture.

Solutrean *adj* relating to characteristic stone and flintwork from the Upper Paleolithic in areas of Spain and France. It is named after the site at Solutré near Mâcon.

solvable *adj* capable of being solved.—**solvability** *n.*

solve *vt* to work out the answer to; to clear up, resolve.

solvent *adj* capable of dissolving a substance; able to pay all debts. * *n* a liquid that dissolves substances.—**solvency** *n.*

solvent abuse *n* the deliberate inhalation of fumes from solvents (such as in glue and polish) to become intoxicated.

Solzhenitsyn *n* **Aleksandr Isayevich** (1918–) Russian novelist and historian who exposed the wrongs of Russian society in works such as *One Day in the Life of Ivan Denisovich* (1962). He won the Nobel Prize for Literature in 1970.

som *n* the standard monetary unit of Kyrgyzstan.

SOM *abbr* = Society of Occupational Medicine.

soma *n* (*pl* **somatas** *or* **somas**) all of an organism except the germ cells.

SOMA *abbr* = Sharing of Missionaries Abroad; Society of Medical Authors.

Somali *n* (*pl* **Somalis** *or* **Somali**) a native or inhabitant of Somalia; the Somali language.—*also adj.*—**Somalian** *adj.*

Somalia *n* a republic lying on the horn of Africa's east coast.

Somali shilling *n* the standard monetary unit of Somalia.

somatic *adj* of or relating to the body, as opposed to the mind; (*med*) of or relating to the non-reproductive parts of the body. —**somatically** *adv.*

somato- *or* **somat-** *prefix* body.

somatotype *n* physical build, body type.

somber *adj* dark, gloomy, or dull; dismal; sad.—**somberly** *adv.*—**somberness** *n.*

sombrero *n* (*pl* **sombreros**) a wide-brimmed hat with a high crown, worn esp in Spanish-speaking countries.

Sombrero Galaxy *n* a spiral galaxy in the constellation Virgo, which is edge-on to Earth, making its structure difficult to view.

some *adj* certain but not specified or known; of a certain unspecified quantity, degree, etc; a little; (*inf*) remarkable, striking, etc. * *pron* a certain unspecified quantity, number, etc.

-some *adj suffix* apt to, e.g., *tiresome*. * *n suffix* a group of, e.g., *foursome*.

somebody *n* (*pl* **somebodies**) an unspecified person; an important person. * *pron* someone.

someday *adv* at some future day or time.

somehow *adv* in a way or by a method not known or stated.

someone *n* somebody.—*also pron.*

someplace *adv* somewhere.

Somerled *n* (*d.* 1164) king of (the Isle of) Man (1158–1164). He was the seventh king of Man and became the first Lord of the Isles after expelling the Norsemen in 1140. He is considered to be the founder of the powerful MacDonald clan.

somersault *n* a forward or backward roll head over heels along the ground or in mid-air.—*also vi.*

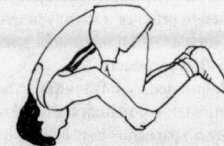

something *n, pron* a thing not definitely known, understood, etc; an important or notable thing. * *adv* to some degree.

sometime *adj* former. * *adv* at some unspecified future date. * *adj* having been formerly; being so occasionally or in only some respects.

sometimes *adv* at times, now and then.

someway *adv* in a certain unspecified manner.

somewhat *adv* to some extent, degree, etc; a little.

somewhere, somewheres *adv* in, to, or at some place not known or specified.

Sommaruga *n* **Giuseppe** (*b.* 1867) Italian architect, whose notable works include the Palazzo Castiglioni, Milan.

sommelier *n* a wine waiter.

somnambulate *vi* to get up and walk while asleep.—**somnambulant** *adj.*—**somnambulation** *n.*

somnambulism *n* the practice of walking in one's sleep.—**somnambulist** *n.*—**somnambulistic** *adj.*

somnolent *adj* sleepy, drowsy.—**somnolence, somnolency** *n.*

Somnos or **Somnus** *n* (*Roman myth*) the equivalent of Hypnos, the Greek god of sleep.

son *n* a male offspring or descendant.

son. *abbr* (*music*) = sonata.

sonar *n* an apparatus that detects underwater objects by means of reflecting sound waves.

sonata *n* (*mus*) a composition for a solo instrument, usu the piano.

sonata form *n* (*mus*) a method of arranging and constructing music that is commonly used (since *c.* 1750) for symphonies, sonatas, concertos, etc.

sonata-rondo form *n* (*mus*) a type of rondo, popular with such composers as Beethoven, which is a combination of rondo form and sonata form.

sonatina *n* (*mus*) a short sonata.

sondage *n* (*archeo*) a deep inspection trench.

sonde *n* a device for collecting scientific data in the upper atmosphere.

Sondheim *n* **Stephen** (1930–) American composer and lyric-writer. He wrote the lyrics for the musical *West Side Story*, and his own compositions include the shows *Company, Sweeney Todd*, and *A Little Night Music*.

sone *n* a unit of loudness equivalent to 40 phons.

son et lumière *n* an evening entertainment staged at historical sites and buildings using lighting displays, music, and recorded speech to illuminate the history of the place.

song *n* a piece of music composed for the voice; the act or process of singing; the call of certain birds.

song and dance *n* (*inf*) a fuss; a long, involved story.

songbird *n* a bird with a musical call.

song cycle *n* (*mus*) a set of songs that have a common theme or have words by a single poet.

song form *see* **ternary form**.

"Song Of Iowa, The" *n* the official song of the American State, Iowa.

Song of Solomon *n* (*Bible*) a book forming part of the Hebrew Scriptures, a collection of poems and bridal songs, pagan and sensuous, in praise of sexual love between man and woman.—*also* **Song of Songs**.

Song of the Earth *n* a song cycle by Gustave Mahler, for mezzo-soprano, tenor, and orchestra, first performed in 1908. The words are a translation of ancient Chinese poems.

songster *n* a singer; a songbird—**songstress** *nf.*

sonic *adj* of, producing, or involving sound waves.—**sonically** *adv.*

sonic barrier *n* the increase in air resistance experienced by objects traveling close to the speed of sound, the sound barrier.

sonic boom *n* an explosive sound produced by the shock wave when an aircraft, etc reaches supersonic speed.

sonic mapping *n* the use of an echo sounder to produce a map showing the depths of the sea.

son-in-law *n* (*pl* **sons-in-law**) a daughter's husband.

sonnet *n* a rhyming poem in a single stanza of 14 lines.

sonneteer *n* a composer of sonnets.

sonny *n* (*pl* **sonnies**) a patronizing form of address to a boy.

sonobuoy *n* a buoy used to detect underwater sounds and transmit them by radio to surface vessels.

sonorous *adj* giving out sound; full, rich, or deep in sound.—**sonorously** *adv.*—**sonorousness** *n.*

SONRA *abbr* = Society of Newfoundland Radio Amateurs.

Sons of Mil Espaine *see* **Mil Espaine, Sons of**.

soon *adv* in a short time; before long; **sooner or later** at some future unspecified time, eventually.

soot *n* a black powder produced from flames.—**sooty** *adj.*

soothe *vt* to calm or comfort; to alleviate; to relieve (pain, etc).—**soothing** *adj.*—**soothingly** *adv.*

soothsayer *n* a person who predicts events.

sop *n* a piece of bread or other food dipped in liquid before being eaten; a concession or a bribe offered to appease or cajole. * *vt* (**sopping, sopped**) to dip (bread, etc) into liquid. * *vi* to be soaked.

sop. *abbr* = soprano.

SOP *abbr* = significant other person; standard operating procedure; sum of products.

soph *abbr* = sophomore.

sophism *n* a clever but fallacious argument.—**sophistry** *n.*—**sophist** *n.*—**sophistic** or **sophistical** *adj.*

sophisticated *adj* refined; worldly-wise; intelligent; complex.—**sophistication** *n.*

Sophocles *n* (*c.* 496–406 BC) Greek dramatist, whose extant plays include *Antigone*.

sophomore *n* a second-year student at college or high school.—**sophomoric** *adj.*

soporific *adj* inducing sleep; sleepy.

sopping *adj* wet through.

soppy *adj* (**soppier, soppiest**) wet; (*inf*) sickly sentimental.—**soppily** *adv.*—**soppiness** *n.*

sopra *n* (*mus*) above, as in *come sopra* (as above).

sopranino *n* (*pl* **sopraninos**) a musical instrument of the highest pitch in its class.

soprano *n* (*pl* **sopranos** or **soprani**) the highest singing voice of females or boys; a person who sings soprano.

Sopwith *n* **Sir Thomas [Octave Murdoch]** (1888–1989) English aeronautical engineer, and designer of the Sopwith Camel, a successful fighter plane of World War I.

SOR *abbr* = sale or return.

sorbet *n* a flavored water ice; sherbet.

sorcerer *n* person who uses magic powers; a magician or wizard.—**sorceress** *nf.*

sorcery *n* (*pl* **sorceries**) the practice of magic, esp with the assistance of evil spirits.

sordid *adj* filthy, squalid; vile; base; selfish.—**sordidly** *adv.*—**sordidness** *n.*

sordino *n* (*pl* **sordini**) a mute for a stringed or brass musical instrument.

sore *n* a painful or tender injury or wound; an ulcer or boil; grief; a cause of distress. * *adj* painful; tender; distressed.—**soreness** *n.*

sorehead *n* (*inf*) an angry, disgruntled person.

sorely *adv* seriously, urgently.

SORG *abbr* = Stratospheric Ozone Review Group.

sorghum *n* any of a genus of tropical cereal grasses grown for fodder.

sorority *n* (*pl* **sororities**) a society of women university students.

Soroti *n* a city in Uganda.

sorrel[1] *n* a color between orange-brown and light brown; an animal, esp a horse, of this color.

sorrel[2] *n* a herb with bitter leaves used in salads.

sorrow *n* sadness; regret; an expression of grief. * *vi* to mourn, grieve.

sorrowful *adj* full of, showing or causing sorrow.—**sorrowfully** *adv.*—**sorrowfulness** *n.*

sorry *adj* (**sorrier, sorriest**) feeling pity, sympathy, remorse, or regret; pitiful; poor.—**sorrily** *adv.*—**sorriness** *n.*

sort *n* a class, kind, or variety; quality or type. * *vt* to arrange according to kind; to classify; (*comput*) to organize (data) into a particular order; (*with* **out**) to find a solution to, resolve; to disentangle; to organize, discipline; (*inf*) to punish, attack violently.—**sorter** *n.*

sorted *adj* (*sl*) fully prepared or organized; put in order.

sortie *n* a sudden attack by troops from a besieged position; one mission by a single military plane.

sort key *n* (*comput*) the field name in a database by which a sort is conducted.

sort order *n* (*comput*) the way in which a sort organizes data.

SOS *n* an international signal code of distress; an urgent call for help or rescue.

sos *abbr* (*Latin*) = *si opus sit*, "if necessary."

SoS *abbr* = Secretary of State.

SOS *abbr* = Save Our Seatrout (Republic of Ireland); (*Brit*) Save Our Shires; Service or Services of Supply; Society of Schoolmasters; (*Brit*) Stars' Organisation for Spastics.

so-so *adj* not good but not bad, middling. * *adv* average, indifferently.

sospirando *adj* (*mus*) sighing.

sost. or **sosten.** *abbr* = sostenuto.

sostenuto *adj* (*mus*) sustained.

sot *n* a habitual drunkard.

soteriology *n* (*theol*) the doctrine of salvation, esp through Jesus Christ.—**soteriological** *adj.*

Sothis *n* Egyptian goddess of the star Sirius. The heliacal (before the sunrise) rising of this star was incorporated into the Egyptian calendar

sotto voce *adv* in an undertone.

Sottsass *n* **Ettore** (1917–) Austrian designer, who in 1980 created the Memphis furniture and furnishings group.

sou *n* (*pl* **sous**) (*formerly*) a French coin of little value; a very small sum of money.

Sou. *abbr* = Southern.

soubrette *n* a minor female role in a comedy, esp a pert lady's maid; a saucy young woman.

soubriquet *see* **sobriquet**.

soufflé *n* a baked dish made light and puffy by adding beaten egg whites before baking.—*also adj.*

Soufflot *n* **Jacques G** (1713–80) French architect, whose notable works include Hotel Dieu, Lyons.

sough *vi* to make a moaning sound like the wind.—*also n.*

sought *see* **seek**.

souk *n* an open-air market in Muslim countries.

soul *n* a person's spirit; the seat of the emotions, desires; essence; character; a human being. * *adj* characteristic of African Americans.

S

soul-destroying *adj* extremely boring, depressing.

soul food *n* (*inf*) traditional food (e.g., yams, chitterlings) eaten by African-American people of the Southern US.

soulful *adj* expressing profound sentiment.—**soulfully** *adv*.—**soulfulness** *n*.

soulless *adj* devoid of emotion; bleak; dull.

soul mate *n* a person, such as a lover or close friend, with whom one bonds deeply.

soul music *n* music derived from African-American gospel singing marked by intensity of feeling and closely related to rhythm and blues.

soul-searching *n* close examination of one's conscience, motives, etc.

soum[1] *n* (*mus*) a Burmese harp.

soum[2] *n* currency of Uzbekistan.

sound[1] *adj* healthy; free from injury or damage; substantial; stable; (*sleep*) deep; solid; thorough.—**soundly** *adv*.—**soundness** *n*.

sound[2] *n* a narrow channel of water connecting two seas or between a mainland and an island.

sound[3] *n* vibrations transmitted through the air and detected by the ear; the sensation of hearing; any audible noise; the impression given by something; (*phys*) the effect upon the ear created by air vibrations with a frequency between 20 Hz (hertz) and 20 kKz (20,000 Hz); (*mus*) in acoustics, tones resulting from regular vibrations as opposed to noise; (*med*) an instrument that resembles a rod with a curved end, used to explore a body cavity, e.g., the bladder, or to dilate strictures. * *vi* to make a sound; to give a summons by sound. * *vt* to cause to make a sound; to voice; to make (a signal or order) by sound; (*with off*) (*inf*) to complain loudly.

sound barrier *n* the increase in air resistance experienced by objects traveling close to the speed of sound, the sonic barrier.

sound board *n* a thin board in certain musical instruments that resonates to enhance the sound; a sounding board; (*comput*) an add-on board for personal computers that gives digital-sound capabilities to a computer.

soundbox *n* the hollow resonating cavity of a musical instrument such as a guitar or violin.

sound effects *npl* artificial sounds used for dramatic purposes in plays, television shows, movies, etc.

sound hole *n* the opening in the belly (upper surface) of a stringed instrument, e.g., the F-shaped holes in a violin or the round hole in a guitar.

sounding[1] *n* measurement of the depth of water; a test or sampling, e.g., of public opinion.

sounding[2] *adj* resounding.

sounding board *n* a thin board placed behind a platform to direct the sound at the audience; a sound board; a person or thing used to test reaction to a new idea or plan.

sounding line *n* a line marked at regular intervals for sounding.

soundpost *n* (*mus*) a piece of wood connecting the belly (upper surface) of a stringed instrument to the back, which helps to distribute vibrations through the body of the instrument.

soundproof *adj* unable to be penetrated by sound. * *vt* to make soundproof by insulation, etc.

sound system *n* a means of producing sound, e.g., speech; a hi-fi or public-address system.

soundtrack *n* the sound accompanying a film; the area on motion-picture film that carries the sound recording.

soup *n* a liquid food made from boiling meat, fish, vegetables, etc, in water; (*inf*) a difficult or embarrassing situation. * *vt* (*with up*) (*inf*) to increase the power and performance of the engine of (a vehicle).—**soupy** *adj*.

soupçon *n* a slight flavor; a trace.

soup kitchen *n* a place where soup and other food is dispensed to homeless and destitute people.

soupspoon *n* a spoon with a rounded bowl for eating soup.

sour *adj* having a sharp, biting taste; spoiled by fermentation; bad-tempered; distasteful or unpleasant; (*soil*) acid in reaction. * *vti* to make or become sour.—**sourly** *adv*.—**sourness** *n*.

source *n* a spring forming the head of a stream; an origin or cause; a person, book, etc, that provides information. * *vti* (*inf*) to find a supplier (for); to identify a source (of).

source and application/uses of funds *n* an accounting statement that indicates the sources from which a company has derived its funds and the uses to which these funds have been put during a specified trading period.

source code *n* (*comput*) the instructions that a programmer creates when writing a program, which are then compiled into machine code before the computer can run the program.

source program *n* (*comput*) an original program that has been translated into machine code.

sour cream *n* cream deliberately soured by bacteria and used in sauces, dressings, etc.

sourdough *n* dough used in more than one baking to save on fresh yeast; a prospector in North America who lived on bread made from sourdough.

sour grapes *n sing* pretending to dislike something because it cannot be obtained or achieved by oneself.

sourpuss *n* (*inf*) a gloomy person.

Sousa *n* **John Philip** (1854–1932) American bandmaster and composer, who formed a successful military-style band that toured the world giving concerts.

souse *vt* to immerse in water or other liquid; to saturate; to pickle or steep in a marinade; (*sl*) to make drunk. * *vi* to become saturated or immersed. * *n* the act of sousing; something pickled; pickling liquid; (*sl*) a drunkard.

Sousse *n* a city in Tunisia.

soutane *n* a cassock.

souterrain *n* (*archeo*) a stone gallery below ground level, found in the highlands of Britain and Ireland.

south *n* the direction to one's right when facing the direction of the rising sun; the region, country, continent, etc, lying relatively in that direction. * *adj*, *adv* facing toward or situated in the south.

South Africa *n* a republic that lies at the southern tip of the African continent.

South Carolina (SC) *n* a state of the United States of America (USA) of which the capital is Columbia.

South Dakota (SD) *n* a state of the United States of America (USA) of which the capital is Pierre.

Southdown *n* a breed of hornless sheep that yields wool and esp meat.

southeast *n* the point on a compass midway between south and east. * *adj*, *adv* at, toward, or from the southeast.

southeasterly *adj*, *adv* toward or from the southeast. * *n* (*pl* **southeasterlies**) a wind from the southeast.

southeastern *adj* in, toward, or from the southeast; inhabiting or characteristic of the southeast.—**southeasterner** *n*.

southerly *adj* in, toward, or from the south. * *n* (*pl* **southerlies**) a wind from the south.

southern *adj* in, toward, or from the south; inhabiting or characteristic of the south.—**southernmost** *adj*.

Southern Cross *n* (*astron*) a constellation of the southern hemisphere comprising a cross of four stars, identified by its position to the west of two bright stars A and B Centauri.

southerner *n* an inhabitant of the south.

southern lights *npl* the aurora australis.

Southey *n* **Robert** (1774–1843) English poet, closely associated with Wordsworth and Coleridge, who was appointed British poet laureate in 1813.

Southey's tubes *npl* very fine tubes for drawing off fluid, e.g., from subcutaneous tissue.

southpaw *n* (*inf*) a left-handed boxer; a left-handed person.—*also adj*.

South Pole *n* the most southerly point on the Earth's axis; the most southerly point on the celestial sphere; (*without caps*) the pole of a magnet that points south.

southward *adj* toward the south.

southwest *n* the point on a compass midway between south and west. * *adj*, *adv* at, toward, or from the southwest.

southwester *n* a strong wind from the southwest.

southwesterly *adj*, *adv* toward or from the southwest. * *n* (*pl* **southwesterlies**) a wind from the southwest.

southwestern *adj* in, toward, or from the southwest; inhabiting or characteristic of the southwest.—**southwesterner** *n*.

souvenir *n* a keepsake, a memento.

sov *abbr* = shut-off valve.

SOV *abbr* = subject-object-verb.

sovereign *adj* supreme in authority or rank; (*country, state, etc*) independent. * *n* a supreme ruler; a monarch.—**sovereignty** *n*.

soviet *n* a workers' council in the former USSR.

sovietism *n* a political system of which the soviet is the unit.

sow[1] *n* an adult female pig.

sow[2] *vt* (**sowing, sowed,** *pp* **sown** *or* **sowed**) to plant or scatter (seed) on or in the ground; to disseminate; to implant.—**sower** *n*.

sou'wester *n* a waterproof hat with a wide brim at the back, worn by sailors.

Soweto *n* a city south of Johannesburg in South Africa. * *abbr* = So(uth) we(stern) To(wnships).

soybean *n* a type of bean (orig from Asia), used as a source of food and oil.

Soyinka *n* **Wole** (1934–) Nigerian poet, novelist, dramatist, and critic, who worked in London in the late 1950s. He supported the Biafran side in the Nigerian Civil War and was imprisoned, *The Man Died: Prison Memoirs* describing his experiences there. He was awarded the Nobel Prize for Literature in 1986.

soy sauce *n* a dark, salty sauce made from fermented soybeans.

sozzled *adj* (*inf*) drunk.

sp *abbr* = self-propelled; (*Latin*) *sine prole*, "without issue"; species; stop payment.

sp. *abbr* = special; species; specific; specimen; spelling; spirit; spiritus.

s.p. *abbr* = single pole; (*astron*) sub polo; supra protest.

Sp. *abbr* = Spain; Spaniard; Spanish.

SP *abbr* = Shining Path; Socialist Party; starting price; submarine patrol.

spa *n* a mineral spring; a resort where there is a mineral spring.

s.p.a. *abbr* (*marine ins*) = subject to partial average.

SPA *abbr* = Saudi Press Agency; (*Brit*) Scottish Pipers' Association; (*Brit*) Scottish Pistol Association; (*Brit*) Scottish Publishers' Association; Singapore People's Alliance; Society of St Peter Apostle for Native Clergy.

SPAB *abbr* = Society for the Protection of Ancient Buildings.

SPAC *abbr* = Standing Pharmaceutical Advisory Committee.

space *n* the limitless three-dimensional expanse within which all objects exist; outer space; a specific area; an interval, an empty area; room; an unoccupied area or seat. * *vt* to arrange at intervals.

Space Age *n* the era when space exploration has become possible.

space-age *adj* of or pertaining to the Space Age; modern.

space bar *n* the long bar on a typewriter or computer keyboard for inserting spaces.

spacecraft *n* (*pl* **spacecraft**) a vehicle for travel in outer space.

spaced-out or **spaced** adj (sl) high on drugs.

space frame n (archit) a three-dimensional structure designed to span large spaces with few or no supporting columns.

spaceman n (pl **spacemen**) a person who travels in outer space; an alien.—**spacewoman** nf (pl **spacewomen**).

space platform see **space station**.

space probe n an unmanned rocket equipped for exploring outer space.

spaceship n a crewed spacecraft.

space shuttle n a manned spacecraft designed as a re-usable ferry between the earth and a space station.

space station n a manned artificial satellite designed to orbit the Earth and serve as a permanent base for space exploration.—also **space platform**.

spacesuit n a sealed and pressurized suit worn by astronauts in space.

space-time (continuum) n (phys) the four-dimensional co-ordinate system comprising the three spatial and one temporal co-ordinates which together define a continuum in which any particle or event may be located.

space velocity n (astron) a star's movement and direction in three-dimensional space.

spacewalk n a period of time spent by an astronaut floating in space outside a spacecraft. * vi to walk in space.—**spacewalker** n.

spacious adj large in extent; roomy.—**spaciously** adv.—**spaciousness** n.

spade[1] n a tool with a broad blade and a handle, used for digging.

spade[2] n a black symbol resembling a stylized spearhead marking one of the four suits of playing cards; a card of this suit.

spadework n routine preliminary work.

spadix n (pl **spadixes** or **spadices**) a spike of flowers clustered around a fleshy stem and enclosed in a spathe.

spaghetti n pasta made in thin, solid strings.

spaghetti western n a type of violent cowboy movie, usu shot on location in Italy or Spain, which became popular in the 1960s.

Spain n a constitutional monarchy situated in southwest Europe and occupying the greater part of the Iberian Peninsula, which it shares with Portugal. It includes the Balearic Islands in the Mediterranean Sea, the Canary Islands in the Atlantic Ocean, and the enclaves of Ceuta and Melilla on the coast of Morocco in North Africa.

spake (arch) pt of **speak**.

spam n (comput) junk mail in e-mail transmissions.

Spam n (trademark) tinned pork luncheon meat.

span n a unit of length equal to a hand's breadth (about 9 inches); the full extent between any two limits, such as the ends of a bridge or arch. * vt (**spanning, spanned**) to extend across.

Span. abbr = Spanish.

SPANA abbr = Society for the Protection of Animals in North Africa.

spandex n an elastic textile fiber made from polyurethane.

spandrel n the space between the right or left shoulder of an arch and the rectangular wall or molding enclosing it.

spangle n a sequin or other small piece of shiny decoration; any small, glittering particle. * vt to decorate with spangles. * vi to sparkle with or like spangles.—**spangly** adj.

Spaniard n a native or inhabitant of Spain.

spaniel n any of various breeds of dog with large, drooping ears and a long, silky coat.

Spanish adj of or pertaining to Spain. * n the language of Spain and Spanish America; the people of Spain.

Spanish-American adj of or pertaining to Spanish America (the countries in South and Central America where Spanish is spoken). * n a native or inhabitant of a Spanish-American country.

Spanish fly n a European blister beetle; a substance prepared from dried Spanish fly (cantharides), which purportedly acts as an aphrodisiac.

Spanish guitar n a type of classical acoustic guitar music; a guitar used to play this.

Spanish omelette n an omelette containing chopped vegetables such as onions, tomatoes, pimentoes, etc.

Spanish onion n a large onion with a mild flavor.

spank vt to slap with the flat of the hand, esp on the buttocks.—also n.

spanking adj (inf) very impressive, large, smart, etc; (inf) brisk, lively.—also adv.

spanner n a tool with a hole or (often adjustable) jaws to grip and turn nuts or bolts, a wrench.

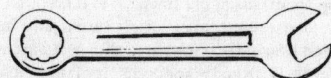

spar[1] n a pole supporting the rigging of a ship; one of the main structural members of the wing of an airplane.

spar[2] vi (**sparring, sparred**) to box using gentle blows, as in training; to argue.—also n.

sparc abbr = scalable processor architecture.

spare vt to refrain from harming or killing; to afford; to make (something, e.g., time) available. * adj kept as an extra, additional; scanty. * n a spare part; a spare tire.—**sparely** adv.—**spareness** n.

sparerib n a pork rib with most of the meat cut away.

spare tyre n (Brit, inf) a roll of excess fat around the waist.

sparing adj frugal, economical.—**sparingly** adv.—**sparingness** n.

spark n a fiery or glowing particle thrown off by burning material or by friction; a flash of light from an electrical discharge; a trace. * vt to stir up; to activate. * vi to give off sparks.

Spark n Muriel [Sarah] (1918–) Scottish novelist, whose novels are usu comic and satirical, with a strong element of the fantastic or supernatural, as in Memento Mori and The Ballad of Peckham Rye. Her best-known novel is The Prime of Miss Jean Brodie.

sparking plug n a spark plug.

sparkle n a spark; vivacity. * vi to shine; to glitter; (water, wine) to effervesce; to be lively or witty.

sparkler n a handheld firework that throws off brilliant sparks; (inf) a diamond.

sparkling wine n a wine made effervescent artificially by carbon dioxide gas or naturally by secondary fermentation.

spark plug n a device that produces a spark to ignite the explosive mixture in an internal-combustion engine.—also **sparking plug**.

sparring partner n (boxing) a partner who stands in as an opponent for training purposes; a person with whom one regularly argues.

sparrow n any of various small brownish songbirds related to the finch.

sparse adj spread out thinly; scanty.—**sparsely** adv.—**sparseness** or **sparsity** n.

Sparta n a city of ancient Greece, the capital of Laconia and of the Spartan state, and the chief city in the Peloponnese.—also **Lacedaemon**.

Spartan adj of or pertaining to Sparta; rigorously severe.

Sparti npl (Greek myth) the "sown men", the name given to the armed men who arose from the dragon's teeth sown by Cadmus.

SPAS abbr (Latin) = Societatis Philosophicae Americanae Socius "Member of the American Philosophical Society."

spasm n a sudden, involuntary muscular contraction; any sudden burst (of emotion or activity).—**spasmodic** adj intermittent; of or like a spasm.—**spasmodically** adv.

spasmolytic n a drug that reduces spasms (in smooth muscle).

Spassky n Boris Vasilyevich (1937–) Russian chess player, and world champion (1969–72).

spastic n a person who suffers from cerebral palsy. * adj affected by muscle spasm.

spastic colon see **irritable bowel syndrome**.

spasticity n an increase in the state of readiness of muscle fibers to contract (or an increase in the normal partial contraction) with an increased resistance to stretch. Movement requires great effort with a lack of normal co-ordination.—also **muscular hypertonicity**.

spastic paralysis n weakness of a limb, characterized by involuntary muscular contraction and loss of muscular function.

spat[1] see **spit**[2].

spat[2] n a gaiter covering the ankle and instep and fastening under the shoe.

spat[3] n a young oyster or other bivalve mollusk.

spat[4] n a petty argument or quarrel. * vi to have a petty argument.

spate n a large amount; a sudden outburst (as of words); a sudden flood.

spathe n a leafy part that encloses the floral spikes of certain flowers.

spatial adj relating to space.—**spatially** adv.

spatiotemporal adj of, involving, or occurring in both space and time; of or pertaining to space-time.

spa town n a town that has grown up around mineral springs.

spatter vti to scatter or spurt out in drops; to splash.—also n.

spatula n a tool with a broad, flexible blade for spreading or mixing foods, paints, etc.; (med) an instrument used to hold down the tongue when the throat is being examined; (archeo) a multipurpose tool with a broad, thin blade, usu made of bone.

spatulate adj shaped like a spatula.

spawn n a mass of eggs deposited by fish, frogs, or amphibians; offspring. * vti to lay (eggs); to produce, esp in great quantity.

spay vt to sterilize (a female animal) by removing the ovaries.

SPBA abbr (Brit) = Scottish Pipe Band Association.

SP boat abbr = submarine patrol boat.

SPBP abbr = Society for the Preservation of Birds of Prey.

SPBW abbr = Society for the Preservation of Beers from the Wood.

SPC abbr = Seed Production Committee; Sherry Producers' Committee; Society for Prevention of Crime; Society of Pension Consultants; Southern Pacific Commission; stored program control.

SPCA abbr = Society for the Prevention of Cruelty to Animals.

SPCC abbr = Society for the Prevention of Cruelty to Children.

SPCK abbr = Society for Promoting Christian Knowledge.

SPDA abbr = single-premium deferred annuity.

SPE abbr = Society for Photographic Education; Society for Pure English.

speak vi (**speaking, spoke**, pp **spoken**) to utter words; to talk; to converse (with); to deliver a speech; to be suggestive of something; to produce a characteristic sound; (with out, up) to speak loudly; to express an opinion frankly.—**speakable** adj.

speakeasy n (pl **speakeasies**) a club where alcoholic drink was sold illegally during the Prohibition era in the US in the 1920s.

speaker n a person who speaks, esp before an audience; the presiding official in a legislative assembly; a loudspeaker.

speaking clock n a recorded telephone message which gives the time.

spear n a weapon with a long shaft and a sharp point; a blade or shoot (of grass, broccoli, etc). * vt to pierce with a spear.

spearhead *n* the pointed head of a spear; the leading person or group in an attack or other action. * *vt* to serve as a leader of.

spearmint *n* a common mint plant which yields an oil used for flavoring.

spear-thrower *n* (*archeo*) an extension of the arm that enables the spear to be thrown further.

spec. *abbr* = special; specially; specification.

SPEC *abbr* = South Pacific Bureau for Economic Co-operation.

specchia *n* a form of burial monument in southern Italy, commonly a stone cairn.

special *adj* distinguished; uncommon; designed for a particular purpose; peculiar to one person or thing.—**specially** *adv*.

Special Branch *n* the division of the British police force that deals with political security.

special delivery *n* fast delivery of mail for an extra fee.

special effects *npl* illusions created for a movie or television show by trick camerawork or props; (*mus*) any extraordinary sounds, such as cow bells, that may be required of an orchestra, or part of an orchestra, to satisfy the demands of a composer.

special handling *n* parcel-post or fourth-class mail treated as first class for an extra fee.

special-interest group *n* (*comput*) a group of like-minded users who regularly get together to discuss their chosen topic on-line on an Internet connection.

specialist *n* a person who concentrates on a particular area of study or activity, esp in medicine.

specialize *vi* to concentrate on a particular area of study or activity. * *vt* to adapt to a particular use or purpose.—**specialization** *n*.

special licence *n* (*Brit*) a license allowing a marriage to take place without regard to the normal legal requirements.

special pleading *n* (*law*) the allegation of new facts in an action as opposed to a direct denial or admission of the opposition evidence; arguments that concentrate on the positive as opposed to the negative aspects of a case.

specialty *n* (*pl* **specialties**) a special skill or interest; a special product.

speciation *n* the evolution of a species.—**speciate** *vi*.

specie *n* money in coin.

species *n* (*pl* **species**) a class of plants or animals with the same main characteristics, enabling interbreeding; a distinct kind or sort; (*mus*) in the teaching of strict counterpoint, a rhythmic pattern in which one voice part can be combined with another.

specif. *abbr* = specifically.

specific *adj* explicit; definite; of a particular kind. * *n* a characteristic quality or influence; a drug effective in treating a particular disease.—**specifically** *adv*.—**specificity** *n*.

specific gravity *n* the ratio of the density of a substance to that of the same volume of water.

specific heat capacity *n* the heat required to raise the temperature of a unit of mass of a given substance by one degree.

specification *n* a requirement; (*pl*) a detailed description of dimensions, materials, etc of something.

specify *vt* (**specifying, specified**) to state specifically; to set down as a condition.—**specifier** *n*.

specimen *n* (*plant, animal, etc*) an example of a particular species; a sample; (*inf*) a person.

specious *adj* apparently true, but in fact false.—**speciously** *adv*.—**speciousness** *n*.

speck *n* a small spot; a fleck.

speckle *n* a small mark of a different color. * *vt* to mark with speckles.

speckle interferometry *n* a technique for measuring small angles, which utilizes the principle of interference of light.

specs *npl* specifications; (*inf*) spectacles.

SPECT *abbr* = single photon emission computed tomography.

spectacle *n* an unusual or interesting scene; a large public show; an object of derision or ridicule; (*pl*) a pair of glasses.—**spectacled** *adj*.

spectacular *adj* impressive; astonishing.—**spectacularly** *adv*.

spectate *vi* to be a spectator.

spectator *n* an onlooker.

spectator sport *n* a sport that attracts mostly spectators rather than participants.

specter *n* an apparition or ghost; a haunting mental image.

spectra *see* **spectrum**.

spectral *adj* of or like a specter; of or produced by a spectrum.—**spectrally** *adv*.—**spectrality** *n*.

spectral line *n* a line of emission or absorption, occupying a narrow wavelength band in a spectrum.

spectral type *n* a classification system for stars, based upon the spectrum of light they emit.

spectrograph *n* a device for producing and recording spectra.—**spectrographic** *adj*.

spectrography *n* heating a small sample until it vaporizes, then analyzing the light emitted to reveal the elements present.

spectroheliogram *n* (*astron*) an image of the sun obtained using a spectroheliograph.

spectroheliograph *n* (*astron*) an instrument for photographing the sun using a single wavelength of light.

spectrohelioscope *n* (*astron*) a device that is essentially the same as a spectroheliograph but that permits an image of the sun to be viewed in light of one wavelength.

spectrometer *n* a spectroscope used to measure spectra.—**spectrometric** *adj*.—**spectrometry** *n*.

spectroscope *n* an instrument for generating and examining spectra.—**spectroscopic** *adj*.—**spectroscopically** *adv*.—**spectroscopy** *n*.

spectroscopic binary *n* a binary star determined as such by the nature of its spectral lines.

spectroscopy *n* the generation, study, and interpretation of spectra using spectroscopes (which includes spectrometers, spectrographs, etc).

spectrum *n* (*pl* **spectra**) the range of color that is produced when a white light is passed through a prism; any similar distribution of wave frequencies; a broad range.

specular reflector *n* in remote sensing, a surface that reflects electromagnetic radiation without scattering or diffusing it, e.g. a still water surface.

speculate *vi* to theorize, conjecture; to make investments in the hope of making a profit.—**speculation** *n*.—**speculator** *n*.

speculative *adj* of or based on speculation; engaging in speculation in finance, etc.—**speculatively** *adv*.

speculum *n* (*pl* **specula** *or* **speculums**) a medical instrument for dilating and examining a bodily passage or cavity; a mirror used as a reflector in an optical instrument such as a telescope.

sped *see* **speed**.

speech *n* the action or power of speaking; a public address or talk; language, dialect.

speechify *vi* (**speechifying, speechified**) to make a speech or speeches, esp in a dull or pompous manner.—**speechifier** *n*.

speechless *adj* unable to speak; silent, as from shock; impossible to express in words.—**speechlessly** *adv*.—**speechlessness** *n*.

speech recognition *n* (*comput*) technology in which the spoken word is converted into signals that can be converted into commands for a computer to follow.

speech synthesis *n* (*comput*) the process by which the computer translates text into computer-generated output that simulates human speech.

speech therapy *n* treatment of people who are unable to speak coherently.

speed *n* quickness; rapidity or rate of motion; (*phys*) the ratio of distance covered by a body moving in a straight line or continuous curve to the time required to cover that distance; (*photog*) the sensitivity of film to light; (*sl*) an amphetamine drug. * *vi* (**speeding, sped** *or* **speeded**) to go quickly, hurry; to drive a vehicle at an illegally high speed.

Speed *abbr* (*Brit*) = Scottish Partnership in Electronics for Effective Distribution.

speedball *n* (*sl*) a mixture of heroin and cocaine or amphetamines.

speeding *n* the driving of a vehicle at an illegally high or dangerous speed.

speed limit *n* a legal maximum or minimum speed at which a vehicle may travel on specified roads.

speed of light *n* a universal and absolute value, independent of the speed of the observer, 186,281 miles per second.

speedometer *n* an instrument in a motor vehicle for measuring its speed.

speed reading *n* a system of reading rapidly by skimming the text.

speed trap *n* a stretch of road under surveillance by police, usu with radar devices, to catch speeding motorists.

speedway *n* the sport of racing light motorcycles around dirt or cinder tracks; a stadium for motorcycle racing; a road reserved for fast traffic.

speedwell *n* any of various plants of the figwort family with small blue or white flowers.

speedy *adj* (**speedier, speediest**) quick; prompt.—**speedily** *adv*.—**speediness** *n*.

speleology *n* the scientific study of caves.—**speleological** *adj*.—**speleologist** *n*.

spell[1] *n* a sequence of words used to perform magic; fascination.

spell[2] *vt* (**spelling, spelt** *or* **spelled**) to name or write down in correct order the letters to form (a word); (*letters*) to form (a word) when placed in the correct order; to indicate; (*with* out) to read slowly and painstakingly; to explain in detail; to discern, realize the meaning of. * *vi* to spell words.

spell[3] *n* a usu indefinite period of time; a period of duty in a certain occupation or activity. * *vt* to relieve, stand in for.

spellbound *adj* entranced, enthralled.

spell checker *n* (*comput*) a utility program or part of a larger application that individually checks each word in a document against a dictionary file.

spelling bee *n* a spelling contest.

spelt *see* **spell**[2].

spelunker *n* a person whose hobby is exploring caves.—**spelunking** *n*.

Spence *n* Sir **Basil** (1907–76) Indian-born Scottish architect, who designed Coventry Cathedral.

Spencer *n* 1. **Lady Diana** *see* **Diana** 2. **Sir Stanley** (1891–1959) English painter.

spend *vt* (**spending, spent**) to pay out (money); to concentrate (one's time or energy) on an activity; to pass (time); to use up. * *vi* to pay out money.—**spender** *n*.

Spender *n* Sir **Stephen [Harold]** (1909–95) English poet and critic, who was a close associate of Auden in the 1930s and whose poem "The Pylons" resulted in the derisive label of "Pylon poets" being applied to Spender and other poets of the era.

spendthrift *n* a person who spends money wastefully or extravagantly.

Spengler *n* **Oswald** (1880–1936) German philosopher, whose historicist study *The Decline of the West* (1918–22) argued that civilizations rise and fall in inexorable cycles and that Western civilization could thus be expected to decay according to the same immutable laws that destroyed previous civilizations.

Spenser *n* **Edmund** (c. 1552–99) English poet, noted particularly for his allegorical poem *The Faerie Queene*.

spent[1] *see* **spend**.

spent[2] *adj* consumed, used up; physically drained, exhausted.

Speos *n* (*Egypt*) a temple cut into rock, like those at Abu Simbel and Beni-Hasan.

sperm *n* semen; the male reproductive cell.

spermaceti *n* a waxy substance derived from the oil in the head of a sperm whale.

spermatic *adj* pertaining to, consisting of, or conveying sperm.

spermatid *n* any of the four male gametes that form into a spermatozoon.

spermat(o)- or **sperm(o)-** *prefix* sperm.

spermatocyte *n* a cell that develops into a male germ cell.

spermatogenesis *n* the formation and development of spermatozoa in the testis.—**spermatogenetic** *adj*.

spermatogonium *n* (*pl* **spermatogonia**) an immature male germ cell.

spermatophyte *n* a plant that produces seeds.—**spermatophytic** *adj*.

spermatozoon *n* (*pl* **spermatozoa**) any of the male reproductive cells present in the semen.

spermicide *n* a substance that destroys sperm.—**spermicidal** *adj*.

sperm oil *n* oil obtained from the head of the sperm whale.

sperm whale *n* a large whale with a blunt head which is hunted for its oil and spermaceti.

SPES *abbr* = South Place Ethical Society.

SPET *abbr* = single photon emission tomography.

spew *vti* to vomit; to flow or gush forth. * *n* something spewed.

SPF *abbr* = (*Brit*) Scottish Pensioners' Forum; (*Brit*) Scottish Police Federation; South Pacific Forum; sun protection factor.

SPG *abbr* = Society for the Propagation of the Gospel; Special Patrol Group.

SPGA *abbr* (*Brit*) = Scottish Professional Golfers' Association.

SPGB *abbr* (*Brit*) = Socialist Party of Great Britain.

sp. gr. *abbr* = specific gravity.

sphagnum *n* a genus of moss which grows in bogs and is a major constituent of peat.

sphalerite *see* **blende**.

sphenoid *adj* wedge-shaped; of or pertaining to the sphenoid bone. * *n* a sphenoid bone.

sphenoid bone *n* a wedge-shaped bone at the base of the skull.

sphere *n* a ball, globe, or other perfectly round object; a field of activity or interest; a social class.—**spherical** or **spheric** *adj*.—**spherically** *adv*.

spherical aberration *n* an imperfection in a lens or mirror in which light rays do not all converge at the same point because parts of the lens or mirror are at different distances from the optic axis and have different focal lengths.

spheroid *n* a figure that is nearly a sphere.

spherometer *n* an instrument for measuring the curvature of spherical surfaces.

spherule *n* a small sphere.

sphincter *n* a ring-shaped muscle controlling the opening and closing of an orifice.

sphinx *n* (*with cap*) (*Greek myth*) a monster with a lion's body and human head, which killed travelers who gave the wrong answer to a riddle; (*without cap*) any of various massive statues with a lion's body and human head erected by the ancient Egyptians; a mysterious or enigmatic person.

sp. ht. *abbr* = specific heat.

sphygmograph *n* a device that records variations in blood pressure and pulse.—**sphygmographic** *adj*.—**sphygmography** *n*.

sphygmomanometer *n* a device for measuring arterial blood pressure.

spianato *adj* (*mus*) even, smooth.

spicate *adj* (*flowers, leaves*) spiked, pointed.

spicato *n* (*pl* **spicatos**) (*mus*) (a musical piece or passage played using) a technique in which the bow is made to rebound lightly off the strings of an instrument.—*also adj*.

spice *n* an aromatic vegetable substance used for flavoring and seasoning food; these substances collectively; something that adds zest or interest. * *vt* to flavor with spice; to add zest to.

spicebush *n* an aromatic North American plant.

spick-and-span *adj* scrupulously clean and tidy.

spicule *n* a small needle-like body in the skeleton of sponges, corals, etc; a jet of hot gas erupting from the surface of the sun.

spicy *adj* (**spicier, spiciest**) flavored with spice; pungent; (*inf*) somewhat scandalous or indecent.—**spicily** *adv*.—**spiciness** *n*.

spider *n* a small, wingless creature (arachnid) with eight legs and abdominal spinnerets for spinning silk threads to make webs.

spider crab *n* any of various crabs with triangular bodies and very long legs.

spider monkey *n* a monkey of South and Central America with a slender body and long limbs.

spiderwort *n* tradescantia.

spidery *adj* thin, and angular, like a spider's legs.

spied *see* **spy**.

spiel *n* glib talk intended to cajole or persuade.—*also vi*.

Spielberg *n* **Steven** (1947–) American movie director and producer, whose movies include *Jaws* (1975), *Close Encounters of the Third Kind* (1977), *E.T.* (1982) and *Raiders of the Lost Ark* (1981).

spiffing *adj* (*sl*) (*arch*) excellent.

spiffy *adj* (**spiffier, spiffiest**) smart, elegant.

spigot *n* a small stopper or tap for a cask; a tap.

SPII *abbr* = (*Brit*) Scottish Pig Industry Initiative; Seed and Plant Improvement Institute (Iran).

spike *n* long heavy nail; a sharp-pointed projection, as on a shoe to prevent slipping; an ear of corn, etc; a cluster of stalkless flowers arranged on a long stem; (*comput*) a surge of electricity that at best causes a system crash or at worst can burn out components inside the computer. * *vt* to pierce with a spike.—**spiky** *adj*.

spike heel *n* a high pointed heel used in women's shoes.

spikenard *n* (a fragrant oil derived from) an Indian aromatic plant.

spilikin *see* **spillikin**.

spill[1] *vti* (**spilling, spilled** or **spilt**) to cause, esp unintentionally, to flow out of a container; to shed (blood). * *n* something spilled.—**spillage** *n*.

spill[2] *n* a splinter or thin strip of wood or twisted paper for lighting a fire, etc.

spillikin *n* a sliver of wood, cardboard, or plastic.—*also* **spilikin**.

spillway *n* a channel for surplus water from a dam, etc.

spilt *see* **spill**[1].

spin *vt* (**spinning, spun**) to rotate rapidly; to draw out and twist (fibers) into (thread or yarn); (*spiders, silkworm, etc*) to make a web or cocoon; to draw out (a story) to a great length; (*with* out) to prolong, extend; to cause (money, etc) to last longer. * *vi* to seem to be spinning from dizziness; (*wheels*) to turn rapidly without imparting forward motion. * *n* a swift rotation; (*inf*) a brief, fast ride in a vehicle; (*astron*) the angular momentum of an elementary particle or nucleus; an emphasis or slant imparted to information, proposals, or policies.

spina bifida *n* a congenital abnormality in the formation of the spine, causing the meninges to protrude, and associated with partial paralysis.

spinach *n* a plant with large, green, edible leaves.

spinal *adj* of or relating to the spine or spinal cord.—**spinally** *adv*.

spinal anesthesia *n* the loss of sensation in a part of the body as a result of spinal injury.—*also* **subarachnoid anesthesia.**

spinal column *n* the skeleton of jointed vertebrae and interconnecting cartilaginous tissue that surrounds and protects the spinal cord.—*also* **spine, backbone**.

spinal cord *n* the cord of nerves enclosed by the spinal column.

spindle *n* the notched rod by which thread is twisted in spinning; a pin around which machinery turns.

spindly *adj* (**spindlier, spindliest**) tall and slender; frail.

spindrift *n* sea spray.

spine *n* a sharp, stiff projection, as a thorn of the cactus or quill of a porcupine; a spinal column; the backbone of a book.

spine-chiller *n* a book, movie, etc that inspires terror.—**spine-chilling** *adj*.

spineless *adj* lacking a spine; weak-willed; irresolute.—**spinelessly** *adv*.—**spinelessness** *n*.

spinet *n* a type of small harpsichord.

spinifex *n* any of several coarse Australian grasses with spiny seed heads or spiked leaves.

spinnaker *n* a large triangular sail sometimes carried by racing yachts.

spinner *n* a revolving fishing lure; (*cricket*) a ball bowled with a spin, or a bowler who does this.

spinneret *n* an organ in spiders and other insects for producing silk threads.

spinning wheel *n* a small household machine with a wheel-driven spindle for spinning yarn from fiber.

spin-off *n* a product or benefit derived incidentally from existing research and development.

spinose *adj* (*plants*) spiny.

Spinoza *n* **Baruch** (1632–77) Dutch philosopher, whose great work is his posthumously published *Ethics* (1677), in which he rejects the dualism of René Descartes and argues for a virtually pantheistic deity.

spinster *n* an unmarried woman.

spiny *adj* (**spinier, spiniest**) covered with spines or thorns; troublesome.

spiny anteater *n* the echidna.

spiny lobster *n* any of several large edible crustaceans with a spiny shell.

spiracle *n* a respiratory aperture in various insects and some fishes; the blowhole in whales.

spiral *adj* winding around in a continuous curve up or down a center or pole. * *n* a helix; a spiral line or shape; a continuous expansion or decrease, e.g., in inflation. * *vi* to move up or down in a spiral curve; to increase or decrease steadily.

spiral galaxy *n* a galaxy in which two arms consisting of new stars spiral outward from an ellipsoidal nucleus of old stars.

spire *n* the tapering point of a steeple.

spirea *n* any of various plants of the rose family having clusters of small white or pink flowers.

spirillum *n* (*pl* **spirilla**) a bacterium with a curved or spiral body.

spirit *n* soul; a supernatural being, as a ghost, angel, etc; (*pl*) disposition; mood; vivacity, courage, etc; real meaning; essential quality; (*usu pl*) distilled alcoholic liquor. * *vt* to carry (away, off, etc) secretly and swiftly.

spirit. *abbr* (*Italian*) = *spiritoso*, "lively" (music).

spirited *adj* full of life; animated.—**spiritedly** *adv*.—**spiritedness** *n*.

spirit level *n* a glass tube filled with liquid containing an air bubble and mounted in a frame, used for testing whether a surface is level.

spirito *n* (*mus*) spirit, so *con spirito* means "with spirit."

spiritual *adj* of the soul; religious; sacred. * *n* an emotional religious song, originating among the Black slaves in the American South.—**spirituality** *n*.—**spiritually** *adv*.

spiritualism *n* the belief that the spirits of the dead can communicate with the living, as through mediums.—**spiritualist** *n*.

spirochete *n* any of a genus of slender, spiral-shaped bacteria that includes those causing syphilis.

spirograph *n* a device that records respiratory movements.—**spirographic** *adj*.

spirometer *n* an instrument used to test how the lungs are working by recording the volume of air inhaled and exhaled.

spirt *see* **spurt**.

spit[1] *n* a pointed, iron rod on which meat is roasted; a long, narrow strip of land projecting into the water. * *vt* (**spitting, spitted**) to fix as on a spit, impale.

spit[2] *vt* (**spitting, spit**) to eject from the mouth; to utter with scorn. * *vi* to expel saliva from the mouth; (*hot fat*) to splutter; to rain lightly. * *n* saliva.

spit and polish *n* (*inf*) obsession with neatness and cleanliness, esp in the military services.

spite *n* ill will; malice. * *vt* to annoy spitefully, vex.—**spiteful** *adj*.

spitting image *n* (*inf*) a person who almost exactly resembles another.

spittle *n* saliva ejected from the mouth.

spittoon *n* a usu metal pan for spitting into, a cuspidor.

spiv *n* (*Brit, sl*) a person of smart appearance who lives by shady dealings, esp on the black market.

SPKC *abbr* = Small Pig Keepers' Council.

spkr. *abbr* = sprinkler.

spl *abbr* (*Latin*) = *sine prole legitima*, "without legitimate issue."

splanchnic *adj* of or pertaining to the viscera.

splash *vti* to spatter with liquid; to move with a splash; to display prominently; (*with* **down**) to land (a spacecraft) on water. * *n* something splashed; a patch of color; a small amount, esp of a mixer added to an alcoholic drink.—**splashy** *adj*.

splashdown *n* (the scheduled time of) the landing of a spacecraft on the ocean.

splatter *vti* to splash, spatter.—*also n*.

splay *vti* to turn out at an angle; to spread out. —*n* (*archit*) the sloping edge around a doorway or window which expands the opening along the depth of the wall.

spleen *n* a large lymphatic organ in the upper left part of the abdomen which modifies the blood structure; spitefulness; ill humor.

splendid *adj* brilliant; magnificent; (*inf*) very good.—**splendidly** *adv*.—**splendidness** *n*.

splendiferous *adj* (*inf*) splendid.

splendor *n* brilliance; magnificence; grandeur.—**splendorous** *or* **splendrous** *adj*.

splenectomy *n* (*pl* **splenectomies**) removal of the spleen, possibly because of rupture and bleeding.

splenetic *adj* of or pertaining to the spleen; spiteful, irritable.—**splenetically** *adv*.

splenic *adj* of, pertaining to, or in the spleen.

splenius *n* (*pl* **splenii**) either of the two muscles at either side of the back of the neck that move the head.—**splenial** *adj*.

splenomegaly *n* distension of the spleen.

SPLF *abbr* = Society for the Preservation of Life from Fire.

splice *vt* to unite (two ends of a rope) by intertwining the strands; to connect (two pieces of timber) by overlapping.—*also n*.

spline *n* a key or slot in a shaft that fits into grooves in a surrounding sleeve and locks the two together.

splint *n* a rigid structure used to immobilize and support a fractured limb; a splinter of wood for lighting fires. * *vt* to put in splints.

splinter *n* a thin, sharp piece of wood, glass, or metal broken off. * *vti* to break off into splinters.—**splintery** *adj*.

splinter group *n* a small group that has split off from the main body.

split infinitive *n* (*gram*) an infinitive with another word between *to* and the verb.

split *vti* (**splitting, split**) to break apart (usu into two pieces); to separate into factions; to divide into shares; to burst or tear. * *n* the act or process of splitting; a narrow gap made (as if) by splitting; a dessert consisting of sliced fruit, esp banana, with ice cream, nuts, etc; (*often pl*) the act of extending the legs in opposite directions and lowering the body to the floor. * *adj* divided; torn; fractured.

Split *n* a city in Croatia.

split-capital investment trust *n* a kind of investment trust that has a limited life, the equity capital being split into various classes of income shares and capital shares.

split-level *adj* (*building*) having rooms or areas in one part less than a full story higher than another that adjoins them.

split personality *n* instability in mood or behavior; a condition of having two or more distinct personalities.

split-screen *n* (*cinema, television*) a technique involving the simultaneous projection of different images onto separate areas of the screen.

split second *n* a very brief moment, an instant.—**split-second** *adj*.

split shift *n* a shift in which the working hours are divided into two distinct periods.

splodge, splotch *n* a large, irregular spot, stain, or smear. * *vt* to mark with a splodge or splotch.—**splodgy** *or* **splotchy** *adj*.

splurge *vi* to spend lavishly (on); to show off. * *n* an extravagant display, esp of wealth.

splutter *vi* to spit out food or drops of liquid noisily; to utter words confusedly and hurriedly.—*also n*.

spm *abbr* (*Latin*) = *sine prole mascula*, "without male issue."

SPM *abbr* = short particular meter.

SPMA *abbr* = (*Brit*) Scottish Modern Pentathlon Association; Sewage Plant Manufacturers' Association; Shoe Pattern Manufacturers' Association.

SPMO *abbr* = Senior Principal Medical Officer.

SPMU *abbr* (*Brit*) = Society of Professional Musicians in Ulster.

SPNM *abbr* = Society for the Promotion of New Music.

sp. nov. *abbr* (*Latin*) = *species nova*, "new species."

SPNR *abbr* = Society for the Promotion of Nature Reserves.

SPOA *abbr* (*Brit*) = Scottish Plant Owners' Association; Scottish Prison Officers' Association.

Spock *n* **Dr** [Benjamin McLane] (1903–98) American pediatrician, whose theories on the raising of infants were popular in the 1960s.

Spohr *n* **Ludwig (Louis)** (1784–1859) German violinist, composer, conductor, and teacher, whose works include nine symphonies, ten operas (e.g., *Faust*), and numerous miscellaneous pieces for violin, piano, and harp.

spoil *vt* (**spoiling, spoiled** *or* **spoilt**) to damage as to make useless, etc; to impair the enjoyment, etc, of; to overindulge (a child). * *vi* to become spoiled; to decay, etc, as food. * *npl* booty, valuables seized in war; the opportunities for financial gain from holding public office.

spoiler *n* a projecting structure on an aircraft wing that increases drag to reduce lift; any similar structure for increasing the stability of vehicles at high speed.

spoil-sport *n* (*inf*) a person who spoils the fun of others.

spoilt *see* **spoil**.

spoke1, spoken *see* **speak**.

spoke[2] *n* any of the braces extending from the hub to the rim of a wheel.

spokeshave *n* a small two-handled plane used for smoothing curved surfaces.

spokesman *n* (*pl* **spokesmen**) a person authorized to speak in behalf of others.—**spokeswoman** *nf* (*pl* **spokeswomen**).

spondylitis *n* inflammation of the vertebrae.

spondylosis *n* degeneration of joints and the intervertebral disks of the spine, producing pain in the neck and lumbar region, where the joints may actually restrict movement.

sponge *n* a plant-like marine animal with an internal skeleton of elastic interlacing horny fibers; a piece of natural or manmade sponge for washing or cleaning. * *vt* to wipe with a sponge. * *vi* (*inf*) to scrounge.—**sponginess** *n*.—**spongy** *adj*.

sponge cake *n* a sweet cake with a light porous texture.

spongiform encephalopathy *n* a neurological disease that is caused by a slow virus and results in a spongy degeneration of the brain with progressive dementia. *See* **Creutzfeldt-Jakob disease**.

sponson *n* a projecting gun mounting on a ship or tank, etc to allow forward fire; an air-filled projection on the hull of a seaplane to provide stability.

sponsor *n* a person or organization that pays the expenses connected with an artistic production or sports event in return for advertizing; a business firm, etc that pays for a radio or TV show advertizing its product; the issuing house that handles a new issue of shares for a company. * *vt* to act as sponsor for.—**sponsorship** *n*.

spontaneity *n* (*pl* **spontaneities**) the quality of being spontaneous; a spontaneous action, etc.

spontaneous *adj* arising naturally; unpremeditated.—**spontaneously** *adv*.—**spontaneousness** *n*.

spontaneous combustion *n* the self-igniting of a substance through internal chemical processes such as oxidation.

spontaneous generation *n* abiogenesis.

Spontini *n* **Gasparo Luigi Pacifico** (1774–1851) Italian composer whose best-known works include the spectacular operas *La Vestale* and *Fernand Cortez*.

spoof *n* (*sl*) a hoax or joke; a light satire.—*also vti*.

SPOOF *abbr* = Society for the Perpetration of Outrageous Farces.

spook *n* (*inf*) a ghost; (*inf*) a spy. * *vt* to frighten.—**spooky** *adj*.

spool *n* a cylinder, bobbin, or reel, upon which thread, photographic film, etc, are wound. * *vt* to wind on a spool.

spooler *n* (*comput*) a utility program that is used to facilitate printing.

spoon *n* a utensil with a shallow bowl and a handle, for eating, stirring, etc.—**spoonful** *n*.

spoonbill *n* any of various wading birds with flattened bills.

spoonerism *n* the accidental transposition of the initial letters or opening syllables of two or more words with amusing results, e.g., *half-warmed fish* for *half-formed wish*.

spoonfeed *vt* (**spoonfeeding, spoonfed**) to feed (a baby, etc) with a spoon; to spoil; to provide (a person) with ideas and information without requiring any effort on his or her part.

spoor *n* a trail, esp of a wild animal. * *vti* to track (something) by a spoor.

Sporades *npl* two groups of small islands in the Greek Archipelago, one in the northern Aegean Sea, the other lying scattered to the east of the Cyclades.

sporadic *adj* occurring here and there; intermittent.—**sporadically** *adv*.

sporangium n (pl **sporangia**) (in fungi, etc) an organ or part in which asexual spores are produced.

spore n an asexual reproductive body produced by algae, fungi, and ferns, capable of giving rise to new individuals.

SPORE abbr = Society for the Preservation of the Rain-Forest Environment.

sporogenesis n the formation of spores in plants and animals.—**sporogenous** adj.

sporozoan n any of a group of spore-producing parasitic protozoans that includes the malaria parasite.

sporran n an ornamental pouch worn in front of the kilt as part of traditional Highland dress in Scotland.

sport n an athletic game or pastime, often competitive and involving physical capability; good-humored joking; (inf) a person regarded as fair and abiding by the rules. * vi to play, frolic. * vt (inf) to display, flaunt.

sporting adj interested in, concerned with, or suitable for sport; exhibiting sportsmanship; willing to take a risk.—**sportingly** adv.

sportive adj playful.—**sportively** adv.—**sportiveness** n.

sports car n a small, low, open, usu two-seater vehicle with sleek looks, designed for fast speeds.

sportscast n a sports broadcast.—**sportscaster** n.

sportsman n (pl **sportsmen**) a person engaged in sport; a person who plays by the rules, is fair, is a good loser, etc.—**sportswoman** nf (pl **sportswomen**).—**sportsmanlike** or **sportsmanly** adj.—**sportsmanship** n.

sports medicine n the branch of medicine dealing with sports injuries.

sportswear n clothing worn for sports and recreation.

sporty adj (**sportier**, **sportiest**) (inf) fond of sport; flashy, ostentatious.—**sportily** adv.—**sportiness** n.

sporule n a tiny spore.

spot n a small area differing in color, etc, from the surrounding area; a stain, speck, etc; a taint on character or reputation; a small quantity or amount; a locality; (inf) a difficult or embarrassing situation; a place on an entertainment program; a spotlight. * vt (**spotting**, **spotted**) to mark with spots; (inf) to identify, recognize; to glimpse.

spot check n a sudden random examination.—**spot-check** vt.

spotless adj immaculate.—**spotlessly** adv.—**spotlessness** n.

spotlight n a powerful light used to illuminate a small area; intense public attention. * vt (**spotlighting**, **spotlighted** or **spotlit**) to illuminate with a spotlight; to focus attention on.

spot market n a market that makes provision for the buying and selling of securities, commodities, or foreign currencies for immediate delivery.

spot month n the month in which goods bought on the basis of a futures contract will become available for delivery.

spot on adj (inf) absolutely right.

spotted dick n a steamed pudding made with suet and currants.

spotty adj (**spottier**, **spottiest**) marked with spots, esp on the skin; intermittent, uneven.—**spottily** adv.—**spottiness** n.

spot-weld vt to join (two pieces of metal) with circular welds.—**spot-welder** n.—**spot welding** n.

spouse n (one's) husband or wife.

spout vt to eject in a strong jet or spurts.—vi (inf) to drone on boringly. * n a projecting lip or tube for pouring out liquids.

spp abbr = species (pl).

SPP abbr = (Brit) Seed Potato Promotions of Northern Ireland; sub-pubic prostatectomy.

SPPA abbr (Brit) = Scottish Pre-School Play Association.

s.p.q.r. abbr = small profits, quick returns.

SPQR abbr (Latin) = Senatus Populusque Romanus, "the Senate and People of Rome."

SPR abbr = Society for Psychical Research.

sprain n a wrenching of a joint by sudden twisting or tearing of ligaments.—also vt.

sprang see **spring**.

sprat n a small food fish related to the herring; a small or young herring.

Spratling n William (1900–67) American architect and silversmith, whose handcrafted wares were ordered by movie stars and presidents, including Orson Welles and Lyndon Johnson.

sprawl vi to lie down with the limbs stretched out in an untidy manner; to spread out in a straggling way. * n a sprawling position.

spray[1] n fine particles of a liquid; mist; an aerosol or atomizer. * vti to direct a spray (on); to apply as a spray.

spray[2] n a number of flowers on one branch; a decorative flower arrangement; an ornament resembling this.

spray gun n a device for applying paint, varnish, etc in the form of a spray.

SPRC abbr = Society for the Prevention and Relief of Cancer.

spread vt (**spreading**, **spread**) to extend; to unfold, open; to disseminate; to distribute; to apply (a coating, e.g., butter). * vi to expand in all directions. * n an expanse; (inf) a feast; food which can be spread on bread; a bed cover; (com) the difference between the bid price (or buying price) and the offer price (or selling price) of a security, commodity, or foreign currency; (com) the simultaneous buying and selling of commodity futures.

spread eagle n an emblem of an eagle with wings and legs stretched out.

spread-eagle vt to place with the limbs outstretched.—**spread-eagled** adj.

spreadsheet n a computer program that allows easy entry and manipulation of text and figures, used for accounting and financial planning.

Sprechgesang n (mus) a type of singing that is half speech.

spree n (inf) excessive indulgence, e.g., in spending money, alcohol consumption, etc.

spree killer n a person who kills a group or number of people in an unpremeditated assault at a single location.

SPRI abbr = Scott Polar Research Institute.

sprier see **spry**.

sprig n a twig with leaves on it.

sprightly adj (**sprightlier**, **sprightliest**) full of life or energy.—**sprightliness** n.

spring vi (**springing**, **sprang** or **sprung**, pp **sprung**) to move suddenly, as by elastic force; to arise suddenly; to originate. * vt to cause to spring up, cause to operate suddenly. * n a leap; the season between winter and summer; a coiled piece of wire that springs back to its original shape when stretched; the source of a stream.

spring balance n a device that measures weight by the tension of a spring linked to a pointer on a calibrated scale.—also **spring scale**.

springbok n a South African gazelle.

spring chicken n a young chicken from two to ten months old; (inf) a young, inexperienced person.

spring-clean vti (Brit) to clean (a house, etc) thoroughly.—**spring clean** n.

springe n a snare for catching small animals.

Springfield n the capital city of Illinois, a state of the USA.

spring onion n (Brit) a scallion.

spring roll n a Chinese savory snack comprising a mixture of beansprouts, chopped meat, etc rolled in a thin pancake and fried.

spring scale see **spring balance**.

springtail n any of various small, wingless, leaping insects.

spring tide n a high tide that occurs at the full or new moon.

springtime n the season of spring; the earliest and most promising period in the life of something or someone.

springy adj (**springier**, **springiest**) elastic, resilient; light, spongy.—**springily** adv.—**springiness** n.

sprinkle vt to scatter in droplets or particles (on something).—also n.

sprinkler n a nozzle for spraying water; a fire-extinguishing system that operates automatically on detection of smoke or heat.

sprinkling n a small quantity scattered randomly.

sprint n a short run or race at full speed. * vi to go at top speed.—**sprinter** n.

sprint abbr = solid-propellant rocket-intercept missile.

sprit n a small spar which runs from the mast to the outer upper corner of a sail.

sprite n an elf or imp; a dainty person.

spritsail n a sail extended by a sprit.

spritzer n a drink made with wine, usu white, and soda water.

s-process n (astron) a process of nucleosynthesis that, in contrast to the r-process, is slow.

sprocket n a wheel with a row of teeth that engage the holes in a chain, or a reel of film, in order to turn it.

sprout n a new shoot on a plant; a small cabbage-like vegetable. * vt to put forth (shoots). * vi to begin to grow.

spruce[1] adj smart, neat, trim. * vt to smarten.

spruce[2] n an evergreen tree of the pine family with a conical head and soft, light wood.

sprue or **psilosis** n a composite deficiency disease because of lack of food being absorbed as a result of a disease of the intestine or a metabolic disorder that means fats cannot be absorbed.

sprung see **spring**.

spry adj (**sprier**, **spriest** or **spryer**, **spryest**) vigorous, agile.—**spryly** adv.—**spryness** n.

s.p.s. abbr (Latin) = sine prole superstite, "without surviving issue."

SPS abbr = (Brit) Scottish Painters' Society; (Brit) Scottish Prison Society; Society of Portrait Sculptors.

SPSO abbr = Senior Principal Scientific Officer.

spt. abbr = seaport.

SPTA abbr = Small Potteries Trade Association.

SPTC abbr = (Brit) Scottish Parent-Teacher Council; Single Parent Travel Club.

SPUC abbr = Society for the Protection of the Unborn Child.

spud n a small narrow digging tool; (inf) a potato. * vt (**spudding**, **spudded**) to dig with a spud.—**spudder** n.

spume n foam; surf; froth.

spun see **spin**.

spunk n a spark, a match; (sl) pluck, courage.

spunky adj (**spunkier**, **spunkiest**) full of courage; spirited.—**spunkily** adv.—**spunkiness** n.

spun silk n a shiny material made from silk waste.

spur n a small metal wheel on a rider's heel, with sharp points for urging on the horse; encouragement, stimulus; a hard sharp projection; (archit) a supporting strut; (archit) a sloping buttress; (archit) an ornamental carved feature, often foliage, found between the plinth and the circular base molding above; (archit) a projection from a wall that has some protective purpose. * vt (**spurring**, **spurred**) to urge on.

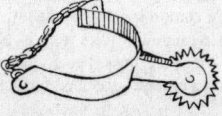

spurge *n* any of various plants that produce a bitter, milky juice.

spurious *adj* not legitimate or genuine; false.—**spuriously** *adv.*—**spuriousness** *n.*

spurn *vt* to reject with disdain. * *n* disdainful rejection.

spur stone *n* (*archit*) a stone projecting from the corner of a building to prevent damage from passing traffic.

spurt *vt* to gush forth in a sudden stream or jet. * *n* a sudden stream or jet; a burst of activity.—*also* **spirt.**

sputnik *n* the name used for a series of artificial satellites launched by the former Soviet Union in the 1950s and 1960s (Russian for "traveling companion").

sputter *vi* to splutter.—*also n.*

sputum *n* saliva and mucus.

SPVD *abbr* = Society for the Prevention of Venereal Disease.

sp. vol. *abbr* = specific volume.

spy *n* (*pl* **spies**) a secret agent employed to collect information on rivals. * *vi* (**spying, spied**) (*usu with* **on**) to keep under secret surveillance, act as a spy. * *vt* to catch sight of.

spyglass *n* a small telescope.

spyhole *n* a peephole, as in a front door.

sq *abbr* = sequence; squadron; square.

sq *abbr* = square; stereophonic-quadrophonic.

sq. *abbr* = sequence; (*Latin*) *sequens* or *sequentes* or *sequentia*, "the following."

Sq. *abbr* = Squadron.

SQA *abbr* = (*Brit*) Scottish Qualifications Authority; software quality assurance.

SQL *abbr* = standard *or* structured query language.

SQMS *abbr* = Staff Quartermaster Sergeant.

SqnQMS *abbr* = Squadron Sergeant Major.

SqO *abbr* = Squadron Officer.

sqq. *abbr* (*Latin*) = *sequentes* or *sequentia*, "the following."

squab *n* (*pl* **squabs** *or* **squab**) a young bird, esp a pigeon; a stuffed cushion; a short, fat person. * *adj* (*bird*) unfledged; short and fat.

squabble *vi* to quarrel noisily. * *n* a noisy, petty quarrel.—*also n.*

squad *n* a small group of soldiers that form a working unit; a section of a police force; (*sport*) a group of players from which a team is selected.

squad car *n* a police patrol vehicle.

squadron *n* a unit of warships, cavalry, military aircraft, etc.

squalid *adj* filthy; neglected; sordid; degrading.—**squalidly** *adv.*—**squalidness** *n.*

squall *vi* to cry out loudly like a baby. * *n* a loud cry; a violent gust of wind.

squalor *n* foulness; dirt; filth.

squama *n* (*pl* **squamae**) (*biol*) (something resembling) a scale.

squander *vt* to spend extravagantly or wastefully.

square *n* a shape with four sides of equal length and four right angles; an open space in a town, surrounded by buildings; (*inf*) an old-fashioned person; an instrument for drawing right angles; the product of a number multiplied by itself. * *adj* square-shaped; forming a square; forming a right angle (with); (*financial account*) settled; fair, honest; equal in score; (*inf*) old-fashioned. * *vt* to make square; to multiply (a quantity) by itself; (*with* **away**) (*inf*) to put in order, tidy up. * *vi* to agree.—**squarely** *adv.*—**squareness** *n.*

square bracket *n* either of a pair of written or printed characters [ ] used to enclose text or in mathematical expressions.

square dance *n* any of various dances in which the participants join hands to form squares.—**square-dance** *vi.*

square meal *n* a meal of satisfying quantity.

square measure *n* the measure of an area; the square of a linear measure.

square piano *n* a piano in a square case.

square root *n* a number that when multiplied by itself produces a given number (*2 is the square root of 4*).

squash[1] *vt* to squeeze, press, or crush; to suppress. * *vi* to squelch; to crowd. * *n* a crushed mass; a crowd of people pressed together; a fruit-flavored drink; a game played in a walled court with rackets and rubber ball.—**squashy** *adj.*

squash[2] *n* (*pl* **squashes** *or* **squash**) a marrow or gourd eaten as a vegetable.

SQUASH *abbr* = Squatters' Action for Secure Homes.

squat *vi* (**squatting, squatted**) to crouch down upon the heels; to occupy land or property, without permission or title. * *adj* short and dumpy. * *n* the act of squatting; a house that is occupied by squatters.

squatter *n* a person who squats.

squaw *n* a Native American woman.

squawk *n* a loud, raucous call or cry, as of a bird; (*inf*) a loud protest.—*also vi.*

squeak *vi* to make a high-pitched cry. * *n* a squeaky noise.—**squeaker** *n.*—**squeaky** *adj.*

squeaky-clean *adj* spotless; above reproach.

squeal *vi* to make a shrill and prolonged cry or sound; (*sl*) to be an informer; to protest.

squeamish *adj* easily nauseated; easily shocked or disgusted.—**squeamishly** *adv.*—**squeamishness** *n.*

squeegee *n* a tool with a rubber-edged blade for scraping away excess water from a surface, esp a window. * *vt* (**squeegeeing, squeegeed**) to wipe clean with a squeegee.

squeeze *vt* to press firmly, compress; to grasp tightly; to hug; to force (through, into) by pressing; to extract liquid or juice from by pressure; to obtain (money, etc) by force, to harass. * *n* squeezing or being squeezed; a hug; a small amount squeezed from something; a crowding together; financial pressure or hardship.—**squeezable** *adj.*

squelch *vi* to walk through soft, wet ground, making a sucking noise. * *vt* to crush or squash completely. * *n* a squelching sound.

squib *n* a small firework that fizzes and then explodes; a short, witty attack in speech or writing, a lampoon.

squid *n* (*pl* **squids** *or* **squid**) an edible mollusk, related to the cuttlefish, with a long body and ten arms.

squid *abbr* = superconducting quantum interference device.

squiffy *adj* (**squiffier, squiffiest**) (*Brit*) slightly drunk.

squiggle *n* a short, wavy line, esp handwritten. * *vi* to squirm; to wriggle.—**squiggly** *adj.*

squill *n* a Mediterranean plant of the lily family; a seashore variety of this whose bulbs were formerly used medicinally.

squint *vi* to half close or cross the eyes; to glance sideways. * *n* crossed eyes, as caused by a visual disorder; a glance sideways; (*inf*) a look; (*archit*) an opening cut at an angle through the wall of a church or a pier to permit a view of the altar. * *adj* squinting; (*inf*) crooked.

squire *n* a country gentleman, esp the leading landowner in a district.

squirm *vi* to writhe; to wriggle; to feel embarrassed or ashamed.

squirrel *n* (*pl* **squirrels** *or* **squirrel**) a bushy-tailed rodent with gray or reddish fur which lives in trees and feeds on nuts. * *vt* (*usu with* **away**) to hoard.

squirrel cage *n* a small cylindrical cage that is rotated by a small animal running inside; the rotor of an induction motor with cylindrically arranged copper bars.

squirt *vt* to eject (liquid) in a jet. * *vi* to spurt. * *n* a jet of liquid; (*inf*) an insignificant person.

squirt gun *n* a water pistol.

squish *vt* to crush, esp so as to produce a squelching sound. * *vi* to make or move with a squelching sound. * *n* a soft, squelching sound.—**squishy** *adj.*

Sr *symbol* (*chem*) = strontium (element).

sr *abbr* = self-rising.

s/r *abbr* = sale or return.

Sr *abbr* = Senior; Señor; Sir; Sister.

SR *abbr* = Saunders Roe; Senior Registrar; Shipping Receipt; Sons of the Revolution; Southern Region.

Sra. *abbr* = Señora.

SRA *abbr* = Snail Racing Association; Squash Rackets Association.

sram *abbr* = short-range attack missile.

SRAM *abbr* = static random access memory.

SRAP *abbr* (*Brit*) = Scottish Rent Assessment Panel.

SRBM *abbr* = short-range ballistic missile.

SRC *abbr* = Science Research Council; (*Brit*) Scottish Refugee Council; Sheriff Court Rules Council; (*Spanish*) *Sociedad Regolar Collectiva*, "partnership"; Student Representative Council.

srcc *abbr* = strikes, riots, and civil commotions.

SRCh *abbr* = State Registered Chiropodist.

SRCN *abbr* = State Registered Children's Nurse.

SRD *abbr* = Safety and Reliability Directorate; (*Brit*) State Registered Dietician.

SRDE *abbr* = Signals Research and Development Establishment.

SRE *abbr* (*Latin*) = *Sancta Romana Ecclesia*, "Holy Roman Church."

Sreng *n* (*Irish Celtic myth*) a Fir Bholg warrior who was despatched as an ambassador to have talks with the Tuatha De Danann when they landed with their invading force in Ireland.

SRG *abbr* = Strategic Research Group.

SRGC *abbr* (*Brit*) = Scottish Rock Garden Club.

SRHE *abbr* = Society for Research into Higher Education.

SRI *abbr* = (*Latin*) *Sacrum Romanum Imperium*, "Holy Roman Empire"; Saudi Arabian riyal.

Sri Lanka *n* an island republic lying in the Indian Ocean just off the southeastern tip of India, from which it is separated by the Palk Strait.

Sri Lankan rupee *n* currency of Sri Lanka.

SRIS *abbr* = Science Reference Information Service.

SRM *abbr* = short-range missile.

SRMN *abbr* (*Brit*) = State Registered Mental Nurse.

SRN *abbr* (*Brit*) = State Registered Nurse.

sRNA *abbr* = soluble ribonucleic acid.

SRNA *abbr* = Shipbuilders' and Repairers' National Association.

SRO *abbr* = (*Brit*) Scottish Record Office; self-regulatory organization; single room occupancy; Society of Registration Officers; standing room only; statutory rules and orders.

SRP *abbr* = Society for Radiological Protection; Society for Recorder Players; (*Brit*) State Registered Physiotherapist; suggested retail price.

SRPA *abbr* = Squash Rackets Professional Association.

SRPS *abbr* (*Brit*) = Scottish Railway Preservation Society.

SRR *abbr* = Society for Research in Rehabilitation.

SRS *abbr* = (*Brit*) Scottish Record Society; (*Brit*) Scottish Reformation Society; (*Brit*) Scottish Rhododendron Society; (*Brit*) (*Latin*) *Societatis Regiae Sodalis*, "Fellow of the Royal Society"; Surgical Research Society; Swiss Railways Society.

Srta. *abbr* = Señorita.

SRU *abbr* (*Brit*) = Scottish Research into UFOs; Scottish Rugby Union.

SRWS *abbr* (*Brit*) = Scottish Rights of Way Society.

ss. *abbr* (*Latin*) = *semis*, "one half."

SS *abbr* = Saints; (*Latin*) *Sancti*, "Saints"; (*Latin*) *Sanctissimus*, "Most Holy"; (*German*) *Schutzstaffel*, "protection group" (Nazi special police force); scilicet; screw steamer; Secretary of State; Secret Service; Social Security; Spastics Society; steamship; Statistical Society; Stereoscopic Society; Sunday School; (*Latin*) *supra scriptum*, "written above"; surface-to-surface (missile, etc).

SSA *abbr* = School Secretaries' Association; (*Brit*) Scottish Schoolmasters' Asssociation; (*Brit*) Scottish Skateboard Association; (*Brit*) Scottish Sound Archive; Side-Saddle Association; Silver Steel Association; Sisters of Saint Anne; Social Security Administration; (*Brit*) Society of Scottish Artists; standard spending assessment.

SSAC *abbr* = (*Brit*) Scottish Society for Autistic Children; (*Brit*) Scottish Sub-Aqua Club; Social Security Advisory Committee.

SSAD *abbr* (*Brit*) = Scottish Sports Association for People with Disabilities.

SSAE *abbr* = stamped, self-addressed envelope.

SSAFA *abbr* = Soldiers', Sailors', and Airmen's Families' Association.

SSAP *abbr* = Statement of Standard Accounting Practice.

SSB *abbr* (*Latin*) = *Sacrae Scripturae, Baccalaureus*, "Bachelor of Sacred Scripture."

SSC *abbr* = (*Brit*) Scottish Schoolboys' Club; (*Brit*) Scottish Ski Club; (*Brit*) Scottish Society of Composers; (*Brit*) Scottish Sports Council; Secretarial Studies Certificate; short service commission; Solicitor, Supreme Court; Surgical Society of China.

SSCA *abbr* = (*Brit*) Scottish Ship Chandlers' Association; Social Science Computing Association.

SSCR *abbr* (*Brit*) = Scottish Society for Crop Research.

SSD *abbr* = (*Latin*) *Sacrae Scripturae Doctor*, "Doctor of Sacred Scripture"; (*Latin*) *Sanctissimus Dominus*, "the most holy lord" (pope); Social Services Department.

SSE *abbr* = south-southeast.

SSEC *abbr* (*Brit*) = Secondary Schools Examinations Council.

SSEES *abbr* = School of Slavonic and East European Studies.

SSEG *abbr* (*Brit*) = Scottish Solar Energy Group.

SSF *abbr* = (*Brit*) Scottish Surfing Federation; Society for the Study of Fertility; Society of Saint Francis; Society of Shoe Fitters.

SSFA *abbr* (*Brit*) = Scottish Schools' Football Association; Shetland Salmon Farmers' Association.

SSFTA *abbr* (*Brit*) = Scottish Soft Fruit Trade Association.

SSGA *abbr* (*Brit*) = Scottish Salmon Growers' Association; Scottish Shellfish Growers' Association.

SSGBP *abbr* = Society of Snuff Grinders, Blenders, and Purveyors.

SSHA *abbr* (*Brit*) = Scottish Special Housing Association.

SSHC *abbr* = Society to Support Home Confinement.

SSI *abbr* = Sculptors' Society of Ireland; site of scientific interest; Social Services Inspectorate; site of scientific interest; Supplemental Security Income Program.

SSJE *abbr* = Society of Saint John the Evangelist.

SSL *abbr* (*Latin*) = *Sacrae Scripturae Licentiatus*, "Licentiate of Sacred Scripture."

SSLH *abbr* (*Brit*) = Society for the Study of Labour History.

SSM *abbr* = Saturday, Sunday, Monday; Staff Sergeant Major; surface-to-surface missile.

SSMH *abbr* (*Brit*) = Scottish Society for the Mentally Handicapped.

SSN *abbr* = severely subnormal; standard serial numer.

SSNTA (*Brit*) = Scottish Seed and Nursery Trade Association.

SSO *abbr* = Senior Supply Officer.

SSP *abbr* = (*Brit*) Scottish Socialist Party; (*Brit*) Scottish Society of Playwrights; statutory sick pay.

SSPCA *abbr* (*Brit*) = Scottish Society for the Prevention of Cruelty to Animals.

SSPS *abbr* (*Brit*) = Sheffield Sawmakers' Protection Society.

SSPWB *abbr* (*Brit*) = Scottish Society for the Protection of Wild Birds.

SSR *abbr* = Soviet Socialist Republic.

SSRA *abbr* (*Brit*) = Scottish Seaweed Research Association; Scottish Squash Rackets Association.

SSRC *abbr* = Social Science Research Council.

SSRI *abbr* = selective serotonin uptake inhibitor (an antidepressant drug).

SSS *abbr* = (*Brit*) Secretary of State for Scotland; Selective Service System; Ship Stamp Society; sick sinus syndrome; Simplifield Spelling Society; Sunday Shakespeare Society; standard scratch score.

SSSA *abbr* = (*Brit*) Scottish Salmon Smokers' Association; (*Brit*) Scottish Schools Swimming Association; Synthetic Sports Surfaces Association.

SSSI *abbr* = site of special scientific interest; Soil Science Society of Ireland.

SSSU *abbr* (*Brit*) = Scottish Speed Skating Union.

SST *abbr* = (*Brit*) Scottish Scenic Trust; (*Brit*) Scottish Sculpture Trust; supersonic transport.

SSTA *abbr* (*Brit*) = Scottish Secondary Teachers' Association.

S star *n* a red giant type of star that is similar to an M star but has bands of zirconium oxide.

SSU *abbr* = Sunday School Union.

SSW *abbr* = south-south-west.

SSWA *abbr* (*Brit*) = Scottish Solway Wildfowlers' Association.

st. *abbr* = stanza; stet; stone (weight); strophe.

s.t. *abbr* (*mus*) = shipping ticket; short ton.

St *abbr* = Saint.

St. *abbr* = Saturday; Statute(s); Strait; stratus; Street.

ST *abbr* = septic tank; Standard Time; Summer Time; Superintendent of Transportation.

sta. *abbr* = stationary; stator.

Sta. *abbr* = Santa; Station.

STA *abbr* = Sail Training Association; (*Brit*) Scottish Textile Association; (*Brit*) Scottish Trampoline Association; Solar Trade Association; Supersonic Tunnel Association (Sweden); Swimming Teachers' Association.

StAAA *abbr* (*Brit*) = St Andrew's Ambulance Association.

stab *vt* (**stabbing, stabbed**) to injure with a knife or pointed weapon; to pain suddenly and sharply. * *vi* to thrust at (as if) with a pointed weapon. * *n* an act or instance of stabbing; a wound made by stabbing; a sudden sensation, as of emotion, pain, etc; (*inf*) an attempt.

Stabat Mater *n* "His Mother stood," the initial words of a verse from the Gospel account of the Crucifixion.

stabile *n* an abstract sculpture resembling a mobile but stationary.

stability *see* **stable**[1].

stabilize *vti* to make or become stable or steady.—**stabilization** *n*.

stabilizer *n* a device for stabilizing an aircraft, ship, bicycle, etc.

stable[1] *adj* steady or firm; firmly established; permanent; not decomposing readily.—**stability** *n*.

stable[2] *n* a building where horses or cattle are kept; a group of racehorses belonging to one owner; a group of people, such as writers, performers, etc, working for or trained by a specific establishment. * *vti* to put, keep, or live in a stable.

stacc. *abbr* (*Italian*) = *staccato*, "detached" (music).

staccato *adj* (*musical notes*) short, abrupt; (*speech*) sharp, abrupt, disconnected. * *adv* in a staccato manner.

stack *n* a large neatly arranged pile (of hay, papers, CDs, etc); a chimney stack; a high, steep rock pillar close to a cliff but separated from it by the sea, formed when the arch joining it to a cliff collapses; (*inf*) a large amount of; a number of aircraft circling an airport waiting for permission to land. * *vt* to pile or arrange in a stack.

staddle stones *npl* (*archit*) mushroom-shaped stones supporting wooden structures such as hay barns or granaries.

stadium *n* (*pl* **stadiums** or **stadia**) a sports ground surrounded by tiers of seats; (*archit*) in ancient Greece, a running track.

staff *n* (*pl* **staves**) a strong stick or pole; (*mus*) one of the five horizontal lines upon which music is written (—*also* **stave**); (*pl* **staffs**) a body of officers who help a commanding officer or perform special duties; the workers employed in an establishment; the teachers or lecturers of an educational institution. * *vt* to provide with staff.

stag *n* a full-grown male deer; (*stock exch*) a person who applies for a large number of shares in a new share issue in the hope that the demand for the new shares will be in excess of the supply of the shares and that this will lead to an increase in the price of the shares when trading begins. * *adj* (*party*) for men only.

stag beetle *n* any of various beetles with large, pincer-like mandibles.

stage *n* a degree or step in a process; a raised platform, esp for acting on; (*with* **the**) the theater, the theatrical calling; any field of action or setting; a portion of a journey; a propulsion unit of a space rocket discarded when its fuel is spent. * *vt* to perform (a play) on the stage; to plan or organize (an event).

stagecoach *n* a four-wheeled vehicle drawn by horses, which formerly carried passengers or mail.

stagecraft *n* skill in writing or staging plays.

stage direction *n* an instruction in the text of a play (regarding characterization, movement, lighting, etc) for an actor or director.

stage door *n* the back entrance to a theater used by the staff and players.

stage fright *n* nervousness at appearing before an audience.

stagehand *n* a person who handles scenery or lighting in a drama production.

stage left *n* the area of a stage to the left of an actor facing the audience.

stage-manage *vt* to act as stage manager of; to organize or direct from behind the scenes.

stage manager *n* a person responsible for the stage arrangements prior to and during the performance of a play.

stage right *n* the area of a stage to the right of an actor facing the audience.

stage-struck *adj* obsessed with theater and the idea of becoming an actor.

stage whisper *n* a loud whisper made by an actor and intentionally audible to the audience.

stagey *see* **stagy**.

stagflation *n* an economic situation characterized by a combination of high inflation and stagnant or declining output and employment.

stagger *vi* to walk unsteadily, totter. * *vt* to astound; to give a shock to; to arrange so as not to overlap; to alternate.

staggering *adj* astounding.—**staggeringly** *adv*.

staging *n* a temporary platform, esp horizontal planking supported by scaffolding.

staging area *n* an assembly point for troops in transit.

staging post *n* a regular stopover point on a long route.

stagnant *adj* (*water*) not flowing, standing still with a revolting smell; unchanging, dull.—**stagnancy** *n*.

S

stagnant loop syndrome *n* (*med*) a condition in which a segment of the small intestine is discontinuous with the rest or when there is an obstruction, either of which causes slow movement through the intestines.

stagnate *vi* to be or become stagnant.—**stagnation** *n*.

stag party *n* a party for men only, usu given for one who is due to be married shortly.

STAGS *abbr* (*Brit*) = sterling accruable government securities.

stagy, stagey *adj* (**stagier, stagiest**) theatrical, dramatic.

staid *adj* sober; sedate; old-fashioned.—**staidly** *adv*.—**staidness** *n*.

stain *vt* to dye; to discolor with spots of something that cannot be removed. * *vi* to become stained; to produce stains. * *n* a discolored mark; a moral blemish; a dye or liquid for staining materials, e.g., wood.

stained glass *n* colored glass used in windows.

stainless *adj* free from stain; (*materials*) resistant to staining.—**stainlessly** *adv*.

stainless steel *n* a type of steel resistant to tarnishing and corrosion.

stair *n* a flight of stairs; a single step; (*pl*) a stairway.

staircase *n* a flight of stairs with banisters.

stairway *n* a staircase.

stairwell *n* the vertical shaft for a staircase.

stake¹ *n* a sharpened, metal or wooden post driven into the ground, as a marker or fence post; a post to which persons were tied for execution by burning; this form of execution. * *vt* to support with, tie or tether to a stake; to mark out (land) with stakes; (*with* **out**) to put under surveillance.

stake² *vt* to bet; (*inf*) to provide with money or resources. * *n* a bet; a financial interest; (*pl*) money risked on a race; (*pl*) the prize in a race

stakeholder *n* (*com*) a person who has an interest in the operation and performance of a company.

stakeout *n* surveillance, esp by police; premises under surveillance.

stalactite *n* an icicle-like calcium deposit hanging from the roof of a cave.

stalag *n* a German prisoner-of-war camp in World War II.

stalagmite *n* a cylindrical deposit projecting upward from the floor of a cave, caused by the dripping of water and lime from the roof.

stale *adj* deteriorated from age; tainted; musty; stagnant; jaded.—**staleness** *n*.

stale cheque *n* (*Brit*) a check that has not been presented for payment within a six-month period and so will not be honored by banks.

stalemate *n* (*chess*) a situation in which a king can only be moved in and out of check, thus causing a draw; a deadlock.—*also vt*.

Stalin *n* **Joseph** [**Josef Vissarionovich Dzhugashvili**] (1879–1953) Soviet dictator, who assumed absolute power following the Bolshevik Revolution. His regime was marked by relentless purges of his enemies. His forces occupied Eastern Europe following Hitler's defeat.

Stalinism *n* the theory and practice of authoritarian rule associated with Joseph Stalin.—**Stalinist** *n, adj*.

stalk¹ *n* the stem of a plant.

stalk² *vi* to stride in a stiff or angry way. * *vt* to hunt (game or prey) stealthily.—**stalker** *n*.

stalking-horse *n* a means of concealing true intentions; a candidate standing in an election to confuse the opposition or test the amount of prospective support for the real candidate in whose favor the stand-in then withdraws.

stall¹ *n* a compartment for one animal in a stable; a table or stand for the display or sale of goods; a stalling of an engine; (*aircraft*) a loss of lift and downward plunge due to an excessive decrease in airspeed; (*archit*) a fixed seat in a church or cathedral, usu covered partially at the back and/or sides; (*pl*) (*Brit*) the seats on the ground floor of a theater. * *vti* (*vehicle engine*) to stop or cause to stop suddenly, e.g., by misuse of the clutch; (*aircraft*) to lose or cause to lose lift because of an excessive reduction in airspeed.

stall² *vi* to play for time. * *vt* to postpone or delay. * *n* (*inf*) any action used in stalling.

stallion *n* an uncastrated male horse, esp one kept for breeding.

stalwart *adj* strong, sturdy; resolute; dependable. * *n* a loyal, hard-working supporter.

stamen *n* (*pl* **stamens** *or* **stamina**) the pollen-bearing part of a flower.

sta. mi. *abbr* = statute miles.

stamina *n* strength; staying power.

staminate *adj* (*plants*) having or producing stamens.

Stamitz *n* **Karl** (1745–1801) German-born violinist and composer of Czech descent. His works include 70 symphonies, a symphony for two orchestras, and two operas. His father, Johann, and brother, Anton, were also noted musicians.

stammer *vi* to pause or falter in speaking; to stutter.—*also n*.—**stammerer** *n*.

stamp *vt* to put a mark on; to imprint with an official seal; to affix a postage stamp to; (*with* **out**) to extinguish by stamping; to suppress or eradicate by force. * *vi* to bring the foot down heavily (on); * *n* a postage stamp; the mark canceling a postage stamp; a block for imprinting.

stamp duty *or* **stamp tax** *n* a tax on some types of legal documents.

stampede *n* an impulsive rush of a panic-stricken herd; a rush of a crowd.—*also vti*.

stamping ground *n* (*inf*) a favorite or habitual meeting place.

stance *n* posture; the attitude taken in a given situation,

stanch *see* **staunch**².

stanchion *n* an upright post, pillar, rod. or similar support. * *vt* to provide with a stanchion.

stand *vi* (**standing, stood**) to be in an upright position; to be on or rise to one's feet; to make resistance; to remain unchanged; to endure, tolerate; to reach a deadlock; (*with* **by**) to look on without interfering; to be available for use if required; (*with* **down**) to withdraw, resign; to leave a witness box after testifying in court; (*soldier*) to go off duty; (*with* **off**) to remain at a distance; to reach a stalemate; (*with* **up**) to rise to one's feet. * *vt* to put upright; to endure, tolerate; (*with* **by**) to remain loyal to, defend; (*with* **off**) to (cause to) keep at a distance; to lay off (employees) temporarily; (*with* **up**) to resist; to withstand criticism, close examination, etc; (*inf*) to fail to keep an appointment with. * *n* a strong opinion; a standing position; a standstill; (*pl*) a structure for taxis awaiting hire; (*pl*) a structure for spectators; the place taken by a witness for testifying in court; a piece of furniture for hanging things from; a stall or booth for a small retail business; a grouping of trees of the same type in a forest.

stand-alone *n, adj* (*comput*) (denoting) a computer system that is self-contained and has only the hardware and software required by the user.

standard *n* a flag, banner, or emblem; an upright pole, a pillar; an authorized weight or measure; a criterion; an established or accepted level of achievement; (*comput*) a pre-defined set of guidelines that is set by the manufacturers to determine the type of interface between a peripheral device and the computer and the way the device communicates with the processor; (*pl*) moral principles. * *adj* serving as a standard; typical; (*comput*) denoting a standard.

standard atmosphere *n* an accepted condition of the atmosphere for use in calibrating instruments and measuring altitudes. The most commonly accepted standard atmosphere is based on a surface temperature of 59°F and surface pressure of 1013.25 millibars or 760 millimeters of mercury.

standard-bearer *n* a person who carries a standard; the leader of a particular cause or party.

standard cost *n* an estimated product cost that indicates in advance of production what a product ought to cost on the basis of reasonably efficient operations.

standard gauge *n* a railroad gauge of 4 feet 8 inches.

standardize *vt* to make standard; to reduce to a standard.—**standardization** *n*. —**standardizer** *n*.

standard of living *n* the level of material comforts enjoyed by an individual, family, group, or community.

standard time *n* the time, based on the sun's position at noon, that is used for timekeeping within a country calculated at a meridian that is roughly central to the country. Very large countries, such as the USA, have several time zones.

stand-by *n* (*pl* **stand-bys**) a person or thing held in readiness for use in an emergency, etc.—*also adj*.

stand-in *n* a substitute; a person who takes the place of an actor during the preparation of a scene or in stunts.—*also vi*.

standing *n* status or reputation; length of service, duration. * *adj* upright; permanent; (*jump*) performed from a stationary position.

standing army *n* a permanent body of paid soldiers as maintained by a nation.

standing order *n* an instruction to a bank by a depositor to pay fixed amounts at regular intervals (for bills, etc); a regulation governing conduct, procedure, etc in an organization or assembly.

standing wave *n* (*phys*) a disturbance produced when two similar wave motions are transmitted in opposite directions at the same time.

standoff *n* a deadlock, stalemate.

standoffish *adj* aloof, reserved.

standpipe *n* a vertical pipe with a tap providing an external water supply.

standpoint *n* a point of view, opinion.

standstill *n* a complete halt.

stand-up *adj* (*collar*) upright; (*fight*) furious; (*comedian*) telling jokes standing alone in front of an audience.

Stanford *n* **Charles Villiers** (1852–1924) Irish-born composer, remembered for his opera *Shamus O'Brien*, and his 3rd (*Irish*) symphony.

Stanislavsky *n* **Konstantin** (1863–1938) Russian director and actor and co-founder of the Moscow Art Theatre in 1897. His theory of acting (method acting) has been influential.

stank *see* **stink**.

Stanley¹ *n* capital city of Falkland Islands.

Stanley² *n* **John** (1713–86) English composer and famous organist, blind from early childhood. His works include concertos for strings, pieces for flute, and compositions for organ.

stannic *adj* of or containing (tetravalent) tin.

stannous *adj* of or containing (bivalent) tin.

stanza *n* a group of lines that form a division of a poem.

stapes *n* small bone (stirrup) of the middle ear.

staphylococcus *n* (*pl* **staphylococci**) any of a group of minute spherical bacteria of the genus *Staphylococcus* that are normally present on skin and mucous membranes.

staple¹ *n* a principal commodity of trade or industry of a region or nation; a main constituent. * *adj* chief.

staple² *n* a U-shaped, thin piece of wire for fastening. * *vt* to fasten with a staple.

star *n* any one of the celestial bodies, esp those visible by night, which appear as small points of light, including planets, comets, meteors, and less commonly the sun and moon; a figure with five points; an exceptionally successful or skillful person; a famous actor, actress, musician, etc. * *vti* (**starring, starred**) to feature or be featured as a star.

Star Carr *n* a Mesolithic site a few miles south of Scarborough in England.

star catalog *n* a database on stars, providing observations and information concerning position, magnitude, and related properties.

star cluster *n* a group of stars thought to have the same origin.

star dot star *n* (*comput*) (*inf*) the wildcard search command where *.* finds all files because the asterisk can represent any set of characters.

star network *n* (*comput*) a representation of a network where the network server is located in a central position and the user stations are connected around this central point and not to one another.

Star of David *n* a six-pointed star formed by two intersecting triangles, a hexagram.

Star-Spangled Banner *n* (*with the*) the national anthem of the USA; the Stars and Stripes.

star warrior *n* one who advocates the US's Strategic Defense Initiative.

Star Wars *n sing* the popular name for the Strategic Defense Initiative.

starboard *n* the right side of a ship or aircraft when facing the bow.

starburst galaxy *n* a galaxy in which there is a very high rate of star formation occurring, with an associated and very high production of infrared radiation.

starch *n* a white, tasteless food substance found in potatoes, cereal, etc; a fabric stiffener based on this. * *vt* to stiffen with starch.—**starchy** *adj*.

Starck *n* Philippe (1949–) Prolific French designer, whose products are notable also for their unusual names.

star-crossed *adj* ill-fated; unfortunate.

stardom *n* the fame and status enjoyed by celebrities or stars.

stardust *n* a large cluster of distant stars appearing as dust; a feeling of romance.

stare *vi* to gaze fixedly, as in horror, astonishment, etc; to glare. * *n* a fixed gaze.

starfish *n* (*pl* **starfish** *or* **starfishes**) an echinoderm consisting of a central disk from which five arms radiate outward.

stargaze *vi* to look at the stars; to daydream.

stark *adj* bare; plain; blunt; utter. * *adv* completely.—**starkly** *adv*.—**starkness** *n*.

stark-naked *or* **starkers** *adj* (*inf*) completely naked.

starlet *n* a young actress regarded as a potential star.

starling *n* any of a family of small songbirds, esp a common European bird with black plumage tinged with green that congregates in large groups.

Starn *n* (*Irish Celtic myth*) a son of Sera and brother of Partholan.

Starov *n* Ivan Y (1744–1808) Russian architect, whose notable works include Tauride Palace, St Petersburg.

Starr *n* Ringo [Richard Starkey] (1940–) English rock drummer and singer. He was the Beatles' drummer (1962–70), and occasionally sang on their records, notably "Yellow Submarine."

starry-eyed *adj* dreamy, impractical, overly optimistic.

Stars and Stripes *n sing* 1. (*with the*) the national flag of the USA consisting of 13 alternate red-and-white stripes and a blue square filled with white stars representing the individual states.—*also* **Star-Spangled Banner**. 2. (*with The*) the song officially adopted as the US national anthem in 1931, with words written by Francis Scott Key in 1814 to a tune by John Stafford Smith.

star-studded *adj* featuring many celebrities.

start *vi* to commence, begin; to jump involuntarily, from fright. * *vt* to begin. * *n* a beginning; a slight, involuntary body movement; a career opening.

START *abbr* = Strategic Arms Reduction Talks *or* Treaty.

start bit *n* (*comput*) the initial bit sent in serial communications that indicates to the receiving computer that the byte of data is about to be sent.

starter *n* a person who starts something, esp an official who signals the beginning of a race; a competitor in a race; the first course of a meal; a small electric motor used to start an internal-combustion engine (—*also* **self-starter**).

starting block *n* one of a pair of angled wooden or metal pads or blocks against which a sprinter braces the feet in crouch starts.

starting gate *n* (*horseracing*) a removable barrier holding each horse in line and which is raised to start a race.

starting grid *n* (*motor racing*) the numbered grid where drivers line up at the start of a race, position being determined by the times gained in practice laps.

starting price *n* (*esp horseracing*) the final odds on a horse offered by bookmakers at the start of a race.

starting stalls *npl* the metal enclosures for horses at the starting line with gates that spring open simultaneously to start the race.

startle *vt* to cause to be frightened or surprised.—**startling** *adj*.

start-up disk *n* (*comput*) a disk that contains the operating system code required to start the computer.

starve *vi* to die or suffer from a lack of food. * *vt* deprive (a person) of food; to deprive of (anything necessary).—**starvation** *n*.

STAS *abbr* (*Brit*) = Scottish Training Advisory Service.

stash *vt* to hide (money, etc) for future use. * *n* a hiding place; something hidden; (*sl*) drugs hidden for personal consumption.

stasis *n* (*pl* **stases**) a stoppage in the flow of bodily fluids, e.g. blood; a state of balance or inactivity.

Stasov *n* Vasily P (*b.* 1769) Russian architect, whose notable works include Moscow Gate.

stat. *abbr* = statuary; statue; statute(s).

Stat. *or* **Stat.atL.** *abbr* = Statutes at Large.

state *n* condition; frame of mind; position in society; ceremonial style; (*with cap*) an area or community with its own government, or forming a federation under a sovereign government. * *adj* of the state or State; public; ceremonial. * *vt* to express in words; to specify, declare officially.

statecraft *n* the art of government; statesmanship.

state department *n* the government department that handles foreign affairs; foreign office.

State House *n* the building that houses a state legislature in the US.

stateless *adj* not having a nationality.—**statelessness** *n*.

stately *adj* (**statelier, stateliest**) dignified; majestic.—**stateliness** *n*.

stately home *n* a large country mansion, usu of historical interest, which is open to the public.

statement *n* a formal announcement; a declaration; a document showing one's bank balance.

statement of account *n* (*com*) a document that records the nature and value of the products that have been supplied and also records any amounts of money that are still owed.

"State Of Maine Song" *n* the song of the American state, Maine.

state-of-the-art *adj* using the most advanced technology yet possible.

stateroom *n* a luxury private cabin in a ship; a large room in a palace used for state occasions.

States *n sing or pl* the USA.

state school *n* (*Brit*) any school funded by the state which provides free education.

stateside *adj* of, in, or to the USA.—*also adv*.

statesman *n* (*pl* **statesmen**) a well-known and experienced politician.—**statesmanship** *n*.

state tax lien *n* (*law*) a lien filed by the State of Texas against any real estate owned by a person who has failed to pay all of his or her state, city, or metropolitan transit-authority sales taxes in the county in which the lien is filed.

static *adj* fixed; stationary; at rest. * *n* electrical interference causing noise on radio or TV.

static electricity *n* electricity which is stationary as opposed to flowing in a current.

statics *n sing* the branch of mechanics dealing with the forces that produce a state of equilibrium.

station *n* a train or bus terminal or stop; headquarters (of the emergency services); military headquarters; (*inf*) a TV channel; position in society, standing. * *vt* to assign to a post, place, office.

stationary *adj* not moving.

stationary orbit *n* (*astron*) the orbit of a satellite around a body such that the satellite stays above a fixed point about the latter's equator.

stationer *n* a dealer in stationery, office supplies, etc.

stationery *n* writing materials, esp paper and envelopes.

stationery document *n* (*comput*) see **stylesheet**.

station house *n* a building that houses police or fire services.

stationmaster *n* the senior official in charge of a train station.

station wagon *n* a car with extra carrying space reached through a rear door.

statism *n* the concentration of economic and political power in the state.—**statist** *n*.

statistic *n* a fact obtained from analyzing information expressed in numbers.

statistics *n sing* the branch of mathematics dealing with the collection, analysis, and presentation of numerical data.—**statistical** *adj*.—**statistician** *n*.

stator *n* the stationary part of a motor or generator.

statoscope *n* a sensitive aneroid barometer for indicating minute fluctuations in pressure, used in altimeters in aircraft.

statuary *n* (*pl* **statuaries**) statues collectively.

statue *n* a representation of a human or animal form that is carved or molded.

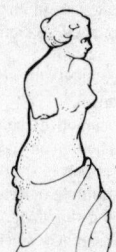

statue menhir *n* an upright slab upon which is carved a rudimentary human figure.

statuesque *adj* like a statue.—**statuesquely** *adv*.—**statuesqueness** *n*.

statuette *n* a small statue, figurine.

stature *n* the standing height of a person; level of attainment.

status *n* (*pl* **statuses**) social or professional position or standing; prestige; condition or standing from the point of view of the law, position of affairs.

status quo *n* the existing state of affairs.

status symbol *n* a possession that indicates high social standing, wealth, etc.

statute *n* a law enacted by a legislature; a regulation.

statute book *n* a register of statutes enacted by a legislature.

statute law n law enacted by a legislature.

statute mile n (formal) a mile.

statute of limitations n a statute that restricts the period of time in which proceedings may be brought to enforce a right or punish an offense.

statutory adj established, regulated, or required by statute.

statutory audit n an audit of a company's financial records.

statutory books npl the financial records that a company is required to keep.

statutory meeting n a meeting that is held by a company in accordance with the relevant legislation, usu the annual general meeting of shareholders.

statutory offense n a crime as established by statute.

statutory rape n sexual intercourse with a female who is below the statutory age of consent.

Stauffenberg n **Count Berthold von** (1907–44) German soldier. He was one of the chief conspirators in the 20 July 1944 assassination attempt on Adolf Hitler, shortly after which he was executed.

STAUK abbr = Seed Trade Association of the United Kingdom.

staunch[1] adj loyal; dependable.—**staunchly** adv.—**staunchness** n.

staunch[2] vt to stem the flow of (blood, etc). * vi to cease to flow.—also **stanch**.

Stavanger n a city in the Kingdom of Norway.

stave n a piece of wood of a cask or barrel; (mus) a staff. * vt (**staving, staved** or **stove**) (usu with **in**) to smash or dent inward.

staves see **staff**.

STAWRS abbr = Simplified Tax and Wage Reporting System

stay[1] n a rope supporting a mast; (archit) a structural diagonal bar, trace, or strut used to prevent movement in a structure.

stay[2] vi to remain in a place; to wait; to reside temporarily. * vt to support; to endure; to stop, restrain. * n a suspension of legal proceedings; a short time spent as a visitor or guest.

stay-at-home n a quiet, placid, unadventurous person.—also adj.

staying power n stamina.

STB abbr = (Latin) Sacrae Theologiae Baccalaureus, "Bachelor of Sacred Theology"; (Latin) Scientiae Theologiae Baccalaureus, "Bachelor of Theology"; (Brit) Scottish Tourist Board; set-top box (for digital TV); Surface Transportation Board.

St Bernard n a Saint Bernard dog.

STC abbr = Scandinavian Trade Centre; short-title catalog; Standard Telephones and Cables Limited; subject to contract; Surgical Textiles Conference.

St. Cu. abbr = stratocumulus.

std. abbr = standard.

STD abbr = (Latin) Sacrae Theologiae Doctor, "Doctor of Sacred Theology"; (Latin) Scientiae Theologicae Doctor, "Doctor of Theology"; sexually transmitted disease; Society of Teachers of the Deaf; (Brit) subscriber trunk dialling.

Stdy. abbr = Saturday.

STE abbr = Society of Telecom Executives.

steadfast adj firm, fixed; resolute.—**steadfastly** adv.—**steadfastness** n.

steady adj (**steadier, steadiest**) firm, stable; regular, constant; calm, unexcitable. * n (pl **steadies**) (inf) a regular boyfriend or girlfriend. * vti (**steadying, steadied**) to make or become steady.—**steadily** adv.—**steadiness** n.

steady-state theory n the theory that the universe remains in a steady equilibrium as matter is continuously created as it expands.

steak n a slice of meat, esp beef or fish, for grilling or frying.

steakhouse n a restaurant that specializes in steaks.

steal vt (**stealing, stole,** pp **stolen**) to take from someone dishonestly; to obtain secretly. * n (inf) an unbelievable bargain.

stealth n a manner of moving quietly and secretly.

Stealth technology n the development, in great secrecy, of a new type of military aircraft.

stealthy adj (**stealthier, stealthiest**) acting or performed in a quiet, secret manner; unobtrusive, furtive.—**stealthily** adv.—**stealthiness** n.

steam n the hot mist or vapor created by boiling water. * vi to give off steam; to move by steam power; (sl) to take part in illegal steaming; (with **up**) (glasses, windows) to become covered in condensation. * vt to cook with steam. * adj driven by steam.

steam bath n a room or enclosure filled with steam for bathing in.

steamboat n a boat powered by steam.

steam engine n a stationary or locomotive engine powered by steam.

steamer n a pan with a perforated bottom for cooking by steam; a ship propelled by steam engines; (sl) one who takes part in steaming.

steaming n (sl) the practice of multiple mugging by a gang of youths who move rapidly down a street, mugging and shiplifting.

steam iron n an electric iron that can heat water to use as steam which is emitted through the face to improve pressing.

steamroller n a vehicle with heavy rollers for pressing down road surfaces; an overpowering person or thing. * vt to crush (as if) with a steamroller; to obtain or influence by overpowering force.

steamy adj (**steamier, steamiest**) full of steam; (inf) erotic.—**steamily** adv.—**steaminess** n.

stearic acid n a fatty acid derived from solid fats and used for making candles and soap.

steatite n soapstone.

steato- prefix fat.

steed n (arch, poet) a horse.

steel n an alloy of iron and carbon; strength or courage. * adj of or like steel. * vt to cover with steel; to harden; to nerve (oneself).

steel band n a band that uses percussion instruments made from oil drums.

steel drum n (mus) a percussion instrument ("pan") made by West Indian musicians (particularly from Trinidad) out of discarded oil drums. Each drum can be tuned to play a range of notes by beating and heat-treating different sections of the "head," i.e., the top, of the drum.

Steele n **Sir Richard** (1672–1729) Anglo-Irish essayist and dramatist, who was a close associate of Addison, with whom he was chief contributor to The Tatler (1709–11) and The Spectator (1711–12).

steel gray n a bluish-gray color.

steel wool n a compact mass of steel fibers used for scouring and polishing.

steely adj (**steelier, steeliest**) of or like steel; hard, relentless.—**steeliness** n.

steelyard n a balance using a pivoted graduated arm along which a weight slides.

steenbok n (pl **steenboks** or **steenbok**) any of a genus of small antelopes of central and southern Africa.

steep[1] adj sloping sharply; (inf) excessive, exorbitant.—**steeply** adv.—**steepness** n.

steep[2] vti to soak or be soaked in a liquid; to saturate; to imbue.—also n.

steepen vti to make or become steeper.

steeple n a tower of a church, with or without a spire; the spire alone.

steeplechase n a horse race across country or on a course over jumps; a track race over hurdles and water jumps.—**steeplechaser** n.

steeplejack n a person who climbs and repairs tall chimneys.

steer[1] n a castrated male of the cattle family.

steer[2] vti to direct (a vehicle, ship, bicycle, etc) in the correct direction of travel.

steerage n the cheapest berths on a passenger ship.

steerageway n a rate of forward motion that allows a vessel to be steered.

steering n the mechanism that controls the direction of a ship, vehicle, etc.

steering committee n a committee that organizes the content and order of business for a legislative assembly.

steering wheel n a wheel used for controlling the direction of a vehicle, ship, etc.

stegosaur or **stegosaurus** n (pl **stegosaurs** or **stegosauri**) any of various plant-eating dinosaurs with armored body plates.

Steichen n **Edward** (1879–1973) Luxembourg-born American photographer. He was a founder of the Photo-Secession group with Alfred Stieglitz and others, and organized The Family of Man (1955) photography exhibition, which was highly influential in its portrayal of the unity of mankind.

stein n an earthenware beer mug, often with a hinged lid.

Stein[1] n **Gertrude** (1874–1946) American writer, whose works include Three Lives (1908).

Stein[2] n **Jock [John]** (1922–85) Scottish soccer player and manager. He was manager of Glasgow Celtic (1965–78) and manager of the Scotland team.

Steinbeck n **John [Ernst]** (1902–68) American novelist, who achieved great success with his novels about America's rural poor, e.g., Of Mice and Men and Grapes of Wrath. He was awarded the Nobel Prize for Literature in 1962.

Steiner n **Rudolf** (1861–1925) Austrian philosopher, who formed his own movement of "anthroposophy" in 1912.

Steinway & Sons n (mus) a firm of piano manufacturers founded by Heinrich Steinweg (Henry Steinway) in New York in 1853.

stele n (pl **stelae** or **steles**) an upright slab of stone with inscriptions dating from prehistoric times; an inscribed commemorative slab placed on the front of a building; the vascular tissue in the stems and roots of plants.

stellar adj of or composed of stars.

stellar evolution n (astron) the various stages of the life of a star, which begins with the creation of the star from the condensation of gas, primarily hydrogen.

stellar vault n (archit) an ornate vault with a star-shaped pattern created by intersecting ribs, liernes, and tiercerons.

stellar wind n an outpouring of matter from a hot star which is particularly large for red giants and ultraviolet stars, where the winds flow at vast speeds.

stellate or **stellated** adj of, resembling, or composed of stars.

stellular adj filled with or composed of small stars; star-shaped.

St Elmo's fire n a flame-like electric discharge from a ship's mast and rigging in thundery weather.—also **corposant**.

stem[1] n a plant stalk; the upright slender part of anything, such as a wineglass; the root of a word; (mus) the line, or "tail," attached to the head of all notes smaller than a whole note. * vi (**stemming, stemmed**) to originate (from).

stem[2] vt (**stemming, stemmed**) to stop or check (the flow or tide).

STEM abbr = scanning transmission electron microscopy.

stench n a foul odor.

stencil n a pierced sheet of card or metal for reproducing letters by applying paint; a design so made. * vti to produce (letters, etc) or designs using a stencil.—**stenciler** n.

Stendhal n [Henri Beyle] (1788–1842) French novelist and critic, noted for his great mastery of character analysis in such historical novels as The Red and the Black and The Charterhouse of Parma.

Sten gun n a light sub-machine gun.

stenography n shorthand.—**stenographer** n.

stenosis n (pl **stenoses**) an abnormal narrowing of a bodily passage or orifice.—**stenotic** adj.

stent n a device used in surgery to help the healing of two structures that have been joined by draining away the contents.

stentorian *adj* (*voice*) loud, booming.

step *n* one movement of the foot ahead in walking, running, or dancing; a pace; a grade or degree; a stage toward a goal; one tread of a stair, rung of a ladder. * *vti* (**stepping, stepped**) to take a step or a number of paces.

step- *prefix* related by remarriage of a spouse or parent.

stepbrother *n* a son of one's step-parent from a former marriage.

stepchild *n* (*pl* **stepchildren**) a stepson or stepdaughter.

stepdaughter *n* the daughter of one's spouse from a former marriage.

stepfather *n* the husband of one's remarried mother.

stephanotis *n* a tropical climbing plant with fragrant white flowers.

Stephen *n* 1. **Saint** (first century) one of seven deacons appointed by the Apostles to relieve them of the routine duties of giving alms; the first Christian martyr. His feast day is 26 December. 2. (1096–1154) king of England (1135–1154). The son of Stephen, Count of Blois, and Adela, daughter of William the Conqueror. Succeeded by Henry II, the first of the Plantagenet kings.

stepladder *n* a short, portable ladder with flat steps fixed within a frame.

stepmother *n* the wife of one's remarried father.

step-parent *n* a stepfather or stepmother.

steppe *n* a vast, grassy, treeless plain.

stepping stone *n* a stone or stones allowing a stream, puddle, etc to be crossed by foot; a means of advancing toward some end.

stepsister *n* the daughter of one's step-parent from a former marriage

stepson *n* the son of one's spouse from a former marriage

step-trenching *n* (*archeo*) a method of excavation in which a large area narrows with depth by means of a number of large steps.

ster. *abbr* = sterling.

steradian *n* a unit of solid angular measurement.

stere *n* a unit equal to one cubic meter (35.3 cubic feet), used for measuring timber.

stereo *n* (*pl* **stereos**) a hi-fi with two loudspeakers; stereophonic sound. * *adj* stereophonic.

stereo. *abbr* = stereotype.

stereochemistry *n* the study of the composition and properties of matter in relation to the spatial arrangement of atoms in molecules.

stereograph *n* two almost identical images that when superimposed and viewed through a stereoscope produce a three-dimensional picture.

stereophonic *adj* (*sound-reproduction system*) using two separate channels for recording and transmission to create a spatial effect.—**stereophonically** *adv*.—**stereophony** *n*.

stereoscope *n* an optical device that blends two images viewed from a slightly different aspect into a single three-dimensional picture.—**stereoscopic** *adj*.

stereoscopy *n* viewing objects in three dimensions.

stereotaxis *n* (*biol*) the movement or reaction of an organism due to its contact with a solid body.

stereotype *n* a fixed, general image of a person or thing shared by many people.—*also vt*.

steric *adj* of or pertaining to the spatial arrangement of atoms in a molecule.

sterile *adj* unable to produce offspring, fruit, seeds, or spores; fruitless; free from germs.—**sterility** *n*.

sterilize *vt* to render incapable of reproduction; to free from germs.—**sterilization** *n*.—**sterilizer** *n*.

sterling *n* the British system of money. * *adj* of excellent character.

stern[1] *adj* severe; austere, harsh.—**sternly** *adv*.—**sternness** *n*.

stern[2] *n* the rear part of a boat or ship.

Stern *n* **Isaac** (1920–) a Russian-born violinist, who has lived in the USA since childhood. He made his first public appearance (in the USA) at the age of 15 and has remained a premier solo performer ever since.

Sterne *n* **Laurence** (1713–68) Irish-born English novelist, whose wildly eccentric "novel," *The Life and Opinions of Tristram Shandy*, created a sensation in the 1760s with its deliberately disordered narrative, lack of plot, and practical jokes on the reader.

sternum *n* (*pl* **sterna** *or* **sternums**) the breastbone.

sternutation *n* sneezing.

sternutator *n* a substance that induces sneezing, tears, etc, such as a gas used in riot control.

steroid *n* any of a large number of compounds sharing the same chemical structure, including sterols and many hormones; any of a group of lipids with a characteristic structure comprising four carbon rings fused together.

sterol *n* any of various solid steroid alcohols, such as cholesterol, found in plants and animals.

stertorous *adj* characterized by heavy breathing or snoring sounds.—**stertorously** *adv*.—**stertorousness** *n*.

stesso *adj* (*mus*) same, so *lo stesso tempo* means "the same speed."

stet *interj* a proofreading direction meaning that deleted matter marked by a row of dots should remain. * *vt* (**stetting, stetted**) to mark (text) in this way.

stethoscope *n* an instrument used to detect body sounds.—**stethoscopic** *adj*.

stetson *n* a man's felt hat with a broad brim and high crown.

Steuben *n* American glasswork manufacturer founded in 1903, and an important center for the study of glass-making.

stevedore *n* a laborer who loads and unloads ships.

Stevens *n* 1. **Brooks** (1911–) American industrial designer of the first outboard motor and the 1950 Harley-Davidson motorcycle. 2. **Wallace** (1878–1955) American poet, whose collections include *Harmonium*, *The Man with the Blue Guitar*, and *Collected Poems*. He also published a book of essays, *The Necessary Angel*, and the posthumous *Opus Posthumous*.

Stevens-Johnson syndrome *n* a common hypersensitivity reaction to sulfonamide antibiotics, and a form of erythema that produces skin lesions, in which the eyes and mucosa may ulcerate.

Stevenson *n* 1. **Adlai E[wing]** (1900–65) American Democrat politician. A noted liberal and intellectual, who was much respected abroad, he stood twice against Dwight D Eisenhower as the Democratic presidential candidate (1952, 1956). His campaign speeches were published as *Call to Greatness* (1954) and *What I Think* (1956). 2. **Robert Louis [Balfour]** (1850–94) Scottish novelist, poet, and essayist, whose works include *Treasure Island* (1883), *Travels with a Donkey in the Cevennes* (1879) and *The Strange Case of Dr Jekyll and Mr Hyde* (1886).

Stevenson screen *n* a box designed to protect meteorological instruments from conditions that might lead to inaccurate readings.

stew *n* a meal of cooked meat with vegetables. * *vt* to cook slowly.

steward *n* a manager (of property); a race organizer; a person who serves food on an aircraft or ship and looks after passengers.

stewardess *n* a woman who serves food on an aircraft or ship and looks after passengers.

Stewart *n* 1. **Jackie [John Young Stewart]** (1939–) Scottish racing driver, and world champion (1969, 1971, and 1973). 2. **J[ohn] I[nnes] M[ackintosh]** [pen name **Michael Innes**] (1906–94) Scottish novelist and critic, who published around 30 detective novels featuring Inspector John Appleby. Under his own name, he published several notable works of criticism, most notably *Eight Modern Writers*. 3. **[Lady] Mary [Florence Elinor]** (1916–) British writer of thrillers and children's adventure stories.

St. Ex. *abbr* = Stock Exchange.

stg. *abbr* = sterling.

stge. *abbr* = storage.

STGWU *abbr* (*Brit*) = Scottish Transport and General Workers' Union.

STH *abbr* = somatrophic hormone.

St Helena *n* a volcanic island in the south Atlantic Ocean, which is a British overseas territory and an administrative center for the islands of Tristan da Cunha to the south and Ascension Island to the north.

Sthenelus *n* (*Greek myth*) one of the Epigoni, who captured Thebes and who fought at Troy.

Stheno *see* Gorgons.

stick[1] *vt* (**sticking, stuck**) to pierce or stab; to attach with glue, adhesive tape, etc; (*with* **up**) (*inf*) to rob at gunpoint. * *vi* to cling to, adhere; to stay close to; to be held up; (*with* **around**) (*inf*) to wait in the vicinity, linger; (*with* **by**) to remain faithful to; to stay close to.

stick[2] *n* a broken-off shoot or branch of a tree; a walking stick; a hockey stick; a rod.

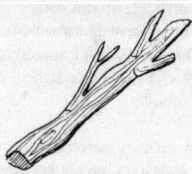

sticker *n* an adhesive label or poster.

sticking plaster *n* (*Brit*) an adhesive bandage.

stick insect *n* a wingless insect with a long, thin body resembling a twig.

stick-in-the-mud *n* (*inf*) a person who feels threatened by new ideas or situations.

stickleback *n* any of various small freshwater fishes with sharp spines on the back.

stickler *n* a person who is scrupulous or obstinate about something.

stick-up *n* (*inf*) a robbery at gunpoint.

sticky *adj* (**stickier, stickiest**) covered with adhesive or something sweet; (*weather*) warm and humid; (*inf*) difficult.—**stickily** *adv*.—**stickiness** *n*.

sticky end *n* (*inf*) an unpleasant death.

sticky wicket *n* (*cricket*) a damp wicket that is difficult to bat on; (*inf*) an awkward or unpleasant situation.

Stieglitz *n* **Alfred** (1864–1946) American photographer, who formed the Photo-Secession group with Edward Steichen, which became a highly influential force for establishing photography as an art form. He also founded the magazine *Camera Work* (1903–17).

stiff *adj* not flexible or supple; rigid; firm; moving with difficulty; having aching joints and muscles; formal, unfriendly; (*drink*) potent; (*breeze*) strong; (*penalty*) severe. * *n* (*sl*) a corpse. * *adv* utterly.—**stiffly** *adv*.—**stiffness** *n*.

stiffen *vti* to make or become stiff.—**stiffener** *n*.

stiff-necked *adj* stubborn, aloof.

stifle *vt* to suffocate; to smother; to suppress, hold back.

stifling *adj* excessively hot and stuffy.

stigma *n* (*pl* **stigmas** *or* **stigmata**) a social disgrace; the part of a flower that receives pollen; (*Christianity*) marks resembling the wounds of Christ thought to appear on the bodies of saintly people.

stigmatize *vt* to brand as bad or disgraceful.—**stigmatization** *n*.

stilbestrol *n* a synthetic estrogen that relieves menstrual disorders and menopausal symptoms and is helpful in treating breast and prostate cancers.

stile *n* a step, or set of steps, for climbing over a wall or fence.

stiletto *n* (*pl* **stilettos**) a small, slender dagger; a pointed tool for piercing holes in leather, etc; a high heel tapering to a point on a woman's shoe. * *vt* (**stilettoeing, stilettoed**) to stab with a stiletto.

still[1] *adj* motionless; calm; silent; (*drink*) not carbonated. * *n* a single photograph taken from a movie. * *vti* to make or become still. * *adv* continuously; nevertheless.—**stillness** *n*.

still[2] *n* an apparatus for distilling liquids, esp spirits.

stillbirth *n* the birth of any child that provides no evidence of life.

stillborn *adj* born dead; (*idea, project, etc*) a failure from the start, abortive.

still life *n* (*pl* **still lifes**) a painting of inanimate objects, such as flowers, fruit, etc.

Still's disease *n* a chronic arthritis in children, affecting several joints, with fever and a red rash.

stilt *n* either of a pair of poles with footrests on which one can walk, as in a circus; a supporting column.

stilted *adj* (*speech, writing*) pompous, unnaturally formal; (*conversation*) forced, intermittent.

Stilton *n* a blue-veined cheese with a strong flavor.

STIM *abbr* = scanning transmission ion microscope.

stimulant *n* a drug, drink, or food that increases one's heart rate and body activity.

stimulate *vt* to excite, arouse.—**stimulation** *n*.

stimulus *n* (*pl* **stimuli**) something that acts as an incentive; an agent that arouses or provokes a response in a living organism.

sting *n* a sharp, pointed organ of a bee, wasp, etc, or hair on a plant, used for injecting poison; a skin wound caused by injected poison from an insect or plant; (*sl*) a swindle. * *vt* to wound with a sting; to cause to suffer mentally; to goad, incite; (*sl*) to cheat by overcharging. * *vi* to feel a sharp pain.

stingray *n* any of various rays with a whiplike tail bearing sharp venomous spines.

stingy *adj* (**stingier, stingiest**) miserly, mean.—**stingily** *adv*.—**stinginess** *n*.

stink *vi* (**stinking, stank** or **stunk**, *pp* **stunk**) to give out an offensive smell; (*sl*) to possess something in an excessive amount; (*sl*) to be extremely bad in quality. * *n* a foul smell.

stink bomb *n* a small glass capsule that releases a foul smell when broken, used for practical jokes.

stinker *n* (*inf*) an offensive person or thing; (*inf*) something difficult or unpleasant.

stinkhorn *n* a type of foul-smelling fungus.

stinko *adj* (*sl*) drunk.

stinkweed *n* any of various plants with pungent scents.

stint *vt* to be frugal in the supply or allowance of something. * *vi* to be frugal or miserly. * *n* a fixed period or quantity of work; a limitation, restriction.

stipe *n* a short stalk or stem of a plant, esp of a mushroom.

stipend *n* a regular payment of money as wages or for expenses, esp to a clergyman.

stipendiary *adj* of or receiving a stipend. * *n* (*pl* **stipendiaries**) a person who receives a stipend.

stipple *vt* to engrave, paint, draw, etc, in tiny dots.

stipulate *vt* to specify as a condition of an agreement.—**stipulation** *n*.

stir[1] *vt* (**stirring, stirred**) to mix, as with a spoon; to rouse; to stimulate, excite; (*with* **up**) to agitate, instigate. * *vi* to be disturbed; to move oneself; to be active. * *n* a stirring movement; tumult.

stir[2] *n* (*sl*) prison.

STIR *abbr* = surplus to immediate requirements.

stir-fry *vt* to cook (chopped vegetables, etc) by stirring rapidly in hot oil in a wok or frying pan.

Stirling *n* **James** (*b.* 1926) English architect, whose notable works include Neuestaatsgalerie, Stuttgart.

stirring *adj* rousing, exciting.—**stirringly** *adv*.

stirrup *n* a strap and flat-bottomed ring hanging from a saddle, for a rider's foot.

stirrup cup *n* a farewell drink, orig given to a rider on horseback before departure.

stirrup pump *n* a small portable water pump held steady by a stirrup-shaped foot bracket, used for fire-fighting.

stitch *n* a single in-and-out movement of a threaded needle in sewing; a single loop of a yarn in knitting or crocheting; a sudden, sharp pain, esp in the side. * *vti* to sew.

stk. *abbr* = stock.

STL *abbr* (*Latin*) = *Sacrae Theologiae Lector*, "Reader *in Sacred Theology*"; *Sacrae Theologiae Licentiatus*, "Licentiate of Sacred Theology."

stlg. *abbr* = sterling.

STLO *abbr* = Scientific and Technical Liaison Officer.

STM *abbr* = (*Latin*) *Sacrae Theologiae Magister*, "Master of Sacred Theology"; scanning tunneling microscope; (*Latin*) *Scientiae Theologicae Magister*, "Master of Theology"; scientific, technical, and medical; short-term memory.

STO *abbr* = (*Brit*) Scottish Tenants' Organization; senior technical officer.

stoat *n* a small European mammal related to the weasel.

stochastic *adj* random; involving chance or probability.

stock *n* raw material; goods on hand; shares of corporate capital, or the certificates showing such ownership; lineage, family, race; a store; the cattle, horses, etc, kept on a farm; the broth obtained by boiling meat, bones, and vegetables as a foundation for soup, etc. * *vt* to supply; to keep in store. * *adj* standard; hackneyed.

stockade *n* a defensive enclosure or barrier of stakes fixed in the ground.

stock appreciation *n* the amount by which the stock-in-trade of a company has increased over a given period.

stockbroker *n* a person who deals in stocks.

stock car *n* a standard-production automobile modified for racing.

stock certificate *n* a document proving ownership of one or more shares in the capital stock of a company.

stock control *n* the process of regulating the stock-in-trade of a company so that there is an adequate level maintained to meet requirements and the level is not unnecessarily high.

stock depreciation *n* the amount by which the stock-in-trade of a company has decreased over a given period of time.

stock exchange or **stock market** *n* the market for dealing in stocks and shares.

Stockhausen *n* **Karlheinz** (1928–) German composer, who is regarded as the leading exponent of twelve-tone music.

stockholder *n* an owner of corporate stock.

Stockholm *n* capital city of Sweden.

stocking *n* a sock; a nylon covering for a woman's leg, supported by a garter belt.

stocking filler *n* a gift suitable for a Christmas stocking.

stock-in-trade *n* the goods that a company has for the purpose of carrying out its business activities; the goods or services that a company offers for sale.

stock market *see* **stock exchange**.

stockpile *n* a reserve supply of essentials.—*also vt*.

stock-still *adv* motionless.

stocktaking *n* making an inventory of goods on hand (in a store, warehouse, etc); evaluating one's present condition, resources, etc.

stock valuation *n* the setting of a money value on the various components of a firm's stock-in-trade.

stock watering *n* the creation of more shares by a company than is justifiable by the value of the company's tangible assets.

stocky *adj* (**stockier, stockiest**) short and sturdy.—**stockily** *adv*.—**stockiness** *n*.

stockyard *n* a yard for holding cattle, sheep, pigs, etc before they are sold, transported, or slaughtered.

stodge *n* (*inf*) heavy, starchy food.

stodgy *adj* (**stodgier, stodgiest**) (*food*) thick, heavy, and indigestible; uninteresting.—**stodgily** *adv*.—**stodginess** *n*.

stoic *n* a person who suffers hardship without showing emotion.—**stoical** *adj*.—**stoically** *adv*.—**stoicism** *n*.

stoichiometry *n* (*chem*) an aspect of chemistry that deals with the proportion of elements (or chemical equivalents) making pure compounds.

stoke *vt* to stir and feed (a fire) with fuel.

Stoker *n* **Bram [Abraham]** (1847–1912) Irish novelist and short-story writer, noted primarily for the novel *Dracula*, which has been filmed many times and remains one of the classic horror stories of all times.

Stokowski *n* **Leopold** (1882–1977) British-born American conductor, best known for his work with Walt Disney on the movie *Fantasia*.

STOL *abbr* = short take-off and landing, a system that allows an aircraft to take off and land within a short distance.

stole[1] *see* **steal**.

stole[2] *n* a long scarf or piece of fur worn on the shoulders.

stolen *see* **steal**.

stolid *adj* impassive; unemotional.—**stolidity** *n*.—**stolidly** *adv*.

STOLVCD *abbr* = short take-off and landing, vertical climb and descent.

stoma *n* (*pl* **stomata**) a minute aperture in the epidermis of a plant for the passage of gases; an orifice or mouth-like opening; a permanent surgical opening, esp in the abdominal wall.

stomach *n* the organ where food is digested; the belly. * *vt* to put up with.

stomach pump *n* a suction pump that empties the contents of the stomach through a long tube inserted orally.

stomata *see* **stoma**.

stomatitis *n* inflammation of the mouth.

stomatology *n* the branch of medicine concerned with the mouth.—**stomatological** *adj*.

stomp *vti* to walk with heavy steps; to stamp. * *n* an early jazz dance; (*mus*) a blues composition in which the beat is literally stomped on the floor.

stone *n* a small lump of rock; a precious stone or gem; the hard seed of a fruit; (*pl* **stone**) a unit of weight (14 lb./6.35 kg). * *vt* to throw stones at; to remove stones from (fruit).

Stone *n* 1. **Edward Durrell** (1902–78) American architect, whose notable works include the US Embassy, New Delhi. 2. **Oliver** (1946–) American movie director, whose movies include *Platoon* (1986), for which he won an Academy Award, *Wall Street* (1987), and *JKF* (1991).

Stone Age *n* the prehistoric age of human culture characterized by the use of stone tools and weapons.

stone circle *n* a circle made of standing stones, assumed to be for ceremonial and religious purposes.

stoned *adj* (*inf*) under the influence of drink or drugs.

stone-deaf *adj* utterly deaf.

stonefish *n* (*pl* **stonefish** or **stonefishes**) a venomous tropical fish with markings that resemble a stone on the seabed.

Stonehenge *n* a prehistoric stone circle in Wiltshire, England, possibly constructed 2500–1500 BC. Believed to have religious or astronomical purposes. According to Celtic mythology, Myrddin is said to have had Stonehenge built with stones brought from Ireland. In Ireland, they had formed the Giants' Ring on Mount Killaraus.

stone's throw *n* a short distance.

stonewall *vi* to obstruct or hinder, esp in politics and government.

stonewashed *adj* (*clothes*) made to appear worn and faded by the abrasive action of pumice particles.

stony, stoney *adj* (**stonier, stoniest**) of, like, or full of stones; unfeeling, heartless.—**stonily** *adv*.—**stoniness** *n*.

stony-broke *adj* (*inf*) completely without money.

stony-hearted *adj* unfeeling, cruel.—**stony-heartedness** *n*.

stony-iron meteorite *n* a meteorite comprising metallic and stony components.

stony meteorite *n* a meteorite composed mainly of rock-forming silicates, including pyroxene, olivine, and plagioclase, with some nickel-iron.

stood *see* **stand**.

stooge *n* (*sl*) a performer who feeds lines to a comedian; a person subordinate to or dominated by another; a stool pigeon. * *vi* to act as a stooge.

stool *n* a seat or a support for the back when sitting, with no back or arms; matter evacuated from the bowels.

stool pigeon *n* a police informer.

stoop[1] *vti* to bend the body forward and downward; to degrade oneself; to deign.—*also n*.

stoop[2] *n* a porch or small landing with stairs at the entrance to a house or building.

stooped *adj* hunched.

stop *vt* (**stopping, stopped**) to halt; to prevent; to intercept; to plug, block. * *vi* to cease; to come to an end; to stay. * *n* an act or instance of stopping; an impediment; (a knob controlling) a set of organ pipes; any of the standard settings of the aperture in a camera lens, f-stop; a regular stopping place for a bus or train; a punctuation mark, esp full stop; (*archit*) the projecting stone, often carved, against which features such as hood-molds end.

STOP *abbr* = suction termination of pregnancy.

stop bath *n* a mildy acidic solution used to halt the development of a negative print, plate, etc.

stop bit *n* (*comput*) the final bit sent in serial communications, which indicates to the receiving computer that the byte of data has been sent.

stopcock *n* a device for regulating the flow of liquid in a pipe.

Stopes *n* **Marie [Charlotte Carmichael]** (1880–1958) British scientist, and pioneer of birth control.

stopgap *n* a temporary substitute, expedient.

stoplight *n* a red light on a traffic signal warning vehicles to halt; a brake light.

stopover *n* a short break in a journey.

STOPP *abbr* = Society of Teachers Opposed to Physical Punishment.

stoppage *n* stopping or being stopped; an obstruction; a deduction from pay; a concerted cessation of work by employees, as during a strike.

Stoppard *n* **Tom** (1937–) Czech-born British dramatist, whose plays include *Rosencrantz and Guildenstern Are Dead*.

stop payment *n* an order by a depositor to a bank not to honor a check written by the depositor.

stopper *n* a cork, a bung.

stopping *n* (*mus*) on stringed instruments, the placing of fingers on a string to shorten its effective length and raise its pitch.

stop press *n* (the space reserved for) an item of last-minute news added to a newspaper after printing has begun.

stop-ridge *n* a transverse ridge on the face of a flat ax, designed to redistribute the impact.

stop sign *n* a road sign that orders vehicles to stop.

stopwatch *n* a watch that can be started and stopped, used for timing sporting events.

stor. *abbr* = storage.

Storace *n* **Stephen** (1763–96) English composer who traveled Europe (meeting Mozart in the process). His works include operas (such as *No Song, No Supper*), chamber music and songs.

storage *n* storing or being stored; an area reserved for storing; (*comput*) the storing of data in a computer memory or on disk, tape, etc.

storage battery *n* an accumulator.

storage capacity *n* the maximum amount of information that can be held in computer memory or a storage device.

storage device *n* a piece of computer equipment, such as a hard disk, used to store data.

storage heater *n* a radiator which accumulates heat during periods of off-peak electricity.

store *n* a building were retail goods are sold or services provided; a large supply of goods for future use; a warehouse. * *vt* to set aside; to put in a warehouse, etc; (*comput*) to put (data) into a computer memory or onto a storage device.

store-bought *adj* purchased from a store, as opposed to being homemade.

store card *n* (*Brit*) a charge card issued by a store or chain of stores for the purchase of goods there only.

storehouse *n* a place for storing things; a rich source or supply.

stores record card *n* a record that is kept by a company for each item of stock-in-trade.

stork *n* a long-necked, long-legged wading bird.

storksbill *n* any of several plants of the geranium family with pink or purple flowers.

storm *n* a heavy fall of rain, snow, etc with strong winds; a violent commotion; a furore; (*mil*) an attack on a fortified place. * *vt* to rush, invade. * *vi* to be angry; to rain or snow hard.—**stormy** *adj*.

stormbound *adj* affected or confined by storms.

storm door *or* **storm window** *n* an extra external door or window for protection against severe weather.

storm surge *n* extreme storm conditions caused by a combination of very low pressure at sea, high winds, and spring tides, leading to extensive damage on land.

storm trooper *n* a member of the Sturmabteilung, a semi-military group of the German Nazi party (1924–45) notorious for its violence; a member of a shock troop.

Storting, Storthing *n* the parliament of Norway.

story[1] *n* (*pl* **stories**) a narrative of real or imaginary events; a plot of a literary work; an anecdote; an account; (*inf*) a lie; a news article.

story[2] *n* (*pl* **stories**) a horizontal division of a building; a set of rooms occupying this space.

storyboard *n* (*movies, television*) a sequence of drawings or photographs showing the images to be shot to film for a particular story.

stotin *see* **tolar**.

stotinka *n* a monetary unit of Bulgaria, equal to one hundredth of a lev.

stout *adj* strong; short and plump; sturdy. * *n* strong, dark beer.—**stoutly** *adv*.—**stoutness** *n*.

stouthearted *adj* brave.—**stoutheartedly** *adv*.

stove[1] *n* a cooker; heating apparatus.

stove[2] *see* **stave**.

stow *vt* to store or pack in an orderly way.

stowage *n* stowing or being stowed; goods in storage; a place for storage or the charge for this.

stowaway *n* a person who hides on a ship, aircraft, etc to avoid paying the fare.

Stowe *n* **Mrs Harriet [Elizabeth] Beecher** (1811–96) American novelist, best known for her anti-slavery novel *Uncle Tom's Cabin, or, Life Among the Lowly* (1852).

stp *abbr* = standard temperature and pressure.

STP *abbr* = (*Latin*) *Sacrae Theologiae Professor*, "Professor of Sacred Theology"; scientifically treated petroleum (slang name for a hallucinogenic drug).

str *abbr* = surplus to requirements.

str. *abbr* (*mus*) = steamer; stringed (instruments); string(s).

strabismus *n* a squint.

straddle *vt* to have one leg or support on either side of.

Stradella *n* **Alessandro** (1642–82) Italian composer, singer, and violinist, who was murdered for eloping with a nobleman's mistress. His works include six oratorios and assorted sonatas and concertos.

Stradivari *n* **Antonio**, also known as **Antonius Stradivarius** (1644–1737) Italian violin-maker, whose instruments are unsurpassed for the quality of their sound. He was taught the craft by Amati and founded his own business in Cremona.

strafe *vt* to machine-gun (troops, vehicles, etc) from the air.—*also n*.

straggle *vi* to stray; to wander.—**straggler** *n*.—**straggly** *adj*.

straight *adj* (*line*) continuing in one direction, not curved or bent; direct; honest; (*sl*) heterosexual; (*alcoholic drinks*) neat, not diluted. * *adv* directly; without delay. * *n* being straight; a straight line, form, or position; a straight part of a racetrack; (*poker*) a hand containing five cards in sequence.—**straightness** *n*.

straight and narrow *n* (*inf*) the honest and virtuous way of life.

straight angle *n* an angle of 180°.

straightaway *adv* without delay.

straightedge *n* a length of wood, metal, etc used to rule or test for accurate straight lines.

straighten *vti* to make or become straight; (*with* **out**) to make or become less confused or entangled; to resolve.

straight face *n* a face betraying no signs of emotion, esp amusement.—**straight-faced** *adj*.

straight fight *n* a contest between only two candidates.

straight flush *n* (*poker*) five cards of the same suit in sequence.

straightforward *adj* honest, open; simple; easy.—**straightforwardly** *adv*.—**straightforwardness** *n*.

straightjacket *see* **straitjacket**.

straight-laced *see* **strait-laced**.

straight man *n* a person who acts as a stooge to a comedian.

straight-out *adj* (*inf*) honest, direct; thorough.

strain[1] *vt* to tax; to stretch; to over-exert; to stress; to injure (a muscle) by over-stretching; to drain or sieve (food). * *n* over-exertion; tension; an injury from straining; (*phys*) distortion produced by forces acting on a material.

strain[2] *n* a plant or animal within a species having a common characteristic; a trait; a trace.

strained *adj* (*action, behavior*) produced by excessive effort; (*mood, atmosphere*) tense, worried.

strainer *n* a sieve or colander used for straining liquids, pasta, tea, etc.

strait *n* a channel of sea linking two larger seas; (*usu pl*) difficulty, distress.

straitjacket *n* a coat-like device for restraining violent people; something that restricts or limits.—*also vt*. —*also* **straightjacket**.

strait-laced *adj* prim, morally strict.—*also* **straight-laced**.

strand¹ *vt* to run aground; to leave helpless, without transport or money.

strand² *n* a single piece of thread or wire twisted together to make a rope or cable; a tress of hair.—*also vt*.

strange *adj* peculiar; odd; unknown; unfamiliar.—**strangely** *adv*.—**strangeness** *n*.

stranger *n* a person who is unknown; a new arrival to a place, town, social gathering, etc; a person who is unfamiliar with or ignorant of something.

strangle *vt* to kill by compressing the windpipe, choke; to stifle, suppress.—**strangler** *n*.

stranglehold *n* (*wrestling*) a grip that presses an opponent's windpipe; a powerful restrictive force or influence.

strangles *n sing* an infectious bacterial disease of horses that inflames the respiratory tract, equine distemper.

strangulate *vt* to strangle; to compress (e.g., a blood vessel or the intestine) so as to cause a blockage. * *vi* to become strangulated.—**strangulation** *n*.

strangury *n* slow, painful urination.

strap *n* a narrow strip of leather or cloth for carrying or holding (a bag, etc); a fastening, as on a shoe or wristwatch; a triple option on a security or commodity market, consisting of one "put" option and two "call" options at the same price and for the same period. * *vti* (**strapping**, **strapped**) to fasten with a strap; to beat with a strap.

straphanger *n* (*inf*) a standing passenger in a bus or train, etc.

strapping *adj* tall, well-built. * *n* (*med*) the application of layers of adhesive plaster to cover part of the body and maintain moderate pressure so as to prevent too much movement and provide rest, as with fractured ribs.

strapwork *n* (*archit*) a surface ornamentation consisting of interlaced decorated bands with moldings at the edges of the bands.

Strasberg *n* **Lee** (1901–82) American theatrical director, who adopted and adapted the theories of Stanislavsky to develop method acting, a style of acting that achieved world fame through students such as James Dean and Marlon Brando.

Strasbourg *n* a city in France.

strata *see* **stratum**.

stratagem *n* a clever action planned to deceive or outwit an enemy.

strategic *or* **strategical** *adj* of, relating to, or important in strategy; (*weapons*) designed to strike at the enemy's homeland, not for use on the battlefield.—**strategically** *adv*.

strategic alliance *n* (*com*) a pooling of the resources and skills of two or more companies to enable them to engage effectively in a business activity.

Strategic Defense Initiative *n* (*formerly*) the US government's proposed deployment of satellites armed with laser devices to destroy enemy missiles.

strategic fit *n* (*com*) the extent to which a new area of business activity in a company will fit with the current business activities of the company or what has been seen as its future scope.

strategic group *n* (*com*) a group of companies within a market or within an industry in which each company pursues broadly similar policies in relation to product, pricing, etc.

strategy *n* (*pl* **strategies**) the planning and conduct of war; a political, economic, or business policy.—**strategist** *n*.

strath *n* (*Scot*) a wide, flat river valley.

strathspey *n* (the music for) a type of Scottish dance with slow, gliding steps.

straticulate *adj* (*rocks*) having thin strata.

stratified *adj* arranged or deposited in strata or layers.—**stratification** *n*.

stratigraphy *n* (the scientific study of) the composition and order of rock strata.—**stratigraphic** *adj*.

stratocumulus *n* (*pl* **stratocumuli**) layers of dark cloud in dense, round masses.

stratopause *n* the top of the stratosphere.

stratosphere *n* a layer of the earth's atmosphere above 6 miles, in which temperature increases with height.—**stratospheric** *adj*.

stratum *n* (*pl* **strata** *or* **stratums**) a layer of sedimentary rock; a level (of society).

stratus *n* (*pl* **strati**) a continuous horizontal layer of cloud.

Straub *n* **Marianne** (1909–) Swiss weaver, who revitalized the flagging Welsh weaving industry.

Strauss *n* 1. **Eduard** (1835–1916) Austrian composer, and the youngest brother of Johann Strauss "the younger." He, too, composed waltzes. 2. **Johann "the elder"** (1804–49) an Austrian conductor and composer, whose works include various waltzes as well as other pieces. 3. **Johann "the younger"** (1825–99) Austrian violinist, conductor, and composer, best known for his Viennese waltzes, e.g. the "Blue Danube." 4. **Joseph** (1827–70) Austrian composer, and younger brother of Johann Strauss "the younger." He also composed dance music. 5. **Richard** (1864–1949) German composer and conductor, whose works include *Also Sprach Zarathustra*, several operas, and *Four Last Songs*.

Stravinsky *n* **Igor Fyodorovich** (1882–1971) Russian composer, who composed ballet scores for Diaghilev, e.g. *Petrushka* (1911).

straw *n* the stalks of threshed grain; a tube for sucking up a drink.

strawberry *n* (*pl* **strawberries**) a soft, red fruit used in desserts and jam.

strawberry-blonde *adj* (*hair*) reddish blonde. * *n* a woman with hair of this color.

strawberry mark *n* an irregular blood-colored birth mark.

strawberry tree *n* a European evergreen tree bearing fruit resembling strawberries.

straw poll *n* an unofficial poll to assess public opinion.

stray *vi* to wander; to deviate; to digress. * *n* a domestic animal that has become lost. * *adj* random.

streak *n* a line or long mark of contrasting color; a flash of lightning; a characteristic, a trace. * *vti* to mark with or form streaks; to run naked in public as a prank.—**streaker** *n*.

streaky *adj* (**streakier**, **streakiest**) marked with streaks; (*bacon*) having alternate layers of fat and lean.

stream *n* a small river, brook, etc; a flow of liquid; anything flowing and continuous, * *vi* to flow, gush.

streamer *n* a banner; a long decorative ribbon.

streamline *vt* to shape (an automobile, a boat, etc) in a way that lessens resistance through air or water; to make more efficient, simplify.—**streamlined** *adj*.

stream of consciousness *n* a fluxive method of narration in which characters voice their feelings with no authorial comment and no orthodox dialog or description.

Streep *n* **Meryl [Mary Louise]** (1949–) American actress, whose movies include *Kramer vs Kramer* (1979) and *Sophie's Choice* (1982), for both of which she won Academy Awards.

street *n* a public road in a town or city lined with houses; such a road with its buildings and pavements; the people living, working, etc, along a given street. * *adj* pertaining to urban youth culture.

Street *n* **George E** (*b*. 1824) English architect, whose notable works include All Saints' Church, Clifton, Bristol, England.

streetcar *n* an electrically powered vehicle for public transport, which travels along rails set into the ground, a tram.

street cred *or* **street credibility** *n* the mastery of the style and ways or urban culture.

street fighter *n* (*sl*) a person who is tough and combative.

street furniture *n* (*Brit*) the items seen on streets, such as railings and street lamps.

street price *n* (*comput*) the price at which a computer or other hardware can be bought as compared with the official retail price set by the manufacturer.

street value *n* the value of a commodity, esp an illegal drug, in terms of the price charged to the ultimate users.

streetwalker *n* a prostitute who solicits in the streets.

streetwise *adj* (*inf*) experienced in surviving or avoiding the potential dangers of urban life.

Streichquartett *n* (*mus*) a string quartet.

Streisand *n* **Barbra [Barbara Joan]** (1942–) American singer and actress, and winner of several awards, including an Academy Award for her role in *Funny Girl* (1968).

strength *n* the state or quality of being physically or mentally strong; power of exerting or withstanding pressure, stress, force; potency; effectiveness.

strengthen *vti* to make or become stronger.

strenuous *adj* vigorous; requiring exertion.—**strenuously** *adv*.—**strenuousness** *n*.

strep *n* (*inf*) a streptococcus.

strepitoso *adv* (*mus*) in a boisterous manner.

streptococcus *n* (*pl* **streptococci**) any of a genus of spherical bacteria occurring in chains of different length.

streptokinase *n* an enzyme that is produced by streptococci and causes fibrin to undergo lysis.

streptomycin *n* an antibiotic derived from a soil bacterium, used in the treatment of infections such as tuberculosis.

stress *n* pressure; mental or physical tension or strain; emphasis; (*phys*) a system of forces producing or sustaining a strain. * *vt* to exert pressure on; to emphasize.

stressed skin construction *n* (*archit*) a method of construction in which an outer skin is fastened to a framework to form an integrated unit.

stress fracture *n* a fracture created by making excessive demands on the body, commonly occurring in sport.

stretch *vt* to extend, draw out. * *vi* to extend, spread; to extend the limbs or body; to be capable of expanding, as in elastic material. * *n* the act of stretching or instance of being stretched; the capacity for being stretched; an expanse of time or space; (*sl*) a period of imprisonment.—**stretchy** *adj*.

stretcher *n* a portable frame for carrying the sick or injured.

stretch mark *n* (*usu pl*) a mark left on the skin after rapid expansion, esp on the abdomen after pregnancy.

stretto *adj* (*mus*) close together, i.e., denoting a quickening of tempo.

Strettweg *n* a location in Austria where a unique bronze wagon model was discovered. It is thought to date from the seventh century BC and thus belongs to the early Celtic period or Hallstatt culture.

strew *vt* (**strewing**, **strewed**, *pp* **strewn** *or* **strewed**) to scatter; to spread.

strewth *interj* used to express surprise or alarm.

STRG *abbr* (*Brit*) = Scottish Tory Reform Group.

striation *n* any of a series of parallel grooves, scratches, ridges, or lines on a surface.—**striated** *adj*.

stricken *adj* suffering (from an illness); afflicted, as by something painful.

Strickland *n* **William** (1787–1854) American architect, whose notable works include Tennessee State Capitol, Nashville.

strict *adj* harsh, firm; enforcing rules rigorously; rigid.—**strictly** *adv*.—**strictness** *n*.

stricture *n* harsh criticism, censure; (*med*) a narrowing of a passage in the body, e.g., the urethra, esophagus, or ureter.

stride *vi* (**striding, strode**, *pp* **stridden**) to walk with long steps. * *vt* to straddle.—*also n.*

strident *adj* loud and harsh.—**stridency** *n.*—**stridently** *adv.*

stridulate *vi* (*insects*) to make a chirping or scraping sound.

strife *n* a fight, quarrel; struggle.

strike *vt* (**striking, struck**) to hit; to crash into; (*mil*) to attack; to ignite (a match) by friction; (*disease, etc*) to afflict suddenly; to come upon, esp unexpectedly; to delete; (*clock*) to indicate by sounding; to assume (e.g., an attitude); to occur to; to produce (a medal or coin) by stamping; to lower or take down (a flag or tent); to come upon (oil, ore, etc) by drilling or excavation; (*with* **down**) to afflict or cause to die suddenly; (*with* **off**) to delete or erase from a list, etc; to prevent from continuing in a profession, esp due to malpractice; to sever or separate from (as if with a blow); (*with* **out**) to erase or delete; (*with* **up**) to cause to begin, bring about. * *vi* to cease work to enforce a demand, e.g., for higher wages or better working conditions; (*with* **out**) to begin on a journey; (*baseball*) to be put out on strikes; (*inf*) to be completely unsuccessful; (*with* **up**) (*orchestra, band*) to begin to play or sing. * *n* a stoppage of work; a military attack; (*geol*) the direction of a horizontal line, measured with a compass, on an inclined plane, e.g., a rock bedding plane.

strikebound *adj* (*factory, etc*) closed or paralyzed by striking workers.

strikebreaker *n* a person who continues work while colleagues are on strike; a person hired to replace a striking worker.—**strikebreaking** *n, adj.*

strike pay *n* (*Brit*) money paid to workers on strike from union funds.

striker *n* a worker who is on strike; a mechanism that strikes, as in a clock; (*soccer*) a forward player whose primary role is to score goals.

striking *adj* impressive.—**strikingly** *adv.*

striking platform *n* the part of a piece of flint or stone that is struck to knock off a blade or flake.

Strindberg *n* **Johan August** (1849–1912) Swedish dramatist and novelist, whose plays include *Miss Julie* (1888) and *The Ghost Sonata* (1907).

Strine *n* Australian English (a humorous rendering of the Australian pronunciation of *Australian*).

string *n* a thin length of cord or twine used for tying, fastening, etc; a stretched length of catgut, wire, or other material in a musical instrument; (*comput*) a series of characters that can be used as a basis for a search; (*pl*) the stringed instruments in an orchestra; their players; a line or series of things. * *vt* (**stringing, strung**) to thread on a string; (*with* **up**) (*sl*) to kill by hanging. * *vi* (*with* **along**) (*inf*) to appear to agree (with); to accompany; to deceive, esp to gain time.

string. *abbr* = stringendo.

string bean *n* the edible immature green pod of the kidney bean, green bean; (*sl*) a tall thin person.

stringed *adj* (*musical instruments*) having strings.

stringendo *adj* (*mus*) increasing in tension, often with accelerated tempo.

stringent *adj* strict.—**stringently** *adv.*—**stringency** *n.*

stringer *n* a horizontal support in a structure; a long, horizontal brace to strengthen a framework, as in an aircraft fuselage; a journalist or photographer temporarily employed by a newspaper, magazine, or news service to cover a particular area.

string quartet *n* (a piece of music written for) a musical ensemble comprising two violins, one viola, and one cello.

string tie *n* a narrow tie.

stringy *adj* (**stringier, stringiest**) of or resembling string; (*meat, etc*) fibrous, chewy; (*physique*) sinewy.

strip *vt* (**stripping, stripped**) to peel off; to divest; to take away removable parts of. * *vi* to undress. * *n* a long, narrow piece (of cloth, land, etc); an airstrip or runway; (*stock exch*) a triple option on a security or commodity market, consisting of one "call" option and two "put" options at the same price and for the same period.

strip cartoon *n* a series of drawings in a newspaper, etc that tell a story.

strip club *n* a nightclub that features striptease artists.

stripe *n* a narrow band of a different color from the background; a chevron worn on a military uniform to indicate rank. * *vt* to mark with a stripe.—**striped** *adj.*—**stripy** *adj.*

strip lighting *n* lighting using long fluorescent tubes.

stripling *n* a youth, boy.

strip mining *n* mining by surface excavation, opencast mining.

stripper *n* a striptease artist; a device or solvent that removes paint.

striptease *n* an erotic show where a performer removes his or her clothes slowly and seductively to music.

strive *vi* (**striving, strove**, *pp* **striven**) to endeavor earnestly, labor hard; to struggle, contend.

STRIVE *abbr* = Society for the Preservation of Rural Industries and Village Enterprises.

strobe *n* (*inf*) a stroboscope.

strobe lighting *n* (the equipment used to produce) high-intensity flashing light.

stroboscope *n* a device for observing motion by making the subject visible at prescribed intervals using a synchronized flashing light.

strode *see* **stride**.

stroganoff *n* sliced beef cooked with mushrooms and onions in a sour-cream sauce.

Stroh violin *n* (*mus*) a violin made of metal (invented by Charles Stroh in 1901), which incorporates a trumpet bell and does not have a normal violin body.

stroke[1] *n* a blow or hit; (*med*) a seizure; the sound of a clock; (*sport*) an act of hitting a ball; a manner of swimming; the sweep of an oar in rowing; a movement of a pen, pencil, or paintbrush.

stroke[2] *vt* to caress; to do so as a sign of affection.

stroke play *n* (*golf*) scoring by the number of strokes taken.

stroll *vi* to walk leisurely, saunter. * *n* a leisurely walk for pleasure.

stroller *n* a wheeled metal-and-canvas chair for a small child.

stroma *n* (*pl* **stromata**) (*bot*) any tissue that functions as a framework in plant cells.

Strömgren sphere *n* the spherical envelope to a hot star of type O or B that contains ionized gas, mainly hydrogen with helium.

strong *adj* physically or mentally powerful; potent; intense; healthy; convincing; powerfully affecting the sense of smell or taste, pungent. * *adv* effectively, vigorously.—**strongly** *adv.*

strong-arm *adj* using unwarranted physical force.

strongbox *n* a solid, secure container for valuables.

strong drink *n* alcoholic drink.

stronghold *n* a fortress; a center of strength or support.

strong-minded *adj* resolute, determined.—**strong-mindedly** *adv.*—**strong-mindedness** *n.*

strong point *n* something at which one excels.

strongroom *n* a room specially designed to keep money and valuables secure from theft or fire, etc.

strontium *n* a soft metallic element. * symbol Sr.

strop *n* a strip of leather for sharpening a razor. * *vt* (**stropping, stropped**) to sharpen using a strop.

strophe *n* a stanza or movement of a Greek chorus alternating with the antistrophe sung when moving to the left.—**strophic** *adj.*

strophism *n* (*bot*) the twisting of a stalk as it grows in response to a stimulus from a particular direction, e.g., light.

stroppy *adj* (**stroppier, stroppiest**) (*inf*) surly, angry; quarrelsome.

strove *see* **strive**.

struck *see* **strike**.

structural formula *n* (*chem*) a formula providing information on the atoms present in a molecule and the way that they are bound together, i.e., an indication of the structure.

structuralism *n* a view of the social sciences, literature, linguistics, etc, which stresses the importance of inherent underlying hierarchical structures, interrelationships and patterns of organization.—**structuralist** *n.*

structure *n* organization; construction; arrangement of parts in an organism or of atoms in a molecule of a substance; system, framework; order. * *vt* to organize, arrange; to build up.—**structural** *adj.*—**structurally** *adv.*

structured programming language *n* (*comput*) a computer-programming language that encourages the programmer to think logically about the purpose of the program, e.g., C, Pascal and Ada.

structured query language *n* (*comput*) a set of 30 commands used to assist users in obtaining information from a database. * *abbr* SQL.

strudel *n* very thin pastry rolled up with a fruit filling and baked.

struggle *vi* to move strenuously so as to escape; to strive; to fight; to exert strength; to make one's way (along, through, up, etc) with difficulty. * *n* a violent effort; a fight.

strum *vt* (**strumming, strummed**) to play on (a guitar, etc), by moving the thumb across the strings.

struma *n* (*pl* **strumae**) enlargement of the thyroid gland; goiter.

strumpet *n* (*arch*) a prostitute.

strung *see* **string**.

strung-up *adj* (*inf*) tense, anxious.

strut[1] *vi* (**strutting, strutted**) to walk in a proud or pompous manner.

strut[2] *n* a brace or structural support; (*archit*) a structural element that prevents two other elements from moving toward each other. * *vt* to brace.

struthious *adj* (*birds*) related to or resembling the ostrich.

strychnine *n* a poison used in very small quantities as a stimulant.

STS *abbr* (*Brit*) = Scottish Tartans Society; Scottish Text Society.

STSF *abbr* (*Brit*) = Scottish Target Shooting Federation.

STSO *abbr* = Senior Technical Staff Officer.

STT *abbr* = Sacred Trees Trust; (*Brit*) Scottish Tree Trust.

STTA *abbr* (*Brit*) = Scottish Table Tennis Association.

St. Tr. *abbr* = State Trials.

STUA *abbr* (*Brit*) = Scottish Trust for Underwater Archaeology.

Stuart *n* 1. **Prince Charles Edward [Louis Philip]** (1720–88) [also known as Bonnie Prince Charlie or the Young Pretender]. He led the Jacobite revolt against the Hanoverian King George III in 1745, fleeing Scotland after defeat at Culloden in 1746. 2. **James** (*b.* 1713) English architect, whose notable works include the temple, Hagley.

S

stub *n* a short piece left after the larger part has been removed or used; the counterfoil of a check, receipt, etc. * *vt* (**stubbing, stubbed**) to knock (one's toe or foot) painfully; to extinguish (a cigarette).

stubble *n* the stubs or stumps left in the ground when a crop has been harvested; any short, bristly growth, as of beard.—**stubbly** *adj*.

stubborn *adj* obstinate; persevering; determined, inflexible.—**stubbornly** *adv*.—**stubbornness** *n*.

Stubbs *n* George (1724–1806) English painter and engraver, best known for his paintings of horses, as shown in his book *Anatomy of the Horse* (1766). His works include *Mares and Foals by a River* (1763–68) and *Horses Attacked by a Lion* (1770).

stubby *adj* (**stubbier, stubbiest**) short and thick. * *n* (*pl* **stubbies**) (*Austral sl*) a small bottle of beer.

STUC *abbr* (*Brit*) = Scottish Trades Union Congress.

stucco *n* (*pl* **stuccoes, stuccos**) a type of cement or plaster used to coat and decorate outside surfaces of walls. * *vt* (**stuccoing, stuccoed**) to decorate or finish with stucco.

stuck *see* **stick**.

Stuck *n* (*mus*) a piece.

stuck-up *adj* (*inf*) conceited; proud; snobbish.

stud[1] *n* a male animal, esp a horse, kept for breeding; a collection of horses and mares for breeding; a farm or stable for stud animals.

stud[2] *n* a large-headed nail; an ornamental fastener; (*archit*) a secondary vertical timber in the walls of a timber-framed building. * *vt* (**studding, studded**) to cover with studs.

stud. *abbr* = student.

studbook *n* a written record of the pedigree of a thoroughbred horse, dog, etc.

student *n* a person who studies or investigates a particular subject; a person who is enrolled for study at a school, college, or university.

StudentIEIE *abbr* = Student of the Institution of Electrical and Electronic Incorporated Engineers.

StudentIMechIE *abbr* = Student of the Institution of Mechanical Incorporated Engineers.

StudIAP *abbr* = Student of the Institution of Analysts and Programmers.

studied *adj* carefully planned.—**studiedly** *adv*.—**studiedness** *n*.

StudIManf *abbr* = Student Member of the Institute of Manufacturing.

StudIMS *abbr* = Student of the Institute of Management Specialists.

studio *n* (*pl* **studios**) the workshop of an artist, photographer, or musician; (*pl*) a building where motion pictures are made; a room where television or radio shows are recorded.

studio apartment *n* a small apartment with one main room, a kitchen, and a bathroom.

studio couch *n* a couch resembling a divan that can be converted into a bed.

studious *adj* given to study; careful.—**studiously** *adv*.—**studiousness** *n*.

StudProfBTM *abbr* = Student of Professional, Business, and Technical Management.

StudSE *abbr* = Student of the Society of Engineers.

StudSElec *abbr* = Student of the Society of Electroscience.

StudWeldI *abbr* = Student of the Welding Institute.

study *vt* (**studying, studied**) to observe and investigate (e.g., phenomena) closely; to learn (e.g., a language); to scrutinize; to follow a course (at college, etc). * *n* (*pl* **studies**) the process of studying; a detailed investigation and analysis of a subject; the written report of a study of something; a room for studying.

stuff *n* material; matter; textile fabrics; cloth, esp when woolen; personal possessions generally. * *vt* to cram, fill.

stuffed shirt *n* (*inf*) a pretentious or pompous person.

stuffing *n* material used to stuff or fill anything; a seasoned mixture put inside poultry, meat, vegetables, etc before cooking.

stuffy *adj* (**stuffier, stuffiest**) badly ventilated; lacking in fresh air; dull, uninspired.—**stuffily** *adv*.—**stuffiness** *n*.

stultify *vt* (**stultifying, stultified**) to make ineffectual or futile.—**stultification** *n*.

stumble *vi* to trip up or lose balance when walking; to falter; (*with* **across, on**) to discover by chance. * *n* a trip; a blunder.

stumbling block *n* an obstacle to further progress.

stump *n* the part of a tree remaining in the ground after the trunk has been felled; the part of a limb or tooth that remains after the larger part is cut off or destroyed. * *vt* (*inf*) to confuse, baffle. * *vi* to campaign for an election.

Stumpf *n* 1. **Axel** (1957–) German designer, who works in Berlin in an avant-garde manner. 2. **Bill** (1936–) American industrial designer, who designed the 1984 *Ethospace* open-plan office system.

stumpy *adj* (**stumpier, stumpiest**) short and thick.—**stumpiness** *n*.

stun *vt* (**stunning, stunned**) to render unconscious due to a fall or heavy blow; to surprise completely; to shock.

stung *see* **sting**.

stun gun *n* a type of gun that emits high-voltage electricity to stun victims.

stunk *see* **stink**.

stunner *n* (*inf*) a strikingly attractive or impressive person or thing.

stunning *adj* (*inf*) strikingly attractive.—**stunningly** *adv*.

stunt[1] *vt* to prevent the growth of, dwarf.

stunt[2] *n* a daring or spectacular feat; a project designed to attract attention. * *vi* to carry out stunts.

stuntman *n* (*pl* **stuntmen**) a man employed to replace an actor during dangerous scenes and stunts.—**stuntwoman** *nf* (*pl* **stuntwomen**).

stupa *n* a domed shrine holding Buddhist relics.

stupefy *vt* (**stupefying, stupefied**) to dull the senses of.—**stupefaction** *n*.

stupendous *adj* wonderful, astonishing.—**stupendously** *adv*.

stupid *adj* lacking in understanding or common sense; silly; foolish; stunned.—**stupidity** *n*.—**stupidly** *adv*.

stupor *n* extreme lethargy; mental dullness.

sturdy *adj* (**sturdier, sturdiest**) firm; strong, robust.—**sturdily** *adv*.—**sturdiness** *n*.

sturgeon *n* any of various large food fishes whose roe is also eaten as caviare.

Sturmabteilung *see* **storm trooper**.

stutter *vi* to stammer.—*also n*.

Stuttgart *n* a city in Germany.

STV *abbr* = single transferable vote.

sty[1], **stye** *n* (*pl* **sties**) an inflamed swelling on the eyelid.

sty[2] *n* (*pl* **sties**) a pen for pigs; any filthy place.

style *n* the manner of writing, painting, composing music peculiar to an individual or group; fashion, elegance. * *vt* to design or shape (e.g., hair).—**styler** *n*.

stylesheet *n* (*comput*) a file that has been saved with all the formatting required for a particular task.—*also* **stationery document**.

stylish *adj* having style; fashionable.—**stylishly** *adv*.—**stylishness** *n*.

stylist *n* a person who writes, paints, etc, with attention to style; a designer; a hairdresser.

stylistic *adj* of literary or artistic style.—**stylistically** *adv*.

stylize *vt* to give a conventional style to.—**stylization** *n*.—**stylizer** *n*.

stylobate *n* (*archit*) the base upon which a colonnade stands; (*archit*) the top step of the stepped base of a Greek temple.

stylus *n* (*pl* **styluses** *or* **styli**) the device attached to the cartridge on the arm of a phonograph that rests in the groove of a record and transmits the vibrations that are converted to sound; (*comput*) a device resembling a pen that is used as an input device on a graphics tablet, screen, or personal digital assistant

stymie *n* (*pl* **stymies**) (*golf*) a situation in which a ball is obstructed by another ball between it and the hole. * *vt* (**stymieing, stymied**) to obstruct, hinder.

S-type asteroid *n* (*astron*) an asteroid type common in the inner asteroid belt, thought to contain silicates.

styptic *adj* acting to stop bleeding by contracting the blood vessels. * *n* a styptic drug.

styrene *n* a liquid hydrocarbon used in making rubber and plastics.

Styx *n* (*Classical myth*) the name of the principal river in the underworld.

s.u. *abbr* (*transp*) = set up.

Su. *abbr* = Sunday.

SU *abbr* = Scripture Union; (*elect*) Siemens Unit (of resistance); Soviet Union; Supporters' Union.

Suaebhard *n* (*d.* 692) king of Kent (690–692). Joint ruler with Wihtred.

Sualtam *n* (*Irish Celtic myth*) the mortal father of Cuchulainn. The night before his wedding to Deichtire, the god Lugh carried her off and slept with her, and Setanta (Cuchulainn) was later born.

Suantrade *n* (*Irish Celtic myth*) one of the harpists of Uaithne who made such sad music that men died while listening.

suave *adj* charming, polite.—**suavely** *adv*.—**suaveness** *n*.

suavity *n* (*pl* **suavities**) politeness; urbanity; a suave action, comment, etc.

sub *n* (*inf*) a submarine; a substitute; a subscription; a subeditor.

sub. *abbr* = subaltern; substitute(s); suburb; suburban.

sub. *abbr* (*Italian*) = *subito*, "suddenly."

sub- *prefix* under, below; subordinate, next in rank to.

sub-agent *n* a person or company employed to buy and sell goods in behalf of an agent, thus being the agent of an agent.

subaltern *n* a commissioned officer in the British army ranking below captain. * *adj* inferior in rank or status.

subaqua *adj* of or pertaining to underwater sports.

subarachnoid anaesthesia *see* **spinal anesthesia**.

subarachnoid hemorrhage *n* bleeding into the subarachnoid space, often because of a ruptured cerebral aneurysm.

subarachnoid space *n* the space between the arachnoid and pia mater meninges covering the brain and spinal cord.

sub-Arctic *adj* near to, but outside, the Arctic Circle.

subatomic *adj* smaller than an atom; occurring within an atom.

SUBAW *abbr* (*Brit*) = Scottish Union of Bakers and Allied Workers.

subconscious *adj* happening without one's awareness. * *n* the part of the mind that is active without one's conscious awareness.—**subconsciously** *adv*.—**subconsciousness** *n*.

subcontinent *n* a land mass having great size but smaller than any of the usu recognized continents.

subcontract *n* a secondary contract, under which work or supply of materials is let out to a firm other than the main party of the contract.—*also vt*.—**subcontractor** *n*.

subculture *n* a distinct group with its own customs, language, dress, etc within an existing culture.

subcutaneous *adj* under the skin.—**subcutaneously** *adv*.

subdirectory *n* (*pl* **subdirectories**) (*comput*) a directory within a directory.

subdivide *vt* to further divide (what has already been divided). * *vi* to divide or be divided into parts.—**subdivision** *n*.

subdominant *n* (*mus*) the fourth note of the major or minor scale.

subduction zone *n* (*geol*) an essential component of the concept of plate tectonics.

subdue *vt* to dominate; to render submissive; to repress (e.g., a desire, an impulse); to soften, tone down (e.g., color, etc).

subdural *adj* below the dura mater, esp denoting the space between this and the arachnoid meninges around the brain.

subdwarf *n* a smaller and fainter star that forms a band below those in the main sequence on the Hertzsprung-Russell diagram.

subeditor *n* a person who checks and corrects newspaper articles.—**subedit** *vt*.

subgiant *n* a giant star that lies between the main sequence and the giants on the Hertzsprung-Russell diagram, smaller and less luminous than giants of the same spectral type.

subhead or **subheading** *n* a heading associated with a subdivision of a text.

subhuman *adj* (*animal*) lower down the evolutionary scale than mankind; less than human.

subito *adv* (*mus*) suddenly, as in *piano subito* (suddenly soft).

subj. *abbr* = subject; subjective; subjectively; subjunctive.

subject *adj* (*with* to) under the power (of); liable (to). * *n* a person under the power of another; a citizen; a topic; a theme; the scheme or idea of a work of art; a musical theme (a substantial group of notes) on which a composition or part of a composition is constructed, e.g., the first and second subjects in the exposition in sonata form; (*mus*) the subject in a fugue; (*mus*) the leading voice (first part) of a fugue. * *vt* to bring under control; to make liable; to cause to undergo.—**subjection** *n*.

subjective *adj* determined by one's own mind or consciousness; relating to reality as perceived and not independent of the mind; arising from one's own thoughts and emotions, personal.—**subjectively** *adv*.—**subjectivity** *n*.

sub judice *adv* being decided by a court.

subjugate *vt* to overpower, conquer.—**subjugation** *n*.

subjunctive *adj* denoting that mood of a verb which expresses doubt, condition, wish, or hope. * *n* the subjunctive mood.

sublet *vt* (**subletting, sublet**) to let (a property which one is renting) to another.

sublimation *n* (*chem*) the formation of a vapor directly from a solid, without going through the liquid phase.

sublime *adj* noble; exalted.—**sublimely** *adv*.—**sublimity** *n*.

subliminal *adj* beneath or beyond the conscious awareness.—**subliminally** *adv*.

subliminal advertizing *n* advertizing using subliminal images to influence the viewer unconsciously.

sublittoral zone *n* the zone of the sea that stretches from the lowest mark of ordinary tides to the edge of the continental shelf.

sub-machine gun *n* a light automatic or semiautomatic gun designed to be fired from the hip or shoulder.

submarine *adj* underwater, esp under the sea. * *n* a naval vessel capable of being propelled under water, esp for firing torpedoes or missiles.

submediant *n* (*mus*) the sixth note of the major or minor scale.

submenu *n* (*comput*) a secondary menu that appears as a set of options associated with an option chosen in the main menu.

submerge or **submerse** *vt* to plunge or sink under water; to cover, hide.—**submergence** or **submersion** *n*.

submerged coast *n* a coastline formed by a rise in sea level or by the land sinking, featuring valleys, rias, or fjords.

submersible *adj* capable of being submerged. * *n* an underwater vessel used for exploration or construction work.

submillimeter-wave astronomy *n* astronomy that involves the study of electromagnetic radiation with a wavelength of 0.3 to 1 millimeter.

submission *n* an act of submitting; something submitted, such as an idea or proposal; the state of being submissive or compliant; the act of referring something for another's consideration, criticism, etc.—**submissively** *adv*.—**submissiveness** *n*.

submit *vt* (**submitting, submitted**) to surrender (oneself) to another person or force; to refer to another for consideration or judgment; to offer as an opinion. * *vi* to yield, surrender.

subnormal *adj* less than normal; having low intelligence.—**subnormality** *n*.—**subnormally** *adv*.

subordinate *adj* secondary; lower in order, rank. * *n* a subordinate person. * *vt* to put in a lower position or rank.—**subordination** *n*.

subordinated debt *n* a debt that can be claimed by an unsecured creditor on the liquidation of a company only after the claims of secured creditors have been met.

subordination agreement *n* (*law*) an agreement between two parties, the debtor and the beneficiary of a new lien or a previously existing lien, which makes that lien secondary or inferior to another lien.

suborn *vt* to persuade to commit perjury or some other illegal act.

subphrenic abscess *n* an abscess occurring beneath the diaphragm and commonly on the right side.

subpoena *n* a written legal order requiring the attendance of a person in court. * *vt* (**subpoenaing, subpoenaed**) to serve with a subpoena.

subrogation *n* the right of an insurer to take over any other methods that the insured person may have recourse to for acquiring compensation for the same occurrence, after the insured person has received any compensation due by the insurer.

sub rosa *adv* in secret.

subroutine *n* a self-contained section of a computer program that performs a particular task as many times as required by the main program.

subscribe *vt* to pay to receive regular copies (of a magazine, etc); * *vi* (*with* to) to donate money to (a charity, campaign); to support or agree with (an opinion or faith.—**subscription** *n*.

subscriber *n* a person who subscribes; (*com*) a person who is a signatory of a memorandum of association of a new company, who pays for a specified quantity of shares, and who is involved in appointing the first directors of the company.

subscriber trunk dialing *n* a service that allows users to dial long-distance calls directly.

subscript *n* a character written or printed below another character.—*also adj*.

subscription shares *npl* the shares bought by the initial subscribers to a company.

subsec. *abbr* = subsection.

subsequent *adj* occurring or following after.—**subsequently** *adv*.

subservient *adj* obsequious; servile; subordinate.—**subservience** *n*.—**subserviently** *adv*.

subside *vi* to sink or fall to the bottom; to settle; to diminish; to abate.—**subsidence** *n*.

subsidiarity *n* the devolution of decision making or control to the lowest effective level.

subsidiary *adj* secondary; supplementary; (*company*) owned or controlled by another. * *n* (*pl* **subsidiaries**) an accessory, an auxiliary; a business owned by another.—**subsidiarily** *adv*.

subsidiary company *n* a company that is owned by another company.

subsidiary theme *n* (*mus*) any theme that is less important than the main theme or themes of a composition.

subsidize *vt* to aid or support with a subsidy.—**subsidization** *n*.—**subsidizer** *n*.

subsidy *n* (*pl* **subsidies**) government financial aid to a private person or company to assist an enterprise.

subsist *vi* to exist; to continue; to manage to keep oneself alive (on).

subsistence *n* existence; livelihood.—**subsistent** *adj*.

subsistence economy *n* an undeveloped economy in which people barter goods rather than buy and sell using cash.

subsistence farming *n* a form of farming where all the produce goes to support the household and there is none left over for sale.

subsoil *n* the layer of soil lying immediately beneath the surface soil.

subsonic *adj* traveling at a speed less than that of sound.

subst. *abbr* = substantive; substitute.

substance *n* matter (such as powder, liquid); the essential nature or part; significance.

substantial *adj* of considerable value or size; important; strongly built.—**substantiality** *n*.—**substantially** *adv*.

substantiate *vt* to prove, verify.—**substantiation** *n*.

substitute *vti* (*with* for) to put or act in place of another person or thing; to replace (by). * *n* a person or thing that serves in place of another.—*also adj*.—**substitution** *n*.

substitution *n* the act of substituting; (*chem*) a reaction in which an atom or group in a molecule is replaced by another atom or group, often hydrogen by a halogen, hydroxyl, etc.

substrate *n* (*biol*) the surface upon which an organism lives and from which it may derive its food; (*chem*) a substance in a reaction that is catalyzed by an enzyme; (*electronics*) the single crystal or semiconductor used as the base on which an integrated circuit or transistor is printed.

substructure *n* a foundation or supporting framework.

subsume *vt* to include in a larger group or category.

subterfuge *n* a trick employed to conceal something.

subterranean *adj* below the surface of the earth; concealed.

subtitle *n* an explanatory, usu secondary, title to a book; a printed translation superimposed on a foreign language movie.—*also vt*.

subtle *adj* delicate; slight; not noticeable; difficult to define, put into words; ingenious.—**subtleness** *n*.—**subtly** *adv*.

subtlety *n* (*pl* **subtleties**) subtleness; a fine distinction.

subtotal *n* the sum of part of a series of figures. * *vt* to sum in part.

subtract *vti* to take away or deduct (one quantity from another).—**subtraction** *n*.

subtropical *adj* of or characteristic of the regions bordering on the tropics.

subtropical high *n* an area of almost constant high pressure about 30° north and south of the Equator.

suburb *n* a residential district on the outskirts of a large town or city.—**suburban** *adj*.—**suburbia** *n*.

suburbanite *n* a person who lives in a suburb.

subversion *n* the act of undermining the authority of a government, institution, etc; collapse, ruin.

subversive *adj* liable to subvert established authority. * *n* a person who engages in subversive activities.—**subversively** *adv*.—**subversiveness** *n*.

subvert *vt* to overthrow or ruin (something established); to corrupt, as in morals.

subway *n* an underground metropolitan electric railroad; a passage under a street.

subzero *adj* (*temperature*) lower than zero.

Succat *n* either the childhood name or the nickname of St Patrick.

succeed *vt* to come after, follow; to take the place of. * *vi* to accomplish what is attempted; to be successful.

success *n* the gaining of wealth, fame, etc; the favorable outcome (of anything attempted); a successful person or action.

successful *adj* having success.—**successfully** *adv*.—**successfulness** *n*.

succession *n* following in sequence; a number of persons or things following in order; the act or process of succeeding to a title, throne, etc; the line of descent to succeed to something.

successive *adj* following in sequence.—**successively** *adv*.—**successiveness** *n*.

successor *n* a person who succeeds another, as to an office.

succinct *adj* clear, concise.—**succinctly** *adv*.—**succinctness** *n*.

succor *n* (a person or thing that provides) help, support, esp in time of need. * *vt* to provide such help.

succotash *n* a cooked mixture of sweetcorn and lima beans.

succubus or **succuba** *n* (*pl* **succubi** or **succubae**) a female demon thought to have sexual intercourse with sleeping men.

succulent *adj* juicy; moist and tasty; (*plant*) having fleshy tissue. * *n* a succulent plant (such as a cactus).—**succulence** or **succulency** *n*.—**succulently** *adv*.

succumb *vi* to yield to superior strength or overpowering desire; to die.

Sucellus *n* (*Gaulish Celtic myth*) "good striker"; a god who is often depicted as carrying a long-handled mallet, has a wine cask or drinking vessel near, and is often accompanied by a dog.

such *adj* of a specified kind (e.g., *such people, such a movie*); so great. * *adv* so; very.

suchlike *adj* of similar kind.

suck *vt* to draw (a liquid or air) into the mouth; to dissolve or roll about in the mouth (a candy, etc); (*with* **in**, **up**, etc) to draw in as if by sucking.—*also n*.

sucker *n* (*sl*) a person who is easily taken in or deceived; a cup-shaped piece of rubber that adheres to surfaces.

suckle *vt* to feed at the breast or udder.

suckling *n* a young animal that is not yet weaned.

Suckling *n* **Sir John** (1609–41) English poet and dramatist. The best known of his lyrics is the charming "Ballad upon a Wedding." Most of his works are included in the posthumous collection, *Fragmenta Aura*.

sucks *interj* (*sl*) used to express disappointment.

SUCL *abbr* (*transp*) = set up in carloads.

sucre *n* the monetary unit of Ecuador.

Sucre *n* the legal capital of Bolivia.

sucrose *n* sugar.

suction *n* the act or process of sucking; the exertion of a force to form a vacuum.

Sudan *n* a republic in Africa, lying just south of the Tropic of Cancer in northeast Africa.

Sudanese dinar *n* currency of the Sudan.

sudd *n* in northeast Africa, a mass of floating vegetation that has broken away from nearby swamps.

sudden *adj* happening quickly and unexpectedly, abrupt.—**suddenly** *adv*.—**suddenness** *n*.

sudden death *n* (*sport*) extra time in a tied match, the winner being the next to score or take a point.

sudden infant death syndrome *n* the sudden death of a baby, often occurring overnight, from unknown causes. * *abbr* SIDS.—*also* **cot death**.

SuDoc *abbr* = Superintendent of Documents

suds *npl* the bubbles or foam on the surface of soapy water.—**sudsy** *adj*.

SUDS *abbr* = sudden unexplained death syndrome.

sue *vt* (**suing, sued**) to bring a legal action against.

Süe *n* **Louis** (1875–1968) French architect and painter, who designed German-influenced furniture in the first years of this century.

suede, suède *n* leather finished with a soft nap.

suet *n* white, solid fat in animal tissue, used in cooking.

Suez *n* a city in Egypt.

suf., suff. *abbr* = suffix.

suffer *vt* to undergo; to endure; to experience. * *vi* to feel pain or distress.—**sufferer** *n*.—**suffering** *n*.

sufferable *adj* endurable.—**sufferably** *adv*.

sufferance *n* reluctant tolerance, tacit permission; endurance.

suffice *vi* to be sufficient or adequate (for some purpose).

sufficient *adj* enough; adequate.—**sufficiency** *n*.—**sufficiently** *adv*.

suffix *n* (*pl* **suffixes**) a letter, syllable, or syllables added to the end of a word to modify its meaning or to form a new derivative.

suffocate *vti* to kill or be killed by depriving of oxygen or by inhaling a poisonous gas; to feel hot and uncomfortable due to lack of air; to prevent from developing.—**suffocation** *n*.

suffrage *n* the right to vote.

suffragette *n* esp in the UK, a campaigner for women's right to vote in the early years of the 20th century.

suffuse *vt* to spread over or fill, as with color or light.—**suffusion** *n*.

sugar *n* a sweet, white, crystalline substance obtained from sugar cane and sugar beet * *vi* to sweeten.

sugar beet *n* a type of beet from which sugar is extracted.

sugar cane *n* a tall grass with stout canes grown as a source of sugar.

sugar daddy *n* a wealthy and usu elderly man who lavishes gifts on an attractive young woman.

sugar maple *n* a North American maple tree used as a source of wood and of sugar from its sweet sap.

sugary *adj* resembling or containing sugar; cloyingly sweet in manner, content, etc.—**sugariness** *n*.

suggest *vt* to put forward for consideration; to bring to one's mind; to evoke.—**suggestion** *n*.

suggestible *adj* easily influenced by others.—**suggestibility** *n*.

suggestive *adj* evocative; rather indecent, risqué.—**suggestively** *adv*.—**suggestiveness** *n*.

Suharto *n* **Thojib N J** (1921–) Indonesian general and statesman, who launched a brutal campaign of repression against communists and other dissidents in the mid-1960s, and assumed executive power in 1967 after president **Achmed Sukarno** or **Soekarno** (1901–70), the first president of Indonesia, resigned in his favor.

suicidal *adj* of, pertaining to, suicide; liable to commit suicide; destructive of one's own interests.—**suicidally** *adv*.

suicide *n* a person who kills himself or herself intentionally; the act or instance of killing oneself intentionally; ruin of one's own interests.

suicide gene *n* a gene having bacteria that end its life cycle.

sui generis *adj* unique.

suit *n* a set of matching garments, such as a coat and pants or skirt; one of the four sets of 13 playing cards; a lawsuit. * *vt* to be appropriate for or to; to be convenient or acceptable to.

suitable *adj* fitting; convenient (to or for).—**suitably** *adv*.—**suitability** *n*.

suitcase *n* a portable, oblong traveling case.

suite *n* a number of followers or attendants; a set, esp of rooms, furniture, pieces of music; (*comput*) a collection of several programs that fit together to provide a comprehensive set of tools, including, e.g., a word-processing program, a spreadsheet, an organizer, a database, a communications program, and a presentation program.

suitor *n* a man who courts a woman; (*law*) a person who brings a lawsuit.

Suk *n* **Josef** (1874–1935) Czech composer, violinist, and viola player who was the son-in-law of Dvořák. He composed two symphonies and, among other works, symphonic poems.

Sukarno *see* **Suharto.**

Sukhumi *n* a city in Georgia.

sukiyaki *n* a Japanese dish of thinly sliced beef, vegetables, and seafood, cooked rapidly in soy sauce, saké, etc, at the table.

sul, sull' *prep* (*mus*) on, over, as in *sul ponticello* (over the bridge), in violin bowing.

SULCL *abbr* (*transp*) = set up in less than carloads.

sulf- *prefix* sulfur.

sulfa drug *n* any of various sulfonamide drugs used for treating bacterial infections.

sulfate *n* a salt of sulfuric acid.

sulfonamide *n* any of a group of compounds that are amides of sulfonic acid, such as the sulfa drugs.

sulfonic acid *n* any of a group strong organic acids used in the manufacture of drugs, dyes, and detergents.

sulfur *n* a yellow non-metallic element that is inflammable and has a strong odor. * symbol S.— **sulfuric** *adj*.

sulfur dioxide *n* a pungent toxic gas used in various industrial processes that is a major air pollutant.

sulfuric acid *n* a powerfully corrosive acid.

Sulis *n* (*Celtic myth*) the goddess who presided over the healing spring at Bath, England was Sulis. One of the British Celtic water deities and a goddess of healing. The Romans named the town that is now Bath after her, "Aquae Sulis." From the time of the arrival of the Romans, Sulis began to be identified with the classical goddess Minerva.

sulk *vi* to be sullen.

sulky *adj* (**sulkier, sulkiest**) bad-tempered, quiet, and sullen, because of resentment.—**sulkily** *adv*.—**sulkiness** *n*.

sullen *adj* moody and silent; gloomy, dull.—**sullenly** *adv*.—**sullenness** *n*.

Sullivan *n* **Sir Arthur** (1842–1900) English composer, whose collaboration with W S Gilbert resulted in the "Savoy operas," e.g., *The Pirates of Penzance* and *The Gondoliers*, of which there are 13 in all.

sully *vt* (**sullying , sullied**) to blemish, defile the purity of. * *n* (*pl* **sullies**) a tarnish or stain.

sultan *n* a ruler, esp of a Muslim state.

sultana *n* a dried white grape used in cooking; the wife or female relative of a sultan.

sultanate *n* a country or region ruled by a sultan; the office or authority of a sultan.

sultry *adj* (**sultrier, sultriest**) (*weather*) very hot, humid, and close; sensual; passionate.—**sultrily** *adv*.—**sultriness** *n*.

sum *n* the result of two or more things added together; the total, aggregate; a quantity of money; essence, gist. * *vt* (**summing, summed**) (*usu with* **up**) to add; to encapsulate; to summarize.

sum *n* the standard monetary unit of Uzbekistan.

sum. *abbr* (*Latin*) = *sumat*, "let him take"; *sumendum*, "let it be taken."

SUM *abbr* = surface-to-underwater missile.

Sumer *n* an area of lower Mesopotamia between Babylon and the Persian Gulf, the site of the first civilization *c*. 3500 BC.

summarize *vt* to make or be a summary of.—**summarization** *n*.—**summarizer** *n*.

summary *adj* concise; performed quickly, without formality. * *n* (*pl* **summaries**) a brief account of the main points of something.—**summarily** *adv*.—**summariness** *n*.

summary financial statement *n* (*com*) a shortened version of a company's annual accounts.

summation *n* the act of finding a sum or total; the result of summation; a summary; the summing-up of an argument, esp by a lawyer before a jury.

summer *n* the warmest season of the year, between spring and autumn.—**summery** *adj*.

summerhouse *n* a small building in a garden, used as a shady retreat in summer.

Summers *n* **Gerald** (1899–1987) British furniture designer, who rivaled the great continental designers in the 1930s.

summer school *n* an academic course held during the summer.

summer stock *n* theatrical productions produced by small repertory companies during the summer.

summing-up *n* a concluding summary of the points in a speech, argument, etc; a review of the main evidence made by a judge to the jury before it considers its verdict.

summit *n* the highest point, the peak; a meeting of world leaders.

summitry *n* the practice of convening, or style of conducting, summit conferences.

summon *vt* to order to appear, esp in court; to convene; to gather (strength, enthusiasm, etc).

summons *n* (*pl* **summonses**) a call to appear (in court). * *vt* to serve with a summons.

sumo *n* traditional Japanese wrestling.

sump *n* a section of the crankcase under an engine for the oil to drain into to form a reservoir.

sumptuous *adj* lavish; luxurious.—**sumptuously** *adv*.—**sumptuousness** *n*.

Sumqayit *n* a a city in Azerbaijan.

sun *n* the star around which the Earth and other planets revolve, which gives light and heat to the solar system; the sunshine. * *vt* (**sunning, sunned**) to expose (oneself) to the sun's rays.

Sun Yat-sen *or* **Sun Zhong Shan** *n* (1866–1925) Chinese nationalist leader and statesman, who played a leading role in the overthrow of the Manchu dynasty and became the first president of the Republic of China in 1911–12.

Sun. *or* **Sund.** *abbr* = Sunday.

sunbaked *adj* baked hard by exposure to the sun.

sunbathe *vi* to lie in the rays of the sun or a sun lamp to get a suntan.—**sunbather** *n*.

sunbeam *n* a ray of sunlight.

sunburn *n* inflammation of the skin from exposure to sunlight.—*also vt*.

sunburst *n* a sudden flash of sunlight; a pattern resembling the sun surrounded by rays; a brooch with a design resembling this.

sundae *n* a serving of ice cream covered with a topping of fruit, syrup, nuts, etc.

Sunday *n* the day of the week after Saturday, regarded as a day of worship by Christians; a newspaper published on a Sunday.

Sunday best *n* best clothes kept for wearing on Sundays.

Sunday driver *n* a person who only drives at weekends; a slow and overly careful driver.

Sunday school *n* a class for religious instruction held on Sundays.

sun deck *n* the upper deck of a ship that catches most of the sun; a terrace used for sunbathing.

sundew *n* any of various bog plants with sticky hairs that trap insects.

sundial *n* a device that shows the time by casting a shadow on a graduated dial.

sundown *n* sunset.

sundry *adj* miscellaneous, various. * *n* (*pl* **sundries**) (*pl*) miscellaneous small things.

sunflower *n* a tall plant with large, yellow flowers whose seeds yield oil.

sung *see* **sing**.

sunglasses *npl* tinted glasses to protect the eyes from sunlight.

sungrazer *n* (*astron*) a comet that passes through the sun's outer layers.

sunk *see* **sink**.

sunk capital *n* (*com*) the value of a company's funds no longer available to that company because the money has been spent on assets that are useless or unrealizable.

sunk costs *n* (*com*) the cost of durable items paid for by a company when these items can be treated as assets in the account books.

sunlamp *n* an electric lamp that produces ultra-violet rays for tanning the skin.

Sunna *n* the body of Islamic doctrine accepted by orthodox Muslims as based on the life and teachings of Mohammed.

Sunni *n* the branch of Islam that accepts the orthodoxy of the Sunna.—**Sunnite** *n*.

sunny *adj* (**sunnier, sunniest**) (*weather*) bright with sunshine; (*person, mood*) cheerful.—**sunnily** *adv*.—**sunniness** *n*.

sunrise *n* dawn.

sunrise industry *n* a high-technology industry with a bright future.

sunroof *n* a panel in the roof of an automobile that slides open.

SUNS *abbr* = sonic underwater navigation system.

sunset *n* dusk.

sunshine *n* the light and heat from the sun.

sunshine recorder *or* **Campbell-Stokes recorder** *n* an apparatus comprising a glass sphere that focuses the sun's rays on card recording the duration of the sunshine.

sunspot *n* a dark patch sometimes visible on the sun's surface; (*inf*) a holiday resort with guaranteed sunshine.

sunstroke *n* illness caused by exposure to the sun.

suntan *n* browning of the skin by the sun.—**suntanned** *adj*.

suntrap *n* a sunny sheltered spot.

SUNY *abbr* = State University of New York.

sup. *abbr* = superfine; superior; superlative; supine; supplement; supplementary; supply; (*Latin*) *supra*, "above"; supreme.

Sup. C. *or* **Sup. Ct.** *abbr* = Superior Court; Supreme Court.

super *adj* (*inf*) fantastic, excellent; (*inf*) a superintendent, as in the police. * *n* a variety of high-octane gas.

super. *abbr* = superfine; superior.

super- *prefix* above, on the top of; extremely, excessively; greater in size, quality, etc.

superable *adj* able to be overcome.—**superably** *adv*.

superannuate *vt* to pension off on account of old age or illness.

superannuation *n* regular contributions from employees' wages toward a pension scheme.

superb *adj* grand; excellent; of the highest quality.—**superbly** *adv*.

supercharge *vt* to increase the power of (an engine) by using a device that supplies air or fuel in increased quantities by raising the intake pressure; to charge (the atmosphere, a conversation, etc) with excess tension or emotion.—**supercharger** *n*.

supercilious *adj* arrogant; haughty, disdainful.—**superciliously** *adv*.—**superciliousness** *n*.

supercluster *n* (*astron*) a structure that is hundreds of millions of light years across and which consists of a grouping of several clusters of galaxies.

super computer *n* (*comput*) a computer designed to execute very complex calculations at very high speeds.

superconductivity *n* (*phys*) the complete loss of electrical resistance exhibited by certain materials at very low temperatures.—**superconducting** *or* **superconductive** *adj*.—**superconduction** *n*.—**superconductor** *n*.

supercool *vt* to cool (a liquid, etc) below freezing without solidification or crystallization.

superdelegate *n* a delegate to a Democratic Party convention, appointed rather than elected.

superego *n* (*pl* **superegos**) (*psychol*) the division of the unconscious mind that functions as a conscience.

superficial *adj* near the surface; slight, not profound; (*person*) shallow in nature.—**superficiality** *n*.—**superficially** *adv*.

superfluidity *n* (*phys*) the flowing of a fluid without friction.

superfluous *adj* exceeding what is required; unnecessary.—**superfluity** *n*.

supergiant *n* (*astron*) a star of enormous size and brightness with a low density.

superglue *n* an adhesive that forms strong bonds instantly.

supergrass *n* an informer who incriminates a large number of people.

superheat *vt* to heat above boiling point without vaporization; to heat (a vapor) above boiling point without boiling occurring.

superhigh frequency *n* a radio frequency between 30 000 and 3000 megahertz.

superhuman *adj* surpassing normal human strength or abilities; divine.

superimpose *vt* to put or lay upon something else.

superintend *vt* to have the charge and direction of; to control, manage.

superintendent *n* a person who manages or supervises; a director; a British police officer next above the rank of inspector.

superior *adj* higher in place, quality, rank, or excellence; greater in number or power. * *n* a person of higher rank.—**superiority** *n*.

superiority complex *n* an inflated opinion of one's own abilities and merits.

superl. *abbr* = superlative.

superlative *adj* of outstanding quality; (*gram*) denoting the extreme degree of comparison of adjectives and adverbs.—**superlatively** *adv*.

supermajority provisions *npl* (*com*) provisions in the rules of a company that require more than the usual simple majority of its members when voting is taking place on certain motions.

superman *n* (*pl* **supermen**) a person of outstanding abilities and achievements.

supermarket *n* a large self-service store selling food and household goods.

supernatural *adj* relating to things that cannot be explained by nature; involving ghosts, spirits, etc.—**supernaturally** *adv*.

supernova *n* (*pl* **supernovae** *or* **supernovas**) (*astron*) a star that explodes temporarily, burning with an intensity one hundred million times that of the sun.

supernova remnant *n* (*astron*) the material blown out of an expanding star at the time of a supernova.

supernumerary *adj* extra; beyond the usual number. * *n* (*pl* **supernumeraries**) an extra person or thing.

superpose *vt* to place (a geometric figure) on top of another so that their outlines coincide; to lay (something) on top of something else.—**superposition** *n*.

superpower *n* a nation with great economic and military strength.

supersaturation *n* (*phys*) the state of a solution when it contains more dissolved solute than is required to produce a saturated solution.

superscript *n* a character written or printed above another character.—*also adj*.

supersede *vt* to take the place of, replace.

supersmart card *n* a smart card equipped with a screen and a keyboard, allowing interaction with the user.

supersonic *adj* faster than the speed of sound.—**supersonically** *adv*.

superstar *n* (*inf*) a famous movie actor, musician, or sportsperson.

superstition *n* an irrational belief based on ignorance or fear.—**superstitious** *adj*.

superstore *n* a very large supermarket.

superstructure *n* a structure above or on something else, as above the base or foundation, e.g., above the main deck of a ship.

Super Tuesday *n* the Tuesday, usu in March, on which a number of states, with over half of all the delegates, hold primary elections for the selection of Presidential candidates.

super VGA *n* (*comput*) a graphics display standard that can display from 800 pixels by 600 vertical lines to 1024 pixels by 768 lines with 256 colors.

supervise *vti* to have charge of, direct, superintend.—**supervision** *n*.

supervisor *n* one who supervises; an overseer, an inspector.—**supervisory** *adj*.

superwoman *n* (*pl* **superwomen**) a woman of outstanding abilities and achievements.

supine *adj* lying on the back; lazy, indigent.—**supinely** *adv*.

supp. *or* **suppl.** *abbr* = supplement.

Suppé *n* **Franz von** (1819–95) Dalmatian-born composer and conductor of Belgian descent, who is best remembered for his satirical songs, his operettas, and his overture *Poet and the Peasant*.

supper *n* a meal taken in the evening, esp when dinner is eaten at midday; an evening social event; the food served at a supper; a light meal served late in the evening.

supplant *vt* to replace; to remove in order to replace with something else.

supple *adj* flexible, easily bent; lithe; (*mind*) adaptable.—**suppleness** *n*.

supplement *n* an addition or extra amount (usu of money); an additional section of a book, periodical, or newspaper. * *vt* to add to.—**supplemental** *adj*.

supplicate *vt* to entreat earnestly to (a person) or for (something). * *vi* to make a humble petition.— **supplication** *n*.—**supplicatory** *adj*.

supply *vt* (**supplying, supplied**) to provide, meet (a deficiency or a need); to fill (a vacant place). * *n* (*pl* **supplies**) a stock; (*econ*) the availability of goods or services; (*pl*) provisions.—**supplier** *n*.

supply and demand *n* (*econ*) quantities available and required that regulate market price.

supply chain *n* (*econ*) a series of stages in a supply process through which a particular set of goods or services moves.

support *vt* to hold up, bear; to tolerate, withstand; to assist; to advocate (a cause, policy); to provide for financially. * *n* a means of support; maintenance.

supporter *n* a person who backs a political party, sports team, etc.

suppose *vt* to assume; to presume as true without definite knowledge; to think probable; to expect. * *vi* to conjecture.

supposed *adj* believed to be on available evidence.

supposedly *adv* allegedly.

supposition *n* an assumption, a hypothesis.

suppositious *adj* hypothetical.

suppository *n* (*pl* **suppositories**) a cone or cylinder of medicated soluble material for insertion into the rectum or vagina.

suppress *vt* to crush, put an end to (e.g., a rebellion); to restrain (a person); to subdue.—**suppression** *n*.—**suppressor** *n*.

suppurate *vi* to form or discharge pus.—**suppuration** *n*.—**suppurative** *adj*.

supr. *abbr* = supreme.

supra *prefix* above, situated above; over; beyond.

supranational *adj* transcending national boundaries or interests.

suprarenal gland *see* **adrenal gland**.

supremacist *n* a person who advocates the supremacy of a particular group.

supreme *adj* of highest power; greatest; final; ultimate.—**supremacy** *n*.

Supreme Court *n* the highest judicial body in a nation or state.

supremo *n* (*pl* **supremos**) (*inf*) the person in overall charge, a boss.

Supt *abbr* = superintendent.

Surabaya *n* a city in Indonesia.

surcharge *vt* to overcharge (a person); to charge an additional sum; to overload. * *n* an additional tax or charge; an additional or excessive charge.

surd *n* (*math*) a number containing an irrational root; an irrational number.

sure *adj* certain; without doubt; reliable, inevitable; secure; safe; dependable. * *adv* certainly.

sure-fire *adj* (*inf*) certain to succeed.

sure-footed *adj* not liable to slip or fall; unlikely to make a mistake.

surely *adv* certainly; securely; it is to be hoped or expected that.

sure thing *n* (*inf*) something assured of success. * *interj* yes, of course.

surety *n* (*pl* **sureties**) a person who undertakes responsibility for the fulfillment of another's debt; security given as a guarantee of payment of a debt.

surf *n* the waves of the sea breaking on the shore or a reef.

surf *abbr* = spent unreprocessed fuel.

surface *n* the exterior face of an object; any of the faces of a solid; the uppermost level of sea or land; a flat area, such as the top of a table; superficial features. * *adj* superficial; external. * *vt* to cover with a surface, as in paving. * *vi* to rise to the surface of water.

surface mail *n* mail transported by land or sea.

surface tension *n* (*phys*) the tension created by forces of attraction between molecules in a liquid, resulting in an apparent elastic membrane over the surface of the liquid.

surface wind *n* (*meteorol*) the wind as measured close to the Earth's surface.

surfactant *or* **surface-active agent** *n* (*chem*) a compound that reduces the surface tension of its solvent, e.g., a detergent in water.

surfactant *see* **respiratory distress syndrome**.

surfboard *n* a long, narrow board used in the sport of surfing.

surfeit *n* an excessive amount.

surfing *n* the sport of riding in toward shore on the crest of a wave, esp on a surfboard.

surg. *abbr* = surgeon; surgery; surgical.

surge *n* the rolling of the sea, as after a large wave; a sudden, strong increase, as of power; (*astron*) a solar prominence occurring as an ejection of material from the chromosphere into the corona in a spiked form —*also vi*.

surgeon *n* a medical specialist who practices surgery.

surge protector *n* (*comput*) a device placed between a computer and the mains power supply to protect the computer from momentary increases in the voltage of the power supply.

surgery *n* (*pl* **surgeries**) the treatment of diseases or injuries by manual or instrumental operations; (*Brit*) the consulting room of a doctor or dentist; (*Brit*) the daily period when a doctor is available for consultation; (*Brit*) the regular period when an MP, lawyer, etc is available for consultation.—**surgical** *adj*.—**surgically** *adv*.

Surg. Gen. *abbr* = Surgeon General.

surgical spirit *n* methylated spirit used for sterilizing.

Suriname *n* a republic in northeast South America, formerly Dutch Guiana.

Suriname guilder *n* currency of Suriname.

surly *adj* (**surlier, surliest**) ill-tempered, rude.—**surlily** *adv*.—**surliness** *n*.

surmise *n* a guess, a conjecture. * *vt* to infer the existence of from partial evidence.

surmount *vt* to overcome; to rise above.

surname *n* the family name. * *vt* to give a surname to.

surpass *vt* to outdo, outshine; to excel; to exceed.

surpassing *adj* exceptional; greatly exceeding others.—**surpassingly** *adv*.

surplice *n* a loose, white, wide-sleeved clerical garment worn by members of the clergy and choristers.

surplus *n* (*pl* **surpluses**) an amount in excess of what is required; an excess of revenues over expenditure in a financial year.

surprise *n* the act of catching unawares; an unexpected gift or event; astonishment. * *vt* to cause to feel astonished; to attack unexpectedly; to take unawares.—**surprising** *adj*.—**surprisingly** *adv*.

surreal *adj* bizarre.

surrealism *n* a movement in art characterized by the expression of the activities of the unconscious mind and dream elements.—**surrealist** *n*.—**surrealistic** *adj*.

surrender *vt* to relinquish or give up (possession or power). * *vi* to give oneself up to an enemy.—*also n*.

surrender value *n* (*ins*) the sum of money that is handed over by an insurance company to the holder of a life-insurance policy who has canceled it before it has reached the end of the contracted period.

surreptitious *adj* done by stealth; clandestine, secret.—**surreptitiously** *adv*.

Surrey *n* **Earl of [Henry Howard]** (*c.* 1517–47) English poet, soldier, and courtier, whose translations of parts of Virgil's *Aeneid*, *Tottel's Miscellany*, were the first printed blank verse in English.

surrogacy *or* **surrogate motherhood** *n* a practice in which a woman bears a child for a childless couple.

surrogate *n* a person or thing acting as a substitute for another person or thing.—*also adj*.

surrogate mother *n* a woman who bears a child in behalf of a childless couple.

surround *vt* to encircle on all or nearly all sides; (*mil*) to encircle. * *n* a border around the edge of something.

surroundings *npl* the conditions, objects, etc around a person or thing; the environment.

surtax *n* an additional tax, esp on income above a prescribed level.—*also vt*.

Surtees *n* **Robert Smith** (1803–64) English sports journalist, creator of a series of novels mainly concerned with the sporting life of the foxhunting grocer, Mr Jorrocks, e.g. *Jorrocks' Jaunts* and *Jollies and Handley Cross*.

surtitle *n* a caption projected onto a screen above the stage during an opera as a translation of the libretto or to explain some detail of the action.—*also vt*.

surv *abbr* = standard underwater research vessel.

surv. *abbr* = surveying; surveyor.

surveillance *n* a secret watch kept over a person, esp a suspect.

survey *vt* (**surveying, surveyed**) to take a general view of; to appraise; to examine carefully; to measure and make a map of (an area). * *n* (*pl* **surveys**) a detailed study, as by gathering information and analyzing it, a general view; the process of surveying an area or a house.

surveyor *n* a person who surveys land or buildings.

Surv.-Gen. *abbr* = Surveyor General.

survival *n* surviving; a person or thing that survives; a relic.

survive *vt* to live after the death of (another person); to come through alive. * *vi* to remain alive (after experiencing a dangerous situation); to continue, endure.—**survivor** *n*.

SUS *abbr* = (*Brit*) Scottish Union of Students.

Susa *n* the capital of ancient Susiana in Iran, and the site of an impressive tell.

susceptible *adj* (*with* **to**) ready or liable to be affected by; impressionable.—**susceptibility** *n*.—**susceptibly** *adv*.

sushi *n* a Japanese dish of small cakes of cold rice with various toppings, esp raw fish.

suspect *vt* to mistrust; to believe to be guilty; to think probable. * *n* a person under suspicion. * *adj* open to suspicion.

suspend *vt* to hang; to discontinue, or cease temporarily; to postpone; to debar temporarily from a privilege, etc.

suspended animation *n* a cessation of the vital functions in an organism, esp though freezing.

suspended sentence *n* a sentence that does not come into force unless a further offense is committed.

suspender *n* (*Brit*) a fastener for holding up stockings; (*pl*) straps worn over the shoulders to hold up pants.

suspender belt *n* (*Brit*) a garter belt.

suspense *n* mental anxiety or uncertainty; excitement.

suspense account *n* a temporary account in the financial records of a company or organization that records balances to correct errors or to allow for balances that have not yet been finalized.

suspension *n* suspending or being suspended; a temporary interruption or postponement; a temporary removal from office, privileges, etc; the system of springs, shock absorbers, etc that support a vehicle on its axles; (*chem*) a dispersion of fine particles in a liquid; (*mus*) a device used in harmony in which a note sounded in one chord is sustained while a subsequent chord is played or sung, producing a dissonance which is then resolved.

suspicion *n* the act of suspecting; a belief formed or held without sure proof; mistrust; a trace.—**suspicious** *adj*.—**suspiciously** *adv*.

Süssmayer *n* **Franz Xavier** (1766–1803) Austrian composer, who was a pupil of Mozart and Salieri. His compositions include Masses, cantatas, and music for the theater. He became a friend of Mozart and completed his *Requiem*, obtaining final instructions at Mozart's deathbed.

sustain *vt* to hold up, support; to maintain; to suffer (e.g., an injury); to nourish.

sustaining pedal *see* **piano**.

sustenance *n* nourishment.

SUT *abbr* = Society for Underwater Technology.

Sutherland *n* 1. **Graham [Vivian]** (1903–80) English painter, and official war artist (1941–45). 2. **Dame Joan** (1926–) Australian soprano.

suttee *n* (*Hinduism*) (*formerly*) the practice of a widow throwing herself on her husband's funeral pyre; this custom.—*also* **sati**.

Sutton Hoo *n* a site in Suffolk, England, consisting of over a dozen mounds with graves.

suture *n* a stitch holding together a wound after surgery; (*med*) a type of joint across which there is no movement, e.g., in the skull.—*also vt*.

Suva *n* capital city of Fiji.

Suzman *n* **Helen** (1917–) South African politician. She became an MP for the liberal United (later Progressive, then Democratic) Party in 1953, retiring in 1989. She has been a long and consistent campaigner against apartheid.

Suzuki, *n* **Daisetsu Teitaro** (1870–1966) Japanese Buddhist philosopher, whose works on Zen Buddhism, such as *Studies in Zen* (1955), played a key role in popularizing the principles of Zen Buddhism in the West.

sv *abbr* = (*Latin*) *sub verbo*, "under the word"; (*Latin*) *sub voce*, "under the heading."

s/v *abbr* = surrender value.

SV *abbr* = (*Latin*) *Sancta Virgo*, "Holy Virgin"; (*Latin*) *Sanctitas Vestra*, "Your Holiness"; simian virus; Sons of Veterans.

SVA *abbr* (*Brit*) = Scottish Volleyball Association.

SVC *abbr* = superior vena cava.

SVD *abbr* = swine vesicular disease.

svelte *adj* slim and elegant.

Svendsen *n* **Johan Severin** (1842–1911) Norwegian composer, violinist, and conductor. Having been a virtuoso violin player, he turned to composing while studying in Leipzig, where he was influenced by Wagner. He wrote orchestral works, including two symphonies.

S-VHS *abbr* = Super Video Home System.

SVO *abbr* (*gram*) = subject, verb, object.

SVP *abbr* (*French*) = *s'il vous plaît*, "please"; Society of Saint Vincent de Paul.

svr *abbr* (*Latin*) = *spiritus vini rectificatus*, "rectified spirit of wine."

SVS *abbr* = Society of Visiting Scientists; still-camera video system.

s.v.t. *abbr* (*Latin*) = *spiritus vini tenuior* " proof spirit of wine."

sw. *abbr* = swell organ; switch.

s.w. *abbr* = sent wrong.

Sw. *abbr* = Sweden; Swedish.

SW *abbr* = Samaritans Worldwide; short wave; small women's (size of clothing); southwest(ern).

S/W *abbr* = software.

SWA *abbr* = (*Brit*) Scotch Whisky Association; (*Brit*) Scottish Whitebait Association; (*Brit*) Scottish Women's Aid; Society of Women Artists; Sports Writers' Association; Steel Window Association.

SWA *abbr* = Southwest Africa.

swab *n* a wad of absorbent material, usu cotton, used to clean wounds, take specimens, etc; a mop.—*also vt*.

SWACS *abbr* = Space Warning and Control System.

swaddle *vt* to bind tightly, envelop; to wrap (a baby) in swaddling clothes.

swaddling clothes *npl* narrow strips of cloth used to wrap and restrain an infant.

swag *n* (*sl*) loot.

swagger *vi* to strut; to brag loudly. * *n* boastfulness; swinging gait.

Swahili *n* a language spoken in Kenya, Tanzania and other parts of east Africa; (*pl* **Swahilis, Swahili**) a member of a people speaking this language who live mainly in Zanzibar.

swain *n* (*poet*) a male suitor or lover.

Swakopmund *n* a city in Namibia.

Swalfred *n* (*d. c.*712) king of Essex (695–709). Succeeded his father, Sebbi, and ruled jointly with his brother, Sigeherd.

swalk *abbr* = sealed with a loving kiss.

swallow[1] *n* a small migratory bird with long wings and a forked tail.

swallow[2] *vt* to cause food and drink to move from the mouth to the stomach; to endure; to engulf; (*inf*) to accept gullibly; (*emotion, etc*) to repress.—*also n*.

swallow dive *n* a dive executed with the back arched and arms outstretched at the start.

swam *see* **swim**.

swami *n* (*pl* **swamies, swamis**) a Hindu religious teacher.

swamp *n* wet, spongy land; bog. * *vt* to overwhelm; to flood as with water.—**swampy** *adj*.

swan *n* a large, usu white, bird with a very long neck, that lives on rivers and lakes. * *vi* (**swanning, swanned**) (*inf*) to wander aimlessly.

swan dive *n* a swallow dive.

swank *vi* (*inf*) to show off.—*also n*.—**swanky** *adj*.

swap *vti* (**swapping, swapped**) (*inf*) to trade, barter. * *n* (*inf*) the act of exchanging one thing for another.—*also* **swop**.

swap file *n* (*comput*) a file held on the hard disk, and used when a computer's RAM is not large enough to store the full program. The computer processor moves information between the RAM and the swap file as required.

SWAPO, Swapo *abbr* South West Africa People's Organization.

sward *n* (an area of land with) a surface of short grass.

swarm *n* a colony of migrating bees; a moving mass, crowd or throng. * *vi* to move in great numbers; to teem.

swarthy *adj* (**swarthier, swarthiest**) dark-complexioned.—**swarthiness** *n*.

swash *n* the powerful movement of water up a beach from a breaking wave.

swashbuckling *adj* swaggering; exciting, adventurous.—**swashbuckler** *n*.

swastika *n* an ancient symbol formed by a cross with the ends of the arms bent at right-angles, used by Nazi Germany.

swat *vt* (**swatting, swatted**) (*inf*) to hit with a sharp blow; to swipe.—*also n*.—**swatter** *n*.

swath *n* the width of one sweep of a scythe or other mowing device; a strip, row, etc, mowed; a broad strip.

swathe *vt* to bind or wrap around, as with a bandage; to envelop, enclose. * *n* the strip of the Earth's surface that is scanned by a sensor in an orbiting satellite.

sway *vi* to swing or move from one side to the other or to and fro; to lean to one side; to vacillate in judgment or opinion. * *n* influence; control.

Swaziland *n* a monarchy almost entirely within the borders of the Republic of South Africa but with a short border in the east with Mozambique.

swb *abbr* = short wheelbase.

swbd. *abbr* = switchboard.

SWbS *abbr* = southwest by south.

SWbW *abbr* = southwest by west.

SWCL *abbr* (*Brit*) = Scottish Wildlife and Countryside Link.

SWE *abbr* = Society of Wood Engravers.

swear *vi* (**swearing, swore**, *pp* **sworn**) to make a solemn affirmation, promise, etc, calling God as a witness; to give evidence on oath; to curse, blaspheme, or use obscene language; to vow; (*with* **off**) to promise abstinence from. * *vt* (*with* **in**) to appoint to an office by the administration of an oath.

swearword *n* a profane or obscene expression.

sweat *n* perspiration; (*inf*) hard work; (*inf*) a state of eagerness, anxiety.—*also vti*.—**sweaty** *adj*.

sweatband *n* a strip of material in a hat, or worn on the wrist or around the forehead, to absorb sweat.

sweater *n* a knitted garment for the upper body.

sweat glands *npl* the glands in the epidermis of skin that project into the dermis and are under the control of the sympathetic nervous system. *See also* **perspiration**.

sweating assets *npl* (*econ*) the process of increasing the profits that are generated by a company's assets in situations in which the return on capital has been found to be inadequate.

sweatpants *npl* loose-fitting pants with a drawstring waist and elasticated ankles.

sweatshirt *n* a loose, collarless, heavy cotton, long-sleeved top.

sweatshop *n* a small factory or workshop where employees work long hours at low wages in poor conditions.

Swed. *abbr* = Sweden; Swedish.

swede *n* a round root vegetable with yellow flesh.

Swede *n* a native of Sweden.

Sweden *n* a constitutional monarchy that occupies the larger and longer eastern section of the Scandinavian Peninsula.

Swedish *adj* pertaining to Sweden, its people, or their language. * *n* the language of Sweden.

Sweelinck *n* **Jan Pieterszoon** (1562–1621) Dutch composer, organist, and harpsichordist, who became an influential teacher of Dutch and German composers.

sweep *vt* (**sweeping, swept**) to clean with a broom; to remove (rubbish or dirt) with a brush. * *vi* to pass by swiftly. * *n* a movement, esp in an arc; a stroke; scope, range; a sweepstake.

sweeper *n* a person who sweeps, esp the roads; (*soccer*) (*inf*) a player positioned before the goalkeeper to collect loose balls, tackle attacking players, etc.

sweep facility *n* a facility by which a bank automatically transfers a customer's funds to whichever account will bring in most interest.

sweeping *adj* wide-ranging; indiscriminate.—**sweepingly** *adv*.

sweepstake *or* **sweepstakes** *n* a lottery in which the prize constitutes all the money staked; a horse race, etc in which the winner receives the entire prize.

sweet *adj* having a taste like sugar; pleasing to other senses; gentle; kind. * *n* (*Brit*) a small piece of candy; (*Brit*) a dessert.—**sweetly** *adv*.—**sweetness** *n*.

sweet-and-sour *adj* (*food*) cooked in a sauce containing sugar and vinegar or lemon juice.

sweetbread *n* the pancreas or thymus gland of an animal, cooked as food.

sweet brier *n* a Eurasian rose with pink flowers.

sweet cicely *n* an aromatic European plant with small, white flowers; the aniseed-flavored leaves of this, once used in cookery.

sweet clover *n* a species of sweet-scented trefoil or clover, with clusters of small, yellow or white flowers; melilot.

sweetcorn *n* maize, corn on the cob.

sweeten *vti* to make or become sweet or sweeter; to mollify.

sweetener *n* a sweetening substance that contains no sugar; (*sl*) a bribe.

sweetheart *n* a lover.

sweetie *n* sweetheart, darling; (*inf*) a kindly, pleasant person; (*Brit, inf*) a small piece of candy;.

sweetmeat *n* a piece of candy, a preserve, a small cake, or other sugary delicacy.

sweet pea *n* a climbing garden plant cultivated for its large, fragrant blooms.

sweet pepper *n* (a plant bearing) a large fruit with thick, fleshy walls, eaten ripe (red) or unripe (green).

sweet potato *n* (a tropical climbing plant with) a large edible tuberous root.

sweet william *n* a widely grown Eurasian plant with clusters of white, red, pink, or purple flowers.

sweet-talk *vt* (*inf*) to flatter, cajole.—**sweet talk** *n*.

swell *vi* (**swelling, swelled,** *pp* **swollen** *or* **swelled**) to increase in size or volume; to rise into waves; to bulge out. * *n* the movement of the sea; a bulge; a gradual increase in the loudness of a musical note; (*inf*) a socially prominent person. * *adj* excellent.

swelling *n* inflammation.

swell organ *n* (*mus*) a manual on an organ. The notes played on this manual can become louder and softer by the opening and closing of the shutters on the swell box that encloses the pipes.

swelter *vi* to suffer from heat. * *n* humid, oppressive heat.

sweltering *adj* uncomfortably hot.

swept *see* **sweep**.

sweptback *adj* (*aircraft wing*) slanting backward.

sweptwing *adj* (*aircraft*) having sweptback wings.

swerve *vi* to turn aside suddenly from a line or course; to veer.—*also n*.

SWET *abbr* (*Brit*) = Society of West End Theatres.

Sweyn Forkbeard *n* (d. 1014) king of England, Norway and Demark. Reigned (England) from 1013–1014. The son of Harold Bluetooth of Denmark and Queen Gunild, he built his North Sea empire through conquest and marriage. He had two sons; Harold IV of Denmark and Canute, later to be king of England.

SWF *abbr* = single white female.

SWFA *abbr* (*Brit*) = Scottish Women's Football Association.

swg *or* **SWG** *abbr* = standard wire gauge.

swg. *or* **swtg.** *abbr* = switching.

SWG *abbr* (*Brit*) = Song Writers' Guild of Great Britain.

SWHA *abbr* (*Brit*) = Scottish Women's Hockey Association.

SWI *abbr* (*Brit*) = Scottish Woollen Industry.

swift *adj* moving with great speed; rapid. * *n* a swallow-like bird.—**swiftly** *adv*.—**swiftness** *n*.

Swift *n* **Jonathan** (1667–1745) Anglo-Irish divine, poet, and satirist, whose masterpiece is *Gulliver's Travels* (1726).

swig *vt* (**swigging, swigged**) (*inf*) to take a long drink, esp from a bottle.—*also n*.

swill *vti* to drink greedily; to guzzle; to rinse with a large amount of water. * *n* liquid refuse fed to pigs.

swim *vi* (**swimming, swam,** *pp* **swum**) to move through water by using limbs or fins; to be dizzy; (*with* **with**) to be flooded (with). * *n* the act of swimming.—**swimmer** *n*.

swimmingly *adv* (*inf*) easily, without effort.

swimming pool *n* an artificial outdoor or covered pool used for swimming in.

swimsuit *n* a one-piece garment for swimming in.

Swinburne *n* **Algernon [Charles]** (1837–1909) English poet and critic, noted for his sensuous verse. His poems, e.g., *Poems and Ballads*, created a public scandal for their sexuality and for the author's dislike of Christianity and sympathy for paganism.

swindle *vti* to cheat (someone) out of money or property.—*also n*.—**swindler** *n*.

swindle sheet *n* (*sl*) an expenses form.

swine *n* (*pl* **swine**) a pig; (*inf*) a contemptible person; (*inf*) an unpleasant thing.

swine fever *n* a viral infection of pigs.

swineherd *n* a person who looks after pigs.

swing *vi* (**swinging, swung**) to sway or move to and fro, as an object hanging in the air; to pivot; to shift from one mood or opinion to another; to play swing music; (*music*) to have a lively rhythm; (*sl*) to be hanged. * *vt* to whirl; to influence; to achieve, bring about. * *n* a swinging, curving, or rhythmic movement; a suspended seat for swinging in; a shift from one condition to another; a type of popular jazz played by a large band and characterized by a lively, steady rhythm.

swing *abbr* = sterling warrant into gilt-edged stock.

swingeing *adj* drastic, severe.

swinging *adj* (*inf*) up-to-date; lively.

swinging door *n* a hinged door that opens in or out and swings to of itself.

swing-wing *adj* of or pertaining to an aircraft with movable wings that are swept back at high speeds and moved forward for approach and landing.—*also n*.

swipe *n* (*inf*) a hard, sweeping blow. * *vt* (*inf*) to hit with a swipe; (*sl*) to steal.

swirl *vti* to turn with a whirling motion.—*also n*.

swish *vi* to move with a soft, whistling, hissing sound. * *n* a swishing sound. * *adj* (*inf*) smart, fashionable.

Swiss *adj* of or belonging to Switzerland. * *n* (*pl* **Swiss**) a native of Switzerland.

Swiss chard *n* an edible beet with thick stalks and large leaves.

Swiss cheese *n* a hard cheese with large holes.

Swiss Franc *n* currency of Switzerland and the Principality of Liechtenstein.

swiss roll *n* (*Brit*) a thin sponge cake spread with a layer of jam and/or cream and rolled up.

switch *n* a control for turning on and off an electrical device; a sudden change; a swap. * *vt* to shift, change, swap; to turn on or off (an electrical device).

switchback *n* a zigzag road in a mountain region; a roller coaster.

switchblade *n* a flick knife.

switchboard *n* an installation in a building where telephone calls are connected.

switching *n* (*com*) the use of the money acquired from the sale of one investment in order to purchase another investment; the process of exporting and importing goods through a third country where the type of currency used to pay for the goods can be exchanged into another currency that is acceptable to the seller; the intervention of a country in the international currency market in order to prevent an undue outflow of its currency.

switching cost *n* (*com*) a method of making sure that a customer will be involved in additional expenditure if he or she switches to the product or service of a different supplier.

Swithhelm *n* (d. 665) king of Essex (660–665). Succeeded by his son, Sebbi and his brother, Sighere, who ruled jointly.

Swithin *n* **Saint** (c. 805–862) English Ecclesiastic; bishop of Winchester; built and restored churches and built a bridge over the Itchen on the east side of Winchester. His feast day is 15 July.

Swithred *n* king of Essex, Britain (746–758). He made Colchester the capital of his kingdom.

Switzerland *n* a landlocked federal republic in central Europe, sharing its borders with France, Italy, Austria, Liechtenstein, and Germany.

swivel *n* a coupling that permits parts to rotate. * *vi* to turn (as if) on a pin or pivot.

swl *abbr* = safe working load.

SWLA *abbr* = Society of Wildlife Artists.

SWLG *abbr* (*Brit*) = Scottish Wild Land Group.

SWM *abbr* = single white male.

SWMF *abbr* (*com*) = South Wales Miners' Federation.

SWOA *abbr* (*com*) = Scottish Woodland Owners' Association.

swollen *see* **swell**.

swoon *vi* to faint.—*also n*.

swoop *vt* to carry off abruptly. * *vi* (*usu with* **down**) to make a sudden attack, as a bird in hunting.—*also n*.

swop *see* **swap**.

sword *n* a weapon with a long blade and a handle at one end.

sword dance *n* a dance in which swords are brandished or placed on the ground and stepped between.

swordfish *n* (*pl* **swordfish** *or* **swordfishes**) a large marine fish with a sword-like, upper jaw.

swordplay *n* fighting with swords; verbal combat.

swordsman *n* (*pl* **swordsmen**) a person skilled in the use of a sword.

swordstick *n* a walking stick concealing a sword.

swore, sworn *see* **swear**.

swot *vi* (**swotting, swotted**) (*inf*) to study hard for an examination. * *n* (*inf*) a person who studies hard.

SWOT *abbr* = strengths, weaknesses, opportunities, and threats (product-marketing analysis).

SWOT analysis *n* the analysis of the internal strengths and weaknesses of a product or company and the external opportunities that are open to it, along with the potential threats it faces.

swp *abbr* = safe working pressure.

SWP *abbr* = Socialist Workers' Party.

SWPF *abbr* = single white professional female.

SWR *abbr* = standing-wave ratio.

SWRI *abbr* (*Brit*) = Scottish Women's Rural Institutes.

SWS *abbr* = Society of Wetland Scientists; static water supply.

SWT *abbr* (*Brit*) = Scottish Wildlife Trust.

Swtz. *or* **Swit.** *abbr* = Switzerland.

swum *see* **swim**.

swung *see* **swing**.

SX *abbr* = Sundays excepted.

SY *abbr* = steam yacht.

Sybaris *n* an ancient Greek city of lower Italy, on the Gulf of Tarentum, the first Greek colony, whose inhabitants were proverbial for their lives of luxury.—**Sybarite** *n*.—**Sybaritic** *adj*.

sycamore *n* a Eurasian maple tree; an American plane tree; a tree of Africa and Asia bearing a fruit resembling a fig.

sycophant *n* a person who flatters and praises powerful people to win their favor.—**sycophancy** *n*.—**sycophantic** *adj*.

Sydenham's chorea *see* **chorea**.

Sydney *n* a city in Australia.

SYHA *abbr* (*Brit*) = Scottish Youth Hostels Association.

syllabary *n* a writing system in which a syllable (vowel and consonant) is represented by a symbol.

syllabi *see* **syllabus**.

syllabic *adj* consisting of syllables; articulated in syllables.

syllable *n* a word or part of a word uttered in a single sound; one or more letters written to represent a spoken syllable.

syllabub, sillabub *n* a cold dessert made with sweetened whipped cream flavored with sherry, wine, lemon juice, etc.

syllabus *n* (*pl* **syllabuses** *or* **syllabi**) a summary or outline of a course of study or of examination requirements; the subjects studied for a particular course.

syllogism *n* a form of reasoning consisting of a major premise, a minor premise, and a conclusion, e.g., *All men must die; I am a man; therefore I must die*.

sylph *n* a slim girl or woman.

sym. *abbr* = symbol; symmetrical; (*mus*) symphony.

symbiosis *n* a mutually advantageous partnership between two interdependent plant or animal species.—**symbiotic** *adj*.

symbiotic star *n* a variable star that shows spectral features of both a cool star and hot gases from a B star.

symbol *n* a representation; an object used to represent something abstract; an arbitrary or conventional sign standing for a quality, process, relation, etc, as in music, chemistry, or mathematics.

symbolic *or* **symbolical** *adj* of, using, or constituting a symbol.—**symbolically** *adv*.

symbolism *n* the use of symbols; a system of symbolic representation.—**symbolist** *n*.

symbolize *vt* to be a symbol of; to represent by a symbol.—**symbolization** *n*.—**symbolizer** *n*.

symbol retailer *n* a voluntary retailer.

symmetrical *or* **symmetric** *adj* having symmetry.—**symmetrically** *adv*.

symmetry *n* (*pl* **symmetries**) the corresponding arrangement of one part to another in size, shape, and position; balance or harmony of form resulting from this.

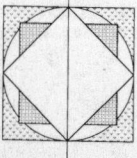

sympathetic *adj* having sympathy; compassionate; (*med*) (*symptom, disease*) occurring as a result of disease elsewhere in the body, e.g., injury of one eye and a related inflammation in the other.—**sympathetically** *adv*.

sympathetic nervous system *n* a part of the autonomic nervous system whose functions include raising the heartbeat rate, constricting blood vessels, and inhibiting saliva secretion.

sympathetic strings *npl* (*mus*) strings on certain instruments (such as the sitar) that are not plucked or bowed but are set in sympathetic vibration and produce a note without being touched, when the same note is played on a "melody" string.

sympathize *vi* (*with* **with**) to feel sympathy (for); to commiserate (with); to be in sympathy (with).—**sympathizer** *n*.—**sympathizingly** *adv*.

sympathy *n* (*pl* **sympathies**) agreement of ideas and opinions; compassion; (*pl*) support for an action or cause.

symphonic poem *n* (*mus*) an orchestral composition, a form of program music, usu in one movement, which attempts to interpret or describe an emotion, idea, or story.

Symphonie fantastique *n* an orchestral work in five movements by Berlioz (1830).

symphony *n* (*pl* **symphonies**) an orchestral composition in several movements; a large orchestra for playing symphonic works.—**symphonic** *adj*.—**symphonically** *adv*.

Symplegades *see* **Clashing Rocks**.

symposium *n* (*pl* **symposiums** *or* **symposia**) a conference at which several specialists deliver short addresses on a topic; an anthology of scholarly essays.

symptom *n* a bodily sensation experienced by a patient indicative of a particular disease; an indication.

symptomatic *adj* of, being, or relating to symptoms; indicative.—**symptomatically** *adv*.

syn. *abbr* = synonym; synonymous; synonymy.

syn- *prefix* together.

synagogue *n* a building where Jews assemble for worship and religious study.

synapse *n* the point at which a nerve impulse is transmitted between neurons.

sync, synch *n* (*inf*) synchronization. * *vti* (*inf*) to synchronize.

synchromesh *adj* (*gear system*) incorporating a device that regulates the revolving parts in a gear so that they are at the same speed when brought into contact. * *n* a gear system using this.

synchronize *vt* to adjust (watches) to show the same time. * *vi* to occur at the same time and speed.—**synchronization** *n*.—**synchronizer** *n*.

synchronous *adj* occurring at the same time; (*comput*) (*method of communication*) synchronized with electronic signals produced by a computer. *See also* **parallel port**.—**synchronously** *adv*.—**synchronousness** *n*.

synchrotron radiation *n* electromagnetic radiation given out when electrons with very high energy pass through a magnetic field almost at the speed of light.

syncline *n* a downfold fold of rocks shaped like a basin, with the younger strata uppermost (in the center).

syncopate *vt* (*mus*) to modify beats in (a musical piece) by displacing the rhythmical accents from strong beats to weak ones and vice versa.—**syncopation** *n*.

syncope *n* fainting; a temporary loss of consciousness because of a fall in blood pressure and a reduced supply of blood to the brain.

syndactyly *n* a congenital effect in which there is a fusion of fingers or toes.

syndicate *n* an association of individuals or corporations formed for a project requiring much capital; any group, as of criminals, organized for some undertaking; an organization selling articles or features to many newspapers, etc. * *vt* to manage as or form into a syndicate; to sell (an article, etc) through a syndicate. * *vi* to form a syndicate.—**syndication** *n*.

syndicated loan *n* a loan that is supplied by a number of financial institutions collectively.

syndrome *n* a characteristic pattern of signs and symptoms of a disease.

synergist *n* a muscle that works in conjunction with another muscle; a drug that combines with another drug, the two having a greater effect when taken together than separately.—**synergism** *n*.—**synergistic** *adj*.

synergy *n* synergism; (*com*) the possibility that the merger of two individual companies will produce a combined operation of greater productivity and efficiency.—**synergetic** *or* **synergistic** *adj*.

synesis *n* (*gram*) a construction in harmony with its sense rather than with strict syntax, e.g., "a large number were present."

synesthesia *n* a sensation produced in a part of the body other than the part stimulated; a subjective sensation of a sense different from the sense stimulated.—**synesthetic** *adj*.

Synge *n* [**Edmund**] **J**[**ohn**] **M**[**illington**] (1871–1909) Irish dramatist, whose plays of Irish peasant life were performed at the Abbey Theatre in Dublin. His masterpiece is the *The Playboy of the Western World*.

synod *n* a council of members of a church that meets to discuss religious issues.

synonym *n* a word that has the same, or similar, meaning as another or others in the same language.

synonymous *adj* having the same meaning; equivalent.—**synonymously** *adv*.

synonymy *n* (*pl* **synonymies**) the condition of being synonymous; a system or collection of synonyms; the use of synonyms for emphasis, e.g., "in any shape or form."

synop. *abbr* = synopsis.

synopsis *n* (*pl* **synopses**) a summary or brief review of a subject.

synoptic chart *n* a weather map showing atmospheric pressure, temperature, wind speed and direction, cloud cover, and precipitation for a given area at a specific time.

synovia *n* a thick fluid that lubricates the joints and tendons.—**synovial** *adj*.

synovial membrane *or* **synovium** *n* the inner membrane of a capsule enclosing a joint that moves freely.

synovitis *n* inflammation of the membrane around a joint.

synovium *see* **synovial membrane**.

synpotic image *n* the image of a large part of the Earth's surface.

syntax *n* (*gram*) the arrangement of words in the sentences and phrases of language; the rules governing this; (*comput*) the set of rules that govern the way in which a command is given to a computer so that it recognizes the command and proceeds accordingly.—**syntactic** *adj*.—**syntactically** *adv*.

syntax error *n* (*comput*) an error resulting from the incorrect spelling of a command or in the way the commands are entered.

synth *n* a synthesizer.

synthesis *n* (*pl* **syntheses**) the process of combining separate elements of thought into a whole; the production of a compound by a chemical reaction.

synthesize *vti* to combine into a whole.

synthesizer *n* an electronic device producing music and sounds by using a computer to combine individual sounds previously recorded.

synthetic *adj* produced by chemical synthesis; artificial.—**synthetically** *adv*.

SYP *abbr* = Society of Young Publishers.

syphilis *n* a contagious, infectious, sexually transmitted disease.—**syphilitic** *adj*.

syphon *see* **siphon**.

syr. *abbr* = (*pharm*) syrup; (*Latin*) *syrupus*, "syrup."

Syr. *abbr* = Syria; Syriac; Syrian.

Syria *or* **the Syrian Arab Republic** *n* a country in southwest Asia, which borders on the Mediterranean Sea in the west.

Syrian *n* a native or inhabitant of Syria; the Arabic dialect spoken there.—*also adj*.

Syrian Pound *n* currency of the Syrian Arab Republic.

syringe *n* a hollow tube with a plunger at one end and a sharp needle at the other by which liquids are injected or withdrawn, esp in medicine. * *vt* to inject or cleanse with a syringe.

syrinx *n* (*pl* **syringes**) the vocal organ in birds.

Syrinx *n* (*Greek myth*) an Arcadian nymph, who, pursued by Pan, fled into a river and was changed into a reed of which Pan then made his pipes.

syrup *n* a thick, sweet substance made by boiling sugar with water; the concentrated juice of a fruit or plant; (*med*) a mixture of sugar, water, and drug, used for the easy administration of medications that may taste unpleasant.—**syrupy** *adj*.

SYSOP *abbr* (*comput*) = SYStem OPerator.

syst. *abbr* = system.

systaltic *adj* (*heart, etc*) alternately expanding and contracting; pulsating.

system *n* a method of working or organizing by following a set of rules; routine; organization; structure; a political regime; an arrangement of parts fitting together; (*comput*) all the necessary hardware and software required in an installation, all of which is interconnected and set up to work together (central processing unit, disk drives, monitor, printer, keyboard, etc).

systematic *adj* constituting or based on a system; according to a system.—**systematically** *adv*.

systematize *vt* to arrange according to a system.—**systematization** *n*.—**systematizer** *n*.

system date *n* (*comput*) the date that is held in a computer's internal memory, protected by a battery backup so that it is not lost when the computer is switched off.

system disk *n* (*comput*) a disk containing the operating system and all related files. It can be a floppy or a hard disk.

system error *n* (*comput*) an error that occurs at the system level of operation of a computer, as opposed to a user-generated error.

systemic *adj* (*poison, infection, etc*) of or affecting the entire body; (*insecticide, etc*) designed to be taken up into the plant tissues.—**systemically** *adv*.

systemic lupus erythematosus *n* a chronic inflammatory disease of connective tissues, believed to be an autoimmune disease. *See also* **lupus**.

systemize *vt* to systematize.—**systemization** *n*.

system program *n* (*comput*) *see* **ROM**.

system prompt *n* (*comput*) an indicator to show that the operating system is ready to accept a command.

systems analysis *n* analysis of a particular task or operation to determine how computer hardware and software may best perform it.—**systems analyst** *n*.

system software *n* (*comput*) the group of codes that the computer requires to start up, including the operating system, which controls all the major functions of the computer.

systole *n* the regular contractions of the chambers of the heart by which the circulation of blood is maintained.—**systolic** *adj*.

systolic blood pressure *n* (*physiol*) the pressure generated by the left ventricle of the heart at the peak of its contraction.

Szasz *n* **Thomas Stephen** (1920–) Hungarian-born American psychiatrist, who argued that mental illness is in reality a myth fostered as an agent of repression in such works as *The Myth of Mental Illness* (1961). He also attacked R D Laing and the anti-psychiatry movement in *Schizophrenia: The Sacred Symbol of Psychiatry* (1979).

Szeged *n* a city in Hungary.

Szekely *n* **Martin** (1956–) French furniture designer, who began as a copper-plate engraver and worked extensively in stark black carbon steel.

Szymanowski *n* **Karol** (1882–1937) Polish composer who is considered the father of modern Polish music. His works include operas (such as *King Roger)* the ballet *Harnasie*, four symphonies, and many pieces of chamber music.

T

t,T *n* the 20th letter of the English alphabet; something shaped like a T.

T *symbol* (*chem*) tritium.

t *abbr* = tare; temperature; tense; tera-; (*French*) *tome*, "volume"; ton or tonne; transitive; troy.

t. *abbr* = (*Italian*) (*music*) *tace*, "be silent"; tare; target; telephone; temperature; tempo; (*Latin*) *tempore*, "in the time of"; tenor; (*gram*) tense; (*geom*) tensor; territorial; territory; time; tome; (*Latin*) *tomus*, "volume"; ton or tonne; (*French*) *tonneau*, "ton" (metric); town; township; transit; transitive; trillo; tun; tutti.

T *abbr* = tablespoon; (*chem*) tantalum; temperature on the absolute scale; tenor; (*phys*) (surface) tension; tesla; thousand (car mileage); time; Thursday; Tuesday.

T. *abbr* = (*astron*) temporary magnitude; Testament; triangle; (*Brit law*) Trinity Term; Tuesday; Turkish; Turkish (pounds).

Ta *symbol* (*chem*) tantalum (element).

ta *abbr* = target area; time and attendance.

t.a. *abbr* (*Latin*) = *testantibus actis*, "as the acts show."

TA *abbr* = Traffic Auditor; Transactional Analysis; Transport Association; (*Brit mil*) Territorial Army; Tricycle Association; teaching assistant.

TA & VRA *abbr* (*Brit mil*) = Territorial, Auxiliary and Volunteer Reserve Association.

tab[1] *n* tabulator; tablet. * *vt* (**tabbing, tabbed**) to tabulate.

tab[2] *n* a small tag, label, or flap; (*inf*) a bill, as for expenses. * *vt* (**tabbing, tabbed**) to fix a tab on.

tab. *abbr* = tables.

TAA *abbr* = (*Brit mil*) Territorial Army Association; Ticket Agents Association; Trade Adjustment Assistance; Trans-Antarctic Association; Trans-Australia Airlines; Tropical Agriculture Association.

TAB *abbr* (*med*) = typhoid-paratyphoid A and B, a vaccine obtained from salmonella bacteria and used in the treatment of typhoid and the A and B strains of paratyphoid.

tabard *n* a short armless tunic, esp one bearing a coat of arms and worn by a herald or by a knight over his armor; a sleeveless garment shaped like this worn by women.

Tabasco *n* (*trademark*) a very hot red pepper sauce.

tabbouleh *n* an Arabic salad made with vegetables, spices, lemon juice, and cracked wheat.

tabby *n* (*pl* **tabbies**) a domestic cat with a striped coat, esp a female; a heavy watered silk. * *adj* striped in brown or grey. * *vt* (**tabbying, tabbied**) to pattern (silk) with a wavy pattern.

tabernacle *n* a place of worship; a decorative recess with a canopy in which the holy sacraments are placed; an ornamental receptacle containing the holy sacraments.—**tabernacular** *adj*.

Tabernacle *n* (*Bible*) the tent which contained the Ark of the Covenant. It was carried by the Hebrews as they wandered through the wilderness. *See also* **Horns of the Altar**.

Tabernacles *n* **Feast of the** an eight-day Jewish feast.

tabes *n* (*pl* **tabes**) wasting caused by chronic disease.—**tabetic** *adj*, *n*.

tabes dorsalis *n* (*med*) paralysis caused by syphilis at an advanced stage when it attacks the spinal cord. *See also* **locomotor ataxia**.

Tabitha *n* (*Bible*) Aramaic for the Greek Dorcas, or dove. *See also* **Dorcas**.

tab key *n* (*comput*) a key that is used to move text to the right by a preset number of spaces.

tabla *n* (*mus*) a pair of Indian drums, beaten by the hands, which are often used to accompany the sitar in classical Indian music.

tablature *n* (*mus*) musical notation indicating the strings, frets, fingering, rhythm, etc, to be used, esp for the lute.

table[1] *n* a piece of furniture consisting of a slab or board on legs; the people seated round a table; supply of food; a flat surface; a level area; a slab or tablet in a wall; an inscription on this; a list of facts and figures arranged in columns for reference or comparison; a folding leaf of a backgammon board; **at table** having a meal; **on the table** (*legislative bill, etc*) postponed, often indefinitely; **to turn the tables on** to put (an opponent) in a position of disadvantage previously held by oneself. * *vt* to submit, to put forward; to postpone indefinitely; to lay on a table. * *adj* of, on or at a table.

table[2] *n* (*mus*) an alternative name for the upper surface or belly of members of the violin family.

tableau *n* (*pl* **tableaux, tableaus**) a dramatic or graphic representation of a group or scene; a tableau vivant.

tableau vivant *n* (*pl* **tableaux vivants**) a representation of an historical scene by people in costume posed silently and motionless.

tablecloth *n* a cloth for covering a table.

table d'hôte *n* (*pl* **tables d'hôte**) a meal at a fixed price for a set number of courses.—*also adj*.

tableland *n* an expanse of flat elevated land, a plateau.

tablespoon *n* a large serving spoon; a unit of measure in cooking.

tablespoonful *n* (**tablespoonfuls**) the amount a tablespoon holds.

tablet *n* a pad of paper; a medicinal pill; a cake of solid substance, such as soap; a slab of stone.

table tennis *n* a game like tennis played on a table with small bats and a ball.

tableware *n* dishes, cutlery, etc for use at mealtimes.

tabloid *n* a small-format newspaper characterized by emphasis on photographs and news in condensed form.

TABMAC *abbr* = The All British Martial Arts Council.

taboo, tabu *n* (*pl* **taboos, tabus**) a religious or social prohibition of the use or practice of something; the thing prohibited. * *adj* forbidden from use, mention, etc. * *vt* (**tabooing, tabooed** or **tabuing, tabued**) to forbid by social or personal influence the use, practice or mention of something or contact with someone.

tabor, tabour *n* (*mus*) a small drum formerly used to accompany a pipe, both instruments being played by the same person.

Tabriz *n* city in Islamic Republic of Iran.

tab stop *n* (*comput*) the point where the cursor stops when the tab key is pressed.

tabular *adj* like a table, flat; arranged in the form of a table; calculated with a table.—**tabularly** *adv*.

tabula rasa *n* (*pl* **tabulae rasae**) the mind when regarded as in its original state and clear of impressions; a fresh start.

tabulate *vt* to arrange (written material) in tabular form.—**tabulation** *n*

tabulator *n* a device that sets stops to locate columns on a typewriter or word processor.

TAC *abbr* = Tactical Air Command; Theatres Advisory Council; Tobacco Advisory Council.

TACAC *abbr* = Trans Atlantic Committee on Agricultural Change.

tacamahac *n* (any tree yielding) any of various pungent gum resins used esp in incense.

tacan *abbr* = tactical air navigation.

tace *adj* (*mus*) (*Italian*) "silent."

tacet *vi* (*mus*) a direction on a musical score indicating that from this point a particular instrument is not to play.

tachism *n* a form of action painting using random blobs of color.

tachistoscope *n* a device for projecting visual information onto a screen for a split second only, used in the study of perception and learning.

tacho- *prefix* speed.

tachograph *n* a device in motor vehicles, esp lorries, to record speed and time of travel.

tachometer *n* an instrument for measuring the speed of rotation of a shaft, as in a vehicle engine.

tachy- *prefix* rapid or accelerated.

tachycardia *n* (*med*) increased rate of heartbeat, which may be caused naturally, as with exercise, or be symptomatic of disease.

tachygraphy *n* shorthand, esp as used in ancient Greece and Rome.

tachymeter *n* a surveying instrument for measuring long distances rapidly.

tachyon *n* (*phys*) a theoretical elementary particle that can travel faster than light.

tacit *adj* implied without really being spoken; understood.—**tacitly** *adv*.—**tacitness** *n*.

taciturn *adj* habitually silent and reserved.—**taciturnity** *n*.

tack[1] *n* a short, flat-headed nail; (*naut*) the course of a sailing ship; a course of action, approach; adhesiveness; a horse's harness, including saddle and bridle. * *vi* to change direction. * *vt* to fasten with tacks.

tack[2] *n* (*inf*) food.

Tackett *n* **La Gardo** (1911–94) American ceramicist and teacher whose work with his students led to the formation of architectural pottery in 1950.

tackle *n* a system of ropes and pulleys for lifting; equipment; rigging; (*sport*) an act of grabbing and stopping an opponent. * *vt* to attend to (*task, etc*), undertake; to confront (*a person*); (*sport*) to challenge with a tackle.

tacky[1] *adj* (**tackier, tackiest**) sticky (*paint, etc*).

tacky[2] *adj* (**tackier, tackiest**) (*inf*) shabby; ostentatious, and vulgar; seedy.—**tackiness** *n*.

tact *n* discretion in managing the feelings of others.—**tactful** *adj*.—**tactless** *adj*.

tactical voting *n* the strategy in elections of voting for the candidate most likely to defeat the favorite, rather than voting for one's preferred choice.

tactics *n sing* stratagem; ploy; the science or art of maneuvering troops in the presence of the enemy.—**tactical** *adj*.—**tactician** *n*.

tactile *adj* relating to, or having a sense of touch.

tad *n* (*inf*) a small boy; (*inf*) a tiny quantity; a bit.

tadpole *n* the larva of a frog or toad, esp at the stage when the head and tail have developed.

Taegu *n* city in the Republic of Korea.

Taeuber-Arp *n* **Sophie** (1889–1943) Swiss artist and designer and wife of Jean Arp.

TAFE *abbr* = Technical and Further Education.

Tafelmusik *n* (*mus*) (*German*) "table music," i.e. music sung during a banquet as an entertainment.

TAFF *abbr* = Take-Away and Fast Food Federation.

taffeta *n* a thin glossy fabric with a silky luster.

taffrail *n* the rail at the stern of a ship.

Taft *n* **William Howard** (1857–1930) American Republican statesman. He became the 27th president of the US (1909–13) in succession to Theodore Roosevelt. More conservative in his policies than Roosevelt, he alienated the reformist wing of the Republican Party. He was appointed chief justice of the Supreme Court (1921–30), and became a noted isolationist in the 1930s.

tag[1] *n* a strip or label for identification. * *vt* to attach a tag; to mark with a tag. * *vi* (*with* **onto, after, along**) to trail along (behind).

tag[2] *n* a children's chasing game; (*baseball*) the putting out of a runner by touching him with the ball. * *vt* (**tagging, tagged**) to touch another player in a game of tag; to put a runner out by touching him with the ball.

TAG *abbr* = Towpaths Action Group.

tag end *n* the final part of something.

Tages *n* (*Roman myth*) a grandson of Jupiter.

tagged image file format *see* TIFF.

tagliatelle *n* pasta in narrow ribbons.

Tagore *n* **Rabindranath** (1861–1941) Indian poet and philosopher who also wrote plays, essays and novels and short stories. Regarded by many Bengalis as their greatest writer, he was awarded the 1913 Nobel prize for literature. He was knighted in 1915, but repudiated the title in 1919 as a protest against the Amritsar Massacre.

TAH *abbr* = total abdominal hysterectomy.

tahini *n* a thick paste of ground sesame seeds.

Tahitian *adj* of or pertaining to the South Pacific island of Tahiti, its people or language. * *n* a native of Tahiti; the Polynesian language spoken in Tahiti.

Tahoua *n* city in Niger.

tahr *n* a type of Himalayan wild goat.

t'ai chi ch'uan *or* **t'ai chi** *n* a Chinese form of exercise using movements designed to improve balance and coordination.

taiga *n* (*geog*) the belt of coniferous forest dominated by spruces and firs extending across the subarctic regions of Eurasia and North America.

tail[1] *n* the appendage of an animal growing from the rear, generally hanging loose; the rear part of anything; (*pl*) the side of a coin without a head on it; (*inf*) a person who keeps another under surveillance, esp a detective. * *vti* to follow closely, to shadow; (*with* **off, away**) to (cause to) dwindle.

tail[2] *n* (*mus*) the stem attached to the head of a minim (half note), or a smaller note.

tailback *n* a long queue of traffic behind an obstruction; in football, the offensive back farthest from the line of scrimmage.

tailboard *n* a hinged or removable section at the rear of a motor vehicle.

tail coat *n* a man's black or gray coat cut horizontally just below the waist at the front with two long tails at the back.

tail-end *adj* tardy; being the last in line. * *n* the last.

tailgate *n* the hinged board at the rear of a truck that can be let down or removed. * *vti* to drive dangerously close behind (another vehicle).—**tailgater** *n*.

taillight *n* a red warning light at the rear of a motor vehicle.

tailor *n* a person who makes and repairs outer garments, esp. men's suits. * *vi* to work as a tailor. * *vt* to adapt to fit a particular requirement.

tailor-made *adj* specially designed for a particular purpose or person.

tail piece *n* (*mus*) the piece of wood at the base of a violin to which the strings are attached.

tail pin *n* (*mus*) the metal rod at the bottom of a cello or double bass that can be pulled out to adjust the height of the instrument above the floor.

tailpipe *n* a pipe at the rear of jet engine or motor vehicle for discharging exhaust gases.

tailplane *n* a small stabilizing wing at the rear of an aircraft, a horizontal stabilizer.

tailspin *n* a spiraling nose dive; (*inf*) a state of chaos.

tailstock *n* the adjustable part of a lathe that supports the free end of a workpiece.

tail rotor *n* the small propeller at the rear of a helicopter that counteracts the tendency of the body to spin in the opposite direction to the main rotor blades.

Tailtinn *n* (*Irish Celtic myth*) the battle at which the sons of Mil Espaine defeated the Tuatha De Danann for the second time.

tailwind *n* a wind in the same direction as a ship or aircraft is traveling.

T'ai-nan *n* a city in Taiwan.

Tain Bo Cuailnge *n* (*Irish Celtic myth*) the quest of Medb, queen of Connacht, for the Donn Cuailnge, the great brown bull of Ulster.

taint *vt* to contaminate; to infect. * *vi* to be corrupted or disgraced. * *n* a stain; corruption.

taipan[1] *n* a powerful businessman operating in Hong Kong or China.

taipan[2] *n* a venomous Australian snake.

T'ai-pei *n* capital city of Taiwan.

Taiwan *n* [**Republic of China**] the largest of a group of islands located in the Pacific Ocean, about 100 miles or 161 kilometers off the southeast coast of mainland China, across the Taiwan Strait.

Ta'izz *n* city in Yemen.

Tajikistan *n* a republic in central Asia bounded by China in the east, Afghanistan to the south, Uzbekistan to the west, and Kyrgyzstan to the north.

Tajik rouble *n* currency of Tajikistan.

taka *n* the standard monetary unit of Bangladesh, made up of 100 paisa.

take *vb* (**taking, took,** *pp* **taken**) *vt* to lay hold of; to grasp or seize; to gain, win; to choose, select; (*attitude, pose*) to adopt; to understand; to consume; to accept or agree to; to lead or carry with one; to use as a means of travel; (*math*) to subtract (from); to use; to steal; (*gram*) to be used with; to endure calmly; (*with* **apart**) to dismantle; to criticize; (*with* **back**) to retract, withdraw (a promise, etc); (*with* **down**) to write down; to dismantle; to humiliate; (*with* **for**) (*inf*) to mistakenly believe to be; (*with* **in**) to understand, perceive; to include; to make a garment smaller by altering seams, etc; to offer accommodation to; (*inf*) to swindle, deceive; (*with* **on**) to employ as labor; to assume or acquire; to agree to do (something); to fight against; (*with* **out**) to extract; to obtain, procure; to escort; (*sl*) to kill; (*with* **up**) to begin as a business or hobby; to accept an offer or invitation; to occupy (time or space); to act as a patron to; to shorten (a garment); to interrupt or criticize; to absorb. * *vi* (*plant, etc*) to start growing successfully; to become effective; to catch on; to have recourse to; to go to; (*with* **after**) to resemble in appearance, character, etc; (*with* **on**) (*inf*) to become upset or distraught; (*with* **to**) to escape to as a refuge; to acquire a liking for; to adopt as a habit; (*with* **up**) to resume, continue further. * *n* (*film, TV*) the amount of film used without stopping the camera when shooting.

takeaway *n* a takeout.

take-home pay *n* pay remaining after all deductions, such as income tax, have been made.

taken *see* **take**.

takeoff *n* the process of an aircraft becoming airborne; (*inf*) an amusing impression or caricature of another person.

takeout, take-out *n* a cooked meal that is sold for consumption outside the premises; a shop or restaurant that provides such meals.—*also adj*.

takeover *n* the taking over of control; (*com*) an attempt to take control of a company by making an offer to buy shares at a specified price.—*also adj*.

taking *adj* attractive, charming; (*inf*) catching, contagious. * *n* the act of one that takes; (*pl*) earnings; profits.

Takt *n* (*mus*) (*German*) "time," so *im Takt* means "in time."

tal *abbr* = traffic and accident loss.

tal. *abbr* (*Latin*) = *talis*, "such a one."

tal. qual. *abbr* (*Latin*) = *talis qualis*, "as they come," of average quality.

tala *n* currency of Western Samoa. *See* **sene**.

talatat blocks *n* (*Egypt*) the small blocks of sandstone used for rapid building during the Amarna Period (from the Arabic meaning "three hand-widths").

talayot *n* a type of stone building, unique to the islands of Minorca and Majorca; (*hist*) the name given to a Bronze and Iron Age culture.

Talbert *n* **Bruce J** (1838–81) British architect of the Corn Exchange Hall in Dundee. He became one of the leading designers of the aesthetic movement.

talc *n* a type of smooth mineral used in ceramics and talcum powder; talcum powder.

talcum powder *n* perfumed powdered talc for the skin.

tale *n* a narrative or story; a fictitious account, a lie; idle or malicious gossip.

talent *n* any innate or special aptitude.—**talented** *adj*.

talent scout *n* a person employed to recruit talented people for professional careers in sport, entertainment, etc.

talent show *n* a show that gives amateurs a chance to perform in the hope of attracting interest from professionals.

Taliesin *n* 1. (*Welsh Celtic myth*) the son of Cerridwen. 2. a historical figure, noted for his poetic powers.

talik *n* (*geog*) a layer of unfrozen ground between the permafrost and the upper layer that freezes and thaws.

talipot *n* a palm tree of the East Indies with large leaves used for roofing, umbrellas, etc.

talisman *n* (*pl* **talismans**) an object or charm supposed to ward off evil and bring good luck; an amulet.

Talisman *abbr* = Transfer Accounting Lodgement for Investors and Stock Management.

talk *vt* to speak; to know how to speak (a language); to discuss or speak of (something); to influence by talking; (*with* **down**) to silence or override (a speaker, argument, etc) by talking loudly; to radio instructions to (an aircraft) so that it may land safely; (*with* **into**) to persuade by argument or talking; (*with* **out**) to resolve by discussion; (*with* **round**) to persuade by talking. * *vi* to converse; to discuss; to gossip; to divulge information; (*with* **back**) to reply impudently; (*with* **down**) to speak in a condescending manner (to); (*with* **round**) to discuss (a subject) without reaching any conclusion; (*with* **shop**) to discuss work, esp after working hours. * *n* a discussion; a lecture; gossip; (*pl*) negotiations.

talkative *adj* given to talking a great deal.

talkback *n* a two-way communication system in a TV studio.

talkie *n* (*inf*) an early motion-picture film with sound.

talking book *n* a recording of a book for the blind.

talking head *n* the head and shoulders of a person on television talking directly to the camera without using visual material.

talking picture *n* a talkie.

talking point *n* a subject for conversation or discussion; something that lends support to an argument.

talking-to *n* a reprimand, lecture.

talk show *n* a television or radio program with informal interviews and conversation, a chat show.

tall *adj* above average in height; (*inf*) exaggerated (*story*).—**tallness** *n*.

Tallahassee *n* capital city of Florida, a state of the USA.

tallboy *n* a high chest of drawers on legs, a highboy.

Tallinn *n* capital city of Estonia.

Tallis *n* **Thomas** (*c*.1505–85) English composer and organist, considered to be one of the most important of his era.

tallith *n* (*pl* **tallithim**) a fringed shawl worn by Jewish men during religious services.

tall order *n* (*inf*) a request that is difficult to fulfill.

tallow *n* solid animal fat used to make soap, candles, etc.

tall ship *n* a square-rigged sailing vessel.

tall story *n* (*inf*) an exaggerated or unbelievable account

tally *n* (*pl* **tallies**) reckoning, account; one score in a game. * *vi* (**tallying, tallied**) to correspond; to keep score.

tally-ho *n* the cry of a person at a fox hunt when sighting the quarry.—*also vti*.

Talman *n* **William** (1650–) English architect. His notable works include Chatsworth House, south and east front.

Talmud *n* the body of Jewish law.—**Talmudic** *adj*.

talon[1] *n* a claw of an animal, esp a bird of prey.

talon[2] *n* (*mus*) (*French*) the "nut" or heel of a bow.

Talorcen *n* (*d.* 657) king of the Picts; the son of Eanfrith of Bernicia.

Talorgen *n* (*d.* 787) king of the Picts (785–787).

Talthybius *n* (*Greek myth*) the chief herald of the Greek forces in the Trojan War.

talus[1] *n* (*pl* **tali**) *n* (*anat*) the ankle bone, which articulates with the lower leg bones (tibia and fibula) above and also with the heel bone (calcaneus) below. *See also* **tarsus**.

talus[2] *n* (*pl* **taluses**) scree; the sloping side of a wall.

TAM *abbr* = Television Audience Measurement; tactical air missile.

tamale *n* a Mexican dish of minced meat with crushed maize and seasonings.

Tamale *n* city in Ghana.

tamandua *n* a small tree-dwelling anteater of Central and South America.

tamarack *n* (the wood of) any of various North American larches.

tamarin *n* any of numerous small monkeys of South America resembling marmosets.

tamarind *n* a tropical evergreen tree bearing a pulpy fruit used for food, in beverages, and in laxative preparations.

tamarisk *n* any of a genus of evergreen trees and shrubs of Mediterranean and tropical regions with tiny leaves and numerous clusters of pink or white flowers.

TAMBA *abbr* = Twins and Multiple Births Association.

tambala *n* a monetary unit of Malawi, equal to one hundredth of a kwacha.

Tambo *n* **Oliver** (1917–93) South African politician. He joined the African National Congress in 1944, and when the ANC was banned in 1960 left South Africa to set up an expatriate section. During Mandela's imprisonment, he was the ANC's acting president (1967–77) and president (1977–91).

tambour *n* (*mus*) a drum; (an embroidery produced on) a circular frame for holding fabric taut during embroidery; a rolling top on a desk or cabinet made from thin strips of wood on a canvas backing. * *vt* to embroider using a tambour.

tamboura, tambura *n* (*mus*) an Indian stringed instrument used to provide a drone as accompaniment to singing.

tambourin *n* a dance of Provence in France; a narrow drum played along with a pipe, as the accompaniment to dancing; (*mus*) a lively 18th-century piece in the style of the folk-dance from Provence, usually in 2/4 time.

tambourine *n* (*mus*) a percussion hand instrument made of skin stretched over a circular frame with small jingling metal discs around the edge.

tambura *see* **tamboura**.

tame *adj* not wild, domesticated; compliant; dull, uninteresting. * *vt* to domesticate esp an animal; to subdue; to soften.

Tamil *n* a member of a people inhabiting southeastern India and Sri Lanka; the language they speak.—*also adj*.

tam-o'-shanter *n* a tight-fitting Scottish woolen or cloth beret with a full crown and a pompom on top.

tamoxifen *n* a drug used in the treatment of certain breast cancers.

tamp *vt* to pack down firmly with a series of blows; to pack (a blast-hole) with sand or earth above the explosive charge.

tamper *vi* to meddle (with); to interfere (with).

Tampere *n* city in Finland.

tampion *n* (*mil*) a plug for the muzzle of a gun.

tampon[1] *n* a firm plug of cotton wool inserted in the vagina during menstruation.

tampon[2] *n* a plug of compressed gauze inserted into a wound or cavity to absorb blood.

tampon[3] *n* (*mus*) a type of drumstick which has a head at each end, held in the middle to produce a drum roll.

tam-tam *n* (*mus*) a large bronze gong of Chinese origin.

tan *n* a yellowish-brown color; suntan. * *vti* (**tanning, tanned**) to acquire a suntan through sunbathing; to convert tan or hide into leather using tannin; (*inf*) to thrash.

tan., tan *abbr* = tangent.

TAN *abbr* = Third Age Network.

tanager *n* any of numerous American woodland songbirds, the male of which has vividly colored plumage.

Tanaka *n* **Kakuei** (1918–) Japanese politician and prime minister (1972–74). He established diplomatic relations with Communist China, but was forced to resign following charges of taking bribes from Lockheed, for which he was tried (1983) and imprisoned.

Tanaquil *n* the wife of Lucius Tarquinius Priscus, the fifth king of Rome.

tanbark *n* bark, esp from the oak, used as a source of tannin.

TANCA *abbr* = Technical Assistance to Non-Commonwealth Countries.

T & A *abbr* = tonsils and adenoids.

T & AVR *abbr* (*Brit mil*) = Territorial Army Volunteer Reserve.

t & b *abbr* = top and bottom.

t & e *abbr* = test and evaluation; tired and emotional (drunk); travel and entertainment; trial and error.

tandem *n* a bicycle for two riders, sitting one behind the other.

t & g *abbr* = tongued and grooved.

T & G *abbr* = Transport and General Workers' Union.

t & o *abbr* = taken and offered.

tandoori *n* an Indian method of cooking meat, vegetables, and bread using a large clay oven.

t & p *abbr* = theft and pilferage.

T & RA *abbr* = Tennis and Rackets Association.

t & s *abbr* = toilet and shower.

T & SG *abbr* = Television and Screenwriters' Guild.

T & T *abbr* = taxed and tested (of second-hand cars); Trinidad and Tobago.

tang[1] *n* sharp smell or a strong taste.—**tangy** *adj*.

tang[2] *n* a thin projecting piece at the base of the blade of a metal tool or weapon which anchors it within the handle.

Tanga *n* town in Tanzania.

Tange *n* **Kenzo** (1913–) Japanese architect. Influenced by Le Corbusier and by traditional Japanese building styles, his buildings include the Hiroshima Peace Center (1949–55) and St Mary's Cathedral in Tokyo (1965).

tangent *n* (*geom*) a straight line that just touches the circumference of a circle; a function of an angle in a right-angled triangle, defined as the ratio of the side opposite the angle to the length of the side adjacent to it. * *adj* touching at one point.

tangential *adj* of superficial relevance; digressive.

tangerine *n* a small, sweet orange with a loose skin; the color of this.—*also adj*.

tangible *adj* capable of being felt, seen or noticed; substantial; real.—**tangibility** *n*.

Tangier *n* a city in Morocco.

tangle *n* a mass of hair, string or wire knotted together confusedly; a complication. * *vt* to intertwine in a mass, to snarl; to entangle, complicate. * *vi* to become tangled or complicated; (*with* with) to become involved in argument with.

tango *n* (*pl* **tangos**) (*mus*) a Latin-American dance in moderately slow 2/4 time, originating from Argentina. It makes use of syncopated rhythms and became popular in Europe in the 1920s. * *vi* (**tangoing, tangoed**) to dance the tango.

tangram *n* a Chinese puzzle made from a square cut into a rhomboid, a square, and five triangles, which can be combined to produce different figures.

tanh *abbr* (*math*) = hyperbolic tangent.

Tanis *n* a settlement and nome capital in the eastern Delta region of Egypt, home town of the Ramessides of the 19th and 20th Dynasties.

tank *n* a large container for storing liquids or gases; an armored combat vehicle, mounted with guns and having caterpillar tracks.

tanka *n* (*pl* **tankas, tanka**) a Japanese verse form with five lines.

tankage *n* the capacity of a tank; the storing of oil, etc in tanks.

tankard *n* a tall, one-handled drinking mug, often with a hinged lid.

tanked *adj* (*sl*) extremely drunk.

tanker *n* a large ship or truck for transporting oil and other liquids.

tank engine *n* a steam locomotive that carries its own water supplies instead of using a tender.

tank top *n* a sleeveless pullover with a low neck.

tanner *n* a person who tans skins.

tannery *n* (*pl* **tanneries**) a place where hides are tanned.

tannic acid *n* tannin.

tannic *adj* of, resembling, or derived from tan or tannin.

tannin *n* a yellow or brown chemical found in plants or tea, used in tanning.

Tansley *n* **Sir Arthur George** (1871–1955) English botanist. One of the pioneers of the study of plant ecology, his works include *Practical Plant Ecology* (1923) and *The British Islands and Their Vegetation* (1939).

tansy *n* (*pl* **tansies**) any of numerous aromatic plants with yellow flowers and finely divided leaves, once used for seasoning and as a medicine.

tantalize *vt* to tease or torment by presenting something greatly desired, but keeping it inaccessible.

tantalum *n* (*chem*) a hard metallic element of the vanadium family, esp used for hardening alloys.

tantalus *n* a cabinet or case where bottles of spirit may be locked up yet remain visible.

Tantalus *n* (*Greek myth*) a king who offended the gods and was punished in a lake whose waters receded from his lips when he attempted to drink, where the fruit overhead withdrew when he attempted to eat, and where a huge rock threatened to fall and crush him.

tantamount *adj* equivalent (to) in effect; as good as.

tantara *n* the sound of a horn or trumpet playing a fanfare.

tanto *n* (*mus*) (*Italian*) "so much" as in *allegro non tanto*, meaning "quick, but not too quick."

tantrum *n* a childish fit of bad temper.

Tanz *n* (*mus*) (*German*) "dance."

Tanzania *n* a republic on the east coast of central southern Africa, comprising a large mainland area and the islands of Pemba and Zanzibar.

Tanzanian shilling *n* currency of Tanzania.

Tao *n* the spirit of creative harmony in the universe; the path of virtuous conduct in harmony with the natural order.

Taoiseach *n* the prime minister of the Republic of Ireland.

Taoism *n* a Chinese religious and philosophical system advocating a simple passive life in harmony with the natural order.

tap[1] *n* a quick, light blow or touch; a piece of metal attached to the heel or toe of a shoe for reinforcement or to tap-dance. * *vti* (**tapping, tapped**) to strike lightly; to make a tapping sound.

tap[2] *n* a device controlling the flow of liquid through a pipe or from a container, a faucet. * *vt* (**tapping, tapped**) to pierce in order to draw fluid from; to connect a secret listening device to a telephone; (*inf*) to ask for money from; (*resources, etc*) to draw on.

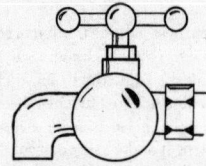

tap dance *n* a dance in which the feet are used to tap out a rhythm. Tap dancing was made popular by Fred Astaire's performances in films during the 1930s. Special shoes with steel plates at the toe and heel are usually worn. * *vi* to perform a tap dance.—**tap-dancer** *n*.—**tap-dancing** *n*.

tap issue *n* (*Brit*) the issue of government securities or bills to selected market makers, usually with a view to influencing the price of gilts.

tap root *n* (*bot*) a main root that grows vertically downwards and has small lateral roots.

tap shoe *n* one of a pair of shoes with metal taps on the heel and toe, used for tap-dancing.

tap stock *n* a gilt-edged security from an issue that has not been fully subscribed that is then released onto the market gradually when its market price attains predetermined levels.

tape *n* a strong, narrow strip of cloth, paper, etc, used for tying, binding, etc; tape measure; magnetic tape, as in a cassette or videotape. * *vt* to wrap with tape; to record on magnetic tape.

tape deck *n* a tape recorder in a hi-fi system.

tape measure *n* a tape marked in inches or centimeters for measuring.

tape player *n* a self-contained tape recorder.

taper *n* a long thin candle. * *vti* to make or become gradually narrower toward one end.—**tapering** *adj*.

tape recorder *n* a machine used for recording and reproducing sounds or music on magnetic tape, esp as part of a hi-fi system, a tape deck.

tape recording *n* a recording made on magnetic tape.

tapestry *n* (*pl* **tapestries**) a heavy fabric woven with patterns or figures, used for wall hangings and furnishings.

tapeworm *n* a tape-like, parasitic, intestinal worm.

taphonomy *n* (*archeo*) the study of bones with a view to discovering what has happened to them since they were deposited.

tapioca *n* a glutinous starch extracted from the root of the cassava and used in puddings, etc.

Tapiovaara *n* Ilmari (1914–95) Finnish interior and furniture designer who was one of the pioneers of knock-down furniture.

tapir *n* (*pl* **tapirs, tapir**) a South American hoofed mammal with a short flexible proboscis.

tappet *n* a projecting arm or lever, e.g. a cam, that moves or is moved by another part in a machine.

taproom *n* a bar.

taps *n sing* a call on a bugle at a military camp signaling lights out; any similar signal, as at a military funeral.

tar[1] *n* a thick, dark, viscous substance obtained from wood, coal, peat, etc, used for surfacing roads. * *vt* to coat with tar.—**tarry** *adj*.

tar[2] *n* (*inf*) a sailor.

Tara *n* town in County Meath, Ireland; for many centuries the most sacred place in Ireland, and the main residence of the high kings, the ancient site dating back to 2000 BC. It was regarded as the Celtic capital of Ireland.

taramasalata *n* a pale pink fish-roe paste served as a starter.

Taranis *n* (*Celtic myth*) the Celtic thunder god equated with the Roman god, Jupiter.

tarantella *n* (the music for) a very fast, wild folk dance from southern Italy, in 6/8 time and gradually increasing in speed. Chopin used the form in a concert piece.

Taranto *n* a coastal city in southern Italy, settled from the Neolithic period.

tarantula *n* (*pl* **tarantulas, tarantulae**) a large, hairy spider with a poisonous bite that is painful but not deadly.

Tarawa *n* capital city of Kiribati.

Taraxippus *n* (*Greek myth*) a round altar located near a very dangerous spot on the racecourse at Olympia.

Tarbhfeis *n* (*Irish Celtic myth*) "the bull feast," a ceremony associated with the selection of the high kings of Ireland.

tarboosh, tarbush *n* a brimless red cap resembling a fez worn by Muslim men.

Tardenosian *adj* relating to a Mesolithic culture of southern France that emerged *c*.6000 BC from the earlier Sauveterrian.

tardy *adj* (**tardier, tardiest**) slow; later than expected.—**tardily** *adv*.—**tardiness** *n*.

tare[1] *n* (the seed of) a type of vetch plant.

tare[2] *n* (an allowance for) the weight of the wrapping or container in which goods are packed; the weight of an unloaded goods vehicle. * *vt* to weigh in order to calculate the tare.

target *n* a mark to aim at, esp in shooting; an objective or ambition; (*comput*) the destination for a copied file.

target cell *n* (*biol*) an abnormal form of red blood cell that is large and has a ringed appearance when stained and viewed microscopically, resembling a target.

target company *n* (*com*) a company that has been targeted by an individual or company as the target of a takeover bid.

target market *n* (*com*) the segment of a market at which a firm directs its marketing thrust.

tariff *n* a tax on imports or exports; a list of prices in a hotel; the rate of charge for public services, such as gas or electricity.

Tarkington *n* [Newton] Booth (1869–1946) American novelist and dramatist, remembered chiefly for his novel of midwest life, *The Magnificent Ambersons*, which was made into a major film by Orson Welles.

Tarkovsky *n* Andrei (1932–86) Russian film director. The simplest of his seven feature films is his first, *Ivan's Childhood* (1962). His later films steadily become more complex and allegorical, e.g. *Andrei Rublev* (1966) and his two films made in exile from the USSR, *Nostalgia* (1983) and *The Sacrifice* (1986).

tarlatan, tarletan *n* a type of thin stiff cotton fabric.

Tarmac, Tarmacadam *n* a material for surfacing roads made from crushed stones and tar; an airport runway. * *vti* (**tarmacking, tarmacked**) to lay down a tarmac surface.

tarn *n* (*Brit*) a small mountain lake.

tarnation (*inf*) a euphemism for damnation.

tarnish *vi* for metal, to lose its luster or discolor due to exposure to the air. * *vt* to taint a reputation.—*also n*.

taro *n* (*pl* **taros**) (the edible root of) a tropical Asian plant.

TARO *abbr* (*Brit mil*) = Territorial Army Reserve of Officers.

tarot *n* a game played with 22 pictorial cards, which are also used for fortune-telling.

tar paper *n* a heavy paper coated with tar, used in the construction of buildings.

tarpaulin *n* canvas cloth coated with a waterproof substance.

Tarpeian Rock *n* a precipitous rock forming part of the Captoline Hill at Rome over which people convicted of treason were hurled.

tarpon *n* (*pl* **tarpon, tarpons**) a large silvery fish hunted for sport.

Tarquinius Superbus *n* Lucius [Tarquin the Proud] the last of the legendary kings of Rome who, according to tradition, reigned from 534 to 510 BC.

tarragon *n* an aromatic herb used for flavoring.

tarry *vi* (**tarrying, tarried**) to delay or dawdle; to linger; to wait briefly.

TARS *abbr* = The Arthur Ransome Society.

tarsus *n* (*pl* **tarsi**) (*anat*) the small bones of the ankle and the heel in vertebrates; the plate of tissue that stiffens the eyelid.—**tarsal** *adj, n*.

Tarsus *n* a town in southern Turkey, the birthplace of St Paul.

tart. *abbr* = tartaric.

tart[1] *adj* having a sour, sharp taste; sharp, severe (*speech*).—**tartly** *adv*.—**tartness** *n*.

tart[2] *n* an open pastry case containing fruit, jam, or custard; (*inf*) a prostitute. * *vt* (*with* up) (*inf*) to dress cheaply and gaudily; to decorate, esp cheaply.

tartan *n* a woolen cloth with a checkered pattern, esp in Scotland and Ireland, having a distinctive design for each clan.

tartar *n* a hard, yellow, crusty deposit which forms on the teeth; a salty deposit on the sides of wine casks.

tartare sauce, tartar sauce *n* a mayonnaise sauce with chopped capers, herbs, etc, eaten esp with fish.

tartaric acid *n* (*chem*) an organic acid obtained from grapes and many other fruits.

Tartarus *n* (*Greek myth*) a deep and sunless abyss as far below Hades as earth is below Heaven.

Tartessus *n* an ancient city near Gades (now Cadiz) in Spain.

Tartini *n* Giuseppe (1692-1770) an Italian violinist, composer, and teacher. His works include many violin concertos, sonatas (such as *The Devil's Trill*), symphonies, and church music.

TAS *abbr* = true air speed.

TASC *abbr* = Transportation Administrative Service Center

TASHA abbr = Tranquilizer Anxiety Stress Help Association.

Tashkent n capital city of Uzbekistan.

task n a specific amount of work to be done; a chore.

task force n a small unit with a specific mission, usu military.

taskmaster n a person who demands constant hard work.

Tasm. abbr = Tasmania.

TASM abbr = tactical air-to-surface missile.

Tasmanian devil n a burrowing flesh-eating marsupial of Tasmania with a black coat and long tail.

TASS abbr = Technical, Administrative and Supervisory Section.

tassel n an ornamental tuft of silken threads decorating soft furnishings, clothes, etc; a growth that looks like this, esp on corn. * vb (**tasseling, tasseled** or **tasselling, tasselled**) vt to decorate with tassels. * vi (plant) to grow tassels.

taste vt to perceive (a flavor) by taking into the mouth; to try by eating and drinking a little; to sample; to experience. * vi to try by the mouth; to have a specific flavor. * n the sense by which flavors are perceived; a small portion; the ability to recognize what is beautiful, attractive, etc; liking; a brief experience.

taste bud n (anat) any of the small projecting sensory organs on the tongue's surface by which taste is perceived.

tasteful adj showing good taste.—**tastefully** adv.—**tastefulness** n.

tasteless adj without taste, bland; in bad taste.—**tastelessly** adv.

taster n a person skilled in determining the balance of flavors in a product, esp tea, wine; a device for tasting or sampling; (formerly) a person who tasted food before it was served to a king, etc.

tasto n (mus) (Italian) the keyboard of a piano or the finger-board of a stringed instrument.

tasty adj (**tastier, tastiest**) savory; having a pleasant flavor.

tat vi (**tatting, tatted**) vi to do tatting. * vt to make by tatting.

TAT abbr = thematic apperception test; tired all the time; transatlantic telephone cable; Tree Advice Trust.

ta-ta (Brit) (inf) goodbye.

tatami n (pl **tatamis, tatami**) straw matting used as a floor covering, esp in Japan.

Tate n 1. **[John Orley] Allen** (1899–1979) American poet and critic who supported the concept of a local sense of identity against the corrupting abstract notion of "America." His Collected Poems was published in 1977. 2. **Nahum** (1652–1715) English poet and dramatist, whose notorious version of Shakespeare's King Lear gave the play a happy ending.

TATHS abbr = Tool and Trades History Society.

Tati n Jacques [Jacques Tatischeff] (1908–82) French actor and film director. He became an international comedy star with his Monsieur Hulot creation, an engagingly incompetent character hopelessly at odds with the modern world.

Tatius, Titus n a king of the Sabines who led his troops against Rome to take vengeance on the abduction of the Sabine women by the Romans.

tatter n a torn or ragged piece of cloth.—**tattered** adj.

tatterdemalion n a person wearing ragged clothes, a ragamuffin.—also adj.

tatting n (the process of making) a type of delicate handmade lace.

tattle n (a) gossip. * vi to gossip. * vt to reveal (secrets, etc) by gossiping.

tattletale n a gossip. * adj telltale.

tattoo[1] n (pl **tattoos**) a continuous beating of a drum; a military display of exercises and music.

tattoo[2] vt (**tattooing, tattooed**) to make permanent patterns or pictures on the skin by pricking and marking with dyes. * n (pl **tattoos**) marks made on the skin in this way.

tatty adj (**tattier, tattiest**) shabby, ragged.

Tatum n 1. **Art[hur]** (1910–56) American jazz pianist. Blind in one eye and partially sighted in the other, he was largely self-taught on the piano and became an acclaimed virtuoso of jazz piano music in the "swing" mode. 2. **Edward Lawrie** (1909–75) American biochemist. He shared the 1958 Nobel prize for physiology or medicine with George Wells Beadle and Lederberg.

tau n the 19th letter of the Greek alphabet.

taught see **teach**.

taula n a T-shaped monument consisting of a horizontal stone slab supported on a single vertical monolith or pillar.

TAUN abbr = Technical Assistance of the United Nations.

taunt vt to provoke with mockery or contempt; to tease. * n an insult.

taupe n, adj (a) brownish-gray.

Taurians npl the ancient inhabitants of the Tauric Chersonese, the peninsula on the north coast of the Black Sea, now known as the Crimea.

taurine n of or like a bull.

tauromachy n the art or practice of bullfighting.

Taurus A n (astron) the radio source belonging to the Crab nebula within the constellation Taurus.

Taurus n (astrol) The Bull, the second of the twelve signs of the zodiac; a constellation situated near Orion and partly within the Milky Way in the northern hemisphere.—**Taurean** adj.

TAURUS abbr (stock exch) = Transfer and Automated Registration of Uncertified Stock.

taut adj stretched tight; tense; stressed.

tauten vti to make or become taut.

tauto- (also **taut-**) prefix same.

tautog n a large North American food fish related to the wrasse.

tautology n (pl **tautologies**) a statement that uses different words to repeat the same thing.—**tautological, tautologous** adj.

tautomerism n (chem) a special case of structural isomerism, often called dynamic isomerism, when a compound exists as a mixture of two forms, or isomers, in equilibrium.

Tavener n **John Kenneth** (1944–) English composer . He studied under Lennox Berkeley, and is noted particularly for his religious compositions, e.g. the opera Thérèse (1973–76).

tavern n a place licensed to sell alcoholic drinks; an inn.

taverna n a Greek hotel with its own bar; a Greek restaurant.

Taverner n **John** (c.1490-1545) an important English composer who taught at Oxford University and is best known for his religious works (chiefly Masses and Magnificats).

TAVR abbr (Brit) = Territorial and Army Volunteer Reserve.

TAVRA abbr (Brit) = Territorial, Auxiliary and Volunteer Reserve Association.

taw abbr = twice a week.

tawdry adj (**tawdrier, tawdriest**) showy, cheap, and of poor quality.

Taweret n an Egyptian goddess with a hippopotamus head, credited with bringing babies to childless women and thus often portrayed on charms and amulets.

tawny adj yellowish brown.

tawny owl n a European owl with brown plumage.

tawse n (Scot) a leather strap with a slit end formerly used for punishing schoolchildren.

tax n a rate imposed by the government on property or persons to raise revenues; a strain. * vt to impose a tax (upon); to strain.

tax avoidance n a method of legally minimizing tax liabilities by taking maximum advantage of tax allowances and tax relief.

tax burden n the total amount of tax that is sustained by an individual, company, or organization.

tax evasion n the process of trying to avoid paying tax by various illegal means.

tax exile n a person who lives abroad to avoid paying high taxes.

tax haven a country that imposes a low rate of taxes and thus attracts tax exiles as residents.

tax rebate n a repayment of tax paid.

tax relief n a deduction from a taxable amount that is allowed by law.

tax return n a form on which a taxpayer makes an annual statement of income and related circumstances so that the appropriate tax liability can be assessed.

tax shelter n a financial arrangement to minimize tax liability.

tax therapist n a tax adviser who helps with the completion of income tax forms.

tax year see **fiscal year**.

taxa see **taxon**.

taxable adj able or liable to be taxed.

taxable income n the amount of a person's income that is liable to taxation after the deduction of any income tax allowances to which the person is entitled.

taxation n the act of levying taxes; the amount raised as tax.

tax-deductible adj referring to an amount of money that can be deducted from income or profits before the amount that is subject to tax is established.

tax-free adj exempt from taxes.

taxi n (pl **taxis**) a taxicab. * vi (**taxiing** or **taxying, taxied**) to move an aircraft along the runway before takeoff or after landing.

taxicab n a car, usu fitted with a taximeter, that may be hired to transport passengers.

taxidermy n the art of preparing and stuffing the skins of animals ready for exhibiting.—**taxidermist** n.

taximeter n a meter fitted into a taxi to record the time taken for a journey.

taxis n (pl **taxes**) (biol) a movement in a simple organism (e.g., a bacterium) in response to certain external stimulii; (med) the restoration of a displaced part by manual pressure.

taxiway n a marked route from a terminal to a runway along which an aircraft taxis.

taxon n (pl **taxa**) any taxonomic group or category.

taxonomy n (the science of) the classification of living things into groups based on similarities of biological origin, design, function, etc.

taxpayer n a person who or an organization that pays taxes.

Taÿgete n (Greek myth) the nymph of Mount Taÿgetus.

Taÿgetus n a range of mountains in Greece that divided ancient Messenia from Laconia.

Taylor n 1. **A[lan] J[ohn] P[ercivale]** (1906–90) English historian. His works include The Origins of the Second World War (1961) and The Trouble Makers (1957). 2. **Elizabeth** (1932–) English-born American stage and film actress. Among the films she made are National Velvet (1944), Butterfield 8 (1960) and Who's Afraid of Virginia Woolf? (1966), the last two earning her oscars. 3. **Jeremy** (1613–67) English bishop and theologian whose works include The Rule and Exercises of Holy Living and The Rule and Exercises of Holy Dying. 4. **Michael** (1927–86) American interior and furniture designer who had many show-business clients. 5. **Zachary** (1784–1850) 12th president of the US (1849–50), who succeeded Polk.

Tb symbol (chem) terbium (element).

tb, t.b. abbr = trial balance; tubercle bacillus; tuberculosis

TB abbr = Tariff Bureau; torpedo boat; tubercle bacillus; tuberculosis.

TB, tbyte abbr (comput) = terabyte.

tba abbr = to be advised/agreed/announced; tires, batteries, accessories.

TBA abbr = Tea Buyers' Association; Teaching Brothers' Association; Thoroughbred Breeders Association; Tropical Biology Association.

tb & s abbr = top, bottom, and sides.

tbcf abbr = to be called for.

tbd *abbr* = to be determined.

TBD *abbr* (*naut*) = torpedo-boat destroyer.

TBF *abbr* = Teachers' Benevolent Fund.

TBI *abbr* = throttle-body injection; total body irradiation.

T'bilisi *n* capital city of Georgia.

tbl *abbr* = through bill of lading.

TBM *abbr* = tactical ballistic missile; tuberculous meningitis.

TBO *abbr* = time between overhauls.

TBOAA *abbr* = Tuna Boat Owners Association of Australia.

T-bone steak *n* a large sirloin steak containing a T-shaped bone.

tbs. (also **tbsp.**) *abbr* = tablespoon; tablespoonful.

TBT *abbr* = tributyl tin.

tbyte *see* **TB**.

Tc *symbol* (*chem*) technetium (element).**tc** *abbr* = time check; true course.

tc. *abbr* = tierce; tierces.

t.c., TC *abbr* (*mus*) (*Italian*) = *tre corde*, "three strings," (direction to release left-hand pedal of piano).

TC *abbr* = Tandem Club; Technician Certificate; Trusteeship Council (UN); travelers' check.

TCA *abbr* = Technician in Costing and Accounting; Tertiary Colleges Association; Textile Converters Association; tricyclic antidepressant.

TCAS *abbr* = Three Counties Agricultural Society.

TCB *abbr* = Thames Conservancy Board; tumor cell burden.

TCBM *abbr* = trans-continental ballistic missile.

TCC *abbr* = Textile Conservation Center; Toxic Chemicals Committee.

TCCB (*Brit*) *abbr* = Test and County Cricket Board.

TCD *abbr* = Trinity College, Dublin.

TCDD *abbr* = tetrachlorobenzodioxin (an environmental pollutant).

TCE *abbr* = trichloroethylene (a solvent).

T-cell *n* (*biol*) a type of white blood cell that forms in the bone marrow and moves to the thymus gland, situated in the thorax.—*also* **T-lymphocyte**.

TCert *abbr* = Teacher's Certificate.

tcf *abbr* = trillion cubic feet.

TCF *abbr* = Touring Club de France.

TCGF *abbr* = T-cell growth factor.

Tchaikovsky *n* **Peter Ilyich** (1840–93) The outstanding Russian composer of the 19th century. Notable for his strong melodic sense and rejection of an overtly nationalistic and "folk" approach to composition.

TCI *abbr* = Tall Clubs International; Tasmanian Confederation of Industries; Touring Club Italiano; Tree Council of Ireland.

TCJCC *abbr* = Trades Councils Joint Consultative Committee.

TCL *abbr* = Trinity College of Music, London.

T-CLL *abbr* = T-cell chronic lymphatic leukemia.

TCM *abbr* = Trinity College of Music, London.

TCMB *abbr* = Tomato and Cucumber Marketing Board.

TCP *abbr* = transmission control protocol; trichlorophenylmethyliodisalicyl (an antiseptic).

TCP or **IP** *abbr* (*comput*) = Transmission Control Protocol or Internet Protocol, a cross-platform communications protocol that allows computers with different operating systems to communicate.

TCPA *abbr* = Town and Country Planning Association.

tcs. *abbr* = tierces.

td *abbr* = technical data; test data; time delay.

TD *abbr* = (Irish) *Teachda Dála*, "Member of the Dáil"; Teaching Diploma; Technician Diploma; (Brit *mil*) *Territori*al Decoration or Decorations; Traffic Director; Treasury Decision or Department; Tunisian Dinar (unit of currency); tardative dyskinesia; technical drawing.

T/D *abbr* = time deposit.

TDA *abbr* = Tableware Distributors' Association; Timber Development Association; Timber Drying Association; Trade and Development Agency

TD&RA *abbr* = Twist Drill and Reamer Association.

TDCR *abbr* = Teacher's Diploma of the College of Radiographers.

TDD *abbr* = telecommunications device for the deaf.

TDDL *abbr* = time-division data link.

TDE *abbr* = total digestible energy.

TDG *abbr* = Timeshare Developers Group.

TDL *abbr* = tunable diode laser.

TDM *abbr* = time-division multiplexing.

TDMA *abbr* = time-division multiple access.

TDN *abbr* = total digestible nutrients.

TDP *abbr* = technical development plan.

tdr *abbr* (*French*) = *tous droits réservés*, "all rights reserved."

TDRSS *abbr* = tracking and data-relay satellite system.

tds *abbr* (*Latin*) = *ter die sumendus*, "to be taken thrice daily."

Te *symbol* (*chem*) tellurium (element).

te *abbr* = thermal efficiency.

t/e *abbr* = time expired; twin-engined.

TE *abbr* = Topographical Engineer.

tea *n* a shrub growing in China, India, Sri Lanka, etc; its dried, shredded leaves, which are infused in boiling water for a beverage; in UK, a light meal taken in mid-afternoon; a main meal taken in the early evening.

tea bag *n* a small porous bag containing tea leaves for infusing.

tea ball *n* a perforated metal ball that holds tea leaves to make tea.

TEAC *abbr* = Technical Education Advisory Council.

tea caddy *n* an airtight container for storing tea.

teach *vt* (**teaching**, **taught**) to impart knowledge to; to give lessons (to); to train; to help to learn. * *vi* to give instruction, esp as a profession.—**teachable** *adj*.

TEACH *abbr* = Teacher Education Admissions Clearing House.

teacher *n* a person who instructs others, esp as an occupation.

tea chest *n* a large wooden box used to transport tea.

teach-in *n* an informal conference at a university or college with lectures and discussions on a topical issue.

teaching *n* the profession or practice of being a teacher; the act of giving instruction.

teaching fellow *n* a postgraduate student who undertakes teaching responsibilities in return for tuition, accommodation, etc.—**teaching fellowship** *n*.

teaching hospital *n* a hospital where medical students are taught and trained.

tea cloth *n* a tea towel for drying dishes; a dishtowel.

tea cozy *n* a cover for a teapot to keep the contents warm.

teacup *n* a small cup for drinking tea.

Teague *n* **Walter Dorwin** (1883–1960) American industrial designer who, with Frank del Guidice, designed the Boeing 707 and 727 airline interiors.

teak *n* a type of hard wood from an East Indian tree.

teakettle *n* a kettle with a handle and spout for boiling water to make tea.

teal *n* (*pl* **teal, teals**) a small freshwater duck; a dark greenish blue.

team *n* a group of people participating in a sport together; a group of people working together; two or more animals pulling a vehicle. * *vi* (*with* **up**) to join in cooperative activity.

teammate *n* a colleague, a fellow team member.

team spirit *n* willingness to work harmoniously within a group.

teamster *n* a truck driver.

teamwork *n* cooperation of individuals for the benefit of the team; the ability of a team to work together.

tea party *n* a social gathering at which tea is served.

teapot *n* a vessel in which tea is made.

teapoy *n* a three-legged stand or table.

tear[1] *n* a drop of salty liquid appearing in the eyes when crying or when the eyes are smarting; anything tear-shaped.

tear[2] *vb* (**tearing, tore,** *pp* **torn**) *vt* to pull apart by force; to split; to lacerate; (*with* **down**) to destroy, demolish. * *vi* to move with speed; (*with* **into**) (*inf*) to attack physically or verbally. * *n* a hole or split.

TEAR *abbr* = The Evangelical Alliance Relief Fund.

tearaway *n* an impetuous, violent person.

teardrop *n* a tear. * *adj* shaped like a tear.

tearful *adj* weeping; sad.—**tearfully** *adv*.

tear gas *n* gas that irritates the eyes and nasal passages, used in riot control.

tearing *adj* overwhelming, violent.

tearjerker *n* a strongly sentimental book, film, play, etc.

tearoom or **teashop** *n* a restaurant where tea and light refreshments are served.

tea rose *n* any of numerous garden bush roses descended from a Chinese rose and valued for their large tea-scented blooms.

tease *vt* to separate the fibers of; to torment or irritate; to taunt playfully. * *n* a person who teases or torments; (*inf*) a flirt.—**teaser** *n*.

teasel, teazel, teazle *n* any of various plants with prickly leaves and flower heads formerly dried and used to raise a nap on woolen cloth; an implement used for this purpose.

tea service or **tea set** *n* the set of cups and saucers, etc for serving tea.

teashop *n* a tearoom.

teaspoon *n* a small spoon for use with a teacup or as a measure; the amount measured by this.—**teaspoonful** *n*.

teat *n* the nipple on a breast or udder; the mouthpiece of a baby's feeding bottle.

tea towel or **tea cloth** *n* a towel for drying dishes; a dishtowel.

TEC *abbr* = The Executive Council; Total Environment Center; Training and Enterprise Council.

tech. *abbr* = technical; technically; technology.

Tech(CEI) *abbr* = Technician (Council of Engineering Institutions).

Tech Duinn *n* (*Irish Celtic myth*) the name given to an island off the southwest coast of Ireland. It was believed to be the home of Donn, the god of the dead.

technetium *n* an artificially produced metallic element whose radioisotope is used in radiotherapy.

technical *adj* relating to or specializing in practical, industrial, mechanical or applied sciences; (*expression, etc*) belonging to or peculiar to a particular field of activity.—**technically** *adv*.

technicality *n* (*pl* **technicalities**) a petty formality or technical point.

technical knockout *n* a decision by a referee to end a fight because a boxer is too badly hurt to continue.

technical reserves *npl* (*com*) the assets that are held by an insurance company against future claims or losses.

technician *n* a person skilled in the practice of any art, esp in practical work with scientific equipment.

Technicolor *n* (*trademark*) the production of color film by combining identical scenes with different primary colors into a single print.

technique *n* method of performing a particular task; knack.

techno- *prefix* technical; technological.

technocracy *n* (*pl* **technocracies**) government by technical experts.— **technocrat** *n*. —**technocratic** *adj*.

technol. *abbr* = technological; technologically; technology.

technology *n* (*pl* **technologies**) the application of mechanical and applied sciences to industrial use.—**technological** *adj*.—**technologist** *n*.

TechRMS *abbr* = Technological Qualification in Microscopy.

TechWeldI *abbr* = Technician of the Welding Institute.

techy *see* **tetchy**.

tectonic *adj* of or relating to building or construction; (*geol*) concerned with earth movements, as involved in folding and faulting.

tectonics *n sing* the art or science of constructing buildings, etc; the study of the forces that shape the earth's geological structure.

Tedco *abbr* = Thames Estuary Development Company.

teddy *n* (*pl* **teddies**) a woman's one-piece undergarment.

teddy bear *n* a stuffed toy bear.

tedious *adj* monotonous; boring.—**tediously** *adv*.—**tedium** *n*.

TEDIS *abbr* = Trade Electronic Data Interchange System.

tee *n* the place from where the first stroke is played at each hole on a golf course; a small peg from which a ball is driven. * *vti* to position (the ball) on the tee; (*with* **off**) to hit a golf ball from a tee.

TEE *abbr* = Telecommunications Engineering Establishment; Trans-Europe Express; total energy expenditure.

teem[1] *vi* (*with* **with**) to be prolific or abundant in.

teem[2] *vi* to pour (with rain).

teen *n* a teenager. * *adj* teenage.

teenager *n* (*inf*) a person who is in his or her teens.

teens *npl* the years of one's life from thirteen to nineteen.—**teenage, teenaged** *adj*.

teeny *adj* (**teenier, teeniest**) (*inf*) tiny.

teenybopper *n* a young girl who avidly follows the latest fashions in clothes and pop music.

teepee *see* **tepee**.

tee shirt *see* **T-shirt**.

teeter *vi* to move or stand unsteadily.

teeth *see* **tooth**.

teethe *vi* to cut one's first teeth.

teething *n* the condition in babies of the first growth of teeth.

teething ring *n* a hard ring for a teething baby to chew on.

teething troubles *npl* problems encountered in the early stages of a project, etc; pain caused by growing teeth.

teetotaler, teetotaller *n* a person who abstains from alcoholic drinks.—**teetotal** *adj*.

TEF *abbr* = Textile Employers' Federation.

TEFL *abbr* = Teaching English as a Foreign Language.

Teflon *n* (*trademark*) polytetrafluoroethylene, a coating for pots and pans that prevents food sticking.

teg, t.e.g. *abbr* = top edges gilt.

Tegea *n* a city of southeast Arcadia, the principal city of Arcadia in ancient times.

Tegucigalpa *n* capital city of Honduras.

tegument *n* an outer covering; an integument.

Tehran *n* capital city of the Islamic Republic of Iran.

Tehuacan Valley *n* an arid valley in Puebla, Mexico, in which the very dry conditions have led to the remarkable preservation of organic material.

Teilhard de Chardin *n* Pierre (1881–1955) French Jesuit theologian, philosopher, and paleontologist. He developed a theory of evolution, described in *The Phenomenon of Man* (1955) and other works. The church refused to let his books be published in his lifetime.

Teiresias, Tiresisas *n* (*Greek myth*) a Theban seer who was changed into a woman as a youth and was later turned back into a man.

Te Kanawa *n* Dame Kiri (1944-) a New Zealand soprano who is especially famous for roles in operas by Verdi, Mozart, and Richard Strauss.

Tekoa *n* (*Bible*) home of the prophet Amos, who was a shepherd there.

tektite *n* (*geol*) a spherical glassy object found in various parts of the world and thought to be of meteoric origin.

tel. *abbr* = telegram; telegraph; telegraphic; telephone.

TEL *abbr* = tetraethyl lead (petrol additive).

tel-, tele- *prefix* at a distance; from.

telamon *n* (*archit*) a figure or half-figure of a man, used in place of a column or pilaster to support an entablature, an atlas.

Telamon *n* (*myth*) a hero, one of the Argonauts and one of the hunters of the Calydonian Boar.

Tel Aviv (Tel Aviv-Yafo) *n* capital city of Israel.

Tel. Bn. *abbr* = Telegraph Battalion.

telecast *vt* to broadcast by television. * *n* a television broadcast.—**telecaster** *n*.

telecom, telecoms *n* short for telecommunications.

telecommunication *n communication of* information over long distances by telephone and radio.

telecommunications *npl* (*comput*) the use of the telephone systems, either land lines or satellite, to transmit information (voice, video or computer data).

telecommute *vi* (*comput*) to work from a home base rather than commute to the office, using a modem to communicate and transmit material between the two.

teledu *n* a mammal of Java and Sumatra resembling the badger and related to the skunk, which releases a foul-smelling liquid when threatened.

telefilm *n* a motion picture produced for television.

teleg. *abbr* = telegram; telegraph; telegraphic; telegraphy.

telegenic *adj* suitable for television in content or appearance.

telegram *n* a message sent by telegraph.

telegraph *n* a system for transmitting messages over long distances using electricity, wires, and a code. * *vt* to transmit by telegraph.—**telegraphic** *adj*.— **telegraphy** *n*.

telekinesis *n* the movement of objects using pure thought without the application of physical force.—**telekinetic** *adj*.

Telemachus *n* (*Greek myth*) the son of Odysseus and Penelope.

Telemann *n* Georg Philipp (1681-1767) German composer who became friendly with Bach. His works include 44 Passions, 40 operas, 600 French overtures, and numerous pieces of chamber music.

telemark *n* a skiing turn in which one ski is placed ahead of the other and then angled gradually inward.

telemeter *n* any instrument that measures or records events and transmits the data to a distant receiver; a device for measuring distances. * *vt* to gather and transmit data from a distance.

telemetry *n* the use of radio waves to transmit, register and record the readings of an instrument at a distance.

telencephalon *n* (*anat*) the frontal brain including the cerebrum, parts of the hypothalamus and the third ventricle.—**telencephalic** *adj*.

teleology *n* the philosophical doctrine that explains nature or natural processes in terms of purpose or design.—**teleological** *adj*.— **teleologist** *n*.

telepathy *n* the communication between people's minds of thoughts and feelings, without the need for speech or proximity.—**telepathic** *adj*.

telephone *n* an instrument that enables speech to be transmitted by means of electric currents or radio waves. * *vt* to call by telephone.

telephone book *or* **telephone directory** *n* a book listing the names, addresses, and telephone numbers of subscribers in a given area.

telephone booth *n* a cubicle for paid public use of a telephone.

telephone directory *see* **telephone book**.

telephone exchange *n* the main telephone office of a district, where calls are connected.

telephone number *n* a number that identifies a particular telephone and is used in making a connection with it.

telephone operator *or* **telephonist** *n* a person who operates a telephone switchboard.

telephone selling *n* (*com*) a method of direct marketing in which the seller of a product makes an initial contact with a potential customer.

telephonist *see* **telephone operator**.

telephony *n* the system by which sounds are transmitted by telephone.—**telephonic** *adj*.

telephotography *n* the use of a telephoto lens to photograph distant objects.

telephoto lens *n* a camera lens that magnifies distant objects.

Telephus *n* (*Greek myth*) a son of Heracles and Auge, who was raised by a hind, and who was reunited with his mother with the help of the Delphic oracle.

teleprinter *n* a teletypewriter.

TelePrompTer *n* (*trademark*) a prompting device used in TV, etc, which provides speakers with a script that remains invisible to the audience; an autocue.

telesales *npl* (*com*) selling products and services by telephone.

telescope *n* a tubular optical instrument for viewing objects at a distance.

telescopic *adj* of or like a telescope; that can be viewed by through a telescope.— **telescopically** *adv*.

telesthesia *n* supposed perception of objects or events beyond the normal range of the senses.—*also* **telesthesia**.—**telesthetic** *adj*.

Telesto *n* (*astron*) a small moon or satellite of the planet Saturn, discovered in 1980.

Teletext *n* (*trademark*) written information transmitted non-interactively to television viewers.

telethon *n* (*media*) a long television extravaganza that encourages viewers to send in money for a charitable cause.

Teletype *n* (*trademark*) a teleprinter.

teletypewriter *n* a telegraph apparatus with a keyboard that transmits and a printer that receives messages over a distance.

televangelist *n* a person, usu a minister of the Christian Pentecostal church, who conducts television shows to preach the church's message and seek donations.

televise *vt* to transmit by television.

television *n* the transmission of visual images and accompanying sound through electrical and sound waves; a television receiving set; television broadcasting.

teleworker *see* **telecommute**.

telex *n* a communication system whereby subscribers hire teletypewriters for transmitting messages. * *vt* to transmit by telex.

Telford *n* Thomas (1757–1834) Scottish architect. His notable works include Dean Bridge, Edinburgh, and the Caledonian Canal.

telic *adj* having a purpose.

tell[1] *vb* (**telling, told**) *vt* to narrate; to disclose; to inform; to notify; to instruct; to distinguish; (*with* **off**) (*inf*) to reprimand; to count off and assign to a duty. * *vi* to tell tales, to inform on; to produce a marked effect.

tell[2] *n* (*archeo*) a mound found in the Middle East that is formed from the accumulated debris of thousands of years of human occupation.

teller *n* a bank clerk; a person appointed to count votes in an election.

Teller *n* Edward (1908–) Hungarian-born American physicist who settled in the US in 1935, where he became one of the leading figures in the development of nuclear weapons at Los Alamos.

telling *adj* having great impact.

telltale *n* a person who tells tales about others. * *adj* revealing what is meant to be hidden.

tellurian *adj* of the earth. * *n* an inhabitant of the earth.

telluric *adj* of or in the earth or soil; of or containing (high valency) tellurium.

tellurium *n* (*chem*) a brittle nonmetallic element related to sulfur and selenium.

tellurometer *n* an electronic instrument for measuring distances using microwaves.

Tellus *n* in Roman mythology, the earth and the goddess of the earth, the equivalent of the Greek, Ge.—*also* **Terra.**

telly *n* (*pl* **tellies**) (*Brit inf*) television.

Telnet *n, vti* (*trademark*) (*comput*) the main Internet protocol for creating a connection to other remote computers and Internet locations worldwide.

TELO *abbr* = Tamil Elam Liberation Organization.

telo-, tel- *prefix* end.

telophase *n* (*biol*) the last and fourth stage of meiosis or mitosis in eukaryotic cells.

Telphusa *n* (*Greek myth*) a spring in Boeotia, the site of an ancient oracle; the nymph of the spring.

TEM *abbr* = transmission electron microscopy.

temenos *n* (*archit*) the sacred area around a temple.

temerity *n* rashness.

temp *n* (*inf*) a temporary employee.

temp. *abbr* = temperance; temperature; temporal; temporary; (*Latin*) *tempore*, "in the time of."

Tempe *n* a valley of northern Greece, in Thessaly, between Mount Olympus and Mount Ossa.

temper[1] *n* a frame of mind; a fit of anger. * *vt* to tone down, moderate; to heat and cool steel repeatedly to bring to the correct hardness.

temper[2] *n* material added to clay to give a pottery object added durability during and after firing.

tempera *n* (a method of painting using) powdered pigments mixed with an emulsion, esp egg yolk and water; a painting done in tempera; opaque watercolor used for posters.

temperament[1] *n* one's disposition.

temperament[2] *n* (*mus*) the way in which intervals between musical notes have been altered.

temperamental *adj* easily irritated; erratic.—**temperamentally** *adv*.

temperance *n* moderation; abstinence from alcohol.

temperate *adj* mild or moderate in temperature; (behavior) moderate, self-controlled.

temperate climate *n* a moderate climate with no extremes of temperature, most likely to be found in maritime areas in mid latitudes.

temperate zone *n* the region between the tropic of Cancer and the Arctic Circle, or between the tropic of Capricorn and the Antarctic Circle.

temperature *n* degree of heat or cold against a standard scale; body heat above the normal.

tempered *adj* (*chem*) hardened to the correct degree; having a certain disposition or temper; moderated, qualified.

tempest *n* a violent storm.

tempestuous *adj* stormy; violent; passionate.

tempi *see* **tempo.**

Templar *abbr* = Tactical Expert Mission Planner (military computer).

template[1] *n* a pattern, gauge, or mould used as a guide esp in cutting metal, stone, or plastic.

template[2] (*archit*) a block of stone set at the top of a rubble wall or brick pier to spread the weight of overlying beams.

template[3] (*comput*) a document that is prewritten and formatted and ready for final editing or adjustment before printing.

temple[1] *n* a sacred building constructed for the purpose of worship and containing a statue of a god

temple[2] *n* the side of the head above the level of the eye and the ear.

Temple of Jerusalem *n* the center of Jewish worship for a thousand years. Solomon's Temple was destroyed in 587 BC; the second building was completed about 515 BC and desecrated in the second century BC; the third was a reconstruction of the second. *See also* **Solomon; Zerubbabel; Herod; Priest; High Priest.**

Temple *n* Shirley (1928–) American film actress and Republican politician; became the world's leading child film star with films such as *Dimples* (1936); later she developed a career in politics under her married name of Shirley Temple Black.

Templier *n* Raymond (1891–1968) French jewelry designer who joined the long-established family firm in 1912.

tempo *n* (*pl* **tempos, tempi**) (*mus*) the speed at which music is meant to be played; rate of any activity.

temporal[1] *adj* relating to time; secular, civil.

temporal[2] *adj* of or relating to the temples of the head.

temporality *n* (*pl* **temporalities**) the state or condition of being temporal; a secular or civil authority or power.

temporal lobe *n* (*anat*) a lobe on each side of the cerebral hemisphere associated with hearing and speech.

temporal lobe epilepsy *n* epilepsy that is centered within the temporal lobe, caused by disease within the cerebral cortex.

temporary *adj* lasting or used for a limited time only; not permanent.—**temporarily** *adv*.

temporize *vi* to delay in order to gain time; to act to fit the occasion.—**temporization** *n*. —**temporizer** *n*.

temp. prim. *abbr* (*music*) (*Italian*) = *tempo primo*, "original speed."

tempt *vt* to entice to do wrong; to invite, attract, induce.—**tempter** *n*. —**temptress** *nf*.

temptation *n* the act of tempting or the state of being tempted; something or someone that tempts.

tempting *adj* attractive, inviting.

tempura *n* a Japanese dish of seafood or vegetables fried in batter.

ten *adj, n* the cardinal number next above nine. * *symbol* 10, X, x.

ten. *abbr* = tenement; tenor; tenuto.

tenable *adj* capable of being believed, held, or defended.

tenacious *adj* grasping firmly; persistent; retentive; adhesive.

tenacity *n* the state or quality of being tenacious; doggedness, obstinacy; adhesiveness, stickiness.

tenaculum *n* (*pl* **tenacula**) (*med*) a hooked surgical instrument for seizing and holding parts, such as arteries.

tenancy *n* (*pl* **tenancies**) the temporary possession by a tenant of another's property; the period of this.

tenant *n* a person who pays rent to occupy a house or apartment or for the use of land or buildings; an occupant.

tenant farmer *n* a farmer who works land owned by someone else to whom he pays rent.

Ten Commandments *see* **Commandments.**

tench *n* (*pl* **tench**) a freshwater fish of the carp family.

tend[1] *vt* to take care of; to attend (to).

tend[2] *vi* to be inclined; to move in a specific direction.

tendency *n* (*pl* **tendencies**) an inclination or leaning.

tendentious, tendencious *adj* showing bias, not impartial.—**tendentiousness, tendenciousness** *n*.

tender[1] *adj* soft, delicate; fragile; painful, sore; sensitive; sympathetic.—**tenderly** *adv*.—**tenderness** *n*.

tender[2] *n* (*com*) an offer to provide goods or services at a fixed price. * *vi* to make an offer. * *vt* to present for acceptance; to offer as payment.

tender[3] *n* a railroad car attached to locomotives to carry fuel and water; a small ship that brings stores to a larger one.

tenderfoot *n* a newcomer to rough, outdoor life; an inexperienced beginner.

tenderhearted *n* having a compassionate, loving, or sensitive disposition.—**tenderheartedly** *adv*.—**tenderheartedness** *n*.

tenderize *vt* to make meat more tender by pounding or by adding a substance that softens.—**tenderization** *n*. —**tenderizer** *n*.

tenderloin *n* a cut of meat from between the ribs and sirloin.

tendon *n* (*anat*) fibrous tissue attaching a muscle to a bone.

tendonitis *n* inflammation of a tendon, which often results from excessive or unaccustomed exercise but may also result from infection.

tendril *n* (*bot*) a thread-like shoot of a climbing plant by which it attaches itself for support.

Tenedos *n* a Greek island in the Aegean Sea, on the west coast of Turkey.

tenement *n* a building divided into apartments, each occupied by a separate owner or tenant.

tenesmus *n* (*med*) an urgent but ineffectual attempt to urinate or void the bowels.

tenet *n* a belief or doctrine.

tenfold *adj, adv* 10 times as much or as many; composed of 10 parts.

ten-gallon hat *n* a wide-brimmed hat with a high crown, esp worn by cowboys.

tenge *n* the standard monetary unit of Kazakhstan.

Teng Hsiao-p'ing *see* **Deng Xiao Ping.**

tenia *n* (*pl* **teniae**) (*archit*) a thin fillet molding separating the architrave from the frieze in the Greek Doric order.

teniasis *n* (*med*) infestation with tapeworms.

Tenn. *abbr* = Tennessee.

tenner *n* (*inf*) a ten-dollar bill; a ten-pound note.

Tennesse *n* a state of the USA, of which the capital is Nashville.

Tennessee Waltz *n* The the song of the American state, Tennesse.

tennis *n* a game for two or four people, played by hitting a ball over a net with a racket.

tennis court *n* a court surfaced with clay, asphalt or grass on which tennis is played.

tennis elbow *n* (*med*) stiffness and pain in the elbow joint due to excessive exercise, such as playing tennis.

Tennstedt n **Klaus** (1926–) a German conductor and violinist. He has worked with many noted orchestras and is known for his interpretations of the works of Mahler.

Tennyson n **Alfred Lord [1st Baron Tennyson]** (1809–92) English poet who first came to public notice with *Poems, Chiefly Lyrical*. He was appointed British poet laureate in succession to Wordsworth in 1850.

Tenochtitlán n capital city of the Aztecs built on islands in the Valley of Mexico.

tenon n a projection on the end of a piece of wood for connecting with a mortise. * vt to form a tenon; to connect using a tenon and mortise.

tenon saw n a fine-toothed saw with a sturdy back used for cutting tenons, etc.

tenor[1] adj (*mus*) indicates the range of an instrument, between an alto member of the family and a bass, e.g. tenor saxophone. * n the highest adult male voice, higher than a baritone and lower than an alto; a man who sings tenor; the reciting note in psalm singing; an obsolete term for a viola (tenor violin).

tenor[2] n a general purpose or intent.

tenor[3] n (*com*) the time that has to elapse before a bill of exchange becomes due for payment.

tenor clef n (*mus*) a C clef placed so as to designate the fourth line of the staff as middle C.

tenor drum n (*mus*) a drum, frequently used in military bands, between a side drum and bass drum in size and pitch, and without snares.

tenosynovitis n inflammation of the tendons in a joint through repetitive movements of the joint concerned.

tenpin n a bowling pin used in tenpins.

tenpin bowling n in UK, tenpins.

tenpins n *sing* a bowling game involving the rolling of a large bowl along a lane to knock over as many as possible of ten pins.

tenrec n any of various related mammals of Madagascar resembling shrews.

TENS *abbr* = transcutaneous electrical nerve stimulation.

tense[1] adj stretched, taut; apprehensive; nervous, and highly strung. * vti to make or become tense.—**tensely** adv.—**tenseness** n.

tense[2] n (*gram*) the verb form that indicates the time of an action or the existence of a state.

tensile adj of or relating to tension; stretchable.

tensile strength n the greatest stress a material can bear without breaking.

tensimeter n an instrument that measures differences in vapor pressures.

tensiometer n an instrument for measuring tensile strength; an instrument for comparing vapor pressures in different liquids; an instrument for measuring the surface tension of a liquid; an instrument for measuring the moisture content of soil.

tension n the act of stretching; the state of being stretched; (*between forces, etc*) opposition; stress; mental strain.

tensor n (*anat*) any muscle that stretches or tightens a body part.

tens. str. *abbr* = tensile strength.

tent n a portable shelter of canvas, plastic, or other waterproof fabric, which is erected on poles and fixed to the ground by ropes and pegs.

tentacle n a long, slender, flexible growth near the mouth of invertebrates, used for feeling, grasping, or handling.

tentative adj provisional; not definite.—**tentatively** adv.—**tentativeness** n.

tent caterpillar n any of various voracious caterpillars that build large silken webs in trees.

tenterhook n one of a series of hooks on which cloth is stretched to dry; (*pl*) (*with on*) in a tense or anxious state.

tenth adj the last of ten; being one of ten equal parts. * n one of ten equal parts.

tenuous adj slight, flimsy, insubstantial.—**tenuousness** n.

tenure n the holding of property or a position; the period of time which a position lasts; a permanent position, usu granted after holding a job for a number of years.—**tenured** adj.

tenuto n (*mus*) (*Italian*) "held" a term which indicates that a note should be held for its full value, or in some cases, even longer.

Tenzing Norgay *see* **Hillary, Edmund**.

teocalli n (*pl* **teocallis**) the pyramid-shaped bases supporting Aztec temples.

Teotihuacán n the most important city in ancient Mexico. At its peak it may have been home to as many as 200,000 people.

tepee n a cone-shaped, North American Indian tent formed of skins; a wigwam.—*also* **teepee**.

tepid adj slightly warm, lukewarm.

TEPP *abbr* = tetraethyl pyrophosphate (pesticide).

tequila n a spirit distilled from a Mexican agave plant; the plant itself.

ter. *abbr* = terrace; territory.

ter- *prefix* three times; third; three.

tera- *prefix* (*comput*) a prefix representing one trillion (10^{12}). * *symbol* T.

terabyte, TB, tbyte n (*comput*) a measurement of memory capacity that is approx one trillion bytes. The actual number is 1,099,511,627,776 bytes.

Terah n (*Bible*) father of Abraham.

Teraphim n (*Bible*) primitive idols probably used as charms to bring good luck. They may also have served as title-deeds to family property.

terat., teratol. *abbr* = teratology.

terato- *prefix* monster.

teratogen n (*med*) a substance or disease or any other factor that causes the production of abnormalities in a fetus.

teratogenesis n the processes that result in the development of physical abnormalities in a fetus.

teratoma n (*med*) a tumor that is composed of unusual tissues not normally found at that site and derived from partially developed embryological cells.

terbium n (*chem*) a metallic element of the rare earth group.

tercel *see* **tiercel**.

tercentenary n (*pl* **tercentenaries**) a three hundredth anniversary.—*also adj*.

Tercom *abbr* = terrain contour matching.

terebene n (*chem*) a liquid hydrocarbon derived from oil of turpentine and sulfuric acid used in making varnishes, as an antiseptic and in medicines.

terebinth n a European tree that yields a resinous liquid.

terebinthine n of or pertaining to the terebinth; of or like turpentine.

teredo n (*pl* **teredos, teredines**) a burrowing mollusk, the shipworm.

Terence n [**Publius Terentius Afer**] (*c*.190–159 BC) Roman dramatist whose six comedies are all extant and, like those of Plautus, are adaptations of Greek originals.

Teresa of Avila n **Saint** (1515–1582) Spanish nun and mystic. She founded a convent of strict Carmelite nuns at Avila 1562. Her writings: *The Way of Perfection, Foundations*, and *The Interior Castle*, are classics in the literature of mysticism. Her feast day is October 15.

terete adj having a smooth cylindrical shape.

Tereus n (*Greek myth*) the husband of Procne, who seduced her sister Philomela, and then cut out Philomela's tongue when she threatened to tell.

tergiversate vi to switch allegiances; to be evasive, to equivocate.

term[1] n a limit; any prescribed period of time; a division of an academic year; a word or expression, esp in a specialized field of knowledge; (*pl*) mutual relationship between people; (*pl*) conditions of a contract, etc. * vt to call, designate.

term[2], **termini,** *or* **terminal figure** n (*archit*) a pedestal narrower at the base than the top, which is carved into a figure or may carry a sculptured bust. See **caryatid**.

term. *abbr* = terminal; termination.

termagant n a shrewish, nagging woman.

terminal[1] adj being or situated at the end or extremity; (*disease*) fatal, incurable.

terminal[2] n a bus, coach, or railroad station at the end of the line; the point at which an electrical current enters or leaves a device; (*comput*) a device with a keyboard and monitor for inputting or viewing data from a computer.—**terminally** adv.

terminal emulation n (*comput*) a procedure whereby a terminal or personal computer acts like another in order that communications can take place between computers.

terminal value n the value of an investment at the end of an investment period, taking into account the specified rate of interest.

terminal velocity n (*phys*) the greatest speed reached by a projected or falling object; the speed of a projectile when it reaches its target.

terminate vti to bring to or come to an end.—**termination** n.

terminator n (*astron*) the boundary between the hemisphere of a planet or moon which is lit up by the sun, and that which is facing away and lies in darkness.

terminology n (*pl* **terminologies**) the terms used in any specialized subject.

terminus n (*pl* **termini, terminuses**) the final part; a limit; end of a transportation line.

termitarium n (*pl* **termitaria**) a termite's nest.

termite n a wood-eating, white, ant-like insect.

TermNet *abbr* = International Network for Terminology.

term paper n a major essay submitted by a school or college student at the end of a term.

terms of trade npl a form of price index that indicates the ratio of a country's export process relative to its import prices.

tern n a small, black and white sea bird.

ternary adj in three parts; (*number system*) using three as a base.

ternary form n (*mus*) a term applied to a piece of music that is divided into three self-contained parts, with the first and third sections bearing strong similarities.

ternary time *see* **triple time**.

terp n (*archeo*) an earth mound built in the coastal areas of Holland and Germany on which a settlement was sited.

terpene n (*chem*) any of various hydrocarbons present in the essential oils of plants, esp conifers.

Terpsichore n (*Greek myth*) one of the nine Muses, dedicated to lyric poetry and dance.

Terpsichorean adj pertaining to dancing, or to Terpsichore, the Muse of dancing and choral song in classical myth.

terr. *abbr* = terrace; territory.

terra firma n solid ground; the earth.

terra incognita n an unexplored or unknown area or country.

Terra *see* **Tellus**.

terrace n a raised level area of earth, often part of a slope; an unroofed paved area adjoining a house; a row of houses; a patio or balcony. * vt to make into a terrace.

terracotta n a brownish-red clay used for making flower pots and statues, which is baked but not glazed; a brown-red color.

terrain n the surface features of a tract of land; (*fig*) field of activity.

terramara n (*archeo*) the local Italian name in the Po valley for an accumulated mound of debris that is the remains of a Bronze Age settlement.

terrapin n an aquatic North American turtle.

terrarium n (*pl* **terraria, terrariums**) an enclosure for small land animals; a glass container for plants.

terrazzo n mosaic flooring in the form of marble chips set in mortar and highly polished.

terrestrial *adj* relating to, or existing on, the earth; earthly; representing the earth; being on land rather than on the water.

terrestrial radiation *n* the heat radiated from the earth.

terrible *adj* causing great fear; dreadful; (*inf*) very unpleasant.

terribly *adv* frighteningly; (*inf*) very.

terrier *n* a type of small, active dog.

terrific *adj* of great size; (*inf*) excellent.

terrify *vt* (**terrifying, terrified**) to fill with terror, to frighten greatly.

terrine *n* an earthenware dish for pâté; pâté or similar food served in this.

territorial *adj* relating to or owned by a territory. * *n* (*Brit*) (*with cap*) a member of the Territorial Army, a British volunteer reserve force.

territorial waters *or* **territorial seas** *n* the coastal waters with the sea-bed below and the air above them that a state claims as its own.

territory *n* (*pl* **territories**) an area under the jurisdiction of a city or state; a wide tract of land; an area assigned to a salesman; an area of knowledge.

terror *n* great fear; an object or person inspiring fear or dread.

terrorism *n* the use of terror and violence to intimidate.— **terrorist** *n*.

terrorize *vt* to terrify; to control by terror.—**terrorization** *n*.

terry *n* (*pl* **terries**) a cloth with an uncut pile made of looped threads.

Terry *n* [Dame] **Ellen Alice** (1847–1928) English actress whose stage career began in 1856 at the age of nine in a Shakespeare production by Charles Kean, and ended in 1925.

terse *adj* abrupt, to the point, concise.—**tersely** *adv*.

tertian *adj* (med) of fever, occurring on alternate days.

tertiary *adj* third.

terzett, terzetto *n* (*mus*) (*Italian*) an instrumental or vocal trio.

TES *abbr* = *Times Educational Supplement*.

TESCO *abbr* = British supermarket chain founded by T E Stockwell and J Cohen.

TESL *abbr* = Teaching of English as a Second Language.

tesla *n* the SI unit of magnetic flux density.

TESOL *abbr* = Teachers of English to Speakers of Other Languages.

TESSA *abbr* (*Brit*) = Tax-Exempt Special Savings Account.

tessellated *adj* resembling mosaic.

tessera *n* (*pl* **tesserae**) a piece of marble, glass, etc used in a mosaic.

Tessin *n* **Nicodemus** (1615–81) Swedish architect. His notable works include Göteborg Town Hall.

tessitura *n* (*mus*) (*Italian*), "texture," a term that indicates whether the majority of notes in a piece are high up or low down in the range of a voice (or instrument).

test *n* an examination; trial; a chemical reaction to test a substance or to test for an illness; a series of questions or exercises. * *vt* to examine critically.

Test. *abbr* = Testament.

Testa *n* **Angelo** (1921–) American fabric designer of the 1941 *Little Man* abstract floral fabric, hailed as a new direction in fabric design.

testament *n* a will; proof; tribute; (*arch*) a covenant made by God with men; (*with cap*) one of the two main parts of the Bible.

testate *adj* having made and left a will.

testator *n* a person who leaves a will.

test ban *n* an agreement between nations to limit or abandon tests of nuclear weapons.

test-bed *n* an area designed for testing machinery.

test case *n* a legal action that establishes a precedent.

test-drive *vt* (**test-driving, test-drove,** *pp* **test-driven**) to go for a short drive in a car, etc, to assess its performance.

tested *adj* subjected to testing.

tester *n* (*archit*) a canopy situated above a pulpit, throne, tomb, bed, or other structure.

testicle, testis (*pl* **testes**) *n* (*anat*) one of the pair of male sex organs that are situated within the scrotum. They produce sperm and secrete the hormone testosterone.

testify *vi* (**testifying, testified**) to give evidence under oath; to serve as witness (to); (*with* **to**) to be evidence of. * *vt* to be evidence of.

testimonial *adj* relating to a testimony. * *n* a recommendation of one's character or abilities.

testimony *n* (*pl* **testimonies**) evidence; declaration of truth or fact.

testis *see* **testicle**.

test marketing *n* (*com*) the process of launching a new product by testing it out in a restricted geographical area or among a restricted sample of consumers.

test match *n* one of a series of international cricket or Rugby football matches.

testosterone *n* a steroid hormone secreted by the testes that promotes the development of male characteristics. *See also* **androgen**.

test pilot *n* someone who flies new types of aircraft to test their performance and characteristics.

test tube *n* a cylinder of thin glass closed at one end, used in scientific experiments.

test-tube baby *n* a baby which develops from an ovum fertilized outside the mother's body and replaced in the womb. *See also* **in vitro fertilization**.

testy *adj* (**testier, testiest**) touchy, irritable.

tetanus *or* **lockjaw** *n* (*med*) an intense and painful spasm of muscles, caused by the infection of a wound by bacteria

tetchy *adj* (**tetchier, tetchiest**) irritable, touchy.—*also* **techy**.—**tetchily** *adv*.—**tetchiness** *n*.

tête-à-tête *n* (*pl* **tête-à-têtes, tête-à-tête**) a private conversation between two people.

tether *n* a rope or chain for tying an animal; the limit of one's endurance. * *vt* to fasten with a tether; to limit.

Tethys[1] *n* (*Greek myth*) a female Titan, who married her brother Oceanus and became the mother of all the river-gods and of their three thousand sisters, the Oceanids.

Tethys[2] *n* (*astron*) a moon or satellite of the planet Saturn, first discovered in 1684 by Giovanni Cassini.

tetra-, tetr- *prefix* four.

tetrachloride *n* (*chem*) a chloride containing four atoms of chlorine.

tetrachord *n* (*mus*) a group of four notes.

tetracycline *n* an antibiotic that is obtained both naturally and synthetically and is used to treat rickettsial, viral, and bacterial infections, e.g. relapsing fever.

tetragon *n* a plane figure with four angles and four sides.—**tetragonal** *adj*.—**tetragonally** *adv*.

tetrahedron *n* (*pl* **tetrahedrons, tetrahedra**) a solid figure enclosed by four plane faces of triangular shape.

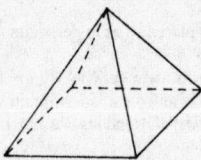

tetrahydroamino-acridine *n* a drug currently being tried out for use in the treatment of Alzheimer's disease.

tetrahydrocannabinol *n* (*chem*) a natural compound that is the main intoxicant in cannabis and can also be produced synthetically.

tetralogy *n* (*pl* **tetralogies**) a series of four related works, such as novels or plays.

Tetrarch *n* ruler of a fourth part of a province in Roman times.

tetravalent *adj* (*chem*) having a valency of four.

Teucer *n* (*Greek myth*) a hero who was the best archer with the Greek forces in the Trojan War.

Teut. *abbr* = Teuton; Teutonic.

Teutates *n* (*Gaulish Celtic myth*) tribal deity.

Teuthras *n* (*Greek myth*) king of Mysia, who received Auge and brought up her son Telephus.

Teutonic *adj* of Germanic peoples or their language.

TeV *abbr* = (*phys*) tera-electron volt.

tewt *abbr* = tactical exercise without troops.

Tex. *abbr* = Texan; Texas.

Texas *n* a state of the USA, of which the capital is Austin.

Texas, Our Texas *n* the song of the American state, Texas.

Tex-Mex *adj* of or pertaining to a Texan version of something Mexican, such as food or music.

text *n* the main part of a printed work; the original or exact wording; a passage from the Bible forming the basis of a sermon; a subject or topic; a textbook.

text alignment *n* (*comput*) the justification of text in a word processing or page layout document.

textbook *n* a book used as a basis for instruction.

text chart *n* (*comput*) a slide presentation that contains no graphics but consists only of text, e.g. showing a menu list of items.

text editor *n* (*comput*) a basic word processing program that is used mainly for writing computer programs and batch files, with very limited facilities for formatting and printing.

text file *n* (*comput*) a file that contains only ASCII characters and no formatting, used mainly for transfer of information between different programs or computers.

textile *n* a woven fabric or cloth. * *adj* relating to the making of fabrics.

text message *n* a typed piece of text that can be sent by a cellular phone.

Text Rec *abbr* (*Latin*) = *textus receptus*, "received text."

textual *adj* of or relating to a text; contained in or based on a text; (*operation, etc*) exactly as planned according to theory or calculation.

textual criticism *n* the study of a written work (e.g., the Bible) to establish the original text; the close reading and analysis of any literary work.

texture *n* the characteristic appearance, arrangement or feel of a thing; the way in which threads in a material are interwoven.—**textural** *adj*.

text wrap *see* **wrap around type**.

Teyrnon *n* (*Irish Celtic myth*) lord of Gwent Is-Coed. He is best known as the foster father of Pryderi, whom he named Gwri.

tf *abbr* = tax-free.

TFA *abbr* = Tenant Farmers' Association; Texas Forestry Association; Textile Finishers' Association; The Freedom Association; total fatty acids.

TFAP *abbr* = Tropical Forestry Action Plan.

TFC *abbr* = Tasmanian Forestry Commission.

TFOF *abbr* = Taxi Fleet Operators" Federation.

tfr *abbr* = transfer.

TFS *abbr* (med) = testicular feminization syndrome.

TFSC *abbr* = Turkish Federated State of Cyprus.

TFSK *abbr* = Turkish Federated State of Kibris (Cyprus).

TFSR *abbr* = Tools For Self Reliance.

TFTA *abbr* = Traditional Farm-Fresh Turkey Association.

TFU *abbr* = telecommunications flying unit.

TFX *abbr* = tactical fighter, experimental.

t.g. *abbr* = type genus.

TG *abbr* = (*Brit*) Tate Gallery; transformational grammar.

TGA *abbr* = Timber Growers Association; Tropical Growers Association.

TGAT *abbr* = Task Group on Assessment and Testing.

tgb *abbr* = tongued, grooved, and beaded.

TGE *abbr* (*med*) = transmissible gastroenteritis.

TGF *abbr* = transforming growth factor.

TGI *abbr* = Target Group Index; Tory Green Initiative.

TGIA *abbr* = Toy and Giftware Importers' Association.

TGIF *abbr* (*inf*) = Thank God it's Friday.

TGUK *abbr* = Timber Growers United Kingdom Limited.

TGV *abbr* (*French*) = *Train à Grande Vitesse*, "High Speed Train."

TGWU *abbr* = (*Brit*) Transport and General Workers' Union.

Th *symbol* (*chem*) thorium (element).

Th. *abbr* = Thursday.

TH *abbr* = Territory of Hawaii.

Th-A *symbol* (*chem*) thorium A.

THA *abbr* = tetrahydroamino-acridine.

Thackeray *n* **William Makepeace** (1811–63) Indian-born English novelist and essayist, noted particularly for witty social satire, e.g. *The Book of Snobs* (1846–47).

Thaddeus *n* (*Bible*) one of the twelve disciples of Jesus; some ancient versions read Lebbaeus, or Lebbaeus called Thaddaeus. *See* **Jude.**

Thai *n* (*pl* **Thais, Thai**) a native or inhabitant of Thailand; the language of Thailand.—*also adj.*

Thailand *n* a constitutional monarchy, formerly known as Siam, located in southeast Asia.

thalamus *n* (*pl* **thalami**) (*anat*) one of a pair of masses of gray matter located within each side of the forebrain. Each is a center for coordinating and relaying the sensory information concerned with all the senses, apart from that of smell.

Thalassa *n* (*astron*) a small moon or satellite of the planet Neptune, discovered by the Voyager 2 space probe in 1989.

thalassemia *n* an inherited form of anemia in which there is an abnormality in the hemoglobin. The disease is widespread throughout the Mediterranean, Asia, and Africa.—*also* **Cooley's anemia.**

thalassic *adj* of or relating to or situated near the sea, esp a small inland sea.

Thaleia, Thalia[1] *n* (*Greek myth*) one of the nine Muses, dedicated to comedy.

Thaleia, Thalia[2] (*Greek myth*) one of the Graces.

thalidomide *n* a sedative drug withdrawn from use when it was discovered to cause malformation in unborn babies.

thallium *n* (*chem*) a soft white poisonous metallic element.

thalweg *n* the long profile of a river valley or the line of the deepest part of the stream.

than *conj* introducing the second element of a comparison.

thanatology *n* the scientific study of death.

Thanatos *n* (*Greek myth*) death and the personification of death.

thank *vt* to express gratitude to or appreciation for. * *npl* an expression of gratitude.—**thankful** *adj.*—**thankfully** *adv.*

thankless *adj* without thanks; unappreciated; fruitless, unrewarding.—**thanklessness** *n.*

thanksgiving *n* the act of giving thanks; a prayer of gratitude to God; (*with cap*) Thanksgiving Day.

Thanksgiving Day *n* a legal holiday observed on the fourth Thursday of November in the US, and on the second Monday of October in Canada.

thank-you *n* an expression of gratitude.

Thant *n* **U** (1909–74) Burmese diplomat. He succeeded Hammarskjöld as secretary general of the United Nations (1961–72), and was widely admired for his role as a tactful mediator, most notably during the Cuban missile crisis.

Tharshish *n* possibly a ship-building or trading port somewhere in the ancient Mediterranean.

Thasus *n* the most northerly island in the Aegean Sea, a few miles south of the Macedonian coast.

that *demons adj, pron* (*pl* **those**) the (one) there or then, esp the latter or more distant thing. * *rel pron* who or which. * *conj* introducing noun clause or adverbial clause of purpose or consequence, because, in order that; (*preceded by* **so, such**) as a result.

thatch *n* roofing straw, heather, reeds, etc held in place by stones, poles or wires. * *vt* to cover a roof with thatch.

Thatcher *n* **Baroness Margaret Hilda** (1925–) English Conservative stateswoman. She was the first woman to lead a major British political party and was prime minister from 1979 until she resigned in 1990. During this period she launched an ideological crusade ("Thatcherism") against socialism.

thaumatology *n* (*pl* **thaumatologies**) the study of miracles; a discourse on miracles.

thaumaturge, thaumaturgist *n* a miracle-worker; a magician.—**thaumaturgy** *n.*

thaw *vi* to melt or grow liquid; to become friendly. *vt* to cause to melt. * *n* the melting of ice or snow by warm weather.

Th-B *symbol* (*chem*) thorium B.

ThB *abbr* (*Latin*) = *Theologiae Baccalaureus*, "Bachelor of Theology."

THB *abbr* = Traditional Housing Bureau.

THC *abbr* (*chem*) = tetrahydrocannabinol (component of cannabis).

ThD *abbr* (*Latin*) = *Theologiae Doctor*, "Doctor of Theology."

THD *abbr* = total harmonic distortion.

the *demons adj* denoting a particular person or thing. * *adv* used before comparative adjectives or adverbs for emphasis.

THE *abbr* = Technical Help to Exporters.

theat. *abbr* = theatrical.

theater, theatre *n* a building where plays and operas are performed; the theatrical world as a whole; field of operations; a setting for important events;

theater-in-the-round *n* a theater with seats arranged in a circle around the stage area.

theater of cruelty *n* a form of theater that uses non-verbal means of communication to project the pain and loss fostered by the modern world, subverting the idea of art as a set of concepts separate from real life.

theater of the absurd *n* a form of theater that characterizes the human condition as one of helplessness in the face of an irrational universe.

theatrical *adj* relating to the theater; melodramatic, affected.—**theatrically** *adv.*

theatricals *npl* performances of drama, esp by amateurs.

thebe *see* **pula.**

Thebe *n* (*astron*) a small moon or satellite of the planet Jupiter, discovered in 1979.

Thebes *n* (*Egypt*) modern Luxor; in the decline of the Egyptian Old Kingdom, in the period after 2475 BC, Thebes became a capital city, controlling a great area of the Nile Valley and sometimes the entire country.

Thebes *n* a city of ancient Greece, the principal city of Boeotia.

thee *pron* the objective case of **thou.**

theft *n* act or crime of stealing.

theine *n* caffeine.

their *poss adj* of or belonging to them; his, hers, its.

theirs *poss pron* of or belonging to them; his, hers, its.

theism *n* belief in the existence of a God or gods, esp God as the supernatural Creator of the universe.—**theist** *n.*—**theistic** *adj.*

Th-Em *abbr* (*chem*) = thorium emanation.

them *pron* the objective case of **they.**

thematic map *n* a map designed to show particular attributes, e.g. population, climate or oil wells, rather than physical features such as mountains or rivers.

theme *n* (*mus*) the melody, or other musical material, that forms the basis of a work or a movement and which may be varied or developed; the main subject of a discussion; an idea or motif in a work; a short essay; a style adopted for an exhibition, activity, etc.—**thematic** *adj.*

theme park *n* a leisure area in which the buildings and settings follow a particular theme, e.g. a period in history.

theme song *n* (*mus*) a recurring melody in a film score or musical that is associated with the work or a particular character; a signature tune.

Themis *n* (*Greek myth*) a female Titan, the goddess of order, law, and justice.

themselves *pron* the reflexive form of **they** or **them.**

then *adv* at that time; afterward; immediately; next in time. * *conj* for that reason; in that case.

thenar *n* (*anat*) the ball of the thumb; the palm of the hand.

thence *adv* from that time or place; for that reason.

thenceforth *adv* from that time on; thereafter.

thenceforward, thenceforwards *adv* thenceforth.

theo-, (*also* **the-**) *prefix* god.

theobromine *n* (*chem, med*) an alkaloid similar to caffeine present in cacao beans and tea, used in treating heart disease.

theocracy *n* (*pl* **theocracies**) (a state having) government by a deity or priesthood.—**theocrat** *n.*—**theocratic** *adj.*

Theocritus *n* (c.310–250 BC) Greek poet whose work established the standard frame of the pastoral: shepherds and shepherdesses singing to one another of their loves in a world of peace and plenty in which the sun always shines.

theodolite *n* a surveying instrument for measuring angles, consisting of a small telescope, a spirit level, and a compass, all of which are mounted on a tripod.

Theodore *n* **Saint** (c. 602–90) Greek monk from Tarsus in Cilicia; archbishop of Canterbury (667). Theodore's framework of the Catholic church survived the upheavals of the sixteenth century and is still the basis of the diocesan system of the Church of England. His feast day is September 19.

theol. *abbr* = theologian; theological; theology.

theologian *n* a person who studies and interprets religious texts, etc; a teacher of theology.

theology *n* (*pl* **theologies**) the study of God and of religious doctrine and matters of divinity.—**theological, theologic** *adj.*—**theologically** *adv.*

Theoph. *abbr* = Theophilus; Theophrastus.

Theophilus *n* (*Bible*) the "most excellent" official to whom the Gospel of Luke and the Acts of the Apostles are addressed by their author.

theor. *abbr* = theorem.

theorem *n* (*philos*) a proposition that can be proved from accepted principles; law or principle.

theoretical, theoretic *adj* of or based on theory, not practical application; hypothetical; conjectural.—**theoretically** *adv.*

theoretician *n* a person who concentrates on the theoretical basis of a subject.

theoretics *npl* the speculative parts of a science.

theorize *vi* to form theories; to speculate.—**theorist, theorizer** *n.*—**theorization** *n.*

theory *n* (*pl* **theories**) an explanation or system of anything; ideas and abstract principles of a science or art; speculation; a hypothesis.

T

theos. *abbr* = theosophical; theosophist; theosophy.

Thera *n* a volcanic island in the Aegean Sea north of Crete.—*also* **Santorini**.

therap. *abbr* (*med*) = therapeutic or therapeutics.

therapeutic, therapeutical *adj* relating to the treatment of disease; beneficial.—**therapeutically** *adv*.

therapeutics *npl* the area of medicine concerned with the various methods of healing and treatment.

therapy *n* (*pl* **therapies**) (*med*) the treatment of physical or mental illness.—**therapist** *n*.

there *adv* in, at, or to, that place or point; in that respect; in that matter.

thereabout, thereabouts *adv* at or near that place or number.

thereafter *adv* after that; according to that.

thereagainst *adv* in opposition to; contrary to.

thereat *adv* at that place; at such time.

thereby *adv* by that means.

therefore *adv* for that or this reason; consequently.

therefrom *adv* (*arch*) from that or it; from that time or place.

therein *adv* in that place or respect.

thereof *adv* of this or that; because of that.

thereon *adv* on that or it; immediately following that.

Theresa of Calcutta *n* **Mother [Agnes Gonxha Bojaxhiu]** (1910–97) Yugoslavian-born (of Albanian parentage) Roman Catholic nun and missionary. She founded the Order of the Missionaries of Charity in 1950. Venerated by many people as a living saint, her work in Calcutta with orphans and with the dying led to her being awarded the 1979 Nobel Peace Prize.

Theresa of Lisieux *n* **Saint** (1873–97) French Carmelite nun; noted for her autobiography, *The Story of a Soul*. She was canonized in 1925. Her feast day is October 1.

thereupon *adv* immediately after that.

therm *n* a measurement of heat.

therm. *abbr* = thermometer.

thermal (*also* **thermic**) *adj* generating heat; hot; warm; (*underwear*) of a knitted material with air spaces for insulation. * *n* a strong upcurrent of warm air used by gliding birds and glider pilots to gain height.

thermal conductivity *n* (*phys*) a measure of the rate of heat flow along a body by conduction.

thermal depression *n* (*meterol*) an area of low pressure that occurs in continental interiors.

thermal erosion *n* (*geol*) the erosion caused when a frozen river thaws and undercuts its banks; the mass movement of ground when permafrost thaws.

thermal expansion (*also* **thermal fracture**) *n* (*geol*) the cracking that takes place in rocks subject to large daily temperature changes, due to the various constituents of the rock expanding and contracting at different rates.—*also* **thermal fracture**.

thermal metamorphism *or* **contact metamorphism** *n* (*geol*) the process of metamorphism that occurs when rocks are intruded by an igneous body and the rocks are recrystallized in response to the heat.

thermal printer *n* (*comput*) a printer that uses heat to form an image on special paper, often used by fax machines.

thermal radiation *n* electromagnetic radiation resulting from the high temperature of a body.

thermal sensing *n* in remote sensing, when the sensor picks up heat being radiated from a feature, so enabling remote sensing to be carried out in cloudy conditions or in darkness.

thermion *n* (*chem*) an electron emitted by a material at high temperature.

thermionic *adj* (*chem*) of, pertaining to, or worked by, thermions, esp a tube.

thermistor *n* (*elect*) a semiconductor device whose resistance varies inversely with a change in temperature.

thermo- (*also* **therm-**) *prefix* heat.

thermochemistry *n* the branch of chemistry dealing with the heat changes of chemical reactions.

thermocline *n* the layer of water in the oceans or deep lakes that separates the warmer surface water from cold, deep water. It is a zone approximately one to three kilometers deep where temperatures fall sharply.

thermocouple *n* (*elect*) a device that generates a thermoelectric effect between two dissimilar semiconductors, used in measuring temperature differences.

thermodynamics *n* (*phys*) the branch of physics concerned with the relationship between heat and other forms of energy.

thermoelectric, thermoelectrical *adj* (*phys*) of or derived from electricity generated by difference of temperature.—**thermoelectricity** *n*.

thermograph *n* (*med*) a thermometer that records continuously, and where the recording is usually achieved by means of an electrical device.

thermography *n* a method of recording the heat produced by different areas of the body, using photographic film sensitive to infrared radiation; *n* the use of heat sensors in an aircraft to detect changes in ground surface temperature. Sometimes these indicate a buried archeological structure.

thermoluminescence[1] *n* a method of dating minerals that is similar to the radiocarbon technique, but is applied to material that has been burnt or fired.

thermoluminescence[2] *n* (*physics*) a phenomenon whereby a material gives out light upon heating, due to electrons being freed from defects in crystals;

thermolysis *n* (*chem*) breakdown of a compound or molecule by heat.

thermometer *n* an instrument for measuring temperature.

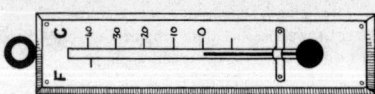

thermonuclear *adj* (*phys*) of or relating to nuclear fusion or nuclear weapons that utilize fusion reactions.

thermoplastic *adj* becoming soft and malleable when heated. * *n* a resin or synthetic plastic that can be heated, molded, and cooled without appreciable change of its properties.

Thermos *n* (*trademark*) a brand of vacuum bottle.

thermosphere *n* the atmospheric layer between the mesosphere and the exosphere.

thermostat *n* an automatic device for regulating temperatures.

thermotropism *n* (bot) the growth of a plant in the direction of a heat source.—**thermotropic** *adj*.—**thermotropically** *adv*.

third party *n* a person other than the two principals; a bystander.

Theroux *n* **Paul Edward** (1941–) American writer whose works include *The Old Patagonian Express: By Train Through the Americas* (1979).

Thersander *n* (*Greek myth*) a hero, one of the Epigoni, who fought and was killed at Troy.

Thersites *n* (*Greek myth*) a Greek soldier in the Trojan War, who mocked and criticized the Greek leaders, and was killed by Achilles.

THES *abbr* (Brit) = *Times Higher Education Supplement*.

Thesaur. Amer. Septent. Sigil. *abbr* (*Latin*) = *Thesaurus Americae Septentrionis Sigillum*, "Seal of the Treasury of North America" or Seal of the US Treasury.

thesaurus *n* a reference book or computer file that lists alternative meanings for words, i.e. synonyms.

these *see* **this**.

Theseus *n* (*Greek myth*) a king of Athens and famous hero, who killed the Minotaur and performed many other exploits.

thesis *n* (*pl* **theses**) a dissertation written as part of an academic degree; a theory expressed as a statement for discussion.

thespian *adj* (*theatre*) of or pertaining to drama. * *n* an actor or actress.

Thess. *abbr* = Thessalonians; Thessaly.

Thessalonians *n* **the First and Second Letters of Paul to the** (*Bible*) similar letters in which Paul urges the recipients to stand firm in the face of suffering, and considers what happens to believers who die before the second coming of Christ.

Thessalonica *n* wealthy and important trading and seaport city in northern Greece.

Thessaloníki *n* a city in Greece.

Thessaly *n* a northeastern area of Greece, whose major cities in ancient times were Larissa, Pharsalus, and Pherae.

theta *n* the eighth letter of the Greek alphabet.

Thetis *n* (*Greek myth*) a divinity, the wife of Peleus and mother of Achilles.

they *pers pron, pl of* **he**, **she** *or* **it**.

they'd = they would; they had.

they'll = they will; they shall.

they're = they are.

they've = they have.

THF *abbr* = Trust House Forte (a British hotel and restaurant chain).

THG *abbr* = Telecommunications Heritage Group.

THI *abbr* = temperature-humidity index.

thiamine, thiamin *n* vitamin B, present in a wide variety of plants and animals and essential for normal metabolism and nerve function.

thick *adj* dense; viscous; fat, broad; abundant, closely set; in quick succession; crowded; (*inf*) stupid. * *adv* closely; frequently.

thicken *vti* to make or become thick.—**thickener** *n*.

thicket *n* a small group of trees or shrubs growing thickly and closely together.

thickhead *n* (*inf*) an ignorant person, an idiot.—**thickheaded** *adj*.

thickness *n* being thick; the dimension other than length or width; a layer.

thickset *adj* having a short, stocky body.

thick-skinned *adj* not sensitive; not easily offended.

thick-witted *adj* stupid.

thief *n* (*pl* **thieves**) a person who steals.

Thierrat *n* **Augustin** (1798–1870) French painter who became a professor of painting and later of floral design at the Lyon École des Beaux-Arts.

Thiersch's graft *n* a type of skin graft in which thin strips of skin are taken from one part of the body and placed on the wound that is required to be healed.

Thiès *n* a city in Senegal.

thieve *vti* to steal.

thigh *n* the thick fleshy part of the leg from the hip to the knee.

thighbone *n* the femur.

thimble *n* a cap or cover worn to protect the finger when sewing.

thimbleful *n* what a thimble contains, a tiny amount.

Thimphu *n* capital city of Bhuta.

thin *adj* (**thinner, thinnest**) narrow; slim; lean; sparse, weak, watery; (*material*) fine; not dense. * *vt* to make thin; to make less crowded; to water down.—**thinly** *adv*.—**thinness** *n*.

thine *pron* an old-fashioned word for **yours**.

thing *n* an inanimate object; an event; an action; (*pl*) possessions; (*inf*) an obsession.

thingamabob, thingumabob *n* (*inf*) something or someone the name of which has been forgotten, is unknown, or is hard to categorize, etc.—*also* **thingamajig, thingumajig, thingummy, thingie**.

Thinite Period *n* (3150–2700 BC) the era of the first two Egyptian dynasties, from the name of the kings' city of origin near Abydos.

think *vi* (**thinking, thought**) to exercise the mind in order to make a decision; to revolve ideas in the mind, to ponder; to remember; to consider; * *vt* to judge, to believe or consider; (*with* **up**) to concoct, devise; (*with* **over**) to ponder, to consider the costs and benefits of.—**thinker** *n*.

thinking *adj* capable of using thought, rational; intelligent. * *n* the process of using thought; opinion, reasoning.

think-tank *n* (*inf*) a group of experts convened to analyze and advise on ways of handling a particular problem.

thin market *n* in the stock exchange, a market in which the price of the relevant commodity, currency, etc, may be subject to change if transactions of a sizeable nature take place.

thinner *n* a substance, such as turpentine, added to paint, varnish, etc, to thin it.

thin-skinned *adj* overly sensitive to criticism; easily offended.

third *adj* the last of three; being one of three equal parts. * *n* one of three equal parts.

third class *n* a class of mail in the US and Canadian postal systems that includes all printed matter, except periodicals, weighing below a certain amount and unsealed; the cheapest accommodation on a ship, aircraft, etc.—**third-class** *adj, adv*.

third degree *n* the use of torture, bullying, or rough questioning to obtain information.

third-degree burn *n* (*med*) a severe burn which destroys surface and underlying tissue and may involve loss of fluid and shock.

third generation *adj* (*comput*) an era in computing around the mid 1960s when the transistor was replaced by integrated circuits and disk storage and on-line terminals were introduced.

thirdly *adv* in the third place; as a third point.

third party insurance *n* insurance that relates to someone other than the insurer or the policy-holder and occurs when there is a legal obligation to others to be taken into consideration.

third party vendor *n* (*comput*) a business that buys computer equipment and accessories from a manufacturer and sells to the end user.

third person *n* grammatical forms, such as pronouns and verbs, used when referring to the person or thing spoken or written of, not to the person speaking or writing or to the person or persons addressed.

third rail *n* a metal rail that carries the current to an electric locomotive.

third-rate *adj* inferior.

Third World *n* the underdeveloped countries of the world (usu refers to those in Africa, Asia and South America).

thirst *n* a craving for drink; a longing. * *vi* to feel thirst; to have a longing.

thirsty *adj* (**thirstier, thirstiest**) having a desire to drink; dry, arid; longing or craving for.—**thirstily** *adv*.—**thirstiness** *n*.

thirteen *adj, n* three and ten.—**thirteenth** *adj, n*.

thirty *adj, n* (*pl* **thirties**) three times ten.—**thirtieth** *adj, n*.

thirty-second note *n* (*mus*) a note with a time value of one thirty-secondth of a whole note, a demisemiquaver.

this *demons pron* (*pl* **these**) *or adj* denoting a person or thing near, just mentioned, or about to be mentioned.

Thisbe *see* **Pyramus**.

thistle *n* a wild plant with prickly leaves and a purple flower.

thistledown *n* the feathery cluster of seeds produced by the thistle.

thither *adv* (*arch*) to or toward that place.

thixotropy *n* (*phys*) the property of some fluids that are very viscous until a stress is applied, when the fluid flows more easily.

Th M, ThM *abbr* (Latin) = *Theologiae Magister*, "Master of Theology."

tho, tho' *conj, adv* (*inf*) though.

tholos *n* (*pl* **tholoi**) (*archeo*) a circular building from ancient Greece with a beehive-shaped central chamber and a conical or domed roof.

Thomas *n* Saint [**Didymus** or **Doubting Thomas**] (*Bible*) one of the twelve Apostles. After the Resurrection he would not believe he had seen Jesus till he had seen his wounds. The patron saint of architects. His feast day is July 3.

Thomas à Becket *see* **Becket, Thomas à**.

Thomas Aquinas *n* Saint (*c*.1225–74) Italian theologian and philosopher whose writings are a cornerstone in the teachings of the Roman Catholic Church.

Thomas *n* Dylan [**Marlais**] (1914–53) Welsh poet whose best-known single work is *Under Milk Wood* (1954), a radio drama in poetic prose. His exuberant, hard drinking persona ultimately led to his death in New York. 2. [**Philip**] **Edward** (1878–1917) English poet; encouraged to write poetry by Robert Frost. Killed in action (1915) before the publication of his *Poems* (1917). 3. **R[onald] S[tuart]** (1913–2000) Welsh poet regarded as one of the foremost religious poets of modern

times. His poems display a deep concern for the bleak and often spiritually barren way of life of the poor of rural Wales.

Thompson *n* 1. **Emma** (1959–) English TV and film actress. 2. **Flora** [**Jane**] (1876–1947) English author, noted for her autobiographical trilogy, in one volume as *Lark Rise to Candleford*. 3. **Francis** (1859–1907) English poet who was rescued from opium addiction by Alice Meynell. Her poems are intensely spiritual with elaborate imagery. 4. **Jim** (1906–76) American novelist whose crime novels are in the tradition of seedy determinism.

Thomson *n* 1. **Alexander "Greek"** (1817–) Scottish architect. His notable works include the St Vincent Street Church, Glasgow. 2. **Sir George Paget** (1892–1975) English physicist. He shared the 1937 Nobel prize for physics with the American physicist Clinton Joseph Davisson for their (independent) discovery of the diffraction of electrons by crystals. 3. **James** (1700–1748) Scottish poet and dramatist whose most famous poems are *The Seasons* and *The Castle of Indolence*. 4. **James** (1834–82) Scottish poet, chiefly remembered for his poem "City of Dreadful Night," a long, nightmarish vision of a decaying city. 5. **Sir Joseph John** (1856–1940) English physicist. He was awarded the 1906 Nobel prize for physics for his discovery (1906) of the electron. 6. **Roy Herbert [1st Baron Thomson of Fleet]** (1894–1976) Canadian-born British newspaper proprietor. After acquiring a fortune in the oil trade, he began buying radio stations and newspapers in Canada in the 1930s, subsequently expanding into the US and Britain. 7. **Virgil** (1896–1989) an American composer and music critic of great originality. His works include operas, ballets, film music, chamber music, and many songs.

Thonet *n* **Michael** (1796–1871) German furniture maker and designer who became one of the most innovative 19th-century furniture designers.

thong *n* a piece or strap of leather to lash things together; the lash of a whip; a sandal held on the foot by a thong passing between the toes and fixed to a strap passing over the top of the foot.

Thor *n* (*Norse myth*) the god of thunder.

thoracic *adj* pertaining to the chest, e.g. the thoracic duct.

thoracocentesis *or* **pleuracentesis** *n* (*med*) the withdrawal, by means of a hollow needle inserted through the chest wall, of fluid from the pleural cavity.

thorax *n* (*pl* **thoraxes, thoraces**) the part of the body enclosed by the ribs; the chest; in insects, the middle one of the three chief divisions of the body—**thoracic** *adj*.

Thoreau *n* **Henry David** (1817–62) American philosopher, and friend of Emerson, whose advocacy of self-sufficiency and passive resistance to tyranny has been very influential.

thorium *n* (*chem*) a radioactive metallic element used in industry and as a nuclear fuel.

thorn *n* (*bot*) a shrub or small tree having thorns, esp hawthorn; a sharp point or prickle on the stem of a plant or the branch of a tree.

Thorndike *n* **Dame Sybil** (1882–1976) English actress. Notable for her long acting career, from 1904 to the late 60s, she created many roles, including Shaw's *Saint Joan* (1924).

Thornthwaite climate classification *n* a classification of climates based on characteristic vegetations and associated precipitation. *See also* **Köppen classification**.

thorny *adj* (**thornier, thorniest**) prickly; (*problem*) knotty.

thoron *n* (*chem*) a gas, a radioactive isotope of radon.

thorough *adj* complete, very detailed and painstaking, exhaustive.—**thoroughness** *n*.

thorough bass *see* **figured bass**.

thoroughbred *adj* bred from pure stock. * *n* a pedigree animal, esp a horse.

thoroughfare *n* a way through; a public highway, road; right of passing through.

thoroughgoing *adj* very thorough; out-and-out.

thoroughly *adv* completely, fully; entirely, absolutely.

Thorpe *n* [**John**] **Jeremy** (1929–) British Liberal politician; leader of the Liberal Party (1967–76).

those *adj, pron* plural of that.

Thoth *n* an early rival to Ra, the Egyptian sun-god, as creator of Egypt (and hence the world).

thou[1] *pron* (*arch*) an old-fashioned word for **you**.

thou[2] *n* (*pl* **thous, thou**) (*inf*) a thousand; a thousandth of an inch.

though *conj* yet, even if; * *adv* however; nevertheless.

thought *n* the act of thinking; reasoning; serious consideration; an idea; opinions collectively; design, intention. * *pt, pp* of **think**.

thoughtful *adj* pensive; considerate.

thoughtless *adj* without thought; inconsiderate.

thought-out *adj* produced by or resulting from careful thinking and consideration.

thought-provoking *adj* stimulating thought.

thousand *adj* ten times one hundred; (*pl*) denoting any large but unspecified number. * *n* the number 1000.—**thousandth** *adj, n*.

Thousand and One Nights, The *see* **Arabian Nights' Entertainments**.

thp *abbr* = thrust horsepower.

THR *abbr* (*med*) = total hip replacement.

Thrace *n* now a part of northern Greece together with European Turkey. In ancient geography, it was separated from Asia by the Propontis, and its two narrow channels, the Bosporus and the Hellespont.

thrall *n* the condition of being controlled or ruled by another; slavery; a slave; a person with a ruling need or passion. * *vt* to enslave.

thrash *vt* to beat soundly; to defeat; (*with* **out**) to discuss thoroughly, until agreement is reached. * *vi* to thresh grain; to writhe.

thrashing *n* a beating or flogging; punishment.

thread *n* a fine strand or filament; a long thin piece of cotton, silk or nylon for sewing; the spiral part of a screw; (*of reasoning*) a line; (*comput*) a link between an article in a newsgroup and any responses to that article.* *vt* to pass a thread through the eye of a needle; to make one's way (through).

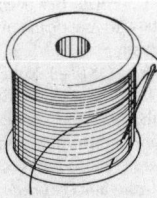

threadbare *adj* worn, shabby.

threadworm *n* (*zool*) a long slender worm, parasitic in humans and pigs.

threat *n* a declaration of an intention to inflict harm or punishment upon another.

threaten *vti* to utter threats to; to portend.

threatening *adj* menacing, intimidating; warning; ominous, sinister.—**threateningly** *adv*.

three *adj, n* the cardinal number next above two. * *symbol* 3, III, iii.

Three Age System *n* a system devised by Christian Thomsen (1788–1865) for dividing prehistory into the Stone Age, Bronze Age, and Iron Age.

three Rs *npl* reading, writing and arithmetic, regarded as the basis of learning.

three-dimensional, three-D, 3-D *adj* having or seeming to have length, breadth and depth.

three-dimensional spreadsheet *n* (*comput*) a spreadsheet program that consists of several layers of related pages or worksheets.

threefold *adj, adv* three times as much or as many; composed of three parts.

three-mile limit *n* a limit of three miles around the coast of a state regarded as territorial waters.

three-point landing *n* an aircraft landing in which the two main wheels and nose wheel or tail wheel touch down at the same time.

three-quarter *adj* being three quarters of the normal size or length. * *n* (*sport*) one of usu four attacking players in rugby football used particularly for running with the ball.

three-ring circus *n* a circus with three rings for simultaneous performances; an extraordinary or exciting spectacle; a state of chaos or confusion.

threescore *n* (*arch*) sixty.—*also adj*.

threesome *n* a group of three; a game for three people.

three-wheeler *n* a vehicle with three wheels.

threnody, threnode *n* (*pl* **threnodies, threnodes**) (*mus*) a song or speech of lamentation, esp on a person's death.

thresh *vti* to beat out (grain) from (husks).

threshold *n* the sill at the door of a building; doorway, entrance; the starting point, beginning.

threshold agreement *n* an agreement that workers' pay will be increased by a specified amount if the rate of inflation goes above a specified amount in a given period.

threshold population *n* the minimum population required for the provision of goods or services.

threw *see* **throw**.

thrice *adv* three times.

thrift *n* careful management of money.—**thrifty** *adj*.

thrift shop *n* a shop that sells used clothing and other items to raise money for charity.

thriftless *adj* worthless; careless or wasteful of money.—**thriftlessness** *n*.—**thriftlessly** *adv*.

thrill *vti* to tingle with pleasure or excitement. * *n* a sensation of pleasure and excitement; a trembling or quiver.

thriller *n* a novel, film, or play depicting an exciting story of mystery and suspense.

thrilling *adj* exciting, gripping.

thrips *n* (*pl* **thrips**) any of various small insects with sucking mouthparts that feed on and damage plants.

thrive *vi* (**thriving, thrived** *or* **throve**, *pp* **thrived** *or* **thriven**) to prosper, to be successful; to grow vigorously.—**thriving** *adj*.

thro, thro' *prep, adv* (*inf*) through.

throat *n* the front part of the neck; the passage from the back of the mouth to the top part of the tubes into the lungs and stomach; an entrance.

throaty *adj* (**throatier, throatiest**) hoarse; guttural; deep, husky.—**throatily** *adv*.

throb *vi* (**throbbing, throbbed**) to beat or pulsate rhythmically, with more than usual force; to vibrate, beat.—*also n*.

throes *npl* violent pangs or pain.

thrombin *n* (*biol*) an enzyme that contributes to blood clotting. *See also* **coagulation**.

thrombocyte *n* a blood platelet.

thromboembolism *n* (*med*) a blood clot (thrombus) that forms in one part of the circulation, usually a deep vein in the leg, and becomes lodged elsewhere, causing a total blockage.

thrombolysis *n* (*med*) the dissolving of blood clots by enzyme activity.

thrombophlebitis *n* (*med*) inflammation of the wall of a vein along with clot formation in the affected section of the vessel.

thrombosis *n* (*pl* **thromboses**) (*med*) the forming of a blood clot in the heart or in a blood-vessel.

thrombus *n* (*pl* **thrombi**) (*med*) the blood clot that blocks a vessel in thrombosis.

throne *n* a chair of state occupied by a monarch; sovereign power. * *vt* to place on a throne.

throng *n* a crowd. * *vti* to crowd, congregate.

throstle *n* (*arch*) any of various Old World thrushes.

throttle *n* a valve controlling the flow of fuel or steam to an engine. * *vt* to regulate the speed of (an engine) using a throttle; to choke or strangle.

through *prep* from one side or end to the other; into and then out of; covering all parts; from beginning to end of; by means of; in consequence of; up to and including. * *adv* from one end or side to the other; completely. * *adj* going without interruption; unobstructed.

throughout *prep* in every part of; from beginning to end. * *adv* everywhere; at every moment.

throughput *n* (*comput*) the amount of material processed in a particular period, esp by a computer.

throughway *see* **thruway**.

throve *see* **thrive**.

throw *vt* (**throwing, threw**, *pp* **thrown**) to hurl, to fling; to cast off; (*party*) to hold; (*inf*) to confuse or disconcert; (*with* **off**) to cast off, discard, abandon; to distract, elude; to produce in a casual manner; to confuse, disconcert; (*with* **out**) to discard, reject; to dismiss or eject, esp forcibly; to emit, give forth; to construct out from a main section; to confuse, distract; (*with* **over**) to abandon, jilt; (*with* **together**) to assemble hurriedly or carelessly; to bring (people) into casual contact; (*with* **up**) to raise quickly; to resign from, abandon; to build hurriedly; to produce; (*inf*) to vomit. * *vi* to cast or hurl through the air (with the arm and wrist); to cast dice; (*with* **up**) (*inf*) to vomit. * *n* the act of throwing; the distance to which anything can be thrown; a cast of dice.

throwaway *adj* disposable.

throwback *n* a reversion to an earlier or more primitive type.

throw-in *n* a throw from touch to resume play in soccer, rugby football, etc.

thrown *see* **throw**.

thru *prep* (*sl*) through.

thrum *vi* (**thrumming, thrummed**) to strum; to beat incessantly.

thrush[1] *n* a songbird with a brown back and spotted breast.

thrush[2] *n* (*med*) a fungal disease occurring in the mouths of babies or in women's vaginas.

thrust *vti* (**thrusting, thrust**) to push with force; to stab, pierce; to force into a situation. * *n* a forceful push or stab; pressure; the driving force of a propeller; forward movement; the point or basic meaning; (*geol*) a fault inclined at a low angle in which the sense of movement is reversed, i.e. one block moves up the thrust plane over the underlying block.

thruway *n* (*transp*) an expressway.—*also* **throughway**.

THT *abbr* (*Brit*) = Terence Higgins Trust.

thud *n* a dull, heavy sound, caused by a blow or a heavy object falling. * *vi* (**thudding, thudded**) to make such a sound.

thug *n* a violent and rough person, esp a criminal.

thuggery *n* rough and violent behavior.

Thule *n* relating to a widespread Inuit culture that existed *c*. 500–1300 .

thulium *n* (*chem*) a malleable metallic element of the rare-earth group.

thumb *n* the first, short, thick finger of the human hand. * *vt* (*book*) to turn (the pages) idly.

thumbed *adj* worn by use.

thumb index *n* a series of semicircular notches cut in the edge of a book for easier reference to particular parts.

thumbnail *n* the nail of the thumb. * *adj* concise.

thumbnut *n* a wing nut.

thumbprint *n* an impression made by the thumb, esp for identification.

thumbs down *n* a sign of refusal or failure.

thumbscrew *n* an instrument of torture that crushes the thumbs; a screw with a modified head for tightening with the finger and thumb.

thumbs up *n* an indication of approval or encouragement.

thumbtack *n* a flat-headed pin used for fastening paper, drawings, etc, a drawing pin.

thump *n* a heavy blow; a thud. * *vi* to throb or beat violently. * *vt* to strike with something heavy.

thumping *adj* (*inf*) very great.

thunder *n* the rumbling noise that accompanies lightning flashes, due to the sudden heating and expansion of the air caused by the electrical discharge; any similar sound. * *vi* to sound as thunder. * *vt* (*words*) to utter loudly. *See also* **lightning**.

thunderbolt *n* a flash of lightning accompanied by thunder; anything sudden and shocking.

thunderclap *n* a loud bang of thunder.

thundercloud *n* an electrically charged cloud that produces thunder and lightning.

thundering *adj* (*inf*) unusually great, excessive.

thunderous *adj* very loud; producing thunder.

thunder stick *or* **bullroarer** *or* **whizzer** *n* (*mus*) an instrument consisting of a flat piece of wood fastened to a piece of string. When the piece of wood is whirled around the head, it creates a roaring sound.

thunderstorm *n* a storm of thunder, lightning and heavy rain or hail caused by unstable conditions in the atmosphere.

thunderstruck *adj* astonished.

thundery *adj* indicating thunder.

Thur., Thurs. *abbr* = Thursday.

Thurber *n* James [Grover] (1894–1961) American humorist, cartoonist and essayist, much of whose work first appeared in *The New Yorker*, including his most famous story, "The Secret Life of Walter Mitty."

thurible *n* a censer.

Thursday *n* the fifth day of the week.

thus *adv* in this or that way; to this degree or extent; so; therefore.

thwack *vti* to hit hard, whack. * *n* a heavy blow, whack; the sound of this.

thwart *vt* to prevent, to frustrate.

thy *poss adj* an old-fashioned word for **your**.

Thyestes *n* (*Greek myth*) a son of Pelops, who seduced the wife of his brother Atreus, who, in revenge, served up to him the body of his own son at a feast.

thyme *n* a herb with small leaves used for flavoring savory food.

thymol *n* a substance obtained from thyme and used as a fungicide and antiseptic.

thymus *n* (*pl* **thymuses, thymi**) (*anat*) a gland, divided into two lobes, that is present in the neck and forms a vital part of the body's response to infection.

thyristor *n* any of various semiconductor devices that act as switches or rectifiers.

thyroid *or* **thyroid gland** *n* (*anat*) the gland in the neck affecting growth and metabolism. *See also* **cretinism**

thyroidectomy *n* (*med*) surgical removal of the thyroid gland.

thyrotoxic adenoma *n* (*med*) a form of thyrotoxicosis or Graves' disease.

thyrotropin (also **thyrotrophin**) *n* a hormone secreted by the pituitary gland that stimulates the thyroid gland.

thyroxine *n* an important hormone produced by the thyroid gland and used medically to treat conditions resulting from underactivity of this gland, e.g. cretinism.

thyrsus *n* (*pl* **thyrsi**) (*Greek myth*) a pole that was carried by maenads and satyrs while taking part in revels associated with Dionysus in ancient Greece.

ti *n* the seventh note of the scale in solmization.

'tis (*poet*) = it is.

Ti *symbol* (*chem*) titanium (element).

TI *abbr* = Textile Institute; Toastmasters International; thermal imaging.

TIA *abbr* = Telecommunications Industry Association.

Tianjin *n* a city in China.

tiara *n* a semicircular crown decorated with jewels.

TIB *abbr* (*Brit*) = Tourist Information Bureau.

Tiber *n* a river of Italy, rising in the Apennines in Tuscany, flowing through Rome and into the Mediterranean.

Tiberias *n* Sea of (*Bible*) alternative name for the Sea of Galilee.

Tiberius *n* [Tiberius Claudius Nero] (42 BC–AD 37) Roman emperor. A much respected soldier, his reign became increasingly despotic and he ruled Rome from his refuge on Capri from AD 26.

tibia *n* (*pl* **tibiae, tibias**) (*anat*) the inner and thicker of the two bones between the knee and the ankle; the shinbone.

TIBOR *abbr* = Tokyo Inter-Bank Offered Rate.

tic *n* (*med*) any involuntary, regularly repeated, spasmodic contraction of a muscle.

TIC *abbr* = Timber Industries Confederation; Tourist Information Center.

TICCIH *abbr* = The International Committee for the Conservation of the Industrial Heritage.

tick[1] *n* a check mark (√) to check off items on a list or to indicate correctness; the sound of a clock; (*sl*) a moment; (*comput*) a single beat of the microchip that determines the number of instructions that a chip can process, usu one instruction per tick. * *vi* to make a regular series of short sounds; to beat, as a clock; (*inf*) to work, function; (*with over*) (*engine*) to idle; to function routinely. * *vt* (*often with off*) to check off, as items in a list.

tick[2] *n* a small bloodsucking insect that lives on people and animals.

ticker *n* a telegraphic device that receives and outputs stock-market prices on a paper tape; any similar device operated electronically and outputting to a display monitor; (*inf*) the heart; (*inf*) a watch.

ticker tape *n* a continuous length of paper tape output from a telegraphic ticker.

ticket *n* a printed card, etc, that gives one a right of travel or entry; a label on merchandise giving size, price, etc.

tickle *vt* to touch lightly to provoke pleasure or laughter; to please or delight.

ticklish, tickly *adj* sensitive to being tickled; easily offended; difficult or delicate.

tick-tack-toe *n sing* a game in which two players place noughts and crosses into squares on a grid with nine spaces, the winner being the first to form a row of three noughts or crosses.

ticktock *n* a ticking sound, esp of a clock. * *vi* to make such a sound.

tid, t.i.d. *abbr* (*Latin*) = *ter in die*, "three times a day."

tidal *adj* relating to, or having, tides.

tidal wave *n* a large wave as a result of high winds with spring tides; a huge destructive wave caused by earthquakes; something overwhelming.

tidbit *see* **titbit**.

tiddly *adj* (**tiddlier, tiddliest**) (*inf*) very small; (*inf*) slightly drunk.

tiddlywinks (also **tiddledywinks**) *npl* a game whose object is to flick small plastic discs into a container by snapping them with a larger disc.

tide *n* the regular rise and fall of the seas, oceans, etc, usu twice a day, caused by the gravitational effect of the moon and sun; a current of water; a tendency; a flood. * *vt* (*with over*) to help along temporarily.

tide rip *n* a rip current.

tidemark *n* the highest or lowest point reached by the sea.

tidewater *n* water overflowing land at flood tide; water that is affected by the tide.

tidings *npl* news, information.

tidy *adj* (**tidier, tidiest**) neat; orderly. * *vt* to make neat; to put things in order.—**tidily** *adv*.—**tidiness** *n*.

tie *n* a knot, bow, etc; a bond; a long narrow piece of cloth worn with a shirt; necktie; an equality in score; (*mus*) a curved line that joins two notes of the same pitch together, indicating that they should be played as one long note. * *vi* to score the same number of points (as an opponent); (*with in*) to be linked in a certain way; (*with up*) to dock (a vessel). * *vt* (**tying, tied**) to bind; to fasten with a string or thread; to make a bow or knot in; to restrict; (*with in*) to link with something; (*with up*) to fasten tightly (as if) with cord, string, etc; to connect, link; to invest money, etc, so as to make it unavailable for alternative uses; to preoccupy, distract.

tie beam *n* a horizontal beam that holds parts of a structure together.

tiebreaker, tiebreak *n* any means of deciding a contest which has ended in a draw, such as an extra game, hole, question, etc.

tie-dyeing, tie-dye *n* a method of producing patterns on textiles by tying or knotting parts of the fabric to limit the amount of dye absorbed.

tie-in *n* a link or connection; a book linked to a film or TV series.

tie line *n* a telephone link between two private branch exchanges.

tiepin *n* a decorative pin used to secure the ends of a tie to a shirt.

Tiepolo *n* Giambattista (1696–1770) Italian artist and the greatest decorative fresco painter of the rococo period.

tier *n* a row or rank in a series when several rows are placed one above another.

tier. *abbr* (*meas*) = tierce.

tiercel *n* a male of various hawks, esp as used in falconry.—*also* **tercel**.

tierceron *n* (*archit*) a secondary rib in a vault which arises from the vault and springs to the ridge riborn

tie-up *n* a link, connection; a standstill.

tif *abbr* = telephone interference factor.

TIF *abbr* = Theatre Investment Fund.

tiff *n* a petty quarrel or disagreement. * *vi* to quarrel; to be in a huff.

TIFF, Tiff *abbr* (*comput*) = Tagged Image File Format. A standard relating to graphic images, which are made up of a series of dots. *See also* **bitmap**.

Tiffany *n* 1. Charles Louis (1812–1902) American design entrepreneur who started out with a fancy goods and stationery store on Broadway with John B Young. 2. Louis Comfort (1848–1933) American glassmaker and interior designer who founded the Tiffany Glass Company. His Favrile glass became the epitome of the art nouveau style.

TIG *abbr* (*chem*) = tungsten inert gas.

tiger *n* a large, fierce carnivorous animal of the cat family, having orange and black stripes.—**tigress** *nf*.

tiger beetle *n* any of numerous predatory beetles with powerful mandibles and spotted wing cases.

tiger cat *n* an ocelot or similar medium-sized wildcat with a striped coat.

tiger lily *n* a lily of China and Japan cultivated for its dark-spotted orange flowers.

tiger moth *n* any of various large moths marked with stripes or spots.

Tigernmas *n* (*Irish Celtic myth*) an Irish king who may have had some historical connections. He supposedly introduced the worship of Cenn Cruiach to Ireland. This worship involved human sacrifice on the feast of Samhain.

tiger's eye, tigereye *n* a brownish-yellow gemstone.

tiger shark *n* a large shark of warm waters with a striped or spotted skin.

tiger snake *n* an aggressive poisonous Australian snake with striped markings.

Tighina *n* a city in Moldova (Moldavia).

tight *adj* taut; fitting closely; not leaky; constricted; miserly; difficult; providing little space or time for variance; (*contest*) close; (*inf*) drunk.

tighten *vti* to make or grow tight or tighter.

tightfisted *adj* miserly.

tightknit *adj* tightly integrated.

tight-lipped *adj* having the lips firmly pressed together, as from annoyance; taciturn.

tightrope *n* a taut rope on which acrobats walk.

tights *npl* (*Brit*) a one-piece garment covering the legs and lower body, panty hose.

tightwad *n* a miser; a person who is mean with money.

tigon, tiglon *n* the hybrid offspring of a tiger and a lioness.

Tigris *n* river in Western Asia. *See also* **Euphrates**.

TIH *abbr* = Their Imperial Highnesses.

TIIAL *abbr* = The International Institute of Applied Linguistics.

Tijuana *n* a city in Mexico.

tike *see* **tyke**.

tilde *n* a sign ~ placed above a letter to indicate a nasal sound, as in Spanish *señor*.

tile *n* a thin slab of baked clay used for covering roofs, floors, etc. * *vt* to cover with tiles; (*comput*) to set windows in a side by side fashion on the desktop. *See also* **cascading windows**.

till[1] *n* a drawer inside a cash register for keeping money.

till² *prep* until. * *conj* until.

till³ *vt* (*land*) to cultivate for raising crops, as by ploughing.

till⁴ *n* sediment deposited as a result of the action of glacial ice without water as an agent.

tiller *n* (*naut*) the handle or lever for turning a rudder in order to steer a boat.

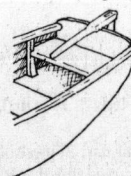

Tillich *n* **Paul [Johannes]** (1886–1965) German-born American theologian and philosopher who became a critic of the Nazis. His works include The Courage To Be (1952) and Systematic Theology (1951–63).

TILS *abbr* = Technical Information and Library Service.

tilt *n* a slope or angle. * *vi* to slope, incline, slant. * *vt* to raise one end of.

TIM *abbr* = time is money.

timber *n* wood when used as building material; a beam; trees collectively. * *vt* to provide with timber or beams.

timbale *n* a mixture of meat or fish with cream cooked in a mould lined with vegetables or pastry.

timbered *adj* (*archit*) having wooden beams on the exterior.

timber framing *n* (*archit*) a framework of vertical and horizontal timbers, the intervening spaces being infilled with other materials.

timber hitch *n* a knot used to tie a rope, etc to a log or spar.

timber lacing *n* (*archeo*) a latticework of timbers around which a stone wall or earthwork was built up.

timber line *see* **tree line**.

timber truss *n* (*archit*) a roof constructed from a framework of timbers called the truss. It is open on the inside, i.e. the beams can be viewed from the room below.

timber wolf *n* (*zool*) a type of large gray North American wolf.

timbre *n* (*mus*) (*French*) the quality of a tone, or the characteristic sound of a voice or musical instrument.

time¹ *n* the past, present, and future; a particular moment; hour of the day; an opportunity; the right moment; duration; occasion. * *vt* to regulate as to time; to measure or record the duration of.

time² *n* (*mus*) the rhythmic pattern (number of beats in a bar) of a piece of music, as indicated by the time signature.

time and motion study *n* (*com*) the study of working procedures to improve efficiency.

time bomb *n* a bomb designed to explode at a predetermined time; something with a potentially delayed reaction.

time capsule *n* a container holding objects representative of contemporary society and culture buried until discovered in the future.

timecard *n* (*com*) a card used in a time clock for recording an employee's arrival and departure.

time clock *n* (*com*) a device that records the times of arrival and departure of an employee on a card.

time-consuming *adj* using up or taking a lot of time.

time deposit *n* (*com*) a deposit of money in an account in a commercial bank that bears interest and that is deposited for a specified period.

time exposure *n* exposure of a photographic film for usu several seconds; a photograph taken in this way.

time-honored *adj* traditional, in accordance with venerable customs.

time immemorial *n* the far distant past beyond memory or record.

timekeeper *n* a person or instrument that records or keeps time; an employee who records the hours worked by others.—**timekeeping** *n*.

time lag *n* the interval between two connected events.

time-lapse photography *n* a technique of filming very slow action, such as plant growth, by taking single frames at fixed intervals and then running them at normal speed.

timeless *adj* eternal; ageless.

timely *adj* at the right time, opportune.—**timeliness** *n*.

time-names *or* **rhythm-names** *n* (*mus*) a French method of teaching time and rhythm in which beats are given names, such as "ta", "ta-te" etc.

time-out *n* a suspension of play to rest, discuss tactics, etc; a brief rest period.

timepiece *n* a clock or watch.

timer *n* a device for measuring, recording or controlling time; a device for controlling lights, heating, etc by setting an electrical clock to regulate their operations.

time scale *see* **dating**.

timeserver *n* a person whose opinions, behavior, etc, follow current fashions.—**timeserving** *adj, n*.

timeshare *n* joint ownership of holiday accommodation by several people with each occupying the same premises in turn for short periods.

time sharing *n* (*comput*) a technique for sharing resources in a multi-user system.

time sheet *n* (*com*) a document on which are recorded the tasks undertaken by a worker and the amount of time that has been spent on each task.

time signature *n* (*mus*) a sign on a musical staff indicating the number of beats per bar and time value of each beat.

timetable *n* a list of times of arrivals and departures of trains, airplanes, etc; a schedule showing a planned order or sequence.

time value *n* in the stock exchange, the market value of an option over and above its intrinsic value.

timeworn *adj* dilapidated; old-fashioned, hackneyed.

time zone *n* a geographical area or north-south band of the earth's surface throughout which the same standard time is used. *See also* **standard time**; **International Date Line**.

timid *adj* shy; lacking confidence.—**timidity** *n*.—**timidly** *adv*.

timing *n* the control and expression of speech or actions to create the best effect, esp in the theater, etc.

Timisoara *n* a city in Romania.

timocracy *n* (*pl* **timocracies**) a form of government in which ownership of property is required to hold office.

Timon *n* (*Bible*) one of seven men of good repute chosen to help the daily distribution of food in the early church. *See also* **Stephen**.

timorous *adj* timid, fearful.—**timorously** *adv*.—**timorousness** *n*.

Timothy *n* (*Bible*) a disciple of St Paul. They met in Lystra in Asia Minor on Paul's second journey.

Timothy *n* **the First and Second Letters of Paul to** (*Bible*) together with the letter to Titus these are known as the Pastoral Letters, and contain advice about the day-to-day oversight of the church.

Timp. *abbr* (*music*) = timpani.

timpani, tympani *or* **kettledrums** *npl* (*mus*) the main orchestral percussion instruments, consisting of bowl-shaped shells over which the membrane is stretched. They can also be tuned by means of screws, which alter the tension of the membrane.—**timpanist** *n*.—*also* **tympany, tympany**.

TIMS *abbr* = The Institute of Management Science.

tin *n* (*chem*) a malleable metallic element; a container of tin, a can. * *adj* made of tin or tin plate. * *vt* (**tinning, tinned**) to put food into a tin.

Tincommius *n* (*fl*.15) king of the Atrebates tribe. One of Commius's three sons who divided their father's kingdom and used the title of *Rex*, meaning "king."

tin ear *n* (*inf*) damaged or insensitive hearing.

tin god *n* a self-important person; a person who is undeservedly venerated.

Tin Pan Alley *n* (*mus*) the nickname given to West 28th Street, New York, where the popular-song publishing business used to be situated. It consequently became a slang expression for the popular music industry.

tin plate *n* thin sheets of iron or steel plated with tin.—**tin-plate** *adj*.

tin whistle *or* **penny whistle** *n* (*mus*) a metal whistle-flute, similar to a recorder, but with six finger holes. It produces high-pitched sounds and is commonly used to play folk music.

Tinbergen *n* 1. **Jan** (1903–94) Dutch economist who shared the 1969 Nobel prize for economics with the Norwegian economist Ragnar Frisch for their work in the field of econometrics. 2. **Niko[laas]** (1907–88) Dutch ethologist and brother of Jan Tinbergen who shared the 1973 Nobel prize for physiology or medicine with Lorenz and Karl von Frisch for his studies of animal behavior.

tinct. *abbr* = tincture.

tinctorial *adj* pertaining to coloring, dyeing, or staining.

tincture *n* (*med*) an extract of a substance in a solution of alcohol for medicinal use; a color, hue, tint; a hint of flavor or aroma; (*her*) a heraldic color. * *vt* to tint with a color.

tinder *n* dry wood for lighting a fire from a spark.

tinderbox *n* a metal box with tinder, flint, and steel for making a spark; an unstable or potentially explosive person, thing or situation.

tine *n* a slender projecting point, as the prong of a fork or point of an antler.

tinea *n* (*med*) a fungal skin condition, esp ringworm.

tinfoil *n* baking foil for wrapping food; silver paper.

ting¹ *n* a high sharp ringing sound. * *vi* to make this sound.

ting² *n* a pottery or bronze bowl, standing on three small legs, that was common in ancient China.

tinge *vt* to tint or color. * *n* a slight tint, color or flavor.

tingle *vi* to feel a prickling, itching or stinging sensation. * *n* a prickling sensation; a thrill.—**tinglingly** *adv*.—**tingly** *adj*.

tinhorn *n* (*sl*) a small-time gambler; a mediocre person. * *adj* cheap and showy.

tinker *n* (*formerly*) a traveling mender of pots, pans etc. * *vi* to fiddle with; to attempt to repair.

tinkle *vi* to make a sound like a small bell ringing; to clink, to jingle; to clink repeatedly. * *n* a tinkling sound; (*inf*) a telephone call.

tinnitus *n* (*med*) a continuous ringing or roaring sound in the ears caused by an infection, etc.

tinny *adj* (**tinnier, tinniest**) of or resembling tin; flimsy in construction or appearance; of food, having a metallic taste; having a high metallic sound.

tinpot *adj* (*inf*) cheap, inferior; petty, mediocre.

tinsel *n* a shiny Christmas decoration made of long pieces of thread wound round with thin strips of metal or plastic foil; something showy but of low value. * *adj* cheaply showy, flashy. * *vt* (**tinseling, tinseled** *or* **tinselling, tinselled**) to adorn with tinsel.

Tinseltown *n* (*inf*) Hollywood.

tinsmith *n* a person who works with tin or tin plate.

tint *n* a shade of any color, esp a pale one; a tinge; a hair dye. * *vt* to color or tinge.

tintinnabulation *n* (the sound of) a ringing of bells.

Tintoretto *n* **Jacopo** (1518–94) Venetian painter noted for his dynamic use of lighting and highlighting.

tiny *adj* (**tinier, tiniest**) very small.

-tion *n suffix* indicating action, state, condition, process, etc.

tip[1] *n* (*Brit*) a garbage dump. * *vti* (**tipping, tipped**) to tilt or cause to tilt; to overturn; to empty (out, into, etc); to dump garbage etc;

tip[2] *n* the pointed end of anything; the end, as of a billiard cue, etc. * *vt* (**tipping, tipped**) to put a tip on.

tip[3] *n* an inside piece of information; a helpful hint. * *vt* to give a helpful hint or inside information to.

tip[4] *n* a gratuity. * *vt*i to give a gratuity to, as a waiter, etc

tip[5] *n* a light tap; in baseball, a ball that is lightly touched by the bat.

TIP *abbr* = terminal interface processor.

tipi *see* **teepee**.

tip-off *n* a warning based on inside information.

Tippett *n* **Sir Michael Kemp** (1905–98) English composer. His works include several operas, symphonies, song cycles, and chamber music.

tipple *vi* to drink alcohol regularly in small quantities. * *n* an alcoholic drink.

tipster *n* a person who gives horse-racing tips.

tipsy *adj* (**tipsier, tipsiest**) slightly drunk.

tiptoe *vi* (**tiptoeing, tiptoed**) to walk very quietly or carefully.

tiptop *adj* excellent. * *adv* at the peak of condition. * *n* the best; the highest point.

TIR *abbr* (*French*) = *Transports Internationaux Routiers*, "International Road Transport."

tirade *n* a long angry speech of censure or criticism.

Tirane *n* capital city of Albania.

Tiraspol *n* a city in Moldova (Moldavia).

TIRC *abbr* = Tobacco Industry Research Committee.

tire[1] *vt* to exhaust the strength of, to weary. * *vi* to become weary; to lose patience; to become bored.

tire[2] *n* (*transp*) a protective, usu rubber, covering around the rim of a wheel.

tired *adj* weary, sleepy; hackneyed, conventional, flat; (*with* **of**) exasperated by, bored with.

tireless *adj* never wearying.—**tirelessly** *adv*.—**tirelessness** *n*.

Tiresias *see* **Teiresias**.

tiresome *adj* tedious.

Tir na mBan *n* (*Irish Celtic myth*) an Otherworld country, an island that was populated entirely by women.

Tir na Og *or* **Tir na Nog** *n* (*Irish Celtic myth*) an Otherworld realm in which people are forever young. It is thus sometimes known as the "land of the forever young" or the "land of youth."

tiro *see* **tyro**.

Tiryns *n* a very ancient city of Greece, in the plain of Argolis.

TIS *abbr* = Technical Information Service.

Tisiphone *n* (*Greek myth*) one of the three Furies, the others being Alecto and Megaera.

tissue *n* thin, absorbent paper used as a disposable handkerchief, etc; a very finely woven fabric; (*anat*) a mass of organic cells of a similar structure and function; (*anat*) one of the primary layers composing any of the parts of the body, consisting of a large number of cells with a similar structure and function, e.g. connective tissue; (*biol*) a group of cells with a similar function that aggregate to form an organ.

tissue culture *n* (*biol*) the culture or growth, outside the body, of tissues of living organisms.

Tisza *adj* relating to a culture from the end of the Danubian period, centered east of the Tisza river in the Danube region *c*.4000 BC.

tit. *abbr* = title.

tit[1] *n* a songbird such as a blue tit or great tit.

tit[2] *n* (*vulg*) a woman's breast.

titan *n* a person of enormous strength, size or ability.

Titan *n* (*astron*) the largest moon or satellite of the planet Saturn, discovered in 1655.

titanic *adj* monumental; huge.

titanium dioxide *n* (*chem*) a white powder used chiefly as a pigment.

titanium *n* (*chem*) a strong, malleable, and ductile metal that resembles iron. It is used to make lightweight alloys.

Titannia *n* (*astron*) the largest moon or satellite of the planet Uranus, discovered in 1787.

Titans *npl* (*Greek myth*) the six sons and six daughters of Uranus (Heaven) and Ge (Earth). They were Oceanus, Coeus, Crius, Hyperion, Iapetus, Cronos, Theia, Rhea, Themis, Mnemosyne, Phoebe, and Tethys.

titbit, tidbit *n* a tasty morsel of food; a choice item of information.

tit for tat *n* an equivalent given in retaliation.

tithe *n* a tenth part of agricultural produce, formerly allotted for the maintenance of the clergy and other church purposes. * *vti* to pay a tithe.

Tithonus *n* (*Greek myth*) a mortal who obtained immortality but not eternal youth.

Titian *n* [**Tiziano Vecelli**] (*c*.1490–1576) Venetian painter, one of the great figures of world art. His powerful and richly colored works include *Bacchus and Ariadne* (1523), *Charles V at Mehlberg* (1548), and *The Rape of Europa* (1562).

titillate *vt* to tickle; to arouse or excite pleasurably.

titillation *n* the act of titillating; the condition of being titillated; a pleasurable feeling, esp sexual.

Titius-Bode Law *n* a mathematical law that enables the approximate distances of the planets from the sun to be predicted.

titivate, tittivate *vti* to smarten up.

title *n* the name of a book, play, piece of music, work of art, etc; the heading of a section of a book; a name denoting nobility or rank or office held, or attached to a personal name; (*law*) that which gives a legal right (to possession).

title bar *n* (*comput*) a shaded bar containing the name of the active file, shown at the top of an on screen window in GUI systems.

titled *adj* having a title.

title deed *n* a legal document that proves the ownership of land and/or property on it.

title page *n* the page of a book containing its title and usually the author's and publisher's names.

title role *n* the character in a play, film, etc after whom it is named.

Tito *n* **Marshal [Josip Broz]** (1892–1980) Yugoslav statesman. He became secretary general of the Yugoslav Communist Party in 1937, and in 1941 organized a partisan force to fight the German occupying forces. After the war, he established a Communist government and broke with Stalin.

titrate *vt* (*chem*) to measure by titration.

titration *n* (*chem*) a method of determining the amount of a constituent in a solution by adding a known quantity of a reagent.

titer *n* (*chem*) the concentration of a substance in a solution as determined by titration.

titter *vi* to giggle, snigger. * *n* a suppressed laugh.

tittle-tattle *n* idle chat, empty gossip.

titular *adj* having, or relating to, a title; existing in name or title only.

Titus *n* (*Bible*) a Greek companion and fellow-worker of Paul, who affectionately called him "my brother Titus."

Titus *n* **the Letter of Paul to** (*Bible*) one of the Pastoral Letters, it is largely concerned with the rule and order of the Christian church towards the end of the first century. *See also* **Timothy, Letters**.

TIU *abbr* = Telecommunications International Union.

Tiy *n* a notable Egyptian queen of the New Kingdom, principal wife to the Pharaoh Amenophis III and mother of Akhenaten (18th Dynasty).

tizzy *n* (*inf*) a state of confusion or agitation.

TJ *abbr* = triple jump (athletics).

TJA *abbr* = Table Jellies Association.

TKO *abbr* = technical knockout, in boxing, etc.

Tl *symbol* (*chem*) thallium (element).

tl *abbr* = total loss.

TL *abbr* = thermoluminescent.

T/L *abbr* = time loan.

TLA *abbr* = Toy Libraries Association.

TLC *abbr* = tender loving care; thin-layer chromatography; total lung capacity.

TLG *abbr* = Theatrical Ladies' Guild.

TLMI *abbr* = The Leprosy Mission International.

tlo, t.l.o. *abbr* = total loss only.

TLO *abbr* = Technical Liaison Officer.

TLR *abbr* = twin-lens reflex (camera).

TLRS *abbr* = Tramway and Light Railway Society.

tls. *abbr* = taels.

TLS *abbr* (*Brit*) = *Times Literary Supplement*.

TLU *abbr* = table look-up.

T-lymphocyte *see* **T-cell**.

Tm *symbol* (*chem*) thulium (element).

tm, t.m. *abbr* = true mean.

TM *abbr* = Their Majesties; Traffic Manager; Trainmaster; tactical missile; technical manual; (*com*) trade mark; transcendental meditation; trench mortar.

TMA abbr = Telecommunications Managers' Association; Theatrical Management Association.

TMBA *abbr* = Teacher Member of the British Arts; Twins and Multiple Births Association.

TMC *abbr* = Tourism Ministers Council.

TMD *abbr* = theatre missile defense.

TML *abbr* = three-mile limit.

TMO *abbr* = telegraphic money order.

TMPDF *abbr* = Trade Marks, Patterns and Designs Federation.

TMS *abbr* = The Minerals, Metals and Materials Society; Tramway Museum Society.

tmv *abbr* = true mean value.

Tn *symbol* (*chem*) thoron.

tn *abbr* = telephone number.

tn. *abbr* = ton.

Tn, Tn. *abbr* = train.

TN *abbr* = trade name; true north; Tennessee.

TNA *abbr* (*chem*) = tetranitroaniline.

TNC *abbr* = transnational corporation.

TNF *abbr* = transnecrosis factor.

TNIMBM *abbr* = Technicians of the Institute of Maintenance and Building Management.

TNM *abbr* = tactical nuclear missile.

TNPG *abbr* = The Nuclear Power Group.

TNT *abbr* = (*chem*) trinitrotoluene; (*chem*) trinitrotoluol.

TNTC *abbr* = too numerous to count.

TNW *abbr* = tactical nuclear warfare; theatre nuclear weapon.

TNX *abbr* (*chem*) = trinitroxylene.

to *prep* in the direction of; toward; as far as; expressing the purpose of an action; indicating the infinitive; introducing the indirect object; in comparison with. * *adv* toward.

t.o. *abbr* = turn over; turnover.

t/o *abbr* = take off; turnover.

TO *abbr* = Tax Officer; Transport Officer; telegraph office; turn over.

toad *n* an amphibious reptile, like a frog, but having a drier skin and spending less time in water.

toadflax *n* a common perennial plant with yellow and orange flowers.

toadstool *n* a mushroom, esp a poisonous or inedible one.

toady *n* (*pl* **toadies**) a person who flatters insincerely, a sycophant. * *vi* (**toadying, toadied**) (*with* **to**) to act in a servile manner.

Toamasina *n* city in Madagascar.

to and fro *adj* forward and backward; here and there.—**toing and froing** *n*.

toast *vt* to brown over a fire or in a toaster; to warm; to drink to the health of. * *n* toasted bread; the sentiment or person to which one drinks.

toaster *n* a person who toasts; a thing that toasts, esp an electrical appliance for toasting.

toastmaster *n* the proposer of toasts at public dinners.—**toastmistress** *nf*.

ToB *abbr* (*Brit*) = Tour of Britain (cycling).

tobacco *n* (*pl* **tobaccos, tobaccoes**) (*bot*) a plant whose dried leaves are used for smoking, chewing, or snuff.

tobacconist *n* a person or shop that sells cigarettes, etc.

Tobiah *n* (*Bible*) an Ammonite, partly Jewish, leader who did everything he could to prevent the rebuilding of the walls of Jerusalem. *See also* **Nehemiah**.

toboggan *n* a sledge, sled.

toby (jug) *n* (*pl* **tobies, toby jugs**) a mug in the shape of a man with a three-cornered hat.

toccata *n* (*mus*) a piece of music for keyboard in a free style with rapid runs.

Toc H *abbr* = Talbot House (originally telegraphic code for TH, Talbot House being the London headquarters of the charity).

tocopherol *n* vitamin E, present in wheat-germ oil, egg yolk, etc.

tocsin *n* an alarm bell; a warning signal.

tod *abbr* = time of delivery.

today *n* this day; the present age. * *adv* on this day; nowadays.

Todd *n* **Alexander Robertus [Baron Todd of Trumpington]** (1907–) Scottish biochemist who was awarded the 1957 Nobel prize for chemistry for his research into the chemical structure of nucleotides.

toddle *vi* to walk with short, unsteady, steps, as a child who is learning to walk.

toddler *n* a young child.

toddy *n* (*pl* **toddies**) a drink of whisky or brandy, sugar, and hot water.

to-do *n* (*pl* **to-dos**) (*inf*) a fuss, commotion, quarrel.

toe *n* one of the five digits on the foot; the part of the shoe or sock that covers the toes.

TOE *abbr* = Theatre of Everything.

toea *n* a monetary unit of Papua New Guinea, equivalent to one hundredth of a kina.

toe cap *n* a reinforced covering on the toe of a shoe or boot.

TOEFL *abbr* = Test of English as a Foreign Language.

toehold *n* a small ledge, crack, etc used in climbing; any slight means of support or access; a wrestling hold in which an opponent's foot is twisted.

toenail *n* the thin, hard covering on the end of the toes.

toffee (also **toffy**) *n* (*pl* **toffees, toffies**) a sweet of brittle but tender texture made by boiling sugar and butter together.

toffee apple *n* an apple coated with toffee and eaten from a stick.

toffee-nosed *adj* (*inf*) pretentious, patronizing, arrogant.

Toft *n* **Charles** (*c.*1831–1909) British potter and metalworker who became involved in the revival of the 16th-century French "Henri II" ware.

tofu *n* unfermented soya bean curd, used in cooking.

tog[1] *n* (*pl*) (*inf*) clothes. * *vt* (**togging, togged**) (*inf*) to dress.

tog[2] *n* in UK, an official measurement of the warmth of a duvet, quilt, etc.

toga *n* (*hist*) a piece of cloth draped around the body, as worn by citizens in ancient Rome.

together *adv* in one place or group; in cooperation with; in unison; jointly.

toggle *n* a peg attached to a rope to prevent it from passing through a loop or knot; a button of this form; (*comput*) a software instruction for starting or stopping a style, etc. * *vt* to fasten with a toggle.

toggle switch *n* an electrical device for opening or closing a circuit.

Togliatti *n* **Palmiro** (1893–1964) Italian Communist politician. He helped found the Italian Communist Party and became party secretary (1926–64). He helped build the Italian communist party into the largest in western Europe.

Togo *n* a small republic with a narrow coastal plain on the Gulf of Guinea in West Africa.

Togodummus *n* (*fl.*50) a high king of the British tribes; son of Cunobelinus and brother of Caradoc.

toil *vi* to work strenuously; to move with great effort. * *n* hard work.

toilet *n* a lavatory; the room containing a lavatory; the act of washing and dressing oneself.

toilet paper *or* **toilet tissue** *n* an absorbent paper, usu wound around a cardboard cylinder, for cleansing after defecation or urination,

toilet water *n* a diluted perfume.

toiletry *n* (*pl* **toiletries**) a lotion, perfume, etc used in washing and dressing oneself.

Tojo *n* **Hideki** (1885–1948) Japanese soldier. He became minister of war (1940–44) and prime minister (1941–44). He was executed as a war criminal.

token *n* a symbol, sign; an indication; a metal disc for a slot machine; a souvenir; a gift voucher. * *adj* nominal; symbolic.

tokenism *n* the making of only a token effort.

token passing *n, vt* (*comput*) a protocol in which tokens move around a network. When a node wants to send a message over the network it has to obtain a free token. The node that controls the token controls the network until the message has been passed and acknowledged.

token ring network *n* (*comput*) a local area network that uses token passing technology as the basis for communications.

Tokyo *n* capital city of Japan.

ToL *abbr* (*Brit*) = Tower of London.

TOL *abbr* = Tree of Life.

tolar *n* the standard monetary unit of Slovenia, made up of 100 stotin.

tolbooth *n* (*Scot*) a town hall; a jail.

told *see* **tell**.

tolerable *adj* bearable; fairly good.—**tolerably** *adv*.

tolerance *n* open-mindedness; forbearance; (*med*) ability to resist the action of a drug, etc; ability of a substance to endure heat, stress, etc without damage.

tolerant *adj* able to put up with the beliefs, actions, etc of others; broad-minded; showing tolerance to a drug, etc; capable of enduring stress, etc.

tolerate *vt* to endure, put up with, suffer.

Toliara *n* a city in Madagascar.

Tolkien *n* **J[ohn] R[onald] R[euel]** (1892–1973) South African-born British fantasy writer and scholar whose best-known works are *The Hobbit* and *Lord of the Rings*.

toll[1] *n* money levied for passing over a bridge or road; a charge for a service, such as a long-distance telephone call; the number of people killed in an accident or disaster.

toll[2] *vt* (*bell*) to ring slowly and repeatedly, as a funeral bell. * *vi* to sound, as a bell. * *n* the sound of a bell when tolling.

tollbooth, tolbooth *n* a booth where money is paid to pass over a bridge, road, etc.

toll call *n* a telephone call charged at higher than the standard or local rate.

tollgate *n* a gate where money is paid to pass over a bridge, road, etc.

Tollund *n* a Danish peat bog from which was recovered the well-preserved body of an Iron Age man.

Tollund Man *n* the body of a man discovered in a peat bog in Denmark in 1950. He is thought to have been placed in the bog around 500 bc. He had been garroted and was wearing only a leather cap and girdle.

Tolstoy *n* **Count Leo Nikolaevich** (1828–1910) Russian novelist, dramatist, short-story writer, and philosopher. He wrote a remarkable autobiographical trilogy, *Childhood* (1852), *Boyhood* (1854), and *Youth* (1857). His novels *War and Peace* (1863–69) and *Anna Karenina* (1875–77) are frequently described as the greatest of all novels.

Toltec *n* a group of peoples who flourished in Mexico *c.*1000.

toluene *n* (*chem*) a flammable hydrocarbon derived from petroleum and coal tar used as a solvent and in organic synthesis.

tom *n* a male animal, esp a cat.

Tom, Dick and Harry *n* an ordinary person, anybody taken at random.

tomahawk *n* a light axe used by Native Americans.

tomato *n* (*pl* **tomatoes**) a plant with red pulpy fruit used as a vegetable.

tomb *n* a vault in the earth for the burial of the dead.

tombolo *n* a sand or shingle spit that connects an island to the mainland.

tomboy *n* a girl who likes rough outdoor activities.

tombstone *n* a memorial stone over a grave.

tomcat *n* a male cat.

tome *n* a large, heavy book, esp a scholarly one.

-tome *n suffix* a cutting instrument.

tomfool *n* a fool.

tomfoolery *n* (*pl* **tomfooleries**) foolish behavior; nonsense.

tommy gun *n* a (Thompson) sub-machine gun.

Tommy *n* (*pl* **Tommies**) (*inf*) a private in the British army.

tommyrot *n* complete nonsense.

tomography *n* a technique using X-rays or ultrasound so that pictures of slices of the body are obtained at different levels to build up a three-dimensional image.

tomorrow *n* the day after today; the future.—*also adv*.

tomtit *n* (*zool*) any of various small tits, esp a blue tit.

tom-tom *n* (*mus*) a long small-headed drum usually beaten with the hands.

-tomy *n suffix* surgical incision.

ton *n* a unit of weight equivalent to 2,000 pounds in US or 2,240 pounds in UK; (*pl*) (*inf*) a great quantity.

tonal *n* of or pertaining to tone; having a key.

tonality *n* (*pl* **tonalities**); the scheme of colors and tones in a painting; (*mus*) the character of a musical composition in relation to scale or key; a system of tones.

tone *n* the quality of a sound; pitch or inflection of the voice; color, shade; body condition; (*mus*) an interval comprising two semitones; a musical note; in plainsong, a melody. * *vti* to give tone to; to harmonize (with); (*with* **down**) to (become) moderate in tone; (*with* **up**) to make or become healthier, tighter, etc.

tone arm *n* the tracking arm in a record player that holds the cartridge and stylus.

tone-deaf *adj* insensitive to differences in musical pitch.

tone poem *see* **symphonic poem**.

toner *n* a cosmetic used on the skin for various effects; (*photog*) a chemical used to alter the tone of a photograph; the ink particles used in various reprographic devices such as laser printers and photocopiers.

tong *n* a Chinese-American secret society.

Tonga *n* a constitutional monarchy comprising a low limestone chain of islands in the east and a higher volcanic chain in the west about 20° south of the Equator and just west of the International Date Line in the Pacific Ocean.

tongs *npl* an instrument consisting of two arms that are hinged, used for grasping and lifting.

tongue *n* the soft, moveable organ in the mouth, used in tasting, swallowing, and speech; the ability to speak; a language; a piece of leather under the laces of a shoe; a jet of flame; the tongue of an animal served as food; the catch of a buckle.

tongue-lash *vt* to scold, rebuke severely.—**tongue lashing** *n*.

tongue-tied *adj* speechless.

tongue-twister *n* a sequence of words that it is difficult to pronounce quickly and clearly.

tonguing *n* (*mus*) in the playing of a wind instrument, this means interrupting the flow of breath with the tongue so that detached notes are played, or the first note of a phrase is distinguished.

tonic[1] *n* a medicine that improves physical well-being; something that imparts vigor; a carbonated mineral water with a bitter taste. * *adj* relating to tones or sounds.

tonic[2] *n* (*mus*) the first note of a major or minor scale.

tonic sol-fa *n* (*mus*) a system of notation and sight-singing used in training, in which notes are sung to syllables. The notes of the major scale are: doh, re, me, fah, soh, la, te, doh (doh is always the tonic, whatever the key). The system was pioneered in England by John Curwen in the mid-19th century.

tonight *n* this night; the night or evening of the present day.—*also adv*.

tonn. *abbr* = tonnage.

tonnage *n* (*transp*) a merchant ship's capacity measured in tons; the weight of its cargo; the amount of shipping of a country or port; merchant ships collectively; a duty levied on ships based on tonnage or capacity.

tonne *n* metric ton, 1,000 kg.

tonometer *n* (*mus*) a device, such as a tuning fork, for measuring the pitch of tones.

tonsil *n* (*anat*) one of the two oval organs of soft tissue situated one on each side of the throat.

tonsillectomy *n* (*pl* **tonsillectomies**) (*med*) a surgical operation to remove the tonsils.

tonsillitis *n* (*med*) inflammation of the tonsils caused by bacterial or viral infection.

tonsils *n* (*anat*) the two small masses of lymphoid tissue situated on either side at the back of the mouth.

tonsure *n* shaving part of the head to denote a clerical state in certain churches and religious orders; the shaved area itself. * *vt* to give a tonsure to (a monk, etc).—**tonsured** *adj*.

tontine *n* a financial scheme whereby each participant contributes an equal sum to a fund that is eventually awarded to the person who survives all the others.

Tony *n* (*pl* **Tonys, Tonies**) an annual award for excellence in the theater.

too *adv* in addition; also; likewise; extremely; very.

TOO *abbr* = time of origin; to order only.

took *see* **take**.

tool *n* an implement that is used by hand; a means for achieving any purpose.

toolbar *n* (*comput*) an editable strip of buttons that appears at the top of the screen, used to select commands without using menus.

toolbox *n* (*comput*) a set of prewritten programs or routines used by programmers for incorporation into larger programs.

tooling *n* a design or decoration made with a tool, as on leather.

tool-maker *n* a person who repairs and maintains precision machine tools.

toolroom *n* an area in a factory, machine shop, etc where tools are kept or repaired.

toot *vi* to hoot a car horn, whistle, etc in short blasts. * *n* a hoot.—*also vt*.

tooth *n* (*pl* **teeth**) one of the white, bone-like structures arranged in rows in the mouth, used in biting and chewing; the palate; a tooth-like projection on a comb, saw, or wheel.

toothache *n* a pain in a tooth.

toothbrush *n* a small brush for cleaning teeth.

toothed whale *n* any of various whales with simple teeth, such as dolphins.

toothpaste *n* a paste for cleaning teeth, used with a toothbrush.

toothpick *n* a sliver of wood or plastic for removing food particles from between the teeth.

tooth powder *n* a powder used for cleaning the teeth.

toothsome *adj* appetizing.

toothy *adj* (**toothier, toothiest**) having or revealing prominent teeth.

top[1] *n* the highest, or uppermost, part or surface of anything; the highest in rank; the crown of the head; the lid. * *adj* highest; greatest. * *vt* to cover on the top; to remove the top of or from; to rise above; to surpass; (*with* **up**) to raise up to the full capacity or amount.

top[2] *n* a child's toy, which is spun on its pointed base.

TOP *abbr* = temporarily out of print; (*med*) termination of pregnancy.

Topa *n* (*Irish Celtic myth*) a manservant of Partholan who was seduced by the wife of Partholan and so who may have been the father of Rury.

topaz *n* any of various yellow gems.

top brass *npl* (*mil inf*) the highest-ranking military or other officials.

topcoat *n* an overcoat.

top dog *n* (*inf*) the leader, the most important person.

top down programming *n* (*comput*) a method of designing programs, starting with a basic statement of the program's main objectives, which is then divided into sub-objectives, and so on.

top drawer *n* (*inf*) the most prominent people in society.

tope[1] *vi* to consume alcoholic drink in excessive quantities.—**toper** *n*.

tope[2] *n* a small gray European shark.

topee *n* a pith helmet.—*also* **topi**.

Topeka *n* the capital city of Kansas, a state of the USA.

top flight *adj* excellent, of the highest quality.

topgallant *n* a mast or sail above a topmast.—*also adj*.

top gear *n* the highest gear in a motor vehicle; maximum speed or activity.

top hat *n* a man's tall, silk hat.

top-heavy *adj* having an upper part too heavy for the lower, causing instability.

tophi *see* **gout**.

topi *see* **topee**.

topiary *adj* pertaining to the art or practice of trimming bushes and trees into ornamental shapes. * *n* (**topiaries**) a tree or bush shaped in this way.

top secret *adj* highly confidential.

topic *n* a subject for discussion; the theme of a speech or writing.

TOPIC *abbr* = Teletext Output Price Information Computer.

topical *adj* of current interest.

topknot *n* a tuft of hair or knot of ribbons on the head.

topless *adj* lacking a top; of a garment, revealing the breasts; wearing such a garment.

topmast *n* a mast next above the lowest mast.

topmost *adj* nearest the top, highest.

topnotch *adj* (*inf*) excellent.

topo- (also **top-**) *prefix* place; locality.

topocentric coordinates *n* (*astron*) the coordinates of a heavenly body when measured from the earth's surface.

topog. *abbr* = topographical; topography.

topography *n* (*pl* **topographies**) the study or description of surface features of a place on maps or charts; the surface features of the earth, whether natural or artificial.—**topographer** *n*.—**topographical** *adj*.

topological map *n* a map drawn up to show a particular feature rather than to give an overall impression of an area. Distance, scale, and relative orientation are not particularly important; clear, uncluttered presentation is.

topology *n* the study of a particular locality; the study of the properties of geometric figures that are unaffected by distortion; (*comput*) a local area network layout.—**topological** *adj*.—**topologist** *n*.

topping *n* a top layer, esp a sauce for food.

topple *vi* to fall over. * *vt* to cause to overbalance and fall; (*government*) to overthrow.

TOPS *abbr* = Theatre Organ Preservation Society; Training Opportunities Scheme.

topsail *n* a square sail next above the lowest sail on a mast.

topside *n* the upper side; a boneless cut of beef; the open or upper decks of a ship. * *adv* on top.

topsoil *n* the upper, more fertile layers of soil above the subsoil.

topspin *n* a spin imparted to a ball that makes it travel faster or higher.

topsy-turvy *adj, adv* turned upside down; in confusion.

tor *n* a small hill rising abruptly from the smoother hill slopes surrounding it.

tor *abbr* = time of receipt.

Torach *see* **Tory Island**.

Torah *n* (a scroll containing) the Pentateuch; Jewish sacred writings and teachings collectively.

torc *n* a decorative open-ended metal ring designed to be worn around the neck which was usually in the form of a twisted "rope" of gold or bronze; torcs were often a sign of nobility or high status.

torch *n* a flashlight; a device for giving off a hot flame.—**torchlight** *n*.

torchbearer *n* a person carrying a torch; a leader, source of inspiration.

torch song *n* a sentimental song about the sufferings of love.—**torch singer** *n*.

Torc Triath *n* (*Irish Celtic myth*) the king of the boars.

tore *see* **tear**.

toreador *n* a bullfighter, esp on horseback.

torero *n* (*pl* **toreros**) a bullfighter, esp one who fights on foot.

torii *n* (*pl* **torii**) a gateway to a Japanese Shinto temple.

torment *n* torture, anguish; a source of pain. * *vt* to afflict with extreme pain, physical or mental.—**tormentor, tormenter** *n*.

torn *see* **tear**[2].

tornado *n* (*pl* **tornadoes, tornados**) a violently whirling column of air seen as a funnel-shaped cloud that usu destroys everything in its narrow path.

toroid *n* (a solid enclosed by) a surface generated by a circle rotated about a line in the same plane as but not intersecting the circle.—**toroidal** *adj*.

Toronto *n* a city in Canada.

torpedo *n* (*pl* **torpedoes**) a self-propelled submarine offensive weapon, carrying an explosive charge. * *vt* to attack, hit, or destroy with torpedo(es).

torpedo boat *n* a small high-speed warship from which torpedoes are launched.

torpid *adj* lethargic, sluggish.—**torpidity** *n*.

torpor *n* a state of physical and mental sluggishness.

torque *n* (*physics*) a force that causes rotation around a central point, such as an axle.

torr *n* (*pl* **torr**) a unit of pressure equal to 133.322 newtons per square meter.

torre *n* (*archeo*) a Corsican name for Bronze Age towers constructed of Cyclopean masonry.

torrent *n* a rushing stream; a flood of words.—**torrential** *adj*.

torrid *adj* burning, parched or scorched with heat; passionate.—**torridity, torridness** *n*.

Torroja *n* **Eduardo** (1899–) Spanish architect. His notable works include the Algeciras Market Hall.

Tórshavn *n* capital city of the Faeroe Islands.

torsi *see* **torso**.

torsion *n* a twisting effect on an object when equal forces are applied at both ends but in opposite directions; (*med*) a twisting of the whole or part of an organ that impairs the nerve and blood supply.

torsk *n* (*pl* **torsk, torsks**) a large marine food fish related to the cod.

torso *n* (*pl* **torsos, torsi**) (*anat*) the trunk of the human body.

tort *n* (*law*) a private or civil wrong.

torte *n* a rich cake or tart filled with cream, fruit, etc.

Tortelier *n* **Paul** (1914-90) a French cellist and composer, who played with many of the world's leading orchestras. His son, Jan Pascal Tortelier, is a noted violinist and conductor.

tortellini *n* small stuffed pasta shapes.

torticollis *see* **wryneck**.

tortilla *n* a round thin maize pancake usually eaten hot with a topping or filling.

tortoise *n* a slow-moving reptile with a dome-shaped shell into which it can withdraw.

tortoiseshell *n* a brown and yellow color.

tortricid *n* any of a family of moths whose larvae live in nests of rolled-up leaves.

tortuous *adj* full of twists, involved.—**tortuously** *adv*.

torture *n* subjection to severe physical or mental pain to extort a confession, or as a punishment.—*also vt*.—**torturer** *n*.

torus *n* (*pl* **tori**) (*archit*) a convex semicircular molding, esp at the base of a column; (*geom*) a donut-shaped ring that is generated by rotating a circle about an axis.

torus *n*; —**toric** *adj*.

Torvill, Jayne (1957–) and **Dean, Christopher** (1958–) English ice-dance skaters. They became world champions (1981–83), European champions (1981–82, 1984) and Olympic champions (1984).

Tory *n* (*pl* **Tories**) a member of the Conservative Party in UK politics; an American supporter of the British during the American Revolution.—*also adj*.

Tory Island *n* (*Irish Celtic myth*) an island on which the Fomorii had a stronghold; the name derives from the word *torach*, meaning a watchtower, and the island is sometimes referred to as Torach.

tos *abbr* = temporarily out of stock; terms of service.

Toscanini *n* **Arturo** (1867–1957) Italian conductor. Regarded as one of the most authoritarian conductors of all time, he was renowned for his fanatical devotion to authenticity and disdain for showy interpretation of the score. His forte was Italian and German opera.

tosh *n* (*sl*) nonsense.

Toshiba *abbr* (*Japanese*) = *Tokyo Shibaura Denki KK*, "Tokyo Shibaura Electrical Corporation."

toss *vt* to throw up; to pitch; to fling; (*head*) to throw back; (*with off*) to produce, write, perform, etc, quickly and easily; to drink in one gulp. * v *i* to be tossed about; to move restlessly; (*with up*) to spin a coin to decide a question by the side that falls uppermost. * *n* the act of tossing or being tossed; a pitch; a fall.

toss-up *n* the throwing of a coin to decide a question; an even chance.

tosto *n* (*mus*) (*Italian*), "rapid," as in *piu tosto*, "quicker".

tot *abbr* = time over target.

tot[1] *n* anything little, esp a child; (*Brit*) a small measure of spirits.

tot[2] *vt* (**totting, totted**) (*with up*) to add up or total.

total *adj* whole, complete; absolute. * *n* the whole sum; the entire amount. * *vt* (**totaling, totaled** *or* **totalling, totalled**) to add up.—**totally** *adv*.

total absorption costing *n* (*com*) a method of calculating production costs that takes account not only of direct costs such as labor and materials but also others borne by the company, such as administrative costs.

total assets *npl* (*com*) the combined amount of a company's fixed assets and current assets.

totalitarian *adj* relating to a system of government in which one political group maintains complete control, esp under a dictator.—**totalitarianism** *n*.

totality *n* (*pl* **totalities**) the whole amount.

totalizator *n* a machine for registering bets and computing the odds and payoff, as at a racetrack.

tote[1] *n* (*inf*) totalizator.

tote[2] *vt* to carry.

tote bag *n* (*inf*) a large bag for shopping or other items.

totem *n* an object regarded as a symbol and treated with respect by a particular group of people.

totem pole *n* a large pole carved with totemic symbols used in rituals by certain Native American tribes.

totter *vi* to walk unsteadily; to shake or sway as if about to fall.—**tottery** *adj*.

toucan *n* a fruit-eating South American bird with an immense, brightly colored beak.

touch *n* the sense by which something is perceived through contact; the act of touching; a trace; understanding; a special quality or skill. * *vi* to be in contact; to be adjacent; to allude to. * *vt* to come in contact with, esp with the hand or fingers; to reach; to affect with emotion; to tinge or tint; to border on; (*sl*) to ask for money (from); (*with off*) to cause to explode, as with a lighted match; to cause (violence, a riot, etc) to start; (*with up*) to improve by making minor alterations or additions to.

touch-and-go *adj* precarious, risky.

touchdown *n* the moment when an aircraft or spaceship lands; (*sport*) a placing of the ball on the ground to score in American or rugby football.

touché *interj* (*fencing*) used to acknowledge an opponent's hit; an acknowledgement of a valid or accomplished reply, remark, witty comment, etc.

touched *adj* emotionally affected; mentally disturbed.

touching *adj* affecting, moving. * *prep* concerning, in respect of.

touch judge *n* a linesman in Rugby football.

touchline *n* (*sport*) the side boundary of a pitch.

touchmark *n* a maker's distinguishing mark on pewter.

touchpaper *n* paper impregnated with a slow-burning substance used to ignite fireworks.

touch sensitive display *n* (*comput*) a type of screen with a pressure sensitive panel in front of the screen, often used for public information access.

touchstone *n* a siliceous stone used to test gold and silver from the marks they make on it; any test or standard of genuineness.

touch-type *vi* to type quickly and accurately without looking at the keyboard.—**touch-typist** *n*.

touchwood *n* dry rotten wood useful for tinder.

touchy *adj* (**touchier, touchiest**) irritable; very risky.

tough *adj* strong; durable; hardy; rough and violent; difficult; (*inf*) unlucky.—**toughen** *vti*.—**toughness** *n*.

tough-minded *adj* realistic; unsentimental.

Toulouse *n* a city in France.

Toulouse-Lautrec *n* **Henri [Marie Raymond] de** (1864–1901) French painter and graphic artist associated with the art nouveau movement. His subjects were café clientele, prostitutes, and cabaret performers around Montmartre, as in *In the Parlor at the Rue des Moulins* (1894).

toupee *n* a wig or section of hair to cover a bald spot, esp worn by men.

tour de force *n* (*pl* **tours de force**) an outstanding achievement or performance.

tour *n* a turn, period, etc as of military duty; a long trip, as for sightseeing. * *vti* to go on a tour (through).

touraco *n* (*pl* **touracos**) any of a family of brightly colored crested birds native to Africa.

tourelle *n* (*archit*) a turret projecting out from the wall on corbels.

tourism *n* traveling for pleasure; the business of catering for people who do this; the encouragement of touring.

tourist *n* one who makes a tour, a sightseer, traveling for pleasure.—*also adj*.

tourist class *n* economy accommodation, as on a ship, aircraft, etc.

touristy *adj* (*inf*) full of or designed for tourists.

tourmaline *n* (*chem*) a silicate mineral of various colors used in jewelry and electronic equipment.

tournament *n* a sporting event involving a number of competitors and a series of games.

tournedos *n* (*pl* **tournedos**) a thick round fillet of beef steak.

Tourneur *n* **Cyril** (*c*.1575–1626) English dramatist and author of *The Atheist's Tragedy* and possibly of *The Revenger's Tragedy*.

tourniquet *n* (*med*) a length of bandage, rubber tube, cord, etc, tied tightly around a limb to stop bleeding in an emergency.

tour operator *n* a company that specializes in offering package tours.

tousle *vt* to make untidy, ruffle, make tangled (esp hair).

tout *vti* (*inf*) to praise highly; (*inf*) to sell betting tips on (race horses); (*inf*) to solicit business in a brazen way. * *n* (*inf*) a person who does so.

tovarish, tovarich *n* (*Russian*) a comrade.

tow *vt* to pull or drag with a rope. * *n* the act of towing; a towrope.

TOW *abbr* = tug of war.

TOWA *abbr* = Tug of War Association.

towage *n* the act of towing; the charge made for it.

toward, towards *prep* in the direction of; concerning; just before; as a contribution to.

towel *n* an absorbent cloth for drying the skin after it is washed, and for other purposes; **to throw in the towel** to admit defeat. * *vti* (**toweling, toweled** *or* **towelling, towelled**) to rub (oneself) with a towel.

towelette *n* a small moistened tissue for cleaning the face, etc.

toweling *n* cloth for towels; a rubbing with a towel.

tower *n* a tall, narrow building, standing alone or forming part of another; a fortress. * *vi* (*with* **over**) to rise above; to loom.

tower block *n* (*Brit*) a tall office or residential building.

tower house *n* (*archit*) a medieval Scottish fortified house with two or more floors, the main hall being set above ground level.

towering *adj* immensely tall; powerful; impressive; intense.

tower system *n* (*comput*) a computer system in which the electronics, disk drives, etc, are contained in a box resembling a tower. *See also* **mini tower**.

town *n* a densely populated urban center, smaller than a city and larger than a village; the people of a town.

town hall *n* a large building housing the offices of the town council, often with a hall for public meetings.

town house *n* a two or three-story house with a garage below, usu one of a row; a house in a fashionable area; one's house in town.

townie *n* (*pl* **townies**) a person who lives in a city or town as opposed to the countryside.—*also* **towny**.

town planning *n* the design and construction of the total physical and social environment of a town.

Townsend *n* **Charles H** (1851–28) English architect. His notable works include the Horniman Museum, London.

township *n* a division of a county in many US states, constituting a unit of local government; in South Africa, an urban area formerly reserved for Blacks.

towny *see* **townie**.

towpath *n* the footpath beside a river or canal.

towrope, towline *n* a strong rope or cable for towing a wheeled vehicle, ship, etc.

tow truck *or* **breakdown truck** *n* a vehicle for towing away smashed or damaged cars, etc.

tox., toxicol. *abbr* = toxicology.

tox-, toxic-, toxico- *prefix* poison.

toxemia *n* (*med*) a type of blood poisoning resulting from the toxins produced by rapidly multiplying bacteria at a localized site of infection, such as an abscess.—**toxemic,** *adj*.

toxic *adj* poisonous; harmful; deadly.—**toxicity** *n*.

toxicant *n* a poison. * *adj* poisonous.

toxicology *n* the scientific study of poisons, their effects and antidotes.—**toxicologic, toxicological** *adj*.—**toxicologist** *n*.

toxic shock syndrome *n* (*med*) a state of acute shock as a result of septicemia and caused by toxins produced by staphylococcal bacteria.

toxin *n* a poison produced by bacteria and by many species of plant and also present in snake venom.

toxocariasis *n* (*med*) a disease caused by the larvae of roundworms, which normally infect the domestic dog and cat but can be passed to humans if they swallow material contaminated with eggs in infected feces.

toxoid *n* (*med*) a toxin of reduced power used in vaccines to stimulate the production of antitoxins.

toxoplasmosis *n* (*med*) a disease affecting the central nervous system caused by a parasitic worm.

toy *n* an object for children to play with; a replica; a miniature. * *vi* to trifle; to flirt.

toyboy *n* (*inf*) the younger male lover of an older woman.

Toynbee *n* **Arnold [Joseph]** (1889–1975) English historian. His major work is *A Study of History* (1934–61), which compares civilizations past and present in terms of a rhythmic process of growth and decay.

tp abbr = target practice; teaching practice.

tp. abbr = township.

t.p. abbr = title page.

TP *abbr* = to pay; third party.

T/P *abbr* = title page.

tPA *abbr* = tissue plasminogen activator.

TPA *abbr* = Taiwan Pineapple Association; Tea Packers' Association; Tea Producers' Association; The Pizza Association; Turkish Peace Association.

tpd *abbr* = tons per day.

tph *abbr* = tons per hour.

tpi *abbr* = teeth/tracks/turns/threads per inch.

TPI *abbr* = tax and prices index.

tpm *abbr* = tons per minute.

t.p.m. *abbr* = title page mutilated.

TPN *abbr* = total parenteral nutrition.

TPR *abbr* = temperature, pulse, respiration.

TPS *abbr* = Tax Payers' Society; Thomas Paine Society.

t.p.w. *abbr* = title page wanting.

TQM *abbr* = total quality management.

tr. *abbr* = trace; transactions; transitive; translated; translation; translator; transpose; treasurer; (*Italian*) *trillo*, "trill"; trills; trustee.

Tr. *abbr* = Troop.

TR, t.r. *abbr* = tempore regis; teste Rege; (shipping) tons registered.

TR *abbr* = (*Brit mil*) Territorial Reserve; transmit-receive.

T/R *abbr* = transmitter-receiver; trust receipt.

TRA *abbr* = The Reclamation Association; Thoroughbred Racing Association.

trabeated *adj* (*archit*) of a post and lintel type construction as in the buildings of ancient Classical Greece.

trace *n* a mark etc left by a person, animal, or thing; a barely perceptible footprint; a small quantity. * *vt* to follow by tracks; to discover the whereabouts of; (*map, etc*) to copy by following the lines on transparent paper.

Trace *abbr* = test equipment for rapid automatic check-out evaluation (prior to take-off).

traceable *adj* able to be traced.—**traceably** *adv*.

trace element *n* (*chem*) an element that occurs in very small quantities in rocks, but which can be detected by geochemical analysis; (*med*) an element essential in nutrition but only in minute amounts.

trace element analysis *n* analysis of minute quantities of elements in metal ores, minerals, and rocks. This frequently identifies the original source of the material.

tracer *n* a projectile that glows or leaves a smoke trail allowing its flight to be observed; a radioisotope introduced into the body whose course can be traced by a detector for diagnostic purposes; (*med*) a substance that is marked so that when it is introduced into the body its progress can be followed.

tracery *n* (*archit*) the decorative intersecting ornamental wood or stonework in Gothic windows, screens, etc.

trace fossil *n* (*geol*) a sedimentary structure, due in some way to the presence or activity of an organism.

trachea *n* (*pl* **tracheae**) the air passage from the mouth to the lungs, the windpipe.

tracheitis *n* (*med*) inflammation of the trachea, often accompanying a viral infection of the upper respiratory tract.

tracheo-, (also trache-) *prefix* trachea.

tracheostomy, tracheotomy *n* (*med*) a surgical procedure in which a hole is made in the trachea to allow direct access of air to the lower respiratory passages.

trachoma *n* (*med*) an infectious eye disease caused by a virus that leads to scarring and eventual blindness.—**trachomatous** *adj*.

Trachonitis *n* (*Bible*) area of Palestine, north of Galilee, ruled by Philip, the tetrarch in NT times.

trachyte *n* (*geol*) a type of light-colored volcanic rock.

tracing *n* a copy of a drawing, etc made by tracing.

tracing paper *n* transparent paper used for tracing.

track *n* a mark left; a footprint; parallel steel rails on which trains run; a course for running or racing; sports performed on a track, as running, hurdling; the band on which the wheels of a tractor or tank run; one piece of music on a record; a sound track (*comput*) one of a number of concentric circles on a floppy or hard disk, encoded during formatting; a particular area on the disk for data storage. * *vt* to follow the tracks of; to follow by radar and record position of a satellite, etc; (*with* **down**) to find by tracking.

track-and-field *adj* denoting various competitive athletic events (as running, jumping, weight-throwing) performed on a track and adjacent field.

trackball *n* (*comput*) an input device similar to a mouse that is turned upside down, whereby the ball is moved within a static unit.

tracker *n* a person who follows by tracking footprints, etc; a dog that follows a scent.

track event *n* an athletic event that takes place on a running track.

track record *n* (*inf*) a record of the past achievements or failures of someone or something.

track shoe *n* a spiked running shoe.

tracking station *n* a place that uses radio or radar antennae to follow the course of objects in space or the atmosphere.

tracklaying *adj* having an endless loop of metal track around the wheels.

trackpad *n* (*comput*) a square pad embedded in the case of a laptop computer. Moving the finger over it moves the cursor on the screen.

tracks per inch, tpi *adj* (*comput*) a measure of the density of data storage on floppy disks.

tracksuit *n* a loose suit worn by athletes to keep warm.

tract[1] *n* an expanse of land or water; a part of a bodily system or organ.

tract[2] *n* a treatise.

tractable *adj* easily worked; easily taught; docile.

traction *n* act or state of drawing and pulling; (*med*) the use of weights to pull on a muscle, etc, to correct an abnormal condition.

tractor *n* a motor vehicle for pulling heavy loads and farming machinery.

tractor feed *adj* (*comput*) a mechanism used in dot matrix printers to push the paper past the print head, where sprockets engage in prepunched perforations at the edges of the paper.

Tracy *n* **Spencer** (1900–1967) American film actor. He won two Oscars in a row, for *Captains Courageous* (1937) and *Boy's Town* (1938). He had a long personal and professional relationship with Katharine Hepburn.

trad *adj* (*inf*) traditional. * *n* traditional jazz.

trade *n* buying and selling (of commodities); commerce; occupation; customers; business. * *vi* to buy and sell; to exchange; (*with* on) to take advantage of.—**trader** *n*.

trade association *n* (*com*) an organization formed to represent the interests of firms that operate in the same industry.

trade credit *n* (*com*) a system which allows a customer time to pay for goods received.

trade cycle *n* (*com*) a recurrent fluctuation in economic activity between boom and slump.

trade discount *n* (*com*) a reduction in the usual price of goods or services to customers because they buy regularly and in bulk.

trade gap *n* (*com*) the difference in value between a country's imports and exports when imports are the greater.

trade-in *n* a used item given in part payment when buying a replacement.

trademark *n* a name used on a product by a manufacturer to distinguish it from its competitors, esp when legally protected.—*also vt*.

trade-off *n* the exchange or substitution of one thing or priority for another, often as a compromise.

trade price *n* (*com*) the price paid to a wholesaler or manufacturer by a retailer.

tradescantia *n* any of a genus of common houseplants cultivated for their variegated foliage.

tradesman *n* (*pl* **tradesmen**) a shopkeeper; a skilled worker.

trade show *n* a gathering of the members of a particular industry at which goods and services are displayed and promoted and at which business contacts are made.

trade union *n* (*Brit*) a labor union.

trade winds *n* mainly easterly winds that blow from the subtropics to the equator.

trading *n* the act of buying and selling (goods, etc).—*also adj*.

trading account *n* (*com*) the section of a profit and loss account in which the cost of sales of goods is set against the sales revenue raised by the goods in order to calculate the amount of the gross profit.

trading post *n* a general store in a sparsely populated region.

trading profit *n* (*com*) the profit arising from the trading operations of a company, excluding such items as directors' fees, auditors' fees, interest, etc.

trading stamp *n* a stamp with a specified value given away with certain retail purchases, which can be exchanged for goods when enough have been collected.

tradition *n* the handing down from generation to generation of opinions and practices; the belief or practice thus passed on; custom.—**traditional** *adj*.—**traditionally** *adv*.

trad jazz *n* (*mus*) literally, "traditional jazz"; a term referring to the type of comparatively simple jazz with a strong melody, as played in New Orleans, which preceded the development of bebop.

traduce *vt* to speak badly of; to misrepresent.

traffic *n* trade; the movement or number of vehicles, pedestrians, etc, along a street, etc. * *vi* (**trafficking, trafficked**) to do business (esp. in illegal drugs).

traffic circle *n* a junction of thoroughfares where traffic circulates one way to ease progress, a roundabout.

traffic island *n* a raised area in the centre of a road to guide traffic and provide refuge for pedestrians crossing.

traffic jam *n* a stoppage of traffic due to congestion.

traffic light *n* one of a set of colored lights used to control traffic at street crossings, etc.

traffic pattern *n* a network of air lanes above an airport to which aircraft are restricted.

trag. *abbr* = tragedy; tragic.

tragacanth *n* a gum obtained from a species of spiny leguminous plants used in pharmacy and in calico printing.

tragedian *n* an actor who plays mainly tragic roles.—**tragedienne** *nf*.

tragedy *n* (*pl* **tragedies**) a play or drama that is serious and sad, and the climax a catastrophe; an accident or situation involving death or suffering.—**tragic** *adj*.—**tragically** *adv*.

tragicomedy *n* a dramatic or literary work which combines tragic and comic elements; a situation or event with tragic and comic aspects.

Traherne *n* **Thomas** (1637–74) English poet and author of religious meditations. The manuscript of his *Centuries of Meditations*, which includes many beautiful mystical passages, was discovered on a London bookstall in 1896 and published in 1908.

trail *n* a path or track; the scent of an animal; something left in the wake (e.g., *a trail of smoke*). * *vi* to hang or drag loosely behind; (*plant*) to climb; (*with* off *or* away) to grow weaker or dimmer. * *vt* to drag along the ground;

to have in its wake; to follow behind; to advertise a film, event, or program beforehand.

trailblazer *n* a person who blazes a trail; a pioneer in a particular field.

trailer *n* a large enclosed vehicle equipped to be lived in and able to be pulled by a car, a large vehicle designed to be towed by a truck, etc; a motor home; an advertisement for a film or television program.

trailer park *n* an area available for rent to motor homes, caravans, etc, usu with electricity, water, etc, piped in.

trailing edge *n* the rear edge of an aerofoil.

train *n* a series of railroad cars pulled by a locomotive; a sequence; the back part of a dress that trails along the floor; a retinue. *vt* to teach, to guide; to tame for use, as animals; to prepare for racing, etc; (*gun, etc*) to aim. * *vi* to do exercise or preparation.

trained *adj* skilled.

trainee *n* a person who is being trained.

trainer *n* a coach or instructor; a person who prepares athletes, horses etc for competition.

training *n* practical instruction; a course of physical exercises.

training school *n* an institution for training in vocational subjects, e.g. teaching, nursing.

training ship *n* a moored vessel on which people are taught seamanship.

train oil *n* oil obtained from whale blubber.

train surfing *n* the practice of clinging onto the outside of a moving train for kicks.—**train surfer** *n*.

traipse *n* a tiring walk, a trudge. * *vi* to walk wearily, trudge about.

trait *n* a characteristic feature.

traitor *n* a person who commits treason or betrays his country, friends, etc.—**traitorous** *adj*.

trajectory *n* (*pl* **trajectories**) the path of an object, such as a bullet, moving through space.

tram[1] *n* a small wagon running on rails in a mine; a streetcar; a cable car.

tram[2] *n* a double twisted thread used in some silks.

trammel *n* a type of net for catching birds or fish; (*often pl*) a hindrance to freedom of movement or action; an instrument for drawing ellipses. * *vt* (**trammeling, trammeled** *or* **trammelling, trammelled**) to trap, catch; to hinder, restrict.

tramp *n* a vagrant; (*sl*) a prostitute. * *vti* to walk heavily; to tread or trample; to wander about as a tramp.

trample *vti* to tread under foot.

trampoline *n* a sheet of strong canvas stretched tightly on a frame, used in acrobatic tumbling.

trance *n* a state of unconsciousness, induced by hypnosis, in which some of the powers of the waking body, such as response to commands, may be retained.

tranche *n* (*com*) a portion of something, esp a sum of money or issue of shares.

tranchet *n* (*archeo*) a stone tool with a chisel-shaped blade produced by striking off a flake.

tranquil *adj* quiet, calm, peaceful.—**tranquilly** *adv*.

tranquility *n* the state of being tranquil; calmness.

tranquilize *vt* to make tranquil, esp by administering a drug.— **tranquilization** *n*.

tranquilizer *n* a drug that has a soothing and calming effect, relieving stress and anxiety.

tranquillo *n* (*mus*) (*Italian*), "calm."

trans. *abbr* = transactions; transferred; (*elec*) transformer; transitive; translated; translation; translator; transportation; transpose.

trans- *prefix* through; across; on the other side of.

transact *vt* (*com*) to conduct or carry out.

transaction *n* the act of transacting; something transacted, esp a business deal; (*pl*) a record of the proceedings of a society.

transaction costs *npl* (*com*) the costs that are associated with the process of buying and selling.

transaction exposure *n* (*com*) the extent of the risk that the cost of a transaction will alter between the date on which the transaction is carried out and the date of settlement.

transalpine *adj* beyond (usu north) of the Alps.

transatlantic *adj* crossing the Atlantic Ocean; across, beyond the Atlantic.

transceiver *n* a combined radio transmitter and receiver.

transcend *vt* to rise above or beyond; to surpass.—**transcendent** *adj*.

transcendental *adj* beyond physical experience; surpassing; supernatural.—**transcendentally** *adv*.

transcendental meditation *n* a technique for emptying and refreshing the mind by repeating a mantra.

transcendentalism *n* (*philos*) a philosophy compounded of generalized mysticism and optimism.

transcontinental *adj* extending or traveling across a continent.—**transcontinentally** *adv*.

transcribe *vt* to write out fully from notes or a tape recording; to make a phonetic transcription; to arrange a piece of music for an instrument other than the one it was written for.

transcript *n* a written or printed copy made by transcribing; an official copy of proceedings, etc.

transcription *n* the act of transcribing; something transcribed, esp a piece of music;

a transcript; a recording made for broadcasting; (*genetics*) the formation of an RNA molecule from one strand of a DNA molecule.

transducer *n* (*phys*) a device that converts one form of energy into another, often a physical quantity into an electrical signal, as in microphones and photocells.

transect *n* (*geog*) a transverse section across a region to show relationships between soils, vegetation and the character of the land surface.

transept *n* (*archit*) one of the two wings of a church, at right angles to the nave.

transepted gallery grave *n* (*archeo*) a form of gallery grave with additional small recesses off the primary burial chamber.

transf., transfd. *abbr* = transferred.

transfer *vt* (**transferring, transferred**) to carry, convey, from one place to another; (*comput*) to move information from disk to memory and vice versa; (*law*) to make over (property) to another; (*com*) to move money from the control of one institution to another. * *vi* to change to another bus, etc. * *n* the act of transferring; the state of being transferred; someone or something that is transferred; a design that can be moved from one surface to another.—**transferable** *adj*.

transferase *n* (*chem*) an enzyme that catalyzes the transfer of chemical groups between molecules, e.g. acyl transferase.

transfer deed *n* a document that is used to record the transfer of property, including shares, from one person to another.

transference *n* the act of transferring; the state of being transferred; (*psychol*) the redirection of emotion under analysis, usu toward the analyst.

transfer price *n* (*com*) the internal price at which raw materials, components, or finished products are transacted between the divisions of a company.

transfer RNA *n* one of the three major classes of RNA that functions as the carrier of amino acids to ribosomes, where the polypeptide chains of proteins are formed.

transfiguration *n* a change in appearance, esp to a more spiritual or exalted form; (*eccles*) (*with cap*) (the festival commemorating) the change in the appearance of Christ as described in the Gospels.

transfigure *vt* to transform or become transformed in appearance, esp for the better.

transfix *vt* to impale with a sharp weapon; to paralyze with shock or horror.

transform *vti* to change the shape, appearance, or condition of; to convert.—**transformation** *n*.

transformer *n* a device for changing the voltage of an alternating current.

transfusion *n* (*med*) the injection of blood into the veins of a sick or injured person.—**transfuse** *vt*.

transgress *vti* to break or violate (a moral law or code of behavior); to overstep (a limit).—**transgressor** *n*.

transgression *n* the act of transgressing; infringement of a rule, etc; a sin.

transhumance *n* the seasonal movement of people and animals between winter and summer pastures, e.g. to use an alp. The people have two abodes and are therefore not nomads.

transient *adj* temporary; of short duration, momentary.—**transience** *n*.

Transient Lunar Phenomenon *or* **TLP** *n* (*astron*) a passing and short-lived change in the appearance of some surface features on the moon, such as colored patches or glows, or obscuring of the detail of features.

transistor *n* a semiconductor device that is used in three main ways: as a switch, as a rectifier, and as an amplifier creating strong signals from weak ones.

transit *n* a passing over or through; conveyance of people or goods; (*astron*) movement of a small body across the disk of a larger body (to an observer on earth) as with a satellite moving across its parent planet.

transit camp *n* temporary accommodation for soldiers, refugees, etc.

transit circle *or* **meridian circle** *n* the circle made by an optical telescope which is fixed so that it can only swing in a vertical north–south plane.

transition *n* passage from one place or state to another; change; (*mus*) the changing from one key to another during the course of a composition; (*mus*) a passage linking two sections of a piece, which often involves a change of key.—**transitional** *adj*.

transition element *n* (*chem*) one of the elements in the periodic table that is characterized by an incomplete inner electron shell and a variable valency.

transition point *n* (*chem*) the point at which a substance may exist in more than one solid form, in equilibrium.

transitive *adj* (*gram*) denoting a verb that requires a direct object; of or relating to transition.—**transitively** *adv*.—**transitivity** *n*.

transitory *adj* lasting only a short time.—**transitorily** *adv*.——**transitoriness** *n*.

transl. *abbr* = translated; translation, translations.

translate *vti* to express in another language; to explain, interpret; (*comput*) to change a file that has been saved in one file format to another so that the file can be opened in a different program.—**translator** *n*.

translation *n* the act of translating; something translated into another language or state; an interpretation; the synthesis of proteins in a ribosome that has messenger RNA attached to it.

transliterate *vt* to convert a word, etc into the corresponding characters of another alphabet.—**transliteration** *n*.

translucent *adj* allowing light to pass through, but not transparent.—**translucence** *n*.

transmigrate *vi* of the soul, to pass into the body of another person after death; to migrate.

transmission *n* the act of transmitting; something transmitted; a system using gears, etc, to transfer power from an engine to a moving part, esp wheels of a vehicle; a radio or television broadcast.

transmit *vt* (**transmitting, transmitted**) to send from one place or person to another; to communicate; to convey; to send out radio or television signals.

transmitter *n* an apparatus for broadcasting television or radio programs.

transmogrify *vt* (**transmogrifying, transmogrified**) to change shape, esp in a bizarre or comic manner.—**transmogrification** *n*.

transmute *vt* to change into a different form or substance.—**transmutation** *n*.

transnational *n* extending beyond national boundaries.

transoceanic *adj* on or from the other side of ocean; crossing the ocean.

transom *n* (*archit*) a horizontal bar across a window or between a door and a window over it; a fanlight; any of several transverse beams supporting and strengthening the stern of a vessel.

transp. *abbr* = transportation.

transparency *n* (*pl* **transparencies**) the state of being transparent; a slide.

transparent *adj* that may be easily seen through; clear, easily understood.—**transparently** *adv*.—**transparentness** *n*.

transpiration *n* (*biol*) the loss of water vapor from pores in the leaves of plants.

transpire *vti* to emit, to pass off through the pores of the skin; to exhale (moisture); of news, to become known, to leak out; (*inf*) to happen.—**transpiration** *n*.

transplant *vt* to remove and plant in another place; to remove an organ from one person and transfer it to another.—*also n*.

transplantation *n* (*med*) the transfer of an organ or tissue from one person to another (allotransplant) or within the body of an individual (autotransplant), i.e. skin and bone grafting.

transponder *n* a device that automatically transmits a radio signal on receiving a predetermined signal.

transport *vt* to convey from one place to another; to enrapture. * *n* the system of transporting goods or passengers; the conveyance of troops and their equipment by sea or land; a vehicle for this purpose.—**transportable** *adj*.—**transportation** *n*.

transpose *vt* to put into a different order; to interchange; (*mus*) to change the key of. * *vti* to move one term or element from one side of an equation to the other with a corresponding reversal in sign.—**transposition** *n*.

transposing instruments *n* (*mus*) instruments which sound notes different from those actually written down, e.g. a piece of music in E flat for the B flat clarinet would actually be written in F.

transposition *n* (*mus*) the changing of the pitch of a composition, e.g. to suit the voice range of a singer.

transputer *n* (*comput*) a fast microchip comprising a 32-bit microprocessor which is used as a component in compact supercomputers.

transsexual *n* a person born of one sex who identifies psychologically with the opposite sex.—**transsexualism** *n*.

transubstantiation *n* the doctrine, esp in RC church, that the bread and wine of the communion are transformed into the body and blood of Christ when consecrated, although their appearance remains unchanged.

transuranic *adj* (*chem*) having an atomic number greater than that of uranium.

transverse *adj* crosswise.—**transversely** *adv*.

transverse arch *n* (*archit*) an arch which separates the bay of one vault from the next, the division being marked by a rib running transversely.

transverse wave *n* (*phys*) a wave in which the vibration occurs at right angles to the direction of wave propagation.

transvestite *n* a person who gains sexual pleasure from wearing the clothes of the opposite sex.—**transvestism** *n*.

trap *n* a mechanical device or pit for snaring animals; an ambush; a trick to catch someone out; (*transp*) a two-wheeled horsedrawn carriage. * *vt* (**trapping, trapped**) to catch in a trap; to trick.

trapdoor *n* a hinged or sliding door in a roof, ceiling, or floor.

trapdoor spider *n* any of various spiders that build silk-lined traps in the ground covered by a hinged lid of earth and silk.

trapeze *n* a gymnastic apparatus consisting of a horizontal bar suspended by two parallel ropes.

trapezium *n* (*pl* **trapeziums, trapezia**) a quadrilateral in which none of the sides are parallel; (*Brit*) a quadrilateral in which two of the sides are parallel.—**trapezial** *adj*.

Trapezium *n* (*astron*) an open cluster of very young stars, dust, and gas lying in the Orion nebula.

trapezoid *n* a quadrilateral in which two of the sides are parallel; (*Brit*) a quadrilateral in which none of the sides are parallel.

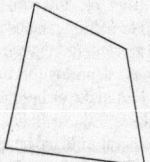

trapper *n* a person who traps animals, esp for their skins.

trappings *npl* trimmings; additions; ornaments.

Traquair *n* **Phoebe Anna** (1852–1936) Irish-born enameler, jewelry and tapestry designer who was the first woman to be appointed honorary member of the Royal Scottish Academy.

trash *n* nonsense; refuse; rubbish.

trash can *n* a container for household refuse, a garbage can.

trashy *adj* (**trashier, trashiest**) of poor quality.—**trashiness** *n*.

trattoria *n* (*pl* **trattorias, trattorie**) an Italian restaurant.

trauma[1] *n* (*psych*) an emotional shock brought about by a harmful and upsetting circumstance.— **traumatic** *adj*.

trauma[2] *n* (*med*) an event that causes physical damage, such as a fracture.— **traumatic** *adj*.

trav. *abbr* = traveler; travels.

travail *n* painful physical effort; the pain of childbirth. * *vi* to suffer through physical effort, esp in childbirth.

travel *vb* (**traveling, traveled** or **travelling, travelled**) *vi* to journey or move from one place to another. * *vt* to journey across, through. * *n* journey.

travel agency *n* an agency through which one can book travel, make travel arrangements.—**travel agent** *n*.

traveler, traveller *n* a person who travels; a salesman who travels for a company.

traveler's check *n* a draft purchased from a bank, etc signed at the time of purchase and signed again at the time of cashing.

travelog *n* a film or illustrated lecture on travel.

travel sickness *see* **motion sickness**.

Traven *n* B [**Albert Otto Max Feige**] (*c*.1882–1969) German-born American novelist. He wrote adventure novels, of which the best known are *The Death Ship* and *The Treasure of the Sierra Madre*.

traverse *n* a horizontal move in rock climbing, skiing, etc. * *vt* to cross.

travertine *n* (*chem*) a mineral comprising mostly calcium carbonate, used for building.

travesty *n* (*pl* **travesties**) a misrepresentation; a poor imitation; a parody.

travois *n* (*pl* **travois**) a simple sled formerly used by Native Americans, comprising two trailing poles supporting a board or net and dragged by a dog or horse; a similar contraption for dragging logs.

trawl *vti* to fish by dragging a large net behind a fishing boat.

trawler *n* a boat used for trawling.

tray *n* a flat board, or sheet of metal or plastic, surrounded by a rim, used for carrying food or drink.

TRB culture *n* (*archeo*) the earliest Neolithic culture in northern Europe and southern Scandinavia. It emerged *c*.4000 BC.

TRC *abbr* (*Brit*) = Thames Rowing Club.

TrCo *abbr* = Trust Company.

trcs. *abbr* = tierces.

TRDA *abbr* = Timber Research and Development Association.

treacherous *adj* untrustworthy, disloyal; unstable, dangerous.

treachery *n* (*pl* **treacheries**) disloyalty, betrayal of trust.

treacle *n* a thick sticky substance obtained during the refining of sugar.—**treacly** *adj*.

tread *n* a step, way of walking; the part of a shoe, wheel, or tire that touches the ground. * *vti* (**treading, trod**, *pp* **trodden**) to step or walk on, along, in, over, or across; to crush or squash (with the feet); to trample (on).

treadle *n* a foot lever or pedal on a machine.

treadmill *n* a grind; a monotonous routine.

treas. *abbr* = treasurer, treasury.

treason *n* the crime of betraying one's government or attempting to overthrow it; treachery.—**treasonable** *adj*.

treasr. *abbr* = treasurer.

treasure *n* wealth and riches hoarded up; a person or thing much valued. * *vt* to hoard up; to prize greatly.

treasure hunt *n* a game in which players follow clues to locate a hidden object.

treasurer *n* a person appointed to take charge of the finances of a society, government, or city.

treasure-trove *n* (*law*) valuable items such as gold and silver found buried and of unknown ownership; any valuable find.

treasury *n* (*pl* **treasuries**) a place where valuable objects are deposited; the funds or revenues of a government.

Treasury bill *n* a bill of exchange that is issued by the Bank of England on the authority of the UK government.

treat *n* an entertainment paid for by another person; a pleasure seldom indulged; a unusual cause of enjoyment. * *vt* to deal with or regard; to subject to the action of a chemical; to apply medical treatment to; to pay for another person's entertainment; to deal with in speech or writing.

treatise *n* a formal essay in which a subject is treated systematically.

treatment *n* the application of drugs, etc, to a patient; the manner of dealing with a person or thing, esp in a novel or painting; behavior toward someone.

treaty *n* (*pl* **treaties**) a formal agreement between states.

treble *adj* triple, threefold; (*mus*) denoting the treble. * *n* the highest range of musical notes in singing. * *vti* to make or become three times as much.

treble clef *n* (*mus*) a clef that places G above middle C on the second line of the staff.

trebuchet *n* (*hist*) a type of medieval military catapult used in sieges.

trecento *n* the 14th century, esp in reference to Italian art and literature.

tree *n* a tall, woody, perennial plant having a single trunk, branches, and leaves.

tree creeper *n* any of various small songbirds with curved beaks for prizing insects from tree trunks.

tree farm *n* a tree-growing area producing a managed and continuous output of timber.

tree fern *n* a large tropical fern with a woody stem.

tree frog *n* any of various frogs that inhabit trees.

tree line *n* the height or latitude beyond which no trees grow on mountains or in cold regions.—*also* **timber line**.

tree structure *n* (*comput*) a way of organizing directories on a disk that shows the core or main directory at the top with the various subdirectories and sub-subdirectories extending branchlike from it.

tree surgeon *n* a person skilled in saving diseased or damaged trees.—**tree surgery** *n*.

tree toad *n* a tree frog.

trefoil *n* any of various plants with three leaflets; an ornament or design resembling this.

trek *vi* (**trekking, trekked**) to travel slowly or laboriously; (*inf*) to go on foot (to). * *n* a long and difficult journey; a migration.

trellis *n* a structure of latticework, for supporting climbing plants, etc.— **trelliswork** *n*.

trem *abbr* = transport emergency.

trem. *abbr* = tremolo.

tremble *vi* to shake, shiver from cold or fear; to quiver.—*also n*.

trembler *n* a device that makes or breaks an electric circuit when subject to vibration.

tremendous *adj* awe-inspiring; very large or great; (*inf*) wonderful; marvelous.

tremolando *n* (*mus*) (*Italian*), "trembling."

tremolo *n* (*pl* **tremolos**) (*mus*) (*Italian*) the rapid repetition of a single note, or the rapid alternation between two or more notes; a device that produces this effect, as in an organ.

tremor *n* a vibration; (*med*) an involuntary movement of a muscle. *See also* **chorea; multiple sclerosis; Parkinsonism**.

tremulous *adj* quivering; agitated.

trench *n* a long narrow channel in the earth, used for drainage; such an excavation made for military purposes.

trenchant *adj* keen; incisive; effective.

trench coat *n* a waterproof coat.

trencher *n* a wooden board formerly used for serving food.

trencherman *n* a person who eats heartily.

trench fever *n* (*med*) an infectious disease transmitted by the body louse.

trench foot *n* (*med*) a degenerative condition of the feet caused by prolonged immersion in cold water.

trench mouth *n* (*med*) a contagious viral disease causing ulceration of the mucous membrane of the mouth.—*also* **Vincent's angina**.

trend *n* tendency; a current style or fashion.

trendsetter *n* a person who starts a new fashion.

trendy *adj* (**trendier, trendiest**) (*inf*) fashionable. * *n* (*pl* **trendies**) (*inf*) a person who tries to be fashionable.—**trendily** *adv*.—**trendiness** *n*.

Trenton *n* capital city of New Jersey, a state of the USA.

trepan *n* (*med*) a primitive form of trephine. * *vt* (**trepanning, trepanned**) to cut with a trepan.

trepang *n* a type of large sea cucumber dried and used in Chinese cookery, bêche-de-mer.

trepanning *n* (*med*) early surgery in which a small piece of bone was removed from a person's skull.

trephine *n* (*med*) a surgical saw for removing circular sections of bone, esp from the skull. * *vt* to cut with a trephine.

trepidation *n* a state of fear or anxiety.

trespass *vi* to intrude upon another person's property without their permission; to encroach upon, or infringe, another's rights. * *n* act of trespassing.— **trespasser** *n*.

tress *n* a lock, braid, or plait of hair.

trestle *n* a wooden framework for supporting a table top or scaffold boards.

Trevelyan *n* **George Macaulay** (1876–1962) English historian. His works include *History of England* (1926), *English Social History* (1944), and several biographies, e.g. *Grey of Falloden* (1937).

Trevor *n* **William** [**William Trevor Cox**] (1928–) Irish novelist and short-story writer whose highly regarded fiction includes the novels, *The Old Boys* and *Fools of Fortune*, and the short-story collections, *Angels at the Ritz* and *Beyond the Pale*.

trews *npl* tight-fitting tartan trousers.

trey *n* three spots or the number three on a dice, domino, or playing card.

Trezzini *n* **Domenico** (1670–) Swiss architect whose notable works include the Cathedral of St Peter and Paul, St Petersburg.

trf *abbr* = tuned radio frequency.

TRF *abbr* = Trail Riders Fellowship.

TRFA *abbr* = Trussed Rafter Fabricators' Association.

trfr. *abbr* = transfer.

TRG *abbr* = Tertiary Research Group; Tory Reform Group.

TRH *abbr* = Their Royal Highnesses; thyrotrophin-releasing hormone.

tri- *prefix* having, made up of, or containing three or three parts; every third.

TRI *abbr* = Thrombosis Research Institute; Tin Research Institute; Toxics Release Inventory.

triad[1] *n* a group or set of three, a trio; (*mus*) a chord of three notes that includes a third and a fifth.

triad[2] *n* (*Egypt*) a traditional triple grouping of Egyptian deities, usually father, mother and son (as in Amun, Mut and Khonsu).

triage *n* (*med*) the sorting and treatment of the wounded according to chance of survival.

trial *n* a test or experiment; judicial examination; an attempt; a preliminary race, game in a competition; suffering; hardship; a person causing annoyance.

trial and error *n* solving problems through trying various solutions and rejecting the least successful.

trial balance *n* (*com*) a listing of the balances on the accounts of a company with the debit balances on one side and the credit balances on the other.

trial balloon *n* a balloon used for atmospheric tests, such as measuring wind velocity; a scheme devised to test public opinion.

trial marriage *n* the living together beforehand of a man and woman intending to marry for the purpose of determining compatibility.

Trial of Jesus *n* (*Bible*) although there was insufficient evidence at his trial to convict Jesus, when he responded to a question that he was the Christ, the high priest called for the death sentence for blasphemy. *See also* **Barabas; Caiaphas; Council.**

trial run *n* an opportunity to test something before purchase, as a vehicle; a rehearsal.

triangle *n* (*math*) a plane figure with three angles and three sides; (*mus*) a percussion instrument consisting of a triangular metal bar beaten with a metal stick.—**triangular** *adj*.

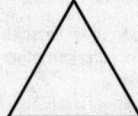

triangulate *vt* to divide into triangles; to make triangular; to survey by dividing an area into a network of triangles.—**triangulation** *n*.

triangulation *n* the method used for carrying out a topographical survey using trigonometry.

Triangulum Australe *or* **The Southern Triangle** *n* (*astron*) a small but prominent constellation lying in the southern hemisphere, partly within the Milky Way and near Crux.

Triangulum Galaxy *n* (*astron*) a spiral galaxy situated within the Triangulum constellation. It is the third largest member of the local group and is at a distance of 2.7 million light years.

Triangulum *or* **the Triangle** *n* (*astron*) a small but prominent constellation lying in the northern hemisphere. It is near Perseus and between Aries and Andromeda.

triathlon *n* an athletic event in which contestants compete in swimming, cycling, and running.

triatomic *adj* (*chem*) having three atoms in the molecule.

tribadism *n* simulated heterosexual intercourse by lesbians, with one partner lying on top of the other.

tribe *n* a group of people of the same race, sharing the same customs, religion, language, or land.—**tribal** *adj*.—**tribesman** *n*.

Tribel *n* Annie (1933–) French furniture designer who joined Atelier d'Urbanisme et d'Architecture in 1962.

tribo- *prefix* friction.

triboelectricity *n* electricity generated by friction.

tribology *n* (*phys*) the study of friction, lubrication, and wear, as occurs when two surfaces are in contact in relative motion.

triboluminescence *n* (*phys*) luminescence caused by friction.—**triboluminescent** *adj*.

tribulation *n* distress, difficulty, hardship.

tribunal *n* a court of justice; a committee that investigates and decides on a particular problem.

tribune[1] *n* in ancient Rome, a magistrate appointed to protect the rights of common people; a champion of the people.

tribune[2] *n* a raised platform or dais from which speeches are delivered.

tribune[3] (*archit*) the apse of a basilica or a church built on the basilican plan; a gallery in a church.

tributary *n* (*pl* **tributaries**) a stream or river flowing into a larger one.

tribute *n* a speech, gift, or action to show one's respect or thanks to someone; a payment made at certain intervals by one nation to another in return for peace.

tricentenary *n* (*pl* **tricentenaries**) a tricentennial.—*also adj*.

tricentennial *adj* lasting, or happening every, 300 years. * *n* an anniversary of 300 years; a period of 300 years.

triceps *n* (*pl* **tricepses, triceps**) (*anat*) any three-headed muscle, esp the large muscle that extends the forearm.

trichiasis *n* (*med*) a condition of having in-growing eyelashes which irritate the eyeball.

trichina *n* (*pl* **trichinae**) a hair-like parasitic worm that infests the intestines and muscles of pigs and humans.

trichinosis *n* (*med*) a disease in humans caused by infestation of muscular tissues by trichinae.

tricho-, trich- *prefix* hair; filament.

trichology *n* the medical study and treatment of hair diseases.—**trichologist** *n*.

trichomoniasis *n* (*med*) either of two types of infection caused by a protozoan organism that either attacks the digestive system, causing dysentery, or causes vaginal inflammation and discharge.

trichorrhoea *n* (*med*) the medical name for the falling out of hair, which may be caused by disease, such as typhoid fever or scarlet fever, or has no apparent cause.

trichosis *n* (*med*) any disease of the hair.

trichotomy *n* (*pl* **trichotomies**) a division into three parts or categories.—**trichotomous** *adj*.

trichromatic of, involving, or combining three colors; (*med*) of or having normal color vision.—**trichromatism** *n*.

trick *n* fraud; deception; a mischievous plan or joke; a magical illusion; a clever feat; skill, knack; the playing cards won in a round. * *adj* using fraud or clever contrivance to deceive. * *vt* to deceive, cheat.—**trickster** *n*.

trickery *n* (*pl* **trickeries**) the practice or an act of using underhand methods to achieve an aim; deception.

trickle *vti* to flow or cause to flow in drops or in a small stream.—*also n*.

trickle-down *adj* denoting a theory in economics that financial incentives to big business will percolate through to small businesses and individuals.

trick or treat *n* a Halloween tradition in which children dress in costumes, call on their neighbors and threaten to do mischief if refused presents of sweets, apples, nuts, money, etc.

tricky *adj* (**trickier, trickiest**) complicated, difficult to handle; risky; cunning, deceitful.—**trickily** *adv*.—**trickiness** *n*.

tricolor *n* a flag with three stripes of different colors.

tricorn *adj* having three horns or corners. * *n* a three-cornered hat.

tricuspid *adj* having three cusps, flaps, points, or segments. * *n* a tooth with three cusps.

tricuspid valve *n* (*anat*) a valve that has three flaps or cusps and controls the passage of blood from the right atrium to the right ventricle of the heart and normally prevents back flow.

tricycle *n* a three-wheeled pedal cycle, esp for children.

Tri De Dana *n* (*Irish Celtic myth*) the triad of gods associated with craftsmanship. They were Creidhne, Goibhniu and Luchta. They forged and repaired the magical weapons of the Tuatha De Danann.

trident *n* three-pronged spear.

tridentate, tridental *adj* having three teeth or prongs.

tried[1] *see* **try**.

tried[2] *adj* tested; trustworthy.

triennial *adj* happening every third year; lasting for three years.

triennium *n* (*pl* **trienniums, triennia**) a period of three years.

trier *n* one who tries.

Trifid nebula *n* (*astron*) an emission nebula, consisting of a huge cloud of ionized hydrogen, situated in the constellation Sagittarius.

trifle *n* anything of little value; a dessert of whipped cream, custard, sponge cake, sherry, etc. * *vi* to treat lightly; to dally.

trifling *adj* insignificant.

trifocal *adj* having three focuses or focal lengths. * *npl* glasses with trifocal lenses.

trifurcate, trifurcated *adj* having three branches or forks.

trig., trigon) *abbr* = trigonometric; trigonometrical; trigonometry.

trigeminal nerve *n* (*anat*) the fifth and largest of the cranial nerves, involved in the relaying and perception of sensations (temperature, touch, pain, etc) from the whole of the face and mouth, and also in controlling the muscles involved in chewing.—*also adj*.

trigeminal neuralgia *n* (*med*) a severe form of neuralgia that can affect all the divisions of the trigeminal nerve.—*also* **tic douloureux**

trigger *n* a catch that when pulled activates the firing mechanism of a gun. * *vt* (*with* **off**) to initiate; to set (off).

trigger-happy *adj* too eager to resort to firearms or violence; rash, aggressive.

triglycerides *n* fats consisting of three fatty acid molecules combined with glycerol, which are the form in which the body stores fat.

triglyph *n* (*archit*) a stone block in a Doric frieze carved with three vertical grooves called glyphs.

trigonometric function *n* (*math*) any of various functions (e.g., sine, cosine, tangent) expressed as ratios of the sides of a right-angled triangle.

trigonometry *n* the branch of mathematics concerned with calculating the angles of triangles or the lengths of their sides.

trike *n* (*inf*) a tricycle.

trilateral *adj* having three sides.

trilby *n* (*pl* **trilbies**) a soft felt hat with a fold in the crown.

trilingual *adj* speaking three languages; written in three languages.—**trilingualism** *n*.

trilithon *n* (*archeo*) an archway of two large vertical stones with a slab or lintel across the top.

trill *n* (*mus*) an ornament in which a note is rapidly alternated with the note above used in both vocal and instrumental pieces. * *vti* to sing or play with a tremulous tone; (*a bird*) to make a shrill, warbling sound.

Trilling *n* Lionel (1905–75) American critic whose collection of essays, *The Liberal Imagination*, was very influential in its concern for locating literary criticism as something central to Western, liberal culture.

trillion *n* a million million (10^{12}); (*Brit*) formerly a million million million (10^{18}); (*inf*) (*pl*) a very large number.

trilobite *n* any of a group of extinct Paleozoic marine arthropods with a body in three sections.

trilogy *n* (*pl* **trilogies**) any series of three related literary or operatic works.

trim *adj* (**trimmer, trimmest**) in good condition; tidy, neat; slim. * *n* a decorative edging; a haircut that tidies; (*archit*) a trimming that finishes the edge of a surface or opening. * *vt* to neaten; to cut or prune; to decorate; to balance the weight of cargo in a ship or aircraft.

trimaran *n* (*naut*) a boat with three hulls.

trimester¹ *n* a period of three months; a division of the academic year in certain colleges and universities.

trimester² *n* (*med*) the first three months of pregnancy.

trimming *n* decorative part of clothing; (*pl*) accompaniments.

Trin. *abbr* = Trinity.

Trincomalee *n* a city in Sri Lanka.

trinh *n* a monetary unit of Vietnam, equal to one thousandth of a dong.

Trinidad and Tobago *n* a republic, which is the most southerly of the Lesser Antilles group, situated off the Orinoco Delta in northeastern Venezuela.

Trinidad and Tobago dollar *n* currency of Trinidad and Tobago.

trinitrotoluene *n* (*chem*) a solid yellow chemical substance used as a high explosive.

trinity *n* (*pl* **trinities**) a group of three; (*eccles*) (*with cap*) in Christianity, the union of Father, Son, and Holy Spirit in one God.

trinket *n* a small or worthless ornament.

trinomial *adj* having three terms. * *n* (*math*) a polynomial consisting of three terms.

Trinovantes *n* the tribal name given to the Britons who were said to be inhabiting London, and the territory to the north of there, at the time of the second invasion of Julius Caesar in 54 BC.

trio *n* (*mus*) a group of three performers; a piece of music written for such a group; (*mus*) the middle section of a minuet, as found in sonatas, symphonies etc.

triode *n* (*elect*) an electronic valve or semiconductor device with three electrodes.

trip *vb* (**tripping, tripped**) *vi* to move or tread lightly; to stumble and fall; to make a blunder. * *vt* (*often with* **up**) to cause to stumble; to activate a trip. * *n* a stumble; a journey, tour, or voyage; a slip; a mistake; a light step; a mechanical switch; (*sl*) a hallucinatory experience under the influence of a drug.

tripartite *adj* made up of or divided into three parts; involving or binding three parties.

tripe *n* the stomach lining of a ruminant, prepared for cooking; (*inf*) rubbish, nonsense.

triplane *n* an aircraft with three wings positioned one above the other.

triple *adj* threefold; three times as many. * *vti* to treble.

triple-alpha process *n* (*astron*) a nuclear fusion reaction that occurs in the interior of a star once all the hydrogen in the core has been used up and the temperature has climbed to 100 million degrees.

triple jump *n* an athletic event in which a competitor makes a hop, step, and jump in succession.

triple spin CD ROM *n* (*comput*) a CD ROM drive that operates three times faster than a standard CD ROM drive.

triplet *n* one of three children born at one birth; (*mus*) a group of three notes played in the time of two notes.

triplicate *adj* threefold.

tripod *n* a three-legged stand, as for supporting a camera.

Tripoli (Tarabulus) *n* capital city of Libya.

Tripoli (Trablous) *n* a city in the Lebanon.

tripper *n* a tourist; a trip switch.

Triptolemus *n* (*Greek myth*) a prince of Eleusis, who flew in a chariot drawn by winged dragons and sowed grain all over the earth. He was worshiped in the Eleusinian Mysteries.

triptych *n* a picture consisting of three panels fixed or hinged side by side.

tripwire *n* a concealed wire that sets off a bomb, booby trap, etc when tripped over.

trireme *n* (*hist*) an ancient Greek galley with three banks of oars.

trisect *vt* to divide into three (equal) parts.—**trisection** *n*.

trishaw *n* a rickshaw.

triskelion *n* (*pl* **triskelia**) a symbol consisting of three bent limbs or branches radiating from a centre.

trismus *n* (*med*) lockjaw.

trisomy *n* (*med*) the abnormal condition in which an organism has three chromosomes rather than the normal pair for one type of chromosome.

trisyllable *n* a word of three syllables.

trit. *abbr* = triturate.

trite *adj* dull; hackneyed.

tritium *n* (chem) a radioactive isotope of hydrogen.

triton *n* any of various marine gastropod mollusks having a heavy spiral shell.

Triton¹ *n* (*Greek myth*) the name of certain sea-gods, with the body of a human above and a fish below.

Triton² *n* (*astron*) the largest moon or satellite of the planet Neptune, first seen in 1846, just after the discovery of Neptune itself.

tritone *n* (*mus*) an interval consisting of three whole tones.

triturate *vt* to crush or grind into a fine powder.—**trituration** *n*.

triumph *n* a victory; success; a great achievement. * *vi* to win a victory or success; to rejoice over a victory.—**triumphal** *adj*.

triumphal arch *n* (*archit*) a free-standing arch built to commemorate a victory.

triumphant *adj* feeling or showing triumph; celebratory; victorious.— **triumphantly** *adv*.

triumvir *n* (*pl* **triumvirs, triumviri**) a member of a ruling body of three persons.

triumvirate *n* the office of a triumvir; joint rule by three persons.

trivalent *adj* (*chem*) having a valency of three.

trivet *n* a three-legged metal stand for supporting hot dishes.

trivia *npl* unimportant details.

trivial *adj* unimportant; commonplace.

triviality *n* (*pl* **trivialities**) a trifle, detail; the state of being trivial.

-trix *n suffix* female.

TRM *abbr* = trademark.

tRNA, t-RNA *abbr* (*chem*) = transfer ribonucleic acid (RNA).

TRNC *abbr* = Turkish Republic of Northern Cyprus.

TRO *abbr* = Temporary Restraining Order.

Troad *n* (*hist*) an area of Asia Minor which took its name from its main city, Troy.

Troas *n* (*hist*) seaport city of Asia Minor, on the Aegean; a Roman colony in NT times.

TROBI *abbr* (*Brit*) = Tree Register of the British Isles.

trocar *n* (*med*) a pointed instrument for inserting drainage tubes into bodily cavities.

trochal *adj* wheel-shaped.

troche *n* (*med*) a medicinal lozenge.

trochee *n* (*poet*) a metrical foot comprising one long syllable followed by one short syllable.

trod, trodden *see* **tread**.

troglodyte *n* a cave dweller.

troika *n* a Russian vehicle drawn by three horses harnessed abreast; a triumvirate.

Troilus *n* (*Greek myth*) a son of Hecuba and either Priam or Apollo, who was killed by Achilles during the Trojan War.

Trojan Group *n* (*astron*) two groups of asteroids which share the orbit of the planet Jupiter around the sun.

Trojan horse¹ *n* (*Greek myth*) a wooden horse constructed by the Greeks to gain entrance to Troy undetected.

Trojan horse² *n* (*comput*) a program that appears to perform a valid function but, in fact, contains hidden codes that can cause damage to the system that runs the program, but does not replicate itself or infect other files as a virus does.

Trojan War *n* (*Greek myth*) a war waged against the city of Troy by a league of Greek leaders. The Trojans withstood the Greek forces for ten years, and were only defeated by the stratagem of the wooden horse.

troll *n* a supernatural creature dwelling in a cave, hill, etc.

trolley *n* (*pl* **trolleys**) a table on wheels for carrying or serving food; a cart for transporting luggage; a cart for carrying shopping in a supermarket; a device that transmits electric current from an overhead wire to a motor vehicle, such as a trolleybus.

trolleybus, trolley car *n* a bus that sometimes runs on rails and is powered by electricity from overhead wires.

trollop *n* a slovenly woman; a prostitute.—**trollopy** *adj*.

Trollope *n* 1. **Anthony** (1815–82) English novelist, whose more than 50 books are dominated by two main novel sequences: the "Barsetshire" novels and the "Palliser" novels. 2. **Frances** (1780–1863), mother of Anthony, English author whose most notable work is a bad-tempered (and very successful) study of American life, *Domestic Manners of the Americans*. 3. **Joanna** (1943–) English novelist whose novels include *The Choir* and *Next of Kin*.

tromba marina *n* (*mus*) a long, stringed instrument of the 15th century, also known as a "sea-trumpet". It consisted of a long, tapered box with one string mounted on top that was played with a bow. Inside the box were some twenty sympathetic strings.

trombone *n* (*mus*) brass musical wind instrument whose length is varied with a U-shaped sliding section. Tenor and bass trombones are often used in orchestras.

Tromsö *n* a city in the Kingdom of Norway.

Trondheim *n* a city in the Kingdom of Norway.

troop *n* a crowd of people; (*mil*) a group of soldiers within a cavalry regiment; (*pl*) armed forces; soldiers. * *vi* to go in a crowd.

trooper *n* a cavalryman; a mounted policeman or a state policeman.

troopship *n* a ship used to transport military forces.

trop. *abbr* = tropic; tropical.

trope *n* a word or phrase used in a figurative sense; (*mus*) an addition of music or words to traditional plainsong liturgy.

-trope *n suffix* turning, being attracted toward.

trophic *adj* (*med*) relating to nutrition.

tropho- (also **troph-**) *prefix* nutrition.

trophy *n* (*pl* **trophies**) a cup or shield won as a prize in a competition or contest; a memento, as taken in battle or hunting.

-trophy *n suffix* growth, nutrition.

tropic *n* (*geog*) one of the two parallel lines of latitude north and south of the equator; (*pl*) the regions lying between these lines.

-tropic *adj suffix* turning to or responding to an external stimulus.

tropical *adj* relating to the tropics; (*weather*) hot and humid.

tropical air mass *n* an air mass formed in the subtropical anticyclone belt bringing warmer weather as it moves away from the Equator, either northwards or southwards.

tropical climate *n* a climate in which mean monthly temperatures are always above 68°F (20°C) although conditions vary according to altitude and rainfall.

tropical cyclone *n* a low pressure system with very strong winds occurring within the tropics.

tropical fish *n* any of numerous species of usu brightly colored fish popular in aquariums.

tropical rainforest *n* a forest occurring in tropical areas of heavy rainfall.

tropical storm *n* a cyclone in the tropics with wind speeds less than that of a hurricane.

tropism *n* growth of a plant organ in a particular direction due to an external stimulus, e.g. touch, light.

-tropism, -tropy *n suffix* turning or developing in response to an external stimulus.

tropo- *prefix* turning or changing.

tropopause *n* the region between the troposphere and stratosphere.

troposphere *n* the earth's atmosphere between the surface and the tropopause (the boundary with the stratosphere). It contains most of the water vapor and is where most weather features occur.

-tropous *adj suffix* turning away.

troppo *n* (*mus*) (*Italian*), "too much," as in *allegro non troppo,* meaning "fast but not too fast."

Tros *n* (*Greek myth*) the king after whom Troy was named.

trot *vi* (**trotting, trotted**) (*horse*) to go, lifting the feet higher than in walking and moving at a faster rate. * *vt* (*with* **out**) (*inf*) to produce or display repeatedly, esp for others" approval; to produce in a trite or careless manner. * *n* the gait of a horse; a brisk pace.

Trotsky n Leon [Lev Davidovich Bronstein] (1879–1940) Russian revolutionary and Marxist theorist.

trotter *n* a horse trained for fast trotting; the foot of an animal, esp a pig.

troubadour *n* a minstrel; a poet or singer.

trouble *vti* to cause trouble to; to worry; to pain; to upset; to cause inconvenience; to take pains (to). * *n* an anxiety; a medical condition causing pain; a problem; unrest or disturbance.—**troublesome** *adj*.

troublemaker *n* a person who makes trouble.

troubleshoot *vti* (*comput*) to investigate the reason for a particular occurrence or malfunction in a computer system.

troubleshooter *n* a person whose work is to locate and eliminate a source of trouble or conflict.—**troubleshooting** *n*.

trough *n* a long, narrow container for water or animal feed; a channel in the ground; the lowest part of a wave between two crests; (*geog*) a U-shaped valley that has been gouged out by glacial erosion; an elongated area of low barometric pressure;.

trounce *vt* to defeat completely.

troupe *n* a traveling company, esp of actors, dancers, or acrobats.—**trouper** *n*.

trousers *npl* an item of clothing covering the body from waist to ankle, with two tubes of material for the legs; pants.

trousseau *n* (*pl* **trousseaux, trousseaus**) the clothes and linen a bride collects for her marriage.

trout *n* (*pl* **trout**) a game fish of the salmon family living in fresh water.

trove *see* **treasure trove**.

trowel *n* a hand tool for gardening; a flat-bladed tool for spreading cement, etc.

troy (**weight**) *n* a system for weighing precious stones and metals, in which one pound = 12 ounces and one ounce = 20 pennyweights or 480 grains.

Troy *n* a site near Hissarlik in Turkey which was rediscovered in 1871 by Heinrich Schliemann. Excavation has revealed that the city was rebuilt nine times.—**Trojan** *adj*.

TRRL *abbr* = Transport and Road Research Library.

trs. *abbr* = transpose; trustees.

TRSR *abbr* = taxi and runway surveillance radar.

TRSSGM *abbr* = tactical range surface-to-surface guided missile.

truant *n* a pupil who is absent from school without permission. * *vi* to play truant.—also *adj*.—**truancy** *n*.

truce *n* an agreement between two armies or states to suspend hostilities.

truck *n* a heavy motor vehicle for transporting goods; a vehicle open at the back for moving goods or animals. * *vi* to drive a truck. * *vt* (*goods*) to convey by truck.

trucker *n* a truck driver.

truculent *adj* sullen; aggressive.—**truculence** *n*. —**truculently** *adv*.

Trudeau *n* Pierre [Elliott] (1919–2000) Canadian Liberal politician. He became an MP in 1965 and was prime minister (1968–79, 1980–84). He retired from politics in 1985.

trudge *vti* to travel on foot, heavily or wearily. * *n* a tiring walk.

true *adj* (**truer, truest**) conforming with fact; correct, accurate; genuine; loyal; perfectly in tune. * *adv* truthfully; rightly.

true-blue *adj* staunchly loyal or committed.—**true blue** *n*.

truelove *n* a sweetheart.

Trueman *n* Freddy [Frederick Sewards Trueman] (1931–) English cricketer. A notable fast bowler and batsman, he played in 67 Tests.

true north and true south *n* the direction of the geographic north or south pole from the observer. It differs from the direction of the magnetic poles.

TrueType *n, adj* (*trademark*) (*comput*) a scalable font technology that displays on-screen fonts exactly as the printer prints them, and does not require any special printer processors, making it portable between systems.

Truffaut *n* François (1932–84) French film director, critic and actor; one of the Cahiers du Cinema group of film critics. His films include Jules et Jim (1961) and *The Last Metro* (1980).

truffle *n* a round, edible underground fungus; a sweet made with chocolate, butter, and sugar.

truism *n* a self-evident truth.

Trujillo *n* a city in Peru.

truly *adv* completely; genuinely; to a great degree.

Truman *n* **Harry S** (1884–1972) American Democratic statesman. He became 33rd president of the US (1945–52) after Franklin D. Roosevelt's death.

trump *n* the suit that is chosen to have the highest value in one game of cards. * *vt* to play a trump card on; (with up) to invent maliciously, fabricate (an accusation, etc).

trump card *n* any card of a suit chosen as trump; an advantageous action, resource, etc.

trumpery *adj* worthless. * *n* (*pl* **trumperies**) foolish talk, nonsense; a worthless article.

trumpet *n* (*mus*) a brass wind instrument consisting of a long tube with a flared end and three buttons; any number of very different wind instruments that are found all over the world.* *vti* to proclaim loudly.—**trumpeter** *n*.

trumpeter swan *n* a rare wild North American swan with a black bill.

truncate *vt* to cut the top end off; to shorten; (*comput*) to cut off part of an entry (a number or character string) so that it fits a predefined space or is easier to process.—**truncation** *n*.

truncheon *n* a short, thick club carried by a policeman.

trundle *vt* (*an object*) to push or pull on wheels. * *vi* to move along slowly.

trunk *n* the main stem of a tree; the torso; the main body of anything; the proboscis of an elephant; a strong box or chest for clothes, etc, esp on a journey; storage space at the rear of a car; (*pl*) a man's short, light pants for swimming.

trunk line *n* a transportation system handling through traffic; a communications system.

trunk road *n* a main road.

trunnion *n* one of a pair of projections used to support an object.

truss *n* (*med*) a device that consists of a pad attached to a belt with spring straps to maintain its position, worn under clothing to support a hernia; (*archit*) a number of timbers joined together to form a frame to carry other timbers. * *vt* to bind (up).

trust *n* firm belief in the truth of anything, faith in a person; confidence in; custody; a financial arrangement by which assets are held and managed by the trustee for the benefit of some other person, called the beneficiary; (*com*) a business syndicate. * *adj* held in trust. * *vti* to have confidence in; to believe.—**trustful** *adj*.

trust company *n* (*com*) a company that functions as a corporate and personal trustee.

trustee *see* **trust**.

trust fund *n* (*com*) a fund that consists of the assets belonging to a trust.

trustworthy *adj* reliable, dependable.

trusty *adj* (**trustier, trustiest**) trustworthy, faithful. * *n* a prisoner granted special privileges as a trustworthy person.—**trustily** *adv*.—**trustiness** *n*.

truth *n* that which is true, factual or genuine; agreement with reality.

truthful *adj* telling the truth; accurate, realistic; honest, frank.—**truthfulness** *n*.

try *vb* (**trying, tried**) *vt* to test the result or effect by experiment; to determine judicially; to put strain on; (*with* **on**) to put (a garment) on to check the fit, etc; (*inf*) to attempt to deceive somebody; (*with* **out**) to test (someone) for a job, etc. * *vi* to attempt; to make an effort; (*with* **out**) to undergo a test (for a job, team, etc). * *n* (*pl* **tries**) an attempt, an effort; (*rugby football*) a score made with a touchdown.

trying *adj* causing annoyance, exasperating.—**tryingly** *adv*.—**tryingness** *n*.

try-on *n* (*inf*) a trying on of clothes to check the fit; an attempt to deceive.

tryout *n* an experimental test; an audition for a theatrical part; a test for a position in a team.

trypanosome *n* any of genus of parasitic worms that infest the blood of animals and humans and can cause sleeping sickness.

trypanosomiasis *n* (*med*) (a disease caused by) infection with trypanosomes. *See also* **sleeping sickness**.

trypsin *n* (*med*) an enzyme in the pancreas involved in digestion.—**tryptic** *adj*.

tryptophan, tryptophane *n* an amino acid found in proteins which is essential to life.

try square *n* an L-shaped instrument for drawing and testing right angles.

tryst *n* an appointment to meet secretly.

ts *abbr* = tensile strength.

t.s. *abbr* = tensile strength; test solution; transport and supply; (paper) tubsized.

t/s *abbr* = transshipment.

TS *abbr* = Television Society; Theosophical Society; Tolkien Society; Tourism Society; Training Ship; transsexual; typescript.

TSA *abbr* = The Securities Association; Tourette Syndrome Association; Training Services Agency; Trust for the Study of Adolescence Limited; Tuberous Sclerosis Association of Great Britain; (*med*) tumour-specific antigen.

tsar *n* the title of the emperors of Russia until 1917, and sovereigns of certain other Slav nations; a powerful person.—*also* **czar, tzar**.

tsarevitch *n* the eldest son of a tsar.—*also* **czarevitch, tzarevitch**.

tsarina, tsaritsa *n* the wife of a tsar; an empress.—*also* **czarina, tzarina**.

TSB *abbr* = Textile Statistics Bureau; (*Brit*) Trustee Savings Bank.

TSBA *abbr* (*Brit*) = Trustee Savings Banks Association.

Tschichold *n* Jan (1902–74) German typographer and design theorist who designed many innovative posters and books.

TSE *abbr* = transmissible spongiform encephalopathy.

tsetse fly *n* a fly that feeds on blood and transmits diseases.

Tsetserleg *n* a city in Mongolia.

TSFA *abbr* = The Securities and Futures Authority.

TSG *abbr* = Tibet Support Group.

TSgt *abbr* = Technical Sergeant.

TSH *abbr* = Their Serene Highnesses; (*med*) thyroid-stimulating hormone.

T-shirt *n* a short-sleeved casual cotton top.—*also* **tee-shirt**.

TSH-RF *abbr* = (*med*) thyroid-stimulating-hormone-releasing factor.

tsi *abbr* = tons per square inch.

TSI *abbr* = Transportation Safety Institute

TSO *abbr* = Trading Standards Officer; TRICARE Support Office; town sub-office.

tsp. *abbr* = teaspoon.

TSP *abbr* = Thrift Savings Plan; textured soya protein.

T-square *n* a T-shaped instrument for drawing and determining right angles.

t.s.r. *abbr* = traveling stock reserve.

TSR *abbr* = Trans-Siberian Railway; tactical strike reconnaissance; terminate and stay resident.

TSRB *abbr* = Top Salaries Review Body.

TSS *abbr* = Turner's Syndrome Society; time-sharing system; toxic shock syndrome.

TSSA *abbr* = Transport Salaried Staffs Association.

TSU *abbr* = this side up.

tsunami *n* (*pl* **tsunamis, tsunami**) a large sea wave produced by underwater earthquakes or volcanic eruptions.—**tsunamic** *adj.*

tsvp, TSVP *abbr* (*French*) = *Tournez, s'il vous plaît*, "Please turn over."

TSW *abbr* (*Brit*) = Television South West.

TT *abbr* = Transport Trust; teetotal; telegraphic transfer; time trial; tuberculin tested.

T Tauri star *n* (*astron*) a type of very young star or protostar that has just condensed out of the interstellar medium, and is rapidly throwing off material and contracting.

T Tauri wind *n* (*astron*) a rapid outflowing of material from a T Tauri star, resembling a solar wind but with a much greater loss of matter.

TTAW *abbr* (*Brit*) = Table Tennis Association of Wales.

TTBT *abbr* = Threshold Test Ban Treaty.

TTF *abbr* = Timber Trade Federation.

TTFN *abbr* = ta-ta for now.

t.t.l. *abbr* = to take leave.

TTL *abbr* = through the lens.

TTNS *abbr* (*Brit*) = The Times Network Systems (database system for schools).

TTRA *abbr* (*Brit*) = Tourist Trophy Riders' Association.

TTS *abbr* = Transport Ticket Society; teletypesetting.

TTT *abbr* = team time trial.

TTTA *abbr* = Timber Trade Training Association.

T type asteroid *n* (*astron*) an asteroid belonging to a class that has a very low albedo.

Tu. *abbr* = Tuesday.

TU *abbr* = Tupolev (Soviet aircraft manufacturer); (*Brit*) trade union; transmission unit.

TUA abbr = Telecommunications Users' Association; Tractor Users Association.

Tuan mac Carell *n* (*Irish Celtic myth*) the son of Starn, brother of Partholan. He is supposed to have survived a plague that destroyed most other people and to have been reborn as a stag.

Tuatha De Danann *n* (*Irish Celtic myth*) "people of the goddess Danu" the gods of pre-Christian Ireland. When the Tuatha De Danann arrived in Ireland, they fought two great battles, the first against the previous invaders, the Fir Bholg, and the second against the Fomorii.

tub *n* a circular container, made of staves and hoops; a bathtub.

tuba *n* (*mus*) a large brass instrument of bass pitch.

tubal *n* of or relating to a tube, esp the bronchial or Fallopian tubes.

tubby *adj* (**tubbier, tubbiest**) plump.

TUBCS *abbr* = Trade Union Badge Collectors' Society.

tube *n* a long, thin, hollow pipe; a soft metal or plastic cylinder in which thick liquids or pastes, such as toothpaste, are stored; (*inf*) in London, the underground railway system.—**tubular** *adj.*

TUBE *abbr* = The Union of Bookmakers' Employees.

tubeless tire *n* a tire that remains airtight without requiring an inner tube.

tuber *n* (*bot*) the swollen, fleshy root of a plant where reserves of food are stored up, as a potato.

tubercle *n* (*med*) a small rounded knob on a bone, or a minute nodular tissue that is characteristic of tuberculosis.

tubercle bacillus *n* a bacterium that causes tuberculosis.

tuberculate *adj* (*med*) affected with tubercles.—**tuberculation** *n.*

tuberculin *n* (*med*) a sterile liquid prepared with weakened tubercle bacillus and used in the diagnosis of tuberculosis.

tuberculosis *n* (*med*) a group of infections caused by the bacillus *Mycobacterium tuberculosis*, of which pulmonary tuberculosis of the lungs (consumption or phthisis) is the best-known form.

tubercular *adj.*

tuberose *n* a bulbous Mexican plant with fragrant white flowers.

tuberous *adj* forming or resembling tubers.

tubing *n* tubes collectively; a length of tube; the material from which tubes are made; a circular fabric.

tub-thumper *n* a passionate or aggressive public speaker.

tubular bells *npl* (*mus*) an orchestral percussion instrument consisting of a set of long metal tubes played with a mallet to simulate the sounds of bells.

tubule *n* (*anat*) a small tube-like structure in the body, as in the kidney, testicle, etc.

TUC *abbr* (*Brit*) = Trades Union Congress.

Tucana *or* **The Toucan** *n* (*astron*) a constellation in the southern hemisphere, first depicted in 1603 in the star atlas of Johann Bayer. It lies near Grus (The Crane) and contains the Small Magellanic Cloud.

TUCC *abbr* (*Brit*) = Trades Union Congress General Council.

tuck *vt* to draw or gather together in a fold; (*with* **up**) to wrap snugly. * *vi* (*inf*) (*with* **into**) to eat greedily. * *n* a fold in a garment.

tucker *vt* (*inf*) to exhaust, tire (out).

Tuckwell *n* **Barry** (1931-) an Australian horn-player who has lived in Britain since 1951. He has played as a soloist with many leading chamber orchestras and has formed his own quintet, known as the Tuckwell Wing Quintet.

Tue., Tues. *abbr* = Tuesday.

Tuesday *n* the third day of the week.

tufa *n* (*geol*) a type of porous rock deposited from springs.

tuff *n* (*geol*) a type of volcanic rock composed of fused lava ash.

tuffet *n* a small low seat; a clump of grass.

tuft *n* a bunch of grass, hair, or feathers held together at the base; a clump.

TUG *abbr* = Telephone Users' Group.

tug *vti* (**tugging, tugged**) to pull with effort or to drag along. * *n* a strong pull; a tugboat.

tugboat *n* a small powerful boat for towing ships.

tug of love *n* a conflict over the custody of a child between separated parents, etc.

tug of war *n* a contest in which two teams tug on opposite ends of a rope to pull the opposing team over a central line; a struggle for supremacy between two opponents.

tugrik *n* the standard monetary unit of Mongolia, made up of 100 mongos.

TUI *abbr* = Trade Unions International of Public and Allied Employees.

TUIAFPW *abbr* = Trade Unions International of Agricultural, Forestry and Plantation Workers.

Tuireann *n* (*Irish Celtic myth*) 1. the wife of Illan. When she was pregnant, she was turned into a wolfhound by her husband's mistress. Instead of giving birth to children, Tuireann gave birth to two wolfhounds, Bran and Sgeolan, who became the faithful hunting hounds of Fionn mac Cumhaill. 2. *See* **Tuirenn**.

Tuirenn *or* **Tuireann** *n* (*Irish Celtic myth*) the father of Brian, Iuchar and Iucharba, possibly by the goddess Brigid.

TUIREG *abbr* = Trade Unions International Research and Education Group.

tuition *n* teaching, instruction.

TUIWC *abbr* = Trade Unions International of Workers in Commerce.

TUIWE *abbr* = Trade Unions International of Workers in Energy.

tulip *n* a highly-colored cup-shaped flower grown from bulbs.

tulip tree *n* a North American tree with large tulip-shaped flowers.

tulipwood *n* the soft white wood of the tulip tree used in making furniture.

tulle *n* a delicate semi-transparent fabric of rayon, silk, etc, used for scarves and veils.

Tullus Hostilius *n* (*hist*) the third legendary king of Rome and successor to Numa Pompilius.

Tully–Fisher relation *n* (*astron*) a method of determining the distances of remote spiral galaxies which was devised in 1977 by B Tully and R Fisher.

tumbaga *n* an alloy of copper and gold which was extensively used for metal work in South America.

tumble *vi* to fall over; to roll or to twist the body, as an acrobat; (*with* **to**) (*inf*) to discover (a secret, etc); to understand. * *vt* to push or cause to fall. * *n* a fall; a somersault.

tumbledown *adj* dilapidated, crumbling.

tumble-dry *vt* (*clothes*) to dry by rotating with warm air in a machine.—**tumble dryer** *n.*

tumbler *n* a large drinking glass without a handle or stem; an acrobat.

tumbler switch *n* a simple electrical switch used in lighting.

tumbleweed *n* a plant that detaches from its roots and is blown around by the wind.

tumbrel, tumbril *n* a farm cart that tips up to deposit its load; (*hist*) a cart of similar design used to carry prisoners to the guillotine during the French Revolution.

tumescent *adj* swollen or beginning to swell.

tumid *adj* swollen, distended; pompous, bombastic.—**tumidly** *adv.*—**tumidity** *n.*

tummy *n* (*pl* **tummies**) (*inf*) stomach.

tumor *n* (*med*) an abnormal swelling in any part of the body, which consists of an unusual growth of tissue and may be malignant or benign.

tumult *n* a commotion; an uproar.

tumultuous *adj* disorderly; rowdy, noisy; restless.—**tumultuously** *adv.*—**tumultuousness** *n.*

tumulus *n* (*pl* **tumuli**) (*archeo*) another name for a burial mound or cairn.

Tumulus culture *n* (*archeo*) a Bronze Age culture, centered originally in Bavaria, which flourished 1800–1500 BC.

tun *n* a large wine or beer cask; a unit of capacity equal to about 252 wine gallons (954 liters).

tuna *n* (*pl* **tuna, tunas**) a large ocean fish of the mackerel group.

tundra *n* the treeless region between the snow and ice of the Arctic and the northern extent of tree growth, found in northern Canada, Alaska, northern Siberia and northern Scandinavia.

tune *n* a melody; correct musical pitch; harmony. * *vt* (*musical instrument*) to adjust the notes of; (*radio, TV etc*) to adjust the resonant frequency, etc, to a particular value; (*with* **up**) to adjust an engine to improve its performance. * *vi* (*with* **up**) to adjust (musical instruments) to a common pitch before playing.—**tuneful** *adj.*—**tunefully** *adv.*

tuner *n* a person who tunes musical instruments; a device that tunes a radio or television receiver.

tune-up *n* an adjustment of a musical instrument to correct pitch or of an engine to improve its performance.

tungsten *n* (*chem*) a hard malleable grayish-white metallic element used in lamps, etc, and in alloys with steel.

Tunguska event *n* an enormous and violent explosion which took place in the Tunguska region of Siberia in 1908 on June 30, believed to have been caused by the explosion of a meteorite, comet nucleus or asteroid 5.3 miles above the earth's surface.

tunic *n* a hip or knee-length loose, usu belted blouse-like garment; a close-fitting jacket worn by soldiers and policemen.

tunicate *n* any of a group of small primitive marine animals with sac-shaped bodies enclosed in a thick membrane. * *adj* having or enclosed in a membrane; (*bulbs*) made up from concentric layers of tissue.

tuning see **tune**.

tuning fork *n* (*mus*) a two-pronged steel device which, when tapped, will sound a single, "pure" note. It was invented by John Shore in 1711 and is used to tune instruments etc.

Tunis *n* capital city of Tunisia.

Tunisia *n* a republic in north Africa that lies on the south coast of the Mediterranean Sea.

tunnel *n* an underground passage, esp one for cars or trains underneath a river or town center. * *vb* (**tunneling, tunneled** *or* **tunnelling, tunnelled**) *vt* to make a way through. * *vi* to make a tunnel.

tunnel handle *n* a "handle" made by piercing two holes through the side of a pot so that the fingers can be inserted.

tunnel vision *n* (*med*) a condition in which peripheral vision is impaired; a narrowness of viewpoint due to preoccupation with a single idea, plan, etc.

tunny *n* (*pl* **tunnies, tunny**) tuna.

tuppence *n* twopence.

Tupper *n* **Earl** (1907–83) American chemist who founded Tupper Plastic in 1942 and devised the "Tupperware Party" method of marketing.

Tura *n* (*Egypt*) a site at the apex of the Delta, on the eastern bank from Saqqara in Egypt; much of the best building limestone came from the famous quarries at this site.

turban *n* a headdress consisting of cloth wound in folds around the head worn by men; a woman's hat of this shape.

turbid *adj* muddy; dense; thick.—**turbidity** *n*. —**turbidly** *adv*.

turbidite *n* (*geol*) a sedimentary rock type, deposited by a turbidity current, which reveals clear layers of sediment, the heaviest at the bottom

turbidity current *n* a current in water that is loaded with sediment, producing a gravity-controlled body of water and sediment that is denser than the surrounding water.

turbine *n* a machine in which power is produced when the forced passage of steam, water, etc causes blades to rotate.

turbo- *prefix* of, driven or powered by a turbine.

turbocharger *n* a supercharger driven by a turbine powered by the exhaust gases of an engine.

turbofan *n* a jet engine with a large fan that forces air out with the exhaust gases to increase thrust; an aircraft with such engines; the fan in such an engine.

turbogenerator *n* an electrical generator driven by a steam turbine.

turbojet *n* (an aircraft with) a turbojet engine.

turbojet engine *n* a gas turbine that provides propulsive power from a jet of hot exhaust gases.

turboprop *n* a jet aircraft engine that also operates a turbine-driven air compressor.

turbot *n* (*pl* **turbot, turbots**) a large, flat, round edible fish.

turbulence *n* a state of confusion and disorder; instability causing gusty air currents.

turbulent *adj* disturbed, in violent commotion.

turd *n* (*vulg*) a piece of excrement; (*vulg sl*) a despicable person.

tureen *n* a large dish for serving soup, etc.

turf *n* (*pl* **turfs, turves**) the surface layer of grass and its roots; (sport) (*with* **the**) a racetrack in horse racing. * *vt* to cover with turf; (*with* **out**) (*inf*) to eject forcibly, throw out.

turf line *n* (*archeo*) a darker layer in an excavation trench which marks the presence of buried turf.

turf war *n* a dispute over an area, or land claimed by one party as being under its control in the face of the claims of another individual or group.

Turgenev *n* **Ivan Sergeyevich** (1818–83) Russian novelist, short-story writer and dramatist. The best known of his plays is A *Month in the Country* (1850).

turgid *adj* swollen; pompous, bombastic.—**turgidity** *n*.—**turgidly** *adv*.

Turin, Torino *n* a city in Italy.

Turin Canon *n* an Egyptian king list, written on a fragmentary papyrus roll, now preserved in the Egyptian Museum, Turin.

Turing *n* **Alan Mathison** (1912–54) English mathematician; developed the concept of an idealized computer called the "Universal Automaton" (later known as the "Turing Machine"); worked on the "Enigma" code-breaking project at Bletchley Park in World War II.

Turk *n* a native or inhabitant of Turkey; any speaker of a Turkic language.

Turk. *abbr* = Turkey; Turkish.

turkey *n* (*pl* **turkeys, turkey**) a large bird farmed for its meat.

Turkey *n* a republic spanning the continents of Europe and Asia.

turkey buzzard *n* an American vulture.

turkey cock *n* a male turkey.

Turkey red *n* (a cotton fabric of) a bright red color.

Turkic *n* a branch of the Altaic family of languages including Turkish, Tartar, etc.— **Turkic**, adj

Turkish *adj* pertaining to Turkey, its people or their language. * *n* the official language of Turkey.

Turkish bath *n* a bath with steam rooms, showers, massage, etc.

Turkish coffee *n* strong black (usu sweetened) coffee.

Turkish delight *n* a jelly-like flower-flavored sweet covered with icing sugar.

Turkish lira *n* currency of Turkey.

Turkmenbashi *n* city in Turkmenistan.

Turkmenistan *n* a central Asian republic of the former USSR.

Turks and Caicos Islands *n* a British Crown Colony comprising two island groups which form the southeastern archipelago of the Bahamas in the Atlantic Ocean.

Turk's-cap lily *n* a variety of lily with purple-red flowers found in Europe and Asia; martagon lily.

Turku *n* a city in Finland.

turmeric *n* a tropical Indian plant; the powdered stem of this plant used as a yellow coloring agent and curry spice.

turmoil *n* agitation; disturbance, confusion.

turn *vi* to revolve; to go in the opposite direction; to depend on; to appeal (to) for help; to direct (thought or attention) away from; to change in character; to be shaped on the lathe; (*with* **off**) to leave or deviate from a road, etc; (*with* **in**) (*inf*) to retire to bed for the night; (*with* **on**) to depend on; (*sl*) to take drugs; (*with* **to**) to begin a task; (*with* **up**) to appear, arrive; to find unexpectedly; to happen without warning. * *vt* to change the position or direction of by revolving; to reverse; to transform; (*age, etc*) to have just passed; to change or convert; to invert; (*with* **off**) to cause to cease operating (as if) by flicking a switch, turning a knob, etc; (*inf*) to cause a person to lose interest in or develop a dislike for something; (*with* **down**) to reduce the volume or intensity of (sound, brightness, etc); to refuse, decline; to fold down (sheets, a collar, etc); (*with* **in**) to deliver; to produce, record (a performance, score, etc); (*with* **on**) to cause to begin operating (as if) by flicking a switch, turning a knob, etc; (*sl*) to arouse or excite, esp sexually; (*sl*) to introduce (a person) to drugs; (*with* **up**) to discover, uncover; to increase the volume or intensity of (sound, brightness, etc). * *n* a rotation; new direction or tendency; a place in sequence; a turning point, crisis; performer's act; an act of kindness or malice; a bend.

turnabout *n* a reversal of position, opinion, attitude, etc.

turnbuckle *n* a mechanical link with a screw thread at one end and a swivel at the other, used for tightening a threaded wire or rope.

turncoat *n* a deserter, renegade.

turner *n* a person who operates a lathe.

Turner *n* 1. **Joseph Mallord William** (1775–1851) English painter whose most notable works include *The Fighting Téméraire (1839)*. 2. **Tina** [Annie Mae Bullock] (1940–) American singer. A performer of long-lasting popularity, her albums include *Private Dancer* (1984).

Turner's syndrome *n* (*med*) a genetic disorder affecting females in which there is only one X-chromosome instead of the usual two.

turning *n* a road, path, etc that leads off from a main way; the point where it leads off; a bend; the art of shaping objects on a lathe. * *n* an object so made; (*pl*) waste produced on a lathe.

turning point *n* the point at which a significant change occurs.

turnip *n* (*bot*) a plant with a large white or yellow root, cultivated as a vegetable.

turnout *n* a gathering of people.

turnover *n* the volume of business transacted in a given period; a fruit or meat pasty; the rate of replacement of workers.

turnpike *n* a toll road, esp one that is an expressway.

turnround *n* (the time required to complete) the unloading and reloading of a ship, aircraft, etc.

turn-round rate *n* in the stock exchange, the total cost of a transaction on a commodity market.

turnstile *n* a mechanical gate across a footpath or entrance which admits only one person at a time.

turntable *n* a circular, horizontal revolving platform, as in a record player.

turn-up *n* (*Brit*) the cuff of a trouser; (*inf*) a surprise.

Turnus *n* (*Roman myth*) king of the Rutulians, who fought against and was killed by Aeneas after his landing in Italy.

turp *abbr* = (*med*) trans-urethral resection of the prostate.

turpentine *n* an oily resin secreted by coniferous trees, used as a solvent and thinner for paints.—*also* **turps**.

turpentine tree *n* a terebinth or related tree that yields a turpentine.

turpitude *n* depravity; wickedness.

turps *n sing* (*inf*) turpentine.

turquoise *n* an opaque greenish-blue mineral, valued as a gem; the color of turquoise.—*also adj*.

turret *n* a small tower on a building rising above it; a dome or revolving structure for guns, as on a warship, tank, or airplane.—**turreted** *adj*.

turtle *n* any of an order of land, freshwater, or marine reptiles having a soft body encased in a hard shell; **to turn turtle** to turn upside down.

turtledove *n* a brown dove with speckled wings and a dark tail, noted for its cooing and its care for its partner and young.

turtleneck *n* a high close-fitting neckline on a sweater.

turves *see* **turf**.

tus. *abbr* = tussis.

tusk *n* a long, projecting tooth on either side of the mouth, as of the elephant.—**tusked** *adj*.

tusker *n* an animal with tusks.

tussle *n* a scuffle.

tussock *n* a dense tuft of grass.

Tutankhamen, Tutankhamun *n* (1361–1352 BC) a boy king of ancient Egypt. His tomb survived unviolated until 1922, when it was discovered and opened by Howard Carter; its magnificence stunned the world.

tutelage *n* guardianship; guidance by a tutor.

Tuthmosis I *n* Egyptian pharaoh of the 18th Dynasty (ruled 1506–1493 BC).

Tuthmosis II *n* Egyptian pharaoh of the 18th Dynasty (ruled 1493–1479 BC); son of Tuthmosis I.

Tuthmosis III *n* Egyptian pharaoh of the 18th Dynasty (ruled 1479–1425 BC); one of the great kings of Egypt, who acceded at the age of six; son of Tuthmosis II.

Tuthmosis IV *n* Egyptian pharaoh of the 18th Dynasty (ruled 1401–1390 BC); succeeded Amenophis II.

tutor *n* a private teacher who instructs pupils individually; (*Brit*) a member of staff responsible for the supervision and teaching of students. * *vt* to instruct; to act as a tutor.

tutorial *n* a period of tuition by a tutor to an individual or a small group. * *adj* of or pertaining to a tutor.

tutti *adj, adv* (*mus*) all together, to be performed by the whole orchestra. * *n* a musical piece or passage so performed.

tutti-frutti *n* (*pl* **tutti-fruttis**) (*Italian*) a type of ice cream containing pieces of chopped candied fruits.

tut-tut *interj* an exclamation of impatience or mild disapproval. * *vi* (**tut-tutting, tut-tutted**) to express disapproval or impatience by uttering "tut-tut."

tutu *n* a short, projecting, layered skirt worn by a ballerina.

tutulus *n* a circular, bronze, decorative object worn by women during the Bronze Age in Denmark; a short, defensive ditch across the approach to a Roman camp.

Tuvalu *n* a constitutional monarchy located just north of Fiji in the South Pacific, comprising nine coral atolls.

Tuvalu dollar, Australian dollar *n* currency of Tuvalu.

tu-whit tu-whoo *interj* an imitation of the cry of an owl.

tuxedo, tux *n* a man's semi-formal suit with a tailless jacket.

tuyère *n* the ceramic tip of a blowtube used in the smelting of copper in South America.

Tuzla *n* city in Bosnia-Herzegovina.

TV *abbr* = television; transvestism; transvestite.

TVA *abbr* = Tennessee Valley Authority; (*French*) *taxe sur la valeur ajoutée*, "value-added tax."

TVE *abbr* = Television Trust for the Environment.

TVP *abbr* = textured vegetable protein (a meat substitute used in vegetarian dishes).

TVRO *abbr* = television, receive only (type of antenna).

TVU *abbr* (*Brit*) = Thames Valley University.

TWA *abbr* = Tibetan Women's Association; Trans-World Airlines.

twaddle *n* utter rubbish in speech or writing. * *vi* to speak or write twaddle.

twain[1] *adj, n* (*arch*) two.

twain[2] *n* (*comput*) a standard that allows a document to be scanned without leaving the application into which the image is to be inserted.

Twain *n* Mark [**Samuel Langhorne Clemens**] (1835–1910) American novelist, short-story writer and humorist. His two most famous novels are The Adventures of Tom Sawyer (1876) and The Adventures of Huckleberry Finn (1884).

twang *n* a sharp, vibrant sound, as of a taut string when plucked; a nasal tone of voice. * *vt* to make a twanging sound.

'twas (*poet*) = it was.

twat *n* an idiot; (*vulg*) the female genitals.

tweak *vt* to twist, pinch, or pull with sudden jerks. * *n* a sharp pinch or twist.

twee *adj* (*inf*) excessively quaint, affected.

tweed *n* a twilled woolen fabric used in making clothes.

'tween *prep* (*arch*) between.

tweet *interj* an imitation of the chirp of a small bird. * *vi* to make this sound.

tweeter *n* a small loudspeaker for reproducing high-frequency sounds.

tweezers *n sing* small pincers used for plucking.

twelfth *adj* the last of twelve; being one of twelve equal parts.

Twelfth Day *n* (*eccles*) Epiphany.

twelfth man *n* the reserve member of a cricket team.

Twelfth Night *n* (*eccles*) the evening of Epiphany, the twelfth day after Christmas, January 6.

twelve *adj* the cardinal number next after eleven. * *symbol* 12, XII, xii.

twelvemo *n* a book of sheets folded into twelve leaves; this book size.—*also* **duodecimo**.

twelve-tone *adj* (*mus*) pertaining to a type of serial music using only the twelve semitones of the chromatic scale as a tone row for compositions.

twenty *adj, n* two times ten. * *n* (*pl* **twenties**). * *symbol* 20, XX, xx.—**twentieth** *adj*.

twenty-one *n* pontoon (card game); blackjack.

twenty-twenty, 20/20 *adj* normal vision

'twere (*poet*) = it were.

twerp *n* (*inf*) a foolish or contemptible person.—*also* **twirp**.

TWh *abbr* = terawatt hour.

twice *adv* two times; two times as much; doubly.

twiddle *vt* to twirl or fiddle with idly.

TWIF *abbr* = Tug of War International Federation.

twig[1] *n* a small branch or shoot of a tree.—**twiggy** *adj*.

twig[2] *vti* (**twigging, twigged**) (*inf*) to grasp the meaning of.

twilight *n* a period after sunset and before sunrise when the sky is partially lit up by scattered light rays from the sun; the final stages of something.

twilight area *n* a rundown area in a city.

twilit *adj* lit by twilight.

twill *n* a cloth woven in such a way as to produce diagonal lines across it.—**twilled** *adj*.

TWIMC *abbr* = to whom it may concern.

twin *n* either of two persons or animals born at the same birth; one thing resembling another. * *adj* double; very like another; consisting of two parts nearly alike. * *vt* (**twinning, twinned**) to pair together.

twin bed *n* one of a pair of single beds.

twine *n* a string of twisted fibers or hemp. * *vti* to twist together; to wind around.

twin-engined *adj* (*mech*) having two engines.

twinge *n* a sudden, stabbing pain; an emotional pang.

twinkle *vi* to sparkle; to flicker.

twinkling *n* a wink; an instant; the shining of the stars.

twin-screw *adj* having two propellers.

twinset *n* a jumper and cardigan designed to be worn together.

twin-tub *n* a washing machine with two drums, one for washing and the other for spin-drying.

twirl *vt* to whirl; to rotate; to wind or twist. * *vi* to turn around rapidly.

twirp *see* **twerp**.

twist *vt* to unite by winding together; to coil; to confuse or distort (the meaning of); to bend. * *vi* to revolve; to writhe. * *n* the act or result of twisting; a twist of thread; a curve or bend; an unexpected event; a wrench.

twister *n* a waterspout or a tornado; (*inf*) a dishonest person, a swindler.

twisty *adj* (**twistier, twistiest**) winding.

twit[1] *vt* (**twitting, twitted**) to tease or reproach. * *n* a nervous state.

twit[2] *n* (*Brit inf*) a silly or foolish person.

twitch *vt* to pull with a sudden jerk. * *vi* to be suddenly jerked. * *n* a sudden muscular spasm.

twitter *n* a chirp, as of a bird. * *vi* to chirp.

two *adj, n* the cardinal number next above one. * *symbol* 2, II, ii.

TWOC *abbr* = taking without owner's consent.

two-cycle *see* **two-stroke**.

two-dimensional *adj* of or having two dimensions; lacking (the illusion of) depth.

two-edged *adj* having two cutting edges; (*remark, etc*) double-edged.

two-faced *adj* deceitful, hypocritical.

twofold *adj* multiplied by two; double. * *adv* doubly.

two-handed *adj* having or needing two hands; ambidextrous; requiring two people.

twopence *n* the sum of two pence; (*Brit*) a coin of this value; something of little value.—*also* **tuppence**.

two-piece *n* a garment consisting of two separate matching bits.—*also adj*.

two-ply *adj* made of two thicknesses or strands.

twosome *n* a group of two; a game for two people.

Twosre *n* (*Egypt*) the last female king of Egypt (ruled 1196–1188 BC); she took power in the turbulent and anarchic period at the end of the 19th Dynasty, after the death of her stepson, Siptah.

two-step *n* (*mus*) the music for) a ballroom dance in duple time.

two-stroke *n, adj* of an internal combustion engine, having a piston which makes two strokes for every explosion.—*also* **two-cycle**.

two-tier tender offer *n* (*com*) a tender offer in a takeover bid in which a high initial offer is made to shareholders for enough shares to be acquired by the bidder to ensure a controlling interest in the company. This is followed by an offer to purchase the rest of the shares at a lower price.

two-time *vti* (*sl*) to be unfaithful to (a lover, etc); to double-cross.—**two-timer** *n*.

two-tone *adj* of two colors or shades of the same color; of sirens, etc, having two notes.

two-way *adj* allowing movement or operation in two (opposite) directions; involving two participants; involving mutual obligation; of radio, capable of transmitting and receiving messages.

two-way mirror *n* a sheet of glass that reflects as a mirror on one side but can be seen through from the other.

'twould (*poet*) = it would.

twp. *abbr* = township.

TWR *abbr* = Trans World Radio.

Twrch Trwyth *n* (*Welsh Celtic myth*) a fierce boar who had been a king before being transformed. In Irish Celtic mythology, Torc Triath was his equivalent.

TWS *abbr* = Tasmanian Wilderness Society; The Wilderness Society; The Wildlife Society.

TWU *abbr* = Theatre Writers' Union; Tobacco Workers' Union.

TX *abbr* = Texas.

Ty. *abbr* = Territory.

Tyche *n* (*Greek myth*) the personification of chance or luck, the equivalent of the Roman Fortuna.

Tycho's star *n* (*astron*) a supernova of type I, situated in the constellation Cassiopeia, first seen in 1572 and carefully studied by Tycho Brae.

tycoon *n* a powerful industrialist, etc.

tyke *n* a (mongrel) dog; (*inf*) a cheeky child.—*also* **tike**.

Tyler *n* **John** (1790–1862) 10th president of the US (1841–45).

Tylwyth Teg *n* (*Welsh Celtic myth*) the collective name given to the people of Gwyn ap Nudd.

tympani *see* **timpani**.

tympanic bone *n* (*anat*) a bone enclosing part of the middle ear and supporting the tympanic membrane.

tympanic membrane *n* (*anat*) the eardrum, which separates the middle and outer ears and vibrates in response to sound waves.

tympanites *n* (*med*) distension of the abdomen caused by the accumulation of gas in the intestine.—**tympanitic** *adj*.

tympanum *n* (*pl* **tympanums, tympana**) (*anat*) the cavity of the middle ear; the tympanic membrane, eardrum; (*archit*) the space between the lintel of a doorway and the enclosing arch; (*archit*) the (recessed) triangular face of a pediment.

Tynan *n* **Kenneth [Peacock]** (1927–80) English theatre critic noted for his sharp wit and vigorous promotion of the new "kitchen sink" drama of the mid–1950s.

Tyndale *n* **William** (*c*.1495–1536) English humanist and principal translator of the Authorized Version of the Bible who was burnt at the stake for his Protestant beliefs. *See also* **More, Sir Thomas**.

Tyndareus *n* (*Greek myth*) a king of Sparta and husband of Leda.

typ., typo., typog. *abbr* = typographer; typographic; typographical; typography.

type *n* a kind, class or group; sort; model; a block of metal for printing letters; style of print. * *vt* to write by means of a typewriter; to classify.

-type *n suffix* of the form specified; printing process.

type ahead buffer *n* (*comput*) a memory buffer that stores the characters being typed on the keyboard so that they can be processed by the RAM when the processor is free.

typecast *vt* (**typecasting, typecast**) to cast in the same role repeatedly because of physical appearance, etc.

typeface *n* the printing surface of a type character; a particular design of a set of type characters.

typescript *n* a typed copy of a book, document, etc.

typeset *vt* (**typesetting, typeset**) to set in type.—**typesetter** *n*.

type site *n* (*archeo*) the site, often the first one to be discovered, that yields typical artifacts of a particular culture and after which that culture is usually named.

type style *n* refers to the weight of type or the slope of the type as opposed to the size of the type or the typeface.

typewriter *n* a keyboard machine for printing characters.

typhoid *or* **typhoid fever** *n* (*med*) a severe infectious disease of the digestive system acquired by ingesting contaminated food or water. * *adj* of or pertaining to typhoid fever.—*also* **typhoidal**.

Typhon, Typhoeus *n* (*Greek myth*) a monster, described sometimes as a destructive hurricane and sometimes as a fire-breathing giant with a hundred heads and terrifying eyes and voices.

typhoon *n* a violent tropical cyclone originating in the western Pacific.

typhus *or* **typhus fever** *n* (*med*) a highly contagious acute disease spread by body lice and characterized by fever, a rash and headache.—**typhous** *adj*.

typical *adj* representative of a particular type; characteristic.—**typicality** *n*.—**typically** *adv*.

typify *vt* (**typifying, typified**) to characterize.—**typification** *n*.

typist *n* a person who uses a typewriter, esp as a job.

typo *n* (*pl* **typos**) (*inf*) a typographical error.

typography *n* the way in which printed material is designed or set for printing.—**typographic, typographical** *adj*.

typology *n* the study of types of objects, etc, for classification purposes.

tyrannicide *n* (a person responsible for) the killing of a tyrant.

tyrannize *vi* to exercise power (over) in a vicious and oppressive manner. * *vt* to crush, oppress.—**tyrannizer** *n*.

tyrannosaur, tyrannosaurus *n* a large carnivorous dinosaur of the Cretaceous period which stood on powerful hind legs.

tyranny *n* (*pl* **tyrannies**) the government or authority of a tyrant; harshness; oppression.

tyrant *n* a person who uses his or her power arbitrarily and oppressively; a despot.—**tyrannical** *adj*.

Tyre *n* (*hist*) ancient seaport and trading city of the Phoenicians on an island off the coast of Palestine. It survived the attack of many enemies but eventually fell to Alexander the Great.

tyro *n* (*pl* **tyros**) a novice, a beginner.—*also* **tiro**.

Tyro *n* (*Greek myth*) the mother of Pelias and Neleus by Poseidon.

Tyrolienne *n* (*mus*) folksong of the Tyrol; song accompanied with dancing.

Tyrrhenian Sea *n* the name given to that part of the Mediterranean Sea which is enclosed between the Islands of Corsica and Sardinia on the west, the Italian Peninsula on the east, and Sicily on the south.

Tyson *n* **Mike [Michael Gerald]** (1966–) American boxer and world heavyweight champion (1987–90).

Tytila *n* (*d. c*.593) king of East Anglia (*c*.578–593); the successor of Wuffa.

tzar, tzarevitch, tzarina *see* **tsar, tsarevitch, tzarina**.

Tzara *n* **Tristan [Samuel Rosenstock]** (1896–1963) Romanian-born French poet and essayist who was one of the founders of Dada. Tzara's best-known volume of poetry is *Approximate Man*.

tzatsiki *n* a Greek dip made from plain yogurt, shredded cucumber, and mint.

tzetze *n* (*mus*) Abyssinian instrument similar to the guitar, formed of a long carved neck attached to a gourd. It has frets and one string, usually made of the tough fiber of a palm tree.

T

U

u, U *n* the 21st letter of the English alphabet; something shaped like a U.

U *symbol* (*chem*) uranium; (the) versor (part of a quaternion); prefixed as *Uq* (*math*).

u *abbr* = uncle; united atomic mass unit; unit; university; upper.

U *abbr* = Universal (film censorship classification); union; unionist; united; university; upper-class.

ua *abbr* = unauthorized absence; under age.

UA *abbr* = United Artists; Urostomy Association.

u/a, U/A *abbr* (*marine ins*) = underwriting account.

UAC *abbr* = Ulster Automobile Club.

UAE *abbr* = United Arab Emirates.

Uaithne *n* (*Irish Celtic myth*) 1. the harp of the Daghda. It was a magic instrument and would play only when it was asked to do so by one of the Daghda. 2. the name of the Daghda's harpist.

UAM *abbr* = underwater-to-air missile.

u & lc *abbr* = upper and lower case.

u & o *abbr* = use and occupancy.

UAOD *abbr* = United Ancient Order of Druids.

UAR *abbr* = United Arab Republic.

uas *abbr* = upper air space.

UAS *abbr* = Union of African States.

Uath mac Imoman *n* (*Irish Celtic myth*) warrior said to have been able to turn himself into any shape. He was asked to decide whether Cuchulainn, Laoghaire or Conall was the greatest warrior in the whole of Ireland.

Uathach *n* (*Irish Celtic myth*) the daughter of Scathach, a female prophet and warrior; Cuchulainn's mistress and perhaps his wife.

UAU *abbr* = Universities Athletic Union.

uAwg *abbr* (*German*) = *um Antwort wird gebeten*, "reply requested."

ubac *n* the side of a valley that is shaded, and less likely to be used for growing crops or for housing.

UBF *abbr* = Union of British Fascists.

ubiety *n* the state of being in a specific place.

ubiquitous *adj* existing, or seeming to exist everywhere at once.—**ubiquity** *n*.

U-boat *n* a German submarine.

Ubon Ratchathani *n* city in Thailand.

UBR *abbr* = Uniform Business Rate.

UBS *abbr* = United Bible Societies.

uc, u.c. *abbr* = (*Italian*) *una corda*, "one string" (direction to depress the left-hand pedal of piano); (*print*) upper case.

u/c *abbr* = undercharge.

UC *abbr* = University College; Upper Canada.

UCA *abbr* = Ulster Chemists Association; Ulster Curers Association.

UCAR *abbr* = Union of Central African Republics.

UCAS *abbr* = Universities and Colleges Admissions Service.

UCATT *abbr* = Union of Construction, Allied Trades and Technicians.

UCC *abbr* = Ulster Countryside Commission; Union Carbide Corporation; Universal Copyright Convention; University College Cork.

UCCA *abbr* = Universities' Central Council on Admissions.

UCI *abbr* (*French*) = *Union Cycliste Internationale*, International Cycling Union.

UCL *abbr* (*Brit*) = University College London.

UCLA *abbr* = University of California at Los Angeles.

UCM *abbr* = University Christian Movement.

UCR *abbr* = unconditioned reflex.

UCS *abbr* = unconditioned stimulus.

UCSW *abbr* = Union of Country Sports Workers.

UCT *abbr* = United Commercial Travelers (of America).

UCV *abbr* = United Confederate Veterans.

UCW *abbr* = Union of Communication Workers.

UCWRE *abbr* = Underwater Countermeasures and Weapons Research Establishment.

ud *abbr* = unfair dismissal; (*Latin*) *ut dictum*, "as said."

UD *abbr* = United Dairies.

UDA *abbr* = Ulster Defence Association.

UDC *abbr* = United Daughters of the Confederacy; Universal Decimal Classification; Urban Development Corporation; Urban District Council.

udder *n* a milk-secreting organ containing two or more teats, as in cows.

UDF *abbr* = Ulster Defence Force; United Democratic Front (South Africa).

UDHR *abbr* = Universal Declaration of Human Rights.

UDI *abbr* = Universal Declaration of Independence.

UDM *abbr* = Union of Democratic Mineworkers.

UDR *abbr* = Ulster Defence Regiment.

UDT *abbr* = United Dominions Trust.

UDUP *abbr* = Ulster Democratic Unionist Party.

UEA *abbr* = Universal Esperanto Association; (*Brit*) University of East Anglia.

UEFA *abbr* = Union of European Football Associations.

UEL *abbr* (*Canada*) = United Empire Loyalist.

Uen *n* (*d. c.*839) king of the Picts, Britain (837–839).

UEPS *abbr* = United Elvis Presley Society.

UER *abbr* = university entrance requirements.

u/f *abbr* = unfurnished.

UF *abbr* = United Free Church.

UFAW *abbr* = Universities Federation for Animal Welfare.

UFC *abbr* = United Free Church (Scotland); Universities Funding Council.

UFF *abbr* = Ulster Freedom Fighters; Ulster Furniture Federation.

UFO *abbr* = unidentified flying object.

ufology *n* the study of UFOs.—**ufologist** *n*.

UFORA *abbr* = Unidentified Flying Objects Research Association.

u/g *abbr* = underground.

Ugaine Mor *n* (6th century BC) semi-legendary high king of Ireland. He is supposed to have ruled the whole of Ireland and part of Western Europe, particularly Gaul. On Ugaine's death, Ireland was divided into twenty-five parts among his children, and this system lasted for three hundred years.

Uganda *n* a landlocked republic in east central Africa.

Uganda shilling *n* currency of Uganda.

UGC *abbr* = University Grants Committee.

ugh *interj* an expression of disgust, dislike, or horror.

ugli, ugli fruit *n* (*pl* **uglis, uglies**) a citrus fruit that is a cross between a grapefruit and a tangerine.

ugly *adj* (**uglier, ugliest**) unsightly; unattractive; repulsive; ill tempered.—**ugliness** *n*.

ugly duckling *n* an initially unpromising person or thing that turns out successfully.

UHF *abbr* = Ulster Historical Foundation; ultra-high frequency.

uh-huh *interj* used to indicate assent or agreement.

UHT *abbr* = ultra-heat treated (milk or cream); ultra high temperature.

UHV *abbr* = ultra high vacuum.

ui, u.i. *abbr* (*Latin*) = *ut infra*, "as below."

UI *abbr* = Understanding Industry.

UIA *abbr* = Ultrasonic Industry Association.

Uigreann *n* (*Irish Celtic myth*) warrior who fought Cumhaill, the father of Fionn mac Cumhaill because of Cumhaill's abduction of Muirne.

UJD *abbr* (*Latin*) = *Utriusque Juris Doctor*, "Doctor of Both Laws" (canon and civil).

UK *abbr* = United Kingdom (of Great Britain and Ireland).

UKA *abbr* = Ulster King of Arms.

UKADGE *abbr* = United Kingdom Air Defence Ground Environment.

UKAEA *abbr* = United Kingdom Atomic Energy Authority.

UKAFFP *abbr* = United Kingdom Association of Frozen Food Producers.

UKAFMM *abbr* = United Kingdom Association of Fish Meal Manufacturers.

UKASS *abbr* = United Kingdom Association of Suggestion Schemes.

UKCC *abbr* = United Kingdom Central Council for Nursing, Midwifery, and Health Visiting.

UKCTA *abbr* = United Kingdom Commercial Travellers Association.

UKCVCC *abbr* = United Kingdom Computer Virus Control Centre.

ukelele, ukulele *n* a small, four-stringed guitar.

UKFA *abbr* = United Kingdom Fellmongers Association.

UKFC *abbr* = United Kingdom Fortifications Club.

UKFFCA *abbr* = United Kingdom Freight Forwarders Container Association.

UKFR *abbr* = United Kingdom Feline Register.

UKgal *abbr* = United Kingdom gallon.

UKHA *abbr* = United Kingdom Harp Association; United Kingdom Housekeepers Association.

UKIAS *abbr* = United Kingdom Immigrants' Advisory Service.

UKJGA *abbr* = United Kingdom Jute Goods Association.

UKJSA *abbr* = United Kingdom Jet Ski Association.

UKPA *abbr* = United Kingdom Pilots' Association.

UKPIA *abbr* = United Kingdom Petroleum Industry Association Limited.

UKPMA *abbr* = United Kingdom Preserves Manufacturers Association.

Ukr. *abbr* = Ukraine.

Ukraine *n* a republic in eastern Europe, sharing borders with Moldova, Hungary, Slovakia, Poland, Belarus, and Russia.

UKSCC *abbr* = United Kingdom Spoon Collectors Club.

UKSIA *abbr* = United Kingdom Sugar Industry Association.

UKTA *abbr* = United Kingdom Tea Association.

UKWGF *abbr* = United Kingdom Wool Growers Federation.

UKWWA *abbr* = United Kingdom Wood Wool Association.

ul *abbr* = upper limit.

UL *abbr* = university library.

ULA *abbr* = Ulster Launderers Association; uncommitted logic array.

Ulaanbaatar *n* capital city of Mongolia.

Ulaid *n* the original Irish name for Ulster.

Ulbricht *n* **Walter** (1893–1973) East German Communist politician. He left Germany for the Soviet Union in 1933, returning in 1945 in the wake of the Red Army. As general secretary of the East German Socialist Unity (i.e. Communist) Party (1946–71), he supervised the sovietization of East German society, crushed the Berlin workers' rebellion of 1953 and built the Berlin Wall in 1961.

ULCC *abbr* = ultra-large crude carrier (oil tanker).

ulcer *n* an open sore on the surface of the skin or a mucous membrane.—**ulcerous** *adj*. *See* **duodenal ulcer; gastric ulcer; peptic ulcer**.

ulcerate *vti* to make or become ulcerous.

-ule *n suffix* smallness.

ulema *n* (a member of) a body of Muslim theologians and religious scholars.

-ulent *adj suffix* abundant.

ULF *abbr* = ultra-low frequency.

ullage *n* the amount by which a container (e.g., a barrel) is less than full.

ULM *abbr* = universal logic module.

ULMS *abbr* = underwater long-range missile system.

ulna *n* (*pl* **ulnas, ulnae**) the longer and thinner of the two bones in the human forearm; the corresponding bone in the forelimb of other vertebrates.—**ulnar** *adj*.

ulnar nerve *n* a nerve in the forearm that passes close to the skin surface at the elbow.

ulotrichous *adj* having woolly or curly hair.

ULS *abbr* = unsecured loan stock.

ulster *n* a long heavy double-breasted overcoat with a belt.

Ulster *n* former province of Ireland, now divided between Northern Ireland and the Republic of Ireland; (*Irish Celtic legend*) one of the five provinces into which the Fir Bholg divided Ireland.

Ulsterman *n* (*pl* **Ulstermen**) a native or inhabitant of Ulster.—**Ulsterwoman** (*pl* **Ulsterwomen**) *nf*.

ult. *abbr* = ultimate/ly.

ulterior *adj* (*motives*) hidden, not evident; subsequent.

ultima *n* the last syllable of a word.

ultimate *adj* last; final; most significant; essential. * *n* the most significant thing.—**ultimately** *adv*.

ultimatum *n* (*pl* **ultimatums, ultimata**) the final proposal, condition, or terms in negotiations.

ultimogeniture *n* (*law*) inheritance by the youngest son.

ulto. *abbr* (*Latin*) = *ultimo*, "in the last" (month).

ult. praes. *abbr* (*Latin*) = *ultimo, ultimus*, or *ultimum praescriptus*, "prescribed last time."

ultra *adj* extreme, uncompromising. * *n* an extremist.

ULTRA *abbr* = Unrelated Live Transplant Regulatory Authority.

ultra- *prefix* beyond.

ultrabasic rock *n* (*chem*) an igneous rock that contains many silicate minerals of iron and magnesium, such as amphiboles and pyroxenes, and with silica occurring as quartz.

ultracentrifuge *n* (*phys*) a special centrifuge machine that generates high centrifugal forces as it is capable of spinning at speeds of up to 50,000 revolutions per minute.

ultraconservative *adj* deeply conservative or reactionary. * *n* a reactionary person.

ultrafiche *n* a type of high-density microfiche containing a very large number of microcopies.

ultrahigh frequency *n* a radio frequency in the range between 300 megahertz and 3000 megahertz.

ultraism *n* the advocacy of extreme action.—**ultraist** *n*.

ultramarine *adj* deep blue. * *n* a blue pigment; a vivid, deep blue.

ultramicroscope *n* an optical device for viewing tiny particles undetectable by a conventional microscope.—**ultramicroscopic** *adj*.

ultramodern *adj* extremely modern.— **ultramodernism** *n*. —**ultramodernist** *n*. —**ultramodernistic** *adj*.

ultrashort *adj* (*radio wave*) having a wavelength less than 10 meters.

ultrasonic *adj* (*waves, vibrations*) having a frequency beyond the human ear's audible range.

ultrasound *n* ultrasonic waves used in medical diagnosis and therapy.

ultraviolet *adj* of light waves, shorter than the wavelengths of visible light and longer than X-rays.

ultraviolet astronomy *n* the observation and recording of electromagnetic radiation from stellar or other sources, which lies in the wavelength band range of 91.2 to 320 nanometers.

ultraviolet light *n* ultraviolet radiation.

ultraviolet radiation *n* (*phys*) a form of radiation that occurs beyond the violet end of the visible light spectrum of electromagnetic waves.

ultravirus *n* a virus small enough to pass through the finest filter.

ululate *vi* to howl or wail, as with pain or grief.—**ululant** *adj*.—**ululation** *n*.

ULV *abbr* = ultra low volume.

Ulysses, Ulixes *n* the Latin name of Odysseus.

um *interj* expressing hesitation, uncertainty, etc.

um. *abbr* = unmarried.

umano *n* (*mus*) (*Italian*) "human," as *voce umano*, the human voice.

umbel *n* a flower-cluster characteristic of plants of the carrot family, in which the stalks grow from the same place on the main stem producing an umbrella effect.—**umbellate** *adj*.

umbelliferous *adj* of or pertaining to a family of plants and shrubs bearing umbels, including carrots, parsley, and fennel.—**umbellifer** *n*.

umber *n* a brown pigment. * *adj* dark brown.

umbilical *n* of, pertaining to, near, or resembling the navel.

umbilical cord *n* the vascular tube connecting a fetus with the placenta through which oxygen and nutrients are passed.

umbilicate, umbilicated *n* depressed or shaped like a navel; having an umbilicus.—**umbilication** *n*.

umbilicus *n* (*pl* **umbilici**) the navel; a navel-shaped depression on a plant or animal.

umbo *n* (*pl* **umbones, umbos**) the boss in the center of a shield; a rounded anatomical protrusion.

umbra *n* (*pl* **umbrae, umbras**) an area of total shadow, esp during an eclipse; the dark center of a sunspot.—**umbral** *adj*.

umbrage *n* resentment; offence.

umbrella *n* a cloth-covered collapsible frame carried in the hand for protection from rain or sun; a general protection.

Umbriel *n* a moon or satellite of the planet Uranus, which was first observed by W Lassell in 1851.

UMDS *abbr* = United Medical and Dental Schools.

UMFC *abbr* = United Methodist Free Churches.

umiak *n* an Inuit (Eskimo) boat made from hide stretched over a wooden frame.—*also* **oomiak**.

UMIST *abbr* (*Brit*) = University of Manchester Institute of Science and Technology.

umlaut *n* the mark (¨) placed over a vowel in German and other languages to modify its sound; the change of a vowel brought about by its assimilation to another vowel.

umpire *n* an official who enforces the rules in sport; an arbitrator.—*also vti*.

umpteen *adj* (*inf*) an undetermined large number.—**umpteenth** *adj*.

'un, un *pron* (*dial*) one.

UN, U.N. *abbr* = United Nations.

un- *prefix* not; opposite of; contrary to; reversal of an action or state.

UNA *abbr* = United Nations Association.

unable *adj* not able; lacking the strength, skill, power, or opportunity (to do something).

unabsorbed costs *n* (*com*)in a production process, that part of the overhead costs not covered by the revenue it brings in when the output goes below a specified level.

unaccountable *adj* inexplicable, puzzling; not to be called to account for one's actions.

unaccustomed *adj* (*with to*) not used (to); not usual or familiar.

una corda *adj, adv* (*mus*) (*piano*) to be played with the soft pedal depressed.

unadorned *adj* not adorned; plain.

unadulterated *adj* pure, unmixed.

unadvised *adj* unwise, imprudent; not advised.—**unadvisedly** *adv*.

unaffected *adj* sincere, frank, without pretension; not influenced or affected.—**unaffectedly** *adv*.

un-American *adj* contrary to US customs, ideals, or interests.—**un-Americanism** *n*.

unanimous *adj* showing complete agreement.—**unanimity** *n*. —**unanimously** *adv*.

unanswerable *adj* (*logic, argument, etc*) not able to be refuted; (*question*) not able to be answered.

unapproachable *adj* aloof, unfriendly; impossible to reach; not to be equaled or rivaled.

unappropriated profit *n* (*com*) the portion of the profit made by a company that is neither assigned to a specific purpose nor allocated to the payment of dividends.

unapt *adj* (*usu with for*) not suitable, unqualified; (*usu with to*) not apt.— **unaptly** *adv*.—**unaptness** *n*.

unarmed *adj* not in possession of weapons; defenseless.

unashamed *adj* feeling no guilt; bold.— **unashamedly** *adv*.—**unashamedness** *n*.

unasked *adj* not asked or asked for; not invited or requested; spontaneous. * *adv* of one's own accord; without prompting.

unassailable *adj* not open to attack; not open to criticism or doubt.

unassuming *adj* unpretentious; modest.

unattached *adj* unmarried, not engaged to be married; not belonging to a particular group, organization, etc.

unattended *adj* not supervised; not accompanied.

unauthorized *adj* not endorsed by authority.

unavailing *adj* futile, hopeless.—**unavailingly** *adv*.

unavoidable *adj* bound to happen, inevitable; necessary, compulsory.—**unavoidably** *adv*.

unaware *adj* not conscious or aware (of); ignorant (of).

unawares *adv* by surprise; unexpectedly, without warning.

unbalanced *adj* mentally unstable; having bias or over-representing a particular view, group, interest, etc; (*bookkeeping*) not having equal debit and credit totals.

Un Ballo in Maschera *see* **Masked Ball, A**.

unbd. *abbr* (*bookbinding*) = unbound.

unbearable *adj* intolerable, not able to be endured.—**unbearably** *adv*.

unbeatable *adj* impossible to beat; outstanding, excellent.

unbeaten *adj* not beaten, unsurpassed.

unbecoming *adj* (*clothes, make-up, etc*) not enhancing the wearer's appearance; (*behavior*) not suitable or seemly.

unbeknown *adj* (*with* **to**) happening without (a person's) knowledge.

unbelief *n* disbelief, skepticism, esp in religious matters.

unbelievable *adj* not able to be believed; incredible.—**unbelievably** *adv*.

unbeliever *n* a person who does not believe, esp in a religion.

unbelieving *adj* lacking belief; skeptical.—**unbelievingly** *adv*.

unbend *vb* (**unbending, unbent**) *vt* to straighten from a bent shape; to release or untie (e.g., a rope). * *vi* to become more relaxed, affable, or informal in manner.

unbending *adj* severe, stern; inflexible, unchanging; rigid in behavior or attitude.

unbiased, unbiassed *adj* without prejudice or bias; impartial, even-handed, disinterested.

unbidden *adj* not commanded, asked for, or invited.

unblushing *adj* shameless, impudent.—**unblushingly** *adv*.

unborn *adj* not yet born; still to appear or happen in the future.

unbosom *vt* to reveal the thoughts or feelings of (oneself).

unbounded *adj* without limits.

unbowed *adj* not bowed; not subdued, free.

unbridled *adj* unrestrained; (*horse*) having no bridle.

UNBRO *abbr* = United Nations Border Relief Operation.

unbroken *adj* whole, in one piece; continuous, uninterrupted; (*record*) not yet beaten; (*horses, etc*) wild, untamed; organized, disciplined.

unbundling *n* (*com*) an informal term used to describe the selling of many of the subsidiary companies of a conglomerate, often on takeover and sometimes with a view to paying for the takeover.

unburden *vt* to reveal or confess one's troubles, secrets, etc to another in order to relieve the mind; to take off a burden.

unbutton *vt* to unfasten the buttons of (a garment).

unbuttoned *adj* unfastened; (*inf*) free, uninhibited.

uncalled-for *adj* unnecessary, unwanted, unwarranted.

uncanny *adj* (**uncannier, uncanniest**) odd; unexpected; suggestive of supernatural powers; unearthly.

UNCAST *abbr* = United Nations Conference on the Applications of Science and Technology.

UNCED *abbr* = United Nations Conference on Environment and Development.

unceremonious *adj* without ceremony, informal; abrupt, rude.—**unceremoniously** *adv*.

uncertain *adj* not knowing accurately, doubtful; (*with* **of**) not confident or sure; not fixed, variable, changeable.—**uncertainty** *n*.

uncertainty principle *n* (*phys*) the principle that it is impossible to determine accurately both the position and momentum of an elementary particle simultaneously.—*also* **Heisenberg uncertainty principle**.

uncharted *adj* not marked on a map; unsurveyed, unexplored.

unchristian *adj* contrary to Christian belief or principle; savage, pagan.

uncial *adj* written in or resembling large rounded capital letters as used in early medieval Greek and Latin manuscripts. * *n* an uncial character or manuscript.

uncinate *adj* (*plant, animal*) having a hook-shaped part.

uncircumcised *adj* not circumcised; not Jewish; impure.—**uncircumcision** *n*.

UNCITRAL *abbr* = United Nations Commission on International Trade law.

uncivil *adj* lacking in manners, impolite.—**uncivility** *n*.

uncivilized *adj* not civilized, unsophisticated; remote, wild.

uncle *n* the brother of one's father or mother; the husband of one's aunt.

unclean *adj* not clean, contaminated; ceremonially defiled.

Uncle Sam *n* the government of the US personified.

Uncle Tom *n* (*derog*) a Black person who acts in a servile manner to white people.

unclothe *vt* (**unclothing, unclothed** *or* **unclad**) to remove the clothes from; to uncover.

UNCLS *abbr* = United Nations Conference on the Law of the Sea.

uncoil *vti* to (cause to) unwind.

uncomfortable *adj* causing discomfort; feeling discomfort or unease.

uncommitted *adj* not bound to a particular cause, belief or course of action.

uncommon *adj* rare, unusual; extraordinary.

uncommonly *adv* hardly ever; exceptionally, particularly.

uncommunicative *adj* not willing to talk or express an opinion, etc; reserved.

uncompromising *adj* not prepared to compromise; inflexible, obstinate.

unconcern *n* indifference.

unconcerned *adj* not involved in or concerned with; not troubled.

unconditional *adj* without restrictions or conditions, absolute.

unconformity *n* (*geol*) a break in the deposition of sedimentary rocks, allowing erosion of previously formed rock before eventual deposition of further sediments.

unconscionable *adj* unscrupulous; unreasonable.—**unconscionably** *adv*.

unconscious *adj* not aware (of); lacking normal perception by the senses, insensible; unintentional. * *n* the deepest level of mind containing feelings and emotions of which one is unaware and unable to control.—**unconsciously** *adv*.

unconsciousness *n* the state of being without the senses, as when knocked out.

unconstitutional *adj* contrary to the constitution of a country.—**unconstitutionality** *n*.

unconventional *adj* not bound by social rules or conventions.—**unconventionally** *adv*.

uncork *vt* to pull the cork from a bottle; (*emotions, desires, etc*) to unleash, give vent to.

uncouple *vti* to disconnect or become disconnected.

uncouth *adj* lacking in manners; rough; rude.—**uncouthness** *n*.

uncover *vt* to remove the cover from; to reveal or expose; to remove one's hat in greeting or out of respect.

uncovered *adj* not having a cover; revealed; not having any insurance or security; with one's hat removed out of respect, etc.

UNCRO *abbr* = United Nations Confidence-Restoring Operation (in Croatia).

UNCSTD *abbr* = United Nations Conference on Science and Technology for Development.

UNCTAD *abbr* = United Nations Conference on Trade and Development.

unction *n* an anointing, as for medical or religious purposes; anything that soothes or comforts; affected sincerity.

unctuous *adj* oily; smarmy; too suave; insincerely charming.—**unctuously** *adv*.—**unctuousness** *n*.

uncurl *vti* to straighten; to straighten up, relax.

uncut *adj* not cut; (*book*) not having the folds of the leaves trimmed or slit; (*gemstone*) not cut into shape; not abridged.

undaunted *adj* fearless; not discouraged.—**undauntedly** *adv*.

UNDCP *abbr* = United Nations International Drug Control Program.

undecagon *n* a polygon with eleven sides.

undeceive *vt* to free from deception or error.

undecided *adj* doubtful, hesitant; (*solution, etc*) not determined.—**undecidedly** *adv*.

undelete program *n* (*comput*) a utility program that is used to restore files that have been deleted from a disk, possibly by accident. *See also* **recover**.

undemonstrative *adj* not demonstrative, reserved; calm.—**undemonstratively** *adv*.— **undemonstrativeness** *n*.

undeniable *adj* readily apparent, obviously true; unquestionably excellent.

under *prep* lower than; beneath the surface of; below; covered by; subject to; less than, falling short of. * *adv* beneath, below, lower down. * *adj* lower in position, degree, or rank; subordinate.

under- *prefix* beneath, below.

underachieve *vi* to perform less well than expected given one's potential.—**underachiever** *n*.

underact *vt* to perform (a dramatic role) without proper conviction or emphasis.

underage *adj* below the normal or legal age.

underarm *adj* of, for, in, or used on the area under the arm, or armpit; done with the hand below the level of the elbow or shoulder.

underbelly *n* (*pl* **underbellies**) the underside of an animal, etc; the most vulnerable part of something.

underbid *vb* (**underbidding, underbid**) *vt* to bid a lower amount than (rivals); (*bridge, etc*) to bid less than the strength of the hand merits. * *vi* to bid too low.

undercapitalized *adj* (*business*) having insufficient capital to operate efficiently.—**undercapitalization** *n*.

undercarriage *n* the landing gear of an airplane; a car's supporting framework.

undercharge *vt* to charge below the fair price.

underclass *n* those least privileged people in society who fall outside the normal social scale, characterized by poverty, unemployment, poor education, social instability, etc.

underclothes *npl* underwear.—*also* **underclothing**.

undercoat *n* a coat of paint, etc, applied as a base below another; a growth of hair or fur under another; a coat worn under an overcoat.

undercover *adj* done or operating secretly.

undercroft *n* (*archit*) a vaulted chamber for storage which may be completely or partly underground.

undercurrent *n* a hidden current under water; an emotion, opinion, etc, not apparent.

undercut *vt* (**undercutting, undercut**) to charge less than a competitor; to undermine.

underdeveloped *adj* not fully grown, immature; (*societies*) having an inadequate social and political infrastructure for sustained economic growth; (*film*) not processed long enough to form a proper image.

underdog *n* the loser in an encounter, contest, etc; a person in an inferior position.

underdone *adj* not sufficiently or completely cooked.

underdressed *adj* wearing clothes that are too informal for a particular occasion.

underemployed *adj* not fully or most efficiently employed.

underestimate *vti* to set too low an estimate on or for. * *n* too low an estimate.

underexpose *vt* (*photog*) to fail to expose (film) to light sufficiently long to produce a good image.—**underexposed** *adj*.—**underexposure** *n*.

underfelt *n* a layer of thick felt between a carpet and floor.

underfit stream *or* **misfit stream** *n* a stream that has narrower meander belts and shorter meander wavelengths than would be expected in the valley in which it flows, possibly evidence of a change in climate.

underfoot *adv* underneath the foot or feet; on the ground.

undergarment *n* a piece of underwear or clothing worn beneath other outer clothing.

undergo *vt* (**undergoing, underwent,** *pp* **undergone**) to experience, suffer, endure.

undergraduate *n* a student at a college or university studying for a first degree.

underground *adj* situated under the surface of the ground; secret; of noncommercial newspapers, movies, etc that are unconventional, radical, etc. * *n* a secret group working for the overthrow of the government or the expulsion of occupying forces; an underground railway system; a subway.

undergrowth *n* shrubs, plants, etc growing beneath trees.

underhand *adv* (*sport*) with an underarm motion; underhandedly.

underhanded *adj* sly, secret, deceptive.—**underhandedly** *adv*.

underlay *n* a material, lining laid beneath another for support; felt or rubber laid beneath a carpet for insulation, etc.

underlie *vt* (**underlying, underlay,** *pp* **underlain**) to be situated under; to form the basis of.

underline *vt* to put a line underneath; to emphasize.

underling *n* a person of inferior rank or status to someone else; a subordinate.

underlying *adj* existing, but hard to detect; fundamental, supporting.

undermentioned *adj* mentioned below or later in the text.

undermine *vt* to wear away, or weaken; to injure or weaken, esp by subtle or insidious means.

underneath *adv* under. * *adj* lower. * *n* the underside.—*also prep*.

undernourished *adj* consuming or supplied with less than the minimum quantity of food necessary for normal health and growth.

underpants *npl* pants worn as an undergarment by men and boys, shorts.

underpass *n* a section of road running beneath another road, a railway, etc.

underpin *vt* to strengthen or support from beneath.

underpinning *n* the material used to support a structure, the foundation.

underplay *vt* to perform (a dramatic role) with restraint; to play down the importance of.

underprivileged *adj* lacking the basic rights of other members of society; poor.

underproof *adj* containing less alcohol per volume than proof spirit.

underrate *vt* to undervalue, to underestimate.

underscore *vt* to draw a line under; to emphasize.

undersea *adj, adv* below the surface of the sea.

underseal *n* a protective layer of tar, etc applied to the underside of a vehicle. * *vt* to apply this protective layer.

undersecretary *n* (*pl* **undersecretaries**) a senior civil servant in Great Britain; in US, a secretary immediately subordinate to a principal.

undersell *vt* (**underselling, undersold**) to sell at a reduced price; to sell at a price lower than (someone else); to promote with moderation.

undersexed *adj* having a weaker than normal sex drive.

undershirt *n* a sleeveless undergarment for the upper body, a vest.

undershoot *vti* (**undershooting, undershot**) to (cause to) land short of a runway; to shoot short of a target.

underside *n* the lower surface.

undersigned *adj* signed at the end. * *n* a person who signs his or her name at the end of a document.

undersized *adj* less than usual size.

underskirt *n* a woman's undergarment worn beneath the skirt, a petticoat.

underslung *adj* suspended from above; (*vehicle chassis*) suspended below the axles.

undersong *n* (*mus*) a chorus or burden of a song.

understand *vb* (**understanding, understood**) *vt* to comprehend; to realize; to believe; to assume; to know thoroughly (e.g. a language); to accept; to be sympathetic with. * *vi* to comprehend; to believe.—**understandable** *adj*.

understanding *n* comprehension; compassion, sympathy; personal opinion, viewpoint; mutual agreement. * *adj* sympathetic.

understate *vt* to state something in restrained terms; to represent as less than is the case.—**understatement** *n*.

understudy *vti* (**understudying, understudied**) to learn a role or part so as to be able to replace (the actor playing it); to act as an understudy (to).—*also n*.

undertake *vt* (**undertaking, undertook,** *pp* **undertaken**) to attempt to; to agree to; to commit oneself; to promise; to guarantee.

undertaker *n* a funeral director.

undertaking *n* enterprise; task; promise; obligation.

under-the-counter *adj* reserved for special customers only; secret, furtive.

under-the-table *adj* hidden, illegal.

underthings *npl* underwear.

undertone *n* a hushed tone of voice; an undercurrent of feeling; a pale color.

undertow *n* the backwash from a breaking wave; an undercurrent moving in a different direction from the surface current.

undervalue *vt* (**undervaluing, undervalued**) to put too low a price or value on.—**undervaluation** *n*.

underwater *adj* being carried on under the surface of the water, esp the sea; submerged; below the water line of a vessel.—*also adv*.

under way *adv* in or into motion or progress.

underwear *n* garments worn underneath one's outer clothes, next to the skin.

underweight *adj* weighing less than normal or necessary.

underwent *see* **undergo**.

underwhelm *vt* to disappoint.

underworld *n* criminals as an organized group; (*myth*) Hades.

underwrite *vt* to agree to finance (an undertaking, etc); to sign one's name to (an insurance policy), thus assuming liability. * *vi* to work as an underwriter.—**underwriter** *n*.

undesirable *adj* not desirable; not pleasant; objectionable.—**undesirability** *n*.—**undesirably** *adv*.

undetermined *adj* not yet decided; not discovered.

undies *npl* (*inf*) women's underwear.

undifferentiated marketing *n* a (*com*) marketing strategy that aims to exploit the widest possible market.

undo *vt* (**undoing, undid,** *pp* **undone**) to untie or unwrap; to reverse (what has been done); to bring ruin on; (*comput*) a command available in programs that reverses the effect of the previous command given.

undocumented *adj* (*comput*) features of programs that have not been documented in the program manual.

UNDOF *abbr* = United Nations Disengagement Observer Force.

undone *adj* not done; not fastened or tied.

undoubted *adj* without doubt; definite, certain.—**undoubtedly** *adv*.

UNDP *abbr* = United Nations Development Program.

undreamed, undreamt *n* (*with of*) not thought of or imagined.

undress *vt* to remove the clothes from. * *vi* to take off one's clothes.

undressed *adj* not dressed, partially or informally clothed; (*wound*) not bandaged; (*food*) not prepared for serving; (*hides*) not processed.

UNDRO *abbr* = United Nations Disaster Relief Organization.

Undry *n* (*Irish Celtic myth*) the magic cauldron of the Daghda. It had an unlimited supply of food that was never used up, no matter how many people ate from it.

undue *adj* improper; excessive.

undulant fever *see* **brucellosis**.

undulate *vti* to move or cause to move like waves; to have or cause to have a wavy form or surface.

undulation *n* a wavelike form or motion.

unduly *adv* too; excessively; improperly.

undying *adj* eternal.

unearned *adj* (*income*) not earned by labor or skill; undeserved.

unearth *vt* to dig up from the earth; to discover; to reveal.

unearthly *adj* mysterious; eerie; supernatural; absurd, unreasonable.

uneasy *adj* uncomfortable; restless; anxious; disquieting.—**uneasily** *adv*.—**uneasiness** *n*.

uneatable *adj* (*food*) not edible, esp because of its condition or appearance.

uneconomic *adj* wasteful; unprofitable.

UNEF *abbr* = United Nations Emergency Force.

unemployable *adj* not fit or acceptable for work.

unemployed *adj* not having a job, out of work.—**unemployment** *n*.

UNEP *abbr* = United Nations Environment Program.

unequal *adj* not equal; not regular or uniform; not sufficiently strong or able.—**unequally** *adv*.

unequalled, unequaled *adj* not equaled; supreme.

unequal voices *n* (*mus*) voices of mixed qualities such as those of men and women in chorus.

unequivocal *adj* unambiguous; plain; clear.—**unequivocally** *adv*.

unerring *adj* sure, unfailing.

UNESCO *abbr* = United Nations Educational, Scientific and Cultural Organization.

uneven *adj* not level or smooth; variable; not divisible by two without leaving a remainder.—**unevenness** *n*.

uneventful *adj* ordinary, routine.—**uneventfully** *adv*.

unexampled *adj* without precedent or comparison.

unexceptionable *adj* irreproachable.

unexceptional *adj* ordinary, normal.

unexpected *adj* not looked for, unforeseen.—**unexpectedly** *adv*.

unfailing *adj* not failing or giving up; persistent; constant; dependable.—**unfailingly** *adv*.

unfair *adj* unjust; unequal; against the rules.—**unfairly** *adv*.—**unfairness** *n*.

unfair dismissal *n* the unfair termination of an employee's employment by an employer.

unfaithful *adj* disloyal; not abiding by a promise; adulterous.—**unfaithfully** *adv*.—**unfaithfulness** *n*.

unfamiliar *adj* not known, strange; (*with* **with**) not familiar.

UNFAO *abbr* = United Nations Food and Agriculture Organization.

unfasten *vt* to open or become opened; to undo or become undone; to loose, loosen.

unfathomable *adj* not able to be measured; incomprehensible.

U

unfavorable, unfavourable *adj* negative, disapproving; adverse.

unfeeling *adj* callous, hardhearted.—**unfeelingly** *adv*.

Unficyp *abbr* = United Nations Force in Cyprus.

unfinished *adj* not finished, incomplete; in the making; crude, sketchy.

unfit *adj* unsuitable; in bad physical condition.

unflappable *adj* (*inf*) calm, not easily agitated.

unflinching *adj* calm, steadfast.—**unflinchingly** *adv*.

unfold *vti* to open or spread out; to become revealed; to develop.

unforeseen *adj* unsuspected.

unforgettable *adj* never to be forgotten; fixed in the mind; impressive; exceptional.—**unforgettably** *adv*.

unformatted *adj* (*comput*) a term indicating that an item of magnetic media requires formatting prior to being put into operation.

unfortunate *adj* unlucky; disastrous; regrettable. * *n* an unlucky person.

unfortunately *adv* regrettably, unluckily, unhappily.

unfounded *adj* groundless; baseless.

UNFPA *abbr* = United Nations Fund for Population Activities.

unfreeze *vti* (**unfreezing, unfroze, unfrozen**) to (cause to) thaw; to remove restrictions on (wage or price rises, etc).

unfrock *vt* to remove (a person in holy orders) from ecclesiastical office.

unfurl *vti* to open; to unfold.

ung. *abbr* (*Latin*) = *unguentum*, "ointment."

UNGA *abbr* = United Nations General Assembly.

ungainly *adj* (**ungainlier, ungainliest**) awkward; clumsy.—**ungainliness** *n*.

Ungers *n* Oswald Mathias (1926–) German architect whose furniture and carpet designs are based on geometric forms.

ungodly *adj* (**ungodlier, ungodliest**) not religious; sinful; wicked; (*inf*) outrageous.

ungovernable *adj* not able to be controlled or restrained.

unguarded *adj* without protection, vulnerable; open to attack; careless; candid, frank.—**unguardedly** *adv*.

unguent *n* a lubricant or ointment.

unguis *n* a fingernail or toenail.

ungula *adj* a term meaning relating to the fingernails or toenails.

ungulate *n, adj* (an animal) having hooves.

unhallowed *adj* not consecrated; sinful.

unhappy *adj* (**unhappier, unhappiest**) not happy or fortunate; sad; wretched; not suitable.—**unhappily** *adv*.—**unhappiness** *n*.

UNHCR *abbr* = United Nations High Commission for Refugees; United Nations High Commissioner for Refugees.

unhealthy *adj* (**unhealthier, unhealthiest**) not healthy or fit, sick; encouraging or resulting from poor health; harmful, degrading; dangerous.—**unhealthily** *adv*.—**unhealthiness** *n*.

unheard *adj* not heard; not listened to.

unheard-of *adj* not known before; without precedent.

unhinge *vt* to make crazy, derange.

unholy *adj* (**unholier, unholiest**) wicked; (*inf*) outrageous, enormous.

unhook *vt* to remove from a hook; to unfasten the hooks of (a garment).

UNHQ *abbr* = United Nations Headquarters.

uni *n* (*inf*) university.

uni- *prefix* one; single.

unicameral *adj* of or having only one legislative chamber.—**unicamerally** *adv*.

UNICEF *abbr* = United Nations International Children's Emergency Fund, now United Nations Children's Fund.

unicellular *adj* (*microorganisms, etc*) consisting of a single cell.—**unicellularity** *n*.

UNICOR *abbr* = Federal Prison Industries, Inc.

unicorn *n* an imaginary creature with a body like a horse and a single horn on the forehead.

unicycle *n* a pedal-driven cycle with a single wheel, used by circus and street entertainers.

unidirectional *adj* involving, going in, or operating in one direction only.

UNIDO *abbr* = United Nations Industrial Development Organization.

UNIFIL *abbr* = United Nations Interim Force in Lebanon.

uniform *adj* unchanging in form; consistent; identical. * *n* the distinctive clothes worn by members of the same organization, such as soldiers, schoolchildren.—**uniformly** *adv*.

uniform commercial code *n* (*law*) a secure financial transaction like a mortgage or a deed of trust.

uniform delivered pricing *n* (*com*) the cost of an item will be the same, regardless of the distance of the retail outlets from the central warehouses.

uniformity *n* (*pl* **uniformities**) the state of being consistent or the same; dullness, monotony.

unify *vt* (**unifying, unified**) to make into one; to unite.—**unification** *n*.

UNIKOM *abbr* = United Nations Iraq-Kuwait Observation Mission.

unilateral *adj* involving one only of several parties; not reciprocal.—**unilateralism** *n*. —**unilaterally** *adv*.

unimpeachable *adj* completely honest, truthful, etc; irreproachable.—**unimpeachably** *adv*.

uninhibited *adj* not repressed or restrained; relaxed, spontaneous.—**uninhibitedly** *adv*.

uninterested *adj* lacking interest; not concerned, indifferent.—**uninterestedly** *adv*.

uninterruptable power supply *or* **UPS** *n* (*comput*) a power supply that switches to an alternative power source, such as a battery, in the event of the main supply crashing, thus preserving data.

union *n* the act of uniting; a combination of several things; a confederation of individuals or groups; marriage; a trades union.

unionist *n* an advocate or supporter of union or unionism.—**unionism** *n*.

unionize *vt* to organize (employees) into a trade union.—**unionization** *n*.

Union Jack *n* the national flag of the UK.

uniparous *adj* (*zool*) producing a single egg or a single offspring at birth; (*bot*) producing one axis.

unipolar *adj* of, produced by, or having a single electric or magnetic pole.—**unipolarity** *n*.

unique *adj* without equal; the only one of its kind.—**uniquely** *adv*.

unis. *abbr* = unison.

unisex *adj* of a style that can be worn by both sexes.

unisexual *adj* of one sex only; having male or female sex organs but not both.—**unisexually** *adv*.—**unisexuality** *n*.

unison *n* accordance of sound, concord, harmony; **in unison** simultaneously, in agreement, in harmony.

unit *n* the smallest whole number, one; a single or whole entity; (*measurement*) a standard amount; an establishment or group of people who carry out a specific function; a piece of furniture fitting together with other pieces.—**unitary** *adj*.

Unit. *abbr* = Unitarian; Unitarianism.

UNITA *abbr* (*Portuguese*) = *União Nacional por Independência Total de Angola*, "National Union for the Total Independence of Angola."

unit cost *n* (*com*) the cost of a unit of production or sales in the expenditure of a company, arrived at by dividing the total production cost by the number of units involved.

unite *vti* to join into one, to combine; to be unified in purpose.

United Arab Emirates *or* **UAE** *n* a federation of seven oil-rich sheikdoms located in The Gulf.

United Kingdom of Great Britain and Northern Ireland *or* **UK** *n* a constitutional monarchy situated in northwest Europe and comprising England, Wales, Scotland and the six counties of Northern Ireland.

United Nations *n sing or pl* an international organization of nations for world peace and security formed in 1945.

United States *n* a federation of states, esp the United States of America.

United States of America *n* a federal republic consisting of 50 states and the District of Columbia.

unit price *n* (*com*) the price paid per unit of product or article purchased or the price charged per unit of article or product sold.

unit pricing *n* (*com*) the practice of indicating on a product pack not only the price per product pack but also the price per unit by weight, volume, or pack.

unit trust *n* a company that manages a range of investments on behalf of members of the public whose interests are looked after by an independent trust.

unity[1] *n* (*pl* **unities**) oneness; harmony; concord; (*math*) the number or numeral one; a quantity assuming the value of one.

unity[2] *n* any one of the three classical and neoclassical principles of dramatic construction, derived from Aristotle's *Poetics*, that require that a play's action should be restricted to a single plot (unity of action), its location restricted to one place (unity of place) and its events restricted to a single day (unity of time).

Unius *n* (*Irish Celtic myth*) the name of the river over which Morrigan stood with one foot on each bank when she was making love to the Daghda.

univ. *abbr* = universal; universally; university.

Univ. *abbr* = Universalist.

univallate *n* (*archeo*) having just one rampart.

universal *adj* widespread; general; relating to all the world or the universe; relating to or applicable to all mankind.—**universally** *adv*.—**universality** *n* (*pl* **universalities**).

universal indicator *n* (*chem*) a mixture of certain substances, which will change color to show the changing pH of a solution.

universal joint *or* **universal coupling** *n* a linkage between two rotating shafts that allows movement in all directions.

universal suffrage *n* suffrage for all adults.

universal time *n* a precise measurement of time, designated UT, which is related very closely to the mean daily movement of the sun.

universe *n* all existing things; (*astron*) the totality of space, stars, planets, and other forms of matter and energy; the world.

university *n* (*pl* **universities**) an institution of higher education which confers bachelors' and higher degrees; the campus or staff of a university.

UNIX *n* (*comput*) an operating system suitable for a wide range of computers from mainframes to personal computers.

unjust *adj* not characterized by justice; not fair.—**unjustly** *adv*.—**unjustness** *n*.

unkempt *adj* uncombed; slovenly, disheveled.

unkind *adj* lacking in kindness or sympathy; harsh; cruel.—**unkindly** *adv*.—**unkindness** *n*.

unknown *adj* not known; not famous; not understood; with an unknown value. * *n* an unknown person or thing.

unleaded *adj* (*gasoline*) not mixed with tetraethyl lead.

unleash *vt* to release from a leash; to free from restraint.

unleavened *adj* (*bread, etc*) made without yeast or other raising agent.

Unleavened Bread, the Feast of *see* **Passover**.

unless *conj* if not; except that.

unlettered *adj* illiterate.

unlike *adj* not the same, dissimilar. * *prep* not like; not characteristic of.—**unlikeness** *n*.

unlikely *adj* improbable; unpromising.

unlimited *adj* without limits; boundless; not restricted.—**unlimitedly** *adv*.

unlisted *adj* not on a list; ex-directory.

unload *vti* to remove a load, discharge freight from a truck, ship, etc; to relieve of or express troubles, etc; to dispose of, dump; to empty, esp a gun.

unlock *vt* (*door, lock, etc*) to unfasten; to let loose; to reveal; to release.

unloose, unloosen *vt* to relax (a grip, etc); to release, free; to untie.

unlovely *n* ugly, unpleasant.—**unloveliness** *n*.

unlucky *adj* (**unluckier, unluckiest**) not lucky, not fortunate; likely to bring misfortune; regrettable.

unman *vt* (**unmanning, unmanned**) to weaken the nerve or courage of; to make effeminate.

unmanly *adj* weak, cowardly; effeminate.—**unmanliness** *n*.

unmanned *adj* (*spacecraft, etc*) not manned, operated by remote control.

unmannerly *adj* lacking good manners; rude.—**unmannerliness** *n*.

unmask *vti* to remove the mask from; to expose, show up.

unmentionable *adj* too bad, shocking, embarrassing, etc to be mentioned.

unmentionables *npl* underwear.

unmistakable, unmistakeable *adj* obvious, clear.—**unmistakably, unmistakeably** *adv*.

unmitigated *adj* unqualified, absolute.

UNMOGIP *abbr* = United Nations Military Observer Group in India and Pakistan.

unmoved *adj* not touched by emotion, calm.

unnatural *adj* abnormal; contrary to nature; artificial; affected; strange; wicked.—**unnaturally** *adv*.

unnecessary *adj* not necessary.—**unnecessarily** *adv*.—**unnecessariness** *n*.

unnerve *vt* to cause to lose courage, strength, confidence; to frighten.

unnumbered *adj* countless; not having a number.

UNO *abbr* = United Nations Organization.

unobtrusive *adj* modest, staying in the background.

unoccupied *adj* not occupied, empty; unemployed.

Unosom *abbr* = United Nations Operation in Somalia.

unpack *vti* (*suitcase, etc*) to remove the contents of; (*container, etc*) to take things out of; to unload.

unpaid *adj* not paid; working voluntarily without a salary.

unparalleled *adj* having no equal, unmatched.

unparliamentary *adj* contrary to parliamentary procedure or practice.

unpeg *vt* (**unpegging, unpegged**) to remove a peg from; to unfasten.

unperson *n* a person (e.g. a political dissident) whose existence is officially ignored or denied.

unpick *vt* to undo the stitching of.

unplaced *adj* not placed; not among the first three at the end of a race.

unpleasant *adj* not pleasing or agreeable; nasty; objectionable.—**unpleasantly** *adv*.—**unpleasantness** *n*.

unplug *vt* (**unplugging, unplugged**) to remove an electrical plug from a socket, to disconnect; to rid of an obstruction.

unplumbed *adj* not plumbed; not fully investigated or explored.

unpopular *adj* disliked; lacking general approval.—**unpopularity** *n*.

unprecedented *adj* having no precedent; unparalleled.

unprejudiced *adj* not prejudiced, impartial.

unprepared *adj* not prepared beforehand; not ready or equipped.—**unpreparedly** *adv*.— **unpreparedness** *n*.

unprepossessing *adj* unattractive, repellent.

unpretentious *adj* modest, not boasting.

unprincipled *adj* lacking scruples.

unprintable *adj* too bad, libelous, obscene, etc to be printed.

unprofessional *adj* contrary to professional etiquette.—**unprofessionally** *adv*.

Unprofor *abbr* = United Nations Protection Force (in Bosnia, Croatia, etc).

unprotected software *n* (*comput*) software that can be copied from the original program disks on to other floppy disks or onto a hard disk. *See also* **copy protection**.

unputdownable *adj* (*book*) grippingly readable.

unqualified *adj* lacking recognized qualifications; not equal to; not restricted, complete.

unquestionable *adj* certain, not disputed.—**unquestionably** *adv*.

unquestioned *adj* not called into question; indisputable.

unquiet *adj* turbulent, disordered; nervous, agitated.—**unquietly** *adv*.—**unquietness** *n*.

unquote *interj* used when speaking to indicate the end of a direct quotation.

unquoted company *n* a company whose securities are not usu available to members of the public on a stock exchange.

unquoted securities *npl* securities that are not traded on a stock exchange or securities for which no price is regularly quoted.

unravel *vt* (**unraveling, unraveled** *or* **unravelling, unravelled**) to disentangle; to solve.

unread *adj* not read (yet); unfamiliar with a specified subject; illiterate.

unreadable *adj* illegible; not worth reading.

unreal *adj* not real; imaginary, fanciful; false, insincere.

unreason *n* absence of reason in thought or action.

unreasonable *adj* contrary to reason; lacking reason; immoderate; excessive.—**unreasonably** *adv*.

unreasoning *adj* lacking reason, irrational.

UNREF *abbr* = United Nations Refugee Emergency Fund.

unrelenting *adj* relentless; continuous.—**unrelentingly** *adv*.

unremitting *adj* incessant.

unrequited *adj* not reciprocated, not returned.

unreserved *adj* not reserved; frank, demonstrative; absolute, entire; not booked.

unreservedly *adv* without conditions; openly.

unrest *n* uneasiness; anxiety; angry discontent verging on revolt.

UNRFNRE *abbr* = United Nations Revolving Fund for Natural Resource Exploration.

unrighteous *adj* sinful, wicked.

unrivaled, unrivalled *adj* without equal, peerless.

unroll *vti* to open out or down from a roll; to unfold; to straighten out; to reveal or become revealed.

UNRRA *abbr* = United Nations Relief and Rehabilitation Administration.

unruffled *adj* cool and calm; still, smooth.

unruly *adj* (**unrulier, unruliest**) hard to control, restrain, or keep in order; disobedient.

UNRWA *abbr* = United Nations Relief and Works Agency (for Palestinian refugees).

unsaddle *vt* to take the saddle from; to unseat. * *vi* to remove the saddle from a horse.

unsaid *adj* not said or expressed.

unsaturated *adj* (*chemical substance*) having double or triple bonds and therefore able to form products by chemical addition; (*vegetable fats*) containing fatty acids with double bonds.—**unsaturation** *n*.

unsavory, unsavoury *adj* distasteful; disagreeable; offensive.

UNSC *abbr* = United Nations Security Council; United Nations Social Commission.

unscathed *adj* unharmed.

UNSCOM *abbr* = United Nations Special Commission.

unscramble *vt* to disentangle; (*a scrambled message*) to make intelligible.

unscrew *vti* to remove a screw from; (*lid, etc*) to loosen by turning.

unscrupulous *adj* without principles.

unseasonable *n* (*weather*) unusual for the season of the year; untimely.—**unseasonableness** *n*. —**unseasonably** *adv*.

unseat *vt* to dislodge from a seat, saddle, etc; to remove from office.

unsecured loan *n* a loan for which the borrower has no collateral security.

unseeded *adj* (*tennis players, etc*) not ranked among the top players in the preliminary rounds of a competition.

unseemly *adj* unbecoming; inappropriate.

unseen *adj* concealed, hidden; not seen or read beforehand.

unselfish *adj* not selfish; thinking of others before oneself.—**unselfishly** *adv*.—**unselfishness** *n*.

unsettle *vti* to disturb, disrupt, or disorder.

unsettled *adj* changeable; lacking stability; unpredictable; not concluded.

UNSG *abbr* = United Nations Secretary General.

unsheathe *vt* to draw (a weapon) from a sheath.

unsightly *adj* unattractive; ugly.

unskilled *adj* without special skill or training.

unskillful, unskilful *adj* clumsy, awkward.

unsociable *n* antisocial; reserved.

unsocial *n* averse to social activities; (*working hours*) outside the normal working day.

unsolicited *adj* not asked for.

unsophisticated *adj* naïve, inexperienced; simple; pure, unadulterated.

unsound *adj* flimsy, not stable; defective, flawed; in poor health; not sane.—**unsoundly** *adv*.—**unsoundness** *n*.

unsparing *adj* profuse, lavish; severe.

unspeakable *adj* bad beyond words, indescribable.

unstable *adj* easily upset; mentally unbalanced; irresolute.

unsteady *adj* (**unsteadier, unsteadiest**) shaky, reeling; vacillating.—**unsteadily** *adv*.

unstop *vt* (**unstopping, unstopped**) to remove the stopper from; to free from an obstruction.

unstressed *adj* (*vowel, syllable, word, etc*) not pronounced with stress; not emphasized; not under stress.

unstrung *adj* emotionally distressed.

unstudied *adj* natural; unaffected in manner.

unsubstantial *adj* lacking weight, flimsy; of doubtful factual validity.

unsullied *adj* not stained, pure.

unsung *adj* not acclaimed or celebrated.

unswerving *adj* not deviating; constant, unchanging.

untangle *vt* to rid of tangles, unravel; to sort out.

untaught *adj* not educated or trained; not acquired by teaching.

UNTC *abbr* = United Nations Trusteeship Council.

untenable *adj* not able to be justified or defended.—**untenability** *n*.

unthinkable *adj* inconceivable; out of the question; improbable.—**unthinkably** *adv*.

unthinking *adj* unable to think; thoughtless, inconsiderate.—**unthinkingly** *adv*.

untidy *adj* (**untidier, untidiest**) not neat, disordered. * *vt* (**untidying, untidied**) to make untidy.—**untidily** *adv*.

U

untie vt (**untying, untied**) to undo a knot in, unfasten.

until prep up to the time of; before. * conj up to the time when or that; to the point, degree, etc that; before.

untimely adj premature; inopportune.

unto prep (arch) to.

untold adj not told; too great to be counted; immeasurable.

untouchable adj unable to be touched or handled; exempt from criticism or control; lying beyond reach.

untoward adj unseemly; unfavorable; adverse.

untrue adj incorrect, false; not faithful, disloyal; inaccurate.

untruth n falsehood; a lie.

untruthful adj telling lies; false.

UNTSO abbr = United Nations Truce Supervision Organization.

UNTT abbr = United Nations Trust Territory.

untutored adj lacking (refined) education.

Unuist n a king of the Picts, Britain; the brother of Drest IV; reigned from 820–834.

unused adj not (yet) used; (with to) not accustomed (to something).

unusual adj uncommon; rare.

unutterable adj impossible to express in words.—**unutterably** adv.

unvarnished adj not varnished; plain, direct; not embellished.

unveil vt to reveal; to disclose.

unwaged adj not paid a wage; unemployed.

unwarrantable adj indefensible.

unwarranted adj not authorized.

unwary adj lacking caution; heedless, gullible; unguarded.—**unwarily** adv.

UNWCC abbr = United Nations War Crimes Commission.

unwelcome adj not welcome, not invited; disagreeable; unpleasant.

unwell adj ill, not well; (inf) suffering from a hangover.

unwholesome adj harmful to physical, mental, or moral health and well-being; ill-looking; (food) of poor quality.—**unwholesomeness** n.

unwieldy adj not easily moved or handled, as because of large size; awkward.—**unwieldily** adv.—**unwieldiness** n.

unwilling adj not willing, reluctant; said or done with reluctance.—**unwillingly** adv.—**unwillingness** n.

unwind vt to untangle; to undo. * vi to relax.

unwise adj lacking wisdom; imprudent.—**unwisely** adv.

unwitting adj not knowing; unintentional.—**unwittingly** adv.

unworldly adj spiritual, not concerned with the material world.

unworthy adj (**unworthier, unworthiest**) not deserving.

unwritten adj not written or printed; traditional; oral.

unwritten law n law based on custom or mores rather than legislative enactment.

UNY abbr = United Nations of Yoga.

up adv to, toward, in or on a higher place; to a later period; so as to be even with in time, degree, etc. * prep from a lower to a higher point on or along. * adj moving or directed upward; at an end; (inf) well-informed. * vt (**upping, upped**) to raise; to increase; to take up. * n ascent; high point.

up abbr = under proof (alcohol).

up. abbr = upper.

UP abbr = Union Pacific; United Presbyterian; United Press; University Press.

UPA abbr = United Printers Association.

up-and-coming adj promising for the future; likely to succeed.

upas n a Javanese tree that yields a poisonous sap.

upbeat n (mus) an unaccented beat in the last bar. * adj (inf) cheerful, optimistic.

upbraid vt to rebuke severely; to reproach.

upbringing n the process of educating and nurturing (a child).

UPC abbr = United Presbyterian Church; Universal Postal Convention; Universal Product Code.

upcountry adv towards the interior of a country, inland.

update vt to bring up to date.

Updike n **John Hoyer** (1932–) American novelist, short-stor y writer, and poet whose best-known work is the "Rabbit" sequence, e.g. *Rabbit, Run*. His other works include the novels *The Centaur* and short-story collections, e.g. *Pigeon Feathers and Other Stories*.

updraught, updraft n a upward flow of air or other gas.

upend vti to turn or become turned on end; to upset or transform completely.

upfront adj honest, open. * adv (money) paid in advance.

upgrade vt to improve, raise to a higher grade.

upheaval n radical or violent change.

uphill adj ascending, rising; difficult, arduous. * adv up a slope or hill; against difficulties.

uphold vt (**upholding, upheld**) to support, sustain; to defend.

upholster vt (furniture) to fit with stuffing, springs, covering, etc.—**upholsterer** n.

upholstery n (pl **upholsteries**) materials used to make a soft covering esp for a seat.

UPI abbr = United Press International.

Upjohn n **Richard** (1802–78) English architect whose notable works include Trinity Church, New York.

upkeep n maintenance; the cost of it.

upland n an area of high ground. * adj of or pertaining to uplands.

uplift vt to raise, lift up; to improve the moral, cultural, spiritual, etc standard or condition of. * n a moral, cultural, spiritual, etc improvement.

upload vt (comput) to copy a file from your computer to another computer connected through the telecommunication system. See also **download**.

upmarket adj of or appealing to wealthier buyers.

upmost see **uppermost**.

UPNI abbr = Unionist Party of Northern Ireland.

UPOA abbr = Ulster Public Officers Association.

upon prep on, on top of.

UPOW abbr = Union of Post Office Workers.

upper adj farther up; higher in position, rank, status. * n the part of a boot or shoe above the sole; (sl) a drug used as a stimulant.

upper case n capital letters.—**upper-case** adj.

upper class n people occupying the highest social rank.—**also** adj.

upper crust n (inf) the aristocracy.

uppercut n an upward swinging punch to the chin.—**also** vb.

Upper Egypt n the long, narrow valley of the Nile from Memphis to the first cataract, forming one of the original two lands that comprised the ancient Egyptian kingdom. Its chief center was Thebes.

upper hand n the position of control, advantage.

upper house, chamber n one of the two houses of a bicameral legislature, such as the British House of Lords or US Senate.

uppermost adj at the top; highest in importance. * adv into the highest position, etc.—**also upmost**.

uppity adj (inf) snobbish, arrogant.

Uppsala n city in Sweden.

upright adj vertical, in an erect position; righteous, honest, just. * n a vertical post or support. * adv vertically.

uprising n a revolt; a rebellion.

uproar n a noisy disturbance; a commotion; an outcry.

uproarious adj making or marked by an uproar; extremely funny; (laughter) boisterous.—**uproariously** adv.

uproot vt to tear out by the roots; to remove from established surroundings.

UPS abbr = uninterruptible power supply.

upset[1] vt (**upsetting, upset**) to overturn; to spill; to disturb; to put out of order; to distress; to overthrow; to make physically sick.

upset[2] n an unexpected defeat; distress or its cause. * adj distressed; confused; defeated.

upshot n the conclusion; the result.

upside down adj inverted; the wrong way up; (inf) topsy turvy.

upsilon n the 20th letter of the Greek alphabet.

upslope fog n an advection fog that occurs in upland areas.

upstage vt to draw attention to oneself. * adv to the rear of the stage.

upstairs adv up the stairs; to an upper level or story. * n an upper floor.

upstanding adj honest; of good character; in a standing position.

upstart n a person who has suddenly risen to a position of wealth and power; an arrogant person.

upstate n the mostly northern areas of a US state. * adv, adj towards, in, or pertaining to this area of a US state.

upstream adv, adj in the direction from which a stream is flowing.

upstroke n an upward stroke, as of a pen, paintbrush, piston, etc.

upsurge n a sudden rise or swell.

upswing n an upward swing or movement; an improvement, esp in the state of the economy.

uptake n a taking up; a shaft or pipe for carrying smoke upwards; (inf) understanding.

uptight adj (inf) very tense, nervous, etc.

up-to-date adj modern; fashionable.

upturn n an upward trend; an (economic) improvement. * vt to turn upside down.

UPU abbr = Universal Postal Union.

UPUP abbr = Ulster Popular Unionist Party.

uPVC abbr = unplasticised polyvinyl chloride.

UPW abbr = Union of Post Office Workers.

upward, upwards adj from a lower to a higher place.—**also** adv.

upward compatibility adj (comput) the ability of an application program to run under a more advanced computer or operating system than it was originally designed for.

upwardly-mobile adj aspiring to improve one's social and economic status.—**upward mobility** n.

upwelling n the means by which cold, nutrient-rich deep sea currents rise through the ocean to the warmer surface layers.

upwind adj, adv in the direction from which the wind is blowing.

UQ abbr = University of Queensland.

Ur n (Bible) a very old center of early civilization in Mesopotamia near the mouth of the Euphrates; it is first named as the place from which Abraham and his father Terah, and their household set out for Haran. See also **Mesopatania**.

Ur symbol (chem) uranium.

UR abbr = Uniform Regulations; unconditioned reflex.

URA abbr = Urban Regeneration Agency.

uraeus n (Egypt) an ornamental serpent worn on the brow, emblematic of the snake-goddess Wadjet or Buto, and symbol of kingship from the early Lower Egypt kingdom. See also **regalia**.

Urania n (Greek myth) one of the nine Muses, who presided over astronomy.

uranium n a metallic element used as a source of nuclear energy.

uranium series dating n an absolute dating method based on the radioactive decay of uranium isotopes.

urano- *prefix* sky; the heavens.

uranography *n* the description and mapping of the stars, etc by astronomers.— **uranographer** *n*. —**uranographic** *adj*.

Uranus[1] *n* the seventh planet from the sun.

Uranus[2] *n* (*Greek myth*) the sky and the god of the sky.

urate *n* a salt or ester of uric acid.—**uratic** *adj*.

uratemia *n* (*med*) the presence in the blood of urate compounds, associated with gout, when urates are deposited in the body.

urban *adj* of or relating to a city.—**urbanization, urbanisation** *n*.

Urban *n* **Joseph** (1872–1933) Austrian painter and architect who was also the first designer to use modern and Art Deco designs for movies.

Urban VIII *n* **[Maffei Barberini]** (1568–1644) Italian pope (1623–44). He developed his diplomatic skills as a papal envoy to France, befriended writers and scholars (among them Galileo Galilei), established the papal summer residence at Castel Gandolfo, and used his influence to establish members of his family in important positions.

urban decay *n* the older, rundown part of a city where housing has become dilapidated and vandalism and petty crime are common.

urban diseconomies *n* the disadvantages of urban life, e.g. traffic congestion, pollution, higher rates, and higher house insurance.

urbane *adj* sophisticated; refined.—**urbanity** *n*.

urban guerrilla *n* a terrorist who operates in a town or city.

urbanite *n* a person who lives in a town or city.

urban renewal *n* rehabilitation of dilapidated city areas, as by housing construction and slum clearance.

URBM *abbr* = ultimate-range ballistic missile.

URC *abbr* = United Reformed Church.

urchin *n* a raggedly dressed mischievous child; a sea urchin.

urea *n* a soluble crystalline compound present in urine produced by protein metabolism.

ureaplasma *n* microorganisms responsible for diseases such as prostatitis, nonspecific urethritis, infertility, and neonatal death.

uremia, uraemia *n* the accumulation of waste products in the blood that are normally passed in the urine.

ureter *n* a tube that carries urine from the kidney to the bladder or cloaca.

ureterectomy *n* surgical excision of the ureter, usu with the removal of the associated kidney.

ureteritis *n* inflammation of the ureter, which usu occurs with bladder inflammations.

ureteroenterostomy *n* the creation by surgery of a link between the ureter and the bowel, thus bypassing the bladder.

ureteroplasty *n* reconstruction of a damaged or diseased ureter by surgery, using tissue from the bowel or from the bladder.

ureteroscope *n* an instrument introduced into a dilated ureter often to locate a stone or remove stone fragments created by the ultrasonic destruction of a larger stone.

ureterostomy *n* the creation of an external opening to the ureter whereby the ureter is brought to the surface to permit drainage.

ureterotomy *n* an incision into the ureter, commonly to remove a stone.

urethra *n* the duct carrying urine out of the bladder.

urethritis *n* inflammation of the urethra.

uretic *adj* of or pertaining to the urine.

Urey *n* **Harold Clayton** (1893–1981) American chemist who was awarded the 1934 Nobel prize for chemistry for his isolation of the heavy hydrogen isotope, deuterium. He worked on the production of heavy water during World War II.

URF *abbr* = uterine relaxing factor.

urge *vt* to drive forward; to press, plead with. * *n* an impulse, yearning.

Urgench *n* city in Uzbekistan.

urgency *n* (*pl* **urgencies**) the quality or condition of being urgent; compelling need; importance.

urgent *adj* impelling; persistent; calling for immediate attention.—**urgently** *adv*.

-urgy *n suffix* technology; technique.

urh-heen *n* (*mus*) a Chinese violin.

URI *abbr* = upper respiratory infection.

-uria *n suffix* diseased condition of the urine.

Uriah *n* (*Bible*) David committed adultery with Bathsheba, the wife of Uriah the Hittite, and then arranged for Uriah to be sent to the front battle line where he was killed. *See also* **Bathsheba; David; Nathan**.

uric *adj* of, present in, or derived from urine.

uric acid *n* a white odorless substance found in the urine of birds, reptiles, and some mammals.

Urien *n* British king of Rheged (reigned late 5th century); descended from King Coel, who ruled this kingdom around the Solway Firth, Scotland. He is said to have been the father of Owain.

urim and thummim *n* (*Bible*) objects put in the breastpiece worn by the high priest and used in casting lots to determine the will of God.

urinal *n* a bowl or trough for urination in public lavatories.

urinalysis *n* (*pl* **urinalyses**) the chemical analysis of urine for signs of disease.

urinary organs *n* the kidneys, ureters, bladder, and urethra responsible for the extraction of components from the blood to form urine, its storage, and periodic discharge from the body.

urinary tract *n* the system of ducts that permits movement of urine out of the body from the kidneys, i.e. the ureters, bladder, and urethra.

urinate *vi* to pass urine.

urination *n* the discharge of urine from the body via the urethra, begun by a voluntary relaxation of the sphincter muscle below the bladder.—*also* **micturition**.

urine *n* a yellowish fluid excreted by the kidneys and conveyed to the bladder.— **urinary** *adj*.

urine retention *n* the condition when urine is produced by the kidneys but it is retained in the bladder because of an obstruction or a weakness in the bladder.

urinogenital *adj* urogenital.

Uris *n* **Leon M[arcus]** (1924–) American novelist whose best known work is *Exodus* (1958).

URL *abbr* (*comput*) = Uniform Response Locator. Identifies the location of files on servers.

urn *n* a vase or large vessel; a receptacle for preserving the ashes of the dead; a large metal container for boiling water for tea or coffee.

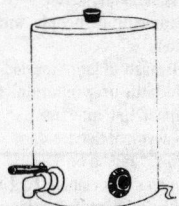

urnfield *n* (*archeo*) a cemetery of cremation graves with ashes in urns.

Urnfield cultures *n* (*archeo*) Bronze Age cultures in Europe which made use of urnfields.

uro-, ur- *prefix* urine; urinary tract.

urogenital, urinogenital *adj* of or pertaining to the urinary and reproductive organs.—*also* **genitourinary**.

urology *n* the medical study and treatment of urogenital diseases.—**urologist** *n*. — **urological** *adj*.

uroscopy *n* the diagnosis of diseases by the examination of the patient's urine.

Ursa Major *n* **[The Great Bear]** a constellation in the northern hemisphere which is one of the most familiar and easily recognized.

Ursa Minor *n* **[The Little Bear]** a constellation in the northern hemisphere, described by Ptolemy in AD 140, and containing the north celestial pole.

ursine *adj* of or resembling a bear.

Ursula *n* **Saint** (4th century) legendary British princess. To avoid marriage, she is said to have asked to travel for three years with 11,000 maidens. On their return journey, they were massacred by the Huns of Cologne. Her feast day is October 21.

URT *abbr* = upper respiratory tract.

Urtext *n* (*mus*) (*German*) "original text."

URTI *abbr* = upper respiratory tract infection.

urticaria *n* an allergic reaction which produces raised itchy whitish patches on the skin.—*also* **hives; nettle rash**.

URTU *abbr* = United Road Transport Union.

Uru. *abbr* = Uruguay.

Uruguay *n* a republic in South America, lying to the south of Brazil on the east coast of the continent.

us *pron* the objective case of **we**.

us *abbr* (*Latin*) = ut supra, "as above."

u/s *abbr* = unserviceable; useless.

US *abbr* = Uncle Sam; Under-Secretary; United Service; United States; unconditioned stimulus.

USA *abbr* = United States Army; United States of America.

USAB *abbr* = United States Animal Bank.

USAF *abbr* = United States Air Force.

USAFA *abbr* = United States Air Force Academy.

usage *n* customary use; practice, custom; use of language.

USAID *abbr* = United States Agency for International Development.

US Army *abbr* = United States Army.

USBA *abbr* = United States Badminton Association; United States Brewers Association.

USC *abbr* = Ulster Special Constabulary; United States of Colombia.

U.S.C. *abbr* = United States Code.

USCC, USCCt *abbr* = United States Circuit Court.

USCCR *abbr* = United States Commission on Civil Rights.

USCG *abbr* = United States Coast Guard.

Uscias *n* (*Irish Celtic myth*) one of the four wizards who taught their magic to the Tuatha De Danann before they came to Ireland, the others being Esias, Morfessa and Simias.

USCL *abbr* = United Society for Christian Literature.

USCSOI *abbr* = US Customs Service Office of Investigation.

USDA *abbr* = United States Department of Agriculture.

USDAW *abbr* = Union of Shop, Distributive and Allied Workers.

USDistCt *abbr* = United States District Court.

U

US Dollar *n* currency of the United States of America (USA), Guam, Northern Mariana Islands, Palau, Puerto Rico, British Virgin Islands, Federated States of Micronesia, Marshall Islands, US Virgin Islands, Turks and Caicos Islands.

USDOC *abbr* = United States Department of Commerce.

use[1] *vt* to put to some purpose; to utilize; to exploit (a person); to partake of (drink, drugs, tobacco, etc).—**usable, useable** *adj*.

use[2] *n* act of using or putting to a purpose; usage; usefulness; need (for); advantage; practice, custom.

USec *abbr* = Under-Secretary.

used *adj* not new; second-hand.

useful *adj* able to be used to good effect; (*inf*) capable, commendable.—**usefully** *adv*.

useless *adj* having no use.—**uselessly** *adv*.—**uselessness** *n*.

Usenet *n* (*comput*) a collection of all the newsgroups.

user *n* one who uses; (*inf*) a drug addict; (*comput*) the person who is operating the computer.

user-defined *adj* (*comput*) a selection of preferences chosen by the user of a computer.

user-friendly *adj* easy to understand and operate.

user group *n* (*comput*) a gathering of people with similar objectives who communicate through computers.

Userkaf *n* first king of the Fifth Dynasty of Egypt (period ranged from 2510–2460).

user interface *n* a means by which the user communicates with the computer, e.g. graphical user interface, command line interface.

USES *abbr* = United States Employment Service.

usf *abbr* (*German*) = *und so fort*, "and so on."

USFA *abbr* = Ulster Sea Fishermen's Association; US Fire Administration.

USFWS *abbr* = United States Fish and Wildlife Service.

USG *abbr* = United States Government.

USGA *abbr* = United States Golf Association.

USGS *abbr* = United States Geological Survey.

U-shaped valley *or* **glaciated valley** *n* a valley created by a glacier that occupied the whole valley, rather than just the valley floor, over-steepening the sides and widening it.

usher *n* one who shows people to their seats in a theater, church, etc; a doorkeeper in a law court. * *vt* to escort to seats, etc.

usherette *nf* a woman who directs people to their seats in a cinema.

USHG *abbr* = United States Home Guard.

USI *abbr* = United Service Institution; Union of Students in Ireland.

USIA *abbr* = United States Information Agency.

USIP *abbr* = United States Institute of Peace.

USITC *abbr* = United States International Trade Commission.

USL *abbr* = United States Legation.

USM *abbr* = United States Mail; United States Marine; underwater-to-surface missile; unlisted securities market.

USMA *abbr* = United States Military Academy.

USMC *abbr* = United States Marine Corps.

USMHS *abbr* = United States Marine Hospital Service.

USMS *abbr* = United States Marshals Service.

USN *abbr* = United States Navy.

USNA *abbr* = United States National Army; United States Naval Academy.

USNCB *abbr* = United States National Central Bureau of INTERPOL.

USNG *abbr* = United States National Guard.

USNRF *abbr* = United States Naval Reserve Force.

USP, U S Pharm. *abbr* = United States Pharmacopoeia.

USPG *abbr* = United Society for the Propagation of the Gospel.

USPHS *abbr* = United States Public Health Service.

USPO *abbr* = United States Post Office.

USPS *abbr* = United States Postal Service.

USR *abbr* = United States Reserves.

USRCS *abbr* = United States Revenue Cutter Service.

USS *abbr* = Under-Secretary of State; United Seamen's Service; United States Scouts; United States Senate; United States Ship; United States Standard; Universities Superannuation Scheme; ultrasound scanning.

USSC, USSCt. *abbr* = United States Supreme Court.

USSR *abbr* = (*formerly*) Union of Soviet Socialist Republics.

USSS *abbr* = United States Steamship.

Ustinov *n* Sir Peter [Alexander] (1921–) British actor , director, dramatist, and raconteur (of Russian-French parentage).

USTR *abbr* = United States Trade Representative.

usu. *abbr* = usual; usually.

usual *adj* customary; ordinary; normal.—**usually** *adv*.

usurer *n* a person who lends money at an excessively high rate of interest.

usurp *vt* to seize or appropriate unlawfully.—**usurper** *n*.

usury *n* (*pl* **usuries**) the practice of taking excessive interest on a loan; an excessive interest rate.

USV *abbr* = United States Volunteers.

usw *abbr* (*German*) = *und so weiter*, "and so forth."

USW *abbr* = ultrashort waves; ultrasonic waves.

USWD *abbr* = Undersurface Warfare Division.

UT *abbr* = University of Tasmania; Utah; unit trust; urinary tract.

UTA *abbr* = Ulster Transport Authority; Unit Trust Association; United Typothetae of America.

Utah *or* **UT** *n* a state of the USA, of which the capital is Salt Lake City.

"Utah, We Love Thee" *n* the song of the American state, Utah.

UTC *abbr* = Unitary Tax Campaign; Universal Time Coordinates; University Training Corps.

ut dict. *abbr* (*Latin*) = *ut dictum*, "as directed."

utensil *n* an implement or container, esp one for use in the kitchen.

uterine *adj* relating to the uterus.

uterus *n* (*pl* **uteri**) the female organ in which offspring are developed until birth, the womb.—**uterine** *adj*.

UTI *abbr* = urinary tract infection.

utilitarian *adj* designed to be of practical use.

utilitarianism *n* the ethical doctrine that the criterion of right action is that which produces the greatest happiness for the greatest number.

utility *n* (*pl* **utilities**) usefulness; a public service, such as telephone, electricity, etc; a company providing such a service.

utility program *n* (*comput*) a program that helps the user to obtain the most benefit from a computer system by performing routine tasks, e.g. copying data from one file to another. *See also* **desk accessory**.

utility room *n* a room containing laundry appliances, heating equipment, etc.

utilize *vt* to make practical use of.—**utilization** *n*.

utmost *adj* of the greatest degree or amount; furthest. * *n* the most possible.

utopia *n* a imaginary society or place considered to be ideal or perfect.—**utopian** *adj*, *n*.

Utopian novel *n* a novel set in a supposedly ideally organized state.

UTS *abbr* = ultimate tensile strength.

ut sup. *abbr* (*Latin*) = *ut supra*, "as above."

utter[1] *adj* absolute; complete.

utter[2] *vt* to say; to speak.—**utterance** *n*.

utterly *adv* completely.

Utzon *n* **Jørn** (1918–) Danish architect and town planner whose best-known building is the Sydney Opera House.

UU *abbr* = Ulster Unionist.

Uuencode *n* (*comput*) a program used to convert a file into an ASCII file so that it can be transmitted as a text message.

UUM *abbr* = underwater-to-underwater missile.

UUP *abbr* = Ulster Unionist Party.

Uurad *n* (*d*. 842) a king of the Picts, Britain (839–842). Four of his sons claimed the throne after him.

UUUP *abbr* = United Ulster Unionist Party.

uuV *abbr* (*German*) = *unter üblichem Vorbehalt*, "errors and omissions excepted."

UV *abbr* = ultraviolet.

UVA *abbr* = ultraviolet radiation A.

UVAF *abbr* = Unemployed Voluntary Action Fund.

UVB *abbr* = ultraviolet radiation B.

UVC *abbr* = ultraviolet radiation C.

uvea *n* the middle pigmented layer of the eye, consisting of the iris, choroid, and ciliary body.

uveitis *n* inflammation of any part of the uvea of the eye.

UVF *abbr* = Ulster Volunteer Force.

UVL *abbr* = ultraviolet light.

UVR *abbr* = ultraviolet radiation.

uvula *n* (*pl* **uvulas, uvulae**) the fleshy tissue suspended in the back of the throat over the back part of the tongue.

u/w *abbr* = underwater; unladen weight.

U/w *abbr* = underwriter.

UWA *abbr* = University of Western Australia.

UWC *abbr* = Unemployed Workers' Charter.

UWCE *abbr* = Underwater Weapons and Countermeasures Establishment.

UWE *abbr* = University of the West of England.

UWEAMA *abbr* = Under Water Equipment & Apparel Manufacturers' Association.

UWIST *abbr* = University of Wales Institute of Science and Technology.

UWRA *abbr* = Urban Water Research Association.

UWT *abbr* = Urban Wildlife Trust.

U-X *symbol* (*chem*) uranium X.

UXB *abbr* = unexploded bomb.

uxorious *adj* excessively fond of one's wife; doting.—**uxoriously** *adv*.—**uxoriousness** *n*.

U-Y *symbol* (*chem*) uranium Y.

Uzbekistan *n* a central Asian republic of the former USSR, which declared itself independent in 1991. The Republic of Uzbekistan shares borders with Turkmenistan in the west, Kyrgyzstan, Tajikistan, and Afghanistan and it encompasses the southern half of the Aral Sea.

Uzzah *n* (*Bible*) driver of the cart carrying the Ark when it was brought from the house of Abinadab by David; the oxen stumbled and Uzzah put out his hand to steady the Ark, but was struck dead for this sacrilegious act. *See also* **Ark of the Covenant**.

Uzziah *n* [Azariah]; reigned in Jerusalem 783–742 BC, the most prosperous period of the kingdom of Judah; he was an able and powerful ruler, but contracted leprosy, considered a punishment from God.

V

v, V *n* the 22nd letter of the English alphabet; something shaped like a V.
V *symbol* (*chem*) vanadium.
v *abbr* = vacuum; (*Latin*) *vel*, "or"; velocity; verb; verse; verso; versus; vertical; very; (*Latin*) *vide*, "see"; volume; (*German*) *von*, "of"; vowel.
v. *abbr* = valve; ventral; version; vicar; vice-; village; vision; vocative; voice; voltage; volunteers; vena.
V *abbr* = 5 in Roman numerals; (*math*) vector; velocity; (*chem*) vicinal; victory; volt(s); (*mus*) verte, violin, violino, violini, voce, voci, volta, volti.
V42 bis *n* (*comput*) a data compression and error correction standard used for communications between modems.
va *abbr* = verb active; verbal adjective; viola.
v.a. *abbr* = verb active; verbal adjective; (*Latin*) *vixit annos*, " he *or* she lived . . . years."
v/a *abbr* = voucher attached.
VA *abbr* = Department of Veterans Affairs; Vicar Apostolic; Vice Admiral; Virginia (*also* **Va**); Volunteer Artillery.
va & i *abbr* = verb active and intransitive.
VAB *abbr* = Voluntary Agencies Bureau.
vac *n* (*inf*) a vacation.
vac *abbr* = vacuum.
vacancy *n* (*pl* **vacancies**) emptiness; an unoccupied job or position.
vacant *adj* empty; unoccupied; (*expression*) blank.—**vacantly** *adv*.—**vacantness** *n*.
vacate *vt* to leave empty; to give up possession of.
vacation *n* a period away from work, school, etc for travel, rest or recreation; a period of the year when universities, colleges and law courts are closed. * *vi* to go on holiday.
vacationer, vacationist *n* a person on vacation, a holiday-maker.
Vaccarini *n* **Giovan B** (1702–) Italian architect whose notable works include Catania Cathedral.
vaccinal *adj* pertaining to or caused by a vaccine or vaccination.
vaccinate *vt* to inoculate with vaccine as a protection against a disease.—**vaccinator** *n*.
vaccination *n* inoculation with a vaccine; the resulting scar; the production of immunity to a disease by inoculation with a vaccine or a specially prepared material that stimulates the production of antibodies.
vaccine *n* a modified and hence harmless virus or other microorganism used for inoculation to give immunity from certain diseases by stimulating antibody production; cowpox virus used in this way against smallpox; (*comput*) a utility program designed to prevent a
computer virus from attacking a system.
vaccinia *n* (*med*) cowpox.—**vaccinial** *adj*.
vacillate *vi* to waver, to show indecision; to fluctuate.—**vacillation** *n*. —**vacillator** *n*.
vacuity *n* (*pl* **vacuities**) emptiness; a vacant state of mind or expression; absence of matter; a vacuum; idleness; lack; an inane remark.
vacuole *n* (*biol*) a small cell or cavity filled with fluid in the interior of organic cells or protoplasm.—**vacuolate, vacuolated** *adj*.
vacuous *adj* empty; lacking intelligence, mindless.—**vacuously** *adv*.—**vacuousness** *n*.
vacuum *n* (*pl* **vacuums, vacua**) a region devoid of all matter; a region in which gas is present at low pressure; a vacuum cleaner. * *vt* to clean with a vacuum cleaner. * *adj* of, having or creating a vacuum; working by suction or maintenance of a partial vacuum.
vacuum bottle, vacuum flask *n* a container for keeping liquids hot or cold.
vacuum cleaner *n* an electrical appliance for removing dust from carpets, etc, by suction.—**vacuum-clean** *vt*.

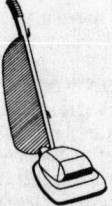

vacuum distillation *n* (*chem*) distillation performed under reduced pressure.
vacuum-packed *adj* sealed in an airtight packet from which the air has been removed.

VAD *abbr* = Voluntary Aid Detachment.
vade mecum *n* (*pl* **vade mecums**) a handbook or manual, etc for ready reference, usu of a size to fit in a pocket.
VAdm *abbr* = Vice Admiral.
vadose *adj* pertaining to the layer above the surface of the water table and immediately below the surface of the ground.
Vaduz *n* capital city of the Principality of Liechtenstein.
vagabond *n* a vagrant; a wandering, homeless person.—**vagabondage** *n*. —**vagabondism** *n*.
vagal *adj* of, pertaining to, affected or controlled by the vagus nerve.
vagary *n* (*pl* **vagaries**) unpredictable or erratic behavior or actions; a whim.—**vagarious** *adj*.
vagina *n* (**vaginas, vaginae**) in female mammals and humans, the canal connecting the uterus and the external sex organs.—**vaginal** *adj*.
vaginate, vaginated *adj* (*bot*) (*plant anat*) sheathed; with a vagina or sheath.
vaginitis *n* inflammation of the vagina as a result of infection or deficiency in diet or poor hygiene.
vago *n* (*mus*) (*Italian*) with a vague, indefinite expression.
vagotomy *n* (*med*) the cutting of fibers of the vagus nerve to the stomach.
vagrancy *n* (*pl* **vagrancies**) the habits and life of a vagrant; wandering without a settled home.
vagrant *n* a person who has no settled home, a tramp. * *adj* wandering, roaming; wayward.—**vagrantly** *adv*.
vague *adj* unclear; indistinct, imprecise; (*person*) absent-minded.—**vaguely** *adv*.—**vagueness** *n*.
vagus *n* (*pl* **vagi**) vagus nerve.
vagus nerve *n* the tenth cranial nerve, which supplies the muscles for swallowing, and carries the taste sensation from the mouth.
vail[1] *vti* (*arch*) to lower, to let fall; to take off (a hat) in respect.
vail[2] *n* (*arch*) a gratuity, a tip.
vain *adj* conceited; excessively concerned with one's appearance; senseless; futile; worthless; **in vain** to no purpose.—**vainly** *adv*.—**vainness** *n*.
vainglorious *adj* elated by one's achievements; boastful; showy.—**vaingloriously** *adv*.—**vaingloriousness** *n*.
vainglory *n* (*pl* **vainglories**) excessive vanity; boastfulness; showiness.
vair *n* a fur trimming on medieval robes, probably of Russian squirrel; (*her*) fur represented by small shields, colored white and blue alternately.
val. *abbr* = valentine; value.
Val. *abbr* = Valenciennes (lace).
valance *n* a decorative cover for the base of a bed; a canopy for a window frame to hide rods, etc; a pelmet.—**valanced** *adj*.
Valdiva *n* (*archeo*) an archeological site and name of a culture that flourished in coastal Ecuador, 3800–1700 BC.
vale[1] *n* a valley.
vale[2] *interj*, *n* (*arch*) farewell.
valediction *n* a saying farewell; a taking leave; an instance of this; a speech made at this time.
valedictorian *n* a college student appointed on grounds of merit to deliver the valedictory oration on Commencement day.
valedictory *adj* uttered or bestowed on saying farewell; shown, performed or done by way of valediction. * *n* (*pl* **valedictories**) a valedictory oration; a statement or speech made on leaving a position, etc.
valence, valency *n* (*pl* **valences, valencies**) (*chem*) the power of elements to combine; the number of atoms of hydrogen that an atom or group can combine with to form a compound.
valence electron, valency electron *n* (*chem*) one of the electrons present in the outermost shell of an atom of a corresponding element.
Valencia[1] *n* a city in Spain.
Valencia[2] *n* a city in Venezuela.
Valenciennes (lace) *n* an ornate type of bobbin lace, formerly made of linen, now usu of cotton.
-valent *adj suffix* having a specified number of valences, e.g., *univalent*.
Valentien *n* **Anna Marie** (1862–1950) and **Albert R** (1847–1925) American ceramicists who set up the Valentien Pottery, active until 1914.
valentine *n* a lover or sweetheart chosen on St Valentine's Day, February 14; a card or gift sent on that day.
Valentine *n* **Saint** (*d*. 270) Roman priest imprisoned during the reign of Claudius II for assisting his fellow Christians throughout the persecution. He refused to renounce his faith, and was beaten with clubs and beheaded. His feast day is February 14.

Valentino *n* **Rudolph** [Rodolfo Guglielmi di Valentina d'Antonguolla] (1895–1926) Italian-born American film actor. He became the leading screen personification of the romantic hero in such films as *The Four Horsemen of the Apocalypse* (1921) and *The Son of the Sheik* (1926).

valerian *n* a herb with a root formerly used for medicinal purposes; the root of this used as a sedative.

Valéry *n* **Paul** (1871–1945) French poet and critic associated with the symbolist movement, volumes of whose poetry include *The Young Fate* and *Graveyard by the Sea*.

valet *n* a manservant; a steward in a hotel or on board ship. * *vt* to attend (someone) as a valet. * *vi* to work as a valet.

Valletta *n* capital city of Malta.

valetudinarian, valetudinary *n* (*pl* **valetudinarians, valetudinaries**) a person who is overly preoccupied with his or her own health, a hypochondriac; a chronic invalid. * *adj* of ill health; sickly; seeking to recover health—**valetudinarianism** *n*.

valgus *adj* (*med*) deviating outwards from the vertical middle line of the body. * *n* (*pl* **valguses**) a deformity caused by a twisting from the middle line of the body, e.g., bow-legs.

Valhalla *n* (*Scandinavian myth*) the palace or hall of immortality in which the souls of heroes slain in battle dwell.—*also* **Walhalla**.

valiant *adj* courageous; brave.—**valiance, valiancy** *n*. —**valiantly** *adv*.

valid *adj* based on facts; (*objection, etc*) sound; legally acceptable; binding.—**validity** *n*. —**validly** *adv*.

validate *vt* to corroborate; to legalize.—**validation** *n*.

valine *n* an amino acid formed by the digestion of protein.

valise *n* a small case, usu of a size large enough to carry what is needed for an overnight visit.

Valkyrie *n* (*Scandinavian myth*) one of the twelve Norse war goddesses, handmaidens of Odin, who selected those who were worthy to be slain in battle and led them to Valhalla.—*also* **Walkyrie**.

vallation *n* a defensive wall; a rampart; the act of building this.

vallecula *n* (*pl* **valleculae**) (*anat*) a cleft or depressed area; (*bot*) a groove, a deep wrinkle.—**vallecular, valleculate** *adj*.

valley *n* (*pl* **valleys**) low land between hills or mountains usu with a river or stream flowing along its bottom; something resembling a valley, e.g., the angle where two sloping sides of a roof meet.

Valley *n* **The** capital city of Anguilla.

valley glacier *n* a glacier situated in an upland preglacial valley.

Valley of the Kings *n* funerary site for the kings of ancient Egypt used for 400 years; a steep-sided, rocky valley in the arid hills on the west bank of the Nile, opposite Thebes.

Valley of the Queens *n* funerary site at Thebes, in the hills above Medinet Habu and close to Deir el Medina, where queens' tombs were situated.

valley train *n* a deposit of sand, gravel and pebbles stretching along the sides of a valley for a considerable distance in front of the snout of a glacier.

valley wind *n* the wind generated in a valley as air is warmed by the sun during the day and cooled at night.

valonia *n* a large, dried acorn cup, or unripened acorn, from a particular kind of oak tree, used in tanning, dying, ink-making, etc.

valor *n* courage; bravery (in battle).—*also* **valour.**

valorous *adj* (*person*) valiant, courageous; (*action*) characterized by valor.—**valorously** *adv*.—**valorousness** *n*.

valorize *vt* to give an arbitrary price to (something) under government control.—**valorization** *n*.

Valparaiso *n* a city in Chile.

valse *n* a waltz, often used in the titles of musical compositions.

valuable *adj* having considerable importance or monetary worth. * *n* a personal possession of value, esp jewelry; (*pl*) valuable possessions.—**valuably** *adv*.

valuate *vt* to estimate the worth of, to value.—**valuator** *n*.

valuation *n* the act of valuing or valuating; an estimated price or worth; an estimation.—**valuational** *adj*.

value *n* worth, merit, importance; market value; purchasing power; relative worth; (*comput*) a numeric cell entry in a spreadsheet program; (*pl*) moral principles. * *vt* (**valuing, valued**) to estimate the worth of; to regard highly; to prize.—**valuer** *n*.

value added *n* (*com*) the value that is added to a company's bought-in materials and services by the company's own efforts, such as production and marketing.

value-added statement *n* (*com*) a form of accounting statement that indicates the value added accumulated by a company in the course of an accounting period and how this wealth has been allocated.

value-added tax *or* **VAT** *n* an indirect tax levied by the UK government on value added to goods or services.

value analysis *n* (*com*) a detailed examination and evaluation of a product's design or production with a view to ensuring that it is as economically and efficiently produced as possible.

value chain *n* (*com*) the chain of activities and processes by which a firm buys in materials or components, manufactures a product or creates a service, markets it and provides after-sales service.

value judgment *n* a subjective or unwarranted judgment.

valued *adj* estimated; esteemed; prized.

valueless *adj* without value; worthless.—**valuelessness** *n*.

valuta *n* the value of one currency in terms of another.

valvar *see* **valvular**.

valvate *adj* having, resembling, or operating by means of a valve or valves; (*bot*) (*petals*) meeting at the edges without overlapping.

valve *n* a device for controlling the flow of a gas or liquid through a pipe; (*anat*) a tube allowing blood to flow in one direction only; (*mus*) a device on a brass instrument for increasing the length of the tube and thus altering the pitch being played.

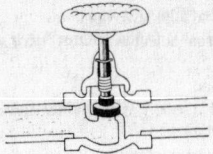

valvotomy *n* an operation undertaken to open a heart valve and render it functional.

valvular *adj* of, affecting a valve or valves, esp of the heart; acting like a valve; shaped like a valve; operating by means of a valve or valves.

valvular heart disease *n* a disease that affects mainly the aortic valve and mitral valve, which may narrow or weaken. *See* **aortic stenosis; stenosis**.

valvule, valvelet *n* a little valve; anything resembling this.

valvulitis *n* inflammation of the valves, esp of the heart.

vambrace *n* plate armor for the forearm.

VAMH *abbr* = Voluntary Association for Mental Health.

vamoose, vamose *vi* (*sl*) to make off quickly, to decamp.

vamp[1] *n* the part of a sock, boot or shoe covering the front of the foot; anything patched up or refurbished; an improvised musical accompaniment made up of chords. * *vt* to provide with a (new) vamp; to mend or repair; (*with* **up**) to renovate; (*mus*) to improvise.—**vamper** *n*.

vamp[2] *n* a seductive woman. * *vt* to fascinate or exploit by seducing. * *vi* to act as a vamp.

vampire *n* (*folklore*) a dead creature that by night leaves its grave to suck the blood of living people; a person who preys on others, an extortioner; a vampire bat.—**vampiric** *adj*.

vampire bat *n* a tropical American blood-sucking bat.

vampirism *n* belief in vampires; bloodsucking, or other acts associated with vampires.

VAMW *abbr* = Voluntary Association for Mental Welfare.

van[1] *n* a covered motor vehicle for transporting goods, etc.

van[2] *n* the vanguard.

VAN *abbr* = Voluntary Arts Network; value-added network.

vanadium *n* a rare soft white metallic element used in steel alloys.—**vanadic** *adj*.

Van Alen *n* **William** (1883–1954) American architect whose signature building was the wildly creative Chrysler Building in New York, begun in 1928.

Van Allen *n* **James Alfred** (1914–) American physicist who discovered the Van Allen radiation belts outside the earth's atmosphere.

Van Allen radiation belts *n* (*phys*) two belts of radiation consisting of charged particles (electrons and protons) trapped in the earth's magnetic field and forming two belts around the earth.

Vanbrugh *n* **Sir John** (1664–1726) English dramatist and architect, noted for his witty comedies, e.g. *The Relapse*, *The Provok'd Wife*, and *The Confederacy*. He was also an architect of note, the most famous of his buildings being Blenheim Palace.

Van Buren *n* **Martin** (1782–1862) American Democrat politician and 8th president of the US (1837–41).

Vancouver *n* a city in Canada.

V & A *abbr* = Victoria and Albert Museum.

vandal *n* a person who wilfully or ignorantly damages property; (*with cap*) a member of a Germanic tribe that sacked Rome (AD 455). * *adj* of, acting like a vandal; characterized by vandalism or lack of culture.

vandalism *n* the ruthless destruction or spoiling of anything beautiful or venerable; barbarous, ignorant or inartistic treatment.—**vandalistic** *adj*.

vandalize *vt* to carry out an act of vandalism.—**vandalization** *n*.

Van de Graaf generator *n* a machine that continuously separates electrostatic charges and in so doing produces a very high voltage.

van den Broeke *n* **Floris** (1945–) Dutch furniture designer who was one of the fashionable designers of the 1960s.

Van der Post *n* **Sir Laurens** [Jan] (1906–97) South African novelist, travel writer, and mystic whose novels include *The Seed and the Sower* (1963), filmed as *Merry Christmas, Mr Lawrence*. His travel books include *The Lost World of the Kalahari*.

van der Waals' force *n* a weak attractive force between two neighbouring atoms.

van de Velde *n* **Henry Clemens** (1863–1957) Belgian architect whose own house was a classic of the Art Nouveau style.

v & l *abbr* = vodka and lime.

van Doesburg *n* **Theo** (1883–1931) Dutch architect who was one of the founding members of the **De Stijl** group.

v & t *abbr* = vodka and tonic.

v & v *abbr* = verification and validation.

Vandyke beard *n* a small pointed beard.

Vandyke collar *n* a wide, white collar of lace or sewed work, with a deeply indented edge.

vane *n* a blade at the top of a spire, etc to show wind direction; a weather vane; a blade on a windmill or propeller.

van Eyck *n* **Jan** (*c*.1385–1441) Dutch painter. A master in the medium of oil painting, he was court painter to Philip, Duke of Burgundy from 1425 to *c*.1430. His paintings are both realistic and charged with a serene, spiritual atmosphere, as in the *Arnolfini Marriage* (1434).

vang *n* (*naut*) a guy rope from the end of a gaff to the deck, used for steadying the extremity of the peak of a gaff to the side of a ship; a rope running from the boom of a mainsail to the deck, used to keep the boom lowered.

Van Gogh *n* **Vincent** (1853–90) Dutch painter. Uncompromising from the start, his art was thoroughly unacademic in its realistic subject matter and bold, expressionistic style.

vanguard *n* the front part of an army; the leading position of any movement.

vanilla *n* extract from the orchid pod used as a flavoring.—**vanillic** *adj* from vanilla.

vanish *vi* to disappear from sight, to become invisible, esp in a rapid and mysterious manner; to fade away; to cease to exist; (*math*) (*numbers, quantities*) to become zero.—**vanisher** *n*.

vanishing cream *n* a cleansing or foundation cream for make-up that is colorless when applied to the face.

vanishing point *n* the point at which parallel lines viewed in perspective appear to converge; the point at which something disappears.

vanity *n* (*pl* **vanities**) a fruitless endeavor; worthlessness; empty pride or conceit; love of indiscriminate admiration; an idle matter or show; a worthless or unfounded idea or statement; emptiness, lightness.

vanity case, vanity box *n* a small case used for carrying cosmetics, etc.

vanquish *vt* to conquer; to defeat; to overcome, to subdue.—**vanquisher** *n*. — **vanquishment** *n*.

VANS *abbr* = value-added network service.

vantage *n* a favorable position; a position allowing a clear view or understanding.

Vanuatu *n* a parliamentary republic, formerly known as the New Hebrides, comprising some 12 islands and 60 islets in the Pacific Ocean. Vanuatu has been independent since 1980.

Vanvitelli *n* **Luigi** (1700–) Italian architect whose notable works include the palace at Caserta, Naples.

vanward *adj* towards the front, in the van. * *adv* forward, towards the front.

vapid *adj* flavorless, flat, insipid; dull, lifeless.—**vapidity** *n*. —**vapidly** *adv*.

vapor *n* the gaseous state of a substance normally liquid or solid; particles of water or smoke in the air; (*pl*) hysteria. * *vi* to pass off in vapor, vaporize; to boast.—*also* **vapour**.

vaporish *adj* like vapour; full of vapor; (*arch*) in a state of depression and lethargy.—*also* **vapourish**.—**vaporishness, vapourishness** *n*.

vaporize *vt* to change into vapor.—**vaporization** *n*. —**vaporizer** *n*.

vaporizer *n* a device that produces a mist of liquid medication for inhalation commonly used to treat asthma.

vaporous *adj* in the form of or like vapor; foggy, steamy; unreal, fanciful.—**vaporously** *adv*.—**vaporosity** *n*.

vapor pressure *n* (*phys*) the pressure exerted by a vapor whether in a mixture of gases or by itself; the part of the atmospheric pressure that is due to water molecules contained in the atmosphere.

vapor trail *n* condensed vapor left in the wake of an aircraft exhaust appearing as a white trail in the sky.

vapour *see* **vapor**.

vapourish *see* **vaporish**.

vapourware *n* (*comput*) software under development that is marketed in advance of its release.

vaquero *n* (*pl* **vaqueros**) a hersdman in the southwest USA; a cowboy.

var. *abbr* = variant; variation; variety; variometer; various.

Vardy *n* **John** (1718–) English architect. His notable works include Spencer House, London.

varec *n* the ash left after burning kelp.

Varèse *n* **Edgard** (1883–1965) French-born American composer and conductor.

His (usually orchestral) compositions are noted for their combination of the extreme registers of instruments with taped and electronic sounds.

Vargas Llosa *n* **[Jorge] Mario [Pedro]** (1936–) Peruvian novelist whose works, e.g. *The War of the End of the World* and *The Storyteller*, often feature radical restructuring of time, space, and even character identity within the narrative, and have some affinities with magic realism.

variable *adj* liable to change; not constant. * *n* (*math*) a changing quantity that can have different values, as opposed to a constant.—**variability** *n*. —**variably** *adv*.

variable cost *n* (*com*) an item of business expenditure that tends to vary directly with the level of output.

variable overheads *npl* (*com*) the business overheads or indirect costs that vary proportionately with the level of output.

variable star *n* a star with physical properties (e.g., brightness) which vary over the course of time, both on a regular and irregular basis.

variance *n* disagreement, dissension; variation; tendency to vary; (*law*) a discrepancy between two statements or documents; (*accounts*) the difference between the budgeted levels of cost for a business activity or income from it and the actual cost or income that was achieved; **at variance** in conflict.

variant *adj* different; differing from an accepted or normal type, text, etc. * *n* a variant form or reading.

variation *n* a varying or being varied; alteration; deviation from a standard or type; diversity; deviation of the magnetic needle from true north; the measure of this; (*gram*) inflexion; (*mus*) repetition of a theme or melody with modifications.—**variational** *adj*.

varicella *n* (*med*) chickenpox.—**varicelloid** *adj*.

varices *see* **varix**.

varicocele *n* a swelling of the veins of the scrotum or of the spermatic cord.

varicolored, varicoloured *adj* variegated, particolored; of several colors.

varicose *adj* (*veins*) abnormally swollen and dilated.— **varicosis** *n*.—**varicosity** *n*.

varicose ulcer *n* an ulcer on the lower leg that is difficult to heal because of poor circulation.

varicose veins *n* veins that have become stretched, distended, and twisted.

varied *adj* showing variety, changing; partially changed; various; variegated.—**variedly** *adv*.

variegate *vt* to mark with different colors or tints; to dapple, streak; to cause to diversify.

variegated *adj* marked with different colors.

variegation *n* the condition of being variegated; diversity of colors.

variety *n* (*pl* **varieties**) diversity; an assortment.—**varietal** *adj*.

variety show *n* an entertainment made up of various acts, such as songs, comedy turns, etc.

variform *adj* having various forms.

variola *n* (*med*) smallpox.—**variolar** *adj*.

variolate *adj* having shallow, pitted depressions similar to those left on the skin after smallpox. * *vt* to inoculate with smallpox virus.—**variolation** *n*.

variole *n* a whitish spot or round mass consisting of radiating threads of crystal.

variolite *n* a kind of igneous rock with whitish spots, made up of clustered varioles.—**variolitic** *adj*.

varioloid *n* smallpox modified by vaccination or other means of acquired partial immunity. * *adj* like smallpox.

variorum *n* an edition of the works of an author with notes by various commentators.—*also* *adj*.

various *adj* varied, different; several.—**variously** *adv*.

varix *n* (*pl* **varices**) (*med*) a varicose vein; a twisted, dilated artery.

var. lect. *abbr* = varia lectio.

varlet *n* a scoundrel; (*arch*) a servant, attendant, or page of a knight.

varmint *n* (*dial*) a rascal; an offensive or trying person or animal; (*hunting sl*) the fox.

Varna *n* a city in Bulgaria.

varnish *n* a sticky liquid which dries and forms a hard, glossy coating. * *vt* to coat with varnish.—**varnisher** *n*.

VARS *abbr* = Visual Artists Rights Society.

varsity *n* (*pl* **varsities**) (*Brit, NZ inf*) university.

varus *n* (*pl* **varuses**) a deformity caused by a turning in towards the vertical midline of the body, e.g., pigeon toes.

varve *n* a lacustrine deposit, near to ice sheets, of banded clays, silts and sands. The rhythmically banded sediments were deposited annually in lakes at the edge of ice sheets.

vary *vti* (**varying, varied**) to change, to diversify, modify; to become altered.—**varyingly** *adv*.

vas *n* (*pl* **vasa**) a vessel or duct, especially one carrying blood, lymph or sperm.

VAS *abbr* (*Brit*) = Vasectomy Advancement Society of Great Britain.

Vasari *n* **Giorgio** (1511–74) Italian glass painter who worked closely with Michelangelo and Raphael. He also designed the Uffizi in Florence.

VASCAR *abbr* = visual average speed computer and recorded (speed-trap device).

vascular *adj* (*biol*) of, consisting of, or containing vessels as part of a structure of animal and vegetable organisms for conveying blood, sap, etc.—**vascularity** *n*.

vasculitis *n* (*med*) inflammation of the blood vessels, which may cause damage to their linings and narrowing.

vasculum *n* (*pl* **vascula, vasculums**) a botanist's specimen box.

vas deferens *n* (*pl* **vasa deferentia**) one of the two tubes that join the testes to the ejaculatory duct via the prostate gland; the spermatic duct. *See* **testicle**.

vase *n* a vessel for displaying flowers.

vasectomy *n* (*pl* **vasectomies**) male sterilization involving the cutting of the vas deferens.

Vaseline *n* (*trademark*) petroleum jelly used as a lubricant.

vasoconstriction *n* (*med*) the narrowing of blood vessels with a consequent reduction in blood supply to the tissues.

vasoconstrictor *n* a nerve, drug, etc that constricts blood vessels.—**vasoconstrictive** *adj*.

vasodilation, vasodilatation *n* (*med*) the increase in diameter of blood vessels, producing a lowering of blood pressure and increased flow.

vasodilator *n* a nerve, drug, etc that dilates blood vessels.—**vasodilative** *adj*.

vasomotor *adj* (*nerve, drug, etc*) pertaining to or controlling the diameter of blood vessels.

vasopressin *n* a hormone of the pituitary gland that constricts blood vessels and reduces urine secretion by increasing the quantity of water reabsorbed by the kidney.—*also* **antidiuretic hormone.**

vasovagal attack *n* fainting, precipitated by a slowing of the heart and a fall in blood pressure.

vasovasostomy *n* the reversal of vasectomy.

vassal *n* a servant; dependant; subordinate.

vassalage *n* the state of being a vassal; the obligations associated with such a state; servitude; dependence; (*rare*) vassals collectively.

Vassos *n* **John** (1898–1985) Greek illustrator who was a pioneer in the use of applied psychology to determine the effectiveness of labels, packages and containers.

vast *adj* immense.—**vastly** *adv*.—*n* **vastness.**

vasty (**vastier, vastiest**) *adj* (*arch*) vast.

vat *n* a large barrel or tank. * *vt* (**vatting, vatted**) to put in a vat; to treat in a vat.

Vat. *abbr* = Vatican.

VAT *abbr* = value added tax.

vatic, vatical *adj* of, or relating to a prophet or prophecy.

Vatican *n* the residence of the pope in Rome; papal authority.

Vatican City *n* a papal state lying in the heart of Rome in Italy. It is the world's smallest independent state and headquarters of the Roman Catholic Church; capital city of Vatican City.

Vatican City Lira *n* currency of Vatican City.

Vaticanism *n* (*often derog*) the doctrine of Papal supremacy and infallibility.

vaticination *n* a prophecy.

Vatu *n* currency of Vanuatu.

vaudeville *n* (*mus*) (*French*) originally a type of popular, satirical song sung by Parisian street musicians. In the 19th century, stage performances with songs and dances were called "vaudevilles" and the term came to describe music hall shows.

Vaughan *n* **Henry** (1621–95) Welsh poet best known for his collection of mystical religious verse, *Silex Scintillans*.

Vaughan Williams *n* **Ralph** (1872–1958) English composer. His works include nine symphonies, opera, ballets, choral works, piano music, and chamber music.

vault[1] *n* an arched ceiling or roof; a burial chamber; a strongroom for valuables; a cellar.—**vaulted** *adj*.

vault[2] *vti* to leap or jump over an obstacle. * *n* a leap.—**vaulter** *n*.

vaulting[1] *n* (*arch*) arched work in a building, etc.

vaulting[2] *adj* overly confident; to an exaggerated degree; used in the act of leaping over.

vaulting shaft *n* (*archit*) the upright, vertical shaft from which the main ribs in a vault spring.

vaunt *vti* to display boastfully; to brag. * *n* a boast.—**vaunter** *n*.—**vauntingly** *adv*.

v. aux. *abbr* = verb auxiliary.

vavasour, vavasor, vavassor *n* (*feudalism*) the tenant of a baron or lord who is that lord's vassal and who in turn has other vassals under him.

Vavilov *n* **Nikolai Ivanovich** (1887–1943) Russian botanist and plant geneticist. He developed a "principle of diversity," which states that the original source of a cultivated plant will be found to lie within the area containing the greatest diversity of the plant.

vb. *abbr* = verb.

VB *abbr* = Veterans' Bureau.

vb. a. *abbr* = verbal adjective.

VBA *abbr* = Veterans Benefits Administration.

VBBA *abbr* = Vietnam-British Business Association.

VBF *abbr* = Vinegar Brewers Federation.

VBRA *abbr* = Vehicle Builders and Repairers Association.

vb.n. *abbr* = verbal noun.

vc. *abbr* = violoncello.

VC *abbr* = Vatican City; Veterinary Corps; Volunteer Corps; Vickers Commercial (used in names of aircraft manufactured by them, e.g. VC10); Victoria Cross; Viet Cong; vice-chairman; vice-chancellor; vice-consul.

VCA *abbr* = Vehicle Certification Association.

VCAA *abbr* = Veteran and Classic Aeroplane Association.

VC&GCA *abbr* (*Brit*) = Victoria Cross and George Cross Association.

VCC *abbr* = Veteran Car Club of Great Britain.

VCH *abbr* = Victoria County History.

VCPA *abbr* = Vintage and Classic Power Craft Association.

VCPS *abbr* = Video Copyright Protection Society.

VCR *abbr* = video cassette recorder.

VCT *abbr* = Vintage Charities Trust.

v.d. *abbr* = vapor density; various dates.

VD *abbr* = Volunteer (Officers') Decoration; venereal disease.

v. def. *abbr* = verb defective.

v. dep. *abbr* = verb deponent.

VDH *abbr* (*med*) = valvular disease of the heart.

VDI *abbr* (*comput*) = virtual device interface.

VDJ *abbr* = video disk jockey.

VDQS *abbr* (*French*) = *vin délimité de qualité supérieure*, "quality wine from a specified region."

VDR *abbr* = video-disk recording.

VDRL *abbr* = Venereal Disease Reference Laboratory Test.

VDS *abbr* (*Scot*) = Volunteer Development Scotland.

VDT *abbr* (*comput*) = Video Display Terminal. *See* **VDU**.

VDU *abbr* (*comput*) = visual display unit, or monitor or screen or video display terminal.

VE *abbr* = Victory in Europe (at the end of World War II); vaginal examination.

veal *n* the edible flesh of a calf.

Veblen *n* **Thorstein** (1857–1929) American economist (of Norwegian parentage). Regarded as the founder of the school of institutional economics. His works include *The Theory of the Leisure Class* (1899) and *The Theory of Business Enterprise* (1904).

vector *n* (*phys*) a physical quantity having both direction and magnitude, e.g. displacement, acceleration, etc; an aircraft's or missile's course; (*biol*) a piece of DNA that transmits a parasitic disease.—**vectorial** *adj*.

vector graphics *npl* (*comput*) *see* **object oriented graphics**.

Veda *n* (any of) the oldest sacred books or collection of hymns of the Hindus, written in old Sanskrit and of great antiquity.—**Vedic** *adj*.

Vedanta *n* a Hindu philosophy based on the Veda, postulating that the world of the senses is based on an illusion.—**Vedantic** *adj*.

vedette *n* a small patrol boat (—*also* **vedette boat**); a mounted sentry in advance of an outpost (—*also* **vidette**).

Vedic *adj* pertaining to the Veda, or to the old Sanskrit in which these were written; pertaining to the original Indo-Europeans of India.

veer *vi* (*wind*) to move in a clockwise direction; i.e. in the northern hemisphere from north to east and vice versa in the southern hemisphere; to swing around; to change from one mood or opinion to another.—**veeringly** *adv*.

veery *n* (*pl* **veeries**) a tawny North American thrush.

veg. *abbr* = vegetable(s).

VEGA *abbr* = Vegetarian Economy and Green Agriculture.

Vega *or* **Alpha Lyrae** *or* μ **Lyr** *n* the fifth brightest star in the sky, in the constellation Lyra.

Vega Carpio *n* **Lope de** (1562–1635) Spanish poet and dramatist whose eventful life included service in the Spanish Armada in 1588, and, near the end of his life, in the Spanish Inquisition.

vegan *n* a strict vegetarian who consumes no animal or dairy products.

vegetable *n* a herbaceous plant grown for food; (*inf*) a person who has suffered brain damage. * *adj* of, relating to or derived from plants.

vegetal *adj* of growth and vital functions; vegetable.

vegetarian *n* a person who consumes a diet that excludes meat and fish. * *adj* of vegetarians; consisting wholly of vegetables.

vegetarianism *n* the doctrine or practice of vegetarians; abstention from meating meat, fish, or other animal products.

vegetate *vi* to grow like a plant; to sprout; to lead a mentally inactive, aimless life.

vegetation *n* vegetable growth; plants in general.—**vegetational** *adj*.

vegetative, vegetive *adj* (*plants*) growing or having the power of growing, or producing growth in; (*way of life*) dull, passive, uneventful; (*reproduction*) asexual; referring to functions other than sexual reproduction.

vegetative propagation *n* (*bot*) a type of reproduction in which the non-sexual organs of the plant are capable of producing progeny.

vehement *adj* passionate; forceful; furious.—**vehemence, vehemency** *n*.—**vehemently** *adv*.

vehicle *n* a conveyance, such as a car, bus or truck, for carrying people or goods on land; a means of transmission for ideas, impressions, etc; a medium; (*med*) a substance in which a strong medicine can be administered palatably.—**vehicular** *adj*.

Veii *n* an ancient Etruscan city north of Rome.

veil *n* a thin fabric worn over the head or face of a woman; a nun's headdress; anything that conceals; a velum. * *vt* to put on a veil; to cover; to conceal, dissemble.

veiled *adj* covered with or wearing a veil; shrouded in a veil; concealed, hidden, covert; not openly declared; (*sound, voice*) indistinct, muffled.

vein *n* (*anat*) any thin-walled vessel that carries blood back from the body to the heart; (*geol*) a sheet-like feature usually occupying a fracture (crack) or fissure within a rock, which is infilled with mineral deposits; (*bot*) a branching rib in a leaf; a streak of different color, as in marble, cheese, etc; a style or mood (*serious vein*). * *vt* to streak.—**veiny** *adj*.

veinlet *n* a small vein.

veinprint *n* the pattern of veins on the back of the hand, which is unique to an individual.

vel. *abbr* = vellum.

Vela *or* **The Sail** *n* a constellation in the southern hemisphere situated partly within the Milky Way and earlier identified in the 1700s as one of the parts of a much larger constellation, Argo Navis (The Ship).

velamen *n* (*pl* **velamina**) (*anat*) an outer membrane or epidermis; a velum; (*bot*) a thick, moisture-absorbing aerial root, consisting of dead cells, found on some plants.

Vela pulsar *n* a young pulsar, about 10,000 years old, occurring in the constellation Vela.

velar *adj* of the velum or soft palate; (*phonetics*) pronounced with the back of the tongue touching the soft palate. * *n* a velar sound.

velarium *n* (*pl* **velaria**) in ancient Rome, the great awning that stretched over open theaters.

Velázquez, Velàsquez *n* Diego Roderiguez de Silva y (1599–1660) Spanish painter. Influenced by Titian and Tintoretto. His works include the portrait of *Pope Innocent X* and *Surrender of Breda*.

Velcro *n* (*trademark*) a nylon material made of matching strips of tiny hooks and pile that are easily pressed together or pulled apart.

veld, veldt the Afrikaans term for the naturally occurring open grasslands of South Africa, further classified according to altitude.

velites *n* in ancient Rome, a lightly armed soldier, usu from the poorer section of society.

velleity *n* (*pl* **velleities**) (*arch*) the lowest degree of desire, mere inclination.

vellum *n* fine parchment; a good quality writing paper.

veloce *adv* (*mus*) very quickly.

velocipede *n* an early form of bicycle, propelled by striking the toes on the road; any early form of bicycle or tricycle.

velocity *n* (*pl* **velocities**) the rate of change of position of any object; speed.

velocity of light *n* (*phys*) the vector quantity for light traveling through a given medium.

velodrome *n* an arena with a banked cycle-racing track.

velour, velours *n* a velvet-like fabric.

velouté *n* a rich white sauce or soup, with a basis of egg yolks, cream and stock.

velum *n* (*pl* **vela**) (*anat*) the soft palate; any body structure resembling a veil; (*bot, zool*) a membranous covering or organ, such as the membranous covering of certain molluscs or that covering a developing mushroom.

velure *n* a kind of plush or velvet-like material; a velvet pad for smoothing a silk hat.

velutinous *adj* (*bot*) thickly covered with short hairs, velvety.

velvet *n* a fabric made from silk, rayon, etc with a soft, thick pile; anything like velvet in texture.

velveteen *n* a cotton cloth with a pile like velvet.

velvety *adj* soft to the touch; mellow.

Ven. *abbr* = Venerable; Venice.

vena *n* (*pl* **venae**) (*anat*) a vein.

vena cava *n* (*pl* **venae cavae**) (*anat*) one of the two major veins that empty blood into the right chamber of the heart in air-breathing vertebrates.

venal *adj* corrupt; willing to accept bribes.—**venality** *n*. —**venally** *adv*.

venatic, venatical *adj* of or pertaining to hunting; (*people*) likely to engage in hunting.

venation *n* the arrangement of veins in a leaf or an insect's wing; these veins collectively.—**venational** *adj*.

vend *vt* to sell, to offer for sale; to peddle; (*rare*) to state or disseminate (an opinion, etc).

vendace *n* (*pl* **vendaces, vendace**) either of two types of small European freshwater fish.

vendee *n* (*law*) a buyer; someone to whom something has been sold.

vendetta *n* the taking of private vengeance; a feud.—**vendettist** *n*.

vendible *adj* saleable; (*arch*) venal. * *n* (*usu pl*) something that is saleable.

vending machine *n* a coin-operated machine which dispenses goods.

vendor, vender *n* a seller; a machine that ejects goods, etc, after a required amount of coins has been inserted.

veneer *n* an overlay of fine wood or plastic; a superficial appearance. * *vt* to cover with veneer.

venerable *adj* worthy of reverence or respect.—**venerability** *n*. —**venerably** *adv*.

Venerable Bede *see* **Bede**.

venerate *vt* to revere; to respect.—**venerator** *n*.

veneration *n* a venerating or being venerated; respect mingled with awe, deep reverence.

venereal *adj* (*disease*) resulting from sexual intercourse.

venereal disease *n* any of various diseases, such as syphilis or HIV/AIDS, transmitted by sexual contact.—*also* **sexually transmitted disease**.

venery[1] *n* (*arch*) hunting, usu with hounds, the chase.

venery[2] *n* (*arch*) sexual indulgence, the pursuit of sexual gratification.

venesection *n* the operation of opening a vein; phlebotomy.

Venet. *abbr* = Venetian.

Venetian blind *n* a window blind formed of long thin horizontal slips of wood that can be pivoted.

Venez. *abbr* = Venezuela.

Venezuela *n* a federal republic in South America.

vengeance *n* the act of taking revenge; retribution; **with a vengeance** to a high degree; and no mistake.

vengeful *adj* bent on vengeance; vindictive.—**vengefully** *adv* **vengefulness** *n*.

venial *adj* (*sin*) forgivable, excusable, not very wrong; (*sin*) not entailing damnation.—**veniality** *n*. —**venially** *adv*.

venison *n* the edible flesh of the deer.

Venite *n* (*mus*) (*Latin*) (*Anglican church*) the 95th Psalm, used as a canticle at Matins; the music for this.

venography *n* examination of veins using X-rays after injection of a radio-opaque substance.—*also* **phlebography**.

venom *n* the poison of a snake, wasp, etc; spite, malice, rancor.

venomous *adj* secreting venom; malicious, spiteful.—**venomously** *adv*.—**venomousness** *n*.

venose *adj* having many veins, veiny; venous; (*plant*) with a surface of vein-like ridges.

venosity *n* the state of being abnormally venose; (*blood vessels, organs*) the condition of containing too much blood.

venous *adj* pertaining to, contained in, or consisting of veins or blood.—**venously** *adv*.—**venousness** *n*.

venous blood *n* blood carried to the heart in veins, distinguishable from arterial blood by its darker color.

vent[1] *n* a small opening or slit; an outlet or flue for the escape of fumes; an opening in a volcano leading down to the magma chamber through which lava is ejected during an eruption - some volcanoes have a single central vent, others have a line of vents. * *vt* to release; (*temper*) to give expression to.—**venter** *n*.

vent[2] *n* a slit in the back of a coat, often forming a flap; an opening in a battlemented wall.

ventage *n* a finger-hole of a flute or similar instrument; a small opening, an outlet.

ventail *n* the part of a helmet protecting the lower part of the face.

venter *n* (*anat, zool*) the belly or abdomen of vertebrates; the part of a muscle that swells outwards; (*bot*) the swollen base of that part of some plants containing the egg cell; (*law*) the womb.

ventilate *vt* to supply with fresh air; to oxygenate (the blood); to make public; to submit to discussion.—**ventilative** *adj*.

ventilation *n* the act of ventilating; the state of being ventilated; free discussion; (*med*) the means whereby air passes into and out of the lungs, aided by movement of the diaphragm.

ventilator *n* an appliance for ventilating a room, etc; (*med*) a device for enabling a patient to breathe normally.

ventouse *n* a machine used in childbirth, comprising a suction cup to be attached to the head of the fetus enabling it to be gently pulled out of the uterus. It is an alternative to the use of forceps.—*also* **vacuum extractor**.

ventral *adj* (*anat*) the term used to describe anything relating to the front, abdominal part of the body or a hollow structure; (*bot*) of, pertaining to, or located on that part of a plant facing towards the stem, esp a leaf. **ventricle** *n* a small cavity; (*biol*) one of the lower chambers of the heart, which pumps blood; one of the four cavities of the brain.—**ventricular** *adj*.

ventricose, ventricous *adj* (*biol*) swelling, esp on one side only.—**ventricosity** *n*.

ventricular fibrillation *n* a rapid arrhythmia of the ventricle, which is dangerous.

ventriloquism, ventriloquy *n* the act or art of speaking so that the sounds appear to come from a source other than the actual speaker.—**ventriloquial** *adj*.—**ventriloquist** *n*. —**ventriloquistic** *adj*.

ventriloquize *vi* to practise ventriloquism.

venture *n* a dangerous expedition; a risky undertaking. * *vti* to risk; to dare.—**venturer** *n*.

venture capital *n* capital provided either in the form of share capital or loan capital to finance a business venture that is considered to present a higher financial risk than usual.

venturesome *adj* daring, rash; risky, hazardous.—**venturesomely** *adv*.—**venturesomeness** *n*.

Venturi effect *n* the effect that a narrowing channel has on the velocity of a current of gas or liquid.

Venturi *n* Robert (1925–) American architect. His notable works include extension to National Gallery, London.

venue *n* the place of an action or event.

venule *n* a tiny vein that collects blood from the capillaries.

Venus[1] *n* (*Roman myth*) the goddess of love; a beautiful woman.

Venus[2] *n* (*astron*) the planet second from the sun, that can sometimes be seen as a bright star in the morning or evening

Venus figurines *n* stylized small obese female figurines which were made by Upper Paleolithic peoples in central Europe and Russia.

ver. *abbr* = verse, *or* verses.

veracious *adj* observant of the truth, truthful; honest; true, accurate.—**veraciously** *adv*.—**veraciousness** *n*.

veracity *n* (*pl* **veracities**) habitual observance of the truth; correspondence with the truth or facts; a truthful statement, a truth.

veranda, verandah *n* a roofed porch, supported by light pillars.

veratrine *n* a poisonous mixture of alkaloids from plants of the hellebore family, formerly used medically, to relieve neuralgia or as a counter-irritant.

verb *n* (*gram*) the part of speech that expresses an action, a process, state or condition or mode of being.

verb. sap. *abbr* (*Latin*) = *verbum sapienti sat est*, "a word is sufficient to the wise."

verbal *adj* of, concerned with or expressed in words; spoken, not written; literal; (*gram*) of, pertaining to or characteristic of a verb.—**verbally** *adv*.

verbalism *n* something expressed in words; a word or phrase; excessive attention to wording rather than content; meaningless phrases or sentences resulting from this.

verbalist *n* one skilled with words; one who concentrates on words rather than content.—**verbalistic** *adj*.

verbalize *vt* to put into words; to make into a verb.—**verbalization** *n*.

verbatim *adj, adv* (*Latin*) "word for word."

verbena *n* any of various kinds of ornamental fragrant plant, usu found in America, with red, white or purple flowers; any similar type of plant.

verbiage *n* more words than are needed for clarity, wordiness; the use of too many words.

verbify *vti* (**verbifying, verbified**) to convert (a noun, etc) into a verb; to be verbose.

verbose *adj* using more words than are necessary; overloaded with words.—**verbosely** *adv*.—**verbosity** *n*.

verdant *adj* (*grass, foliage*) green and fresh; covered with grass; inexperienced, gullible.—**verdancy** *n*. —**verdantly** *adv*.

verderer *n* (*formerly*) in England, an official who had charge of the royal forests and was responsible for maintaining peace in them.

Verdi *n* **Giuseppe** (1813–1901) Italian composer of opera who started his musical career as an organist. Notable for the operas, *Rigoletto* (1851), *Il Trovatore* (1853), *La Traviata* (1853), and *Aida* (1871).

verdict *n* the decision of a jury at the end of a trial; decision, judgment.

verdigris *n* a greenish deposit that forms on copper or brass.

verdure *n* green vegetation; greenness; freshness; the freshness and healthy growth of vegetation.—**verdurous** *adj*.—**verdurousness** *n*.

verge[1] *n* the brink; the extreme edge or margin; a grass border beside a road; a staff or wand as an emblem of office; the spindle of a watch balance; (*archit*) a projecting edge of roof tiles or slates.

verge[2] *vi* to incline, descend; (*with* **on**) to border on, to be on the verge of.

verger *n* an official who has care of the interior of a church; a staff bearer of a bishop, etc.

Vergil *see* **Virgil**.

Vergottini *n* **Bruno** (1935–) Italian industrial designer who started his career in 1968 in fashion as well as industrial and interior design.

veridical *adj* truthful, veracious; (*psychol*) of or pertaining to events in dreams that in retrospect appear to have foretold the future.

verifiable *adj* capable of being verified.—**verifiability** *n*.

verification *n* the act of proving to be true; confirmation; the state of being verified; a marshaling of facts, etc that proves the truth of, e.g. a theory; (*law*) (*formerly*) a short affidavit at the end of a pleading indicating that the pleader is willing to supply proof.

verify *vt* (**verifying, verified**) to confirm the truth of, to check; to substantiate, to bear out; (*law*) to authenticate or support by proofs; (*comput*) a computer procedure that ensures that an operation was completed correctly.—**verifiable** *adj*.—**verification** *n*. —**verifier** *n*.

verily *adv* (*arch*) in truth, certainly.

verisimilitude *n* the appearance of truth, probability.—**verisimilar** *adj*.

verismo *n* (*mus*) (*Italian*) a type of opera concerned with representing contemporary life of ordinary people in an honest and realistic way, e.g. Mascagni's *Cavalleria rusticana*.

veritable *adj* real, genuine.—**veritably** *adv*.

verity *n* (*pl* **verities**) the quality or state of being true; a truth; a true fact, reality.

verjuice *n* an acidic liquor expressed from unripe grapes, apples, etc formerly used in sauces; sourness, tartness.

Verlaine *n* **Paul** (1844–96) French poet, regarded with his lover Rimbaud as an early symbolist. Their affair ended when Verlaine shot and wounded Rimbaud, spending two years in prison for the deed. Collections of Verlaine's verse include *Saturnian Poems*, the religious poems of *Wisdom*, and *Romances Without Words*.

Verm. *abbr* = Vermont.

Vermeer *n* **Jan [Johannes]** (1632–75) Dutch painter. He is best remembered for his small-scale intimate interior scenes, carefully composed and lit, usually by daylight through a window, e.g. *Woman in Blue reading a Letter*.

vermeil *n* silver-gilt, or any other metal gilded; (*poet*) vermilion. * *adj* of a bright red color.

vermicelli *n* a pasta similar to spaghetti but in finer strings.

vermicide *n* a substance for killing worms.—**vermicidal** *adj*.

vermicular *adj* vermiform; vermiculate; worm-like; pertaining to or caused by worms.

vermiculate *adj* moving like a worm; worm-eaten; adorned with wavy lines; (*thoughts*) constantly recurring, casuistic. * *vt* to mark with close wavy lines.—**vermiculation** *n*.

vermiform *adj* worm-shaped.

vermiform appendix *n* the worm-shaped structure attached to the cecum vestigially in humans and certain other mammals, the appendix.

vermifuge *n* a drug that expels intestinal worms.

vermilion, vermillion *n* a bright scarlet color. * *adj* of this color.

vermin *n* (*used as pl*) pests, such as insects and rodents; persons dangerous to society.

vermination *n* the breeding or spread of vermin, worms or larvae; infestation with vermin, worms or larvae.

verminous *adj* infested with, caused by, or like vermin.

Vermont *or* **VT** *n* a state of the USA, of which the capital is Montpelier.

vermouth *n* a white wine flavoured with herbs, used in cocktails and as an aperitif.

vernacular *n* the commonly spoken language or dialect of a country or region. * *adj* native.—**vernacularly** *adv*.

vernacularism *n* vernacular usage; a vernacular word or expression.

vernal *adj* of, appearing in, relating to, or suggestive of the spring.—**vernally** *adv*.

vernation *n* (*bot*) the arrangement of leaves within a bud.

Verne *n* **Jules** (1828–1905) French novelist, whose innovative fantasy novels, e.g. *Voyage to the Centre of the Earth* and *20,000 Leagues Under the Sea*, are regarded as the earliest great science fiction novels.

vernier *n* a small sliding scale attached to a larger fixed scale, with gradations to indicate minute subdivisions of the smallest divisions on the main fixed scale; an additional apparatus used to fine-tune or adjust an instrument. * *adj* of, pertaining to, or having a vernier.

Veronal (*trademark*) *n* a sedative or hypnotic drug; barbitone.

veronica[1] *n* any of several plants with blue, pink or white flowers, incl speedwell.

veronica[2] *n* (*RC Church*) the image of Christ's face that in legend appeared on a handkerchief given to him by St Veronica as he went to his crucifixion; this handkerchief; any similar image of Christ's face on a cloth.

veronica[3] *n* (*bullfighting*) a maneuvre by a matador in which he swings the cape slowly before the bull while standing still.

verruca *n* (*pl* **verrucae, verrucas**) a wart on the hand or foot; (*biol*) a wart-like excrescence.—**verrucose, verrucous** *adj*.

vers *abbr* = versine.

vers libre *n* verse with no regular metrical system; free verse.

versatile *adj* turning readily from one occupation to another, adaptable; talented in many different ways; variable, fickle, changeable; (*biol*) able to move or turn freely.—**versatilely** *adv*.—**versatility** *n*.

verse *n* a line of poetry; a stanza of a poem; a metrical composition, esp of a light nature; a short section of a chapter in the Bible. * *vti* to make verses (about).

versed *adj* skilled or learned in a subject.

versicle *n* a short verse or text sung by priest and congregation alternately in a liturgical service.

versicolor, versicolour *adj* parti-coloured; changeable in colour, iridescent.

versification *n* verse-making; the meter or verses of a poem; the conversion of prose into verse.

versify *vti* (**versifying, versified**) to write poetry or verse; to turn into verse.—**versifier** *n*.

version *n* a translation from one language into another; a particular account or description; (*med*) the procedure to move a fetus in the uterus to a more normal position to make delivery easier.—*also* **turning**—**versional** *adj*.

version number *n* (*comput*) the number assigned to a version or release of a program, amended each time the author revises the program.

verso *n* (*pl* **versos**) a left-hand, even-numbered page of a book, the back of the recto; the back of a printed sheet; the reverse of a coin.

versus *prep* against; in contrast to.

vert *n* (*English law*) (*formerly*) the right to collect whatever grows and bears a green leaf in a forest; green vegetation; (*her*) green.

vert. *abbr* = vertebrata; vertebrate; vertical.

vertebra *n* (*pl* **vertebrae, vertebras**) one of the interconnecting bones of the spinal column.—**vertebral** *adj*.

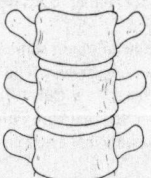

vertebrate *n* an animal with a backbone. * *adj* having a backbone; of the vertebrates.

vertebration *n* division into vertebrae or vertebrae-like segments.

vertex *n* (*pl* **vertexes, vertices**) the topmost point; apex; (*anat*) the crown of the head; (*geom*) the point at which two sides of a polygon or the planes of a solid intersect.

vertical *adj* perpendicular to the horizon; upright. * *n* a vertical line or plane.—**verticality** *n*. —**vertically** *adv*.

vertical disintegration *n* (*com*) the disintegration of a vertical marketing system as a consequence of the withdrawal of a company from one stage of the system.

vertical marketing system *n* (*com*) a distribution system in which the relevant parties, the producers, the wholesalers and the retailers are part of a unified structure.

vertical takeoff and landing *see* **VTOL**.

verticil *n* a whorl-like arrangement of leaves or flowers around a stem

verticillate *adj* (*biol*) arranged in a whorl-like pattern.—**verticillately** *adv*.—**verticillation** *n*.

vertiginous *adj* revolving, rotary; giddy; causing giddiness; whirling.—**vertiginously** *adv*.—**vertiginousness** *n*.

vertigo *n* (*pl* **vertigoes, vertigines**) a sensation of dizziness and sickness caused by a disorder of the sense of balance.—**vertiginous** *adj*.

vertu *see* **virtu**.

Vertumnus, Vortumnus *n* (*Roman myth*) a god of fertility, particularly with regard to crops and the changing of the seasons.

Verulanium *n* (*hist*) an important town in Roman Britain, situated at modern St Albans, that flourished AD 100–300.

vervain *n* a perennial European with clusters of tiny bluish-purple flowers.

verve *n* enthusiasm; liveliness; energy.

vervet *n* a small African monkey with dark hands and feet and yellowish or greenish coat.

Verwoerd *n* **Hendrik Frensch** (1901–66) South African politician and prime minister (1958–66) who fostered apartheid, banned the African National Congress (1960) and took South Africa out of the Commonwealth (1961).

very *adj* complete; absolute; same. * *adv* extremely; truly; really.

very high frequency *n* a radio frequency between 300 and 30 megahertz.

Very light *n* a colored flare fired from a Very pistol as a signal at sea or to give temporary light.

ves. *abbr* = vessel.

VES *abbr* = Voluntary Euthanasia Society.

VESA *abbr* (*comput*) = Video Electronics Standards Association (a grouping of manufacturers who have devised standards to ensure that computers and VDUs are compatible).

vesica *n* (*pl* **vesicae**) (*anat*) the bladder, esp the urinary bladder; (*art*) a pointed oval halo used as an aureole in medieval sculpture or painting.—**vesical** *adj*.

vesicant, vesicatory *n* (*pl* **vesicants, vesicatories**) a substance (e.g., mustard gas) that causes blistering, with applications in chemical warfare. * *adj* raising blisters.

vesicate *vt* to raise blisters on. * *vi* to become blistered.—**vesication** *n*.

vesicle *n* a small blister; a small cyst or sac; (*anat*) a bladder-like vessel or cavity, esp one filled with serous fluid; (*geol*) a cavity in rock formed by gases during solidification; (*bot*) a small sac found in some seaweeds and aquatic plants.—**vesicular** *adj*.

vesicular breathing *n* soft, normal sounds of breathing heard in the lung by means of a stethoscope.

vesper *n* (*arch*) evening; (*with cap*) the evening star; (*Anglican Church*) evensong; (*RC Church*) the sixth of the canonical hours. * *adj* pertaining to evening or vespers.

vespertine, vespertinal *adj* of evening; (*bot*) opening in the evening; (*zool*) active in the evening; (*astron*) setting about sunset.

vespiary *n* (*pl* **vespiaries**) a nest of wasps or hornets.

vespine *adj* of, pertaining to, or like a wasp or wasps.

vessel *n* a container; a ship or boat; (*med*) a tube in the body along which fluids pass.

vest *n* a waist-length sleeveless garment worn under a jacket; a sleeveless undergarment worn next to the skin, a singlet; a waistcoat. * *vt* to place or settle (power, authority, etc); (*with* **in**) to confer or be conferred on; to invest with a right to.

vesta *n* a short match of wax or wood, lit by friction.

Vesta[1] *n* (*astron*) the third-largest known asteroid, discovered in the early 1800s, and the only asteroid to be sometimes bright enough to be detected by the naked eye.

Vesta[2] *n* (*Roman myth*) the goddess of the hearth and the household fire, the Roman equivalent of the Greek, Hestia.

vestal *adj* pertaining to or sacred to the goddess Vesta; vowed to chastity, pure. * *n* a vestal virgin; a virgin.

vestal virgin *n* one of the six virgin priestesses who tended the sacred fire on the altar of the temple of Vesta, in ancient Rome.

vested *adj* (*law*) having permanent entitlement to the possession or use of property, now and in the future, ratified by law or custom; (*priest, etc*) clothed in ecclesiastical vestments.

vested interest *n* (*law*) a permanent entitlement to the possession and use of property, now and in the future; a strong reason for acting in a certain way, usu for personal gain; (*usu pl*) people in such a state.

vestibule *n* an entrance hall or lobby; a covered entrance at the end of a rail carriage; (*anat*) a communicating channel.—**vestibular** *adj*.

vestige *n* a hint; a trace; a rudimentary survival of a former organ; a particle.—**vestigial** *adj*.—**vestigially** *adv*.

vestigial *adj* (*med*) the term applied to an organ that has progressively, over a long time, lost its function and structure to become rudimentary.

vestment *n* a garment or robe, esp that worn by a priest or official.—**vestmental** *adj*.

vestry *n* (*pl* **vestries**) a room in a church where vestments, etc are kept and parochial meetings held; a meeting for parish business.—**vestral** *adj*.

vestryman *n* (*pl* **vestrymen**) a member of a vestry elected by the parishioners.

vesture *n* (*arch*) clothing; something that clothes, a covering; (*law*) everything growing on someone's land apart from trees; something obtained from land, such as wheat. * (*arch*) *vt* to clothe.

vesuvianite *n* a mineral of a green, brown or yellow color, similar to the garnet, idocrase.

vet *n* a veterinary surgeon. * *vt* (**vetting, vetted**) to examine, check for errors, etc.

vet. *abbr* = veteran; veterinarian; veterinary.

vetch *n* a common leguminous climbing plant with blue or purple flowers and a stem with tendrils, found in temperate climates and used for green fodder; any similar plant.

vetchling *n* a climbing plant like a vetch mainly found in northern temperate regions with angled or winged stems with tendrils and gaudy flowers.

veter. *abbr* = veterinary.

veteran *adj* old, experienced; having served in the armed forces. * *n* a person who has served in the armed forces; a person who has given long service in a particular activity.

veterinarian, veterinary surgeon *n* a person trained in treating sick or injured animals.

veterinary *adj* of or dealing with diseases of domestic animals.

VetMB *abbr* = Bachelor of Veterinary Medicine.

veto *n* (*pl* **vetoes**) the right of a person or group to prohibit an action or legislation; a prohibition. * *vt* (**vetoing, vetoed**) to refuse to agree to; to prohibit.—**vetoer** *n*.

VETS *abbr* = Veterans' Employment and Training Service

vex *vt* to annoy; to puzzle, confuse.—**vexer** *n*. —**vexingly** *adv*.

vexation *n* a vexing or being vexed; an annoying thing; irritation, distress.

vexatious *adj* causing vexation; annoying; troublesome; harassing; (*litigation*) designed merely to annoy.—**vexatiously** *adv*.

vexed *adj* annoyed; (*question*) much debated.—**vexedly** *adv*.—**vexedness** *n*.

vexillum *n* (*pl* **vexilla**) (*bot*) the largest petal found on flowers of the plant family to which the sweet pea and similar plants belong; (*zool*) the vane of a feather.

v.f. *abbr* = *verba fecit*.

VF *abbr* = ventricular fibrillation; video frequency; voice frequency.

VFM *abbr* = value for money.

VFW *abbr* = Veterans of Foreign Wars of the US.

vg *abbr* = very good.

VG *abbr* = Vicar-General.

VGA *abbr* = video graphics array.

VGC *abbr* (*Brit*) = Vintage Glider Club of Great Britain.

VGLI *abbr* = Veterans' Group Life Insurance

VGSOH *abbr* = very good sense of humour.

VHA *abbr* = Veterans Health Administration

vhc *abbr* = very highly commended.

VHD *abbr* = video high density.

VHE *abbr* = very high energy.

VHF *abbr* = very high frequency.

VHS *abbr* = video home system.

VHT *abbr* = very high temperature.

Vi *symbol* (*chem*) virginium.

vi *abbr* = verb intransitive; (*Latin*) *vide infra*, "see below."

VI *abbr* = Virgin Islands.

VI *abbr* (*Latin*) = *virgo intacta*, "virgin."

via *prep* by way of.

VIA *abbr* = Visually Impaired Association.

viable *adj* capable of growing or developing; able to live separately; workable; practicable.—**viability** *n*. —**viably** *adv*.

viaduct *n* a road or railway carried by a bridge with arches over a valley, river, etc.

vial *n* a small bottle for medicines, etc; a phial.

via media *n* a middle course between extremes; a compromise.

viand *n* an article of food. (*pl*) meat ready to be cooked; food.

viaticum *n* (*pl* **viatica, viaticums**) (*RC Church*) the Eucharist administered to someone whose death is or might be imminent; (*rare*) an allowance or provisions given to a person setting out on a journey.

vibes *npl* (*sl*) vibrations; vibraphone.

vibraculum *n* (*pl* **vibracula**) (*zool*) a whip-like appendage by which some polyzoans ward off parasites.

vibrant *adj* vibrating; resonant; bright; lively.—**vibrancy** *n*. —**vibrantly** *adv*.

vibraphone *or* **vibes** *n* (*mus*) an American instrument, similar to the glockenspiel, which consists of a series of metal bars which are struck with mallets. —**vibraphonist** *n*.

vibrate *vti* to shake; to move quickly backwards and forwards; to quiver; to oscillate; to resound.—**vibratingly** *adv*.

vibratile *adj* capable of or characterized by vibrating.—**vibratility** *n*.

vibration *n* a vibrating or being vibrated; oscillation; resonance; vacillation; (*usu pl*) an emotional reaction instinctively sensed; (*phys*) the rapid alternating of particles caused by the disturbance of equilibrium; (*mus*) a term in acoustics, for the wave-like motion by which a musical tone is produced. Sound vibrations are mechanical; radio vibrations are electro-magnetic and inaudible.—**vibrational** *adj*.

vibrative *adj* vibratory.

vibrato *n* (*pl* **vibratos**) (*mus*) (*Italian*) a pulsating effect obtained by rapid variation of emphasis on the same tone.

vibrator *n* the vibrating part in various instruments; a dildo.

vibratory *adj* vibrating; consisting of or causing vibrations.

vibrio *n* (*pl* **vibrios**) a spiral or curved, rod-like bacillus.—**vibrioid** *adj*.

vibrissa *n* (*pl* **vibrissae**) a sensitive whisker on an animal's face; any of the bristle-like feathers found in the beak area of certain insect-eating birds.

viburnum *n* any of several shrubs or trees, incl the guelder rose, with red or black berry-like fruits, found in various temperate and sub-tropical regions; the dried bark from some of these, sometimes used medicinally.

vic. *abbr* = vicar; vicarage.

vicar *n* a parish priest; a clergyman in charge of a chapel.

vicarage *n* the residence of a vicar.

vicarial *adj* of, pertaining to, or acting as a vicar, vicars or a vicariate; (*ecclesiastical functions*) delegated, vicarious.

vicariate, vicarate *n* the rank, office, or district of a vicar.

vicarious *adj* substitute; obtained second-hand by listening to or watching another person's experiences.—**vicariously** *adv*.—**vicariousness** *n*.

vice[1] *n* an evil action or habit; a grave moral fault; great wickedness; a serious defect, a blemish.

vice[2] *n* a clamping device with jaws, used for holding objects firmly.—*also* **vise**.

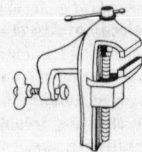

vice- *prefix* one who acts in place of or as a deputy to another.

Vice Adm. *abbr* = Vice Admiral.

vice admiral *n* a rank of naval officer next below admiral.

vice chairman *n* (*pl* **vice chairmen**) one who takes the chair in a chairman's absence.

vice chancelor *n* the chief executive officer of a university.

vice consul *n* a person who acts in place of a consul in a subordinate district, etc.

vicegerent *n adj* a person holding delegated power or ruling as another's deputy.—*also adj*.—**vicegerency** *n*.

viceinnial *adj* lasting twenty years; happening every twenty years.

Vicente de Oliveira *n* Mateus (1710) P ortuguese architect. His notable works include the palace of Queluz.

vice president *n* a deputy or assistant president.

viceregal *adj* of or relating to a viceroy; (*Austral, NZ*) of or relating to a governor general.

vicereine *n* a viceroy's wife.

viceroy *n* one who rules a country or province as a representative of a king or queen.

viceroyalty, viceroyship *n* (*pl* **viceroyalties, viceroyships**) the office or term of a viceroy.

vice versa *adv* conversely; the other way round.

vichyssoise *n* leek and potato soup consumed cold.

Vichy water *n* a mineral water from Vichy in France.

vicinage *n* a surrounding district, a neighborhood; the people of a neighborhood; proximity.

vicinal *adj* neighboring; adjacent; (*chem*) resembling or substituting for a crystal face or form; denoting substituted atoms on adjacent atoms in a molecule.

vicinity *n* (*pl* **vicinities**) a nearby area; proximity.

vicious *adj* cruel; violent; malicious; ferocious.—**viciously** *adv*.—**viciousness** *n*.

vicissitude *n* a change of circumstances or fortune; (*pl*) ups and downs.—**vicissitudinary, vicissitudinous** *adj*.

Vickers *n* Jon (1926–) a Canadian tenor who is especially famous for his roles in Wagner and Verdi operas.

Vico *n* Giovanni Battista (1668–1744) Italian philosopher. His *Scienza Nuova* (1725), a remarkably original work which posits a cyclical rise and fall for civilizations as human nature evolves through cultural and linguistic changes, was largely ignored until the 19th century.

victim *n* a person who has been killed or injured by an action beyond his or her control; a dupe.

victimize *vt* to make a victim of, to cause to suffer.—**victimization** *n*.—**victimizer** *n*.

victor *n* a winner; a conqueror.

victoria *n* a light, open, four-wheeled, two-seater carriage; a giant South American water-lily; a victoria plum.

Victoria[1] *n* capital city of Seychelles.

Victoria[2] *n* (1819–1901) queen of the United Kingdom of Great Britain and Ireland; from 1876 Empress of India (1837–1901). Married in 1840 to her cousin, Prince Albert of Saxe-Coburg.

Victoria[3] *n* Tomas Luis de (*c*.1548–1611) an outstanding Spanish composer of polyphonic music, who was also a priest. He held various church positions in Rome before returning to Madrid.

victoria plum *n* a large purplish-red sweet variety of plum.

Victorian *adj* of or living in the reign of Queen Victoria; old-fashioned, prudish.

victorious *adj* having won in battle or contest; emblematic of victory; triumphant.—**victoriously** *adv*.

victory *n* (*pl* **victories**) triumph in battle; success; achievement.

victual *n* (*usu pl*) food, provisions. * *vt* (**victualing, victualed** *or* **victualling, victualled**) to supply with food; to take in provisions.

victualer, victualler *n* (*formerly*) a supplier of provisions, esp to an army; a provision ship; an innkeeper.

vicuña, vicuna *n* a South American animal similar to the llama with a fine, long, reddish silky fleece; cloth made from this fleece.

vid. *abbr* (*Latin*) = *vide*, "see."

VID *abbr* = virtual image display.

Vidal *n* [Eugene Luther] Gore (1925–) American novelist, dramatist and critic. His American historical fiction provides an unofficial and waspishly entertaining alternative history of the US and its leaders.

vide (*Latin*) "see."

vide infra (*Latin*) "see later" (in this book).

videlicet *adv* that is to say, namely.

video *n* (*pl* **videos**) the transmission or recording of television programs or films, using a television set and a video recorder and tape. * *vt* (**videoing, videoed**) to record on video tape.

video adapter *n* (*comput*) the electronic card that generates the graphic output that is displayed on a VDU.

video card *n* (*comput*) see **video adapter**.

video cassette *n* a cassette containing video tape.

videoconferencing *n* an electronic system that allows people in different locations to hold a discussion in which they can see each other as well as speak to each other.

video disk *n* (*comput*) a high storage optical storage device used for pictures, movies and sound.

video RAM *see* **VRAM**.

video recorder *n* the machine on which video cassettes are played or recorded.

video tape *n* a magnetic tape on which images and sounds can be recorded for reproduction on television.—**video-tape** *vt*.

vide supra (*Latin*) "see earlier" (in this book).

vidette *see* **vedette**.

vidkid *n* a child who is addicted to watching television or video.

vie *vi* (**vying, vied**) to contend or strive for superiority.—**vier** *n*.

Vienna *n* capital city of Austria.

Vienna State Opera *n* (*mus*) one of the world's leading opera companies. Its famous conductors have included Gluck, Donizetti, Mahler, Karajan.

Vientiane *n* capital city of Laos.

vierhandig *n* (*mus*) (*German*) "Four-handed," i.e. a piano duet.

Vietnam *n* a long narrow socialist republic in southeast Asia which runs down the coast of the South China Sea.

view *n* sight; range of vision; inspection, examination; intention; scene; opinion; (*comput*) an on-screen display of the contents of a file or part of a file * *vt* to see; to consider; to examine intellectually.

viewer *n* a person who views, esp television; an optical device used in viewing.

viewfinder *n* a device in a camera showing the view to be photographed.

viewless *adj* without a view; (*poet*) invisible, unseen.

viewpoint *n* opinion; a place from which something can be viewed, esp a scenic panorama.

vigil *n* keeping watch at night.

vigilance *n* a being vigilant; watchfulness; alertness.

vigilant *adj* on the watch to discover and avoid danger, watchful; alert; cautious.—**vigilantly** *adv*.

vigilante *n* a self-appointed law enforcer.

vignette *n* a small picture or design in a book without a line framing it; a picture, the edges of which shade off gradually into the background; a short word sketch. * *vt* to depict in vignette; to shade off into the background.—**vignettist** *n*.

Vignola *n* Giacomo B (1507–) Italian architect. His notable works include the Villa Giulia, Rome.

Vignon *n* Pierre A (1762–) F rench architect. His notable works include the Madeleine, Paris.

vigor *n* physical or mental strength; vitality.—*also* **vigour**.

vigoroso *adv* (*mus*) with vigor.

vigorous *adj* full of vigour; powerful; lusty.—**vigorously** *adv*.—**vigorousness** *n*.

vigour *see* **vigor**.

Viking *n* one of the Norse pirates who ravaged the coasts of Europe from the 8th–10th centuries.

vil. *abbr* = village.

Vila *n* capital city of Vanuatu.

vilayet *n* a province of Turkey.

vile *adj* wicked; evil; offensive; very bad.—**vilely** *adv*.—**vileness** *n*.

vilify *vt* (**vilifying, vilified**) to malign.—**vilification** *n*.—**vilifier** *n*.

villa *n* a large country or suburban house.

Villa *n* Pancho [Francisco Villa, originally Doroteo Arango] (*c*.1877–1923) Mexican revolutionary. A former bandit, his forces aided Zapata in the seizure of Mexico City (1914–15). Villa's forces sparked off the US invasion of 1916–17 by killing some US civilians.

village *n* a collection of houses smaller than a town.

villager *n* an inhabitant of a village.

Village Romeo and Juliet *n* **A** an opera by Delius who also wrote the libretto. It was first performed in 1907.

villain *n* a scoundrel; the main evil character in a play, film or novel; (*arch*) a boor.

villainous *adj* depraved, evil, wicked; very bad, wretched.—**villainously** *adv*.—**villainousness** *n*.

villainy *n* (*pl* **villainies**) great wickedness; an atrocious crime.

Villa-Lobos *n* **Heitor** (1887–1959) Brazilian composer and conductor. When he was 18, he joined an expedition up the Amazon to collect folk music. He settled in Paris (1923–30), where his work, combining elements of traditional Brazilian music with the European classical tradition, became highly popular.

villanella *n* (*pl* **villanelle**) (*mus*) (*Italian*) literally, a "rustic song", a popular part-song of the 17th century.

villanelle *n* a poem of 19 lines in six stanzas rhymed aba aba aba aba aba abaa, the 6th, 12th and 18th lines being the same as the first, and the 9th, 15th and 19th the same as the third.

Villanovans *n* an Iron Age people who emerged in Tuscany *c.*900 BC and spread to the area around Bologna.

Villanueva *n* **Juan de** (1739–) Spanish architect. His notable works include the Prado Museum, Madrid.

villein *n* (*hist*) a feudal tenant of the lowest class, a serf.

Villeroy et Boch *n* German ceramics and glassware manufacturer, located at Mettlach.

villi *see* **villus**.

Villiers *n* **George [2nd Duke of Buckingham]** (1606–67) English poet, dramatist, and courtier whose main claim to literary fame is his superb send-up of the conventions of the heroic tragedy genre, *The Rehearsal*, written in collaboration with others, which mercilessly satirizes Dryden. The play was updated by Sheridan as *The Critic*.

Villon *n* **François** (*c.*1431–63) French poet, who seems to have had a violent, unstable personality. He was banished from Paris in 1463, nothing being known of him after this date. Two main collections of his work survive: *Le Lais* or *Little Testament*, and *Testament* or *Great Testament*, the latter including the remarkable "Ballad of Ladies of Long Ago," with its haunting refrain, "Mais où sont les neiges d'antan?" ("But where are the snows of yesteryear?").

villous, villose *adj* covered with villi; (*bot*) covered with long, thin, soft hairs.

villus *n* (*pl* **villi**) (*biol*) the velvety fiber of the mucous membrane of the intestine; (*bot*) the soft hair covering a fruit or flower.—**villosity**.

Vilnius *n* capital city of Lithuania.

vim *n* (*sl*) energy, force.

vimineous *adj* (*bot*) of or producing long flexible shoots.

v. imp. *abbr* = verb impersonal.

vina *n* (*mus*) a seven-stringed Indian musical instrument.

vinaceous *adj* of the color of wine; wine-red.

Viña del Mar *n* city in Chile.

vinaigrette *n* a salad dressing made from oil, vinegar and seasoning.

Vinca *n* (*archeo*) a tell near Belgrade in Serbia with evidence of a long period of Neolithic occupation.

Vincent *n* **René** (1879–1936) French ceramicist and illustrator who drew illustrations for *La Vie Parisienne* and *L'Illustration*.

Vincent *n* **Saint** (*d.* 304)a Spanish Christian; his feast day is January 22.

Vincent de Paul *n* **Saint** (1576–1660) French Roman Catholic priest associated with great works of charity. His feast day is September 27.

Vincent's angina *n* (*med*)a former name for ulcerative gingivitis and ulcerative inflammation of the throat, caused by bacteria.

vincible *adj* capable of being conquered or overcome.—**vincibility** *n*.

vinculum *n* (*pl* **vincula**) (*anat*) a ligament; (*math*) a horizontal line over quantities having the effect of a parenthesis; (*print*) a brace; a bond of union, a tie.

vindicate *vt* to establish the existence or truth of, to justify; to clear of charges, to absolve from blame.—**vindicable** *adj*.—**vindicator** *n*. —**vindicatory** *adj*.

vindication *n* a vindicating or being vindicated; an event, fact, evidence, etc that justifies a deed or claim.

vindictive *adj* vengeful; spiteful; (*damages*) exemplary, punitive.—**vindictively** *adv*.—**vindictiveness** *n*.

vine *n* any climbing plant, or its stem; a grapevine; a sphere of activity, esp spiritual or mental endeavour.

vinedresser *n* a person who cultivates vines.

vinegar *n* a sour-tasting liquid containing acetic acid, used as a condiment and preservative.

vinegary *adj* of or like vinegar; sour; ill-tempered.

vinery *n* (*pl* **vineries**) a place where grapes are grown or wine is made.

vineyard *n* a plantation of grapevines.

vingt-et-un *n* a gambling game with cards in which players try to obtain points better than the banker's but not more than 21.—*also* **blackjack, pontoon, twenty-one.**

vinic *adj* contained in or obtained from wine.

viniculture *n* the cultivation of vines and manufacture of wine, viticulture.—**vinicultural** *adj*.—**viniculturist** *n*.

viniferous *adj* wine-producing.

vinificator *n* in winemaking, an apparatus for collecting alcoholic vapors.

vin ordinaire *n* (*pl* **vins ordinaires**) the ordinary table wine of France.

vinous *adj* of, pertaining to, or having the qualities of wine; like wine; wine-colored; inspired by wine.—**vinosity** *n*.

vintage *n* the grape harvest of one season; wine, esp of good quality, made in a particular year; wine of a particular region; the product of a particular period. * *adj* (*cars*) classic; (*wine*) of a specified year and of good quality; (*play*) characteristic of the best.

vintager *n* a gatherer of grapes in a wine harvest.

vintner *n* a wine merchant.

vinyl *n* a strong plastic used in floor coverings, furniture and records, etc.

viol *n* (*mus*) a family of medieval six-stringed instruments played with a bow which were widely used in the 16th and 17th centuries; originally a general term for any bowed stringed instrument; now the name of the alto member of the violin family.

viola[1] *n* (*mus*) a stringed instrument of the violin family, and tuned a fifth below it.

viola[2] *n* (*mus*) any of several plants of the genus that includes violets and pansies.

violable *adj* capable of being violated or broken.

violaceous *adj* of violet color or family.

viola da braccio *n* (*mus*) (*Italian*) literally, an "arm viol"; a generic term for any stringed instrument played on the arm. It came to mean a violin or viola.

viola da gamba *n* (*mus*) (*Italian*) literally, a "leg viol"; a term originally used of those members of the viol family played vertically between the legs or on the lap, but it came to be used exclusively for the bass viol.

viola d'amore *n* (*mus*) (*Italian*) literally, a "love viol," i.e. a tenor viol with seven strings (instead of six) and seven or fourteen sympathetic strings. It is so called because it had a particularly sweet tone.

violate *vt* to break or infringe (an agreement); to rape; to disturb (one's privacy).—**violative** *adj*.—**violator** *n*.

violation *n* the act of violating, infringing, or injuring; rape; outrage; an act of irreverence or profanation.

violence *n* physical force intended to cause injury or destruction; natural force; passion, intensity.

violent *adj* urged or driven by force; vehement; impetuous; forcible; furious; severe.—**violently** *adv*.

violet *n* a small plant with bluish-purple flowers; a bluish-purple color.

violetta *n* (*mus*) a small viol.

violin *n* (*mus*) a stringed instrument, played with a bow, which was introduced in the 16th century. It was developed independently of the viol from the medieval fiddle. It has no frets and just four strings.

violinist *n* (*mus*) a person who plays the violin.

violino primo *n* (*mus*) (*Italian*) a first violin.

violino principale *n* (*mus*) (*Italian*) a solo violin or leader.

violino ripieno *n* (*mus*) (*Italian*) a violin part required only to fill in and strengthen the whole.

violino secondo *n* (*mus*) (*Italian*) a second violin.

violist *n* (*mus*) a player of a viol or viola.

Viollet-le-Duc *n* **Eugène Emanuel** (1814–79) French architect and historian who restored ancient buildings, including Notre-Dame from 1845 to 1865.

violoncellist *n* (*mus*) a performer on the violoncello.

violoncello *n* (*mus*) the tenor of the violin family, normally abbreviated to "cello," dating from the 16th century. It is held vertically between the legs of the seated player, and the tail pin rests on the ground. It has four strings, which are played with a bow.

violone *n* the largest type of viol, corresponding to the double-bass.

VIP *abbr* = very important person.

viper *n* a common European venomous snake.—**viperine** *adj*.

viperous, viperish *adj* viper-like; malignant.

VIR *abbr* (*Brit*) (*Latin*) = *Victoria Imperatrix Regina*, "Victoria, Empress and Queen."

virago *n* (*pl* **viragoes, viragos**) a bad-tempered woman.

viral *adj* of or caused by a virus.

viral hemorrhagic fever *n* a viral disease with a high mortality rate.

viral pneumonia *n* an acute lung infection caused by one of a number of viruses. *See* **pneumonia**.

Virbius *n* (*Roman myth*) a minor god and companion of Diana.

virelay, virelai *n* an old French form of poem with short lines and two rhymes variously arranged.

virement *n* (*accounts*) a practice that is allowed under some forms of budgetary control by which overspending under one budget expenditure heading in a company may be offset by underspending under another budget expenditure heading.

vireo *n* (*pl* **vireos**) a small greenish American singing bird.

virescence *n* the state of being virescent, esp in place of the normal color of petals.

virescent *adj* beginning to be green; greenish.

V

Virg. *abbr* = Virginia.

virga *n* (*meteorol*) a feature relating to certain cloud formations where trails of precipitation fall beneath the cloud but evaporate before reaching the ground.

virgate[1] *adj* (*bot*) slim and straight.

virgate[2] *n* an old English unit of land equal to approx 30 acres.

Virgil, **Vergil** *n* [Publius Vergilius Maro] (70–19 BC) Roman poet. His works include the ten pastoral poems *Eclogues* or *Bucolics*, the *Georgics* (poems on agricultural subjects that celebrate the rural way of life), and his masterpiece, the *Aeneid* (an epic poem in 12 books that charts the progress of the Trojan hero Aeneas from the fall of Troy to the founding of the Roman state).

virgin *n* a person (esp a woman) who has never had sexual intercourse; (*with cap*) Mary, the mother of Christ; a painting or statue of her. * *adj* chaste; pure; untouched.

virginal[1] *adj* of or pertaining to a virgin or virginity; befitting a virgin; chaste, pure, innocent; fresh, unsullied, untouched.

virginal[2] *n* (*mus*) a keyboard instrument dating from the 16th century in which the strings are plucked by quills. It was similar to the harpsichord, except that it had an oblong body with strings running parallel to the keyboard; the word has also been used to describe any member of the harpsichord family.

Virginia or **VG** *n* a state of the USA, of which the capital is Richmond.

Virgin Islands *n* British a British overseas territory comprising four large islands and 36 islets and cays, lying at the northwestern end of the Lesser Antilles in the Caribbean Sea.

Virgin Islands *n* US a self-governing US territory, comprising a group of 50 volcanic islands, which are part of the Virgin Islands group in the northwest of the Lesser Antilles in the Caribbean Sea.

virginity *n* the state of being a virgin; the state of being chaste, untouched, etc.

Virgo[1] *n* the Virgin, a constellation containing a cluster of faint galaxies known as the Virgo cluster.

Virgo[2] *n* the 6th sign of the zodiac.—**Virgoan** *adj*.

Virgo A *n* a very strong source of radio emission associated with a large, elliptical galaxy designated M87 in the Virgo cluster.

Virgo Cluster *n* a vast cluster of about 2,500 galaxies in the constellation Virgo, three quarters of which are spiral.

virgo intacta *n* (*pl* **virgines intactae**) (*law*) a girl or woman who is a virgin.

virgulate *adj* rod-shaped.

virgule *n* a small rod; a slanting punctuation mark (/), a solidus.

viridescent *adj* greenish; turning green.— **viridescence** *n*.

viridity *n* greenness; freshness.

virile *adj* of a mature man, manly; strong, forceful; sexually potent.—**virility** *n*.

virology *n* the study of viruses.

v. irr. *abbr* = verb irregular.

virtu *n* a love or knowledge of the fine arts, connoisseurship; artistic excellence, fine workmanship; the quality of appealing to a collector; artistic objects, antiques, curios, etc, collectively.—*also* **vertu**.

virtual *adj* in effect or essence, though not in fact or strict definition; (*comput*) denoting memory, making use of an external memory to increase capacity.

virtual drive *n* (*comput*) part of a computer's internal memory that is defined to act like a disk drive, from where data can be accessed very quickly by the main processor.

virtually *adv* to all intents and purposes, practically.

virtual machine *n* (*comput*) a computerized version of a computer that acts as if the computer was real and can actually run applications.

virtual memory or **VM** *n* (*comput*) the use of disk drive storage to extend the RAM of a computer.

virtual reality *n* (*comput*) a computer-generated environment that allows the user to experience various aspects of life without actually undergoing them.

virtue *n* moral excellence; any admirable quality; chastity; merit.

virtuoso *n* (*pl* **virtuosos**, **virtuosi**) a person highly skilled in an activity, esp in playing a musical instrument; the word was formerly synonymous with "amateur". * *adj* skilled, masterly in technique.—**virtuosic** *adj*.—**virtuosity** *n*.

virtuous *adj* righteous; upright; pure.—**virtuously** *adv*.—**virtuousness** *n*.

virulence *n* (*med*) the ability of bacteria or viruses to cause disease, measured by the number of people infected, the speed with which they spread through the body, etc.

virulent *adj* (*disease*) deadly; extremely poisonous; hostile; vicious.— **virulence** *n*. —**virulently** *adv*.

virus *n* (*pl* **viruses**) a very simple microorganism capable of replicating within living cells, producing disease; the disease caused by a virus; a harmful influence; (*comput*) a program designed to cause damage to systems that the virus infects, which can spread quickly through computer and telecommunication systems by copying itself.

VIS *abbr* = Veterinary Investigation Service.

visa *n* an endorsement on a passport allowing the bearer to travel in the country of the government issuing it. * *vt* (**visaing**, **visaed**) to mark with a visa; to grant a visa to.

visage *n* the face; the countenance; appearance.

visard *see* **vizard**.

vis-à-vis *prep* opposite to; in face of. * *adj, adv* facing. * *n* the person opposite; a counterpart.

viscacha *n* a South American burrowing rodent, that looks like a large chinchilla.— *also* **vizcacha**.

viscera *npl* (*sing* **viscus**) the large internal organs of the animal body, the entrails.

visceral *adj* of, pertaining to, or affecting the viscera; pertaining to or touching deeply inward feelings.—**viscerally** *adv*.

viscid *adj* (*leaves*) covered with a sticky layer; (*fluids*) thick, glutinous.—**viscidity** *n* —**viscidly** *adv*.

viscometer, **viscosimeter** *n* an instrument for measuring viscosity.

Visconti [di Modrone] *n* Count Luchino (1906–76) Italian film director. An aristocrat, he became a Marxist in the 1930s. His films include *The Leopard* (1963), *The Damned* (1969) and *Death in Venice* (1971), the latter two starring Dirk Bogarde.

viscose *n* a form of cellulose used in making artificial silk.

viscosity *n* (*pl* **viscosities**) the property or state of being sticky or glutinous; (*phys*) a property of fluids that indicates their resistance to flow.

viscount *n* in Britain, a title of nobility next below an earl.—**viscountess** *nf*.

viscountcy *n* (*pl* **viscountcies**) the rank of a viscount.

viscous *adj* sticky, thick; having viscosity.—**viscously** *adv*.—**viscousness** *n*.

viscus *see* **viscera**.

vise *see* **vice**.

Vishnevskaya, Galina *see* **Rostropovich, Mstislav**.

visibility *n* (*pl* **visibilities**) clearness of seeing or being seen; the degree of clearness of the atmosphere.

visible *adj* able to be seen, perceptible; apparent, evident.—**visibleness** *n*. — **visibly** *adv*.

visible control *n* (*com*) a technique used in production to make any defects visible to employees.

visibles *npl* (*com*) exports and imports in the form of goods rather than services, the latter being invisibles.

visible speech *n* a phonetic alphabet representing the actual movements of the vocal organs and used in teaching the deaf.

vision *n* the power of seeing, sight; a supernatural appearance; a revelation; foresight; imagination; a mental concept; a person, scene, etc of unusual beauty; something seen in a dream or trance.—**visional** *adj*.

visionary *adj* imaginative; having foresight; existing in imagination only, not real. * *n* (*pl* **visionaries**) an imaginative person; a dreamer; an idealist, a mystic.

visit *vt* to go to see; to pay a call upon a person or place; to stay with or at; to punish or reward with. * *vi* to see or meet someone regularly. * *n* the act of going to see, a call.—**visitable** *adj*.

visitant *n* a migratory bird; a visitor, esp a pilgrim; a ghost. * *adj* (*arch*) visiting.

visitation *n* a visit by a superior; a punitive act of God; an official visit; right of access of a divorced parent to his or her children; a large migration of animals; (*with cap*) the visit paid by the Virgin Mary to Elizabeth (Luke 1:39*ff*); a picture representing the event; the day on which this is commemorated, 2 July.— **visitational** *adj*.

visiting card *n* a small card with a person's name on it, left when paying visits.

visitor *n* a person who visits; a caller; a tourist; a migratory bird pausing in transit; an official acting as an inspector and adviser.

visor *n* a movable part of a helmet protecting the face; the peak of a cap.—*also* **vizor**.—**visored** *adj*.

vista *n* a view, as from a high place; a mental picture.—**vistaed**, **vista'd** *adj*.

VISTA *abbr* = Volunteers in Service to America

visual *adj* having, producing, or relating to vision or sight; perceptible, visible; (*knowledge*) attained by sight or vision; (*impressions, etc*) based upon something seen; of the nature of, producing or conveying a picture in the mind; (*phys*) optical. * *n* a piece of graphic material used for display or to convey a concept, etc; (*pl*) the visual aspect of a film, etc.—**visually** *adv*.

visual aid *n* a film, slide or overhead projector, etc used to aid teaching.

visual binary *n* (*astron*) a binary star in which the two members are far enough apart to be visible separately when viewed with an appropriate telescope, or even with the naked eye.

visual display unit *see* **VDU**.

visualize *vt* to form a mental picture of; to make visible to the mind or imagination. * *vi* to construct a visual image in the mind.—**visualization** *n*. —**visualizer** *n*.

vital *adj* of, connected with or necessary to life; essential; lively, animated; fundamental; (*wound, error*) fatal. * *n* (*pl*) the bodily organs essential for life.— **vitally** *adv*.

vital capacity *n* (*med*) the largest volume of air that can be exhaled after breathing in deeply.

vitalism *n* the belief that life cannot be explained as resulting wholly from physical and chemical processes, but must include some other vital non-material force or process.—**vitalist** *n*. —**vitalistic** *adj*.

vitality *n* (*pl* **vitalities**) vigor, hold on life; spirits; animation; capacity to last, durability.

vitalize *vt* to give life to; to animate; to make vigorous.—**vitalization** *n*.

vital statistics *npl* data recording births, deaths, marriages, etc used in compiling population statistics; (*inf*) the measurements of a woman's figure.

vitamin *n* one of several organic substances occurring naturally in foods, which are essential for good health.—**vitaminic** *adj*.

vitamin A *n* a fat-soluble vitamin essential for vision in dim light, growth, and the maintenance of mucous tissue.

vitamin B *n* a group of vitamins that, although they are not related chemically, are often found in the same types of food.

vitamin B₁, thiamine *n* a vitamin a deficiency of which leads to beri-beri.

vitamin B₂, riboflavin *n* a vitamin important in tissue respiration (enzyme reactions in cells) although a deficiency is not serious.

vitamin B₃, pantothenic acid *n* a vitamin that occurs widely in foods and is therefore unlikely to be lacking in the diet.

vitamin B₆, pyridoxine *n* a vitamin that is important in the metabolism of several amino acids.

vitamin B₁₂, cyanocobalamin *n* an important vitamin in the synthesis and production of red blood cells (erythrocytes). A deficiency produces anemia and degeneration of the nervous system.

vitamin C, ascorbic acid *n* a vitamin the deficiency of which leads to fragility of tendons, blood vessels, and skin, all characteristic of scurvy. The presence of ascorbic acid is believed to assist the uptake of iron during digestion.

vitamin D *n* a vitamin that is produced by the action of sunlight on the skin. It is vital in the control of blood calcium levels. A deficiency leads to rickets and osteomalacia.

vitamin E *n* a group of compounds thought to prevent damage to cell membranes. A deficiency is unusual because of its widespread occurrence in foods.

vitamin H *see* **biotin.**

vitamin K *n* a vitamin synthesized by bacteria in the large intestine that is essential for the clotting of blood.

vitel. *abbr* = vitellus.

vitellin *n* a protein forming the major component in the yolk of birds' eggs.

vitelline *adj* of or pertaining to egg yolk; of a yellow color close to the shade of egg yolk.

vitiate *vt* to make faulty or ineffective; to taint; to deprave; to invalidate or annul (a legal document, etc).—**vitiation** *n*. —**vitiator** *n*.

viticulture *n* the science of grapes and grape-growing.—**viticulturer, viticulturist** *n*. —**viticultural** *adj*.

vitreous *adj* of like or obtained from glass; of the vitreous body.—**vitreousness** *n*.

vitreous body, vitreous humor *n* the jelly-like substance occurring between the lens and the retina in the eye.

vitrescence *n* the quality of being vitrescent; the process of changing something, such as a crystalline material, into glass.

vitrescent *adj* capable of being made into or becoming like glass.

vitric *adj* glass-like.

vitrified fort *n* a fort that has been set alight so that the stones of the walls have vitrified and fused together.

vitrify *vt* (**vitrifying, vitrified**) to convert into glass or a glass-like substance.—**vitrifiable** *adj*.—**vitrification, vitrifaction** *n*.

vitriol *n* sulphuric acid; savage criticism. * *vt* (**vitrioling, vitrioled** *or* **vitriolling, vitriolled**) to throw vitriol over, to poison with vitriol.

vitriolic *adj* of or relating to vitriol; scathing, bitter.

vitriolize *vt* to harm by throwing vitriol over; to change into vitriol; to use vitriol in or as a part of the processing of something.—**vitriolization** *n*.

Vitruvius Pollio *n* Marcus a first century Roman architect and writer on architecture.

Vitsyebsk *n* city in Belarus.

vitta *n* (*pl* **vittae**) (*bot*) an oil tube in the fruit of some plants, e.g., parsley; (*zool*) a colored stripe.—**vittate** *adj*.

vituline *adj* of, like, calves or veal.

vituperate *vt* to berate; to abuse verbally.—**vituperative** *adj*.—**vituperator** *n*.

vituperation *n* the act of vituperating; blame, censure, reproof; the expression of this in abusive or violent language.

viv. *abbr* = vivace.

viva *interj* long live, hurrah for. *n* in UK, an oral examination, a viva voce. * *vt* (**vivas** *or* **viva's, vivaing, vivaed** *or* **viva'd**) to examine orally.

vivace *adv* (*mus*) (*Italian*) in a lively manner; with spirit.

vivacious *adj* lively; animated; spirited.—**vivaciously** *adv*.—**vivaciousness** *n*.

vivacity *n* (*pl* **vivacities**) vivaciousness; animation of the mind or disposition; liveliness of conception or perception; spirited conduct, manner or speech; brilliancy of light or color.

Vivaldi *n* **Antonio** (1675-1741) an Italian composer and violinist who was ordained as a priest in 1703. His music had an impact on Bach and was revived during the 19th century, his four concertos for violin, which are collectively known as *The Four Seasons*, becoming especially popular.

vivamente *n* (*mus*) (*Italian*) "in a lively way."

vivarium *n* (*pl* **vivariums, vivaria**) a place for keeping animals in their natural state for research or observation.

viva voce *adj, adv* orally, by word of mouth. * *n* an oral examination, a viva.

vivid *adj* brightly colored; graphic; lively; intense.—**vividly** *adv*.—**vividness** *n*.

vivify *vt* (**vivifying, vivified**) to give life to; to make more lively or more vivid.—**vivification** *n*. —**vivifier** *n*.

viviparous *adj* (*zool*) giving birth to young that have developed inside the body, as do most mammals.—**viviparity** *n*. —**viviparously** *adv*.

vivisect *vt* to subject to vivisection.—**vivisector** *n*.

vivisection *n* the practice of performing surgical operations on living animals for scientific research.—**vivisectional** *adj*.

vivisectionist *n* a person who practises or approves of vivisection.

vivo *n* (*mus*) (*Italian*) "lively."

Vix *n* **Princess of** (*c.*6th century BC) a Celtic princess buried in a barrow at Vix in Burgundy in France. Her grave with its grave goods, which was excavated in 1953, significantly added to knowledge of the Celts.

vix. *abbr* (*Latin*) = *vixit*, "lived."

vixen *n* a female fox; a malicious or shrewish woman.—**vixenish** *adj*.

viz. *abbr* (*Latin*) = *videlicet*, "namely."

vizard *n* (*arch*) a mask or other object that disguises; a visor.—*also* **visard.**

vizcacha *see* **vischacha.**

vizier, vizir *n* a minister of state or high official in Muslim countries, esp in the Ottoman Empire.

vizierate *n* the status, authority or (term of) office of a vizier.

vizor *see* **visor.**

VJ *abbr* = Victory over Japan (at the end of World War II); video jockey.

vl *abbr* (*Latin*) = *varia lectio*, "variant reading."

vl. *abbr* (*mus*) = violin.

vla. *abbr* (*mus*) = viola.

VLBC *abbr* = very large bulk carrier (ship).

VLBW *abbr* = very low birth weight.

VLCC *abbr* = very large crude carrier (oil tanker).

VLCD *abbr* = very low calorie diet.

VLDB *abbr* = very large database.

VLDL *abbr* = very low density lipoprotein.

VLF *abbr* = very low frequency.

VLLW *abbr* = very low level waste (nuclear).

Vlorë *n* city in Albania.

VLSI *abbr* = very large scale integration.

vm. *abbr* = voltmeter.

VM *abbr* = Virgin Mary; virtual machine.

v/m. *abbr* = volts per meter.

VM/CMS *abbr* = Virtual Machine Conversational Monitor System.

VMD *abbr* = (*Latin*) *Veterinariae Medicinae Doctor*, "Doctor of Veterinary Medicine"; Veterinary Medicines Directorate.

VMG *abbr* = Voluntary Movement Group.

VMH *abbr* = Victoria Medal of Honour.

VMM *abbr* = Volunteer Missionary Movement.

VMS *abbr* = Virtual Machine System.

vmt *abbr* = very many thanks.

vn. *abbr* = violin.

v.n. *abbr* = verb neuter; (*Latin*) *vicario nomine*, "as representative" *or* substitute.

VNA *abbr* = Vietnam News Agency.

vo. *abbr* = verso.

VO *abbr* = Veterinary Officer; voice over.

VOA *abbr* = Voice of America (radio station of the US Information Agency).

voc. *abbr* = vocative.

VOCA *abbr* = Visiting Orchestras Consultative Association.

vocab. *abbr* = vocabulary.

vocable *n* (*linguistics*) a word looked on as a pattern of characters or sounds with no regard to meaning; a sound; a vowel. * *adj* able to be spoken.

vocabulary *n* (*pl* **vocabularies**) an alphabetical list of words with their meanings; the words of a language; an individual's command or use of particular words.

vocal *adj* of, for, endowed with, relating to, or produced by the voice; outspoken, noisy; (*phonetics*) having a vowel function. * *n* a vowel; (*pl*) music for the voice, not another instrument.—**vocally** *adv*.

vocal chords *npl* either of two pairs of elastic membranous folds in the larynx, esp the lower pair, which vibrate and produce sound when air is expelled over them.

vocalic *adj* of, like or containing vowels.

vocalist *n* a singer.

vocalization *n* (*mus*) control of the voice and vocal sounds, and the method of producing and phrasing notes with the voice.

vocalize *n* a vocal exercise to improve flexibility and control of the voice in which a singer sings to one vowel sound. *vti* to express with the voice; to articulate, utter distinctly; to use the singing voice; to sing to vowel sounds; to write with vowels or vowel points.—**vocalization** *n*. —**vocalizer** *n*.

vocal score *see* **score.**

vocation *n* a calling to a particular career or occupation, esp to a religious life; a sense of fitness for a particular career.

vocational *adj* of or relating to a vocation or occupation; providing special training for a particular career.—**vocationally** *adv*.

vocative *adj* used, involved in or pertaining to loud utterances to attract attention; (*gram*) denoting the case of a noun, adjective, or pronoun used in addressing a person in some inflected languages, e.g., Latin. * *n* (*gram*) a vocative case or form.

voce *n* (*mus*) (*Italian*) "voice," as in *voce di petto*, "chest voice."

vociferant *adj* clamorous, noisy. * *n* a clamorous, noisy person.

vociferate *vti* to speak loudly and insistently, to clamor; to shout, to bawl.—**vociferation** *n*. —**vociferator** *n*.

vociferous *adj* clamorous, noisy.—**vociferously** *adv*.—**vociferousness** *n*.

vodka *n* a spirit distilled from rye, potatoes, etc.

vogue *n* the fashion at a specified time; popularity. * *adj* fashionable, in vogue.—**voguish** *adj*.

voice *n* sound from the mouth; sound produced by speaking or singing; the quality of this; the power of speech; utterance; expressed opinion, vote; (*gram*) the forms of a verb showing the relation of subject to action; (*phonetics*) a sound uttered with vibration of the vocal chords not with mere breath; (*mus*) (1) the three categories of adult male voice (bass, baritone and tenor); the three female categories (contralto, mezzo-soprano and soprano); and the two boy categories (treble and alto). (2) parts in contrapuntal compositions, traditionally termed "voices." * *vt* to express; to speak; (*mus*) to regulate so as to give the correct tone; (*phonetics*) to utter with the voice, to make sonant.—**voicer** *n*.

voice/data switch *n* (*comput*) a switch that identifies the type of call being received over a telephone line and routes the call to the appropriate device so that voice calls go to a telephone and fax calls to a fax machine.

voiced *adj* having a voice, esp of a specified kind, quality or tone; (*phonetics*) uttered with the voice or vibration of the vocal chords, sonant.

voiceful *adj* (*poet*) having a voice; sonorous.

voiceless *adj* speechless, dumb; (*phonetics*) not voiced.—**voicelessly** *adv*.—**voicelessness** *n*.

voice mail *n* (*comput*) a system that stores voice communication on disk and can replay the message on command.

voice messaging *n* the use of answering machines attached to telephones to store messages until it is possible or convenient for the recipient to receive the messages.

voice-over *n* the voice of an unseen narrator, esp in a film, TV commercial, etc.

voice recognition *n* (*comput*) the ability of a computer to recognize a voice, translate it into a digital pattern and reproduce the pattern as text or as computer generated speech.

voice synthesis *see* **speech synthesis**.

void *adj* unoccupied, empty; not legally binding; having no cards of a particular suit. * *n* an empty space, a vacuum; vacancy, sense of loss. * *vt* to discharge, to emit; empty; to make invalid.—**voidable** *adj*.—**voider** *n*.

voidance *n* the act of voiding or evacuating; emptiness; the annulment of a legal deed.

voided *adj* (*her*) having the inner part of a figure cut away, leaving only the outer edges; being, or having been caused to be, empty.

voile *n* a light, sheer fabric of silk, rayon, etc used for dresses, scarves, etc.

vol. *abbr* = volcanic; volcano; volume; volunteer.

Volans *or* **The Flying Fish** *n* a small, faint constellation in the southern hemisphere situated near the Large Magellanic Cloud.

volant *adj* flying; able to fly; (*her*) appearing to fly; (*poet*) nimble.

Volapuk, Volapük *n* an artificial language taking elements from English, French, German, Latin, etc invented in 1880 and intended for international commercial use.—**Volapukist, Volapükist** *n*.

volar *adj* (*anat*) of the palm of the hand or sole of the foot.

volatile *adj* evaporating very quickly; changeable, fickle; unstable; light-hearted, mercurial; flighty; (*chem*) denoting any substance that can easily change from the solid or liquid state to its vapor; (*comput*) having a memory that loses data when power is disconnected.—**volatility** *n*.

volatile storage *n* (*comput*) storage of which the contents are lost when power is removed, e.g. the RAM.

volatilize *vti* to turn into vapour, to (cause to) evaporate. —**volatilization** *n*.

vol-au-vent *n* a case of light puff pastry filled with a savory sauce.

volc. *abbr* = volcano.

volcanic *adj* of, like or due to the action of a volcano; violent, intense.—**volcanically** *adv*.

volcanic bomb *n* (*geol*) a lump of lava thrown out from a volcano that can take one of several shapes depending upon the type of lava, the degree of solidification and its flight through the air.

volcanic vent *n* (*geol*) the pipe that connects a volcanic crater with the source of magma.

volcanism *n* volcanic action.—*also* **vulcanism**.

volcanize *vt* to subject to volcanic heat; to cause to change by means of volcanic heat.—**volcanization** *n*.

volcano *n* (*geol*) (*pl* **volcanoes, volcanos**) a natural vent or opening in the earth's crust that is connected by a pipe, or *conduit*, to a chamber at a depth that contains magma; lava, volcanic gases, steam and ash may be ejected.

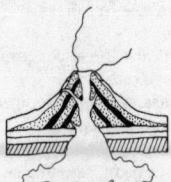

volcanology *n* the science of volcanoes and the occurrences associated with them.—*also* **vulcanology**.—**volcanological, vulcanological** *adj*.—**volcanologist, vulcanologist** *n*.

vole[1] *n* a small rat-like rodent with a short tail.

vole[2] *vt* to win all the tricks in a deal. * *n* a slam.

volitant *adj* able to fly, volant; flying, or otherwise moving about, in a rapid, nimble fashion.

volition *n* the exercise of the will; choice.—**volitional** *adj*.

volitive *adj* pertaining to or having the power of will; (*gram*) desiderative; expressing a wish or intention.

Volkmann's contracture *n* a condition often caused by pressure from a cast or tight bandage on the arm.

volley *n* (*pl* volleys) the multiple discharge of many missiles or small arms; a barrage; (*tennis, volleyball*) the return of the ball before it reaches the ground. * *vt* (**volleying, volleyed**) to return (a ball) before it hits the ground.—**volleyer** *n*.

volleyball *n* a team game played by hitting a large inflated ball over a net with the hands; the ball used.

vols. *abbr* = volumes.

Volscians, Volsci *n* (*hist*) an ancient Italian tribe who lived in Latium.

volt[1] *n* the circular gait of a horse in dressage; (fencing) a leap to avoid a thrust.

volt[2] *n* (*elect*) the unit of measure of the force of an electrical current; the unit of potential difference.

volta *n* (*pl* **volte**) a lively 16th-century Italian dance; (*mus*) 1. music in triple time, originally written to accompany such a dance; 2. a particular time as specified.

voltage *n* (*elect*) electrical energy that moves a charge around a circuit, measured in volts.

voltaic *adj* pertaining to electricity generated by chemical action or galvanism; galvanic.

Voltaire *n* [**François Marie Arouet**] (1694–1778) French philosopher, poet, historian, essayist, dramatist, and essayist. An important French philosopher of the enlightenment, his most influential work is the *Philosophical Letters* (1734) while other works include the novel *Candide* (1759).

voltaism *n* galvanism; electricity generated by chemical action.

voltameter *n* an instrument for measuring an electric charge; a coulombmeter.

volte-face *n* (*pl* **volte-faces, volte-face**) a change to an opposite opinion or direction.

volti subito *n* (*mus*) (*Italian*) "turn over quickly" (of a page).

voltmeter *n* an instrument for measuring voltage.

voluble *adj* speaking with a great flow of words, fluent; (*arch*) revolving, rotating; (*bot*) twining.—**volubility** *n*. —**volubly** *adv*.

volubleness *n* excessive fluency of speech.

volume *n* (*phys*) the amount of space occupied by an object or substance; quantity, amount; intensity of sound; a book; one book of a series.—**volumed** *adj*.

volume label *n* (*comput*) a name that identifies the disk, given when the disk is formatted. *See* **format**.

volumeter *n* an instrument for measuring the volume of a gas, liquid, or solid.

volumetric *adj* of or relating to measurement by volume.—**volumetrically** *adv*.

volumetric analysis *n* (*chem*) chemical analysis that uses standard solutions of known concentrations to calculate a particular constituent present in another solution, using titration.

voluminous *adj* of great size or bulk; (*writings*) capable of filling many volumes; (*clothes*) ample, loose.—**voluminosity** *n*. —**voluminously** *adv*.

voluntarism *n* the theory that the will is dominant over the intellect; a belief in voluntary participation not compulsion in a course of action; voluntaryism.—**voluntaryist** *n*.

voluntary *adj* spontaneous, deliberate; without remuneration; supported by voluntary effort; having free will; (*law*) acting gratuitously or from choice, not because of any legal compulsion or argument; (*muscles*) controlled by conscious effort; designed; pertaining to voluntaryism.* *n* (*pl* **voluntaries**) (*mus*) (1) improvised piece of instrumental music (16th century). (2) an organ solo (sometimes improvised) played before and after an Anglican service; (*arch*) a volunteer.—**voluntarily** *adv*.—**voluntariness** *n*.

voluntary arrangement *n* (*com*) a system by which companies in financial difficulty may come to an arrangement with their creditors to pay off their debts and make their own arrangements to resolve their financial difficulties rather than having to undertake a winding-up process.

voluntaryism *n* the theory that churches, schools, etc should depend on voluntary contributions, not state aid.—**voluntarist** *n*. —**voluntaristic** *adj*.

voluntary muscle *n* muscle that is under conscious control, e.g. those operating the skeleton.—*also* **striated muscle**

voluntary retailer *or* **symbol retailer** *n* (*com*) an independent retailer who joins together with other independent retailers so that they can buy in large quantities from wholesalers at much lower prices than they could achieve without this cooperation.

volunteer *n* a person who carries out work voluntarily; a person who freely undertakes military service. * *vti* to offer unasked; to come forward, enlist or serve voluntarily.

voluptuary *n* (*pl* **voluptuaries**) a person given up to bodily pleasures or the enjoyment of luxury, a sensualist. * *adj* exciting sensual desire; devoted to pleasures of the senses; voluptuous; luxurious.

voluptuous *adj* excessively fond of pleasure; having an attractive figure; luxurious; exciting sensual desire.—**voluptuously** *adv*.—**voluptuousness** *n*.

volute *n* a spiral; a whorl; anything shaped to resemble a spiral or otherwise convoluted form; a spiral, scroll-shaped ornament, esp on an Ionic capital, a helix; a tropical shellfish with a spiral shell; any of the whorls found on the shells of snails; an auxiliary curved part of an engine that collects waste gases or liquids from that engine. * *adj* spiral-shaped; (*machinery*) moving spirally; (*bot*) rolled up. (—*also* **voluted**).

volution *n* a spiral; a convoluted or turning shape or movement; any of the whorls of a shell.

volvox *n* a genus of round, hollow microscopic plants having a rotatory motion, found in ponds, etc.

volvulus *n* a twisting of part of the intestine, which usually results in some obstruction that may reduce the blood supply, ending in gangrene.

vomer *n* the flat, slender bone separating the nostrils in mammals.

vomit *vi* to eject the contents of the stomach through the mouth, to spew. * *n* matter ejected from the stomach when vomiting.—**vomiter** *n*.

vomitive *adj* of or causing vomiting. * *n* an emetic.

vomitory *adj* vomitive. * *n* (*pl* **vomitories**) an emetic; an aperture for vomited matter; any opening through which something is ejected; in ancient Rome, a corridor from a street entrance to a tier of seats in an amphitheater. (—*also* **vomitorium**).

vomiturition *n* violent retching; repeated vomiting.

von Braun *n* **Wernher** (1912–77) German-born American rocket engineer. The technical director (1937–45) of the German rocket project at Peenemunde in World War II, he designed the V–1 and V–2 rocket bombs that were launched in random attacks against southern England in 1944. Captured by the US, he was put to work on US rocket research, including the development of the Saturn moon rockets.

Vonnegut *n* **Kurt Jnr** (1922–) American novelist, essayist, and short-stor y writer whose science fiction fables include *The Sirens of Titan*, *Cat's Cradle*, and *Slaughterhouse-Five* (1969), which is generally regarded as his masterpiece.

von Neumann *n* **John** (1903–57) Hungarian-born American mathematician. He was one of the founders of the theory of games, i.e. the application of statistical logic to the choice of game strategies. He also made significant contributions to quantum theory and to computer research, and was a consultant on the development of the atom bomb.

von Recklinghausen's disease *n* a congenital disorder, in which soft tissue tumors form along nerves and beneath the skin.

voodoo *n* (*pl* **voodoos**) a religious cult in the West Indies, based on a belief in sorcery, etc; one who practices voodoo. * *vt* (**voodooing, voodooed**) to affect by voodoo.

voodooism *n* the beliefs and practices of voodoo.—**voodooist** *n*. —**voodooistic** *adj*.

VOP *abbr* = very oldest procurable (of spirits).

voracious *adj* eager to devour (food, literature etc); very greedy.—**voraciously** *adv*.—**voracity** *n*.

Voroshilov *n* **Klimenti Yefremovich** (1881–1969) Soviet military leader and statesman. A Red Army commander in the civil war, he was commissar for defence (1925–40), in charge of the Red Army. He became president (1953–60) after his friend Stalin's death.

vortex *n* (*pl* **vortexes, vortices**) a whirlpool; a powerful eddy; a whirlwind; a whirling motion or mass.—**vortical** *adj*.—**vortically** *adv*.

vorticella *n* (*pl* **vorticellae**) any of a genus of ciliated, bell-shaped animalcules.

vorticism *n* an art movement in which cubist techniques were amalgamated with that aspect of futurism expressing reservations about the quality of contemporary life, and its reliance on machines, so that objects were presented so as to give the effect of an assemblage of vortices; the English variant of futurism, its adherents including writers such as Wyndham Lewis and Ezra Pound.—**vorticist** *n*.

Vortigern *n* a British tribal king of Kent (reigned *c*.450). "Vortigern," the title used for an overlord, also came to be used as the name of the tribal leader who is thought to have asked mercenaries from Jutland to help him fight off attacks from northern Picts.

vortiginous *adj* whirling, vortical; vortex-like.

Vortumnus *see* **Vertumnus**.

VOSCO *abbr* = Vietnam Ocean Shipping Company.

vostro *n* a bank account in a UK bank held by a foreign bank.

votary *n* (*pl* **votaries**) a person vowed to religious service or worship; an ardent follower, a devotee of a person, religion, occupation, idea, etc.—*also* **votarist**. * *adj* ardently devoted to a deity or saint.

vote *n* an indication of a choice or opinion as to a matter on which one has a right to be consulted; a ballot; decision by a majority; the right to vote; franchise. * *vi* to cast one's vote. * *vt* to elect (to office).—**votable, voteable** *adj*.

voter *n* a person with a right to vote, esp one who uses it.

voting shares *npl* shares in a company that give the holder of them the right to vote at the annual general meeting of the company or at any extraordinary meetings of the company that may be called.

votive *adj* given, consecrated, or promised by vow; (*RC Church*) voluntary, given by free will not by prescription.

votive deposit *n* an object or group of objects given as an offering to a god.

vouch *vt* to provide evidence or proof of. * *vi* to give assurance; to guarantee.

voucher *n* a written record of a transaction; a receipt; a token that can be exchanged for something else.

vouchsafe *vt* to give, to grant; to condescend (to).—**vouchsafement** *n*.

voussoir *n* (*archit*) a wedge-shaped block of stone which forms the curve of an arch.

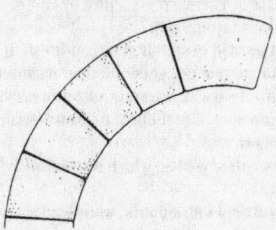

vow *n* a solemn or binding promise. * *vt* to promise; to resolve.—**vower** *n*.

vowel *n* an open speech sound produced by continuous passage of the breath; a letter representing such a sound, as *a, e, i, o, u*. * *adj* of or constituting a vowel.— **vowelless** *adj*.

vowelize *vt* to insert vowel points in (usu something written in Hebrew).— **vowelization** *n*.

vowel point *n* a diacritical mark indicating a vowel in Hebrew, Arabic, etc.

vox *n* (*pl* **voces**) a voice; a sound.

vox humana *n* an organ stop with tones like the human voice.

vox pop. *abbr* (*Latin*) = *vox populi*, "voice of the people."

voyage *n* a long journey, esp by ship or spacecraft. * *vi* to journey.—**voyager** *n*.

voyageur *n* a Canadian boatman working for a fur-trading company, esp if covering an area inland; any boatman, trapper or guide, esp in Northern Canada.

voyeur *n* a person who is sexually gratified from watching sexual acts or objects; a peeping Tom.—**voyeurism** *n*. —**voyeuristic** *adj*.

Voysey *n* **Charles Francis Annesley** (1857–1941) British architect who designed H G Wells' Spade House, Sandgate, Kent.

vp *abbr* = vanishing point; verb passive.

v.p. *abbr* = various places of publication (*bibliography*).

VP *abbr* = Vice-President; verb phrase.

VPA *abbr* = Vegetable Protein Association.

VPC *abbr* (*French*) = *vente par correspondance*, "mail order."

vpd *abbr* = vehicles per day.

vph *abbr* = vehicles per hour.

VPO *abbr* = Vienna Philharmonic Orchestra.

vps *abbr* = vibrations per second.

vr *abbr* = variant reading; verb reflexive.

v.r. *abbr* = variant or various reading; verb reflexive.

VR *abbr* = (*Latin*) *Victoria Regina*, "Queen Victoria"; Volunteer Reserve; virtual reality; vulcanised rubber.

vraisemblance *n* an appearance of truth, verisimilitude.

VRAM *abbr* (*comput*) = Video random-access memory (RAM). RAM used in conjunction with a video card together to enhance the performance of video displays.

V. Rev. *abbr* = Very Reverend.

VRH *abbr* = Volunteer Reading Help.

VRI *abbr* = (*Latin*) *Victoria Regina et Imperatrix*, "Victoria, Queen and Empress"; viral respiratory infection.

VRO *abbr* = vehicle registration office.

VRS *abbr* = Virtual Reality Society.

vs *abbr* = (*Latin*) *versus*, "against"; (*Latin*) *vide supra*, "see above"; (*Italian*) (*mus*) *volti subito*, "turn over quickly."

vs. (*Latin*) *abbr* = *versus*, "against."

v.s. *abbr* = (*Latin*) *vide supra*, "see above"; visible supply; (*Italian*) (*mus*) *volti subito*, "turn over quickly"; volumetric solution.

VS *abbr* = Vegetarian Society; Veterinary Surgeon; The Victorian Society.

VSAM *abbr* = virtual storage access method.

VSC *abbr* = Volunteer Staff Corps.

VSCC *abbr* = Vintage Sports Car Club.

VSD *abbr* = ventricular septal defect.

V-shaped valley *n* a valley that has been created by river erosion, giving it evenly sloping sides, in contrast to U-shaped or glaciated valleys, which have much steeper sides.

VSI *abbr* = Vegetarian Society of Ireland.

VSL *abbr* = Venture Scout Leader.

VSO *abbr* = Vienna State Opera; Voluntary Service Overseas; very superior old (of spirits).

VSOP *abbr* = very superior old pale (brandy, etc).

VSR *abbr* = very special reserve (of wine, etc).

VSS *abbr* = versions; vital signs stable.

VSTOL *abbr* = vertical and short take-off and landing.

VSUK *abbr* = Vegetarian Society of the United Kingdom Limited.

vt, v.t. *abbr* = verb transitive.

VT, Vt *abbr* = Vermont.

VT *abbr* = ventricular tachycardia; (*Latin*) *Vetus Testamentum*, "Old Testament."

VTC *abbr* (*Brit*) = Volunteer Training Corps.

V

VTO *abbr* = vertical take-off.

VTOHL *abbr* = vertical take-off, horizontal landing.

VTOL *abbr* = vertical take-off and landing.

VTOVL *abbr* = vertical take-off, vertical landing.

VTR *abbr* = videotape recorder.

V-type asteroid *n* a class of asteroid represented by only one known example, Vesta.

VU *abbr* = varicose ulcer; volume unit.

vug, vugh *n* (*mining*) a small cavity, often crystal-lined, in a lode or rock.

Vuitton *n* **Louis** French luggage designer and manufacturer.

Vulcan *n* (*Roman myth*) the god of fire and smiths corresponding to the Greek god, Hephaestus; (*arch*) a planet once thought to orbit Mercury.

vulcanism *see* **volcanism.**

vulcanite *n* a hard, vulcanized rubber, which is resistant to the effects of chemicals, ebonite.

vulcanize *vt* to treat (rubber) with sulphur, white lead and other substances at high temperatures under pressure to improve its strength and elasticity or render it hard and non-elastic; to change the properties of (any material) in a similar way.— **vulcanization** *n.*

vulcanology *see* **volcanology.**

vulg. *abbr* = vulgar; vulgarly.

Vulg., Vul. *abbr* = Vulgate.

vulgar *adj* of the common people; vernacular; unrefined, in bad taste; coarse; offensive, indecent.—**vulgarly** *adv.*—**vulgarness** *n.*

vulgar fraction *n* (*math*) an ordinary fraction with one number over the other.

vulgarian *n* a vulgar pretentious person, esp one who shows of his or her wealth.

vulgarism *n* a crude expression; coarseness.

vulgarity *n* (*pl* **vulgarities**) coarseness of manners or language; a vulgar phrase, expression, act, etc.

vulgarize *vt* to debase; to popularize.—**vulgarization** *n.* —**vulgarizer** *n.*

Vulgate *n* a 4th–century Latin version of the Bible made by St Jerome, by combining text from the original language material and an earlier Latin text derived from the Greek; (*RC Church*) a revised form of this used as the authorized version. * *adj* pertaining to, or contained in, the Vulgate.

vulnerable *adj* capable of being wounded physically or mentally; open to persuasion; easily influenced; open to attack, assailable; (*contract bridge*) having won one game and liable to doubled penalties.—**vulnerability** *n.* —**vulnerably** *adv.*

vulnerary *adj* used for healing wounds. * *n* (*pl* **vulneraries**) a drug, ointment, etc, used in this way.

vulpine, vulpecular *adj* pertaining to, like, or characteristic of a fox; cunning.

vulture *n* a large bird of prey having no feathers on the neck or head and feeding chiefly on carrion; a rapacious person.

vulturine, vulturous *adj* vulture-like.

vulva (*pl* **vulvae, vulvas**) *n* the external female genitalia, comprising two pairs of fleshy folds (labia) surrounding the opening of the vagina.—**vulval, vulvar, vulvate** *adj.*

vulvectomy *n* surgical removal of the vulva.

vulviform *adj* like a cleft with projecting edges.

vulvitis *n* inflammation of the vulva.

vulvovaginitis *n* inflammation of both the vulva and vagina.

vv *abbr* = vice versa.

vv. *abbr* = verses; violins.

VV Cephei star *n* a class of gigantic binary stars of which there are few known examples.

vv. ll. *abbr* = *variae lectiones.*

VVO *abbr* = very, very old (of brandy, etc).

VW *abbr* = Very Worshipful; (*German*) *Volkswagen,* "People's Car."

vy *abbr* = various years.

vying *see* **vie.**

vyse *n* (*archit*) a spiral staircase.

W

w, W *n* the 23rd letter of the English alphabet.

W *symbol* (*chem*) tungsten.

w *abbr* = wicket; widow; word.

w, w. *abbr* = wanting; warden; warehousing; watt; week(s); weight; western; wide; width; wife; with; won; (*phys*) work.

W, W. *abbr* = Wales; Washington; Wednesday; Welsh; watt(s); west; western; white; winter; women; (clothing size) women's.

w.a., WA *abbr* = (*marine ins*) with average.

WA *abbr* = Washington; West Africa; Western Australia; Willwriters Association.

WAA *abbr* = Women's Auxiliary Association.

WAAA *abbr* = Women's Amateur Athletic Association.

WAAC *abbr* = Women's Army Auxiliary Corps.

WAAE *abbr* = World Association for Adult Education.

WAAF *abbr* = Women's Auxiliary Air Force.

WAB *abbr* = Wales Advisory Body for Local Authority Higher Education.

WABA *abbr* = Welsh Amateur Basketball Association; Welsh Amateur Boxing Association.

WAC *abbr* = Women's Army Corps.

WACA *abbr* = World Airlines Clubs Association.

WACCC *abbr* = Worldwide Air Cargo Commodity Classification.

wacky *adj* (**wackier, wackiest**) (*sl*) crazy, eccentric.—**wackily** *adv*.—**wackiness** *n*.

wad *n* a small, soft mass, as of cotton or paper; a bundle of paper money.

WAD *abbr* = World Association of Detectives.

wadding *n* any soft material for use in padding, packing, etc.

waddle *vi* to walk with short steps and sway from side to side, as a duck.—*also n*.

waddy *n* (*pl* **waddies**) a club with a thickened head used as a weapon by Australian Aborigines. * *vt* (**waddying, waddied**) to hit with a waddy.

wade *vti* to walk through water; to pass (through) with difficulty.

wader *n* a bird that wades, e.g. the heron; (*pl*) high waterproof boots worn by anglers.

wadi, wady *n* a channel of a stream in North Africa which is dry except in the rainy season.

Wadjet *n* (*Egypt*) a serpent-goddess, protector of the Upper Egypt nome called after her, with the cult center at Buto.

waf *abbr* = with all faults.

WAF *abbr* = Women in the Air Force.

WAFA *abbr* = World Association of Flower Arrangers.

WAFB *abbr* = Workers Aid for Bosnia.

wafer *n* a thin crisp cracker or biscuit; (*Christianity*) the disc of unleavened bread used in the Eucharist.

waffle[1] *n* a thick, crisp pancake baked in a waffle iron.

waffle[2] *vi* (*esp Brit inf*) to speak or write at length without saying anything substantial.

waffle iron *n* a metal cooking utensil with two hinged metal parts that close and impress a square pattern on a waffle.

WAfr, W. Afr. *abbr* = West Africa.

waft *vt* to drift or float through the air. * *n* a breath, scent, or sound carried through the air.

wag[1] *vti* (**wagging, wagged**) to move rapidly from side to side or up and down (as of a finger, tail).—*also n*.

wag[2] *n* a joker, a wit.

WAG *abbr* = Writers' and Artists' Guild.

WAGA *abbr* = Welsh Amateur Gymnastic Association.

WAGBI *abbr* = Wildfowl Association of Great Britain and Ireland.

WAGC *abbr* = World Amateur Golf Council.

wage *vt* to carry on, esp war. * *n* (*often pl*) payment for work or services.

wage differential *n* the difference in wage rates between different groups of workers.

wage drift *n* the tendency for the actual earnings of workers to rise faster than increases in wage rates would suggest.

wage earner *n* a person who works for wages.

wage freeze *n* a fixing by government of wages at their existing levels in an effort to control inflation.

Wagenfeld *n* Wilhelm (1900–90) German architect and industrial designer whose 1939 *Oberweimer* set of glasses outsold any other set of glasses made worldwide.

Wagenseil *n* Georg Christoph (1715–77) an Austrian composer and keyboard player who was a pupil of Fux. He became a court composer in Vienna and his works include symphonies, concertos, oratorios, and operas.

wager *n* a bet. * *vti* to bet.

wage restraint *n* under a wage restraint policy, the government tries to get the unions and workers to accept only small wage increases.

WAGGGS *abbr* = World Association of Girl Guides and Girl Scouts.

waggle *vti* to wag.—*also n*.

Wagner *n* [Wilhelm] Richard (1813–83) German composer whose works include the opera *Tannhäuser* (1845) and the *Ring of the Niebelung* cycle (1876).

Wagnerian *n* of or resembling the music of Richard Wagner, characterized by dramatic grandeur and emotional intensity.

wagon *n* a four-wheeled vehicle pulled by a horse or tractor, for carrying heavy goods.

wagoner *n* a driver of a wagon.

wagon-lit *n* (*pl* **wagons-lits**) a sleeping-car on a European train.

wagtail *n* any of numerous small birds with tails that jerk constantly.

wah-wah *n* the sound of a trumpet, etc when alternately muted and unmuted; a pedal or lever used with an electric guitar, etc to imitate this sound.

WAIA *abbr* = World Association of Introduction Agencies.

waif *n* a homeless, neglected child.

WAIF *abbr* = World Adoption International Fund.

wail *vi* to make a long, loud cry of sorrow or grief; to howl, to moan.—*also n*.

wain *n* (*poet*) a farm wagon.

wainscot *n* wooden paneling on the interior of a wall.—*also* **wainscoting**. * *vt* to line (a wall) with a wainscot.

wainwright *n* a person who builds wagons.

WAIS *abbr* (*comput*) = Wide Area Information Server. A server system specialized in searching databases.

waist *n* the narrowest part of the human trunk, between the ribs and the hips; the narrow part of anything that is wider at the ends; the part of a garment covering the waist.

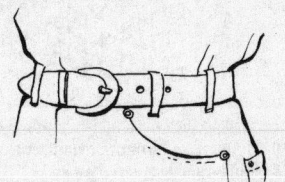

waistband *n* a band of material (on a skirt, trousers, etc) that strengthens and completes the waist.

waistcoat *n* (*Brit*) a waist-length, sleeveless garment worn immediately under a suit jacket; a vest.

waistline *n* the narrowest part of the waist; its measurement; the seam that joins the bodice and skirt of a dress, etc; the level of this.

wait *vti* to stay, or to be, in expectation or readiness; to defer or to be postponed; to remain; (*with at or on*) to serve food at a meal. * *n* act or period of waiting.

waiter *n* a man or woman who serves at table, as in a restaurant.—**waitress** *nf*.

waiting *n* the act of remaining inactive or stationary; a period of waiting. * *adj* of or pertaining to a wait; in attendance.

waiting game *n* a delay in acting or deciding in order to benefit from more favorable circumstances later.

waiting list *n* a list of people applying for or waiting to obtain something.

waiting room *n* a room for people to wait in at a station, hospital, etc.

waiting time *n* (*com*) the period of time during which the operators of machines, or the machines themselves, are not working because they are waiting for materials, repairs, etc.

wait state *n* (*comput*) the interval programmed into a computer during which the microprocessor waits for the RAM to catch up.

waive *vt* to refrain from enforcing; to relinquish voluntarily.

waiver *n* (*law*) a waiving of a right, claim etc.

WAJ *abbr* = World Association of Judges.

wake[1] *vb* (**waking, woke**, *pp* **woken**) *vi* to emerge from sleep; to become awake. * *vt* to rouse from sleep. * *n* a watch or vigil beside a corpse, on the eve of the burial.—**wakeful** *adj*.—**waken** *vti*.

wake[2] *n* the waves or foamy water left in the track of a ship; a trail.

Walcott *n* Derek [Anton] (1930–) St Lucian-born West Indian poet and dramatist, and winner of the 1992 Nobel prize for literature.

Waldheim *n* Kurt (1918–) Austrian diplomat who became secretary-general of the United Nations (1972–82) and president of Austria (1986–). Revelations about his role in Nazi genocide in Yugoslavia during the war surfaced in the late 1980s.

Waldteufel *n* Emil (1837-1915) a French composer and pianist. He wrote many dances, mainly waltzes, which include *The Skater's Waltz* and *Espana*.

wale *n* a ridge or mark on the body, a weal; a ridge on a ribbed material such as corduroy; a heavy plank along a ship's side.

Walesa *n* **Lech** (1943–) Polish trade union leader and statesman; became leader of Solidarity in 1980; Solidarity was banned in 1981 and he was imprisoned (1981–82); won the 1983 Nobel peace prize. In the first free elections in eastern Europe (1989) since the 1940s, he became president of a Solidarity government.

Walhalla *see* **Valhalla**.

walk *vi* to travel on foot with alternate steps; (*with* **out**) to leave suddenly; to go on strike; (*with* **on**) to abandon, jilt. * *vt* to pass through or over; (*a dog*) to exercise; to escort on foot. * *n* the act of walking; distance walked over; gait; a ramble or stroll; a profession.—**walker** *n*.

walkabout *n* a ceremonial wander through the Australian bush made periodically by an Aborigine; an informal stroll through a crowd by a politician, celebrity, etc.

walker *n* one who walks; a tubular metal frame with rubber feet, used as a walking aid by the elderly or disabled; a similar frame used by babies who are learning to walk.

Walker *n* **Alice Malsenior** (1944–) American writer whose novels include the Pulitzer prizewinning work, *The Color Purple* (1982).

walkie-talkie, walky-talky *n* (*pl* **walkie-talkies, walky-talkies**) a portable two-way radio transmitter and receiver.

walk-in *adj* (*cupboard*) large enough to enter and move around in.

walking *adj* able to walk; appearing to walk; ambulatory; marked by traveling on foot (*walking holiday*); intended for walkers (*walking boots*); in animate form (*walking bomb*). * *n* the act of walking; gait; the condition of a track, etc.

walking papers *n* (*sl*) notice of dismissal.

walking stick *n* a stick used in walking, a cane.

Walkman *n* (*trademark*) a small portable cassette player (and sometimes radio) used with earphones.

walk-on *n* a small (esp non-speaking) part in a play.

walkout *n* a strike; a sudden departure.

walkover *n* an unopposed or easy victory; a horse race with only one starter.

walk-through *n* a rehearsal.

walkway *n* road, path, etc, for pedestrians only.

Walkyrie *see* **Valkyrie**.

wall *n* a vertical structure of brick, stone, etc for enclosing, dividing, or protecting. * *vt* to enclose with a wall; to close up with a wall.

Wall *n* **James E** (*d*. 1917) American furniture manufacturer who produced pieces made from imported bamboo and lacquered panels.

wallaby *n* (*pl* **wallabies, wallaby**) a small kangaroo-like animal.

Wallace *n* **Alfred Russel** (1823–1913) Welsh naturalist. Independently of Darwin, he devised a theory of evolution by natural selection. His works include *Geographical Distribution of Animals* (1876) and *Man's Place in the Universe* (1898).

wallah, walla *n* (*inf*) a person with a specified job or responsibility.

wallaroo *n* (*pl* **wallaroos, wallaroo**) a type of large kangaroo.

walled *adj* having walls; surrounded or protected as if by walls; fortified.

Waller *n* **Fats [Thomas Wright Waller]** (1904–43) American jazz pianist and composer and an exponent of the "stride" school of jazz piano; he was noted for his humorous lyrics.

wallet *n* a flat pocketbook for paper money, cards etc.

walleye *n* an eye with an opaque cornea; any eye with a pale or white iris; a squint in which an eye turns outward.

wallflower *n* a fragrant plant with red or yellow flowers; a person who does not dance for lack of a partner.

Wallis *n* **Sir Barnes [Neville]** (1887–1979) English aeronautical engineer who was the designer of the "bouncing bombs" used in the "Dambuster" bombing raids of 1943.

Wallis and Futuna Islands *n* a French overseas territory in the southern central Pacific comprising two island groups 142 miles or 230 kilometers apart.

Walloon *n* a member of a French-speaking people of southern Belgium and adjacent areas of France; the French dialect of Walloons.—*also adj*.

wallop *vt* (*inf*) to beat or defeat soundly; (*inf*) to strike hard. * *n* (*inf*) a hard blow.

walloping *adj* (*inf*) large, massive. * *n* (*inf*) a thrashing, a defeat.

wallow *vi* (*animal*) to roll about in mud; to indulge oneself in emotion.—*also n*.

wallpaper *n* decorated paper for covering the walls of a room; (*comput*) an on-screen design that acts as a backdrop to the icons, windows, etc.

wall-plate *n* (*archit*) in roofing, a timber laid along the top of the wall to which the ends of the rafters are fastened.

Wall Street *n* a street in New York where the Stock Exchange is situated; the center of American finance.

wall-to-wall *adj* (*carpet*) covering the whole area of a room; (*inf*) nonstop, continuous.

wally *n* (*pl* **wallies**) (*Brit sl*) an idiot.

walnut *n* a tree producing an edible nut with a round shell and wrinkled seed; its nut; its wood used for furniture.

Walpole *n* 1. **Horace [4th Earl of Oxford]** (1717–97) English author, noted for his vast correspondence and for his fascination with the "Gothic." His novel, *The Castle of Otranto*, was the first major Gothic novel. 2. **Sir Hugh** (1884–1941) English novelist whose best-known work is a sequence of historical novels set in northwest England, the *Herries Chronicle*. 3. **Sir Robert [1st Earl of Orford]** (1676–1745) English statesman. As chancellor and first lord of the treasury he was, effectively, Britain's first prime minister (1721–42).

walrus *n* (*pl* **walruses, walrus**) a large, thick-skinned aquatic animal, related to the seals, having long canine teeth and coarse whiskers.

walrus moustache *n* a thick drooping moustache.

Walter *n* **Bruno [Bruno Walter Schlesinger]** (1876–1962) German-born American conductor particularly associated with the works of Mahler.

Walton *n* 1. **Alan** (1891–1948) British painter, decorator, and architect who set up a textile company with his brother in 1925. 2. **Izaak** (1593–1683) English author best known for his hugely popular work *The Compleat Angler*, which is both a treatise on the art of angling and a celebration of the quiet life. 3. **Sir William [Turner]** (1902–83) English composer.

Walton, Sir Earnest *see* **Cockcroft, Sir John Douglas**.

waltz *n* a piece of music with three beats to the bar; a whirling or slowly circling dance. * *vi* to dance a waltz.

WAM *abbr* = Working Association of Mothers.

WAMF *abbr* = Welsh Amateur Music Federation.

wampum *n* polished shells strung like beads formerly used as money by North American Indians.

WAMS *abbr* = World Association of Military Surgeons.

WAMT *abbr* = Women and Manual Trades.

wan *adj* (**wanner, wannest**) pale and sickly; feeble or weak.—**wanly** *adv*.—**wanness** *n*.

wan *abbr* = wide-area network.

WAN *see* **wide area network**.

wand *n* a magician's rod.

wander *vi* to ramble with no definite destination; to go astray; to lose concentration.—*also n*.

wandering Jew *n* any of various trailing or climbing plants; (*with cap*) a legendary figure condemned by Christ to roam the world until the Day of Judgement as punishment for an insult.

Wandering Rocks *npl* (*Greek myth*) mobile rocks in the sea that destroyed ships that attempted to pass between them.—*also* **Planctae**.

wanderlust *n* a compelling desire for travel.

W & M *abbr* = William and Mary.

w. and r. *abbr* (*transp*) = water and rail.

w & s *abbr* = whisky and soda.

w & t *abbr* = wear and tear.

wane *vi* to decrease, esp of the moon; to decline. * *n* decrease, decline.

wangle *vti* (*inf*) to achieve (something) by devious means.

waning slope *n* the low, slightly concave slope at the foot of a hill.

wank *vi* (*Brit vulg*) to masturbate.—*also n*.

wanker *n* (*Brit vulg*) a person who masturbates; (*derog*) a stupid, contemptible or worthless person.

wannabee *n* (*sl*) a person who wants to be someone or something else.

want *n* lack; poverty. * *vt* to need; to require; to lack; to wish (for).

want ad *n* (*inf*) a newspaper or magazine advertisement requesting an item, job, etc.

wanted *adj* sought after.

wanting *adj* lacking.

wanton *adj* malicious; willful; sexually provocative.

WAO *abbr* = World Association for Orphans and Abandoned Children.

WAPA *abbr* = Western Area Power Administration.

WAPC *abbr* = Women Against Pit Closures.

wapiti *n* (*pl* **wapitis**) a large deer of North America.

war *n* military conflict between nations or parties; a conflict; a contest. * *vi* (**warring, warred**) to make war.

WAR *abbr* = Women Against Rape; Workers Against Racism.

warble *vi* to sing with trills and runs; to sing like a bird.

warble fly *n* a species of fly the larvae of which burrow under the skin of cattle causing painful lumps.

warbler *n* any of a family of small Old World songbirds which includes the nightingale and robin.

war bride *n* a woman who marries a soldier during wartime, esp one from overseas.

Warburg *n* **Otto Heinrich** (1883–1970) German biochemist and cell physiologist. His work on cell metabolism and respiration, with particular reference to cancer research, earned him two Nobel prizes for physiology or medicine (1931, 1944).

WARC *abbr* = Women's Amateur Rowing Council; World Administrative Radio Conference; World Alliance of Reformed Churches.

war chest *n* money accumulated to finance war; a fund accumulated to pursue a specific goal, e.g. a political campaign.

war correspondent *n* a journalist who reports from the front line in a war.

war crime *n* a crime committed in wartime (such as mistreatment of prisoners) which violates conventional notions of decency.

war cry *n* a rallying call in battle; a party catchword.

ward *n* a section of a hospital; an electoral district; a division of a prison; a child placed under the supervision of a court. * *vt* (*with* **off**) to repel; to fend off.—**wardship** *n*.

Ward *n* 1. **Dame Barbara Mary [Baroness Jackson of Lodsworth]** (1914–81) English economist and conservationist; a highly influential advocate of conservation and fair distribution of the earth's resources during the 1960s. 2. **Mrs Humphrey [Mary Augustus Ward]** (1851–1920) English novelist whose best-known novel, *Robert Ellsmere*, is a study of religious commitment that inspired much public debate. 3. **Neville** (1922–) British interior designer who designed the exterior of the Design Centre in London.

-ward, -wards *adj suffix* indicating a certain direction.

war dance *n* a ritual dance before or after battle as practiced by certain North American Indian tribes.

warden *n* an official; a person in charge of a building or home; a prison governor;

warder *n* (*Brit*) a prison officer.

ward heeler *n* (*sl*) a local political hanger-on for a politician.

wardrobe *n* a cupboard for clothes; one's clothes.

wardroom *n* a room in a warship for use by officers with the exception of the captain.

ware *n* (*pl*) merchandise, goods for sale; pottery.

warehouse *n* a building for storing goods.

warehouse club *n* a large scale members-only retail outlet which offers product at discount.

warehousing[1] *n* the storage of goods in a warehouse.

warehousing[2] *n* the building up of a shareholding in a company before a takeover bid by purchasing small lots of shares and keeping them in the names of nominees so that the purchaser can remain anonymous.

warfare *n* armed hostilities; conflict.

warfarin *n* a crystalline substance used in medicine as an anticoagulant and also as a poison to kill rodents.

war game *n* a simulated battle or tactical exercise using models or computers for military training; a re-enactment of a battle using model soldiers.

warhead *n* the section of a missile containing the explosive.

Warhol *n* **Andy [Andrew Warhola]** (1930–87) American pop artist and film-maker who was the prime exponent of pop art in the early 1960s with his deliberately mundane works, e.g. reproductions of Campbell's soup.

warhorse *n* a horse used in battle; (*inf*) a veteran of military or political conflict.

warlike *adj* hostile.

war loan *n* a type of government stock issued in wartime to raise funds for the war effort.

warlock *n* a sorcerer, a magician.

Warlock *n* **Peter [Philip Heseltine]** (1894–1930) English composer and writer whose works include many songs and choral compositions, e.g. *The Curlew*, and orchestral pieces, including the *Capriol Suite*.

warlord *n* a military leader or ruler of (part of) a country.

warm *adj* moderately hot; friendly, kind; (*colors*) rich; enthusiastic. * *vt* to make warm. * *vi* to become enthusiastic (about). —**warmly** *adv*.—**warmth** *n*.

warm-blooded *adj* having a constant and relatively high temperature; passionate.

warm boot *n* (*comput*) a system restart that is initiated usu because a system error has occurred during operations. *See also* **bootstrapping**.

warmed-over *adj* not fresh; reheated.

warm front *n* the edge of an advancing mass of warm air.

warm-hearted *adj* kind, sympathetic; affectionate.

warming pan *n* a long-handled (usu copper) pan filled with hot coals and formerly used to warm a bed.

warmonger *n* a person who incites war, esp for personal gain; warrior, a fighting soldier.

warm-up *n* a period of exercise or practice before a race, etc.

warn *vt* to notify of danger; to caution or advise (against).—**warning** *n*.

warp[1] *vti* to twist out of shape; to distort; to corrupt. * *n* the threads arranged lengthwise on a loom across which other threads are passed.

warp[2] *n* the very fine-grained sediments found in tidal estuaries.

war paint *n* paint smeared on the face and body by North American Indians before entering battle; (*inf*) formal or ceremonial dress, regalia; (*inf*) cosmetics.

warpath *n* the route used by a war party of North American Indians; (*with* **on the**) on a hostile expedition; (*with* **on the**) (*inf*) angry.

warped *adj* distorted, twisted; embittered.

warplane *n* an aircraft for use in combat.

warrant[1] *vt* to guarantee; to justify. * *n* a document giving authorization; a writ for arrest.

warrant[2] *n* a security that gives the holder the right to purchase shares in a company at a specified set price at a future date.

warrantee *n* somebody to whom a warrant is given.

warrant officer *n* a person in the armed services holding a rank between commissioned officers and NCOs.

warrantor *n* a person or company that offers a warranty.

warranty[1] *n* (*pl* **warranties**) a pledge to replace something if it is not as represented, a guarantee.

warranty[2] *n* (*pl* **warranties**) a condition included in an insurance policy, the breach of which may result in the insurer's refusal to meet a claim, even if this claim is not directly related to the breach.

warranty deed *n* (*law*) a legal document conveying interest in real property, with the grantor warranting or guaranteeing the property.

warren *n* an area in which rabbits breed.

Warren *n* **Robert Penn** (1905–89) American poet, novelist, and critic, the best known of whose novels is *All the King's Men*, which charts the progress of a demagogic politician (based on Governor Huey Long of Louisiana) in the southern USA.

War Requiem *n* an ambitious choral work by Britten for choirs, organ, solo voices, and chamber orchestra. The piece consists of alternating settings of poems by Wilfred Owen and the Requiem Mass. It was first performed in 1962.

warring *adj* engaged in war.

warrior *n* a soldier, fighter.

Warsaw, Warszawa *n* capital city of Poland.

warship *n* a ship equipped for war.

wart, verruca *n* a small, hard projection on the skin.—**warty** *adj*.

wart hog *n* an African wild pig with warty lumps on the face, large tusks, and thick coarse hair.

wartime *adj, n* (of) a period or time of war.

Warton *n* **Thomas** (1728–90) English poet who was professor of poetry at Oxford University (1757–67) and poet laureate from 1785. He is best known for his *History of English Poetry*, the first such work of any depth and important for its collection of works by early poets such as Chaucer, Spenser, and Dante.

wary *adj* (**warier, wariest**) watchful; cautious.—**warily** *adv*.—**wariness** *n*.

was *see* **be**.

WAS *abbr* = World Aquaculture Society; World Archaeological Society; World Association for Sexology.

WASA *abbr* = Welsh Amateur Swimming Association.

WASAC *abbr* = Welsh Association of Sub Aqua Clubs.

wash[1] *vti* to cleanse with water and soap; to flow against or over; to sweep along by the action of water; to separate gold, etc, from earth by washing; to cover with a thin coat of metal or paint; (*with* **down**) to wash thoroughly from top to bottom; to take a drink of liquid to help in swallowing food; (*with* **out**) to (cause to) fade by laundering; to rain out; (*with* **up**) to wash one's face and hands; * *n* a washing; the break of waves on the shore; the waves left behind by a boat; a liquid used for washing.

wash[2] *n* the name given to coarse-textured alluvial material.

wash[3] *n* the movement downslope of surface soil by rain.

Wash. *abbr* = Washington.

WASH *abbr* = Women Against Sexual Harassment.

washable *adj* able to be washed without damage.—**washability** *n*.

washboard *n* a corrugated board used (esp *formerly*) for scrubbing clothes.

washbowl, washbasin *n* a basin or bowl, esp a bathroom fixture, for use in washing one's hands, etc.—*also* **wash-hand basin**.

washcloth *n* a cloth used for washing the face or body.

washed-out *adj* faded in color; fatigued.

washed-up *adj* unsuccessful, ineffective; unpromising.

washer *n* a flat ring of metal, rubber, etc, to give tightness to joints; a washing machine.

washing *n* the act of cleansing with water; a number of items washed together.

washing machine *n* a device for washing clothes.

washing powder *n* a powdered detergent formulated for washing fabrics.

washing soda *n* sodium carbonate dissolved in water used for washing and cleaning.

Washington or WA *n* a state of the USA, of which the capital is Olympia.

Washington *n* **George** (1732–99) American general and 1st president of the United States (1789–97).

Washington DC *n* capital city of the USA; the capital city of the District of Columbia, a state of the USA.

"Washington, My Home" *n* the song of the American state of Washington.

washing-up *n* (*Brit*) the washing of dishes and cutlery after a meal; the dishes and cutlery waiting to be washed.

washland *n* a flood plain with artificial embankments into which a river can be diverted in order to prevent flooding and damage further downstream.

washout *n* (*sl*) a failure.

washroom *n* cloakroom, lavatory.

washstand *n* a piece of furniture for holding a bowl and jug of water used for washing.

washtub *n* a large tub used for washing clothes.

washy *adj* (**washier, washiest**) weak, watery; pale; lacking in strength or vigor.—**washiness** *n*.

wasn't = was not.

wasp *n* a winged insect with a black and yellow striped body, which can sting.

Wasp, WASP *n* an American of northern European, esp British, descent and Protestant upbringing, regarded as belonging to the most privileged group in American society (White Anglo-Saxon Protestant).

waspish *adj* sharp in speech or manner, irritable.

wasp waist *n* a very slender waist.

wassail *n* (*formerly*) a toast made at festivities; a festive celebration with a lot of drinking and merriment; spiced ale or mulled wine served (esp formerly) at Christmas or other festive occasions. * *vi* to make merry.

W

Wassermann test *n* a blood test used to diagnose syphilis.

wastage *n* anything lost by use or natural decay; wasteful or avoidable loss of something valuable.

waste *adj* useless; left over; uncultivated or uninhabited. * *vt* to ravage; to squander; to use foolishly; to fail to use. * *vi* to lose strength, etc as by disease. * *n* uncultivated or uninhabited land; discarded material, garbage, excrement.—**wasteful** *adj*.—**wastefully** *adv*.—**wastefulness** *n*.

wastebasket *n* a receptacle for waste paper.

wasted *adj* ravaged, devastated; not used to best advantage; weak, emaciated; (*sl*) dead, killed; (*sl*) showing the effects of alcohol or drug abuse.

wasteland *n* a piece of barren or uncultivated land; a desolate region; something (e.g. a period of time, relationship) lacking in moral, spiritual, emotional, etc vitality.

wastepaper *n* paper discarded as waste.

wastepipe *n* a pipe carrying off used water from sinks, baths, etc.

waster[1] *n* a wasteful person or thing; a good-for-nothing.

waster[2] *n* (*archeo*) a shard, pot, or part of a pot thrown away after firing because of a fault.

wasting asset *n* a non-renewable resource such as a coal mine.

wastrel *n* a vagabond; a waster, idler.

WASWC *abbr* = World Association of Soil and Water Conservation.

WATA *abbr* = World Association of Travel Agents.

watch *n* surveillance; close observation; vigil; guard; a small timepiece worn on the wrist, etc; a period of duty on a ship * *vi* to look with attention; to wait for; to keep vigil. * *vt* to keep one's eyes fixed on; to guard; to tend; to observe closely; (*chance, etc*) to wait for.—**watcher** *n*. —**watchful** *adj*.—**watchfully** *adv*.—**watchfulness** *n*.

WATCH *abbr* = Watch Trust for Environmental Education.

watchband *n* a strap of leather, etc, for securing a watch to the wrist.

watchcase *n* a protective metal casing for a watch mechanism.

watchdog *n* a dog that guards property; a person or group that monitors safety, standards, etc.

watchmaker *n* a person who makes and repairs watches.

watchman *n* (*pl* **watchmen**) a person who guards a building or other property.

watch night *n* a religious service on New Year's Eve.

watchtower *n* a tower for a sentry to keep watch from.

watchword *n* a password.

water *n* the substance H_2O, a clear, thin liquid, lacking taste or smell, and essential for life; any body of it, as the ocean, a lake, river, etc; bodily secretions such as tears, urine. * *vt* to moisten with water; to irrigate; to dilute with water; (*with* **down**) to dilute; to reduce in strength or effectiveness. * *vi* (*eyes*) to smart; to salivate; to take in water.

water balance *n* (*meteorol*) the movement of water, on a global scale, between the atmosphere and the ground surface.

water bed *n* a bed with a water-filled mattress.

water bird *n* any swimming or wading bird.

water biscuit *n* a thin, crisp biscuit, usu served with cheese.

water blister *n* a blister on the skin filled with watery fluid instead of blood.

water boatman *n* any of various aquatic bugs adapted for swimming.

waterborne *adj* floating on or traveling by water.

waterbuck *n* an African antelope which lives in swampy areas.

water buffalo *n* a common domesticated Asian buffalo.

water cannon *n* an apparatus for pumping water at high pressure to disperse crowds.

water chestnut *n* an Asian aquatic plant with edible nutlike fruit; (the edible tuber of) a Chinese plant with a succulent root.

water clock *n* a clock with a mechanism operated by flowing or dripping water.

water-closet *n* a lavatory.

watercolor, watercolour *n* (*Brit*) a water-soluble paint; a picture painted with watercolors.

water-cooled *adj* (*engine etc*) cooled by the circulation of water.

water cooler *n* a device for dispensing chilled drinking water.

watercourse *n* (a channel for) a stream, river, or canal.

watercraft *n* skill in handling boats and other vessels; a vessel traveling by water.

watercress *n* a plant growing in ponds and streams, used in a salad.

water cure *n* hydropathy.

water diviner *n* a person who searches for water using a divining rod.

waterfall *n* a fall of water over a precipice or down a hill.

water flea *n* any of numerous tiny freshwater crustaceans.

Waterford *n* city in the Republic of Ireland.

waterfowl *n* (*pl* **waterfowl**) a bird that frequents lakes, rivers, etc, esp a duck.

waterfront *n* an area alongside a body of water, esp a docks.

water gas *n* a toxic inflammable mixture of carbon monoxide and hydrogen produced by passing steam over hot carbon, used as a fuel.

water glass *n* a solution of sodium or potassium silicate in water used as a protective coating and to preserve eggs.

water hammer *n* (the sound of) the concussion of water in a pipe when a blockage is suddenly dislodged.

water hole *n* a water-filled hollow where animals drink.

Waterhouse *n* 1. **Alfred** (1830–1905) English architect. His notable works include the Natural History Museum, the Prudential Building, and St Paul's School, London. 2. **George Marsden** (1824–1906) English-born New Zealand statesman; prime minister of New Zealand (1872–73). 3. **Keith** (1929–) English writer best known for his novel Billy Liar (1959).

water hyacinth *n* a floating aquatic plant of tropical America that often blocks waterways with its dense growth.

water ice *n* an iced dessert made from frozen water, sugar, and a flavoring.

watering can *n* a container with a spout for watering plants.

watering hole *n* (*inf*) a bar or pub.

watering place *n* a place where animals or people can obtain water; a spa resort.

water jacket *n* a casing filled with water used for cooling machinery.

water jump *n* a ditch filled with water used as an obstacle in a steeplechase and other sporting contests.

water level *n* the surface level of water in a reservoir, etc.

water lily *n* any of a family of plants with large floating leaves and showy flowers.

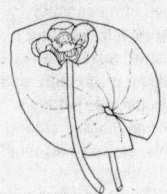

waterline *n* a line up to which a ship's hull is submerged.

waterlogged *adj* soaked or saturated with water.

water main *n* a main pipe or conduit for carrying water.

watermark *n* a line marking the height to which water has risen; a mark impressed on paper which can only be seen when held up to the light.

water meadow *n* a flat area beside a river that is subject to flooding from time to time, usu in winter.

watermelon *n* a large fruit with a hard green rind and edible red watery flesh.

water mill *n* a mill operated by a water wheel.

water on the brain *see* **hydrocephalus**.

water pistol *n* a toy gun that shoots a stream of water.

water polo *n* a game played in water by two teams of seven swimmers with the aim of scoring by hitting a ball into the opponents' goal.

water power *n* the power of falling or moving water used to operate machinery or generate electricity.

waterproof *adj* impervious to water; watertight.—*also vt*.

water-repellent *adj* (*fabrics, etc*) treated with a substance that prevents penetration by water.

water-resistant *adj* (*fabrics, etc*) designed to resist water penetration as long as possible.

watershed *n* a turning point; (*geog*) the boundary between two drainage basins, usu running along the highest ground where the head streams of rivers rise.

waterside *n* the edge of a body of water.

water-skiing *n* the sport of planing on water by being towed by a motorboat—**water-skier** *n*.

water snake *n* any of numerous snakes that live in or near water, esp a nonvenomous freshwater snake of the genus *Natrix*.

water softener *n* a device or chemical designed to counteract chemicals that cause hardness in water.

water-soluble *adj* capable of dissolving in water.

water spaniel *n* a breed of large curly-coated spaniel used in hunting waterfowl.

waterspout *n* a pipe for draining water; a tall column of water formed by a whirlwind and reaching from the sea to the clouds.

water table *n* the level below which the ground is saturated with water.

watertight *adj* not allowing water to pass through; foolproof.

water tower *n* an elevated tank or reservoir to allow water to be supplied under pressure.

waterway *n* a navigable channel of water.

water wheel *n* a wheel designed to be turned by running water and used to drive machinery; a wheel used for raising water.

water wings *npl* inflatable rubber floats worn on the arms of those learning to swim.

waterworks *n* (*as sing*) an establishment that supplies water to a district; (*pl: inf*) the urinary system; (*inf*) tears.

waterworn *adj* rubbed smooth by the action of water.

watery *adj* thin, diluted.

Watson *n* 1. **James Dewey** (1928–) American biologist. He and F rancis Crick discovered the "double helix" structure of DNA and shared the 1962 Nobel prize for physiology or medicine with Maurice Wilkins. 2. **John B[roadus]** (1878–1958) American psychologist. He became the leading theorist and proponent of behaviorism. His works include *Behavior—An Introduction to Comparative Psychology* (1914). *See also* **Skinner**.

Watson-Watt *n* **Sir Robert Alexander** (1892–1973) Scottish physicist who was responsible for the development of radar.

watt *n* a unit of electrical power.

Watt *n* **James** (1736–1819) Scottish engineer. His improvements to the hitherto unreliable steam engine led directly to the rapid expansion of the industrial revolution. The watt, a unit of power, is named after him.

wattage *n* amount of electrical power.

Watteau *n* **Jean-Antoine** (1684–1721) French painter and an outstanding exponent of rococo art.

watt-hr. *abbr* = watt-hour, watt-hours.

wattle *n* (material for) a framework of stakes or poles interwoven with thin branches, twigs, etc formerly used for fencing and building; a loose flap of skin hanging from the necks of certain birds and lizards; an Australian acacia tree with small brightly-colored flowers. * *vt* to build of or with wattle; to interweave or interlace (with sticks, etc) to make a light frame.

wattle and daub *n* (*archit*) a method of wall construction using branches or thin laths (the wattles) upon which is plastered clay or mud (the daub).

Watts, Charlie *see* **Jagger, Mick.**

Waugh *n* Evelyn [**Arthur St John**] (1903–66) English novelist known for his brilliant satires. His novels include *Brideshead Revisited* (1945).

WAVA *abbr* = World Association of Veteran Athletes.

wave *n* an undulation traveling on the surface of water; the form in which light and sound are thought to travel; an increase or upsurge (e.g., of crime); a hair curl; a movement of the hand in greeting or farewell. * *vti* to move freely backward and forward; to flutter; to undulate; to move the hand to and fro in greeting, farewell, etc; (*with* **down**) to signal (a vehicle, etc) to stop with a wave.— **wavy** *adj.*

wave band *n* a range of radio frequencies or wavelengths.

wave base *n* the depth at which there is no motion caused by the wave at the surface.

waveguide *n* a metal tube used to guide microwaves along a particular path.

wavelength *n* the distance between the crests of successive waves of light or sound; radio frequency.

wavelet *n* a small wave.

wave mechanics *n sing* (*physics*) the theory in quantum mechanics that describes the behavior of elementary particles in terms of their wave properties.

waver *vi* to hesitate; to falter.—**waverer** *n.*

wave refraction *n* the process whereby waves bend so that they are parallel to the shore when they break on to it.

wax[1] *n* beeswax; an oily substance used to make candles, polish, etc * *vt* to rub, polish, cover, or treat with wax.

wax[2] *vi* to increase in strength, size, etc.

waxen *adj* made of wax; pale and smooth like wax.

wax paper *n* paper that has been rendered moistureproof by treating with wax.

waxwork *n* a figure or model formed of wax; (*pl*) an exhibition of such figures.

waxy *adj* (**waxier, waxiest**) consisting of or like wax; adhesive.—**waxily** *adv.*—**waxiness** *n.*

way *n* path, route; road; distance; room to advance; direction; state; means; possibility; manner of living; (*pl*) habits.

waybill *n* a document with list of goods and shipping instructions accompanying a shipment.

WAYC *abbr* = Welsh Association of Youth Clubs.

wayfarer *n* a traveler.

waylay *vt* (**waylaying, waylaid**) to lie in wait for; to accost.

Wayne *n* John [**Marion Michael Morrison**] (1907–79) American film actor best known as the star of many classic westerns.

way-out *adj* (*inf*) unconventional, unusual; amazing.

-ways *adv suffix* indicating a certain direction or manner.

ways and means *npl* the methods used to accomplish something; the revenues and means of raising revenues for the use of government.

wayside *n* the side of or land adjacent to a road.

wayward *adj* willful, stubborn; unpredictable.—**waywardness** *n.*

w.b. *abbr* = warehouse book; water ballast; westbound.

Wb *abbr* = (*phys*) weber.

WB *abbr* = Warner Brothers; Water Board; Weather Bureau; Women's Bureau; World Bank; World Brotherhood.

W/B *abbr* = waybill.

WBA *abbr* = (*Brit*) West Bromwich Albion; World Boxing Association; World Bowling Association; whole body activity.

WBC *abbr* = World Boxing Council; white blood cell.

WBCS *abbr* = Welsh Black Cattle Society.

WBF *abbr* = World Bridge Federation.

wbi *abbr* = will be issued.

WbN *abbr* = west by north.

WBO *abbr* = World Boxing Organization.

WBR *abbr* = whole body radiation.

WbS *abbr* = west by south.

WBS *abbr* = whole body scan.

WBU *abbr* = Welsh Badminton Union; Welsh Baseball Union.

wc, w.c. *abbr* = without charge.

WC *abbr* = (*Brit*) water-closet; Wesleyan Chapel; West Central.

W/C, W/Cdr *abbr* = Wing Commander.

wca *abbr* = worst-case analysis.

WCA *abbr* = Wholesale Caterers' Alliance; Women's Christian Association; Women's Cricket Association; Wood Carvers Association; World Calendar Association.

WCC *abbr* = Wales Craft Council; War Crimes Commission; Welsh Consumer Council; World Cheerleader Council; World Council of Churches; World Cultural Council.

WCCL *abbr* = Welsh Council for Civil Liberties.

WCF *abbr* = World Congress of Faiths; World Curling Federation.

WCMMF *abbr* = World Congress of Man-Made Fibers.

WCP *abbr* = World Council of Peace; World Court Project.

WCRA *abbr* = Women's Cycle Racing Association.

WCS *abbr* = Wilkie Collins Society.

WCT *abbr* = Women Caring Trust; World Championship Tennis.

WCTU *abbr* = Woman's Christian Temperance Union.

WCU *abbr* = Welsh Chess Union; World Conservative Union.

WD *abbr* = War Department; Works Department.

2-w/d *abbr* = two-wheel drive.

4-w/d *abbr* = four-wheel drive.

WDA *abbr* = Well Drillers Association; Welsh Development Agency; World Dredging Association.

WDC *abbr* = Woman Detective Constable; World Darts Council; World Disarmament Campaign.

WDS *abbr* = Woman Detective Sergeant.

we *pron pl* of I; I and others.

w/e *abbr* = weekend; week ending.

We. *abbr* = Wednesday.

WEA *abbr* = Workers's Educational Association.

weak *adj* lacking power or strength; feeble; ineffectual.—**weakness** *n.*

weaken *vti* to make or grow weaker.

weak interaction *n* (*physics*) an interaction between elementary particles that is responsible for certain particle decay processes.

weak-kneed *adj* (*inf*) submissive, easily intimidated.

weakling *n* a person who lacks strength of character.

weakly *adj* (**weaklier, weakliest**) not robust; sickly. * *adv* in a weak manner, feebly.

weak-minded *adj* lacking in determination; feeble-minded.

weal *n* a raised mark on the skin left by a blow with a lash.

wealth *n* a large amount of possessions or money; affluence; an abundance (of).— **wealthy** *adj.*

wealth tax *n* a direct tax levied by a government on a person's private assets.

wealth-consuming sector *n* (*com*) the service industries that are able to exist when a community can earn enough money to pay for them.

wealth-creating sector *n* (*com*) manufacturing industries where raw materials are refined and made into items that can be sold at a profit.

wean *vt* (*baby, animal*) to replace the mother's milk with other nourishment; to dissuade (from indulging a habit).

WEAN *abbr* = Women's Earth Action Network.

weapon *n* any instrument used in fighting.

weaponry *n* weapons collectively.

wear *vb* (**wearing, wore,** *pp* **worn**) *vt* to have on the body as clothing; (*hair, etc*) to arrange in a particular way; to display; to rub away; to impair by use; to exhaust, tire; (*with* **down**) to overcome gradually through persistent pressure; (*with* **out**) to tire or exhaust. * *vi* to be impaired by use or time; to be spent tediously; (*with* **off**) to become gradually weaker in effect; (*with* **out**) to make or become worthless through prolonged use. * *n* deterioration from frequent use; articles worn.—**wearer** *n.*

wearable *adj* suitable to be worn.

wear and tear *n* deterioration or depreciation from everyday use.

wearing *adj* exhausting, tiresome, oppressive.

weary *adj* (**wearier, weariest**) tired; bored. * *vti* (**wearying, wearied**) to make or become tired.—**weariness** *n.*—**wearisome** *adj.*

weasel *n* a small carnivorous animal with a long slender body and reddish fur.

weasel words *npl* (*inf*) evasive or misleading talk.

weather *n* atmospheric conditions, such as temperature, rainfall, cloudiness, etc. * *vt* to expose to the action of the weather; to survive. * *vi* to withstand the weather.

weather-beaten *adj* worn or damaged by the weather; hardened or bronzed through exposure to the weather.

weatherboard *n* a sloping, usu overlapping, timber board used as external cladding for a wall or roof.—**weatherboarding** *n.*

weather-bound *adj* delayed or postponed due to bad weather.

weathercock *n* a weather vane in the form of a cock to show the wind direction.

weathered *adj* affected or seasoned by exposure to the weather; (*rocks*) altered in shape by erosion; (*roof*) having a sloped surface to allow rainwater to escape.

weather eye *n* an eye trained to observe changes in the weather; (*inf*) an alert or watchful gaze.

weatherglass *n* a barometer.

weathering *n* the erosion of rocks through the action of the wind, rain, frost, etc; (*archit*) the sloping surface of a sill, parapet etc which throws off rainwater; the degradation of building materials due to action of the weather.

weatherman *n* (*pl* **weathermen**) a weather forecaster on radio or television who is usually also a professional meteorologist.

weather map *n* a chart showing weather conditions over a particular area for a specified period.

weatherproof *adj* designed to withstand exposure to weather without damage or deterioration.—*also vt.*

weather station *n* a meteorological post for collecting, recording, and transmitting data on weather conditions.

weather vane *n* a device attached to a tall structure to indicate wind direction.

weave *vb* (**weaving, wove,** *pp* **woven**) *vt* to interlace threads in a loom to form fabric; to construct. * *vi* to make a way through (e.g., a crowd), to zigzag.— **weaver** *n*.

weaverbird *n* any of various Old World songbirds that build nests of interwoven grass, twigs, etc, including the house sparrow.

web *n* a woven fabric; the fine threads spun by a spider; the membrane joining the digits of birds, animals; (*archit*) in a vault, the cell or bay between ribs.

Webb *n* 1. **Sir Aston** (1849–1930) English architect. His notable works include the east front of Buckingham Palace and the Victoria and Albert Museum, London. 2. **Beatrice [Potter]** (1858–1943) and **Sidney James [Baron Passfield]** (1859–1947) English social reformers and economists. They co-founded the London School of Economics (1895) and founded the *New Statesman* (1913). 3. **Philip** (1831–1915) British architect who in 1861 went into partnership with William Morris.

webbed *adj* (*ducks, etc*) having the digits connected by a fold of skin.

webbed fingers *see* syndactyly.

webbing *n* a strong narrow woven fabric of jute, cotton, etc, used for straps and belts; anything forming a web.

Web browser *see* browser.

weber *n* the SI unit of magnetic flux.

Weber *n* 1. **Carl Maria Ernst von** (1786–1826) German composer, conductor, and pianist. 2. **Karl Emanuel Martin** (1889–1963) German designer who opened his own studio in Hollywood in 1927. 3. **Max** (1864–1920) German sociologist who is regarded as one of the founders of sociology.

Webern *n* **Anton von** (1883–1945) Austrian composer; a leading exponent of the serial form of composition.

Weber's test *n* the assessment of a person's deafness by using a tuning fork the stem of which is placed on the forehead or maxillary incisors and if the hearing is normal, the sound is equal in both ears.

Webster *n* 1. **John** (*c*.1578–1632) English dramatist noted for the tragedy *The Duchess of Malfi*. 2. **Noah** (1758–1843) American lexicographer and philologist noted for his work *An American Dictionary of the English Language* (1828) in which he established Americanisms and American usages.

wed *vti* (**wedding, wedded** *or* **wed**) to marry; to join closely.

we'd = we had; we would.

Wed, Wed. *abbr* = Wednesday.

WEDA *abbr* = Wholesale Egg Distributors Association; Wholesale Engineering Distributors Association.

wedded *adj* of or resulting from marriage; devoted (to art, etc).

wedding *n* marriage; the ceremony of marriage.

wedding cake *n* an ornately decorated rich fruit cake, usu in three tiers, served at a wedding.

wedding ring *n* a band of gold or platinum used at a wedding and worn to show marital status.

wedge *n* a v-shaped block of wood or metal for splitting or fastening; a wedge-shaped object. * *vti* to split or secure with a wedge; to thrust (in) tightly; to become fixed tightly.

wedge-shaped gallery grave *n* (*archeo*) a Megalithic chamber tomb found in Ireland in which the burial chamber forms a gallery.

wedlock *n* marriage.

Wednesday *n* fourth day of the week, between Tuesday and Thursday.

wee[1] *adj* (*Scot*) small, tiny.

wee[2] *n* (*inf*) the act of passing urine; urine. * *vt* (*inf*) to pass urine.—*also* **wee-wee**.

weed *n* any undesired plant, esp one that crowds out desired plants; (*sl*) marijuana; (*pl*) a widow's black mourning clothes. * *vt* to remove weeds; (*with* **out**) to remove or eliminate (something superfluous or harmful).

weedkiller *n* a chemical or hormonal substance used to kill weeds.

weedy *adj* (**weedier, weediest**) full of weeds; (*inf*) thin and scrawny.

week *n* the period of seven consecutive days, esp from Sunday to Sunday.

weekday *n* a day of the week other than Saturday or Sunday.

weekend, week-end *n* the period from Friday night to Sunday night—*also adj*.

weekly *adj* happening once a week or every week.

weeknight *n* the evening or night of a weekday.

Weeks, Feast of *see* Pentecost.

weeny *adj* (**weenier, weeniest**) (*inf*) tiny, minute.

weep *vti* (**weeping, wept**) to shed tears, to cry; (*wound*) to ooze.

weepie *n* (*inf*) a sentimental film.

weeping *n* the act of weeping. * *adj* shedding tears; exuding moisture; (*tree*) with drooping branches.—**weepingly** *adv*.

weeping willow *n* a Chinese willow tree with slender drooping branches.

weepy *adj* (**weepier, weepiest**) tearful; prone to crying.—**weepily** *adv*.— **weepiness** *n*.

weevil *n* a beetle which feeds on plants and crops.

wee-wee *see* **wee**[2].

wef *abbr* = with effect from.

weft *n* the yarn woven across the lengthwise threads in a loom.—*also* **woof**.

weigh *vt* to measure the weight of; to consider carefully; (*with* **down**) to weight; to oppress; (*with* **up**) to assess, make a judgment about (a person, thing, etc). * *vi* to have weight; to be burdensome; (*with* **in**) (*boxer, wrestler*) to be weighed before a bout; (*jockey*) to be weighed after a race; (*inf*) to make a contribution to (e.g., an argument).

weighbridge *n* a large scale consisting of a metal plate set into the road onto which vehicles are driven to be weighed.

weigh-in *n* (*sports*) the checking of the weight of a contestant, esp of a jockey after a race or of a boxer before a bout.

weight *n* the amount which anything weighs; influence; any unit of heaviness. * *vt* to attach a weight to.

weightlessness *n* the state of having no or little reaction to gravity, esp in space travel.

weight lifting *n* the sport of lifting weights of a specific amount in a particular way.—**weight lifter** *n*.

weight training *n* physical exercise involving lifting heavy weights.

weight watcher *n* a person on a diet to lose weight.

weighty *adj* (**weightier, weightiest**) heavy; serious.—**weightily** *adv*.

Weil *n* 1. **Daniel** (1953–) Ar gentinean architect who worked in London designing a range of designer clocks and radios for his own company, Parenthesis.2. **Simone** (1909–43) French philosopher who worked for the French Resistance in London, and starved herself to death in sympathy with Nazi Camp internees.

Weill *n* **Kurt** (1900–50) German composer noted for his collaborations with Brecht, e.g. *The Threepenny Opera* (1928). He fled from Germany in 1935, settling in the US.

Weil's disease *see* leptospyrosis.

Weinberg *n* **Steven** (1933–) American physicist. He devised a theor y of the unity of the forces operating on elementary particles (now called the Weinberg-Salam theory) that was independently arrived at by the Pakistani physicist Abdus Salam, and later developed by the American physicist Sheldon Glashow. All three shared the 1979 Nobel prize for physics.

Weinberger *n* **Casper Willard** (1917–) American politician; defense secretar y during Reagan's administration; resigned in 1987.

weir *n* a low dam across a river which controls the flow of water.

weird *adj* unearthly, mysterious; eerie; bizarre.—**weirdly** *adv*.

weirdo, weirdie *n* (*pl* **weirdos, weirdies**) (*inf*) an eccentric person.

Weismuller *n* **Johnny** (1903–84) American swimmer and film star. He was the first man to swim 100 meters in less than a minute, 440 yards in under five minutes. He won five Olympic gold medals (1921–28) and achieved further fame starring as Tarzan in 19 films in the 1930s and 40s. He is credited with inventing the Tarzan "yodel."

Weizmann *n* **Chaim [Azriel]** (1874–1952) Russian-born chemist and Israeli statesman who participated in the negotiations for a Jewish homeland and became the first president of Israel (1949–52).

welch *see* welsh.

Welch *n* **Robert Radford** (1929–) British product designer and silversmith.

welcome *adj* gladly received; pleasing. * *n* reception of a person or thing. * *vt* to greet kindly.

weld *vt* to unite, as metal by heating until fused or soft enough to hammer together; to join closely. * *n* a welded joint.

Weldon *n* **Fay** (1933–) English novelist whose novels, which belong with the feminist "consciousness-raising" fictions that began to emerge in the 1970s, include *Female Friends* and *The Cloning of Joanna May*.

welfare *n* wellbeing; health; assistance or financial aid granted to the poor, the unemployed, etc.

welfare state *n* a state in which the government assumes responsibility for the health and social security of its citizens.

well[1] *n* a spring; a hole bored in the ground to provide a source of water, oil, gas, etc; the open space in the middle of a staircase * *vi* to pour forth.

well[2] *adj* (**better, best**) agreeable; comfortable; in good health. * *adv* in a proper, satisfactory, or excellent manner; thoroughly; prosperously; with good reason; to a considerable degree; fully. * *interj* an expression of surprise, etc.

we'll = we will; we shall.

well-advised *adj* acting with good sense; carefully thought out.

well-appointed *adj* fully equipped or furnished.

well-balanced *adj* sensible, sane.

well-being *n* condition of being well or contented; welfare.

well-bred *adj* well brought up; of good stock.

well-connected *adj* having powerful friends or relatives.

well-disposed *adj* favorable, feeling kindly (toward).

well-done *adj* performed with skill; thoroughly cooked, as meat.

Welles *n* **[George] Orson** (1915–85) American stage and film director, and actor who achieved notoriety in 1938 with his radio production of Wells's *War of the Worlds*, causing mass panic in the US. He co-wrote, produced and directed *Citizen Kane* and his acting roles include Harry Lime in *The Third Man*.

well-favored, well-favoured *adj* attractive.

well-found *adj* fully equipped.

well-founded *adj* borne out by facts.

well-groomed *adj* clean and tidy in dress and appearance.

well-grounded *adj* well instructed in a subject.

wellhead *n* the source of a stream, spring, etc; a source, origin.

well-heeled *adj* (*inf*) wealthy.

wellies *npl* (*Brit inf*) wellingtons.

well-informed *adj* knowledgeable on a wide range of subjects; possessing reliable information on a specific matter.

Wellington *n* capital city of New Zealand.

Wellington *n* 1st Duke of [**Arthur Wellesley**] (1769–1852) Anglo-Irish soldier and statesman, and Tory prime minister (1828–30). Nicknamed the "Iron Duke," he led the Allied forces to victory against Napoleon at Waterloo in 1815.

wellington (boot) *n* a rubber, waterproof boot.

well-intentioned *adj* having good intentions (but often without producing good results).

well-knit *adj* firm, compact.

well-known *adj* widely known, famous; known fully.

well-mannered *adj* having or showing good manners; polite.

well-meaning *adj* having good intentions (but often without producing good results).

well-nigh *adv* almost.

well-off *adj* in comfortable circumstances; prosperous.

well-preserved *adj* well looked after; remaining youthful in appearance.

well-read *adj* having read widely and deeply.

well-rounded *adj* having a pleasantly curved or rounded shape; full, complete.

Wells *n* H[**erbert**] G[**eorge**] (1866–1946) English novelist and short-story writer whose science fiction works include several classics, e.g. *The War of the Worlds* (1898).

well-spoken *adj* spoken clearly and eloquently; spoken in a pleasing manner.

well-thought-of *adj* having a good reputation.

well-thumbed *adj* (*book*) marked by frequent handling.

well-to-do *adj* prosperous.

well-wisher *n* a person who is sympathetic to another person, cause, etc.

well-worn *adj* showing signs of wear; (*phrase, etc*) trite, hackneyed.

welsh *vti* to avoid paying a gambling debt; to run off without paying.—*also* **welch**.—**welsher, welcher** *n*.

Welsh *adj* relating to the people of Wales or their language.—*also n*.

Welsh corgi *n* a corgi.

Welsh dresser *n* a dresser with drawers and cupboards below and open shelves above.

Welsh rabbit, Welsh rarebit *n* melted cheese on toast.

welt *n* a band or strip to strengthen a seam; a weal.

welter *vi* to roll or wallow. * *n* a jumble.

welterweight *n* a professional boxer weighing 140–147 pounds; a wrestler weighing 154–172 pounds.

wen *n* a benign skin tumor, esp on the scalp.

WEN *abbr* = Women's Environmental Network.

wench *n* (*used facetiously*) a girl or young woman.

wend *vt* to amble, to saunter.

Wendy house *n* (*Brit*) a toy house for children to play in.

Weni *n* (*Egypt*) an Egyptian courtier and high official of the Sixth Dynasty. He served under the first three pharaohs of the dynasty but is particularly associated with Pepy I.

Wenis *n* (*Egypt*) last Egyptian pharaoh of the Fifth Dynasty; his rule, ending around 2460 BC, is generally taken to mark the end of the classic period of the Old Kingdom.

Wensleydale *n* a mild crumbly English cheese.

went *see* **go**.

wept *see* **weep**.

Wepwawet *n* (*Egypt*) a deity of the underworld, a jackal- or wolf-headed god, the "opener of the ways." His origin was as the nome deity of Asyut, and, with Anubis, he was recognized as protector of the necropolis at Abydos.

were *see* **be**.

we're = we are.

weren't = were not.

werewolf *n* (*pl* **werewolves**) an imaginary person able to transform himself for a time into a wolf.

Werthheim's hysterectomy *n* a major form of hysterectomy undertaken to deal with uterine or ovarian cancer.

WES *abbr* = Waterways Experiment Station; Western Equestrian Society; Women's Engineering Society; Writing Equipment Society.

Wesley *n* 1. **Charles** (1707–88) English Methodist preacher and brother of John Wesley, founder of the Methodist movement, he also wrote over 5000 hymns, including "Hark, the Herald Angels sing." 2. **John** (1703–91) English preacher and evangelist; he formed a small group of devout Anglicans who subsequently became known as the "Methodists." This name was used to describe the expanding movement, which remained within the Church of England in Wesley's lifetime.

Wessex *n* (*hist*) a kingdom centered on the upper Thames valley in England, founded around the 6th century.

west *n* the direction of the sun at sunset; one of the four points of the compass; the region in the west of any country; (*with cap*) Europe and the Western Hemisphere. * *adj* situated in, or toward the west. * *adv* in or to the west.

West *n* 1. **Mae** (1892–1980) American vaudeville artist, dramatist, and film actress. She became renowned for her wit and sexuality in such films as *She Done Him Wrong*. 2. **Nathanael** [**Nathan Weinstein**] (1903–40) American novelist whose macabre novels have as their main theme the souring of the American dream, e.g. *Miss Lonelyhearts* and *The Day of the Locust*. 3. **Dame Rebecca** [**Cecily Isabel**

Fairfield] (1892–1983) Anglo-Irish novelist and journalist, whose novels include *The Return of the Soldier* and *The Birds Fall Down*.

West Bay *n* major town in Cayman Islands.

westerly *adj* toward the west; blowing from the west. * *n* (*pl* **westerlies**) a wind blowing from the west.—*also adv*.

western *adj* of or in the west. * *n* a film, novel, etc about the usu pre-20th century American West.

westerner *n* a person from the west.

Western Hemisphere *n* that half of the earth containing North and South America.

westernize *vti* to make or become familiar with the ideas, institutions, customs, etc of the West.—**westernization** *n*.

westernmost *adj* farthest west.

Western Sahara *n* a republic in west African with a coastline on the Atlantic Ocean.

Western Samoa *n* a constitutional monarchy, lying in the Polynesian sector of the Pacific Ocean about 447 miles or 720 kilometers northeast of Fiji. It consists of seven small islands and two larger volcanic islands.

"West Virginia" *n* the song of the American state, West Virginia.

West Virginia *or* **WV** *n* a state of the USA, of which the capital is Charlestown.

westward *adj* toward the west.—*also adv*.—**westwards** *adv*.

west wind drift *n* a slow movement of ocean water eastwards; known in the Pacific as the North Pacific current and in the North Atlantic as the Gulf Stream.

wet *adj* (**wetter, wettest**) covered or saturated with water or other liquid; rainy; misty; not yet dry. * *n* water or other liquid; rain or rainy weather. * *vti* (**wetting, wet** *or* **wetted**) to soak; to moisten.—**wetness** *n*.

WET *abbr* = Western European Time.

wet blanket *n* (*inf*) a person who dampens the enthusiasm of others.

wet dream *n* an erotic dream causing orgasm.

wet nurse *n* a woman employed to care for or suckle another's child.

wet-nurse *vt* to act as a wet nurse; (*inf*) to devote constant attention to (a person).

wet rot *n* (*Brit*) decay in timber caused by a fungus; any of various fungi that cause rot in damp timber.

wet suit *n* a close-fitting suit worn by divers, etc, to retain body heat.

WEU *abbr* = Western European Union.

we've = we have.

wf, w.f. *abbr* = wing forward; (*printing*) wrong font.

WFA *abbr* = White Fish Authority; Women's Football Association; Workers' Film Association.

WFAS *abbr* = World Federation of Acupuncture Societies.

WFB *abbr* = World Fellowship of Buddhists.

WFC *abbr* = World Feminist Commission; World Food Council.

WFD *abbr* = World Federation of the Deaf.

WFE *abbr* = Women for Freedom in Europe.

WFEO *abbr* = World Federation of Engineering Organizations.

WFH *abbr* = Wages for Housework; World Federation of Healing.

WFLOE *abbr* = Women For Life On Earth.

WFP *abbr* = World Food Program.

WFS *abbr* = Wild Flower Society; Women for Socialism; World Food Security.

WFSS *abbr* = Welsh Folk Song Society.

WFT *abbr* = Winged Fellowship Trust.

WFTT *abbr* = World Federation of Twinned Towns.

WFTU *abbr* = World Federation of Trade Unions.

WFU *abbr* = Women's Farming Union.

wg *abbr* = water gauge; wire gauge.

WG *abbr* = Welsh Guards.

WGAS *abbr* = Wholesale Grocers Association of Scotland.

WGer, W. Ger. *abbr* = West Germany.

WGF *abbr* = Women's Gas Federation and Young Homemakers.

WGGB *abbr* = Writers Guild of Great Britain.

WGU *abbr* = Welsh Golfing Union.

wh *abbr* = wing half.

wh, whr. *abbr* = watt-hour.

WHA *abbr* = Welsh Hockey Association; Western Horsemen's Association of Great Britain.

whack *vti* (*inf*) to strike sharply, esp making a sound. * *n* (*inf*) a sharp blow.

whacking *adj* (*Brit inf*) enormous. * *adv* (*inf*) very, extremely.

whale *n* a very large sea mammal that breathes through a blowhole, and resembles a fish in shape. * *vi* to hunt whales.

whalebone *n* a horny substance forming plates in the upper jaws of toothless whales; a piece of this formerly used for stiffening undergarments.

whalebone whale *n* any of various large whales that have whalebone plates instead of teeth which are used to filter plankton for food.

whaler *n* a person or a ship employed in hunting whales.

whaling *n* the practice of hunting whales for food, oil, etc.

wham *n* (the sound of) a heavy blow. * *vti* (**whamming, whammed**) to hit or cause to hit with a loud noise.

WHAM *abbr* = Women, Heritage and Museums.

whang *n* (the sound of) a forceful blow. * *vti* to hit or cause to hit with force.

wharf *n* (*pl* **wharfs, wharves**) a platform for loading and unloading ships in harbor.

wharfage *n* (the charge for) the use of a wharf; wharves collectively.

wharfinger *n* the owner or manager of a wharf.

Wharton *n* **Edith Newbold** (1862–1937) American writer whose novels include *The House of Mirth* (1905).

what *adj* of what sort, how much, how great. * *relative pron* that which; as much or many as. * *interj* used as an expression of surprise or astonishment.

whatever *pron* anything that; no matter what.

what if analysis *n* (*comput*) a procedure using a spreadsheet to explore the effect of changes in one input into a calculation.

whatnot *n* (*inf*) something or someone the name of which has been forgotten, is unknown or is hard to categorize; a set of open shelves for ornaments, photographs, etc.

whatsit *n* (*inf*) something or someone the name of which has been forgotten, is unknown or is hard to categorize.

whatsoever *adj* whatever.

whb *abbr* = wash-hand basin.

WHC *abbr* = Women's Health Concern.

WHD *abbr* = Wage and Hour Division.

wheal *see* **weal**.

wheat *n* a cereal grain usu ground into flour for bread.

wheatear *n* a small gray and white migratory thrush.

wheaten *adj* made from the grain or flour of wheat; pale yellow in color.

wheat germ *n* the kernel of a grain of wheat, high in nutritive value.

wheatmeal *adj, n* (made from) brown flour with a high proportion of wheat grain.

whee *interj* used to express joy or delight.

wheedle *vt* to persuade, to cajole (into); to coax with flattery.

wheel *n* a solid disc or circular rim turning on an axle; a steering wheel; (*pl*) the moving forces. * *vt* to transport on wheels. * *vi* to turn round or on an axis; to move in a circular direction, as a bird.

wheelbarrow *n* a cart with one wheel in front and two handles and legs at the rear.

wheelbase *n* the distance between the front and rear axles of a vehicle.

wheelchair *n* a chair with large wheels for invalids.

wheel clamp *n* (*Brit*) a device that prevents an illegally parked car from being driven away until a fine is paid to release it.—*also vt*.

Wheeler *n* **Sir [Robert Eric] Mortimer** (1890–1976) Scottish archaeologist. His works include *Archaeology and the Earth* (1954) and an autobiography, *Still Digging* (1955).

wheeler-dealer *n* (*inf*) a shrewd operator in business, politics, etc.

wheelhouse *n* (*archeo*) a circular building with inner dividing walls arranged like the spokes of a wheel.

wheelie *n* a stunt in which a bicycle or motorcycle is ridden for a distance with the front wheel off the ground.

wheelwright *n* a person who makes and repairs wheels for a living.

wheeze *vi* to breathe with a rasping sound; to breathe with difficulty.—*also n*.

wheezy *adj* (**wheezier, wheeziest**) making a wheezing sound.—**wheezily** *adv*.—**wheeziness** *n*.

whelk *n* a shellfish with a snail-like shell.

whelp *n* the young of various animals, esp a dog; an impudent child. * *vt* to give birth to (a puppy, etc). * *vi* (*bitch*) to bring forth young.

when *adv* at what or which time * *conj* at the time at which; although; *relative pron* at which.

whence *adv* from what place.—*also conj*.

whenever *adv, conj* at whatever time.

whensoever *conj, adv* whenever.

where *adv* at which or what place; to which place; from what source; *relative pron* in or to which.

whereabouts *adv* near or at what place; about where. * *n* approximate location.

whereas *conj* since; on the contrary.

whereby *adv* by which.—*also conj*.

wherein *adv* (*formal*) in what; how. * *conj* in which; where.

whereof *adv, conj* (*arch*) of what or which.

whereon *adv, conj* (*arch*) on what or which.

wheresoever *adv* (*emphatic*) wherever.

"Where the Columbines Grow" *n* the official song of the American state of Colorado.

whereto *adv, conj* (*formal*) to what or which.

whereupon *adv* at which point; upon which.

wherever *adv* at or to whatever place.

wherewithal *n* the means or resources.

whet *vt* (**whetting, whetted**) to sharpen by rubbing, to stimulate.

whether *conj* introducing an alternative possibility or condition.

whetstone *n* a stone for sharpening the edges of tools; something that sharpens or stimulates.

whew *interj* an exclamation of astonishment, amazement, relief, etc.

whey *n* the watery part of milk that is separated from the curds in sour milk.

whf. *abbr* = wharf.

WHI *abbr* = Welsh Hearing Institute.

which *adj* what one (of) * *pron* which person or thing; that. * *relative pron* person or thing referred to.

whichever *pron* whatever one that; whether one or the other; no matter which.— *also adj*.

whichsoever *adj, pron* (*arch*) whichever.

whiff *n* a sudden puff of air, smoke or odor.

while *n* a period of time. * *conj* during the time that; whereas; although. * *vt* to pass (the time) pleasantly.

whilst *conj* (*esp Brit*) while.

whim *n* a fancy; an irrational thought.

whimper *vi* to make a low, unhappy cry.—*also n*.

whimsical *adj* unusual, odd, fantastic.—**whimsicality** *n*.

whimsy, whimsey *n* (*pl* **whimsies, whimseys**) a fanciful notion, a whim.

whine *vi* (*dog*) to make a long, high-pitched cry; (*person*) to complain childishly. * *n* a plaintive cry.

whinge *vi* to moan, complain.—*also n*.

whinny *vi* (**whinnying, whinnied**) to neigh softly.—*also n*.

whip *n* a piece of leather attached to a handle used for punishing people or driving on animals; an officer in parliament who maintains party discipline. * *vb* (**whipping, whipped**) *vt* to move, pull, throw, etc suddenly; to strike, as with a lash; (*eggs, etc*) to beat into a froth; (*with* **up**) to stir into action, excite; (*inf*) to produce in a hurry. * *vi* to move rapidly.

whipcord *n* a strong cord of tightly twisted strands used for whips; a cotton or worsted fabric with diagonal ridges.

whip hand *n* (*usu with* **the**) the dominant position.

whiplash *n* a stroke with a whip; a neck injury when the head is jerked forward and backward.

whipped cream *n* cream that has been stiffened by beating, used as a topping for desserts, etc.

whippersnapper *n* an insignificant but impudent young person.

whippet *n* a small racing dog like a greyhound.

whipping boy *n* a person who is constantly punished for the mistakes of others, a scapegoat.

Whipple's disease *n* a rare disease of the intestines, resulting in malabsorption of food.

whippoorwill *n* a nocturnal American bird with a distinctive call.

whip-round *n* (*Brit inf*) an appeal among friends for contributions.

whipsaw *n* any of various types of saw with a long flexible blade. * *vt* to cut with a whipsaw; to defeat (someone) by acting jointly with another; to get the better of (someone) in two ways at once, esp by winning two different bets in a single play at faro.

whipstock *n* the handle of a whip.

whir, whirr *n* a humming or buzzing sound. * *vti* (**whirring, whirred**) to revolve with a buzzing noise.

whirl *n* a swift turning; confusion, commotion; (*inf*) an attempt or try. * *vti* to turn around rapidly; to spin.

whirligig *n* a spinning top.

whirlpool *n* a circular current or vortex of water.

whirlpool bath *n* a bath with a device that swirls water.

Whirlpool galaxy *n* a spiral galaxy (M51; NGC 5194), first described in 1845, lying at a distance of 13 million light years from the earth in the constellation of Canes Venatia.

whirlwind *n* a whirling column of air; rapid activity.

whisk *vt* to make a quick sweeping movement; (*eggs, cream*) to beat, whip. * *vi* to move nimbly and efficiently. * *n* a kitchen utensil for whisking; (*inf*) a small amount.

whisker *n* any of the sensory bristles on the face of a cat, etc; (*pl*) the hair growing on a man's face, esp the cheeks.—**whiskered** *adj*.

whiskey *n* whisky distilled in the US or Ireland.

whiskey-jack *see* **Canada jay**.

whisky *n* (*pl* **whiskies**) a spirit distilled from barley or rye.

whisper *vti* to speak softly; to spread a rumor. * *n* a hushed tone; a hint, trace.

whist *n* a card game for four players in two sides, each side attempting to win the greater number of the 13 tricks.

whistle *vti* to make a shrill sound by forcing the breath through the lips; to make a similar sound with a whistle; (*wind*) to move with a shrill sound; (*with* **for**) (*inf*) to demand or hope for in vain. * *n* a whistling sound; a musical instrument; a metal tube that is blown to make a shrill warning sound.

Whistler *n* 1. **James Abbott McNeill** (1834–1903) US painter who settled in London; he was influenced by the Pre-Raphaelites and by Japanese art. His works include *Arrangement in Grey and Black*, a portrait of his mother. 2. **Rex** (1904–44) British theater designer and *trompe d'oeil* muralist.

whistle stop *n* a minor railroad station where trains stop only on signal; a brief appearance by a candidate on tour during an election campaign.

whit *n* the tiniest possible amount.

Whit *see* **Whitsuntide**.

white *adj* of the color of snow; pure; bright; (*skin*) light-colored. * *n* the color white; the white part of an egg or the eye.

White *n* 1. **Andrew Dickson** *see* **Cornell, Ezra**. 2. **Patrick [Victor Martindale]** (1912–90) English-born Australian novelist who was awarded the Nobel prize for literature in 1973. His historical novels, e.g. *The Tree of Man*, are set in the Australian outback and describe the suffering and struggles of settlers and explorers of the wilderness. 3. **T[erence] H[anbury]** (1906–64) English novelist whose trilogy on the Arthurian legends, published in one volume as *The Once and Future King*, is the most popular and entertaining of the modern versions of the Arthur myth. The first volume of the trilogy, *The Sword in the Stone*, is regarded as a classic of children's literature.

white ant *n* a termite.

whitebait *n* (*pl* **whitebait**) the edible young of the herring and sprat.

white birch *n* (the wood of) a North American birch with a white paper-like bark; (the wood of) a European birch with a silvery-white bark.

white blood cell *n* a leucocyte.

whitecap *n* a wave with a white foamy crest.

white-collar *adj* of office and professional workers.

white dwarf *n* a small faint star of high density.

white elephant *n* a thing of little use.

whiteface *n* white facial make-up as worn by circus clowns.

white feather *n* a symbol of cowardice.

white fibrous tissue *n* tissue consisting of fibers of collagen which forms ligaments, sinews, and scar tissue, and also occurs in the skin.

white flag *n* a flag of plain white material used to signify surrender or arrange a truce.

whitefly *n* (*pl* **whiteflies**) any of various small insects that feed on and injure plants.

white gold *n* a pale alloy of gold chiefly with platinum and palladium.

white goods *npl* household appliances, as refrigerators, etc; household linen, as sheets, towels, etc.

Whitehall *n* the British government; departmental government.

Whitehead *n* 1. **A[lfred] N[orth]** (1861–1947) English mathematician and philosopher. With his pupil, Bertrand Russell, he wrote *Principia Mathematica* (1910–13), a highly acclaimed work that was described as the most important contribution to the study of logic since Aristotle. 2. **William** (1715–85) English dramatist who became poet laureate in 1757, attracting satirical comment to which he replied in *A Charge to the Poets*.

white heat *n* an intense heat accompanied by the emission of white light from a substance; (*inf*) intense excitement or emotion.

white hope *n* (*inf*) a person who is expected to win fame for his or her community, country, etc.

white-hot *adj* of a temperature so hot that white light is emitted; intensely passionate.

White House *n* the official residence of the president of the US; the US presidency.

white knight *n* (*com*) in a situation involving a takeover bid, a person or company that makes a bid that is more welcome than a previous bid that was seen as unacceptable or unwelcome in some way.

white lead *n* a white solid of mostly lead carbonate, esp used in pigments.

white leg *see* **thrombophlebitis**.

white lie *n* a harmless lie, esp as uttered out of politeness.

white light *n* light, e.g. sunlight, that contains approximately equal proportions of the whole spectrum of visible radiation.

white matter *n* whitish tissue in the brain and spinal cord composed of nerve fibers.

white meat *n* a light-colored meat such as poultry or veal.

white metal *n* an alloy, esp of tin, used in bearings, domestic utensils, etc.

White Mount *n* (*Brit Celtic myth*) one of the major druidic sites in London, England; the head of the Bendigeid Vran was buried there by Manawydan fab Llyr, Pryderi and others. The supposed founder of London, Brutus, was also buried there.

whiten *vti* to make or become white; to bleach.

White Nile *n* the longer of the two branches of the River Nile, rising in Lake Victoria in Central Africa.

white noise *n* sound that contains approximately equal proportions of all the audible frequencies.

whiteout *n* a weather condition when heavy cloud and snow reflect most of the available light and greatly reduce visibility.

white paper *n* a government document detailing proposed legislation.

white pine *n* (the wood of) a tall pine native to northeastern America, with leaves in clusters of five; (the wood of) any of various trees resembling this.

white sauce *n* a sauce made with butter, flour and seasonings mixed with milk, cream, or stock.

white slave *n* a woman or girl held against her will and forced into prostitution.

white spirit *n* (*Brit*) a colorless inflammable liquid distilled from petroleum and used as a solvent and thinner for paint.

white supremacy *n* belief in the superiority of white people.—**white supremacist** *n*, *adj*.

white-tailed deer *n* a type of North American deer with a long white tail.

white tie *n* a white bow tie worn as part of a man's formal evening dress.—**white-tie** *adj*.

White Walls *n* in ancient Egypt, an early name for the site that was later called Memphis.

whitewash *n* a mixture of lime and water, used for whitening walls; concealment of the truth.—*also vt*.

white water *n* water with a foaming surface, as in rapids.

white whale *n* the beluga.

white wine *n* wine made from green grapes or from skinned black grapes.

whitewood *n* (any of various trees yielding) a light-colored wood.

whitey *n* (*pl* **whities**) (*derog*) in US, a Black person's term for a white person.

whither *adv* to what or which place.

whiting *n* (*pl* **whitings, whiting**) an edible saltwater fish of the cod family.

Whitlam *n* **[Edward] Gough** (1916–) Australian Labour politician. He became prime minister (1972–75), and was dismissed by Sir John Kerr, the governor-general, for refusing to call a general election. Labour was defeated in the ensuing election, and Whitlam retired from parliament in 1978.

whitlow *n* a painful inflammation at the end of a finger or toe.

Whitman *n* **Walt[er]** (1819–92) American poet whose collection *Leaves of Grass*, (1855) is regarded as the most important volume of poems in American literature.

Whitsun *adj* (*Christianity*) of, observed on, or pertaining to Whit Sunday or Whitsuntide. * *n* Whitsuntide.

Whit Sunday *n* (*Christianity*) the seventh Sunday after Easter, Pentecost.

Whitsuntide *n* (*Christianity*) the week beginning with Whit Sunday.—*also* **Whit**.

Whittier *n* **John Greenleaf** (1807–92) American poet whose strong Quaker principles pervade his work, which, like Whitman's, celebrates the common people of America. His verse was enormously popular, and his antislavery poems, e.g. *Voices of Freedom*, contributed significantly to the abolitionist cause.

whittle *vt* to pare or cut thin shavings from (wood); (*with* **away** *or* **down**) to reduce.

Whittle *n* **Sir Frank** (1907–96) English aeronautical engineer who designed the first operational jet engine for aircraft, first used in 1941.

whiz, whizz *vi* (**whizzing, whizzed**) to make a humming sound. * *n* (*pl* **whizzes**) a humming sound; (*inf*) an expert.

whiz kid, whizz kid *n* (*inf*) a person of extraordinary achievements given their relatively young age.

WHL *abbr* = World Hypertension League.

WHML *abbr* = Wellcome Historical Medical Library.

who *pron* what or which person; that.

WHO *abbr* = World Health Organization.

whoa *interj* a command given, esp to a horse, to slow down or come to a halt.

who'd = who would.

whodunit, whodunnit *n* (*inf*) a detective novel, play, etc.

whoever *pron* anyone who; whatever person.

whole *adj* not broken, intact; containing the total amount, number, etc; complete. * *n* the entire amount; a thing complete in itself.

wholefood *n* unrefined food, free from additives.

wholehearted *adj* sincere, single-minded, enthusiastic.—**wholeheartedly** *adv*.

whole hog *n* (*inf*) the complete amount or extent.

whole-life policy *n* a life-insurance policy, under the tenets of which a specified amount of money is paid on the death of the person whose life has been insured.

wholemeal *adj* (*Brit*) *see* **wholewheat**.

whole milk *n* milk from which nothing has been removed.

whole note *n* (*mus*) a note with a time value equal to two half notes.—*also* **semibreve**.

whole number *n* a number without fractions; an integer.

wholesale *n* selling of goods, usu at lower prices and in quantity, to a retailer.

wholesaler *n* (*com*) a distributor who buys goods in relatively large quantities from manufacturers, stores them and sells them on in smaller quantities to retailers.

wholesome *adj* healthy; mentally beneficial.—**wholesomeness** *n*.

whole-tone scale *n* (*mus*) a scale in which all the intervals are whole-tones, i.e. two half steps (semitones).

wholewheat *adj* (*esp US flour*) made from the entire wheat kernel.—*also* **wholemeal**.

who'll = who will; who shall.

wholly *adv* completely.

whom *pron* objective case of **who**.

whomever *pron* the objective form of **whoever**.

whoop *n* a loud cry of excitement; (*med*) the noisy and characteristic drawing in of breath following a coughing attack in whooping cough.

whoopee *interj* used to express wild excitement. * *n* boisterous fun.

whoopee cushion *n* a joke cushion that emits a rude noise when sat on.

whooping cough *n* an infectious disease, esp of children, causing coughing spasms.

whoops *interj* (*inf*) an exclamation of surprise or apology.

whoosh *n* a rushing or hissing sound. * *vi* to make or move with such a sound.

whop *vt* (**whopping, whopped**) to beat, thrash; to defeat completely.

whopper *n* (*inf*) a large specimen.—**whopping** *adj*.

whore *n* a prostitute.

whorehouse *n* a brothel.

whoremonger *n* a person who uses the services of whores.—*also* **whoremaster**.

Whorf *n* **Benjamin Lee** (1897–1941) American linguist. Influenced by the German-born American linguist Edward Sapir, he devised what became known as the Sapir-Whorf hypothesis. This asserts that "users of markedly different grammars . . . arrive at somewhat different views of the world." His theory derives from his comparison between the Hopi language and "standard average European" language.

whorl *n* a ring of leaves or petals round a stem; a single turn of a spiral; something shaped like a spiral; the central ridges of a fingerprint forming a complete circle.

whortleberry *n* a bilberry.

who's = who is.

whose *pron* the possessive case of **who** or **which**.

whosoever *pron* (*arch*) whoever.

who's who *n* a reference book containing the names and brief biographical details of famous or important people.

WHPU *abbr* = Welsh Homing Pigeon Union.

WHRA *abbr* = Welwyn Hall Research Association.

WHS *abbr* = Wesley Historical Society.

WHSC *abbr* = West Highland Steamer Club.

why *adv* for what cause or reason? * *interj* exclamation of surprise. * *n* (*pl* **whys**) a cause.

whydah *n* any of various African weaverbirds with black and white plumage.

w.i. *abbr* = (*stock exch.*) when issued; wrought iron.

WI *abbr* = Wisconsin; West Indies; (*Brit*) Women's Institute.

WIA *abbr* = Willow Importers Association; World Interfaith Association; wounded in action.

WIAC *abbr* = Women's International Art Club.

WIBA *abbr* = Welsh Indoor Bowls Association.

WIC *abbr* = Women, Infants and Children, Special supplemental food program for.

wick *n* a cord, as in a candle or lamp, that supplies fuel to the flame.

wicked *adj* evil, immoral, sinful.—**wickedly** *adv.*—**wickedness** *n*.

wicker *n* a long, thin, flexible twig; such twigs woven together, as in making baskets.—**wickerwork** *n*.

wicket *n* a small door or gate; (*croquet*) any of the small wire arches through which the balls must be hit; (*cricket*) the stumps at which the bowler aims the ball; the area between the bowler and the batsman; a batsman's innings.

wicketkeeper *n* (*cricket*) the fielder standing immediately behind the wicket.

widdershins *see* **withershins**.

wide *adj* broad; extensive; of a definite distance from side to side; (*with* **of**) far from the aim; open fully. * *n* (*cricket*) a ball bowled beyond the reach of the batsman.—**widely** *adv*.

wide-angle *adj* (*photog*) with an angle of view of 60 degrees or more.

wide area network *or* **WAN** *n* (*comput*) a computer network that connects computers over long distances using telephone lines or satellite communications.

wide-awake *adj* fully awake; ready, alert.

wide-eyed *adj* astonished; innocent.

widen *vti* to make or grow wide or wider.

widespread *adj* widely extended; general.

widget *n* (*inf*) a small device or gadget the name of which is lost or forgotten; a whatsit.

Widor *n* **Charles Marie Jean Albert** (1845–1937) a French composer and organist who taught at the Paris Conservatoire. His works include operas, ten organ "symphonies" (his famous toccata comes from the 5th), piano concertos, and chamber music.

widow *n* a woman whose husband has died. * *vt* to cause to become a widow.—**widowhood** *n*.

widower *n* a man whose wife has died.

widow's peak *n* a pointed growth of hair in the middle of the forehead.

width *n* breadth.

wield *vt* (*a weapon, etc*) to brandish; to exercise power.

Wiener *n* **Norbert** (1894–1964) American mathematician. Advised by his tutor, Bertrand Russell, to study mathematics, he coined the term "cybernetics" for the feedback mechanism in electronics, the theory of which is expanded in works such as *Cybernetics* (1948).

Wiener Werksätte *n* established by Moser, a member of the breakaway artists' group, the Vienna Secession, the Wiener Werkstätte became a center for progressive design around 1905.

Wieslthier *n* **Valerie** (1895–1945) Austrian designer who was head of the ceramic workshop of the Wiener Werkstätte.

wife *n* (*pl* **wives**) a married woman.

wig *n* an artificial covering of real or synthetic hair for the head.

wigeon, widgeon *n* a Eurasian wild duck the male of which has a gingery head.

wigging *n* (*Brit inf*) a severe reprimand.

wiggle *vti* to move from side to side with jerky movements.

Wiglaf *n* a king of Mercia, Britain (827–840). He was expelled by the powerful Egbert of Wessex in 827 but regained the throne within a year.

Wigmore Hall *n* (*mus*) a concert hall in Wigmore Street, London, which was famous for its chamber concerts and recitals. It was built in 1910.

WIGS *abbr* = Women in German Studies.

wigwag *vb* (**wigwagging, wigwagged**) *vi* to move back and forth; to send a signal by means of flag semaphore. * *vt* to signal by wigwagging; to cause (something) to move back and forth. * *n* (the message sent using) a system of signaling with flags.

wigwam *n* a North American Indian conical shelter.

Wihtred *n* a king of Kent, Britain (690–725). Ruled jointly with Suaebhard to 692 and married three times.

WIIU *abbr* = Workers' International Industrial Union.

WIL *abbr* = Workers International League.

Wilberforce *n* **William** (1759–1833) English philanthropist and politician who campaigned to end the British slave trade until its abolition in 1807.

Wilberforce, Samuel *see* **Huxley, Thomas Henry**.

wilco *interj* used in telecommunications to indicate that a message is received and being acted upon.

Wilcox *n* **Ella Wheeler** (1850–1919) American poet whose prolifically produced verses, in the collection *Poems of Passion*, were enormously popular in their day. Her appeal was due to a blend of sentimentalism and everyday "common sense," exemplified in her best-known lines "Laugh and the world laughs with you; Weep, and you weep alone" ("Solitude").

wild *adj* in its natural state; not tamed or cultivated; uncivilized; lacking control; disorderly; furious.—**wildly** *adv.*—**wildness** *n*.

WILD *abbr* = International Wilderness Leadership Foundation.

wild boar *n* a wild pig with tusks, of Europe and Asia.

wildcat *adj* (*strike*) unofficial. * *n* a fierce, undomesticated cat.

wild card *n* (*card games*) a card with an arbitrary value determined by the holder; (*sport*) a team that has not qualified for a competition but is allowed to take part; (*comput*) a special character that is substituted for another character or range of characters in a search, e.g. an asterisk for zero or any number of characters, a question mark for one character; (*sl*) an unpredictable element.

Wilde *n* **Oscar [Fingal O'Flahertie Wills]** (1854–1900) Irish dramatist, poet, essayist, and wit, who was famously jailed for homosexuality (1895–97). His poetry includes *The Ballad of Reading Gaol* and his plays include *The Importance of Being Earnest* (1895).

wildebeest *n* (*pl* **wildebeests, wildebeest**) a gnu.

Wilder *n* **1. Billy [Samuel Wilder]** (1906–) Austrian-born American film director and screenwriter who won oscars for *The Lost Weekend*, *Sunset Boulevard* and *The Apartment*. **2. Thornton [Niven]** (1897–1975) American novelist and dramatist whose best-known novel is *The Bridge of San Luis Rey*, a historical novel set in 18th-century Peru. His fiction is, for the most part, an optimistic celebration of the lives of ordinary people.

wilderness *n* an uncultivated and desolate place.

wild-eyed *adj* staring angrily or crazily.

wildfire *n* a fire that spreads fast and is hard to put out.

wildfowl *n* any bird that is hunted for game, esp waterbirds such as ducks and geese.

wild-goose chase *n* a futile pursuit of something.

wilding *n* (the fruit of) any uncultivated plant; a wild animal; (*sl*) a violent rampage though the streets by a teenage gang.

wildlife *n* animals in the wild.

wild oat *n* (*usu pl*) a Eurasian grass related to cultivated oats; (*pl*) youthful excesses.

wild rice *n* a North American grass that bears edible grains; its grain.

Wild West *n* the western US during the lawless period of early settlement.

wile *n* a trick, craftiness.

Wilfrid *n* **Saint** (634–709) Northumbrian nobleman who abandoned Celtic customs and adhered to those of Rome; became archbishop of York. He was a creative artist who knew how to create splendid effects through art and religious ceremonial. His feast day is October 12.

wilful *see* **willful**.

Wilkins *n* **1. Maurice Hugh Frederick** (1916–) New Zealand physicist and biologist whose research resulted in Crick and Watson's discovery of the "double helix" structure of DNA, for which all three shared the 1962 Nobel prize for physics. **2. William** (1778–1839) English architect. His notable works include Downing College, Cambridge.

will[1] *n* power of choosing or determining; desire; determination; attitude, disposition; a legal document directing the disposal of one's property after death. * *vt* to bequeath; to command.

will[2] *aux vb* used in constructions with 2nd and 3rd persons; used to show futurity, determination, obligation.

Willaert *n* **Adrian** (*c*.1485–1562) Flemish composer who went to live and work in Venice. His works include Masses, motets, and various instrumental pieces.

Willemstad *n* capital city of the Netherlands Antilles.

willful *adj* stubborn; done intentionally.—*also* **wilful**.—**willfully, wilfully** *adv.*—**willfulness, wilfulness** *n*.

William I *n* **[the Conqueror]** (1027–87) duke of Normandy and king of England.

The illegitimate son of Robert, Duke of Normandy, he invaded England after Harold II became king and defeated the English forces at the Battle of Hastings. He launched a ferocious assault upon rebels in the North of England in 1069, and ordered the compilation of the Domesday book in 1086.

William I *n* [**the Lion**] (1143–1214) king of Scots (1165–1214). The brother of Malcolm IV and the grandson of David I, he became king at the age of 22. His first act as king was to attempt to reclaim Northumbria, which had been taken from Scotland by Henry II in 1157.

William II *n* [**Rufus**] (1056–1100) king of England (1087–1100). The third son of William I and Matilda of Flanders, he was born in Normandy and gained the nickname "Rufus" on account of his florid complexion.

William III *n* [**William of Orange**] (1650–1702 king of England, Scotland and Ireland (respectively as William III, II and I) (1689–1702).

William IV *n* (1765–1837) king of the United Kingdom of Great Britain and Ireland (1830–37). He was succeeded by his niece, Victoria, in 1837.

Williams *n* 1. **Charles** (1886–1945) English poet, novelist, and critic whose highly individual supernatural thrillers, e.g. *War in Heaven*, *Descent into Hell*, and *All Hallows Eve*, have a devoted following. 2. **Shirley** [**Vivien Teresa Brittain**] (1930–) English politician. She became a Labor MP in 1964, and formed the Social Democratic Party with Jenkins, Owen and Rodgers in 1981, becoming the party's first elected MP (1981–83). She retired from politics to become a professor at Harvard University. 3. **Tennessee** [**Thomas Lanier Williams**] (1911–83) American dramatist whose plays, lurid melodramas about sexual and social frustration in the Deep South, include *The Glass Menagerie*, *A Streetcar Named Desire*, and *Cat on a Hot Tin Roof*, and *The Night of the Iguana*. 4. **William Carlos** (1883–1963) American poet, novelist, and short-story writer.

Williamson *n* **Malcolm** (1931–) Australian-born British composer . Master of the Queen's Music since 1975, his works include several operas, e.g. *Our Man in Havana* (1963), and music for film and television, and for children.

willies *npl* (with **the**) nervousness, jumpiness.

willing *adj* ready, inclined; eager.—**willingly** *adv*.—**willingness** *n*.

will-o'-the-wisp *n* a pale phosphorescent glow sometimes seen over marshy areas and thought to be caused by combustion of gas from decaying organic matter; an elusive person or thing.

willow *n* a tree or shrub with slender, flexible branches; the wood of the willow.

willowherb *n* any of various plants of the evening-primrose family with pink or white flowers.

willow pattern *n* a traditional oriental-style design on china tableware consisting of a scene with figures and a willow tree, usu in blue on a white background.

willowy *adj* flexible, graceful.

willpower *n* the ability to control one's emotions and actions.

willy-nilly *adv* whether desired or not.

Wilmot, John *see* **Rochester, 2nd Earl of**.

Wilmotte *n* **Jean-Michel** (1948–) F rench interior architect with an impressive list of commissions including a bedroom for President Mitterand.

Wilm's tumor *n* a tumor of the kidney (nephroblastoma) in infancy.

Wilson *n* 1. **Sir Angus** (1913–91) South African-born English novelist and short-story writer whose fictions are sharply observed satires within a wide variety of social settings. His novels include *Hemlock and After*, and *The Old Men at the Zoo*. 2. **Colin** [**Henry**] (1931–) English novelist and critic who wrote studies of existentialist writers, e.g. Camus and Sartre. 3. **Edmund** (1895–1972) American critic, poet, and dramatist whose main critical work is *Axel's Castle*, an influential study of symbolist writers. 4. **Sir** [**James**] **Harold** [**Baron of Rievaulx**] (1916–95) English Labour statesman; prime minister (1964–70, 1974–76); he defended US policy on Vietnam; resigned in 1976. 5. **Harriette** (1786–1846) English author and courtesan. Her *Memoirs of Harriette Wilson* (1825) created a public scandal by naming and discussing her various "protectors," associates and acquaintances, many of them prominent men. 6. [**Thomas**] **Woodrow** (1856–1924) American Democratic statesman. He became 28th president of the USA (1913–21). Re-elected in 1916 on a policy of neutrality, he declared war on Germany following the sinking of US vessels by U-boats.

wilt *vi* to become limp, as from heat; (*plant*) to droop; to become weak or faint.

wily *adj* (**wilier, wiliest**) crafty; sly.—**wiliness** *n*.

WIM *abbr* = Women in Management; Women in Media; Women in Medicine.

WIMA *abbr* = Women's International Motorcycle Association; World International Medical Association.

wimp *n* (*inf*) a weak or ineffectual person.

WIMP, Wimp (*acronym*) (*comput*) a graphical interface using Windows, Icons, Mice and Pull-down menus that makes a computer easier to use.

wimple *n* a linen or silk cloth draped round the head and neck but leaving the face uncovered, worn by women in medieval times and still used by some nuns.

win *vti* (**winning, won**) to gain with effort; to succeed in a contest; to gain e.g. by luck; to achieve influence over; (*with* **over**) to gain the support or affection of (someone). * *n* a success.

wince *vi* to shrink back; to flinch (as in pain).—*also n*.

winch *n* a hoisting machine. * *vt* to hoist or lower with a winch.

wind[1] *n* a current of air; breath; scent of game; (*inf*) flatulence; tendency; (*mus*) wind instrument(s). * *vt* (**winding, winded**) to cause to be short of breath; to perceive by scent.

wind[2] *vb* (**winding, wound**) *vt* to turn by cranking; to tighten the spring of a clock; to coil around something else; to encircle or cover, as with a bandage; (*with* **down**)

to lower by winding a handle, etc. * *vi* to turn, to twist, to meander; (*with* **down**) to diminish in power or intensity; to slacken; to relax.

windage *n* the difference between the bore of a gun and the diameter of the projectile; (an allowance for) the deflection of a projectile caused by the wind.

windbag *n* (*inf*) a person who talks a lot of rubbish.

windblown *adj* blown or shaped by the wind.

windbreak *n* a shelter that breaks the force of the wind, as a line of trees.

windburn *n* redness and soreness of the skin due to the wind.

windcheater *n* a warm hooded jacket of windproof material.

wind-chill *n* a measure of the effect of low temperature combined with wind.

winded *adj* out of breath.

winder *n* one who or that which winds; a winding apparatus; a key for winding a spring-driven mechanism; a step in a spiral staircase.

windfall *n* fruit blown off a tree; any unexpected gain, esp financial.

windfall gain *n* an exceptional gain that arises from an unexpected change in the financial market conditions which has helped to raise the price of a financial security, stock, or asset.

Windhoek *n* capital city of Namibia.

winding *adj* meandering.

winding sheet *n* a sheet used to wrap a body for burial.

wind instrument *n* a musical instrument played by blowing into it or passing an air current through it.

windjammer *n* a large fast merchant sailing vessel.

windlass *n* any of various devices for hoisting, hauling, or lifting using a rope or chain wound round a motorized drum. * *vt* to hoist, etc using a windlass.

wind machine *n* a device used in film and theater to produce realistic wind effects.

windmill *n* a machine operated by the force of the wind turning a set of sails.

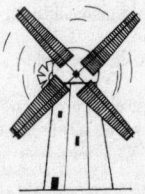

window[1] *n* a framework containing glass in the opening in a wall of a building, or in a vehicle, etc, for air and light.

window[2] *n* a financial opportunity, such as a chance to invest in something profitable, which may be available only for a limited time and so should be taken advantage of.

window[3] *n* a period of the day during which interbank clearances and transfers may be carried out.

window[4] *n* (*comput*) an on-screen frame, usu rectangular in shape, that contains the display of a file.

window box *n* a narrow box on a windowsill for growing flowers, etc.

windowdressing *n* the arrangement of goods in a shop window; ornamentation intended to disguise the true nature of something.

windowpane *n* the glass in a window.

Windows (*trademark*) or **Microsoft Windows** (*trademark*)] *n* (*comput*) a comprehensive software facility that utilizes the GUI features that were developed by Macintosh (*trademark*).

window-shopping *n* the occupation of looking at goods for sale without buying them.—**window-shopper** *n*.

windowsill *n* a sill beneath a window.

windpipe *n* the air passage from the mouth to the lungs, the trachea.

wind rose *n* a diagram to illustrate the frequency with which wind blows from various specified directions in a given period of time.

wind shadow *n* a zone of quiet air in the lee of an object or windbreak.

windshield or **windscreen** *n* a protective shield of glass in the front of a vehicle.

windshield wiper or **windscreen wiper** *n* a metal blade with a rubber edge that removes rain, etc, from a windscreen.

windsock[1] *n* a canvas cylinder flown from an airport mast to show the direction of the wind.—*also* **drogue**.

windsock[2] *n* a covering for a microphone that prevents wind noise.

Windsor *n* **Duke of** (1894–1972) English monarch (1936). He succeeded his father, George V, to the throne, but abdicated to marry the American divorcée, Wallis Simpson.

windsurfing *n* the sport of skimming along the surface of the water standing on a surfboard fitted with a sail.

windswept *adj* exposed to the wind; disheveled.

wind tunnel *n* an apparatus for maintaining a constant force of air current to test the aerodynamics of an aircraft, etc.

wind-up *n* the conclusion.

windward *adv*, *adj* toward the direction where the wind blows from.

windy *adj* (**windier, windiest**) exposed to the winds; stormy; verbose.

wine *n* fermented grape juice used as an alcoholic beverage; the fermented juice of other fruits or plants.

wine bar *n* a bar that serves wine and food.

wine box *n* wine sold in a box with a small tap for pouring.

W

wine cellar *n* a place for storing wines, ideally a cool cellar; a stock of stored wines.

wine cooler *n* a vessel that is filled with ice for cooling wine bottles.

wine-colored *adj* dark purplish-red.

wineglass *n* a glass, usu with a stem, for drinking wine.

winegrower *n* a person who grows vines and makes wine.

wine press *n* (a place containing) equipment for squeezing juice from grapes to make wine.

winery *n* (*pl* **wineries**) a place where wine is made.

wineskin *n* the skin of an animal, esp a goat, sewn into a bag for holding wine.

wing *n* the forelimb of a bird, bat, or insect, by which it flies; the main lateral surface of an airplane; a projecting part of a building; the side of a stage; a section of a political party. * *vti* to make one's way swiftly; to wound without killing.

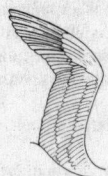

WING *abbr* = Work Injured Nurses Group.

Wingate *n* **Orde [Charles] Major-General** (1903–44) English soldier. In 1942, he organized the "Chindits," specially trained jungle troops who caused much disruption to the Japanese supply lines during the Burma campaign in World War II. He died in a plane crash.

wing chair *n* an armchair with high sides for excluding draughts.

wing collar *n* a stiff upturned shirt collar with the points turned down.

wingding *n* (*inf*) a wild party; a real or pretended fit.

wing nut *n* a nut that is tightened manually using flat wings that project on each side.

wingspan, wingspread *n* the width of a bird or airplane between the tips of the wings.

wink *vi* to quickly open and close one's eye; to give a hint by winking; (*with* **at**) to disregard; to allow (something normally prohibited) to happen. * *n* the act of winking; an instant.

winkle¹ *n* a periwinkle.

winkle² *n* an edible sea snail. * *vt* (*with* **out**) (*inf*) to extract, prise out; to uncover, disclose.

winkle-pickers *npl* shoes or boots with sharp pointed toes.

winner *n* one that wins; (*inf*) a person or thing that is assured of success.

winning *n* a victory; (*pl*) money won in gambling. * *adj* charming.

Winnipeg *n* a city in Canada.

winnow *vt* to separate out the chaff from (the grain) by blowing air across it; to analyze.

wino *n* (*pl* **winos**) (*inf*) a down-and-out addicted to cheap wine.

winsome *adj* charming, pleasing.

winter *n* the coldest season of the year: in the northern hemisphere from November or December to January or February. * *vi* to spend the winter.

wintergreen *n* any of various evergreen plants or shrubs; an aromatic essential oil from these formerly used in medicine.

winterize *vt* to prepare something (e.g., a car) to withstand winter weather.— **winterization** *n*.

Winterreise *n* **Die ["The Winter Journey"]** a cycle of 24 songs by Schubert, to words by W Miller. The songs tell the story of a lovelorn young man.

winter sports *npl* sports that take place on ice or snow, such as skiing.

wintry, wintery *adj* (**wintrier, wintriest**) typical of winter, cold, stormy, snowy; unfriendly, frigid.

winy *adj* (**winier, winiest**) tasting like or resembling wine.

WIP *abbr* = work in progress.

wipe *vt* to rub a surface with a cloth in order to clean or dry it; (*with* **out**) to remove; to erase; to kill off; to destroy. * *n* a wiping.

wiper *n* a person or thing that wipes; a windscreen wiper.

WIPO *abbr* = World Intellectual Property Organization.

WIR *abbr* = White Irish Resistance.

wire *n* a flexible thread of metal; a length of this; (*horse racing*) the finish line of a race; a telegram. * *adj* formed of wire. * *vt* to fasten, furnish, connect, etc, with wire; to send a telegram.

wired *adj* (*sl*) wearing a hidden electronic recording or listening device; (*sl*) nervous or edgy, esp as a result of taking a stimulating drug.

wire-haired *adj* (*dogs, etc*) having a coat of stiff hairs.

wireless *n* (*formerly*) a radio.

wire service *n* a news agency that sends out news to television and radio stations.

wiretap *vb* (**wiretapping, wiretapped**) *vi* to connect to a telephone wire in order to listen in to a private conversation. * *vt* to tap (a telephone).— **wiretapper** *n*.

wireworm *n* the filament-like larva of certain beetles which infest and destroy plant roots.

wiring *n* a system of wires used in an electrical device or circuit.

Wirkkala *n* **Tapio** (1915–85) one of Finland's greatest glass designers, designing for the Littala glassworks from 1947.

wiry *adj* (**wirier, wiriest**) lean, supple, and sinewy.— **wiriness** *n*.

Wis. *or* **Wisc.** *abbr* = Wisconsin.

WISA *abbr* = West Indies Sugar Association; West Indies Shipping Corporation.

Wisconsin *or* **WI** *n* a state of the USA, of which the capital is Madison.

Wisd. *abbr* = Wisdom (Book of).

wisdom *n* the ability to use knowledge; sound judgment.

wisdom tooth *n* one of four teeth set at the end of each side of the upper and lower jaw in humans and grown last.

wise *adj* having knowledge or common sense; learned; prudent. * *vti* (*with* **up**) (*inf*) (to cause) to become informed or aware.— **wisely** *adv*.

-wise *adv suffix* direction or manner; concerning.

wiseacre *n* a person who pretends to be clever or wise, a know-all.

wisecrack *n* (*inf*) a witty or sarcastic remark.—*also vi*.

wise guy *n* (*inf*) a person who is always making critical or sarcastic comments.

wise use *n* a policy designed to protect the use of natural resources and promote environmental awareness.

wish *vti* to long for; to express a desire. * *n* desire; thing desired.

wishbone *n* the forked bone at the front of the breastbone of a bird consisting of the fused clavicles.

wishful *adj* having a wish; hopeful.

wishful thinking *n* the mistaken belief that one's wishes correspond to reality.

wishy-washy *adj* weak, thin, feeble.

wisp *n* a thin strand; a small bunch, as of hay; anything slender.—**wispy** *adj*.

wisteria, wistaria *n* a purple-flowered climbing plant.

wistful *adj* pensive; sad; yearning.—**wistfully** *adv*.—**wistfulness** *n*.

wit *n* (*speech, writing*) the facility of combining ideas with humorous effect; a person with this ability; (*pl*) ability to think quickly.

WITA *abbr* = Women's International Tennis Association.

witch *n* a woman who practices magic and is considered to a have dealings with the devil.

witchcraft *n* the practice of magic.

witch doctor *n* a man in certain tribes who appears to be able to cure sickness or cause harm to people.

witchery *n* (*pl* **witcheries**) witchcraft; fascination.

witch hazel *n* any of a genus of North American shrubs with yellow flowers; a soothing lotion made from the bark of this applied to lumps, bruises, skin rashes, etc.

witch hunt *n* a campaign of harassment of those with dissenting opinions; the search for and persecution of those accused of witchcraft.

witching *adj* of or suitable for witchcraft.

with *prep* denoting nearness or agreement; in the company of; in the same direction as; among; by means of; possessing.

withal *adv* (*arch*) as well; moreover.

withdraw *vb* (**withdrawing, withdrew**, *pp* **withdrawn**) *vt* to draw back or away; to remove; to retract. * *vi* to retire; to retreat.—**withdrawal** *n*.

withdrawal symptoms *npl* a characteristic feature when someone stops using a drug upon which he or she is dependent.

withdrawn *adj* introverted, reserved; remote.

wither *vi* to fade or become limp or dry, as of a plant. * *vt* to cause to dry up or fade.

withers *npl* the ridge between the shoulder blades of a horse.

withershins *adv* counter-clockwise.—*also* **widdershins**.

withhold *vt* (**withholding, withheld**) to hold back; to deduct; to restrain; to refuse to grant.

withholding tax *n* tax that is deducted at source from dividend or interest payments.

within *prep* inside; not exceeding; not beyond.

without *prep* outside or out of; beyond; not having, lacking. * *adv* outside.

withstand *vt* (**withstanding, withstood**) to oppose or resist, esp successfully; to endure.

witless *adj* foolish, stupid; not witty.

witness *n* a person who gives evidence or attests a signing; testimony (of a fact). * *vt* to have first-hand knowledge of; to see; to be the scene of; to serve as evidence of; to attest a signing. * *vi* to testify.

witness stand, witness box *n* an enclosure for witnesses in a court of law.

Wittgenstein *n* **Ludwig [Josef Johann]** (1889–1951) Austrian-born British philosopher whose *Philosophical Investigations* were published posthumously.

witticism *n* a witty remark.

wittingly *adv* knowingly.

witty *adj* (**wittier, wittiest**) full of wit.—**wittily** *adv*.—**wittiness** *n*.

wives *see* **wife**.

wizard¹ *n* a magician; a man who practices witchcraft or magic; an expert.— **wizardry** *n*.

wizard² *n* (*comput*) a computerized expert system that leads the user through the sometimes complex process of creating a document, query etc.

wizened *adj* dried up, wrinkled, shriveled.

WJC *abbr* = World Jewish Congress.

WJCB *abbr* = World Jersey Cattle Bureau.

WJEC *abbr* = Welsh Joint Education Committee.

WJFITB *abbr* = Wool, Jute, and Flax Industry Training Board.

wk, wk. *abbr* = week.

w.k. *abbr* = well-known.

WKA *abbr* = Warp Knitters Association.

wks. *abbr* = weeks; works.

w.l., WL *abbr* = waiting list, wavelength.

WLA *abbr* = Women's Land Army; World Literary Academy.

WLF *abbr* = Women's Liberal Federation.

W. lon., W. long. *abbr* = west longitude.

WLM *abbr* = Women's Liberation Movement.

WLR *abbr* = Weekly Law Reports.

WLS *abbr* = Welsh Language Society.

WLSS *abbr* = Wheelchair Loan Service Scotland.

WLTM *abbr* = would like to meet.

wm., Wm. *abbr* = wattmeter.

WM *abbr* = well maintained; white male.

WMA *abbr* = Wallcovering Manufacturers Association; Waterheaters Manufacturers Association; Weather Modification Association; Workers' Music Association; Working Mothers' Association; World Media Association.

WMAC *abbr* = West Midlands Advisory Council for Further Education.

WMC *abbr* = Working Men's Club; World Methodist Council; World Mining Congress.

WMCCSA *abbr* = World Masters Cross Country Ski Association.

WMCIU *abbr* = Working Men's Club and Institute Union Limited.

WMF *abbr* = Waste Management Forum; World Memorial Fund for Disaster Relief.

wmk. *abbr* = watermark.

WMM *abbr* = World Movement of Mothers.

WMO *abbr* = World Meteorological Organization.

wmp *abbr* = with much pleasure.

WMRL *abbr* = Water Management Research Laboratory.

WMS *abbr* = Welsh Mines Society; Wesleyan Missionary Society.

WNA *abbr* = Welsh Netball Association.

WNB *abbr* = weekly news bill.

WNCCC *abbr* = Women's Nationwide Cancer Control Campaign Limited.

wndp *abbr* = with no down payment.

WNE *abbr* = Welsh National Eisteddfod.

WNET *abbr* = Women's Network for Entrepreneurial Training.

wnl *abbr* = within normal limits.

WNO *abbr* = Welsh National Opera.

WNP *abbr* = Welsh National Party; wire nonpayment.

w.n.w., WNW *abbr* = west-northwest.

wo *abbr* = walkover; written order.

w/o *abbr* = without; written off.

WO *abbr* = War Office; warrant officer; wireless operator.

woad *n* (a blue dye obtained from the leaves of) a European plant of the mustard family.

WOAR *abbr* = Women Organized Against Rape.

wobble *vi* to sway unsteadily from side to side; to waver, to hesitate.—**wobbly** *adj*.

woc *abbr* = without compensation.

wocs *abbr* = waiting on cement setting.

Wodehouse *n* P[elham] G[renville] (1881–1975) English novelist and short-story writer who created the characters Bertie Wooster and his butler, Jeeves. He became a US citizen in 1955.

wodge *n* (*Brit inf*) a thick slice or chunk of something.

woe *n* grief, misery; (*pl*) misfortune.—**woeful** *adj*.—**woefully** *adv*.

woebegone *adj* sorrowful.

wog *n* (*Brit offensive*) a non-white person.

wok *n* a large, metal, hemispherical pan used for Chinese-style cooking.

woke, woken *see* **wake**[1].

wolf *n* (*pl* **wolves**) a wild animal of the dog family that hunts in packs; a flirtatious man.

Wolf *n* Hugo (1860–1903) Austrian composer who had a fanatical respect for Wagner. His works include many song cycles, two operas, and chamber music.

wolfcall *n* a whistle made by a man when seeing an attractive woman.—*also* **wolf whistle**.

Wolfe *n* 1. Thomas [Clayton] (1900–1938) American novelist whose major achievement is a huge four-volume series of largely autobiographical novels, i.e. *Look Homeward, Angel, Of Time and the River, The Web and the Rock*, and *You Can't Go Home Again*. 2. Tom [Thomas Kennerly Jr] (1931–) American journalist and writer whose novels include *The Electric Kool-Aid Acid Test* (1968).

Wolff Olins *n* a British design studio established in 1955 in London.

wolfhound *n* any of several types of large dog formerly used to hunt wolves.

wolfram *n* tungsten; wolframite.

wolframite *n* a mineral that is the chief ore of tungsten and also contains iron and manganese.

Wolf-Rayet star *n* one of a class of rare, extremely luminous and exceptionally hot stars.

Wolf sunspot number (R) *n* an indication of the amount of sunspot activity on the solar disc, introduced in 1848 by Rudolf Wolf, now superseded by the International Sunspot number (RI).

wolf whistle *see* **wolf call**.

Wolsey *n* Cardinal Thomas (*c*.1475–1530) English cleric, archbishop of York and lord chancellor. His failure to secure an annulment of Henry VIII's marriage led to his dismissal.

wolverine *n* a voracious carnivorous animal of northern forests of Europe, North America, and Asia with thick black fur.

wolves *see* **wolf**.

woman *n* (*pl* **women**) an adult human female; the female sex.

womanhood *n* the state of being a woman.

womanish *n* resembling a woman; suitable for women.

womanize *vi* to pursue women for sex.—**womanizer** *n*.

womankind *n* female human beings; women collectively, esp as distinct from men.

womanly *adj* having the qualities of a woman.

womb *n* the female organ in which offspring are developed until birth, the uterus; any womb-like cavity; a place where something is produced.

wombat *n* an Australian marsupial mammal resembling a small bear.

women *see* **woman**.

womenfolk *npl* women collectively; the female members of a family, group or community.

Women's Institute *n* (*esp Brit*) an organization for women which engages in various social and cultural activities.

Women's Movement *n* a feminist movement seeking to end male domination of women in society.

won[1] *n* the standard monetary unit of North and South Korea made up of 100 chon.

won[2] *see* **win**.

won't = will not.

wonder *n* a feeling of surprise or astonishment; something that excites such a feeling; a prodigy. * *vi* to feel wonder; to be curious; to speculate; to marvel.

Wonder *n* Stevie [Steveland Judkins] (1950–) American soul, rock and pop singer, and pianist. Blind since infancy, he achieved fame early and has had long-lasting success.

wonderful *adj* marvelous.—**wonderfully** *adv*.

wonderland *n* a land full of marvels.

wonderment *n* astonishment, awe; curiosity.

wondrous *adj* (*poet*) wonderful, marvelous.

wonky *adj* (**wonkier, wonkiest**) (*sl*) crooked, unsteady.

Wonsan *n* a city in the Democratic People's Republic of Korea.

wont *adj* accustomed; inclined. * *n* habit.

woo *vt* (**wooing, wooed**) to seek to attract with a view to marriage; to court; to solicit eagerly.—**wooer** *n*.

WoO *abbr* (*German*) = Werke ohne Opuszahl, "works without an opus number" (Beethoven's unpublished works).

wood *n* the hard fibrous substance under the bark of trees; trees cut or sawn, timber; a thick growth of trees.

Wood *n* 1. Sir Henry [Joseph] (1869–1940) English conductor and founder of the London Promenade Concerts (the "Proms") in 1895. 2. John (Elder) (1704–54), English architect. His notable works include Queen Square and others, Bath. 3. John (Younger) (1728–82) English architect. His notable works include Royal Crescent, Bath.

wood alcohol *n* methanol.

woodbine *n* wild honeysuckle.

woodchuck *n* a North American marmot with thick reddish-brown fur.—*also* **groundhog**.

woodcock *n* a game bird related to the snipe.

woodcraft *n* skill in living and surviving in the forest, esp hunting; skill at woodwork.

woodcut *n* an engraving made on wood; a print made from this.

woodcutter *n* a person whose job is to cut down trees.

wooded *adj* covered with trees.

wooden *adj* made of wood; stiff.

wood engraving *n* the art of engraving illustrations on wood; (a print taken from) a piece of engraved wood.

woodenhead *n* (*inf*) a foolish person.

Woodhenge *n* a site and sacred monument in Wiltshire, England, near Stonehenge.

woodland *n* land covered with trees.

Woodland culture *n* a mix of similar cultures from eastern North America. Living in forests and by water, agricultural life was established by *c*.1250 BC.

woodlouse *n* (*pl* **woodlice**) a small ground-dwelling wingless crustacean with a segmented body that can roll itself into a ball.

woodman *n* (*pl* **woodmen**) a forester or woodcutter.

wood nymph *n* (*Greek myth*) a nymph of the woods, a dryad.

woodpecker *n* a bird that pecks holes in trees to extract insects.

wood pigeon *n* a large European wild pigeon with white patches of feathers on the body and neck.

woodpile *n* a pile of wood, esp firewood.

wood pulp *n* wood that has been pulped and treated for papermaking.

Woods *n* Tiger (1975–) American golfer of prodigious ability and winner of many major titles after turning professional in 1996.

wood screw *n* a pointed metal screw with an external thread and slotted head designed to be driven into wood with a screwdriver.

woodshed *n* a small shed for storing wood (e.g., firewood), tools, gardening equipment, etc.

woodsman *n* (*pl* **woodsmen**) a person who lives and works in a wood; a woodman.

woodwind *n* section of an orchestra in which wind instruments, originally made of wood, are played.

woodwork *n* carpentry.

woodworm *n* (*esp Brit*) an insect larva that bores into wood; the damage in furniture so caused.

woody *adj* (**woodier, woodiest**) covered in trees.

woof[1] *n* the horizontal threads crossing the warp in a woven fabric.

woof[2] *interj* a noise like the bark of a dog. * *vi* to make this sound.

woofer *n* a loudspeaker.

wool *n* the fleece of sheep and other animals; thread or yarn spun from the coats of sheep; cloth made from this yarn.

woolen, woollen *adj* made of wool.

Woolf *n* [**Adeline**] **Virginia** (1882–1941) English novelist and critic whose novels include *To the Lighthouse*.

woolgathering *n* idle daydreaming.— **woolgather** *vi*.—**woolgatherer** *n*.

woolly bear *n* a large furry caterpillar produced by the tiger moth.

woolsack *n* the official seat of the Lord Chancellor in the British House of Lords (formerly made from a large sack of wool).

woolsorter's disease *n* a former name for anthrax.

Woolworth *n* **Frank Winfield** (1852–1919) American businessman and founder of the F W Woolworth chain of stores.

wooly, woolly *adj* (**woolier, wooliest** *or* **woollier, woolliest**) of, like or covered with wool; indistinct, blurred; muddled. * *n* (*pl* **woollies**) (*inf*) a woolen garment.—**wooliness, woolliness** *n*.

woozy *adj* (**woozier, wooziest**) (*inf*) mentally confused, dazed; dizzy, nauseous.

wop *n* (*derog*) an Italian.

word *n* a single unit of language in speech or writing; talk, discussion; a message; a promise; a command; information; a password; (*pl*) lyrics; (*pl*) a quarrel. * *vt* to put into words, to phrase; to flatter.

word blindness *n* alexia or dyslexia.

word count *n* (*comput*) a feature of many programs that provides the user with the total number of words contained in a document.

word for word *adj*, *adv* (*a translation, etc*) using exactly the same words, verbatim.

wording *n* the way in which words are used, esp in written form; a choice of words.

word-perfect *adj* able to repeat something without mistake.—*also* **letter-perfect**.

wordplay *n* verbal wit or repartee.

word processing *n, vt* (*comput*) a method of document preparation, storage, and editing, using a microcomputer/personal computer.

word processor *n* computer software that allows the input, formatting, storage, and printing of text electronically; the hardware, including microprocessor, monitor, keyboard, and printer, required to operate word-processing software.

Wordsworth *n* 1. **Dorothy** (1771–1855) English writer, sister of William Wordsworth. She kept journals which were not published until after her death. The most famous of these is the *Grasmere Journal*, which contains many superb passages describing people and landscapes that her brother used as the basis for some of his poems. 2. **William** (1770–1850) English poet. He met Coleridge in 1795 and they published their great joint volume *Lyrical Ballads* in 1798. He became poet laureate in 1843.

word wrap *n* (*comput*) a feature of word processing programs that automatically moves words down to the next line if they go beyond the right-hand margin.

wordy *adj* (**wordier, wordiest**) verbose.

wore *see* **wear**.

work[1] *n* employment, occupation; a task; the product of work; manner of working; place of work; a literary composition; (*pl*) a factory, plant. * *vi* to be employed, to have a job; to operate (a machine, etc); to produce effects; (*with* **on**) to (attempt to) persuade by persistent effort; (*with* **out**) to undertake a regular, planned series of exercises. * *vt* to effect, to achieve; (*with* **off**) to eliminate though effort; (*with* **over**) to examine closely; (*inf*) to assault violently. —**workable** *adj*.—**worker** *n*.

work[2] *n* (*physics*) the transfer of energy (i.e., the changing of energy into a different form) as in potential energy into kinetic energy or chemical energy into heat energy.

workaday *adj* suited for working days; ordinary, mundane.

workaholic *n* a person with a compulsive need to work.

workbench *n* a bench designed for woodworking, metalworking, etc.

workbook *n* an exercise book with spaces for answers to set questions; (*comput*) a three-dimensional spreadsheet.

workbox *n* a box for holding material and tools for work.

workday *see* **working day**.

workers' cooperative *n* a form of business organization that is owned and controlled by those who work in it.

work ethic *n* belief in the moral value of work.

work force *n* the number of workers who are engaged in a particular industry; the total number of workers who are potentially available.

work group *n* (*comput*) a small group of employees assigned to work together on a specific project.

workhorse *n* a horse used for work on a farm; (*inf*) a person or thing that works the hardest in an organization, business, etc.

workhouse *n* (*formerly*) in UK, a public institution for paupers; in US, a prison for petty offenders whose sentences are served by manual labor.

working *adj* spent in or used for work; functioning. * *n* operation; mode of operation; (*pl*) the manner of functioning or operating; (*pl*) the parts of a mine that are worked.

working capital *n* liquid capital available for the daily operation of a business.

working class *n* people who work for wages, esp manual workers; proletariat.— *also adj*.

working day *or* **workday** *n* a day for working as opposed to a holiday; the number of hours spent working during the day.

working drawing *n* a plan or drawing used to guide a builder, engineer, etc during the actual construction.

working party *n* (*esp Brit*) a committee established to investigate a particular problem.

work in progress *n* goods that are still in the production or assembly process in a company.

workload *n* the amount of work done or required to be done in a particular period.

workman *n* (*pl* **workmen**) a person employed in manual labor; a person who works in a particular manner.

workmanlike *adj* skillful.

workmanship *n* technical skill; the way a thing is made, style.

workmate *n* (*Brit*) a colleague with whom one works.

work of art *n* a fine painting, sculpture, building, etc; something that has the aesthetic qualities of a work of art.

work-out *n* a session of strenuous physical exercises.

workroom *n* a room for work, a workshop.

worksheet *n* (*comput*) a matrix of rows and columns in a spreadsheet program into which are entered headings, numbers, and formulae.

workshop *n* a room or building where work is done; a seminar for specified intensive study, work, etc.

workshy *adj* (*Brit*) disinclined to work.

work station *n* a place in an office, esp a desk equipped with a computer terminal, where a single person works; (*comput*) a desktop computer in a local area network that serves as an access point to the network.

work study *n* a system of techniques used to analyze human work processes.

worktop *n* (*Brit*) an area in a kitchen, usu with a laminated surface, where food is prepared.

work-to-rule *n* (*Brit*) industrial action in which employees adhere strictly to rules and regulations in the workplace with the aim of slowing production.—**work to rule** *vi*.

world *n* the planet earth and its inhabitants; mankind; the universe; a sphere of existence; the public.

worldbeater *n* someone or something surpassing all others, a champion.— **worldbeating** *adj*.

world-class *adj* of the highest quality in the world.

World Cup *n* an international soccer championship competition held very four years, alternately in Europe and North or South America, the national teams being selected through a series of preliminary tournaments.

worldly *adj* (**worldlier, worldliest**) earthly, rather than spiritual; material; experienced.

world music *n* popular music of or combining ethnic styles from various different countries around the world.

world power *n* a country that is powerful enough to influence international politics.

World Series *n* an annual competition (best of seven games) between the winning teams of the two major North American baseball leagues.

world-shaking *adj* of momentous significance.

World War I *n* a war (1914–18) in which Belgium, France, Italy, Japan, Russia, UK, US, and other allies defeated Germany, Austria, Bulgaria, and Turkey.

World War II *n* a war (1939–45) in which France, UK, US, USSR, and other allies defeated Germany, Italy, and Japan.

world-weary *adj* tired of life.

worldwide *adj* universal.

worldwide web *n* (*comput*) a hypertext-based document retrieval system linked to the Internet.

worm *n* an earthworm; an insect larva; the thread of a screw. * *vt* to work (oneself into a position) slowly or secretly; to extract information by slow and persistent means.

WORM (*acronym*) (*comput*) *w*rite once *r*ead *m*any times: an optical disk that stores information which cannot then be overwritten, used for data archiving and backup.

worm-eaten *adj* eaten into (as if) by worms; decayed; antiquated.

Wormley *n* **Edward** (1907–95) American furniture designer who worked in Chicago and New York.

worms *n sing* any disease or condition caused by infestation with parasitic worms.

worm's-eye view *n* the view from the very bottom or humblest position.

Wormt *abbr* = write once, read many times.

wormwood *n* a European plant that yields a bitter oil used in making absinthe; (something causing) bitterness.

wormy *adj* (**wormier, wormiest**) infested with or eaten by worms; resembling a worm; full of holes caused by burrowing worms.

worn *see* **wear**.

worn-out *adj* (*machine, etc*) past its useful life; (*person*) depressed, tired.

worriment *n* (*inf*) worry, anxiety.

worrisome *adj* causing worry; prone to anxiety.

worry *vb* (**worrying, worried**) *vt* to bother, pester, harass. * *vi* to be uneasy or anxious; to fret. * *n* (*pl* **worries**) a cause or feeling of anxiety.—**worrier** *n*.

worry beads *npl* a string of beads fiddled with for comfort or to relieve tension.

worse *adj* (*compar of* **bad** *and* **ill**) less favorable; not so well as before. * *adv* with great severity.—**worsen** *vti*.

worship *n* religious adoration; a religious ritual, e.g. prayers; devotion. * *vb* (**worshiping, worshiped** *or* **worshipping, worshipped**) *vt* to adore or idolize. * *vi* to participate in a religious service.—**worshiper, worshipper** *n*.

worshipful *adj* feeling or displaying worship or respect; (*with cap*) in UK, used as a title of respect for various high-ranking officials.

worst *adj* (*superl of* **bad** *or* **ill**; *see also* **worse**) bad or ill in the highest degree; of the lowest quality. * *adv* to the worst degree. * *n* the least good part.

worst-case *adj* being, or taking account of, the worst possible situation or outcome (*worst-case scenario*).

worsted *n* twisted thread or yarn made from long, combed wool.

worth *n* value; price; excellence; importance. * *adj* equal in value to; meriting.

worthless *adj* valueless; useless; of bad character.—**worthlessness** *n*.

worthwhile *adj* important or rewarding enough to justify the effort.

worthy *adj* (**worthier, worthiest**) virtuous; deserving. * *n* (*pl* **worthies**) a worthy person, a local celebrity.—**worthily** *adv*.

Wosac *abbr* = worldwide synchronization of atomic clocks.

WOSB *abbr* = War Office Selection Board.

Wouk *n* **Herman** (1915–) American novelist whose books include *The Caine Mutiny* (1951).

would *see* **will**[2].

would-be *adj* aspiring or professing to be.

wouldn't = would not.

wound[1] *n* any cut, bruise, hurt, or injury caused to the skin; hurt feelings. * *vt* to injure.

wound[2] *see* **wind**[2].

wove, woven *see* **weave**.

wow *interj* exclamation of astonishment. * *n* (*sl*) a success.

WOW *abbr* = War on Want; Wider Opportunities for Women; Women Against the Ordination of Women; World of Water; waiting on weather.

wp *abbr* = weather permitting.

wp. *abbr* = worship.

w.p. *abbr* = wire payment.

WP *abbr* = Warsaw Pact; Workers Party (Ireland); word processing; word processor.

w.p.a. *abbr* = (*marine ins*) with particular average.

WPA *abbr* = Water Polo Association; Wire Products Association; World Pheasant Association; World Presbyterian Alliance.

wpb *abbr* = wastepaper basket.

WPBS *abbr* = Welsh Plant Breeding Station.

WPBSA *abbr* = World Professional Billiards and Snooker Association.

WPC *abbr* = Welsh Pricing Committee; Woman Police Constable; World Print Council.

WPCS *abbr* = Welsh Pony and Cob Society; White Park Cattle Society.

wpful. *abbr* = worshipful.

WPG *abbr* = Workers Power Group.

WPGA *abbr* = Women's Professional Golf Association.

WPI *abbr* = wholesale price index.

wpm *abbr* = words per minute.

WPM *abbr* = World Presbyterian Missions.

WPMSF *abbr* = World Professional Marathon Swimming Federation.

WPO *abbr* = World Ploughing Organization.

WPRA *abbr* = Waste Paper Recovery Association.

WPS *abbr* = Wireless Preservation Society and National Wireless Museum.

wr. *abbr* = writing paper.

w.r. *abbr* = warehouse receipts; (*ins*) war risk.

WR *abbr* = Western Region; West Riding (former part of Yorkshire); (*Latin*) *Wilhelmus Rex*, "King William."

WRA *abbr* = Windsurfing Retailers Association.

WRAAC *abbr* = Women's Royal Australian Army Corps.

WRAAF *abbr* = Women's Royal Australian Air Force.

WRAC *abbr* = Women's Royal Army Corps.

wrack[1] *n* destruction; **wrack and ruin** (the remains of) something destroyed.

wrack[2] *n* seaweed deposited on the shore.

WRAF *abbr* = Women's Royal Air Force.

WRAG *abbr* = Welsh Railways Action Group.

wraith *n* an apparition of a living person, supposedly a sign of impending death; any ghost.

wrangle *vi* to argue; to dispute noisily. * *n* a noisy argument.

wrap *vt* (**wrapping, wrapped**) to fold (paper) around (a present, purchase etc); to wind (around); to enfold; (*with* **up**) to enclose in paper; (*inf*) to make the final arrangements for. * *vi* (*with* **up**) to put warm clothes on; (*inf*) to be quiet. * *n* a shawl.

wrap around type *n* (*comput*) type that is contoured so that it surrounds a graphic item in a document.

wrapper *n* one who or that which wraps; a book jacket; a light dressing gown.

wrasse *n* a marine food fish with thick lips and brilliant coloration.

wrath *n* intense anger; rage.—**wrathful** *adj*.

Wratinsky *n* 1. **Paul** (1756–1808) an Austrian violinist, composer, and conductor. His compositions include much forgotten dramatic music, 12 symphonies, chamber music, and the opera, *Oberon*. 2. **Anton Wratinsky** (1761–1808) brother of Paul Wratinsky, he was a violinist and conductor.

WRB *abbr* = Water Resources Board.

WRBS *abbr* = Wholesale and Retail Bakers of Scotland.

WRC *abbr* = Water Research Center; Women's Resource Center.

WRDC *abbr* = White Rose Dollmakers' Circle; Wool Research and Development Corporation.

wreak *vt* to inflict or exact (e.g., vengeance, havoc).

wreath *n* (*pl* **wreaths**) a twisted ring of leaves, flowers, etc; something like this in shape.

wreathe *vti* to form into a wreath; to decorate with wreaths; to move or coil in wreaths.

wreck *n* accidental destruction of a ship; a badly damaged ship; a run-down person or thing. * *vt* to destroy; to ruin.

wreckage *n* the process of wrecking; remnants from a wreck.

wrecked *adj* (*sl*) intoxicated by alcohol or drugs; exhausted.

wrecker *n* a person who causes a wreck; a demolition worker; a breakdown van.

wren *n* small brownish songbird, with a short erect tail.

Wren *n* **Sir Christopher** (1632–1723) English architect who was commissioned to rebuild St Paul's Cathedral (completed 1710) after the Great Fire of London in 1666. He also designed many other new London churches.

wrench *vt* to give something a violent pull or twist; to injure with a twist, to sprain; to distort. * *n* a forceful twist; a sprain; a spanner; emotional upset caused by parting.

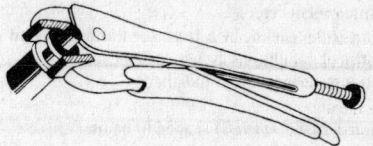

wrest *vt* to take with force (from); to seize; to obtain by toil.

wrestle *vti* to fight by holding and trying to throw one's opponent down; to struggle. * *n* a contest in which the opponents wrestle.—**wrestler** *n*.

wrestling *n* the skill or sport of fighting by grappling and trying to throw each other to the ground.

wretch *n* a miserable or pitied person; a despised and scorned person.

wretched *adj* very miserable; in poor circumstances; despicable.—**wretchedly** *adv*.—**wretchedness** *n*.

WRF *abbr* = World Rehabilitation Fund; World Runner Foundation.

WRG *abbr* = Waterway Recovery Group.

WRI *abbr* = Women's Rural Institute; war risks insurance.

wrier, wriest *see* **wry**.

wriggle *vi* to move with a twisting motion; to squirm, to writhe; to use evasive tricks.—*also n*.—**wriggler** *n*.—**wriggly** *adj*.

wright *n* a maker (as in *playwright*), a builder (as in *shipwright*).

Wright *n* 1. **Frank Lloyd** (1867–1959) America's greatest architect, designer, and theorist, who revolutionized the approach to design. His notable works include the Larkin Building, Buffalo; the Imperial Hotel, Tokyo; the Guggenheim Museum, New York. 2. **Orville** (1871–1948) and **Wilbur** (1867–1912) American aviators and brothers who designed and built the first heavier-than-air flying machine. 3. **Russel** (1904–76) important American designer of domestic goods and the first designer to have his name credited in the manufacturer's advertising.

wring *vt* (**wringing, wrung**) to twist; to compress by twisting in order to squeeze water from; to pain; to obtain forcibly.

wrinkle *n* a small crease or fold on a surface. * *vti* to make or become wrinkled.

wrist *n* the joint connecting the hand with the forearm.

wristband *n* the cuff of a sleeve that covers the wrist; a band round the wrist that absorbs sweat.

wristguard *or* **bracer** *n* (*archeo*) a plate of stone or bone fastened to the wrist of a bowman to prevent injury from the bow string.

wristwatch *n* a watch worn on a bracelet or strap around the wrist.

writ *n* (*law*) a written court order.

write[1] *vb* (**writing, wrote,** *pp* **written**) *vt* to form letters on paper with a pen or pencil; to express in writing; to compose (a letter, music, literary work, etc); to communicate by letter; (*with* **off**) to cancel a bad debt as a loss; (*inf*) to damage (a vehicle) beyond repair; (*with* **down**) *vt* to put in writing; to harm or demean (a person) in writing; (*with* **up**) to describe, update, or put into finished form by writing; to praise or publicize in writing. * *vi* to be a writer; (*with* **down to** *or* **for**) to write in a simplified style for a less educated taste.

write[2] *vti* (*comput*) an operation of the central processing unit that records information on to a computer's RAM or secondary storage media such as disk drives.

write-off *n* a debt canceled as a loss; (*inf*) a badly damaged car.

write/protect *vti* (*comput*) to protect a file or disk so that a user cannot modify or erase its data.

writer *n* an author; a scribe or clerk.

writer's cramp *n* painful spasms or paralysis in the thumb and fingers from excessive writing.

write-up *n* a published report or review, esp a favorable one.

writhe *vi* to twist the body violently, as in pain; to squirm (under, at).

writing *n* the act of forming letters on paper, etc; a written document; authorship; (*pl*) literary works.

writing-down allowance *n* (*com*) a capital allowance, introduced in 1993, available for plant and machinery used in trade in the UK.

writing paper *n* paper treated to accept ink and used esp for letters.

written *see* **write**.

written-down value *n* the accounting value of a fixed asset in a firm's balance sheet. This value represents the original initial cost minus any cumulative depreciation.

WRM *abbr* = World Rainforest Movement.

WRN *abbr* = Woman Returners Network.

Wrnach *n* (*Welsh Celtic myth*) a giant who owned a sword that Culhwch had to get hold of as one of the tasks imposed on him by Yspaddaden. Cet obtained the sword by trickery and killed Wrnach.

WRNR *abbr* = Women's Royal Naval Reserve.

WRNS *abbr* = Women's Royal Naval Service.

wrnt. *abbr* = warrant.

WRO *abbr* = war risks only.

Wroclaw *n* city in Poland.

wrong *adj* not right, incorrect; mistaken, misinformed; immoral. * *n* harm; injury done to another. * *adv* incorrectly. * *vt* to do wrong to.—**wrongly** *adv*.

wrongdoer *n* a person who breaks (moral) laws.—**wrongdoing** *n*.

wrongful *adj* unwarranted, unjust.—**wrongfully** *adv*.

wrongful dismissal *n* the dismissal of an employee which contravenes the terms of his or her employment contract.

wrongful trading *n* the trading by a company during a period when it has no reasonable chance of avoiding insolvency or liquidation.

wrong-headed *adj* stubborn; of poor judgment.

wrote *see* **write**.

wrought *adj* formed; made; (*metals*) shaped by hammering, etc.

wrought iron *n* iron that is forged or rolled, not cast.

WRP *abbr* = Workers' Revolutionary Party.

WRRA *abbr* = Women's Road Records Association (cycling).

WRSA *abbr* = World Rabbit Science Association.

WRST *abbr* = World Rainforest Survival Trust.

wrt *abbr* = with respect to.

WRU *abbr* = Welsh Rugby Union.

wrung *see* **wring**.

WRVS *abbr* = Women's Royal Voluntary Service.

wry *adj* (**wryer, wryest** *or* **wrier, wriest**) twisted, contorted; ironic.—**wryly** *adv*.—**wryness** *n*.

wryneck *n* (*med*) the condition when the head is twisted to one side because of a scar contracting or, more commonly, excessive muscle contraction.—*also* **torticollis**.

WS *abbr* = The Wilderness Society; Web Society; Writer to the Signet.

WSA *abbr* = Water Services Association; West of Scotland Agricultural College; Wine & Spirit Association of Great Britain and Northern Ireland; Women Sport Australia; World Service Authority.

WSAS *abbr* = Wine and Spirit Association of Scotland.

WSAVA *abbr* = World Small Animal Veterinary Association.

WSB *abbr* = World Scout Bureau.

WSBA *abbr* = Welsh Schools Basketball Association.

WSC *abbr* = Welfare State Campaign; Western Sahara Campaign; World Series Cricket; World Spiritual Council.

WSCA *abbr* = Welsh Schools Cricket Association.

WSF *abbr* = Women's Sports Foundation; World Scout Foundation.

WSGF *abbr* = Welsh Seed Growers Federation.

WSJ *abbr* = *Wall Street Journal*.

WSMR *abbr* = White Sands Missile Range.

WSO *abbr* = World Sikh Organization; World Simulation Organization.

WSPA *abbr* = World Society for Protection of Animals.

WSPU *abbr* = Women's Social and Political Union.

WSRS *abbr* = Wildlife Sound Recording Society.

WSS *abbr* = World Ship Society.

WSSA *abbr* = Weed Science Society of America; Welsh Secondary Schools Association.

w.s.w., WSW *abbr* = west-southwest.

wt, wt. *abbr* = weight.

w/t *abbr* = wireless telegraphy.

WT *abbr* = weekly takings.

WTA *abbr* = Women's Tennis Association.

WTB *abbr* = Wales Tourist Board.

WTN *abbr* = Worldwide Television News.

WTO *abbr* = Warsaw Treaty Organization.

WTO, WTrO *abbr* = World Trade Organization.

WToO *abbr* = World Tourism Organization.

WTT *abbr* = World Team Tennis.

WTUC *abbr* = World Trade Union Conference.

WU *abbr* = Women's Union.

Wuffa *n* (*d. c.*578) a king of East Anglia, Britain (571–*c*.578); considered to be the first king of the East Angles.

Wuhan *n* a city in China.

Wulfhere *n* (*d.* 675) a king of Mercia, Britain (657–675); a younger brother of Peada.

Wulfstan *n* Saint (1009–95) English monk; the last of the Anglo-Saxon saints; bishop of Worcester (1062). Fought the slave trade in Bristol; enforced the discipline of priestly celibacy. His feast day is January 19.

wunderkind *n* (*pl* **wunderkinder, wunderkinds**) a child prodigy; a whizz kid.

WUR *abbr* = World University Roundtable.

wurst *n* any of various types of spicy sausage from Germany or Austria.

w/v *abbr* = weight in volume.

W. Va. *abbr* = West Virginia.

WVRSC *abbr* = Wholesale Vegetable and Root Seeds Committee.

WVS *abbr* = Women's Voluntary Service.

w/w *abbr* = wall to wall; weight for weight.

WW *abbr* = world war.

W/W *abbr* = warehouse warrant.

WWI *abbr* = World War I.

WWII abbr = World War II.

WWA *abbr* = War Widows Association of Great Britain; Welsh Water Authority; World Wrestling Federation; Woven Wire Association.

WWGBP *abbr* = World Working Group on Birds of Prey and Owls (Germany).

WWHA *abbr* = Welsh Women's Hockey Association.

WWO *abbr* = Wing Warrant Officer.

WWOOF *abbr* = Working Weekends on Organic Farms.

WWP *abbr* = World Wide Peace.

WWSU *abbr* = World Water Ski Union.

WWT *abbr* = Wildfowl & Wetlands Trust.

WWTA *abbr* = Welsh Weight Training Association; Woolen and Worsted Trades Association.

WWW *abbr* = Women Welcome Women; World Weather Watch; (Internet) World Wide Web.

WWWC *abbr* = World Without War Council.

WX *abbr* = (clothing size) Women's Extra.

WY *abbr* = Wyoming.

Wyatt *n* 1. **Benjamin D** (1775–1850) English architect. His notable works include Drury Lane Theatre, London. 2. **James** (1746–1813) English architect. His notable works include Castle Coole, Northern Ireland. 3. **Samuel** (*b.* 1737) English architect. His notable works include Doddington Hall, Cheshire. 4. **Sir Thomas** (1503–42) English poet and diplomat whose main claim to literary fame rests on several striking love poems and his role as popularizer of the sonnet form in English.

WYC *abbr* = World Youth Choir.

Wycherley *n* **William** (1641–1715) English dramatist whose two best-known comedies are *The Country Wife* and *The Plain Dealer*.

Wyman, Bill *see* **Jagger, Mick**.

Wyndham *n* **John** [John Wyndham Parkes Lucas Benton Harris] (1903–69) novelist and short-story writer whose best-known works are the science fiction novels *The Day of the Triffids*, *The Kraken Wakes*, *The Midwich Cuckoos*, and *Trouble with Lichen*.

Wyo., Wy. *abbr* = Wyoming.

"Wyoming" *n* the official song of the American state of Wyoming.

Wyoming *or* **WY** *n* a state of the USA of which the capital is Cheyenne.

WYSA *abbr* = Woolen Yarn Spinners Association.

WYSIWYG *adj* (*acronym*) (*comput*) *w*hat *y*ou *s*ee *i*s *w*hat *y*ou *g*et: meaning that the layout and style of text, etc, on screen will be exactly as printed out.

WZO *abbr* = World Zionist Organization.

X

x, X *n* the 24th letter of the English alphabet; something shaped like an X; the mark used by an illiterate person to represent a signature; a mark (on a map) to show a particular spot.

x *symbol* (*math*) the x-axis or a coordinate along the x-axis; ex, as in ex coupon, ex dividend, etc

X *symbol* Christ (from the shape of chi, the Greek capital initial letter of *Christos*); Christian; (*chem*) xenon (element); (*chem*) a univalent negative radical, in formulae; the Roman numeral for 10; (*Brit*) former film censorship classification which limited viewing to those over 18, now replaced by the symbol 18; an unknown or mysterious factor; (*math*) unknown quantity; a symbol indicating error.

xanth-, xantho- *prefix* yellow.

Xanthe *n* (*Greek myth*) one of the daughters of Oceanus.

xanthein *n* a soluble yellow pigment found in plant tissue.

xanthelasma *n* yellow fatty deposit in the eyelids and skin around the eyes.

xanthic *adj* yellowish; of or relating to xanthine.

xanthine *n* an insoluble yellow pigment found in plant tissue; a yellowish-white crystalline compound allied to uric acid; a derivative of this.

Xanthippe *n* the wife of Socrates (*fl.*5th century BC); a quarrelsome scolding wife.

xantho-, xanth- *prefix* yellow.

xanthochroid *adj* blond and blue-eyed with fair white skin. * *n* an xanthochroid person.

xanthochromia *n* a yellow coloring, e.g. the skin in jaundice or the cerebrospinal fluid when it contains hemoglobin breakdown products.

xanthoma *n* (*pl* **xanthomas, xanthomata**) a small yellow tumor in the skin caused by deposits of lipids.—**xanthomatous** *adj*.

xanthophyll *n* (*bot*) an orange or yellow pigment in autumn leaves.—**xanthophyllous** *adj*.

xanthopsia *n* a disturbance in vision causing everything to appear yellow.

xanthosis *n* a yellow pigmentation of the skin in diabetes, etc.

xanthous *adj* yellow.

Xanthus[1] *n* (*Greek myth*) a king of the Pelasgians at Argos, who later settled in the island of Lesbos.

Xanthus[2] **and Balius** *n* (*Greek myth*) the immortal horses of Achilles.

x-axis *n* (*pl* **x-axes**) the reference axis of a graph along which the x coordinate is measured.

x-c *abbr* = cross-country (skiing).

x-c., x-cp., XC *abbr* = ex coupon.

X-chromosome *n* one of the pair (with the Y-chromosome) of sex chromosomes that occur in females.

xcut. *abbr* = crosscut.

x-d., x-div., XD *abbr* = ex dividend.

XDR *abbr* = extended dynamic range (cassettes).

Xe *symbol* (*chem*) xenon.

xebec *n* a small three-masted Mediterranean sailing vessel with lateen sails.

Xenakis *n* **Lannis** (1922–) a Romanian-born, Greek composer who trained to be an architect in Paris.

xeno-, xen- *prefix* strange; foreign.

xenolith *n* (*geol*) a rock occurring in a system of rocks to which it does not belong.

xenomorphic *adj* (*mineral grain*) abnormal in shape owing to the pressure of adjacent minerals in rock.

xenon *n* a heavy inert colorless odorless gaseous element found in tiny quantities in the atmosphere.

xenophobia *n* fear or dislike of strangers or foreigners.—**xenophobe** *n*. —**xenophobic** *adj*.

Xenophon *n* (*c*.435–354 BC) Greek soldier and historian. He led the Greek forces back through Persian territory in its 1,500-mile march to the Black Sea, a journey described in his *Anabasis*. His other works include a history of Greece, *Hellenics*.

xer-, xero- *prefix* dryness.

xeroderma, xerodermia *n* dryness of the skin caused by a deficiency in secretions from the sebaceous glands.

xerography *n* photocopying by using light to form an electrostatic image on a photoconductive plate to which toner powder adheres, the particles then being fused by heat and the image transferred onto paper.—**xerographic** *adj*.—**xerographically** *adv*.

xerophilous *adj* (*plant*) drought-loving; adapted to a dry climate.—**xerophily** *n*.

xerophthalmia *n* a disease of the eye with dryness and ulceration of the cornea, caused by vitamin deficiency.—**xerophthalmic** *adj*.

xerophyte *n* a xerophilous plant, e.g. cactus, that has adapted for growth with a limited water supply.—**xerophytic** *adj*.

xerostomia *n* abnormal dryness of the mouth caused by failure of the salivary glands.

Xerox *n* (*trademark*) a photocopying process using xerography; the copy produced by this. * *vt* to produce a copy in this way.

Xerxes I *n* Egyptian pharaoh of the 27th Dynasty who ruled 486–465 BC.

x-height *n* (*print*) the height of the letter x in lowercase.

Xhosa *n* (*pl* **Xhosa, Xhosas**) a member of a Negroid people of southern Africa; the Bantu language of these people.

xi *n* (*pl* **xis**) the 14th letter of the Greek alphabet.

x-i., x-int., X.i. *abbr* = ex interest.

xiphisternum *n* (*pl* **xiphisterna**) (*anat, zool*) the lowest part of the breastbone, the xiphoid process.—**xiphisternal** *adj*.

xiphoid *adj* sword-shaped. * *n* the xiphoid process.

xiphoid process, xiphoid cartilage *n* the xiphisternum.

xlwb *abbr* = extra long wheelbase.

Xm., Xmas *abbr* = Christmas.

XML *abbr* (*comput*) = eXtensible Markup Language. A markup language for documents which enables the use of SGML on the worldwide web.

xmodem *n* (*comput*) an asynchronous file transfer protocol that facilitates error-free transmission of computer files through the telephone system.

XMS *abbr* (*comput*) = eXtended Memory Specification. A set of guidelines that standardize the method a programmer can use to access memory above 1,024 kilobytes.

xn *abbr* = ex new (without the right to new shares).

Xn. *abbr* = Christian.

x-n., X-N. *abbr* = ex new.

Xnty. *abbr* = Christianity.

Xois *n* (*Egypt*) a settlement in the Nile Delta, between Busiris and Buto; the home of the 14th Dynasty of Egyptian pharaohs.

XON/XOFF *n* (*comput*) a method of communicating between modems. *See also* **communications settings; handshaking**.

xr *abbr* = ex rights.

XR *abbr* = X-ray.

X-ray, x-ray *n* radiation of very short wavelengths, capable of penetrating solid bodies, and printing on a photographic plate a shadow picture of objects not permeable by light rays. * *vt* to photograph by X-rays.

X-ray astronomy *n* the study of distant bodies in space that are emitting X-rays, detected by the satellite ROSAT, launched in 1990.

X-ray binary *n* the most common source of bright galactic X-rays, derived from binary stars, in which one of the pair is a degenerate star such as a white dwarf, black hole, or neutron star.

X-ray burster *n* a source of cosmic X-rays, characterized by intense bursts of activity of a random nature.

X-ray diffraction *n* a method of analysis in which a beam of X-rays of a certain wavelength is fired at a crystal. It has been used in archeology to study Neolithic jade and pottery.

X-ray florescence spectrometry *n* an analytical technique used to determine the elements in a sample by bombarding it with X-rays and measuring the light given out by its atoms.

XRT *abbr* = X-ray therapy.

X-rts. *abbr* = ex-rights.

xs *abbr* = expenses.

XS *abbr* = cross-section.

XST *abbr* = experimental Stealth technology.

Xt. *abbr* = Christ.

Xtian. *abbr* = Christian.

Xty. *abbr* = Christianity.

Xuthus *n* (*Greek myth*) a king of the Peloponnese, and the father of Achaeus and Ion.

xw *abbr* = ex warrants.

xylem *n* the woody vegetable tissue in plants that conducts water and gives support.

xylo-, xyl- *prefix* wood.

xylograph *n* a wood engraving; an impression made from a wood block.

xylography *n* the art of making wood engravings or making woodcuts; the art of printing from wood blocks.—**xylographer** *n*. —**xylographic** *adj*.—**xylographically** *adv*.

xyloid *adj* like wood.

xylophagous *adj* (*insects*) wood-eating.

xylophone *n* a percussion instrument consisting of a series of wooden bars which are struck with small hammers.—**xylophonic** *adj*.

xylophonist *n* a performer on a xylophone.

xylotomous *adj* (*insects*) boring into or cutting wood.

x-y plotter *n* (*comput*) a printer that creates a drawing by plotting *x* and *y* coordinates provided by the application program, commonly used for CAD drawings, architectural drawings, and blueprints.

Y

y, Y *n* the 25th letter of the English alphabet; something shaped like a Y.

y *symbol* (*math*) the second unknown quantity.

Y *symbol* (*chem*) yttrium.

y. *abbr* = yard/s; year/s; (*elec*) admittance.

Y *abbr* = (*Japanese currency*) yen ; (*Chinese currency*) yuan.

Y2K *abbr* = Year 2000.

YAA *abbr* = Yachtsmens Association of America.

yabber *n* (*Austral sl*) talk, esp in broken English. * *vti* to talk.

yacht *n* a sailing or mechanically driven vessel, used for pleasure cruises or racing. * *vi* to race or cruise in a yacht.—yachting *n*. —yachtsman *n* (*pl* yachtsmen). —yachtswoman *nf* (*pl* yachtswomen).

yackety-yak *n* (*sl*) persistent trivial chatter.

YAF *abbr* = Young Americans for Freedom.

yah *sentence substitution* an informal word for yes;*interj* expressing derision;

yahoo *n* (*pl* yahoos) a crude, vicious person.

Yahweh, Yahveh *n* Jehovah.

yak[1] *n* a domesticated species of ox found in Tibet having horns and long hair.

yak[2] *n* (*sl*) persistent trivial talk or chatter. * *vi* (yakking, yakked) to talk in this way.

Yale lock *n* (*trademark*) a type of cylinder lock for doors.

yam *n* the edible, starchy tuberous root of a tropical climbing plant; sweet potato.

Yamaguchi *n* Kazama (1946–) Japanese industrial designer who became known for his lighting and vehicle body designs.

Yamasaki *n* Minoru (1912–86) American architect. His notable works include the American Concrete Institute, Detroit.

yamen *n* (*formerly*) the official residence of a Chinese mandarin.

yammer *vi* (*inf*) to whimper or whine constantly; (*inf*) to complain loudly and persistently. * *n* (*inf*) a whining or complaining sound.

Yamo *n* (1959–) Algerian designer whose 1990 table ser vice for Christofle was widely distributed.

Yamoussoukro *n* capital city of Côte D'Ivoire.

Yanagi *n* Sori (1915–) Japanese industrial designer whose best-known piece of wooden furniture was his 1955 *Butterfly* stool.

yang kin *n* (*mus*) a Chinese instrument furnished with brass strings which are struck with two little hammers, like a dulcimer.

Yang Shao *adj* relating to a Neolithic culture that flourished in the valley of the Yellow River in China from *c*.5000 BC.

yank *vti* to pull suddenly, to jerk. * *n* a sudden sharp pull.

Yank *n* (*inf*) a Yankee.

Yankee *n* (*inf*) a citizen of the US, an American.

Yankee bond *n* a bond issued in the USA by a foreign borrower.

"Yankee Doodle" *n* the official song of the American state of Connecticut.

Yaoundé *n* capital city of Cameroon.

yap *vi* (yapping, yapped) to yelp, bark; (*sl*) to talk constantly, esp in a noisy or irritating manner.

YAPLO *abbr* (*Brit*) = Yorkshire Association of Power Loom Workers.

yapok, yapock *n* a tropical American aquatic marsupial with webbed hind feet, thick fur, and a long tail.

YAR *abbr* = Yemen Arab Republic.

yard[1] *n* a unit of measure of three feet and equivalent to 0.9144 meters; (*naut*) a spar hung across a mast to support a sail.

yard[2] *n* an enclosed concrete area, esp near a building; an enclosure for a commercial activity (e.g., a shipyard); an area of ground for growing herbs, fruits, flowers, or vegetables, usu attached to a house, a garden; an area with tracks for the making up of trains, servicing of locomotives, etc.

yardage[1] *n* a length measured in yards.

yardage[2] *n* the use of a yard; the charge made for this.

yardang *n* a long ridge of rock, lying along the direction of the prevailing wind in a desert, formed as the wind removes all the loose material on either side of it.

yardarm *n* (*naut*) either half of a yard.

yard goods *npl* fabrics of a standard width sold by the yard.

yardman *n* (*pl* yardmen) a worker in a railroad yard.

yardmaster *n* the manager of a railroad yard.

yardstick *n* a standard used in judging.

yare *adj* ready; active, brisk; (*yacht, etc*) easily handled.

yarmulke *n* a skullcap worn by Jewish men at prayer and by Orthodox male Jews at all times.

yarn *n* fibers of wool, cotton, etc spun into strands for weaving, knitting, etc; (*inf*) a tale or story. * *vi* to tell a yarn; to talk at length.

yarrow *n* a strongly scented astringent herb with clusters of small flowers.

YASGB *abbr* = Youth Association of Synagogues in Great Britain.

yashmak, yashmac *n* a veil worn by Muslim women, showing only the eyes.

yataghan, yatagan *n* a short curved Turkish sword without a guard.

yatter *vi* (*sl*) to gabble, to chatter.—*also n*.

yauld *adj* (*Scot*) active; alert.

yaupon *n* an American evergreen shrub of the holly family.

yaw *vi* (*ship, aircraft*) to deviate from a course; (*aircraft*) to turn from side to side about the vertical axis. * *vt* to cause to yaw. * *n* a yawing movement or course.

yawl *n* a two-masted sailing vessel with its aftermast at the stern.

yawn *vi* to open the jaws involuntarily and inhale, as from drowsiness; to gape.—*also n*.

yawning *adj* gaping; wide-open; drowsy.—yawningly *adv*.

yawp *vi* to cry harshly, to scream; (*sl*) to speak foolishly. * *n* such a cry or talk.

yaws *n sing* a tropical disease causing ulceration of the skin, frambesia.

y-axis *n* (*pl* y-axes) the reference axis of a graph along which the y-coordinate is measured.

Yayoi *n* the Bronze-Iron Age period in Japan, which began *c*.250 BC, following on from the Jomon period.

Yazlikaya *n* (*archeo*) a natural cleft in the cliffs near Boghaz Köy, Turkey, the faces of which are carved with relief figures and hieroglyphics dating to *c*.1300 BC.

yazoo *n* a tributary that is prevented from joining a main stream by levees that it cannot breach; after running parallel to the main stream, it will eventually find a suitable junction and be able to join the main river.

Yb *symbol* (*chem*) ytterbium.

YB *abbr* = Year Book.

YC *abbr* = Young Conservative; yacht club; youth club.

YCA *abbr* = Yacht Charter Association; Yacht Cruising Association.

YC & UO *abbr* = Young Conservation and Unionist Organization.

YCF *abbr* = Yacht Club de France.

Y-chromosome *n* one of the pair (with the X-chromosome) of sex chromosomes that occur in males. *See also* X-chromosome.

yclept *adj* (*arch*) named.

YCND *abbr* = Youth Campaign for Nuclear Disarmament.

yd., yds *abbr* = yard/s.

YD *abbr* = Youth Defense.

YDS *abbr* (*Brit*) = Yorkshire Dialect Society.

ye[1] *pron* (*arch*) you (the person addressed and others) the old method of printing the.

ye[2] *definite article* (*arch*) the.

YE *abbr* = Your Excellency.

yea *adv, n* (*arch*) yes.

yeah *sentence substitute* (*inf*) yes.

yean *vi* (*sheep, goat*) to bring forth (a lamb or kid).

yeanling *n* a lamb or kid.

year *n* a period of 12 months, or 365 or 366 days, beginning with January 1 and ending with December 31; a period of approximately 12 months.

yearb. *abbr* = yearbook.

yearbook *n* an annual publication reviewing the events of the previous year or bringing information up to date.

yearling *n* an animal a year old or in its second year.

yearling bond *n* a bond that is issued by a local authority and is redeemable one year after the issuing of it.

yearlong *adj* lasting a year.

yearly *adj* occurring every year; lasting a year. * *adv* once a year; from year to year.

yearn *vi* to feel desire (for); to long for.—yearning *n*.

yeast *n* a fungus that causes alcoholic fermentation, used in brewing and baking.

yeasty *adj* (yeastier, yeastiest) smelling of or containing yeast.—yeastiness *n*.

Yeats *n* 1. W[illiam] B[utler] (1865–1939) Anglo-Irish poet and dramatist and winner of the 1923 Nobel prize for literature. 2. Jack [John Butler] (1870–1957) brother of William Butler Yeats and an illustrator.

yegg, yegman *n* (*pl* **yeggs, yegmen**) (*sl*) a safecracker, a criminal.

yeld *adj* (*Scot*) barren, giving no milk.

yell *vti* to shout loudly; to scream; to emit a yell. * *n* a loud shout; a concerted cheer by supporters, students, etc, at a game.

yellow *adj* of the color of lemons, egg yolk, etc; having a yellowish skin; (*inf*) cowardly. * *n* the color yellow. * *vi* to become or turn yellow.

yellow-belly *n* (*pl* **yellow-bellies**) (*sl*) a coward.—**yellow-bellied** *adj*.

yellow fever *n* an infectious tropical fever caused by a virus transmitted by certain mosquitoes.

yellow fibrous tissue *n* tissue composed of the fibers of the protein elastin.

yellowhammer *n* a small European bird with a yellow head, neck, and breast.

yellow jacket *n* an American hornet or wasp with yellow markings.

yellow pages *npl* (part of) a telephone directory that lists business subscribers under different categories according to the type of service offered.

yellow spot *n* (*anat*) the point of acutest vision in the retina.

yellow streak *n* (*inf*) a cowardly nature.

yellowwood *n* an American tree; its wood, which yields a yellow dye.

yelp *vti* to utter a sharp, shrill cry or bark.—*also n*.

Yeltsin *n* **Boris Nikolayevich** (1931–) Russian politician and a former Politburo member; elected to the Congress of People's deputies in 1989; became president in 1990; re-elected in 1996; resigned in 1999 and succeeded by Vladimir Putin.

Yemen *n* a republic bounded by Saudi Arabia in the north, Oman in the east, the Gulf of Aden in the south and the Red Sea in the west.

yen[1] *n* (*pl* **yen**) the monetary unit of Japan. *See also* **riel; sen**.

yen[2] *n* (*inf*) a yearning, an ambition.

yeo. *abbr* = yeomanry.

yeoman *n* (*pl* **yeomen**) (*formerly*) a farmer who cultivated his own land; a non-commissioned officer in the navy, marines.

yeomanly *adj* of or like a yeoman; workmanlike.—*also adv*.

yeoman of the guard *n* a member of the British sovereign's veteran bodyguard.

yeomanry *n* yeomen collectively; in UK, a volunteer cavalry force raised from country districts as a home guard (1761–1907) now part of the Territorial Army.

yeoman service *n* effective assistance.

yep *sentence substitute* (*inf*) yes.

yerba (maté) *n* an infusion of dried leaves of the maté, which makes a mildly stimulating tea.

Yerevan *n* capital city of Armenia.

yes *sentence substitute* a word of affirmation or consent.

YES *abbr* = Youth Employment Service; Youth Enterprise Scheme; Young Entomologists Society.

yes man *n* a servile, fawning, sycophantic person.

yester *adv* (*rare*) of yesterday.

yesterday *n* the day before today; the recent past. * *adv* on the day before today; recently.

yet *adv* still; so far; even. * *conj* nevertheless; however; still.

YET *abbr* = Young Explorers Trust.

yeti *n* a mysterious animal thought to live high in the Himalayan mountains but never seen.—*also* **abominable snowman**.

Yevtushenko *n* **Yevgenii Aleksandrovich** (1933–) Russian poet. His best-known poem is *Babi Yar* (1962), a denunciation not only of the Nazi crimes against the Jews, but also of Russian anti-semitism.

yew *n* an evergreen tree or shrub with thin, sharp leaves and red berries.

YFC *abbr* = Young Farmers' Club.

YFCU *abbr* = Young Farmers' Clubs of Ulster.

Y-fronts *npl* (*trademark*) men's underpants with an inverted Y-shaped opening at the front.

Ygdrasil, Yggdrasil *n* (*Norse myth*) an ash tree whose roots and branches bind together earth, heaven, and hell.

YH *abbr* = youth hostel.

YHA *abbr* = Yacht Harbor Association; Youth Hostels Association.

YHAFHE *abbr* = Yorkshire and Humberside Association for Further and Higher Education.

YHANI *abbr* = Youth Hostels Association of Northern Ireland.

YHC *abbr* = Young Herpetologists Club.

yid *n* (*derog*) a Jew.

Yiddish *n* a mixed German and Hebrew dialect spoken by European Jews.

yield *vt* to resign; to give forth, to produce, as a crop, result, profit, etc. * *vi* to submit; to give way to physical force, to surrender. * *n* the amount yielded; the profit or return on a financial investment.

yip *n* a cry, an exclamation. * *vi* (**yipping, yipped**) to utter a yip.

yippee *interj* used to express exuberant delight.

YJA *abbr* = Yachting Journalists' Association; Young Journalists' Association.

ylang-ylang *n* a Malaysian tree with fragrant flowers; a perfume made from the flowers.

YLGN *abbr* = Young Labor Green Network.

YMBA *abbr* = Yacht and Motor Boat Association.

YMCA *abbr* = Young Men's Christian Association.

Y M Cath A *abbr* = Young Men's Catholic Association.

YMCK *abbr* (*comput*) = yellow, magenta (red), cyan (blue) and black. The basic colors used in printing.

YMCU *abbr* = Young Men's Christian Union.

YMFS *abbr* = Young Men's Friendly Society.

YMHA *abbr* = Young Men's Hebrew Association.

ymodem *n* (*comput*) an asynchronous file transfer protocol that is similar to xmodem but sends files in batches of 1,024k as opposed to 128k.

yn. *abbr* = (*Japanese currency*) yen.

Ynawag *n* (*Welsh Celtic myth*) one of the seven survivors of the expedition led by Bendigeid Vran or Bran the Blessed against Matholwch, then king of Ireland, to rescue Branwen.

yo *abbr* = year old.

yob, yobbo *n* (*pl* **yobs, yobbos**) (*sl*) a young lout, a hooligan.

yob *abbr* = year of birth.

yod *abbr* = year of death.

yodel *vti* (**yodeling, yodeled** *or* **yodelling, yodelled**) to sing, alternating from the ordinary voice to falsetto.—**yodeler, yodeller** *n*.

yoga *n* a system of exercises for attaining bodily and mental control and well-being.—**yogic** *adj*.

yogi *n* (*pl* **yogis, yogin**) a person skilled in yoga.

yogurt, yoghurt *n* a semi-liquid food made from milk curdled by bacteria.

yo-heave-ho *interj* (*formerly*) a cry made by sailors while heaving anchor, etc.

yoicks *interj* a foxhunting cry urging on the hounds.

yoke *n* a bond or tie; slavery; the wooden frame joining oxen to make them pull together; part of a garment that is fitted below the neck. * *vt* to put a yoke on; to join together.

yokel *n* (*derog*) a country person who is regarded as unsophisticated and simple-minded.

Yokohama *n* major city in Japan.

yolk *n* the yellow part of an egg.

yolk sac *n* the membrane enclosing an egg yolk.

yom *abbr* = year of marriage.

Yom Kippur *n* an annual Jewish holiday marked by fasting and prayer.—*also* **Day of Atonement**.

yomp *vi* to march laboriously carrying heavy equipment, esp over rough terrain.

yon *adj, adv* (*dial*) yonder, over there.

yonder *adv* over there.

Yonge *n* **Charlotte M[ary]** (1823–1901) English novelist. *The Heir of Radclyffe* is the only one of her many novels that is still regularly printed.

YOP *abbr* = Youth Opportunities Program.

yore *n* time long past.

Yorkist *n* an adherent of the royal house of York in England, esp during the Wars of the Roses (1455–85).—*also adj*.

Yorkshire pudding *n* a baked pudding made from batter and traditionally eaten with roast beef.

Yorkshire terrier *n* a small shaggy breed of terrier with a long coat of bluish gray and tan hair.

you *pron* (*gram*) 2nd person singular or plural; the person or persons spoken to.

you'd = you would; you had.

you'll = you will; you shall.

Youmans *n* **Vincent** (1898–1946) an American composer who is best known for his musicals, e.g.*No! No! Nanette* and *Hit the Deck*.

young *adj* in the early period of life; in the first part of growth; new; inexperienced. * *n* young people; offspring.

Young *n* 1. **Dennis** (1917–) British furniture and industrial designer whose best-known piece is the 1947 *Shell Chair*. 2. **Roland** (1887–1953) British film actor whose films include *Topper* (1937) and *Topper Returns* (1941).

youngling *n* (*poet*) a young child or animal.

youngster *n* a young person; a youth.

your *poss adj* of or belonging to or done by you.

you're = you are.

yours *poss pron* of or belonging to you.

yourself *pron* (*pl* **yourselves**) the emphatic and reflexive form of **you**.

youth *n* the period between childhood and adulthood; young people collectively; the early stages of something; a young man or boy.—**youthful** *adj*.—**youthfully** *adv*.

youth hostel *n* a supervised lodging for usu young travelers.

you've = you have.

yowl *n* a loud mournful cry, esp from pain.—*also vi*.

yo-yo *n* (*pl* **yo-yos**) a hand-held toy made of a flat spool which can be made to wind up and down a piece of string.

YPSCE *abbr* = Young People's Society of Christian Endeavor.

YPTES *abbr* = Young People's Trust for Endangered Species.

yr *abbr* = year; younger; your.

YRC *abbr* = Youth Rights Campaign.

yrs *abbr* = years; yours.

YSA *abbr* = Young Socialist Alliance.

Y

YSAU *abbr* = Young Swimmers Athletic Union.

Yspaddaden *n* (*Welsh Celtic myth*) "chief giant"; according to legend, he had such huge, heavy eyelids that they had to be propped open by metal supports before he could see anything. He was the father of Olwen.

Yt *symbol* (*chem*) yttrium.

YT *abbr* = Yukon Territory.

YTA *abbr* = Young Theater Association.

ytd *abbr* = year to date.

YTS *abbr* = Youth Training Scheme.

ytterbium *n* a soft metallic element of the lanthanide series.

yttrium *n* a metallic element used in alloys and lasers.

YTV *abbr* = Yorkshire Television.

YU *abbr* = Yale University.

yuan *n* (*pl* **yuan**) the monetary unit of the People's Republic of China.

Yuc. *abbr* = Yucatán.

yucca *n* a plant with stiff, spear-like leaves and white flowers.

yuck *interj* (*sl*) expressing disgust.

yucky *adj* (**yuckier, yuckiest**) (*sl*) disgusting.

Yugoslavia, Jugoslavia or **FRY** *n* a federal republic comprising only Serbia and Montenegro, which are the largest and the smallest of the six republics of the former Yugoslavia.

Yukawa *n* **Hideki** (1907–81) Japanese physicist. In 1949, he became the first Japanese to be awarded the Nobel prize for physics for his prediction (in 1935) of the meson within the atomic nucleus.

yu kin *n* (*mus*) a Chinese variety of guitar, also called "Moon Guitar."

Yukon time *n* the 9th time zone west of Greenwich covering the Yukon Territory.

yule *n* Christmas.

Yule log *n* a large log traditionally burnt in the fire on Christmas Eve.

yuletide *n* the Christmas festival or season.

yummy *adj* (**yummier, yummiest**) (*inf*) tasty, pleasing. * *interj* yum-yum.

yum-yum *interj* used to express pleasure, esp when eating.

yup *adv* (*inf*) yes.

yuppie, yuppy *n* (*inf*) any young professional regarded as affluent, ambitious, materialistic, etc.

yurt *n* a circular portable tent of skins used by the Mongolian nomads of Siberia.

YW or **YWCA** *abbr* = Young Women's Christian Association.

YWCTU *abbr* = Young Women's Christian Temperance Union.

Ywerit *n* (*Welsh Celtic myth*) the father of Bendigeid Vran or Bran the Blessed.

YWHA *abbr* = Young Women's Hebrew Association.

YY Orionis star *n* one of a number of variable stars that may be a subclass of T Tauri stars.

Z

z, Z *n* the 26th letter of the English alphabet; something shaped like a Z; (*math*) the third unknown quantity.

z (*symbol*) (*math*) an algebraic variable; the z-axis.

Z (*symbol*) (*physics*) impedance; (*chem*) atomic number; (*astron*) zenith distance.

z, z. *abbr* = zenith; zero; zone.

ZAAA *abbr* = Zambia Amateur Athletics Association.

zabaglione *n* a dessert of whipped egg yolks, sugar, and marsala wine.

Zacchaeus *n* (*Bible*) chief tax-collector in Jericho. When Jesus visited the city, Zacchaeus climbed a tree to see him; Jesus saw him and invited himself to Zacchaeus' house; this act made him unclean to orthodox Jews.

Zacharias *see* **Zechariah**.

Zacynthos, Zakynthus *n* one of the islands lying off the western coast of the Greek Peloponnese; modern Zante.

ZADCA *abbr* = Zinc Alloy Die Casters' Association.

Zadok *n* (*Bible*) priest who lived in the time of David and Solomon and gave his loyalty and considerable political support to the royal house; later high priests of Judaism claimed descent from Zadok.

Zagreb *n* capital city of Croatia.

Zaide *n* (*mus*) Mozart's two-act operetta, to a book by Schachtner, composed about 1780, was never performed.

Zaira *n* (*mus*) Vincenzo Bellini's three-act opera, to a book by Romani, was first performed in Parma on May 10, 1829.

zaire *n* the standard monetary unit of the Democratic Republic of Congo (formerly Zaïre), being made up of 100 makuta (*sing* likuta).

Zaïrese *n* a native or inhabitant of the African republic of Zaïre.—*also adj.*

Zakharov *n* **Andreyan D** (*b.* 1761–) Russian architect. His notable works include the Admiralty in Leningrad.

Zambia *n* a republic located in central southern Africa.

Zamboanga *n* city in Philippines.

zamindar *n* (*hist*) in India, a district tax collector under the Mogul empire; a landowner paying land tax.—*also* **zemindar**.

Zamyatin *n* **Yevgeny Ivanovich** (1884–1937) Russian novelist, short-story writer, dramatist, and critic whose best-known work is the grim anti-Utopian novel *We*.

Zandonai *n* **Riccardo** (1883–1944) Italian composer who composed operas in a verismo style. His operas include *Il grillo del Focolare* and *Francesca da Rimini*.

Zangwill *n* **Israel** (1864–1926) English novelist, dramatist, and journalist, best known for his novel of Jewish life in the London slums, *Children of the Ghetto*.

Zanini *n* **Marco** (1954–) Italian architect who has designed several collections of furniture with Ettore Sottsass Associati and the Memphis company.

ZANU *abbr* = Zimbabwe African National Union.

Zanuck *n* **Darryl F[rancis]** (1902–79) American film producer. He began his Hollywood career as a scriptwriter, becoming a producer in 1927, and was one of the founders of 20th-Century Fox (1935). The many films he produced include *The Jazz Singer* (1927), *Little Caesar* (1930), and *The Grapes of Wrath* (1940).

zany *adj* (**zanier, zaniest**) comical; eccentric.—**zanily** *adv.*—**zaniness** *n.*

Zanzibar *n* a town on the island of Zanzibar.

Zanzibar Island *n* part of Tanzania, an island off the coast of Tanzania.

zap *vb* (**zapping, zapped**) *vt* to attack; to kill; to bombard; (*comput*) to get rid of data. * *vi* to rush around.

Zapata *n* **Emiliano** (1879–1919) Mexican revolutionary. An Indian tenant farmer, he led (1910–19) a guerrilla campaign against the Mexican government in the name of land reform. He was assassinated by a government agent. *See also* **Villa**.

Zapf *n* **Otto** (1931–) important German industrial designer of system furniture for Knoll.

Zapf Dingbats *n* (*comput*) a set of decorative symbols developed by Herman Zapf, a German typeface designer.

Zapotec *n* (*hist*) a people who occupied the valley of Oaxaca, Mexico by AD 300.

Zappa *n* **Frank** (1940–93) American rock musician and Czech diplomat.

zappy *adj* (**zappier, zappiest**) (*sl*) energetic, snappy.

ZAPU *abbr* = Zimbabwe African People's Union.

Zaragoza *n* city in Spain.

zareba, zariba *n* in northern East Africa, a stockade made of thorn hedges as a protection against wild animals or enemies; a place so protected.

zarf *n* an ornamental holder for a coffee cup used in Arab countries.

Zarqa *n* a city in the Hashemite Kingdom of Jordan.

zarzuela *n* a traditional Spanish one-act comic opera with a satirical theme and including dialogue.

Zátopek *n* **Emil** (1922–) Czech athlete. One of the greatest long-distance runners of all time, he won the 5,000 and 10,000 meters, and the marathon in the 1952 Olympics.

Zawi Chemi Shanidar *n* an archeological site in northern Iraq in which there is possible evidence for the very early domestication of sheep (9000 BC).

z-axis *n* the reference axis of a three-dimensional coordinate system, along which the z-coordinate is measured.

zB *abbr* (*German*) = *zum Beispiel*, "for example."

ZB *abbr* = Zen Buddhism.

ZCCT *abbr* = Zoo Check Charitable Trust.

ZDA *abbr* = Zinc Development Association.

zeal *n* fervent devotion; fanaticism.

zealot *n* an extreme partisan, a fanatic.

Zealots *n* (*Bible*) the Zealots were a fanatical nationalist party in Palestine in the time of Jesus; they wanted to win independence from the Romans by armed rebellion.

zealous *adj* full of zeal; ardent.—**zealously** *adv.*—**zealousness** *n.*

Zebedee *n* (*Bible*) a fisherman of Galilee and father of James and John, disciples of Jesus; his wife may have been one of the women of Galilee who went with Jesus to Jerusalem, and witnessed the Crucifixion.

zebra *n* (*pl* **zebras, zebra**) a black and white striped wild animal related to the horse.—**zebrine** *adj.*

zebra crossing *n* (*Brit inf*) a street crossing for pedestrians marked by black and white strips on the road.

zebu *n* (*pl* **zebus, zebu**) an Asian and African ox with a prominent hump and a large dewlap.

Zech. *abbr* = Zechariah.

Zechariah, Zacharias *n* the father of John the Baptist.

Zechariah *n* **the Book of** (*Bible*) consists of two parts: eight dream-visions aimed at inspiring people with a purpose and a hope in the ideal Jerusalem; followed by prophetic oracles, mainly in poetic form and obscure.

zed *n* (the pronunciation of) the letter z in the UK.

Zedekiah *n* (*Bible*) after sacking Jerusalem, Nebuchadrezzar made Zedekiah his vassal king; after a second siege the walls were breached in 587 BC and Zedekiah was caught and taken to captivity in Babylon; it was the end of the royal house of David and the kingdom of Judah.

zedoary *n* an aromatic substance like ginger made from the root stock of an Indian plant.

zee *n* (*pl* **zees**) (the pronunciation of) the letter z in US.

Zeeman effect *n* an effect that is noticed when atoms in a magnetic field give off or absorb radiation.

Zeffirelli *n* **Franco** (1923–93) Italian stage and film director and designer whose films include *Romeo and Juliet*.

zeg *abbr* = zero economic growth.

Zeitgeist *n* the spirit of the time; the beliefs, attitudes, tastes, etc, of a particular period.

Zelmira *n* (*mus*) Rossini's two-act opera, to a book by Tottola, was first performed in Naples on February 16, 1822.

zelo *n* (*mus*) (*Italian*) "zeal."

zelosamente *n* (*mus*) (*Italian*) "zealously" or "ardently."

Zelus *n* (*Greek myth*) the personification of zeal or strife.

zemindar *see* **zamindar**.

zemstvo *n* (*pl* **zemstvos, zemstva**) a local elective assembly in the old Russian empire.

Zen *n* a Japanese Buddhist sect that emphasizes self-awareness and self-mastery as the means to enlightenment.

zenana *n* the part of the house reserved for women and girls in a Muslim household.

Zend-Avesta *n* the sacred writings of the Zoroastrians.

zenith *n* the point at which the sun or moon appears to be exactly overhead; peak, summit (of ambition, etc).

zenith distance *n* (*astron*) the angular distance of a heavenly body from the zenith.

zeolites *npl* (*geol*) a group of aluminum silicates of sodium, potassium, calcium, and barium that contain loosely held water that can be removed by heating and regained by exposure to water.

Zeph. *abbr* = Zephaniah.

Zephaniah *n* (*Bible*) prophet of the OT, a descendant of King Hezekiah of Judah who lived and prophesied in Jerusalem in the days of Josiah.

Zephaniah *n* **the Book of** (*Bible*) a collection of short oracles warning repeatedly of the day of God's punishment about to fall on the wicked priests, officials, and citizens of Jerusalem.

zephyr *n* a soft, gentle breeze; a very thin woolen material; a garment made of this.

Zephyrus *n* (*Greek myth*) the god of the west wind.

zeppelin *n* a rigid, cigar-shaped airship.

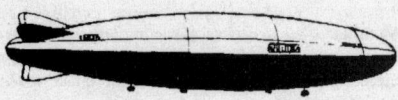

zero *n* (*pl* **zeros, zeroes**) the symbol 0; nothing; the lowest point; freezing point, 0 degrees Celsius. * *vi* (*with* **in**) (*inf*) to focus attention on (a problem, subject, etc); (*inf*) to converge upon; (*with* **in on**) to concentrate fire (from a weapon) on a specific target.

zero-based budgeting *n* a system of budgeting that involves the preparation of a budget from a zero base, i.e. starting from the initial assumption that there is no commitment to spend on any activity and that every item of expenditure on every activity has to be justified.

zero gravity *n* weightlessness.

zero hour *n* the time at which something is scheduled to begin.

zero population growth *n* a condition in which the number of live births in a particular population equals the number of deaths, resulting in a stable population.

zero-rated *adj* applied to goods and services that, although taxable, are currently subject to a tax rate of zero.

Zerubbabel *n* (*Bible*) a descendant of David and the second last reigning king of Judah before the Exile.

zest *n* the outer part of the skin of an orange or lemon used to give flavor; enthusiasm; excitement.—**zestful** *adj*.—**zestfully** *adv*.—**zestfulness** *n*.

zeta *n* the sixth letter of the Greek alphabet.

Zetes and Calais *n* (*Greek myth*) the twin sons of Boreas, the north wind and god of the north wind, known as the Boreades.

Zethus *n* (*Greek myth*) the son of Zeus and Antiope and twin brother of Amphion.

zeuge *n* (*pl* **zeugen**) a rock or yardang in a desert, the base of which has been undercut by wind erosion.

zeugma *n* a figure of speech in which a word is used with two others, to only one of which it properly applies.—**zeugmatic** *adj*.

Zeus *n* (*Greek myth*) the king of the gods.

Zeuxippe *n* (*Greek myth*) a naiad, mother of Procne and Philomela and twin sons, Erechtheus and Butes.

ZG *abbr* = Zoological Garden/s.

Zhivkov *n* **Todor** (1911–98) Bulgarian Communist statesman; prime minister (1962–71); president (1971–89).

Zhou En Lai *see* **Chou En-lai**.

Zhukov *n* **Georgi Konstantinovich** (1895–1974) Russian soldier. Zhukov's forces repulsed the Germans from the suburbs of Moscow, successfully defended Leningrad and captured the German 6th Army at Stalingrad. He took Warsaw in September 1944 and Berlin in May 1945.

Zia ul-Haq *n* **Mohammed** (1924–88) Pakistani general. He led the military coup against Zulfikar **Bhutto** in 1977 and became president (1978–88). He opposed the Soviet invasion of Afghanistan (1979) and pursued a domestic policy designed to make Pakistan a totally Islamic culture. His death in a plane crash is generally assumed to have been due to sabotage.

zidovudine *n* an antiviral drug used to treat HIV infection. Although it slows the growth of the HIV, it does not effect a cure.

Ziegfeld *n* **Florenz** (1869–1932) American theater manager. His spectacular revues (the "Ziegfeld Follies") were produced annually (1907–31) and were designed as the American equivalent of the *Folies Bergères* in Paris.

Zift *abbr* = zygote intrafallopian transfer.

ziggurat *n* a Sumerian tower temple.

zigzag *n* a series of short, sharp angles in alternate directions. * *adj* having sharp turns. * *vti* (**zigzagging, zigzagged**) to move or form in a zigzag.

zilch, zilcho *n* (*sl*) nothing.

zillah *n* (*hist*) an administrative district in India during British rule.

zillion *n* (*pl* **zillion, zillions**) (*inf*) an indefinitely large number or quantity.

Zilina *n* city in the Slovak Republic.

Zimb *abbr* = Zimbabwe.

Zimbabwe *n* a landlocked republic in southern Africa.

Zimbabwean *n* a native or inhabitant of the African republic of Zimbabwe.—*also adj*.

Zimbabwe Dollar *n* currency of Zimbabwe.

zimbalom *see* **dulcimer**.

Zimmer *n* (*trademark*) a frame of tubular metal used by the infirm as a walking aid.

Zimmerman *n* **Marie** (1878–1972) American metalworker who used Egyptian, Far Eastern, and Greek art as inspiration for her jewelry.

Zimmermann *n* **Dominikus** (1685–) German architect. His notable works include the Frauenkirche, Günzburg.

zinc *n* a bluish-white metallic element used in alloys and batteries. * *vt* (**zincing, zinced** *or* **zincking, zincked**) to coat with zinc.—**zincic** *adj*.

zincograph *n* a design in relief on a zinc plate; a print made from this. * *vti* to etch on zinc; to reproduce in this way.—**zincographer** *n*. —**zincographic** *adj*.—**zincography** *n*.

Zinder *n* city in Niger.

zing *n* (*inf*) a high-pitched buzz; (*inf*) vitality, exuberance. * *vi* (*inf*) to move with a zinging sound.

Zingarelli *n* **Niccolò Antonio** (1752–1837) an Italian composer of thirty-one operas, (such as *Berenice*, his last and most popular) and church music.

zinnia *n* a tropical American plant with showy flowers.

Zinoviev *n* **Grigori Yevseevich** (1883–1936) Russian politician. He became chairman of the Comintern (1919–26) and Politburo member (1921–26). He allied himself with **Stalin** against **Trotsky** and was subsequently himself purged by Stalin in 1927 and executed in 1936 after a show trial.

Zion *n* (*Bible*) the original hilltop fortress captured by David, which became the oldest part of Jerusalem. Zion came to be known as the city of David and eventually the name was applied to the whole of the enlarged sacred city.

Zionism *n* a movement formerly to resettle Jews in Palestine as their national home, now concerned with the development of Israel.—**Zionist** *n, adj*.—**Zionistic** *adj*.

zip[1] *n* a light whizzing sound of a bullet, etc; (*sl*) brisk energy; a slide fastener on clothing, bags, etc with interlocking teeth, a zipper. * *vb* (**zipping, zipped**) *vi* to move at high speed, to dart. * *vt* to fasten with a zip.

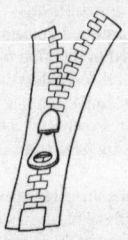

zip[2] *vt* (*comput*) to compress files so that they utilize less space on a disk.

ZIP *abbr* = Zone Improvement Plan.

ZIP Code *n* (*trademark*) a postcode that uses digits to denote an area.

zipper *n* a zip.

zippy *adj* (**zippier, zippiest**) speedy; energetic.

zircon *n* a variously colored hard translucent mineral, some varieties of which are cut as gemstones.

zirconium *n* a metallic element found in zircon and used in alloys.

zit *n* (*sl*) a pimple, spot.

zither *n* a musical instrument with 30–45 strings over a shallow sounding box played by plucking.—**zitherist** *n*.

zloty *n* (*pl* **zlotys, zloty**) the monetary unit of Poland.

zmodem *n* (*comput*) a fast and popular modem file transfer protocol.

Zn *symbol* (*chem*) zinc.

ZO *abbr* = Zionist Organization.

zodiac *n* an imaginary belt in the heavens along which the sun, moon, and chief planets appear to move, divided crosswise into twelve equal areas, called "signs of the zodiac," each named after a constellation; a diagram representing this.—**zodiacal** *adj*.

zodiacal light *n* a luminous triangular tract of sky sometimes seen before dawn or after dusk, esp in the tropics.

zoetrope *n* a toy with a revolving cylinder showing a series of pictures in apparent motion.

-zoic *adj suffix* (*animal*) having a specified kind of existence; (*geol*) belonging to an era with a particular form of life.

Zola *n* **Emile** (1840–1902) French novelist. He was a prominent exponent of naturalism in the novel, and a propagandist for social justice.

Zollinger-Ellison syndrome *n* (*med*) an uncommon disorder resulting in diarrhea and multiple peptic ulcers caused by a pancreatic tumor or enlarged pancreas.

Zollverein *n* in the 19th century, a union of German states with common customs tariffs against outside countries and free trade among themselves; any customs union.

Zomba *n* city in Malawi.

zombie, zombi *n* (*pl* **zombies**) a person who is lifeless and apathetic; an automaton.

zonate, zonated *adj* (*bot, zool*) marked with bands.

zone *n* a region, area; a subdivision; any area with a specified use or restriction; (*comput*) a subgroup of networked computers in a local area network. * *vt* to divide or mark off into zones; to designate as a zone; to encircle with a zone.—**zonal** *adj*.

zone pricing *n* (*com*) a form of pricing system used by some companies by which their market area is divided into zones, usually those customers who live in a zone farthest from the company's headquarters or main warehouse paying more than those who live nearest.

zonked *adj* (*sl*) intoxicated by drugs or alcohol; (*sl*) exhausted.

zoo *n* (*pl* **zoos**) a place where a collection of living wild animals is kept for public showing.

zoo-, zo- *prefix* animals.

zoochem. *abbr* = zoochemical; zoochemistry.

zoochemistry *n* the chemistry of the constituents of animal bodies.—**zoochemical** *adj*.

zoogeog. *abbr* = zoogeographical; zoogeography.

zoogeography *n* the science of the geographical distribution of animals.—**zoogeographer** *n*. —**zoogeographic, zoogeographical** *adj*.

zoography *n* descriptive zoology.—**zoographic, zoographical** *adj*.

zooid *adj* resembling but not completely being an animal or plant. * *n* a zooid organism; an animal organism produced by fission; (*corals, etc*) a member of a compound organism.

zool. *abbr* = zoological; zoology.

zoological garden *n* a zoo.

zoologist *n* a person who studies animals and animal behavior.

zoology *n* (*pl* **zoologies**) the study of animals with regard to their classification, structure, and habits.—**zoological** *adj*.—**zoologically** *adv*.

zoom *vi* to go quickly, to speed; to climb upward sharply in an airplane; to rise rapidly; (*photog*) to focus in on an object using a zoom lens; (*comput*) to enlarge or reduce the size of a page on screen for easier viewing. * *n* the act of zooming; a zoom lens.

zoom box *n* (*comput*) a small box positioned at the edge of a screen window that is used to zoom a window.

zoom lens *n* (*photog*) a camera lens that makes distant objects appear closer without moving the camera.

zoomorphism *n* the representation (esp of a deity) in the form of or with the attributes of an animal.—**zoomorphic** *adj*.

zoonosis (*pl* **zoonoses**) *n* an infectious animal disease that can also be transmitted to humans.

zooph. *abbr* = zoophytological; zoophytology.

zoophobia *n* an unnatural and strong fear of animals.

zoophyte *n* any animal (e.g., coral, a sponge) that resembles a plant.—**zoophytic** *adj*.

zootomy *n* animal anatomy; the dissection of animals.—**zootomical** *adj*.—**zootomist** *n*.

zorille, zoril *n* a small African mammal that resembles and smells like a skunk.

Zoroastrianism *n* a religious system founded by the Persian prophet Zoroaster (*c*.628–551 BC), based on the recognition of the dual principle of good and evil.—**Zoroastrian** *n, adj*.

Zoser *or* **Djoser** *n* Egyptian pharaoh of the Third Dynasty (period from 2700–2625 BC).

Zouave *n* (*formerly*) a soldier in a French-Algerian infantry unit characterized by a colorful eastern-style uniform; a soldier in a similar unit, esp a Union Army unit of the American Civil War.

zounds *interj* (*arch*) expressing anger and astonishment.

ZPDA *abbr* = Zinc Pigment Development Association.

zpg *abbr* = zero population growth.

Zr *symbol* (*chem*) zirconium.

ZS *abbr* = Zoological Society.

Z-score *n* a statistic that has been devised to try to summarize the susceptibility of a business to failure.

ZSI *abbr* = Zoological Society of Ireland.

ZSL *abbr* = Zoological Society of London.

ZST *abbr* = Zone Standard Time.

ZTDC *abbr* = Zimbabwe Tourist Development Corporation.

zucchetto *n* (*pl* **zucchettos**) a skullcap worn by Roman Catholic ecclesiastics, which varies in color according to rank (black for a priest, purple for a bishop, red for a cardinal, white for the Pope).

zucchini *npl n* a type of small vegetable marrow.—*also* **courgette**.

Zuckerman *n* **Baron Solly** (1904–83) South African-born British zoologist. He was chief scientific adviser to the British government (1964–71). Noted for his work on primates, his books include *The Social Life of Monkeys and Apes* (1932) and the essay collection *Man and Aggression* (1968).

Zulu *n* (*pl* **Zulus, Zulu**) a member of a Negroid people of South Africa, or their language.—*also adj*.

ZUM *abbr* = Zimbabwe Unity Movement.

Zürich *n* city in Switzerland.

zurna *n* (*mus*) a Turkish wind instrument similar in character to the oboe.

Zweig *n* **Stefan** (1881–1942) Austrian biographer, dramatist, essayist, poet, and novelist (British citizen from 1938). He was Jewish and a pacifist, and died by his own hand.

Zwicky *n* **Stefan** (1952–) Swiss interior and furniture designer who worked for Olivetti before setting up his own studio in 1983.

zwieback *n* a thin rusk.

Zwingli *n* **Huldreich Ulrich** (1484–1531) Swiss religious reformer.

zyg-, zygo- *prefix* yoked, paired.

zygodactyl *adj* (*bird*) with the toes in pairs, two pointing forward and two backward. * *n* a zygodactyl bird, e.g. the parrot.—**zygodactylous** *adj*.

zygomatic arch *n* (*anat*) the arch of bone on either side of the face, below the eyes.

zygomatic bone *n* (*anat*) a facial bone and one of a pair of bones that form the prominence of the cheeks.

zygomorphic, zygomorphous *adj* (*flowers*) bilaterally symmetrical.—**zygomorphism, zygomorphy** *n*.

zygospore *n* a spore formed from the fusion of gametes.—**zygosporic** *adj*.

zygote *n* the cell formed by the union of an ovum and a sperm; the developing organism from such a cell.

zymogen *n* (*biochem*) a form of an enzyme that is inactive.

zymosis *n* (*pl* **zymoses**) an infectious disease caused by a virus or organism that acts like a ferment; fermentation.

zymotic *adj* caused by or relating to an infection or an infectious disease; producing fermentation.

zymurgy *n* the chemistry of fermentation in brewing, etc.

ZZ Ceti star *n* one of a number of pulsating, variable white dwarf stars resembling the one after which they are named, ZZ Ceti.

Z

Appendix I
Grammar and Usage

abbreviations are shortened forms of words usually used as a space-saving technique and becoming increasingly common in modern usage. They cause problems with regard to punctuation. The common question asked is whether the letters of an abbreviation should be separated by periods. In modern usage the tendency is to omit periods from abbreviations. This is most true of abbreviations involving initial capital letters, as in TUC, EEC and USA. In such cases periods should definitely not be used if one or some of the initial letters do not belong to a full word. Thus television is abbreviated to TV and educationally subnormal to ESN.

There are usually no periods in abbreviations involving the first and last letters of a word (contractions) Dr, Mr, Rd, St, but this is a matter of taste.

Abbreviations involving the first few letters of a word, as in "Prof" (Professor) are the most likely to have periods, as in "Feb." (February) but again this is now a matter of taste. These are mostly formed by adding lower-case *s*, as in Drs, JPs, TVs. Note the absence of apostrophes.

antonym refers to a word that is the opposite of another word. Thus "black" is an antonym for "white," "cowardly" is an antonym for "courageous," "dull" is an antonym for "bright" and "fast" is an antonym for "slow."

apostrophe[1] is a figure of speech which takes the form of a rhetorical address to an absent or dead person or to a personified thing, as in "O Romeo! Romeo! wherefore art thou, Romeo?" and "Oh Peace, why have you deserted us?"
apostrophe[2] is a form of punctuation that is mainly used to indicate possession. Many spelling errors center on the position of the apostrophe in relation to *s*.

Possessive nouns are usually formed by adding *'s* to the singular noun, as in "the girl's mother," and "Peter's car"; by adding an apostrophe to plural nouns that end in *s*, as in "all the teachers' cars"; by adding *'s* to irregular plural nouns that do not end in *s*, as in "women's shoes."

In the possessive form of a name or singular noun that ends in *s*, *x* or *z*, the apostrophe may or may not be followed by *s*. In words of one syllable the final *s* is usually added, as in "James's house," "the fox's lair," "Roz's dress." The final *s* is most frequently omitted in names, particularly in names of three or more syllables, as in "Euripides' plays." In many cases the presence or absence of final *s* is a matter of convention.

The apostrophe is also used to indicate omitted letters in contracted forms of words, as in "can't" and "you've." They are sometimes used to indicate missing century numbers in dates, as in "the '60s and '70s," but are not used at the end of decades, etc, as in "1960s," not "1960's."

Generally apostrophes are no longer used to indicate omitted letters in shortened forms that are in common use, as in "phone" and "flu."

Apostrophes are often omitted wrongly in modern usage, particularly in the media and by advertisers, as in "womens hairdressers," "childrens helpings." In addition, apostrophes are frequently added erroneously (as in "potato's for sale" and "Beware of the dog's"). This is partly because people are unsure about when and when not to use them and partly because of a modern tendency to punctuate as little as possible.

brackets are used to enclose information that is in some way additional to the main statement. The information so enclosed is called *parenthesis* and the pair of brackets enclosing it can be known as *parentheses*. The information that is enclosed in the brackets is purely supplementary or explanatory in nature and could be removed without changing the overall basic meaning or grammatical completeness of the statement. **Brackets**, like *commas* and *dashes*, interrupt the flow of the main statement but **brackets** indicate a more definite or clear-cut interruption. The fact that they are more visually obvious emphasizes this.

Material within brackets can be one word, as in "In a local wine bar we had some delicious crepes (pancakes)" and "They didn't have the chutzpah (nerve) to challenge her." It can also take the form of dates, as in "Robert Louis Stevenson (1850–94) wrote *Treasure Island*" and "*Animal Farm* was written by George Orwell (1903–50)."

The material within brackets can also take the form of a phrase, as in "They served lasagne (a kind of pasta) and some delicious veal" and "They were drinking Calvados (a kind of brandy made from apples)" or in the form of a clause, as in "We were to have supper (or so they called it) later in the evening" and "They went for a walk round the loch (as a lake is called in Scotland) before taking their departure."

It can also take the form of a complete sentence, as in "He was determined (we don't know why) to tackle the problem alone" and "She made it clear (nothing could be more clear) that she was not interested in the offer." Sentences that appear in brackets in the middle of a sentence are not usually given an initial capital letter or a period, as in "They very much desired (she had no idea why) to purchase her house." If the material within brackets comes at the end of a sentence the period comes outside the second bracket, as in "For some reason we agreed to visit her at home (we had no idea where she lived)."

If the material in the brackets is a sentence which comes between two other sentences it is treated like a normal sentence with an initial capital letter and a closing period, as in "He never seems to do any studying. (He is always either asleep or watching television.) Yet he does brilliantly in his exams." Punctuation of the main statement is unaffected by the presence of the brackets and their enclosed material except that any punctuation that would have followed the word before the first bracket follows the second bracket, as in "He lives in a place (I am not sure exactly where), that is miles from anywhere.

There are various shapes of brackets. Round brackets are the most common type. Square brackets are sometimes used to enclose information that is contained inside other information already in brackets, as in "(Christopher Marlowe [1564–93] was a contemporary of Shakespeare)" or in a piece of writing where round brackets have already been used for some other purpose. Thus in a dictionary if round brackets are used to separate off the pronunciation, square brackets are sometimes used to separate off the etymologies.

Square brackets are also used for editorial comments in a scholarly work where the material within brackets is more of an intrusion to the flow of the main statement than is normerly the case with bracketed material. Angle brackets and brace brackets tend to be used in more scholarly or technical contexts.

capital letters are much less common than lower-case letters. They are used as the initial letter of proper nouns. Thus names of countries, rivers, mountains, cities, etc. Thus we find Africa, Mount Everest, River Nile, Paris, etc. The first names and surnames of people have initial capital letters, as in John Black and Mary Brown. Initial capital letters are used for the days of the week, as in Tuesday and Wednesday, for the months of the year, as in May and October, public and religious holidays, as in Easter Sunday, Ramadan and Hanaku. Initial capital letters are used for the books of the Bible.

Points of the compass are spelt with an initial capital letter if they are part of a specific geographical feature or region, as in South Africa.

Initial capital letters are usually used in the titles of books. Only the main words are capitalized. Prepositions, determiners and the articles are left in lower-case, unless they form the first word of the title, as in *A Room with a View* and *For Whom the Bell Tolls*.

Initial capital letters are necessary in tradenames, as in Hoover, Jacuzzi, Xerox and Kodak. Note that verbs formed from trade names are not spelt with an initial capital letter.

The first word in a sentence is spelt with a capital letter, as in "We heard them come in. They made very little noise. However, we are light sleepers.."

For capital letters in abbreviation see ABBREVIATIONS.

colon is a punctuation mark (:) which is used within a sentence to explain, interpret, clarify or amplify what has gone before it. "The standard of school work here is extremely high: it is almost university standard," "The fuel bills are giving cause for concern: they are almost double last year's." "We have some new information: the allies have landed." A capital letter is not usually used after the colon in this context.

The **colon** is also used to introduce lists or long quotations, as in "The recipe says we need: tomatoes, peppers, courgettes, garlic, oregano and basil," "The boy has a huge list of things he needs for school: blazer, trousers, shirts, sweater, ties, shoes, tennis shoes, rugby boots, sports clothes and leisure wear" and "One of his favourite quotations was: 'If music be the food of love play on' ."

The **colon** is sometimes used in numerals, as in "7:30 a.m.," "1:20:01" and "a ratio of 7:3." It is used in the titles of some books, for example where there is a subtitle or explanatory title, as in "The Dark Years: the Economy in the 1930s."

In informal writing, the dash is sometimes used instead of the colon, Indeed the dash tends to be overused for this purpose.

comma is a very common punctuation mark. In modern usage there is a tendency to adopt a system of minimal punctuation and the comma is one of the casualties of this new attitude. Most people use the comma considerably less frequently than was formerly the case.

However there are certain situations in which the comma is still commonly used. One of these concerns lists. The individual items in a series of three or more items are separated by commas. Whether a comma is put before the "and" which follows the second-last item is now a matter of choice. Some people dislike the use of a comma after "and" in this situation, and it was formerly considered wrong. Examples of lists include— "At the sports club we can play tennis, squash, badminton and table tennis," "We need to buy bread, milk, fruit and sugar," and "They are studying French, German, Spanish and Russian." The individual items in a list can be quite long, as in "We opened the door, let ourselves in, fed the cat and started to cook a meal" and "They consulted the map, planned the trip, got some foreign currency and were gone before we realized it." Confusion may arise if the last item in the list contains "and" in its own right, as in "In the restaurant they served ham salad, shepherd's pie, pie and chips and omelette. In such cases it as well to put a comma before the "and."

In cases where there is a list of adjectives before a noun, the use of commas is now optional although it was formerly standard practice. Thus both "She wore a long, red, sequinned dress" and "She wore a long red sequinned dress" are used. When the adjective immediately before the noun has a closer relationship with it than the other adjectives no comma should be used, as in "a beautiful old Spanish village."

The **comma** is used to separate clauses or phrases that are parenthetical or naturally cut off from the rest of a sentence, as in "My mother, who was of Irish extraction, was very superstitious." In such a sentence the clause within the commas can be removed without altering the basic meaning. Care should be taken to include both commas. Commas are not normally used to separate main clauses and relative clauses, as in "The woman whom I met was my friend's sister." Nor are they usually used to separate main clauses and subordinate clauses, as in "He left when we arrived" and "They came to the party although we didn't expect them to." If the subordinate clause precedes the main clause, it is sometimes followed by a comma, especially if it is a reasonably long clause, as in "Although we stopped and thought about it, we still made the wrong decision." If the clause is quite short, or if it is a short phrase, a comma is not usually inserted, as in "Although it rained we had a good vacation" and "Although poor they were happy." The use of commas to separate such words and expression from the rest of the sentence to which they are related is optional. Thus one can write "However, he could be right" or "However he could be right." The longer the expression is, the more likely it is to have a comma after it, as in "On the other hand, we may decide not to go."

Commas are always used to separate terms of address, interjections or question tags from the rest of the sentence, as in "Please come this way, Ms Brown, and make yourself at home," "Now, ladies, what can I get you?" and "It's cold today, isn't it?"

Commas may be used to separate main clauses joined by a coordinating conjunction, but this is not usual if the clauses have the same subject or object, as in "She swept the floor and dusted the table." In cases where the subjects are different and the clauses are fairly long, it is best to insert a comma, as in "They took all the furniture with them, and she was left with nothing."

A **comma** can be inserted to avoid repeating a verb in the second of two clauses, as in "he plays golf and tennis, his brother football."

dash is a punctuation mark in the form of a short line that indicates a short break in the continuity of a sentence, as in "He has never been any trouble at school—quite the reverse," "I was amazed when he turned up—I thought he was still abroad." In such situations it serves the same purpose as brackets, except that it is frequently considered more informal. The dash should be used sparingly. Depending on it too much can lead to careless writing with ideas set down at random rather than turned into a piece of coherent prose.

The **dash** can be used to emphasize a word or phrase, as in "They said good-bye then—forever." It can also be used to add a remark to the end of a sentence, as in "They had absolutely no money—a regular state of affairs towards the end of the month." The **dash** can also be used to introduce a statement that amplifies or explains what has been said, as in "The burglars took everything of value—her jewellery, the silver, the TV set, her hi-fi and several hundred pounds." It can be used to summarize what has gone before, as in "Disease, poverty, ignorance—these are the problems facing us."

The **dash** is also used to introduce an afterthought, as in "You can come with me—but you might not want to." It can also introduce a sharp change of subject, as in "I'm just making tea—what was that noise?" It can also be used to introduce some kind of balance in a sentence, as in "It's going to take two of us to get this table out of here—one to move it and one to hold the door open."

Dashes are sometimes found in pairs. A pair of dashes acts in much the same way as a set of round brackets. A pair of dashes can be used to indicate a break in a sentence, as in "We prayed—prayed as we had never prayed before—that the children would be safe," "It was—on reflection—his best performance yet," and "He introduced me to his wife—an attractive pleasant woman—before he left."

Dashes are used to indicate hesitant speech, as in "I don't—well—maybe—you could be right." They can be used to indicate the omission of part of a word or name, as in "It's none of your b— business," "He's having an affair with Mrs D—."

They can also be used between points in time or space, as in "Chicago–New York" and "1750–1790."

ellipsis indicates omission of some kind. It can refer to the omission of words from a statement because they are thought to be obvious from the context. In many cases it involves using an auxiliary verb on its own rather than a full verb, as in "Jane won't accept it but Mary will" and "They would go if they could." In such cases the full form of "Jane won't accept it but Mary will accept it" and "They would go if they could go" would sound unnatural and repetitive. This is common in spoken English. Some sentences containing an ellipsis sound clumsy as well as ungrammatical, as in "This is as good, or perhaps even better than that," where "as" is omitted after "good" and in "People have and still do express their disapproval about it," where "expressed" is omitted after "have." Care should be taken to avoid ellipsis if the use of it is going to be ambiguous or clumsy.

Ellipsis is often used to indicate an omission from a quoted passage. If part of a passage is quoted and there is a gap before the next piece of the same passage is required to be quoted an **ellipsis** is used in the form of three dots. If the part of the passage quoted does not start at the beginning of a sentence the ellipsis precedes it.

exclamation is a word, phrase or sentence called out with strong feeling of some kind. It is marked by an **exclamation mark** which occurs at the end of the exclamation, as in "Get lost!," "What a nerve!," "Help!," "Ouch!" "Well I never!," "What a disaster!," "I'm tired of all this!" and "Let me out of here!" An **exclamatory question** is a sentence that is interrogative in form but is an exclamation in meaning, as in "Isn't the baby beautiful!" and "Isn't it lovely!."

homonym refers to a word which has the same sound and often the same spelling as another word but which differs in meaning – more correctly classified as homographs or homophones. Examples include:

"bill," a noun meaning "a written statement of money owed," as in "You must pay the bill for the conversion work immediately," or a "written or printed advertisement," as in "We were asked to deliver handbills advertising the play."

"bill," a noun meaning "a bird's beak," as in "The seagull has injured its bill."

"fair," an adjective meaning "attractive," as in "fair young women"; "light in colour," as in "She has fair hair"; "fine, not raining," as in "I hope it keeps fair"; "just, free from prejudice," as in "We felt that the referee came to a fair decision."

"fair," a noun meaning "a market held regularly in the same place, often with stalls, entertainments and rides" (now often simply applying to an event with entertainments and rides without the market), as in "He won a coconut at the fair"; "a trade exhibition," as in "the Frankfurt Book Fair."

hyphen refers to a small stroke used to join two words together or to indicate that a word has been broken at the end of a line because of lack of space. It is used in a variety of situations.

The **hyphen** is used as the prefixed element in a proper noun, as in "pre-Christian," "post-Renaissance," "anti-British," "anti-Semitic," "pro-French" and "pro-Marxism." It is also used before dates or numbers, as in "pre-1914," "pre-1066," "post-1920," "post-1745." It is also used before abbreviations, as in "anti-EEC" and "anti-TUC."

The **hyphen** is used for clarification. Some words are ambiguous without the presence of a hyphen. For example, "re-cover," as in "re-cover a chair," is spelt with a hyphen to differentiate it from "recover," as in "The accident victim is likely to recover." Similarly, it is used in "re-form," meaning "to form again," as in "They have decided to re-form the society which closed last year," to differentiate the word from "reform," meaning "to improve, to become better behaved," as in "He was wild as a young man but he has reformed now." Similarly "re-count" in the sense of "count again" , as in "re-count the number of votes cast," is spelt with a hyphen to differentiate it from "recount" in the sense of "tell," as in "recount what happened on the night of the accident."

The **hyphen** was formerly used to separate a prefix from the main element of a word if the main element begins with a vowel, as in "pre-eminent," but there is a growing tendency in modern usage to omit the **hyphen** in such cases. At the moment both "pre-eminent" and "preeminent" are found. However, if the omission of the **hyphen** results in double i, the **hyphen** is usually retained, as in "anti-inflationary" and "semi-insulated."

The **hyphen** was formerly used in words formed with the prefix *non-*, as in "non-functional," "non-political," "non-flammable" and "non-pollutant." However there is a growing tendency to omit the hyphen in such cases, as in "nonfunctional" and "nonpollutant." At the moment both forms of such words are common.

The **hyphen** is usually used with "ex-" in the sense of "former," as in "ex-wife" and "ex-president."

The **hyphen** is usually used when "self-" is prefixed to words, as in "self-styled," "a self-starter" and "self-evident."

Use or non-use of the **hyphen** is often a matter of choice, house style or frequency of usage, as in "drawing-room" or "drawing room." and "dining-room" or "dining room." There is a modern tendency to punctuate less frequently than was formerly the case and so in modern usage use of the **hyphen** in such expressions is less frequent. The length of compounds often affects the inclusion or omission of the hyphen. Compounds of two short elements that are well-established words tend not to be hyphenated, as in "bedroom" and "toothbrush." Compound words with longer elements are more likely to be hyphenated, as in "engine-driver" and "carpet-layer."

Some fixed compounds of two or three or more words are always hyphenated, as in "son-in-law," "good-for-nothing" and "devil-may-care."

Some compounds formed from phrasal verbs are sometimes hyphenated and sometimes not. Thus both "take-over" and "takeover" are common, and "run-down" and "rundown" are both common. Again the use of the hyphen is a matter of choice. However some words formed from phrasal verbs are usually spelt without a hyphen, as in "breakthrough."

Compound adjectives consisting of two elements, the second of which ends in -*ed*, are usually hyphenated, as in "heavy-hearted," "fair-haired," "fair-minded" and "long-legged."

Compound adjectives when they are used before nouns are usually hyphenated, as in "gas-fired central heating," "oil-based paints," "solar-heated buildings" and "chocolate-coated cookies."

Compounds containing some adverbs are usually hyphenated, sometimes to avoid ambiguity, as in "his best-known opera," a "well-known singer," "an ill-considered venture" and "a half-planned scheme."

Generally adjectives and participles preceded by an adverb are not hyphenated if the adverb ends in -*ly*, as in "a highly talented singer," "neatly pressed clothes" and "beautifully dressed young women."

In the case of two or more compound hyphenated adjectives with the same second element qualifying the same noun, the common element need not be repeated but the **hyphen** should be, as in "two- and three-bedroom houses" and "long- and short-haired dogs."

The **hyphen** is used in compound numerals from 21 to 99 when they are written in full, as in "thirty-five gallons," "forty-four years," "sixty-seven kilometers" and "two hundred and forty-five kilometers." Compound numbers such as "three hundred" and "two thousand" are not hyphenated.

Hyphens are used in fractions, as in "three-quarters" and "seven-eighths."

Hyphens are also used in such number phrases as "a seventeenth-century play," "a sixteenth-century church," "a five-year contract" and a "third-year student."

The other use of **hyphens** is to break words at the ends of lines. Formerly people were more careful about where they broke words. Previously, words were broken up according to etymological principles but there is a growing tendency to break words according to how they are pronounced. Some dictionaries or spelling dictionaries give help with the division and hyphenation of individual words. General points are that one-syllable words should not be divided and words should not be broken after the first letter of a word or before the last letter. Care should be taken not to break up words, for example by forming elements that are words in their own right, in such a way as to mislead the reader. Thus divisions such as "the-rapist" and "mans-laughter" should be avoided.

italic type refers to a sloping typeface that is used for a variety of purposes. It is used to differentiate a piece of text from the main text, which is usually in Roman type. For example, it is used sometimes for the titles of books, newspapers, magazines, plays, films, musical works and works of art, as in "he is a regular reader of *The Times*," "She reads *The New Yorker*," "Have you read *Animal Farm* by George Orwell," "He has never seen a production of Shakespeare's *Othello*," "We went to hear Handel's *Messiah*," "*Mona Lisa* is a famous painting." Sometimes such titles are put in quotation marks rather than in italic.

Italic type is also sometimes used for the names of ships, trains, etc, as in "the launch of *The Queen Elizabeth II*," "She once sailed in *The Queen Mary*" and "Their train was called *The Flying Scotsman*."

Italic type is also used for the Latin names of plants and animals, as in "of the genus *Lilium*," "trees of the genus *Pyrus*, *Panthera pardus* and *Canis lupus*."

Italic type is sometimes used for foreign words that have been adopted into the English language but have never been fully integrated. Examples include *bête noire*, *raison d'être*, *inter alia* and *Weltschmerz*.

Italic type can also sometimes be used to draw attention to a particular word, phrase or passage, as in "How do you pronounce *formidable*?," or to emphasize a word or phrase, as in "Is he *still* in the same job?"

numbers can be written in either figures or words. It is largely a matter of taste which method is adopted. As long as the method is consistent it does not really matter. Some establishments, such as a publishing house or a newspaper office, will have a house style. For example, some of them prefer to have numbers up to 10 written in words, as in "They have two boys and three girls." If this system is adopted, guidance should be sought as to whether a mixture of figures and words in the same sentence is acceptable, as in "We have 12 cups but only six saucers," or whether the rule should be broken in such situations as "We have twelve cups but only six saucers."

period is a punctuation mark consisting of a small dot. Its principal use is to end a sentence that is not a question or an exclamation, as in "They spent the money.," "She is studying hard.," "He has been declared redundant and is very upset." and "Because she is shy, she rarely goes to parties."

The **period** is used in decimal fractions, as in "4.5 meters" and "12.2 litres." It can also be used in dates, as in "1.20.01," and times, as in "3.15 tomorrow afternoon."

In modern usage the tendency is to omit **periods** from abbreviations. This is most true of abbreviations involving initial capital letters as in TUC, BBC, EEC and USA. In such cases periods should definitely not be used if one or some of the initial letters do not belong to a full word. Thus, television is abbreviated to TV and educationally subnormal to ESN.

There are usually no periods in abbreviations involving the first and letters of a word (contractions) Dr, Mr, Rd, St, but this is a matter of taste.

Abbreviations involving the first few letters of a word, as in "Prof" (Professor) are the most likely to have periods, as in "Feb." (February), but again this is now a matter of taste.

The **period** can also be called **point** or **period**.

question mark refers to the punctuation mark that is placed at the end of a question or interrogative sentence, as in "Who is he?," "Where are they?," "Why have they gone?," "Whereabouts are they?," "When are you going?" and "What did he say?." The **question mark** is sometimes known as the "query."

quotation marks, also known as *inverted commas* or *quotes*, are used in *direct speech*. **Quotation marks** are also used to enclose titles of newspaper articles, book chapters, short stories, poems, songs, articles in periodicals and essays. **Quotation marks** may consist of a set of single inverted commas or a set of double inverted commas. If a title, etc, is to be enclosed in quotation marks and the title is part of a piece of writing already in quotation marks for some other reason, such as being part of direct speech, then the quotation marks round the title should be in the type of quotation marks opposite to the other ones. Thus if the piece of writing is in single quotation marks then the title should be in double quotation marks. If the piece of prose is in double quotation marks the title should be in single quotation marks. Examples include "Have you read 'My Last Duchess' by Robert Browning?" and "Can you sing 'Auld Lang Syne'?"

semi-colon is a rather formal form of punctuation. It is mainly used between clauses that are not joined by any form of conjunction, as in "We had a wonderful vacation; sadly they did not," "She was my sister; she was also my best friend" and "He was a marvelous friend; he is much missed." A dash is sometimes used instead of a semi-colon but this more informal.

The **semi-colon** is also used to form subsets in a long list or series of names so that the said list seems less complex, as in "The young man who wants to be a journalist has applied everywhere. He has applied to *The Times* in London; *The Globe and Mail* in Toronto; *The Age* in Melbourne; *The Tribune* in Chicago."

The **semi-colon** is also sometimes used before "however," "nevertheless" "hence," etc, as in "We have extra seats for the concert; however you must not feel obliged to come."

synonym refers to a word which has the same meaning as another of the same language, or a word denoting a very similar description but perhaps differing in some senses, or in a range of applications. Synonyms for the verb "believe" would include: "accept," "consider," "count on," "guess," "judge" etc.

PARTS OF SPEECH

These define the ways in which words can be used in different contexts:

active voice is one of two voices that verbs are divided into, the other being PASSIVE VOICE. In verbs in the active voice, commonly called *active verbs*, the subject of the verb performs the action described by the verb. Thus, in the sentence "The boy threw the ball," "throw" is in the active voice since the subject of the verb (the boy) is doing the throwing. Similarly, in the sentence "Her mother was driving the car," "driving" is in the active voice since it is the subject of the sentence (her mother) that is doing the driving. Similarly, in the sentence "We saw the cows in the field," "saw" is the active voice since it is the subject of the sentence (we) that is doing the seeing. *See also* PASSIVE VOICE.

adjective is a word that describes or gives information about a noun or pronoun. It is said to qualify a noun or pronoun since it limits the word it describes in some way, by making it more specific. Thus, adding the adjective "red" to "book" limits "book," since it means we can forget about books of any other color. Similarly, adding "large" to "book" limits it, since it means we can forget about books of any other size.

Adjectives tell us something about the color, size, number, quality, or classification of a noun or pronoun, as in "purple dress," "jet-black hair," "bluish eyes"; "tiny baby," "large houses," "biggish gardens," "massive estates"; five children," "twenty questions," "seventy-five books"; "sad people," "joyful occasions," "delicious food," "civil engineering," "nuclear physics," "modern languages," "Elizabethan drama."

Several adjectives may modify one noun or pronoun, as in "the small, black cat," "an enormous, red-brick, Victorian house." The order in which they appear is flexible and can vary according to the emphasis one wishes to place on the various adjectives. However, a common sequence is size, quality, color and classification, as in "a small, beautiful, pink wild rose" and "a large, ugly, grey office building."

Adjectives do not change their form. They remain the same whether the noun to which they refer is singular or plural, or masculine or feminine. All the above examples of adjectives come before the noun, but not all adjectives do so.

Many **adjectives** are formed from either the past participles of verbs, and so end in *-ed*, or from the present participles and so end in *-ing*. Examples of adjectives ending in *-ed* include "annoyed," "blackened," "colored," "damaged," "escaped," "fallen," "guarded," "heated," "identified," "jailed," "knotted," "labeled," "mixed," "numbered," "opened," "pleated," "recorded," "satisfied," "taped," "used," "varied," "walled," "zoned." Examples of adjectives ending in *-ing* include "amusing," "boring," "captivating," "demanding," "enchanting," "fading," "grating," "horrifying," "identifying," "jarring," "kneeling," "labouring," "manufacturing," "nursing," "operating," "parting," "quivering," "racing," "satisfying," "telling," "undermining," "worrying," "yielding."

Several **adjectives** end in *-ical* and are formed by adding *-al* to certain nouns ending in *-ic*. Examples include "arithmetical," "comical," "critical," "cynical," "fanatical," "logical," "magical," "musical," "mystical" and "sceptical." Sometimes the adjectives ending in *-ical* are formed from nouns that end in *-ics*. These include "acoustical," "ethical," "hysterical," "statistical" and "tropical." Several adjectives end in *-ic* and are formed from nouns ending in *-ics*. These include "acoustic," "acrobatic," "aerobic," "athletic," "economic," "electronic," "genetic," "gymnastic," "histrionic" and "linguistic."

Other common adjectival endings include *-ful*, as in "beautiful," "dreadful," "eventful," "graceful," "hateful," "tearful" and "youthful." They also include *-less*, as in "clueless," "graceless," "hatless," "meaningless" and "sunless."

Many adjectives end in *-able* and many end in *-ible*. There are often spelling problems with such adjectives. The following adjectives are likely to be misspelt:

Some adjectives in *-able*:

abominable	definable	impeccable	readable
acceptable	delectable	implacable	recognizable
adaptable	demonstrable	impracticable	regrettable
adorable	dependable	impressionable	renewable

advisable	desirable	indescribable	reputable
agreeable	discreditable	indispensable	sizeable
amiable	disreputable	inimitable	stoppable
approachable	durable	insufferable	tenable
available	enviable	lamentable	tolerable
bearable	excitable	manageable	transferable
beatable	excusable	measurable	understandable
believable	expendable	memorable	unmistakable
blameable	foreseeable	nameable	usable
calculable	forgettable	non-flammable	variable
capable	forgivable	objectionable	viable
changeable	healable	operable	washable
comfortable	hearable	palpable	wearable
commendable	immovable	pleasurable	winnable
conceivable	impassable	preferable	workable

Some adjectives ending in *-ible*:

accessible	credible	expressible	irascible
admissible	defensible	fallible	negligible
audible	destructible	feasible	perceptible
collapsible	digestible	flexible	permissible
combustible	discernible	forcible	possible
compatible	divisible	gullible	repressible
comprehensible	edible	indelible	reproducible
contemptible	exhaustible	intelligible	

adverb is a word that adds to our information about a verb, as in "work rapidly"; about an adjective, as in "an extremely beautiful young woman"; or about another adverb, as in "sleeping very soundly." **Adverbs** are said to modify the words to which they apply since they limit the words in some way and make them more specific. Thus, adding "slowly" to "walk," as in "They walked slowly down the hill," limits the verb "walk" since all other forms of "walk," such as "quickly," "lazily," etc, have been discarded.

There are several different kinds of **adverbs**, categorized according to the information they provide about the word they modify. They include adverbs of time, adverbs of place, adverbs of manner, adverbs of degree, adverbs of frequency, adverbs of probability, adverbs of duration, and interrogative adverbs.

Adverbs of time tell us when something happened and include such words as "now," "then," "later," "soon," "afterwards," "yesterday," etc, as in "He is due to arrive now," I will call you later," "She had a rest and went out afterwards," "They left yesterday."

Adverbs of place tell us where something happened and include such words as "there," "here," "somewhere," "anywhere," "thereabouts," "abroad," "outdoors," "overhead," "underground," "hither and thither," etc, as in "I haven"t been there," "They couldn't see her anywhere," "His family live abroad," and "We heard a noise overhead."

Adverbs of manner tell us how something happens and include a wide range of possibilities. Frequently adverbs in this category are formed by adding *-ly* to an adjective. Examples of these include:

adjective	adverb	adjective	adverb
anxious	anxiously	mean	meanly
bad	badly	narrow	narrowly
cautious	cautiously	pale	palely
dumb	dumbly	quick	quickly
elegant	elegantly	soothing	soothingly
fearless	fearlessly	tough	toughly
hot	hotly	unwilling	unwillingly
interested	interestedly	vain	vainly
joking	jokingly	weak	weakly
lame	lamely		

Some adjectives have to be modified in some way before the suffix *-ly* is added to form the adverbs. For example, in adjectives ending in *-y*, the *y* changes to *i* before *-ly* is added. Examples of these include:

adjective	adverb	adjective	adverb
angry	angrily	happy	happily
busy	busily	merry	merrily
canny	cannily	pretty	prettily
dry	drily	silly	sillily
easy	easily	tatty	tattily
funny	funnily	weary	wearily

Note the exceptions "shyly," "slyly," "wryly."

Adjectives ending in *-e* frequently drop the *e* before adding *-ly*. Examples of these include:

adjective	adverb	adjective	adverb
able	ably	peaceable	peaceably
feeble	feebly	true	truly
gentle	gently	unintelligble	unintelligibly

Suffixes other than *-ly* that may be added to adjectives to form **adverbs of manner** include *-wards*, as in "backwards," "heavenwards"; *-ways*, as in "edgeways," "sideways"; *-wise*, as in "clockwise," "moneywise."

Some **adverbs of manner** may take the same form as the adjectives to which they correspond. These include "fast," "hard," "solo," "straight," "wrong," as in "She took the wrong book" and "Don"t get me wrong."

Adverbs of degree tells us the degree, extent or intensity of something that

happens and include "hugely," "immensely," "moderately," "adequately," "greatly," "strongly," "tremendously," "profoundly," "totally," "entirely," "perfectly," "partially," "practically," "virtually," "almost," as in "They enjoyed the show hugely," "The office was not adequately equipped," "We strongly disapprove of such behavior," "He was totally unaware of the facts," "They are virtually penniless."

Adverbs of frequency are used to tell us how often something happens and include "never," "rarely," "seldom," "infrequently," "occasionally," "periodically," "intermittently," "sometimes," "often," "frequently," "regularly," "normally," "always," "constantly," "continually," as in "She never eats breakfast," "We go to the movies occasionally," "He goes to the dentist regularly," "Normally they travel by bus," "He is in pain constantly."

Adverbs of probability tells us how often something happens and include "probably," "possibly," "conceivably," "perhaps," "maybe," "presumably," "hopefully," "definitely," "certainly," "indubitably," "doubtless," as in "You will probably see them there," "He may conceivably pass the exam this time," "Presumably they know that she is leaving," "Hopefully the news will be good," "I am definitely not going," "He is indubitably a criminal."

Adverbs of duration tell us how long something takes or lasts and include "briefly," "temporarily," "long," "indefinitely," "always," "permanently," "forever," as in "We stopped briefly for coffee," "Have you known her long?," "Her face is permanently disfigured," "They have parted forever."

Adverbs of emphasis add emphasis to the action described by the verb and include "absolutely," "certainly," "positively," "quite," "really," "simply," "just," as in "They absolutely detest each other," "He positively adores her," "She really wants to be forgiven," "I simply must go now."

Interrogative adverbs ask questions and include "where," "when," "how," and "why," as in "Where are you going?," "When will you be back?," "How will you get there?," "Why have they asked you to go?" They are placed at the beginning of sentences, and such sentences always end with a question mark.

adverbial clauses are subordinate clauses that modify the main or principal clause by adding information about time, place, concession, condition, manner, purpose and result. They usually follow the main clause but most of them can be put in front of the main clause for reason of emphasis or style.

auxiliary verb refers to a verb which is used in forming tenses, moods and voices of other verbs. These include "be," "do" and "have."

The verb "to be" is used as an **auxiliary verb** with the *-ing* form of the main verb to form the continuous present tense, as in "They are living abroad just now" and "We were thinking of going on vacation but we changed our minds."

The verb "to be" is used as an **auxiliary verb** with the past participle of the main verb to form the passive voice, as in "Her hands were covered in blood" and "These toys are manufactured in China."

The verb "to have" is used as an **auxiliary verb** along with the past participle of the main verb to form the perfect tenses, as in "They have filled the post," "She had realized her mistake" and "They wished that they had gone earlier."

The verb "to be" is used as an **auxiliary verb** along with the main verb to form negative sentences, as in "She is not accepting the job." The verb "to do" is used as an **auxiliary verb** along with the main verb to form negative sentences, as in "he does not believe her." It is also used along with the main verb to form questions, as in "Does he know that she's gone?" and to form sentences in which the verb is emphasized, as in "She *does* want to go."

complex sentence refers to a type of sentence in which there is a main clause and one or more subordinate clauses. The sentence "We went to visit him although he had been unfriendly to us" is a complex sentence since it is composed of a main clause and one subordinate clause ("although he had been unfriendly to us"). The sentence "We wondered where he had gone and why he was upset" is a complex sentence since it has a main clause and two subordinate clauses ("where he had gone" and "why he was upset").

conjunctions are of two types. Coordinating conjunctions join units of equal status, as in "bread and butter," "We asked for some food and we got it." A subordinating conjunction joins a dependent or subordinating clause to main verbs: in "We asked him why he was there," "why he was there" is a subordinate clause and thus "why" is a subordinating conjunction.

definite article is a term for "the," which is the most frequently used word in the English language. "The" is used to refer back to a person or thing that has already been mentioned, as in "Jack and Jill built a model. The model was of a ship" and "We've bought a car. It was the cheapest car we could find."

"The" can be used to make a general statement about all things of a particular type, as in "The computer has lead to the loss of many jobs" and "The car has caused damage to the environment." "The" can be used to refer to a whole class or group, as in "the Italians," "the Browns" and "the younger generation."

"The" can also be used to refer to services or systems, as in "They are not on the phone." It can be used to refer to the name of a musical instrument when someone's ability to play it is being referred to, as in "Her son is learning to play the violin."

"The" indicates a person or thing to be the only one, as in the Bible, the King of Spain, the White House, the Palace of Westminster and the President of the United States.

"The" can be used instead of a possessive determiner to refer to parts of the body, as in "She took him by the arm" and "The dog bit him on the leg."

"The" is used in front of superlative adjectives, as in "the largest amount of money" and "the most beautiful woman." It can also be used to indicate that a person or thing is unique or exceptional, as in "the political debater of his generation." In this last sense "the" is pronounced "thee."

finite clause is a clause which contains a "finite verb," as in "when she sees him," "after she had defeated him," and "as they were sitting there."

finite verb is a verb that has a tense and has a subject with which it agrees in number and person. For example "cries" is finite in the sentence "The child cries most of the time," and "looks" is finite in the sentence "The old man looks ill." However "go" in the sentence "He wants to go" is non-finite since it has no variation of tense and does not have a subject. Similarly in the sentence "Sitting on the river-bank, he was lost in thought," "sitting" is non-finite.

first person refers to the person who is speaking or writing when referring to himself or herself. The **first person** pronouns are "I," "me," "myself" and "mine," with the plural forms being "we," "us," "ourselves" and "ours." Examples include "She said, '*I* am going home' ," " '*I* am going shopping,' he said' ," " '*We* have very little money left,' she said to her husband," and "He said, '*We* shall have to leave now if we are to get there on time' ." The first person determiners are "my" and "our," as in "I have forgotten to bring *my* notebook" and "We must remember to bring *our* books home."

he is a personal pronoun and is used as the subject of a sentence or clause to refer to a man, boy, etc. It is thus said to be a "masculine" personal pronoun. Since he refers to a third party and does not refer to the speaker or the person being addressed , it is a "third-person pronoun." Examples include "James is quite nice but he can be boring," "Bob has got a new job and he is very pleased" and "He is rich but his parents are very poor."

He traditionally was used not only to refer to nouns relating to the masculine sex but also to nouns that are now regarded as being neutral or of "dual gender." Such nouns include "architect," "artist," "athlete," "doctor," "passenger," "parent," "pupil," "singer," "student." Without further information from the context it is impossible to know to which sex such nouns are referring. In modern usage it is regarded as sexist to assume such words to be masculine by using **he** to refer to one of them unless the context indicates that the noun in question refers to a man or boy. Formerly it was considered acceptable to write or say "Send a message to the architect who designed the building that he is to attend the meeting" whether or not the writer or speaker knew that the architect was a man. Similarly it was considered acceptable to write or say "Please tell the doctor that he is to come straight away" whether or not the speaker or writer knew that the doctor was in fact a man. Nowadays this convention is considered sexist. In order to avoid sexism it is possible to use the convention "he/she," as in "Every student was told that he/she was to be smartly dressed for the occasion," "Each passenger was informed that he/she was to arrive ten minutes before the coach was due to leave" and "Tell the doctor that he/she is required urgently." However this convention is regarded by some people as being clumsy, particularly in spoken English or in informal written English. Some people prefer to be ungrammatical and use the plural personal pronoun "they" instead of "he/she" in certain situations, as in "Every passenger was told that they had to arrive ten minutes before the coach was due to leave" and "Every student was advised that they should apply for a college place by March." In some cases it may be possible to rephrase sentences and avoid being either sexist or ungrammatical, as in "All the passengers were told that they should arrive ten minutes before the coach was due to leave" and "All students were advised that they should apply for a college place by March."

her is a personal pronoun. It is the third person singular, is feminine in gender and acts as the object in a sentence, as in "We saw her yesterday," "I don't know her," "He hardly ever sees her," "Please give this book to her," "Our daughter sometimes plays with her" and "We do not want her to come to the meeting." *See* HE.

hers is a personal pronoun. It is the third person singular, feminine in gender and is in the possessive case. "The car is not hers," "I have forgotten my book but I don't want to borrow hers," "This is my seat and that is hers," and "These clothes are hers." *See* HIS; HER.

him is the third person masculine personal pronoun when used as the object of a sentence or clause, as in "She shot him," "When the police caught the thief they arrested him" and "His parents punished him after the boy stole the money." Traditionally **him** was used to apply not only to masculine nouns, such as "man" and "boy," but also to nouns that are said to be "of dual gender." These include "architect," "artist," "parent," "passenger," "pupil" and "student." Without further information from the context, it is not possible for the speaker or writer to know the sex of the person referred to by one of these words. Formerly it was acceptable to write or say "The artist must bring an easel with him" and "Each student must bring food with him." In modern usage this convention is considered sexist and there is a modern convention that "him/her" should be used instead to avoid sexism, as in "The artist must bring an easel with him/her" and "Each student must bring food with him/her." This convention is felt by some people to be clumsy, particularly in spoken and in informal English, and some people prefer to be ungrammatical and use the plural personal pronoun "them" instead, as in "The artist must bring an

easel with them" and "Each student must bring food with them." In some situations it is possible to avoid being either sexist or ungrammatical by rephrasing the sentence, as in "All artists must bring easels with them" and "All students must bring food with them. *See* HE.

his is the third personal masculine pronoun when used to indicate possession, as in "He has hurt his leg," "The boy has taken his books home" and "Where has your father left his tools?" Traditionally **his** was used to refer not only to masculine nouns, such as "man," "boy," etc, but to what are known as nouns "of dual gender." These include "architect," "artist," "parent," "passenger," "pupil" and "student." Without further information from the context it is not possible for the speaker or the writer to know the sex of the person referred to by one of these words. Formerly it was considered acceptable to use **his** in such situations, as in "Every student has to supply his own sports equipment" and "Every passenger is responsible for his own luggage." In modern usage this is now considered sexist and there is a modern convention that "his/her" should be used instead to avoid sexism, as in "Every student has to supply his/her own sports equipment" and "Every passenger is responsible for his/her own luggage." This convention is felt by some people to be clumsy, particularly when used in spoken or informal written English. Some people prefer to be ungrammatical and use the plural personal pronoun "their," as in "Every student must supply their own sports equipment" and "Every passenger is to be responsible for their own luggage." In some situations it is possible to avoid being sexist, clumsy and ungrammatical by rephrasing the sentence, as in "All students must supply their own sports equipment" and "All passengers are to be responsible for their own luggage."

indefinite article: **a** and **an** are the forms of the indefinite article. The form **a** is used before words that begin with a consonant sound, as in "a box," "a garden," "a road," "a wall." The form **an** is used before words that begin with a vowel sound, as in "an apple," "an easel," "an ostrich," "an uncle." Note that it is the sound of the initial letter that matters and not the spelling. Thus **a** is used before words beginning with a *u* when they are pronounced with a *y* sound as though it were a consonant, as "a unit," "a usual occurrence." Similarly, **an** is used, for example, before words beginning with the letter *h* where this is not pronounced, as in "an heir," "an hour," "an honest man."

Formerly it was quite common to use **an** before words that begin with an *h* sound and also begin with an unstressed syllable, as in "an hotel (ho-tel)," "an historic (his-tor-ik) occasion," "an hereditary (her-ed-it-ary) disease." It is now more usual nowadays to use **a** in such cases and ignore the question of the unstressed syllable.

intransitive verb refers to a verb that does not take a "direct object," as in "Snow fell yesterday," "The children played in the sand," "The path climbed steeply," "Time will tell," "The situation worsened," "Things improved" and "Prices increased." Many verbs can be either transitive or intransitive, according to the context. Thus "play" is **intransitive** in the sentence "The children played in the sand" but "transitive" in the sentence "The boy plays the piano." Similarly "climb" is intransitive in the sentence "The path climbs steeply" but transitive in the sentence "The mountaineers climbed Everest." Similarly "tell" is **intransitive** in the sentence "Time will tell" but "transitive" in the sentence "He will tell his life story."

irregular verbs are verbs that do not conform to the usual pattern of verbs in that some of their forms deviate from what one would expect if the pattern of regular verbs was being followed. There are four main forms of a regular verb—the infinitive or "base" form, as in "hint," "halt," "hate" and "haul"; the "third-person singular" form as "hints," "halts," "hates" and "hauls"; the *-ing* form or "present participle," as "hinting," halting," "hating" and "hauling"; the *-ed* form or "past tense" or "past participle," as "hinted," halted," "hated" and "hauled."

Irregular verbs deviate in some way from that pattern, in particular from the pattern of adding *-ed* to the past tense and past participle. They fall into several categories.

One category concerns those which have the same form in the past tense and past participle forms as the infinitive and do not end in *-ed*, like regular verbs. These include:

infinitive	past tense	past participle
bet	bet	bet
burst	burst	burst
cast	cast	cast
cost	cost	cost
cut	cut	cut
hit	hit	hit
hurt	hurt	hurt
let	let	let
put	put	put
run	run	run
set	set	set
shed	shed	shed
shut	shut	shut
slit	slit	slit
split	split	split
spread	spread	spread

Some **irregular verbs** have two past tenses and two past participles which are the same, as in:

infinitive	past tense	past participle
burn	burned, burnt	burned, burnt

infinitive	past tense	past participle
dream	dreamed, dreamt	dreamed, dreamt
dwell	dwelled, dwelt	dwelled, dwelt
hang	hanged, hung	hanged, hung
kneel	kneeled, knelt	kneeled, knelt
lean	leaned, leant	leaned, leant
leap	leaped, leapt	leaped, leapt
learn	learned, learnt	learned, learnt
light	lighted, lit	lighted, lit
smell	smelled, smelt	smelled, smelt
speed	speeded, sped	speeded, sped
spill	spilled, spilt	spilled, spilt
spoil	spoiled, spoilt	spoiled, spoilt
weave	weaved, woven	weaved, woven
wet	wetted, wet	wetted, wet

Some **irregular verbs** have past tenses which do not end in *-ed* and have the same form as the past participle. These include:

infinitive	past tense	past participle
become	became	became
bend	bent	bent
bleed	bled	bled
breed	bred	bred
build	built	built
cling	clung	clung
come	came	came
dig	dug	dug
feel	felt	felt
fight	fought	fought
find	found	found
flee	fled	fled
fling	flung	flung
get	got	gotten
grind	ground	ground
hear	heard	heard
hold	held	held
keep	kept	kept
lay	laid	laid
lead	led	led
leave	left	left
lend	lent	lent
lose	lost	lost
make	made	made
mean	meant	meant
meet	met	met
pay	paid	paid
rend	rent	rent
say	said	said
seek	sought	sought
sell	sold	sold
send	sent	sent
shine	shone	shone
shoe	shod	shod
sit	sat	sat
sleep	slept	slept
slide	slid	slid
sling	slung	slung
slink	slunk	slunk
spend	spent	spent
spin	spun	spun
stand	stood	stood
stick	stuck	stuck
sting	stung	stung
strike	struck	struck
string	strung	strung
sweep	swept	swept
swing	swung	swung
teach	taught	taught
tell	told	told
think	thought	thought
understand	understood	understood
weep	wept	wept
win	won	won
wring	wrung	wrung

Some **irregular verbs** have regular past tense forms but two possible past participles, one of which is regular. These include:

infinitive	past tense	past participle
mow	mowed	mowed, mown
prove	proved	proved, proven
sew	sewed	sewn, sewed
show	showed	showed, shown
sow	sowed	sowed, sown
swell	swelled	swelled, swollen

Some **irregular verbs** have past tenses and past participles that are different from each other and different from the infinitive. These include:

infinitive	past tense	past participle
arise	arose	arisen
awake	awoke	awoken
bear	bore	borne
begin	began	begun

bid	bade	bidden
bite	bit	bitten
blow	blew	blown
break	broke	broken
choose	chose	chosen
do	did	done
draw	drew	drawn
drink	drank	drunk
drive	drove	driven
eat	ate	eaten
fall	fell	fallen
fly	flew	flown
forbear	forbore	forborne
forbid	forbade	forbidden
forgive	forgave	forgiven
forget	forgot	forgotten
forsake	forsook	forsaken
freeze	froze	frozen
forswear	forswore	forsworn
give	gave	given
go	went	gone
grow	grew	grown
hew	hewed	hewn
hide	hid	hidden
know	knew	known
lie	lay	lain
ride	rode	ridden
ring	rang	rung
saw	sawed	sawn
see	saw	seen
rise	rose	risen
shake	shook	shaken
shrink	shrank	shrunk
slay	slew	slain
speak	spoke	spoken
spring	sprang	sprung
steal	stole	stolen
stink	stank	stunk
strew	strewed	strewn
stride	strode	stridden
strive	strove	striven
swear	swore	sworn
swim	swam	swum
take	took	taken
tear	tore	torn
throw	threw	thrown
tread	trod	trodden
wake	woken	woke
wear	wore	worn
write	written	wrote

major sentence can be used to refer to a sentence that contains at least one subject and a finite verb, as in "We are going" and "They won." They frequently have more elements than this, as in "They bought a car," "We lost the match," "They arrived yesterday" and "We are going away next week." They are sometimes described as "regular" because they divide into certain structural patterns, a subject, finite verb, adverb or adverbial, etc. The opposite of a **major sentence** is called a "minor sentence," "irregular sentence" or "fragmentary sentence." These include interjections such as "Ouch!" and "How terrible"; formula expressions, such as "Good morning" and "Well done"; and short forms of longer expressions, as in "Traffic diverted," "Shop closed," "No dogs" and "Flooding ahead." Such short forms could be rephrased to become "major sentences," as in "Traffic has been diverted because of roadworks," "The shop is closed on Sundays," "The owner does not allow dogs in her shop" and "There was flooding ahead on the motorway."

modal verb refers to a type of "auxiliary verb" that "helps" the main verb to express a range of meanings including, for example, such meanings as possibility, probability, wants, wishes, necessity, permission, suggestions, etc. The main modal verbs are "can," "could"; "may," "might"; "will," "would"; "shall," "should"; "must." Modal verbs have only one form. They have no *-s* form in the third person singular, no infinitive and no participles. Examples of modal verbs include "He cannot read and write," "She could go if she wanted to" (expressing ability); "You can have another cookie," "You may answer the question" (expressing permission); "We may see her on the way to the station," "We might get there by nightfall" (expressing possibility); "Will you have some wine?," "Would you take a seat?" (expressing an offer or invitation); "We should arrive by dawn," "That must be a record" (expressing probability and certainty); "You may prefer to wait," "You might like to leave instructions" (expressing suggestion); "Can you find the time to phone him for me?," "Could you give him a message?" (expressing instructions and requests); "They must leave at once," "We must get there on time" (expressing necessity).

modifier refers to a word, or group of words, that "modifies" or affects the meaning of another word in some way, usually by adding more information about it. **Modifiers** are frequently used with nouns. They can be adjectives, as in "He works in the *main* building" and "They need a *larger* house." **Modifiers** of nouns can be nouns themselves, as in "the *theatre* profession," "the *publishing* industry" and "*singing* tuition." They can also be place names, as in "a *Paris* cafe" and "the *London* underground" or adverbs of place and direction, as in "a *downstairs* cloakroom."

Adverbs, adjectives and pronouns can be accompanied by **modifiers.** Examples of modifiers with adverbs include "walking *amazingly* quickly" and "stopping *incredibly* abruptly." Examples of modifiers with adjectives include "a *really* warm day" and "a *deliriously* happy child." Examples of modifiers with pronouns include "*almost* no one there" and "*practically* everyone present." The examples given above are all "pre-modifiers."

mood refers to one of the categories into which verbs are divided. The verb moods are "indicative," "imperative" and "subjunctive." The indicative makes a statement, as in "He lives in France," "They have two children" and "It's starting to rain." The "imperative" is used for giving orders or making requests, as in "Shut that door!," and "Please bring me some coffee." The subjunctive was originally a term in Latin grammar and expressed a wish, supposition, doubt, improbability or other non-factual statement. It is used in English for hypothetical statements and certain formal "that" clauses, as in "If I were you I would have nothing to do with it," "If you were to go now you would arrive on time," and "It was his lawyer who suggested that he sue the firm." The word **mood** arose because it was said to indicate the verb's attitude or viewpoint.

non-finite clause is a clause which contains a "non-finite verb." Thus in the sentence "He works hard to earn a living," "to earn a living" is a non-finite clause since "to earn" is an infinitive and so a non-finite verb. Similarly in the sentence "Getting there was a problem," "getting there" is a non-finite clause, "getting" being a present participle and so a non-finite verb.

non-finite verb is one which shows no variation in tense and which has no subject. The non-finite verb forms include the infinitive form, as in "go," the present participle and gerund, as in "going," and the past participle, as in "gone."

noun indicates the name of something or someone. Thus "anchor," "baker," "cat," "elephant," "foot," "gate," "lake," "pear," "shoe," "trunk" and "wallet" are all nouns. There are various categories of nouns.

noun clause refers to a "subordinate clause" which performs a function in a sentence similar to a noun or noun phrase. It can act as the subject, object or complement of a main clause. In the sentence "Where he goes is his own business," "where he goes" is a **noun clause**. In the sentence "They asked why he objected," "why he objected" is a **noun clause**. A **noun clause** is also known as a nominal clause.

noun phrase refers to a group of words containing a noun as its main word and functioning like a noun in a sentence. Thus it can function as the subject, object or complement of a sentence. In the sentence "The large black dog bit him," "the large black dog" is a **noun phrase** and in the sentence "They bought a house with a garden," "with a garden" is a **noun phrase**. In the sentence "She is a complete fool," "a complete fool" is a noun phrase.

passive voice designates the voice of a verb whereby the subject is the recipient of the action of the verb. Thus, in the sentence "Mary was kicked by her brother," "Mary" is the receiver of the "kick" and so "kick" is in the passive voice. Had it been in the active voice it would have been "Her brother kicked Mary." Thus "the brother" is the subject and not the receiver of the action.

personal pronouns are used to refer back to someone or something that has already been mentioned. The personal pronouns are divided into subject pronouns, object, pronouns and possessive pronouns. They are also categorized according to "person." *See* FIRST PERSON, SECOND PERSON and THIRD PERSON.

prepositions are words which relate two elements of a sentence, clause or phrase together. They show how the elements relate in time or space and generally precede the words which they "govern." Words governed by **prepositions** are nouns or pronouns. **Prepositions** are often very short words, as "at," "in," "on," "to," "before" and "after." Some complex prepositions consist of two words, as "ahead of," "instead of," "apart from," and some consist of three, as "with reference to," "in accordance with" and "in addition to." Examples of **prepositions** in sentences include "The cat sat on the mat," "We were at a concert," "They are in shock," "She arrived before me" and "Apart from you she has no friends."

pronoun is a word that takes the place of a noun or a noun phrase.

second person refers to the person or thing to whom one is talking. The term is applied to personal pronouns. The second person singular whether acting as the subject of a sentence is "you," as in "I told you so," "We informed you of our decision" and "They might have asked you sooner." The **second person** personal pronoun does not alter its form in the plural in English, unlike in some languages. The possessive form of the **second person** pronoun is "yours" whether singular or plural, as in "He said to the boys 'These books are not yours' " and "This pen must be yours."

sentence is at the head of the hierarchy of grammar. All the other elements, such as words, phrases and clauses go to make up sentences. It is difficult to define a sentence. In terms of recognizing a sentence visually it can be described as beginning with a capital letter and ending with a period, or with an equivalent to the period, such as an exclamation mark. It is a unit of grammar that can stand alone and make sense and obeys certain grammatical rules, such as usually having a subject and a predicate, as in "The girl banged the door," where "the girl" is the subject and "the door" is the predicate.

simple sentence is a sentence which cannot be broken down into other clauses. It generally contains a finite verb. Simple sentences include "The man stole the car," "She nudged him" and "He kicked the ball."

tense is used to show the time at which the action of a verb takes place. One of the tenses in English is the "present tense." It is used to indicate an action now going on or a state now existing. A distinction can be made between the "habitual present," which marks habitual or repeated actions or recurring events, and the "stative present," which indicates something that is true at all times. Examples of "habitual present" include "He works long hours" and "She walks to work." Examples of the stative tense include "The world is round" and "Everyone must die eventually."

The progressive present or continuous present is formed with the verb "to be" and the present participle, as in, "He is walking to the next village," "They are thinking about leaving" ,'She was driving along the road when she saw him" and "They were worrying about the state of the economy."

The "past tense" refers to an action or state which has taken place before the present time. In the case of "irregular verbs" it is formed by adding *-ed* to the base form of the verb, as in "fear/feared," "look/looked," and "turn/turned." For the past tense of "irregular verbs," *see* IRREGULAR VERBS.

The "future tense" refers to an action or state that will take place at some time in the future. It is formed with "will" and "shall." Traditionally "will" was used with the second and third person pronouns ("you," "he/she/it," "they") and "shall" with the first person ("I" and "we"), as in "You will be bored," "He will soon be home," "They will leave tomorrow," "I shall buy some bread" and "We shall go by train." Also traditionally "shall" was used with the second and third persons to indicate emphasis, insistence, determination, refusal, etc., as in "You shall go to the ball" and "He shall not be admitted." "Will" was used with the first person in the same way, as in "I will get even with him."

In modern usage "will" is generally used for the first person as well as for second and third, as in "I will see you tomorrow" and "We will be there soon" and "shall" is used for emphasis, insistence, etc. for first, second and third persons.

The "future tense" can also be formed with the use of "be about to" or "be going to," as in "We were about to leave" and "They were going to look for a house.

Other tenses include the "perfect tense" which is formed using the verb "to have" and the past participle. In the case of "regular verbs" the "past participle" is formed by adding "ed" to the base form of the verb. For the past participles of "irregular verbs" see irregular verbs. Examples of the "perfect tense" include "He has played his last match," "We have traveled all day" and "They have thought a lot about it."

The "past perfect tense" or "pluperfect tense" is formed using the verb "to have" and the past participle, as in "She had no idea that he was dead," and "They had felt unhappy about the situation."

The "future perfect" is formed using the verb "to have" and the past participle, as in "He will have arrived by now."

third person refers to a third party not the speaker or the person or thing being spoken to. Note that "person" in this context can refer to things or people. "Person" in this sense applies to personal pronouns. The third person singular forms are "he," "she" and "it" when the subject of a sentence or clause, as in "She will win" and "It will be fine." The third person singular forms are "him," "her," "it" when the object, as in "His behavior hurt her" and "She meant it." The third person plural is "they" when the subject, as in "They have left" and "They were angry" and "them" when the object, as in "His words made them angry" and "We accompanied them."

The possessive forms of the singular are "his," "hers" and "its," as in "he played his guitar" and "The dog hurt its leg" and the possessive form of the plural is theirs,as in "That car is theirs" and "They say that the book is theirs."

transitive verb is a verb which takes a direct object. In the sentence "The boy broke the window" "window" is a "direct object" and so "broke" (break) is a transitive verb. In the sentence "She eats fruit" "fruit" is a "direct object" and so "eat" is a transitive verb. In the sentence "They kill enemy soldiers" "enemy soldiers" is a "direct object" and so "kill" is a transitive verb." See INTRANSITIVE VERB.

verb is often known as a "doing" word. Although this is rather restrictive ,since it tends to preclude auxiliary verbs, modal verbs, etc. the verb is the word in a sentence that is most concerned with the action and is usually essential to the structure of the sentence. **Verbs** "inflect" and indicate tense, voice, mood, number, number and person. Most of the information on **Verbs** has been placed under related entries. See ACTIVE, PASSIVE, VOICE, AUXILIARY VERB, MODAL VERB, MOOD, FINITE VERB, NON-FINITE VERB, TRANSITIVE VERB, INTRANSITIVE VERB and IRREGULAR VERB.

verb phrase refers to a group of verb forms which has the same function as a single verb. Examples include "have been raining," "must have been lying," should not have been doing and "has been seen doing."

voice is one of the categories that describes verbs. It involves two different ways of looking at the action of verbs. It is divided into "active voice" and "passive voice." See ACTIVE VOICE and PASSIVE VOICE.

Appendix II
Proof Correction Marks

The conventional system of reader's marks should be used when preparing manuscripts or when checking proofs. The marks below are those most commonly used. The correction should be clearly marked within the text, and in the margin. When several corrections within the same line are required the marks should be separated by a clear vertical or diagonal line.

Marginal mark	Meaning	Corresponding marks in the text
ℐ	Delete (take out)	Strike through words or letters to be taken out
ℐ̰	Delete and close up	Strike through and place ◠ above and below words or letters to be taken out
#ⱡ	Insert space	Caret mark ⋏ in required position
stet	Leave as printed	Dots under letters or words which are to remain
caps	Change to capital letters	Three lines under letters or words to be altered
s.c.	Change to small capitals	Two lines under letters or words to be altered
caps & s.c.	Use capital letters for initial letters and small capitals for remainder of words	Three lines under initial letters and two lines under remainder of the words
l.c.	Change to lower case	Encircle letters to be changed
bold	Change to bold type	Wavy line under letters or words to be altered
ital.	Change to italics	Line under letters or words affected
rom.	Change to roman type	Encircle words to be altered
w.f.	Wrong font — replace by letter of correct font	Encircle letter to be altered
ઈ	Inverted type	Encircle letter to be altered
eq #	Make spacing equal	∟ between words
less #	Reduce space	∟ between words
trs.	Transpose the order of letters or words	⌐⌐⌐ between letters or words (numbering when necessary)
□ⱡ	Indent one em	⌐
‖	Correct the vertical alignment	As marginal mark
═	Straighten lines	As marginal mark, drawn through lines to be straightened
n.p.	Begin a new paragraph	⌐ before first word of new paragraph
run on	No fresh paragraph here	Connecting line between paragraphs
spell out	The abbreviation or figure to be spelt out in full	Encircle words or figures to be altered
out – see copy	Insert omitted portion of copy	Caret mark ⋏ in required position
⊙ⱡ	Insert period	" "
⸝ⱡ	Insert comma	" "
⊙ⱡ	Insert colon	" "
⸵ⱡ	Insert semicolon	" "
ⱶⱡ	Insert hyphen	" "
⸮ⱡ	Insert interrogation mark	" "
em ⱡ	Insert one-em rule	" "
ⵑⱡ	Insert exclamation mark	" "
⸰	Insert apostrophe	" "
⸰²	Insert superior figure	" "
₂⸰	Insert inferior figure	" "
"	Insert quotation marks	" "
⸢⸣ⱡ	Insert a three-dot leader	" "
?	Refer to author	Encircle words, etc., affected
c/⸴	Insert parentheses	Caret marks in required positions
⸢/⸥	Insert brackets	" "

Appendix III
The United States of America

The States: capital, postal abbreviation, area, population, motto, capital, flower, bird and nickname

Alabama (AL)
Area (sq miles): 51,705. Area (sq km): 133,915
Population: 4,352,000
Motto: Crossroads of America
Capital: Montgomery
State flower: Camellia
State bird: Yellowhammer
Nicknames: Heart of Dixie; Camellia State

Alaska (AK)
Area (sq miles): 591,004. Area (sq km): 1,530,693
Population: 614,000
Motto: North to the future
Capital: Juneau
State flower: Forget-me-not
State bird: Willow ptarmigan
Nickname: The Last Frontier

Arizona (AZ)
Area (sq miles): 114,000. Area (sq km): 295,259
Population: 4,668,000
Motto: *Diat Deus* ("God enriches")
Capital: Phoenix
State flower: Saguaro
State bird: Cactus wren
Nickname: Grand Canyon State

Arkansas (AR)
Area (sq miles): 53,187. Area (sq km): 137,754
Population: 2,538,000
Motto: *Regnat Populus* ("The people rule")
Capital: Little Rock
State flower: Apple blossom
State bird: Mockingbird
Nickname: Land of Opportunity

California (CA)
Area (sq miles): 158,706. Area (sq km): 411,047
Population: 32,670,000
Motto: *Eureka* ("I have found it")
Capital: Sacramento
State flower: Golden poppy
State bird: California valley quail
Nickname: Golden State

Colorado (CO)
Area (sq miles): 104,091. Area (sq km): 269,594
Population: 3,971,000
Motto: *Nil sine numine* ("Nothing without providence")
Capital: Denver
State flower: Blue (Rocky Mountain) Colombine
State bird: Lark Bunting
Nickname: Centennial State

Connecticut (CT)
Area (sq miles): 5,018. Area (sq km): 12,997
Population: 3,275,000
Motto: *Qui transtulit sustinet* ("He who transplanted still sustains")
Capital: Hartford
State flower: Mountain laurel
State bird: American robin
Nicknames: Constitution State; Nutmeg State

Delaware (DE)
Area (sq miles): 2,044. Area (sq km): 5,294
Population: 745,000
Motto: Liberty and independence
Capital: Dover
State flower: Peach blossom
State bird: Blue hen chicken
Nickname: First State; Diamond State

District of Columbia (DC)
Area (sq miles): 68. Area (sq km): 108.8
Population: 606,900
Motto: *Justitia omnibus* ("Justice for all")
Capital: Washington
State flower: American beauty rose
State bird: Wood thrush
Nickname: Capital city

Florida (FL)
Area (sq miles): 58,664. Area (sq km): 151,939
Population: 14,916,000
Motto: in God we trust
Capital: Tallahassee
State flower: Orange blossom
State bird: Mockingbird
Nickname: Sunshine State

Georgia (GA)
Area (sq miles): 58,910. Area (sq km): 152,576
Population: 7,643,000
Motto: Wisdom, justice and moderation
Capital: Atlanta
State flower: Cherokee rose
State bird: Brown thrasher
Nickname: Peace State; Empire State of the South

Hawaii (HI)
Area (sq miles): 6,471. Area (sq km): 16,760
Population: 1,194,000
Motto: The life of the land is perpetuated in righteousness
Capital: Honolulu
State flower: Hibiscus
State bird: Nene Goose/Hawaiian Goose
Nickname: Aloha State

Idaho (ID)
Area (sq miles): 83,564. Area (sq km): 216,430
Population: 1,229,000
Motto: *Esto perpetua* ("It is perpetual")
Capital: Boise
State flower: Syringa
State bird: Mountain bluebird
Nickname: Gem State

Illinois (IL)
Area (sq miles): 57,871. Area (sq km): 149, 885
Population: 12,046,000
Motto: State sovereignty — national union
Capital: Springfield
State flower: Native violet
State bird: Cardinal
Nickname: Prairie State

Indiana (IN)
Area (sq miles): 36,413. Area (sq km): 94,309
Population: 5,900,000
Motto: Crossroads of America
Capital: Indianapolis
State flower: Peony
State bird: Cardinal
Nickname: Hoosier State

Iowa (IA)
Area (sq miles): 56,275. Area (sq km): 145,752
Population: 2,863,000
Motto: Our liberties we prize and our rights we will maintain
Capital: Des Moines
State flower: Wild rose
State bird: Goldfinch
Nickname: Hawkeye State

The United States of America

Kansas (KS)
Area (sq miles): 82,277. Area (sq km): 213,096
Population: 2,629,000
Motto: *Ad astra per aspera* ("To the stars through difficulties")
Capital: Topeka
State flower: Sunflower
State bird: Western meadowlark
Nickname: Sunflower State

Kentucky (KY)
Area (sq miles): 40,409. Area (sq km): 104,659
Population: 3,937,000
Motto: United we stand, divided we fall
Capital: Frankfort
State flower: Goldenrod
State bird: Kentucky cardinal
Nickname: Bluegrass State

Louisiana (LA)
Area (sq miles): 47,752. Area (sq km): 123,677
Population: 4,369,000
Motto: Union, justice, and confidence
Capital: Baton Rouge
State flower: Magnolia
State bird: Eastern brown pelican
Nickname: Pelican State

Maine (ME)
Area (sq miles): 33,265. Area (sq km): 86,156
Population: 1,245,000
Motto: *Dirigo* ("I direct")
Capital: Augusta
State flower: White Pine cone and tassel
State bird: Chickadee
Nickname: Pine Tree State

Maryland (MD)
Area (sq miles): 10,460. Area (sq km): 27,091
Population: 5,135,000
Motto: *Fatti maschi, parole femine* ("Many deeds, womanly words")
Capital: Annapolis
State flower: Black-eyed Susan
State bird: Baltimore oriole
Nickname: Old line state; Free State

Massachusetts (MA)
Area (sq miles): 8,284. Area (sq km): 21,455
Population: 6,148,000
Motto: *Ense petit placidam sub libertate* ("By the sword we seek peace, but peace only")
Capital: Boston
State flower: Mayflower
State bird: Chickadee
Nickname: Bay State; Colony State.

Michigan (MI)
Area (sq miles): 97,102. Area (sq km): 251,493
Population: 9,818,000
Motto: *Si quaeris peninsulam amoenam* ("If you seek a pleasant peninsula, look about you").
Capital: Lansing
State flower: Apple Blossom
State bird: Robin
Nicknames: Great Lake State; Wolverine State

Minnesota (MN)
Area (sq miles): 86,614. Area (sq km): 224,329
Population: 4,726,000
Motto: *L'Etoile du nord* ("Star of the North")
Capital: St Paul
State flower: Pink and white lady's slipper
State bird: Common loon
Nicknames: North Star State; Gopher State

Mississippi (MS)
Area (sq miles): 47,689. Area (sq km): 123,514
Population: 2,752,000
Motto: *Virtute et armis* ("By valor and arms").
Capital: Jackson
State flower: Magnolia
State bird: Mockingbird
Nickname: Magnolia State

Missouri (MO)
Area (sq miles): 69,697. Area (sq km): 180,415
Population: 5,439,000
Motto: *Salus populi suprema lex esto* ("The welfare of the people shall be the supreme law")
Capital: Jefferson City
State flower: Hawthorn
State bird: Bluebird
Nickname: Show-Me-State

Montana (MT)
Area (sq miles): 147,046. Area (sq km): 380,847
Population: 881,000
Motto: *Oro y plata* ("Gold and silver").
Capital: Helena
State flower: Bitterroot
State bird: Western meadowlark
Nickname: Treasure State

Nebraska (NE)
Area (sq miles): 77,355. Area (sq km): 200,349
Population: 1,663,000
Motto: Equality before the law
Capital: Lincoln
State flower: Goldenrod
State bird: Western Meadowlark
Nickname: Cornhusker State

Nevada (NV)
Area (sq miles): 110,561. Area (sq km): 286,352
Population: 1,745,000
Motto: All for our country
Capital: Carson City
State flower: Sagebrush
State bird: Mountain Bluebird
Nickname: Sagebrush State; Battle-Born State

New Hampshire (NH)
Area (sq miles): 9,279. Area (sq km): 24,032
Population: 1,185,000
Motto: Live free or die
Capital: Concord
State flower: Purple lilac
State bird: Purple finch
Nickname: Granite State

New Jersey (NJ)
Area (sq miles): 7,787. Area (sq km): 20,168
Population: 8,116,000
Motto: Liberty and prosperity
Capital: Trenton
State flower: Purple violet
State bird: Eastern goldfinch
Nickname: Garden State

New Mexico (NM)
Area (sq miles): 121,593. Area (sq km): 314,924
Population: 1,737,000
Motto: *Crescit eundo* ("It grows as it goes").
Capital: Santa Fe
State flower: Yucca
State bird: Roadrunner
Nickname: Land of Enchantment

New York (NY)
Area (sq miles): 52,735. Area (sq km): 136,583
Population: 18,176,000
Motto: *Excelsior* ("ever upward")
Capital: Albany
State flower: Rose (any color)
State bird: Bluebird
Nickname: Empire State

North Carolina (NC)
Area (sq miles): 52,669. Area (sq km): 136,412
Population: 7,547,000
Motto: *Esse quam videri* ("To be rather than to seem")
Capital: Raleigh
State flower: Dogwood
State bird: Cardinal
Nickname: Tar Heel State; Old North State

The United States of America

North Dakota (ND)
Area (sq miles): 70,702. Area (sq km): 183,117
Population: 639,000
Motto: Liberty and union, now and forever, one and inseparable
Capital: Bismarck
State flower: Wild prairie rose
State bird: Western Meadowlark
Nickname: Peace Garden State

Ohio (OH)
Area (sq miles): 44,787. Area (sq km): 115,998
Population: 11,210,000
Motto: With God all things are possible
Capital: Columbus
State flower: Scarlet carnation
State bird: Cardinal
Nickname: Buckeye State

Oklahoma (OK)
Area (sq miles): 69,956. Area (sq km): 181,185
Population: 3,347,000
Motto: *Labor omnia vincit* ("Labor conquers all things")
Capital: Oklahoma City
State flower: Mistletoe
State bird: Scissor-tailed flycatcher
Nickname: Sooner State

Oregon (OR)
Area (sq miles): 97,073. Area (sq km): 251,418
Population: 3,282,000
Motto: The union
Capital: Salem
State flower: Oregon grape
State bird: Western meadowlark
Nickname: Beaver State

Pennsylvania (PA)
Area (sq miles): 46,063. Area (sq km): 119,251
Population: 12,002,000
Motto: Virtue, liberty and independence
Capital: Harrisburg
State flower: Mountain laurel
State bird: Ruffed grouse
Nickname: Keystone State

Rhode Island (RI)
Area (sq miles): 1,212. Area (sq km): 3,139
Population: 989,000
Motto: Hope
Capital: Providence
State flower: Violet
State bird: Rhode Island hen
Nickname: Little Rhody; Ocean State

South Carolina (SC)
Area (sq miles): 31,113. Area (sq km): 80,852
Population: 3,836,000
Motto: *Dum spiro spero* ("While I breathe, hope")
Capital: Columbia
State flower: Carolina jessamine
State bird: Carolina wren
Nickname: Palmetto State

South Dakota (SD)
Area (sq miles): 77,116. Area (sq km): 199,730
Population: 739,000
Motto: Under God, the people rule
Capital: Pierre
State flower: Pasque flower
State bird: Ring-knecked Pheasant
Nickname: Coyote State; Sunshine State

Tennessee (TN)
Area (sq miles): 42,144. Area (sq km): 109,152
Population: 5,431,000
Motto: Agriculture and commerce
Capital: Nashville
State flower: Iris
State bird: Mockingbird
Nickname: Volunteer State

Texas (TX)
Area (sq miles): 266,807. Area (sq km): 691,027
Population: 19,760,000
Motto: Friendship
Capital: Austin
State bird: Mockingbird
Nickname: Lone Star State

Utah (UT)
Area (sq miles): 84,899. Area (sq km): 219,887
Population: 2,010,000
Motto: Industry
Capital: Salt Lake City
State flower: Sego lily
State bird: Seagull
Nickname: Beehive State

Vermont (VT)
Area (sq miles): 9,614. Area (sq km): 24,900
Population: 591,000
Motto: Freedom and unity
Capital: Montpelier
State flower: Red clover
State bird: Thrush
Nickname: Green Mountain State

Virginia (VA)
Area (sq miles): 40,767. Area (sq km): 105,586
Population: 6,792,000
Motto: *Sic semper tyannis* ("Thus always to tyrants")
Capital: Richmond
State flower: Flowering dogwood
State bird: Cardinal
Nickname: Old Dominion

Washington (WA)
Area (sq miles): 68,139. Area (sq km): 176,479
Population: 5,690,000
Motto: *Alki* ("By and by")
Capital: Olympia
State flower: Rhododendron
State bird: Willow Goldfinch
Nickname: Evergreen State

West Virginia (WV)
Area (sq miles): 24,231. Area (sq km): 62,758
Population: 1,812,000
Motto: *Montani semper liberi* ("Mountaineers are always free")
Capital: Charlestown
State flower: Rhododendron
State bird: Cardinal
Nickname: Mountain State

Wisconsin (WI)
Area (sq miles): 66,215. Area (sq km): 171,496
Population: 5,224,000
Motto: Forward
Capital: Madison
State flower: Wood violet
State bird: Robin
Nickname: Badger State

Wyoming (WY)
Area (sq miles): 97,809. Area (sq km): 253,324
Population: 481,000
Motto: Equal rights
Capital: Cheyenne
State flower: Indian paintbrush
State bird: Meadowlark
Nickname: Equality State

Commonwealth: Puerto Rico (PR)
Area (sq miles): 3,349. Area (sq km): 8,647
Population: 3,829,000
Motto: *Joannes est nomen eius* ("John is his name")
Capital: San Juan
State flower: Maga
State bird: Reinita
Nickname: Equality State

The Declaration of Independence

IN CONGRESS, July 4, 1776.

The unanimous Declaration of the thirteen united States of America,

When in the Course of human events, it becomes necessary for one people to dissolve the political bands which have connected them with another, and to assume among the powers of the earth, the separate and equal station to which the Laws of Nature and of Nature's God entitle them, a decent respect to the opinions of mankind requires that they should declare the causes which impel them to the separation.

We hold these truths to be self-evident, that all men are created equal, that they are endowed by their Creator with certain unalienable Rights, that among these are Life, Liberty and the pursuit of Happiness.—That to secure these rights, Governments are instituted among Men, deriving their just powers from the consent of the governed, —That whenever any Form of Government becomes destructive of these ends, it is the Right of the People to alter or to abolish it, and to institute new Government, laying its foundation on such principles and organizing its powers in such form, as to them shall seem most likely to effect their Safety and Happiness. Prudence, indeed, will dictate that Governments long established should not be changed for light and transient causes; and accordingly all experience hath shewn, that mankind are more disposed to suffer, while evils are sufferable, than to right themselves by abolishing the forms to which they are accustomed. But when a long train of abuses and usurpations, pursuing invariably the same Object evinces a design to reduce them under absolute Despotism, it is their right, it is their duty, to throw off such Government, and to provide new Guards for their future security.—Such has been the patient sufferance of these Colonies; and such is now the necessity which constrains them to alter their former Systems of Government. The history of the present King of Great Britain is a history of repeated injuries and usurpations, all having in direct object the establishment of an absolute Tyranny over these States. To prove this, let Facts be submitted to a candid world.

He has refused his Assent to Laws, the most wholesome and necessary for the public good.

He has forbidden his Governors to pass Laws of immediate and pressing importance, unless suspended in their operation till his Assent should be obtained; and when so suspended, he has utterly neglected to attend to them.

He has refused to pass other Laws for the accommodation of large districts of people, unless those people would relinquish the right of Representation in the Legislature, a right inestimable to them and formidable to tyrants only.

He has called together legislative bodies at places unusual, uncomfortable, and distant from the depository of their public Records, for the sole purpose of fatiguing them into compliance with his measures.

He has dissolved Representative Houses repeatedly, for opposing with manly firmness his invasions on the rights of the people.

He has refused for a long time, after such dissolutions, to cause others to be elected; whereby the Legislative powers, incapable of Annihilation, have returned to the People at large for their exercise; the State remaining in the mean time exposed to all the dangers of invasion from without, and convulsions within.

He has endeavoured to prevent the population of these States; for that purpose obstructing the Laws for Naturalization of Foreigners; refusing to pass others to encourage their migrations hither, and raising the conditions of new Appropriations of Lands.

He has obstructed the Administration of Justice, by refusing his Assent to Laws for establishing Judiciary powers.

He has made Judges dependent on his Will alone, for the tenure of their offices, and the amount and payment of their salaries.

He has erected a multitude of New Offices, and sent hither swarms of Officers to harass our people, and eat out their substance.

He has kept among us, in times of peace, Standing Armies without the Consent of our legislatures.

He has affected to render the Military independent of and superior to the Civil power.

He has combined with others to subject us to a jurisdiction foreign to our constitution, and unacknowledged by our laws; giving his Assent to their Acts of pretended Legislation:

For Quartering large bodies of armed troops among us:

For protecting them, by a mock Trial, from punishment for any Murders which they should commit on the Inhabitants of these States:

For cutting off our Trade with all parts of the world:

For imposing Taxes on us without our Consent:

For depriving us in many cases, of the benefits of Trial by Jury:

For transporting us beyond Seas to be tried for pretended offences

For abolishing the free System of English Laws in a neighbouring Province, establishing therein an Arbitrary government, and enlarging its Boundaries so as to render it at once an example and fit instrument for introducing the same absolute rule into these Colonies:

For taking away our Charters, abolishing our most valuable Laws, and altering fundamentally the Forms of our Governments:

For suspending our own Legislatures, and declaring themselves invested with power to legislate for us in all cases whatsoever.

He has abdicated Government here, by declaring us out of his Protection and waging War against us.

He has plundered our seas, ravaged our Coasts, burnt our towns, and destroyed the lives of our people.

He is at this time transporting large Armies of foreign Mercenaries to compleat the works of death, desolation and tyranny, already begun with circumstances of Cruelty & perfidy scarcely paralleled in the most barbarous ages, and totally unworthy of the Head of a civilized nation.

He has constrained our fellow Citizens taken Captive on the high Seas to bear Arms against their Country, to become the executioners of their friends and Brethren, or to fall themselves by their Hands.

He has excited domestic insurrections amongst us, and has endeavoured to bring on the inhabitants of our frontiers, the merciless Indian Savages, whose known rule of warfare, is an undistinguished destruction of all ages, sexes and conditions.

In every stage of these Oppressions We have Petitioned for Redress in the most humble terms: Our repeated Petitions have been answered only by repeated injury. A Prince whose character is thus marked by every act which may define a Tyrant, is unfit to be the ruler of a free people.

Nor have We been wanting in attentions to our British brethren. We have warned them from time to time of attempts by their legislature to extend an unwarrantable jurisdiction over us. We have reminded them of the circumstances of our emigration and settlement here. We have appealed to their native justice and magnanimity, and we have conjured them by the ties of our common kindred to disavow these usurpations, which, would inevitably interrupt our connections and correspondence. They too have been deaf to the voice of justice and of consanguinity. We must, therefore, acquiesce in the necessity, which denounces our Separation, and hold them, as we hold the rest of mankind, Enemies in War, in Peace Friends.

We, therefore, the Representatives of the united States of America, in General Congress, Assembled, appealing to the Supreme Judge of the world for the rectitude of our intentions, do, in the Name, and by Authority of the good People of these Colonies, solemnly publish and declare, That these United Colonies are, and of Right ought to be Free and Independent States; that they are Absolved from all Allegiance to the British Crown, and that all political connection between them and the State of Great Britain, is and ought to be totally dissolved; and that as Free and Independent States, they have full Power to levy War, conclude Peace, contract Alliances, establish Commerce, and to do all other Acts and Things which Independent States may of right do. And for the support of this Declaration, with a firm reliance on the protection of divine Providence, we mutually pledge to each other our Lives, our Fortunes and our sacred Honor.

The 56 signatures on the Declaration appear in the positions indicated:

Column 1
Georgia: Button Gwinnett, Lyman Hall, George Walton.

Column 2
North Carolina: William Hooper, Joseph Hewes, John Penn.
South Carolina: Edward Rutledge, Thomas Heyward, Jr., Thomas Lynch, Jr., Arthur Middleton.

Column 3
Massachusetts: John Hancock.
Maryland: Samuel Chase, William Paca, Thomas Stone, Charles Carroll of Carrollton.
Virginia: George Wythe, Richard Henry Lee, Thomas Jefferson, Benjamin Harrison, Thomas Nelson, Jr., Francis Lightfoot Lee, Carter Braxton.

Column 4
Pennsylvania: Robert Morris, Benjamin Rush, Benjamin Franklin, John Morton, George Clymer, James Smith, George Taylor, James Wilson, George Ross.
Delaware: Caesar Rodney, George Read, Thomas McKean.

Column 5
New York: William Floyd, Philip Livingston, Francis Lewis, Lewis Morris.

New Jersey: Richard Stockton, John Witherspoon, Francis Hopkinson, John Hart, Abraham Clark.

Column 6
New Hampshire: Josiah Bartlett, William Whipple.
Massachusetts: Samuel Adams, John Adams, Robert Treat Paine, Elbridge Gerry.
Rhode Island: Stephen Hopkins, William Ellery.
Connecticut: Roger Sherman, Samuel Huntington, William Williams, Oliver Wolcott. New Hampshire: Matthew Thornton.

The United States of America

PRESIDENTS AND VICE PRESIDENTS OF THE UNITED STATES

President	Term	Year of Birth–Death	Party	Vice President	Year of Birth–Death	Congresses
1. George Washington	4/30/1789–3/3/1797	1732–1799	F	John Adams	1735–1826	1, 2, 3, 4
2. John Adams	3/4/1797–3/3/1801	1735–1826	F	Thomas Jefferson	1743–1826	5, 6
3. Thomas Jefferson	3/4/1801–3/3/1805	1743–1826	D–R	Aaron Burr	1756–1836	7, 8
	3/4/1805–3/3/1809			George Clinton	1739–1812	9, 10
4. James Madison	3/4/1809–3/3/1813	1751–1836	D–R	George Clinton	1739–1812	11, 12
	3/4/1813–3/3/1817			Elbridge Gerry	1744–1814	13, 14
5. James Monroe	3/4/1817–3/3/1825	1758–1835	D–R	Daniel D. Tompkins	1774–1825	15, 16, 17, 18
6. John Quincy Adams	3/4/1825–3/3/1829	1767–1848	D–R	John C. Calhoun	1782–1850	19, 20
7. Andrew Jackson	3/4/1829–3/3/1833	1767–1845	D	John C. Calhoun	1782–1850	21, 22
	3/4/1833–3/3/1837			Martin Van Buren	1782–1862	23, 24
8. Martin Van Buren	3/4/1837–3/3/1841	1782–1862	D	Richard M. Johnson	1780–1850	25, 26
9. William Henry Harrison	3/4/1841–4/4/1841	1773–1841	W	John Tyler	1790–1862	27
10. John Tyler	4/6/1841–3/3/1845	1790–1862	W	(No Vice President)		27, 28
11. James K. Polk	3/4/1845–3/3/1849	1795–1849	D	George M. Dallas	1792–1864	29, 30
12. Zachary Taylor	3/4/1849–7/9/1850	1784–1850	W	Millard Fillmore	1800–1874	31
13. Millard Fillmore	7/10/1850–3/3/1853	1800–1874	W	(No Vice President)		31, 32
14. Franklin Pierce	3/4/1853–3/3/1857	1804–1869	D	William R. King	1786–1853	33, 34
15. James Buchanan	3/4/1857–3/3/1861	1791–1868	D	John C. Breckinridge	1821–1875	35, 36
16. Abraham Lincoln	3/4/1861–3/3/1865	1809–1865	R	Hannibal Hamlin	1809–1891	37, 38
	3/4/1865–4/15/1865			Andrew Johnson	1808–1875	39
17. Andrew Johnson	4/15/1865–3/3/1869	1808–1875	D	(No Vice President)		39, 40
18. Ulysses S. Grant	3/4/1869–3/3/1873	1822–1885	R	Schuyler Colfax	1823–1885	41, 42
	3/4/1873–3/3/1877			Henry Wilson	1812–1875	43, 44
19. Rutherford B. Hayes	3/4/1877–3/3/1881	1822–1893	R	William A. Wheeler	1819–1887	45, 46
20. James Garfield	3/4/1881–9/19/1881	1831–1881	R	Chester A. Arthur	1829–1886	47
21. Chester A. Arthur	9/20/1881–3/3/1885	1829–1886	R	(No Vice President)		47, 48
22. Grover Cleveland	3/4/1885–3/3/1889	1837–1908	D	Thomas A. Hendricks	1819–1885	49, 50
23. Benjamin Harrison	3/4/1889–3/3/1893	1833–1901	R	Levi P. Morton	1824–1920	51, 52
24. Grover Cleveland	3/4/1893–3/3/1897	1837–1908	D	Adlai E. Stevenson	1835–1914	53, 54
25. William McKinley	3/4/1897–3/3/1901	1843–1901	R	Garret A. Hobart	1844–1899	55, 56
	3/4/1901–9/14/1901			Theodore Roosevelt	1858–1919	57
26. Theodore Roosevelt	9/14/1901–3/3/1905	1858–1919	R	Charles W. Fairbanks	1852–1918	57, 58
	3/4/1905–3/3/1909			Charles W. Fairbanks	1852–1918	59, 60
27. William H. Taft	3/4/1909–3/3/1913	1857–1930	R	James S. Sherman	1855–1912	61, 62
28. Woodrow Wilson	3/4/1913–3/3/1921	1856–1924	D	Thomas R. Marshall	1854–1925	63, 64, 65, 66
29. Warren G. Harding	3/4/1921–8/2/1923	1865–1923	R	Calvin Coolidge	1872–1933	67, 68
30. Calvin Coolidge	8/3/1923–3/3/1925	1872–1933	R	Charles G. Dawes	1865–1951	68
	3/4/1925–3/3/1929			Charles G. Dawes	1865–1951	69, 70
31. Herbert C. Hoover	3/4/1929–3/3/1933	1874–1964	R	Charles Curtis	1860–1936	71, 72
32. Franklin D. Roosevelt	3/4/1933–1/20/1941	1882–1945	D	John N. Garner	1868–1967	73, 74, 75, 76
	1/20/1941–1/20/1945			Henry A. Wallace	1888–1965	77, 78
	1/20/1945–4/12/1945			Harry S. Truman	1884–1972	79
33. Harry S. Truman	4/12/1945–1/20/1949	1884–1972	D	Alben W. Barkley	1877–1956	79, 80
	1/20/1949–1/20/1953			Alben W. Barkley	1877–1956	81, 82
34. Dwight D. Eisenhower	1/20/1953–1/20/1961	1890–1969	R	Richard M. Nixon	1913–1994	83, 84, 85, 86
35. John F. Kennedy	1/20/1961–11/22/1963	1917–1963	D	Lyndon B. Johnson	1908–1973	87, 88
36. Lyndon B. Johnson	11/22/1963–1/20/1965	1908–1965	D	Hubert H. Humphrey	1911–1978	88
	1/20/1965–1/20/1969			Hubert H. Humphrey	1911–1978	89, 90
37. Richard M. Nixon	1/20/1969–1/20/1973	1913–1994	R	Spiro T. Agnew	1918–1996	91, 92
	1/20/1793–8/9/1974			Spiro T. Agnew*	1918–1996	93
				Gerald R. Ford	1913–	93
38. Gerald R. Ford	8/9/1974–1/20/1977	1913–	R	Nelson A. Rockefeller	1908–1979	93, 94
39. James (Jimmy) Carter	1/20/1977–1/20/1981	1924–	D	Walter F. Mondale	1928–	95, 96
40. Ronald Reagan	1/20/1981–1/20/1989	1911–	R	George H. W. Bush	1924–	97, 98, 99, 100
41. George H. W. Bush	1/20/1989–1/20/1993	1924–	R	J. Danforth Quayle	1947–	101, 102
42. William Clinton	1/20/1993–1/20/2001	1946–	D	Albert A. Gore, Jr.	1948–	103, 104, 105, 106
43. George W. Bush	1/20/2001–	1946–	R	Richard Cheney	1941–	107

* Spiro T. Agnew resigned on October 10, 1973. Gerald R. Ford was inaugurated December 6, 1973.

F: Federalist   D–R: Democratic Republican   D: Democratic   W: Whig   R: Republican

Appendix IV
Countries of the World

Afghanistan
Area: 652,090 square kilometers or 251,773 square miles
Population: 20,883,000
Capital: Kabul
Other major cities: Herat, Kandahar, Mazar-e-Sharif
Form of government: Republic
Religions: Sunni Islam, Shia Islam
Currency: Afghani

Albania
Area: 28,748 square kilometers or 11,009 square miles
Population: 3,670,000
Capital: Tirane
Other major cities: Durrès, Shkodèr, Vlorë
Form of government: Socialist Republic
Religion: Constitutionally atheist but mainly Sunni Islam
Currency: Lek

Algeria
Area: 2,381,741 square kilometers or 919,595 square miles
Population: 29,168,000
Capital: Algiers (Alger)
Other major cities: Oran, Constantine, Annaba
Form of government: Republic
Religion: Sunni Islam
Currency: Algerian Dinar

American Samoa
Area: 199 square kilometers or 77 square miles
Population: 56,000
Capital: Pago Pago
Form of government: Unincorporated Territory of the USA
Religion: Christianity
Currency: US Dollar

Andorra
Area: 453 square kilometers or 175 square miles
Population: 65,877
Capital: Andorra la Vella
Form of government: Republic
Religion: Roman Catholicism
Currency: Franc, Peseta

Angola
Area: 1,246,700 square kilometers or 481,354 square miles
Population: 11,185,000
Capital: Luanda
Other major cities: Huambo, Lobito, Benguela, Lubango
Form of government: People's Republic
Religions: Roman Catholicism, Animism
Currency: Kwanza

Anguilla
Area: 96 square kilometers or 37 square miles
Population: 12,394
Capital: The Valley
Form of government: British Overseas Territory
Religion: Christianity
Currency: East Caribbean Dollar

Antigua and Barbuda
Area: 442 square kilometers or 171 square miles
Population: 66,000
Capital: St John's
Form of government: Constitutional Monarchy
Religion: Christianity (mainly Anglicanism)
Currency: East Caribbean Dollar

Argentina
Area: 2,780,400 square kilometers or 1,073,518 square miles
Population: 35,220,000
Capital: Buenos Aires
Other major cities: Cordoba, Rosario, Mar del Plata, Mendoza, La Plata, Salta
Form of government: Federal Republic
Religion: Roman Catholicism
Currency: Peso

Armenia
Area: 29,800 square kilometers or 11,506 square miles
Population: 3,893,000
Capital: Yerevan
Other major city: Kunmayr (Gyumri)
Form of government: Republic
Religion: Armenian Orthodox
Currency: Dram

Aruba
Area: 193 square kilometers or 75 square miles
Population: 87,000
Capital: Oranjestad
Form of government: Self-governing Dutch Territory
Religion: Christianity
Currency: Aruban Florin

Australia
Area: 7,741,220 square kilometers or 2,988,902 square miles
Population: 18,871,800
Capital: Canberra
Other major cities: Adelaide, Brisbane, Melbourne, Perth, Sydney
Form of government: Consitutional Monarchy
Religion: Christianity
Currency: Australian Dollar

Austria
Area: 83,859 square kilometers or 32,378 square miles
Population: 8,106,000
Capital: Vienna
Other major cities: Graz, Linz, Salzburg, Innsbruck
Form of government: Federal Republic
Religion: Roman Catholicism
Currency: Schilling

Azerbaijan
Area: 86,600 square kilometers or 33,436 square miles
Population: 7,625,000
Capital: Baku
Other major city: Sumqayit
Form of government: Republic
Religions: Shia Islam, Sunni Islam, Russian Orthodox
Currency: Manat

Bahamas
Area: 13,878 square kilometers or 5,358 square miles
Population: 284,000
Capital: Nassau
Other important city: Freeport
Form of government: Constitutional Monarchy
Religion: Christianity
Currency: Bahamian Dollar

Bahrain
Area: 694 square kilometers or 268 square miles
Population: 599,000
Capital: Manama (Al Manamah)
Form of government: Hereditary Monarchy
Religions: Shia Islam, Sunni Islam
Currency: Bahrain Dinar

Bangladesh
Area: 143,998 square kilometers or 55,598 square miles
Population: 120,073,000
Capital: Dhaka
Other cities: Chittagong, Khulna, Narayanganj, Saidpur
Form of government: Republic
Religion: Sunni Islam
Currency: Taka

Barbados
Area: 430 square kilometers or 166 square miles
Population: 265,000
Capital: Bridgetown
Form of government: Constitutional Monarchy
Religions: Anglicanism, Methodism
Currency: Barbados Dollar

Belarus
Area: 207,600 square kilometers or 80,155 square miles
Population: 10,203,000
Capital: Minsk
Other major cities: Homyel (Gomel), Vitsyebsk, Mahilyov
Form of government: Republic
Religions: Russian Orthodox, Roman Catholicism
Currency: Rouble

Belgium
Area: 30,519 square kilometers or 11,783 square miles
Population: 10,159,000
Capital: Brussels
Other major cities: Antwerp, Charleroi, Ghent, Liège, Oostende
Form of government: Constitutional Monarchy
Religion: Roman Catholicism
Currency: Belgian Franc

Belize
Area: 22,696 square kilometers or 8,763 square miles
Population: 222,000
Capital: Belmopan
Other major city: Belize City
Form of government: Constitutional Monarchy
Religions: Roman Catholicism, Protestantism
Currency: Belize Dollar

Benin
Area: 112,622 square kilometers or 43,484 square miles
Population: 5,563,000
Capital: Porto Novo
Other major city: Cotonou
Form of government: Republic
Religions: Animism, Roman Catholicism, Sunni Islam, Christianity
Currency: CFA Franc

Bermuda
Area: 53 square kilometers or 20 square miles
Population: 64,000
Capital: Hamilton
Form of government: British Overseas Territory
Religions: Protestantism, Roman Catholicism
Currency: Bermuda Dollar

Bhutan
Area: 47,000 square kilometers or 18,147 square miles
Population: 1,812,000
Capital: Thimphu
Form of government: Constitutional Monarchy
Religions: Buddhism, Hinduism
Currency: Ngultrum

Bolivia
Area: 1,098,581 square kilometers or 424,165 square miles
Population: 8,140,000
Capital: La Paz (administrative), Sucre (legal)
Other major cities: Cochabamba, Santa Cruz, Oruro, Potosi
Form of government: Republic
Religion: Roman Catholicism
Currency: Boliviano

Bosnia-Herzegovina
Area: 51,129 square kilometers or 19,735 square miles
Population: 4,510,000
Capital: Sarajevo
Other major cities: Banja Luka, Mostar, Tuzla
Form of government: Republic
Religions: Eastern Orthodox, Sunni Islam, Roman Catholicism
Currency: Dinar

Botswana
Area: 581,730 square kilometers or 224,607 square miles
Population: 1,490,000
Capital: Gaborone
Other cities: Francistown, Molepolole, Mahalapye
Form of government: Republic
Religions: Animism, Christianity
Currency: Pula

Brazil
Area: 8,547,403 square kilometers or 3,300,171square miles
Population: 157,872,000
Capital: Brasília
Other major cities: Belem, Belo Horizonte, Curitiba, Porto Alegre, Recife,
 Rio de Janeiro, Salvador, São Paulo
Form of government: Federal Republic
Religion: Roman Catholicism
Currency: Cruzeiro

Brunei
Area: 5,765 square kilometers or 2,226 square miles
Population: 300,000
Capital: Bandar Seri Begawan
Other major cities: Kuala Belait, Seria
Form of government: Monarchy (Sultanate)
Religion: Sunni Islam
Currency: Brunei Dollar

Bulgaria
Area: 110,912 square kilometers or 42,823 square miles
Population: 8,356,000
Capital: Sofiya
Other major cities: Burgas, Plovdiv, Ruse, Varna
Form of government: Republic
Religion: Eastern Orthodox
Currency: Lev

Burkina Faso
Area: 274,000 square kilometers or 105,792 square miles
Population: 10,780,000
Capital: Ouagadougou
Other major cities: Bobo-Dioulasso, Koudougou
Form of government: Republic
Religions: Animism, Sunni Islam
Currency: CFA Franc

Burundi
Area: 27,834 square kilometers or 10,747 square miles
Population: 6,088,000
Capital: Bujumbura
Form of government: Republic
Religion: Roman Catholicism
Currency: Burundi Franc

Cambodia
Area: 181,035 square kilometers or 69,898 square miles
Population: 10,273,000
Capital: Phnom-Penh
Other major cities: Battambang, Kampong Cham
Form of government: People's Republic
Religion: Buddhism
Currency: Riel

Cameroon
Area: 475,442 square kilometers or 183,569 square miles
Population: 13,560,000
Capital: Yaoundé
Other major city: Douala
Form of government: Republic
Religions: Animism, Roman Catholicism, Sunni Islam
Currency: CFA Franc

Canada
Area: 9,970,610 square kilometers or 3,849,674 square miles
Population: 29,964,000
Capital: Ottawa
Other major cities: Calgary, Toronto, Montréal, Vancouver, Québec City,
 Winnipeg
Form of government: Federal Parliamentary State
Religions: Roman Catholicism, United Church of Canada,
 Anglicanism
Currency: Canadian Dollar

Cape Verde
Area: 4,033 square kilometers or 1,557 square miles
Population: 396,000
Capital: Praia
Form of government: Republic
Religion: Roman Catholicism
Currency: Cape Verde Escudo

Countries of the World

Cayman Islands
Area: 264 square kilometers or 102 square miles
Population: 38,000
Capital: George Town
Other main town: West Bay
Form of government: British Overseas Territory
Religion: Christianity
Currency: Cayman Islands Dollar

Central African Republic
Area: 622,984 square kilometers or 240,535 square miles
Population: 3,344,000
Capital: Bangui
Other major cities: Bambari, Bangassou
Form of government: Republic
Religions: Animism, Roman Catholicism
Currency: CFA Franc

Chad
Area: 1,284,000 square kilometers or 495,755 square miles
Population: 6,515,000
Capital: N'Djamena
Other major cities: Sarh, Moundou, Abéché
Form of government: Republic
Religions: Sunni Islam, Animism
Currency: CFA Franc

Chile
Area: 756,626 square kilometers or 292,135 square miles
Population: 14,419,000
Capital: Santiago
Other major cities: Arica, Concepcion, Valparaiso, Viña del Mar
Form of government: Republic
Religion: Roman Catholicism
Currency: Chilean Peso

China, or The People's Republic of China
Area: 9,596,961 square kilometers or 3,705,408 square miles
Population: 1,246,871,951
Capital: Beijing (Peking)
Other major cities: Chengdu, Guangzhou, Harbin, Shanghai, Tianjin, Wuhan
Form of government: People's Republic
Religions: Buddhism, Confucianism, Taoism
Currency: Yuan

Colombia
Area: 1,138,914 square kilometers or 439,737 square miles
Population: 35,626,000
Capital: Bogotá
Other major cities: Barranquilla, Cali, Cartagena, Medellin
Form of government: Republic
Religion: Roman Catholicism
Currency: Colombian Pesov

Comoros
Area: 1,865 square kilometers or 720 square miles (excluding Mayotte)
Population: 538,000
Capital: Moroni
Other towns: Dornoni, Fomboni, Mutsamudu, Mitsamiouli
Form of government: Federal Islamic Republic
Religion: Sunni Islam
Currency: Comorian Franc

Congo
Area: 342,000 square kilometers or 132,047 square miles
Population: 2,668,000
Capital: Brazzaville
Other major city: Pointe-Noire
Form of government: Republic
Religions: Christianity, Animism
Currency: CFA Franc

Congo, The Democratic Republic of (DRC)
Area: 2,344,858 square kilometers or 905,355 square miles
Population: 46,812,000
Capital: Kinshasa
Other major cities: Bukavu, Lubumbashi, Mbuji-Mayi, Kananga, Kisangani
Form of government: Republic
Religions: Roman Catholicism, Protestantism, Islam
Currency: Congolese Franc

Costa Rica
Area: 51,100 square kilometers or 19,730 square miles
Population: 3,398,000
Capital: San José
Other major cities: Alajuela, Límon, Puntarenas
Form of government: Republic
Religion: Roman Catholicism
Currency: Colon

Côte D'Ivoire
Area: 322,463 square kilometers or 124,504 square miles
Population: 14,781,000
Capital: Yamoussoukro
Other major cities: Abidjan, Bouaké, Daloa
Form of government: Republic
Religions: Animism, Sunni Islam, Roman Catholicism
Currency: CFA Franc

Croatia
Area: 56,538 square kilometers or 21,824 square miles
Population: 4,501,000
Capital: Zagreb
Other major cities: Osijek, Rijeka, Split
Form of government: Republic
Religions: Roman Catholicism, Eastern Orthodox
Currency: Kuna

Cuba
Area: 110,861 square kilometers or 42,804 square miles
Population: 11,019,000
Capital: Havana
Other major cities: Camaguey, Holguin, Santa Clara, Santiago de Cuba
Form of government: Socialist Republic
Religion: Roman Catholicism
Currency: Cuban Peso

Cyprus
Area: 9,251 square kilometers or 3,572 square miles
Population: 756,000
Capital: Nicosia
Other major cities: Famagusta, Limassol, Larnaca
Form of government: Republic
Religions: Greek Orthodox, Sunni Islam
Currency: Cyprus Pound

Czech Republic
Area: 78,864 square kilometers or 30,450 square miles
Population: 10,315,000
Capital: Prague (Praha)
Other major cities: Brno, Olomouc, Ostrava, Plzen
Form of government: Republic
Religions: Roman Catholicism, Protestantism
Currency: Koruna

Denmark
Area: 43,094 square kilometers or 16,639 square miles
Population: 5,262,000 (excluding the Faeroe Islands)
Capital: Copenhagen (København)
Other major cities: Ålborg, Århus, Odense
Form of government: Constitutional Monarchy
Religion: Lutheranism
Currency: Danish Krone

Djibouti
Area: 23,200 square kilometers or 8,958 square miles
Population: 3,280,000
Capital: Djibouti
Form of government: Republic
Religion: Sunni Islam
Currency: Djibouti Franc

Dominica
Area: 751 square kilometers or 290 square miles
Population: 74,000
Capital: Roseau
Form of government: Republic
Religion: Roman Catholicism
Currency: East Caribbean Dollar

Countries of the World

Dominican Republic
Area: 48,734 square kilometers or 18,816 square miles
Population: 8,052,000
Capital: Santo Domingo
Other cities: Barahona, Santiago, San Pedro de Macoris
Form of government: Republic
Religion: Roman Catholicism
Currency: Dominican Peso

Ecuador
Area: 283,561 square kilometers or 109,484 square miles
Population: 11,698,000
Capital: Quito
Other major cities: Guayaquil, Cuenca, Manta
Form of government: Republic
Religion: Roman Catholicism
Currency: Sucre

Egypt
Area: 1,001,449 square kilometers or 386,662 square miles
Population: 60,603,000
Capital: Cairo (El Qâhira)
Other major cities: Alexandria (El Iskandarîya), Giza (El Gîza), Port Said, Suez
Form of government: Republic
Religions: Sunni Islam, Christianity
Currency: Egyptian Pound

El Salvador
Area: 21,041 square kilometers or 8,124 square miles
Population: 5,796,000
Capital: San Salvador
Other major cities: Santa Ana, San Miguel,
Form of government: Republic
Religion: Roman Catholicism
Currency: Colón

Equatorial Guinea
Area: 28,051 square kilometers or 10,831 square miles
Population: 410,000
Capital: Malabo
Other major town: Bata
Form of government: Republic
Religion: Roman Catholicism
Currency: CFA Franc

Eritrea
Area: 28,051 square kilometers or 10,831 square miles
Population: 410,000
Capital: Malabo
Other major town: Bata
Form of government: Republic
Religion: Roman Catholicism
Currency: CFA Franc

Estonia
Area: 45,227 square kilometers or 17,413 square miles.
Population: 1,453,844
Capital: Tallinn
Other major cities: Narva, Pärnu
Form of government: Republic
Religions: Eastern Orthodox, Lutheranism
Currency: Kroon

Ethiopia
Area: 1,104,300 square kilometers or 426,373 square miles
Population: 58,506,000
Capital: Addis Ababa (Adis Abeba)
Other major towns: Dire Dawa, Gonder, Jima
Form of government: Federation
Religions: Ethiopian Orthodox, Sunni Islam
Currency: Ethiopian Birr

Falkland Islands
Area: 12,173 square kilometers or 4,700 square miles
Population: 2,221
Capital: Stanley
Form of government: British Crown Colony
Religion: Christianity
Currency: Falkland Islands Pound

Faeroe (Faroe) Islands
Area: 1,399 square kilometers or 540 square miles
Population: 47,000
Capital: Tørshavn
Form of government: Self-governing Region of Denmark
Religion: Lutheranism
Currency: Danish Krone

Fiji
Area: 18,274 square kilometers or 7,056 square miles
Population: 797,000
Capital: Suva
Form of government: Republic
Religions: Christianity, Hinduism
Currency: Fijian Dollar

Finland
Area: 338,145 square kilometers or 130,559 square miles
Population: 5,125,000
Capital: Helsinki (Helsingfors)
Other major cities: Turku, Tampere
Form of government: Republic
Religion: Lutheranism
Currency: Markka

France
Area: 551,500 square kilometers or 212,935 square miles
Population: 58,375,000
Capital: Paris
Other major cities: Bordeaux, Lyon, Marseille, Nantes, Nice, Toulouse, Strasbourg
Form of government: Republic
Religion: Roman Catholicism   Currency: Franc

French Guiana or Guyane
Area: 90,000 square kilometers or 34,749 square miles
Population: 153,000
Capital: Cayenne
Form of government: French Overseas Department
Religion: Roman Catholicism   Currency: Franc

French Polynesia
Area: 4,000 square kilometers or 1,544 square miles
Population: 223,000
Capital: Papeete
Form of government: Overseas Territory of France
Religions: Protestantism, Roman Catholicism
Currency: Franc

Gabon
Area: 267,668 square kilometers or 103,347 square miles
Population: 1,106,000
Capital: Libreville
Other major city: Port Gentil
Form of government: Republic
Religions: Roman Catholicism, Animism
Currency: CFA Franc

Gambia
Area: 11,295 square kilometers or 4,361 square miles
Population: 1,141,000
Capital: Banjul
Form of government: Republic
Religions: Sunni Islam, Christianity   Currency: Dalasi

Georgia
Area: 69,700 square kilometers or 26,911 square miles
Population: 5,411,000
Capital: T'bilisi
Other major cities: Sukhumi, Batumi
Form of government: Republic
Religions: Georgian and Russian Orthodox, Islam
Currency: Lari

Germany
Area: 356,733 square kilometers or 137,735 square miles
Population: 81,912,000
Capital: Berlin, Bonn (seat of government)
Other major cities: Cologne (Köln), Dortmund, Düsseldorf, Essen, Frankfurt, Hamburg, Leipzig, Munich (München), Stuttgart
Form of government: Republic
Religions: Lutheranism, Roman Catholicism
Currency: Deutsche Mark

Countries of the World

Ghana
Area: 238,537 square kilometers or 92,100 square miles
Population: 17,459,350
Capital: Accra
Other major cities: Sekondi-Takoradi, Kumasi, Tamale
Form of government: Republic
Religions: Protestantism, Animism, Roman Catholicism
Currency: Cedi

Gibraltar
Area: 6.5 square kilometers or 2.5 square miles
Population: 27,192
Capital: Gibraltar
Form of government: Self-governing British Colony
Religion: Christianity
Currency: Gibraltar Pound

Greece
Area: 131,957 square kilometers or 50,949 square miles
Population: 10,475,000
Capital: Athens (Athínai)
Other major cities: Iráklion, Lárisa, Patras (Patrai), Piraeus (Piraiévs), Thessaloníki
Form of government: Republic
Religion: Greek Orthodox
Currency: Drachma

Greenland
Area: 2,175,600 square kilometers or 840,000 square miles
Population: 58,200
Capital: Godthåb (Nuuk)
Form of government: Self-governing Region of Denmark
Religion: Lutheranism
Currency: Danish Krone

Grenada
Area: 344 square kilometers or 133 square miles
Population: 92,000
Capital: St George's
Form of government: Independent State within the Commonwealth
Religions: Roman Catholicism, Anglicanism, Methodism
Currency: East Caribbean Dollar

Guadelope
Area: 1,705 square kilometers or 658 square miles
Population: 431,000
Capital: Basse-Terre
Other main town: Pointe-à-Pitre
Form of government: French Overseas Department
Religion: Roman Catholicism
Currency: Franc

Guam
Area: 549 square kilometers or 212 square miles
Population: 153,000
Capital: Agana
Form of government: Unincorporated Territory of the USA
Religion: Roman Catholicism
Currency: US dollar

Guatemala
Area: 108,889 square kilometers or 42,042 square miles
Population: 10,928,000
Capital: Guatemala City
Other cities: Cobán, Puerto Barrios, Quezaltenango
Form of government: Republic
Religion: Roman Catholicism   Currency: Quetza

Guinea
Area: 245,857 square kilometers or 94,926 square miles
Population: 7,518,000
Capital: Conakry
Other major cities: Kankan, Kindia, Labé
Form of government: Republic
Religion: Sunni Islam   Currency: Guinea Franc

Guinea-Bissau
Area: 36,125 square kilometers or 13,948 square miles
Population: 1,091,000
Capital: Bissau
Form of government: Republic
Religions: Animism, Sunni Islam
Currency: Peso

Guyana
Area: 214,969 square kilometers or 83,000 square miles
Population: 838,000
Capital: Georgetown
Other cities: Linden, New Amsterdam
Form of government: Cooperative Republic
Religions: Hinduism, Protestantism, Roman Catholicism
Currency: Guyana Dollar

Haiti
Area: 27,750 square kilometers or 10,714 square miles
Population: 7,336,000
Capital: Port-au-Prince
Other towns: Cap-Haïtien, Les Cayes, Gonaïves
Form of government: Republic
Religions: Roman Catholicism, Voodooism
Currency: Gourde

Honduras
Area: 112,088 square kilometers or 43,277 square miles
Population: 6,140,000
Capital: Tegucigalpa
Other cities: San Pedro Sula, La Ceiba, Puerto Cortés
Form of government: Republic
Religion: Roman Catholicism
Currency: Lempira

Hong Kong
Area: 1,075 square kilometers or 415 square miles
Population: 6,687,200
Form of government: Special Autonomous Province of China
Religions: Buddhism, Taoism, Christianity
Currency: Hong Kong Dollar

Hungary
Area: 93,032 square kilometers or 35,920 square miles
Population: 10,193,000
Capital: Budapest
Other major cities: Debrecen, Miskolc, Pécs, Szeged
Form of government: Republic
Religions: Roman Catholicism, Calvinism, Lutheranism
Currency: Forint

Iceland
Area: 103,000 square kilometers or 39,769 square miles
Population: 275,277
Capital: Reykjavík
Other major cities: Akureyri, Kópavogur
Form of government: Republic
Religion: Lutheranism
Currency: Icelandic Króna

India
Area: 3,287,590 square kilometers or 1,269,346 square miles
Population: 970,930,000
Capital: New Delhi
Other major cities: Ahmadabad, Bangalore, Bombay, Calcutta, Delhi, Madras, Hyderabad, Kanpur
Form of government: Federal Republic, Secular Democracy
Religions: Hinduism, Islam, Sikkism, Christianity, Jainism, Buddhism
Currency: Rupee

Indonesia
Area: 1,904,569 square kilometers or 735,358 square miles
Population: 196,813,000
Capital: Jakarta
Other major cities: Bandung, Medan, Palembang, Semarang, Surabaya
Form of government: Republic
Religions: Sunni Islam, Christianity, Hinduism
Currency: Rupiah

Iran, Islamic Republic of
Area: 1,648,195 square kilometers or 634,293 square miles
Population: 61,128,000
Capital: Tehran
Other major cities: Esfahan, Mashhad, Tabriz
Government: Islamic Republic
Religion: Shia Islam
Currency: Rial

Countries of the World

Iraq
Area: 438,317 square kilometers or 169,235 square miles
Population: 20,607,000
Capital: Baghdad
Other major cities: Al-Basrah, Al Mawsil
Form of government: Republic
Religions: Shia Islam, Sunni Islam
Currency: Iraqi Dinar

Ireland, Republic of
Area: 70,284 square kilometers or 27,137 square miles
Population: 3,626,087
Capital: Dublin
Other major cities: Cork, Galway, Limerick, Waterford
Form of government: Republic
Religion: Roman Catholicism
Currency: Punt = 100 Pighne

Israel
Area: 21,056 square kilometers or 8,130 square miles
Population: 6,100,000
Capital: Tel Aviv (Tel Aviv-Yafo)
Other major cities: Jerusalem, Haifa
Form of government: Republic
Religions: Judaism, Sunni Islam, Christianity
Currency: New Israeli Shekel

Italy
Area: 301,268 square kilometers or 116,320 square miles
Population: 57,339,000
Capital: Rome (Roma)
Other major cities: Milan (Milano), Naples (Napoli), Turin
 (Torino), Genoa (Genova), Palermo, Florence (Firenze)
Form of government: Republic
Religion: Roman Catholicism
Currency: Lira

Jamaica
Area: 10,990 square kilometers or 4,243 square miles
Population: 2,491,000
Capital: Kingston
Other town: Montego Bay
Form of government: Constitutional Monarchy
Religions: Anglicanism, Roman Catholicism, Protestantism
Currency: Jamaican Dollar

Japan
Area: 377,801 square kilometers or 145,870 square miles
Population: 125,761,000
Capital: Tokyo
Other major cities: Osaka, Nagoya, Sapporo, Kobe, Kyoto, Yokohama
Form of government: Constitutional Monarchy
Religions: Shintoism, Buddhism, Christianity
Currency: Yen

Jordan, Hashemite Kingdom of
Area: 97,740 square kilometers or 37,738 square miles
Population: 5,581,000
Capital: Amman
Other major cities: Aqaba, Zarqa, Irbid
Form of government: Constitutional Monarchy
Religion: Sunni Islam
Currency: Jordanian Dinar

Kazakhstan
Area: 2,717,300 square kilometers or 1,049,156 square miles
Population: 15,671,000
Capital: Astana
Other major city: Almaty
Form of government: Republic
Religion: Sunni Islam
Currency: Tenge

Kenya
Area: 580,367 square kilometers or
Population: 31,806,000
Capital: Nairobi
Other towns: Mombasa, Eldoret, Kisumu, Nakuru
Form of government: Republic
Religions: Roman Catholicism, Protestantism, other Christianity, Animism
Currency: Kenya Shilling

Kiribati
Area: 726 square kilometers or 280 square miles
Population: 80,000
Capital: Tarawa
Government: Republic
Religions: Roman Catholicism, Protestantism
Currency: Australian Dollar

Korea or Democratic People's Republic of Korea
Area: 120,538 square kilometers or 46,540 square miles
Population: 22,466,000
Capital: Pyongyang
Other cities: Chongjin, Wonsan, Hamhung
Form of government: Socialist Republic
Religions: Buddhism, Confucianism, Chondogyo (a combination of Taoism and Confucianism)
Currency: Won

Korea, Republic of
Area: 99,373 square kilometers or 38,368 square miles
Population: 46,430,000
Capital: Seoul (Soul)
Other major cities: Pusan, Taegu
Form of government: Republic
Religions: Buddhism, Christianity, Confucianism, Chondogyo (a combination of Taoism and Confucianism) Unification Church
Currency: Won

Kuwait
Area: 17,818 square kilometers or 6,880 square miles
Population: 1,866,104
Capital: Kuwait City (Al Kuwayt)
Government: Constitutional Monarchy
Religions: Sunni Islam, Shia Islam
Currency: Kuwaiti Dinar

Kyrgyzstan
Area: 198,500 square kilometers or 76,641 square miles
Population: 4,575,000
Capital: Bishkek
Other major city: Osh
Government: Republic
Religion: Sunni Islam
Currency: Som

Laos
Area: 236,800 square kilometers or 91,429 square miles
Population: 5,035,000
Capital: Vientiane
Other major cities: Luang Prabang, Savannakhét, Paksé
Form of government: People's Republic
Religion: Buddhism
Currency: New Kip

Latvia
Area: 64,600 square kilometers or 24,942 square miles
Population: 2,491,000
Capital: Riga
Other cities: Liepaja, Daugavpils
Form of government: Republic
Religion: Lutheranism
Currency: Lat

Lebanon
Area: 10,400 square kilometers or 4,015 square miles
Population: 3,084,900
Capital: Beirut (Beyrouth)
Other important cities: Tripoli (Trablous), Sidon (Saïda),
Form of government: Republic
Religions: Shia Islam, Sunni Islam, Christianity
Currency: Lebanese Pound

Lesotho
Area: 30,355 square kilometers or 11,720 square miles
Population: 2,078,000
Capital: Maseru
Form of government: Constitutional Monarchy
Religions: Roman Catholicism, other Christianity
Currency: Loti

Countries of the World

Liberia
Area: 111,369 square kilometers or 43,000 square miles
Population: 2,820,000
Capital: Monrovia
Other major city: Buchanan
Form of government: Republic
Religions: Animism, Sunni Islam, Christianity
Currency: Liberian Dollar

Libya
Area: 1,759,540 square kilometers or 679,362 square miles
Population: 4,389,739
Capital: Tripoli (Tarabulus)
Other major cities: Banghazi, Misrâtah
Form of government: Socialist People's Republic
Religion: Sunni Islam
Currency: Libyan Dinar

Liechtenstein, Principality of
Area: 160 square kilometers or 62 square miles
Population: 31,320
Capital: Vaduz
Form of government: Constitutional Monarchy (Principality)
Religion: Roman Catholicism
Currency: Swiss Franc

Lithuania
Area: 65,200 square kilometers or 25,174 square miles
Population: 3,701,300
Capital: Vilnius
Other major cities: Kaunas, Klaipeda, Siauliai,
Form of government: Republic
Religion: Roman Catholicism
Currency: Litas

Luxembourg, Grand Duchy of
Area: 2,586 square kilometers or 998 square miles
Population: 412,000
Capital: Luxembourg City
Other cities: Esch-sur-Algette, Differdange, Dudelange
Form of government: Constitutional Monarchy (Duchy)
Religion: Roman Catholicism
Currency: Luxembourg Franc

Macao or Macau
Area: 18 square kilometers or 7 square miles
Population: 440,000
Capital: Macao
Form of government: Special Adminstrative Region under Chinese
 Sovereignity
Religions: Buddhism, Roman Catholicism
Currency: Pataca

Macedonia, Former Yugoslav Republic of (FYROM)
Area: 25,713 square kilometers or 9,928 square miles
Population: 2,174,00
Capital: Skopje
Other cities: Kumanovo, Ohrid
Form of government: Republic
Religions: Eastern Orthodox, Islam
Currency: Dinar

Madagascar
Area: 587,041 square kilometers or 226,658 square miles
Population: 15,353,000
Capital: Antananarivo
Other major cities: Fianarantsoa, Mahajanga, Toamasina, Toliara
Form of government: Republic
Religions: Animism, Roman Catholicism, Protestantism
Currency: Franc Malgache

Malawi
Area: 118,484 square kilometers or 45,747 square miles
Population: 10,114,000
Capital: Lilongwe
Other cities: Blantyre, Zomba
Form of government: Republic
Religions: Animism, Roman Catholicism, Presbyterianism
Currency: Kwacha

Malaysia
Area: 329,758 square kilometers or 127,320 square miles
Population: 20,581,000
Capital: Kuala Lumpur
Other major cities: Ipoh, George Town, Johor Baharu
Form of government: Federal Constitutional Monarchy
Religion: Islam
Currency: Ringgit or Malaysian Dollar

Maldives
Area: 298 square kilometers or 115 square miles
Population: 263,000
Capital: Malé
Form of government: Republic
Religion: Sunni Islam   Currency: Rufiyaa

Mali
Area: 1,240,192 square kilometers or 478,841 square miles
Population: 11,134,000
Capital: Bamako
Other towns: Gao, Kayes, Ségou, Mopti, Sikasso
Form of government: Republic
Religions: Sunni Islam, Animism
Currency: CFA Franc

Malta
Area: 316 square kilometers or 122 square miles
Population: 376,513
Capital: Valletta
Form of government: Republic
Religion: Roman Catholicism
Currency: Maltese Pound

Marshall Islands
Area: 181 square kilometers or 70 square miles
Population: 58,000
Capital: Dalap-Uliga-Darrit (on Majuro Atoll)
Form of government: Republic in free
association with the USA
Religion: Protestantism
Currency: US Dollar

Martinique
Area: 1,102 square kilometers or 425 square miles
Population: 384,000
Capital: Fort-de-France
Form of government: Overseas Department of France
Religion: Roman Catholicism
 Currency: French Franc

Mauritania or the Islamic Republic of Mauritania
Area: 1,025,520 square kilometers or 395,956 square miles
Population: 2,351,000
Capital: Nouakchott
Other major cities: Kaédi, Nouadhibou
Form of government: Republic
Religion: Sunni Islam   Currency: Ouguiya

Mauritius
Area: 2,040 square kilometers or 788 square miles
Population: 1,160,000
Capital: Port Louis
Form of government: Republic
Religions: Hinduism, Roman Catholicism, Sunni Islam
Currency: Mauritian Rupee

Mexico
Area: 1,958,201 square kilometers or 756,066 square miles
Population: 96,578,000
Capital: Mexico City
Other major cities: Guadalajara, León, Monterrey, Puebla,
 Tijuana
Form of government: Federal Republic
Religion: Roman Catholicism
Currency: Mexican Peso

Micronesia, Federated States of
Area: 702 square kilometers or 271 square miles
Population: 109,000
Capital: Palikir
Form of government: Republic
Religion: Christianity
Currency: US Dollar

Moldova (Moldavia)
Area: 33,700 square kilometers or 13,012 square miles
Population: 4,327,000
Capital: Chisinau
Other cities: Tiraspol, Tighina, Bel'tsy
Form of government: Republic
Religion: Russian Orthodox
Currency: Leu

Monaco
Area: 1 square kilometre or 0.4 square miles
Population: 32,000
Capital: Monaco
Form of government: Constitutional Monarchy
Religion: Roman Catholicism
Currency: French Franc

Mongolia
Area: 1,566,500 square kilometers or 604,829 square miles
Population: 2,354,000
Capital: Ulaanbaatar
Other cities: Altay, Saynshand, Hovd, Choybalsan, Tsetserleg
Form of government: Republic
Religions: Buddhism, Shamanism, Islam
Currency: Tughrik

Montserrat
Area: 102 square kilometers or 39 square miles
Population: 4,500
Capital: Plymouth
Form of government: British Overseas Territory
Religion: Christianity
Currency: East Caribbean Dollar

Morocco
Area: 446,550 square kilometers or 172,414 square miles
Population: 27,623,000
Capital: Rabat
Other major cities: Casablanca (Dar el Beida), Fès, Marrakech, Tanger
Form of government: Constitutional Monarchy
Religion: Sunni Islam
Currency: Dirham

Mozambique
Area: 799,380 square kilometers or 309,496 square miles
Population: 16,916,000
Capital: Maputo
Other towns: Beira, Nampula
Form of government: Republic
Religions: Animism, Roman Catholicism, Sunni Islam
Currency: Metical

Myanmar, Union of
Area: 676,578 square kilometers or 261,228 square miles
Population: 45,922,000
Capital: Rangoon (Yangon)
Other major cities: Mandalay, Moulmein, Pegu
Form of government: Republic
Religion: Buddhism
Currency: Kyat

Namibia
Area: 824,292 square kilometers or 318,261 square miles
Population: 1,575,000
Capital: Windhoek
Other cities: Swakopmund, Lüderitz
Form of government: Republic
Religions: Lutheranism, Roman Catholicism, other Christianity
Currency: Namibian Dollar

Nauru
Area: 21 square kilometers or 8 square miles
Population: 11,000
Capital: Nauru
Form of government: Republic
Religions: Protestantism, Roman Catholicism
Currency: Australian Dollar

Nepal, Kingdom of
Area: 147,181 square kilometers or 56,827 square miles
Population: 21,127,000
Capital: Kathmandu
Other city: Biratnagar
Form of government: Constitutional Monarchy
Religions: Hinduism, Buddhism
Currency: Nepalese Rupee

Netherlands
Area: 40,844 square kilometers or 15,770 square miles
Population: 15,517,000
Capital: Amsterdam
Seat of government: The Hague (s'Gravenhage)
Other major cities: Rotterdam, Eindhoven
Form of government: Constitutional Monarchy
Religions: Roman Catholicism, Dutch Reform, Calvinism
Currency: Guilder

Netherlands Antilles
Area: 800 square kilometers or 309 square miles
Population: 207,333
Capital: Willemstad
Form of government: Self-governing Dutch Territory
Religion: Roman Catholicism
Currency: Netherlands Antilles Guilder

New Caledonia or Nouvelle Calédonie
Area: 18,575 square kilometers or 7,172 square miles
Population: 189,000
Capital: Noumea
Form of government: French Overseas Territory
Religion: Roman Catholicism
Currency: Franc

New Zealand
Area: 270,534 square kilometers or 104,454 square miles
Population: 3,681,546
Capital: Wellington
Other major cities: Auckland, Christchurch, Dunedin, Hamilton
Form of government: Constitutional Monarchy
Religions: Anglicanism, Roman Catholicism, Presbyterianism
Currency: New Zealand Dollar

Nicaragua
Area: 130,668 square kilometers or 50,193 square miles
Population: 4,663,000
Form of government: Republic
Capital: Managua
Other cities: Matagalpa, León, Granada
Religion: Roman Catholicism
Currency: Córdoba Oro

Niger
Area: 1,267,000 square kilometers or 489,191 square miles
Population: 9,465,000
Capital: Niamey
Other major cities: Agadez, Maradi, Tahoua, Zinder
Form of government: Republic
Religion: Sunni Islam
Currency: CFA Franc

Nigeria
Area: 923,768 square kilometers or 356,669 square miles
Population: 115,120,000
Capital: Abuja
Other major cities: Lagos, Onitsha, Enugu, Ibadan, Kano, Ogbomosho
Form of government: Federal Republic
Religions: Sunni Islam, Christianity
Currency: Naira

Northern Mariana Islands
Area: 464 square kilometers or 179 square miles
Population: 49,000
Capital: Saipan
Form of government: Commonwealth in union with the USA
Religion: Roman Catholicism
Currency: US Dollar

Countries of the World

Norway, Kingdom of
Area: 323,877 square kilometers or 125,050 square miles
Population: 4,445,460
Capital: Oslo
Other major cities: Bergen, Trondheim, Stavanger, Kristiansand, Tromsö
Form of government: Constitutional Monarchy
Religion: Lutheranism
Currency: Norwegian Krone

Oman, or the Sultanate of Oman
Area: 309,500 square kilometers or 119,498 square miles
Population: 2,302,000
Capital: Muscat (Masqat)
Other towns: Salalah, Al Khaburah, Matrah
Form of government: Monarchy
Religions: Ibadi Islam, Sunni Islam
Currency: Rial Omani

Pakistan, or the Islamic Republic of Pakistan
Area: 796,095 square kilometers or 307,374 square miles
Population: 134,146,000
Capital: Islamabad
Other major cities: Faisalabad, Hyderabad, Karachi,
Lahore, Rawalpindi
Form of government: Federal Islamic Republic
Religions: Sunni Islam, Shia Islam
Currency: Pakistan Rupee

Palau
Area: 459 square kilometers or 177 square miles
Population: 17,000
Capital: Koror
Form of government: Free Associated Republic (USA)
Religions: Roman Catholicism and Modekngei
Currency: US Dollar

Palestine
Area:
 Gaza 360 square kilometers or146 square miles
 Jericho 70 square kilometers or 27 square miles
 West Bank 5,860 square kilometers or 2,269 square miles
Population:
 Gaza 924,200
 Jericho 20,600
 West Bank 2,050,000
Form of government: Republic with limited powers
Religions: Sunni Islam, Shia Islam, Eastern Catholicism
Currency: None (Israeli and Jordanian currency used)

Panama
Area: 75,517 square kilometers or 29,157 square miles
Population: 2,674,000
Capital: Panama City
Other major cities: Colón, Puerto Armuelles, David
Form of government: Republic
Religion: Roman Catholicism
Currency: Balboa

Papua New Guinea
Area: 462,840 square kilometers or 178,704 square miles
Population: 4,400,000
Capital: Port Moresby
Form of government: Republic
Religions: Protestantism, Roman Catholicism
Currency: Kina

Paraguay
Area: 406,752 square kilometers or 157,048 square miles
Population: 4,955,000
Capital: Asunción
Other major cities: Concepción, Ciudad del Este, Encarnación
Form of government: Republic
Religion: Roman Catholicism
Currency: Guaraní

Peru
Area: 1,285,216 square kilometers or 496,225 square miles
Population: 25,015,000
Capital: Lima
Other major cities: Arequipa, Callao, Chiclayo, Cuzco, Trujillo
Form of government: Republic
Religion: Roman Catholicism
Currency: Nuevo Sol

Philippines
Area: 300,000 square kilometers or 115,831 square miles
Population: 71,899,000
Capital: Manila
Other cities: Cebu, Davao, Quezon City, Zamboanga
Form of government: Republic
Religions: Sunni Islam, Roman Catholicism, Animism
Currency: Philippine Peso

Pitcairn Islands
Area: 5 square kilometers or 2 square miles
Population: 54
Form of government: British Overseas Territory
Religion: Seventh Day Adventism
Currency: New Zealand Dollar

Poland
Area: 323,250 square kilometers or 124,808 square miles
Population: 38,628,000
Capital: Warsaw (Warszawa)
Other major cities: Gdansk, Kraków, Lódz, Poznan, Wroclaw
Form of government: Republic
Religion: Roman Catholicism
Currency: Zloty

Portugal
Area: 91,982 square kilometers or 35,514 square miles
Population: 9,920,760
Capital: Lisbon (Lisboa)
Other major cities: Braga, Coimbra, Faro, Porto, Setúbal
Form of government: Republic
Religion: Roman Catholicism
Currency: Escudo

Puerto Rico
Area: 8,875 square kilometers or 3,427 square miles
Population: 3,736,000
Capital: San Juan
Form of government: Self-governing Commonwealth (in association with the USA)
Religions: Roman Catholicism, Protestantism
Currency: US Dollar

Qatar
Area: 11,000 square kilometers or 4,247 square miles
Population: 558,000
Capital: Doha (Ad Dawhah)
Form of government: Absolute Monarchy
Religion: Wahhabi Sunni Islam
Currency: Qatar Riyal

Réunion
Area: 2,510 square kilometers or 969 square miles
Population: 664,000
Capital: St Denis
Form of government: French Overseas Department
Religion: Roman Catholicism
Currency: Franc

Romania
Area: 238,391 square kilometers or 92,043 square miles
Population: 22,520,000
Capital: Bucharest (Bucuresti)
Other major cities: Brasov, Constanta, Galati, Iasi, Timisoara, Craiova, Brâila, Arad, Ploiesti
Form of government: Republic
Religions: Romanian Orthodox, Roman Catholicism
Currency: Leu

Russia or the Russian Federation
Area: 17,075,400 square kilometers or 6,592,850 square miles
Population: 146,100,000
Capital: Moscow (Moskva)
Other major cities: St Petersburg (Sankt Peterburg), Nizhniy Novgorod, Novosibirsk, Samara
Form of government: Republic
Religions: Russian Orthodox, Sunni Islam, Shia Islam, Roman Catholicism
Currency: Rouble

Countries of the World

Rwanda
Area: 26,338 square kilometers or 10,169 square miles
Population: 5,397,000
Capital: Kigali
Other major city: Butare
Form of government: Republic
Religions: Roman Catholicism, Animism
Currency: Rwanda Franc

St Helena
Area: 122 square kilometers or 47 square miles
Population: 5,157
Capital: Jamestown
Form of government: British Overseas Territory
Currency: St Helena Pound

St Kitts and Nevis
Area: 261 square kilometers or 101 square miles
Population: 41,000
Capital: Basseterre
Other major city: Charlestown
Form of government: Constitutional Monarchy
Religions: Anglicanism, Methodism
Currency: East Caribbean Dollar

St Lucia
Area: 622 square kilometers or 240 square miles
Population: 144,000
Capital: Castries
Form of government: Constitutional Monarchy
Religion: Roman Catholicism
Currency: East Caribbean Dollar

St Vincent and the Grenadines
Area: 388 square kilometers or 150 square miles
Population: 113,000
Capital: Kingstown
Form of government: Constitutional Monarchy
Religions: Anglicanism, Methodism, Roman Catholicism
Currency: East Caribbean Dollar

San Marino
Area: 61 square kilometers or 24 square miles
Population: 25,000
Capital: San Marino
Other towns: Borgo Maggiore, Serravalle
Form of government: Republic
Religion: Roman Catholicism
Currency: Lira

Saõ Tomé and Príncipe
Area: 964 square kilometers or 372 square miles
Population: 135,000
Capital: São Tomé
Form of government: Republic
Religion: Roman Catholicism
Currency: Dobra

Saudi Arabia
Area: 2,149,690 square kilometers or 830,000 square miles
Population: 18,836,000
Capital: Riyadh (Ar Riyād)
Other major cities: Ad Dammam, Mecca (Makkah), Jeddah(Jiddah), Medina (Al Madinah)
Form of government: Monarchy
Religions: Sunni Islam, Shia Islam
Currency: Riyal

Senegal
Area: 196,722 square kilometers or 75,955 square miles
Population: 8,572,000
Capital: Dakar
Other major cities: Kaolack, Thiès, St Louis
Form of government: Republic
Religions: Sunni Islam, Roman Catholicism
Currency: CFA Franc

Seychelles
Area: 455 square kilometers or 175 square miles
Population: 76,000
Capital: Victoria
Form of government: Republic
Religion: Roman Catholicism   Currency: Seychelles Rupee

Sierra Leone
Area: 71,740 square kilometers or 27,699 square miles
Population: 4,297,000
Capital: Freetown
Other city: Bo
Form of government: Republic
Religions: Animism, Sunni Islam, Christianity
Currency: Leone

Singapore
Area: 618 square kilometers or 239 square miles
Population: 3,044,000
Capital: Singapore
Form of government: Parliamentary Democracy
Religions: Buddhism, Sunni Islam, Christianity, Hinduism
Currency: Singapore Dollar

Slovakia or the Slovak Republic
Area: 49,035 square kilometers or 18,928 square miles
Population: 5,374,000
Capital: Bratislava
Other major cities: Kosice, Zilina, Nitra
Form of government: Republic
Religion: Roman Catholicism   Currency: Slovak Koruna

Slovenia
Area: 20,256 square kilometers or 7,821 square miles
Population: 1,991,000
Capital: Ljubljana
Other major cities: Maribor, Kranj
Form of government: Republic
Religion: Roman Catholicism   Currency: Tolar

Solomon Islands
Area: 28,896 square kilometers or 11,157 square miles
Population: 391,000
Capital: Honiara
Form of government: Parliamentary Democracy within the Commonwealth
Religion: Christianity
Currency: Solomon Islands Dollar

Somalia
Area: 637,657 square kilometers or 246,201 square miles
Population: 9,822,000
Capital: Mogadishu (Muqdisho)
Other major towns: Hargeysa, Burco
Form of government: Republic
Religion: Sunni Islam   Currency: Somali Shilling

South Africa
Area: 1,221,037 square kilometers or 471,445 square miles
Population: 42,393,000
Capital: Pretoria (administrative), Cape Town (legislative)
Other major cities: Johannesburg, Durban, Port Elizabeth, Soweto
Form of government: Republic
Religions: Christianity, Hinduism, Islam
Currency: Rand

Spain
Area: 505,992 square kilometers or 195,365 square miles
Population: 39,270,400
Capital: Madrid
Other major cities: Barcelona, Valencia, Sevilla, Zaragoza, Malaga, Bilbao
Form of government: Constitutional Monarchy
Religion: Roman Catholicism   Currency: Peseta

Sri Lanka
Area: 65,610 square kilometers or 25,332 square miles
Population: 18,354,000
Capital: Colombo
Other major cities: Trincomalee, Jaffna, Kandy, Moratuwa
Form of government: Republic
Religions: Buddhism, Hinduism, Christianity, Sunni Islam
Currency: Sri Lankan Rupee

Sudan
Area: 2,505,813 square kilometers or 967,500 square miles
Population: 27,291,000
Capital: Khartoum (El Khartum)
Other major cities: Omdurman, Khartoum North, Port Sudan
Form of government: Republic
Religions: Sunni Islam, Animism, Christianity
Currency: Sudanese Dinar

Countries of the World

Suriname

Area: 163,265 square kilometers or 63,037 square miles
Population: 423,000
Capital: Paramaribo
Form of government: Republic
Religions: Hinduism, Roman Catholicism, Sunni Islam
Currency: Suriname Guilder

Swaziland

Area: 17,364 square kilometers or 6,704 square miles
Population: 938,700
Capital: Mbabane
Other towns: Big Bend, Manzini, Mankayane, Lobamba
Form of government: Monarchy
Religions: Christianity, Animism
Currency: Lilangeni

Sweden

Area: 449,964 square kilometers or 173,732 square miles
Population: 8,843,000
Capital: Stockholm
Other major cities: Göteborg, Malmö, Uppsala, Örebro, Linköping
Form of government: Constitutional Monarchy
Religion: Lutheranism
Currency: Krona

Switzerland

Area: 41,284 square kilometers or 15,940 square miles
Population: 7,076,000
Capital: Bern
Other major cities: Zürich, Basle (Basel), Geneva (Genève), Lausanne
Form of government: Federal Republic
Religions: Roman Catholicism, Protestantism
Currency: Swiss franc

Syria or the Syrian Arab Republic

Area: 185,180 square kilometers or 71,498 square miles
Population: 14,619,000
Capital: Damascus (Dimashq)
Other cities: Halab, Hims, Dar'a
Form of government: Republic
Religion: Sunni Islam
Currency: Syrian Pound

Taiwan, Republic of China

Area: 35,742 square kilometers or 13,800 square miles
Population: 21,854,273
Capital: T'ai-pei
Other major cities: Kao-hsiung, T'ai-nan, Chang-hua, Chi-lung
Form of government: Republic
Religions: Taoism, Buddhism, Christianity
Currency: New Taiwan Dollar

Tajikistan

Area: 143,100 square kilometers or 55,251 square miles
Population: 5,919,000
Capital: Dushanbe
Other major city: Khujand
Form of government: Republic
Religion: Shia Islam
Currency: Tajik Rouble

Tanzania

Area: 938,000 square kilometers or 362,162 square miles
Population: 30,799,100
Capital: Dodoma
Other towns: Dar es Salaam, Zanzibar, Mwanza, Tanga
Form of government: Republic
Religions: Sunni Islam, Roman Catholicism, Anglicanism, Hinduism
Currency: Tanzanian Shilling

Thailand

Area: 513,115 square kilometers or 198,115 square miles
Population: 60,206,000
Capital: Bangkok (Krung Thep)
Other major cities: Chiang Mai, Nakhon Ratchasima, Ubon Ratchathani
Form of government: Constitutional Monarchy
Religions: Buddhism, Sunni Islam
Currency: Baht

Togo

Area: 56,785 square kilometers or 21,925 square miles
Population: 4,201,000
Capital: Lomé
Other major city: Sokodé
Form of government: Republic
Religions: Animism, Roman Catholicism, Sunni Islam
Currency: CFA Franc

Tonga

Area: 747 square kilometers or 288 square miles
Population: 99,000
Capital: Nuku'alofa
Form of government: Constitutional Monarchy
Religions: Methodism, Roman Catholicism
Currency: Pa'anga

Trinidad and Tobago

Area: 5,130 square kilometers or 1,981 square miles
Population: 1,297,000
Capital: Port of Spain
Other towns: San Fernando, Arima
Form of government: Republic
Religions: Roman Catholicism, Hinduism, Anglicanism, Sunni Islam
Currency: Trinidad and Tobago Dollar

Tunisia

Area: 162,155 square kilometers or 62,592 square miles
Population: 9,092,000
Capital: Tunis
Other major cities: Sfax, Bizerte, Sousse
Form of government: Republic
Religion: Sunni Islam   Currency: Dinar

Turkey

Area: 774,815 square kilometers or 299,158 square miles
Population: 62,697,000
Capital: Ankara
Other major cities: Istanbul, Izmir, Adana, Bursa
Form of government: Republic
Religion: Sunni Islam   Currency: Turkish Lira

Turkmenistan

Area: 488,100 square kilometers or 188,456 square miles
Population: 4,569,000
Capital: Ashkhabad (Ashgabat)
Other cities: Chardzhou, Mary, Turkmenbashi
Form of government: Republic
Religion: Sunni Islam   Currency: Manat

Turks and Caicos Islands

Area: 430 square kilometers or 166 square miles
Population: 23,000
Capital: Grand Turk
Form of government: British Crown Colony
Religion: Christianity   Currency: US Dollar

Tuvalu

Area: 26 square kilometers or 10 square miles
Population: 10,000
Capital: Funafuti
Form of government: Constitutional Monarchy
Religion: Protestantism
Currency: Tuvalu Dollar/Australian Dollar

Uganda

Area: 241,038 square kilometers or 93,065 square miles
Population: 19,848,000
Capital: Kampala
Other cities: Entebbe, Jinja, Soroti, Mbale
Form of government: Republic
Religions: Roman Catholicism, Protestantism, Animism, Sunni Islam
Currency: Uganda Shilling

Ukraine

Area: 603,700 square kilometers or 233,090 square miles
Population: 51,094,000
Capital: Kiev (Kiyev)
Other major cities: Dnepropetrovsk, Donetsk, Khar'kov, Odessa, Lugansk, Sevastopol (in the Crimea)
Form of government: Republic
Religions: Eastern Orthodox, Roman Catholicism
Currency: Rouble

Countries of the World

United Arab Emirates (UAE)
Area: 83,600 square kilometers or 32,278 square miles
Population: 2,260,000
Capital: Abu Zabi (Abu Dhabi)
Other major cities: Dubai (Dubayy), Sharjah, Ras al Khaymah
Form of government: Monarchy
Religion: Sunni Islam   Currency: Dirham

United Kingdom of Great Britain and Northern Ireland (UK)
Area: 244,101 square kilometers or 94,248 square miles
Population: 58,784,000
Capital: London
Other major cities: Birmingham, Manchester, Glasgow, Liverpool, Edinburgh, Cardiff, Belfast
Form of government: Constitutional Monarchy
Religions: Anglicanism, Roman Catholicism, Presbyterianism, Methodism
Currency: Pound Sterling

United States of America (USA)
Area: 9,158,960 square kilometers or 3,536,278 square miles
Population: 270,298,524
Capital: Washington DC
Other major cities: New York, Chicago, Detroit, Houston, Los Angeles, Philadelphia, San Diego, San Francisco
Form of government: Federal Republic
Religions: Protestantism, Roman Catholicism, Judaism, Eastern Orthodox
Currency: US Dollar

Uruguay
Area: 177,414 square kilometers or 68,500 square miles
Population: 3,203,000
Capital: Montevideo
Other major cities: Salto, Melo
Form of government: Republic
Religions: Roman Catholicism, Protestantism
Currency: Peso Uruguayos

Uzbekistan
Area: 447,400 square kilometers or 172,742 square miles
Population: 24,000,000
Capital: Tashkent
Other cities: Urgench, Nukus, Bukhara, Samarkand
Form of government: Republic
Religions: Sunni Islam, Eastern Orthodox
Currency: Soum

Vanuatu
Area: 12,189 square kilometers or 4,706 square miles
Population: 169,000
Capital: Vila
Form of government: Republic
Religion: Roman Catholicism   Currency: Vatu

Vatican City
Area: 0.44 square kilometers or 0.2 square miles
Population: 1000
Capital: Vatican City
Form of government: Papal Commission
Religion: Roman Catholicism
Currency: Vatican City Lira

Venezuela
Area: 912,050 square kilometers or 352,145 square miles
Population: 22,710,000
Capital: Caracas
Other major cities: Maracaibo, Valencia, Barquisimeto
Form of government: Federal Republic
Religion: Roman Catholicism
Currency: Bolívar

Vietnam
Area: 331,689 square kilometers or 128,066 square miles
Population: 75,181,000
Capital: Hanoi
Other major cities: Ho Chi Minh City, Haiphong, Hué, Dà Nang
Form of government: Socialist Republic
Religions: Buddhism, Taoism, Roman Catholicsm
Currency: New Dong

Virgin Islands, British
Area: 151 square kilometers or 58 square miles
Population: 19,000
Capital: Road Town
Form of government: British Overseas Territory
Religion: Protestantism
Currency: US Dollar

Virgin Islands, US
Area: 347 square kilometers or 134 square miles
Population: 106,000
Capital: Charlotte Amalie
Form of government: Self-governing US Territory
Religion: Protestantism
Currency: US Dollar

Wallis and Futuna Islands
Area: 200 square kilometers or 77 square miles
Population: 15,000
Capital: Mata-Uru
Form of government: French Overseas Territory
Religion: Roman Catholicism
Currency: Franc

Western Sahara
Area: 266,000 square kilometers or 102,703 square miles
Population: 266,000
Capital: Laâyoune (El Aaiún)
Form of government: Republic (de facto controlled by Morocco)
Religion: Sunni Islam
Currency: Moroccan Dirham

Western Samoa
Area: 2,831 square kilometers or 1,093 square miles
Population: 166,000
Capital: Apia
Form of government: Constitutional Monarchy
Religion: Protestantism
Currency: Tala

Yemen
Area: 527,968 square kilometers or 203,850 square miles
Population: 15,919,000
Capital: San'a
Commercial capital: Aden (Adan)
Other cities: Al Hudaydah, Ta'izz
Form of government: Republic
Religions: Zaidism, Shia Islam, Sunni Islam
Currency: Riyal

Yugoslavia (FRY)
Area: 102,173 square kilometers or 39,449 square miles
Population: 10,574,000
Capital: Belgrade (Beograd)
Other cities: Nis, Novi Sad, Pristina
Form of government: Federal Republic
Religions: Eastern Orthodox, Islam
Currency: New Dinar

Zambia
Area: 752,618 square kilometers or 290,587 square miles
Population: 8,275,000
Capital: Lusaka
Other cities: Kitwe, Ndola, Mufulira
Form of government: Republic
Religions: Christianity, Animism
Currency: Kwacha

Zimbabwe
Area: 390,757 square kilometers or 150,872 square miles
Population: 11,908,000
Capital: Harare
Other cities: Bulawayo, Mutare, Gweru
Form of government: Republic
Religions: Animism, Anglicanism, Roman Catholicism
Currency: Zimbabwe Dollar

Countries of the World

WORLD TIME ZONES

At 12:00 noon, Greenwich Mean Time, the standard time is:

PLACE	LOCAL TIME	PLACE	LOCAL TIME
Addis Ababa (Ethiopia)	4pm	Karachi (Pakistan)	5pm
Alexandria (Egypt)	2pm	Lima (Peru)	7am
Amsterdam (Netherlands)	1pm	Lisbon (Portugal)	12 noon
Anchorage (USA)	2am	Los Angeles (USA)	4am
Athens (Greece)	2pm	Madrid (Spain)	1pm
Auckland (New Zealand)	12 midnight	Manila (Philippines)	8pm
Baghdad (Iraq)	3pm	Mecca (Saudi Arabia)	3pm
Bangkok (Thailand)	7pm	Melbourne (Australia)	10pm
Barcelona (Spain)	1pm	Mexico City (Mexico)	6am
Beijing (China)	8pm	Montreal (Canada)	7am
Belfast (N. Ireland)	12 noon	Moscow (Russian Fed.)	3pm
Belgrade (Fed. Rep. of Yugoslavia)	1pm	New York (USA)	7am
Berlin (Germany)	1pm	Oslo (Norway)	1pm
Bogotá (Colombia)	7am	Paris (France)	1pm
Bombay (India)	5.30pm	Perth (Australia)	8pm
Brussels (Belgium)	1pm	Prague (Czech Republic)	1pm
Bucharest (Romania)	2pm	Rangoon (Burma)	6.30pm
Budapest (Hungary)	1pm	Rio de Janeiro	9am
Buenos Aires (Argentina)	9am	Rome (Italy)	1pm
Calcutta (India)	5.30pm	St Petersburg (Russian Fed.)	3pm
Cape Town (South Africa)	2pm	Santiago (Chile)	8am
Caracas (Venezuela)	8am	Seoul (Republic of Korea)	9pm
Casablanca (Morocco)	12 noon	Shanghai (China)	8pm
Chicago (USA)	6am	Singapore (Singapore)	8pm
Copenhagen (Denmark)	2pm	Stockholm (Sweden)	1pm
Dacca (Bangladesh)	6pm	Sydney (Australia)	10pm
Darwin (Australia)	9.30pm	Tashkent (Uzbekistan)	6pm
Delhi (India)	5.30pm	Tehran (Iran)	3.30pm
Denver (USA)	5am	Tel Aviv (Israel)	2pm
Geneva (Switzerland)	1pm	Tokyo (Japan)	9pm
Havana (Cuba)	7am	Valparaíso (Chile)	8am
Helsinki (Finland)	2pm	Vancouver (Canada)	4am
Ho Chi Minh City (Vietnam)	7pm	Vienna (Austria)	1pm
Hong Kong (Hong Kong)	8pm	Vladivostock (Russian Fed.)	10pm
Istanbul (Turkey)	2pm	Warsaw (Poland)	1pm
Jakarta (Indonesia)	7pm	Wellington (New Zealand)	12 midnight
Jerusalem (Israel)	2pm	Zurich (Switzerland)	1pm
Johannesburg (South Africa)	2pm		

THE EARTH'S VITAL STATISTICS

Age:	Approx 4600 million years	Volume of the oceans:	1321 million cubic km (317 million cubic miles)
Weight:	Approx 5.976×10^{21} tonnes	Average height of land:	840 m (2756 ft) above sea level
Diameter:	Pole to Pole through the centre of the Earth 12,713 km (7900 miles)	Average depth of ocean:	3808 m (12 493 ft) below sea level
	Across the Equator through the centre of the Earth 12,756 km (7926 miles)	Density:	5.52 times water
		Mean temperature:	22°C (72°F)
		Length of year:	365.25 days
Circumference:	Around the Poles 40,008 km (24,861 miles)	Length of one rotation:	23 hours 56 minutes
	Around the Equator 40,091 km (24,912 miles)	Mean distance from Sun:	149 600 000 km (92,960,000 miles)
Area:	Land 148,326,000 sq km (57,268,700 sq miles) 29% of surface	Mean velocity in orbit:	29.8 km (18.5 miles) per second
	Water 361,740,000 sq km (139,667,810 sq miles) 71% of surface	Escape velocity:	11.2 km (6.96 miles) per second
		Atmosphere:	Main constituents: nitrogen (78.5%), oxygen (21%)
Volume:	1,084,000 million cubic km (260,160 million cubic miles)	Crust:	Main constituents: oxygen (47%), silicon (28%), aluminium (8%), iron (5%).

CONTINENTS OF THE WORLD

	Highest Point		Area	
	(m)	(ft)	(sq km)	(sq miles)
Asia	8848	29,028	43,608,000	16,833,000
Africa	5895	19,340	30,335,000	11,710,000
North & Central America	6194	20,320	25,349,000	9,785,000
South America	6960	22,834	17,611,000	6,798,000
Antarctica	5140	16,863	14,000,000	5,400,000
Europe	5642	18,510	10,498,000	4,052,000
Oceania	4205	13,796	8,900,000	3,400,000

OCEANS OF THE WORLD

	Maximum Depth		Area	
	(m)	(ft)	(sq km)	(sq miles)
Pacific	11,033	36,198	165,384,000	63,838,000
Atlantic	8381	27,496	82,217,000	31,736,000
Indian	8047	26,401	73,481,000	28,364,000
Arctic	5450	17,880	14,056,000	5,426,000

PRINCIPAL RIVERS OF THE WORLD

Name (location)	Length (km)	(miles)	Name (location)	Length (km)	(miles)
Nile (Africa)	6695	4160	Kama (Europe)	2028	1260
Amazon (S Amer)	6516	4050	Xingú (S Amer)	2012	1250
Yangtze (Asia)	6380	3965	Columbia (N Amer)	1950	1210
Mississippi-Missouri (N Amer)	6019	3740	Juruá (S Amer)	1932	1200
Ob-Irtysh (Asia)	5570	3460	Peace (N Amer)	1923	1195
Yenisel-Angara (Asia)	5553	3450	Tigris (Asia)	1900	1180
Hwang Ho (Asia)	5464	3395	Don (Europe)	1870	1165
Zaïre (Africa)	4667	2900	Pechora (Europe)	1814	1127
Mekong (Asia)	4426	2750	Araguaya (S Amer)	1771	1100
Amur (Asia)	4416	2744	Snake (N Amer)	1670	1038
Lena (Asia)	4400	2730	Red (N Amer)	1639	1018
Mackenzie (N Amer)	4250	2640	Churchill (N Amer)	1610	1000
Niger (Africa)	4032	2505	Marañón (S Amer)	1610	1000
Paraná (S Amer)	4000	2485	Pilcomayo (S Amer)	1610	1000
Missouri (N Amer)	3969	2466	Ucayali (S Amer)	1610	1000
Mississippi (N Amer)	3779	2348	Uruguay (S Amer)	1610	1000
Murray-Darling (Australia)	3750	2330	Magdalena (S Amer)	1529	950
Volga (Europe)	3686	2290	Oka (Europe)	1481	920
Madeira (S Amer)	3203	1990	Canadian (N Amer)	1459	906
St. Lawrence (N Amer)	3203	1990	Godavari (Asia)	1449	900
Yukon (N Amer)	3187	1980	Parnaíba (S Amer)	1449	900
Indus (Asia)	3180	1975	Dnestr (Europe)	1411	877
Syrdar'ya (Asia)	3079	1913	Brazos (N Amer)	1401	870
Salween (Asia)	3060	1901	Fraser (N Amer)	1368	850
Darling (Australia)	3057	1900	Salado (S Amer)	1368	850
Rio Grande (N Amer)	3034	1885	Rhine (Europe)	1320	825
São Francisco (S Amer)	2897	1800	Narmada (Asia)	1288	800
Danube (Europe)	2850	1770	Tobol (Asia)	1288	800
Brahmaputra (Asia)	2840	1765	Athabaska (N Amer)	1231	765
Euphrates (Asia)	2815	1750	Pecos (N Amer)	1183	735
Pará-Tocantins (S Amer)	2752	1710	Green (N Amer)	1175	730
Zambezi (Africa)	2650	1650	Elbe (Europe)	1160	720
Amudar'ya (Asia)	2620	1630	Ottawa (N Amer)	1121	696
Paraguay (South America)	2600	1615	White (N Amer)	1111	690
Nelson-Saskatchewan (N Amer)	2570	1600	Cumberland (N Amer)	1106	687
Ural (Asia)	2534	1575	Yellowstone (N Amer)	1080	671
Kolyma (Asia)	2513	1562	Donets (Europe)	1079	670
Ganges (Asia)	2510	1560	Tennessee (N Amer)	1050	652
Orinoco (South America)	2500	1555	Vistula (Europe)	1014	630
Arkansas (N Amer)	2350	1460	Loire (Europe)	1012	629
Colorado (N Amer)	2330	1450	Tagus (Europe)	1006	625
Xi Jiang (Asia)	2300	1437	Tisza (Europe)	997	619
Dnepr (Europe)	2285	1420	North Platte (N Amer)	995	618
Negro (S Amer)	2254	1400	Ouachita (N Amer)	974	605
Aldan (Asia)	2242	1393	Sava (Europe)	940	584
Irrawaddy (Asia)	2150	1335	Neman (Europe)	937	582
Ohio (N Amer)	2102	1306	Oder (Europe)	910	565
Orange (Africa)	2090	1299			

PRINCIPAL MOUNTAINS OF THE WORLD

Name (location)	Height (m)	Height (ft)	Name (location)	Height (m)	Height (ft)
Everest (Tibet-Nepal)	8848	29,028	Ras Dashan (Ethiopia)	4620	15,158
Godwin-Austen or K2			Belukha (Kazakhstan)	4506	14,783
(Kashmir-Sinkiang)	8611	28,250	Markham (Antarctica)	4350	14,271
Kangchenjunga (Nepal-India)	8587	28,170	Meru (Tanzania)	4566	14,979
Makalu (Nepal)	8463	27,766	Hubbard (Alaska–Yukon)	4557	14,950
Dhaulagiri (Nepal)	8167	26,795	Kirkpatrick (Antarctica)	4528	14,855
Nanga Parbat (India)	8125	26,657	Karisimbi (Rwanda–Zaire)	4508	14,787
Annapurna (Nepal)	8091	26,545	Weisshorn (Switzerland)	4505	14,780
Gosainthan (Tibet)	8012	26,286	Matterhorn/Mont Cervin		
Nanda Devi (India)	7816	25,643	(Switzerland–Italy)	4477	14,690
Kamet (India)	7756	25,446	Whitney (California)	4418	14,495
Namcha Barwa (Tibet)	7756	25,446	Elbert (Colorado)	4399	14,431
Gurla Mandhata (Tibet)	7728	25,355	Massive Mount (Colorado)	4397	14,424
Kongur (China)	7720	25,325	Harvard (Colorado)	4396	14,420
Tirich Mir (Pakistan)	7691	25,230	Rainier or Tacoma (Washington)	4392	14,410
Minya Kanka (China)	7556	24,790	Williamson (California)	4382	14,375
Kula Kangri (Tibet)	7555	24,784	La Plata (Colorado)	4371	14,340
Muztagh Ata (China)	7546	24,757	Blanca Peak (Colorado)	4364	14,317
Kommunizma (Tajikistan)	7495	24,590	Uncompahgre (Colorado)	4361	14,306
Pobedy (Russian Fed.–China)	7439	24,406	Crestone (Colorado)	4356	14,291
Chomo Lhari (Bhutan–Tibet)	7313	23,992	Lincoln (Colorado)	4354	14,284
Api (Nepal)	7132	23,399	Grays (Colorado)	4351	14,274
Lenina (Kyrgyzstan-Tajikistan)	7134	23,405	Evans (Colorado)	4347	14,260
Aconcagua (Argentina)	6960	22,834	Longs (Colorado)	4345	14,255
Ojos del Salado (Argentina)	6908	22,664	White (California)	4343	14,246
Tupungato (Argentina–Chile)	6801	22,310	Colima (Mexico)	4340	14,236
Mercedario (Argentina)	6770	22,211	Shavano (Colorado)	4337	14,229
Huascarán (Peru)	6769	22,205	Princeton (Colorado)	4327	14,196
Llullaillaco (Chile)	6723	22,057	Yale (Colorado)	4327	14,196
Neradas de Cachi (Argentina)	6720	22,047	Elgon (Uganda-Kenya)	4321	14,176
Kailas (Tibet)	6714	22,027	Shasta (California)	4317	14,162
Incahuasi (Argentina)	6709	22,011	Grand Combin (Switzerland)	4314	14,153
Tengri Khan (Kyrgyzstan)	6695	21,965	San Luis (Colorado)	4312	14,146
Sajama (Bolivia)	6542	21,463	Batu (Ethiopia)	4307	14,130
Illampu (Bolivia)	6485	21,276	Pikes Peak (Colorado)	4301	14,110
Antofalla (Argentina)	6441	21,129	Snowmass (Colorado)	4291	14,077
Illimani (Bolivia)	6402	21,004	Culebra (Colorado)	4286	14,070
Chimborazo (Ecuador)	6310	20,702	Sunlight (Colorado)	4284	14,053
McKinley (Alaska)	6194	20,320	Split (California)	4283	14,051
Copiapo or Azifre (Chile)	6080	19,947	Redcloud (Colorado)	4278	14,034
Logan (Yukon, Canada)	6051	19,524	Finsteraarhorn (Switzerland)	4274	14,022
Cotopaxi (Ecuador)	5896	19,344	Wrangell (Alaska)	4269	14,005
Kilimanjaro (Tanzania)	5895	19,340	Mount of the Holy Cross (Colorado)	4266	13,996
Ollagüe (Chile-Bolivia)	5868	19,250	Humphreys (California)	4259	13,972
Cerro del Potro (Argentina–Chile)	5830	19,127	Ouray (Colorado)	4254	13,955
Misti (Peru)	5822	19,101	Guna (Ethiopia)	4231	13,881
Cayambe (Ecuador)	5797	19,016	Mauna Kea (Hawaii)	4205	13,796
Huila (Colombia)	5750	18,865	Gannet (Wyoming)	4202	13,785
Citlaltepi (Mexico)	5699	18,697	Hayes (Alaska)	4188	13,740
Demavend (Iran)	5664	18,582	Fremont (Wyoming)	4185	13,730
Elbrus (Russian Fed.)	5642	18,510	Sidley (Antarctica)	4181	13,717
St Elias (Alaska, Canada)	5489	18,008	Mauna Loa (Hawaii)	4169	13,677
Popocatepetl (Mexico)	5453	17,887	Jungfrau (Switzerland)	4158	13,642
Cerro Lejfa (Chile)	5360	17585	Kings (Utah)	4124	13,528
Foraker (Alaska)	5304	17,400	Kinabalu (Sabah)	4102	13,455
Maipo (Argentina–Chile)	5290	17,355	Cameroon (Cameroon)	4095	13,435
Ixtaccihuati (Mexico)	5286	17,342	Fridtjof Nansen (Antarctica)	4068	13,346
Lucania (Yukon, Canada)	5228	17,150	Tacaná (Mexico–Guatemala)	4064	13,333
Tomila (Colombia)	5215	17,109	Bernina (Switzerland)	4049	13,284
Dykh Tau (Russian Fed.)	5203	17,070	Summit (Colorado)	4046	13,272
Kenya (Kenya)	5200	17,058	Waddington (British Columbia, Canada)	4042	13,262
Ararat (Turkey)	5165	16,945	Lister (Antarctica)	4025	13,205
Vinson Massif (Antarctica)	5140	16,863	Cloud Peak (Wyoming)	4016	13,176
Kazbek (Georgia)	5047	16,558	Yu Shan (Taiwan)	3997	13,113
Blackburn (Alaska)	5037	16,523	Truchas (New Mexico)	3994	13,102
Jaya (Irian Jaya, Indonesia)	5030	16,502	Wheeler (Nevada)	3981	13,058
Sanford (Alaska)	4941	16,208	Robson (British Columbia, Canada)	3954	12,972
Klyucheveyskava (Russian Fed.)	4750	15,584	Granite (Montana)	3902	12,799
Mont Blanc (France–Italy)	4808	15,774	Borah (Idaho)	3858	12,655
Domuyo (Argentina)	4800	15,748	Baldy (New Mexico)	3848	12,623
Vancouver (Alaska–Yukon, Canada)	4786	15,700	Monte Viso (Italy)	3847	12,621
Trikora (West Irian, Indonesia)	4750	15,584	Kerinci (Sumatra)	3805	12,483
Fairweather (Alaska–Brit. Columbia,			Grossglockner (Austria)	3797	12,460
Canada)	4670	15,320	Erebus (Antarctica)	3794	12,447
Monte Rosa (Switzerland–Italy)	4634	15,203	Excelsior (California)	3790	12,434

Appendix V
Weights and Measures: Conversions and Equivalents

Measurement of mass or weight

avoirdupois

		metric equivalent
	1 grain (gr)	= 64.8 mg
	1 dram (dr)	= 1.772 g
16 drams	= 1 ounce (oz.) = 28.3495 g	
16 oz (= 7000 gr.)	= 1 pound (lb)	= 0.4536 kg
100 lb	= 1 short hundredweight	= 45.3592 kg
112 lb	= 1 long hundredweight	= 50.8024 kg
2,000 lb	= 1 short ton	= 0.9072 kg
2,240 lb	= 1 long ton	= 1.01605 tonnes

metric

		avoirdupois equivalent
	1 milligram (mg)	0.015 gr
10 mg	= 1 centigram	0.154 gr
10 cg	= 1 decigram (dg)	1.543 gr
10 dg	= 1 gram (g)	15.43 gr = 0.035 oz
10 g	= 1 decagram (dag)	= 0.353 oz
10 dag	= 1 hectogram (hg)	= 3.527 oz
10 hg	= 1 kilogram (kg)	= 2.205 lb
1000 kg	= 1 tonne (metric ton)	= 0.984 (long) ton
		= 2204.62 lb

Troy weight

		metric equivalent
	1 grain	= 0.065 g
4 grains	= 1 carat of gold or silver	= 0.2592 g
6 carats	= 1 pennyweight (dwt)	= 1.5552 g
20 dwt	= 1 ounce (oz)	= 31.1035 g
12 oz	= 1 pound (lb)	= 373.242 g
25 lb	= 1 quarter (qr)	= 9.331 kg
100 lb	= 1 hundredweight (cwt)	= 37.324 kg
20 cwt	= 1 ton of gold or silver	= 746.68 kg

Note: the grain troy is the same as the grain avoirdupois, but the pound troy contains 5760 grains, the pound avoirdupois 7000 grains. Jewels are not weighed by this measure.

Linear measure

		metric equivalent
	1 inch (in)	= 25.4 mm
12 in	= 1 foot (ft)	= 0.305 m
3 ft	= 1 yard (yd)	= 0.914 m
2 yds	= 6 ft = 1 fathom (fm)	= 1.829 m
5.5 yds	= 16.5 ft = 1 rod	= 5.029 m
4 rod	= 22 yds = 66 ft = 1 chain	= 20.12 m
10 chain	= 220 yds = 660 ft = 1 furlong (fur.)	= 0.201 km
8 fur.	= 1760 yds = 5280 ft = 1 (statute) mile (mi)	= 1.609 km
3 mi	= 1 league	= 4.827 km

metric

		U.S. equivalent
	1 millimeter (mm)	= 0.0394 in
10 mm	= 1 centimeter (cm)	= 0.3937 in
10 cm	= 1 decimeter (dm)	= 3.937 in
10 dm	= 1 meter (m)	= 39.37 in
10 m	= 1 decameter (dam)	= 10.94 yds
10 dam	= 1 hectometer (hm)	= 109.4 yds
10 hm	= 1 kilometer (km)	= 0.621 mi

Surveyor's measure

Surveyor's linear units

		metric equivalent
1 link	= 7.92 in	= 20.117 cm
25 links = 1 rod	= 5.50 yds	= 5.029 m
100 links = 1 chain	= 22 yds	= 20.12 m
10 chains = 1 furlong (fur.)	= 220 yds	= 0.201 m
80 chains = 8 fur.	= 1 mile (mi)	= 1.609 km

Surveyor's square units

	metric equivalent
100 x 100 links or 10,000 sq. links	= 1 sq. chain = 484 sq. yds = 404.7 m²
4 x 4 poles or 16 sq. poles	= 1 sq. chain
22 x 22 yds or 484 sq. yds	= 1 sq. chain
100,000 sq. links or 10 sq. chains	= 1 acre = 4840 sq. yds = 0.4047 ha

Square measure

		metric equivalent
	1 square inch (sq. in)	= 6.4516 cm²
144 sq. in.	= 1 square foot (sq. ft)	= 0.0929 m²
9 sq. ft.	= 1 square yard (sq. yd)	= 0.8361 m²
30¼ sq. yds.	= 1 square perch	= 25.29 m²
40 sq. perch	= 1 rood	= 0.1012
4 roods or 4840 sq. yds	= 1 acre	= 04.047 ha
640 acres	= 1 square mile (sq. mi)	= 2.5900 km²

metric units		U.S. equivalent
	1 square millimeter (mm²)	= 0.0016 sq. in
100 mm²	= 1 square centimeter (cm²)	= 0.1550 sq. in
100 cm²	= 1 square decimeter (dm²)	= 15.500 sq. in
100 dm²	= 1 square meter (m²)	= 10.7639 sq. ft
		(= 1.1959 sq. yds)
100 m²	= 1 square decameter (dam²)	= 1076.3910 sq. ft
100 dam²	= 1 square hectometer (hm²)	= 0.0039 sq. mi
100 hm²	= 1 square kilometer (km²)	= 0.3861 sq. mi

*Note: The square hectometer is also known as a *hectare* (ha.).

The hectare can be sub-divided into *ares*:

metric units		
100 m²	= 1 are	= 119.59 sq. yds
1000 m²	= 10 ares = 1 dekare	= 1195.9 sq. yds
10,000 m²	= 100 ares = 1 hectare	= 2.471 acres

Cubic measure

		metric equivalent
	1 cubic inch (cu. in)	= 16.39 cm³
1728 cu. in	= 1 cubic foot (cu. ft)	= 0.0283 m³
27 cu. ft	= 1 cubic yard (cu. yd)	= 0.7646 m³

		metric units
1000 cubic millimeters (mm³)	= 1 cubic centimeter (cm³)	= 0.0610 cu. in
1000 cubic centimeters (cm³)	= 1 cubic decimeter (dm³)	= 610 cu. in
1000 cubic decimeters (dm³)	= 1 cubic meter (m³)	= 35.3147 cu. ft

The *stere* is also used, in particular as a unit of measurement for timber:

1 cubic meter	= 1 stere	= 35.3147 cu. ft
10 decisteres	= 1 stere	= 35.3147 cu. ft
10 steres	= 1 decastere	= 353.1467 cu. ft
		(= 13.0795 cu. yds)

Liquid measure

		metric equivalent
	1 fluid ounce (fl. oz)	= 29.573 ml
4 fl. oz	= 1 gill	= 118.291 ml
4 gills	= 1 pint (pt)	= 473.163 ml
2 pt	= 1 quart (qt)	= 0.9461
4 qt	= 1 gallon (gal)	= 3.7851

U.S. and British equivalents

U.S.	British
1 fluid ounce	1.0408 fl oz
1 pint	0.8327 pt
1 gallon	0.8327 gal

metric units		
10 milliliters (ml)	= 1 centiliter (cl)	= 0.0211 pt
10 cl	= 1 deciliter (dl)	= 0.211 pt
10 dl	= 1 liter (l)	= 2.11 pt
		(= 0.264 gal)
10 l	= 1 decaliter (dal)	2.64 gal
10 dal	= 1 hectoliter (hl)	26.4 gal
10 hl	= kiloliter (kl)	264.0 gal

Weights and Measures: Conversions and Equivalents

Temperature

Equations for conversion

$$°\text{Fahrenheit} = (9/5 \times x°\text{C}) + 32 \qquad °\text{Centigrade} = 5/9 \times (x°\text{F} - 32)$$
$$°\text{Kelvin} = x°\text{C} + 273.15$$

Some equivalents

	Centigrade	Fahrenheit
Normal temperature of the human body	36.9°C	98.4°F
Freezing point	0°C	32°F
Boiling point	100°C	212°F

Table of equivalents

Fahrenheit	Centigrade	Centigrade	Fahrenheit
100°C	212°C	30°C	86°F
90°C	194°F	20°C	68°F
80°C	176°F	10°C	50°F
70°C	158°F	0°C	32°F
60°C	140°F	-10°C	14°F
50°C	122°F	-20°C	4°F
40°C	104°F	-30°C	-22°F

Approximate oven temperatures

Description	Electric °C	°F	Gas no. (equiv. °F)
very cool	107°	225°	1/4 (240°)
	121°	250°	1/2 (265°)
cool	135°	275°	1 (290°)
	149°	300°	2 (310°)
warm	163°	325°	3 (335°)
moderate	177°	350°	4 (355°)
fairly hot	191°	375°	5 (375°)
	204°	400°	6 (400°)
hot	218°	425°	7 (425°)
very hot	232°	450°	8 (450°)
	246°	475°	9 (470°)

Clothing Sizes

Women: Dresses, Coats, Skirts/Junior Sizes Misses Sizes

American	7	9	11	13	15	8	10	12	14	16	18
British	9	11	13	15	17	10	12	14	16	18	20
Continental	34	36	38	40	42	38	40	42	44	46	48

Women: Blouses, Sweaters

American	10	12	14	16	18	20
British	32	34	36	38	40	42
Continental	38	40	42	44	46	48

Women: Shoes

American	4½	5	5½	6	6½	7	7½	8	8½	9	9½
British	3	3½	4	4½	5	5½	6	6½	7	7½	8
Continental	35½	36	36½	37	37½	38	38½	39	39½	40	40½

Children:

American	3	4	5	6	6X
British	18	20	22	24	26
Continental	98	104	110	116	122

(For older children, sizes usually correspond with their ages)

Children: Shoes

American	8	9	10	11	12	13	1	2	3
British	7	8	9	10	11	12	13	1	2
Continental	24	25	27	28	29	30	32	33	34

Men: Suits

American	34	35	36	37	38	39	40	41	42
British	34	35	36	37	38	39	40	41	42
Continental	44	46	48	49½	51	52½	54	55½	57

Men: Shirts

American	14½	15	15½	16	16½	17	17½	18
British	14½	15	15½	16	16½	17	17½	18
Continental	37	38	39	41	42	43	44	45

Metric Tyre Pressure Conversion Chart

Pounds per sq in	Kilograms per sq cm	Kilo Pascals (kPa)	(Atmospheres)
14	0.98	96.6	0.95
16	1.12	110.4	1.08
18	1.26	124.2	1.22
20	1.40	138.0	1.36
22	1.54	151.8	1.49
24	1.68	165.6	1.63
26	1.83	179.4	1.76
28	1.96	193.2	1.90
30	2.10	207.0	2.04
32	2.24	220.8	2.16
36	2.52	248.4	2.44
40	2.80	276.0	2.72
50	3.50	345.0	3.40
55	3.85	379.5	3.74
60	4.20	414.0	4.08
65	4.55	448.5	4.42

Mile/kilometer

Miles	Kilometers	Kilometers	Miles
1	1.6	1	0.6
2	3.2	2	1.2
3	4.8	3	1.8
4	6.4	4	2.4
5	8.0	5	3.1
6	9.6	6	3.7
7	11.2	7	4.3
8	12.8	8	4.9
9	14.4	9	5.5
10	16.0	10	6.2
20	32.1	20	12.4
30	48.2	30	18.6
40	64.3	40	24.8
50	80.4	50	31.0
60	96.5	60	37.2
70	112.6	70	43.4
80	128.7	80	49.7
90	144.8	90	55.9
100	160.9	100	62.1
1000	1,609	1,000	621

For approximate conversions:

Miles – Kilometers: divide by 5, then multiply by 8

Kilometers – Miles: divide by 8, multiply by 5

Numeration

Arabic	Roman	Ordinal	Binary
1	I	1st first	1
2	II	2nd second	10
3	III	3rd third	11
4	IV	4th fourth	100
5	V	5th fifth	101
6	VI	6th sixth	110
7	VII	7th seventh	111
8	VIII	8th eighth	1000
9	IX	9th ninth	1001
10	X	10th tenth	1010
11	XI	11th eleventh	1011
12	XII	12th twelfth	1100
13	XIII	13th thirteenth	1101
14	XIV	14th fourteenth	1110
15	XV	15th fifteenth	1111
16	XVI	16th sixteenth	10000
17	XVII	17th seventeenth	10001
18	XVIII	18th eighteenth	10010
19	XIX	19th nineteenth	10011
20	XX	20th twentieth	10100
21	XXI	21st twenty-first	10101
29	XXIX	29th twenty-ninth	11101
30	XXX	30th thirtieth	11110
32	XXXII	32nd thirty-second	100000
40	XL	40th	101000
50	L	50th	110010
60	LX	60th	111100
64	LXIV	64th	1000000
90	XC	90th	1011010
99	XCIX	99th	1100011
100	C	100th	1100100
128	CXXVIII	128th	10000000
200	CC	200th	11001000
256	CCLVI	256th	100000000
300	CCC	300th	100101100
400	CD	400th	110010000
500	D	500th	111110100
900	CM	900th	1110000100
1000	M	1000th thousandth	1111110100
1024	MXXIV	1024th	10000000000
1500	MD	1500th fifteen hundredth	10111011100
4000	MV	4000th	111110100000
5000	V	5000th	1001110001000
10,000	X	10,000th	10011100010000
100,000	C	100,000th	11000011010100000
1,000,000	M	1,000,000th millionth	$10^{500,000}$

CHEMICAL ELEMENTS

An element is a substance not separable by ordinary chemical means into substances different from itself. Fewer than a hundred elements occur naturally, the others can only be made artificially.

Name	Symbol	Atomic number	Atomic weight	Valency
Actinium	Ac	89	(227)	
Aluminum	Al	13	26.98154	3
Americium	Am	95	(243)	3,4,5,6
Antimony	Sb	51	121.75	3,5
Argon	Ar	18	39.948	0
Arsenic	As	33	74.9216	3,5
Astatine	At	85	(210)	1,3,5,7
Barium	Ba	56	137.34	2
Berkelium	Bk	97	(247)	3,4
Beryllium	Be	4	9.01218	2
Bismuth	Bi	83	208.9804	3,5
Boron	B	5	10.81	3
Bromine	Br	35	79.904	1,3,5,7
Cadmium	Cd	48	112.40	2
Caesium	Cs	55	132.9054	1
Calcium	Ca	20	40.08	2
Californium	Cf	98	(251)	
Carbon	C	6	12.011	2.4
Cerium	Ce	58	140.12	3.4
Chlorine	Cl	17	35.453	1,3,5,7
Chromium	Cr	24	51.996	2,3,6
Cobalt	Co	27	58.9332	2,3
Copper	Cu	29	63.546	1,2
Curium	Cm	96	(247)	3
Dysprosium	Dy	66	162.50	3
Einsteinium	Es	99	(254)	
Erbium	Er	68	167.26	3
Europium	Eu	63	151.96	2,3
Fermium	Fm	100	(257)	
Fluorine	F	9	18.99840	1
Francium	Fr	87	(223)	1
Gadolinium	Gd	64	157.25	3
Gallium	Ga	31	69.72	2,3
Germanium	Ge	32	72.59	4
Gold	Au	79	196.9665	1,3
Hafnium	Hf	72	178.49	4
Hahnium	Ha	105		
Helium	He	2	4.00260	0
Holmium	Ho	67	164.9304	3
Hydrogen	H	1	1.0079	1
Iridium	In	49	114.82	3
Iodine	I	53	126.9045	1,3,5,7
Irdium	Ir	77	192.22	3,4
Iron	Fe	26	55.847	2,3
Krypton	Kr	36	83.80	0
Lanthanum	La	57	138.9055	3
Lawrencium	Lr	103	(260)	
Lead	Pb	82	207.2	2,4
Lithium	Li	3	6.941	1
Lutetium	Lu	71	174.97	3
Magnesium	Mg	12	24.305	2
Manganese	Mn	25	54.9380	2,3,4,6,7
Mendelevium	Md	101	(258)	
Mercury	Hg	80	200.59	1,2
Molybdenum	Mo	42	95.94	3,4,6
Neodymium	Nd	60	144.24	3
Neon	Ne	10	20.179	0
Neptunium	Np	93	237.0482	4,5,6
Nickel	Ni	28	58.70	2,3
Niobium	Nb	41	92.9064	3,5
Nitrogen	N	7	14.0067	3,5
Nobelium	No	102	(255)	
Osmium	Os	76	190.2	2,3,4,8
Oxygen	O	8	15.9994	2
Palladium	Pd	46	106.4	2,4,6
Phosphorus	P	15	30.97376	3,5
Platinum	Pt	78	195.09	2,4
Plutonium	Pu	94	(244)	3,4,5,6
Polonium	Po	84	(209)	
Potassium	K	19	39.098	1
Praseodymium	Pr	59	140.9077	3
Promethium	Pm	61	(145)	3
Protactinium	Pa	91	231.0359	
Radium	Ra	88	226.0254	2
Radon	Rn	86	(222)	0
Rhenium	Re	75	186.207	
Rhodium	Rh	45	102.9055	3
Rubidium	Rb	37	85.4678	1
Ruthenium	Ru	44	101.07	3,4,6,8
Rutherfordium	Ru	104		
Samarium	Sm	62	105.4	2,3
Scandium	Sc	21	44.9559	3
Selenium	Se	34	78.96	2,4,6
Silicon	Si	14	28.086	4
Silver	Ag	47	107.868	1
Sodium	Na	11	22.98977	1
Strontium	Sr	38	87.62	2
Sulphur	S	16	32.06	2,4,6
Tantalum	Ta	73	180.9479	5
Technetium	Tc	43	(97)	6,7
Tellurium	Te	52	127.60	2,4,6
Terbium	Tb	65	158.9254	3
Thallium	Tl	81	204.37	1,3
Thorium	Th	90	232.0381	4
Thulium	Tm	69	168.9342	3
Tin	Sn	50	118.69	2,4
Titanium	Ti	22	47.90	3,4
Tungsten (Wolfram)	W	74	183.85	6
Uranium	U	92	238.029	4,6
Vanadium	V	23	50.9414	3,5
Xenon	Xe	54	131.30	0
Ytterbium	Yb	70	173.04	2,3
Yttrium	Y	39	88.9059	3
Zinc	Zn	30	65.38	2
Zirconium	Zr	40	91.22	4

TIME

Periods of Time

annual	yearly
biannual	twice a year
bicentennial	every 200 years
biennial	every two years
bimonthly	every two months; twice a month
biweekly	every two weeks; twice a week
centennial	every 100 years
decennial	every 10 years
diurnal	daily
duodecennial	every 12 years
millennial	every 1,000 years
millennium	a thousand years
novennial	every nine years
octennial	every eight years
perennial	year after year
quadrennial	every four years
quadricentennial	every 400 years
quincentennial	every 500 years
quindecennial	every 15 years
quinquennial	every 5 years
semiannual	every six months
semicentennial	every 50 years
semidiurnal	twice a day
semiweekly	twice a week
septennial	every seven years
sesquicentennial	every 150 years
sexennial	every six years
thrice weekly	three times a week
tricennial	every 30 years
triennial	every three years
trimonthly	every three months
triweekly	every three weeks; three times a week
undecennial	every 11 years
vicennial	every 20 years

Traditional Anniversary Names

1st	Paper	14th	Ivory
2nd	Cotton	15th	Crystal
3rd	Leather	20th	China
4th	Fruit, flowers	25th	Silver
5th	Wood	30th	Pearl
6th	Iron, sugar	35th	Coral
7th	Wool, copper	40th	Ruby
8th	Bronze	45th	Sapphire
9th	Pottery	50th	Golden
10th	Tin, aluminium	55th	Emerald
11th	Steel	60th	Diamond
12th	Silk, fine linen	75th	Diamond
13th	Lace		

Birthstones

Month	Biblical	Present
January	Garnet	Garnet
February	Amethyst	Amethyst
March	Jasper	Aquamarine, Bloodstone
April	Sapphire	Diamond
May	Chalcedony, Carnelian, Agate	Emerald, chrysoprase
June	Emerald	Pearl, moonstone, alexandrite
July	Onyx	Ruby, carnelian
August	Carnelian	Peridot, sardonyx
September	Chrysolite	Sapphire, lapis luzuli
October	Aquamarine, Beryl	Opal, tourmaline
November	Topaz	Topaz
December	Ruby	Turquoise, zircon

Days of the Week

Day	Derivation	Abbreviation
Sunday	The Sun	Sun. or S.
Monday	The Moon	Mon. or M.
Tuesday	Tiu, Norse God of War	Tues. or T.
Wednesday	Woden, Anglo-Saxon chief of Gods	Wed. or W.
Thursday	Thor, Norse God of Thunder	Thurs. or Th.
Friday	Frigg, Norse Goddess	Fri. or F.
Saturday	Saturn, Roman God of Harvests	Sat. or Sa.

Months of the Year

Month	Derivation	Abbreviation
January	Janus, Roman God of Doors and Gates	Jan.
February	Februa, Roman period of purification	Feb.
March	Mars, Roman God of War	Mar.
April	Aperire, Latin for "to open"	Apr.
May	Maia, Roman Goddess of Spring and Growth	My.
June	Juno, Roman Goddess of Marriage	Jun. or Je.
July	Julius Caesar	Jul. or Jy.
August	Augustus, First Emperor of Rome	Aug.
September	Septem, Latin for "seven"	Sept. or Sep.
October	Octo, Latin for "eight"	Oct.
November	Novem, Latin for "nine"	Nov.
December	Decem, Latin for "ten"	Dec.

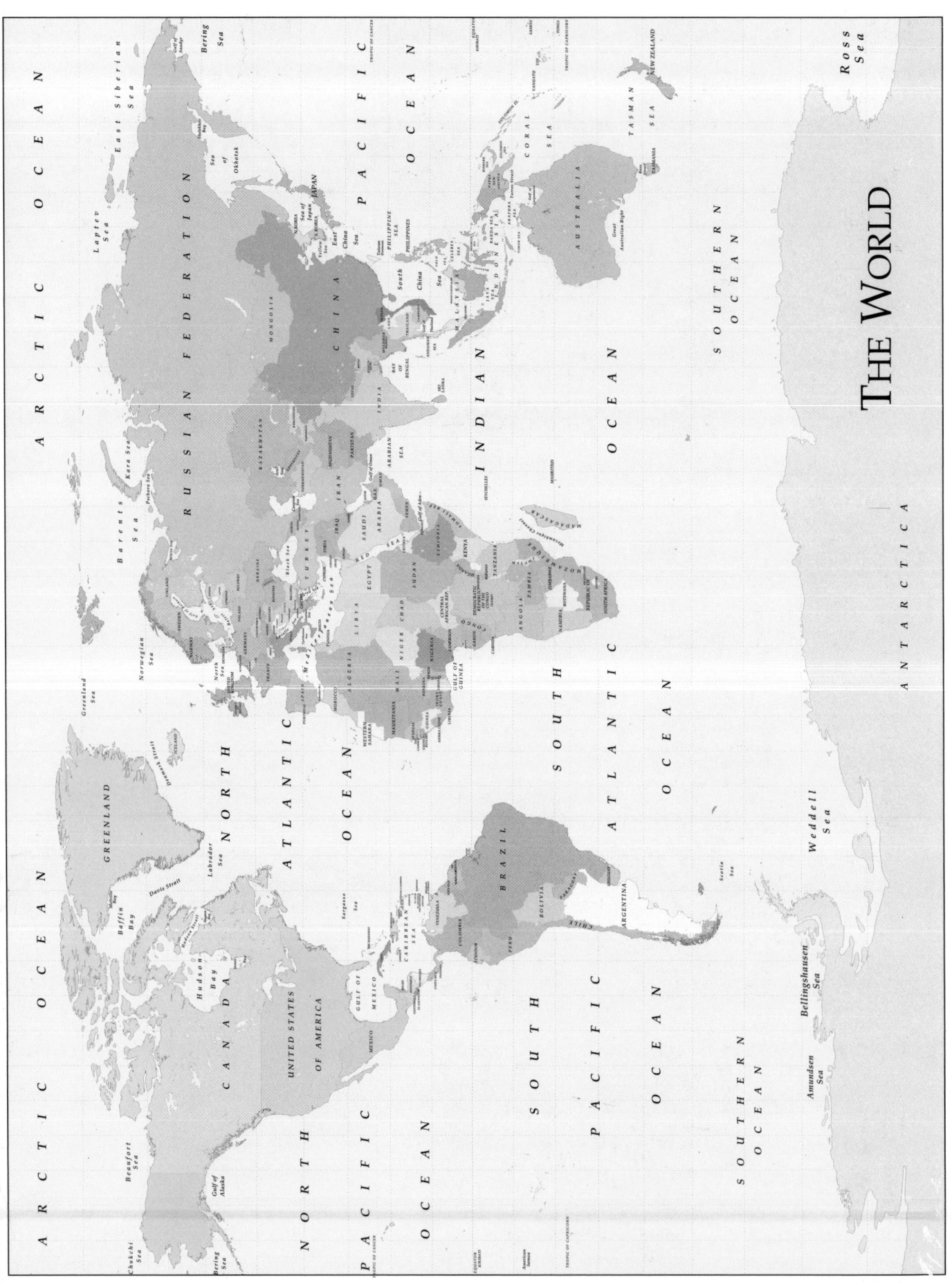

THE WORLD